KU-826-041

PEARS

CYCLOPAEDIA

1971–72

A BOOK OF BACKGROUND INFORMATION
AND REFERENCE FOR EVERYDAY USE

EDITOR

L. MARY BARKER

B.Sc.Lond.

Eightieth edition

The Editor desires to express her gratitude to readers for their
criticisms and suggestions and to all those who in one way or
another have contributed to the making of this edition.   Correspondence should be addressed to the Editor at 'Middlemarch',
Halstead, Sevenoaks, Kent.

First published 1897

7207 0385 9

*Printed and Bound in Great Britain by Richard Clay (The Chaucer Press), Ltd.,
Bungay, Suffolk*

© *1971 by Pelham Books Ltd.*

CONTENTS

CONTENTS

INDEX

Some of the sections are alphabetically arranged and index themselves. Their contents are not included here except where it is anticipated some special difficulty in reference may arise. Each section has a letter and, where appropriate, the column is given in brackets after the page number, *e.g.*, F8(1), G26(2). The sections " Greek Myths and Legends ", " Medical Matters " and " The World of Music " have each a separate index and glossary.

HISTORICAL EVENTS

Chronicle of events from the earliest times to the present day. For events in pre-history the reader may also like to consult the Geological Time Scale in Part IV and the sub-section "The Earliest Men and their Dates" in Part V of the Science Section.

CHRONICLE OF EVENTS

Note.—For classical history and for the past millennium most dates are well established. For other periods there is sometimes considerable uncertainty. Many of the dates in ancient history are either dubious or approximate, sometimes both.

B.C.   **PREHISTORY**

B.C.	
5,000,000,000	Age of Earth.
3,300,000,000	Earliest known rocks (found in Rhodesia and Manitoba).
2,000,000,000	Life appears.
600,000,000	First large-scale occurrence of fossils.
30,000,000	Earliest ape fossils (Oligovene period—Fayum, Egypt).
20,000,000	Early ape fossils (Miocene period—*Proconsul*, E. Africa).
1,700,000	Earliest known hominids (Lower Pleistocene—*Australopithecus*, and *Homo habilis* S. Africa, E. Africa.) Oldowan culture—first stage of Palaeolithic or Old Stone Age (hunting and food-gathering) which persisted until end of Ice Age, *c.* 8,000 B.C.
400,000	*Homo erectus* stage (Java, China, Africa) with crude chopping tools and early hand-axes. Heidelberg jaw, Vertezöllös remains (Europe).
180,000	Ancestors of Neandertalers and *Homo sapiens*, with advanced hand-axes (Europe: Steinheim and Swanscombe).
70,000	Neandertalers (Europe, Asia, N. Africa). Rhodesian Man (S. Africa). Solo Man (Java). Flake tools.
40,000	First cold phase ends. Neandertal race becoming extinct.
30,000	Second cold phase. *Homo sapiens* (modern man). Implements show significant advances: small knife-blades, engraving tools. Paintings and sculpture; magic rites and ceremonies. Cro-Magnons with Aurignacian culture.
18,000	Final culmination of last ice age. Aurignacian culture dying out to be replaced by Solutrean and then by the Magdalenian cultures. Great flowering of Palaeolithic art.
15,000	First immigrants from Asia to cross Behring Straits?
8,000	Last glaciers in Britain disappeared. Proto-Neolithic in Middle East. Agricultural settlements (*e.g.*, Jericho). Settled way of life leading eventually to such skills as weaving, metallurgy; inventions as ox-drawn plough, wheeled cart.
5,000	Britain becomes an island (land connection with continent severed by melting ice-sheets).

B.C. **CIVILISATION IN THE MIDDLE EAST**

4000	Susa founded.
3500	Sumerian civilisation flourishes. Cuneiform writing.
3000	First Egyptian Dynasty. Hieratic writing already perfected. Early Minoan Age (Crete). Pictorial writing, copper, silver, gold in use. Early Mycenean civilisation begins.
2980	Memphis capital of Egypt.

B.C.

2870	First settlements at Troy.
2850	Golden Age of China begins (legendary).
2700	Great Pyramid age in Egypt begins.
2400	Aryan migrations. Sargon founds Agade: Semitic empire.
2205	Hsia Dynasty begins in China (legendary).
2200	Middle Minoan Age; pottery, linear writing in pen and ink.
1900	Bronze Age begins in Britain. Stonehenge (1860–1560 B.C.).
1760	Shang Dynasty begins in China (dated traditionally 1760–1122 B.C.).
1750	Aryan invasion of Mesopotamia.
1720	Hyksos conquest of Egypt. War chariots introduced.
1700	Code of Hammurabi at Babylon.
1600	Late Minoan Age: bronze in use.
1550	Sack of Babylon by Hittites.
1546	18th Dynasty in Egypt commences. Civilisation at peak (under Thotmes III, 1490). Chronology more certain.
1500	Powerful Mitanni (Aryan) kingdom in Asia Minor. Phoenicia thriving—trade with Egypt and Babylonia. Vedic literature in India.
1450	Zenith of Minoan civilisation.
1400	Ugarit (N. Syria) culture at its zenith. Cretan civilisation ends: Knossos burnt. Temple at Luxor built.
1377	Amenhotep IV (Ikhnaton), the " heretic " Pharaoh.
1350	Zenith of Hittite civilisation.
1300	Israelite oppression (Rameses II). Phoenician settlements—Hellas and Spain (Cadiz). Tyre flourishing.
1250	Assyrian conquest in Babylon: dominant in Western Asia.
1230	Exodus of Israelites from Egypt.
1200	Attacks on Egypt by " Peoples of the Sea ". Downfall of Hittite kingdom. Siege of Troy (Homeric). Beginning of sea-power of independent Phoenician cities. Probably all these are connected with Achaean and other migrations in Aegean area.
1122	Chou Dynasty begins in China (870 years).
1115	Magnetic needle reputed in China.
1028	Establishment of kingship in Israel (Saul).
1000	Jerusalem capital of Israel. David king. *Rig Veda* (India).
961	Solomon begins temple at Jerusalem.
900	Probably period of writing of Homer's epics.
893	Assyrian chronological records begin.
850	Foundation of Carthage (traditional).
781	Chinese record of an eclipse.
776	First Olympiad to be used for chronological purposes.
753	Foundation of Rome (traditional).
750	Greek colonists settling in Southern Italy.
745	Accession of Tiglath-Pileser III; Assyrian Power at its height. Deportation of subject peoples (Israel 722).
683	Kingship abolished in Athens.
625	Neo-Babylonian (Chaldean) Empire (Nineveh destroyed 612).

B.C.

621 Publication of Athenian laws by Draco.

610 Spartan constitution, made rigid after Messenian Wars; later attributed to Lycurgus.

594 Athenian constitution reformed by Solon.

586 Jerusalem taken by Babylonians. Inhabitants exiled till 538.

561 Pisistratus tyrant of Athens.

560 Accession of Croesus—great prosperity of Lydia.

538 Babylon taken by Persians: Empire founded by Cyrus, soon covers almost all of civilised Middle East.

509 Foundation of Roman Republic (traditional).

508 Democratic constitution proclaimed in Athens.

500 Etruscans at height of their power in Northern Italy. Iron age beginning in Britain.

GREAT AGE OF GREECE

499 Revolt of Ionian Greek cities against Persian king Darius.

494 Secession of Plebeians from Rome. Tribunes established.

490 Battle of Marathon: Athenian repulse of Persian attack.

480 Death of Buddha. Battle of Thermopylae: Spartans under Leonidas wiped out by Persians. Battle of Salamis: Persian fleet defeated by Athenians under Themistocles; Persian invasion of Greece halted.

479 Battles of Plataea and Mycale: Greek victories by land and sea respectively destroy Persian invasion force. Death of Confucius.

477 League of Delos founded by Athens for defence against Persia; soon becomes Athenian Empire. (467 Naxos kept in by force.)

461 Pericles comes to power in Athens.

458 Cincinnatus saves Rome (traditional).

456 Death of Aeschylus.

447 Building of Parthenon begun.

431 Death of Phidias. Outbreak of Great Peloponnesian War between Athens and Sparta. Pericles "Funeral Oration" (according to Thucydides).

425 Death of Herodotus.

416 Massacre of Melos by Athenians.

415 Sicilian Expedition: flight of Alcibiades from Athens to Sparta.

413 Loss of entire Athenian expeditionary force at Syracuse.

406 Death of Euripides and Sophocles.

405 Battle of Aegospotami: Athenian navy destroyed by Sparta.

404 Athenian surrender to Sparta: beginning of Spartan hegemony in Greece.

403 Beginning of epoch of Warring States in China.

400 Death of Thucydides, Greek historian (?).

399 Execution of Socrates.

390 Occupation of Rome by Gauls under Brennus.

371 Battle of Leuctra: Spartans defeated by Thebans: beginning of Theban hegemony in Greece.

370 Death of Hippocrates of Cos (?).

347 Death of Plato.

338 Battle of Chaeronea: Greek city-states defeated by Philip II of Macedon, who becomes supreme in Greece.

336 Assassination of Philip of Macedon: accession of Alexander.

334 Alexander's invasion of Persian Empire. Battle of Granicus, first victory.

333 Battle of Issus: Alexander defeats Darius of Persia.

332 Alexander's siege and capture of Tyre, occupation of Egypt.

B.C.

331 Battle of Arbela (Gaugamela)—final defeat of Darius.

330 Death of Darius and end of Persian Empire. Alexander heir to civilisations of Middle East.

326 Battle of Hydaspes: Alexander conquers the Punjab.

323 Death of Alexander at Babylon. Beginning of Hellenistic Age in Middle East and Eastern Mediterranean. Ptolemy I founds dynasty in Egypt. Alexandria becomes intellectual centre of Hellenic world.

322 Death of Demosthenes.

321 Death of Aristotle. Maurya dynasty unites N. India.

312 Seleucus I founds dynasty in Asia.

300 Zeno the Stoic, Epicurus and Euclid flourishing.

ROME: CONQUESTS AND DECAY OF REPUBLICAN INSTITUTIONS

290 End of Third Samnite War. Rome dominates Central Italy.

275 Battle of Beneventum: Rome finally defeats Pyrrhus and the Greek cities of Southern Italy. Rome dominates all Italy.

274 Asoka becomes ruler of two-thirds of Indian sub-continent.

264 Beginning of First Punic War (Rome v. Carthage).

260 Battle of Mylae: first great Roman naval victory.

255 Defeat and capture of Regulus by Carthaginians.

250 "La Tène" Iron Age people invade Britain.

241 End of First Punic War. Sicily becomes first Province of Rome.

221 Kingdom of Ch'in completes conquest of all Chinese states, under Shih Huang Tih.

218 Outbreak of Second Punic War: Hannibal crosses Alps.

216 Battle of Cannae: Hannibal wipes out great Roman army.

214 Great Wall of China constructed (by linking existing walls).

213 Burning of Chinese classics.

212 Capture of Syracuse by Romans and death of Archimedes.

207 Battle of Metaurus: defeat and death of Hasdrubal. End of Hannibal's hopes of overcoming Rome.

205 Roman provinces organised in Spain.

202 Former or Eastern Han Dynasty in China. Battle of Zama: Hannibal defeated by Scipio Africanus.

201 End of Second Punic War. Rome dominates Western Mediterranean.

196 After defeating Macedon, Rome proclaims independence of Greek city-states. Death of Eratosthenes the geographer (?).

160 Death in battle of Judas Maccabaeus: Jewish revolt against Seleucids continues successfully.

149 Outbreak of Third Punic War.

146 Carthage destroyed. Roman province of Africa formed. Roman provinces of Macedonia and Achaea formed, and most of remainder of Greece reduced to vassal status.

134 First Servile War: Revolt of slaves in Sicily under Eunus. Suppressed 132.

133 Siege and destruction of Numantia by Romans. Tiberius Gracchus Tribune. Attempted land reforms. Murdered 132.

129 Roman province of Asia formed from lands bequeathed by Attalus of Pergamum.

124 Chinese Grand College to train Civil Service officials.

123 Caius Gracchus Tribune. Attempted land reforms. Murdered 121.

110 Chinese expansion to include most of southeast of modern China, under Emperor Wu Ti. Commercial activity in Indian Ocean.

B.C.

106 Jugurtha captured by Marius and Sulla.

104 Second Servile War: revolt of slaves in Sicily under Tryphon and Athenion. Suppressed 101.

102 Chinese expedition to Ferghana and possible knowledge of West.

101 Battle of Vercellae: Marius ends threat of Cimbri to Rome.

91 Social War: revolt of Italian cities against Rome. Suppressed 88. Roman franchise granted to most Italians.

88 Civil Wars of Marius and Sulla begin.

87 Massacre in Rome by Marius.

82 Proscriptions in Rome by Sulla.

75 Belgic invasion of south-eastern Britain.

73 Third Servile War: revolt of slaves in southern Italy under Spartacus the gladiator. Suppressed 71.

63 Conspiracy of Catiline exposed by Cicero.

60 First Triumvirate: Pompey, Caesar, Crassus.

58 Beginning of Caesar's conquest of Gaul.

55 Caesar's first British expedition: second, 54.

53 Battle of Carrhae: destruction of Roman army under Crassus by Persians.

52 Revolt of Vercingetorix against Caesar.

50 Migration to Britain of Commius and his followers.

49 Caesar crosses the Rubicon. Beginning of war against Pompey and the Senate.

48 Battle of Pharsalus: defeat of Pompey by Caesar.

46 Caesar's calendar reforms.

44 Murder of Caesar.

43 Second Triumvirate: Antony, Octavian, Lepidus.

42 Battle of Philippi: defeat and death of Brutus and his associates.

31 Battle of Actium: naval victory of Octavian over Antony and Cleopatra. Octavian unchallenged master of the Roman world.

THE ROMAN EMPIRE

27 Octavian given the title of Augustus by the Senate.

19 Death of Virgil.

8 Death of Horace.

6 Birth of Jesus Christ. (?)

A.D.

6 Civil Service Examination system in China.

9 Radical reforms by Emperor Wang Mang. Annihilation of Roman army under Varus by Teutonic tribesmen under Arminius.

10 Cunobelinus reigning over much of south-east Britain from Colchester.

14 Death of Augustus.

17 Death of Livy.

18 Death of Ovid.

25 Beginning of Later or Eastern Han Dynasty in China.

29 Crucifixion of Christ (?).

43 Roman invasion of Britain under Aulus Plautius.

51 Caractacus taken to Rome as prisoner.

60 Revolt of Boudicca.

63 Death of St. Paul.

64 Great Fire of Rome.

65 Death of Seneca.

66 Jews of Palestine rebelled against Roman rule.

68 Death of Nero—end of Julio-Claudian line of Roman Emperors.

70 Jerusalem taken and Jewish revolt suppressed by Titus.

79 Destruction of Pompeii and Herculaneum by eruption of Vesuvius.

A.D.

80 Completion of Colosseum (Flavian Amphitheatre).

83 Battle of Mons Graupius: Agricola crushes Caledonians.

96 Accession of Nerva: first of the "Five Good Emperors."

97 Chinese expedition under Kang Yin (lieutenant of Pan Ch'ao) penetrates to Persian Gulf.

117 Death of Trajan, accession of Hadrian. Roman Empire at its greatest extent.

122 Beginning of Hadrian's Wall (Tyne–Solway) by Aulus Platorius Nepos.

135 Suppression of Bar-Cochba's revolt and Dispersion of Jews.

142 Construction of Antonine Wall (Forth–Clyde) by Quintus Lollius Urbicus.

180 Death of Marcus Aurelius, last of the "Five Good Emperors." Beginning of the "Decline" of the Roman Empire (Gibbon).

193 Praetorian guards murder Emperor Pertinax, sell Empire to highest bidder (Didius Julianus).

196 Clodius Albinus, governor, withdraws forces from Britain to support his attempt to become Emperor. Northern Britain overrun by barbarians.

208 Septimius Severus visits Britain to punish Caledonians (death at York 211).

212 Edict of Caracalla. Roman citizenship conferred on all free inhabitants of Empire.

220 End of Han Dynasty: China divided and frequently invaded for next three centuries.

227 Sassanid Empire in Persia.

230 Emperor Sujin—Japanese history emerging from legendary stage.

251 Goths defeat and kill Emperor Decius.

259 Break-away "Gallic Empire" set up: suppressed 273.

273 Defeat of Zenobia and destruction of Palmyra by Emperor Aurelian.

284 Accession of Diocletian, who reorganises Roman Empire (293) with rigid social laws and heavy taxation.

287 Carausius attempts to found independent "Empire of Britain": suppressed 297.

306 Constantine proclaimed Emperor at York.

313 Edict of Milan. Christianity tolerated in Roman Empire.

320 Gupta dynasty reunites India.

325 Council of Nicaea: first general Council of the Church.

367 Successful attack on Britain by Picts, Scots, Saxons.

369 Restoration of Roman authority in Britain by Theodosius.

378 Battle of Adrianople: Goths defeat and kill Eastern Roman Emperor Valens.

383 Magnus Maximus withdraws forces from Britain to support his attempt to conquer north-western part of Empire.

388 Magnus Maximus defeated and killed in Italy.

395 Death of Emperor Theodosius the Great: the division of the Empire into East and West at his death proves eventually to be the final one.

406 Usurper Constantine III withdraws forces from Britain to support his claims: probable end of Roman military occupation of Britain.

410 Sack of Rome by Alaric the Goth. Emperor Honorius tells Britons to arrange for their own defence.

THE BARBARIAN INVASIONS

415 Visigoths begin conquest of Spain.

419 Visigothic kingdom of Toulouse recognised by Roman government.

429 Vandals begin conquest of North Africa.

432 St. Patrick begins mission in Ireland.

A.D.

446 " Groans of the Britons "—last appeal to Rome (traditional).

451 Châlons: Attila the Hun repelled from Gaul by mixed Roman–Barbarian forces.

452 Attila's raid into Italy: destruction of Aquilea and foundation of Venice by refugees.

455 Rome pillaged by Vandals.

476 Romulus Augustulus, last Western Roman Emperor, deposed by Odovacar: conventionally the end of the Western Roman Empire.

481 Clovis becomes King of the Franks, who eventually conquer Gaul (d. 511).

493 Theodoric founds Ostrogothic Kingdom in Italy (d. 526).

515 Battle of Mount Badon: West Saxon advance halted by Britons, perhaps led by Arthur (?).

BYZANTIUM AND ISLAM

527 Accession of Justinian I (d. 565).

529 Code of Civil Law published by Justinian. Rule of St. Benedict put into practice at Monte Cassino (traditional).

534 Byzantines under Belisarius reconquer North Africa from Vandals.

552 Byzantine reconquest of Italy complete.

563 St. Columba founds mission in Iona.

568 Lombard Kingdom founded in Italy.

570 Birth of Mohammed.

577 Battle of Deorham: West Saxon advance resumed.

589 Reunion of China under Southern Ch'en dynasty

590 Gregory the Great becomes Pope.

597 St. Augustine lands in Kent.

605 Grand Canal of China constructed.

618 T'ang Dynasty in China: their administrative system lasts in essentials for 1,300 years.

622 Hejira or flight from Mecca to Medina of Mohammed: beginning of Mohammedan era.

627 Battle of Nineveh: Persians crushed by Byzantines under Heraclius.

632 Death of Mohammed: all Arabia now Moslem. Accession of Abu Bakr, the first Caliph.

634 Battle of Heavenfield: Oswald becomes king of Northumbria, brings in Celtic Christianity.

638 Jerusalem captured by Moslems.

641 Battle of Mehawand: Persia conquered by Moslems.

643 Alexandria taken by Moslems.

645 Downfall of Soga clan in Japan, after establishing Buddhism: beginning of period of imitation of Chinese culture.

650 Slav occupation of Balkans now complete.

663 Synod of Whitby: Roman Christianity triumphs over Celtic Christianity in England.

685 Nectansmere: end of Northumbrian dominance in England.

698 Carthage taken by Moslems.

711 Tarik leads successful Moslem invasion of Spain.

718 Failure of second and greatest Moslem attack on Constantinople. Pelayo founds Christian kingdom of Asturias in Northern Spain.

726 Byzantine Emperor Leo III begins Iconoclast movement: opposed by Pope Gregory II, and an important cause of difference between Roman and Byzantine churches.

THE HOLY ROMAN EMPIRE AND THE TRIUMPH OF CHRISTIANITY IN EUROPE: NORSEMEN AND NORMANS

732 Tours: Moslem western advance halted by Charles Martel.

735 Death of Bede.

750 Beginning of Abbasid Caliphate (replacing Omayyads).

A.D.

751 Pepin King of the Franks: founds Carolingian dynasty. Ravenna taken by Lombards: end of Byzantine power in the West.

754 Pepin promises central Italy to Pope: beginning of temporal power of the Papacy.

778 Roncesvalles: defeat and death of Roland.

786 Accession of Haroun-al-Rashid in Baghdad.

793 Sack of Lindisfarne: Viking attacks on Britain begin.

795 Death of Offa: end of Mercian dominance in England.

800 Coronation of Charlemagne as Holy Roman Emperor.

814 Death of Charlemagne: division of his empire.

825 Ellandun: Egbert defeats Mercians and Wessex becomes leading kingdom in England.

827 Moslem invasion of Sicily.

840 Moslems capture Bari and occupy much of Southern Italy.

843 Treaty of Verdun: final division of Carolingian Empire, and beginning of France and Germany as separate states.

844 Kenneth MacAlpin becomes king of Picts as well as Scots: the kingdom of Alban.

862 Rurik founds Viking state in Russia: first at Novgorod, later at Kiev.

866 Fujiwara period begins in Japan. Viking " Great Army " in England: Northumbria, East Anglia and Mercia subsequently overwhelmed.

868 Earliest dated printed book in China.

872 Harold Fairhair King of Norway.

874 Iceland settled by Norsemen.

885-6 Viking attack on Paris.

893 Simeon founds first Bulgar Empire in Balkans.

896 Arpad and the Magyars in Hungary.

899 Death of Alfred the Great.

900 Ghana at the height of its power in North West Africa.

910 Abbey of Cluny founded: monastic reforms spread from here.

911 Rolf (or Rollo) becomes ruler of Normandy.

912 Accession of Abderrahman III: the most splendid period of the Omayyad Caliphate of Cordova (d. 961).

923 Brandenburg taken from the Slavs by Henry the Fowler, first of the Saxon Holy Roman Emperors.

929 Death of Wenceslas, Christian King of Bohemia.

937 Battle of Brunanburh: crowning victory of Athelstan. West Saxon kings now masters of England.

955 Battle of Lechfeld: Magyars finally defeated by Otto the Great and settle in Hungary.

960 Beginning of Sung Dynasty in China.

965 Harold Bluetooth, king of Denmark, accepts Christianity.

966 Mieszko I, king of Poland, accepts Christianity.

968 Fatimids begin their rule in Egypt.

982 Discovery of Greenland by Norsemen.

987 Hugh Capet king of France: founder of Capetian dynasty.

988 Vladimir of Kiev accepts Christianity.

991 Battle of Maldon: defeat of Byrhtnoth of Essex by Vikings—renewed Viking raids on England.

993 Olof Skutkonung, king of Sweden, accepts Christianity.

1000 Leif Ericsson discovers North America.

1001 Coronation of St. Stephen of Hungary with crown sent by the Pope.

1002 Massacre of St. Brice's Day: attempt by Ethelred to exterminate Danes in England.

A.D.

1014 Battle of Clontarf: victory of Irish under Brian Boru over Vikings.

1016 Canute becomes king of England; builds short-lived Danish " empire."

1018 Byzantines under Basil II complete subjection of Bulgars.

1040 Attempts to implement Truce of God from about this time.

1046 Normans under Robert Guiscard in southern Italy.

1054 Beginning of Almoravid (Moslem) conquests in West Africa.

1060 Normans invade Sicily.

1066 Norman conquest of England under William I.

1069 Reforms of Wang An-Shih in China.

THE CRUSADES

1071 Manzikert: Seljuk Turks destroy Byzantine army and overrun Anatolia.

1073 Hildebrand (Gregory VII) becomes Pope. Church discipline and Papal authority enforced.

1075 Seljuk Turks capture Jerusalem.

1076 Kumbi, capital of Ghana, sacked by Almoravids: subsequent break-up of Ghana Empire.

1084 Carthusians founded by St. Bruno at Chartreuse.

1086 Compilation of Domesday Book.

1094 El Cid takes Valencia.

1095 Council of Clermont: Urban II preaches First Crusade.

1098 Cistercians founded by St. Robert at Citeaux.

1099 First Crusade under Godfrey of Bouillon takes Jerusalem.

1100 Death of William Rufus in the New Forest. Baldwin I: Latin Kingdom of Jerusalem founded.

1106 Tinchebrai: Henry I of England acquires Normandy, captures his brother Robert.

1115 Abelard teaching at Paris. St. Bernard founds monastery at Clairvaux.

1119 Order of Knights Templars founded.

1120 Loss of the White Ship and heir to English throne.

1122 Concordat of Worms: Pope and Emperor compromise on the Investiture Controversy, but continue to quarrel over other matters (Guelfs and Ghibellines).

1135 Stephen takes English crown: civil wars with Matilda and anarchy ensue.

1143 Alfonso Henriques proclaimed first king of Portugal.

1144 Moslems take Christian stronghold of Edessa.

1148 Second Crusade fails to capture Damascus.

1150 Carmelites founded about this time by Berthold.

1152 Accession of Emperor Frederick Barbarossa.

1154 Henry of Anjou succeeds Stephen: first of Plantagenet kings of England.

1161 Explosives used in warfare in China.

1169 Strongbow invades Ireland: beginning of Anglo-Norman rule. Saladin ruling in Egypt.

1170 Murder of Thomas Becket in Canterbury cathedral.

1171 Spanish knightly Order of Santiago founded.

1176 Battle of Legnano: Frederick Barbarossa defeated by the Lombard League. Italian autonomy established.

1185 Kamakura Period in Japan: epoch of feudalism: until 1333.

1187 Hattin: destruction of Latin kingdom of Jerusalem by Saladin.

A.D.

1189 Third Crusade launched: leaders—Frederick Barbarossa, Philip Augustus of France, Richard Lionheart of England.

1191 Capture of Acre by Crusaders.

1192 End of Third Crusade without regaining Jerusalem. Richard I seized and held to ransom in Austria on return journey.

1198 Innocent III becomes Pope.

1202 Fourth Crusade, diverted by Venetians, takes Zara from Byzantines.

1204 Fourth Crusade captures Constantinople, founds Latin Empire. King John of England loses Normandy to France.

1206 Temujin proclaimed Gengiz Khan (Very Mighty King) of all the Mongols: soon controls all of Central Asia.

1208 Albigensian Crusade launched: the first against Christians.

1212 Battle of Las Navas de Tolosa: decisive victory of Spaniards over Moors. The Children's Crusade.

THE CULMINATION OF THE MIDDLE AGES

1215 Fourth Lateran Council: the authority of the mediaeval Church and Papacy at its zenith. Dominicans recognised by the Pope. Magna Carta extorted by barons from John.

1223 Franciscans recognised by the Pope.

1229 Emperor Frederick II, through diplomacy, recognised by Moslems as King of Jerusalem.

1230 Teutonic Knights established in Prussia.

1237 Golden Horde (Mongols) begin subjugation of Russia.

1241 Mongol incursions into Central Europe.

1250 St. Louis of France captured on his Crusade in Egypt. Mamelukes become rulers of Egypt. Mandingo king declares his independence of Ghana and embraces Islam.

1256 Conference of Baltic ports; the first form of the Hanseatic League.

1258 Provisions of Oxford: barons under Simon de Montfort force reforms on Henry III of England. Baghdad destroyed by Mongols.

1260 Kublai Khan ruling in China.

1264 Battle of Lewes: Montfort's party become rulers of England.

1265 Simon de Montfort's Parliament. Battle of Evesham: defeat and death of de Montfort.

1274 Death of Thomas Aquinas.

1281 Repulse of Mongol attack on Japan.

1282 Sicilian Vespers: rising of Sicilians against French ruler.

1284 Completion of Edward I of England's conquest of Wales.

1290 Expulsion of Jews from England. Death of Maid of Norway: Edward I begins attempts to rule Scotland.

1291 Fall of Acre: end of Crusading in Holy Land. Everlasting League of Uri: beginnings of Swiss Confederation.

1294 Death of Roger Bacon, the founder of experimental science. Death of Kublai Khan: unity of Mongol Empire now only nominal.

1295 " Model Parliament " of Edward I (anticipated in 1275).

1308 Death of Duns Scotus.

THE DECLINE OF THE MIDDLE AGES

1309 Papacy moves to Avignon: beginning of the Babylonish Captivity.

1312 Suppression of Templars by king of France and Pope.

1314 Battle of Bannockburn: victory of Robert Bruce secures Scottish independence.

1321 Death of Dante.

1325 Zenith of Mandingo Empire of Mali (North West Africa) under Mansa Musa; superseded at end of 15th century by Songhai empire.

1327 Deposition of Edward II; subsequently murdered.

A.D.

1336 Ashikaga Period in Japan: great feudal lords semi-independent of authority of Shogun.

1337 Death of Giotto.

1338 Beginning of Hundred Years' War between England and France.

1340 Battle of Sluys: English capture French fleet.

1344 Swabian League: weakness of Imperial authority in Germany obliges towns to form leagues for mutual protection.

1346 Battles of Crecy and Neville's Cross: spectacular English victories over French and Scots.

1347 Calais taken by Edward III of England. Cola di Rienzi attempts to reform government of Rome: killed 1354.

1348 Black Death reaches Europe (England 1349, Scotland 1350).

1351 Statute of Labourers: attempt by English Parliament to freeze wages.

1353 Statute of Praemunire: restraints placed on Papal intervention in England.

1354 Ottoman Turks make first settlement in Europe, at Gallipoli.

1355 Death of Stephen Dushan: collapse of Serbian Empire which he had built.

1356 Battle of Poitiers: capture of King John of France by Black Prince. "Golden Bull" regulates Imperial elections in such a way as to place power in the hands of the German princes: valid until 1806.

1358 The Jacquerie: rising of French peasants.

1360 Peace of Bretigny: Edward III makes great territorial gains in France.

1362 English becomes the official language in Parliament and the Law Courts.

1363 Timur (Tamerlane) begins his career of conquest in Asia.

1368 Ming Dynasty in China.

1370 Bertrand du Guesclin Constable of France: regains much territory from the English. Peace of Stralsund: Hansa in complete control of Baltic Sea.

1377 Pope returns to Rome: End of Babylonish Captivity.

1378 Disputed Papal Election: Beginning of Great Schism.

1380 Battle of Chioggia: decisive victory of Venice over Genoa. Battle of Kulikovo: Dmitri Donskoi of Moscow wins first major Russian victory over Golden Horde.

1381 Peasants' Revolt in England under Wat Tyler.

1384 Death of John Wyclif.

1385 Battle of Aljubarotta: Portugal safeguards independence from Castile.

1386 Battle of Sempach: Swiss safeguard independence from Habsburgs. Jagiello (Vladislav V) unites Lithuania and Poland.

1389 Battle of Kossovo: crushing defeat of Serbs and neighbouring nations by Turks.

1396 Battle of Nicopolis: "the last crusade" annihilated by Turks.

1397 Union of Kalmar: Denmark, Norway and Sweden united under one crown: dissolved 1448.

1398 Timur invades and pillages Northern India.

1399 Richard II deposed by Henry IV: first of the Lancastrian kings of England.

1400 Owen Glendower revolts in Wales. Death of Chaucer.

1401 De Haeretico Comburendo: the burning of heretics made legal in England.

1410 Battle of Tannenberg: Poles and Lithuanians break power of Teutonic Knights.

1415 Battle of Agincourt: great success of Henry V of England in France. Council of Constance ends Great Schism, burns John Hus.

1420 Treaty of Troyes: English claims to French throne recognised. Hussite Wars begin: Bohemian heretics defend themselves successfully.

A.D.

1429 Relief of Orleans by Joan of Arc.

1431 Burning of Joan of Arc.

1433 Rounding of Cape Bojador: first great achievement in exploration ordered by Henry the Navigator.

1434 Cosimo dei Medici begins his family's control of Florence.

1435 Congress of Arras: Burgundians withdraw support from England, in favour of France.

1438 Albert I becomes Emperor—the first Habsburg Emperor.

1440 Death of Jan van Eyck.

1450 Rebellion of Jack Cade against government of Henry VI of England.

1453 Battle of Castillon: final English defeat and end of Hundred Years' War. Constantinople taken by Turks: end of Byzantine or Eastern Roman Empire.

RENAISSANCE, DISCOVERIES, "NEW MONARCHIES"

1454 First dated printing from movable types in Europe: Papal indulgence printed at Mainz.

1455 First battle of St. Albans: beginning of Wars of the Roses.

1458 Mathias Corvinus becomes king of Hungary. George of Podiebrad becomes king of Bohemia.

1461 Battle of Towton: Yorkist victory in a particularly bloody battle. Louis XI becomes king of France.

1467 Charles the Bold becomes Duke of Burgundy.

1469 Marriage of Ferdinand of Aragon with Isabella of Castile: union of the main kingdoms of Spain. Lorenzo the Magnificent becomes ruler of Florence.

1470 Warwick ("The Kingmaker") turns Lancastrian, dethrones Edward IV.

1471 Return of Edward IV: Lancastrians crushed at Barnet and Tewkesbury. Ivan III of Moscow takes Novgorod: Muscovy rising to supremacy in Russia.

1476 Caxton sets up his press at Westminster.

1477 Battle of Nancy: defeat and death of Charles the Bold: end of the greatness of Burgundy.

1479 Pazzi conspiracy against the Medici in Florence.

1481 Inquisition becomes active in Castile (1484 in Aragon).

1485 Battle of Bosworth Field: beginning of Tudor period in England.

1487 Lambert Simnel's rising fails.

1488 Bartholomew Diaz rounds Cape of Good Hope.

1491 Brittany acquired by King of France (by marriage).

1492 Rodrigo Borgia becomes Pope Alexander VI. Granada, last Moorish foothold in Western Europe, conquered by Spain. Christopher Columbus discovers the West Indies.

1493 Sonni Ali brings Songhai Empire to height of its prestige: Timbuktu renowned centre of literary culture.

1494 Italy invaded by French led by Charles VIII: beginning of Italian Wars and "modern" European diplomacy and international relations. Treaty of Tordesillas: Spain and Portugal agree to divide unexplored part of world: subsequently approved by Pope.

1496 Hapsburg-Spanish marriages: foundation of later empires.

1497 Perkin Warbeck captured by Henry VII (hanged 1499). John Cabot discovers Newfoundland.

1498 Savonarola burned. Vasco da Gama at Calicut: the sea route to India found.

1499 Amerigo Vespucci charts part of the South American coast.

A.D.
1500 Brazil discovered by Pedro Cabral.

1503 Casa de Contratación established at Seville; beginnings of Spanish colonial government. Fall of Caesar Borgia.

1507 Affonso de Albuquerque becomes Viceroy of Portuguese Empire in the East.

1513 Accession of Pope Leo X, zenith of Renaissance Papacy. Machiavelli writes *The Prince*. Balboa discovers the Pacific (South Sea). Battle of Flodden: James IV of Scotland defeated and killed by English.

1514 Battle of Chaldiran: Turkish victory begins long series of wars between Turkish and Persian Empires.

REFORMATION, HAPSBURG–VALOIS WARS

1515 Francis I becomes king of France: victory of Marignano ends legend of Swiss invincibility. Thomas Wolsey becomes Lord Chancellor of England and Cardinal.

1516 Algiers taken by Barbarossa; beginning of the Corsairs.

1517 Martin Luther nails up his Ninety-five Theses: beginning of the Reformation. Turks conquer Egypt.

1519 Charles V inherits Hapsburg lands and elected emperor. Magellan begins first circumnavigation of the world. Death of Leonardo da Vinci.

1520 Suleiman the Magnificent becomes Sultan; Turkish power at its height. Field of Cloth of Gold; celebrated diplomatic meeting, spectacular but with no results.

1521 Mexico conquered by Hernando Cortes. Belgrade taken by the Turks. Diet of Worms: Luther commits himself irrevocably. Charles V divides his dominions: Austrian and Spanish Hapsburgs.

1522 Rhodes taken by the Turks; Knights of St. John move to Malta. Election of Adrian VI, last non-Italian Pope.

1523 Swedes expel Danish overlords, elect Gustavus Vasa King.   [(1525).

1524 Peasants' War in Germany (suppressed
1525 Battle of Pavia: defeat and capture of Francis I by Imperialists.

1526 Battle of Mohács: Turkish victory ends Hungarian independence. Foundation of Danubian Hapsburg Monarchy (Hungarian and Bohemian crowns united with Austrian patrimony of Hapsburgs): Holy Roman Empire prolonged for 300 years. Battle of Panipat: Babar begins Moslem conquest of India, founds Mogul Empire.

1527 Sack of Rome by Imperialists. Italy under control of Charles V.

1529 Siege of Vienna by the Turks. Peace of Cambrai; pause in Hapsburg–Valois struggle, end of serious French intervention in Italy. Diet of Speyer: origin of the name Protestant.

1532 Peru conquered by Francisco Pizarro.

1533 Ivan IV (the Terrible) becomes Tsar. Marriage of Henry VIII and Catherine of Aragon declared null.

1534 Act of Supremacy: Henry VIII asserts control over English Church.

1535 Coverdale's English Bible printed. Execution of Thomas More and John Fisher.

1536 Execution of Anne Boleyn. Dissolution of smaller Monasteries by Henry VIII and Thomas Cromwell (remainder dissolved 1539). Pilgrimage of Grace: Northern rising because of religious grievances.   [de Quesada.

1538 Chibchas of Bogota conquered by Gonzalo

1540 Francisco de Coronado begins explorations in North America. Society of Jesus recognised by Pope.

1541 John Calvin regains authority in Geneva.

1542 First Portuguese reach Japan. New Laws of the Indies: first attempt to legislate for welfare of colonial natives, by Spanish government.

1543 Death of Copernicus.   [Reformation.

1545 Opening of Council of Trent: the Counter-

A.D.
1547 Death of Henry VIII: Somerset Protector in the name of the boy king, Edward VI.

1549 First English Book of Common Prayer. Kett's Rebellion in Norfolk, because of economic grievances.

1550 Deposition of Protector Somerset: Northumberland rules England.

1553 Lady Jane Grey proclaimed Queen by Northumberland on death of Edward VI: Mary I succeeds. Servetus burned by Calvin.

1555 Latimer and Ridley burned by Mary. Religious Peace of Augsburg: policy of *cuius regio, eius religio* accepted in Germany.

1556 Charles V abdicates imperial powers in favour of brother Ferdinand. Cranmer burned. Akbar becomes Mogul Emperor (d. 1605).

1557 Macao becomes permanent Portuguese port in China.

1558 Calais lost by English to French. Elizabeth I becomes Queen of England.

1559 Peace of Cateau-Cambrésis: end of Hapsburg–Valois duel.

RELIGIOUS WARS

1561 Mary, Queen of Scots, returns to Scotland.

1562 First War of Religion in France: wars continue intermittently until 1598.

1563 Thirty-nine Articles define Elizabethan Church settlement.

1564 Birth of Shakespeare; death of Michelangelo.

1565 Malta beats off Turks.

1567 Deposition of Mary, Queen of Scots. Alva in the Netherlands: severe rule.

1568 Flight of Mary, Queen of Scots, to England: imprisonment. San Juan de Ulua: defeat of Hawkins, and end of his slave-trading voyages. Beginning of Anglo-Spanish maritime feud. Revolt of Moriscos of Granada (suppressed 1570).   [England.

1569 Rebellion of Northern Earls (Catholic) in

1570 Elizabeth I anathematised by Pope.

1571 Battle of Lepanto: spectacular defeat of Turkish sea-power by Don John of Austria. Bornu (or Kanem) in Central Sudan at its zenith under Idris III.

1572 Dutch "Sea Beggars" take Brill. Massacre of St. Bartholomew in France. Polish Crown elective again, on death of Sigismund II.

1576 Catholic League formed in France, led by Guise family.   [1580).

1577 Drake begins voyage round world (returns

1578 Battle of Alcazar-Quivir: death of King Sebastian of Portugal. Parma re-establishes Spanish rule in Southern Netherlands.

1579 Union of Utrecht: seven northern provinces of Netherlands form what becomes Dutch Republic. Death of Grand Vizier Sokolli: decline of Turkish power begins.

1580 Philip II of Spain becomes king of Portugal.

1582 Gregorian Calendar (or New Style) introduced by Pope Gregory XIII.

1584 Assassination of William the Silent.

1585 Hidéyoshi Dictator of Japan: unification of the country. English intervention in Spanish–Dutch War.

1587 Execution of Mary, Queen of Scots. Drake "singes King of Spain's beard." Shah Abbas I (the Great) becomes ruler of Persia (d. 1629).

1588 Spanish Armada defeated.

1589 Death of Catherine de' Medici, Queen-Mother of France.

1591 Songhai Empire destroyed by troops from Morocco.

1593 Henry IV of France becomes Catholic.

1598 Edict of Nantes: French Protestants guaranteed liberty of worship. End of French Wars of Religion.

1600 English East India Company founded. Tokugawa Period begins in Japan (Ieyasu takes title of Shogun, 1603): lasts until 1868.

A.D.

1601 Rebellion and execution of Earl of Essex. Elizabethan Poor Law.

1602 Dutch East India Company founded.

1603 Irish revolts finally suppressed by Mountjoy. Accession of James VI of Scotland as James I of England: Union of English and Scottish Crowns.

1604 Hampton Court Conference: James I disappoints Puritans.

1605 Gunpowder Plot.

1607 Virginia colonised by London company: Jamestown founded.

1608 Quebec founded by Champlain.

1609 Twelve Years' Truce between Spain and United Provinces: Dutch independence in fact secured. Expulsion of Moriscos from Spain.

1610 Assassination of Henry IV of France.

1611 Plantation of Ulster with English and Scottish colonists. Authorised Version of the Bible in England.

1613 Michael Romanov becomes Czar: the first of the dynasty.

1614 Napier publishes his explanation of logarithms.

1616 Death of Shakespeare and Cervantes. Edict of Inquisition against Galileo's astronomy.

1618 "Defenestration of Prague": Bohemian assertion of independence begins Thirty Years' War.

1620 Pilgrim Fathers settle in New England.

1624 "Massacre of Amboina": English driven out of spice islands by Dutch. Richelieu becomes Chief Minister in France.

1628 Murder of Duke of Buckingham. Petition of Right by Commons to Charles I. Fall of La Rochelle: French Protestants lose political power. Harvey publishes his work on the circulation of blood.

1629 Charles I begins Personal Rule.

1630 Gustavus Adolphus of Sweden enters Thirty Years' War, turns tide against Imperialists.

1631 Sack of Magdeburg, one of the worst incidents of the Thirty Years' War.

1632 Battle of Lützen: death of Gustavus Adolphus.

1633 William Laud appointed Archbishop of Canterbury. Thomas Wentworth takes up his post as Lord Deputy of Ireland.

1634 Dismissal and murder of Imperialist general Wallenstein.

1635 John Hampden refuses to pay Ship Money.

1636 Japanese forbidden to go abroad.

1637 Russian pioneers reach shores of Pacific.

1638 Covenant widely signed in Scotland.

1639 First Bishops' War: Charles I comes to terms with Scots.

1640 Second Bishops' War: Charles I defeated by Scots. Long Parliament begins: abolition of Royal prerogatives. Great Elector (Frederick William) becomes ruler of Brandenburg. Revolt of Catalonia (finally suppressed 1659). Revolt of Portugal: Duke of Braganza proclaimed king.

1641 Japanese exclude all foreigners (except for small Dutch trading fleet). Massacre of Protestants in Ireland. Wentworth (Earl of Strafford) executed. Grand Remonstrance of Commons to Charles I.

1642 Charles I attempts to arrest the Five Members. Outbreak of English Civil War: first general engagement, Edgehill. Death of Richelieu.

1643 Mazarin becomes Chief Minister of France. Battle of Rocroi: French victory, end of Spanish reputation for invincibility. English Parliament agrees to Solemn League and Covenant, secures services of Scots army.

1644 Marston Moor: decisive battle of English Civil War. North lost to Charles I. Tippemuir: Montrose begins victorious Royalist

A.D.

campaign in Scotland. Ch'ing Dynasty (Manchu) in China.

1645 Formation of New Model Army. Naseby: main Royalist army crushed. Battle of Philiphaugh: Montrose's army destroyed.

1646 Charles I surrenders to Scots.

1647 Charles I handed over to Parliament. Charles I seized by Army. Charles I flees to Carisbrooke Castle.

1648 Second Civil War: New Model Army defeats Scots and Royalists. "Pride's Purge": Parliament refashioned by Army. Peace of Westphalia ends Thirty Years' War.

ASCENDANCY OF FRANCE

1649 Charles I executed. England governed as Commonwealth. Cromwell in Ireland. New Code of Laws in Russia completes establishment of serfdom.

1651 Battle of Worcester: Cromwell's final victory, now master of all Britain. First English Navigation Act. Hobbes' *Leviathan* published.

1652 Foundation of Cape Colony by Dutch under Van Riebeek. First Anglo-Dutch War begins (ends 1654).

1653 Cromwell dissolves Rump, becomes Protector.

1655 Major-Generals appointed to supervise districts of England. Jamaica seized by English.

1656 Grand Vizier Kiuprili: revival of Turkish government.

1658 Death of Cromwell.

1659 Peace of the Pyrenees: France replaces Spain as greatest power in Western Europe.

1660 Restoration of monarchy in Britain: Charles II. Royal Society founded.

1661 Death of Mazarin: Louis XIV now rules in person. "Clarendon Code"; beginning of persecution of Non-conformists in England.

1664 New York taken by English: Second Anglo-Dutch War ensues (ends 1667).

1665 Great Plague of London.

1666 Great Fire of London. Newton's discovery of law of gravitation.

1667 Dutch fleet in the Medway. War of Devolution begins: first of Louis XIV's aggressions.

1668 Portuguese Independence recognised by Spain.

1669 Death of Rembrandt.

1670 Secret Treaty of Dover between Charles II and Louis XIV. Revolt of peasants and Don Cossacks under Stenka Razin (suppressed 1671).

1672 Third Anglo-Dutch War begins (ends 1674). Murder of De Witt brothers: William of Orange becomes leader of Dutch against French invasion.

1673 Test Act deprives English Catholics and Non-conformists of public offices. Death of Molière.

1675 Battle of Fehrbellin: Swedes defeated by Great Elector; rise of Prussian military power.

1678 "Popish Plot" of Titus Oates utilised by Shaftesbury and the Whigs to bring pressure on Charles II.

1679 Bothwell Brig: suppression of Scottish Covenanters. Habeas Corpus Act passed.

1680 Chambers of Reunion: Louis XIV uses legal arguments to complete annexation of Alsace.

1681 Oxford Parliament: Charles II overcomes his opponents, begins to rule without Parliament.

1683 Rye House Plot. Siege of Vienna by the Turks: last major Turkish attack on Europe.

1685 Sedgemoor: Monmouth's rebellion crushed by James II. Revocation of Edict of Nantes: persecution of French Protestants by Louis XIV.

A.D.

1675 Greenwich Royal Observatory founded.

1688 Seven Bishops protest against James II's policy of toleration, and are acquitted. William of Orange lands in England: flight of James II. "The Glorious Revolution."

1689 Derry relieved: failure of James II to subdue Irish Protestants. Killiecrankie: death of Dundee and collapse of Highland rising. Bill of Rights defines liberties established by "Glorious Revolution."

1690 Locke's *Two Treatises on Government* published. Beachy Head: French victory over Anglo-Dutch fleet. Boyne: defeat of James II by William III.

1691 Capitulation of Limerick: surrender of Irish supporters of James II on conditions which are not fulfilled.

1692 Massacre of Glencoe: Government's "lesson" to Highlanders. La Hogue: Anglo-Dutch fleet regains command of the sea.

1693 National Debt of England begun.

1694 Bank of England founded.

1695 Press licensing abandoned: freedom of the press in England.

1696 Peter the Great sole Czar.

1697 Peace of Ryswyck between Louis XIV and William III. Peter journeys "incognito" to the West.

1699 Treaty of Karlowitz: great Turkish concessions to Austrians. Death of Racine.

1700 Great Northern War, involving all Baltic powers, begins (ends 1721). Battle of Narva: Russians defeated by Charles XII of Sweden. Death of Charles II of Spain: under French influence Louis XIV's grandson Philip of Anjou named successor.

1701 War of the Spanish Succession begins. Hungarian revolt led by Francis Rakoczi against Austrians. Elector of Brandenburg receives title of King of Prussia. Act of Settlement establishes Protestant Hanoverian Succession in England.

1703 Methuen Treaty between England and Portugal. St. Petersburg founded.

1704 Gibraltar taken by Rooke. Blenheim: Marlborough stops France from winning war.

1706 Ramillies: Marlborough's second great victory. Turin: Eugene defeats French in Italy.

1707 Almanza: Anglo-Austrian forces in Spain defeated by French under Berwick. Act of Union: English and Scottish Parliaments united. Death of Aurungzib, last powerful Mogul.

1708 Oudenarde: Marlborough's third great victory.

1709 Pultava: Charles XII's invasion of Russia smashed by Peter the Great. Malplaquet: Marlborough's fourth great victory—at great cost in lives.

1710 Tory government in England.

1711 Dismissal of Marlborough.

1713 Peace of Utrecht: England makes advantageous peace with Louis XIV. Bourbon king of Spain grants Asiento (monopoly of Spanish American slave trade) to England.

1714 Peace of Rastatt between France and Austria. Death of Queen Anne: accession of George I. Beginning of Hanoverian Dynasty in Britain. Whig oligarchy rules.

1715 Jacobite Rising defeated at Preston and Sheriffmuir. Death of Louis XIV. France under Regent Orleans.

ENLIGHTENED DESPOTS: FIRST BRITISH EMPIRE

1716 Septennial Act: English Parliament prolongs its life from three to seven years.

1717 Belgrade taken by Austrians under Eugene.

1720 Collapse of Law's system of banking ("Mississippi Bubble") in France. "South Se Bubble" in England.

A.D.

1721 Robert Walpole becomes first Prime Minister. Peace of Nystad: Sweden no longer a major power at end of Great Northern War. Russian gains.

1723 Death of Christopher Wren.

1727 First Indemnity Act for Non-conformists.

1729 Methodists begin at Oxford.

1730 Resignation from government of Townshend, who becomes agricultural pioneer.

1733 First Family Compact between Bourbon kings of France and Spain. Withdrawal of Walpole's Excise Bill. John Kay invents flying shuttle, first of the great textile inventions. Jethro Tell publishes *The Horse-Hoing Husbandry*, advocating new agricultural methods.

1738 Lorraine ceded to France.

1739 Nadir Shah with Persian army sacks Delhi, ruins Mogul power. War of Jenkins' Ear begins between Spain and Britain.

1740 Frederick II (the Great) becomes king of Prussia. Maria Theresa succeeds to Austrian dominions. Frederick siezes Silesia, begins War of the Austrian Succession.

1742 Fall of Walpole.

1743 Dettingen: George II, last British king to command his army in the field, defeats French.

1745 Fontenoy: Duke of Cumberland defeated by Marshal Saxe. Jacobite Rebellion under Prince Charles Edward: initial success, victory of Prestonpans, march to Derby.

1746 Culloden: Jacobites destroyed by Cumberland.

1748 Treaty of Aix-la-Chapelle: Frederick retains Silesia, elsewhere status quo.

1750 Death of J. S. Bach.

1751 First volume of the *Encyclopédie* published in France. Clive takes and holds Arcot: checks plans of Dupleix in Southern India. Chinese conquest of Tibet.

1752 Britain adopts New Style calendar.

1753 British Museum begun by government purchase of Sloane's collection.

1755 Lisbon earthquake. Braddock's defeat and death at the hands of French and Indians.

1756 Diplomatic Revolution (alliance of Austria with France) achieved by Kaunitz; Britain and Prussia perforce became allies. Seven Years' War begins. Minorca taken from British by French (Byng executed 1757). Black Hole of Calcutta: suffocation of many British prisoners.

1757 Pitt Secretary of State, main influence in British government. Rossbach: one of Frederick II's numerous victories against heavy odds. Plassey: Clive conquers Bengal.

1759 "Year of Victories" for Britain: Quebec, Minden, Lagos, Quiberon Bay. James Brindley designs Worsley-Manchester Canal: the beginning of this form of transport in Britain. Voltaire publishes *Candide*. Death of Handel.

1760 Wandewash: decisive defeat of French in India, by Coote.

1761 Panipat: Mahrattas heavily defeated by Afghans. Fall of Pitt.

1762 Catherine II (the Great) becomes Czarina. Rousseau's *Social Contract* and *Emile* published.

1763 Peace of Paris: British colonial gains, First British Empire at its height. Peace of Hubertusburg: Frederick II retains his gains. Pontiac's Conspiracy: failure of Red Indian attempt to destroy British power.

1764 John Wilkes expelled from Commons. James Hargreaves invents spinning jenny.

1766 Henry Cavendish proves hydrogen to be an element.

1768 Royal Academy of Arts founded.

1769 Richard Arkwright erects spinning mill (invention of water frame).

1770 Struensee comes to power in Denmark (executed 1772). "Boston Massacre." James Cook discovers New South Wales.

1772 First Partition of Poland between Russia, Prussia, and Austria.

A.D.
1773 Society of Jesus suppressed by Pope (restored 1814). Revolt led by Pugachov in Russia (suppressed 1775). "Boston Tea Party."

1774 Warren Hastings appointed first Governor-General of India. Treaty of Kutchuk Kainarji: great Turkish concessions to Russia. Karl Scheele discovers chlorine. Joseph Priestley's discovery of oxygen.

1775 Watt and Boulton in partnership at Soho Engineering Works, Birmingham. Lexington: first action in American War of Independence.

1776 American Declaration of Independence. Adam Smith's *Wealth of Nations* published.

1777 Saratoga: surrender of British army under Burgoyne to Americans.

1779 Beginning of great Franco-Spanish siege of Gibraltar (raised finally, 1783). Samuel Crompton invents spinning mule.

1780 Joseph II assumes sole power in Austria. Armed neutrality of maritime nations to restrain British interference with shipping.

1781 Joseph II introduces religious toleration, abolishes serfdom in Austria. Yorktown: surrender of British under Cornwallis to American and French forces.

1782 Battle of the Saints: Rodney's victory saves British West Indies.

1783 Treaty of Versailles: American independence recognised. Pitt the Younger becomes Prime Minister of Britain. First flights in hot-air (Montgolfier) and hydrogen (Charles) balloons.

1784 Death of Dr. Samuel Johnson.

1785 Edmund Cartwright invents the power loom.

1787 American Constitution drafted.

1788 Impeachment of Warren Hastings begins (ends 1795).

FRENCH REVOLUTION AND NAPOLEON

1789 Washington first President of U.S.A. French Revolution begins. Storming of the Bastille (July 14).

1790 Civil constitution of the Clergy in France.

1791 Flight of Louis XVI and Marie Antoinette to Varennes.

1792 Battle of Valmy: French Revolution saved from intervention of European kings. Denmark becomes first country to prohibit slave trade. France becomes a Republic.

1793 Louis XVI beheaded. Second partition of Poland.

1794 "Glorious First of June." Fall of Robespierre and end of Jacobin Republic. Negro revolt in Haiti led by Toussaint L'Ouverture.

1795 The Directory established. "Whiff of Grapeshot": Napoleon Bonaparte disperses Paris mob, Oct. 5. Batavian Republic set up by France.

1796 First Italian campaign of Bonaparte: victories of Lodi, Arcola.

1797 Treaty of Campo Formio: Bonaparte compels Austria to make peace. Britain left to fight France alone.

1798 Bonaparte goes to Egypt. Battle of the Nile. Vinegar Hill rebellion in Ireland suppressed.

1799 New coalition against France: Suvorov and Russians victorious in Italy. Bonaparte returns to France. *Coup d'état* of Brumaire, Nov. 9. Consulate set up.

1800 Parliamentary Union of Great Britain and Ireland.

1801 Treaty of Lunéville: Austria makes peace; great French gains in Germany.

1802 Peace of Amiens between Britain and France. *Charlotte Dundas*, first practical steamship, on Clyde.

1803 Insurrection in Ireland under Robert Emmet. Britain again at war with France.

A.D.
1804 Bonaparte becomes Emperor. Spain declares war against Great Britain. Serbian revolt against Turks under Kara George.

1805 Battle of Trafalgar, Nelson's great victory and death, Oct. 21. Battle of Austerlitz, Dec. 2.

1806 Death of Pitt, Jan. 23. Confederation of the Rhine: Napoleon's reorganisation of Germany, July 12. End of Holy Roman Empire, Aug. 6. Prussia overthrown at Jena. Napoleon declares Great Britain in a state of blockade—"Continental System."

1807 Slave trade abolished in British Empire. Treaty of Tilsit: with Alexander of Russia his friend, Napoleon controls all of Europe. Occupation of Portugal by French, to enforce Continental Blockade.

1808 Occupation of Spain by French. Spanish rising: guerrilla warfare. Peninsular War begins. Battle of Vimeiro (defeat of French by Wellington), Aug. 21.

1809 Battle of Corunna and death of Sir John Moore, Jan. 16. Attempted risings in Germany against Napoleon: Austria renews war. Treaty of Schönbrunn, Oct. 14.

1810 Self-government established in Argentina: first South American state to become independent of Spain.

1811 Massacre of Mamelukes at Cairo. Luddite riots.

1812 Retreat from Moscow: destruction of Napoleon's Grand Army.

1813 War of Liberation starts in Germany. Defeat of French by Wellington at Vitoria, June 21.

1814 Soult defeated by Wellington at Toulouse, April 10. Abdication of Napoleon, April 11; Louis XVIII king of France. Congress of Vienna (concluded June 1815) under guidance of Metternich. Resettlement of Europe, usually by restoration of kings. Germanic Confederation under Austrian supervision. Poland ruled by Czar. Kingdom of Netherlands to include Belgium.

THE OLD ORDER RESTORED

1815 Escape of Napoleon from Elba. Battle of Waterloo, June 18. Corn Law in Britain to safeguard agricultural interests by keeping up prices. Quadruple Alliance (Austria, Russia, Prussia, Britain) to maintain Vienna settlement and hold regular meetings (" Congress System ") —frequently confused with Holy Alliance, which was simply a declaration of Christian principles. Napoleon sent to St. Helena, Oct. 16.

1818 Bernadotte made king of Sweden (Charles XIV), Feb. 6.

1819 Singapore founded by Stamford Raffles. Beginnings of Zollverein (Customs Union) in Germany under Prussian influence. Parliamentary reform meeting at Manchester dispersed by military (" Peterloo "), Aug. 16.

1820 Death of George III, Jan. 29.

1821 Death of Napoleon at St. Helena, May 5.

1822 Congress of Verona: congress system breaks down with refusal of Britain (Canning) to intervene against revolutions.

1823 "Monroe Doctrine" announced by U.S.A. President, Dec. 2.

1824 Repeal of Combination Acts in Britain which had forbidden Trades Unions. Charles X king of France.

1825 Independence of all Spanish American mainland now achieved. Nicholas I Czar of Russia. First railway, Stockton to Darlington, opened.

1826 First crossing of Atlantic under steam by Dutch ship *Curaçao*. Menai suspension bridge opened.

1827 Battle of Navarino, Turkish and Egyptian fleet destroyed. Death of Beethoven.

1828 Death of Chaka, great Zulu conqueror.

1829 Greece independent. Catholic Emancipation Act in Britain. Metropolitan Police established.

A.D.

1830 Death of George IV, June 26. Louis Philippe ousts Charles X. Belgium breaks away from Holland. Russian Poland revolts ineffectually.

1831 First Reform Bill introduced by Lord John Russell. Leopold of Saxe-Coburg becomes king of independent Belgium. British Association founded. Faraday discovers electromagnetic induction.

1832 Reform Bill passed, June 7. Walter Scott, Jeremy Bentham, and Goethe die. Electric telegraph invented by Morse.

1833 Beginning of "Oxford Movement" in English Church. First government grant made to English schools. First British Factory Act.

1834 Poor Law Amendment Act: tightening up of relief in Britain. "Tolpuddle Martyrs" victimised to discourage British working-class movement. Carlist wars begin in Spain.

1835 Municipal Reform Act revises British local government. The word "socialism" first used. "Tamworth Manifesto" of Peel defines aims of Conservative Party.

1836 People's Charter states programme of Chartists. Great Trek of Boers from British South African territory. Texas achieves independence of Mexico.

1837 Queen Victoria succeeds to the throne.

1838 National Gallery opened.

1839 First Afghan war begins. Chartist riots at Birmingham and Newport. Anti-Corn Law League founded. Aden annexed by Britain.

1840 Penny postage instituted. Queen Victoria marries Prince Albert of Saxe-Coburg-Gotha. "Opium War" with China begins. Union Act gives Canada responsible government. Last convicts landed in New South Wales.

1841 Hong Kong acquired by Britain.

1842 Chartists present second national petition and put themselves at the head of strikes.

1846 Repeal of the Corn Laws. Peel resigns.

1847 British Museum opened.

REVOLUTIONS AND NEW NATIONS

1848 Monster meeting of Chartists on Kennington Common, procession abandoned, Apr. 10. General revolutionary movement throughout the Continent. Louis Philippe abdicates: French Republic proclaimed. Swiss Federal Constitution established after defeat of Sonderbund (Catholic secession movement). Rising in Vienna: flight of Metternich, accession of Francis Joseph. Nationalist risings in Bohemia and Hungary. Frankfurt Parliament: attempt to unite Germany on liberal principles. Communist Manifesto produced by Marx and Engels. U.S.A. makes great territorial gains from Mexico. Gold discovered in California.

1849 Collapse of revolutionary movements. Rome republic besieged by French (June 3), defended by Garibaldi, holds out until July 2. Austrians take Venice, Aug. 22. Repeal of old Navigation Laws. Punjab annexed by Britain.

1850 Cavour becomes Prime Minister of Piedmont. Don Pacifico affair; privileges of British citizenship at their highest defended by Palmerston.

1851 Great Exhibition in Hyde Park. First satisfactory submarine telegraph cable between Dover and Calais laid. Gold discovered in Australia.

1852 Independence of Transvaal recognised by Britain. Napoleon III Emperor of the French.

1853 Perry lands in Japan: beginning of Western influence. Russia and Turkey at war.

1854 War declared against Russia by France and Britain. Allied armies land in Crimea, Sept. 14 (Alma, Siege of Sevastopol, Balaklava, Inkerman). Orange Free State set up.

1855 Sardinia joins Britain and France against Russia. Fall of Sevastopol and end of Crimean War. Alexander II Czar of Russia.

A.D.

1856 Peace Treaty signed at Paris. Bessemer invents process for large-scale production of steel. Livingstone completes journey across Africa.

1857 Indian Mutiny. Relief of Lucknow. Canton captured by English and French.

1858 *Great Eastern* launched. Crown assumes government of India. Treaty of Aigun, by which China cedes Amur region to Russia.

1859 Darwin publishes *Origin of Species*. French support for Piedmont in war with Austria (Magenta, Solferino). Piedmont receives Lombardy. Harper's Ferry raid: John Brown hanged, Dec. 2.

1860 Garibaldi and the Thousand Redshirts in Sicily and Naples; most of Italy united to Piedmont. Vladivostok founded; Russia strongly established on N.W. Pacific.

1861 Abraham Lincoln takes office as Pres. of U.S. American Civil War commences with 11 states breaking away to form Southern Confederacy. Bull Run (July 21) Confederate success ends Federal hopes of easy victory. Victor Emmanuel proclaimed by first Italian Parliament as king of Italy. Emancipation of Serfs in Russia. Death of Prince Albert, Dec. 14.

1862 Bismarck becomes leading minister in Prussia. Garibaldi attempts to seize Rome but wounded at Aspromonte, Aug. 29. Cotton famine in Lancashire.

1863 Polish rising against Russia (suppressed 1864). French in Mexico. Battle of Gettysburg, July 1–3. Maximilian of Austria made emperor of Mexico.

1864 Cession of Schleswig-Holstein to Prussia and Austria. First Socialist International formed. Taiping rebellion in China ended. Federal army enters Atlanta, Sept. 2: General Sherman captures Savannah (" From Atlanta to the sea "), Dec. 22. Geneva Convention originated.

1865 Death of Cobden, Apr. 2. General Lee surrenders to Grant, Apr. 9. Lincoln assassinated, Apr. 14. Thirteenth Amendment to Constitution: slavery abolished in U.S. Death of Palmerston, Oct. 18. Lister introduces antiseptic surgery in Glasgow. Tashkent becomes centre of Russian expansion in Central Asia. Mendel experiments on heredity. William Booth founds Salvation Army.

1866 Austro-Prussian War over Schleswig-Holstein ("Seven Weeks War"). Prussian victory at Sadowa (July 3). Venice secured for Italy, who had, however, been defeated by Austrians at Custozza (June 24) and Lissa (July 20). Treaty of Prague, Aug. 23.

1867 North German Confederation founded. Emperor Maximilian of Mexico shot. Dominion of Canada established. Russia sells Alaska to America for $7 million. Garibaldi makes second attempt to seize Rome, but defeated by Pope with French support at Mentana, Nov. 3. Second Parliamentary Reform Bill passed (Disraeli "dished the Whigs").

1868 Shogunate abolished in Japan: Meiji period of rapid Westernisation under Imperial leadership begins. Ten Years' War (1868–78); struggle for Cuban independence from Spain. Disraeli succeeds Derby as Prime Minister but defeated in general election by Gladstone, Nov.

1869 General Grant, Pres. of U.S. Irish Church disestablished. Suez Canal formally opened.

1870 Napoleon III declares war against Prussia. French defeated at Woerth, Gravelotte, and Sedan. Paris besieged. Rome and Papal states annexed to kingdom of Italy. Irish Land Act passed. Forster's Education Act puts elementary education within reach of all British children. Papal Infallibility announced.

1871 William I of Prussia proclaimed emperor of Germany at Versailles, Jan. 18. Paris capitulates, Jan. 28. Commune of Paris proclaimed, Mar. 28. Peace signed at Frankfurt-on-Main, May 10. Government troops enter Paris and

A.D.

crush Communards, May 28. Thiers President of the Republic, Aug. 31. Mont Cenis tunnel opened. Trade Unions in Britain legalised.

RIVAL IMPERIAL POWERS

1872 Ballot introduced in Britain. Death of Mazzini, Mar. 10.

1873 Death of Livingstone, May 4. Ashanti war.

1874 Disraeli succeeds Gladstone as Prime Minister.

1875 England purchases Khedive's shares in Suez Canal, Nov.

1876 Bulgarian massacres. Serbo-Turkish war. Bell invents the telephone. Custer defeated and killed in last large-scale Red Indian success. Porfirio Diaz in power in Mexico (until 1911).

1877 Victoria declared Empress of India. Transvaal annexed to British Empire. War between Russia and Turkey. Satsuma rebellion in Japan: final unsuccessful attempt to halt new ideas.

1878 Congress of Berlin: general Balkan settlement. Cyprus ceded to Britain. Second war with Afghanistan (ended 1880). Edison and Swan produce first successful incandescent electric light.

1879 Dual control (Britain and France) in Egypt. Zulu War. Gladstone's Midlothian Campaign. Tay Bridge destroyed, Dec. 28.

1880 Beaconsfield ministry succeeded by second Gladstone ministry. Transvaal declared a republic.

1881 British defeat at Majuba: independence of Transvaal recognised. France occupies Tunis. Gambetta becomes Prime Minister of France. Revolt of the Mahdi in the Sudan. Pasteur's famous immunisation experiment to show that inoculated animals can survive anthrax.

1882 Lord Frederick Cavendish, Irish Secretary, assassinated in Phoenix Park, Dublin, May 6. Triple Alliance (Germany, Austria, Italy) first formed. Alexandria bombarded, July 11. Cairo occupied by British troops, Sept. 14.

1883 National Insurance begun in Germany. Death of Wagner.

1884 Wolseley heads expedition to Khartoum to rescue Gordon. French establish complete protectorate in Indo-China. Evelyn Baring takes over administration of Egypt. Russians capture Merv. Berlin Conference defines rights of European Powers in Africa. Third Parliamentary Reform Bill. Parsons invents his turbine. Greenwich meridian internationally recognised as prime meridian. Fabian Society founded.

1885 Khartoum captured; Gordon slain, Jan. 26.

1886 Upper Burma annexed by Britain. Home Rule Bill defeated in Commons. All Indians in U.S.A. now in Reservations. Daimler produces his first motor car. Completion of Canadian Pacific Railway. Gold discovered in the Transvaal.

1887 Queen Victoria's Jubilee celebration, June 21.

1888 William II German Emperor. County Councils set up in Britain.

1889 Mayerling: tragic death of Prince Rudolf of Austria, Jan. 30. Flight of General Boulanger, after attempting to become master of France. Second Socialist International set up. Great London dock strike, Aug. 15–Sept. 16. Parnell Commission concludes sittings, Nov. 23 (129th day).

1890 Parnell ruined by divorce case: Irish politicians split. Sherman Anti-Trust Law: first attempt in U.S.A. to break cartels. Opening of Forth Bridge, Mar. 4. Bismarck resigns, Mar. 17, Caprivi succeeds. Heligoland ceded to Germany.

1891 The United States of Brazil formed.

1892 Panama Canal financial scandals in France.

1893 Home Rule Bill passes third reading in Commons, Sept. 1: Lords reject Bill, Sept. 8.

1894 Opening of Manchester Ship Canal, Jan. 1.

A.D.

Gladstone resigns, Mar. 3, Lord Rosebery succeeds. Armenian massacres by Turks: repeated at intervals for next quarter of century. Japan declares war against China. Dreyfus convicted of treason.

1895 Opening of Kiel canal, June 21. Rosebery resigns, June 22; Salisbury Ministry succeeds. Treaty of Shimonoseki: Japan gets Formosa, free hand in Korea. New Cuban revolution breaks out against Spanish. Marconi sends message over a mile by wireless. Röntgen discovers X-rays. Freud publishes his first work on psycho-analysis. Jameson Raid, Dec. 29.

1896 Jameson raiders defeated by Boers, Jan. 1. Adowa: Italian disaster at hands of Abyssinians, the first major defeat of a white colonising power by " natives."

1897 Cretan revolt leads to Greek–Turkish War. Hawaii annexed by U.S.A. Queen Victoria's Diamond Jubilee, June 22.

1898 Port Arthur ceded to Russia. Spanish–American War. *Maine*, U.S. warship, blown up in Havana harbour. Treaty of Paris, Dec. 10: Cuba freed, Puerto Rico and Guam ceded to U.S.A., Philippines surrendered for $20 million. Death of Gladstone, May 19. Battle of Omdurman, decisive defeat of Mahdists, Sept. 2. Empress of Austria assassinated, Sept. 10. The Curies discover Radium.

1899 Boer War begins, Oct. 10. Gold discovered in the Klondyke.

1900 Boers attack Ladysmith, Jan. 6. Battle of Spion Kop, Buller repulsed with severe losses, Jan. 24. Relief of Kimberley, Feb. 15. Ladysmith relieved, Feb. 28. Mafeking relieved May 17. Boxer outbreak in China, May. Annexation of Orange Free State, May 26. Roberts occupies Johannesburg, May 31. " Khaki Election." Annexation of the Transvaal, Oct. 25. Australian Commonwealth proclaimed, Dec. 30.

1901 Queen Victoria dies, Jan. 22. Trans-Siberian Railway opened for single-track traffic.

1902 Anglo-Japanese Alliance, Jan. 30. Death of Cecil Rhodes, Mar. 26. Treaty of Vereeniging ends Boer War, May 31.

1903 Congo scandal: celebrated case of misrule and exploitation. Royal family of Serbia assassinated, June 11. First controlled flight in heavier-than-air machine—Orville and Wilbur Wright at Kitty Hawk, U.S.A., Dec. 17.

1904 Russo-Japanese War begins, Feb. 8. Japanese victory at Yalu River, May 1. British forces under Younghusband reach Lhasa, Aug. 3. Treaty with Tibet signed at Lhasa, Sept. 7.

1905 Port Arthur falls to Japanese, Jan. 3. " Bloody Sunday " massacre at St. Petersburg, Jan. 22. Destruction of Russian fleet under Rozhdestvenski at Tsushima by Admiral Togo (May). Treaty of Portsmouth (U.S.A.) ends Russo-Japanese war. Separation of Church and State in France. Norway separates itself from Sweden.

1906 General strike in Russia. San Francisco destroyed by earthquake and fire, Apr. 18. Simplon tunnel opened for railway traffic, June 1. First Duma (Parliament with limited powers) in Russia. Liberal " landslide " majority in Britain: Labour M.P.s appear. Movement for Women's Suffrage becomes active in Britain. Algeciras Conference: Franco-German crisis resolved in favour of France. Death of Ibsen. Vitamins discovered by F. G. Hopkins.

1907 New Zealand becomes a dominion.

1908 Annexation of Congo by Belgium. Young Turk revolution. Annexation of Bosnia and Herzegovina by Austria: severe rebuff for Russia. Asquith becomes Prime Minister of Britain.

1909 Old Age Pensions in Britain. Peary reaches North Pole. Blériot makes first cross-Channel flight. House of Lords rejects Lloyd George's budget. Union of South Africa formed. Henry Ford concentrates on producing Model T chassis: beginnings of cheap motors.

A.D.

1910 Accession of George V on death of Edward VII, May 6. Liberals win two General Elections. Labour Exchanges established in Britain. Death of Tolstoy and Florence Nightingale.

1911 Parliament Act: power of Lords decisively reduced. British M.P.s paid for first time. National Insurance in Britain. Great British rail strike. Tripoli taken from Turkey by Italy. Chinese Revolution. Amundsen reaches South Pole, Dec. 14.

1912 China becomes a Republic under Sun Yat Sen. *Titanic* disaster off Cape Race, Apr. 14–15. Great British coal strike. Scott's last expedition. Outbreak of Balkan Wars.

1913 Treaty of Bucharest: most of Turkey-in-Europe divided among Balkan states.

FIRST WORLD WAR

1914 Archduke Francis Ferdinand, heir to the Hapsburg thrones, assassinated at Sarajevo, June 28. Austria–Hungary declares war against Serbia, July 28. Germany declares war against Russia, Aug. 1. Germany declares war against France, Aug. 3. German invasion of Belgium: Great Britain declares war against Germany, Aug. 4. Great Britain declares war on Austria–Hungary, Aug. 12. British Expeditionary Force concentrated before Mauberge, Aug. 20. Battle of Mons: Japan declared war on Germany, Aug. 23. Battle of the Marne, Sept. 5–9. Trench warfare began on Aisne salient, Sept. 16. Three British cruisers (*Aboukir, Hogue,* and *Cressy*) sunk by one U-boat, Sept. 22. First Battle of Ypres, Oct. 12–Nov. 11. Raiding of German cruiser *Emden* until destroyed, Nov. 9. Battle of Coronel: German cruisers *Scharnhorst* and *Gneisenau* sink British cruisers *Good Hope* and *Monmouth*, Nov. 1. Great Britain declares war against Turkey, Nov. 5. Destruction of German squadron off Falkland Is., Dec. 8. British protectorate over Egypt proclaimed, Dec. 17. First Zeppelin appeared over British coast, Dec. 29.

1915 Turkish army defeated in Caucasus, Jan 5. Great Britain declared blockade of Germany, Mar. 1. Battle of Neuve Chapelle, Mar. 10–13. Naval attack on Dardanelles called off, Mar. 22. First landing of British, Australian, New Zealand troops on Gallipoli Peninsula, Apr. 25. Second Battle of Ypres, Apr. 22–May 25: Germans first used gas. Sinking of *Lusitania*, May 7. Battle of Aubers Ridge, May 9–25. Italy declares war on Austria, May 22. British Coalition Government formed, May 26. Italian army crosses Isonzo, June 2. Zeppelin destroyed by R. A. J. Warneford, June 7. Second landing of Allied troops at Suvla Bay. Italy declares war on Turkey, Aug. 20. Turks defeated at Kut-el-Amara, Sept 28. Serbia conquered by Austria and Bulgaria, Nov. 28. French and British troops occupy Salonika, Dec. 13. British troops withdraw from Anzac and Suvla, Dec. 20.

1916 Evacuation of Gallipoli completed, Jan 8. Opening of Battle of Verdun, Feb. 21. Sinn Fein rising in Ireland, Apr. 24. First Daylight Saving Bill passed. Fall of Kut, Apr. 29. Battle of Jutland, May 31. Brusilov's offensive in Galicia begins, June 4. Kitchener drowned when *Hampshire* struck mine, June 5. Battle of the Somme, July 1–Nov. 13: British losses: 420,000. Italians capture Gorizia, Aug. 10. Hindenburg and Ludendorff chiefs of German staff, Aug. 27. Rumania declares war against Austria and Germany, Aug. 27. Tanks first used by British, Sept. 15. Death of Francis Joseph of Austria, Nov. 21. Lloyd George forms War Cabinet, Dec. 6. Joffre replaced by Nivelle, early Dec.

1917 Unrestricted submarine warfare begins, Feb. 1. British troops occupy Baghdad, Mar. 11. Revolution in Russia, Mar. 12. U.S.A. declares war on Germany, April 6. Battle of Arras, Apr. 9–14: Vimy Ridge taken by Canadians, Apr. 10. Pétain replaced Nivelle, May 15. Messines Ridge taken by British, June 7. First American contingents arrive in France, June 26. Allenby assumes Palestine

A.D.

command, June 29. Third Battle of Ypres opened, July 31. Russia proclaimed a Republic, Sept. 15. British victory on Passchendaele Ridge, Oct. 4. French victory on the Aisne, Oct. 23. Caporetto: Italians severely defeated by Austrians. Oct. 24. Bolshevik Revolution, Nov. 7 (Oct. 25 O.S.). Passchendaele captured by British, Nov. 6. Balfour declaration recognised Palestine as "a national home" for the Jews, Nov. 8. Hindenburg Lines smashed on 10-mile front, Nov. 20. Fall of Jerusalem, Dec. 9. Russo-German armistice signed, Dec. 15.

1918 Treaty of Bresh-Litovsk, Mar. 3. German offensive against British opened on Somme, Mar. 21. Battle of Arras, Mar. 21–Apr. 4. Second German offensive against British, Apr. 9–25. British naval raid on Zeebrugge and Ostend, Apr. 23. Foch appointed C.-in-C. Allied armies, Apr. 14. Peace signed between Rumania and Central Powers, May 7. *Vindictive* sunk in Ostend harbour, May 9. Last German offensive against French, July 15. British, Canadians, and Australians attack in front of Amiens, Aug. 8. Allenby destroyed last Turkish army at Megiddo, Sept. 19. Bulgarians signed armistice, Sept. 29. General Allied offensive in West began, Sept. 26. Germans accepted Wilson's Fourteen Points, Oct. 23. Great Italian advance, Oct. 24. Turkey surrenders, Oct 30. Austria accepts imposed terms, Nov. 3. Popular government in Poland (Lubin), Nov. 7. Revolutionary movement begins in Germany, Nov. 8. Kaiser abdicates and escapes to Holland, Nov. 9. Armistice signed by Germans, Nov. 11.

THE TWENTIES AND THIRTIES

1919 Peace Conference in Paris, Jan. 18. Total eclipse of the sun, as predicted by Einstein, March 29. First direct flight across Atlantic by Sir J. Alcock and Sir A. W. Brown, June 15. Interned German fleet scuttled at Scapa Flow, June 19. Treaty of Peace with Germany signed at Versailles, June 28. Treaty of St. Germain: break-up of Austrian Empire, Sept. 10.

1920 Peace Treaty ratified in Paris. First meeting of League of Nations, from which Germany, Austria, Russia, and Turkey are excluded, and at which the U.S.A. is not represented. Prohibition in U.S.A. Peace Treaty with Turkey signed at Sèvres: Ottoman Empire broken up, Aug. 10. Degrees first open to women at Oxford Univ., Oct. 14.

1921 Riots in Egypt, May 23. In complete disregard of the League of Nations, Greece makes war on Turkey. Heligoland fortresses demolished, Oct. 14. Irish Free State set up by Peace Treaty with Britain, Dec. 6.

1922 Four-Power Pacific Treaty ratified by U.S. Senate, Mar. 24. Heavy fighting in Dublin, the Four Courts blown up, July 2. Defeat of Greek armies by the Turks, Aug.–Sept. Mussolini's Fascist "March on Rome," Oct. 28.

1923 French troops despatched to Ruhr, Jan. 11. Treaty of Lausanne, July 24. Earthquake in Japan, Tokio and Yokohama in ruins, Sept. 1. Rhine Republic proclaimed, Bavaria defies the Reich, Oct. 20. Turkish Republic proclaimed: Kemal Pasha, first President, Oct. 29.

1924 Lenin dies, Jan. 21. First Labour Ministry in Britain under MacDonald, Jan. 22; lasts 9 months. George II of Greece deposed and a Republic declared, Mar. 25. Dawes Plan accepted by London conference; Ruhr evacuation agreed to, Aug. 16.

1925 Hindenburg elected German President, Mar. 26. Treaty of Locarno signed in London, Dec. 1. Summer Time Act made permanent.

1926 Ibn Saud proclaimed king of the Hedjaz in Jeddah, Jan. 11. Evacuation of Cologne by British forces, Jan. 31. General strike in Britain.

1927 Canberra, the new capital of Australian Commonwealth, inaugurated, May 9. Lindbergh flies Atlantic alone, May 21.

1928 Earthquake in Greece, Corinth destroyed, Apr. 23. Capt. Kingsford-Smith flies the

A.D.

Pacific, June 9. General Nobile rescued by aeroplane from Arctic one month after disaster, June 24. Kellogg Pact accepted by Gt. Britain, July 18. German airship with 60 persons crosses Atlantic, Oct. 15. Women in Britain enfranchised.

1929 King Amanullah of Afghanistan abdicates, Jan. 14. Second Labour Ministry under Mac-Donald. Graf Zeppelin makes numerous successful inter-continental flights. Commander Byrd flies over South Pole, Nov. 30. American slump and Wall Street crash.

1930 *R.101* destroyed in France on first flight to India, 48 lives lost, Oct. 5—end of British interest in airships.

1931 Great floods in China. Resignation of Labour Government and formation of Coalition under MacDonald.

1932 Manchuria erected into Japanese puppet state of Manchukuo, Feb. 18. Sydney Harbour Bridge opened, Mar. 19. Ottawa Imperial Conference.

1933 Hitler appointed Chancellor by Hindenburg, Jan. 30, and step by step gains supreme control. German Reichstag set on fire, Feb. 27.

1934 Dollfuss, Austrian Chancellor, murdered by Austrian Nazis, July 25. Death of Hindenburg, Aug. 2. Hitler becomes Dictator.

1935 Saar plebiscite for return to Germany, Jan. 13. Baldwin succeeds MacDonald as Prime Minister, June 7. War begins between Italy and Abyssinia, Oct. 3. Ineffectual economic "sanctions" by League of Nations against Italy, Nov. 18.

1936 Accession of King Edward VIII, Jan. 20. Repudiation of Locarno Treaty by Germany, Mar. 7. Remilitarization of Rhineland, Mar. 8. Italian troops occupy Addis Ababa, May 5. Civil War breaks out in Spain, July 18. King Edward VIII abdicates after a reign of 325 days, Dec. 10. The Duke of York succeeds his brother as King George VI, Dec. 12.

1937 Coalition Ministry under Chamberlain, May 28. Japanese begin attempted conquest of China—" China incident," July 7.

1938 Singapore naval base opened, Feb. 14. Austria annexed by Germany, Mar. 13. British navy mobilised, Sept. 28. Munich Agreement between Chamberlain, Daladier, Hitler, and Mussolini, Sept. 29.

1939

February 27 Great Britain recognises General Franco's Government.

March 16 Bohemia and Moravia annexed by Hitler and proclaimed a German Protectorate. **22** Memel ceded to Germany by Lithuania. **28** Anti-Polish press campaign begun by Germany.

April 1 Spanish War ends. **7** Italy seizes Albania. **14** First British talks with Russia. **27** Conscription introduced in Great Britain. **28** Hitler denounces Anglo-German Naval agreement and the Polish Non-Aggression Treaty.

May 12 Great Britain signs defensive agreement with Turkey. **22** Italy and Germany sign pact. **23** France and Turkey sign defensive agreement. **25** Anglo-Polish treaty signed in London.

July 10 Chamberlain re-affirms British pledge to Poland.

August 23 German-Soviet Pact signed by von Ribbentrop. **25** Japan breaks away from the Anti-Comintern Pact. **28** Holland mobilises. **31** British fleet mobilised.

SECOND WORLD WAR

September 1 Poland invaded by German forces. Great Britain and France mobilise. **1–4** Evacuation schemes put in motion in England and Wales: 1,200,000 persons moved. **2** Compulsory military service for all men in Britain aged 18 to 41. **3** War declared (11 a.m.) between Britain and Germany as from 5 p.m. **4** British liner *Athenia* sunk by submarine. R.A.F. raid the Kiel Canal entrance and bomb German warships. **6** First enemy air raid on Britain. **8** Russia mobilises. Russian troops on Polish border. **11** British troops on French soil. **17**

A.D.

Russian troops cross the Polish frontier along its entire length. Russian and German troops meet near Brest Litovsk. **27** Capitulation of Warsaw. **29** Nazi–Soviet pact signed in Moscow approving partition of Poland.

October 14 *Royal Oak* sunk in Scapa Flow with a loss of 810 lives.

November 8 Bomb explosion in the Bürgerbräukeller at Munich after Hitler's speech. Germans using magnetic mines. **29** Diplomatic relations between Russia and Finland severed. **30** Finland attacked by Russia.

December 11 Italy leaves the League of Nations. **13** Battle of the River Plate: engagement of German warship *Admiral Graf Spee* by H.M. cruisers *Exeter*, *Ajax*, and *Achilles*. **14** Rejection by Russia of the League of Nations' offer of mediation in the Russo-Finnish war. Russia expelled from the League of Nations. **18** *Admiral Graf Spee* scuttles herself in the entrance of Montevideo harbour.

1940

February 14 Finnish advanced posts captured by Russians. **16** 299 British prisoners taken off the German Naval Auxiliary *Altmark* in Norwegian waters. **26** Finns lose the island fortress of Koivisto. Finns retreat from Petsamo.

March 12 British ships to be fitted with a protective device against magnetic mines. Finland concludes a peace treaty whereby she cedes to Russia the Karelian Isthmus, the town of Vipuri and a military base on Hango Peninsula.

April 9 Invasion of Denmark and Norway by Germany. **15** British troops arrive in Norway. **19** British soldiers land in the Faroes.

May 2 British troops withdrawn from Norway. **10** Holland, Belgium and Luxembourg invaded by German forces. Parachute troops landed near Rotterdam. British troops cross the Belgian border. British troops land in Iceland. Rotterdam bombed. **11** National Government formed under Churchill. **13** Queen Wilhelmina arrives in London. **14** Rotterdam captured. Holland ceases fighting. Allied troops land near Narvik. **17** Belgian Government moves to Ostend. **24** German forces enter Boulogne. **27** Belgian army capitulates on the order of King Leopold. British forces to be withdrawn from Flanders. Narvik captured by Allied forces. **29** Ostend, Ypres, Lille and other Belgian and French towns lost to the Germans.

June Evacuation of British army from Dunkirk (May 27–June 4): 299 British warships and 420 other vessels under constant attack evacuate 335,490 officers and men. **5** Hitler proclaims a war of total annihilation against his enemies. **8** German armoured forces penetrate French defences in the West near Rouen. **10** Italy declares war on Great Britain and France. **14** Paris captured by German forces. **15** Soviet troops occupy Lithuania, Latvia and Estonia. **22** French delegates accept terms for an Armistice. **25** Hostilities in France cease at 12.35 a.m.

July 1 Channel Islands occupied by Germany. **3** French naval squadron at Oran immobilised. **10** Battle of Britain began.

August 19 British withdrew from British Somaliland. **25** British began night bombing of Germany.

September 6 King Carol of Rumania abdicates in favour of his son Michael. **7** London sustains severe damage in the largest aerial attack since war commenced. **15** Battle of Britain ends with British victory: German aeroplanes destroyed, 1,733; R.A.F. losses, 915. **23** Japanese troops enter Indo-China.

October 7 German troops enter Rumania. **28** Greece rejects an Italian ultimatum.

November 1 Greeks repel Italian attacks. **5** H.M.S. *Jervis Bay* lost defending Atlantic convoy from German warship *Admiral Scheer*. **11** Italian fleet at Taranto crippled by Fleet Air Arm. **14** Coventry heavily attacked, the Cathedral destroyed. **22** Albanian town of Koritza captured by the Greeks.

December 2 Bristol heavily bombed. **11** Sidi Barrani captured by British forces: beginning

A.D.

of Wavell's destruction of Italian forces in Cyrenaica. 29 City of London severely burned by incendiary bombs: Guildhall and eight Wren Churches destroyed.

1941

January 5 Bardia captured. 22 Tobruk captured by Australian troops.

February 7 Benghazi captured. 26 Mogadishu, capital of Italian Somaliland, occupied by Imperial troops. German mechanised troops in Libya.

March 4 British raid Lofoten Islands. 11 U.S. Lease and Lend Bill signed by Roosevelt. 27 Keren—main battle in British conquest of Abyssinia and Somaliland. 28 Cape Matapan: Italian fleet routed by British. 30 Rommel opens attack in N. Africa.

April 4 Addis Ababa entered by Imperial troops. 6 Greece and Yugoslavia invaded by German troops. 8 Massawa capitulates. 11 Belgrade occupied by German forces. 13 Bardia given up by British. Tobruk holds out. 24 Empire forces withdrawing from Greece. 27 Athens captured by the Germans.

May 2 Evacuation from Greece completed. 10 Rudolf Hess descends by parachute in Scotland. 20 Crete invaded by German air-borne troops. 24 H.M.S. *Hood* sunk. 27 German battleship *Bismarck* sunk; British forces withdraw from Crete.

June 2 Clothes rationing commences. 4 William II (ex-Kaiser of Germany) dies. 18 Treaty of friendship between Turkey and Germany signed. 22 Germany attacks Russia. 24 Russia loses Brest Litovsk.

July 3 Palmyra (Syria) surrenders to Allied forces. 7 U.S. forces arrive in Iceland. 9 General Dentz, the French High Commissioner in Syria, asks for Armistice terms. 25 Fighting round Smolensk.

August 25 British and Russian troops enter Persia. 27 The Dnepropetrovsk dam blown up by the Russians.

September 18 Crimea cut off from mainland. 19 Kiev entered by Germans.

October 6 German attack on Moscow. 16 Soviet Government leaves Moscow. Odessa occupied by German and Rumanian troops. 19 Taganrog on Sea of Azov captured by Germans. 26 Kharkov captured by the Germans.

November 14 *Ark Royal* sunk. 18 Libyan battle opens: Eighth Army's first offensive. 23 Bardia and Fort Capuzzo captured by British. 24 H.M.S. *Dunedin* torpedoed. 25 H.M.S. *Barham* sunk. 30 Russians re-take Rostov.

December 1 Points rationing scheme in force in Britain. 4 German attack on Moscow halted. 7 Japanese attack on Pearl Harbour. 8 Japanese forces land in Malaya. 9 British forces in Tobruk relieved. 10 H.M.S. *Repulse* and *Prince of Wales* sunk off Malaya by Japanese. Phillippines invaded by Japanese. 25 Hongkong surrenders to Japanese.

1942

January 2 Manila and Cavite taken by Japanese. 23 Japanese forces land in New Guinea and the Solomon Islands.

February 9 Soap rationed. 12 Escape through English Channel of German ships *Scharnhorst*, *Gneisenau*, and *Prinz Eugen*. 15 Singapore surrenders to Japanese. 27 Battle of Java Seas.

March 9 Surrender of Java to Japanese.

April 15 George Cross awarded to the island of Malta.

May 4-8 Battle of Coral Sea. 7 Madagascar invaded by British forces. 7 U.S. forces sink 11 Japanese warships off the Solomon Islands. 30 Over 1,000 bombers raid Cologne. Canterbury bombed.

June 3-7 Midway Island: U.S. naval victory turns tide in Pacific. 20 Tobruk captured by the Germans.

July 16 R.A.F. make first daylight raid on the Ruhr.

August 6 Germans advancing towards the Caucasus. 10 American forces land in the Solomon

A.D.

Islands. 11 Malta convoy action (loss of H.M.S. *Eagle*, *Manchester*, *Cairo*, and one destroyer). 19 Raid on Dieppe. 23-25 Battle of Solomons.

September 6 Germans halted at Stalingrad.

October 23 El Alamein: Allied offensive opens in Egypt.

November 4 Rommel's army in full retreat. 5 Red Army holding firm at Stalingrad. 7 Allied invasion of N. Africa. 27 German forces enter Toulon. French Fleet scuttled.

December 2 First self-sustained, controlled nuclear chain reaction in uranium took place on a Chicago tennis court. 24 Admiral Darlan assassinated.

1943

January 6 German armies in the Caucasus and the Don elbow in retreat. 18 Leningrad 16-month siege ended. 23 Tripoli occupied by the Eighth Army. 27 American bombers make their first attack on Germany. 31 Remnants of the German army outside Stalingrad surrender.

February 9 Guadalcanal Island cleared of Japanese troops. 16 Kharkov retaken by the Russians.

March 1-3 Battle of Bismarck Sea. 23 8th Army penetrates the Mareth Line.

May 7 Tunis and Bizerta captured by Allies. 12 All organised German resistance in Tunisia ceases. 16 Dams in the Ruhr breached by the R.A.F. 22 Moscow dissolves the Comintern.

June 3 French Committee for National Liberation formed in Algiers.

July 10 Allied invasion of Sicily. 25 Mussolini overthrown. 28 Fascist Party in Italy dissolved.

August 17 Sicily in Allied hands.

September 3 Italian mainland invaded. 7 Italy surrenders. 9 British and American troops land near Naples. 10 Rome seized by the Germans. 14 Salamaua captured from the Japanese. 23 *Tirpitz* severely damaged (sunk Nov. 12, 1944). 25 Smolensk taken by the Russians.

October 1 Naples taken. 25 Russians capture Dnepropetrovsk and Dneprodzerzhinck.

November 6 Kiev taken by the Russians. 26 Second Battle of Solomons. 28 Churchill, Roosevelt, and Stalin meet in Teheran.

December 2 Men between 18 and 25 to be directed to the mining industry by ballot in Britain. 26 Sinking of German battleship *Scharnhorst*.

1944

January 22 Allied landings at Anzio. 28 Argentina breaks with the Axis Powers.

February 1 American forces land on the Marshall Islands. 2 Russians penetrate Estonia.

March 15 Cassino (Italy) destroyed by Allied bombers.

May 9 Sevastopol captured by Russians. 18 Capture of Cassino and Abbey by Allies. 19 50 Allied officers shot after escaping from a German prison camp. 30 Battle for Rome commences.

June 4 Allied forces enter Rome. King of Italy signs decree transferring his powers to Prince Umberto, his son. 6 *D-Day*: invasion of Europe (over 4,000 ships in invasion fleet). 7 Defeat of Japanese thrust at India, outside Imphal. 9 Heavy fighting near Caen. 12 First V-1 falls on England. 18 Cherbourg peninsula cut by the Americans. Russians break through the Mannerheim Line.

July 3 Minsk captured by Russians. 9 Caen captured by Allies. 20 " Bomb plot " on Hitler' life. 21 Guam captured by Americans.

August 1 Uprising in Warsaw. 4 Myitkyina falls to Allied forces. 15 Allied forces land in southern France. 23 Paris liberated. Marseilles taken. Rumania surrenders. 25 Rumania declares war on Germany.

September 3 Allies in Belgium. 4 Antwerp and Brussels taken by Allies. Holland entered. Finland " ceases fire." 6 Bulgaria asks for an armistice. 7 Boulogne entered by Allies. Bulgaria declares war on Germany. 8 First V-2 falls on England. 11 Allied forces fighting on

A.D.

Reich territory. **17** Allied air-borne troops land near Arnhem. **22** First Battle of Philippines.

October 3 Warsaw rising crushed by the Germans. **5** British troops land on the mainland of Greece. **14** Athens occupied by Allies. **15** Hungary asks for armistice terms. **20** Aachen captured by the Americans. **25** Battle of Leyte Gulf: end of Japanese sea-power. **28** Second Battle of Philippines.

December 6 Civil war breaks out in Athens. **16** German forces counter-attack in the Ardennes: last German offensive in the West. **26** Budapest encircled by Russians.

1945

January 5 Organized fighting in Athens ceases. **11** U.S. forces land on Island of Luzon. **17** Warsaw captured by the Russians. **21** Russian troops in Silesia. **23** Burma road to China re-opened.

February 4 Yalta conference. **14** Bombing of Dresden. **19** Americans land on Iwojima Island.

March 6 Cologne captured by Allies.

April 1 U.S. Invasion of Okinawa. **5** Russian Government denounces the Soviet-Japan neutrality pact. Japanese Cabinet resigns. **11** Russian Army enters Vienna after 7-day battle. **12** Death of President Roosevelt. **25** Berlin surrounded by Russian troops. **27** Russians and Americans link up in Germany. **28** Mussolini and his mistress shot by Italian partisans. **30** Hitler killed himself and his mistress.

May 2 German armies in Italy surrender. Berlin captured by the Russians. **3** Rangoon captured by British. **4** German forces in N.W. Germany, Holland and Denmark surrender. **8** End of World War II against Germany officially declared to be one minute past midnight (Tuesday). **28** Naval air attacks on Japan.

June 26 United Nations Charter signed at San Francisco.

July 5 Polish Government in Warsaw recognised by Allies. **26** Labour Party remarkably successful in General Election.

August 6 Atomic bomb first used against Japan: Hiroshima laid waste. **8** Russia declares war against Japan. **9** Russia advances into Manchuria. Nagasaki target for atomic bomb No. 2. **14** Japan surrenders unconditionally to the Allies. **17** Lend-Lease terminated.

September 2 Victory over Japan celebrated: end of Second World War.

" COLD WAR ": AFRO-ASIAN INDEPENDENCE

October 9 U.S.A. to keep secret of manufacture of atomic bomb. **15** Laval executed.

November 20 Trial of major war criminals opens at Nuremberg.

1946

February 1 Mr. Trygve Lie elected Secretary-General of UNO.

April 19 League of Nations formally wound up.

June 5 Italy votes for Republic. **30** United States atom bomb tests at Bikini.

July 13 United States House of Representatives approves loan to Britain. British H.Q. in Jerusalem blown up. **24** Underwater atom bomb test at Bikini.

August 1 Peace Conference opens in Paris.

September 6 United Nations F.A.O. considers establishment of World Food Board.

October 16 Nuremberg sentences on Nazis carried out, Goering commits suicide. **23** General Assembly of the United Nations opens in New York.

November 10 Communists head poll in French General Elections.

December 2 Agreement signed for economic fusion of British and American zones in Germany.

A.D.

1947

January 1 British coal industry nationalised. **14** M. Vincent-Auriol elected first President of Fourth Republic.

March 15 Floods in England worst recorded. **24** Netherlands Government and Indonesian Cabinet sign agreement in Batavia for a United States of Indonesia.

April 1 School leaving age raised to 15 in Great Britain.

June 5 Inauguration of " Marshall Aid ".

August 3 Dutch military action in Indonesia ends. **15** India and Pakistan assume Dominion Status. Viscount Mountbatten appointed Governor-General of India and Mr. Jinnah Governor-General of Pakistan. **29** Palestine Committee agrees British Mandate should end, majority report recommends partition.

September 22 First Atlantic automatic flight by U.S. pilotless aircraft.

October 6 Cominform, new international Communist organization, set up in Belgrade.

November 20 Marriage of Princess Elizabeth. **29** Palestine Committee of U.N. Assembly votes in favour of partition of Palestine into Jewish and Arab States.

December 15 Breakdown of 4-Power Conference on Germany. **30** King Michael of Rumania abdicates; Rumania becomes a People's Republic.

1948

January 1 British Railways nationalised. **4** Burma becomes independent Republic. **30** Mahatma Gandhi assassinated in New Delhi.

February 1 New Malayan federal constitution comes into force. **4** Ceylon Independence Act. **25** New Czechoslovak Government formed under Communist leadership.

March 10 Death of Jan Masaryk.

April 1 British electricity industry nationalised. **5** First European Aid shipments sail from America. **16** O.E.E.C. established.

May 3 Mr. Rajagopalachari appointed Gov.-Gen. of India in succession to Earl Mountbatten. **14** British Mandate for Palestine ended at midnight. Jews proclaim new State of Israel.

June 28 Yugoslavia expelled from Cominform; " Titoism " denounced.

July 1 " Berlin Airlift ": American, British and French zones of Berlin supplied by air. **23** Malayan Communist party outlawed. **29** Bread rationing in Great Britain ends.

August 15 Republic of Korea proclaimed.

September 3 Death of Dr. Benes. **11** Death of Mohammed Ali Jinnah. **17** Count Bernadotte, U.N. Mediator for Palestine, assassinated.

October 30 Chinese Communist forces capture Mukden.

November 3 Mr. Truman elected U.S. President. **14** Birth of a son to Princess Elizabeth.

December 21 Republic of Ireland Bill signed in Dublin.

1949

March 15 Clothes rationing ends in Great Britain. **31** Russia protests against Atlantic Pact.

April 1 Newfoundland becomes part of Canada.

May 1 Gas Industry nationalised. **3** Ten-power conference in London establishes Council of Europe. **12** Berlin blockade lifted.

August 24 North Atlantic Treaty comes into force.

September 12 Professor Theodor Heuss elected first President of West German Republic. **21** General Mao Tse-Tung proclaims People's Republic of China.

October 2 Russia recognises newly-established Chinese People's Republic. **11** Herr Wilhelm Pieck elected first President of East German Republic.

December 8 Chinese Nationalist Government leaves mainland and sets up H.Q. in Formosa. **27** United States of Indonesia come into being.

1950

January 6 Britain recognizes Communist Government of China ; **24** Dr. Rajendra Prasad elected

A.D.

first President of Indian Republic; 26 New Constitution of Indian Republic comes into force.

February 14 30-year treaty of alliance between Russia and China signed in Moscow; 23 Labour Party wins General Election with narrow majority.

March 5 Lord Boyd Orr warns world that communism spreads where hunger prevails; 22 First of U.S. super-fortresses arrives in Norfolk.

April 1 Italy takes over from Britain administration of Somaliland; 13 First shipment of military aid to France under N.A. Pact unloaded at Cherbourg.

May 1 New Chinese marriage law abolishes polygamy and child marriages and gives both sexes equal rights; 19 Points rationing ends in Britain after 8 years; 25 Middle East Tripartite Declaration by Britain, France, and U.S.A.; 26 Petrol rationing ends in Britain.

June 25 N. Korean troops advance into S. Korea; Security Council calls for cease fire; 27 Pres. Truman orders U.S. air, and sea forces to support S. Korea and protect Formosa; U.N. Commission in Korea proposes neutral mediator; military assistance to S. Korea endorsed by Security Council; 30 Pres. Truman authorizes use of American ground troops in Korea.

July 2 American troops land in S. Korea; 8 Gen. MacArthur designated C.-in-C. of U.N. forces in Korea.

August 1 Security Council meets under chairmanship of M. Malik, the Soviet delegate; 7 American forces in Korea open offensive and halt drive on Pusan; 15 Princess Elizabeth gives birth to a daughter; severe earthquake in Assam; 17 Independence Day in Indonesia.

September 6 British troops in action in Korea; 9 Soap rationing ends in Britain.

October 9 U.N. forces across the 38th parallel in strength; 19 Sir Stafford Cripps retires from public life on account of illness; Pyongyang, N. Korean capital, captured by U.N. forces; 21 Princess Anne Elizabeth Alice Louise christened; 26 New Chamber of House of Commons opened at Westminster; 29 King Gustav V of Sweden dies.

November 2 Death of George Bernard Shaw aged 94; 6 Chinese forces from Manchuria reported fighting in Korea.

December 3 Mr. Attlee flies to Washington for talks with Pres. Truman; 4 Pyongyang occupied by Chinese; 19 Gen. Eisenhower appointed Supreme Commander of West European Defence Forces set up by Atlantic Powers; 25 Stone of Scone stolen from Westminster Abbey.

1951

January 30 U.N. Assembly rejects resolution of 12 Asian and Arab nations calling for 7-nation conference for peaceful settlement of Korean question; 31 Decree confiscating property of Alfred Krupp cancelled.

February 15 Vesting date for Iron and Steel.

April 11 Gen. MacArthur relieved of all his commands by Pres. Truman and replaced by Lt.-Gen. Ridgway; 13 Coronation Stone returned to Westminster Abbey.

May 2 Persian oil industry nationalized; Germany admitted to Council of Europe; 3 H.M. the King opens Festival of Britain from steps of St. Paul's.

June 23 M. Malik, Russian delegate to the U.N., appeals for settlement of Korean war.

July 1 Colombo plan comes into force; 9 State of war between Britain and Germany officially ended; 10 Armistice negotiations open at Kaesong; 17 King Leopold abdicates in favour of his son Baudouin, who becomes fifth King of the Belgians; 20 King Abdullah of Jordan assassinated.

September 1 Tripartite Security Treaty between U.S.A., Australia, and New Zealand signed in San Francisco; 8 Japanese Peace Treaty—to which Russia, China, and India are not

A.D.

parties—signed at San Francisco; Security Pact between Japan and U.S.A., providing for retention of American forces in Japan, also signed; 23 H.M. the King undergoes successful operation; 30 Festival of Britain ends.

October 8 Princess Elizabeth and Duke of Edinburgh leave for Canadian tour; 15 Egyptian Parliament passes unanimously Bills abrogating Anglo-Egyptian treaty of 1936 and 1899 Sudan Condominion Agreement; 16 Assassination of Liaquat Ali Khan; 25 General Election won by Conservatives with small majority.

November 5 Mr. Attlee receives the Order of Merit.

December 17 London foreign-exchange market reopens after 12 years; 24 Libya becomes independent state; 31 I.R.O. closes down.

1952

January 2 Mutual Security Agency replaces Economic Co-operation Administration; 31 Princess Elizabeth and Duke of Edinburgh leave London on first stage of Commonwealth tour.

February 6 King George VI died at Sandringham aged 56; 7 Queen Elizabeth II and the Duke of Edinburgh arrive home by air from Kenya; 15 Funeral of King George VI at Windsor; 21 Identity cards abolished.

March 20 South African Supreme Court rules invalid Dr. Malan's Act which places Cape coloured voters on separate electoral register.

April 11 H.M. the Queen declares that she wishes her children and descendants to bear the name of Windsor; 21 Death of Sir Stafford Cripps in Switzerland; 28 Japan regains status as sovereign and independent power.

May 5 H.M. the Queen takes up residence at Buckingham Palace; 27 Treaty setting up European Defence Community signed in Paris.

June 23 Power plants along Yalu River attacked by U.S. aircraft in biggest raid of Korean war.

July 7 American ship *United States* wins Atlantic Blue Riband; 19 Fifteenth Olympic Games held in Helsinki; 23 Military *coup d'état* takes place in Cairo.

August 1 Ratification of Bonn Agreement, by which W. Germany again becomes independent nation, and Treaty of Paris, which sets up the European Defence Community, approved by Government against Labour opposition; 16 Severe thunderstorms in Somerset and N. Devon cause rivers to flood; W. Lyn changes course bringing devastation to Lynmouth; 26 Passive resistance campaign against racial laws in S. Africa gains momentum.

September 2 Sir William Slim appointed Gov.-Gen. of Australia (from 1953); 8 New Egyptian Cabinet appoints Gen. Neguib military Gov.-Gen. of Egypt and approves land reforms.

October 3 Britain's first atomic weapon exploded in Monte Bello Islands, off N.W. Australia; 5 Tea derationed and decontrolled; 20 State of emergency declared in Kenya as a result of Mau Mau activities.

November 1 Reported explosion of U.S. hydrogen bomb at Eniwetok atoll in mid-Pacific; 4 Gen. Eisenhower, Republican Candidate, wins sweeping victory in American Presidential election.

December 29 Fish recently caught off Madagascar confirmed as species of the prehistoric Coelacanth.

1953

January 20 Inauguration of General Eisenhower as 34th President of the United States; 31 Violent N.E. gales combined with surging high tides caused extensive flooding with loss of life along coasts of eastern England, the Netherlands, and Belgium.

February 4 Sweet rationing ended; 23 War-time deserters in Britain granted amnesty.

March 6 Marshal Stalin died, aged 74; 24 Death of Queen Mary at Marlborough House, aged 85; 31 Mr. Dag Hammarskjöld elected U.N. Sec.-Gen. in succession to Mr. Trygve Lie.

April 15 Dr. Malan's National Party again returned to power in S. Africa with increased

A.D.

majority; **24** Mr. Churchill created a Knight of the Garter by the Queen.

May 4 Duke of Edinburgh received his pilot's "wings"; **29** E. P. Hillary and Sherpa Tenzing of the Everest Expedition led by Colonel John Hunt reached summit of Everest (29,002 ft.).

June 2 Coronation of H.M. Elizabeth II in Westminster Abbey amid scenes of magnificent pageantry; ceremony televised; **26** Republic of Egypt accorded *de facto* recognition by Britain.

July 4 German–Austrian Expedition reached summit of Nanga Parbat in the Himalayas; **13** De-nationalisation of British steel industry; **14** Royal Assent given to Central African Federation Bill; **27** Korean Armistice signed at Panmunjom.

August 9–12 Disastrous earthquakes in Greek Ionian Islands; **12** Explosion of Russian hydrogen bomb reported.

September 17 Bank rate reduced from 4 to 3½ per cent; **23** Royal Commission on Capital Punishment recommended that juries should decide whether death sentence or life imprisonment should be imposed on prisoners found guilty of murder, and that the M'Naghten Rules on insanity should be abrogated or amended; **26** Sugar rationing ended after nearly 14 years; **30** Professor Piccard in his bathyscaphe dived 10,000 ft. off Italian coast.

October 15 Sir Winston Churchill awarded 1953 Nobel Prize for Literature.

November 11 Great bell at Notre Dame rung by electricity for first time; **21** Piltdown skull, discovered in Sussex in 1911, found by anthropologists to be partial hoax; **23** The Queen and Duke of Edinburgh left in stratocruiser *Canopus* on first stage of 6-months' tour of Commonwealth.

December 1 Agreement signed for laying first transatlantic telephone cable; **23** M. René Coty elected Pres. of France at the 13th ballot; L. P. Beria, former chief of Soviet Secret Police, and six associates sentenced to death and shot; **25** The Queen gave her Christmas broadcast from Auckland; **31** Mildest December for 20 years, and before that for over 200 years.

1954

January 9 Self-government began in the Sudan; **12** M. Le Trouquer (Socialist) elected President of French National Assembly on retirement of M. Herriot; **16** M. René Coty became President of France in succession to M. Vincent Auriol; **31** Intense cold covered most of Europe.

February 3 The Queen and the Duke of Edinburgh arrived in Australia; First Parliament of newly formed Federation of Rhodesia and Nyasaland opened in Salisbury; **5** Britain's first "breeder" pile in operation at Harwell.

March 1 American hydrogen bomb exploded at Bikini; **22** London gold market reopened after 15 years.

April 1 The Queen and the Duke of Edinburgh left Australia; **3** Oxford won 100th Boat Race; **21** Russia joined UNESCO; **26** Conference on Far East opened in Palais des Nations, Geneva, Mr. Chou En-lai representing China; Russia joined I.L.O.

May 6 Roger Bannister ran the mile in under 4 min., the first man in the world to do so; **7** Fortress of Dien Bien Phu fell to Viet-Minh after siege of 8 weeks and final battle of 20 hours; **11** Bank rate reduced from 3½ to 3 per cent; **15** The Queen and the Duke of Edinburgh returned from their six-months' tour of the Commonwealth; **13** Liverpool Cotton Exchange re-opened

June 1 Television licence fee raised from £2 to £3 a year; **2** Mr. John A. Costello (Fine Gael) elected Prime Minister of Ireland; **17** Indo-Chinese crisis brought M. Mendès-France to power in France; **22** First all-African Cabinet in British Africa appointed in the Gold Coast; **27** First electric power station using atomic energy began working in Soviet Union; **30** Eclipse of the sun.

July 3 All food rationing ended in Britain; **8** Mr. Nehru opened the world's longest canal

A.D.

(Bhakra–Nangal hydro-electric project); **27** Agreement reached in Cairo for withdrawal of British troops from Suez Canal Zone; **31** K2 (Mount Godwin Austen), second highest peak in the world, climbed by Italian team led by Prof. Ardito Desio of Milan Univ.

August 5 Persian oil dispute settled; **11** Cessation of hostilities in Indo-China after 8 years of fighting.

September 14 Sheffield–Manchester electrified railway opened.

October 14 Mr. Anthony Eden created a Knight of the Garter by the Queen; **19** Anglo-Egyptian Suez Canal Agreement.

November 1 French settlements in India passed under Indian control; **22** Death of Andrei Vyshinsky; **30** Sir Winston Churchill celebrated his 80th birthday and was presented by both Houses of Parliament with a portrait of himself by Graham Sutherland.

1955

January 27 Bank rate increased from 3 to 3½ per cent; **31** Princess Margaret left for tour of W. Indies.

February 8 Marshal Bulganin succeeded Mr. Malenkov as chairman of the Soviet Council of Ministers; **15** Plans to build 12 atomic power stations in Britain during next 10 years announced; **17** Britain to proceed with manufacture of hydrogen bombs; **24** Bank rate raised to 4½ per cent and restrictions on hire purchase announced; Dr. Albert Schweitzer appointed honorary member of the Order of Merit; Turco-Iraqi pact signed at Baghdad (Britain, Pakistan, and Persia acceded later).

April 5 Sir Winston Churchill resigned as Prime Minister; **6** Sir Anthony Eden succeeded as Prime Minister; **18** Afro-Asian conference (29 nations) opened at Bandung; Death of Dr. Albert Einstein; **29** Signor Gronchi elected President of Italy.

May 5 Ratification of London and Paris agreements completed; Germany attained full sovereignty and Western European Union came into being; **26** British general election resulted in Conservative majority of 59.

June 15 U.S. and Britain agreed to co-operate on atomic energy; **16** Revolt against the Perón government in Argentina.

July 9 Leading world scientists issued appeal for renunciation of war because of possible effects of hydrogen bomb; **18** Four-Power conference opened in Geneva (Pres. Eisenhower, Sir Anthony Eden, M. Faure, Marshal Bulganin), the first meeting between heads of Government since Potsdam, 1945; **27** Austrian State Treaty came into force.

August 8 International conference on peaceful uses of atomic energy opened in Geneva (1200 scientists from 72 countries attended).

September 16 Universal Copyright convention came into force, bringing U.S. into agreement with European countries; **19** General Perón resigned after rebels threatened to bombard Buenos Aires; **22** Independent television service began.

October 2 City of London became a "smokeless zone"; **12** British and Soviet warships exchanged courtesy visits; **20** Syria and Egypt signed mutual defence treaty; **23** Referendum on Saar European Statute gave victory to pro-German parties.

November 5 Vienna State Opera House re-opened; **23** *Hamlet* played on Russian stage by British company, the first since Tsarist times.

December 7 Mr. Attlee announced his retirement and was created an earl; **12** Completion of 830-mile pipeline through Urals, crossing 6 rivers; **14** Mr. Hugh Gaitskell elected leader of the Parl. Labour Party; **18** Anglo-American offer of financial assistance to Egypt in building Aswan High Dam; **24** In Christmas broadcast the Pope spoke of need to suspend nuclear test explosions.

1956

January 1 Sudan proclaimed an independent republic; **27** The Queen and the Duke of Edin-

A.D.
burgh left by air for 3 weeks' tour of Nigeria;
200th anniversary of birth of Mozart celebrated;
Terrorist activity in Cyprus increasing.

February 1 Britain had coldest day since 1895;
13 Referendum in Malta resulted in vote in
favour of integration with Britain; **16** House
of Commons rejected by majority of 31 Government motion to retain death penalty; Bank
rate increased from 4½ to 5½ per cent. (highest
since 1932); **23** Remarkable sunflare caused
increased cosmic radiation and long-wave radio
disturbances; **25** M. Khrushchev in speech to
Congress of Russian Communist Party denounced Stalin.

March 2 King Hussein of Jordan discharged
Lieut.-Gen. J. B. Glubb; **5** Telephone weather
forecast began; **9** Archbishop Makarios with
leaders of Enosis movement in Cyprus deported
to the Seychelles; **23** The Queen laid foundation
stone of new Coventry Cathedral; Pakistan
proclaimed an Islamic Republic within the
Commonwealth.

April 6 Earl Attlee created Knight of the Garter;
11 Five-day week for Civil Servants announced;
18 Cease-fire between Israel and Egypt came
into force; **29** French occupation of Indo-China
ended after 80 years.

May 23 First atomic power station in Britain
started working at Calder Hall; **24** 2,500th
anniversary of the death of Buddha celebrated
in India; **31** May was the sunniest month at
Kew since 1922 and the driest since 1896.

June 3 Third-class travel abolished on British
Railways to conform to continental practice;
13 Last British troops left Suez; **24** Col. Nasser
elected Pres. of Egypt.

July 20 Britain joined U.S.A. in withdrawing offer
to help Egypt finance Aswan High Dam; **26**
Pres. Nasser announced nationalisation of Suez
Canal Company.

August 30 French troops arrived in Cyprus.

September 25 Newly-laid submarine telephone
cable linking Britain and America opened to
public service.

October 3 Bolshoi Ballet danced at Covent Garden;
15 Duke of Edinburgh left on world tour; **16**
Prime Minister left with For. Sec. for Paris
meeting; **17** The Queen opened Calder Hall, the
world's first nuclear power station for commercial use; **19-21** New liberalised policy adopted
by Central Committee of Polish United Workers'
Party; M. Gomulka elected first secretary; **23**
Insurrection broke out in Budapest and spread
throughout country; **28** Pres. Eisenhower
called upon Israel not to "endanger the peace";
29 Israeli forces invaded Egypt and after 5 days'
fighting had control of Sinai peninsula, heavy
fighting at Abu Aweigila; **30** Britain and France
issued 12-hour ultimatum to Israel and Egypt
to cease fighting; Britain and France vetoed
US resolution in Security Council calling upon
Israel to withdraw behind armistice line; **31**
Anglo-French offensive launched against
military targets in Egypt.

November 2 UN Gen. Assembly called for
immediate cease fire in Egypt; **4** Canadian
resolution calling for international UN force
for Middle East adopted; Soviet forces launched
attack on Budapest to crush uprising; **5**
Anglo-French airborne troops landed at Port
Said; **6** Seaborne troops landed at Port Said;
Pres. Eisenhower re-elected President with
Congress controlled by Democrats; Anglo-
French forces ceased fire at midnight; **7** Egypt
accepted cease fire on UN conditions; **15**
UN Emergency Force left Naples for Suez;
16 Suez Canal blocked by 49 ships; **17** First
refugees from Hungary arrived in Britain; **22**
Duke of Edinburgh opened 16th Olympic
Games in Melbourne; **20** Sir Anthony Eden
flew to Jamaica for rest cure; **24** UN for third
time called upon Britain, France, and Israel to
withdraw troops from Egypt.

December 5 140 people arrested in S. Africa for
alleged treason; Anglo-French forces began to
leave Port Said; **19** Lord Radcliffe's proposals
for a constitution for Cyprus published; **29**
Suez Canal clearing operation by UN salvage
fleet began.

A.D.
1957
January 1 Anglo-Egyptian treaty of 1954 abro-
gated by Pres. Nasser as from October 31, 1956;
Saar became tenth *Land* of German Federal
Republic; Road Traffic Act came into force; **5**
Eisenhower Doctrine for Middle East an-
nounced; **9** Resignation of Sir Anthony Eden
as Prime Minister; **10** Mr. Harold Macmillan
appointed Prime Minister; **16** Sadlers Wells
Ballet group combined to form The Royal
Ballet; Death of Signor Toscanini; **20** Mr.
Gomulka's National Unity Front overwhelm-
ingly returned in Polish general election;
India's first atomic reactor, *Apsara*, inaugu-
rated; **31** Trans-Iranian oil pipeline from
Abadan to Teheran (600 m.) completed.

February 7 Bank Rate reduced from 5½ to 5 per
cent; **15** Mr. Gromyko replaced Mr. Shepilov
as Soviet Foreign Minister; **16** The Queen flew
to Portugal on State visit and joined Duke of
Edinburgh there who had just completed
World tour; **22** Duke of Edinburgh granted
title of Prince of the United Kingdom; **26**
Indian resolution adopted by UN for "peaceful, democratic, and just solution" of Cyprus
problem.

March 1 Mass protest in Tokio against nuclear
weapon tests in Pacific; **5** Fianna Fail party
under Mr. de Valera secured absolute majority
in general election; **6** Ghana celebrated independence; Israeli withdrawal from Sinai
completed; **11** Warning by WHO of genetic
effects of radiation; **13** Anglo-Jordanian treaty
of 1948 ended; **21** Homicide Act in force
(death penalty retained only for five categories
of "capital murder"); **25** European Common
Market and Euratom treaties signed by France,
Germany, Italy, and Benelux countries.

April 3 British Labour Party called for abolition
of H-bomb tests; **4** No further call-ups for
National Service after 1960; **8** The Queen and
Prince Philip arrived in France on State visit;
9 Suez Canal cleared and opened to all shipping;
11 Agreement signed in London granting full
internal self-government to Singapore from Jan.
1, 1958; **17** Archbishop Makarios arrived in
Athens from exile; During the month appeals
were made by the Pope, Dr. Schweitzer and
Mr. Nehru for the banning of nuclear tests and
weapons.

May 14 Petrol rationing (imposed 17.12.56)
ended; **15** First British H-bomb exploded in
Central Pacific near Christmas I.; **16** M. Spaak
succeeded Lord Ismay as NATO Sec. Gen.;
18 The Queen and Prince Philip left for State
visit to Denmark; **20** Death of Dr. Gilbert
Murray.

June 1 New Copyright Act came into force; First
drawing of Premium Bond prizes; **17** Historic
decisions taken by US Supreme Court on
matters relating to civil liberties; **19** Completion of British H-bomb tests in Pacific; **30**
The IGY opened at midnight.

July 1 Women voted for the first time in Egypt's
first general election since revolution of 1952;
17 Electricity Bill enacted appointing new Central Electricity Generating Board and Electricity Council in place of Central Electricity
Authority; **18** President Mao Tse-tung's
famous "Let 100 flowers blossom and 100
schools of thought contend" speech published;
25 Tunisia declared a republic; **31** Federation
of Malaya Independence Act received Royal
Assent.

August 1 Sir Christopher Hinton appointed chairman of new C.E.G.B., responsible for new
nuclear power stations; **31** Royal Charter
granted to Tangier by King of Morocco.

September 6 Disarmament discussions in London
ended without agreement; **15** German general
election (Dr. Adenauer re-elected Chancellor
Oct. 22); **19** Bank Rate raised from 5 to 7 per
cent.; **20** Death of Jean Sibelius, the Finnish
composer; **30** Network Three introduced by
B.B.C.

October 4 First earth satellite launched by Russia
(180 lb. sphere, 23 in. diameter); **10** U.S.A.
abolished fingerprinting for foreign visitors
staying less than a year; **11** Largest radio tele-

A.D.

scope in world went into operation at Jodrell Bank for Manchester University; 14 The Queen opened Canadian Parliament in Ottawa; New road–rail double-decker bridge over Yangtse, one of largest in world, opened to traffic; 17 Endorsement of cheques no longer necessary save when negotiated.

November 3 Second earth satellite weighing half a ton launched into space by Russia with dog on board; 16 Russia announced construction of "scientific city" of 12 research institutes in Siberia; 20 Britain's first export order for nuclear power station for Northern Italy announced.

December 1 Latin 26-letter alphabet to be adopted in China; 4 Ninety people killed in rail ay accident in fog at Lewisham; 6 Attempt to launch earth satellite in the U.S.A. failed; *Sputnik I* completed its thousandth circuit of the Earth; 25 The Queen's Christmas broadcast televised for the first time; 31 The *Sputniks* were still circling the Earth, the first being expected to fall in the first days of January.

1958

January 1 Treaties establishing EEC (Common Market) and EAEC (Euratom) came into force; Metric system of weights and measures adopted throughout Japan; 3 Inauguration of West Indian Federation; Sir Edmund Hillary and New Zealand party reached South Pole; 4 *Sputnik I* disintegrated after completing 1,367 circuits of the Earth and travelling 43 million miles; 6 First non-stop flight across Antarctica by single-engine British aircraft (1,600 miles in 10 hr. 57 min.); Mr. Thorneycroft resigned from Government after disagreement in Cabinet over pruning Budget estimates; 7 Mr. Macmillan left for six-week tour of Commonwealth; 8 Summit talks proposed by Marshal Bulganin and Notes sent to 19 States; 13 Over 9,000 scientists from 44 countries petition UN Sec. Gen. to end nuclear weapons tests; 20 Dr. Vivian Fuchs, leader of Commonwealth expedition, reached South Pole; 24 Announcement that Harwell scientists working with ZETA had passed first milestone on road towards power from nuclear fusion; 28 Abolition of licensed prostitution in Italy; 31 First American earth satellite *Explorer I* (30·8 lb.) successfully launched.

February 1 Union of Egypt and Syria in the United Arab Republic; 5 Continuation of Antarctic research for at least 5 years after end of IGY announced; 8 French aircraft bombed Tunisian frontier village of Sakhiet; 14 Merger of Iraq and Jordan under name of Arab Federation; 19 Worst colliery disaster in Indian history in West Bengal; 25 Restoration plans for Stonehenge announced; Campaign for Nuclear Disarmament launched under presidency of Lord Russell.

March 2 IGY Commonwealth Trans-Antarctic Expedition, led by Dr. Vivian Fuchs, completed first crossing of Antarctic (2,200 miles in 99 days); 8 Federal union between UAR and Yemen established; 14 Birth of Prince Albert of Monaco; Small test satellite, *Beta 1958*, successfully launched by US Navy; 20 Bank rate reduced from 7 to 6 per cent; 21 Opening of London planetarium, the first of its kind in Britain; 26 Third US earth satellite, *Explorer III*, successfully launched; 27 M. Khrushchev elected Prime Minister in succession to M. Bulganin; 31 Russian resolution to suspend nuclear tests; other powers invited to follow suit.

April 1 Abolition of legalised prostitution in Japan; 4 Campaign for Nuclear Disarmament organised 50-mile protest march from London to Atomic Weapons Research Establishment at Aldermaston, Berkshire; 14 *Sputnik II* disintegrated over Caribbean, having completed 2,370 circuits of the Earth and travelled 62 million miles; 17 Nationalist Party of S. Africa returned with increased majority; Sir Grantley Adams elected first Prime Minister of the new West Indian Federation; 22 Princess Margaret opened the new Federal Parliament in Trinidad.

A.D.

May 1 Intense radiation belt in outer space discovered by US *Explorer* earth satellite; 10 Anti-government disturbances in Lebanon; 13 Military and colonist insurrection in Algeria; President of Italy paid state visit to Britain; 15 *Sputnik III* launched under IGY programme; New college to be built at Cambridge University (Churchill College); 22 Further reduction in Bank Rate to 5½ per cent.; 24 Nuclear reactor at Dounreay began working; 29 General de Gaulle accepted invitation to form a "Government of national safety."

June 1 General de Gaulle became Prime Minister of France; Clean Air Act banning emission of dark smoke came into force; 9 Gatwick Airport opened by the Queen; 19 Further cut in Bank Rate from 5½ to 5 per cent.; New British plan for Cyprus announced; 20 London bus strike ended after 7 weeks; 21 Greek Government rejected British plan for Cyprus; 23 Ghana to be declared a republic.

July 1 Conference of scientists, including Russian delegation, met at Geneva to discuss ways of detecting nuclear tests; 14 Iraq monarchy overthrown, King Faisal assassinated; establishment of Republic announced; 15 US marines landed in Lebanon; 17 British troops flown to Amman in response to King Hussein's appeal; 24 First life barons and baronesses under Life Peerages Act named; 26 H.M. the Queen created her son, Charles, Prince of Wales; 31 British Prime Minister sent appeal to all Cypriots to end violence.

August 1 British Government recognised Republic of Iraq; 5 U.S. nuclear submarine *Nautilus* surfaced after having passed under North Pole; 7 Litter Act came into force in Britain; 14 Bank Rate reduced from 5 to 4½ per cent.; 17 First attempt by America to launch moon rocket failed; Britain to resume nuclear tests on Christmas Island; 23 Bombardment by Chinese of Quemoy (Formosa Strait); 29 More American warships join Seventh Fleet in Formosa Strait.

September 1 International conference on peaceful uses of atomic energy opened in Geneva; 7 Britain successfully fired its first ballistic rocket (Black Knight) from Woomera; 15 Ambassadors of America and China met in Warsaw for discussions on Formosa crisis; 16 Relaxations in hire-purchase; 29 Referendum resulted in overwhelming victory for General de Gaulle; Lord Goddard retired as Lord Chief Justice; succeeded by Lord Justice Parker; Gen. Sir Francis Festing succeeded Field-Marshal Sir Gerald Templer as Chief of the Imperial General Staff.

October 1 India began change to metric system; 2 French Guinea proclaimed Republic of Guinea after overwhelming vote for independence in French referendum; 8 Martial law in Pakistan; 9 Death of Pope Pius XII at age of 82; 11 The London weeklies *John Bull* and *Illustrated* merged; US *Pioneer* space-rocket successfully launched (but failed to reach moon); 21 First women peers introduced to House of Lords; 28 State opening of Parliament and Queen's Speech televised; Cardinal Roncalli, Patriarch of Venice, elected as Pope John XXIII at age of 76; 31 Conference opened in Geneva (Russia, Britain, and the United States) on suspension of nuclear tests.

November 20 Bank Rate reduced from 4½ to 4 per cent.; 21 Work started on Forth road bridge, the largest suspension bridge in Europe; 27 Russian plan for withdrawal of troops and demilitarised free Berlin.

December 8 Last of four nuclear reactors at Calder Hall brought into operation; 17 Chinese leader, Mao Tse-tung, to resign as chairman of Republic but to retain party office; 18 US 4-ton missile fired into orbit; Empire Day to be known in future as Commonwealth Day; 21 General de Gaulle elected President of France; 27 Partial convertibility between £ and $ announced; UAR and Russia signed agreement on Russian co-operation in Aswan high dam project; 28 General de Gaulle announced devaluation of the franc; 31 IGY officially came to an end.

A.D.
1959

January 1 Batista Government in Cuba overthrown by revolutionary movement under Dr. Fidel Castro; **2** Russia launched planet round the sun (*Lunik I*); **3** Alaska became 49th state of American Union; **4** Mr. Mikoyan, Soviet Dep. Prime Min., arrived in Washington on 16-day visit; Rioting in Leopoldville; **7** Britain recognised new Cuban Government; **8** Gen. de Gaulle installed as first Pres. of Fifth French Republic; **10** Russian proposal for conference of 28 nations to draw up German Peace Treaty; **25** Oecumenical Council, the first since 1870, convened by Pope John XXIII.

February 1 Votes for women rejected by Swiss national poll; **9** New research reactor to be built at Windscale, Cumberland; **11** M. Vincent Auriol resigned from French Socialist Party; **21** Mr. Macmillan arrived in Moscow on official visit; **23** Archbishop Makarios returned to Cyprus after 3-year exile; Cyprus to become a republic with Greek Pres. and Turkish Vice-Pres.; **26** State of emergency declared in Southern Rhodesia; **27** Riots in Malta dockyard due to dismissal of workers.

March 3 American *Pioneer IV* went into planetary orbit round sun; State of emergency declared in Nyasaland; British scientists isolated basic molecule of penicillin; **17** Uprising in Lhasa against Chinese rule; Flight of Dalai Lama to India; **24** Iraq withdrew from Baghdad Pact.

April 5 Panchen Lama arrived in Lhasa to take over local government of Tibet; **8** Chair of Criminology founded at Cambridge; **14-16** Worst flood disaster of century in S. America; **23** British heart specialists in Moscow to demonstrate heart surgery; **27** Liu Shao-ch'i succeeded Mao Tse-tung as Chairman (President) of Chinese People's Republic.

May 1 Opening of Rajendra Bridge (6,074 ft.) over Ganges at Hathidah (Bihar); **2** First Scottish nuclear power-station opened at Chapelcross; **15** Jodrell Bank radioed message to United States via moon; **28** Opening of Mermaid Theatre in City of London; **30** Auckland Harbour Bridge officially opened; **31** World's population (2,800 millions) increasing at rate of 45 millions a year.

June 8 U.S. Post Office made first successful delivery of mail by guided missile; **17** Mr. de Valera elected Pres. of Rep. of Ireland; Serious riots in African townships in Durban; **18** Five-year plan for Scottish Highlands announced; **24** World record price (£275,000) paid at Sotheby's for Rubens' *The Adoration of the Magi*; **26** St. Lawrence Seaway formally opened by the Queen and Pres. Eisenhower; **29** Norwegian Halden nuclear reactor in operation;

July 3 Italy to build nuclear submarine *Guglielmo Marconi*; Tancarville road bridge near Le Havre, longest suspension bridge in Europe, opened; **4** Transatlantic record flight set up by Vickers *Vanguard* turbo-prop airliner (2,500 m. in 5½ hrs.); **5** Recovery in good condition of 3 animals from outer space; **7** Litter Act passed making it an offence to drop litter (fine up to £10); **21** Launching of first nuclear merchant ship *Savannah* by Mrs. Eisenhower; **28** £100 tax-free annuity for V.C. holders.

August 16 The Street Offences Act came into force; **21** Baghdad Pact renamed Central Treaty Organisation; **22** First round-the-world service by British airliners inaugurated; **23** Announcement of plan for oil-pipeline network between Soviet Union and East European countries (completion 1963).

September 11 British loan made available for Malta dockyard. **13** Russia launched *Lunik II* which landed on moon; **15** Soviet atomic icebreaker *Lenin* made maiden voyage into Baltic; **25** Mr. Bandaranaike, Prime Min. of Ceylon, assassinated; **27** Typhoon in W. Japan (5,000 killed and missing, 1,000,000 homeless).

October 4 Russia fired *Lunik III*, which took photographs of back of moon; **8** General Election returned Conservatives with 100 overall majority; **10** End of one of longest droughts ever recorded in Britain; **24** Opening of new

A.D.
airport for Wellington, N.Z.; **29** Dublin's famous Abbey Theatre to be rebuilt (destroyed by fire 1951).

November 1 Basic travel allowance for British tourists ended (foreign currency up to £250 a year and further amounts on application to Bank of England); **2** First section of London-Yorkshire motorway (M1) opened to traffic; **5** Philip Noel-Baker awarded Nobel Peace Prize; **8** Sudan and U.A.R. signed agreement on distribution of Nile waters; **17** Announcement of discovery by American scientists of submarine plateau in Arctic Ocean; **19** Bank of England announced introduction of new series of bank notes (10s., £1, £5, £10); **14** Dounreay fast breeder reactor went into operation; **21** British book exhibition opened in Moscow; **24** CERN's proton synchrotron at Geneva went into full operation generating 24,000 million electron volts (24 GeV.); **27** Duke of Edinburgh opened Ghana's Academy of Learning in Accra; **28** Naval dockyard at Hong Kong closed after 80 years; **30** Inauguration of Italy's first nuclear research reactor; Pink Zone traffic plan went into operation in London.

December 1 Anglo-Russian cultural agreement signed in London; **12**-power treaty on Antarctica signed in Washington; State of emergency in Cyprus ended; Bursting of dam at Fréjus killed 384 people; Pres. Eisenhower began tour of Europe, Asia, and Middle East; **5** Opening of 400-mile Sahara pipeline by French Prime Minister; **6** Inauguration of Panchet Hill Dam on Damodar R., Bihar; **10** Raising of school-leaving age to 16 recommended by Crowther Report; **14** Archbishop Makarios elected first Pres. of Cyprus; **15** New world speed record of 1,520 m.p.h. set up by U.S. Air Force pilot; **21** Marriage of Shah of Persia to Miss Farah Diba; **26** Soviet Antarctic expedition reached South Pole; **28** Jugoslavia's first nuclear reactor went into operation; Tokyo reported that in 1959 38 people died in hospital from 1945 Hiroshima atomic bomb attack.

1960

January 1 Republic of Cameroun (formerly French Cameroons) became independent state. **4** Albert Camus, French writer, killed in car crash. **7** Hirfanli Dam in Turkey opened, largest in Europe. **9** Work begun on Aswan High Dam. **12** State of emergency ended in Kenya after 8 years; **13** Mr. Aleksander Soldatov appointed to succeed Mr. J. Malik as Soviet Ambassador to Britain. **21** Bank rate increased to 5%. **23** M. Jacques Piccard and an American naval officer descended 7 miles under Pacific in Marianas Trench. **24** Army rising in Algeria. **29** Broadcast of Pres. de Gaulle to nation contributed to collapse of military revolt.

February 3 Mr. Macmillan addressed S. African Parliament (famous "wind of change" speech). **4** Announcement that American university had made radar contact with Sun. **13** First French atomic test in Sahara. **17** British agreement to U.S. ballistic missile early-warning system at Fylingdales Moor, Yorkshire. **19** Prince Andrew born. **29** Agadir destroyed by earthquake.

March 17 New £1 notes issued in Britain. **18** Last steam locomotive of British Railways named. **21** Sharpeville shooting in S. Africa when police fired on African gathering. **23** Mr. Khrushchev in Paris. **30** State of emergency in S. Africa.

April 1 U.N. Security Council adopted resolution deploring shootings in S. Africa. Dr. Hastings Banda, Pres. of proscribed Nyasaland African Congress, released from detention in S. Rhodesia. **5** Pres. de Gaulle on state visit to Britain. **9** Attempt on life of Dr. Verwoerd. **13** *Blue Streak* as military weapon abandoned. **27** Rep. of Togo (former Togoland) came into being as independent state.

May 1 U.S. aircraft engaged in military reconnaissance flight over Soviet territory shot down. **6** Wedding of Princess Margaret and Mr. A. Armstrong-Jones in Westminster Abbey. **7** U.S. to resume underground nuclear tests; Tal beat Botvinnik in world chess championship; Mr.

A.D.

Leonid Brezhnev succeeded Marshal Voroshilov as Pres. of Soviet Union. **16** Opening and breakdown of Summit conference in Paris. **17** Queen Elizabeth The Queen Mother officially opened Kariba Dam. **21** Earthquake disaster in Chile. **25** Everest climbed by 3 Chinese by northern slope. Army seized control in Turkey. End of U.S. foreign aid to Cuba. **30** Death of Boris Pasternak.

June 10 Britain's first guided-missile destroyer *Devonshire* launched. Britain's nuclear power programme to be slowed down. **23** Bank rate raised to 6%. **25** Completion of second Saharan oil pipe-line (Edjelé to La Skirra on Tunisian coast). **26** British rule in Somaliland ended; Madagascar became independent state within French Community. **29** House of Commons rejected Wolfenden Committee's recommendations on homosexuality. **30** Belgian Congo became independent as the Congo Republic (Pres. M. Kasavubu, Prime Min. M. Lumumba).

July 1 Ghana proclaimed a Republic; Somali Republic came into being (merging of former British Somaliland and Italian Somaliland). **6** Army mutiny in Congo. Death of Aneurin Bevan. **11** Ivory Coast, Dahomey, Niger, and Upper Volta became independent. M. Tshombe, Congolese privincial leader, declared Katanga independent. M. Lumumba asked for U.N. help in reorganising mutinous *Force publique*. **12** Congo (French), Chad and Central African Rep. became independent. **14** Sec. Council called for withdrawal of Belgian troops from Congo. **19–26** Royal Society Tercentenary celebrations.

August 2 Rawalpindi capital of Pakistan instead of Karachi. **8** Military *coup d'état* in Laos. **9** Sec. Council called on Belgium to withdraw troops from Katanga and authorised U.N. troops to replace them. **16** End of British rule in Cyprus which becomes independent Republic. **25** Olympic Games opened in Rome. **29** Prime Minister of Jordan assassinated.

September 5 Announcement by Pres. Kasavubu that he had dismissed M. Lumumba as Prime Minister of Congo. **14** M. Lumumba appealed to U.N. for protection. **19** India and Pakistan signed Indus Waters Treaty. **23** Mr. Khrushchev led Soviet delegation to U.N. General Assembly in New York and criticised U.N. operations in Congo.

October 1 Federation of Nigeria became independent state and a Member of the Commonwealth. **5** Labour Party Conference voted against Party's official defence policy. **14** Turkish trials of members of Menderes régime began. **21** Royal Navy's first nuclear submarine *Dreadnought* launched at Barrow-in-Furness by the Queen. **27** Bank rate reduced to 5½%.

November 1 U.S. *Polaris* missile-firing submarines to have base on Clyde. **3** Mr. Gaitskell re-elected leader of Parliamentary Labour Party. **9** Senator John Kennedy elected Pres. of United States. **28** Islamic Republic of Mauritania proclaimed its independence.

December 1 Capture of M. Lumumba by Col. Mobutu's forces. **2** Archbishop of Canterbury visited the Pope at the Vatican. **8** Bank rate reduced to 5%. **14** Fighting in Vientiane, cap. of Laos, between right-wing and left-wing forces. **15** Marriage of King Baudouin of Belgium. **17** Revolt in Ethiopia crushed. **21** Strikes in Belgium. **27** Union of Ghana, Guinea, and Mali. **31** Farthing ceased to be legal tender.

1961

January 18 M. Lumumba, first Prime Min. of the independent Congo, sent to Katanga for imprisonment. **20** The Queen and the Duke of Edinburgh left for tour of India, Pakistan. Nepal and Iran; Mr. John Kennedy took office as 35th Pres. of the United States. **23** Portuguese liner *Santa Maria* seized in Caribbean by armed insurgents under Captain Henrique Galvão as protest against Salazar dictatorship. **26** Full diplomatic relations resumed between Britain and United Arab Republic. **31** M. Spaak resigned as Sec.-Gen. of Nato.

A.D.

February 1 Increased National Health Service prescription charges announced. **3** Capt. Galvão hands over *Santa Maria* to Commander of Brazilian Navy in Recife. **5** Riots in Angola. **13** Death of M. Lumumba announced (violent demonstrations in many countries). **15** Total eclipse of the sun visible from Europe. **21** U.N. authorised the use of force " if necessary, in the last resort " to prevent civil war in Congo; measures also to be taken for withdrawal of all foreign military personnel and mercenaries. **26** Death of King Mohammed V of Morocco; succeeded by elder son who becomes King Hassan II.

March 8 First of American nuclear-powered submarines carrying Polaris missiles arrived at Holy Loch; Death of Sir Thomas Beecham. **12** First winter ascent of the Eiger. **14** The New English Bible (New Testament) published. **15** Uprising of tribal groups in Angola, Portuguese murdered; brutal retaliation of Portuguese by burning and bombing. **25** Russian satellite with dog aboard launched and brought safely back to earth. **29** Four-year South African treason trial ended with acquittal of accused. **31** The Nore Command ceased to exist.

April 9 Death of former King Zog of Albania. **11** Opening of trial of Adolf Eichmann in Jerusalem. **12** Major Yuri Gagarin made first flight into space and back. **17** Unsuccessful invasion of Cuba by rebel forces. **22** Insurrection of part of French army in Algeria: State of emergency declared in France. **23** Census held in Great Britain. **24** Gen. de Gaulle ordered blockade of Algeria. **25** Both sides in Laos agreed to cease-fire. **26** Collapse of mutiny in Algeria. **27** Independence of Sierra Leone.

May 1 Betting and Gaming Act came into force in Britain; betting shops opened. **5** Commander Alan Shepard made first American flight into space; The Queen and the Duke of Edinburgh visited Pope John XXIII at the Vatican. **12** Botvinnik regained world chess championship from Tal. **16** International conference on Laos opened in Geneva; Army in South Korea seized power. **17** Guildford Cathedral consecrated. **19** British Trade Fair in Moscow opened (M. Khrushchev present). **20** Talks opened at Evian between French government and Algerian provincial government (broke down July 18). **31** Gen. Trujillo, dictator of Dominican Republic, assassinated; South Africa became a Republic and withdrew from British Commonwealth.

June 1 N. Cameroons became part of Nigeria. **3** Meeting of Pres. Kennedy and M. Khrushchev in Vienna. **9** Security Council voted for Afro-Asian resolution calling upon Portugal to end repressive measures in Angola. **24** Promulgation by Pope John XXIII of new constitution for the Knights of Malta. **27** Enthronement of Dr. Ramsey as Archbishop of Canterbury in Canterbury Cathedral. **30** Portuguese refused to stop repressive measures in Angola.

July 1 British forces landed in Kuwait following appeal from ruler. **2** Death of Ernest Hemingway. **7** Soviet Trade Exhibition opened in London. **11** Major Yuri Gagarin, Russian pioneer of space travel, welcomed in London. **18** Over £9 million raised in Britain for 1960 World Refugee Year. **19** Fighting began between French and Tunisian forces over Bizerta naval base; Announcement of U.K.–U.S. agreement to establish Missile Defence Alarm (Midas) Station at Kirkbride, Cumberland. **21** U.S. launched its second space traveller (Capt. V. Grissom) 118 m. high, flight time 16 mins.; New Runcorn-Widnes Bridge opened over Mersey and Manchester Ship Canal (third largest span of its kind in the world and the largest span arch in Europe). **24** Bank rate rose from 5 to 7%. **30** Israel began construction of deep-sea port at Asdod.

August 4 International Monetary Fund placed £714 million at Bitain's disposal. **6** Major Titov, Russia's second space man, circled earth 17 times before landing back near Moscow 25 hours later. **13** Soviet sector of Berlin sealed off from Western sectors. **14** Jomo Kenyatta

A.D.

became a free man again. **15** U.N. recognised M. Adoula's government as the central government of the Congo. **16** Dr. Hastings Banda's Malawi Congress Party won control in the Nyasaland Legislative Assembly. **30** No agreement reached at Geneva on banning of nuclear tests. **31** Soviet announcement of resumption of nuclear weapons tests.

September 5 International conference on preservation of wild life opened at Arusha, Tanganyika; U.S. to resume underground nuclear tests. **18** Mr. Hammarskjöld killed in plane crash when flying from Leopoldville, Congo, to Ndola, N. Rhodesia, to meet M. Tshombe in effort to arrange cease-fire between U.N. and Katanga forces. **28** Syria seceded from the United Arab Republic (the latter name to continue to be used by Egypt).

October 1 S. Cameroons gained independence as part of Cameroun. **3** Mr. A. Armstrong-Jones created Earl of Snowdon. **4** Labour Party Conference voted against Polaris bases and German troops in Britain. **5** Bank rate reduced to 6½%. **10** Volcanic eruption on Tristan da Cunha: whole population evacuated to Britain. **21** U.S. put into space, amid world-wide protest, 350 million copper needles for reflecting radio signals (they failed to disperse into orbit). **23** Nobel Peace Prize for 1960 awarded to South African, Albert Luthuli, former Zulu chief; that for 1961 posthumously to Dag Hammarskjöld. **30** Russia tested a bomb of over 60 megatons amid world-wide protest. **31** Hurricane struck British Honduras, Belize devastated; Stalin's body removed from the Lenin Mausoleum in Red Square; Australia's new radio telescope at Parkes, N.S.W. officially commissioned by Gov.-Gen.

November 1 Boy scouts permitted to wear long trousers. **2** Bank rate reduced to 6%. **3** U Thant, Burma's chief representative at U.N., elected Acting Sec.-Gen. of U.N.; Birth of son to Princess Margaret and Lord Snowdon; Government refused to save Doric arch at Euston station. **7** Dr. Adenauer re-elected Chancellor of Fed. German Rep. for fourth time. **8** Official negotiations for entry of Britain into Common Market opened in Brussels; Wales votes for Sunday opening. **9** The Queen and the Duke of Edinburgh left for tour of Ghana, Liberia, and Sierra Leone. **20** Admission of Russian Orthodox Church to World Council of Churches meeting at New Delhi. **28** South Africa's apartheid policy condemned by U.N.

December 8 Cross-Channel submarine cable linking electricity systems of England and France officially inaugurated. **9** Tanganyika became independent sovereign state within British Commonwealth; Russia broke off diplomatic relations with Albania. **15** Adolf Eichmann sentenced to death by Israeli court for crimes against the Jewish people and against humanity; Mr. Macmillan and Pres. Kennedy met in Bermuda. **17** Indian troops took over Portuguese colony of Goa. **19** Decimal coinage accepted in principle by British government. **20** Mr. Adoula and Mr. Tshombe agreed on Katanga's subordinate status. **27** Belgium and the Congo resumed diplomatic relations.

1962

January 1 Western Samoa became independent. **10** Avalanche disaster in Peru. **11** Smallpox outbreak in Britain. **15** Centigrade first used in weather forecasts. **16** Death of R. H. Tawney. **24** T.U.C. decided to join "Neddy". **27** New world record for mile by New Zealander Peter Snell (3 min. 54·4 secs.). **30** Birth of son to King Hussein of Jordan.

February 11 Death of Lord Birkett. **20** American first manned orbital flight.

March 7 Franco-Algerian negotiations began at Evian; Publication of Royal College of Physician's Report on dangers to health from cigarette smoking. **8** Bank rate reduced from 6 to 5½%. **14** Opening of 17-nation disarmament conference at Geneva. **19** End of Algerian war. **28** Inauguration of Marlborough

A.D.

House, built by Wren, as Commonwealth Centre.

April 1 Government's "pay pause" ended. **2** "Panda" crossings in operation in number of British towns. **5** Completion of Gt. St. Bernard road tunnel. **7** Strike in Asturias—first of many throughout Spain. **8** French people voted in referendum approving Algerian peace settlement. **11** Pres. Kennedy condemned U.S. steel industry for raising prices. **13** International agreement (40 countries) to stop oil pollution of seas and beaches. **20** Gen. Salan, O.A.S. leader, arrested by French in Algiers. **25** U.S. began new series of atmospheric nuclear tests in Pacific. **26** Britain's first satellite, *Ariel*, launched from Cape Canaveral; Bank rate down from 5 to 4½%. **30** Norway applied to join Common Market.

May 6 Signor Segni elected Pres. of Italy; Canonisation of St. Martin de Porres of Lima (d. 1639), first mulatto saint of the R.C. church. **8** Trolleybuses ran for last time in London. **13** Dr. Radhakrishnan elected Pres. of India. **25** Consecration of new Coventry Cathedral. **29** Dawley, Shropshire, designated new town. **31** Eichmann executed in Israel; Dissolution of The West Indies Federation.

June 5 Creation of University of Lagos, Nigeria. **14** Creation of European Space Research Organisation (ESRO). **15** Nuclear power station at Berkeley, Glos., began electricity supply to national grid. **18** The *Flying Scotsman* made centenary journey; Conservatives (Mr. Diefenbaker) won Canadian general election by small majority. **23** Cease-fire in Laos. **24** Opening of Punjabi University, India. **28** U.N. called for more liberal constitution for S. Rhodesia.

July 1 Burundi and Rwanda became independent; After 132 years French colonial rule in Algeria ended; Commonwealth Immigrants Act came into force. **3** Plan for British national theatre and opera house accepted by L.C.C. and Government. **5** Independence celebrated in Algeria. **8** Pres. de Gaulle and Chan. Adenauer attended Mass in Rheims cathedral. **10** *Telstar*, first experimental satellite in space communication, launched—first live television between U.S. and Europe. **20** Death of G. M. Trevelyan, the historian. **25** Opening of new civic centre at Plymouth. **26** Government announce setting up of "Nicky". **30** Archbishop of Canterbury visited Moscow. **31** Rendezvous of U.S. nuclear submarines at North Pole.

August 5 Russia began series of atmospheric nuclear tests; Death of Marilyn Monroe, at age 36. **5** Jamaica became independent. **10** Abandonment of *Blue Water* missile. **11** British mountaineers scaled Russia's highest peak (Mt. Communism). **11** and **12** Russia launched two men into orbit (64 orbits and 48 orbits). **13** British travel allowances further eased from £250 a year to £250 a journey. **14** Completion of Mont Blanc tunnel (7½ m.). **17** Pres. Kennedy's Bill on medical care rejected by Senate. **20** Government approval for construction of new underground railway between Victoria and Walthamstow. **21** Maiden voyage of *Savannah*, world's first nuclear-powered merchant ship. **27** U.S. *Mariner II* launched towards Venus. **31** Trinidad and Tobago became independent.

September 3 Opening of Trans-Canada highway (4,800 m. from St. John's, Newfoundland, to Victoria, B.C.). **7** Life presidency for Dr. Nkrumah. **15** In exchange of Notes Iran assured Russia that no foreign rocket bases would be permitted. **20** Zimbabwe African People's Union banned in S. Rhodesia; Fighting between Chinese and Indian troops on disputed N.E. frontier. **27** Overthrow of Imamate and republic proclaimed in Yemen. **29** Canada launched her first satellite, the *Alouette*, into orbit. **30** U.S. troops enforced Fed. Government's order that Negro student should enrol at Mississippi State University.

October 3 6-orbit flight of U.S. astronaut. **9** Uganda became independent. **11** 21st Oecumenical Council opened at St. Peter's, Rome.

A.D.

17 Opening of Hyde Park Corner underpass; Electricity for national grid generated at Dounreay reactor. 24 Commencement of U.S. naval quarantine of Cuba. 28 Dismantling of missile base in Cuba agreed upon by Russia; Gen. de Gaulle won referendum for his proposal for direct election of President.

November 1 Russia sent spacecraft on 7-month journey to Mars. 6 Admiralty announced record ocean depth by H.M.S. *Cook* in Mindanao trench (37,782 ft); Opening of Commonwealth Institute (replaces Imperial Institute, S. Kensington). 18 Death of Niels Bohr. 20 Cuba blockade ended. 21 Cease-fire declaration by China on Sino-Indian border dispute (no further hostilities occurred after this date). 29 Announcement of new Indo-Pakistan negotiations on Kashmir. 30 U Thant unanimously elected Sec.-Gen. of U.N.

December 5 Soviet-American space research co-operation agreement; Uprising in British prot. of Brunei in protest to joining Fed. of Malaysia; British nuclear device exploded underground in Nevada. 9 Tanganyika became republic and Dr. Julius Nyerere its first president. 12 British troops in control of Brunei uprising. 14 Signals from *Mariner II* as it passed within 21,000 miles of Venus; Eritrea became province of Ethiopia; N. Rhodesia's first African dominated government formed. 15 Sir Edgar Whitehead's party lost to right-wing party in S. Rhodesian general election. 17 Mr. Macmillan left for meeting with Pres. Kennedy at Nassau, Bahamas. 21 U.S. decision to abandon *Skybolt*; offer of *Polaris* missiles for British submarines to form part of multilateral Nato nuclear force. 23 M. Fedorenko succeeded M. Zorin as Soviet perm. rep. at U.N. 25 Europe snowbound with freezing temperatures. 28 Agreement in principle reached between China and Pakistan defining mutual boundary. 29 Southern England swept by blizzard. 30 Worst snowstorms in England since 1881. 31 British Transport Commission replaced by British Railways Board (created by Transport Act, 1962), with Dr. Beeching as chairman.

1963

January 2 Gen. Lemnitzer succeeded Gen. Norstad as Supreme Allied Commander, Europe. 3 Bank rate reduced from 4½ to 4 per cent. 14 Gen. de Gaulle's press conference repulsing Britain's entry to EEC and rejecting U.S. Polaris offer. 15 Official ending of Katanga secession. 18 Death of Hugh Gaitskell; Aden acceded to Fed. of S. Arabia. 29 Britain was refused entry to EEC; Death of Robert Frost, the American poet.

February 1 Nyasaland became self-governing protectorate. 5 Death of Lord Samuel. 6 Shipping restrictions on Cuba announced by U.S. Government. 8 Overthrow of Iraq government and execution of Gen. Kassim. 12 Seventeen-nation disarmament conference resumed in Geneva. 14 Harold Wilson elected leader of Labour Party. 19 Bali volcano disaster (others followed March 19, May 19). Earthquake in Barce, Libya. 22 Unemployment figures showed 878,356, highest since 1947.

March 5–6 First frost-free night in Britain since Dec. 22. 8 Syrian government overthrown by military coup. 17 Typhoid broke out in Zermatt; First of Tristan da Cunha islanders returned home. 27 Publication of Beeching Report on British Railways.

April 5 Opening of Berkley and Bradwell civil nuclear power stations. 6 Polaris missile agreement signed between U.S. and Britain. 8 Mr. Diefenbaker's Conservative Party defeated by Liberals in Canadian general election. 9 Honorary American citizenship conferred on Sir Winston Churchill. 10 Pope John XXIII published his encyclical *Pacem in Terris*; New Zealand to change to decimal coinage in 1967; Loss of U.S. nuclear submarine *Thresher* with 129 lives. 17 Commissioning of Royal Navy's first nuclear-powered submarine, H.M.S. *Dreadnought*. 20 Execution of Julian Grimau, Spanish communist leader.

A.D.

May 1 End of Dutch East Indies: New Guinea (West Irian) handed to Indonesia. 15 Twenty-two-orbit flight of Major Cooper of U.S. Air Force. 16 Radio contact lost with Soviet *Mars I* launched Nov. 1962. 20 Petrosian won world chess title from Botvinnik; Life presidency for Pres. Sukarno of Indonesia.

June 1 Death of Pope John XXIII; new internal self-government constitution for Kenya came into force with Jomo Kenyatta as Kenya's first Prime Minister. 11 Iraq resumed war against Kurds. 12 Rioting on big scale in Georgetown, British Guiana. 14–19 Bykovsky-Tereshkova space flights (first woman astronaut). 16 Resignation of Mr. Ben-Gurion announced. 20 House of Commons censure on Mr. John Profumo, former Sec. of State for War. 24 Zanzibar achieved internal self-government. 28 Inauguration in Nairobi of Univ. of East Africa. 30 Pope Paul VI crowned.

July 2 Franco-German Treaty of Co-operation came into force. 5 Sino-Soviet ideological talks began. 9 State visit of King and Queen of Greece to Britain. 26 Skopje destroyed by earthquake. 29 Pres. de Gaulle rejected Moscow test-ban treaty. 31 The Peerage Bill received the Royal Assent; Security Council called on member states to impose partial arms embargo on Portugal.

August 1 Under Criminal Justice Act, 1961, minimum prison age raised to 17. 3 First successful solo climb on north wall of Eiger by Michel Darbellay, a Swiss mountain guide. 5 Partial nuclear-test-ban treaty signed in Moscow by America, Russia, and Britain. 7 Security Council resolution to stop sale and shipment of arms to S. Africa. 8 Glasgow-London mail train robbery (£2·5 million). 9 Caernarvon declared royal borough (first in Wales). 16 Announcement of American-Soviet weather-and communications-satellite programme. 20 Mr. Khrushchev visited Yugoslavia. 21 Buddhists arrested and martial law imposed in South Vietnam. 28 Great Negro "freedom march" on Washington. 31 Death of George Braque, the French painter; The "hot line" linking Kremlin with White House went into service.

September 5 Soviet-American co-operation in cosmic ray research in Antarctica announced. 15 Ben Bella elected first President of Algeria. 16 New state of Malaysia (Malaya, Singapore, North Borneo (now Sabah), and Sarawak) came into being. 17 Malaysia broke off diplomatic relations with Indonesia; Flyingdales ballistic missile early warning station came into operation. 18 New Australian decimal currency to be introduced Feb. 1966 (unit to be called the dollar). 19 Anglo-French report recommended rail tunnel as Channel link. 21 Reform of Roman Catholic Curia announced by Pope Paul VI. 23 Report on decimal currency advocated division of £1 into 100 units. 25 Denning report on Profumo affair published. 29 Reopening of Vatican Council; First buildings of University of East Anglia opened at Norwich.

October 1 Nigeria became a republic within the Commonwealth with Dr. Azikiwe its first President; Algeria nationalised French-owned land 3 Honduras government overthrown by Army. 4 Hurricane Flora struck the Caribbean. 9 Viaont dam disaster (N. Italy); the Kubaka of Buganda became first President of Uganda. 15 Dr. Adenauer retired after 14 years as Chancellor of Fed. German Republic; succeeded by Prof. Ludwig Erhard. 18 Mr. Macmillan resigned as Prime Minister; succeeded by the Earl of Home; French sent cat into space and brought it safely back. 23 Robbins report on higher education published.

November 1 Diem oligarchy of S. Vietnam overthrown by military coup; First executions in S. Africa under the Sabotage Act of 1963. 7 Eleven German miners rescued after a fortnight underground; Sir Alec Douglas-Home elected at Kinross and W. Perthshire. 9 Train and mine disasters in Japan. 13 Death of Dr. Margaret Murray, the archaeologist, at age 100. 16 Greece began to release Communist prisoners

A.D.

taken during last war. **17** Temples of Abu Simbel to be removed and re-sited. **18** Opening of Dartford–Purfleet tunnel, linking Kent and Essex under Thames. **22** Assassination of President Kennedy in Dallas, Texas; Vice-President Lyndon Johnson sworn in as new President. **27** Publication of Buchanan report.

December 3 Britain's second nuclear submarine, the *Valiant*, launched. **4** Second session of Vatican Council ended; Closure of Woolwich Arsenal announced. **10** Zanzibar became an independent state within the Commonwealth. **12** Kenya became an independent state within the Commonwealth. **22** Greek liner *Lakonia* caught fire and sank on Christmas cruise, 250 miles W. of Gibraltar. **31** Dissolution of Federation of Rhodesia and Nyasaland.

1964

January 4–6 Pope Paul made pilgrimage to Holy Land: first meeting between Pope and Patriarch of Constantinople since 1439. **9** Rioting in Panama. **12** Republican régime in Zanzibar. **20** Army mutiny in Tanganyika. **27** France recognized China; School-leaving age to be raised to 16 in 1970–71. **28** Riots in Salisbury, S. Rhodesia, after trial of Joshua Nkomo.

February 6 Anglo-French agreement on rail Channel tunnel announced. **11** Fighting between Greeks and Turks at Limassol, Cyprus. **27** Bank rate raised from 4 to 5%.

March 4 August Bank holiday in 1965 and 1966 to be moved to last Monday in month. **6** Death of King Paul of the Hellenes; son proclaimed King Constantine XIII. **10** Birth of Prince Edward. **11** S. Africa withdrew from I.L.O. **19** Opening of Great St. Bernard tunnel. **24** Stansted, Essex, provisionally chosen as site of London's third airport. **25** Plinth at Runnymede and scholarship fund for study in U.S. to be memorials to President Kennedy. **27** U.N. peacekeeping force in Cyprus operational; Britain's second space satellite, *Ariel* 2, launched in Virginia; Severe earthquake and tidal wave in Alaska.

April 4 Dr. Leakey confirmed discovery in Tanganyika of *Homo habilis*; heavy fighting in Cyprus between Greek and Turkish communities. **5** Death of General MacArthur. **8** Shaikh Abdullah, former Prime Minister of Kashmir, released by Indian Government. **9** First Greater London Council election: Labour 64, Conservatives 36. **10** Mr. Macmillan declined earldom and Order of the Garter. **13** Mr. Ian Smith became Prime Minister of S. Rhodesia on resignation of Mr. Winston Field. **16** Sentences totalling 307 years passed on 12 men found guilty in mail train robbery trial (two subsequently escaped from prison). **21** Opening of BBC-2. **23** Shakespeare quatercentenary celebrations. **27** Tanganyika and Zanzibar united (United Republic of Tanzania).

May 1 Birth of a daughter to Princess Margaret and Lord Snowdon. **9** Mr. Khrushchev's first visit to Egypt (completion of first stage Aswan High Dam). **22** State of emergency declared in British Guiana. **26** Typhoid outbreak in Aberdeen. **27** Death of Jawaharlal Nehru.

June 2 Mr. Lal Bahadur Shastri elected Prime Minister of India. **3** Senator Barry Goldwater of Arizona defeated Mr. Nelson Rockefeller, Governor of New York, in Republican Party's primary election in California. **5** First flight into space of Britain's *Blue Streak* rocket (fired from Woomera). **9** Death of Lord Beaverbrook. **12** Life imprisonment imposed on Nelson Mandela and others in Rivonia trial, Pretoria; 20-year treaty of friendship signed between Soviet Union and E. Germany. **30** Last U.N. troops left Congo.

July 2 Enactment of U.S. Civil Rights Bill. **3–4** Foreign ministers of Iran, Pakistan and Turkey agreed to form Regional Co-operation for Development (R.C.D.) group. **6** Nyasaland be-

A.D.

came independent state of Malawi. **10** M. Tshombe succeeded M. Adoula as Prime Minister of the Congo. **12** Death of Maurice Thorez, French communist leader. **15** Mr. Mikoyan succeeded Mr. Brezhnev as President of the Soviet Union. **17** Court of Session, Edinburgh, ruled that Harris Tweed must be wholly made in Outer Hebrides; Mr. Donald Campbell broke land-speed record on Lake Eyre with 403·1 m.p.h. **27** Last appearance of Sir Winston Churchill in House of Commons. **31** American *Ranger* 7 hit moon after sending back over 4,000 pictures of surface.

August 2 U.S. destroyer attacked by N. Vietnam torpedo boats off coast of N. Vietnam. **4** Nine French miners rescued after being trapped underground at Champagnole for 8 days; Bodies of three murdered civil rights workers found near Philadelphia, Mississippi. **5** Congolese rebels captured Stanleyville; U.S. air raid on N. Vietnam. **13** General Grivas, former EOKA leader, took over supreme command of Cypriot National Guard. **13** Common Market set up by Arab League (Iraq, Jordan, Kuwait, Syria and U.A.R.) to come into force Jan. 1965. **21** Death of Togliatti, Italian Communist leader.

September 2 Indonesian landings in Malaya. **4** Opening of new Forth bridge (largest suspension bridge in Europe). **7** People's Republic of the Congo declared by Congolese rebels. **14** Third session of Vatican Council opened (closed 21 Nov.). **20** Gen. de Gaulle began his tour of S. America. **21** Malta became independent state within the British Commonwealth after 164 years of British rule. **22** Hunterston nuclear power station opened. **28** Maiden flight of supersonic TSR 2; Death of Harpo Marx, the great film comedian.

October 5 The Queen and the Duke of Edinburgh arrived in Canada on week's visit. **10** Opening of Olympic Games in Tokyo. **12** Soviet 3-man spaceship launched on 24-hour flight; First shipment of liquid methane from Saharan oilfield to Britain. **14** 1964 Nobel Peace Prize awarded to Dr. Martin Luther King. **15** Mr. Khruschev replaced in posts of First Secretary of the CPSU and Prime Minister by Mr. Brezhnev and Mr. Kosygin respectively; General election in Britain: Labour won with overall majority of five. **16** Mr. Harold Wilson became Prime Minister; China exploded an atomic device. **22** M. Jean-Paul Sartre declined Nobel Prize for Literature which had been awarded him. **24** Northern Rhodesia achieved independence as Republic of Zambia with Kenneth Kaunda as its first President; S. Rhodesia became officially known as Rhodesia. **26** Government proposed 15% import surcharge and export tax rebate to deal with balance of payments crisis. **29** Nobel Prize for Chemistry awarded to Prof. Dorothy Hodgkin.

November 2 Deposition of King Saud of Saudi Arabia and accession of his brother Faisal. **3** U.S. Presidential election: sweeping victory for President Johnson over Senator Goldwater. **5** Mr. Chou En-lai in Moscow for 47th anniversary of October revolution; Cease-fire in Yemen after two years of civil strife. **10** Australia to introduce selective compulsory service for military service overseas. **12** Grand Duchess Charlotte of Luxembourg abdicated after 45 years' rule in favour of her son. **17** Government to ban export of arms to S. Africa. **23** Bank rate rose from 5 to 7%. **21** Opening of Verrazano-Narrows bridge spanning mouth of New York harbour, the world's longest bridge. **24** Belgian paratroops landed at Stanleyville to rescue rebel-held hostages.

December 1 Death of J. B. S. Haldane. **2** The Pope welcomed in Bombay. **5** Bishopsgate railway goods depot destroyed by fire, two customs officers dying in blaze. **12** Kenya became Republic within Commonwealth with Mr. Kenyatta as first President. **16** Statement of Intent on productivity, prices and incomes signed by Government, T.U.C. and Employers' organisations. **17** Free prescriptions from 1 February 1965. **28** Signor Saragat elected

A.D.

President of Italy. **31** Mr. Donald Campbell broke world water-speed record with speed of 276·33 m.p.h. on Lake Dumbleyung in W. Australia.

1965

January 7 Indonesia withdrew from U.N. **15** Child's body found (Dec. 11, 1964) in coffin in Stepney identified as that of Lady Anne Mowbray (1472–81), child wife of Richard, Duke of York (one of Princes in the Tower); remains reinterred in Westminster Abbey; Prime Minister of Burundi assassinated. **20** Lyndon Baines Johnson inaugurated as 36th President of U.S. **21** Prime Minister of Iran assassinated. **24** Death of Sir Winston Churchill. **26** Hindi became official language of India with English an additional official tongue. **31** National Health prescription charges ended.

February 1 The Queen and Duke of Edinburgh in Ethiopia on state visit. **4** Lysenko dismissed as Director of Institute of Genetics. **7** First U.S. retaliatory raids against N. Vietnam. **17** Pres. Johnson announced U.S. would continue " actions that are justified as necessary for defence of S. Vietnam." **18** Gambia became independent as 21st member of the Br. Commonwealth. **24** U.S. piloted jets bombed Vietcong in S. Vietnam. **25** Dr. Heenan, Archbishop of Westminster, created a cardinal.

March 3 Remains of Roger Casement, from Pentonville Prison, reburied in Dublin; Seretse Khama became Bechuanaland's first Prime Minister. **7** First of 3,500 American marines landed in S. Vietnam. **18** Alexei Leonov became first man to leave a spaceship and float in space. **19** Record price of 760,000 guineas paid at Christie's for Rembrandt's *Titus*. **23** First successful two-man manœuvring flight by Grissom and Young in *Gemini III*; Dr. Dorothy Hodgkin awarded Order of Merit. **24** Successful completion of U.S. *Ranger* moon shot programme. **25** Defeat of Mrs. Bandaranaike in Ceylon elections; Mr. Senanayake became Prime Minister. **28** Death of the Princess Royal; Earthquake in Chile.

April 1 Younger brother of King Hussein made heir to Jordan throne in place of his 3-year-old son. **6** Launching of *Early Bird* commercial communication satellite; Cancellation of TSR 2. **9** Fighting broke out between Indian and Pakistan forces in Rann of Kutch. **11** Tornadoes in mid-western U.S. killed 278 people. **23** Opening of 250-mile Pennine Way, Britain's first long-distance footpath from Edale in Derbyshire to Kirk Yetholm in Roxburghshire. **24** Outbreak of civil war in Dominican Republic. **27** Import surcharge of 15 per cent reduced to 10 per cent. **28** Landing of American troops in Dominican Republic. **29** Australian troops to be sent to S. Vietnam.

May 8 Arrest of Sheik Abdullah on return to India from tour abroad; Spanish confirmation that one of bodies found near Portuguese border in Feb. was that of General Delgado, Portuguese opposition leader. **11** Cyclone and tidal wave disaster in E. Pakistan killing 16,000 people. **13** Conservatives made big gains in U.K. local government elections. **14** Inauguration of Kennedy memorial at Runnymede; China exploded second atomic bomb. **15** Completion of Benmore power station and Cook Strait cable—part of New Zealand's 10-year power development scheme. **17** Britain and France to co-operate in developing two military aircraft; 31 miners killed in Welsh colliery disaster. **18** The Queen and the Duke of Edinburgh on 10-day state visit to Fed. German Republic. **20–29** Indian ascents of Everest. **28** 267 miners killed in Indian colliery disaster.

June 1 237 miners killed in Japanese colliery explosion. **3** Bank rate reduced to 6 per cent; Launching of U.S. *Gemini IV* with McDivitt and White; the latter walked in space for 20 min. **4–7** Visit of Mr. Chou En-lai to Tanzania. **7** 128 miners killed in Jugoslav mine disaster. **9** World record for mile broken by M. Jazy of France (3 min. 53·6 sec.). **17** Opening of Commonwealth Prime Ministers' Conference

A.D.

in London. **19** Pres. Ben Bella of Algeria deposed by Revolutionary Council under Col. Boumedienne. **22** 700th anniversary of Parliament celebrated. **28** *Early Bird* went into commerical service (poised 23,000 miles above Atlantic between Brazil and Africa). **30** Cease-fire agreement in Rann of Kutch signed.

July 8 Another mail train robber escaped from prison. **6** Inauguration of SRC radiotelescope at Lord's Bridge, Cambridge. **11** Mme. Furtseva, Soviet Minister of Culture, visited Britain. **14** Adlai Stevenson died in London, suddenly. **14** Mme. Vaucher climbed north wall of Matterhorn, the first woman to do so. **15** First close-up pictures of Mars successfully transmitted to earth by U.S. *Mariner IV* across 134 million miles; King Constantine of Greece dismissed his Prime Minister, Mr. Papandreou. **16** Opening of Mont Blanc tunnel. **19** Death of Syngman Rhee, former Pres. of S. Korea. **20** Malawi to become a republic on July 6, 1966. **22** Sir Alec Douglas-Home resigned as leader of the Conservative Party; succeeded by Mr. Edward Heath (July 28). **26** Maldive Islands became independent. **29** Rebuilding of London Bridge planned; Appointment of Lord Casey as Governor-General of Australia. **30** U.S. Medical Care for the Aged Bill passed.

August 1 Radio and television licence fees increased; Television ban on cigarette advertising. **3** Creation of a new award " The Queen's Award to Industry " for export and technological achievement; M. Malraux, French Minister of Culture, met Mao Tse-tung in Peking. **5** Clashes on Kashmir border. **6** U.S. Voting Rights Bill passed. **9** Singapore seceded from Malaysia; Marriage between Moslems and Communists forbidden in U.A.R. **11** Negro riots in Los Angeles. **12** Appointment of first woman High Court judge. **21** U.S. *Gemini V* (Cooper and Conrad) launched (landed Aug. 29 after 120 orbits). **24** Pres. Nasser and King Faisal signed cease-fire agreement in Yemen.

September 1 Pakistan forces crossed Kashmir cease-fire line. **2** Death of Sir Harry Hylton-Foster, Speaker of the House of Commons. **5** Death of Dr. Albert Schweitzer. **6** Indian forces invaded W. Pakistan and bombed Lahore. **12** American division 20,000 strong landed in S. Vietnam; General election in Norway: Labour Government defeated. **14** Second Vatican Council reconvened for 4th session. **16** Publication of Government's White Paper, *The National Plan*, covering Britain's economic development 1964–70. **21** British Petroleum oil rig *Sea Gem* struck oil in North Sea. **22** Cease-fire in Indo-Pakistan war.

October 1 Attempt to overthrow Pres. Sukarno of Indonesia; reprisals against communists. **3** First international symposium on water desalination met in Washington. **4** The Pope flew to New York and addressed the U.N. Assembly; First Commonwealth Medical Conference met in Edinburgh. **6** Sir Robert Menzies appointed Lord Warden of the Cinque Ports. **8** Talks in London on Rhodesian independence ended without agreement. **11** Publication of Vinland Map, the only known example of mediæval Norse cartography. **13** Pres. Kasavubu of the Congo dismissed Mr. Tshombe. **17** Demonstrations throughout U.S. and in London against war in Vietnam. **19** Dr. Erhard re-elected Chancellor of Fed. Rep. of Germany. **22** Pakistan and India accept cease-fire call of Security Council. **26** Dr. Horace King elected Speaker of House of Commons—the first Labour Speaker. **28** Parliament passed Bill abolishing death penalty for murder.

November 1 Severe gales swept Britain. **8** New British colony of British Indian Ocean Territory set up. **11** Mr. Ian Smith of Rhodesia signed unilateral declaration of independence; Britain declared rebel regime illegal and introduced economic sanctions. **15** New land speed record of 600·6 m.p.h. set up in Utah by jet-powered car. **20** Security Council called on all states to sever economic relations with Rhodesia, and urged oil embargo. **25** General Mobuto

A.D.

deposed Pres. Kasavubu. 25 France launched her first earth satellite. 27 Pres. Kaunda of Zambia asked Britain to send troops to Kariba.

December 1 R.A.F. Javelins arrived in Zambia. 4 *Gemini VII* (Borman and Lovell) launched. 6 Russia increased her defence expenditure. 8 The Second Vatican Council closed. 9 Mr. Mikoyan retired as President of the Soviet Union; replaced by Mr. Nikolai Podgorny. 15 Rendezvous in orbit between *Geminis VI* and *VII*; Tanzania and Guinea broke off diplomatic relations with Britain over Rhodesia. 16 Mr. Wilson addressed the U.N. Assembly; Dead Sea Scrolls exhibited at British Museum. 17 Britain imposed oil embargo on Rhodesia; New forms of service for Anglican Church published. 19 General de Gaulle re-elected French President. 22 Christmas truce in Vietnam; Death of Richard Dimbleby, the B.B.C. commentator; 70 m.p.h. speed limit on British roads came into force. 27 Oil rig *Sea Gem* collapsed in North Sea; 5 killed, 8 missing. 28 900th anniversary of Westminster Abbey celebrated.

1966

January 3 Indo-Pakistani summit talks in Tashkent with Mr. Kosygin as host. 9 Violent rioting in Nigeria. 10 Sudden death of Mr. Shastri in Tashkent. 11 Opening of Lagos Commonwealth Conference under chairmanship of Fed. Prime Min. of Nigeria. 12 Death of Alberto Giacometti, sculptor and painter. 15 Army coup in Nigeria: Fed. Prime Min. killed. 16 General Ironsi, C.-in-C. of Nigerian army, took over command to restore law and order; Death of Sergei Korolyov, Russian space scientist. 18 Arrival in London of Sir Hugh Beadle, Chief Justice of Rhodesia, for talks with British Government. 21 Smith regime in Rhodesia rejected Royal Prerogative commuting death sentences on two Africans. 22 Opening of Volta River project in Ghana. 24 Air India *Boeing* crashed into Mont Blanc: 177 killed, including Homi Bhabha, the Indian nuclear physicist. 31 U.S. bombing of N. Vietnam resumed after 37 days; British Government banned all trade with Rhodesia; Russia launched *Luna* 9.

February 2 Successful soft landing on moon by *Luna* 9; tracked by Jodrell Bank radio telescope. 5 Pres. Johnson went to Honolulu to review Vietnam with other American leaders. 9 Britain to build prototype fast reactor (PFR) at Dounreay in Caithness. 17 Britain protested to S. Africa over petrol supplies to Rhodesia. 23 Military coup in Damascus (ninth in Syria in 17 years). Death of Vicky (Victor Weisz), political cartoonist. 24 Army coup in Ghana while Dr. Nkrumah absent in Far East.

March 1 Britain to adopt decimal currency in 1971; Russian rocket landed on Venus. 2 Dr. Nkrumah arrived in Guinea from Moscow; Britain protested to Portugal over oil storage tanks being built in Mozambique to pump oil to Rhodesia. 3 Pres. Sékou Touré of Guinea appointed Dr. Nkrumah executive head of state. 4 Britain recognised new régime in Ghana; Canadian *DC 9* crashed near Tokyo: 64 killed. 5 BOAC *Boeing* crashed near Tokyo: 124 killed; Nelson pillar in O'Connell Street, Dublin, blown up. 8 Severe earthquake in Hopeh, N. China. 9 U Thant called for cessation of bombing in N. Vietnam and for participation of Vietcong in any peaceful settlement. 10 Marriage of Princess Beatrix of the Netherlands and Herr Claus von Amsberg; U.S. to establish world-wide satellite communications system by 1968, based on *Early Bird*. 11 Chi-Chi, the London Zoo's giant panda, flew to Moscow for union with An-An of the Moscow Zoo. 23 Historic meeting in Rome of Archbishop of Canterbury and the Pope. 25 Two of the team climbing north face of the Eiger reached summit. 31 British General Election: Labour victory with overall majority of 97.

April 3 Soviet *Luna* 10 became the first lunar orbiter (orbital period: 2 hr., 58 min., 15 sec.). 5 Britain warned Portugal of consequences of

A.D.

allowing oil to be pumped from port of Beira to Rhodesia. 6 Greek Government withdrew registration from oil-tanker *Joanna V* off Beira. 7 Recovery of U.S. hydrogen bomb lost off coast of Spain. 9 U.N. Security Council passed resolution authorising British Government " to prevent by the use of force if necessary the arrival at Beira of vessels reasonably believed to be carrying oil destined for Rhodesia." 10 C.-in-C., British Forces in Middle East, instructed to stop any ship going to Beira with oil for Rhodesia: *Manuela* intercepted and boarded by British naval party and escorted away from Beira; Death of Evelyn Waugh, the novelist. 11 Students and militant Buddhists intensified campaign for return to civilian rule in S. Vietnam. 21 Opening of Parliament televised for first time. 30 Official support from Chou En-lai for " cultural revolution " to wipe out " bourgeois ideology " in all fields of culture.

May 9 China exploded third nuclear device. 14 Death of Lady Megan Lloyd George. 16 Seaman's strike began (ended 1 July—biggest strike in England since the war and the first of its kind since 1911). 18 Talks between Britain and Spain opened over Gibraltar. 26 British Guiana became independent state of Guyana.

June 1 Peace talks between Malayasia and Indonesia: restoration of friendly relations. 2 American *Surveyor I* made soft landing on Moon; De Valera re-elected President of Irish Republic. 6 *Gemini* 9, manned by 2 astronauts, recovered after 45 orbits, making most accurate return to earth yet: 2 hour space walk. 11 Commonwealth Day (the Queen's official birthday) to be observed on this date in future. 27 Death of Arthur Waley, translator from Chinese and Japanese.

July 3 Resignation of Mr. Frank Cousins as Minister of Technology over prices and incomes policy. 5 Indonesian People's Consultative Assembly deprived Dr. Sukarno of life-presidency. 6 Malawi became a Republic within Commonwealth with Dr. Banda as its first President. 7 Sino-Tanzanian co-operation in joint shipping line; Inauguration of Eurochemic plant at Mol in Belgium. 8 British industrial exhibition opened in Moscow. 14 Bank rate raised from 6 to 7 per cent; In first by-election since General Election, Labour lost seat in Carmarthen to Welsh Nationalist. 16 Prime Minister in Moscow for talks with Mr. Kosygin and for British industrial exhibition. 18 International Court of Justice at the Hague ruled in favour of S. Africa: no violation of mandate of S.W. Africa. 20 Prime Minister announced 6-month freeze on wages, salaries, and prices. 21 Successful landing of *Gemini 10*: docking manoeuvre and space walk. 24 Common Market completed its agricultural policy; free trade by 1 July 1968. 25 Report that Mao Tse-tung had swum 9 miles in Yangtze R. in 65 minutes. 27 Retirement of M. Spaak from political life. 29 Mutiny by section of Nigerian army; General Ironsi later reported to have been killed; U.S. aircraft attacked oil depots near Hanoi and Haiphong. 30 World Cup won by England: West Germany defeated 4–2.

August 1–2 Plenary session of Central Committee of Chinese Communist Party: Marshal Lin Piao officially recognised as Mao Tse-tung's successor. 3 Post Office to become public corporation in 1969. 4 Sir Edmund Compton named Britain's first Parliamentary Commissioner (Ombudsman). New plan for rebuilding Piccadilly Circus published. 7 Opening of Salazar Bridge spanning Tagus River (longest suspension bridge in Europe). 10 American *Orbiter I* launched—first U.S. moon satellite; Public inspection of Cabinet and other official documents to be allowed after 30 years instead of present 50; Cabinet reshuffle: Mr. George Brown became Foreign Secretary. 11 Indonesian–Malaysian peace agreement signed in Djakarta. 17 New world mile record: J. Ryun of Kansas Univ. (3 min. 15·3 sec.). 18 Mass rally of Chinese Red Guards in Peking celebrating the " cultural revolution," attended by Mao Tse-tung, Lin Piao, and Chou En-lai; Tay road bridge opened (longest road bridge in Britain: 7,356 feet be-

A.D.

tween anchorages); Earthquake in E. Turkey: over 2,000 killed. 27 Francis Chichester set sail round world: arrived Sydney 12 Dec. 31 Decree restoring federal system of government to Nigeria announced.

September 1 Britannia airliner crashed at Ljubljana in Yugoslavia: 95 killed. 4 President de Gaulle's suggestion that U.S. should withdraw from Vietnam prior to peace negotiations rejected. 5 Selective Employment Tax came into force. 6 Dr. Verwoerd assassinated in Parliament, Cape Town. 8 Opening of new Severn road bridge (centre span 3,230 ft., side spans 1,000 ft.). Pakistan and Malaysia agreed to resume diplomatic relations (broken off 1965). 11 Dr. Immanuel Jakobovits elected Chief Rabbi of Commonwealth in succession to Dr. Jacob Brodie; Fourth French nuclear device exploded over Mururoa testing site in S. Pacific. 13 Mr. John Vorster chosen as S. Africa's new Prime Minister. 15 German submarine *Hai* sank off Dogger Bank. 16 Opening of new Metropolitan Opera House at Lincoln Centre, New York; Launching at Barrow of H.M.S. *Resolution*, Britain's first Polaris submarine. 17 Red Guards warned by Chou En-lai not to interfere with the economy. 19 Inauguration of Paris–Shanghai air service: Civil Rights Bill providing housing integration defeated in U.S. Senate. 25 Congolese Government troops regained control of Kisangani. 28 Indonesia resumed U.N. membership. 30 Sir Seretse Khama became first President of Republic of Botswana.

October 1 Release of Speer and von Schirach from Spandau, leaving only Rudolf Hess there. 2 Heavy casualties after cyclone and tidal wave struck E. Pakistan; Many deaths in path of hurrican Inez in Caribbean. 4 Basutoland became independent kingdom of Lesotho. 5 Part 4 of 1966 Prices and Incomes Act came into effect, giving Government power to freeze wages and prices. 21 Aberfan disaster: avalanche of sludge from coal tip slid down upon South Wales mining village killing 144, including 116 children in school. 26 Brussels chosen as new headquarters of NATO Council. 27 China's fourth nuclear test. 28 Channel Tunnel to be built and opened to traffic by 1975 (subject to satisfactory solution of problems involved); Indonesia readmitted to U.N.

November 4 Italian floods: torrential rain caused Arno to burst its banks into city of Florence; Venice flooded after highest tide for 200 years. 9 " Hot line " between Paris and Moscow. 22 Organic Law of Spanish State provided for appointment of Prime Minister. 25 Security Council censured Israel for military attack on border villages of S.W. Jordan on 13 Nov. 23 Red Guards demanded dismissal of Liu Shao-Ch'i, China's Head of State. 26 Opening of the Rance barrage; Australian General Election: Liberal–County Party Coalition Government led by Mr. Harold Holt returned; New Zealand General Election: Mr. Keith Holyoake's National Party returned. 29 King Ntare of Burundi overthrown while in Congo: republic proclaimed. 30 Resignation of Dr. Erhard, Western German Chancellor; Barbados (British dependency since 1627) became independent.

December 1 Mr. Kosygin in France for 8-day visit: Dr. Kiesinger (Christian Democratic Union) took office as Chancellor of German Federal Republic with Herr Willi Brandt (Social Democratic Union) as Foreign Sec. 2 Meeting of Prime Minister and Mr. Ian Smith of Rhodesia on board H.M.S. *Tiger* off Gibraltar: working document prepared; U Thant re-elected U.N. Sec.-Gen. for further 5 years. 5 Mr. Ian Smith and colleagues rejected working document. 7 Opening of first stage of Roseires dam on Blue Nile, Sudan. 16 U.N. Security Council voted for British resolution for mandatory sanctions (including oil) against Rhodesia. 28 China exploded her fifth nuclear bomb. 29 Death of Lord Brain, authority on nervous diseases. 31 Death of Mr. Christian Herter, former U.S. Sec. of State.

A.D.

1967

January 4 Turkish oil pipeline opened, from Batman to Iskenderun on Black Sea coast; Donald Campbell killed at Coniston while trying to break own water speed record. 10 General Election in Bahamas (first all-Negro Cabinet took office Jan. 16 under Mr. Lynden O. Pindling). 11 Last detachment of British troops left Sarawak. 13 Army took over power without bloodshed in Togo. 15 Prime Minister and Foreign Secretary in Rome for first round of Common Market talks. 16 Britain and France agreed to go ahead with swing-wing military aircraft (French withdrew on 5 July) and to collaborate in building helicopters. 18 Mr. Jeremy Thorpe, M.P. for North Devon, elected Leader of Liberal Party following resignation of Mr. Grimond. 20 Agreement on Soviet–Japanese air service between Moscow and Tokyo via Siberia. 26 Bank rate reduced from 7 to 6½ per cent. 27 Death of Marshal Juin; Three American astronauts killed in fire in cabin during ground test at Cape Kennedy.

February 2 Direct peace talks between U.S. and N. Vietnam proposed by Pres. Johnson in letter to Pres. Ho Chi Minh. 5 Launching of *Vittorio Veneto*, Italy's first guided missile cruiser. 6 Mr. Kosygin arrived in London for 8-day visit. 7 Bush fire in Tasmania: 62 lives lost and heavy damage to homes and farms. 8 Inauguration of Bhutan's first hydroelectric station at Thimpu. 9 Historic meeting between H.M. the Queen and Mr. Kosygin at Buckingham Palace. 13 Agreement on establishment of a " hot line " between Kremlin and 10 Downing Street. 15 President Ho Chi Minh replies to Pres. Johnson: stipulated cessation of U.S. bombing raids against N. Vietnam prior to talks; Chinese authorities ordered dissolution of all " revolutionary organisations " and return of their members to their own provinces. 19 Death of Robert Oppenheimer, the American physicist, " father of the atom bomb." 22 Mr. Sangster succeeded Sir Alexander Bustamente as Prime Minister of Jamaica; Pres. Sukarno of Indonesia surrendered rule to Gen. Suharto. 23 Trinidad and Tobago first Commonwealth member to join OAS (Organisation of American States). 25 Launching at Birkenhead of Britain's second Polaris submarine, H.M.S. *Renown*. 26 Congress Party returned to power in Indian elections but lost 8 states. 27 International treaty banning nuclear weapons from outer space and prohibiting use of Moon and other celestial bodies signed in London, Moscow, and Washington.

March 1 Opening of London's new concert hall: Queen Elizabeth Hall adjoining Royal Festival Hall. 6 Death of Zoltán Kodály, the Hungarian composer. 9 Confirmation that American planes based on Thailand were bombing N. Vietnam. 12 Mrs. Indira Gandhi re-elected Prime Minister of India; Launching of Italy's first submarine since the war, the *Enrico Toti*. 13 In French general elections Gaullists gained bare majority in National Assembly: Death of Sir Frank Worrell the West Indies cricketer; £ sterling reached strongest position for year on foreign exchange markets. 14 U Thant proposed plan for bringing peace to Vietnam. 15 Announcement that American bombing of N. Vietnam would continue. 16 Bank rate reduced to 6 per cent. 18 *Torrey Canyon* (American owned, flying Liberian flag) ran aground on Seven Stones reef off Land's End with 120,000 tons of crude oil aboard. 20 Sir Francis Chichester in *Gipsy Moth IV* rounded Cape Horn. 22 Army in Sierra Leone siezed power. 28 High explosives dropped on *Torrey Canyon* by Royal Navy Buccaneer aircraft successful in releasing oil from wreck and setting fire to it; U Thant made public his revised peace proposals: (1) general standstill truce; (2) preliminary talks between those concerned; (3) reconvening of 1954 Geneva conference; Pope Paul issued encyclical *Populorum Progressio* on duties of rich nations towards poor nations. 29 Launching of France's first nuclear submarine, *Le Redoutable*; Last link of South-East Asia Commonwealth cable system (SEACOM)

A.D.

inaugurated by the Queen. **31** Death of Marshal Malinovsky, defender of Stalingrad, at age of 68.

April 5 Oil from *Torrey Canyon* reached Cherbourg peninsula. **13** Conservatives gained landslide victory in GLC elections. **19** Death of Konrad Adenauer. **21** Army coup in Greece (suspension of parliamentary democracy); Stalin's daughter arrived in New York. **23** Colonel Vladimir Komarov, the Soviet cosmonaut, killed (parachute failure after completion of test flight). **27** Crown Princess Beatrix of the Netherlands gave birth to a son; Opening in Montreal of Expo 67—Canada's 100th birthday international fair.

May 2 Prime Minister's statement to Commons: Britain to apply to join the Common Market. **4** Bank rate reduced to 5½ per cent. **6** Disturbances in Hong Kong. **8** Dr. Zakir Hussain elected President of India, the first Muslim to hold that office. **11** Britain presented application to join Common Market. **14** Opening of Liverpool's new Roman Catholic cathedral. **15** First day of new Spanish restrictions on air space around Gibraltar. **19** U Thant complied with Pres. Nasser's request to remove U.N. peace force from Egypt–Israel border. **22** Egypt closed Straits of Tiran to Israeli shipping; Japan joined European Nuclear Energy Agency's Reactor programme at Halden in Norway. **23** J. Ryun (U.S.A.) broke his own world mile record, 3 min. 51·1 sec. **28** Francis Chichester arrived in Plymouth. **30** Secession of Eastern Nigeria (Biafra) from Federation of Nigeria; Jordan and Egypt concluded 5-year defence agreement similar to that signed by Egypt and Syria in 1966.

June 1 General Moshe Dayan appointed Defence Minister of Israel. **3** 160 people killed in two British air crashes: at Perpignan in France and at Stockport the following day. **5** Outbreak of 6-day war in Middle East: lightning attack by Israel caused severe Arab losses and capture of Gaza strip, Sinai, Jordanian territory west of R. Jordan and small area of Syria. **6** East African Economic Community Treaty signed (Kenya, Tanzania, Uganda). **8** U.N. called for immediate cease-fire in the Middle East. **8–9** More riots in Hong Kong. **9** Pres. Nasser offered his resignation, but later withdrew it; France extended fishing limit around French coasts to 12 miles. **10** Fighting in Middle East ceased following U.N. Security Council's cease-fire resolutions; Soviet Union broke off diplomatic relations with Israel. **11** Israeli cargo ship sailed through Strait of Tiran. **12** Soviet Union launched Venus spacecraft. **14** Security Council rejected Soviet motion condemning Israel for aggression. **17** China exploded her first hydrogen bomb. **19** Pres. Nasser took over as Prime Minister; Mr. Kosygin addressed U.N. General Assembly. **20** Mutiny of South Arabian troops. **23** Meetings between Pres. Johnson and Mr. Kosygin in Glassboro, New Jersey. **23–24** More violent outbreaks in Hong Kong. **26** Council of Ministers of E.E.C. decided to refer British application for membership to Commission of the Communities; Mr. Kosygin visited Cuba; U.S.A. and Panama agreed on new treaties concerning Panama Canal and possible new sea-level canal. **27** Ron Clarke of Australia set world 2-mile record of 8 min. 19·8 sec. at Vaesteras, Sweden. **28** Israel took over control of Old City of Jerusalem. **29** Queen Elizabeth and Duke of Edinburgh arrived in Ottawa on week's visit to Canada. **30** End of period of severe economic restraint in Britain.

July 1 Mr. Tshombe arrested in Algeria after having been kidnapped in mid-flight; Colour television (first in Europe) began on B.B.C. 2. **2** Third French nuclear test at Mururoa atoll in Pacific (previous ones, 6 and 27 June). **3** Coronation of King Taufa'-ahau Tupou IV of Tonga. **4** Emergency Special Session of U.N. General Assembly (convened at request of Soviet Union on 17 June) called on Israel to rescind measures taken to change status of Jerusalem and to alleviate suffering resulting from Arab–Israel hostilities. **7** Francis Chichester knighted by the Queen at Greenwich. **8** Police post at Sha

A.D.

Tay Kok, Hong Kong, attacked by demonstrators from China. **10** New fast passenger service fully operative on completion of electrification between Waterloo, Southampton, and Bournemouth: use of steam traction eliminated in Southern Region of British Rail; New Zealand changed over to decimal currency. **12** Negro riot in Newark, N.J.; Motorway speed limit in Britain to remain at 70 m.p.h. **13** Public Records Act, 1967, reduced from 50 to 30 years the period for which public records are closed to public inspection (Act came into operation Jan. 1968). **14** The Decimal Currency Act, 1967, came into operation, providing for the introduction of decimal currency in Britain in 1971. **15** *Lake Palourde*, sister ship of *Torrey Canyon*, arrested at Singapore as surety for oil pollution damage. **17** U.N. observers began operating on Arab–Israeli cease-fire line; London's first supersonic boom tests. **18** Government announcement of cuts in defence commitments: planned withdrawal East of Suez by mid-1970s. **20** Recommendation by Latey Committee that legal age of majority should be 18. **21** Albert Luthuli killed in railway accident in South Africa. **22** Earthquake in N.W. Turkey. **23** Urban Negro riot in Detroit. **24** Pres. de Gaulle rebuked by Mr. Pearson for using Quebec separatist slogan, *Vive Quebec libre*, in speech in Montreal; visit cut short. **25** Pope Paul visited Istanbul, Izmir, and Ephesus (first papal visit since A.D. 711). **28** Vesting day of the National Steel Corporation.

August 3 National Coal Board blamed in Aberfan tribunal report for the disaster; Lord Roben's offer of resignation not accepted by Minister of Power. **13** U.S. bombed N. Vietnam 10 miles from Chinese border. **17** U Thant asked U.S. to suspend bombing of N. Vietnam for 3 or 4 weeks. **21** Britain began phased withdrawal of British forces from Aden and S. Arabia.

September 1 Death of Ilya Ehrenburg, the Soviet writer. **3** Chinese Red Guards ordered to cease violence; Sweden's traffic changed from left to right. **10** Gibraltar referendum result: overwhelming vote to stay with Britain. **18** Merseyside and London dockers went on strike with the ending of the casual work system; U.S. announced its decision to deploy an anti-ballistic missile system against China. **20** Launching on Clydebank of Cunard liner *Queen Elizabeth II*, largest passenger liner built in Britain since the war. **26** Agreement for construction of European airbus signed in Bonn by Britain, France, and Fed. Rep. of Germany. **27** *Queen Mary* arrived at Southampton at end of her last transatlantic voyage (sold for £1·2 million to the city of Long Beach, California).

October 2 H.M.S. *Resolution*, Britain's first Polaris submarine, commissioned. London Bridge put up for sale (work began on new bridge, Nov. 6). **8** Death of Lord Attlee. **9** Provisions of Road Safety Act dealing with drink and driving came into force: it is an offence to drive after drinking if the amount of alcohol in the blood-stream exceeds the prescribed limit of 80 milligrams per 100 millilitres of blood; Che Guevara, Cuban revolutionary leader, killed in guerrilla fighting in Bolivian jungle. **10** Outer Space Treaty ratified by 93 countries. **13** Tyne toll tunnel opened by the Queen: crosses lower Tyne at Jarrow, linking motorways in Northumberland and Durham. **16** Opening of new NATO H.Q. at Evère, Brussels. **18** Russian craft (*Venus 4*) made first soft-landing on Venus. **19** American space probe *Mariner 5* passed within 2,000 miles of Venus; Bank rate increased from 5½ to 6 per cent. **21** Israeli destroyer *Eilat* sunk off Sinai coast by missile boats of Egyptian Navy. **22** Big demonstrations against Vietnam war in Washington, London, and other capitals. **24** Israeli bombardment of Egypt's Suez oil refineries. **25** Foot-and-mouth epidemic began at Oswestry. **26** Coronation of Shah of Iran; Government decision not to build national library on proposed Bloomsbury site; Anglo-French agreement on joint production of helicopters. **30** Canadian Expo 67 closed: total attendance for the 6 months—50,360,648; Old age pensions and other benefits increased in

A.D.

Britain: First automatic link-up and separation of unmanned spacecraft by Russian *Cosmos 186* and *Cosmos 188*.

November 9 Bank rate increased from 6 to 6½ per cent; Successful launching of U.S. giant *Saturn 5* rocket. **14** The Queen paid state visit to Malta. **17** Régis Debray, French Marxist writer, sentenced to 30 years' imprisonment for guerrilla activities in Bolivia. **18** Devaluation of £ sterling by 14·3 per cent ($2.80 to $2.40 to the £); Bank rate increased from 6½ to 8 per cent. **20** Professor Blackett and Sir William Walton appointed to the Order of Merit. **22** House of Lords ruled that barristers could not be sued for professional negligence; Security Council unanimously adopted British resolution requiring withdrawal of Israeli forces from occupied Arab territories and an end to all belligerency; Britain abandoned plan to build staging post on island of Aldabra (unique wild life sanctuary). **23** Indus water project inaugurated with opening of Mangla Dam on the Jhelum R., W. Pakistan, one of biggest in world. **26** Lisbon and suburbs flooded: death roll 464. **27** Gen. de Gaulle in press conference ruled out early Common Market negotiations with Britain; 8-week unofficial London dock strike ended. **29** Aden became independent as the Republic of South Yemen. **30** Greece, Turkey, and Cyprus agreed on peace plan for settlement of Cyprus issue.

December 1 Inauguration by Queen of Isaac Newton telescope at Royal Observatory, Herstmonceux, the biggest in Europe; world record price of 560,000 guineas paid for Monet's impressionist painting *La Terrasse à Sainte-Adresse* at Christie's. **3** First human heart transplant operation took place at Cape Town. **13** King Constantine attempted unsuccessfully to overthrow the Greek military junta. **14** Ban on arms to S. Africa reaffirmed by Prime Minister. **17** Mr. Harold Holt, Australian Prime Minister, drowned in swimming accident. **19** France voted against negotiations for Britain's entry to Common Market: Britain stated application would not be withdrawn. **20** Diplomatic relations resumed between Britain and Egypt. **29** Statement by N. Vietnam Foreign Minister that N. Vietnam ready to hold talks with U.S. once bombing of N. Vietnam ceased.

1968

January 9 U.S. *Surveyor* spacecraft soft-landed on moon; Departure of Cardinal Ottaviani from Roman Curia; Senator John G. Gorton elected Prime Minister of Australia. **14-15** Violent earthquake tremors in W. Sicily. **16** Prime Minister's announcement of cuts in public expenditure to release resources from home to export. **19** Anglo-Soviet agreement for scientific and technological cooperation signed in London. **23** Seizure by N. Korea of *USS Pueblo* on intelligence mission off N. Korean coast.

February 11-12 U Thant in Moscow and London for talks on Vietnam. **13** U.S. planes bombed outskirts of Saigon: 10,500 more American troops to be sent to Vietnam. **18** Second Communist offensive in Vietnam; U.S. "San Antonio formula" rejected by N. Vietnam (Pres. Johnson's offer of 19 Sept. 1967 to halt bombing of N. Vietnam on condition that peace talks would follow and no military advantage would be taken of the pause); Introduction of British Standard Time. **19** Rann of Kutch tribunal decision: nine-tenths to India; one-tenth to Pakistan. **24** Battle of Hué: end of 25-day defence by Vietcong guerrillas.

March 2 The Queen exercised royal prerogative of mercy in respect of 3 Africans under sentence of death in Rhodesia. **3** Government White Paper on foot-and-mouth epidemic: 2,339 farms affected; 422,900 animals slaughtered; circumstantial evidence that virus came from lamb imported from Argentina. **6** Africans in Rhodesia hanged in defiance of the Queen's reprieve. **12** Mauritius became independent. **14** Speculative rush for gold in leading financial centres: U.S. Bank rate raised from 4½ to 5 per cent. **15** Stock Exchange closed and Bank

A.D.

Holiday declared in Britain; Resignation of Mr. George Brown as Foreign Secretary. **17-18** Summit meeting in Washington of Western central bankers: two-tier system for gold agreed (deals between central banks at $35 an ounce, commercial deals at free price); London gold pool dissolved. **20** Mr. Roy Jenkins's first Budget. **21** Bank rate reduced to 7½ per cent. **22** Resignation of Pres. Novotny of Czechoslovakia; American battle deaths in Vietnam since 1961: 20,000 (3,000 since Tet (lunar new year) offensive); General Westmoreland, American field commander in Vietnam, recalled to Washington to become U.S. Army Chief of Staff at Pentagon. **27** Yuri Gagarin killed in air crash. **30** Money Conference in Stockholm: agreement to launch special drawing rights scheme in face of French non-cooperation. **31** Pres. Johnson announced his decision to abdicate presidency in January, to limit bombing of Vietnam, and to initiate peace moves.

April 1 Death of Russian physicist, Prof. Lev Laudau, Nobel Prize winner. **4** Assassination of Martin Luther King at Memphis, Tennessee. **8** N. Vietnam agreed to direct talks with U.S. **13** Tanzania first country to recognise Biafra–Nigeria's secessionist eastern region. **16** Britain decided to withdraw from ELDO. **17** Lake Havasu City in Arizona to be site for London Bridge. **20** Pierre Trudeau became Canada's new Liberal Prime Minister. **28** Extreme right-wing N.P.D. Party won 12 seats in state parliament of Baden-Württemberg.

May 3 Pres. Johnson accepted a N. Vietnam proposal to meet in Paris on 10 May for preliminary talks; Student riots in Latin quarter of Paris. **10** Violent clashes between students and police: 500 security police led charge through barricades. **13** Vietnam peace talks began in Paris. **17** French workers occupied factories. **18** Pres. de Gaulle cut short Rumanian tour to return to Paris. **19** Parliamentary elections in Italy: Christian Democrats and Communists largest parties in both Chamber of Deputies and Senate. **22** French National Assembly adopted amnesty law after trade unions had declared their readiness to negotiate with employers and Government. **29** UN Security Council adopted resolution imposing comprehensive mandatory sanctions on Rhodesia. **31** Dissolution of French National Assembly.

June 5 Senator Robert Kennedy shot in Los Angeles; he died the next day. **10** National Health prescription charge of 2/6d introduced. **12** Death of Sir Herbert Read. **14** Restrictions on entry into Britain by anyone connected with illegal régime in Rhodesia. **15** Warsaw Pact manoeuvres in Czechoslovakia. **26** Liberal Party, led by Mr. Pierre Trudeau, won Canadian general election. **30** In French general election Gaullists won increased majority.

July 1 All tariffs on industrial goods traded between EEC members abolished and a common external tariff came into effect. **4** Fourth assembly of World Council of Churches opened at Uppsala; Mr. Alec Rose landed at Portsmouth after sailing single-handed round the world in *Lively Lady*; he was knighted the next day. **10** M. Couve de Murville replaced M. Pompidou as Prime Minister of France. **22** New 1,058-mile oil pipeline from Dar es Salaam, Tanzania, to Ndola, Zambia, in operation. **26** Government decision to remove Aberfan tips. **28** Death of Otto Hahn, the German physicist; serious student riots in Mexico City. **29** The Pope issued encyclical *Humanae vitae* condemning all forms of artificial birth control; Four-day summit conference opened between Czech and Soviet leaders at Cierna.

August 3 Meeting in Bratislava between Czech leaders and leading personalities from Bulgaria, East Germany, Hungary, Poland and the Soviet Union; Death of Marshal Rokossovsky, Russian military hero of Second World War. **5** Talks between both sides in Nigerian civil war at Addis Ababa (adjourned 9 Sept. without agreement). **20** Soviet forces with contingents from Bulgaria, East Germany, Hungary and Poland entered Czechoslovakia. **22** The Pope

A.D.

visited Bogota, Colombia, the first papal visit to Latin America in its 450 years of connection with Roman Catholic Church. 27 End of four-day talks in Moscow between Soviet and Czech leaders: Czech leaders gave certain undertakings to Moscow in order to secure withdrawal of Soviet troops; Death of Princess Marina, Duchess of Kent. 28 Tear gas and clubs used by Chicago police against demonstrators at Democratic National Convention. 31 Major earthquake in Khorassan province NE Iran.

September 6 Swaziland became independent. 11 Departure of Russian troops from Prague. 13 From 1 July 1969 banks in England and Wales to close on Saturdays; the Appellate Division of the High Court of Rhodesia ruled that the 1965 constitution was legal. 15 Worst flooding in England since 1953 (rain caused by warm air from S. France meeting cold air from Scandinavia over SE England). 16 Two-tier postal system began in Britain. 19 Bank rate reduced from 7½ to 7 per cent. 21–22 Clashes between students and police in Mexico City. 22 Successful recovery of Soviet spacecraft *Zond 5* in Indian Ocean, after research voyage round moon; Inauguration of reconstructed Abu Simbel temple on new site above Lake Nasser. 26 The Theatres Act, abolishing censorship, came into force; Professor Marcello Caetano appointed Prime Minister of Portugal because of illness of Dr. Salazar. 27 French again vetoed British entry into Common Market.

October 1 Federal Nigerian troops captured Okigwi, having taken Aba and Owerri in Sept. 5 Clashes between police and crowds in Londonderry: beginning of disturbances and riots in N. Ireland. 9 British Prime Minister and Mr. Ian Smith discussed proposals for settlement of Rhodesian question on HMS *Fearless* off Gibraltar (talks ended in disagreement). 11 U.S. 3-man moon rocket *Apollo 7* successfully launched on 10-day orbital test manoeuvres. 12 Olympic Games opened in Mexico City; Fernando Po and Rio Muni, dependencies of Spain, became independent as Rep. of Equatorial Guinea. 14 The Queen opened new Euston station. 16 Visit of Soviet Prime Minister, Mr. Kosygin, to Prague: treaty signed providing for stationing of Soviet troops in Czechoslovakia. 27 Czechoslovakia became a two-state federation; Massive demonstration march in London against Vietnam war. 31 President Johnson ordered halt to bombing of N. Vietnam.

November 1 Pres. Liu Shao-chi expelled from Chinese Communist Party. 4 NLF delegation arrived in Paris. 5 Presidential elections in U.S. gave victory to Mr. Richard Nixon, Republican. 12 Credit restrictions in France: Bank rate raised from 5 to 6 per cent; Major policy statement by Mr. Brezhnev at Polish Party Congress —" a threat to a Socialist country is a threat to all Socialist countries." 11 Maldive Islands became a republic. 15 New Greek Constitution came into force with increased power for Prime Minister, Mr. Papadopoulos. 19 Germany refused to revalue the Deutsche Mark. 20 Meeting of Group of Ten countries in Bonn to deal with speculative movements. 22 Standby credit of 2,000 million dollars arranged for support of franc; higher taxation in Britain, totalling £250 million; France did not devalue but introduced stringent measures of exchange control and economies; Mexican students ended their four-months strike. 26 Death of Upton Sinclair, the American novelist. 29 Serious rioting in Rawalpindi. 30 Civil rights disturbances in Armagh.

December 1 Pres. Ayub Khan agreed to students' educational demands; Bishop of Cadiz condemned wage and working conditions in southern Spain in pastoral letter; Civil rights demonstrations in Armagh. 2 Two pipelines blown up carrying water over Welsh border. 8 Royal naval dockyard in Singapore formally handed over to authorities there. 10 Mandate of UN Force in Cyprus extended to June 1969. 20 Launching of HMS *Churchill*, Britain's eighth nuclear submarine. 21–27 *Apollo 8* moon mission (Borman, Lovell and Anders made first lunar orbits). 27 China tested thermonuclear

A.D.

weapon. 28 Following attack (26th) by Arabs on two Israeli airliners at Athens, Israeli commandos retaliated by wrecking 13 Arab aircraft at Beirut airport. 31 Successful maiden flight of Soviet TU-144 supersonic airliner (rival to Anglo-French Concorde).

1969

January 1–4 People's Democracy march from Belfast to Londonderry. 4 Spanish enclave of Ifni ceded to Morocco. 5 Soviet Venus probe launched. 7 Opening of Commonwealth Prime Ministers Conference in London. 16 First manned docking operation in orbiting flight by Soviet *Soyuz 4* and *Soyuz 5*. 16 Vietnam peace talks in Paris resumed after 2 months. 20 Spain extended her territorial waters from 6 to 12 miles. 20 State of emergency throughout Spain; UN Sec. Council decided to add Russian and Spanish to its working languages (hitherto English and French).

February 3 Assassination of Dr. Edourdo Mondlane, Mozambique nationalist leader. 12–13 Visit of Mr. Wilson to Bonn and W. Berlin. 16 Inauguration of Kainji Dam on Niger River, Nigeria. 18 Attack by Arabs on Israeli airliner at Zurich airport; Opening of submarine cable between Cape Town and Lisbon. 19 Death of Lady Asquith. 20 Kilimanjaro climbed by 8 blind Africans. 22 Vietnam Tet offensive began. 23–March 2 Visit of President Nixon to European capitals; Death of former King Saud of Saudi-Arabia. 24 U.S. *Mariner* Mars spacecraft launched. 26 Death of Mr. Eshkal, Prime Minister of Israel. 28 Bank rate raised to 8 per cent.

March 2 Successful maiden flight of French-built Concorde at Toulouse. Mrs. Golda Meir chosen as Israel's Prime Minister. Sino-Soviet border clash on Ussuri river. 3 *Apollo 9* launched on 10-day earth orbital test mission. 5 Dr. Gustav Heinemann elected W. Germany's first Social Democratic President by Federal Assembly meeting in W. Berlin. 7 Opening of Victoria line (first underground railway to be built in London for over 60 years). 9 General Riad, Egyptian Chief of Staff, killed during 3-hour artillery battle with Israel along Suez canal. 11 Milton Keynes to be site for Britain's Open University. 13 Alaskan oil deposit found by British Petroleum. 14 Mortgage rate in Britain increased to 8½ per cent. 16 Mrs. Martin Luther King preached at St. Paul's, the first woman to do so. 18 U.S. offensive in S. Vietnam; 1969 Geneva Conference opened; Longhope lifeboat disaster. 19 British troops landed with no opposition on Anguilla. 25 Resignation of Pres. Ayub Khan: Gen. Yahya Khan, C.-in-C. Pakistan Army took over power. 27 Mr. Wilson in Lagos on fact-finding mission. 28 Death of General Eisenhower; Visit of Lord Caradon to Anguilla.

April 1 Opening of China's ninth Communist Party congress in Peking. 9 Successful maiden flight of British-built Concorde. 14 Lin Piao declared Mao's successor. 17 Mr. Dubcek replaced as First Secretary of Czechoslovak Communist Party by Dr. Husak (Mr. Dubcek later elected Chairman of the Federal Assembly). 21 British army units to guard key points in Northern Ireland. 23 President Saragat of Italy on 8-day state visit to Britain; Biafran capital of Umuahia captured by Federal forces. 25 Owerri recaptured by Biafrans. 28 General de Gaulle resigned as President of France after vote defeat in referendum; Anglo-Italian declaration of policy on Europe signed in London; Mr. Terence O'Neill resigned as Prime Minister of Northern Ireland.

May 1 Secrecy oath taken by new cardinals in final consistory ceremony not to reveal any instructions given to them by the Pope; Major James Chichester-Clark became Prime Minister of Northern Ireland. 2 *Queen Elizabeth 2* sailed on her maiden voyage. 3 Death of Dr. Zakir Husain, India's President. 12 Conservatives gained 957 seats in urban and borough elections

A.D.

in England and Wales; Representation of the People Act 1969 came into operation (voting age now 18). **16–17** Landings of Soviet *Venus 5* and *Venus 6* on surface of planet (220 million-mile flight, 4½ months). **18–26** U.S. *Apollo 10* moon flight (Stafford, Young, Cernan). **21** Lord Ritchie-Calder appointed Chairman of Metrication Board. **27** Hungary first Warsaw pact country to ratify nuclear non-proliferation treaty. **30** Colony of Gibraltar renamed City of Gibraltar.

June 5 World Communist conference opened in Kremlin by Mr. Brezhnev. **8** Spain closed its frontier with Gibraltar; Conference on Midway I. between Pres. Nixon and Pres. Thieu of S. Vietnam: withdrawal of 25,000 U.S. troops announced. **10** Provisional Revolutionary Government set up by Vietcong in S. Vietnam; Cambridge to establish a social science tripos. **15** M. Georges Pompidou elected 19th President of France on the second ballot. **16** Death of Field-Marshal Earl Alexander. **17** Boris Spassky became new world chess champion, beating former champion Tigran Petrosian. **18** Government's plans to put legal restraints on unofficial strikers dropped in return for T.U.C. pledge to deal with unconstitutional disputes. **20** Pollution of Rhine: millions of fish killed. **24** Resignation of Sir Humphrey Gibbs as Governor of Rhodesia; closure of Rhodesia House in London announced. **25** U.S. Senate adopted resolution calling upon executive branch not to commit American troops or financial resources to foreign countries without approval of Congress. **29** Death of M. Tshombe. U.S. troops in Vietnam: 539,000 including 263,000 for ground combat.

July 1 Investiture of Prince Charles as 21st Prince of Wales at Caernarvon Castle; Dr. Gustav Heinemann took office as Pres. of Fed. Rep. of Germany. **3** U.N. Security Council censured measures taken by Israel to change status of Jerusalem. **5** Assassination in Nairobi of Mr. Tom Mboya. **8** Church of England rejected scheme for unity with Methodist Church while Methodists accepted union; Tate Gallery to have new gallery on adjacent site. **9** Egypt extended full diplomatic recognition to E. Germany. **13** Launching of Soviet unmanned *Luna 15*; Renewed violence in Londonderry. **14** Inauguration of first earth-satellite communications station in Middle East (near Manama, Bahrain I.); First major contingent of U.S. troops began withdrawal from S. Vietnam. **15–20** President of Finland, Dr. Urho Kekkonen, paid state visit to Britain. **21** Two U.S. astronauts, Armstrong and Aldrin, first men to land on the moon (3.56 a.m. B.S.T.). **22** Prince Juan Carlos of Bourbon-Parma named future King of Spain by General Franco. **23** Commissioner Erik Wickberg, a Swede, elected General of Salvation Army. **24** Splashdown in Pacific of *Apollo 11* capsule (Armstrong, Aldrin and Collins aboard, after 195 hours in space). **31** U.S. *Mariner 6* took photos of large areas of Mars which were televised back to Earth; Pope Paul visited Kampala, Uganda, to consecrate new shrine to Ugandan Catholics martyred there in 1886; Halfpennies ceased to be legal tender in Britain.

August 8 French franc devalued by 12½ per cent. **9** Sino-Soviet agreement on border river navigation after meeting at Khabarovsk. **11** President Kaunda announced plans for increased government control of economy and for reform of state institutions. **12** Apprentice boys march in Londonderry followed by 3-day street battle. **14** British troops on duty in Ulster. **16** Mr. V. V. Giri, Acting President, successful in Indian presidential election. **17** Eiger climbed by six Japanese mountaineers. **18** Hurricane Camille which began as African rainstorm swept across Mississippi Gulf, killing over 400 people. **19** British Army took over responsibility for police and security in Northern Ireland. **22** Arrival in Pakistan of first Chinese trade caravan using re-opened " silk route " from China over Karakoram range. **29** General election in Ghana: Dr. Busia (Progress Party) became Prime Minister.

A.D.

September 1 King Idris of Libya deposed by military junta. **3** Death of Ho Chi Minh, President of North Vietnam since 1945. **10** Barricades in Belfast dismantled and Army's " peace line " erected; Cameron Report *Disturbances in Northern Ireland* issued. **11** Meeting in Peking between Soviet and Chinese Prime Ministers, Mr. Kosygin and Mr. Chou En-lai. **15** Pres. Nixon announced withdrawal by mid-December of further 35,000 troops from S. Vietnam. **17** Pres. Suharto named West Irian as a province of Indonesia. **21** U.S. s.s. *Manhattan* first commercial vessel to navigate the Northwest Passage; Indian troops called in to quell religious riots in Ahmedabad. **23** Mr. Ton Duc Thang elected President of North Vietnam; China carried out its first underground nuclear test. **24** Official opening of earth satellite station in Hong Kong, with first " live " television transmission between Hong Kong and Washington. **28** General election in Federal Republic of Germany: Herr Willy Brandt, leading a coalition of Social Democrats (S.P.D.) and Free Democrats (F.D.P.) elected Chancellor. **29** China exploded a new hydrogen bomb. **30** Peking Radio said China was ready to settle border dispute with Soviet Union by negotiations; U.S. announced withdrawal of 6,000 troops from Thailand in next nine months.

October 1 Vesting day for new Post Office Corporation (Postmaster-General became known as Minister for Posts and Telecommunications). **10** Hunt Committee report on Northern Ireland recommended disarming Royal Ulster Constabulary and disbanding B specials; Sir Arthur Young, commissioner of the City of London police, took over command of the R.U.C. **11** Mr. Tung Pi-Wu appointed President of China in place of Mr. Liu Shao-chi. **11–13** Group flight by Soviet *Soyuz* spacecraft—first experiment in space welding. **13** Vatican's international synod of Bishops opened in Rome. **14** The seven-sided 50p (10s.) piece introduced. **15** Mr. Dubcek resigned as President of Czechoslovak Federal Assembly; Peaceful demonstration by millions of Americans against Vietnam war. **20** Talks started in Peking on Soviet–Chinese border dispute. **23** Britain banned cyclamates with effect from Jan. 1, 1970. **24** Deutsche Mark revalued upwards at 3·66 to the U.S. dollar (old rate DM 4.00 = $1). **27** St. Vincent received status of Associated State.

November 11 France decided to take part in project to build particle accelerator (reduced from 300 GeV to 200 GeV) under auspices of CERN (Britain withdrew in June 1968); Owners of *Torrey Canyon* agreed to pay £1·5 million each to British and French governments for claims for oil damage in 1967. **14** Launching of *Apollo 12* (Conrad, Gordon, Bean): second human landing on moon 19th; splashdown 24th; Colour programmes began in London on B.B.C. I and I.T.V. **15** Agreement signed between Tanzania, Zambia and China on construction of 1,100-mile railway from Dar es Salaam to Zambia's copperbelt. **17** Strategic arms limitation talks (SALT) between U.S. and Soviet Union opened in Helsinki. **18** European Commission of Human Rights presented confidential report to Ministerial Committee of Council of Europe on alleged violation of human rights in Greece. **21** U.S. to return Okinawa to Japan in 1972. **24** Rudolf Hess, last of Nazi war criminals in gaol, moved temporarily to British Army hospital; Soviet Union and U.S. ratified nuclear non-proliferation treaty. **25** U.S. renounced use of biological warfare. **28** W. Germany signed non-proliferation treaty— the ninety-fifth country to do so.

December 1–2 Summit meeting of E.E.C. at The Hague: agreement on negotiations for British entry by end of June 1970. **2** Death of Marshal Voroshilov, former Pres. of Soviet Union. **4** Quarantine in Britain extended from six to eight months. **10** Soviet Union pledged support for Arab countries in Arab–Israel conflict. **11** Launching in Britain of European Conservation Year, emphasising need to improve air, water and general environment; For

A.D.

first time since Jan. 1968 U.S. and Chinese diplomats met for discussion in Warsaw. **12** Greece withdrew from Council of Europe. **15** Pres. Nixon announced withdrawal before 15 April 1970 of further 50,000 troops from Vietnam (a total of 115,500 since he became President). **16** House of Commons voted for permanent abolition of death penalty: 158 majority. **18** House of Lords also voted to end hanging: 46 majority. **19** Relaxation of U.S. trading restrictions with China. **27** In Japanese general election ruling Liberal Democratic Party won sweeping victory: the Komeito (Clean Government) Party gained additional 22 seats and Japanese Socialist Party lost 44. **30** New constitution adopted by Congo (Brazzaville) based on Marxist–Leninist principles; country to be known as the People's Republic of the Congo.

1970

January 1 Limit of £10 over-the-counter withdrawals from post office savings accounts raised to £20. **11** Federal Nigerian troops captured Owerri; flight from Biafra of Gen. Ojukwu. **12** Gen. Effiong proclaimed end of secession. **13** Sikh policemen in Britain won right to wear turbans instead of helmets. **19** Dutch pastoral council of Roman Catholic church passed motion in favour of voluntary celibacy; Inauguration of Tarapur atomic power station, 100 m. north of Bombay, largest single atomic power station in Asia. **21** Stalin's daughter Svetlana deprived of Soviet citizenship. **27** Miss Peggy Herbison, Labour M.P., appointed first woman Lord High Commissioner of the Church of Scotland. **30** Demonstrations in Indian state of Hariana in protest against Government's decision to allot the joint city capital of Chandigarh to the Sikh majority of Punjab.

February 1 Pope reaffirmed that celibacy was a fundamental law of the Latin church and rejected demands of Dutch bishops for abolition of strict law of priestly celibacy; Serious clash between Syria and Israel on Golan Heights cease-fire line. **3** Bertrand Russell died at his home at Plas Penrhyn in N. Wales; Mr. Dubcek received by President Sunay of Turkey as Ambassador of Czechoslovakia. **5** Public Order (Amendment) Act, 1970 (Northern Ireland) enacted. **9** Duke of Edinburgh and Prince of Wales attended Conservation conference in Strasbourg. **10** Government White Paper on the economic consequences of British membership of the Common Market published; Supreme Court of India restored 14 major nationalised banks to their original owners and declared the State's takeover of banking to be illegal and unconstitutional. **11** Japan launched her first earth satellite—*Rising Sun I*. **12** Israeli air attack on metal plant near Cairo killed 70 Egyptian civilians and wounded 100; Jordan Government agreed to suspend measures decreed earlier to restrict activities of Palestinian guerrillas. **15** Opening of Eilat–Ashkelon oil pipeline (Gulf of Akaba to Mediterranean) bypassing Suez Canal; Death of Lord Dowding (Chief of Fighter Command during Battle of Britain). **17** Mrs. Meir, Israel's Prime Minister, offered to halt attacks if Egypt agreed to respect the cease-fire. **21** Israel-bound Swissair Coronado airliner exploded killing 47 people aboard. **22** Guyana became a co-operative republic.

March 2 The Queen left London for 40,000 mile tour of Fiji, Tonga, New Zealand and Australia; Herr Willy Brandt, W. German Chancellor, on official vist to Britain; Rhodesia severed last link with Britain with proclamation of republic. **4** French submarine *Eurydice* lost off Toulon with 57 men aboard. Herr Willy Brandt made honorary Doctor of Civil Law by Oxford University. **5** Entry into force of the Treaty on the Non-Proliferation of Nuclear Weapons; Bank rate reduced ½ per cent to 7½ per cent; Possibility of new Thames tunnel from Thamesmead to Barking. **6** German bank rate raised by 1½ per cent to 7½ per cent; Teachers' strike ended with pay settlement with Burnham Com-

A.D.

mittee. **7** Total solar eclipse seen in Mexico and on television screens. **8** Archbishop Makarios narrowly escaped assassination by gunman. **9** U.S. consulate in Salisbury to be closed, leaving only those of S. Africa and Portugal. **10** U Thant, U.N. Sec.-Gen., warned that life on earth can be preserved only by international surveillance, consultation and action on environmental matters; France successfully fired her Diamant B rocket from new space centre at Kourou, French Guiana. **11** War with Kurds ends in Iraq: autonomy, representation in Parliament, recognition of Kurdish as official language in areas of Kurdish majorities; Royal family in Wellington, New Zealand. **14** Prince Sihanouk in Moscow for talks on Cambodian situation. **15** Expo-70, first world fair in Asia, opened near Osaka, Japan; Assassination of Mr. Georgadjis, Cypriot Minister of the Interior, former Eoka leader. **15** Publication of the *New English Bible*, a new translation, not a revision of an existing translation; Mr. Kosygin, Soviet Prime Minister, sent a message to Pres. Nixon calling for halt to U.S. armed intervention in Laos. **18** Prince Sihanouk overthrown by right-wing coup; U.N. Security Council passed resolution making it mandatory for member states to interrupt immediately all transportation to and from Rhodesia; diplomatic, trade and military relations to be severed. **19** Meeting of Federal Chancellor and East German Prime Minister at Erfurt. **22** Publication of Rhodesian Church's letter *Crisis for Conscience* criticising recent legislation of illegal regime in Rhodesia. **23** South Africa banned from 1970 Davis Cup tennis competition. **24** Commons rejected by only 7 votes Conservative M.P.'s bill to make murders of policemen serve at least 30 years in gaol. **25** Regulations limiting noise levels of aircraft to come into effect 1 Jan. 1971. **25** Public Schools Commission under chairmanship of Professor David Donnison recommended that Britain's 177 direct-grant schools should become comprehensive and abolish fees. **27** Soviet troops to stay in Czechoslovakia for "defence of the Western frontier of the Socialist community". **28** Earthquake in Turkish town of Gediz. **30** The Queen arrived in Sydney, first visit to Australia since 1963.

April 1 Death of Marshal Timoshenko, Red Army leader; Murder of Count von Spreti, West German Ambassador to Guatemala, by guerrilla kidnappers. **7** Government decision to rehouse Museum library on south side of Gt. Russell street. **8** Joint Chinese–North Korean communiqué published on America's new Asian policy which gives a privileged rôle to Japan. **30** Egyptian schoolchildren killed during Israeli bombing raid in Nile delta. **9** County council elections in England and Wales: Conservatives made net gain of 74 seats; Labour net loss of 11; Labour gained control of ILEA; G.L.C. remains under Tory control in ratio of 65–35 (excluding 16 aldermanic seats). **10** U.S. Senate Foreign Relations Committee voted unanimously to repeal the Tonking Bay resolution of 1964 which Pres. Johnson used to justify his involvement of more than 500,000 American troops in Vietnam war. **15** Bank rate reduced to 7 per cent; Greece condemned at Council of Europe meeting in Strasbourg for repeated violations of the European Convention on Human Rights. **18** Splashdown of *Apollo 13* (Lovell, Haise and Swigert) after most complex rescue operation in history. **20** British sixpence to be retained as legal tender for at least 2 years after Decimal Day. **21** Reported mutiny in Trinidad's Army; Death of Dr. Enid Starkie, authority on French literature and poetry; President Nixon announced withdrawal of another 150,000 American troops from Vietnam within a year. **22** Lenin's centenary celebrations; General election in South Africa for 2·2 million white voters. **24** China launched her first satellite (380 lb). **25** Russia launched 8 Cosmos research satellites from one carrier rocket. **28** ELDO decided to abandon British *Blue Streak* rocket for the new Europa III launcher in favour of French rocket. **30** U.S. combat troops crossed into Cambodia.

A.D.

May 1 Pres. Obote of Uganda announced nationalisation of all important export businesses. **4** Four students at the American Kent State University shot dead by National guard during anti-war demonstration; Royal family returned from Commonwealth tour of Australasia. **6** New 20-year treaty of friendship, cooperation and mutual assistance between Czechoslovakia and Soviet Union signed in Prague. **7** Italian regional elections: socialists in stronger position. **8** In borough elections in England and Wales Labour made net gains of 443 seats. **9** U.A.R. became a full contracting member of GATT. **12** U.N. Security Council adopted resolution condemning Israel military action in Lebanon; Beginning of Danube floods in Rumania which caused 161 deaths. **15** South Africa expelled from International Olympic Committee. **18** Illegal student demonstration in Johannesburg in protest against detention without charge, for over a year, of 22 Africans. **21** Herr Brandt and Herr Stoph held second round talks at Kassel. **22** Britain cancelled South African cricket tour. **25** Foreign banks in the Sudan nationalised. **28-30** Emperor Haile Selassie of Ethiopia paid official visit to Soviet Union. **31** Earthquake in N. Peru: more than 50,000 people killed and 800,000 homeless; France successfully carried out biggest explosion in current nuclear test series in Pacific.

June 4 Tonga became an independent state within the Commonwealth. **7** Fighting, lasting several days, broke out in Jordan between Government troops and Palestinian guerrillas. **9** Agreement signed by Pres. of Kenya and Emperor of Ethiopia on boundary between the two countries. **11** Drought (over 8 weeks) in Borrowdale, one of wettest regions of Britain; Seathwaite had warmest night in Britain for 100 years; Inauguration of Zululand Territorial Authority, second of eight " Bantustans " to be created in S. Africa. **15** Pres. Kaunda announced that no more coal would be imported from Rhodesia since enough was being produced within Zambia. **17** Oil discovered by U.S. consortium off coast of Ghana. **18** General election in Britain: Conservatives won with overall majority of 30 (Conservatives 330, Labour 287, Liberals 6). **19** Record orbital space flight by Soviet cosmonauts in *Soyuz 9* (17 days, 17 hours). **21** Death of ex-President Sukarno of Indonesia; Brazil won world cup 4-1 over Italy. **22** France and Spain signed 5-year military cooperation agreement; Voting age in U.S.A. reduced from 21 to 18. **23** Arrival at Bristol of Brunel's steamship *Great Britain* after 8,000-mile tow from Falklands to be restored to original appearance as when launched in 1843). **26** Mr. Dubcek expelled from Czechoslovak Communist Party; Anti-pollution legislation protecting Arctic waters enacted by Canada. **27-28** Violent disturbances in Belfast and Londonderry; additional troops flown in. **29** Conservative Government announced removal of restrictions on sale of council houses; Britain made its third application to join Common Market; Issue of circular 10/70 announcing Conservative policy on secondary school education: circular 10/65 (issued by Labour Government) withdrawn, thus stopping evolution towards comprehensive schools. **20-July 17** Visit of Pres. Nasser to Soviet Union. The warmest June since 1858 over most of the Midlands.

July 1 Administrative division of West Pakistan into four provinces (Baluchistan, North-West Frontier, Sind and Punjab) came into operation. **2** Queen's speech contained proposals for trade union reform, tax cuts, stricter immigration control and abolition of Land Commission. **5** Señor Luis Alvarez of the ruling Institutional Revolutionary Party elected President of Mexico (he took office on 1 Dec.); Death sentence passed by military tribunal in Cambodia after trial, *in absentia*, of former Head of State, Prince Sihanouk. **5-16** Royal visit to Canada. **6** Sir Alec Douglas-Home, Foreign and Commonwealth Secretary, told Commons of Government's intention to resume the sale of arms to S. Africa which had been abandoned

A.D.

by Labour Government in 1964. **20** Death of Mr. Iain Macleod, Chancellor of the Exchequer. **23** First bill of new Parliament enacted to give pensions to people over 80 who were not insured under present state scheme; Two CS gas cannisters thrown into Commons chamber from Strangers' Gallery; **27** Death of Dr. Salazar, Prime Minister of Portugal, 1932-68. **30** Damages totalling £485,528 awarded in High Court to 28 deformed thalidomide children and their parents. **31** Himachal Pradesh, previously administered by Central Government, to become 18th state of India (later, Manipur, Tripura and Meghalaya also granted full statehood).

August 2 Inter-island ferry sank in squall off Nevis, W.I.: more than 100 people missing; During further disturbances in Belfast, Army fired rubber bullets. **7** Under U.S. peace initiative (the " Roger's Plan ") " standstill " cease-fire agreed between U.A.R. and Israel came into force along Suez Canal. **10** Mr. Maudling, Home Secretary, warned that direct rule from Westminster would be imposed unless programme of reform went forward. **12** German–Soviet non-aggression treaty signed in Moscow by the Federal Chancellor, Herr Brandt, and Soviet Prime Minister, Mr. Kosygin. **13** Israel complained that Egypt had violated cease-fire by moving missiles near Suez Canal. **14** Conclusion of second round of strategic arms limitation talks (SALT) between U.S.A. and Soviet Union in Vienna. **19** Sino–Soviet trade talks began in Khabarovsk, Soviet Far East. **23** All marches in N. Ireland banned until Jan. 1971. **23-Sept. 6** Second plenary session of Ninth Central Committee of the Communist Party of China held in Peking, with Chairman Mao Tse-tung presiding. **25** Indirect talks between U.A.R., Israel and Jordan opened in New York, under auspices of Dr. Jarring, the U.N. mediator. **26** Government of the Sudan announced nationalisation of the Press. **28** Western Samoa became a member of the Commonwealth. **31** Mr. Edward Akufo-Addo elected Pres. of Ghana.

September 1-3 Eighth summit conference of Heads of State and Government of O.A.U. in Addis Ababa, under chairmanship of Pres. Kaunda, opened with address by U.N. Sec.-Gen.: agreed that delegation should be sent to make representations to Britain, France, Italy and W. Germany on question of arms sales to S. Africa. **1-4** Conference of 14 West African countries held in Dakar established West African Rice Development Association. **2** Britain's Black Arrow rocket failed at Woomera to put its satellite into orbit. **4** World Council of Churches proposed financial aid to African guerrillas. **6, 9, 12** Four hijackings of planes by Arab guerrillas. **7** Princely order in India abolished by presidential decree. **8-10** Third summit conference of non-aligned countries held in Lusaka (Zambia), Pres. Tito of Yugoslavia playing important part. **17** Jordan civil war began: house to house fighting in Amman between King Hussein's army and Palestinian guerrillas. **13** World exhibition, Expo '70, closed in Osaka, Japan (British Pavilion had 8,576,600 visitors, 13 per cent of total attendance). **19** Syrian Palestine Liberation Army units intervened in fighting in Jordan. **21** U.S. Senate defeated by 55 votes to 39 on motion to cut off all funds for U.S. forces in Vietnam and neighbouring countries by 31 Dec. 1971. **22** Resumption of U.S. arms aid to Greece announced; Tunku Abdel Rahman resigned as Prime Minister of Malaysia (succeeded by Tun Abdul Razak). **24** Soviet unmanned *Luna 16* brought back moon rock samples from Sea of Fertility; Commander Jacques Cousteau, French undersea explorer, outlined to Council of Europe 5-point programme to deal with sea pollution. **27** Agreement to end civil war in Jordan signed in Cairo by King Hussein and Mr. Yassir Arafat, chairman of the Central Committee of the Palestine Liberation Organisation, and representatives of eight Arab states; Pope proclaimed St. Teresa of Avila (1515–82) Doctor of the Church

A.D.
(Doctorate was later conferred on St. Catherine of Siena (1347–80). **28** Sudden death of President Nasser (Mr. Anwar Sadat was later elected President of the U.A.R.).

October 1 Gen. Gowen of Nigeria announced nine-point programme pending return to civilian rule by 1976. **5, 10** Quebec kidnappings of British diplomat and provincial minister by extreme separatist group. **10** Fiji became independent and a member of the Commonwealth after 96 years of British rule. **13** Canada and China established diplomatic relations. **15** Canonisation of 40 16th and 17th cent. English and Welsh martyrs. **17** Murder of Mr. Laporte kidnapped on 10 Oct. **24** Dr. Salvador Allende became president of Chile, the first Marxist socialist in Latin America to arrive in power by democratic means.

November 6 Mt. Cook climbed by New Zealanders. **8** Lord Cromer appointed to succeed Mr. John Freeman as British ambassador in Washington. **9** Death of General de Gaulle. **12** Cyclone and tidal wave struck E. Pakistan in Brahmaputra–Ganges delta: 200,000 deaths, 2 million homeless. **17** Russia's *Luna 17* landed on moon equipped with 8-wheeled moon-walker which moved over surface, inaugurating a new stage in lunar exploration. **20** For the first time U.N. voted to admit China but majority was less than required two-thirds. **21** U.S. bombing of N. Vietnam resumed after 2-year halt. **24** U.N. Security Council demanded immediate cessation of armed attack against Republic of Guinea and withdrawal of mercenaries. **25** Arrival of U.N. mission in Conakry to investigate alleged invasion of mercenaries under Portuguese leadership. **30** People's Republic of South Yemen to be known as People's Democratic Republic of Yemen.

December 2 Britain to return to G.M.T. in winter months (clocks to be put back 31 Oct. 1971). **3** Release from captivity of Mr. James Cross, British diplomat kidnapped 5 Oct. **4** The bustard reintroduced into England where it has not bred for over 150 years. **7** Herr Brandt (W. Germany) and Mr. Gomulka (Poland) signed treaty recognising Oder–Neisse boundary; Pakistan held first free elections. **8** Earthquake in N. Peru: 82 people killed. **15** Soviet *Venus 7* spacecraft (launched 17 Aug.) landed and made first transmission of scientific information from surface of another planet, recording surface temperature of *c.* 480° C, and atmospheric pressure 100 times greater than on earth; Sir Alan Marre to succeed Sir Edmund Compton as Ombudsman from 31 March 1971. **18** For first time in Italian history divorce became legally possible after parliamentary approval of a bill first proposed in 1966: Vatican opposition. **20** Mr. Gomulka resigned: succeeded by Mr. Edward Gierek. **23** Marxist writer, Regis Debray, freed in Bolivia. **30** General Franco commuted death sentences on 6 Basque nationalists. **31** Russian Supreme Court granted reprieve to 2 Jews sentenced to be shot in Leningrad hijacking trial.

1971

January 1 U.S.A. entered its 11th year in Vietnam war: American deaths since 1 Jan. 1961: *c.* 53,000; 60,000 troops to be withdrawn by 1 May, leaving 284,000 in Vietnam; Divorce Reform Act 1969 came into force; 38 miners killed in Kentucky mine disaster. **2** Ibrox Park (Glasgow) disaster: 66 football spectators killed and 200 injured. **3** The Open University went on the air for the first time. **5** Resignation of Lord Robens, chairman of the National Coal Board, confirmed. **8** Dr. Jarring in Israel for talks with Israeli leaders. **10** January temperature records broken in London (15° C), highest recorded, and Cairngorms (16° C). **14** Opening of 1971 Commonwealth Conference in Singapore. **15** Opening of Aswan High Dam. **19** Post Office workers' strike began. **22** Commonwealth Conference ended with agreement on a Declaration of

A.D.
Principles, the opening paragraph of which read: "The Commonwealth of nations is a voluntary association of independent sovereign states, each responsible for its own policies, consulting and cooperating in the common interests of their peoples and in the promotion of international understanding and world peace." **25** Pres. Obote of Uganda deposed (on way back from Commonwealth Conference) by Maj.-Gen. Idi Amin, Army and Air Force commander. **28** Indian Ocean cyclone caused severe flooding in N. Mozambique. **31** Launch of *Apollo 14* to moon (Shepard, Roosa, Mitchell).

February 4 Troop reinforcements sent to Belfast following night of violence; Financial collapse of Rolls Royce. **7** Male referendum in Switzerland gave women right to vote in national elections. **8** S. Vietnamese troops supported by American air and artillery support crossed into Laos. **9** Apollo 14 astronauts back on earth; Earthquake in San Fernando valley, N. of Los Angeles. **11** Seabed treaty signed by Britain, U.S. and Soviet Union; Second Reading in Commons of Rolls Royce (Purchase) Bill nationalising company's vital assets. **14** Western oil companies signed agreement in Tehran which will increase revenues to six producing countries in the Gulf. **15** Decimal Day in Britain. **17** Local government reform proposals published by Government: two-level structure of counties and districts for England and Wales. **18** Unemployment in U.K. (inc. N. Ireland) 761,154. **20** S. Vietnamese reverse in Laos. **21** New London Bridge opened for pedestrians; March of over 100,000 trade unionists in London in protest against Government's Industrial Relations Bill. **22** Tornadoes hit southern states of U.S., especially Mississippi delta communities; British government approved sale to S. Africa of 7 Westland Wasp naval helicopters (delivery 1972–3), despite UN Security Council's embargo on arms to S. Africa. **24** Immigration Bill published which will place Commonwealth citizens and aliens under a single system of immigration control. **25** S. Vietnamese drive in Laos halted.

March 1 1-day strike by 1·5 million craftsmen in engineering plants in Britain in protest against Industrial Relations Bill. **2** Labour's motion criticising supply of arms to S. Africa defeated in Commons by 311 votes to 275. **4** Mr. Maudling, Home Secretary, addressed joint session of Northern Ireland Parliament in Stormont. **10** Mr. Gorton resigned as Prime Minister of Australia; replaced by Mr. William Mahor; Murder of 3 young soldiers in Belfast. **11** Landslide victory for Mrs. Gandhi in Indian general election. **18** More troops (1,300) to be sent to N. Ireland, bringing total to 9,700; Unemployment figure in Britain (inc. N. Ireland) reached 794,300. **19** S. Vietnamese withdrawal from Laos began; Landslide N.E. of Lima: 1,000 dead. **20** Resignation of Major Chichester-Clark as Prime Minister of N. Ireland (succeeded by Mr. Brian Faulkner). **25** Bengali uprising in E. Pakistan under Shaikh Mujibar; Resignation of Mr. George Woodcock from chairmanship of Commission on Industrial Relations. **29** Lieut. Calley convicted of murder of 22 people in S. Vietnamese village of May Lai during massacre (16 March 1968) of unarmed civilians by American soldiers. **30** Mr. Brezhnev at 24th Party Congress called for conference of five nuclear powers (U.S., France, Britain, China, Soviet Union) to discuss nuclear disarmament; At Geneva Soviet Union agreed to outlaw germ warfare. **31** Indian Parliament called for ending of use of force and "the massacre of defenceless people" in E. Pakistan.

April 1 Bank rate reduced from 7 to 6 per cent. **6** Death of Stravinsky. **13** Table tennis teams in Peking from U.S., Canada, Colombia, Nigeria and England. **14** Direct telephone link with China reopened after 22 years. **17** Egypt, Syria and Libya formed new Federation of Arab republics. **23** Launching of *Soyuz 10* (with 3 cosmonauts) to dock with Salyut space station in technical experiment to develop permanent base above Earth.

PROMINENT PEOPLE

Glimpses of some of the famous people in the history of the world. See also Section E for composers; Section I for contemporary dramatists; Section M for novelists and poets of the twentieth century.

PROMINENT PEOPLE

A

Abel, Sir Frederick (1826–1902), English military chemist, an authority on explosives. He and his friend James Dewar patented the propellant cordite (*see* L27).

Abelard, Peter (1079–1142), one of the founders of scholastic moral theology, b. at Pallet (Palais) near Nantes. He lectured in Paris, where he was sought by students, though persecuted for alleged heresy. His main achievement was to discuss where others asserted. His love for Héloïse, a woman of learning, ended in tragic separation and in a famous correspondence.

Abercrombie, Lascelles (1881–1938), English poet and critic.

Abercrombie, Sir Patrick (1879–1957), architect and town-planner, brother of the above. He was consulted on the replanning of Plymouth, Hull, Bath and other cities and produced a plan for Greater London, 1943.

Acheson, Dean Gooderham (b. 1893), U.S. Secretary of State in the Truman administration, 1949–53.

Acton, 1st Baron (John Emerich Edward Dalberg Acton) (1834–1902), English historian. He planned the *Cambridge Modern History*.

Adam, Robert (1728–92), architect, one of four Scottish brothers. He developed a characteristic style in planning and decoration and his achievements in interior design include Harewood House, Yorks.; Osterley Park, Middlesex; Syon House, Middlesex; Kedleston Hall, Derbyshire; Luton Hoo, Bedfordshire; and Kenwood.

Adams, John (1735–1826), succeeded Washington as president of the U.S.A. He was the first of the republic's ambassadors to England.

Adams, John Couch (1819–92), English mathematician and astronomer. He shared credit for the discovery of the planet Neptune (1846) with the French astonomer Leverrier, working independently.

Adams, Samuel (1722–1803), American revolutionary statesman, b. Boston. He advocated " no taxation without representation " as early as 1765; promoted the " Boston tea-party "; and in 1776 signed the Declaration of Independence.

Adams, William (c. 1564–1620), navigator, b. Gillingham, Kent; the first Englishman to visit Japan. He found favour with the emperor Ieyasu, and an English and Dutch trading settlement was established till 1616.

Addams, Jane (1860–1935), American sociologist who founded Hull House, Chicago, in 1889.

Addison, Joseph (1672–1719), writer and Whig politician. He contributed to the *Tatler*, and was co-founder with Steele of the *Spectator*.

Adelard of Bath (c. 1090–c. 1150), English mathematician who translated into Latin the *Arithmetic* of Al-Kwarizmi and so introduced the Arabic numerals to the West (*see* L7).

Adenauer, Konrad (1876–1967), chancellor of the West German Federal Republic, 1949–63; founder and chairman of the Christian Democratic Party, 1945–66. To a defeated Germany he gave stable constitutional government and a place in the Western alliance. He promoted reconciliation with France but resisted accommodation with Russia.

Adler, Alfred (1870–1937), Austrian psychiatrist, founder of the school of individual psychology. An earlier pupil of Freud, he broke away in 1911, rejecting the emphasis on sex, regarding man's main problem as a struggle for power to compensate for feelings of inferiority. *See* Adlerian psychology, Section J.

Adrian, 1st. Baron (Edgar Douglas Adrian) (b. 1889), English physiologist. He shared with Sherrington the 1932 Nobel prize for medicine for work on the electrical nature of the nerve impulse. Pres. Royal Society 1950–5; Pres. British Association 1954; Chancellor Leicester Univ. 1957–; Chancellor Cambridge Univ. 1967–; O.M. 1942.

Adrian IV (Nicholas Breakspear) (d. 1159), pope 1154–59, the only English pope, b. near St. Albans. He crowned Frederick Barbarossa Holy Roman Emperor. Granted overlordship of Ireland to Henry II.

Aeschylus (525–456 B.C.), founder of Greek tragic drama. Of the many plays he wrote, only seven have come down to us, including *The Seven against Thebes*, *Prometheus Bound*, and a trilogy on Orestes.

Aesop (? 6th cent. B.C.), semi-legendary fabulist, originally a slave. The fables attributed to him probably have many origins.

Agassiz, Louis (1807–73), Swiss-American embryologist, author of *Lectures on Comparative Embryology*, intended for laymen, *Researches on Fossil Fishes*, and *Studies on Glaciers*. He was an opponent of Darwinian evolution.

Agricola, Gnaeus Julius (37–93), Roman governor of Britain, who subdued the country except for the Scottish highlands. His son-in-law Tacitus wrote his life.

Agrippa, Marcus Vipsanius (63–12 B.C.), Roman general.

Ahmad Khan, Sir Syed (1817–98), Indian educationist and social reformer who founded what is now the Aligarh Muslim University.

Airy, Sir George Biddell (1801–92), English mathematician who was astronomer royal for over 40 years, 1835–81. He set up a magnetic observatory at Greenwich.

Akbar, Jalal-ud-din Mohammed (1542–1605), Mogul emperor of India, son of Humayun. He extended the imperial power over much of India, stabilised the administration, promoted commerce and learning; and, though a Muslim, respected Hindu culture and tolerated Christian missions. His reign saw a flowering of Mogul culture.

Alanbrooke, 1st Viscount (Alan Francis Brooke) (1883–1963), British field-marshal; chief of the imperial general staff 1941–46. Sir Arthur Bryant's *The Turn of the Tide* and *Triumph in the West* are based on his war diaries.

Alarcón, Pedro Antonio de (1883–91), Spanish novelist. His short story, *El Sombrero de tres picos* (The Three-Cornered Hat) became the subject of Falla's ballet and of Hugo Wolf's opera *Der Corregidor*.

Alaric I (376–410), Visigothic chief who, as first auxiliary to the Roman emperor Theodosius, later attacked the empire and sacked Rome in 410.

Alban, St. (d. c. 303), proto-martyr of Britain, converted by a priest to whom he had given shelter. He suffered under Diocletian at Verulam (now St. Albans), where in the 8th cent. King Offa of Mercia founded the abbey of that name.

Albert, Prince Consort (1819–61), son of the Duke of Saxe-Coburg-Gotha, married Queen Victoria in 1840. He helped the queen with political duties, projected the international exhibition of 1851, and in 1861 in a dispute with the United States advised a conciliatory attitude which averted war. He died of typhoid fever and is commemorated by the Albert Memorial in Kensington Gardens.

Albertus Magnus (Albert the Great) (1206–80), Dominican scholastic philosopher, b. Swabia. His interest in nature as an independent observer marked the awakening of the scientific spirit. Among his pupils was Thomas Aquinas.

Alcibiades (c. 450–404 B.C.), Athenian general and statesman. Pupil and friend of Socrates, he was an egoist whose career brought Athens disaster. He was murdered in Phrygia.

Alcott, Louisa May (1832–88), American author of books for girls, notably *Little Women*.

Alcuin (735–804), English scholar, who settled on the continent and helped Charlemagne with the promotion of education. *See* Monasticism, Section J.

Aldred (d. 1069), Saxon archbishop of York who crowned William the Conqueror.

Aldrich, Henry (1647–1710), English composer of church music, theologian and architect. He designed Peckwater quadrangle at Christ Church, the chapel of Trinity College, and All Saint's Church, Oxford, and wrote the " Bonny Christ Church bells."

Alekhine, Alexander (1892–1946), world chess champion, 1927–35, 1937–46. He was born in Moscow and became a French citizen after the Russian revolution.

Alembert, Jean le Rond d' (1717–83), French mathematician and philosopher, one of the encyclopaedists, a leading representative of the Enlightenment.

Alexander of Tunis, Earl of (Harold Leofric George Alexander) (1891–1969), British field-marshal, b. Ireland. Directed retreat at Dunkirk 1940, and Burma 1942; C.-in-C. Allied Armies in Italy 1943–4; Supreme Allied Commander, Mediterranean 1944–5. Governor-general of Canada 1946–52.

Alexander II (1818–81), reforming Tsar of Russia, succeeded his father Nicholas in 1855. In 1861 he emancipated the serfs and in 1865 established provincial elective assemblies. Later his government became reactionary, and he was assassinated by Nihilists.

Alexander the Great (356–323 B.C.), Greek conqueror. Educated by Aristotle, he succeeded his father Philip as king of Macedon in 336 B.C. He led the Greek states against Persia; and, crossing the Hellespont, he defeated Darius and sacked Persepolis. He captured Egypt and founded Alexandria. He penetrated to India. D. at Babylon. Centuries later legends formed round him.

Alexandra, Queen (1844–1925), daughter of Christian IX of Denmark, married the Prince of Wales (afterwards Edward VII) 1863.

Alfieri, Vittorio, Count (1749–1803), Italian poet and dramatist.

Alfonso the Wise (1221–84), king of Leon and Castile, known for his code of laws and his planetary tables. He caused the first general history of Spain to be written. Dethroned 1282.

Alfred the Great (849–99), king of Wessex who became a national figure. From the outset he had to repel Danish invaders. After years of effort he won the battle of Ethandun (Edington), and subsequently, probably in 886, made peace with Guthrum, leaving to the Danes the north and east. He built ships, was an able administrator, and promoted education, his own translations from the Latin being part of the earliest English literature.

Al-Kwarizimi (fl. *c.* 830), Persian mathematician said to have given algebra its name.

Allenby, 1st Viscount (Edmund Henry Hynman Allenby) (1861–1936), British general. He served on the Western front 1914–16, commanded in Palestine 1917–18, capturing Jerusalem on 9 December 1917.

Alleyne, Edward (1566–1626), actor and founder of Dulwich College.

Al-Mamun (813–33), caliph of Baghdad, son of Harun-al-Rashid. He built an observatory at Baghdad where observations were long recorded.

Ampère, André Marie (1775–1836), French physicist who propounded the theory that magnetism is the result of molecular electric currents. The unit of electric current is named after him.

Amundsen, Roald (1872–1928), Norwegian explorer, the first to navigate the north-west passage and to reach the south pole. Sailing in the fishing smack *Gjoa*, he made the north-west passage in 3 years, 1903–6, and in 1911 sailed to the antarctic in the *Fram*, reaching the pole on 14 December 1911, a month before his English rival Scott. His attempt to rescue Nobile after his crash in the airship *Italia* cost him his life.

Anacreon (*c.* 560–475 B.C.), Greek lyric poet.

Anaxagoras (488–428 B.C.), Ionian philosopher who came to Athens 464 B.C. and inspired Pericles and the poet Euripides with his love of science. His rational theories outraged religious opinion, and, like Socrates (who differed from him) he was indicted for impiety.

Anaximander (611–547 B.C.), Miletan philosopher, pupil of Thales, the first among the Greeks to make geographical maps, and to speculate on the origin of the heavenly bodies. He introduced the sun-dial from Babylon or Egypt.

Anaximenes (b. *c.* 570 B.C.), the last of the Milesian school founded by Thales. For him the primal substance was air and he was the first to see the differences between substances in quantitative terms.

Andersen, Hans Christian (1805–75), Danish writer, especially of fairy tales such as *The Little Mermaid* and *The Ugly Duckling*, which are still widely read. He also wrote an autobiography *Mit Livs Eventyr*.

Anderson, Elizabeth Garrett (1836–1917), one of the first English women to enter the medical profession. She practised in London for many years and later became mayor of Aldeburgh, her native town, the first woman to hold the office of mayor.

Andrea del Sarto (1487–1531), Italian painter, b. Florence, the son of a tailor. Known as the "faultless painter," he painted religious frescoes and other works, his *Sculptor* being in the National Gallery.

Andrée, Salomon August (1854–97), Swedish explorer who attempted in 1897 to reach the north pole by balloon. In 1930 a Norwegian scientific expedition discovered the remains of the Andrée expedition on White Island, including a log-book, sketch maps, and diaries.

Andrew, St. one of the apostles of Jesus, brother of Simon Peter, whose festival is observed on 30 November. He became the patron saint of Scotland in the 8th cent.

Angelico, Fra (1387–1455), Italian painter. An exquisite colourist, Fra Giovanni (his Dominican name) painted especially religious frescoes, mainly at Florence and Rome.

Angell, Sir Norman (1872–1967), political commentator, author of *The Great Illusion* (1910), in which he argued that war could no longer pay, and *The Money Game* (1918). Nobel peace prize 1933.

Ångström, Anders Jöns (1814–74), Swedish physicist who studied heat, magnetism, and spectroscopy; hence the angstrom unit used for measuring the wavelength of light.

Anne, Queen (1665–1714), Queen of Gt. Britain and Ireland. A daughter of James II, she succeeded William III in 1702. The act of union with Scotland was passed in 1707. A well-intentioned woman without marked ability, she was influenced by favourites, at first by the Duchess of Marlborough, but in the main she was guided by Tory and high church principles (she established Queen Anne's Bounty to improve church finances). Her reign was notable for literary output (Swift, Pope, Addison, Steele, Defoe), developments in science (Newton), architecture (Wren, Vanbrugh), and for the Duke of Marlborough's victories in war.

Anouilh, Jean (b. 1910), French playwright. *See* Section I.

Anselm, St. (1033–1109), Italian scholar who succeeded Lanfranc as archbishop of Canterbury. He resisted William II, but was able to work with the latter's successor, Henry I.

Anson, 1st Baron (George Anson) (1697–1762), English admiral who sailed round the world 1740–44, his squadron being reduced during the voyage from seven ships to one. An account was compiled by his chaplain.

Antoninus Pius (86–161), Roman emperor, successor of Hadrian. In his reign, which was peaceful, the Antonine wall between the Forth and the Clyde was built to protect Britain from northern attack.

Antonius Marcus (Mark Antony) (*c.* 83–30 B.C.), Roman triumvir. He supported Caesar, and after the latter's death was opposed by Brutus and Cassius, and defeated by Octavian; committed suicide. His association with the Egyptian queen Cleopatra is the subject of Shakespeare's play.

Antony, St. (*c.* 251–356), early promoter of the monastic life. B. in Upper Egypt, he retired into the desert, where he was tempted, but attracted disciples and founded a monastery. Took part in the Council of Nicaea 325. (From his supposed help against erysipelas derives its name of St. Antony's fire.)

Apelles, 4th cent. B.C., Greek painter whose chief paintings, which have not survived, were of Alexander the Great holding a thunderbolt and of Aphrodite rising from the sea.

Apollinaire, Guillaume (Wilhelm Apollinaris Kostrowitzi) (1880–1918), French poet representative of the restless and experimental period in the arts before the first world war. He invented the term *surrealism*. B. Rome of Polish extraction.

Apollonius of Perga (fl. 220 B.C.), Greek mathematician of the Alexandrian school, remembered for his conic sections; introduced the terms *ellipse, parabola,* and *hyperbola.*

Apollonius Rhodius (fl. 250 B.C.), scholar and poet of Alexandria and Rhodes, librarian at Alexandria. His epic *Argonautica* is about the Argonaut heroes.

Appert, Nicholas (1752–1841), sometimes known as François Appert, invented the method of preserving animal and vegetable foods by means of hermetically sealed cans or tins, and paved the way for the creation of a vast world industry.

Appleton, Sir Edward Victor (1892–1965), English physicist, best known as the discoverer of the ionised region of the upper atmosphere which became known as the Appleton layer. His researches led to the development of radar. Nobel prizewinner 1947.

Aquinas, Thomas, St. (c. 1225–74), scholastic philosopher and Dominican friar of Italian birth, whose philosophico-theological system (called Thomism) is still accepted by Catholic ecclesiastics. He understood Aristotle well and interpreted his thought in accord with Christian teaching. His most important works are *Summa contra Gentiles* and *Summa theologica. See also* God and Man, Section J.

Arago, Dominique François Jean (1786–1853), French astronomer and physicist, remembered for his discoveries in electromagnetism and optics.

Archimedes (287–212 B.C.), Greek mathematician, b. Syracuse, son of an astronomer; remembered for his contributions to pure mathematics, mechanics, and hydrostatics, notably the Archimedean screw for raising water, the conception of specific gravity, the doctrine of levers, and the measurement of curved areas. Not less than his scientific knowledge was his practical skill. He was killed by the Romans in the siege of Syracuse.

Argand, Aimé (1755–1803), Swiss physician, inventor of the lamp bearing his name, which was the first to admit a current of air to increase the power of the flame, by use of a chimney glass and circular wick.

Ariosto, Ludovico (1474–1533), Italian poet, author of *Orlando Furioso.*

Aristides (d. c. 468 B.C.), Athenian general and statesman, called "the just"; fought at Marathon.

Aristippus (c. 435–356 B.C.), founder of the Cyrenaic school of philosophy. He taught that man should aim at pleasure, but held that the pleasant was identical with the good.

Aristophanes (c. 444–c. 385 B.C.), Greek dramatist and comic poet, who satirised Athenian life. Among his plays are *The Clouds* and *The Birds.*

Aristotle (384–322 B.C.), Greek philosopher, pupil of Plato, after whose death in 347 he left Athens to become tutor to the young prince Alexander of Macedon. Subsequently at Athens he established his famous school in the garden known as the *Lyceum,* where he lectured in the *peripatos* (cloister) which gave his school of philosophy its name *Peripatetic.* He took the whole field of knowledge as his subject, giving it unity, and providing a philosophy which held its own for 2,000 years.

Arkwright, Sir Richard (1732–92), English inventor. A native of Preston, and originally a barber, he experimented with cotton-spinning machines. His "water frame" (run by water power), patented in 1769, was an early step in the industrial revolution. In 1790 he made use of Boulton and Watt's steam-engine. Rioters sacked one of his mills in 1779.

Arne, Thomas Augustine (1710–78), English composer, remembered for *Rule, Britannia!* (from a masque called *Alfred*), and for Shakespearean songs such as *Where the bee sucks.* He also wrote operas (women singers appeared in *Judith* in 1761) and oratorios.

Arnold, Matthew (1822–88), English poet, critic, and educational reformer; son of Thomas. Among his poems is *The Scholar Gipsy.*

Arnold, Thomas (1795–1842), English headmaster, whose influence at Rugby gave it a high position among public schools.

Arrhenius, Svante August (1859–1927), Swedish chemist, one of the founders of modern physical chemistry. Received 1903 Nobel prize for originating the theory of electrolytic dissociation (ionisation).

Artaxerxes, the name borne by several ancient Persian kings. The first Artaxerxes, son of Xerxes, reigned 464–424 B.C.; he was succeeded by Darius II 424–404 B.C., who was followed by Artaxerxes II, who reigned until 358 B.C. Artaxerxes III, the last to bear the name, was a cruel and treacherous man and was poisoned in 338 B.C.

Arthur (c. 600), fabled Celtic warrior, first referred to in the 9th cent. chronicle of Nennius, who speaks of his 12 victories over the invading Saxons. In mediaeval times his legend developed an extensive literature, woven together by Sir Thomas Mallory in his *Morte d'Arthur,* printed in 1485. Excavations are currently proceeding at South Cadbury, Somerset, the supposed site of his seat, Camelot.

Arundel, Thomas (1353–1414), archbishop of Canterbury 1396, and for a time lord chancellor. An enemy of heresy, he persecuted the Lollards.

Aske, Robert, leader of the Pilgrimage of Grace 1536, directed against the Henrician Reformation; executed 1537.

Asoka (273–32 B.C.), Indian emperor and upholder of Buddhism. At first he expanded his empire by conquest, but on being converted to Buddhism rejected war and aimed at the good of his people. He sent Buddhist missionaries as far as Ceylon and Syria. Art flourished, and many rock inscriptions commemorate his doings.

Asquith, Herbert Henry, 1st Earl of Oxford and Asquith (1852–1928), Liberal prime minister 1908–16, having previously served under Gladstone. His government enacted social reforms including old-age pensions (1908) and unemployment insurance (1911), but as a war minister he had to give way to Lloyd George. He resigned leadership of his party in 1926. His daughter Violet (1887–1969), an eloquent speaker, was created a life peeress in 1964.

Asser, a Welsh monk of the 9th cent., traditionally author of a life of King Alfred.

Astor, John Jacob (1763–1848), founder of the millionaire family, was a native of Heidelberg, emigrated to America, and made a fortune by trading in fur.

Astor, Viscountess (Nancy Witcher Astor, *née* Langhorne) (1879–1964), the first woman M.P. to take her seat in the House of Commons, an American by birth, wife of the 2nd Viscount Astor.

Atatürk, Kemal (1881–1938), builder of modern Turkey. A fine soldier, he defended the Dardanelles against the British in 1915 and drove the Greeks out of Turkey in 1922. President of the Turkish republic, and virtually dictator, 1923–38.

Athanasius, St. (296–373), upholder of the doctrine of the Trinity against Arius, who denied the divinity of Christ. He was bishop of Alexandria. He is not now thought the author of the creed which bears his name.

Athelstan (895–940), grandson of Alfred the Great, was crowned king of England in 925, and was the first ruler of all England.

Atherstone, William Guybon (1813–98), South African geologist and an originator of the South African diamond industry.

Attila (406–53), invading king of the Huns from Asia. He defeated the Roman emperor Theodosius, and entered Gaul, but was defeated in 451 near Châlons-sur-Marne.

Attlee, 1st Earl (Clement Richard Attlee) (1883–1967), Labour prime minister 1945–51, having served as deputy to Churchill 1942–5. Called to the Bar in 1905, he lectured at the London School of Economics 1913–23, was mayor of

Stepney 1919, and parliamentary leader of his party 1935–55. His government helped to create a welfare society and granted independence to India. His writings include an autobiography, *As it Happened*, and *Empire into Commonwealth*.

Auchinleck, Sir Claude John Eyre (b. 1884), British field-marshal; G.O.C. North Norway 1940; C.-in-C. India 1941, 1943–7; Middle East 1941–2.

Auden, Wystan Hugh (b. 1907), poet, b. in England and naturalised an American. Succeeded C. Day Lewis as professor of poetry at Oxford 1956–61. *See* Section M, Part II.

Auer, Leopold (1845–1930), Hungarian violinist and teacher; Mischa Elman and Jascha Heifetz were among his pupils.

Augustine of Canterbury, St. (d. *c.* 605), first archbishop of Canterbury. He was sent from Rome in 597 by Gregory the Great to convert the English peoples.

Augustus, Caius Octavianus (63 B.C.–A.D. 14), first Roman emperor. Nephew of Julius Caesar, he was for 12 years triumvir with Mark Antony and Lepidus; then reigned alone. His reign was notable for peace, and for writers like Horace and Virgil; hence Augustan age for a great period in literature (the title Augustus was given him by the Senate).

Aurelius, Marcus Antonius. *See* Marcus Aurelius Antoninus.

Auriol, Vincent (1884–1966), French politician. He voted against surrender in 1940, was interned and escaped to London in 1943. President of the Fourth Republic 1947–54.

Aurangzeb (1618–1707), Mogul emperor of India. Son of Shah Jehan, he obtained power by acting against his father and brothers. In his long reign the Mogul empire reached its fullest extent; but he estranged Hindus and Sikhs; and when he died his authority was in dispute and the Mogul empire broke up.

Austen, Jane (1775–1817), author of *Emma*, *Mansfield Park*, *Northanger Abbey*, *Persuasion*, *Pride and Prejudice*, and *Sense and Sensibility*. Though confining herself to the personal relations of the English middle classes, she combined artistry, accuracy, imaginative power, satiric humour, sense, and genuine feeling with the ability to create a range of living characters. She spent the first 25 years of her life at her father's Hampshire vicarage. She was unmarried.

Austin, 1st Baron (Herbert Austin) (1886–1941), English motor manufacturer, pioneer of the small car—the 7-horsepower car—which he put on the market in 1921.

Avenzoar (Ibn Zuhr) (*c.* 1090–1162), Arab physician, b. Seville. His chief work was the *Tasir*.

Averroës (Ibn Rushd) (1126–98), Arab philosopher, b. Cordova. He believed in the eternity of the world (not as a single act of creation as demanded by the current theology of Islam, Christianity and Judaism, but as a continuous process) and in the eternity of a universal intelligence, indivisible but shared in by all. He expounded Aristotle to his countrymen, but his teaching was modified by Neoplatonism. He was a friend of Avenzoar.

Avicenna (Ali ibn-Sina) (980–1037), Arab philosopher and physician, of Bokhara, whose influence on mediaeval Europe was chiefly through his *Canon of Medicine*, in which he attempted to systematise all the medical knowledge up to his time.

Avogadro, Amedeo (1776–1856), Italian physicist, remembered for his hypothesis, since known as Avogadro's Law, that equal volumes of gases under identical conditions of temperature and pressure contain the same number of molecules.

Avon, Earl of. *See* Eden, Anthony.

Ayrton, William Edward (1847–1908), English electrical engineer, inventor of a number of electrical measuring instruments. His first wife, **Matilda Chaplin Ayrton** (1846–83), was one of the first woman doctors, and his second wife, **Hertha Ayrton** (1854–1923), became known for her scientific work on the electric arc and sand ripples and for her work for woman suffrage.

Ayub Khan, Mohammed (b. 1907), Pakistani military leader; president of Pakistan, 1958–69.

Azikiwe, Nnamdi (b. 1904), Nigerian statesman; president of Nigeria, 1963–6.

B

Baber, Babar or Babur (Zahir ud-din Mohammed) (1483–1530), founder of the Mogul dynasty which ruled northern India for nearly three centuries; a descendant of Tamerlane.

Bach, Johann Sebastian (1685–1750), composer. B. at Eisenach, Germany, he was successively violinist, church organist, and chief court musician. It was as organist at the Thomaskirche, Leipzig, that he composed the St. Matthew and the St. John Passion and the B minor Mass. His work was in the school of the contrapuntal style (especially the fugue and the chorale); after his day it lost favour, but during the last century it has gained ground continually. Personally he was contented and unworldly, but latterly became blind. His family was connected with music for seven generations. *See* Section E.

Bach, Karl Philipp Emmanuel (1714–88), 3rd son of the above, and one of the first experimenters in the symphonic and sonata forms.

Backhaus, Wilhelm (1884–1969), German pianist, gifted in interpreting classical and romantic concertos.

Bacon, Francis, Lord Verulam (1561–1626), English philosopher. He threw over Aristotelian deductive logic for the inductive method (*see* Baconian method, Section J); remembered for the impulse his writings gave to the foundation of the Royal Society (*c.* 1662). His chief work is the *Novum Organum*. His career as statesman under Elizabeth and James I was brought to an end by charges of corruption.

Bacon, Roger (*c.* 1219/20–1294), founder of English philosophy, advocate of the value of observation and experiment in science. He first studied arts at Oxford but when he returned from lecturing in Paris he devoted himself to experimental science, especially alchemy and optics. He became a Franciscan friar in 1257. After his death he acquired a reputation for necromancy which was undeserved.

Baden-Powell, 1st Baron (Robert Stephenson Smyth Baden-Powell) (1857–1941), founder of Boy Scouts (1908) and Girl Guides (1910) to promote good citizenship in the rising generation; Chief Scout of the World 1921–41. As a young cavalry officer in the South African war he defended Mafeking.

Baer, Karl Ernst von (1792–1876), German naturalist, b. Estonia, founder of the science of embryology. He discovered the mammalian ovum (1827). An opponent of Darwin's theory.

Baffin, William (1584–1622), British navigator and explorer who in 1616 discovered the bay which separates the north-east coast of Canada from Greenland, which bears his name.

Bagehot, Walter (1826–77), English economist and journalist, editor of *The Economist*. Among his works are *The English Constitution* and *Lombard Street*.

Baird, John Logie (1888–1946), Scottish television pioneer, inventor of the televisor and the noctovisor.

Baker, Sir Benjamin (1840–1907), English civil engineer. With Sir John Fowler he built the Forth bridge and the London Metropolitan railway. He designed the vessel which brought Cleopatra's Needle to London. In Egypt he was consulting engineer for the Aswan dam.

Baker, Sir Herbert (1862–1946), English architect who designed the Bank of England, Rhodes house, Oxford, and, with Sir E. Lutyens, New Delhi.

Bakst, Léon (1868–1924), Russian painter who designed scenery and costumes for Diaghilev's ballets.

Baldwin of Bewdley, 1st Earl (Stanley Baldwin) (1867–1947), Conservative prime minister, 1923–4, 1924–9, and 1935–7. His handling of the crisis over Edward VIII's proposed marriage ended with the king's abdication.

Balewa, Sir Abubakar Tafawa (1912–66), federal prime minister of Nigeria, 1960–6; murdered during the crisis of January 1966.

Balfour, 1st Earl (Arthur James Balfour) (1848–1930), statesman and writer. He was Conservative prime minister 1902–5. As foreign secretary under Lloyd George, he was responsible for a declaration on Palestine.

Balliol, John de (d. 1269), founder of Balliol College, Oxford; a regent for Scotland; sided with Henry III against his barons.

Balliol, John de (1249–1315), king of Scotland. Son of the above, he claimed the throne against Robert Bruce and was chosen by the arbitrator, Edward I of England, whose overlordship he acknowledged. Later, on renouncing homage, he was taken captive and d. in retirement. His son Edward Balliol (d. 1363) obtained the kingdom for a time, acknowledging Edward III of England and surrendering Lothian; but retired on an annuity, 1356.

Ball, John (d. 1381), English priest and a leader of the Peasants' Revolt, after which he was executed. The couplet *When Adam delved, and Eve span, Who was then the gentleman?* is attributed to him.

Balzac, Honoré de (1799–1850), French novelist of wide influence, and author of over eighty novels to which he gave the covering title of *La Comédie Humaine*, depicting the appetites and passions of the new social class born of the revolution and Napoleon.

Bancroft, Sir Squire (1841–1926), Victorian actor-manager.

Bandaranaike, Solomon West Ridgway Dias (1899–1959), socialist prime minister of Ceylon from 1956 until his assassination in 1959. His widow, Mrs. Sirimawo Bandaranaike, became the world's first woman prime minister, 1960–5.

Banks, Sir Joseph (1743–1820), an amateur scientist of wealth who accompanied Captain Cook on his expedition to the Pacific 1768–76. He left botanical collections to the British Museum.

Banting, Sir Frederick Grant (1891–1941), Canadian physician who with C. H. Best discovered insulin.

Bantock, Sir Granville (1868–1946), composer of songs, orchestral and choral music.

Barbarossa. *See* Frederick I.

Barbarossa (Ital. = red beard), surname of two brothers who were Barbary pirates: Uruz (c. 1474–1518), was killed by Spaniards, and Khaireddin (c. 1483–1546) conquered Tunis for the Turks and died in Constantinople.

Barbirolli, Sir John (1899–1970), conductor of the Hallé Orchestra 1943–70; succeeded Toscanini as conductor of the New York Philharmonic Symphony Orchestra 1937–42.

Barbusse, Henri (1874–1935), French writer, author of the war novel *Le Feu*, which portrays in a starkly vivid way the experience of the common soldier.

Barham, Richard Harris (1788–1845), English humorist, author of *The Ingoldsby Legends*, written under his pen-name of Thomas Ingoldsby. His best known poem is *The Jackdaw of Rheims*.

Barnardo, Thomas John (1845–1905), founder of homes for orphan-waifs; devoted himself to the protection, education, and advancement of destitute children.

Barrie, Sir James Matthew (1860–1937), Scottish author and dramatist. His novels include *A Window in Thrums*. Among his plays are *Dear Brutus*, *The Admirable Crichton*, and *Peter Pan* which gained great popularity with children.

Barrow, Isaac (1630–77), divine and mathematician, tutor of Sir Isaac Newton.

Barry, Sir Charles (1795–1860), architect of the houses of parliament at Westminster, the details of which were contributed by his assistant A. W. Pugin.

Barth, Karl (1886–1968), Swiss theologian, described by the late Pope John as a Protestant St. Thomas Aquinas.

Bartók, Bela (1881–1945), Hungarian composer. From an early age he was deeply interested in folk-song which inspired his researches into Hungarian and Rumanian peasant music. He left for America in 1940, where he lived precariously and apparently unhappily until the end of the war made a return possible, regrettably too late. *See* Section E.

Bartolommeo, Fra (di Paolo) (1475–1517), Italian painter. At first influenced by Savonarola, he later resumed painting. Some of his best work is at Lucca.

Bartolozzi, Francesco (1725–1815), Italian engraver, who settled in England and became a founder-member of the Royal Academy; noted for his stipple engravings.

Bashkirtseff, Marie (1860–84), Russian painter and writer of a diary.

Bassi, Agostino (1773–1856), Italian amateur microscopist who first suggested that infectious diseases might be caused by the invasion of the body by micro-organisms.

Batten, Jean Gardner (b. 1909), New Zealand airwoman who flew solo from England to Australia in 1934.

Baudelaire, Charles Pierre (1821–67), French poet of originality and sensitivity, best known for his *Les Fleurs du Mal*. His life was darkened by poverty and ill-health.

Bax, Sir Arnold (1883–1953), composer of numerous piano compositions, songs, and chamber works.

Baxter, Richard (1615–91), presbyterian divine and author; imprisoned after the Restoration. He wrote an autobiography.

Bayard, Pierre de Terrail, Seigneur de (c. 1474–1524), French knight, known as the " chevalier sans peur et sans reproche." He fought in campaigns against Italy and fell at the battle of Romagnano.

Bayle, Pierre (1647–1706), French philosopher, author of the *Dictionnaire historique et critique* (1697). His sceptical views influenced Voltaire and the encyclopedists of the 18th cent.

Baylis, Lilian Mary (1874–1937), manager of the Old Vic theatre from 1898 and of Sadler's Wells from 1931. Promoter of Shakespeare and of opera in English.

Beaconsfield. *See* Disraeli.

Beardsley, Aubrey Vincent (1872–98), black-and-white artist, who in a brief life published much work, some of it controversial (as in the *Yellow Book*).

Beatty, 1st Earl (David Beatty) (1871–1936), British admiral; succeeded Jellicoe as commander of the Grand Fleet 1916–19. Commanding the British battlecruisers, he fought the German fleet on 28 August 1914 in the Heligoland Bight, and on 31 May 1916 off Jutland.

Beaufort, Sir Francis (1774–1857), hydrographer of the navy, who introduced the wind scale (1805) which bears his name. *See* Section N.

Beaumont, Francis (1584–1616), and Fletcher, John (1579–1625), joint authors of many plays, including *The Maid's Tragedy* and *Philaster*.

Beaverbrook, 1st Baron (William Maxwell Aitken) (1879–1964), British newspaper owner and politician, a Canadian by birth. He gave energetic service as minister of aircraft production 1940–1. He controlled the *Daily Express*, *Sunday Express*, and *Evening Standard*, which sponsored his political campaigns.

Becket, Thomas (1118?–70), saint and martyr. An able chancellor, 1155–62, on becoming archbishop of Canterbury he made the position of the church his first care; and, coming into conflict with Henry II, was murdered in Canterbury cathedral. His shrine became a place of pilgrimage.

Beckett, Samuel (b. 1906), Anglo-Irish dramatist and novelist. Nobel prizewinner 1969. *See* Sections I and M.

Becquerel, Antoine Henri (1852–1908), French physicist who in 1896 discovered radioactivity in uranium. Shared with the Curies the 1903 Nobel prize in physics.

Bede, the Venerable (673–735), English historian and scholar; lived at Jarrow. His chief work is his *Ecclesiastical History* to 731.

Beecham, Sir Thomas (1879–1961), English conductor and impresario. Founded the London Philharmonic Orchestra in 1931; introduced into England the operas of Richard Strauss, Russian operas, and the Diaghilev ballet; championed the music of Delius. Pub. Frederick Delius's biography, 1959; Memoirs, *A Mingled Chime*.

Beecher, Henry Ward (1813–87), American preacher and lecturer, whose church was at Brooklyn.

Beerbohm, Sir Max (1872–1956), critic and caricaturist, master of irony and satire. His works include *Zuleika Dobson* and *A Christmas Garland*, and he contributed to the *Saturday Review*.

Beethoven, Ludwig van (1770–1827), composer. B. at Bonn (his father being a tenor singer at the Elector's court), at 17 he went to Vienna, was recognised by Mozart, and eventually settled there; he never married, and gradually became deaf. In the development from simplicity to complexity of musical treatment, he stands midway between Mozart and Wagner; but in him were uniquely combined the power to feel and the mastery of musical resources necessary to express his feelings. Between the years 1805 and 1808 he composed some of his greatest works: the oratorio *Mount of Olives*, the opera *Fidelio*, and the *Pastoral* and *Eroica* symphonies besides a number of concertos, sonatas, and songs. The symphonies, nine in number, rank as the greatest ever written and the pianoforte sonatas and string quartets are unequalled in beauty. He died in Vienna at the age of 56. *See Section E.*

Behring, Emil von (1854–1917), German bacteriologist, founder of the science of immunology. Nobel prizewinner 1901.

Behring, Vitus (1680–1741), Danish navigator who entered the Russian service and in 1728 discovered the strait which bears his name.

Belisarius (505–65), Roman general under Justinian who fought against the Vandals, Ostrogoths, and Persians.

Bell, Alexander Graham (1847–1922), inventor, b. Edinburgh, emigrated to Canada in 1870, later becoming an American citizen. In 1876 he exhibited an invention which was developed into the telephone. He devoted attention to the education of deaf-mutes.

Bell, Gertrude Margaret Lowthian (1868–1926), the "uncrowned queen of Arabia," was a traveller in the Middle East; her knowledge proved of service to the British government in the first world war.

Bellamy, Edward (1850–98), American author of *Looking Backward*, a prophetic utopian novel.

Bellini, family of Venetian painters: Jacopo (*c.* 1400–70) and his two sons, **Gentile** (1429–1507), whose works include the *Adoration of the Magi* (National Gallery); and **Giovanni** (*c.* 1429–1516), brother-in-law of Mantegna, and teacher of Giorgione and Titian, who continued his tradition of light and colour.

Bellini, Vincenzo (1801–35), Italian operatic composer; b. Sicily. His melodies were admired by Chopin. His best-known operas are *I Capuleti ed i Montecchi, La Sonnambula, Norma* and *I Puritani. See Section E.*

Belloc, Hilaire (1870–1953), versatile writer whose works include *The Bad Child's Book of Beasts, The Path to Rome, Hills and the Sea, Cautionary Tales,* and historical studies of Danton, Robespierre, and Richelieu. In France, he became a British subject in 1902.

Belzoni, Giovanni Battista (1778–1823), Egyptologist. B. at Padua, he settled in England in 1803. His first interest was in hydraulics, and for this purpose he went to Egypt to Mehemet Ali. There he explored Thebes, Abu Simbel, and one of the pyramids, sending some sculptures to the British Museum.

Benavente y Martínez, Jacinto (1866–1954), Spanish dramatist, whose plays include *Los Intereses Creados* (Bonds of Interest). Nobel prizewinner 1922.

Benedict, St. (*c.* 480–*c.* 550), patriarch of western monasticism. B. at Nursia, and at first a hermit at Subiaco, he attracted numerous followers and grouped them in twelve monasteries. Later he went to Monte Cassino, where he formulated the Benedictine rule, of wide application in Western Christendom. *See Monasticism, Section J.*

Benes, Eduard (1884–1948), Czechoslovak statesman; co-founder with Thomas Masaryk of the Czech Republic after the break-up of the Austro-Hungarian monarchy (1918).

Ben Gurion, David (b. 1886), Zionist leader. He helped organise the Jewish Legion in 1918, and was prominently connected with the Labour movement in Palestine in between the world wars. Prime minister of Israel 1948–63.

Bennett, Enoch Arnold (1867–1931), English author, who wrote of the pottery towns where he was brought up. His novels include *The Old Wives' Tale, Clayhanger,* and *Hilda Lessways.* He also wrote plays, including *Milestones, The Great Adventure,* and *Mr. Prohack.*

Bennett, James Gordon (1841–1918), proprietor of the *New York Herald.* He sent out Stanley on an expedition to find Livingstone.

Bentham, Jeremy (1748–1832), utilitarian philosopher and writer on jurisprudence. His main works are *Government* and *Principles of Morals and Legislation.*

Bentley, Richard (1662–1742), classical scholar who did pioneer work in textual criticism.

Benz, Karl (1884–1929), German engineer whose motor car produced in 1885 was one of the first to be driven by an internal combustion engine.

Béranger, Jean Pierre de (1780–1857), popular French song-writer, whose compositions were often written to serve some passing political purpose.

Beresford, 1st Viscount (William Carr Beresford) (1768–1854), British general. He fought under Wellington in the Peninsular War and reorganised the Portuguese army.

Berg, Alban (1885–1935), Austrian composer whose best-known work is the three-act opera *Wozzeck,* based upon a drama by Buchner, which has become a modern classic.

Bergson, Henri Louis (1859–1941), French philosopher, exponent of the theory of creative evolution and the life force. Nobel prizewinner 1927. *See* **Vitalism, Section J.**

Bériot, Charles Auguste de (1802–70), Belgian violinist, whose wife was the operatic contralto Malibran. His son, **Charles Wilfrid de Bériot** (1833–1914) was a pianist and the teacher of Ravel.

Berkeley, George (1685–1753), idealist philosopher and critic of Locke. His spiritual outlook led him to believe that reality exists only in the eye of God, that it is undiscoverable by science, though it can be revealed by religion. His chief work is *Alciphron.* He was a master of prose. Of Irish birth, he became bishop of Cloyne.

Berlin, Irving (b. 1888), American composer of popular songs, b. Russia; pioneer of both ragtime and jazz music. His songs include *Alexander's Rag-time Band, Always, What'll I do?;* his musicals include *Annie Get your Gun* and *Call me Madam.*

Berlin, Sir Isaiah (b. 1909), British university teacher, b. Riga; Chichele Prof. of Social and Political Theory at Oxford 1957–67. His works include *Karl Marx, The Hedgehog and the Fox,* and *The Age of Enlightenment.*

Berlioz, Hector (1803–69), composer. B. near Grenoble, the son of a doctor, his romantic sensibility, taste for the grand (as in his *Requiem*), and response to literary influence made him a prime figure in the French romantic movement. His works include the symphony *Romeo and Juliet,* and the operas *Benevenuto Cellini* and *Beatrice and Benedict.* His first wife was an Irish actress, Harriet Smithson, whom he met while she was playing Shakespearean parts in Rome. *See Section E.*

Bernadotte, Count Folke (1895–1948), nephew of the late King Gustav of Sweden. U.N. mediator for Palestine 1947. Assassinated by Jewish terrorists.

Bernadotte, Jean Baptiste (1764–1844), a French commander who served under Napoleon, and in 1810 was chosen heir to the throne of Sweden. In 1818 he succeeded as Charles XIV.

Bernal, John Desmond (b. 1901), physicist, b. Ireland. Prof. of Physics, Birkbeck College, Univ. of London, 1937–63, Prof. of Crystallography, 1963–8. Author of *The Social Functions of Science, Science in History, The Origin of Life.* Lenin peace prize 1953.

Bernard, Claude (1813–78), French physiologist whose discoveries though not of immediate application paved the way for the work of Pavlov and Hopkins.

Bernard of Menthon (923–1008), patron saint of mountaineers. He founded Alpine hospices in the passes that bear his name.

Bernard, St. (1090–1153), abbot of Clairvaux, which became a chief centre of the Cistercian order. This order aimed at seclusion and austerity, and practised manual work. His writings had wide influence in Europe.

Bernhardt, Sarah (1844–1923), French tragedienne, b. Paris, daughter of a Dutch jewess. She became a member of the Comédie Française after the siege of Paris. Her first performance in London was in 1879. Her successes included *Phèdre, La Dame aux Camélias, Fédora, Théodora,* and *La Tosca,* and she produced and played in Racine and Molière.

Best, Charles Herbert (b. 1899), Canadian physiologist, who with F. G. Banting discovered the use of insulin in the treatment of diabetes.

Berthelot, Marcellin Pierre Eugène (1827–1907), French chemist and politician. He was the first to produce organic compounds synthetically.

Berzelius, Jöns Jakob (1779–1848), Swedish chemist, founder of electrochemical theory. His work was mainly concerned with the exact determination of atomic and molecular weights and he devised the system of chemical symbols in use today.

Bessemer, Sir Henry (1813–98), inventor of the process of converting cast-iron direct into steel. This revolutionised steel manufacture, reducing the cost of production and extending the use of steel.

Bevan, Aneurin (1897–1960), British socialist politician, architect of the National Health Service which came into operation in 1948.

Beveridge, 1st Baron (William Henry Beveridge) (1879–1963), British economist. Drew up the Beveridge Plan, published in 1942, which formed the basis of the present social security services.

Bevin, Ernest (1881–1951), British trade union leader, who later became a forceful foreign secretary. He was assistant general secretary of the Dockers Union, later general secretary of the Transport and General Workers Union; Minister of Labour 1940–5, and Foreign Secretary 1945–51.

Beyle, Marie Henri. *See* Stendhal.

Bhave, Vinova (b. 1895), Indian reformer, leader of the Sarvodaya movement. A follower of Gandhi, in 1951 he began a walking mission to persuade landlords to help landless peasants. In four years 4 million acres of land were redistributed.

Bichat, Marie François Xavier (1771–1802), French physiologist whose study of tissues founded modern histology. His theory was that life is " the sum of the forces that restrict death."

Biddle, John (1615–62), unitarian. He taught in Gloucester; was several times imprisoned for his controversial writings; and died of fever contracted in prison. *See also* **Unitarianism, Section J.**

Binyon, Laurence (1869–1943), poet, art critic, and orientalist, who worked at the British Museum 1893–1933.

Birch, Samuel John Lamorna (1869–1955), English landscape painter in watercolour, known for his Cornish and Australian studies.

Birkbeck, George (1776–1841), founder of mechanics' institutes, first at Glasgow, later in London; founder also of University College, London.

Birkenhead, 1st Earl of (Frederick Edwin Smith) (1872–1930), English lawyer and politician; lord chancellor 1919–22; secretary for India 1924–8.

Bishop, Sir Henry Rowley (1786–1855), English composer who wrote *Home, sweet Home*, glees, and operas.

Bismarck, Otto Eduard Leopold von, Prince Bismarck, Duke of Lauenburg (1815–98), Prusso-German diplomat and statesman, chief architect of the German empire. He was of Junker family. As Prussian ambassador at St. Petersburg (1859–62) and at Paris (1862), he learned to assess the European situation. He was recalled to Berlin by the king to become chief Prussian minister; and when the house of representatives would not pass a military bill he closed the house. He used a dispute over Schleswig-Holstein to bring about the defeat of Austria at Königgratz in 1866; and he provoked the Franco-Prussian war of 1870–1 when France was defeated at Sedan. Germany then became united under the military leadership of Prussia, with the king as emperor, instead of by the slower processes of democracy. He presided over the Berlin Congress of European powers in 1878. In 1884 he began a colonial policy. His authoritarian system, in spite of its inherent defects, was at least based on cautious and accurate assessment of power politics. This factor was not understood by William II, who succeeded as emperor in 1888, and dismissed the " iron chancellor " in 1890.

Bizet, Georges (1838–75), properly **Alexandre César Léopold,** French composer, chiefly remembered for his opera *Carmen* from the story by Merimée.

Björnson, Björnstjerne (1832–1910), Norwegian poet, dramatist and novelist. His work provides an image of Norwegian life from the period of the sagas (*Kong Sverre*) to contemporary problems (*Over Aevne*), and he wrote the national anthem.

Black, Joseph (1728–90), Scottish chemist. A professor first at Glasgow, later at Edinburgh, he was the first to undertake a detailed study of a chemical reaction. He laid the foundation of the quantitative science of heat and his discovery of latent heat was applied by Watt in improving his steam-engine.

Blackett, Baron (Patrick Maynard Stuart Blackett) (b. 1897), British physicist whose work on nuclear and cosmic ray physics gained him a Nobel prize in 1948. Author of *Military and Political Consequences of Atomic Energy* (1948), *Lectures on Rock Magnetism* (1956), *Studies of War* (1962). Pres. British Association 1957; Pres. Royal Society 1966–70; O.M. 1967.

Blackmore, Richard Doddridge (1825–1900), English novelist and author of *Lorna Doone*.

Blackstone, Sir William (1723–80), English judge. His *Commentaries on the Laws of England* is a classic.

Blackwood, Algernon (1869–1951), English novelist and writer of short stories.

Blackwood, William (1776–1834), originator of *Blackwood's Magazine*.

Blair, Robert (1699–1746), Scottish poet, author of *The Grave*.

Blake, Robert (1599–1657), Parliamentary general and an admiral in the Cromwellian navy in the Dutch and Spanish wars.

Blake, William (1757–1827), English poet, mystic, and artist, son of a hosier in Carnaby market, Soho. A solitary, and deeply religious man, he had a hatred of materialism. He produced his own books, engraving on copper plates both the text of his poems and the illustrations. His *Book of Job* is a masterpiece in line-engraving in metal, his poems range from the mystical and almost incomprehensible to the delightfully simple *Songs of Innocence*. He has been called " the great teacher of the modern western world." His art is in many ways reminiscent of that of another rebel of the same day, the Spanish painter Goya.

Blanqui, Louis Auguste (1805–81), French revolutionary leader, master of insurrection. He invented the term " dictatorship of the proletariat," and his social theories, stressing the class struggle, influenced Marx. Active in 1830, 1848, and 1871, he spent 37 years in prison.

Blériot, Louis (1872–1936), French airman; the first to fly the English Channel from Calais to Dover, on 25 July 1909.

Bligh, William (1754–1817), sailor, b. Plymouth. He accompanied Cook 1772–4, and discovered bread-fruit; but was in 1789 cast adrift from *The Bounty* by his mutinous crew. As governor of New South Wales (1806) he fought to suppress the rum traffic.

Blind, Karl (1826–1907), German agitator, b. Mannheim. He was active in the German risings of 1848, and imprisoned; but escaped and settled in England, remaining in touch with men like Mazzini and Louis Blanc.

Bliss, Sir Arthur (b. 1891), English composer; succeeded Sir Arnold Bax as Master of the Queen's Musick 1953.

Bloch, Ernest (1880–1959), composer, whose music is characterised by Jewish and oriental themes. B. in Geneva, he became a naturalised American.

Blondin, Charles (1824–97), French rope performer, who crossed the Niagara Falls on a tight-rope.

Blücher, Gebhard Leberecht von (1742–1819), Prussian general. He fought against Napoleon, especially at Lützen and Leipzig; and he completed Wellington's victory at Waterloo by his timely arrival.

Blum, Léon (1872–1950), French statesman, leader of the French Socialist Party. His efforts strengthened the growth of the Popular Front and the campaign against appeasement of Hitler. He held office only briefly and was interned in Germany 1940–5.

Blunden, Edmund Charles (b. 1896), English poet and critic; professor of poetry at Oxford 1966–8.

Blunt, Wilfrid Scawan (1840–1922), English poet and political writer who championed Egyptian, Indian, and Irish independence.

Boadicea (Boudicca), queen of the Iceni in eastern Britain, who fought against the Roman invaders, but was defeated in A.D. 61 and killed herself.

Boccaccio, Giovanni (1313–75), Italian author, father of the novel. He is chiefly known for his *Decameron* (set in the neighbourhood of Florence during the plague), and for his life of Dante.

Boccherini, Luigi (1743–1805), Italian cellist and composer of chamber music. He settled in Madrid.

Bode, Johann Ehlert (1747–1826), German astronomer remembered for his theoretical calculation (known as Bode's law) of the proportionate distances of the planets from the sun. *See* L16.

Boethius (480–524), Roman scientific writer who translated the logical works of Aristotle and provided the dark ages with some elementary mathematical treatises.

Bohr, Niels Henrik David (1885–1962), Danish nuclear physicist whose researches into the structure of the atom gave him great authority in the world of theoretical physics. With Rutherford he applied the quantum theory to the study of atomic processes. Nobel prizewinner 1922.

Boieldieu, François Adrien (1775–1834), French composer especially of operas, including *La Dame blanche*.

Boileau-Despréaux, Nicolas (1636–1711), French literary critic and poet, best known for his *Satires*.

Boito, Arrigo (1842–1918), Italian poet and composer; he wrote the libretti of *Otello* and *Falstaff* for Verdi.

Boleyn, Anne (1507–36), queen of Henry VIII and mother of Queen Elizabeth. She was maid-in-waiting to Catherine of Aragon and her successor when Catherine's marriage was annulled. She failed to produce a male heir and was beheaded on a charge of adultery.

Bolivar, Simón (1783–1830), South American revolutionist, called the Liberator, b. Caracas. He led independence movements in the north-west of South America against Spanish rule, aiming at a South American federation. He founded Grand Colombia (now Venezuela, Colombia, Panama, Ecuador). He died poor, of tuberculosis, but is revered as a Latin-American hero.

Bonaventura, St. (1221–74), Franciscan theologian, b. Orvieto. His mystical theory of knowledge was in the Augustinian tradition.

Bondfield, Margaret Grace (1873–1953), as minister of Labour, 1929–31, she was the first woman to enter the cabinet and to be a member of the privy council.

Bondi, Hermann (b. 1919), British mathematician and astronomer, b. Vienna; chief scientist to the Min. of Defence, 1971– ; associated with the steady state theory of the universe. *See* F5.

Bone, Sir Muirhead (1876–1953), architectural draughtsman and etcher, b. Glasgow; excelled in dry-point and drawings of intricate scaffolding; official war artist in both world wars.

Bonheur, Rose (1822–99), French painter of animals.

Boniface, St. (680–754), apostle of Germany. B. at Credition, Devon, his name being Wynfrith, he became a Benedictine monk, and went as missionary to Friesland, securing papal approval. He founded Fulda Abbey and became archbishop of Mainz, but was martyred.

Bonnard, Pierre (1867–1947), French painter of landscapes, still life, and nudes, a colourist and skilled draughtsman.

Booth, Edwin Thomas (1833–93), American Shakespearean actor, brother of John Wilkes Booth who assassinated President Lincoln.

Booth, William (1829–1912), founder and first general of the Salvation Army, b. Nottingham. In 1865, with the help of his wife, Catherine Booth, he began mission work in the East End of London, which led to the creation in 1878 of the Salvation Army on military lines. He developed branches in many parts of the world.

His son Bramwell (d. 1929) and his daughter Evangeline were among his successors. *See also* Salvation Army, Section J.

Borges, Jorge Luis (b. 1899), Argentine poet, critic, and short story writer. Some of his work has been translated into English, including the collection *Labyrinths* (1962).

Borgia, Caesar (1476–1507), Italian general. The son of Pope Alexander VI, at 17 he was suspected of murdering his brother. He became captain-general of the church, and made himself master of Romagna, the Marches, and Umbria. Banished by Pope Julius II, he met his death fighting in Spain.

Borlaug, Norman Ernest (b. 1914), American wheat scientist, responsible for the "green revolution" which is transforming the agricultural prospects of the less-developed countries of the world. Nobel prize for peace 1970.

Borodin, Alexander Porfyrievich (1833–87), Russian composer who taught chemistry and founded a school of medicine for women. In a busy professional life he wrote two symphonies, two string quartets, the symphonic sketch *In the Steppes of Central Asia* and the opera *Prince Igor*. *See* Section E.

Borrow, George Henry (1803–81), English author, for many years agent for the British and Foreign Bible Society; in the course of his wanderings he studied gypsy life and wrote of his experiences in *Lavengro, Romany Rye, Bible in Spain*.

Bose, Subhas Chandra (1897–1945), Indian nationalist leader; killed in a plane crash.

Boswell, James (1740–95), Scottish author of *The Life of Dr. Johnson*, with whom he spent some years in intimacy. His own journals and letters recently published form an extensive literary collection.

Botha, Louis (1862–1919), South African soldier and statesman. In command of Transvaal forces 1899–1902 in the Boer war, he became prime minister of the Transvaal in 1907, and first premier of the Union of South Africa in 1910. In the 1914–18 war he conquered territory then under German rule.

Bottesini, Giovanni (1821–89), Italian double-bass player.

Botticelli, Sandro (c. 1445–1510), Italian painter. He worked under Fra Lippo Lippi, and was influenced by Savonarola. His art is delicate and poetic. His *Birth of Venus* is in the Uffizi Gallery, Florence, and his *Mars and Venus* in the National Gallery. He illustrated Dante's *Inferno*.

Bottomley, Horatio (1860–1933), English politician, journalist, and notorious financier, who died in poverty after serving a prison sentence for fraud.

Botvinnik, Mikhail (b. 1911), Russian chess player; world champion 1948–57, 1958–60, 1961–3. Retired 1965.

Boughton, Rutland (1878–1960), English composer of the opera *The Immortal Hour*, and writer on the history and philosophy of music.

Boult, Sir Adrian (b. 1889), conductor of the London Philharmonic Orchestra 1950–7, and of the B.B.C. Symphony Orchestra 1930–50. Musical Director B.B.C. 1930–42.

Boulton, Matthew (1728–1809), engineer who in partnership with James Watt manufactured steam-engines at his Soho works near Birmingham. He also minted a new copper coinage for Great Britain.

Bowdler, Thomas (1754–1825), issued for family reading expurgated editions of Shakespeare and Gibbon, hence the term " bowdlerise."

Boyce, William (1710–79), London organist and composer, who also collected the works of English church composers. He was master of the orchestra for George III.

Boyd Orr, 1st Baron (John Boyd Orr) (b. 1880), British physiologist and nutritional expert. Director-general World Food and Agricultural Organisation 1945–8. Chancellor Glasgow Univ. 1946. Nobel prizewinner 1949.

Boyle, Robert (1627–91), English scientist who with Robert Hooke laid the foundations of the modern sciences of chemistry and physics. He established the law which states that the volume of a gas varies inversely as the pressure upon it, provided temperature is constant. His chief work is the *Sceptical Chymist* (1661).

Bradley, Omar Nelson (b. 1893), American general. In the second world war he commanded in Tunis, Sicily, and Normandy, and was made chief of staff in 1948. Retired 1953.

Bradman, Sir Donald George (b. 1908), Australian cricketer who captained Australia in test matches against England 1936–48.

Bragg, Sir William Henry (1862–1942), English physicist. He held the chair of physics at Adelaide, Leeds, and London, and was professor of chemistry at the Royal Institution 1923–42. Pres. Royal Society 1935–40.

Bragg, Sir William Lawrence (b. 1890), son of the above. He succeeded Rutherford at the Cavendish laboratory, Cambridge, 1938–53. Dir. Royal Institution 1954–66. Shared with his father the 1915 Nobel prize for their fundamental work on X-rays and crystal structure.

Brahe, Tycho (1546–1601), Danish astronomer. At his island observatory at Uraniborg, provided by his sovereign, he carried out systematic observations which enabled Kepler to work out his planetary laws.

Brahms, Johannes (1833–97), composer. B. in Hamburg (son of a double-bass player), he did not marry, and led a simple life devoted to music; latterly he lived in Vienna. He was a friend of the Schumanns. His work, while classical in form, is romantic in temper. *See* Section E.

Braille, Louis (1809–52), French educationist, who, as teacher of the blind, perfected his system of reading and writing for the blind. As the result of an accident when he was three years old he was himself blind.

Bramah, Joseph (1749–1814), English inventor of the safety-lock and hydraulic press which bear his name. He also invented the water-closet (1778) and a machine for printing the serial numbers on bank-notes.

Brandes, Georg Morris Cohen (1842–1927), Danish literary critic who exerted a vitalising influence on literature and art.

Brandt, Willy (b. 1913), first social democratic chancellor of the Federal Republic of Germany, 1969– .

Brangwyn, Sir Frank (1867–1956), artist of Welsh extraction, b. Bruges; first worked for William Morris making cartoons for textiles; he excelled in murals and in etching.

Breakspear, Nicholas. *See* Adrian IV.

Brecht, Bertold (1898–1959), German dramatist and poet, whose cynical and satirical works are characteristic of the period between the two world wars. He left Germany in 1933 for Russia, went to the U.S.A. in 1941, and returned to East Germany after the war. His plays include *Die Dreigroschenoper* (with music by Kurt Weill). *See* Section I.

Brennan, Louis (1853–1932), inventor, b. Ireland. His inventions include a gyro-directed torpedo and a mono-rail locomotive on the gyroscope principle.

Breton, Andrée (1896–1966), French poet, founder of the surrealist literary movement in France and a close friend of Apollinaire.

Brewster, Sir David (1781–1868), Scottish physicist, noted for his research into the polarisation of light; invented the kaleidoscope. He helped to found the British Association for the Advancement of Science.

Brezhnev, Leonid Ilyich (b. 1906), succeeded Khrushchev as First Secretary of the Soviet Communist Party in 1964; formerly Pres. of the Supreme Soviet of the U.S.S.R.

Bridges, 1st Baron (Edward Bridges) (1892–1969), son of Robert Bridges. He was from 1945 permanent secretary to the Treasury and head of the civil service.

Bridges, Robert (1844–1930), poet laureate 1913–30. His *Testament of Beauty* (1929) has been called "a compendium of the wisdom, learning and experience of an artistic spirit."

Bridgewater, 3rd Duke of (Francis Egerton) (1736–1803), founder of British inland navigation by his canal, to the design of James Brindley (*q.v.*) from Manchester to his coal mines at Worsley, later extended to join the Mersey at Runcorn.

Bridie, James (pseudonym of Osborne Henry Mavor) (1888–1951), Scottish author and dramatist. The first of his many successful plays was *The Anatomist*, produced in 1931.

Other plays include *Tobias and the Angel*, *Jonah and the Whale*, *Mr. Bolfrey*, *Dr. Angelus*.

Brieux, Eugène (1858–1932), French dramatist whose realistic plays deal with social evils, such as venereal disease in *Les Avariés* (Damaged Goods).

Bright, Sir Charles Tilston (1832–88), English telegraph engineer who supervised the laying of the British telegraph network and the Atlantic cables (1856–8).

Bright, John (1811–89), radical Quaker statesman and orator; friend of Cobden, with whom he promoted the movement for free trade.

Brindley, James (1716–72), English canal builder, b. Derbyshire, of poor parents, apprenticed as a millwright. He was employed by the Duke of Bridgewater (*q.v.*) and designed and constructed the Bridgewater canal, carrying it over the R. Irwell by an aqueduct, the first of its kind. He also built the Grand Trunk canal linking the Mersey with the Trent.

Britten, Edward Benjamin (b. 1913), English composer, closely associated with the Aldeburgh festival. O.M. 1965. *See* Section E.

Broca, Paul (1824–80), French pathologist, anthropologist and pioneer in neuro-surgery. He localised the seat of speech in the brain and originated methods for measuring brain and skull ratios.

Broch, Hermann (1886–1951), Austrian novelist, author of the trilogy *The Sleepwalkers*. Lived in U.S.A. after 1938.

Broglie, prominent family of Piedmontese origin; **Victor Maurice** (1647–1727), and **François Marie** (1671–1745) were marshals of France; **Louis Victor, Prince de Broglie** (b. 1892) received the Nobel prize for his work on quantum mechanics, and his brother **Maurice, Duc de Broglie** (1875–1960), also a physicist, is noted for his work on the ionisation of gases, radioactivity, and X-rays.

Brontë, Charlotte (1816–55), forceful novelist, daughter of an Anglican clergyman of Irish descent, incumbent of Haworth, Yorkshire. She published under a pseudonym *Jane Eyre*, which was at once successful, and was followed by *Shirley* and *Villette*. Her sister **Emily** (1818–48) wrote poetry and also *Wuthering Heights*; and **Anne** (1820–49) wrote *Agnes Grey*.

Brooke, Rupert (1887–1915), English poet who died during the first world war, whose works, though few, showed promise and include the poems *Grantchester* and *If I Should Die*.

Brougham and Vaux, 1st Baron (Henry Peter Brougham) (1778–1868), English legal reformer; advocate of Queen Caroline against George IV; helped to found London university.

Brown, Sir Arthur Whitten (1886–1948), together with Sir John Alcock (d. 1919) in 1919 made the first transatlantic flight, crossing from Newfoundland to Ireland in 16 hr. 12 min.

Brown, John (1800–59), American abolitionist. His action in inciting Negro slaves to rebel in 1859 led to the civil war. He was hanged after failing to hold the U.S. arsenal at Harper's Ferry which he had captured. Known as "Old Brown of Osawatomie" and regarded as a martyr.

Browne, Charles Farrer (1834–67), American humourist who wrote under the pseudonym of Artemus Ward.

Browne, Hablot Knight (1815–82), English artist, the "Phiz" of many book illustrations, including Dickens's *Pickwick Papers* and other novels.

Browne, Sir Thomas (1605–82), author of *Religio Medici*, was a London physician and antiquary.

Browning, Elizabeth Barrett (1806–61), English poet. Owing to an injury in childhood, she spent her youth lying on her back, but her meeting with Robert Browning, whom she married, brought a remarkable recovery. In her lifetime her works were more read than those of her husband. They include *Cry of the Children*, *Sonnets from the Portuguese*, and *Aurora Leigh*.

Browning, Robert (1812–89), English poet. Because of his involved style his reputation grew only slowly. In *Strafford* and *The Blot on the 'Scutcheon* he attempted drama also. He married Elizabeth Barrett and lived mainly abroad. His works include *Dramatis Personae* and *The Ring and The Book*.

Bruce, Robert (1274–1329), Scottish national leader against Edward I and Edward II of England. Crowned king in 1306, after years of struggle he defeated Edward II at Bannockburn in 1314.

Bruch, Max (1838–1920), German composer and conductor, best known for his G minor violin concerto.

Bruckner, Anton (1824–96), Austrian composer and organist. *See* Section E.

Brummell, George Bryan (1778–1840), " Beau Brummell," fashion leader and friend of the Prince Regent (George IV).

Brunel, Isambard Kingdom (1806–59), English civil engineer, son of Sir Marc Isambard Brunel (1769–1849), whom he assisted in building the Thames (Rotherhithe) tunnel. He was engineer of the Great Western Railway and built the ocean liners, the *Great Western*, the *Great Britain* (brought back from the Falkland Is. to Bristol in 1970), and the *Great Eastern*. His other works include the Clifton suspension bridge over the R. Avon at Bristol and the Royal Albert bridge over the R. Tamar at Saltash.

Brunelleschi, Filippo (1377–1446), Italian architect, b. Florence; he adapted the ideals of the Roman period. Examples of his work in Florence include the Pitti Palace, the churches of San Lorenzo and San Spirito, and the cathedral dome (the biggest in Europe).

Bruno, Giordano (1548–1600), Italian philosopher. A Dominican friar, he came to favour the astronomical views of Copernicus and was burnt at the stake.

Bruno, St. (*c.* 1032–1101), German monk, founder in 1084 of the Carthusian order at La Grande Chartreuse in the French Alps.

Brutus, Marcus Junius (85–42 B.C.), conspirator against Julius Caesar; later committed suicide.

Buchanan, George (1506–82), Scottish humanist who spent most of his life in France lecturing and writing Latin poems, plays, and treatises. Montaigne, Mary Queen of Scots, and James VI of Scotland were his pupils at various times.

Buchman, Frank Nathan David (1878–1961), American evangelist, founder of the Oxford Group Movement. *See* Moral Re-Armament, Section J.

Buchner, Eduard (1860–1917), German chemist, remembered for his work on the chemistry of fermentation. Nobel prizewinner 1907.

Büchner, Georg (1813–37), German dramatist. Dying at 24, his limited output (principally *Dantons Tod* and the fragment *Wozzeck*) is marked by power and maturity.

Buckle, Henry Thomas (1821–62), author of *The History of Civilisation in England*.

Buddha. *See* Gautama, Siddhartha.

Budge, Sir Ernest Alfred Wallis (1857–1934), archaeologist who conducted excavations in Mesopotamia and Egypt.

Buffon, Georges-Louis Leclerc, Comte de (1707–88), French naturalist, author of the *Histoire naturelle* (44 vols., 1749–1804).

Bulganin, Nikolai Alexandrovich (b. 1895), Soviet prime minister 1955–8; defence minister 1947–9, 1953–5. Retired 1960.

Bull, John (*c.* 1562–1628), English composer; possibly composer of *God save the Queen*.

Bülow, Hans Guido von (1830–94), German pianist and conductor. He married Liszt's daughter Cosima, who later left him to marry Wagner.

Bunsen, Robert Wilhelm (1811–99), German chemist, discoverer of the metals caesium and rubidium, and inventor of the Bunsen burner, battery, and pump. Made important observations in spectrum analysis.

Bunyan, John (1628–88), was originally a travelling tinker and is believed to have served in the Parliamentary army. He joined an Independent church in Bedford in 1655 and became a popular preacher. After the Restoration he was thrown into prison, and there wrote *The Pilgrim's Progress*. Of his 60 works, the best known after *Pilgrim's Progress* are *The Holy War*, *Grace Abounding*, and *Mr. Badman*. *See also* Allegory, Section M, Part V.

Burckhardt, Jacob Christoph (1818–97), Swiss historian, author of *The Civilisation of the Renaissance in Italy*.

Burghley, 1st Baron (William Cecil) (1520–98), English statesman. After holding office under

her two predecessors, he was Queen Elizabeth I's secretary of state, 1558–72, and lord high treasurer, 1572–98.

Burke, Edmund (1729–97), Whig writer and political philosopher. B. in Dublin, he became secretary to Lord Rockingham and entered parliament in 1765. He advocated the emancipation (though not the independence) of the American colonies; and better administration in India; but was against the French revolution.

Burnet, Gilbert (1643–1715), bishop of Salisbury, b. Edinburgh. He wrote a *History of his Own Times*, which deals with many events of which he had personal knowledge.

Burnet, Sir John James (1859–1938), architect, b. Glasgow. The north front of the British Museum (King Edward's galleries) is his most important work in London.

Burney, Fanny (Madame D'Arblay) (1752–1840), originator of the simple novel of home life. Daughter of the organist, Dr. Burney, she published *Evelina* in 1778, and this brought her into court and literary society. She also wrote *Cecilia* and *Camilla*.

Burns, Robert (1759–96), Scottish poet. The son of a cottar, his first poems published in 1786 were at once successful, and he bought a farm. The farm failed, but he had a post as exciseman, and continued to write simply with tenderness and humour. Among his best known poems are *Auld Lang Syne*, *Scots wa hae*, *Comin' through the rye*, and *The Banks of Doon*.

Burton, Sir Richard Francis (1821–90), British explorer and orientalist, who made a pilgrimage to Mecca and Medina in 1853 disguised as a Moslem. He explored Central Africa and translated the *Arabian Nights* (16 vols.).

Burton, Robert (1577–1640), English clergyman and scholar, author of *The Anatomy of Melancholy*.

Busoni, Ferruccio Benvenuto (1866–1920), pianist and composer of three operas (the last *Dr. Faust*, unfinished at his death), much orchestral and chamber music, and works for the piano. B. in Empoli, he lived in Germany. *See* Section E.

Butler, Joseph (1692–1752), English bishop, remembered for his *Analogy of Religion*, published in 1736 in reply to deistic attacks.

Butler, Nicholas Murray (1862–1947), American educationist who shared with the sociologist Jane Addams the 1931 Nobel peace prize.

Butler, Baron (Richard Austen Butler) (b. 1902), Conservative politician who brought in the Education Act of 1944 and helped secure Conservative acceptance of the welfare state. He took a leading part in drafting the *Industrial Charter* of 1947. " Butskellism " was the term applied to Conservative social and economic policies of the early fifties. Master of Trinity College, Cambridge, 1965. Life peer 1965.

Butler, Samuel (1612–80), English verse-satirist, author of the poem *Hudibras* against the Puritans.

Butler, Samuel (1835–1902), English novelist and satirist, author of *Erewhon* and its sequel *Erewhon Revisited*. Other works include *The Fair Haven*, *Life and Habit*, and *Evolution Old and New*, in which he attacked Darwinism. His autobiographical novel *The Way of All Flesh* and his *Notebooks* were published after his death. He exhibited regularly at the Academy and was also a musician.

Butt, Clara (1872–1936), English contralto; made her début in London in 1892. She married Kennerly Rumford in 1900.

Buxton, Sir Thomas Fowell (1786–1845), English social reformer; succeeded Wilberforce as leader of the anti-slavery group in parliament.

Buys Ballot, Christoph Henrich Diedrich (1877–90), Dutch meteorologist who formulated the law which bears his name (an observer with back to wind in northern hemisphere has lower pressure to left; in southern hemisphere to right).

Byrd, Richard Evelyn (1888–1957), American rear-admiral, explorer and aviator. He flew over the north pole, 1926; and in 1929 made the first flight over the south pole. He made other polar expeditions in 1925, 1933–5, 1939 and 1946.

Byrd, William (1543–1623), English composer of church music, sacred choral music, string music, vocal and instrumental music; and a founder of the school of English madrigalists. He was organist of Lincoln cathedral at 20 and later of Queen Elizabeth's chapel royal. *See* Section E.

Byron, 6th Baron (George Gordon Byron) (1788–1824), English romantic poet who influenced European literature and thought. At 20 he published *Hours of Idleness*, which was violently attacked by the *Edinburgh Review*. This provoked his retaliatory *English Bards and Scotch Reviewers*, which caused a sensation. His *Childe Harold's Pilgrimage* appeared in 1812. His married life was unhappy. He went to help the Greeks in their struggle for independence and died at Missolonghi. *See also* Romantic Movement, Section J.

C

Cable, George Washington (1844–1925), American author and social critic, b. New Orleans, whose writings reflect the colour problems of his day: *Ole Creol Days, The Silent South*.

Cabot, John (1425–*c.* 1500), Genoese explorer who settled in Bristol and sailed westwards under letters-patent from Henry VII of England in 1497. Discovered Newfoundland and Nova Scotia, believing them to be part of Asia, and may have reached the mainland of America before Columbus did. His son:

Cabot, Sebastian (1474–1557), was born in Venice, and in 1509 in search of a north-west passage to Asia sailed as far as Hudson Bay. Entered Spanish service in 1512, and spent several years exploring the Plate and Parana rivers. Re-entered English service in 1548 and organised expedition to seek a north-east passage to India, which resulted in trade with Russia. English claim to North America is founded on the voyages of the Cabots.

Cabral, Pedro Alvarez (*c.* 1467–*c.* 1520), Portuguese navigator, friend of Vasco da Gama, discovered Brazil, which he named "Terra da Santa Cruz."

Cadbury, George (1839–1922), liberal Quaker philanthropist of Cadbury Bros., mainly responsible for the pioneer garden city of Bournville.

Cadogan, Sir Alexander (1884–1968), English diplomat. He helped to draft the charter of the United Nations organisation and became Gt. Britain's representative on the Security Council.

Caedmon, the first English Christian poet, lived in the 7th cent. and, according to Bede, was first a cowherd and later a monk at Whitby. His poetry was based on the scriptures.

Caesar, Caius Julius (*c.* 101–44 B.C.), Roman general and writer. Under the declining republic, he was assigned in 61 the province of Gaul; in the course of pacifying it he invaded Britain (55 B.C.). Opposition in Rome to his career, mainly from Pompey, provoked him in 49 to the defiance of crossing the Rubicon with his army. He defeated Pompey, whom he pursued to Egypt, where he established Cleopatra as queen. At Rome he became dictator, and his reforms include the Julian calendar. He was murdered in 44. His career paved the way for Rome becoming an empire under his nephew Octavian. His writings are masterly accounts of his wars.

Calderón de la Barca, Pedro (1600–81), Spanish dramatist, representative of contemporary Spanish thought, who also wrote court spectacles for Philip IV. Among his best-known works are *La Vida es Sueño* and *El divino Orfeo*.

Callas, Maria Meneghini (b. 1923), Greek opera singer; made her professional debut in 1947 at Verona; especially successful in *Norma*.

Calvin, John (1509–64), French Protestant reformer and theologian. B. in Picardy, he broke with the Roman Catholic church about 1533, and subsequently settled in Geneva, where from 1541 he established a theocratic regime of strict morality. His theology was published in his *Institutes*; while, like Luther, he accepted justification by faith without works, he also believed in predestination. His doctrines spread on the continent, in Scotland and to some extent in England. *See* Calvinism, Section J.

Camden, William (1551–1623), English antiquary and historian. His *Britannia* appeared in 1586.

Cameron, Sir David Young (1865–1945), Scottish etcher and landscape painter.

Cameron, Richard (1648–80), Scottish preacher who revolted in defence of the Solemn League and Covenant and was killed at Airds Moss (Ayrshire).

Cameron, Verney Lovett (1844–94), English explorer, the first to cross the African continent from east to west. He surveyed Lake Tanganyika and in 1872 went out to find Livingstone.

Camillus, Marcus Furius (4th cent. B.C.), Roman general. When the Gauls attacked in 387 B.C., he was made dictator and defeated them.

Cammaerts, Emile (1878–1953), Belgian poet who settled in England (1908) to become the first professor of Belgian studies in the university of London.

Camões, Luis Vaz de (1524–80), Portuguese poet, author of *Os Lusiadas*, an epic of Portuguese history and discovery.

Campbell, Colin, 1st Baron Clyde (1792–1863), Scottish general who was commander-in-chief in India during the Mutiny.

Campbell, Sir Malcolm (1885–1948), racing driver who held the land-speed record of 301 mile/h (1935) and water-speed record of 141·7 mile/h (1939). His son, Donald held the water-speed record of 276·33 mile/h (1964); killed in 1967 at Coniston.

Campbell, Mrs. Patrick (Beatrice Stella Tanner) (1865–1940), English actress of beauty and wit, friend of G. B. Shaw.

Campbell, Thomas (1777–1844), Scottish poet, who at 22 published *The Pleasures of Hope*. His war poems include *Ye Mariners of England* and *The Battle of the Baltic*. He was one of the founders of University College, London.

Campbell-Bannerman, Sir Henry (1836–1908), Liberal statesman, prime minister 1905–8. His ministry included Asquith, Lloyd George, and Churchill.

Camus, Albert (1913–60), French writer, native of Algiers. He was active in the resistance movement; and later set himself the task of elucidating values. His best-known novels are *L'Étranger, La Peste, L'Homme revolté*. In 1957 he received the Nobel prize for his "penetrating seriousness" which has "thrown light on the problems of human conscience." Killed in car crash. *See also* Section I.

Canaletto (Antonio Canal) (1697–1768), Italian artist. B. at Venice, he painted views of his city. From 1746 to 1756 he worked mainly in London. Some of his work is in the National Gallery, and there is a collection at Windsor.

Canning, George (1770–1827), English statesman. He was an advocate of Catholic emancipation, and was the first to recognise the free states of South America.

Cannizzaro, Stanislao (1826–1910), Italian chemist who carried forward the work of Avogadro in distinguishing between molecular and atomic weights.

Canova, Antonio (1757–1822), Italian sculptor. B. at Venice, he infused grace into the classical style.

Canton, John (1718–72), English physicist and schoolmaster, the first to verify in England Franklin's experiments on the identity of lightning with electricity. He was the first to demonstrate that water is compressible and produced a new phosphorescent body (Canton's phosphorus) by calcining oyster shells with sulphur.

Canute (*c.* 994–1035), king of the English, Danes and Norwegians. The son of a Danish king, after some years of fighting he established himself as king of England and ruled with wisdom and firmness.

Capablanca, José Raoul (1888–1942), Cuban chess player, world champion from 1921 to 1927 when he was beaten by Alekhine.

Caractacus or Caradoc, a king in west Britain, who resisted the Romans in the first century. After capture he was freed by the emperor Claudius.

Carey, William (1761–1834), first Baptist missionary to India. An Oriental scholar, he published 24 translations of the scriptures.

Carissimi, Giacomo (1604–74), Italian composer, b. near Rome. He introduced more instrumental variety into the cantata and oratorio, and brought the recitative to perfection. His *Jephtha* is still in print, and there are collections of his works at Paris and Oxford. *See* **Section E.**

Carlyle, Thomas (1795–1881), Scottish author. Of peasant stock, he went to Edinburgh university, but later lived mainly in England where he lectured. He married Jane Welsh. His individual views pervade his historical writing. His best known works include *Sartor Resartus*, *Heroes and Hero Worship*, *Cromwell's Letters and Speeches*, and the *French Revolution*.

Carnegie, Andrew (1835–1919), philanthropist b. Dunfermline; emigrated to America in 1848; and after early struggles he established the Carnegie iron works, from which he retired in 1901 with a fortune. He made munificent gifts to Free Libraries and other educational work.

Carnot, Lazare Nicolas Marguerite (1753–1823), French military engineer, prominent in the French revolutionary wars, 1792–1802. His son, **Sadi Carnot** (1796–1832), was a physicist and engineer who worked on the motive power of heat, establishing the principle that heat and work are reversible conditions. *See* **F17.**

Caroline, Queen (1768–1821), was married to George IV when he was Prince of Wales. They soon separated, but when he became king in 1820, she tried to assert her position. The question came before parliament. In spite of some public sympathy she was unsuccessful.

Carrel, Alexis (1873–1944), American surgeon who won the Nobel prize in 1912 for his success in suturing blood vessels in transfusion and in transplantation of organs. A Frenchman by birth, he returned to France in 1939.

Carroll, Lewis. *See* **Dodgson, Charles Lutwidge.**

Carson, Baron (Edward Henry Carson) (1854–1935), Irish barrister, solicitor-general for Ireland 1892; attorney general 1915; first lord of the admiralty 1916–17; member of the war cabinet 1917–18. He led a semi-militant organisation against Home Rule.

Carter, Howard (1873–1939), Egyptologist who was associated with the 5th Earl of Carnarvon in discovering in 1922 the tomb of Tutankhamun.

Carter, Jacques (1494–1557), French navigator, b. St. Malo, who explored Canada, especially the gulf and river of St. Lawrence.

Cartwright, Edmund (1743–1823), English inventor of the power-loom, and also of a wool-combing machine, important steps in the weaving side of the textile revolution.

Cartwright, John (1740–1824), brother of the above; reformer and agitator against slavery.

Caruso, Enrico (1873–1921), Italian tenor, b. Naples.

Carver, George Washington (1864–1943), American Negro agricultural chemist of world repute.

Casabianca, Louis de (c. 1752–98), captain of the French flagship *L'Orient* at the Battle of the Nile. He and his ten-year-old son died together in the burning ship.

Casals, Pablo (b. 1876), Spanish cellist and conductor. He exiled himself from Spain in 1938 as a protest against dictatorship.

Casanova de Seingalt, Giacomo (1725–98), Italian adventurer, author of licentious memoirs.

Cassatt, Mary (1845–1926), American artist who settled in France and was a friend of Degas. She painted women and children, and aroused American interest in Impressionism.

Cassini, French family of Italian origin, distinguished for work in astronomy and geography. Through four generations (1671–1793) they were heads of the Paris Observatory.

Cassius, Caius Longinus, Roman general who opposed the dictatorship of Julius Caesar, and took part in his murder. He died in 42 B.C. after being defeated by Mark Antony.

Castlereagh, Viscount (Robert Stewart Castlereagh) (1769–1822), British minister of war and foreign secretary, who took a leading part in the Napoleonic wars. He was however unpopular and committed suicide.

Castro, Fidel (b. 1927), Cuban revolutionary. After two unsuccessful attempts he succeeded in 1959 in overthrowing a police-state. He has initiated reforms in agriculture, industry, and education, and repulsed American economic

dominance. His acceptance of Russian support led to the " missiles crisis " of 1962.

Catchpool, E. St. John (b. 1890), first secretary of the English Youth Hostels Association, 1930–50; president of the International Federation, 1938–50.

Catherine, St. (4th cent.). Traditionally a virgin martyr in Alexandria, though not mentioned before the 10th cent. Legend represents her as tied to a wheel; hence " St. Catherine's wheel."

Catherine de' Medici (1519–89), Italian-born wife of Henry II and mother of three French kings (she was regent for Charles IX). Her antagonism to the Protestants may have led to the massacre of St. Bartholomew's day. She was able, and appreciated art and literature, but was unscrupulous and cruel.

Catherine of Aragon (1485–1536), first wife of Henry VIII of England, was daughter of Ferdinand and Isabella of Spain, and mother of Mary Tudor. When Henry VIII attempted to obtain papal dissolution of their marriage, and subsequently obtained an English declaration of its nullity (thus precipitating a movement towards the Reformation) she bore herself with dignity during her retirement.

Catherine the Great (1729–96), Empress Catherine II of Russia. Daughter of a German prince, she married in 1745 the future Peter III, a weakling, later deposed and murdered. Intelligent, cultivated, autocratic, she proved a capable ruler for a time but was hampered and opposed by the landed interests and, despite plans for reform, her reign was marked by imperialist expansion and extension of serfdom.

Cato, Marcus Porcius (234–149 B.C.), Roman statesman and writer. His tenure of office as censor was characterised by austerity and conservatism. He advocated opposition to Carthage. His writings deal with agriculture and history.

Catullus, Caius Valerius (c. 84–54 B.C.), Roman poet who wrote lyrics to Lesbia. His poems show sincere feeling and also Greek influence.

Cavell, Edith Louisa (1865–1915), English nurse who cared for friend and foe in Brussels in 1914–15, but was executed by the Germans for helping Allied fugitives to escape.

Cavendish, Henry (1731–1810), English scientist, a contemporary of Black, Priestley, Scheele, and Lavoisier, remembered for his investigations into the nature of gases. He discovered hydrogen and the chemical composition of water. He was the first to determine the weights of equal volumes of gases.

Cavour, Camillo Benso di (1810–61), Italian statesman, who, as premier of Piedmont, helped to bring about the unification of Italy.

Caxton, William (1422–91), first English printer, probably learnt printing at Cologne, and later set up a printing press at Westminster.

Cecil of Chelwood, 1st Viscount (Robert Cecil) (1864–1958), English politician who helped draft the Charter of the League of Nations. Nobel prize for peace 1937.

Cecilia, St. (2nd or 3rd cent.), patron saint of music. Tradition in the 5th cent. says that she converted her husband, and after her martyrdom was buried in a catacomb. She is often represented playing the organ.

Cellini, Benvenuto (1500–71), Italian sculptor and goldsmith. B. at Florence, he worked for some years in Rome. His bronze statue *Perseus with the head of Medusa* is at Florence. His life was adventurous and he wrote an *Autobiography* which is revealing of himself and his time.

Celsius, Anders (1701–44), Swedish physicist and astronomer who invented the centigrade thermometer.

Ceresole, Pierre (1879–1945), Swiss founder of International Voluntary Service. He was by profession a teacher of engineering, and his pacifism led him to become a Quaker.

Cervantes, Saavedra Miguel de (1547–1616), Spanish novelist and dramatist, b. at Alcalà de Haneres. He was injured at the battle of Lepanto, and thereafter struggled to earn a livelihood from literature. His *Don Quixote* describes the adventures of a poor gentleman, confused in mind, who on his horse Rosinante with his squire Sancho Panza seeks adventures; it satirised chivalry, but is also a permanent criticism of life. Of his plays only two survive.

Cézanne, Paul (1839–1906), French painter, b. in Aix-en-Provence, the son of a wealthy banker and tradesman. He developed a highly original style, using colour and tone in such a way as to increase the impression of depth. He said that he wanted "to make of Impressionism something solid and durable, like the art of the Museums." Like Giotto, six hundred years before, he more than any other artist determined the course European painting was to take. *La Vielle au Chapelet* and *Les Grandes Baigneuses* are in the National Gallery. He was a friend of Zola.

Chadwick, Sir James (b. 1891), English physicist, one of Rutherford's collaborators in the field of atomic research. Discovered the neutron in 1932, one of the main steps in the discovery of the fission process which led to the production of the atom bomb.

Chagall, Marc (b. 1889), Russian painter, b. at Vitebsk of Jewish parents, the forerunner of surrealism. He lives in Paris.

Chaliapin, Fedor Ivanovich (1873–1938), Russian opera singer, a bass with dramatic gifts.

Chamberlain, Joseph (1836–1914), English statesman. He began with municipal work in Birmingham. At first a Liberal under Gladstone, he became Conservative. He opposed Home Rule for Ireland, and was the first advocate of a partial return to protection.

Chamberlain, Neville (1869–1940), son of Joseph. He was prime minister 1937–40, when he appeased Hitler by the Munich agreement of 1938.

Chambers, Sir William (1726–96) British architect, b. Stockholm. He rebuilt Somerset House and designed the pagoda in Kew Gardens.

Chaminade, Cécile (1857–1944), French pianist and composer.

Champlain, Samuel de (1567–1635), French navigator who founded Quebec (1608), and discovered the lake known by his name.

Chantrey, Sir Francis Legatt (1781–1841), English sculptor who contributed statues to Westminster Abbey and St. Paul's. He left a fortune to the Royal Academy for the purchase of works of British art. The collection is in the Tate Gallery.

Chaplin, Charles Spencer (b. 1889), first international screen star, with more than 40 years' achievement. B. in London, his mother was a music-hall singer and he made his début at five. In 1910 he went to the United States; and with the Keystone Company in Los Angeles (1914–15) he made films in which his early hardships are reflected in humour and sadness. His films include *Shoulder Arms*, *The Kid*, *The Gold Rush*, *City Lights*, *The Great Dictator*, *Modern Times*, and *Limelight*. In 1953 he went to live in Switzerland. *Autobiography* (1964).

Chapman, George (1559–1634), Elizabethan poet, dramatist, and translator of the *Iliad* and *Odyssey*. His best-known play is *Bussy d'Ambois*.

Chapman, Sydney (1888–1970), English mathematician and geophysicist, noted for his work on the kinetic theory of gases, geomagnetism, and solar and ionospheric physics. He was president of the special committee of the I.G.Y., 1957–8. An upper layer of the atmosphere and a crater on the far side of the moon are named after him.

Charcot, Jean Baptiste (1867–1936), French explorer, who in 1903–5 and 1908–10 commanded expeditions to the south polar regions. Charcot island in the Antarctic is named after him.

Chardin, Jean Baptiste Siméon (1699–1779), French painter of still life and interior domestic scenes.

Chares (c. 300 B.C.), Greek worker in bronze from Rhodes, sculptor of the Colossus of Rhodes, one of the seven wonders of the world, which was destroyed in the earthquake of 225 B.C.

Charlemagne (742–814), Charles the Great. From being King of the Franks, he came to govern an empire comprising Gaul, Italy, and large parts of Spain and Germany, and was crowned Holy Roman Emperor.

Charles, Jacques Alexandre César (1746–1823), French physicist, the first to use hydrogen gas in balloons and who anticipated Guy-Lussac's law on the expansion of gases.

Charles Edward (Stuart) (1720–88), the Young Pretender (i.e., claimant of the English throne),

grandson of James II, led an unsuccessful rising in 1745 and died in exile.

Charles I (1600–49), King of England, Scotland, and Ireland, succeeded his father James I in 1625. Personally sincere, and having an appreciation of art, he was yet ill-fitted to cope with the political problems of his time. His marriage with the French princess Henrietta Maria was unpopular. He supported Archbishop Laud's strict Anglicanism, and he also attempted to rule without parliament. Defeated in the Civil War which broke out in 1642, he spun out negotiations for a settlement till he was beheaded in 1649.

Charles II (1630–85), King of England, Scotland, and Ireland, son of Charles I; after the Civil War escaped to France, and returned in 1660 when the monarchy was restored. His religious sympathies were Roman Catholic and his personal life was amorous; but in political matters he was shrewd and realistic, and contrived not to " go on his travels " again. He promoted the development of the navy, but had to accept the laws enforcing religious conformity imposed by parliament.

Charles V (1500–58), Hapsburg ruler, succeeded his grandfather, Maximilian I, as emperor of the Holy Roman Empire, and as heir to Ferdinand and Isabella succeeded to the Spanish crown. His rivalry with Francis I of France led to prolonged war. He crushed a revolt of peasants in 1525. He presided in 1521 at the Diet before which Luther appeared, after which religious struggle continued in Germany till the Augsburg settlement of 1555. In this year he retired to a monastery in Spain.

Charles XII of Sweden (1682–1718), a brave but rash and ambitious general. He repelled Russian attacks at Narva in 1700, but subsequently pursuing military adventure he was defeated by Peter the Great at Poltava in 1709; and on invading Norway was killed at a siege.

Chateaubriand, François René, Vicomte de (1768–1848), French writer and diplomat. In a varied career he was at first an emigré, and later served as diplomat under both Napoleon and Louis XVIII. He was a friend of Mme. Recamier. His writings include *Mémoires d'outre-tombe*.

Chatham, 1st Earl of (William Pitt) (1708–78), English statesman and orator. His energetic conduct of the Seven Years War was an important contribution to English victory and to acquisitions in Canada and India at the peace (1763), though by then he was out of office. In the dispute with the American colonies he upheld their right to resist imposed taxation, and collapsed while making a last speech on this dispute.

Chatterton, Thomas (1752–70), English poet who tried to pass off his writings as newly discovered ancient manuscripts and killed himself at the age of 17.

Chaucer, Geoffrey (1340?–1400), English poet. His main work, *The Canterbury Tales*, gives a vivid picture of contemporary life.

Chekov, Anton (1860–1904), Russian dramatist and short-story writer, whose plays include *The Cherry Orchard*, *Uncle Vanya*, and *The Three Sisters*. His stories include *The Steppe*, *The Sleepyhead*, *The Post*, *The Student*, and *The Bishop*. He was of humble origin and while a student at Moscow supported his family by writing humorous sketches and tales.

Cherubini, Luigi (1760–1842), Italian-born musician, for many years director of the Paris Conservatoire and composer of operas and church music.

Chesterfield, 4th Earl of (Philip Dormer Stanhope) (1694–1773), English statesman, whose *Letters* to his natural son, Philip Stanhope, are full of grace, wit, and worldly wisdom.

Chesterton, Gilbert Keith (1874–1936), English essayist, novelist and poet, who also wrote studies of Charles Dickens and Robert Browning. His best-known works include *The Napoleon of Notting Hill* and *The Ballad of the White Horse*.

Chevalier, Albert (1861–1923), English music-hall comedian known for his coster sketches.

Chevalier, Maurice (b. 1889), French stage and film actor.

Chiang Kai-shek (b. 1887), Chinese general. He at first fought for Sun Yat-sen. After the latter's death (1925), as commander of the

Kuomintang army, he attempted to unite China; but (involved as he was with business interests) he was more anxious to defeat the Communists than to repel the Japanese adventure in Manchuria in 1931. He was unable to establish peace and a stable, progressive régime; and in 1949 retired to Formosa after military defeat by the Communists. His wife is Mayling Soong.

Chichester, Sir Francis (b. 1902), English seaman, who sailed his *Gipsy Moth IV* into Sydney harbour in 1966 after a 107-day voyage from Plymouth, and back again round the Horn.

Chippendale, Thomas (1718–79), designer of furniture, b. Otley, Yorks. His designs are shown in *The Gentleman and Cabinet Maker's Director*, 1754.

Chirico, Giorgio de (b. 1888), painter associated with the surrealist school, born in Greece of Italian parents.

Chomsky, Noam (b. 1908), American theoretical linguist, professor of Linguistics, Massachusetts Institute of Technology; inventor of transformational grammar.

Chopin, Frédéric François (1810–49), Polish pianist and composer, son of a French father and Polish mother. He has been called "the poet of the piano" because of the originality and delicacy of his playing. He enjoyed Paris intellectual and musical society, was a friend of George Sand, and played in numerous concerts all over Europe. He died of consumption. *See* Section E.

Chou-En-lai (b. 1898), Chinese revolutionary statesman. He organised revolt in Shanghai in 1927 and later joined forces with Mao Tse-tung, becoming prime minister of the new China in 1949. At the Geneva conference of 1954 he helped to secure peace in Indo-China.

Chrysostom, St. John (c. 347–407), preacher. Chrysostom means golden-mouthed. First at Antioch, and later as patriarch of Constantinople, he was an eloquent teacher; but by outspokenness he lost the Empress Eudoxia's favour and died from ill-treatment.

Churchill, Lord Randolph Henry Spencer (1849–95), Conservative politician, who held brief office only. He was father of Winston Churchill.

Churchill, Sir Winston Leonard Spencer (1874–1965), British statesman and author, son of the last-named. He entered parliament in 1900. He served as a junior officer with the British forces abroad; and during the Boer War he acted as war correspondent. He held the following ministerial posts; Under-Secretary for the Colonies 1905–8; President of the Board of Trade 1908–10; Home Secretary 1910–11; First Lord of the Admiralty 1911–15, 1939–40; Chancellor of the Duchy of Lancaster 1915; Minister of Munitions 1917; Minister of War 1918–21; Minister of Air 1919–21; Secretary of State for the Colonies 1921–2; Chancellor of the Exchequer 1924–9; Prime Minister and Minister of Defence 1940–5; Prime Minister 1951–5. He was rector or chancellor of three universities. Cast in the heroic mould, he lived a full life. His main achievement was as leader of the British people in the second world war. His writings include a biography of his ancestor, Marlborough, and histories of the first and second world wars. He exhibited at the Royal Academy. Hon. American citizenship conferred 1963.

Chulalongkorn, Phra Paramindr Maha (1853–1910), Siamese reforming monarch.

Cibber, Colley (1671–1757), a London actor and dramatist. His best comedies are *The Careless Husband* and *Love's Last Shift*. He wrote an autobiography.

Cicero, Marcus Tullius (106–43 B.C.), Roman orator and philosopher, many of whose letters and speeches survive. He held political office but was killed by the troops of the triumvirate.

Cid (El Campeador) (c. 1035–99), name given to the Spanish knight Rodrigo Diaz, a soldier of fortune who fought against Moors and Christians alike. Myth made him a national hero of knightly and Christian virtue.

Cierva, Juan de la (1895–1936), Spanish engineer who invented the autogiro.

Cimabue, Giovanni (Cenni di Pepo) (1240–1302), early Florentine painter. His only certain work is the St. John in Pisa cathedral.

Cimarosa, Domenico (1749–1801), Italian composer. His best-known opera is *Il Matrimonio Segreto*. He held revolutionary views.

Cimon (c. 512–449 B.C.), Athenian statesman and general, son of Miltiades. He defeated the Persian fleet at the mouth of the Eurymedon in 468. He worked for cooperation with other states, including Sparta.

Cipriani, Giambattista (1727–85), Italian painter of historical subjects who worked in London; a founder member of the Royal Academy.

Clair, René (b. 1898), French film producer, whose early films, full of wit and satire, include *Sous les Toits de Paris* and *À Nous la Liberté*.

Clare, John (1793–1864), Northamptonshire labourer who became a poet. *Poems Descriptive of Rural Life and Scenery*, and *The Village Minstrel* were among his publications. He died in the county lunatic asylum.

Clarendon, 1st Earl of (Edward Hyde) (1609–74), English statesman and historian. He was for some years chancellor to Charles II, and his daughter married the future James II, but he fell and died in exile. He wrote a *History of the Rebellion*.

Clark, Baron (Kenneth McKenzie Clark) (b. 1903), English art historian. He was director of the National Gallery 1934–45, Slade professor of fine arts at Oxford 1946–50, and chairman of the Arts Council 1953–60. Life peer 1969.

Clarkson, Thomas (1760–1846) devoted his life to the abolition of slavery and shares with Wilberforce credit for the passing of the Act of 1807 abolishing the British slave trade.

Claude Lorrain (Gellée) (1600–82), French landscape painter. B. near Nancy, he settled in Rome. A close student of nature, he excelled in depicting sunrise or sunset, and founded a "picturesque" tradition.

Claudius (10 B.C.–A.D. 54), Roman emperor. After the murder of Caligula, he was proclaimed emperor almost accidentally by the Praetorian Guard. He was a sensible administrator. In his time the empire was extended to include Britain, Thrace, and Mauretania. He was probably poisoned by his wife Agrippina.

Clausewitz, Karl von (1780–1831), German military expert whose *Vom Kriege*, expounding his theories on war, dominated Prussia in the 19th cent.

Clemenceau, Georges (1841–1929), French statesman of radical views; twice premier, 1906–9, 1917–20. He was a defender of Dreyfus. In old age he presided at the peace conference of 1919, where he was hostile to Germany ("the Tiger").

Clemens, Samuel Langhorne. *See* **Twain, Mark.**

Cleopatra (69–30 B.C.), daughter of Ptolemy XI, the sixth queen of Egypt by that name, a brilliant, ambitious woman. In 51 she became joint sovereign with her younger brother Ptolemy XII. She was banished to Syria, but, obtaining the help of Caesar, regained the kingdom. She and Caesar became lovers, and in 47 she bore him a son Caesarion (later Ptolemy XIV). After Caesar's murder she returned to Egypt. She met the triumvir Mark Antony and bore him twins; he deserted his wife and broke with his brother-in-law Octavian (later Augustus). Antony and Cleopatra were, however defeated in 31 B.C.; Antony fell upon his sword, and Cleopatra killed herself with an asp bite. Her life inspired Shakespeare's *Antony and Cleopatra* and Shaw's *Caesar and Cleopatra*.

Clive, 1st Baron (Robert Clive) (1725–74), English general who helped to lay the foundations of English power in India. B. near Market Drayton, he entered the service of the East India Company. He contemplated suicide, but Anglo-French rivalry, culminating in the Seven Years War, gave scope for his military powers in the siege of Arcot and the battle of Plassey. As a governor he showed administrative capacity. In his later life he was poor and unpopular.

Clovis (c. 465–511), Merovingian king of the Franks and a convert to Christianity. He defeated the Burgundians and West Goths, and fixed his court at Paris.

Clyde, Lord. *See* **Campbell, Colin.**

Cobbett, William (1763–1835), English controversialist. He is chiefly known for his *Rural Rides*, but also published a weekly *Political Register* from 1802.

Cobden, Richard (1804–65), English advocate of free trade. The son of a Sussex farmer, he led agitation against the laws restricting import of corn, and they were repealed in 1846. He was impoverished by his public work and was helped by subscription.

Cochrane, Thomas, 10th Earl of Dundonald (1775–1860), British seaman, who crippled a French fleet in Biscay (1809), aided the liberation of Chile and Peru from Spanish rule (1819–22), of Brazil from Portuguese rule (1823–5), and assisted the Greeks in their struggle to throw off the Turkish yoke (1827).

Cockcroft, Sir John Douglas (1897–1967), Cambridge nuclear physicist who shared with E.T.S. Walton the 1951 Nobel prize. They had worked together at Cambridge in the historic " atom-splitting " experiments beginning with the transmutation of lithium into boron. He was directly involved in Britain's first nuclear power programmes.

Cockerell, Christopher (b. 1910), English inventor of the hovercraft, which works on the aircushioning principle. *See* **L57.**

Cocteau, Jean (1891–1963), French writer and artist in widely varied forms of art.

Cody, Samuel Franklin (1861–1913), American aviator, the first man to fly in Britain (1,390 ft. on 16 Oct. 1908). He became a British subject in 1909. Killed while flying.

Cody, William Frederick (1846–1917), American showman, known as " Buffalo Bill," whose Wild West Show toured America and Europe.

Cohn, Ferdinand Julius (1828–98) German botanist, founder of the science of bacteriology.

Coke, Sir Edward (1552–1634), English legal author, judge, and rival of Francis Bacon. His legal works are his *Reports* and *Institutes.*

Colbert, Jean Baptiste (1619–83), French statesman under Louis XIV, who fostered new industries, encouraged commerce, reformed the finances and established the navy on a sound basis. A patron of literature, science, and art.

Cole, George Douglas Howard (1889–1959), English economist and political journalist, professor of social and political theory at Oxford, 1944–57. Among his writings are *The Intelligent Man's Guide through World Chaos,* and *A History of Socialist Thought* (5 vols.).

Coleridge, Samuel Taylor (1772–1834), English poet, critic, and friend of Wordsworth, with whom he published *Lyrical Ballads.* His poems include *The Ancient Mariner, Christabel,* and *Kubla Khan.* His literary criticism is still valuable.

Coleridge-Taylor, Samuel (1875–1912), English composer, the son of a West African doctor practising in London and an Englishwoman. He is best known for his Hiawatha trilogy.

Colet, John (c. 1467–1519), English humanist and divine, founded St. Paul's School (1512). As scholar and friend of Erasmus he helped to bring the new learning to England.

Colette (Sidonie Gabrielle Claudine Colette) (1873–1954), French author of the *Claudine* stories, *Chéri* and *La Fin de Chéri.*

Collier, John (1850–1934), English painter noted for his " problem " pictures.

Collingwood, 1st Baron (Cuthbert Collingwood) (1750–1810), British admiral whose ship, the *Royal Sovereign,* led the fleet to battle at Trafalgar, and who on Nelson's death assumed command.

Collingwood, Robin George (1889–1943), English philosopher, historian, and archaeologist, associated with Oxford from 1908 to 1941. His philosophical thought is best studied in *Speculum Mentis, Essay on Philosophical Method, Idea of Nature,* and *Idea of History.*

Collins, Michael (1890–1922), Irish politician and Sinn Fein leader. He successfully organised guerrilla warfare, and mainly negotiated the treaty with Britain in 1921, but was killed in a Republican ambush on his return.

Collins, William (1788–1847), English landscape and figure painter.

Collins, William Wilkie (1824–89), son of the above; practically the first English novelist to deal with the detection of crime. *The Woman in White* appeared in 1860.

Colt, Samuel (1814–62), of Hartford, Connecticut,

invented the revolver in 1835. It was used in the war with Mexico.

Columba, St. (521–97), founder of the monastery of Iona, b. Ireland. From his island shrine he made missionary journeys to the Highlands of Scotland.

Columbanus, St. (c. 540–615), Irish abbot who founded a number of monasteries in continental Europe. *See* Monasticism, Section J.

Columbus, Christopher (c. 1446–1506), Italian navigator, who, prevailing upon Ferdinand and Isabella of Spain to bear the expense of an expedition, in 1492 discovered the Bahamas, Cuba, and other West Indian islands. In 1498 he landed on the lowlands of S. America.

Comenius, John Amos (1592–1670), Czech educationist and pastor, advocate of the " direct " method of teaching languages, of the use of pictures in education, and of equality of educational opportunity for girls.

Compton, Arthur Holly (1892–1962), American physicist whose work on X-rays established what is known as the Compton effect (1923). While professor of physics at the university of Chicago (1923–45) he helped to develop the atomic bomb. Nobel prizewinner 1927.

Compton, Karl Taylor (1887–1954), scientist-administrator, brother of the above. Pres. Massachusetts Institute of Technology 1930–48.

Compton-Burnett, Ivy (1884–1969), English novelist whose books deal with family relationships and include *Pastors and Masters, Men and Wives, A House and Its Head, Manservant and Maidservant. See* Section M, Part I.

Comte, August (1798–1857), French philosopher, founder of positivism. *See* Positivism, Section J.

Condé, Louis, Prince de (1621–86), French general who defeated Spain at Rocroi in 1643.

Confucius or **K'ung Fu-tse** (c. 551–478 B.C.), Chinese philosopher, founder of the system of cosmology, politics, and ethics known as Confucianism. He was not concerned with the supernatural, but appealed to reason and taught love and respect of one's fellows, superiority to ambition, charity, forgiveness, and repentance. *See* Confucianism, Section J.

Congreve, William (1670–1729), Restoration dramatist, whose witty plays include *The Way of the World* and *Love for Love.*

Conrad, Joseph (1857–1924), English novelist of Polish birth, whose parents were exiled to France for political reasons. He became master mariner in the British merchant service, and began to write novels after he left the sea in 1884. His novels include *Almayer's Folly, Lord Jim, Nostromo. See* Section M, Part I.

Conscience, Hendrik Henri (1812–83), Flemish novelist who wrote *The Lion of Flanders.*

Constable, John (1776–1837), English landscape painter, b. East Bergholt, Suffolk. Unlike his contemporary Turner, who journeyed over the continent with his sketchbook, he found his scenes within a few miles of his home. His work was more popular in France than in England at the time and affected the Barbizon school and Delacroix. Examples of his work are in the National Gallery (including *The Hay Wain, Flatford Mill,* and *The Cornfield),* the Victoria and Albert, and the Tate (*The Valley Farm).*

Constant, Jean Joseph Benjamin (1845–1902), French painter of portraits and Oriental subjects.

Constantine (274–338), called " the Great ", the first Christian Roman emperor. He was proclaimed at York by the army in 306. He stabilised the empire after a period of decline, and founded a new capital at Constantinople. A Christian council was held under his auspices at Nicaea in 325, and he was baptised on his death-bed.

Constantine I (1868–1923), King of Greece 1913–17, and 1920. He married Princess Sophia of Prussia, sister of the Kaiser.

Cook, James (1728–79), English navigator, son of an agricultural labourer. He entered the Royal Navy and gained a high reputation for his scientific skill. He made voyages of discovery to New Zealand and Australia in the ships under his command, *Endeavour, Resolution,* and *Adventure.* He anchored at Botany Bay in 1770 on his first voyage and gave it that name because of the interesting plants found on its shores. He also surveyed the Newfoundland coast. In an attempt to find the north-west passage he was murdered at Hawaii.

Cooper, Sir Astley Paston (1768–1841), English surgeon and author of medical textbooks.

Cooper, James Fenimore (1789–1851), American novelist, who produced stirring stories of adventure, among them *The Spy*, *The Last of the Mohicans*, *The Pathfinder*, and *The Deer Slayer*.

Cooper, Samuel (1609–72), English miniaturist, represented with his brother Alexander (d. 1660) in the Victoria and Albert Museum. Among his miniatures is a portrait of Cromwell.

Copernicus, Nicolas (1473–1543), founder of modern astronomy, b. at Torun in Poland. He studied at Cracow and at a number of Italian universities before settling at Frauenburg in 1512 where he became canon of the cathedral. More of a student than a practical astronomer, he spent most of his private life seeking a new theory of the heavenly bodies. In his *On the Revolution of the Celestial Orbs*, published after his death, he broke with the past and put forward the novel theory that the planets, including the earth, revolve round the sun.

Coppée, François Joachim (1842–1908), French poet, novelist and dramatist.

Coquelin, Benoit Constant (1841–1909), and Coquelin, Ernest (1848–1909), (Coquelin aîné et cadet), brothers, were leading lights of the French theatre.

Corelli, Arcangelo (1653–1713), Italian composer and violinist, who established the form of the concerto grosso. *See* Section E.

Corneille, Pierre (1606–84), French dramatist, who ranks with Racine as a master of classical tragedy. *Le Cid*, *Polyeucte*, and *Le Menteur* marked a new era in French dramatic production.

Cornwallis, 1st Marquess (Charles Cornwallis) (1738–1805), British general who commanded the British forces which surrendered to the Americans at Yorktown in 1781, thus ending the war of independence. He was twice governor-general of India.

Corot, Jean Baptiste (1796–1875), French landscape painter.

Correggio, Antonio Allegri da (1494–1534), Italian painter, b. Correggio. His style anticipates the baroque. His *Ecce Homo* is in the National Gallery.

Cortés, Hernando (1485–1547), Spanish adventurer, b. Medellín, Extremadura, who captured Mexico for Spain, crushing an ancient civilisation.

Coulton, George Gordon (1858–1947), scholar and historian of the Middle Ages. In his *Five Centuries of Religion* he sets forth his interpretation of monastic history in England from the Conquest to the Reformation.

Couperin, a family of French musicians who were organists at St. Gervais, Paris, from about 1650 till 1826. François Couperin (1668–1733), called "Couperin the Great," is the best known today for his harpsichord music.

Cousin, Victor (1792–1867), French educationist and philosopher, founder of the eclectic school.

Cousins, Samuel (1801–87), English mezzotint engraver of plates after Reynolds, Millais, Landseer, and Hogarth.

Cousteau, Jacques-Yves (b. 1910), French underwater explorer, pioneer of aqualung diving.

Couve de Murville, Maurice (b. 1900), French diplomat; General de Gaulle's foreign minister 1958–68.

Coverdale, Miles (1488–1568), one of the early English reformers, b. Yorkshire, later to become bishop of Exeter. He assisted Tyndale in translating the Pentateuch and completed his own translation of the Bible in 1535. The Psalms still used in the Prayer Book and many of the phrases in the authorised version of 1611 are from his translation.

Cowper, William (1731–1800), English religious poet. His work is characterised by simplicity and tenderness. His best-known poems are *John Gilpin* and *The Task*.

Cox, David (1783–1859), English landscape painter. A collection of his works is in the Birmingham Gallery and the Tate Gallery.

Crabbe, George (1754–1832), English narrative poet of grim humour; author of *The Village* and *The Borough*.

Craig, Edward Gordon (1872–1966), son of Ellen Terry, producer and author of books on stagecraft.

Cranmer, Thomas (1489–1556), archbishop of Canterbury under Henry VIII, and Edward VI; an ardent promoter of the Reformation. On Mary's accession he at first consented to return to the old faith, but when called upon to make public avowal of his recantation, refused, and was burnt at the stake. His contributions were the English Bible and Book of Common Prayer.

Crichton, James (1560–82), Scottish adventurer who for his scholarly accomplishments was called "the admirable Crichton." He was killed in a brawl.

Cripps, Sir Stafford (1889–1952), British Labour statesman. A successful barrister, he relinquished practice for public work. As chancellor of the exchequer in post-war Britain, his programme was one of austerity, but his able exposition and single-minded purpose won him general support. Ill-health terminated his career.

Crispi, Francesco (1819–1901), Italian statesman, who aided Garibaldi and was later premier.

Crispin, St. (*c.* 285), martyr with his brother. By tradition they were Roman and became shoemakers, hence patron saints of shoemaking.

Croce, Benedetto (1886–1952), Italian philosopher and critic. His philosophy is expounded in the four volumes of *Filosofia dello Spirito* (which has been translated into English). He founded and edited *La Critica* in 1903, a review of literature, history, and philosophy. He was strongly opposed to fascism.

Croesus (d. *c.* 546 B.C.), last king of Lydia, reputed to be of immense wealth. Conquered and condemned to death by Cyrus, he was reprieved when Cyrus heard him recall Solon's saying "Call no man happy till he is dead."

Crome, John (1769–1821), English landscape painter, b. Norwich.

Cromer, 1st Earl of (Evelyn Baring) (1841–1917), British diplomat who, as British comptroller-general in Egypt from 1883 to 1907, did much to maintain order, improve the finances, and promote development. His *Modern Egypt* appeared in 1908.

Crompton, Samuel (1753–1827), English inventor of the spinning-mule (1779), which substituted machinery for hand work. He was b. near Bolton, a farmer's son, and benefited little by his invention.

Cromwell, Oliver (1599–1658), Protector of the commonwealth of England, Scotland, and Ireland. B. at Huntingdon, he represented Huntingdon in parliament. When civil war broke out, he served under the Earl of Essex; and then reorganised the parliamentary army, winning victories at Marston Moor and Naseby. Tortuous negotiations with Charles I could not be brought to an end, and he promoted the king's trial and execution in 1649. He defeated the Scots at Dunbar. When continued difficulties beset government he became Protector in 1653, but was soon obliged to govern by major-generals. His handling of Ireland enhanced the difficulties of that country. An able general and a strong character, he was personally tolerant (an Independent), sincere and devout; but he found himself in the revolutionary's dilemma—that there is no easy exit from a revolutionary situation; thus paradoxically he provoked English aversion to military rule.

Cromwell, Richard (1626–1712), son of the above, and his successor in the protectorate.

Cromwell, Thomas (1485–1540), English statesman, who succeeded Wolsey in the service of Henry VIII, and carried out the dissolution of the monasteries, but on his fall from favour he was executed.

Crookes, Sir William (1832–1919), English physicist who discovered the element thallium (1861) and invented the Crookes tube (1874) which was used by J. J. Thomson and others in their researches into the conduction of electricity in gases. He was also an authority on sanitation.

Cruikshank, George (1792–1878), caricaturist and book illustrator, whose work includes illustrations to *Grimm's Fairy Tales*, and *Oliver Twist*. Collections of his work are in the British Museum and the Victoria and Albert Museum.

Cummings, Bruce Frederick (1889–1917), English

zoologist and author of *Journal of a Disappointed Man.*

Cunard, Sir Samuel (1787–1865), founder of the Cunard line of steam ships. He was born in Nova Scotia, of a Welsh family of Quakers.

Cunningham of Hyndhope, 1st Viscount (Andrew Browne Cunningham) (1883–1963), British admiral in two world wars, b. Edinburgh. He served as commander-in-chief, Mediterranean, 1939–42 and Feb.–Oct. 1943; naval commander-in-chief for the Allied assault on North Africa 1942; first sea lord 1943–6.

Curie, Marie Sklodowska (1867–1934), first great woman scientist, b. Poland. Her father was a professor of physics at Warsaw. She came to Paris to study at the Sorbonne and married **Pierre Curie** (1859–1906), professor of physics. Thus began a fruitful collaborative career that led to the discovery of radium for which they shared the 1903 Nobel prize for physics. In 1911 Mme. Curie received the Nobel prize for chemistry. Pierre Curie was killed in an accident. *See also* Joliot-Curie.

Curzon of Kedleston, 1st Marquess (George Nathaniel Curzon) (1859–1925), statesman and administrator; viceroy of India 1898–1905; member of Lloyd George's war cabinet 1916–18; foreign secretary 1919–24.

Cuthbert, St. (*c.* 635–87), Celtic monk who became prior of Old Melrose (on the Tweed) and later of Lindisfarne. For a time he lived in seclusion on one of the Farne islands. The story of his life we owe to Bede.

Cuvier, Georges (1769–1832), French naturalist, noted for his sytem of classification of animals and his studies in comparative anatomy. His *Le Règne Animal* (1819) was a standard work for many years.

Cuyp, Albert (1620–91), Dutch landscape painter of sea and river views.

Cyprian, St. (d. 258), bishop of Carthage, and early Christian writer who was martyred.

Cyrus (559–529 B.C.), Persian emperor. He founded the Achæmenid line, having defeated the Medes. By conquering Lydia and Babylonia, he controlled Asia Minor. He was a wise and tolerant ruler, allowing the Jews to rebuild their temple.

D

Daguerre, Louis Jacques Mandé (1789–1851), French photographic pioneer, who invented the daguerrotype process. *See* L29.

Daimler, Gottlieb (1834–90), German inventor, with N. A. Otto of Cologne, of the Otto gas engine. The Mercédès car, exhibited at Paris in 1900, was named after his daughter.

Dale, Sir Henry Hallett (1875–1968), English physiologist. He shared the 1936 Nobel prize for medicine for his work on the chemical transmission of nerve impulses.

Dalhousie, 1st Marquess of (James Andrew Broun Ramsay) (1812–60), governor-general of India. He annexed the Punjab and later other states; opened the civil service to Indians and acted against suttee.

Dalton, John (1766–1844), English chemist and mathematician, a Quaker teacher of Manchester. In 1808 in the first number of his *New System of Chemical Philosophy* (1808–27) the modern chemical atomic theory was first propounded by him. According to this the atoms of the chemical elements are qualitatively different from one another. *See* Section F, Part II.

Damien, Father (1840–89), Belgian missionary priest, originally named Joseph de Veuster, who, witnessing the sufferings of the lepers confined on the Hawaiian island of Molokai, obtained permission to take charge, and remained there until he himself died of leprosy.

Damocles, 5th cent. B.C., Syracusan flatterer who pronounced the tyrant Dionysius the happiest of men. To illustrate the uncertainty of life, Dionysius invited him to a banquet, where a naked sword hung over his head by a hair. Hence the expression "Sword of Damocles" to mean impending danger or threat.

Damrosch, Walter Johannes (1862–1950), American conductor and composer, b. Breslau Prussia. He promoted musical development in the U.S., especially while conductor of the New York Symphony Society which his father, **Leopold Damrosch** (1832–1885) had founded in 1878.

D'Annunzio, Gabriele (1863–1938), Italian poet, dramatist and nationalist. In 1919 he led a raid on Fiume and seized it, but was eventually forced to surrender. His bodyguard wore the black shirt which was to be the uniform of the Fascists.

Dante Alighieri (1265–1321), Italian poet, a figure of world literature. He was b. at Florence in a troubled period. Though he saw her but once or twice, he loved a lady whom he called Beatrice, who is believed to have been Bice Portinari who married Simone di Bardi; she died in 1290, after which Dante wrote his *Vita Nuova*. His next work *Convivio* was philosophical. He joined the party of the Bianchi, attained municipal office, but was imprisoned and in 1301 fled. His *Divina Commedia* is a description of hell, purgatory, and heaven, a work of moral edification, replete with symbolism. He d. at Ravenna.

Danton, Georges Jacques (1759–94), French revolutionary. To his eloquent lead in 1792 was largely due the defeat of the foreign forces attempting to quell the revolution. He was a member of the committee of public safety, and sought to modify the extremists, but was displaced by Robespierre and was subsequently executed.

D'Arblay. *See* Burney.

Darius I (548–486 B.C.), Persian king and founder of Persepolis. He extended the borders of the Persian empire beyond the Indus, and reorganised it into satrapies. He declared " God's plan for the earth is not turmoil but peace, prosperity and good government." On clashing with the Greeks, however, he was defeated at Marathon. **Darius II** was a natural son of Artaxerxes I and d. 405 B.C. **Darius III** (d. 331 B.C.) was the last of the Persian kings, and was defeated by Alexander and assassinated.

Darling, Grace Horsley (1815–42), English heroine who by putting off in a small boat from the lighthouse on one of the Farne islands, of which her father was keeper, saved the shipwrecked crew of the *Forfarshire.*

Darnley, Henry Stewart, Lord (1545–67), second husband of Mary, Queen of Scots (1565). He plotted the murder of her secretary, Rizzio, and was subsequently himself murdered. Through his son James I he is the ancestor of the Stuart monarchs.

Darwin, Charles Robert (1809–82), English naturalist, b. Shrewsbury, one of the pioneers of experimental biology. After returning from his formative voyage round the world as naturalist on the *Beagle* (1831–6), he spent nearly twenty years building up evidence for his theory of evolution before publishing it in *The Origin of Species* (1859). In it he argued that the evolution of present-day morphology had been built up by the gradual and opportunistic mechanism of natural selection. His ideas though welcomed by biologists aroused bitter controversy. *See* Section F, Part IV.

Daudet, Alphonse (1840–97), French writer who covered a wide range and whose works include *Lettres de mon Moulin, Robert Helmont,* and *Tartarin de Tarascon.*

D'Avenant, Sir William (1606–68), English dramatist, and author of the first attempt at English opera, *Siege of Rhodes* (the music for which was composed by Charles Coleman and George Hudson).

David I (1084–1153), King of Scotland. As uncle of Matilda, daughter of Henry I of England, he supported her claim to the English crown, but was defeated. In Scotland he promoted unity and development.

David II (1324–71), King of Scotland. He was son of Robert Bruce. In invading England he was captured at Neville's Cross, 1346.

David, Sir Edgeworth (1858–1934), Australian geologist who accompanied Shackleton's antarctic expedition, 1907–9, leading the party that reached the south magnetic pole.

David, Jacques Louis (1748–1825), French painter of classical subjects and an ardent republican.

David, St., patron saint of Wales who lived in south Wales in the 6th cent.

Davidson, 1st Baron (Randall Thomas Davidson) (1848–1930), archbishop of Canterbury, 1903–28.

Davies, Sir Walford (1869–1941), English organist, composer, and broadcaster on music.

Davies, William Henry (1871–1940), Welsh poet. He spent some years tramping, both in England and America, and his work shows knowledge of and love for nature. He wrote Autobiography of a Super Tramp.

Da Vinci. See Leonardo.

Davis, Jefferson (1808–89), American civil war leader. B. in Kentucky, he was made president of the Confederate States when the civil war broke out. After the war he was tried for treason, but discharged. He wrote The Rise and Fall of the Confederate Government.

Davis, John (c. 1550–1605), Elizabethan explorer and discoverer of Davis's Strait, the channel between the Atlantic and Arctic oceans on the west of Greenland. Invented the backstaff, or Davis's quadrant.

Davitt, Michael (1846–1906), Irish nationalist. The son of a peasant who later came to England, he joined the Fenians, and in 1870 was sentenced to penal servitude. On his release he helped to found the Land League in 1879; was again imprisoned; and wrote Leaves from a Prison Diary. He was subsequently returned to parliament.

Davy, Sir Humphry (1778–1829), English chemist, b. Penzance. Much of his work found practical application, e.g., the miner's safety lamp which still bears his name. His Elements of Agricultural Chemistry (1813) contains the first use in English of the word "element." He took Michael Faraday as his assistant at the Royal Institution.

Dawber, Sir Guy (1861–1938), English architect. As chairman of the Council for the Preservation of Rural England, he did much to bring about the restoration of buildings throughout the country.

Day Lewis, Cecil (b. 1904), poet and critic; professor or poetry at Oxford 1951–6. He succeeded Masefield as poet laureate in 1968. See Section M, Part II.

Debussy, Claude Achille (1862–1918), composer and leader of the French Impressionist school in music. Among his works are Suite bergamasque, containing the popular Clair de lune; L'Après-midi d'un Faune, inspired by the poem of Mallarmé, and La Mer. He also wrote an opera Pelléas et Mélisande based on Maeterlinck's drama. See also Section E.

Defoe, Daniel (1660–1731), English political writer; also author of Robinson Crusoe, Moll Flanders, and a Tour of Gt. Britain. His Shortest Way with Dissenters brought him imprisonment.

De Forest, Lee (1873–1961), American inventor who was the first to use alternating-current transmission, and improved the thermionic valve detector by which wireless and sound films were made possible.

Degas, Edgar (1834–1917), French Impressionist painter and sculptor, son of a banker. He painted subjects from everyday life—dancers, café life, the racecourse.

De Gasperi, Alcide (1881–1954), Italian politician who founded the Christian Democrat Party and worked for European federation; prime minister 1945–53.

De Gaulle. See Gaulle, Charles de.

De Havilland, Sir Geoffrey (1882–1965), pioneer of civil and military aviation in Britain; designer of the famous Moth machines. His son was killed in 1946 while testing a plane.

Delacroix, Ferdinand Victor Eugène (1798–1863), French painter of the Romantic school.

De la Mare, Walter John (1873–1956), English poet and novelist whose work has a characteristic charm. Much of it was written for children.

Deiane, John Thadeus (1817–79), editor of The Times, 1841–77, who did much to establish that paper's standing.

Delaroche, Paul (1797–1856), French historical painter.

Delibes, Clément Philibert Léo (1836–91), French composer of much graceful music, including operas, of which Lakmé is the best known, and ballets, among them Coppélia.

Delius, Frederick (1862–1934), English composer

of German parentage. His music, highly idiosyncratic in idiom, was more readily received in Germany than in England until promoted by Sir Thomas Beecham. See Section E.

Democritus (c. 470–c. 400 B.C.), one of the first scientific thinkers, pupil of Leucippus (fl. c. 440 B.C.). He took an atomic view of matter, denied the existence of mind as a separate entity, and counted happiness and inner tranquility as important moral principles. His attitude was not shared by his contemporary, Socrates, nor by Plato and Aristotle, but was accepted by Epicurus. The atomic theory thus passed into the background for many centuries.

Demosthenes (385–322 B.C.), Greek orator who, by his Philippics, roused the Athenians to resist the growing power of Philip of Macedon.

De Quincey, Thomas (1785–1859), English essayist and critic; friend of Wordsworth and Southey. He wrote Confessions of an Opium-eater.

De Reszke, Jean (1853–1925) and De Reszke, Edouard (1856–1917), Polish operatic singers, the first a tenor, the second a baritone.

Derwentwater, 3rd Earl of (James Radcliffe) (1689–1716), leader of the English Jacobite movement for placing the pretender on the throne. He was defeated at Preston in 1715 and beheaded.

Descartes, René (1596–1650), French mathematician, pioneer of modern philosophy. Unconvinced by scholastic tradition and theological dogma, he sought to get back to why anything can be said to be true, which turned out to be a fruitful line of thought. The basis of his Cartesian philosophy is summed up in his own words, cogito, ergo sum (I think, therefore I am).

Desmoulins, Camille (1760–94), French revolutionary. He represented Paris in the National Convention, and wrote witty and sarcastic pamphlets and periodicals. He was an ally of Danton, and when Robespierre came to power he was arrested and executed on the same day as Danton.

Deutscher, Isaac (1907–67), Marxist historian, biographer of Stalin and Trotsky. B. in Poland, he joined the outlawed Polish Communist Party but was expelled for his anti-Stalinist views. In 1939 he came to London.

De Valéra, Eamon (b. 1882), Irish statesman. b. New York, son of a Spanish father and an Irish mother. He was brought up in Limerick and was imprisoned for his part in the Easter rising of 1916. He opposed the treaty of 1921; and in 1926, when the republican Fianna Fáil was founded, he became its president. Fianna Fáil won the election of 1932, and he then became president of the Executive Council, 1932–8, and prime minister, 1938–48, 1951–4, 1957–9. He promoted Irish neutrality in the second world war, encouraged the use of the Irish language, and in spite of early intransigence his leadership has been moderate.

de Valois, Dame Ninette (b. 1898), Irish-born ballet dancer and choreographer. She toured Europe with Diaghilev, 1923–5, and in 1931 founded the Sadlers Wells Ballet School (now Royal Ballet School), of which she became director. Autobiography (1957).

Dewar, Sir James (1842–1923), chemist and physicist, a native of Kincardine. He succeeded in liquefying hydrogen, and invented the vacuum flask. The explosive cordite was the joint invention of himself and Sir Frederick Abel.

Dewey, John (1859–1952), American philosopher, psychologist, and educationist. A follower of William James, he was an exponent of pragmatism.

De Wit, Jan (1625–72), Dutch republican statesman, who carried on war with England and later negotiated the Triple Alliance, but was overthrown by the Orange Party and murdered.

Diaghilev, Sergei Pavlovich (1872–1929), Russian ballet impressario and founder of the Russian ballet. Among those associated with him are Anna Pavlova, Vaslav Nijinsky, Tamara Karsavina, Leonide Massine, Michel Fokine, the choreographer, L. N. Bakst, the painter, and Igor Stravinsky, the composer.

Dickens, Charles (1812–70), popular English novelist of the 19th cent., with enormous output and capacity for vivid story-telling. Of humble origin, he was extremely successful.

His best-known works are perhaps *Pickwick Papers, Oliver Twist, A Christmas Carol* (this influenced the observance of Christmas), *Dombey and Son, David Copperfield, Little Dorrit,* and *Great Expectations.* He gave public readings from his works.

Dickinson, Emily (1830–86), American poet whose writing has a mystic quality. She lived a cloistered life and published almost nothing in her lifetime.

Dickinson, Goldworthy Lowes (1863–1932), English author, an interpreter and upholder of the Greek view of life.

Diderot, Denis (1713–84), French man of letters, critic of art and literature, and editor of the *Encyclopédie* (1713–84) to which many writers of the Enlightenment contributed.

Diemen, Anthony van (1593–1645), Dutch promoter of exploration. As governor-general in the Far East, he promoted Dutch trade and influence; and despatched Abel Tasman, who in 1642 discovered New Zealand and Van Diemen's Land (now Tasmania).

Diesel, Rudolf (1858–1913), German engineer, inventor of an internal combustion engine which he patented in 1893. *See also* L81.

Diocletian (245–313), Roman emperor and persecutor of Christianity. He divided the empire under a system of joint rule; later abdicated; and built a palace in Dalmatia.

Diogenes (412–322 B.C.), Greek cynic philosopher who lived in a tub and told Alexander to get out of his sunshine. He sought virtue and moral freedom in liberation from desire.

Dionysius the elder and younger, tyrants of Syracuse in the 4th cent. B.C.

Dirac, Paul Adrien Maurice (b. 1902), English physicist who shared with Erwin Schrödinger the 1933 Nobel prize for their work in developing Heisenberg's theory of quantum mechanics. *See Section F, Part II.*

Disney, Walter Elias (1901–66), American film cartoonist, creator of Mickey Mouse. He is known for his *Silly Symphonies, Snow White and the Seven Dwarfs,* and *Pinocchio.*

Disraeli, Benjamin, Earl of Beaconsfield (1804–81), English statesman and novelist who helped to form modern Conservatism in England. The son of Isaac (*q.v.*), he published his first novel at 21, and later *Coningsby* and *Sibyl,* which helped to rouse the social conscience. He entered parliament in 1837 and was prime minister 1868 and 1874–80, when he arranged the purchase of shares in the Suez canal. He was rival of Gladstone and friend of Queen Victoria.

Disraeli, Isaac (1766–1848), father of Benjamin (*q.v.*) and author of *Curiosities of Literature.*

Dobson, Austin (1840–1921), English writer of light verse and of 18th cent. biography.

Dodgson, Charles Lutwidge (1832–98), English writer. Under the pseudonym Lewis Carroll, he wrote poems and books for children, including *Alice in Wonderland.* In private life he was a lecturer in mathematics at Oxford.

Dolci, Carlo (1616–86), one of the last Florentine painters.

Dolci, Danilo (b. 1925), Italian architect who since 1952 has dedicated himself to the rehabilitation of the people of Sicily in their desperate poverty.

Dominic, St. (1170–1221), founder of the Friars Preachers or Black Friars. B. in Castile, he and his followers sought to teach the ignorant. In 1216 they were formed into an order and vowed to poverty. The order spread through Europe.

Domitian (Titus Flavius Domitianus) (A.D. 51–96), Roman emperor, son of Vespasian. He ruled despotically, aroused the hatred of the senate, and was assassinated as a result of a palace conspiracy.

Donatello (Donato di Niccolò) (c. 1386–1466), Italian sculptor, b. Florence, son of Niccolò di Betto di Bardo. He was the founder of modern sculpture, producing statues independent of a background, designed to stand in the open to be viewed from all angles. Among his masterpieces are the statues of *St. George* and *David* (in the Bargello, Florence) and his equestrian *Gattamelata* in Padua, the first bronze horse to be cast in the Renaissance.

Donizetti, Gaetano (1797–1848), Italian composer. The best-known of his sixty operas are *Lucia*

di Lammermoor, La Fille du Régiment, and *Don Pasquale. See* **Section E.**

Donne, John (1572–1631), English metaphysical poet and preacher (dean of St. Paul's). His poems and sermons, marked by passion, wit, and profundity of thought have received full publicity only in the present century.

Doré, Gustave (1833–83), French artist who painted scriptural subjects and illustrated Dante, Milton, and Tennyson.

Dostoyevsky, Feodor Mikhailovich (1821–81), Russian novelist, b. Moscow. As a result of his revolutionary activity he was sent to hard labour in Siberia. In his books, which include *Crime and Punishment, The Brothers Karamazov, The Idiot,* and *The Possessed,* he explored the dark places of the human spirit to a degree not previously attempted.

Douglas of Kirtleside, 1st Baron (William Sholto Douglas) (1893–1969), British airman; commanded Fighter command, 1940–2, Coastal command, 1944–5. A Labour peer.

Douglas, Norman (1868–1952), novelist and travel writer. A Scot, born in Austria, he made his home on the Mediterranean. His works include *South Wind.*

Douglas-Home, Sir Alexander Frederick (b. 1903), Conservative prime minister, 1963–4; foreign and commonwealth secretary, 1970–.

Doulton, Sir Henry (1820–97), English potter and the inventor of Doulton ware.

Dowden, Edward (1843–1913), English literary critic and Shakespearian scholar.

Dowding, 1st Baron (Hugh Caswell Tremenheere Dowding) (1882–1970), British airman; commanded Fighter command during the Battle of Britain period (1940).

Dowland, John (c. 1563–1626), English composer of songs with lute accompaniment. His son Robert succeeded him as Court lutanist to Charles I.

Doyle, Sir Arthur Conan (1859–1930), English writer, creator of the detective Sherlock Holmes and of his friend and foil, Dr. Watson. He also wrote historical novels.

Doyle, Richard (1824–83), humorous artist on the staff of *Punch.*

D'Oyly Carte, Richard (1844–1901), English theatrical manager, who built the Savoy theatre and there produced Gilbert and Sullivan operas. The D'Oyly Carte company played in many countries.

Drake, Sir Francis (c. 1540–96), English seaman. In 1577–80 he sailed round the world in the *Golden Hind.* In 1587 he destroyed a number of Spanish ships in Cadiz harbour; and under Lord Howard he helped to defeat the Spanish Armada in 1588.

Draper, John William (1811–82), American chemist, b. near Liverpool. He was the first, using Daguerre's process, to take a successful photograph of the human face (1840) and of the moon.

Dreiser, Theodore (1871–1935), American novelist of austere realism, author of *An American Tragedy.*

Dreyfus, Alfred (1859–1935), French victim of injustice. Of Jewish parentage, in 1894 he was accused of divulging secrets to a foreign power, and was sentenced by a military secret tribunal to imprisonment for life on Devil's Island in French Guiana. At a new trial in 1899 he was again found guilty. Efforts continued to be made on his behalf, and in 1906 he was entirely exonerated, restored to his rank in the army, and made a Chevalier of the Legion of Honour.

Drinkwater, John (1882–1937), English poet and playwright. His plays include *Abraham Lincoln* and *Oliver Cromwell.*

Drummond, William (1585–1649), Scottish poet and Royalist pamphleteer. He was laird of Hawthornden.

Drury, Alfred (1857–1944), English, sculptor especially of statues of Queen Victoria at Bradford and Portsmouth.

Dryden, John (1631–1700), prolific English poet and dramatist, who also wrote political satire (*Absalom and Achitophel*). He was hostile to the revolution of 1688, and thereafter mainly translated classical writers, including Virgil.

Du Barry, Marie Jeanne Bécu, Comtesse (1746–93), mistress of Louis XV of France and guillotined by the revolutionary tribunal.

B21

Du Chaillu, Paul Belloni (1835–1903), traveller in Africa, who in 1861 and 1867 published accounts of his explorations. A French-American.

Dufferin and Ava, 1st Marquess of (Frederick Temple Hamilton-Temple Blackwood) (1826–1902), British diplomat, writer, and governor-general of Canada and viceroy of India.

Dulles, John Foster (1888–1959), U.S. Secretary of State in the Republican administration 1953–9. His foreign policy was inflexibly opposed to negotiation with Russia and to U.S. recognition of China.

Dumas, Alexandre (1802–70), French romantic novelist, among whose many works are *The Three Musketeers* and *The Count of Monte Cristo*.

Dumas, Alexandre (1824–95), French dramatist, son of the above; author of *La Dame aux Camélias*.

Du Maurier, George (1834–96), contributor to *Punch* and author of *Trilby*.

Dundee, 1st Viscount (John Graham of Claverhouse), (1648–89), Scottish soldier ("Bonnie Dundee"). Employed to suppress the covenanters, he was defeated at Drumclog, but victorious at Bothwell Brig. At the revolution of 1688 he supported James II, and was killed in the (victorious) battle of Killiecrankie.

Dundonald, Earl of. *See* Cochrane, Thomas.

Duns Scotus, John (c. 1265–1308), Scottish scholastic philosopher, b. at Maxton near Roxburgh, opponent of Thomas Aquinas. He joined the Franciscans, studied and taught at Oxford and Paris, and probably d. at Cologne. He challenged the harmony of faith and reason.

Dunstable, John (c. 1380–1453), the earliest English composer known by name. He was a contemporary of the Netherlands composers Dufay and Binchois. *See* Section E.

Dunstan, St. (908–88), reforming archbishop of Canterbury. He lived through seven reigns from Athelstan to Ethelred, and was adviser especially to Edgar. Under him Glastonbury Abbey became a centre of religious teaching.

Dupleix, Joseph François (1697–1763), French governor in India. He extended French influence and power in the Carnatic, but his plans were frustrated by his English opponent, Clive. He was recalled in 1754 and died in poverty.

Dürer, Albrecht (1471–1528), German painter and engraver. B. at Nuremberg, he was (like his Italian contemporary, Leonardo) a man of intellectual curiosity and scientific insight. His best work is in his copper engravings, woodcuts, and drawings; the former include *The Knight, Melancholia*, and *St. Jerome in his Study*. He may be regarded as the founder of the German school and a pioneer of etching. Examples of his work are in the British Museum. He was the friend of Luther and Melanchton.

Durham, Earl of (John George Lambton) (1792–1840), served as governor-general of Canada after the disturbances of 1837, and in 1839 presented to parliament the *Durham Report*, which laid down the principle of colonial self-government.

Duse, Elenora (1861–1924), Italian tragedienne.

Duval, Claude (1643–70), notorious highwayman who came to England from Normandy and was eventually hanged at Tyburn.

Dvořák, Antonin (1844–1904), Czech composer whose music is rich in folk-song melodies of his native Bohemia. In 1884 he conducted his *Stabat Mater* in London. His *New World* symphony was composed in New York, where he was head of the National Conservatoire (1892–5). *See* Section E.

Dyson, Sir Frank Watson (1868–1939), English astronomer who was astronomer royal 1910–33, and astronomer royal for Scotland 1905–10.

Dyson, Sir George (1883–1964), English composer and writer. In *The New Music* he analyses the technique of modern schools of composition. He composed several choral works such as *The Canterbury Pilgrims* and *Nebuchadnezzar*.

E

Eastlake, Sir Charles Lock (1793–1865), English painter of historical and religious works.

Eastman, George (1854–1932), American inventor of the roll photographic film and the Kodak camera. His philanthropies were estimated at over $100 million.

Eck, Johann von (1486–1543), German Catholic theologian and opponent of Luther.

Eddington, Sir Arthur Stanley (1882–1944), English astronomer (Greenwich observatory 1906–13; Cambridge observatory 1914–44). His works include *The Nature of the Physical World*.

Eddy, Mrs. Mary Baker (1821–1910), American founder of the Church of Christ Scientist. Her *Science and Health with Key to the Scriptures* was published in 1875. *See* Christian Science, Section J.

Edelinck, Gerard (1640–1707), Flemish engraver, b. Antwerp, the first to reproduce in print the colour, as well as the form, of a picture.

Eden, Robert Anthony, 1st Earl of Avon (b. 1897), British statesman. He entered parliament in 1923; became foreign secretary in 1935 (resigning in 1938 over Chamberlain's rebuff to President Roosevelt); deputy prime minister in 1951; and succeeded Sir Winston Churchill in 1955. His Suez policy divided the country. He resigned for health reasons in 1957. Memoirs, *Facing the Dictators; The Reckoning*; and *Full Circle*. Earldom conferred 1961. Chancellor, Birmingham Univ.

Edgar (943–75), King of England 959–75. He was advised by Archbishop Dunstan.

Edgar Atheling (c. 1060–c. 1130), was the lawful heir of Edward the Confessor, but in the Norman invasion he was unable to maintain his claim.

Edgeworth, Maria (1767–1849), Irish novelist, whose stories include *Castle Rackrent, The Absentee*, and *Belinda*.

Edinburgh, Duke of (Philip Mountbatten) (b. 1921), consort of Queen Elizabeth II. He relinquished his right of accession to the thrones of Greece and Denmark on his naturalisation in 1947 when he took the name of Mountbatten. He is the great-great-grandson of Queen Victoria, grandson of Admiral Prince Louis of Battenberg, and nephew of Earl Mountbatten of Burma. Pres. British Association 1951–2. Chancellor, Universities of Edinburgh, Wales, and Salford.

Edison, Thomas Alva (1847–1931), American inventor of the transmitter and receiver for the automatic telegraph; the phonograph; the first practical incandescent lamp; and many devices for the electrical distribution of light and power. From being a newsboy on the railway and later a telegraph clerk, he became a master at applying scientific principles to practical ends. He set up a research laboratory (originally a barn) at Menlo Park, New Jersey, where his inventions were tested out.

Edmund II (Ironside) (980–1016), the son of Ethelred, king of the English, made a compact with Canute to divide England, but soon afterwards died.

Edward the Confessor (c. 1004–1066), English king who preceded the Norman Conquest and founded Westminster Abbey. He was canonised in 1161.

Edward the Elder (c. 870–c. 924), son of Alfred, succeeded him as king of the West Saxons in 899. He overcame the Danes and reoccupied the northern counties.

Edward I (1239–1307), King of England, succeeded his father Henry in 1272. Able and energetic, his legislation influenced the development of the land law, and he summoned parliamentary assemblies. A soldier, he conquered Wales, building castles, but could not maintain his hold on Scotland.

Edward II (1284–1327), succeeded his father Edward I as king of England in 1307 and was defeated by the Scots at Bannockburn. Weak and inept, he was murdered in 1327.

Edward III (1312–77), succeeded his father Edward II as king of England in 1327. Popular and ambitious for military glory, he began the Hundred Years War with France. He fostered the woollen industry. Latterly he became senile.

Edward IV (1442–83), able but dissolute Yorkist leader whose reign brought about a revival in the power of the monarchy, in English sea power, and in foreign trade (in which he himself took part). Spent 1470–71 in exile. Began rebuilding of St. George's chapel, Windsor. Patron of Caxton.

Edward V (1470–83), succeeded his father Edward IV at the age of 12 and was a pawn in the quarrels of baronial relatives. He and his brother were shut up in the Tower by his uncle, Richard, Duke of Gloucester, and there probably murdered, though exact proof has not been established.

Edward VI (1537–53), succeeded his father, Henry VIII, as king of England when in his tenth year. He was delicate and studious, and his government was carried on successively by the Dukes of Somerset and Northumberland; while under Archbishop Cranmer the prayer book was issued. He was induced to name Lady Jane Grey his successor.

Edward VII (1841–1910), King of England. The son of Queen Victoria, he married Princess Alexandra of Denmark in 1863, and succeeded his mother in 1901. Interested mainly in social life and in international contacts, he visited India in 1875 and travelled much in Europe.

Edward VIII (b. 1894), King of England, succeeded his father George V in 1936, and abdicated later that year because of disagreement over his proposed marriage. He was created Duke of Windsor, and was governor of the Bahamas 1940–45.

Ehrlich, Paul (1854–1915), German bacteriologist, who at Frankfurt-on-Main carried out work in immunology. He discovered salvarsan for the treatment of syphilis. Nobel prizewinner 1908.

Eiffel, Alexandre Gustave (1832–1923), French engineer, one of the first to employ compressed air caissons in bridge building. Among his works are the Eiffel Tower (1887–9) and the Panama Canal locks.

Einstein, Albert (1879–1955), mathematical physicist whose theory of relativity superseded Newton's theory of gravitation. He was born in Ulm of Jewish parents, lived for many years in Switzerland, and held a succession of professorial chairs at Zurich, Prague, and Berlin. In 1921 he was awarded the Nobel prize for his work in quantum theory. He was driven by the Nazis to seek asylum in America and became professor at the Institute for Advanced Study at Princeton 1933–45. In August 1939 at the request of a group of scientists he wrote to President Roosevelt warning of the danger of uranium research in Germany and stressing the urgency of investigating the possible use of atomic energy in bombs. *See* **Relativity, Section F, Part II.**

Eisenhower, Dwight David (1890–1969), American general and statesman. He was C.-in-C. Allied Forces, N. Africa, 1942–3; and in the European theatre of operations, 1943–5; and was Republican President, 1953–61.

Eisenstein, Sergei Mikhailovich (1898–1948), Russian film director of *The Battleship Potemkin*, *Alexander Nevsky*, and *Ivan the Terrible*.

Eleanor, Queen of Edward I. After her death in 1290 the king had memorial crosses erected at the twelve places where her body rested on its way from Grantham to Westminster.

Elgar, Sir Edward (1857–1934), English composer, especially of choral-orchestral works for festivals. His oratorios include *The Kingdom*, *The Apostles*, and *The Dream of Gerontius*; he also wrote *Enigma Variations*, and the tone-poem *Falstaff*. *See* **Section E.**

Elgin, 7th Earl of (Thomas Bruce) (1766–1841), British diplomat who, with the object of saving them, conveyed some sculptures from the Parthenon in Athens to the British Museum.

Eliot, George (1819–80), the pen-name of Mary Ann (later Marion) Evans, whose novels include *Adam Bede*, *The Mill on the Floss*, *Silas Marner*, *Middlemarch*, and *Daniel Deronda*. Her works show deep insight. She lived with the writer George Lewes from 1854 until his death 25 years later. (Although Lewes had been deserted by his wife it was then not possible to obtain a divorce). She brought up his three children.

Eliot, Thomas Stearns (1888–1965), poet and critic. He was born in St. Louis, Missouri, and became a British subject in 1927. His poems include *Prufrock and Other Observations*, *The Waste Land*, *The Hollow Men*, *Ash Wednesday*, *Four Quartets*; his verse dramas *Murder in the Cathedral* and *The Family Reunion*. He described himself as "classicist in literature, royalist in politics, and Anglo-Catholic in religion". Nobel prizewinner 1948. *See* **Sections I and M (Part II).**

Elizabeth (b. 1900), Queen Consort of George VI, daughter of the 14th Earl of Strathmore. Before her marriage in 1923 she was Lady Elizabeth Angela Marguerite Bowes-Lyon. Chancellor, Universities of London and Dundee.

Elizabeth I (1533–1603), Queen of England, daughter of Henry VIII, succeeded her sister Mary in 1558. Politically and intellectually able and firm, though personally vain and capricious, she chose to serve her able men such as William Cecil; and her long reign was one of stability, victory over the Spanish, and adventure in the New World; while the Church of England was established, and literary output prepared the way for Shakespeare; it was however marred by the execution of Mary, Queen of Scots.

Elizabeth II (Elizabeth Alexandra Mary of Windsor) (b. 1926), Queen of England, ascended the throne in February 1952 on the death of her father George VI. Her Consort, Prince Philip, Duke of Edinburgh, is the son of Prince Andrew of Greece and a descendant of the Danish royal family. They have four children: Charles, Prince of Wales (b. 1948), Princess Anne (b. 1950), Prince Andrew (b. 1960), and Prince Edward (b. 1964).

Ellis, Havelock (1859–1939), Englsh writer whose *Studies in the Psychology of Sex* was influential in changing the public attitude towards sex. His books were published in America long before they were in England.

Emerson, Ralph Waldo (1803–82), American poet and essayist, b. Boston, member of the transcendentalist group of thinkers. Among his best-known poems are *Woodnotes*, *Threnody*, *Terminus*, *Brahma*, *The Problem*.

Emin Pasha, the name adopted by Eduard Schnitzer (1840–92), a German explorer associated with Gen. Charles Gordon in the Sudan as a medical officer; and governor of the Equatorial Province 1878–89, when he was menaced by the Mahdi and rescued by Stanley. He has contributed greatly to African studies.

Emmet, Robert (1778–1803), Irish patriot, led the rising of 1803, was betrayed, and executed.

Empedocles (*c.* 500–*c.* 430 B.C.), Greek philosopher, b. Agrigentum in Sicily, founder of a school of medicine which regarded the heart as the seat of life, an idea which passed to Aristotle, as did his idea that all matter was composed of four elements: earth, air, fire, and water.

Engels, Friedrich (1820–95), German socialist, son of a wealthy textile manufacturer, lifelong friend of Karl Marx, with whom he collaborated in writing the *Communist Manifesto* of 1848. Through him Marx acquired his knowledge of English labour conditions.

Epicurus of Samos (342–270 B.C.), refounded the atomic view of matter put forward by Democritus, and held that peace of mind comes through freedom from fear, the two main sources of which he regarded as religion and fear of death. The Epicureans were a rival sect to the Peripetics and Stoics.

Epstein, Sir Jacob (1880–1959), sculptor, b. New York of Russian–Polish parents. His work includes *Rima*, in Hyde Park; *Day* and *Night* on the building of London Underground headquarters; *Genesis*, exhibited in 1931; *Lazarus*, in New College, Oxford; the *Madonna and Child* group in Cavendish Square, London; the figure of *Christ in Majesty* in aluminium in Llandaff cathedral; a sculpture for the T.U.C. headquarters in London; and a bronze group for Coventry cathedral.

Erasmus, Desiderius (1466–1536), Dutch Renaissance humanist, who spent several years in England and was the friend of Dean Colet and Sir Thomas More. He aimed at ecclesiastical reform from within and scorned the old scholastic teaching. He thus prepared the way for Luther. His *Praise of Folly* is still read.

Erhard, Ludwig (b. 1897), German economist and politician; succeeded Adenauer as Chancellor of the West German Federal Republic, 1963–7.

Ericsson, John (1803–89), Swedish engineer who entered into competition with George Stephenson in the first famous trial of locomotives.

Essex, 2nd Earl of (Robert Devereux) (1566–1601), favourite of Queen Elizabeth I in her old age. Unsuccessful as governor-general of Ireland, he returned to England against the Queen's wish; plotted; and was executed.

Ethelbert, King of Kent at the close of the 6th cent., accepted Christianity on the mission of St. Augustine.

Ethelred II (c. 968–1016), King of England. Unable to organise resistance against the Danish raids, he was called the Unready (from Old Eng. uraed = without counsel).

Etty, William (1787–1849), English artist of historical and classical subjects.

Eucken, Rudolf Christoph (1846–1926), German philosopher of activism, which puts personal ethical effort above intellectual idealism. Nobel prizewinner 1908.

Euler, Leonhard (1707–83), Swiss mathematician, remembered especially for his work in optics and on the calculus of variations. He was called by Catherine I to St. Petersburg, where he was professor, 1730–41, and by Frederick the Great to Berlin, where he remained from 1741 till 1766. He became blind but continued his work.

Euripides (480–406 B.C.), Greek tragic dramatist, who is known to have written about 80 plays, of which 18 are preserved, including *Alcestis*, *Medea*, *Iphigenia*, and *Orestes*. He displayed a sceptical attitude towards the myths.

Eusebius (264–340), ecclesiastical historian. His *Ecclesiastical History* gives the history of the Christian church to 324. He also wrote a general history, *Chronicon*.

Evans, Sir Arthur John (1851–1941), English archaeologist, known for his excavations at Knossos in Crete and his discovery of the pre-Phoenician script.

Evans, Dame Edith Mary (b. 1888), versatile English actress who made her first appearance as Cressida in *Troilus and Cressida* in 1912.

Evelyn, John (1620–1706), cultured English diarist who gives brilliant portraits of contemporaries. He also wrote *Sylva*, a manual of arboriculture.

Eyck, Jan van (c. 1389–1441), Flemish painter, whose best-known work is the altarpiece in Ghent cathedral. His brother **Hubert** (c. 1370–1426) is associated with him.

F

Fabius, the name of an ancient Roman family who over many generations played an important part in early Roman history. **Quintus Fabius Maximus Verrucosus** (d. 203 B.C.) saved Rome from Hannibal by strategic evasion of battle; hence his name *Cunctator* (delayer), and the term Fabian policy.

Fabre, Jean Henri Casimir (1823–1915), French naturalist, whose study of the habits of insects were delightfully recorded in his *Souvenirs entomologiques*.

Faed, name of two Scottish genre painters, **Thomas** (1826–1900), and **John** (1819–1902). A third brother, **James**, engraved their works.

Fahrenheit, Gabriel Daniel (1686–1736), German physicist, b. Danzig. He introduced c. 1715 the mercury thermometer and fixed thermometric standards.

Fairbairn, Sir William (1789–1874), Scottish engineer. In 1817 he took the lead in using iron in shipbuilding.

Fairfax, 3rd Baron (Thomas Fairfax) (1612–71), parliamentary general in the English civil war, and victor of Marston Moor. In 1650 he withdrew into private life.

Falla, Manuel (1876–1946), Spanish composer whose music is highly individual with a strong folk-song element. *See Section E.*

Faraday, Michael (1791–1867), English experimental physicist, founder of the science of electromagnetism. He was the son of a Yorkshire blacksmith and at 13 became apprenticed to a bookseller in London. In 1813 he became laboratory assistant to Sir Humphry Davy at the Royal Institution, succeeding him as professor of chemistry in 1833. He set himself the problem of finding the connections between the forces of light, heat, electricity, and magnetism and his discoveries form the basis of the modern electrical industry. He inaugurated the Christmas lectures for juvenile audiences at the Royal Institution.

Farman, Henri (1874–1958) French aviator, one of the pioneers of aviation, and a designer and builder of aeroplanes.

Farouk I (1920–65), King of Egypt, 1936–52. He was forced to abdicate as a result of the military coup of 1952.

Farrar, Frederick William (1831–1903), English clergyman, author of the schoolboy story *Eric*.

Faulkner, William (1897–1962), American novelist, whose series of novels, *The Sound and the Fury*, *As I Lay Dying*, *Light in August*, *Sanctuary*, depict the American South. Nobel prizewinner 1949. *See Section M, Part I.*

Fauré, Gabriel Urbain (1845–1924), French composer and teacher. His works include chamber music, nocturnes, and barcarolles for piano, an opera *Pénélope*, some exquisite songs, and *Requiem*. Ravel was among his pupils. *See Section E.*

Fawcett, Millicent Garrett (1847–1929), educational reformer and leader of the movement for women's suffrage; one of the founders of Newnham College, Cambridge. She was the wife of the blind Liberal politician and economist, Henry Fawcett (1833–84).

Fawkes, Guy (1570–1606), a Yorkshire catholic, who with Catesby and other conspirators planned the Gunpowder Plot. Although warned, he persisted and was captured and hanged. *See L51.*

Fénelon, François de Salignac de la Mothe (1651–1715), archbishop of Cambrai and author of *Telemachus*.

Ferdinand V of Aragon (1452–1516), who married Isabella of Castile, and with her reigned over Spain, saw the Moors expelled from Spain, equipped Columbus for the discoveries that led to Spain's vast colonial possessions, and instituted the Inquisition.

Ferguson, James (1710–76), Scottish astronomer who, from being a shepherd-boy, educated himself in astronomy, mathematics, and portrait painting.

Fermi, Enrico (1901–54), Italian nuclear physicist whose research contributed to the harnessing of atomic energy and the development of the atomic bomb. He postulated the existence of the neutrino and discovered the element Neptunium. Nobel prizewinner 1938.

Fichte, Johann Gottlieb (1762–1814), German philosopher of the nationalistic Romantic school who prepared the way for modern totalitarianism.

Field, John (1782–1837), Irish composer of nocturnes, pupil of Clementi and teacher of Glinka. His work served as a model for Chopin.

Fielding, Henry (1707–54), English novelist, author of *Tom Jones*, *Joseph Andrews*, and *Amelia*, as well as plays.

Fildes, Sir Luke (1844–1927), English painter and woodcut-designer.

Finsen, Niels Ryberg (1860–1904), Danish physician who established an institute for light therapy and invented the Finsen ultra-violet lamp. Nobel prizewinner 1903.

Firdausi, pen-name of Abu'l Kasim Mansur (940–1020), Persian poet, author of the epic *Shah-Nama* or Book of Kings.

Fisher of Lambeth, Baron (Geoffrey Francis Fisher), (b. 1887), archbishop of Canterbury, 1945–61; Headmaster of Repton School, 1914–32.

Fisher, Herbert Albert Laurens (1865–1940), English historian and educational reformer; author of *A History of Europe*.

Fisher, Sir Ronald Aylmer (1890–1962), British scientist who revolutionised both genetics and the philosophy of experimentation by founding the modern corpus of mathematical statistics.

FitzGerald, Edward (1809–83), English poet who translated the *Rubáiyát* of Omar Khayyam (1859).

Fitzroy, Robert (1805–65), British meteorologist who introduced the system of storm warnings which were the beginning of weather forecasts.

Flammarion, Camille (1842–1925), French astronomer, noted for his popular lectures and books which include *L'Astronomie Populaire*.

Flamsteed, John (1646–1719), the first English astronomer royal, for whom Charles II built an observatory at Greenwich (1675) where he worked for 44 years.

Flaubert, Gustave (1821–80), French novelist, and creator of *Madame Bovary*. His perfection of style was attained through unremitting effort. Other works were *Salammbô*, *L'Education sentimentale*, and *Bouvard et Pécuchet*.

Flaxman, John (1755–1826), English sculptor, b. York, employed as modeller by Josiah Wedgwood. He then took to monumental sculpture.

Flecker, James Elroy (1884–1915), English poet whose works include *Golden Journey to Samarkand*, *Hassan* (staged in London, 1923), and *Don Juan*, as well as many lyrics.

Fleming, Sir Alexander (1881–1955), Scottish bacteriologist who discovered the antibacterial enzyme lysozyme in 1922 and penicillin in 1928. Full recognition came during the war when Florey separated the drug now used for treatment from the original penicillin. Awarded Nobel prize for medicine jointly with Florey and Chain, 1945.

Fleming, Sir Ambrose (1849–1945), British scientist whose invention of the raido valve in 1904 revolutionised radio telegraphy and solved problems of radio-telephony. This eventually made possible high quality sound transmission, and thus led to broadcasting and television.

Fletcher, John (1579–1625), English dramatist who collaborated with Francis Beaumont (*q.v.*) in writing many pieces for the stage.

Flinders, Matthew (1774–1814), English navigator and explorer who made discoveries in and around Australia. He sailed through Bass Strait, so called in honour of his surgeon.

Florey, Baron (Howard Walter Florey) (1898–1968), British pathologist, b. Australia. Shared 1945 Nobel prize with Fleming and Chain for work on penicillin.

Foch, Ferdinand (1851–1929), French general. In the first world war he halted the German advance at the Marne (1914), and was engaged in the battles of Ypres (1914 and 1915) and the Somme (1916). In 1918 he became supreme commander of the British, French, and American armies and dictated the terms of Allied victory.

Fokine, Michel (1880–1944), Russian dancer, choreographer to Diaghilev's company, and creator of *Les Sylphides*, *Prince Igor*, *Scheherazade*, *Firebird*, and *The Spectre of the Rose*.

Fokker, Anthony (1890–1939), Dutch aircraft engineer, b. Java. The Fokker factory in Germany made warplanes for the Germans in the first world war.

Fonteyn, Dame Margot (Mme. Roberto de Arias) (b. 1919), prima ballerina of the Royal Ballet and acclaimed foremost English dancer.

Ford, Henry (1863–1947), founder of Ford Motor Company (1903), of which he was president until 1919, when he was succeeded by his son, Edsel B. Ford (1893–1943). He was the pioneer of the cheap motor car.

Forester, Cecil Scott (b. 1899), English novelist, author of the *Captain Hornblower* series.

Forster, Edward Morgan (1879–1970), English novelist, author of *The Longest Journey*, *A Room with a View*, *Howards End*, *A Passage to India*. O.M. 1969. *See* Section M, Part I.

Foscari, Francesco (*c.* 1372–1457), Doge of Venice and victor over Milan.

Fourier, Charles (1772–1837), French socialist who propounded a system of associated enterprise which although utopian stimulated social reform.

Fourier, Jean Baptiste Joseph (1768–1830), French mathematical physicist. He played an active part in politics, holding administrative posts in Egypt and Isère, yet finding time for his own research, especially on the flow of heat along a conductor.

Fowler, Sir John (1817–98), was the engineer of the first underground railway (the London Metropolitan) and with his partner, Sir Benjamin Baker, of the Forth bridge.

Fox, Charles James (1749–1806), English Whig statesman. Son of the 1st Lord Holland, he entered parliament at 19. He held office only for brief periods between 1770 and 1806, but he upheld the liberal causes of the day (American independence, the French revolution, and parliamentary reform), and was one of the impeachers of Warren Hastings. During a period of war and reaction his leadership inspired younger men.

Fox, George (1624–91), founder of the Society of Friends, son of a weaver of Fenny Drayton, Leicestershire.

Foxe, John (1516–87), English martyrologist, author of *History of the Acts and Monuments of the Church* (better known as *Foxe's Book of Martyrs*).

Frampton, Sir George James (1860–1928), English sculptor of the Peter Pan statue in Kensington Gardens and the Edith Cavell memorial.

France, Anatole (1844–1924), French writer, especially of short stories. Nobel prizewinner 1921.

Francis I (1494–1547), King of France. Brilliant but ambitious and adventurous, he fostered learning and art, and met Henry VIII at the Field of the Cloth of Gold. His rivalry with the Emperor Charles V involved France in prolonged war, especially in Italy (he was captured at Pavia, 1525). He persecuted the Protestants.

Francis of Assisi, St. (1181/2–1226), founder of the Franciscan Order. Son of a wealthy cloth merchant, in 1208 he turned from a life of pleasure to poverty and the complete observance of Christ's teaching. He and his friars went about preaching the gospel by word and example, and the brotherhood increased rapidly. He was said to have received the stigmata (marks of Christ's five wounds) in 1224. His last years were spent in illness. He was canonised in 1228.

Francis, Sir Philip (1740–1818), English politician, reputed author of the *Letters of Junius*.

Franck, César Auguste (1822–90), composer and organist, b. at Liége in Belgium. His music is romantic, mystical, and personal in idiom. Much of his composition is for the organ. *See* Section E.

Franco, Francisco (b. 1892), Spanish general and dictator. He led the Fascist rebellion against the Republican government (1936) and with German and Italian help ended the civil war (1939), since when he has been ruler of Spain.

Franklin, Benjamin (1706–90), American statesman. B. at Boston, he was at first a printer and journalist. He then took an interest in electricity, explained lightning as of electrical origin, and invented the lightning conductor. He was active in promoting the Declaration of Independence in 1773; he negotiated French support; and helped to frame the American constitution.

Franklin, Sir John (1786–1847), English Arctic explorer. His expedition in the *Erebus* and the *Terror* to find the north-west passage ended disastrously, and all attempts to find survivors failed.

Fraunhofer, Joseph von (1787–1826), optical instrument-maker of Munich, the first to map the dark lines of the solar spectrum named after him.

Frazer, Sir James George (1854–1941), Scottish anthropologist, b. Glasgow; author of *The Golden Bough*.

Frederick I (*c.* 1123–90), Holy Roman Emperor, nicknamed Barbarossa. A strong personality, he sought to impose his will on the city-states of northern Italy and the papacy, and was defeated at Legnano in 1176 but was more successful with a conciliatory policy (1183). He had also to contend with opposition at home. He died on the third crusade.

Frederick II (1194–1250), Holy Roman Emperor, grandson of the above, and son of the heiress of Sicily. Brilliant and enlightened, he attracted to his court in Sicily Jewish, Mohammedan, and Christian scholars; founded the university of Naples; was a patron of the medical school of Salerno; wrote a treatise on falconry; and commissioned a code of laws. Politically he was less successful, having trouble with the Lombard cities, and being involved with the papacy especially as regards his delay in going on crusade; but after negotiations with the sultan of Egypt he actually was crowned king of Jerusalem.

Frederick II (the Great) (1712–86), King of Prussia. Having inherited from his father a well-drilled army, in 1740 he seized Silesia from Austria, and retained it through the resulting war and the Seven Years war. He also took part in the partition of Poland. An able administrator and an outstanding general, he made Prussia powerful and strengthened its military tradition. He corresponded with Voltaire and he also played the flute.

Freud, Sigmund (1856–1939), psychiatrist and founder of psychoanalysis; b. Moravia, studied medicine in Vienna, where he lived until 1938 when the Nazi invasion of Austria sent him into exile in London where he died. His theories of the mind, based on years of investigation, illumined the way we think about ourselves, and had immense influence upon modern thought. *See* Psychoanalysis, Section J.

French, Sir John, 1st Earl of Ypres (1852–1925), first British commander-in-chief in the first world war; replaced by Sir Douglas Haig in 1915.

Friese-Greene, William (1855–1921), English inventor of the cinematograph. His first film was shown in 1890. He died in poverty.

Frobisher, Sir Martin (1535–94), first British navigator to seek the north-west passage from the Atlantic to the Pacific through the Arctic seas. He is commemorated in Frobisher's Strait. He also fought against the Spanish Armada.

Froebel, Friedrich Wilhelm August (1782–1852), German educational reformer, founder of the Kindergarten system.

Froissart, Jean (1337–1410), French author of *Chronicles* covering the history of Western Europe from 1307 to 1400, one of the chief sources for the history of the first half of the Hundred Years war.

Frost, Robert (1874–1963), American poet, author of *Stopping by Woods on a Snowy Evening, Birches, The Death of the Hired Man, After Apple-Picking.*

Froude, James Anthony (1818–94), English historian and biographer of Carlyle.

Fry, Christopher (b. 1907), English poet and dramatist of Quaker family; author of *The Lady's Not for Burning, Venus Observed,* and *The Dark is Light Enough. See* Section I.

Fry, Elizabeth (1780–1845), English prison reformer. She lived at Norwich and belonged to the Society of Friends.

Fry, Roger (1866–1934), English art critic and painter; introduced the work of Cézanne and the post-impressionists in England; author of *Vision and Design.*

Fuchs, Leonard (1501–66), German naturalist whose compendium of medicinal plants was for long a standard work. He was professor of medicine at Tübingen and the genus *Fuchsia* is named after him.

Fuchs, Sir Vivian Ernest (b. 1908), British geologist and explorer; leader of the British Commonwealth Trans-Antarctic Expedition 1957–8, the first to cross the Antarctic continent.

Fuller, Thomas (1608–61), English antiquarian and divine, author of *Worthies of England* and a *Church History of Britain.*

Fulton, Robert (1765–1815), American engineer who experimented in the application of steam to navigation, and in 1807 launched the *Clermont* on the Hudson.

Furniss, Harry (1854–1925), caricaturist, b. Wexford. He came to London as a young man, served on the staff of *Punch* and illustrated the works of Dickens and Thackeray.

G

Gade, Niels Vilhelm (1817–90), Danish composer. While studying at Leipzig he met Mendelssohn, whom he succeeded as conductor of the Gewandhaus orchestra.

Gagarin, Yuri Alexeyevich (1934–68), Soviet cosmonaut, the first man to be launched into space and brought safely back (12 April 1961). His flight was made in the front portion of a multi-

stage rocket which made a single circuit of the earth in 108 min. Later he was killed in an air crash.

Gainsborough, Thomas (1727–88), English landscape and portrait painter, b. at Sudbury in Suffolk. His portraits are marked by informality and grace; examples are in the Tate Gallery.

Gaiseric or Genseric (c. 390–477), king of the Vandals, the ablest of the barbarian invaders of the Roman empire. He led his people from Spain into Africa, took Carthage, gained control of the Mediterranean by his pirate fleets, and sacked Rome in 455. He was a bigoted Arian.

Gaitskell, Hugh Todd Naylor (1906–63), Labour politician and economist. He wrote *Money and Everyday Life* (1939). He represented Leeds South from 1945; was chancellor of the exchequer 1950–1; and leader of the Labour opposition 1955–63.

Galbraith, John Kenneth (b. 1908), American university professor of economics, b. Canada; author of *The Affluent Society* (1958), *The Liberal Hour* (1960), *The New Industrial State* (1967). He was ambassador to India 1961–3.

Galdós, Benito Pérez. *See* Pérez Galdós.

Galen, Claudius (131–201), physician, b. Pergamum (Asia Minor) of Greek parents. He systematised medical knowledge with his idea of purposive creation by the will of God; and thus discouraged original investigation. Many of his treatises survive, and his influence lasted for more than a thousand years.

Galileo (1564–1642), Italian scientist whose experimental-mathematical methods in the pursuit of scientific truth laid the foundations of modern science. He became professor of mathematics at Pisa university when he was 25 and lectured at Padua for 18 years. He made a number of fundamental discoveries, *e.g.*, in regard to the hydrostatic balance, thermometer, magnet, telescope, and foreshadowed Newton's laws of motion. He detected the four major satellites of Jupiter, the ring of Saturn, and the spots of the sun. He proved the superiority of the Copernican over the Ptolemaic theory, and was imprisoned for so doing. He died the year Newton was born.

Galsworthy, John (1867–1933), English novelist and playwright, author of a series of novels dealing with the history of an upper middle-class family. Nobel prizewinner 1932.

Galton, Sir Francis (1822–1911), founder of eugenics, cousin of Darwin. His early work, *Meteorographica* (1863), contains the basis of the modern weather chart. He also devised finger-print identification, and was one of the first to apply mathematics to biological problems.

Galvani, Luigi (1737–98), Italian physician and physiologist, whose experiments at Bologna demonstrated the principle of animal electricity.

Gama, Vasco da (c. 1460–1524), Portuguese navigator who discovered the sea route to India in 1498 by doubling the Cape of Good Hope.

Gandhi, Indira (b. 1917), daughter of Nehru, succeeded Shastri in 1966 to become India's first woman prime minister.

Gandhi, Mohandas Kamamchand (Mahatma) (1869–1948), Indian patriot, social reformer and moral teacher. From 1893 to 1914 he lived in South Africa opposing discrimination against Indians. In the movement for Indian independence after 1914 he dominated Congress, instituted civil disobedience, and advocated non-violence; and he sought to free India from caste. After independence he strove to promote the co-operation of all Indians but was assassinated on his way to a prayer meeting. His teaching of non-violence has had influence outside India.

Garbo, Greta (b. 1905), Swedish film actress of poetical quality. Her films included *Queen Christina* and *Ninotchka.*

Garcia, Manuel de Popolo Vicente (1775–1832), Spanish tenor, composer, and singing master. His son **Manuel Patricio Rodriguez** (1805–1906) was tutor to Jenny Lind. Both his daughters (Mme. Malibran and Mme. Viardot) were operatic singers, and his grandson and great-grandson baritones.

Garcia Lorca, Federico. *See* Lorca.

Gardiner, Samuel Rawson (1829–1902), English historian of the Stuart period.

Garibaldi, Giuseppe (1807–82), Italian soldier and patriot, who with Mazzini and Cavour created a united Italy. In 1834 he was condemned to death for helping in a republican plot to seize Genoa, but escaped to S. America. He returned in 1848 to fight for Mazzini but was again forced to flee. In 1851 he returned and gave his support to Cavour, taking part in the Austrian war of 1859. In 1860 with a thousand volunteers he freed Sicily, took Naples, and handed over the Two Sicilies to Victor Emmanuel who was proclaimed king.

Garrick, David (1717–79), English actor and theatrical manager. Brought up at Lichfield, he was taught by Samuel Johnson. He became a highly successful and versatile actor.

Garrison, William Lloyd (1805–79), American philanthropist who worked for the abolition of slavery.

Gaskell, Mrs. Elizabeth Cleghorn (1810–65), English novelist, author of *Mary Barton*, *Cranford*, and a *Life of Charlotte Brontë*.

Gaulle, Charles de (1890–1970), French general and statesman, son of a headmaster of a Jesuit school; first president of the Fifth Republic 1959–69. He fought in the first world war until his capture in 1916. In the second world war he refused to surrender (1940) and raised and led the Free French forces, with headquarters in England. He came to political power in 1958; allowed Algerian independence in 1962 in face of an army and civilian revolt, initiated closer ties with West Germany (Franco-German treaty 1963), recognised Communist China, withdrew from NATO, building his own nuclear force, vetoed Britain's entry into the Common Market (1963 and 1967); and based his government on personal prestige and use of the referendum in place of parliamentary approval. He was taken by surprise by the rising of students and workers in 1968 and resigned after losing the referendum in 1969. He lived to complete only the first volume of his memoirs.

Gauss, Karl Friedrich (1777–1855), German mathematician. He spent most of his life at the university of Göttingen where he set up the first special observatory for terrestrial magnetism. He made major contributions to astronomy, mathematics, and physics. The unit of magnetic induction is named after him.

Gautama, Siddhartha (Buddha, the enlightened) (c. 563–c. 483 B.C.). B. near Benares, a rajah's son, he gave himself up to the religious life and attracted many disciples. Concerned with man's sorrow and suffering, he planned a movement which could be universally shared, in which kindness to others, including animals, took a leading part. His teaching is summarised in the "four noble truths" and the "eightfold path" (see Buddhism, Section J). After his death his teaching spread (with the help of the King Asoka) over much of India and through eastern Asia as far as Japan, and developed varying schools of thought. Buddhism is tolerant and also maintains that the good of the part is that of the whole; hence it is wrong to harm another or take life.

Gautier, Théophile (1811–72), French poet and novelist, author of *Mademoiselle de Maupin*.

Gay, John (1685–1732), English poet, author of *The Beggar's Opera* (set to music by Pepusch) and *Polly*.

Gay-Lussac, Joseph Louis (1778–1850), French chemist, who showed that when gases combine their relative volumes bear a simple numerical relation to each other and to the volume of their product, if gaseous (1808), e.g., one volume of oxygen combines with two volumes of hydrogen to form two volumes of water vapour.

Ged, William (1690–1749), Scottish printer who patented stereotyping.

Geddes, Sir Patrick (1854–1932), Scottish biologist and a pioneer in town and regional planning, who invented the term conurbation.

Geikie, Sir Archibald (1835–1924), Scottish geologist. His brother James specialised in glacial geology.

Genghiz Khan (1162–1227), Mongol conqueror. After years of struggle to make good his succession to his father, he overran the greater part of Asia bringing devastation wherever he went.

Geoffrey of Monmouth (1100–54), chronicler, b. Monmouth, later bishop of St. Asaph. His chronicle drew on his creative imagination.

George I (1660–1727), became King of Great Britain in 1714 as descendant of James I. His chief minister was Sir Robert Walpole. Himself personally undistinguished, his reign saw political development; and in spite of the Jacobite threat (rising in 1715) it began a period of dynastic stability.

George II (1685–1760), son of the above, succeeded in 1727, and survived a more serious Jacobite rising in 1745. His long reign helped the development of constitutional government, for he kept within the limitations of his powers and capacity; and it saw the extension of English power in India and North America.

George III (1738–1820), grandson of George II, reigned 1760–1820. Sincere and well-intentioned, but not politically able, he suffered from mental illness due to intermittent porphyria. His reign saw a clash with John Wilkes, the rise of Methodism, and agrarian and industrial revolution; also the loss of the American colonies, the extension and the questioning of English power in India (Warren Hastings), and prolonged French wars.

George IV (1762–1830), eldest son of George III, reigned 1820–30, having become Prince Regent in 1812. Styled "the first gentleman of Europe," he is remembered for his interest in art and architecture. His married life was unfortunate, and the monarchy was at a low ebb; while his reign was a time of distress and of demand for reform.

George V (1865–1936), was the second son of Edward VII and Queen Alexandra, but became heir to the English throne on the death of his elder brother in 1892. He joined the Navy as a cadet in 1877. In 1893 he married Princess Mary of Teck. He succeeded in 1910 and discharged his office conscientiously. In 1931 he began the royal broadcast on Christmas Day and in 1935 celebrated his silver jubilee. His reign included the Kaiser's war, the emergence of the Irish Free State, and the first Labour government.

George VI (1895–1952), second son of George V, was called to the throne in 1936 on the abdication of his elder brother, Edward VIII. His personal qualities gained wide respect. His reign was marked by Hitler's war and rapid social change.

George, Henry (1839–97), American political economist whose " single tax " on land values as a means of solving economic problems is expounded in his *Progress and Poverty* (1879).

George St., patron saint of England, adopted by Edward III. He is believed to have been martyred by Diocletian at Nicomedia in 303 (and not, as believed by Gibbon, to be confused with George of Cappadocia). The story of his fight with the dragon is of late date.

Gershwin, George (1898–1937), American jazz pianist and song-writer, composer of *Rhapsody in Blue* and the Negro folk-opera *Porgy and Bess*.

Gesner, Conrad (1516–65), Swiss naturalist, b. Zurich. In a series of magnificently illustrated volumes he gave a complete description of the animal and vegetable kingdoms.

Ghiberti, Lorenzo (1378–1455), Florentine sculptor whose bronze doors, beautifying the baptistery in Florence, were described by Michelangelo as fit for the gates of paradise.

Ghirlandaio, Domenico (1449–94), Florentine painter. Most of his frescoes are in Florence, including the cycle of the life of the Virgin and the Baptist in S. Maria Novella. Michelangelo began his apprenticeship in his workshop.

Giacometti, Alberto (1901–66), Swiss sculptor and painter, who worked mainly in Paris and produced abstract symbolic constructions.

Gibbon, Edward (1737–94), English historian of the *Decline and Fall of the Roman Empire*.

Gibbons, Grinling (1648–1720), English wood-carver and sculptor, b. Rotterdam, was brought to the notice of Charles II by Evelyn, the diarist. The choir stalls of St. Paul's and the carving in the Wren library at Trinity College, Cambridge, are his work.

Gibbons, Orlando (1583–1625), English composer

of church music, organist at the chapel royal. See also **Section E.**

Gide, André (1869–1951), French writer of many short novels in which he gives expression to his struggle to escape from his protestant upbringing (*Strait is the Gate, The Counterfeiters*). In his memoir *Si le grain ne meurt* he tells the story of his life up to his marriage. The narratives of his journeys in Africa led to a reform in French colonial policy. Nobel prizewinner 1947.

Gielgud, Sir John (b. 1904), English actor and producer, member of the Terry family, to whom the present popularity of Shakespeare is largely due. See **Section I, Part I.**

Gigli, Beniamino (1890–1957), Italian operatic tenor.

Gilbert, Sir Alfred (1854–1934), English sculptor and goldsmith. His sculptures include *Eros* in Piccadilly Circus.

Gilbert, Sir Humphrey (1537–83), English navigator. He was knighted by Queen Elizabeth for service in Ireland. In 1583 he discovered Newfoundland, but was drowned the same year.

Gilbert, William (1540–1603), English physician to Queen Elizabeth. His book *On the Magnet*, published in Latin in 1600, was the first major original contribution to science published in England.

Gilbert, Sir William Schwenck (1836–1911), English humorist and librettist of the Gilbert and Sullivan light operas. First known as author of the *Bab Ballads*, from 1871 he collaborated with Sir Arthur Sullivan, his wit and satire finding appropriate accompaniment in Sullivan's music. Their operas include *H.M.S. Pinafore, Patience, Iolanthe, The Mikado, The Gondoliers*, and *The Yeoman of the Guard*.

Gill, Eric (1881–1940), English sculptor and engraver, whose works include the *Stations of the Cross* (Westminster Cathedral), *Prospero and Ariel* (Broadcasting House), *Christ Driving the Money-changers from the Temple* (Leeds University). He also worked as a designer for printing (Gill Sans type). and the George VI stamps were his designs.

Gillray, James (1757–1815), English caricaturist who produced upwards of a thousand political cartoons.

Giotto di Bondone (1267–1337), Florentine artist. A pupil of Cimabue, he continued the development away from Byzantine tradition towards greater naturalism. His frescoes survive in the churches of Assisi, Padua, and Florence. He designed the western front of the cathedral at Florence and the campanile.

Gissing, George Robert (1857–1903), English novelist whose works deal with the degrading effect of poverty. The best known is *New Grub Street.*

Giulio Romano or Giulio Pippi (*c.* 1492–1546), Italian artist, was a pupil of Raphael. He was also an engineer and architect.

Gladstone, William Ewart (1809–98), English Liberal statesman. B. at Liverpool, he entered parliament in 1832 as a Tory and held office under Peel. From 1852 he served several terms as chancellor of the exchequer and was Liberal prime minister 1868–74, when his legislation included the education act of 1870, the ballot act, the disestablishment of the Church of Ireland and an Irish land act. In 1874 when Disraeli came to power, he temporarily withdrew, but made a come-back in 1876 with his Mid-Lothian campaign. He was again prime minister 1880–5, 1886 and 1892–4; he carried a parliamentary reform act, and advocated home rule for Ireland but was not able to carry it. His long life was one of moral stature and increasing advocacy of liberal causes. He was also a classical scholar and a writer on church matters.

Glazunov, Alexander Constantinovich (1865–1936), Russian composer, pupil of Rimsky-Korsakov. The first of his eight symphonies was composed when he was 16.

Glendower, Owen (*c.* 1350–*c.* 1416), Welsh chief, who conducted guerrilla warfare on the English border, and figures in Shakespeare's *Henry IV.*

Glinka, Mikhail Ivanovich (1804–57), Russian composer, first of the national school, best known for his operas, *A Life for the Tsar*, and

Russlan and Ludmilla, based on a poem by Pushkin. See **Section E.**

Gluck, Christoph Wilibald (1714–87), German composer, important in the development of opera. He studied in Prague, Vienna and Italy, and his first operas were in the Italian tradition; but with *Orfeo ed Euridice* (1762) his style became more dramatic. There followed *Alceste, Armide*, and *Iphigénie en Tauride* (his best-known work). See **Section E.**

Goddard, Baron (Rayner Goddard) (b. 1877), Lord Chief Justice of England, 1946–58.

Godfrey of Bouillon (*c.* 1061–1100), Crusader on the first crusade, was proclaimed King of Jerusalem, but declined the title for that of Protector of the Holy Sepulchre.

Godiva, Lady (1040–80), English benefactress. According to tradition, she obtained from her husband Leofric, Earl of Chester, concessions for the people of Coventry by riding naked through the town.

Godwin, Earl of the West Saxons (d. 1053), was the father of Edith, wife of King Edward the Confessor, and of Harold, last Saxon king.

Godwin, William (1756–1836), English political writer and philosoper, author of *Political Justice* (which criticised many contemporary institutions) and a novel *Caleb Williams*. He married Mary Wollstonecraft (1759–97), author of *A Vindication of the Rights of Women*; and their daughter, Mary Wollstonecraft Godwin (1797–1851) wrote *Frankenstein* and married Shelley.

Goethe, Johann Wolfgang von (1749–1832), German poet and thinker. B. at Frankfurt-on-Main, his first notable work was a romantic play, *Götz von Berlichingen*, followed by a novel *Werthers Leiden*. In 1776 he became privy councillor to the Duke of Weimar, whom he served for many years. He had wide-ranging interests, and made discoveries in anatomy and in botany. Among his later writings are the play *Iphigénie* and the novel *Wilhelm Meister*, and he wrote many lyrics. His best-known work however is *Faust*, which was composed over many years; its theme is man's search for happiness. In later life he was a friend of Schiller.

Gogol, Nikolai Vasilievich (1809–52), Russian novelist and dramatist. His comedy, *The Government Inspector*, satirised provincial bureaucracy; and his novel, *Dead Souls*, deals with malpractice in the supposed purchase of dead serfs.

Goldsmith, Oliver (1728–74), Irish poet, dramatist and novelist. The son of a poor curate, he came to London in 1756, and eventually joined the circle of Dr. Johnson. He is best known for his novel *The Vicar of Wakefield* and his play *She Stoops to Conquer.*

Goncourt, Edmond Louis Antoine Huot de (1822–96) and **Jules Alfred Huot de** (1830–70), French brothers, remembered for their *Journal des Goncourts*, an intimate account of Parisian society spanning 40 years, and of documentary interest.

Góngora y Argote, Luis de (1561–1627), Spanish poet, b. Cordova. In *Polifemo* and *Soledades* he attempted to express the core of poetry in new experimental forms.

Goodyear, Charles (1800–60), American inventor who discovered the art of vulcanising rubber.

Goossens, Sir Eugene (1893–1962), English conductor and composer of Belgian descent. His compositions include the operas *Judith* and *Don Juan de Mañara*; brother of Léon, oboe virtuoso, and of Sidonie and Marie Goossens, harpists.

Gordon, Charles George (1833–85), Scottish soldier. After service in the Crimea and China, in 1873 he was made governor of the Equatorial provinces of Egypt; and he was a notable governor of the Sudan, 1877–80. When a rising was led by the Mahdi, he was sent out in 1884 to the garrisons in rebel territory and was killed at Khartoum.

Gordon, Lord George (1751–93), agitator, led No-Popery riots in London in 1780.

Gorky, Maxim (Alexey Maximovich Peshkov) (1868–1936), Russian writer. From the age of ten he worked at many trades from scullion on a Volga steamboat to railway guard, while learning to write; see *My Childhood*. His early work was romantic. He spent many

B28

years abroad, but returned in 1928, a supporter of the Soviet regime. His later work is marked by social realism.

Gorton, John Gray (b. 1912), leader of Australian Liberal Party and prime minister 1968–71.

Gosse, Sir Edmund (1849–1928), English poet and critic, known for his literary studies of the 17th and 18th centuries; and for his memoir *Father and Son*.

Gounod, Charles François (1818–93), French composer, known for his operas *Faust* and *Roméo et Juliette*, though his lyrical gifts are shown in earlier works, such as *Le Médicin malgré lui* and *Mireille*.

Gower, John (1325–1408), English poet of the time of Chaucer, author of *Confessio Amantis*.

Goya y Lucientes, Francisco José (1746–1828), Spanish painter and etcher. His portraits are characterised by ruthless realism, and his etchings in the *Horrors of War* by hatred of cruelty and reaction. His frescoes are to be found in Madrid and at Saragossa. Examples of his work are in the National Gallery.

Grace, William Gilbert (1848–1915), English cricketer who scored 54,896 runs, including 126 centuries, and took 2,876 wickets. Scored 1,000 runs in May 1895; and three times made over 300 runs in an innings.

Grahame, Kenneth (1859–1932), Scottish writer of books for children, including *The Golden Age*, *Dream Days*, and *Wind in the Willows*.

Grahame-White, Claude (1879–1959), aviator and engineer, the first Englishman to gain an aviator's certificate, 1909.

Grant, Ulysses Simpson (1822–85), American general of the civil war, and president of the United States from 1869 to 1876.

Granville-Barker, Harley (1877–1946), English dramatist, actor, and producer, who promoted the plays of Ibsen, Shaw, and other serious writers. His own works include *The Voysey Inheritance*.

Grattan, Henry (1746–1820), Irish statesman, who struggled for Irish legislative independence and for Catholic emancipation (though himself a Protestant) and parliamentary reform; but unsuccessfully.

Graves, Robert Ranke (b. 1895), English writer, author of *Goodbye to All That*, written after the first world war; and of *I Claudius* and *Claudius the God*; besides poetry.

Gray, Thomas (1716–71), English poet, author of *Elegy written in a Country Churchyard* and *Ode on a Distant Prospect of Eton College*.

Greeley, Horace (1811–72), American newspaper editor, founder of the New York *Tribune* (1841).

Green, John Richard (1837–83), English historian, author of *Short History of the English People*.

Greenaway, Kate (1846–1901), English artist of children, especially for book illustrations.

Greene, Graham (b. 1904), English novelist and journalist, whose novels (*The Heart of the Matter*, *Brighton Rock*, *The Quiet American*, *Our Man in Havana*, *A Burnt-out Case*), like his plays (*The Complaisant Lover*) and films (*Fallen Idol*, *The Third Man*) deal with moral problems in a modern setting from a Catholic standpoint. *See also* Section M, Part I.

Gregory, St. (c. 240–332), converted King Tiridates of Armenia and was thus founder of the Armenian church.

Gregory I (the Great), St. (c. 540–604), Pope 590–604, was the last great Latin Father and the forerunner of scholasticism. The main founder of the temporal power and the political influence of the papacy, he also maintained the spiritual claims of Rome, enforcing discipline, encouraging monasticism, defining doctrine, and adding to the music, liturgy, and canons of the Church. It was he who sent Augustine on a mission to England.

Gregory VII (Hildebrand) (c. 1020–85), Pope 1073–85. He strove for papal omnipotence within the church and for a high standard in the priesthood (especially by stamping out simony and clerical marriage). He also upheld the papacy against the Holy Roman Empire, and the emperor Henry IV did penance for three days in the snow at Canossa; but he had not quite the vision of Gregory I of an ideal theocracy embracing all states.

Gregory XIII (1502–85), Pope 1572–85; introduced the Gregorian calendar.

Gregory, James (1638–75), Scottish mathematician. He invented a reflecting telescope and was the first to show how the distance of the sun could be deduced by observations of the passage of Venus across the disc of the sun. Successive generations of the family reached distinction.

Grenville, Sir Richard (1541–91), English sea captain, who with his one ship engaged a fleet of Spanish war vessels off Flores in 1591, an exploit celebrated in Tennyson's ballad *The Revenge*.

Gresham, Sir Thomas (1519–79), English financier and founder of the Royal Exchange. Son of a Lord Mayor of London, he was an astute moneyfinder for four successive sovereigns, including Queen Elizabeth I. " Gresham's Law " is the statement that bad money drives out good.

Greuze, Jean Baptiste (1725–1805), French artist, known especially for his studies of girls. His *Girl with Doves* is in the Wallace Collection.

Grey, 2nd Earl (Charles Grey) (1764–1845), British Whig statesman under whose premiership were passed the Reform Bill of 1832, a bill abolishing slavery throughout the British Empire (1833), and the Poor Law Amendment Act, 1834.

Grey, Lady Jane (1537–54), Queen of England for a few days. The daughter of the Duke of Suffolk, she was put forward as queen by Protestant leaders on the death of her cousin, Edward VI; but overcome by the legal claimant, Mary Tudor, and executed.

Grieg, Edvard Hagerup (1843–1907), Norwegian composer, b. Bergen. He presented the characteristics of his country's music with strong accentuation. He is best known for his incidental music to *Peer Gynt*.

Griffin, Bernard William (1899–1956), Roman catholic archbishop of Westminster from 1944 until his death.

Griffith, Arthur (1872–1922), the first president of the Irish Free State, 1921; founder of the *Sinn Fein* movement.

Griffith, David Wark (1880–1948), American film producer, who introduced the close-up, the flash-back, and developed leading actors. His films include *Birth of a Nation*, and *Broken Blossoms*.

Grimm, the brothers Jakob Ludwig Karl (1785–1863), and **Wilhelm Karl** (1786–1859), German philologists and folk-lorists, best known for their *Fairy Tales*. Jakob published a notable philological dictionary, *Deutsche Grammatik*. The brothers also projected the vast *Deutsches Wörterbuch* which was completed by German scholars in 1961.

Grimthorpe, 1st Baron (Edmund Beckett Denison) (1816–1905), horologist who invented the double three-legged escapement for Big Ben (1854). For long known as Sir Edmund Beckett.

Gromyko, Andrei Andreevich (b. 1908), Russian diplomat who has served as foreign minister since 1957. He was ambassador to Britain 1952–3.

Grossmith, George (1847–1912), English actor. With his brother, Weedon Grossmith, he wrote *Diary of a Nobody*. His son, George Grossmith (1874–1935) was a comedian and introduced revue and cabaret entertainment into England.

Grote, George (1794–1871), English historian, author of a *History of Greece*.

Grotius (Huig van Groot) (1583–1645), Dutch jurist, the founder of international law. He was condemned to life imprisonment for religious reasons, but escaped to Paris, where he wrote *De Jure Belli et Pacis*.

Grouchy, Emmanuel, Marquis de (1766–1847), French general, who served under Napoleon; and after Waterloo led the defeated army back to Paris.

Grove, Sir George (1820–1900), English musicologist, author of *Dictionary of Music and Musicians*. By profession he was a civil engineer.

Guedalla, Philip (1889–1944), English historian, author of *The Second Empire*, *Palmertson*, and *The Hundred Days*.

Guevara, Ernesto " Che " (1928–67), revolutionary hero, b. Argentina. He took part in the Cuban guerrilla war and became a minister in the Cuban government 1959–65. He was killed while leading a band of guerrillas against American-trained Bolivian troops. (" Che " is Argentine for " chum ".)

Guido Reni (1575–1642), Italian painter of the Bolognese school whose works are characteristic of the Italian baroque of his period and include the *Aurora* fresco in the Rospigliosi palace at Rome, and *Crucifixion of St. Peter* (Vatican).

Gustavus Adolphus (1594–1632), King of Sweden, the " Lion of the North." After a campaign in Poland he entered the Thirty Years' war in support of Swedish interests and Protestant distress, won the battle of Breitenfeld in 1631 and was killed in action the next year.

Gutenberg, Johann (*c.* 1400–68), German printer, b. Mainz, the first European to print with movable types cast in moulds. The earliest book printed by him was the Mazarin Bible (*see* L76).

Guy, Thomas (1644–1724), English philanthropist. A printer, he made money by speculation; and in 1722 founded Guy's Hospital in Southwark.

Gwynne, Nell (*c.* 1650–87), mistress of Charles II of England. Of Hereford origin, she sold oranges in London and became a comedienne at Drury Lane.

H

Haakon VII (1872–1957), King of Norway, was a Danish prince and elected on the separation of Norway from Sweden in 1905. He resisted the Nazi occupation.

Hadley, George (1685–1768). He developed Halley's theory of the trade winds by taking into account the effect of the earth's rotation and the displacement of air by tropical heat (1735).

Hadrian (76–138), Roman emperor. An able general, he suppressed revolts, and he was also a lover of the arts. He visited Britain and in A.D. 121 built a wall to protect it from the Picts and Scots.

Hafiz, pseudonym of Shams ad-Din Mohammed (d. *c.* 1388), Persian lyrical poet. His principal work is the *Divan*, a collection of short sonnets called *ghazals*. The sobriquet *Hafiz*, meaning one who remembers, is applied to anyone who has learned the Koran by heart.

Hahn, Otto (1879–1968), German chemist and physicist, chief discoverer of uranium fission, the phenomenon on which nuclear power and the atom bomb are based.

Hahnemann, Samuel Christian Friedrich (1755–1843), German physician who founded homoeopathy (treatment of disease by small doses of drugs that in health produce similar symptoms).

Haig, Douglas, 1st Earl of Bermersyde (1861–1928), British field-marshal, b. Edinburgh. He replaced French as commander-in-chief in France, 1915–19, leading the offensive in August 1918; and after the war presided over the British Legion.

Haile Selasse I (b. 1891), Emperor of Ethiopia since 1930. He spent the years of the Italian occupation 1936–41 in England.

Hakluyt, Richard (1553–1616), English writer on maritime discovery. B. in Herefordshire, he spent some time in Paris. From 1582 (when *Divers Voyages* appeared), he devoted his life to collection and publishing accounts of English navigators, thus giving further impetus to discovery.

Haldane, John Burdon Sanderson (1892–1964), biologist and geneticist, noted not only for his work in mathematical evolutionary theory but for explaining science to the layman. He emigrated to India in 1957. He was the son of John Scott Haldane (1860–1936), b. Edinburgh, who studied the effect of industrial occupations upon health.

Haldane, 1st Viscount (Richard Burdon Haldane) (1856–1928), British Liberal statesman. As war minister in 1905 he reorganised the army and founded the Territorials.

Halévy, Ludovic (1834–1903) French playwright, who collaborated with Henri Meilhac in writing libretti for Offenbach and Bizet.

Halifax, 1st Earl of (Edward Frederick Lindley Wood) (1881–1959), British Conservative politician; foreign secretary during the period of appeasement of Germany; as Lord Irwin, viceroy of India 1926–31.

Halifax, 1st Marquess of (George Savile) (1633–95),

English politician of changeable views, who wrote *Character of a Trimmer*.

Hallam, Henry (1777–1859), English historian, best known for his *Constitutional History*. He was father of Arthur Hallam, friend of Tennyson.

Hallé, Sir Charles (1819–95), German-born pianist and conductor, who settled in Manchester and organised an orchestra of high-class talent. He married the violinist Wilhelmine Neruda.

Halley, Edmond (1656–1742), English astronomer royal 1720–42. He published observations on the planets and comets, being the first to predict the return of a comet (*see* L26). He furthered Newton's work on gravitation, setting aside his own researches. He made the first magnetic survey of the oceans from the naval vessel *Paramour*, 1698–1700. His meteorological observations led to his publication of the first map of the winds of the globe (1686).

Hale, George Ellery (1868–1935), American astronomer, after whom is named the 200-inch reflecting telescope on Mount Palomar.

Hals, Frans (*c.* 1580–1666), Dutch portrait painter, b. at Mechlin. He is best known for his *Laughing Cavalier* in the Wallace Collection, and for other portraits in the Louvre and at Amsterdam.

Hamilton, Alexander (1755–1804), American statesman and economist. With Madison and Jay he wrote the *Federalist* (1787). As secretary of the Treasury (1789–95) he put Washington's government on a firm financial footing and planned a national bank. He was the leader of the federalists, a party hostile to Jefferson. He was killed in a duel.

Hamilton, Emma, Lady (*née* Lyon) (*c.* 1765–1815), a beauty of humble birth who, after several liaisons, was married in 1791 to Sir William Hamilton, British ambassador at Naples. There she met Nelson, and later bore him a child, Horatia.

Hammarskjöld, Dag (1905–61), world statesman. After an academic and political career in Sweden, in 1953 he became secretary-general of the United Nations, and aimed at extending its influence for peace, especially by initiating a U.N. emergency force in the Middle East. He was killed in an air crash while attempting to mediate in a dispute between the Congo and the secessionist province of Katanga. Posthumous Nobel peace prize.

Hammond, John Lawrence (1872–1949), English historian of social and industrial history, whose works (with his wife Barbara) include *The Town Labourer* and *The Village Labourer*.

Hampden, John (1594–1643), English parliamentarian and civil war leader. He refused to pay Charles I's illegal ship money in 1636. When civil war broke out, he raised a regiment and was killed on Chalgrove Field.

Hamsun, Knut, pen-name of Knut Pedersen (1859–1952), Norwegian author who in his youth struggled for existence, visited America twice and earned his living by casual labour. His *Markens Gröde* (Growth of the Soil) gained him the Nobel prize in 1920.

Handel, George Frederick (1685–1759), German composer, son of a barber-surgeon to the Duke of Saxony; born the same year as Bach. He spent much of his life in England composing operas and oratorios. His operas, of which there are over 40, include *Atalanta*, *Berenice* and *Serse*, and his oratorios, of which there are 32, include *Saul*, *Israel in Egypt*, *Samson*, *Messiah*, *Judas Maccabaeus*, and *Jehptha*. Eight years before he died he became blind and relied upon his old friend and copyist John Christopher Smith to commit his music to paper. *See* **Section E.**

Hannibal (247–182 B.C.), Carthaginian general. He fought two wars against Rome. In the first he conquered southern Spain. In the second he overran Gaul, crossed the Alps, and defeated the Romans in successive battles, especially at Cannae. Thereafter his forces were worn down by Roman delaying tactics; he was defeated by Scipio at Zama and later poisoned himself.

Harcourt, Sir William Vernon (1827–1904), Liberal politician who revised death duties.

Hardicanute (1019–42), son of Canute, and last Danish king of England.

Hardie, James Keir (1856–1915), Scottish Labour leader, one of the founders of the Labour party.

He first worked in a coal-pit; in 1882 became a journalist; and in 1892 was the first socialist to be elected to the House of Commons (for West Ham – South). He edited the *Labour Leader* 1887–1904. He was the first chairman of the parliamentary Labour party, 1906. A pacifist, he opposed the Boer war.

Hardy, Thomas (1840–1928), English novelist and poet, was trained as an architect and practised for some time, but became known in 1871 with *Desperate Remedies*. In 1874 his *Far from the Madding Crowd* was published. Following that came a series of novels, including *The Trumpet Major*, *The Mayor of Casterbridge*, *Tess of the D'Urbervilles*, and *Jude the Obscure*. In 1908 he completed a dramatic poem, *The Dynasts*, whose central figure is Napoleon. His underlying theme is man's struggle against neutral forces, and he depicts the Wessex countryside.

Hargreaves, James (1720–78), English inventor, b. Blackburn. His spinning-jenny was invented in 1764 and became widely used, though his own was broken by spinners in 1768 and his invention brought him no profit.

Harkness, Edward Stephen (1874–1940), American banker and philanthropist, who in 1930 founded the Pilgrim Trust in Gt. Britain.

Harley, Robert, 1st Earl of Oxford and Mortimer (1661–1724), English statesman and collector of MSS. He held office under Queen Anne, and brought a European war to an end with the treaty of Utrecht. After the Hanoverian succession he lived in retirement, and formed the MSS. collection, now in the British Museum, which bears his name.

Harold II (1022–66), last Saxon king of England, was son of Earl Godwin. He was chosen king in succession to Edward the Confessor. He had at once to meet a dual invasion. He defeated the Norwegian king at Stamford Bridge; but was himself defeated and killed at Hastings by William the Conqueror of Normandy.

Harriman, William Averell (b. 1891), American public official. He was adviser to President Roosevelt and later presidents especially on Marshall Aid and in connection with foreign affairs generally.

Harris, Joel Chandler (1848–1908), American author, creator of Uncle Remus and Brer Rabbit in Negro folk-tales.

Harrison, Frederic (1831–1923), English philosopher and lawyer, author of *The Meaning of History* and *The Philosophy of Common Sense.* He was president of the Positivist committee. *See* Positivism, Section J.

Harrison, John (1692–1776)—" Longitude Harrison," English inventor of the chronometer. It was however too complicated for maritime use and was simplified by others, taking its present form in 1785.

Harte, Francis Bret (1839–1902), American author, who wrote of mining life in California.

Harty, Sir Hamilton (1880–1941), composer and for some years conductor of the Hallé orchestra; b. County Down.

Harun al-Rashid (Aaron the Upright) (763–809), 5th Abbasid caliph of Baghdad. His court was a centre for art and learning, but he governed mainly through his vizier until the latter lost favour and was executed in 803. The *Arabian Nights* associated with him are stories collected several centuries later.

Harvey, William (1578–1657), English physician and discoverer of the circulation of the blood. B. at Folkestone, he studied at Padua while Galileo was there, and was physician to James I and Charles I. His treatise on circulation was published in Latin in 1628.

Hastings, Warren (1732–1818), English administrator in India. As governor-general for the East India Company he revised the finances, improved administration and put down disorder. On his return to England he was impeached for alleged corruption, and, though acquitted, lost his fortune in his own defence. Later however he received a grant from the company. Though he suffered unduly, his trial was important for the future as setting a high standard for Indian administration.

Hauptmann, Gerhart (1862–1946), German dramatist and novelist. B. in Silesia, he lived at first in Berlin and later abroad. His play *The Weavers* deals with a revolt of 1844 and has a collective hero. Other works include *Die versunkene Glocke*, *Der arme Heinrich*, and *Rose Bernd.* Nobel prizewinner 1912.

Havelock, Sir Henry (1795–1857), British general who helped to put down the Indian mutiny.

Hawke, 1st Baron (Edward Hawke) (1705–81), English admiral, who in 1759 defeated the French at Quiberon in a tremendous storm.

Hawkins, Sir John (1532–95), English sailor and slave-trader. In 1562 he was the first Englishman to traffic in slaves. He helped to defeat the Spanish Armada in 1588.

Hawthorne, Nathaniel (1804–64), American author. His works include *The Marble Faun*, *The Scarlet Letter*, and *The House of the Seven Gables.*

Haydn, Franz Joseph (1732–1805), Austrian composer, belongs to the classical period of Bach, Handel, and Mozart. He has been given the title " father of the symphony ". Much of his life was spent as musical director to the princely Hungarian house of Esterhazy. In 1791 and again in 1794 he visited London, where he conducted his Salomon symphonies. His two great oratorios, *The Creation* and *The Seasons*, were written in his old age. *See* **Section E.**

Hazlitt, William (1778–1830), English essayist and critic. His writings include *The Characters of Shakespeare's Plays*, *Table Talk*, and *The Spirit of the Age.* His grandson William Carew Hazlitt (1834–1913) was a bibliographer and writer.

Hearst, William Randolph (1863–1951), American newspaper proprietor who built up a large newspaper empire.

Heath, Edward Richard George (b. 1916), leader of the Conservative party since 1965, and prime minister since 1970. He entered parliament in 1950.

Hedin, Sven Anders (1865–1952), Swedish explorer of Central Asia; wrote *My Life as Explorer.*

Heenan, John Carmel (b. 1905), English Roman Catholic prelate, archbishop of Westminster since 1963; member of Sacred College (1965).

Hegel, Georg Wilhelm Friedrich (1770–1831), German idealist philosopher, b. Stuttgart, whose name is associated with the dialectic method of reasoning with its sequence of thesis –antitheses–synthesis. He studied theology at Tübingen with his friend Schelling. He taught philosophy at Jena, Nuremberg, Heidelberg, and Berlin. He produced an abstract philosophical system which was influenced by his early interest in mysticism and his Prussian patriotism. His doctrines were very influential in the 19th cent. and led to modern totalitarianism. He died of cholera. *See* Dialectical Materialism, Section J.

Heidenstam, Verner von (1859–1940), Swedish author and poet, leader of a new romantic movement. Nobel prizewinner 1916.

Heifetz, Jascha (b. 1901), Russian-born violinist who became a naturalised American. He was the first musician to win a reputation in England by gramophone records before a personal appearance.

Heine, Heinrich (1797–1856), German lyric poet, b. Düsseldorf of Jewish parents. He lived mostly in Paris. His poems show profound beauty and subtlety of thought, but the satire and sometimes bitterness of his writings excited antagonism.

Helmholtz, Hermann von (1821–94), German physiologist. He published his *Erhaltung der Kraft* (Conservation of Energy) in 1847, the same year that Joule gave the first clear exposition of the principle of energy.

Héloïse (c. 1101–64), beloved of Abelard (*q.v.*) Her letters to him are extant.

Hemingway, Ernest (1898–1961), American novelist of new technique and wide influence. His works include *A Farewell to Arms*, *Death in the Afternoon*, *For Whom the Bell Tolls*, and *The Old Man and the Sea.* Nobel prizewinner 1954. He committed suicide. *See* Section M, Part I.

Henderson, Arthur (1863–1935), British Labour politician, b. Glasgow. He worked mainly for disarmament, and was president of the World Disarmament Conference, 1932–5. Nobel peace prize 1934.

Henrietta Maria (1609–69), the daughter of Henry IV of France and wife of Charles I.

Henry, Joseph (1797–1878), American physicist and schoolteacher who independently of Faraday discovered the principle of the induced current. The weather-reporting system he set up at the Smithsonian Institution led to the creation of the U.S. Weather Bureau.

Henry I (1068–1135), King of England. The youngest son of William the Conqueror, he ascended the throne during the absence on crusade of his elder brother Robert of Normandy. His long reign brought order and progress, not entirely destroyed by the anarchy under his successor Stephen.

Henry II (1133–89), King of England. He was son of Matilda, daughter of Henry I, and Geoffrey Plantagenet, count of Anjou; and his lands stretched to the Pyrenees. He was a strong ruler to whom we largely owe the establishment of the common law system (*see* D7) and permanent administrative reforms. His conflict with the Church brought about the murder of his archbishop Becket, a man of resolute character; and his later life was troubled by his unruly sons.

Henry III (1207–72), King of England, succeeded his father John in 1216. Himself devout and simple, his long reign was troubled by a partly factious baronial opposition.

Henry IV (1367–1413), grandson of Edward III and heir to the Duchy of Lancaster, became king of England in 1399. More solid and practical than his cousin Richard II, whom he had supplanted, he consolidated the government.

Henry V (1387–1422), son of Henry IV, succeeded his father as king of England in 1413. A successful commander, he renewed the French war and won the battle of Agincourt, but died young.

Henry VI (1421–71), son of Henry V, succeeded his father as king of England in 1422 as a baby. Gentle and retiring, he inherited a losing war with France. He founded Eton, and King's College, Cambridge. The Yorkist line claimed the crown from his (the Lancastrian) line, and the Wars of the Roses led to his deposition and death.

Henry VII (1457–1509) succeeded Richard III as king of England after defeating him in 1485. The first Tudor king, he was firm and shrewd, even avaricious; he built Henry VII's chapel in Westminster Abbey, and encouraged John Cabot to sail to North America.

Henry VIII (1491–1547), King of England, succeeded his father Henry VII in 1509. A prince of the Renaissance, skilled in music and sports, he loved the sea and built up the navy. His minister Cardinal Wolsey fell when Henry, seeking divorce to obtain a legal heir, rejected papal supremacy and dissolved the monasteries. Ruthless and ostentatious, he executed Sir Thomas More, spent his father's accumulation, and in spite of six marriages left a delicate son to succeed.

Henry IV of France (Henry of Navarre) (1553–1610). Prior to becoming king, he was the leader of the Huguenots; and although on being crowned he became a Catholic, he protected the Protestants by the Edict of Nantes. He then became a national king, but was later assassinated by Ravaillac, a religious fanatic.

Henry the Navigator (1394–1460), Portuguese promoter of discovery, son of John I. His sailors discovered Madeira and the Azores.

Henschel, Sir George (1850–1934), singer, composer, and conductor. B. in Breslau, he became a naturalised Englishman in 1890. Founder and conductor of the London Symphony Concerts (1886).

Hepplewhite, George (d. 1786), English cabinetmaker whose name is identified with the style which followed the Chippendale period.

Heraclitus of Ephesus (*c.* 540–475 B.C.), Greek philosopher. His discovery of a changing world (he lived in an age of social revolution when the ancient tribal aristocracy was beginning to give way to democracy) influenced the philosophies of Parmenides, Democritus, Plato, and Aristotle, and later, of Hegel.

Herbert, George (1593–1633), the most purely devotional of English poets.

Hereward the Wake, the last Saxon leader to hold out against the Normans. His base in the fens was captured in 1071 but he escaped. His exploits were written up by Kingsley.

Herod the Great (*c.* 73–4 B.C.). At first governor of Galilee under the Romans, he obtained the title of king of Judaea in 31 B.C. The massacre of the Innocents reported in the New Testament is in keeping with his historical character.

Herodotus (*c.* 485–425 B.C.), Greek historian, called by Cicero the father of history. He travelled widely collecting historical evidence.

Herrick, Robert (1591–1674), English lyric poet. His poems include *Gather ye rose buds, Cherry ripe,* and *Oberon's Feast.*

Herriot, Edouard (1872–1957), French Radical-Socialist statesman. A scholar, mayor of Lyons for more than a generation, three times prime minister, he resisted the German occupation, and was president of the National Assembly 1947–54.

Herschel, Sir John (1792–1871), British astronomer who continued his father's researches and also pioneered photography, a term introduced by him.

Herschel, Sir William (1738–1822), German-born astronomer who came to England from Hanover as a musician; father of the above. Unrivalled as an observer, and with telescopes of his own making he investigated the distribution of stars in the Milky Way and concluded that some of the nebulae he could see were separate star systems external to the Milky Way. He discovered the planet Uranus in 1781. His sister, **Caroline Lucretia** (1750–1848), compiled a catalogue of the clusters and nebulae discovered by him.

Hertz, Heinrich Rudolf (1857–95), German physicist, whose laboratory experiments confirmed Maxwell's electromagnetic theory of waves and yielded useful information about their behaviour.

Herzl, Theodor (1860–1904), founder of modern political Zionism, was b. Budapest. He convened a congress at Basle in 1897.

Hesiod (fl. *c.* 735 B.C.) Greek poet, author of *Work and Days,* which tells of life in the country.

Hill, Octavia (1838–1912), English social reformer concerned with the housing conditions of the poor, a pioneer in slum clearance in London.

Hill, Sir Rowland (1795–1879), originator of the penny postal system. He was secretary to the Postmaster-General 1846–54, then chief secretary to the Post Office until 1864.

Hindemith, Paul (1895–1963), German composer and viola player. He is associated with the movement for *Gebrauchsmusik,* which regarded music as a social expression. He incurred Nazi hostility and his later life was spent abroad. His numerous and varied works include sonatas, chamber works, songs, operas, ballet music, symphonies, and the oratorio *Das Unauförliche. See* Section E.

Hindenburg, Paul von (1847–1934), German field-marshal. In 1914 he defeated the Russians at Tannenberg. In his old age a national hero, he was president of the German Reich, 1925–34.

Hinshelwood, Sir Cyril Norman (1897–1967), English chemist. He shared with Prof. Semenov of Russia the 1956 Nobel prize for chemistry for researches into the mechanism of chemical reactions. Pres. Royal Society, 1955–60.

Hinton of Bankside, Baron (Christopher Hinton) (b. 1901), as managing director of the industrial group of the U.K. Atomic Energy Authority he played an important part in the building of Calder Hall. Chancellor University of Bath.

Hippocrates of Chios (fl. *c.* 430 B.C.), Greek mathematician, the first to compile a work on the elements of geometry.

Hippocrates of Cos (469–399 B.C.), Greek physician, whose writings are lost, but who is believed to have established medical schools in Athens and elsewhere, and to have contributed towards a scientific separation of medicine from superstition. Traditionally he is the embodiment of the ideal physician.

Hirohito, Emperor of Japan (b. 1901), acceded to the throne in 1926. In 1946 he renounced his legendary divinity.

Hitler, Adolf (1889–1945), German dictator, founder of National Socialism, b. in Austria, son of a customs official. He worked in Vienna as an artisan and already held antisemitic views. In 1912 he came to Munich; enlisted in Bavarian infantry at outbreak of the Kaiser's war. At the end of the war conditions in Germany favoured the growth of a fascist movement and under his leadership the National Socialist (Nazi) party climbed to power. He became Reich chancellor in 1933 and on the death of Hindenburg in 1934 Führer; and commander-in-chief Wehrmacht 1935. Under his regime working class movements were ruthlessly destroyed; all opponents—communists, socialists, Jews—were persecuted and murdered. By terrorism and propaganda the German state was welded into a powerful machine for aggression. There followed the occupation of the Rhineland (1936), the annexation of Austria and Czechoslovakia (1938–9), the invasion of Poland and declaration of war by Great Britain and France (1939), the invasion of Russia (1941). Final defeat came in 1945; on 30 April he committed suicide as the Russian troops closed in on Berlin.

Hobbes, Thomas (1588–1679), English philosopher who published *Leviathan* in 1651. He favoured strong government and supported the supremacy of the state, but his arguments aroused antagonism even among royalists. He was a child of his age in his enthusiasm for scientific enquiry.

Hobhouse, Leonard Trelawney (1864–1929), English sociologist. His books include *The Theory of Knowledge*, *Morals in Evolution*, and *Development and Purpose*.

Ho Chi-minh (1892–1969), leader of the Vietnam revolutionary nationalist party of Indo-China, which struggled for independence from France during and after the second world war. His main purpose was to weld together the nationalistic and communistic elements in Vietnam. As president of North Vietnam he fought to extend his control over South Vietnam, defying the United States.

Hodgkin, Alan Lloyd (b. 1914), British biophysicist working in the field of nerve impulse conduction. During the second world war he worked on the development of radar. Pres. Royal Society, 1970. Nobel prizewinner 1970.

Hodgkin, Dorothy Crowfoot (b. 1910), the third woman to win the Nobel prize in chemistry, awarded in 1964 for her X-ray analysis to elucidate the structure of complex molecules, notably penicillin and vitamin B–12. She and her team at the Dept. of Molecular Biophysics at Oxford succeeded in 1969 in determining the crystalline structure of insulin. Chancellor Bristol Univ.; Order of Merit (1965).

Hogarth, William (1697–1764), English engraver and painter, who satirised his time with character, humour, and power, especially in his *Harlot's Progress*, *Rake's Progress*, *Marriage à la Mode*, *Industry and Idleness*, and *The March to Finchley*.

Hogg, Quintin (1845–1903), educationist and philanthropist who purchased the old Polytechnic Institution in 1882 and turned it into a popular college providing education at moderate rates. His grandson, Lord Hailsham, became lord chancellor in the 1970 Conservative administration.

Hokusai, Katsushika (1760–1849), Japanese artist of the Ukiyo-e (popular school). He excelled in landscapes.

Holbein, Hans, the elder (c. 1465–1524), German painter, b. Augsburg, father of:

Holbein, Hans, the younger (1497–1543), German painter, b. Augsburg; settled in London 1532. He won the favour of Henry VIII, for whom he painted many portraits. He is also known for his series *The Dance of Death*.

Holden, Charles (1875–1960), British architect, designer of public buildings, including British Medical Asscn. Building, London; Underground Head Offices; Univ. of London Senate House.

Holden, Sir Isaac (1807–97), British inventor of woolcombing machinery.

Hölderlin, Johann Christian Friedrich (1770–1843), German poet, friend of Hegel. His works include the novel *Hyperion* and the elegy *Menon's laments for Diotima*. In his middle years his mind became unhinged.

Holford, Baron (William Graham Holford) (b. 1907), British architect and town-planner; planned post-war redevelopment of City of London, including precincts of St. Pauls.

Holmes, Oliver Wendell (1809–94), American author. His writings include *Autocrat of the Breakfast Table*, *The Professor at the Breakfast Table*, and *The Poet at the Breakfast Table*.

Holst, Gustav Theodore (1874–1934), British composer of Swedish descent whose compositions include *The Planets* suite, *The Hymn of Jesus*, an opera *The Perfect Fool*, and a choral symphony. He was outstanding as a teacher. See Section E.

Holyoake, George Jacob (1817–1906), English social reformer and secularist. He wrote a history of the co-operative movement.

Holyoake, Keith Jacka (b. 1904), New Zealand politician and farmer; prime minister since 1960.

Homer, (c. 700 B.C.), epic poet. He is supposed to have been a Greek who lived at Chios or Smyrna, and has been regarded as the author of the *Iliad* and the *Odyssey*, though this is tradition rather than ascertained fact. See H3.

Hood, 1st Viscount (Samuel Hood) (1724–1816), British admiral who in 1793 was in command of the Mediterranean fleet and occupied Toulon.

Hood, Thomas (1799–1845), English poet. His poems include *The Song of the Shirt*, *The Dream of Eugene Aram* and *The Bridge of Sighs*. He was also a humourist and punster.

Hooke, Robert (1635–1703), English physicist. His inventions include the balance spring of watches. He was also an architect and drew up a plan for rebuilding London after the Great Fire. His *Diary* is published.

Hooker, Richard (1554–1600), English theologian, author of *Ecclesiastical Polity*. He was Master of the Temple, 1585–91. For his choice of words he was known as "Judicious Hooker".

Hopkins, Sir Frederick Gowland (1861–1947), English biochemist, pioneer in biochemical and nutritional research. He first drew attention to the substances later known as vitamins. Pres. Royal Society 1930–5. Nobel prize 1929.

Hopkins, Gerard Manley (1844–89), English poet of religious experience and of a style new in his day.

Hopkins, Harry (1890–1946), Franklin Roosevelt's personal assistant at foreign conferences, and in the New Deal and Lend-Lease.

Hopkinson, John (1849–98), English engineer. By developing the theory of alternating current and of the magnetic current in dynamos he paved the way to the common use of electricity.

Hoppner, John (1758–1810), English portrait painter, b. Whitechapel, of German parents.

Horace (Quintus Horatius Flaccus) (65–8 B.C.), Roman satirist and poet, son of a Greek freedman. He wrote *Satires*, *Epodes*, *Odes*, and *Epistles*. He fought on the republican side at Philippi, but lived to become poet laureat to Augustus.

Horniman, Annie Elizabeth Fredericka (1830–1937), founder of the modern repertory system in England. Her father F. J. Horniman founded the Horniman museum.

Houdini, Harry (Erich Weiss) (1874–1926), American illusionist, son of a Hungarian rabbi. He was famed for his escapes from handcuffs.

Houseman, Alfred Edward (1859–1936), English poet, author of *A Shropshire Lad*; he was also a classical scholar. His brother Laurence (1865–1959) was a playwright and wrote *Little Plays of St. Francis* and *Victoria Regina*.

Howard, John (1726–90), English prison reformer. Imprisoned in France in wartime, he subsequently investigated English prisons, securing reforms; and later also continental prisons, dying in Russia of gaol fever.

Howard of Effingham, 2nd Baron (Charles Howard) (1536–1624), afterwards Earl of Nottingham; commanded the fleet which defeated the Spanish Armada (1588), and took part in the capture of Cadiz (1596).

Howe, Elias (1819–67), American inventor of the sewing machine.

Howe, Julia Ward (1819–1910), American suffragette, author of *Mine eyes have seen the glory*.

Howe, 1st Earl (Richard Howe) (1726–99), British admiral whose victories over the French in two wars included that off Ushant on 1 June 1794 ("the glorious first of June").

Howells, William Dean (1837–1920), American novelist, author of *A Modern Instance*, *The Rise of Silas Lapham* and *Indian Summer*.

Hubble, Edwin Powell (1889–1953), American astronomer, noted for his work on extragalactic nebulae. With the 100-inch telescope on Mount Wilson he detected the Cepheid variables in Andromeda. *See also* **The Expanding Universe, F4.**

Hudson, Henry (*c.* 1550–1611), English navigator credited with the discovery of the Hudson river and Hudson Bay, where mutineers turned him adrift to die.

Hudson, William Henry (1841–1922), naturalist, b. Buenos Aires of American parents, naturalised in England (1900). His books include *The Purple Land*, *Green Mansions*, and *Far Away and Long Ago*. Hyde Park bird sanctuary, containing *Rima* by Epstein, was established in his memory.

Huggins, Sir William (1824–1910), British astronomer who pioneered in spectroscopic photography, and was helped by his wife, Margaret Lindsay Murray (1848–1915).

Hughes, Thomas (1822–96), English novelist, author of *Tom Brown's Schooldays*, which is based on Rugby school.

Hugo, Victor Marie (1802–85), French poet, dramatist, and novelist, who headed the Romantic movement in France in the early 19th cent. His dramas include *Hernani*, *Lucrèce Borgia*, *Ruy Blas*, and *Le Roi s'amuse*. Of his novels *Notre Dame* belongs to his early period, *Les Misérables*, *Les Travailleurs de la mer*, and *L'Homme qui rit* were written while he was living in exile in Guernsey. Less well known is his skill as a graphic artist.

Hull, Sir Richard Amyatt (b. 1907), British field-marshal; C.I.G.S. 1961–5; Chief of Defence Staff 1965–7.

Humboldt, Friedrich Heinrich Alexander, Baron von (1769–1859), German naturalist and explorer whose researches are recorded in *Voyage de Humboldt et Bonpland* (23 vols., 1805–34), and *Kosmos* (5 vols., 1845–62).

Hume, David (1711–76), Scottish philosopher who developed the empiricism of Locke into the scepticism inherent in it. His main works are *Treatise of Human Nature* and *Dialogues Concerning Natural Religion*. He also wrote a *History of England*.

Hunt, Holman (1827–1910), English artist, one of the founders of the Pre-Raphaelite movement. His best-known picture is *The Light of the World*.

Hunt, Baron (John Hunt) (b. 1910), leader of the 1953 British Everest Expedition when Tenzing and Hillary reached the summit; director of the Duke of Edinburgh's Award Scheme, 1956–66.

Hunt, Leigh (1784–1859), English poet and essayist. In 1813 he was fined and imprisoned for libelling the Prince Regent in *The Examiner*. He was a friend of Keats and Shelley.

Huxley, Thomas Henry (1825–95), English biologist, b. Ealing. He started life as assistant-surgeon on H.M.S. *Rattlesnake* and during the voyage (1846–50) studied marine organisms. After the publication of Darwin's *Origin of Species* he became an ardent evolutionist and gave the first recognisably modern lecture on the origin of life to the British Association in 1870. He coined the term " agnostic " to distinguish a person who does not know whether God exists or not from the atheist who asserts there is no God. By his popular lectures and vigorous writings, *e.g.*, *Man's Place in Nature*, he made a real attempt to interest the public in the importance of science.

Huygens, Christian (1629–95), Dutch mathematician, physicist, and astronomer, son of the poet Constantijn Huygens (1596–1687); discovered the rings of Saturn, invented the pendulum clock, and developed the wave theory of light in opposition to the corpuscular theory of Newton.

Hyde, Douglas (1860–1949), Irish scholar, historian, poet, and folk-lorist; first president of Eire in the 1937 constitution, 1938–45.

Hypatia of Alexandria, the only woman mathematician of antiquity. She excited the enmity of Christian fanatics, who raised an agitation against her, and she was murdered in A.D. 415.

I

Ibrahim Pasha (1789–1848), Egyptian viceroy, adopted as his son by Mehemet Ali.

Ibsen, Henrik Johan (1828–1906), Norwegian playwright and poet, who dealt with social and psychological problems and revolutionised the European theatre. His chief works are *Ghosts*, *The Wild Duck*, *The Master Builder*, *A Doll's House*, *Hedda Gabler* and the poetic drama, *Peer Gynt*. See **The Background of Modern Drama, Section I, Part I.**

Inge, William Ralph (1860–1954), English divine, dean of St. Paul's and called " the gloomy dean." His books include *Outspoken Essays*.

Ingersoll, Robert Green (1833–99), American orator and lawyer, known as " the great agnostic."

Ingres, Jean Auguste Dominique (1780–1867), French historical and classical painter. His paintings include *La grande odalisque* in the Louvre.

Innocent III (*c.* 1160–1216), Pope 1198–1216. He asserted the power and moral force of the papacy over the Emperor Otto IV, Philip II of France, and John of England. He launched the fourth crusade, encouraged the crusade against the Albigensian heretics, and held the 4th Lateran council. His pontificate marks the zenith of the mediaeval papacy.

Inonü, Ismet (b. 1884), Turkish soldier and statesman. He was leader of the Republican People's Party founded by Kemal Atatürk; premier 1923–38; and president 1938–50 and 1961–5.

Iqbal, Sir Muhammad (1875–1938), poet-philosopher, b. Sialkot (Pakistan). He wrote both poetry and prose in Urdu, Persian, and English, and his work is marked by mystic nationalism.

Ireland, John (1879–1962), English composer, popularly known for his setting of Masefield's *Sea Fever*, but also a composer of chamber music and sonatas for pianoforte and violin.

Irving, Sir Henry (1838–1905), English actor. At the Lyceum theatre from 1871, later with Ellen Terry, he gave notable Shakespearean performances, especially as Shylock and Malvolio.

Irving, Washington (1783–1859), American essayist, whose works include *Tales of a Traveller* and *The Sketch Book*, also biographies.

Isabella of Castile (1451–1504), reigned jointly with her husband, Ferdinand V of Aragon, over a united Spain, from which the Moors and the Jews were expelled. During their reign the New World was discovered.

Ismail Pasha (1830–95), grandson of Mehemet Ali, was Khedive of Egypt, and became virtually independent of the Sultan. Under him the Suez canal was made, but his financial recklessness led to Anglo-French control and to his own abdication.

Ismay, 1st Baron (Hastings Lionel Ismay) (1887–1965), British general who was chief of staff to Sir Winston Churchill in the second world war, and later the first secretary-general of NATO.

Israels, Joseph (1824–1911), Dutch genre painter.

Ito, Hirobumi, Prince (1841–1909), Japanese statesman, four times premier, who helped to modernise his country. He was assassinated by a Korean.

Ivan the Great (1440–1505) brought the scattered provinces of Muscovy under one control and put an end to Tartar rule.

Ivan the Terrible (1530–84), crowned as first Tsar of Russia in 1547, was an autocratic ruler who consolidated and expanded Russia and entered into trading relations with Queen Elizabeth. He killed his own son.

J

Jacks, Lawrence Pearsall (1860–1955), English Unitarian philosopher. His works include an autobiography *Confessions of an Octogenarian*.

Jackson, Andrew (1767–1845), American general who was twice president of the United States.

Jackson, Thomas Jonathan (1824–63), " Stonewall Jackson," was general on the Southern side in the American Civil War; killed at Chancellorsville.

Jacobs, William Wymark (1863–1943), English novelist of humour, especially of East End riverside life.

Jacquard, Joseph Marie (1752–1834), French inventor whose loom provided an effective method of weaving designs.

Jagellons, Lithuanian–Polish dynasty, which ruled Poland 1386–1572.

Jahangir (1569–1627), 3rd Mogul emperor and patron of art.

James I (1566–1625), King of England (1603–25) and, as James VI, King of Scotland (1567–1625). He was the son of Mary Stuart and succeeded to the English throne on the death of Elizabeth I. His reign saw the Gunpowder Plot of 1605 and the publication of the Authorised Version of the Bible, but it also marked an increasingly critical attitude of the puritans towards the established church. Personally more of a scholar than a man of action, he was described as " the wisest fool in Christendom."

James II (1633–1701), King of England and, as James VII, King of Scotland (1685–88), was the younger son of Charles I. Personally honest, and an able admiral, he lacked political understanding; and when, having put down Monmouth's rebellion, he tried and failed to obtain better conditions for his fellow Roman Catholics, he was obliged in 1688 to flee the country.

James, Henry (1843–1916), American novelist, brother of William. He lived mainly in England. His work is noted for intellectual subtlety and characterisation, and includes *The American, Daisy Miller, The Portrait of a Lady, What Maisie Knew*, and *The Spoils of Poynton*. See also **Section M, Part I**.

James, William (1842–1910), American psychologist and philosopher, brother of Henry. He was a protagonist of the theory of pragmatism developed by his friend C. S. Peirce, and invented the doctrine which he called "radical empiricism." His major works are *The Principles of Psychology, The Will to Believe*, and *The Meaning of Truth*. See also **Pragmatism, Section J**.

Janáček, Leoš (1854–1928), Czech composer and conductor, and student of folk music, b. in Moravia, son of a village schoolmaster, creator of a national style. His best-known opera is *Jenufa*. See **Section E**.

Jefferies, Richard (1848–87), English naturalist of poetic perception, b. in Wiltshire, author of *Gamekeeper at Home* and *The Life of the Fields*.

Jefferson, Thomas (1743–1826), American president, 1801–9. He created the Republican Party, by which the federalists, led by Hamilton, were overthrown, and helped to draft the Declaration of Independence. He tried unsuccessfully to bring an end to slavery.

Jeffreys, 1st Baron (George Jeffreys) (1648–89), English judge who held the " bloody assize " after Monmouth's unsuccessful rebellion. In 1688 he was sent to the Tower and there died.

Jellicoe, 1st Earl (John Rushworth Jellicoe) (1859–1935), British admiral. He fought the uncertain battle of Jutland in 1916, after which the German fleet remained in harbour. He was later governor-general of New Zealand.

Jenghiz Khan. See **Genghiz Khan**.

Jenner, Edward (1749–1823), English physician, b. in Glos., pupil of John Hunter. His discovery of vaccination against smallpox (1798) helped to lay the foundations of modern immunology.

Jerome, Jerome Klapka (1859–1927), English humorous writer, author of *Three Men in a Boat*.

Jerome, St. (c. 342–420), scholar, who settled at Bethlehem, and whose translation of the Bible into Latin (the Vulgate) became for centuries the standard use.

Jesus Christ (c. 6 B.C.–A.D. 29), founder of Christianity, was born at Bethlehem in Judaea in a critical period of Jewish history. The firstborn of his mother Mary, he was said to be miraculously conceived, Joseph being his fosterfather. His home was at Nazareth in Galilee, but when he was about 30 he began a 3-year mission. His teaching is summarised in the Sermon on the Mount, and its main theme is love, especially for the poor and downtrodden. He was later crucified. The main source of his life is the New Testament. The title " Christ "

comes from the Greek word *christos* = anointed, which is the Greek translation of the Hebrew title *Messiah*. Modern dating has amended the probable year of his birth.

Jiménez, Juan Ramón (1881–1958), Spanish lyric poet, author of *Platero y Yo*. Nobel prizewinner 1956.

Jinnah, Mohammed Ali (1876–1948), Pakistani statesman. B. at Karachi, he became president of the Muslim League, and succeeded in 1947 in establishing the Dominion of Pakistan, becoming its first governor-general.

Joachim, Joseph (1831–1907), Hungarian violinist and composer.

Joan of Arc, St. (1412–31), French patriot. Of peasant parentage (she was b. at Domrémy), she believed herself called to save France from English domination; and by her efforts Charles VII was crowned at Rheims in 1429. Captured by the English, she was burned as a heretic; but canonised in 1920.

Joffre, Joseph Jacques Césaire (1852–1931), French general. He was commander-in-chief of the French army in the 1914–18 war.

John, St., the Baptist (executed A.D. 28), the forerunner of Jesus Christ.

John, St., the Evangelist, one of the twelve apostles of Jesus Christ, a Galilean fisherman, son of Zebedee and brother of James; traditionally author of the fourth Gospel.

John (1167–1216), youngest son of Henry II, was King of England from 1199. Able but erratic and arbitrary, he lost Normandy. Baronial opposition to him, under the influence of Archbishop Stephen Langton, acquired a national character, and in 1215 he was obliged to seal Magna Carta (see **L74**).

John of Gaunt (1340–99), Duke of Lancaster, son of Edward III and father of Henry IV.

John XXIII (1881–1963), elected Pope in 1958, succeeding Pius XII, was formerly Cardinal Angelo Giuseppe Roncalli, patriarch of Venice. He sought to bring the Church closer to modern needs and to promote Christian unity. His teaching is given in his encyclicals, *Mater et Magistra* and *Pacem in Terris*. He held an Ecumenical Council in 1962.

John, Augustus (1878–1961), British painter and etcher, b. in Wales; noted for his portraits, especially of Lloyd George, Bernard Shaw, and T. E. Lawrence.

Johnson, Amy (1904–41), was the first woman aviator to fly solo from England to Australia. She lost her life serving in the Air Transport Auxiliary in the second world war.

Johnson, Lyndon Baines (b. 1908), President of the United States, 1963–9. He became president on Kennedy's assassination, and followed a progressive policy at home, but his achievements were clouded by the war in Vietnam.

Johnson, Samuel (1709–84), English lexicographer and man of letters, b. at Lichfield. His *Dictionary* was published in 1755, and was followed by *Rasselas, The Idler* (a periodical), and *Lives of the Poets*. He was a focus of London literary life of his day, and his biographer, James Boswell, has vividly portrayed his circle.

Johnston, Sir Harry (1858–1927), British explorer who led an expedition to Kilimanjaro.

Jókai, Mór (1825–1904), Hungarian novelist, author of *Black Diamonds*.

Joliot-Curie, Jean Frédéric (1900–58), and his wife **Irène** (1896–1956), French scientists who discovered artificial radioactivity. Nobel prizewinners 1935. Joliot Curie was one of the discoverers of nuclear fission. Irène was the daughter of Pierre and Marie Curie. Both were communists, and both died from cancer caused by their work.

Jones, Ernest Charles (1819–69), English Chartist leader and poet.

Jones, Sir Harold Spencer (1890–1960), British astronomer; astronomer royal, 1933–55. His major research was to determine the mean distance of the earth from the sun, 93,004,000 miles.

Jones, Inigo (1573–1652), English architect who introduced the Palladian style to London, where his buildings include the banqueting hall in Whitehall and the queen's house at Greenwich. He also introduced the proscenium arch and movable scenery on the English stage.

Jonson, Ben (1573–1637), English poet and

dramatist. His plays include *Every Man in his Humour*, *Volpone*, and *The Alchemist*; and his poems *Drink to me only with thine eyes*. He also produced court masques.

Josephine, Empress (1763–1814), wife of Napoleon I, *née* de la Pagerie, she was previously married to the Vicomte de Beauharnais. She was divorced from Napoleon in 1809.

Josephus, Flavius (38–c.100), Jewish historian, author of *History of the Jewish War* and *Jewish Antiquities*.

Joule, James Prescott (1818–89), English physicist, pupil of Dalton, who researched on electro-magnetism and determined the mechanical equivalent of heat. *See* L65.

Jowett, Benjamin (1817–93), English scholar. He translated Plato's *Dialogues*, and he was an influential Master of Balliol College, Oxford.

Jowitt, Earl (William Allen Jowitt) (1885–1957), British Labour politician and lord chancellor. He wrote *The Strange Case of Alger Hiss*.

Joyce, James (1882–1941), Irish author, b. Dublin. His *Ulysses* gives a microscopic picture of a day in the life of two Irishmen, and flouted the conventions of his day. Other works include *Portrait of the Artist* and *Finnegan's Wake*. *See* Section M, Part I.

Juin, Alphonse (1888–1967), French general who took part in the Allied invasion of Tunisia and the Italian campaign in the second world war.

Julian the Apostate (331–63), Roman emperor who tried to restore paganism in the empire. He was killed in war against Persia.

Jung, Carl Gustav (1875–1961), Swiss psychiatrist. A former pupil of Freud, he later formulated his own system of analytical psychology. *See* Section J.

Junot, Andoche (1771–1813), French general defeated by Wellington in the Peninsular War.

Jusserand, Jean Jules (1855–1932), French author and diplomat, who wrote on English literature and wayfaring life in the Middle Ages.

Justinian I (483–565), Roman emperor in the East. He and his wife Theodora beautified Constantinople, and his general Belisarius was successful in war. He codified Roman law.

Juvenal (60–140), Roman poet and Stoic, remembered for his *Satires*.

K

Kafka, Franz (1883–1924), German-speaking Jewish writer, b. Prague, whose introspective work, the bulk of which was not published till after his early death from tuberculosis, has had a notable influence on later schools, especially the surrealists. It includes the three novels *The Trial*, *The Castle*, and *America*, and some short stories. *See* Section M, Part I

Kālidāsa (c. A.D. 400), chief figure in classic Sanskrit literature. No facts are known about his life and date, but certain evidence places him in the 5th cent. Seven of his works survive: two lyrics, *Ritu-samhara* (The Seasons), and *Megha-dūta* (Cloud Messenger); two epics, *Raghu-vamśa* (Dynasty of Raghu) and *Kumāra-sambhava* (Birth of the War-god); and three dramas, *Śakuntalā*, *Mālavikāgnimitra*, and *Vikramorvaśiya*.

Kant, Immanuel (1724–1804), German philosopher, author of *Critique of Pure Reason* (1781), *Critique of Practical Reason* (1788), and *Critique of Judgement* (1790). He came from a Pietist family of Königsberg, where he lectured, but the Prussian government forbade his lectures as anti-Lutheran. He was influenced by the writings of his neighbour Hamann (*see* Romanticism, Section J) and by Rousseau and Hume, and his own work was of immense influence in shaping future liberal thought. He believed in the freedom of man to make his own decisions and considered the exploitation of man as the worst evil. In *Perpetual Peace* he advocated a world federation of states.

Kapitsa, Pyotr (b. 1894), Russian physicist who worked on atomic research with Rutherford and returned to Russia in 1935. Director of the Institute for Physical Problems, Academy of Sciences of the U.S.S.R.

Kauffmann, Angelica (1741–1807), Anglo-Swiss painter, a foundation member of the Royal Academy and the first woman R.A.

Kaulbach, Wilhelm von (1805–74), German painter who illustrated the works of Goethe and Schiller.

Kaunda, Kenneth (b. 1924), African leader of international standing, son of Christian missionaries. He has been president of Zambia since independence in 1964.

Kean, Edmund (1787–1833), English tragic actor. He made his name as Shylock.

Kean, Charles John (1811–68), English actor-manager, son of Edmund. He married Ellen Tree and in the 1850s played with her in spectacular revivals at the Princess's Theatre, London.

Keats, John (1795–1821), English poet who in his short life produced poems notable for richness of imagination and beauty of thought. They include *Odes*, *Isabella*, and *The Eve of St. Agnes*.

Keble, John (1792–1866), English clergyman associated with the Tractarian movement and author of *The Christian Year*. *See* Tractarianism, Section J.

Keller, Helen Adams (1880–1968), American author and lecturer who overcame great physical handicaps (blind and deaf before the age of two) to live an active and useful life.

Kelvin of Largs, 1st Baron (William Thomson) (1824–1907), British mathematician and physicist, b. Belfast, known for his work on heat and thermodynamics, and contributions to electrical science and submarine telegraphy. In the domain of heat he stands to Joule as Maxwell stands to Faraday in the history of electrical science, both bringing pre-eminently mathematical minds to bear on the results of experimental discoveries. He introduced the Kelvin or Absolute scale of temperature and was one of the original members of the Order of Merit.

Kemble, Fanny (1809–93), English actress. She came of a noted theatrical family, her father and uncle respectively being the actors Charles Kemble and John Philip Kemble, and her aunt, Mrs. Siddons.

Kempenfelt, Richard (1718–82), English admiral, who sank with his ship the *Royal George* together with 600 of the ship's company off Spithead through a shifting of the guns which caused it to capsize.

Kempis, Thomas à (1380–1471), name by which the German mystic Thomas Hammerken was known, was a monk of the Augustinian order, whose life was mainly spent at a monastery near Zwolle. He was the author of *The Imitation of Christ*.

Kennedy, John Fitzgerald (1917–63), President of the U.S.A., 1961–3, the youngest and the first Roman Catholic to be elected; son of a financier. He had world-wide pre-eminence and gave the American people a sense of purpose to meet the challenges of a scientific age. He opposed racial discrimination and initiated a new era in East–West relations; but his foreign policy sowed the seeds of the Vietnam war. He was assassinated in 1963, and his brother Robert in 1968 while campaigning for the presidency.

Kent, William (1684–1748), English painter, furniture designer, landscape gardener, and architect, protégé of Lord Burlington, whose buildings include the great hall at Holkham and the Horse Guards, Whitehall.

Kenyatta, Jomo (b. 1893), African leader who became president of Kenya in 1964.

Kepler, Johann (1571–1630), German astronomer and mystic, for a short time assistant to Tycho Brahe whose measurements he used in working out his laws of planetary motion, which are: 1. Planets move round the sun not in circles, but in ellipses, the sun being one of the foci. 2. A planet moves not uniformly but in such a way that a line drawn from it to the sun sweeps out equal areas of the ellipse in equal times. 3. The squares of the period of revolution round the sun are proportional to the cubes of the distances. The explanation of these laws was given by Newton; they dealt a death-blow to Aristotelian cosmology.

Keyes, 1st Baron (Roger John Brownlow Keyes) (1872–1945), British admiral who led the raid on Zeebrugge in 1918.

Keynes, 1st Baron (John Maynard Keynes) (1883–1946), British economist, who was a Treasury representative at the Versailles peace conference, and published his views in *The Economic Consequences of the Peace*. His *Treatise on Money* (1930) and *The General Theory of Employment, Interest and Money* (1936) influenced economic thought all over the world. *See also* G19(2).

Khrushchev, Nikita Sergeyevich (b. 1894), Russian statesman who became leader of the Soviet Union soon after the death of Stalin; first secretary of the Soviet Communist Party, 1953–64; prime minister, 1958–64. After the harsh years of the Stalinist régime he pursued a policy of relaxation both in home and foreign affairs. Relations with America improved but those with China became strained. Advances were made in scientific achievement, notably in the field of space research. In 1964 his posts were taken over by Leonid Brezhnev (first secretary) and Alexei Kosygin (prime minister).

Kierkegaard, Sören (1813–55), Danish philosopher and religious thinker, whose views have influenced contemporary existentialism. His main work is *Either–Or*.

King, Martin Luther (1929–68), American clergyman and Negro integration leader; awarded the 1964 Nobel peace prize for his consistent support of the principle of non-violence in the coloured people's struggle for civil rights. Assassinated at Memphis, Tennessee.

King, Mackenzie (1874–1950), prime minister of Canada, 1921–5, 1926–30, and 1935–48.

Kingsley, Charles (1819–75), English clergyman and novelist, author of *Hypatia, Westward Ho!, Hereward the Wake* and *The Water Babies*, a children's book.

Kipling, Rudyard (1865–1936), English writer, b. Bombay. His vivid work, popular in his day, portrays contemporary English rule in India, and thus is now less in favour, but won the Nobel prize in 1907; it includes *Kim* and *Stalky and Co.* Among his books for children are *Just So Stories* and the *Jungle Books*.

Kirchhoff, Gustav Robert (1824–87), German mathematical physicist, who with R. W. Bunsen discovered that in the gaseous state each chemical substance emits its own characteristic spectrum (1859). He was able to explain Fraunhofer's map of the solar spectrum. Using the spectroscope, he and Bunsen discovered the elements caesium and rubidium.

Kitchener of Khartoum, 1st Earl (Horatio Herbert Kitchener) (1850–1916), English general. In 1898 he won back the Sudan for Egypt by his victory at Omdurman. He served in the South African war; and in the first world war he was secretary of war, 1914–16. He was drowned on his way to Russia.

Klee, Paul (1879–1940), Swiss artist, whose paintings, in a restless, experimental period, are small-scale, delicate dream-world fantasies of poetical content.

Klemperer, Otto (b. 1885), German-born conductor, internationally known. Expelled by the Nazis he became an American citizen and returned to Europe in 1946.

Kneller, Sir Godfrey (1646–1723), portrait painter, b. at Lübeck, who settled in England and was patronised by English sovereigns from Charles II to George I.

Knox, John (1505–72), Scottish reformer, b. near Haddington. While in exile at Geneva he was influenced by Calvin. On return to Scotland he was a leader of the reforming party against Mary, Queen of Scots. He wrote a *History of the Reformation in Scotland*.

Koch, Robert (1843–1910), German bacteriologist who discovered the bacillus of tuberculosis. He also worked on cholera and on cattle diseases.

Kodály, Zoltán (1882–1967), Hungarian composer and teacher. He worked with Bartok in the collection of folk-tunes and his compositions include the choral work *Psalmus Hungaricus*, the orchestral suite *Hary Janos*, and the symphony in C, written in 1961. *See* **Section E.**

Kokoschka, Oskar (b. 1886), Austrian portrait and landscape painter, a rare interpretative artist, who, after teaching in Dresden, in 1938 settled in England.

Koniev, Ivan Stepanovich (b. 1898), Russian general in the second world war.

Korolyov, Sergei (1907–66), Russian space scientist, who designed the world's first earth satellite, the first manned spaceship and the first moon rocket.

Kosciusko, Tadeusz (1746–1817), Polish patriot. After experience gained in America in the War of Independence, he led his countrymen against Russia in 1792 and 1794 in opposition to the partition of Poland and was temporarily successful.

Kossuth, Louis (1802–94), Hungarian patriot, who in 1848 led a rising of his countrymen against the Hapsburg dynasty, but had to flee to Turkey and later to England.

Kosygin, Alexei Nikolayevich (b. 1904), succeeded Nikita Khrushchev as chairman of the Council of Ministers of the U.S.S.R. (prime minister) in 1964; formerly a deputy chairman of the State Economic Planning Commission, Gosplan.

Kreisler, Fritz (1875–1962), Austrian violinist, who composed violin music and an operetta. He became an American citizen in 1943.

Krenek, Ernst (b. 1900), Austrian composer of partly Czech descent, whose compositions cover a wide range, including the jazz opera *Jonny spielt auf*. He settled in America in 1938.

Kropotkin, Peter, Prince (1842–1921), Russian anarchist, geographer and explorer, who was imprisoned for favouring the political action of a working men's association, but escaped to England. He wrote on socialistic and geographical subjects. Returned to Russia in 1917.

Kruger, Stephanus Johannes Paulus (1825–1904), Boer leader, who in 1881 was appointed head of the provisional government against Britain, and later president. When the war of 1899–1902 turned against the Boers, he vainly sought help in Europe.

Krupp, Alfred (1812–87), founder of the German gun factories at Essen. He installed in a disused factory left him by his father a new steam-engine from England, began to make cast steel, and from 1844 specialised in armaments. The firm's factories made the Big Bertha guns which shelled Paris in 1918. His great-grandson Alfried (b. 1907) was tried as a war criminal in 1948.

Krylov, Ivan Andreyevich (1768–1844), Russian writer of fables who has been called the Russian La Fontaine.

Kubelik, Jan (1880–1940), Czech violinist, son of a gardener at Michle, near Prague, who at the age of 12 played in public. His son Rafael (b. 1914), a conductor of international repute, was musical director of the Royal Opera House, Covent Garden, 1955–8.

Kublai Khan (1216–94), grandson of Genghiz Khan, was the first Mongol emperor of China. He extended the Mongol empire by conquest, and lived in unparalleled splendour. His court was described by Marco Polo and is the subject of a poem by Coleridge.

L

Lablanche, Luigi (1794–1858), singer and actor, b. Naples, who was singing tutor to Queen Victoria.

La Fayette, Marie Joseph Paul Roch Yves Gilbert du Motier, Marquis de (1757–1834), French soldier and statesman. He fought for the colonists in the American War of Independence; and in the 1789 French revolution he proposed a declaration of rights and was commander of the National Guard till his moderation made him unpopular. When the monarchy was restored he was an opposition leader, and took part in the revolution of 1830.

La Fontaine, Jean de (1621–95), French poet and fabulist, b. in Champagne, a friend of Molière, Boileau, and Racine, all brilliant writers of the reign of Louis XIV.

Lagerlöf, Selma (1858–1940), Swedish novelist and first woman member of the Swedish Academy. Nobel prizewinner 1909.

Lagrange, Joseph Louis, Comte (1736–1813)

French mathematician, of Turin and Paris, whose interest in astronomy led him to distinguish two types of disturbance of members of the solar system, the periodic and the secular. He was called by Frederick the Great to Berlin to succeed Euler.

Lalande, Joseph Jerome LeFrançais de (1732–1807), French astronomer, author of *Traité d'astronomie*.

Lamarck, Jean Baptiste Pierre Antoine de Monet de (1744–1829), French biologist whose explanation of evolution was that new organs are brought into being by the needs of the organism in adapting to its environment and that the new facilities can be passed on to the offspring through heredity. *See* **The Evolution of Organisms, Section F, Part IV.**

Lamb, Charles (1775–1834), English essayist, b. London. A clerk in the East India Office, he devoted his life to his sister Mary, who was of unstable mind. He is chiefly known for his *Essays of Elia*, and his letters, which have a blend of humour and tenderness.

Lamb, Sir Horace (1849–1934), English mathematician, writer of a standard work on hydrodynamics.

Lambert, Constant (1905–51), English composer and critic, and conductor of Sadler's Wells ballet. His *Rio Grande* is in jazz idiom.

Landor, Walter Savage (1775–1864), English writer, b. Warwick. He is chiefly remembered for his *Imaginary Conversations* and for his poems. Of intractable temper, he lived for some years in Italy.

Landseer, Sir Edwin (1802–73), English animal painter, b. London. He painted the *Monarch of the Glen* and designed the lions in Trafalgar Square.

Lane, Edward William (1801–76), English Arabic scholar, translator of the *Arabian Nights*.

Lanfranc (*c.* 1005–89), ecclesiastic. B. at Pavia, he became a prior in Normandy, and in 1070 archbishop of Canterbury, in which office he was energetic.

Lang, Andrew (1844–1912), versatile Scottish man of letters, whose large output includes *Myth, Ritual and Religion*, poems, fairy-tales, and fiction.

Lang, 1st Baron (Cosmo Gordon Lang) (1864–1945), was archbishop of Canterbury, 1828–42.

Langland, William (1330?–1400?), English poet, probably educated at Malvern, author of *Piers the Plowman*.

Langton, Stephen (1151–1228), archbishop of Canterbury, and adviser to the insurgent barons who induced King John to sign Magna Carta.

Lansbury, George (1859–1940), British Labour politician, founder of the *Daily Herald*. He improved London's amenities.

Lâo-Tsze (old philosopher) (*c.* 600 B.C.), traditional founder of Taoism in China. *See* **Section J.**

Laplace, Pierre Simon, Marquis de (1749–1827), French mathematician and astronomer, author of *Celestial Mechanics* (1799–1825). He advanced the hypothesis that the solar system had condensed out of a vast rotating gaseous nebula.

La Rochefoucauld, François, Duc de (1613–80), French writer, author of *Reflections and Moral Maxims*.

Lasker, Emanuel (1868–1941), German chess player, world champion, 1894–1921.

Lassalle, Ferdinand (1825–64), German socialist who took part in the revolutionary movement of 1848 and organised workers to press for political rights.

Lassus, Orlandus (Lasso, Orlando di). (*c.* 1532–94), Flemish composer and choirmaster, contemporary of Palestrina, writer of *chansons*, madrigals, and sacred music. *See* **Section E.**

Latimer, Hugh (*c.* 1485–1555), English Protestant martyr, became bishop of Worcester in 1535, and was executed under Queen Mary.

Laud, William (1573–1645), archbishop of Canterbury and adviser to Charles I. His attempts to get conformity for his high church policy made him unpopular and he was impeached and beheaded.

Lauder, Sir Harry (1870–1950), Scottish comic singer of wide popularity. He also wrote *Roamin' in the Gloamin'*.

Laval, Pierre (1883–1945), French politician who collaborated with the German occupation in

the second world war and was subsequently tried and executed.

Lavery, Sir John (1856–1941), Irish portrait painter.

Lavoisier, Antoine Laurent (1743–94), French chemist, b. Paris, was the first to establish the fact that combustion is a form of chemical action. We owe the word *oxygen* to him.

Law, Andrew Bonar (1858–1923), Conservative politician, prime minister 1922–3.

Lawrence, David Herbert (1885–1930), English poet and novelist, b. Notts., a miner's son. He tried to interpret emotion on a deeper level of consciousness. His works, which have had wide influence, include *The White Peacock*, *Sons and Lovers*, *The Rainbow*, *Women in Love*, and *Lady Chatterley's Lover*; also plays. *See* Sections **I** and **M** (Part I).

Lawrence, Sir Thomas (1769–1830), English portrait painter.

Lawrence, Thomas Edward (1888–1935) (Lawrence of Arabia), British soldier who led the Arabs against the Turks in the war of 1914–18, and wrote *The Seven Pillars of Wisdom*.

Leacock, Stephen (1869–1944), Canadian humorist.

Leavis, Frank Raymond (b. 1895), British critic, who edited *Strutiny*, 1932–63, and whose works include *The Great Tradition*; *D. H. Lawrence, Novelist*: and *Anna Karenina and Other Essays*.

Lecky, William Edward Hartpole (1838–1903), Irish historian, author of *England in the Eighteenth Century*.

Leclerc, Jacques Philippe (Philippe, Comte de Hautecloque) (1902–47), French general. He led a Free French force in Africa in the second world war and liberated Paris in 1944. He died in a plane crash.

Le Corbusier (1887–1965), pseudonym of Charles Édouard Jeanneret, Swiss architect, whose books and work (especially his Unité d'Habitation at Marseilles and the new Punjab capital at Chandigarh) have widely influenced town-planning.

Lee of Fareham, 1st Viscount (Arthur Hamilton Lee) (1868–1947), British politician who presented Chequers Court to the nation as prime minister's residence.

Lee, Robert Edward (1807–70), American Confederate general in the Civil War, who made the surrender at Appomattox.

Lee, Sir Sidney (1859–1926), English critic, and joint editor of the *Dictionary of National Biography*.

Leech, John (1817–64), humorist artist, b. London, of Irish descent, contributed to *Punch*.

Leibnitz, Gottfried Wilhelm (1646–1716), German philosopher and mathematician, who invented the differential and integral calculus (1684) independently of Newton whose previous work on the same subject was not published until 1687. It was Leibnitz's nomenclature that is universally adopted.

Leicester, Earl of (Robert Dudley) (1538–88), English soldier, commanded English troops in the Netherlands, 1585–7, without much success, and in 1588 commanded forces assembled against the Armada. He was husband of Amy Robsart.

Leif Ericsson (fl. 1000), discoverer of Vinland on the north-east coast of America; b. Iceland, son of the Norse explorer, Eric the Red, who colonised Greenland.

Leighton, 1st Baron (Robert Leighton) (1830–96), English painter of wide popularity, whose works include *Paolo and Francesca*. He was also a sculptor.

Lely, Sir Peter (Pieter van der Faes) (1618–80), Dutch painter who settled in London and painted court portraits.

Lenin (Vladimir Ilyich Ulyanov) (1870–1924), Russian revolutionary leader and statesman. From 1893 to 1917 he worked underground in Russia and abroad for the revolutionary cause. During this time the Social-Democratic party was formed; within it developed an uncompromising revolutionary group, the Bolsheviks, and of this group Lenin was the leading spirit. In April 1917 he and his fellow exiles returned; after the November revolution he headed the new government, having to face both war and anarchy. In 1922 his "new economic policy " somewhat modified the intensive drive towards planned industrial development. He was born

B38

in Simbirsk (now Ulyanovsk) on the middle Volga, the son of the local inspector of education. His body lies embalmed in Red Square, Moscow.

Leonardo da Vinci (1452–1519), Italian artist and man of science, son of a Florentine lawyer and a peasant. He described himself (when applying to Lodovico Sforza, Duke of Milan, for the post of city planner) as painter, architect, philosopher, poet, composer, sculptor, athlete, mathematician, inventor, and anatomist. His artistic output is small in quantity, and he is best known for his *Last Supper* in the refectory of Santa Maria delle Grazie in Milan and his *Mona Lisa* in the Louvre. He recorded his scientific work in unpublished notebooks written from right to left in mirror writing. The anatomy of the body (himself carrying out dissections), the growth of the child in the womb, the laws of waves and currents, and the laws of flight, all were studied by this astonishing man who believed nothing but had to see for himself. Although he was much admired, few people in his time had any notion of his universal genius.

Leoncavallo, Ruggiero (1858–1919), Italian composer of the opera *Pagliacci*.

Leonidas was king of Sparta at the time of the invasion of Greece by Xerxes (480 B.C.), and led the defence of the pass of Thermopylae, where he fell.

Lermontov, Mikhail Yurevich (1814–41), Russian poet and novelist, exiled to the Caucasus for a revolutionary poem addressed to Tsar Nicholas I on the death of Pushkin. He has been called the poet of the Caucasus. His novel *A Hero of Our Time* was written at St. Petersburg. He lost his life in a duel.

Le Sage, Alain René (1668–1747), French author, b. in Brittany, who wrote *Gil Blas* and *Le Diable Boiteux*. He was also a dramatist and his plays include *Turcaret*.

Lesseps, Ferdinand, Vicomte de (1805–94), French engineer who while serving as vice-consul at Alexandria conceived a scheme for a canal across the Suez isthmus; the work was completed in 1869. He also projected the original Panama canal scheme, which failed.

Lessing, Gotthold Ephraim (1729–81), German philosopher, dramatist, and critic, noted for his critical work *Laokoon* and his play *Minna von Barnhelm*.

Leucippus (fl. 440 B.C.), Greek philosopher, founder with Democritus of atomism, a theory of matter more nearly that of modern science than any put forward in ancient times. One of his sayings survives: "Naught occurs at random, but everything for a reason and of necessity."

Leverhulme, 1st Viscount (William Hesketh Lever) (1851–1925), British industrialist and philanthropist. He founded Lever Bros. which later became Unilever Ltd., and was a practical exponent of industrial partnership. He gave Lancaster House to the nation.

Leverrier, Urbain Jean Joseph (1811–77), French astronomer who, working independently of J. C. Adams of Cambridge, anticipated the existence of the planet Neptune which was later revealed by telescopic search.

Lévi-Strauss, Claude (b. 1908), French social anthropologist, b. Belgium, trained in philosophy and law, exponent of the theory of symbolic structures. His works include *Les structures élémentaires de la parenté* (1949), *Tristes tropiques* (1955), and *Mythologiques* (3 vols., 1964–7).

Lewis, Cecil Day. *See* Day Lewis, Cecil.

Lewis, Sinclair (1885–1951), American writer of novels satirising small-town life and philistinism. His works include *Main Street*, *Babbitt* (hence the term Babbitry), and *Elmer Gantry*. Nobel prizewinner 1931.

Liaquat Ali Khan (1895–1951), leader of the Moslem League (1946) and first premier of Pakistan in 1947. He was assassinated.

Lie, Trygve (1896–1968), Norwegian politician who became secretary-general of the United Nations, 1946–52.

Li Hung Chang (1823–1901), Chinese statesman, who though enlightened was unable to secure much modernisation and had to cede Formosa to Japan in 1895.

Lilburne, John (1614–57), English agitator and

pamphleteer, leader of the Levellers in the Civil War period.

Linacre, Thomas (c. 1460–1524), English humanist and physician, who translated Galen's works and founded the College of Physicians.

Lincoln, Abraham (1809–65), American president. B. in Kentucky, he became a lawyer and was returned to Congress from Illinois in 1846. He was a leader of the Republican party which was formed in 1856 to oppose slavery. He became president in 1861, in which year the Confederate States proposed to withdraw from the Union, and war broke out. The phrase "government of the people, by the people, for the people" comes from his Gettysburg speech of 1863. He was assassinated in 1865.

Lind, Jenny (1820–87), Swedish singer, popular in Europe, and known as the Swedish nightingale. She founded musical scholarships.

Linnaeus (1707–78), Swedish botanist, remembered for his system of defining living things by two Latin names, the first being its *genus*, and the second its *species*. His method is expounded in *Philosophia Botanica* (1751). In 1757 he was ennobled as Karl von Linné. *See* Classification of Organisms, Section F, Part IV.

Lippi, Fra Filippo (1406–69), Italian artist, b. Florence. Frescoes in Prato cathedral are his main work. His son **Filippino** (1457–1504) finished Masaccio's frescoes in the Carmine, Florence, and executed others, for instance in Santa Maria Novella.

Lippmann, Gabriel (1845–1921), French physicist who invented a capillary electrometer and was a pioneer in colour photography. Nobel prizewinner 1908.

Lippmann, Walter (b. 1889), American journalist of influence, writing for the New York *Herald Tribune*, 1931–62.

Lipton, Sir Thomas Johnstone (1850–1931), Scottish business man and philanthropist. B. Glasgow, he emigrated to America, but returned to Scotland and established extensive chain-stores for groceries. He unsuccessfully competed in yachting for the America's Cup.

Lister, Baron (Joseph Lister) (1827–1912), English surgeon, son of J. J. Lister (1786–1869), an amateur microscopist. He founded antiseptic surgery (1865) which greatly reduced mortality in hospitals.

Liszt, Franz (1811–86), Hungarian pianist and composer. His daughter Cosima became the wife of Hans von Bülow and later of Wagner. *See* Section E.

Litvinov, Maxim (1876–1952), Russian diplomat, of revolutionary origin, who first as ambassador in London, then as commissar for foreign affairs, and 1941–3 ambassador to the U.S., gained respect and understanding for his country.

Livingstone, David (1813–73), Scottish explorer in Africa. He discovered the course of the Zambesi, the Victoria Falls and Lake Nyasa (now Lake Malawi), and roused opinion against the slave trade. At one time believed lost, he was found by the American Stanley.

Lloyd-George of Dwyfor, 1st Earl (David Lloyd George) (1863–1945), Liberal statesman of Welsh origin. He was M.P. for Caernarvon, 1890–1944; and as chancellor of the exchequer he introduced social insurance, 1908–11. The war of 1914–18 obliged him to become a war premier (superseding Asquith), and he was subsequently one of the main figures at the peace conference. In 1921 he conceded the Irish Free State. His daughter, Lady Megan Lloyd George, was M.P. for many years, latterly for the Labour Party.

Locke, John (1632–1704), English liberal philosopher and founder of empiricism, the doctrine that all knowledge is derived from experience. His chief work in theoretical philosophy, *Essay Concerning Human Understanding*, was written just before the revolution of 1688 and published in 1690. Other writings include *Letters on Toleration*, *Treatises on Government*, and *Education*.

Lombroso, Cesare (1836–1909), Italian criminologist, whose *L'uomo delinquente* maintained the existence of a criminal type distinguishable from the normal.

Lomonosov, Mikhail Vasilievich (1711–65), Russian philologist and poet who systematised Russian grammar and orthography.

London, Jack (1876–1916), American author of adventure tales such as *Call of the Wild*.

Longfellow, Henry Wadsworth (1807–82), American poet, popular in his lifetime, author of *The Golden Legend* and *Hiawatha*.

Lope de Vega Carpio, Félix (1562–1635), Spanish writer of immense output. First a ballad-writer, he took to play-writing and founded the Spanish drama. The number of his plays is said to have been 1,500, the earlier ones historical, the later ones dealing with everyday life; but most are lost.

Lorca, Federico Garcia (1899–1936), Spanish poet and dramatist of Andalusia. Among his works are *Llanto por Ignacio Sánchez Mejías*, an unforgettable lament on the death of a bullfighter, and *Cancion de Jinete* with its haunting refrain, " Cordoba, far away and alone." He was brutally murdered by Franco sympathisers at the outbreak of the civil war.

Louis IX (1214–70), St. Louis, King of France. Of saintly character (as described in Joinville's *Memoirs*), he also carried out practical reforms. He died on crusade.

Louis XIV (1638–1715), King of France. A despotic ruler, builder of Versailles, he also dominated the Europe of his day; but he sowed the seeds of future trouble for France by his exhausting wars. He revoked the Edict of Nantes which had given religious freedom to the Huguenots since 1598. His reign, however, was a great period for literature.

Louis XV (1710–74), King of France. Extravagant and self-indulgent, his reign marked a declining period for the monarchy, but produced some fine art.

Louis XVI (1754–93), King of France. Well-meaning but incapable, this king saw the outbreak of the French revolution of 1789, in which he and his queen Marie Antoinette were executed.

Louis, Joe (Joseph Louis Barrow) (b. 1914), American Negro boxer, who became world heavyweight champion in 1936, successfully defending his title 25 times.

Low, Archibald Montgomery (1888–1956), British scientist who worked in varied fields, including wireless, television, and anti-aircraft and anti-tank apparatus.

Low, Sir David (1891–1963), British cartoonist, b. New Zealand, associated with the *Evening Standard* and later the *Guardian*; creator of Colonel Blimp.

Lowell, Robert (b. 1917), American poet, author of the verse play *The Old Glory*, and *Life Studies*, an autobiographical volume in verse and prose. *See* Section M, Part II.

Loyola, St. Ignatius (1491–1556), Spanish founder of the Jesuits, a missionary order working directly under the Pope.

Lucretius (99–55 B.C.), Roman poet, author of *De natura rerum*, a long philosophical poem advocating moral truth without religious belief.

Ludendorff, Erich (1865–1937), German general who directed German strategy in the first world war.

Lugard, 1st Baron (Frederick John Dealtry Lugard) (1858–1945), British colonial administrator in Africa, especially Nigeria, and exponent of the system of indirect rule through native chiefs.

Luther, Martin (1483–1546), German Protestant reformer. After spending time in a monastery, he was ordained priest (1507), and lectured at Wittenberg university. In 1517 he protested against the sale of indulgences; and when summoned before the Diet of Worms made a memorable defence. He was protected by the Elector of Saxony, and translated the Bible. German Protestantism culminated in the Augsburg confession (1530). *See also* Lutheranism, Section J.

Luthuli, Albert (1899–1967), African non-violent resistance leader an ex-Zulu chief. Killed in train accident. Nobel prize for peace 1960.

Lutyens, Sir Edwin Landseer (1869–1944), English architect both of country houses and public buildings; designed the cenotaph, Whitehall, and Liverpool Roman catholic cathedral.

Lukács, Georg (b. 1885), Hungarian writer, Marxist thinker and literary critic. His ideas are expounded in *History and Class Consciousness* (1923), *Studies in European Realism* (1946, Eng. tr. 1950), *The Historical Novel* (1955; Eng. tr. 1962).

Lyell, Sir Charles (1797–1875), Scottish geologist, whose *Principles of Geology* (1830–33) postulated gradual geological change and helped to shape Darwin's ideas. His terminology—Pliocene (*Greek* = more recent), Miocene (less recent) and Eocene (dawn)—is still in use.

Lysenko, Trofim (b. 1898), Russian biologist who maintained that environmental experiences can change heredity somewhat in the manner suggested by Lamarck. After the death of Stalin his theories were severely criticised.

Lytton, 1st Baron (Edward George Earle Lytton Bulwer-Lytton) (1803–73), English novelist and playwright, author of *The Last Days of Pompeii*.

M

Macadam, John Loudon (1756–1836), Scottish inventor of the " macadamising " system of road repair.

MacArthur, Douglas (1880–1964), American general. He defended the Philippines against the Japanese in the second world war, and was relieved of his command in 1951 in the Korean war.

Macaulay of Rothley, 1st Baron (Thomas Babbington Macaulay) (1800–59), English historian, poet and Indian civil servant. His poems include *Lays of Ancient Rome*. In India he was mainly responsible for education being given in English.

Macaulay, Zachary (1768–1838), anti-slavery agitator, father of the above.

Macbeth (d. 1057), Scottish king, married Gruoch, granddaughter of Kenneth, king of Alban. He was mormaer of Moray, succeeding Duncan in 1040 after killing him in fair fight. His reign of seventeen years was prosperous, but he was killed by Duncan's son, Malcolm, in 1057. Shakespeare's play is based on the inaccurate *Chronicle* of Holinshed.

MacDiarmid, Hugh (b. 1892), pseudonym of Christopher Murray Grieve, Scottish poet, leader of the Scottish literary renaissance; author of *A Drunk Man Looks at the Thistle*.

Macdonald, Flora (1722–90), Scottish Jacobite heroine who saved the life of Prince Charles Edward after the defeat at Culloden Moor in 1746.

Macdonald, Sir John Alexander (1815–91), Canadian statesman, first prime minister of the Dominion of Canada.

Macdonald, James Ramsay (1866–1937), Labour politician of Scottish origin, premier 1924 and 1929–31; also of a coalition 1931–5. His action over the financial crisis of 1931 divided his party.

Macdonald, Malcolm (b. 1901), son of above, has held positions overseas in the Commonwealth, the last as special representative in Africa.

McDougall, William (1871–1938), British psychologist who settled in America. He opposed Behaviourism, and his works include *Introduction to Social Psychology* and *Outline of Psychology*.

Machiavelli, Niccolò (1467–1527), Florentine Renaissance diplomat and theorist of the modern state. His book *The Prince* (1513), dedicated to Lorenzo the Magnificent, is concerned with the reality of politics—what rulers must do to retain power. His *Discourses* is more republican and liberal.

Mackail, John William (1859–1945), British classical scholar, translator of the *Odyssey*.

Mackenzie, Sir Compton (b. 1883), British writer, whose works include *Carnival, Sinister Street*, and a monumental autobiography.

McLuhan, Herbert Marshall (b. 1911), Canadian author of a number of books on contemporary communications, including *The Gutenberg Galaxy, The Mechanical Bride*. *See* Section J.

Macmillan, Harold (b. 1894), British Conservative politician, premier 1957–63. He has held several offices, and his " wind of change " speech (1960) hailed African independence. Chancellor of Oxford University (1960).

McMillan, Margaret (1860–1931), Scottish educational reformer, b. New York, and pioneer (with her sister Rachel) of child welfare work in London and of open-air nursery schools.

Macneice, Louis (1907–63), British poet, playwright, and translator. *See* Section M, Part II.

Macready, William Charles (1793–1873), British actor and manager, especially associated with Shakespearean roles.

Maeterlinck, Maurice (1862–1949), Belgian man of letters, whose plays include *La Princesse Maleine*, *Pelléas et Mélisande*, and *L'Oiseau Bleu*. Nobel prizewinner 1911. He also did scientific work on bees.

Magellan, Ferdinand (*c.* 1480–1521). Portuguese navigator, and commander of the first expedition (1519) to sail round the world.

Mahler, Gustav (1860–1911), Austrian composer and conductor; a writer of symphonies and songs, a classical romantic, much influenced by Anton Bruckner and Wagner. *See* Section E.

Mahavira, Vardhamana Jnatriputra (6th cent. B.C.), Indian historical (as opposed to legendary) founder of Jainism, which teaches the sacredness of all life. *See* Jainism, Section J.

Maintenon, Françoise d'Aubigne, Marquise de (1635–1719), second wife of Louis XIV. Her first husband was the poet Scarron. On the king's death she retired to a home for poor girls which she had founded.

Makarios III (b. 1913), Greek Orthodox archbishop and Cypriot national leader. Deported by the British to the Seychelles in 1956, he returned in 1957 to become president of the newly independent republic in 1960.

Malibran, Marie Félicité (1808–36), Spanish mezzo-soprano.

Malik, Yakov Alexandrovich (b. 1906), Soviet diplomat; permanent representative at U.N. 1949–52, 1967– ; ambassador to Britain 1953–60; deputy foreign minister 1960–7.

Malory, Sir Thomas (*c.* 1430–71), English writer. From earlier sources and legends of King Arthur and the Knights of the Round Table, he compiled the *Morte d'Arthur* printed by Caxton in 1485.

Malraux, André (b. 1895), French novelist whose works include *La Condition humaine*, *L'Espoir*, and *Psychologie de l'art* (tr. in 2 vols., *Museum without Walls*, and *The Creative Act*).

Malthus, Thomas Robert (1766–1834), English clergyman and economist who in his gloomy essay *The Principle of Population* contended that population tends to increase faster than the means of subsistence and that its growth could only be checked by moral restraint or by disease and war.

Manet, Édouard (1832–83), French painter. His Impressionist pictures include *Olympia* and *Un bar aux Folies-Bergère* (the latter at the Courtauld).

Mann, Thomas (1875–1955), German writer who won world recognition at the age of 25 with his novel *Buddenbrooks*. His liberal humanistic outlook had developed sufficiently by 1930 for him to expose national socialism. He left Germany in 1933 to live in Switzerland, then settled in the U.S. Other works are *The Magic Mountain*, and the *Joseph* tetralogy. Nobel prizewinner 1929.

Mann, Tom (1856–1941), British Labour leader for more than fifty years.

Manning, Henry Edward (1808–92), English cardinal; archbishop of Westminster 1865–92. He was an Anglican churchman before he entered the church of Rome.

Mansfield, Katherine (1890–1923), short-story writer, b. Wellington, New Zealand, whose work was influenced by the short stories of Chekov. Her second husband was John Middleton Murry, literary critic.

Manson, Sir Patrick (1844–1922), Scottish physician, the first to formulate the hypothesis that the malarial parasite was transmitted by the mosquito. His joint work with Sir Ronald Ross rendered habitable vast areas of the earth hitherto closed.

Manuzio, Aldo Pio (1450–1515), Italian printer. founder of the Aldine press in Venice, which for just over a century issued books famed for their beautiful type and bindings.

Manzoni, Alessandro (1785–1873), Italian novelist and poet, b. Milan, whose historical novel *I*

Promessi Sposi (The Betrothed) won European reputation.

Mao Tse-tung (b. 1893), Chinese national and Communist leader. B. in Hunan, of rural origin but university training, he understood how to win peasant support for a national and progressive movement. Attacked by Chiang Kai-shek, he led his followers by the " long march " to N.W. China, whence later they issued to defeat both Japanese and Chiang and proclaim a People's Republic in 1949, and later to promote the " great leap forward ". He resigned the chairmanship of the republic in 1959, but came to the fore again in 1966–8 leading the cultural revolution.

Marat, Jean Paul (1743–93), French revolution leader, largely responsible for the reign of terror, and assassinated by Charlotte Corday.

Marconi, Guglielmo, Marchese (1874–1937), Italian inventor and electrical engineer who developed the use of radio waves as a practical means of communication. In 1895 he sent long-wave signals over a distance of a mile, and in 1901 received in Newfoundland the first transatlantic signals sent out by his station in Cornwall, thus making the discovery that radio waves can bend around the spherically-shaped earth. Nobel prizewinner 1909.

Marco Polo. *See* Polo, Marco.

Marcus Aurelius Antoninus (121–80), Roman emperor and Stoic philosopher of lofty character, whose *Meditations* are still read.

Marcuse, Herbert (b. 1898), political philosopher. B. Berlin, he emigrated to the U.S. during the Nazi regime. A critic of Western industrial society, he sees the international student protest movement as the agent of revolutionary change.

Maria Theresa (1717–80), Empress, daughter of the Hapsburg Charles VI. Able and of strong character, she fought unsuccessfully to save Silesia from Prussian annexation. She promoted reforms in her dominions. She married the Duke of Lorraine and had 16 children.

Marie Antoinette (1755–93), Queen of France, was daughter of the above and wife of Louis XVI; accused of treason, she and her husband were beheaded in the French revolution.

Marie Louise (1791–1847), daughter of Francis I of Austria, became the wife of Napoleon and bore him a son (Napoleon II).

Marius, Caius (157–86 B.C.), Roman general who defended Gaul from invasion; later civil war forced him to flee from Rome, and on his return he took terrible revenge.

Mark Antony. *See* Antonius, Marcus.

Marlborough, 1st Duke of (John Churchill) (1650–1722), English general, victor of Blenheim, Ramillies, Oudenarde and Malplaquet. His wife, Sarah Jennings, was a favourite of Queen Anne.

Marlowe, Christopher (1564–93), English dramatist and precursor of Shakespeare. His plays include *Dr. Faustus*, *Tamburlaine the Great*, *Edward II*, and *The Jew of Malta*. His early death was due to a tavern brawl.

Marryat, Frederick (1792–1848), English author of sea and adventure stories, including *Peter Simple*, *Mr. Midshipman Easy*, and *Masterman Ready*. He was a captain in the Royal Navy.

Marshall, George Catlett (1880–1959), American general. He was U.S. chief of staff 1939–45, and originated the Marshall Aid plan for European reconstruction. Nobel prize for peace 1953.

Martial, Marcus Valerius (*c.* 40–104), Roman poet, b. in Spain. He is mainly remembered for his epigrams.

Marvell, Andrew (1620–78), English poet and political writer. He was Milton's assistant and wrote mainly during the commonwealth.

Marx, Karl (1818–83), German founder of modern international communism, b. Trier of Jewish parentage. He studied law, philosophy and history at the universities of Bonn and Berlin, and later took up the study of economics. In conjunction with his friend Engels he wrote the *Communist Manifesto* of 1848 for the Communist League of which he was the leader. Because of his revolutionary activities he was forced to leave the continent and in 1849 settled in London. Here, mainly while living at 28 Dean Street, Soho, he wrote *Das Kapital*, a deep analysis of the economic laws that govern modern society. In 1864 he helped to found the first International. He ranks as one of the most original and influential thinkers of modern times. He was buried at Highgate cemetery. See Marxism, Section J.

Mary I (1516–58), Queen of England, was daughter of Henry VIII and Catherine of Aragon. A Roman Catholic, she reversed the religious changes made by her father and brother, and about 300 Protestants were put to death. She married Philip of Spain.

Mary II (1662–94), Queen of England with her husband the Dutch William III. As daughter of James II, she was invited to succeed after the revolution of 1688 and expelled her father.

Mary Stuart, Queen of Scots (1542–87), daughter of James V of Scotland and Mary of Guise, she laid claim to the English succession. She was imprisoned in England by Elizabeth and beheaded. Her husbands were the dauphin of France (d. 1560), Lord Darnley (murdered 1566) and Bothwell.

Masaryk, Jan Garrigue (1886–1948), Czech diplomat. The son of Thomas, he was Czech minister in London 1925–38, and foreign secretary while his government was in exile in London and after it returned to Prague, 1940–8.

Masaryk, Thomas Garrigue (1850–1937), Czech statesman and independence leader. He was the first president of Czechoslovakia, 1918–35.

Mascagni, Pietro (1863–1945), Italian composer of Cavalleria Rusticana.

Masefield, John (1878–1967), English poet. His best-known works are Salt-Water Ballads (as a boy he ran away to sea), and Reynard the Fox. He became poet laureate in 1930.

Maskelyne, John Nevil (1839–1917), English illusionist. He also exposed spiritualistic frauds.

Massenet, Jules Émile Frédéric (1842–1912), French composer of songs, orchestral suites, oratorios, and operas, among them Manon and Thaïs.

Massine, Léonide (b. 1896), Russian dancer, one of Diaghilev's choreographers. In 1944 he became a U.S. citizen.

Masters, Edgar Lee (1869–1950), American poet remembered for his Spoon River Anthology.

Matisse, Henri (1869–1954), French painter, member of a group known as Les Fauves (the wild beasts) for their use of violent colour and colour variation to express form and relief. A number of his paintings are in the Moscow Museum of Western Art.

Matsys (Massys), Quentin (1466–1530), Flemish painter, b. Louvain, settled Antwerp; he worked at a time when Italian influence was gaining ground. His Money-changer and his Wife is in the Louvre.

Maugham, William Somerset (1874–1965), British writer, b. Paris. He practised as a doctor till the success of Liza of Lambeth (1897), followed by Of Human Bondage. He was a master of the short story and his work reflects his travels in the East. In both world wars he served as a British agent.

Maupassant, Guy de (1850–93), French writer whose novels and short stories show penetrating realism. His stories include Boule de Suif, La Maison Tellier, and La Peur.

Mauriac, François (1885–1970), French writer whose novels deal with moral problems and include Le Baiser au Lépreux and the play Asmodée. Nobel prizewinner 1952.

Maurois, André (Émile Herzog) (1885–1967), French writer whose works include lives of Shelley and Disraeli.

Maxim, Sir Hiram Stevens (1840–1916), American inventor of the automatic quick-firing gun, perfected in London.

Maxton, James (1885–1946), Scottish Labour politician and pacifist; entered parliament 1922; chairman of I.L.P. 1926–31, 1934–9.

Maxwell, James Clerk (1831–79), Scottish physicist. He wrote his first scientific paper at 15, and after teaching in Aberdeen and London became first Cavendish professor of experimental physics at Cambridge. His mathematical mind, working on the discoveries of Faraday and others, gave physics a celebrated set of equations for the basic laws of electricity and magnetism. His work revolutionised fundamental physics. See Section F, Part II.

Mazarin, Jules (1602–61), cardinal and minister of France was b. in Italy. In spite of opposition from the nobles, he continued Richelieu's work of building up a strong centralised monarchy.

Mazeppa, Ivan Stepanovich (1644–1709), Cossack nobleman, b. Ukraine (then part of Poland, before E. Ukraine passed to Russia, 1667). He fought unsuccessfully for independence allying himself with Charles XII of Sweden against Peter I of Russia (Poltava, 1709). According to legend he was punished for intrigue by being tied to the back of a wild horse and sent into the steppes. Byron wrote a poem about him.

Mazzini, Giuseppe (1805–72), Italian patriot. B. Genoa, he advocated a free and united Italy, and from Marseilles he published a journal, Young Italy. Expelled from the continent, he took refuge in London in 1837. In 1848 he returned to Italy, and became dictator of the short-lived Roman republic, which was put down by French forces. His contribution to Italian unity was that of preparing the way.

Medawar, Sir Peter Brien (b. 1915), British zoologist, author of The Art of the Soluble and The Future of Man; president of the British Association 1969. Nobel prizewinner 1960.

Medici, Florentine family of merchants and bankers who were politically powerful and who patronised the arts. Cosimo the Elder (1389–1464) was for over 30 years virtual ruler of Florence. His grandson, Lorenzo the Magnificent (1449–92), poet, friend of artists and scholars, governed with munificence. His grandson, Lorenzo, was father of Catherine de' Medici, Queen of France (q.v.). A later Cosimo (1519–74) was an able Duke of Florence and then Grand-Duke of Tuscany, which title the Medicis held until 1737.

Méhul, Etienne Nicolas (1763–1817), French operatic composer. Joseph is his masterpiece.

Meitner, Lise (1878–1969), co-worker of Otto Hahn (q.v.) who interpreted his results (1939) as a fission process. A Jewish refugee scientist from Germany, she became a Swedish citizen in 1949.

Melanchthon, Philip (1497–1560), German religious reformer, who assisted Luther, and wrote the first Protestant theological work, Loci communes. He drew up the Augsburg confession (1530).

Melba, Nellie (Helen Porter Mitchell) (1861–1931), Australian soprano of international repute, b. near Melbourne.

Melbourne, 2nd Viscount (William Lamb) (1779–1848), English Whig statesman, was premier at the accession of Queen Victoria.

Mendel, Gregor Johann (1822–84), Austrian botanist. After entering the Augustinian monastery at Brünn he became abbot and taught natural history in the school. His main interest was the study of inheritance, and his elaborate observations of the common garden pea resulted in the law of heredity which bears his name. His hypothesis was published in 1866 but no attention was given to it until 1900. See Section F, Part IV.

Mendeleyev, Dmitri Ivanovich (1834–1907), Russian chemist, first to discover the critical temperatures. He formulated the periodic law of atomic weights (1869) and drew up the periodic table, predicting the properties of elements which might fill the gaps, Element 101 is named after him.

Mendelssohn-Bartholdy, Felix (1809–47), German composer, grandson of Moses Mendelssohn, philosopher. He belongs with Chopin and Schumann to the early 19th cent. classic-romantic school, and his music has delicacy and melodic beauty. He was conductor of the Gewandhaus concerts at Leipzig for a time and often visited England. See Section E.

Mendès-France, Pierre (b. 1907), French politician, premier 1954–5, but defeated on his North African policy. He was a critic of de Gaulle.

Menuhin, Yehudi (b. 1916), American violinist, b. New York of Jewish parentage. He first appeared as soloist at the age of seven and has international repute.

Menzies, Sir Robert Gordon (b. 1894), Australian Liberal statesman, premier 1939–41, 1949–66.

Mercator, Gerhardus (Gerhard Kremer) (1512–94), Flemish geographer who pioneered the making of accurate navigational maps. He worked out the map which bears his name in which meridians and parallels of latitude cross each other at right angles, enabling compass bearings to be drawn as straight lines.

Meredith, George (1828–1909), English writer, b. Portsmouth. His novels include *The Ordeal of Richard Feverel*, *The Egoist*, *Evan Harrington*, *Diana of the Crossways*, and *The Amazing Marriage*. His poetry has had renewed attention; the main works are *Modern Love* and *Poems and Lyrics of the Joy of Earth*.

Mesmer, Friedrich Anton (1733–1815), Austrian founder of mesmerism, or animal magnetism. *See* Mesmerism, Section J.

Mestrovic, Ivan (1883–1962), Yugoslav sculptor of international repute. He designed the temple at Kossovo. He later lived in England, and examples of his work are in London museums.

Metastasio, Pietro (Pietro Bonaventura Trapassi) (1698–1782), Italian librettist who lived in Vienna and provided texts for Gluck, Handel, Haydn, and Mozart.

Mechnikov, Ilya (1845–1916), Russian biologist who discovered that by " phagocytosis " certain white blood cells are capable of ingesting harmful substances such as bacteria (*see* Diseases of the Blood, Section P). For his work on immunity he shared the 1908 Nobel prize for medicine.

Michelangelo (Michelagniolo Buonarroti) (1475–1564), Italian painter, sculptor and poet. Of a poor but genteel Tuscan family, his first interest in sculpture came through his nurse, wife-of a stone-cutter. He was apprenticed to Domenico Ghirlandaio. Like Leonardo, he studied anatomy, but instead of spreading his talents over a wide field, he became obsessed with the problem of how to represent the human body. In him, classical idealism, mediaeval religious belief, and renaissance energy met. Perhaps his most impressive work is the ceiling of the Sistine Chapel (a surface of about 6,000 square feet), the *Last Judgement* behind the chapel altar, his marble *Pietà* (St. Peter's) the statue of *David* (Academy, Florence), the great figure of *Moses* (San Pietro in Vincoli, Rome), and the four allegorical figures *Day*, *Night*, *Dawn*, *Twilight* (intended for the tombs of the Medici family at San Lorenzo, Florence).

Michelet, Jules (1798–1874), French historian who wrote a history of France in 24 vols. and of the revolution in 7 vols.

Michelson, Albert Abraham (1852–1931), American physicist, b. Poland. He collaborated with E. W. Morley in an experiment to determine ether drift, the negative result of which was important for Einstein. Nobel prizewinner 1907. *See* Relativity, Section F, Part II.

Mickiewicz, Adam (1798–1855), Polish revolutionary poet, author of *The Ancestors* and *Pan Tadeusz*.

Mill, John Stuart (1806–73), English philosopher. A member of Bentham's utilitarian school, he later modified some of its tenets. His main work is *On Liberty*, which advocates social as well as political freedom and warns against the tyranny of the majority. *The Subjection of Women* supported women's rights. He also wrote *Principles of Political Economy*. He was godfather to Bertrand Russell.

Millais, Sir John Everett (1829–96), English artist, in his earlier years a pre-Raphaelite (*Ophelia*). His later works include *The Boyhood of Raleigh* and *Chill October*. He married Mrs. Ruskin after the annulment of her marriage.

Millet, Jean François (1814–75), French painter of rural life, sometimes in sombre mood; his works include *The Angelus*.

Millikan, Robert Andrews (1868–1954), American physicist, who determined the charge on the electron and discovered cosmic rays. Nobel prizewinner 1923.

Milne, Alan Alexander (1882–1956), English humorist and poet whose work for children is still widely read.

Milner, 1st Viscount (Alfred Milner) (1854–1925), British administrator, especially in South Africa; author of *England in Egypt*.

Miltiades (d. 489 B.C.), one of the leaders of the Athenian army against the Persians at Marathon.

Milton, John (1608–74), English poet, author of *Paradise Lost*. B. in London, he wrote while still at Cambridge *L'Allegro*, *Il Penseroso*, *Comus*, and *Lycidas*. The Civil War diverted his energies for years to the parliamentary and political struggle, but during this period he defended in *Areopagitica* the freedom of the press. After he had become blind he wrote *Paradise Lost* and a sonnet *On His Blindness*.

Minot, George Richards (1885–1950), who with W. P. Murphy discovered the curative properties of liver in pernicious anaemia. Shared Nobel prize 1934.

Mirabeau, Gabriel, Honoré Victor Riquetti, Comte de (1749–91), French revolutionary leader. His writings and speeches contributed to the revolution of 1789.

Mistral, Frédéric (1830–1914), French poet, and founder of a Provençal renaissance. His works include *Lou Tresor dòu Félibrige* and a Provençal dictionary. Nobel prizewinner 1904.

Mithridates (c. 132–63 B.C.), King of Pontus, in Asia Minor; after early successes against the Romans was defeated by Pompey.

Modigliani, Amedeo (1884–1920), Italian painter and sculptor, b. Livorno. His portraits and figure studies tend to elongation and simplification. He lived mainly in Paris, in poverty illness and disillusionment.

Moffat, James (1870–1944), Scottish divine who translated the Bible into modern English.

Mohammed (570–632), the founder of Islam, the religion of the Moslems, fled from Mecca to Medina in 622, from which date the Mohammedan era opens. By his constant preaching and proclaiming of the one and only deity Allah, he gathered round him a small and loyal, hard-fighting band of followers and was able to return to Mecca eight years later, an acknowledged conqueror. The sacred book of Islam, the *Koran*—though presented by him as an original revelation from the angel Gabriel—may in the main be traced to biblical and rabbinical sources. *See* Islam, Section J.

Molière (Jean Baptiste Poquelin) (1622–73), French playwright. B. in Paris, he gained experience as a strolling player, and subsequently in Paris, partly in the king's service, he wrote an unsurpassed series of plays varying from farce as in *Les Précieuses ridicules* to high comedy. Among his plays are *Tartuffe*, *Le Misanthrope*, *Le Bourgeois gentilhomme*, *Le Malade imaginaire*, and *Le Médécin malgré lui*.

Molotov, Vyacheslav Mikhailovich (b. 1890), Russian diplomat. He succeeded Litvinov as commissar for foreign affairs, 1939–49, and was chief representative of the Soviet Union at numerous post-war conferences. Expelled from the Communist Party 1964. He changed his name from Scriabin to Molotov (the hammer) early in his career to escape the imperial police.

Moltke, Helmuth, Count von (1800–91), Prussian general and chief of staff (1858–88) during the period when Prussia used success in three wars to unite Germany.

Mond, Ludwig (1838–1909), German chemist who in 1867 settled in England as an alkali manufacturer and in partnership with John Brunner successfully manufactured soda by the Solvay process.

Monet, Claude (1840–1926), French painter, leader of the Impressionists, the term being derived in 1874 from his landscape *Impression soleil levant*. He liked painting a subject in the open air at different times of day to show variation in light.

Monier-Williams, Sir Monier (1819–99), English Sanskrit scholar whose works include grammars, dictionaries, and editions of the *Sákuntalá*.

Monk, George, 1st Duke of Albemarle (1608–69), English general and admiral, whose reputation and moderation were mainly responsible for the return of Charles II in 1660.

Monmouth, Duke of (James Scott) (1649–85), English pretender, natural son of Charles II; centre of anti-Catholic feeling against succession of Duke of York (later James II). His troops, mostly peasants, were routed at Sedgemoor (1685) by John Churchill (later Duke of Marlborough). Beheaded on Tower Hill.

Monnet, Jean (b. 1888), French political economist, " father of the Common Market." He drafted the Monnet plan for French economic recovery (1947) and the plan for the establishment of the European Coal and Steel Community, of which he was president 1952–5.

Monroe, James (1758–1831), president of the U.S. He negociated the purchase of Louisiana from France in 1803, and propounded the doctrine that the American continent should not be colonised by a European power. (At that time however the U.S. could not have enforced it.)

Montagu, Lady Mary Wortley (1689–1762), English writer. From Constantinople where her husband was ambassador she wrote *Letters* of which a complete edition was published 1965–7. She introduced England to the idea of inoculation against smallpox.

Montaigne, Michel de (1533–92), French essayist of enquiring, sceptical, and tolerant mind.

Montcalm, Louis Joseph, Marquis de (1712–59), French general, who unsuccessfully commanded the French at Quebec against Wolfe.

Montesquieu, Charles de Secondat, Baron de la Brède et de (1689–1755), French philosopher. His works include *Lettres persanes*, a satire on contemporary life; and *L'Esprit des Lois*, giving his political philosophy. The latter was based largely, but to some extent mistakenly, on English practice, and its influence led the U.S. constitution to separate the executive (President) from the legislature (Congress).

Montessori, Maria (1860–1952), Italian educationist, who developed an educational system based on spontaneity.

Monteverdi, Claudio (1567–1643), Italian composer who pioneered in opera. His chief dramatic work is *Orfeo* (1608). *See* Section E.

Montezuma II (1466–1520), last emperor of Mexico when the Spanish under Cortes invaded.

Montfort, Simon de, Earl of Leicester (*c.* 1208–65), English statesman. He led the barons in revolt against the ineffective rule of Henry III, but he differed from other rebels in that he summoned a parliamentary assembly to which for the first time representatives came from the towns. He was killed at Evesham.

Montgolfier, the name of two brothers, Joseph Michel (1740–1810) and Jacques Etienne (1745–99), French aeronauts who constructed the first practical balloon, which flew 6 miles.

Montgomery of Alamein, 1st Viscount (Bernard Law Montgomery) (b. 1887), British field-marshal; commanded 8th Army in North Africa, Sicily, and Italy, 1942–4; commander-in-chief, British Group of Armies and Allied Armies in Northern France, 1944. He served as Deputy Supreme Allied Commander Europe (NATO), 1951–8. His memoirs were published in 1958.

Montrose, Marquess of (James Graham) (1612–50), Scottish general. In the Civil War he raised the Highland clansmen for Charles I and won the battles of Tippermuir, Inverlochy, and Kilsyth; but was finally defeated and executed. He was also a poet.

Moody, Dwight Lyman (1837–99), American revivalist preacher, associated with Ira D. Sankey, the " American singing pilgrim."

Moore, George (1852–1933), Irish novelist, author of *Confessions of a Young Man*, *Esther Waters*, and *Evelyn Innes*.

Moore, Henry (b. 1898), English sculptor in semi-abstract style, son of a Yorkshire coalminer. Examples of his work are to be seen in the Tate Gallery, St. Matthew's Church, Northampton, the Unesco building in Paris, and on an outside site opposite the House of Lords. O.M. 1963.

Moore, Sir John (1761–1809), British general, who trained the infantry for the Spanish Peninsular campaigns and conducted a brilliant retreat to Corunna, where he was mortally wounded after defeating the French under Soult.

Moore, Thomas (1779–1852), Irish poet, author of *Irish Melodies*, *Lalla Rookh* (oriental stories), and *The Epicurean* (novel). He also wrote a life of Byron.

More, Sir Thomas (1478–1535), English writer and statesman. In 1529 he succeeded Wolsey as lord chancellor, but on his refusal to recognise Henry VIII as head of the church he was executed. His *Utopia* describes an ideal state. He was canonised 1935.

Morgan, Sir Henry (*c.* 1635–88), Welsh buccaneer who operated in the Caribbean against the Spaniards, capturing and plundering Panama in 1671. Knighted by Charles II and made deputy-governor of Jamaica.

Morgan, John Pierpont (1837–1913), American

financier who built the family fortunes into a vast industrial empire.

Morland, George (1763–1804), English painter of rural life. His *Inside of a Stable* is in the National Gallery

Morley, 1st Viscount (John Morley) (1838–1923), English biographer and Liberal politician. He held political office, but is mainly remembered for his life of Gladstone. He also wrote on Voltaire, Rousseau, Burke, and Cobden.

Morley, Thomas (*c.* 1557–1603), English composer of madrigals, noted also for his settings of some of Shakespeare's songs. He was a pupil of Byrd, organist of St. Paul's cathedral, and wrote *Plaine and Easie Introduction to Practicall Music* (1597) which was used for 200 years.

Morris, William (1834–96), English poet and craftsman. His hatred of 19th-cent. ugliness, his belief in human equality, and in freedom and happiness for all, combined to make him a socialist, and he accomplished much for the improvement of domestic decoration. He was a popular lecturer, founded the Socialist League and the Kelmscott Press.

Morrison of Lambeth, Baron (Herbert Morrison) (1888–1965), British Labour statesman. From being an errand-boy, he rose to become leader of the London County Council. During the war he was home secretary, and he was deputy prime minister in a period of notable legislation, 1945–51.

Morse, Samuel Finley Breese (1791–1872), American pioneer in electromagnetic telegraphy and inventor of the dot-and-dash code that bears his name. He was originally an artist.

Mountbatten of Burma, 1st Earl (Louis Mountbatten) (b. 1900), British admiral and statesman. In the second world war he became chief of combined operations in 1942. As last viceroy of India, he carried through the transfer of power to Indian hands in 1947 and was the first governor-general of the dominion. He became first sea lord in 1955 and was chief of defence staff 1959–65.

Mozart, Wolfgang Amadeus (1756–91), Austrian composer. B. Salzburg, he began his career at four and toured Europe at six. In 1781 he settled in Vienna, where he became a friend of Haydn and where his best music was written. His genius lies in the effortless outpouring of all forms of music, in the ever-flowing melodies, in the consistent beauty and symmetry of his compositions, and in the exactness of his method. Among the loveliest and grandest works in instrumental music are his three great symphonies in E flat, G minor, and C (called the " Jupiter "), all written in six weeks in 1788. Three of the greatest operas in musical history are his *Marriage of Figaro* (1786), *Don Giovanni* (1787), and *The Magic Flute* (1791). His last composition, written under the shadow of death, was the *Requiem Mass*, a work of tragic beauty. *See* Section E.

Müller, Sir Ferdinand (1825–96), German-born botanist who emigrated to Australia, where he was director of the Melbourne Botanical Gardens, 1857–73, and whence he introduced the eucalyptus into Europe.

Mumford, Lewis (b. 1895), American writer on town-planning and social problems. His works include a tetralogy: *Technics and Civilisation*, *The Culture of Cities*, *The Condition of Man*, and *The Conduct of Life*; *The Myth of the Machine*, and *The Urban Prospect*.

Munkacsy, Michael von (1844–1900), Hungarian painter of historical subjects.

Munnings, Sir Alfred (1878–1959), English painter, especially of horses and sporting subjects.

Murdock, William (1754–1839), Scottish engineer and inventor, the first to make practical use of coal gas as an illuminating agent (introduced at the Soho works, Birmingham, 1800).

Murillo, Bartolomé Esteban (1617–82), Spanish painter, b. Seville, where he founded an Academy. His early works, such as *Two Peasant Boys* (Dulwich) show peasant and street life; his later paintings are religious, *e.g.*, the *Immaculate Conception* in the Prado.

Murray, Gilbert (1866–1957), classical scholar of Australian birth who settled in England. A teacher of Greek at the universities of Glasgow and Oxford, he translated Greek drama so as to bring it within the reach of the general pub lic. His interest in the classics was begun by an English master's enthusiasm at his country school at Mittagong, New South Wales. He was a strong supporter of the League of Nations and the United Nations.

Mussolini, Benito (1883–1945), Fascist dictator of Italy 1922–43. From 1935 an aggressive foreign policy (Abyssinia and Spain) was at first successful, and in June 1940 he entered the war on the side of Hitler. Defeat in North Africa and the invasion of Sicily caused the collapse of his government. He was shot dead by partisans while attempting to escape to Switzerland.

Mussorgsky, Modest Petrovich (1839–81), Russian composer whose masterpeice is the opera *Boris Godunov* after the play by Pushkin. His piano suite *Pictures at an Exhibition* was orchestrated by Ravel. *See Section E.*

N

Nanak (1469–1538), Indian guru or teacher, who tried to put an end to religious strife, teaching that " God is one, whether he be Allah or Rama." His followers are the Sikhs. *See* Sikhism, Section J.

Nansen, Fridtjof (1861–1930), Norwegian explorer. In 1893 his north polar expedition reached the highest latitude till then attained—86° 14'. He published an account called *Farthest North.* He was active in Russian famine relief, 1921. Nobel peace prize 1922.

Napier, John (1550–1617), Scottish mathematician, b. Edinburgh, invented logarithms (published 1614) and the modern notation of fractions, improvements in the methods of mathematical expression which helped to advance cosmology and physics.

Napoleon I (Bonaparte) (1769–1821), French emperor and general, of Corsican birth (Ajaccio). Trained in French military schools, he became prominent in the early years of the revolution, with uncertainty at home and war abroad. In 1796 he became commander of the army in Italy and defeated the Austrians, so that France obtained control of Lombardy. He then led an expedition to Egypt but Nelson destroyed his fleet. After further Italian victories, he made a *coup d'état* in 1799, and in 1804 became emperor. Against continuing European opposition, he defeated the Austrians at Austerlitz, and his power in Europe was such that he made his brothers Joseph, Louis, and Jerome kings of Naples, Holland, and Westphalia; but in Spain he provoked the Peninsular War, and his armies were gradually driven back by the Spanish, helped by Wellington; while his invasion of Russia in 1812 ended in a disastrous retreat from Moscow; and in 1814 the Allies forced him to abdicate and retire to Elba. He emerged again in 1815 to be defeated at Waterloo and exiled to St. Helena. His government at home was firm and promoted some reforms (*e.g.*, legal codification), but the country was weakened by his wars. In Europe, in spite of the suffering caused by war, there was some spread of French revolutionary ideas, and equally a reaction against them on the part of authority. The imperial idea lingered in France, and Napoleon's remains were brought to Paris in 1840. He married first Josephine Beauharnais and second Marie Louise of Austria.

Napoleon II (1811–32), son of Napoleon I and Marie Louise.

Napoleon III (1808–73), son of Napoleon I's brother Louis. He returned to France in the revolution of 1848, and in 1851 came to power by a *coup d'état*. In his reign Paris was remodelled. His foreign policy was adventurous (the Crimean war, intervention in Mexico, war against Austria and Italy); but when he was manoeuvred by Bismarck into the Franco-Prussian war and defeated at Sedan he lost his throne and retired to England. His wife was the Spanish Eugénie de Montijo.

Nash, John (1752–1835), English architect who planned Regent Street, laid out Regent's Park, enlarged Buckingham Palace, and designed Marble Arch and the Brighton Pavilion.

Nash, Paul (1889–1946), English painter and designer, official war artist in both world wars. Best known pictures are *The Menin Road* of 1918 and *Totes Meer* of 1941.

Nash, Walter (1882–1968), New Zealand Labour politician; prime minister 1957–60.

Nasmyth, James (1808–90), Scottish inventor of the steam-hammer, which became indispensable in all large iron and engineering works.

Nasser, Gamal Abdel (1918–70), leader of modern Egypt and of the Arab world. He led the 1952 army coup that deposed King Farouk, becoming president of the first Egyptian Republic in 1956 and of the United Arab Republic in 1958. His nationalisation of the Suez Canal in 1956 precipitated a short-lived attack by Britain and France. Israeli-Arab hostility led to the June war of 1967. He carried out reforms to bring his people out of feudal backwardness, including the building (with Russian help and finance) of the Aswan High Dam.

Needham, Joseph (b. 1900), British biochemist, historian of science, orientalist, author of the historical work *Science and Civilisation in China* (7 vols., 1954–).

Nehru, Pandit Jawaharlal (1889–1964), Indian national leader and statesman, first prime minister and minister of foreign affairs when India became independent in 1947. He studied at Harrow and Cambridge, and was for many years a leading member of the Congress Party, during which time he was frequently imprisoned for political activity. He played a part in the final negotiations for independence. Under his leadership India made technical, industrial, and social advances. In world affairs his influence was for peace and non-alignment.

Nelson, 1st Viscount (Horatio Nelson) (1758–1805), English admiral. Son of a Norfolk clergyman, he went to sea at 12 and became a captain in 1793. In the French revolutionary wars he lost his right eye in 1794 and his right arm in 1797. Rear-admiral in 1797, he defeated the French at Aboukir Bay in 1798. He was also at the bombardment of Copenhagen in 1801. In 1805 he destroyed the French fleet at Trafalgar, in which battle he was killed. His daring and decision made him a notable commander. He loved Emma Hamilton.

Nenni, Pietro (b. 1891), Italian socialist politician. He became secretary-general of his party in 1944, and was deputy prime minister, 1963–8.

Nernst, Walther Hermann (1864–1941), German scientist who established the third law of thermodynamics that dealt with the behaviour of matter at temperatures approaching absolute zero. Nobel prizewinner 1920.

Nero, Claudius Caesar (A.D. 37–68), Roman emperor, the adopted son of Claudius. He was weak and licentious and persecuted Christians. In his reign occurred the fire of Rome.

Newcomen, Thomas (1663–1729), English inventor, one of the first to put a steam-engine into practical operation. In 1705 he patented his invention, which was the pumping-engine used in Cornish mines until the adoption of Watt's engine.

Newman, Ernest (1868–1959), English music critic, whose chief work is the *Life of Richard Wagner.* He also wrote *A Musical Critic's Holiday.*

Newman, John Henry (1801–90), English priest and writer, who became a cardinal of the Roman church in 1879, and was a founder of the Oxford Movement. He is best remembered by his *Apologia pro Vita Sua* in which he described the development of his religious thought. He wrote *Lead, kindly Light,* set to music 30 years later by J. B. Dykes, and *The Dream of Gerontius,* set to music of Elgar. *See* Tractarianism, Section J.

Newton, Sir Isaac (1642–1727), English scientist, b. Woolsthorpe, Lincs. (the year Galileo died). He studied at Cambridge but was at home during the plague years 1665 and 1666 when he busied himself with problems concerned with optics and gravitation. Through his tutor Isaac Barrow he was appointed to the Lucasian chair of mathematics at Cambridge in 1669 and remained there until 1696 when he was appointed Warden, and later Master of the Mint. He was a secret Unitarian and did not marry. His three great discoveries were to show that white light could be separated into a sequence of coloured components forming the visible spectrum; to use the calculus (invented by him independently of Leibnitz) to investigate the forces of nature in a quantitative way; and to show by his theory of gravitation (for which Copernicus, Kepler and Galileo had prepared the way) that the universe was regulated by simple mathematical laws. His vision was set forth in the *Philosophiae Naturalis Principia Mathematica* of 1687, usually called the *Principia*. It was not until 200 years later that Einstein showed there could be another theory of celestial mechanics.

Ney, Michel (1769–1815), French general who served under Napoleon, especially at Jena, Borodino, and Waterloo.

Nicholas II (1868–1918), last emperor and Tsar of Russia, son of Alexander III. His reign was marked by an unsuccessful war with Japan (1904–5), and by the 1914–18 war. Ineffective and lacking ability, he set up a Duma in 1906 too late for real reform. Revolution broke out in 1917 and he and his family were shot in July 1918.

Nicholas, St. (4th cent.), bishop of Myra, is associated with Christmas under the corruption of Santa Claus.

Nicholson, Sir William (1872–1949), English artist known for his portraits and woodcuts. His son, **Ben Nicholson, O.M.**, (b. 1894) is noted for his abstract paintings.

Nicolson, Sir Harold (1886–1968), English diplomat, author, and critic. His works include *King George V*; and *Diaries and Letters*. His wife was the novelist **Victoria Sackville-West** (1892–1962).

Niemöller, Martin (b. 1892), German Lutheran pastor who opposed the Nazi regime and was confined in a concentration camp. He was president of the World Council of Churches in 1961.

Nietzsche, Friedrich Wilhelm (1844–1900), German philosopher, in his younger years influenced by Wagner and Schopenhauer. His teaching that only the strong ought to survive and his doctrine of the superman are expounded in *Thus spake Zarathustra, Beyond Good and Evil*, and *The Will to Power*.

Nightingale, Florence (1820–1910), English nurse and pioneer of hospital reform, who during the Crimean war organised in face of considerable official opposition a nursing service to relieve the sufferings of the British soldiers, who called her "the lady with the lamp." Her system was adopted and developed in all parts of the world.

Nijinsky, Vaslav (1892–1950), Russian dancer, one of the company which included Pavlova, Karsavina and Fokine, brought by Diaghilev to Paris and London before the 1914–18 war. In *Les Sylphides, Spectre de la Rose* and *L'Après-midi d'un Faune* he won a supreme place among male dancers.

Nikisch, Arthur (1855–1922), Hungarian conductor of the Boston Symphony Orchestra, 1889–93. He was piano-accompanist to the Lieder singer, Elena Gerhardt.

Nimitz, Chester William (1885–1966), American admiral, commanded in the Pacific 1941–5; chief of naval operations 1945–7.

Nixon, Richard Milhous (b. 1913), Republican president of the U.S., 1969– ; elected to Congress, 1946; to Senate, 1951; vice-president, 1952; re-elected, 1956; received Republican presidential nomination in 1960 when Kennedy won with a narrow majority.

Nkrumah, Kwame (b. 1909), Ghanaian leader, first premier of Ghana when his country achieved independence in 1957 and president in 1960. His government was spectacular and he promoted the Pan-African movement; but unsound finance and dictatorial methods led to his overthrow in 1966.

Nobel, Alfred Bernhard (1833–96), Swedish inventor and philanthropist. An engineer and chemist who discovered dynamite, he amassed a large fortune from the manufacture of explosives; and bequeathed a fund for annual prizes to those who each year have contributed most to the benefit of mankind in the fields of physics, chemistry, physiology or medicine, literature and peace. See L126–8.

North, Frederick (1732–92), favourite minister of George III who held the premiership from 1770 to 1782. (He held the courtesy title of Lord

North from 1752.) His incompetent foreign policy led to the American war of independence.

Northcliffe, 1st Viscount (Alfred Charles Harmsworth) (1865–1922), British journalist and newspaper proprietor, b. near Dublin. He began *Answers* in 1888 with his brother Harold, (later Lord Rothermere). In 1894 they bought the *Evening News*, and in 1896 the *Daily Mail*. In 1908 he took over *The Times*.

Northumberland, John Dudley, Duke of (1502–53), English politician who attempted to secure for his daughter-in-law Lady Jane Grey the succession to the throne after Edward VI.

Nostradamus or **Michel de Notre Dame** (1503–66), French astrologer and physician, known for his prophecies in *Centuries*.

Novalis, the pseudonym of Baron Friedrich von Hardenberg (1772–1801), German romantic poet and novelist, whose chief work is the unfinished *Heinrich von Ofterdingen*.

Nuffield, 1st Viscount (William Richard Morris) (1877–1963), British motor-car manufacturer and philanthropist, and until he retired in 1952 chairman of Morris Motors Ltd. He provided large sums for the advancement of medicine in the university of Oxford, for Nuffield College, and in 1943 established the Nuffield Foundation, endowing it with £10 million.

Nyerere, Julius (b. 1922), Tanzanian leader. He became first premier of Tanganyika when it became independent in 1961; and president in 1962. In 1964 he negotiated its union with Zanzibar.

O

Oates, Lawrence Edward (1880–1912), English antartic explorer. He joined Scott's expedition of 1910, and was one of the five to reach the south pole; but on the return journey, being crippled by frost-bite, he walked out into the blizzard to die.

Oates, Titus (1649–1705), English informer and agitator against Roman catholics.

O'Casey, Sean (1884–1964), Irish dramatist whose plays include *Juno and the Paycock, The Silver Tassie, Red Roses for Me*, and *Oak Leaves and Lavender*.

Occam (**Ockham**), **William of** (c. 1270–1349), English scholar and philosopher and one of the most original thinkers of all time. He belonged to the Order of Franciscans, violently opposed the temporal power of the Pope, espoused the cause of nominalism and laid the foundations of modern theories of government and theological scepticism. See Occam's razor, Section J.

O'Connell, Daniel (1775–1847), Irish national leader. A barrister, he formed the Catholic Association in 1823 to fight elections; his followers aimed at the repeal of the Act of Union with England, and formed a Repeal Association in 1840; but the formation of the Young Ireland party, the potato famine, and ill-health undermined his position and he died in exile.

O'Connor, Feargus (1794–1855), working-class leader in England, of Irish birth. He presented the Chartist petition in 1848.

O'Connor, Thomas Power (1848–1929), Irish nationalist and journalist, sat in parliament 1880–1929 and founded the *Star*.

Oersted, Hans Christian (1777–1851), Danish physicist who discovered the connection between electricity and magnetism.

Offa (d. 796), king of Mercia (mid-England), was the leading English king of his day, and built a defensive dyke from the Dee to the Wye.

Offenbach, Jacques (1819–80), German–Jewish composer, b. Cologne, settled at Paris, and is mainly known for his light operas, especially *Tales of Hoffmann*.

Ohm, Georg Simon (1787–1854), German physicist, professor at Munich, who in 1826 formulated the law of electric current, known as Ohm's law, one of the foundation stones in electrical science. See L86.

Olivier, Baron (Laurence Kerr Olivier) (b. 1907), British actor and director, especially in Shakespearean roles. He has also produced, directed, and played in films, including *Henry V, Hamlet,* and *Richard III.* In 1962 he was appointed director of the National Theatre and in 1970 received a life peerage.

Oman, Sir Charles William (1860–1946), English historian, especially of mediaeval warfare and of the Peninsular War. He also wrote memoirs.

Omar ibn al Khattab (581–644), adviser to Mahomet, succeeded Abu Bakr as 2nd caliph. In his reign Islam became an imperial power. He died at the hands of a foreign slave.

Omar Khayyám (*c.* 1050–1123), Persian poet and mathematician, called Khayyám (tent-maker) because of his father's occupation. His fame as a scientist has been eclipsed by his *Rubaiyat,* made known to English readers by Edward FitzGerald in 1859.

O'Neill, Eugene Gladstone (1888–1953), American playwright who, after spending his adventurous youth in sailing, gold-prospecting, and journalism, first won success in 1914 with the one-act play, *Thirst.* His later plays include *Anna Christie, Strange Interlude, Mourning Becomes Electra, The Iceman Cometh.* Nobel prizewinner 1936. *See also* Section I.

Orchardson, Sir William Quiller (1835–1910), Scottish painter, b. Edinburgh, best known for his *Napoleon I on board H.M.S. Bellerophon* and *Ophelia.*

Origen (*c.* 185–254), Christian philosopher and Biblical scholar, who taught at Alexandria and Caesarea, and was imprisoned and tortured in the persecution of Decius, 250. He drew on Greek philosophy as well as on the Hebrew scriptures in his exposition of Christian doctrine.

Orpen, Sir William (1878–1931), British painter of portraits, conversation pieces, and pictures of the 1914–18 war.

Ortega y Gasset, José (1883–1955), Spanish philosopher and essayist, known for his *Tema de Nuestro Tiempo* and *La Rebelión de Las Masas.*

Orwell, George (Eric Arthur Blair) (1903–50), English satirist, b. India, author of *Animal Farm* and *Nineteen Eighty-Four.*

Osler, Sir William (1849–1919), Canadian physician and medical historian, authority on diseases of the blood and spleen.

Ossietzky, Carl von (1889–1938), German pacifist leader after the first world war; sent by Hitler to a concentration camp. Nobel peace prize 1935.

Oswald, St. (*c.* 605–42), won the Northumbrian throne by battle in 633 and introduced Christianity there.

Otto I (the Great) (912–73), founder of the Holy Roman Empire (he was crowned king of the Germans in 936 and emperor at Rome in 962). The son of Henry I, he built up a strong position in Italy (as regards the papacy) and in Germany where he established the East Mark (Austria).

Otto, Nikolaus August (1832–91), German engineer and inventor of the four-stroke cycle that bears his name.

Ouida (Louise de la Ramée) (1939–1908), English novelist of French extraction, whose romantic stories include *Under Two Flags.*

Ovid (43 B.C.–A.D. 18), Latin poet (Publius Ovidius Naso), chiefly remembered for his *Art of Love* and *Metamorphoses.* He died in exile.

Owen, Robert (1771–1858), Welsh pioneer socialist, b. Montgomeryshire. As manager, and later owner, of New Lanark cotton mills he tried to put his philanthropic views into effect; other communities on co-operative lines were founded in Hampshire and in America (New Harmony, Indiana) but although unsuccessful they were influential in many directions. He challenged the doctrine of *laissez-faire,* inaugurated socialism and the co-operative movement, and foresaw the problems of industrial development.

P

Pachmann, Vladimir de (1848–1933), Russian pianist gifted in the playing of Chopin.

Paderewski, Ignace Jan (1860–1941), Polish pianist and nationalist. He represented his country at Versailles and was the first premier of a reconstituted Poland. He died in exile in the second world war.

Paganini, Niccolo (1782–1840), Italian violinist and virtuoso who revolutionised violin technique.

Paine, Thomas (1737–1809), English-born radical political writer. He spent the years 1774–87 in America helping the American revolutionary cause and holding various offices. On his return to England he wrote *The Rights of Man,* was condemned for treason, and had to flee to France. There he entered French politics, was sent to prison, and wrote *The Age of Reason,* advocating deism. His last years were spent in poverty in America.

Palestrina, Giovanni Pierluigi da (*c.* 1525–94), Italian composer of unaccompanied church music and madrigals. *See* Section E.

Palgrave, Sir Francis (1788–1861), English historian and archivist, an early editor of record series. His son Francis Turner Palgrave (1824–97) was a poet and critic and edited *The Golden Treasury;* while another son, William Gifford Palgrave (1826–88) was a traveller and diplomat.

Palissy, Bernard (*c.* 1510–89), French potter who discovered the art of producing white enamel, after which he set up a porcelain factory in Paris which was patronised by royalty.

Palladio, Andrea (1508–80), Italian architect, b. Padua, whose style was modelled on Roman architecture (symmetrical planning and harmonic proportions) and had wide influence.

Palmer, Samuel (1805–81), English landscape painter and etcher, follower of Blake whom he met in 1824. His *Bright Cloud* and *In a Shoreham Garden* are in the Victoria and Albert Museum.

Palmerston, 3rd Viscount (Henry John Temple) (1784–1865), English Whig statesman. At first a Tory, he was later Whig foreign secretary for many years, and prime minister 1855 and 1859–65. His vigorous foreign policy wherever possible took the lead and bluntly asserted English rights.

Pancras, St. (d. 304), patron saint of children, was (according to tradition) baptised in Rome where he was put to death at the age of fourteen in the persecution under Diocletian.

Pandit, Vijaya Lakshmi (b. 1900), sister of Nehru, was India's first ambassador to the Soviet Union (1947–9), and to the U.S. (1949–51), and the first woman to be elected president of the U.N. General Assembly (1954).

Panizzi, Sir Anthony (1797–1879), Italian bibliographer and nationalist. Taking refuge in England after 1821, he became in 1856 chief librarian of the British Museum, undertook a new catalogue and designed the reading room.

Pankhurst, Emmeline (1858–1928), English suffragette who, with her daughters Christabel and Sylvia, worked for women's suffrage, organising the Women's Social and Political Union.

Papin, Denis (1647–1714), French physicist and inventor. He invented the condensing pump, and was a pioneer in the development of the steam-engine. Not being a mechanic, he made all his experiments by means of models.

Paracelsus (Theophrastus Bombastus von Hohenheim) (1493–1541), Swiss physician whose speculations though muddled served to reform medical thought. He criticised the established authorities, Galen and Aristotle, and experimented and made new chemical compounds. His earliest printed work was *Practica* (1529).

Park, Mungo (1771–1806), Scottish explorer in west Africa, where he lost his life. He wrote *Travels in the Interior of Africa* (1799).

Parker, Joseph (1830–1902), English Congregational preacher, especially at what later became the City Temple.

Parnell, Charles Stewart (1846–91), Irish national leader. To draw attention to Ireland's problems, he used obstruction in parliament. He was president of the Land League but was not implicated in crimes committed by some members. His party supported Gladstone, who became converted to Home Rule. His citation in divorce proceedings brought his political career to an end.

Parry, Sir William Edward (1790–1855), English explorer and naval commander in the Arctic, where he was sent to protect fisheries and also tried to reach the north pole.

Parsons, Sir Charles Algernon (1854–1931),

English inventor of the steam-turbine, who built the first turbine-driven steamship in 1897.

Pascal, Blaise (1623–62), Frenchman of varied gifts, b. at Clermont-Ferrand. At first a mathematician, he patented a calculating machine. His *Lettres provinciales* influenced Voltaire. In 1654 he turned to religion, and his incomplete religious writings were published posthumously as *Pensées. See also* Jansenism, Section J.

Pasternak, Boris Leonidovich (1890–1960), Russian poet and writer. B. Moscow, he published his first poems in 1931. For some years his time was spent in translating foreign literature, but in 1958 his novel *Dr. Zhivago*, which describes the Russian revolution and is in the Russian narrative tradition, was published abroad, though banned in the Soviet Union. He was awarded a Nobel prize but obliged to decline it.

Pasteur, Louis (1822–95), French chemist, whose work was inspired by an interest in the chemistry of life. His researches on fermentation led to the science of bacteriology and his investigations into infectious diseases and their prevention to the science of immunology. The pathological–bacteriological import of his researches came about mainly through his disciples (Lister, Roux, and others) and not directly, though all founded on his early non-medical investigations on organisms of fermentation, etc., which were of great importance in industry, and fundamentally. He spent most of his life as director of scientific studies at the Ecole Normale at Paris. The Institute Pasteur was founded in 1888. *See also* Immunology, Section P.

Patmore, Coventry (1823–96), English poet. *The Angel in the House* deals with domesticity. Later he became a Roman catholic, and *The Unknown Eros* is characterised by erotic mysticism.

Patrick, St. (*c.* 389–*c.* 461), apostle of Ireland, was born in Britain or Gaul, and after some time on the continent (taken thither after his capture by pirates) went as missionary to Ireland, where after years of teaching and a visit to Rome he fixed his see at Armagh. He wrote *Confessions.*

Patti, Adelina (1843–1919), coloratura soprano, b. in Madrid of Italian parents, and of international repute.

Paul, St. (*c.* A.D. 10–*c.* 67), Jew to whom was mainly due the extension of Christianity in Europe. B. Tarsus (in Asia Minor), he was a Pharisee, and became converted about A.D. 37. His missionary journeys took him to the Roman provinces of Asia, Macedonia, and Greece (Rome had already had Christian teaching); and his epistles form nearly half the New Testament and were written before the gospels. He helped to develop both the organisation of the early church and its teaching. The date order of his epistles is to some extent conjectural. It is believed that he was executed in Rome. His Hebrew name was Saul.

Paul VI (Giovanni Battista Montini) (b. 1897), elected Pope in 1963 on the death of John XXIII. He was formerly archbishop of Milan. He visited the Holy Land in 1964.

Pavlov, Ivan Petrovich (1849–1936), Russian physiologist, known for his scientific experimental work on animal behaviour, particularly conditioned reflexes and the relation between psychological stress and brain function. Nobel prizewinner 1904.

Pavlova, Anna (1885–1941), Russian ballerina, b. St. Petersburg, excelling in the roles of *Giselle* and the *Dying Swan.*

Peabody, George (1795–1869), American philanthropist, a successful merchant who lived mainly in London. He supported exploration and education.

Peacock, Thomas Love (1785–1866), English novelist, b. Weymouth. His work, which is mainly satirical, includes *Headlong Hall* and *Nightmare Abbey.*

Pearson, Lester Bowles (b. 1897), Canadian politician, served as minister for external affairs 1948–57, and prime minister 1963–8. He has supported the United Nations. Nobel peace prize 1957.

Peary, Robert Edwin (1856–1920), American arctic explorer, discoverer of the north pole (1909).

Peel, Sir Robert (1788–1850), English Conservative statesman, b. in Lancashire, son of a manufacturer. He first held office in 1811. With Wellington he enacted toleration for Roman catholics in 1829. As home secretary he reorganised London police. He developed a new policy of Conservatism, and in 1846, largely as a result of the Irish famine, he repealed the corn laws which protected English agriculture. He died from a riding accident.

Peirce, Charles Sanders (1839–1914), American philosopher, founder of the theory of pragmatism which was later developed by his friend William James. *See* Pragmatism, Section J.

Penfield, Wilder Graves (b. 1891), Canadian brain surgeon, author of *The Cerebral Cortex of Man, Epilepsy and the Functional Anatomy of the Human Brain.*

Penn, William (1644–1718), English Quaker and founder of Pennsylvania. The son of Admiral William Penn, he persisted in becoming a Quaker, and on receiving for his father's services a crown grant in North America he founded there Pennsylvania. He wrote *No Cross, No Crown.*

Penney, Baron (William George Penney) (b. 1909), British scientist. After 23 years in atomic research and development he returned to academic life in 1967 to become Rector of Imperial College. His nuclear research team at A.E.A. developed the advanced gas-cooled reactor (A.G.R.) chosen for the Dungeness " B " and Hinkley Point " B " power stations.

Pepys, Samuel (1633–1703), English diarist and naval administrator. His diary, 1660–69, was kept in cipher and not deciphered till 1825. It gives vivid personal details and covers the plague and fire of London. (The first complete and unexpurgated version of the diary was issued in 1970.)

Pereda, José Maria de (1833–1906), Spanish regional novelist (around his native Santander).

Pérez Galdós, Benito (1843–1920), Spanish novelist and dramatist, who has been compared to Balzac for his close study and portrayal of all social classes, especially in the series of 46 short historical novels *Episodios nacionales.* His longer novels, *Novelas españolas contemporáneas,* some of which are translated, number 31.

Pergolesi, Giovanni Battista (1710–36), Italian composer, best known for his humourous opera *La Serva Padrona* and his *Stabat Mater.*

Pericles (*c.* 490–429 B.C.), Athenian statesman, general, and orator, who raised Athens to the point of its fullest prosperity, and greatest beauty, with the Parthenon, Erechtheum, and other buildings; but he died in the plague which followed the outbreak of the Peloponnesian war.

Perkin, Sir William Henry (1838–1907), English chemist, b. London, who while seeking to make a substitute for quinine discovered in 1856 the first artificial aniline dye, mauve. His son, **W. H. Perkin** (1860–1929) was an organic chemist of note.

Perrin, Francis (b. 1901), French scientist and socialist; succeeded Joliot-Curie as High Commr. of Atomic Energy, 1951–; professor of Atomic Physics, Collège de France, 1946–. Nobel prizewinner 1926.

Persius Flaccus Aulus (A.D. 34–62), Roman satirist and Stoic philosopher.

Perugino, Pietro (1446–1524), Italian artist. He worked in the Sistine Chapel at Rome and he taught Raphael.

Pestalozzi, Johann Heinrich (1746–1827), Swiss educational reformer whose theories laid the foundation of modern primary education. His teaching methods were far in advance of his time. He wrote *How Gertrude Educates Her Children.*

Pétain, Henri Philippe (1856–1951), French general and later collaborator. In the first world war he was in command at Verdun, and between the wars he sponsored the Maginot line. In the second world war, when French resistance collapsed, he came to terms with Germany and headed an administration at Vichy. After the war he was sentenced to life imprisonment.

Peter I, the Great (1672–1725), emperor of Russia. Son of Alexei, he succeeded his brother after some difficulty. He reorganised the army, and, after coming to Deptford to learn shipbuilding, he created a navy. To some extent he westernised Russian social life, and created a new capital at St. Petersburg (1703). In war with Charles XII of Sweden he was at first defeated, but later victorious at Poltava (1709). He married a peasant, Catherine, who succeeded him.

Peter the Hermit (c. 1050–1115), French monk who preached the First Crusade, originated by pope Urban II at the council of Clermont. He went on the crusade himself, but gave up at Antioch.

Petrarch, Francesco (1304–74), Italian poet, son of a Florentine exile. He is chiefly remembered for his poems *To Laura*, but he was also a scholar who paved the way for the Renaissance.

Petrie, Sir Flinders (1853–1942), British egyptologist. He excavated in Britain (1875–90), Egypt (1880–1924), and Palestine 1927–38). See his *Seventy Years of Archaeology*.

Phidias (5th cent. B.C.), Greek sculptor especially in gold, ivory and bronze, worked at Athens for Pericles. No certain examples of his work are extant, but the Elgin marbles in the British Museum may be from his designs.

Philip II of France (1165–1223), son of Louis VII. He went on the Third Crusade with Richard I of England, but in France is mainly remembered for firm government, the recovery of Normandy from England, and the beautifying of Paris.

Philip II of Macedonia (382–336 B.C.), a successful commander, made his the leading military kingdom in Greece and was father of Alexander the Great.

Philip II of Spain (1527–98), succeeded his father Charles V in Spain and the Netherlands, also in Spanish interests overseas. In the Netherlands his strict Roman catholic policy provoked a revolt which ended in 1579 in the independence of the United Provinces. He married Mary Tudor of England; and after her death sent the ill-fated Armada against Elizabeth in 1588.

Philip V of Spain (1683–1746), first Bourbon king, succeeded his uncle Charles II and was grandson of Louis XIV. His accession provoked European war.

Phillip, Arthur (1738–1814), first governor of New South Wales. Under his command the first fleet of 717 convicts set sail from Britain to Australia, and with the founding of Sydney in 1788 colonisation of the whole country began.

Phillips, Stephen (1868–1915), English poet who wrote verse dramas, including *Paolo and Francesca*.

Piast, first Polish dynasty in Poland until the 14th cent. and until the 17th cent. in Silesia.

Piazzi, Giuseppe (1746–1826), Italian astronomer who discovered Ceres, the first of the asteroids to be seen by man.

Picasso, Pablo Ruiz (b. 1881) Spanish painter, b. Málaga; received his early training in Catalonia and settled in Paris in 1903. He and Braque were the originators of Cubism (c. 1909). His influence over contemporary art is comparable with that exercised by Cézanne (q.v.) over the artists of his time. Perhaps the best-known single work is his mural *Guernica*, painted at the time of the Spanish civil war, expressing the artist's loathing of fascism and the horrors of war. His genius has also found scope in sculpture, ceramics, and the graphic arts, and he has designed decor costumes for the ballet.

Piccard, Auguste (1884–1962), Swiss physicist, noted for balloon ascents into the stratosphere and for submarine research. In 1960 his son Jacques made a descent of over 7 miles in the Marianas trench in the western Pacific in a bathyscaphe designed and built by his father.

Pilsudski, Joseph (1867–1935), Polish soldier and statesman who in 1919 attempted by force to restore Poland's 1772 frontiers but was driven back. From 1926 he was dictator.

Pindar (522–443 B.C.), Greek lyric poet.

Pinero, Sir Arthur Wing (1885–1934), English dramatist whose plays include *Dandy Dick*, *The Second Mrs. Tanqueray* and *Mid-Channel*.

Pirandello, Luigi (1867–1936), Italian dramatist and novelist whose plays include *Six Characters in Search of an Author*. Nobel prizewinner 1934.

Pissarro, Camille (1830–1903), French impressionist painter of landscapes; studied under Corot.

Pitman, Sir Isaac (1813–97) b. Trowbridge, English inventor of a system of phonographic shorthand.

Pitt, William (1759–1806), English statesman. Younger son of the Earl of Chatham, he entered parliament at 21 and became prime minister at 24 in 1783 when parties were divided and the American war had been lost. He rose to the position, and held office with scarcely a break till his death. An able finance minister, he introduced reforms, and would have gone further, but Napoleon's meteoric rise obliged him to lead European allies in a long struggle against France. He died worn out by his efforts.

Pius, XII (1876–1958), elected Pope 1939. As Eugenio Pacelli, he was papal nuncio in Germany and later papal secretary of state. It has been argued that, as Pope in wartime, he could have taken a stronger line against Nazi war crimes.

Pizarro, Francisco (c. 1478–1541), Spanish adventurer, b. Trujillo. After Columbus's discoveries, he conquered Peru for Spain, overthrowing the Inca empire. He was murdered by his men.

Planck, Max (1857–1947), German mathematical physicist, b. Kiel, whose main work was on thermodynamics. In 1900 he invented a mathematical formula to account for some properties of the thermal radiation from a hot body which has since played an important role in physics. Nobel prizewinner 1918. *See* Quantum theory, F13.

Plato (427–347 B.C.), Athenian philosopher, pupil of Socrates, teacher of Aristotle. He founded a school at Athens under the name of the Academy, where he taught philosophy and mathematics. His great work is his *Dialogues*, which includes the *Republic*, the longest and most celebrated. His known writings have come down to us and contitutes one of the most influential bodies of work in history. *See also* Mind and Matter, Section J.

Playfair, 1st Baron (Lyon Playfair) (1818–98), a far-sighted Victorian who stood for the greater recognition of science in national life. He forsook his profession as professor of chemistry at Edinburgh to enter parliament. Pres. British Association 1885.

Plimsoll, Samuel (1824–98), English social reformer, b. Bristol. He realised the evil of overloading unseaworthy ships, and as M.P. for Derby he procured the passing of the Merchant Shipping Act, 1876 which imposed a line (the Plimsoll Mark) above which no ship must sink while loading.

Pliny the Elder (A.D. 23–79), Roman naturalist, author of a *Natural History*. He died of fumes and exhaustion while investigating the eruption of Vesuvius. His nephew, Pliny the Younger (A.D. 62–113), wrote *Letters* notable for their charm and the insight they give into Roman life.

Plotinus (c. 203–c. 262), Greek philosopher, was the founder of Neoplatonism, which had considerable influence on early Christian thought. *See also* God and Man, Section J.

Plutarch (c. 46–120), Greek biographer, whose *Lives* portray 46 leading historical figures (in pairs, a Greek and a Roman whose careers were similar). Although based on myth his *Life of Lycurgus* about life in Sparta had a profound influence on later writers, e.g., Rousseau and the romantic philosophers. He was educated at Athens but visited Rome.

Poe, Edgar Allen (1809–40), American poet and story-writer, b. Boston, Mss. His poems include *The Raven* and *To Helen*, and his stories, often weird and fantastic, include *Tales of the Grotesque and Arabesque.*

Poincaré, Raymond Nicolas (1860–1934), French statesman. He was president 1913–20, and as prime minister occupied the Ruhr in 1923.

Pole, Reginald (1500–58), archbishop of Canterbury, cardinal of the Roman church and antagonist of the reformation. He opposed Henry VIII's divorce and went abroad in 1532, writing *De Unitate Ecclesiastica*; as a result of which his mother, Countess of Salisbury, and other relatives were executed. Under Queen Mary Tudor he became archbishop and died when she did.

Pollard, Albert Frederick (1869–1948), English historian, especially of the Tudor period, and first director of the Institute of Historical Research.

Polo, Marco (1256–1323), Venetian traveller, who made journeys through China, India, and other eastern countries, visiting the court of Kubla Khan, and publishing an account of his travels.

Pompadour, Jeanne Antoine Poisson, Marquise de (1721–64), mistress of Louis XV of France, who exercised disastrous political influence.

Pompey (106–48 B.C.), Roman commander, who cleared the Mediterranean of pirates, and became triumvir with Caesar and Crassus.

Pompidou, Georges Jean Raymond (b. 1911), French administrator and politician who succeeded de Gaulle as president of France in 1969.

Pope, Alexander (1688–1744), English poet, b. London, of a Roman catholic family, and largely self-educated. His brilliant satire was frequently directed against his contemporaries. He is especially remembered for *The Rape of the Locke*, *The Dunciad*, *Essay on Criticism*, and *Essay on Man*.

Pound, Ezra Loomis (b. 1885), American poet and writer on varied subjects, a controversial figure. He is noted for his translations of Provençal, Latin, Chinese, French, and Italian poets.

Poussin, Nicolas (1593–1665), French painter. He lived in Rome 1624–40, 1642–65. His *Golden Calf* is in the National Gallery.

Powys, John Cowper (1872–1964), English writer, best known for his novel *Wolf Solent* and his essays *The Meaning of Culture* and *A Philosophy of Solitude*. His brothers, **Theodore Francis** (1875–1953) and **Llewelyn** (1884–1939) were also original writers.

Prasad, Rajendra (1884–1963), Indian statesman, first president of the Republic of India, 1950–62.

Praxiteles (4th cent. B.C.), Greek sculptor, whose main surviving work is *Hermes carrying Dionysus*.

Preece, Sir William Henry (1834–1913), Welsh electrical engineer, associated with the expansion of wireless telegraphy and telephony in the United Kingdom. He was connected with Marconi and introduced the block system.

Prescott, William Hickling (1796–1859), American historian, especially of Mexico, Peru, and of some European subjects.

Prichard, James Cowles (1786–1848), English ethnologist who perceived that people should be studied as a whole. His works include *Researches into the Physical History of Mankind* and *The Natural History of Man*. He practised medicine.

Priestley, John Boynton (b. 1894), English critic, novelist, and playwright, b. Bradford. His works include the novels *The Good Companions*, *Angel Pavement*, and the plays *Dangerous Corner*, *Time and the Conways*, *I Have Been Here Before*, and *The Linden Tree*.

Priestley, Joseph (1733–1804), English chemist who worked on gases, and shared with Scheele the discovery of oxygen. A presbyterian minister, he was for his time an advanced thinker. In 1794 he settled in America. Biography: *Adventurer in Science and Champion of Truth* by F. W. Gibbs (1965).

Prior, Matthew (1664–1721), English poet. In early life he was a diplomat. He was a neat epigrammatist and writer of occasional pieces. His works include *The City Mouse and Country Mouse* and *Four Dialogues of the Dead*.

Prokofiev, Serge Sergeyevich (1891–1953), Russian composer, whose music has a strong folk-song element, rich in melody and invention. He has written operas: *The Love of Three Oranges*, *The Betrothal in a Nunnery*, *War and Peace*; ballets: *Romeo and Juliet*, *Cinderella*; symphonies, chamber music, and the music for Eisenstein's films *Alexander Nevsky*, *Ivan the Terrible*. *See* Section E.

Protagoras (c. 480–411 B.C.), Greek philosopher, chief of the Sophists, noted for his scepticism and disbelief in objective truth, and for his doctrine that "man is the measure of all things."

Proudhon, Pierre Joseph (1809–65), French socialist. In 1840 he propounded the view that property is theft. His main work is *Système des contradictions économiques* (1846). He was frequently in prison.

Proust, Marcel (1871–1922), French psychological novelist, author of a series of novels known under the title of *À la recherche du temps perdu*. His works have been admirably translated into English by C. K. Scott Moncrieff. *See* Section M, Part I.

Prud'hon, Pierre Paul (1758–1823), French portrait painter, a favourite of both Napoleon's empresses.

Ptolemy of Alexandria (Claudius Ptolemaeus) (fl. A.D. 140), astronomer and founder of scientific cartography. In the *Almagest* he attempted a mathematical presentation of the paths along which the planets appear to move in the heavens. His other great work was his *Geographical Outline*.

Puccini, Giacomo (1858–1924), Italian composer, b. Lucca, whose operas include *Manon Lescaut*, *La Bohème*, *Tosca*, *Madam Butterfly*, and *Turandot* (completed by a friend).

Purcell, Henry (1658–95), English composer, b. Westminster, son of a court musician. He became organist of the chapel royal and composer to Charles II. His best works are vocal and choral. He also wrote for the stage. *See* Section E.

Pusey, Edward Bouverie (1800–82), English theologian, a leader of the Oxford or Tractarian movement with Keble and at first also with Newman, till the latter became Roman catholic. The movement aimed at revival. *See* Tractarianism, Section J.

Pushkin, Alexander (1799–1837), Russian writer, b. Moscow, whose place in Russian literature ranks with Shakespeare's in English. He wrote in many forms—lyrical poetry and narrative verse, drama, folk-tales and short stories. Musicians have used his works as plots for operas—the fairy romance *Russlan and Ludmilla* was dramatised by Glinka; the verse novel *Eugene Onegin* and the short story *The Queen of Spades* were adapted by Tchaikovsky, and the tragic drama *Boris Godunov* formed the subject of Mussorgsky's opera. Like Lermontov, who too was exiled, he was inspired by the wild beauty of the Caucasus. He was killed in a duel defending his wife's honour.

Pym, John (1584–1643), English parliamentary leader in opposition to Charles I. He promoted the impeachment of the king's advisers, Strafford and Laud.

Pythagoras (c. 582–500 B.C.), Greek philosopher, b. on the island of Samos, off the Turkish mainland, which he left c. 530 to settle at Croton, a Greek city in southern Italy. He was a mystic and mathematician, and founded a brotherhood who saw in numbers the key to the understanding of the universe.

Q

Quasimodo, Salvatore (1901–68), Italian poet of humanity and liberal views whose works include *La vita non e sogno*. Nobel prizewinner 1959.

Quesnay, François (1694–1774), French economist, founder of the physiocratic school who believed in *laizzez-faire* and influenced the thought of Adam Smith. *See* Physiocrats, Section J.

Quiller-Couch, Sir Arthur Thomas (1863–1944), English man of letters, b. Bodmin, known as "Q." He edited the *Oxford Book of English Verse* and his works include *From a Cornish window*.

R

Rabelais, François (c. 1495–1553), French satirist. At first in religious orders, he late studied medicine and practised at Lyons. His works, mainly published under a pseudonym, are full of riotous mirth, wit and wisdom. The main ones are *Gargantua* and *Pantagruel*.

Rachel, Elisa (Elisa Felix) (1821–58), Alsatian-Jewish tragic actress. Her chief triumph was in Racine's *Phèdre*.

Rachmaninov, Sergey Vasilyevich (1873–1943), Russian composer and pianist, b. Nijni-Novgorod (now Gorki), best known for his piano music, especially his *Prelude*. After the Russian revolution he settled in America. *See* Section E.

Racine, Jean (1639–99), French tragic poet whose dramas include *Andromaque*, *Iphigénie* and *Phèdre*. An orphan, he was brought up by grandparents who sent him to Port Royal school where he acquired a love of the classics. In Paris he became a friend of Molière, whose company acted his first play, and of Boileau, with whom he became joint historiographer to Louis XIV. *Esther* and *Athalie* were written for Madame de Maintenon's schoolgirls.

Rackham, Arthur (1867–1939), English artist and book-illustrator, especially of fairy tales.

Radhakrishnan, Sir Sarvepalli (b. 1888), Indian philosopher and statesman, vice-president of India 1952–62, president 1962–7. He was at one time a professor at Oxford, and was chairman of Unesco in 1949. His works include *Indian Philosophy*.

Raeburn, Sir Henry (1756–1823), Scottish portrait painter, whose style was founded on that of Reynolds. His sitters included Scott.

Raffles, Sir Thomas Stamford (1781–1826), English colonial administrator who founded a settlement at Singapore in 1819. He was also a naturalist, and founded the London Zoo, being first president.

Raikes, Robert (1735–1811), English educational pioneer, whose lead in the teaching of children at Gloucester on Sundays led to an extensive Sunday School movement.

Raleigh, Sir Walter (1552–1618), adventurer and writer. He found favour at the court of Elizabeth I, helped to put down the Irish rebellion of 1580, and in 1584 began the colonisation of Virginia, introducing potatoes and tobacco to the British Isles. At the accession of James I he lost favour and was sent to the Tower, where he wrote his *History of the World*. Released in 1615 to lead an expedition to the Orinoco, he was executed when it failed.

Raman, Sir Chandrasekhara Venkata (1888–1970), Indian physicist whose main work has been in spectroscopy. For his research on the diffusion of light and discovery of the " Raman effect " (a phenomenon of scattered light rays) he was awarded the 1930 Nobel prize.

Rameau, Jean Philippe (1683–1764), French composer and church organist whose works on musical theory influenced musical development in the 18th cent.

Ramón y Cajal, Santiago (1852–1934), Spanish histologist who made discoveries in the structure of the nervous system. Shared 1906 Nobel prize.

Ramsay, Sir William (1852–1916), Scottish chemist, and discoverer with Lord Rayleigh of argon. Later he discovered helium and other inert gases, which he called neon, krypton, and xenon. Nobel prizewinner 1904.

Ramsey, Arthur Michael (b. 1904), archbishop of Canterbury, 1961. His previous career was: professor of divinity at Cambridge 1950–2; bishop of Durham 1952–6; archbishop of York 1956–61. In 1970 he preached in South Africa.

Ranke, Leopold von (1795–1886), German historian, one of the first to base his work on methodical research. His chief work is a *History of the Popes*.

Raphael (Raffaello Santi) (1483–1520) of Urbino was the youngest of the three great artists of the High Renaissance. He was taught at Perugia by Perugino, and then at Florence he came under the influence of Leonardo and Michelangelo. Raphael's Madonnas, remarkable for their simplicity and grace, include the *Madonna of the Grand Duke* (Palazzo Pitti, Florence), the *Sistine Madonna* (Dresden), the *Madonna with the Goldfinch* (Uffizi, Florence), and the *Ansidei Madonna* (National Gallery, London). He painted the frescoes on the walls of the Stanza della Segnatura in the Vatican, those in the adjoining rooms, and elsewhere, and his finest portrait is that of Castiglione. After the death of Bramante he was appointed architect in charge of the rebuilding of St. Peter's.

Rasputin, Grigori Yefimovich (1871–1916), Russian peasant monk, who at the court of Nicholas II exerted a malign influence over the Tsarina through his apparent ability to improve the health of the sickly Tsarevich Alexis. He was murdered by a group of nobles.

Rathbone, Eleanor (1872–1946), social reformer who championed women's pensions and in her book *The Disinherited Family* set out the case for family allowances.

Ravel, Maurice (1875–1937), French composer, pupil of Fauré, one of the leaders of the impressionist movement. He wrote chamber music, piano pieces, songs, and ballet music, including *Daphnis et Chloé*, specially commissioned by Diaghilev. *See* Section E.

Rawlinson, Sir Henry Creswicke (1810–95), English diplomat and archaeologist. He made Assyrian collections now in the British Museum and translated the Behistun inscription of the Persian king Darius. He also wrote on cuneiform inscriptions and on Assyrian history.

Ray, John (1627–1705), English naturalist. A blacksmith's son, he went to Cambridge, travelled in Europe, and produced a classification of plants. He also wrote on zoology.

Rayleigh, 3rd Baron (John William Strutt) (1842–1919), English mathematician and physicist. He studied sound and the wave theory of light; and with Sir William Ramsay discovered argon. Nobel prizewinner 1904.

Read, Sir Herbert (1893–1968), English poet and art critic. His writings include *Collected Poems*, *The Meaning of Art*, and an autobiography, *Annals of Innocence and Experience*.

Reade, Charles (1814–84), English novelist. His chief work is *The Cloister and the Hearth*. He also wrote *Peg Woffington*, *It is Never too Late to Mend*, and *Griffith Gaunt*, aimed at social abuses. He tried unsuccessfully to write plays.

Réaumur, René Antoine Ferchault de (1683–1757), French naturalist who invented a thermometer of eighty degrees, using alcohol.

Récamier, Jeanne Françoise (née Bernard) (1777–1849), French beauty and holder of a noted salon. Her husband was a banker.

Regnault, Henri Victor (1810–78), French chemist and physicist, who worked on gases, latent heat, and steam-engines.

Reith, 1st Baron (John Charles Walsham Reith) (b. 1889), Scottish civil engineer, first director-general of the British Broadcasting Corporation 1927–38.

Rembrandt (Rembrandt Harmenszoon van Rijn) (1606–69), Dutch painter and etcher, b. Leiden, a miller's son, one of the most individual and prolific artists of any period. His output includes portraits, landscapes, large groups, etchings, and drawings. He settled in Amsterdam establishing his reputation with *The Anatomy Lesson*, painted in 1632. In 1634 he married Saskia, a burgomaster's daughter. *The Night Watch* was painted in 1642; it was not well received and Saskia died the same year, leaving the infant Titus. The path from relative wealth to lonely old age is depicted in his self-portraits. Caring little for convention or formal beauty, his work is characterised by bold realism and spiritual beauty, by vitality and simplicity. His understanding of the play of colour and the effects of light can give his pictures a mystical beauty, as in the atmospheric painting *The Mill*. His figures, even for religious pictures, were taken from real life, the Jews in the etching *Christ Healing* from the Jewish quarter where he lived. He met the misfortunes of later life by withdrawing from society and it was during this period of detachment that he produced his greatest works in portraiture, landscape, and biblical story.

Renan, Ernest (1823–92), French writer who, though unable to accept the orthodox viewpoint, wrote much on religious themes, especially a *Life of Jesus*.

Reni, Guido. *See* Guido Reni.

Rennie, John (1761–1821), Scottish civil engineer who built the old Waterloo and Southwark bridges and designed the granite London bridge which stood until recently. He also designed docks at London, Liverpool, Leith Dublin, and Hull; constructed Plymouth breakwater; made canals and drained fens.

Renoir, Pierre Auguste (1841–1919), French impressionist painter, b. Limoges. His works include portraits, still-life, landscapes, and groups, including *La Loge*, *Les Parapluies*, *La première Sortie*, *La Place Pigalle*. He was later crippled with arthritis.

Reuther, Paul Julius, Freiherr von (1816–99), German pioneer of telegraphic press service, who in 1851 fixed his headquarters in London.

Reymont, Vladislav Stanislav (1868–1925), Polish novelist, author of *The Peasants*. Nobel prizewinner 1924.

Reynolds, Sir Joshua (1723–92), English portrait painter, b. Plympton, Devon. His portraits, which include *Mrs. Siddons*, are remarkable for expressiveness and colour and he was a sympathetic painter of children. He was first president of the R.A. from 1768 till his death.

Rhodes, Cecil John (1853–1902), English empire-builder. B. at Bishop's Stortford, he went to South Africa for health reasons and there prospered at the diamond mines. He became prime minister of what was then Cape Colony and secured British extension in what is now Rhodesia. He withdrew from politics after the failure of the ill-advised Jameson Raid of 1896 into the Transvaal. He bequeathed large sums to found scholarships at Oxford for overseas students.

Ricardo, David (1772–1823), English political economist of Jewish descent. By occupation a London stockbroker, he wrote a useful work, *Principles of Political Economy*.

Richard I (1157–99), succeeded his father Henry II as king of England in 1189. A patron of troubadours and a soldier (Lion-heart), he went on the third Crusade and took Acre, but could not recover Jerusalem from Saladin. On his return journey across Europe he was imprisoned and ransomed. He was killed in war with France.

Richard II (1367–1400), son of the Black Prince, succeeded his grandfather Edward III as king of England in 1377. Artistic and able, but erratic and egocentric, he personally at the age of fourteen met the Peasants' Revolt in 1381, making untenable promises. Latterly his rule became increasingly arbitrary, and he was deposed and imprisoned in 1399.

Richard III (1452–85), King of England, succeeded his brother, the Yorkist, Edward IV, in 1483, and is believed to have murdered his two nephews in the Tower. Shortly afterwards he was defeated and killed at Bosworth by the invading Earl of Richmond, who as Henry VII brought to an end the Wars of the Roses. Richard's character is disputed, but he was able and might have been a successful ruler.

Richardson, Sir Albert Edward (1880–1964), British architect, author of *Georgian Architecture*.

Richardson, Sir Owen Williams (1879–1959), English physicist who worked on thermionics, or emission of electricity from hot bodies. Nobel prizewinner 1928.

Richardson, Sir Ralph David (b. 1902), English actor who has worked at the old Vic, on the West End stage, and at Stratford-on-Avon, and appeared in films, including *South Riding, Anna Karenina*, and *The Fallen Idol*.

Richardson, Samuel (1689–1761), English author of *Pamela, Clarissa*, and *The History of Sir Charles Grandison*, exercised considerable influence on the development of the novel.

Richelieu, Armand Jean du Plessis, Duc de (1585–1642), French statesman, cardinal of the Roman church. As minister to Louis XIII from 1624 till his death, he built up the power of the French crown at home in central government, and by his military preparedness and active foreign policy gave France a lead in Europe.

Ridley, Nicholas (1500–55), English Protestant martyr, bishop of Rochester and later of London, was burnt with Latimer under Queen Mary Tudor.

Rienzi, Cola di (1313–54), Italian patriot, b. Rome, led a popular rising in 1347 and for seven months reigned as tribune, but had to flee, was imprisoned, and eventually murdered.

Rilke, Rainer Maria (1872–1926), German lyric poet, b. Prague. His work, marked by beauty of style, culminated in the *Duino Elegies* and *Sonnets to Orpheus*, both written in 1922, which gave a new musicality to German verse. His visits to Russia in 1899 and 1900 and his admiration for Rodin (who had been his wife's teacher) influenced his artistic career.

Rimbaud, Jean Nicolas Arthur (1854–91), French poet, b. Charleville, on the Meuse. In his brief poetic career (4 years from about the age of 16) he prepared the way for symbolism (*Bateau ivre, Les Illuminations*) and anticipated Freud (*Les deserts de l'amour*). He became intimate with Verlaine and at 18 had completed his memoirs, *Une saison en enfer*. He died at Marseilles.

Rimsky-Korsakov, Nikolai Andreyevich (1844–1908), Russian composer whose works include the operas *The Maid of Pskov, The Snow Maiden, Le Coq d'or*, and the symbolic suite *Scheherezade*. He was a brilliant orchestrator and re-scored many works, including Borodin's *Prince Igor*.

Rizzio, David (1533?–66), Italian musician and secretary of Mary, Queen of Scots. He was murdered in her presence at Holyrood by her jealous husband, Darnley.

Robbia, Luca Della (1400–82), Florentine sculptor, who introduced enamelled terra-cotta work.

Roberts of Kandahar, 1st Earl (Frederick Sleigh Roberts) (1832–1914), British general. He took part in the suppression of the Indian Mutiny, in the Afghan war (relieving Kandahar), and when put in command in South Africa in the Boer War he relieved Kimberley and advanced to Pretoria.

Robertson, Sir William (1860–1933), the only British soldier to rise from private to field-marshal. His son, **Brian Hubert, 1st Baron** (b. 1896) served in both world wars and was chairman of the British Transport Commission, 1953–61.

Robeson, Paul Le Roy (b. 1898), American Negro singer, b. Princeton, is especially known for his singing of Negro spirituals, and has appeared in works ranging from *Showboat* to *Othello*.

Robespierre, Maximilien Marie Isidoire de (1758–94), French revolutionary. A country advocate, b. Arras, he was in 1789 elected to the States General and in 1792 to the Convention. He became a leader of the Jacobins, the more extreme party which came to power under stress of war and after the king's execution in 1793. In this crisis, the Committee of Public Safety, of which he was a member and which used his reputation as a cloak, sent many to the guillotine. He opposed the cult of Reason and inaugurated the worship of the Supreme Being. In the reaction from the reign of terror he was denounced, tried to escape, but was guillotined.

Robinson, William Heath (1872–1944), English cartoonist and book-illustrator, especially known for his fantastically humorous drawings of machines.

Rob Roy (Robert McGregor) (1671–1734), Scottish freebooter who helped the poor at the expense of the rich, and played a lone hand in the troubled times of the Jacobite rising of 1715.

Robsart, Amy (1532–60), English victim (it is believed) of murder. The wife of Robert Dudley, Earl of Leicester, she was found dead at Cumnor Place. Her death was used by Scott in *Kenilworth*.

Rockefeller, John Davison (1839–1937), American philanthropist, b. Richford, N.Y. He settled in Cleveland, Ohio, and with his brother William founded the Standard Oil Company, making a fortune. His philanthropic enterprises are carried on by the Rockefeller Foundation. Nelson Rockefeller, elected governor of New York, 1958, 1962, 1966, is his grandson.

Rodin, Auguste (1841–1917), French sculptor, b. Paris. His best-known works include *Le Penseur, Les Bourgeois de Calais*, the statues of Balzac and Victor Hugo, and *La Porte d'Enfer*, a huge bronze door for the Musée des Arts Décoratifs, which was still unfinished at his death.

Rodney, 1st Baron (George Rodney) (1719–92), English admiral, who served in the Seven Years War and the War of American Independence; in the latter war he defeated the French fleet under de Grasse.

Roland de la Platière, Manon Jeanne (1754–93), a leading figure in the French revolution. Her husband Jean Marie (1734–93), belonged to the more moderate or Girondist party, and when threatened escaped: but she was imprisoned and executed. She wrote *Letters* and *Memoirs*.

Rolland, Romain (1866–1944), French author, whose main work is a ten-volume novel, *Jean-Christophe*, the biography of a German musician, based on the life of Beethoven, and a study of contemporary French and German civilisation. Nobel prizewinner 1915.

Romilly, Sir Samuel (1757–1818), English lawyer

D (80th Ed.)

and law-reformer, who aimed at mitigating the severity of the criminal law.

Rommel, Erwin (1891–1944), German general. He took part in the 1940 invasion of France, and was later successful in commanding the Afrika Korps till 1944. He committed suicide.

Romney, George (1734–1802), English artist, b. in Lancashire. He painted chiefly portraits, especially of Lady Hamilton, and lived mainly in London, but returned to Kendal to die.

Röntgen, Wilhelm Konrad von (1845–1923), German scientist who in 1895 discovered X-rays. Nobel prizewinner 1901.

Roosevelt, Franklin Delano (1882–1945), American statesman, a distant cousin of Theodore Roosevelt. During the first world war he held office under Wilson, and though stricken with poliomyelitis in 1921 continued his political career, becoming governor of New York in 1929 and U.S. president in 1933 (the first to hold office for more than two terms), till his death. A Democrat, he met the economic crisis of 1933 with a policy for a " New Deal " (*see* L83). He strove in vain to ward off war. Towards other American countries his attitude was that of " good neighbour ". After Pearl Harbour, he energetically prosecuted the war, holding meetings with Churchill and Stalin, and adopting a " lend-lease " policy for arms. He kept contact with his people by " fireside talks ". His wife Eleanor (1884–1962) was a public figure in her own right, and was chairman of the U.N. Human Rights Commission 1947–51.

Roosevelt, Theodore (1858–1919), American president. Popular because of his exploits in the Spanish-American war, he was appointed Republican vice-president in 1900, becoming president when McKinley was assassinated, and was re-elected 1905. He promoted the regulation of trusts; and his promotion of peace between Russia and Japan gained the Nobel prize, 1906.

Rops, Félicien (1833–98), Belgian artist, known for his often satirical lithographs and etchings.

Ross, Sir James Clark (1800–62), Scottish explorer of polar regions, who accompanied his uncle Sir John, and himself discovered the north magnetic pole in 1831. He commanded the *Erebus* and *Terror* to the antarctic (1839–43), where his discoveries included the Ross ice barrier.

Ross, Sir John (1777–1856), Scottish explorer of polar regions, uncle of the above. He searched for the north-west passage and discovered Boothia peninsula.

Ross, Sir Ronald (1857–1932), British physician, b. India, who discovered the malaria parasite. He was in the Indian medical service, and later taught tropical medicine in England. Nobel prizewinner 1902.

Rossetti, Dante Gabriel (1828–82), English poet and painter, son of Gabriele (1783–1852), an exiled Italian author who settled in London in 1842. With Millais, Holman Hunt and others he formed the Pre-Raphaelite brotherhood which returned to pre-Renaissance art forms. His model was often his wife, Elizabeth Siddal. His poems include *The Blessed Damozel*. His sister Christina Georgina (1830–94) wrote poetry, including *Goblin Market*.

Rossini, Gioacchino Antonio (1792–1868), Italian operatic composer. *See* Section E.

Rostand, Edmond (1868–1918), French dramatist, whose *Cyrano de Bergerac* created a sensation in 1898.

Rothenstein, Sir William (1872–1945), English portrait painter. His son, Sir John (b. 1901), is an art historian and until 1964 was director of the Tate Gallery; he has written an autobiography.

Rothschild, Meyer Amschel (1743–1812), German financier, founder of a banking family, b. Frankfurt. His five sons controlled branches at Frankfurt, Vienna, Naples, Paris and London (Nathan Meyer, 1777–1836). Nathan's son, Lionel (1808–70), was the first Jewish member of the House of Commons.

Roubiliac, Louis François (1695–1762), French sculptor who settled in London and carved a statue of Handel for Vauxhall gardens and one of Newton for Trinity College, Cambridge.

Rouget de Lisle, Claude Joseph (1760–1836), French poet, author of words and music of the *Marseillaise*, revolutionary and national anthem.

Rousseau, Henri (1844–1910), French " Sunday " painter, called " Le Douanier " because on weekdays he was a customs official. According to him, he had served as regimental bandsman in Mexico which may account for his exotic settings and jungle scenes.

Rousseau, Jean-Jacques (1712–78), French political philosopher and educationist, b. Geneva, herald of the romantic movement. After a hard childhood he met Mme de Warens who for some years befriended him. In 1741 he went to Paris where he met Diderot and contributed articles on music and political economy to the *Encyclopédie. La nouvelle Héloïse* appeared in 1760, *Emile*, and *Le Contrat Social* in 1762. *Emile* is a treatise on education according to " natural " principles and *Le Contrat Social*, his main work, sets forth his political theory. It begins, " Man is born free and everywhere he is in chains." Both books offended the authorities and he had to flee, spending some time in England. Later he was able to return to France. His views on conduct and government did much to stimulate the movement leading to the French Revolution. *See also* Education, Section J.

Rubens, Sir Peter Paul (1577–1640), Flemish painter. B. in exile, his family returned to Antwerp in 1587. He studied in Italy and visited Spain. His range was wide, his compositions vigorous, and he was a remarkable colourist. *Peace and War, The Rape of the Sabines*, and *The Felt Hat* are in the National Gallery. He was knighted by Charles I.

Rubenstein, Anton Grigorovich (1829–94). Russian pianist and composer, who helped to found the conservatoire at St. Petersburg (Leningrad); as did his brother Nicholas (1835–81) at Moscow.

Rücker, Sir Arthur (1848–1915), English physicist, who made two magnetic surveys of the British Isles, 1886, and 1891.

Ruisdael, Jacob van (c. 1628–82), Dutch painter of landscapes, b. Haarlem. Several of his works are in the National Gallery, including *Coast of Scheveningen* and *Landscape with ruins*. He was also a fine etcher.

Rupert, Prince (1619–82), general, son of Frederick of Bohemia and his wife Elizabeth, daughter of James I of England. He commanded the Royalist cavalry in the English civil war, but was too impetuous for lasting success. At sea he was defeated by Blake. He improved the art of mezzotinting and was the first governor of the Hudson's Bay Company.

Rusk, Dean (b. 1909), American politician, who has held various posts especially in connection with foreign affairs; a former Rhodes scholar.

Ruskin, John (1819–1900), English author and art critic, b. London. His *Modern Painters* in 5 volumes was issued over a period of years, the first volume having a strong defence of Turner. He helped to establish the Pre-Raphaelites. Other notable works include *The Seven Lamps of Architecture, The Stones of Venice* and *Praeterita. Unto this Last* develops his views on social problems, and he tried to use his wealth for education and for non-profitmaking enterprises. Ruskin College at Oxford, the first residential college for working people, is named after him. In 1848 he married Euphemia Gray, but in 1854 she obtained a decree of nullity and later married Millais.

Russell, 3rd Earl (Bertrand Arthur William Russell) (1872–1970), English philosopher, mathematician, and essayist, celebrated for his work in the field of logic and the theory of knowledge, and remembered for his moral courage, belief in human reason and his championship of liberal ideas. He published more than 60 books, including *The Principles of Mathematics* (1903), *Principia Mathematica* (in collaboration with A. N. Whitehead; 3 vols., 1910–13), *The Problem of Philosophy* (1912), *Mysticism and Logic* (1918), *The Analysis of Mind* (1921), *An Inquiry into Meaning and Truth* (1940), *History of Western Philosophy* (1945), and a number on ethics and social questions. His *Autobiography* (3 vols.) appeared 1967–9. He was the grandson of Lord John Russell and John Stuart Mill was his godfather. Nobel prize for literature 1950; O.M. 1949.

Russell, 1st Earl (John Russell), (1792–1878), English statesman, third son of the 6th Duke of Bedford. He had a large share in carrying the parliamentary reform bill of 1832. He was Whig prime minister 1846–52 and 1865–6. He was also a historian and biographer.

Russell of Killowen, 1st Baron (Charles Russell), British lawyer, b. Ireland; lord chief justice 1894–1900. He defended Parnell.

Rutherford, 1st Baron (Ernest Rutherford) (1871–1937), British physicist, b. New Zealand, eminent in the field of atomic research. His experiments were conducted at Manchester and Cambridge and attracted young scientists from all over the world. In 1911 he announced his nuclear theory of the atom and in 1918 succeeded in splitting the atom. His work prepared the way for future nuclear research.

Ruysdael, Jacob van. See Ruisdael.

Ruyter, Michiel Adrianszoon de (1607–76), Dutch admiral who ranks with Nelson. He fought against England and in 1667 caused alarm by sailing up the Medway as far as Rochester and up the Thames as far as Gravesend. He was mortally wounded at Messina.

S

Sachs, Hans (1494–1576), German poet, b. Nuremberg. A shoemaker, he wrote over 6,000 pieces, some dealing with everyday life, many (including *Die Wittenbergische Nachtigall*) inspired by the Reformation.

Sachs, Julius von (1832–97), German botanist, founder of experimental plant physiology. He demonstrated that chlorophyll is formed in chloroplasts only in light (*see* F28).

Sadi or Saadi (Muslih Addin) (c. 1184–1292), Persian poet, b. Shiraz, best known for his *Gulistan* (Flower Garden), which has been translated into English.

Sainte-Beuve, Charles Augustin (1804–69), French critic, b. Boulogne. He studied medicine, abandoning it for journalism, and after attempting to write poetry, turned to literary criticism. His work reveals the wide range of his intellectual experience and includes *Causeries du lundi* and *Histoire de Port-Royal.* He was sometimes in political trouble for upholding freedom of thought.

Saint-Just, Antoine (1767–94), French revolutionary, a follower of Robespierre and executed with him.

St. Laurent, Louis Stephen (b. 1882), Canadian politician, prime minister 1948–57.

Saint-Saëns, Charles Camile (1835–1921), French composer, for 20 years organist at the Madeleine. His compositions include symphonic and chamber music and the opera *Samson et Dalila,* which was produced by Liszt at Weimar in 1877. *See* Section E.

Saint-Simon, Claude, Comte de (1760–1825), French socialist, who in his *L'Industrie* and *Nouveau christianisme* prepared the way for much later thought.

Saintsbury, George Edward (1845–1933), English critic and literary historian.

Sala, George Augustus (1828–95), English journalist who contributed to (among others) *Household Words* and was a notable foreign correspondent.

Saladin (Salah-ad-din) (1137–93), sultan of Egypt and Syria and founder of a dynasty, who in 1187 defeated the Christians near Tiberias and took Jerusalem. This gave rise to the unsuccessful Third Crusade, in which Richard I of England joined. His great qualities were admired by his opponents, and his administration left many tangible signs in such matters as roads and canals.

Salazar, Antonio d'Oliveira (1889–1970), Portuguese dictator, having first been premier in 1932, a new constitution being adopted in 1933. He gave Portugal stability, but refused to bow to nationalism in Portuguese Africa and India.

Salda, František (1867–1937), Czech critic, essayist and poet who has profoundly influenced Czech thought.

Salimbene de Adamo (1221–c.1228), mediaeval chronicler, b. Parma, whose vivid description of life in the 13th cent. is embodied in his *Cronica.*

Salisbury, 3rd Marquess (Robert Arthur Salisbury)

(1830–1903), English Conservative statesman, prime minister 1885–6, 1886–92, 1895–1902, mainly remembered for his conduct of foreign affairs during a critical period, culminating in the Boer War. His grandson, **Robert Arthur, 5th Marquess** (b. 1893), has led the Conservative opposition in the House of Lords.

Samuel, 1st Viscount (Herbert Samuel) (1870–1963) British Liberal statesman of Jewish parentage. He published philosophical works, including *Practical Ethics.*

Sand, George (1804–76), pseudonym of the French writer Armandine Lucie Dupin. Her publications are extensive and varied, and include the novel *Mauprat,* rural studies, and an autobiography *Histoire de ma vie.* She was associated with Alfred de Musset and Chopin.

Sandow, Eugene (1867–1925), German "strong man" who opened an Institute of Health in London.

Sanger, Frederick (b. 1918), British scientist noted for his work on the chemical structure of the protein insulin. Nobel prizewinner 1958.

Sankey, Ira David (1840–1908), American evangelist and composer, associated with Moody.

San Martin, José de (1778–1850), South American national leader in securing independence from Spanish rule to his native Argentina, Chile and Peru.

Santayana, George (1863–1952), American philosopher and poet, b. Madrid, of Spanish parentage. He was professor of philosophy at Harvard, 1907–12. His books include *The Sense of Beauty, The Life of Reason,* and *The Realms of Being.*

Santos-Dumont, Alberto (1873–1932), Brazilian aeronaut who in 1898 flew a cylindrical balloon with a gasoline engine. In 1909 he built a monoplane.

Sappho of Lesbos (fl. early 6th cent. B.C.), Greek poetess, of whose love poems few remain.

Sardou, Victorien (1831–1908), French dramatist popular in his day. Sarah Bernhardt created famous parts in *Fédora, Théodora* and *La Tosca*; *Robespierre* and *Dante* were written for Irving.

Sargent, John Singer (1856–1922), American painter, b. Florence, who worked mainly in England, especially on portraits.

Sargent, Sir Malcolm (1895–1967), British conductor, b. Stamford, who conducted the Promenade Concerts from 1950 till his death, and succeeded Sir Adrian Boult as conductor of the B.B.C. Symphony Orchestra, 1950–7.

Sartre, Jean-Paul (b. 1905), French existentialist philosopher, left-wing intellectual, dramatist, essayist and novelist. His major philosophical work is *L'Etre et le Néant* and his plays include *Les Mouches, Huis Clos, Crime passionel, La Putain respectueuse,* and *Les Séquestrés d'Altona.* He was awarded (though he declined it) the 1964 Nobel prize. *See* Section I.

Sassoon, Siegfried (1886–1967), English poet and writer with a hatred of war. He is mainly known for *The Memoirs of a Foxhunting Man,* the first part of the *Memoirs of George Sherston.*

Savonarola, Girolamo (1452–98), Florentine preacher and reformer, a Dominican friar, who denounced vice and corruption not only in society but also in the Church itself, especially attacking Pope Alexander VI. He was excommunicated, imprisoned, and with two of his companions hanged in public. His passion for reform made him impatient of opposition and incapable of compromise, yet he was a notable figure and commands the respect of later ages. George Eliot's *Romola* portrays him.

Scarlatti, Alessandro (1659–1725), Italian musician who founded the Neopolitan school of opera. He composed over 100 operas, 200 masses, and over 700 cantatas and oratorios. His son **Domenico** (1685–1757) was a harpsichord virtuoso whose work influenced the evolution of the sonata. The chief years of his life were spent at the Spanish court in Madrid. *See* Section E.

Scheele, Carl Wilhelm (1742–86), Swedish chemist, discoverer of many chemical substances, including oxygen (c. 1773–but published in 1777 after the publication of Priestley's studies).

Schiaparelli, Giovanni Virginio (1835–1910), Italian astronomer, noted for having detected certain dark markings on the surface of the planet Mars which he called canals.

Schiller, Johann Christoph Friedrich von (1759–1805), German dramatist and poet, b. Marbach in Württemberg, began life as a military surgeon. His play *The Robbers* with a revolutionary theme was successful in 1782 in Mannheim. After a stay at Dresden, where he wrote *Don Carlos*, and at Jena, where he wrote a history of the Thirty Years War, he became the friend of Goethe and removed to Weimar, where he wrote *Wallenstein, Mary Stuart, The Maid of Orleans* and *William Tell*, but died young. He is a leading figure in the European romantic movement.

Schirrmann, Richard (1874–1961), German originator of youth hostels. A schoolmaster, in 1907 he converted his schoolroom during holidays to a dormitory. The Verband für deutsche Jugendherbergen was founded in 1913, and the International Youth Hostels Federation in 1932, with Schirrmann as first president.

Schlegel, Friedrich von (1772–1829), German critic, b. Hanover, prominent among the founders of German romanticism, whose revolutionary and germinating ideas influenced early 19th cent. thought. His brother, **August Wilhelm** (1767–1845), made remarkable translations of Shakespeare (which established Shakespeare in Germany), Dante, Calderón, and Camões.

Schliemann, Heinrich (1822–90), German archaeologist, who discovered Troy and excavated Mycenae. *See* H3.

Schnabel, Artur (1882–1951), American pianist of Austrian birth, regarded as a leading exponent of Beethoven's pianoforte sonatas.

Schoenberg, Arnold (1874–1951), Austrian composer of Jewish parentage who in 1933 was exiled by the Nazi regime and settled in America, teaching at Boston and Los Angeles. Among his works are the choral orchestral *Gurre-Lieder* and *Pierrot Lunaire*, a cycle of 21 poems for voice and chamber music. *See* Section E.

Schopenhauer, Arthur (1788–1860), German philosopher, b. Danzig, important historically for his pessimism, and his doctrine that will is superior to knowledge. His chief work is *The World as Will and Idea*. He regarded his contemporary Hegel as a charlatan.

Schubert, Franz Peter (1797–1828), Austrian composer, b. Vienna, the son of a schoolmaster, and a contemporary of Beethoven. He wrote not only symphonies, sonatas, string quartets, choral music and masses, but also over 600 songs of unsurpassed lyrical beauty. He might almost be called the creator of the German *Lied* as known today. He died in poverty in Vienna at 31 before his musical genius could reach its full flowering. *See* Section E.

Schumann, Robert Alexander (1810–56), composer of the early 19th cent. German romantic school. He wrote much chamber music, four symphonies, a piano concerto, and choral music, but it is his early piano pieces and songs that give constant delight. His wife **Clara** (1819–96) was one of the outstanding pianists of her time, especially as interpreter of Chopin. *See* Section E.

Schweitzer, Albert (1875–1965), Alsatian medical missionary, theologian, musician and philosopher, b. at Kayersberg. After publishing learned works, he resigned a promising European career to found at Lambaréné in French Equatorial Africa a hospital to fight leprosy and sleeping sickness and made it a centre of service to Africans. His funds were raised by periodic organ recitals in Europe. His motivation was not patronage but atonement. Nobel peace prize 1952. O.M. 1955.

Scipio, Publius Cornelius (237–183 B.C.), Roman general in the second Punic War, known as Scipio Africanus the elder. Scipio Africanus the younger (185–129 B.C.) was an adoptive relative and an implacable opponent of Carthage (destroyed 146).

Scott, Charles Prestwich (1846–1931), English newspaper editor. Under his editorship (1872–1929) the *Manchester Guardian* became a leading journal.

Scott, Sir George Gilbert (1811–78), English architect in the Gothic revival. He restored many churches and designed the Albert Memorial and the Martyrs' Memorial at Oxford.

Scott, Sir Giles Gilbert (1880–1960), English architect, grandson of above, designed the Anglican cathedral at Liverpool and planned the new Waterloo bridge.

Scott, Robert Falcon (1868–1912), English antarctic explorer. He led two expeditions: one 1901–4 which discovered King Edward VII Land; and another in 1910 which reached the south pole and found the Amundsen records; but while returning the party was overtaken by blizzards and the survivors died from starvation and exposure 11 miles from a depot. *See also* Antarctic exploration, L6. His son, **Peter Scott** (b. 1909), is an artist and ornithologist, founder of the Severn Wild Fowl Trust.

Scott, Sir Walter (1771–1832), Scottish novelist and poet, b. Edinburgh. He was educated for the law, but came to know and love the Border country and his interests were literary; and in 1802–3 he issued a collection of ballads, *Border Minstrelsy*. Poems such as *Marmion* and *The Lady of the Lake* followed. His novels appeared anonymously, beginning with *Waverley* in 1814; and continuing with *Guy Mannering, The Antiquary, Old Mortality, Rob Roy*, and the *Heart of Midlothian*. From 1819 he turned also to English history, with *Ivanhoe* and *Kenilworth*. In 1826 he became bankrupt, largely as the fault of his publishing partner, and worked heroically to clear off debts.

Scott-Paine, Hubert (1891–1954), pioneer in the design and construction of aircraft and sea-craft.

Scriabin, Alexander (1872–1915), Russian composer and pianist, who relied to some extent on extra-musical factors such as religion, and in *Prometheus* tried to unite music and philosophy. *See* Section E.

Seeley, Sir John Robert (1834–95), English historian, author of a life of Christ, *Ecce Homo*.

Segovia, Andrés (b. 1894), Spanish concert-guitarist. He has adapted works by Bach, Haydn, Mozart, and other classical composers to the guitar.

Selfridge, Harry Gordon (1858–1947), American-born merchant who in 1909 opened a new style of department store in Oxford Street.

Semmelweis, Ignaz Philipp (1818–65), Hungarian obstetrician, a pioneer in the use of antiseptic methods, thus reducing the incidence of puerperal fever.

Seneca, Lucius Annaeus (c. 4 B.C.–A.D. 56), Roman stoic philosopher who was tutor to Nero, but lost favour and was sentenced to take his own life.

Senefelder, Alois (1772–1834), Bavarian inventor of lithography about 1796.

Severus, Lucius Septimius (146–211), Roman emperor, and a successful general. On a visit to Britain he suppressed a revolt, repaired Hadrian's wall, and died at York.

Sévigné, Marie de Rabutin-Chantal, Marquise de (1626–96), French woman of letters. Her letters to her daughter Françoise written in an unaffected elegance of style give a moving picture of fashionable society in 17th cent. France.

Sgambati, Giovanni (1841–1914), Italian pianist (pupil of Liszt), composer and teacher, who revived interest in classical instrumental music in an age of opera.

Shackleton, Sir Ernest Henry (1874–1922), British explorer, who made four antarctic expeditions; that of 1909 reached within 100 miles of the south pole. He died on his last expedition.

Shaftesbury, 7th Earl of (Anthony Ashley Cooper) (1801–85), English philanthropist largely responsible for legislation reducing the misery of the industrial revolution. He was for 40 years chairman of the Ragged Schools Union.

Shakespeare, William (1564–1616), England's greatest poet and dramatist, b. Stratford-on-Avon. Little is known of his career up to his eighteenth year, when he married Anne Hathaway. He came to London at the height of the English renaissance and soon became connected with the Globe theatre as actor and playwright. Thirty-eight plays comprise the Shakespeare canon. Thirty-six were printed in the First Folio of 1623 (the first collected edition of his dramatic works), of which eighteen had been published during his lifetime in the so-called Quartos. *Love's Labour's Lost* and *The Comedy of Errors* seem to have been among the earliest, being followed by *The Two Gentlemen of Verona*, and *Romeo and Juliet*. Then followed *Henry VI, Richard III, Richard II, Titus Andronicus, The Taming of the Shrew, King John, The*

B55

Merchant of Venice, A Midsummer Night's Dream, All's Well that Ends Well, Henry IV, The Merry Wives of Windsor, Henry V, Much Ado about Nothing, As You Like It, Twelfth Night. Then came some of his greatest plays, *Julius Cæsar, Hamlet, Troilus and Cressida, Othello, Measure for Measure, Macbeth, King Lear, Timon of Athens, Pericles, Antony and Cleopatra, Coriolanus, Cymbeline, A Winter's Tale, The Tempest, Henry VIII.* and *The Two Noble Kinsmen.* In mastery of language, in understanding of character, and in dramatic perception, he has never been surpassed. Fresh interpretation of his work continues. *See* Section I.

Sharp, Granville (1735–1813), English abolitionist of slavery, and founder of the colony of Sierra Leone.

Shastri, Shri Lal Bahadur (1904–66), Indian politician who became prime minister of India after the death of Nehru in 1964. He died of a heart attack at the end of the Soviet-sponsored Tashkent talks.

Shaw, George Bernard (1856–1950), Irish dramatist who conquered England by his wit and exposure of hypocrisy, cant, and national weaknesses, and whose individual opinions found expression in musical criticism, socialist pamphlets and plays. His plays include *Man and Superman, Heartbreak House, Back to Methuselah, Saint Joan, The Apple Cart,* and *Buoyant Billions,* and most have important prefaces. In 1884 he joined the newly-born Fabian Society. Nobel prizewinner 1925.

Shelley, Percy Bysshe (1792–1822), English poet, b. Horsham. He was a master of language and of literary form, and a passionate advocate of freedom and of new thought. Sent down from Oxford for his pamphlet *The Necessity of Atheism,* he came under the influence of William Godwin; and, after his first marriage came to an unhappy end, married the latter's daughter, Mary Wollstonecraft, herself a writer. In the same year began his friendship with Byron. His works include *The Revolt of Islam,* the *Masque of Anarchy* (an indictment of Castlereagh), *The Cenci* (a play on evil), and *Prometheus Unbound,* besides lyrics such as *To a Skylark* and *Ode to the West Wind.* He was accidentally drowned while sailing near Spezzia.

Sheppard, Hugh Richard (Dick) (1880–1937), Anglican divine and pacifist. He made St. Martin-in-the-Fields a centre of social service and also founded the Peace Pledge Union.

Sheraton, Thomas (1751–1806), English cabinetmaker, b. Stockton, whose *Cabinetmaker's Book* promoted neo-classical designs.

Sheridan, Richard Brinsley (1751–1816), British dramatist, b. Dublin. He was a brilliant writer of comedies, especially *The Rivals, The Duenna, The School for Scandal,* and *The Critic.* He acquired and rebuilt Drury Lane theatre, which reopened in 1794, but was burnt down in 1809; and this, with his lack of business sense, brought him to poverty, in spite of his friends' efforts to help him. He was also in parliament where he made some notable speeches.

Sherman, William Tecumseh (1820–91), American general, who served especially in the Civil War. He took part in the battles of Bull Run and Shiloh, was appointed in 1864 to the command of the southwest, and with 65,000 men marched across Georgia to the sea. In 1865 he accepted Johnston's surrender.

Sherrington, Sir Charles Scott (1875–1952), English scientist, an authority on the physiology of the nervous system. His research led to advances in brain surgery. His principal work is *Integrative Action of the Nervous System* (1906). Shared with E. D. Adrian the 1932 Nobel prize.

Shirley, James (1596–1666), English dramatist. His tragedies include *The Traitor,* and his comedies *Hyde Park.* His death was hastened by the Great Fire.

Sholokhov, Mikhail Aleksandrovich (b. 1905), Russian novelist, author of *And Quiet Flows the Don.* Nobel prizewinner 1965.

Shostakovich, Dmitri (b. 1906), Russian composer, whose music is complex, profound, and deeply significant of the Soviet age in which he lives. His works include operas, ballets, symphonies, chamber music, and music for films. Hero of Soviet Labour 1966. *See* Section E.

Sibelius, Jean (1865–1957), Finnish composer, imbued with national feeling. His works include seven symphonies, a violin concerto, and several tone poems, notably *Finlandia,* and some based on the Finnish poem *Kalevala. See* Section E.

Sickert, Walter Richard (1860–1942), British artist, b. Munich. He was influenced by Degas, and has himself influenced later painters. His *Ennui* is in the Tate Gallery.

Siddons, Sarah (1755–1831), English actress especially in tragic parts. She was daughter of the manager Roger Kemble and her reputation was almost unbounded.

Sidgwick, Henry (1838–1900), English philosopher who wrote *Methods of Ethics,* and who also promoted women's education, especially in the foundation of Newnham and Girton colleges.

Sidney, Sir Philip (1554–86), English poet and writer, best remembered for his *Arcadia, Apologie for Poetrie,* and *Astrophel and Stella,* all published after his death. He was killed at the battle of Zutphen, where he passed a cup of water to another, saying " Thy necessity is greater than mine."

Siemens, Sir William (1823–83), German-born electrical engineer who settled in England and constructed many overland and submarine telegraphs. He was brother of **Werner von Siemens,** founder of the firm of Siemens-Halske.

Sienkiewicz, Henryk (1846–1916), Polish novelist and short-story writer; best known of his historical novels is *Quo Vadis?.* Nobel prizewinner 1905.

Sikorski, Vladislav (1881–1943), Polish general and statesman, prime minister of the Polish government in exile (1939) and commander-in-chief of the Polish forces. Killed in an aircraft accident at Gibraltar.

Simpson, Sir James Young (1811–70), Scottish obstetrician who initiated the use of chloroform in childbirth.

Sinclair, Upton (1878–1968), American novelist whose documentary novel *The Jungle* on the Chicago slaughter yards caused a sensation in 1906.

Singer, Isaac Merritt (1811–75), American mechanical engineer who improved early forms of the sewing-machine and patented a single-thread and chain-stitch machine.

Sisley, Alfred (1839–99), French impressionist painter of English origin, who painted some enchanting landscapes, such as *Meadows in Spring* in the Tate Gallery. He was influenced by Corot and Manet.

Sitwell, Edith (1887–1964), English poet, a great experimenter in verse forms. *Gold Coast Customs, Façade* (set to music by William Walton) and *Still Falls the Rain* are probably best known. She had two brothers, Osbert (1892–1919) and **Sacheverell** (b. 1900), both poets and critics. *See also* Section M, Part II.

Slim, 1st Viscount (William Slim) (1891–1970), British general. He commanded the 14th Army in Burma, was chief of the Imperial General Staff 1948–52, and governor-general of Australia 1953–60.

Sloane, Sir Hans (1660–1753), British collector, b. Ireland. He practised in London as a physician. His library of 50,000 volumes and his collection of MSS. and botanical specimens were offered under his will to the nation and formed the beginning of the British Museum.

Slowacki, Julius (1809–49), Polish romantic poet, a revolutionary, he lived in exile in Paris. His work includes the poetic drama *Kordian, Balladyna* and *Lilli Weneda,* written in the style of Shakespeare; and the unfinished poem *King Spirit* which reveals his later mystical tendencies.

Smeaton, John (1724–92), English engineer; he rebuilt Eddystone lighthouse (1756–59), improved Newcomen's steam-engine, and did important work on bridges, harbours, and canals. He also invented an improved blowing apparatus for iron-smelting.

Smetana, Bedřich (1824–84), Czech composer, creator of a national style. He was principal conductor of the Prague National Theatre, for which he wrote most of his operas, including *The Bartered Bride* and *The Kiss.* Best known of his other compositions are the cycle of symphonic poems *My Country* and the string quartets *From My Life*. He became totally deaf in 1874, suffered a mental breakdown, and died in an asylum. *See* Section E.

Smiles, Samuel (1812–1904), Scottish writer, b. Haddington, in early life a medical practitioner, remembered for *Self Help* (1859), and his biographies of engineers of the industrial revolution.

Smith, Adam (1723–90), Scottish economist, b. Kirkcaldy. In Edinburgh he published *Moral Sentiments*. Later he moved to London, and his *Wealth of Nations* (1776) is the first serious work in political economy.

Smith, Sir Grafton Elliot (1871–1937), Australian anatomist who did research on the structure of the mammalian brain. His works include *The Evolution of Man*.

Smith, John (1580–1631), English adventurer who in 1605 went on a colonising expedition to Virginia and was saved from death by the Red Indian Pocahontas.

Smith, Joseph (1805–44), American founder of the Mormons. He claimed that the *Book of Mormon* was revealed to him. In 1838 feeling against the Mormons culminated in a rising and Smith was murdered. He was succeeded by Brigham Young. *See* Mormonism, Section J.

Smith, Sydney (1771–1845), Anglican divine and journalist, who founded the *Edinburgh Review* and supported Catholic emancipation.

Smith, William (1769–1839), English surveyor and geologist, the first to map the rock strata of England and to identify the fossils peculiar to each layer.

Smith, Sir William Alexander (1854–1914), Scottish founder of the Boy's Brigade (1883), the oldest national organisation for boys in Britain.

Smith, William Robertson (1846–94), Scottish biblical scholar whose " Bible " contribution to the 9th edition of *The Encyclopaedia Britannica* resulted in an unsuccessful prosecution for heresy.

Smollett, Tobias George (1721–71), Scottish novelist whose work is characterised by satire and coarse humour. His main novels are *Roderick Random*, *Peregrine Pickle*, and *Humphrey Clinker*.

Smuts, Jan Christian (1870–1950), South African statesman and soldier. B. in Cape Colony, during the Boer War he fought on the Boer side. He became premier of the Union in 1919 and worked for cooperation within the Commonwealth and in the world, but his party was defeated in 1948 by the Nationalists under Malan.

Smyth, Ethel Mary (1858–1944), English composer and suffragette. Her main works are operas (*The Wreckers* and *The Boatswain's Mate*) and a *Mass in D*. She studied at the Leipzig Conservatory.

Snow, Baron (Charles Percy Snow) (b. 1905), English physicist and novelist, author of the essay *The Two Cultures of the Scientific Revolution*, and a sequence of novels *Strangers and Brothers* (11 vols.). *See* Section M, Part I.

Snyders, Frans (1597–1657), Flemish still-life and animal painter who studied under Breughel.

Soane, Sir John (1753–1837), English architect who designed the Bank of England. He left the nation his house and library in Lincoln's Inn Fields (Soane Museum).

Sobieski, John III (1624–96), elected king of Poland 1674, defended his country from the Turks.

Socinus or **Sozzini, Laelius** (1525–62), Italian founder of the sect of Socinians, with his nephew Faustus (1539–1604). Their teachings resemble those of Unitarians.

Socrates (470–399 B.C.), Greek philosopher and intellectual leader, was the son of a sculptor of Athens. He distinguished himself in three campaigns (Potidaea, Delium, and Amphipolis). Returning to Athens, he devoted himself to study and intellectual enquiry, attracting many followers; through these, especially Xenophon and Plato, we know of his teachings, for he wrote nothing. In 399 B.C. he was charged with impiety and with corrupting the young, found guilty, and accordingly died by drinking hemlock; see Plato's *Apology, Crito,* and *Phaedo.*

Soddy, Frederick (1877–1956), English chemist, who in Glasgow about 1912 laid the foundation of the isotope theory, before the physicists became prominent in that field. Nobel prizewinner 1921.

Solon (638–558 B.C.), Athenian lawgiver, who in a time of economic distress cancelled outstanding debts, and introduced some democratic changes.

Solzhenitsyn, Alexander Isayevich (b. 1919), Russian novelist, author of *One Day in the Life of Ivan Denisovich*, a documentary novel depicting life in one of Stalin's prison camps where he spent many years of his life. He was expelled from the Soviet Writers' Union in 1969. Nobel prizewinner 1970.

Somerset, Duke of (Edward Seymour) (1506–52), lord protector of England in the time of the young Edward VI, but he fell from power and was executed.

Sophocles (495–406 B.C.), Athenian dramatist, who was awarded the prize over Aeschylus in 468. Of over a hundred plays of his, the only extant ones are *Oedipus the King, Oedipus at Colonus, Antigone, Electra, Trachiniae, Ajax,* and *Philoctetes.*

Sorel, Georges (1847–1922), French advocate of revolutionary syndicalism, author of *Reflections on Violence* (1905). The irrational aspects of his philosophy (derived from Bergson) appealed to Mussolini and the Fascists.

Soult, Nicolas Jean de Dieu (1769–1851), French general who fought under Napoleon in Switzerland and Italy, at Austerlitz, and in the Peninsular War.

Sousa, John Philip (1854–1932), American bandmaster and composer of some stirring marches.

Southey, Robert (1774–1843), English poet and historian. In 1803 he settled near Coleridge at Keswick, and in 1813 became poet laureate. His best work was in prose: histories of Brazil and of the Peninsular War; lives of Nelson, Wesley, and others.

Southwell, Robert (1561–95), English poet and Jesuit martyr, beatified 1929. His poems include *The Burning Babe.*

Spaak, Paul Henri (b. 1899), Belgian statesman, first president of the U.N. General Assembly in 1946, and of the Assembly of the Council of Europe, 1949–51; secretary-general of Nato, 1957–61.

Spartacus (d. 71 B.C.), Thracian rebel. A Roman slave and gladiator in Capua, he escaped and headed a slave insurrection, routing several Roman armies, but was defeated and killed by Crassus.

Speke, John Hanning (1827–64), British explorer. In 1858 he discovered the Victoria Nyanza; and in 1860 with J. A. Grant traced the Nile flowing out of it.

Spence, Sir Basil Urwin (b. 1907), Scottish architect, mainly known for the new Coventry cathedral, and for Hampstead civic centre. He has also brought a new approach to university buildings. O.M. 1962.

Spencer, Herbert (1820–1903), English philosopher. B. Derby, he was at first a civil engineer, then a journalist (sub-editor of the *Economist*), when he wrote *Social Statics*. His *Principles of Psychology* (1855), published four years before Darwin's *Origin of Species*, expounded doctrines of evolution. His ten-volume *System of Synthetic Philosophy* was issued over a period of thirty years.

Spencer, Sir Stanley (1891–1959), English artist of visionary power. His two pictures of the *Resurrection* are in the Tate Gallery. He also painted Cookham regatta.

Spengler, Oswald (1880–1936), German historicist who held that every culture is destined to a waxing and waning life cycle and that the West European culture was entering its period of decline. His principal work is *The Decline of the West*. His views prepared the way for national socialism.

Spenser, Edmund (1552–99), English poet, b. London and educated at Cambridge. His *Shepheards Calender* appeared in 1579. In 1580 he went to Ireland as the lord deputy's secretary, and later acquired Kilcolman castle, where he wrote most of his main work, *The Faerie Queene*. His castle was burnt in an insurrection in 1598, when he returned to London. He is called " the poet's poet."

Spinoza, Baruch (1632–77), Dutch philosopher, b. Amsterdam, whose parents came to Holland from Portugal to escape the Inquisition. An independent thinker, his criticism of the Scriptures led to his being excommunicated from the synagogue. He supported himself by grinding and polishing lenses. He owed much to Descartes but was mainly concerned with religion and virtue. His philosophical theories are set out in the *Ethics* which was published posthumously. In the light of modern science his metaphysic cannot be accepted but his moral teaching has enduring validity. *See also* God and Man, Section J.

Spofforth, Reginald (1770–1827), English writer of glees, including *Hail, Smiling Morn.*

Spurgeon, Charles Haddon (1834–92), English Baptist who preached at the vast Metropolitan Tabernacle, London, from 1861 (burnt down 1898).

Staël, Anne Louise, Baronne de Staël-Holstein (1766–1817), French writer. Daughter of the finance minister, Necker, she married the Swedish ambassador, and kept a salon. Her *Lettres sur Rousseau* appeared in 1788. After the revolution she lived partly abroad, partly in France, and after a visit to Italy wrote her novel *Corinne* (1807).

Stalin (Joseph Vissarionovich Djugashvili) (1879–1953), Soviet statesman who for nearly 30 years was leader of the Russian people. He originally studied at Tiflis for the priesthood, but became an active revolutionary and took part in the civil war after 1917. After Lenin's death, he ousted Trotsky and became the outstanding figure. He modernised agriculture on socialist lines by ruthless means, and his series of five-year plans from 1929 made Russia an industrial power. On the German invasion in 1941 he assumed military leadership; and later attended Allied war conferences. After his death some of his methods and the "personality cult" were denounced by Khrushchev, and this had far-reaching results in other Communist countries. In his attack on "official" Marxism, George Lukács says Stalin "turned Marxism on its head" by making it into theories and strategies which fitted his own tactics of the day.

Stanford, Sir Charles Villiers (1852–1924), Irish composer of instrumental, choral, operatic, and other music.

Stanley, Sir Henry Morton (1841–1904), British explorer, b. Denbigh. He fought for the Confederates in the American Civil War. He then became a correspondent for the *New York Herald*, was commissioned to find Livingstone, and did so in 1871 at Ujiji, and with him explored Lake Tanganyika. In 1879 he founded the Congo Free State under the Belgian king. His works include *Through the Dark Continent* and an *Autobiography.*

Steele, Sir Richard (1672–1729), British essayist, b. Dublin. He founded the *Tatler* (1709–11), to which Addison also contributed, and later the *Spectator* (1711–12) and the *Guardian* (1713). He also wrote plays and had a minor political career.

Steen, Jan (1626–79), Dutch genre painter, b. Leiden, son of a brewer. *The Music Lesson* and *Skittle Alley* are in the National Gallery, the *Lute Player* in the Wallace collection.

Steer, Philip Wilson (1860–1942), English painter, especially of landscapes and of portraits.

Stefansson, Vilhjalmur (1879–1962), Canadian arctic explorer of Icelandic parentage; his publications include *Unsolved Mysteries of the Arctic.*

Stein, Sir Aurel (1862–1943), British archaeologist, b. Budapest. He held archaeological posts under the Indian government and explored Chinese Turkestan.

Stendhal, pseudonym of Marie Henri Beyle (1783–1842), French novelist, b. Grenoble. He was with Napoleon's army in the Russian campaign of 1812, spent several years in Italy, and after the revolution of 1830 was appointed consul at Trieste, and afterwards at Civitavecchia. In his plots he recreates historical and social events with imaginative realism and delineates character with searching psychological insight. His main works are *Le Rouge et le Noir*, and *La Chartreuse de Parme.*

Stephen (1105–54), usurped the crown of England from Henry I's daughter in 1135; and, after anarchy, retained it till his death.

Stephen, Sir Leslie (1832–1904), English writer, critic, and biographer. He edited the *Cornhill Magazine* (1871–82), and the *Dictionary of National Biography* (1882–91), and was the father of Virginia Woolf.

Stephenson, George (1781–1848), English engineer, inventor of the locomotive, b. at Wylam near Newcastle, a colliery fireman's son. As enginewright at Killingworth colliery he made his first locomotive in 1814 to haul coal from mines. In 1821 he became engineer to the Stockton and Darlington Railway, which opened in 1825 with the first steam passenger train, travelling at 12 miles an hour. His *Rocket* at 30 miles an hour won the prize of £500 in 1829 for the Liverpool–Manchester Railway. He also discovered the principle on which Davy's safety lamp was based.

Stephenson, Robert (1803–59), English engineer, son of the above, engineered railway lines in England and abroad, and built many bridges including the Menai and Conway tubular bridges and others overseas.

Sterne, Laurence (1713–68), English novelist and humorist. His main works are *Tristram Shandy* and *A Sentimental Journey.* He led a wandering and unconventional life, dying in poverty. His work helped to develop the novel.

Stevenson, Adlai (1900–65), American politician, an efficient governor of Illinois, 1949–53; and ambassador to the U.N., 1960–5.

Stevenson, Robert (1772–1850), Scottish engineer and builder of lighthouses, who invented "intermittent" and "flashing" lights.

Stevenson, Robert Louis (1850–94), Scottish author, b. Edinburgh. He suffered from ill-health and eventually settled in Samoa. His main works are *Travels with a Donkey, Treasure Island, Kidnapped, Dr. Jekyll and Mr. Hyde*, and *The Master of Ballantrae.*

Stinnes, Hugo (1870–1924), German industrialist who built up a huge coalmining, iron and steel, and transport business, and later entered politics.

Stoker, Bram (Abraham Stoker) (1847–1912), Irish author of the horror story *Dracula* and *Personal Reminiscences of Henry Irving.*

Stokes, Sir George Gabriel (1819–1903), Irish mathematician and physicist to whom is due the modern theory of viscous fluids and the discovery that rays beyond the violet end of the spectrum (the ultra-violet rays) produce fluorescence in certain substances.

Stopes, Marie Carmichael (1880–1958), English pioneer advocate of birth control. Her *Married Love* appeared in 1918, and she pioneered birth control clinics.

Stowe, Harriet Beecher (1811–96), American authoress of *Uncle Tom's Cabin* (1852), written to expose slavery.

Strachey, John St. Loe (1901–63), English Labour politician and writer. He held office under Attlee, 1945–51, and his publications include *The Menace of Fascism.*

Stradivari, Antonio (1644–1737), Italian maker of violins, b. Cremona, first in his art.

Strafford, 1st Earl of (Thomas Wentworth) (1593–1641), English statesman. He supported Charles I with a "thorough" policy, both as president of the north and as lord deputy in Ireland, where he introduced flax. His efficiency made him a special target when parliament met, and he was impeached and executed.

Strauss, David Friedrich (1808–74), German theologian, whose *Life of Jesus* attempted to prove that the gospels are based on myths.

Strauss, family of Viennese musicians. **Johann Strauss** (1804–49), the elder, was a composer of dance music, who with Joseph Lanner established the Viennese waltz tradition. His son, **Johann Strauss** (1825–99), the younger, although not so good a violinist or conductor as his father, was the composer of over 400 waltzes, which include *The Blue Danube* and *Tales from the Vienna Woods.* Two of his brothers, Josef Strauss (1827–70) and Eduard Strauss (1835–1916) were also composers and conductors.

Strauss, Richard (1864–1949), German composer and conductor, the son of a horn player in the opera orchestra at Munich. He succeeded von Bülow as court musical director at Meiningen. His works include the operas *Salome, Elektra*, and *Der Rosenkavalier.* the symphonic poems *Don Juan, Till Eulenspiegel*, and *Don Quixote*, and many songs of lyrical beauty. *See* Section E.

Stravinsky, Igor (b. 1882), Russian composer and conductor, pupil of Rimsky-Korsakov. His ballets, *The Fire Bird* (1910) *Petrushka* (1911), representative of his early romantic style, and the revolutionary *The Rite of Spring*, which caused a furore in 1913, were written for the ballet impresario Diaghilev. He adopted a neo-classical style in later works, for example, in the ballets *Pulcinella* and *Apollo Musagetes* and the opera-oratorio *Oedipus Rex*. He brought new vigour and freedom to rhythm and younger composers have been much influenced by his music. He became a French citizen in 1934 and a U.S. citizen in 1945. *See* Section E.

Strindberg, Johan August (1849–1912), Swedish writer of intense creative energy. His work is subjective and reflects his personal conflicts. He married three times but never happily. He produced some 55 plays as well as novels, stories, poems, and critical essays. *Lucky Peter, Gustav Adolf, Till Damascus, The Father, Miss Julie* are some of his plays.

Suckling, Sir John (1609–42), English poet, author of *Why so pale and wan?* He invented crib-bage.

Sudermann, Hermann (1857–1928), German writer of plays and novels, including *Frau Sorge* (translated as Dame Care).

Sulaiman the Magnificent (1494–1566), sultan of Turkey, conquerer, and patron of art and learning, who dominated the eastern Mediterranean but failed to capture Malta.

Sullivan, Sir Arthur Seymour (1842–1900), Irish composer, mainly known for the music he wrote for light operas with W. S. Gilbert as librettist, especially *The Pirates of Penzance, Patience, The Mikado, The Yeomen of the Guard* and *The Gondoliers*. He also wrote sacred music which was popular at the time. He and a friend discovered Schubert's lost *Rosamunde* music.

Sully, Maximilien de Béthune, Duc de (1560–1641), French statesman, finance minister to Henry IV. He also left *Memoirs*.

Sun Yat Sen (1867–1925), Chinese revolutionary, idealist and humanitarian. He graduated in medicine at Hong Kong, but after a rising failed in 1895 he lived abroad, planning further attempts, which succeeded in 1911 when the Manchus were overthrown and he became president. He soon resigned in favour of Yuan Shih-kai. His "Three Principles" were nationalism, democracy, and livelihood.

Sutherland, Graham Vivian (b. 1903), British artist. He painted the 80th birthday portrait of Sir Winston Churchill for parliament, and designed the tapestry for Coventry cathedral. O.M. 1960.

Swedenborg, Emanuel (1689–1772), Swedish author of *Arcana Coelestia, The Apocalypse Revealed, Four Preliminary Doctrines*, and *The True Christian Religion*. He claimed that his soul had been permitted to travel into hell, purgatory, and heaven. His works became the scriptures of the sect named Swedenborgians.

Sweelinck, Jan Pieterszoon (1562–1621), Dutch organist and composer of sacred music. In his fugues he made independent use of the pedals, and prepared the way for Bach. *See* Section E.

Swift, Jonathan (1667–1745), English satirist, b. Dublin of English parents. He crossed to England in 1688 to become secretary to Sir William Temple, and took Anglican orders, but did not obtain promotion. His *Tale of a Tub* and *The Battle of the Books* appeared in 1704. At first active in Whig politics, he became Tory in 1710, writing powerful tracts such as *Conduct of the Allies* (1711). In 1714 he retired to Ireland as Dean of St. Patrick's. His devoted women friends followed him—Hester Johnson (d. 1728), the Stella of his *Journal*, and Esther Vanhomrigh (d. 1723), the Vanessa of his poetry. Here he wrote his best work, including *Gulliver's Travels* (1726) and *The Drapier's Letters*.

Swinburne, Algernon Charles (1837–1909), English poet and critic. He first won attention with a play, *Atalanta in Calydon*, in 1865, followed by *Poems and Ballads*. Later followed *Songs before Sunrise, Bothwell*, and *Mary Stuart*. His criticism includes an essay on Blake.

Swithin, St. (d. 862), English saint, bishop of Winchester. Violent rain for 40 days fell in 971 when his body was to be removed to the new cathedral; hence the superstition as to rain on 15 July.

Symonds, John Addington (1840–93), English author who wrote on the Italian Renaissance.

Synge, John Millington (1871–1909), Irish poet and playwright, author of *Riders to the Sea* and *The Playboy of the Western World*. He was a director of the Abbey Theatre.

Szymanowski, Karol (1882–1937), Polish composer and director of the Warsaw conservatoire.

T

Tacitus, Gains Cornelius (*c.* 55–120), Roman historian. His chief works are a life of his father-in-law Agricola, and his *Histories* and *Annals*.

Taft, William Howard (1857–1930), United States president, 1909–13.

Tagore, Sir Rabindranath (1861–1941), Indian poet and philosopher who tried to blend east and west. His works include the play *Chitra*. Nobel prize 1913 (first Asian recipient).

Talbot, William Henry Fox (1800–77), English pioneer of photography which he developed independently of Daguerre. He also deciphered the cuneiform inscriptions at Nineveh.

Talleyrand-Périgord, Charles Maurice de (1754–1838), French politician and diplomat, led a mission to England in 1792 and was foreign minister from 1797 until 1807. He represented France at the Congress of Vienna.

Tallis, Thomas (*c.* 1510–85), English musician, with Byrd joint organist to the chapel royal under Elizabeth. He composed some of the finest of our church music.

Tamerlane (Timur the Lame) (1336–1405), Mongol conqueror. Ruler of Samarkand, he conquered Iran, Transcaucasia, Iraq, Armenia, and Georgia, and invaded India and Syria. He defeated the Turks at Angora, but died marching towards China. A ruthless conqueror, he was also a patron of literature and the arts. The line of rulers descended from him are the Timurids. He is the subject of a play by Marlowe.

Tarkington, Booth (1869–1946), American author of *Monsieur Beaucaire*.

Tarquinius: two kings of Rome came from this Etruscan family; Lucius the Elder (d. 578 B.C.); and Lucius Superbus, or the proud, (d. 510 B.C.) whose tyranny provoked a successful rising and brought an end to the monarchy.

Tartini, Giuseppe (1692–1770), Italian violinist, who wrote *Trillo del Diavolo*. He discovered the "third sound" resulting from two notes sounded together, a scientific explanation of which was later given by Helmholtz.

Tasman, Abel Janszoon (1603–59), Dutch navigator despatched by Van Diemen. He discovered Tasmania or Van Diemen's Land, and New Zealand, in 1642.

Tasso, Torquato (1544–95), Italian epic poet, b. Sorrento, author of *Gerusalemme Liberata*. He also wrote plays, *Aminta* and *Torrismondo*.

Tawney, Richard Henry (1880–1962), English historian, b. Calcutta, pioneer of adult education, and leader of socialist thought—the first critic of the affluent society. His works include *The Acquisitive Society, Equality, Religion and the Rise of Capitalism*.

Taylor, Sir Geoffrey Ingram (b. 1886), British scientist, noted for his work on aerodynamics, hydrodynamics, and the structure of metals. O.M. 1969.

Taylor, Jeremy (1613–67), English divine, b. Cambridge, author of many religious works, of which the chief are *Holy Living* and *Holy Dying*.

Tchaikovsky, Peter Ilyich (1840–93), Russian composer. His music is melodious and emotional and he excelled in several branches of composition. Among his works are the operas *Eugene Onegin* and *The Queen of Spades* (both from stories by Pushkin), symphonies, including the *Little Russian* and the *Pathétique*, ballets, including *Swan Lake, The Sleeping Beauty*, and *The Nutcracker*, the fantasies *Romeo and Juliet*, and *Francesca da Rimini*, the piano concerto in B flat minor, the violin concerto in D, and numerous songs. *See* Section E.

Tedder, 1st Baron (Arthur William Tedder) (1890–1967), British air marshal. From 1940 he reorganised the Middle East Air Force and later became deputy supreme commander under

Eisenhower for the invasion of Europe. He wrote an autobiography.

Teilhard de Chardin, Pierre (1881–1955), French palæontologist and religious philosopher. He went on palæontological expeditions in Asia, but his research did not conform to Jesuit orthodoxy, and his main works were published posthumously, *The Phenomenon of Man* and *Le Milieu Divin*.

Telemann, Georg Philipp (1681–1767), German composer, b. Magdeburg. His output in all fields of music was extensive; and his vitality and originality of form are appreciated today after a long period of neglect. He held appointments in several German towns.

Telford, Thomas (1757–1834), Scottish engineer, originally a stonemason. He built bridges (two over the Severn and the Menai suspension bridge), canals (the Ellesmere and Caledonian canals), roads, and docks.

Tell, William, legendary Swiss patriot, reputedly required by the Austrian governor Gessler to shoot an apple from his son's head, and the subject of a play by Schiller. The story is late, but the Swiss confederation did first arise in the 14th cent. with Schwyz, Uri, and Unterwalden.

Temple, Frederick (1821–1902), English divine. He was headmaster of Rugby, 1857–69, and archbishop of Canterbury, 1897–1902. He wrote controversial *Essays and Reviews* and supported Irish disestablishment.

Temple, William (1881–1944), English ecclesiastic, son of above, was a leading moral force in social matters and a worker for ecumenism. He was headmaster of Repton, 1910–14, and became archbishop of Canterbury in 1942.

Temple, Sir William (1628–99), English diplomat and writer, was instrumental in bringing about the marriage of Princess Mary with William of Orange. He married Dorothy Osborne, the letter-writer, and Swift was his secretary.

Templewood, 1st Viscount (Samuel John Gurney Hoare) (1880–1959), British Conservative politician. He piloted the India Act through the Commons while secretary for India, 1931–5; and as foreign secretary he negotiated an abortive pact with Laval. He was an advocate of penal reform.

Teniers, David, the elder (1582–1649), **and the younger** (1610–94), Flemish painters of rural life and landscape. The elder lived at Antwerp and the younger at Brussels.

Tenniel, Sir John (1820–1914), English book illustrator, especially for *Alice in Wonderland* and *Punch*.

Tennyson, 1st Baron (Alfred Tennyson) (1809–92), English poet, b. Somersby, Lincs. He had a mastery of language, and his publications extended over 60 years, mirroring much of his age. *In Memoriam* reflects his grief for his friend Arthur Hallam. Apart from his lyrics, his longer works include *The Princess, Maud, Idylls of the King,* and *Enoch Arden.* Interest in his work is returning.

Terence, Publius Terentius Afer (c. 184–159 B.C.), a Latin poet and dramatist, an African (Berber), who rose from the position of a slave.

Teresa, St. (1515–82), influential Spanish religious reformer and writer, b. Avila, a woman of boundless energy and spiritual strength. She entered the Carmelite order about 1534, established a reformed order in 1562 (St. Joseph's, Avila), and also founded, with the help of St. John of the Cross, houses for friars. Her writings which rank high in mystical literature include *The Way of Perfection* and *The Interior Castle.* She was canonised 40 years after her death.

Terry, Ellen Alice (Mrs. James Carew) (1848–1928), English actress, especially in Shakespearean parts with Sir Henry Irving, and in the plays of her friend Bernard Shaw.

Tertullian, Quintus (c. 160–220), Carthaginian theologian whose works, especially *Apologeticum,* have profoundly influenced Christian thought.

Tettrazzini, Luisa (1871–1940), Italian soprano, especially successful in *Lucia di Lammermoor.*

Tetzel, John (c. 1465–1519), German Dominican preacher, whose sale of indulgences for St. Peter's building fund provoked Luther.

Thackeray, William Makepeace (1811–63), English novelist, b. Calcutta, author of *Vanity Fair,* *Pendennis, Esmond, The Newcomes, The Virginians, Philip,* and *Lovel the Widower.* He edited the *Cornhill Magazine* from the first number in 1860, his most notable contributions being *Roundabout Papers.* He also wrote *Yellowplush Papers, The Book of Snobs,* and *The Four Georges* (lectures given in the United States).

Thales of Miletus (c. 624–565 B.C.), earliest of the Greek scientists, he created a sensation by his prediction of an eclipse of the sun, which was visible at Miletus in 585 B.C. He looked upon water as the basis of all material things, and in his mathematical work was the first to enunciate natural laws. *See also* **God and Man, Section J.**

Thant, Sithu U (b. 1909), Burmese diplomat; secretary-general of the United Nations since 1962.

Themistocles (c. 523–458 B.C.), Athenian soldier and statesman. He fortified the harbour of Piraeus and created a navy, defeating the Persians at Salamis in 480 B.C. He prepared the way for later greatness, but fell from power and died in exile.

Theocritus (c. 310–250 B.C.), Greek poet, especially of pastoral subjects. His short poems came to be called *Idylls.*

Theodoric the Great (455–526), King of the East Goths, who conquered Italy. Himself an Arian, he practised toleration, and his long reign was peaceful and prosperous.

Theodosius the Great (346–95), Roman emperor of the East (the Empire being divided in 364). He was baptised as a Trinitarian, issuing edicts against the Arians, and after a judicial massacre at Thessalonica he did penance to (St.) Ambrose.

Theophrastus (c. 372–287 B.C.), Greek philosopher, who succeeded Aristotle as teacher at Athens and inherited his library. He is best known for his botanical works and his *Characters* (moral studies).

Thibaud, Jacques (1880–1953), French violinist, killed in an air crash.

Thierry, Augustin (1795–1856), French historian, known for his *History of the Norman Conquest.*

Thiers, Louis Adolphe (1797–1877), French statesman and historian. After a varied political career, he became president in 1871, helping to revive France after defeat. He wrote a history of the Revolution.

Thomas, Dylan (1914–53), Welsh poet, whose highly individual *Eighteen Poems* (1934) brought him instant recognition. There followed *Twenty-five Poems* and *Deaths and Entrances.* *Under Milk Wood,* a play for voices, has more general appeal. *See* **Section M, Part II.**

Thompson, Sir D'Arcy Wentworth (1860–1948), Scottish zoologist whose *On Growth and Form* (1917), written in lucid and elegant style, has influenced biological science. He was also a classical scholar.

Thomson, Sir George Paget (b. 1892), English physicist, son of Sir J. J. Thomson; author of *The Atom, Theory and Practice of Electron Diffraction, The Inspiration of Science.* Nobel prizewinner 1937.

Thomson, James (1700–48), Scottish poet who wrote *The Seasons* and *The Castle of Indolence.*

Thomson, James (1834–82), poet and essayist, b. near Glasgow, who wrote *The City of Dreadful Night.*

Thomson, Sir Joseph John (1856–1940), English physicist and mathematician, leader of a group of researchers at the Cavendish laboratory, Cambridge. He established in 1897 that cathode-rays were moving particles whose speed and specific charge could be measured. He called them corpuscles but the name was changed to electrons. This work was followed up by the study of positive rays which led to the discovery of isotopes, the existence of which had earlier been suggested by Soddy. Nobel prizewinner 1906. *See also* **Section F, Part II.**

Thoreau, Henry David (1817–62), American essayist and nature-lover, who rebelled against society and lived for a time in a solitary hut. His chief work is *Walden.* He was a friend of Emerson.

Thorez, Maurice (1900–64), French communist leader from 1930 and especially after the second world war.

Thorndike, Dame Sybil (b. 1885), English actress. She made her début in 1904, and has played in Greek tragedies, in the plays of Shakespeare and Shaw, and in Grand Guignol. Her husband was Sir Lewis Casson.

Thornycroft, Sir William Hamo (1850–1925), English sculptor, whose works include a statue of General Gordon in Trafalgar Square.

Thorpe, Sir Thomas Edward (1845–1925), English chemist who researched in inorganic chemistry and with his friend Arthur Rücker made a magnetic survey of the British Isles.

Thorwaldsen, Bertel (1770–1844), Danish sculptor whose works include the Cambridge statue of Byron.

Thucydides (c. 460–399 B.C.), Greek historian, especially of the Peloponnesian War in which he himself fought. He was not merely a chronicler, but saw the significance of events and tried to give an impartial account. The speeches attributed by him to leaders include the beautiful funeral oration of Pericles.

Tiberius, Claudius (42 B.C.–A.D. 37), Roman emperor who succeeded Augustus. His early reign was successful but his later years were marked by tragedy and perhaps insanity. He is the Tiberius of Luke 3.1.

Tillett, Benjamin (1860–1943), English trade-union leader, especially of a dockers' strike in 1889 and a transport-workers' strike in 1911.

Tillotson, John (1630–94), English divine, a noted preacher who became archbishop of Canterbury in 1691.

Timur. See Tamerlane.

Tindal, Matthew (1655–1733), English deist, author of Christianity as old as the Creation.

Tintoretto (1518–94), Venetian painter whose aim it was to unite the colouring of Titian with the drawing of Michelangelo. His numerous paintings, mostly of religious subjects, were executed with great speed, some of them on enormous canvasses. His Origin of the Milky Way is in the National Gallery. His name was Jacopo Robusti, and he was called Il Tintoretto (little dyer) after his father's trade.

Tippett, Sir Michael Kemp (b. 1905), English composer whose works include the operas The Midsummer Marriage, King Priam, and Knot Garden, and the song-cycles Boyhood's End and The Heart's Assurance. See Section E.

Titian (Tiziano Vecelli) (c. 1487–1576), Venetian painter. He studied under the Bellinis and was influenced by Giorgione, for example, in his frescoes at Padua. His mature style is one of dynamic composition and full colour, as in his Bacchus and Ariadne (National Gallery). Among his principal works are Sacred and Profane Love (Borghese Gallery, Rome), and some in the Prado, Madrid.

Tito (Josif Broz) (b. 1892), Yugoslav leader, b. near Klanjec. In 1941 he organised partisan forces against the Axis invaders. In 1945 he became the first communist prime minister and in 1953 president. He has successfully pursued an independent line for his country.

Titus (A.D. 39–81), Roman emperor, son of Vespasian, brought the Jewish war to a close with the capture of Jerusalem. He completed the Colosseum.

Tizard, Sir Henry Thomas (1885–1959), English scientist and administrator. He was chairman of the Scientific Survey of Air Defence (later known as the Tizard Committee) that encouraged the birth of radar before the second world war and turned it into a successful defence weapon. He was chief scientific adviser to the government, 1947–52.

Tocqueville, Alexis, Comte de (1805–59), French liberal politician and historian, author of Democracy in America, still relevant reading.

Todd, 1st Baron (Alexander Robertus Todd) (b. 1907), Scottish biochemist, noted for his work on the structure of nucleic acids. Nobel prizewinner 1957.

Tolstoy, Leo Nikolayevich, Count (1828–1910), Russian writer and philosopher, b. Yasnaya Polyana. Of noble family, he entered the army and fought in the Crimean War. Beginning with simple, natural accounts of his early life (Childhood and Boyhood), he proceeded to articles on the war, and so eventually to perhaps his best work, the long novel War and Peace, followed by Anna Karenina. Increasingly pre-

occupied with social problems, he freed his serfs before this was done officially, and refused to take advantage of his wealth. His later works include The Kreutzer Sonata and Resurrection. By many he was regarded as a moral teacher.

Tooke, John Horne (1736–1812), English politician and pamphleteer, was a supporter of Wilkes and later of Pitt. He was tried for high treason, but was acquitted.

Toole, John Lawrence (1832–1906), English comedian.

Torquemada, Tomas de (1420–98), first inquisitor-general of Spain.

Torricelli, Evangelista (1608–47), Italian physicist, pupil of Galileo. He invented the barometer and improved both microscope and telescope.

Toscanini, Arturo (1867–1957), Italian conductor, b. Parma. He had a remarkable musical memory, and was at the same time exacting and self-effacing. He spent the second world war in exile.

Toulouse-Lautrec, Henri de (1864–1901), French painter, whose pictures portray with stark realism certain aspects of Parisian life in the nineties, especially the Moulin Rouge series. Many are in the Musée Lautrec at Albi.

Tovey, Sir Donald Francis (1875–1940), English pianist and composer. His compositions include chamber music, a piano concerto, and an opera The Bride of Dionysus; and his writings Essays in Musical Analysis.

Toynbee, Arnold (1852–83), English historian and social reformer. The settlement Toynbee Hall was founded in his memory.

Toynbee, Arnold Joseph (b. 1889), nephew of above, English historian, known mainly for his 10-volume Study of History. He was for 30 years director of the Institute of International Affairs.

Traherne, Thomas (c. 1636–74), English religious poet, b. Hereford; author also of Centuries of Meditations.

Trajan (c. 53–117), Roman emperor, was a successful general and firm administrator. He was born in Spain.

Tree, Sir Herbert Beerbohm (1853–1917), English actor-manager of the Haymarket theatre until 1897 when he built His Majesty's theatre. Sir Max Beerbohm was his half-brother.

Trenchard, 1st Viscount (Hugh Montague Trenchard) (1873–1956), British air-marshal. He served with the Royal Flying Corps in the first world war and became the first air marshal of the R.A.F. He was largely responsible for the R.A.F. college at Cranwell and was also concerned in establishing Hendon police college.

Trent, 1st Baron (Jesse Boot) (1850–1931), British drug manufacturer, b. Nottingham. He built up the largest pharmaceutical retail trade in the world, and was a benefactor of Nottingham and its university.

Trevelyan, George Macaulay (1876–1962), English historian, known for his History of England and English Social History.

Trevelyan, Sir George Otto (1838–1928), English liberal politician, father of above. He wrote a life of his uncle Lord Macaulay.

Trevithick, Richard (1771–1833), English mining engineer and inventor, b. near Redruth, Cornwall. His most important invention was a high-pressure steam-engine (1801).

Trollope, Anthony (1815–82), English novelist. His early life was a struggle, the family being supported by his mother's writings. His own career was in the post office, but by strict industry he produced many novels especially portraying clerical life (the Barchester series) and political life (the Phineas Finn series).

Trotsky, Leo (Lev Davidovich Bronstein) (1879–1940), Russian revolutionary, b. of Jewish parents in the Ukraine, one of the leaders of the Bolshevik revolution. As commissar of foreign affairs under Lenin he led the Russian delegation at the Brest-Litovsk conference. He differed from Stalin on policy, believing in "permanent revolution," according to which socialism could not be achieved in Russia without revolutions elsewhere, and was dismissed from office in 1925 and expelled from the Communist party in 1927. In 1929 he took up exile in Mexico where he was assassinated.

Trudeau, Pierre Eliott (b. 1919), Liberal prime minister of Canada since 1968.

Truman, Harry S. (b. 1884), U.S. President, 1945–53. He inherited the presidency on Roosevelt's death in 1945 when he took the decision to drop the first atom bomb, and he won the election of 1948. He intervened in Korea, dismissed General MacArthur, and aimed at raising standards in underdeveloped countries.

Tulsi Das (1532–1623), Indian poet whose masterpiece *Rām-Charit-Mānas* (popularly known as the *Rāmayana* and based on the Sanskrit epic of Vālmiki) is venerated by all Hindus as the Bible is in the West.

Turenne, Henri de la Tour d'Auvergne, Vicomte de (1611–75), French commander who was successful in the Thirty Years' War.

Turgenev, Ivan Sergeyvich (1818–83), Russian novelist, friend of Gogol and Tolstoy, who spent part of his life in exile. His works include *Fathers and Children*, *Smoke*, and *Virgin Soil*. He coined the term nihilist.

Turner, Joseph Mallord William (1775–1851), English landscape painter, b. London, a barber's son. He entered the Royal Academy and was at first a topographical watercolourist. Later he turned to oil and became a master of light and colour, achieving magical effects, especially in depicting the reflection of light in water. His works include *Crossing the Brook*, *Dido building Carthage*, *The Fighting Temeraire*, *Rain, Steam and Speed*. He also made thousands of colour studies. He encountered violent criticism as his style became more abstract which led to Ruskin's passionate defence of him in *Modern Painters*. He bequeathed his work to the nation (National and Tate Galleries, and the British Museum).

Tussaud, Marie (1760–1850), Swiss modeller in wax who learnt from her uncle in Paris, married a Frenchman, and later came to England where she set up a permanent exhibition.

Tutankhamun (d. *c.* 1340), Egyptian pharaoh of the 18th dynasty, son-in-law of Ikhnaton, whose tomb was discovered by Howard Carter in 1922, with the mummy and gold sarcophagus intact. He died when he was 18.

Twain, Mark (Samuel Langhorne Clemens) (1835–1910), American humorist. His *Innocents Abroad* was the result of a trip to Europe. His works include *A Tramp Abroad*, *Tom Sawyer*, *Huckleberry Finn*, and *Pudd'nhead Wilson*.

Tweedsmuir, 1st Baron (John Buchan) (1875–1940), Scottish author of biographies, historical novels, and adventure stories, including *Montrose* and *Thirty-nine Steps*. He was governor-general of Canada 1935–40.

Tyler, Wat (d. 1381), English peasant leader. He was chosen leader of the Peasants' Revolt of 1381 (due to various causes), and parleyed at Smithfield with the young king Richard II, but was killed.

Tyndale, William (*c.* 1494–1536), English religious reformer, translator of the Bible. He had to go abroad, where he visited Luther and his New Testament was printed at Worms. When copies entered England they were suppressed by the bishops (1526). His Pentateuch was printed at Antwerp, but he did not complete the Old Testament. He was betrayed, arrested, and executed. Unlike Wyclif, who worked from Latin texts, he translated mainly from the original Hebrew and Greek and his work was later to become the basis of the Authorised Version of the Bible.

Tyndall, John (1829–93), Irish physicist whose wide interests led him to research on heat, light, and sound, and on bacteria-free air and sterilisation. He discovered why the sky is blue (Tyndall effect) and pioneered popular scientific writing, *e.g.*, *Heat as a Mode of Motion*.

U

Unamuno, Miguel de (1864–1936), Spanish philosopher, poet, essayist, and novelist, author of *El Sentimiento Trágico de la Vida* (The Tragic Sense of Life).

Ulanova, Galina (b. 1910), Russian ballerina, who made her début in 1928, is a leading exponent of the art. She danced in Florence in 1951 and London in 1956.

Undset, Sigrid (1882–1949), Norwegian novelist, daughter of an antiquary, author of *Jenny*, *Kristin Lavransdatter*, and *Olav Audunsson*. Nobel prizewinner 1928.

Unwin, Sir Raymond (1863–1940), English architect of the first garden city at Letchworth.

Ursula, St., said in late legend to have been killed by Huns at Cologne with many companions while on pilgrimage. It took rise from a 4th cent. inscription which simply referred to virgin martyrs.

Usher or Ussher, James (1581–1656), Irish divine who in 1625 became archbishop of Armagh, and whose writings include a long-accepted chronology, which placed the creation at 4004 B.C.

V

Valentine, St., was a Christian martyr of the reign of the emperor Claudius II (d. A.D. 270). The custom of sending valentines may be connected with the pagan festival of Lupercalia.

Vanbrugh, Sir John (1664–1726), English architect and playwright. His buildings include Blenheim Palace and his plays *The Provok'd Wife*.

Vancouver, George (1758–98), British navigator who served under Captain Cook, also doing survey work, and who sailed round Vancouver island.

Vanderbilt, Cornelius (1794–1877), American merchant and railway speculator who amassed a fortune and founded a university at Nashville. His son, **William Henry Vanderbilt** (1821–85), inherited and added to it.

Van Dyck, Sir Anthony (1599–1641), Flemish painter, b. Antwerp. He studied under Rubens, travelled in Italy, and then settled in England with an annuity from Charles I. He excelled in portraits, especially of Charles I and Henrietta Maria, and of their court.

Vane, Sir Henry (1613–62), English parliamentary leader during the civil war period, though not involved in the execution of Charles I. He was executed in 1662.

Van Gogh, Vincent (1853–90), Dutch painter of some of the most colourful pictures ever created. With passionate intensity of feeling he painted without pause whatever he found around him—landscapes, still life, portraits; his was a truly personal art. His life was one of pain, sorrow, and often despair, and in the end he committed suicide.

Van Loon, Hendrik Willem (1882–1944), Dutch-born American popular historian who in 1922 published *The Story of Mankind*.

Vauban, Sebastien de Prestre de (1633–1707), French military engineer, whose skill in siege works (*e.g.*, at Maestrict 1673) was a factor in the expansive wars of Louis XIV. He protected France with fortresses and also invented the socket bayonet.

Vaughan Williams, Ralph (1872–1958), English composer, b. Gloucestershire. After Charterhouse and Cambridge he studied music in Berlin under Max Bruch and, later in Paris, under Ravel. He wrote nine symphonies besides a number of choral and orchestral works, operas (including *Hugh the Drover*, *Riders to the Sea*), ballets, chamber music, and songs. He showed great interest in folk tunes. *See* Section E.

Velasquez, Diego (*c.* 1460–1524), Spanish conquistador, first governor of Cuba.

Velasquez, Diego Rodriguez de Silva y (1599–1660), Spanish painter, b. Seville, especially of portraits at the court of Philip IV, and also of classical and historical subjects. He made two visits to Italy (1629–31, 1649–51), studying the Venetian painters, especially Titian, which hastened the development of his style. Among his masterpeices are *The Maids of Honour*, *The Tapestry Weavers* (both in the Prado), the Rokeby Venus and a portrait of Philip IV (both in the National Gallery), the landscape views from the Villa Medici (Prado) and *Juan de Pareja* (sold in London in 1970 for £2·25 million).

Venizelos, Eleutherios (1864–1936), Greek statesman, b. Crete. He became prime minister in 1910 and held this office intermittently. He promoted the Balkan League (1912), forced the king's abdication (1917), and brought Greece

into the war on the Allied side, securing territorial concessions at the peace conference, but
his expansionist policy in Turkish Asia failed.

Verdi, Giuseppe (1813–1901), Italian composer,
b. near Busseto in the province of Parma. His
early works include *Nabucco*, *Ernani*, *I Due
Foscani*, and *Macbeth*; a middle period is represented by *Rigoletto*, *Il Trovatore*, *La Traviata*,
Un Ballo in Maschera, and *Don Carlos*; to the
last period of his life belong *Aïda*, *Otello*, and
Falstaff (produced when he was 80). See
Section E.

Verlaine, Paul (1844–96), French poet, one of the
first of the symbolists, also known for his
memoirs and confessions. His works include
Poèmes saturniens, *Fêtes galantes*, *Sagesse*, and
Romances sans paroles. He was imprisoned
for two years in Belgium for shooting and
wounding his friend Rimbaud. He died in
poverty in Paris.

Vermeer, Jan (1632–75), Dutch painter, b. Delft.
His main paintings are of domestic interiors,
which he makes into works of art, as in *Lady
at the Virginals* (National Gallery). His reputation has grown during the last century.

Verne, Jules (1828–1905), French writer of science
fiction, including *Five Weeks in a Balloon*,
Twenty Thousand Leagues Under the Sea,
Round the World in Eighty Days.

Vernier, Pierre (1580–1637), French inventor of
the small sliding scale which enables readings
on a graduated scale to be taken to a fraction
of a division.

Veronese, Paolo (1528–88), Italian painter of the
Venetian school, whose works include *Marriage
Feast at Cana in Galilee*, *The Feast in the House
of Simon*, and *The Presentation of the Family of
Darius to Alexander*. His *Adoration of the Magi*
is in the National Gallery.

Veronica, St., legendary woman who was said to
hand her kerchief to Christ on the way to Calvary, to wipe his brow, and his impression was
left on the kerchief. In its present form her
legend dates from the 14th cent.

Verwoerd, Hendrik Frensch (1901–66), South
African politician, b. Amsterdam, exponent of
the policy of apartheid; prime minister 1958–
66. He was assassinated.

Vespasian, Titus Flavius (A.D. 9–70), Roman emperor. He was sent by Nero to put down the
Jews and was proclaimed by the legions. He
began the Colosseum.

Vespucci, Amerigo (1451–1512), Florentine explorer, naturalised in Spain, contractor at
Seville for Columbus. He later explored
Venezuela. The use of his name for the continent arose through a mistake.

Victor Emmanuel II (1820–78), first king of Italy.
King of Sardinia, he was proclaimed king of
Italy in 1861 after the Austrians had been de-
feated and Garibaldi had succeeded in the south.
Rome was added in 1870.

Victoria (1819–1901), Queen of Great Britain, was
granddaughter of George III and succeeded an
uncle in 1837. In 1840 she married Prince
Albert of Saxe-Coburg-Gotha, who died in
1861. Conscientious, hardworking, and of
strict moral standards, she had by the end of a
long life (jubilees 1887 and 1897) won the affection and respect of her subjects in a unique
degree. Her reign saw industrial expansion,
growing humanitarianism, literary output, and
in the main prolonged peace; and by its close
the British empire and British world power had
reached their highest point.

Villeneuve, Pierre de (1763–1806), French admiral who was defeated by Nelson at Trafalgar
and captured along with his ship, the *Bucentaure*.

Villon, François (1431–?1463), French poet, b.
Paris, who lived at a turbulent time at the close
of the Hundred Years War. After fatally
stabbing a man in 1455 he joined the *conquil-
lards*, a criminal organisation. They had a
secret language (the *jargon*) and it was for them
that he composed his ballads. His extant
works consist of the *Petit Testament* (1456),
originally called *Le Lais*, and the *Grand Testament* (1461), masterpieces of mediaeval verse.

Virgil (Publius Vergilius Maro) (70–19 B.C.),
Roman epic poet, b. at Andes near Mantua, he
went to Rome to obtain redress for the military
confiscation of his farm. He was patronised
by Maecenas, and wrote his pastoral *Eclogues*,

followed by his *Georgics*. His best-known work,
the *Aeneid*, deals with the wanderings of Aeneas
after the fall of Troy till his establishment of a
kingdom in Italy.

Vitus, St., Roman Catholic martyr, who lived in
the 4th cent. His cultus is associated with
physical health, and he is invoked against con-
vulsive disorder.

Vivaldi, Antonio (c. 1675–1743), Venetian composer, violin master at the Ospedal della Pieta.
His output of orchestral works was prolific and
Bach arranged some of his violin pieces for the
harpsichord. His reputation, long disparaged,
has grown immensely in recent years. See
Section E.

Volta, Alessandro (1745–1827), Italian physicist of
Pavia, who, working on the results of Galvani,
invented the voltaic pile, the first instrument for
producing an electric current. It provided a
new means for the decomposition of certain
substances. His name was given to the volt,
the unit of electrical potential difference.

Voltaire (François Marie Arouet) (1694–1778),
French philosopher and writer. His first essays
offended the authorities, and he spent the years
1726–9 in England, where he wrote some of his
dramas. Returning to France, he published
his *Philosophical Letters*, which aroused the
enmity of the priesthood. At this juncture,
the Marquise du Châtelet offered him the
asylum of her castle of Cirey, and for the next
15 years he made this his home, writing there
his *Discources of Man*, *Essay on the Morals and
Spirit of Nations*, *Age of Louis XIV*, etc. The
marquise was a mathematician and taught him
some science, thus helping him in his interpretation of Newton's *Principia*. To Voltaire we
owe the story of the falling apple, also the
dictum that Admiral Byng was shot "pour
encourager les autres." He spent the years
1750–3 in Berlin at the invitation of Frederick
the Great. In challenging accepted beliefs and
traditions he prepared the way for the French
revolution.

Vondel, Joost van den (1587–1679), Dutch poet
who lived at Amsterdam. Most of his dramas
are on biblical subjects, and the two most
famous are *Jephtha* and *Lucifer*.

Voroshilov, Klimentiv Efremovich (1881–1969),
Soviet general who commanded the Leningrad
defences in 1941, and was U.S.S.R. president,
1953–60.

Vyshinsky, Andrei Yanuarievich (1883–1954),
Soviet jurist and diplomat; conducted the prosecution of the Moscow treason trials, 1936–8;
represented Russian interests abroad and at
U.N.

W

Wade, George (1673–1738), English general and
military engineer who, after the rising of 1715,
pacified the Scottish highlands, constructing
military roads and bridges. In the 1745 rising
Prince Charles' forces evaded him.

Wagner, Richard (1813–83), German composer,
b. Leipzig. He achieved a new type of musical
expression in his operas by the complete union
of music and drama. He made use of the *Leit-
motif* and was his own librettist. His originality and modernism aroused a good deal of opposition, and he was exiled for some years.
But he was supported by loyal friends, including Liszt, the young King Ludwig of Bavaria,
and the philosopher Nietzsche. He began the
music of the *Ring des Nibelungen* in 1853, but it
was not until 1876 that the whole of the drama
(Rheingold, Valkyrie, Siegfried, Götterdäm-
merung) was performed at Bayreuth under the
conductor Hans Richter. Other operas are
The Flying Dutchman, *Rienzi*, *Tannhäuser*,
Lohengrin, *Tristan und Isolde*, *Die Meistersinger von Nürnberg*, and *Parsifal*, a religious
drama. He married Liszt's daughter Cosima,
formerly wife of his friend Hans von Bülow.
See Section E.

Waley, Arthur (1889–1966), English orientalist,
known for his translations of Chinese and Japanese poetry and prose, being the first to bring the
literature of those countries to the western
world.

B63

Walker, George (1618–90), hero of the siege of Londonderry in 1688, who kept the besiegers at bay for 105 days.

Wallace, Alfred Russel (1823–1913), British naturalist, b. Usk, Monmouth, joint author with Darwin of the theory of natural selection. In 1858, while down with illness in the Moluccas, he sent a draft of his theory to Darwin in England who was amazed to find that it closely agreed with his own theory of evolution which he was on the point of publishing. The result was a reading of a joint paper to the Linnean Society.

Wallace, Edgar (1875–1932), English novelist and playwright, known for his detective thrillers.

Wallace, Sir Richard (1818–90), English art collector and philanthropist, whose widow bequeathed his collection to the nation (Wallace Collection, Manchester Square, London).

Wallace, Sir William (c. 1274–1305), Scottish patriot. He withstood Edward I, at first successfully, but was defeated at Falkirk and executed.

Wallenstein, Albrecht von (1583–1634), German soldier and statesman during the Thirty Years War. An able administrator of his own estates, he sought the unity of Germany, but was distrusted and eventually assassinated.

Waller, Edmund (1606–87), English poet of polished simplicity, author of *Go, lovely rose.* He was able to agree with both parliamentarians and royalists.

Walpole, Horace, 4th Earl of Orford (1717–97), younger son of Sir Robert Walpole, English writer, chiefly remembered for his *Letters,* his *Castle of Otranto,* and his " Gothic " house at Strawberry Hill.

Walpole, Sir Hugh Seymour (1884–1941), English novelist, b. New Zealand. His works include *Fortitude, The Dark Forest,* and *The Herries Chronicle.*

Walpole, Sir Robert, 1st Earl of Orford (1676–1745), English Whig statesman, who came to office soon after the Hanoverian succession and is considered the first prime minister—a good finance minister, a peace minister, and a "house of commons man."

Walter, Bruno (1876–1962), German–American conductor, especially of Haydn, Mozart, and Mahler.

Walter, John (1776–1847), English newspaper editor. Under him *The Times,* founded by his father John Walter (1739–1812), attained a leading position.

Walton, Izaak (1593–1683), English writer, especially remembered for *The Compleat Angler.* He also wrote biographies of Donne, Hooker, and George Herbert.

Walton, Sir William Turner (b. 1902), English composer, whose works include concertos for string instruments, two symphonies, two coronation marches, *Façade* (setting to Edith Sitwell's poem), and an oratorio, *Belshazzar's Feast.* O.M. 1967.

Warbeck, Perkin (1474–99), Flemish impostor, b. Tournai, who claimed to be the younger son of Edward IV with French and Scottish backing, but failed and was executed.

Warwick, Earl of (Richard Neville) (c. 1428–71), " the kingmaker." At first on the Yorkist side in the Wars of the Roses, he proclaimed Edward IV king; but later changed sides and restored the Lancastrian Henry VI. He was killed at Barnet.

Washington, Booker Taliaferro (1858–1915), American Negro educationist, author of *Up from Slavery.* He became principal of Tuskegee Institute, Alabama.

Washington, George (1732–99), first U.S. president. B. in Virginia, of a family which originated from Northamptonshire, he served against the French in the Seven Years War. When the dispute between the British government and the Americans over taxation came to a head, he proved a successful general, and Cornwallis's surrender to him at Yorktown in 1781 virtually ended the war. In 1787 he presided over the Philadelphia convention which formulated the constitution, and was president 1789–97. He was both a general and a leader of men.

Watson, John Broadus (1878–1958), American psychologist, an exponent of behaviourism. *See* Behaviourism, Section J.

Watson-Watt, Sir Robert (b. 1892), Scottish physicist, who played a major part in the development of radar.

Watt, James (1736–1819), Scottish engineer and inventor, b. Greenock. He made important improvements to Newcomen's steam-engine by inventing a separate condenser (applying Black's discoveries (1761–4) on latent heat) and other devices based on scientific knowledge of the properties of steam. He was given support by Matthew Boulton, a capitalist, and settled down in Birmingham with him. He defined one horse-power as the rate at which work is done when 33,000 lb are raised one foot in one minute. He also constructed a press for copying manuscripts. The watt as a unit of power is named after him.

Watteau, Jean Antoine (1684–1721), French painter. He painted pastoral idylls in court dress. His works include *Embarquement pour Cythère* in the Louvre.

Watts, George Frederick (1817–1904), English painter of allegorical pictures and portraits. His works include *Love and Death,* and *Hope.*

Watts, Isaac (1674–1748), English hymn-writer, author of *O God, our help in ages past.*

Watts-Dunton, Walter Theodore (1836–1914), English poet and critic, friend of Swinburne whom he looked after until his death in 1909. His works include *The Coming of Love* and *Aylwin.*

Waugh, Evelyn (1902–66), English satirical writer, author of *Vile Bodies, The Loved One, Brideshead Revisited, Life of Edmund Campion, The Ordeal of Gilbert Pinfold,* and an autobiography, *A Little Learning. See* Section M, Part I.

Wavell, 1st Earl (Archibald Percival Wavell) (1883–1950), British general. He served in the first great war on Allenby's staff and in the second he commanded in the Middle East 1939–41, defeating the Italians; and in India 1941–3. He was viceroy of India 1943–7.

Webb, Sir Aston (1849–1930), English architect who designed the new front of Buckingham Palace, and the Admiralty arch.

Webb, Matthew (1848–83), English swimmer, the first to swim the English Channel (1875).

Webb, Sidney James, Baron Passfield (1859–1947), and his wife Beatrice, née Potter (1858–1943), English social reformers and historians. They combined careful investigation of social problems (their books include *History of Trade Unionism* and *English Local Government*) with work for the future; they were members of the Fabian Society, launched the *New Statesman,* and helped to set up the London School of Economics. He held office in Labour governments.

Weber, Carl Maria Friedrich Ernst von (1786–1826), German composer, who laid the foundation of German romantic opera. His reputation rests principally on his three operas, *Der Freischütz, Euryanthe,* and *Oberon.* He was also an able pianist, conductor, and musical director. *See* Section E.

Webster, Daniel (1782–1852), American statesman and orator. He held office more than once and negotiated the Ashburton Treaty which settled the Maine–Canada boundary.

Webster, Noah (1758–1843), American lexicographer, who published an *American dictionary of the English language.*

Wedgwood, Dame Cicely Veronica (b. 1910). English historian, author of *William the Silent, Thomas Wentworth, The Thirty Years' War, The King's Peace, The Trial of Charles I;* a member of the Staffordshire pottery family. O.M. 1969.

Wedgwood, Josiah (1730–95), English potter, who at his Etruria works near Hanley produced from a new ware (patented 1763) pottery to classical designs by Flaxman, and gave pottery a new impetus.

Weill, Kurt (1900–50), German composer of satirical, surrealist operas, including *Die Dreigroschenoper* (librettist Brecht), and musical comedies, including *Lady in the Dark* and *One Touch of Venus.* In 1936 he settled in the United States. *See* Section E.

Weingartner, Felix (1863–1942), Austrian conductor, also a composer and writer of a text book on conducting.

Weismann, August (1834–1914), German biologist. He worked on the question of individual variability in evolution, stressing the continuity of the germ plasm and rejecting the idea of inheritance of acquired characteristics.

Weizmann, Chaim (1874–1952), Israeli leader, b. Pinsk. He came to England in 1903 and taught biochemistry at Manchester. He helped to secure the Balfour Declaration (1917), promising a Jewish national home, and was for many years president of the Zionists. In 1948 he became first president of Israel.

Wellesley, Marquess (Richard Colley Wellesley) (1760–1842), British administrator. He was a successful governor-general of India, and was brother of the Duke of Wellington.

Wellington, 1st Duke of (Arthur Wellesley) (1769–1852), British general. B. in Ireland, he joined the army and gained experience in India. In the Peninsular War he successfully wore down and drove out the invading French. When Napoleon escaped from Elba, Wellington defeated him at Waterloo. Thereafter he took some part in politics as a Tory, but in the last resort was capable of accepting change.

Wells, Herbert George (1866–1946), English author. B. London, he was at first a teacher. He believed in progress through science, and became one of the most influential writers of his time. His long series of books includes romances of the Jules Verne variety (*The Time Machine*, *The Island of Dr. Moreau*, *The Invisible Man*), sociological autobiography (*Love and Mr. Lewisham*, *Kipps*, *Tono-Bungay*, *The History of Mr. Polly*, *Mr. Britling Sees it Through*), and popular education (*Outline of History*, *The Science of Life*, *The Work, Wealth and Happiness of Mankind*, *The Shape of Things to Come*, *The Fate of Homo Sapiens*). He was an early and successful educator of the common man. He was also a founder member of the Fabian Society.

Wesley, Charles (1707–88), English hymnwriter. He was the companion of his brother John, and wrote over 5,500 hymns, including *Love divine* and *Jesu, lover of my soul*.

Wesley, John (1703–91), English evangelist and founder of Methodism (at first a nickname applied to friends of himself and his brother), b. at Epworth. After a trip to Georgia and after encountering Moravian influence, he began to teach on tour, covering in over 50 years more than 200,000 miles and preaching over 40,000 sermons. He made religion a live force to many ignorant folk of humble station who could only be reached by a new and direct challenge. He made a feature of the Sunday school and increased the use of music (the brothers' first hymnbook appeared in 1739). He did not plan separation from the Anglican church, though it was implicit in his ordination of a missionary, and it took place after his death. *See also* Methodism, Section J.

Westermarck, Edward Alexander (1862–1939), Finnish sociologist. His works include *History of Human Marriage, Origin and Development of the Moral Ideas*, and *The Oedipus Complex*.

Westinghouse, George (1846–1914), American engineer who invented an air-brake for railways (1868) called by his name, and pioneered the use of high tension alternating current for the transmission of electric power.

Westmacott, Sir Richard (1775–1856), English sculptor of Achilles in Hyde Park.

Wharton, Edith (1862–1937), American novelist and friend of Henry James. Her works include *House of Mirth* and *Custom of the Country*.

Whately, Richard (1787–1863), English archbishop of Dublin. He wrote treatises on *Rhetoric* and *Logic*.

Wheatstone, Sir Charles (1802–75), English physicist, one of the first to recognise Ohm's law. In 1837 he (with W. F. Cooke) patented an electric telegraph. He also introduced the microphone.

Wheeler, Sir Charles (b. 1892), English sculptor, especially on buildings. His autobiography is *High Relief*. P.R.A., 1956–66.

Whistler, James Abbott McNeill (1834–1903), American artist. B. at Lowell, he studied in Paris and settled in England. He reacted against the conventions of his day, and Ruskin's uncomprehending criticism of his work resulted in a lawsuit. Among his main works are studies of the Thames, and a portrait of his mother, now in the Louvre.

White, Sir George Stuart (1835–1912), British general who defended Ladysmith in the South African War.

Whitefield, George (1714–70), English evangelist, b. Gloucester. He was at first associated with the Wesleys, but differed from them on predestination. His supporters built him a "Tabernacle" in London, and he had other chapels elsewhere, but founded no lasting sect.

Whitgift, John (1530–1604), archbishop of Canterbury in the time of Elizabeth I (from 1583). His policy helped to clarify and strengthen the Anglican church.

Whitman, Walt (1819–92), American poet, b. Long Island. He led a wandering life and did hospital work in the Civil War. He aimed at forming a new and free American outlook. His works include *Leaves of Grass, Drum Taps*, and *Democratic Views*.

Whittier, John Greenleaf (1807–92), American Quaker poet, b. Haverhill, Mass. He wrote against slavery (*Justice and Expediency*), turning to poetry after the Civil War, especially remembered for *Snow-bound*. His religious poems have become hymns, including *Dear Lord and Father of Mankind*.

Whittington, Richard (c. 1358–1423), English merchant. Son of a Gloucestershire knight, he became a London mercer and was mayor of London 1398, 1406, 1419. He left his fortune to charity. The cat legend is part of European folklore.

Whittle, Sir Frank (b. 1907), pioneer in the field of jet propulsion. The first flights of Gloster jet propelled aeroplanes with Whittle engine took place in May 1941.

Whymper, Edward (1840–1911), English wood-engraver and mountaineer. He was the first to climb the Matterhorn. His books include *Scrambles amongst the Alps*.

Wiggin, Kate Douglas (1856–1925), American novelist, author of *Rebecca of Sunnybrook Farm*.

Wilberforce, William (1759–1833), English philanthropist, b. Hull. He was the parliamentary leader of the campaign against the slave trade, abolished in 1807. He then worked against slavery itself, but that further step was only taken in the year of his death.

Wilcox, Ella Wheeler (1855–1919), American writer of romantic sentimental verse.

Wilde, Oscar Fingall (1854–1900), Irish author and dramatist, son of a Dublin surgeon and leader of the cult of art for art's sake. His works include poems, fairy-tales, short stories, and witty comedies—*Lady Windermere's Fan, A Woman of No Importance, The Ideal Husband*, and *The Importance of Being Earnest*. In a libel action he was convicted of homosexual practices and imprisoned for two years, when he wrote *The Ballad of Reading Gaol*.

Wilder, Thornton Niven (b. 1897), American author and playwright. Among his books are *The Bridge of San Luis Rey* and *Ides of March*.

Wilkes, John (1727–97), English politician. A Whig, he violently attacked George III in his paper the *North Briton*, and as a result of unsuccessful proceedings against him, general warrants were determined illegal. He was again in trouble for obscene libel; his defiance of authority brought him popularity, and he was four times re-elected to parliament but refused his seat, until his opponents gave way. His motives were mixed, but he helped to establish freedom of the press.

Willcocks, Sir William (1852–1932), British engineer, b. India, who carried out irrigation works in India, Egypt, South Africa, and Mesopotamia. He built the Aswan dam (1898–1902).

Willett, William (1856–1915), English advocate of " daylight savings," adopted after his death.

William I of England (1027–87), the " Conqueror ", Duke of Normandy, claimed the English throne as successor to Edward the Confessor, and defeated Harold II at Hastings in 1066. An able commander and a firm ruler, he crushed Saxon resistance, especially in the north, transferred most of the land to his Norman followers, and drew England into closer relations with the continent, as did his archbishop Lanfranc. He ordered the Domesday survey (*see* L32).

William II of England (1056–1100), the Conqueror's son, surnamed Rufus, succeeded in 1187. Capricious and self-indulgent, his reign was troubled, and he was shot (by accident or design) while hunting in the New Forest.

William III of England (1650–1702), King of England, Scotland, and Ireland (1689–1702), son of William II of Orange and Mary, daughter of Charles I. He married Mary, daughter of the Duke of York (later James II) while stadtholder of Holland. In 1688, when James had abdicated and fled the country, he was invited to succeed and he and Mary became joint king and queen. The revolution of 1688 brought to England tolerance of Protestant worship, but William was mainly concerned with war against France, brought to an end in 1697.

William IV of England (1765–1837), third son of George III, succeeded his brother George IV in 1830, and was called the " sailor king." In his reign the parliamentary reform bill of 1832 and other reform measures were carried without obstruction from him.

William I of Germany (1797–1888), King of Prussia and first German emperor. He succeeded to the throne in 1861 and continued resistance to reform, appointing Bismarck as chief minister, and supporting him through the Austro-Prussian and Franco-Prussian wars. His personal character was simple and unassuming.

William II of Germany, the Kaiser (1859–1941), King of Prussia and German emperor from 1888, was grandson of William I and of Queen Victoria. He was intelligent but impetuous, and believed in military power. He dismissed Bismarck. In 1914 his support of Austria helped to precipitate European war, and the resulting defeat brought his abdication, after which he lived in retirement at Doorn in Holland.

William the Silent (1533–1584), Dutch national leader. Prince of Orange, he led the revolt of the Protestant Netherlands against the rule of the Spanish Philip II. The union of the northern provinces was accomplished in 1579, and Spanish rule was renounced by 1584, in which year William was assassinated.

Williams, Sir George (1821–1905), founder of the Young Men's Christian Association.

Williams, Emlyn (b. 1905), Welsh actor-playwright and producer, author of *Night must Fall*, *The Corn is Green* and *The Light of Heart*. He has also given readings from Dickens and Dylan Thomas.

Wilson, James Harold (b. 1916), British Labour statesman. He entered parliament in 1945 as member for Ormskirk and was elected for Huyton in 1950. He became leader of the Labour Party in 1963 after the death of Gaitskell and was prime minister 1964–70. His government enacted a series of social reforms and succeeded in strengthening Britain's international economic position but courted unpopularity by taking the necessary restrictive measures. Faced with Rhodesian U.D.I., he tried to keep open negotiations without compromising on principle. He refused to send troops to Vietnam and to supply arms to South Africa. He prepared for entry into the European Economic Community.

Wilson, Richard (1714–82), British landscape painter, b. Montgomeryshire, who pioneered a freer style than the old classicism.

Wilson, Thomas Woodrow (1856–1924), American statesman. He was U.S. president 1913–21, brought America into the first world war and advocated the League of Nations, but was not a successful negotiator at the peace conference and could not carry his country into the League. His administration introduced prohibition and women's suffrage.

Wingate, Orde Charles (1903–44), leader of the Chindit forces engaged behind the Japanese lines in Burma during the second world war.

Winifred, St., the 7th cent. patron saint of North Wales, said in late legend to have been killed by her rejected suitor, Prince Caradoc, but restored by her uncle.

Wiseman, Nicholas Patrick (1802–65), cardinal, b. in Spain of an Irish family. In 1850 on the restoration in England of the Roman Catholic hierarchy he became first archbishop of Westminster, and reorganised and developed his church in Great Britain.

Wodehouse, Pelham Grenville (b. 1881), English humorist, creator of Jeeves in the Bertie Wooster stories. He is now an American citizen.

Wolf, Friedrich August (1759–1824), German classical scholar, a founder of scientific classical philology.

Wolf, Hugo (1860–1903), Austrian song-writer. In his settings of over 300 German lyrics, including many of Mörike and Goethe, he achieved complete union of poetry and music. *See* Section E.

Wolfe, James (1727–59), British general, b. Westerham. He showed early promise in the Seven Years' War, and was given command of the expedition against Quebec, which in spite of its strong position he captured, but lost his life.

Wolsey, Thomas (c. 1475–1530), English cardinal. A butcher's son at Ipswich, he entered the church, becoming archbishop of York and cardinal, while in the same year (1515) he became Henry VIII's lord chancellor. He was thus powerful and wealthy, and he founded Christ Church (Cardinal) College, Oxford. But in spite of his ability he was unable to secure papal sanction for the king's divorce from Catherine of Aragon, and fell from power and died.

Wood, Sir Henry Joseph (1869–1944), English conductor, founder of the Promenade Concerts which he conducted from 1895 till his death.

Woodcock, George (b. 1904), English trade union leader, T.U.C. general secretary 1960–69. He is chairman of the Commission on Industrial Relations set up by the Labour government in 1969.

Woodville, Elizabeth (1437–91), wife of Edward IV. Her daughter Elizabeth married Henry VII.

Woolf, Virginia (1882–1941), English writer, daughter of Sir Leslie Stephen and wife of Leonard Woolf with whom she founded the Hogarth Press. Her works develop the stream-of-consciousness technique and include *To the Lighthouse*, *Mrs. Dalloway*, *The Waves*, *A Room of One's Own*. *See* Section M, Part I.

Woolley, Sir Richard van der Riet (b. 1906), succeeded Sir Harold Spencer Jones as astronomer royal (England) in 1956.

Wootton of Abinger, Baroness (Barbara Frances Wootton) (b. 1897), English social scientist; chairman Metropolitan Juvenile Courts 1946–62; deputy speaker of the House of Lords 1966. Her works include *Social Science and Social Pathology*, *Crime and the Criminal Law*, and an autobiography *In a world I never made*.

Wordsworth, William (1770–1850), English poet, b. Cockermouth. He went to Cambridge, and in 1798 with Coleridge issued *Lyrical Ballads*, a return to simplicity in English poetry. He settled at Grasmere with his sister Dorothy (1771–1855), to whose insight his poems owe much. Among his best works are his sonnets and his *Ode on the Intimations of Immortality*, besides his *Prelude*.

Wren, Sir Christopher (1632–1723), English architect, b. Wiltshire. After the great fire (1666) he prepared an abortive plan for rebuilding London, but did in fact rebuild St. Paul's and more than fifty other city churches, including St. Stephen, Walbrook, and St. Mary-le-Bow. Other works include Chelsea Hospital, portions of Greenwich Hospital, the Sheldonian theatre, Oxford, and Queen's College library, Oxford. He had wide scientific interests (he was professor of mathematics at Gresham College, London, and professor of astronomy at Oxford) and helped to found the Royal Society.

Wright, Frank Lloyd (1869–1959), American architect, initiator of horizontal strip and all-glass design. His influence has spread over the world. His buildings include the Imperial Hotel, Tokio, and the Guggenheim Museum, New York.

Wright, Orville (1871–1948), American airman who with his brother Wilbur (1867–1912) in 1903 was the first to make a controlled sustained flight in a powered heavier-than-air machine, flying a length of 852 ft. at Kitty Hawk, N.C.

Wyatt, James (1746–1813), English architect who built Fonthill Abbey.

Wyatt, Sir Thomas (1503–42), English poet who introduced the sonnet from Italy. He was also a diplomat.

Wyatt, Sir Thomas the younger (c. 1520–54), son of above, unsuccessfully led a revolt against Queen Mary on behalf of Lady Jane Grey.

Wycherley, William (1640–1715), English dramatist of the Restoration period. A master of satiric comedy, his plays include *Love in a Wood*, *The Plain Dealer*, and (the best-known) *The Country Wife*.

Wyclif, John (*c.* 1320–84), English religious reformer. He taught at Oxford, later becoming rector of Lutterworth. He insisted on inward religion and attacked those practices which he thought had become mechanical. His followers, called Lollards, were suppressed, partly for political reasons. The Wyclif Bible, the first and literal translation of the Latin Vulgate into English, was mainly the work of his academic followers at Oxford.

Wykeham, William of (1324–1404), English churchman. He held office under Edward III and became bishop of Winchester in 1367. He founded New College, Oxford, and Winchester School, and improved Winchester cathedral.

Wyllie, William Lionel (1851–1931), English marine painter of *The Thames Below London Bridge*.

Wyspianski, Stanislav (1869–1907), Polish poet, dramatist and painter. His plays *The Wedding*, *Liberation*, and *November Night* treat of national themes.

X

Xavier, St. Francis (1506–52), "apostle of the Indies," b. at Xavero in the Basque country. He was associated with Loyola in founding the Jesuits, and undertook missionary journeys to Goa, Ceylon, and Japan. He died while planning another to China.

Xenophon (444–359 B.C.), Athenian general and historian. He commanded Greek mercenaries under the Persian Cyrus, and on the latter's death safely marched the Ten Thousand home through hostile country. His chief works are the *Anabasis*, the *Hellenica*, and *Cyropaedia*.

Xerxes (*c.* 519–465 B.C.), King of Persia, was son of the first Darius. In 481 B.C. he started on an expedition against Greece when, according to Herodotus, he had a combined army and navy of over two and a half million men. He defeated the Spartans at Thermopylae, but his fleet was overcome at Salamis. He reigned from 485 to 465 B.C. and met his death by assassination.

Ximénes de Cisneros, Francisco (1436–1517), Spanish statesman and churchman. He became cardinal in 1507; carried out monastic reforms; and directed preparation of a polyglot bible, the *Complutensian*; but as inquisitor-general he was fanatical against heresy. He was adviser to Queen Isabella; in 1506 regent for Queen Juana; and himself directed an expedition to conquer Oran and extirpate piracy.

Y

Yeats, William Butler (1865–1939), Irish lyric poet and playwright, b. near Dublin, a leader of the Irish literary revival. His plays were performed in the Abbey Theatre (which with Lady Gregory (1852–1932) he helped to found), and include *Cathleen Ni Houlihan*, *The Hour Glass*, and *Deidre*. His poetry is discussed in **Section M, Part II**. A complete edition of the *Collected Poems* appeared in 1950.

Yonge, Charlotte Mary (1823–1901), English novelist. Influenced by Keble, she wrote novels which faithfully reflect some aspects of Victorian life; one such is *The Daisy Chain*. She also wrote historical fiction such as *The Dove in the Eagle's Nest*.

Young, Brigham (1801–77), American Mormon leader, and president in 1844 after the founder's death. He was a main founder of Salt Lake City. He practised polygamy. *See also* **Mormonism, Section J**.

Young, Francis Brett (1884–1954), English novelist, author of *My Brother Jonathan* and *Dr. Bradley remembers*.

Young, James (1811–83), Scottish chemist, b. Glasgow, whose experiments led to the manufacture of paraffin oil and solid paraffin on a large scale.

Young, Thomas (1773–1829), English physicist, physician and egyptologist, b. Somerset, of Quaker family. He established the wave theory of light and its essential principle of interference, put forward a theory of colour vision, and was the first to describe astigmatism of the eye. He was also largely responsible for deciphering the inscriptions on the Rosetta stone.

Younghusband, Sir Francis Edward (1863–1942), English explorer and religious leader. He explored Manchuria and Tibet, and wrote on India and Central Asia. He founded the World Congress of Faiths in 1936 (*see* **Section J**).

Ypres, 1st Earl of. *See* **French**.

Ysaÿe, Eugène (1858–1929), Belgian violinist and conductor, noted chiefly for his playing of the works of Bach and César Franck.

Yukawa, Hideki (b. 1907), Japanese physicist, who received the 1949 Nobel prize for predicting (1935) the existence of the meson.

Z

Zadkiel (angel in rabbinical lore), pseudonym of two astrologers: William Lilly (1602–81) and Richard James Morrison (1794–1874).

Zadkine, Ossip (b. 1890), Russian sculptor in France, who makes play with light on concave surfaces. His works include *Orpheus* and the public monument *The Destruction of Rotterdam*.

Zaharoff, Sir Basil (1849–1936), armaments magnate and financier, b. Anatolia of Greek parents. He was influential in the first world war.

Zamenhof, Ludwig Lazarus (1859–1917), Polish-Jew who invented Esperanto. He was by profession an occulist.

Zeno of Citium (?342–270 B.C.), philosopher, founder of the Stoic system. He left Cyprus to teach in Athens.

Zeppelin, Ferdinand, Count von (1838–1917), German inventor of the dirigible airship, 1897–1900. It was used in the first world war.

Zeromski, Stefan (1864–1925), Polish novelist, author of *The Homeless*, *The Ashes*, *The Fight with Satan*.

Zhukov, Georgi Konstantinovich (b. 1896), Soviet general, who led the defence of Moscow and Stalingrad and lifted the siege of Leningrad in the second world war, and accepted the German surrender in 1945. He continued to be active till 1957.

Zhukovsky, Vasily Andreyevich (1783–1852), Russian poet and translator of German and English poets. For many years he was tutor to the future Tsar Alexander II.

Zola, Emile Edouard (1840–1902), French novelist, b. Paris, of Italian descent. His series, *Les Rougon-Macquart*, portrays in a score of volumes the fortunes of one family in many aspects and in realistic manner. He had the moral courage to champion Dreyfus.

Zorn, Anders Leonhard (1860–1920), Swedish sculptor, etcher, and painter.

Zoroaster (Zarathustra) (fl. 6th cent. B.C.), Persian founder of the Parsee religion. He was a monotheist, and saw the world as a struggle between good (Ahura Mazda) and evil (Ahriman). *See* **Zoroastrianism, Section J**.

Zoshchenko, Mikhail (1895–1958), Russian writer of humorous short stories, which include *The Woman who could not Read and other Tales* and *The Wonderful Dog and other Stories*.

Zosimus (fl. *c.* 300), the first known alchemist. He lived in Alexandria.

Zuccarelli, Francesco (1702–88), Italian artist of fanciful landscapes. He spent many years in London and was elected a founder member of the R.A. (1768).

Zuckermann, Sir Solly (b. 1904), British biologist; chief scientific adviser to British governments. His publications include *Scientists and War* and *The Frontiers of Public and Private Science*. O.M. 1968.

Zwingli, Ulrich (1484–1531), Swiss religious reformer. He taught mainly at Zurich, where he issued a list of reformed doctrines, less extreme than those of Calvin.

Zwirner, Ernst Friedrich (1802–61), German architect who restored Cologne cathdral.

BACKGROUND TO PUBLIC AFFAIRS

This section is in two parts. The first is a narrative of political events in Britain since the war and of some significant events around the world. The second part explains the structure of our own political institutions and the main international ones.

TABLE OF CONTENTS

BACKGROUND TO PUBLIC AFFAIRS

This section is in two parts. The first describes some major events since the war and carries the story to 1971. The second part describes our own political institutions, the Commonwealth, the United Nations, Western and other International Organisations.

I. NARRATIVE OF POLITICAL EVENTS

BRITAIN: POLITICAL BACKGROUND.

Brief Historical Survey.

The end of the Great War marked a watershed in British political life. The Representation of the People Act of 1918 gave the vote to all men over the age of 21 and to women over 30, the franchise being extended to women over 21 in 1928. Thus began a new era of mass participation in politics. The newly enfranchised working classes were catered for by a specifically working-class party, the Labour party, and the next decades were to see the virtual eclipse of the other radical party, the Liberals. However, from the mud of Flanders Britain moved into the quagmire of economic depression, each government, no matter what its political hue, seeming to be in the grip of economic forces beyond its control.

Effective demand for goods remained, year in, year out, far below the productive capacity of the economy, and as a result unemployment was always high. Between 1921 and 1939 it never dropped below the million mark, and in the depths of the world slump, in 1932, it nearly reached 3 million out of a total insured labour force of 12·5 million. One worker in four was out of a job, and in some of the depressed areas it was nearer one in three. Even the rearmament drive of 1937–8 failed to end the depression, though it did bring some revival of demand for the products of heavy industry, and it was not until 1940 that unemployment finally disappeared.

In the inter-war period Britain had, considering its unemployment, not been too badly off, for three main reasons. First, we had long been industrialised, so that the chronic under-investment of the period in the means of production had not the effects it would have had on a nation without our stock of capital goods. Second, although throughout the period we were losing ground in overseas markets to our competitors, the terms of trade grew more favourable for us, so that the same volume of exports could pay for a far higher volume of imports than it could have done in 1913—or than it has ever done since the war. That was not much comfort to those dependent for their living on an exporting industry; but it did mean that falling exports brought no serious balance-of-payments problems. And, third, in those days Britain was still the owner of vast overseas assets, which brought in a steady large investment to pay for imports, and which could, if necessary, be drawn on to finance any deficit in the balance of payments.

The Effect of the War.

The war changed all this. The export trade was slashed to a third of its pre-war level, the overseas assets were sold off, and large debts incurred in their place. Investment in, and even maintenance of, capital goods had to be put off. Finally, the war brought to an end the favourable turn in the terms of trade. In 1945 they were much worse than in 1938; and from 1945 to 1951 they steadily turned against us.

As a result, the first five years after the war were years of chronic excess of demand—of demand for more investment to make good the neglect of decades, of demand for more consumption to bring to an end the austerity of wartime and to

allow families to replenish their depleted stocks of household goods, and of demand for exports to meet the unfavourable turn in the terms of trade and to allow us to start paying off the debts incurred in the war. Immediately the problem was an impossible one; without American aid we would have been bankrupt. But gradually as production picked up demand began to come under control once more, and it did seem as if by 1950 the most pressing immediate problems had been successfully surmounted. There were still many relics of the war—housing was still inadequate, the roads and railways were neglected, rationing was still with us, prices were not yet stable, and there were still shortages of many important materials.

Attlee's First Labour Government.

The Labour party left the National government after the overthrow of Germany in May 1945, rejecting overtures from Churchill to continue the coalition. Faced with this re-emergence of party politics, the "caretaker" government had no choice but to call a general election to ascertain which party should lead the nation along the path to peace. The Conservative party campaigned on the slogan "Let Churchill finish the job," Labour on a vigorous programme of social and economic reform. The electorate, remembering the dismal thirties and perhaps intuitively recognising Churchill's greatness as a warrior but his unsuitability to lead in time of peace, as well as desiring radical social changes, returned Clement Attlee with a majority of 146 over all other parties. The Labour party became the majority party for the first time in its history (on its two previous occasions in office, 1924 and 1929–31, it was dependent upon Liberal support). The Conservatives, with 213 seats, fell to their lowest ebb since 1906, and the Liberals, formerly one of the two great parties, captured only 12 seats.

The cabinet (of 20) included Ernest Bevin (Foreign Secretary), former docker and leader of the Transport and General Workers' Union, Aneurin Bevan (Minister of Health), ex-miner from South Wales, Herbert Morrison (Lord President of the Council and deputy Prime Minister), Ellen Wilkinson (Minister of Education), Hugh Dalton (Chancellor of the Exchequer), Sir Stafford Cripps (President of the Board of Trade). Harold Wilson and Hugh Gaitskell, junior ministers at the Ministries of Public Works and Fuel and Power respectively, both Oxford economists, were later to become leaders of their party. The Prime Minister himself, Clement Attlee, educated at Haileybury and Oxford, had done social work in the East End of London, becoming Mayor of Stepney, before entering parliament in 1922. To these men fell the task of shaping post-war Britain.

Although Britain emerged from the war with new industries ready for expansion and a much increased labour force, much of her pre-war capital wealth had been destroyed and urgent action was required to replace worn-out capital equipment and turn industrial resources to peace-time production. To conserve vital resources, a programme of rationing and austerity was introduced. Both trade unions and manufacturers cooperated in holding down wages and prices, the former at least encouraged by the economic and social reforms of the new government.

Public Ownership.

The Labour party was doctrinally committed to some degree of nationalisation, though the exact amount was, and is, a matter of dispute within the party. One of its first acts in 1946 was to nationalise the Bank of England. This had previously been subject to a high degree of central control, and little objection was raised by the Opposition. The nationalisation of the coal industry the same year excited more debate. However, this industry, even before the war, had been subject to governmental intervention, and during the war had been stripped of its capital, worn-out machines not having been replaced. It is significant here that the form of public ownership was not that of a government department, nor control by workers, but responsibility was vested in a semi-independent public board, the National Coal Board. This showed the essentially moderate, pragmatic nature of the nationalisation programme, which continued with the taking into public ownership by 1951 of the electricity- and gas-supply services, the railways, the ports and docks, a large section of road goods transport and some road passenger transport, the canals, the major part of civil aviation, the cable and wireless services, and the major part of the iron and steel industry. The Conservatives after their return to power in 1951 denationalised iron and steel and the major part of the nationalised road goods transport service, but left the other nationalisations undisturbed, though they in certain respects altered the administrative structure set up by the Labour government.

Building the Welfare State.

The immediate post-war years saw the laying of the foundations of the welfare state. The provisions of the Butler Education Act of 1944 were put into operation, greatly expanding facilities and improving the opportunity for each child no matter what its background to enjoy the benefits of higher education. Child allowances were introduced along with a rise in old-age pensions. For a long time doctors and others who had studied the subject of medical care had felt that a national medical service was essential in order to make the best use of hospitals and to bring the full range of modern medicine within the reach of everyone. It was to meet these needs that the National Health Service Act was passed in 1946. The new health service came into operation in July 1948 and proved to be one of the greatest experiments in health care ever undertaken and was watched critically by countries all over the world. For the first time in our history every man, woman, and child in the country, was entitled to free medical care.

Measures were also taken relating to the distribution of industry so as to avoid the pockets of unemployment in certain areas. All this added up to a fundamental restructuring of British society, comparable only to the Liberal reforms of 1906–14.

Foreign Affairs.

When the war ended there was still an abundance of goodwill towards the Soviet Union, but a number of political factors worked the other way and it was allowed to evaporate. As Churchill put it in his famous speech at Fulton, Missouri (1946): "From Stettin on the Baltic to Trieste on the Adriatic an Iron Curtain has descended across the continent." The failure of the nations to make treaties of peace or arrangements for general disarmament, and the continuing loss of confidence between the Soviet Union and the West led to an increase of armaments and defensive pacts on both sides. The United States and Western Europe formed the North Atlantic Treaty Organisation (NATO) and the Russians on their side organised the communist countries by a Warsaw Pact. The old system of a balance of power centred on Europe had col-

lapsed to give way to a new period in world politics dominated by the two great power blocs, the United States and the Soviet Union, and based on nuclear deterrence. *See also* **C41, C38.**

In the Middle East, Britain was one of the guarantors of the new state of Israel carving out land where the Jewish population could settle. The land was taken from the Arabs, with what consequences the Arab–Israeli war of June 1967 showed. *See* **C12.**

Of our former colonies, India (1947), Burma (1948), and Ceylon (1948) received their independence. Burma, while maintaining the closest links with Britain, decided not to follow the example of India, and left the Commonwealth.

Attlee's Second Government and the Korean War.

By 1950 the electorate had lost much of its enthusiasm for radical change and the government, having passed its most important measures, was running out of steam. This possibly explains why a government which had not lost a single by-election was returned with a majority of only six. Among the new men returned for the Conservative party in this parliament were Edward Heath, Iain Macleod, Reginald Maudling, and Enoch Powell, all four to become ministers and Mr. Heath, a prime minister. The government struggled on, handicapped by its small majority, and facing the problems of the Korean war, which put an end to any impression that the economy was under control. Prices of raw materials and food shot up, and a large favourable balance on international trade rapidly turned into a far larger unfavourable balance. A serious price inflation got under way, and the policy of wage restraint collapsed. On top of that came the rearmament programme to meet the military threat of communism. Gaitskell, who had succeeded the dying Cripps at the Exchequer, imposed charges on dentures and spectacles supplied under the national health service, which led to the resignation of Aneurin Bevan, the minister who had piloted the scheme through all its stages in parliament, John Freeman, later to become British Ambassador to Washington, and Harold Wilson, then President of the Board of Trade. Attlee asked for a dissolution and an election in October 1951.

The Conservatives Regain Power, 1951.

The Labour party secured the highest total poll that it or any other party had received in a general election—14 million votes. The Conservatives received a quarter of a million less; but they secured a majority of seats. This anomaly was due to the peculiarities of the electoral system, which piles up large (and useless) majorities for both sides in safe seats. The new cabinet was led by Churchill and was mainly composed of his old war-time colleagues, with Sir Anthony Eden at the Foreign Office, Harold Macmillan at the Ministry of Housing and Local Government, Walter Monckton at the Ministry of Labour, Lord Cherwell as Paymaster-General, and R. A. Butler, later twice to be denied the highest prize of the leadership, the new Chancellor.

The balance-of-payments crisis which reached its peak in the last months of 1951, just after the defeat of the Labour government, was rapidly brought under control, largely because the prices of raw materials fell almost as quickly as they had risen, but also through the imposition of severe import controls. The unannounced, though very real, abandonment of the grandiose rearmament targets also helped. For this control there was, however, a price to pay—a recession in industry, particularly in textiles, but also in a number of consumer durable industries, which brought the first serious, though limited, return to unemployment. But, as import prices continued to fall, the government soon felt able to take steps to re-expand demand. A more ambitious housing programme was underway, and rationing was being abolished.

George VI died in February 1952. He had succeeded to the throne in difficult circumstances when his elder brother, King Edward VIII, had abdicated in order to marry Mrs. Wallis Simpson, an American. George VI had done much to restore the high esteem in which the monarchy is held in Britain, notably by his courage in staying in London during the Blitz and visiting the bombed areas. His death in 1952 was followed by a period of national mourning—" He was father to us all " was a frequent comment of the times, showing both the sense of loss at his death and the degree to which the life of the royal family has become identified with that of the individual subject. The coronation of his daughter, Queen Elizabeth II, followed in June 1953. On the same day as she was crowned, a British expedition climbed Everest and there were high hopes that a new Elizabethan age was dawning.

The Retirement of Churchill.

On 5 April 1955 Sir Winston Churchill handed over the great seal of office for the last time in a career in politics spanning over half a century, during which he had served two great parties, risen to high office, fallen, returned to lead his country in her finest hour, been rejected, finally to return as a peace-time prime minister. The finest orator of his day, his bulldog stubbornness had been an inspiration during the war. In 1954 he was accorded an honour unique in the annals of British parliamentary history—the presentation by the Commons of a book signed by all M.P.s and a portrait by Graham Sutherland. Perhaps the best description of this man who held the stage of British politics for so long is provided by the words introducing his work on the Second World War: " In War: Resolution. In Defeat: Defiance. In Victory: Magnanimity. In Peace: Goodwill." His successor as premier was Sir Anthony Eden, who had resigned over a difference with Chamberlain in 1938, and gone on to be Churchill's foreign secretary during the war. Eden had been the heir-apparent for a number of years, and was, in terms of the offices he had held, well-equipped to take over the reins of power. His first action was to lead the Conservative party into the general election of 1955.

The Retirement of Attlee.

The Conservatives won the election with an overall majority of 58 seats, gaining 49·7 per cent of the vote compared with Labour's 46·4 per cent, though there was a fall in turnout of nearly 5 per cent. This gave the Conservatives a comfortable majority to govern with, and it seemed as though Eden was set for a long tenure at 10 Downing Street. When parliament assembled four older members, including Dalton, resigned because of their age from the Labour shadow cabinet, and at the end of the year Attlee resigned the leadership.

Attlee had seen the Labour party grow from a party which in 1910 gained 7 per cent of the vote and 42 M.P.s to the party which in 1945 had formed the government and carried through a programme of social and economic reform. If Churchill stood for the " finest hour " in our history, Attlee stood for the social revolution which followed it. He retired to the Lords to become a respected elder statesman until his death in 1967. He was succeeded by Hugh Gaitskell as party leader, the first Labour leader born in this century, a man determined to remodel socialism to fit the new age of technocracy and " welfare capitalism."

The Suez Adventure.

This opened in 1956 with the refusal of Britain and the United States, despite earlier promises, to finance the building of the Aswan High Dam which President Nasser considered necessary for the development of the Egyptian economy. Nasser retaliated by nationalising the Suez Canal. Eden, on his own initiative, and without the full approval of all his cabinet, acted in concert with France to retake the canal zone by force. An American veto and considerable pressure from the United Nations led to the withdrawal of British troops, but a parliamentary storm unparalleled since the days of home rule for Ireland blew up. (It was while we were bombing Egypt that Russia suppressed a revolt in her satellite Hungary). Eden's position was severely under-

mined by this and it led to the resignation of two ministers, Anthony Nutting and Sir Edward Boyle. The Prime Minister himself resigned because of ill-health early in 1957. The new leader of the party was Harold Macmillan, chosen by a process of consultation which by-passed the claim of R. A. Butler. *See also* C12(2).

The Macmillan Years.

The struggle for national solvency continued. In 1955 there had been a renewed balance-of-payments crisis, followed by another in 1956 and an even more severe one in 1957, and with each, fresh measures of restriction on demand had to be introduced. These stringent measures finally brought the balance of payments under control; but as in 1952 the control also brought a recession —rather more severe, but still mild by inter-war standards. Then, as in 1953, the government felt able to take steps to re-expand demand, production responded fast and 1959 was a prosperous year. But there were danger signals. Wage demands were beginning to mount, and, although the reserves were still rising, the balance of trade was more unfavourable than in the crisis years of 1956 and 1957.

The country went to the polls in 1959 for the fourth time in the 1950s, and for the third time the Conservatives won, this time with a handsome overall majority of 100 seats. There was despair in the Labour camp and swift recriminations took place. Gaitskell believed that the party's image was outmoded, and in 1960 decided to fight for the abandonment of Clause 4, the nationalisation clause of the party's constitution. This led to a fierce internal struggle between right and left, which was followed by a further campaign to get Conference to adopt a motion making unilateral nuclear disarmament the official policy of the British Labour party. Gaitskell promised to " fight, fight and fight again " to secure the reversal of this decision, and succeeded the following year.

In July 1961 the Chancellor of the Exchequer, Selwyn Lloyd, called for a pay pause in wages, salaries, and dividend payments. This was the first sign of a prices and incomes policy which was to become the main remedy for inflation in the 1960s. Britain had still not solved its central economic problem—how to reconcile the twin aims of growth and stable prices with a satisfactory balance of payments.

From the middle of 1962 the government seemed dogged by misfortune which, it was doubtless hoped, would be changed by Britain's entry into the Common Market (*see* **Section G, Part IV**). Quickly following Britain's exclusion came the hardships of a severe winter and a sudden increase in unemployment. When the spring came the government were caught in another misfortune, the Profumo affair, involving the resignation of its war minister. This did nothing to still the feeling in the Conservative party that the Prime Minister should make way for a younger man, Macmillan indicated that he hoped to lead the party at the next election. This discordant position was suddenly cut by the Prime Minister's illness, which compelled him to resign. By a coincidence his announcement came (10 October 1963) the day after the annual party conference had opened. The resignation would in any event have caused a great debate in the party, but dropped suddenly into the excited atmosphere of a conference it caused a tumult. How confused the situation was is illustrated by the fact that on the very morning when the Queen sent for Lord Home, then Foreign Secretary, the first headline in *The Times* was " The Queen may send for Mr. Butler today."

Among other important events of Macmillan's premiership were: the explosion of the first British hydrogen bomb; the settlement of the Cyprus dispute; the cancellation of the *Blue Streak* missile programme, and the agreement for U.S. *Polaris* submarines to use Holy Loch; the setting up of the National Economic Development Council; the legalisation of betting shops; the winding up of the Central African Federation; the nuclear test ban treaty; and the establishment of a Federation of Malaysia. A number of Commonwealth countries became independent sovereign states (*see* **K 189**).

Death of Hugh Gaitskell.

The Labour party had just recovered from the internal strife of the early 1960s and was unified for the first time in a decade when Gaitskell died in 1963 at the age of 57. A man of enormous passion for the underdog, he had begun the task of modernising the Labour party and left his successor a legacy of a united party ready to face the challenges of a scientific and technological age. There were three candidates for the succession: George Brown, a former trade unionist who had been very close to Gaitskell, and was deputy leader of the party; James Callaghan, another former trade unionist; and Harold Wilson, an Oxford economist, who had served in Attlee's cabinet. Wilson won.

Election Year 1964.

Parliament's legal term expired in the autumn of 1964 but there remained the question whether Sir Alec Douglas-Home, who had renounced his title in 1963, would go to the country in the spring or in the autumn. Concealing his hand till the last moment Sir Alec decided to wait till the autumn. For many months, therefore, the country discussed the issues involved and thus went through much of the emotions of an election, which, when it came, seemed belated, the people being a little weary of worked-up turmoil by politicians, press, and pollsters. Some of the fire of an election had thus been drawn prematurely, but no general election can lack drama. The government's majority dissolved and Wilson kept the lead in a photo-finish. The resultant position can be seen in the table on a later page. Before leaving this point in our story we must note the coincidence by which, within the very two days on which the results came in, there occurred two events of world-wide importance—the fall of Khrushchev and the explosion by China of an atomic bomb.

Upon accession to office the new government was faced with a prospective balance-of-payments deficit of £700–800 million for 1964. It was estimated that although there should be a considerable improvement in 1965 the deficit would still be at an unacceptable level. The government therefore took measures aimed, first, to deal with the immediate deficit, and, second, to begin the task of dealing with the more intransigent underlying economic problems. These measures are discussed under **Internal Developments, Section G, Part IV.**

Changes in the Conservative Party.

The loss of the election was a cause of grave concern to the Conservative party, and as the opinion polls showed Labour increasing its lead and there were grumblings on the backbenches, Sir Alec resigned. One legacy from his brief leadership was a new system of finding a leader of the party. The undignified display at the Blackpool party conference and complaints that some sections of party opinion had not been consulted, led to demands for change. An electoral system was introduced, the leader being chosen by two bodies: first, the parliamentary party and, second, a group composed of Conservative members of both Houses and the Executive Committee of the National Union. The first leader chosen by the new method was Edward Heath, a man in terms of social background much closer to Mr. Wilson than to Sir Alec. Educated at Chatham House School and Balliol College, Oxford, the new leader of the Opposition had been a foremost proponent of entry to the Common Market and had piloted the Resale Price Maintenance Bill through parliament, which abolished the situation whereby manufacturers could prevent retailers from cutting prices if they so desired. This Bill was finally passed under the Labour government, but the fact that Mr. Heath was prepared to put through a measure which was highly unpopular with his own party showed something of the resolve of the new leader.

The 1966 General Election.

Against all the odds and expectations, Labour had governed for seventeen months with a majority over Conservatives and Liberals fluctuating between five and a mere one. Not only that, but when parliament was dissolved it was entirely at the Prime Minister's own choosing. Such is the unexpected course of political events. It might reasonably have been held, and was indeed maintained by many, that no government, short of a coalition, could exist with a majority of less, say, than a dozen. But Mr. Wilson governed with the air of one commanding a secure majority, for he neither trimmed his controversial programme nor made the slightest gesture towards a coalition with Liberals. And he maintained this course against particularly severe economic circumstances. Mr. Wilson chose to appeal to the country on 31 March 1966 and Labour's recovery was complete. His party gained 47·9 per cent of the vote, compared with 41·9 per cent for the Conservatives. On an average swing of 3·5 per cent, the overall Labour majority in the House of Commons was 96. The Liberal party gained only 8·5 per cent of the vote, though it increased its number of seats to 12. See **General Election Results, C7.**

Unpopular Measures in National Interest.

Almost immediately the government was faced with yet another run on sterling, and in July adopted a package of deflationary cuts in public spending and introduced a prices and incomes " freeze." With the cooperation of both sides of industry the measures worked for a time but with sterling coming under almost unremitting pressure our balance-of-payments position deteriorated and by November 1966 the only alternative to massive deflation and soaring unemployment was devaluation. (See **Section G, Part IV** under **International Developments**). Devaluation, by reducing the price of our exports and making imports more expensive compared with home-produced goods, improved our competitive position in the world markets. However, the wage–price spiral continued to rise, and in July 1968 statutory regulation of prices and incomes was introduced. This piece of legislation was fought tooth and nail by the trade unions, and the compulsory provisions were not renewed when they expired at the end of 1969. The deflationary cuts and devaluation marked a new phase in the turn of public opinion, and by the end of 1968 the polls were putting Conservatives over 20 per cent in the lead. The middle of 1969 saw the beginnings of a turn-round in the economic situation.

Foreign Affairs.

The most pressing problem in this field was obtaining a settlement with Rhodesia, and Mr. Wilson made two dramatic if unavailing attempts to come to agreement with Mr. Smith. (This subject is treated more fully in Part II.) In May 1967 Britain put in her second application to join the Common Market and although in the December France voted against negotiations for British membership, the application remained on the table. In defence, the government decided to abandon the East of Suez policy thus forcing Britain to come to terms with its true position in the world (though the decision was taken on the pragmatic ground of saving defence expenditure). The government refused to supply arms to South Africa, in accordance with a United Nations resolution of 1964. The government felt obliged to intervene in Anguilla, a tiny Caribbean island, which had unilaterally seceded from the St. Kitts union in 1967; it was allegedly becoming a Mafia haunt.

Labour Reforms.

A number of important measures were passed in the six years of Labour's rule. On the social front it repealed the Conservative 1957 Rent Act and provided for higher standards in housing, education, and the health service. It gave parliamentary time from its crowded schedule to abolish capital punishment and private members' bills on abortion (Abortion Act, 1967), homosexuality (Sexual Offences Act, 1967), and divorce (Divorce Reform Act, 1969), were carried through by free votes of parliament. The Children and Young

By-Elections 1945–70

	Total by-elections	Changes	Con. +	Con. −	Lib. +	Lib. −	Lab. +	Lab. −	Others +	Others −
1945–50	52	3	3	—	—	—	—	—	—	3
1950–51	16	—	—	—	—	—	—	—	—	—
1951–55	48	1	1	—	—	—	—	1	—	—
1955–59	52	6	1	4	1	1	4	—	—	1
1959–64	62	9	2	7	1	—	6	2	—	—
1964–66	13	2	1	1	1	—	—	1		
1966–70	38	16	12	1	1	—	—	15	2	

Rise and Fall of the Parties, 1945–70

	1945	1950	1951	1955	1959	1964	1966	1970
Conservative . .	213	298	321	345	365	303	253	330
Labour . .	393	315	295	277	258	317	363	287
Liberal . .	12	9	6	6	9	9	12	6
Independant .	14	—	—	—	—	1	—	—
Others . .	8	3	3	2	—	1 (The Speaker)	2 *	7 *
Total . .	640	625	625	630	630	630	630	630

* Includes The Speaker.

General Election Results, 1945–70

	Electorate and turnout %	Votes cast %	Conservative %	Labour %	Liberal %	Nationalist %	Communist %	Others %
1945	72·7 33,240,391	100 25,085,978	39·8 9,988,306	47·8 11,995,152	9·0 2,248,226	0·6 138,415	0·4 102,760	1·8 433,688
1950	84·0 33,269,770	100 28,772,671	43·5 12,502,567	46·1 13,266,592	9·1 2,621,548	0·6 173,161	0·3 91,746	0·4 117,057
1951	82·5 34,645,573	100 28,595,668	48·0 13,717,538	48·8 13,948,605	2·5 730,556	0·5 145,521	0·1 21,640	0·1 31,808
1955	76·7 34,858,263	100 26,760,498	49·7 13,286,569	46·4 12,404,970	2·7 722,405	0·9 225,591	0·1 33,144	0·2 62,447
1959	78·8 35,397,080	100 27,859,241	49·4 13,749,830	43·8 12,215,538	5·9 1,638,571	0·6 182,788	0·1 30,897	0·2 61,619
1964	77·1 35,892,572	100 27,655,374	43·4 12,001,396	44·1 12,205,814	11·2 3,092,878	0·9 249,866	0·2 45,932	0·2 53 116
1966	75·8 35,964,684	100 27,263,606	41·9 11,418,433	47·9 13,064,951	8·5 2,327,533	1·2 315,431	0·2 62,112	0·3 75,146
1970	72·0 39,384,364	100 28,344,807	46·4 13,144,692	42·9 12,179,166	7·5 2,117,638	1·7 481,812	0·1 38,431	1·4 383,068

Persons Act, 1969, made extensive changes in the legal procedures governing young offenders and provided for a comprehensive system of community homes for children in care, and strengthened the law on private fostering (*see* D41–3). A constitutional change of some importance came with the enfranchisement of the 18-year-olds in 1970. The Countryside Act, 1968, enlarged the functions of the Countryside Commission, conferred new powers on local authorities and other bodies for the management of rural areas and provided greater opportunities for leisure and recreational activities in the countryside. It obliged every government department and public authority to have due concern for amenity. Further, the government outlawed racial discrimination in the Race Relations Acts, 1965, 1968 (*see* D46). In industrial policy, the Transport Act, 1968, provided for a better integration of road and rail transport and for higher standards in road transport. In regional policy, the introduction of investment grants was to aid the setting up of new industry in depressed areas and reduce the disparity between the regions in terms of unemployment. The setting up of the Law Commission was on the initiative of Lord Gardiner (Lord Chancellor), an enthusiastic reformer, and many of its recommendations and fresh legislation resulting from them, have been noted under their various headings in Section D, *e.g.*, Criminal Justice Act, 1967, Criminal Law Act, 1967.

The 1970 General Election.

By 1970 our balance-of-payments position had been transformed from a state of chronic deficit to one of healthy surplus. The rise in economic prosperity was reflected in a swing back to the government. This was very welcome to a party which had lost 15 of the 38 by-elections in the course of the parliament, and made no gains. The local election results were also encouraging, with Labour regaining some of the ground it had lost in earlier years when its representation had been decimated, and it had lost control of strongholds such as Newcastle and Sheffield, as well as the Greater London Council. In this favourable climate, the Prime Minister decided to hold an early election. The date was set for 18 June—the first June election this century. The campaigns of the two parties were very different, Mr. Wilson conducting his in an almost casual fashion, and Mr. Heath trying desperately to bestir the electorate from its illusions of what he called " sham sunshine." The only fireworks in the campaign were provided by Mr. Powell when he wondered whether the statistics on immigration had been falsified deliberately, and Mr. Wedgwood Benn when he accused Mr. Powell of hoisting over Wolverhampton the flag that was " beginning to look suspiciously like the one that fluttered over Dachau and Belsen." On the eve of the poll, a Labour victory seemed certain. The opinion polls, with one exception (Opinion Research Centre) were predicting a Labour victory by margins varying from a 2 to a 9 per cent lead over the Conservatives. The eventual result was a 4·7 per cent swing to the Conservatives and their return to power with an overall majority of 30 over all other parties. The reasons for what appears to be a last-minute change are complex, but the most accepted argument is that the publication of unfavourable trade figures just 3 days before polling day enabled the Conservatives to stir up anxiety about the cost of living and the economy. On 19 June a smiling Mr. Heath stood on the steps of 10 Downing Street and declared: " To govern is to serve. This government will be at the service of all the people, the whole nation. Our purpose is not to divide but to unite and where there are differences to bring reconciliation, to create one nation."

A New Style of Government.

The Heath team was a blend of the old and the new. The senior posts were taken by the older men, notably Sir Alec Douglas-Home at the Foreign Office, Reginald Maudling as Home Secretary, Iain Macleod as Chancellor of the Exchequer, and Quintin Hogg who took back his old title of Lord Hailsham to become Lord Chancellor. The new faces included Anthony Barber who was given special responsibility for negotiations with the Common Market countries, Sir Keith Joseph in charge of social security, and Mrs. Margaret Thatcher in charge of education. Due to the tragic early death of Iain Macleod, so long the party's economic expert, and one of its best frontbench debaters, a few short weeks after achieving his ambition of becoming Chancellor, changes had to be made. His place was taken by Anthony Barber, and in the reshuffle that followed, John Davies entered the cabinet to take over the newly-created empire of Trade and Industry, Geoffrey Rippon being shifted to responsibility for Europe. These changes seemed about the only activities the government were undertaking over the summer months, and they ran into severe criticism for inactivity in the face of mounting inflation. There were some moves in foreign policy, negotiations being opened for at least a partial restoration of the British presence East of Suez, and exploratory talks on the restoration of arms supplies to South Africa. In October, the Chancellor introduced a mini-Budget, curbing expenditure and promising a reduction in income tax as from April 1971. This seems to have done little to curb the round of wage increases, and December saw a strike of the electricity workers, following an earlier one in which the dustmen, pitted against the government, received most of what they were asking for. The electricity workers' claim was settled by a court of inquiry (Wilberforce), but at the time of writing (February 1971) the postal workers were out and the motor car industry was also having labour problems. We have yet to see the government's more short-term solution to this turbulent problem, but its long-term policy is contained in the Industrial Relations Bill, at present before parliament. This is being disputed by the Labour party and the trade union movement. In foreign affairs too the government is taking a line different from that of its predecessors. In particular, the decision on the supply of arms to South Africa has caused an uproar, and judging from the remarks of African leaders at the recent Commonwealth Prime Ministers' Conference in Singapore, the future of the Commonwealth may be in danger. *See also* Part II under Central and Local Government, and Section G, Part IV, under Internal Developments.

Northern Ireland.

Northern Ireland went to the polls in June 1970 along with the rest of Britain to elect its 12 representatives at Westminster. The Ulster Unionists took 8 of the 12 seats with Antrim (North) going to the Rev. Ian Paisley of the breakaway Protestant Unionist party, Fermanagh and South Tyrone being captured by the Civil Rights leader, Frank McManus, Miss Devlin holding on in Mid-Ulster, and Gerry Fitt consolidating his gain of 1966 in Belfast (West).

General Elections, 1935–70

	Unionist	Others
1935	10	2
1945	9	3
1950	10	2
1951	9	3
1955	10	2
1959	12	—
1964	12	—
1966	11	1
1970	9 *	3

* includes 1 Protestant Unionist.

The state of the parties, after the parliamentary by-elections of April 1970, in the Northern Ireland parliament at Stormont, was:

Unionists	29
Independent Unionists	8
Protestant Unionists	2
Nationalists	5
N. I. Labour	2
Republican Labour	2
Independents	4

Unlike England, where an alternating-party system exists, Northern Ireland has had a one-party government for 50 years, a major factor in the present situation. *See also* C30(1).

The United Kingdom government sent troops to Northern Ireland in 1969 to curb the violence between the Roman Catholic and Protestant communities. Both Labour and Conservative governments have declared that there will be no change in the constitutional relations between Northern Ireland and Great Britain without the consent of the parliament of Northern Ireland, that attempts to impose political views by gun rule will be crushed, and that the British government stands as guarantor of Stormont's programme of reform to redress communal grievances.

Although the underlying situation has improved and communal strife is less acute as the reforms agreed between Westminster and Stormont take effect, terrorist activity has continued.

Mr. Brian Faulkner heads the new Stormont Cabinet following the resignation of Major Chichester-Clark in March 1971.

WESTERN EUROPE.

France and de Gaulle.

In 1958 General de Gaulle, who had had a brief period of power in 1945–46, established a semi-presidential system with himself as President, taking certain powers away from Parliament and thus opening France's Fifth Republic next year. The President's seven-year term ended in December 1965 and although he had then reached the age of seventy-five he submitted himself for re-election and won with 55·2 per cent of the votes. During his first term of office he steadily brought the war in Algeria to an end, despite all the hopes reposed in him that he would suppress the independence movement. This was a tremendously courageous achievement; and what was equally courageous he brought France through the threat of civil war precipitated by those who were for continuing force upon Algeria. The drive to economic recovery had, it is true, commenced before he came to power. But on the political side he reasserted French spirit and struck out upon a lonely path, building his nuclear force without receiving technical knowledge from America (as we had).

The Right to Participate in Decisions.

Recovery having been accomplished by 1958, de Gaulle was determined that France should "assume its historic rôle in world affairs." She could therefore no longer assent to delegating to the U.S. exclusive authority to make the vital decisions for the defence of the free world everywhere in the world. He wanted not only the right to participate but the official and public recognition of that right by the creation of a three-power organisation to take joint decisions on global problems. The United States declined. Next year came de Gaulle's next step—the withdrawal of naval units from NATO's Mediterranean Command. The following year, 1959, de Gaulle announced that France would proceed to build an independent national atomic force. In 1962 when Kennedy proposed Atlantic partnership with Europe, de Gaulle replied with a plan to group the Western European nations into "an organisation that would be one of the three powers of the planet." In January 1963 de Gaulle rejected an offer by Kennedy to make American *Polaris* missiles available to them but to be assigned to a multilateral Atlantic force. Macmillan accepted a similar offer at the Nassau Conference. The division between de Gaulle and Macmillan was thereupon wide open. At the beginning of 1963 the General slammed the door to the Common Market in Macmillan's face and refused to sign the atomic test-ban treaty. Exactly a year later de Gaulle recognised Communist China which must have angered the United States deeply. In 1965 de Gaulle left SEATO, the south-east Asia Treaty Organisation; and next year NATO was asked to remove its headquarters from France.

A Crisis of Government, May–June 1968.

The student rising of May 1968 touched off a nationwide wave of unrest. The most violent battles raged in the Latin Quarter between students and riot police. An eye-witness said it might have been in the days of the Commune. Universities were occupied by militant students and factories by workers. Mass strikes, involving more than 2 million workers, paralysed the French economy for much of May and part of June.

The immediate aim of the French students had been to force changes in the running of their universities and their grievances were very real. But this discontent in the academic field overlapped with political and ideological discontents and gave expression to the dissatisfaction felt by thousands of young people whether at universities or not. They are discontented with present-day Western civilisation, with paternalism, and demand the right to question and dissent.

Sweeping Guallist Victory.

On May 24 President de Gaulle announced his intention of holding a referendum asking the people for a mandate to reform the nation's economic, social, and educational institutions, the reforms to include participation by workers in the running of the factories and by students in the running of the universities. However, after a visit to the French forces in Western Germany on May 29 (kept secret at the time) and a Cabinet meeting the next day, the President dissolved the National Assembly and the referendum was dropped. Instead a general election was held on May 31 and a new government under the premiership of M. Pompidou was formed. There was a gradual return to work after demands for higher wages had been met and by mid-June the student occupation of the universities had ended. The revolutionary students' organisations that had taken part in the revolution—anarchist, Trotskyite, Maoist, Castroist, and Daniel Cohn Bendit's " Movement of March 22 " were dissolved under a law of 1936. The elections resulted in a sweeping victory for the Gaullists. The Federation of the Left and the Communist Party lost half their seats in the Assembly. M. Mendès-France was rejected by his parliamentary constituency of Grenoble. A new " Union of the Defence of the Republic " was set up as the official Gaullist organisation.

Resignation of de Gaulle.

Early in 1969 de Gaulle decided to attack the French Senate. Not by parliamentary means, but by his favoured method of direct appeal to the electorate through a referendum he sought to take away what were left of its decision-making powers leaving it with only consultative functions. Under his proposals, if the office of President of the Republic became vacant its functions would be exercised temporarily by the Prime Minister and not by the President of the Senate, as laid down by the Constitution. At the same time he sought to reorganise the country into regions. The French people were asked to say " Yes " or " No " to these two major constitutional changes and de Gaulle made it clear that a defeat in the referendum would mean his resignation. If the sweeping victory for de Gaulle in the 1968 election was due to the fear of civil war (as it was in 1958 and in 1961–62), in 1969 there was no threat of chaos and the referendum took place in a period of calm. Contrary to most predictions, the French people voted against the proposed reforms: " Non " won by 11,945,149 (53·18 per cent) to 10,512,469 (46·81 per cent). Paris and other large cities showed large " Non " majorities. On the morning of 28 April 1969 de Gaulle issued a communiqué which read: " I am ceasing to exercise my functions as President of the Republic. This decision takes effect from mid-day today."

De Gaulle's resignation led immediately to fresh presidential elections, the main contenders being M. Pompidou (Gaullist), M. Poher (Centre, and acting-President), and M. Duclos (Communist).

M. Pompidou was elected on the second ballot, the Communists abstaining.

Death of de Gaulle.

General de Gaulle died on 11 November 1970 from a heart attack at his home at Colombey-les-Deux-Eglises, the village where he was buried, at his own request, with a minimum of ceremony. He was 79. De Gaulle was a leader of great courtesy and wit, but he was always an isolated leader and his judgments were always impressive because of this detachment. His purely political gifts were of a high order for a man who entered politics at 50. However, his mastery of words and his certainty that his was the right way led to contradictions which his enemies made capital of. De Gaulle's solid achievement is that the constitutional changes which he introduced remain. So does the party which he created to assist him in maintaining power. And while there have been changes (French hostility to Britain's joining the Common Market has been reversed) Gaullism remains a powerful political force.

Adenauer and Western Germany.

A notable personal achievement of the last two decades was Dr. Konrad Adenauer's Chancellorship of the West German Federal Republic for fourteen years until his retirement in October 1963 at the age of 86. He gave to a people who had not known democratic government for 15 years a new confidence and self respect. He committed himself to constitutional government despite the fact that he was a natural autocrat. Under him Germany enjoyed the first period of stable government since the First World War. As a consequence of this new confidence Germany rebuilt prosperity from decay. His work in building a special relationship with France, culminating in a treaty of friendship, was a dramatic contrast to the long tradition of enmity with France through which he had lived. But while he succeeded in building his country into the Western community he remained intransigent over East Germany; and since a solution must be found it remained for a more imaginative successor to grapple with it.

Erhard and Kiesinger.

In September 1966, when financial troubles were developing, Dr. Erhard, Chancellor, tried to amend the constitution so as to curb the financial powers of the Länder. For this he needed a two-thirds majority in the Bundestag, which he could not secure. His place was taken by Dr. Kurt Kiesinger, Germany's third post-war Chancellor who was able to take office only by the fact that the Social Democrats (SPD) agreed to join the Christian Democrats (CDU). Dr. Erhard had become Chancellor in 1963 as the most popular politician in the country; he left when Germany's rôle in world affairs was undecided and its internal political future dangerously uncertain. Erhard was a determined opponent of hysterical nationalism and was a loyal supporter of the Atlantic Alliance—indeed it was held that he encouraged ties with the United States at the expense of the Franco-German friendship treaty, which had not lived up to the hopes reposed in it. It was this factor which accounted for the enmity of the Bavarian wing of the Christian Democrats called the Christian Social Union (CSU), the party of Herr Strauss. The CSU put its weight behind Dr. Kiesinger's nomination for the Federal Chancellorship and Herr Strauss was suitably rewarded with a Cabinet post.

The End of Christian Democratic Rule, 1969.

The first break in CDU supremacy occurred in March 1969 when the Liberal Free Democrats (FDP) decided to back the SPD nominee for President, Dr. Heinemann, who was elected by the Federal Assembly by 512 votes to 506. The second break came with the general election at the end of September when the SPD made significant gains in both votes and seats.

	1969		1965	
	Seats*	Votes percentage	Seats*	Votes percentage
CDU/ CSU	242	46·1	245	47·6
SPD	224	42·7	202	39·3
FDP	30	5·8	49	9·5
NDP	—	4·3	—	2·0
Others	—	1·1	—	1·6

*Excluding West Berlin (non-voting) representatives.

Despite widespread publicity the extreme right-wing NPD failed to qualify for any seats since it polled less than 5 per cent of the total votes. Thus the three-party system remained. The third break occurred in October 1969 when the SPD and FDP leaders agreed to form a coalition government with Herr Brandt, the SPD leader, as Chancellor, and Herr Scheel, the FDP leader, as Foreign Minister.

Efforts to Improve Relations Between the Two Germanies.

During 1970 there were two meetings between Chancellor Brandt and the East German Prime Minister, Herr Stoph. Herr Brandt's visit to the town of Erfurt in March was noteworthy when several thousand young East Germans massed in his support outside the conference hotel. However, the significance of the meeting was that it took place at all, rather than in anything it produced. The return meeting in Kassel in May showed that Herr Brandt had accepted the existence of two separate states within the German nation. However, this fell short of East Germany's demand for complete recognition by Bonn. Six months of silence followed before talks were resumed, this time at a lower level. The signs are that the Russians wish to consolidate the status quo in Eastern Europe while the Allies hope for positive improvement allowing West Berliners greater access to the East. A treaty signed by West Berlin and the Soviet Union in Moscow in May stated that borders of all European countries are inviolable, including that between the Federal and the Democratic republics. Bonn implies that frontiers can still be changed by mutual agreement. But the treaty still awaits ratification and this depends on a satisfactory outcome of Four Power talks on Berlin.

Greece.

Fearing the confidently expected victory at the elections of 28 May 1967 of the Centre Union, dictatorial power was seized by the Right in the preceding month. Many politicians, journalists, and others were arrested, no charges in many cases being preferred. A rigid press censorship was imposed. The 26-year-old King was confronted with an immensely difficult task, the colonels of the Right junta not wishing for his abdication although they would have pressed forward with their policy even if he had. The new régime was naturally susceptible to foreign opinion. But a very important key was held by the U.S. since Greece has been described as an American protectorate. But the Council of Europe gave the Greek government a warning. Four members countries complained that the new Greek régime had violated eight articles of the European Convention on Human Rights. The Council warned Greece that unless the government ceased to repudiate the values which the council exists to uphold Greece would be suspended or expelled.

The critical position of the King came to a head in December 1967 when after an abortive attempt to free himself of the military junta he went into exile at Rome.

In December 1969, Greece withdrew from the Council of Europe when it became clear that a majority of the 18 member states had decided to vote for her suspension. This followed a report by the council which described the Greek régime as "undemocratic, illiberal, authoritarian and repressive." There is still no real sign of a return to democracy and the régime of Mr. Papadopoulis is still in control after four years. Mr. Papadopoulis managed to get the supply of heavy arms from the United States resumed in 1970 without naming a date for elections. But elections, as stipulated under the Greek constitution, would be far from free: candidates would have to be approved and party programmes would have to be vetted by the constitutional court. Would politicians, faced with these restrictions, stand? Campbell Page, the *Guardian*'s specialist on Greek affairs argues (Feb. 1971) that "absenteeism never pays in Greek politics and only guarantees deeper obscurity." One possibility is the emergence of a party uniting all elements opposed to Mr. Papadopoulis, which would have the prospect of sizeable electoral victories. The stress of foreign pressure—the U.S. is likely to reappraise its diplomatic policy in Greece this year—and his growing unpopularity among Greeks have weakened the prime minister's position. The question of how long he will last is now a serious one.

EASTERN EUROPE.

A Turning Point in Soviet History.

In 1961 Khrushchev publicly and dramatically completed the process which he had begun in 1956, of drawing a line under the Stalin régime and finally rejecting the cult of Stalin. This change was symbolised by the removal of Stalin's body from the mausoleum at the Kremlin. At the same time Khrushchev was confronted by an external challenge to his leadership of the Communist world—by China who believed that Russia was moving steadily away from classical communist doctrine.

Stalin had made the Soviet Union a modern industrial society and a great armed power. But the arbitrary bureaucracy through which this had been achieved had, in Khrushchev's view, overrun itself. Radical changes became essential and Khrushchev attempted various steps—the scaling down of the secret police; the rebuilding of the administrative apparatus; the opening up of virgin lands; and a new theory that war was not inevitable. The legacy of the Stalinist era had been the concept of the "monolithic" party, that is to say, a party which, however torn by internal conflict, must never allow any open division of opinion and free debate, much less the formation of any groups expounding distinctive views. In the light of the trials of authors in 1966–7 the view was bound to be taken outside Russia that the process of deStalinisation had not gone quickly enough.

Khrushchev Leaves the Political Scene.

The career of Nikita Khrushchev as Soviet Prime Minister and Leader of the Communist Party came to an end—to the surprise of the world—in October 1964. Stalin had died in 1953 and the struggle for succession then continued for five years, when Khrushchev emerged with supreme authority. Upon Stalin's death a triumvirate of successors, Malenkov, Molotov, and Beria had decided to give the post of party chief—First Secretary—to Khrushchev, then a relatively harmless outsider, or so he was deemed by them. Beria, the all powerful police chief, was executed as a spy in 1953, Malenkov was forced to give up the premiership in 1954 and three years later both he and Molotov were expelled from the Central Committee. Khrushchev thereupon emerged with supreme powers, and became the talkative and jocular leader whom the world knew.

The Pattern of Change in Leadership.

The student of affairs may be puzzled by the strains and dislocations which occur upon a change of leadership in Russia. But this is less surprising when it is remembered that there is no constitutional manner of embodying a change of opinion or policy in an alternative party or group of men. It will be seen from the diagram of events that after Lenin's death control was divided between the Secretary of the Party and the Premier for seventeen years, until Stalin combined both posts. After Stalin's death in 1953 control was again split (except for ten days) for another five years until, in 1953, Khrushchev who had been Secretary for five years combined the two posts again until 1964. The pattern repeated itself in 1964, Kosygin becoming Premier and Brezhnev Secretary. A meeting of the Supreme Soviet in 1965 confirmed the principle of collective leadership. At the 23rd Soviet Party Congress held in April 1966 it was decided that the Praesidium of the Central Committee should go back to being the Politburo and the First Secretary should revert to General Secretary. The 24th Party Congress held in April 1971 voted to enlarge the Politburo from 11 to 15, which will make retirements possible over the next year or two without any high-level dismissals. The new Politburo, in order of precedence, is as follows: Brezhnev (General Secretary), Podgorny (President of the Soviet Union), Kosygin (Prime Minister), Suslov (the Party's theoretician), Kirilenko, Pelshe, Mazurov, Polyansky, Shelest, Vorono, Shelepin, Grishin, Kunayev, Shcherbitsky, and Kulakov. Brezhnev, Suslov, Kirilenko and Kulakov, by virtue of their joint membership of both Secretariat and the Politburo, appear to form a powerful group within the Soviet leadership.

> Lenin 1917–24
>
> *Premier:* Rykov 1924–30
> *Premier:* Molotov 1930–41
> *Secretary:* Stalin 1922–53
>
> *Premier and Secretary*
> Stalin 1941–53
>
> | Malenkov | Beria | Molotov |
> |---|---|---|
> | | (*Triumvirate*) | |
> | | 1953 | |
>
> *Premier and Secretary*
> Malenkov (10 days in 1953)
>
> *Premier:* Malenkov 1953–55
> *Premier:* Bulganin 1955–58
> *Secretary:* Khrushchev 1953–64
>
> *Premier and Secretary*
> Khrushchev 1958–64
>
> *Premier:* Kosygin 1964
> *Secretary:* Brezhnev 1964

Russian Military Intervention in Czechoslovakia.

In March 1968, when public pressures had secured the removal of President Novotny of Czechoslovakia, it was thought that a genuinely democratic form of communism could be evolved in a communist country and that the Czech example would encourage other Communist countries to reform themselves. But the Soviet Union did not see the new liberalisation policy like that, but rather as preparation for a counter-revolution leading Czechoslovakia back to capitalism. In July, Mr. Brezhnev said that the Soviet Union could not be indifferent to the building of socialism in other socialist countries, and referred to the Hungarian 1956 uprising. Leaders of the Warsaw Pact countries sent a letter to the Czechoslovak party saying that they were deeply disturbed by recent events in Czechoslovakia. The allegations were refuted by the Czechoslovak Presidium and Mr. Dubcek broadcast to the nation reaffirming that "we have no alternative but to complete the profound democratic and socialist changes in our life, together with the people." Talks between the Czechoslovak Presidium and the Soviet Politburo opened at Cierna at the end of July 1968 and at the beginning of August another meeting was held at Bratislava. Afterwards Mr. Dubcek, in a television broadcast, said that the meetings had opened up new scope for the revival process in Czechoslovakia. Then, without the knowledge of the President of the Republic, Russian forces, with contingents from East Germany, Poland Hungary, and Bulgaria, entered Czechoslovakia on the night 20–21 August. The Czech Presidium appealed to all citizens to maintain calm and not to put up resistance to the invading troops.

The Soviet Union justified the military intervention on the grounds that a departure from Marxism–Leninism by a communist country affects all others. This view has been challenged by those who argue that Marx and Lenin accepted the theory of different paths towards socialism.

The New Policy.

Since the Soviet-led invasion of August 1968 there has been a continuous growth of Russian influence over Czechoslovak national affairs, particularly through the removal from office of the principal figures associated with the reform movement. In April 1969 Mr. Dubcek was replaced as First Secretary of the Czechoslovak Communist Party by Dr. Gustav Husak. At the same time Mr. Smrkovsky lost his position as a member of the Presidium. Speaking at the World Communist Conference, held in Moscow in June, Dr. Husak described the new policy of his country after January 1968 as seeking to effect " a transition from bureaucratic centralism to a broader socialist democracy." But in the process the rôle of the Communist Party had been weakened and a situation arose in which " naïvety and romantic political ideas were prevalent as well as cheap gestures and non-class slogans about freedom, democracy, humanitarianism and the will of the people. . . ." During 1970, the party purge continued with the expulsion of Mr. Dubcek, former party leader, and by September roughly one fifth of party members had either resigned or been expelled. Yet, unlike Hungary in 1956, the revisionists did not put former leaders on trial in spite of pressure on Dr. Husak from party hardliners.

World Communist Conference, 1969.

After more than a year's preparation the first international conference of Communist parties since 1960 met in Moscow in June 1969. It was attended by delegates from 75 parties. Among the countries not represented were China, North Vietnam, North Korea, Yugoslavia, and Albania; the Cuban and Swedish delegates attended as observers only. The final document made no direct reference to Soviet criticisms of China nor to the invasion of Czechoslovakia, although these issues were no doubt in the minds of many delegates. The conference dealt with the problem of how to reconcile the principle of sovereign independence with the principle of proletarian internationalism and mutual solidarity. Signor Enrico Berlinguer for the Italian Communist party emphasised the importance of ending the disagreement with China. Account must be taken of the economic realities of Chinese society and China's rôle in the world. " The policy of peaceful coexistence and the anti-imperialist struggle need China's positive contribution. . . . China obviously carries great weight in the international situation. That is why we think it necessary to make an effort to understand the changes taking place in China." Signor Berlinguer went on to say that it is necessary to thrash out all problems frankly and freely, and to recognise and fully respect each party's independence in its search for its own way to socialism. The most striking feature of the document was the assertion that " there is no leading centre of the Communist movement," in contrast to the statement issued by the 1960 Moscow conference that the Soviet party was " the universally recognised vanguard of the world Communist movement." At the same time it asserted that " the defence of socialism is the international duty of Communists."

Sino-Soviet Relations.

During 1970 there was some improvement in Sino-Soviet relations. There was an exchange of ambassadors between Moscow and Peking and, in the autumn, a new trade pact was signed.

THE MIDDLE EAST.

Nasser and the New Egypt.

A new factor in the Middle East was introduced when the Egyptian Army revolted in 1952, overthrowing the monarchy, leading two years later to the emergence of Nasser as Prime Minister. In that year Nasser secured the agreement whereby all British forces were to leave the Suez Canal Zone by 1956. Egypt did not become a democracy in any Western sense but the government runs all the basic enterprises of the country. In 1956 Nasser internationalised the Suez Canal Company as a reply to the withdrawal by the United States of its offer to finance the High Dam at Aswan. The attack by the British and French on Egypt followed, causing serious disagreement with the United States, which inspired international action to rescue Egypt. It was in obedience to a demand by the UN Assembly that Britain, France, and Israel withdrew from the attack on Egypt and an international force of about 6,000 men was organised to help avert further conflict. When, in April 1957, the canal was cleared and in use Egypt not only insisted on full control of the canal but on the right to bar Israeli trade from the canal. Egypt and Saudi Arabia said they would resume blockading the Gulf of Aqaba (a N.E. arm of the Red Sea), but in fact Israeli ships subsequently got through to their previously blockaded port of Eilat. A small UN force remained on the Gaza–Eilat armistice line.

The closure of the canal in the summer of 1967 cost Britain's balance of payments about £20 million a month, since oil had to be brought more expensively from non-Middle East areas. " The growth of big tankers," said Mr. Wilson, " may very soon make the Suez Canal a rather pathetic irrelevance." But all the same he declared it as intolerable that any nation should keep the canal closed to international shipping.

The Middle East War of 1967.

The third Arab–Israeli war began on 5 June 1967. In the words of The Times: " What began as the usual spring exercises of the Syrian army, shelling Israeli settlements in Galilee, ended with the complete overthrow of the Middle Eastern balance of power." Israel destroyed the air forces of Egypt, Jordan, and Syria in a few hours, destroyed their three armies in six days, occupying all Sinai to the banks of the Suez Canal (which was therefore closed), the west bank of the Jordan, and the Syrian hills above Galilee. The war was a disaster for Britain, who, with America, was blamed for a catastrophe which, in the view of The Times, the Arabs had " brought on their own heads." Among other results, the Russians moved permanently into the Middle East, backing the Arabs. The toll of human misery was, and remains, too immense to imagine: at least 300,000 new and old refugees fleeing the occupied territories. And despite the cost of this human and material loss and distress the problem of Israeli–Arab hostility remains unresolved.

UN Appoints Envoy to the Middle East.

Thanks to the efforts of Lord Caradon, who was then British Ambassador to the UN, the members of the Security Council in November 1967 reached agreement, and unanimously, to send a special emissary to the Middle East, Mr. Gunnar Jarring, a Swedish diplomat, whose mastery of twelve languages includes Arabic. An active Arab scholar, he was not known to have sympathies one way or the other in the Middle East. Nasser criticised the Security Council's resolution to send Jarring as inadequate and Syria rejected it. Nasser repeated the formula he had declared at the Arab summit conference in September of " no peace, no recognition and no negotiations." The chief obstacle faced by the UN mediator was the mistrust by each side of the other's motives and ultimate intentions.

The Israeli case remains that peace can only be achieved through a negotiated settlement between the parties directly affected, which involves recognition of Israel as a nation-state. Furthermore, since neither the UN nor the four Powers can of themselves guarantee a settlement, Israel, in the interim period, must rely on her own resources to maintain her existence. The Arab governments have continued to insist that Israel must first withdraw from the occupied areas before a settlement can be considered and even before recognition can be accepted. The Palestinian *fedayeen* organisations, of which *Al Fatah* is the principal body, go further and refuse to accept the state of Israel at all.

The Spread of Violence.

The fighting continued in 1970, until the U.S. produced a peace initiative which led to a cease-fire between Egypt, Jordan, and Israel from 7 August. On 28 September, the Arabs and Egypt lost their leader, President Nasser, who died of a heart attack. Nasser was the first Arab leader to respond favourably to any Middle East peace proposal from the West. The U.S. offer was for a three-month cease fire along the Suez Canal, and mediation through Dr. Jarring on the implementation of UN resolution 242 which calls for Israeli withdrawal. Israel accepted this plan after long consultations with Washington; so did Jordan and Lebanon. But peace hopes were shattered when Israel withdrew from the talks after accusing Egypt and the Soviet Union of moving missiles into the standstill zone. The charge was denied by Egypt, and both sides agreed to a further three months' extension, with President Sadat (Nasser's successor) warning that Israel must produce a timetable for withdrawal from the occupied territories.

Palestinian guerrillas have been predictably hostile to the proposals which they feared would frustrate their plan to establish a democratic state of Palestine in place of Israel. This exacerbated the conflict between the guerrillas and King Hussein's army, the guerrillas having used Jordan as the base for attacks on Israel. Jordan has consistently borne the brunt of Israeli retaliation. The Popular Front for the Liberation of Palestine (PFLP), a small well-organised *fedayeen* organisation, attempted to break the cease-fire and usurp King Hussein's rule and wrest leadership of the guerrilla movement from Al Fatah by hi-jacking 400 people in three aircraft to a disused airfield in northern Jordan. This was in September 1970. Most passengers were released, but 43 Europeans were held hostage after the aircraft had been blown up. After ten days of fighting, in which there were up to 10,000 casualties, President Nasser prevailed on King Hussein and Yasser Arafat, leader of Al Fatah, to sign a peace agreement. The President died the next day.

Subsequently, the smaller guerrilla groups dwindled and Al Fatah has emerged as a moderate movement. The most hopeful sign in 1971 comes from President Sadat who indicated for the first time that Egypt would be prepared to sign a contractual peace treaty with Israel guaranteeing her inviolability and independence within secure and recognised boundaries. He also said that Egypt would recognise Israel's freedom of navigation in the Suez Canal. Israel's reply at the time of writing (March 1971) while likely to include a rejection of a retreat to the borders before the Six Day war, may include the first tentative offer of a map-redrawing. Observers agree that Mrs. Meir may agree to cede that part of the Sinai peninsula west of a line from El-Arish to Sharm-el-Sheikh.

ASIA.

The independence and unity of India on the one hand and the emergence in China of the Central People's Republic on the other form, with the Vietnam war, the three important political features of Asia. India and China have lived, historically speaking, in different worlds; their experiences at the hands of the West have been different; their recent developments and their present political systems are entirely dissimilar—the one a democracy and the other authoritarian.

Indian Changes under British Rule.

The pattern of India's development after independence had been set during British rule. The main features were: the concept of law and the rule of law; a civil service superior to any known before in Asia; a system of education introduced as far back as 1835; English as a common language; and the growth of an intelligentsia (to use a word with a Russian origin) with a humanistic outlook and responsive to Western ideals and traditions. Important consequences followed from these changes. They enabled Hindu society to reform itself on the basis of modern ideas; to create an educated leadership; to modernise Indian languages; and to introduce modern science to India.

Leadership Since Independence.

That the dissolution of British rule was made so peacefully, a miracle of modern times, was due principally to Gandhi who associated nationalism with ethical concepts, summed up in the term " Gandhism " and denoting pacifism, the value of the individual soul and humane ideas. He made India conscious of the social reforms which needed to be made and created the discipline to make a democracy able to carry them through. Gandhi's ideal of religious unity, though disrupted by the partition into the two states, Pakistan and India, made it possible for the new India to be a secular state, in which all religious and minorities had equal rights.

Nehru, India's first prime minister, symbolised India's highest aspirations. As a disciple of Gandhi he revered him; but his political outlook had been different. He was an enlightened liberal working towards a modernised rational, democratic, secular state enjoying both the benefits of large-scale scientific organisation and the spiritual good of individual liberty. Under great strains this way and that he maintained neutrality in the face of world power blocs and embodied in his politics characteristics from differing régimes. He overtowered everybody in Indian public life and was one of the few great figures on the world stage.

Shastri succeeded Nehru. Lal Bahadur was born in 1903 into a caste lower than the Brahmins but equally dedicated to learning; " Shastri " is in fact the title of the degree he received. His air of gentleness was enhanced by his small size; and even by his adversaries in India he was regarded as a good, kind, and tolerant man. He faced problems as complex as any statesman, in the world's biggest, hungriest, and restless democracy. One of his biggest decisions was not to follow China in the nuclear weapons race.

Mrs. Indira Gandhi became Prime Minister of India in January 1966 upon Mr. Shastri's death at the Tashkent conference. Her father was Nehru and she must be regarded as the only daughter in history to have succeeded her father. She is not a relation of Mahatma Gandhi. In Indian families women have always been very highly regarded and India is one of the very few countries where nothing stands in the way of a woman going to the very top. Mahatma Gandhi so far back as 1929 had been uncompromising on women's rights and after Indian independence Hindu law was changed to satisfy his requirements on the status of women. Thus it was Gandhi who took women into politics and paved the way for the election in 1966 of Mrs. Gandhi, the world's most powerful woman. (Mrs. Bandaranaike of Ceylon holds the distinction of being the first woman Prime Minister in history.) Mrs. Gandhi is more radical than both her father Nehru and Mr. Shastri but clings to no " ism " and will confront each problem individually. Among those round Shastri who helped to guide India, she was by far the most cosmopolitan. Educated in Switzerland and at Oxford, she travelled widely with her father and as his hostess met many world leaders. Her family is Hindu and there is no doubt that she shares her father's devotion to the ideal of a secular state. She faced, on election, many difficulties; she promised to honour the agreement with Pakistan reached only a few days earlier at Tashkent where Mr. Shastri died, and she announced her willingness to negotiate with China if favourable conditions are created.

The Indian Elections, 1967.

The monopoly of power enjoyed by the Congress Party of Gandhi and Nehru over India for twenty years was dramatically broken in March 1967. Between 60 and 70 per cent of the Indian electorate of 240 million used their vote. Half Mrs. Indira Gandhi's Congress Cabinet lost their seats, as well as three of the most powerful Congress Party leaders. Several State Governments were overturned. The result represented therefore an emphatic protest vote against continued Congress rule rather than a positive choice of a clear alternative vote. The protest vote went to whichever party seemed locally most capable of turning Congress out. The Congress Party was left with a very thin majority, but it remained the largest single party in the country.

A Congress Deeply Divided.

Differences on economic policies within the Congress Party came to a head in July 1969 when Mrs. Gandhi chose to revive the issue of bank nationalisation in sharp form. Two years earlier, in July 1967, the leadership, divided on outright nationalisation, settled on a compromise formula and introduced " social controls " on both banking and insurance. On 20 July Mrs. Gandhi nationalised the country's 14 large banks by ordinance, relieved Mr. Desai of the finance portfolio, as he differed with her on economic policy, and swiftly piloted the bill through Parliament. In her broadcast to the nation she said that the nationalisation of the banks would herald in a new era in carrying out the Party's policies. She emphasised that this did not mean " an era of nationalisation." Mrs. Gandhi's action was supported by Congress radicals, communists, and socialists, and by the people at large. Big business and the two right-wing parties, the Swatantra Party and the Jan Sangh, condemned it as " a treacherous act against the constitution." In an unexpected judgment the Supreme Court of India in February 1970 restored the 14 nationalised banks to their original owners. The court found that the Government had excluded foreign and minor banks from the scope of the Act passed in 1969 and said that this amounted to discrimination under the constitution. Two courses seemed open to Mrs. Gandhi: to amend the constitution, for which she would need a two-thirds majority, or to enact new legislation to comply with the Supreme Court's objections.

The fiercely fought Presidential election in August 1969 marked a further stage in the conflict between the Prime Minister and her opponents. Mr. V. V. Giri, the Acting President, defeated Mr. N. S. Reddy, the nominee of the " syndicate "— an inner group of party leaders consisting of older and more conservative elements in the Congress party. The intention of the Indian constitution was to make the President a figurehead but events are working to make him more powerful. Mr. Giri, who was 75 at the time, is a distinguished trade union leader.

A New Direction.

Indian democracy survived the split in Congress during 1970, the year of Mrs. Gandhi's supremacy. In spite of leading a minority government she received larger votes of confidence from parliament than she did when Congress was united. This surge of confidence led her to call elections in March 1971.

An alliance of four main opposition parties formed to prevent vote-splitting with the slogan " Oust Indira ". Its components were: Jan Sangh (Hindu Nationalist); the Opposing Congress; SSP (Socialist), and the Swatantra (Free Enterprise).

There was no doubt that Mrs. Gandhi would win the election but the margin was expected to be narrow. In the event, she achieved a landslide victory which more than made up for the losses sustained by the Congress Party in the 1967 elections, before it split into two factions in 1969. Of an electorate of 280 million, more than 100 million went to the polls. Mrs. Gandhi called her victory a mandate for socialism. When opening the first session of the new Indian Parliament, President Giri said the government would immediately launch schemes for the vigorous implementation of the land reform laws, and abolish the privy purses and privileges of former rulers through constitutional measures. Radical plans were outlined to combat unemployment, and to increase production in public and private sectors. A mid-term reappraisal of the present five-year plan would be made.

Pakistan.

Pakistan's economy is still based largely on agriculture, the principal food crops being rice and wheat, and the main cash crops being jute, cotton, and tea. Industry—including cotton and jute textiles, cement, fertilisers, and oil and natural gas production—has been developing fairly rapidly, and employment in manufacturing and other non-agricultural occupations is rising. Economic development has experienced a number of setbacks in recent years. In 1965 the outbreak of hostilities with India led to a sharp increase in defence expenditure and an interruption in the flow of foreign aid, thus drastically reducing for a time the funds available for economic investment. Immediately afterwards the country was faced with two successive seasons of drought and flood with consequent harvest shortfalls, so that scarce foreign exchange had to be used for increased imports of food. The political unrest which led to President Ayub Khan's resignation and his replacement by President Yahya Khan placed the economy under further strain.

A major political crisis had developed in November 1968 following the arrest of Mr. Bhutto (former Foreign Minister and leader of the left-wing People's Party) and student demands for educational reforms. On 3 February 1969 the Opposition parties rejected President Ayub Khan's offer of talks on constitutional reform unless he first ended the state of emergency (in being since September 1965) and released all political prisoners. Faced with mounting agitation throughout the country Ayub Khan decided to negotiate with the Opposition and from then on swift steps have been taken to restore parliamentary democracy in Pakistan. We give the sequence of events:

1969

February 17. State of emergency revoked by presidential proclamation.

February 21. President Ayub Khan announced that he would not be a candidate in the next presidential election.

February 26. Opening session in Rawalpindi of talks between President Ayub Khan and the leaders of the main Opposition parties.

March 13. President Ayub Khan agreed to introduce legislation to restore parliamentary government and universal adult suffrage.

March 25. Ayub Khan announced his resignation from the presidency and handed over administration to General Yahya Khan, C.-in-C. of the Army, who proclaimed martial law, abrogated the constitution, dissolved the National Assembly and removed governors and ministers from office.

March 31. General Yahya Khan assumed the presidency, saying he would act as Head of State until a new constitution had been framed by the elected representatives of the people.

November 28. President Yahya Khan announced that elections would be held on 5 October 1970.

1970

In March, President Yahya Khan announced a new provincial system for Pakistan which freed the political parties and absorbed the country in a long and violent election campaign. A new 5-year plan was also announced to stimulate economic recovery. And the year saw also the worst floods of the century in East Pakistan. The fourth 5-year plan was launched on July 1, promising an outlay of 70,500 million rupees with a growth target of 7·5 per cent for East Pakistan and 5·5 per cent for the West. But this scheme quickly suffered a blow when the Aid-to-Pakistan consortium, meeting in Paris, postponed a request for 500 million dollars, making it dependent on progress towards democracy. In spite of this cold shoulder from the U.S., France, and Britain, Yahya Khan was able to secure substantial promises of interest-free loans and plant from China and the Soviet Union.

President Khan's return from Peking coincided with the floods which killed at least 200,000 in the Ganges delta area in East Pakistan. The disaster postponed to December the first national elections in the country's 23 years of independence. The result of the election (electorate 56 million; 26 parties fielded candidates) was not the expected multiplicity of factions which would have allowed Yahya to continue to rule. Two clear leaders emerged. In East Pakistan, Shaikh Mujibur Rahman of the Awami League had a clear majority while Mr. Bhutto of the People's Party triumphed in the West. However, disagreement on the status of the National Assembly led the President to postpone its first meeting in March 1971.

Bangla Desh (Bengal Nation) was the name chosen by Shaikh Mujibur Rahman for an independent East Pakistan but in April 1971 President Khan sent West Pakistan Army units to crush the independence movement. The result was carnage.

China.

It is only in the last fifty years that the people of China have emerged from centuries of exploitation. It is very difficult for a Western observer to appreciate the dramatic changes which followed the overthrow of the repressive dynasty in 1911 and the advent of the Republic next year. The new leader, Sun Yat Sen, a great idealist and humanitarian, pitted himself against the age-long combination of landlords, military men, and reactionary scholars. For all his achievements Sun failed; or rather Sun's party, the Kuomintang, failed him. Power passed to the military remnants of the old Imperial army and Sun did not succeed in giving his party teeth for militant action for reform. Unfortunately, two years after Sun's death in 1925 his successor General Chiang Kai-shek opened an anti-Communist drive.

Sun's exhortations had been taken to heart by a poet and a scholar, Mao Tse-tung, son of a yeoman farmer from Hunan in the heart of China. Mao's success in raising peasant armies established his pre-eminence as a leader. The countryside helped the Communists to develop honest government. The peasants were ready to work in field and forge. They created a people's army superior to all other armies in Chinese history.

Mao Tse-tung and Other Leaders.

Mao's reputation is based upon his ability first as a military theorist (of guerrilla warfare); second as a political philosopher (adapting Marxism to Chinese needs); and, third, as a more ardent champion of world revolution than the Russian leaders. Chou En-lai, the premier of the State Council, is the best known of Chinese leaders in the outside world and also knows the outside world better than his colleagues. Until the recent upheavals Mr. Liu Shao-ch'i was Mao's right-hand man and his heir-apparent. But now the Defence Minister, Marshal Lin Piao, or Vice-chairman Lin, as he is called, is Mao's chosen successor. This was formally stated in the new constitution that came before the Ninth Party congress in 1969. His devotion to Maoism is beyond doubt. Mr. Tung Pi-Wu was appointed President in place of Mr. Liu Shao-chi.

China's Cultural Revolution

What were the features of China's cultural revolution, as it was called, of which so much was heard in 1966 and 1967? We first briefly indicate the main elements: (1) it was an organised demonstration of the young; (2) it was in favour of Mao Tse-tung; (3) it disseminated Mao's essential

teaching; (4) it was intended to keep alive revolutionary fervour; (5) it thus engendered a sense of China's special path of development; and (6) it emphasised opposition to "revisionism" leading to "bourgeois decay" as, it was said, had occurred in Russia. When Mao himself in December 1965 gave the first hint of a coming purge he styled it a "cultural revolution" against bourgeois and revisionist elements. Let us amplify the main elements in the movement.

The organisation was directed to the under-25s who joined in mammoth demonstrations. Slogans and portraits of Mao Tse-tung appeared everywhere. Huge crowds of young people with red armbands thronged the streets in general excitement. Red Guards took a prominent part. This tremendous emotional support for Papa Mao gave that leader (then 73) the assurance that his choice of successor would be accepted with confidence. Mao's essential teaching was disseminated by millions of copies of a little 300-page book of his selected writings, in a red plastic cover, carried by almost everyone and universally quoted, discussed, and preached. An objective of the movement was to stimulate the young who might otherwise take for granted the achievements of their elders made possible only by their past suffering and hunger. The revolution must be uninterrupted; the class struggle continued. This revolution was set upon a special path, being opposed to the super-Japan western-type technological society. At the same time the cultural revolution emphasised opposition to bourgeois attitudes and encouragement of revolutionary fervour. Beyond all this the young were urged to show initiative, to make suggestions for improvements, not to be afraid to criticise. The upheaval was described as a militant and not a militarist movement; the weapons being the tongue, the pen and the brush justified, it was argued, the description of the revolution as a cultural one. But it developed into violent struggles between revolutionaries and reactionaries and then between the revolutionaries themselves. Mr. Chou En-lai warned that industrial production was being seriously affected. The situation remained very confused until 1968 when there was a gradual return to moderation. Of the 17 surviving members of the Politburo elected at the eighth Communist Party congress of 1956, 13 were declared "bourgeois reactionaries" during the cultural revolution. President Liu Shao-chi was among those expelled from the party. That era of turmoil is now over and Mao in order to fulfil his dream of a powerful, industrialised China has united the country once again.

Ninth Party Congress.

The ninth congress of the Chinese Communist Party, the first held since 1958, took place in Peking during April 1969. It was held in conditions of great secrecy and was attended by over 1,500 delegates. "One remembers writing a year ago," wrote Mr. Richard Harris in *The Times* of 17 September 1969, "that all would be clear when the dilatory Chinese leaders finally got down to their ninth party congress. Well, if the ninth congress revealed anything to the delegates it was certainly not passed on to the outside world. Unlike the eighth party congress which published in due course all the reports and the main speeches, the ninth released only Lin Piao's largely retrospective report and a flaccid communiqué."

Sino-Soviet Border Incidents.

Serious clashes took place in March 1969 between Chinese and Russian troops on the Ussuri river boundary for control of the river islands. The region was once Chinese, ceded to Russia in 1858. From this far eastern extremity of the frontier with the Soviet Union runs for 4,000 miles (almost 7,000 miles if one includes Mongolia) to the great mountain chains of the Pamirs. China has wanted to renegotiate her borders ever since 1949 and amicable boundary settlements have been made with Afghanistan, Burma, Pakistan, Nepal, and Outer Mongolia. China entered into negotiations with the Soviet Union in 1964, being willing to take the Treaties of 1858 and 1860 as the basis for a settlement, but without success.

Steps in the Conflict.

1969

March 2. First of a series of clashes over Daman-sky (or Chen Pao) Island on Ussuri river.

March 29. Soviet Note invited China to resume frontier negotiations, broken off in 1964.

May 2. Clashes in Sinkiang border area.

May 11. China accepted Russian proposal to resume regular meetings of Sino-Soviet commission for navigation on border rivers. The commission was convened at Khabarovsk on 18 June.

May 24. China maintained that negotiations should be held for the " overall settlement of the Sino-Soviet boundary question and the conclusion of a new equal treaty to replace the old unequal one."

August 9. Sino-Soviet agreement on border river navigation announced.

September 13. Soviet troops reported to have crossed frontier into Sinkiang and inflicted casualties. Soviet Union and China exchanged protest Notes.

September 30. Peking radio said China was ready to settle the border dispute with the Soviet Union by negotiations.

1970

There were no major border incidents during the year. Some observers detected a faint mellowing in the relations between the two countries, as evidenced by the exchange of ambassadors by Moscow and Peking. It is difficult to chart any firm progress in the talks which have been going on intermittently to settle ideological differences.

A Break in the Clouds.

There were signs in the spring of 1971 of improving relations between China and the West. At a reception in Peking on 14 April for visiting " ping-pong " teams from the United States, Canada, Britain, Colombia, and Nigeria, the Chinese Prime Minister, Chou En-lai, spoke of a new page in the history of relations between their peoples and the Chinese people. On the same day, U Thant, UN Secretary-General, suggested that the time had come for a conference of the major Powers, with China playing her full part; President Nixon issued a five-point plan for the resumption of contact between the U.S. and China, embracing new links in trade and travel, with the removal of many restrictions; and telephone services between London and Shanghai were reopened after a lapse of 22 years.

China Tests Nuclear Missiles.

In October 1966 without giving details of the weapon, China announced she had tested a guided missile with a nuclear warhead, thus conforming roughly to the timetable for the development of her missile-nuclear capability anticipated by U.S. Intelligence studies. The Chinese announcement reiterated the assurance that China would never be the first to use nuclear weapons. China exploded her eighth nuclear device in December 1968 and in September 1969 carried out her first underground nuclear test and exploded a new hydrogen bomb. In April 1970 China launched her first satellite (singing the song " East is Red ") into orbit, a development which reinforces the argument that China should be brought into arms control discussions.

Vietnam.

In 1941 the Vichy Government in France gave Japan, who was our fighting enemy in the Second World War, permission to use French Indo-China as a base against us. Resistance groups were formed to win back independence and to overthrow both French and Japanese fascists. Japan collapsed in 1945, when the only organised troops were controlled by Ho Chi-minh, a Communist,

who set up a Democratic Republic in the northern part of Vietnam. France was bent upon restoring her colonial empire in the south and next year war broke out between the French and Ho Chi-minh. Readers will remember the dramatic siege and capture by Ho's forces of the fort of Dien Bien Phu in 1954. As a result of a 14-nation conference on Indo-China at Geneva in the same year Vietnam was partitioned after a cease-fire, the country to be united after free elections. Laos and Cambodia became independent.

A declaration taking note of the agreement was signed by the following nations who took part: U.K., France, China, Russia, Cambodia, Laos, and North Vietnam. Unfortunately the United States refused to sign the agreement and South Vietnam refused to hold elections, but both affirmed that they would not use force to upset the agreement. There was thus a crystallisation into two Vietnams—Ho Chi-minh's Hanoi régime in the North and that of the Catholic nationalist Ngo Dinh Diem at Saigon in the South. The Diem régime was corrupt but John Foster Dulles sent in men and materials to prop it up. By 1960 the Communist guerrillas in the South, known as the Vietcong, had set up a National Liberation Front. For eight or nine years a civil war was waged in South Vietnam against a very unpopular dictatorship. All that time it received United States military support and phrases like " the defence of freedom " in Vietnam are to be construed in the light of that fact. It is true, of course, that the North had been helping the rebels in the South. The position became increasingly untenable, and in 1963 the Buddhists rioted against the ruling Roman Catholic minority. The Diem régime which had savagely persecuted the Buddhists was overthrown by the military, the first of a number of military coups. In August 1964 two vessels of the U.S. fleet were alleged to have been attacked in the Gulf of Tonking (off the North Vietnam coast) and American planes bombed North Vietnam installations as retaliation. This was the first of a series of bombing raids. At first the U.S. Government said that these were tit-for-tat raids but this specific basis was superseded by unrelated attacks. In March 1965 the American Ambassador in South Vietnam said that pressure against Hanoi would continue " until the enemy gives in." In June 1965 the State Department gave authority to the American military commander to use troops in offensive operations against the Vietcong. An inquiry conducted by the U.S. Senate Foreign Relations Committee in 1968 made it doubtful whether the alleged attacks on the two U.S. destroyers in the Gulf of Tonking had ever taken place. This put a question mark against the constitutional legality of the war, as Congress had never declared war on North Vietnam.

There have been many attempts to bring about peace negotiations. In December 1967 N. Vietnam said peace talks would follow if the U.S. stopped their bombing unconditionally. In January 1968 President Johnson reaffirmed his San Antonio speech of September 1967 to halt bombing of N. Vietnam on condition that peace talks would follow and no military advantage would be taken of the pause. The San Antonio formula was dismissed by N. Vietnam as being a delaying tactic. N. Vietnam again stressed the necessity for the withdrawal of U.S. forces and said peace talks would begin as soon as the U.S. " has proved that it has really stopped unconditionally the bombings and all other acts of war against N. Vietnam." Meanwhile the Tet (lunar new year) Vietcong offensive developed into a major campaign, covering practically the whole of S. Vietnam.

Mr. Robert McNamara left as Defence Secretary in 1968. He had become a counsellor of coolness and restraint; he rationed General Westmoreland in the supply of troops; and he opposed some escalations, which happened, like the bombing of Hanoi and Haiphong. General Westmoreland, who took over as field commander in Vietnam in 1964, was recalled to Washington in March 1968 to become U.S. Army Chief of Staff at the Pentagon. A major review of the Vietnam situation took place in Washington made necessary by the military, political and psychological impact of the Vietcong Tet offensive. After being advised by his officials that a military solution was impossible and that the only possible political solution was a negotiated settlement, President Johnson in March 1968 announced his partial bombing pause. Peace talks began in Paris in May, and by January 1969 the U.S., S. Vietnam, N. Vietnam, and the National Liberation Front (NLF) were sitting round a table, but because of fundamental differences between the two sides little progress has been made.

A Sketch of Ho Chi Minh.

Relatively little has been written about Ho Chi Minh who died on 3 September 1969, at the age of 79, and this is remarkable of a man whose country has figured so dramatically and tragically in post-war history. Let us therefore take a brief look at him; first, by recalling some of the external facts about him and, second, by a word of interpretation of his achievements and efforts. He had been President of Vietnam since 1945, and this innings must be in the running for a world record. In 1911, as a young man of 21, he went abroad and for thirty years remained an exile from his native land. In France, in England, and elsewhere he studied the world-wide struggle against colonialism and saw the problem he was particularly interested in—the oppression in Vietnam—as part of the widespread colonial exploitation. Thus the Russian Revolution must have made a great impression upon him, illustrating that great changes were possible. Though for this reason he was sympathetic to communism his first concern was the anti-colonial revolution in Vietnam. His main purpose therefore from 1945 was to weld together the two elements in Vietnam of nationalism and communism. By unusual powers of organisation he was successful in this. The evidence is that he did make a genuine and protracted attempt to negotiate independence with the French in 1945–46 and was prepared to make many concessions. The determination of the French to regain control of Indo-China after the Second World War must be regarded as one of the most tragic mistakes of the period. The special character of his achievement is the dove-tailing of the national and communistic elements in Vietnam; and the balance between the two has been skilfully maintained, however uneasy it may seem. Flowing from this was Ho's refusal to take sides in the Sino-Soviet conflict. His attempt to bind together nationalistic and communistic elements has been the more remarkable when it is seen that Vietnam is the only country in South-east Asia where this has been possible, the Communists having been checked in Malaya, in Burma, in Cambodia, and in the Philippines.

Steps in Vietnam History.

1940   Japanese invasion. France withdrew.

1942–5   Vietnamese engage in guerrilla war on invaders, Nationalists and Communists joining forces.

1945   Japan withdrew and Nationalists declare Vietnam independent.
Potsdam agreement makes Britain and China responsible for administration of Vietnam.

1946   Britain invites French to help and then withdraws leaving French in charge. Terrorist attacks on French who made massive reprisals against civilians.

1949   French install Bao Dai as national leader.

1954   French defeated at Dien Bien Phu by the Viet Minh. Geneva Agreements.

1955   Boa Dai persuaded by U.S. to replace his prime minister by Hgo Dinh Diem (American educated Catholic) who in 1956 refutes Geneva Agreements and refuses elections.

1960–3   Three years of increasing conflict between Diem and the National Liberation Front formed to oppose the Diem régime.

1963   Neutral Buddhists appeal to Government for elections. Diem attacks Buddhists. Diem assassinated.

1964   August 2. Gulf of Tongking incident. Prompted Congress to give Pres. Johnson authority to step up American military intervention in S.E. Asia.

1965   February. Large-scale air raids on N. Vietnam opened.

1966   January. Major military operations by U.S. in the south.
March 18. Hanoi bombed for the first time.

1967   February. Bombing of N. Vietnam increased.
May. Fighting in the demilitarised zone running between N. and S. Vietnam.
August. Bombing near Chinese Border.

1968   January-February. Tet offensive: co-ordinated Vietcong attack on cities in S. Vietnam, including Saigon.
March 31. Pres. Johnson announced partial bombing pause.
May. Beginning of peace talks in Paris between U.S. and N. Vietnam.

1969   January 25. Full-scale peace talks open (U.S., S. Vietnam, N. Vietnam, NLF).
July 14. First major contingent of U.S. troops began withdrawal from S. Vietnam.
September 3. Death of Ho Chi Minh.
September 16. President Nixon announced withdrawal by mid-December of further 35,000 troops.
September 23. Mr. Ton Duc Thang elected President of North Vietnam.
December 15. President Nixon announced withdrawal of 50,000 more American troops before 15 April 1970.

1970   March 18. Prince Sihanouk, Cambodian head of state, overthrown in right-wing coup.
April 30. U.S. combat troops invaded Cambodia.
June 29. Last rearguard U.S. units withdrawn from Cambodia, one day ahead of President Nixon's deadline.

1971   February 8. 5,000 S. Vietnamese troops, supported by U.S. helicopters and fighter bombers—but not ground forces—invaded Laos to cut the Ho Chi Minh Trail.
February 25. S. Vietnamese drive in Laos halted.
April. American withdrawal from S. Vietnam well advanced.

Basic Facts about Vietnam.

The population is 32 million (N. 15·5, S. 16·5). Racially they are cousins of the Chinese and their culture is largely derived from China. Nevertheless they are ancient enemies of the Chinese. They are Confucians in their social attitudes. The main religion is Buddhism 70–80 per cent, Roman Catholic 7 per cent. The land area is 129,000 square miles (N. 63,000, S. 66,000). The leading figures in North Vietnam are Ton Duc Thang who succeeded Ho Chi Minh as President, Pham Van Dong, the Prime Minister, Le Duan, First Secretary of the Party, Truong Chink, the Party ideologist, and General Giap, the Defence Minister. The Government of S. Vietnam had been formed by military coup and as a result of a limited election in 1967 the President is Lt.-General Nguyen Van Thieu and the Vice-President Air Vice-Marshal Nguyen Cao Ky.

AFRICA.

The Civil War in Nigeria.

The civil war began in July 1967 after the secession of the Eastern Region under its Ibo leader, Colonel Ojuku. This region became known as

Biafra. Federal troops, under the head of the
Federal Military Government, General Gowon,
advanced into Biafra and cut the secessionists off
from the sea and confined them to the Ibo heartland. Margery Perham, writing in *The Listener*
(19 September 1968) explained that there was a
very wide difference between the Ibo way of life
and that of the other major tribes in Nigeria—the
Hausa and the Yoruba. "This difference
seemed to matter less when all the tribes were held
together within the overarching structure of the
British government. But with independence, with
the full tribal competition for power and economic
advance, certain deep rivalries began to appear."
The Hausa (Muslim) and the Yoruba (Muslim and
Christian) both belong to old civilisations and are
grouped in large city states, the Ibos (mostly
Roman Catholic) are poorer, thirsty for education
and eager for change. The tension between the
main tribal groups led to the assassination in 1966
by Ibo officers of the Hausa Prime Minister,
Abubakar Tafewa Balewa. General Ironi, an
Ibo soldier, tried to impose a unitary system of
government, but was murdered by non-Ibo
soldiers. This tragic civil war, seen by millions
on their television screens, evoked a response for
practical action and Lord Hunt and his mission
were successful in organising help.

The Federal Military Government said that
military operations would cease immediately if
Colonel Ojukwu and his associates would agree to
renounce secession, remain part of Nigeria and
accept the new structure of the Federation based
on the 12 states, including the South Eastern and
Rivers States.

The end of the civil war after a period of
apparent stalemate came in the space of a few
days at the beginning of 1970. Federal troops
captured Owerri, headquarters of the secessionist
régime, together with Uli airstrip through which
relief supplies had reached Biafra. Colonel
Ojukwu departed, leaving Colonel Effiong in
charge of affairs. Colonel Effiong called on his
troops to stop fighting and sued for peace. The
civil war was formally ended on 15 January. The
conduct of the Federal Military Government and
of Federal forces was reported to be notable for
its generosity and spirit of reconciliation. Predictions of vengeance, and even genocide against
the Ibo people, which had gained a wide currency,
largely as a result of "Biafran" propaganda,
were in the event proved to be unfounded. As
soon as the fighting was over, the Nigerian
Government set about the task of relieving hunger
and suffering in the war-affected areas. While
accepting many of the offers of aid which flowed
in from friendly countries, the Government kept
the administration of the relief programme firmly
in its own hands.

The Assassination of Verwoerd.

Dr. Verwoerd, who was murdered in September
1966, while the members of the Commonwealth
were assembled in Conference in London, was the
man who gave form and substance to the idea of
apartheid, led South Africa into a republic and
took her out of the Commonwealth. He studied
applied psychology in Germany and on return
took an interest in politics, organising in 1936 a
protest against the admission to South Africa of a
shipload of Jews fleeing from Germany. He
became a power behind the scenes in the Nationalist Party which, in 1948, ousted the Smuts régime
on the slogan of apartheid. He succeeded J. G.
Strydom as Premier in 1959, a year after being
elected to the House of Assembly. The Bantu
Self Government Act of 1960 provided for the
division of the non-white population into tribal
units, the abolition of their existing representation
in Parliament and the creation of self-governing
"native states." But the aim of apartheid, the
physical separation of races is, apart from other
objections, a dishonest myth, as the economy cannot be run without black labour. The call by The
Pan-African Organisation for a nationwide campaign against the law requiring all African men to
carry passes for identification led to the massacre
by the police at Sharpeville. Verwoerd banned
the two major African political movements, the
African National Congress and the Pan-African
Congress and most African leaders were sent to
prison, proscribed or fled. Verwoerd was born in

Holland, a land noted for its enlightened policy of
racial integration; but after his return to South
Africa from Germany he held the separation of
races to be blessed by scriptural authority and, as
a follower of the Dutch Reformed Church, carried
his philosophy into politics.

Dissension among the Nationalists.

A split occurred in the ruling Nationalist Party
when Dr. Hertzog was dismissed by Mr. Vorster as
Minister of Health in August 1969; two other
members of the South African House of Assembly
were expelled from the party organisation, and
another resigned. They became known as the
verkrampte (rigidly conservative) as opposed to the
verligte (enlightened). They formed the break-
away extreme Right-wing Herstigte (Reformed)
National Party.

In the general election held in April 1970 Dr.
Hertzog and his co-extremists were defeated.
Mr. Vorster's Nationalist Party lost nine seats to
Sir de Villiers Graaf's United Party and suffered
a reduction of majorities over a wide front. Mrs.
Helen Suzman tripled her majority but remained
the only representative of the Liberal Progressive
Party in Parliament. Interpreting the results for
The Observer, Anthony Sampson (author of
Anatomy of Britain, and *The New Europeans*)
said it would be a misreading of the situation to
suppose that Mr. Vorster as a result of the defeat
of the *verkramptes* and of the gains of the United
Party would pursue a more "liberal" internal
policy. "Mr. Vorster and Sir de Villiers Graaf
have been moving for years, almost in step, towards the Right; and in many practical respects
the two main white parties are in a coalition.
There is nothing self-correcting in the South
African political system; as in Rhodesia, the exclusion of the majority from the vote leads to a
steady, almost unopposed, move to the Right."
The word *verligte* may not therefore imply any
relaxation of apartheid, police powers, and ruthless repression of the black population but rather
a realisation that for South Africa to maintain her
economic growth she must make more use of
skilled black labour, expand trade with black
Africa, and improve her relations with Europe
and America. The sports boycott has a significance far beyond the game itself.

Violence and Southern Africa.

Violence has begun to erupt over southern
Africa. The indecisiveness over Rhodesia, the
absence of serious economic pressure on South
Africa and on the Portuguese, whatever the
reasons for this policy, have encouraged those
ready to use violence. And this applies to the
advocates of violence on both sides, black and
white. The guerrilla has suddenly become a
reckonable factor, said Colin Legum, in a part of
the world where, until a few years ago, black violence was unknown. Guerrillas are operating in
South-West Africa, in Angola, in Mozambique,
and in Rhodesia. Until 1966 President Kaunda
of Zambia—opposed to violence—was successful
in denying guerrillas even passage through Zambia.
But he has been unable to resist pressures. In
this new and menacing situation Dr. Banda,
President of Malawi, is in an anomalous position.
He has ranged himself with the White Suprema-
cists against the guerrillas by opening diplomatic
relations with South Africa. He has become a
Black ally of the White Front.

Rhodesia.—*See* Part II.

THE UNITED STATES.
Assassination of Kennedy.

The Assassination of President Kennedy in
November 1963 at Dallas, Texas, shocked the
entire world. The world recognised the growing
mastery which this young man had shown during
his three years of office in leadership and commitment to policies which promised increasing
conciliation among nations. His youthfulness

had galvanised hope in a world in which political decisions were so widely in the hands of leaders past their prime. He was the youngest elected American President (43) when he succeeded Eisenhower at the White House in January 1961, Eisenhower being then America's oldest President. Kennedy had had difficulties with Congress; and it was reassuring, therefore, that Lyndon B. Johnson, who as Vice-President automatically succeeded Kennedy, should have had the reputation of being a skilful negotiator in Congressional matters.

Cuba and the United States.

In 1961 the United States broke off diplomatic relations with Cuba with whom relations had been strained since the Castro revolution of 1959. Shortly afterwards two U.S. aeroplanes, but manned by Cubans, attacked the principal military bases near Havana, the capital. Two days later 1,500 invaders, Cuban exiles—armed, trained and largely controlled by U.S. agencies—landed on the island but were driven back. The United States intelligence service had assumed that the Cuban people would rise against Dr. Castro directly they heard of the landing. Controversy broke out in the States. Confidence in the new Kennedy administration was shaken for the affair was fundamentally alien to the American character. Relations were more bitter than ever, and, by the end of 1961, Cuba became a Communist state in the full sense.

The Crisis of the Autumn of 1962.

The world came to the brink of war during the last week of October 1962. President Kennedy had pledged the United States to take measures to oppose the creation of offensive military power in Cuba. On 22 October, upon alleged evidence of offensive Soviet missile sites there, he announced a blockade of ships (or more precisely a quarantine of ships) carrying weapons to Cuba. Some Soviet ships altered course thus avoiding a direct confrontation. The United Nations made proposals to both sides in preparation for talks; and shortly afterwards Khrushchev decided to dismantle Soviet missile bases in Cuba and ship " offensive weapons " back to the Soviet Union, the United States agreeing to give assurances against an invasion of Cuba which had been threatened.

The Presidential Election, 1968.

The mid-term Congressional elections of 1966 rehabilitated the Republican Party which had been so sundered by the rout of Goldwater in 1964. It chose as its Presidential candidate Richard Nixon (who had once been Vice-President and a Presidential candidate). On the Democratic side the candidature of Lyndon Johnson was first challenged by Senator Eugene McCarthy, who took his stand upon the criticism of America's war in Vietnam, and by Senator Robert Kennedy who was later assassinated. The President announced to the nation on 31 March that he would initiate peace moves in Vietnam and lay down the presidency in January. This dramatic turn of events threw the presidential race into confusion. Vice-President Humphrey then entered the lists to become the chosen candidate for the Democratic Party. It was one of the most closely contested presidential elections in American history, Nixon, the Republican candidate, having a majority of only 499,704 over Humphrey in a total poll of 72 million. Although securing only a small majority of the popular vote Nixon obtained 301 votes in the Electoral College against Humphrey's 191. In January 1969 he became the 37th President of the United States.

The Nixon Administration.

President Nixon's second State of the Union message on 25 February 1971, was in fact a comprehensive statement on U.S. foreign policy. On Vietnam, he pointed out the reduction in American forces from 500,000 to under 300,000; a reduction in the casualty rate from 278 to over 50 deaths a week, and the halving of the cost of

the war to American taxpayers. The President maintained that the extension of the conflict into Cambodia in 1970 had conclusively demonstrated " not only the tactical success of the operations but also their strategic purpose in reducing U.S. involvement in Vietnam."

The Nixon Doctrine.

The 65,000-word document contained also a tentative assessment of this policy,which involves the restriction of aid for friends and allies overseas who are victims of aggression or internal subversion, to military or economic aid but not, unless treaty obligations require it, U.S. troops. Mr. Nixon commented: " The Nixon Doctrine is a philosophy of invigorated partnership, not a synonym for American withdrawal." Its positive achievements, he said, were evidenced by the reduction of troops in Korea, Japan, Okinawa and Thailand.

Defence.

Mr. Nixon said that a fresh review of the need for the Safeguard anti-ballistic missile defence system had recently been completed. Defence secretary, Mr. Melvin Laird, would ask Congress for funds to finance the third stage of the project. This, as some observers were quick to point out, in spite of a slowdown in the deployment by the Soviet Union of SS–9 missiles, and the continuing SALT talks. *See also* C20(2).

The Problem of Violence.

The two final reports of the President's National Committee on the Causes and Prevention of Violence, set up by President Johnson in 1968 after the assassination of Senator Robert Kennedy, were issued in 1969. Participating in the studies were historians, political scientists, anthropologists, psychiatrists, psychologists, sociologists, and lawyers. The first report, issued in June 1969, said that Americans had " become a rather bloody-minded people in both action and reaction " and that " in total magnitude of strife the United States ranks first among the 17 Western democracies and since 1948 had been one of the half-dozen most tumultuous nations in the world." In suggesting methods to overcome violence in society the final report issued in December 1969 stated: " The way in which we can make the greatest progress toward reducing violence in America, is by taking the actions necessary to improve the conditions of family and community life for all who live in our cities, and especially for the poor who are concentrated in the ghetto slums. . . ." The report concluded: " When in man's long history other great civilisations fell, it was less often from external assault than from internal decay. . . . While serious external dangers remain, the graver threats today are internal: haphazard urbanisation, racial discrimination, disfiguring of the environment, unprecedented interdependence, the dislocation of human identity and motivation created by an affluent society—all resulting in a rising tide of individual and group violence. The greatness and durability of most civilisations has been finally determined by how they have responded to these challenges from within. Ours will be no exception."

THE THREAT OF NUCLEAR CONFLICT.

Terms Used.

A deterrent is a weapons system capable of causing such a degree of destruction to an attacker that it would be too high a price for him to pay for any advantages sought. Of course, the attacker may not know what destruction the deterrent could cause, so that what is important is not the owner's estimate of his deterrent but the potential aggressor's estimate of it. Furthermore, deterrent forces must be able to strike back after an aggressor's missile attack. So there is a distinction between first and second strike weapons. The nuclear deterrent is said to be the ultimate deterrent, because nuclear weapons are the most advanced form of weapon.

The nuclear or thermonuclear bomb means a bomb or a missile with an explosive power measured in megatons, *i.e.*, one million times more powerful than bombs used during the Second World War. A ten megaton bomb contains the equivalent of a train of railway wagons filled with high explosive stretching from London to New York—and of course fall-out with its genetic effects.

The independent bomb. Independence, in this context, means the right and ability to launch a force alone against an aggressor. For this it is necessary to own and control thermonuclear weapons and be able to deliver them. The ability to deliver weapons, without which they are useless as a deterrent, raises crucial difficulties.

It is argued that the bomb, like earlier types of armament, is the ultimate guarantee of the nation's security; that without it we should not reach the conference table with other great powers; that it gives us freedom of action and, as such, is a safeguard against the possibility of a change in American policies which might leave us unprotected. The facts and policy of an independent nuclear deterrent have been seriously challenged.

ABM is the anti-ballistics missile defence system, whereby missiles are launched to destroy the missiles of the enemy—anti-missile missiles. Both the U.S.S.R. and U.S.A. are developing an ABM system.

MIRV is the American multiple independent re-entry vehicle which when it re-enters the atmosphere fires off up to 10 warheads, each of them aimed with precision at a different target. Its purpose is to penetrate an anti-missile defence.

SS-9 is the large Soviet missile with a warhead capable of destroying the American Minuteman forces.

Other terms. *Escalation* is a term used for the belief that once a conflict begins which involves nuclear powers, the contesting parties are riding on an escalator from which there is no escape and rising to an all-out thermonuclear war. A weapon is said to be *credible* when it is trustworthy and it can be believed in for its purposes: thus it is sometimes said that the U.K. manned bomber force is credible only for a first strike. *Conventional* weapons and forces are other than nuclear. Atomic devices are described as *tactical* when they are in support of ground forces and *strategic* when they are part of an all-out major strike force.

The Partial Nuclear Test-Ban Treaty.

This important treaty was signed in Moscow in August 1963 between Britain, the U.S.A., and the U.S.S.R. who undertook not to conduct nuclear tests in three out of four possible spheres—in the atmosphere, in outer space and under water. The fourth possibility—underground tests—was not touched by the Treaty, but it declares that agreement on such tests remains a desirable aim. There has been little hope of extending the test-ban treaty to underground explosions, despite the appeal of the United States to Russia to agree. The U.S. and Britain still disagree with Russia over the question of identifying the nature of all underground explosions. The Western Powers insist that no foolproof method has yet been devised and they cannot therefore accept a ban on nuclear underground explosions without a limited number of on the spot inspections. But this is just what Russia is opposed to, on the grounds that this would amount to espionage.

Treaty to Prevent Spread of Nuclear Weapons.

Ever since 1960 there had been talks on how to prevent the proliferation of the bomb and the round of talks, which ended in August 1966, finished without any substantial new progress. The stumbling block was Russia's suspicions that despite declarations by America the arrangements to be made for the future of NATO would give Germany a finger on the nuclear trigger. Talks were resumed at the 18-power Conference at Geneva in February, 1967 where a draft treaty was tabled by the U.S. and U.S.S.R. By March 1968 a single text, sponsored by both the U.S.S.R. and U.S. emerged, containing a number of additions to meet at least some of the demands that had been put forward by the non-nuclear Powers. This joint U.S.–Soviet draft treaty was sent to the UN General Assembly where it was adopted in June by 95 votes to 4, with 21 abstentions. One of the countries that voted against was India—the American-Soviet joint offer of guarantees did not appear to provide the cast-iron protection that India might like against China.

The Nuclear Non-Proliferation Treaty flowing from this agreed draft was signed in London, Moscow, and Washington on 1 July 1968. Britain was the first nuclear weapon power to ratify the treaty on 27 November 1968. It came into force on 5 March 1970.

Nuclear Missile Race.

America's decision to enter the anti-ballistic missile defence system was announced in September 1967 after the Russians had already begun work on their ABM system around Moscow. Under the old plan there were to be ABM sites around some 15 to 20 cities including Boston, Chicago, Seattle, and San Francisco. But there was strong protest from American civilians who were against spending money on more weapons when so much needed to be done in urban development. The present modified system is designed to protect the Minuteman sites. It was described as essentially a " safeguard " programme to strengthen the American deterrent. At the same time the U.S. is increasing its offensive capability by improving the accuracy of its MIRVs as a counter to the powerful Russian SS-9s. *See also* Defence, C19.

Strategic Arms Limitation Talks.

These talks, begun in Helsinki in 1969, were resumed hopefully in 1970. Moscow did not obstruct U.S. moves to start peace talks on the Middle East. But U.S. distrust of the Soviet Union was apparent again by the end of the year. It was a year which has seen the failing of any prospect of an early agreement. Observers say that the two sides are still far apart, but little of the substance of the talks has been revealed.

Outer Space for Peaceful Developments.

An international treaty to preserve outer space for peaceful purposes was completed in December 1966. It was described by President Johnson as " the most important arms control development since the limited test-ban treaty of 1963." Mr. Johnson first proposed such a treaty in May 1966 since when there had been extensive talks between the U.S. and Russia, the only two powers which are seriously involved in space research. The drafting of the treaty was prepared by the United Nations. It provides for rights of exploration in space for all countries; no claims of sovereignty over celestial bodies; no orbiting of weapons of mass destruction (already provided for in an earlier UN resolution); the preservation of space and all celestial bodies for peaceful purposes; and other procedures for peaceful co-operation among nations in space and in the exploration of space.

Seabed Treaty.

A treaty was signed in February 1971 by the three nuclear powers, Britain, the U.S., and Russia, and by 64 other countries, banning nuclear weapons from the seabed.

II. POLITICAL STRUCTURES AND INSTITUTIONS

HOW BRITAIN GOVERNS HERSELF.

1. THE BRITISH CONSTITUTION.

Strictly there is no British Constitution. There is no single document which contains all the rules regulating the operation of our system of government. Indeed many of these rules have not been written down. But this is not to say that there are no constitutional rules. Some are to be found in Acts of Parliament, such as the Representation of the People Acts and the Government of Ireland Act of 1920, but these have no special validity which distinguish them from Acts which relate to less important aspects of our national life. Even those which have never been written down can be fairly clearly delineated at any particular time. Therefore, although the task is made more difficult by the absence of a formal constitution, it is still possible to outline the working of our system of government.

One consequence of the lack of a written constitution has been the gradual evolution of the system over the centuries without any sharp breaks in continuity. Thus, although there have been fundamental changes, for instance in the role of the monarch, many of these changes have not been recorded in any formal manner. Survivals from past ages remain to confuse the student such that it is necessary to distinguish between what Bagehot, writing in the 19th cent., called the " efficient " and " dignified " elements, those parts which were important in the actual running of the country and those parts which remained in existence but now only had a symbolic role.

It is not possible to attach a single label to our system of government which serves to distinguish it from others. A number of labels—monarchical, parliamentary, unitary, and democratic—provide a reasonably accurate short description: monarchical in the sense that the Queen is Head of State although she now only plays a formal part in the conduct of the government, acting always on the advice of her ministers; parliamentary both in the sense that Parliament is the sovereign law-making body and that the government is formed out of Parliament and dependent on its continuing support; unitary in the sense that Parliament is ultimately responsible for all parts of the United Kingdom although it may have chosen to delegate some of its powers to other institutions; and democratic in the sense that the House of Commons is elected on a basis of universal adult suffrage.

In the absence of the safeguard of a written constitution, democracy is preserved by the ordinary law, by the political organisation of the people, by custom and by rights which depend on the capacity of the people to sustain them. It is manifested in universal adult suffrage, the rule of the majority and the right to oppose. Thus all citizens, male and female, over the age of eighteen have the right to elect their own member of Parliament and to vote in local elections. Secondly, it is accepted that the majority has the right to rule subject to a number of safeguards, in particular the right of the minority to oppose. This consideration is vital to a true democracy and opposition is so essentially a part of our system that the Leader of the Opposition is paid a salary by the Government.

Although their functions overlap, the three organs of government are easily distinguishable:

    (i) The legislature, consisting of the Queen in Parliament.

    (ii) The executive, consisting of the Cabinet and other ministers in charge of government departments staffed by civil servants, local authorities, and a number of statutory boards, such as the National Coal Board and the Post Office, responsible for the administration of particular services.

    (iii) The Judiciary.

2. CENTRAL GOVERNMENT.

A. STRUCTURE.

I. THE QUEEN.

The Queen's tenure of the Crown holds for life (unless she abdicates), it is hereditary and it is held by statutory right. The Queen is a constitutional monarch; she took an oath at her Coronation to rule according to the laws and customs of the people. In law, she is head of the executive, an integral part of the legislature and the head of the judiciary as well as being commander-in-chief of the armed forces and temporal head of the Church of England. Thus the Queen appoints the prime minister and legally other ministers only assume office on receiving their seals of office from the Queen. Equally, her assent is necessary before a bill, passed by the House of Commons and the House of Lords, becomes an Act of Parliament. In practice, however, the Queen's role is now purely formal. She reigns but she does not rule. She has no freedom of choice in the selection of a prime minister and the power of veto of legislation is never exercised. In all important respects she acts only on the advice of her ministers. In effect the United Kingdom is governed by Her Majesty's Government in the name of the Queen. However, the Queen still plays an important role socially as the Head of State. Member countries of the Commonwealth (except Malaysia, Lesotho, Swaziland, Tonga and those which are republics) owe allegiance to the Queen and she is represented by a resident Governor-General. All members of the Commonwealth recognise the Queen as Head of the Commonwealth.

II. PARLIAMENT.

Parliament consists of the Queen, the House of Lords and the House of Commons. Collectively they form the legislature. Over the centuries the balance between the three elements has changed such that the Queen only remains a part of the legislature in a formal sense and that the House of Commons, as the popularly elected lower House, has established its paramountcy over the House of Lords, composed of lords spiritual and lords temporal. The maximum life of a Parliament is five years but, on the advice of the prime minister, the Queen may dissolve Parliament and issue a proclamation calling for the election of a new Parliament. Parliament is adjourned from day to day while in session. At the end of a session (usually 12 months in length) it is prorogued. At the expiry of its life it is dissolved.

(a) The Parties.

To understand the operation of our system of government it is essential to appreciate the importance of the party system. The party system emerged in the latter half of the seventeenth century as Parliament gained the right to be the law-making body. Since then there has basically been a two-party system, at different times Cavaliers and Roundheads, Tories and Whigs, Conservatives and Liberals, and, since the 1930s, Conservatives and Labour. Parties exist to form governments and the path to this goal lies in the House of Commons, for the party which obtains a majority of seats has the right to have its leaders form the government. The other party forms Her Majesty's Opposition. To this end parties are highly disciplined and coherent organisations. Once elected the majority's main function is to sustain the government in power. The minority accepts that, because of the rigidity of the party system, it is unlikely to defeat the government in the Commons and therefore sees its role as one of criticising government policy and setting forth an alternative programme which it hopes will win the support of the electorate at the next election. Thus the party system is a major explanation of the relationship between the executive and the legislature and of the role of Parliament.

(b) The House of Lords.

The House of Lords is the oldest second chamber in the world and the most hereditary in its character. It is composed of the lords temporal and the lords spiritual. The former includes all peers who inherited their titles and who have not disclaimed their peerages under the Peerage Act 1963, all peers created for their own life-times under the provisions of the Life Peerages Act 1958 and the Lords of Appeal appointed to assist the House in its judicial duties. The lords spiritual are the 26 most senior bishops. The hereditary element is still large but of declining importance especially as a result of the more frequent attendance of the life peers and peeresses. This has tended to reduce the overwhelming majority which the Conservative party used to enjoy and which constitutes a threat to legislation in the final year of a Labour government. However, the unrepresentative character of the House of Lords has limited its usefulness. Its role is to ease the work-load of an over-burdened House of Commons but not to thwart its will. It still performs a useful function in the legislative process by examining some bills in detail and initiating bills on non-controversial subjects but its part is limited by the Parliament Acts of 1911 and 1949 (see Legislation below). It also serves as the highest Court of Appeal. Finally the House of Lords is a forum where men and women, distinguished in all fields of national life, can discuss issues of importance free from the reins of party discipline.

(c) The House of Commons.

The House of Commons is a representative assembly consisting of 630 M.P.s elected by simple majority in single-member constituencies. Although our system of government is rightly described as parliamentary, this does not mean that Parliament governs. Because of the party system the initiative in government lies elsewhere—in the Cabinet. But Parliament, and especially the Commons, has important functions to play not only as the assembly to which the government is ultimately responsible but also in legitimising legislation, in voting money and in acting as a body in which complaints may be raised.

1. Legislation.—The law of the United Kingdom consists of common law, statute law and equity (see D7–8). Statute law is that part which is made by Parliament and enshrined in Acts of Parliament or statutes of the realm. Any member of Parliament may present a bill after giving formal notice, provided that it does not propose the expenditure of public money, but the principal bills are introduced by the government based upon its programme outlined at the beginning of each session in the Queen's Speech. In certain cases it is customary for the government to consult interests affected before publicly announcing the details of proposed legislation. In many cases the government will publish either a Green Paper which sets out proposals which are still in a formative stage and to which the government is not committed, or a White Paper which outlines the basic objectives of policy and describes the framework in which it is believed the policy should develop. Where legislation is complex and affects many people this pre-legislative consultative process can be very important.

Bills may originate in either House, unless they deal with finance or representation when they are always introduced in the Commons. The First Reading is just a formality. The House begins its examination at the Second Reading when the general principles are debated and voted. If they are approved, the bill is then referred for detailed clause-by-clause examination either to a standing committee or by a committee of the Whole House. (see Committees of the House below). After the Committee Stage comes the Report Stage when the House considers the bill as reported to it by the committee and decides whether any further changes in individual clauses should be made. The final stage is the Third Reading when the House considers the bill as a whole and votes whether, as amended, it should become law. If passed, it is sent to the Lords where it must go through the same stages. Once passed by both Houses the bill is sent to the Queen for Royal Assent.

The Lords cannot require the Commons to agree to amendments; nor can they delay a bill indefinitely. They have no power in respect of money bills; and since the passing of the Parliament Act of 1949 any other public bill which has been passed in the Commons in two successive sessions may be presented for Royal Assent without the consent of the Lords provided that a year has elapsed between the date of the Second Reading of the bill in the Commons and the date on which it was finally passed in that House.

2. Money Functions of the Commons.—The second function of the Commons (and one of its earliest in history) is to provide the State with money. The government cannot raise money by taxation (or in any other way) or spend money without the authority of Parliament; and this power of authority belongs exclusively to the Commons. The House can vote money only on the demand and on the responsibility of a minister of the Crown. The financial procedures of the House are discussed in **Public Expenditure Procedure** below.

3. Critical Functions of the Commons.—There are a number of opportunities for the Opposition and the Government's own back-benchers to criticise government policy. They can question ministers on the floor of the House and have the right to ask a supplementary question to the reply. They can table motions for debate which may help to mould public opinion. They can speak in debates and can raise issues which do not involve public expenditure on the adjournment, or under the 10-minute rule, or by promoting private members' bills (subject to success in the ballot for places). Ultimately this position is based on the ability of the Commons to withdraw its support from a government, by voting a motion of no confidence which would entail its resignation. If it resigns then a general election, probably geared to the issue in question, will result if the prime minister advises the Queen to dissolve Parliament. But a defeat on a motion of confidence does not necessarily result in a general election if an alternative government based on a majority of members is readily available. Because of the predominance of two parties, it is many years since such a situation has arisen in this country. Should such conditions recur, however, back-bench M.P.s would find they were able to exercise considerable powers which for a long time have lain dormant.

To assist it in its critical role Parliament has, since 1967, had a new officer, the Parliamentary Commissioner for Administration, commonly known as the Ombudsman. His function is to investigate complaints of maladministration which are referred to him by M.P.s on behalf of their constituents. In establishing such a post, the House recognised that there were deficiencies in the method of investigating by questions and letters to ministers.

4. Committees of the House.—The House of Commons uses committees to assist it in its work in a number of different ways:

1. Standing Committees.—A standing committee is a miniature of the House itself, reflecting its party composition, and consists of between 20 and 50 M.P.s. Its function is to examine the Committee Stage of legislation. Some bills are not sent to a standing committee but are examined by a committee of the Whole House which consists of all M.P.s but working under special rules of procedure, for instance enabling an M.P. to speak more than once to the same question.

2. Select Committees.—A select committee is a body with special powers and privileges to which the House has delegated its authority in a special way for the purpose of discovering information, examining witnesses, sifting evidence and drawing up conclusions which are reported to the House. As well as ad hoc select committees there are a number of sessional select committees which are almost permanent bodies (such as the Committee of Public Accounts, the Estimates Committee and the Committee of Privileges). (*See* **Specialised Committees, C24(2)**).

(3) **Joint Committees.**—A joint committee consists of members of both Houses. It is really a select committee of the Commons deliberating with a select committee of the Lords and is used to save duplication of effort, usually on uncontentious matters.

(4) **Private Bill Committees.**—A private bill is a special kind of legislation conferring particular powers on any person or body of persons, such as local authorities, in excess of the general law. Private Bill committees deal with the Committee Stage of such bills.

III. THE EXECUTIVE.

The executive work of central government is performed by the prime minister and the other ministers of the Crown. The power of executive action is not given to a government department as a corporate body but to the minister individually who is responsible for the exercise of his duties legally to the Queen and politically to Parliament. All ministers must be members of either the Commons or the Lords.

At the head of the government structure is the Cabinet which is responsible for defining the broad lines of policy of the government and for coordinating its work in different fields. It consists of the leading members of the majority party in the Commons, selected by the prime minister, most of whom are heads of government departments which are staffed by civil servants and responsible for the implementation of government policy in particular fields. In addition there are usually a number of ministers without departmental responsibilities. Its normal size is about 20. Although legally the Cabinet has no corporate constitutional existence, ministers being individually responsible for the exercise of governmental powers, politically it is accepted that the Cabinet is collectively responsible for government policy. Thus the Cabinet acts as one man and a minister who disagrees with the Cabinet must either resign or remain silent.

The head of the government is the prime minister. He is the leader of the majority party in the House of Commons and is responsible for choosing the other members of the government. He takes the chair at meetings of the Cabinet and, while he has few specific responsibilities, not having a department of his own (although the present Prime Minister is also Minister for the Civil Service), he takes a lead on most of the important aspects of government policy. It is now argued by some commentators that the prime minister is so powerful that he is able to dominate his Cabinet such that they are his servants rather than his colleagues.

Although both the Cabinet and the office of prime minister have long histories it is only recently that they have been given formal recognition in law. The fundamental rules of the working of the executive remain informal and within limits vary according to political circumstances.

1. The Civil Service.

The Civil Service is the body of permanent officials who, working in the different departments and ministries, administer the policy of the central government. It consists of some 700,000 people (2·7 per cent of the working population) of whom 490,000 are non-industrial civil servants and the rest industrial workers in places such as the Royal Ordnance Factories and the Royal Naval Dockyards. It is important to realise that seven out of every ten civil servants work outside London, mainly in the regional and local offices of departments such as Health and Social Security, Employment, and Inland Revenue.

The political head of each department is a minister. Very often the minister has no special knowledge or experience in the field to which he is appointed and his tenure of office may be fairly short-lived. Great responsibility therefore falls on the shoulders of the permanent civil servants in his department. They have to ensure that he receives all the relevant facts on which to base decisions and usually he will seek their advice before reaching a decision. The precise relationship between a minister and his senior civil service advisers is a complex and subtle one. On the one hand they are entirely his servants in that he alone is responsible for everything that goes on in the department and he alone can be called to account in Parliament. Civil servants remain largely anonymous and their relationship with their minister is a confidential one. On the other hand the expertise and experience of senior civil servants is such that he depends on them and they can dominate a minister who is not sure of his own mind and who is not backed by the Cabinet as a whole. However, the distinguishing feature of the British Civil Service is that at all levels it is non-political in the sense that it serves both political parties impartially.

The non-industrial Civil Service is divided at present into occupational groups known as " classes." On the administrative side there are three Service-wide classes, The Administrative Class (2,800), the Executive Class (51,500) and the Clerical Class (155,000).

(a) The Fulton Reforms.

The most recent inquiry into the Civil Service was carried out by the Fulton Committee who in 1968 reported that while the Civil Service had many strengths, it was felt to be inadequate in six main respects. These were:

    (*a*) It was still too much based on the philosophy of the amateur (or " generalist " or " all-rounder "). This was most evident in the Administrative Class, which holds the dominant position in the service.

    (*b*) The present system of classes in the service (there are over 1,400, each for the most part with its own separate pay and career structure) seriously impeded its work.

    (*c*) Scientists, engineers, and members of other specialist classes were frequently given neither the full responsibilities and opportunities nor the corresponding authority they ought to have.

    (*d*) Too few civil servants were skilled managers.

    (*e*) There was not enough contact between the service and the community it is there to serve.

    (*f*) Personnel management and career planning were inadequate.

The Committee went on to recommend:

(1) The establishment of a new Civil Service Department to absorb the recruitment and selection functions of the present Civil Service Commission, and to take over the responsibilities for central management of the Service at present carried by the Treasury, but on an expanded scale. The new Department to be accountable to the prime minister with day-to-day responsibility delegated to a non-departmental minister of Cabinet rank. The official head of the new Department (the Permanent Secretary) to be designated Head of the Home Civil Service.

(2) The abolition of the class system in Civil Service. All classes to be abolished and replaced by a single managerial class of civil servant combining the present Administrative and Executive classes. A unified grading structure to cover the entire Civil Service, each post graded by the technique of job evaluation.

(3) The development of greater professionalism in the Service. Professional and technical officers (*i.e.*, specialists) to be given more training in management and opportunities for greater responsibility and wider careers. Administrators to develop a fuller professionalism by specialising, especially in their early years, in particular areas of government, *e.g.*, in economic and financial affairs or social policy.

(4) The establishment of a Civil Service College to provide training courses in management and organisation, and in research. Not restricted to civil servants.

(5) In addition to the permanent secretary, who has overall responsibility, under the minister, for the running of a department, the minister should also have a senior policy adviser who would normally be head of the planning and research unit to be set up within departments for major long-term policy planning. The main task of the new adviser would be to look to and prepare for the future and to ensure that current policy decisions were taken with as full recognition as possible of likely future developments.

(6) The delegation to departments of a larger rôle in recruitment and the speeding up of re-cruitment procedures.

(7) The devotion of more resources to the career management of all civil servants so that they have the opportunity of advancing on their merits.

(8) The encouragement of greater mobility between the Civil Service and other employments through a reform of the restrictions on the trans-fer of pensions. The Committee recommend an expanded " late entry," temporary appointments, short-term exchanges of staff, freer movement out of the Service.

(b) Implementation.

(1) The Civil Service Department was estab-lished in November 1968 on the lines proposed by the Committee.

(2) The Government accepts the abolition of classes and the introduction of a unified grading structure. As interim measures while such a structure is developed, jobs at the top of the Service have been made open to all classes, and on 1 January 1971 the Administrative, Executive and Clerical Classes were to be merged.

(3) The Civil Service College started running courses in autumn 1970 in two residential centres at Sunningdale Park and Edinburgh. In addition the Centre for Administrative Studies in Regent's Park has been expanded.

IV. THE JUDICIARY.

The judiciary is responsible for the interpreta-tion of statutes and the determination of the com-mon law. Judicial functions are exercised quite separately from legislative or executive functions. However there are some links in personnel. Judges are appointed by the Queen acting on the advice of ministers but to safeguard their inde-pendence all senior judges can only be removed by the Sovereign on an address presented by both Houses of Parliament. The Lord Chancellor, the head of the judiciary, is the only political appointment who, as a member of the Cabinet, resigns his position with a change of government. He also serves as Speaker of the House of Lords. The Lords of Appeal are members of the House of Lords. See English Law, D7-9.

B. REFORM OF GOVERNMENT.

1. Machinery of Government.

In October 1970 the Government published a White Paper entitled *The Reorganisation of Central Government* (Cmnd. 4506), the first official publication on the machinery of government since the Report of the Haldane Committee of 1918. It proposed a number of changes in the division of functions between departments and the establish-ment of a new central policy review staff. Con-tinuing the developments of recent years towards the unification of functions within single depart-ments, as seen, for instance, in the Ministry of Defence and the Department of Health and Social Security, the White Paper proposed the merging of the Ministry of Technology and the Board of Trade in a new Department of Trade and Industry and the creation of a new Department of

the Environment by integrating the Ministry of Housing and Local Government, the Ministry of Transport, and the Ministry of Public Building and Works. A number of other minor changes in ministerial responsibilities and departmental organisation were also proposed. By the end of 1970 all these changes had been effected.

The other most important feature of the White Paper was the establishment of a small, multi-disciplinary central review staff within the Cabinet Office. Under the supervision of the Prime Minister it is to work for ministers collectively outlining for the Cabinet as a whole the wider implications of every Government programme. A novel concept in British Government it is not possible at this stage to predict how it will operate. The intention, however, was that the review staff should act as a counter-balancing force for mem-bers of the Cabinet when considering the proposals of individual ministers who had the backing of their departmental staffs. The Prime Minister has appointed Lord Rothschild to head the new unit.

2. Public Expenditure Procedure.

Since 1945 growing attention has been paid to the planning of public expenditure both as a result of its increasing size and because of its vital role in the management of the economy. New tech-niques for the planning and examination of public expenditure have been adopted by the spending departments and by the Treasury. However, Parliament's scrutiny of government spending has not kept pace with these developments. The House of Commons still considers expenditure on an annual cash basis, its procedure being centred around the annual voting of Supply. Most government expenditure, however, requires planning over a number of years ahead. The House has no machinery for examining the long-term priorities and resource implications of public expenditure.

This situation was examined by the Select Committee on Procedure during the 1968–69 Session. It received a large amount of written evidence, including a Green Paper published by the government, *Public Expenditure: A New Presentation* (Cmnd. 4017). This announced that the government intended to publish an annual White Paper, towards the end of the calendar year, which would present to Parliament the results of the government's consideration of the prospects for public expenditure, bringing out the main implications for resources over the period ahead. It was intended that the White Paper should be debated and that this annual discussion should come to occupy as important a place as is now occupied by the annual Budget debate. The Report of the Select Committee in July 1969 welcomed the government's proposals and also recommended that the Estimates Committee, at present operating under restricting terms of reference and precluded from direct examination of policy, be changed to a Select Committee on Expenditure with general terms of reference, " to consider public expenditure".

The first such White Paper was published in December 1969 as *Public Expenditure 1968–69 to 1973–74* (Cmnd. 4234). It set out the govern-ment's plans for public expenditure for the finan-cial year 1969–70 and for the next two years. It also gave allocations of expenditure on a pro-visional and approximate basis for 1972–3 and 1973–4. The White Paper was debated in the House of Commons on 21 and 22 January 1970. The proposal for a Select Committee on Expendi-ture was considered by the new government in 1970 and its conclusions published as a Green Paper (*see* below).

3. Specialised Committees.

In 1966, as one of the procedural reforms intro-duced by Mr. Crossman, the Leader of the House, the government proposed the establishment of a number of specialised select committees to in-vestigate particular areas of policy or the activities of particular departments. Between 1966 and 1970 six such committees were appointed and they produced a large number of reports. On taking office, the Conservative government announced that it would review this experiment, especially in the light of the Report of the Select Committee on Procedure which recommended the establishment of a Select Committee on Expenditure to replace the Estimates Committee.

In October 1970 the results of this review were published as a Green Paper *Select Committees of the House of Commons* (Cmnd. 4507). It proposed a dual system of some specialised committees and an expenditure committee. On the one hand the Select Committee on Nationalised Industries was to be retained along with a number of specialised committees dealing with particular subjects but not with individual departments. The Estimates Committee was also to be enlarged and transformed into an Expenditure Committee which would focus not on the Supply Estimates but on the longer-term and wider implications of public expenditure as a whole and which would not be barred from considering the policies behind the figures. It would be organised into sub-committees covering different subject areas. It was intended to establish the Expenditure Committee early in 1971. At the end of 1970 select committees on Nationalised Industries, Race Relations and Immigration, Science and Technology, and Scottish Affairs had been appointed.

4. Commission on the Constitution.

In February 1969 a Royal Commission was appointed under the chairmanship of Lord Crowther with the following terms of reference: " To examine the present functions of the central legislature and government in relation to the several countries, nations and regions of the United Kingdom: to consider, having regard to the development in local government organisation and in the administrative and other relationships between the various parts of the United Kingdom and to the interests of the prosperity and good government of our people under the Crown, whether any changes are desirable in these functions or otherwise in present constitutional and economic relations; to consider also, whether any changes are desirable in the constitutional and economic relationships between the United Kingdom and the Channel Islands and the Isle of Man." It is expected to report in late 1971 or early 1972.

C. THE WORKING OF GOVERNMENT 1970.

Two of the most important policies advocated by the Conservative Party in Opposition and during the election campaign were reform of industrial relations and reductions in public expenditure. Immediately on assuming office steps were taken to put these policies into practice.

1. Industrial Relations Reform.

Industrial relations have been in the forefront of political controversy for a number of years, particularly since the Report of the Donovan Commission in 1968. In 1969 the Labour government proposed an Industrial Relations Bill based on its White Paper, *In Place of Strife* (Cmnd. 3623), but after prolonged discussions with the TUC it agreed to abandon it in favour of the TUC's pledge to take action itself to deal with strikes. At the time the Conservative party announced that they did not regard this solution as adequate and during the election campaign they made clear their intention to introduce a comprehensive bill during the first session of the new Parliament.

Their proposals were published as a Consultative Document by the Department of Employment in October 1970. In some respects they resemble those of the Labour government, for instance in cases of national emergency there is provision for a compulsory cooling-off period and for the holding of strike ballots, but in other respects they differ substantially. The two basic principles behind their proposals are that collective agreements should be legally binding and enforceable, unless the parties to the agreement expressly declare otherwise, and secondly that a Code of Industrial Relations Practice should be drawn up which would list a number of unfair industrial

actions. To enforce these provisions the government proposes to establish two new statutory agencies and to strengthen a third. A new system of courts for dealing with industrial relations questions is to be created consisting of a National Industrial Relations Court, of equivalent status to the High Court, and at a lower level of Industrial Tribunals. The courts would be able to award compensation, up to a limit of £100,000 in the case of large trade unions, and they could make orders to refrain from unfair industrial action. Secondly, a Registrar of Trade Unions and Employers' Associations is to be appointed to ensure that the two sides' rules are up to standard and are upheld. To qualify for the legal benefits and immunities under the Act, a trade union must secure authorisation by registering with the Registrar. Thirdly, the government intends to put the Commission on Industrial Relations, at present constituted as a Royal Commission, on a statutory basis and to give it new powers and added responsibilities. The government also propose that each worker should have the right both to join and not to join a union, that periods of notice of dismissal should increase with length of service, that workers should have the right of appeal to an Industrial Tribunal if they consider they have been unfairly dismissed, that the pre-entry closed shop should be outlawed and that large firms should give regular shareholders-type reports to their employees.

These proposals were contained in an Industrial Relations Bill which passed its Second Reading in the House of Commons on 15 December 1970. The government hope that the Bill will be presented for Royal Assent in July 1971 and intend that it should come into effect in 1973.

2. Cuts in Public Expenditure.

During the 1970 summer recess the Government undertook a thoroughgoing examination of the work of government and other public authorities. This review was based on a belief that the government was intervening too much in the life of the nation and that too high a proportion of the nation's resources were committed to public expenditure. Its main objectives were to reduce the sphere of government so that it could concentrate its activities and its expenditure on those tasks which it alone could perform and to enable both private industry and the individual citizen to enjoy greater freedom from government interference. The first results of this review were announced in a ministerial statement by the Chancellor of the Exchequer on 27 October 1970. The main features of the government's decisions were a more selective approach to the social services and a general withdrawal in its relations with private industry. In the former category the government proposed to end cheap welfare milk and the supply of free milk to pupils over the age of 7, to abolish the present system of housing subsidies, rents and rebates substituting a system which would give help where it was most needed, to raise the charge for school meals, to fix the charge for dental treatment at about half the cost of the service provided and to relate the charge for prescriptions more closely to their cost and as an interim measure to raise the charge to 20p per item. Some of the money saved in this way is to be spent in giving a new benefit to one of the poorest sections of the community. The Family Income Supplement is to be paid, in addition to existing benefits, to poor families with children where the wage earner is in full-time work, the level of benefit being based on a simple test of income. In the latter category the government proposed to end the Industrial Reorganisation Corporation, to discontinue the Regional Employment Premium by the end of 1974 and to abolish investment grants, replacing them with a system of tax allowances and reductions. Other cuts in public expenditure included the introduction of a system of import levies, of charges for admission to national museums and galleries and the elimination of the grant to London commuter services and to the Consumer Council. Some of the resources released in this way were to be used to increase expenditure on educational building, especially for the replacement and modernisation of primary schools, to develop the health and welfare services, especially for the elderly and the mentally handicapped, and to increase slightly the overseas aid programme.

Although some of the decisions were put into effect immediately, many were announcements of the long-term intentions of the government. *See also* Section G, Part IV, under Internal Developments.

3. Recent Legislation.

The legislative output of Parliament in 1970 was limited as a result of the dissolution in May. A number of major bills, such as the National Superannuation and Social Insurance Bill, the Ports Bill, the Commission for Industry and Manpower Bill and the Education Bill, were lost for this reason. Among the Acts which reached the statute book before the dissolution were the following:

Administration of Justice Act 1970, makes important alterations in the jurisdiction of the High Court and abolishes the power of imprisonment for civil debt. *See* D6.

Equal Pay (No. 2) Act 1970, makes discrimination in pay and terms and conditions of employment on grounds of sex illegal by the end of 1975.

Chronically Sick and Disabled Persons Act 1970, provides for a large number of measures to improve the welfare of chronically sick and disabled persons. A private member's bill, introduced by Mr. Alfred Morris, it was hailed as a charter for the disabled. In particular, it makes the provision of a number of services, formerly permissive, mandatory upon local authorities.

Local Authorities Social Services Act 1970, unifies the administration of the personal social services within each local authority area in England and Wales, thus implementing the main recommendation of the Seebohm Committee (Cmnd. 3703).

Matrimonial Proceedings and Property Act 1970, following the passage of the Divorce Reform Act in 1969, it increases the power of the courts in dealing with a spouse's property on the breakdown of a marriage, allowing the courts to re-allocate family assets. *See* D33.

Police Act 1970 and Ulster Defence Regiment Act 1970, together implement the recommendation of Lord Hunt's Advisory Committee on the Police in Northern Ireland that the police and military roles should be separated. The Acts disbanded the " B " Specials and removed military duties from the Royal Ulster Constabulary and provided for a voluntary police reserve to assist the RUC and a locally recruited part-time force under the command of GOC Northern Ireland to support the regular military forces.

Murder (Abolition of Death Penalty) Act 1965. The Act provided for the abolition of the death penalty until July 1970. In December 1969 both Houses approved resolutions extending the abolition indefinitely. *See* D10(1).

The following Acts and Orders are among those already passed by the new Parliament:

National Insurance (Old Persons' and Widows' Pensions and Attendance Allowance) Act 1970, provides retirement pensions for those who were excluded by their age from participation in the national insurance scheme which came into operation in 1948, widows' pensions for certain younger widows and an allowance for the seriously ill who require constant attention or supervision.

Parliamentary Constituencies Orders 1970, implementing the recommendations of the Boundary Commissioners.

British Standard Time Act 1968. The order which would have made British Standard Time permanent was rejected. From 1971 there will be a return to Greenwich Mean Time during the winter.

The Queen's Speech (July 1970) contained proposals to reform industrial relations, to abolish the Land Commission, to alter the administration of justice in accordance with the recommendations of the Royal Commission on Assizes and Quarter Sessions and to bring the arrangements for admitting Commonwealth citizens into Britain for employment into line with the arrangements for aliens. Among the bills which had passed their Second Reading by the end of 1970 were the Industrial Relations Bill, the Family Income Supplement Bill, the Local Government (Qualification of Members) Bill, the Misuse of Drugs Bill and the Unsolicited Goods and Services Bill.

II. LOCAL GOVERNMENT.

Local government is the creation of Parliament. The structure and boundaries of local authorities are laid down by Parliament and they may only exercise those powers which Parliament either commands or permits them to exercise. Their functions include responsibility for all education except the universities, most personal health and welfare services, public health, environmental planning, traffic and transport, in all cases subject to some central government control. England and Wales (outside the Greater London area) are at present divided into county boroughs and administrative counties. The structure, as the chart shows, is split vertically: on the one side are the administrative counties subdivided into county districts—non-county boroughs, urban districts, and rural districts, the last-named being further divided into parishes; and on the other side are the county boroughs (mostly with populations of over 75,000), local government being in the hands of one authority, the county borough council. In Scotland there are 33 county councils (two pairs being combined for certain purposes), 201 town councils (including 4 counties of cities) and 196 district councils (2 counties not being divided into districts). The Greater London area is administered by the councils of 32 London boroughs and the City of London, and by the Greater London Council.

Local Government in England and Wales

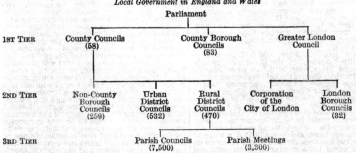

Parliament

1ST TIER	County Councils (58)		County Borough Councils (83)		Greater London Council
2ND TIER	Non-County Borough Councils (259)	Urban District Councils (532)	Rural District Councils (470)	Corporation of the City of London	London Borough Councils (32)
3RD TIER		Parish Councils (7,500)	Parish Meetings (3,300)		

1. Local Government in Greater London.

The London Government Act, 1963, involved the abolition of the London County Council and the Middlesex County Council, and parts of Essex, Surrey, Kent, and Hertfordshire have been incorporated in Greater London, which now covers the whole of the continuously developed area within the green belt. The system came fully into effect on 1 April 1965.

The London Boroughs.—There are 32 London boroughs and the population of each is between 170,000 and 340,000. Broadly speaking the new boroughs are responsible for all the important personal services such as housing, health, and welfare. Each council has a maximum of 60 directly elected councillors, plus aldermen up to one-sixth, making a maximum of 70. The councillors retire together every three years (one year after the GLC elections). The independent position of the City of London remains unchanged and it has the powers of a borough.

The Greater London Council, a directly elected body, carries out functions which need to be planned and administered over Greater London as a whole and consists of 100 councillors and 16 aldermen. The new councils in Greater London came into existence as local authorities when they were elected—the GLC on 9 April 1964, and the London borough councils on 7 May 1964—and from then until 1 April 1965 the new authorities and the old continued side by side. On 1 April 1965 the new councils took over their full functions and the older authorities ceased to exist.

Elections for the Greater London Council.—For the first three elections held in 1964, 1967, and 1970, each of the 32 London boroughs was also the electoral area and returned two, three, or four councillors, according to the size of the electorate in each area. These electoral arrangements may, however, be changed for future elections and it is possible that the number of electoral areas will be increased and will probably return one councillor only, based upon the new Parliamentary constituencies as envisaged in the London Government Act, 1963.

The Powers of London Boroughs.—Each London borough is a housing authority although the Greater London Council is the "overspill" authority. Local development plans are drawn up by the boroughs (within the framework of the overall development plan of the GLC) and the boroughs are responsible for dealing with applications for planning permission. They are wholly responsible for a wide range of personal health services and welfare services for the elderly, the sick and the handicapped, and children's services. The GLC will complete the LCC housing programme and, for the time being, inherits the LCC stock of houses (about 230,000) and will eventually transfer them to the boroughs.

Education in Greater London.—In Inner London, virtually the ex-LCC area, education is the responsibility of a special committee of the Greater London Council, the Inner London Education Authority, consisting of members of the GLC elected from the central area together with a representative of each London borough council, and of the City of London. The ILEA maintains the education service and decides the amount of money needed to be raised by precepts on Inner London borough councils and by borrowing. The education committee established by the ILEA consists of the members of the Authority together with 16 other persons chosen from people experienced in education. The unique arrangements for education in Inner London preserve the continuity of the service which has developed since 1870 as a unity without regard to local boundary divisions. In the Outer London area education is the responsibility of the borough council.

Highways and Traffic.—The GLC is the traffic authority for the whole of Greater London. "Metropolitan roads" come under the GLC and the new boroughs take the remaining roads except trunk roads which the Ministry of Transport continues to look after. In 1970 the GLC took over responsibility for London Transport.

Other Functions.—The GLC is responsible for fire and ambulance services, for refuse disposal and main sewerage. It is responsible also for places like the Royal Festival Hall, the Crystal Palace, the LCC museums, and Kenwood House.

Greater London Development Plan.—A report, *Tomorrow's London*, published by the GLC in November 1969, tells of plans to improve the quality of living within the Greater London area, while preserving the position and status of the capital. The council is concerned not only with providing better amenities for those who live and work in London, but also for those who visit the capital.

The population of Greater London declined between 1939 and 1969 from 8·6 million to 7·9 million. Ninety thousand more people leave the capital each year than come to settle there. The report says the aim is not to have the largest population in the world—" we cheerfully cede this distinction to New York, Tokyo, or São Paulo "—but to concentrate on beauty and amenity. The council affirmed its intention to preserve London's " green belt " (an area of countryside surrounding the city, in which building is severely restricted). In December 1969 the Secretary of State for Local Government and Regional Planning, Mr. Anthony Crosland, announced his intention to appoint a committee of inquiry into the Greater London Development Plan, which he described as " comprehensive, complex, and controversial."

2. Proposals for the Reform of Local Government: Report of Royal Commission.

1. England (except London).

The proposals for the reform of local government in England outside the Greater London area were published on 11 June 1969 (Cmnd. 4039). The Royal Commission was set up in 1966 under the chairmanship of Lord Redcliffe-Maud and took evidence from 2,156 witnesses. Their findings were contained in three volumes, comprising the main report, Mr. Derek Senior's substantial memorandum of dissent, and research appendices.

The structure of local government in England and Wales dates from the 1880s. The report began by pointing out the need for reform; the need for the structure of local government to catch up with the effects of scientific discovery and industrial progress which have so rapidly re-shaped our lives; and the need for local self-government to assist the individual at a time when huge unrepresentative organisations seem to control our lives. Local government should be the means whereby citizens bring their views to bear on public problems which touch most nearly to personal domestic life. There was a need for a new structure and a new map. " If local self-government withers, the roots of democracy grow dry." The Royal Commission said local government must do four things:

    (i) perform specific tasks efficiently;

    (ii) attract and hold the attention of citizens;

    (iii) develop strength to deal with central government as a partner;

    (iv) adapt itself to the changing pattern of people's lives, work, movements, shopping arrangements, etc.

It found that the present system was suffering from three major defects:

    (i) local government areas do not fit the present-day pattern of life and work in modern England. The gap will widen as social economic and technological changes quicken;

    (ii) the division between county boroughs and counties, which was intended in 1888 to reflect the separation of town and country has made the planning of development and transportation impossible. The result has often been an atmosphere of hostility between county boroughs and counties;

(iii) the division of responsibility between county councils and county district councils in the counties means that services which should be in the hands of one authority are fragmented among several. The difficulty of meeting comprehensively the needs of families and individuals is thus greatly increased.

These faults in turn make people feel local government cannot help them, make Parliament doubt the ability of local government to function effectively while the variety in type of authority makes a single local government lobby almost impossible to achieve for negotiation with the government.

The Royal Commission's solution was based on the following general principles:

(i) areas should be so defined that they enable electors and councillors to have a sense of common purpose;

(ii) areas should be based on the inter-dependence of town and country;

(iii) impersonal services (e.g., planning, transport, and major development) should be in the hands of one authority;

In these areas responsibilities would be allocated at two levels, the main metropolitan authority being responsible for planning, transport, and major development. Smaller district authorities (7 in Birmingham, 4 in Liverpool, and 9 in Manchester) would have responsibility for education, social services, health, and housing.

Below the new unitary authorities, existing councils (ranging from city councils, like Leeds, to parish councils) could remain, but their purpose would be mainly to act as a sounding-board of public opinion. In this purely advisory capacity they would have authority only in minor matters like car parks and community halls unless the new local authority agreed to devolve precise powers.

Above the new authorities would be 8 provinces with advisory powers only, unless given more on the recommendation of the Constitutional Commission, which has yet to report. They would take over the job being done by the regional economic planning councils. They would prepare provincial plans which might be binding on the local authorities. Their members would be selected by the local authorities with provision for substantial co-option and they would be unpaid.

On financial matters, the Royal Commission urged that the opportunity offered by re-organisation be taken to examine the short-

Province	No. of authorities		Area (mile²)	Population (1968)
	Unitary areas	Met. areas		
North East	5		3,639	2,749,000
Yorkshire	10		5,631	4,849,000
North-West	6	2	5,402	6,990,000
West Midlands	4	1	5,169	5,164,000
East Midlands	4		4,574	3,017,000
South-West	8		9,408	4,061,000
East Anglia	4		5,889	1,990,000
South-East (excl. Greater London)	17		10,003	9,289,000
	58	3		38,109,000

(iv) all personal services (e.g., education, social services, health, and housing), should be in the hands of one authority;

(v) if possible both the impersonal and the personal group of services should be in the hands of a single authority;

(vi) authorities should be larger than most existing county boroughs if they are to command the resources in revenue and manpower they need;

(vii) the size of authorities is bound to vary but a minimum population of 250,000 is desirable;

(viii) councillors should be able to keep in touch with electors and thus for personal services an authority ought not to exceed a million persons;

(ix) where the area required for planning and other impersonal services contains too large a population for the personal services, there should be a two-tier system established, akin to that already in operation in Greater London;

(x) wherever possible, the new system should respect the traditions and loyalties of the present system.

These principles, in application, led to the recommendation that the existing 1,210 local authorities in England (79 county boroughs, 45 county councils, 227 non-county boroughs, 449 urban districts, and 410 rural districts) should be replaced by:

58 single-tier all-purpose authorities, called unitary authorities, and

3 metropolitan authorities covering the Birmingham, Liverpool, and Manchester conurbations.

comings of present-day local government finance and to remove them. Pointing out that the Exchequer currently accounts for 52 per cent of all local government expenditure, the Royal Commission emphasised that unless local taxation of all types were reformed and expanded, the new authorities would be cramped and handicapped.

In his memorandum of dissent, Mr. Derek Senior argued that England's highly diversified community structure does not lend itself to a pattern of unitary authorities with a pre-determined range of population size. He believes that the areas suitable for the planning and execution of regional development and those for the administration of the social services have little correlation. Accordingly, he recommends that a two-level structure of local government be introduced with 35 regional development authorities controlling planning, transport, investment, police, education, and 148 second level authorities controlling health, welfare, child care, housing management, consumer protection and all other functions involving personal contact with the citizen.

Although the Conservative government does not accept the recommendations of the Royal Commission, the Secretary of State for the Environment emphasised that its report must be the starting point for any discussion of local government reform.

Government Proposals.—The Government's own proposals for reform were published as a White Paper Local Government in England (Cmnd. 4584) in February 1971. The government rejects the unitary principle which Redcliffe-Maud recommended for England, outside the metro-politan areas, and proposes to establish a two-tier system throughout the country based on 44 counties outside Greater London. If the plans are put into effect the present framework of county councils and their districts and county boroughs consisting in all of about 1200 authorities will be replaced by a uniform two-level structure of counties and districts numbering only 370 authorities. Existing county boundaries are to be retained wherever possible although certain counties such as Huntingdon and Peterborough, Hereford, Rutland and Cumberland and Westmorland will not survive as separate counties. Within the counties existing boroughs and districts will be rationalised to provide districts with resources to enable them to carry out efficiently their responsibilities. The bigger cities and towns, will retain their identities but smaller towns will be joined with associated rural areas to form new districts. Districts will continue to vary in size but the minimum population is expected to be 40,000.

All local government functions in relation to education, personal social services, highways, traffic and transport, police and fire services are to be exercised by the county authorities. The district authorities are to be responsible for housing and local amenity functions. Planning is to be divided between the two tiers, the majority of planning control decisions being taken by the district authorities within the broad planning policies established by the county authorities. A unified planning staff will advise both tiers.

A different pattern is proposed for six predominantly urban areas, the metropolitan areas, which must be treated as single entities for important functions such as land-use planning and transport. Metropolitan counties are proposed for Merseyside, South-East Lancashire and North-East Cheshire (Selnec), the West Midlands, West Yorkshire, South Yorkshire and the Tyne and Wear area and the boundaries of these areas are drawn so as to include all the main areas of continuous development and some immediately adjacent areas. Within the metropolitan counties the districts are large enough in population and resources and sufficiently compact in size to be responsible for education and personal social services.

The Government's proposals for the boundaries of the new counties everywhere and of the new districts in the metropolitan counties were published in a departmental circular issued to local authorities for consultation. Within the new counties outside the metropolitan areas, the Government intend to establish a Local Government Boundary Commission to make recommendations regarding the final pattern of the new districts.

The Government aim to introduce a bill to put its proposals into effect during the 1971–72 session. The boundaries of the counties and the metropolitan districts will be laid down in the bill and elections could be held in spring 1973. Parliament could give effect to the district boundaries by order at the end of 1972 and elections for these authorities could be held towards the end of 1973. The new councils would take over from the existing authorities on 1 April 1974.

2. Scotland.

The Royal Commission set up in 1966 under the chairmanship of Lord Wheatley published its report on 25 September 1969. Its description of the defects of the existing system made similar reading to the Maud report. The old unreformed structure had led to a loss of power at the local level, to confusion, hostility between different types of authorities, and, above all, to loss of credibility and status in the eyes of the public. The Commission considered the main requirements of a radically reformed system to be better planning, so making it possible to organise and provide better services for the public, and more effective local democracy. To this end the majority recommended the replacement of the existing 430 authorities (4 cities, 33 county councils, 21 large burghs, 176 small burghs, 196 district councils) by a two-tier system consisting of 7 regions and 37 districts.

A two-tier system of local government in Scotland, consisting of a regional level and a district level of authorities, independently elected and having their own range of functions and their own means of raising finance but working closely together in many spheres, is the main recommendation of the Commission. It also proposes that provision should be made for " neighbourhood " community councils, which would not be local

authorities proper, but would complement the local government structure.

It is proposed that the seven regional authorities (first-tier) should be responsible for the major services, *i.e.*, the major planning and related services (including industrial development, transportation and roads, water, sewerage, redevelopment, new towns, control of the countryside, and tourism); the personal social services (education, social work, and health); housing; the protective services (police, fire, and civil defence); and the impersonal services (such as refuse disposal, coast protection, weights and measures and consumer protection, registration of births, deaths and marriages, and registration of electors).

For the second tier a majority of the Commission expressed a clear preference for the "shire" level, as representative of communities " quite wide in area and relatively self-contained." At this level it recommends the creation of 37 district authorities with responsibility for local planning and related services, building control, housing improvement and ancillary housing functions, local aspects of civil defence, parks and recreation (concurrently with the regional authorities), libraries, environmental health services, and the administration of justice.

The Commission proposed that council elections should take place every four years, with elections to district and regional authorities staggered so that an election would be held every two years; that there should be one council member for each electoral division at the regional and district levels; that councillors should be paid a salary.

As in England, there were notes of dissent mainly from Miss H. Anderson M.P. (Conservative) and Mr. Russell Johnson M.P. (Liberal). These included: (i) all planning should be the responsibility of regional councils, thereby enabling the district councils to be smaller, more numerous (101 in place of 37) and closer to the public; (ii) Orkney, Shetland, and Western Isles should each become all-purpose authorities on the ground that geographically they are distinct and different from the rest of Scotland, (iii) Argyll should be included in the West Region and not the Highlands.

Government Proposals.—The Government's proposals for Scotland were published in a White Paper *Reform of Local Government in Scotland* (Cmnd. 4583). Broadly it accepts the structure of regional and district authorities recommended by the Commission. A further region, covering the Borders, has been added so that there will be 8 in all and, in order to reduce the size of some of the districts in the more remote areas, the Government proposes to increase the number from 37 to 49. The isles of Orkney and Shetland will become virtually all-purpose authorities.

The other important difference is that the district authorities are to be given additional functions in particular in relation to housing, thereby unifying responsibility for the building, management and improvement of housing.

The proposed timetable is a year behind that for England and Wales. Legislation will be introduced in the 1972–73 session, elections will be held in 1974 and the new authorities will be fully operational by 1975.

3. Wales.

Local government in Wales was not included in the terms of reference of the Redcliffe-Maud commission as plans for reform were already far-advanced. However the Labour government had difficulty in finalising these plans, producing two schemes in 1967 and 1970. The Conservative government published its proposals as a consultative document *The Reform of Local Government in Wales*. It proposes that, as in England, local government functions should be divided between 7 large counties and their districts, of which there would be 36 in all. The major differences between this structure and that proposed by the Labour government are in South-East Wales where unitary authorities centred on Cardiff, Swansea and Newport are replaced by a two-tier structure and in North Wales where an additional county is to be created. The timetable for the introduction of the new system is the same as that for England.

4. Northern Ireland.

Northern Ireland is governed under the Government of Ireland Act 1920 which created the Northern Ireland Parliament at Stormont. The Act confers on Stormont extensive powers for regulating the affairs of Northern Ireland but excludes certain matters from its jurisdiction, such as foreign relations and defence, customs and excise and income tax which remain the responsibility of the United Kingdom Parliament. Because of these reserved powers, 12 M.P.s continue to be returned by Northern Ireland constituencies to Westminster. Although in some respects this system is akin to a federal situation, the United Kingdom Parliament retains power to suspend the Government of Ireland Act.

For those matters within the jurisdiction of the Northern Ireland Parliament, the government of Northern Ireland exercises executive powers. The Queen is represented by a Governor.

Local Government—At present local government is exercised by 1 county borough council, 6 county councils, 9 non-county borough councils, 24 urban district councils, 26 rural district councils and 2 development commissions exercising municipal functions. Between 1966 and 1969 plans were agreed for reform of local government but events were overtaken by the disturbances in summer 1969 and the decision in October 1969 to transfer responsibility for housing from local government to a central housing authority. The Minister of Development appointed a Review Body which reported in June 1970. It proposed a two-tier structure similar to that recommended by the Wheatley Commission for Scotland. Stormont would be the regional authority with responsibility for education, personal social services, highways and traffic, with 26 elected district councils exercising more local functions.

THE COMMONWEALTH.

The Commonwealth.

The Commonwealth is a grouping of most of the successor states of the British Empire and is usually described, following the terms of the Statute of Westminster, 1931, as a " free association." It consists at present of 31 independent sovereign states, together with a number of dependencies, mostly small islands which are dependencies of Britain, Australia, or New Zealand. Fiji and Tonga became member states of the Commonwealth in 1970, and Western Samoa was formally admitted in the same year. Successor states of the Empire which are not part of the Commonwealth include Burma, Eire, Sudan, South Africa, and South Yemen (formerly the Federation of South Arabia).

The Nature of the Commonwealth.

The Commonwealth is not a federation, and has no central government, defence force, or judiciary. It is a grouping of states which continues to be useful to members for a wide variety of reasons. It is the only major association of states which links countries of the developed and under-developed world. A web of technical associations, education exchanges, and cultural and personal links, holds it loosely together. Geopolitically, its main segments are Britain and the three older " dominions " (Australia, New Zealand, and Canada); South Asia (India, Pakistan, Ceylon) whose peoples account for most of the quarter of the world's population who live in Commonwealth countries; and those countries of former British Africa which have not left the Commonwealth.

The Sovereign and the Commonwealth.

The Queen's legislative power in the parliaments of the Commonwealth is a formality—she reigns, though she does not rule; but she provides the element of continuity in the administration. The Queen is, therefore, Queen of the United Kingdom, Canada, Australia, New Zealand, Ceylon, Jamaica, Trinidad and Tobago, Sierra Leone, Malta, Fiji, Barbados and Mauritius, all of whom owe her allegiance, and she is the symbol of their free association in the Commonwealth. Those countries which are Republics (India, Pakistan, Ghana, Cyprus, Nigeria, Tanzania, Zambia, Malawi, Botswana, Uganda, Singapore, Kenya, Gambia, and Guyana) with Presidents as Head of State; Malaysia, which has one of the Malay Rulers as Head of State; Lesotho, Swaziland, and Tonga, which have their own monarchs, do not owe allegiance to the Queen. All members accept her as the symbol of the free association of member nations of the Commonwealth and as such Head of the Commonwealth.

The Colonies.

As stated in the opening passage of this outline, the United Kingdom, in common with other members of the Commonwealth, has certain dependencies which are described as " The Colonies." But this is a loose term, for " the Colonies " are not really all Colonies in the strict sense. What are loosely spoken of as Colonies are properly divided into Colonies, Protectorates, Protected States, Trust Territories etc.

Definitions.—*Colony.*—A territory belonging by settlement, conquest, or annexation to the British Crown.

Protectorate.—A territory not formally annexed, but in respect of which, by treaty, grant, usage, sufferance, and other lawful means Her Majesty has power and jurisdiction.

Protected State.—A territory under a ruler which enjoys Her Majesty's protection, over whose foreign affairs she exercises control, but in respect of whose internal affairs she does not exercise jurisdiction.

Trust Territory.—A territory administered by the United Kingdom Government under the trusteeship system of the United Nations.

Condominium.—A territory over which responsibility is shared by two administering powers.

Leased Territories.—This term applies only to that part of the mainland of China which was in 1898 leased to Great Britain for ninety-nine years and is administered by the Government of Hong Kong.

Associated State.—A former colonial territory which has entered into a free and voluntary association with Britain to become self-governing in all matters except for external affairs and defence. The term applies to six of the East Caribbean islands—Antigua, St. Kitts–Nevis–Anguilla, and the four Windward islands of Dominica, St. Lucia, St. Vincent, and Grenada. *See also* C6(2).

Responsibility of the British Government.

The British Government is responsible for the affairs of Colonies (properly called Crown Colonies) both internal and external, and for their defence, and their peoples are British subjects. Protectorates are governed in the same way as Colonies, but have not been annexed. The peoples of Protectorates are not British subjects but British-protected persons. In the case of an Associated State the British Government is responsible for defence and external relations, though it may confer upon the Associated State's government authority to deal with specific matters of foreign affairs.

The future of some of the remaining dependencies of Britain is unclear. Many are so small that it is doubted whether they could ever be viable as independent states, and indeed that doubt applies to some of the smaller states which have already achieved independence. In the case of British Honduras, independence has been delayed because of the political problem represented by the Guatemalan claim to the territory.

The Countries of the Commonwealth.—At the end of the Gazetteer is a list of all the countries of the Commonwealth showing their land area and recent estimates of population. The list distinguishes between the sovereign members and the British dependent territories, and classifies the latter according to the kind of dependency. Not all the British dependencies come exactly within the definition either of Colony or Protectorate, since, for historical reasons, many come partly under one heading, partly under another.

The Commonwealth Secretariat.

This body was established in 1965, with headquarters in London. It acts as a central source of information for Commonwealth members, and prepares the ground for Commonwealth meetings and functions. The Secretary General is Mr. Arnold Smith, a former Canadian diplomat. As might have been expected, the Secretariat has attempted only the most discreet initiatives in relation to major Commonwealth problems such as the Nigerian civil war, Rhodesian U.D.I., and arms sales to South Africa.

Commonwealth Problems.

Britain's attitude to Southern African questions has been for years and remains the principal issue dividing the Commonwealth. With the coming to power of a Conservative government, which has announced the intention of resuming arms sales to South Africa, the focus has moved away from the continued existence of a rebel régime in Rhodesia to what African and Asian Commonwealth countries see as Britain's continued support for a régime of white domination in South Africa. Britain's support of the Nigerian federal military government in the Nigerian war also alienated some African Commonwealth states, but with the end of that war in January, 1970, criticism of Britain's attitude has faded.

There is also the long-standing problem of the hostility between India and Pakistan, but this has long since ceased to be regarded as an issue amenable to British or Commonwealth mediation.

British entry into the Common Market represents a particularly pressing problem for New Zealand and the West Indies because of their dependence on agricultural exports to Britain.

Finally, British attitudes to immigration and particularly to the plight of East African Asians who hold British passports but are nevertheless barred from freely entering Britain, have come in for extensive criticism in Asian and African Commonwealth countries.

Rebellion in Rhodesia.

The dissolution in December 1963 of the Federation of Rhodesia and Nyasaland led to the independence of Northern Rhodesia (as Zambia) and of Nyasaland (as Malawi) and left Southern Rhodesia, renamed Rhodesia, as a self-governing colony. Rhodesia's white, minority Government pressed for complete independence. The Rhodesian Front, under the Prime Ministership of both Mr. Winston Field and Mr. Ian Smith, had insisted that Rhodesia had an immediate right to independence based on (a) the fact that it had been self-governing for forty years, and (b) that this was morally, if not indeed explicitly but privately, promised by British Ministers when the Rhodesian Federation was broken up. The British Government, both under Conservative and Labour rule, specified only that while Rhodesia should move to independence like any other self-governing dependency, it should be under a constitution broadly acceptable to the people as a whole and should provide for a peaceful transition to majority rule. This principle was elaborated in a statement of five conditions set out in the following paragraph. It was not said by either party that independence could not be granted to Rhodesia until a government elected on a franchise wide enough to be described as a government " of the majority " is actually in power. But that majority rule must be the precondition was asserted by the two Rhodesian African leaders (divided, but both in prison), by the African States, by the United Nations, and by some Commonwealth countries.

Five Conditions for Independence of Rhodesia.— In the protracted negotiations between Mr. Smith and Mr. Wilson to reach a settlement in 1965 the latter took his stand on the following five conditions:—

    1. a guarantee of unimpeded progress towards the majority rule already envisaged in the 1961 Constitution;

    2. a guarantee of no retrogressive amendments of the 1961 Constitution;

    3. an immediate improvement in the political status of the African population;

    4. progress towards the elimination of racial discrimination; and

    5. the overriding requirement that Britain must be satisfied that any proposed basis for independence would be acceptable to the Rhodesian population as a whole.

The British Government offered to co-operate in a crash programme of education for Africans to fit them to take an effective share in the economic and political life of the country within the span of, possibly, a decade.

Unilateral Declaration of Independence.—The long pressure for independence from 1963 to 1965 reached its climax on 11 November 1965, when Mr. Ian Smith declared the independence of Rhodesia; and the British Government were confronted by an act of rebellion. (U.D.I. became known as I.D.I., the illegal Declaration). The rebels protested their loyalty to the Sovereign, whose commands, however, they were repudiating. African opinion was outraged, and among the countries which broke off relations with Britain were two Commonwealth countries (Ghana and Tanzania), Mauritania, Guinea, Mali, the Sudan, Algeria, and the Congo (Brazzaville). Britain ruled out, from the start, the use of force; but Mr. Wilson embarked on a policy of graduated economic sanctions, including an oil embargo: the objective being the emergence, under economic hardship, of a liberal alternative to the Smith régime. The United Nations took the view that the 1961 constitution had broken down and that the decrees signed upon I.D.I. amounted to the destruction of all safeguards for the rule of law and for human rights in the 1961 constitution and earlier legislation.

There are many aspects of the complex position in Rhodesia, and several interpretations can be given. But one central fact must be stated simply: nearly five million Africans remain subordinate to 230,000 whites. The implications of the rebellion go far beyond Rhodesia. It has exacerbated the whole problem of race division in Africa. As such it has aroused strong feelings in black African countries and has strained the Commonwealth (on the multi-racial character of which Britain has set such store). The rebellion exacerbates in particular the threatening confrontation between black African countries and South Africa and Portugal.

Commonwealth Conference 1966 and Rhodesia.

—At the Conference of September 1966 it was decided to give the Rhodesian Front régime a final chance of a negotiated settlement with Britain. If the offer were rejected Britain undertook to sponsor jointly mandatory sanctions at the UN, withdraw all previous proposals for a constitutional settlement, and not grant independence before majority rule was achieved. The final offers by Britain had to be accepted before a fixed date.

It was agreed that the British Government would not recommend to Parliament any constitutional settlement which did not conform with six principles. These six principles were the five conditions for independence set out in an earlier paragraph together with a sixth, namely: no oppression of the majority by the minority or of the minority by the majority.

The Ride on the " Tiger."—After secret " talks about talks " between officials during the summer of 1966 Mr. Wilson and Mr. Smith had talks on 2 December on board H.M.S. *Tiger* off Gibraltar and prepared a working document which the Rhodesian Cabinet rejected three days later; and on the 16th the UN Security Council voted on a British resolution for mandatory sanctions including oil.

The " Fearless " Talks.—Mr. Wilson and Mr. Smith met on H.M.S. *Fearless* in Gibraltar harbour on 9 October 1968 in yet another attempt to settle the dispute. But the talks ended on the 13th with disagreement on the fundamental issues still remaining. On 18 November the proposals based on the *Fearless* talks were rejected by Rhodesia. The white minority in the crisis affecting their country had found themselves unready to give the African majority reasonable prospects of education, jobs, political and civil rights. It was clear that what Mr. Smith objected to was majority rule in Rhodesia at any time. In the House of Commons debate of 22 October 1968 the Prime Minister emphasised that the limit of what Britain could offer to reach a settlement with the illegal régime in Rhodesia had been reached.

Commonwealth Conference 1969.

During the discussions at the Commonwealth Prime Ministers' Conference held in London in January 1969, Britain was criticised for abandoning the principle of no independence before majority rule (NIBMAR) in putting forward to Mr. Smith the *Fearless* proposals. The majority view was that these proposals should be withdrawn. But Mr. Wilson could not accept that view. The *Fearless* terms were still on offer to Rhodesia. He considered that it would be right, if it proved possible, to give the people of Rhodesia as a whole an opportunity to decide for themselves whether or not they wished for a settlement which would be fully consistent with the Six Principles laid down by successive British governments. Any such settlement would need to be clearly shown to be the wish of the Rhodesian people as a whole. If that took place, he would consult his Commonwealth colleagues about the NIBMAR commitment. He emphasised, however, that a settlement based on the Six Principles would not be possible if it were shown that there could be no genuine test of its acceptability in present circumstances in Rhodesia.

New Constitution and Republican Form of Government.

A referendum held in Rhodesia in June 1969 supported the illegal régime's proposed new constitution and republican form of government. It was opposed by the two African opposition parties, the Centre Party, Dr. Palley, the Independent M.P., the former GOC of the Rhodesian Army, Lord Malvern and Sir Roy Welensky, both former Prime Ministers of the Central African Federation, business and trade union organisations, and by the Christian churches except the Dutch Reformed church. On the other hand, the Rhodesian Conservative Association condemned the proposals for not going far enough. Despite this opposition, both proposals received large majorities, viz:

for a republic:	Yes	61,130
	No	14,372
for the new constitution	Yes	54,724
	No	20,776

Of the electorate of 81,000 Europeans and 6,645 Africans, some 75,500 cast their votes.

The new constitution follows in most respects the régime's constitutional proposals of May 1969, but additionally lays down that the Head of State shall be a President. The legislature would consist of a Senate (containing 10 European, 10 African chiefs paid by the Government, and 3 appointed members irrespective of race) and a lower House (50 Europeans, 8 chiefs, and 8 elected African members). The composition of the Senate is of special importance as the Declaration of Rights embodied in the régime's constitution would not be subject to jurisdiction in the courts; it would be for the Senate only to decide whether any particular piece of legislation contravened that declaration of rights.

Speaking in the House of Commons on 16 October 1969, the British Foreign and Commonwealth Secretary said such a constitution, giving exceptional voting rights to a particular section of the community by virtue of wealth or education, could be justified—if it could be justified in any circumstances—only if the régime which promulgated it made it overwhelmingly clear that it was giving the less privileged community every possible opportunity to improve its education, to become more prosperous. But, he continued, " ten times as much was at present spent on the education of a European child as on the education of an African child, and while about 11 per cent of European children moved from primary to secondary schools, only 1 per cent of Africans did so. As for the ownership of land, the 230,000 Europeans would own rather more land than the 4,800,000 Africans. If the African happened to advance to the position where he might increase his wealth and voting rights in a town, then we find that the redefinition of areas in the town is such as to operate solidly to the disadvantage of the African who seeks either to be a shopkeeper or a professional man." It was a constitution " which at the very best and on the most favourable interpretation nobody could say is not really racial; it is related to education and income . . . and, at the same time, makes it impossible for the less privileged race to advance in education and income."

The Opposition spokesman on Foreign and Commonwealth affairs in the House of Commons supported the Foreign and Commonwealth Secretary in declaring that Britain could not be a party to Mr. Smith's proposed constitution for Rhodesia if it were adopted, and that there would have to be a change of attitude in Salisbury if there were to be a negotiated settlement. *The Times* in its leader of 18 June 1969 said the real issue in Rhodesia " is an illiberal constitution wholly alien to British traditions—illiberal not just because it repudiates any eventual majority rule and all the six principles, but because in its provisions it clearly opens the door to the type of administrative tyranny and police power that characterise the South African system."

Sir Humphrey Gibbs announced his resignation as Governor on 24 June 1969 and Rhodesia House in London was closed the same day. On 2 March 1970 the illegal régime declared itself a republic.

Talks about Talks.

The Conservative government came to power committed to make one last try at reaching a settlement with Rhodesia. Mr. Heath said in September 1970 that the government wanted to find " a sensible and just solution to the Rhodesian problem." Shortly afterwards, Mr. Smith told a British TV team that he hoped Rhodesia would " never degenerate to the system of one man, one vote . . ." The fifth anniversary of U.D.I. was celebrated with a military parade and fly-past. It appears that neither Britain nor the Rhodesian régime believes there is any real chance of success. Sir Alec Douglas-Home, the Foreign Secretary, told parliament in November 1970 that talks about talks had begun.

Arms Sales to South Africa.

The incoming Labour government in November 1964 announced that it would honour a UN embargo on arms sales to South Africa, although weapons already ordered by that country would be delivered. From that time until the Conservative general election victory of 1970, no arms other than these were supplied (with some small exceptions) and South Africa made a series of protests that Britain had violated the terms of the Simonstown Agreement. The agreement has to do with British–South African naval co-operation in the event of war. The Conservative party in opposition, however, made it clear that it would wish in power to sell arms to South Africa for external defence.

Opposition to the resumption of arms sales built up quickly after it became clear that the Conservative government intended to lift the ban on sales. Tanzania in July 1970 said that she would withdraw from the Commonwealth if sales were resumed. Later Tanzania, Zambia, and Uganda announced they would follow a common course of action, and, in December President Obote of Uganda made it clear that, for Uganda, this would also mean withdrawal from the Commonwealth. In July Sir Alec Douglas-Home, the new Foreign Secretary, had told the Commons that a final decision would be postponed until after talks with some Commonwealth countries and with South Africa itself. The prime ministers of both Canada and India wrote personal letters to Mr. Heath asking him to reconsider his planned policy, and the United States, too, indicated that she was strongly opposed.

Mr. Wilson said in September 1970 that Labour would in office repudiate any arms deal with South Africa. President Julius Nyerere of Tanzania had talks with Mr. Heath in October, and President Kenneth Kaunda of Zambia met the British prime minister a few weeks later. President Kaunda at that time suggested that rather than withdrawing from the Commonwealth, his country would argue for Britain's expulsion, should arms sales be resumed.

Commonwealth Conference 1971.

The Commonwealth Prime Ministers' meeting in Singapore in January 1971 was dominated by the question of arms sales to South Africa. Britain maintained that she was entitled to sell arms under the agreement which allows the British navy to use the base at Simonstown. Opposition from the black African states hardened during a bitter debate over a document which President Kaunda of Zambia presented to the conference, in which he attempted to define the general attitude of Commonwealth members to the major issues of our time, including racial prejudice and discrimination. Mr. Heath would not agree to the phrase in this declaration of principles which read " No country will afford to régimes which practise racial discrimination assistance which directly contributes to the pursuit or consolidation of this evil policy," because it conflicted with his idea that Britain must be free to determine her own policies and he argued that the Commonwealth was bound by nothing save ties of friendship. A face-saving compromise was reached by the insertion of the words " in its own judgment " (between " which " and " directly ").

Mr. Heath agreed also to the setting up of an eight-nation study group to consider the security of the strategic sea routes in the Indian Ocean. The group was due to meet in London in mid-1971. However, in February the British government decided that it was legally bound to supply helicopters and spare parts to the South Africa government under the Simonstown Agreement. Thus the purpose of the study group disintegrated and several members withdrew as a protest. The bitterness of the conference over Britain's attitude to arms sales to South Africa has led several observers to doubt whether ever again there will be a similar gathering of Commonwealth prime ministers.

Australia, New Zealand and South East Asia.

The new Conservative government announced in October 1970 that Britain would maintain a small military force in Malaysia and Singapore, thus reversing the previous government's policy of a complete withdrawal East of Suez by the end of 1971. The British units—one infantry battalion, a few helicopters and maritime reconaissance aircraft, and some frigates and destroyers—will be part of a five-nation force also including units from Singapore, Malaysia, Australia, and New Zealand. Talks to define the arrangements for this proposed defence grouping were due to be held early in 1971. Numerous problems face the new grouping, one related to the fact that Mr. John Gorton, when Australian prime minister, had refused to commit his country to aid Malaysia in her dispute with the Philippines over the status of Sabah. The principal potential threat facing Malaysia and Singapore is internal Communist subversion and there may be fears that Australian, British and New Zealand involvement could lead to a Vietnam type situation. There are also worries that the British and Australian troops might be

drawn into communal war between Malays and Chinese.

The clear involvement of Australia and New Zealand in South-East Asia since the war has had its effect on their domestic affairs. In the early and middle sixties both Australian and New Zealand opinion was broadly in agreement with their governments' support for Malaysian and Singapore's efforts to consolidate their new nationhood and also for the support given by both governments to the South Vietnamese government, including troops. As a result, the Liberal/Country coalition in Australia and the National Party in New Zealand were able to consolidate and extend their power at the expense of the Labour Party in each country. During 1968 and 1969 Labour opposition to participation in the Vietnam war increased in strength; this feeling combined with new leadership within each Labour party and, in Australia in particular, a feeling that the ruling party had " lost its steam, " and had a " long run, " combined to make it appear that in 1969 there would be a change of government in each country. But this did not happen. In New Zealand the National Party just maintained its lead and in Australia the Liberal/Country coalition obtained 66 seats against 59 for Labour. Labour polled just under 47 per cent of the total vote, and it would appear that the government was saved partly by the second preference votes cast for the Democratic Labour Party and partly by its ability to win a majority of marginal seats. Following a crisis in the Liberal party in March 1971, the two top ministers changed places, Mr. William McMahon taking over the premiership and Mr. Gorton the Defence portfolio. Elections are due to be held in 1972.

The greater participation in Asian affairs appears slowly to be moderating Australia's traditional immigration policies. Since 1945 some three million people have settled in the country, of which almost half have had assisted passages. Over half have come from Britain and more than 100,000 from each of Italy, Greece, the Netherlands, and Germany. Of greater interest, perhaps, is the fact that more than 50,000 have been admitted from Asian and African countries including 16,000 Chinese and Japanese.

Canada.

The relationship between the English-speaking and the French-speaking communities remains Canada's principal political problem. The Quebec elections in the spring of 1970, which gave the Quebec Liberal Party, committed to federalism, a clear majority, also saw the separatist Parti Quebecois take 25 per cent of the popular vote. Nevertheless, the improving economic situation in the French-speaking province and the security of the provincial Liberal government seemed to justify the hope that the separatist issue was on its way to cooling off. The kidnapping by the Front de Liberation du Quebec of a British trade commissioner and the Quebec minister of Labour, Mr. Pierre Laporte, showed that some elements in the separatist movement had no intention of conceding ground gracefully. Mr. Pierre Trudeau, the Canadian prime minister, invoked Canada's War Emergency Act, declaring that a state of " apprehended insurrection " existed in the province. Shortly afterwards the corpse of Mr. Laporte was discovered by police. Mr. James Cross, the British trade commissioner, was later released by his captors. As Quebec returned painfully to normal, the general view was that the Quebec separatist movement had been seriously weakened by the kidnappings and the murder of Mr. Laporte.

Conferences were held in 1968 and 1969 between the Federal Prime Minister and the ten Provincial Prime Ministers, and committees have been set up covering the following subjects: official languages, fundamental rights, division of powers, reduction of regional disparities, and the reform of the Senate (upper House). During 1969 the Official Languages Bill was enacted. The new Act provides for equality between the two languages at federal level in parliament and government, in the issue of public instruments in the public services and courts. Bilingual districts could be established wherever the minority reached 10 per cent of the population and a Commission of Official Languages was to act as watchdog. At the same time care was taken to ensure that the federal civil service would not be closed to entrants able to speak English only.

THE UNITED NATIONS.

Charter of the United Nations.

The Charter of the United Nations was signed on June 26, 1945. The purposes of the United Nations can be divided into four groups (security, justice, welfare, and human rights) and the nations undertook to carry out four main duties (to settle disputes peacefully, to refrain from treating or using force, to assist in carrying out the Charter, and not to assist an aggressor). The UN affirms faith in the human rights of all without distinction of race, language, sex, or religion.

Membership of the United Nations.

The UN had one hundred and twenty-seven member countries in 1971. They were:

Afghanistan	Kuwait
Albania	Laos
Algeria	Lebanon
Argentina	Lesotho
Australia	Liberia
Austria	Libya
Barbados	Luxembourg
Belgium	Malagasy Republic
Bolivia	Malta
Botswana	Malawi
Brazil	Malaysia
Bulgaria	Maldive Islands
Burma	Mali
Burundi	Mauritania
Byelorussian S.S.R.	Mauritius
Cambodia	Mexico
Cameroun	Mongolia
Canada	Morocco
Central African Republic	Nepal
	Netherlands
Ceylon	New Zealand
Chad	Nicaragua
Chile	Niger
China (Taiwan)	Nigeria
Colombia	Norway
Congo (Brazzaville)	Pakistan
Congo (Kinshasa)	Panama
Costa Rica	Paraguay
Cuba	Peru
Cyprus	Philippines
Czechoslovakia	Poland
Dahomey	Portugal
Denmark	Roumania
Dominican Republic	Rwanda
Ecuador	Saudi Arabia
El Salvador	Senegal
Equatorial Guinea	Sierra Leone
Ethiopia	Singapore
Fiji	Somalia
Finland	South Africa
France	Spain
Gabon	Sudan
Gambia	Swaziland
Ghana	Sweden
Greece	Syria
Guatemala	Tanzania
Guinea	Thailand
Guyana	Togo
Haiti	Trinidad and Tobago
Honduras	Tunisia
Hungary	Turkey
Iceland	Uganda
India	Ukrainian S.S.R.
Indonesia	United Arab Republic
Iran	U.S.S.R.
Iraq	United Kingdom
Ireland	United States
Israel	Uruguay
Italy	Venezuela
Ivory Coast	Voltaic Republic
Jamaica	Yemen
Japan	Yemen, Southern
Jordan	Yugoslavia
Kenya	Zambia

The membership includes 29 members of Commonwealth countries, representing one quarter of the world's population. The African group is numerically the strongest, with a membership of 39 (excluding S. Africa). Twelve member states are communist. The following countries are not members: China, Switzerland, East Germany, West Germany, North Korea, South Korea, North Vietnam, South Vietnam, Liechtenstein, Monaco.

Major Organs of the UN.

The UN has six major organs: (1) a General Assembly, (2) a Security Council, (3) an Economic and Social Council, (4) a Trusteeship Council, (5) an International Court of Justice, and (6) a Secretariat. It is especially the inclusion of the third body on this list (with all the Commissions and specialised agencies which stem from it) which makes the UN more broad and balanced than the League of Nations.

General Assembly.

The General Assembly occupies a central position in the structure of the UN. But its business is quite distinct from the Security Council. It meets once a year. The Assembly can consider the general principles of co-operation for peace and security and disarmament and regulation of armaments. It can discuss any question concerning peace and security brought before it. It makes recommendations, but any question upon which action is necessary must be referred to the Security Council. The carrying out of its humanitarian work is the function of the Economic and Social Council (dealt with below) which it elects and supervises. Further, the Assembly controls the purse.

Principal Organs of the United Nations.

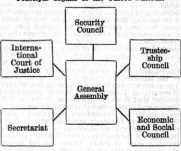

The Security Council.

The aims of the UN are wide—from feeding starving peoples to encouraging self-government in backward areas—but it cannot advance towards the noble objectives set out in the Preambles unless peace is maintained. The principal organ to preserve peace and security is the Security Council. The size of the Security Council was enlarged from 11 to 15 with effect from January 1966. Five seats are permanently occupied by Great Britain, the U.S.A., the U.S.S.R., China, and France. The China which is represented in the UN and on the Security Council is not, however, the Republic of China (or Communist China). It is the régime of Chiang-kai-Shek, who occupies Formosa. The other seats are normally elected for two years by the General Assembly. The ten temporary members are: Argentina, Belgium, Italy, Japan, Somalia (retiring at end of 1972), and Burundi, Nicaragua, Poland, Sierra Leone, and Syria (retiring at the end of 1971). The Security Council sits continuously. It has two functions: (1) to promote the peaceful settlement of disputes and (2) to stop aggression. Under the Charter, parties to a dispute have already promised not to use force, to settle their quarrels peaceably, and to refer their dispute to the Security Council if they really cannot reach a peaceful settlement. On its side the Council can call on the parties to settle disputes peacefully, it can investigate any situation likely to cause a breach of the peace, and at any stage it can recommend a solution.

The Veto.

At this point we must deal with the veto, which applies to substantive questions. The number of affirmative votes required for adopting decisions on substantive matters is 9, including the votes of the five permanent members. In other words if any one of the permanent members says " No " to the use of force, even after a full investigation, the Council cannot use force to settle the dispute. Thus when it comes to imposing sanctions for a breach of the peace the assent is required of the Great Powers, and one of them may of course be a party to the dispute. If the Great Powers imposed sanctions on each other it would mean a major war in which the present UN would disappear. Partly in order to overcome the difficulty of the veto the Assembly set up a Committee to remain in permanent session consisting of one representative of each member. It is known as the Little Assembly, its formal title being the Interim Committee.

The Uniting for Peace Resolution, 1950.

The General Assembly had always been able to discuss matters of peace and security, although it could not make recommendations about them if they were being considered by the Security Council. But in 1950, after the Korean crisis, a new decision was taken by the General Assembly whereby if there were some threat or breach of the peace on which the Security Council was in deadlock, the Assembly, on a vote of seven members of the Security Council, could consider it immediately and make a recommendation about it. This decision, to which Russia and four other countries were opposed, was called the " Uniting for Peace " resolution. By this resolution, too, the Assembly can be called together within twenty-four hours. It was the standing Interim Assembly which considered the Israeli–Egyptian dispute in November 1956.

The Economic and Social Council.

The UN pledged themselves to a broad humanitarian policy of which the following are salient points: to promote higher standards of living; full employment; the conditions of economic and social progress; solutions of international economic, social, health, and other related problems; educational co-operation; universal respect for human rights; and the fundamental freedoms for all. The main business of the Economic and Social Council is to carry out this broad policy. The size of the Council was increased from 18 to 27 with effect from January 1966. To tackle these huge problems the Council established a number of important commissions and bodies, the principal being the following:—

Regional Economic Commissions

Economic Commission for Europe (ECE)

Economic Commission for Asia and the Far East (ECAFE)

Economic Commission for Latin America (ECLA)

Economic Commission for Africa (ECA)

Functional Commissions

Disarmament
Statistics
Population
Social
Human Rights
Status of Women
Narcotic Drugs

Special Bodies

UN Children's Fund (UNICEF)

Commissioner for Refugees

Conference on Trade and Development (UNCTAD)

Industrial Development Organisation (UNIDO)

Intergovernment Agencies (previously called Specialised Agencies).—The agencies are organisations established by intergovernmental agreements, and their activities as a rule are co-ordinated by the Economic and Social Council. The list of the fifteen Agencies are given below.

International Atomic Energy Agency (IAEA)

International Labour Organisation (ILO)

Food and Agriculture Organisation (FAO)

UN Educational, Scientific and Cultural Organisation (UNESCO)

World Health Organisation (WHO)

World Bank (Bank)

International Finance Corporation (IFC)

International Monetary Fund (FUND)

International Development Association (IDA)

International Civil Aviation Organisation (ICAO)

Universal Postal Union (UPU)

International Telecommunication Union (ITU)

World Meteorological Organisation (WMO)

Inter-Governmental Maritime Consultative Committee (IMCO)

General Agreement on Tariffs and Trade (GATT)

Several of these organisations were at work before the UN was set up. One such body is the ILO.

A Peace Force.

Since its inception in 1945, the United Nations has been called on only four times for military action—in Korea (1950), in Egypt (1956), in the Congo (1960) and in Cyprus (1964). Korea was really an American " containment " action under the covering of the UN. In other operations, the number of troops ranged from 6,000 to 20,000. Apart from military action, the UN has sent observers or " presences " to various parts of the world, mainly to the Middle and Far East, to facilitate settlement of disputes. Thus to maintain a standby force of 20,000 men, when it might be needed so rarely, would be a waste, apart from problems of bases, control, and equipment. Two ideas about the best kind of peace force hold the field. They are:—

(1) the earmarking of national military units; and

(2) a permanent multiracial force.

The cogent arguments for a permanent UN Military Force can be studied in *United Nations Forces* by D. W. Bowett, pub. by Stevens in 1967.

A United Nations Success: Technical Assistance.

That the United Nations is something more than a place of talk is proved by a glance at the history of its programme of Technical Assistance. The object of this aid is to help countries to develop their economic and political independence; and, since this must be a truly co-operative venture, receiving countries must not only invite the experts but actively participate in projects they undertake both with money and with local personnel—even the poorest being encouraged to make a contribution. A major reform was made in 1966 by the simplification of the existing systems of capital and technical aid by the United Nations. The two main channels of aid were fused—the UN Special Fund and the UN Technical Assistance Board—to become a single Council for a UN Development Programme (UNDP). *See also* Underdeveloped Economies, Section G, Part III.

Unicef.

Of all the United Nations agencies Unicef has most caught public imagination. In the early years of the war the attempt began to make amends to children whose early years had been shattered by war; and during the quarter century since Unicef has been bringing aid to millions all over Africa and Asia. Unicef does not draw directly on United Nations funds but voluntary help from Governments and individuals. There have been two developments of policy:

(1) a change in 1950 from post-war relief work to programmes of help for mothers and children in developing countries; and

(2) from 1960, an emphasis on education and vocational training rather than pure survival projects.

Human Rights.

The 20th anniversary of the adoption and proclamation of the Universal Declaration of Human Rights by the General Assembly on 10 December 1948 was marked by the observance of the year 1968 as International Year for Human Rights. There seemed, however, in 1968, a good deal to deplore as well as to celebrate. There had been a good deal of thinking on the subject and over two decades numerous conventions had been drawn up. But there had, unfortunately, been a good deal of obstruction and non-co-operation; and in 1968 the situation of slaves, political prisoners, and minorities of all kind was distressing. Let us take these two parts of the problem in turn—the resolution for improvement and the actuality.

Declarations and Conventions on Human Rights.

Every member of the UN endorsed the Universal Declaration of Human Rights. It marked the determination to prevent the recurrence of the genocide and brutality which occurred in the Second World War. Out of it sprang a Commission on Human Rights and numerous other Declarations and Conventions. Thus the European Convention on Human Rights prescribed that " no one shall be subjected to torture or to inhuman or degrading treatment or punishment " and there has been established a European Court on Human Rights. Among subsequent Declarations have been those on:

(1) Granting of Independence to Colonial Countries and Peoples.

(2) Elimination of All Forms of Racial Discrimination.

and among Conventions have been those on:

(3) Abolition of Slavery, the Slave Trade, and Institutions and Practices Similar to Slavery.

(4) Abolition of Forced Labour.

(5) Discrimination in respect of Employment and Occupation.

(6) Equal remuneration of Men and Women Workers.

(7) Freedom of Association and Protection of the Right to Organise.

(8) Discrimination in Education.

(9) Prevention and Punishment of the Crime of Genocide.

(10) Political Rights of Women.

Drafts were being prepared for Covenants or Conventions on:

(11) Civil and Political Rights; Economic, Social, and Cultural Rights.

(12) Elimination of All Forms of Religious Intolerance.

(13) Freedom of Information.

But after conventions are adopted at UNO they need to be ratified; thereafter signed; thereafter nations need to take the necessary action to enable the provisions to be put into force; and finally to put them into force. These are the stages between declaration of intent and fulfilment. As U Thant has said: "The mere adoption of various covenants and international agreements is not enough by itself." We need, therefore, to temper enthusiasm for intentions with critical regard for what is actually happening.

The Persistence of Slavery.

Slavery persists today in five forms defined in the UN Supplementary Convention on the Abolition of Slavery (1956), namely chattel slavery, serfdom, debt bondage, sham adoption, and servile forms of marriage. The Anti-Slavery Society (for the Protection of Human Rights) stated in 1967 that it has recent information of the existence of one or more of these forms of slavery in thirty countries in the " free world." Apart from servile marriage the other forms probably embrace between one or two million people. This exploitation can only be fought when governments legislate against it and their officials and people uphold the law. To encourage them to do so is the main function of the Anti-Slavery Society. Founded so far back as 1823 it is the principal organisation in the world working to end slavery; and it has consultative status at the Economic and Social Council at UNO. It supports the setting up of machinery to implement the slavery conventions called for in October 1967 by the Int. Commission on Prevention of discrimination and Protection of Minorities. Besides the eradication of slavery in all its forms the Society's aims include the abolition of labour systems resembling slavery and the protection and advancement of aboriginal and primitive peoples. The address of the Anti-Slavery Society is Denison House, Vauxhall Bridge Road, S.W.1.

The Anatomy of the United Nations.

Some ironical changes have taken place in the UN since its inception. At the outset the Security Council was built as the organ through which the Great Powers would together discharge their collective responsibility as policemen. They were the superior powers. They had the authority and the means to act as the big policemen to keep others in order. But this assumed that the big five permanent members would agree and act in concert. This is just what they did not do. As a result, in 1950, by Anglo-Saxon device, the General Assembly was mobilised to ensure action when action was vetoed in the Security Council. But over the last decade the Assembly has grown both in numbers and in the independence of its views. It is not at all as interested in the conflict with Communism as those assumed who vested it with additional power: it is more interested in colonialism. So those who gave the Assembly this additional strength would like to reverse the position. But here we confront another difficulty. China, one must expect (and hope), will join the Security Council. That will make the unity in that body which is vitally necessary for peacekeeping even more difficult. The prospect of Communist China becoming a member of the UN advanced in November 1970 when a resolution to admit Peking and expel Formosa secured a majority of two votes. This was the first time Communist China had won a majority for admission. But the effect of the American-backed formula declaring the issue an " important question " means that Peking's admission requires a two-thirds majority. There were signs at the Assembly's 25th session that the " important question " formula may not for much longer win a majority of votes. If the formula were rejected Peking's admission would be conditional only on a simple majority.

The General Assembly's 25th Session.

This centenary session, which was held in New York in the autumn of 1970, attracted numerous heads of state, but the achievements of the session were, as expected, limited. The most important shift was in the vote over the admission of Communist China already mentioned.

The 1970s were declared a "Second UN Development Decade," under which the developed countries are to be asked to contribute 1 per cent of their gross national product to overseas aid, and a corps of UN volunteers, on Peace Corps lines, is to be set up. Few experts expect that more than a handful of the developed nations will actually make the recommended diversion of resources to overseas aid.

A draft treaty banning the use of the seabed for weapons of mass destruction was approved by the Assembly. The draft treaty has, however, been widely criticised on the grounds that it bans something which none of the nuclear powers actually want to do. Neither of the two nuclear powers has any plans for fixed nuclear weapons on the seabed, considering submarine launched missiles technically and strategically preferable.

The African group put forward numerous resolutions condemning apartheid and white minority rule in South Africa, Rhodesia, and the Portuguese colonies. Condemnation of apartheid was one of the points in the 25th anniversary declaration. The existing arms embargo in South Africa was strengthened. The British prime minister, Mr. Edward Heath, managed, however, to avoid all mention of his government's plans to sell arms to South Africa in his speeches to the General Assembly. The French, however, announced a ban on the sale of certain categories of weapons to South Africa.

The Assembly also, in various resolutions, put pressure on Israel to resume unconditionally the indirect negotiations with the Arab countries which earlier in 1970 had been broken off by Israel, on the grounds that the Egyptians had violated the Suez standstill by deploying missiles near the Suez Canal.

WESTERN EUROPEAN ORGANISATIONS.

1. Introduction.

This outline is an attempt to explain the various organisations through which European countries are trying to co-operate. The destruction in Europe in the Second World War emphasised the need for greater union, both for recovery and for defence. A bewildering array of organisations has sprung up. They differ in form, in function, and in membership. Some overlap in function. Some are much less effective than others. The edifice is not, moreover, built on a single harmonious plan. Beneath the edifice are two different kinds of foundations, that is to say, two rival theories. These two theories (the federalist and the functionalist) are explained as the story unfolds. The story traces four main streams—the military, the political, the economic, and the scientific and technological—and describes the bodies which evolved in each stream.

Historic Origin of European Unity.

Sully, the famous Minister of Henry IV, King of France, outlined, in 1633, a proposal for achieving European unity and putting an end to war in Europe. He called it the "Grand Design." It was revived in modern dress by Monsieur Briand, the French Prime Minister, in 1929. During the War (1943) the concept of a United Europe which should be created after victory was won was outlined by Sir Winston Churchill: and he returned to the subject in his famous speech at Zurich University in 1946.

Two Starting Points: European Recovery Programme and the Brussels Treaty.

There were two main sources of the present numerous European bodies. The first was the European Recovery Programme in 1947 (ERP), and the second was the Brussels Treaty of 1948.

The European Recovery Plan was popularly known as the Marshall Plan, as it was the result of the invitation made in 1947 by Mr. Marshall (then U.S. Secretary of State) to the European countries to draft a programme to put Europe on her feet economically. The U.S.A. was ready to give this aid, and it was in its own interest as well to do so, if the countries concerned would agree on co-operation and plan their needs. In March 1948 the countries concerned created the Organisation for European Economic Co-operation (OEEC) to administer the programme of aid. This body was replaced by the Organisation for European Co-operation and Development in 1961.

The Brussels Treaty, 1948, was the other main source of the West European organisations. In March 1948 Britain, France, and the Benelux countries (Belgium, Holland, and Luxembourg), agreed at Brussels to pursue a common policy on economic, political, and military collaboration, and to promote a better understanding of the principles which form the basis of the common civilisation of Western Europe. It also provided for the creation of a Consultative Council. This Council, when formed, was the Council of Europe, and it is described below, together with an account of all the organisations which stemmed from the Treaty. Italy and the German Federal Republic joined the Brussels Treaty Organisation in May 1955, which then became the Western European Union.

2. Military Organisations.

The Brussels Treaty and the Western Union Defence Organisation.

As we have seen, under the Brussels Treaty, so far back as 1948, the five Western Powers concerned pledged themselves to military collaboration; and in the same year they formed the Western Union Defence Organisation. At that time policy was being framed by a fear of a revival of German aggression. But in time this fear was replaced by distrust of the Soviet Union. There were two developments. In the course of seven years the Western Union Defence Organisation was transformed by the inclusion of the German Federal Republic itself and of Italy into a larger body called the Western European Union. How this change came about is described in the following paragraphs, which tell the story of the creation of the new Federal Republic of Germany, the proposal for a European Defence Community (which did not materialise), and the eventual emergence of Western European Union (in 1955). The second sequel of a military character of the Brussels Treaty was the creation of the North Atlantic Treaty Organisation (NATO). Whereas WEU is a regional organisation, NATO has an even larger range, as its members include Canada and the U.S.A. An account of NATO follows the story, to which we now turn, of the emergence of the new German Republic and its eventual incorporation in WEU.

Government of Germany after the War.

As a result of Germany's unconditional surrender on June 5, 1945, all power in Germany was transferred to the Governments of the four principal Allies. By decisions at Potsdam in 1945 that power was exercised by the Commanders-in-Chief of the U.S.A., the United Kingdom the Soviet Union, and France, each being responsible in his own zone of occupation. On matters affecting Germany as a whole, the four would be jointly responsible as members of the Control Council. Berlin was divided into four sectors of occupation.

The London Conference 1947 of the four Foreign Ministers concerned failed to agree on a joint German settlement. Unfortunately, the effect was to set in motion political and economic developments which were speedily to make Germany the battleground of the conflict of ideas between Soviet Russia and the Western Powers. The Allied Control Council could no longer function efficiently; and by the end of 1948 four-Power rule had virtually collapsed and the partition of Germany was complete. A federal Parliament and Government were formed in Western Germany. The Soviet zone prepared a rival form of Government for East Germany.

Western Germany's New Status.—In May 1952 the German problem acquired a new complexion, when the so-called "Contractual Agreements" were signed by the three Allied Powers and Western Germany at Bonn. These Agreements did not form a Peace Treaty, but they attempted to define how W. Germany and the three Allied Governments should work together. Sovereignty was to be restored to Germany and she was to enter a military alliance with France. Indeed, a Treaty called the European Defence Treaty was drawn up between the four Powers, with Italy and the Benelux countries, which was to fit German Armed Forces into a Western European system. But this system, called the European Defence Community, never came to fruition as such, owing to the refusal of France to ratify the Treaty in 1954.

Collapse of EDC.—With the collapse of EDC there was a halt to the idea of a Political Community designed to embrace both the proposed EDC and the existing European Coal and Steel Community. It was logical that these two Communities formed by the same countries should not have separate institutions but should take their place within a single political community.

The London Nine Power Conference and the Paris Agreements, 1954.—Nine Powers met in London to devise a substitute for EDC. They were Belgium, Canada, France the German Federal Republic, Italy, Luxembourg, Netherlands, United Kingdom, and the U.S.A. The Conference considered how to assure full association of the German Federal Republic with the West and the German defence contribution. All the decisions which were reached formed part of one general settlement and these were embodied in agreements signed shortly afterwards in Paris. These decisions included the following:—

1. The occupation of W. Germany by Great Britain, the U.S.A., and France should end.

2. The German Federal Republic and Italy should join the Brussels Treaty Organisation.

3. The W. German Republic was admitted to the North Atlantic Treaty Organisation (NATO).

Western European Union.

These agreements took effect on May 5, 1955, when the occupation régime in Western Germany ended and the Republic attained full sovereignty and independence. At the same time the Republic became a member of the Western European Union (the expanded Brussels Treaty Organisation), which came into formal being on May 5, 1955, and also of NATO, to which we now turn. The WEU includes the EEC countries *and* Britain and is therefore a useful forum for consultation and discussion. The activities of the WEU were boycotted by France in 1969.

The North Atlantic Treaty, 1949.

The founder members of this Pact (which widened the scope of the Brussels Treaty) were Great Britain, the U.S.A., Canada, France, Holland, Belgium, and Luxembourg. The parties agreed that an armed attack against one or more of them in Europe or North America shall be considered an attack against them all and consequently they agreed that if such an armed attack occurs, each of them, in exercise of the right of individual or collective self-defence recognised by the Charter of the UN, will assist the party so attacked.

NATO Policies and Plans.

The NATO Ministerial Council met twice in 1970. NATO policies still continue to be based, sometimes rather uneasily, on the twin concepts of defence and détente. The move towards some kind of détente with the East continued when the May ministerial meeting agreed to a sounding out of Warsaw Pact members on the possibility of a European security conference and mutual force reductions. At the ministerial meeting in December 1970 NATO defined its attitudes more precisely, agreeing that preparatory talks on East-West security should be held once there was a settlement in Berlin. Such talks would also be conditional, the meeting decided, on evidence of progress in "other current talks," meaning the Strategic Arms Limitation Talks between the Soviet Union and the U.S.A. and the talks between West and East Germany. The Soviet Union, anxious for a European security conference, removed one obstacle during 1970 by indicating that it would not oppose American and Canadian participation in any European security talks.

Force levels continue to be a major worry for the Alliance, whose conventional strength is so inferior to that of the Soviet bloc as to lead to a dangerous, and sometimes not very credible, reliance on nuclear weapons. One long-standing fear of the European members, that the U.S. would greatly reduce its forces in Europe, was assuaged in 1970 when President Nixon pledged the U.S. to maintain and improve U.S. forces in Europe. The *quid pro quo* for this commitment emerged at the December ministerial meeting in the form of a West German plan for European members to increase their NATO budgets over the next five years by £375 million. Britain, however, has so far refused to commit itself to an increased financial contribution, maintaining that her contribution of additional units during 1970 is an adequate substitute.

NATO, which up to the time of the Soviet invasion of Czechoslovakia, was evolving towards peace policies concerned with economic and technical co-operation with the East and joint attempts to tackle such all-Europe problems as pollution, has since then reverted strongly to its military role. The basic problems of the future are, of course, no longer seen as related to a possible massive Soviet attack, but to breakdowns or uprisings within Eastern Europe. The fear is that such internal struggles could spill over into more general war. If the West wishes to influence Soviet policy within Communist and neutral Europe, the conventional strength of NATO is of more importance than the nuclear deterrent.

3. Political and Economic Organisations.

The European Economic Community.

The EEC was formed in 1958, growing out of the European Coal and Steel Community, a supranational body set up in 1950 for the co-ordination of coal and steel production in West Germany, Belgium, Holland, Luxembourg, France, and Italy. It has been a notable economic success. The 1970s have seen it complete a common agricultural policy, meet its goals on internal and external tariffs (by 1968), and take the first steps towards a common monetary policy. The EEC is unquestionably the strongest and most significant of all European organisations and the only one which provides any sort of basis for West European unity. Other bodies, such as the Council of Europe and the European Free Trade Area (EFTA) as well as regional associations like the Nordic Council and the Benelux Economic Union now stand outside the mainstream of European political and economic development. Others still, like the Organisation for Economic Co-operation and Development, the successor to the Organisation for European Economic Co-operation (OEEC), have so expanded their terms of reference as to have ceased to be solely European organisations. *See also* **C39–40.**

The Council of Europe.

This body was formed in 1949 and now has 18 member nations. The agreement of 1949 set up a Committee of Ministers and a Consultative

Assembly, forming together a Council of Europe. Headquarters are at Strasbourg.

The Consultative Assembly is the deliberative organ of the Council and is empowered to debate and make recommendations upon any matter which (i) is referred to it by the Committee of Ministers with a request for its opinion, or (ii) has been approved by the Committee. The Assembly consists of 147 members elected by their national parliaments. Originally the members were seated in alphabetical order of names; today they sit grouped in political parties irrespective of their nationality. The Committee of Ministers is the Council's executive organ and is not responsible to the Assembly, but merely reports to it.

Future Role of the Council.—The Council remains in doubt about its future role, particularly if Britain and other candidate nations for Common Market entry are admitted. Its condemnation of Greece in 1970 demonstrated that it has a claim to be the collective voice of European democratic opinion. But criticisms that it is no more than a talk shop and that the EEC and even NATO can better discharge many of the tasks it has attempted continue. The best reply to such criticisms has been that there remains a wide area outside the present scope of NATO and the EEC—an area encompassing, for example, human rights, the law, social policy, education, pollution—where the Council can play a key co-ordinating role. The Council has a reasonably impressive record in some of these areas. Examples are its encouragement of reciprocal social service arrangements between European countries, the co-ordination of medical standards, and its general work on the harmonisation of law.

A European Free Trade Area.

When the Six were discussing the Common Market the British Government declared (1956) that they would consider joining a free-trade area in Europe. Although she would not join the Common Market scheme itself, she would consider sharing in the stage-by-stage reduction of inter-European tariffs on all non-agricultural goods. They would not attempt (unlike the Six) to standardise their own tariff walls in relation to the world outside the European free-trade area. Such a free-trade area would be independently controlled with permanent co-ordination with EEC. In November 1958 France rejected the British proposals for linking the six European common-market nations with the eleven other OEEC countries in a free-trade area. It appeared to the French impossible to establish a free-trade area between the six treaty powers and the other eleven OEEC countries without a single customs tariff between all of them and the outside world and without measures of harmonisation in the economic and social sphere.

The European Free Trade Association.

Thereupon seven countries outside the area of the Six formed a European Free Trade Association. They were Great Britain, Austria, Denmark, Norway, Portugal, Sweden, and Switzerland, and they agreed upon a plan at Stockholm in November 1959. Inside the free-trade area comprising these seven countries it was contemplated that there would eventually be no internal tariffs or quotas, but member states would retain separate external systems. The Seven, upon the foundation of their Association, immediately offered friendly co-operation to the existing Common Market. When EFTA was formed, its member nations confidently expected that the EEC would soon see the error of its ways and agree to the creation of a vast European free trade zone. In the event, EFTA members saw their error first, with three members of the original seven starting negotiations with the EEC in 1961. The same three once again began negotiations with the EEC in June 1970. If Britain, Denmark, Norway, and Ireland (not a member of EFTA) do succeed in joining the Common Market, EFTA can be expected to swiftly wither away. In late 1970, the EEC opened negotiations with Portugal, Iceland, and Finland in an attempt to find arrangements which would soften the blow of British entry. Sweden, Switzerland, and Austria are also working

for some form of association with EEC. (Finland is an associate member of EFTA and Iceland a recently joined full member.)

The Organisation for European Economic Co-operation (OEEC).

We now turn to the third stream, the economic. We have seen that OEEC was created to administer American (Marshall) aid. But it needed also to re-create a sound European economy. The allocation of aid continued until 1952; but the practice of mutual consultation on economic matters continued in order to carry out long-term programmes. Owing to the nature of its original task of distributing Marshall Aid, the U.S.A. and Canada became associate members of the Organisation. In 1961 these two countries formed with members of OEEC the Organisation for Economic Co-operation which replaced OEEC and is described below.

Organisation for Economic Co-operation and Development.

This body has taken the place of OEEC. Canada and the United States, who were associated members of OEEC, joined with the eighteen member countries of that body to set up OECD. The convention was signed in Paris in December 1960, and the new body came into existence in the autumn of 1961. Thus Canada and the U.S.A. join in facing the broader objectives and the new tasks of today, namely to achieve in Europe the highest sustainable economic growth, employment, and standard of living; to contribute to economic development; and to expand world trade on a multilateral and non-discriminatory basis, in accordance with international obligations. The scope of OECD has been further widened by the accession to membership of Japan.

Economic Commission of Europe.

ECE was the first of the great regional commissions to be set up by UNO. It was created in 1947 to concert action for the economic reconstruction of Europe, and it was hoped to strengthen economic co-operation between all European members of UNO. Russia and some of the Communist Eastern European countries are members of ECE, and it is the only European organisation where the Western bloc and Soviet powers can meet for discussion and action.

4. The Development of the Common Market.

The Treaty of Rome, 1958, which had established the European Economic Community defined (in Articles 2 and 3) the principles and objects for which the Community is to work. Those articles specify in detail the steps for creating a Common Market, for approximating the economic policies of member States, the promotion of harmonious development of economic activities, and raising the standard of living. But the aim of " closer relations between its member States " is stated without elaboration. It is into this gap that speculation is poured. No limit is set in the Treaty to the process of integration; on the other hand there is no commitment to join a Federation of Europe. While member States commit themselves to a common policy on a number of economic issues there will be co-ordination of national policies designed to take account of the needs of the rest of the Community.

The Organs of EEC.

The machinery of government of the European Economic Community (into which is now integrated the machinery for ECSC and Euratom) consists of:

1. The Council

2. The Commission

3. The Court

4. The Parliament or Assembly

5. The Economic and Social Committee (for the Common Market and Euratom): and

6. The Consultative Committee (for ECSC).

7. The Ambassadors of the member Governments.

The meetings of Ambassadors form unofficial permanent liaison between Council and Commission. Let us examine the chief official organs.

The Council issues regulations and decisions which are, upon issue, binding in law on all member States. It consists of one member from each member State (normally a Cabinet Minister). Decisions require either unanimity or a qualified majority, weighted as follows:

France	4 votes
Germany	,,
Italy	,,
Belgium	2 votes
Holland	,,
Luxembourg	1 vote

The Council represents national interests. "If federation is unity in diversity, the Commission represents the unity and the Council the diversity. The balancing of individual interests and Community interests is accomplished by discussions between these institutions, culminating in the meetings of the Council of Ministers" (the words of Walter Hallstein, former President of the European Community).

The Commission.—Whereas the Council consists of politicians the Commission consists of permanent officials. It has 14 members—3 each from France, the German Federal Republic, and Italy; 2 each from Belgium and the Netherlands; and 1 from Luxembourg. They are the custodians of the supranational idea and are pledged to complete independence from national control. The business of the Commission is to further the general purposes of the treaties of the Communities and decisions are by majority vote. From the Commission flow two streams:—

(a) Proposals, which it sends to the Council.

(b) Under powers of its own:—

1. Decisions to named countries and binding on them.

2. Directives to named countries to achieve certain results, without specifying the means.

3. Recommendations and Opinions, which are not binding.

4. Authorisations without which many things are forbidden.

The Court, whose procedure is wholly Continental, consists of seven Judges appointed by Governments for a maximum of six years. Its word is final on the interpretation of the Treaty, on the rules made under the Treaty, and on the legality of all the actions of the organs of the Community.

Expansion of the EEC.

Britain opened negotiations in June 1970 on its third attempt to join the Common Market. The application had been made by the previous Labour government, but it fell to the new Conservative government to actually begin the talks. The hope was at that time that the talks on British entry, and on the entry of her fellow candidates, Denmark, Norway, and Eire, could be completed by mid-1971. At the time of going to press Britain had secured useful but marginal agreements on the marketing of some agricultural products and agreement in principle on associate status for African Commonwealth countries and Gibraltar. It had also secured agreement to have a single five-year period for adaptation in both the industrial and agricultural fields. But discussion on the vital details of the timetable for raising food prices and adapting the industrial customs union had not been settled. The British budget proposals had made it clear to the Six that Britain was unlikely to agree to make contributions to the Community exchequer in the early years that would endanger her own balance of payments.

Doubts in Britain.

Opposition to British entry grew in this country as the prospects for entry became more favourable. It is considered possible that, faced with a final decision, a majority of the Labour Party might be against entry.

The Future of the EEC.

Complicating the negotiations for an expansion of the EEC are various unresolved issues about the future development of the organisation. In late 1970, the Council of Ministers, for the third consecutive year, deferred reform of common agricultural policy. The Council also failed to agree on the Werner Plan for monetary and economic union. This report outlined three stages for achieving monetary and economic union by 1980. If the recommendations were carried out more power would be vested in the Commission and in the European Parliament so that decisions would create a common currency, common tax policies, and common economic guidelines could be effectively taken. *See also* Section G, Part IV.

Beyond these immediate and pressing problems, lie other questions, such as the harmonisation of European foreign policies and defence policies. Nuclear weapons pooling by Britain and France would in itself raise serious issues, since Germany is unable to participate in any nuclear force and an agreement between France and Britain might well alienate Germany at a time when its own *Ostpolitik* is modifying its commitment to Western Europe.

5. Scientific and Technological Organisations.

Euratom is the short title of the European Atomic Energy Community (EAEC) formed in 1957 to further the use of nuclear energy in Europe for peaceful purposes and to ensure that Europe does not lag behind in the atomic revolution. The negotiation for this Community opened at the same time, in 1956, as that for the Common Market and the Treaty for it was signed at Rome on 25 March 1957, when the Treaty for the Common Market was signed. Prior to the merger in July 1967 of the three executive bodies of the Common Market, Euratom, and the Coal and Steel Community into a single Community and of the three Councils into a single Council, Euratom was supervised by its own Commission. Euratom's role is to ensure that the Community undertakes the research necessary for the development of nuclear energy not only for power, but also through the use of radioisotopes and radioactive sources, for agricultural, industrial, and medical purposes. It has joined international projects such as the European Nuclear Energy Agency (ENEA) *Dragon* project at Winfrith, Dorset, which is sponsored by OECD.

The Six Co-ordinate on Scientific and Technological Policies.—The Council of Ministers in 1967 reached agreement on a procedure for such co-ordination. Existing co-operation in international organisations included ELDO (European Rocket Launcher Development Organisation)

ESRO (European Space Research Organisation), and CERN (European Nuclear Research Centre) in all of which the Six are associated with Britain. (But in 1968 Britain announced its withdrawal from ELDO when the present development programme ends in 1972.) The urgency of the general problem of co-operation has been sharpened by growing anxiety in Europe generally about the consequences of a technological gap, the difficulties actually encountered in *ad hoc* co-operation—in the aero-space sector, for example —and the extensive overlapping of effort and expenditure.

OTHER GROUPINGS OF STATES.

1. Military Alliances.

NATO—The principal Western defence organisation with prime responsibility for opposing Communist forces in Europe. *See* **C38**.

The Warsaw Pact, formed in 1955, groups the Soviet Union, Bulgaria, Czechoslovakia, East Germany, Hungary, Poland, and Roumania. Its full title is the Eastern European Mutual Assistance Treaty.

ANZUS Council, a loose military alliance grouping Australia, New Zealand, and the United States.

Central Treaty Organisation (CENTO), The successor to the Baghdad Pact alliance of 1955, CENTO groups Great Britain, Iran, Pakistan, and Turkey, with the US as an associate member. It is regarded as of limited effectiveness.

South East Asia Treaty Organisation was formed in 1955 and groups Australia, France, Great Britain, New Zealand, Pakistan, the Philippines, Siam, and the United States. France, Pakistan, and Britain have virtually withdrawn.

2. Organisations of the Third World.

The Third World is the name given to those countries representing the less privileged part of the world, most of them forming part of neither the Western (Capitalist) bloc nor the Eastern (Communist) bloc. They are sometimes called " non-aligned " or " uncommitted nations."
They have three permanent organisations:

    (*a*) **The Afro-Asian People's Solidarity Council** (1957);

    (*b*) **The Afro-Asian Organisation for Economic Co-operation** (1958); and

    (*c*) **The Three Continents Solidarity Organisation** (1966).

The Bandung Conference of 1955 in Indonesia was the first inter-continental conference of the so-called coloured peoples in the history of the world. It adopted a Declaration on Problems of Dependent Peoples that colonialism was an evil and should be brought to an end. It also adopted a Declaration on World Peace and Co-operation, involving five principles of peaceful coexistence.
Other conferences of the Third World have been:

The Belgrade Conference of 1961 was attended by 25 countries and adopted a 27-point declaration containing their common views on international problems and an " Appeal for Peace " addressed particularly to the U.S.A. and the U.S.S.R.

The Cairo Conference of 1964 at which 47 countries attended. Neo-colonialism and imperialism in all forms were condemned particularly in South Africa. '

3. Regional, Political, and Economic Groupings.

EEC—the principal European political and economic grouping. *See* **C38(2), C39(2)**.

Comecon, The Council for Mutual Economic Assistance, groups the Soviet Union, the East European Warsaw Pact members, and Outer Mongolia. Its aim is to co-ordinate and integrate members' economies, but the organisation has been under considerable strain in recent years.

Organisation of American States groups 23 American countries, of which one, Cuba, has been suspended. Its central organ is the Pan-American Union.

The Organisation of Central American States (OCAS) was set up in 1951. Members: Costa Rica, El Salvador, Guatemala, Honduras, Nicaragua.

Latin American Free Trade Association (LAFTA) was formed in 1960 and now comprises 11 nations —Argentina, Bolivia, Brazil, Chile, Colombia, Ecuador, Mexico, Paraguay, Peru, Uruguay, Venezuela.

The Arab League with its seat at Cairo comprises Algeria, Iraq, Jordan, Kuwait, Lebanon, Libya, Morocco, Saudi Arabia, Sudan, Syrian Arab Republic, Tunisia, United Arab Republic and Yemen. A " Pact of the Union of Arab States " was signed in 1945 by representatives of Egypt, Iraq, Lebanon, Saudi Arabia, Syria, Transjordan, and Yemen. Later adherents were Libya, Sudan, Tunisia, Morocco, Kuwait, and Algeria.

The Organisation of African Unity (OAU) was constituted at Addis Ababa in 1963. All independent countries in Africa, except South Africa, are members of the OAU.
There are a number of regional organisations in Africa such as: (1) **the East African Common Services Organisation** (1962) for Kenya, Tanzania, and Uganda, and (2) **the West African Common Market** (1967) comprising twelve countries— Dahomey, Ghana, Ivory Coast, Liberia, Mali, Mauritania, Niger, Nigeria, Senegal, Sierra Leone, Togo, and Upper Volta.

The Colombo Plan, owing its inception in 1951 to the Commonwealth Consultative Committee, is a plan for the economic development of South and South East Asia. It was originally adopted for development programmes in India, Pakistan, Ceylon, Malaya, Singapore, North Borneo, and Sarawak, but the scheme has been widened to include non-Commonwealth countries, and the U.S.A. has agreed to join Australia, Britain, Canada, and New Zealand in making available aid within the framework of the Colombo Plan.

Organisation Commune Africaine et Malgache (OCAM) groups 13 French-speaking African countries and Malagasy. A regional organisation within OAU.

HEATH'S CONSERVATIVE GOVERNMENT
(as re-formed October 1970)

Prime Minister and First Lord of the Treasury—Edward Heath.
Secretary of State for the Home Department—Reginald Maudling.
Secretary of State for Foreign and Commonwealth Affairs—Sir Alec Douglas-Home.
Chancellor of the Exchequer—Anthony Barber.
Lord Chancellor—Lord Hailsham.
Lord President of the Council—William Whitelaw.
Secretary of State for Defence—Lord Carrington.
Secretary of State for Social Services—Sir Keith Joseph.
Chancellor of the Duchy of Lancaster—Geoffrey Rippon.
(Minister in charge of European negotiations).
Secretary of State for Trade and Industry and President of the Board of Trade—John Davies.
Secretary of State for Employment—Robert Carr.
Secretary of State for Education and Science—Margaret Thatcher.
Secretary of State for Scotland—Gordon Campbell.
Lord Privy Seal—Earl Jellicoe.
Secretary of State for the Environment—Peter Walker.
Secretary of State for Wales—Peter Thomas.
Minister of Agriculture, Fisheries, and Food—James Prior.

Speaker of the House of Commons—J. Selwyn Lloyd.
Leader of the Opposition—Harold Wilson.

MINISTERS NOT IN THE CABINET

Minister for Trade—Michael Noble.
Minister for Industry—Sir John Eden.
Minister of Aviation Supply—Frederick Corfield.
(this Ministry is being transferred to the Ministry of Defence)
Minister for Housing and Reconstruction—Julian Amery.
Minister for Transport Industries—John Peyton.
Minister for Local Government and Development—Graham Page.
Parliamentary Secretary, Treasury (Chief Whip)—Francis Pym.
Minister of Overseas Development—Richard Wood.
Paymaster-General—Viscount Eccles.
(Minister with special responsibility for the arts)
Ministers of State, Home Office—Richard Sharples, Lord Windlesham.
Minister of State, Foreign and Commonwealth Office—Joseph Godber.
Chief Secretary to the Treasury—Patrick Jenkin.
Minister of State, Treasury—Terence Higgins.
Minister of State, Ministry of Defence—Lord Balniel.
Minister of State, Department of Health and Social Security—Lord Aberdare.
Minister of State, Department of Employment—Paul Bryan.
Minister of State, Scottish Office—Lady Tweedsmuir.
Minister of Posts and Telecommunications—Christopher Chataway.
Minister of State, Welsh Office—James Gibson-Watt.
Lord Commissioner of H.M. Treasury and Parliamentary Secretary, Civil Service Department—David Howell.
Minister without Portfolio—Lord Drumalbyn.

Law Officers:

Attorney-General—Sir Peter Rawlinson.
Solicitor-General—Sir Geoffrey Howe.
Lord Advocate—Norman Wylie.
Solicitor-General for Scotland—David Brand.

ENGLISH LAW

A concise survey of the English legal system, its history and development from early times, with further detail of some particular branches of the law which are of practical interest to the ordinary citizen.

TABLE OF CONTENTS

ENGLISH LAW

A.—The Sources

Comprising

COMMON LAW		CASE LAW	STATUTE LAW	

B.—The Sub-divisions

I. CONSTITUTIONAL LAW.	II. CRIMINAL LAW, dealing with the relations between the individual and the State.	III. STATUS.	IV. LAW OF PERSONS,* dealing with the relations between one individual citizen and another, established—	V. LAW OF PROPERTY.*
Main Principles: 1. The Supremacy of Parliament. 2. The Rule of Law. (a) *The Legislature*: The franchise, elections, Parliamentary procedure, relations between Lords and Commons, Bills and Acts. (b) *The Executive*: The Crown, the Ministry, Government Departments and their powers. (c) *The Judiciary*: The Courts and their functions, the Judges, means of controlling the Executive and inferior courts. (d) *Local Government*: County, Borough, Urban and Rural District and Parish Councils and their powers. See also Section C, Part II.	A. Grave offences against— 1. *Public Order*: Treason, sedition, riot, blasphemy, obscenity, forgery, bigamy, perjury. 2. *Persons*: Homicide, assault, sexual offences. 3. *Property*: Theft, burglary, dishonestly obtaining property by deception, blackmail. Subsidiary matters: (a) Criminal responsibility. (b) Unconsummated Crimes. (c) Joint Crimes. (d) Punishment and its purpose. B. *Petty Offences, e.g.,* Road Traffic, Factories and Shops, Sale of Food, etc., (dealt with by J.P.s).	1. Nationality. 2. Domicil. 3. Marriage and Divorce. 4. Minority 5. Lunacy. 6. Bankruptcy. 7. Corporations. 8. Adoption. 9. Legitimacy.	*EQUITY** 1. *By act of parties (Law of Contract)*: (1) Simple Contracts. (2) Deeds: (a) *Capacity of parties.* (b) *When writing necessary.* (c) *Mistake.* (d) *Misrepresentation.* (e) *Duress and undue influence.* (f) *Illegality.* (g) *Breach.* 2. *By Law (Law of Tort)*: Civil Wrongs committed against— (1) *The Person*: Trespass, assault, malicious prosecution, and false imprisonment. (2) *Land*: Trespass, Nuisance. (3) *Other Property*: Trespass, Conversion. (4) *Persons towards whom there is a duty to take care*: Negligence. (5) *Reputation (libel or slander)*: Defamation. (6) *Personal and Trade Relationships*: Trade molestation and— (a) *Liability.* (b) *Immunity.* (c) *Effect of Death.* (d) *Remedies.*	IN GENERAL: 1. *Living Persons*: (Effect of Status on Ownership). 2. *Deceased Persons*: (Wills and Intestacies, Probate and Administration.) IN LAND (Immoveable Property): 1. Freeholds (Settlements). 2. Leaseholds. 3. Mortgages. 4. Title. 5. Joint Ownership. IN OTHER PROPERTY (Moveable Property): 1. Chattels. 2. Things in action.

* *Note:* Equity is applied only in matters of civil law relating to persons and property. It has no application to constitutional or criminal law.

THE SYSTEM OF ENGLISH COURTS

I. CIVIL COURTS

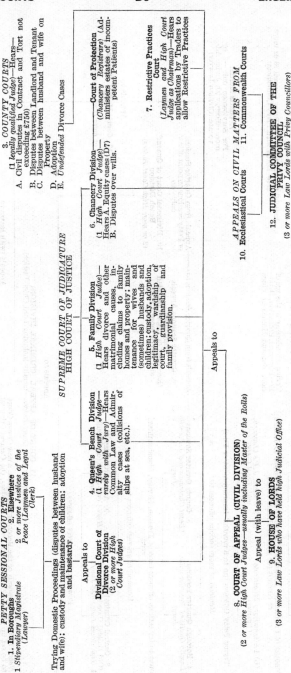

PETTY SESSIONAL COURTS
1. *In Boroughs* — 1 *Stipendiary Magistrate* (*Lawyer*)
2. *Elsewhere* — 2 or more *Justices of the Peace* (*Laymen and Legal Clerk*)

Trying Domestic Proceedings (disputes between husband and wife); custody and maintenance of children; adoption and bastardy

Appeals to

Divisional Court of Divorce Division
(2 or more High Court Judges)

3. *COUNTY COURTS*
(1 *legally qualified Judge*) — Hears —
A. Civil disputes in Contract and Tort not exceeding £750)
B. Disputes between Landlord and Tenant
C. Disputes between husband and wife on Property
D. Adoption
E. *Undefended* Divorce Cases

Court of Protection
(*Chancery Registrars*) (Administers estates of incompetent Patients)

7. **Restrictive Practices Court**
(*Laymen and High Court Judge as Chairman*) — Hears applications by Traders to allow Restrictive Practices

SUPREME COURT OF JUDICATURE
HIGH COURT OF JUSTICE

4. **Queen's Bench Division**
(1 *High Court Judge rarely with Jury*) — Hears Common Law and Admiralty cases (collisions of ships at sea, etc.).

5. **Family Division**
(1 *High Court Judge*) — Hears divorce and other matrimonial causes, including claims to family homes and property; maintenance for wives and (sometimes) husbands and children; custody, adoption, legitimacy, wardship of court, guardianship and family provision.

6. **Chancery Division**
(1 *High Court Judge*) — Hears A. Equity cases (D7)
B. Disputes over wills.

Appeals to

8. **COURT OF APPEAL (CIVIL DIVISION)**
(2 or more High Court Judges—*usually including Master of the Rolls*)

Appeal (with leave) to

9. **HOUSE OF LORDS**
(3 or more Law Lords who have held high Judicial Office)

APPEALS ON CIVIL MATTERS FROM
10. Ecclesiastical Courts   11. Commonwealth Courts

12. **JUDICIAL COMMITTEE OF THE PRIVY COUNCIL**
(3 or more Law Lords with Privy Councillors)

Note: (1) The Administration of Justice Act, 1969, permits appeals, in certain cases, *direct* from the High Court to the House of Lords, to save expense.
(2) The institution of the Family Division and consequential changes in the other Divisions were, at the time of writing, expected in the spring of 1971.

II. CRIMINAL COURTS

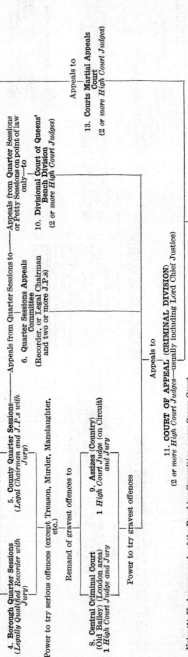

PETTY SESSIONAL COURTS

1. In Boroughs

(A) 1 *Stipendiary Magistrate*

(B) 1 *Stipendiary Magistrate* (*Lawyer*)

2. Elsewhere

(A) 1 *Justice of the Peace*

(B) 2 *or more, J.P.s* (*Laymen, with Legal Clerk*)

Conduct of Preliminary Hearings of grave offences—Power to dismiss or commit for trial to Higher Court

Trying Petty Offences (up to 6 months' Imprisonment or Fine)

Remand of more serious offences to

3. Juvenile Courts

Specially qualified Stipendiary or 2 or more J.P.s

Trying offenders up to the age of 17—Dismissal, Probation, Detention, Remand Homes or Fines

4. Borough Quarter Sessions
(*Legally Qualified Recorder with Jury*)

5. County Quarter Sessions
(*Legal Chairman and J.P.s with Jury*)

Power to try serious offences (except Treason, Murder, Manslaughter, etc.)

Remand of gravest offences to

Appeals from Quarter Sessions to

6. Quarter Sessions Appeals Committee
(Recorder; or Legal Chairman and two or more J.P.s)

Appeals from Quarter Sessions or Petty Sessions on point of law only—to

10. Divisional Court of Queens' Bench Division
(2 *or more High Court Judges*)

8. Central Criminal Court
(Old Bailey) (London area)
1 *High Court Judge and Jury*

9. Assizes (Country)
1 *High Court Judge* (on Circuit) *and Jury*

Power to try gravest offences

Appeals to

11. COURT OF APPEAL (CRIMINAL DIVISION)
—usually including Lord Chief Justice
(2 *or more High Court Judges*)

Appeals (with leave) to

12. HOUSE OF LORDS
(3 *or more Law Lords who have held high Judicial Office*)

14. Ecclesiastical Courts

15. Commonwealth Courts

Appeals (with leave to)

Judicial Committee of the Privy Council (3 or more Law Lords with Privy Councillors)

7. Courts Martial

For Servicemen only—3 or more officers with Judge Advocate (Civilian Lawyer)

Appeals to

13. Courts Martial Appeals Court
(2 *or more High Court Judges*)

Note: (1) Under proposals of the Beeching Committee a new Crown Court is to be set up to absorb the criminal work of Assizes, the Central Criminal Court, and the Borough and County Quarter Sessions.
(2) The Lord Chancellor may by order (after consultation with local authorities) direct that Assizes shall no longer be held for certain places (Administration of Justice Act, 1970). Other minor modifications have been made in the staffing of the Court of Appeal (Criminal Division). These changes came into force on 1 July 1970.

ENGLISH LAW

THE Table set out on D4 shows in concise form:

I. The Sources
II. The Subdivisions

of the Law of England. The intention is to give a general picture of the whole system in tabular form, to explain briefly what the Table represents, and finally to deal, in slightly more detail, with a few selected subjects which may be of particular interest to the ordinary reader.

A word of warning is necessary. Learned text-books have been written on every one of the many subjects referred to in the Table, and the application of the law in any particular case is a matter for the professional expert. The following pages do not claim to do more than to make a brief survey of the whole field of English Law, for the general guidance and interest of the ordinary citizen.

The system of English Courts, as restructured under the Administration of Justice Act, 1970, is set out in tabular form on D5 and D6.

I. THE SOURCES OF ENGLISH LAW

The citizen who desires to make some acquaintance with the English Legal System must begin by disabusing himself of several popular fallacies: for example, that it is a fixed and unalterable code, that it is strictly logical, that it is coldly impersonal and uninfluenced by human factors. The history and practice of the law display precisely the opposite characteristics.

1. COMMON LAW AND CASE LAW.

The English Legal System is a living organism, not a dead, static code. The system as we know it began to develop in the 12th cent., when Henry II extended the practice of sending the royal judges about the country " on circuit," to deal with crimes and disputes, and to adapt and give official authority to the best of the local customs, some of which had been in force since Anglo-Saxon days. The judges did this by empirical methods—that is, by practical, common-sense decisions on the actual cases brought before them, and by setting out their reasoning in detail. Simple records of the most important decisions were kept from the earliest times; as the centuries passed, the gradual elaboration of a system of law-reporting ensured that the facts of significant cases, the reasoned judgments delivered on those facts, and the principles those judgments enshrined, should be recorded and preserved; at the same time the doctrine of precedent—the rule that those principles, enunciated by a superior court, should be followed by all courts inferior to it—ensured consistency throughout the country. Thus there was gradually developed a body of principles—living, growing, and adaptable to new sets of facts as they arose: principles, moreover, which rose above local differences of custom and became common to the whole Realm. Hence the expression *common law*.

Case Law. The system we have described is by no means a thing of the past; it is still in force today. New circumstances are continually arising; cases come before the judges for decision, and it frequently happens that the principles laid down in the past do not apply precisely, in all respects, to the particular facts in point. When this occurs it is the judge's right and duty to interpret and adapt the principle to the new facts before him; his judgment is reported, and his reasoning made clear. The adapted principle of that judgment becomes part of the law of England; it must be followed by all inferior courts; and it will not be ignored or abandoned by courts of the same rank, or any superior court, without reasoned argument and careful consideration. Thus the practising lawyer can never sit back with the comfortable assurance that he has " completed " his studies; he must continually keep his knowledge up to date. The practice of law is not based on rigid rules, but is the art of applying the known principles to the facts of new cases as they arise.

In July 1966 the House of Lords (the Supreme Court of Appeal) announced that it would henceforth regard itself as free to depart from its own previous decisions when it appeared right to do so, though this power would be sparingly used.

2. EQUITY.

But the English genius for practical improvisation has never excluded spiritual and ethical motives of conduct. For hundreds of years the Church was a great power in the land, extending its influence far beyond the strictly ecclesiastical sphere. The great church-leaders of the past took an important part in the secular activities of government and administration; from an early date the King's Chancellor was an ecclesiastic. The Chancellor was not only the King's Secretary of State and Keeper of the royal seal: as royal chaplain he was " Keeper of the King's conscience." It was to him, therefore, that the King turned for advice on matters of state where ethical and moral considerations were involved.

All human institutions are fallible, and the rough-and-ready methods of the early common law sometimes fell short of those ideals of abstract justice that inspire men's minds. Despite, or perhaps because of, its practical outlook, the common law tended to become circumscribed by its own precedents. As the machinery of justice became more elaborately organised, the idealistic doctrine—" Where there is a right there is a remedy "—was apt to degenerate, in practice, into the realistic but soulless form—" Where there is a legal remedy, there is a legal right." Too close an adherence to legal formalities led sometimes to a denial of justice. This was particularly so for the weak, who could not help themselves—feeble-minded persons, tricked or cajoled into " legally " signing away their property; minors unconscionably treated by guardians who, having got legal custody (under a will or otherwise) of a minor's inheritance, refused to honour their solemn trust; borrowers who, having delayed beyond the date fixed for the repayment of a loan, found themselves deprived, under the strict terms of the mortgage deed, of property many times more valuable which they had pledged only as security. For such cases as these the common-law courts provided no remedy, since the victims had suffered no actual illegality. Petitions were therefore sent to the King, " the father of his people," begging him to right such wrongs; and the question of redress was delegated by the King to his Chancellor. The Chancellor had no power directly to revoke or interfere with the decisions of the royal judges by depriving the oppressive party of the property he had " legally " acquired, but he could, and did, insist that that party should not enjoy such acquisition, unconscionably, for his own sole advantage. The defaulting guardian, though he continued legally to hold the minor's property, was compelled to use it for the minor's benefit; the oppressive creditor, who had legally got possession of or sold the debtor's estate, was permitted to take out of the proceeds the amount of his loan, with reasonable interest and expenses, but must hand back the balance to the debtor. Thus the Chancellor administered a kind of *abstract justice*, based upon the promptings of conscience, and not on legalistic nature. He dealt with these cases in his own court—the Chancellor or Chancery—where the yardstick was *equity*—that which was right or fair. And over the centuries the principles on which the Court of Chancery acted became crystallised into a set of rules which followed their own precedents and made conscientious conduct their guiding star.

Naturally enough, the activities of the Court of Chancery were viewed with jealousy and misgiving by the royal judges of the Common Law Courts, and many were the clashes between the two. Equity, however, had come to stay, and the two systems were administered independently until as late as 1873. In that year Parliament passed the Supreme Court of Judicature Act, which (in effect) fused the two systems into one. By means of that and subsequent legislation there was constituted *one High Court of Justice*, of which the *Queen's Bench Division*, the *Chancery Division*, and the *Probate*, *Divorce* and *Admiralty Division* were component parts. The first-named was concerned primarily with common-law suits, the second with equitable matters; but both these Divisions must have regard to both common law and equitable principles. In case of a conflict of principles, those of equity are to prevail. The last-named Division (for historical reasons) dealt with the diverse subjects of wills and intestacies, matrimonial suits, and disputes relating to ships at sea. Criminal cases fall within the jurisdiction of the Queen's Bench Division, but are dealt with in special courts (*see* **D6**). The criminal law (in strict fairness to accused persons) must be absolutely certain and clearly defined; it is administered on strict legalistic principles, from which the doctrines of equity are excluded.

By the Administration of Justice Act, 1970, the system of courts was revised. A new *Family Division* deals with all matrimonial and family matters (*see* **D5**); probate work is taken over by the Chancery Division, while Admiralty work is dealt with by a special section of the Queen's Bench Division.

3. STATUTE LAW.

While, as we have shown, the Courts have the function of interpreting and adapting the prin-

ciples of law laid down in earlier times, they cannot legislate—*i.e.*, the Judge cannot make new laws, or repeal or amend old laws, even when changes are rendered desirable by developing social conditions. The law-making body, or *Legislature*, is *Parliament*. A *Statute* or *Act of Parliament* is the joint act of the Queen, the House of Lords, and the House of Commons; while each of these three " Estates of the Realm " has its own functions, new law can be made, and old law repealed, only by these three Estates acting together, *i.e.*, by Parliament, or by some person or body of persons to whom Parliament has delegated authority to make rules having the force of law. Parliament is free of control by any written constitution or any person or body of persons whatsoever; an Act of Parliament must be enforced by all courts as the law of the land, unless and until it is repealed or amended by Parliament itself. Parliament is not bound by the Acts of a previous parliament, which it is free to repeal or amend as occasion may require. It is equally free to modify the rules of the common law and the rules of equity, however firmly entrenched; but those rules, unless and until modified by parliamentary legislation, continue to guide the Judges both in their interpretation and enforcement of *Statute Law*—*i.e.*, the body of Acts of Parliament still in force for the time being—and in their decisions on those common-law and equitable rules which the Statute Law has left untouched. For example, the Peerage Act, 1963, enables a peer to renounce his title and to become a commoner for all purposes, including voting for, and standing as, a candidate for the House of Commons. By the Law Commission Act, 1965, a body of Commissioners was appointed: (1) to consider various branches of the law; (2) to consolidate and codify the law wherever possible; (3) to draft reforms on certain subjects. The Commission's Fifth Report, issued late in 1970, reviews recommendations for the first five years of its activities and is referred to under various headings in the text that follows.

THE ENGLISH LEGAL SYSTEM.

These three main streams—*common law* (and *case law*), *equity*, and *statute law*—have flowed throughout the centuries, sometimes independently and sometimes in conjunction, to feed the waters of that great river which is the English Legal System.

II. THE SUBDIVISIONS OF ENGLISH LAW

I. CONSTITUTIONAL LAW.

This is that part of the English Legal System which relates to four main branches of national administration:—

    (a) *The Legislature*—*i.e.*, the law-making body known as Parliament.

    (b) *The Executive*—*i.e.*, the Government and the functions of its various components.

    (c) *The Judiciary*—*i.e.*, the Judges, their Courts and powers.

    (d) *Local Government*—*i.e.*, the Local Authorities and their powers.

The two main principles of the Constitution are:—

1. The Supremacy of Parliament.—*I.e.*, there is nothing that Parliament cannot lawfully do, and there is no person or body of persons above Parliament. Its Acts cannot be unconstitutional, since it can itself modify the Constitution at will. Its Acts for the time being in force are the law of the land, and nobody can question their validity.

2. The Rule of Law.—This means that no person or body of persons is above the law of the land, and

that there is one system of law, and one system alone, for everybody. This principle was reaffirmed by the Court of Appeal in the Enfield schools cases in August 1967—ministries and local councils must obey the law like everybody else. There is not in England, as there is in some other states, a special system of law and special courts for scrutinising the acts of ministers, civil servants, or other functionaries; such persons are bound by the same rules of conduct as other citizens. A complaint by a private citizen against a Secretary of State or a Commissioner of Police is investigated by the same courts, and under the same legal rules, as a complaint against another private citizen. Any apparent exception will be found to result from some special provision in an Act of Parliament itself. For example, the Army Act sets up a code of conduct for officers and soldiers, and does not apply to civilians; but that code is part of the Law of England because it is contained in an Act of Parliament—a code which (incidentally) remains valid only if it is confirmed by Parliament in every successive year. Again, the Emergency Powers (Defence) Act, 1939, conferred upon the Crown and its Ministers extensive powers, during the last War, to make Defence Regulations which should have the force of law; but the Act itself had to be passed by Parliament with the proper formalities. Such Regulations derive their legal and binding effect solely from the powers delegated by Parliament; and the High

Court of Justice is competent to scrutinise, and frequently does scrutinise, the wording of the Regulations and the manner in which those powers are exercised, and so satisfy itself that the Minister concerned is not attempting to exceed the authority which Parliament has vested in him—in other words, to protect the citizen against the arbitrary abuse of lawful powers and against their unlawful enlargement. Delegated legislation is always subject to such control; parliamentary legislation is not, since nobody can question the validity of an Act of Parliament. But the interpretation of any Act of Parliament—the ascertainment of its legal meaning and effect—is one of the proper functions of the Courts. By an Act of Parliament in 1966 an office new to the British Constitution was set up—that of Parliamentary Commissioner or Ombudsman (a name borrowed from a Scandinavian institution) to whom complaints of injustice by Government departments may be made.

II. CRIMINAL LAW.

This is that part of the English Legal System which deals with the relations between the individual citizen and society as a whole. Thus, if A murders or robs B, the question of redress is not one merely for B or his family; the victim cannot, in a civilised community, be permitted " to take the law into his own hands," nor can it be left to him to decide what action should be taken against the offender—otherwise blood-feuds and public disorder would result. For that reason it has been the law for centuries past that, in the case of offences (1) against public order, (2) against the person and (3) against property, the State (representing society as a whoie) itself intervenes and prosecutes the offender, for the purpose of upholding public order and vindicating the rule of law by inflicting punishment upon him—not for the purpose of compensating the injured party (which, as will be seen below, is the contrasting function of Civil Law). But recent legislation includes power to make payment of compensation for personal injuries to victims of violent crime. For offences against public order, *see* D44–6.

The two main categories of Crime (as the Tables (**D4, 6**) show) are:—

(*a*) **Grave, Indictable, or Arrestable Offences,** which are dealt with at Assizes, the Central Criminal Court, and Quarter Sessions, and which carry severe penalties—death or lengthy sentences of imprisonment (death only for treason in time of war). (*See also* **D10–11.**) Proposals have been made to re-arrange the Criminal Courts. (*See* **D6.**)

(*b*) **Petty** or (now) **Non-arrestable Offences,** which are dealt with in Magistrates' Courts, and are punishable by light sentences of imprisonment or by fines (with short sentences in the alternative). Examples of this latter class are (*e.g.*, under the Road Traffic Acts) driving without due care and attention, exceeding the speed-limit, causing an obstruction, etc. (*See also* Justices of the Peace, **D43–4.**)

Examples of (a) **Grave, Indictable, or Arrestable Offences** are set out in the Table (**D4**) under the three main headings of:

(1) Offences against Public Order;

(2) Offences against the Person; and

(3) Offences against Property.

In connection with all these categories of offences the Criminal Law is concerned with the following general considerations:—

(*a*) **Criminal Responsibility.**—*I.e.,* the primary principle that every person is presumed (until the contrary is proved) to be sane, provided that his acts are voluntary (*i.e.,* intentional). It would, for example, be absurd for a man, accused of wounding another person by shooting, to plead that he did not intend, when he discharged the firearm at the other person, to do him any bodily

harm. On the other hand, it would be outrageous to convict and punish a child of four who, without understanding the wrongfulness of his behaviour, picked up and took away some attractive and valuable object from a shopcounter; a lunatic who killed somebody under an insane delusion that the victim was a wild beast; a boy (like Oliver Twist) who was compelled, by force or violent threats, to break into a house, or a man who took an overcoat from a public cloakroom, honestly but mistakenly believing it to be his own. In none of these last illustrations is the act a voluntary one in the sense that there was the intention to do something wrong. To the rule that an act is not a crime unless it is intentional in this sense there are a few rare exceptions—cases where an Act of Parliament has expressly and clearly made some form of conduct punishable in itself, whether it was intentional or not; for example, during the War, permitting a light to be visible in black-out hours was punishable, even if it was unintentional and involuntary on the part of the accused. And *see* **Criminal Justice Act, 1967, D10.**

Intention must not be confused with *motive*. For example, in what has become known as " mercy-killing "—*i.e.,* taking the life of a person suffering from a painful and incurable disease—the killer is often actuated by a good motive—the desire to relieve hopeless suffering; but the intention is to kill, and the act is therefore a crime. (It is not necessary for the prosecution to prove any motive.)

The *burden of proof* in criminal cases is on the prosecution, *i.e.,* it is the duty of the prosecution to prove the accused guilty; not the duty of the accused to prove his innocence. The accused is presumed to be innocent unless and until his guilt is proved to the reasonable satisfaction of a jury. The jury are the sole judges of the true facts of the case, and their verdict had to be unanimous until recently; but by the Criminal Justice Act, 1967, it may now be by a majority of 10 to 2. The Act also contains a clause for major changes in committal proceedings by magistrates. *See below,* **D10.**

(*b*) **Unconsummated Crimes.**—*I.e., attempts* to commit crimes which are frustrated by some outside event or by some person's intervention. For obvious reasons the attempt to commit a grave crime is itself an offence for which the offender can be prosecuted and, if convicted of the attempt, punished by fine or imprisonment. *Incitement*, by one person, of another to commit a crime, and *conspiracy* between two or more persons to commit a crime, are usually offences in themselves, whether the incitement or the conspiracy proves successful or not.

(*c*) **Joint Crimes** are those in which two or more persons take part. Such participation may arise in different ways. A *principal in the first degree* is the man who commits the actual offence with *guilty intention* (see (a) above), or who induces its commission by some other person who himself does not understand what he is doing. A *principal in the second degree* is one who *aids and abets* the guilty perpetrator at the time when the crime is committed. An *accessory before the fact* is one who *instigates* or *helps to prepare* the commission of the crime by another person, though not himself present when that other person commits it. In most cases all these three classes of participants in a crime are equally guilty, and liable to the same punishment, provided that all of them shared the same common criminal purpose. (Thus, if two armed burglars break into a house, with their weapons drawn, and one of them shoots and kills the householder, both will be guilty of murder; while the accomplice who helped to plan the burglary will be equally guilty if the plan included the carrying of loaded weapons.)

(*d*) **Punishment and its Purpose.**—The purpose of punishment is fourfold:—

(i) *Retribution*—to demonstrate to the community in general that crime " does not pay " and thus to uphold the rule of law and to prevent the deterioration of public morals;

(ii) *Prevention*—to restrain offenders, so far as possible, from repeating their crimes by keeping them in custody;

(iii) *Reformation*—to make them, so far as possible, better citizens by means of moral and ethical training—teaching them to " go straight "; and

(iv) *Deterrence*—to inspire among offenders and would-be offenders a fear of and a healthy respect for the law and the strength of society as a whole, which it protects.

There has been much controversy on the relative importance of these four functions of punishment. Until comparatively recent times *deterrence* was considered the primary function, and punishments were correspondingly severe and, by modern standards, savage. Experience has shown, however, that crime is not effectively reduced merely by severity of punishment, but rather by the certainty or probability of detection and conviction. And, particularly during the past half-century, *reformation* of the offender, whenever possible, has become a paramount aim, not only on grounds of humanity, but also for the purpose of reducing the wastage of human material which can frequently be salved from a life of crime if it is taken in hand, firmly but kindly, at an early stage (*see* D47). The Children and Young Persons Act, 1969, makes radical reforms in the law and practice relating to children hitherto brought before Juvenile Courts. A summary of the Act appears on D41–3.

(e) **Insanity.**—If a person does an act which, if *voluntary* or *intentional*, would constitute a *crime* (*see* **Criminal Responsibility, D9**), and his legal advisers put forward a defence of insanity, he can still be convicted unless he can prove, to the satisfaction of a jury, that he was " suffering from such a defect of reason, due to disease of the mind, as not to know the nature and quality of the act he was doing, or (if he did not know this) not to know that what he was doing was wrong." Medical men, psychologists, and social reformers have long regarded this rule (which has been in force since 1843) as too severe. It was a rule applicable to all crimes; but the controversy became associated in the public mind chiefly with *murder*. The rule was amended by section 2 of the Homicide Act, 1957; but only in its application to murder cases. It is now provided that " a person who kills (or is a party to the killing of) another shall not be convicted of murder if he was suffering from such abnormality of mind as substantially impaired his mental responsibility for his acts and omissions in doing, or being a party to the killing." (It does not matter whether the " abnormality of mind " arises from " a condition of arrested or retarded development of mind," or from " any inherent causes," or is " induced by disease or injury.") The Act goes on to provide that a person who, under the old law, would have been convicted of murder shall instead be liable to be convicted of *manslaughter*.

In other crimes, where the accused person is clearly proved to have been insane at the time the crime was committed, the verdict is now " Not guilty by reason of insanity."

The **Murder (Abolition of Death Penalty) Act, 1965,** provides that no person shall suffer death for murder; a person convicted of murder shall be sentenced to imprisonment for life. In passing sentence the Court may declare the minimum period which it recommends the Home Secretary to allow to elapse before he orders the murderer's release on licence. The Act was to continue in force until 31 July 1970, and then expire unless both Houses of Parliament passed contrary resolutions. On a free vote in December 1969 both Houses reaffirmed that capital punishment for murder should be abolished.

The **Criminal Justice Act, 1967** revolutionises many provisions of criminal law and procedure:— Magistrates or J.P.s conducting a preliminary inquiry to determine whether there is a *prima facie* case for Quarter Sessions, Assizes or the Central Criminal Court (D6) may commit an accused for trial on written evidence, signed by the witness(es) who made the statement, and declared by them to be true, provided that a copy is handed to the defendant(s), solicitor, or counsel, none of whom objects; but only if the accused is represented by counsel or solicitor. (The statement must be read over to any person who cannot read it.) If the witness is under the age of majority, it must state his age. (The purpose is to save time.) In any case the Court may require such witness to give evidence by word of mouth, either on its own initiative or on the request of any party. The same applies to the trial itself, and admissions are to be good evidence.

Although the examining justices must sit in open Court, no report of the proceedings may be published, unless (a) one of the accused so requests, or (b) the magistrates discharge the accused, or (c) a brief summary of matters excluding evidence is printed. Penalty for unauthorised publication is £500. (Note: The purpose of these provisions is to avoid prejudice to the accused at the main trial.) Notice of discharge or committal must be displayed after the preliminary hearing. Any permitted publication is privileged.

A Court shall not be bound to infer intention or foresight of the results of the accused's actions, but in every case shall decide whether that particular accused did intend or foresee them, on the whole of the evidence. (This reverses a decision in 1962, Director of Public Prosecutions v. Smith, where the House of Lords inferred an intent to kill from the mere fact that the accused accelerated a car and drove with a policeman clinging to the bonnet.)

Notice of the defence of alibi must be given to the prosecutor at least 7 days before the end of the committal proceedings, except with leave of the Court. (This is intended to avoid an alibi being " sprung " on the prosecutor at the last moment, when he cannot disprove it.)

Verdicts of juries need no longer be unanimous. If there are not less than 11 jurors, 10 may return a verdict; if there are 10, 9 may do so. But the jury must be allowed at least 2 hours for deliberation. Persons who have served a term of at least 3 months imprisonment (or in a borstal), summarily, or who have been sentenced to at least 5 years or for life (which usually means about 12 years), are disqualified from serving on a jury—penalty £25; but a verdict is not to be held void because of such disqualification.

Magistrates hearing an offence carrying not more than six months imprisonment may no longer refuse bail to an accused over seventeen, on remand or committal, or in certain other cases. No J.P. may take part in the trial if he knows of previous convictions (to avoid prejudice). A constable may arrest without warrant any person who he believes is likely to break his bail. If the J.P.s refuse bail, the accused may apply for bail to the High Court. A Magistrates' Court shall not sentence an accused to imprisonment in his absence. Magistrates may now impose fines up to £400 (instead of £100). Imprisonment in default of payment is abolished, except when the accused has means to pay but will not. Instead, enforcement shall be by seizing his goods, or by deduction from his earnings.

Preventive detention and corrective training are abolished as is also corporal punishment in prisons. Suspended sentences may be passed and *must* be if the term is for not over 6 months (except in special cases). If the accused commits a further offence, he may have to serve the suspended sentence. The Home Secretary may make rules requiring a " Social inquiry report " before sentence. Deportation of a Commonwealth immigrant may be substituted for imprisonment for life.

There is now power to release prisoners on licence, to revoke such licence, to remand or release young offenders to or from detention or approved schools.

The **Criminal Law Act, 1967.** The old distinction into felonies and misdemeanours is abolished; the expressions " indictable " and " summary " offences are retained, but for some purposes offences are divided into " arrestable " and " non-arrestable " offences. Arrestable offences are those for which (i) the sentence is fixed by law; those for which (ii) the offender is liable to five years imprisonment, and those which (iii) there has been an attempt (D9(2)–(b)) to commit. Arrestable offences, therefore, now include practically every variety of grave crime. Others are known as non-arrestable offences.

The old offence of being an accessory after the fact (except in treason) is abolished; instead, a new offence of " assisting offenders " is created by the Criminal Law Act providing that " where a person has committed an arrestable offence, any other person who, knowing or believing him to be guilty, does, without lawful authority or reasonable excuse, any act with intent to impede his apprehension or prosecution " shall be liable to periods of imprisonment proportionate to the sentence for the main offence. Where the arrestable offence is itself triable summarily (i.e., by a Magistrates' Court) with the defendant's consent, then the offence of " assisting " is also so triable. But the proceedings may be brought only by or with the consent of the Director of Public Prosecutions. A husband or wife has no special exemption.

A new crime of " concealing arrestable offences " is created. In effect the new offence amounts to the prohibition of accepting a bribe in consideration of such concealment, and the consent of the Director of Public Prosecutions must be obtained beforehand, if a prosecution is contemplated. The defendant must know or believe that his information might be of material assistance in securing the conviction of an offender. But the common law rule that " you may show mercy but shall not sell mercy " is modified, so that it is not unlawful to agree not to prosecute or give information on condition that the offender makes good any loss or injury caused by his offence, or makes reasonable compensation for it. It remains unlawful to help to conceal any act of treason.

A new summary offence is created under the Act—the making of false reports to cause wasteful employment of the time of the police in regard to any kind of alleged offence.

Power is given to award compensation to the injured party, in case of any indictable offence, up to the sum of £400 (but compensation for damage due to an accident arising out of the presence of a motor vehicle on a road is excluded; such claims are covered by compulsory insurance). Such compensation may be awarded by the Court trying the offence.

Powers of arrest: Any person may now arrest (i) anyone who is in the act, or whom he suspects to be in the act, of committing an arrestable offence, and (ii) where an arrestable offence has been committed, anyone who is guilty, or whom he suspects to be guilty, of the offence. A constable may without warrant arrest (i) where he suspects with reasonable cause that an arrestable offence has been committed, anyone whom he, with reasonable cause, suspects to be guilty, and (ii) anyone who is about to commit, or whom the constable, with reasonable cause, suspects to be about to commit an arrestable offence. Common law powers of arrest, such as to prevent violence or breach of the peace (D38), are unaffected by the new Act. A constable may enter (if necessary by force) and search any place where anyone (whom he has the right to arrest) is or where, with reasonable cause, he suspects him to be. A person may use such force as is reasonable in the circumstances in the prevention of crime or in effecting or assisting in the lawful arrest of offenders or suspected offenders or of persons unlawfully at large. (This power is not restricted to constables, nor in actual terms to indictable offences; but the words " such force as is reasonable in the circumstances " prevent or, by implication, forbid the use of force for arrest in the case of trivial offences.)

The common law offence of *receiving* is defined as follows: " A person shall be treated as receiving property if he dishonestly undertakes or assists in its detention, removal, or realisation by or for the benefit of another or if he arranges so to do." The common law crimes of theft, and similar offences, codified in the Larceny Act, 1916, have now been recodified, expanded, and more clearly defined by the Theft Act, 1968.

III. STATUS.

A person's *Status—i.e.,* his legal position in society—affects his legal rights and duties in most civil matters and, in some few cases, in criminal matters too (*see* Criminal Responsibility, D9(1)).

1. **Nationality,** in this connection, means British Nationality under the British Nationality Acts, the latest of which was passed in 1965. By the 1948 Act the term " Commonwealth Citizen " was created which can be used as an alternative to British Subject. A person may be a British subject by birth, by naturalisation, by marriage, or by registration, though under the Act of 1948 a woman who was not a British subject before marriage does not automatically acquire British nationality merely by reason of her marriage to a British subject. The law and the courts of this country can determine whether a person is a *British subject* or an *alien*; they cannot determine whether or not he is a citizen of some particular foreign state, since that is a matter for the law of the foreign state concerned. Generally speaking, in times of peace, an alien in this country has the same rights and duties as a British subject, except that an alien has no right to vote in parliamentary or municipal elections, and that some professions (*e.g.,* that of a solicitor) are closed to him. By the Act of 1964, a person who is stateless may apply to be registered as a citizen of the U.K. and Colonies if either parent was such a citizen when he was born, or if the place of his birth is within the U.K. and Colonies at the time of his application. By the Act of 1965 alien wives of those British subjects who are not citizens of any Commonwealth country may be registered as British subjects.

2. **Domicil** means the country where a person has his permanent home without any present intention of changing it. His *domicil of origin* is that of his parents while he is a minor; at the age of majority he is free to acquire a new domicil by making his permanent home elsewhere. Domicil is of particular importance in matters of—

3. **Marriage and Divorce.**—English law generally regards as valid a marriage ceremony carried out in this country after the proper preliminaries and with the proper formalities, whatever the nationality or domicil of the parties. English law also accepts the validity of a marriage ceremony which has been carried out abroad according to the law of the country where it took place. But if one party or the other has an English domicil, the *status of the marriage as an institution* must depend on English law, whether the ceremony was in proper form or not. For example, a man who has his permanent home in England cannot evade the English rule against consanguinity by going through a ceremony of marriage, in Ruritania, with his mother's sister—even if such a marriage is lawful by Ruritanian law, and even if the ceremony has been carried out with the usual Ruritanian formalities, it is still null and void by the law of England. The English court will not, generally speaking, grant a divorce to a man who is domiciled abroad, since the law of the country which is his permanent home may not recognise this divorce, or perhaps any divorce, as valid; and it is improper that he should be regarded as a single man in England and a married man in his homeland. Similarly, English law *will* generally recognise the validity of a divorce granted by the proper court of his domicil (*i.e.,* of the state where he had his permanent home at the time) or of a divorce which the law of his domicil regards as valid, even if it was granted by a court elsewhere—and that whether he is a British subject or not. Under recent court decisions, English law may also recognise a divorce granted by the court of a country with which he has some *genuine connection.* But a person, whatever his nationality, whose per-

manent home is in England will not be regarded
here as validly divorced merely because he has
spent a few weeks in **Angria**, where divorce procedure is simple, and has been granted a decree
there. His status—married or single—generally
depends on the law of his domicil—*i.e.*, the law of
the country which is his permanent home. (*See
also* **D34**(1).)

4. Minority is the status of a person under the
age of majority (now eighteen). A minor cannot
vote at elections; he cannot hold freehold or leasehold property, and he cannot be made bankrupt.
(In exceptional cases where the debt is for " necessaries " (**D14**(1), a bankruptcy notice may be
issued against a minor.) If he enters into certain
kinds of contracts during his minority he can
repudiate them, if he so desires, up to a reasonable time after his majority. He cannot make a
valid will, and his rights under another person's
will or settlement cannot be compromised or
altered without the leave of the High Court. A
minor cannot make a valid marriage without consent of his parent or guardian, or of the appropriate
court. His rights are now the special care of the
Family Division of the High Court, which will
protect those rights according to the Rules of
Equity (*see* **D8**(1)). The Family Law Reform Act,
1969, has reduced the age of majority to eighteen
for all purposes, including the parliamentary vote
and marriage without parental consent.
" Minor " and " minority " may now be used in all
cases instead of " infant " and " infancy."

5. Lunacy, in the broad legal sense, is the status
of a person who is " incapable, by reason of un-
soundness of mind, of managing his affairs."
" Lunacy " in this sense is not necessarily identical
with any of the mental conditions to which such
psychological terms as " insanity," " imbecility,"
" idiocy," and the like are applied; there need
be no actual mental disease. When a person
becomes incapable, for this reason, of managing
his affairs, the law, in order to protect both him
and society at large, changes his status by putting
the custody of his person, or the control of his
property, or both, into reliable hands. Such
matters come under the supervision of the Chancery Division, since one of the functions of Equity
(see above) is to protect those who cannot help
themselves. Certification of " insanity " (in the
psychological sense) is not necessary; but with
the proper medical certificate and legal safeguards the *patient* (as he must be called) may be
removed to a mental hospital. Some reliable
person (usually a near relative) may be appointed,
by an Order of the *Court of Protection* (a branch
of the Chancery Division), as *Receiver* to look after
property. The Receiver's duties are to look after
the property and income of the patient, pay his
debts and defray the expenses of his maintenance
and medical care, and generally to deal with the
patient's property on the patient's behalf.
Periodical accounts must be submitted to the
Court, which will scrutinise them strictly and at
once intervene if there appears to be any irregularity on the part of the Receiver. If there is no
relative to take the responsibility, the *Official
Solicitor* at the Royal Courts of Justice will be
appointed as Receiver, with the same duties and
liabilities.

Apart from these matters of administration, a
person of unsound mind is regarded as incapable
of making a valid will, of entering into a legal
agreement, or of dealing with his property. None
of these transactions is valid unless the person
concerned understood the nature and effect of
what he was doing; and whether he did understand or not is a question of *evidence* in every
individual case; medical and other witnesses must
testify to his conduct and demeanour at the time
when he entered into the transaction in question.
If the Court comes to the conclusion that he was
unable to understand the nature and effect of the
transaction, the Court will *rescind*—*i.e.*, set aside
or cancel—the transaction, even though it was in
proper legal form. By the Administration of
Justice Act, 1969 the Court of Protection may now
authorise the execution of a will or codicil for the
patient.

6. Bankruptcy is the creation of Statute Law—
there was no common law of bankruptcy. It is
the status of a person (the " debtor ") who is
insolvent—*i.e.*, who is unable to pay his debts
(exceeding £50) as they fall due. By the appropriate procedure the State takes the management
of the debtor's property out of his hands and
places it in the hands of the *Official Receiver*,
whose duty it is to realise it and (subject to certain
privileged claims) to distribute it proportionately
among his creditors. The procedure is that one
of the creditors files at the Bankruptcy Court a
bankruptcy petition, on which the Court may
make a receiving order, which has the effect of
transferring the legal management of the debtor's
property to the Official Receiver. That official
investigates the debtor's finances and draws up an
account, called a *statement of affairs*, showing the
debtor's liabilities and assets. There is a meeting
of creditors and a public examination of the debtor
in Court, as a result of which the Court may either
discharge the receiving order (on the debtor's
showing that he can pay his debts, if he is given
time, or persuade the general body of creditors
to accept his proposals for a *composition* of so
much in the £), or the Court may adjudicate the
debtor a bankrupt. In the latter case it is open
to the creditors either to leave the management
of the debtor's property in the Official Receiver's
hands or themselves to appoint a *trustee in bankruptcy* (usually an accountant) nominated by
some or all of them, and that trustee takes over
the management of the debtor's affairs. The
debtor is bound, under penalty, to give full
information about his affairs to the Official
Receiver and the trustee in bankruptcy: he
cannot, while he is a bankrupt, sit or vote in
Parliament or act as a Justice of the Peace or in
certain other offices. He will be committing an
offence if he conceals any property or debt or
falsifies his books of account, if he obtains property
on credit or secures credit of £10 or more without
disclosing his status, if he trades without such
disclosure or fails to keep proper books of account,
or if he leaves or attempts to leave the country,
taking with him property, worth £20 or more,
which ought to be divided among his creditors.
It is also an offence for him to transfer property
with intent to defraud any creditor, and any such
transaction may be set aside by the Court.

7. A Corporation or Incorporated Body is an
association of persons recognised by Act of
Parliament, or by its Charter, as one single legal
entity. It may be a *chartered* or a *statutory
corporation* (*e.g.*, the British Broadcasting Corporation or the London Transport Board), a *local
authority* (*e.g.*, the Greater London Council or
the Westminster City Council), or a *company*
incorporated under the Companies Act, 1948, or
one of the earlier Companies Acts. Generally
speaking, a corporation of any kind has power
only to do such things as it is given power to do
by its Charter or by the Act of Parliament under
which it was constituted; if it goes beyond that
power it is behaving *ultra vires*—" beyond its
powers "—and such acts on its part will be
regarded by the Courts as null and void. The
Court may also restrain the corporation by
injunction—an Order forbidding it to act in such
a manner.

Every corporation, being a single legal entity,
is a legal *person* distinct from the individuals who
are its members. Thus the corporation itself can
take proceedings, or have proceedings brought
against it, in the Civil Courts, and it may itself
be prosecuted in the Criminal Courts, if it commits
an offence, and be liable to a fine. No personal
liability rests upon its individual members,
directors, or officers unless they have personally
done something unlawful or aided and abetted the
corporation in its wrongdoing. The corporation
itself can enter into a legal agreement with one or
more of its members or a member of the public,
and any person injured by its acts can enforce
his legal rights against the property or assets of
the corporation, which are distinct from the
property or assets of the individuals who compose
it.

A *company* is usually a commercial concern and
generally takes advantage of the principle of
limited liability, in which case the last word in

its name must be the word "Limited." The principle is that, in the event of the company's becoming insolvent, none of its members can be compelled to contribute to its funds a larger sum than the sum which he agreed to pay for his shares, however large the indebtedness of the company itself. Every company must file at the Companies Registry a *Memorandum of Association*, setting out its name, the situation of its registered office, its objects (beyond which it has no power to act), its capital, and whether or not it is *limited*. It should also file its *Articles of Association*, setting out its rules of management, the method of issuing, allotting, and transferring its shares, the procedure for meetings, the powers and duties of its directors and other officers, and similar matters. If and when its objects have been fully achieved, or if it is desired to discontinue its activities, or if it becomes insolvent, it will be wound up and dissolved. The winding-up is undertaken by a *Liquidator* whose duties are similar to those of the trustee in bankruptcy. The liquidator may be nominated by the members of the company or, in case of the company's insolvency, by some or all of the creditors, and the liquidator's appointment must be confirmed at a special meeting. If the winding-up of an insolvent company takes more than a year the liquidator must report annually to the Board of Trade, the Government Department which watches the interests of the persons concerned.

8. Adoption. *See* D38–41.
9. Legitimacy. *See* D35–7.

IV. The CIVIL LAW or LAW OF PERSONS.

This deals with the relations between one individual citizen and another, and their mutual rights and duties. If A makes a business agreement with B, and breaks it, or if A walks without permission across B's field of new-mown hay, B will be able to secure *redress* against A by proceedings in a court of law. But in neither case is it necessary for the State to intervene, by way of prosecution, to punish A for what he has done, since no offence against society at large, and no violation of public order, or the rule of law, has arisen. The issue is one merely between A and B; B may choose to ignore the wrong done to him, or he may negotiate amicably with A for the payment of compensation, or, if this fails, he may as plaintiff sue A as defendant in a civil action for *damages*. Unlike a criminal prosecution, undertaken by the State for the preservation of public order and vindication of the rule of law, with a view to punishing the offender, the civil action will be brought, if B so chooses, by B himself for the purpose of recovering compensation in money for the harm he has suffered and (in some cases) of obtaining an *injunction*—a Court Order prohibiting A from continuing his wrongful conduct. Again, a criminal prosecution will not be discontinued even at the request of the injured party, since the State itself is interested to see justice done; but a civil action can be discontinued by B at whatever stage he desires, with or without an agreement for the payment of damages in compensation.

These relations between one individual and another, interference with which may give rise to a civil action for damages or injunction, may arise in two alternative ways:—from the acts of the parties themselves, or from the operation of law. Hitherto evidence of a criminal conviction has not been admitted in civil cases, but this rule is abolished by the Civil Evidence Act, 1968. The onus of proving that the conviction was wrong lies on the accused.

1. Law of Contract.

The relations between individuals which arise from the acts of the parties themselves are usually brought about by a *contract*—*i.e.*, by an agreement between them. A contract may be (*a*) expressed in words, as where A agrees to buy B's motor-car for £400, on certain stated conditions, or (*b*) implied by conduct, as where A calls a taxi and tells the driver to take him to a certain address. (*a*) In the former case, particularly if the contract is put into writing, the parties will normally have

expressed all the necessary terms and conditions. (*b*) In the latter case it is *implied* by A's conduct, and understood by law and custom, that A will be expected to pay, at the end of the journey, the amount of the fare recorded by the taximeter; it is not a necessary for the driver to stipulate those terms in advance. Everybody, several times in the course of each day, enters into an implied contract of this kind—when he steps on an omnibus to go to his work, when he orders a meal in a restaurant, when he tells the grocer to deliver goods to his house, and so on.

Simple Contracts and Deeds.

(1) A **Simple Contract** is a contract *expressed in words* (whether in writing or not) without the formalities of a *deed* (*see below*), or a contract *implied by conduct*. There is no legal contract (*a*) unless there is complete certainty on the terms; (*b*) unless the basis of the agreement is lawful; and (*c*) unless both parties are legally capable of entering into it (*see above*, Status), and (*d*) in complete agreement on their intentions. And the agreement is not enforceable (*e*) unless there is some *consideration*, *i.e.*, some *quid pro quo*, expressed or implied, on either side. (The Law Commission, however, is considering the abolition of *consideration* as essential to every contract.) Thus (*a*) a promise by A that he will buy B's motor-car cannot be enforced by either side unless the price is mentioned, nor (*b*) if the car has been stolen by B, nor (*c*) if A is of unsound mind, nor (*d*) if B owns two cars, and A is thinking of the Ford, while B intends to sell the Austin. Again (*e*) a promise by C, during the course of the year's work, that he will give his employee, D, a Christmas box of £5 is not enforceable by D unless he has made a promise, or done something in return. If C tells D that he will give D the £5 at Christmas on condition that D puts in certain extra time over and above his normal working-hours, and D complies or promises to comply, that compliance, or promise of compliance, will be sufficient consideration to turn A's promise into an enforceable contract. There need be nothing at all in writing, except in a few cases laid down by law; in all other cases the only value of a written agreement, signed by both parties, is that it provides clear evidence of the terms that were agreed. A written contract requires a sixpenny revenue stamp if it is to be produced as evidence in a court of law. (The Law Commission is recommending a code to cover the whole law of contract.)

(2) A **Deed** (broadly speaking) is a contract or other written document, *signed*, *sealed*, and *delivered* by the parties. The formalities of affixing one's seal to a legal document, and pronouncing the formula, "I deliver this as my act and deed," have emphasised the significance and solemnity of certain important transactions for many centuries past; and even persons who were unable to write their names were capable of carrying out the formalities of *sealing* and *delivery*. The legal requirement that deeds should also be *signed* was imposed only in 1925, by section 73 (1) of the Law of Property Act. The chief practical distinction between a simple contract and a deed is that a *deed requires no consideration* to make it enforceable. The special formalities which constitute the *execution* of a deed (*i.e.*, signing, sealing, and delivery) take the place of that moral obligation which (in a simple contract) the common law required to be satisfied by consideration on the part of the person to whom the promise was made. For this reason a deed is required in a case where A makes a promise to B which he desires to render enforceable without any corresponding promise by B to A, and also in a case where A desires to make B a gift of property of such a nature that it cannot be physically handed over. This second case arises particularly where the subject of the gift is land or buildings; in fact, by a provision of the Law of Property Act, 1925, a deed is always necessary to transfer the ownership of any freehold or leasehold property, and also to grant a tenancy for a term of more than three years. The transfer of a legal right of some kind (*e.g.*, a share in a company or the claim to moneys under an insurance policy) is generally effected by deed.

In connection with the Law of Contract the following subsidiary matters must be considered:—

Subsidiary Matters.

(a) **Capacity of Parties.**—The question whether a party to a contract is legally capable of entering into it usually depends on that party's status (*see above*):—

(1) **Nationality.**—Nothing turns on this, except that no commercial contract can be made with an alien enemy in time of war.

(2) **Domicil.**—Where the two or more parties to a contract have their permanent homes in different countries it is a wise precaution for them to state, in the contract, under which country's law and by which country's courts, in case of a dispute, its terms are to be construed. If they omit to do so, and some dispute is brought before the English Court, it will endeavour to decide, by considering the wording of the contract, the language in which it is written, the domicil of the parties, and the general circumstances in which the contract was made, what legal system the parties intended to apply and by what court they intended is to be judged. Sometimes it will decide the dispute according to the rules of the foreign law.

(3) **Marriage and Divorce.**—There is now no practical difference in contractual capacity between single persons, married persons, and divorcees.

(4) **Minority.**—It is not (generally speaking) impossible for a minor to enter into a valid contract, but he will be entitled to repudiate it at any time up to the date of his majority (or a reasonable period after that) unless the contract is (a) clearly for the minor's benefit on the whole (*e.g.*, professional articles or an agreement for apprenticeship), or (b) for the provision of necessaries—*i.e.*, food, drink, clothing, or services which are necessary to the minor in his particular station in life. (The origin of this latter rule is probably the practical consideration that, in earlier times, few people would have taken the risk of providing a minor, on credit, with the bare necessities of life if they had been precluded from suing him for reasonable payment.)

(5) **Lunacy.**—A party to a contract who knows that the other party is of unsound mind will not be permitted to hold the latter to his bargain.

(6) **Bankruptcy.**—A bankrupt cannot make a valid agreement to deal with his property in a manner which contravenes the law of Bankruptcy.

(7) **Corporations.**—Whether a corporation is capable of entering into a particular contract depends upon the legal powers conferred by the Charter or Act of Parliament under which it was constituted, or (if a company) by its Memorandum of Association. If the matter to which the contract relates is of grave importance it will usually signify its adherence to the contract by affixing its seal with the formalities laid down by its Rules or Articles of Association. If it is an everyday or trivial matter the corporation will normally enter into a contract through some agent (*e.g.*, its Town Clerk, Director, or Secretary, as the case may be) who is empowered to sign or speak on its behalf.

(8) and (9) Neither adoption nor legitimacy (or illegitimacy) affects a party's capacity to enter into a contract.

(b) **When Writing is Necessary.**—There are certain exceptions, laid down by Act of Parliament, to the rule that a contract is enforceable even if made only by word of mouth or implied by conduct. The Statute of Frauds, 1677, provided that contracts of these exceptional kinds cannot be enforced by action in the Courts " unless the agreement upon which such action shall be brought, or some memorandum or note thereof, shall be in writing, and signed by the party to be charged therewith, or some other person thereunto by him lawfully authorised "—these last words mean an *agent*. It is not necessary that the whole of the agreement shall be formally set down in writing; but there must be a written and signed record of all the *essential terms*.

(i) A Guarantee.—*I.e.*, a promise by A to B in the form—" Please lend money (or supply goods) to C, and if C does not pay you I will." A's promise by word of mouth cannot be enforced against him.

This provision of the Statute of Frauds still holds good.

(ii) An *agreement* for the *sale or disposition of land* (or *buildings*) or of any interest in land (or buildings). We have already stated that the actual transfer of a freehold or leasehold interest must be effected by deed. This is not the same as an agreement to sell or dispose of land or buildings; a *transfer* effects an immediate change of ownership, while an *agreement to sell* binds the party who signs it to make a transfer of ownership at some future time. Such an agreement need not be in the form of a deed, but its essential terms must be in writing.

Some other parts of the Statute of Frauds have been repealed: that contained in (ii) above has been replaced by a similar provision set out in section 40 of the Law of Property Act, 1925.

(iii) *A bill of exchange or promissory note* must be in writing, by virtue of section 3 of the Bills of Exchange Act, 1882.

(iv) A contract of *Marine Insurance* is inadmissible in evidence unless it is embodied in a marine policy as laid down in the Marine Insurance Act, 1906, sections 22–24, with all relevant conditions fully specified, and duly signed by or on behalf of the insurer.

(v) By the Contracts of Employment Act, 1963 (in force since July 1964), it is the duty of an employer (not later than 13 weeks after the employment commenced) to hand his employee a written statement of particulars of the employment (period, wage, working hours, and what length of notice is required for termination).

(c) **Mistake.**—Suppose that John Brown wants his portrait painted by a famous artist called William Brush, of whom he has heard but whom he has never met. He looks up " William Brush " in the directory and writes to him, at the address shown, offering him 100 guineas to paint the portrait. Suppose that particular " William Brush " is not the artist at all but a stockbroker of the same name. Even if that William Brush accepts Brown's offer, their apparent agreement will not constitute a valid contract, since Brown's mistake as to Brush's identity is so fundamental that it destroys the very basis of the agreement. Where there is a mistake of this kind, " going to the very root of the agreement," no valid contract has, in the eyes of the law, been made. In other special cases equity may, on the ground of conscience, relieve one or both parties from liability under a concluded contract by *rectification* (*i.e.*, by correcting the terms they have inadvertently recorded) or by *rescission* (*i.e.*, by cancellation of the contract). It is not every mistake that will lead to these results; either the mistake must have been *fundamental* or the circumstances must have been such that it would be *unconscientious* for one party or the other to try to enforce his apparent rights.

(d) **Misrepresentation.**—Equity, on similar grounds, has often relieved a party from liability under a contract into which he has been induced to enter through a *representation* by the other party which is *substantially false*—*i.e.*, a statement which is misleading on some essential point. Whether the misrepresentation was deliberate or innocent, the deceived party will usually be able to have the contract set aside—*i.e.*, cancelled.

Suppose, for example, Jones wants to insure his life with the Markshire Insurance Company. Before issuing the policy, which is the contract between them, the Company will ask Jones—"Have you ever suffered from any serious illness?" Suppose Jones says "No," though he did in fact suffer from tuberculosis five years ago. Even if the policy contains a promise by the Company to pay Jones's widow £5000 upon Jones's death, the Company will be entitled to refuse to pay when that event happens; it has been induced to enter into the contract through Jones's misrepresentation.

By the Misrepresentation Act, 1967, if a person enters into a contract (later than April, 1967, when the Act became law) after a misrepresentation has been made by the other party, and (a) the misrepresentation has become a term of the contract, or (b) the contract has been carried out, or both, then, if under the old law he would have been entitled to rescind (i.e., cancel) the contract without alleging fraud, he shall be entitled to do so, in spite of (a) and (b). (Under the old law, once the contract had been carried out, his only remedy was damages, if he had suffered loss.) It is now provided that where such misrepresentation has been made to a person as a result of which he has suffered loss, then the other party shall be liable to damages even if there was no fraud (i.e., deliberate deceit), unless he proves that he believed, on reasonable grounds, up to the date of the contract, that his representations were true. In any case the Court may award damages instead of, or in addition to, rescission, if the Court thinks it equitable to do so, whether the misrepresentation was innocent or fraudulent.

If an agreement is made containing a clause excluding or restricting liability for misrepresentation, that clause shall be ineffective unless the Court thinks it fair and reasonable. In sales of goods rescission and/or damages are to be available to the buyer even after he has become the owner of the goods. And he is not deemed to have accepted them until he has been afforded and has had a reasonable opportunity of inspecting them to ascertain whether they conform to the contract or not.

(Note: This Act is expected to remove abuses, particularly at some auction sales, where the sellers, in their catalogues, have been reckless in attributing a work of art to a particular artist, and have excluded liability for misdescription in the contract.)

(e) **Duress** means compulsion by *threats* or *force.* If a man has been compelled in this manner to put his name to a contract it is *voidable* by him at any time—*i.e.,* he may repudiate it on the ground of duress, and will be upheld by law in doing so. *Undue influence* means influence exerted by A upon B to such an extent that B could not have exercised any free and independent will in doing a particular act. Equity has always been jealous to protect certain classes of persons from this kind of influence; it goes so far as to presume that there has been undue influence where a guardian has got some benefit out of his ward, a parent from his child who is under (or only just over) majority, a doctor from his patient, a solicitor from his client, or a priest from his parishioner. In most of such cases the onus is upon the person in the influential position, who has obtained the benefit, to prove that there was no undue influence; it is not for the other person to prove that his mind was wrongfully influenced by the former.

(f) **Illegality** of contract arises where the parties have agreed to do an act (i) forbidden by law or (ii) contrary to "public policy." (i) The former includes not only an agreement to commit a crime, but also an agreement to do an act which might be harmful to a third party and give him a right of action for breach of contract or tort. The courts will obviously not lend their assistance to a plaintiff who complains that the defendant has refused to honour his agreement to do something unlawful, whether (for example) the agreement was to burgle a house or merely to write a libellous article about another person. (ii) Even if the act agreed upon was not actually unlawful, the courts will refuse to enforce the agreement if it was to do something which is regarded as harmful to the community. It is not, for example, a

crime for a man and a woman to live together without being married, nor is it even "unlawful" in the civil sense that such a way of life gives the one a right of action against the other; but no court would enforce an agreement by a woman to become a man's mistress, nor an agreement by the man to maintain her in return.

(g) **Breach of Contract** occurs when one of the parties breaks his promise and neglects or refuses to perform his duty under the contract. Breach by one party entitles the other party to sue for *damages,* the amount of which is usually assessed so as to compensate the latter for the *actual loss* he has suffered. The object is to put the injured party, so far as money can do it, into the position he would have been in had the contract not been broken. From 1 January 1971 the Law Reform (Misc. Provns.) Act, 1970, has abolished breach of promise suits.

(1) *Damages* have always been the common-law remedy for breach of contract. In special cases, however, equity may grant two other remedies in addition to, or in substitution for, damages; but only where equity regards damages as an insufficient compensation. These additional remedies are:—

(2) *Specific Performance.—I.e.,* an order, to the party in breach, actually to carry out what he contracted to do. In practice this remedy is confined to: (i) contracts for the sale or letting of land or buildings, and (ii) contracts for the sale of some article of a special nature which cannot be replaced by spending money in the open market —for example, the sale of an original painting by Rembrandt. The remedy of specific performance is never granted to enforce a contract for personal services, since it would be impossible for the court to supervise the carrying out of such a contract.

(3) *Injunction.—I.e.,* an order by the court to the party in default *prohibiting him* from carrying out some positive act which would constitute a breach of contract. For example, where a singer has entered into a contract to work, for a certain period, only under the management of one particular impresario and no other, the court may order the singer not to offer or engage her services elsewhere during that period. Disobedience to an injunction constitutes *contempt of court,* and is punishable by fine or imprisonment.

2. Law of Tort.

This branch of the law deals with the relations, between one individual citizen and another, which arise from the operation of the law itself, without the necessity for the parties to do any act to put them into legal relations with one another. As was pointed out above (D13(1)), if A and B are to be linked in a contractual relationship, each of them must take some step to bring that relationship about. No such step, however, is necessary in connection with the matters dealt with by the Law of Tort. Everybody has a right to expect that his person and his property shall be inviolable by other private citizens; he also has a right to expect others to refrain from attacks upon his character and his business reputation. These rights do not arise from any agreement or other act on his part, but from the general principles of the law.

A *tort* is the violation of such a right, which entitles the injured party to bring a civil action for damages to compensate for the injury he has suffered. The word *tort* (in French "wrong") is derived from the Latin *tortus* meaning "twisted" or "distorted."

It will be seen from the Table (D4) that some torts (*e.g.,* assault) may also be crimes—that is, they may entitle the injured party either to bring a civil action for damages or to prosecute the offending party and have him punished by a criminal court in cases where the offending party's action is liable to harm the community at large; a personal assault, for example, may lead in some circumstances to general disorder, and in that event it will become a matter for intervention by the State through the criminal courts (*see* **D6**). This section, however, deals only with the *civil remedies* which, as in breaches of contract, are primarily *damages* and sometimes *injunction*.

Trespass is a wrongful act committed by one citizen, against the will of another citizen, either against the latter's person or in disturbance of his possession of land or other property.

The Law Commission has made proposals for new legislation to make it a criminal offence to destroy or damage any property without lawful excuse, especially if that would endanger life, to threaten to do such an act, or to possess anything by which property could be destroyed or damaged (July 1970).

(1) Trespass against the Person may be by way of *assault*, *battery*, or *false imprisonment*. An *assault* is an attempt to do violence to the person of another; if the act is fully consummated it becomes a battery. Thus it is an assault for one man to shake his fist in the face of another, or to adopt a threatening attitude towards another, or deliberately to set his dog on another person. If the first person actually strikes the other person, or if the dog, encouraged by the first person, actually bites or harms the other person, that is a *battery*. In order to constitute an assault or battery, and to render the trespasser liable to an action for damages, his act must be *deliberate*. It is not assault and battery if A accidentally knocks against B in a crowd, with the result that B falls and is injured. The act by the trespasser must also be against the will of the person injured. Thus an operation performed by a surgeon, though it may seriously affect the body of the other person, is not an assault or battery if the other person has consented to the operation; but such an operation, performed without the other person's consent may amount to an assault or battery.

Certain acts which would in the ordinary way constitute assault or battery are excusable; it is recognised, for example, by the common law, that a parent or a teacher has the right to inflict reasonable chastisement upon a child or pupil in his care, and provided that the chastisement is not excessive the child or pupil has no right of action. If, however, the chastisement results in serious injury or amounts to brutal violence, then the person inflicting it will be liable to an action for damages. (The present Government is considering abolition of corporal punishment in schools.)

False imprisonment means the *unlawful restraint* of one person by another. It need not amount to actually locking up a person in a room; it is sufficient if his freedom of movement is *totally restrained* either by confinement or by the use of force or threat of force. It should be noted that the restraint must be unlawful; it is not, for example, unlawful for a police officer to arrest a person engaged in committing a crime, or a person whom the officer has reasonable grounds for suspecting of committing, or being about to commit, a violent crime. Even a private citizen may lawfully arrest a person who has actually committed a violent crime or whose behaviour has led to a breach of the peace (*see* **D11(1)**).

The tort of *malicious prosecution* is committed by a person who makes a criminal charge against another person where the proceedings terminate in the acquittal of the latter, where the first person was actuated by spite or ill-will, where there was no reasonable or proper cause for the proceedings, and where the second person has suffered damage as a result. The essence of the tort is *malice* on the part of the person who brought the criminal charge; it is not sufficient that he was honestly mistaken.

(2) Trespass to Land arises whenever one person *enters unlawfully* upon land or a building in the possession of another person. Two important points should be noted, as several popular fallacies exist about this tort. First, trespass to land is not in the ordinary case a crime, unless there is some Act of Parliament which makes the trespass a criminal offence (for example, under certain statutes it is a criminal offence for an unauthorised person to cross a railway-line or to enter a Govern-

ment airfield from which considerations of security require unauthorised persons to be excluded). Secondly, it is not necessary, to constitute a trespass, that actual damage should be done to the land or building on which the trespasser has set foot. The essence of the tort is interference with the possession of the other party, and this may arise by merely walking across his field, or throwing refuse upon it, or placing or erecting anything on the land without the other party's consent; any act of physical interference suffices.

(3) Nuisance.—The *tort of nuisance* arises when an occupier of land or premises does something there which substantially interferes with the enjoyment by a neighbouring occupier of his land or premises. In trespass (*see above*) the interference must be physical; this is not so in cases of nuisance. For example, it is a nuisance if A allows his factory chimney to emit volumes of thick smoke which drifts continually into B's house or garden, or for A to carry on, in a building belonging to him, a trade or process which causes noxious smells or disturbing vibrations liable to interfere with B's enjoyment of his property. It is not, however, every such act that gives rise to an action for nuisance; there must be a certain amount of " give and take," particularly in urban areas, but people must not use their premises in an unreasonable or wilfully annoying manner. Thus it has been held that a teacher of music who had pupils singing in her house for several hours a day and on several days a week, which caused considerable disturbance to the person next door, was not committing a nuisance, since it was not unreasonable for her to use her house in this manner. On the other hand, when the person next door retaliated by clashing domestic implements and deliberately making as much noise as possible while the lessons were going on, he was held to have committed a nuisance because his conduct was unreasonable and wilfully annoying. But every case depends upon its own special facts. A building contractor who keeps a pneumatic drill going outside a private house, in connection with building operations, is not liable to an action for nuisance, provided that the use of the drill is necessary to the work, that it is confined to reasonable working hours and limited to a temporary period; but if the owner of a motor-cycle were to keep its engine running, merely to demonstrate its power, outside his own garage for several hours a day, and on several days a week, his neighbours could claim that that was (in law) a nuisance. The Noise Abatement Act, 1960, gives rights to local councils (on their own initiative or on complaint by three householders) to order reduction of unnecessary noise (including loudspeakers) in streets, parks and gardens, and to prosecute offenders.

All the above examples may be classed as *private nuisances*, and they are torts but not crimes. There is, however, another class, known as *public nuisances*, which become criminal offences if they are liable to injure the public in general. Examples of these are leaving an unlighted obstruction on a public road, blocking a public footpath, or allowing a building to get into such a state of disrepair that it causes a danger to users of the public highway. In such cases the person causing the public nuisance may be prosecuted and punished and, moreover, any individual citizen injured by such conduct may have a right to bring a civil action for damages.

(4) Trespass to Goods is an unlawful disturbance by A of B's lawful possession of his goods. Such disturbance may arise by seizure or removal of the goods without the owner's consent or by conduct causing damage to the goods. It follows that every theft of goods is also a trespass; but for the preservation of public morality it is laid down that, if there is a criminal element in the conduct of the wrongdoer which makes his trespass theft, the injured party cannot bring a civil action for damages unless the thief has first been prosecuted in a criminal court.

The *tort of detinue* consists in the wrongful

detention by one person of another's goods and his failure or refusal to deliver them up when demanded.

The *tort of conversion* or *trover* arises when A wrongfully appropriates the goods of B to his own use or to the use of another person, depriving the owner of them permanently or for a substantial time, or destroying them. These torts of *detinue* and *conversion* can be committed only against goods or articles of property; they cannot arise from interference with fixtures permanently attached to a building, growing crops or trees; but these torts may be committed if, after such things have been removed or cut down, the wrongdoer detains or converts them to his own use.

(5) Negligence in law has a very specialised meaning; it is not " neglect " or " carelessness " in the ordinary sense, but failure to take such care as the circumstances of the particular case demand. In the *tort of negligence* there are two essential elements—first, a *legal duty* to exercise proper care and, secondly, *a failure* to take such care. No action for negligence can be brought by A against B, even if B has been grossly careless, unless the relations between the parties were such that B was under that legal duty towards A. Moreover, the degree of care which A is entitled to expect from B will vary according to the nature of those relations.

One obvious example where the legal duty of care arises is among persons using the roads. All of us have the right to use the roads for the purpose of travelling, on foot or in some vehicle, and the manner in which each of us exercises that right will obviously affect the safety and comfort of other road-users. There is therefore a *legal duty of care* upon every road-user (under the common law, and quite apart from the provisions of Acts of Parliament relating to motor-cars) to exercise his right to walk or drive with due regard to the similar rights of other road-users. And, equally obviously, the *standard* or *degree of care* which it is reasonable to expect from the driver of a powerful car is higher than that which is expected from a pedestrian, since the amount of damage which will be caused by carelessness on the part of the driver is very much greater than that which the pedestrian is capable of inflicting.

We are not here referring to offences under the Road Traffic Acts, for which drivers or pedestrians may be prosecuted and punished under the criminal law. Careless or reckless driving or walking may be a criminal offence under those Acts, even if it has caused no injury to any person or property. In cases where such injury has been caused the test to be applied, in determining whether the injured person can sue and recover damages against the other party, is whether that other party has fallen short of the standard of care reasonably to be expected from him. It is true that disobedience to a provision of the Road Traffic Acts, or neglect of the Highway Code, may constitute evidence helping to prove that the latter party was lacking in the proper standard of care required of him; but there may be other circumstances which show that he was negligent in law, and liable to an action by the injured party for damages, even though he committed no criminal offence.

There are many other relationships where the duty to take care arises. One of these is the relation between the occupier of premises and persons coming on to the premises, whether they have a right to be there or not. Towards trespassers (*see above*) the duty of the occupier is merely a negative one—he must not " set a trap "—*i.e.*, he must not deliberately do anything calculated to cause injury, nor must he do any act which, if done carelessly, is reasonably likely to cause injury. If he knows a trespasser is on the premises he must warn him before he does any dangerous act; the fact that the trespasser has no lawful right to be there does not entitle the occupier (for example) to weaken the supports of a bridge or set off an explosion without warning. If the occupier does so, he will be liable to be sued for damages, in an action for negligence, even by a trespasser who is injured as a result. (The Law Commission has recommended that ownership or use of dangerous things, dangerous activities, and damage by animals be penalised by civil action. Damages are to be assessed on a broader basis.)

The other rules, relating to the duty of care owed by an occupier to persons coming on to his premises are now contained in the Occupier's Liability Act, 1957.

The occupier's duty towards a trespasser remains unchanged. The Act, however, abolishes the former distinction between an *invitee* and a *licensee*, both of whom it describes by the new term, *visitor*. The principal rules are:—

1. The occupier owes the same duty (" the common duty of care ") to all his visitors, except in so far as he is free to, and does, extend, restrict, modify, or exclude his duty, to any visitor, by agreement or otherwise.

2. The " common duty of care " means a duty to take such care as in all the circumstances is *reasonable*, to see that the visitor will be *reasonably safe* in using the premises for the purpose for which he is invited or permitted to be there.

There are subsidiary rules—*e.g.*, that an occupier must expect children to be less careful than adults, and that a person " in the exercise of his calling " (*e.g.*, window-cleaner) can be expected to appreciate and guard against special risks incidental to that calling. And a landlord of premises, if he is under a legal obligation towards his tenant to keep the premises in repair, is to owe to visitors the same duty as if the landlord were the occupier, so far as concerns dangers arising from his default in carrying out that obligation. One of the matters recommended by the Law Commission is the creation of a right of redress, for purchasers and visitors injured by defects in a building, against vendors and landlords.

Among the classes of persons upon whom the law imposes a duty to take care are those who practise a profession or calling which, from its nature, demands some special skill, ability, and experience. A man who is advised or treated by a physician, surgeon, or dentist, or who consults a lawyer or an architect, is entitled to expect him both to possess and to exercise a reasonable degree of such skill, ability, and experience. If the professional man falls short of the *proper standard*, the patient or client may bring against him an action for damages on account of his negligence. But a mere error of judgment on a difficult point does not amount to negligence, provided that the professional man possesses the proper standard of knowledge and skill and has used them carefully and conscientiously to the best of his ability. And he is not liable, by virtue of his professional status, to an action of negligence for something he has done while acting otherwise than in his professional capacity—*e.g.*, a solicitor who is asked to express an opinion on the value of a house (which is no part of his professional duty). (But a barrister cannot be sued for negligence in the conduct of a case in court.)

(6) Defamation.—The tort of *defamation* is committed by a person who *attacks the reputation* of another by " publishing " a false and defamatory statement concerning him to a third party. If the defamatory statement is in writing or some other permanent form (*e.g.*, a picture, a film, or a gramophone record), then the action will be for *libel*. If the defamatory statement is in spoken words or some other non-permanent form (*e.g.*, by signs or gestures) it will be *slander*.

Another important distinction must be observed at the outset. In cases of libel the person whose reputation has been attacked may sue for damages without proof of " special damage "—*i.e.*, proof that he has *suffered actual harm* from the libellous statement; while in slander no action can normally be brought *unless special damage* can be proved. There are, however, five exceptional cases where such proof is unnecessary, *viz.*, in slanders:—

(*a*) disparaging a person in the way of his business, profession, or office of profit (*e.g.*, saying of a doctor that " he is ignorant of the first principles of medicine ");

(b) imputing dishonesty to a person holding an office of honour (e.g., saying of a Councillor that " he gives contracts to his friends ");

(c) imputing that a person has committed a crime punishable by imprisonment (e.g., saying of a man " he is no better than a thief ");

(d) imputing that a person is suffering from a contagious disease of a disgraceful kind (especially a venereal disease);

(e) imputing unchastity to a woman or girl.

In these five cases " publication " of the slander alone is sufficient to give rise to an action, without proof of special damage; for slanders of other kinds no action can be brought unless special damage can be proved.

Note also that no action can succeed, either in libel or slander, inless the statement complained of is (1) false, and (2) defamatory and unless (3) there has been publication to a third party. (1) The statement must be false " in substance and in fact "; if it is substantially true the person complaining has suffered no injury, recognised by law, to his right to the inviolacy of his reputation. (2) The statement must be defamatory—i.e., it must be one which " tends to lower him in the estimation of right-thinking members of the community," or which is " calculated to expose him to hatred, ridicule, or contempt." (3) Publication, in this context, means simply making known the defamatory statement to at least one third party. If the defamatory statement is conveyed only to the person defamed, and to no one else, there is no " publication," and the person defamed has no civil remedy.

In one exceptional case—where a defamatory statement, in writing, is likely to lead to a breach of the peace—the person making it may be prosecuted for the offence of criminal libel, for the purpose not of compensating the injured party, but of upholding law and order (D9(1)). In this exceptional case the truth of the statement (see above) is no defence, and publication to a third party is not necessary to secure a conviction. But there is no such offence as " criminal slander."

If a defamatory statement is made reflecting on a class of persons generally (e.g., an attack on " Methodists " or " coloured people " or " moneylenders ") that will not entitle a person who happens to belong to that class to bring an action unless he can show that he personally was aimed at and defamed. (But under the Race Relations Act of 1965 it is now an offence to stir up hatred on the ground of colour.) The family of a deceased person cannot bring an action for a libel or slander upon the reputation of the deceased.

If the person sued puts forward the defence that the words he used were " not published of and concerning " the person bringing the action, the question must be decided whether those to whom the statement was published could reasonably understand it to refer to him. If such understanding is reasonable, then it is no defence for the person who made the statement to show that he did not in fact intend to refer to the other person, or even that the latter's existence was unknown to him.

Some statements are defamatory in their natural and primary sense (e.g., " John Brief is a thoroughly dishonest lawyer "); others may appear unexceptionable if looked at literally, but may have a defamatory meaning in a particular context, or in particular circumstances known to the persons to whom they are published (e.g., " I hear Mrs. B has left her doctor a lot of money. A fine kind of doctor he is ! "). In cases of the latter kind the person who claims that the published words are defamatory of him must plead an innuendo—i.e., he must set out, in his statement of claim, the meaning in which he alleges the words complained of were used. It will be the duty of the judge to decide, as a matter of law, whether the words are capable of bearing that meaning; the jury will have to decide, as a question of fact, whether the words complained of did actually convey that meaning to those who heard or read

them. There are several recognised defences to actions of libel or slander:—

(1) Justification.—A plea that the words complained of were substantially true. Once the words have been shown to be defamatory, it is for the person who used them to prove their truth—not for the party injured to prove them false.

(2) Absolute Privilege.—By common law, or by Act of Parliament, defamatory words used on certain particular occasions, though published to third parties, cannot give rise to any right of action. The occasion is " absolutely privileged.' No party to any legal proceedings, nor any witness counsel, or member of the jury, nor of course the judge, can be called upon to answer for any words he has used during the proceedings, however spiteful, and however harmful they may have been to the reputation of any other person. The rule applies to pleadings (i.e., allegations in writing filed at the court) as well as to statements made in court by word of mouth.

Similar protection applies to words spoken in Parliament by a member of either House (though words spoken outside either House are not protected). And under the Parliamentary Paper Act, 1840, those who publish (in the ordinary sense of the word) the proceedings of either House by its authority, are protected in the same way so are official communications, on affairs of State made by a minister to the Monarch, or by one officer of State to another in the course of his official duty. To all these absolute privilege ap plies.

(3) Qualified Privilege.—Apart from the case just mentioned, there are other occasions which are privileged, not absolutely, but in a qualified sense. The nature of the qualification will be explained below; meanwhile it may be said that a privileged occasion of this latter kind arise whenever the person making a communication has an interest, or a legal, social, or moral duty to make it, and the person to whom it is made has a corresponding interest or duty to receive it. A common example is a reference given, about the character of a servant, by a former to a prospec tive employer; another is a report made, on the commercial credit of a trader, by one person who has dealt with him to another who intends to do so Other occasions of qualified privilege are reports of judicial proceedings, of public meetings, and of the proceedings of municipal or other public bodies.

Such occasions are privileged to this extent an with this qualification—that there was no malice (i.e., spite or other improper motive) in the mind of the person when he made the communication If there was malice, then the fact that the occasion was one of qualified privilege will not protect him from an action for damages at the suit of the person defamed. In any such action it is the duty of the judge to decide, as a question of law, whether the occasion was one of qualified privilege; it is for the jury to decide, as a matter of fact, whether the defendant was malicious in what he wrote or spoke. (Contrast occasions of absolute privilege where the presence or absence of malice is im material.)

(4) Fair Comment " on a matter of public interest."—This form of defence is most commonly employed by newspapermen, reviewers, and critics. If this defence is to succeed, the words t which it relates must be really comment (i.e expressions of opinion, not statements of fact) the comment must be concerned with a matter of public interest (e.g., a book, a play, a musical per formance, a political speech, or the public action of men in the public eye—but not their private lives). Lastly, the comment must be fair—and cannot be fair if it is actuated by malice in the min of the commentator. If he has mingled with hi comment some statement of fact, and that state ment is inaccurate or misleading, that in itself wil prevent the comment from being regarded as fai The onus is on the defendant who is pleading fai comment to establish that what he is seeking t defend is really comment, that the matter on which he commented was one of public interest (not, fo example, private scandal), and that the commen is not based on any misstatement of facts or other

vise unfair. Dishonest or insincere comment cannot be fair; but on the other hand, an honest belief in the commentator's mind that his comment was fair is not enough for a successful defence. The comment must be fair *in fact*.

The usual remedy in actions of libel and slander is damages—a sum of money sufficient (in the jury's view) to compensate a man for the harm his reputation has suffered. In certain rare cases the Court may, in its discretion, grant an injunction ordering the defendant not to publish or not to repeat the publication of a libel.

The Defamation Act, 1952, reduced the risk of legal proceedings against anyone who *innocently* published " a libel. The " publisher " may make an *offer of amends, i.e.,* an offer to " publish " *correction and apology,* and to take practicable steps to *notify* those who have received copies of any defamatory document. (*a*) If the offer is accepted and the promise performed, the party defamed cannot bring, or continue, an action for libel or slander. (*b*) If the offer is rejected, then the " publisher," in any action taken against him, may plead, in defence, that the words were published " innocently, and that the offer of amends was made as soon as practicable. *Innocent* publication means: (1) that the " publisher " did not intend the defamatory words to refer to the other party, and knew of no reason why they might be understood to refer to him; or (2) that the words were not in themselves defamatory, and that the " publisher " knew of no reason why they might be understood to defame the other party; also that, in either case, the " publisher " exercised all reasonable care in regard to its publication."

V. THE LAW OF PROPERTY.

1. In General.

(1) **Living Persons.**—The special rights and disabilities which affect the ownership and disposal of property by certain classes of persons have been already dealt with under the heading of *Status* (D11–13). It is unnecessary to add anything here on the law of property in general, so far as living persons are concerned; but different rules are applicable (as will be seen below) to the ownership and disposal of land and buildings as compared with property of other kinds. The reason for this main distinction is that the former are, in their nature, immoveable and cannot be physically transferred, as can money and " chattels " (*i.e.,* animals and tangible objects which are capable of being owned). In addition, there is a third class—certain *intangible things* which can be owned and dealt with—for example, the right to be paid a debt, a share or stock in a company, an insurance policy, or a patent; these are known as *things in action,* and they can be transferred only in certain formal ways, which will be described below.

(2) **Deceased Persons.**—It is obvious that the law of any civilised community must make provision, not only for the transfer by a living person of his property, but also for the transmission of that property (his " estate ") upon his death. English Law permits every person who is not disqualified by minority or lunacy (**D12(1)**) to give directions, during his lifetime, as to the disposal of his estate upon his death; he can do this by means of a *will*. If he leaves no valid will he is said to die *intestate*, and in that event the law itself lays down how his estate is to be distributed. A concise survey of the law governing the estates of deceased persons is given below. (Some of these rules have been modified, so far as *domicil* is concerned, by the Wills Act, 1963.)

Wills and Intestacies.—The law of wills is highly technical; much trouble can be caused by a home-made " will, and it is wise to seek a solicitor's advice. It is only possible here to outline the *formalities* necessary to make a valid will, and the *procedure* to be adopted after a death. The rules stated are those under English law—applicable to England and Wales, but not Scotland or Northern Ireland.

(1) **The Nature of a Will.**—The person making a will—the *testator*—sets down how he wishes his property to be disposed of after his death, and states the names of the persons (the *executors*) who are to attend to its disposal.

The executors may be, but need not be, some or all of the persons whom the testator desires to benefit under his will. One executor alone is sufficient in law; but if that one dies before he (or she) has completed his duties, delay and difficulty may arise. It is therefore better to appoint at least two executors; if one dies, the other has full powers to continue the work. If the testator's *estate* (that is, his property) is large, it may be best to appoint a bank as executor; all banks have trustee departments which are experienced in such matters. They have scales of charges for executorship work, which will be supplied on request. An executor is not permitted to charge for his work, unless the will authorises him to do so —a thoughtful provision for a complicated estate. Nor is the executor bound to accept the executorship when death occurs.

A will " speaks from death "—that is, it has no legal effect until the testator dies; it can be *revoked* (that is, cancelled) in various ways, or alterations can be made by *codicil*, which is really a supplementary will. Further, the property to which it relates is that of the testator at the date of his death, which may be more or less than what he owns at the date when the will is made. The will can be revoked or varied as often as desired to suit changing circumstances; its provisions are not final until death.

Generally speaking, a testator may make whatever provisions, in regard to his or her property and the persons to be benefited, he or she thinks fit. He or she may even direct that his or her wife, husband, or children are to be deprived of all benefit from the estate; but, if he or she does so, it will be well to give the reasons, either in the will itself, or in a signed, witnessed, and dated document, which should be left with the will.

Under Acts of 1938, 1952, 1965, 1966, and 1969 a husband or wife, an unmarried daughter or son under majority, or a son or daughter, either natural or adopted, " under disability " (that is, one who for some reason is incapable of looking after himself or herself), who is not adequately provided for under the will, may apply to the Court for " reasonable provision for maintenance " out of the estate; the Court has power either to refuse the application or to grant the applicant whatever maintenance it thinks fit. In making its decision the Court will take note of the testator's reasons for his failure to provide for the applicant in question. Similar rules now apply to former husbands and wives, to the surviving spouse of a void marriage, and to illegitimate children (*see* D36(1)).

If a person dies without leaving a valid will, he is said to die *intestate*. In that case somebody (usually the husband or wife or next of kin) must apply to the Probate Registry (at Somerset House in London or in the nearest District Registry elsewhere) to be appointed *administrator*. An administrator has the same rights and duties as an executor. If there are children under majority, and in certain other cases, there must be at least two administrators, and the procedure on death is more involved and troublesome than where executors have been appointed by will. Further, as the testator has not directed what is to happen to his property, the law has laid down an *order of succession*, which the administrators must observe. The intestate's husband or wife is then entitled first to the *personal effects* (furniture, household goods, motor-cars, books, etc.); next, to the whole of the estate, if there are no children or near relatives, or, if there are, and the estate is large enough, the first £8,750, and, after that, the husband or wife and children have certain rights in the remainder of the estate, if any, details of which can be found in the Intestates' Estates Act, 1952, and the Family Provision Act, 1966. If there is no husband or wife, or no children, or neither, the next of kin of the intestate will benefit in order of nearness of their relationship to the deceased. By the Family Reform Act, 1969, illegitimate children have the same rights to succeed to property on an intestacy as legitimate children.

It is always prudent to make a will, however simple, since by doing so the testator exercises control over the disposal of his property and saves considerable trouble for his family.

(2) The Execution of a Will.

The formalities must be strictly observed, except in the case of soldiers, sailors, and airmen on active service (including members of the Women's Services and nurses), for whom informal directions, even in a letter or by word of mouth, are sufficient. For all other testators, inattention to the formalities may render the will invalid, and will in any case cause considerable trouble and expense.

The will must be in writing—*i.e.*, not by word of mouth—handwritten, typewritten, or printed, but the wording need not be in legal or formal language, so long as it clearly identifies the testator, the executors, the various kinds of property dealt with, and the persons to be benefited. It should also state the following formalities have been carried out when it was executed—that is, signed by the testator and *attested*—*i.e.*, witnessed by two competent persons:

(*a*) The will must be signed by the testator, or by some other person in his presence and by his direction. If the testator can write, his usual signature will suffice; if he is illiterate or too unwell to sign in full, he may make his " mark " or his initials alone. If he is incapable of holding a pen, someone else may sign for the testator, provided he is present at the time and authorises the signature. If the testator is blind or otherwise incapable of reading the will, it should be read over to him before his signature or mark is placed on it, and the fact of his blindness should be mentioned in the final clause. *See also* **D12, end of (5).**

(*b*) The signature or mark must be at the foot or end of the will. This means (i) nothing added below the testator's signature, and (ii) nothing written anywhere on the document after the testator himself has finished signing, will be valid, except the signatures, addresses, and descriptions of the witnesses. If, therefore, at the last minute the testator desires some addition, alteration, or deletion to be made, he and the same witnesses must sign or put their initials against the addition, alteration, or deletion, which otherwise will be ignored.

(*c*) The testator's signature must be made or (if he cannot sign) acknowledged in the presence of two witnesses, who must both be present at the same time. Any persons may be witnesses, so long as they are capable of understanding what is going on. They need not read the will or know its contents; but if either of them is a person who is to take a benefit under the will, or the husband or wife of such a person, he or she will lose that benefit. It is therefore safest to call in witnesses who are strangers to the testator. Both witnesses must be present together when the testator signs (or acknowledges) his signature; it will not be a valid attestation if first one witness, and then the other, is called into the room.

(*d*) The witnesses must sign the will in the presence of the testator. Either witness may, if necessary, sign by mark or initial, but no other person may sign on his behalf. For identification purposes it is usual and desirable for the witnesses to add their addresses and occupations, in case of a subsequent dispute which may necessitate their being found to give evidence.

If the will consists of several pages, they should be fastened together before execution, and the signatures of the testator and witnesses should appear at the end of every page, not to satisfy the rules set out above, but as evidence that every page formed part of the will when it was executed.

It is desirable (though not legally essential) that the will should bear, just above the signatures of the witnesses, an *attestation clause*—that is, a formal statement that these formalities have been carried out. The usual wording of this clause will be found in the example shown below.

All these rules apply in exactly the same way to a *codicil*, which is a supplementary document amending the will in part, *e.g.*, by adding a new legacy.

(3) The Contents of a Will.

The opening words should clearly identify the testator by his full names, occupation or description, present address and (if possible) other recent addresses, and declare that this is his *Last Will*. It is sometimes found at death that a testator has a banking account or stocks and shares registered in his name at some past address, and in such cases the bank or company concerned, wishing to be sure that his identity is clear, may insist upon a sworn statement to the effect that he is the same person as the person they knew as customer or shareholder. (*See* example below.)

Next follows the *revocation clause*—a declaration that the will now being made *revokes* (that is cancels) all previous wills and codicils. If this is not inserted, doubts may arise after death as to whether the new provisions are intended to be substituted for, or merely to supplement, provisions in an older will. If it is intended that the older will is to remain valid in part, that should be clearly stated. If the document now being executed is a *codicil*, it should be described as such and the date of the original will to which it is codicil should be mentioned, and also which part of the original will are being *confirmed*, to stand good, and which *revoked*.

The next clause should appoint the executors who must be identified by their full names and descriptions or addresses. " My brother John, " " my son Charles," or " my mother " will suffice since only one person could possibly answer to any of these descriptions; but " my wife " is not enough without giving her names in full, since it does not follow that the person who is the testator's wife at the time of his death was necessarily his wife when the will was made.

Next follow the directions for disposal of the testator's property. *Bequests or legacies of particular articles* (" my pearl necklace," " my oak bedroom suite ") or of particular investments (" my 3% War Stock ")—these are *specific legacies* —must clearly identify exactly what is being bequeathed. In the case of land or a house, the full description should be given—" my leasehold house and grounds at 31, Acacia Road, Redhill in the County of Surrey," or " my freehold farm known as ' Newlands ' at Northgate in the County of Derby." The words " I devise " are the technical words appropriate to freeholds: " I bequeath " to all other kinds of property: the effect is the same. (Bequests or legacies of sums of money—*pecuniary legacies*—should preferably be stated in words rather than figures; if figures are used the accidental omission of a nought may be disastrous.)

Finally, there is the clause that deals with the *residue* of the Estate—that is to say, whatever will remain after the executors have paid the funeral expenses, death duties (if any), legal and other fees, the testator's debts, and the pecuniary legacies he has bequeathed, and after the specific bequests have been handed over to those entitled. Such a clause is necessary because no testator can be sure, when he makes his will, that he has disposed exactly of everything of which he may die possessed, or that all the persons to whom he has made bequests will necessarily be alive, when he dies. In general, the death of such a person— *legatee*—before the testator causes that person's legacy to lapse; but if there is a bequest of the residue for division among a number of persons no harm is done; the *lapsed legacy*, being left over and undisposed of, leaves the residue to be divided among the surviving *residuary legatees*. The expression " such of the following persons who may survive me " may be properly used.

At the time of writing (Nov. 1970), a Committee is considering the possible relaxation of some of these strict rules.

(4) Revocation and Revival.

A will or codicil may be *revoked* (*i.e.*, cancelled) by " burning, tearing, or otherwise destroying " it with the intention of revoking. Destruction by accident, or without the testator's desire to revoke it, is in effective, and if a copy exists, its provisions may be put forward as still valid. The revocation clause in a later will (*see above*) will be equally effective to revoke an earlier will; or some part of the earlier will may be revoked by a later codicil clearly referring to that part.

A will is also revoked—generally speaking—by subsequent marriage, since the law assumes that, if the testator who is newly married had had time for or given thought to the matter, he would have altered his will. If he did not do so after marriage, he will die intestate.

If a testator makes Will A, and later on Will B containing a revocation clause, Will A is revoked—*i.e.*, cancelled. But if Will B is in turn revoked by Will C, that does not *revive*—*i.e.*, revalidate—Will A, unless Will C says, in so many words, that "Will A is hereby revived."

By the Act of 1969 (**D19**(2)) the words "child," "children" in a will include illegitimate as well as legitimate children (unless otherwise stated).

SPECIMEN WILL

I, JOHN SMITH of 31 Acacia Road Redhill in the County of Surrey Company Director[1] HEREBY REVOKE[2] all wills and testamentary documents[3] heretofore made by me AND DECLARE this to be my LAST WILL.

1. I APPOINT my wife JANE SMITH[4] and my Solicitor EDWARD JONES to be jointly the Executors of this my Will.

2. I DEVISE my freehold farm known as "Newlands" situate at Northgate in the County of Derby unto my son JAMES SMITH in fee simple.[5]

3. I BEQUEATH the following specific legacies:[6]

(1) To my son THOMAS SMITH any motor-car of which I may be the owner[7] at the date of my death.

(2) To my said son JAMES SMITH all my shares in the Company known as John Smith & Sons Limited.

(3) To my said wife all my personal chattels[8] not hereby or by any codicil hereto otherwise bequeathed[9] for her own absolute use and benefit.[10]

(4) I BEQUEATH the following pecuniary[11] legacies:

(1) To my daughter JULIA SMITH the sum of TWO THOUSAND POUNDS.

(2) To my secretary EVELYN ROBINSON the sum of ONE HUNDRED POUNDS.

5. I DEVISE AND BEQUEATH all the residue[12] of my real and personal estate whatsoever and wheresoever not hereby disposed of as to my freeholds in fee simple[5] and as to my personal estate absolutely unto my said wife JANE SMITH for her own absolute use and benefit.[10]

6. I DIRECT that any executor of this my Will being a Solicitor or a person engaged in any profession or business may be so employed and act and shall be entitled to make all proper professional charges[13] for any work done by him or his firm in connection with my Estate including work which an executor not being a Solicitor or a person engaged as aforesaid could have done personally.

IN WITNESS whereof I the said JOHN SMITH the Testator have to this my LAST WILL set my hand this twelfth day of April One Thousand Nine Hundred and Seventy.

[14] SIGNED AND ACKNOWLEDGED by the above-named JOHN SMITH the Testator as and for his LAST WILL in the presence of us both present at the same time who at his request in his presence and in the presence of each other have hereunto subscribed our names as witnesses: } John Smith

    George Matthews,
       6, Elm Road,
          Redhill, Surrey.

  Chauffeur.

    Ida Gray,
       10, Oaktree Road,
          Redhill, Surrey.

  Children's Nurse.

[1] Profession is usually inserted for identification purposes.

[2] Revocation Clause—cancels all previous wills and codicils.

[3] "Testamentary documents"—includes both wills and codicils.

[4] Wife's name should be mentioned—he may have a different wife by the time he dies.

[5] "In fee simple"—technical words showing that the entire freehold interest is disposed of.

[6] "Specific legacies"—*i.e.*, legacies of actually specified things.

[7] Not "my motor-car"; he may sell his present car before he dies and perhaps buy a new one, in which case there might be a dispute as to whether he meant only the car he owned at the date of his will.

[8] This expression is defined in the Administration of Estates Act, 1925. It includes furniture plate, china, wines, cigars, books, and other personal effects. It is better to use a word clearly defined by Act of Parliament than a vague word like "possessions."

[9] *i.e.*, all personal effects which the Testator has not left or will not leave to anybody else.

[10] These words show clearly that, although the wife is one of the Executors, with the duty of clearing up the estate for the benefit of all the persons to be benefited, these particular bequests are for her own personal benefit.

[11] "Pecuniary"—*i.e.*, money.

[12] "Residue"—everything left after all the other gifts have been disposed of, and debts paid.

[13] Charging Clause, without which the Executor who is a solicitor would not be able to charge for his work on the Estate.

[14] This is the proper form of attestation clause—*i.e.*, the clause showing that the proper formalities for signing and witnessing were observed.

Probate and Letters of Administration.—It is a peculiarity of the English system that a deceased person's estate, upon his death, does not "vest in" (*i.e.*, fall into the possession of) the persons to whom he has left it by will, or among whom it has by law to be distributed (the "beneficiaries"); the estate vests, in the first instance, in his executor or executors, if he has appointed any such. (If he has made no such appointment, then, pending the appointment of administrator or administrators (**D19**(2)), the estate vests (for the time being) in the Presiding Judge of the Family Division of the High Court of Justice; that Judge has no duties in relation to the estate; but any notices that would, if there were executors, have to be served upon them, must be served for the time being upon him.) The generic name that applies both to executors and administrators, when their title has been lawfully recognised, is *legal personal representatives*; that is to say they are recognised by law as representing the deceased person, for all purposes under the law of property, and for most purposes under the law of contract and the law of tort. Generally speaking, the deceased person's rights and liabilities are transmitted to his legal personal representatives, and can be enforced by or against them as soon as they have taken out a grant of probate or of letters of administration. (Small estates are dealt with more simply.)

The " grant," in either case, is a document issued by one of the Registries and bearing the seal of the Family Division of the High Court and the signature of one of its Registrars. It states the deceased's name and address, the date and place of his death, and either (1) that his last will has been proved and registered in the Registry concerned, or (2) that he died intestate (as the case may be); that (in the former case) the executors, or (in the latter case) the administrators, whose names, addresses, and descriptions are given, are entitled to administer (*i.e.*, to deal with) all the estate which " vests in " them by law; and the document concludes by certifying that an Inland Revenue Affidavit has been delivered, showing the gross and net values of the estate and the amount of estate duty and interest (if any) paid. Where a will has been " proved," a photostat copy of the will is bound up inside the " grant "; if no will has been " proved " the " grant " consists of a single sheet bearing the above-mentioned particulars. It is important to note that, in either case, the title of the legal personal representatives (*i.e.*, their legal right to deal with the estate) is evidenced by the " grant " —*i.e.*, the document by which the Court's authority is conferred upon them—and not directly by the terms of the will or by their relationship (if any) to the deceased. Anybody, for example, who is purchasing property of the deceased from the legal personal representatives is required only to satisfy himself that probate or letters of administration have been granted to them; such a purchaser is not in the least concerned with the terms of the will.

Whenever any *formal transaction* has to be carried out in connection with the deceased person's estate the " grant " must be produced; this applies in particular to dealings with land or buildings, " things in action " (*see* D27(2)), the initiation, defence, or continuation of legal proceedings for the benefit of the estate, and the transfer of the deceased's contractual rights. There are, however, a number of *informal acts* which the persons (if any) appointed by the will to be executors, or the nearest relatives who intend to apply for letters of administration, may properly do before the issue of the " grant "; these include such common-sense matters as arranging the funeral, safeguarding and insuring documents and valuables, feeding livestock, locking up premises, and preserving property which would deteriorate if neglected. All persons should, however, take care not to sell or dispose of any part of the estate before the " grant " is issued; a person who, without lawful authority, meddles with the estate may find himself regarded as *executor de son tort*—*i.e.*, placed in the position of an executor by his own wrongdoing—and thereby bound to meet the liabilities of the deceased person, and pay the death duties (if any), for which he ought to have provided. Even a person named in the will as executor takes a risk if he does more than the most urgently necessary acts before probate, since it may turn out that that will is, for some technical reason, invalid, or some later will may come to light in which he is not named.

Not more than four persons can apply for a grant of probate or letters of administration. If therefore the will names more than four executors, the persons named will have to decide among themselves which of them are to apply. Even if there are no more than four, none of them is compelled to apply, unless he has already meddled with the estate; he can renounce his right by signing a form of renunciation. If the deceased has appointed no executor by will, one or more (not exceeding four) of the next-of-kin can apply

for letters of administration. Apart from the special cases (D19(2)) in which there must be at least two administrators, no grant will be made to any more distant relative of the deceased unless and until all nearer relatives have renounced their rights or been " cleared off "; this last expression means that it must be clearly shown that they are dead or for some other reason are incapable of acting as administrators. (The order of priority among the relatives entitled to take out a grant is: (1) husband or wife; (2) children and their " remoter issue " (*i.e.*, grandchildren, great-grandchildren, etc.); (3) parents; (4) brothers and sisters and issue of deceased brothers and sisters; (5) half-brothers and half-sisters and issue of deceased half-brothers and half-sisters; (6) grandparents, and so forth.)

It has been said above that the property of a deceased person " vests " on his death in his executor or executors, if any; if there are no executors it " vests " in his administrators as soon as they have been duly constituted as such by the " grant." In law these legal personal representatives (executors or administrators) have the same powers of disposing of the deceased's property as if they were the owners of that property in the fullest sense; but in accordance with the rules of equity (*see* D7) they must exercise their powers of disposal strictly in accordance with what is *just* and *conscionable*—*i.e.*, they must distribute the property itself, or sell it and distribute the net proceeds, as laid down by the terms of the will (if any); in case of an intestacy, as laid down by the law of succession, as set out in the Intestates' Estates Act, 1952, and the Family Provision Act, 1966. That strict exercise of their powers which conscience demands will be enforced, in case of need, by the Chancery Division of the High Court of Justice (*see* D8), at the suit of any beneficiary under the will or intestacy. But purchasers and persons other than the beneficiaries can safely deal with the legal personal representatives as though they were legal owners of the deceased's property, provided the " grant " is produced as evidence of their powers.

The procedure in applying for a grant of probate or letters of administration is that the applicants must make a valuation of the various kinds of property of which the estate consists; the value of each item is to be the value on the date of death. (It is not usually necessary to employ a licensed valuer, though this may be helpful if the estate includes valuable jewellery, antiques, or works of art.) An *Inland Revenue Affidavit*, for death-duty purposes, must be completed and sworn before a Commissioner for Oaths. This document is one of a number of printed forms (varying according to the nature and composition of the estate, and obtainable from Somerset House, the Estate Duty Office, and certain principal post offices). It is divided into headed columns showing (*a*) the descriptions and the values of the various parts of the estate (*e.g.*, cash at bank, Government securities, stocks and shares, furniture and effects, and so forth); a separate section shows (*b*) the funeral expenses and the debts which the deceased left owing. The *gross estate* consists of the items under (*a*); the *net estate* is calculated by deducting those under (*b*) from the gross total (the cost of a tombstone cannot be deducted).

In the simplest cases estate duty is payable on the net estate, according to a sliding scale; but no duty is payable on an estate of £10,000 or less. (In all but the simplest cases it would be wise to consult a solicitor, as the law relating to estate duty is excessively complicated.)

Another part of the document sets out particulars of the deceased and of the applicants, and the kind of grant required. The document, when sworn, must be forwarded to the Estate Duty Office, who will assess the duty payable (if any) and interest on such duty from the date of death. This must be paid in full before proceeding further, except the part of the duty that relates to freehold property, which may be paid by instalments. (The deceased's bank will usually grant a loan or overdraft for the purpose of such payment.) When the duty has been paid the Inland Revenue Affidavit will be returned to the applicants receipted.

The second document required is the *Form of*

Oath for Executors or Administrators. This gives particulars of the deceased and of the applicants, as before, and declares either (*a*) that they believe the " paper writing " before them to be the deceased's last will, or (*b*) that the deceased died intestate; in either case they declare their relationship (if any) to the deceased, and the capacity in which they apply (*e.g.*, " the executors named in the will," or " the lawful widow of the deceased," or as the case may be); and they swear to administer the estate (the gross amount of which they mention) according to law, and to produce proper accounts whenever called upon to do so. This Oath must also be sworn before a Commissioner.

If there is a will it must now be signed (for identification purposes) by the applicants and the Commissioner for Oaths. If there is no will a third document is required, known as an *Administration Bond.* This is a printed form which must be completed and signed, sealed, and delivered (*see* D13(2)) by the applicants and two *sureties*—*i.e.*, independent persons who are willing to guarantee that the applicants will carry out their duties according to law, under the penalty of forfeiting double the value of the estate if there is any default. (In practice, an insurance company will usually undertake the duty of surety for a reasonable premium, and in that event no other surety is required.) The Bond must be executed (*i.e.*, signed, sealed, and delivered by the individual sureties, or sealed by the insurance company, and also signed, sealed, and delivered by the applicants) before a Commissioner for Oaths.

Finally, the applicants must take to the Principal Registry of the Family Division at Somerset House or to one of the District Registries outside London, (*a*) the receipted Inland Revenue Affidavit; (*b*) the duly sworn Oath for Executors or Administrators; (*c*) either the will (if any), duly marked with the signatures of the applicants and the Commissioner, or the Administration Bond, duly executed. If there is no hitch, the grant of probate or letters of administration will usually be posted to the applicants (or their solicitor) within about fourteen days.

(For the convenience of persons who have no legal adviser, there is a Personal Applications Department, situated in Bush House, Aldwych, W.C.2, where the officials are extremely helpful in answering questions and showing applicants how to complete the forms. But in most cases trouble and delay will be avoided by employing a solicitor.)

II. Property in Land (Immoveable Property).

Although the *logical distinction* preserved in the legal systems of other countries is between property in land and buildings and property of other kinds (" immoveables " and " moveables "), English law has from an early date made the more artificial distinction between *real property* or *realty* (*i.e.*, freeholds) and *personal property* or *personalty* (*i.e.*, leasehold land and property of all other kinds). The reason is historical. In early times, if the possession of freehold land was withheld from its rightful owner, his remedy was an action for recovery of the actual thing withheld—*i.e.*, the freehold land itself—and that very thing (in Latin, *res*) would be restored to the owner under an order of the Court. On the other hand, when property of other kinds (including leaseholds) was withheld from its rightful owner, his remedy was an action against the wrongdoer, in which the remedy would be the award of damages against the wrongdoer personally (*in personam*)—not an order for the restoration of the actual goods or other property withheld. Although that distinction in the remedies is no longer generally applicable, the terms (realty and personalty) have been retained.

1. Realty or Freehold Property.—The difficulties of this branch of the law are due principally to historical reasons which go back to the Feudal System. In a very practical sense that System recognised only the Monarch as the *owner* of land; those who held it from him were *tenants* (in French, " holders "). If the tenancy was one

which was not limited to expire at the end of a fixed period it was known as " an estate in fee simple "—*i.e.*, a *freehold*; a tenancy which was for a fixed period only was known as " a term of years absolute," or a *leasehold*.

When the Feudal System came to an end this distinction remained. A freehold estate in land is still an interest which has no fixed expiry date; and the freeholder, out of that unlimited interest, can " carve," as it were, fixed leasehold terms, during which tenants will hold the land of him.

The property legislation of 1925 profoundly changed and simplified the law. Until the end of 1925 one important characteristic of the freehold estate was that of *primogeniture*—the rule that, on the death of the freeholder intestate, the freehold passed intact to his eldest son or (if he left no son) to his eldest male heir. This was abolished by the Administration of Estates Act, 1925, which enacted that, in the event of a person's dying intestate after 31 December 1925, the whole of his property (realty as well as personalty) should devolve upon his legal personal representatives (D22(1)); and that it should, as one whole, be sold and converted into money so far as necessary for the payment of the deceased's funeral expenses, and debts, death duties, administration expenses, and for distribution among his next of kin. The eldest son, or heir, has no longer any special privilege.

Settlements.—On the other hand, a freeholder (whom we will call Charles), having a freehold estate in land—*i.e.*, an interest which has no expiry date—can *during his lifetime* create successive interests to take effect one by one. Charles can, if he so desires, *settle* his freehold estate to be enjoyed by himself during his lifetime; after his own death, by his eldest son George during that son's lifetime; then by his second son John, during John's lifetime, and finally by George's son Peter " in fee simple." The successive interests of Charles, George, and John are called *life interests*; the ultimate, future freehold interest, reserved for Peter to enjoy after the deaths of his grandfather, his father, and his uncle, is called a *remainder*. Both the life interests and the remainder are *rights of property* to which Charles, George, John, and Peter become entitled immediately the settlement is made—that is, they are present rights to the future enjoyment of the property, and those rights can be dealt with at any time, even before they " fall into possession." Since Charles, George, and John must some time die, Peter knows now that his freehold remainder must come, some time, to him or his personal representatives and, through them, to his next of kin (*see above*); for even if he dies young, while George and John are still alive, his right will not be " defeated " but will be preserved for those to whom his property may eventually pass under his will or intestacy. Therefore that *present right to future enjoyment* is a piece of property which Peter can deal with *now*, unless he is a minor, or unless he is restricted by the terms of the settlement from doing so. George and John can, if they are so minded, do the same with their life interests—that is, they can *now* sell to another person, for hard cash, their present rights of future enjoyment, or they can mortgage (*i.e.*, pledge) those rights against a loan, on the understanding that they will get back those rights when the loan is repaid.

To watch over these successive interests, and to preserve the rights of the ultimate successor, Charles appoints *trustees* of the settlement, whose duty it is to act impartially by all the beneficiaries. A trust corporation (usually one of the bank trustee companies), which never dies, or at least two individuals, may act as trustees. The Trustee Act, 1925, provides for the appointment, by a simple procedure, of new trustees to take the place of those who die, become unfit, or unwilling to go on acting, etc. In the last resort the Chancery Division of the High Court (the guardian of equity) has power to make such an appointment; for " equity never lacks a trustee."

In order to enable landed property to be freely disposed of, it is provided by the Settled Land Act, 1925, that the person who is for the time being enjoying the current life interest (*see above*) has power to sell the entire freehold estate if he so desires. Nevertheless, the scheme of interests under the settlement is not defeated, for the purchaser from the tenant for life must pay the purchase-money not to him but to the trustees; they must invest the money in safe investments, and carry out the provisions of the trust with the necessary modifications. Each tenant for life will then receive the interest or dividends on the investments during his lifetime, just as formerly he would have received the rents and profits of the land during his lifetime; while the *remainderman* (Peter) will ultimately come into the *capital* of the trust fund (*i.e.*, the investments themselves) in lieu of the freehold interest. (By the terms of a 1961 Act, half the investments may consist of stocks or shares in commercial concerns recommended by a stockbroker or other competent adviser.)

2. Leaseholds.—We have seen above that the freeholder, out of his estate which is unlimited in time, can " carve " fixed *terms of years absolute* or *leasehold* estates. These terms may be of any length; the most common are terms of 999 and 99 years. The document by which such a term is granted is called a *lease*; the person granting the term is the *landlord* or *lessor*; the person to whom it is granted is the *tenant* or *lessee*. But the lessor, by the grant of a lease, has not given up *all* interest in the land. The lessor's freehold estate is unlimited in time; when, therefore, the leasehold term (however long) comes to an end, the right to possession and enjoyment of the land will revert to the freeholder. That right, known as a *reversion*, is again a present right to future enjoyment and, as such, a piece of property which the freeholder can, if he wishes, dispose of now. The " sale of a reversion " is, in fact, equivalent to the sale of the freehold subject to an existing lease; it confers upon the purchaser the lessor's right to receive rent from the lessee throughout the leasehold term, and at the expiration of that term to repossess and enjoy the land without limit of time.

The lessee has a legal estate in the land for a fixed term of years, and he in turn (unless prohibited by the provisions of his lease) can grant sub-terms to expire at any time before his own head-term. This is a process which can be repeated, in turn, by each lessee, underlessee, sub-underlessee, and so forth, who will become respectively the underlessor, sub-underlessor, and so forth, of the person to whom the next subordinate interest is granted. Thus Michael, the freeholder, by granting to James a term of 999 years, leaves himself with a *freehold reversion* which will revert, at the expiration of the 999 years, into the possession of the then freeholder. James, by the grant of an underlease, can carve (out of his leasehold term of 999 years) a sub-term of 99 years in favour of William, whose underlessor or landlord he becomes, leaving himself with a *leasehold reversion*, of 900 years. William, in his turn, can grant to Anne a sub-underlease for 21 years, leaving himself a leasehold reversion of 78 years, and so forth. The relationship of lessor and lessee, or landlord and tenant, subsists between William and Anne, James and William, Michael and James; this relationship is one of *privity of estate* as well as *privity of contract*. The former phrase means that each of these pairs of individuals is linked by their *mutual interest in the same term of years* as above described. The latter phrase, privity of contract, means that the *link is contractual*—it arises from the agreement between Michael and James contained in the headlease, the agreement in the underlease between James and William, and that in the sub-underlease between William and Anne. But between Anne and James, between William and Michael, there is no relationship of any kind, neither of contract nor of estate; Michael can look only to James, James to William, and William to Anne, to carry out the terms of the respective tenancies.

In certain circumstances, however, there may be privity of estate between two parties without privity of contract. Suppose Michael *conveys* (*i.e.*, transfers) his freehold reversion, during the subsistence of James's lease, to Robert. Thereby Robert will take over all Michael's rights; *i.e.*, he will become lessor, in place of Michael, to James as lessee, as well as being entitled to possession of the freehold when James's lease expires. Between Robert and James there will be privity

of estate, arising from their mutual interest in the term of 999 years (as lessor and lessee respectively); but there is between them no privity of contract, for Robert and James have made no agreement with one another. The distinction may in certain circumstances be important.

The Form and Contents of a Lease.—A lease for a term of more than three years must be made by deed (D13(2)) between the lessor and the lessee. It names and describes the parties, and sets forth that, in return for an annual rent (and sometimes on payment, in addition, of a lump sum called a premium), the lessor *demises* (*i.e.*, lets) to the lessee, for a term of so many years from such and such a date, the land in question with the buildings erected thereon. (In the law of property the buildings go with the land on which they stand.) Then follow the *lessee's covenants*—the promises which he is to perform: to pay the rent by stipulated instalments , on certain dates; to pay rates, taxes, and other outgoings on the property; to put and keep the property in full repair; to paint the inside and the outside of the buildings at stated times; to keep the property insured, to its full value, in the names of the lessor and himself; to permit the lessor periodically to inspect the condition of the property; to carry out repairs which the lessor, as a result of such inspections, may call upon him to carry out. These are some of the stock clauses; but every individual lease must be carefully studied in order to ascertain what the lessee's obligations are.

Next come the *lessor's covenants*—the promises which the lessor is to perform; the chief of these is that, if the lessee carries out his part of the bargain, the lessor will permit him " quiet enjoyment " of the property without disturbance during the term. Some leases also contain *stipulations* binding on both parties; for example, a stipulation that the rent shall be reduced or suspended if the property is damaged or destroyed by fire, and sometimes an arbitration clause. At the end of most leases comes a *proviso*, for the protection of the lessor, to the effect that he shall be entitled to expel the lessee, and to re-enter and repossess the property, if the lessee ceases to pay his rent or to perform his covenants as required, or in the event of the lessee's bankruptcy. (But he cannot do so without leave of a Court.)

One copy of the lease (the *original*) is signed, sealed, and delivered (D13(2)) by the lessor, and handed over to the lessee as evidence of his *title* to the leasehold interest. The other copy (the *counterpart*) is signed, sealed, and delivered by the lessee, and handed over to the lessor as evidence of his entitlement to the rent and to the performance of the covenants by the lessee. The counterpart requires a stamp (impressed by the Stamp Duty Branch of the Inland Revenue) of only five shillings; but the original must be stamped at the rate of 5s. for every £50 of the rent in leases not exceeding 7 years (and at higher rates in longer leases). If the rent exceeds £50, 10s. per £50 of any premium is payable also. No stamp duty is payable on rents up to £100 in short leases.

3. Statutory Reforms in Law of Landlord and Tenant.—The above text on Leaseholds and Leases sets out the common law rules. But, at various times since 1920, Parliament has considerably amended and added to those rules—particularly to protect (1) tenants of trade, business and professional premises, and (2) tenants of dwellings of comparatively low rateable value.

1. Business Tenancies.—Under the Landlord and Tenant Act, 1954, Part II (and cases decided under it), as amended by the Law of Property Act 1969, *security of tenure* is granted (under certain conditions) to a lessee or underlessee who occupies premises for the purpose of a trade, business, profession or employment carried on by him on the premises. (We shall refer to such premises as " the holding ".) The holding may not be used as business premises, and there is no security, if the lease or tenancy agreement prohibits such use as such, unless permission has been given by the lessee's (or underlessee's) landlord to that effect *Tenancies excluded* from protection include agri

ultural holdings, mining leases, on-licensed premises (except certain hotels and restaurants) nd tenancies not exceeding six months, unless he tenant and the person who carried on the same usiness there before him have occupied the premises for more than twelve months altogether.

A holding is protected by the Act by the provision that the tenancy does not automatically ome to an end on the date specified in the original ease, but only (i) if the landlord gives to the tenant ot less than six nor more than twelve months otice in writing to terminate the tenancy; (ii) if he tenant gives to the landlord, within a similar eriod, a request for a new tenancy; (iii) where the enancy is for a fixed period, if the tenant gives at east three months notice (expiring at the end of he period or on any quarter day afterwards) that e does not want the tenancy continued; (iv) if it s a periodic tenancy (from month to month or year o year), the tenant gives the landlord notice to uit, of the full legal length; (v) if the tenancy is urrendered or (vi) if the tenancy is forfeited which can be done by the landlord only on a Court pplication). In cases (i) and (ii), the parties may gree to fresh terms for a new tenancy. It is vital n such cases that the time-table laid down in the ct shall be adhered to, and the advice of a olicitor should be sought at least twelve months efore the end of the lease; if any request or application is out of time, the Court cannot help the arty in question. The twelve months or six ionths notice of termination must not expire arlier than the date of expiry of the original lease.

Where (i) the landlord serves the notice of ermination: (a) it must require the tenant, within wo months of the notice being given, to notify he landlord whether or not he is willing to give p possession on the specified date; (b) it must tate whether or not the landlord will oppose an pplication to the Court for a new tenancy, and if) on what grounds. Four of the grounds are that he tenant has neglected repairs or payment of ent for which he is liable or committed some other reach of his lease, or that the landlord has offered easonable alternative accommodation. Three irther grounds are: (e) that the existing tenancy an underlease of part of premises held under the eadlease, and the separate lettings would produce lower total rent than if the whole were let to-ether; (f) that on the termination of the current enancy the landlord intends to demolish and recontruct the holding or a substantial part, and could ot reasonably do so without obtaining possession f the whole; but not if the tenant is willing to ive the landlord access to do the work, or to ccept a new tenancy of part of the holding; (g) nally, that on the termination of the current enancy, the landlord intends to occupy the holdig for the purposes of a business to be carried on y him, or as his residence. (But the landlord ay not oppose the grant of a new lease on this nal ground if his interest was purchased or eated within five years immediately preceding ie termination of the lease.)

If the tenant prefers to request a new tenancy, e must propose not more than twelve nor less an six months from the date of request; but ot earlier than the date of expiry of his existing ase. The tenant must also propose the period the new lease, the rent he is willing to pay and e other particulars of the proposed new tenancy. he tenant cannot make such request (a) if the ndlord has already served a termination notice, (b) if the tenant has served notice to quit; nor n either (a) or (b) take place after the tenant's quest for a new tenancy.

Within two months after a tenant's request, the ndlord must serve on the tenant notice stating which of the above grounds (if any) he will pose the Court's grant of a new tenancy. The rties cannot make any agreement to the effect at the Act shall not apply, without the court's ave at the time the tenancy was granted.

The next step is for the tenant, not less than two onths nor more than four months after the landrd's termination notice or the tenant's request r a new tenancy, to apply to the County Court, ich must grant him a new tenancy on such terms the parties may agree on or the Court thinks fit, less the landlord establishes any of the above ounds of objection. If the landlord's objections e false, the Court will grant the tenant damages. If the landlord establishes any of grounds (e),

(f) or (g), so that the Court canno grant a new tenancy, the Court orders the landlord to pay to the tenant compensation for disturbance, or the parties may agree on the amount of compensation without Court action. If the tenant has carried on business on the holding for the whole of fourteen years preceding the termination, the compensation is twice the net rateable value: if for a lesser period, a sum equal to the rateable value.

If the above procedure is carried out, the old tenancy continues in effect until the final disposal of the case even if the lease has expired meanwhile, but a fair rent may be fixed by the Court for the interim period of the proceedings. "Final disposal " includes any necessary time for appeal.

2. Residential Tenancies.—The Rent Acts, 1965–68, as partially amended by the Housing Act, 1969 (D47–8), restore the security of tenure which had been undermined by the 1957 Rent Act. It is now an offence for a landlord to evict a tenant from "protected" premises without a Court order. The 1957 Rent Act allowed "protected" rents to become decontrolled when the premises were relet. The Acts of 1965–68 stipulate that the vacation of a "protected" property will result not in decontrol, but in conversion on reletting to a "regulated" tenancy under the new Acts, unless it is a "controlled" tenancy of rateable value not over £40 in London or £30 elsewhere. Both "regulated" and "controlled" tenancies are "protected."

Under the Acts of 1965–68 security of tenure is provided for "regulated" dwellings with rateable values (A) above the "controlled" figures (see above) and up to £400 a year in the Metropolitan Police District and £200 elsewhere, to which the rules summarised in the next paragraph apply, except increases permitted as a result of landlords' improvements under the 1969 Act (as to which see D48). (B) Those tenancies still "controlled" are roughly the same as those to which the old Rent Restriction provisions of 1920–39 continue to apply.

Rent officers or assessment committees can revise rents in category (a). Tenancies under (a) are called "regulated tenancies." Certain statutory tenancies of formerly requisitioned dwellings (which would have expired on 31 March 1966) are continued after that date as regulated tenancies. Occupiers who are not tenants (i.e., those in occupation necessarily because of their employment, such as caretakers) are included under the term "tenants." A tenancy of which a non-profit-making Housing Association is landlord is exempt from regulation.

The task of the rent officers and rent assessment committees is to fix fair rents on application of landlord or tenant, or both, in counties, county boroughs, London boroughs and the City of London. They are to take into account all the circumstances, age, character, locality and state of repair of the dwelling; but disrepair due to the tenant's neglect and improvements by the tenant are to be disregarded, as is also any great demand (exceeding supply) of dwellings in the district. The fixed rents are to be registered, and must include payments for furniture and services (if any). If the landlord pays rates, that fact is to be noted, and the registered rent plus the rates may be recovered from the tenant. If the cost of services, or of repairs to be done by the landlord, is a variable sum, the registered terms must say so. The landlord cannot lawfully recover more than the registered rent. taking the above variations into account.

It is unlawful for any person (with intent to cause the residential occupier to give up occupation or to refrain from pursuing his rights or remedies) to do anything calculated to interfere with his peace or comfort or persistently to withdraw or withhold services reasonably required for occupation. "Residential occupier" means a person occupying the premises as a residence, either by contract or by any Act of Parliament. The penalty is a fine up to £100 or imprisonment up to six months or both, before the magistrates, for a first offence, and a fine up to £500 or the imprisonment, or both, for a subsequent conviction. The occupier, even if the premises are not "protected" (i.e., not subject to the Rent Restrictions Acts or certain other statutes) cannot lawfully be evicted even when the tenancy has terminated and the occupier continues to reside there, without leave of the Court. In default, the owner is liable, on conviction before the magistrates, to a fine up to £100 or six months' imprisonment or both—unless he can prove that he reasonably believed that the occupier had ceased to reside in the premises. Occupiers protected are the tenant or former tenant, a lawful subtenant, and the widow or widower, or any member of the family of either, residing with the occupier at his death.

The demand for or taking of a premium as a condition of the grant, renewal, continuance or transfer of a protected tenancy (in addition to the rent) is forbidden (except in case of expenses, paid by the outgoing tenant, for a period after the transfer, or improvements he has paid for, or as a refund to the outgoing tenant of any reasonable premium which he himself paid on taking possession, or (if part of the premises are business premises) for goodwill transferred to the incoming tenant. There are also restrictions on the demand for, or taking of a premium in relation to a protected tenancy; broadly speaking, a premium is lawful only if the tenancy or its continuance is for more than seven years—and then only if the registered rent is higher than the rent payable under the tenancy.

There are wide provisions regarding the protection of occupiers of furnished dwellings and regarding mortgages.

Under the Leasehold Reform Act, 1967, a tenant-occupier of a long leasehold house, in which he resides, can acquire on fair terms the freehold or a lease extended for fifty years. " Long " means a tenancy originally granted for more than twenty-one years. But the tenancy must be at a low rent —i.e., not exceeding two-thirds of the rateable value. The fair terms are ascertained by an elaborate formula (sec. 9). The tenant must have occupied the house as his main or only residence for not less than five years.

(For Housing Act, 1969, see **D47–8**.)

4. Mortgages.—The word mortgage is Norman-French; its literal meaning is " dead pledge." The process of mortgaging land and buildings is roughly analogous to that of pawning a piece of jewellery as security for a loan of money—with the important difference that the land cannot, of course, be physically handed over to the lender (as can the jewellery) to be kept in his custody until the loan is repaid. But a pledge and a mortgage have this in common—that the parties intend no change of ownership; the borrower (the mortgagor) is and remains owner of the property after, as well as before, the transaction. In exchange for a loan of a certain sum, the lender (the mortgagee) temporarily enjoys a charge upon property worth (it may be) much more than that sum, as security for the repayment of the loan, with the stipulated interest, at the stipulated time. The borrower is still the property-owner.

Because of the essential immoveability of land, the mortgage transaction is effected by a mortgage deed, which sets out the terms on which the loan is granted. Generally speaking, the borrower (the mortgagor) is permitted to remain in possession of the mortgaged property unless and until he fails to pay an instalment of interest or to repay the capital when called upon, or unless and until he breaks some condition of the mortgage deed. In early times such failure was often the signal for the lender (the mortgagee) to oust him permanently from possession, and even to deprive him of ownership of the property. But the courts of equity, as we have seen (**D7**(2)), gradually evolved the rule that it was unconscionable for the lender to enrich himself, at a low cost to himself, from a transaction in which the intention of the parties was to pledge the property temporarily as a security, not to sell it permanently for a small sum. Hence was evolved the concept known as the equity of redemption—the rule that, even after the legal date fixed by the deed for repayment of the loan and for freeing the property from the mortgage, the borrower should still remain entitled to redeem the property (i.e., to free it from the charge) by tendering to the lender the balance of the loan, with all interest and costs to date; and that the lender should thereupon be bound to give the borrower full and unfettered rights over the property, free from all the conditions of the

mortgage, and in the same state as it was in originally. The lender must get no collateral (or additional) advantage of a permanent kind once the loan, interest, and costs were paid off; and this is still the law today.

The law, as stated above, has established the principle that the borrower who mortgages his freehold or leasehold interest, as security for a loan of money, shall not be deprived of his ownership, but shall retain such ownership after the execution of the mortgage deed. That deed is in the first place, a contract or agreement under which the borrower promises to repay the loan to the lender, with interest at a certain rate, in one sum or by instalments, and meanwhile, for the lender's protection, to keep the property insured, in proper repair, and so forth. But that is not all; it is clearly important that the lender should, in addition, be granted an interest in the property itself—an interest which will enable him to take actual possession of the property, if need be, to enforce his rights, much as the pawn-broker has the right to possession (though not ownership) of the pledged article until the loan is repaid.

The Law of Property Act, 1925, devised a method of giving the lender a legal estate in the property while still preserving the rights of ownership of the borrower. That Act provides that the grant of a mortgage of land, in whatever form it is effected, shall confer upon the lender a term of years absolute—i.e., a legal estate in the land itself, which the lender can deal with by sale, and which will be transmitted, as an interest in land, to his legal personal representatives upon his death. It is further provided that, on the final discharge of the mortgage (i.e., the repayment of the loan, with all interest and expenses due to the mortgagee), that term of years shall cease and be extinguished, the borrower thereafter continuing to hold his freehold or leasehold estate free from the mortgage term of years, and free also from all the conditions of the mortgage deed.

In such a scheme it was necessary to distinguish the term of years conferred by the mortgage from any term of years absolute which might be conferred upon a lessee or under a lessee by way of a lease or tenancy (see **D24**(1) Leaseholds). For the purpose of such distinction the Act provides that, if the mortgagor's (the borrower's) legal estate is a freehold, the mortgage deed confers upon the mortgagee (the lender) term of 3000 years, thus leaving to the mortgagor legal reversion to commence after the expiration of that term (since the freehold estate is not limited to expire at any particular time). And if the mortgagor's legal estate is a leasehold, due to expire at the end of a fixed period, the mortgage deed confers upon the mortgagee a term of years to expire ten days before the leasehold term, thus again leaving the mortgagor with a legal reversion (in this case of ten days only).

In this way each party has a legal estate in the land itself, quite apart from the contractual rights and obligations in regard to the loan, which can be enforced by and against him personally. The mortgagor can sell his freehold subject to the mortgage term and the obligations of the mortgage deed; the mortgagee can sell his mortgage term with the benefit of the rights that go with it. The sale of a freehold (whether subject to mortgage or not) is effected by a deed called conveyance; the sale of a leasehold is effected by deed called an assignment. The mortgage term can be dealt with in a deed called a transfer of mortgage. In every case the purchaser takes over the vendor's legal estate in the land, subject to, or with the benefit of, the personal obligations or rights in the original deed. In case of the death of the mortgagee or mortgagor, the legal estate in question, and the rights or obligations, are transmitted to his personal representatives.

Finally, it should be mentioned that, as a additional safeguard, the title deeds (evidencing the mortgagor's freehold or leasehold title) must be handed over to the mortgagee when the mortgage deed is executed, as part of the latter's security. The mortgagor must take care to get them back when he redeems the property by paying off the loan, interest, and expenses.

5. Title.—(a) Evidence of title.—Before freehold or leasehold property changes hands, it is the duty of the purchaser's solicitor to *investigate title*— *i.e.*, to satisfy himself that the vendor has a proper title himself and a proper right to convey or assign. Generally speaking, the purchaser's solicitor must go through the deeds (evidencing sales, transmissions on death, grants of leases, grants and redemptions of mortgages) for at least fifteen years back; he must check every step in the *devolution of title* (*i.e.*, every change in ownership) and make *requisitions* (*i.e.*, demand explanations) on any point which is doubtful. This is still the system over the greater part of the country. No stamp duty is payable on conveyances up to £5,500; from £5,500 to £7,000 is 10s. per cent; after that it rises to £1 per cent.

(*b*) Registration of Title.—With a view, however, to simplifying such procedure the Land Registration Acts have provided for a different system. In areas to which an Order in Council has made the system applicable, registration of title is *compulsory* upon any sale of freeholds, or of leaseholds having more than forty years to run. Under the Land Registration Act, 1966, this system is gradually being extended over the whole country. Registration is effected in the following way: one of a number of District Registries investigates the title of every freehold or leasehold sold after the appropriate date, *once and for all.* If they are satisfied that it is in order, they register the owner as *registered proprietor* of the land with *absolute title* to his freehold, *absolute* or *good leasehold title* to his leasehold. (These kinds of titles indicate that the title is unexceptionable, but if there is a slight doubt the proprietor may be granted a *qualified title*; and if he is in possession of the land he may be granted a *possessory title*, which signifies little more than the fact of possession. The Chief Land Registrar is empowered, however, to convert possessory titles into absolute or good leasehold titles, after fifteen years in the case of freeholds, and after ten years in the case of leaseholds. He may convert qualified titles at any time, according to circumstances.)

The Land Registry issues to the registered proprietor a *land certificate*, certifying (on behalf of the Government) that a registered title of the appropriate kind has been granted. In any further transactions relating to that particular land the purchaser's solicitor need not concern himself with the original deeds save in exceptional cases; he can generally rely upon the certified statements made in the land certificate, on which the name of the new registered proprietor is entered by the Land Registry officials when a transfer in his favour, or the grant of a lease to him, is lodged at the Registry. There are appropriate sections in the land certificate for registration of a mortgage and the particulars of the mortgagee for the time being.

6. Joint Ownership.—If two or more persons are the owners of freehold or leasehold property, that does not mean that A owns one part of the land and buildings, and B and C other parts; the effect is that all of them *jointly own the whole.* (The analogy will be clear if the reader considers the case of a motor-car owned jointly by A, B, and C; clearly all three own the entire car between them; it cannot be said that A owns the engine, B the chassis, and C the body.) The Law of Property Act, 1925, recognises such joint ownership of land by means of a device known as a *trust for sale.* The respective rights of A, B, and C (equal or unequal) can be fully enforced only if and when the property is *sold* and the net proceeds of sale, in money, divided up in the proper proportions; and any or all of the joint owners can insist upon such sale or division for the purpose of obtaining their proper shares. But, while the property remains unsold, all the joint owners have rights according to the proportions of their shares; if, for example, the property is let, the net rents, after paying for repairs and other expenses, must be divided between them in those proportions. Up to four persons can jointly own a freehold or leasehold legal estate in land; if more than four are entitled to the *beneficial interest*, then four of their number only must hold the *legal estate*, and equity will enforce the *beneficial rights* of all against the legal owners. A purchaser from joint owners of the legal estate is concerned only with

the latters' *legal title*; provided he hands over the purchase-money to them (not being less than two), or somebody authorised by them, the purchaser is not responsible for what they may do with that money. If those legal owners, from whom the purchaser buys, fail to pay over the proper shares to those beneficially interested, it is for the latter to enforce their rights against the vendors, who have sold the legal estate, by action in the Chancery Division, the guardian of equity. The purchaser's title to the land itself is not affected by the vendors' failure properly to carry out the terms of the trust for sale, so long as the legal estate has been properly transferred to him and he has paid the purchase-money to not less than two legal owners.

III. Property Other than Land (Moveables).

1. Chattels.—Chattels are *concrete things* which can be the subject of ownership, other than land or buildings, and other than objects so closely affixed to land or buildings that they are regarded as part thereof (*e.g.*, growing crops and trees, or " landlord's fixtures " built into some structure or so closely attached that they cannot be removed without serious damage to the structure).

In the ordinary way chattels can be sold or given away without any special legal formalities— merely by *physical transfer*—*i.e.*, by the owner handing them over to somebody else. If a chattel is to be *mortgaged* as security for a loan, the procedure differs according to whether the person pledging it (the borrower) is or is not to retain *possession* of the chattel. (His *ownership*, in either case is not disturbed.)

(*a*) If, as happens when an article is *pawned*, the borrower is not to keep the article in his possession, he hands it over to the pawnbroker, who hands him in exchange the agreed loan and a pawn-ticket. On production of the pawn-ticket, and the repayment of the loan with the stipulated interest, the borrower is entitled to receive the article back. (Provision is made by law for cases where the borrower defaults in payment, or where an unreasonable time elapses before he seeks to redeem what he has pledged.)

(*b*) If, however, the arrangement is that the borrower is to retain possession of the mortgaged article (as may happen if he borrows from a moneylender on the security of his furniture), then the borrower must execute and hand to the lender a document called a *bill of sale.* The law relating to such a document is extremely complex; but the most important provision is that the lender cannot enforce his rights unless he *registers* the bill of sale, at the Bankruptcy Court, in a register which any member of the public can inspect for a small charge. If then some member of the public desires to purchase the article from the person in whose possession it remains, but has reason to suspect that that person, though he may be the owner, has mortgaged it to a money-lender, it is open to the proposing purchaser to inspect the register of bills of sale to satisfy himself on the point. If he finds an entry against the owner's name, he will be wise not to proceed with the transaction. If he finds no such entry, and has no reason to believe the owner to be bankrupt, he can usually assume that there is nothing to prevent the person in possession from passing a good title to him. The proposed purchaser can also inspect the register of bankruptcies in order to see whether the vendor has the right to sell (*see* D12(2)).

2. Things in Action.—These (*see* (D19(1)) are *intangible rights* which can be owned and dealt with but, because of their abstract nature, cannot be physically transferred. If Brown owes Jones £50, Jones (the creditor) can transfer to Robinson the right to collect the £50 from Brown. Jones does this by a document called an *assignment* of the debt and (most important) by giving *written notice* to Brown (the debtor) that Robinson is now the creditor instead of Jones.

Similarly, if Jones owns ten shares in Brown & Co., Ltd., Jones will hold a *share certificate*—*i.e.*, a document certifying the amount of his shareholding. He has certain rights in the company, but these depend upon the company's *memo-*

randum and articles (D12(2)) and upon the *registration* of his name in the company's register of shareholders. The share certificate is only *evidence* of his rights—it is not in itself a piece of property, and the physical handing over of the certificate will effect nothing unless Jones executes a *share transfer* in Robinson's favour and Robinson sends it to the company for registration, together with the old share certificate in Jones's name. After registration of Robinson's name, the company will destroy the old certificate and issue a fresh one to him.

Again, if Jones has insured his life with the Brown Life Assurance Society, he will have received a *policy* which is *evidence* of the right of his legal personal representatives to be paid £1000 on Jones's death. If Jones wishes, during his lifetime, to transfer that benefit to Robinson, he can do so, but it will not suffice for him merely to hand Robinson the policy. To transfer the *rights* under the policy he must execute an *assignment* in which

it is stated that Jones, being the policy-holder and entitled to certain rights thereunder, now assigns those rights to Robinson. But no transfer of those rights will have been effected until Robinson has *notified* the Assurance Society of what has been done and sent it the policy and the assignment for *registration* in its books.

These examples illustrate the principle, set out in the Law of Property Act, 1925, that an *unconditional assignment*, in writing, by a person (the assignor) entitled to any debt or other thing in action, in favour of another person (the assignee), if *notice in writing* is given *to the debtor* or other person on whom the obligation rests (in the above examples, to Brown, the Company, and the Assurance Society), shall entitle the assignee to all the assignor's rights, including the right to enforce those rights by action in the Courts, without calling upon the co-operation of the assignor in whom the right to the debt, or other thing in action, was originally vested.

III. FURTHER DETAIL ON SOME BRANCHES OF THE LAW

DIVORCE AND OTHER MATRIMONIAL CAUSES

1. HISTORICAL SKETCH.

The anomalies in this branch of the Law of England, and the legalistic attitude of the Courts to the subject, are principally due to historical reasons. For centuries the Church of Rome was the supreme ecclesiastical authority, and the law of that Church (Canon Law) applied to *matrimonial causes*—that is to say, disputes relating to any marriage and the mutual rights and duties of the spouses. Marriage was indissoluble—that is, there was no such thing as divorce in the modern sense of breaking the legal tie. But the Ecclesiastical Courts, which alone administered the matrimonial law before 1858, might for certain reasons grant a *decree of nullity* (a declaration that a particular " marriage " was null and void). In other cases they might grant what is now called a *legal separation* (known, in those days as a " divorce *a mensa et thoro*," *i.e.*, banishment from bed and board); this latter decree, however, did not dissolve the marriage bond, but merely gave judicial sanction to the spouses' living apart from each other, and regulated the terms of the separation. After the Reformation the Ecclesiastical Courts continued to deal with matrimonial causes on the same legal principles as before.

As a result of the Acts of Supremacy passed in the reigns of Henry VIII and Elizabeth I, the Sovereign was declared to be the supreme governor of the Realm in all spiritual and ecclesiastical, as well as temporal, causes. This royal supremacy, exercised constitutionally through Parliament, was part of the law of the land; since there was no limitation upon the power of Parliament (see D8), special Acts were passed, from time to time, to effect that which neither the Ecclesiastical nor the Civil Courts then had jurisdiction to do, *viz.*, to break the marriage tie itself. A divorce of this kind, known as " divorce *a vinculo matrimonii* " (a divorce from the marriage bond) was rare, for the procedure was cumbersome and expensive. Except by the passing of a special Act of Parliament, there was no means of getting a marriage dissolved before the year 1858.

The Matrimonial Causes Act, 1857, transferred the jurisdiction in matrimonial matters from the Ecclesiastical Courts to the new Civil " Court for Divorce and Matrimonial Causes "; but perpetuated the old ecclesiastical practice with regard to nullity suits and judicial separation (formerly known as " divorce *a mensa et thoro* "). Apart from this rearrangement, the Act took the revolutionary step of conferring upon this Court a new judicial power—that of granting a divorce in the modern sense of a complete dissolution of marriage. As we have seen (D8), the Supreme Court of Judicature Act, 1873, and subsequent legislation, set up one single High Court of Justice, of which the Probate, Divorce, and Admiralty Division formed part, taking over (with other work) the jurisdiction which had been conferred in 1857 upon the " Court for Divorce and Matri-

monial Causes." This jurisdiction, formerly in the hands of the Probate, Divorce, and Admiralty Division is now allocated to the new Family Division which will deal with cases affecting the family generally. Great changes have been effected by statute (notably in 1923, 1925, 1937, 1950, 1963, 1965, 1967, 1969, and 1970) extending the grounds for divorce and the jurisdiction of the Court; but in the interpretation and adaptation of principles the great body of case law (see D7), which enshrined the principles and practice of the old Ecclesiastical Courts is not without its influence today. The principles of equity (see D7), however, have not modified the strict legalism of this branch of the law; equity has no application to the law of matrimonial causes (except for resort to injunction (see D15) and for the protection of the wife's person or property).

2. POWERS OF INFERIOR COURTS— SUMMARY JURISDICTION.

Concurrently with the jurisdiction of the Divorce Division of the High Court, Magistrates' Courts now have power (Matrimonial Proceedings (Magistrates' Courts) Act, 1960, and Rules made thereunder) to grant relief (by a *matrimonial order*) to either spouse (the *complainant*) in certain cases of misconduct on the part of the other spouse (the *defendant*). The procedure is simpler, quicker and cheaper than in the High Court. A Magistrates' Court may grant a matrimonial order; if such order provides (*a*) that the complainant shall be no longer bound to cohabit with the defendant, that has the same effect as a High Court decree of judicial separation (see D32). A Magistrates' Court may also provide (*b*) that the husband shall pay the wife (or (*c*) where the husband's earning capacity is impaired by age, illness, mental or physical disablement, that the wife shall pay the husband) such weekly maintenance as the Court thinks reasonable *plus* (*h*) weekly payments for each dependent child; (*d*) the child's custody (up to 16 years of age) may be granted to the complainant or (*e*) to a county council or county borough council or (in special circumstances) (*f*) such child may be ordered to be placed under the supervision of an independent person (such as a probation officer) and (*g*) access to the child may be granted to either spouse or to any parent. (There are special provisions relating to (*d*), (*e*) and (*f*). The former limits of £7. 10s. for wife or husband and of £2. 10s. for a child were repealed by the Maintenance Orders Act, 1968.

Either spouse may apply for relief on the ground that the defendant—

    (1) has *deserted* the complainant;

    (2) has been guilty of *persistent cruelty* to the complainant or an infant child of the complainant or of the family (see D30(2));

(3) has been convicted (i) on indictment (i.e., by a jury) of any *assault* on the complainant, or (ii) by a Magistrates' Court of certain offences (involving imprisonment for not less than one month) *against the person* of the complainant, or (iii) of a *sexual offence* (or an attempt thereat) against an infant child of either spouse who is a child of the family;

(4) has committed *adultery*;

(5) while knowingly suffering from *venereal disease*, has insisted upon sexual intercourse with the complainant, or permitted such intercourse without the complainant being aware of such disease;

(6) is a *habitual drunkard* or a *drug addict*;

(7) being the husband, has compelled the wife, or led her, *to submit to prostitution*;

(8) being the husband, has wilfully *neglected to provide reasonable maintenance* for the wife or any dependant child of the family;

(9) being the wife (in case (c) above) has *wilfully neglected to provide*, or make a reasonable contribution to, *reasonable maintenance* for the husband or any dependant child of the family, having regard to any resources of the spouses.

A Magistrates' Court has jurisdiction to hear any such complaint if either spouse ordinarily resides in the Court district, or (except in (3) above) if the cause of complaint arose in that district, or (in case (3)) if the offence or attempt arose in that district. Jurisdiction is also exercisable if the complainant resides in England and the parties last resided together in England (even if the defendant now resides in Scotland or Northern Ireland), or if the defendant resides in England though the complainant resides in Scotland or Northern Ireland. The Court may order the costs of the application to be paid by either party.

The general rule is that a complaint under (4) above must be made within six months of the date when the act of adultery first became known to the complainant. A complaint on any other grounds must generally be made within six months of the ground of the complaint arising, unless the complainant was abroad at the time; but this time limit does not apply to such continuing offences as desertion (*see below*) or wilful neglect to maintain.

These "domestic proceedings," as they are termed, may be heard before one stipendiary (legally qualified magistrate) or not more than three justices of the peace, including, so far as practicable, both a man and a woman. The hearing is in private, the public being excluded, and newspapers are prohibited from publishing details; "domestic proceedings" must be dealt with separately from other matters, and reports from probation officers may be received on the subject of any attempted reconciliation or on the means of the parties. The same applies (under an Act of 1968) to appeals to the High Court from a Magistrates' Court's hearing of a matrimonial case (*see* "Appeals" below). In general, the magistrates should apply the same general principles as are applied in the Divorce Division; lay justices of the peace are advised on the law by their legally qualified clerk.

A Magistrates' Court, however, has no power to grant a divorce or to annul a marriage; the jurisdiction to make such a decree is in the hands of the Family Division of the High Court of Justice and, since 1967, of certain "designated" County Courts in undefended cases. Generally speaking, the law relating to domestic proceedings in Magistrates' Courts now (November 1970) remains unchanged, but in the High Court and designated County Courts there have been far-reaching reforms.

A maintenance order may be enforced by committing the defendant to prison if his failure to comply with the order is shown to be due to wilful refusal or culpable neglect, and if he has fallen into arrears. But this is the final resort if enforcement fails by "attachment of earnings," *i.e.*, an order to employers to deduct the debt from the debtor's wages. Arrears becoming due more than a year before application for enforcement in the High Court or designated County Courts (see (1) below) may be remitted or made payable by instalments.

No order is enforceable while a wife is residing with her husband, and no order may be made on the application of a complainant where it is proved that he or she has been guilty of adultery, unless the defendant condoned or connived at (*see below*), or by his wilful neglect or misconduct conduced to (*i.e.*, tended to lead to), the adultery. An order already granted will be *discharged* (*i.e.*, its effect will be terminated) on proof of the complainant's adultery, or on proof that the spouses voluntarily resumed cohabitation, except for any one period of not more than 3 months with a view to effecting a reconciliation.

If a matrimonial cause is pending in the Family Division of the High Court, no application for a separation or maintenance order ought to be dealt with by a Magistrates' Court. And a Magistrates' Court may refuse to make any order when the suit in question would, in its opinion, be more conveniently dealt with by the Family Division.

By the Matrimonial Proceedings and Property Act, 1970, a maintenance order will be discharged by the remarriage of the party in whose favour it was made; and the Court may order overpayments to be refunded.

Appeals. A Magistrates' Court has power "to state a case," upon *a point of law* (not a question of *fact*) arising on the application, for decision by a Divisional Court consisting of two or more judges of the Family Division. And an appeal from a Divisional Court lies to the Court of Appeal, by leave of either the former or the latter.

3. MATRIMONIAL CAUSES in the HIGH COURT and UNDEFENDED DIVORCE CASES in DESIGNATED COUNTY COURTS.

(1) Constitution of the Courts.

The President of the Family Division and not less than three other High Court Judges attached to that Division are the permanent judges for Matrimonial Causes. They sit both at the Royal Courts of Justice in London and at Assizes. (*See* reference to proposed new Family Division of High Court (**D28(2)**.) Certainly subsidiary duties are performed by the seven Registrars of the Principal Registry of the Division at Somerset House, and by District Registrars in the principal cities of England and Wales. The Matrimonial Causes Act, 1967, permits designated County Courts to grant divorces in undefended cases.

(2) Practice and Procedure.

In contrast to "domestic proceedings" in Magistrates' Courts, the Judges of the Family Division or of designated County Courts sit normally in open court, though they have power to sit *in camera* (in private) where the ends of justice so require. In *nullity proceedings*, however, it is provided by statute that evidence on the question of sexual incapacity must be heard *in camera* unless the Judge is satisfied that the ends of justice require such evidence to be heard in open court. Press publicity is limited by statute to certain matters and the publication of indecent matter may give rise to prosecution, in any matrimonial proceedings.

In general, practice and procedure in the Family Division and designated County Courts are governed by statute, by rules of Court framed by a judicial committee under statutory authority, and by the principles and practice of the old Ecclesiastical Courts—except in proceedings for dissolution of marriage, which the old Courts could not entertain (*see* **D28(1)**).

(3) Relief and Grounds for Relief.

(a)—**Nullity of Marriage.** The High Court has power to declare a "marriage" null and void in two main classes of case:

(i) "*Marriages*" *Void from their Inception* —*i.e.*, where one of the parties had another husband or wife living at the time of the ceremony; where there was a mistake as to the nature of the ceremony, or the identity of the other party; where one party had been declared of *unsound mind* and was detained as a lunatic at the time of the ceremony; where the parties were within the *prohibited degrees* of relationship (*e.g.*, brother and sister, or uncle and niece); or where the ceremony was not in due form, or was a mock " marriage."

(ii) *Marriages which are Voidable—i.e.*, which stand good unless and until one party or the other (" the Petitioner ") successfully petitions the Court for annulment—*i.e.*, where either party was sexually impotent at the date of the ceremony; where either party has wilfully refused to consummate the marriage; where the marriage was induced by threats or fear or duress (*i.e.*, force), or where one spouse was intoxicated at the time of the ceremony.

The Act of 1965 added certain other grounds: (*a*) where either party was, at the time of the ceremony, in fact of unsound mind but had not been declared so, or was then a mental defective, or then subject to recurrent fits of insanity or epilepsy; (*b*) where the other spouse was, at the time of the marriage, suffering from venereal disease in a communicable form; and (*c*) where the wife was, at the time of the marriage, pregnant by some person other than the petitioning husband. But in those last cases (*a*), (*b*), and (*c*) the Court must not grant a decree unless it is satisfied that the petitioner was, at the time of the marriage, ignorant of the facts alleged; that the proceedings were instituted within a year of the marriage, and that there has been no sexual intercourse between the parties, with the consent of the petitioner, since he or she discovered that there were grounds for a decree of nullity.

Where a " marriage " is void (*see above*) the law regards it as never having taken place at all. Where it is voidable, the decree annuls the marriage retrospectively from its inception; but certain transactions between the parties while they actually remained married are validated, and the Court has power to order maintenance for the woman; and any child who would in the normal way have been the legitimate child of the parties remains legitimate, notwithstanding the annulment.

Sterility—*i.e.*, inability to produce children—is not, in itself, a ground for annulment of the marriage. If the impotence of one spouse appears to be curable without danger the Court may, before pronouncing a decree, require that opportunity for cure be first given. If he or she refuses to undergo examination or treatment the Court may infer, after hearing the other party's evidence, that impotence exists. The petitioning husband or wife may ask for a nullity decree on the ground of his or her own impotence, provided he or she did not know of it at the time of the marriage. And there have been recent cases in which both partners have been granted decrees.

Apart from the one-year rule (mentioned in the last paragraph but two) in certain cases, delay (however long) in petitioning for nullity is no bar to the grant of a decree.

(b) Divorce—(i) *Its Nature and Purpose.*— Divorce means the breaking of the legal tie of marriage by a decree of the Court. There has been much controversy on the subject.

We have to start by facing the unpalatable truth that some marriages do break down in fact. The symptoms of break-down may be continual strife, and sometimes violence, between the spouses, so long as they continue to live together; or there may be an actual breaking-up of the home because one or the other finds the situation intolerable and leaves. The function of the law should be to deal with this state of affairs as best it can, paying due regard: (*a*) to the interests of the children (if any) who are innocent parties to the dispute: (*b*) to the interests of the spouses and of any third party involved; (*c*) to the interests of public decency and the safeguarding of family life generally.

Divorce is the drastic *remedy* provided by the civil law in the case of a marriage which has already *broken down in fact*; the availability of divorce does not bring about the break-down, any more than the availability of surgical treatment can be said to bring about ill-health. A marriage may break down—that is to say, the " kernel " of the marriage, the mutual respect and affection between the spouses, has withered away; only an empty shell—the legal tie—continues to subsist between them. How should this situation be dealt with by law?

It is common ground, among both the upholders of the orthodox view and those who advocated reform, first that every possible effort should be made, by private individuals and public institutions, to effect a reconciliation, if at all possible. Such efforts are favoured by the law, and excellent work is done to this end by religious organisations, medical men, probation officers, and such institutions as the Marriage Guidance Council.

Secondly, it is common ground that, if such efforts are unsuccessful and the breach proves irreparable in fact, the interest of the children " of the family " should be paramount, and no pains should be spared to secure their proper care and maintenance. The Matrimonial Proceedings and Property Act, 1970, defines a " child of the family " as (*a*) a child of both parties, and (*b*) any other child, not boarded out with them by a local authority or voluntary organisation, who has been treated by both parties as a child of the family. There are elaborate provisions for the protection of all such children (**D33**(1)); the welfare of the children is the *paramount consideration*, irrespective of the rights and wrongs as between the parents. Nobody will deny that, once the marriage has broken down *in fact*, the children will suffer to some extent; but it does not follow that they would suffer less if the legal tie between the parents were preserved, or if the home, with its atmosphere of strife, and perhaps of violence, were kept together at all costs—even assuming such a thing were possible. A divorce may not be granted unless the Judge has made an order declaring whether he is satisfied that all possible arrangements have been made for the care and upbringing of the children, that the only children of the family are those named in the order, that the arrangements are satisfactory or the best that can be devised, or that there are no " children of the family." A decree absolute made *without such order* is void. But if circumstances make it desirable to grant the decree absolute without delay, although arrangements for the children have not been finalised, the Court may make an order to that effect, accepting an undertaking from one or both parties to bring the question back before the Court at the earliest opportunity. In the last-named case, nobody is entitled to question the validity of the decree once the Judge's *order* is made.

The Divorce Reform Act, 1969, has revolutionised the law. The old attitude, that divorce is a " penalty " upon the " guilty " party, has been abolished. From 1 January 1971 (when the new Act came into force) only one ground for filing a divorce petition by either party (the " petitioner ") will exist, *viz.*, that the marriage has *irretrievably broken down—i.e.*, that it is impossible for the couple to go on living together as man and wife. After long debate Parliament decided that, to prove such breakdown, it would be impracticable for the Courts to investigate the whole history of the marriage, which would require lengthy evidence from both parties, perhaps lasting for days. The Act therefore provides five points of evidence on one of which the petitioner must satisfy the Court; " satisfy " means that he or she must convince the Court " on a balance of probabilities "—*not* (as in criminal cases (**D9**(2)) " beyond all reasonable doubt." One of the five following points of evidence must be proved:

(*a*) that the respondent (the other party to the proceedings) has committed adultery and the petitioner finds it intolerable to live with him or her;

(*b*) that the respondent has behaved in such a way that the petitioner cannot reasonably be expected to live with him or her;

(*c*) that the respondent has deserted the petitioner for a continuous period of at least two years immediately preceding the petition;

(d) that the parties have lived apart for a continuous period of at least two years immediately preceding the petition *and* the respondent consents to the grant of a divorce;

(e) that the parties have lived apart for a continuous period of at least five years immediately preceding the petition;

(f) finally, to cover those cases where one of the spouses has disappeared and not been heard of for many years:

> Any married person who alleges that reasonable grounds exist for supposing the other party to be dead may petition the Court to have it presumed that the other party is dead and to have the marriage dissolved.

No petition for divorce on any ground may be presented until the expiration of three years from the date of the marriage, unless a Judge is satisfied that there is a case of exceptional hardship upon the Petitioner or exceptional depravity on the part of the Respondent. Whether there is such a case is a question for the Judge's discretion upon the evidence brought before him. Concealment or misrepresentation by the petitioner may result in dismissal of the petition, or postponement of the decree absolute until three years have elapsed since the marriage. The Judge must also have regard to the interests of any " child of the family " (**D**30(2)).

As to the above-mentioned grounds for divorce:

(a) *Adultery* means *voluntary sexual intercourse* between a husband and a woman who is not his wife, or between a wife and a man who is not her husband. (A woman who has been raped—*i.e.*, forced to have intercourse with another man against her will—is not guilty of adultery.) For obvious reasons, direct evidence of the act of adultery is rare, and the Court may infer from circumstantial evidence that adultery has taken place. But adultery alone is not sufficient unless the court is " satisfied " that the petitioner " finds it intolerable " to live with the Respondent. The test for this will probably be the state of the petitioner's own feelings.

(b) In place of evidence of the former offence of " cruelty," (i) the Court must now be " satisfied " that the respondent has (ii) behaved in such a way that (iii) the petitioner cannot reasonably be expected to live with him or her. Until there have been cases decided on this ground, it is impossible to say how the Courts will consider (ii) and (iii). " Misbehaviour " is a much more vague idea than " cruelty," which had been explained in many reported cases to mean " conduct causing danger to life, limb, or health " (bodily or mental) " or giving rise to a reasonable apprehension of such dangers." But the new (ii) and (iii) seem to depend, not on the petitioner's feelings, but on the Judge's opinion whether his or her unwillingness to go on living with the respondent is " reasonable," in the particular case before him, or not. When " cruelty " was the basis, the question was *not* " Would other people describe the respondent's conduct as 'cruel'?" but " Has this particular husband been 'cruel' to this particular wife, or *vice versa*?"; this question was for the decision of the Judge. Also, in other legal connections, *reasonableness* is a matter for the Court to decide; and in (iii) (*above*) the words " *be expected* to live " seem to indicate that the new paragraph will be similarly interpreted.

(c) *Desertion* means, primarily, the intentional permanent abandonment, by one spouse of the other, without that other's consent, and without reasonable cause. Therefore there is no desertion in such cases (for example) as: (i) where a husband cannot live with his wife because he is serving a sentence of imprisonment; (ii) where a husband leaves his wife for a short time for necessary business or family reasons, intending to return to her; (iii) while a separation continues with the consent of both parties; (iv) where the spouse who abandoned the other had just cause to do so.

Indeed, in certain cases under (c) the doctrine known as constructive desertion may apply against the other spouse, if he or she has (figuratively speaking) driven the first spouse away. *Constructive desertion* means, not " deser-

tion " in the literal sense of walking out of the matrimonial home, but conduct on the part of one party which is intended to force, and virtually forces, the other party to leave him or her. Thus, if a husband brings his mistress to live with him in the matrimonial home and, as a result, his wife leaves him, not only is the wife innocent of desertion in the legal sense, but the husband is himself guilty of constructive desertion; it will be presumed against him that he intended to terminate his marital association, and he has in fact *carried out that intention.* Such a case illustrates the principle that there are *two elements* in the legal meaning of *desertion*—the act of physical separation and the intention to bring normal married life to an end.

In order to bring about desertion it is not necessary that the spouses should cease to live under the same roof; " desertion is not withdrawal from a place, but from a state of things." It is sufficient that the Respondent has withdrawn from, or forced the other to withdraw from life together " in the same household."

It should also be noted that desertion is not a single act but a continuous state of affairs. The Petitioner must prove that desertion without cause continued during the entire period of two years required by law as the basis of a divorce petition. Although (*see above*) desertion in the legal sense must be without the consent of the petitioning spouse, recent judicial decisions have tended to dispense with the requirement that the deserted party must prove a *continuing desire* for the deserting party to return, and a *continuing willingness* to receive and reinstate the deserting party, during the entire period of two years preceding the commencement of proceedings; in other words, once the latter party's *original act* and *intention of deserting* has been proved, that intention is presumed to have continued, unless there is evidence to the contrary. A matrimonial order made by a Magistrates' Court (*see* (**D**28(2)) does not necessarily prevent the period of desertion from running, unless the order contains a clause, deliberately inserted, to the effect that " the parties shall no longer be bound to cohabit." (And the insertion of such a clause is rare.) Nor does a decree of judicial separation made by the High Court (**D**32(2)); but in both cases the period of living apart (two years) must precede such order or decree.

If the deserting party makes an offer to return to the matrimonial home it is the duty of the other party to receive him (or her) back and to resume normal married life together, if the offer to return is genuine and if no other matrimonial offence has been committed by the deserting party. Whether such an offer is " genuine " is a question of fact, to be decided on all the evidence; it will generally be a wise safeguard for a deserted party who receives such an offer to take legal advice before accepting or rejecting it: for if rejection of the offer subsequently proves to have been unjustified, he (or she) may become the deserting party. This situation, again, arises from the legal view that " desertion " consists of two elements—the *act* and the *intention* of deserting.

An honest and reasonable belief, by one spouse, that the other spouse has committed, or is committing, adultery, if such a belief is induced by the other spouse's conduct, may be " just cause " for the first spouse to refuse to live together, and prevent him (or her) from being regarded as the deserting party.

(d) This paragraph provides for new evidence of " breakdown "—*viz.*, that the parties have lived apart for at least two years continuously, immediately before the petition, and that the respondent consents to a divorce. Up to 31 December 1970 the old law continued to apply —that an agreed separation afforded no ground for divorce; Parliament and the Courts for many years set their faces against " divorce by consent." But, from 1 January 1971 " living apart " for two years, even by mutual agreement, though not amounting to desertion (**D**30(2)–(c)), will be regarded as evidence that the marriage has irretrievably broken down (**D**30(2)) and enable the Courts to grant a divorce. It no longer matters whether the parties ceased to live together through the fault of one or both, or whether the separation is due to incompatibility, so long as both consent to divorce.

(e) This paragraph provides for further new evidence of breakdown—*viz.*, that the parties have lived apart for at least five years continuously, immediately before the petition; it does not matter (except as stated below) whether the respondent consents or not, or which party, if any, is at fault. This is the most controversial of the new grounds. It is likely that many husbands, or wives, who have deserted their spouses and have hitherto failed to persuade the deserted party to divorce the other spouse, will take advantage of this new ground. To understand this change in the law it must be remembered that the new *sole ground for divorce* is *irretrievable breakdown* of the marriage; if the parties have not lived together for five years it will be obvious that the marriage has broken down beyond repair.

However, the Act provides certain safeguards against injustice, and favours reconciliation whenever possible:

(1) It is the Court's duty, in all cases, to inquire, "so far as it reasonably can," into the facts alleged by each side; *unless, unless*, the Court is satisfied that there is *no irretrievable breakdown*, it shall grant a divorce.

(2) In case (e) above, the respondent may oppose a grant on the ground that divorce would result in " grave financial or other hardship " to him or her and that it would, in all the circumstances, be wrong to dissolve the marriage. If there is such opposition, and (e) is the only ground for divorce which the Court would otherwise grant, it shall consider all the circumstances, including the parties' conduct, their interests and those of the children concerned (*e.g.*, a new irregular union or the birth of illegitimate children); if the Court feels that a divorce would result in such hardship (as mentioned above) and that in all the circumstances it would be wrong to dissolve the marriage, it shall dismiss the petition. Thus, in case (e), the Judge will have a discretion to grant or refuse a divorce. " Hardship " includes the loss of any benefit which the respondent might acquire if the marriage continued (*e.g.*, widow's pension rights on the petitioner's death *may* be such a " benefit " if it is a loss special to the particular case).

(3) In case (d) (divorce by consent after two years' separation) the Court may, after decree *nisi* and before decree absolute (D32(2)), on the Respondent's application, rescind (*i.e.*, cancel) the decree if it is satisfied that the Petitioner misled the Respondent (whether intentionally or not) on any matter connected with his or her consent.

(4) In cases (d) or (e) the Respondent may request the Court to consider his or her financial position; the Court must then pay regard to all the circumstances (age, health, conduct, earning power, financial resources and obligations of both parties, and of the Respondent as they are likely to be, after a divorce, if the Petitioner dies first). The Court shall not grant a decree absolute unless satisfied that the Petitioner need not make financial provision for the Respondent, or that any financial provision made is fair and reasonable, or the best that can be made in the circumstances (perhaps, *e.g.*, that the Petitioner has a new family to maintain). Nevertheless the Court may, if it thinks fit, proceed with the case if it appears that circumstances render it desirable to grant the decree absolute without delay and if the Petitioner has given a satisfactory undertaking to make approved financial provisions for the Respondent.

(5) In all cases any agreement or arrangement between the parties may be referred to the Court for its approval. The Judge again has a discretion.

(6) The Petitioner's solicitor must certify whether he has discussed with the Petitioner (in all cases) the possibility of reconciliation and given him or her names and addresses of persons qualified to help to bring the parties together. If at any time the Court feels there is such a possibility, it may adjourn the proceedings for that purpose.

(7) Even if, after the Petitioner's knowledge of the Respondent's adultery, or experience of mis-behaviour or desertion, the parties live together for total period(s) of six months or less (in Magistrates' Courts three months or less), with a view to reconciliation, such period(s) shall be disregarded; the same applies if the ground is " living apart " for 2 years or 5 years ((d) or (e) above); nor is the period of desertion broken ((c) above) by the six months' trial period(s).

(8) But if the parties continue to resume life together, after such knowledge of adultery, for more than six months (in Magistrates' Courts three months), that adultery cannot be relied on under (a).

Damages for Adultery.—The petitioner's right to claim such damages, under the old law, was abolished, from 1 January 1971, by the Law Reform (Miscellaneous Provisions) Act, 1970.

Restitution of Conjugal Rights.—This form of action has been abolished, on the Law Commission's recommendation, from 1 January 1971, by section 20 of the Matrimonial Proceedings and Property Act. 1970.

Judicial Separation.—A petition for this form of relief may be presented by either spouse on any of the grounds for which a divorce petition (*see above*) might have been presented; but on such a petition the Court is not required to consider whether the marriage has irretrievably broken down. The effect of the decree (as in the case of a similar order made by a Magistrates' Court) is that the Petitioner is no longer bound to live with the Respondent, and cannot therefore be regarded as a deserting party. (The legal bond of marriage remains in force; the procedure is therefore often employed by a spouse who does not desire divorce, perhaps for reasons of conscience, perhaps merely so as not to allow the other party freedom to marry somebody else.) It is, however, open to a Petitioner, who has obtained a decree of judicial separation, to petition for divorce, on the same facts, at a later date—provided that three years have elapsed since the date of the marriage (*see* D31(1)).

Decree Nisi and Decree Absolute.—When the case comes on for trial the Judge will hear the evidence of the Petitioner and his or her witnesses, and legal argument on his or her behalf; if the case is defended by the Respondent spouse, or by the Co-respondent (*i.e.*, any man accused, in the petition, of adultery with a Respondent wife), or by any woman named in the petition as having committed adultery with a Respondent husband, the Judge will hear their evidence and legal argument on their behalf. The Judge, if not satisfied on one of the points (a) to (f) (D30–1) in a case of divorce or judicial separation, must dismiss the petition, in which event the married status of the parties will remain unchanged. If the Judge is satisfied on one of the points mentioned he will, in a suit for judicial separation, pronounce a final decree; in a suit for divorce he will pronounce a decree unless he is satisfied, *on all the evidence*, that the marriage has not broken down irretrievably.

In a suit for nullity or divorce, the Judge will pronounce a decree *nisi*—*i.e.*, an order that the marriage is to be annulled or dissolved unless (*nisi*), before that event takes place, some cause is shown to the Court why final annulment or dissolution ought not to be permitted. Intervention for this purpose may be made by an official known as the *Queen's Proctor*, or by any member of the public. Such interventions after decree *nisi* are rare, but may be made, in divorce cases, on the ground, for example, that some material fact, was concealed from the Court at the hearing. (And see D30(2)—orders regarding " children of the family.")

If such intervention succeeds, the decree *nisi* will be rescinded (*i.e.*, cancelled) and the parties will retain their former status. If there is no such intervention, or if such intervention is dismissed, then the marriage will be finally annulled or dissolved on application (on a special form), at the Divorce Registry concerned, by or on behalf of the Petitioner, not earlier than *three months* after the decree *nisi* (unless the Court fixes a shorter time by special order). If the Petitioner does not make such an application, then the Respondent may do so after the lapse of a *further three months* (*i.e.*, six months after the date of the decree *nisi*), and the Court has power to grant or refuse such application or to deal with the case as it thinks fit.

The decree which finally annuls or dissolves the marriage is called a *decree absolute*. Unless and until it is granted, the marriage tie still subsists; the decree *nisi* does *not* terminate the status of husband and wife. But the *decree absolute* does terminate that status, leaving both parties free to marry again.

Custody of Children.—Apart from the general power of the Family Division, as guardian of equity (**D7**), to protect the person and the property of any minor (**D12**) and of the Local Authority under the Children and Young Persons Act, 1969, (even though there may be no matrimonial proceedings between its parents), and apart from the additional powers of that Division and of Magistrates' Courts, under the Guardianship of Infant Act, 1925, to appoint a guardian or guardians for any infant and to make orders for either parent to have access to the infant (*i.e.*, to see it periodically) and for the infant's maintenance, the Family Division itself may make orders for the custody, maintenance, and education of the children of the family in any matrimonial proceedings, and give directions for placing them under the protection of the Court, and for access to them by either or both of the parties. The expression " children of the family " includes children lawfully adopted by both husband and wife, children of a bigamous " marriage " which has given rise to nullity proceedings (**D29**), and also children born before the marriage of their parents and legitimated by that (subsequent) marriage. The new definition of the term, which is very wide, is stated in **D30**(2). The Court may make such orders and give such directions at any time after proceedings have been commenced for nullity, divorce, or judicial separation; it may make interim orders, and give interim directions, from time to time during the proceedings. It is, however, unusual for the Divorce Division to make orders for custody of or access to any child over the age of sixteen (since such orders would be difficult to enforce).

In all such proceedings, in whatever court they may be taken, the paramount consideration is the welfare of the children—not the punishment of either parent, nor any privilege of the father as against the mother, or *vice versa*. (It is, for example, unusual for the Court to deprive the mother of the custody of a very young child, even though she has committed, or is living in, adultery —unless, of course, she is neglecting the child or is a " bad mother " in the widest sense.) In some cases, for good reason, both parents may be passed over, and the custody of the child may be given to some third party, or to a local authority.

Financial Provision.—The Matrimonial Proceedings and Property Act, 1970, makes very detailed new provision for the maintenance of a divorced spouse and/or for " children of the family " (**D30**(2)).

Apart from the *occupation rights* in, or the transfer of, the matrimonial home (**D34**(2)), the Act provides that a spouse who does " substantial " (*i.e.*, important and lasting) work, or contributes substantially in money "or money's worth" to the other spouse's property (not merely the matrimonial home), shall acquire such a share of the beneficial interest in that property as may seem just to a Court dealing with the matter. Jurisdiction in such property disputes is given to the High Court as well as a County Court, even if the marriage has been dissolved or annulled within the past 3 years.

If spouses are *judicially separated* (not divorced), when one of them dies *intestate* (**D19**(2)), that one's estate shall devolve (*i.e.*, be dealt with) as if the surviving spouse were already dead (but not in case of a Magistrates' Court separation order— **D29**(1)).

The old expressions "alimony " and "maintenance pending suit " are abolished. All financial assistance to a spouse or children during or after the termination of matrimonial proceedings is known as "ancillary relief" (*i.e.*, subsidiary), and it may consist of " periodical payments" (so much per week or per month) or " lump sum(s) " (one or more payments of a substantial amount). The Court has power to order such periodical payments during the proceedings for the respondent spouse and children of the family as it thinks reasonable. On granting a decree the Court may order the petitioner to make to the respondent (*a*) such periodical payments as the order may specify and/or (*b*) to secure such payments to the Court's satisfaction (by deposit of a capital sum to produce enough interest to satisfy the periodical payments) and/or (*c*) to pay to the other spouse such lump sum or sums, in one amount or by instalments, as the Court may specify, to enable the other spouse to meet liabilities " reasonably incurred " (perhaps including legal expenses) in maintaining him or herself or any child of the family. Such order may (at the Court's discretion) be made (*a*) before or on granting the decree, or at any time afterwards; (*b*) even if the proceedings are dismissed, forthwith or within a reasonable period. If any child of the family is over 18, payments may be ordered direct to him or her. The Court has now the new power to order (*a*) one spouse to transfer to the other, or for the benefit of a child of the family, some specified property, or (*b*) to settle (**D23**(2)) such property for the benefit of the other spouse or any such child, or (*c*) to vary any voluntary settlement made between the spouses before or after marriage, whether by will or otherwise, or (*d*) to extinguish or reduce the interest of either spouse under such settlement.

In deciding the nature of such ancillary relief (see above), the Court must consider all the circumstances of the case, including (*a*) income, earning capacity, property and other financial resources of each spouse; (*b*) financial needs, obligations and responsibilities which each spouse has or is likely to have in future (*e.g.*, responsibility for a new wife and children); (*c*) the family's living standard before the marriage broke down; (*d*) ages of the spouses and duration of the marriage; (*e*) either spouse's physical or mental disability (if any); (*f*) each spouse's contribution to the family's welfare; (*g*) the value of any prospective benefit which a spouse may lose by divorce or annulment (**D32**(2)). The Court shall so exercise its powers as to place the parties, so far as practicable and just (having regard to their conduct), in the financial position they would have been in if there had been no breakdown. In addition, in regard to any child of the family, the Court shall have regard to the way in which that child was being or was expected, before the breakdown, to be educated or trained; whether and to what extent each spouse assumed responsibility for the child's maintenance, whether he or she knew the child was not his or hers, and the liability of any other person to maintain the child. Similar provisions apply if, without divorce, nullity or separation, a responsible spouse is found by the Court to have wilfully neglected to provide reasonable maintenance to the other spouse or any child of the family for whom it was reasonable to expect the spouse responsible to provide.

If the Court considers that *any* child of the family needs immediate financial assistance, but it is not yet possible to decide how much and for how long, the Court may order the spouse responsible temporarily to make such reasonable payments as the Court thinks fit. The maximum period of such ancillary provision (*a*) for a spouse, is the joint lives of the spouses or (*b*) the other spouse's remarriage (if earlier). For a child of the family the maximum age is usually 18 or (if earlier) the child's birthday next following the upper limit of compulsory school age (soon to be 16); but the relief may be extended beyond 18 if the child is receiving education or being trained for a trade, profession, or vocation (*e.g.*, an articled clerk or apprentice) until the death of the person liable, except for arrears. The Court may vary or discharge any of such orders. Legal personal representatives (**D22**(1)) of a deceased spouse are not liable for distributing his or her estate after the expiry of 6 months from probate or letters of administration (**D22**(1)), without regard to the possibility of variation; but the child may make a claim against the beneficiaries of the estate for any sum which became due not more than one year earlier.

The Act also contains elaborate provisions for the variation, extension or discharge of voluntary maintenance agreements made between the parties; such changes may sometimes be made by Magistrates as well as by the High Court. There are also safeguards to prevent any party responsible from evading his or her responsibilities by entering into transactions of certain kinds, which the Court may set aside (*i.e.*, cancel).

It will be seen, from this necessarily concise summary of the details of the Act, that very considerable powers and duties are conferred upon the Courts to enable them to order proper provision to be made for the victims, whether spouses or children, of any breakdown of marriage. Although such breakdown may now be followed by divorce (whoever is at fault), that does not mean that the welfare of dependents, whether adults or children, can be neglected by the person to whom divorce, annulment, or separation is granted.

Domicil.—It has been explained above (**D11**) why the English Court will not, generally speaking, grant a divorce to a man who is domiciled abroad. Since the domicil of a wife is the same as that of her husband (even if she has not lived with him for many years), the refusal of the English court to accept jurisdiction has caused hardship in many cases. To mitigate this hardship the Matrimonial Causes Act, 1965 (not repealed) conferred upon the Divorce Division an additional statutory jurisdiction in the following cases, in favour of a wife, even if her husband is not domiciled in England:

(*a*) In any matrimonial proceedings, other than for a " decree of presumption of death and dissolution of marriage " (*see below*), if: (i) the wife has been deserted by her husband, or the husband has been deported from the United Kingdom as an alien; and (ii) immediately before the desertion or deportation the husband was domiciled in England.

(*b*) In proceedings for divorce or nullity, if: (i) the wife is resident (*i.e.*, actually living for the time being) in England; and (ii) has been ordinarily resident there for a period of three years immediately preceding the commencement of the proceedings; and (iii) the husband is not domiciled in any other part of the United Kingdom, or in the Channel Islands or the Isle of Man. (The two last-named territories have their own separate systems of law.)

(*c*) In proceedings for a decree of " presumption of death and dissolution of marriage ": the husband is presumed by law (for the purpose of ascertaining the wife's domicil) to have died " immediately after the last occasion when she knew, or had reason to believe him, to be living." (Thus the wife can acquire an English domicil of her own as from that date.)

(*d*) Recent cases have decided that the English courts shall have the right to recognise a divorce granted by the court of a foreign country with which the petitioner has some " genuine connection " (*e.g.*, that he or she was born or is resident there, even if not domiciled there (*see* **D11**(2)) at the time of the foreign divorce.

And, under the Matrimonial Causes (War Marriages) Act, 1944;

(*e*) In the special case of marriages celebrated during the Second World War, where: (i) the husband was, at the time of the marriage, domiciled outside the United Kingdom; (ii) the wife was, immediately before the marriage, domiciled in England; and (iii) the parties never resided together in the country which was the husband's domicil at the time of the marriage, the Divorce Division may deal with proceedings for divorce or nullity as if both parties were at all material times domiciled in England. (This provision was to cover the special cases of soldiers from the Dominions or Colonies, the United States or other foreign countries, who while stationed here during the War, married English girls and had to go back to their own countries, leaving their wives behind —in some instances without communicating with them again.) (This Act applies only to marriages between 3 September 1939 and 1 June 1950.)

Housekeeping Allowances.—If any question arises as to the right of a husband or wife to money derived from any allowance made by the husband for housekeeping, or any similar expenses, or to any property acquired out of such money, the money or property (in the absence of agreement to the contrary) shall be treated as belonging to them both in equal shares. (The old rule was that the wife's savings out of housekeeping allowances belonged to the husband.)

Matrimonial Homes.—The Matrimonial Homes Act, 1967, protects the rights of either spouse to remain in occupation of the matrimonial home, even if it belongs to the other spouse. If already *in occupation*, he or she is not to be evicted except with leave of the Court; if not in occupation, he or she may enter and occupy the home. The Court has power to enforce, restrict or terminate these rights, having regard to the conduct of both spouses, their needs and financial resources, those of the children, and all the circumstances. The Court's powers include the right to except part of the home from a spouse's occupation, to order one spouse in occupation to make periodical payments in respect of such occupation, and to impose on either obligations for repairing, maintaining or discharging liabilities on the home. Any payment made by the occupying spouse towards satisfaction of the other spouse's liabilities for rent, rates, mortgage payments, etc., shall count as if it were made by the other spouse. Occupation of the home by one spouse shall be treated as possession by the other spouse if he or she is protected by the Rent Control provisions (**D25**(2)); but this shall not affect any right of the occupying spouse against the other under any Act or Order. These rights are to last only so long as the marriage subsists, unless provision is made for such rights to be a charge on the other spouse's ownership or lease, or the Court makes an order (under the Matrimonial Proceedings and Property Act, 1970) for transfer of *ownership* of the home to the other spouse, or to settle it (**D23**(2)) for her or his benefit. In deciding how (if at all) to exercise this power, the Court must have regard to each party's contribution to the family's welfare, " including looking after the home and caring for the family," not necessarily by payment in money.

If one spouse is entitled in law to occupy the house as owner or lessee, the other spouse's rights of occupation shall be a charge on the first spouse's title (**D26**(2)), from the date of acquisition of the right, the marriage, and the coming into force of the Act. The right shall be terminated (*a*) by death of the second spouse, or (*b*) by the termination of the marriage (unless the Court otherwise orders). Any surrender of ownership or tenancy shall be subject to these rights; so also shall bankruptcy of the owner or lessee. The rights on any one home may be registered at the Land Registry for the second spouse's protection; only a mortgagee (**D26**) can enforce his rights against both spouses.

If the owner or lessee contracts to sell or let his legal estate (**D27**(1)) in the home, such registered charge must be cancelled before vacant possession can be promised. The Chief Land Registrar shall cancel the charge if either spouse is dead, or on a divorce or nullity decree (**D32**(2), or under a Court Order. A spouse entitled to such protection may release his or her rights in writing.

If the Rent Control Acts (**D25**(2)) apply, and there is a *decree absolute* (**D32**(2)) of divorce or nullity, the Court may direct that the ownership or lease be transferred to the former spouse if he or she was not already owner or lessee, and the originally protected spouse shall no longer be protected. Or the Court may direct that both spouses, together or separately, shall be liable for any obligations in respect of the home; but the landlord must have an opportunity of being heard by the Court. (This paragraph does not affect the rights referred to in the first paragraph).

(*Note:* Broadly, these provisions *prevent* a husband or wife who is owner or lessee of the matrimonial home from turning out the other spouse after the marriage has broken up.)

LEGITIMACY AND ILLEGITIMACY

Until about 40 years ago illegitimacy (or "bastardy") was regarded as a disgrace both for mother and child; it also brought great financial disadvantages. This state of affairs has been gradually remedied, and today the rights of an illegitimate child are almost the same as those of the legitimate.

I. The Status.

From very early times legitimacy and illegitimacy have been questions of status (D11(2)); in the legal systems of most countries it was based on the Latin maxim *Mater semper certa est; pater incertus* that is, "it is always certain who is a child's mother, but who is its father is uncertain." The reason is obvious; midwives, doctors, or relatives are nearly always present when a child is born, and actually see the child issuing from the mother's body. But, even when a child is born to a married woman living with her husband—still more when she is unmarried—doubts may arise as to the father's identity, since no third party is present when sexual intercourse takes place, and there is always a *possibility* that even an apparently "respectable" married woman may have had sexual relations with some other man, as well as with her husband, at about the same time (about 270–300 days) before the birth. Therefore the question of "paternity" (fatherhood) is one of *inference and deduction*; although in the vast majority of cases where married couples are living happily together, no question arises; the husband takes it for granted that the wife's child is his. But there are some wives who commit adultery (D31(1)), and some have relations with a man other than the husband, as well as with him, at about the time of conception. In such cases the wife may herself be uncertain which of the two men has fathered her child. In nearly all legal systems the relevant date to establish legitimacy (as we shall see) is nearly always the date of the child's *birth*, even if it occurs only a few weeks after marriage, so that intercourse between a man and an unmarried girl may produce a legitimate child provided it is born at any time after the marriage takes place. (In England it is estimated that a substantial proportion of brides are already pregnant on the wedding-day; but this does not normally prevent the child from being born legitimate, unless the husband (more rarely the wife) produces *clear evidence* that he is not the father.)

In the Canon Law of the early Catholic Church these considerations gave rise to the second maxim—*pater est quem nuptiae demonstrant*, that is, "fatherhood is proved by marriage." This prevented a man not married with the blessing of the Church to the mother at the date of the child's birth, from being regarded as the legal father; though *civil law* quite early recognised that (1) not the man who was the husband when the child was born, but some other man, was the "natural" father if the wife had been unfaithful; (2) if the mother was still unmarried when the child was born, there was a "natural" father (who might or might not be easily found, and willing or unwilling to marry the mother *after the birth*). In both cases the child was and is, illegitimate: obviously (1) is more difficult to prove if husband and wife are or were living together at the date of birth or conception than (2) where the *facts* of the mother's unmarried status when the child is born, and of the actual birth taking place, are easily proved by witnesses. For these reasons the civil law, quite early in history, abandoned the Church's rule that "fatherhood is proved by marriage." There was a legal presumption (1) that the husband living with a married woman at the date of birth was the father of the child, however soon after the marriage the birth took place and the child was regarded as legitimate unless clear evidence could be produced to disprove the presumption beyond all reasonable doubt (as in criminal law—D9(2)); (2) that a child born to an unmarried woman was illegitimate.

II. Instances.

Many people famous in history have been born illegitimate. Charlemagne (742–814), emperor of the Holy Roman Empire, had no less than four mistresses, as well as four wives; all the former bore him illegitimate children, many of whom became rulers or princes of great States. William I of England (" the Conqueror ") was the bastard son of Duke Robert (nicknamed " the Devil ") of Normandy; his mother was the daughter of a tanner. In the 12th century Sir Robert Faulconbridge was the reputed father of an illegitimate son; in Shakespeare's play *King John* he is called " Philip the Bastard " and was suspected to be the illegitimate son of Richard I (*Cœur de Lion*); in the play he is shown as a noble character, a great warrior, and patriot. Don Juan of Austria, victor in the Battle of Lepanto (1571), when the allied Christian fleets defeated the Turkish (Moslem) armada, was the bastard son of the Hapsburg emperor, Charles V.

III. Legitimation.

As there is nothing that our Parliament cannot lawfully do (D8(1)), it did on rare occasions pass *Acts to legitimate bastard children* of great families. One such Act in the reign of Richard II (1381–99) legitimated the bastard offspring of John of Gaunt, Duke of Lancaster, but without giving them the right of succession to the Crown. King Charles II was the natural father of many bastard sons, by different mistresses, several of whom were raised to the peerage, among them the Dukes of Grafton, St. Albans, Richmond, Monmouth, and Buccleuch.

Moreover, for about a century past, that part of our legal system known as "private international law" has recognised that, since legitimacy is a question of status, which in turn depends on *domicil* (D11(2)), if the father of a bastard was, at the date of its birth, domiciled in a foreign country under the law of which the child could be legitimated by the subsequent marriage of its parents, then English law would recognise the child as legitimate either from its date of birth or from the date of the marriage. In Scotland the same rule operated, but only from the marriage date. But, apart from such exceptional foreign cases, there was no way under English law, until 1927, of legitimating a bastard except by an Act of Parliament which very few could succeed in getting passed.

IV. Disabilities of Illegitimacy.

Until comparatively recent times the social and legal disabilities of an illegitimate child were considerable. He was *filius nullius*, that is, "nobody's child" since he had no lawful and (often) no known father. Socially, he lived under a lifelong stigma which made him a kind of second-class citizen, for puritanical and narrow-minded people often imputed to the child the "sin" of its mother; the sufferings of such a child have been graphically described by Charles Dickens in the persons of Oliver Twist and Esther Summerson in *Bleak House*. Under the Poor Law Act 1830 a mother was legally obliged to maintain her illegitimate child up to the age of 16 or (if it was a girl) until its marriage. But in those days an unmarried mother, besides the disgrace of her position, found it difficult, or impossible to find a situation which would allow her to maintain herself and keep the child with her; adoption (D38–41) was then unknown, so that in too many cases the child, and often the mother too, found themselves in the workhouse. Even if the father was known and traced, there was then (as between him and the mother) no duty for proper maintenance, unless he voluntarily made a binding contract (D13(1)) with her to contribute to the child's support; but this came to an end on the mother's death.

Although there was legislation, dating back to 1576, requiring the natural father of the child (if he could be traced) to share the mother's financial responsibility, this remained, for nearly three centuries, intimately bound up with the Poor Law—the object being, not to give the mother a legal remedy against him, but to prevent the cost of the child's maintenance from falling on the Parish.

V. Removal of Financial Disabilities.

Not until the Bastardy Act 1845 was the mother given an independent remedy against the "putative" (supposed) father without the intervention of the Poor Law authorities. By the Act of 1845, amended in 1872–3, 1914, 1918, 1923, 1957, and 1960, the mother has been able to issue a summons, before a magistrate or J.P. (**D43**), against the putative father; assuming she could prove his paternity she could get an order (now called an "affiliation order") for him to pay a sum, raised in 1957 to a maximum of 50/- a week, towards the child's maintenance up to the age of 16. By the Maintenance Orders Act 1960 this maximum was abolished, and the sum awarded is now entirely in the court's discretion, depending on the means and conduct of the parties. The application may be made before the birth, but cannot be entertained if made later than 12 months after the birth, unless the putative father has, within those 12 months, paid money for its maintenance. Either party may appeal against the order, its amount or its refusal from the magistrate or J.P.s to Quarter Sessions (**D6**) or, on a point of law only, to the Divisional Court (**D5**). The applicant must be a "single woman"; but the courts have generously interpreted these words to include a widow, a divorced woman, or a married woman living apart from her husband, provided the child is clearly illegitimate. Thus a bastard child is now financially protected during the lifetime of its mother, or its father if the case can be proved against him, up to the age of 16.

It was still the law until recently that this protection ceased on the death of the responsible parent; but, by Part II of the Family Law Reform Act 1969 (with effect from 1 January 1970), on the death of such a parent intestate (without a will—**D19(1)**), an illegitimate child shares equally with any legitimate children in the intestate parent's estate and, *vice versa*, the parents from an intestate illegitimate child. If there *is* a will, the words "child," "son," "daughter," "mother," "father," and other words implying kinship, are to include kinship through illegitimacy as well as legitimacy. Executors and administrators (**D22(1)**) of the deceased who have distributed the estate, in ignorance of the existence of illegitimate children, among the legitimate persons entitled to benefit are not liable to the former who may, however, "follow the property into the hands of" those who have received it and claim their lawful share from the latter. The right of certain illegitimate—as well as legitimate—"dependants" to claim "reasonable" provision from the estate of a testator who has made no provision or insufficient provision for them has already been noted (**D19(2)**). The same right has now (1970) been given to children of a void marriage (**D30(1**)) and to the surviving spouse of such a marriage. Thus the financial disabilities of bastardy are abolished.

VI. Removal of Social Disabilities.

The Legitimacy Act 1926, for the first time in English legal history, permitted "legitimation by subsequent marriage of the parents." It provided that if the natural parents of an illegitimate child (the father being domiciled (**D11(2)**) in England or Wales) should marry or have married each other *after the child's birth*, the child was "legitimated"—*i.e.*, it became legitimate from 1 January 1927 (when the Act came into force) or from the date of the marriage, whichever was later. The birth of such a child could be reregistered as legitimate with the Registrar of Births, Marriages, and Deaths, but failure to reregister did not prevent legitimation. However, the subsequent marriage of the natural parents could not, under that Act, legitimate the child if one of them was married to a third party at the

date of the child's birth; this remained the law until the exception was abolished by the Legitimacy Act 1959 (as from 29 October of that year); the 1959 Act also provided that any child of a void marriage (**D30(1)**), whenever born, should be treated as the legitimate child of its parents if, at the time of the sexual intercourse resulting in the birth, or the date of the marriage, if later both or either of the parents "reasonably" believed the marriage was valid. Thus there is now practically no social disability attaching to an illegitimate child.

VII. Evidence of Paternity.

We have seen (I., above) that, while maternity is easily *provable*, fatherhood is not; that (1) the man who was the husband of a married woman when a child was born was, for many centuries, regarded as its father, and the child as legitimate, unless there was clear evidence to the contrary; (2) the child of a "single" woman, including one living apart from her husband at the date of birth, was generally regarded as illegitimate. But, in the past forty years or so, questions have often arisen in the courts not only whether a child is legitimate or not, but who is its *natural* father. Such questions might arise (1) where the child's mother is married and living with her husband, but is shown to have committed adultery at the presumed time of conception, in which case the husband may deny his paternity; (2) where the child's mother is unmarried but has had intercourse with more than one man at about that time. *Direct evidence* of fatherhood is hard to come by.

In 1924, when many financial and social disabilities attached to illegitimacy, the House of Lords, on appeal (**D5**), decided the case of *Russell* v. *Russell*. In the lower courts the husband had denied paternity of the child born to his wife, although they were living together at the time of conception, by giving evidence, in a divorce suit on the grounds of the wife's alleged adultery, of sexual practices between him and his wife not amounting (as he said) to proper intercourse sufficient to beget a child. The Lords decided that it was indecent and intolerable that evidence of non-intercourse between a married couple, living together, should be given by either of them tending to bastardise a child born in wedlock. That decision, binding on all courts (**D7(1)**) became part of the law of England; it was so strictly interpreted that even during the second world war neither husband nor wife could give evidence of "non-access" (*i.e.*, husband and wife not living together) even if the husband had been abroad, when the child was conceived, on active service, though the country's defence authorities, or strangers who knew the facts, could do so. This rule remained in force until it was abolished by the Law Reform (Miscellaneous Provisions) Act 1949 (now sec. 43 of the Matrimonial Causes Act 1965). Similarly, for the protection of a child born in wedlock while the spouses were living together, the legal presumption that (I., above) such a child was legitimate, unless the contrary was proved "beyond all reasonable doubt," held good until the passing of the Family Law Reform Act 1969, sec. 26 of which provides that "any presumption of law as to the legitimacy or illegitimacy of any person may in any civil proceedings be rebutted" (*i.e.*, "contradicted") "by evidence which shows that it is more probable than not that that person is illegitimate or legitimate, as the case may be, and it shall not be necessary to prove that fact beyond reasonable doubt in order to rebut the presumption."

VIII. Blood Tests.

The reasons for these relaxations of the strict rules of law relating to proof of illegitimacy are principally that (1) the disabilities of illegitimacy (V and VI above) have now practically disappeared; (2) the progress of medical science has, in the past 20 years, made it possible for specialists to say, with a 70 per cent. degree of probability that a particular man is *not the father* of a particular child. Since 1901 researches of the serologist Dr. Landsteiner and his successors have been developed and have now reached a point where, by investigating the blood groups (*see* index to Section P) of a child, its mother, and one or more men, a specialist can say, with comparative certainty (*a*) that a particular man is not the father of a particular child, or (*b*), with almost complete certainty, that of two men one is less likely to be the father than the other. Without going into medical technicalities it can be said that, if it is found that a child's blood contains some constituent or characteristic absent from the blood of both its mother and her husband, or of the putative father, *he cannot be the natural father* of the child.

In the past twenty years evidence based on *voluntary* blood tests has become acceptable by the courts (*a*) in cases involving the suspected adultery of a wife and non-paternity of her husband; (*b*) in cases where a "single" woman has given birth to a child and it is uncertain what man is its father. Where *all the parties willingly* have submitted themselves and the child for blood tests, no difficulty arises; the results of the tests are part of the evidence, admissible in the court hearing the case. But these tests cannot prove *who is* the father, but only *who is not.* Nevertheless, such tests have in recent years become a valuable source of evidence, provided that *all parties* involved have submitted to tests.

The difficulties begin (*a*) if one or more of the parties refuses to submit himself or herself for a test, or (*b*) if the person having custody of the child refuses to have it blood-tested. To obtain a blood sample only a very slight surgical operation is required; but (*a*) in the case of an adult even the slightest surgical operation performed on him or her without consent would be an assault and battery (**D16(1)**); therefore the courts, and the Law Commission, have resolutely set their faces against physical compulsion or punishment of any kind for refusal to take a test. But the Family Law Reform Act, Part III (which will not come into force until the Lord Chancellor exercises the power that the Act gives him (**D8–9**) to bring it into operation when he thinks fit—probably not before the spring of 1971) confers on the courts power to "direct" the use of blood tests, on the application of any party, whenever the paternity of a child has to be determined in any civil proceedings. Part III of the Act briefly sets out the proposed procedure and confers power on the Home Secretary to issue regulations (**D8–9**) on the details. But the Act lays it down that (1) no blood sample is to be taken from any person without his consent, if he is over 16, (2) in which case his consent shall be as valid as if he had attained his majority (**D12(1)**). (3) A blood sample may be taken from anybody under 16 (not suffering from mental disorder) with the consent of the person having his or her care and control. (4) If a person is suffering from mental disorder and cannot understand the "nature and purpose" of blood tests, the person having his care and control must consent, and the medical practitioner in charge of his case must certify that taking a blood sample will not prejudice his care and treatment.

But what if a person over 16, not suffering from mental disorder, fails or refuses to obey the court's direction to take any step to enable blood tests to be made? The answer appears in sec. 23 of the Act; in such event "the court may draw such inferences, if any, from that fact as may appear proper in the circumstances." It is also provided that if in any proceedings in which paternity is to be determined the court gives a direction for a blood test to be taken, and any party involved, who would normally be entitled to rely on the presumption of law that a child is legitimate, fails to take any step required of him to give effect to the direction, the court may adjourn to enable him to take that step; if at the end of the adjournment he has unreasonably failed to take it, the court may dismiss his claim for relief notwithstanding the absence of evidence to rebut the presumption. And if a person named in a direction fails to consent to the taking of a blood sample from any person of whom he has care and control, he shall be deemed to have failed to take such a step. In other words the court may draw the conclusion that the person refusing is doing so because he fears that the test, if made, would be against his or her case. So, for example, if a married mother refuses to submit herself or her child to a blood

test, the court may assume that it is because she fears that such a test might help to provide evidence that her husband is not the father, and so forth. These rules should help to deter adult parties from refusing to comply with the court's direction in a case where a child's paternity is disputed.

(*b*) As regards minors under 16, particularly *children of tender years,* there have been, both before and since the Act was passed but before Part III has come into force, conflicting decisions in the High Court and the Court of Appeal on the question whether it is right and proper for the courts to direct the taking of a blood test on a young child, especially if it is under 4 or 5 years old. Since equity (**D7(2)**) took a special interest in the welfare of young children who could not protect themselves—an interest which it exercised, before the Judicature Act 1873 (**D8(1)**) through the old Court of Chancery but, after that Act, through any High Court Judge (**D8(1)**)—it has been customary, in any case concerning the custody, upbringing, or welfare of a young child, to appoint a guardian *ad litem* (" for the purposes of the case ") to argue, on the child's behalf, its own interests, which may be different from those of its mother or father (*see* (*a*), above). As a result of such arguments, in various cases, some Judges have held (i) that it can never be equitable (**D7(2)**) to order a blood test on a child born in wedlock which may help to provide evidence that "its mother was lying when she said her husband was the father," and that it is almost certainly not the offspring of the husband but of an adulterer. (ii) Conversely, other Judges have felt that, in all doubtful cases, the child itself will at some time be anxious to know who is its natural father—a question which ought not to be decided by the court on *partial evidence*—excluding the scientific and up-to-date evidence of blood tests—assuming that all the adult parties are willing to submit themselves to tests; above all, that if a woman is suspected of adultery, her husband will leave the court with a sense of grievance and injustice, and never treat the child as his own, in a fatherly way, if such clear, up-to-date, scientific evidence is excluded.

Two such cases, *W.* v. *W.* and *S.* v. *S.*, in which majorities of two Judges to one, in different Courts of Appeal, had given conflicting decisions, came before the House of Lords (**D5**) in July 1970. The five Law Lords unanimously decided in favour of view (ii), above. Lord Reid, who delivered the principal speech, dealt with the whole history of the subject which we have outlined above, and emphasised that the former financial and social disabilities of illegitimacy have now practically disappeared. "In large towns nobody knows or cares whether a newcomer is legitimate or illegitimate; one hopes that prejudice is decreasing. Some children may grow up sensitive or resentful at having been born illegitimate; others not. No one can foretell whether the child would resent the evidence having been suppressed or not. . . . On the whole it is better that 'the truth should out.' Courts should permit blood tests on a young child unless satisfied that it would be against the child's interest—' a young child,' because, as soon as it was old enough to understand, it would generally be unwise to submit it to the test against its will. The court must protect the child, but it is not really doing so by banning a test on some vague or shadowy conjecture that it might turn out to its disadvantage. A parent can lawfully use constraint to his young child if it is not cruel or oppressive; so why cannot the court? "

Lords Reid and Hodson added some words which have left part of the question in doubt. They did not believe that Part III of the Act was intended to grant power, to magistrates' courts (in affiliation cases) and "designated" county courts (**D29(2)**) in undefended divorces, to order blood tests on young children, as the rights of protection formerly exercised by the Court of Chancery had been transferred by the Judicature Acts (**D8(1)**) only to the High Court. There is, however, nothing in the 1969 Act which defines or restricts the meaning of "the court", nor in the Law Commission's recommendations. The resolution of this doubt must await the Lord Chancellor's order (above), probably in the spring of 1971, and the Act may be amended.

ADOPTION OF CHILDREN

Adoption is the act of a person who takes upon himself the position of parent to a child who is not in law his own legitimate child. It has been for centuries very common in India and most Continental countries, and for over a hundred years in most parts of the United States. It was recognised by the laws of Greece and Rome from early times. Julius Caesar adopted his grand-nephew Octavian (afterwards the Emperor Augustus) in 46 B.C. But there was no provision for adoption under the Common Law of England (D4); the transfer of parental rights and duties in respect of a child to another person was unknown to our law until 1926, when the first of a series of Adoption Acts was passed. There have been a number of amendments since then. The present law is mainly contained in the Adoption Acts 1958 and 1968. " Informal adoption," outside the Acts, is invalid. (But under the Adoption Act, 1968, adoptions effected under the law of certain foreign countries may be recognised by the English courts.)

The procedure for adoption is as follows:

(1) Approach by would-be adopters to a registered Adoption Society or Local Authority for help in adopting a child, and explanations of their qualifications.

(2) Investigations of suitability of persons and home, including medical matters, and notification to parent(s) of eventual need for formal consent and effects of Order when made.

(3) Informal consent of parents or guardian to handing over of child to would-be-adopters " on trial."

(4) Actual handing over of child to would-be adopters " on trial."

(5) Formal application by would-be adopters to a Court.

(6) Formal consent of parents to adoption.

(7) Hearing by the Court. If an Order is refused, and there is no appeal, the child must be returned to its parent(s), or to the Local Authority if the parents are unsuitable. There may be an appeal, while the child is still in the hands of the Applicants, to the Court of Appeal and the House of Lords. If the original application, or appeal, succeeds, an Order is made. Then, and only then is the child adopted.

We shall now explain the sequence in more detail.

Applications for Adoption.—The would-be adopters (the " Applicants ") normally approach a registered Adoption Society, a County Council or County Borough Council to make and participate in adoption arrangements, which must eventually be confirmed by an Order of the High Court, a County Court, or a Magistrates' Court hearing juvenile cases. The Adoption Society or Local Authority carefully investigates the suitability of the Applicants, interviews them and sees their home, and ascertains the religion in which the parents wish the child to be brought up. The Applicants must produce a certificate from a registered medical practitioner to the effect that they are in good health, as must the parents of the child to certify that its health is good. The Society or Local Authority must hand the parents a memorandum, in ordinary language, explaining the effects of an Adoption Order if made by the Court, and calling attention to the parents' formal consent being eventually required. Such consent may be withdrawn at any time before the Order is actually made, but may be dispensed with by the Court on special grounds (see below).

If all these preliminary matters are satisfactory the Society or Council may hand the child over provisionally to the Applicants for a " trial period " of not less than three consecutive months preceding the Order, if made; but no period is counted before the child is six weeks old. No maximum period is laid down by law within which the Applicants must apply to the Court. This is regarded by reformers as a serious defect in procedure. They consider that there should be a maximum period of (say) six months, within which the Applicants must apply to the Court for an Order, and the parents should be compelled to decide within that period whether or not they are prepared to give formal written consent to the proposed adoption. (The Home Secretary appointed the Houghton Committee in 1969 to consider the law, policy, and procedure on the adoption of children. The review will include such issues as whether relatives should be able to apply for guardianship instead of adoption, the relation between adoption law and that part of guardianship law which gives the natural father of an illegitimate child the right to apply for custody, and, in particular, the position of long-term foster parents who wish to keep a child permanently against the wishes of the natural parents. The Committee has published its preliminary proposals as a " working paper " for consideration and comment by all persons and institutions interested. A brief summary of these preliminary proposals is given at the end of this article (D40–1).

Formal consent may be dispensed with by the Court if a parent, or his or her wife or husband, cannot be found, is incapable of consenting, or is living apart in what seems likely to be a permanent separation. A parent's consent may also be dispensed with if he or she has abandoned, neglected, or ill-treated the child, or is " unreasonably " refusing consent. If the parent does not attend the Court hearing, that consent must be given in writing, witnessed by a J.P., County Court officer, or Magistrate's Clerk; or outside England by a British Consul or Vice-Consul or foreign Notary.

None of the provisions relating to consent applies to the proposed adoption of a child who is not a U.K. national; but such adoption must conform to the internal law of the country of which he is a national (Act of 1968).

As soon as an application to the Court is filed by the Applicants, the Official Solicitor (or, in Magistrates' Court cases, the Children's Officer of the Local Authority) is appointed the child's guardian ad litem (i.e., a guardian for the purpose of the proceedings, who looks after the interests of the child without regard to those of anybody else). If no appointment for the Court hearing is made within 15 days from the application to the Court, the guardian ad litem must apply for the Court's directions. (This is a new rule, to avoid executive delay.) The Court then hears the case in camera (i.e., in private, the public not being admitted) and has a complete discretion either to make or to refuse an Adoption Order. If refused, and there is no appeal, the child must be returned to its parent(s) or, if they are unsuitable, placed in the care of the Local Authority. If an Order is made or the Applicant(s) successfully appeal, the child remains with the Applicant(s): only on the making of an Adoption Order by the Court is the child legally adopted.

Adoption Orders.—The High Court (Family Division), a County Court, or a Magistrates' Juvenile Court may make an Adoption Order authorising an Applicant, in the prescribed manner, to adopt a child. An Order may be made on the application of two spouses jointly, or by one spouse with the consent of the other spouse; but in no other case may an Order be made in favour of more than one person. (Dispensing with consent—see above.) An Order may be made authorising the adoption of an illegitimate or legitimated child, or the re-adoption of an already adopted child (e.g., in case of the death of the Adopter(s)), by his or her mother or natural father, either alone or jointly with his or her spouse: this facilitates the adoption of illegitimate or legitimated children and puts them (for record purposes) on a par with legitimate children who have been adopted. (A legitimated child is one born out of wedlock, but whose parents have subsequently married.)

An adoption Order may not generally be made

in England unless the Applicant and the child are living in England. (But see Act of 1968, above.) Nor may an Order be made unless the Applicant (or one of two Applicants) is: (*a*) the mother or father of the illegitimate or legitimated child (with the other parent's consent); or (*b*) a "relative," *i.e.*, a grandparent, brother, sister, uncle, or aunt of the child, or a person who would be such relative if the child were the legitimate child of its mother or father, or of former adopters, and such relative is aged 21 or over; or (*c*) in any other case, is 25 years old or more. On the application of a sole male Applicant to adopt a female child, no Order may be made unless the Court is satisfied that there are "special circumstances" justifying an Adoption Order "as an exceptional measure."

No Adoption Order may be made unless the child has been continuously in the care and possession of the Applicant for at least three consecutive months immediately preceding the Order (not counting any time before the infant is six weeks old); this is subject to the safeguards detailed below as to supervision of a "protected child." (But in the case of Applicants domiciled (**D11**) outside Great Britain, who desire to adopt an infant under the law of the country of domicil, and to obtain a provisional Adoption Order in England, the child may be taken or sent abroad for the purpose first mentioned and the period of three consecutive months is extended to six.) Except where one of the Applicants is a parent of the child, no Order is to be made in respect of that child who, at the hearing, is below the upper limit of the compulsory school age, unless the Applicant has given notice, in writing, to the Local Authority of his intention, at least three months (in cases of provisional adoption, six months) before the Court Hearing.

Formal Consents Required.—No Order may be ordinarily made without the consent of every person who is a parent or guardian of the child (which may be given either unconditionally or subject to conditions as to the religion in which the parent or guardian requires the child to be brought up). Even so, the consent of the parent or guardian may be dispensed with (*see above*). Where a parent or guardian has given informal consent without knowing the identity of the Applicant(s), and subsequently withdraws his or her consent solely on this ground, he or she is deemed to be withholding consent "unreasonably." (*See also* Act of 1968, above, and preliminary proposals of the Home Office Houghton Committee (**D40**).)

Matters on which the Court must be satisfied.—Before making the Order the Court must be satisfied:

(*a*) that every person whose consent is necessary, and has not been dispensed with, has consented to and understands the nature and effect of the proposed Adoption Order; in particular that every parent understands that the effect will be to deprive him or her permanently of his or her parental rights;

(*b*) that the proposed Order will be for the child's welfare;

(*c*) that the Applicant has not received or agreed to receive, and that no person has made or given, or agreed to make or give, any payment or other reward, in consideration of the adoption, except such as the Court may sanction (if any).

As to (*a*), the Court must have regard to the Applicant's health, to be evidenced by the certificate of a fully registered medical practitioner; the Court shall also give due consideration to the wishes of the child, having regard to his or her age and understanding. The Court may impose such terms and conditions as it thinks fit, including a requirement that the adopter shall make such financial provision for the child as is just and expedient. It may postpone a decision on the application and make an interim order giving the Applicant custody of the child for a probationary period not exceeding two years, upon such terms as it may think fit, for the maintenance, education, and supervision of the child's welfare. The same rules apply to an interim order for custody, as to consent and dispensing with consent, as for a final

Adoption Order; but the Court may not make an interim order without the three months' care and possession and notice to the Local Authority as are provided above. An interim custody order for less than two years may be extended to the full two years, but no longer. An interim order for custody is not an Adoption Order.

Procedure and Appeals.—To safeguard the child's interests during the hearing the Court has to appoint a guardian *ad litem* (*see Applications for Adoption*, para 5).

Effects of Adoption Orders.—Upon an Order being made, all rights, duties, obligations, and liabilities of the parents or guardians in relation to custody, maintenance, and education of the child, including rights to appoint a guardian by will, to consent or refuse consent to its marriage, shall be extinguished: and all such rights, etc., shall be exercisable by, and enforceable against, the Adopter(s) as if the child were his, her, or their legitimate child, and the child shall stand to the Adopter(s) in the same position. If two spouses are the Adopters, they shall stand to each other and to the child (for the purpose of court orders for custody, maintenance of and right of access (**D33**(1)) as if they were the lawful father and mother, and the child shall stand to them in the same relation.

For the purpose of the marriage laws, an Adopter and Adoptee shall be regarded as if they were within the prohibited degrees of blood relationship—even if a later Adoption Order is made in favour of another person (*i.e.*, an Adopter may not in any circumstances marry the Adoptee).

Succession to Property.—If, after an Adoption Order, the Adopter or Adoptee dies without a will in respect of any property, the property shall devolve as if the Adoptee were the lawful child of the Adopter (**D21–3**) and not the child of any other person. In any disposition of property made by will, codicil or settlement (**D21, 23**) after an Adoption Order, a reference to the "child or children" of the Adopter shall include a reference to the Adoptee (unless the contrary intention appears). The will or codicil is treated as having been made at the Adopter's death. But any reference to the "child or children" of the natural parents (or either of them) shall not include a reference to the Adoptee. And any reference to a "relative" of the Adoptee shall (unless the contrary intention appears) be regarded as a reference to the person who would be such a relative if the Adopter were his lawful parent. (But these provisions do not apply to any dignity or title of honour—*e.g.*, a hereditary peerage.)

For the purposes of the Administration of Estates Act, 1925 (**D21–3**), an Adoptee shall be regarded as a brother or sister of any child or adopted child of the Adopter. Executors and administrators (**D21–3**) are not liable if they distribute the estate of the Adopter without ascertaining that no Adoption Order has been made; but the Adoptee may sue the beneficiary for the Adoptee's share of the property; if there has been more than one Adoption Order, the earlier adoption shall be disregarded.

Citizenship.—If the Adoptee was not a citizen of the United Kingdom and Colonies (**D11**) but the Adopter or male Adopter is, the Adoptee shall be such a citizen as from the date of the Adoption Order.

Registration.—The Registrar-General is to keep an Adopted Children's Register, to contain authorised entries but no others. A certified copy of the entries counts as evidence; the index may be searched by anybody, who may obtain a certified copy of any entry. No other record may be seen by the public without a Court Order. Every entry shows only its number, date, and country of birth of the child, the name and adopted surname of the child and of the Adopters, the date of the Adoption Order and of the Court, the date of entry, and signature of the Registrar. The word "adopted" or "re-adopted" is written against the name of the child in the Register of Births;

but this shall be cancelled if an Adoption Order is refused or an appeal against adoption succeeds.

If a child adopted by its mother or natural father is subsequently legitimated by their marriage, the Court of Adoption may, on their application, revoke the Adoption Order and the entries in the register and any certificate shall be cancelled (and the parents' names substituted).

Local Authorities and Adoption Societies.—Except for the Local Authorities or registered Adoption Societies mentioned at the commencement of *Applications for Adoption,* para 1, no other body may make adoption arrangements; and even the authorised bodies may not place the child in the care and possession of a would-be adopter if the last-named person could not lawfully adopt him, under the penalty of a fine of £100 or six months' imprisonment; and the Court may order the child to be returned to his parent(s) or guardian(s) or to the Local Authority or registered Adoption Society. There are strict provisions as to which Adoption Societies may be registered or struck off the register, and as to appeals.

Care and Possession of Infants awaiting Adoption.—While an application is pending, a parent or guardian who has assented may not, without the court's leave, remove the infant from the care and possession of the Applicant; the Court will not give leave without considering the infant's welfare. The parent(s) or guardian(s) may not take back an infant, in the care and possession of any Applicant, before the actual Adoption Order, and must give written notice to the Authority or Society (before an Adoption Order is made) of the parent's or guardian's intention to part with the child, in which case the child must be handed to the Applicant(s) through the Authority or the Society. Only in cases where the adoption application is refused by the Court or on appeal, may the child be returned to or retained by the parent or guardian.

Supervision.—Where arrangements have been made for placing a child, below the upper limit of compulsory school age, in the care and possession of a " stranger," or where notice of intention to apply for an Adoption Order is given, then the child is known as a " protected child " while it is in the care and possession of a " stranger "; but not if it is in an Approved School or some other home under the Children's Acts. The child ceases to be a " protected child " at the age of 18, or on the making of an Adoption Order. It is the duty of every Local Authority to see that every " protected child " is periodically visited by its officers, who shall satisfy themselves of the child's well-being and give such advice as may be needed. The officers must produce a document of authority, and may then inspect any premises where the child is kept or to be kept. It is the duty of any " stranger " to give notice of all arrangements with regard to " protected children," including any change of address, and particulars of the name, sex, date and place of birth, and name and address of the parent(s) or guardian(s) or person(s) from whom the child is received. In the event of a " protected child's " death, the person(s) having care and possession must give written notice to the Authority. If neither the Local Authority nor a registered Adoption Society took part in the arrangements and it appears to the Authority that such arrangements would be detrimental to the child, the Authority may in writing prohibit the proposed Adopters from keeping the child in any premises, subject to appeal to a Juvenile Court. If the Court is satisfied that a " protected child " is received or about to be received by an unfit person, or in non-approved premises, the Court may order his removal to a place of safety until he can be restored to his parent(s) or guardian(s) or relative(s). On proof that there is imminent danger to the child's health or well-being, this power may be exercised by a J.P. A Local Authority may receive any child so removed (even if not a " protected child " and even if he is over 17) informing the parent(s) or guardian(s) of what has been done. There are heavy penalties for any contravention by a " stranger " of these provisions.

A warrant may be issued, in the event of refusal to allow a visit, or the inspection of premises by an authorised person.

General.—It is generally unlawful to give any payment in consideration of the adoption of a child, any grant of consent (*i.e.,* formal or informal) in connection therewith, the transfer of care and possession, the making of arrangements for adoption—penalty, fine £100 and/or six months' imprisonment; but this does not apply to payment of a registered Adoption Society's expenses, or any payment authorised by a Court. No advertisement may be published indicating the desire of the parent(s) or guardian(s) to have his, her, or their child adopted, that a person desires to adopt a child, or that any person (except a Local Authority or registered Adoption Society) can make such arrangements—penalty, fine £50.

Detailed Court Rules have been made for the carrying out of these arrangements.

There are five Schedules to the 1958 Act. Schedule III, the most important, sets out the nature and purposes of the Regulations which every Adoption Society must have.

> Every Adoption Society must set up a " case committee " of not less than three, to consider each individual case.
>
> No child shall be delivered to the proposed Adopter until the latter has been interviewed by the case committee, who must inspect the premises where the child is to live permanently after all the reports have been considered.
>
> Every Society must furnish a report on its activities and the prescribed accounts.
>
> Provision must be made for the care and supervision of any child placed with a Society with a view to adoption.
>
> There is a prohibition of or restriction upon disclosure of records kept by the Society, and provision for their safe keeping.

Home Office (Houghton) Committee's Preliminary Proposals (October 1970).—One unsatisfactory feature of the present law is that the Courts have held, in certain cases, that the rights of natural parents to oppose an adoption order or to withdraw consent already given, at the last moment, just when the Court is about to make an order, must be preserved; this has meant that the welfare of the child is not at present the first and paramount consideration in adoption as it is in cases of custody (**D33**(1)) and guardianship (Guardianship of Infants Act 1925, sec. 1).

(1) The Committee recognises that the child's need, above all, is for security; especially if a conflict arises between the natural parents and the would-be adopters, the Committee's first proposal is that the law should be changed so as to ensure that the welfare of the child comes first, having regard to the family's situation as a whole. The child's welfare cannot be regarded in isolation from the family generally, including brothers, sisters and other relatives, as well as parents. (Some readers may remember the unhappiness of the little Fanny Price, in Jane Austen's *Mansfield Park,* on being taken away to be brought up by her rich aunt and uncle, miles from her home, and separated for a long time from her brothers and sisters.) If, on consideration in this light, the best long-term solution for the child's welfare consists in severing parental and family ties permanently, the law should not stand in the way; the long-term welfare of the child should be the first and paramount consideration. The length of time he may have been with foster-parents or would-be adopters is one, but not the only, important factor; his emotional relationship with his natural family must also be considered in each individual case.

(2) Further consideration should be given to the possibility of allowances and subsidies for guardians and adopters in approved cases. (At present any form of payment is illegal.)

(3) When placing a child with would-be adopters, the local authority or adoption society

should pay some regard to the natural parent(s)' wishes as to the religion in which the child should be brought up; but the law should cease to permit them to make that question a condition of their consent to an adoption order.

(4) Although the number of adoption orders registered in England, Wales and Scotland rose from 14,668 in 1958 to 26,986 in 1968, it fell slightly, in 1969, to 26,049. It appears that a higher proportion of unmarried mothers are keeping their babies; and the tendency to reduction in the number adopted may be accentuated by the increasing use of contraceptives (*e.g.*, " the pill ") and the legalisation of abortion in certain circumstances. There is required a nationally available adoption service, focusing primarily on the needs of children, and forming an integral part of the comprehensive social services. Every local authority should secure the provision of such a service in its own area, as part of child care. The system of registration of voluntary adoption societies should be retained and strengthened. The placing of a child, with a view to adoption, with non-relatives should be permitted only to local authorities and authorised adoption societies.

(5) (*a*) The present minimum " trial period " of three months, during which the child must reside with would-be adopters before they can apply for an order (**D38**(2)), should be extended to one year, and the consent of the local authority should always be obtained. (*b*) If, for five years or more, they have cared for a child, they should have an absolute right to apply to the Court for an adoption order—in either case irrespective of the views of the natural parent(s). Change (*a*) is desirable because local authorities or voluntary organisations sometimes place a child with foster-parents in cases where the natural parents have no thought of giving up their parental rights and responsibilities (*e.g.*, because they are temporarily unable to secure living accommodation suitably extensive for the size of their families, but have every intention of keeping the child with them as soon as they find a suitable home), (*b*) is desirable in order to prevent the risk of causing the child or the would-be adopters to feel insecure.

(6) New provisions should be made by law for finalising the consent of the natural parent(s), not at the time when the Court is about to make the order, but before the date of the hearing—in some cases even before the child is placed with would-be adopters. This would be in the interests of the child both by diminishing the risk of his removal from the adoptive home at a late stage and also by lessening the anxiety of those who wish to adopt him—an anxiety which in itself can harm the child's developing relationship with its adoptive parents. But it is essential that there be safe-guards to ensure that the consent of the natural parent(s) is given freely, with full understanding of its implications; also that arrangements for the child's welfare be provided for if adoption is not approved.

(7) The child should always be told, as he grows up, that he has been adopted, and his curiosity about his natural parents satisfied. More than one-third of all adoptions are by unmarried mothers or other relatives; these are fundamentally different from adoption by strangers. In the former kind of adoption the adopters already belong to the child's own family, and are often already caring for him; this makes it harder to achieve " openness " between the adopters and the child. In the (few) cases where a child is adopted by his unmarried mother or (more rarely) unmarried father, attempts by this means to conceal his illegitimacy from him or from the world at large (**D40**(1)) coupled with registration of the adoption and the issue of a new certificate instead of the birth certificate), are likely to be damaging to him, rather than helpful, in the long run—*see also Illegitimacy*, **D35**. And the apparent advantage of permitting such adoptions is outweighed by the disadvantages of cutting any link which exists with the other parent by means of " access " (**D33**(1)), and transforming a natural into an artificial relationship. In any case, the unmarried mother already has custody and is responsible for him by law. Therefore it is doubtful whether it should still be permissible for a natural parent to adopt his or her own child.

(8) But, to replace adoptions of this special kind, opportunities for custody and guardianship should be extended. Such orders are not necessarily permanent in their effect, and do not extinguish the legal rights and responsibilities of natural parents; they are therefore more appropriate in cases ((5) above) where the natural parents are temporarily unable to have the child with them because of overcrowded accommodation. Guardianship has the advantage of conferring on the child the security which he needs, since the guardian cannot be ousted without a Court order. It does not bewilder a child who has already got to know his natural parent(s); and there is no reason why a guardian, if otherwise qualified, should not later be able to apply for adoption. A step-parent (after death or divorce of the natural parent) should be able to adopt the illegitimate child of his or her spouse, provided this does not affect the latter's legal position as parent.

These preliminary proposals will be considered and discussed by professional people and others interested in the subject, so that the Committee's final proposals may be published by the end of 1971, to enable new legislation to be prepared.

TREATMENT OF JUVENILES IN NEED OF CARE

Quite apart from the protection and welfare provisions for " children of the family " affected by matrimonial disputes (**D33**(1)), revolutionary provisions have been made by Part I of the Children & Young Persons Act, 1969, for the " treatment " (a word which has taken the place of " punishment ") of delinquent or other *children* (under the age of 14) and *young persons* (between 14 and 17) in need of care. Part II of the Act deals with accommodation for children committed to the care of local authorities and foster-children. In 1933 the minimum age of *criminal responsibility* (the age at which the law regards them as responsible for delinquent behaviour) was raised from 7 to 8 years; by the Children & Young Persons Act, 1963, it was again increased to 10. The Act of 1969 provides for raising the minimum age at which a child *may be prosecuted* (at present 10). The Government has announced its intention to specify the age of 12 as the age below which a child may not be prosecuted (but see last para. but one, **D42**(2)).

Part I of the 1969 Act came mainly into force on 1 January 1971; other parts will take effect when the Home Secretary makes an authorised order. The Act was based on two Government White Papers (proposals for discussion and state-ments of intention)—*The Child, the Family and the Young Offender* (1965) and *Children in Trouble* (1968), and the Report of the Committee on Children and Young Persons (1960). The first proposed setting up " Family Councils " in place of Juvenile Courts; but this created so much controversy that it was dropped. But the basic aim of reform has been fulfilled—to remove the stigma of criminality from " children " in trouble up to the age of 14. Instead of a prosecution (**D9**(1)) for what, in an adult, would be a criminal offence, a local authority, a constable, or an officer of the National Society for the Prevention of Cruelty to Children (" a qualified person ") may bring a child before a Juvenile Court (staffed by specially qualified and selected magistrates) in " care proceedings ". The need for " care and control " is a test which governs all the conditions (*a*) to (*f*) below. Such proceedings may be put in motion in cases of (*a*) truancy; (*b*) suspected offences (other than homicide); (*c*) children and young persons " beyond control " of their parents or guardians; (*d*) children and young persons who are ill-treated or neglected or who are in moral danger where, in addition, they are in need of care and control which they are unlikely to receive unless the Court makes an order. " Truancy " cases must be brought by a local education authority. (A child under 5 need never appear before a court, though his parents or guardians must be present at the hearing.) In the case of a child or young person who is found to be in need of care and control (if he or she is not over 16 and is not or has not been married), the Court may make one of the following orders: (1) requiring a parent or guardian to enter into a recognisance (i.e., an undertaking supported by the penalty of forfeiting a sum of money if the condition is not fulfilled) to take proper care of him and exercise proper control over him; (2) a supervision order (see below); (3) a care order (see below); (4) a hospital order; or (5) a guardianship order. In all cases notice of the proceedings must be given to the local authority where the child or young person resides (unless it is the local authority itself which is taking the proceedings).

These care proceedings are (for the purpose of evidence) regarded as civil not criminal, except in (b), above, where the alleged offence must be proved " beyond all reasonable doubt " (D9(2)); other cases may be proved on " a balance of probabilities " (since no question of fault on the part of the child or young person may arise). In case (b), in addition to one of the orders (1) to (5), the Court may order the young person, if an offence is proved against him, or his parents or guardians (if they conduced to the offence by neglect), or under the parents or guardians of a child to pay compensation up to £100 to any injured party. An appeal lies to quarter sessions (D6).

The Act further provides that private prosecutions of children and young persons for alleged offences are prohibited; Court proceedings may be started only by " a qualified informant "—and then only if that informant is satisfied that the case could not adequately be dealt with by a parent, teacher, or other person, by means of a police constable's caution or by action on the part of the local authority (which must be consulted in all cases) without proceedings. Full information of the offender's age must be given to the Court in a written statement, which must also certify the points above mentioned in this paragraph; if it fails to do so the Court shall quash (i.e., cancel) the proceedings. If the accused is under 17 he shall be tried summarily (i.e., by the Juvenile Court itself)—not sent for trial by judge and jury, except in cases of (i) homicide, (ii) certain grave crimes attracting long periods of detention (see below), or (iii) a joint charge together with another person of 17 or over and the Court thinks that justice requires that they both be committed together for trial by judge and jury, in any of which cases they shall be so committed. If the accused is found guilty summarily, he may be fined up to £50, placed on probation or under supervision, or sent to detention for 3 months or less. The Act makes provision for the minimum age for borstal training to be raised from 15 to 17, if and when the Home Secretary makes an order to that effect. A child convicted of homicide, or a young person convicted of any offence for which, if an adult, he could be sent to prison, may be placed under a care or supervision order, or his parent or guardian may be ordered to enter into a recognisance (see above).

If a police inspector, or higher officer, swears before a J.P. that a young person is suspected of an offence which, in the case of an adult, is punishable with imprisonment, and the issue of prosecution has to be decided, the J.P. may issue a summons for his attendance, or a warrant for his arrest, for the purpose of bringing him before a Court, which may order his finger- and palm-prints to be taken. Existing provisions for subsequent destruction of such prints, in certain circumstances, in the case of an adult, apply also to such young persons.

It is the duty of the local authority concerned to supply the Court with information as to home surroundings, school record, health and character, to assist the Court in its decision. Existing restrictions on newspaper reports of Court proceedings against a child or young person (which might identify him) are extended to young persons of any age below 18, and to appeals, unless the Court decides to waive the restrictions " to avoid injustice to the child or young person accused."

A supervision order is an order for supervision by a local authority or probation officer, and may include a requirement that the child or young person shall (i) reside with a named individual who agrees to take charge of him, or (ii) live for a specified period in a specified place and to present himself to a specified person at specified times and places and to participate in activities on specified days. But the total periods under (ii) shall not exceed 90 days in all.

Further, if the Court is satisfied on medical evidence that the mental condition of the child or young person is susceptible to medical treatment (e.g., in drug offences)—though without the need for detention—the Court may order him to submit to treatment by a qualified medical practitioner, or as a non-resident patient in a specified place, or as a resident patient in a hospital or nursing-home; but if he has attained 14 years of age, not unless he consents. No such requirement shall continue in force after the age of 18. Any supervisor's duty is to advise, assist, and befriend. The Court may vary or discharge such orders from time to time. If the child or young person is over 18, and the Court finds that he has failed to comply with any condition imposed, it may fine him up to £20; if it discharges the order it may impose any punishment which it could have imposed if it had had power to try him for the offence leading to the supervision order. If and when a doctor certifies that the treatment should be extended or varied, or is not effective or no longer necessary, the doctor shall so report to the supervisor; he shall notify the Court, which may cancel or vary the requirement. In most of such cases the supervised person must be brought before the Court; if he does not attend on summons, he may be arrested on warrant and, while awaiting the hearing, detained for not more than 72 hours. A supervision order shall cease to have effect at the end of 3 years, or the attaining by the supervised person of the age of 18, unless previously discharged.

Part I of the Act also contains detailed requirements for the appointments by the " children's regional planning committee " of supervisors and arrangements for supervision, for committal to the local authority's care, the local authority's powers and duties (similar to those possessed by a parent or guardian), including arrangements for visits by an independent person to advise and befriend him. The Act also lays down details for release, as well as for detention; in emergency cases detention without warrant or sentence must not exceed 8 days, which applies equally to a child so arrested otherwise than for homicide. Detention may be in a " community home." There are penalties, by fine up to £20, for absence from premises where a supervised person has been ordered to remain, and for anybody who knowingly compels, persuades, or assists him to " go absent."

Part II of the Act, regulating conditions of accommodation in community homes, and of those boarded out with foster-parents (in both cases regular inspections must be held), was brought into force on 1 December 1969. The provisions are very detailed; every local authority must see that foster-children are regularly visited and take steps to see to their safety and well-being.

Community homes constitute a single legal category of establishment for all children in care, replacing (when the Act is fully operational) the existing separate categories of approved schools, remand homes and probation hostels. They would be planned by regional committees, established by groups of local authorities, sometimes in partnership with voluntary organisations.

Many of the provisions detailed above have not yet been brought into force, and indeed may be phased into operation so that different ages may be specified for different purposes. It should be noted that the Government has announced that it does not intend to bring into force the section which restricts the right to prosecute a young person (see above), nor does it intend to seek to raise the minimum age for prosecution to 12 until satisfied that local authority social work departments can cope with the increased burden; and that there is no intention of raising the age above 12.

The reorganisation of Central Government has led to many of the responsibilities in this field being transferred from the Home Office to the Department of Health & Social Security.

A Home Office White Paper of December 1970 stated that the number of children in England and Wales in the care of local authorities on 31 March 1970 was 71,210; of voluntary organisations 12,475. Of the former total, 5,411 (though in the care of local authorities), are accommodated in voluntary homes. The corresponding figures for 1969 were 70,188 and 13,434 respectively. The slight decrease in the voluntary figure does not imply that these organisations play any less important part than in the past in the pattern of services available to children and their families.

JUSTICES OF THE PEACE

Sentencing Policy.—The arrangements, announced at the end of May 1964, by the Lord Chief Justice, "for the purpose of achieving greater uniformity of sentencing policy and a deeper understanding of the many social factors involved," comprise the organisation of more and longer conferences of all holders of judicial office, including justices of the peace, chairmen of quarter sessions, recorders and High Court judges. Working parties, in groups, consider case histories of "offenders," and later meet to discuss the sentences which each group would have passed if these cases had come before them in court. On the same day it was announced from Downing Street that a Royal Commission was being appointed (under the chairmanship of Lord Amory (former Chancellor of the Exchequer)),

"to conduct a fundamental review of penal methods, the concepts and purposes which should underlie the punishment and treatment of offenders in England and Wales; to report how far they are realized by the penalties and methods of treatment available, and whether any changes are desirable in these, or in the arrangements and responsibility for selecting the sentences to be imposed on particular offenders; and to review the work of the services and institutions dealing with offenders and the responsibility for their administrations, and to make recommendations."

Some of the Commission's recommendations are incorporated in the Criminal Justice Act, 1967 (D10, and the Criminal Law Act, 1967 (D10–11)).

Compulsory Training of New J.P.s.—Early in June 1964 the Lord Chancellor announced new arrangements for the *compulsory* training and instruction of newly-appointed justices of the peace, and fresh attempts to stop "glaring instances of inadequate, excessive or inconsistent sentences." An advisory council has re-organised the present scheme for voluntary training (which started in 1950), and every newly-appointed justice gives an undertaking not to try cases, without the Lord Chancellor's authority, until he or she has been through a compulsory course. The course includes attending as observers in their own and other courts and at quarter sessions, and visits to prisons, borstals, and similar institutions.

General Duties of J.P.s.—All these announcements have focused attention upon the work of justices of the peace—the unpaid, lay magistrates throughout the country who deal with the largest proportion of criminal offences, in various courts. Other manifold duties fall upon them—the appointment of special constables, certain matters relating to highways, the grant and renewal of licences for the sale of intoxicating liquors, "domestic proceedings" (matrimonial orders between husband and wife), custody of children and affiliation and adoption orders. Certain magistrates—both laymen and lawyers—with special qualifications sit in juvenile courts to deal with offences by and against young people, and with the committing of young people to the care of approved persons or authorities, whenever the young people are in need of care and protection.

Although, therefore, the criminal jurisdiction of J.P.s (as they are generally known) is by no means the full extent of their duties, it is this criminal jurisdiction which has been most frequently in the public eye; and the three announcements mentioned above relate only to that aspect of the J.P.s' duties. Neither historically nor currently are J.P.s expected to be lawyers; the clerk of the court, who advises them on points of law, is nearly always a solicitor; and at quarter sessions the chairman and deputy chairman are usually barristers or solicitors of not less than ten years' standing, with special qualifications for the task.

Procedure and Powers.—For "domestic proceedings" and in juvenile courts (outside the City of London and the metropolitan stipendiary court area, where full-time, legally-qualified, paid magistrates preside), not more than three J.P.s should sit, including both a man and a woman, whenever practicable. For other duties not more than seven J.P.s (and, preferably, not more than five, and an odd, not even, number) should sit. The election of a chairman and a number of deputy-chairmen is held by the J.P.s in October; those elected hold office for one year from January 1, and are eligible for re-election. All sittings are held in public, except in "domestic proceedings," custody, guardianship and adoption cases; and in these and in juvenile courts the press, though not usually excluded, are not permitted to identify the parties by name or address, or to publish evidence of an indecent character.

The powers of one single J.P., sitting alone, are restricted to adjourning a trial, remanding a prisoner in custody or on bail, and taking recognisances. An information charging an offence may be laid before him; if it is in writing, and substantiated on oath, he may issue a warrant; in a civil matter, in similar circumstances, he may issue a summons. Search warrants may, in most cases, be issued by a single J.P., and so may a summons or warrant requiring the attendance of a witness. A stipendiary (legally-qualified, paid, full-time magistrate) is not so limited; he has all the powers of a court of summary jurisdiction (*i.e.*, two or more J.P.s sitting together).

Criminal Jurisdiction.—Except in those instances in which a special limit of time is prescribed by a particular Act of Parliament, no information may be laid (in regard to a criminal offence), nor complaint (in a civil case) after the lapse of six months from the date when the offence was committed or the matter of complaint arose. The J.P.s' criminal jurisdiction covers (1) the trial of "summary offences" (minor offences triable by a magistrates' court other than under (2) below) punishable by a maximum of six months imprisonment for one offence, or a fine (in general) not exceeding £100. The jurisdiction also extends to (2) certain "indictable" (or "arrestable") offences which may be tried summarily if the accused consents; in such cases the maximum punishments are 6 months imprisonment or a fine not exceeding £400, or both, for one such offence, or 12 months imprisonment for two or more such offences. There are also (3) certain petty offences which the accused or the prosecution may elect to be tried on indictment, before a jury at quarter sessions. No offender under the age of 17 may be sentenced to imprisonment by a court of summary jurisdiction; but such young offender may be sent to a detention centre. Alternatively, he may be committed, in custody, to quarter sessions for sentence to a period of borstal training. First offenders should not be sent to prison; they are frequently placed on probation or given suspended sentences D(10(2)).

One J.P. or more may sit as a court of preliminary enquiry to determine whether there is a *prima facie* case (*i.e.*, one that calls for a defence) against an accused which will require his being indicted before a jury. For this purpose the J.P.s take depositions (that is, evidence given (*see* D10(2)) under oath, by prosecution witnesses, and reduced to writing and signed by each witness who has given it). If the J.P.s decide, at the end of the hearing, that the prosecution has disclosed no *prima facie* case, the accused is discharged; if there is such a case, then after due warning to the accused that he is not obliged to say anything but that, if he does answer the charge, anything he says will be written down and may be used in evidence at his trial, he is committed for trial, on bail or in custody (according to the gravity of the charge), at quarter sessions or assizes. (For restrictions on newspaper reports of such proceedings, see Criminal Justice Act, 1967 (**D10**(2)).)

History of the Office of J.P.—The above is by no means an exhaustive account of the duties of J.P.s and of the procedure before them; but sufficient has been said to indicate the vital importance of their work. The office is both honorary and honourable; as early as 1327, in the reign of Edward III, the King appointed " conservators " of the peace within his Kingdom; and the Justices of the Peace Act, 1361, in the same reign, determined " what sort of persons should be Justices of the Peace and what authority they should have." From that day to this their duties have gradually become more difficult and extensive, as society has grown more complex. It would seem that, while there are many advantages in leaving the trial of the less grave offences to lay magistrates (as J.P.s are) the system, which for over six centuries has prominently figured in our penal practice, will be brought up to date and made more efficient by the proposed compulsory training. The only doubts have arisen on the ground that persons " of the best of reputation in the counties " (Act of 1344), who are prepared

to give their time, without remuneration, to these public-spirited duties, may find it difficult, or in some cases impossible, to attend courses of training, in their spare time, in addition.

Recruitment of J.P.s.—The Lord Chancellor in his 1965 presidential address to the Magistrates' Association at Guildhall, London, said he would like to see the J.P.s recruited from more varied walks of life. " The strength of the lay magistracy," he said, " is dependent on the ordinary man and woman realising that the Benches reflect all shades of opinion and are not representative of one section only." He said he would also like to see more coloured magistrates appointed. " There are now two coloured justices serving on the Bench and these appointments have both been tremendously successful." The Lord Chief Justice, in October 1970, said that J.P.s should be empowered to give up to 12 months' prison sentences for violent crimes. He advocated reconsideration of compulsorily suspended sentences during which many people commit further offences. *See also* **D10**(2).

Justices of the Peace Act, 1968. By this Act *ex officio* J.P.s are abolished, except for the Lord Mayor and aldermen of the City of London, who may still sit together with lay justices appointed by the Lord Chancellor.

FREE SPEECH AND PUBLIC ORDER

In the constitution of our parliamentary democracy (*see* **D8**) certain unwritten rules have been recognised for about three centuries past. These rules, which are not always easy to reconcile, may be summarised as follows:

(1) **Free Speech.**—Free and open discussion, *within the law*, ought to be permitted, both in private and in public, of all political, social, moral and religious questions.

(2) **Unpopular Opinions.**—Unpopular or minority opinions, lawfully expressed, privately or publicly, by act or word, do not become unlawful merely because their expression may induce other people to commit unlawful acts.

(3) **Provocation.**—Every man is presumed to *intend* the natural consequences of his acts; hence, the use of threatening, abusive or insulting language or behaviour, if it is naturally provocative of disorder, is unlawful.

(4) **Public Order.**—The *preservation of public order* is of paramount importance; a magistrate or police officer, or any person (*see* **D11**(1)) has a right and duty to take any steps necessary to stop a breach of the peace taking place, or to prevent a breach which he reasonably apprehends.

These rules have recently been widely discussed, as a result of the activities of political extremists who make a special feature of propaganda against racial or religious minorities. Some of their meetings and marches have been accompanied by grave public disorder.

Until comparatively recent times the whole subject depended upon common law decisions (**D7**), not statute law (**D8**). For example:

Unlawful Assembly is a common law offence, constituted by an assembly of three or more persons, intending either to commit a crime by open force, or to carry out any common purpose, whether lawful or unlawful, in such manner as to give firm and courageous persons in the neighbourhood reasonable grounds to apprehend a breach of the peace in consequence of the assembly. (The words " any *common* purpose, *whether lawful or unlawful*," should be noted.)

Sedition is a common law crime, which includes the doing of *acts* or the speaking of *words* with the *intention* of promoting feelings of ill-will or hostility between different classes of the Queen's subjects. If the words or acts (whatever the intention) have a *direct tendency* to cause unlawful meetings or disturbances, they are seditious, since

" a man is presumed to intend the natural consequences of his acts " (*see* (3), *above*). This does not mean that there must be no full and free discussion, nor that there is any prohibition upon criticism, or even censure; but there must be *no malignity*, nor any imputation of *corrupt or malicious motives*, such as to incite people to take the law into their own hands and to provoke them to tumult and disorder.

With these principles in mind, let us consider some actual cases (decided during the past ninety years) in which these rules have been applied.

Beatty v. Gillbanks (1882) arose from the activities of the newly-founded Salvation Army, which was " an association for carrying out religious exercises among themselves, and for a religious revival among certain classes of the community." Its leaders formed their followers into *processions* which marched through the streets of Weston-super-Mare, with *bands and banners*, collecting people as they marched back to their hall, where *prayer-meetings* were held. They were opposed on several occasions by an organisation calling itself the " Skeleton Army," which objected to these religious exercises. In consequence, disorders frequently arose, and the Salvation Army leaders were charged with " unlawfully and tumultuously assembling to the disturbance of the peace." The Magistrates bound them over to be of good behaviour; the Salvation Army appealed to the High Court.

The Judges decided that the Magistrates were wrong. " Everyone must be taken to intend the natural consequences of his acts " ((3), *above*) " and if this disturbance of the peace was the natural consequence of the Salvation Army's activities, they would have been liable, and the Magistrates would have been right to bind them over. But the evidence does not support this contention. . . . There was nothing in their conduct which was either tumultuous or against the peace; on the contrary, the evidence shows the disturbances were caused by other people, antagonistic to them. What has happened here is that an *unlawful organisation* has assumed to itself the right to *prevent* the Salvation Army from *lawfully assembling*, and the decision of the Magistrates amounts to this—that a man may be convicted for doing a lawful act if he knows that his doing it may cause another to do an unlawful act. There is no authority for such a proposition."

Wise v. Dunning (1902) is a contrasting case. A fanatical Protestant clergyman had, on several occasions, held meetings in parts of Liverpool containing a strong Roman Catholic population. At these meetings he had used offensive, violent, and provocative language, attacking the Pope and the Roman Catholic Church. In consequence, breaches of the peace had occurred, and the Liverpool Magistrate had bound him over to be of good behaviour. The Protestant clergyman appealed to the High Court, protesting that there was no evidence that he had committed or intended to commit a breach of the peace, and that the Magistrate's decision (as in the earlier case) was wrong. But the Judges upheld the Magistrate's decision and dismissed the appeal. The Lord Chief Justice said " there was abundant evidence that, in the public streets, he had used *language which was abusive*, which had *caused an obstruction*, and that he intended to do *similar acts* in another place." The two other Judges said that every case depends upon its own *facts* and *evidence*:

> " The law does not as a rule regard an illegal act as being the natural consequence of a temptation held out to commit it; but ... the cases show that *the law regards the infirmity of human temper* to the extent of considering that a breach of the peace, although an illegal act, may be the *natural consequence of insulting or abusive* language or conduct."

The clergyman's behaviour (unlike that of the Salvation Army leaders in the earlier case) was in itself violently provocative; therefore the Magistrate was justified in binding him over, " under preventive power " to stop breaches of the peace, which were the " natural result " of his behaviour.

Both the above cases, as it happened, dealt with religious controversies. But the same rules apply in controversies of other kinds.

Duncan v. Jones (1936) was concerned with provocation on a *political* and *social* question. There was grave unemployment at the time, and feelings between the unemployed, and their supporters, against the Government, and its policies, ran high. Mrs. Jones had held a meeting of unemployed men right opposite an unemployment training-centre: she had made a speech strongly attacking the Government's policy, and a disturbance had followed. Fourteen months later, when she appeared at the same place for the same purpose, the Police Superintendent forbade her to hold the meeting there. She insisted on doing so, stepped on her box, and began to address the bystanders. It was not, at that stage, suggested that she was obstructing the highway, or inciting anybody to commit a breach of the peace. Nevertheless she was *convicted of obstructing* the Superintendent *in the execution of his duty*, and her conviction was upheld by the High Court. " She must have known (from earlier experience) the *natural consequence* of holding such a meeting at that place; the Superintendent *reasonably apprehended a breach of the peace*; it therefore became *his duty to prevent it*, and she was guilty of *obstructing him in carrying out that duty*."

The Public Order Act, 1936.—In the period preceding the Second World War, extremist political organisations held meetings at which they wore political uniforms and used " strongarm " tactics similar to those in vogue among the Italian Fascists and German Nazis. They also indulged, like the Nazis, in virulent propaganda calculated to stir up racial hatred. As a result of the explosion of public feelings, in the existing state of international tension, grave disorders took place in London and other cities. The situation was discussed in both Houses of Parliament and it was generally agreed that the law required to be clarified and strengthened. On December 18, 1936, the Public Order Act received the Royal Assent, and came into force on January 1, 1937.

Prohibition of Political Uniforms.—Section 1 of the Act (subject to certain exceptions) forbids the wearing, in a public place or at a public meeting, of uniform signifying the wearer's association with a political organisation, or with the promotion of a political object. (The exceptions are " ceremonial, anniversary or other special occasions " on which the Chief Officer of Police may permit

a relaxation of the prohibition (with the Home Secretary's consent) only if he is satisfied that no risk of public disorder is likely to be involved.)

Prohibition of Quasi-Military Organisations.—Section 2 makes it an offence to participate in the control or management of an association whose members are (a) organised or trained or equipped to enable them to be employed " in usurping the functions of the police or of the armed forces of the Crown," or (b) organised and trained, or organised and equipped as follows; either (i) for the purpose of the use or display of physical force in promoting a political object, or (ii) in such manner as to arouse reasonable apprehension that they are organised, and either trained or equipped, for the purpose described in (i). (It was under (b) (ii) that two of the leaders of a present-day extremist political organisation were convicted and sentenced to imprisonment in October, 1962, at the Central Criminal Court; their appeals were dismissed.) The consent of the Attorney-General (the Senior Law Officer of the Crown) is required before a prosecution under Section 2 can be instituted. In certain circumstances a High Court Order may be made to search the premises of the organisation and to impound its property.

Preservation of Public Order on the Occasion of Processions.—Section 3 confers powers for this purpose, as follows:

(1) On a *Chief Officer of Police*, if he has reasonable grounds for apprehending that a procession may occasion serious public disorder (having regard to time, place and circumstances), power to impose on the organisers or participants in the procession such conditions as appear necessary for preserving public order (including the route of the procession and power to prohibit it from entering any " public place "); but no conditions restricting the display of flags, banners or emblems are to be imposed unless they are reasonably necessary to prevent risk of a breach of the peace.

(2) On a *Borough or Urban District Council* (if the Chief Officer of Police believes that his powers under (1) (*above*) will not suffice to prevent serious public disorder, and on application by him) power to make an Order (with the consent of the Home Secretary) prohibiting all public processions, or certain classes of public processions in the area for a period not exceeding three months. (This power does not apply within the City of London or the Metropolitan Police Area, as to which *see* (3) (*below*).)

(3) On the *Commissioner of the City of London Police*, and the *Commissioner of Metropolitan Police*, a power similar to that described in (2) (*above*), and on similar conditions. Thus, within the London Area the Police Authorities, and in urban areas outside London the Local Authorities, are given power to prohibit processions (or " marches ") on the conditions described in (2) above.

It is an offence for anybody knowingly to fail to comply with any Order or condition imposed, or to organise or assist in organising a public procession in contravention of the Section.

Prohibition of Offensive Weapons.—By Section 4, anybody is guilty of an offence if he has with him any offensive weapon at a public meeting or on the occasion of a public procession, without lawful authority. (Note the words " *on the occasion of* a public procession "; it is *not only those taking part* in the procession, *but also bystanders*, who may commit this offence.) " Lawful authority " extends to servants of the Crown, Members of Parliament or of a Local Authority (acting as such), police officers, members of Fire Brigades or Cadet Corps, and so forth.

Prohibition of Offensive Conduct Conducive to Breaches of the Peace.—Section 5 (as now amended by the Race Relations Act, 1965) reads—" Any person who in any public place or at any public meeting (a) uses threatening, abusive or insulting words or behaviour, or (b) distributes or displays any writing, sign or visible representation which is threatening, abusive or insulting with intent to provoke a breach of the peace, or whereby a breach of the peace is likely to be occasioned, shall be guilty of an offence."

Disorderly Conduct at a Public Meeting.—Section 6 refers to the Public Meeting Act, 1908. Section 1 of the 1908 Act makes it an offence for a person to *act in a disorderly manner* at a *lawful* public meeting for the purpose of *preventing the trans-action of the meeting's business.* Section 6 of the 1936 Act gives power to a constable, if he reason-ably suspects an offence under the 1908 Act, to demand of the suspected offender his name and address (provided that the chairman of the meet-requests him to do so). If the suspected offender refuses or fails to give his name and address, or gives a false name and address, he commits an offence, and the constable may arrest him without warrant. (Note that, to qualify for protection, the public meeting must in the first place, be *lawful.*) Section 6 of the 1936 Act has been con-siderably extended and strengthened by Section 6 of the Race Relations Act, 1965, for stirring up hatred on grounds of race or colour. The Public Order Act, 1963, has greatly increased the penalties under Section 5 of the Act of 1936 and Section 1 of the Act of 1908; but an undertaking has been given by the Home Office that the new Act will not be used to suppress mere " heckling " at a public meeting. *See also* Race Relations Act, 1968, *below.*

Jordan v. Burgoyne (1963) was similar to *Wise v. Dunning* (1902), except that the 1963 case was concerned with section 5 of the Public Order Act, 1936. At a public meeting in Trafalgar Square, to an audience of 5,000, which included many Jews, Colin Jordan used the words—" Hitler was right. Our real enemies—the people we should have

fought—were not the National Socialists of Ger-many, but World Jewry and its associates." There was *complete disorder* and a general surge towards the speaker by the crowd, but they were restrained by the police, under Superintendent Burgoyne; and 20 arrests were made while the crowd was being dispersed.

Before the Bow Street Magistrate Jordan was convicted and sentenced to imprisonment, for " *using at a public meeting insulting words whereby a breach of the peace was likely to be occasioned.*" He appealed to Quarter Sessions, who found as a fact that, though the words were highly insulting, they were not likely to lead ordinary responsible persons to commit breaches of the peace; they therefore allowed Jordan's appeal against con-viction. The prosecution then asked for " a case to be stated " for the High Court on the question whether the words in section 5 could properly be interpreted to mean " likely to lead to a breach of the peace by ordinary citizens."

The Lord Chief Justice, with two other Judges, decided that Quarter Sessions were wrong. The test was not whether the insulting words were likely to cause a breach of the peace by a *hypo-thetical audience,* whatever their creed, faith, race, or political views; in any case the Judges imagined that any *reasonable citizen would be provoked* beyond endurance. But this was an Act to keep order in public places, and " a speaker must *take his audience as he finds it.* If those words to that audience are likely to provoke a breach of the peace, the speaker is guilty of an offence. The right of free speech is not in question; he may express his views as strongly as he likes, but he must not threaten, abuse or insult that audience." The case was sent back to Quarter Sessions with a direction to find the offence proved, and to dismiss Jordan's appeal from the Magistrate's convic-tion. *See* D6.

RACE RELATIONS

It is already a criminal offence, under the Race Relations Act, 1965, to stir up hatred on grounds of race or colour. The Race Relations Act of 1968 is not penal in its remedies, but makes " discrimination " a civil wrong, giving rise (in the first place) to conciliation (*see below*) by regional committees, and (if these fail) to damages (D16(1)) or injunction (D15(2)) or both. A person who feels there has been discrimination against him can complain, in writing or by word of mouth, or someone else, authorised by him in writing, can complain on his behalf, within two months of the discriminatory act, to the local conciliation com-mittee or to the Race Relations Board direct. The Act applies to discrimination on grounds of race, colour, or ethnic or national origins. Un-lawful discrimination means treating a person less favourably than others, on any of the above grounds; " separate but equal " treatment (*e.g.,* segregation) counts as less favourable treatment.

It is unlawful for anyone providing the public with goods, facilities, or services to discriminate by refusing, or deliberately omitting to provide, any-body with goods, *etc.,* of the like quality, in the like manner, or on the like terms as are normally made available to others. Examples are—access to and use of any place which the public may enter; facilities for entertainment, a recreation or refreshment; accommodation in a hotel, board-ing-house, *etc.;* facilities for banking, insurance-grants, loans, credit, or finance; for education, instruction, or training, or the services of any trade, profession, business, local or other authority. But hotels, *etc.,* are exempted if the landlord or some of his immediate family live on the premises; or where there is not normally accommodation for more than twelve persons in the first two years of the Act, or six persons thereafter, besides the landlord and some of his family.

It is also unlawful to discriminate in employ-ment—terms, recruitment, training, promotion, dismissal, or conditions of work; also to refuse to employ a person, on grounds of race, *etc.,* on work of any description which is available and for which he is qualified (though employers *may* treat employees differently by reason of seniority, ability, or educational standards). During the second two years of the Act, commencing 14 November 1970, employers of less than ten

employees are exempted; for the following two years the limit will be abolished. And if an employer " discriminates " in good faith for the purpose of preserving " a reasonable balance " of different groups, the discrimination is not un-lawful; but " reasonable balance " must be be-tween (1) those who (of whatever race, colour, *etc.*) were born, or wholly or partly educated, in Britain and (2) others, whatever their race, *etc.* Other exemptions are *inside* employees in a private household (*e.g., au pair* girls) but not *outside* employees (*e.g.,* builders); employment wholly or mainly outside Britain, in any country, ship, or aircraft; in a British ship if persons of different races, *etc.,* would otherwise have to share sleeping, mess, or sanitary accommodation; or where race, *etc.,* is a *bona fide* qualification (*e.g.,* waiters in a Chinese restaurant).

It is unlawful for any organisation of employers or workers to discriminate in admitting members, benefits of membership, or expulsion; in selling or letting all types of premises (including furnished or unfurnished living accommodation, business premises, or land). The prohibition applies equally to property-owners (including companies), estate-agents, developers, and local authorities (*e.g.,* borough councils)—unless (1) the person offering accommodation (" the landlord ") lives in the premises and shares facilities with others, and (2) there is accommodation for not more than two households besides the landlord; or (3) the land-lord, wholly occupying the premises, sells without any advertisement or estate-agent. It is also unlawful to publish or display any discriminatory advertisements or notice. Until 13 November 1970 boarding- and lodging-houses were included in (1) and (2) if there was not accommodation for more than 12 persons other than the landlord's household; from 14 November 1970, the number was reduced to six.

Anybody who deliberately aids, induces, or incites another unlawfully to discriminate will be equally liable—*e.g.,* neighbours who put pressure on a vendor to prevent sale of his house to a coloured, *etc.,* person. (But incitement to *racial hatred* is still a crime (D45(1).)

If a regional committee or the Race Relations Board thinks, on investigation of a complaint, there has been unlawful discrimination, it will try by private conciliation to settle the complaint and to get the discriminator to give a satisfactory written assurance for the future. Only if such assurance is refused will court proceedings arise. The Board will proceed in one of the special county courts (D5), where the judge will be assisted by two assessors. The court may grant an injunction to restrain future unlawful discrimination, or damages for actual or potential loss suffered by the victim, or both. Disobedience will mean a penalty for contempt of court. Employment complaints are an exception; they will be first referred to the Department of Employment and Productivity, which will try to settle by conciliation if there is suitable machinery. If the complainant is dissatisfied, he can appeal to the Board, which can then apply for injunction or damages for actual loss and loss of opportunity (compensation for lost benefit which the complainant might have expected).

ADDITIONAL DETAILS ON CRIMINAL LAW (PUNISHMENT)

(See D10).

OVERCROWDING IN PRISONS—POSSIBLE REMEDIES

It has long been recognised that the country's prisons, many of which were built more than a century ago, are extremely congested, partly because of the increase in convictions during the past 20 years (from 20,000 to 40,000), and partly because the present accommodation is not adapted to modern ideas of reformative treatment (D10(1)). In November 1970 the Home Office Parliamentary Under-Secretary outlined a double approach to the problem. First, the prison building and modernisation programme is to be pressed on as fast as possible. Secondly, the Government is looking into new alternative forms of punishment and treatment. This, however, requires the understanding and approval of public opinion; the Home Office must stress that it does not safeguard the general community to herd men into old-fashioned prisons, sleeping two or three in a one-man cell, which prevents the use of reformative methods and makes prisons places that train men for further crime rather than try to reform them to live in the general community.

This second plan—to find suitable alternative methods of treatment—will necessitate increasing the probation and after-care service from its strength of 3,400 (November 1970) to 4,700 officers by 1975. The cost of training them, and of paying them adequate salaries, will be provided by the Government; if, however, the present trend of crime increase continues, convicted men will be hardened and more difficult for probation officers to deal with. However, three working groups of consultants are considering how the proposed enlarged services can best be used.

The prison population can be divided roughly into two—(1) those whose offences and conduct show clearly the need for secure detention (*see* D(10(1))—" Prevention "); (2) those who could be dealt with adequately in ways which do not segregate them from their families and general society, who may be reformed by help and guidance (D10(1)—" Reformation "). and thus avoid drifting into " recidivism "—*i.e.*, continual repetition of crime.

Division (2) may be treated in three possible ways:

(*a*) A scheme of part-time community service by offenders, to be run by probation officers and voluntary (charitable) agencies. This would be purposeful, which prison-life is not; offenders would be encouraged, under supervision, to make some repayment to the general community for the injury and damage they have done (*see also* D11(1)—Compensation). If this succeeded, it would avoid the enormous problems of adjustment to civilian life for prisoners who intend " to go straight " at the end of their sentence. But many practical problems are involved and are being investigated.

(*b*) A scheme combining a fine with a compulsory term of probation. It is recognised that this has the disadvantage of changing the present basis of the relationship between the probation officer and the offender, which is very important. But there is bound, in any case, to be an element of compulsion in practice if supervision by probation officers is to play its part in a new system of substitutes for prison. Investigation has started.

(*c*) A scheme of " intermediate treatment "—compulsory attendance at day or evening centres, or in hostels, where offenders can receive constant guidance and support. In 1970 the Home Office began an experiment to extend the scope of approved probation hostels (previously provided only for treatment of juveniles in need of care—D41) to men up to 30 or even 35 years of age. The Courts are already using these new facilities for some men with criminal records who would otherwise have been sent to prison. Voluntarily run hostels for after-care are already in use; a similar system should be tried to keep men out of prison. Investigation proceeds.

Further suggestions, being considered, are (*i*) extending the temporary release of prisoners " on parole ", and (*ii*) relaxing the censorship of letters at " open " prisons. This latter is already partially in force at one " open " prison. And (*iii*) the " home leave " scheme, which now applies, towards the end of a sentence, for certain prisoners serving five years or more, may be extended to some serving three years or more.

Since this pronouncement the tragic fact has emerged that, among the greatly increased total prison population (see above) there were about 13,500 mentally disturbed persons in 1969, compared with 6,000 in 1961. For these men prison is totally unsuitable: they need long-term medical or psychiatric treatment; but only three hostels are at present (November 1970) suitable, holding only about 150 patients. Part of the difficulty is that prisons are the responsibility of the Home Office, mental hostels or hospitals of the Department of Health; there is now no legal power to confine such mentally disturbed persons in mental hospitals if they do not choose to stay; if they abscond and commit further offences, they can be sent only to prison, and from there to mental hospitals again. To prevent this process from being constantly repeated, the law should be changed, so that such unfortunates may be securely held in mental hostels or hospitals during their treatment. (This is quite apart from places like Broadmoor, where persons found " not guilty by reason of insanity " (D10(1)) of murder are confined " during the Queen's pleasure "—*i.e.*, until (if ever) they are no longer dangerous.)

ADDITIONAL DETAILS ON LAW OF LANDLORD AND TENANT

(See D26(1)).

THE HOUSING ACT, 1969, AND A BRIEF FORECAST OF EXPECTED REFORM.

The object of the very lengthy 1969 Act was to increase the availability of housing accommodation at reasonable and fair rents. It was argued that, before the Act, landlords of dwellings *controlled* by the old Rent Restrictions Acts—a control perpetuated by the Acts of 1965–1968 for premises of very low rateable value (D25(2)) were unwilling either to let them, because of the poor return, or to put or keep them in a good state of repair, with proper amenities of a modern kind.

Accordingly, Parts I and II of the 1969 Act allow local authorities (referred to below as " councils ") to provide financial assistance for

CRITICAL

landlords of such dwellings, whether houses or flats, towards the cost of conversions and improvements, and coin the term "improvement areas" which the councils may declare some districts to be and advertise the facilities available.

Parts III and IV deal with rents of improved accommodation, in dwellings occupied by one or more families; further details of these Parts are given below.

Part V is concerned with slum-clearance—a problem tackled (never quite successfully) by many governments in the past.

Part VI gives councils power to *insist* on repair of old-fashioned houses without proper amenities, to make advances for such repairs, and (if necessary) to make improvements by agreement with, and at the expense of, the owner. It is estimated that, when the Act came into force, 1·8 million dwellings were unfit for habitation; a further 4·5 million lacked "standard amenities" (see below) or were in need of repairs costing at least £125 each. Councils are also required periodically to review housing conditions in their areas.

The size of the problem is due to many causes—not only the "freezing" of *controlled rents* at very low levels, but also the earlier age at which young people leave home to found their own families, the inability of the few who still occupy big, old-fashioned houses to procure domestic help to enable them to keep such a house going as a single unit, with the result that some rooms are disused or let off as apartments in a dilapidated and unsuitable state.

In the brief account of Parts III and IV below the separate units into which a larger house or flat may be divided are called "dwellings." The entire Act has 91 sections and ten schedules; all, therefore, that can be done here is to give a short summary of some of its important provisions as they affect landlords and tenants.

The Department of the Environment (formerly the Ministry of Housing & Local Government) has issued two booklets for the guidance of landlords, tenants, and lodgers (the terms used where more than one family occupies a single unit)—(1) *House Improvements & Rents* and (2) *Phasing of Rent Increases*. These booklets contain simple questions and answers to some of the problems arising under the Act. But they are *not official statement of law*, the complications of which will necessitate consultation with a solicitor if a dispute arises.

Part III has as its main purpose the increase of rented accommodation by offering landlords incentives, by way of higher rents, to improve those dwellings still controlled by the Rent Restrictions Acts (D25(2)) by installing certain "standard amenities" (see below) which may enable them to be converted into "regulated tenancies" under the Rent Act, 1968, at "fair" rents higher than the old "controlled" rents (D25(2)). Such conversion may take place when the landlord has satisfied "the qualifying conditions"—*i.e.*, that the dwelling (*a*) is provided with all *standard amenities* for the exclusive use of its occupants; (*b*) is in good repair (disregarding internal decoration), having regard to its age, character, and locality; (*c*) is in all other respects fit for human habitation. If satisfied on these points the council may, on the landlord's application, issue a "qualification certificate" to that effect, whereupon (in most cases) a tenancy becomes a regulated tenancy to which the "fair rent" provisions apply.

Standard amenities are a fixed bath or shower, wash-hand basin and sink, with hot and cold water supplies to all, water-closet indoors (or "readily accessible" from the dwelling). Bath or shower should be in a bathroom; if this is not practicable, they may be in any room except a bedroom. The qualification certificate shall not be issued unless—(i) the dwelling has, at all times since 25 August 1969, been provided with standard amenities or (ii) works to provide them were begun before that date; (iii) the landlord, except with the council's written consent, uses each dwelling for the purposes of private occupation (not business), must not be charging a rent higher than the legal rent, and no premium may be paid or asked by him or any tenant. (There are some other conditions for which reference must be made to the Act.) The application must state the name of the tenant under the existing controlled tenancy, what works are necessary to satisfy the conditions, with plans and specifications. The council must serve on the tenant a notice (1) that he may, within 28 days, complain that the dwelling does not satisfy the conditions, and (2) explaining the effect of the Act. If the tenant makes no complaint, and the council finds that the qualifying conditions are met, it will issue a certificate; if the tenant makes such a complaint, and the council finds it justified, it must refuse the landlord a certificate; in either case it must notify the tenant of the result.

If (under (*ii*) above) the application was made before the works were completed but the council thinks the dwelling will satisfy the qualifying conditions after completion, it may *provisionally approve* the applicant's request and issue a certificate accordingly, sending a copy to the tenant, whose consent must be obtained both before and after the works are completed. In such cases, in order to obtain a *fair rent certificate*, the landlord must apply to the rent officer (D25(2)), with copies of plans and specifications; the officer's certificate specifies the fair rent which may be charged under a regulated tenancy if the works are properly completed. When the council has inspected the dwelling, and is satisfied that the fair rent certificate, and is satisfied that the dwelling meets the qualifying conditions, it shall issue a qualification certificate and send the tenant a copy. After such conversion from a controlled to a regulated tenancy, the landlord applies to the rent officer for registration of the fair rent. If the council refuses a certificate or provisional approval, it must give the landlord its written reasons.

A landlord who has been refused, or a tenant who thinks the council's certificate was wrongly issued, may appeal to the County Court which, after inspection and consideration, may refuse or allow the appeal, with or without conditions. If the council's certificate is "quashed" (*i.e.*, cancelled), any fair rent registration shall be deleted and shall be regarded as never having been effective.

Where the council gave only provisional approval—(*ii*) above—the tenancy shall remain controlled until the full certificate is issued. In certain circumstances some rent increases permitted by the 1968 Act (D25(2)) may be disallowed if the above procedure has not been followed, or may be recovered only in stages as laid down in the Act. The tenant's consent must be sought for the works to be carried out; if it is refused, the County Court may consider the dispute (giving regard particularly to the tenant's accommodation while the works are being done) and make an order, with or without conditions, accordingly. But it shall make no order empowering the landlord to enter and do the works if the rating authority certifies that the tenant's income is within the "rate relief limits" specified in the Act.

Part IV of the Act relates to houses "in multiple occupation"—*i.e.*, dwellings occupied by persons who do not form one single household (the former definition was "occupied by members of more than one family"). This Part of the Act enables councils to make orders applying a "management code" for such dwellings, to ensure that there are proper means of escape from fire, gives directions to reduce or prevent overcrowding in houses in multiple occupation, the keeping of registers thereof by the council, its powers to make "control orders" followed by "compulsory purchase orders", and a list of offences and penalties. For further detail the Act must be consulted.

In November 1970 the new Minister announced plans to speed up the system of housing grants (under Part I). At the same time he promised revised schemes to remedy the housing problem in the worst areas by removing inequalities between tenants of council and private dwellings, extending the "fair rent" principle to both, to operate a *rent rebate* system for needy tenants of both classes, to take energetic steps for slum-clearance by assisting councils and private landlords to improve or rebuild. Further statements of the Government's intentions will be issued after discussion with councils; but it will probably be 1972 or later before the further legislation which will be needed can be passed. Thus the 1969 Act is likely to be considerably amended in due course.

THE
WORLD OF
MUSIC

The art of music as it has developed in the Western world, with a glossary of musical terms and an index to composers.

TABLE OF CONTENTS

THE WORLD OF MUSIC

In writing this section no special knowledge on the part of the reader is assumed; it is for those who want to know about the history of music, how different styles evolved, and how one composer influenced another. It is a background to music as the science section is a background to science, and just as the latter cannot show the reader the colours of the spectrum but only tell of Newton's experiments and of the relationship between colour and wavelength, so in this section we can only describe man's achievements in the world of sound. But knowing something about a composer, his work, and when he lived can help to bring fuller understanding and enjoyment when listening to his music.

The section is in three parts:

I. Historical Narrative and Discussion

II. Glossary of Musical Terms

III. Index to Composers

I. HISTORICAL NARRATIVE AND DISCUSSION

The history of music, like that of any people or art, is not one of uninterrupted progress towards some ideal perfection. For five centuries or more music in the West has achieved peaks of accomplishment in one style or another before society has dictated or composers have felt the need for something new and different. Thus Wagner's music-drama *Parsifal*, lasting five hours, is not necessarily a more rewarding work than what Monteverdi achieved in *Orfeo* 250 years earlier. More complex yes, more rewarding—well, that is for the listener to judge.

We must keep this in mind when considering the development of music from a starting point of, say, Gregorian chant down to the complicated structures of a Schoenberg in our own day. In this development there is no true dividing line between one period and another, nor must simplifying terms such as "classical" or "romantic" be taken too literally.

The earliest history of Western music as we know it today is closely bound up with the Church, for music had to be provided for services. The earliest Christian music was influenced by Greek songs, few of which unfortunately have survived, and by the music of synagogues, where the art of chanting originated. The modal system of the ancient Greeks was highly organised. The earliest Greek scale was known from A to A and the four descending notes A,G,F,E became the basis of their musical theory, and it is from them that Western music learned to call notes after the letters of the alphabet. A scale can begin on any note and always includes two semitones upon which much of the character of a melody depends.

The Greek modes were based on the white notes only; the Dorian, Phrygian, Lydian, and Mixolydian began respectively on E,D,C, and B. Their character was thus decided by the position of the semitones, and they formed the basis, often corrupted, of the mediaeval modes. This system was transmitted through Latin writers such as Boethius and Cassiodorus, and through Arabic writers. The eight Church modes were not established until the 8th or 9th cent. These plagal modes, as they are called, started in each case, for technical reasons, a fourth below the authentic modes.

By the end of the 6th cent. Gregorian chant had developed so far that some sort of permanent record was required. *Neumes*, signs placed over the Latin text, were the earliest attempt at musical notation. Gradually lines came into use until a four-line stave was established, probably in the 11th and 12th cent., and with them clef signs, although the treble clef as we know it today did not appear until the 13th cent.

And what is this music—plainchant—like? It is an unaccompanied, single line of melody, which, when we have become used to its "antique" flavour is heard to have a wide range of spiritual and emotional expression, not excluding word painting. The texts used came from the Liturgy. These beautiful, extended lines of flowing, flexible melody can still be heard on Sundays in Roman Catholic cathedrals and churches.

Polyphony is Born.

The 10th cent. saw the appearance of a book called *Musica Enchiriadis* (whose authorship is disputed) which introduced theories about unison singing in which the melody is doubled at the fourth or fifth. Organum, or diaphony, is used to describe this method of writing, a term which confusingly could also be used for a kind of singing where melismatic melody was heard over a drone note on the organ. Rules came into fashion defining which intervals were allowed and which parts of the church services could be sung in more than one part. By the time of Guido d'Arezzo (c. 990–1050), a Benedictine monk who helped advance notation, contrary motion was permitted as the cadence was approached, another technical advance. Gradually the voices became more and more independent, and the third, so long considered a discord, came into use. Pérotin, of Notre Dame, was the first composer to write for three and four voices, and he and his great predecessor Léonin were the great masters of early polyphony. The proximity and spikiness of Pérotin's harmony is almost modern-sounding, and as with Gregorian chant, once we have adjusted ourselves to the sound, this music can be a rewarding experience.

Early Secular Music.

In mediaeval France, towards the end of the 11th cent., there developed what has become known as the age of the troubadours, poet-musicians. They were the successors to the *jongleurs*, or jugglers, and minstrels about whom we know little as practically none of their music has survived. The troubadours hymned the beauty of spring and of ladies. Contemporary with them in Germany were the Minnesingers. Their songs were mostly set in three modes. Adam de la Halle (d. 1287), because so much of his music survives, is perhaps the best-known of the troubadours. He was a notable composer of *rondels*, an early form of round, of which the English *Sumer is icumen in*, written by a monk of Reading c. 1226, is a fine example.

Ars Nova.

The term *ars nova* derives partly from writings of Philippe de Vitry (1291–1361) who codified the rules of the old and the new music in a valuable treatise. This *new art* represented a freeing of music from organum and rhythmic modes, and an increase in the shape and form of melodic line. France was the centre of music during the 14th cent. and apart from Philippe de Vitry the leading composer was Guillaume de Machaut (1300–77), who wrote many secular works as well as a polyphonic setting of the Mass. His music is notable for its vigour and tenderness as well as for its technical expertise. Meanwhile in 14th-cent. Italy a quite separate branch of *ars nova* was developing. Imitation and canon were to be noted in the music of Italian composers, and choral forms such as the Ballata, Madrigal (which often included instrumental accompaniment) and Caccia (a two-voice hunting song in canon) were common. The greatest Italian composer of this period was the blind organist and lutenist Francesco di Landini (*c.* 1325–97).

England was less affected by *ars nova* and tended to remain loyal to older forms. Not until the 15th cent. did she begin to make a significant contribution to the history of music. Both John Dunstable (*c.* 1380–1453), who was no less eminent as a mathematician and an astronomer than as a musician, and his contemporary Lionel Power advanced the technique of music by their method of composition (use of the triad, for instance) and mellifluous style. Their musicianship was much appreciated on the Continent. Dunstable did away with the use of *cantus firmus*—a fixed melody—and increased the use of free composition.

After Dunstable the next great figure in European music was Guillaume Dufay (*c.* 1400–74), the most celebrated composer of the Burgundian school. His music is distinguished for its blend of flowing melody, cleverly wrought counterpoint, and tender expressiveness. Much travelled, Dufay was a man of catholic outlook. Together with Dunstable and the Burgundian Gilles Binchois he bridged the gap between 14th cent. *ars nova* and the fully developed polyphony of the 15th cent.

Ars nova composers also showed an interest in secular music and many of their *rondeaux* and *chansons* (those of Binchois particularly) have been preserved. Personality began to play a distinguishing part in composition.

The results of Dufay's good work can be heard in the flowering of the Franco-Netherland school later in the 15th cent. Its two most notable representatives are Ockeghem (*c.* 1420–95) and his pupil Josquin des Prés (*c.* 1450–1521), who carried musical expressiveness even further than Dufay; their work can also be grand and majestic. Indeed Josquin's wide range, from the humorous to the dignified, partially accounts for his justly deserved high reputation. He was a master of counterpoint but tempered his mechanical ingenuity with imaginative insight.

Throughout the Renaissance choral music was breaking away, as we have seen, from its earlier bonds. The mediaeval tradition of having the *cantus firmus* in the tenor went by the board; the use of dissonance, when only two voices were used in mediaeval times, was abandoned in favour of euphony; and all the voices, democratically, came to share the musical lines. Composers also began to respect their texts; where words were previously fitted to the music, the reverse was now the case. In Josquin's music, indeed, we have the first attempts at symbolism: matching verbal ideas with musical ones. The importance of this musical renaissance has been realised only over the past twenty years. At last the Renaissance composers are coming to be seen not merely as historical figures relevant only in so far as their work culminated in the great classical composers, but as masters in their own right, whose music should be nearly as familiar to us as is that of a Mozart or a Beethoven.

With the exception of Dufay, little is known of the lives of the musicians so far mentioned. Most of them were in the service of royal or ducal households where they were in charge of the chapel choir, or else they worked in or around the great cathedrals, teaching at choir-schools. They were well rewarded for their services and their social position was probably high.

The Sixteenth Century.

By the 16th cent. music in England was a steadily expanding art and much encouraged. Music-making in the home was becoming quite the fashion in social circles. The Chapels Royal remained the chief musical centres but the music was changing with the development of new secular forms so that it was not so much religious as a part of life. Composers began their lives as choirboys and received a thoroughgoing education, both theoretical and practical.

Carrying on from where Josquin and his contemporaries left off, Palestrina in Italy, Victoria in Spain, Lassus in the Netherlands, and Byrd in England brought the polyphonic style to its zenith. At the same time came the rise of the madrigalists, first in Italy, then in the Netherlands; and then the beginnings of instrumental music as it came to be known in the succeeding centuries.

The vocal composers began to use chordal (homophonic) as well as contrapuntal (polyphonic) methods of writing—examples are Victoria's *Ave Verum Corpus* and Palestrina's *Stabat Mater*—but polyphony was still the fullest most magnificent instrument of composition, as for instance in Byrd's *O Quam Gloriosum* which shows an eager response to the mood and to the inflection of the words in a kind of vocal orchestration. A feature of all these composers' music, but more especially that of Victoria (*c.* 1535–1611) and Palestrina (1525–94), is its serene simplicity and fervour of utterance. Palestrina was perhaps more spacious in his effects, Victoria the more passionate. How well we can imagine—and sometimes hear—their music resounding down the naves of the great cathedrals of Europe.

The music of Lassus (*c.* 1532–94) is distinguished both in sheer amount and in vitality. His mastery in the field of motets was unrivalled, encompassing a wide range of subject and mood. He and his fellow Flemish composers, Willaert, de Monte and Arcadelt, were also expert in the Madrigal, a form popular in Italy and England as well. The Madrigal was a contrapuntal setting of a poem, usually not longer than twelve lines, in five or six parts. The subject (of the poetry) was usually amorous or pastoral. It was a short-lived, but highly prolific vogue. Orlando Gibbons (1583–1625), Thomas Weelkes (*c.* 1575–1623), and John Wilbye (1574–1638) were the most prominent English exponents.

Instrumental Music.

By the end of the 14th cent. instrumental music began to become something more than mere anonymous dance tunes or primitive organ music. Instruments often accompanied voices, or even replaced them, so that the recorder, lute, viol and spinet indoors, and sackbuts and shawms outdoors, had already been developed by the time instrumental music came to be written down. Gradually a distinction grew up between what was appropriate to the voice and what was suitable for instruments. Byrd, Gibbons, and Giles Farnaby in England, the great blind keyboard player, Cabezón (1510–66) in Spain, and Frescobaldi (1583–1643) in Italy produced valuable instrumental works. Perhaps the *Parthenia* and the *Fitzwilliam Virginal Book*, collections of Early English Keyboard music, give as fair a representative idea as any of the development of instrumental form at this time.

In chamber music musicians often played collections of dance tunes strung together to make a whole; or they chose fantasies (or " fancies ") where a composer altered a tune as he wished. Then there were sets of variations on a ground that is a simple tune played over and over again on a bass viol.

As far as brass instruments are concerned, they were often used on festive occasions in spacious halls or in cathedrals. The Venetian composer Andrea Gabrieli (c. 1510–86) was the first to combine voice and instruments and his son Giovanni Gabrieli (1557–1612) carried the process further to produce sacred symphonies, often using antiphonal effects.

Drama in Music.

Not until the end of the 16th cent. did anyone begin to think about combining drama and music, and so " invent " the new art we know today as opera. A group of artistic intelligentsia met together in Florence and conceived the idea of reviving the ancient declamation of Greek tragedy. They took Greek mythological subjects, cast them in dramatic form, and set them to music, not in the choral polyphonic style of the Madrigal, but with single voices declaiming dialogue in music. The earliest examples of what was called *Dramma per Musica* were Peri's *Daphne* in 1597 (now lost) and his *Eurydice*, in which he co-operated with Caccini. The new style came to its full flowering with the appearance of Monteverdi (1567–1643), whose genius would surely have shone in any age.

Monteverdi's first opera, *Orfeo*, produced in 1607, is a landmark of dramatic expression, and it is nothing less than a catastrophe that so many of his later operas have been lost. His *Orfeo* provides the basic ground work for the operas of the next two centuries: recitative, accompanied recitative, and aria. His last opera *L'Incoronazione di Poppaea*, written when he was at the great age (for those days) of 75, succeeds in its aim of creating a free, fluid form, slipping easily from recitative to arioso and even aria without the strict, closed forms that were to be used in the 17th and 18th cent. He focusses attention to an almost unbelievable extent on character rather than situation. He creates real people with all their faults and foibles—the kittenish, sexually attractive Poppaea, the power-drunk, infatuated Nero, the noble Seneca, and the dignified, rejected empress Octavia. As recent productions have shown these characters leap from the musical page as if they had just been created, each unerringly delineated in musical terms. Only the vocal line, the continuo, and the very incomplete instrumental ritornelli parts have been preserved, but in sensitive, knowledgeable hands tonal variety in the shape of wind and string parts can be added, as we know certain instruments were available to the composer.

Monteverdi's successors were Cavalli (1602–76), Cesti (1623–69) and Stradella (1642–82), who gave the solo voice more and more prominence encouraged by the advent of the castrati's brilliant voices. These artificially created singers had a vogue and popularity similar to " pop " singers of today, fêted wherever they appeared. The aria became more extended and ornate, and dramatic verisimilitude gradually but inexorably took second place to vocal display. An aria was nearly always in *da capo* form, the first section being repeated after a contrasting middle one.

Sixteenth- and Seventeenth-century Church Music.

Of course, the invention of a new dramatic style affected church music too. The concentration on the vertical aspect of music (homophony) as opposed to the horizontal (polyphony) led to the increasing importance of the voice in religious music. In Italy, it is true, there was the late-flowering, great madrigalist Carlo Gesualdo (1560–1614), whose harmonic daring still astonishes us today, but by 1600 the cantata was coming to replace older forms in church music. In its simplest form this was a story told in accompanied recitative. Giacomo Carissimi (c. 1604–74) was one of the first significant composers of this new form. He too was in on the birth of the oratorio, whose forerunner was the *sacra rappresentazione* (mystery or miracle play) of early 16th-cent

Florence. Then in the mid-16th cent. St. Philip Neri brought in elements from popular plays on sacred subjects in his services in Rome, designed to hold the attention of youth—rather as certain parsons have tried with " pop " services today. Emilio di Cavalieri (c. 1550–1602) and Carissimi developed the form adding arias and choral movements, omitting actual representation. Alessandro Scarlatti (1660–1725), whose oratorios bear a close resemblance to his operas, brought oratorio to its zenith in Italy.

Heinrich Schütz (1585–1672), Bach's great predecessor, was the founder of German church music. His historical place has never been called into question but only in recent times have the intrinsic merits of his own music come to be recognised. He studied with Giovanni Gabrieli in his youth and later came under the influence of Monteverdi, so it was not surprising that he brought Italian ideas across the Alps to Germany and wrote the first German opera *Daphne*, now sadly lost. He also introduced his country to the Italian declamatory style and to the new kind of concertato instrumental writing. But his dramatic religious works were his greatest contribution to musical development. He wrote with a devout intensity, bringing to life the scriptural texts by closely allying his urgent music to the words. His three settings of the Passions—Matthew, Luke, and John—paved the way for Bach's even more remarkable works in this genre. Two contemporaries of Schütz, Johann Hermann Schein (1586–1630) and Samuel Scheidt (1587–1654), were both important figures in German Reformation music.

Lully, Purcell, and Seventeenth-century Opera.

France resisted the tide of Italian opera, although paradoxically it was an Italian, Jean-Baptiste Lully (c. 1632–87), who charted the different course of French opera which was from the beginning associated with the court ballet. His musical monopoly during the reign of Louis XIV was put to good use. In his thirteen operas the libretto, usually on classical, allegorical themes, plays a vital part in the composition, which is therefore less clearly divided between recitative and aria than in Italian opera. The orchestration and the ballets assume greater importance than in the traditional Italian form. It was, in short, a more realistic, less stylised art.

In England, opera developed out of the entertainment known as the Masque, a succession of dances, accompanied by voices and instruments and often incorporated in a drama or spectacle. Henry Lawes's (1596–1662) setting of Milton's *Comus* is probably the most famous of these entertainments. The *Venus and Adonis* of John Blow (1649–1708) can be called the first English opera because here the music is gradually gaining the ascendancy over the spoken word. However, it was Purcell (1658–95), Blow's pupil, with *Dido and Aeneas*, who really gave dramatic life to the new medium by giving his characters a true musical personality that was subtler than anything the mere spoken word could achieve. The grief-laden lament of the dying Dido "When I am laid in earth " has an expressive power, achieved by extraordinarily bold harmonic effects, never before and seldom since achieved. The opera was in fact written for a young ladies' boarding school. Purcell followed it with several outstanding semi-operas—such as *The Fairy Queen* (to Dryden's text). His untimely death at the age of 36 probably robbed us of several full-length operas—and perhaps a consequence of this was that English music after him did not develop as it should have done.

His verse anthems and much of his instrumental music, especially the Fantasias, are also rich in imaginative mastery through his original use of harmony and counterpoint. However, a great deal of his pieces were written for a specific occasion and many of the odes are set to impossibly trite texts. At least his genius was partly acknowledged in his own day, and he was appointed organist in Westminster Abbey where he was buried with due pomp. He is said to have died through catching cold when locked out of his own house at night.

Vivaldi and the Rise of Instrumental Music.

Out of the dance suites popular in the 16th cent. and the beginning of the 17th (known in Italy as the *Sonata da Camera*) developed the concerto. This began as two groups of instrumentalists compared and contrasted with each other as in Giovanni Gabrieli's *Sonata piano e forte*. With Arcangelo Corelli (1653–1713) the concerto grosso took a more definite shape, alternating a solo group of instruments with the main body of strings in three or more contrasting movements. Guiseppe Torelli (1658–1709), Francesco Geminiani (1687–1762) and Tommaso Albinoni (1671–1750) were other notable contributors to the form, but none of the composers so far mentioned has today achieved the popularity of the priest Antonio Vivaldi (*c.* 1678–1741), himself a violinist, who had at his disposal the orchestra at the Ospedale della Pieta in Venice. The young women at this music school also contributed the vocal side of the concerts there of which there are many descriptions. One says: " They sing like angels, play the violin, flute, organ, oboe, cello, bassoon—in short no instrument is large enough to frighten them . . . I swear nothing is so charming than to see a young and pretty nun, dressed in white, a sprig of pomegranate blossom behind one ear, leading the orchestra, and beating time with all the grace and precision imaginable." For this body, Vivaldi wrote about 500 concertos which maintain a remarkably even quality, of which " The Four Seasons " are perhaps the most felicitous.

Meanwhile organ music was advancing rapidly in technique. Girolamo Frescobaldi (1583–1643) and Jan Pieterszoon Sweelinck (1562–1621) wrote works that provided the foundation of the Italian and Northern German schools of organ music. Their ricercares gradually developed into the fugue, a vein so richly mined by Bach. Among their successors the most notable figure before Bach was Johann Pachelbel (1653–1706).

Other keyboard music, especially for the harpsichord, was the particular province of France and Jean-Philippe Rameau (1683–1764) and François Couperin (1668–1733) were both masters of keyboard style and harmonic invention.

Bach (1685–1750).

The two giant figures of Bach and Handel bestride the first half of the 18th cent. Their differences are perhaps greater than their similarities. Bach wrote essentially for himself (although of course, he had to satisfy his employers at Cöthen and Leipzig) while Handel was composing to please his wide public. Bach was a provincial, always remaining in central Germany; Handel was widely travelled. Bach was devoutly religious, almost ascetic; Handel was more a man of the world. They never met.

To summarise Bach's vast output in a short space is virtually impossible. One can only try to distil the flavour of his music. He brought the art of polyphony to the highest pitch of mastery that has ever been achieved or is ever likely to be achieved. In his famous " Forty-Eight " and " the Art of the Fugue " he explored all the fugal permutations of the major and minor keys. At the same time his music rose above technical brilliance to achieve, especially in his organ music, the two Passions, many of the church cantatas, and the B minor Mass, intense emotional and expressive power. The cantatas, from his Leipzig appointment (1723) onwards, were integrated into the services. They consisted usually of a chorus based on a Lutheran hymn tune, recitatives, several extended arias, and a concluding chorus usually a straightforward version of the hymn tune in which the congregation joined. There are some two hundred of these works and they contain a wealth of comparatively unknown and sometimes even unrecognised beauties. The St. John and the St. Matthew Passion extend these procedures to a grand scale, an Evangelist telling the new Testament story in vivid recitative, the chorus taking the part of the crowd, soloists pondering in arias on the meaning of the Gospel, and Jesus's words being sung by a bass. Anyone who has heard either of these works well performed cannot help but dismiss from his mind any idea of Bach as a mere dry-as-dust musical mathematician. In the St. Matthew Passion, every suggestion in the text that can possibly be illustrated by a musical equivalent is so illustrated. The Old Testament Pharasaic law is represented by strict musical forms such as the canon; Christ's sayings are given noble arioso life; and the arias reflect truly the New Testament's compassionate message. Technically the work is a marvel; expressively it is eloquent. The B minor Mass, although it contains borrowings from many of his own works, still stands as a satisfying monumental whole in which Bach's choral writing achieved a new richness, the adaptations being in accord with their new setting.

Bach's instrumental music, especially the violin concertos and the unaccompanied works for violin and cello, not only show the immense range of his powers but also contain many of his deeper thoughts, whereas the orchestral suites and the Brandenburg concertos are more extrovert, particularly the rhythmically exuberant fast movements.

Bach closes an era—that of the later contrapuntalists—by achieving the *ne plus ultra* in fugal composition; his last, incomplete work, the Art of the Fugue, is evidence of this.

Handel (1685–1759).

During his lifetime Handel was far more widely recognised as a great composer than Bach, and his music, unlike Bach's, maintained its place in popular esteem until the re-discovery of Bach and the dominance of the symphony placed Handel somewhat in the background.

During the latter part of the 19th cent. Handel's name was mainly associated with mammoth, anachronistic performances of a small sample of his oratorios at the Crystal Palace and elsewhere in England. In his lifetime these works, and all his other works in the genre, were sung by a small choir who were outnumbered by the instrumental players. Over the past few years authentic-sized performances of his oratorios and a revival of interest in his operas have revealed the real Handel, unknown to our grandparents.

The operas were neglected partly because the vocal prowess they required—and which the castrati so brilliantly supplied—was no longer available and because their dramatic life, at least according to 19th- and early 20th-cent. tenets, hardly existed. Now it is realised that this neglect has deprived us of an unending stream of glorious melody and of much daring harmony. But perhaps it is in the hitherto disregarded oratorios, such as *Semele*, that Handel's innate dramatic sense and musical range are to be heard gloriously fulfilled, and the pastoral serenade *Acis and Galatea* is surely one of the most delightful scores ever composed.

Handel was a colourful, imaginative orchestrator, and this can be heard both in his accompaniment to vocal music and in his concerti grossi, op. 3 and 6, the earlier set exploiting a diversity of interesting string and wind combination. In his writing he was at home in a polyphonic or homophonic style as his superb choruses show. His organ concertos, of which he was the "inventor" (to quote a contemporary source), were often played between the acts of his oratorios. They are alternately expressive and exuberant pieces calling for some virtuosity from the player. His occasional works, such as the Water Music and Fireworks Music show his ingenuity in extending the range of the typical 17th cent. suite to serve a particular occasion.

Handel's working life was mostly spent in England where his Italian operas were acclaimed. In the years between his arrival here in 1711 and 1729 he wrote nearly thirty operas. It was only when the public tired of these and his reputation slumped that he turned to oratorio with equal success.

Bach and Handel between them crowned the age of polyphony that had lasted for two hundred years or more. After them, it is hardly surprising that composers began looking for a new style, already anticipated in the music of Rameau and particularly Dominico Scarlatti (1685–1737), whose harpsichord sonatas foreshadowed the classical sonata form that was to dominate music for the next two hundred years. The change in musical style about 1750 was partly the result of a change in musical patronage. Bach was the last great composer to earn his living through being employed by the church. The new patrons were the nobility who liked to have a composer on hand to write for the various evening entertainments of the time. For this purpose the princes and dukes had their own orchestras and their own small opera houses. The music required had to be elegant, formal, galant. Haydn was exceptionally fortunate in having an employer, Prince Nicholas of Esterhazy, who allowed him to write more or less as he wished so that he was able to develop symphonic form into something more than a pleasing way of passing an evening.

The early symphonists, culminating in Haydn, broke away from Bach's contrapuntal treatment of the orchestra. Instruments now came to be treated in a more colourful manner according to their particular timbre. The court of Mannheim had an orchestra of a standard unheard hitherto, and Johann Stamitz (1717–57) and his son Karl (1745–1801) influenced the great composers who were to follow in their footsteps. The composition of their orchestra was flexible, oboes, flutes, and horns often being added to the standard string section. Bach's son Carl Philipp Emanuel (1714–88) added to and developed symphonic and sonata form, especially as regards keys and subjects.

Haydn and Mozart.

These two figures dominate the second half of the 18th cent. as Bach and Handel did the first. In a brief space only a general picture can be presented of their huge output and influence. Of Haydn's 104 symphonies (there may even be others) more than half are worthy of study and hearing. The craftsmanship is always remarkable, the invention ever new. Indeed without Haydn's harmonic daring or his melodic ingenuity, the even greater symphonic thought of Beethoven would have been impossible: Haydn laid the groundwork on which his successor built towering edifices. A work such as the 93rd symphony in D is typical of his mature style with its searching introduction, powerfully wrought, earnestly argued first movement, beautiful Largo and resourceful bustling finale. Haydn did not fight shy of contrapuntal writing: the development section of this symphony's first movement and the finale are evidence of that, but it was only as an integral part of a predominantly homophonic technique.

Mozart's symphonies are not so different in form from Haydn's but—and this must be a subjective judgment—he put more emotional feeling into his. Nobody could listen to the heart-searching first movement of his 40th symphony without being deeply moved. It was in his final three works in the medium that Mozart brought his symphonic art to perfection, and these obviously had an effect on Haydn's later symphonies written after them. For passion and tenderness contained within a classical form these late symphonies, and many other of Mozart's works, have yet to be surpassed.

Haydn, who has been rightly termed "the Father of the Symphony" was also the founder of the string quartet—perhaps the most perfect, because the most exactly balanced, form of musical expression. The four instruments—two violins, viola, and cello—discuss, argue, commune with each other over the whole gamut of feeling. In his quartets Haydn's mastery of structure is even more amazing than in his symphonies. Mozart's quartets (especially the six devoted to Haydn) and even more his quintets achieve miracles of beauty in sound, nowhere more so than in the first movement of the G minor (his most personal key)

quintet. The two late piano quartets show how the piano can be ideally combined with strings. His clarinet quintet is also a masterly work.

Haydn did not leave any concertos of consequence. Mozart's, especially those for piano, are among his greatest works. As a brilliant clavier player himself, he showed a consummate skill in writing for the keyboard. Although the instrument he knew was slightly less advanced than the piano today, his concertos call for virtuosity in execution, yet they are as searching in emotional content as the late symphonies and quartets. Indeed the C major concerto (K. 467) and the C minor (K. 491) may be said to hold the quintessential Mozart. As well as twenty (mature) piano concertos, Mozart wrote six for the violin, four for the horn, and eighteen others, but none of these delightful as they are, can be placed in quite the same class.

Of their church music, Haydn's sixteen masses and his oratorios—The Creation and the Seasons (both late works)—are perhaps more worthy of attention than Mozart's various masses, but we must not forget Mozart's final work—the Requiem or the serene late Motet Ave Verum Corpus.

Eighteenth-century Opera.

Mozart—for many the first great opera composer—did not, of course, create his masterpieces out of nothing. In France, Lully was followed by Rameau (1683–1764), who carried on his tradition of using classical themes but developed a more flexible style of recitative and greatly increased vividness of expression. But it was Gluck (1714–87) who more than anyone broke out of the straitjacket of the now ossified Italian form of opera—dominated by the singer—and showed just what could be achieved in moving human terms. Drama in music really came of age with his Orfeo e Eurydice (1762), Alceste (1767) and Iphigénie en Tauride (1779). His simplicity and poignancy of expression were not lost on Mozart.

Meanwhile in Germany a kind of opera called Singspiel appeared during the 18th cent. Breaking away from classical themes, mundane stories were told in dialogue and music.

Until quite recently Haydn's operas were dismissed as unworthy representations of his genius but, chiefly through the enlightening efforts of the Haydn scholar, H. C. Robins Landon, some of his fifteen surviving works in the medium have been successfully revived. They have proved to be perfectly viable for the stage and, especially in the ensembles, full of that delightful invention to be found in the rest of his opus, if on a less fully developed scale. Still as musical drama they inevitably fall far short of Mozart's achievements, for the younger composer seems to have had an instinctive feeling for the stage. Into his operas he poured his most intense, personal music. He vividly portrays the foibles, desires, loves, and aspirations of mankind.

The earlier, immature stage pieces of his youth led to such works as Lucio Silla (1772) and La Finta Giardiniera (1775) with their first glimpses of the glories to come. His first indubitably great opera is Idomeneo (1781). Despite its unpromisingly static plot, Idomeneo reveals Mozart's stature through its ability to breathe new life into a conventional opera seria form. Though influenced by Gluck it is yet more human and touching in its musical expression. To succeed this Mozart wrote a much more frivolous piece Die Entführung aus dem Serail. Stemming from the Singspiel tradition, it none the less creates real-life characters who have much charming music to sing.

After three lesser pieces Mozart embarked on his four masterpieces—Le Nozze di Figaro (1786), Don Giovanni (1787), Così fan tutte (1790), and Die Zauberflöte (1791).

Figaro, as well as being a delightful comedy, explores more fully than any previous opera situation and character, which find expression in beautiful arias and in two finales of symphonic proportion. In *Don Giovanni*, less satisfactory as a dramatic structure, the range of musical characterisation and insight into human motives is widened still further. *Così* lyrically but humorously expresses the follies of love. Mozart could not help but love his characters and his music for them is at one and the same time amusing and heartfelt. *Die Zauberflöte*—The Magic Flute—displays Mozart's deep-felt love of his fellow men and of truth in an opera of great spiritual strength. Nor has opera any more loveable personality than the birdcatcher Papageno. Mozart's final opera *La Clemenza di Tito*, extolling imperial magnanimity, has never achieved the success or popularity of his other maturer stage works, though it contains much excellent music.

Beethoven.

Mozart was the last major composer to depend, to any large extent, on private patronage for his living, and even he left the service of the Archbishop of Salzburg because he could not stand the restrictions imposed on his freedom. Henceforth composers would have to stand on their own two feet with all the advantages (liberty) and disadvantages (lack of security) that implied. Beethoven (1770–1827) was the first such composer of importance.

Although his work is usually divided into three periods, this division is somewhat too arbitrary, for no other composer in history, with the possible exception of Wagner, has shown such a continual development of his genius. Coming at just the right moment in musical history, he crowned the achievements of Haydn and Mozart with music of the utmost profundity of thought and feeling that looks back to its classical heritage and forward to the romantic movement of the 19th cent. His influence on musical thinking and writing is incalculable.

His first period shows his strong melodic gifts and the beginning of his individuality in developing form and structure to suit his own ends and match his particular genius. Unusual keys are explored, unusual harmonic procedures employed. With the " Eroica " (his third symphony) he established his position as a great composer. The unity of purpose he here achieved within a long and diverse structure is truly staggering, even today. In the first movement alone the structural invention and cogency went far beyond what even Mozart had achieved in his " Jupiter " symphony, and the second movement—a vast funeral March—has an overwhelmingly tragic emotional content. But the " Eroica " was followed by six equally great symphonies, each one as varied, as inventive, as unified as the others. The ninth symphony is significant in both its length and finale. Here Beethoven crowns three superb instrumental movements with a choral movement that, as well as summing up all that has gone before, expresses in music the joy in existence more ecstatically than any other work.

The burning intensity of Beethoven's genius is just as evident in his chamber music. His quartets are the product of a revolutionary age in which the social graces and formal restraint of the 18th cent. were thrown off in a search for a more personal mode of expression. The early op. 18 set, and the Razoumovsky quartets, op. 59, go even beyond the range of Haydn's and Mozart's works in the medium but it was in his late quartets, his final musical testament, that Beethoven refined and distilled his art for posterity. No words can possibly describe their unique quality, but any and every chance should be taken to make their acquaintance: the effort required will be more than amply rewarded.

The early piano concertos do not reach quite this level of attainment, but the last three, together with the violin concerto, are on a par with the finest of the symphonies and quartets, as well as being considerable tests of the performers' technique. The Triple Concerto for piano, violin, and cello is an unusual and rewarding work.

Beethoven's grandest choral work—and one of the most noble in existence—is the Mass in D (*Missa Solemnis*). Its vast scale and sublime utterance often defeat performers, but when it is successfully done there is no more spiritually uplifting experience for the listener. Except perhaps Beethoven's only opera, *Fidelio*. This simple escape story was transformed by Beethoven's creative fire into a universal symbol of liberty, the composer identifying himself with the struggle for freedom from tyranny and release from darkness.

Beethoven lived in a period of war and revolution. A passionate belief in the brotherhood of man and in liberty, he was shocked to find his ideals thrown over by revolutionaries-turned-dictators. His own tragedy of deafness, which came upon him at the moment of his triumph, nearly submerged him, but in the end he won through and produced the string of masterpieces from the " Eroica " onwards. Hope springing from despair, love from hatred, victory over defeat, these are the unquenchable legacies left by Beethoven.

The Romantic Movement.

Inevitably, the Romantic movement in literature that burst forth about 1800 was bound to have its counterpart in music. And so it was. Breaking the classical bonds, composers such as Schubert, Schumann, Liszt, and Berlioz sought a new freedom in musical expression. Form became of less importance than content; and that content often had literary connections. For their purposes a larger orchestra was needed and supplied, but the miniature, the song especially, because of its very personal connotation, was also a favourite form.

Schubert (1797–1828)—described by Liszt as " the most poetic of musicians "—is perhaps the greatest lyrical genius in musical history. In him the Viennese tradition and influence of Haydn, Mozart, and Beethoven reached its zenith. The song was always Schubert's starting point, so it is hardly surprising that his reputation as a song writer has never been impaired but in his symphonic and instrumental works too it is always his inexhaustible fund of melody that first calls for attention. Nobody could listen to his " Trout " quintet, for piano and strings, his octet, his fifth symphony, or his song cycle *Die Schöne Müllerin* without being enchanted and invigorated by the sheer tunefulness of the music. But there is much more to Schubert than this: his understanding of the possibilities of harmonic change, his grasp of orchestral coloration (in the great C major symphony, for instance), his free use of sonata structure.

Although Mozart, Haydn, and Beethoven had all contributed to the song as an art form, it was with Schubert that it achieved its first full flowering. If he had written nothing but his songs, his place in the musical firmament would be assured. With his *Erlkönig* in 1815 the German *Lied* came of age and from then until the end of his life he wrote more than six hundred songs, hardly a dud among them. Whether it is the charm of *Heidenröslein*, the drama of *Der Doppelgänger*, the numbed intensity of the *Winterreise* cycle Schubert unerringly went to the heart of a poet's meaning; indeed he often raised poor verses to an inspired level by his settings. And for the first time the pianist shares a place of equal importance with the singer.

There is only room to mention one or two other composers, some of them wrongly neglected, who were roughly contemporaries of Beethoven and Schubert: the Czech Dussek (1760–1812), who like Beethoven bridges the classical-romantic gulf, Boccherini (1743–1805), the two Italian opera composers Cimarosa (1749–1801) and Paisiello (1740–1816), the Frenchman Méhul (1763–1817) and the German Hummel (1778–1836).

Weber (1784–1826) lacked Beethoven's energy and constructive powers and Schubert's sheer lyrical profundity, but he is an important figure, especially in the field of opera, where his *Der*

Freischütz and *Oberon* led the way to a more flexible, dramatically realistic form of opera. His vivid imagination exactly fitted the new romantic mood abroad. The sheer beauty in the melodic shape of his music is also not to be denied.

Mendelssohn and Schumann.

Mendelssohn (1809–47) was the civilised craftsman among the Romantic composers. A boy genius—many of his finest works were written before he was twenty—he maintained the importance of classical form while imbuing it with his own affectionate brand of poetic sensibility. His third and fourth symphonies—the " Scottish " and " The Italian "—(and possibly the fifth " The Reformation "), his string quartets (some of which go deeper than most of his music), violin concerto, first piano concerto, and of course, the incidental music to " A Midsummer Night's Dream " represent his tidy yet effervescent style at its most winning.

Schumann (1810–1856) is less easy to categorise. His early romantic flame was burnt out by some flaw in his intellectual and/or emotional make-up, and his inspiration seems to have declined in later years. No matter, by then he had given us the marvellous song cycles of 1840, an ever fresh piano concerto, many fine piano solos, including the mercurial, popular *Carnaval* and several symphonies, which, if not structurally perfect, contain much lovely music. The joys and sorrows of love and the feeling for natural beauty are all perfectly mirrored in these charming, lyrical works.

Romantic Giants.

Berlioz (1803–69) and Liszt (1811–86) are the two most typical representative figures of the Romantic era. Both have always been controversial figures, with ardent advocates and opponents either unduly enthusiastic or unfairly derogatory. Berlioz might be termed the perfect painter in music. With an uncanny mastery of orchestral sound he could conjure up the countryside, the supernatural and the historical with the utmost ease. He based his music on the " direct reaction to feeling " and a desire to illustrate literature by musical means. That his technical expertise was not always the equal of his undoubted genius, can be heard in many of his larger works such as the dramatic cantata *The Damnation of Faust* and the dramatic symphony *Romeo and Juliet*, yet most people are willing to overlook the occasional vulgarity for the ineffable beauty of his many fine pages, but brutal cuts in his music, such as are often made in, for instance, his epic opera *The Trojans* only have the effect of reducing the stature of his works. We must accept him, warts and all. Anyone who has seen the two parts of *The Trojans*, presented complete in one evening at Covent Garden, will realise that Berlioz knew what he was about.

His output is not quantitatively large but includes several monumental works, as well as *The Trojans*. The *Requiem* (" Grand Messe des Morts ") requires a tenor solo, huge chorus and orchestra, and brass bands, although Berlioz uses these forces fastidiously. The *Symphonie funèbre et Triomphale*, calls in its original form, for choir, brass, and strings. But Berlioz was just as happy writing on a smaller scale as his exquisite song cycle, to words of Théophile Gautier, *Nuits d'Été*, shows. Gautier perhaps summed up better than anyone Berlioz's singular talent: " In that renaissance of the 1830s Berlioz represents the romantic musical idea, the breaking up of old moulds, the substitution of new forms for unvaried square rhythms, a complex and competent richness of orchestration truth of local colour, unexpected effects in sound, tumultuous and Shakespearian depth of passion, amorous or melancholy dreaminess, longings and questionings of the soul, infinite and mysterious sentiments not to be rendered in words, and that something more than all which escapes language but may be divined in music."

During his lifetime Liszt was fêted and honoured not only by his musical colleagues but by the world at large, which idolised him and his piano. Then his reputation took a plunge from which it has only recently recovered. To be sure much of his early music is glitter and gloss, but his symphonies and tone poems—especially the Faust Symphony, the Dante Symphony (both, of course, inspired by literature), and *Orpheus* and *Prometheus*—and his late piano works show that he was an extraordinary harmonic innovator. The piano sonata in B minor brings his romantic, wilful temperament within a reasonably stable, pianistic form, and as such is a landmark in the repertory of the instrument. Liszt's output was prodigious, but the inquiring listener should explore the more original of his compositions already mentioned to form a true picture of his fertile genius.

Chopin.

Chopin (1810–49) was the master of the keyboard, par excellence. His development of the technical and expressive capabilities of the piano is unique in musical history. His inventive powers were poured out with nervous passionate energy and in a highly individual style through twenty astonishing, possibly agonised years of creative activity before his early death. A Chopin melody, limpid, transparent, singing, can be recognised easily by anyone, but his style gradually developed into something more subtle, more satisfying than pure melody. He took the greatest care of every detail so that any alteration, however small, upsets the perfect balance of his work. His poetic sensibility can be found in any of his works; for his constructive ability we must turn to the Ballades, the B minor Sonata, and the Barcarolle, while the Preludes and Studies blend technical powers and emotional expressiveness in ideal proportions.

Nineteenth-century Opera.

After Mozart's operas and Beethoven's *Fidelio*, the medium might have been expected to decline. Instead it took on a new, if different, lease of life that culminated in Verdi's extraordinary output.

Rossini (1792–1868) created a world of exuberant high spirits in his operatic works that are as cheerful and heart-warming today as they were a hundred or more years ago.

He always worked in and around the lyric theatres of Italy and between 1810 and 1830 poured out a stream of works, not all of which can be expected to be masterpieces. However, *Il Barbiere di Siviglia*, *L'Italiana in Algieri*, *La Cenerentola* and *Le Comte Ory* will always delight audiences as long as opera houses exist. Although these works are difficult to sing really well, their vitality and charm can never be submerged even by poor voices or indifferent staging.

His German contemporaries were critical of his confidence and frivolity, but his works show a consistency of invention and an irresistible tunefulness that anyone might envy. In recent years, there has also been a renewed interest in his more serious operas—*Otello* (1816), *La Gazza Ladra* (1817), *Semiramide* (1823), *La Siège de Corinthe* (1820), and *Guillaume Tell* (1829)—which were certainly surpassed in dramatic power by his successors but which nevertheless are not to be despised or neglected.

William Tell, to give it its more popular title, was his last work for the stage although he lived on for nearly forty years in retirement in Paris, scene of many of his greatest successes. There he enjoyed good living, dispensing *bons mots*, and occasionally composing trifles. An exception is the unpretentious *Petite Messe Solennelle*, written originally for soloists, chorus, a harmonium, and two pianos. Rossini later orchestrated it, but he would not allow it to be performed during his lifetime. The first public performance was on 28 February 1869, as near as possible to the 78th anniversary of the composer's birth on Leap Year Day 1792.

In contrast to the mercurial Rossini, Vincenzo Bellini (1801–1835) was an exquisite, romantic figure dealing with exquisite, romantic stories, an operatic equivalent to Chopin, who much admired him. His delicate, sinuous vocal line (in the arias) and brilliant acrobatics in the final sections (cabalettas) require singers of the utmost accomplishment to do them justice, although his music is never as florid as Rossini's. His most typical and popular works are probably *La Sonnambula* (1831), *Norma* (1831) and *I Puritani* (1835). The first is a tender, homely country story, the second an almost heroic lyrical drama of sacrifice, and the third a rather unsatisfactory historical story redeemed by its appealing music. In the past few years singers of the calibre of Maria Callas, Joan Sutherland, Guiletta Simionato, and Marilyn Horne have brought Bellini's operas a popularity almost equal to that they enjoyed at the time they were written.

Gaetano Donizetti (1797–1848) was an even more prolific operatic composer than Rossini. He wrote at least 75 works, mostly for the Italian stage, several of which, such as *Alfredo il Grande* or *Emilia di Liverpool*, are never likely to be revived, but during the past few years, with the renewed interest in what are called the *Ottocento* operas, many of his serious operas have been resuscitated and found as enjoyable in performance as his more frequently heard comedies.

He was a well-grounded musician and although his invention is often criticised for being too tied to the conventions of his day performances often belie this reputation, his dramatic instinct proving sure. *Lucia di Lammermoor*, because of the chances it offers to a coloratura soprano with tragic pretensions, has always held the stage and of late *Lucrezia Borgia*, *Anna Bolena*, *La Favorita*, and *Poliuto* have all been successfully revived. Of his lighter works, the comedies *L'Elisir d'Amore* and *Don Pasquale* have never declined in popularity. One of his last works was *Linda di Chamounix* (1842) which he wrote for Vienna where it aroused such enthusiasm that the Emperor appointed him Court Composer and Master of the Imperial Chapel.

French Opera.

The taste in Paris was for more and more lavish productions. Following Spontini (1774–1851), whose works were comparatively austere, came Halévy (1799–1862) and Giacomo Meyerbeer (1791–1864) whose operas contain all the ingredients that came to be expected of " Grand Opera "—spectacle, huge ensembles, showpieces for the soloists, and extended, if superfluous ballet. Drawing from Italian, German, and French traditions Meyerbeer's music contained everything the public wanted, yet today they are seldom revived, perhaps because his creative powers were essentially derivative, yet when they *are* given, operas like *Les Huguenots*, *Le Prophète*, and *L'Africaine* still have the power to fascinate and his influence on his successors, notably Wagner, was considerable.

Verdi.

Italian opera in the 19th cent. culminated in the works of Giuseppe Verdi (1813–1901), who rose from a peasant background to become his country's most noted composer, as well as something of a natural hero during the period of the Risorgimento. His earliest works, indeed, often roused his hearers to patriotic fervour. For instance, *Nabucco* (1842), with its theme of an oppressed people seeking deliverance, was treated as a symbol of the Italians' fight for freedom.

Musically, Verdi developed out of all recognition during the course of his long career. The continuously flowing structure of his last two operas *Otello* and *Falstaff* is very far removed from the start-stop formulas, inherited from his predecessors, of his first works, yet even they are touched, in harmonic subtleties, orchestral felicities, and a sense of drama, by a spark of genius, a burning inspiration that sets him apart from all other

operatic composers. *Ernani* (1844), *I due Foscari* (1844), and *Luisa Miller* (1849) all have foretastes of glories to come even if as a whole they are flawed dramas, and these " galley years ", as Verdi himself later described them, gave him the essential know-how to produce his later, greater operas, as well as establishing him incontrovertibly as the most popular Italian composer of the time.

However, it was with *Rigoletto* (1851), *Il Trovatore* (1853), and *La Traviata* (1853) that Verdi first really staked his claim to immortality. In these pieces his increasing dramatic mastery are married to a wonderful flow of lyrical melody, at the same time controlled by a fine musical sensibility. They were followed by four operas— *Simon Boccanegra* (1857), *Un Ballo in Maschera* (1858), *La Forza del Destino* (1862), and *Macbeth* (revised version, 1865)—in which Verdi overcame complexities of story line by his continually developing musical powers. This period is crowned by *Don Carlos* (written for the Paris Opéra, 1867) a masterly exercise in combining private and public situations in a single, grand, and characterful work. In some respects Verdi never surpassed the subtlety of his writing in this opera. *Aïda* (1871) carried on the process but the characterisation in this ever-popular piece is less refined than in *Don Carlos*, if the grandeur of the design is more spectacular.

The success of *Otello* (1887) owes nearly as much to the skill of Boito whose literary ability combined with musical knowledge (he was himself a composer) presented Verdi with an ideal libretto for his seamless music in which the drama moves inevitably to its tragic end. Recitative, aria, ensemble are fused in a single, swiftly moving music-drama, which in its very different way equals that of Wagner. *Falstaff* (1893) achieves the same success in the field of comic opera, a brilliant, mercurial ending to a distinguished career. If Verdi had written only these two final masterpieces his place in musical history would be assured.

Brahms.

Brahms (1833–1897) has justly been described as " a romantic spirit controlled by a classical intellect," for while complying with most of the formal regulations of sonata form he imbued them with an emotional content that accorded with his time. Indeed Schumann declared that he was the " one man who would be singled out to make articulate in an ideal way the highest expression of our time."

Perhaps in his chamber music will be found the quintessence of his art. The piano and clarinet quintets, the two string sextets, the horn trio, and the violin sonatas all are designed on a large scale yet the expression remains intimate, the design and structure clear.

The symphonies and concertos, though, remain his most popular works; they are part of the solid repertory of every orchestra and most piano and violin players in the world. Their high seriousness, constant lyrical beauty, and control of form are deeply satisfying. They do not provide the extremes of passion and excitement provided by his contemporaries, but their study provides continuous absorption and delight. The double concerto for violin and cello deserves a mention as a unique work in music.

Brahms wrote more than two hundred songs in which the desire for melodic beauty takes precedence over the words and meaning. Many are set to poor poetry, but hidden away are still some unexplored treasures, and the Four Serious Songs, at least, are tragic masterpieces. In a lighter vein the two sets of *Liebeslieder Walzer* for four voices are irresistible. The choral Requiem, too, is a fine work.

Bruckner.

In recent years Bruckner's reputation *vis-à-vis* his great contemporary Brahms has been enhanced in England. The old conception of him as a naïve Austrian unable to grasp the fundamentals of symphonic architecture has died hard, and the prevailing popularity of his grandest works is at last gaining him his rightful place in the 19th-cent. firmament. The nine symphonies and the masses are his chief claim to immortality. They contain melodies of unforgettable beauty, symphonic paragraphs of unparalleled grandeur, and an appreciation of formal development that, though different, is as equally valid as that of Brahms. The movements of his symphonies are long and he often pauses, as if for breath and to admire the scenery, before he reaches the climactic peak of his musical journey. His idiom is best approached by a newcomer to his work through the fourth and seventh symphonies as they are perhaps the easiest to understand, but the fifth, sixth, eighth, and ninth (unfinished) are just as beautiful—and cogently argued—once one has acquired the knack, so to speak, of listening to his music. Most of these works are now to be heard in their original form, stripped of the veneer of "improvements" suggested to the diffident composer by his friends.

As well as the masses, which translate Bruckner's symphonic ideas to the choral plain, Bruckner's delightful string quintet is worth investigating.

Wagner.

Praised only this side of idolatry by his admirers, unmercifully criticised by his detractors, Richard Wagner (1813–83) is perhaps the most controversial composer in musical history. And so it was bound to be with such a revolutionary figure, whose writings, other than his music, contain, to say the least, dubious theories and whose operas, composed to his own libretti, broke the bonds of the form as known until his time. His regarded music-drama as a fusion of all the arts—music, literature, painting—in one unity. With *The Ring of the Nibelungs* he achieved his purpose; no other work of art has ever tried to encompass the whole of existence. Today, and surely forever, musicians, philosophers, and writers will argue over its meaning, and each age will reinterpret it according to its own lights.

But before he reached this pinnacle of achievement, Wagner gradually transformed opera—through *Rienzi*, *The Flying Dutchman*, *Tannhäuser*, and *Lohengrin*—so that a new mould was fashioned to take what he wanted to pour into it. He introduced the *Leitmotiv*, a musical theme that could be associated with a particular person, situation, or idea, each time it occurred. Slowly he developed the musical form so that the drama could unfold continuously without breaks for arias. By the time he began to write *Tristan and Isolde* and *Die Meistersinger*, he had perfected his methods and had he never undertaken *The Ring* that tragedy and that comedy would have assured him his place in the musical firmament. Indeed, *Die Meistersinger* is considered a masterpiece even by those who are not willing or prepared to accept the rest of the Wagnerian ethos.

The length and complexity of these operas, and of *Parsifal*, a work of unique beauty in spite of certain *longueurs*, means that it is almost essential to prepare oneself by homework, with libretti and records, before attempting to assimilate them in the opera house. The added effort is well worth while for the ultimate musical satisfaction they bring because Wagner was more than an operatic reformer: he opened up a new harmonic language (especially in the use of chromaticism) that was logically to develop into the atonality of the 20th cent.

Wolf.

As Wagner was the culmination of the 19th cent. symphonic and operatic tradition, so Hugo Wolf (1860–1903) summed up, if he did not surpass, the achievements in song-writing of Schubert Schumann, and Loewe (1796–1869).

Wolf was a lonely pathetic man. He lived much of his life in poverty, and eventually lost his reason and died of an incurable disease. These circumstances account perhaps for his almost feverish bursts of creative activity, which were also the outward sign of his burning genius. His greatest contributions to the art of *Lieder* were his extraordinary insight into the poet's meaning and the harmonic means by which he heightened the expression of the words. He raised the importance of the piano part even higher than had Schumann, and in some of his songs the vocal part takes the form of a free declamation over a repeated idea in the piano. However, in the main the vocal and piano parts are interweaved with great subtlety, and he unerringly matched the very varied moods of the poems he chose to set. His greatest creative period was between early 1888 and early 1890 when songs poured from his pen daily—more than 50 settings of the German poet Mörike, 20 of Eichendorff, more than 50 of Goethe, and more than 40 of Heyse and Geibel (the Spanish Song-book). Later he composed songs from Heyse's Italian Song-book and the three Michelangelo sonnets. And the range of his creative understanding was wide, taking in the almost wild passion of the Spanish songs, the humanity and humour of the Italian love-songs, the titanic power of *Prometheus* (Goethe), the varying moods of the Mörike book, and the intangible power of the Michelangelo sonnets. There are almost inexhaustible riches here for the inquiring mind to discover. Outside Lieder, Wolf's output is small, but it includes a sadly neglected opera, *Der Corregidor*, the Italian Serenade for string quartet (alternatively for small orchestra) and a tone poem *Penthesilea*.

Ernest Newman, his greatest champion, summed up his work most aptly: "Wolf practically never repeats himself in the songs; every character is drawn from the living model. It is a positively Shakespearian imagination that is at work—Protean in its creativeness, inexhaustibly fecund and always functioning from the inside of the character or the scene, not merely making an inventory from the outside."

National Movements.

During the course of the 19th cent., alongside the emergence of national political identity, came the rise of nationalism in music, fertilising traditional Western—that is basically German—musical forms with folk material. Of these groups the Russian is certainly the most important, if not the most vital.

Glinka (1804–57) was the first important Russian composer of the national school and, although his two operas *A Life for the Tsar* (sometimes called *Ivan Susanin*) and *Russlan and Ludmilla* are strongly influenced by Italian models, they do introduce Russian song and harmony into the texture. He undoubtedly influenced Borodin (1833–87), Cui (1835–1918), Balakireff (1837–1910), Mussorgsky (1839–81) and Rimsky-Korsakov (1844–1908)—the so-called "Five" of 19th-cent. Russian music. However, each was very much of an individualist too. Borodin was a lecturer in chemistry who wrote in his spare time. His two symphonies, two string quartets led up to his most notable work, the opera *Prince Igor*, left incomplete at his death. Balakireff, friend and adviser to the rest of the group, wrote little himself, but his orchestral works and the piano fantasia, *Islamey*, are worthy of investigation.

Modest Mussorgsky (1839–81) is today seen as the most important and inspired of "The Five." More than the others he used Russian song and Russian speech as the basis of his operas in which he portrayed the lives and destinies of his own people. Although his capacities were seriously impaired by an uncongenial job, poverty, and drinking, he produced two great operas, *Boris Godunov* and *Khovanshchina*, and another *Sorochintsy Fair* that is immensely enjoyable. *Boris* should be given in its original, with spare orchestration, but more often than not it is heard in Rimsky-Korsakov's more elaborate revision. In any case the opera exists in various versions, none of them necessarily the right one: what is important is to hear it in one or the other because of its great portrayal of Boris's personality set against the background of the Russian people, unforgettably presented in choral outbursts. *Khovanshchina* was completed by Rimsky-Korsakov, *Sorochintsy Fair* by Tcherepnin (although other versions also exist). Mussorgsky's songs explore a new vein of naturalistic vocal declamation. Each of the four *Songs and Dances of Death* is a miniature drama worthy of Wolf, although of course in a quite other idiom. The *Nursery* songs miraculously conjure up a child's world as seen from a child's point of view. Many of the individual songs, the *Sunless* cycle too, should be investigated.

Rimsky-Korsakov (1844–1908) is perhaps a less attractive figure because so much of his music seems heartless or merely decorative, but this judgment is probably made on the strength of hearing *Shéhérazade* and the *Capriccio Espagnol* a few too many times. Such of his 15 operas that are played evince a (literally) fantastic mind and lyrical vein, and it is a pity that *Sadko*, *The Snow Maiden*, and *The Tsar's Bride*, at least, are not heard more often.

Tchaikovsky.

Peter Ilyich Tchaikovsky (1840–93) is a more universally admired figure than any of " The Five " and his music is indubitably closer to the mainstream than theirs in that it adheres more nearly to Western European forms. His popularity is due to his unhesitating appeal to the emotions and to his tender, often pathetic melodic expression. His lyrical gift is stronger than his sense of architecture, as he himself admitted. Yet his later symphonies—the fourth, fifth, and sixth (the *Pathétique*)—are all cogently enough argued and invigorating, as can be heard in the hands of a conductor willing to emphasise their formal power rather than their tendency towards sentimentality: the orchestral craftsmanship is also superb. The three piano concertos and the violin concerto offer rare opportunities for virtuoso display within a reasonably dramatic structure and his various overtures are always exciting to hear.

The three ballets—*The Sleeping Beauty*, *Swan Lake*, and *Nutcracker* show Tchaikovsky's skill on a smaller and perhaps more congenial scale, but only two of his operas—*Eugene Onegin* and *The Queen of Spades*—survive in regular performance. They demonstrate his ability to delineate character and his always eloquent melodic invention. His songs often felicitously capture a passing mood or emotion.

Bohemia (Czechoslovakia).

The Czech national school is dominated by two composers—Smetana (1824–84) and Dvořák (1841–1904). In his own country Smetana holds a unique position as the father of his country's music—which is remarkable when you consider that he lived in a country that was then under Austrian rule and never spoke the Czech language perfectly. Yet his music is filled with the spirit of Czech history and national life, and many of his operas, his most important contribution, deal purely with national subjects. The reawakening of interest in things national, after Austria's defeat by Italy in 1859, led to the establishment of a Provisional Theatre in 1862 and Smetana's first opera *The Brandenburgers in Bohemia* was produced there in 1866, but its success was eclipsed by the enormous popularity of *The Bartered Bride*, which appeared the same year. Its melodic charm, lively characterisation and cosy humour have carried it round the world and it is the one Smetana opera to be in the repertory of most opera houses. However, his next opera *Dalibor* (1868) is considered by some authorities as his masterpiece. It is conceived on a heroic scale, and frequently rises to great dramatic heights. His later operas include *Libuše* (1872) a solemn festival tableau, *The Two Widows* (1874), a delightful comedy, *The Kiss* (1876), *The Secret* (1878), and *The Devil's Wall* (1882).

His main orchestral work *Má Vlast* (My Country), written between 1874 and 1879, is a cycle of six symphonic poems nobly depicting the life and legends of his country. He wrote only three mature chamber works—an elegiac piano trio, written in 1855 in memory of the death of his eldest daughter, and two string quartets, both autobiographical. The first in E minor (1876)—" From My Life "—tells of his youth and aspirations until a terrible, screeching E in *altissimo* describes the onset of deafness; the second in D minor, sadly neglected, was described by the composer as an attempt to explain the " whirlwind of music in the head of one, who has lost his hearing," and was probably influenced by Beethoven's later music.

Dvořák combined a fecund melodic gift with an intelligent grasp of structure. His symphonies and chamber music are mostly written in classical form, yet the works are imbued with a spontaneity and freshness that have not lost one whit of their charm over the years.

He wrote nine symphonies and, although only the last three or four are regularly performed, they are mostly mature works, several of which, for instance No. 7 in D minor (formerly known as No. 2) reach a tragic grandeur at times. They are all orchestrated in a masterly way and are full of delightful detail. Dvořák wanted to show that a Brahms could come out of Bohemia—and he succeeded in doing so while maintaining a definitely individual flavour, strongly influenced by natural rhythms.

He wrote three concertos, one each for piano, violin, and cello. The earlier ones are interesting without being quite in the first flight of the composer's output, but the cello concerto of 1895 is perhaps the composer's crowning achievement—warm, mellifluous, romantic.

He wrote chamber music throughout his long creative life. Some of the early works are weak and derivative, but the later string quartets, the " Dumky " trio, and the piano quartet and quintet are expressive and full of unforced invention. Dvořák felt himself somewhat hampered when setting words, nevertheless his *Stabat Mater* and *Te Deum* are both deeply felt choral works and he wrote songs throughout his career, many of them very fine indeed. He wrote ten operas, but only *Rusalka* (1901) has gained a foothold outside Czechoslavakia.

Janáček.

The Moravian composer Leoš Janáček (1858–1928) spent most of his life in Brno as a working musician. His music has recently come to be recognised as some of the most original written in the past hundred years. His operas, in which he closely followed the inflection of the speech of his native land, are his finest works. Over the score of his last opera, *From the House of the Dead*, he wrote the words " In every human being there is a divine spark " and it is this deep love of humanity that permeates all his works. Of his operas *Kátya Kabanová* (1921) and *The Cunning Little Vixen* (1924), the *Makropoulos Affair* (1926), and *From the House of the Dead* (adapted from a Dostoyevsky novel, 1928) are the most important and they have all been produced in Britain in recent years. His original genius is self-evident in all of them.

Among his orchestral works *Taras Bulba* and *Sinfonietta* should be noted, and his two string quartets, very difficult to play, should be better known. The song cycle, *Diary of one who has disappeared*, for tenor, contralto, and three female voices with piano, and the Glagolithic Mass contain music of much expressive beauty.

Hungary.

The Hungarian musical outburst came somewhat later than that in other countries. Its great figure is Bela Bartók (1881–1945) who, as well as being a national figure, has proved an influential composer in the whole of 20th-cent. music. His mind was full of folk music, but it was transmuted by his strongly personal style and powerful intellect into something highly original. His music is tense and volatile but this restlessness is sometimes relieved by a kind of other-wordly, ethereal lyricism, as in the lovely slow movements of his quartets.

Bartók was affected as much by the musical innovations of Debussy and Stravinsky (see below) as by East European, notably Magyar, folk music and many of his works are an attempt to meld the two.

The most important part of his output is undoubtedly his string quartets which cover most of his creative life. To this intimate form he confided his personal innermost thoughts and in it conducted his most far-reaching musical experiments, thereby extending its boundaries beyond anything previously known. As with Beethoven's late quartets many of Bartók's rely on organic or cyclic development while remaining just within the laws of classical form. As Mosco Carner puts it, "For profundity of thought, imaginative power, logic of structure, diversity of formal details, and enlargement of the technical scope, they stand unrivalled in the field of modern chamber music."

The most important of his orchestral works are the three piano concertos, of which the first two are harsh and uncompromising, and fiendishly difficult to play, while the third, written in 1945, is mellower and more diatonic. The second violin concerto (1937–8) shows the various elements of Bartók's style in full flower, by turns exhuberant, passionate, and brilliant. The *Music for Strings, Percussion and Celesta* (1937) is remarkable for its strange sonorities and its fascinating texture. The *Concerto for Orchestra* (1944) is more immediately appealing and again shows the composer in complete command of a large canvas. Of the piano works *Mikrokosmos* (1935) and the sonata for two pianos and percussion (1937) are especially to be noted.

His chief stage pieces are *The Miraculous Mandarin* (1919), a harsh, cruel ballet which drew appropriately dramatic music from the composer, and the opera *Duke Bluebeard's Castle* (1911), a luscious, original score that makes one regret that he wrote no more operas later in his career.

Kodály (1882–1967) was from early years closely associated with Bartók and with him collected Hungarian folk melodies using many of them in his music. He worked in many forms and the more important of his works are the Peacock Variations for orchestra, the choral *Psalmus Hungaricus* and *Te Deum*, The *Dances of Galánta*, and the opera *Háry János*, and the sonatas for cello and for unaccompanied cello.

Sibelius, Nielsen and Grieg.

Among Scandinavian composers the Finn Jean Sibelius (1865–1957) and the Dane Carl Nielsen (1865–1931) are outstanding. Sibelius is a lone northern figure ploughing his own furrow, oblivious or, at any rate, ignoring the unusual developments that were taking place in Central Europe, yet his seven symphonies are strong as granite, honest, rugged works that will undoubtedly stand the test of time. They are not by any means all similar in mood, or even form. The first is very much influenced by Tchaikovsky and Borodin, the second and third show a more personal style developing, the fourth is terse and tragic, the fifth lyrical, bright, and lucid; the sixth is perhaps most typically Sibelian in its evocation of primeval nature, and the seventh—in one continuous movement—is a more purely abstract piece, notable for its structural logic and the grandness of its themes. The violin concerto is the most easily understood of the composer's main works and has a grateful part for the soloist.

The tone poems *The Swan of Tuonela*, *Pohjola's Daughter*, *En Saga*, *Night Ride and Sunrise*, *The Bard*, and *Tapiola* uncannily evoke the icy words of the legends of the far north, and the primeval forces of nature. Sibelius's one string quartet *Voces Intimae* and many of his songs are worth hearing too. The quality of this enigmatic composer's music has recently been the subject of much argument, but his musical personality is probably strong enough to survive the quirks of fashion.

Carl Nielsen (1865–1931) is another individualist. His six symphonies, like Sibelius's seven, are the most important part of his output, but whereas Sibelius was dealing with a huge, uninhabited northern landscape, Nielsen is more friendly and serene in his music, which is seldom forbidding, always inventive, throwing a new light, through unusual ideas about harmony, structure and tonality, on traditional forms. He also wrote highly individual concertos for the flute and clarinet, four string quartets and two operas—the dramatic, rather Brahmsian *Saul and David* (1902) and a delightful comedy, *Maskarade* (1906), full of lyrical music.

The Norwegian composer Edvard Grieg (1843–1907) was essentially a miniaturist whose range of feeling was not wide but whose music is always gentle and appealing. His most notable works are the romantic piano concerto, the atmospheric incidental music to Ibsen's play *Peer Gynt*, the charming Lyric Suite, and the small piano pieces. Not an important composer, then, but always an attractive one.

Elgar and the English Revival.

After the death of Purcell there is hardly a name in English music worth speaking of until the 19th cent. when Hubert Parry (1848–1918) and Charles Villiers Stanford (1852–1924), actually an Irishman, led a revival. Their music is seldom heard today, but their pioneer work paved the way for Edward Elgar (1857–1934). Although all were influenced by Brahms they nevertheless managed to establish a new English tradition that has been carried on in our own day. Elgar's symphonies are laid out on a grand, leisurely scale and they are both eloquent and exhilarating. His violin concerto has an elegiac slow movement as has the glorious cello concerto and both contain many fine opportunities for the soloist. The cello concerto is as appealing a work as any by Elgar expressing his innermost thoughts. His *Enigma* variations are a series of portraits in sound of his friends, but there is another overall theme to go with them that has never been identified. This has not prevented the work from becoming Elgar's most popular, not surprisingly when one considers its charm and melodiousness. Three other orchestral pieces that should not be neglected are his symphonic study *Falstaff*, a many-sided musical picture of the Fat Knight, and the overtures *Cockaigne*, a happy evocation of London, and *In the South*, inspired by a visit to Italy. His three late chamber works, written when he was 61, are reticent, economic pieces that remove any misconception of Elgar as a bombastic composer. His songs are mostly feeble, but the oratorios, notably *The Dream of Gerontius*, show the composer's ability to control a large canvas. The composer himself wrote over the score of *Gerontius*, "This is the best of me"—a verdict with which we can readily agree.

The French Impressionists.

César Franck (1822–90) was the main figure in mid-19th-cent. musical France and his influence spread even wider than his music of which only the D minor Symphony, the Symphonic Variations for piano and orchestra, the piano quintet, and the violin sonata are likely to be encountered today. The leading French opera composers of that time were Massenet (1842–1912) and Gounod (1818–93).

Concurrently with similar movements in French painting and poetry came the French Impressionist composers at the end of the 19th cent. Their leader—and one of the great seminal forces of modern music—was Claude Debussy (1862–1918). His aim was to capture a mood or sensation and he did that by more or less inventing a fresh system of harmony using a whole-tone scale, unusual chords, and creating in the orchestra new, highly personal textures—there is no mistaking the Debussy idiom once you have heard at least one piece by him. His impressionistic style did not lead him, however, to abandon form as some have suggested, and his main works are just as closely organised as those by classical German composers. His music is sensuous and poetic yet nearly always formally satisfying as well.

His reputation, at least with the general musical public, rests largely on his orchestral music, a few piano pieces and his only opera *Pelléas et Mélisande*. *La Mer* is a scintillating evocation of the sea in all its moods; *Nocturnes*, *Images*, and *Prélude à l'Après midi d'un Faune* exactly suggest different places, times, moods—the " Iberia " and " Gigues " sections of *Images*, calling to mind respectively the spirit of Spain and the flickering light of a rainy English night. *Pelléas*, based on a Symbolist drama by Maeterlinck, tells a story of love, jealousy, and murder in predominantly restrained yet emotionally loaded terms. It is an elusive original work that has no predecessor or successor. Intensely atmospheric, rivetingly beautiful, it weaves an irresistible spell over the listener.

Debussy's chamber music is unjustly neglected. His string quartet (1893) was one of the first works in which he displayed his new and strange world of sound, and the three late sonatas, one for violin, one for cello, and the third for flute, viola, and harp are elliptical, compressed pieces which seem to be questing disjointedly into new regions of sound. His songs too, are worthy of investigation, and his piano music, especially the twenty-four Preludes and some of the shorter pieces, contain some of his most imaginative and original ideas and thoughts.

Gabriel Fauré (1845–1924) is a difficult figure to place. He lived through all kinds of musical revolutions yet they seemed to affect the character of his work very little. He has never been, and is never likely to be, a widely known or popular composer, yet his music has a reticence and delicacy that is very appealing. Despite his dreamy, retiring art he was not a recluse, but a very sociable man.

He was content with forms as he found them, but he imbued them with a very personal, human style. Perhaps his art is best heard in his songs. They are not overtly passionate or dramatic but the long, sinuous melodies and subtle harmonies are exquisitely wrought. Of the song-cycles, *La Bonne Chanson*, *Cinq Mélodies* (Verlaine), *Le Chanson d'Eve*, and *L'Horizon Chimérique* are best known. The last written in 1922, when the composer was seventy-seven, is a beautiful setting of words by a soldier killed in the first World War. There are also many remarkable single songs, many of them settings of poems by Verlaine.

He wrote few orchestral pieces, but the *Ballade* for piano and orchestra and the *Pavane* are among his most typical and delicate compositions, and his outstanding piano music, modelled on Chopin's, includes Nocturnes, Impromptus, and Barcaroles. His chamber music covers more than half a century from the violin sonata of 1876 to the string quartet written the year he died. In that period he composed two piano quartets, two piano quintets, another violin sonata and two cello sonatas, the later works failing to show quite the unforced lyrical grace of the earlier ones. Perhaps Fauré is best approached with the first piano quartet, a charming, easily assimilated work, and the beautiful choral *Requiem*.

Saint-Saëns (1835–1921), an accomplished, cultivated musician, has had a " bad press " but his craftsmanship, as displayed in his symphonies, concertos, and *Samson et Dalila* (one among his 12 operas) is not to be despised.

Henri Duparc (1844–1933), despite a very long life, is known today only for a group of songs he wrote before he was forty. They are among the most emotionally direct yet tasteful melodies ever written. Paul Dukas (1865–1935) is another

figure off the beaten track, as it were. He, too, is known only for a handful of compositions. He was strongly influenced by Vincent d'Indy (1851–1931) and the school who strongly opposed Debussy's new ideas, yet he could not help but come under Debussy's spell. Dukas's one great work is his opera *Ariane et Barbe-Bleue*, the text adapted from a Maeterlinck play written with the composer in mind.

Maurice Ravel (1875–1937), a pupil of Fauré, followed in Debussy's footsteps, although his later pieces were more ascetic. Indeed, he was one of the most fastidious of composers, always seeking, and often finding, artistic perfection. The works he wrote before 1918 are definitely of the Impressionist School and it would be difficult to imagine more beautiful sounds than are to be found in the ballet *Daphnis et Chloé*, in the song-cycle *Shéhérazade*, and the piano fantasy *Gaspard de la Nuit*. His first style was summed up in the A minor piano trio (1915). In his later music Ravel was struggling, not always successfully, to keep up with new developments such as jazz and atonality. The piano concerto, for instance, shows very strongly the influence of jazz.

Outstanding orchestral works of his, other than *Daphnis* are *Rapsodie espagnole* (1907), *La Valse* (1920), a sumptuous evocation of the Vienna waltz, and the ever-popular *Boléro*. Two chamber works, besides the trio, are masterpieces—the string quartet (1902–3) and the Introduction and Allegro for Harp, String Quartet, Flute, and Clarinet. This Septet composed in 1906, ravishes the senses with magical sound.

Ravel's piano pieces are perhaps his most notable contribution to music, combining an extraordinary feeling for the instrument's technical possibilities with the sensibility of a Chopin, and in this field *Jeux d'eau*, *Miroirs*, and *Ma Mère l'Oye*, all written just after the turn of the century, come very close to the perfection of *Gaspard de la Nuit*. His songs show his unusual appreciation of the need to fuse poetic and musical values, and he set exotic poems for preference. The song-cycle *Histoires naturelles* (1906) is an acutely observed setting of five poems about birds and animals; *Cinq Mélodies populaires Grecques* (1907) are charming settings of Greek folk songs; *Trois Poèmes de Mallarmé* (1913), *Chansons Mendècasses* (1926), are suitably exotic settings of three poems by an 18th-cent. Creole poet called Parny. Finally in 1932 came *Don Quichotte à Dulcinée*, three poems by Paul Morand, Ravel's last composition.

Ravel wrote two operas—the slight but moderately amusing *L'Heure espagnole* (1907), nicely orchestrated in a faintly and appropriately Spanish style and *L'Enfant et les Sortilèges* (1925) to a story by Colette, a delicious fantasy about a naughty child who gets his due punishment for tormenting animals and destroying furniture.

Spain.

Felipe Pedrell (1841–1922) has been aptly described as the midwife of Spanish nationalist music. As a musicologist and teacher he strongly influenced the two main composers of the school, Manuel Falla (1876–1946) and Enrique Granados (1867–1916). Falla's output was not large and most of it was written about the time of the first World War. He had spent the years before the war in Paris and there he naturally came under the influence of Debussy. Debussy wrote Spanish music without ever having been to Spain but so true was it that even to Falla, born and bred in Andalusia, it had new things to say. He was able to take something from Debussy and blend it with his own highly individual style, evoking in his music all the passion and gaiety of his native land. Perhaps his most typical works are the two ballets *Love the Magician* (1915) full of Spanish atmosphere, and *The Three-Cornered Hat* (1919). The opera *La Vida Breve* (1905), despite its weak libretto, has much appeal, especially when the leading rôle is sung by such a vibrant artist as Victoria de los Angeles. The Seven Popular Spanish Songs (1914) conjure up the vivacity and smouldering passion at the heart of the country's character, as does *Nights in the Garden of Spain* (1916), an evocative piece for piano and orchestra. His later works, especially the harpsichord concerto of 1926, show Falla tending towards a less ebullient, more neo-classical style. His second opera *Master Peter's Puppet Show* (1923) is a miniaturist work, refined and intense. His third opera *Atlantida*, left unfinished at his death, was completed by his pupil Ernesto Halffter and first staged in 1962. It is a long work, more a dramatic cantata than an opera, and as such a rather unwieldy epic.

Granados, who was drowned when his ship was torpedoed by the Germans in 1916, was perhaps a more restrictedly Spanish composer than Falla, but his music is unfailingly attractive, and surely others of his seven operas, besides *Goyescas* (which is heard occasionally), deserve to be rescued from oblivion. *Goyescas* itself is especially famous for the second interlude and opening of Act III—*La Maja y el Ruiseñor* (The lover and the nightingale), a haunting, sinuous melody for soprano, sometimes heard in its original form as a piano solo. He wrote a set of *Tonadillas*. A tonadilla is a type of Spanish song popular in the 18th cent., and Granados's set ably and enchantingly recaptures a lost age of grace and character. His exciting Spanish Dances are heard in both their piano and orchestral form.

The chief claim to fame of Albéniz (1860–1909) is *Ibéria*, masterly descriptive pieces for piano. Turina (1882–1949), not altogether successfully, attempted a more cosmopolitan style, but his most often heard music, especially that for guitar, is typically Spanish.

The Late German Romantics.

While composers such as Debussy, Sibelius, Stravinsky, and Schoenberg (see below for the latter pair) were striking out along new paths, Richard Strauss (1864–1949) continued in the trend of 19th-cent. German composers; he was the tradition's last great figure. At least two of his operas—*Salome* and *Elektra*—were considered shocking at the time, but today we can hear that they are essentially big-scale, romantic works—natural successors to Wagner's—however startling the harmonies may once have seemed.

If Strauss did not achieve the granite intellectual greatness of Beethoven or Wagner, there is no denying his melodic genius and powers of fertile invention which overlaid the streak of vulgarity and inflation in his musical make-up. His first outstanding achievement was in the field of the symphonic poem, where he carried the work of composers such as Liszt and Berlioz to its logical conclusion. Starting with *Don Juan* in 1888 and ending with *Sinfonia Domestica* in 1903 he wrote a series of kaleidoscopic works, full of enormous vitality, endless melody, and fascinating orchestration. The most easily assimilated—and the most popular—are *Don Juan* and *Till Eulenspiegel* but some of the longer works, notably *Also Sprach Zarathustra* (based on Nietzsche's prose poem) and *Don Quixote* (based, of course, on Cervantes's great work) will reward the persistent, inquiring mind with long hours of enthralled listening. Other works sound somewhat dated in their bombastic over-confidence, though Strauss's skill in composition seldom flagged at this stage of his long creative career. The symphonic poems all tell something of a story usually based on a literary source, but it is not essential to the enjoyment of the music to know what this is, although it may be helpful.

Strauss's reputation is even more solidly based on his fifteen operas, the earliest of which *Guntram* was first performed in 1894, the last, *Capriccio*, in 1942. During these years the essentials of Strauss's style changed little, though it became very much more refined as the years passed. His first operatic period ended with the violent, sensuous tragedies *Salome* (1905) and *Elektra* (1909), the latter being his first collaboration with his chief librettist Hugo von Hofmannsthal. Then came their unique *Der Rosenkavalier* (1911), which

filters the charm and the decadence of 18th-cent. Vienna through early 20th-cent. eyes. This was followed by *Ariadne auf Naxos* (1912). Originally intended to be given after Molière's *Le Bourgeois Gentilhomme*, it was later presented (1916) without the play but with a preceding scene, written by von Hofmannsthal. *Die Frau ohne Schatten* is the most grandiose result of the Strauss-Hofmannsthal partnership. It is a complex psychological allegory, but Strauss's contribution is not on as consistently lofty a level as is his librettist's. *Intermezzo* (1924), which has a libretto by Strauss himself, is a largely autobiographical domestic comedy, which has lately gained in reputation as a compact, charming piece. With *Die Aegyptische Helena* (1928), an opera on a mythical theme, and *Arabella* (1933), another charming Viennese comedy, the Strauss-Hofmannsthal collaboration ended on account of the librettist's death. Strauss then wrote *Die Schweigsame Frau* (1935) to a libretto by Stefan Zweig, based on a play by Ben Jonson, and *Friedenstag* (1938), *Daphne* (1938)—a beautiful opera—and *Die Liebe der Danae* (written 1938–40) with Josef Gregor as librettist. His swan-song was *Capriccio*, a dramatisation of the old argument about the relative importance of words and music in opera. The libretto is by the conductor Clemens Krauss and the opera, a serene, melodious work, was a fit end to a great operatic career.

However, Strauss went on composing till nearly the end of his life, adding a group of late orchestral pieces to his already large catalogue of works. The *Metamorphoses* for 23 solo string instruments, is probably the best of these. During his long creative career he wrote numerous songs, many of them, such as *Morgen*, *Wiegenlied* and *Ruhe, meine Seele* of surpassing beauty.

Other notable figures in German music at this time were Max Reger (1873–1916), a somewhat ponderous but highly accomplished composer who, in a quarter of a century of creative life, wrote more than 150 works, of which his sets of variations, his piano concerto, and chamber music are probably the most impressive. Hans Pfitzner (1869–1949), another German traditionalist, is chiefly remembered today for his opera *Palestrina*, about events, now known to be spurious, in the life of the 16th-cent. Italian composer.

Mahler.

Gustav Mahler (1860–1911), the Austrian Jewish composer, is one of the most important figures in 20th-cent. music. In a sense he bridges the gulf between the late Romantics, who were tending more and more towards chromaticism and away from established key relationships, and the atonalists, who abandoned key signatures entirely. His detractors maintain that his inflation of allegedly banal Viennese beer-house music to unheard-of lengths rules him out of court as a serious writer. His admirers would claim that his music encompasses the whole of life in enormous, valid structures. The truth, if truth there be, perhaps lies somewhere in between: that if his material does not always justify the length of his symphonies, if there are occasional imperfections and *longueurs*, these shortcomings are worth putting up with for the sake of the depth of utterance, the humanity and the poetry of the great pages. He admitted himself that "I cannot do without trivialities," but it is out of these impurities that he forged his titanic victories.

His music is undoubtedly best approached through his songs, where the words force him to discipline his wide-ranging vision. *Lieder eines fahrenden Gesellen* (1884), to his own words, *Kindertotenlieder* (1901–4), to poems by Rückert, and some individual songs perfectly relate words to music, and are all of a poignant loveliness. Similarly *Das Lied von der Erde* (1908), especially the last of the six songs, is a touching farewell to the world, nobly expressed.

The ten symphonies, however, are Mahler's most impressive legacy to posterity. They are almost impossible to characterise briefly so vast are they in terms of both length and variety. The first, fourth and ninth are probably the easiest to grasp but the fifth, sixth and seventh, despite flaws, contain some of his most awe-inspiring conceptions. The second and third, both of which use soloists and chorus, are revolutionary in layout and concept; they both try, inevitably without complete success, to carry out the composer's dictum, " a symphony should be like the world—it must contain everything." The eighth is even more gargantuan, but as in all Mahler's work size does not mean loss of clarity or an overloading of the structure. Part one—a mighty choral invocation—is a visionary setting of the mediaeval hymn *Veni Creator Spiritus*. Part two, which incorporates adagio, scherzo, and finale in one, is a setting of the final scene of Goethe's *Faust*. Until recently all of Mahler's unfinished tenth symphony that was ever performed was the Adagio, but the musicologist and Mahler scholar, Deryck Cooke, has recently completed the symphony to critical and popular acclaim and thus added a noble, and also optimistic epilogue to the Mahler opus. The debate over the quality of Mahler's music is likely to continue: one fact, however, that cannot be gain-said is his popularity with an ever-increasing audience, many of them young people. There must be something in his uncertainty and intense self-inquiry that accords with the mood of today.

Schoenberg and the Second Viennese School.

Arnold Schoenberg (1874–1951) revolutionised Western music by his twelve-note theory—a system which uses all the notes of the chromatic scale " and denies the supremacy of a tonal centre," as Schoenberg himself puts it. This serial technique of composition, as it is commonly called, naturally sounds strange to an ear acclimatised to music written, as it were, with a home base, but Schoenberg and his disciples Berg and Webern showed that the system could produce works that were something more than mere intellectual exercises. None of the more recent advances in music would have been possible, even thinkable, without Schoenberg's pioneer work.

Schoenberg always regarded himself as much as a composer as a theorist or teacher, and his works are supposed to appeal as much to the emotions as to the intellect, although to be understood they do, of course, require the listener's concentrated attention. To appreciate how his ideas developed it is necessary to hear first his pre-atonal music, such as the *Gurrelieder* (1900–1) and *Verklärte Nacht* (1899), in which he carried Wagnerian chromaticism to extreme lengths. The *Gurrelieder*, in particular, is a luxuriant, overblown work that shows the Wagnerian idiom in an advanced stage of decay, in spite of many beautiful pages of music. In his succeeding works the feeling of tonality began to disappear until in the Three Piano Pieces (opus 11), of 1909, he finally rejected tonality, although the new 12-note scheme is not yet evident; traces of the old order can still be heard. The succeeding works were mostly short, highly compressed, and very expressive. Schoenberg was reaching out for a new system, which would " justify the dissonant character of these harmonies and determine their successions." By 1923 he had formulated his 12-note system and the Five Piano Pieces (opus 23), and the Serenade (opus 24) of that year, can thus be considered the first works that used a note-row as the fundamental basis of their composition. Between 1910 and 1915, however, the Russian composer Alexander Scriabin (1872–1915) had attempted to define a new method of composition of his own employing the "mystic chord" of ascending fourths, but his scheme proved comparatively abortive when compared with Schoenberg's. Josef Hauer (1883–1959) also developed a 12-note system which he propounded in 1919 and he always considered himself, rather than Schoenberg, as the true founder of the system. He later worked out a system of tropes (*i.e.*, half-series of six notes).

To return to Schoenberg, in later works he shows much more freedom and assurance in the use of his system. The wind quintet (1924), the variations for orchestra, opus 31 (1927–8), the third (1926), and fourth (1936) string quartets, and the

string trio (1946) are modern classics of their kind: they require concentrated listening and a degree of understanding of the unfamiliar style of composition. The set of songs with piano *Das Buch der hängenden Gärten* (opus 15), written in 1908, *Pierrot Lunaire*, opus 21 (1912) and the Four Songs, opus 22 (1913–14) provide a kind of bridge between tonality and atonality that the adventurous mind should cross. The monodrama *Erwartung* (1909) is another fascinating work, but perhaps the unfinished *Moses and Aaron* (1932) is Schoenberg's masterpiece as its production at Covent Garden in 1965 showed. Here, for certain, the composer matched his obvious intellectual capacities with an evident emotional content and managed to combine *Sprechgesang* (speech-song) and singing with a real degree of success.

It is only in recent years that Schoenberg's music has had a real chance to make its mark through the essential prerequisite of frequent performance. If his idiom now seems approachable, and a reasonably natural outcome of late 19th-cent. developments, it is perhaps because other, more recent composers have extended the boundaries of sound much further.

Schoenberg's two most respected disciples were Anton Webern (1883–1945) and Alban Berg (1885–1935). Webern's output is small, reaching only to opus 31, and many of his works are very brief. They are exquisitely precise, and delicate almost to a fault. He was trying to distil the essence of each note and in so doing carried the 12-note system to its most extreme and cerebral limit. His music has often been described as pointillist in the sense that one note is entirely separated from the next, there being little discernible melody. Beyond Webern's music, there is indeed the sound of nothingness, and he was rightly described during his lifetime as the " composer of the *pianissimo espressivo*". In his later works, Webern tended towards a strict, and often ingenious use of form and the Variations for Orchestra of 1940 are a good example of this and of his delicacy of orchestration. Webern's influence has perhaps been greater than the impact of his own music, even though he has had no direct successor.

Berg's music is much more accessible. Like Webern his total output was not large but nearly all his works are substantial additions to the repertory. He is also the directest link between Mahler and the second Viennese School, as Mahler's music influenced him strongly. He studied with Schoenberg from 1904 to 1910. His music is more intense, more lyrical, and less attenuated in sound than Schoenberg's or Webern's. His humanity and abiding compassion can be heard most strongly in his finest opera *Wozzeck* (1925) and his violin concerto (1935), written as an elegy on the death of Manon Gropius, a beautiful 18-year-old girl. Both works are very carefully designed yet formal considerations are never allowed to submerge feeling, and the note-row is fully integrated into the structure.

Both *Wozzeck* and the unfinished but rewarding *Lulu* are concerned with society's outcasts who are treated with great tenderness in both operas. The later work is entirely dodecaphonic, all the opera's episodes being based on a theme associated with Lulu. Between these operas Berg wrote the highly complex Chamber Concerto for piano, violin, and thirteen wind instruments (1925) and the expressive Lyric Suite (1926). Among his early works the Seven Early Songs (1908–9) and the concert aria *Der Wein* (1929) are notable.

Stravinsky.

Igor Stravinsky (b. 1882) is another vital figure in 20th-cent. music. If his influence has been in quite another and perhaps less drastic direction than Schoenberg's it is hardly less important. Indeed, future musical historians may consider his achievement the more significant. He has been compared with the painter Picasso in his almost hectic desire to keep up with the times, yet, although he has written in a number of very different styles during the past fifty years, every work of his is stamped with his own definitive musical personality. His most revolutionary and seminal work is undoubtedly *The Rite of Spring* (written for the ballet impresario Diaghilev), which caused a furore when it first appeared in 1913, and although it no longer shocks, the rhythmical energy, the fierce angular thematic material, and the sheer virtuosity of the orchestration will always have the power to excite new audiences. Before *The Rite* Stravinsky had written two ballets for Diaghilev—*The Firebird* and *Petrushka*—that are no less filled with vitality and new, albeit not so violent, sounds. During the next thirty years Stravinsky wrote a series of ballet works, gradually becoming more austere and refined in composition. *Apollo* (1928) and *Orpheus* (1947) belong among his most attractive scores.

Stravinsky has not confined himself in stage works to the ballet. *The Nightingale* (1914) is a charming, early opera; *The Soldiers Tale* (1918) is a witty combination of narration, mime, and dance; *Les Noces* (1923) is a concise, original choreographic cantata for soloists and chorus; *Oedipus Rex* (1927) is a dignified version of the Sophocles play, which can be staged or given on the concert platform; either way it is a moving experience. *Perséphone* (1934), a melodrama for reciter, tenor, chorus, and orchestra is an appealing, lucid score. Since the war his most important stage work by far has been *The Rake's Progress* (1951), with a libretto by W. H. Auden and Chester Kallman. This fascinating opera is deliberately based on 18th-cent. forms and the music itself is neo-classical, always attractive, sometimes haunting.

Stravinsky has been no laggard in writing for the concert-platform either. The finest of these works are probably the fervent impressive choral *Symphony of Psalms* (1930), the Violin Concerto (1931) and the aggressive compact Symphony in three movements (1945). Of his chamber music the Octet (1923), a Duo Concertant (1932), and Septet (1952) are probably the most important, but no piece, even the driest and most pedantic, is without redeeming features.

Stravinsky is often thought of as an aloof, detached figure. He has been castigated for his lack of lyrical warmth. But in spite of his own professed desire to drain his music of specific emotion, craftsmanship and originality, often with a strange other-worldly beauty added, are unmistakeably there throughout his many scores. Quirky and annoying he may be, dull never.

Busoni and Puccini.

Italian music in the early part of the century was dominated by two very different composers—Ferruccio Busoni (1866–1924) and Giacomo Puccini (1858–1924). Busoni is a difficult figure to place. His austere, intellectual power is never called in question, but he seldom, if ever, succeeded in translating his technical prowess into altogether successful compositions. We can admire the strength, honesty, and often beauty of such works as his huge piano concerto (1903–4), *Fantasia Contrappuntisca* (1912)—for piano solo—and his unfinished opera *Doktor Faust* without ever capitulating to them entirely. None the less, it has to be admitted that those who have studied his music closely have always fallen completely under his spell. In style his music is anti-Romantic and often neo-Classical yet he was an ardent admirer of Liszt and more especially of Liszt's realisation of the possibilities of the pianoforte. Busoni, himself a great pianist, carried on where Liszt had left off in his own piano music, in which form and expression often find their perfect balance. *Doktor Faust* is undoubtedly his most important opera but *Die Brautwahl* (1908–10) and *Turandot* (1917) have many points of interest too.

Puccini's *Turandot*—his last opera—is a much grander version of the same Gozzi fable and the culmination of this great opera composer's work. His achievement is at an almost directly opposite pole to Busoni's. Not for him the severity or intellectuality of his contemporary. He sought and found an almost ideal fusion of straight-forward lyricism and dramatic truth. His music unerringly follows the pathos and passion of the stories he sets and all his characters " live " as human beings. That, and his abundant flow of easy, soaring melody, are the reasons for his immense popular success, unequalled by any other 20th-cent. composer. Whether it is the pathetic Mimi (*La Bohème*—1896) and Cio-Cio-San, (*Madama Butterfly*—1904), the evil Scarpia, (*Tosca* —1900), the cunning Schicchi (*Gianni Schicchi*— 1918), the ardent Rudolfo (*La Bohème*) and Cavaradossi (*Tosca*), or the ice-cold Turandot (*Turandot*—1926), Puccini's musical characterisation is unfailing. And he backs his *verismo* vocal writing with an orchestral tissue that faithfully reflects the milieu of each opera, for instance, Japanese for *Butterfly*, Chinese for *Turandot*, while never losing his particular brand of Italian warmth. His orchestration is always subtle and luminous.

Other Italian composers who wrote operas in the *verismo* style of Puccini were Leoncavallo (1858– 1919), Mascagni (1863–1945), and Giordano (1867– 1948).

Prokofiev, Shostakovich, and Rachmaninov.

Sergey Prokofiev (1891–1953) spent part of his creative life in his native Russia, part of it (1918– 34) abroad, mostly in Paris. His early music, apart from the popular Classical Symphony (1916– 17) tended to be acid and harsh, but on his return to Russia his style, though still frequently satirical, became warmer, more Romantic. The third piano concerto (1917) and the second symphony (1924) are good examples of the former period, the ballets *Romeo and Juliet* (1935) and *Cinderella* (1941–44) and the fifth (1944) and sixth (1949) symphonies of the latter. His music gives the impression of immense rhythmical energy, as in the outer movements of several of his nine piano sonatas, but this fierce drive is often leavened by the soft, wistful lights of his slow movements. His second string quartet (1941), perhaps, presents all the elements of his music in the kindest light.

His strong leaning towards fantasy and mordant parody is felt in his earlier operas *The Love of the Three Oranges* (1921) and *The Fiery Angel* (1922–25). *War and Peace* (1941–42) was written in the face of strong pressure from the Soviet authorities.

Dmitri Shostakovich (b. 1906) has also suffered from attacks of " formalism ". He had to conform to Stalin's requirements for writing music, but he has survived and continues to produce music of universal appeal, as, for example, his most recent string quartets. Like Prokofiev, his music falls into two very distinct styles: one humorous and spiky, the other intense, very personal and often large-scale in its implications. Not all his symphonies reach the expressive depths of numbers one, five, six, and eight, but they all have rewarding passages and his recent violin and cello concertos are of high quality. He has so far written eleven string quartets, a piano quintet (an attractive piece) and two operas: the satirical *The Nose* (1930) and *Katerina Ismailova* (1934, revised 1959), originally known as " Lady Macbeth of Mstensk." The first performance (outside Russia) of his fourteenth symphony was to be heard at the Aldeburgh festival in 1970.

Although Sergey Rachmaninov (1873–1943) was born in Russia, he left his home country in 1918, disliking the Soviet régime, and lived mostly in Switzerland and the United States. His music is chiefly notable for its Romanticism, nostalgic melody, nervous energy and, in the piano works, its opportunities for displays of virtuosity. The first three piano concertos, the third symphony, the piano preludes, and the Rhapsody on a theme of Paganini, are his most typical and attractive works, and many of his songs are touching and beautiful. He wrote three operas.

Modern French Music.

French music after Debussy and Ravel was dominated by the slighter composers known as *Les Six*, the most important of whom were Arthur

Honegger (1892–1955, Swiss born), Darius Milhaud (b. 1892) and Francis Poulenc (1899–1963). Each has contributed music of some wit and charm to the repertory. They were influenced by Erik Satie (1866–1925), an eccentric but interesting figure, who wrote works with odd titles such as *Three Pear-Shaped Pieces*. His music is entirely unsentimental, often ironic.

Much more revolutionary has been the work of Olivier Messiaen (b. 1908), who has turned to Indian music and, above all, to bird-song for inspiration. He first came to notice as a composer of organ music. Then his *Quatuor pour la fin de temps*, written in captivity between 1940 and 1942, his long piano pieces, based on bird-song (often literally) and his gigantic *Turangalila* symphony show him experimenting with complex rhythms, strange sonorities (using unusual instruments such as the Ondes Martenot in the symphony), and considerably widening music's horizons. Edgar Varèse (1885–1965) cultivated an even broader spectrum of sound, employing electronic instruments to complement and contrast with traditional ones. Pierre Boulez (b. 1925), a pupil of Messiaen, bases his extremely complex works on mathematical relationships. His music, other than that for the piano, mostly calls for a variety of percussion instruments often combined with the soprano voice in evocations of French poetry (Mallarmé in particular). The resulting timbre and sonorities are intriguing even when the intellectual basis of the music is but dimly perceived.

Modern German Music.

Kurt Weill (1900–50) is chiefly known for his socio-politically pointed operas, such as *Die Dreigroschenoper* (1929), *Mahagonny* (1929), *Der Jasager* (1930), and *Happy End* (1929), all effective works on the stage, and for his particular brand of brittle, yet fundamentally romantic music. His influence on later composers has been considerable.

Carl Orff (b. 1895) has written chiefly for the stage. His music is rhythmically insistent, avoids counterpoint, and is deliberately, even self-consciously straightforward. Most frequently heard is his *Carmina Burana*, lively, rumbustious choral settings of mediæval poems.

Paul Hindemith (1895–1964) in his later years wrote in a strictly tonal, often neo-classical idiom, after being one of the most advanced intellectuals of his time. As well as many chamber and orchestral works, he wrote three formidable operas: *Die Harmonie der Welt, Cardillac* and *Mathis der Maler*.

Karlheinz Stockhausen (b. 1928), a pupil of Messiaen, is another extreme innovator. He more than anyone puts electronics to musical use. His scores are a maze of diagrams and instructions, which really need the composer's presence for their true interpretation. It is too early to say whether his music is evidence of a passing vogue or a real step forward in musical ideas.

Hans Werner Henze (b. 1926) has rebelled against the musical climate in Germany, and now lives in Italy, yet his music combines the intellectuality of the modern German schools with the lyricism of Italian music. He has written five symphonies, though none follow the traditional form, and nine operas, among them two impressive large-scale works, *König Hirsch* (1952–55) and *The Bassarids* (1966), to an Auden-Kallman libretto.

American Music.

It was not until the 20th cent. that American music really got under way and an American school came into being. With the possible exception of MacDowell (1861–1908) no earlier composers are remembered or played today. Many composers of the American school have, of course, taken their cue from Europe but the influence of American jazz and folk-song is also recognisable in some of their music. Aaron Copland (b. 1900) is probably the most important figure on the

current scene, and such works as *Appalachian Spring, Billy the Kid*, and his third symphony have gained a certain amount of international recognition and popularity. Samuel Barber (b. 1910) works along traditional lines and his music, like Copland's, is essentially diatonic. He has contributed to all the usual forms (symphony, concerto, sonata), most recently to opera with *Vanessa* (1958) and *Antony and Cleopatra* (1966), which opened the new Metropolitan Opera House in New York's Lincoln Centre. Roy Harris (b. 1898) has written seven symphonies and several concertos, which include folk elements.

Charles Ives (1874–1954) has recently been recognised as the most original American composer. While carrying on a highly successful career in insurance, Ives yet managed to anticipate in his works, all written before 1920, many of the innovations which were later "invented" in Europe. His orchestral music is much influenced by the sounds, such as brass bands, which he heard in his native New England as a boy. His *Three Places in New England* and *The Unanswered Question* have a beautiful, elusive quality about them. In his five symphonies and *Concord* sonata we notice the working of an original mind employing polytonality and polyrhythms in larger and more complex works. An element of improvisation is sometimes introduced, another anticipation of latter-day technique. Ives is unlikely ever to become a popular composer—his music is too complicated and eclectic for that—but his importance as a prophet is surely established.

Modern English School.

The amazing 20th cent. revival of music in England owes much to Ralph Vaughan Williams (1872–1958) and Gustav Holst (1874–1934). Vaughan Williams's music is today suffering a decline in reputation, but the best of his symphonies (one, four, five, and six), his Fantasia on a theme by Tallis, his ballet *Job*, and the best of his choral music have a sturdiness about them that will no doubt weather the whim of passing fashion. His music alternates between the forceful and the contemplative and both moods are expressed in a distinctive musical vocabulary, based on modalism and 16th-cent. polyphony.

Holst was a more enigmatic figure, but his influence has undoubtedly been greater. Only his suite *The Planets* and the choral *The Hymn of Jesus* have established themselves as repertory works, but his bold harmonic experiments and the austerity, even mysticism, of his style as heard in the orchestral pieces *Egdon Heath, Beni Mora*, and the opera *Savitri* are perhaps more typical of this contemplative original composer. His daughter Imogen, a conductor, has done much to promote understanding of her father's music. Contemporaries who deserve much more than a passing reference are John Ireland (1879–1962) and Sir Arnold Bax (1883–1953).

Frederick Delius (1862–1934) was the only important English disciple of the French impressionist school. He lived in France from 1888 onwards. His most important works are the atmospheric tone-poems for orchestra, such as *Brigg Fair*; the vocal and orchestral *A Mass of Life, Sea Drift* and *Appalachia*, and the opera *A Village Romeo and Juliet*.

Of the more recent generation of English composers the most important are undoubtedly Benjamin Britten (b. 1913) Sir Michael Tippett (b. 1905), Alan Rawsthorne (b. 1905), and Sir William Walton (b. 1902). Britten has done more than anyone to establish English music on the forefront of the international stage. Much of his music seems to have an immediate appeal to large audiences and certainly his many stage works have earned him a quite exceptional prestige both at home and abroad. *Peter Grimes* (1945), *Billy Budd* (1951), *Gloriana* (1953), *A Midsummer Night's Dream* (1960) all, in their very different ways, show his consummate mastery of stage technique and the first two are also moving human documents. On a smaller scale he has achieved as much with his chamber operas—*The Rape of Lucretia* (1946), *Albert Herring* (1947), and *The Turn of the Screw* (1954, based on a Henry James novel)—and with the two recent Parables for Church Performance—*Curlew River* (1964) and *The Burning Fiery Furnace* (1966). If he had written nothing else, those dramatic works would have marked him out as a composer of outstanding imaginative gifts.

But there is more—the choral works culminating in the *War Requiem* (1962), his various song cycles written for the tenor Peter Pears, the Serenade for tenor, horn, and string, *Nocturne* for tenor and orchestra, the three Canticles, and the Spring Symphony are further evidence—in very different media—of both his intense emotional commitment and his technical skill. While being strongly influenced by such composers as Schubert, Verdi, Mahler, and Berg, his style is entirely his own: it is a musical personality that manages to combine, as it has been said, " a deep nostalgia for the innocence of childhood, a mercurial sense of humour and a passionate sympathy with the victims of prejudice and misunderstanding."

This last quality is particularly evident also in Tippett's emotional makeup as expressed in his music, especially in one of his earliest successes, the choral work *A Child of Our Time* (1941), which shows both his compassion and his ability to write on a large scale. But Tippett is as much a mystic and searcher as a composer and he is constantly seeking new and different ways of widening his listeners' horizons, as may be heard in the exceedingly complex *Vision of St. Augustine* (1965), which tellingly sets to music the striving to understand the " beyond " of Augustine's words.

Tippett has also sought new means of musical expression as he has shown in his second opera *King Priam* (1962), very spare and pointed in idiom, and in the concerto for orchestra (1962). These works, as well as his piano concerto (1956) and second symphony—a luminous work—and his three string quartets, are very difficult to perform —and to get to know—but the effort to understand the composer's wide-spanning mind is always richly rewarded. However, perhaps a newcomer to his music does better to approach him through the more straightforward earlier works, the concerto for double string orchestra (1939), the Fantasia Concertante on a theme of Corelli (1953) —a lyrically poetic piece—or the song cycles *Boyhood's End* (1943) and *Heart's Assurance* (1957). The quality of his allegorical opera *The Midsummer Marriage* (1952), in spite of its involved libretto (by the composer), is now better appreciated since its revival at Covent Garden. *The Knot Garden*, also concerned with the inner life of the spirit and the external world, was first performed at Covent Garden in 1970. Tippett is an uncompromising individualist, writing without fear or favour, perhaps considerably in advance of his time in thought and achievement.

Rawsthorne's style is admirably direct and honest. Eschewing the latest fashions in music

he has ploughed his own furrow of deeply felt writing. His ideas are argued out with considerable lyrical force, and his astute regard for form does not hide the underlying emotional content of his music nor the touch of wit that pervades some of his more lively movements. Among his most important accomplishments to date are his three string quartets, violin concerto, two piano concertos, and the quintet for piano and wind instruments.

Walton's outstanding contribution was made before the second World War in music that was alternately gay and romantic. The irreverent *Façade* (1923) for speaker and chamber orchestra falls into the former category, the poetic viola concerto (1929) into the second. His first symphony (1934–5) is an arresting, dramatic score, and the oratorio *Belshazzar's Feast* (1931) is a landmark in choral music. Since the war his works have never quite recaptured the same urgency of expression.

Elisabeth Lutyens (b. 1906) is Britain's leading twelve-note composer. For long shunned by the musical establishment, she has now been accepted as an important and seminal figure in the history of 20th-cent. music. Her output has been large and includes numerous works for unusual, small groups of instruments, often combined with a solo voice. Benjamin Frankel (b. 1906), Edmund Rubbra (b. 1901), Sir Arthur Bliss (b. 1891), and Lennox Berkeley (b. 1903) are other composers of note among the senior school of living British composers. Egon Wellesz (b. 1885), Austrian born, settled in this country in 1939. He has written operas, choral works, symphonies, and chamber music, and is still active. There is a thriving junior school of British composers who have already made their mark, among them Alexander Goehr, Richard Rodney Bennett, Malcolm Williamson, and Nicholas Maw, each of whom has written one or more operas.

Where Does the Future Lie?

It is anybody's guess which way music will develop during the next few decades. Are older forms quite outmoded, as some recent innovators suggest, and does the future therefore lie with the electronic music and/or percussive sounds—of Boulez, Stockhausen, Luigi Nono (b. 1924), and their disciples? Or will what has been recognised as musical sound for several generations adapt itself to the new mood abroad? Has atonalism still something to offer or was it a passing phase, already dated and out of fashion? Perhaps the only answer that can be given with certainty is that, as with other centuries, a dozen or so composers' music will survive to delight later generations and that these geniuses will be found among composers who do and say what they must in music without regard to fashion, patronage, or fear of what anyone writes about them. May they be worthy of their rich heritage.

II. GLOSSARY OF MUSICAL TERMS

A. Note of scale, commonly used for tuning instruments.

Absolute Music. Music without any literary descriptive or other kind of reference.

A Capella. Literally " in the church style." Unaccompanied.

Accelerando. Quickening of the pace.

Accidental. The sign which alters a note by a semitone, *i.e.,* ♯ (sharp) raises it; ♭ (flat) lowers it; ♮ restores a note to its original position.

Accompaniment. Instrumental or piano part forming background to a solo voice or instrument that has the melody.

Ad. lib. (L. *ad libitum*). Direction on music that strict time need not be observed.

Adagio. A slow movement or piece.

Aeolian mode. One of the scales in mediæval music, represented by the white keys of the piano from A to A.

Air. A simple tune for voice or instrument.

Alberti bass. Rhythmical accompanying figure made up by splitting a chord. Used extensively in 18th-cent. music and associated with the Italian composer Alberti.

Allegretto. Not quite so fast as *Allegro.*

Allegro. Fast, but not too fast.

Alto. An unusually high type of male voice; also the vocal part sung by women and boys with a low range.

Ambrosian Chant. Plainsong introduced into church music by St. Ambrose, bishop of Milan (d. 397), and differing from Gregorian chant.

Andante. At a walking pace, not so slow as *Adagio* nor as fast as *Allegretto.*

Animato. Lively.

Answer. Second entry in a fugue, usually in the dominant.

Anthem. Composition for use in church during a service by a choir with or without soloists.

Antiphonal. Using groups of instruments or singers placed apart.

Appoggiatura. An ornament consisting of a short note just above or below a note forming part of a chord.

Arabesque. Usually a short piece, highly decorated.

Arco. Direction for string instruments to play with bow.

Aria. Vocal solo, usually in opera or oratorio, often in three sections with the third part being a repeat of the first. An *Arietta* is a shorter, lighter kind of aria.

Arioso. In the style of an aria; halfway between aria and recitative.

Arpeggio. Notes of a chord played in a broken, spread-out manner, as on a harp.

Ars antiqua. The old mediæval music, based on organum and plainsong, before the introduction of *Ars nova* in 14th cent.

Ars nova. Musical style current from 14th cent., more independent than the old style in the part-writing and harmony.

Atonal. Not in any key; hence *Atonality*.

Aubade. Morning song.

Augmentation. The enlargement of a melody by lengthening the musical value of its notes.

Ayre. Old spelling of *air*.

B. Note of scale, represented in Germany by *H*.

Bagatelle. A short, generally light piece of music. Beethoven wrote 26 Bagatelles.

Ballad. Either a narrative song or an 18th-cent. drawing-room song.

Ballade. Instrumental piece in story-telling manner. Chopin wrote 4.

Ballet. Stage entertainment requiring instrumental accompaniment; originated at French court in 16th and 17th cent.

Bar. A metrical division of music; the perpendicular line in musical notation to indicate this.

Barcarolle. A boating-song, in particular one associated with Venetian gondoliers.

Baritone. A male voice, between tenor and bass.

Baroque. A term applied, loosely, to music written in the 17th and 18th cent., roughly corresponding to baroque in architecture.

Bass. The lowest male voice; lowest part of a composition.

Bass Drum. Largest of the drum family, placed upright and struck on the side.

Bassoon. The lowest of the woodwind instruments, uses double reed.

Beat. Music's rhythmic pulse.

Bel canto. Literally " beautiful singing "—in the old Italian style with pure tone and exact phrasing.

Berceuse. Cradle song.

Binary. A piece in two sections is said to be binary in form. The balance is obtained by a second phrase (or section) answering the first.

Bitonality. Use of two keys at once.

Bow. Stick with horsehair stretched across it for playing string instruments.

Brass. Used as a collective noun for all brass or metal instruments.

Breve. Note, rarely used nowadays, with tone value of two semibreves.

Bridge. Wood support over which strings are stretched on a violin, cello, guitar, etc.

Buffo(a). Comic, as in *buffo bass* or *opera buffa*.

C. Note of scale.

Cabaletta. Final, quick section of an aria or duet.

Cadence. A closing phrase of a composition or a passage, coming to rest on tonic (key note).

Cadenza. Solo vocal or instrumental passage, either written or improvised, giving soloist chance to display technical skill to audience.

Calando. Becoming quieter and slower.

Canon. Device in contrapuntal composition whereby a melody is introduced by one voice or instrument then repeated by one or more voices or instruments, either at the same pitch (canon at the unison) or at different intervals (canon at the fifth, for example).

Cantabile. Song-like, therefore flowing and expressive.

Cantata. Vocal work for chorus and/or choir.

Cantilena. Sustained, smooth melodic line.

Cantus firmus. Literally " fixed song." Basic melody from 14th to 17th cent., around which other voices wove contrapuntal parts.

Canzonet. Light songs written in England c. 1600.

Carillon. A set of bells in tower of church, played from a keyboard below.

Carol. Christmas song.

Castrato. Artificially-created male soprano and alto, fashionable in 17th and 18th cent. (The castration of vocally gifted boys prevailed in Italy until the 19th cent.)

Catch. A part-song like a round, in vogue in England from 16th to 19th cent.

Cavatina. An operatic song in one section, or a slow song-like instrumental movement.

Celesta. Keyboard instrument with metal bars struck by hammers.

Cello. Four-stringed instrument, played with bow, with a bass range. Comes between viola and double bass in string family.

Cembalo. Originally the Italian name for the dulcimer, but sometimes applied to the harpsichord.

Chaconne. Vocal or instrumental piece with unvaried bass.

Chamber Music. Music originally intended to be played in a room for three or more players.

Chanson. Type of part-song current in France from 14th to 16th cent.

Chant. Singing of psalms, masses, etc., in plainsong to Latin words in church.

Choir. Body of singers, used either in church or at concerts.

Chorales. German hymn tunes, often made use of by Bach.

Chord. Any combination of notes heard together. *See also* Triad.

Chording. Spacing of intervals in a chord.

Chorus. Substantial body of singers, usually singing in four parts.

Chromatic. Using a scale of nothing but semitones.

Clarinet. Woodwind instrument with single reed in use since mid-18th cent.

Clavichord. Keyboard instrument having strings struck by metal tangents, much in use during 17th and 18th cent. as solo instrument.

Clavier. Used in German (*Klavier*) for piano, in England for any stringed keyboard instrument.

Clef. Sign in stave that fixes place of each note.

Coda. Closing section of movement in Sonata form.

Coloratura. Term to denote florid singing.

Common chord. See Triad.

Common Time. Four crotchets to the bar, 4/4 time.

Compass. Range of notes covered by voice or instruments.

Composition. Piece of music, originated by a composer's own imagination; act of writing such a piece.

Compound time. Any musical metric not in simple time.

Con Brio. With dash.

Concert. Public performance of any music.

Concertato. Writing for several solo instruments to be played together.

Concerto. Work for one or more solo instruments and orchestra.

Concerto grosso. Orchestral work common in 17th and 18th cent. with prominent parts for small groups of instruments.

Concord. Opposite of discord, *i.e.*, notes that when sounded together satisfy the ear. (Conventional term in that its application varies according to the age in which one lives.)

Conduct. To direct a concert with a baton.

Consecutive. Progression of harmonic intervals of like kind.

Consonance. Like Concord.

Continuo. Bass line, used in 17th- and 18th-cent. music, for a keyboard instrument, requiring special skill from performer.

Contralto. A woman's voice with a low range.

Counterpoint. Simultaneous combination of two or more melodies to create a satisfying musical texture. Where one melody is added to another, one is called the other's counterpoint. The adjective of counterpoint is contrapuntal.

Counter-tenor. Another name for male alto.

Courante. A dance in triple time.

Crescendo. Getting louder.

Crook. Detachable section of tubing on brass instruments that change the tuning.

Crotchet. Note that equals two quavers in time value.

Cycle. Set of works, especially songs, intended to be sung as group.

Cyclic form. Form of work in two or more movements in which the same musical themes recur.

Cymbal. Percussion instrument; two plates struck against each other.

D. Note of scale.

Da Capo (abbr. D.C.). A *Da Capo* aria is one in which the whole first section is repeated after a contrasting middle section.

Descant. Additional part (sometimes improvised) sung against a melody.

Development. Working-out section of movement in sonata form. *See* Sonata.

Diatonic. Opposite of chromatic; using proper notes of a major or minor scale.

Diminished. Lessened version of perfect interval. e.g., semitone less than a perfect fifth is a diminished fifth.

Diminuendo. Lessening.

Diminution. Reducing a phrase of melody by shortening time value of notes.

Discord. Opposite of concord, *i.e.* notes that sounded together produce a clash of harmonies.

Dissonance. Like discord.

Divertimento. A piece, usually orchestral, in several movements; like a suite.

Dodecaphonic. Pertaining to 12-note method of composition.

Dominant. Fifth note of major or minor scale above tonic (key) note.

Dorian Mode. One of the scales in mediæval music, represented by the white keys on the piano from D to D.

Dot. Placed over note indicates staccato; placed after note indicates time value to be increased by half.

Double bar. Two upright lines marking the end of a composition or a section of it.

Double bass. Largest and lowest instrument of violin family; played with bow.

Drone bass. Unvarying sustained bass, similar to the permanent bass note of a bagpipe.

Drum. Variety of percussion instruments on which sound is produced by hitting a skin stretched tightly over a hollow cylinder or hemisphere.

Duet. Combination of two performers; composition for such a combination.

Duple time. Time in which main division is two or four.

Dynamics. Gradations of loudness or softness in music.

E. Note of scale.

Electronic. Term used to describe use of electronic sounds in music.

Encore. Request from audience for repeat of work, or extra item in a programme.

English horn (Cor anglais). Woodwind instrument with double reed of oboe family.

Enharmonic. Modulation made by means of change of note between sharps and flats, although note remains the same (E flat becomes D sharp, for example).

Ensemble. Teamwork in performance; item in opera for several singers with or without chorus; a group of performers of no fixed number.

Episode. Section in composition usually divorced from main argument.

Exposition. Setting out of thematic material in a sonata-form composition.

Expression marks. Indication by composer of how he wants his music performed.

F. Note of scale.

False relation. A clash of harmony produced when two notes, such as A natural and A flat, are played simultaneously or immediately following one another.

Falsetto. The kind of singing by male voices above normal register and sounding like an unbroken voice.

Fanfare. Flourish of trumpets.

Fantasy. A piece suggesting free play of composer's imagination, or a piece based on known tunes (folk, operatic, etc.).

Fermata. Pause indicated by sign ⌒ prolonging note beyond its normal length.

Fifth. Interval taking five steps in the scale. A perfect fifth (say, C to G) includes three whole tones and a semitone; a diminished fifth is a semitone less, an augmented fifth a semitone more.

Figure. A short phrase, especially one that is repeated.

Fingering. Use of fingers to play instrument, or the indication above notes to show what fingers should be used.

Flat. Term indicating a lowering of pitch by a semitone, or to describe a performer playing under the note.

Florid. Term used to describe decorative passages.

Flute. Woodwind instrument, blown sideways. It is played through a hole, not a reed. Nowadays, sometimes made of metal.

Folksong. Traditional tune, often in different versions, handed down aurally from generation to generation.

Form. Course or layout of a composition, especially when in various sections.

Fourth. Interval taking four steps in scale. A perfect fourth (say, C to F) includes two whole tones and a semitone. If either note is sharpened or flattened the result is an augmented or a diminished fourth.

Fugato. In the manner of a fugue.

Fugue. Contrapuntal composition for various parts based on one or more subjects treated imitatively but not strictly.

G. Note of scale.

Galant. Used to designate elegant style of 18th-cent. music.

Galliard. Lively dance dating back to 15th cent. or before.

Gavotte. Dance in 4/4 time, beginning on third beat in bar.

Giusto. Strict, proper.

Glee. Short part-song.

Glissando. Rapid sliding scales up and down piano or other instruments.

Glockenspiel. Percussion instrument consisting of tuned steel bars and played with two hammers or keyboard.

Grace note. See Ornament.

Grave. In slow tempo.

Grazioso. Gracefully.

Gregorian Chant. Plainsong collected and supervised mainly by Pope Gregory (d. 604).

Ground bass. Figure on theme used as bass in a composition and constantly repeated without change.

Guitar. Plucked string instrument of Spanish origin, having six strings of three-octave compass.

H. German note-symbol for *B.*

Harmony. Simultaneous sounding of notes so as to make musical sense.

Harp. Plucked string instrument of ancient origin, the strings stretched parallel across its frame. The basic scale of C flat major is altered by a set of pedals.

Harpsichord. Keyboard stringed instrument played by means of keyboard similar to a piano but producing its notes by a plucking, rather than a striking action.

Homophonic. Opposite of polyphonic, *i.e.,* indicated parts move together in a composition, a single melody being accompanied by block chords, as distinct from the contrapuntal movement of different melodies.

Horn. Brass instrument with coiled tubes. Valves introduced in 19th cent. made full chromatic use of instrument possible.

Hymn. Song of praise, especially in church.

Imitation. Repetition, exactly, or at least recognisably, of a previously heard figure.

Impromptu. A short, seemingly improvised piece of music, especially by Schubert or Chopin.

Improvise. To perform according to fancy or imagination, sometimes on a given theme.

In alt. The octave above the treble clef; *in altissimo,* octave above that.

Instrumentation. Writing music for particular instruments, using the composer's knowledge of what sounds well on different instruments.

Interlude. Piece played between two sections of a composition.

Intermezzo. Formerly meant interlude, now often used for pieces played between acts of operas.

Interval. Distance in pitch between notes.

Ionian mode. One of the scales in mediæval music, represented on piano by white keys between C and C. identical therefore to modern C major scale.

Isorhythmic. Term applied to motets of 14th and 15th cent. where rhythm remains strict although melody changes.

Jig. Old dance usually in 6/8 or 12/8 time.

Kettledrum (It. pl. *Timpani*). Drum with skin drawn over a cauldron-shaped receptacle, can be tuned to definite pitch by turning handles on rim, thus tightening or relaxing skin.

Key. Lever by means of which piano, organ, etc., produces note; classification, in relatively modern times, of notes of a scale. Any piece of music in major or minor is in the *key* of its tonic or keynote.

Keyboard. Term used to describe instruments with a continuous row of keys.

Key-signature. Indication on written music, usually at the beginning of each line, of the number of flats or sharps in the key of a composition.

Kitchen Department. Humorous term for percussion section of an orchestra.

Lament. Musical piece of sad or deathly significance.

Largamente. Spaciously.

Largo. Slow.

Leading-motive (Ger. *Leitmotiv*). Short theme, suggesting person, idea, or image, quoted throughout composition to indicate that person, etc.

Legato. In a smooth style (of performance, etc.).

Lento. Slow.

Libretto. Text of an opera.

Lied. (pl. *Lieder*). Song, with special reference to songs by Schubert, Schumann, Brahms, and Wolf.

Lute. String instrument plucked with fingers, used in 15th- and 16th cent. music especially.

Lydian mode. One of the scales in mediæval music, represented by white keys of piano between F and F.

Lyre. Ancient Greek plucked string instrument.

Madrigal. Contrapuntal composition for several voices, especially prominent from 15th to 17th cent.

Maestoso. Stately.

Major. One of the two main scales of the tonal system with semitones between the third and fourth, and the seventh and eighth notes, identical with 16th-cent. Ionian mode.

Mandolin(e). Plucked string instrument of Italian origin.

Manual. A keyboard for the hands, used mostly in connection with the organ.

Master of the King's (or *Queen's*) *Musick.* Title of British court appointment, with no precise duties.

Melisma. Group of notes sung to a single syllable.

Mélodie. Literally a melody or tune; has come to mean a French song (cf. German *Lied*).

Metronome. Small machine in use since the beginning of the 18th cent., to determine the pace of any composition by the beats of the music, *e.g.,* ♩ = 60 at the head of the music indicates sixty crotchets to the minute.

Mezzo, Mezza. (It. = "half") *Mezza voce* means using the half voice (a tone between normal singing and whispering). *Mezzo-soprano,* voice between soprano and contralto.

Minim. Note that equals two crotchets in time value.

Minor. One of the two main scales of the tonal system (cf. major), identical with 16th-cent. Aeolian mode. It has two forms—the harmonic and melodic, the former having a sharpened seventh note, the latter having the sixth and seventh note sharpened.

Minuet. Originally French 18th-cent. dance in triple time, then the usual third movement in symphonic form (with a contrasting trio section) until succeeded by scherzo.

Mixolydian mode. One of the mediaeval scales represented by the white keys on the piano from G to G.

Modes. Scales prevalent in the Middle Ages. *See* Aeolian, Dorian, Ionian, Lydian, Mixolydian, Phrygian.

Modulate. Changing from key to key in a composition, not directly but according to musical "grammar".

Molto. Much, very; thus *allegro molto.*

Motet. Sacred, polyphonic vocal composition. More loosely, any choral composition for use in church but not set to words of the liturgy.

Motive, motif. Short, easily recognised melodic figure.

Motto. Short, well-defined theme recurring throughout a composition, cf. *Idée fixe* in Berlioz's *Symphonie Fantastique.*

Movement. Separate sections of a large-scale composition, each in its own form.

Music drama. Term used to describe Wagner's, and sometimes other large-scale operas.

Mutes. Devices used to damp the sound of various instruments.

Natural (of a note or key). Not sharp or flat.

Neo-classical. Term used to describe music written mostly during the 1920s and 30s in the style of Bach or Mozart.

Ninth. Interval taking nine steps, *e.g.,* from C upwards an octave and a whole tone to D.

Nocturne. Literally a " night-piece ", hence usually of lyrical character.

Nonet. Composition for nine instruments.

Notation. Act of writing down music.

Note. Single sound of specified pitch and duration; symbol to represent this.

Obbligato. Instrumental part having a special or essential rôle in a piece.

Oboe. Woodwind instrument with double reed, descended from hautboy; as such, in use since 16th cent., in modern form since 18th cent.

Octave. Interval taking eight steps of scale, with top and bottom notes having same " name ": C to C is an octave.

Octet. Composition for eight instruments or voices.

Ondes Martenot. Belongs to a class of melodic instruments in which the tone is produced by electrical vibrations controlled by the movement of the hands not touching the instrument.

Opera. Musical work for the stage with singing characters, originated in early years of 17th cent.

Opera seria. Chief operatic form of 17th and 18th cent., usually set to very formal librettos, concerning gods or heroes of ancient history.

Operetta. Lighter type of opera.

Opus. (abbr. *Op.*) With number following *opus* indicates order of a composer's composition.

Oratorio. Vocal work, usually for soloists and choir with instrumental accompaniment, generally with setting of a religious text.

Orchestra. Term to designate large, or largish, body of instrumentalists, originated in 17th cent.

Orchestration. Art of setting out work for instruments of an orchestra. To be distinguished from *Instrumentation* (*q.v.*).

Organ. Elaborate keyboard instrument in which air is blown through pipes by bellows to sound notes. Tone is altered by selection of various stops and, since the 16th cent., a pedal keyboard has also been incorporated.

Organum. In mediæval music a part sung as an accompaniment below or above the melody or plainsong, usually at the interval of a fourth or fifth; also, loosely, this method of singing in parts.

Ornament. Notes that are added to a given melody by composer or performer as an embellishment.

Overture. Instrumental introduction or prelude to larger work, usually opera. Concert overtures are simply that: *i.e.,* work to be played at start of a concert.

Part. Music of one performer in an ensemble; single strand in a composition.

Part-song. Vocal composition in several parts.

Passacaglia. Composition in which a tune is constantly repeated, usually in the bass.

Passage. Section of a composition.

Passion. Musical setting of the New Testament story of Christ's trial and crucifixion.

Pastiche. Piece deliberately written in another composer's style.

Pavan(e). Moderately paced dance dating from 16th cent. or earlier.

Pedal. Held note in bass of composition.

Pentatonic Scale. Scale of five notes—usually piano's five black keys or other notes in the same relation to each other.

Percussion. Collective title for instruments of the orchestra that are sounded by being struck by hand or stick.

Phrygian Mode. One of the scales of mediæval music, represented by the white keys on piano from E to E.

Piano. Soft, abbr. *p*; *pp = pianissimo*, very soft; instrument, invented in 18th cent., having strings struck by hammer, as opposed to the earlier harpsichord where they are plucked. The modern piano has 88 keys and can be either " upright " (vertical) or " grand " (horizontal).

Pianoforte. Almost obsolete full Italian name for the piano.

Pitch. Exact height or depth of a particular musical sound or note.

Pizzicato. Direction for stringed instruments, that the strings should be plucked instead of bowed.

Plainchant, Plainsong. Mediæval church music consisting of single line of melody without harmony or definite rhythm.

Polka. Dance in 2/4 time originating in 19th cent. Bohemia.

Polonaise. Polish dance generally in 3/4 time.

Polyphony. Combination of two or more musical lines as in *counterpoint.*

Polytonality. Simultaneous use of several keys.

Postlude. Closing piece, opposite of Prelude.

Prelude. Introductory piece.

Presto. Very fast. *Prestissimo.* Still faster.

Progression. Movement from one chord to next to make musical sense.

Quartet. Work written for four instruments or voices; group to play or sing such a work.

Quaver. Note that equals two semiquavers or half a crotchet.

Quintet. Work written for five instruments or voices; group to play or sing such a work.

Rallentando. Slowing down.

Recapitulation. Section of composition that repeats original material in something like its original form.

Recitative. Term used for declamation in singing written in ordinary notation but allowing rhythmical licence.

Recorder. Woodwind instrument, forerunner of flute.

Reed. Vibrating tongue of woodwind instruments.

Register. Set of organ pipes controlled by a particular stop; used in reference to different ranges of instrument or voice (*e.g.,* chest register).

Relative. Term used to indicate common key signature of a major and minor key.

Répétiteur. Member of opera house's musical staff who coaches singers in their parts.

Rest. Notation of pauses for instrument in composition, having a definite length like a note.

Retrograde. Term used to describe a melody played backwards.

Rhapsody. Work of no definite kind with a degree of romantic content.

Rhythm. Everything concerned with the time of music (*i.e.,* beats, accent, metre, etc.) as opposed to the pitch side.

Ritornello. Passage, usually instrumental, that recurs in a piece.

Romance, Romanza. Title for piece of vague song-like character.

Romantic. Term used vaguely to describe music of 19th cent. that has other than purely musical source of inspiration.

Rondo. Form in which one section keeps on recurring.

Rubato. Manner of performing a piece without keeping strictly to time.

Sackbut. Early English name for trombone.

Saxophone. Classified as wind instrument, although made of brass, because it uses a reed.

Scale. Progression of adjoining notes upwards or downwards.

Scherzo. One of two middle movements, usually third, in four-movement sonata form. Displaced minuet in this form at beginning of 19th cent.

Score. Copy of any music written in several parts.

Second. Interval taking two steps in scale, *e.g.*, C to D flat, or to D.

Semibreve. Note that equals two minims or half a breve.

Semiquaver. Note that equals half a quaver.

Semitone. Smallest interval commonly used in Western music.

Septet. Composition for seven instruments or voices.

Sequence. Repetition of phrase at a higher or lower pitch.

Serenade. Usually an evening song or instrumental work.

Seventh. Interval taking seven steps in the scale.

Sextet. Composition for six instruments or voices.

Sharp. Term indicating a raising of pitch by a semitone.

Shawm. Primitive woodwind instrument, forerunner of oboe.

Simple time. Division of music into two or four beats.

Sinfonietta. Small symphony.

Sixth. Interval taking six steps in the scale.

Solo. Piece or part of a piece for one performer playing or singing alone.

Sonata. Term to denote a musical form and a type of composition. In *sonata form* a composition is divided into exposition, development and recapitulation. A *sonata* is a piece, usually, for one or more players following that form.

Song. Any short vocal composition.

Soprano. Highest female voice.

Sostenuto. Sustained, broadly.

Sotto voce. Whispered, scarcely audible, applied to vocal as well as instrumental music.

Sprechgesang. (Ger. Speech-song.) Vocal utterance somewhere between speech and song.

Staccato. Perform music in short, detached manner.

Staff. Horizontal lines on which music is usually written.

Stop. Lever by which organ registration can be altered.

String(s). Strands of gut or metal set in vibration to produce musical sounds on string or keyboard instruments. Plural refers to violins, violas, cellos, and basses of orchestra.

Study. Instrumental piece, usually one used for technical exercise or to display technical skill, but often having artistic merits as well (*e.g.* Chopin's).

Subject(s). Theme or group of notes that forms principal idea or ideas in composition.

Suite. Common name for piece in several movements.

Symphony. Orchestral work of serious purpose usually in four movements, occasionally given name (*e.g.*, Beethoven's "Choral" symphony).

Syncopation. Displacement of musical accent.

Tempo. Pace, speed of music.

Tenor. Highest normal male voice.

Ternary. A piece in three sections is said to be in ternary form. The balance is obtained by repeating the first phrase or section (though it need not be exact or complete) after a second of equal importance.

Tessitura. Compass into which voice or instrument comfortably falls.

Theme. Same as *subject* but can also be used for a whole musical statement as in "theme and variations."

Third. Interval taking three steps in scale.

Time. Rhythmical division of music.

Timpani. See Kettledrum.

Toccata. Instrumental piece usually needing rapid, brilliant execution.

Tonality. Key, or feeling for a definite key.

Tone. Quality of musical sound; interval of two semitones.

Tonic Sol-fa. System of musical notation to simplify sight-reading.

Transcribe. Arrange piece for different medium, instrument, or voice than that originally intended.

Transition. Passage that joins two themes of sections of a composition.

Transpose. Perform a piece at different pitch from that originally intended.

Treble. Highest part in vocal composition; high boy's voice.

Triad. A chord consisting of a note with the third and fifth above it, *e.g.*, C–E–G. A common chord is a triad of which the 5th is perfect, e.g., C–E–G or C–E flat–G. Thus major and minor triads are common chords.

Trio. Work written for three instruments or voices; group to play or sing such a work.

Trombone. Brass instrument with slide adjusting length of tube.

Trumpet. Metal instrument of considerable antiquity; modern version has three valves to make it into a chromatic instrument.

Tuba. Deepest-toned brass instrument with three or four valves.

Twelve-note. Technique of composition using full chromatic scale with each note having equal importance. Notes are placed in particular order as the thematic basis of works.

Unison. Two notes sung or played together at same pitch.

Valve. Mechanism, invented in early 19th cent. to add to brass instruments allowing them to play full chromatic scale.

Variation. Varied passage of original theme. Such variations may be closely allied to or depart widely from the theme.

Verismo. Term to describe Italian operas written in "realist" style at the turn of this century.

Vibrato. Rapid fluctuation in pitch of voice or instrument. Exaggerated it is referred to as a "wobble" (of singers) or tremolo.

Viol. String instrument of various sizes in vogue until end of 17th cent.

Viola. Tenor instrument of violin family.

Violin. Musical four-string instrument, played with bow, of violin family, which superseded viol at beginning of 18th cent.

Virginals. English keyboard instrument, similar to harpsichord of 17th and 18th cent.

Vivace. Lively.

Voluntary. Organ piece for church use, but not during service.

Waltz. Dance in triple time, fashionable in 19th cent.

Whole-tone scale. Scale progressing by whole tones. Only two are possible, one beginning on C, the other on C sharp.

Xylophone. Percussion instrument with series of wood bars tuned in a chromatic scale and played with sticks.

Zither. String instrument laid on knees and plucked. Common in Central-European folk music.

III. INDEX TO COMPOSERS

THE WORLD OF SCIENCE

A contemporary picture of scientific discovery, designed to explain some of the most important ideas in astronomy, physics, chemistry, biology, and anthropology, and to give some account of recent research in various fields.

TABLE OF CONTENTS

THE WORLD OF SCIENCE

In Parts I, II, and III the inanimate universe is described. This is the domain of cosmology astronomy, geology, physics, and chemistry. There are already many interesting links which join this realm to that of the living and make it difficult to say where the boundary lies. Nevertheless it is still convenient to accord to the biological and social sciences two separate chapters. Parts IV and V. In Part VI our intention is to give some short accounts of recent developments in both science and technology. They are usually contributed by scientists actively engaged in these, their own special fields.

I. ASTRONOMY AND COSMOLOGY—THE NATURE OF THE UNIVERSE

The universe includes everything from the smallest sub-atomic particle to the mightiest system of stars. The scientific view of the universe (not the only view but the one we are concerned with here) is a remarkable achievement of the human mind, and it is worth considering at the outset what a " scientific view " is, and what is remarkable about it.

A scientific view of something is always an intimate mixture of theories and observed facts, and not an inert mixture but a seething and growing one. The theories are broad general ideas together with arguments based on them. The arguments are designed to show that, if the general ideas are accepted, then this, that, or the other thing ought to be observed. If this, that, or the other actually are observed, then the theory is a good one; if not, then the theoreticians have to think again. Thus theoretical ideas and arguments are continually subjected to the severe test of comparison with the facts, and scientists are proud of the rigour with which this is done. On the other hand, theories often suggest new things to look for, i.e., theories lead to predictions. These predictions are frequently successful, and scientists are entitled to be proud of that too. But it follows that no theory is immutable: any scientific view of any subject may, in principle, be invalidated at any time by the discovery of new facts, though some theories are so soundly based that overthrow does not seem imminent.

A remarkable aspect of the scientific view of the universe is that same principles are supposed to operate throughout the whole vastness of space. Thus the matter and radiation in stars are not different from the matter and radiation on earth, and their laws of behaviour are the same. Therefore theories hard won by studies in terrestrial physics and chemistry laboratories are applied at once to the whole cosmos. Astronomy and cosmology are spectacular extensions of ordinary mechanics and physics.

LOOKING AT THE UNIVERSE.

The universe is observable because signals from it reach us and some manage to penetrate our atmosphere.

First, there are waves of visible light together with invisible rays of somewhat longer (infra-red) and somewhat shorter (ultra-violet) wavelengths. These waves show us the bright astronomical objects and, to make use of them, astronomers have constructed telescopes of great power and precision backed up with cameras, spectroscopes, and numerous auxiliaries. The most powerful telescope, at Mt. Palomar, California, has a 200-inch-diameter mirror. The next major advance in optical telescope performance probably awaits the erection of telescopes on satellites outside the earth's atmosphere, which at present acts as a distorting and only partially transparent curtain.

Secondly, there are radio waves of much longer wavelength than light. These can be detected by sensitive radio receivers with special aerial systems. These are the radio telescopes. The most

well known British one is at Jodrell Bank and it started working in 1957.

Other types of radiation from outer space impinge on the atmosphere. Cosmic radiation consists of very fast-moving fundamental particles, including protons (F14). Cosmic rays are detected by Geiger counters, by the minute tracks they leave on photographic plates, and by other means. The origin of cosmic rays is still uncertain, but many people think they must have an intimate connection with the nature and evolution of the universe itself.

X-rays and neutrinos (F14) from outer space can also be detected, the former especially by satellite-borne detectors and the latter by apparatus buried in deep mines. X-ray astronomy and neutrino astronomy are being born.

By interpreting the signals that reach us by these various routes, astronomers have formed a remarkably detailed picture of its structure. The merest outline of this will now be given.

Great Distances and Large Numbers.

Let us start with nearby objects. This raises at once the question of what " nearness " and " distance " are in astronomy and how they are to be expressed. A convenient unit of distance is the light-year, i.e., the distance that light, travelling at 186,000 miles per second, traverses in one year. Since vast numbers as well as vast distances will enter the question, we need a shorthand for large numbers. Ten times ten times ten will be represented by 10^3; six tens multiplied together (i.e., one million) will be written 10^6, and so on. 10^{14} would mean a hundred million million. One divided by a million (i.e., one-millionth) will be written 10^{-6}; the very small number obtained by dividing one by the product of fourteen tens will be written 10^{-14}. A light-year is $5 \cdot 88 \times 10^{12}$ miles; the radius of an atom is about 10^{-8} cm.

PLANETS, STARS, AND GALAXIES.

The Solar System.

The earth is the third, counting outwards, of nine planets revolving in nearly circular orbits round the sun. Their names and some other particulars are given in the table (F7). The sun and its planets are the main bodies of the solar system. Between Mars and Jupiter revolve numerous chunks of rock called the asteroids; the largest of these, Ceres, is 480 miles across. Apart from these, the solar system is tenuously populated with gas, dust, and small particles of stone and iron. Dust continuously settles on the earth, and frequently small fragments enter the atmosphere, glow, and evaporate; these are meteors or shooting stars. Sometimes larger rocks, called meteorites, hit the earth. Comets are relatively compact swarms of particles—containing ice according to one theory—which travel in elongated orbits round the sun. Their spectacular tails form under the sun's influence when they approach it. Not all comets stay indefinitely in the solar system; some visit us and go off into space for ever.

The sun itself is a dense, roughly spherical mass of glowing matter, 865,000 miles across. Its heat is so intense that the atoms are split into separated electrons and nuclei (*see* **F10**) and matter in such a state is called plasma. At the sun's centre the temperature has the unimaginable value of about 13 million degrees Centigrade (a coal fire is about 800° C). Under such conditions the atomic nuclei frequently collide with one another at great speeds and reactions occur between them. The sun consists largely of hydrogen and, in the very hot plasma, the nuclei of hydrogen atoms interact by a series of reactions whose net result is to turn hydrogen into helium. This is a process which releases energy just as burning does, only these nuclear processes are incomparably more energetic than ordinary burning. In fact, the energy released is great enough to be the source of all the light and heat which the sun has been pouring into space for thousands of millions of years.

Emerging from the sun and streaming past the earth is a " solar wind " of fast-moving electrons and protons (*see* **F10**) whose motion is closely linked with the behaviour of an extensive magnetic field based on the sun. In fact, the region round the sun and extending far into space past the earth is full of complex, fluctuating particle streams and magnetic fields which interact with planetary atmospheres causing, among other things, auroras and magnetic storms.

Stars.

In colour, brightness, age, and size the sun is typical of vast numbers of other stars. Only from the human point of view is there anything special about the sun—it is near enough to give us life. Even the possession of a system of revolving planets is not, according to some modern views, very unusual.

No star can radiate energy at the rate the sun does without undergoing internal changes in the course of time. Consequently stars evolve and old processes in them give rise to new. The exact nature of stellar evolution—so far as it is at present understood—would be too complex to describe here in any detail. It involves expansion and contraction, changes of temperature, changes of colour, and changes in chemical composition as the nuclear processes gradually generate new chemical elements by reactions such as the conversion of hydrogen to helium, helium to neon, neon to magnesium, and so on. The speed of evolution changes from time to time, but is in any case very slow compared with the pace of terrestrial life; nothing very dramatic may occur for hundreds of millions of years. Evidence for the various phases of evolution is therefore obtained by studying many stars, each at a different stage of its life. Thus astronomers recognise many types with charmingly descriptive names, such as blue giants, sub-giants, red and white dwarfs, supergiants.

The path of stellar evolution may be marked by various explosive events. One of these, which occurs in sufficiently large stars, is an enormous explosion in which a substantial amount of the star is blown away into space in the form of high-speed streams of gas. For about a fortnight, such an exploding star will radiate energy 200 million times as fast as the sun. Japanese and Chinese (but not Western) astronomers recorded such an occurrence in A.D. 1054, and the exploding gases, now called the Crab nebula, can still be seen in powerful telescopes and form a cloud six or seven light-years across. While it lasts, the explosion shows up as an abnormally bright star and is called a *supernova*.

Groups of Stars.

It is not surprising that ancient peoples saw pictures in the sky. The constellations, however, are not physically connected groups of stars but just happen to be patterns visible from earth. A conspicuous exception to this is the Milky Way, which a telescope resolves into many millions of separate stars. If we could view the Milky Way from a vast distance and see it as a whole we should observe a rather flat wheel of stars with spiral arms something like the sparks of a rotating Catherine wheel. This system of stars is physically connected by gravitational forces and moves through space as a whole; it is called a *galaxy*.

The galaxy is about 10^5 light-years across and contains roughly 10^{11} stars. An inconspicuous one of these stars near the edge of the wheel is our sun; the prominent stars in our night sky are members of the galaxy that happen to be rather near us. Sirius, the brightest, is only 8·6 light-years away, a trivial distance, astronomically speaking.

The galaxy does not contain stars only, there are also clouds of gas and dust, particularly in the plane of the galaxy. Much of the gas is hydrogen, and its detection is difficult. However, gaseous hydrogen gives out radio waves with a wavelength of 21 cm. Radio telescopes are just the instruments to receive these, and workers in Holland, America, and Australia detected the gas clouds by this means. In 1952 they found that the hydrogen clouds lie in the spiral arms of the galaxy, and this is some of the strongest evidence for the spiral form.

Another important feature of the galactic scene is the weak but enormously extensive magnetic field. This is believed to have an intimate connection with the spiral structure.

Around the spiral arms, and forming part of the galaxy, are numerous globular clusters of stars. These are roughly spherical, abnormally densely packed, collections of stars with many thousands of members. Because of its form and density, a globular cluster may be assumed to have been formed in one process, not star by star. Thus all its stars are the same age. This is of great interest to astronomers, because they can study differences between stars of similar age but different sizes.

Galaxies.

One might be forgiven for assuming that such a vast system as the galaxy is in fact the universe; but this is not so. In the constellation of Andromeda is a famous object which, on close examination, turns out to be another galaxy of size and structure similar to our own. Its distance is given in the table (F7). The Milky Way, the Andromeda Nebula, and a few other smaller galaxies form a cluster of galaxies called the Local Group. Obviously it would not be so named except to distinguish it from other distinct groups, and it is indeed a fact that the universe is populated with *groups*, or *clusters*, of *galaxies*. A cluster may contain two or three galaxies, but some contain thousands. So far as the eye of the telescope and camera can see, there are clusters of galaxies.

On a photograph a galaxy is a nebulous blob without the hard outline that a single star produces. Such nebulæ were formerly thought to be inside the Milky Way, but, after controversy, it was established that many of them were separate distant galaxies. By about 1920 it was known that there were at least half a million galaxies, and with the advent of the 100-in. Mt. Wilson telescope this number rose to 10^8 and is being increased further by the 200-in. telescope which can see out to a distance of 7×10^9 light-years. Through the powerful telescopes the nearer galaxies reveal their inner structures. Photographs of galaxies are among the most beautiful and fascinating photographs ever taken, and readers who have never seen one should hasten to the nearest illustrated astronomy book. Recent careful co-operation between optical and radio-astronomers has revealed that some very remote galaxies are strong sources of radio waves. Sometimes these radio galaxies have unusual structures suggestive of violent disturbance.

The Expanding Universe.

Two discoveries about galaxies are of the utmost importance. One is that, by and large, clusters of galaxies are uniformly distributed through the universe. The other is that the distant galaxies are receding from us.

How is this known? Many readers may be familiar with the Doppler effect first discovered in 1842. Suppose a stationary body emits waves of any kind and we measure their wavelength, finding it to be L ins. Now suppose the body approaches us; the waves are thereby crowded together in the intervening space and the wavelength appears less than L; if the body recedes the wavelength appears greater than L. The Austrian physicist, J. Doppler (1803-53), discovered this behaviour in sound waves, and it explains the well-known change of pitch of a train whistle as it approaches and passes us. The same principle applies to the light. Every atom emits light of definite wavelengths which appear in a spectroscope as a series of coloured lines—a different series for each atom. If the atom is in a receding body all the lines have slightly longer wavelengths than usual, and the amount of the change depends uniquely on the speed. Longer wavelengths mean that the light is redder than usual, so that a light from a receding body shows what is called a " red shift." The speed of recession can be calculated from the amount of red shift.

It was the American astronomer, V. M. Slipher, who first showed (in 1914) that some galaxies emitted light with a red shift. In the 1920s and 1930s the famous astronomer E. Hubble (1889-1953) measured both the distances and red shift of many galaxies and proved what is now known as Hubble's Law. This states that the speed of recession of galaxies is proportional to their distance from us. This does not apply to our neighbours in the Local Group, we and they are keeping together. Hubble's Law has been tested and found to hold for the farthest detectable galaxies; they are about 7×10^9 light-years away and are receding with a speed ⅔ of that of light.

Does this mean that the Local Group is the centre of the universe and that everything else is rushing away from us? No; Hubble's Law would appear just the same from any other cluster of galaxies. Imagine you are in a square on some fabulous chess board which is steadily doubling its size every hour; all other squares double their distances from you in an hour. Therefore the farther squares from you must travel faster than the nearer ones; in fact, Hubble's Law must be obeyed. But anyone standing in any other square would get the same impression.

This extraordinary behaviour of the universe is one of the most exciting discoveries of science. Let us envisage one possible implication. If the galaxies have always been receding, then in the past they must have been closer together. Following this to its conclusion, it seems that all the matter in the universe must have been packed densely together about 10^{10} years ago. Was this really so? The lack of any definite answer to this question is one of the things that makes cosmology so interesting.

Quasars and Pulsars.

In November 1962 Australian radio-astronomers located a strong radio emitter with sufficient precision for the Mt. Palomar optical astronomers to identify it on photographs and examine the nature of its light. The red shift was so great that the object must be exceedingly distant; on the other hand it looked star-like, much smaller than a galaxy. By the beginning of 1967 over a hundred of these objects had been discovered and other characteristics established, such as strong ultra-violet radiation and inconstancy, in some cases, of the rate at which radiation is emitted. Not all of these so-called quasars are strong radio emitters; some show all the other characteristics except radio emission. It has been estimated that the " quiet " kind are about a hundred times more numerous than the radio kind. One great problem here is: how can such relatively small objects generate such inconceivably great amounts of energy that they appear bright at such huge distances? So far this is unanswered; these quasi-stellar objects are a great mystery, though they are generally held to be an important pointer towards a deeper understanding of cosmology.

Late in 1967 while investigating quasars, Cambridge radio-astronomers discovered pulsars, a new type of heavenly body. Their characteristic is the emission of pulses of radio waves every second or so with a repetition rate that is regular to at least 1 part in 10^8. At present they are believed to be peculiar stars hardly bigger than the Earth and situated inside our galaxy.

THE ORIGIN AND DEVELOPMENT OF THE UNIVERSE.

Errors of observation and interpretation occur of course. But there are many checks and repetitions made, so that, on the whole, the descriptive account of the universe would be generally agreed among astronomers. When it comes to inventing theoretical explanations, however, science is on less sure ground, and indeed the theory of the universe is an arena of controversy at present. In most other sciences experiments can be repeated and the same phenomena observed under differing but controlled conditions. This is very helpful. But, by definition, there is only one universe: one cannot repeat it or do experiments with it. On the other hand, it must be remembered that the light from distant galaxies has taken perhaps 10^9 years to reach us, so it tells us what the galaxies were like that number of years ago. Therefore we are not confined simply to describing the present state of the universe; by looking farther into space we are looking farther into the past as well. How, then, does the state of the universe vary with time?

Evolutionary Theories.

One answer to this can be obtained from Einstein's general theory of relativity. Some slight indication of what this theory is about is given on page F15, and its logical development is, of course, a matter for mathematical specialists. It turns out that, if we assume that matter is distributed uniformly throughout space (as observation strongly suggests), then the solutions of Einstein's equations show how the state of the universe may vary with time. Unfortunately there are many possible solutions corresponding to expanding, static, or contracting universes. As we have already seen, the actual universe is expanding, therefore the static and contracting solutions can be ruled out. There is still a multiplicity of expanding possibilities; some correspond to indefinite expansion from an initially very dense state, others to expansion followed by contraction to a dense state followed by expansion and so on repeatedly, i.e., a pulsating universe. The " dense state " is presumably to be identified with the time when the receding galaxies were all concentrated near one another, possibly in some dense conglomeration of atoms. This initial state is thought by some to be the origin of the universe; they would say it has been expanding and evolving ever since. If the universe is pulsating, then sooner or later, gravitational attractions between galaxies will slow the observed recession down and turn it into a mutual approach and so back to the dense state. A straightforward application of the mathematics makes this dense state *infinitely* dense, and presumably something must happen before this inconceivable situation arises. For example, forces between atomic nuclei may play an important part and determine what the dense state (if any) is actually like.

The Steady-State Theory.

A rival theory was proposed in 1948 by Bondi, Gold, and Hoyle. They suggested that the universe is not changing with time; there was no initial dense state and no pulsations; the universe always has been, and always will be, like it is now. This does not mean that no local changes can be observed—this would clearly be contrary to the facts. But it does mean that, on the large scale, the clusters of galaxies have a distribution which is uniform in space and unchanging in time. If the numbers of clusters of galaxies in a large volume of space were counted every few thousand million years the answer would always be the same.

At first sight this appears to contradict outright the observed expansion of the universe. For if the galaxies are receding from one another how can the number in a given volume remain constant? The situation is saved by a bold proposal. It is that matter, in the form of hydrogen atoms, is being *continuously created* throughout space. This gas accumulates in due course into new galaxies, so that as the old ones move apart the young ones appear to keep the numbers up. The necessary amount of continuous creation can be calculated and is equivalent to the appearance of one atom in an average-sized room every 20 million years. If this seems absurdly small, try calculating the rate of creation in tons per second in a sphere of radius 10^9 light-years.

The rate of creation is, however, much too small to have affected any of the laws of ordinary physics. The famous law of the conservation of matter (" matter can neither be created nor destroyed ") is violated, but on such a small scale that physicists, it is said, should not complain. Nevertheless, some do complain and see in this violation a strong point against this theory.

The Formation of Galaxies and Stars.

On any theory of the universe, some explanation has to be found for the existence of clusters of galaxies. In all theories galaxies condense out from dispersed masses of gas, principally hydrogen.

Once a huge gas cloud becomes sufficiently condensed to be separately identifiable as a galaxy, further condensation goes on inside it. It is believed on theoretical grounds that it could not condense into one enormous star but must form many fragments which shrink separately into clusters of stars. In these clusters many stars, perhaps hundreds or thousands or even millions, are born at once. A small cluster, visible to the naked eye, is the Pleiades. The Orion nebula, visible as a hazy blob of glowing gas in the sword of Orion, is the scene of much star-forming activity at present.

According to the evolutionary theory, the " initial dense state " consisted of very hot plasma in a state of overall expansion. The expanding plasma was both cooling and swirling about. The random swirling produces irregularities in the distribution of the hot gas—here it would be rather denser, there rather less dense. If a sufficiently large mass of denser gas happened to occur, then the gravitational attraction between its own particles would hold it together and maintain its permanent identity, even though the rest of the gas continued to swirl and expand. Such a large mass would gradually condense into fragments to become galaxies, the whole mass turning into a cluster of galaxies.

The steady-state view is interestingly and significantly different, for, on this theory, galaxies have always been present, and the problem is one of finding how existing galaxies can generate new ones out of the hydrogen gas which is supposed to be continuously created everywhere. Moreover, this has to be done at just the right rate to maintain the galactic population density constant—otherwise it would not be a *steady-state* theory.

A theoretical proposal allowing for galaxy creation was in fact provided by steady-state cosmologists but will not be outlined here because it now seems that the steady-state theory is losing ground.

The Changing Scene.

The 1960s witnessed revolutionary developments in both observational and theoretical astronomy. By 1966 the attractive simplicity of the original steady-state theory had been obscured by modifications forced upon its protagonists by new evidence or theoretical objections. It is an interesting and significant fact that the apparent demise of the steady-state theory has resulted from a welcome injection into cosmology of the characteristic activity of the other sciences, namely, the comparison of theory with observation. For example, it now seems agreed after some years of uncertainty that remote sources of radio waves are more abundant the weaker their intensity. This strongly suggests that they are more abundant at greater distances. Thus the universe is not *uniform* as the original steady-state theory prescribed. Since greater distances correspond to earlier times, any extra abundance of objects observed at the greater distance means that the universe was denser in its younger days than now. This favours an evolutionary theory of the universe.

The same theory requires that the initial dense state of the universe—aptly christened " the primaeval fireball "—should contain intense

electromagnetic radiation with a distribution of wavelengths characteristic of the high temperature. As the fireball, *i.e.*, the universe, expanded over a period of about 10^{10} years it cooled, and one feature of this process is that the wavelengths of the radiation increase and their distribution becomes characteristic of a much lower temperature. In fact, the wavelengths should now be concentrated round about 1 mm to 1 cm (corresponding to about $-270°$ C) and the radiation should approach the earth uniformly from all directions. Radiation just like this has recently been detected in several laboratories, first by Penzias and Wilson in America during 1965. They used very sensitive radio receivers originally designed to detect signals from artificial satellites. No plausible terrestrial or galactic origin for the radiation has yet been conceived; the waves appear to have something to do with the universe itself. Neither is there a rational basis for the radiation within the steady-state theory which probably receives here its *coup de grâce*. The evolutionary theory survives so far.

The Formation of the Chemical Elements.

A stable nucleus is one that lasts indefinitely because it is not radioactive. There are 274 known kinds of stable atomic nuclei and little likelihood of any more being found. These nuclei are the isotopes (*see* **F10**) of 81 different chemical elements; the other elements, including, for example, uranium and radium are always radioactive. Some elements are rare, others abundant. The most common ones on earth are oxygen, silicon, aluminium, and iron. However, the earth is rather atypical. It is especially deficient in hydrogen, because the gravitational attraction of our small planet was not strong enough to prevent this very light gas from escaping into space.

It is possible to examine the chemical constituents of meteorites and to infer the composition of the sun and other stars from the spectrum of the light they emit. By such means, the conclusion has been reached that 93% of the atoms in our galaxy are hydrogen, 7% are helium; all the other elements together account for about one in a thousand atoms. A glance at the Table of Elements (**F 66**) will show that hydrogen and helium are two of the lightest elements; they are in fact the two simplest.

According to the steady-state theory, hydrogen atoms are constantly being created. The evolutionary theory supposes that the dense initial state was a system of very hot protons and electrons, *i.e.*, split-up hydrogen atoms. In either case, therefore, the problem is to explain how the heavier chemical elements appear in the universe at all. It is here that a fascinating combination of astronomy and nuclear physics is required.

We have already referred to the fact that the energy radiated from the sun originates in nuclear reactions which turn hydrogen into helium. Why is energy given out? To answer this question we note that nuclei are made up of protons and neutrons (*see* **F10**). These particles attract one another strongly—that is why a nucleus holds together. To separate the particles, energy would have to be supplied to overcome the attractive forces. This amount of energy is called *binding energy* and is a definite quantity for every kind of nucleus. Conversely, when the particles are brought together to form a nucleus the binding energy is *released* in the form of radiations and heat. Different nuclei consist of different numbers of particles, therefore the relevant quantity to consider is the *binding energy per particle*. Let us call this B. Then if elements of *high* B are formed out of those of *low* B there is a *release* of energy.

Now B is small (relatively) for light elements like lithium, helium, and carbon; it rises to a maximum for elements of middling atomic weight like iron; it falls again for easily heavy elements like lead, bismuth, and uranium. Consequently, energy is released by forming middleweight elements either by splitting up heavy nuclei (" nuclear fission ") or by joining up light ones (" nuclear fusion ").

It is the latter process, fusion, that is going on in stars. The fusion processes can be studied in physics laboratories by using large accelerating machines to hurl nuclei at one another to make them coalesce. In stars the necessary high velocity of impact occurs because the plasma is so hot. Gradually the hydrogen is turned into helium, and helium into heavier and heavier elements. This supplies the energy that the stars radiate and simultaneously generates the chemical elements.

The very heavy elements present a problem. To form them from middleweight elements, energy has to be *supplied*. Since there is plenty of energy inside a star, a certain small number of heavy nuclei will indeed form, but they will continually undergo fission again under the prevailing intense conditions. How do they ever get away to form cool ordinary elements, like lead and bismuth, in the earth? One view links them with the highly explosive supernovæ, to which we have already referred (**F4 (1)**). If the heavy elements occur in these stars the force of the explosion disperses them into cool outer space before they have time to undergo the fission that would otherwise have been their fate. The heavy elements are thus seen as the dust and debris of stellar catastrophes. This view is in line with the steady-state theory, because supernovæ are always occurring and keeping up the supply of heavy elements. In the evolutionary theory some of the generation of elements is supposed to go on in the very early stages of the initial dense state and to continue in the stars that evolve in the fullness of time. It cannot be claimed that the origin of the chemical elements is completely known, but we have said enough to show that there are plausible theories. Time and more facts will choose between them.

The Formation of the Planets.

Did the sun collect its family of planets one by one as a result of chance encounters in the depths of space? Or was the solar system formed all at once in some generative process? To this fundamental question at least there is a fairly definite answer. The planetary orbits all lie in about the same plane and the planets all revolve the same way round the sun. This could hardly have happened by chance; indeed, it provides almost conclusive evidence for the alternative view. But what was the generative process?

Many ideas have been proposed, and the problem is very intricate. One view is that the sun and its planets formed in a stellar condensation, a feature of which was the pushing outwards from the central sun of a disc of matter which subsequently became the planets. Such a process would be regarded as normal in stars, and not exceptional.

On the other hand, the planets have been attributed to the effect of a passing star whose gravitational attraction drew out from the sun a jet of gaseous matter which condensed into the planets. Such an encounter between stars is very rare and, on this theory, the formation of planets must be an outside chance. This theory is not widely held now.

The connection between stellar and planetary theory is brought out again by the existence on the planets of the heavier chemical elements. How did they get there? If it be true that heavy elements are hurled into space by exploding supernovæ (see above), then at least one such explosion must have mingled its products with the widespread interstellar hydrogen before the planets condensed. At one time Hoyle put forward the view that the sun was once accompanied by another star (there are many such binary systems known to astronomers) and that the sun's partner exploded. Some of the ejected gases, captured by the sun's gravitational attraction, later condensed into planets, while the remnant of the star recoiled from the explosion and got away into space. This explanation was later modified in that the exploding star and the sun need not be a close pair but merely two of a cluster of stars formed at the same time.

Before leaving this subject, where theories are more numerous than firm conclusions, one more question may be raised: was the earth formed hot or cold? There are adherents to both opinions. One side would say that the planets condensed from hot gases, became liquid, and subsequently cooled and solidified, at the surface if not throughout. Others would say that dust, ice, and small particles formed in space first and subsequently accumulated into large bodies, whose temperature rose somewhat later on. With space exploration beginning in earnest, considerable future progress in understanding planetary formation can be anticipated. (*See also* **Section L: Mars, Venus, Planets.**)

THE SOLAR SYSTEM.

Name.	Distance from Sun (millions of miles).	Diameter (thousands of miles).	Average density (water = 1).	Number of Satellites.
Sun	—	865	1·41	—
Mercury . . .	36	3·1	3·73	0
Venus	67	7·6	5·23	0
Earth	93	7·9	5·52	1
Mars	142	4·2	3·94	2
Jupiter . . .	484	85·0	1·34	12
Saturn . . .	887	70·0	0·69	9
Uranus . . .	1785	30·9	1·36	5
Neptune . . .	2797	33·0	1·32	2
Pluto . . .	3670	?	?	0

SOME ASTRONOMICAL DISTANCES.

(1 light-year = $5·88 \times 10^{12}$ miles).

Object.	Distance from Earth (light-years).	Velocity of recession (miles per second).	Object.	Distance from Earth (light-years).	Velocity of recession (miles per second).
Sun	$1·6 \times 10^{-5}$	—	Andromeda Galaxy .	$1·5 \times 10^{6}$	—
Nearest star (Proxima Centauri) . .	4·2	—	Galaxy in Virgo . .	$7·5 \times 10^{7}$	750
Brightest star (Sirius) .	8·6	—	Galaxy in Gt. Bear .	10^{9}	9,300
Pleiades . . .	340	—	Galaxy in Corona Borealis . .	$1·3 \times 10^{9}$	13,400
Centre of Milky Way .	$2·6 \times 10^{4}$	—	Galaxy in Bootes .	$4·5 \times 10^{9}$	24,400
Magellanic clouds (the nearest galaxies) .	$1·6 \times 10^{5}$	—	Very remote quasi-stellar object . .	$\sim 1·5 \times 10^{10}$	$\sim 150,000$

THE EARTH.

Structure.

The earth has the shape of a slightly flattened sphere, with an equatorial radius of 6378 km and a polar radius 21 km less. Its mass can be calculated from Newton's Law of Gravitation and from measurements of the acceleration due to gravity, and is 5.97×10^{24} kg. The average density follows from these two figures and is about 5·5 grams per cubic centimetre. This is nearly twice the density of typical rocks at the surface, so there must be very much denser material somewhere inside, and the earth must have a definite internal structure.

This structure can be investigated using shock waves from earthquakes or large explosions. These are received at recording stations at different distances from their source, having penetrated to varying depths within the earth, and their relative times of arrival and characteristic forms enable the deep structure to be worked out. This consists of three main units, a core at the centre with a radius about half that of the earth, the mantle outside this, and the thin crust, about 35 km thick under the continents and 5 km thick under the oceans, forming a skin surrounding the mantle.

The composition of these three units can be deduced by observation and inference. For example, meteorites which arrive at the earth's surface from other parts of the solar system consist of three main types, composed of iron–nickel alloy, stony silicates, and a mixture of iron and silicates. Could these have originated from the break-up of some planet like the earth? If so, then perhaps the core of the earth is made up of iron–nickel alloy and the mantle of magnesium-rich silicates. Experiments on the physical properties of these materials at high pressures show strong similarities with the measured properties of the earth's interior. In addition, rocks composed of magnesium-rich silicates are found at the earth's surface in places where material seems to have come from great depth, such as in the debris from volcanic explosions. These may be direct samples of the earth's mantle.

Core, Mantle, and Crust.

By these arguments, and by many others, a picture can be built up of the internal structure of the earth. The core is composed of iron-nickel alloy. It is liquid at the outside, but contains a solid inner core of radius about one-fifth of that of the earth. Convection currents flowing in the liquid part give rise to the earth's magnetic field. Outside this the mantle is solid, and is made up mainly of magnesium–iron silicates of various kinds. By studying its physical properties through earthquake wave observations, the mantle may be divided into several zones, of which the most important is the asthenosphere. This is the part of the mantle between 70 and 300 km depth in which volcanic lavas are formed. In this region the mantle is everywhere quite near to the temperature at which it begins to melt, and is thus rather soft compared with the rest of the mantle. The presence of a soft asthenosphere accounts for many of the surface features of the earth, mountain belts and ocean basins, that make it so very different from cratered planets such as the Moon and Mars.

The sharp boundary between mantle and crust is called the Mohorovicic Discontinuity. Above it, the crust is different under continents and oceans. The thick continental crust has a composition that can broadly be called granitic, while the thin oceanic crust is poorer in silicon, sodium, and potassium and richer in calcium, iron, and magnesium. The continental crust has been built up over thousands of millions of years by welding together mountain belts of different ages, while the oceanic crust is made up of basalt lavas and is nowhere older than 250 million years.

Rocks.

Rocks are naturally occurring pieces of the solid earth. If you take a rock and break it up into grains, then separate the grains into different heaps of like grains, each heap will consist of grains of the same *mineral*. For example, the kind of rock called granite can be divided into glassy grains of the mineral quartz, milky white or pink grains of the mineral feldspar, shiny black flakes of the mineral biotite, and shiny colourless flakes of the mineral muscovite. Both biotite and muscovite belong to the mica group of minerals. Each different mineral has a well-defined composition or range of composition, and a definite and characteristic arrangement of the atoms that compose it. There are several thousand known kinds of minerals, but only fifty or so are at all common.

There are three main kinds of rock; igneous rocks, formed by the solidification of molten lava; sedimentary rocks, formed from material laid down under gravity on the earth's surface; and metamorphic rocks, formed by heating or reheating of either of the other kind of rock. Each of these broad groups may be further subdivided. When *igneous rocks* solidify deep inside the earth. they cool slowly and large crystals have time to form. Coarse-grained igneous rocks such as granites are known as plutonic igneous rocks. Conversely the rapidly cooled fine-grained igneous rocks that form the volcanic lavas, such as basalts and rhyolites, are called volcanic igneous rocks. *Sedimentary rocks* can be divided into three kinds: Clastic sediments are those formed from mechanically abraded and transported fragments of pre-existing rocks and include sandstone, mudstone, and clay. Organic sediments are those composed, as are most limestones, of fragments of organically produced material such as shells, wood, and bone. Chemical sediments are formed by direct chemical action and include, most typically, salt deposits formed by evaporation of sea water. *Metamorphic rocks* are more difficult to subdivide. They are usually classified on the basis of their original composition and/or the maximum pressure and temperature to which they have been subjected. Chemical reactions in metamorphic rocks give rise to successions of minerals as the pressure and temperature change, so that examination of a metamorphic rock will often allow one to say how deeply it was buried and how hot it was.

Age of Rocks.

There are two distinct ways of estimating the age of rocks. The first gives the *relative age*. It is based on the principle that in a sequence of sediments, older rocks lie underneath and younger ones above, that igneous rocks are younger than the rocks they intrude, and that folded rocks are formed earlier than the earth movements that fold them. Correlation of a sequence of rocks in one place with those in another is made by fossil faunas and floras. Thus a complete scale of relative ages can be built up, stretching back to the first rocks containing fossils (see the table in Part IV). The *age in years* can, on the other hand, be measured by using radioactive elements (Part II) contained in rocks. If the amount of a radioactive element present is measured, and the amount of the product of radioactive decay can also be found, then, using the known rates of decay, the time since the product started to accumulate (defined for this purpose as the age in years) can be measured. This method is particularly useful for studying rocks that do not contain fossils (igneous and metamorphic rocks, or those too old to contain fossils). By similar methods, the *age of the earth* can be obtained. This turns out to be about 4.75×10^9 years. The rocks containing the first fossils are 2.5–3×10^9 years old, while organised life in abundance first appeared about 0.6×10^9 years ago.

The Continents and the Ocean Floor.

The outer part of the earth, namely, the asthenosphere and the solid mantle and crust overlying it, the lithosphere, is in a state of restless movement, and it is this movement that gives rise to the formation of oceans, continents, and mountain belts. The surface of the earth can be divided into a number of rigid plates of lithosphere, which move apart, or together, or slide past one another. Some of these plates are very large, such as the one which contains all of North America, all of

South America, and about half of the Atlantic Ocean. Others are no more than a few thousand square kilometres in size. But they are all moving about relative to one another like ice floes in pack-ice. Where two plates move apart, hot material rises from the asthenosphere to fill the gap, partly melts, and gives rise to a chain of volcanoes and a thin volcanic crust. This is how ocean basins form and grow larger. In the Atlantic, the Mid-Atlantic Ridge marks the line along which plates are moving apart, and where new ocean is being formed. Long narrow pieces of ocean such as the Red Sea and the Gulf of California mark where a continent has just begun to split apart, and a new ocean is forming. Where two plates slide past one another, a great tear fault results. Such a fault is the San Andreas fault which runs from the Gulf of California to San Francisco. Jerky movement on this fault gave rise to the great San Francisco earthquake of 1906 and could give rise to another earthquake there at any time.

Where two plates move together, the result depends on the nature of the crust forming the plates. If at least one of the plates is oceanic, the oceanic crust dips down into the mantle and slides away to great depths until it eventually merges with the asthenosphere. Along this dipping sheet of crust, strong earthquakes occur and frictional heating of the sheet leads to melting and the production of quantities of lava. Examples of such boundaries are the Andes, where the Pacific Ocean dips beneath South America, and Indonesia, where the Indian Ocean dips below Asia. When both plates are continental, on the other hand, the crust is too thick and bouyant to slide into the mantle, and a collision results, giving rise to a fold mountain chain. Eventually the movement grinds to a halt, the plates weld together, and the fold mountains become dormant. The Himalayas were formed in this way from the recent collision of India and Asia. The evidence that has led to these conclusions is too complex to summarise here. It comes from a study of rock magnetism, earthquakes, the flow of heat from inside the earth and even from the shapes of the continents, that must match across the oceans by which they have been split apart. Confirmation has come from a series of holes drilled in the ocean which has shown how the crust becomes younger towards the centres of the oceans.

Rates of movement of plates have been calculated, ranging from a few millimetres a year to ten centimetres a year. The faster movements can be measured directly on the ground by such simple techniques as looking at the displacement of railway lines, walls, and roads, but the slower ones, and those beneath the oceans must be measured by more indirect geophysical methods. The mechanism by which this movement takes place is still unknown. Are the plates pulled by their sinking edges, or pushed by their rising edges, or moved by some other means? But it cannot be doubted that the movement does happen, and that it holds the key to the development of the earth's crust since the time it was first formed. See **Plate Tectonics, Part VI.**

The Rest.

There is a lot more to the study of the earth than has been possible to set down here. The oceans, the atmosphere, and the rocks of the crust all interact with one another in their development in a complex way. The surface of the earth has gradually changed as life has evolved over thousands of millions of years and ice ages have come and gone, changing the surface again and again. Just as important is the economic potential of the earth, on which we depend for all of our energy and all raw materials. This section has given the basic framework within which such further investigations are carried out, to help the reader understand as he reads more widely.

II. PHYSICS—THE FUNDAMENTAL SCIENCE OF MATTER

WHAT PHYSICS IS ABOUT.

Anyone compelled by curiosity or professional interest to look into contemporary journals of pure physics research is soon struck by the fact that the old text-book division of physics into "heat, light, sound, electricity, and magnetism" has become very blurred. The indispensable periodical of research summaries, *Physics Abstracts*, contains about 3,000 entries a month, under many separate headings. This is very daunting even to the experienced physicist and, as a token of the human effort devoted to one single branch of science, it is impressive for variety, for degree of specialisation, and for sheer volume. How can the main features of this great work be presented to the non-specialist?

Two different, though complementary, sections can be distinguished. First, there is the physics concerned with the properties of matter in bulk, with solids, liquids, and gases, and with those odd but very important substances, such as paints, plastic solutions, and jelly-like material, which are neither properly solid nor liquid. In this vast domain of physics questions like this are asked: Why is iron magnetic, copper not? What happens when solids melt? Why do some liquids flow more easily than others? Why do some things conduct electricity well, others badly, some not at all? During the last century, particularly the last few decades, it has become clear that such questions can be answered only by raising and solving others first. In particular, we must ask: (i) Of what nature are the invisible particles of which matter is composed? and (ii) How are those particles arranged in bulk matter?

The first of these two questions has generated the second major category of modern physics: this is the physics of particles and of the forces that particles exert on each other. In this field, which represents science at its most fundamental, questions like this are asked: If matter is composed of small units or particles, what are they like? How many kinds of particle are there? Do the particles possess mass? electric charge? magnetism? How do the particles influence each other? How can their motion be described and predicted?

Once scientists became convinced that matter did indeed consist of particles, the *arrangement* of the particles in matter became an important question. This is the problem of *structure*. It was discovered, by von Laue in Germany and by W. H. and W. L. Bragg in England, that the structure of solids could be inferred from the way X-rays are reflected. It is well known that X-rays can penetrate solids. In doing so, they encounter successive layers of particles and are reflected from them. The reflections reveal how far apart the layers are and how the particles are arranged in space. This is the technique of X-ray crystallography. By now it has shown that most solid matter is *crystalline, i.e.*, it consists of a regular pattern of particles repeated over and over again to fill the volume of the solid—just as a wallpaper is covered by repeated units of design. The units in a crystal are very small, often about 10^{-8} cm across, and the particles in them are very close together.

Liquids, on the other hand, have no repeated pattern, but consist of particles which are jumbled up, though still very closely packed—like marbles in a bag. In gases, the particles are widely separated and moving rapidly about; the average distance between particles in air is about 10 times that in ordinary solids, and air particles have an average speed of 5×10^4 cm per sec. (1,000 m.p.h.).

In general, therefore, the structure of matter is fairly well understood. This does not mean that structure studies are out of date, but only that now they are devoted to elucidating the structure of particular substances, often extremely complex ones such as are found in living matter. We shall therefore say no more about structure,

but turn to the major divisions of physics introduced above: (i) particles and their forces; (ii)
the properties of matter in bulk.

PARTICLES AND FORCES.

The idea that matter is composed of small
particles, or atoms, originated, it is true, in
classical times. Nevertheless, the modern views
need be traced back no farther than the beginning
of the nineteenth century, when Dalton and his
contemporaries were studying the laws of chemical
combination. By that time the distinctions
between elements, compounds, and mixtures were
already made. Compounds and mixtures are
substances which can be separated into smaller
amounts of chemically distinguishable constituents. Elements (see N34) cannot be so divided.
In a mixture the components may be mixed in
any proportion and sorted out again by non-
chemical means. In a compound the elements
are combined in fixed proportions by weight.
This last fact gives the clue to atomic theory.

Dalton and Atomic Theory.

Dalton pointed out that the fixed combining
weights of elements could easily be explained if
the elements consisted of atoms which combined
in simple numerical ratios, e.g., 1 atom of element
A with one of B, or one of B with two of C, and
so on. For instance, 35·5 g of chlorine combine
with 23·0 g of sodium to make 58·5 g of ordinary
salt. If we assume one atom of chlorine links
with one of sodium, then the atoms themselves
must have weights in the ratio 35·5 to 23·0.
This turns out to be consistent with the combining weights of chlorine and sodium in all other
compounds in which they both take part. Sometimes two elements combine in several different
proportions by weight. But this is easily explained by assuming that the atoms link up in
different numbers, e.g., one iron atom with one
oxygen, or two irons with three oxygens, or three
irons with four oxygens. Then the three different
combining proportions arise from the three different numbers of atoms, using in each case the
same ratio of oxygen atom weight to iron atom weight.

Atomic Weight.

Over the century and a half since Dalton, these
ideas have been repeatedly tested by chemical
experiments. No one now doubts that every
chemical element has atoms of characteristic
weight. By convention the number 12·0000 is
ascribed to carbon and called its " atomic weight."
The atomic weights of other atoms are expressed
by giving their ratio to that of carbon, e.g., hydrogen, 1·008; iron, 55·85. These numbers are only
ratios; the real weight of one single oxygen atom
is $2·7 \times 10^{-23}$ g.

J. J. Thomson and the Electron.

Matter is electrically uncharged in its normal
state, but there exist many well-known ways of
producing electric charges and currents—rubbing
amber, or rotating dynamos, for example. It is
therefore necessary to have some theory of electricity linked to the theory of matter. The fundamental experiment in this field was made by J. J.
Thomson when, in 1897, he discovered the electron.
If you take two metal electrodes sealed inside a
glass vessel, and if the air is suitably pumped out
and a high voltage applied to the electrodes, then
the negative one emits a radiation which causes
the walls of the tube to glow. The rays are called
cathode rays. The discovery of the electron was
essentially a clarification of the nature of cathode
rays. Thomson showed that they were streams of
particles with mass and negative electric charge
and a general behaviour unlike any other atomic
particle known at that time. The importance of
this discovery for the world of science cannot be
overestimated, and its technical progeny are in
every home and factory in radio valves, television
tubes, and other devices.

Rutherford–Bohr Atom.

Since the electrons emerge from matter, they
are presumably parts of atoms. The relation be-

tween the negative electrons and the positively
charged constituents of matter was elucidated by
the great experimenter Rutherford and the great
theoretician Bohr. Their work, just before the
First World War, showed that the positive charge,
together with almost all the mass, is concentrated
in the central core or nucleus of the atom about
which the very light-weight electrons revolve.
The diameter of an atom is about 10^{-8} cm, roughly
one three-hundred-millionth part of an inch. The
central nucleus has a diameter about 10,000 times
smaller still. The nucleus and the electrons hold
together because of the electric attraction between
them.

At this stage work could, and did, go on separately along several different lines:

(i) Electrons could be studied on their own.
Nowadays the handling of beams of electrons
of all sizes and intensities has become a
major industry.

(ii) The nucleus could be treated as a
special problem, and this led to the mid-
century flowering of nuclear physics, to the
atomic bomb, and to nuclear power.

(iii) The behaviour of electrons in the atom
could be analysed; this is the great domain
of atomic physics which spreads into many
other sciences as well.

Volumes have been written about each of these
three fields, but we can spare only a few lines for
each.

The Electron.

Electrons are expelled from solids by light,
heat, electric fields, and other influences. It has
therefore been possible to study beams of electrons
on their own in vacuo. Electrons inside matter,
either as constituents, or temporarily in transit,
can also be observed by their innumerable effects.
These observations all show the particles to be
indistinguishable one from another; all electrons
are the same wherever they come from. They
have a definite mass ($9·11 \times 10^{-28}$ g), a negative electric charge, a magnetic moment, and a
" spin " (intrinsic rotatory motion). No one
has ever subdivided an electron or obtained an
electric charge smaller than that on one electron.
The electronic charge is therefore used as a basic
unit of charge in atomic physics. The electron
has come to be the best known of all the " fundamental particles."

The Nucleus.

The early research programmes in nuclear
physics were greatly facilitated by the occurrence
in nature of certain unstable (radioactive) nuclei
which emit fast-moving fragments. The latter
can be used as projectiles to aim at other nuclei
as targets; the resulting impacts yield much
valuable information. This technique still
dominates nuclear physics, though nowadays the
projectiles are artificially accelerated by one or
other of the large costly machines designed for
the purpose.

The most important early discovery was that
the nucleus consists of two types of fundamental
particle—the positively charged proton and the
electrically neutral neutron. These two are of
nearly equal mass (about 1,800 times that of the
electron), and like electrons, have a magnetic
moment and spin. The proton charge is equal to
the electron charge, though opposite in sign.
Consider a moderately complex nucleus like that
of iron. This usually has 30 neutrons and 26 protons. Its atomic weight therefore depends on the
total number of neutrons plus protons, but the total
charge depends only on the number of protons—
called the atomic number. The latter is denoted
by Z while the total number of neutrons plus
protons is called mass number and denoted by M.
A species of nucleus with given values of Z and
M is called a nuclide. Z is also the number of
electrons in the atom, since the atom as a whole is
electrically neutral. The atomic number determines the chemical nature of the atom (see below),
so that by altering the number of neutrons in a
nucleus we do not change the chemical species.
It is therefore possible to find—and nowadays to

make—nuclei of the same element which nevertheless differ slightly in weight because they have different numbers of neutrons. These are called *isotopes*. Iron isotopes are known with 26, 27, 28, 29, 30, 31, 32, and 33 neutrons, but all have 26 protons. Thus a set of isotopes consists of the various nuclides that have the same Z but different M's.

Stable Nuclides.

The protons and neutrons in a nucleus are bound together by strong forces called *nuclear forces*. In many cases, the forces are so strong that no particles ever escape and the nucleus preserves its identity. There are two hundred and seventy-four different combinations of neutrons and protons of this kind, and they are called the *stable nuclides*. The earth is largely composed of such stable nuclides, because any unstable ones have, in the course of time, spontaneously broken up into stable residues.

Nevertheless, there are some unstable nuclei left on earth. They give rise to the phenomenon of radioactivity which was discovered by Becquerel in 1893.

Unstable Nuclides: Radioactivity.

Becquerel found that certain chemicals containing uranium gave off rays capable of blackening a photographic plate, and shortly afterwards Marie and Pierre Curie discovered more substances, including radium, which produce similar but stronger effects. By now, about fifty chemical elements having radioactive properties are known to exist on earth, some, like radium, being strongly radioactive, others, like potassium, being so weak that the radiations are difficult to detect. These are called the *natural radioactive nuclides*.

The main facts about radioactivity are as follows: it is a *nuclear* phenomenon and (with minor exceptions) proceeds quite independently of whatever the electrons in the atom may be doing. Thus, the radioactivity of an atom is not affected by the chemical combination of the atom with other atoms, nor by ordinary physical influences like temperature and pressure. The radioactivity consists of the emission by the substance of certain kinds of rays. The early workers, Rutherford being the giant among them, distinguished three kinds of rays labelled α, β, and γ. These are described below. Whatever kind of ray is examined, it is found that the radiation from a given sample decreases gradually with time according to a definite law which states that the intensity of radiation decreases by half every T seconds. The number T, called the half-life, is constant for each radioactive material, but varies enormously from substance to substance. For instance, radium decreases its activity by a half every 1,622 years, whereas the half-life of one of the polonium isotopes is about 0.3×10^{-6} sec.

α-, β-, and γ-rays.

The three most well-known types of radioactive emission are quite distinct from one another.

(i) α-rays or α-particles consist of two protons and two neutrons bound together. They are ejected from the radioactive nucleus with one of several well-defined speeds. These speeds are high, often of the order 10^9 cm per sec. Two protons and two neutrons are the constituents of the nucleus of helium, and α-particles are thus fast-moving helium nuclei.

(ii) β-rays are moving electrons. They may emerge from their parent nucleus with any speed from zero to a definite maximum. The maximum speed often approaches that of light, and is different for each isotope. The electron has a positively charged counterpart, the positron (see below), and β-rays are sometimes positrons. To distinguish the two cases, the symbols β^- and β^+ are used. The naturally occurring β-radiations are almost all β^-.

(iii) γ-rays travel with the speed of light because they are in fact electromagnetic waves differing from light only in the extreme shortness of their wavelength. They have no electric charge.

It is unusual, though not unheard of, for the same radioactive substance to emit both α- and β-rays. On the other hand, γ-rays frequently accompany either α- or β-rays.

γ-rays pass through matter easily; in fact, they are extra penetrating X-rays. α-rays can be stopped by thin sheets of tissue paper. α-rays brought to rest pick up a pair of electrons from the surrounding matter and become neutral helium atoms, and helium gas from this source is consequently found imprisoned in certain radioactive rocks. β-rays are intermediate in penetrating power between α- and γ-rays.

We must now try to interpret these observations.

Radioactive Disintegration.

A nucleus is a collection of neutrons and protons interacting with each other and possessing collectively a certain amount of energy. Just as some human organisations lose their coherence if they accept too many members, so nuclei can remain stable only if (i) the total number of particles is not too great, and (ii) neutrons and protons are there in suitable proportions. Radioactive nuclei are the ones for which either or both these conditions do not hold. Sooner or later such nuclei eject a fragment, thus getting rid of some energy they cannot contain. This is called a *radioactive disintegration*, and the fragments are the α-, β-, and γ-rays. α-emission relieves a nucleus of two neutrons and two protons and some energy; γ-emission simply carries off excess energy without altering the number or kind of particles left behind. β-emission is more complicated. There are no electrons normally present in a nucleus, but they are suddenly created and explosively emitted if a neutron changes into a proton; positive electrons are similarly generated if a proton changes into a neutron. β-emission is therefore a mechanism for changing the ratio of protons to neutrons without altering the total number of particles.

Both α- and β-emission change the Z of a nucleus, and the product, or daughter nucleus, is a different chemical element. α-emission also changes the M. It might happen that the daughter nucleus is unstable, in which case it too will disintegrate. Successive generations are produced until a stable one is reached. Part of such a family tree is shown below. The symbols above the arrows show the kind of rays emitted at each stage, the figures are the mass numbers, M, and the names and symbols of chemical elements can be found at the end of the Section, **F66.**

$$U^{238} \xrightarrow{\alpha} Th^{234} \xrightarrow{\beta} Pa^{234} \xrightarrow{\beta} U^{234} \xrightarrow{\alpha} Th^{230} \xrightarrow{\alpha}$$
$$Ra^{226} \xrightarrow{\alpha} Rn^{222} \xrightarrow{\alpha} Po^{218} \xrightarrow{\alpha} Pb^{214} \xrightarrow{\beta} Bi^{214} \xrightarrow{\beta}$$
$$Po^{214} \xrightarrow{\alpha} Pb^{210} \xrightarrow{\beta} Bi^{210} \xrightarrow{\beta} Po^{210} \xrightarrow{\alpha} Pb^{206}$$
$$(Pb^{206} \text{ is stable lead}).$$

This family exists naturally on earth, because the head of the family, U^{238}, has so long a half-life (4.5×10^9 years) that there has not yet been time enough since its formation for it to have disappeared.

Artificial Radioactivity.

Nowadays many new radioactive isotopes can be man-made. All that is required is to alter the M or Z (or both) of a stable isotope to a value which is incompatible with stability. The means for doing this is *bombardment*, i.e., stable nuclei are exposed to the impacts of atomic particles such as streams of protons from an accelerator, the neutrons in an atomic reactor, or simply the α-particles from another radioactive substance. The new material is called an *artificially radioactive isotope*. Artificial radioactivity is not different in kind from that of the naturally radioactive substances, but the half-lives are usually on the short side. Indeed, the isotopes in question would exist in nature but for the fact that their short half-lives ensured their disappearance from the earth long ago.

Suppose a piece of copper is exposed to the intense neutron radiation in an atomic reactor at Harwell.

The more abundant of the two stable isotopes of ordinary copper has thirty-four neutrons and twenty-nine protons (i.e., $Z = 29$, $M = 63$). In the reactor many (not all) of these nuclei absorb a neutron, giving an unstable copper nucleus with $Z = 29$, $M = 64$. When removed from the reactor the specimen is observed to be radioactive with a half-life of 12·8 hours. It is somewhat unusual in that it gives out both β^{-} and β^{+} rays. Some nuclei emit electrons, leaving a daughter nucleus with one more positive charge than copper, i.e., a zinc nucleus ($Z = 30$, $M = 64$). One neutron has become a proton, and the resulting zinc nucleus is stable. The others emit positrons, leaving behind a nucleus in which a proton has been turned into a neutron ($Z = 28$, $M = 64$); this is a stable nickel nucleus. The overall process is one example of the artificial transmutation of the chemical elements which is now a commonplace of nuclear physics. It was first discovered by Irene and Frederick Joliot-Curie in 1934.

Lack of a Complete Theory.

Consider now a collection of, say, one million radioactive nuclei of the same kind. It is impossible to tell exactly when any one of them will disintegrate; it is a matter of chance which ones break up first. All we know is that, after a time equal to the half-life, only a half a million will survive unchanged. In general, the more excess energy a nucleus has, the more likely it is to break up, and therefore the shorter the half-life of that particular nuclear species. In principle, to calculate the half-life theoretically, one would have to have a reliable theory of nuclear forces and energies. This is still being sought after, so it is probably fair to say that while the laws of behaviour of radioactive isotopes are well and accurately known, the *explanation* of this behaviour in terms of the properties of protons and neutrons is by no means complete.

Nuclear Fission—Chain Reaction.

A discovery important not just for nuclear physics but for the whole of mankind was made by Hahn and Strassman in 1939. This was the discovery of nuclear fission in uranium. One of the natural isotopes of uranium is an unstable one, U^{235}, with 143 neutrons and 92 protons. It normally shows its instability by emitting α- and γ-rays. If uranium is bombarded with neutrons, some U^{235} nuclei temporarily gain an extra neutron, which makes them even less stable. This they show by splitting into two roughly equal parts, called fission fragments, together with two or three neutrons. There are two highly important things about this disintegration. One is that the two or three neutrons can promote further disintegrations in other uranium nuclei, and the process can therefore be self-propagating: it is then called a *chain reaction*. The other is that the total mass of the fission products is less than that of the original nucleus. This mass difference does not disappear without trace; it turns into energy according to a formula referred to in a paragraph below (**F15(1)**).

Application of these New Forces.

The world has found two uses for the energy liberated in nuclear chain reactions: the atomic bomb and nuclear power plants. In the first, conditions are arranged to promote and encourage a tremendous and rapid chain reaction leading to an explosion; in the second, the steady liberation of energy in the form of heat is controlled for use in turbines which can generate electricity or provide propulsion. Both uses represent epoch-making technical achievements, but mankind has yet to show itself capable of bearing sanely the burden of responsibility which nuclear physicists have laid upon it. One thing is certain: the discoveries will not cease. Already, other fissionable elements have been made and used; new chemical elements have been created; nuclear plants (" atomic piles ") have stimulated great demands for new materials that will stand the heat and radiation inside the reactor, and this promotes research in other fields of science; irradiation inside an atomic pile gives new and potentially useful properties to old materials;

nuclear power drives ships and submarines. It is difficult to write even briefly about contemporary nuclear physics without feeling keenly the ambiguity of its powerful promises.

Although so much is known about the behaviour of nuclei, the theory of the nucleus leaves much to be desired. What holds the neutrons and protons together? Why are some nuclei more stable than others? It is certain that the forces between neutrons and protons in a nucleus are unlike the electrical attractions between the nucleus as a whole and its surrounding electrons. Nor have they anything to do with gravitation. Indeed, the best description and explanation of nuclear forces is the objective of much of the contemporary research effort in nuclear physics.

Atoms.

A nucleus surrounded by its full complement of electrons is an electrically neutral system called an atom. Neither the atom as a whole, nor its nucleus, counts as a " fundamental particle " because either can be subdivided into more elementary parts, thus:

$$atom \longrightarrow electrons + nucleus \longrightarrow electrons + neutrons + protons$$

The chemical identity of the atoms of a given element, which was Dalton's key idea, depends entirely on the number and motion of the electrons. For example, the simplest element, hydrogen, has one proton for a nucleus, and one electron. The latter is comparatively easily detached or disturbed by the electric forces exerted by neighbouring atoms, consequently hydrogen is reactive chemically, i.e., it readily lends its electron to build chemical structures with other equally co-operative elements. The second element, helium, has a nucleus of two protons and two neutrons; outside are two electrons in a particularly stable arrangement. Indeed, this pair of electrons is so difficult to disarrange that a special name has been coined to cover such cases—*closed shells*. Helium, with its closed shell, will not react chemically with anything. As the nuclear charge increases, different electron arrangements of greater or lesser stability succeed one another, with every so often a closed shell corresponding to one of the chemically inert gases neon, argon, xenon, krypton. *See* **F20 (1)**.

Such considerations, pursued in sufficient detail, enable atomic physics to account for all the differences and similarities among the chemical elements and, in principle at least, for the other facts of chemistry as well.

Ions.

It is possible to remove one or more electrons from an atom, leaving it positively charged. The atom is then said to be *ionised* and is called a *positive ion*. Alternatively, some atoms are capable of accepting electrons above their normal complement, thus becoming negative ions. The behaviour of ions is very important in many fields of physics and chemistry, and some of these will be referred to later.

Molecules.

Electrical attractions of various kinds cause atoms and ions to form compound groups. This is the basis of chemical combination, and the smallest conceivable fragment of compound which still preserves the chemical identity of that compound is called a molecule. Molecules have a wide range of complexity, from simple pairs of atoms to highly intricate spirals and chains composed of thousands of atoms. *See* Part III.

Excited Atoms.

Like the nuclei described above, atoms can be given excess energy and will then return to their ground state with the emission of radiation. The excess energy usually resides in one of the electrons which is executing unusually violent motion. The electron returns to normal by releasing its excess energy in the form of light whose colour is characteristic of the atom involved.

F13

Herein lies the explanation of innumerable natural and technical phenomena, such as the colours of glowing gases whether they exist in the sun and stars, in aurorae, or in street-lamps and neon signs. Herein also lies the reason for the importance of spectroscopy, which is the study of the characteristic radiation from excited atoms; for spectroscopy is not only a useful tool for the chemical identification of elements (" spectroscopic analysis ") but was one of the main routes along which twentieth-century physicists broke through to a knowledge of the inner nature of the atom.

Maxwell and Electromagnetic Waves.

Atoms are held together by the electric attraction of the nucleus for the electrons. Finer details of atomic behaviour depend on the magnetic moments of the particles. Any region of space subject to electric and magnetic influences is called an *electromagnetic field*. Before the discovery of the electron, Maxwell had perfected a general theory of the electromagnetic field, giving to physics a celebrated set of equations which describe satisfactorily almost all electric and magnetic phenomena. *Inter alia*, he proved that disturbances in the electric and magnetic conditions at one place could be propagated to another place through empty space, with a definite velocity, just as sound waves are propagated through air. Such electromagnetic disturbances in transit are called *electromagnetic waves*, and their velocity turned out experimentally to be the same as that of light and radio waves—which was a decisive argument to show that both of these phenomena are themselves electromagnetic waves.

Einstein and Photons.

In the years between about 1900 and 1920 this view was upset by Planck, Einstein, Millikan, and others, who focused attention on phenomena (radiant heat, photoelectricity) in which light behaves like a stream of particles and not at all like waves. A wave and a particle are two quite different things, as anyone will admit after a moment's contemplation of, say, the ripples on a pond and a floating tennis ball. The acute question was: is light like waves or particles? This celebrated dilemma soon multiplied its horns. In 1927 electrons were shown to be quite capable of behaving as waves instead of particles, and this is now known to be true of protons, neutrons, and all other fundamental particles as well.

Theoretical physicists have devised means of having it both ways. To say that light behaves as particles means that the waves of the electromagnetic field cannot have their energy subdivided indefinitely. For waves of a given frequency, there is a certain irreducible quantity of energy that must be involved whenever light interacts with anything. This quantity is the product $h\nu$, where ν is the frequency and h is a constant named after Planck. Each such unit is called a *quantum of the electromagnetic field* or a *photon* and is counted as one of the fundamental particles. Frequencies and wavelengths vary widely; typical wavelengths are: radio—hundreds or thousands of metres; radar—a few centimetres; visible light—5×10^{-5} cm; X-rays—10^{-8} cm.

Elementary Particles.

Nature seems to use four different kinds of force to make one particle interact with another. The weakest force is gravity; while this dominates celestial mechanics its effect inside atoms is negligible compared with the other three. The binding forces inside atoms are *electromagnetic*, *e.g.*, the attraction of nuclei for electrons. Considerably stronger still is the nuclear force which holds the nuclei together and this is called the *strong interaction*. The fourth force is called the *weak interaction* and is intermediate in strength between electromagnetic and gravitational forces. It is responsible for a number of phenomena of which the best known is β-radioactivity.

Particles may respond to some or all of the forces. Protons are involved with all of them but electrons respond to all except the " strong interaction." When new particles are discovered physicists try to find out their fundamental properties and among these is their response (if any) to each kind of force. Some other basic properties are: electric charge (if any), mass (if any), and the speed with which the particle splits up spontaneously into other types.

So many so-called elementary particles have been discovered (about a hundred) that the whole conception of " elementary-ness " has been in question. Are all the particles equally " elementary "? Are some of them excited states or combinations of others? When a family reaches a hundred it becomes difficult to believe they are *all* grandparents. One current trend is away from setting up a hierarchy in which some particles are elementary and some composite and towards treating them all as mutually dependent for their existence. This, however, is a very difficult problem, not yet solved.

A few particles are stable but most decay into products. The lifetimes of unstable particles are extraordinarily short by everyday standards but, even so, some (of about 10^{-17} sec. or upwards) are much longer than others (of about 10^{-22} sec.). The Table on page **F14** contains the stable particles and a *selection* of the moderately unstable ones with brief comments on their properties.

The Table shows a rudimentary classification into four groups: (i) the photon; (ii) leptons—which are particles, lighter than protons, which do not react to the " strong " type of force; (iii) mesons—which are particles, lighter than protons, which are subject to all the kinds of force; (iv) baryons—which include protons, neutrons, and heavier particles, all of which react to the " strong " force. Many of these particles have been produced for the first time in recent years by bombarding matter with beams of high energy particles. Much of this work is done in the large accelerating machines at Brookhaven, New York, and the European Organisation for Nuclear Research, Geneva.

Forming particles into groups is an important matter. It is comparable with arranging chemical elements into the Periodic Table. The pattern does not of itself explain anything but it strongly suggests where to look for explanations. The classification of particles currently favoured is based on the very sophisticated mathematical ideas known as *group theory*. Group theory is a branch of mathematics which is finding increasing application in physics and it had a resounding success recently which illustrates the value of grouping. It turned out that there was no known particle to occupy a vacant position in one of the family groups required by the theory. This particle, the omega minus, was sought and found with exactly the right properties in February 1964. This is reminiscent of finding the missing elements in the Periodic Table. The discovery of omega minus generated much excitement in the scientific world and many physicists believe that a new and deeper understanding of fundamental physics is just round the corner. The corner may be turned if three much sought after but as yet undiscovered particles called the quarks are found. Some theoreticians believe that the properties of all other particles could be explained by the behaviour of the three really fundamental quarks. The latter are hypothetical but are being taken very seriously by those who are trying to detect them experimentally.

It is now accepted that every fundamental particle is a manifestation of the waves of one or other kind of field. Physicists speak of waves, particles, and fields in the same breath or rather the same equation. Little is to be gained by asking if electrons or photons are " really " particles or waves. All one can say is that they are things whose behaviour is predicted and described by certain equations. Those who must visualise can imagine particles in some phenomena and waves in others: neither conception contains the whole truth. Why should the ultimate invisible constituents of matter be forced into one or other category derived from everyday experience? For convenience, however, we shall continue to call these things " elementary particles."

SOME MEMBERS OF THE ATOMIC FAMILY

The numbers in brackets after the name denote first the electric charge and second, the mass. The charge on an electron is counted as −1 unit and the electron mass as +1 unit. Thus (+1, 207) means the particle has a positive charge of 1 unit and a mass 207 times that of the electron.

Photon (0, 0)	A quantum of electromagnetic radiation, *e.g.*, light, X-rays, γ-rays. The concept was introduced by M. Planck in 1900 when he described the emission of light as taking place in " packets " rather than in a steady stream. The energy of a photon is proportional to the frequency of the radiation and inversely proportional to the wavelength.

Leptons

Electron (−1, 1)	Discovered by J. J. Thomson in 1897. The number of orbital electrons in an atom determines its chemical properties. Actual rest mass = $9 \cdot 1 \times 10^{-28}$ g. Emitted as β-rays by some radioactive nuclei. A stable particle.
Positron (+1, 1)	Positive counterpart or, " anti-particle," to the electron. Predicted theoretically by P. A. M. Dirac in 1928 and first discovered in cosmic rays by C. D. Anderson in 1932. Emitted as β-rays by some radioactive nuclei. When positrons and electrons collide they usually annihilate each other and turn into γ-rays; consequently, positrons only last about 10^{-10} sec. within ordinary matter, but are stable in isolation.
Neutrino (0, 0) and Anti-neutrino (0, 0)	These particles travel with the speed of light and are distinguished from one another by the relation of their spin to their direction of motion. A neutrino is emitted with the positron during positive β-decay; and an anti-neutrino with the electron during negative β-decay. Their interaction with matter is extremely slight. First postulated by Pauli in 1933 and detected in 1956. π-meson decay also produces neutrinos and anti-neutrinos but in 1962 it was proved experimentally that these are a different species. Thus there are two kinds of neutrino each with an anti-neutrino. All these particles are distinguished from photons by having different spin.
Muon (±1, 207)	Similar to, but heavier than, the electron and positron; disintegrates into electron (or positron if positive) + neutrino + anti-neutrino.

Mesons

Pion (±1, 273) or (0, 264)	The π-meson. Charged pions decay either into muons and neutrinos or into electrons and neutrinos. Neutral pions decay into γ-rays, into " positron-electron pairs," or both. Pions are intimately connected with nuclear forces, *i.e.*, with the " strong " interaction.
Kaon (±1, 967) or (0, 974)	The K-mesons. These decay in many different ways producing other mesons, electrons, and neutrinos.

Baryons

Proton (+1, 1836·1)	The positively-charged constituent of nuclei; the hydrogen nucleus is one proton. Fast-moving protons occur in cosmic rays. Does not spontaneously disintegrate.
Anti-proton (−1, 1836·1)	Negative anti-particle of the proton. Its existence was long suspected. Artificially produced and detected for the first time in 1955. Will react with the proton to produce pions or kaons.
Neutron (0, 1838·6)	Discovered by J. Chadwick in 1932. The neutral constituent of nuclei. When free it spontaneously disintegrates into a proton, an electron, and an anti-neutrino, after an average lifetime of about 18 minutes. Passes through matter much more easily than charged particles.
Anti-neutron (0, 1838·6)	The anti-particle of the neutron from which it is distinguished by properties connected with its magnetic moment and spin. Will react with neutron to produce pions or kaons.
Lambda Particle (0, 2183)	Discovered in 1947. Decays into proton plus pion.
Sigma Particle (0 or ±1; about 2330)	Various modes of disintegration, producing neutrons, protons, mesons and lambda particles.
Omega Minus (−1, 3270)	Predicted by recent theory and discovered at Brookhaven, New York, in 1964. Still under intensive study.

QUANTUM THEORY AND RELATIVITY.

Quantum Theory.

The point of view of the last paragraph is characteristic of quantum theory, which is the currently accepted fundamental theory of matter and motion. One can reasonably ask at what position in space, exactly, is a particle? Or, what, exactly, is the wavelength of a wave? But the first question cannot be reasonably asked of a wave, nor the second of a particle. Since electrons have something in common with both, one question cannot be answered precisely for electrons without ignoring the other; alternatively, both questions can be given an imprecise answer. As the wavelength of electrons is intimately connected with their speed, one has to accept an accurate knowledge of the speed (wavelength) and ignorance of position, or the converse, or *inaccurate* knowledge of both. This is the famous Heisenberg Uncertainty Principle. Quantum theory is a set of mathematical rules for calculating the behaviour of fundamental particles in accordance with the Uncertainty Principle. In spite of its equivocal-sounding name, the principle has led to an enormous increase in the accuracy with which physical phenomena can be described and predicted. Quantum theory includes all that previous theories did and more.

Quantum theory grew up in the same epoch as the Theory of Relativity. Heroic attempts have been made to combine the two, but with only partial success so far. Relativity is concerned with all motion and all physical laws, but its characteristic manifestations occur only when something is moving with nearly the velocity of light. Quantum theory is likewise all-embracing, but its typical phenomena almost always occur when something on the minute atomic scale is in question. Consequently, the vast majority of everyday mechanics needs no more than the classical theory laid down by Newton, which is neither relativistic nor quantum.

Relativity.

Historically, relativity grew out of attempts to measure the speed with which the earth moved through that hypothetical medium, called the ether, which was supposed at that time to be the bearer of light waves. To take a simple analogy: sound waves travel through still air with a certain definite speed. v. If you move through the air with speed v' towards oncoming sound waves, they will pass you at the speed $v + v'$. Michelson and Morley, in their celebrated experiment of 1887, failed to find the corresponding behaviour on the part of light. This is so important an experiment that it has been repeated, and repeatedly discussed, ever since. In October 1958 the latest and most accurate confirmation of the Michelson–Morley result was announced. It seems as if light always travels with the same speed relative to an observer, however fast he moves relative to anything else. Einstein put it this way: two observers moving with any constant velocity relative to each other will always agree that light travels past them at the same speed; this speed is denoted by c, and is approximately 186,000 miles per second.

This postulate, logically developed, leads to remarkable conclusions. For instance: if you walk from tail to nose of an aircraft at 4 m.p.h. and the plane is receding from me at 300 m.p.h., then you recede from me at 304 m.p.h. " Common sense," Newton, and Einstein would all agree on this. But if you could walk at 0·25c and the plane moved at 0·5c, the Newtonian mechanics would give your recession speed as 0·75c, whereas Einsteinian relativity would give about 0·71c. Although at the everyday speed of 300 m.p.h., the disagreement, though present in principle, is absolutely negligible, at speeds near that of light it becomes very pronounced. Many experiments show that the relativity answer is right.

Equivalence of mass and energy.

Another famous consequence of relativity is the equation $E = mc^2$, connecting energy, E, with mass, m. c is so great that when mass is converted to energy a small mass gives a large energy. The grim demonstration of this was given to the world at Hiroshima; a more hopeful one at Calder Hall, the world's first nuclear power station. The life-giving energy of the sun is derived from nuclear processes which consume mass and deliver energy according to this equation.

Mass and rest mass.

" Mass " is far from being a simple notion. The only complication we shall note here is that the mass of a body is not necessarily constant. A stationary body can be observed to have a mass called its *rest mass*. If the body moves, it has energy of motion and therefore, according to Einstein's mass–energy equation, it increases its mass. Mass thus depends on speed, but in such

a way that there is very little change unless the speed approaches that of light. Many experiments on atomic particles demonstrate this. The interesting question now arises: do all fundamental particles have rest mass? or do some have mass derived solely from their energy? The answer appears to be that photons and neutrinos have no rest mass; all other particles have. The Table on **F14** gives their rest masses.

Special theory of relativity.

The mathematical development of Einstein's ideas, leading to the conclusions just referred to, constitutes the Special Theory of Relativity. Stated more generally, the theory raises the question whether two observers in uniform relative motion could ever detect, as a result of their relative speed, any difference in the physical laws governing matter, motion, and light. To this, Special Relativity answers: No. The detailed theory involves special consideration of the results the two observers would obtain when measuring (i) the spatial distance, and (ii) the time interval, between the same two events. It turns out that they would not agree on these two points. They would agree, however, on the value of a certain quantity made up jointly of the spatial distance and the time interval in a somewhat complex combination. The intimate mixture of space and time in this quantity has led to the treatment of the three space dimensions and time on an equivalent footing. Hence the frequent references to time as the " fourth dimension." Minkowski devised an extremely elegant presentation of relativity theory by using an extension of ordinary geometry to four dimensions. A line drawn in his four-dimensional space represents the path of a particle in space and time, *i.e.*, the whole history of the particle. Thus the movement of particles in the ordinary world is turned into the geometry of lines in Minkowski's four-dimensional world of " space–time."

Relativity and Gravitation.

The apparently innocuous extension of the preceding ideas to include observers in accelerated relative motion opened up new fields of mathematical complexity, but enabled Einstein to bring gravitation into the argument. In speaking of atoms and particles we have not yet mentioned gravity. This is because the electrical and magnetic forces acting between the particles constituting matter are much stronger than the gravitational; gravity need not enter atomic theory at all. But in the discussion of astronomical problems and the movements of large-scale, electrically uncharged bodies, it has been usual, ever since Newton, to say that two bodies of mass m_1 and m_2, separated by a distance r, attract one another with a force proportional to m_1m_2/r^2. This is Newton's inverse square law of gravitation. With this, Newton explained the movements of planets and comets and the falling to earth of the apple from his tree.

The apple's fall is accelerated, and we observe this by noting its position relative to certain marks fixed with respect to us, and by timing it with some sort of clock. This system of location in space and time may be called our " frame of reference." We therefore assert that, in our frame of reference, the apple falls down with an acceleration which Newton saw no alternative but to attribute to a thing called gravitational attraction. Galileo had shown that *all* bodies fall with the same acceleration at all points, and we can now rephrase this by saying that in our frame of reference there is a constant gravitational attraction or *uniform gravitational field*. (This last statement and Galileo's demonstration only refer strictly to points fairly near the earth's surface; at greater distances the gravitational field decreases and is therefore not uniform.)

Now suppose a collection of falling bodies is observed by an intelligent creature, designated C, who inhabits one of them. C has his own frame of reference fixed relative to him. In C's frame neither his own body, nor any of the others, is accelerated, and therefore he has no reason to suppose a gravitational force is acting on them. We have, therefore, the following situation:

(i) in our frame, fixed relative to us, we find all the bodies falling subject to a gravitational pull;

(ii) in C's frame, undergoing accelerated fall relative to us, no gravitational field is apparent.

It looks, therefore, as if one has only to choose the correct frame of reference for the measurements in order to remove the need for any assumptions about the existence of gravitational fields. This is a simple illustration of the connection between gravitation and frames of reference for the measurement of space and time. Einstein's General Theory of Relativity extends this to cover non-uniform gravitational fields and shows that what Newton taught us to call the gravitational field of material bodies is better thought of as a peculiarity of the space and time in the neighbourhood of such bodies. Since space–time, as we mentioned above, can be expressed in geometrical terms, Einstein has transformed the theory of gravitation into an exercise (a difficult one) in the geometry of space–time. Other physicists, in Einstein's tradition, are trying to turn *all* physics into geometry, but no one knows whether this is really feasible.

All this abstruse work is much more than a demonstration of mathematical power and elegance. Observable phenomena which fall outside the scope of Newton's theory of gravitation are accounted for by relativity. One is the small but definite discrepancy between the actual orbit of the planet Mercury and the predictions of Newton's theory. Another is the bending of stellar light rays as they pass close to the sun, an effect which results in the apparent displacement of the position of the star. A third is the effect of a gravitational field on the wavelength of light emitted by atoms. Similar atoms in different places in a gravitational field emit radiations with slightly different wavelengths. For example, the light from an atom in the intense field of a star should have slightly longer wavelength than the corresponding light from an atom on earth. This effect has always proved very difficult to detect with certainty. However, Einstein's prediction was verified with moderate accuracy in 1960 by a very subtle method which was purely terrestrial in its operation. The atoms being compared were placed at the top and bottom of a water tower and the difference in their emission was detected by means that belong rather to nuclear physics than to astronomy.

Quantum Theory and Relativity Combined.

The atomic family table refers to " antiparticles." The theory which first introduced such things in 1934 is due to the Cambridge physicist Dirac and was epoch-making. Dirac conceived an equation to describe the motion of electrons subject to the laws of both quantum theory and relativity. His achievement was thus to synthesise these two great ideas. The spin of the electron was originally a supposition that helped to make sense of spectroscopic observations of light emitted from atoms. Dirac's equation made spin a logical consequence of the union of relativity and quantum theory. Perhaps even more important was the brilliant inference that the equation for the electron implied the existence of another particle having the same mass and spin but with a positive instead of a negative electric charge. This object is called the electron's antiparticle and is now well known as a positron.

A positron and electron can be created simultaneously (" pair production ") and can annihilate each other when they collide.

Every particle is now believed to imply an antiparticle, so it is conceivable that the universe could have been (but isn't) an anti-universe, *i.e.*, all the electrons and protons might have been positrons and antiprotons and so on. The laws of physics would still have been applicable, however.

Not all particles are charged electrically but, when they are, their antiparticles have equal charges of the opposite sign. Whenever charged particles interact the total amount of electric charge is the same before and after whatever events occur. This is called the law of conservation of charge.

Conservation Laws.

Parity. Charge conservation and the conservation of energy (F 17(2)) are only two of a considerable number of conservation laws. Readers who have studied mechanics will also be aware of the conservation of momentum and of angular momentum. A conservation law is the proposition that in the course of physical happenings such and such a quantity is " conserved," *i.e.*, maintains a constant value.

The establishment of conservation laws is playing a great part in our growing understanding of elementary particles although the things that are conserved are somewhat abstruse. One of them is called parity.

Any reader who looks in a mirror knows that the left- and right-hand sides of his face are interchanged in the image. Fortunately mirrors do not also turn the image upside down, but, if they did, the face would then have undergone what is called " a parity transformation." A screwdriver driving a right-handed screw downwards becomes, on parity transformation, a screwdriver driving a left-handed screw upwards. The law of conservation of parity is a way of asserting that any physical process that goes on in the world could equally well go on—obeying the same laws—in a parity transformed world. There is nothing left-handed that does not in principle have a right-handed counterpart.

For many years this belief was strongly held. It came as something of a shock when, in 1957, after theoretical proposals by Lee and Yang in America, Wu and co-workers proved that parity was not always conserved. To understand Wu's experiment, we must recall that nuclei can have intrinsic spin. Suppose the axis of spin were downwards into the page and the rotation were suitable for driving an ordinary screw into the page. Then Wu showed that beta-rays from such a nucleus are emitted *preferentially upwards*, *i.e.*, against the direction of travel of the screw. The parity transformed version of this would have the beta-rays preferentially emitted in the same direction as the travel of the screw and, if parity is conserved, this process would happen too. But it does not. If the beta-rays in the experiment had been emitted in equal numbers up and down, then the parity transformed version would have had this feature too, and thus parity would have been conserved.

Of the four types of force referred to on **F 13(1)**, only the weak interaction does not conserve parity. The whole matter is bound up with the anti-neutrino which is emitted simultaneously with the negative beta-ray. It appears that antineutrinos are always " right-handed " which means that if one could look at an antineutrino receding from us it would be seen to be spinning clockwise.

Modern research on elementary particles is greatly concerned to find out which types of process obey which conservation laws. The parity surprise is only one of the stimulating shocks that this type of work is heir to. It is very much in the tradition of Einstein, part of whose monumental contribution to physics was his demonstration of the need to analyse conservation laws.

Conclusion.

Over a century's development of the atomic ideas has brought a progressive, if jerky, increase in the mathematical precision of the theories. In some fields of particle physics, observations to one part in a million, or even better, can be explained, to that level of accuracy, by the existing theories. At the same time, however, the theories have lost visual definition. An atom as an invisible but none the less solid billiard ball was easy enough; so was a light wave conceived like a sound wave in air. Even after Rutherford, an atom consisting of a miniature solar system merely exchanged the solid billiard ball for a system of revolving billiard balls and was no great obstacle to visualisation. But since quantum theory and the Uncertainty Principle, every unambiguous visualisation of fundamental wave-particles leaves out half the picture, and although the electrons are in the atom, we can no longer represent them in definite orbits. The moral seems to be that visualisation is unnecessary, or at best a partial aid to thought. All the theoretical knowledge is in the equations, and these are very precise. Hence the non-physicists' grumble—that physics is too mathematical these days—has some justification, and hence also the growing distinction in physics between the theoreticians, who are usually mathematically trained, and the experimenters, who can rarely read the papers their theoretical colleagues write, but provide the results for them to write about.

THE PROPERTIES OF MATTER IN BULK.

One of the most obvious and at the same time most wonderful things about the properties of matter is their great variety. Think of air, diamond, mercury, rubber, snow, gold, pitch, asbestos. . . . Even the differences of state of the same chemical substance are remarkable enough, ice, water, and steam, for example. One of the aims of physics is to reach an understanding of all these different properties by explaining them in terms of the behaviour of the particles discussed in the previous section (F9–17). The widespread success with which this imposing programme has been carried out indicates the maturity of physics. It is difficult to think of any major property of matter in bulk for which there is not some attempted theoretical explanation, though future physicists will no doubt regard some present-day theories as rudimentary or incorrect.

Physics, Statistics, and Thermodynamics.

Take a number equal to the population of London, multiply it by itself, and multiply the product by another million. The answer is about the number of molecules in 1 cubic centimetre of ordinary air. They are constantly moving about and colliding with one another. Even if the nature of the molecules and their laws of motion were perfectly understood, it would clearly be impracticable to calculate the exact paths described by each particle of so vast an assembly. This difficulty brought into being a whole branch of physics concerned with calculating the overall or average properties of large numbers of particles. Just as statisticians will provide the average height, income, expectation of life, and so on, of the population of London, without knowing everything about every individual, so statistical physicists can work out average properties of molecules or atoms in large groups. This important branch of physics is called *Statistical Mechanics*. It was founded in the nineteenth century by Maxwell, Boltzmann, and Gibbs and is still being actively developed.

Consider now all the molecules in 1 cubic centimetre of air contained in a small box. They are continually bombarding the walls of the box and bouncing off. This hail of impacts (it is actually about 10^{23} impacts per square centimetre per second) is the cause of the pressure which the gas exerts against the walls of the box. Now suppose we pump air in until there is twice as much as before, though the box is still the same size and at the same temperature. This means that the density of the gas (i.e., the mass of 1 unit of volume) has doubled. We should now expect twice as many impacts per second on the walls as before, and consequently twice the pressure. We therefore arrive at a conclusion that, if the volume and temperature are constant, the pressure of a gas is proportional to its density. This is one of the simplest statistical arguments that can be checked against observation; in fact, it stands the test very well.

Heat, temperature, and energy.

The proviso about the temperature remaining the same is an important one for the following reason. In the nineteenth century there was much discussion about the nature of heat. To Joule we owe the now well-established view that heat is equivalent to mechanical work. In one of his experiments, in the 1840s, the work necessary to rotate paddle wheels against the resistance of water in a tank generated heat that caused a slight rise in the temperature of the water. Joule found out exactly how much work was equivalent to a given quantity of heat. However, one can do other things with work besides generate heat; in particular, work creates motion, as when one pushes a car. Bodies in motion possess a special form of energy, called kinetic energy, which is equal to the work done in accelerating them from a state of rest. We have, then, three closely connected ideas: work, heat, and kinetic energy. Now according to the views of the nineteenth century, which are still accepted, any heat given to a gas simply increases the kinetic energy of its molecules: the hotter the gas, the faster its molecules are moving. If, therefore, the gas in our box is allowed to get hotter, there is an increase in molecular speed, and the impacts on the walls become correspondingly more violent. But this means the pressure increases, so we have another law: if the density remains the same, the pressure increases if the temperature does.

Laws of Thermodynamics.

Such considerations as these have been pursued with great elaboration and subtlety. The notions of heat, temperature, energy, and work—familiar but vague in everyday life—have been given precise definitions, and the relations between them have been enshrined in the Laws of Thermodynamics. Enshrined is perhaps a suitable word, because these laws are so soundly and widely based on experimental results that they have greater prestige than any others in physics. If any proposed physical law comes in conflict with thermodynamics then so much the worse for that law—it has to be revised. It is sometimes asserted that no one is properly educated who does not understand the Second Law of thermodynamics. We cannot, therefore, leave this section without at least stating the two best known thermodynamic laws:

First Law: *If any physical system is given a quantity of heat, and if the system performs some work, then the energy of the system increases by an amount equal to the excess of heat given over work done.* This law asserts that heat, energy, and work are convertible one into the other, and that all such transactions balance exactly. This is one form of a principle accepted as fundamental in all science, viz., the Principle of the Conservation of Energy, according to which energy can never be created or destroyed, but only changed from one form to another.

Second Law: *It is impossible to make an engine which will continuously take heat from a heat source and, by itself, turn it all into an equivalent amount of mechanical work.* In fact, all engines which produce work from heat—steam engines for example—always use only a fraction of the heat they take in and give up the rest to some relatively cool part of the machine. The Second Law makes this obligatory on all work-from-heat devices. This statement of the Second Law has an engineering ring about it and, indeed, it arose from the work of the nineteenth-century French engineer Carnot. Nevertheless, it can be re-phrased in very abstract terms, and has been applied with unbroken success to all fields of science involving the transfer of heat and allied matters. It sets a definite limit to the kinds of physical process that can be conceived to take place. Nothing has been known to contravene it.

The States of Matter.

The molecular motion in gases has been referred to in the previous section. Tacitly it was assumed that each molecule acted independently of all others, except that collisions occurred between them. In reality, molecules exert attractive forces on one another and, if a gas is cooled so that molecular movements become relatively sluggish, a time comes when the attractive forces succeed in drawing the molecules close together to form a liquid. This process is called condensation.

The molecules in a liquid are packed tightly together and they impede each others' movements. On the other hand, movement still persists, and the molecules struggle about like people in a milling crowd. Besides wandering about, the molecules vibrate. These motions represent the energy contained in the liquid.

The fact that the molecules, though irregularly packed, can still slip past one another and move from place to place, explains the essential property of liquids that distinguishes them from solids—ability to flow. As a matter of fact, although the rather vague assertion that in a liquid molecules are irregularly packed would be generally accepted, there is no agreed opinion on what the irregularity is actually like. Indeed, not only the precise structure of liquids, but the theory of liquids in general, is fraught with such considerable mathematical difficulties that the liquid state is much less well understood than the solid or gaseous.

Most solids are crystals. The popular idea of a crystal is of something which has a more or less regular geometrical form with faces that glint in the light—like snowflakes or gems. However, crystallinity really depends on a regular inner pattern of the atoms, and may or may not show itself on the visible surface. A lump of lead, for example, is crystalline, though it may not look it.

The actual arrangement of the atoms in a crystal can be extremely complex. Some are quite simple, however. The largest model of a crystal structure must surely be the 400-ft. "Atomium" building in the 1958 Brussels Exhibition. This consisted of eight balls, representing atoms, situated at the corners of a cube, and one more ball exactly in the middle. Imagine this repeated in all directions so that every ball is the centre of a cube whose corners are the eight neighbouring balls. This is known to crystallographers and physicists as the "body-centred cubic structure"; it is the actual arrangement of atoms in iron, sodium, chromium, and some other metals. If every ball, instead of being the centre of a cube, were the centre of a regular tetrahedron (a solid figure with four equal triangular faces), and had its four neighbours at the corners of the tetrahedron, then we should have the "diamond structure." This is how the carbon atoms are arranged in diamonds.

In crystals the atoms are locked into a regular ordered structure by attractive forces which give the solid its rigidity and prevent it from flowing. The atoms are so close together that any attempt to press them closer involves crushing or distorting the atoms—a process they resist strongly. This explains why solids (and liquids too) are so difficult to compress. Gases can easily be compressed because there is so much space between the molecules.

The distinction between solid and liquid is not so sharp as is commonly supposed. A lump of dough will not bounce, but is plastic; a steel ball-bearing is very elastic and bounces excellently, but one cannot mould it in the fingers. Neither dough nor steel qualifies for description as a liquid. There are, however, substances which can be moulded like plasticine into a ball that will then bounce very well on the floor like an elastic solid, and finally, if left on a flat table, will spread into a pool and drip off the edge like a liquid. There is no point in trying to force such things into rigid categories. One may say instead that for short, sharp impacts the material behaves like an elastic solid, but under long-sustained forces it flows like a liquid. The properties of these, and many other anomalous materials, are increasingly engaging the attention of those who study the science of flow—*rheology*. It is interesting to see how many familiar and important materials exhibit peculiar rheological behaviour—paint, dough, ball-pen ink, cheese, unset cement, and solutions of nylon and other plastics are only a few examples.

Inside a Crystalline Solid.

We now return to our wallpaper analogy of crystal structure and give some free play to our visual imagination.

Suppose we have walls papered with a regular pattern of, say, roses, fuchsias, and green leaves. These represent the different kinds of atoms in the solid. Careful observation shows that the whole pattern is shimmering. The flowers and leaves are not stationary, but are undergoing slight random oscillations about their proper positions. In a crystal these movements are called thermal vibrations, and are never absent. The hotter the crystal, the more the vibration, and at a high enough temperature the vibrations become so great that the atoms get right out of position and the pattern disappears altogether, *i.e.*, the crystal melts. Thermal vibrations are essential to the theory of solids, and are responsible for numerous physical properties.

Next we note something extraordinary about some of the papered walls. On these the paper has been hung in irregular patches fitted together like a not very well-made jig-saw puzzle. Lines of roses which should be vertical are horizontal in some patches, oblique in others. This represents the situation in most ordinary solids, for they consist of many small pieces of crystal irregularly packed together. Such material is called *polycrystalline*, and the small pieces are *crystal grains*. Crystal grains may be almost any size, sometimes visible to the naked eye, as often on galvanised iron.

However, on one wall, we see excellent regularity and no obvious patches at all. The physicist would call this a *single crystal*, and several techniques exist for preparing them. Natural single crystals can be found, and there are some beautiful large single crystals of rock salt. But on examining the single crystal wall closely, we find a number of places where the paperhanger has failed to make adjacent pieces register perfectly—there is a slight disjointedness. This occurs in real single crystals, and the line along which the structure fails to register is called a *dislocation*. These are much studied by physicists because of their bearing on the mechanical properties of solids, on the yielding of metals under strong stress, for instance.

This by no means exhausts the possibilities of the wallpaper analogy; several other phenomena can be found. For example, in a place where there should be a fuchsia there is actually a daffodil—something completely foreign to the pattern. Or perhaps a small wrongly shaped leaf is jammed between the proper leaves in a place that should really be blank. These represent chemical impurity atoms. The first is called *substitutional*, because it occupies the position of an atom that should be there, the second is called *interstitial*, because it does not. Substitutional impurities of indium metal, deliberately added to the semi-conductor silicon, make possible the manufacture of transistors (*see* Section L). Some steels derive their valuable properties from interstitial carbon atoms within the iron pattern.

What physicists call a vacancy would occur if a flower or leaf were simply missing. Remembering that all the atoms are vibrating, we should not be surprised if occasionally an atom jumps into a neighbouring vacancy if there happens to be one, *i.e.*, the atom and the vacancy change places. Later this may occur again. In the course of time, a rose which was near the ceiling may make its way to the floor by jumping into vacant rose positions when they occur near enough. This process, which the physicist calls *diffusion*, is also analogous to the game in which numbers or letters can be moved about in a flat box because there is one vacant space to permit adjustment. The more vacancies there are in a crystal, the faster diffusion occurs. It is, in fact, very slow in solids, but is nevertheless evidence that apparently quiescent materials are really internally active.

Metals, Electricity, and Heat.

There is ample evidence that inside metals there are large numbers of free electrons. To illuminate this statement let us take sodium metal as an example. One single sodium atom has a nucleus with eleven protons; there are therefore eleven electrons in the atom. The outermost one is easily detached, leaving a positively charged sodium ion behind. We may think of these ions arranged in the three-dimensional pattern characteristic of sodium crystals. It is the same as the iron structure previously described. The detached electrons, one per atom, occupy the spaces in between. The usual metaphor is that the structure of ions is permeated by a "gas" of electrons. Like all visualisations of fundamental particles, this must be taken as a rough approximation. The important point is that the electrons in the gas are not bound to individual atoms but may wander freely about the crystal, hindered only by the collisions they make with the vibrating ions.

This is the picture as it appeared to physicists of the first decade of this century, and we can explain many properties of metals with it. Naturally the theory has developed greatly since then, thanks to the great work of Lorentz, Sommerfeld, and Bloch; it now relies heavily on quantum theory, but it is surprising how little violence is done to modern ideas by the simple picture we are using.

The free electrons move randomly in all directions at thousands of miles per hour. If the metal is connected across a battery it experiences an electric field. Electrons are negatively charged particles, and are therefore attracted to the electrically positive end of the metal. They can move through the metal because they are free; this flow is not possible to those electrons which remain bound to the ions. The function of the battery is to keep the flow going and, for as long as it is going, it is the electric current.

The flow of electrons is not unimpeded. They constantly collide with the ions and are deflected from the path of flow. This hindrance is what the electrician calls *electrical resistance*. The electric force, due to the battery or a dynamo, accelerates the electrons, thus giving them extra energy; but they lose this to the ions at collisions because the ions recoil and vibrate more than before. The net effect of innumerable collisions is to increase the thermal vibrations of the ions, *i.e.*, to make the metal hotter. This is the explanation of the fact well known to every user of electric irons: that electric current heats the conductor. If a strong current is passed through a wire, the heating is so great the wire glows, as in electric-light bulbs, or melts and breaks, as in blown fuses.

If one end of a metal rod is heated we soon feel the heat at the other end; metals are excellent thermal conductors. This is because the mobile free electrons carry the heat energy down the rod, passing it on to the ions by colliding with them. Substances without free electrons cannot do this, nor can they conduct electricity well; so we have, in the free electrons, an explanation of the fact that the good electrical conductors are the good heat conductors. For technical purposes, it would be useful to have electrical insulators that would conduct heat well, and *vice versa*; but this is almost a contradiction in terms, and one can only compromise.

Non-conductors and Semi-conductors.

There are some elements, and numerous compounds, in which all the electrons are so tightly bound to their parent atoms that free electron flow is impossible. These materials are electrical and thermal insulators.

Let us return to our sodium atom. It readily loses its outer electron, forming a positive ion. The ion is very stable; indeed, its electron arrangement resembles the "closed shell" belonging to the inert gas neon. The chlorine atom, on the other hand, would have a very stable structure, resembling the inert gas argon, if only it could be given one extra electron to complete the closed shell. If the outer sodium electron were given to a chlorine atom we should have two stable ions, one positive and one negative. These would then attract each other and form a compound. This is just how common salt, sodium chloride, is formed, and its crystals consist of a regular network of alternate sodium and chlorine ions. As all the electrons are bound to ions, it is not surprising that salt will not conduct electricity or heat to any appreciable extent. Not all insulating compounds are built on this pattern, but all have structures which bind the electrons tightly.

We have seen (**F18**) that Nature does not permit a hard-and-fast distinction between solids and liquids; nor does she between conductors and insulators. Over a hundred years ago, Faraday knew of substances which would conduct electricity, but rather badly. A common one is the graphite in pencils. Others are the elements selenium, germanium, and silicon, and a considerable number of compounds. Such substances are called semi-conductors.

Semi-conductors conduct badly because they have so few free electrons, many thousands of times fewer than metals. In very cold germanium—say, 200 degrees below freezing—all the electrons are tightly bound to atoms and the substance is an insulator. It differs from normal insulators in that, on warming it, the gradually increasing thermal vibration of the crystal detaches some of the electrons, for they are only moderately tightly bound. The warmer the crystal becomes, the more of its electrons become detached and the better it conducts electricity. By about the temperature of boiling water, there are so many freed electrons that conduction is moderately good, though less good than in metals. This is basic semi-conductor behaviour. Because transistors can be made of germanium, and because they are of such great technical importance, more knowledge has accumulated about germanium than about any other material. *See also* **Transistor, Section L.**

Magnetism.

The most important thing about magnetism is that it is inseparably connected with electricity. Oersted showed this in July 1820, when he deflected a magnetic compass needle by passing an electric current through a wire near it. Since then, many experiments have shown that wherever a current flows there will certainly be a magnetic field in the surrounding space. The laws of this are very well known now—they are the Maxwell equations previously referred to (**F13**). However, most people first meet magnetism when, as children, they pick up pins with a magnet. Where is the electricity here? and what is a magnet?

The explanation of magnetism exemplifies beautifully the technique of explaining the bulk properties of matter in terms of fundamental particles. In the atoms the electrons are moving, and a moving electric charge constitutes an electric current. Therefore each moving electron is a tiny source of magnetism. It does not immediately follow that every atom is a source of magnetism because it might—and often does—happen that the magnetic effect of different electrons in the atom cancel out. In helium atoms, for example, the two electrons have equal but opposed magnetic effects. Nevertheless, some atoms and ions have a net effect called their *magnetic moment*. This simply means they behave like tiny magnets. Crystals containing such atoms will be magnetic, though the magnetism is much weaker than in ordinary magnets because the different atoms largely annul one another's effects. In a very limited number of crystals, however, the magnetic ions act on one another in a special way which forces all the atomic magnets to point in the same direction. The total effect of many co-operating atoms is very strong and the crystal becomes what we normally call a magnet. Iron acts like this, so do cobalt and nickel, the rarer elements gadolinium and dysprosium, and a fair number of alloys. On the whole, this behaviour, which is called *ferromagnetism*, is very rare. The reason for the co-operation of all the atomic magnets is not explained to everyone's satisfaction yet, though the key idea was given by Heisenberg in 1928.

In the section dealing with the electron it was pointed out that every electron has an *intrinsic* magnetic moment. This is in addition to any effect simply due to the electron's motion round a nucleus. The net effects of ions are therefore partly due to the intrinsic magnetism of electrons. In the ferromagnetic metals the latter is by far the most important contribution. Thus we pick up pins, and benefit from magnets in other ways, because innumerable fundamental particles act in co-operation for reasons that are still somewhat obscure. It is interesting to ask whether the electrons responsible for magnetism are the same free electrons that allow the metals to conduct electricity. It is thought not.

We are accustomed to think of magnets as metallic. Actually the magnet originally discovered by the Chinese was the mineral lodestone, which is a non-metallic oxide of iron. Nowadays a number of non-metallic magnets are made. They are called *ferrites*, and some are insulators and some are semi-conductors. The combination of magnetism and insulation is technically very valuable in radio, radar, and other applications. The explanation of ferrite behaviour is related to that of metallic ferromagnetism, but is not the same.

Conclusion.

The aim of the second part of this account of physics is to show how our conception of fundamental particles allows us to build theories of the properties of matter. This very aim shows that the two " major divisions " of physics referred to at the beginning (**F9**) are divided only in the way that labour is divided by co-operating workers to lighten the task. For the task of physics is a very great one—no less than to explain the behaviour of matter; and since the universe, living and inanimate, is made of matter, physics must necessarily underlie all the other sciences.

III. THE WORLD OF THE CHEMISTS

WHAT CHEMISTRY IS ABOUT.

The science of chemistry is concerned with the properties of atoms, the laws governing their combination to form molecules, and, more generally, with the behaviour of materials composed of large numbers of molecules. Thus chemistry borders on or, rather, interpenetrates physics—a fact illustrated by the existence of professional journals devoted to " chemical physics " and " physical chemistry." Physics is more concerned with the fundamental nature of matter and radiation; chemistry concentrates on the ways in which atoms combine, or can be made to combine, with each other to form innumerable compounds. Chemistry also merges with the life sciences where it deals, as in biochemistry, with the properties of the complex molecular building blocks of living organisms, *e.g.*, proteins, carbohydrates, nucleic acids. Because of its comprehensiveness, the science of chemistry has been subdivided into what were at one time convenient sub-sciences, *e.g.*, organic chemistry, electrochemistry, but here too the borderlines are becoming progressively blurred. Our task here will be to outline some of the ideas in use by present-day chemists.

ELEMENTS AND COMPOUNDS.

Electron Shells and Stability.

The reader will find in Part II a brief description of the atom and definitions of atomic number, atomic weight, isotope, and other terms. The simplest atom is hydrogen (H) with atomic number 1. Some common elements with their chemical symbols and atomic numbers are:— carbon (C) 6; oxygen (O) 8; sodium (Na) 11; chlorine (Cl) 17; calcium (Ca) 20; silver (Ag) 47; and uranium (U) 92. Let us now consider atoms in more detail.

The electrons in atoms move in well-defined *orbits* and the orbits fall into well-defined groups called *shells*. If all the orbits in a shell have electrons actually present in them the shell is *filled* or *closed* and this confers on the shell an unusual stability or inertness. Conversely, unfilled shells lead to activity and the electrons in the incompletely filled shells largely determine the chemical and physical properties of the element and are responsible for the combination of atoms to form molecules. The inner shell, *i.e.*, the one nearest the nucleus, can accommodate only two electrons (the element helium has just that number) and the next two shells can hold eight each. Large atoms, *e.g.*, lead, radium, have many filled shells and, subject to special exceptions, the general rule is that the inner shells are the filled ones and the outer shell may be incomplete. Elements which have equal numbers of electrons in their outer shell resemble each other. Thus the elements with complete electronic shells are chemically unreactive gases, *e.g.*, argon and neon (minor constituents of the atmosphere). Elements with just one electron in the outer shell are highly reactive metals, *e.g.*, sodium and potassium, whereas those with just one electron too few are also reactive but are not metals, *e.g.*, chlorine, bromine, iodine.

Molecules, Ions, and Bonds.

The general tendency of matter is for those changes that are possible to go on happening until a lasting arrangement or *stable state* is reached. Atoms with closed shells are stable but atoms with unfilled shells can achieve stability in several ways, of which two are as follows:

(i) *Electron sharing.*

When atoms share electrons, the resulting structure, composed of several atoms, is known as a molecule. The simplest case is the molecule of hydrogen, composed of two atoms each contributing one electron. Thus each atom will have a share of two electrons which is the number required to fill completely the inner shell. The shared electrons constitute a *chemical bond* and confer stability on the resulting hydrogen molecule.

A more complex molecule is carbon tetrachloride, CCl_4. Here the carbon atom with four electrons in its outer shell is bonded to four chlorine atoms each of which needs one electron to complete a set of eight. Thus by sharing the electrons each of the five atoms can form a complete shell of eight electrons. The properties of the resulting molecular species do not usually bear any resemblance to the constituent atoms. Whereas molecular chlorine is a gas and carbon is a solid, carbon tetrachloride is a liquid which finds application as a dry cleaning fluid.

(ii) *Electron transfer.*

Another method of completing electron shells is by transfer of one or more electrons from an atom with one or two electrons in its outer shell to one with that number too few. Thus sodium, with one electron in its outer shell, will combine with chlorine, deficient in one electron. This results in two electronically stable species (ions), both of which carry electric charges. Thus the sodium will now have a net positive charge of 1 unit (11 protons, 10 electrons), whereas the chlorine has an excess negative charge (17 protons, 18 electrons). Because of these electric charges, solutions of ionic substances conduct electricity and this property is utilised in industrial processes such as electroplating and in the extraction of metals from their ores.

Thus the electrons which participate in the formation of chemical bonds are those in partly-filled shells (valence electrons), and the simplest and most stable type of bonds are those in which two electrons are shared (a covalent bond) and those in which there is a net transfer of electrons (an ionic bond). Sometimes, in order to attain a complete electronic shell, a chemical bond will require the sharing of four or even six electrons. The resulting molecules are highly reactive and will readily, and sometimes violently, combine with other molecules or atoms to achieve the greater stability associated with the two-electron covalent bond.

Molecules must not be envisaged as rigid assemblies of atoms with electrons uniformly distributed around the various nuclei. The properties of molecules are best acccounted for by imagining the atomic nuclei to be vibrating about mean positions the bonds acting like spiral springs, holding the nuclei together. The electrons form a mobile cloud of negative charge which sorrounds the nuclei. The valence electrons, constituting the bond between pairs of atoms, also have no fixed location but fluctuate about mean positions, more or less along the line joining the atoms. Although the electrons are shared, their mean position is not usually halfway between the two

and 46 g of alcohol, both quantities will contain the same number of molecules. Similarly, 1 litre of water with 342 g of sugar dissolved in it, and 1 litre with 58·5 g of salt, will again contain the same number of dissolved molecules because the molecular weights of sugar ($C_{12}H_{22}O_{11}$) and salt (NaCl) are 342 and 58·5 respectively. In each case the number of grams taken is numerically equal to the molecular weight and this amount is called 1 *mole* of a substance or the *gram molecular weight*.

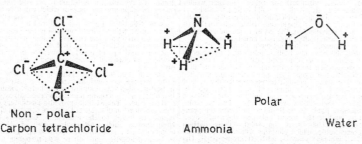

Non - polar
Carbon tetrachloride

Ammonia

Polar

Water

Fig. 1.   The arrangement in space of molecules CCl_4, NH_3, and H_2O.

atoms but depends on the relative atomic sizes and charges. In the carbon-chlorine bond of carbon tetrachloride the valence electrons are subjected to electrical attractions due to 17 positive charges on the chlorine nucleus and 6 positive charges on the carbon nucleus. Although the forces due to the chlorine nucleus are partially compensated by the intervening negative charges of the complete electronic shells, they are stronger than the forces from the carbon nucleus, and the valence electrons are therefore pulled towards the chlorine atom which thus attains a net negative charge, leaving the carbon with a corresponding positive charge. The magnitude of this charge is less than that of an ion, and the carbon–chlorine bond should be symbolised $\overset{+}{C} - \overset{-}{Cl}$ to emphasise that separate positive and negative charges of equal magnitude are embodied in the structure, and are attracting each other as well as causing an electric field outside the molecule.

A pair of equal and opposite charges like this is called a *dipole* and is the electrical analogue of the ordinary magnet which has north and south *poles* instead of charges. Chemical bonds made with dipoles are called *polar bonds*. Most molecules, both simple and complex, are bound with polar bonds, but in the case of CCl_4 the four bonds are symmetrically arranged in space so that the electric effects of the dipoles cancel each other outside the molecule which therefore does not, as a whole, act like a dipole. On the other hand, the bond dipoles in a molecule may not cancel in this way (Fig. 1) in which case the whole molecule will possess the properties of a dipole *e.g.*, when subjected to an electric field it will rotate to align itself with the field just as a compass needle will line up with a magnetic field.

Atomic and Molecular Weights.

The masses of the electron and proton were determined early in the 20th century by ingenious experiments. The electronic mass is extremely small, about 9×10^{-28}g and the mass of a hydrogen atom is $1·7 \times 10^{-24}$g, which indicates that the proton is 1,837 times heavier than the electron and that the mass of the atom is almost completely confined to the nucleus.

The molecular weight of a compound is the sum of the atomic weights (F10) of all the constituent atoms, *e.g.*, water (H_2O) and ethyl alcohol (C_2H_5OH) have molecular weights 18 and 46 respectively. This means that the alcohol molecule weighs more than the water molecule in the ratio 46 to 18. If therefore we take 18 g of water

The word mole may also be used for atoms or ions and means, in general, that amount of molecules (or atoms or ions, as the case may be) such that the total number of them is equal to the number of atoms in 12 g of carbon (F10). This number, called Avogadro's number, is approximately 6×10^{23}. Thus one mole of any substance contains 6×10^{23} molecules of that substance and this fact makes the mole a very useful unit both in theory and practice.

Forces between Molecules.

Something has already been said (F17, 18) about the differences between solids, liquids, and gases and we may now put the question: what forces are responsible for the organisation of molecules in liquids or solids and their disorganisation in the gaseous state? Questions of this kind are of profound interest to chemists, physicists, and biologists.

unpolarized

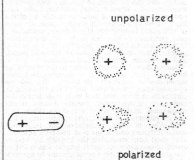

polarized

Fig. 2.   Mutual polarisation of molecules by distortion of their electron clouds.

The forces which act between molecules depend mainly on the fact that the electrons orbiting a molecule form a mobile cloud of negative charge. If a polar molecule is brought up to another molecule, then the latter will become polarised, *i.e.*, its electronic cloud will be displaced with respect to the nucleus. This is shown in Fig. 2 and it is apparent that the formerly non-polar molecule has acquired a temporary polar character. In this state it will be able to polarise other nearby molecules, and the ease with which molecules are polarised depends on how strongly the electrons are held in position by the nuclear charge, and this in turn depends on the mean distance between the nucleus and the electronic cloud. Thus, the larger the molecule, the more easily the electron cloud can be distorted by a nearby dipole and hence the stronger are the intermolecular forces. These forces are attractions or *binding forces.* They can be disrupted by violent vibratory or other motions whose source is heat, as when a solid is first melted and then boiled and its molecules fly off in all directions to form a gas. Since strong attractions are due to ease of polarisation, the latter must influence the melting and boiling points of substances.

As a general rule substances composed of small molecules have low boiling points and are gaseous at room temperature and atmospheric pressure, because when they approach each other during a collision, the forces they exert upon one another are not strong enough to produce cohesion and condensation. Examples of this type of behaviour are hydrogen and helium which boil at −253°C and −269°C respectively. Larger molecules are likely to be liquid at ordinary temperature, and if the forces between them are even stronger, they may be solid. Thus carbon tetrachloride, which contains five atoms, boils at 77°C, whereas glucose, with 24 atoms ($C_6H_{12}O_6$) is a solid, melting at 146°C. Chemical compounds which are ionic in character are usually crystalline solids with high melting points (e.g., common salt, quicklime) because ions, possessing permanent charges, exert stronger forces on one another than do molecules.

Metals and Salts.

It has already been explained that chemical elements are conveniently classified according to the number of electrons in the outer shell, because it is mainly those electrons which participate in chemical reactions and make bonds. Thus elements with 1, 2, or at most 3 electrons in the outer shell (e.g., sodium, calcium, aluminium respectively) will undergo reactions which enable them to lose those electrons, i.e., they will attempt to form ionic compounds. These elements are metallic, and when solid or liquid, conduct heat and electricity. On the other hand, elements which need 1 or 2 electrons to form a complete shell (e.g., chlorine, oxygen respectively) can also form ionic compounds by reacting with a metal, though these elements are themselves classed as non-metals and can be gases, liquids, or solids at room temperature. When a metal atom combines with one or more atoms of non-metal, the resulting ionic compound is termed a salt. Common salts of the metal sodium are the chloride, carbonate, and sulphate. Other examples of industrially important salts are silver bromide (used in photographic films), calcium sulphate (plaster of paris), and magnesium sulphate (epsom salts.)

Metals do not normally occur in the pure state in nature but are found as compounds (ores), sometimes of a complex structure. The science of metallurgy is concerned with the extraction of metals from their ores, and with their properties and uses. Since many metals possess useful mechanical and electrical properties, they find use as materials of construction, and hence the knowledge of their properties and behaviour under different conditions is of great importance. One need only remember the imperfectly understood phenomenon of metal fatigue which led to the crashes of the early Comet aircraft to appreciate how vital is the contribution of metallurgy to the process of engineering.

Although metals can be mixed with other metals to form alloys, the large majority of metallic compounds are the salts in which the metal is present as positive ion (cation), and the negative ion (anion) is composed of one or several non-metallic elements. Common salts are the chloride, bromide, iodide, nitrate, sulphate, phosphate, and carbonate. Metals with simple electron structures can form only one type of ion. Thus sodium, with one outer shell electron forms Na^+ and 1 electron; calcium with two outershell

electrons forms Ca^{++} and 2 electrons. There are, however, a number of metals with more complex electronic structures, involving partially filled inner electronic shells and these can exist in a variety of ionic forms. They include many metals which find application as structural materials, e.g., iron, copper, gold, platinum, nickel, chromium. For instance, iron can exist as Fe^{++} or Fe^{+++} and the process of removing a further electron from Fe^{++} is termed *oxidation*, and any chemical reagent which is capable of bringing about such a process is an *oxidising agent.* Conversely the addition of an electron is called *reduction* and the reagent which can give up an electron is a *reducing agent.* Thus the conversion of Fe^{++} to Fe^{+++} is achieved by an oxidising agent which is itself reduced in the process. Processes involving the transfer of one or several electrons are called Redox (reduction-oxidation) reactions and are of great importance in many branches of chemical technology and biochemical processes.

The non-metals which feature in the anions of salts include the well-known and industrially important elements, sulphur, phosphorus, iodine, bromine, and the common gases oxygen, nitrogen, and chlorine. Table 1 (F23) provides a summary of the classification of a few of the more common elements according to the number of electrons in their outer shell. Although some of these elements, e.g., aluminium, undoubtedly possess metallic properties and others, e.g., nitrogen, are non-metals, the dividing lines are not always so clearly defined and most of the compounds formed by elements near the centre of Table 1 are of the covalent type.

ACIDS AND BASES.

pH Values.

Hydrogen occupies a unique position in Table 1. According to its electronic structure it can be classified with sodium and potassium, as having one electron in its outer shell. It therefore readily forms cations, H^+, but it can hardly be called a metal. Having lost its electron, what remains is a proton (F10), a single positive charge. Thus we can compare sodium chloride, Na^+ Cl^-, with H^+ Cl^-, but whereas sodium chloride exists in the ionic form in the solid and liquid states and in solution, HCl is a covalent gas in the pure state, but readily ionises in solution, because the H^+ does not exist on its own, but attaches itself to a solvent molecule. Thus when HCl is dissolved in water, it ionises and the H^+ combines with the water: $HCl + H_2O \rightarrow (H^+ \ H_2O) + Cl^-$. This is a typical example of what is known as an *acid-base reaction*, an acid being defined as a substance which in solution can produce one or several protons (hydrogen ions), and the base as being a substance which can accept protons from an acid. In the above reaction HCl is the acid and H_2O the base, and the reaction consists of the transfer of the proton from acid to base. Other common acids include sulphuric acid ($2H^+ + SO_4^{--}$) and nitric acid ($H^+ + NO_3^-$). When ammonia (NH_3), a covalent gas, is dissolved in water, an acid base reaction also occurs: $NH_3 + HOH \rightarrow (NH_3.H^+) + OH^-$. Here water acts as acid, since it donates a proton to the ammonia, forming NH_4^+, the ammonium ion. When a proton is removed from water, the remainder, a negatively charged ion, is called the hydroxyl ion, OH^-. It has now been established that water can act either as an acid or a base, and in pure water two molecules of water can react: $H_2O + H_2O = (H^+ \ H_2O) + OH^-$, so that one molecule behaves as an acid and the other as a base. This phenomenon is called self-ionisation and also occurs in other solvents.

The extent to which water ionises is very small, thus 1 litre of " pure " water contains 10^{-7} moles each of H^+ and OH^- ions. However, when a stronger acid, i.e., one that can produce more hydrogen ions than water, is added, the concentration of hydrogen ions increases and that of OH^- ions decreases correspondingly, so that the product of the amounts of H^+ and OH^- ions will always be constant and equal to 10^{-14} (see law of chemical equilibrium). It is important to be able to compare the strengths of acid solutions and this is done by reference to the concentration of hydrogen ions. The numerical measure is obtained by taking minus the logarithm of the hydrogen ion concentration and this number is called the pH value of the solution. Thus in pure water, the hydrogen ion concentration is 10^{-7} moles per litre and the pH value is therefore 7.

Vinegar, which is a dilute solution of acetic acid in water, has a hydrogen ion concentration of about 10^{-4} moles per litre; its pH is 4. Thus, solutions with a pH value below 7 are acidic (they contain an excess of hydrogen ions) and those with a pH value greater than 7 are basic (they contain an excess of OH^- ions). Many chemical and most biological reactions are extremely sensitive to small changes in the pH and steps must frequently be taken to adjust the pH to an optimum value for a given reaction. This is achieved by means of substances known as buffers, which have the capacity of mopping up or producing hydrogen ions and to maintain a constant pH. An example of this buffering action is the prevention of stomach acidity by the use of bicarbonates.

THE HYDROGEN BOND AND WATER.

Where hydrogen is covalently bonded to a small, fairly strongly electronegative atom, i.e., one which requires 1, 2, or 3 electrons to fill its outer shell, the one electron which can be supplied by hydrogen is not shared equally by the two atoms but is pulled closer to the electronegative atom. The most common examples of this phenomenon are liquid water and ice. Here the electronegative atom is oxygen, as shown in Fig. 3. The dots represent the outer shell electrons of oxygen and the crosses the electrons contributed by hydrogen. The oxygen atom 1 exerts a strong pull on the lone electron supplied by the hydrogen, so that at the position of the oxygen atom 2 it appears as though the hydrogen is in fact an ion (H^+), devoid of electrons, and since a pair of electrons of oxygen atom 2 are already pointing in the direction of this hydrogen atom, a weak bond will be formed. Thus the "hydrogen bond" consists of one hydrogen atom

between two oxygen atoms. The actual strength of such a bond is only about 10 per cent of that of an ordinary covalent bond, and not very much energy is required to disrupt it. In terms of most chemical reactions the hydrogen bond is therefore not of great significance, but it is vital in reactions which occur with small changes in energy, i.e., biochemical reactions, where the making and breaking of hydrogen bonds is frequently of supreme importance. It must also be

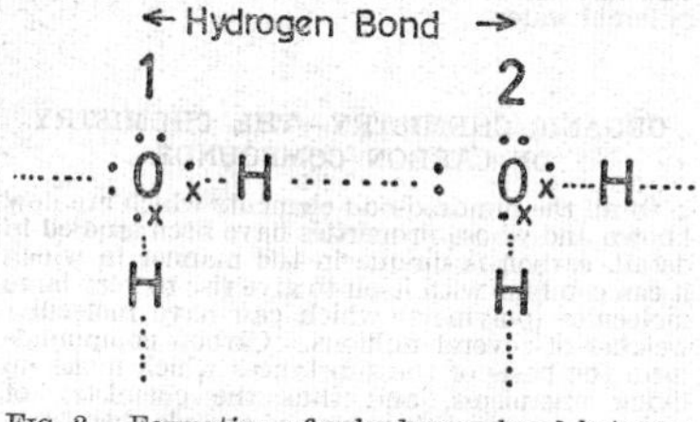

Fig. 3. Formation of a hydrogen bond between neighbouring water molecules.

borne in mind that all biological reactions take place in an aqueous medium which is highly hydrogen-bonded and it is well known that water is the essential substrate for all life processes, although it is not always appreciated that water is also the most anomalous of chemical compounds. It is one of very few substances that are denser in the liquid than in the solid state (ice floats on water) and it is unique in that upon heating the liquid from its melting point to about 4°C, a further contraction takes place. From our discussion on intermolecular forces it is apparent that a chemical compound made up of small molecules, being not very easily polarised, should exist in the gas state at ordinary temperature, and this is the case for other substances whose molecules have approximately the same dimensions as those of

TABLE 1.
ELECTRONS IN OUTER SHELL (VALENCE ELECTRONS)

1	2	3	4	5	6	7	8
Hydrogen							
Sodium	Magnesium Calcium	Aluminium	Carbon Silicon	Nitrogen Phosphorus	Oxygen Sulphur	Chlorine	Neon Argon
Potassium						Bromine	
Silver	Radium					Iodine	

Metals Positive ions	Covalent	Non-metals Negative ions or covalent

TABLE 2

Class of Compound	Elements	Example	Origin or Use
Hydrocarbon	C,H	Octane Benzene	Nat. oil deposit, fuel Coal tar, solvent, and raw material
Alcohols	C,H,O	Ethyl alcohol	Formed by fermentation of sugar
Amides	C,H,O,N	Acetamide	Constituents of synthetic polymers, e.g., nylon
Lipids	C,H,O	Olive oil	Found in plant seeds, used as food energy
Carbohydrates	C,H,O	Sugar, starch, cellulose	Occur in Nature—sources of energy and plan structural materials
Amino acids	C,H,N,O,(S)	Glycine, alanine	Building blocks of proteins
Steroids	C,H,O	Cholesterol	Hormone substances
Terpenes	C,H,O	Geraniol	Occur in Nature—perfumes

water, *viz.*, CO_2 (carbon dioxide), NH_3, and HCl. The abnormal physical properties of water are due to the extensive hydrogen bonding which exists in its liquid and solid forms. Indeed, ice is the most perfectly hydrogen-bonded structure, and liquid water appears to retain some of this regular crystalline order, the main difference being that such crystalline regions are short-lived, forming and melting many million times every second. Nevertheless a snapshot of short enough exposure would no doubt reveal ice-like regions in liquid water.

ORGANIC CHEMISTRY—THE CHEMISTRY OF CARBON COMPOUNDS.

Of all the hundred-odd elements which are now known and whose properties have been studied in detail, carbon is unique in the manner in which it can combine with itself to give rise to very large molecules (polymers) which can have molecular weights of several millions. Carbon compounds form the basis of the substances which make up living organisms, and thus the chemistry of carbon compounds is known as organic chemistry. Reference to Table 1 (F23) shows that carbon is capable of forming 4 covalent bonds, and the simplest organic compound is methane, CH_4 (the main constituent of North Sea gas). The hydrogen atoms are capable of being replaced by other atoms or groups of atoms, including carbon. Thus by replacing one of the C—H bonds by a C—C bond, $CH_3.CH_3$ (or C_2H_6) can be obtained. This process can continue and result in long chains of carbon atoms and the compounds so obtained form a series whose general formula is C_nH_{2n+2}, where n is any whole number. The compound C_8H_{18} is known as octane and forms the basis of petrol. The larger members of the series are the paraffin waxes. Starting again from methane and replacing one hydrogen atom by oxygen + hydrogen so that the carbon is covalently bonded to the oxygen, methyl alcohol, CH_3OH is obtained. Once again this is the first member of a series, the alcohols, whose second member, C_2H_5OH (ethyl alcohol), forms the basis of all alcoholic drinks.

In addition to ordinary 2-electron covalent bonds carbon also forms bonds involving 4 and 6 shared electrons. These bonds are much less stable than the ordinary covalent bonds so that compounds possessing them are extremely re-active. Carbon atom chains can also form side branches or closed rings, usually containing 5 or 6 carbon atoms. Furthermore, the important group of aromatic compounds are based on ben-zene, C_6H_6, in which the 6 carbon atoms form a planar ring and each has one hydrogen atom bonded to it. The remaining electrons form a mobile pool, so that the whole molecule is easily polarised and can be made to react with many other substances. It follows that a large variety of compounds can be obtained using only the elements carbon, hydrogen, and oxygen. If the elements nitrogen, phosphorus, sulphur are in-cluded, as well as chlorine, bromine, and iodine, the number of possible compounds becomes even larger. Table 2 provides some examples of classes of organic compounds and their occur-rence in nature or their industrial application.

To achieve the growth of molecules by the elongation of the carbon chains is not usually feasible technically, although in nature this is a common process, brought about by enzymes (F25(1)). However, some molecules, especially those with four or six electron bonds, can react with one another to form polymers. In addition many molecules can be made to react (condense) to form more complex molecules with the elimi-nation of a simple molecule, such as water or ammonia. Examples of the latter type of poly-mer are the proteins which are composed of amino-acid units (Table 2), the polysaccharides (carbohydrates), such as starch and cellulose, made up of condensed sugar molecules (Table 2), and synthetic condensation polymers of acids and alcohols known as polyesters, *e.g.*, Terylene Additional polymers also figure largely in chemical technology, examples being polyvinyl chloride (PVC), polyolefines (*e.g.*, polythene) and poly-styrene.

CHEMICAL REACTIONS.

Laws Governing Chemical Reactions.

Large amounts of energy are locked up within molecules and some of this energy is used up in chemical reaction. Like other forms of energy (*e.g.*, electrical and mechanical) it is subject to certain laws, such as the law of conservation of energy which states that energy cannot be created or destroyed, but can be converted from one form to another. Thus, part of the chemical energy during the reaction may be converted into heat, and this is frequently the case (F17).

Another very important law deals with the extent to which a chemical reaction will proceed. The reaction of nitrogen with hydrogen, which combine to give ammonia, forms the basis of the fixation of atmospheric nitrogen in the manu-facture of fertilisers. The two gases combine in the molecular ratio of 1:3, two molecules of ammonia being produced, *i.e.*. $N_2 + 3H_2 = 2NH_3$. However, ammonia also decomposes to form nitrogen and hydrogen, and at a certain stage the rates of the two opposing reactions will be equal and the mixture is then said to be at equilibrium. The position of the equilibrium, *i.e.*, the amount of ammonia formed, can be influenced by changes in temperature, pressure, or the amounts of the reacting substances, and the law of chemical equilibrium states that, if any factor governing an equilibrium is altered, then the equilibrium will shift in an attempt to counter the imposed alteration. Thus, in the ammonia synthesis, if ammonia is removed then more nitrogen and hydrogen will react in trying to re-establish the equilibrium. Furthermore, the reaction between hydrogen and nitrogen proceeds with the evo-lution of heat, so, if the temperature of the gas mixture is raised (*i.e.*, heat is added) then the equilibrium will readjust itself in an attempt to nullify the imposed change, and accordingly some ammonia will decompose into hydrogen and nitrogen, because this process *absorbs* heat.

The laws governing the influence of temperature, pressure, and chemical composition on reactions are termed chemical thermodynamics and the effects described can be calculated in quantitative terms. Some of the problems of chemical engineering are concerned with maximising yields of chemical reactions, while at the same time reconciling the necessary conditions with the economics of the process, *e.g.*, cost of plant, materials, and fuel.

One other important consideration is the speed with which chemical reactions proceed, and the time taken to reach equilibrium (chemical kin-etics). This cannot be predicted by the laws of chemical thermodynamics. According to thermo-dynamic calculations, gaseous hydrogen and oxygen will react to form liquid water, but this reaction is so slow that even in a million years not very much water would be formed.

Catalysts.

Molecules react as a result of collisions, during which the energy due to the collision must be channelled into the chemical bond which is to be broken or to be made. Although at ordinary pressure and temperature molecules collide many million times every second, if all these collisions were to result in chemical reaction, then all re-actions would occur with explosive violence. In fact, only a very small number of collisions are of a high enough energy for reaction to take place. This energy, termed the energy of activation, is therefore an important factor controlling the rate of a chemical reaction. The combination of hydrogen and oxygen normally has a large energy of activation and the two gases do not react to form water, although thermodynamics predicts that the reaction is feasible. Reaction rates can be increased, *i.e.*, the activation energy lowered, if certain solids are added, on which one or several of the reacting species are adsorbed. The bond formed between the added solid (*e.g.*, platinum) and the reacting gas is strong enough to weaken other bonds in the molecules, so that, on collision with another molecule, reaction takes place more readily. The solid which itself does not participate in the chemical reaction, is called a *catalyst*. Its function is to promote chemical reactions between substances which, because of the high activation energy, would not react in its absence. Catalysts find applications not only in many industrial processes but are also extensively used by living organisms, where they are called *enzymes*. Current theories hold that the reacting molecule fits into a hole or groove, like a key into a lock, on the enzyme protein where it is held while the reaction takes place; an example of an enzyme catalysed reaction is the breakdown of starch by the body. This consists of several steps, each of which is controlled by its own specific enzyme. These biological catalysts are much more efficient than those used in synthetic reactions, both in their specificity and in the lowering of the energy of activation (*i.e.*, the increase in the reaction rate). Sometimes a foreign molecule which bears a similarity to the molecule whose reaction is to be catalysed, will combine with a catalyst. If this foreign molecule is very strongly held by the catalyst then the latter can no longer perform its function and is said to be poisoned. This is also true for enzymes: *e.g.*, carbon monoxide and cyanides act as poisons by combining with certain important enzymes and thus inhibit the biochemical reactions on which the functioning of organs depends.

SOME USEFUL APPLICATIONS OF CHEMISTRY.

The application of basic chemical and physical principles to the manufacturing industries has led to the technological revolution which began at the turn of the century and is still gathering momentum. Although it is impossible to cover fully the areas in which the chemical sciences find application, a few of the more important fields are noted below:

Electrochemistry.

Electrochemistry deals with processes in which chemical energy is converted into electrical energy or *vice versa*. The most common examples are the dry battery and the lead storage battery (L13), although the generation of electricity by fuel cells (L43) is fast becoming of industrial importance. Conversely, if a current is passed through an ionic solution, a chemical reaction will take place, and this principle is employed in the electrolytic refining of metal ores and in metal plating processes.

Surface Chemistry.

Surface chemistry is based on the fact that solid and liquid surfaces have properties which are different from those of matter in the bulk state. A molecule A situated in the bulk interacts with its neighbours, but the various forces will cancel, as shown in **Fig. 4.** For a molecule B in the

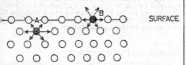

FIG. 4—Surface Forces: molecules within the solid (or liquid) are subject to balanced forces, but for molecules in the surface there is a resultant downward force.

surface there is a net inward pull. The surface is therefore a high energy state and thermodynamics predicts that substances will try to minimise their total surface area. In a liquid this leads to the formation of spherical drops. The solid, on the other hand, will attract vapours and liquids which deposit surface films and thus reduce its surface energy. One application of adsorbed films, catalysis, has already been discussed.

Surface effects become significant in processes where the ratio of surface area to bulk volume is large, for instance, where matter is finely dispersed. This is the case in the technology of paints, printing inks, detergency, dairy products, air and water pollution, and solutions of polymers. The above-mentioned properties are also utilised in processes which involve the deposition of substances on surfaces, *e.g.*, textile finishing (water- and crease-proofing), metal coating, herbicides, cosmetics, and adhesives. Perhaps the most important field in which surface behaviour is one of the determining factors is biology. All living cells are separated from each other by membranes, and nutrients and other chemicals are adsorbed on, and diffuse through, these membranes, the nature and action of which are as yet very imperfectly understood (**F27(1)**).

Photochemistry.

Like other forms of energy, light, both visible and ultraviolet, can cause chemical changes to take place and, conversely, some reactions will give rise to the emission of radiation, *e.g.*, fluorescence. The ultimate source of most of the energy on each is the radiation from the sun which, by the process of photosynthesis (**F28(1)**), can be converted by green plants into the chemical energy stored in coal, oil, and carbohydrates. The mechanism of photosynthesis is one of the most baffling problems in chemical kinetics.

In photography a film of gelatin, in which are embedded small grains of silver bromide, is exposed to light, when a " latent image " is formed. This is believed to consist of submicroscopic specks of silver in some of the grains, but the mechanism of its formation is still uncertain. The latent image can be " developed " into a negative image (silver) which is then " fixed " by dissolving away the unreduced silver bromide.

Analytical Chemistry.

This is an important branch of Chemistry and deals with the identification and quantitative estimation of substances, often in complex mixtures. Where a quantitative analysis is to be achieved, the component under study has first to be separated in the pure state and then a suitable method must be found to determine its concentration in the mixture. In earlier days most analytical techniques were based on chemical reactions which were specific for the compound to be separated. Thus, sodium chloride and sodium sulphate can be separated by making use of the fact that many metal sulphates are insoluble in water, so that if a solution of, say, barium chloride is added to the mixture, barium sulphate will precipitate as solid and can be removed from the sodium chloride by filtration. If the amount of mixture initially used and the amount of precipitated barium sulphate are known, then, from the chemical formulae for barium and sodium sulphates, $BaSO_4$ and Na_2SO_4, it is easy to calculate the percentage of sodium sulphate in the original mixture.

During the last 25 years chemical analytical techniques have gradually been superseded by much more refined physical methods. Most important among these are the spectroscopic methods which can distinguish between small differences in energies associated with the vibrational motions of different chemical bonds. Some of these techniques not only measure energy differences but can detect minute amounts of energy, such as the energy liberated by a burning candle at a distance of 1 mile.

The detection, identification, and sometimes the quantitative estimation of very minor constituents of mixtures is frequently of great importance in industrial processes and products. For instance the presence of 1 g of iron in a ton of edible oil will rapidly cause the oil to turn rancid. Another example of the importance of traces of chemical compounds is provided by flavour and aroma of foodstuffs and perfumes. Frequently the characteristic, agreeable odour of a product is due to minute concentrations of one or several fairly simple organic compounds which at higher concentrations possess a quite unpleasant odour. The isolation of these compounds from natural products such as fruit or flowers and their identification provides a continous challenge to the ingenuity of the analytical chemist.

Conclusion.

It will now be readily seen that the science of chemistry covers a large field which extends from the very simple molecules, such as H_2O, to the complex naturally occurring molecules with molecular weights of several millions. It involves very fundamental studies, ranging from the nature of the forces between atoms and the how and why of apparently simple chemical reactions, to the very applied problems encountered in the manufacture of high-strength construction materials. Among new fields which have developed rapidly during recent years petroleum chemicals rank high. This industry, which is centered on the oil companies, produces a large variety of substances, such as detergents, polymer raw materials, solvents, dyestuffs, fats and waxes, from by-products obtained during oil refining. Pharmaceutical chemistry, too, is rapidly developing and attempts

are being made not only to synthesise new drugs but to gain a better understanding of the mechanism of drug action.

Probably the most significant developments during the next twenty years will occur in the field of biochemistry. The elucidation of the structure and genetic functions of nucleic acids and some proteins has provided the impetus for further investigation into the chemistry and physics of these and other biologically active molecules. Other outstanding problems which may well be solved in the not too distant future include the mechanism of membrane action, muscle contraction and nerve impulse propagation in molecular terms. Where a hundred years ago the sciences of physics, chemistry, and biology parted ways to follow their own separate paths, they are now seen to be converging and the areas of overlap are gradually increasing, as the molecular concepts of chemistry are providing a means of studying biological processes in terms of established physical laws and mechanisms. This part of the story will now be taken up in the section that follows.

IV. BIOLOGY—THE SCIENCE OF LIFE

WHAT BIOLOGY IS ABOUT.

Biology embraces the study of all living things which exist on earth at the present time and also the recognisable remains of those that are extinct. Living things or organisms range from the apparently simple micro-organisms such as viruses and bacteria to the largest animals and plants.

Living Processes.

The enormous variation and complexity of living processes make the task of understanding and defining life a very difficult one. Every living organism undergoes continual physical and chemical changes which, in spite of their diversity, are referred to as the metabolism of the organism. Metabolism involves the processing of food materials, the production of waste products, and all the intermediate stages between these whereby energy and matter are provided for the operation, maintenance, and growth of the organism. These reactions are under very exact chemical or nervous control at every stage and can be slowed down or speeded up as the need arises. Thus the organism can react to changes in the environment in which it lives, adjusting its activities in relation to the external changes. Finally, organisms can reproduce either in an identical or very slightly modified form. In this process new individuals are produced and the species continues to survive. Differences between offspring and parents can, under certain circumstances, act cumulatively over many generations and so form the basis of evolutionary change in which new species of organism are ultimately formed.

Molecular Biology.

It has been evident for many years that the most fundamental aspects of these living processes occur in basic structural units known as cells. We shall examine this level of organisation first before we attempt to look at the larger questions of the organisation of multicellular animals and plants and their interactions in groups or populations. The study of living processes at the molecular and cell level has been given a tremendous impetus in recent years by the advent of new techniques which enable microscopic and submicroscopic parts of cell to be examined. Physicists, chemists, and mathematicians have found themselves working alongside biologists in this field and several of the very notable advances have been made by physical scientists. At this level of organisation the traditional division of Biology into Botany, the study of plants, and Zoology, the study of animals, has little meaning. Even the more recent Genetics, the study of inheritance, Biophysics and Bio-

chemistry, concerned with the physics and chemistry of organisms, and Cytology, the study of cell structure, are losing such identity as they may once have had. Molecular biology is a term frequently used in describing this rapidly expanding and fascinating field of research.

THE CELL.

Cells were first seen in 1665 by Robert Hooke when he looked at a piece of cork under his primitive microscope. It was not until 1839, however, that Schlieden and Schwann produced the cell doctrine which visualised the cell as both the structural and functional unit of living organisation. Exceptions may be found to the cell doctrine. For example, some protozoa, algae, and fungi show very complex internal organisation but are not divided into cells; they are usually called acellular organisms. The viruses also constitute a difficulty since in many ways they are intermediate between living and dead matter. They are absolutely dependent on cells of other organisms for their continued existence. Outside living cells they are inert molecules which may take a crystalline form. Inside a host cell, however, they become disease-producing parasites which multiply and show many of the other properties of living organisms. They are minute and lack the complex organisation usually associated with cells. Notwithstanding their somewhat ambiguous position, the viruses are often treated as though they were single cells or parts of cells and their extreme simplicity has made them ideal material for many types of research at this level. The bacteria also lack some of the properties of cells but the differences are not so clearly defined as they are in the case of viruses.

Structure and Function of Cells.

Though the constituent cells of a multicellular organism are usually specialised to perform particular functions, they have a great many features in common. The cell is often said to be made up of a substance called protoplasm, a term for the fundamental material of life which dates from the 19th cent. Protoplasm has two main constituents, the cytoplasm and the nucleus, and is bounded on the outside by a cell or plasma membrane. Plant cells generally have an additional wall composed primarily of cellulose and used for support. The nucleus is the controlling centre of the cell and has rather limited metabolic capabilities. The cytoplasm contains various subunits which operate to produce energy and new cell structure during the normal metabolism of the cell.

Cells take up the raw materials for metabolism

through the cell membrane from extracellular fluid which surrounds them. The nutrients include carbohydrates, fats, proteins, minerals, vitamins, and water. Fats and carbohydrates are important principally as sources of energy, though both types of compound are found in permanent cell structure. Proteins are complex substances of high molecular weight which contain nitrogen in addition to the carbon, hydrogen, and oxygen found in the other compounds. They are of fundamental importance in the structure and function of the cell and are built up of a number of simple nitrogen-containing organic molecules called amino acids. There are twenty amino acids occurring commonly in nature so that the number of possible combinations in large protein molecules is quite clearly enormous. A group of proteins whose significance is well established are the enzymes which are the catalysts of chemical reactions in living cells. Each enzyme will control and speed up a specific reaction even though it is present in very small amounts and is usually unchanged at the end of the process. A large number of inorganic mineral salts are essential for cells to function normally. Some, such as sodium, potassium, and calcium salts, are needed in considerable quantity; others are required only in trace amounts and these include iron, copper, and manganese. The trace elements are usually important constituents of enzyme systems. Vitamins are also necessary in very small amounts and it seems reasonable to conclude that their function is also a catalytic one in parts of some enzyme systems.

I. CYTOPLASM.

For a long time cytoplasm was thought to be a homogenous and structureless substrate in which enzymes occurred as part of a general colloidal system. With the refinement of techniques such as electron microscopy and ultracentrifugation, more and more identifiable components have been found within the cytoplasm. It now seems certain that the material other than these recognisable particles is not a structureless matrix but a highly organised and variable complex at the molecular level.

Identification of Components: recent techniques.
Ultracentrifuge.

When soft tissues such as liver are ground up in a homogeniser, which usually takes the form of a plunger fitting fairly tightly into a glass tube, the cells are broken up but the smaller particles escape destruction. The particles remain in a highly active biochemical state if the salt concentration of the liquid into which they are released by homogenisation is more or less the same as that within the cell from which they came. Early failures to isolate cell fractions were almost all attributable to osmotic difficulties in which differences of salt concentration led to the movement of water into or out of the particles and to their subsequent destruction. The homogenate can be treated in a centrifuge in which high speed rotation subjects the particles to forces many thousands times greater than gravity. As a result the heaviest particles, such as the nuclei, are deposited first on the bottom of the centrifuge tube. The liquid is then transferred to another tube and the process repeated at a higher speed which brings down slightly lighter particles called mitochondria. The next collection of particles which can be obtained is called the microsomal fraction. By careful use of this technique, biochemists can produce a variety of cell constituents which can be studied in the absence of all the other reacting systems of the cell.

Radioactive Isotopes.

In many of the studies of cell chemistry which have been made on whole cells, on cell fractions, or on isolated enzyme systems, progress has been due in a large part to the availability of isotopes. With the aid of compounds prepared in the laboratory and labelled with the radioactive isotopes of elements such as carbon, hydrogen, nitrogen, oxygen, sulphur, and phosphorus, biochemists can now follow the metabolic fate of

these substances in living organisms. The presence of a radioactive " labelled " element in any of the products of metabolism can be determined by means of Geiger and scintillation counters. The studies involving radioactive isotopes have shown more clearly than any others that living material is never static but is in a state of dynamic equilibrium. Substances are constantly broken down and replaced by other substances so that an organism may appear to be more or less unchanging but its components are always turning over.

Light Microscopy.

Many of the particles which can be isolated and studied have been identified within the living cell by means of the light microscope. Especially useful in this respect have been the phase contrast and interference modifications which make structures of different refractive index visible and do not depend on differences in light absorption as does the ordinary instrument.

Electron Microscope.

In light microscopy true images of particles smaller than the wavelength of light cannot be formed. Great difficulty is experienced in resolving particles much smaller than 0·5 microns (0·0005 millimetre) in size. The electron microscope, which uses a beam of electrons instead of light, is capable of much greater resolution because electrons behave as rays of extremely short wavelengths. Details as fine as 20 Ångstroms (0·002 microns) have been resolved and a tremendous amount of structure has been revealed by this instrument. However, many of the objects which are well known from electron microscope studies have not been isolated nor have functions been ascribed to them. Conversely, much of the biochemistry of cells cannot be linked to known structures. One of the great limitations of the electron microscope is that it can only be used to examine very thin slices of dead material.

X-ray Diffraction.

A method which can reveal a great deal of information about the arrangement of constituent parts in very complex biological molecules is that of X-ray diffraction. In this method X-rays are reflected from regularities in the molecular structure so as to form a pattern characteristic of the structure. Studies of X-ray diffraction patterns can be made on living material so that the internal shape of biological molecules can be worked out and the changes, if any, followed during phases of activity. In many ways X-ray diffraction has been useful in filling the gaps between biochemical studies of molecular behaviour and the essentially static view of cell structure obtained from the electron microscope.

Constituents of Cytoplasm.

The following are some of the particulate and membranous constituents of cytoplasm which have been identified and analysed with varying degrees of success by these and many other techniques:

1. Mitochondria and Oxidation.

Mitochondria vary in shape from cylindrical rods to spheres and in size from 0·2 to 3·0 microns. When seen in the living cell they are in constant motion. The whole structure is enclosed within a thin double membrane, the inner layer of which is thrown into folds extending across the central cavity of the mitochondrion and dividing it into small chambers. The function of mitochondria is to provide energy for the reactions of the rest of the cell. Almost the whole machinery for the oxidation of foodstuffs is to be found in the mitochondria and, as might be expected, is related in some way to the complex structure. Slight damage to the mitochondrion will render it unable to carry out a complete cycle of oxidative processes. Destruction of parts of the double membrane system prevents the production of energy-rich phosphate bonds in adenosine triphosphate (ATP) in which energy is stored and transported about the cell.

The Krebs Cycle.

The oxidative reactions which produce the energy are quite unlike those in which hydrocarbons are burnt in the laboratory. They proceed through a large number of controlled steps during which the energy is slowly evolved. The basic fuel substances, carbohydrates, fats, and proteins, are broken down outside the mitochondria to four major intermediate products which are pyruvic acid, oxalacetic acid, acetic acid and ketoglutaric acid. These acids diffuse into the mitochondria and are oxidised in a cyclical system of reactions called the Krebs or citric acid cycle which ultimately leads to the production of carbon dioxide and water. The actual oxidation of the various compounds participating in the cycle is brought about by a series of enzymes described as an electron transport chain. Oxidation in these cases is essentially a removal of electrons from the substrate, invariably accompanied by an equal number of hydrogen nuclei. The electrons, sometimes with and sometimes without the hydrogen nuclei, are passed from one compound to another until eventually they combine with oxygen to form water. One of the best known electron transport systems is that involving iron-containing substances called cytochromes.

An example of a typical stage in the Krebs cycle is the conversion of succinic acid to fumaric acid under the control of the enzyme succinic dehydrogenase. Both acids are compounds containing four carbon atoms but the latter has two electrons and two hydrogen nuclei fewer than the former which is therefore said to be oxidised during the conversion. The electrons are accepted by the first member of a chain of cytochromes which is thus reduced and the hydrogen is set free as hydrogen ions. The electrons are passed down the chain of cytochromes which are reduced in turn and re-oxidise the earlier members of the chain. In the final stage the reduced cytochrome is oxidised by oxygen which accepts the electrons and combines with the hydrogen ions to form water. These steps produce energy, but this does not all appear as heat because some is used to drive a reaction which consumes energy. The first law of thermodynamics states that such a coupling is necessary if a high energy compound is to be produced. The energy consuming reaction is the conversion of adenosine diphosphate (ADP) to adenosine triphosphate (ATP) with its energy-rich phosphate bond. The whole process is known as oxidative phosphorylation. The mitochondria produce far more energy than they require and the ATP passes into the cytoplasm for use in the rest of the cell.

2. Chloroplasts and Photosynthesis.

Chloroplasts are particles found in cells in the green parts of plants, in fact they contain the green pigment which is called chlorophyll. They are involved in the extremely important process known as photosynthesis in which energy absorbed from light is used to synthesise carbohydrates from carbon dioxide and water, oxygen being formed as a by-product.

Chloroplasts are disc-shaped or flat ellipsoids from 2 to 20 microns across, possessing a complex structure which in many ways is reminiscent of that found in mitochondria. A typical double membrane surrounds the structure and the inside is made up very largely of a stack of discs consisting of paired membranes connected at their ends to form closed systems. This seems to be a further development of the type of lamellated structure seen dividing the central cavity of a mitochondrion. The chlorophylls and other pigments, such as the orange yellow carotenoids, seem to be arranged in layers a single molecule thick in the chloroplast discs so that they are maximally exposed to light.

Photosynthesis.

In photosynthesis there are two somewhat independent sets of reactions, one needing light and the other going on in the dark. The primary process is the absorption of light quanta by the chlorophyll which causes some of the electrons of its molecule to pass from one orbital to another

and thus enter an excited state. It is thought that chlorophyll then loses electrons which pass either to a recently discovered protein called ferrodoxin or to another oxidising agent, plastoquinone. The electrons from plastoquinone are transferred via a complex series of steps involving a cytochrome chain back to the chlorophyll. During these sequences oxygen is liberated from water molecules and energy-rich phosphate bonds are produced. The production of ATP in this reaction, which can only take place in the light, is called photosynthetic phosphorylation and, in this respect, makes plants independent of stored carbohydrate as their primary energy source.

The reactions so far described have not involved carbon dioxide and though it is possible to make the system operate solely in this way it is not usual for it to do so. Normally the electrons from ferrodoxin are passed to another electron accepting system together with hydrogen ions from water. At the same time, as recent isotope studies have revealed, carbon dioxide is combined with a 5-carbon sugar and the resulting compound immediately splits into two molecules of a 3-carbon phosphoglyceric acid. The reduced electron system which has oxidised ferrodoxin now comes into operation and, together with energy from ATP, is used to synthesise sugar and starch from the 3-carbon compounds. The reactions in which carbon dioxide is taken up or " fixed " and then reduced during the formation of sugar can go on in the dark unlike those of photosynthetic phosphorylation described earlier.

The importance of this process whereby plants can make use of the energy in sunlight to fix carbon dioxide and produce carbohydrates is quite clear. The whole animal population of the world, including man, is dependent on plants for food since even the meat-eating carnivores prey upon herbivores. Although scientists continue to make efforts to produce adequate food material from simple compounds, there is still no better machinery known for doing this than the plant cell. Man is dependent on photosynthesis not only for his supplies of food but also for much of

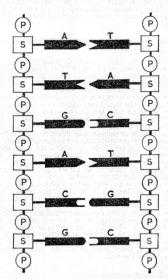

Fig. 1. *Nucleic Acids.* A portion of a DNA molecule showing how it is made up of two strands of nucleotides. Each nucleotide consists of a base which may be Adenine (A), Thymine (T), Guanine (G) or Cytosine (C), united to the Pentose Sugar, Desoxyribose (S), in turn joined to Phosphoric Acid (P). The nucleotides are linked through the phosphoric acid groups. The two strands are held together by hydrogen bonds between bases, adenine linking only with thymine, and guanine only with cytosine.

his fuel, since much of the combustible material removed from the earth is of plant origin. In this respect atomic energy may eventually prove to be an adequate alternative.

3. Endoplasmic reticulum, Ribosomes, and Protein Synthesis.

A network of elaborate and oriented double membranes existing within parts of the cytoplasm can be seen in the electron microscope. In the space between the pairs of double membranes small granules are visible, either free in the space or attached to a membrane. The whole system is called the endoplasmic reticulum. When the cell is homogenised and centrifuged the endoplasmic reticulum appears as the microsomal fraction. Biochemical analysis after separation of the membranous from the granular components reveals that the former is composed largely of phospholipids and cholesterol, which are compounds closely related to fats, and the latter of ribonucleic acid (RNA).

Nucleic Acids.

The term nucleic acid covers a class of substances, usually of great complexity, built up from smaller units called nucleotides. Each nucleotide consists of a base, united to a sugar, in turn united to phosphoric acid. Nucleotides are joined together in a linear fashion by means of the phosphoric acid residues to form a chain from which the bases project at right angles (Fig. 1). Two types of sugar are found in naturally occurring nucleic acids and these are the ribose of RNA

and the desoxyribose of desoxyribonucleic acids (DNA). We shall return to the latter when the nucleus is considered. Four nitrogen-containing bases occur in nucleic acids and in RNA—adenine, cytosine, guanine, and uracil. In DNA the uracil is replaced by thymine.

Protein Synthesis.

There is good evidence that RNA is manufactured exclusively within the nucleus and subsequently moves out into the cytoplasm. Some of it, called ribosomal RNA, unites with protein to form the granules, or ribosomes, of the endoplasmic reticulum. Another form, called messenger RNA, also migrates from the nucleus to associate with ribosomes but does not become incorporated into their permanent structure. It is also well established that the ribosomes are closely linked with protein synthesis in the cell because radioactive amino acids, when fed to an animal, are always found first in the ribosomes before any other cell structure. The specification for a particular protein is not carried on the ribosome which is merely the factory for making these complex molecules. It is thought that messenger RNA carries instructions from the nucleus which specify exactly the protein to be synthesised at a ribosome. This is done by means of a code in which a "triplet" of three nucleotide bases codes one amino acid (Fig. 2). Thus on a long molecule of RNA, three adjacent uracil bases would specify an amino acid called phenylalanine. If these were followed on the RNA molecule by one uracil and two guanines then the amino acid tryptophan would be specified and this would be

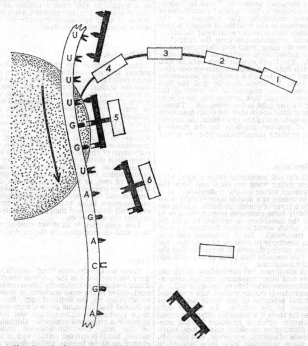

FIG. 2. A portion of a molecule of messenger RNA, associated with a ribosome and synthesising a protein. The base sequence on the messenger RNA has been determined by the helix labelled with the downward pointing arrow in Fig. 3. Adenine specifies Uracil (U), Cytosine specifies Guanine (G), Thymine specifies Adenine (A), and Guanine specifies Cytosine (C). The ribosome is moving down the messenger RNA strand "reading" the triplet code. Amino acid 4, which is phenylalanine specified by UUU, has just been joined to three other amino acids and its carrier RNA released to the cytoplasm. Amino acid 5, tryptophan specified by UGG, is attached to its carrier RNA and in position ready to be joined to the protein chain by the ribosome. Amino acid 6, methionine specified by UAG, is attached to its carrier RNA but has not been brought into position on the messenger RNA strand. Other amino acids and carrier RNA molecules exist free in the cytoplasm and have not yet associated.

F30

joined to the phenylalanine. In this way complex protein molecules can be built up according to instructions emanating from the nucleus for each of the 20 different amino acids. It is far from clear how the amino acids in the cytoplasm are brought into position on the RNA "template" and how they are activated so as to combine and form protein. It is thought that they are first attached, by appropriate enzymes, to small molecules of so-called carrier RNA in the cytoplasm before associating on the template of messenger RNA. The association is then accomplished by a ribosome which moves along the messenger RNA chain, as it were "reading" the code, and taking appropriate carrier RNA-amino acid complexes from the surrounding medium. There are still many gaps in our knowledge of the exact sequence of events.

This system is responsible for building and maintaining much of the organisation of the cytoplasm. All the enzymes, for example, catalysing every reaction within the cell will be specified and built up on the appropriate RNA template. The understanding of protein synthesis is of fundamental importance to the whole of biology and has particular significance in studies on cancer where cell growth becomes abnormal.

4. The Golgi Apparatus.

The characteristic features of the Golgi apparatus are numbers of large vacuoles or spaces, bordered by closely packed layers of double membranes. The latter look very much like the membranes of the endoplasmic reticulum but do not have the ribosome particles along their edge. They are therefore known as "smooth" membranes in contrast to the "rough" membranes of endoplasmic reticulum. The function of the Golgi apparatus is not established though it may be associated with secretory activity of the cell.

The Golgi apparatus has been the subject of controversy for many years and illustrates one of the major difficulties in working at the molecular cell level. The Golgi structure can only be seen through the light and electron microscopes after the cell has been through a number of preparative stages. Many biologists thought that the preparation itself was responsible for creating the Golgi apparatus and that nothing like the objects seen would really exist in the living cell. Though there is now little doubt that the Golgi apparatus is a real constituent of the cytoplasm, the general problem of creating artefacts by the involved treatment in many investigations remains a very real one.

5. Cell Membrane.

Though the cell membrane plays a most vital part in regulating what can enter and leave the cell, it remains rather poorly understood. It is thought to consist of a double layer of lipid molecules with a layer of protein probably outside the lipid. Fairly large molecules seem to be able to penetrate the membrane in relation to their fat solubility, which would support the hypothesis of its lipid framework. Small molecules and ions appear to penetrate in relation to their size, the smaller ones getting through more readily than the larger. This suggests that pores of a certain size exist in the membrane.

The cell membrane has mechanisms which can move ions and other substances against concentration differences either into or out of the cell. A fine microelectrode can be pushed into a cell and the electrical potential of the inside determined with respect to the outside. In all the cells studied so far there is a potential difference across the membrane which is produced by the non-uniform distribution on either side of ions, particularly those of sodium, potassium, and chloride. Though these potentials have been studied in animal and plant cells generally, they are best known from the work on nerve cells where sudden changes in the membrane potential are the basis of nerve impulses. A great deal is now known about the mechanism whereby the potential change, and thus the nerve impulse, is propagated from one end of a nerve to the other. The basic process which produces the nerve impulse in any region of the nerve fibre has been shown to be a sudden increase in permeability of the membrane to sodium ions in that region. A problem of much interest is how such activity can be passed from one nerve to the next, that is to say how a change of potential in one cell membrane can be made to affect an adjacent cell membrane. Such a process is fundamental to the large collections of nerve cells which form the nervous systems of animals. Transmission takes place at a special region called a synapse and when an impulse reaches this region it causes the release of a small amount of chemical transmitter substance which diffuse to the membrane of the adjacent cell. There it combines with the membrane in such a way as to change its permeability to ions and so produce a nerve impulse in the second cell. A number of transmitter substances have now been identified and many of them are related chemically to tranquillisers and other drugs affecting the nervous system.

II. NUCLEUS.

The main regions of the nucleus are the surrounding nuclear membrane, a mass of material known as chromatin, and a small sphere called the nucleolus. The nuclear membrane is a double structure very much like the membranes of the cell surface and endoplasmic reticulum. Suggestions have been made that these membranes are continuous at some regions within the cell. The status of chromatin was in doubt for many years. Light microscope studies reveal very little structure in the nucleus until the time when the cell is preparing for, and undergoing, division or mitosis. At this time a number of discrete double strands, the chromosomes, are revealed by virtue of their chromatin content—the material stains heavily with basic dyes.

Cell Division.

During division the chromosomes behave in regular and recognisable sequence. In the first stage called prophase they appear and at the same time the nuclear membrane breaks down. Next, in metaphase, the chromosomes become arranged across the equator of a splindle-shaped collection of fibrils which appears in the area formerly outlined by the nucleus. Then follows anaphase in which the two threads of each chromosome, the chromatids, move to opposite poles of the spindle. Finally in the last stage, telophase, nuclear membranes are formed round the two separate collections of chromosome material and the cytoplasm itself divides into two. Thus two cells are formed each containing the same number of chromosomes as the parent and the cells enter a period of rest, or interphase, between divisions During interphase the chromatin material disappears and the possibility was considered of the chromosomes being assembled as a prelude to every cell division and then being dispersed in the nuclear sap afterwards.

This suggestion is in direct conflict with the view that chromosomes are the carriers of genes

Genes.

These are the elements which contain all hereditary information and the medium whereby hereditary features are transmitted from one cell to the next, either in the same organism or from parents to offspring via the fertilised egg. Experiments indicated that the same genes always occupy the same position on chromosomes and this really demands a structural continuity through the life of the cell. The chromosomes undoubtedly persist, but it is still not certain why or how they change so as to become visible during division One suggestion has been that the nucleic acids o which they are very largely made up condense during the period of prophase. In the resting nucleus the chromosomes may be much more swollen and occupy much of the nucleus.

The problem that has attracted the most atten tion and is possibly the most fundamental that biology has to offer is that of the nature of the genes. The important material of the genes is known to be desoxyribosenucleic acid (DNA), made up of nucleotides as is RNA, though in this case the bases are adenine, cytosine, guanine, and thymine. The DNA molecule is large and complex. Two long chains of nucleotides are known to coil round in a double helix with the pairs of bases on each helix directed towards one another and linked by means of hydrogen bonds (Fig. 3).

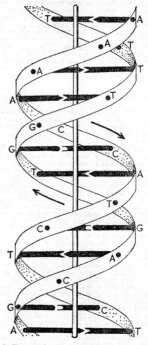

Fig. 3. The actual arrangement of the two nucleotide strands in a double helix, with the bases projecting and linking the two helices as shown.

Furthermore, if adenine is the base on one chain, thymine must be its partner on the other and similarly guanine can link only with cytosine. Because of this pairing off of bases there is sufficient information in a single chain of nucleotides to resynthesise the double helix once more. Thus if we examine a section of a single strand of the helix and find bases in the order adenine, thymine, guanine, adenine, cytosine, we can predict that in similar positions on the other strand we shall find thymine, adenine, cytosine, thymine, guanine. The capacity of one half of a DNA molecule to specify the other half exactly, enables the system to be self-replicating in a way that is essential in a hereditary transmitter and fits in well with what is known of chromosome behaviour during cell division.

Transmission of Genetic Information.

Accepting that DNA is the material of the gene it remains now to examine the nature of the information which it passes from cell to cell and organism to organism. Long before the structure and significance of the DNA molecule was known, geneticists were finding that alterations in a gene, known as a mutation, usually affected a particular chemical reaction and this in turn caused the changes seen in the organism as a whole. The effect was due to the failure to synthesise a necessary enzyme and so the hypothesis "one gene = one enzyme" gathered currency. This view has now been extended to include proteins other than enzymes and it is now certain that specific genes control the synthesis of specific proteins. The DNA of the genes transmits the instructions about protein synthesis to the ribosomes via messenger RNA. In the nucleus, messenger RNA is made with specific base sequences in its molecule by using DNA as the template; thus a group of three adjacent adenine bases in DNA would produce a group of three adjacent urocil bases in the synthesised RNA and this would lead to the specification of phenylalanine at the ribosome as we have seen. Only one of the two strands in the DNA double helix participates in the production of RNA.

Within the nucleus, the nucleolus is believed to play an important part in the synthesis of RNA since its turnover of this material is very rapid. It has been suggested that the nucleolus supplements the RNA produced by chromosomes and acts as the channel through which this material is released to the cytoplasm. There is now some good evidence which points to the nucleolus as the source of ribosomal RNA since cells which lose the nucleolus have no ribosomes.

The processes involved in nuclear control and the transmission of information from cell to cell is summarised in the aphorism "DNA makes RNA and RNA makes protein." The system of carrying that information in the base sequences of DNA molecules has become known as the "genetic code." A remarkable landmark in the study of DNA occurred when, towards the end of 1967, Kornberg and his colleagues managed to synthesise a virus DNA in a test tube. The synthesised molecules proved to be capable of infecting bacteria in the same way that the naturally occurring virus would. The DNA was synthesised using an extracted virus DNA molecule as template and attaching nucleotides by means of appropriate enzymes. The newly made molecules were then separated from the template. It can hardly be claimed that this is the creation of life in a test tube since the template was extracted from a living virus. The experiment suggests many possibilities in experimental modification of the genetic constitution of an organism with all the far reaching ethical consequences.

MULTICELLULAR ORGANISATION.

It is axiomatic, if evolutionary theory is accepted, that in the course of very long periods of time there has been a general change in multicellular organisation from the simple aggregation of cells with little individual differentiation, to the highly specialised and differentiated cells and tissues seen in complex animals and plants. It is fascinating to speculate on the environmental variations and internal mechanisms which together produced this result. The problem is so vast, however, that a complete analysis is impossible and even a statement of the sequence of changes is in many cases highly controversial.

Another aspect of becoming multicellular, where the problems offer more hope of analysis, is that the complex organisation must be built up in the lifetime of each animal or plant from the single-celled stage of the fertilised egg. We have already seen how cells can divide repeatedly, handing on self-replicating chromosomes so that each cell is apparently identical. If this were really so then division of the fertilised egg would result in an unorganised mass of cells showing no differentiation. The essential problems in development are: (1) how is the smooth succession of shape changes produced during cell division so that an appropriate and recognisable end product is reached?; (2) how do the cells differentiate during this temporal sequence so that those which form part of the eye, say, are different from those of liver and blood?

Method of Development.

There are some important differences in the method of development in animals and plants. In animals there tends to be a relatively short period during which the basic structure is produced and after which growth, repair, and replacement may cause adjustment rather than major change. In higher plants, on the other hand, the apical regions of both roots and shoots remain in a permanently embryonic state and add material, which then differentiates, in a continuous process throughout the life of the plant. In spite of these differences—and in any case there are many exceptions—the two main problems in development are essentially similar in both animals and plants.

A great deal of work has been done on animal development since this takes place in a fairly stereotyped way during a short period of time. The fertilised egg of an animal divides in such a way as to form a hollow ball of cells, the blastula, which folds in on itself to produce a two-layered sac, the gastrula. A third layer, the mesoderm, is now added between the two layers, known as ectoderm on the outside, and endoderm on the inside. At this stage much of the animal's basic structure is established. Many aspects of this orderly sequence can be explained in terms of specific adhesive properties of cells, so that a cell will stick to others of the same type but not to unrelated types. Other mechanical properties such as elasticity, particularly in surface layers, are important in maintaining shape and producing appropriate changes during processes when one layer is folded in on another. Why cells should have the different physical properties necessary to produce an integrated whole embryo is not known, but certainly it cannot be thought that every cell has an absolutely fixed constitution and therefore a predetermined role in development. Large parts of developing embryos can be removed in early stages and their places taken by remaining cells so that intact organisms are still produced. One is led to conclude that the surroundings of a cell have a great deal of influence on the way it reacts and that there is a great deal of adaptability in the developing system, especially in its early stages.

Formation of Specialised Tissues.

These points lead us on to the second major question concerning the differences which appear progressively in cells during development so that specialised tissues are ultimately formed. This is essentially a problem in the regulation of gene activity since we know that each cell division produces daughter cells which are genetically identical. It seems likely therefore that instructions are carried on the chromosomes to cope with all requirements of the organism, but that in specialised cells only a small fraction of this full potential is realised. For a long time embryologists have known that egg cytoplasm shows regional differences which make identical nuclei behave differently, and it is thought that regional cytoplasm can in some way control gene activity. Techniques for the transplantation of nuclei in developing frog embryos have been perfected and it has been possible to put a nucleus from an intestinal cell of a tadpole into an enucleate egg. The egg will go on to develop normally even though its nucleus came from a fully specialised cell derived from endoderm. The embryo will form blood and muscle from the mesodermal layer and all the other components of an organism, under the influence of a nucleus which normally would have produced none of these things. One can conclude that all the genes are present, even in the nuclei of specialised cells, but that they have to be placed in a suitable cytoplasmic environment in order to be activated. Similar nuclear transplantation experiments indicate that genes can be " turned off " as well as " turned on " by an appropriate cytoplasmic environment, even though the nuclei come from cells which are so specialised as to stop dividing. The components of cytoplasm which control gene activity are still quite unknown.

A study of cell differentiation and the development of multicellular organisation leads us to the view that, important though the nucleus and its genes are in controlling cell activity, an integrated organism is the result of complex interactions between its constituent cells and between the cytoplasm of those cells and their nuclei.

THE CLASSIFICATION OF ORGANISMS.

It was clear to the biologists of the 17th cent. that animals and plants could be fitted into different groups or species. John Ray, a leading biologist of the day, defined a species as a group of individuals capable of interbreeding within the group. This criterion, with its corollary that a species is reproductively isolated from organisms outside the group, has survived more or less unchanged to the present day. The early workers also saw that some species were very similar to one another while others were obviously dissimilar. Systems of classification based on the similarities and differences were drawn up so that all organisms could be fitted into an orderly scheme and species could be given names in accordance with the scheme. The most famous collector and classifier was the Swede, Linnaeus, who established his reputation in the 1730s. A very large number of animals and plants are known by the names given to them by Linnaeus.

Systematics, as the study of species and of higher groups of classification is called, acquired a new significance after Darwin and the Theory of Evolution. From the biological point of view the most satisfactory classification became one which reflected the evolution of the organisms classified. Such a system, based on the phylogeny or evolutionary history of a group, is called a natural classification. It is not always easy to produce because ancestral types tend to become extinct and the problem then becomes one of reconstructing a whole branching system when only the ends of the branches are known. A great deal of the work on systematics has, of necessity, to be done on museum specimens which may be fossils or material preserved in some way by the collectors. The biological criterion of reproductive isolation cannot be used to define a species when the only available representatives are in a preserved state. In this case the scientist must resort to an assessment of structural differences in an attempt to decide whether two organisms are of different or the same species. It has often been said, unfairly, that such species are subjective concepts which exist only in the mind of the systematist. In recent years computer techniques have been used to compare large numbers of structural differences between groups of animals or plants. Physiological and biochemical characteristics are also becoming part of the armoury of the 20th cent. systematist. All these techniques have led to the realisation that even the species cannot be regarded as a static point in an evolutionary pattern. Some species die out and others arise as conditions in the environment slowly change. This essentially dynamic view of a continually shifting equilibrium between animals, plants and their environment has given rise to what Huxley has aptly called " The New Systematics " in his book of that title.

When the systematist shifts his attention to the higher levels of classification the problems are just as great as at the species level. Different species having features in common can be grouped together into genera, genera into families, families into orders, orders into classes, and classes into phyla. The dividing lines between different groups at all levels is always difficult and in the final analysis somewhat arbitrary since at these levels we do not have any biological criterion such as exists for the species. The evolutionary status of the larger groups is also poorly defined. Many are now recognised to be polyphyletic, which is to say that there are several main evolutionary lines running right through the group.

THE ANIMAL KINGDOM.

The animal kingdom is divided into about 24 large groups or phyla though the number varies between different classifications. Ten of the more important phyla are listed below.

1. Protozoa.—Microscopic, unicellular forms of great variety. Some may have more than one nucleus and others form colonies. Many are able to swim by waving hair like flagella or cilia.

Others move by putting out extensions of the body or pseudopodia into which the rest of the body then flows. Protozoa are found in the sea, in fresh water and in the soil. Some are parasitic and cause important diseases in animals and man such as sleeping sickness and malaria.

2. Porifera.—Sponges. Very primitive multicellular animals whose cells display considerable independence of one another. Largely marine. The body which may become branched and plant-like is supported by a framework of spicules and fibres. The bath sponge is the fibrous skeleton of certain species.

3. Coelenterates.—Hydra, jellyfish, sea anemones, corals. Simple animals which have a body only two cells thick surrounding a gut cavity with a single opening to the outside. Largely marine. Many are colonial. Coral reefs are formed from the calcareous skeletons of these animals.

4. Platyhelminths.—Flatworms, which are free living in water, and liver flukes and tapeworms, which are parasitic. A third, solid block of cells, the mesoderm, has been developed between the two layers of cells seen in the coelenterates. A simple gut may be developed and the reproductive system is complex especially in the parasitic forms.

5. Nematodes.—Roundworms. The body is smooth and pointed at each end. Some of the most numerous and widespread of all animals. Free living in all environments and parasitic in practically all groups of plants and animals. At the same level of complexity as the Platyhelminths.

6. Annelids.—Segmented worms such as earthworms, marine worms and leeches. A system of spaces, the body cavity, is developed in the mesoderm so that movements of the main body of the animal and movements of the gut become more or less independent. Digestive, excretory, circulatory, nervous and reproductive systems are all well developed.

7. Arthropods.—A very large, diverse and important group of animals which includes crustaceans such as crabs, shrimps and water fleas; myriapods, such as centipedes and millepedes; insects; and arachnids, such as spiders and scorpions. The arthropods show many of the developments seen in annelids and in addition they possess a jointed, hard exoskeleton. Paired appendages grow out from the segments of the body and form antennae, mouth parts, walking legs, etc. The muscles within the skeleton are able to exert a fine control over the movement of the appendage. In order to grow these animals have to shed the exoskeleton periodically.

8. Molluscs.—Mussels, clams, oysters, squids, octopods and snails. Complex body form but somewhat different from annelid–arthropod type. Unsegmented body protected by shell which is variously developed in different types. It forms two valves in mussels and oysters, a spiral structure in snails, is reduced and internal in squids and completely lost in octopods.

9. Echinoderms.—Starfish, brittle stars, sea cucumbers, sea urchins, and sea lilies. All marine and all radially symmetrical, usually with five radii. Completely unlike the other advanced, major groups. Circulatory, excretory and nervous systems differently developed. Locomotion and feeding by means of hundreds of tube feet projecting from under surface.

10. Chordates.—Sea squirts, Amphioxus, fish, amphibia, reptiles, birds and mammals. Segmented animals which at some stage in their life have gill slits leading from pharynx to the outside and a supporting notochord from which, in all chordates except sea squirts and Amphioxus, is developed a vertebral column or backbone. Those animals with a backbone are commonly referred to as vertebrates, *all* those without as invertebrates. These are obviously names of convenience having no phylogenetic significance since they lump together totally unrelated phyla in one case and align these with a part of a single phylum in the other. The vertebrates have been investigated more completely than any other animals because of their direct structural and functional relationship with man himself. There are five well defined classes which are listed below. The first vertebrates were the fish and from them came the amphibia. The amphibia gave rise to the reptiles and both birds and mammals evolved from different reptilian stock.

(a) Fish

Cold blooded, aquatic animals breathing by means of gills. Sharks, rays and dogfish belong to a group known as the elasmobranchs characterised by a skeleton made of cartilage. Bony fish, or teleosts, include almost all the fresh water fish and the common marine fish such as cod, mackerel, plaice, herring, etc.

(b) Amphibia

Cold blooded, more or less terrestrial animals which have to return to water to breed. Five fingered limbs are developed in place of the fins of fish. The egg hatches into a tadpole larva which is aquatic and breathes by gills. At metamorphosis the larva changes into the terrestrial adult which possesses lungs. Some amphibia such as the axolotl may become sexually mature as a larva and so never metamorphose into the adult. The class includes newts, salamanders, frogs and toads.

(c) Reptiles

Cold blooded and terrestrial. These animals do not return to water to breed because they have an egg with a relatively impermeable shell containing the food and water requirements of the developing embryo. There is no larval stage. Present day reptiles such as lizards, snakes and crocodiles are all that remains of a tremendous radiation of dinosaur-like creatures which occurred in the Mesozoic (**F44**).

(d) Birds

Warm blooded and adapted for aerial life. The characteristic feathers act both to insulate the body against heat loss and to provide the airfoil surfaces necessary for flight. The birds are an astonishingly uniform group and show less diversity of structure than much lower classification categories (*e.g.*, the teleosts) in other classes. The relationships of the 19,000 or more species of bird are difficult to establish because of this uniformity. It is clear that the flightless forms such as the ostrich are primitive and that the penguins are also in a separate category but the typical modern birds are classified in a large number of rather arbitrary orders. About half of all the known species are placed in one enormous order called the Passeriformes or perching birds.

(e) Mammals

Warm blooded animals which have been successful in a tremendous variety of habitats. Mammals are insulated from the environment by the characteristically hairy and waterproofed skin. They are, with two exceptions, viviporous which means that their young are born alive and in typical mammals at an advanced stage of development. In the marsupials of Australia the young are born at an early stage and transferred to a pouch where they develop further. The two exceptions referred to are primitive monotreme mammals known as the duck-billed platypus and spiny ant-eater and these animals lay eggs. The young of mammals are suckled by means of the milk producing mammary glands. The mammals include aquatic whales and dolphins, hoofed ungulates, flesh eating carnivores, rodents and insectivores, the aerial bats, and the tree climbing primates to which man himself belongs.

THE PHYSIOLOGY OF ANIMALS.

Some basic features of cell organisation have already been dealt with, and in unicellular animals all life processes, such as respiration, movement, growth and reproduction, proceed in the single cell. However in multicellular animals cells are of various types, constituting distinct tissues and organs which perform special functions in the body. Although each cell has its own complex metabolism there must be co-ordination between cells forming special tissues and between the tissues which form the whole organism in order for the body to function efficiently. The study of these functional interrelationships at the tissue and organism level of organisation is the province of the physiologist.

1. Movement, Fibrils and Skeletons.

(a) **Muscles.**—The prime movers in almost all animal movement are large protein molecules in the form of microscopic fibrillar threads. In some way not yet fully understood these fibrils can convert the chemical energy stored in the high energy phosphate bonds of ATP into mechanical energy. In the long, thin cells forming the muscles of animals, it has been discovered that there are two sets of fibrils, one formed of a protein called myosin, the other of actin, arranged in a regular, interdigitating fashion. When the muscle contracts the fibrils slide into one another so that, although the fibrils themselves do not change in length, the muscle as a whole develops tension and shortens. This, the Sliding Filament Theory of Muscle Contraction, was formulated in 1953 by A. F. Huxley, H. E. Huxley and J. Hanson. Fine bridges extend from the myosin fibrils to attach on to the actin and it is here that the conversion of chemical to mechanical energy goes on.

(b) **Skeletons.**—In order for muscles to work effectively it is necessary for them to operate in some sort of skeletal system. Contraction but not relaxation is an active process; muscles must be arranged in antagonistic pairs so that one muscle can extend the other. A skeleton also provides a system of levers so that the muscles can do work against the environment in an efficient manner. A simple type of skeleton found in fairly primitive animals is the hydrostatic system of coelenterates and worms. Here the animal can be thought of as a fluid filled bag or tube which can change shape but whose volume remains constant. By contraction of circular muscles the tube will become long and thin and conversely contraction of longitudinal muscles makes the tube short and fat. Examination of an earthworm will demonstrate how alternating waves of activity of this type passing from head to tail can move the animal over the ground. The earthworm shows an advance over the simplest systems because the hydrostatic tube is broken up into small units by the segmentation of the body. This makes local responses possible. The next advance to be seen is the development in animals such as arthropods and vertebrates of a firm skeleton to which muscles are directly attached. The skeleton can then be used to support the body and to engage the environment. It seems to matter little whether an endoskeleton (vertebrates) or exoskeleton (arthropods) is developed since in both cases a tremendous radiation of fins for swimming, legs for walking and wings for flying can be seen. However in other respects these two types of skeleton show significant differences. The exoskeleton for example offers more protection than the endoskeleton while apparently setting an upper size limit. All the really big animals have endoskeletons.

(c) **Cilia.**—Fibrillar systems are also seen in the fine hair-like cilia which project from the surface of some cells. Cilia are important in a number of ways. They are the organelles of movement in many Protozoa, they are used to produce water currents past the bodies of some aquatic animals, and they are of great importance in moving fluid within the body of almost all animals. They beat in a regular fashion, the effective stroke being accomplished with the cilium held straight out from the surface and the recovery stroke with the cilium flexed at the base. Cilia possess the same structure no matter

where they come from. In transverse section eleven fibrils can be seen which run the whole length of the organelle. Two of the fibrils are single and situated centrally while the other nine are double fibrils arranged in a circle around the periphery of the cilium. Work is still going on in this field, but it has been suggested that the peripheral fibrils are contractile and cause the cilium to bend. The function of the central fibrils is unknown.

2. Nutrition and the Alimentary Canal.

All animals must take in and digest food materials. As well as water they require complex organic substances, proteins, fats and carbohydrates, together with small amounts of salts and vitamins. These materials are obtained by eating the dead bodies of plants and other animals. They are taken into the alimentary canal and there broken down or digested by enzymes into simpler, soluble amino acids, sugars and fatty acids. These substances are absorbed and distributed to various parts of the body where they are used in cell metabolism (F26, 27) or stored for future use.

(a) The Size of Food—Microphagy and Macrophagy.

Many animals, called macrophagous feeders, take in relatively large masses of food. Some such as frogs and snakes swallow their food whole, but many break it up first. Arthropods have modified appendages arranged round the mouth for cutting, some molluscs have a rasp-like radula with which to scrape off particles, and many mammals break up their food with jaws and teeth. The teeth are usually well adapted to the type of food. Carnivores have large, sharp canines, premolars and molars with which to tear the flesh of the prey, fish eating seals have small peg-like teeth to grip the fish and herbivorous ungulates have flat grinding teeth with which they break up hard plant material.

In contrast, microphagous feeders collect small particles of food material from the environment by continuous filtration. In bivalve molluscs and many marine worms water currents are produced by beating cilia. Food is trapped within the confined space through which the water flows by means of a plentiful supply of sticky mucus in the filtering region. Some crustacea use fine hairs to sieve off food material, often from water currents created by the swimming movements. The most startling of filter feeders is the whalebone whale. As the whale swims forward a stream of water flows in at the front of the mouth and out at the sides via sheets of whalebone which filter off the organisms on which the animal feeds. Though macrophagy seems to favour the attainment of larger size there are exceptions! Another type of particulate feeding is seen in those animals which eat deposits of detritus as do many worms. Finally some animals take in only soluble food materials. These fluid feeders include internal parasites like the tapeworm which absorb substances over the surface of the body, and insects such as the aphid with sucking mouth parts.

(b) Reception and Storage.

The food now passes into the alimentary canal which may be fairly simple, straight tube but more usually becomes long and coiled. The gut tube may be divided into several functional components though the divisions must not be regarded as absolute. The first section is usually involved in the selection, by taste, smell and texture, and the reception of food. A lubricating mucus, together with some digestive enzymes, may be added at this stage from glands such as salivary glands. A large crop for food storage occurs in animals as diverse as insects and birds but in mammals this region remains as a simple tube called the oesophagus.

(c) Mixing, Grinding and Early Digestion.

Waves of contraction in the muscles of the gut move the food onwards. This peristaltic action delivers the food to a region known variously in different animals as the stomach, gizzard or gastric mill. Here the further disintegration and mixing with enzymes is accomplished in many forms simply by contraction of the muscle of the stomach wall. Stones may assist the action in the gizzard of birds for example, and more bizarre modifications are seen in some crustaceans and molluscs. In the former there is a complicated gastric mill with grinding surfaces, teeth and a filter, and in the latter a long rod, called the crystalline style, is rotated by ciliary action against a hard pad on the opposite wall of the stomach. In the ruminating mammals such as sheep and cattle the stomach is divided into four chambers. The function of the first two of these is to mix food with a bacterial culture which exists in this region and to regurgitate the cud for further grinding. The bacteria break down plant cell walls and so benefit the host which cannot deal unaided with the main component known as cellulose. The final two chambers of the ruminant stomach are more typical in function.

A variety of digestive enzymes are released into the stomach region. Carbohydrates, fats and proteins are all broken down to some extent. The main enzyme in the stomach of vertebrate animals is a proteinase which works under acid conditions.

(d) Final Digestion and Absorption.

The finely divided food now passes on to the intestine where digestion continues, using enzymes liberated in the preceding region, or under the action of new enzymes released from intestinal glands. In the vertebrates the pancreas secretes a number of enzymes acting on all types of food material, one of the most important being the protein-breaking trypsin. The pancreatic secretion is liberated into the anterior end of the intestine known as the duodenum and operates in an alkaline medium.

Soluble products of the process of digestion are absorbed through the wall of the intestine into the blood stream. Blood vessels carry the food material to the liver where it is put to use in the animal's metabolism or stored as liver glycogen. The surface for absorption is increased by tremendous folding of the intestine interior, seen as fingerlike villi in higher vertebrates or as the so called spiral valve in some fish.

(e) Processing of Waste Material.

The undigested remains of the food now pass through the most posterior regions of the alimentary canal known simply as the hindgut in many forms or as the colon and rectum in others. A major function of this region, particularly in terrestrial animals, is the removal of water so as to conserve this vital material. In the rectum the faeces are formed and stored before being eliminated from the body.

3. Respiration. Gills, Lungs and Tracheae.

The oxidations which consume oxygen and produce carbon dioxide go on at the cellular level as explained earlier (F20). All living cells respire and remain alive only if supplied with oxygen. In a multicellular body, however, many cells are remote from the oxygen of the environment and the need arises for an efficient respiratory system by which oxygen can be taken up and carbon dioxide released. In addition a circulatory system is necessary to transport the oxygen to and from the respiring cells.

(a) Simple Gas Exchange Systems.

Animals such as protozoa which because of their size have a high surface area to volume ratio do not need special structures for gas exchange. Diffusion over the whole body surface ensures an adequate supply of oxygen. Much larger animals such as earthworms also find it possible to rely on diffusion alone, partly because their consumption of oxygen is fairly low, and partly because their bodies are permeable all over. For various reasons most animals restrict the permeability of the outer layers of the body and under these conditions special respiratory areas have to be developed.

(b) Gas Exchange in Water.

Aquatic animals, except those such as whales breathing at the surface, have to obtain their oxygen from the supplies which are dissolved in the water. This presents several problems because water is a dense medium, there is not a lot of oxygen in solution, and its diffusion rate is low. For these reasons there is a surprising functional uniformity in gill systems and they are very different from lungs. Gills are fine, finger-like processes with a good blood supply which are held out in a water stream. The water current is brought very close to the gill filaments so that the length of diffusion pathway for oxygen is minimal. There is a "counter current" flow of water and blood so that the water containing most oxygen comes into contact with the blood just leaving the gill. This ensures that most of the oxygen can be transferred from water to blood through the thin gill cells. The efficiency of "counter current" systems is well known to the engineer but they were invented by aquatic animals long before they were by man. These features can be seen in the gills of molluscs, crustacea and fish. The pumping devices which maintain the water currents also operate economically. Flow is maintained in crustacea by appendages modified to form beating paddles, in many molluscs by ciliary movement, and in fish by the operation of a double pump in mouth and opercular cavities. In almost all cases there is a continuous current over the gills, the water coming in one way and going out another. Thus the animal avoids reversing the flow with the consequent waste of energy in accelerating and decelerating a large mass of water. Fish, for example, take water in at the mouth and force it out through the gill slits (sharks) or operculum (teleosts).

(c) Gas Exchange in Air.

Air breathing animals do not encounter these problems since the medium is less dense, contains a great deal (20%) of oxygen and diffusion rates are high. Lungs are therefore in the form of sacs whose walls are well supplied with blood. The area of the walls may be increased by folding so that the lung becomes spongy and full of minute air spaces called alveoli where the gas exchanges goes on. Only the main airways receive fresh air as the lung expands; oxygen is renewed in the alveoli by diffusion. Ventilation of the lung is accomplished by a tidal flow of air in and out of the same tubular opening known as the trachea. The actual ventilating mechanism varies in different animals. In the amphibia for example air is forced into the lungs when the floor of the mouth is raised with the mouth and nostrils shut. The lungs are emptied by elastic recoil and by lowering the floor of the mouth. Higher vertebrates use a costal pump which changes the volume of chest and lungs by movements of the ribs. This change in volume is further assisted in mammals by the diaphragm, a sheet of muscle which lies beneath the lungs and separates thorax and abdomen. In many animals sound producing organs are associated with the lungs and trachea. The larynx is a vocal organ in frogs, some lizards, and most notably mammals. In birds voice production takes place in the syrinx situated further down at the base of the trachea.

A completely different gas exchanging system is seen in insects. Branching tubes, known as tracheae, run throughout the body and carry oxygen directly to the cells without the intervention of a blood system. The tracheae communicate with the outside world via a series of holes called spiracles. Although the main tubes may be actively ventilated, diffusion in the system accounts for a large part of the movement of oxygen between the outside world and cells.

4. Circulation.

In simple, small animals there is no blood system and dissolved oxygen, nutrients and other materials move about the body solely by diffusion, assisted to a certain extent by streaming movements of protoplasm within the cells. In larger animals a transport system is necessary to convey materials about the body and in many, but not all, it is in the form of a blood system. Blood systems are of two types, closed and open.

(a) Open Systems.

In an open circulatory system blood is pumped from the heart into a few major arteries but these very quickly give way to large tissue spaces or sinuses so that the tissues and organs of the body are directly bathed in blood. Blood flows slowly from the sinuses back to the heart. Both molluscs and arthropods possess an open system. The heart in most arthropods is a long, thin tube in the dorsal part of the body, pumping blood towards the head. Auxiliary muscles may be attached to the heart to pull it out and refill it after the pumping cycle. Mollusc hearts on the other hand are of the chambered type, with thin walled auricles receiving blood from the gills and pumping it to a more muscular ventricle. The ventricle in turn contracts to pump blood to the body. In squids and octopods two auxiliary hearts are seen, receiving blood at low pressure from the body and pumping it through the gills and thence to the main heart.

(b) Closed Systems.

In a closed system blood is pumped round the body in a branching network of arteries, and comes into contact with tissues and cells via very thin walled vessels called capillaries. Substances diffuse into and out of the blood through capillary walls. From capillaries, blood enters the veins and so returns to the heart. Blood flow in the tubes of a closed system is much more brisk and blood pressures tend to be higher than in an open system. In annelids the closed system is fairly simple with a vessel above the gut in which blood moves forward connecting to one below in which blood moves backwards. The blood is pumped by peristaltic contraction of the vessels and this system must be regarded as the precursor of a localised pump. Simple hearts are in fact seen in some annelids.

In vertebrates a well defined heart is always present, situated ventrally at the level of the fore-limbs. In fish there is a single auricle and ventricle and the latter pumps blood directly to the gills. From the gills the blood is collected into a dorsal aorta which then branches to serve the rest of the body. Associated with the development of lungs and loss of gills in the tetrapods, we see a progressive modification of this simple pattern. The most posterior gill vessel is taken over as the lung or pulmonary artery and slowly a completely separate circuit evolves. This involves the division of the single heart into right and left sides, the former pumping blood to the lungs and the latter to the body. In the birds and mammals where the division is complete the system can be seen to be functionally satisfactory. Blood flows along the following route: left auricle to left ventricle, to body, to right auricle, to right ventricle, to lungs, to left auricle, and so on. Thus blood charged with oxygen in the lungs returns to the heart before being pumped to the body. In the lower tetrapods, division of the heart is incomplete and considerable interest centres on the function of these apparently imperfect systems. Amphibian hearts have two auricles but only a single ventricle. In spite of this, evidence is accumulating to show that blood from the lungs and body is not mixed as it passes through the ventricle. A further complication in amphibia is due to the moist skin also being used for gas exchange. Some oxygen is thus contained in blood returning from the body. Reptiles show a further advance in that the ventricle is almost completely divided into two. The system appears still to be functionally inadequate because one of the major arteries to the body leaves from the deoxygenated side along with lung vessels.

(c) Function of the Blood.

Most of the materials transported by the blood such as nutrients, waste materials and hormones are carried in solution in the plasma. The respiratory gases, oxygen and carbon dioxide, are present in greater quantity than would be possible if they were in simple solution. Carbon dioxide is carried in the form of bicarbonate and oxygen combines with blood pigment. The best known blood pigment is haemoglobin which is found in a variety of animals and gives the red colour to blood. When oxygen is present in high concentration, as it is in the lungs, combination occurs to give oxyhaemoglobin. If the concentration of oxygen is low, as it is in the tissues, dissociation occurs and oxygen is given off leaving reduced haemoglobin. Carbon monoxide will combine more readily than oxygen with haemoglobin so that in carbon monoxide poisoning the blood cannot transport oxygen. The haemoglobin of vertebrates is contained in high concentration in red blood corpuscles. The amount of haemoglobin and, hence, oxygen carried is greater than if the pigment is not in corpuscles. In mammals the oxygen carrying capacity of blood is thirty times that of a similar quantity of water. Other blood pigments are the blue haemocyanin found in crustacea and molluscs, and the violet haemerythrin found in some worms. Also present in the blood are various types of white corpuscle which are part of the defence mechanism of the body and ingest invading bacteria. Special blood proteins such as fibrinogen, causing clot formation, and antibodies effective against foreign substances occur in the plasma.

5. Excretion, Ionic Regulation and Kidney Tubules.

As the chemical reactions included under the term metabolism proceed, so numerous waste products accumulate. The most important of these are compounds containing nitrogen, such as ammonia, urea and uric acid, arising from the use of protein as an energy source. In terrestrial animals they are removed from the blood by the kidney. The basic unit of a kidney is the tubule; in worms these tubules are not concentrated into a solid kidney but occur, a pair in every segment, right down the body. The kidney tubule begins with an end sac, corpuscle or funnel which is closely associated with the body cavity or the blood system. Fluid is filtered from the body cavity or blood into the corpuscle whence it passes to the tubule proper. During passage down the tubule, useful materials are reabsorbed through the tubule cells into the blood whereas unwanted materials remain and pass to the outside world.

Although it is usual to think of kidney function being primarily one of nitrogenous excretion, it is quite common to find that in aquatic animals the kidneys are hardly used for this purpose. In these animals the tubules are primarily concerned in regulating the salt and water levels in the body, nitrogenous wastes being eliminated by diffusion through any permeable surface. In fresh water for example all animals have osmotic problems since the body fluids have a much greater osmotic pressure than the environment. Water tends to enter the body and salts tend to leave. Fresh water animals produce large quantities of very dilute urine, filtering off a lot of blood plasma into the tubules but reabsorbing all wanted materials including the invaluable salts. Fresh water crustacea, molluscs and fish all possess tubules of different morphology which show very similar functional properties.

Different environmental conditions impose different demands on the osmotic and ionic regulating machinery. In very dry conditions, such as in deserts, it is obviously of advantage to reabsorb as much water from the tubule as possible. All animals do this but it is interesting that only birds and mammals have discovered the secret of so concentrating the urine that its salt concentration is higher than that in the blood. This is done by means of a hairpin-like loop in the tubule called the Loop of Henle, another example of a counter current device.

6. Co-ordinating Systems.

Overall co-ordination of the animal's body, so that it functions as a whole and reacts appropriately to environmental changes, is largely the province of two systems, one chemical or hormonal, the other nervous. In one respect these are systems for homeostasis, that is for preserving the *status quo*, in spite of considerable environmental fluctuation. Paradoxically they can also initiate change as, for example, one can see in the daily repertoire of complicated behaviour patterns produced by almost any animal.

(a) Nervous Systems.

(i) *Sensory Information.*

Before appropriate reactions can be produced to any stimulus it is necessary to measure its intensity, position, duration and, most important, character. This is done by sense organs which are usually specialised to receive stimuli of a single modality or character. Thus photoreceptors detect light, mechanoreceptors detect mechanical disturbance and chemoreceptors detect specific chemicals. In all cases the sense organs produce a message about the stimulus in the form of nerve impulses (see **F30**–Cell Membrane) which travel up the nerve from the sense organ to the rest of the nervous system. Change of stimulus intensity is usually signalled as a change in frequency of nerve impulses. The position of the sense organ which is active indicates the position of the stimulus within or without the body. The duration of the repeated discharge of nerve impulses indicates the duration of the stimulus.

(ii) *Simple Networks.*

The simplest type of nervous system is the network of interconnected nerve cells (neurones) found in the coelenterates. Branching processes of the nerve cells communicate with neighbouring processes at special regions called synapses (**F30**). Quite complicated behaviour is possible even with this relatively simple system. If a sea anemone is prodded violently it will close up equally violently, showing that activity has spread throughout the network. If it is tickled gently it will respond with local contractions around the site of stimulation. The movements of feeding and locomotion are very delicately performed at appropriate times.

(iii) *Central Nervous Systems.*

In the majority of animals all the nerve cells tend to become collected into a solid mass of tissue referred to as a central nervous system (C.N.S.). Within the mass the nerve cells are interconnected via synapses in the same way as in a nerve net. The connexions with sense organs and muscles are made via long processes called axons. Numbers of axons are usually bound together with connective tissue to form a nerve trunk. In annelids and arthropods the C.N.S. is seen as a ventral cord lying beneath the gut with a swelling or ganglion in each segment of the body. In molluscs, the ganglia are usually more closely grouped around the oesophagus, with the possible provision of a pair of ganglia further back in the viscera. Vertebrates possess a dorsal nerve cord which is uniform in diameter and not ganglionated, though nerves emerge from it in a segmental fashion. The segmental nerves arise in two separate bundles or roots. The dorsal root is made up entirely of sensory nerves conveying information to the C.N.S. The ventral root consists of motor nerves which convey nerve impulses to the muscles of limbs and alimentary canal together with other effector organs such as glands.

(iv) *Reflexes.*

A reflex, in which stimulation of a sense organ or sensory nerve results in the almost immediate contraction of a muscle, is the simplest type of C.N.S. activity. Reflexes have been studied in all animals but the best known ones can be seen in frogs, cats, dogs, and sometimes humans. The very simplest is the stretch reflex, in which a stretched muscle is made to contract by activity coming into the C.N.S. from stretch receptors in the muscle. The activity is relayed directly to the motor neurones of the muscle concerned, making them active and thus causing the muscle to contract. This reflex is monosynaptic, *i.e.* there is only the single synaptic connexion between sensory nerve and motor neurone. The knee jerk in humans is a stretch reflex, the stretch being caused by hitting the muscle tendon as it passes over the knee. Much of the recent work on reflexes has been done on this simple system, notably by Eccles. The flexor reflex, which is seen as the sudden withdrawal of a limb from any painful stimulus, is more complicated. Although the stimuli may vary, the withdrawal response is always accomplished by contraction of flexor muscles which bring the limb in towards the body. The reflex is polysynaptic, *i.e.* several intermediate neurones connect the sensory nerves through to the motor neurones. More complicated still is the scratch reflex in which an animal is made to scratch its flank in response to an irritation or tickling in that region. This reflex demonstrates some of the more involved properties of the C.N.S. For example a dog will continue to scratch for a time after the tickling has stopped, so that the C.N.S. must continue to be active in the absence of sensory stimulation. This has been called after-discharge.

(v) *The Brain.*

The C.N.S. functions in a more complicated way than is suggested by study of the reflexes and most of these higher activities are co-ordinated by the brain. A greater condensation of neurones is seen at the front end of the C.N.S. of all animals because of the larger numbers of sense organs in that region. Brains, which become the dominant part of the C.N.S., can be seen in arthropods, molluscs and vertebrates. The close association with sense organs is illustrated by the vertebrate brain which is divided into three regions: (*a*) forebrain (nose), (*b*) midbrain (eye) and (*c*) hindbrain (ear and taste). However, the brain is much more than a relay station for these stimulus modalities and it receives information from other parts of the body via the spinal cord. All this information is correlated and activity patterns initiated and transmitted to appropriate regions. In lower vertebrates, the roof of the midbrain (the optic tectum) is the important correlation centre and its effectiveness has been well established in studies on instinct and learning in fish. Another region of the brain of importance in all vertebrates is a dorsal upgrowth of the hindbrain called the cerebellum. This is a motor co-ordinating centre which ensures that all activities are performed in a smooth and well balanced way by the muscles and limbs of the body. In reptiles, the forebrain begins to take over the correlation role and in mammals this development reaches its peak in the cerebral cortex. In man the cortex overshadows the rest of the brain and contains some 1,000,000,000 neurones. It is easy to see the magnitude of the problem of understanding a system of this complexity. The bee's brain with far, far fewer cells can initiate complicated behaviour such as the hive dances. The possibilities offered by the human cortex seem vastly greater, though they are often realised in ways which give cause for concern. At the moment it would be quite impossible to build a computer with the properties of the human brain. To do this in the future would depend on major advances in computer technology and even greater advances in the knowledge of central nervous systems.

(b) Hormonal Regulation.

Many aspects of an animal's metabolism are regulated, not by the nervous system, but by specific chemical signals known as hormones which are circulated in the blood stream. Growth, carbohydrate metabolism, salt balance, activity of ovaries and testes and their associated structures, and colour change are all regulated in some way by hormones. The substances are secreted by endocrine glands or ductless glands as they are often called. The important endocrine glands in vertebrates are the thyroid, parathyroid, adrenal, pancreas, the sex glands, and the pituitary.

In the past the endocrine and nervous systems were regarded as exerting an independent control in slightly different functional areas of the body. It is clear now that the integration of the two systems is much greater than was formerly envisaged and in vertebrates is accomplished through the pituitary gland. Secretions of this gland regulate almost all other endocrine glands and the secretions of the pituitary are either produced in the C.N.S. with which it is directly connected or are controlled by C.N.S. secretions. An astonishing, parallel development of other neurosecretory systems, such as those of the pituitary, has been found in a variety of animals and in all types the neurosecretory organ complex is the dominant endocrine gland of the body. In crustacea the so called X organ complex found within the eyestalk, and in insects neurosecretory cells connecting to the corpora cardiaca glands, occupy the functional position of the vertebrate pituitary. They all regulate growth, metabolism and reproductive physiology, either directly or through the mediation of other endocrine glands.

7. Animal Behaviour.

In discussing the nervous system we have already dealt with simple mechanisms such as the reflex. Very much more complicated are the instinctive and learned patterns of behaviour which are studied by animal psychologists and ethologists such as Lorenz and Tinbergen.

(a) Instinct.

Instinct is inborn behaviour which does not have to be learnt and is usually performed in a stereotyped way. For example a gull will retrieve an egg taken out of its nest by shovelling it back with the underside of its beak. The gull will never replace an egg in its nest in any other way, for example by using a wing or leg, and once it has begun a retrieval it will usually continue the movements back to the nest even though the egg is taken away. An instinctive behaviour pattern is triggered off by a particular stimulus or " releaser " which may be a very small part of the total environment. A male stickleback will attack a very crude model with a red belly but will not attack an exact model without it. The red underside appears to be a much more important stimulus than general shape. A particular instinctive pattern cannot always be elicited and the reaction of an animal very largely depends on when the behaviour was last produced. The longer the time that elapses, the easier it is to trigger off the instinctive pattern until eventually it may appear in the absence of an appropriate set of environmental circumstances.

(b) Learning.

Learning is that behaviour acquired during the organism's lifetime as a result of experience. Evidence of learning has been seen in many animals from worms upwards though, as might be expected, the more complicated types of learning are found only in those animals with elaborate nervous systems. A simple type of learning is seen when an animal, upon repeated exposure to a stimulus, gradually decreases the normal response which is usually one of flight, until eventually the response may disappear completely. This process is called habituation. More complex are the conditioned reflexes, which were first discovered by Pavlov. In these an animal can in some way connect a conditioned stimulus such as a bell, with an unconditioned stimulus such as meat, so that eventually it salivates when the bell is rung. Trial and error learning of the type needed to be successful in running a maze is more complicated still. In this there is a retrospective element because the reward is at the end of the maze comes after all the responses. Many animals can run mazes but the white rat has been extensively used in experiments of this nature and there is a huge literature on this one animal. A final category of learning can be called insight learning; in this an animal shows evidence of resolving a new problem without trial and error. This type of learning involves the perception of relations between different parts of the environment and though there may be examples in arthropods and molluscs the clearest evidence of it is seen in the behaviour of birds and mammals.

8. Reproduction.

A single animal may live for a short or long time, but eventually it dies, and the continuance of the species is dependent upon reproduction. Some protozoa, such as *Amoeba*, reproduce asexually by the simple division of the cell to produce two new individuals. Asexual reproduction also occurs in some coelenterates, such as jelly-fish, in which there is an alternation of sexual and asexual generations. However, the vast majority of animals only reproduce sexually.

This involves the fusion of two cells, the gametes, produced by adult individuals, and each zygote thus formed develops into an individual of the next generation. The gametes are of two kinds, the large, spherical, immobile ova produced by the female gonad or ovary and the much smaller motile sperms produced by the male gonad or testis. The motility of the sperms helps them to reach the passive ovum, which contains food reserves to support the early development of the embryo.

Worms.—The flat worms, particularly parasitic forms, have complicated life cycles, and many are hermaphrodite, *i.e.*, each individual has both male and female organs. Cross-fertilisation usually occurs, the sperms from one worm being introduced into the female duct of another. The round worms are unisexual, and internal fertilisation also occurs. Of the annelids the polychaete worms are unisexual, but the ova and sperms are shed into the sea, where fertilisation takes place. However, *Lumbricus* and the leeches are hermaphrodite, cross-fertilisation takes place and the eggs are laid in cocoons.

Arthropods.—Many crustacea are unisexual, though the sedentary barnacles are hermaphrodite. Internal fertilisation may occur, but in the crabs and crayfish pairing takes place and the sperms are deposited on the tail of the female. When the eggs are shed they become fertilised and remain attached to the abdominal appendages. Most crustacea have motile larval stages into which the eggs first develop. In *Daphnia*, the water-flea, parthenogenesis sometimes occurs, *i.e.*, the eggs develop without being fertilised. The sexes are separate in the arachnida and there are usually no larval stages except in the primitive king-crabs. The insects are also unisexual, and the fertilised eggs are laid after copulation. In some, *e.g.*, dragon-flies, an immature nymph similar to the adult is formed, but in flies, beetles, moths, and many others the egg hatches into a larval form. This then develops into a pupa, from which the final adult or imago is produced. In the social ant's nest the workers are sterile females with large heads, reduced eyes, and no wings. The males and queens are winged, and insemination of the latter occurs during the " nuptial " flight.

Molluscs and Echinoderms.—Most lamellibranchs are unisexual, although some species of scallops and oysters are hermaphrodite. There are motile larval forms, and in the swan mussel, *Anodonta*, the larvae develop in the mantle cavity of the parent and when liberated become attached to the gills or fins of fish, where they remain parasitic for some time. Some gasteropods are unisexual, but the slugs and snails are hermaphrodite. In the latter cross-fertilisation occurs, the two approaching snails being stimulated to copulate by firing small sharp darts of calcium carbonate into each other. The echinoderms are unisexual, and fertilisation takes place in the sea. The egg first develops into a ciliated larval form.

Vertebrates.—The sexes are always separate in the vertebrates. In some cartilaginous fish, *e.g.*, dogfish, internal fertilisation occurs and the eggs are laid in protective sacs. In contrast, the bony fish shed ova and sperms into the water, where fertilisation takes place. Although pairing may take place in the amphibia, fertilisation occurs in water, and there is usually an aquatic larval stage. The reptiles, birds, and mammals are independent of water for fertilisation, as copulation takes place and the sperms from the male are introduced directly into the female. Most reptiles and all birds lay eggs with hard shells. Development of the embryo in marsupial mammals begins in the female uterus, but is continued in a ventral pouch which surrounds the teat of the mammary gland. In the two living species of monotreme mammals the eggs are incubated in a similar pouch. Finally, in the eutherian mammals the embryo develops in the female uterus and is born at an advanced stage.

Diversity of Sexual Reproduction.— This brief survey will give some idea of the diversity of sexual reproduction in animals. External fertilisation is very much a matter of chance, and large numbers of gametes are produced which offset the great losses of gametes and embryos that this method involves. Internal fertilisation is more certain, and is also independent of external water—an important factor in land animals. In vertebrates particularly there is increase in the care of the young by the parents, involving the development of characters of behaviour as well as those of structure. Some fish lay their eggs in holes or nests which are protected by the male. Similarly, a few frogs build nests, while others carry the eggs about. The eggs of birds require a constant high temperature for their development, and they are usually incubated by the parents. After hatching the young are fed and guarded by the parents until they can leave the nest and fend for themselves. In the eutherian mammals the embryos are attached to the uterus wall by the placenta, *via* which food materials pass from the mother. The period of gestation is long, and after birth the young are supplied with milk from the mother until they are weaned and can feed themselves. Another feature in mammals is the period of " childhood " during which they play and learn and are protected and fed by their parents. The internal fertilisation, internal development, and care and protection of the young after birth which is so conspicuous in the higher vertebrates results in the reduction of losses during the vulnerable embryonic and young stages, and in consequence relatively few progeny are produced by a pair of individuals.

THE PLANT KINGDOM.

There are various ways in which the main classes of the plant kingdom can be grouped, but a simple, up-to-date arrangement is given in the chart. Vascular plants are often known as the *Tracheophyta* because they all possess woody conducting elements. These are absent in non-vascular plants, and the bacteria, fungi, and algæ are often called *Thallophyta*, i.e., they have a relatively simple plant body or thallus. Many of the bryophytes also possess a thallus, but in some there is a stem bearing leaves, although a true vascular system is absent. Many thallophytes are aquatic. whereas the tracheophytes are mostly land plants in which the development of woody tissues can be related to the attainment of the land habit as the plant kingdom evolved. However, the chart should not be taken as indicating the evolutionary relationships of the various groups. It is more a convenient arrangement which reflects the relative complexity of the plant body.

1. Bacteria.—This is a vast group of minute organisms of very simple structure. They are spherical or rod shaped and may exist as separate cells, some species being motile, or as long chains or irregular masses. Their minute size makes the elucidation of their structure very difficult. There is a wall of complex composition, and cytoplasm which contains glycogen and fat. Electron-microscope studies have revealed the presence of structures which appear to consist of nuclear material. Multiplication is by simple division, which may take place very rapidly. For example, *Bacillus subtilis* can divide every 20 minutes, so that in 8 hours a single cell may give rise to 16 millions. Recent research indicates that a sexual process may also occur. Bacteria can survive unfavourable conditions by producing a

resistant spore within the cell. They do not possess chlorophyll, though a few are pigmented. Most obtain their food already formed, and are thus either saprophytes or parasites. The saprophytic bacteria occupy a vital position in the living world. They are responsible for most of the decay of dead organic matter, and it has been truly said that without them the surface of the earth would soon become completely covered with the dead bodies of animals and plants. Bacteria also play a vital part in the circulation of nitrogen in nature. By breaking down organic material, ammonia is released and ammonium carbonate is formed in the soil. This is oxidised by other bacteria to form nitrates, which can be absorbed by plants again. Yet other bacteria can "fix" atmospheric nitrogen, and one species, *Rhizobium leguminosum*, occurs in the root nodules of plants such as clover and lupins. These plants are often grown on poor soils and ploughed in, thus improving the fertility of the soil. The parasitic bacteria are also of great importance, as they are responsible for many diseases of plants, animals, and man. (*See* **P7(1).**)

2. Fungi.—This is a large group of plants, none of which contain chlorophyll. Hence, like the bacteria, they are either parasites on other living plants and animals or saprophytes which live on dead organic matter. Some are unicellular aquatic plants, but many have a body called a mycelium composed of many branched threads or hyphæ. In the higher fungi (*e.g.*, toadstools, bracket fungi, and puff-balls) complex reproductive structures are formed. All fungi produce spores. In the aquatic species these may be motile, but the majority form minute, airborne spores. The spore output is often very great, and a single mushroom may produce 1,800 million spores. Some fungi are serious diseases of crop plants, such as potato blight and wheat rust.

3. Algæ.—These are essentially aquatic plants which contain chlorophyll. They range from microscopic forms to the large seaweeds. The green algæ (*Chlorophyceæ*) live mostly in fresh water and may be unicellular, motile or non-motile, or filamentous, though a few found in tropical seas are more complex. The brown algæ (*Phæophyceæ*) are mostly seaweeds which possess a brown pigment, fucoxanthin, which masks the green chlorophyll. They include the bladder-wracks (*Fucus*) and kelps (*Laminaria*) of our coasts and the seaweeds which form dense floating masses over hundreds of square miles of the Sargasso Sea. Other groups are the red algæ (*Rhodophyceæ*), mostly seaweeds of delicate form, the unicellular marine diatoms (*Bacillariophyceæ*), and the blue-green algæ (*Cyanophyceæ*). All algæ possess unicellular reproductive organs. Various types of life cycle occur, the most complex being found in the red algæ.

4. Bryophyta.—These are the liverworts (*Hepaticæ*) and the mosses (*Musci*). They are all small plants characterised by a sharply defined life-cycle. This consists of an alternation of generations, the " plant " being a gametophyte bearing sex organs. The latter are multicellular, the female archegonium containing a single stationary ovum and the male antheridium producing many motile sperms. The latter are released and swim in water to the archegonium, where fertilisation takes place. After this a sporophyte is formed

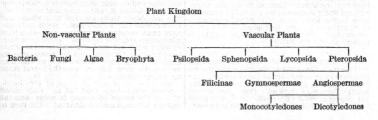

which is always dependent on the gametophyte and never becomes free living. The sporophyte usually consists of an absorbing foot buried in the tissue of the gametophyte and a stalk or seta bearing at the top a single sporangium. In many mosses this is a complex structure with hygroscopic teeth which move apart only when dry, thus releasing the minute spores only when conditions are suitable for their dissemination in the air. The bryophytes are of little economic importance, and may be looked upon as an evolutionary sideline. However, they occupy suitable " niches " in many plant communities, and species of the bog-moss *Sphagnum* cover large areas where rainfall is high.

5. Psilopsida.—This is a small group of primitive, vascular, spore-bearing plants. Its only living representatives are two rare genera of the Southern Hemisphere. However, a number of fossil forms are known from the Devonian period. The best known are those found in the chert at Rhynie in Scotland. The plants are excellently preserved, and their internal structure can be easily seen. They were probably marsh plants with prostrate and erect leafless stems, although *Asteroxylon* had simple leaves.

6. Sphenopsida.—The only living members of this group are about twenty-five species of horsetails (*Equisetum*). In the Carboniferous period many tree forms existed (*e.g., Calamites*), the remains of which are very common in coal deposits.

7. Lycopsida.—In the Carboniferous period the tree clubmosses were also prominent members of the forests (*e.g., Lepidodendron*). They often reached 100 ft. in height, were branched or unbranched, and had large simple leaves. They also had extensive root systems. The only living members belong to a few genera of small herbaceous clubmosses, such as *Lycopodium* and *Selaginella*. Like the true mosses, they have an alternation of generations, but the elaborate plant with stem, leaves, and roots is the sporophyte, and the gametophyte is very small. In *Lycopodium* only one kind of spore is produced, and the resultant gametophyte is bisexual. *Selaginella* produces numerous small microspores which give rise to the very reduced male gametophytes and motile sperms and the few large megaspores which produce the female gametophytes. The latter are formed within the megaspore wall, which splits to allow the sperms to reach the small archegonia.

8. Filicinæ.—These are the true ferns, which in some classifications are put with the horsetails and clubmosses in the Pteridophyta or vascular cryptogams (*i.e.,* vascular plants without seeds). The ferns have a long fossil history, and remains very similar to the living Royal ferns (*Osmunda*) are known from the Carboniferous. The ferns are widespread and particularly abundant in tropical forests. The majority are herbaceous perennial plants, but a few are aquatic, and there are some tree ferns, which may reach 20 ft. in height. Most ferns possess a stem bearing roots and large leaves or fronds. The plant is the sporophyte and produces numerous spores in sporangia borne on the fronds. Each spore gives rise to a minute green free-living gametophyte known as the prothallus, which bears the archegonia and antheridia. After fertilisation a young sporophyte develops, which at first draws nourishment from the prothallus. Thus, as in the *Bryophyta*, external water is essential for the motile sperms to swim in, and there is a clearly defined alternation of generations, but the sporophyte is a complex independent plant, and the gametophyte is reduced though free-living.

9. Gymnospermæ.—These were the dominant land plants in the Mesozoic era, although fossil remains are found as far back as the Devonian. The living members still form large forests in the North Temperate regions. They are mostly tall evergreen trees with roots, stems, and small leaves. The conifers include the pines (*Pinus*),

larches (*Larix*), and yews (*Taxus*). The cycads are a relic group of tropical plants with thick, unbranched trunks and large fern-like leaves. The maiden-hair tree of Japan (*Ginkgo biloba*) has also had a long geological history. Another interesting Gymnosperm is *Metasequoia*, a genus well known to palæobotanists. In 1948 a few living specimens were found in a remote area of China. Seeds were collected and plants are now being grown in botanical gardens all over the world. The Gymnosperms are characterised by the production of " naked " seeds, which are usually borne on cones. The male pollen grains, which are equivalent to the microspores of *Selaginella*, are carried by wind to the ovule of the female cone. The pollen germinates and the pollen tube carries the male gametes to the reduced archegonia borne on the female prothallus, which, unlike those of the ferns, is retained within the ovule on the parent plant. After fertilisation an embryo is formed, the prothallus becomes the food store or endosperm, and the outer part of the ovule becomes the seed coat. The cycads and *Ginkgo* retain a primitive feature in that the male gametes are motile and they swim to the archegonia from the pollen tube.

10. Angiospermæ.—The apparent sudden rise of the Angiosperms in the Cretaceous period is still the " abominable mystery " it was to Darwin. Various suggestions have been put forward, but nothing definite is known about the origin of the group. The Angiosperms or flowering plants are now the dominant group over most of the land surface of the earth, and at least 250,000 species are known. Apart from the natural vegetation, the majority of our crop and garden plants are Angiosperms. They occur in every type of habitat and range in form from gigantic trees to minute plants, such as the duck-weeds. Some are climbers, others succulents, and a number have reverted to the aquatic habit. Although most possess chlorophyll, a few are partial (*e.g.,* Mistletoe) or complete parasites (*e.g.,* Dodder).

Flower, Fruit and Seeds.—The diagnostic feature of the group is the production of seeds, which are completely enclosed within the female part of the flower, the ovary. Basically a flower is a short reproductive shoot which bears several whorls of lateral organs. At the base are several, often green, protective sepals forming the calyx, and above this are the often brightly coloured petals of the corolla. Within this are the stamens of the androecium or male part of the flower. Centrally is the female gynoecium of one or more carpels containing the ovules. The parts of the flower may be free, as in the buttercup, or fused together. In many species the petals are fused (sympetalous), the stamens are borne on the corolla (epipetalous), and the carpels are fused to form a compound gynoecium (syncarpous). The stamens possess anthers, which produce pollen grains. These are shed and carried by insects or wind to the receptive stigmas of the carpels. Each produces a tube which grows down the style to the ovary and enters an ovule. The ovule is a complex structure containing an ovum and a primary endosperm nucleus. Two male nuclei are discharged from the pollen tube, one fuses with the ovum and the other fuses with the primary endosperm nucleus. After this " double fertilisation " an embryo is formed which is embedded in the nutritive endosperm and the outer tissues of the ovule form the seed coat or testa. The ovary of the carpel develops into the fruit containing the seeds. Fruits are of various kinds, being either dehiscent and opening when mature to release the seeds or indehiscent, with a succulent or dry wall. The indehiscent fruits are shed as a whole, and often contain only a single seed. Seeds and fruits show great variation in structure, and often have adaptations assisting dispersal. Some have hairs or wings which aid wind dispersal, whereas others have hooks or are sticky and are transported by animals. Some have flotation devices and may be carried a great distance from the parent plant by water. Seeds vary in size from the microscopic seeds of orchids to those of the double coconut, which may weigh 40 lb. Only about 10% of the weight of a seed is water, and the embryo, although alive, is dormant. The bulk o a seed consists of stored food material, commonly fats or starch and proteins, which may be contained in the endosperm surrounding the embryo, although in some species the endosperm is absorbed during seed development and the food is stored in the one or two swollen seed leaves or cotyledons of the embryo.

Classification of Flowering Plants.— John Ray (1627–1705) was the first botanist to recognise the two great divisions of the Angiosperms—the dicotyledons with two seed leaves and the monocotyledons with only one. This primary division of the flowering plants has stood the test of time and is still recognised. Other differences are also found between the two groups. The dicotyledons usually have net-veined leaves and the floral parts are in fours or fives, whereas the monocotyledons usually have leaves with parallel veins and the floral parts are in threes.

ECOLOGY—THE STUDY OF LIVING ORGANISMS IN THEIR ENVIRONMENT.

So far we have examined biological organisation at the level of the cell through to the whole, multicellular organism. The important branch of biology which deals with the relationship between living organisms and their environment must now be considered. Living organisms and the physical environment in which they exist form what is termed an ecosystem. Obviously it would be possible to regard the whole world as a giant ecosystem, though for purposes of study it would be extremely unrewarding and impractical to adopt such an extreme attitude. A pond, a rocky or sandy shore, a forest, and a peat bog are examples of ecosystems on a somewhat smaller scale, possessing different properties and containing populations of animals and plants that are different both in number of individuals and in species represented. The ecologist seeks to understand why a particular species is present in certain numbers in an ecosystem in terms of that species' interaction with all other living organisms (biotic factors) and with the physical (abiotic) factors of the ecosystem.

1. Abiotic Factors.

All living organisms will show ranges of tolerance for abiotic factors such as temperature, humidity, salinity, oxygen levels, amount of light, etc. Clearly, if any factor in the environment moves outside the range of tolerance of a species, it becomes limiting for that particular species which is then excluded from the environment. Within the range of tolerance there will be an optimum value for each abiotic factor at which a species will survive best.

There is not a firm line separating suitable and unsuitable environments, but rather a steady shift from optimum values into conditions in which an organism finds it more and more difficult to survive. The interaction of different abiotic factors in an environment produces a complex situation which will make the environment suitable for one species but will exclude another species having slightly different abiotic optima from the first, even though the conditions are not outside the tolerance ranges of either species. Thus trout and carp show considerable overlap in the ranges of temperature, oxygenation of the water, and speed of water current in which they can survive and it is possible for both species to live in the same pool or tank. In the wild, however, they tend to form part of different ecosystems because trout have a lower temperature optimum, need more oxygen, and are more active than carp. Trout are found in rapidly-flowing, cool, unpolluted chalk streams whereas carp live best in shallow lakes which are somewhat warmer and rather stagnant.

One of the most important abiotic factors in an environment is the nature of the substrate upon or within which an organism moves and settles.

(a) **The Terrestrial Environment.**—Soil is the commonest substrate for terrestrial organisms.

Particle sizes, ranging from the coarsest gravel soils, through sands and silts to the finely textured clays, have extensive effects on the flora and fauna of any area. Coarsely textured soils are obviously penetrated most easily both by roots and by soil animals. Soils of this type also allow the rapid movement of water and soil gases, but they have the serious disadvantage of poor water retention. The level at which water saturation occurs is known as the water table and is an important abiotic factor. The terrestrial environment tends on the whole to dehydrate organisms and there is always a marked dependence on water supplies.

Soil characteristics also vary with depth. A vertical section through any soil is referred to as its profile and has considerable bearing on the ecosystems in which the soil is involved. The layers, or horizons, of a soil profile vary enormously from one soil to another. Below a surface layer of organic debris one can, in general terms, distinguish a layer of soil from which substances have been leached (A horizon), soil containing the leached-out substances from the layer above (B horizon), the weathered parent material (C horizon), and finally the parent rock or some other stratum beneath the soil (D horizon).

Humus, which is formed from animal and plant remains and is located in the lower parts of the A profile, is of great importance in providing food for soil organisms and chemical elements such as nitrogen, phosphorus, and calcium for plant growth. It is also important in maintaining good soil structure and, though inorganic fertilisers can supply chemical elements, they have little or no effect on structure. Soil requires careful cultivation, and structure is easily disturbed by such things as heavy farm machinery. The smearing of soils by spinning tractor wheels as wet land is ploughed, or the winter harvesting of crops such as sugar beet in adverse conditions, eventually leads to the creation of impermeable layers with the disastrous exclusion of oxygen and oxygen-consuming organisms.

(b) **The Aquatic Environments.**—Marine and freshwater environments together cover more than 75 per cent of the earth's surface and, since they can be occupied throughout their entire depth, offer a much greater volume of living space than does the land. There is only a slight difference between the density of water and of living tissues, so that the bodies of aquatic organisms are very largely supported by the environment and do not need strong woody stems or powerfully muscled limbs to hold them up. Water has a high specific heat, which means that large amounts of heat are needed to raise its temperature. The result is that aquatic environments tend to show much smaller fluctuations in temperature than the terrestrial ones. In general, the larger the volume of water the smaller are the fluctuations in temperature, and so the fauna and flora of the oceans will not show wide temperature tolerance, whereas that of small pools will, but in neither case will the tolerance be so great as that shown by many terrestrial forms. Oxygen and carbon dioxide concentrations are very different in water and in air and this has led in animals to the development of gill systems for gas exchange rather than the lungs, or lung-type structures, of terrestrial forms. Gas concentrations are also variable from one aquatic environment to another, making them suitable for the support of different fauna and flora.

An important difference between the sea and freshwater is seen when their salt concentrations are determined. This is usually done experimentally by measuring the temperature at which the medium freezes, because a well-established relationship exists between the salt concentration in a solution and the extent to which the freezing point is lowered below that of the solvent (in this case distilled water) alone. Thus, whereas freshwater freezes at 0 °C or just below whereas sea water, with its high salt content, freezes at −1·9 °C, and a mixture of half fresh and half sea water freezes at −0·95 °C. Organisms living in fresh or in sea water face quite dissimilar problems in osmotic and ionic regulation. Life evolved originally in the sea and the salt concentration in the blood of marine molluscs, crustaceans, and echinoderms, for example, produces precisely the same freezing point depression as does sea water itself. Marine organisms have, on several occasions in the course of their evolution, moved into freshwater. Representatives of the worms, crustaceans, molluscs, and vertebrates have all independently invaded this very dilute habitat. What is more, all these animals show approximately the same types of modification to cope with the change. Their outer layers, in the main, become impermeable and the salt concentration of their blood is reduced considerably (to a freezing point of $-1 \cdot 0$ °C in fish and to a spectacularly low level in the freshwater mussel, depressing the freezing point to a mere $-0 \cdot 2$ °C). The kidneys become enlarged and produce a large volume of dilute urine. By these means freshwater animals can cut down loss of their salts to the dilute medium and can also remove the large volume of water that enters their bodies by osmosis. It is interesting that all terrestrial vertebrates, including the mammals, have retained a salt concentration in their blood of about half the seawater level and this is partly attributable to their freshwater ancestry. The transition between seawater and freshwater was achieved via brackish water estuaries and the organisms which live under brackish water conditions today are of great interest in showing how tolerance of substantial fluctuations in salinity can be achieved. The ultimate development of salinity tolerance is seen in such animals as the salmon and eel which move from fresh to salt water and back again during their life cycle.

2. Biotic Factors.

(a) **Associations between Organisms.**—No organism can be considered to be independent of any other organism in an ecosystem but in some cases close associations of various types can be developed between different species or different members of the same species.

Commensalism is an association which benefits one member but has little effect on the other. Small organisms can live within the protective covering offered by a larger individual, as, for example, commensal crabs living within the shell of some species of oyster.

Symbiosis is a somewhat closer association in which both members benefit, as do certain species of green algae and the coelenterates in whose body tissues they live. The algae are protected and the coelenterates benefit from the food produced by the photosynthetic plant. Some symbiotic organisms are unable to survive outside the association. The lichens which are associations of algae and fungi, are examples of this type of symbiosis, as are some of the food-processing micro-organisms together with the animals in whose intestinal tracts they live.

Social animals. In some cases animals of the same species form social groups in which co-operative effort and division of labour makes them more successful in exploiting a particular environment. Social development is most obvious among certain insects such as termites, ants, wasps, and bees, and among the vertebrates. Social organisation in these groups may lead to the development of different behaviour patterns and ultimately, as in ants and bees, for example, to the evolution of a variety of structural modifications so that different castes are recognisable.

Parasitism. Not all associations are of mutual benefit and when one organism becomes sufficiently specialised so that it can live successfully on materials extracted from another, the latter is always adversely affected. Parasites, by causing disease in, and sometimes the death of, the host, can influence population growth and size. Important groups are bacteria, protozoa, fungi, nematodes (roundworms), and platyhelminths (tapeworms and liver flukes). Viruses are also important disease-producing agents which are incapable of an independent existence outside the cells of the host and utilise the host cell's metabolic pathways directly to synthesise new virus material.

Many parasites (and other pests which may disturb the comfort and health of man) can now be controlled to some extent, and, for a variety of reasons, such control procedures have extensive effects on the ecosystems involved. The regulation of some bacterial parasites by means of antibiotics, and control of the insect vectors of organisms such as the malaria parasite by means of insecticides, have both been important factors in the increase in human population. Though the beneficial effects of pest control of all types are clear, the process is not without its difficulties and dangers. Indiscriminate use of many chemical agents has led to the development of resistant strains. In any group of organisms, some will naturally be more resistant to a pesticide or antibiotic than others and these will be the survivors of any treatment that is less than totally effective. They will form the breeding stock for subsequent generations and so progressively more and more resistant types will evolve. Thus, there are now many strains of bacteria resistant to penicillin and other antibiotics. Even more alarming is the recent discovery that this resistance can be transferred in an infective way between bacteria of different species. Another complication associated with chemical control is that the agent concerned frequently affects a wide spectrum of organisms, including those that are in no sense injurious to man or his crops. Thus DDT kills bees and other pollinating insects unless its application to a crop is very precisely timed. In addition, the accumulation of quantities of chlorinated hydrocarbons such as DDT in the environment is known to have an injurious effect on organisms other than insects. Because these chemicals are broken down very slowly they now form a serious problem in environmental pollution.

Predation. A less direct association than that between parasite and host is the one which exists between predators and the prey which they capture and kill. However, interactions in both parasitism and predation have features in common, particularly those affecting population numbers. If the abundance of prey increases, the effort and time required for a capture is reduced so that the rate of predation must also go up. Eventually, however, predators do not respond to further increases in prey; because they are satiated, or for some other behavioural reason, a maximum predation rate is reached in a population of a certain size. Increased prey density also tends to result in larger numbers of predators, produced either by aggregation from outside areas or by increased reproduction rate. The density of predators then begins to have its limiting affect on the rate of predation. The total response may lead to stability in numbers but more often periodic oscillations in the number of both predators and prey are seen.

(b) **The Food Factor.**—Plants are the ultimate source of organic food for all animals. The most important food plants are those capable of photosynthesis (F28) in which organic material is synthesised from carbon dioxide and water, using radiant energy from the sun to drive the reaction.

Food Chains. Plants are eaten by herbivores which in turn are eaten by carnivores. It is possible to see many such sequences, called food chains, in all ecosystems. For example, in the open sea, green algae are the important photosynthetic organisms; these are eaten by a small crustacean, *Calanus*, which in turn forms a large part of the diet of the herring. Feeding relationships are usually of much greater complexity than is suggested by a simple food chain. Thus, *Calanus* represents about 20 per cent of the herring's diet but it is also eaten by many other marine animals as well. For example, it forms about 70 per cent of the total diet of larval sand eels. The larval eels are eaten in turn by the herring and may form 40 per cent of its diet. Because an animal's diet is usually quite varied and one species of animal or plant may be part of the food of a wide range of different animals, interactions are set up which are referred to as food webs. The more knowledge there is about a particular food web, the more complex it becomes. However, for general comparative purposes it is possible to disregard the detail of species and to group together all organisms with similar food habits. When this is done a relationship known as pyramid of numbers often appears in which organisms at the base of a food chain (the primary producers) are extremely abundant, while those at the apex (the final consumers) are relatively few in number.

Productivity. The validity of using numbers of individuals in such an analysis is often open to question, especially when ecosystems are to be compared. For example, a comparison between numbers of herring and numbers of whales as final consumers in two pyramidal systems is not very informative. This difficulty is partially overcome by using estimates of the total weight (biomass) of organisms at each level rather than their number. Even this has disadvantages because determinations of biomass give a measure of the amount of material present at any one time (the standing crop) but give no indication of the amount of material being produced or the rate of its production (the productivity). In some parts of the sea, for example, the biomass of small animals forming the zooplankton is greater than that of the plant life or phytoplankton on which it depends for food. This seems to contravene the pyramid concept. However, the rate of production of new material by the phytoplankton is very much greater than by the zooplankton so that, if taken over a year, the total amount of plant material produced would far exceed the total production of animal material. Productivity is a concept of great practical and theoretical importance. It may be determined in terms of the actual organic material produced in an area over a set period of time or, more usefully, in terms of the amounts of energy transferred and stored at each food level, again over a set period of time.

Under natural conditions only 1 to 5 per cent of the light falling on a plant is converted by its photosynthetic system into chemical energy contained in the material of its tissues. Similarly herbivores which consume plants will pass on to their predators only some 10 per cent of the energy contained in the plant material they eat. These low values for photosynthetic efficiency and ecological efficiency respectively are due to the fact that most of the energy appears as heat during the metabolic reactions needed to sustain life and only a small amount is incorporated into new tissue. It is easy to see that the form of a pyramid of numbers can be explained in terms of low ecological efficiency, as can the observation that a food chain rarely has more than five links. The loss of energy at each stage must mean that each succeeding stage becomes smaller and smaller in number and that the number of stages is severely limited.

Human Population and Food. The present very large increase in human population and the predicted rise from 3,300 million in 1968 to 6,000 million in the year 2000 has led to a pressing need for the controlled exploitation of food resources in the world. Consideration of the processes of energy transfer suggests that man should be mainly herbivorous. They also suggest that present agricultural crops, with the possible exception of sugar cane, do not achieve as high a primary productivity as that encountered in some natural ecosystems. Crops rarely achieve complete plant cover of the land throughout the growing season so as to trap the maximum amount of sunlight. It would be necessary to mix crops to do this effectively and there would then be complicated harvesting problems.

If man remains an omnivore, as he almost certainly will, then his domestic food animals will continue to be herbivorous as they are at present, though whether they will be the same herbivores is less easy to predict. Beef cattle raised on grassland convert only 4 per cent of the energy in the plants of their environment into similar chemical energy in their tissues. At the present time

intensive farming practices are being empoyed to improve conversion, usually by harvesting plant material, processing it, and bringing it to the animals which are housed in special buildings. This cuts down on the wastage of plant food because it can be grown under better conditions and less of it is consumed by animals other than the cattle. Careful breeding and the limitation of the period over which livestock is raised to that of maximum growth efficiency have also contributed to conversions of some 35 per cent, achieved in the case of broiler chickens and calves. The moral problems raised by these methods and the circumstances which make them necessary give rise to widespread concern.

Fish are also an important part of man's diet and again an understanding of the ecology of food fish is important in running efficient fisheries. Many populations have gone down so that returns have gone down in spite of intensified fishing effort. The fisheries scientist is concerned to discover the limit at which the maximum number of fish can be taken without depleting the population year by year. Research is also going on into possible methods of enclosing and farming areas of the sea or estuaries.

Population Dynamics.

Factors such as those outlined above interact to determine the size and character of any population of living organism. Study of the numbers of organisms in a population, together with their change and regulation, forms a branch of the subject of considerable practical importance known as population dynamics.

Numbers of animals and plants tend to increase up to the capacity of the environment, at which stage some essential resource will exert a limiting effect. The rate of increase will be determined by the balance between reproduction rate and mortality. As Malthus appreciated, adults of any organism tend to replace themselves by a greater number of progeny and, in the absence of losses by mortality and other factors, there is a vast potential for increase in all populations. If an organism doubles its number in a year, there will be a 1,000-fold increase in 10 years, and a 10 million-fold increase in 20 years. Increase of this type soon leads to shortages and overcrowding so that mortality goes up, the net rate of increase diminishes, and finally an equilibrium is reached with no further increase in number. The change from low to high numbers with the passage of time follows an S-shaped curve, starting slowly becoming faster and faster, and then slowing down to equilibrium.

When a population reaches equilibrium, the numbers are kept at a steady level by factors such as competition for food, refuge, or space. These factors are said to be density-dependent because greater numbers in the population intensify the competition and increase mortality, lower numbers decrease competition and favour survival. Abundance is therefore regulated by density-dependent processes arising from interactions, first, between individuals making up the population, and secondly, between the population under consideration and other populations whose members may be competitors, predators, or food. The level of abundance at which this regulation occurs may vary greatly and will be determined, at least in part, by general environmental factors such as temperature, rainfall, amount of sunlight, the nature of the vegetation, and so on.

Human population is increasing rapidly at the present time, mainly because of the fall in death-rate. Food production is also increasing, but in some areas of the world supply and requirement are so evenly matched that drought or war are inevitably followed by a famine. Though the human population has not yet reached the stage of equilibrium, it is clear that ultimately it must be subject to forces of regulation similar to those that control populations of other organisms. Birth-rate cannot exceed death-rate indefinitely in any living organism. By limiting the size of families it is possible for man to achieve a population equilibrium at levels lower than those at which regulative factors such as famine or aggression must begin to operate. Rational control of birth-rate seems to offer the best chance of averting a global population disaster.

THE GEOLOGICAL RECORD.

The various stages in the history of the earth can be read by the geologists in the strata or layers of rock laid down since the planet began to solidify, and it is in these rocks, too, that the record of life upon earth may be traced.

No Life Rocks.—The earliest rocks in the record are known as the Azoic (no life) rocks, because they show no trace of living things, and these layers are of such thickness that they occupy more than half of the whole record. That is to say, for more than half of the earth's history nothing living existed upon any part of the globe. For millions of years the surface of our planet was nothing but bare rock without soil or sand, swept by hot winds exceeding in violence the wildest tornadoes of today, and drenched by torrential downpours of tropical rain, which, as we have seen elsewhere, gradually tore away the surface to form sandy sediments at the bottom of the seas. In such ancient rocks pushed above the surface by later upheavals we can still trace the marks of primeval oceans as they rippled upon the barren shores or of raindrops which left their imprint perhaps 1,500 million years ago.

Primitive Sea-life.—As we move upwards through the strata, however, traces of life begin to appear and steadily increase as we come to the more recent levels. The earliest signs appear in what is known as the Early Paleozoic Age (or by some writers as the Proterozoic Age), when we find the fossilised remains of small shellfish, sea-weeds, and trilobites—the latter were creatures somewhat like the plant-lice of modern times. All these primitive animals and plants lived in the shallow tidal waters of ancient seas; for as yet life had not invaded either the dry land or the deep oceans. It is, of course, clear that these creatures of Early Paleozoic times were not the first living things: they were merely the first creatures capable of leaving fossilised remains, and without doubt must have had more primitive ancestors—amoebic-like forms, jellyfish, bacteria, and so on whose bodies were too soft to leave any traces in the record of the rocks.

The Age of Fishes.—Towards the end of the Early Paleozoic Era, in what we now know as the Silurian period, there arose a new form of life: the first backboned animals, primitive fishes somewhat similar to the sharks of today; and in the division of the Upper Paleozoic Era known as the Devonian, they had come to multiply so greatly that this is frequently described as the Age of Fishes.

First Land Animals and Plants.—It is about this time, too, that we begin to find traces of animal and plant life upon the dry land. Both animals and plants had acute problems to solve before it became possible for them to live out of water; for both animals and plants had hitherto been supported by the surrounding water and respired by removing oxygen dissolved in the water. In land animals this problem was solved by a long series of adaptations from gills to lungs. Plants were able to invade the land because of the evolution of an impermeable outer cuticle which prevented water loss and also the development of woody tissues which provided support and a water-conducting system for the whole plant body.

Amphibia and Spore-bearing Trees.—The first type of vertebrates (backboned animals) to live upon dry land was the group of amphibia in the Carboniferous Age, which is today represented by the newts, frogs, toads, and salamanders. In all these forms the eggs give rise to a tadpole stage with gills which lives for some time entirely in water. Later the gills give place to a primitive form of lung which enables the animal to live upon land. Even so, amphibia are restricted more or less to swampy or marshy land, and without a damp environment they would dry up and shrivel to death. The most abundant forms of plant life in the Carboniferous period were the tree-like horsetails, clubmosses, and ferns, the fossilised tissues of which are found in the coal measures and are burned as household coal. But these plants also, as in the case of the amphibia, could exist only amongst the swamps and marshes, and life, although it had freed itself from the necessity of existence in the waters of the earth, still had to return to the water in order to reproduce itself. The highlands and the deeper waters of the planet were still empty of living things. Although the Carboniferous period had been a period of warmth and abundance, the Paleozoic Era came to an end with a long cycle of dry and bitterly cold ages. Such long-term climatic changes were due, it is now supposed, to such factors as changes in the earth's orbit, the shifting of its axis of rotation, changes in the shape of the land masses, and so on. Long before the Ice Ages of more recent times, there are records in the rocks of alternating periods of warmth and

THE GEOLOGICAL TIME SCALE

ERAS	PERIODS	AGE (millions of years)	LIFE
CAENOZOIC	Pleistocene	1	Man
	Pliocene		
	Miocene	25	Birds, Mammals and modern plants
	Oligocene		Molluscs
	Eocene	70	
MESOZOIC	Cretaceous	135	Dinosaurs, Cycads; Earliest Birds;
	Jurassic	180	Ammonites and Sea-urchins
	Triassic	225	
PALAEOZOIC	Permian	270	First mammals; Early reptiles
	Carboniferous	350	Amphibians, tree-ferns, first insects
	Devonian	400	Fishes, first land plants
	Silurian	440	Mainly invertebrate animals; no
	Ordovician	500	life on land. Trilobites and
	Cambrian	600	graptolites

PRE-CAMBRIAN (also PROTEROZOIC, ARCHAEOZOIC)　2,000　Life emerges
　　　　　　　　　　　　　　　　　　　　　　　5,000　Age of Earth

cold as far back as the Azoic and Early Paleozoic Eras. This long cold spell at the close of the Paleozoic era came to an end about 220 million years ago, and was succeeded by a long era of widely spread warm conditions—the Mesozoic Era, the so-called Age of Reptiles.

The Mesozoic Era.—The reptiles first appeared in the Permian, but it was during the Mesozoic era that they became the dominant group of animals. The giant reptiles included the stegosaurus, the gigantosaurus, the diplodocus, and many other kinds which were far larger than any land animals living today. Some, for example the diplodocus, were 100 ft. long, although they were vegetarian in habit and were preyed upon by other almost equally huge flesh-eating reptiles. Some species, such as the plesiosaurs and icthyosaurs, became secondarily aquatic, while the pterodactyl possessed wings with which it could glide and perhaps fly short distances. However, they all differed from the amphibia in that they had hard, dry skins, their lungs were more efficient, fertilisation was internal due to the development of copulatory organs, and they laid eggs with hard, protective shells.

It was also during the Mesozoic era that the warm-blooded birds arose. The birds, like the reptiles, lay eggs with hard shells, and they have several internal features found in the reptiles. The fossil bird Archæopteryx, three specimens of which have been found in Germany, lived in the Jurassic period. Although it was obviously a bird, it retained many reptilian features. Earliest mammals are recognised in rocks of the late Palaeozoic but in the Mesozoic considerable evolution of the group took place. The fossil Trituberculata which are also found in the Jurassic, are believed to be related to forms from which both the marsupial and placental mammals arose. Although insects were present as far back as the Carboniferous, it was in the Mesozoic that many of the groups we know today first appeared.

Great changes also took place in the plant cover of the land during this era. The spore-bearing giant horsetails and tree clubmosses declined and were replaced by gymnosperms—trees bearing naked seeds. One large group of these, the cycadeoids, has become extinct, but the conifers and a few of the once abundant cycads still remain. The flowering plants or angiosperms also made their appearance, and towards the end of the Cretaceous their evolution was extremely rapid. In fact, many of the fossil leaves found in rocks of Cretaceous age are indistinguishable from those of some present-day flowering plants.

A New Era.—But, perhaps 150 million years later, all this seemingly everlasting warmth and sunshine, the lush tropical life, the giant reptiles who had ruled the world, were wiped out by a new period of bitter cold which only the hardy species could survive. A new Era known as the Caenozoic was beginning, ushered in by a period of upheaval and volcanic activity, following which the map of the world came to resemble more closely the picture we know today. The cold period may have lasted several million years, and the main species to survive it were those which had come into existence towards the end of the Mesozoic Era, the seed-bearing flowering plants, the birds, and the mammals. The once all-powerful reptiles from this time onwards are represented only by the comparatively few and relatively small reptilian species of today: the snakes, lizards, crocodiles, and alligators. It was at this time, too, that, long after the creation of the mountains of Scotland and Norway (the so-called Caledonian revolution), or even of the Appalachian mountains (the Appalachian revolution), there arose the great masses of the Alps, the Himalayas, the Rocky Mountains, and the Andes. These are the mountain chains of the most recent, the Caenozoic revolution. Initially, as we have seen, the climate of the Caenozoic Era was cold, but the weather grew generally warmer until a new period of abundance was reached, only to be followed at the end of the Pliocene by a period of glacial ages generally known as the First, Second, Third, and Fourth Ice Ages.

THE EVOLUTION OF ORGANISMS.

Introduction.—It is commonly thought that the great 19th cent. naturalist Charles Darwin was the first person to suggest that life had continually evolved. However, the idea that species of living organisms could change over long periods of time was considered by some Greek writers and, much later, by the Frenchmen Buffon and Lamarck at the end of the 18th cent. Further, the work of the 18th cent. geologists such as James Hutton and William Smith provided a basis without which Darwin's contribution would have been impossible. Hutton showed that the earth's surface had undergone prolonged upheavals and volcanic eruptions with consequent changes in sea level. This implied that the earth was much older than had previously been supposed. Smith developed a method of dating the geological strata by means of the fossils found in them and demonstrated that widely different types of animals and plants existed at different periods of the earth's history. As described in the previous section a general picture is presented of the evolution of organisms from the simple to the complex and from the aquatic to the terrestrial environment. These discoveries were in conflict with the Biblical account in the book of Genesis and, although various attempts were made to explain them away or discredit them, it became abundantly clear that through millions of years life has been continually changing, with new species constantly arising and many dying out. Before considering Darwin's major contribution to the theory of evolution it will be appropriate to outline briefly the various lines of evidence which indicate that, in fact, evolution has taken place.

The Evidence for Evolution.—

1. *The Geological Record.*—It has already been pointed out that successively younger rocks contain fossil remains of different and relatively more complex organisms. The spore-bearing plants preceded the gymnosperms and the angiosperms arose much later. Similarly in the vertebrate series the fish appeared before the amphibia which were followed by the reptiles and later by the air breathing, warm-blooded birds and mammals. On a more restricted level the rocks provide even greater support for the occurrence of evolution. For example, the evolution of the horse has been worked out in great detail from the small Eohippus which was about a foot high and had four digits on the forefeet and three on the hind feet to the large one-toed animal living today. However, such complete series are rare and the geological record is very incomplete. There are a number of gaps, particularly between the major groups of organisms. No satisfactory fossil evidence is known of the ancestors of the angiosperms (**F40**) and although some may be discovered it could be that they did not grow in conditions which favoured their preservation as fossils. On the other hand, Archæopteryx provides an indisputable link between the reptiles and the birds.

Another important point should also be made about the age of the geological record. Although we talk about the age of fishes, the age of reptiles and so on it must be emphasised that these are the periods during which particular groups were abundant or even dominant. Each group probably originated many millions of years before it became widespread. Further, some groups, such as the giant reptiles and the seed-ferns, died out completely whereas others, the fishes and true ferns for example, are still common today. However, even in the latter groups there is evidence that they have continued to evolve so that many fishes and ferns that exist today are very different from those of the Devonian and Carboniferous periods (**F44**). On the other hand, the geological record also shows that some species, for example the Maiden-hair tree, have remained unaltered for many millions of years.

2. *Geographical Distribution.*—Nearly all the marsupials or pouched mammals are found in the Australian continent which was cut off from the mainland about 60 million years ago. All the

fossil evidence indicates that at that time the eutherian or placental mammals did not yet exist. The marsupials are the only naturally occurring mammals in Australia (**F33**(2)) but since the isolation of the continent the group has given rise to a large number of species very similar in appearance to those which evolved elsewhere in the world among the eutherian mammals. There are marsupials which look like wolves, dogs, cats and squirrels; yet they have no close biological relationships to these animals. Further, some marsupials such as the kangaroos have evolved which are unlike any other creatures in the rest of the world. Quite clearly the isolation of Australia so long ago has resulted in the evolution of these distinct types. A similar small-scale effect of isolation was studied by Darwin in the Galapagos islands where each has its own distinct flora and fauna which differ also from those of the S. American mainland.

3. *Anatomy.*—The comparative study of the development and mature structure of the mammalian body provides much evidence that all the species have evolved from a single ancestral stock. Although the arm of an ape, the leg of a dog, the flipper of a whale and the wing of a bat appear very different externally they are all built on the same skeletal plan. It would be difficult to explain such similarities unless they had all evolved from a common type. There is also evidence that the early development of an animal recapitulates its biological history to a certain extent. For example, the gill slits found in fish are formed during the early stages in the development of a mammal although later they disappear. Finally, apparently useless vestigial structures sometimes occur which would be inexplicable unless regarded in the light of an evolutionary history. In man a small appendix and vestiges of a third eyelid occur but these are functionless although in other animals such structures are well developed and functional, *e.g.*, the appendix in the rabbit.

4. *Human Selection.*—During his brief history on earth modern man has continually selected and bred animals and plants for his own use. We have only to look at the various breeds of dogs which have been developed from a single wild type to see that under certain circumstances great structural divergence can occur in a species even in a relatively short time.

The Darwinian Theory of Evolution.—Darwin amassed a great deal of information such as that outlined above which convinced him that evolution of life had taken place over millions of years. His was the first real attempt to collect all the evidence scientifically and no other satisfactory alternative explanation of all the facts he presented has been proposed. Perhaps even more important was his attempt to explain *how* evolution had actually occurred. He published his theory after many years of work in his book *The Origin of Species by Means of Natural Selection* in 1859. Some of his ideas have since been modified owing to our increased knowledge of genetics but they are so important that it is worth while recounting the main points of his theory.

1. *The Struggle for Existence.*—It is clear that in nature there is a severe struggle for existence in all animals and plants. Over a period of time the number of individuals of a species in a given community does not vary greatly. This implies that the number of progeny which survive to become mature breeding individuals more or less replaces the number of mature ones that die. Generally speaking the reproductive output of a species is much greater than this. For example, a single large foxglove plant may produce half a million seeds each one of which is potentially capable of giving rise to a new individual. Obviously nearly all the progeny die before reaching maturity and the chance of any single one surviving is very remote.

2. *Variation.*—The individuals of any generation of human beings obviously differ from one another and such differences are found in other organisms. No two animals of the same species (except perhaps for identical twins) are exactly alike and when a large number of individuals are examined it is clear that they vary considerably in structure, colour, activity and so on. Darwin also pointed out that generally these variations were passed on from one generation to the next, for example, the children of tall parents tend to grow tall.

3. *Survival of the Fittest.*—If there is an intense struggle for existence in their natural environment among individuals of a species having different characteristics, those which are best " fitted " to a given set of conditions are most likely to survive to maturity. These will reproduce and the features which enabled them to survive will be passed on to their offspring. This process is liable to continue and a species will become better adapted to its environment.

4. *Natural Selection.*—Over a long period of time the environment of a given species is never stable but will change in various ways. As it does so the characters which best fit the individuals to the changed environment will be selected (not consciously of course) and the species will change. The environment may change only in part of the range of the species and thus lead to divergence and the production of a new species alongside the old one.

Darwin and Lamarck.—Darwin pictured evolution as a slow continuous process with natural selection operating on the small inheritable variations found between the individuals of a species which are undergoing intense competition. This neglects the important effect of the environment on the growth and structure of the individual. It is obvious that external conditions will affect the development of an organism, for example the effect of various soil conditions on the growth of a plant or the amount of food material available to an animal. Lamarck maintained that the characters acquired by an individual owing to the effect of its environment could be passed on to its offspring. Undoubtedly characters are acquired by the individual during its growth but in spite of many attempts to prove otherwise no experiments have been done which prove conclusively that these are inherited by the offspring. Thus Lamarck's theory that evolution has occurred by the inheritance of acquired characters is not generally acceptable today.

Mutation Theory.—The data accumulated by Darwin showed that the variations between individuals of a species are small and graded into one another. If a particular character in a group of individuals is measured it is found that it varies symmetrically about a mean or average, with most values clustered about the mean and with few extreme ones. Darwin himself was worried about this fact because, although selection over a long period of time might shift the position of the mean, he did not see how it could bring about the discontinuity necessary for the establishment of a distinct new species. De Vries in his *Mutation Theory* published in 1901 put forward the view that evolution depends, not on the accumulation of continuous minute variations, but primarily upon large discontinuous variations or mutations. The importance of such spontaneous " sports " was considered by Darwin but he rejected the idea because when they appear they are usually " monstrous ". Such individuals are less " fitted " to their environment and therefore they will not survive to reproduce and give rise to a new species. That mutations are important factors in evolution is undoubtedly true but modern work has shown that the whole problem is far more complex than either Darwin or De Vries supposed.

Mendelism.—It is remarkable that in spite of carrying out many careful experiments on inheritance in plants Darwin did not discover the simple laws which are the basis of modern genetics. Mendel investigated inheritance in the garden pea and published his results in 1865, *i.e.*, at the time that Darwin's work was being widely discussed. However, Mendel's important discoveries were not generally known until 1900. When he crossed a pure breeding tall plant with a pure breeding dwarf plant all the progeny were tall. When these plants were self-pollinated the next genera-

a population and are not diluted or lost. Although they may not be of importance when they first appear they may be so if the selection pressure changes and they become of survival value. Thus specific characters may change or diverge and evolution will take place. His investigations also showed that recombination of factors could give rise to plants with new characteristics. By crossing a pure bred tall plant having round seeds

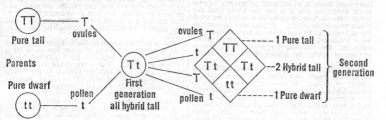

tion consisted of approximately one quarter dwarf plants and three quarters tall. From this and similar experiments Mendel deduced that the "factors" passed from parents to offspring were paired, only one of the pair came from each parent and that one could be dominant over the other. When he dealt with two pairs of characters, *e.g.*, tall or dwarf plants and round or wrinkled seeds, he found that they segregated and recombined independently and in predictable ratios.

The importance of Mendel's work in relation to evolution is that it showed that there was no blending of the characters in the offspring. Mutations can be hidden as recessive characters in

with a dwarf plant having wrinkled seeds he produced in the second generation some tall plants with wrinkled seeds and dwarf plants with round seeds. When a large number of characters are involved it is obvious that considerable variation and recombination occurs upon which natural selection can work.

Mendel was fortunate in his choice of experimental material with its easily recognisable contrasting characters. It is now known that his "factors" are the genes carried by the chromosomes in the nucleus of the cell. At the present time the biochemical basis of heredity is being vigorously investigated. *See* F31.

V. SCIENCES OF MAN

A biologist interested in classification might supplement the account of the animal kingdom in Part IV with the following further description of Man:

> "Man is a member of the order of Primates which is sub-divided into two sub-orders: Prosimii and Anthropoidea. The Prosimii include the lemurs and the Tarsier; the Anthropoidea include the monkeys, the apes and man. The anthropoid apes form a family called Pongidae and the extinct and living forms of man together constitute the family Hominidae. Although these two families constitute one superfamily, the Hominoidea, there are many differences between them in both body form and function. Apes progress by over-arm swinging in trees and they are usually quadrupedal on the ground; hominids habitually stand and walk upright."

But human beings have many remarkable attributes and it is not surprising therefore that besides biologists, scientists of many kinds contribute to the study of man. Even anthropology, which literally means "the study of man" is not a single well-defined science but has become diversified into a number of parts which have complicated connections with biology, archaeology, sociology, history, psychology, and many other studies. Physical anthropology, with which we shall deal first, is much concerned with the description of those physical characteristics of man which distinguish race from race, and man from animals. Such a study is important if we are to learn how man evolved. To describe physical characteristics quantitatively, suitable measurements must be made, *i.e.*, we must have techniques of anthropometry (man measurement). Physical measurement of the body cannot however exhaust the study of man, and therefore we shall also look at some of the current ideas of social anthropology which is one of a number of disciplines concerned

with the study of man in society. There we shall stop, not, of course, because there are no further aspects to consider. Psychology, with its many different approaches, is the study of mind, and something of the nature of mind and mental development will be found in Section Q.

PHYSICAL ANTHROPOLOGY.

The Earliest Men and Their Dates.

Fossil Primates.

Some fossil forms are known both in the Eocene and the Oligocene periods (F44). However, during the Miocene period in East Africa many varieties of Primates appeared, probably as a direct result of major climatic fluctuations in the area. These Miocene primates possessed attributes later to be more fully developed either among the Pongids or among the Hominids. Thus Proconsul, a common form in Miocene East Africa, was less specialised in locomotion and in cranial detail than are the apes of today. During the Miocene some of these East African primates left the trees and learned to walk upright, gradually adapting their pelvic and leg bones to an erect posture. By freeing the arms and hand this opened the way to tool-using and eventually to tool-making also.

Man's Distinctive Attributes.

Man has been variously defined as a large-brained hominid, as a bipedal hominid and also as a maker of tools to a set and regular pattern. These criteria imply both morphological and functional attributes. In tracing man's ancestry we do not find all of these characteristics appearing simultaneously. The further back in time we proceed, the fewer of these attributes are recognisable. Bipedalism is an early feature; the other attributes were to follow later.

The Australopithecinae.

These creatures probably lived during the Pliocene and Lower Pleistocene periods. For many years controversy raged as to whether they were to be classified as Pongid or as Hominid. Many dental features, for example, indicate their hominid affinities and they were, moreover, bipedal. However, their brains were very small and fall within the Pongid range. They might well have used tools, a widespread propensity among many Primates, but it is far less likely that the South African forms were capable of making tools in the manner described. It may well be that the use of bones, teeth and wood as tools might long have predated the use of more durable stone artifacts. On balance, however, the Australopithecinae might be described as the earliest Hominids.

Many fossil remains of the Australopithecinae have been found and they have been given a variety of names. It appears, however, that in South Africa a single genus existed probably with two species. Of these, one is small, generalised and lightly built, and is termed *Australopithecus* or *A. africanus*, while the other is larger, more specialised and robust, and is termed *Paranthropus* or *A. robustus*. It is improbable that either of these South African forms constituted a major source of the later, more advanced hominids.

In the Lower Pleistocene Bed I in the Olduvai Gorge, Tanzania, a fossil rather similar to the more rugged Australopithecines of South Africa was found. *Zinjanthropus boisei*, as it was named, is now frequently referred to as *Australopithecus boisei*. Estimated to be some 1,700,000 years old, this creature was perhaps the earliest tool-maker, but it is likely that *Homo habilis*, a more advanced hominid contemporaneously existing at Olduvai, was the maker of the numerous Oldowan stone tools found in Bed I. Oldowan tools, widely distributed in Africa, represent the first tool-making tradition, and with this culture the Palaeolithic Age begins.

Homo erectus.

Remains are very widespread in the Old World and they represent the next major stage in the evolution of the Hominids. Most finds are dated to the Middle Pleistocene period. The brain is now much larger than in the Australopithecines, though smaller than in modern man. The skull bones are very thick and the skull exhibits massive bony ridges. There is neither a chin nor a forehead present. The first finds were made in Middle Pleistocene deposits in Java by Dr. E. Dubois. This creature, *Pithecanthropus erectus* (*Homo erectus javanensis*) was indisputably erect and walked on two legs. Dr. G. H. R. von Koenigswald discovered more specimens of the same general type in Java and he also found the remains of a Lower Pleistocene more rugged form which he named *P. robustus*. A massive jaw which he found—*Meganthropus palaeojavanicus*—probably represents the Australopithecine stage in Java and has also been named *Paranthropus* (*Australopithecus*) *palaeojavanicus*.

In 1927 and 1929 the first remains of Pekin Man (*Sinanthropus pekinensis*; *Homo erectus pekinensis*) were found in Chou Kou Tien cave near Pekin. These remains were Middle Pleistocene contemporaries of Java Man whom they closely resembled.

Until certain finds were made in East Africa in the nineteen fifties and sixties, particularly at Olduvai, *Homo erectus* remains were only known from the Far East. It had been widely accepted that man originated in Asia and not in Africa, an interpretation that is little supported today. A skull found in the Middle Pleistocene Bed II at Olduvai, as well as certain mandibles found at Ternifine, Algeria, are also without doubt representatives of *Homo erectus*. The Ternifine (*Atlanthropus*) jaws as well as very similar mandibles found at Sidi Abderrahman, near Casablanca, Morocco, are accompanied by hand axes of the so-called Acheulean culture. The Olduvai *Homo erectus* skull dated at approximately 490,000 years was also associated with hand axes.

European fossil remains approximately contemporaneous with Pekin Man include the massive Mauer Jaw found without associated artifacts in 1907 near Heidelberg in Germany. In 1964 and 1965 equally ancient remains were found at Vertezöllös, Hungary, and these are also of the *Homo erectus* type.

Absolute and Relative Dating.

In tracing the emergence of man it is desirable that the various finds should be dated as accurately as possible, both in relative terms and also, if possible, in absolute terms. Various methods have been devised and the results are often expressed by giving the date as so many years B.P. The initials B.P. stand for "before present" and the present conventionally means the year A.D. 1950.

The potassium-argon method, depending on the rate of radioactive decay of potassium to argon is useful for dating material from 230,000 to 26 million years old. For more recent finds up to about 50,000 years old, the Carbon-14 method is appropriate. Dating with this method depends on establishing the ratio of Carbon-14 (the radioactive isotope of Carbon) to Carbon-12—ordinary Carbon. One method of relative dating is called the fluorine method depending as it does on the fact that fossil bones contain fluorine in proportion to their antiquity. Relative dating may also be deduced from the depths at which fossil bones are found in undisturbed strata. Relative dating is also possible from the known sequence of glacial events during the Pleistocene. During this period much of northern Eurasia witnessed four major glacial advances, the so-called ice ages, Günz, Mindel, Riss, and Würm. Milder periods or Interglacials separated the Ice Ages and geological deposits of the glacial and interglacial periods, easily characterised by the remains of the distinctive flora and fauna which they contain, provide a framework for dating fossil man. Thus two human skulls from the second, Mindel–Riss Interglacial (130–180,000 B.P.) are known in Europe, those of Steinheim, Germany, and Swanscombe, Kent. The latter was associated with the Mid-Acheulean hand-axe culture. No artifacts were found with Steinheim man. The Steinheim cranium is much more complete than the Swanscombe remains and in size it approximates to modern man. Some of its morphological features are similar to modern man; others to Neanderthal man. Steinheim could in fact be a generalised ancestor for both these major human types. The Swanscombe bones are sometimes similarly interpreted though they have on occasion been classed as an early form of *Homo sapiens*, pre-dating the Neanderthalians.

Neanderthal Man.

Neanderthaloids are found in Upper Pleistocene times during the early part of the Würm glaciation, particularly in Europe, West and Central Asia, and North Africa. Early discoveries included those in the Neander valley in Germany, Gibraltar, Spy (Belgium), and Krapina (Jugoslavia). Subsequently many other finds were made including, for example, La Chapelle (France), Teshik-Tash (Uzbekistan) Hauna Fteah (Cyrenaica), and Rabat (Morocco).

Early proto-Neanderthalers, such as Steinheim, were followed by the "classic" Neanderthal forms, conventionalised as of brutish appearance, with massive eyebrow ridges, sloping foreheads, long, large, crania and receding chins. The cave of Tabun on Mt. Carmel, Israel, yielded remains of these "classic" forms, while the nearby Skhull cave contained remains of men much more similar to those of today. The remains may represent variation normal within a group or else may indicate that the Neanderthalers interbred with people of modern type, thus producing the Skhull hybrids.

Rhodesian Man, found in 1921, in Broken Hill, Zambia, is clearly neither a Neanderthaler nor a modern type of man. The skull was for long thought to be unique, if not highly aberrant. However, in 1951 a similar skull was found at Saldanha Bay in the Cape Province of South Africa. These are early Upper Pleistocene remains, approximately 40,000 years B.P. Solo Man, in Java, is a not altogether dissimilar and may be the direct descendant of *Homo erectus* in South East Asia. Both Rhodesian and Solo Man are sometimes regarded as variants of the basic Neanderthal type.

Homo Sapiens.

Homo sapiens emerged during the fourth, Würm, glaciation, a process precisely dated by the radiocarbon technique among others. Neanderthal Man seems to have been replaced by *Homo sapiens*, of completely modern appearance, certainly by some 30,000 years B.P.

Neanderthal Man's stone tools were made on flakes, and in Europe constituted the so-called Mousterian industry. Post-Neanderthal men were technically more advanced, their stone tools including small knife blades and engraving tools specialised for different purposes. This is the typical Upper Palaeolithic tool assemblage, of the Aurignacian, Solutrean and Magdalenian, and other tool-making cultures. It was during this Upper Palaeolithic period that man, though still everywhere a hunter and gatherer of foodstuffs, first showed artistic tendencies.

Combe Capelle in southern Central France yielded the earliest known skull (approximately 34,000 years B.P.) of completely modern type in western Eurasia and Africa. The Cromagnon people were somewhat later (20–30,000 years B.P.). Physically, the Cromagnon people were tall, with long heads, very large brain cases and short, broad faces. Approximately similar humans have been found elsewhere, as in the Upper Cave at Chou Kou Tien, and a skull from the Niah Cave in Sarawak dated at about 40,000 years B.P. is the earliest known representative of *Homo sapiens* in Asia. In Java, the descendants of Solo Man may well be the Wadjak people of about 10,000 years B.P. These are similar to the Australian Aborigines and they may be roughly contemporary with a skull from Keilor near Melbourne which indicates that Australia was populated in late Pleistocene or early post-Pleistocene times. Again in Upper Pleistocene Southern Africa there were people with very large brain cases and with features rather like the present-day Bushmen and Hottentots. The Boskop skull is of this type. No skeletons showing characteristic Negro features have been found in Africa before post-Pleistocene times. This suggests a late evolutionary emergence for the Negroes. The Americas were peopled by immigrants from North East Asia some 15–20,000 years ago, and subsequently. Some of the early groups of immigrants have been described as " Archaic White ", as have the Ainu of Northern Japan, but it is more generally accepted that successive waves of Mongoloids moved into the Americas from Asia, the Eskimo being the last group to arrive.

Even today the total number of known fossil human remains is small for the long time span of human evolution and it is very difficult if not impossible as yet to trace the precise ancestry of each of the races of man.

The Races of Man.

The species *Homo sapiens* to which all living men belong is differentiated into local variant populations which are interfertile and not always sharply distinguished from one another. Many attempts have been made to classify mankind into races, usually on the basis of readily visible external features such as head shape, stature, and skin colour. Such formal classifications express real features of human variation but in somewhat artificial if not misleading manner, since the impression is created that the species is naturally partitioned into discrete, discontinuous groups, whereas changes from one region to another are often gradual rather than abrupt transitions. Again all human groups are variable within themselves and populations frequently overlap considerably in quantitative characters, in which case, the distinction between them is best expressed in statistical terms as differences in average values. Discrete variables such as blood groups are usually found in most populations but with different frequencies of occurrence.

A race is best considered as a Mendelian population, that is, as a reproductive community of individuals who share in a common gene pool. Again a race has been defined as a group of people who have the majority of their physical attributes in common. It is manifestly improper to refer to religious or linguistic groupings as races since cultural attributes obviously vary quite independently of the physical features used in race definition.

Three types of Mendelian populations or races are sometimes distinguished: (1) Geographical, (2) Local and (3) Microgeographical or Micro-races.

(1) *Geographical Race.*

This is a collection of Mendelian populations such as occupy whole continents or large islands and separated by major barriers such as mountains and deserts. The Australian Aborigines and the African Negroes provide examples.

(2) *Local Races.*

These are sub-populations within the Geographical Races, frequently corresponding with distinct or isolated breeding populations. They are adapted to local environmental pressures and are maintained by social and physical barriers which prevent gene flow between them. Examples include the tribes within the Amerindian Geographical Race, the Basques, Ainu and Gypsies.

(3) *Micro-races.*

These are the numerous distinct populations which are not clearly bounded breeding populations and can be distinguished only statistically. Their existence is demonstrated by variations in the frequencies of genes within a densely populated country. Many of man's physical attributes, etc. vary from group to group and since these traits have a genetic component, then they also are characteristic of micro-races.

Anthropometry.

This constitutes a system of techniques for the measurement of the skeleton and of the body. From the early 19th cent. onwards anthropometry was an important means of giving quantitative expression to the variation in physical traits among human beings. In fact until fairly recently, anthropometry has been the mainstay of physical anthropology, preoccupied as it was with the problems of evolutionary descent. The measurement of the skeleton was stressed since skeletal remains constitute the most direct evidence of earlier populations. The shape of the living body and of the skeleton can precisely be expressed metrically, but it is usual to use relatively few measurements, and these normally represent the major features, including, for example, stature, shoulder width, head length, and head breadth. The latter two were especially favoured and the cephalic index was obtained by expressing the breadth as a percentage of the length. Long heads, with low cephalic indices (below 75) were termed dolichocephalic, while round heads, with high indices (above 81) were termed brachycephalic.

Anthropometric features are known to vary widely among the world's populations. Thus while the Nilotes of the Sudan have an average stature of 1·78 m the African pygmies average 1·36 m. Dolichocephalic heads are prevalent among Australian Aborigines while brachycephaly is extremely prevalent among the Mongoloid peoples of Asia.

Anthropometric characteristics such as these are not immutable and it has been shown in studies in the United States, Hawaii, and elsewhere that immigrants' offspring rapidly develop bodily changes when compared with their parents or when compared with groups in their homelands. It is impossible to say whether the races of man are becoming more or less heterogeneous as a result of such processes.

Pigmentation.

Hair, skin, and eye colour were traditionally described either in subjective terms or else by reference to matching standards. Both procedures presented serious limitations in reliability and in comparability of results. Recent years have witnessed the use of much more satisfactory objective procedures, involving spectrophotometers in hair and skin colour studies. These instruments record the percentage of light of a number of known specified wavelengths reflected from a surface relative to the reflectance from a pure white surface. In general the darker the specimen, say of hair, the lower the percentage of light which it reflects. Using such instruments precise and reliable quantitative estimations of hair and skin colour are possible; the genetic basis of the traits may be clarified and comprehended and the selective advantages of skin and hair colour may be examined quantitatively. Dark skins confer advantages in hot, sunny areas since they protect the body against the harmful effects of ultraviolet radiation, minimising the incidence of skin cancer for example. Light skins are advantageous in cloudy areas with low insolation since they facilitate the body's synthesis of Vitamin D, thus reducing the incidence of rickets. The correlation between dark pigmentation and high levels of solar radiation is high, but it is impossible to state how much of the geographical distribution of skin colour mirrors the spread of dark- and light-skinned peoples from one or two sources and how much of the patterning is due to independent adaptations in many human groups in the past.

Physiometric Observations.

These cover a range of phenomena including handedness, the ability to taste phenylthiocarbamide (P.T.C.), colour-blindness, and fingerprints. The genetic basis for many of these attributes are well known. Thus red-green colour blindness is a sex-linked character, males being far more frequently affected than females. Within Britain percentages of colour-blind males range from 5·4 in N.E. Scotland to 9·5 in S.W. England. Non-European populations generally exhibit much lower frequencies.

The tasting of P.T.C. is controlled by two genes, T and t, the former being dominant. TT and Tt individuals normally experience a bitter taste sensation when they sip P.T.C. solutions; tt individuals either cannot taste the substance at all or else only in very strong concentrations. The tt individuals are termed Non-tasters; TT and Tt individuals are termed Tasters. High frequencies of Non-tasters (exceeding 38 per cent) occur in parts of Wales and in Orkney, while low values (approximately 24 per cent) occur in North Lancashire and Northumberland. A clue to the selective significance of this trait is provided by the excess of Non-tasters among individuals with nodular goitres (thyroid abnormalities). Non-European populations usually have lower percentages of Non-tasters than the British figures quoted.

Attributes of the Blood.

1. Blood Groups.

Many blood group systems (see Index to Section P) are known today in addition to the ABO system which was the first discovered and which matters so much in blood transfusion. The mode of inheritance of the numerous blood-group substances is known. Blood grouping is relatively simple depending as it does on reactions between antigens on the red blood cells and specified antibodies derived from the blood serum.

The ABO system basically involves three genes, A, B, and O. Every individual inherits two of these genes from parents and so the genotype (genetic constitution) must be one of the following: AA, AO, BB, BO, AB, or OO. O is recessive to both A and B and thus there are four possible phenotypes (genetic constitutions detectable by blood grouping): A, B, AB, and O.

The ABO genes constitute a polymorphic system, that is several genes occur with frequencies such that the least frequent of them occurs with a frequency exceeding that due to mutation alone. Certain selective advantages and disadvantages of the ABO genes in human populations are known. Thus stomach cancers are more frequent among individuals of group A than they are in the population at large. Again, duodenal ulcers are almost 40 per cent more common among persons of blood group O than in individuals of the other ABO groups.

Both on a global and on a local scale, the ABO genes display marked racial variation. Within Britain A varies from 31 per cent to 53 per cent,

increasing in frequency from North to South; O varies from 38–54 per cent, increasing in frequency from South to North. B shows less variation, though it is most prevalent in the Celtic areas. The regional fluctuations are not random but systematic and statistically highly significant despite the enormous migrations within Britain during the last few hundred years, which might well have masked or minimised the underlying variability.

Globally the ABO variation is also striking. Thus the percentage of the blood group B exceeds 30 among the Mongoloids of Central and East Asia but the B gene is virtually absent in the Australian Aborigines, the American Indians and in the Basques. Many Amerindian tribes are 100 per cent O; some others have very high A frequencies.

In the Rhesus blood group system all humans are either Rh+ (DD or Dd) or Rh− (dd) (see Index to Section P). All the Amerindians and Australian Aborigines, and most of the East Asians are Rh+. Rh− individuals are more frequent in western Asia, in parts of Africa and especially in north west Europe where the Rh− percentage is approximately 15. The Basques are distinctive in having a 40 per cent Rh− frequency. Racial variation is partly explained by selection via haemolytic disease of the newborn (erythroblastosis foetalis), whereby Rh+ offspring of Rh− women (possible if the father is Rh+) may die before birth owing to their Rh blood group incompatibility with their mother.

2. Haemoglobins.

Haemoglobin exists in alternative forms in man and these are genetically controlled. The frequencies of some of the genes which control haemoglobins vary markedly among human populations. The principal technique used to show variant haemoglobins is electrophoresis—the movement of charged particles in an electric field.

Normal human haemoglobin comprises two different haemoglobins (A and A2). An interesting variant is haemoglobin S. This may be indicated by electrophoresis and also by a sickling test. Red cells containing haemoglobin S placed in an oxygen-free atmosphere assume sickle shapes. Individuals who have inherited one S gene (AS heterozygotes) have a mild, non-fatal anaemia—the sickle cell trait. Homozygous SS individuals suffer from the severe sickle cell anaemia which is usually fatal before maturity. Some abnormal haemoglobins including S, E, and C have high frequencies and their existence, since all of them are deleterious to some extent, provides opportunities for viewing the action of natural selection and gene flow in human populations. Haemoglobin S reaches very high frequencies among some populations in southern Asia and particularly in much of tropical Africa (10–40 per cent), despite its severe effect on individual viability and fertility. Haemoglobin C is most prevalent in northern Ghana and contiguous areas while Haemoglobin E is found principally in South East Asia, with frequencies as high as 27 per cent in Cambodia.

Homozygous SS individuals hardly ever live to transmit the S gene and without a compensatory effect the gene would be totally lost except for certain cases possibly occurring as mutations. Compensation is through positive selection in favour of AS individuals who are more resistant to and so protected from falciparum malaria. Again AS females might be more fertile than AA females in certain populations, and this again would help to maintain the high S frequencies.

Other polymorphisms include the haptoglobins (proteins that bind the haemoglobin of old and broken-down red blood cells), serum transferrins (proteins in the blood sera used in transporting iron within the body) and the enzyme Glucose-6 phosphate Dehydrogenase (G6PD) and selective agencies are operative on these also.

The non-uniform distribution of blood group haemoglobin, and other gene frequencies in the races of man may be explained in terms of natural selection, gene flow between populations, random genetic drift, the founder principle and the development of geographical and socio-cultural isolation. As a principal agency only natural selection can account for the magnitude of the population differences and for the maintenance of the observed balanced genetic polymorphisms in man. Known frequency distributions suggest that there is some relationship between the environment and the incidence of, for example, the blood group genes. Both the variability and also the geographical gradients for the A and B genes are consistent with the hypothesis that these genes are influenced by environmental selection and it seems unlikely that such a phenomenal relationship is confined to the ABO system. Human populations or races are defined in terms of traits, only some of which have here been indicated, which are brought into being and maintained primarily by natural selection—by the incidence of disease, blood group incompatibilities, diseases of the new born, and by differential fertility.

THE STUDY OF SOCIAL ANTHROPOLOGY.

What the Subject is About.

Social anthropology is concerned with the way men live as members of ordered societies. It has been described as a branch of sociology, or as the sociology of the simpler peoples. Neither description is wholly correct. A social anthropologist seeks to identify the *structure* of the society he studies and the *processes* of social interaction within it. His method is direct contact—what has been called "participant observation." Therefore he must deal with a unit small enough to be manageable with this technique. Nation-states, such as sociologists commonly work among, are too large. Most social anthropologists have done their work in what we call "small-scale" societies; that is, peoples who lacked such media of communication as writing or money, let alone any mechanical means of transport, until these were brought to them from Europe. A social anthropologist may choose to work in some section of a society that possesses those techniques—in the ancient countries of the East or in Europe or America. In that case he confines himself to a microcosm such as a village or a factory. When he is writing of societies alien to his own and that of most of his readers he is obliged to describe their *culture* as well as their social relationships, since without such a description his readers would not be able to picture, or even understand, the social rules that are his main subject of study; this would be superfluous for a sociologist taking modern machine society for granted. Culture has been called the raw material out of which the anthropologist makes his analysis of social structure. It is the sum total of standardised ways of behaving, of lore and technique, of belief and symbolism, characteristic of any given society.

The Notion of Roles.

All the world, as Shakespeare said, is a stage, and this is a key metaphor for social anthropologists. Every individual does indeed play many parts, not consecutively but all together; for every social relationship carries with it the expectation of society that the parties to it will behave in approved ways. Father and children, ruler and subjects, buyers and sellers, husband and wife; every one of these words is the name of a *role* to be played by the person it describes. The playing of roles involves the recognition of claims and obligations as well as appropriate modes of behaviour in personal contacts. All these rules are called *norms*; when they are concerned with rights and obligations they are *jural norms*. A social norm is what people think ought to happen; unlike a statistical norm, it may or may not be what happens in the majority of cases.

Kinship and Marriage.

In societies of simple technology most roles are *ascribed*; that is, the parts people will play in life are given them at birth by the fact of their parentage and of the group in which this makes them members. In other words, the most important principal of organisation is *kinship*. W. H. R. Rivers called this "the social recognition of biological ties." The ties in question can be called genealogical; they all derive from the recognition of common ancestry. Such ties may be fictitious, as when a child is adopted. But in the vast majority of cases the relationships that are recognised are actually biological.

No man can recognise for social purposes all the individuals with whom he has a common ancestor somewhere in the past, or even know of their existence; their number increases with every generation. In every society a selection is made, from the whole universe of genealogically related persons, of certain categories towards which an individual recognises specific obligations and on whom he can make specific claims. Such *corporate groups* of kin have a permanent existence; they recruit new members in each generation in accordance with recognised rules. Kin groups are concerned largely with the transmission of property, and for this and other purposes they recognise the common authority of a senior man; they are also religious groups, performing together rituals directed to their common ancestors.

The common patrimony of a kin group normally consists in land or livestock; in societies of more advanced technology it may be a boat, as in Hong Kong, or even, as in Japan, a family business. It may have non-material resources too, such as the right to supply chiefs or priests for the society as a whole; this may be put conversely as the right to hold political or religious office. Those who share a common patrimony have a common interest in preserving and increasing it. Wrongs done by their members to outsiders are compensated from their collective resources, and they have joint responsibility for seeking compensation if one of their own members is injured, particularly in the case of homicide.

Descent.

Kin groups may be recruited according to a number of principles. A principle widely followed in small-scale societies is that of *unilineal descent*; that is, group membership is derived from one parent only, either the father (*patrilineal* or *agnatic*) or the mother (*matrilineal*). Property is *administered* by men in either system, but in the matrilineal system it is *inherited* from the mother; hence its control passes from a man to the sons of his sisters. In a unilineal system every individual recognises kin linked to him through the parent from whom he does not trace his descent; this is the principle of *complementary filiation*. The complementary kin are *matrilateral* where the descent rule is patrilineal, *patrilateral* where it is matrilineal. A unilineal descent group is called a *lineage*.

Descent can also be traced *cognatically*; that is, all descendants of a common ancestral pair may be recognised as forming one *kindred*. In such a system there is no permanent group patrimony; people inherit a share of the property of both their parents, and this is often conferred upon them when they marry, while their parents are still living. Or all the inhabitants of a village may share rights in its rice-fields or fishing ponds; a man chooses among what kin he will live, but he can have rights in one village only. In such a system there are no continuing groups defined by descent; the permanent group is territorial, consisting in the inhabitants of the village.

Marriage.

Kinship status is defined by legitimate birth, and this in its turn by legal marriage. There are always rules against marriage with specified categories of kin, though these are not necessarily near kin. Some societies consider that the ideal marriage is that between the children of a brother and a sister; if such marriages are repeated through the generations they create a permanent link between two lineages. Marriage between members of the same lineage is nearly always forbidden; this is expressed in the term *lineage exogamy*. The general effect of the prohibitions is to spread widely through a society the links created by marriage; links that impose an obligation of friendship on groups that without them would be mutually hostile.

In a matrilineal system women bear children for their own lineage; it is expected that they should be fathered by a man who has married their mother according to the approved procedure, but a child's lineage membership is not affected by the marriage of its mother. But in a patrilineal society wives must be brought from outside to bear children for the group. Associated with this fact is the payment of *bridewealth*, which used to be mistakenly interpreted as the purchase of wives.

This payment is what fixes the status of a woman's children; all those she bears while the bridewealth is with her lineage are reckoned as the children of the man on whose behalf it was paid, even if he is dead and she is living with another partner. In a matrilineal society the making of gifts is part of the marriage procedure, but they are of slight economic value in comparison with bridewealth. The difference is correlated with the difference in what the husband acquires by the marriage; in both cases he gains the right to his wife's domestic services and sexual fidelity, but where bridewealth is paid he can also count her children as his descendants and call on their labour when he needs it.

In societies where most roles are ascribed by the fact of birth, marriage is the most important field in which there is freedom of choice. But the choice is commonly exercised not by the couple but by their lineage seniors, who are more concerned with alliances between lineages than with the personal feelings of the pair. *Polygamy*, or the simultaneous marriage of a man to more than one woman, is permitted in lineage-based societies; indeed it is the ideal, though only a minority of men attain it. One reason why it is valued is that it enables a man who has the resources necessary for successive bridewealth payments to build up a network of alliances.

Authority Systems.

Every society has some arrangements for the maintenance of order, in the sense that force may be used against those who infringe legitimate rights. In every society theft, adultery, and homicide are treated as offences. Where no individual has authority to punish these on behalf of the community, *self-help* is the approved course. Lineage membership is significant here; a man who is wronged will go with his kin to seek redress (for a theft or adultery) or vengeance (for the homicide of a kinsman). Vengeance can be bought off by the payment of compensation; but because the taking of life is a serious matter in the most turbulent of societies, there must also be a solemn reconciliation, with a sacrifice to the ancestral spirits, between the lineages of killer and victim. The recognition of an appropriate method of dealing with injuries has been described as " the rule of law " in its simplest form.

Within a lineage the senior man is expected to settle quarrels, and the ancestral spirits are believed to punish with sickness juniors who do not listen to him. When quarrels break out between members of different lineages, their elders may meet and seek a solution. Where there is no hereditary authority individuals may attain positions of leadership in virtue of their powers of mediation by persuasion.

In addition to the maintenance of rights, most societies require at some time arrangements for the organisation of collective activities. It is possible for there to be no ascribed role of organiser; in such a case leadership is a matter of competition. Competitive leadership in economic activities is characteristic particularly of the very small societies of New Guinea. What is needed here is not only powers of persuasion but resources to reward the participants. The very important principle, to be discussed later, that every gift ought at some time to be returned, is the basis of their position. A man who can put others in his debt can call upon their labour. It may take a long time to build up the necessary resources for acknowledged leadership, and leadership may be lost to a rival and is not necessarily passed to an heir.

Responsibility both for law and order and for collective activities may be shared on recognised principles among the whole adult male population. This is done where society is organised on the basis of *age*, a system widely found in east and west Africa. In such a system all adult men pass through a series of stages at each of which appropriate tasks are allotted to them. In its simplest form the division is made into ' warriors ' and ' elders '. This principle may be complicated in various ways, but the essence of it is that men in their prime are responsible for activities requiring physical strength, impetuosity, and courage, while their elders have the task of mediating in disputes, discussing public affairs, and performing sacrifices to the ancestors. Men in the warrior grade are the fighting force, and may also have the police functions of summoning disputants and witnesses before the elders, and seizing property from a man who has been adjudged to pay compensation and does not do so voluntarily. Sometimes specific public works are allotted to them, such as rounding up stray cattle or clearing weeds from paths or springs. It is also possible for community responsibilities to be shared in more complicated ways, as for example among the Yakö of Nigeria, where the adherents of particular religious cults are believed to call on the spirit which they worship to punish persons guilty of particular offences.

Where there are hereditary chiefs, both public works and the maintenance of law and order are the responsibility of the chief and his subordinate officials. Resources are accumulated for public purposes by the collection of tribute, and labour is obtained for public works by the recognition of the principle that persons in authority can claim the labour of those subject to them. Expectations are attached to the role of chief as to any other. Chiefs are expected to dispense justice fairly, to be generous to the poor, to reward loyalty, and to be successful in war, and they are reminded of these expectations in the course of the elaborate rituals performed at their accession. The prosperity of the whole land is commonly held to be bound up with the health of the chief and the favourable attitude towards him of supernatural beings. He may be obliged to obey all kinds of ritual restrictions to this end; for example it was believed of the ruler of Ruanda, in east Africa, that he must not bend his knee lest the country be conquered. Chiefs are either themselves responsible for the performance of ritual on behalf of the whole populace or must maintain priests to do this.

Social anthropologists have recently turned their attention to the process of competition for the commanding roles which any society offers. Some would claim to have discarded the idea of structure altogether in favour of that of process; yet the structure must be taken into account as the set of rules in accordance with which the game is played. There are societies where it is the rule that on the death of a chief his sons must fight for the succession to test who is the strongest and has the largest following. There are others where the rule of succession may seem to be clear, and yet there can always be dispute as to who fits it best. Sometimes people pursue the struggle for power by accusing their rivals of witchcraft; sometimes by massing their followers behind them in a show of strength before which their adversaries retire; the first is the method of the Ndembu in western Zambia, the second that of the Pathans in the Swat Valley in Pakistan. Such confrontations occur at moments of crisis, but the process of building up support is going on all the time. The study of these processes is among the most interesting new developments in social anthropology.

Economic Systems.

In societies where money provides a common standard for measuring the relative value of different kinds of goods, people who exchange goods can make very exact calculations of profit and loss. It is often assumed that where there is no such common medium of exchange people do not make any economic calculations, and dispose of their property in ways that are the reverse of businesslike. The principal reason why this assumption is made is the great importance attached in societies of simple technology to the making of gifts. The essential difference between a gift and a commercial exchange is that no return is stipulated. In the commercial world goods are sold, services hired, at a price, and anyone who fails to pay has broken a contract and is liable to be punished. The obligation to return a gift is a moral one. Moreover, to compete in the giving of gifts seems at first sight the very opposite of competition in the acquisition of wealth. But in most societies people who have a surplus of wealth like to have a reputation for generosity; only in the affluent world of machine production people feel the need to have many more material possessions before they begin to think in terms of surplus.

The exchange of gifts plays a particularly large part in the societies of Melanesia, where me[n] form partnerships for the express purpose of giving and receiving valuable objects, and earn prestige at least as much by giving as by receiving. This exchange of valuables, mostly shell ornaments, is so important that it has a name in the language of each society. The first such exchange system to be described by an anthropologist was the *kula* of the Trobriand Islands, observed by Malinowski. An important man had a partner in an island on either side of his own home; from one he received armbands and returned necklaces, from the other he received necklaces and returned armbands. These objects did not become part of a store of wealth for any man; nobody could hold one long before it was time to pass it on to his partner. To receive his gift a man sailed by canoe to his partner's home; he was there welcomed peaceably, and while he was making his formal visit the crew were bartering their goods on the shore with the local populace. Thus the *kula* partnership had the nature of a political alliance; it was a means of maintaining peaceful relations between populations which would otherwise have been hostile.

In the highland area of New Guinea identical objects are exchanged, so that the relative value of amounts given and received can be calculated. In some parts the ideal is that a return gift should be twice the original one. Naturally it is no small achievement to carry on a prolonged series of exchanges at such a rate. Very few men manage it, and those who do are the acknowledged leaders of their community. For each large gift he has made a man wears a little bamboo stick hung round his neck; thus his munificence is publicly proclaimed. A new partnership is initiated by making the minimum gift. Men make these partnerships with others not bound to them by kinship, notably with their relatives by marriage. Each partnership extends the range within which a man can count on friendly treatment. So widespread is the idea that gifts should be repaid, and services rewarded, after some delay, and at the discretion of the man making the return, that where the highland people have taken to growing coffee for sale, the large-scale planters do not pay wages but employ young men for planting who get their return by coming to them later for help in difficulties. Of course the young men would stop giving their work if they judged that the return was not adequate.

Gift-giving, then, is an investment, but not one that produces a direct material return. One anthropologist, R. F. Salisbury, has called it an investment in power. The extreme case of such an uneconomic use of goods was found—before it was forbidden—in the *potlach* of some Indians of the north-west coast of America. There a man who was insulted would challenge the offender to a competition in destruction. Great quantities of fish-oil would be poured on the fire, and sheets of copper thrown into the sea. The challenger was demonstrating how much wealth he could afford to destroy.

Certainly this is not turning resources to material advantage. No more is the giving of a very expensive dinner-party in London or New York. But equally certainly, it is not done without calculation. In the affluent society people display their superior affluence because this demonstrates their prestige rating, just as in the *potlach*; and they keep on good terms, through the hospitality they offer, with people from whom they may later seek a return in professional dealings, rather as in the Melanesian gift-exchanges. The difference between the uses to which resources are put in societies of simple and of complex technology is one only of degree. The proportion that is devoted to securing non-material advantages is higher in the small-scale societies, and so is the proportion of gift-giving to commercial exchange. In gift-giving there is no bargaining, but there is a clear expectation of return. The initiation of new social relationships by the making of gifts is not by any means confined to New Guinea. Bride-wealth which legitimises children is the most widespread example. Pastoral peoples in East Africa also make gifts of stock to selected friends in distant parts. The friend on his home ground is a sponsor for his partner, and he is expected to make return gifts from time to time, and may be asked for a beast if his partner is in difficulties. One could think of such an arrangement as a type of insurance.

A small number of social anthropologists have specialised in the study of the economic systems of small-scale societies, and have asked whether the concepts devised for the analysis of monetary economies—such notions, for example, as capital and credit—can be applied to people who gain their livelihood directly from the resources of their immediate environment. Starting from the assumption that there is always some choice in the allocation of resources, they have observed how these choices are actually made in the societies where they have worked. They have asked how the value of such goods as are obtained by barter is measured; how labour is obtained, how directed and how rewarded for such enterprises as the building of a canoe or a temple, which call for the co-operation of large numbers. They have examined the use of media of exchange, asking how far any of these fulfil the functions that we associate with money.

The general conclusion of these studies is that peoples of simple technology are perfectly capable of rational calculation in the allocation of their resources, even though their calculations are rough by comparison with those of the entrepreneur in an industrial society. They know what to regard as an adequate return when they are bartering goods. They withhold goods from consumption when they are planning an enterprise; that is to say, a man who proposes to initiate such an activity as canoe-building arranges to be able to feed his labour force.

Religion.

At a time when people questioned whether " primitive " societies could be said to have religion, E. B. Tylor offered as a " minimum " definition of religion " the belief in spiritual beings." All societies of simple technology have such beliefs, and think that unseen personalised beings influence the course of nature by direct intervention, causing rain to fall if they are pleased with the actions of men and withholding it if they are angry, sending sickness as a punishment and so forth. In the great majority of such societies the most important spirits to be worshipped are those of dead ancestors. But there may also be a belief in gods responsible for particular aspects of the world, to whom offerings are made for protection or success in their special fields. Many preliterate peoples believe in a 'high god' from whom all other spirits derive their power, and one school of anthropology sees this as evidence of an original state of higher religious consciousness from which man has declined; but this view is not widely held.

Rituals involving groups of people are commonly performed on occasions when changes of status are to be signalised. A child becomes a member of society not by being born, but at a naming or showing ceremony. A youth or girl becomes adult at initiation. Marriage, which makes a couple into potential parents and links their kin groups, is another such ritual.

In funerary rites the dead person is made into an ancestor, and his heir adopts his social personality and his responsibilities. The accession of a man to political office is surrounded by ritual, and chiefs frequently observe annual rites at the time of harvest, when it is the season, not the person, that is changing. These are *confirmatory* rituals, designed to keep society and the world on an even course. When something goes wrong, a drought or epidemic or an individual sickness, *piacular* rituals are performed to make peace with the spirits responsible for the disaster.

An essential aspect of many of these religions is the belief in witchcraft—that is that it is possible for humans to harm one another merely by hating them. Witchcraft supplies an explanation of undeserved misfortune. Diviners employ a multitude of techniques (which anthropologists rather inaccurately call oracles) to detect whether a disaster is a merited punishment or is due to witchcraft.

Every small-scale society has its myths—stories which tell how the world as people know it came to be. Sometimes their ritual re-enacts the myth; often the myth tells how the ritual was first performed and thereby gives a reason for its continuance. Then there are myths telling how death and evil came into the world. Some myths lend authority to the existing social order, and particularly to the claims of ruling groups, by telling how the social structure was divinely ordained. Under the influence of the French anthropologist Lévi-Strauss, many anthropologists are beginning to see both myths and the symbolism of ritual as man's earliest attempt to order intellectually the world of his experience.

Social Change.

No doubt all the societies that anthropologists have studied have been gradually changing throughout the centuries when their history was not recorded. But they experienced nothing like the rapidity of the changes that came to them when they were brought under the rule of European nations and introduced to mass production and a money economy. The effect of this has been in essence to widen the range of choice in the relationships that people can form. A man may choose to be dependent on an employer rather than on work in co-operation with his kin or village mates. He is more likely to rise in the world by going to school and getting a city job than by earning the respect of the villagers or the approval of a chief. Small-scale societies are now becoming merged in larger ones, and the close ties of the isolated village are loosened. In the newly created industrial areas new specialised associations are formed to pursue professional and other interests. The social insurance that kinship provided is lacking, and it has not as yet been replaced by what the state offers in the highly industrialised societies. The minority that has whole-heartedly adopted the values of the industrialised world now produces the political rulers of new states. They are impatient to carry the majority along the same road, but there are profound conflicts of value between them and the still largely illiterate masses.

PART VI. SPECIAL TOPICS

SCIENTIFIC FINDINGS FROM THE APOLLO 11 LUNAR MISSION.

The moon has been an object of scientific study ever since Galileo turned his new telescope on to it in 1609. However, 360 years later a new era began when, on 18 July 1969, two members of the crew of the U.S. Apollo 11 mission stepped down on to the surface of the moon. There they made numerous novel observations, deployed certain notable experimental arrangements, and a few days later safely brought back to their base some 11 kg (24 lb) of lunar rocks and a similar quantity of lunar soil. Before the mission began there had been anxiety that lunar rocks and soil might conceivably carry organisms and spores which could be deadly to earth inhabitants. This was really only a remote possibility for there is no atmosphere on the moon, no water was expected, temperatures at the height of the lunar day could be 150°C and at the middle of the lunar night could well drop much lower even than −150° below zero, and added to that the intense radiations from the sun (not thinned out at all by any atmosphere, as on earth) would act as a fierce sterilising agent on any organisms. However, purely as a precaution, both the crew and the materials retrieved were strictly quarantined for 50 days and subjected to exhaustive biological testing. Plants, animals, and so on were all " infected " with moondust. It turned out to be completely sterile.

This being so a total of 7 kg of the retrieved material was distributed in selected small quantities to 150 scientific laboratories, for a meticulously planned examination; planned with the efficiency of a complex military operation. Most of the laboratories selected, chosen for their expertise and for their specialised equipment, were in the U.S.A.; some fourteen in Great Britain and a small handful in various other countries. Since in most of the laboratories selected, examination of the material was carried out by a multiple team, it will be seen that several hundred specialists, mainly geologists, mineralogists, chemists, and physicists (together with a strong force of technicians) pooled their skills into a well co-ordinated and concentrated attack on this precious unique cargo, which had been brought back at such enormous expense, from the south-western part of a region on the moon known as Mare Tranquillitatis, the location being 0·67° N and 23·49° E; that is to say from practically a lunar equatorial region.

Before the Apollo mission, the U.S. space team had successfully " soft-landed " spacecraft on the moon—the Surveyor craft. These had sent back some very excellent television pictures of the moon's surface which had indicated that the terrain was barren, pitted, and very foreboding. Furthermore, they had shown that, where they landed, the surface was covered with a firm soil capable of supporting some considerable weight. It was such information which encouraged the NASA organisation to go ahead with a landing and in the event this televised information proved to be absolutely reliable. Despite some expressed fears that a landing craft might sink in conjectured lunar dust, this did not happen, for the manned craft on arriving found a firm landing on soil-covered rock. As is now widely known, the astronauts spent several hours on the moon since they were expertly furnished with a fine life-supporting system. Communications were perfect between them (it had to be radio communication, of course, for there is complete silence on the airless moon) and indeed superb television pictures were sent back during the famous " moon-walk." A major objective was the retrieval of lunar material for study.

Three kinds of material were brought back, namely (i) rocks, (ii) fine surface " soil " scooped up into bags, and (iii) two cylindrical " cores " of soil obtained by hammering hollow tubes in to a depth of some 6 inches, the idea being to secure some evidence of stratified layers, if any. Much preparatory work and training went into the design of the collecting tools and the storage packages. In particular, contamination problems were studied, and in the end tools of stainless steel and plastic packings were found best. Since there is no atmosphere on the moon all the objects were effectively picked up in a first-class vacuum. They were therefore sealed in vacuum-tight containers which on return to earth were opened in a vacuum chamber. This was essential for those observations concerned with evaluation of slight gas content in the lunar material.

Considering the relatively trivial quantity of rock and soil recovered an astonishing number of basic scientific findings have already been made. In a conference on progress held in Houston in early January 1970 preliminary findings were announced. The expanded reports from this conference fill 3 massive volumes, a total of some 2,500 closely packed pages of measurements made over an extensive variety of geological, chemical and physical properties. In this article we pick out some of the highlights from this report.

Apparatus on the Moon.

The lunar mission was valuable for reasons other than the retrieval of the precious lunar material. The astronauts made very many notable visual observations which they recorded and brought back a mass of close-up photographs (in colour) showing rocks, etc., in situ before collection, information of very pertinent significance to the practical geologist. (Strictly speaking, one ought to talk of a " selenologist," not of a " geologist "). They noted physical properties of lunar soil, brought back comments on varieties of craters, conducted a brilliant original television transmission seen by the whole world, and successfully deployed three prepared experiments. The first was to set up a seismograph, a recorder of "lunar quakes," an equipment designed to tele-meter back to earth moon-quakes and trembles, if any. This functioned for three weeks and indeed sent back numerous strange signals. It is not clear yet whether these were due to meteor impacts or indeed to gurgling venting of residual fluids from the spacecraft left in the vicinity. The second experiment consisted in setting up a large light-reflector. Later, this functioned in a remarkably successful way. From the base on earth an extremely intense short pulse of light (from a special light source called a "laser") was sent to this reflector and the time taken for the light beam to reach it and get back was measured with the greatest precision. The time is only 2·5 seconds, but it can be measured to within a thousand-millionth of a second by modern devices. Since the speed of light is accurately known, this timing permits of an assessment of the *distance* to the moon with very high accuracy indeed. In fact with the first set of measurements already reported, the moon distance has been measured to within an error of only four metres! This astonishing performance opens up a new era in observing the orbit and wobblings of the moon. In future it is expected that scientists will be able to improve on this precision and measure the distance between the testing station and the reflector to within a mere 6 inches!

The third experiment set up by the astronauts was intended (and succeeded) to measure the constituent atoms in the "solar wind." It has for some time been recognised that the enormous high temperature activity of the sun leads to the hurling out from the sun of a vast "wind" of energetic atoms of various kinds. On earth, these are trapped in the upper atmosphere. The moon has no atmosphere, hence the solar wind atoms arrive on the surface, indeed they bombard it violently. Actually this was at one time considered a possible dangerous hazard for lunar astronauts, but since they were well protected, it proved innocuous. Something of the nature of the solar wind has been assessed by the experiment set up by the Apollo team. A sheet of aluminium foil of area 4 square yards was exposed on the moon to the sun's rays for one and a quarter hours. It received in addition to light the atoms from the solar wind which were caught and trapped in the aluminium. The foil was rolled up and brought back. When heated in a vacuum in the laboratory it released gas which had been trapped and by using highly refined testing methods the solar wind particles could be identified. In particular, atoms of helium, neon, and argon were found as constituents in the solar wind. This fact has had a considerable part to play in other observations carried out to attempt to assess the age of the moon, of which we shall write later. For similar gases have been found in lunar soil and the contribution of solar wind to these plays an important part in calculations made.

Direct Observations made by Astronauts.

On touch-down numerous craters were observed and described. Crater density is practically inversely proportional to size—the smaller the craters, the more abundant they are. In the neighbourhood of descent, craters ranged from 1 foot to 50 feet across. On a grander scale, of course, they range to sizes of hundreds of miles in diameter. The interest lies in the report of the *smaller* features not visible even to the largest telescopes on earth. On landing the engines stirred up a big obscuring stream of surface dust but no lingering cloud was formed. This was to be expected for on the moon, which has no gaseous atmosphere to support fine particles, the curious situation exists that a small piece of dust falls under gravity just as fast as a great boulder. The familiar dust clouds on earth owe their existence entirely to atmospheric support. In like fashion the astronauts noted later that when they kicked dust, it travelled surprisingly far, due both to the low gravity (one-sixth that

on earth) and to the absence of a resisting atmosphere.

Surface colours were reported to be variants of a chalky grey. Many boulders littered the scene. Most craters had raised rims but none were really sharp-edged. A considerable range of rock fragments were noted, some being partially hidden in the soil. Over the whole scene was soil looking like powdered graphite. It proved to cling to clothes and implements. Indeed it made the rocks slippery to foothold but it took very firm well-retained footprints, many of which appear on the surface pictures recorded. The top layer of the soil was distinctly of a lighter grey colour than the rest, the top one inch being quite distinctive. Below this, for some 6 inches, there was a sand-like zone. Later observation on retrieved material showed that the surface layer was largely microscopic particles. The difference in colour with layering is proof that some kind of surface alteration is going on despite absence of weathering (through absence of atmosphere). Possible causes of this are (i) radiation from the sun, (ii) bombardment continuously by micro-meteorites, (iii) changes due to fierce expansions and contractions occasioned by the gross temperature differences experienced once a month between lunar night and day.

Examination of Retrieved Rocks.

Once the retrieved lunar surface material had passed through the very strictly imposed biological quarantine, intensive studies of a considerable range of physical and chemical properties were initiated. Samples were sent for distribution to various laboratories, most of which had prepared in advance for the handling of the material. In the event, many of the researchers received samples of only 5 g each but, despite the relatively small quantities, astonishingly complete reports have appeared. Three distinctive types of material were brought back. The first kind was what the geologist calls crystalline igneous rock, arising in formation through heat processes. The second kind (widespread on earth) goes by the name of breccia. This is material consisting of small crystal fragments cemented together by a subsequent heating process. The third kind of material (usually called "fines") is in effect a soil consisting of quite small particles.

The crystalline igneous rocks appear to be of typical volcanic origin and do not differ outrageously from similar rocks found on the earth. They include many well-known earth minerals, known to the mineralogists as, for example, clinopyroxine, plagioclase, ilmenite, olivine, and so on; some native iron is present also. Very few *new* minerals have been detected although two minor ones appear certain. These include a mineral rich in the metal titanium (it has been named Armalcolite) and a new form of an iron-rich mineral called pyroferroxite. This poverty in new minerals compared with the earth must play its part in later theories about the origin of the moon. They bear on the question of whether the moon was spun off the earth or not.

However, a notable very distinctive feature is the presence of a remarkably large quantity of *glass* on the moon, glass in a variety of shapes and forms. True, some glass is (rarely) found on earth either volcanic in origin, or widely distributed in small individual lumps. The small individual lumps of glass found on earth are called *Tektites*, but none of the lunar glass at all resembles earth tektite glass. Not only is the lunar glass distributed in spatter lumps but in addition many of the retrieved rocks show numerous small glass-lined pits on the surface, pits perhaps two millimetres or more across. One obtains the strong impression that the rocks had been "shot blasted" with many small glass spheres (indeed we believe this is actually the case). Furthermore, on some rocks there are locally thin glass crusts, apparently created by the spatter impact of a larger molten glass globule. Many of the retrieved and observed rocks have rounded edges, as though they have been subjected to some *erosion* process, despite lack of atmosphere or weathering. They look, in fact, as if they had been rounded by a kind of "sand blasting" operation. Chemical examination seems to prove that the glass has been created by direct local melting of the lunar dust and the lunar breccia. However, the basic cause of glass formation remains as yet a problem.

One of the really important findings made on the retrieved minerals is that in *no case* whatsoever were there any crystals present which require *water of crystallization* as part of their structure. All crystals found are what the chemist calls, anhydrous. Clearly there is no water at all on the moon and there was none when the surface rocks were created. This finding is obviously closely associated with questions as to whether or not life existed on the moon in the past. Without air, without water, life as we know it sounds highly improbable.

It is considered by some of the investigators that lunar minerals are more like meteor minerals than earth minerals. Most investigators agree that the Apollo 11 rocks contain appreciably more of the metal titanium than corresponding earth rocks. (This might only be a local factor for the early results of the studies from Apollo 12 differ in this respect. There is less titanium metal than at Apollo 11.) There is plenty of evidence that many of the retrieved lunar minerals have experienced severe shock. When a crystalline material is subjected to severe impact or to a shock wave passing through it from a nearby explosive impact, recognisable deformations take place in the crystal structure. Such evidence together with the existence of a great deal of fragmented angular glass imply that the moon's surface has been exposed to a multitude of meteoric impacts, large and small, in the course of its complex history.

Duplicated chemical analysis shows that more than half of the known elements found on earth occur also in the lunar rock retrieved. This is even more than one could have anticipated from so restricted a region. As yet no *new* elements have been found. The fact that the surface has been exposed for immense ages to those fast particles from outer space called cosmic rays, has created in the surface layers an anticipated degree of radioactivity. This in turn has led to the formation of the atomic products following radioactive disintegrations of atoms.

The Age of the Moon's Surface.

A number of duplicated attempts of various kinds have been made to assess the *age* of the surface of the moon. There is relatively close agreement between the different approaches. The ages of rocks can be found by various methods, the best of these being based on measurements of what are called *isotope abundances*. An analogy might assist the uninitiated here. Suppose we imagine the existence of identical twins who look alike and behave alike but are slightly different in weight, indeed such that we can only distinguish one from the other by weighing. A similar situation happens among atoms. Take a metal like lead, for instance. There are three main kinds of lead atoms, all looking and behaving alike, but differing slightly in weight. These three kinds of atoms, which require special techniques to distinguish one from the other, are called *isotopes* of lead. Practically all types of atoms (whether gases like oxygen, solids like carbon, or metals like iron) have several isotopes. Some isotopes are very stable but others are not so stable. They tend to break up after a time and change to other kinds of atoms. This we call radioactivity and describe the culprit as a *radioactive isotope*. (*See also* **F10–11**).

Now the well-known metal potassium has an isotope which is weakly radioactive and this converts itself slowly into an isotope of the gas argon. The rate of transformation is very slow but it can be derived with certainty from various rules. If this kind of argon isotope be found in close association with potassium (and it cannot be confused with other kinds of argon) then from the amount present it is possible to calculate how long it has taken for the transformation process to have gone on to accumulate this particular amount. Unfortunately the calculation can be upset by the fact that argon is a gas and may drift away from the rock in which it is created. Also we do know that the solar wind is bringing in argon from outside. Nevertheless by this method an age for the rocks on the surface of the moon has been calculated to be about *3,000 million years*, not in fact very different from the age of earth rocks calculated in similar fashion. Another method of calculation involves the radioactive transformation of an isotope of the metal rubidium (found in moon rock) into an isotope of the metal strontium and this has given the quite near value of *3,700 million years*. Finally, the radioactive metal thorium (also in moon rocks) is known to transform itself into the metal lead (*see* **F11(2)**) and this method has given *4,900 million years* for the age. So more or less the result from the three methods lies somewhere between about 3,000 and 5,000 million years, a relatively close agreement. Since earth rocks are of somewhat similar age this information bears closely on the question of the origin of the moon.

One most significant finding is that the concentration of *carbon* is quite low, *i.e.*, some 200 parts per million. The *lunar* carbon in this particular region may even be a good deal less than that, because we can certainly expect some carbon in the solar wind, and in over 3,000 million years the solar wind may have brought in relatively substantial quantities of carbon. This very low carbon content has an important influence on theories as to whether or not there has ever been living material on the moon. Although no evidence of such has yet been found one must needs be cautious, since all the lunar material retrieved comes from one very small region and elsewhere things could be different.

The Lunar Soil.

The returned lunar soil, the fine-grain material, turns out to be of striking and unusual interest. It is grey in colour and a little denser than typical earth soil. It has, of course, no organic content and is a powdery material which sticks to anything with which it comes into contact. On the moon, the top six inches was easily penetrated, after which the soil became more resistant. Microscopic examination of all samples of the returned soil reveals most unexpectedly that perhaps *half* of it consists of finely broken down pieces of glass of varying colours. Included too can be up to a few per cent of finely dispersed free iron. Some of the iron is alloyed with nickel, in the typical fashion of iron in meteorites, and no doubt this has been brought in by outside meteorites. The existence *today* of *free* iron shows that it has remained in a completely airless and waterless situation on the moon. The glass fragments are shiny and show no corrosion either. Yet there is certain evidence which does very strongly suggest that there has been some *mechanical* mixing. This could well arise from prolonged repeated impact from a very large number of small meteoric bombardments over the ages. Such bombardments could also have created the glass, for glass is molten rock and any energetic impacts could locally raise the temperature to melt surface rock into glass. Succeeding impacts could then break down older glass pieces into tiny fragments, if such impacts were repeated often enough. This explanation is supported by the fact that the chemical composition of the soil material resembles that of the surrounding rocks, implying that the dust and soil have been created locally and not brought in from outside the moon, as some have thought. As already mentioned, there is of course *some* meteoric material also present. Some of the soil brought back has acquired magnetism. The cause is problematic as yet, for the moon today has hardly any magnetic field.

Undoubtedly the most striking property of the lunar soil is the presence in it of enormous numbers of small glass spheres (*glass "marbles"*) and equally huge numbers of glass cylinders, egg-shapes, pear-shapes, and dumbbell-shapes. If anything really highlights the special distinctive peculiarity of lunar soil it is these glass objects. Although by weight they only represent a few per cent of the soil mass, because of their very smallness they are there in vast numbers. Different kinds of glass spheres abound. Most are less than 1 millimetre across, although one of the photographs taken on the moon shows such an object about an inch across (the object itself was not retrieved). Both colour and degree of transparency of the glasses vary. The majority are amber coloured, some are grey, and pale greens and blues have also been found. The surfaces of the objects may be shiny and highly specular, or they can be coated with a hard dull layer of moon dust. Many objects have internal voids and vacuoles.

Chemical analysis shows that increasing depth in colour is usually associated with increasing content of titanium metal. The soil itself also contains angular glassy fragments similar in appearance and composition to the obviously melt-formed smooth spherules. Both the irregular grains and the spherules have, on occasion, free iron entrapped; thus such objects can be picked up with a hand magnet. The range of shapes and forms of the glassy objects is surprising. The writer of this article extracted by hand, from a mere 5 g of lunar dust, no less than 200 reasonably sized spherules and other shapes, merely using tweezers. If this be representative it means there are 40,000 such objects per kg of moon dust. But this is vastly outnumbered by the smaller similar objects easy to see under the microscope, which in the writer's sample reach the extraordinary number of 300,000,000 per kg of lunar soil.

Many of the larger spherules have been shown to have once been high-speed projectiles on the moon, probably having been violently ejected at formation as droplets of molten glass, through some fierce impact mechanism. Any satisfactory theory of the origin and formation of the lunar surface will have to account for the glassy spherules. (They are equally abundant at the Apollo 12 site, some 800 miles away.) While the *larger* glass spherules may be splashes from a melt created by impact, the tiny ones may have been formed through melting of glass fragments already in the moon dust, the melting having come about through radiation or conduction heating from some nearby meteoric impact event, of which there must have been vast numbers.

There is a great deal of past history locked up in the lunar soil and further researches and future lunar retrievals may supply the answers.

PLATE TECTONICS—A DYNAMIC MODEL FOR THE EARTH'S OUTER LAYERS.

Over the last few years we have developed a new way of looking at the geology of the earth's surface which gives a much clearer picture than we had before about how such features as ocean basins, continents, and mountain chains are related to one another, and how the earth's surface has developed during the several thousand million years of geological time. This article will explain first what this new model is, and how it works, and then describe the evidence that has persuaded most geologists that it does work. To avoid repetition it is assumed that the reader will consult Part I (F8–9) where the basic structure of the earth is described and technical terms explained. It will also be useful to be ready to turn to the Atlas section for maps of the parts of the world under discussion.

Plate Tectonics.

The surface of the earth can be divided into a number of plates of lithosphere (see **F8**) (hence the name for the theory—tectonics means the study of earth movements). These are rigid internally and active only on their edges. They range in size from a few thousand square km, to plates the size of North America, South America, and half of the Atlantic Ocean taken together. The plates are in constant motion relative to one another, so that any boundary between two plates is of one of three kinds, extensional (the plates are moving apart), compressional (they are moving together), and shearing (they are sliding past one another). These boundaries are marked by strings of earthquakes all concentrated in a

narrow zone, and these are the main locations of earthquakes, those within the plates being few, scattered, and weak. It is at the plate boundaries that geology really happens, where dynamic processes take place. The interiors of plates are marked by slow heavings and sinkings and by quiet deposition of sediment or quiet erosion, less dramatic processes by far than are found at the plate boundaries.

Plates Moving Apart.

At extensional plate boundaries, as the plates of lithosphere move apart, soft mantle material from the asthenosphere (see **F8**) wells up to fill in the gap. As it rises, it partly melts, and the lava comes to the surface as a volcanic scum, leading to the formation of a line of volcanoes along the plate boundary and resulting in a capping of solidified lava about 5 km thick on top of the cooled and rigid asthenosphere which has now become part of the lithosphere. This crust is the thin ocean crust, found everywhere in the deep ocean basins. Extensional plate boundaries thus lead to the formation of new ocean crust, and to the increase in area of the ocean basins. Such processes are happening in most of the world's ocean basins, where extensional plate boundaries are marked by broad gentle rises, such as the Mid-Atlantic Ridge that runs down the centre of the Atlantic Ocean from Iceland to the Azores, past Ascension Island and near Tristan da Cunha. Another great rise of this kind runs from the Red Sea, through the Gulf of Aden, across the Indian Ocean, around the south of Australia and New Zealand, across the Pacific past Easter Island and the Galapagos, ending up in the Gulf of California. Along these rises, and along many smaller ones, the plates are moving apart and creating new ocean crust. Especially interesting are the places such as the Red Sea, the Gulf of Aden, and the Gulf of California where continents have been split apart fairly recently (not more than 20 million years ago) and where new oceans are forming. In other places, such as Baffin Bay, it can be shown that extensional plate boundaries did exist at one time, but are now dormant.

Plates Sliding Past One Another.

Shearing plate boundaries, where plates slide past one another, are perhaps the most approachable kind of plate boundary. If the plates on both sides are continental, as they sometimes are, then shearing plate boundaries are marked by great faults on the earth's surface, which can be visited and inspected directly. Such faults are the San Andreas fault of California, the Alpine fault of New Zealand, and the North Anatolian fault of Turkey. Along these faults the two plates move inexorably past one another. Where the fault slips well, roads, walls, and railways running across it are slowly, steadily displaced at easily measurable rates of up to 10 cm per year. Parts of these faults stick, though, and in such places the stress in the rocks builds up, while the fault does not move. Eventually the stress breaks the blockage with a sudden sharp earthquake which may, if the accumulated strain is enough, be immensely destructive. Such an earthquake was the San Francisco earthquake of 1906 and similar earthquakes are associated with most other shearing boundaries.

Plates Moving Together.

Compressional plate boundaries, where the plates are coming together, are more complicated, but they have fundamental importance in the development of mountain belts and continents. The best approach is to consider the development of some hypothetical compressional boundary from the time it starts until it stops, while drawing parallels with plate boundaries in different stages of development in different parts of the world. Imagine a compressional plate boundary in an ocean basin, so that the crust on both sides of the boundary is oceanic. As compression involves shortening, one of the plates is over-ridden by the other and the over-ridden plate is pushed, or

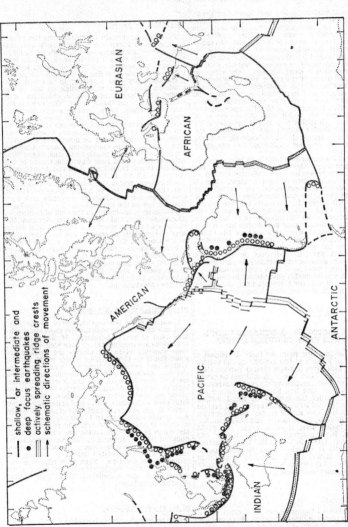

shallow, or intermediate and
deep focus earthquakes
actively spreading ridge crests
schematic directions of movement

Boundaries of plates superimposed on a map of the world. Extensional boundaries are marked by dotted lines within parallel lines,
giving a schematic idea of the rate of extension. Shearing boundaries are marked
Compressional boundaries are marked by full lines associated with circles indicating earthquakes.

slides, down into the mantle. This thrusting involves considerable friction, as might be imagined, and along the descending cold plate is developed a zone of earthquakes that represent fracture of the plate until such depths as it has warmed through enough to be incorporated in the soft asthenosphere. The frictional heating of the down-going slab causes the ocean crust attached to it to melt and form volcanic lava which rises to the surface to form a chain of volcanoes over the descending plate. In this initial stage, then, there is an ocean basin containing a chain of volcanic islands (an island arc), outside which is a deep trench, marking where the down-going plate disappears, and a zone of earthquakes (the Benioff zone) extends from the trench under the island arc. Such simple compressional plate boundaries are found in, for example, the Ryukyu arc between Japan and Formosa, the Caribbean arc in the West Indies, the Aleutian arc in the north Pacific. The next stage in the development of compressional plate boundaries, which may not occur for 100 million years or so, is that eventually a continent arrives at the boundary being carried on the plate which is being consumed. Now plate tectonics only make sense if we make an assumption here, a reasonable sounding one, but one not proved, that continental crust is too thick and too buoyant to be carried down the Benioff plane (i.e., downwards into the mantle) as oceanic crust is carried. At this stage the direction of the downward motion must reverse, so that the oceanic crust previously over-riding is now over-ridden, the island arc becomes welded on to the edge of the continent, and a new downward flow forms dipping under the continent. Now there is a deep trench next to the continental margin, a zone of earthquakes reaching under the continent, and a line of volcanoes along the edge of the continent. The continent has grown, too, by the addition of the island arc to its edge. This process happened a few million years ago when New Guinea collided with the Indonesian island arc, picked up the arc, and reversed the downward flow so that now it dips down under the continental crust of New Guinea. Such a process must also account for the trench along the west coast of South America and the volcanoes in the Andes.

Colliding Continents.

Eventually, at some still later time, a continent approaches carried on the oceanic plate that is now being consumed. This continent will be carrying with it a prism of sediments draped over its edge and on to the nearby ocean crust, formed by erosion of the continents and transport of material into the sea. As the two continents meet, neither can over-ride the other, they collide, squeezing up the prism of sediment between them into a mountain chain, and becoming welded together. The plate boundary is then destroyed, and both plates are joined together into one large one. Such an event is just ending in the Himalayas, where India has collided with Asia. Further in the past Italy collided with Europe to form the Alps, and 400 million years or so ago America collided with Europe to form the Caledonian mountain chain, fragments of which are found today from Spitzbergen through Norway, Greenland, Great Britain, Newfoundland, and as far south as Georgia. This chain was split apart later by the initiation of an extensional boundary that gave rise to the Atlantic Ocean.

This is essentially how plate tectonics works. It provides a new way of looking at changes taking place now, and those that have taken place in the past, and gives a framework that relates oceans, mountain chains, and continents together as different sides of the same process.

As far as can be estimated at present, the rate of creation of new crust at extensional plate boundaries is balanced globally by the rate of destruction of crust at compressional plate boundaries. The surface area of the earth seems to be remaining about the same, but some oceans, such as the Atlantic and the Indian Ocean are growing, while the Pacific is shrinking. The area of the continents is gradually increasing by the welding on of island arcs to their edges, and so the ratio of ocean area to continental area is gradually decreasing. Rates of relative movement between plates can be measured and appear to be between several millimetres and several centimetres per year. Thus the Atlantic at the latitude of the British Isles is widening at a rate of 2 cm per year (= 20 km per million years).

Evidence for Movement.

The evidence that the plates are moving as has been described is rather complex, but some pieces are more easily described than others. The simplest of all is the fit of the continents. Clearly if continents have been split open by extensional plate boundaries, the two edges of the split should match when they are brought together in the direction along which the extensional movement has happened. Such a fit can be demonstrated for the North Atlantic continents, Europe, Scandinavia, Greenland, and North America, and, most spectacularly, for South America and Africa across the South Atlantic. Other fits that have been successful are the two sides of the Red Sea and the Gulf of Aden, and those of the Gulf of California.

It is possible, by examining the records of the earthquake waves from a single earthquake at a large number of receiving stations at different places to determine the orientation of the fracture in the earth, the fault on which the movement of the earthquake has taken place, and the direction of this movement. If plate movement is taking place, then the fault orientation and direction of movement on the fault should be consistent with the predicted plate movement. This is found to be the case wherever it is attempted, and provides a further piece of evidence.

More technical evidence comes from investigating the earth's magnetic field. Surveys by ships towing magnetometers that measure the strength of the earth's magnetic field from place to place show that, parallel to the mid-ocean ridge crests, the postulated extensional plate boundaries, are long linear magnetic anomalies. These are areas in which the magnetic field is either stronger or weaker than is expected, and they are caused by the magnetism of the rocks at the bottom of the oceans. The size of the anomalies observed is greater than would be expected from reasonable variations in the magnetic properties of the rocks, and their origin was for some years a mystery. However, it became clear that the earth's magnetic field had periodically reversed its direction at different times in the past, so that the north magnetic pole became the south magnetic pole and vice versa. Measurements of the direction of magnetisation of volcanic lavas together with determination of their ages by their content of radioactive elements enabled a magnetic time scale to be built up showing epochs in which the magnetic field had the same direction as now separated by epochs in which the field was reversed. The lengths of these epochs in the last 5 million years range from a few thousand years to a few hundred thousand years, and they fall into a characteristic irregular pattern.

Now, if new volcanic crust is being continuously created at extensional plate boundaries, then, when the magnetic field is in one direction a strip of crust magnetised in that direction will be formed, and later, when it reverses, a strip magnetised in the opposite direction will be formed. So a pattern of strips should result reflecting both the magnetic time scale and the rate of extension at that plate boundary. Comparison of the observed linear magnetic anomalies with calculations based on this model showed that by this means the magnetic anomalies could be accounted for without demanding extraordinary magnetic properties in the ocean floor rocks. The anomaly pattern fits the reversal time scale very closely, and is symmetrical on each side of the plate boundary. Thus this is strong evidence that creation of ocean crust at extensional plate boundaries does take place. Conversely, it also allows estimates of the rate of extension to be made wherever magnetic surveys over extensional plate boundaries are available, by comparing the magnetic anomaly pattern with the reversal time scale. By this means the rate of plate movements can be determined.

Finally, there has recently been a series of holes drilled through the sediments in the deep oceans by the American JOIDES project. This has involved positioning a drilling barge using a ring of engines around its circumference, and letting a drill string down through the five or so kilometres of water to the ocean floor, where it drills and cores on instructions from the surface. Two main results relevant to the plate tectonics hypothesis have come out of this project. First, as would be expected on the hypothesis, the oceans are all very young. The oldest sediment so far recovered is no more than 180 million years old, while many continents are more than 2,500 million years old. Second, a series of holes was drilled across the South Atlantic at points where the magnetic anomalies indicated that the ocean crust was of well-defined age, if the plate tectonics hypothesis was correct. The holes drilled through the sediments and into the volcanic rocks beneath, and in each case the date of the oldest sediment in the hole agreed very closely with the date suggested by the magnetic anomalies for the crust at that site. This was concrete evidence of a kind very different from the inferential evidence of magnetic anomalies, earthquake waves, and continental fitting, and finally convinced many geologists who had up to then been uncertain that plate tectonics was a reasonable hypothesis and that plate movements are happening. Some remain unconvinced, but it is probably true to say that most geologists nowadays are willing to use plate tectonics as at least a working hypothesis.

Mechanisms for Plate Movements.

The situation in plate tectonics at the moment is that, while most people are convinced that plate tectonics is a useful way of describing the evolution and development of the earth's surface, very few agree on what forces drive the plates, initiate motion and continue it so inexorably over such long periods of time. For some this is an intellectual stumbling block—unless they can be convinced of a mechanism for plate movements, they are unwilling to agree that plates can move at all. But it is difficult to justify this point of view. The same people find no difficulty in using the Law of Gravitation, even though it is not at all clear how gravity works or why it works in the way it does. However, the search for a mechanism has a certain fascination, and should be touched on for the sake of completeness.

Mechanisms proposed so far fall essentially into three classes, convection currents, pushing mechanisms, and pulling mechanisms. The convection current hypothesis holds that the mantle of the earth is stirred by slow-moving convection currents, and that these are, directly or indirectly, responsible for plate movements. Although the transfer of material in plate movements is rather like convection, with hot material coming up at extensional boundaries and cold material going down at compressional boundaries, the shape of the plates is unlike any reasonable convection flow pattern, and other difficulties are also found. Pushing mechanisms suppose that plates are elevated by expansion in the mantle at extensional boundaries, and then slide off sideways, pushing the rest of the plate ahead. Pulling mechanisms, on the other hand, postulate that as the ocean crust slides down the Benioff zone at converging boundaries, it becomes transformed to a very dense material, which then sinks, pulling the rest of the plate after it.

All of these mechanisms are unsatisfactory in one way or another. Possibly the answer lies in some combination of them, or perhaps in some mechanism yet to be thought of. There does appear, however, to be general agreement that the only source for the energy necessary to move the plates is the heat of the earth's interior, and as this becomes better understood, the mechanisms should become clear.

MUSEUMS OF SCIENCE AND TECHNOLOGY

Aims, Possibilities, and Problems.

A museum has no purpose which is not ultimately educational, and the basic philosophy of a museum man must include the belief that the study of what other people have done and are doing stimulates the intellect and the imagination, and provides signposts (and no entry signs) along the way of a creative life. If such a philosophy seems at variance with some current educational theory, which lays stress on discovering for oneself rather than on learning by the experience of others, and also seems to ignore the marked preference of the young for making their own mistakes, then the museum man must fortify himself by studying the attendance figures. He will find that museums are becoming more popular every year.

It is difficult to discern any trends towards particular types of collections in this increasing popularity. In London, the Science Museum draws the largest attendance, but it has done so for a long time, and there is no sign that there has been a swing away from the Art museums. There is no evidence that increasing popularity is a result of museums being better than they were. Drab, unmodernised galleries are quite as well filled as some colourful and spacious ones, and the Pitti Palace in Florence demonstrates that crowds will still come to a picture gallery where half the pictures on display simply cannot be seen. To a museum man the present situation presents an opportunity rather than a cause for self-congratulation.

Museums of science and technology are in one respect better placed than art museums or museums of local history, when it comes to educating this large and variously motivated public. The things they display not only need interpretation, but can be seen to need it. The Science Museum has a century-old tradition of long and learned labels, the first paragraphs of which may suffice for the less curious, and are devised to do so, while the full extent may even finish with suggestions for further reading. These long labels are sometimes criticised for being aimed at a very small minority of visitors, or on the general ground that a label cannot be devised to suit a wide variety of types of readers, or (perhaps most often) for spoiling the look of the display. There is something in all of these criticisms, but they are more likely to be met by more and better labels than by reducing these to the level of descriptiveness typified by the time honoured phrases " primitive passerine bird " or "Flemish, 15th cent."

Museum Education Departments.

It is not surprising that, among our national museums, the Science Museum and the Natural History Museum should have the busiest education departments concerned with the exploitation of the museum collections for purposes of formal education. Both museums deal largely with subjects which figure in school and university curricula. In the Science Museum, a noticeable consequence of the broadening of educational minds in recent years is the large demand for tours and lectures for history students, and also the frequent requests for lectures on light, colour, materials, and design for art students. This last illustrates the kind of useful extra-curricular activity which becomes possible when the museum education department has a high reputation and a firm base of regular demand upon which to build. The assurance of a large " clientèle " makes it worth while to arrange special series of lectures for older children, given by invited lecturers from industrial or university research departments. It is also possible to arrange a regular programme of scientific films and to offer the general public a range of entertainments on a far more lavish scale than would otherwise be justified.

The growth of the education service in the Science Museum has almost certainly been due to difficulties within the schools. There have been shortages of qualified teachers and of equipment. These shortages have persisted and even grown worse, while science itself has advanced faster than before. This is a situation in which one museum, however great, can do very little, even though it is exploring ways of spreading its influence by publications, by opening its galleries to the television teams, by training teachers and staff for other museums. It is quite clear that every scientific museum in the country, including general museums with considerable scientific, technological or industrial collections, could find work to do in this field.

One important point must be stressed. The education department must not be a poor relation within the museum, grudgingly afforded a little unused space and staffed by seconded teachers widely regarded as unwelcome by the rest of the staff. Such has been the case occasionally in the past, but where the job to be done is of such importance, it must be done by people of high intellectual calibre, whose role in the museum is not merely that of exploiters but no less that of advisers. These are the people who will have the greatest contact with the thoughtful visitors, of all ages, and who will represent the management of the museum in the eyes of most of its public. Their ideas for the improvement of the collections will come from their practical experience of the value of those collections to the most interested people, and their knowledge of the subjects will be enriched by contact with many visitors who have specialised knowledge of those subjects.

What Do the Visitors Want?

Even in the Science Museum, group visits account for less than 10% of total attendance. It would be extremely difficult to do a statistical analysis of the motivations of the rest, and it has not been attempted. Some indications have been given by casual visitors to public lectures on Saturday afternoons. As these represent perhaps 2% of visitors on that day, and a probably unrepresentative sample at that, undue importance cannot be attached to what they said, but, at least, over some years these people have given answers conforming to the same pattern.

There were always a few who had come specially to attend the lecture because they were interested in the subject. They were invariably people who had visited the museum before, most of them frequently. All the rest had come to the lecture because they were in the museum and had seen the lecture publicised within the building. The question then put was: why had they come to the museum? The rather vague answers provided by this predominantly adult set of people suggested that almost all had been before and thought the museum a splendid place. About a third had an evident desire to increase their store of knowledge. The rest simply wished to experience pleasure of a not very intellectual kind, by seeing things of beauty (which are not the sole prerogative of art museums), by seeing other people, by enjoying the comforting sensations of man's greatness and even by feeding national pride. Such motives are not to be despised, and would suffice for poets, novelists, and even painters, but a curious point is that very few of these people made a habit of visiting art museums, whereas, among the more purposeful third this was quite common.

A possible reason for the popularity of the Science Museum, and of other museums such as the Museum of British Transport, with relatively unmotivated visitors, is that such museums approach history, or science, or art, via the workaday world in which they feel at ease and able to contribute some understanding. The art museums start right at the top, with what are usually the products of an élite for an élite, and on the assumption that we needs must love the highest when we see it, devote more care to presentation than to interpretation. The result is often a good deal of public embarrassment. Even though this division of museums into two kinds is an absurd oversimplification, it remains true that practically everything in any museum can be made more accessible to the public by treating it as if it were a scientific mystery rather than a self-evident masterpiece.

Organisation of Collections

The smaller the museum the smaller the problem when it comes to organisation of collections, but the greater the challenge of trying to turn scraps of information into a body of knowledge for the visitor to acquire. No fact contributes to knowledge if it stands alone and a small scientific

H (80th Ed.)

collection requires contextual material if it is to engage the attention of any but the most informed and dedicated student. Many small museums have specialised collections of scientific material, often the gift of a local collector of notability. It is easy to see how such a collection of, for instance, early photographs and equipment can be vitalised by putting it in the context of the history of photography, certainly, but also of optics, of photochemistry, and of art, and by aiming eventually to include cinematography and such aspects as photolithography. In this way even a single collection can enhance its value to the casual or purposeful visitor immeasurably.

The aim of a small museum in the scientific field should be in some way to expand, because there is virtue in sheer size and variety. This adds the element of comparison to that of context and so increases the intellectual stimulus, but, of course, it increases the problems of organisation and of interpretation. The extreme example of this is the Science Museum, where the richness of the collections makes it possible to put most of the objects into several different contexts. However, only one basic set of references can be used for the physical layout of the galleries, so the museum is arranged according to some fifty subject divisions. Even these require some duplication of material.

It is perhaps in unravelling another fifty subjects from the same material that the education service performs a task peculiarly its own. These subjects are partly perfectly obvious academic-type ones, such as electronics, kinematics, or wave mechanics, and lead the student (of electronics, for example) through collections labelled Atomic Physics, Radio and Television, X Rays, Navigation, Time Measurement and Mathematics. They may deal with particular materials, such as rubber or plastics, or with periods of history. Ideally, a museum of great size should have ways of referring its visitors to all these paths of knowledge which lead over many different fields, preferably by means of publications but perhaps also by means of large photographic displays.

A museum which is not too large or too crowded, and which takes its educational function seriously, might well dispense entirely with the practice of imposing a logical physical organisation on its collections. The assumption would have to be made that every visitor would be equipped with the particular guide to suit his requirements. It could be argued that it is more economic to print more guides than to attempt to coax awkward material into possibly unpractical juxtapositions. The advantage from the point of view of display and of convenience within the building would be great, but the intellectual advantage might be still greater. It is becoming increasingly important that young scientists and engineers should not be trained to think along the lines of a single subject or part of a subject, but should be aware of the possibility of other ways of thinking. Not only will this make them better scientists in the first place—it will also equip them better to reapply their scientific training in another field should this be necessary.

Types of Exhibit.

A particular difficulty confronting museums of science and technology is the extraordinary variety and extreme range of size of their objects on view. A locomotive may weigh 100 tons, and an insect be only visible through a microscope. This immediately poses the question of whether a model of the locomotive would not do as well, or a microphotograph of the insect. The answer to this is no, but in some cases it is only no by a narrow margin. It depends upon the visitor. There is a type of visitor who comes to a museum especially to see the real thing. In the case of the insect reality is already once removed by the microscope, but it is still worth while to display one or two in this way, and to back them up with a large collection of photographs of other varieties. In the case of the locomotive, size is of its essence, too, and its beauty (or ugliness) is partly scale dependent, as is all beauty. Its relationship to the men that handled it and crawled about it is historical evidence, and its technology is far more readily grasped in the full size. Finally, at the present time it can be obtained for about half the price of a fine quality model (and if a museum model is not of fine quality it is useless).

There is a type of museum exhibit which is not a proper museum piece at all, but a didactic display or demonstration. One way of using such material is to explain an adjacent museum piece. This is really an extension of the label. The other way of using such demonstration pieces is to arrange a series of them as a complete lesson in some subject. This has been done quite admirably in some museums, but it can be best done in a lecture theatre, with a lecturer who can answer questions. Unless a museum is built specially as a teaching tool, this kind of thing should be planned to put the museum pieces proper into context.

Inevitably, museum pieces will mean different things to different people. A piece of eighteenth century apparatus—a Herschel telescope perhaps —will be an optical instrument to some, a personal relic of a great man to others, a symbol of astronomical discovery, a piece of elegant furniture, or an interesting example of a mechanical handling device to others again. It is all those things, and its presentation and labelling should at least not obscure any of its qualities. Museum objects sometimes reveal fresh qualities when modern developments make the ideas behind them appear prophetic. Exactly this has happened to Babbage's calculating machines in the Science Museum, now seen as the intellectual forerunners of the electronic computer.

A recurring anxiety of the museum man in the scientific field is "how up to date can we be?" A small, specialised museum should try to keep pace with developments in its field, even though this may involve discarding material which eventually proves to have been of ephemeral interest. The public will expect this of the museum. But for an establishment of the size of the Science Museum this is simply impossible. It must be highly selective in its choice of topicalities, not only in trying to judge their long-term significance, but equally in judging their essential suitability for museum treatment. As an example, organ transplant operations, though highly topical recently, simply do not lend themselves to museum display.

What Should the Public Think?

This is the question the museum man should not ask. The museum should present facts. If it cannot avoid opinions then alternative theories must be aired. The museum should not try to impose an itinerary on its visitors or do anything to make a visit less happy for those who come to browse, to make their own discoveries, to watch the children or admire the architecture. The public must feel at home and welcome.

The museum authorities should make sure that the discoveries are there to be made. They should open as many inviting paths of investigation as possible. The paths should be there, and maps should be on sale. The evidence should be on display. If any attempt is made to go beyond this, the public will cease to enjoy the museum.

Science Museums and the Others.

Art museums are full of obviously beautiful things. Historical museums are often enlivened by reconstructed period rooms, bright costumes, and amusing bygones. Museums of science and technology are less well endowed, superficially, in these respects. Therefore their display techniques need to be very advanced. Generally the objects look best by being well lit and austerely presented, but the rooms or galleries require very careful treatment, to give the impression of an agreeable place to be in, with a little curiosity about what is round the corner, but no sense of being hurriedly drawn on. It is better for the visitor to come again than to feel he has to see it all. In the Science Museum, there is no chance that he will ever see it all—it would be a full time job for two years.

The staff of a scientific museum should hope that their visitors visit other museums as well. From textile machinery to woven fabrics is a natural enough progression, as from chemistry to cera-

mics. The arts cannot be properly understood without the sciences, and every artist or craftsman is a technologist too. The visitor who looks at Victorian furniture in one museum and at a Victorian locomotive in another may well decide that the locomotive is the more artistic.

Ultimately all museums which are not solely devoted to natural history are museums of human ideas. As such, they have similarities greater than their differences.

GRAMOPHONE RECORDS PAST AND PRESENT.

Preamble.

For countless centuries, man has sought to make permanent records of his emotions and of the events that have encompassed him. By way of the graphic and tactile arts, at first crude and sketchy but later touching the heights of masterpiece, and by way of the critical achievement of learning to write, man has evolved means of communicating not only with his contemporaries but with future generations also. With time, the earlier technologies of painting oils and printing inks, of engraving and casting, led to the more modern one of photography: the "still" and the "movies". All these developments over aeons of time had one feature in common: they were silent. Even the sheet of music was in some respects no more than the transcript of a speech, a set of instructions for the musician to produce his own version of the composer's first performance, as best he could.

Not surprising then that during the latter half of the nineteenth century, many inventors sought to make permanent records of actual sounds— speech as uttered, music as performed, and songs sung. The concept was essentially the making of a "sound record" which could be caused to *reproduce* the original sound.

Acoustic Recording.

The first fifty years, or thereabouts, of such recording was the era of "acoustic recording." The name, not a very happy one, refers to the use of a direct mechanical linkage between a receptor for the incident sound—invariably a horn terminating in a diaphragm, the latter performing the same function as the ear-drum in that it vibrates in sympathy with the sound pressure vibrations—and a small pointed or chisel-ended tool, the purpose of which is to cut or to indent the surface of the recording medium. The process of converting a quantity of one kind, in this case an alternating "acoustic" pressure, into another, in this case a mechanical vibration, is termed transduction. In the ideal transducer, the changes and variations in its output (the mechanical vibration) are exactly in unison with the changes and variations of its input (the pressure alternation).

Mary Had a Little Lamb: the Phonograph.

All acoustic recording machines made use of such an acoustic-mechanical transducer, in one form or another. Of these precursors of the modern gramophone, the earliest which was in any sense commercially viable was that developed in the U.S.A. by Edison in 1877–8, arising from an earlier experimental apparatus of his, into which he had spoken, and reproduced, a nursery rhyme.

Edison's machine was the Phonograph, in which the cutting tool, a ball-tipped stylus, bore on to a wax cylinder. The cylinder was rotated (by hand originally, later by a clockwork mechanism), and the stylus vibrated in an up-and-down direction so as to indent the wax. Because the wax surface was in motion, it was indented more or less deeply by the stylus to give an undulating track. This mode of recording, named technically "vertical displacement" recording, is often referred to more evocatively as hill-and-dale recording. To produce the sound which initiated the indentations, it was necessary to reverse the function of the transducer. This was done by setting the stylus back to the commencement of the track it had made, and by rotating the cylinder once more. The track itself was made to form a spiral on the surface of the cylinder by attaching the horn and stylus to a lead screw arrangement, identical in principle to that of a screw-cutting lathe.

The Gramophone Proper.

One very serious limitation of the Edison machine was that, although it made a permanent if crude recording, this recording could not be duplicated or copied. In present-day jargon, each recording was " a one-off." Fortunately for the gramophile, there was an almost concurrent introduction of Berliner's Gramophone. This used a transducer similar to that of the Phonograph, but there were important differences. The rotating element was not a cylinder, but a disc; the stylus moved " sideways ", not " up and down ", so as to make a lateral-displacement recording rather than a vertical one; and the recording medium, the disc, was of wax-coated zinc.

The way was now clear to copy recordings: using a technique borrowed from the electrotype trade, the recorded disc was coated with graphite and then thickly electroplated. When the electroplate was peeled off it did, of course, carry the groove pattern in relief, so that it could be used as a die by means of which copy recordings could be pressed. In essence, this is the way in which recordings are copied today, although many refinements to ensure exact copying have been developed. Many curious recipes were at first used for the pressing material, which eventually emerged as one of several mixes of three main ingredients: shellac, lamp black as a lubricant, and a filler such as slate or mica dust. The mixture was necessarily thermoplastic, albeit made up of natural compounds, in order that it could be pressed while hot and soft.

Progress could now be made to improve the basic inventions: better spring-drive motors to give more constant pitch to the recorded sound (spurious pitch variations are referred to, also evocatively, as wow and flutter); changes in the mix of materials used for the pressings, so as to reduce both the background noise, or needle hiss, and also the wear; and many substantial improvements in the transducers.

Since the copy recording or " pressing " could now be played on a separate machine, it was possible to design one transducer—the cutter head—to cut the master recording, and another—called the sound box—to replay the pressings. Much inventive talent was expended in the design of these transducers and their associated acoustic horns.

" Electric Recordings."

The crucial limit to indefinite improvement was the fact that, in the recording process, all the work done in displacing the cutting stylus had to be carried out by the sound wave. Similarly, on replay, the force necessary to actuate the diaphragm of the sound box had to be transmitted (from the driving motor) via the walls of the groove and the needle. All this militated against refinements of design which could yield better high-frequency response, lower non-linearity distortion, and reduced pressures at the needle tip. However, by the mid-nineteen-twenties, the technology of electronics was exploding: the radio valve was being developed and exploited for all communication purposes, so that in 1924 a new form of cutter-head was invented by Maxfield and Harrison. It was essentially an electromagnetically operated stylus, wherein a varying electrical current rather than a sound wave caused the stylus to vibrate. This was an electromechanical transducer, and so a second transducer, an acousti-electrical one, was necessary. The latter already existed as the microphone, the electrical output from which could be magnified by a valve amplifier before it was fed to the cutter head.

Electric recordings, as they were called by the ad. men, facilitated another large improvement in recording quality. The microphone was a comparatively small design problem on the acoustical side and once it had turned the sound waves into corresponding electrical currents, the forces required by the cutting stylus, however large, could be provided by way of the recording amplifier. Furthermore, it became simple to make the degree of amplification, or gain, depend on the sound frequency, so as to compensate for deficiencies in, for example, the cutter head or microphone.

Electrical Pick-ups.

Within the next decade, by the mid-thirties, the equivalent of the electrical sound box—the gramophone pick-up—had also come into common use. This transduced the mechanical vibrations of the needle into electrical signals which could be amplified, and thence made audible in a loudspeaker. Its impact on quality of reproduction was dramatic. The use of frequency-dependent gain could be further extended, not only to correct for deficiencies, but also to record and replay over a much wider spectrum of frequencies. Hitherto, it had not been practicable to reproduce sound much lower in pitch than about the octave below middle C. Primarily this was because, in order to reproduce a sound pressure which is constant at every frequency (in order to give a constant sound intensity), the lateral displacement, or sideways movement, of the stylus must be inversely proportional to frequency. Therein is a fact of acoustical life, and if this inverse frequency law were applied rigorously, it would follow that as the pitch of a sound is lowered, groove displacement would have to increase in proportion. That is, for each octave reduction in frequency, the groove displacement must double! If the low frequencies were not selectively attenuated during recording, one groove would break into its neighbours on fortissimo passages, unless the groove spacing were to be unacceptably coarse. Indeed, the choice of groove spacing was, and to some extent remains, a compromise between groove isolation and length of playing time. So the bass frequencies were attenuated during the recording process; and whereas with acoustic replay there was virtually no simple way of recovering them, the electrical replay chain could be compensated (equalised) to give extra amplification to the low frequencies and thus make good the deficiencies in the low notes.

For the reason explained above, the weight borne by the needle of a sound-box was necessarily large—often many hundreds of grammes. The pick-up, with its succeeding amplifier, could do much better than this, since its needle did not have to move a diaphragm and a large mass of air. Early pick-ups tracked with a playing weight of 10–30 g, and today a weight of 5 g would be thought excessive, 0·5–2 g being usual.

Again, reducing the demand for work to be done by the moving parts of the pick-up meant that these could be very much smaller, lighter, and more freely moving. These reductions in both effective mass and stiffness in turn made it possible, and indeed desirable, to abandon the traditional needle, replacing it by a minute jewelled tip attached directly to the moving part of the transducer. The stylus is then capable of tracing the groove pattern at much shorter wavelengths (higher frequencies) than hitherto. In early days of electrical recording, the highest recorded frequency was probably not much greater than 4 kHz (3 octaves above middle C): at the inner part of a 78 rpm disc, the wavelength is then about 20 micrometres, or 5 thousandths of an inch. Today, despite the reduced turntable speeds, the upper limit of recording is usually not less than 16 kHz, the concomitant wavelength near the inner grooves of a 33⅓ rpm record being less than 3 micrometres, or 0·7 thousandths of an inch.

f.f.r.r.

By the mid-1940s, the limit of the traditional shellac-base pressing had been reached with the introduction of the Decca " full frequency range " recordings. These incorporated a somewhat smaller groove than normal, to improve short-wavelength tracing; a degree of high-frequency pre-emphasis, whereby the higher frequencies are relatively increased, or emphasised, during recording, so allowing a corresponding de-emphasis to be arranged for in the replay amplifier to reduce needle-hiss; a variable-pitch* recording, such that on loud passages the groove spacing is automatically increased, thereby allowing some relaxation of the need to compress the dynamic range; and a modified bass characteristic. These measures produced a worthwhile gain in record quality, but they were within two years to be followed by a comprehensive re-think on the conventional 78 rpm shellac disc.

(*The word " pitch " above is ambiguous in the disc recording context: it can refer to the physical concomitant of frequency or, as here, to the number of grooves per inch of radius, by analogy to screw threads, the pitch of which is the distance between adjacent turns of the thread.)

l.p.

This re-appraisal exercise was carried out by Goldmark of the American Columbia Company. Its object was to increase the playing-time of the disc, so as to minimise the need for breaks in the reproduction of most classical music, and to lessen one of the principal remaining limitations of the disc recording: the need to restrict the range of loudness that could be handled—a limitation known as compressing the dynamic range. Compare an early pre-l.p. recording with a recent version of the same work, and observe how, in the earlier recording, the loud passages are held in check and the soft passages rendered less so. This is volume compression in action, necessary to overcome groove-jumping on the fortissimi and to ride the signal above the surface noise at the pianissimo end of the loudness scale.

The outcome of Goldmark's work was introduced as the Microgroove recording, now simply referred to as the l.p., or long-playing record. The immediate step towards longer playing time is speed reduction, and this was effected by making the speed 33½ rpm instead of 78 rpm, a time gain of 2·3. Speed reduction, however, carries with it the penalty of shorter wave-lengths. To make these more readily traceable by the stylus, the groove profile was considerably reduced in size; it called for a new standard in stylus profiles also. The stylus for the 78 rpm disc had terminated in a spheroidal tip of radius 2·5–3·0 thousandths of an inch. The new styli had tips of radius not more than 1 thousandth inch. A bonus of the smaller groove was that more grooves per inch could be cut, yielding a further useful increase in playing time, which in the event increased from about 4 minutes to about 20 minutes, for a 12-inch disc, a time improvement of 5.

Shorter wavelengths, even if they are made traceable, exacerbate the surface noise problem, because the desired deviations of groove become more comparable with the undesired irregularities stemming from the granularity of the mix. So the shellac/carbon black/filler formulae were abandoned, to be replaced by a modern synthetic thermoplastic, a co-polymer of polyvinyl acetate and polyvinyl chloride (F24(1)). The poly-merised vinyls are at once smoother, more friction-free, and less brittle than the traditional mixes. Their use, particularly if associated with the lubricant lamp-black and a non-granular filler, not only improves the wear properties, but most importantly reduces the surface noise many times; sufficiently, that there could be a downward extension of recording level on quiet parts of the programme, to the benefit of the dynamic range. Variable-pitch recording and h.f. pre-emphasis were perpetuated.

In total, these substantial changes to the gramophone record yielded the following improvements:

    increased playing time
    reduced tracing distortion
    increased dynamic range
    somewhat improved frequency range
    reduced needle-hiss
    reduced breakage-rate.

It is true that l.p. discs are somewhat more vulnerable to the careless finger nail or the dropped pick-up, that they readily acquire an electro-static charge which attracts dust particles, and that dust is more offensive in the microgroove than in the standard groove. But the achievement of their introduction was hardly less significant than the inception of electric recording itself.

As a postscript to this short account of the l.p. disc, the 45 rpm record should be mentioned. It emerged from the Radio Corporation of America a year after the Columbia innovation. It used a similar fine groove and was pressed from similar material. Its speed was technically slightly better than that of the l.p. disc; and its thickened centre, its very large bore and its 7 inch diameter were all tailored to suit a novel automatic record changer with a simple, cheap, and extremely rapid change mechanism. It offered an alternative approach to the long-play problem. The record changer has long since gone out of production, but the discs persist as a medium for short programmes, notably of the pop kind.

" Stereo."

The possibilities of the l.p. record and modern pick-ups were further exploited during the 1950s, when more or less successful attempts were made to diffuse the concentrated source of sound which a single loudspeaker represents. The name given to these ventures is stereophony, and the object is to simulate the distributed source formed by a group of musicians, a stage of actors, and so on, by a limited number of independent signal channels, each terminating in one or more loudspeakers.

The early history of stereophony is bound up with the fact that typical headphones have two earpieces, each of which can supply sound signals to its ear independently of the other. Two microphones in the positions normally occupied by the ears, two signal channels and the two ear-pieces give a very satisfactory sensation of sound location, and the system is named a binaural one.

If, however, loudspeaker facilities are required, and for reasons of personal if not social convenience they usually are, it is necessary to generate stereophonic signals by means more technically sophisticated. This is certainly true if the number of channels is not to be excessive; and there are good commercial reasons why the number of channels is restricted to two.

The fundamental work on the processing of signals to yield two-channel stereophony was done by the late A. D. Blumlein, of E.M.I. Ltd., his original patent being dated 1931. The fertility and soundness of his ideas were stunted by the limitations of contemporary pick-ups and discs; they had to wait on the development of the magnetic tape and the l.p. disc. These having been achieved, stereophonic tapes and discs appeared from 1955 onwards. Stereo discs, surviving some very crude attempts emanating from the U.S.A., are now, at their best, superb.

However the stereo signals are processed in the recording studio, and there is more than one thought on this matter, what is eventually applied to the two-channel recording machine is a pair of signals designated as L and R, for Left and Right, respectively. These two signals separately modulate a single groove by causing the stylus simultaneously to cut what is in effect both a hill-and-dale recording and a lateral recording. The stylus is acted upon by two transducing elements at right angles, so that its vibration is partly vertical and partly lateral. It would seem simplest to make the vertical and lateral recordings carry separately the L and R signals. For a number of technical reasons this is not done. The transducers, mutually at right angles, are each inclined at 45° to the record surface, so that the groove walls, also inclined at 45°, separately receive the L and R information. Replay with an element which is purely lateral-responsive, i.e., a monophonic pick-up, therefore generates a mixed (L + R) signal. The mode is called 45/45 recording.

On replay, the stereo pick-up stylus performs a similar, compound vibration, and its two trans-ducers, similarly at right angles, resolve the motion such that the L and R signals re-appear at the pick-up's two pairs of output terminals. Thereafter the L and R are amplified in identical channels before application to a pair of loud-speaker systems. The designed-for differences in arrival times and intensities of the two signals can then give a subjective effect of sound distribution, valid over a reasonable area in front of the loudspeakers.

Tomorrow.

The superiority of the modern l.p. over the original Berliner records is very clear, in respect of every important performance criterion. The scratchy, sub-telephone quality of the early discs has to be compared with the noise-free, stereophonic sound of the best of the l.p.s, extending as it does over the whole of the audible spectrum, and of quality limited chiefly by the capability of the replay equipment. Is there room for improvement? Does there remain to be heralded another major innovation in the development of the gramophone record?

To prophesy accurately in such matters demands genius or luck. However, it is to be noted that the technical performance of the contemporary disc leaves little room for improvement. It is true that the technique of tracing a pre-cut groove with a stylus carries certain intrinsic distortions with it, all of which introduce spurious harmonic and inharmonic tones not present in the original performance; and one recent development has been the introduction during recording of a kind of inverse distortion which on replay tends to cancel out the replay distortion. But this is refinement, not a major innovation.

Similarly, there is always the quest for increased playing time without sacrifice of quality. It is difficult to see its achievement with the traditional disc-recording medium, in view of the extreme delicacy of pick-up necessary to achieve the prevailing standards of quality at the prevailing record speeds.

It might be felt that a major change could be made—downwards—in the price of records, by some novel production-engineering venture. Yet of the components of the selling price, the production cost is less, sometimes much less, than the sum of the other costs, all of which are unrelated to the recording medium: artists' fees, royalties, publicity, tax, and so on.

The truth is probably that the disc record has nearly reached the end of its technical exploitability, and that it is susceptible to improvements in detail only. The disc has survived competition from other media, notably the magnetic tape, because of its convenience of use in the domestic environment and because it is supported by a massive and long-established production effort, dealing with a similarly large and established repertoire. In short, both manufacturers and the general public know and accept the gramophone record. Other days bring other ways, though. The disc will survive for many years, but not as the medium of the future; the latter may already exist as the coated-plastic tape—or it may await invention.

Appendix.

Some Explanations of Terminology.

The better to appreciate the problem of sound-recording, consider the nature of the sound itself. The ear responds to sound (i.e., it gives the sensation of hearing) by a complicated mechanism which is imperfectly understood, but which certainly originates in the vibration of a diaphragm. This is the ear drum, which is a thin membrane of cartilage completely closing the entrance to the middle ear and to other parts of the hearing system further within the skull. The motion of the ear drum is conveyed by a linkage of three small bones, the ossicles, to the inner ear, wherein a conversion is made from mechanical vibration to nervous signals which are transmitted to the brain. See also Q12–13.

Pitch.

Vibration of the ear drum results from vibration, or periodic alternation, of air pressure. Hence, the source of sound must itself set up air-

pressure variations. Moreover, if the sound is to be audible, and by definition it must be so, the pressure variations must not occur too slowly—the comparatively slow change of pressure with change of altitude, for example, causes a sensation not of sound but of ear blockage. Nor must the variations be too rapid—the "inaudible" dog whistle sets up air-pressure variations which are too frequent to be heard by the human ear, and we enter the realm of ultrasonics (L118). The rate at which the pressure variations recur, called the frequency, is the physical concomitant of the pitch of the sound.

It transpires that the person with average hearing can sense variations occurring not less frequently than about 20 per second and not more frequently than about 15,000 per second, although age and state of health have something to do with the exact range of audible frequencies.

So a requirement of the ideal sound-recording system is that it shall respond to air-pressure fluctuations within the range 20–15,000 Hz (cycles, or complete fluctuations, per second). (With pressure changes there are associated velocity changes, and some recording systems are velocity responsive, rather than pressure responsive. This does not alter the tenor of what is said here about frequency range, etc.)

Loudness.

If it is to simulate the ear, in order that it can later reproduce the sound for the benefit of another ear, the recording system must also cater for the range of loudnesses which the average ear will accept. This range is very large indeed, for the greatest loudness an ear can tolerate without actual pain or damage is set up by a pressure variation at the ear, of a magnitude which is perhaps 10 million times the pressure magnitude corresponding to a sound which is barely audible. This gives a measure of what is often referred to as the "dynamic range" of the recording system. The dynamic range is the difference between the loudest, or highest-level, sound which the system can handle without malfunction, and the smallest signal which it can handle.

Noise.

The question of the very small signals that represent the very quiet sounds arises because of a third important factor which has to be taken into account: this is the residual noise level. A certain level of noise and hum exists inescapably within the recording system, and because sounds which are quiet enough to lie just above, below, or at the noise level are in practice the smallest that can usefully be handled, the dynamic range is reckoned with the noise level as its lower limit.

Distortion.

We are deriving some of the most important features by means of which recording systems can be judged, and in addition to the three referred to above (frequency range, dynamic range, and noise level), there is one other. It is non-linearity distortion. This is a general name given to any imperfection of the system which degrades the way in which the system responds to sounds of various loudnesses. For example, if the original sound doubles in loudness, does the reproduced sound do likewise? If so, there is no non-linearity distortion present. On the other hand, if the reproduced sound does not change in exact proportion to the original, non-linearity distortion exists. The ear is not very tolerant of the effects of non-linearity, which shows itself in the production of spurious sounds which were not present in the original. These spurious signals may be overtones, or harmonics, of components of the original (the so-called harmonic distortion), or they may be inharmonic signals (inter-modulation distortion) which grate even more offensively on the listener's ear. An everyday example of non-linearity distortion at work is the public telephone service: the reproduction at the telephone earpiece is distorted very badly by comparison with the original speech, or indeed by comparison with a reproduced sound of high quality, such as that from a good v.h.f. receiver tuned to a B.B.C. v.h.f. broadcast.

ELEMENTS

Element (Symbol)	Atomic Number	Atomic Weight	Valency	Element (Symbol)	Atomic Number	Atomic Weight	Valency
actinium(Ac)* .	89	227		molybdenum (Mo) . . .	42	95·94	3, 4, 6
aluminium (Al).	13	26·9815	3	neodymium (Nd)	60	144·24	3
americium (Am)*	95	243	3, 4, 5, 6	neon (Ne) . .	10	20·183	0
antimony (Sb) .	51	121·75	3, 5	neptunium (Np)*	93	237	4, 5, 6*
argon (A) . .	18	39·948	0	nickel (Ni) . .	28	58·71	2, 3
arsenic (As). .	33	74·9216	3, 5	niobium (Nb) .	41	92·906	3, 5
astatine (At)* .	85	210	1, 3, 5, 7	nitrogen (N) .	7	14·0067	3, 5
				nobelium (No)*	102	254	
barium (Ba) .	56	137·34	2	osmium (Os) .	76	190·2	2, 3, 4, 8
berkelium (Bk)*	97	249	3, 4	oxygen (O) . .	8	15·9994	2
beryllium (Be) .	4	9·0122	2	palladium (Pd).	46	106·4	2, 4, 6
bismuth (Bi) .	83	208·980	3, 5	phosphorus (P).	15	30·9738	3, 5
boron (B) . .	5	10·811	3	platinum (Pt) .	78	195·09	2, 4
bromine (Br) .	35	79·909	1, 3, 5, 7	plutonium (Pu)*	94	242	3, 4, 5, 6
cadmium (Cd) .	48	112·40	2	polonium (Po)*.	84	242	
calcium (Ca) .	20	40·08	2	potassium (K) .	19	39·102	1
californium (Cf)*	98	249		praseodymium (Pr)	59	140·907	3
carbon (C) . .	6	12·01115	2, 4	promethium (Pm)*	61	145	3
cerium (Ce) .	58	140·12	3, 4	protactinium (Pa)* .	91	231	
caesium (Cs) .	55	132·905	1	radium (Ra)* .	88	226	2
chlorine (Cl) .	17	35·453	1, 3, 5, 7	radon (Rn)* .	86	222	0
chromium (Cr) .	24	51·996	2, 3, 6	rhenium (Re) .	75	186·2	
cobalt (Co) . .	27	58·9332	2, 3	rhodium (Rh) .	45	102·905	3
copper (Cu) .	29	63·54	1, 2	rubidium (Rb) .	37	85·47	1
curium (Cm)* .	96	245	3	ruthenium (Ru)	44	101·07	3, 4, 6, 8
dysprosium (Dy)	66	162·50	3	samarium (Sm)	62	150·35	2, 3
				scandium (Sc) .	21	44·956	3
einsteinium (Es)*	99	254		selenium (Se) .	34	78·96	2, 4, 6
erbium (Er) .	68	167·26	3	silicon (Si) . .	14	28·086	4
europium (Eu) .	63	151·96	2, 3	silver (Ag) . .	47	107·870	1
fermium (Fm)*.	100	252		sodium (Na) .	11	22·9898	1
fluorine (F) . .	9	18·9984	1	strontium (Sr) .	38	87·62	2
francium(Fr)* .	87	223	1	sulphur (S) . .	16	32·064	2, 4, 6
gadolinium (Gd)	64	157·25	3	tantalum (Ta) .	73	180·948	5
gallium (Ga) .	31	69·72	2, 3	technetium (Tc)*	43	99	6, 7
germanium (Ge)	32	72·59	4	tellurium (Te) .	52	127·60	2, 4, 6
gold (Au) . .	79	196·967	1, 3	terbium (Tb) .	65	158·924	3
hafnium (Hf) .	72	178·49	4	thalium (Tl) .	81	204·37	1, 3
helium (He) .	2	4·0026	0	thorium (Th) .	90	232·038	4
holmium (Ho) .	67	164·930	3	thulium (Tm) .	69	168·934	3
hydrogen (H) .	1	1·00797	1	tin (Sn) . .	50	118·69	2, 4
indium (In) .	49	114·82	3	titanium (Ti) .	22	47·90	3, 4
iodine (I) . .	53	126·9044	1, 3, 5, 7	tungsten (see wolfram)			
iridium (Ir) .	77	192·2	3, 4	uranium (U) .	92	238·03	4, 6
iron (Fe) . .	26	55·847	2, 3	vanadium (V) .	23	50·942	3, 5
krypton (Kr) .	36	83·8	0	wolfram (W) .	74	183·85	6
lanthanum (La)	57	138·91	3	xenon (Xe) .	54	131·30	0
lawrencium(Lw)*	103	257		ytterbium (Yb)	70	173·04	2, 3
lead (Pb) . .	82	207·19	2, 4	yttrium (Y) .	39	88·905	3
lithium (Li). .	3	6·939	1	zinc (Zn) . .	30	65·37	2
lutetium (Lu) .	71	174·97	3	zirconium (Zr) .	40	91·22	4
magnesium (Mg)	12	24·312	2				
manganese (Mn)	25	54·9380	2,3,4,6,7				
mendeleevium (Mv)* . .	101	256					
mercury (Hg) .	80	200·59	1, 2				

* In the cases of these elements, which are very rare or not found in nature, but have been artificially prepared, atomic weight in the chemical sense is meaningless; the integral mass of the most stable isotope known is given.

Note: In 1961 the isotope of Carbon-12 replaced Oxygen as a standard, the weight of its atom being taken as exactly 12. This change of standard has meant a slight adjustment in atomic weights from the old chemical scale.

The new elements with an atomic number higher than that of uranium 238 (element 92) are termed Transuranics.

GAS LAWS

Boyle's Law (1662) pV = constant.

Charles' Law (1787) $\dfrac{pV}{T}$ = constant.

Van der Waal's equation $\left(p + \dfrac{a}{V^2}\right)(V - b) = RT$ where a and b are constants.

Adiabatic expansion of a gas pV^{γ} = constant where $\gamma = \dfrac{C_p}{C_v}$.

BACKGROUND TO ECONOMIC EVENTS

The aim of this section is to help the ordinary reader to follow economic events as they happen, and to understand the controversies that accompany them.

TABLE OF CONTENTS

BACKGROUND TO
ECONOMIC EVENTS

This section is divided into four parts. Part I gives a brief description of the most important problems of economic policy. Part II is concerned with a more detailed survey of the British economy and the way in which it operates. In the course of this survey, the specialised terms used by economists are explained, and the attempt is made to present an intelligible summary of the information, facts, and figures relevant to an understanding of economic events. There are five main sub-sections: International Trade and Payments; Production, Employment, and Industry; Incomes, Wages, and Prices; Money, Banking, and Finance; and Economic Aspects of the Public Services. Part III outlines the main economic problems faced by the underdeveloped countries, and the economic policies of Britain and other developed countries towards the underdeveloped world. Some suggestions for further reading are given at the end of Parts II and III. Part IV is written as shortly before publication as possible, and contains a survey of developments in the British economy since 1960.

I. CENTRAL PROBLEMS OF ECONOMIC POLICY

Unemployment.

Between the wars, unemployment was Britain's most urgent economic problem. The level of unemployment varied with the ups and downs of the trade cycle. Quite the worst slump was that of the early 1930s: in 1932, nearly 3 million workers were without a job. But unemployment remained high even in the best years, and in no year between 1919 and 1939 were there fewer than a million workers unemployed. Economists make a distinction between *structural* unemployment and *cyclical* unemployment. Structural unemployment appears when the structure of industry gets out of line with the pattern of demand for industrial products. In Britain, unemployment was particularly severe and persistent in areas which were dependent on the coal, textile, and shipbuilding industries, and some sections of the engineering industry. These industries had been in the forefront of Britain's industrial growth in the 19th cent., and had contributed greatly to the expansion of exports. In areas like South Wales, Tyneside, Clydeside, and Northern Ireland there was little alternative work for those no longer needed in the "staple" industries: new industries were being built up in the inter-war period, but they tended to be located in the relatively prosperous Midlands and South-East England. Cyclical unemployment appears when there is a general decline in the level of demand for goods and services, which leads to a decline in the employment of workers producing those goods and services. In the slump years unemployment was so high because of a combination of structural and cyclical unemployment; in the best years, unemployment was largely structural.

Unemployment means waste. Men willing to work, who could produce valuable goods and services, are idle; the economy produces fewer goods and services than it is capable of producing. Unemployment also means hardship and low standards of living for those out of work, and for their families.

The avoidance of mass unemployment has been accepted as a primary objective of economic policy by all political parties, and there is a wide measure of agreement on the policies which must be applied to ensure that unemployment on the scale of the 1930s never occurs again. Cyclical unemployment has to be tackled by measures to increase total demand and total spending by consumers, by investors, and by the Government. Structural unemployment has to be tackled by inducing new industries to move into areas where other employment is declining, or by inducing labour to move from those areas to areas where there is a demand for its services.

There have been ups and downs in unemployment in the post-war years, but these have been very slight compared to those of the pre-war years. In most post-war years, less than 2 per cent of the working population was unemployed —a sharp contrast with the 11 per cent for 1937 and the 22 per cent for 1932. But there are still areas of the country where structural unemployment is serious. In Northern Ireland, for example, despite the efforts which have been made to attract new industries, unemployment ranged between 6 and 10 per cent in the last decade.

Inflation.

A characteristic of the British economy in post-war years has been a persistent rise in prices and money incomes. For example, between 1959 and 1969, retail prices went up by about 41 per cent, or—expressed as an annual rate—by 3·5 per cent per annum, export prices rose by 30 per cent (or 2·7 per cent per annum), and weekly wage rates by about 52 per cent (4·3 per cent per annum). However, these rates of increase were somewhat slower than the corresponding rates in the immediately post-war decade. This inflation of prices and money incomes is considered undesirable for two main reasons. Firstly, it is associated with an arbitrary redistribution of purchasing power. Prices rise for everyone, but some members of the community are better placed than others to secure increases in their money incomes which offset, or more than offset, the rise in the price of the goods and services they buy. The feeling that particular groups are falling behind, in that their money incomes have not risen as fast as those of other groups, is a source of much unrest and discontent. Secondly, and crucially for the British economy, an inflation of prices makes it more difficult to achieve a satisfactory balance of payments. As prices of our exports rise, it becomes harder to sell them in foreign markets; and as imports become cheap in comparison with goods produced at home there is a tendency to buy more of them.

Two main explanations have been advanced to account for the inflation which has occurred. The first stresses the role of an excess of demand or spending power in the economy—of too much money chasing too few goods, and so leading to a rise in prices. The inflationary problem is seen as the obverse of the cyclical unemployment problem: the latter involves a deficiency of spending, and the former an excess. Those who consider an excess of demand (*demand-pull*) to be an important factor in the inflationary situation favour policies designed to reduce purchasing power: for example, the reduction of spendable income by levying higher taxes, or the reduction of spending financed through borrowing by making credit more expensive or more difficult to get. The second stresses the role of an excessive increase in incomes: it is argued that prices have risen mainly because costs have increased faster than productivity (*cost-push*). Those who take this view favour measures to restrain or control increases in wages, profits, rents, and other forms of income. Neither explanation excludes the other. Many would agree that both demand-pull and cost-push factors have contributed—with different strengths at different times—to the inflationary spiral in prices and incomes, and that measures both to control demand and to restrain or control incomes may be necessary.

But it is easier to specify in general terms the measures needed to combat inflation than it is to apply policies which are successful in practice. In particular, policy measures to restrain or control wage increases are difficult to reconcile with widely-accepted procedures of collective bargaining.

The Balance of Payments.

Britain is heavily dependent on imports. This country must import food: it cannot produce enough food within its borders to feed its population. Many of the raw materials necessary for its industry have to be purchased from abroad. Furthermore, some manufactured goods produced in other countries will be purchased because they are cheaper or more attractive than similar goods produced at home. All these goods, and our imports of services, have to be paid for in foreign currency. Foreign currency is earned by exporting goods and services to other countries. It is not, however, considered sufficient to earn enough foreign currency from our exports to pay for our imports. The objective is to earn considerably more than that, so that we have a surplus of foreign currency available to pay off external debts, to build up our external assets by investing abroad, to enable us to lend and give aid to underdeveloped countries, and to increase our foreign exchange resources.

Since the war, our balance of payments position has been precarious. Exports have increased considerably, but so have imports; and the margin of safety has been so narrow that unfavourable turns of events have led to crises in the balance of payments. In several years, our earnings from the export of goods and services have not even been sufficient to cover our payments for imports, and in no year has the surplus been as large as is considered necessary. With the balance of payments delicately poised even in favourable years, and with corrective action necessary in crisis years, economic policies have been much influenced by our foreign trade problems. It is easy to say that most of the problems would disappear, or would become less urgent, if we could achieve a major expansion of our exports. But most export markets are highly competitive, and we cannot expect to sell more unless the price, quality, and terms of delivery of our goods and services are at least as attractive as those of our rivals in export markets.

Economic Growth.

Taking a longer view, the most important objective of internal economic policy must be to raise the standard of living. The standard of living can increase only if more goods and services are produced per head of population. In a fully-employed economy, the main source of increased output is a higher productivity—output per person—of the working population.

Standards of living in this country have been rising: the output of goods and services per head of population increased by about 25 per cent between 1959 and 1969. Nevertheless, many economists are of the opinion that the rate of growth of output and productivity can be, and

should be, increased. In particular, they point out that our rate of growth compares unfavourably with that achieved by some other countries. The potentialities for higher productivity are enormous. The U.S.A. has the highest standard of living in the world: in many industries, output per person employed is twice or more than yet attained in this country. In order to achieve a higher level of productivity in this country, more and better machinery and capital equipment will have to be installed; also, work will have to be planned, organised, and controlled in such a way as to make more effective use of labour and machinery.

Underdeveloped Countries.

Britain and the other developed countries of the world have important responsibilities towards the underdeveloped countries. The poorest two-thirds of the world's population account for only a sixth of total world income and output, while two-thirds of world income accrue to the richest sixth of world population, a category which includes Britain. The poorest two-thirds suffer from poverty, hunger, malnutrition, debilitating diseases, and widespread illiteracy. To make matters worse, most of the poor countries are experiencing a rapid growth of population. Output has to rise as fast as population just to prevent standards of living from falling, and an increase in standards of living requires an even faster growth of output.

Few underdeveloped countries can hope to solve the increasing problems they face without active and generous help from developed countries. This help must take many forms. Financial aid in the form of grants or loans in order to place resources at the disposal of underdeveloped countries which they would otherwise not be able to obtain; technical aid to assist in the solution of the many technical problems which have to be solved; trading policies which do not hinder underdeveloped countries from getting the imports they need or from selling their exports—these are all activities in which Britain must play her part. In particular, of course, Britain must contribute to the development of the underdeveloped countries of the Commonwealth.

The Inter-relationship of Economic Problems.

Each of the problems briefly described above is extremely complex. The difficulties of achieving successful solutions are further aggravated by the fact that the problems are inter-related in such a way that measures which are helpful for one problem can make others more difficult to solve. For example, a reduction of purchasing power might be considered helpful in the control of inflation, and might ease balance of payments problems by reducing—or slowing down the increase of—imports. But it could also lead to an increase in unemployment, and to a slowing down in the rate of growth of the economy. Or again, a reduction in aid to underdeveloped countries could make it easier to balance our external accounts, but such action could hardly be reconciled with our responsibilities towards underdeveloped countries. In the next section, particular aspects of the British economy are considered in some detail; the final section discusses the main features of the development of the economy since 1960.

II. SURVEY OF THE BRITISH ECONOMY

1. INTERNATIONAL TRADE AND PAYMENTS.

Imports and Exports.

In 1964 the United Kingdom bought from abroad goods to the value of £5,514 million, or just over £100 per head. Food is a large item in this bill, accounting for 32 per cent of the total. Fuel, largely oil, costs about 11 per cent, basic materials for industry 31 per cent, and manufactured goods (a category that includes a large number of semi-manufactured goods bought for

further processing) 36 per cent. This last category of imports has increased sharply in recent years. In 1954 this represented only 20 per cent in an import bill of only £3,359 million. All this can be seen in the table.

There are three main determinants of the level of British imports. One is the competitiveness of British with foreign producers. Britain imports those commodities which—at the current exchange rate between the pound and foreign currencies—can be bought more cheaply from foreign than from home producers. Secondly, the level of imports depends on the extent to which free trade is prevented by tariffs on imported goods or by other devices. Thirdly, as total incomes in the economy expand, there is a general increase in the demand for goods and services, including imports. Therefore imports can be expected to vary directly with the total of incomes in the economy, known as the *national income*.

One would expect that the liberalisation of trade since the early 1950s, together with a decline in the competitiveness of British producers, would have produced an expansion of imports relative to national income. In fact imports as a proportion of national income fell from 23 to 21 per cent between 1954 and 1964. The observed decrease must be explained by the sluggish demand for *primary products* such as food and raw materials. The British spend little of their additional income on imported food, and the development of synthetic substitutes and new products has slowed down the growth in demand for raw materials. Moreover, since the demand for primary products of this sort has been sluggish on a world scale, while supply has increased, their price has fallen in relative terms, and this too has reduced the total cost of British imports.

—fell or stagnated in world markets over the decade.

The Volume of Trade.

Superficially it would appear that any improvement in the terms of trade raises the value of British exports relative to imports. However, this is not always true: faster inflation in this country, leading to a more rapid increase in export prices, would harm rather than help the balance of payments. If the prices of our export goods rise faster than the prices of our competitors in overseas markets, it will become progressively more difficult to sell our exports. Conversely, an inflation in Britain will make it progressively more attractive to buy goods produced abroad. Thus between 1954 and 1964 the value of imports grew slightly faster than the value of exports despite the slower growth of import prices than of export prices. This was because the volume of imports increased by 61 per cent and the volume of exports by only 40 per cent. The trade balance may well be helped by a fall in the price of imported primary products; but the balance of trade

UNITED KINGDOM IMPORTS AND EXPORTS

Imports of goods (c.i.f.)	£ million.		Percentage of total.	
	1954.	1964.	1954.	1964.
Food, drink, and tobacco	1,314	1,773	39	32
Basic materials	1,015	1,119	30	20
Fuels and lubricants	329	585	10	11
Semi-manufactures	513	1,173	15	21
Finished manufactures	174	838	5	15
TOTAL*	3,359	5,514	100	100
Exports of goods (f.o.b.)				
Food, drink, and tobacco	154	283	6	7
Basic materials	101	158	4	4
Fuels and lubricants	151	138	6	3
Metals	338	500	13	12
Engineering products	1,007	1,915	38	45
Textiles	324	275	12	6
Other manufactured goods	490	847	18	20
TOTAL*	2,650	4,254	100	100
Re-exports of imports	98	154	—	—

* The column figures do not add up to the totals because the former exclude postal packages.

Since the exports of one country must be the imports of another, the same factors in reverse, foreign competitiveness, access to foreign markets, and the level of foreign incomes determine the level of British exports. In 1964 these amounted to £4,254 million, of which no less than 83 per cent were manufactures, mainly of engineering products. Thus Britain gains from trade by exporting manufactures, in which she has a *comparative advantage*, in return for food and raw materials, which she is not suited to produce.

The Terms of Trade.

Between 1954 and 1964 the value of British imports rose by 64 per cent and the value of exports by 61 per cent. These changes can be separated into two components, volume and price. Imports rose in price by only 4 per cent, whereas export prices rose by 19 per cent. The ratio of the average price of exports to that of imports is known as the *terms of trade*; and a rise in the price of exports relative to imports indicates an improvement in the terms of trade. Thus when we note in the table that the terms of trade improved by 15 per cent between 1954 and 1964, we mean that in 1964 15 per cent less exports by volume would have been needed to buy the same amount of imports as in 1954. This improvement in the terms of trade reflects the fact that the prices of many primary products—food and raw materials such as wheat, cocoa, rubber, or copper

in manufactures will be worsened by an improvement in their terms of trade.

VISIBLE TRADE: VOLUME AND PRICES

	1961 = 100.		Percentage increase 1954–64.
	1954.	1964.	
Value			
Imports	76	125	64
Exports	72	116	61
Volume			
Imports	74	119	61
Exports	80	112	40
Price			
Imports	103	107	4
Exports	89	106	19
Terms of trade	116	99	15

Over the decade there was a persistent fall in Britain's share of world exports, from 20·0 per cent of exports of manufactures in 1954 to 13·6 per cent in 1964. Her competitors in export markets—and particularly Germany and Japan—were more successful in expanding their exports. Had the prices of British exports risen less rapidly over this period, Britain's share of world exports would have been higher in 1964.

The Balance of Visible Trade.

The balance of (visible) trade is the difference between exports and imports of goods. It is said to be in *surplus* if exports exceed imports and in *deficit* if imports exceed exports. In estimating the balance of trade it is important that imports and exports be valued on the same basis. The normal method in the trade returns is to measure imports *c.i.f.* (cost, insurance, and freight) and exports *f.o.b.* (free on board). In other words import prices are shown to include the costs of transporting them to Britain, and exports are valued at the prices when loaded in British ports. Our table shows both imports and exports *f.o.b.*

In no year except 1958 was there a surplus in the British balance of trade. Moreover, the deficit was particularly big in certain years, 1951, 1955, 1960, and 1964. The deficit of 1951 was largely due to the Korean war which led to a stockpiling of primary products and a startling increase in their prices. The other three years coincided with booms in the British economy. These were periods of very full employment and high demand which could be met only by increased imports. Moreover, there was a building up of raw material stocks which had been depleted during the preceding upswings of the economy.

Invisible Trade, and the Current Balance of Payments.

The chronic deficit in the balance of visible trade has in normal years been offset by a surplus in the *balance of invisible trade*. This surplus derives from four main groups of transactions. The first covers receipts from non-residents *less* payments to non-residents, for services such as shipping and insurance. The second covers receipts from foreign governments in respect of

together. A deficit with non-sterling area countries persisted throughout the 1950s and into the 1960s.

The Long-term Capital Account.

We have seen that Britain earned a surplus on its current balance of payments in most recent years. Yet it is not sufficient for this country to avoid deficits on its current account. The objective is to earn a substantial surplus in order to finance investment in and lending to other countries— particularly the underdeveloped countries of the Commonwealth; to repay debts to foreign countries which have been incurred; and to build up reserves of gold, dollars, and other currencies which can help to tide us over difficult periods. In fact the objective of the Government was to earn current account surpluses of more than £200 million in normal years; and a surplus of this magnitude was only achieved in the exceptionally favourable year 1958.

Between 1954 and 1964 there was a persistent and growing amount of British private investment abroad. Since private foreign investment in Britain also rose, the *balance of long-term capital transactions* did not show a clear trend. Nevertheless it was generally in deficit to the extent of £100–£200 million. As with current transactions there were considerable regional differences. Usually there was a heavy deficit in long-term capital transactions with the sterling area and only minor imbalance with the rest of the world. Thus in 1965 Britain had a deficit with the sterling area of £307 million and a surplus with the rest of the world of £92 million, giving an overall deficit on long-term capital account of £215 million. The net flow of long-term capital to the sterling area neutralised the current account surplus with the sterling area, equal to £313 million; and this was also the tendency in other years.

CURRENT BALANCE OF PAYMENTS
(£ million)

	1951.	1952–54.	1955.	1956–59.	1960.	1961–63.	1964.
Imports (f.o.b.) . .	3,501	2,958	3,432	3,497	4,137	4,166	5,005
Exports (f.o.b.) . .	2,752	2,778	3,076	3,366	3,733	4,058	4,471
Balance of visible trade .	−749	−180	−356	−131	−404	−108	−534
Balance of invisible trade	330	386	283	255	131	170	122
Current balance of payments . .	−419	206	−73	124	−273	62	−412

military bases in the country *less* payments by this country in respect of military bases abroad. The third covers receipts of gifts and grants made to this country, *less* gifts and grants made by this country. The fourth includes all receipts of interest, dividends, and profits earned on overseas investment *less* interest, dividends and profits paid out on foreign investment in this country.

The table shows that in most years the surplus on invisibles exceeded the deficit on visibles, so that Britain earned a surplus on the *current balance of payments*. However, there was a long-run tendency for the surplus on invisibles to decline: net earnings from shipping services fell and Government military expenditure abroad and grants to other countries increased.

The Current Balance of Payments by Regions.

All the figures presented so far refer to Britain's trade with the external world as a whole. These hide a marked pattern of trade. In 1964 just over a third of visible imports and exports came from and went to the countries of the overseas sterling area—comprising the Colonial territories, independent Commonwealth countries other than Canada, British protected states in the Persian Gulf and a few countries such as Burma and South Africa. One reason for Britain's declining share of world trade is that trade within the sterling area has been growing less rapidly than world trade as a whole. Almost 35 per cent of our visible trade was done with Western Europe, and rather less than 17 per cent with North America. The current balance of payments surplus found in normal years is generally made up of a large surplus with sterling area currencies, partially offset by a deficit with all other countries taken

Monetary Movements.

In 1965 Britain had a current account deficit of £104 million and a deficit on long term capital account of £215 million; implying a deficit in the *balance of current and long-term capital transactions* of £319 million. This balance had to be financed either through an increase in liabilities (for example, an increase in the sterling liabilities held by foreigners, or in short-term loans from the International Monetary Fund) or by a reduction in assets (for example a reduction in the gold and dollar reserves). In fact, the gold and foreign currency reserves actually rose in 1965 by £246 million, but the sterling balances increased by £55 million and our debts to the International Monetary Fund by no less than £499 million. Total recorded net monetary movements to meet the deficit amounted to only £232 million, so that there must have been an unrecorded increase in credit equal to £87 million, known as the *balancing item*. Let us consider each of these " financing " transactions in turn.

The Sterling Balances.

Sterling is an international currency, and governments and individuals may hold balances in sterling (*e.g.*, Treasury bills, Government stocks and bank accounts) for many reasons. Sterling area countries reckon to keep a high proportion of their international trade reserves in the form of sterling balances. It is convenient to hold sterling to finance trading transactions because sterling is widely acceptable in settlement of trading debts. Sterling balances will also be held to the extent that they are considered a profitable and safe way of holding liquid assets. It may be profitable to hold sterling if the rate of interest paid on balances in London is higher than that paid in other financial centres. And it may be considered safe to hold sterling if the chances of sterling devaluation (which would automatically reduce the value of the balances in terms of any currency which did not devalue) are thought to be remote.

An increase in the sterling balances enables Britain to finance an adverse balance on current plus long-term capital account without reducing the gold and foreign exchange reserves. Conversely, a reduction in sterling balances can impose a drain on reserves even if there is no adverse balance on current plus long-term capital account.

At the end of 1965 sterling balances held by non-residents (excluding the International Monetary Fund) amounted to £3,470 million; far in excess of Britain's reserves of gold and convertible currencies, equal to £1,070 million. Nearly three-quarters of this amount was held by the rest of the sterling area. However, it is unlikely that Britain would be able to finance a persistent deficit in her balance of payments through a progressive increase in the sterling balances: in the long run the sterling balances will probably be reduced—as indeed they were between 1955 and 1965, by some £200 million. Many under-developed countries of the sterling area will want to run down their sterling balances in order to help finance the imports required for their development programmes (*see also* G33).

Sterling holdings outside the sterling area, and particularly the unofficial (*i.e.*, private) holdings, are highly volatile, in that they may be withdrawn very rapidly if for any reason it is thought less profitable or less safe to hold sterling than some other currency or gold. Since confidence in sterling is weakest (*i.e.*, fear that it will be devalued is greatest) when the balance of payments is in deficit, sterling balances tend to move perversely, so accentuating movement in the reserves. Such was the case in the sterling crisis at the end of 1964. It is ironical that Britain's position as an international currency country makes it more and not less difficult to rely on a running down of reserves to meet a temporary deficit in the balance of payments.

Foreign Exchange Reserves.

The gold and convertible currency reserves are used to finance payments abroad which cannot be financed in any other way: they are a last line of defence in international trade. The reserves held in London belong to the sterling area as a whole, and not just to this country. Members of the sterling area are willing to pay into these central reserves some or all of their net earnings of gold and convertible currencies, in exchange for sterling balances. They do this on the understanding that they can, should they wish to do so, call upon the central reserves by exchanging sterling balances for gold and convertible currencies.

The central reserves of gold and foreign currencies amounted to £1,070 million at the end of 1965; a level which, though higher than in many previous post-war years, was felt to be quite inadequate. There are bound to be imbalances in international trade and payments, and the function of these reserves is to tide over temporary imbalances by increasing reserves in favourable periods and running down reserves in unfavourable periods. If reserves are not sufficient to withstand temporary pressures, measures to protect the reserves will have to be taken—*e.g.*, raising Bank Rate and tightening up monetary policies generally—and these measures may create unemployment and recession, and restrict the growth of the economy.

The International Monetary Fund.

The *International Monetary Fund* (IMF) was set up after the war with the objective of working towards free trade at stable exchange rates. Under the original agreement setting up the Fund, members agreed to make their currencies convertible into other currencies and gold at fixed rates of exchange, and agreed not to impose exchange or import controls without the permission of the Fund. Any alteration in the rates of exchange by more than 10 per cent also requires the per-

mission of the Fund. For many years after the war, the imbalances in world trade—and particularly the acute shortage of dollars—were such that many countries had to invoke the clauses in the agreement which permitted them to impose restrictions during a "transitional" period. Although there is still a long way to go before the Fund reaches its objectives, considerable progress towards them was made during the 1950s. The progressive relaxation of exchange and import controls by this country was paralleled in some other countries, and most of the currencies important in world trade and payments were declared convertible.

The function of the Fund is to make foreign exchange resources available to members who run into balance of payments difficulties. Each member country makes a deposit (called its quota) partly in gold and partly in its own currencies, with the Fund. The size of the deposit is fixed in relation to the country's share in world trade. In return, it is granted certain automatic drawing rights, which entitle it to borrow foreign currencies from the Fund. Furthermore, the Fund has power to make larger loans, and to grant stand-by credits to be drawn on if required. Before the Fund will make such loans and credits available, it has to be satisfied that the borrowing country is taking appropriate action to correct the balance of payments disequilibrium.

In 1956, at the time of the Suez crisis, there was a running down of sterling balances, and Britain negotiated a loan of £202 million from the Fund and an even larger stand-by credit. Again in 1964 and 1965, when there was a severe deficit on current and long-term capital account and heavy speculation against sterling, the Government borrowed from the IMF £369 million in 1964 and £499 million in 1965. In this way the country could ride out crises of confidence in sterling without a severe loss of reserves.

Correcting a Deficit.

If an imbalance in the current plus long-term capital account persists, the deficit cannot be met indefinitely from monetary movements. At some stage the Government must take action to remove the deficit. What action can it take? There are a number of alternatives available, each with its advantages and disadvantages, and economic opinion is by no means unanimous on the choice of policy. Let us consider each of these alternatives in turn.

Variation of the Exchange Rate.

The *exchange rate* is the ruling official rate of exchange of pounds for gold and other currencies. It determines the value of British goods in relation to foreign goods. If the pound is devalued in terms of gold and other currencies, British exports (which are paid for in pounds) become cheaper to foreigners and British imports (paid for by purchasing foreign currency) become more expensive to holders of pounds. In this way *devaluation* can improve the British balance of payments position by encouraging exports and discouraging imports.

But there are certain disadvantages attached to devaluation. The prospect of devaluation results in a speculative outflow of foreign funds, and one devaluation may be taken as a sign that there will be further devaluation in the future. Secondly, the sterling area countries—many of them underdeveloped—will suffer a capital loss because they hold their reserves largely in the form of sterling rather than gold (*but see* G33). Thirdly, the rise in the price of imports of raw materials and consumption goods results in higher costs and prices and then in wage demands to maintain the British standard of living. It is possible that inflation will in this way neutralise the beneficial effects of devaluation.

The pound was devalued in 1949, when an official exchange rate of £1 = $2·8 was established and again in 1967, to a rate of £1 = $2·4.

Exchange Controls and Convertibility.

A currency is fully *convertible* if it can be freely exchanged for any other currency, or for gold, at the ruling official rates of exchange. Exchange controls impose restrictions on convertibility by limiting the powers of holders of a currency to exchange their holdings for other currencies or gold at the official rate of exchange. For many years after the war, for example, there was a world-wide shortage of dollars: if sterling had been convertible, there would have been a rush to convert sterling into dollars, with the consequence that the dollar reserves of the sterling area would soon have been exhausted. In fact, a premature attempt to establish sterling convertibility in 1947 led to such a drain on reserves that strict exchange controls had to be re-imposed.

Exchange controls on residents can be enforced by requiring that earnings of foreign currencies (e.g., the proceeds from the sale of exports) be handed over to the exchange control authority—the Bank of England acts as the Government's agent—in exchange for sterling; and by permitting the exchange of sterling for foreign currencies (e.g., to enable the purchase of imports) only for transactions approved by the exchange control authority. There was a move towards convertibility of sterling during the 1950s, and the sterling held by non-residents was made fully convertible in 1958. Residents, however, continued to be subject to exchange controls.

By restricting convertibility the Government can make it more difficult for funds to move into or out of sterling. In this way the Government can impede capital movements, e.g., British private investment abroad, or flows of short-term capital; or it can restrict current spending abroad, e.g., on foreign holidays.

Import Controls and Tariffs.

Import controls impose limitations on the quantity or value of goods which are permitted to enter a country: tariffs are duties levied on imported goods so that the price of those goods to consumers in a country is higher than the price received by the foreigners supplying the goods. In the early post-war years, this country maintained strict import controls over a wide range of goods. These were gradually dismantled, until in 1959 the last remaining import controls on goods were abandoned, except on habit-forming drugs and some agricultural products and textiles from the Far East—to give a measure of protection to British producers.

All countries impose tariffs. Some tariffs are primarily intended to raise revenue for the Government, and others are primarily intended to protect home industries by raising the price of competing goods from abroad. The rights of countries to raise tariffs, or to operate tariffs in a discriminatory way (i.e., to offer lower tariffs on goods from some sources than on similar goods from other sources), are closely circumscribed by the rules of the General Agreement on Tariffs and Trade (GATT). The object of the GATT is to work towards free trade, especially through a reduction in tariffs. In the post-war period GATT held several major conferences, at which bargaining to reduce tariffs was attended by modest success. The most significant moves towards free trade in this period were on a regional basis.

The disadvantage of introducing import controls or tariffs to correct a deficit in the balance of payments is that the benefits of free trade are lost. Moreover, there is always the possibility of retaliation by Britain's trading partners. Nevertheless, import controls or tariffs may well be preferable to another measure which has been used to correct a deficit, deflation.

Deflation.

Throughout the post-war period the U.K. balance of payments was far from secure. As a result, domestic economic policies were much influenced by balance of payments considerations. Devaluation was turned to only as a last resort. The movement in the 1950s and 1960s was towards greater freedom of trade. By ruling out devaluation and trade restrictions, the authorities had to fall back on deflation of the economy to correct periodic deficits. In other words, the Government took measures to discourage demand and so cut back incomes and employment. By reducing demand in general, the authorities secured a fall in demand for imports. However, it was necessary to cut back national income by many times

the ensuing fall in imports. Deflation is a painful method of correcting a deficit. Not only does it have a direct effect on the level of incomes and employment, but it is also liable to slow down the rate of growth of the economy. This can happen because deflation can weaken the incentive to expand productive capacity by investing in new plant, machinery, and other capital goods.

The problem which faced British policy-makers attempting to raise the rate of economic growth was this: as total demand for goods and services expands, it is difficult to prevent growth in the demand for imports and diversion of exports to the home market, particularly when home industries reach the limit of their productive capacity. Yet if consequent balance of payments difficulties are met by restrictions on total demand, it is difficult to maintain the investment necessary for growth in the productive capacity of the economy. The main need in the late 1960s was the same as that at the start of the 1950s: to achieve an expansion of exports relative to imports so as to secure economic growth without running into balance of payments difficulties.

The international monetary system is partly to blame for the British decisions to resort to periodic deflation of the economy. The use of sterling as a reserve currency has subjected the balance of payments to violent swings in short-term capital flows. Moreover, a world-wide shortage of international liquidity, i.e., gold and foreign exchange reserves, means that countries have an incentive to maintain a surplus in their balance of payments and so increase their reserves. In this situation surplus countries do not help to correct an imbalance in foreign transactions: the burden of correcting the imbalance is placed on the deficit country. If the Government of the deficit country feels itself unable to devalue its currency or to impose trade restrictions, it has to deflate the economy. The existing international monetary system contains a " deflationary bias," which the IMF has at most only ameliorated.

The European Common Market and the European Free Trade Area.

By the end of the 1950s, Europe was divided into two major trading groups: the Common Market, or European Economic Community (EEC) comprising: Belgium, France, Holland, Italy, Luxembourg, and West Germany, and the European Free Trade Association (EFTA) comprising: Austria, Denmark, Norway, Portugal, Sweden, Switzerland, and the United Kingdom.

An account of the negotiations for British entry to the EEC in the 1960s is given in Part IV.

2. EMPLOYMENT, PRODUCTION, AND INVESTMENT.

Population.

In June 1965 the population of the United Kingdom was estimated to be 54·4 million–47·8 million in England and Wales, 5·2 million in Scotland, and 1·5 million in Northern Ireland. The total was still rising slowly, at a rate of about 0·7 per cent per annum. Prediction of future trends is difficult. Before the war it was common to predict that Britain's population would fall later in the century; but these predictions were made at a time when the birth-rate was very low. Since then the birth-rate has risen sharply, and the net reproduction rate (the ratio of the birth-rate of girls less their infant mortality to the population of women of child-bearing age) has been above one in most years since the war. In the near future population will certainly continue to rise slowly as improving medical services raise the average length of life and as the gap between generations shortens.

The Population of Working Age.

Of the total population only some are of working age. Working age is defined as the period between the minimum school leaving age of 15 and retiring age—65 for men and 60 for women. Of course, not all those of working age do work and not all those above working age have retired; nevertheless the ratio between population not of working age and the total is a useful statistic, as it does provide a rough guide to the numbers who have to be supported out of the current national income, but who do not contribute to it. This ratio is rising and will continue to rise. In 1965, 23·3 per cent of the U.K. population was below working age and 15·0 per cent above. By 1980 it is fairly certain that 16 per cent of the population will be above working age; and much more speculatively, it is guessed that 26 per cent will be below. So the population not of working age will rise from 38·3 to 42 per cent. The expected growth in the proportion of the old explains why the proportion on pensions (*see* G24(2) is going to grow steadily. More generally, it is clear that some growth in output per worker will be needed to meet the needs of the increasing proportion of dependants.

The Working Population.

Not all persons of working age actually work, although the vast majority do; but only a part are gainfully employed, *i.e.*, work for wages, salaries, and profits. And it is only those who are gainfully employed who are counted in the working population. Housewives, mothers, and those who give their services gratis to good causes are excluded, unless they also do some work for cash. In 1965, when the total population of Great Britain was 53 million, of whom 32·7 million were of working age, the total working population (including the unemployed who are seeking employment) was only 25·5 million. Of the 17·5 million women of working age only 8·8 million were gainfully employed. So for every person gainfully occupied there was just over one other person to be supported out of the goods and services they provided. One feature of the post-war years was a steady increase in the proportion of persons going out to work. Whereas in 1965, 78 per cent of the working-age population was gainfully employed, in 1955 the figure was only 66 per cent.

or less inevitable. Some seasonal rise in unemployment in the winter must be expected, *e.g.*, in seaside towns, and for this reason unemployment in January is half a per cent or so higher than in June. Moreover, some unemployment is bound to be involved in job-changing and as the demands of industries change. "Full employment" means that there should be about as many jobs vacant as there are workers looking for jobs. A large excess of vacancies is evidence of inflationary pressure in the labour market, for it means that the employers needing workers to meet the demands for their products will have to compete with each other by bidding up wages.

To some extent unemployment figures are misleading, as not all unemployed workers are eligible for unemployment benefit under the National Insurance Scheme. Most married women who go out to work normally opt not to pay the full National Insurance contributions, so that, when they become unemployed, they just drop out of the "working population". Unemployment figures definitely understate the seriousness of recessions, as they do not count all the persons who would like to have, but cannot find, jobs.

Of the 317,000 persons unemployed in mid-1964, 240,000 were men and 77,000 women. Of the men, over half, 147,000, had been unemployed for over eight weeks. Thus long-term unemployment was nearly 1 per cent of the labour force, serious enough for those affected but not the kind of unemployment to be cured easily by reflationary measures.

Regional Unemployment.

A peculiarly dreadful feature of the inter-war years was the emergence of the depressed areas—the regions of the country where a third of the men had not had a job for a year or more. Such extreme regional unemployment has not recurred since 1945: only in Northern Ireland was unemployment very high. Between 1954 and 1964

DISTRIBUTION OF WORKING POPULATION, JUNE 1965
(Thousands)

Basic Industries.		Manufacturing Industries.		Services.	
Agriculture and fishing	486	Food, drink, and tobacco	810	Distribution trades	2,961
Mining and quarrying	624	Chemicals and allied industries	515	Financial, professional, and scientific services	3,045
Construction	1,656	Metal manufacture	632		
Gas, electricity, and water	411	Vehicles	862	Catering, hotels, etc.	612
Transport and communication	1,628	Engineering and other metal goods	2,848	Public administration:	
		Textiles	767	National	545
		Paper printing and publishing	633	Local	758
		Other manufacturing	1,779	Miscellaneous	1,574
Total	4,805	Total	8,846	Total	9,495
Percentage of working population	*20·8*		*38·2*		*41·0*

Most of the working population work for wages or salaries as employees. Of the total for Great Britain in June 1965 of 25·5 million, 1·7 million were employers or self-employed, 0·4 million were in the Forces, and 23·4 million were either employees or unemployed persons looking for work. The table shows the industries in which people work. Some 38 per cent of the total work in manufacturing industry, 2·8 million of these in engineering and allied industries, 21 per cent work in the basic industries, and the remaining 41 per cent are in the so-called service industries.

Employment and Unemployment.

In 1965 an average of 329,000 persons—1·4 per cent of the working population—were unemployed. Even in January 1959, the worst month of the 1950s, the rate rose only to 2·8 per cent, and in February 1963—an exceptional month—to 3·9 per cent. In most post-war years the average was lower than 1·5 per cent. This contrasts with an average figure in 1937, the best year of the 1930s, of 11 per cent, and with a figure of 22 per cent at the bottom of the slump in 1932. Probably 1–1·5 per cent is somewhere near the practicable minimum; for some unemployment is more

unemployment there ranged between 6 and 10 per cent. Nevertheless, regional inequalities exist.

UNEMPLOYMENT AND VACANCIES
(Great Britain, thousands)

	Unemployment. (Annual average.)	Vacancies. (End of period.)	Unemployment as percentage of total employees.
1932*	2,829	n.a.	*22·1*
1937*	1,482	n.a.	*10·9*
1954	285	338	*1·3*
1956	257	279	*1·2*
1958	457	163	*2·1*
1960	360	294	*1·6*
1962	463	157	*2·0*
1964	381	311	*1·6*
1966	360	234	*1·5*
1969	559	249	*2·3*

* Figures relate only to population insured against unemployment.

PERCENTAGE OF WORKERS UNEMPLOYED, BY REGIONS

	February 1963.	February 1965.
London and South-eastern . . .	2·3	1·0
Eastern and Southern .	3·6	1·2
South-western . .	3·8	1·8
Midlands . . .	3·4	0·8
Yorkshire and Lincolnshire . .	3·3	1·2
North-western . .	4·1	1·8
Northern . .	7·1	3·1
Scotland . .	6·2	3·6
Wales . . .	6·0	2·8
North Ireland . .	11·2	6·9
Great Britain . .	*3·9*	*1·6*

DECREASE IN EMPLOYMENT IN SELECTED INDUSTRIES, 1945–65

	Thousands.	Per cent.
Textiles . . .	224	23
Mining and quarrying	242	28
Shipbuilding . .	77	27
Agriculture, forestry, and fishing .	221	21

In February 1963—during a period of recession and also cold weather—the percentage of all workers unemployed in Great Britain was 3·9. But the table shows a lower proportion of the labour force was unemployed in the Midlands and the South, and that there was a much higher percentage of unemployment in the North, in Scotland, and in Northern Ireland. Moreover, the labour shortage of early 1965 was not shared equally: unemployment remained significant in these areas. In this situation checks have to be placed on the economy before full employment is reached, because in the booming areas vacancies far exceed unemployment.

One of the main reasons for the regional pattern of unemployment is that certain industries and services, in which big changes have been taking place, tend to be grouped in specific regions. Most of our early industrial centres had to be established close to coal, iron ore, and adequate water supplies. But employment in many long-established industries has recently been declining. The scale of this contraction can be seen from the table. On the other hand new and growing industries, and their related offices, have been concentrated in Greater London, the South East, and the Midlands. The growth of services, too, has centred on the areas where industry is booming and population is increasing. In the absence of Government intervention, the process would tend to become cumulative, and regional inequalities would grow rather than diminish.

National Income.

Gross domestic income (GDY) is the sum total of incomes received for the services of labour, land, or capital in a country. Gross domestic product (GDP) is the money value of all the goods and services produced in the country. So as to avoid double-counting, only the *value added* at each stage of production is included: firms' purchases are excluded. The revenue from selling the GDP is either paid out to the hired factors of production—labour, land, and capital—or retained in the form of profits. Therefore, provided it is calculated net of taxes on goods produced, GDP must equal GDY. To estimate gross national income from GDY it is necessary to add the net income—such as profits and interest—received from abroad. If an allowance is made for wear and tear of the nation's capital equipment, *i.e.*, for *capital consumption*, we arrive at net national income, better known as the *national income*.

In 1965 the national income of the United King-

dom was £28,280 million, implying a national income per head of £518. In 1955 the corresponding figures had been £15,514 million and £303 per head. However, only part of this increase in value was due to an increase in the quantity of goods and services produced: some of the increase simply reflected a rise in prices. It is important to calculate changes in the volume of output—known as *real output*—as well as changes in its value. Real output is calculated by the statistical device of constructing an index number. This is done by calculating the volume of goods and services provided in each year and then valuing these goods and services at the prices found in one particular year. Thus between 1955 and 1965 the money value of national income rose by 82 per cent; whereas real output increased by only 33 per cent, and the difference represented a rise in prices.

In real terms national income per head rose by 24 per cent between 1955 and 1965, or by 2·2 per cent per annum. National income per head is the most useful indicator of the standard of living. However, this measure is necessarily a crude one. For instance, it cannot take account of new products, *e.g.*, television or the plastic bucket; nor of changes in the distribution of income between rich and the poor; nor of the " quality of life," affected by such things as traffic jams and smokeless zones; nor of the length of the working week.

Industrial Production.

It is fairly easy to measure output in the main manufacturing industries, and in many of the basic industries. It is much more difficult to do so for the service industries: the output of a doctor or a teacher is not easily measured. So each month the Central Statistical Office calculates the *index of industrial production* covering the main " productive " industries. However, this tends to give a false impression of the rate of growth of output, since the industrial sector is the one best placed to raise its output per head and for which demand expands most rapidly. Roughly a 5 per cent increase in industrial output is likely to be accompanied by a 3 per cent increase in GDP, on which the average standard of living depends.

Manufacturing industry accounts for more than three-quarters of industrial production. Within manufacturing industry two industries have expanded most rapidly—chemicals, which includes drugs, plastics, cosmetics, detergents, and oil refining; and vehicles, which includes cars, tractors, commercial vehicles, and aircraft. The slowest growing manufacturing industries are textiles and shipbuilding, which are losing their markets to cheaper competitors. Those industries in which demand has stagnated are also the industries in which output per employee, *i.e.*, productivity, has stagnated.

International Comparisons.

Between 1955 and 1964 Britain's GDP grew less rapidly than that of any other country listed in the table, except the U.S.A. The British economy was also characterised by a relatively slow growth of output per head, *i.e.*, productivity. Many explanations of Britain's poor performance have been suggested, and there is by no means agreement on this matter among economists. It has been argued that the U.K.—like the U.S.A.—has a highly advanced economy, in which there is a relatively high demand for services; and that it is difficult to raise productivity in the large services sector. Another argument is that Britain has been hampered by its slowly growing labour force, which has restricted growth not only in output but also in output per man. The reason given is that an expanding labour force needs to be equipped with additional plant and machinery; so that its capital equipment tends to be newer on average than that used by a static labour force, and thus more up-to-date and efficient.

Some commentators have put the blame on the inefficiency of our business management; some on our educational system, biased towards the humanities; some on the social milieu which looks down on money-making as a career; some on over-manning and other restrictive practices of trade unions. A good deal of attention has

AN INTERNATIONAL GROWTH LEAGUE TABLE

| | Percentage change per annum, 1955–64. | | | Investment as percentage of G.N.P. | |
	Output.	Employment.	Output per head.	Including dwellings.	Excluding dwellings.
Japan . . .	10·4	1·4	8·8	28·8	21·5
W. Germany .	6·3	1·3	5·0	23·7	18·4
Italy . . .	5·7	0·1	5·6	21·6	15·6
Sweden . .	5·4	1·5	3·9	22·8	17·4
France . .	5·2	0·3	4·9	19·2	14·3
Denmark . .	5·0	1·2	3·8	18·7	15·4
Belgium . .	3·6	0·6	3·0	18·4	13·7
U.S.A. . .	3·1	1·1	2·0	17·1	12·2
U.K. . .	3·1	0·5	2·6	15·8	12·7

also been paid to the proportion of output which different countries devote to *investment*, i.e., expenditure on commodities—such as plant and machinery—for use in future production. These investment ratios are shown in the table. With the exception of the U.S.A., all countries have investment ratios considerably higher than in the U.K., with correspondingly higher growth rates of output and productivity. Since investment in dwellings contributes very little to growth, it is appropriate to exclude this investment: however, the same results are obtained. This leads to the hypothesis that Britain's growth rate could be raised if a higher proportion of output were devoted to investment, particularly in plant and machinery. There is probably some truth in many of these explanations, and it is unlikely that any one remedy will be sufficient to raise the British growth rate.

Capital and Automation.

Many of the growing industries are capital-intensive; they use much machinery and equipment per unit of output produced. In chemicals, steel, and, above all, electricity, the plant is extremely expensive. Most of the innovations since the war—nylon, atomic power, electronics, polythene, etc.—require a high capital investment, and cannot pay unless they are worked nearly full-out. One way to achieve this is by shift work, and it may be that a full exploitation of the potentialities of these new industries will require a greater extension of this system of work. And the future holds out prospects of still more intensive requirements for capital as automation spreads. With automation, much of the manual semi-skilled work should come to an end. The new electronic computers will be able to control the machines that actually do the manufacturing operations. "Transfer" machines can read details of the work to be done off a piece of tape; they can adjust themselves to correct mistakes or to adjust for faulty materials.

So far the impact of automation has been small. The main use has been in the office, where electronic computers can carry out far more efficiently much of the routine calculating, recording, and checking operations previously done by clerks. But it will continue to spread, and must do so if the growth in wealth is to continue. The change will come only gradually. But ultimately one can envisage that both in manufacturing industry and in office work the machine will have replaced much of the human effort in work, and even more of its drudgery. The typical manual job will become that of the skilled maintenance man.

This revolution will take many decades to effect. It raises no spectre of widespread redundancy; but it does mean that over the years more and more emphasis will need to be laid on the training of workers for skilled work, and indeed on raising the general level of education. Also over the years the average size of factory is likely to grow as these new methods, if they are to be profitable, have to be used on a large scale. Finally, the prospect is for ever-increasing requirements of capital—and of course for the savings to finance it.

Investment.

In 1965 gross investment in capital assets amounted to £6,252 million. This is about 20 per

cent of the gross national product (GNP). In other words, about one part in five of total production was used to replace old assets or to add to the nation's stock of capital equipment. The addition to the stock of capital assets (net investment) accounts for 60 per cent of gross investment; the remainder is needed to offset the wastage of assets already in use. We have seen (above) that the proportion of total output invested in Britain is lower than in countries with faster growth rates of output and productivity; and there is reason to believe that a higher proportion would improve the growth rate. But a rise in the investment ratio would involve a fall in other forms of expenditure, notably private and public consumption; and this would have to be brought about by increasing taxation or encouraging people to save. In other words, a faster rate of growth—which was achieved by this method would involve a sacrifice in current consumption. A choice must be made between the loss in current consumption and the ensuing gain in future consumption. Of course not all consumption expenditure is equally important to the standard of living: some would argue that if defence expenditure was pruned to permit more investment, there would be no loss to set against the future gain.

Types of Investment.

There are four main kinds of investment: plant and machinery; vehicles; dwellings and other construction. In 1965 the four categories accounted for 37, 10, 21, and 32 per cent respectively of total gross investment. Investment may also be analysed by the purpose for which it is used. It is clear from the table that some sectors are more capital-intensive than others. Manufacturing and social services (such as education and health) take a surprisingly small proportion of total investment; distribution (retail, wholesale, banking, and finance) and public utilities and services take a large proportion. Investment in electricity alone accounts for 10 per cent of the total. Investment in real terms rose most rapidly for social services and for distribution over the decade; manufacturing, other production industries, and transport fared badly.

GROSS INVESTMENT BY PURPOSE, 1965

	Percentage of total 1965.	Percentage increase 1955–65.
Manufacturing . .	21	48
Other production industries	7	36
Transport . .	9	46
Distribution . .	17	127
Public utilities and services . .	20	121
Housing . .	20	62
Other social services .	6	155
Total . .	100	76

The Finance of Investment.

Any business is allowed to charge as a cost the depreciation of its assets. Normal depreciation allowances are based on the original cost of the asset and on its expected useful life. In a time of price inflation depreciation allowances will not provide sufficient finance to permit the replacement of assets at higher prices, and there are many supporters of depreciation allowances being based on replacement costs. Many firms do set aside extra funds specifically to cover these extra replacement costs.

Governments have, however, adopted certain fiscal devices to encourage replacement and investment. Soon after the war initial allowances were introduced. Under this system firms were permitted to charge against profits in the first year of its life 20, or at times 40, per cent of the cost of any new equipment, and the system amounted to a loan of the tax saved in the first year, repaid over the life of the asset. In 1954 initial allowances for machinery were replaced by a system of investment allowances, under which a firm could charge against profits 20 per cent of the cost of any new machine, with the difference that all ordinary depreciation allowances were still chargeable. So the investment allowance was a grant, not a loan, of the saved tax. In 1966 it was announced that initial and investment allowances on new plant and machinery in the key sectors—manufacturing, mining, and shipping—would be replaced by cash grants. Other plant and machinery and industrial building would receive higher initial allowances. In 1970 the new Conservative Government announced that investment grants would be replaced by a system of 60 per cent initial allowances.

Depreciation allowances and government allowances and grants for investment are sufficient to cover the majority of investment (excluding dwellings) by the private sector, and to cover a minor part of public (non-housing) investment. The residue of investment, and housebuilding, has to be provided from savings. Companies rely mainly on retained profits, which are often larger, taking companies as a whole, than their net investment; and so too do the profit-making nationalised industries. Much public investment must be financed by the Treasury.

Monopoly and Competition.

This trend to increasing size and increasing capitalisation has been going on now for many decades, and in the process it has changed the face of British industry. In the early 19th cent. the typical firm was the owner-managed textile mill. Then in the 1860s and 1870s came the discovery of cheap methods of making steel, with the consequential immense growth in the engineering industries. Most of the chemical industry is still newer—some very new—and in these capital-intensive industries the big firm predominates. In some it has become almost a monopoly; no small firm can easily challenge industrial giants like Imperial Chemical Industries, the Dunlop Rubber Company, or Unilever. In others the pattern is of a few firms, all large, as in motor cars, detergents, and steel. Competition goes on, but it has changed its form. In the old days competition was largely by price. Now it is largely by advertising and by variations in the quality and other features of the product—detergents and motor cars being good examples. And in many industries groups of firms producing similar products entered into agreements which had the effect of restricting competition, for example through schemes for price-fixing.

Legislation against Restrictive Practices.

The Restrictive Practices Act of 1956 outlawed many of the main forms of restrictive agreements to prevent competition. Collective price fixing was declared to be illegal unless the industry could show that the practice brought substantial benefit to the public. Collective price-fixing was the the system under which a central association for the industry lays down minimum prices at which members may sell. Usually such a system was backed by arrangements for collective boycotts, under which members of the association would refuse to sell goods to wholesalers or retailers who broke the rules. Often the wholesalers too were in the scheme, and they would collectively refuse to buy from manufacturers who broke the rules. Collective boycotts were also found in industries without collective price-fixing, one common purpose being to make sure that retailers did not sell a manufacturer's products below his recommended price. This form of collective resale price maintenance was also outlawed by the Act. Under the Act any restrictive agreements of several specified kinds had to be registered with the Registrar of Restrictive Practices. He then had to decide whether there was a *prima facie* case for the discontinuation of the agreement, and, if he thought there was, the case was referred to a new Restrictive Practices Court, containing both judicial and lay members.

The Act of 1956 permitted individual manufacturers to enforce *resale price maintenance* (r.p.m.) for their own products. Few suppliers would want the publicity of enforcing r.p.m. through the courts, but individual suppliers could still put some commercial pressure on price-cutters, e.g., by offering less favourable terms or by refusing them supplies. The Resale Prices Act of 1964 prohibited all methods of enforcing minimum resale prices. However, goods which had been registered in due time with the Registrar of restrictive trading agreements or have been approved by the Restrictive Practices Court, were exempted, temporarily in the former case and permanently in the latter. For r.p.m. to be approved by the Court, it must be shown that some ensuing benefit to consumers (*e.g.*, of increased quality or more retail outlets) outweighed any detriment. It is also lawful to withhold supplies to retailers selling goods at a loss to attract customers. The list of applications for exemption is a long one, but the effect of the Act should be lower prices in the shops. It will also mean a more rapid decline of small retailers.

The Restrictive Practices Acts leave untouched the industries where one firm is dominant: these remain the responsibility of the Monopolies Commission, who report on industries referred to them by the Board of Trade, and make recommendations after investigation. The Monopolies and Mergers Act of 1965 strengthened control over monopolies and mergers. With regard to monopolies, the Government wished to provide itself with legal powers of enforcement: previously monopolies had been expected to comply voluntarily with the findings of the Monopolies Commission. The Act also permits the Government to refer a merger or a proposed merger to the Monopolies Commission in cases where the merger would lead to monopoly (defined as control of at least one third of the market) or would increase the power of an existing monopoly, or where the value of the assets taken over exceeds £5 million. But it would be wrong to presume that mergers are always bad: mergers—by facilitating research and other economies of large-scale operation—may increase industrial efficiency. For this reason the Labour Government established an Industrial Reorganisation Corporation to promote the grouping of firms in cases where such grouping would be beneficial to their industry; but in 1970 the Conservative Government decided to wind it up.

Restrictive labour practices—which result in the " over-manning " of plant or the " under-employment " of men—are common in British industry. These stem from such causes as the fear of redundancy and unemployment, anxiety to preserve a craft skill threatened by technical progress, the desire to work at overtime rates, and sometimes just inertia. In the fully-employed economy of the 1960s, redundancy should not be a problem, and under-employed labour is urgently needed elsewhere. The elimination of these restrictive practices requires more enlightened management, more union co-operation, and more Government measures to promote the mobility of labour between occupations.

Nationalised Industries.

Nationalised industry accounts for about 20 per cent of British industry. Local authorities also run some services—largely in bus transport and water provision. With the exception of coal-mining, all these industries are natural monopolies in which the provision of competing services would be obviously wasteful. They are thus obvious candidates for nationalisation. With the exception of steel—nationalised 1951–53 and re-nationalised in 1967—nationalisation has not been extended into manufacturing industry, not even where the existence of a private monopoly might suggest that there was a strong case. But nationalised industries are not free from competition. The railways face competition from road transport, some publicly and some privately owned; the fuel industries compete with each other, and with the privately owned oil industry.

Nationalised industries are supposed to earn enough to cover their costs. In the first ten years the two airways corporations were granted subsidies; but these have now ceased. Costs for a nationalised industry include interest payments on capital—both on the compensation paid to the previous owners and on the rather larger amounts of capital raised since nationalisation. The electricity boards, and to a lesser extent the gas boards, earn something above their costs to finance expansion, but not even then on the scale which is normal practice in private industries. The National Coal Board has accumulated a deficit by not increasing coal prices sufficiently to meet the increasing costs of production. British Rail has been in chronic deficit which it was the object of the Beeching Report to reduce.

The nationalised industries are voracious users of capital, as they are nearly all highly capitalised industries. Until 1956 they raised new capital, when they wanted it, by floating an issue on the Stock Exchange, the issue being guaranteed by the Government. Since then the nationalised industries have drawn directly on the Exchequer for their capital. This system has been attacked on both sides. The advocates of private enterprise have pointed to the strain this puts on the Exchequer, and to the unfairness whereby the nationalised industries get their capital cheaper or more easily than private industry. From the other side, it has been pointed out that the nationalised industries have suffered from their dependence on the Exchequer. In times of balance of payments crises the nationalised industries have been forced by the Government to cut back their planned programmes, sometimes at serious cost in disorganisation.

3. INCOMES, WAGES, AND PRICES.

Personal Income, Spending, and Saving.

National income is a measure of the total income accruing to residents in return for services rendered. It therefore consists of the sum of wages, salaries, profits, and rents. Not all this income accrues to persons. Thus, companies do not distribute all their profits to shareholders: in 1965 undistributed profits amounted to £4,040 million. This is part of national income but not of personal income. On the other hand, some personal incomes are not payments for services rendered. Such incomes are called " transfer incomes " to emphasise that their payment does not add to the national income, but only transfers income from one recipient to another. Included in this category are retirement pensions, children's allowances, National Assistance payments, etc., amounting in 1965 to £2,724 million; and the interest on the National Debt paid out to persons. Total personal income in 1965 was £29,736 million.

The table shows what happened to this income. Direct taxation—income tax and surtax—took about 11 per cent of total personal income, and National Insurance contributions, which being compulsory are in effect a form of tax, took a further 6 per cent. The remainder of personal income—called disposable income—was available for spending or saving. In 1965 total personal savings amounted to 6 per cent of personal income and 8 per cent of personal disposable income.

The other 92 per cent of disposable income was spent on consumption goods and services. Consumption expenditure in turn was broken down in the following way: a quarter on food; an eighth on drink and tobacco; 16 per cent on housing, fuel, and light; 9 per cent on clothing; 8 per cent on durable goods (motor cars, television

sets, refrigerators, etc.); 7 per cent on travel; leaving just over a fifth for other goods and services. Almost as much was spent on drink and tobacco as on housing, fuel, and light. This is partly because drink and tobacco is subject to heavy indirect taxation, which is the name given to taxes which are levied on particular goods and services. Thus nearly three-quarters of expenditure on tobacco goes to the Government. Total indirect taxation on consumers' expenditure amounted to £4,196 million in 1965, though this was offset by subsidies—payments by the Government towards the cost of particular goods and services, mainly some foods and housing—amounting to £508 million.

DISPOSAL OF PERSONAL INCOME, 1965

	£ million.	Percentage.
Total Personal Income .	29,700	100
less:		
Direct Taxes . .	3,390	11
National Insurance contributions. . .	1,690	6
gives:		
Disposable Income . .	24,620	83
Available for:		
Consumption . .	22,710	77
Saving . . .	1,910	6

Types of Personal Income.

Compare the sources of personal income in 1938 and in 1963. We see in the table that income from employment increased considerably, largely owing to a rise in the salary bill. The reason is not that salaries have increased faster than wages, but rather that the number of salaried workers has increased much faster than the number of wage-earners. There has also been an increase in the proportion of incomes derived from public grants—old age pensions, war pensions, sickness benefits, student grants, etc.

SOURCES OF PERSONAL INCOME, 1938 AND 1963
(As percentage of total)

	1938.	1963.
Income from employment of which:	59·5	71
wages . . .	38	39
salaries . . .	18	25
Forces' pay . .	1·5	1·5
employers' contributions* .	2·5	5·5
Income from self-employment of which:	12·5	9
professional persons .	2	1·5
farmers . .	1·5	2
others . . .	9	5
Income from property .	22·5	11·5
Grants from public authorities .	5·5	8·5
Total . . .	100	100

* To National Insurance and other superannuation schemes.

The types of income which have fallen as a proportion of the total are incomes of self employed persons and incomes from property. During the war and for several years afterwards property incomes changed little—the effects of rent control, excess profits tax, and low interest rates were such that these incomes did not rise while other incomes increased sharply. In more recent years there was a rise, as rent control or some property was lifted and as interest rates increased; but nevertheless the share of property incomes in 1963 was only about half of what it had been in 1938. Over this quarter of a century there was a fundamental redistribution of income away from property-owners towards employees.

Incomes by Size.

In 1964 over 70 per cent of income-receivers had incomes under £1,000 and over 90 per cent under £1,500. The remaining 9 per cent with incomes over £1,500 received 27 per cent of the total income, and the top 1 per cent received 8 per cent of the total. Thus Britain is far from being an egalitarian society; income is still very unevenly distributed, but not so unevenly as before the war,

allowance now adds substantially to spending power. As tax rates have risen, it has become increasingly profitable for such classes to claim every expense to which they are conceivably entitled. Particularly important are cars required for business and also used for pleasure.

Second, only in 1965 did capital gains become taxable. If one buys an asset which then rises in value, one has clearly gained extra spending power. Not only have people in Britain been exempt from tax on capital gains, a considerable advantage in periods of boom in ordinary share prices, but also they have been able by a number

BRITISH INCOMES BY SIZE, 1964

Range of incomes before tax.	As percentage of total.			
	Number of incomes.	Incomes before tax.	Incomes after tax.	Rates of tax as percentage.
£50–£250 . . .	14	3	4	0
£250–£500 . . .	22	10	11	2
£500–£1,000 . . .	35	31	33	6
£1,000–£1,500 . . .	20	29	30	9
£1,500–£2,000 . . .	5	11	10	14
£2,000–£3,000 . . .	2	6	5	20
£3,000–£5,000 . . .	1	4	3	27
£5,000– . . .	0·5	6	4	46
Total . . .	27.5m.	£22,885 m.	£20,268 m.	11

when the top 1 per cent received 16 per cent of total income.

Taxes on income are of course highly progressive, rising sharply as income increases. Those with low incomes pay no income tax, and in so far as they are pensioners, no compulsory contributions either. We see from the table that the proportion of income paid in direct taxes rises from 2 per cent in the income bracket £250–£500 to 9 per cent in the bracket £1,000–£1,500 to 46 per cent for incomes exceeding £5,000 per annum.

This tax burden somewhat changes the distribution of incomes. After tax the top 9 per cent received only 23 per cent, and the top 1 per cent only 5·5 per cent of total incomes. But the re-distributive effect of taxation must not be over-stressed; the levelling-up of incomes before tax has been very much more important in making Britain rather more egalitarian than has been any taxation policy.

Income and Spending Power.

In many ways figures for incomes alone substantially over-estimate the degree of equality found in Britain. First, incomes are incomes as defined for income-tax purposes. Any allowed

of devices to convert income into capital gains, and thus avoid paying income tax. Before 1965 various Chancellors of the Exchequer merely tried to close loopholes by making illegal various transactions aimed at tax avoidance.

Distribution of Capital.

Spending power depends not only on income and capital gains but also on the sheer amount of capital owned; and in respect of capital Britain is still far from egalitarian. The only figures are those that arise in connection with the payment of death duties. In 1964/5 those who at death left estates of more than £5,000—just over a fifth of the total numbers dying—owned 77 per cent of the total, and the richest 1 per cent owned 24 per cent of the total. And this in spite of a growing tendency for the rich to pass on their money before death to avoid death duties. Compared with 1938, the main change appears to be that the fairly rich are somewhat more numerous and the extremely rich are somewhat less numerous. The vast majority still own very little, and Britain is far from being a property-owning democracy.

Wages and Salaries.

In 1965 two thirds of personal income was paid in the form either of wages, salaries, or Forces' pay. The distinction between the first two is

DISTRIBUTION OF WEALTH: VALUE OF ESTATES FOR DEATH DUTIES, 1964/5

Size of estate. £,000.	As percentage of total.	
	Number of estates.	Value of estates.
–1	38	3
1–2	17	5
2–3	11	5
3–5	13	10
5–10	11	14
10–25	6	19
25–50	2	15
50–100	1	13
100–	0·4	16
Total	295,798	£1,531 m.

WAGE AND SALARY LEVELS IN MANUFACTURING INDUSTRY
(Earnings per week, October 1969)

	Administrative, Clerical, and Technical Staff.		Wage earners. (Adults only.)
	Monthly paid.	Weekly paid.	
Men .	£35 19s.	£24 9s.	£25 10s.
Women .	£15 14s.	£12 0s.	£12 2s.

expenses are excluded; and for the self-employed and the higher ranks of management the expense

very much a matter of convention; many salary-earners now earn less than wage earners, and the main division is between those salary-earners who are paid monthly and the rest. This we see in the table. Even though weekly-paid staff do not now earn more than wage-earners, they may still in effect be better off: for they generally work shorter hours; are more likely to be covered by private superannuation schemes; and usually work in better conditions.

No regular statistics are collected about salary levels; but every half-year the Department of Employment publishes detailed figures of the actual earnings in one week of wage-earners in a wide range of industries. There is a considerable variation in earnings between industries. Manufacturing industries pay well; and within manufacturing industries, vehicles and paper, printing and publishing pay the highest weekly wages. Public administration (including local government road-men and the like) is a low-wage sector, particularly for men. For women the best paying industry is the buses where there is equal pay for male and female conductors. It should be borne in mind, however, that the average earnings for an industry may disguise a wide dispersion of earnings among firms of the industry and also within firms.

AVERAGE WEEKLY EARNINGS OF MANUAL WORKERS IN CERTAIN INDUSTRIES
(October 1969)

	Men.	Women.
Vehicles . . .	£28 13s.	£14 13s.
Paper, printing, and publishing . . .	£29 2s.	£12 11s.
Chemicals . . .	£25 13s.	£12 2s.
Food, drink, and tobacco	£24 3s.	£11 19s.
Textiles . . .	£22 17s.	£11 18s.
All manufacturing industries* . .	£25 11s.	£12 2s.
Transport and communications (except railways) . .	£25 18s.	£16 17s.
Construction . .	£24 9s.	£11 8s.
Public administration .	£18 9s.	£11 17s.
All industries* .	£24 16s.	£12 2s.

* Including industries not listed.

Differentials.

Women earn on average much less than men, and juveniles usually much less than adults. Before the war the gap was relatively greater. Men, for instance, earned 5·6 times as much in October 1965 as they did in October 1938; but for women the ratio was 6·2 times. Nearly all this narrowing occurred during the war, when it was the common practice for wage advances to take the form of a flat-rate increase to all employees regardless of sex. Since 1950 the practice has altered. The usual thing has been to grant roughly similar percentage increases to all grades, and there has in fact been a slight widening of the gap.

The same narrowing occurred in other differentials. Skilled workers, for instance, were during the war granted the same flat-rate advances as unskilled and there was then and, to some extent, also in the years immediately after the war, a sharp narrowing of the reward for skill in many industries. As for the sex differential, the narrowing has now come to a halt; but it has not been reversed, and wages within the working-class are much less widely spread than they used to be. Some would say the rewards for skill were insufficient; but, on the other hand, the upgrading of the lowest-paid has, together with the reduction in long-term unemployment, been the main means by which the grinding poverty of the worst-off members of society—with all its undesirable consequences, such as malnutrition of children— has been eliminated. Today the really numerous poor are the old, the sick, and the handicapped— and not, as before the war, families with a working head who was earning too little to make ends meet.

Differentials have been a major source of industrial strife in some industries. In engineering there has been continued conflict between unions with membership largely among the skilled and those with membership largely among the semiskilled over what form demands for wage increases should take. On the railways the strife has been even more open.

Overtime and Short-time.

The earnings of any individual worker depend on many factors, and are usually far above the minimum wage-rates payable for a week. They include overtime earnings; and overtime working is common for men. In most weeks about 2 million workers in manufacturing will be working overtime to the extent of 8 to 9 hours. So the average-week in 1969 was 46 hours, which is about 6 hours above the average standard working week without overtime. In the transport industry the average working-week for men was as much as 51 hours. Indeed the average working-week in 1960 was higher than before the war, even though the standard working-week had been reduced. In most industries it was cut by 4 hours soon after the war from 48 to 44 hours, a 42-hour week was introduced between 1960 and 1962, and there was a movement towards a 40-hour standard working-week between 1964 and 1966.

Short-time, the working of less than the standard week, has not been common since the war. It has been important in particular industries at particular times; but even in February 1963, at the bottom of the recession, it was far smaller than overtime. Then 165,000 workers were on an average short-time of 12·5 hours—a total of 2·0 million hours lost, as against 12·3 million hours of overtime in the same week.

Earnings and Rates.

Overtime is not, however, the main reason why earnings exceed minimum wage-rates; for most workers earn very much more than the minimum in the standard working-week. One reason is payment by results, the system of payment under which the worker's wage depends partly on output. The commonest form is still the piecework system, under which pieceworkers are paid a fixed low rate per hour for each hour worked plus a fixed piecework price for each operation performed; but increasingly employers tend to prefer as a more effective incentive some scheme under which the bonus payment is related to the output of a larger group or to that of a whole factory. With payment by results systems—these cover about 40 per cent of the workers in manufacturing industry—earnings rise as productivity rises, and, as usually such workers also participate in advances in wage-rates negotiated between employers and unions, the gap between earnings and wage-rates tends to widen for them. So workers not paid by results press for similar advances for themselves, and in times of booming trade get them under a wide variety of names and forms—merit payments, lieu rates, compensation bonuses, etc.

Between 1959 and 1969 wage-rates rose by 52 per cent and earnings by 80 per cent. The advance in rates was little more than the rise in retail prices—only 11 per cent—so that anyone who actually earned the minimum rate throughout was not much better off. But earnings rose by 39 per cent more than prices, so that the main source of the extra real income of the working-class is to be found in the widening gap between earnings and rates.

Wage Negotiation.

In Britain there were 10·0 million trade union members in 530 unions in 1968. Most of these unions are very small, over 350 having less than 2,500 members, but 19 have a membership of over 100,000. The main job of unions is collective bargaining with employers, and in most industries most employers also belong to associations which bargain collectively on their behalf. Some big firms, however, prefer to remain outside the associations, and strike their own bargain with the unions. Before the war many firms tried to encourage the formation of Company Unions, *i.e.*, of unions confined to employees of a single firm; but this is now uncommon. In some lowly paid trades—catering, baking, dressmaking, and others —minimum wages are fixed by Wages Boards or Councils set up by the Department of Employment; and representatives of the workers and employers, and independent members, meet together to reach agreement on the settlement to be recommended to the Minister. But over most of industry the aim of collective bargaining is to reach voluntary agreement, and the Department of Employment intervenes only when no agreement is reached. Even in the nationalised industries, the Government does not usually intervene unless negotiations between the Boards and the unions break down.

The usual pattern of negotiation is like this. First, the union puts in a claim for an all-round increase, usually much larger than it expects to get. Then after a time the employers reply, often offering a much smaller increase, and sometimes none at all. They then argue round a table until either they reach agreement or they definitely fail to reach agreement. If the latter happens the next step varies considerably from industry to industry. Many industries have their own " conciliation " machinery, in which outsiders try to help the two sides to reach agreement. Some, though not many, also have their own " arbitration " machinery, in which outsiders can recommend a solution of the dispute, which is sometimes binding and sometimes not. It depends on what the two sides have agreed on in advance. Many industries have no machinery of their own and depend on the general facilities the Minister responsible can offer. He may appoint an impartial conciliator; or he may, with the agreement of both parties, refer the matter to the Industrial Court, which arbitrates between the parties; or he may set up a Court of Enquiry which enquires into the dispute and makes recommendations, which are not binding on the parties; or he may decide to do nothing at all, if he judges intervention to be useless. Nor need either unions or employers call him in; the former may opt to put pressure on the employers immediately either by strike action, or by banning overtime or piecework, or by other action.

Thus the British Government traditionally has little power to control wages directly or to impose agreements. The recent attempts to introduce compulsion in wage-determination are described in **Part IV**.

Important Negotiations.

A few negotiations are particularly important in determining how wages rise in a year; for the pattern of later settlements tends roughly to follow those of earlier settlements. Probably the most important of all are those between the Confederation of Engineering and Shipbuilding Unions—an organisation representing 3 million workers—and the Engineering Employers' Federation, as this single negotiation directly affects the wages of 3¼ million workers, and indirectly many more. On several occasions since the war negotiations between these two have broken down, and only finally been settled after a Court of Enquiry had recommended a compromise wage-advance. The Confederation is a special negotiating body comprising all the unions who have members working in the engineering and shipbuilding industries. These include many small, skilled workers' unions, such as the Patternmakers' Union, but they also include, besides the 1-million-strong Amalgamated Engineering Union, the two large general unions, the Transport and General Workers' Union, with about 1½ million members, and the General and Municipal Workers' Union, with not far short of a million. These last two represent the semi-skilled and unskilled workers, and conflict between them and the skilled unions concerning differentials is common.

Another often important negotiation is that between the British Transport Commission and the three railway unions—the large National Union of Railwaymen, representing most grades, the Amalgamated Society of Locomotive Engineers and Firemen, representing the drivers and the firemen, and the Transport Salaried Staffs' Association, representing the ticket collectors, railway clerks, etc. The importance of this negotiation lies in the fact that railwaymen are comparatively badly paid; but, as the Transport Commission runs a deficit, any wage advance has effectively to be paid for by the Government. Time and time again—for example the rise in early 1960 arising out of the Guillebaud Report on railway pay—wage advances have been given to railwaymen with the purpose of trying to narrow the gap between them and other workers; but the advance given to railwaymen then acts as a guide to other settlements, so that the railwaymen remain relatively as badly paid as before.

Strikes.

The strike is the unions' weapon of last resort. Most unions maintain strike funds in order to support their members when they call them out on strike; but these funds are small, and strike pay is usually very much below normal wages. So unions cannot afford to call strikes irresponsibly, and major official strikes are uncommon. In most years there will be one or two, but not more, and the total number of working-days lost is usually negligible—less than one day per head. Even in the industry affected the lost working-days are usually made up in the following weeks by overtime.

Nevertheless, the big strikes are important; for the success or failure of one big strike can affect the results of all the other collective bargaining under way at the time. They can also affect the awards of arbitration tribunals since, in the main, arbitration awards tend to follow the pattern of settlements already made in other industries. There is no purpose in a tribunal trying to be fair if it cannot get its awards accepted. So the settlement reached as a result of a strike often determines the amount by which wage-rates will rise on average over all industries.

Most strikes are neither large nor official, nor about wages. An official strike is one called by a union, usually by decision of the national executive, and is usually the result of a breakdown in collective bargaining about wages. But unofficial strikes called by local leaders with the authorisation of unions are usually about other matters. Few of the big unofficial strikes which have plagued the London Docks since the war were about wages, but usually about some relative triviality that only bore witness to the thoroughly poor state of labour relations in that industry. Much the same may be said about the continual strikes in shipbuilding, many of them caused by demarcation disputes concerning which type of skilled worker. These sort of strikes are really a form of industrial protest, and the employers have to bear their share of the blame.

In 1965 there were in all 2,350 strikes in the United Kingdom; 869,000 workers were directly or indirectly involved, and 2,932,000 working days were lost. This means that the average strike involved 370 workers and lasted over 3 days.

In most industries there are very few strikes. The main strike-prone industries, apart from the mines, are vehicles, shipbuilding, and docks; but even in these the extent of strikes must not be exaggerated. In shipbuilding with the worst record of disputes, losses are only just over one day a year and, if that were all, could safely be ignored. But, of course, strikes are also a symptom of industrial trouble; and it is no accident that in shipbuilding productivity has scarcely improved at all since the war.

Prices and Real Incomes.

The aim of a trade union is to get for its members a higher standard of living, and its success depends on the extent to which wage advances exceed the rise in the cost-of-living. Prices rose very rapidly

WAGES AND PRICES
(1955 = 100)

	Weekly wage-rates.	Weekly earnings.	Index of retail prices.	Real wage-rates.	Real earnings.
1950	73	68	77	96	91
1955	100	100	100	100	100
1960	124	130	114	109	114
1965	151	175	136	112	129
1969	184	224	159	116	141

(by over 30 per cent) between 1949 and 1953, and earnings only just kept ahead in this period. But since then *real earnings* (i.e., command over goods and services of money earnings) have risen steadily. Thus, between 1955 and 1969, the real earnings of a wage-earner rose by 41 per cent.

Real incomes of pensioners and those on National Assistance have gone up too, after the serious erosion of their value in the late 1940s. The retirement pension is still inadequate for a decent life; but that is because when the National Insurance scheme was set up in 1948 it was believed that the nation could not afford anything better, and not because inflation has eroded the value of the pension (see **G 24**). Inflation can no longer be deplored on the main ground that it leads to much hardship. The main danger is that British exports become uncompetitive, and that the balance of payments position deteriorates and puts a brake on the growth of the economy.

Price Changes.

In the calculation of real wages it is usual to make use of the *index of retail prices*, commonly called the cost-of-living index. This index is calculated monthly by the Ministry of Labour, and in a few industries with sliding-scale agreements, wages are adjusted to take account of the index. In other industries the index has naturally had an influence on the course of negotiations. Indeed, up to 1958 it was probably the dominant influence. In no year before then had the annual rise in prices been less than 2 per cent.

in 1951. Since then, however, the dominant trend of import prices has been downwards, and changes in prices of imports cannot be directly blamed for the continuing rise in prices since 1951. The source has to be looked for in the tendency of wages, salaries, profits, and other incomes to rise faster than real output, and this they have done in almost every year since the war.

Wages and Prices.

Wage increases are probably the most important. When a trade union negotiates a wage advance for all or most of the employees in an industry, firms will immediately consider whether they should increase their prices to cover their increased wage-costs. As it is common practice for firms to fix the selling prices of their products by first calculating the direct cost of labour and of materials, and then adding on a percentage to cover overhead costs and profits, they will tend to want to raise their prices not only to cover the cost of the wage advance but also to cover their percentage addition. Moreover, in deciding whether or not their customers will stand for such increases, firms will be influenced by the knowledge that their competitors have to pay the

INDEX OF RETAIL PRICES

(January 1956 = 100)

	1965 Weight.*	Monthly average index.				
		1950.	1955.	1960.	1965.	1969.
Food	311	65	98	107	124	146
Drink	65	} 94	100	98	127	148
Tobacco . . .	76		98	112	146	168
Housing . . .	109	83	98	132	169	206
Fuel and light . .	65	65	92	117	150	181
Durable household goods .	59	80	94	98	107	121
Clothing and footwear .	92	83	98	104	114	125
Transport and vehicles .	105	—	—	118	135	157
Services . . .	63	73	97	115	147	186
Other goods . . .	55	77	96	120	140	170
All items . . .	*1000*	*74*	*97*	*111*	*132*	*155*

* *I.e.*, proportionate importance of item in total expenditure in 1965.

Price changes have not been the same for all types of goods. For instance, between 1956 and 1965, when the total index rose by 32 per cent, housing went up by 69 per cent and fuel and light by 50 per cent; but the prices of food, clothing, drink, and especially durable household goods rose less than the average. Since rent, fuel, and food form a much higher proportion of total expenditure for the poor, and particularly for pensioners, than for most households, it is possible that prices rose more for the poor than for the rich over these years.

The Causes of Price Inflation.

Prices charged in the shops are determined by a great many factors, over many of which the Government has little or no control. First among these is the price of imports. Prices of imported food and raw materials are determined in the world markets, in which Britain is only one of many purchasers. In the raw material markets the U.S.A. is usually the dominant purchaser, and prices depend greatly on the level of economic activity there. In the food markets British purchases are much more important, since the U.S.A. grows most of its own food, and is a large exporter of some foods. Prices in raw material markets are continually changing, and can fluctuate wildly. For instance, the average price of copper rose 40 per cent between 1954 and 1955, and then fell back in 1957 to 10 per cent below its 1954 level. Fluctuations at the time of the Korean War were even more fantastic. The price of wool rose over four times, and then came down just as abruptly to only a quarter above its earlier level; the price of rubber behaved similarly. The large rise in import prices, coming on top of the rise that had been brought about by devaluation, caused the cost-of-living index to shoot up sharply

increased wages too, and will probably therefore be raising their prices. So industry-wide wage advances—and changes in costs of materials—are particularly likely to be passed on to the consumer; and, as wage-earners are also consumers, to generate further demands for wage advances to cover the increased prices. Profits per unit also go up under this tendency to set prices on a *cost-plus* basis; but it is the wage advance which tends to set the spiral off, by providing the opportunity for price increases.

Once this spiral gets going, it is very hard to stop it. In general, the requirement is that wage earnings should not rise faster than productivity (output per man). But, as in some industries productivity is very slow to rise, and as it would be unfair and impracticable to exclude their workers from participating in any general rise in the standard of living, this requirement means that in industries with a rapid growth of productivity wage advances should be kept well below the rate of rise of productivity. For two reasons this is rather difficult. First, rising productivity often raises the wages of some workers in these industries automatically, because they are paid by results or through some incentive scheme. The rise of wages from this source takes the form of a tendency on the part of earnings in these industries to rise faster than wage-rates; but that does not mean that all employees benefit, or that there is any likelihood that the unions in these industries will not press for the same rate of increase in wage-rates as is achieved in the slowly-growing industries. Second, employers in the rapidly-growing industries have far less reason to resist demands for wage increases than those in slowly-growing industries. Indeed, they are quite likely to bid up wages in order to get the labour they need, rather than to try to hold down wages.

There are therefore major problems in preventing a faster rise in wages than in productivity, with its consequence of rising prices. And once a wage-price spiral has started, the problems become more acute because unions and employers become accustomed to substantial annual advances in money wages. A main source of continuing price inflation has been the tendency of money wages to continue to advance at a rate that was appropriate when the cost-of-living was going up sharply, but ceased to be appropriate in later years.

The Stopping of Price Inflation.

There are several possible methods of attack on the inflationary spiral of wages and prices. Perhaps the most fundamental, and certainly the most helpful to other objectives of economic policy, is to achieve a faster rate of productivity growth. The faster the growth of average productivity, the faster can average incomes rise without an increase in average prices. But if wages and other incomes rise more rapidly than productivity, it will be difficult to maintain price stability.

Comprehensive and detailed Government control of wages must probably be ruled out for political and institutional reasons, and so must comprehensive and detailed control of prices. Either would involve a much more " controlled " economy than we have at present, and experience suggests that such detailed control would involve a major loss of flexibility in the economy. At the other extreme, general exhortations to unions to exercise restraint on wages, and to manufacturers to exercise restraint on prices, have probably had little effect.

Various intermediate lines of approach have been or could be tried. In 1948–50, the Government secured the co-operation of the T.U.C. in the wages " freeze ". For a time this was successful, but the increases in prices which followed the devaluation in 1949 made substantial increases in wages unavoidable, and the freeze was abandoned. By setting an example in the nationalised industries over which it has a more direct influence, the Government can encourage employers to take a tougher attitude towards wage claims. This was one strand of policy in the later 1950s. Its disadvantage is the obvious unfairness of a policy which is most likely to be effective in nationalised industries, many of whose workers are relatively badly-paid. Another approach is to lower tariffs or remove quotas on imports, thus exposing some manufacturers at home to tougher competition from abroad. Manufacturers would be less able to raise prices without losing markets, and unions would be less willing to press wage claims if there was a real danger that some of their members would lose their jobs as a consequence. But the gains from a policy which depends for its success on higher imports have to be weighed against its effects on the balance of payments. Or again, many prices in the economy are directly influenced by Government indirect taxation which raises the price of some goods, and Government subsidies which lower the prices of other goods. By manipulating its tax and subsidy policies, the Government can exercise a powerful influence on the price level: though of course any reduction in indirect taxation or increase in subsidies would probably have to be financed by increases in direct taxation, which may in turn have undesirable effects on incentives to harder work and greater effort.

More indirectly, the Government can attempt to control the wage-price spiral by controlling purchasing power through its monetary and fiscal policies. If purchasing power is curbed, manufacturers find it more difficult to raise prices, and the bargaining power of unions may be reduced. In the 1950s, the Government relied heavily on fiscal and more especially monetary policies, the nature of which will be examined in later sections. The main danger is that curbing purchasing power is likely to curb the rise in output and productivity, so that attempts to control the wage-price spiral in this way could result in the stagnation of the economy. Furthermore, there is a danger that some wage increases will continue in periods of stagnation so that inflation cannot be entirely avoided.

It is clear that there is no easy solution—there

are difficulties and disadvantages attaching to every possible measure for controlling price inflation. In Part IV we shall discuss the solutions which have been attempted in the 1960s.

4. MONEY, BANKING, AND FINANCE.

The Radcliffe Report.

In September 1957 the Chancellor set up the Radcliffe Committee to report on the working of Britain's monetary institutions. The report of the committee, published in 1959, contains a detailed description of the monetary institutions of this country, and a systematic appraisal of monetary policies in the 1950s. It is complicated, because the monetary system is complicated; but it is written in terms which can be understood by the layman. Any reader who finds the following account inadequate should consult it.

Money.

In Britain money consists of bank-notes, coinage, and banks' debt. Bank-notes—mainly in denominations of £10, £5, and £1—are issued by the Bank of England, which has been publicly owned since 1946, and which acts in effect as an agent of the Government. We shall see below (**G21**(1)) how commercial banks can also create money.

The total size of the bank-note issue is not a good guide to the amount of purchasing power in the economy. The Bank of England stated in its evidence to the Radcliffe Committee that it was now its policy to issue bank-notes in accordance with the convenience of the public, and not to use this means of controlling the amount of purchasing power. As a result, the various checks on the size of the note issue—in particular the Parliamentary control over the fiduciary issue, i.e., the permitted maximum level of the note issue—have become functionless and may be ignored. An increase in the value of the note issue is now only a symptom and not a cause of inflation.

Determination of Income and Employment.

What matters is the amount of purchasing power available to the public. Most private expenditure is financed out of income—after paying taxes—and most government expenditure out of taxes; but most investment, public and private, and a growing amount of purchases of durable goods by consumers, is not financed out of income, but out of borrowing of one kind or another. And the primary purpose of monetary policy must be to keep the total of this kind of expenditure out of credit in line with the amount of savings private individuals and profit-making companies are prepared to make out of their incomes. For if such investment expenditure exceeds the amount which the community wishes to save out of its current level of income, it means that the total demand for goods and services exceeds total current output. If output cannot be increased because men and machines are already fully-employed, prices and wages and also imports are forced up in response to the demand. If, on the other hand, investment expenditure falls short of saving out of full-employment income, production and employment are reduced below the full-employment level.

There is no automatic mechanism in our economic system which ensures full-employment of resources, and it is the task of Government to balance savings and investment at the right level of employment. This important fact was first established by the great economist J. M. (later Lord) Keynes. Prior to the Great Depression, economists believed that any divergence from full-employment was a temporary phenomenon, which would right itself. However, in the 1930s Keynes produced a new explanation of how income and employment are determined; and so brought about what has come to be known as the *Keynesian Revolution* in economics.

Government Control of Income and Employment.

The Government can control the level of income and employment in various ways. First, in many fields the Government has only very restricted powers to influence behaviour. It cannot compel persons or companies to save; it can only offer them inducements to do so in the form of higher interest rates or of tax concessions on receipts from interest, and their effectiveness is limited. Nor in general has it very much direct power over expenditure out of credit. It can and does control the conditions under which hire-purchase agreements are made—and this does, temporarily at any rate, make a great deal of difference to the amount of goods bought on hire-purchase. It can to a certain extent influence private companies in their investment policies by granting and withdrawing incentives to invest-ment (see G13(1)); but it is doubtful quite how much influence these changes have. And it can, if it chooses, exercise direct control over building, by allowing building only on licence. This power, however, is not now used in order to control the level of investment, but only in order to encourage it in depressed areas and discourage it elsewhere. The only authorities over whose investment the Government does have real control are the nationalised industries; and, as the Radcliffe Committee pointed out, there are obvious dis-advantages in any system whereby investment in public utilities is determined, not by the need for such investment, but by the need to balance savings and investment.

The two main means remaining are fiscal and monetary control. If the Government thinks there is going to be a shortage of private savings it raises more in taxation or reduces its current expenditure and so increases the Budget surplus (see G24(2)). The second form of control is much more complex; in principle, the aims are twofold. One is to keep the amount of credit-creation down (or up) to the required extent; the second is to ensure that the Government gets the share of savings it needs to cover its investment pro-grammes. The complexity arises from the inter-relations between these two tasks.

The Government as Borrower.

The Government is a heavy borrower from the rest of the economy. In 1965 total public borrow-ing—by government, nationalised industries, and local authorities—stood at £38,000 million, equiva-lent to 1·4 times the annual national income. Most of this immense National Debt was built up during the war, when government expenditure far ex-ceeded taxation; but the total continues to advance year by year, owing to the heavy capital requirements of the nationalised industries.

The Government borrows in six main ways. First, the issue of bank-notes is in effect a form of government borrowing. Second, it borrows from foreign governments. Third, it borrows from companies through tax reserve certificates, which are a means by which companies let the Govern-ment have the taxes they would have to pay on profits as the latter are earned, rather than when the taxes legally become due. Fourth, it borrows direct from private individuals through the various forms of national savings. In all forms of national savings the Government pays interest—or in the case of premium bonds prizes in lieu of interest to the winners of the monthly draw—to the holders, who have the right either on demand or at short notice to the repayment of their loans.

Gilt-edged Securities and Treasury Bills.

The fifth and sixth methods of borrowing are through the market. The main method is through the Stock Exchange by the issue of fixed-interest securities, called gilt-edged securities. In 1965 the net amount owing to the public on all such securi-ties was nearly £13,000 million—a third of total public debt. Most gilt-edged securities are pro-mises to repay at a specified date in the future the amount originally borrowed; and in the mean-time to pay a fixed amount of interest each half-year. Some gilt-edged securities are irredeem-able, and consist therefore simply of a promise to pay the interest in perpetuity.

Most gilt-edged securities are held by institu-tions: the banks, discount houses, and other major financial institutions of the country, and foreign governments (whose holdings represent their sterling balances, (see G7(2)); only a fifth of the total being held by private individuals. Gilt-edged securities, unlike national savings, are not liquid assets. Until they become due for replace-ment they can only be sold on the Stock Exchange for what they will fetch, and variations in their market value are quite considerable. Dealings in second-hand securities can have important effects on the economy. Variation in the market price of securities implies an inverse variation in the effective rate of interest which they earn. This in turn can influence the general level of interest rates, hence the amount of investment which it is profitable to carry out, and hence the general level of economic activity.

The sixth form of borrowing is by means of Treasury Bills, of which £2,100 million were out-standing in 1965. A Treasury Bill is an extremely short-term loan to the Government—usually for three months. Each week the Treasury offers for sale some £300 million of these, and a number of specialised institutions bid for them. The difference between their bids and the value of these bonds on repayment is called discount, and is a substitute for interest. These bills play a crucial role in the monetary system, for it is by affecting the rate of discount on Treasury Bills that Bank Rate influences monetary conditions in the economy; but more of that a little later.

Government Borrowing and Liquidity.

Monetary policy consists largely in varying the way in which the Government borrows to finance its expenditure. This is because the form of borrowing affects the amount of liquidity in the economy. All financial institutions have some policy regarding liquidity. In general they try to maintain sufficient reserves either of cash or of assets which can be immediately converted into cash to meet any foreseeable sudden increase in their commitments. But they do not hold all their assets in liquid form. The chance that all their creditors simultaneously demand their money back can be ruled out, and therefore most of them act on the principle that they should maintain cash or other liquid assets to cover some percentage of their total outstanding commit-ments. Whereas currency and Treasury Bills are regarded as liquid assets, government securities and most other forms of government borrowing are illiquid.

If therefore the Government borrows more by issuing currency or Treasury Bills and less by other means, this action increases the amount of liquid assets about and therefore the total lending which financial institutions think it safe to make. And, conversely, if the Government borrows less by issuing currency or Treasury Bills and more by other means, this tends to decrease the total amount of loans which financial institutions are prepared to make. However, government con-trol over the way in which it borrows is circum-scribed. The public can be persuaded to hold more government securities only if the rate of interest earned on securities is increased. In the 1950s the British Government was unable to pre-vent a rapid accumulation of short-term debt, even though it allowed the rate of interest earned by irredeemable government securities to rise from less than 4 per cent in 1950 to over 5 per cent in 1960.

The Commercial Banks.

In the centre of the financial world stand the commercial banks. In England these are known as the London clearing banks. In this country, unlike the United States, the banking system is highly concentrated; there being five main banks with branches in every town. The commercial banks are important because their debts are used by the public as money. Anyone who has a bank current account can sign cheques or withdraw cash on demand up to the limit of his account. Because they can be used as a means of payment just as readily as bank-notes, bank deposits are money.

Commercial banks earn a profit by borrowing funds and then lending part of these funds at higher rates of interest. Because it is unlikely that all deposits will be withdrawn at once, the banks hold only a small proportion of their de-posits in the form of cash. The Bank of England requires them to hold 8 per cent; and we see in the table that in 1965 the average cash ratio was

LONDON CLEARING BANKS, 1965
(£ million)

Liabilities.		Assets.		Percentage of deposits.
Capital and reserves . .	513	Cash . . .	739	8·2
Deposits	8,989	Other liquid assets . .	2,042	22·5
Other	542	" Special deposits " .	56	0·6
		Investments . .	1,087	12·1
		Advances . .	4,653	51·8
		Other . . .	1,467	
Total	10,044	Total . . .	10,044	

8·2 per cent. In addition they hold by convention liquid assets (Treasury bills and money at call and short notice) equal to at least 28 per cent of their deposits; the ratio being 30·7 per cent in 1965. These liquid assets are easily transferable into cash. Their remaining assets are more remunerative; the majority being advances made to the public and earning a rate of interest higher than Bank Rate. In 1965 cash held by the commercial banks amounted to £739 million, whereas the public had deposits with the banks totalling £8,989 million. Thus the banking system can create money: it does so by accepting bank deposits far in excess of the cash held to meet demands for these deposits.

The Control of Commercial Banks.

The first step in any credit squeeze is to put pressure on the commercial banks by reducing their liquidity; so causing them to restrict their advances to would-be investors. This can be done in two main ways. The first is by *open-market operations*, in which the Bank deliberately sells more government stock than it otherwise would. The purchasers pay by cheque, and thus create a debt from the commercial banks to the Bank of England. Such debts have to be settled in cash, and so pressure is put on the banks' liquidity. The second is *Bank Rate*. If Bank Rate is raised it has the immediate effect of raising the rate of discount on Treasury Bills. A high rate of discount on these makes them appear attractive investments to those who do not normally buy them, and the commercial banks find it difficult to get as many of them as they would like. So again there is pressure on the banks' liquidity.

Faced by such pressure, the banks have to take steps to restore their liquidity either by selling securities or by calling in advances. Neither method brings in much cash directly; for since the banks will be paid by cheque rather than in cash, they have to go on until the depletion of deposits caused by the paying of these cheques cuts down the total of deposits to the level where liquid assets once again represent 30 per cent of the total. To this there is one major exception; if the Bank of England buys the securities the banks sell—and the need to ensure an orderly market may force it to do so—then selling securities brings more cash into the banks, and thus enables them to replenish their liquidity.

Since 1958, the monetary authorities have had the power to call upon the banks to make *special deposits* in cash with the Bank of England. Unlike other deposits of the banks with the Bank of England, special deposits cannot be treated as forming part of the liquid assets of commercial banks. This is in effect another way of putting pressure on the liquidity position of banks: the necessity of making such deposits could force them to sell securities or reduce advances. " Special deposits " amounted to 0·6 per cent of the banks' total deposits in 1965.

Bank Advances and Other Credit.

Bank advances are the simplest of all forms of credit; the customer is just given the right to sign cheques beyond his credit account, and interest is charged on the overdraft. In the late 1950s, a new form of advance—the personal loan—was introduced by some banks. These are granted to customers who would not earlier have been regarded as credit-worthy. A higher rate of interest is charged than on ordinary overdrafts, and more specific rules about repayment are laid down.

Most advances, however, are made to business, particularly to small business, and to farmers. In business the common practice is to finance working capital—stocks and work-in-progress—out of bank advances, and to depend on more permanent forms of borrowing for the purchase of fixed capital. But there are no fixed rules; business gets its finance wherever it can, and in fact there is such a variety of ways in which it can get capital that a squeeze on bank advances alone is not as effective as might be expected. Big businesses, in practice, scarcely suffer at all; for they are in the best position to tap other sources of credit. Quite a good example is provided by the hire-purchase finance companies. During the credit squeeze of 1956–58 the banks were asked by the Chancellor of the Exchequer to hold down advances, and in particular not to increase advances to hire-purchase finance companies. They did so; but the companies had no difficulty in getting the money they needed by borrowing direct from the public at high rates of interest. The real sufferers tend to be small businesses and professional people, who do find it hard to obtain credit elsewhere; but even they may be able to do so; for instance, by taking out a mortgage on their property or by buying their equipment on hire-purchase where previously they had paid cash, or by cashing some national savings.

The Radcliffe Committee discussed at length how effective a squeeze on the banks was likely to be, and in general their conclusion was that it was not likely to be very effective, because most borrowers would usually find other sources of credit. The other sources would usually be more expensive; but they thought this mattered very little, as interest payments form only a small part of most business costs, except in very highly capitalised industries, most of which are now publicly owned. Interest does matter in housing; the monthly interest payments due on a mortgage to a building society can go up substantially when the rate of interest goes up, although usually for existing, as opposed to new, mortgages no more money is asked for; instead the term of the mortgage in years is extended. But in hire-purchase, where service charges far exceed the interest element in any loan, interest is of trivial importance.

The Stock Exchange.

The banks through their advances are the main providers of short-term credit; but most long-term credit is provided through the Stock Exchange. In 1965 the total market value of all securities traded on the Stock Exchange was £75,000 million, of which £57,000 million represented stocks or shares in public companies. There are three main types. *Debenture Stock* is simply a fixed-interest loan. *Preference Stock* is a fixed-interest loan, with provisions for waiving the interest if the company fails to earn profits. Preference shareholders cannot get a company declared bankrupt if it does not pay them a dividend; but Debenture holders can. The third type—and much the most important—is *Ordinary Shares*. Nominally the owner of an Ordinary Share is a part-owner of the company concerned, with most of the rights of ownership. He has no right to any particular dividend or interest payment, but only the right to participate in net profits if there are any. In addition to stocks or shares in public companies, British Government gilt-edged securities worth £15,000 million were quoted on the Stock Exchange.

The Return on Financial Assets.

Each type of holding has obvious advantages. The fixed-interest security brings in a guaranteed income; the Ordinary Shareholder has no such guarantee, though in practice during the post-war period the risk of a decline in dividend was small. In a time of inflation the risks attached to holding fixed-interest securities are in some ways greater than those attached to holding Ordinary Shares; for, while Ordinary Shares appreciate in market value when there is inflation, fixed-interest securities tend to fall in market value, because the Government is forced to increase interest rates as an anti-inflationary measure. Furthermore, in the long run the growth of the economy tends, even without inflation, to raise the value of Ordinary Shares by increasing the value of companies. And, lastly, for investors who pay tax at heavy rates on their incomes—and most large personal investors in the Stock Exchange are rich people—capital gains are worth more than income in dividends. So for private investors, the Ordinary Share was a much better bet in the 1950s; and because Ordinary Shares were so popular, the yield on such shares—the ratio of dividends to market value—fell below the yield obtainable on Government securities (see table).

and manipulated in an attempt to control demand. This policy was adhered to by both Governments in the 1960s. We see in the table that the rate on Treasury Bills has kept in line with Bank Rate.

In addition to influencing the cost of credit by manipulating interest rates, the Government influenced the availability of certain sorts of credit through the credit-squeeze. At times it made it more difficult for the banks to extend their lending by operating on the banks' liquidity position, and it also issued more or less strongly-worded " requests " that banks should restrict growth of, or secure a reduction in, their advances.

A form of monetary control which was particularly important after 1950 was the control of hire-purchase. By increasing or lowering the proportion of the price which has to be paid as a down-payment, and by reducing or lengthening the time over which repayments can be made, the Government was able greatly to influence the volume of hire-purchase transactions, and therefore the use of this particular form of credit. These controls, of course, only affect the rather narrow class of goods—cars, furniture, washing-machines, television sets, etc.—for which a substantial proportion of sales are on hire-purchase terms. In consequence, the output of those industries concerned with the manufacture of these goods fluctuated widely.

The Effectiveness of Monetary Controls.

Running through the Radcliffe Report is a scepticism concerning the likely general effective-

PERCENTAGE YIELD ON FINANCIAL ASSETS

	Bank Rate. (range during year)	Treasury bill rate.	Irredeemable government bond rate.	Ordinary Share rate.
1950 . .	2	0·5	3·5	5·3
1955 . .	3–4·5	3·6	4·2	5·4
1960 . .	4–6	4·9	5·4	4·6
1965 . .	6–7	5·9	6·4	5·5
1969 . .	7–8	7·6	8·9	3·9

Most Ordinary Shares are held by private individuals; but increasingly in recent years holdings by insurance companies and pension funds have become more important, because of the growth of private superannuation schemes. Insurance companies and pension funds cannot afford to take risks, so the main bulk of their funds is still invested in fixed-interest securities; but they have shown a growing tendency to increase the proportion of their funds invested in Ordinary Shares. This switch, by lowering the demand for gilt-edged securities relative to Ordinary Shares, contributed to the downward pressure on the prices of gilt-edged securities. Legislation was introduced in 1960 to permit trusts to invest up to 50 per cent of their funds in the Ordinary Shares of large companies. In the same way, this has depressed the yield on Ordinary Shares and raised the yield on gilt-edged.

Historically, the greater security of gilt-edged holdings has normally been reflected in lower yields. If inflation is controlled, or if the prospect of industrial expansion becomes less bright, the demand for gilt-edged may increase and that for Ordinary Shares decrease; and the " normal " pattern of yields may then return.

Survey of Monetary Controls.

The post-war Labour Government pursued a *cheap money* policy. There was no major use of monetary policy as an economic regulator; Bank Rate for instance was kept at 2 per cent throughout, and the rate on Treasury Bills was only ½ per cent. Instead the Government relied on controls and on fiscal measures to keep inflation in check. For this neglect of money controls there was, in fact, a very good case: the pent-up demand for goods was so strong, and the funds available to companies and individuals so large, that monetary restrictions would not have made very much difference. The Conservative Government reintroduced monetary policy in 1951. Bank Rate was raised—reaching a peak in 1957—

ness of monetary policy, both as an anti-deflationary and an anti-inflationary weapon of control. In the former case, it is clearly difficult to encourage spending by making credit more easily available, if business prospects are so poor that no investment looks profitable. In the latter case, the Committee concluded on the use of monetary policy to counter inflation in the 1950s (para. 469).

> " The obstructions to particular channels of finance have had no effect on the pressure of total demand, but have made for much inefficiency in financial organisation."

They went on to add (para 472):

> " We are driven to the conclusion that the more conventional instruments (*e.g.*, Bank rate) have failed to keep the system in smooth balance, but that every now and again the mounting pressure of demand has in one way or another (generally *via* the exchange situation) driven the Government to take action, and that the quick results then required have been mainly concentrated on the hire-purchase front and on investment in the public sector which could be cut by administrative decision. The light engineering industries have been frustrated in their planning, and the public corporations have had almost equally disheartening experience. . . . It is far removed from the smooth and widespread adjustment sometimes claimed as the virtue of monetary action; this is no gentle hand on the steering wheel that keeps a well-driven car in its right place on the road."

However, the Radcliffe Committee did recognise that monetary measures have influenced " confidence " in sterling. A rise in interest rates increased the attractiveness of holding sterling balances, and stern monetary measures were taken as indicative of the Government's intention to solve its problems without recourse to devaluation. In these ways, monetary policy has helped to stem speculative outflows of sterling balances which threatened to impose heavy strains on our reserves. Many commentators feel that these effects provide an important justification for the use of certain forms of monetary controls.

The late 1960s saw a revival of belief in the efficacy of monetary policy (*see* **G40**).

5. ECONOMIC ASPECTS OF THE PUBLIC SERVICES

The Cost of Public Services.

In 1965 total public expenditure was no less than £14,055 million, about £260 per head. Of this total, the central government spent over 60 per cent, the local authorities under 30 per cent, and the nationalised industries' investment programme was responsible for 10 per cent. Total public expenditure almost doubled between 1955 and 1965; and rose as a proportion of the national income from 46 to 50 per cent.

ing expenditure consists of two quite different items. The first, housing subsidies, is a recurrent cost, and represents the difference between the cost of housing, including the cost of borrowing, and rents received on council housing. In 1965 costs exceeded the rents of £324 million by £149 million, so that the average council-house tenant was paying just under 14s. in the £ of the cost of accommodation. Up to 1957 the Government contracted to pay a flat subsidy per year on every council house built. From 1957, Government subsidies were no longer paid on ordinary new council houses, but in 1961 were reintroduced, in a form intended to encourage councils to charge higher rents on their existing houses. The Labour Government substantially increased the subsidy in 1967; it being calculated as the difference between interest payable on new housing at current interest rates and at 4 per cent.

The other part consists of the capital cost of building new houses, £628 million in 1965. This is financed out of borrowing by local authorities. In the early 1950s local authorities were able to borrow from the Government, but they have been

THE COST OF PUBLIC SERVICES
(£ million.)

	1955.	1965.	Percentage increase. 1955–65.	Percentage of total. 1965.
Expenditure:				
Defence	1,567	2,121	35	15·1
Housing	532	934	76	6·6
Environmental services	240	556	132	4·0
Roads, transport, and communication	352	1,005	186	7·2
Education	549	1,567	185	11·1
Child care, school meals, milk, and welfare foods	103	173	68	1·2
National Health Service	579	1,269	119	9·0
National Insurance, pensions, and assistance	993	2,413	143	17·2
Agriculture	188	336	79	2·4
External relations	135	428	217	3·0
Police and prisons	101	247	145	1·8
Debt interest	907	1,457	61	10·4
Other expenditure	842	1,549	84	11·0
Total expenditure	7,088	14,055	98	100·0
Revenue:				
Income taxes	2,287	4,016	76	28·6
Indirect taxes	2,177	3,766	73	26·8
of which: drink	*389*	*588*	*51*	*4·4*
tobacco	*656*	*994*	*52*	*7·1*
Local rates	475	1,230	159	8·8
National Insurance and health contributions	594	1,685	184	12·0
Other revenue	1,472	2,124	44	15·1
Total revenue	7,005	12,821	83	91·2
Net borrowing	83	1,234	—	8·8
Total expenditure	7,088	14,055	98	100·0

The Government collects in revenue considerably more than it spends itself, but transfers funds to the local authorities, to the National Insurance Fund, and to the nationalised industries. The expenditure of the public sector as a whole generally exceeds its revenue, and the difference is met by net borrowing.

A breakdown of public expenditure is shown in the table. Not all categories of expenditure expanded at the same rate: expenditure on roads, transport and communication, education, external relations, and National Insurance, pensions and assistance increased faster than the total; and expenditure on defence, debt interest, child care, the agricultural subsidy, and housing fell behind the total. Nevertheless, defence expenditure accounted for 15 per cent of the total (*i.e.*, 7·5 per cent of national income) in 1965.

Public Housing.

Expenditure on public housing amounted to 6·6 per cent of public expenditure in 1965; this percentage having fallen over the decade. Hous-

increasingly forced to borrow from the market. The two policies of freezing subsidies and making borrowing more difficult have slowed down the expansion of council housing. In 1953, the peak year, councils built 245,000 houses, in 1960 only 128,000 and in 1965, 165,000. Private building has exceeded council building since 1959, and in 1965 council building represented only 40 per cent of the total.

Education.

Educational expenditure rose by no less than 185 per cent between 1955 and 1965; and accounted for just over 11 per cent of public expenditure in 1965. A small part of the increase is explained by the expansion of enrolment; total school enrolment in Britain increased by only 7 per cent over the decade. In addition, expenditure rose because the more expensive types of education—secondary schools and universities—expanded more rapidly. University enrolment increased by 60 per cent over the decade; but the enrolment of 157,000 students in 1965 still did not meet the demand for higher education. Secondary school enrolment also shot up: pupils of school-leaving age (15 or over) as a percentage of the age-group 15–19 nearly doubled in England and Wales. Nevertheless, this proportion was only 19 per cent in 1965. Therefore it is to be expected that expenditure will continue to increase rapidly in the future.

However, quantitative expansion is not enough: there is general recognition that qualitative reform is also needed. It is important to reduce the size of classes—there were on average 29 pupils per teacher in primary schools and 18 in secondary schools in 1965, but these averages cover a wide dispersion; to raise the school-leaving age to 16—scheduled for 1972; to get rid of the gaunt Board Schools inherited from the Victorian era; and to raise teaching standards by improving the conditions for recruitment of teachers.

It is increasingly recognised that education can be an economic investment for the future just as much as capital formation in, say, machinery or roads. There is a " private return " on " investment in education ", which takes the form of higher earnings over the lifetime of the person educated; and there is a " social return " on public resources devoted to education, being the greater contribution to the national product which trained and educated people can make.

Social Security.

Social security benefits come from two sources. The larger part (£1,780 million in 1965) is paid out of the National Insurance and Industrial Injury Funds. These funds are built up largely out of the compulsory weekly National Insurance contributions which most of the adult population have to pay. For employees, both employer and employee pay a contribution, in return for which employees receive rights to pensions, sickness-, unemployment-, and other benefits. The self-employed also pay contributions of smaller size than the sum of the employer's and employee's contribution, and are not entitled to unemployment and one or two other benefits. And most non-employed persons, other than married women and the retired, have to pay still lower contributions and are entitled to even fewer benefits. Weekly contributions include a contribution to the cost of the National Health Service.

The most costly benefit is the retirement pension. The pension is paid as of right on retirement. Individuals may increase their rate of pension by staying on at work after the minimum retiring age of 65 for men or 60 for women; but the number who do so for more than a year is small—partly, but probably not mainly, because most private superannuation schemes lay down a fixed retiring age. Supplementary benefits, on the other hand, are given on proof of need. The high incidence of supplementary benefits—no less than 2·7 million persons received supplementary benefits in 1969 of whom 1·7 million were old-age pensioners—shows that national insurance benefits are often inadequate. It was partly to improve the pensions of those able to afford higher contributions that the scheme for graduated pensions was introduced.

The Finance of Social Security.

The National Insurance Scheme is an odd mixture of insurance and tax. The levels of contributions, when the scheme started in 1948, were fixed on the actuarial principle that contributions by or on behalf of an individual plus a specified State contribution should on average suffice to pay for the benefits to which he was entitled. But the scheme did not allow for inflation, and a succession of increases granted in the rate of pensions has put an end to this actuarial probity. Whenever a bill is introduced to increase pensions the Government Actuary calculates by how much contributions should be raised in order that those who contribute throughout their working lives at the new rates would just earn their right to the new benefits; but the new rates of pensions are granted to all, including those who have already retired. It was always expected that as the number of retired persons grew the fund would move into deficit; but with each rise in pensions the estimated size of the future deficit has risen. The scheme for graduated pensions also had the objective of reducing this deficit.

Graduated Pensions.

Under this scheme, which affects only employees, there are two kinds of workers—*ordinary* and *contracted-out*. In the case of the contracted-out workers, their employer (on whom the decision whether to contract out rests) must institute a private superannuation scheme that gives at least as favourable terms as the new State scheme, including the provision that rights under the scheme should be transferable up to the limits of the State scheme. Transferability is the guarantee that the individual does not lose his pension rights when he changes his job; but one unsatisfactory feature of the private schemes that have existed has been their use to tie employees to their jobs. For ordinary workers the contribution now depends on earnings. Those earning less than £9 a week pay a flat-rate contribution, which is lower than that paid by contracted-out workers. Those earning more than £9 pay in addition a percentage of the amount by which earnings exceed £9 up to a limit of £18 and in return receive the right to an increased pension on retirement.

The scheme is devised partly to encourage private superannuation, which is still largely confined to salaried employees and employees of the State. But one purpose is clear: in return for a promise of higher pensions when they retire, most workers who are contracted-in pay more now, and thus contribute now to the cost of the pensions of the retired. The estimated deficit is eliminated, and indeed the principle is established that the basic rates of contributions should not be fixed on actuarial principles but on the principle that on balance benefits paid in a year should roughly balance receipts. No provision was made for automatically increasing pensions as the cost of living goes up or indeed as the average standard-of-living rises; all changes in rates of benefit still require a new Act of Parliament.

Public Revenue.

We see from the table that, of the sources of revenue, local rates and National Insurance contributions were the most buoyant over the decade. Over 28 per cent of the total public revenue in 1965 came from income tax, which was levied both on individuals and on the undistributed profits of companies. Indirect taxes on goods and services accounted for a further 27 per cent. It is interesting to note that direct and indirect taxation actually fell as a proportion of national income between 1955 and 1965.

Two commodities in particular were heavily taxed: drink and tobacco. Together they accounted for 12 per cent of public revenue. These commodities are singled out partly for social reasons and partly because—in economists' jargon—the demand for them is *inelastic*; *i.e.*, the public reduces its consumption of drink and tobacco only slightly in response to a rise in their price. In 1965 taxation increased the price of cigarettes by 2·3 times; drink by 0·7 times; consumer durables, such as cars and washing machines, by 0·2 times; and food hardly at all. For goods and services in general, tax raised the price by roughly a quarter.

The Budget.

Each year in April the Chancellor of the Exchequer announces his Budget for the coming fiscal year. The most important and most difficult task in drawing up the Budget is to decide on the size of deficit to aim for. The deficit is the excess of public expenditure over public revenue; and it has to be financed by borrowing from the private sector. A large deficit is inflationary: sometimes that may be required to get the economy out of recession. A small deficit—and even more, a surplus—is deflationary, and is a means of holding an inflation in check.

The calculation of the precise deficit or surplus needed is a chancy business; for the level that is required depends on the amount of saving and on the amount of spending out of credit that people intend to do—and this is not easily predictable. It also depends on the change in the foreign balance. Nor can the Chancellor be sure his figures are right: estimating next year's revenue, and even next year's expenditure, by the Government is difficult enough, but he needs to estimate also the likely trends of private income and expenditure, without really reliable information as to what they were in the past year. So it cannot be expected that fiscal policy alone can prevent inflation and deflation.

Nevertheless, fiscal policy—running large deficits when economic activity is low, and small ones when it seems to be excessively high—is the most important action through which the economy can be kept on an even keel. Monetary policy may help; but the decision of the Chancellor on the size of his Budget surplus is the key one.

6. SOURCES OF STATISTICS, AND SOME SUGGESTIONS FOR FURTHER READING

The non-specialist will find that most of the statistics he needs are given in the *Annual Abstract of Statistics*, published every year by Her Majesty's Stationery Office. This comprehensive document includes figures on population, social conditions, education, labour, production, trade and balance of payments, national income and expenditure, wages and prices, and many other topics. For more up-to-date information, reference should be made to the *Monthly Digest of Statistics* which has a similar coverage and gives month-by-month figures. A selection of the more important series, presented in a manner which can more easily be understood by the layman, is given in another Stationery Office publication, *Economic Trends*, also issued monthly.

Even greater detail is given in various other Government publications, e.g. in the Blue Book on *National Income and Expenditure*, published annually; and the *Balance of Payments* White Paper, published twice a year. Fuller information on labour problems is given in the *Employment and Productivity Gazette*, on trade in the *Board of Trade Journal*, and on financial matters in the *Bank of England Quarterly Bulletin*. These three periodicals include discussions on the statistics presented. An important new Government annual publication in 1970 was *Social Trends*, containing articles and detailed statistics on social and economic conditions in Britain.

For an analysis of developments in the economy see the official *Economic Report*, published just before the Budget by the Treasury, and the *Economic Review*, a private publication issued by the National Institute for Economic and Social Research. To explain economic events and policy the Treasury publishes a monthly *Progress Report*, available free of charge to the public.

For a scholarly critique of Government economic policy see J. C. R. Dow, *Management of the British Economy 1945-60* (Cambridge University Press). An excellent, North American, survey of the British economy is found in the Brookings Institution Report, *Britain's Economic Prospects*, edited by Richard E. Caves (George Allen and Unwin). An entertaining account of economic ideas and their application is found in Michael Stewart, *Keynes and After* (Penguin Books). Other Pelicans include Joan Robinson, *Economic Philosophy*, and J. Pen, *Modern Economics*. A thorough explanation of international monetary affairs is given in Fred Hirsch., *Money International* (Allen Lane). E. J. Mishan in *Growth: The Price We Pay* (Staples Press) produces an interesting criticism of economists' and politicians' "obsession" with economic growth and affluence.

III. THE UNDERDEVELOPED ECONOMIES

Income Levels.

Two-thirds of the world's population live in dire poverty—a poverty which can scarcely be imagined by those accustomed to the standards of living attained in the relatively few developed countries of the world. The orders of world inequality may be seen from the table comparing annual income per capita by region, converted into pounds sterling at official exchange rates.

NATIONAL INCOME PER CAPITA BY REGION, 1963.

	(£ p. a.)
North America	882
Oceania	443
Europe	350
Latin America	107
Middle East	93
Africa	43
Asia (excl. Japan)	36

These figures are only very approximate because exchange rates are misleading indicators of purchasing power and because the averages conceal considerable income inequalities within some regions and countries. Nevertheless, it is clear that poverty is widespread in the world. The alleviation of this poverty is widely recognised as the most important economic—and indeed political—task of the second half of the twentieth century.

Peasant Agriculture.

"Underdeveloped" (or "developing" or "less developed" or "poor") countries have predominantly agricultural economies, and peasant *subsistence agriculture* is widespread. In subsistence agriculture the primary object is to produce the food for your own family. Primitive tools and techniques of cultivation are used, and the margin between what can be produced and what is required to support life is narrow: the failure of crops because of drought, or the destruction of crops by floods or pests, can lead to famine unless food is quickly supplied from outside the area affected.

Agricultural production may be kept down by a shortage of land, or by a lack of farming knowledge and skills, or by a lack of funds for investment in land improvements or machinery, or by an unjust system of land tenure which deprives the farmer of incentive to raise his production. In many underdeveloped countries there is considerable potential for increasing agricultural output; but before such increases can be achieved new skills have to be mastered and different techniques of production introduced, investment funds have to be provided, and—in some countries—there must be land reform. If power lies in the hands of landlords and money-lenders who favour the *status quo*, political change must come first.

The Population Problem.

In many underdeveloped countries there is population pressure on the land and much under-employment in the sense that people have insufficient work to keep them occupied for more than part of the day or year. With the application of modern methods of disease control—*e.g.*, the eradication of malaria through DDT spraying —death rates have tended to fall, while birth rates have remained high. Birth rates are kept up by such factors as tradition, social prestige, religion, the need for security in old age, and a lack of facilities for family planning. In consequence, many underdeveloped countries are experiencing an unprecedented population explosion: annual rates of increase of between 2 and 3 per cent, which double population in as little as 35 and 24 years respectively, have been recorded.

The table indicates that over half of the world's population lives in Asia, and that the developed regions account for under a third of the total. Apart from Australasia (into which immigration is high) the developed regions show slower rates of population growth than Africa, Latin America, and Asia. The figures of population density may easily be misinterpreted, since they take no account of the nature of the area, *e.g.*, deserts and lakes are included. But it is clear that Asia is more densely populated than Africa or Latin America. Population density is a hindrance only in agricultural economies: because it is industrialised and has accumulated much capital, Europe can support at a high standard of living a population more concentrated even than that of Asia.

POPULATION SIZE, GROWTH AND DENSITY BY REGION

	Population 1968 (m)	Growth rate 1960–68 (% p.a.)	Density 1968 (per sq. km).
North America	309	1·8	13
Europe	455	0·9	92
USSR	238	1·3	11
Oceania	19	2·1	2
Africa	336	2·4	11
South America	180	2·7	10
Asia	1946	2·0	71
World Total	*3483*	*1·9*	*26*

As a result of rapid population growth the pressure of population on the land has increased, particularly in Asia. Less productive land has been brought into cultivation, and erosion and loss of fertility have become major problems. A substantial increase in output is required to prevent a fall in per capita income as population grows, and an even greater increase is required if living standards are to be improved. Between 1960 and 1967 food production in the developing countries as a group increased by 20 per cent, but per capita food production rose by only 1 per cent. Even in those countries with plenty of land a rapid increase in population diverts scarce investment resources away from directly productive investments such as factories and irrigation projects so as to meet the needs of the expanding population for more schools, hospitals, housing, cities, and other public services.

International Trade.

Almost all underdeveloped countries export primary products (foodstuffs, industrial raw materials, and minerals) and import manufactured goods, especially the capital goods (plant, machinery, and vehicles) required for development. This international division of labour has recently operated to the disadvantage of the underdeveloped countries. The world demand for their primary products has increased only very slowly. This is because people spend just a small part of their additional income on food (e.g., tea, coffee, cocoa), because synthetic substitutes have been developed for many raw materials (e.g., rubber, cotton, jute), because developed countries protect their own agriculture (e.g., sugar) and because demand in the developed countries has moved towards commodities with low raw material content (e.g., from heavy industries to services). In consequence, the general trend has been for the prices of primary products to fall. This was an important cause of the improvement in Britain's terms of trade (see G6). The reverse of the coin was a deterioration in the terms of trade of many underdeveloped countries, i.e., they could now buy fewer imports for a given quantity of exports. Primary commodities exported by developing countries decreased in price on average by 15 per cent over the period 1957–62, and increased by only 4 per cent between 1962 and 1968. Over the period 1957–68 their terms of trade worsened by 12 per cent. This contributed to the shortage of foreign exchange which restricts investment expenditures in many underdeveloped countries.

The prices of various primary products tend to fluctuate violently from one year to another. Many underdeveloped economies depend heavily on the exports of one or two commodities. For instance, coffee is the most important product in Brazil, cotton in Egypt, copper in Zambia, sugar in Cuba, cocoa in Ghana, and rice in Burma. Fluctuations in the world price of its main export cause instability in the export revenues of a country, and this in turn can produce fluctuations in income throughout its domestic economy.

Industrialisation.

In those underdeveloped countries where there is population pressure on the land, alternative employment has to be created in industry or services. Even in countries with a surplus of land, if there is heavy dependence on one or two primary products, industrialisation provides a means of diversifying the economy.

But industrialisation is not an easy course. Because the margin between agricultural production and food consumption is narrow, the surplus from the agricultural sector exchangeable for the products of other sectors—e.g., industry and services— is small; i.e., the demand for the goods and services produced by other sectors is low. A second constraint on industrialisation is imposed by competition from abroad; new industries in an underdeveloped country have to compete with established industries in developed countries, which have the advantage of experience, a trained labour force, and markets big enough for them to reap all the potential economies of large-scale production. On the other hand, underdeveloped countries with their relatively cheap labour may have an advantage in the production of simple labour-intensive products: witness the success of Hong Kong in exporting textiles and plastic products to the developed countries.

Underdeveloped countries can of course take advantage of the technical advances made in the developed countries. But this is not without its drawbacks. Even in countries with cheap labour the most profitable techniques of production in industry are normally highly capital-intensive, so that the amount of investment funds required to equip a worker is often enormous and the amount of employment provided in meeting the local demand for a manufactured product is often small. Hence the argument for developing an *intermediate technology* which is both profitable and suited to the needs of the underdeveloped countries.

Educated Manpower.

Many underdeveloped countries are faced with the dual problem of unskilled labour surpluses and scarcities of skilled and educated manpower. The problem is particularly acute in some of the recently independent countries of Africa. To give an extreme example: at the time of its independence in 1964, Zambia had only 100 Zambian university graduates and 1,200 secondary school graduates in a population of 3·5 million. In such countries the great shortage of educated and skilled people enables them to earn high incomes—with the result that there is a very unequal distribution of income. And even in countries where surpluses have developed, the existence of an international market for professional people like doctors and engineers helps to keep up their earnings: these countries suffer from a " brain drain " to the developed world.

Because teachers are educated people, education in underdeveloped countries can be very expensive. In Uganda in 1965 only 45 per cent of the children in the relevant age-group were at primary school and only 2 per cent were at secondary school. Yet the salary bill paid to their teachers exceeded 2 per cent of the gross domestic product. In such circumstances it is difficult to meet the demands for universal primary education; especially if the sort of primary education provided does not enable children to become better farmers.

Economic development is not just a matter of capital accumulation: it requires also an increase in educated manpower. Not only more knowledge but also new habits and attitudes—e.g., attitudes towards risk-taking, hard work, and thrift. Education—of the right sort and with suitable content—is generally acknowledged to be important for development, although the benefits of education cannot be quantified at all satisfactorily.

Economic Aid.

The gap between living standards in the underdeveloped areas of the world and in the areas already developed has tended to widen in recent years. In the 1950s real income per capita rose in the developed countries by 2·7 per cent per annum on average, and in the underdeveloped countries by 2·3 per cent per annum. It was through a growing world recognition of this situation that the 1960s were designated " The United Nations Development Decade." But between 1960 and 1968 these rates of growth widened to 4·0 and 2·3 per cent per annum respectively. World inequalities increased despite a larger flow of economic assistance from the richer to the poorer nations. The total net flow of economic assistance from Western industrial countries to the developing world was over £5,600 million in 1969. Roughly £2,600 million of this was net private investment, and £3,000 million official Government aid. But whereas total aid increased rapidly in the 1950s, the increase was not continued in the 1960s: total aid in 1966 was no higher than the estimate for 1961. Almost half of the official Government aid in 1969 was contributed by the United States; the other principal donors were France, West Germany, Japan and Britain, in that order.

Aid to underdeveloped countries takes many forms, it serves many purposes, and it is given for many reasons. Underdeveloped countries need aid to provide finance for development projects; to provide foreign exchange with which imports for development purposes can be bought; and to provide the trained manpower and technical knowledge which they lack. The motives of the donor are not always humanitarian. " Aid " can take a military form; it can be used to prop up an incompetent or unjust government, or to buy support in the cold war. Nor is aid always beneficial to the recipient country. It may be wasted on ill-conceived or prestige projects, or cause the Government simply to relax its own efforts. Sometimes schools or hospitals are built with aid but there is a lack of local revenues with which to staff and run these institutions. Concern over donors' motives and instances of waste has led some people to react against aid-giving. However, the correct remedy is not to cut off aid but rather to prevent its misuse.

One form of aid is private investment by firms and individuals from developed countries. These investments—setting up branch factories, for example—are concentrated in those projects which appear profitable to the investor. However, it is a characteristic of underdevelopment that there are few openings for profitable investment. Most of the U.K. private investment overseas, for example, has been concentrated in relatively highly developed countries of the sterling area. Private investment cannot be relied upon to provide an adequate flow of aid.

Donor governments may finance specific projects, or they may contribute to the general pool of funds available for expenditure by the governments of underdeveloped countries. But financial aid is not always enough. Most underdeveloped countries need help and advice in planning their development, to ensure that development possibilities are exploited and that scarce resources are used to best advantage. Hence the many schemes for providing experts by individual countries and by the technical agencies of the United Nations, such as the Food and Agriculture Organisation (FAO), the World Health Organisation (WHO), the International Labour Organization (ILO), the United Nations Educational, Scientific, and Cultural Organisation (UNESCO), the Technical Assistance Board (UNTAB) and so on. Hence also the schemes for educating and training people from the developing countries in universities and colleges in the developed countries.

The International Bank.

The International Bank for Reconstruction and Development (IBRD) known as the *International Bank* or as the *World Bank*, is an agency of the United Nations established in 1945. It has the primary function of making funds available to assist underdeveloped countries. Member nations agree to subscribe quotas—fixed in much the same way as the quotas for the IMF—to the Bank. In fact, only a small proportion of the quotas has been called up by the Bank; the major part of the Fund's resources are borrowed—on the security of the remainder of the quotas—in financial centres: particularly in New York, but also in London and elsewhere.

Usually, loans are made to finance specific projects of investment in underdeveloped countries; and the Bank will normally make a loan only if it is satisfied that the investment will yield a revenue sufficient to enable the payment of interest on the loan, and the repayment of the sum lent. In 1970 the Bank made loans to the value of about £700 million. Thus a sizeable amount of lending is channelled through the Bank, but it is clear that some projects of great value to underdeveloped countries cannot be financed in this way, because they would not yield returns quickly or large enough to meet the Bank's stringent requirements for interest and repayment. Accordingly a new institution, the *International Development Association*, was set up in 1960 with the power to make loans at low rates of interest and with more generous repayment conditions. The IDA contributes (but only on a limited scale) towards the development of education and agriculture.

Unctad.

In 1964 the United Nations Conference on Trade and Development (UNCTAD) was held. For the first time the poorer nations of the world—77 were represented—came together to act as a pressure group on trading matters. The Conference made the following recommendations. Developing countries should be given freer access to world markets for their manufactures and semi-manufactures by the elimination of quotas and tariffs. International commodity agreements should be made for each major primary commodity in world trade, to stabilise commodity prices. Compensation schemes—whereby countries are compensated for the declining prices of their primary products—were recommended for consideration. The conference also resolved that the developed countries should aim to provide at least 1 per cent of their national income as aid for the underdeveloped countries.

Nothing concrete resulted from the 1964 Session: no significant trade measures in favour of the developing countries were taken, and the international transfer of financial resources diminished in relation to the income of the developed countries. A second Session of the Conference was held in 1968. Again, no action resulted from the Session; but the developed countries did accept more firmly the principle of discrimination in favour of developing countries in trade and shipping, and the 1 per cent target for aid.

British Aid.

The table shows how British Government aid to underdeveloped countries has increased in

BRITISH GOVERNMENT AID, 1957/8 TO 1969/70.

Fiscal year	Total aid			Multi-lateral aid £m.	Bilateral Aid		
	£m.	per capita £	as per-centage of GNP		Total £m.	Grants £m.	Loans £m.
1957/8	65	1·3	0·33	3	62	50	12
1960/1	147	2·8	0·65	17	130	60	70
1963/4	173	3·2	0·64	15	158	72	87
1964/5	191	3·5	0·65	16	175	92	83
1965/6	205	3·8	0·66	19	186	93	94
1966/7	215	3·9	0·65	19	196	92	104
1967/8	213	3·9	0·61	24	189	89	100
1968/9	207	3·7	0·56	29	179	92	87
1969/70	217	3·9	0·56	24	194	83	111

recent years. It was fairly constant before 1957/8 but more than tripled to £213 million in the decade following 1957/8. Aid per capita of the British population nearly tripled, and amounted to £3. 18s. per head in 1967/8. However, when aid is expressed as a percentage of the gross national product (GNP), we see that the per- centage increased from 0·33 of 1 per cent in 1957/8 to 0·65 of 1 per cent in 1960/1, remained at that level until 1966/7 and then fell. To be just 1 per cent of GNP, aid would have to be raised by about £100 million. Aid may be divided into multi- lateral aid and bilateral aid. Multilateral aid is given through the medium of the international institutions, such as the IBRD and the IDA; bilateral aid is given directly to the developing countries. Multilateral aid was still only £24 million in 1969/70. The increase in aid since 1957/8 has taken place in bilateral aid. Whereas loans were fairly negligible in 1957/8, they in- creased rapidly, and exceeded grants from 1964/5.

It must be remembered in deciding the terms on which Government aid is provided, that the foreign indebtedness of the developing countries is increasing sharply. About four-fifths of British loans is made available for 20 years or more. Normally the rate of interest on these loans is the rate at which the British Government can borrow on the capital market. However, the Government decided in 1965 to make develop- ment loans free of interest in appropriate cases. About a third of expenditure on aid is formally tied to the purchase of British goods and services. Other aid is not tied formally, and may be used directly to finance local expenditure; but when it is used to finance imports directly, it has to be spent on British goods if these are available on competitive terms. Multilateral aid is untied. The tying of aid tends to raise the costs to develop- ing countries; but it also enables countries with precarious foreign balances—such as Britain—to be more generous.

Aid takes the form not only of financial but also of technical assistance. To co-ordinate and pro- mote technical assistance the Department of Technical Co-operation (DTC) was set up in 1961. British Government expenditure on technical assistance amounted to £44 million in 1969. At the end of 1969 British technical assistance personnel overseas totalled altogether 12,000 (excluding volunteers recruited by voluntary societies); over 1,500 administrators, 5,000 teachers, 1,000 agricultural advisers, 3,000 indus- trial and technological advisers, and 1,200 doctors and medical workers.

In 1964 the Labour Government established an Overseas Development Ministry (ODM), through which all British aid was channelled and co-ordinated; but in 1970 the Conservative Government absorbed the ODM into the Foreign Office. The amount of aid which ought to be provided has become a political issue in some countries such as the United States: thankfully this has not occurred in Britain.

Some Suggestions for Further Reading.

For an introduction to the subject the reader is referred to Jagdish Bhagwati, *The Economics of Underdeveloped Countries* (World University Library). An interesting account of life in rural India is found in Kusum Nair, *Blossoms in the Dust* (Duckworth). On Asia the reader may wish to dip into the three volumes of Gunnar Myrdal entitled *Asian Drama: An Enquiry into the Poverty of Nations* (Alan Lane, The Penguin Press). A helpful introduction to African prob- lems is found in Andrew M. Kamarck, *The Econo- mics of African Development* (Praeger). The Overseas Development Institute has published a number of pamphlets on aid topics, including *The Less Developed Countries in World Trade, British Development Policies*, and *Volunteers in Develop- ment*. The Ministry of Overseas Development has compiled a handbook of *British Aid Statistics* (HMSO). The Report of the Commission on International Development, *Partners in Develop- ment*, (the Pearson Report, 1969) reviews the problems of the less developed countries and makes recommendations for their solution by means of aid policies.

IV. DEVELOPMENTS IN THE BRITISH ECONOMY SINCE 1960.

1. INTERNATIONAL DEVELOPMENTS

The Balance of Payments.

The balance of payments problem dominated events in the British economy in the 1960s. It is therefore important to analyse the balance of pay- ments in some detail, to understand the circum- stances which led to the devaluation of the pound in 1967 and the transformation of the balance of payments after 1968.

Developments may be followed in the table, showing the balance of payments in the new form of presentation introduced in 1970. In the old presentation (*see* G7) a distinction was made be- tween the *basic balance* (current plus long term capital account) and short term *monetary move- ments*. But it became increasingly difficult to make this distinction because of the growing variety and intricacy of capital movements. Instead, a line was drawn between the *total cur- rency flow* (current account plus all capital flows) and *official financing*. If the total currency flow is negative, this means that the authorities have to finance the deficit either by borrowing from the IMF or other monetary authorities or by drawing on the official reserves of gold and foreign exchange.

Developments up to 1964.

(i) The Current Account.

The deterioration in the current balance of pay- ments of well over £400 million between 1959 and 1960 was mainly attributable to an increase of nearly £500 million in imports: exports also in- creased but not by enough to pay for the increased imports. The main cause was the upsurge in demand in 1959–60. During the upsurge, pro- ductive capacity at home became strained, and some goods were imported to supplement home supplies. Stocks of imported goods were run down in 1959 and replenished in 1960. And higher incomes meant higher demands for im- ported goods. These developments might be interpreted as indicating the adverse effects on the balance of payments of internal expansion. No doubt imports will increase as the economy expands; but it can be argued that sudden and very rapid bursts of expansion, as in 1959–60, will have a much greater effect on imports than would a steadier and more sustained growth.

In the following two years, imports were steady at about the 1960 level: the internal economy was relatively stagnant, partly because restrictive measures had been adopted to curb demand at home and protect the balance of payments. Imports were sharply up by over £250 million in 1963 with the rapid expansion of national expendi- ture, but there was a slightly larger increase in the value of exports.

The surplus on invisible trade, which had ex- ceeded £300 million in the early and middle fifties, ranged between £100 and £200 million in the early sixties (*see* G7).

(ii) The Capital Account.

Capital flows may be divided into official long- term capital flows, net private investment, and various monetary movements, *e.g.*, trade credit, changes in the sterling balances (*see* G8) and Euro- dollar transactions (*see* G33). There was a fairly steady official long-term capital outflow in the 1960s and a less steady net private investment abroad.

Most volatile were the monetary movements. For instance, there would have been a large deficit in the currency flow in 1960 had it not been for a substantial inflow of short-term funds (*i.e.*, addi- tions to our short-term liabilities). The sterling balances rose by an unprecedented amount of over £400 million. This was largely due to speculation against the dollar, based on fears that it might be devalued. So great was the inflow

BALANCE OF PAYMENTS 1960–70
(£ million)

	1960	1961	1962	1963	1964	1965	1966	1967	1968	1969	1970
Exports (f.o.b.)	3,732	3,891	3,993	4,282	4,486	4,817	5,182	5,122	6,273	7,061	7,885
Imports (f.o.b.)	4,138	4,043	4,095	4,362	5,005	5,054	5,255	5,674	6,916	7,202	7,882
Visible balance	−406	−152	−102	−80	−519	−237	−73	−552	−643	−141	+3
Invisible balance	+141	+148	+214	+194	+124	+160	+116	+240	+324	+578	+628
Current balance	−265	−4	+112	+114	−395	−77	+43	−312	−319	+437	+631
Official long-term capital	−103	−45	−104	−105	−116	−85	−80	−57	+17	−98	−205
Net private investment	−69	+61	−19	−87	−241	−81	−29	−90	−140	+16	−70
Other capital flows	+431	−326	+128	+89	+68	−142	−499	−413	−887	+67	+907
Balancing item	+299	−25	+75	−69	−11	+32	−26	+201	−81	+321	+157
Total currency flow	+293	−339	+192	−58	−695	−353	−591	−671	−1,410	+743	+1,420
Net borrowing from IMF *	−116	+370	−375	+5	+357	+489	+15	−339	+506	−30	−134
Other net borrowing *	—	—	—	—	+216	+110	+294	+895	+790	−669	−1,161
Transfer from portfolio to reserves *	—	—	—	—	—	—	+316	+204	—	—	—
Change in reserves *	−177	−31	+183	+53	+122	−246	−34	+115	+114	−44	−125
Total official financing *	−293	+339	−192	+58	+695	+353	+591	+671	+1,410	−743	−1,420

* A plus sign denotes a rise in liabilities or a fall in assets, and a minus sign a fall in liabilities or a rise in assets.

that there was a curious combination of a very large deficit on current account and a substantial rise in our reserves of gold and convertible currencies.

The dangers inherent in the financing of deficits through additions to short-term liabilities were vividly demonstrated the following year. Much of the funds which moved in during 1960 was moved out again before July 1961 in a wave of speculation against sterling. The outflow was financed partly by running down reserves of gold and convertible currencies by £280 million between end-1960 and July 1961, and partly through the Basle agreement under which European central banks undertook to build up short-term holdings in centres (London in this case) from which funds were being withdrawn. The rapid drain on the reserves had to be stopped; and the European central banks were not prepared to see their sterling holdings rise much higher. So in July 1961 a series of crisis measures—including the raising of Bank Rate to 7 per cent—were taken, primarily to protect sterling. In addition, arrangements were made to withdraw over £500 million from the IMF with provision for further credits if necessary. In 1962, speculative movements of funds were much less violent. Aided by a substantial improvement in the current balance of payments, Britain was able to complete repayments of its IMF drawing. These repayments did, however, involve a drain on the reserves; and this explains the substantial fall in the reserves over the year.

The 1964 Crisis.

Imports in 1964 were some £640 million higher than in 1963, whereas exports were up by less than £200 million. The remarkable increase in the value of imports cannot be explained simply as a rise in import prices: imports increased by 15 per cent in value and by 11 per cent in volume. Nor can it be seen merely as a response to the expansion of the economy: if imports had done no more than rise in line with output, they would have increased in volume only by about 4 per cent. Part of the explanation lies in the fact that importers were stockbuilding after the depletion of raw material stocks during the boom of 1963. More important, however, is the fact that imports of manufactured goods rose by 28 per cent, or two-thirds of the total rise in import value. This leads us to the conclusion that home producers were losing ground in the British market to foreign competitors. In the same way, the disappointing performance of exports was due, not to lack of overseas demand—world trade in manufactures rose by about 15 per cent in 1964—but to the diminishing competitiveness of British products.

(i) Remedial Measures.

The timing of Government action on the balance of payments position was influenced by the General Election of mid-October. The out-going Government had been concerned with the impending Election, and argued that the deficit was abnormal and could be expected to improve without remedial action. On taking office, the new Government decided that immediate remedial action was necessary. Three courses were possible. It could devalue the pound and so improve the competitive position of British exports and import-substitutes (see G8). But a devaluation was seen to have disadvantages. The price of necessary imports would be increased and this would lower the British standard of living: the ensuing wage demands would make it more difficult to implement an Incomes Policy—which is an alternative method of improving the British competitive position in world markets (see G38). Furthermore, the devaluation of the pound might have necessitated the devaluation of other currencies including the dollar: this would have defeated the purpose of the devaluation. These real arguments against devaluation are not to be confused with the spurious argument that devaluation is somehow morally wrong. A second possible course of action was to reduce imports to a satisfactory level by the deflation of the economy. However, national income would have to fall by a multiple of the required cut in imports. Deflation was rejected because it would cause unemployment and because it was considered to provide only a short-term solution to Britain's economic problems: somehow the foreign imbalance had to be corrected without impeding the growth of output and productivity. A third course of action was to impose import controls or tariffs and export subsidies. Import controls were rejected: for one reason, it would take time to set up the necessary administrative machinery.

So it was that the Government decided upon an additional import tariff and an export subsidy.

Within two weeks of coming to power, the Government announced its measures (which had in fact been investigated by the previous Chancellor). There was to be an immediate but temporary surcharge of 15 per cent on all imports of manufactures and semi-manufactures: the more necessary imports such as foodstuffs and basic raw materials were excluded. A new system of export rebates was introduced, representing the indirect taxes paid in Britain by British exporters, mainly duties on oil, petrol, and vehicle licenses. The value of the rebate averaged 1½ per cent of the value of exports. The import surcharge was critically received by the other EFTA members; it clashed with their objective of eliminating all tariffs by the end of 1966.

Some commentators have argued that Britain should direct its policies towards removing restraints on trade, by cutting tariffs within EFTA or GATT or even unilaterally: lowering tariff barriers will contribute to efficiency by subjecting British industries to stiffer competition. By contrast, it is also possible to argue that we should at times impose greater restraints on imports, so that economic growth can occur without being hampered by balance of payments difficulties. The Government defended its action to the GATT Council in terms of an article in the Treaty which allows parties in balance of payments difficulties to resort to tariff restriction (see G9). Regrettably, the GATT Council declared the import surcharge a violation of the Treaty

*

(ii) Speculation Against Sterling.

The large deficit in non-monetary capital flows in 1964 of £350 million was as remarkable as the deficit on current account. The outflow was due to an increase in private investment abroad; there was no increase in net Government lending. Part of the net private capital outflow in the first half of the year may have been abnormal and part in the second half of 1964 may have been related to the growing current account deficit: portfolio investment in this country was not an attractive proposition, and foreign firms tended to repatriate any funds available.

There was a net monetary capital inflow in the first half of 1964, which financed the growing overall deficit. The crisis arose in the second half of the year, when an outflow of short-term capital —a " flight of hot money "—took place in expectation that a British devaluation would be necessary to cure the worsening imbalance. To protect the reserves, the IMF granted Britain a stand-by credit of £330 million. However, once the feeling developed that the pound would have to be devalued, the process became cumulative: the greater the outflow the more likely it seemed that Britain would be forced to devalue. A great deal of sterling was offered for sale by speculators holding pounds—the " Gnomes of Zurich "—and by British and foreign importers and exporters. In order to prevent the price of sterling from falling below the official minimum limit to the exchange rate of £1 = 2·78 (i.e., to " support sterling ") the Bank of England was itself forced to buy pounds. To do this the Bank had to draw on the country's reserves of gold and foreign exchange. The vast drain on the reserves could not be allowed to continue, and in late November, Bank Rate was raised by 2 per cent to 7 per cent. The aim of this measure was to lure back short-term capital funds with the high rate of interest, and also to convince speculators that the pound would not be devalued. Speculators were not convinced, however, and the crisis continued. Two days later it was announced that an enormous loan totalling £1,070 million would be made available to Britain from all the leading Western central banks. This news was sufficient to slow down the speculative outflow, and by the close of 1964 the selling had come to an end.

Events Leading to Devaluation.

Imports increased a good deal more slowly than output in 1965; rising by only 1 per cent. This was partly because the stockbuilding of 1964 had come to an end, and partly because the import

surcharge held back imports of manufactured consumer goods. The value of exports was 7 per cent higher in 1965 than in 1964, and their volume 5 per cent higher. Thus the current deficit was more than halved, from the record of £400 million in 1964 to just over £100 million in 1965. The deficit on capital account was also cut considerably. Nevertheless, an overall deficit in total currency flow amounting to £350 million in 1965 had to be financed by monetary movements.

The trade balance showed little improvement by mid-1965, and in the third quarter fear of devaluation led to yet another run on sterling, probably as severe as that of November 1964. The Government was again forced to draw on the IMF and to borrow from the United States Federal Reserve Bank. This time, however, the extent of speculation against the pound was successfully concealed. When the trade balance improved rapidly in the second half of 1965, the speculation died away.

However, this progress did not continue into 1966, and confidence in the pound was further upset by the seamen's strike in May and June. Yet another flight of short-term capital occurred; and this led the Government in panic to introduce a policy of deflation, in a package-deal known as the " July measures " (see G41). Only two measures improved the balance of payments directly: a reduction of the personal travel allowance outside the sterling area to £50 per annum and a proposed cut in Government overseas spending. The fall in demand resulting from the deflationary policy, together with a wage-freeze introduced at the same time (see G39), improved the trade balance and actually turned it into a surplus at the end of 1966. But it should be remembered that this improvement was achieved only at the cost of some unemployment of men and machinery and a slower rate of economic growth.

Imports rose in value by over 6 per cent and exports fell in value by nearly 2 per cent between 1966 and 1967. Thus the trade gap which had almost closed in 1966 widened to a record level in 1967. The rise in imports cannot be explained simply by the rise in demand, as incomes rose by only 1 per cent between the two years: the " July measures " were taking effect. One reason for the surge in imports was the removal of the temporary import surcharge in the preceding November, which caused a postponement of purchases until 1967, and reduced the price of imported goods competing with British products. Other reasons were the building up of imported stocks which had been depleted, and the Middle East war in June, which raised the price of essential oil imports. The main reason for the fall in exports was the exceptionally slow growth of world production in 1967: demand in the countries importing British goods was fairly stagnant. Exports were also hit by the dock strikes in September. The deficit in total currency flow over the year was £670 million, of which perhaps £200–400 million was due to speculation. With the trade returns deteriorating, sterling came under almost unremitting speculative pressure from the end of May onwards, reaching a climax in November.

Devaluation of the Pound, 1967.

The Government recognised that action would have to be taken to improve the balance of payments, and to obtain further foreign loans to protect the depleted reserves. The same alternatives were open as in 1964: deflation, import controls, tariffs and devaluation (see G29). Simple deflation to reduce imports was ruled out politically as the economy was now already in recession. Import controls and tariffs would meet with resistance from Britain's competitors and the GATT, and tariffs had been tried in 1964 without success. The Government decided to devalue the pound.

The case for devaluation is a mixed one (see G8 and 29). It makes imports more expensive relative to home-produced goods, and so demand for manufactured goods shifts away from imports; but in the case of food and raw materials, Britain must continue to import these essentials at the higher price because there are no domestic substitutes. It is possible, therefore, that devaluation will actually raise the import bill. However, export receipts should be increased by a greater amount: Britain exports its products in a highly competitive market, so that the reduced price of British goods in terms of foreign currencies should lead to a considerable increase in the amount of exports.

This improvement in the trade balance depends on Britain being able to retain at least part of the price advantage gained by devaluation. However, since devaluation raises the price of imported goods, it raises the cost of living both directly and indirectly, *e.g.*, imported raw materials rise in price, so increasing production costs, which are passed on as higher prices. The trade unions react to this cut in the standard of living by demanding wage increases. In this way a spiralling inflation can occur which entirely neutralises the gain from devaluation. Devaluation makes an incomes policy both more difficult and more important (*see* **G37**).

On November 18, 1967, the pound was devalued by 14·3 per cent, from $2.8 to $2.4 to the £. Devaluation was anticipated by speculators, and on the day before, there was a run on the pound said to be greater than any previously experienced. The devaluation was unfortunately delayed by the need to achieve international co-operation so as to prevent a flurry of competitive devaluations. As it was, only a few minor currencies—including those of Denmark, Hong Kong, Ireland, Jamaica, New Zealand, and Spain—were devalued with sterling. It was also agreed among central bankers that Britain should be given credits of up to $3,000 million, including $1,400 million standby credit from the IMF (*see* **G8**). This credit protected the reserves against speculation; but it would have to be paid back out of balance of payments surpluses over the next few years.

Devaluation increases the demand for domestically produced goods and services: imports are replaced by local substitutes and foreign demand for British goods increases. This switch in demand requires also a switch in scarce resources—labour and capital—into the exporting and import substituting industries, if the new demand is to be met. To release resources for these industries it is necessary to reduce the demand for resources elsewhere in the economy. Accordingly, the devaluation was accompanied by a series of deflationary measures (*see* **G41**).

Improvement after Devaluation.

In his Letter of Intent to the IMF immediately after devaluation the Chancellor stated the Government's aim to improve the balance of payments by at least £500 million a year. However, progress after devaluation was disappointing and fell far short of official expectations. The current account showed a deficit for 1968 of £319 million: no improvement on the deficit for 1967 of £312 million. Moreover, this improvement came on the invisible and long-term capital accounts: the trade gap actually widened considerably. The value of exports rose by 20 per cent between 1967 and 1968, 8 per cent in price and 12 per cent in volume. But less than half of the increase in volume was due to devaluation, since world trade was growing rapidly. Despite the devaluation the volume of imports rose by no less than 7 per cent, outstripping the growth of output, and largely because of devaluation import prices rose by 11 per cent; so that imports increased in value by 18 per cent.

The balance of payments was transformed in 1969, improving strongly throughout the year. One reason for the improvement was a statistical correction: the discovery that exports had been systematically under-recorded for some years and that this had reached a level of over £100 million by 1969. But this does not mean that our much discussed balance of payments difficulties could be dismissed as a statistical illusion. The volume of exports grew by no less than 8 per cent between 1968 and 1969, mainly owing to the rapid increase in world trade. However, the British share of world exports fell by an unusually small amount. Imports rose in volume by only 2 per cent, being held back in part by the slackening of output growth and a decline in stock-building. Another contributory factor may have been the *import deposit* scheme, introduced by the Government in November 1968, by which importers were required to deposit with H.M. Customs for a period of six

months money equal to half (later 40 and then 30 per cent) of the value of certain imports. The improvement in the balance of payments enabled the Government at the start of 1970 to abolish the restrictions on expenditure by British residents on travel outside the Sterling Area, and at the end of 1970 to abolish the import deposit scheme. Between 1969 and 1970 exports grew in volume by 5·5 per cent and in value by 12 per cent; but this was slower than the growth of world exports as a whole. British imports also grew rapidly; the increase in volume (7 per cent) being far greater than the increase in the real income of the economy (1·5 per cent). For only the seventh time since 1800, Britain's visible trade was actually in surplus in 1970!

The surplus on current account was no less than £440 million in 1969 and £631 million in 1970. But this improvement in current account after 1968 came more from invisibles than from trade. In 1969 the surplus on the invisible account was £580 million and in 1970 £628 million; the most improved components being private services (*e.g.*, financial, insurance, and travel services) and net income from abroad. The total currency flow was transformed from an enormous deficit in 1968 (when the authorities borrowed £1,300 million) to a large surplus of £740 million in 1969 and one of £1,420 million in 1970.

Was the improvement in the balance of payments after 1968 an indication that the policy of devaluation had eventually succeeded? The efficacy of devaluation can only be judged after a few years, and then with difficulty since we need to know what would have happened in the absence of devaluation. Economists have not produced a unanimous answer. It was still possible that in 1971 a reflation of the economy and the expected stock-building (raising imports), the slower growth of world trade (curtailing exports), and an accelerated wage–price spiral of inflation (reducing competitiveness) would renew the balance of payments difficulties that had dogged the economy in the 1960s.

Britain's Debt Repayments.

At the end of 1968 the British Government had short- and medium-term debts outstanding to central banks and the IMF of no less than £3,360 million. This represented about 10 per cent of the national income in 1968 and compared with gold and foreign exchange reserves of only £1,010 million. In 1969, however, the surplus on the current account, the inflow of short-term funds and a large positive " balancing item " reflecting unrecorded transactions (*see* the table on **G29**) enabled the Government to reduce its indebtedness by £700 million. The continued improvement in the balance of payments in 1970 and the first allocation of Special Drawing Rights (*see* **G33**) enabled the Chancellor to announce in his April budget that the outstanding debts were down to £1,650 million while the reserves stood at £1,130 million. By December 1970 outstanding debts had fallen to £1,370 million and the reserves were £1,180 million.

Overseas Investment.

At the end of 1967 the total stock of private long-term investment by the United Kingdom overseas was estimated at £11,500 million and investment by overseas companies in the United Kingdom at £4,965 million. In that year the United Kingdom received income of £1,019 million from its overseas investments and paid out £600 million on foreign investments in the United Kingdom, *i.e.*, the net income from interest, dividends and profits was £419 million. Investment abroad takes the form of portfolio investment (on foreign stocks or bonds) or direct investment (by British companies in their overseas affiliates). Well over half of this direct investment now takes the form of profits not remitted by affiliates.

The table indicates that United Kingdom investment abroad rose sharply in the second half of the 1960s despite the policy of requiring " voluntary restraint " on investment in the developed sterling area countries. However, foreign investment in the U.K. also rose rapidly: there was actually a net inflow of investment in 1969. At the same time interest, profits and dividends from British-owned private capital overseas also

PRIVATE FOREIGN INVESTMENT AND RETURNS

	1961–65 *	1966	1967	1968	1969	1970
Private foreign investment:						
Foreign investment in U.K.	252	274	366	587	678	665
U.K. investment abroad	325	303	456	727	652	735
Net investment abroad	73	29	90	140	−16	70
Private sector interest, profits and dividends:						
Credits	791	910	919	1,060	1,263	1,309
Debits	289	361	370	500	470	513
Net income from abroad	502	549	549	560	793	796

* Annual averages.

increased, partly as a result of devaluation raising their sterling value; net private income from abroad being no less than £800 million in 1970.

Should the British Government encourage or discourage private investment abroad? In 1967 and 1968 Professor Reddaway published his Reports on this subject, prepared for the Confederation of British Industry. He concluded that for every £100 of British direct private investment overseas, British exports would immediately increase by about £11, *i.e.*, there would be an initial drain on the balance of payments of £89. The average rate of profit on capital after overseas tax would thereafter be about £8 per annum, or only £5 if capital appreciation was allowed for. In arriving at a policy for foreign investment the short-term balance of payments loss must be weighed against the long-term gain. The importance of the short-term considerations depends on the state of the balance of payments, *e.g.*, if more investment overseas at a time of deficit causes the Government to take deflationary measures, the national cost is great.

The International Monetary System.

(i) International Liquidity.

Imbalance in payments between countries is financed by transfers of gold or foreign exchange (*see* G8). These reserves of gold and foreign exchange are known as *international liquidity*. Their basic characteristic is general acceptability: they can perform their function only if they retain the confidence of those engaged in international transactions. Unless it is ultimately convertible into goods and services, gold has merely an industrial and ornamental value. But since most central banks are prepared to buy and sell gold at a fixed price in terms of their local currency, confidence in gold is maintained.

Two *international reserve currencies* have emerged to supplement gold: the pound and the dollar. The pound has performed this function since World War I, but the dollar has become the main reserve currency since World War II. Surplus countries are prepared to hold short-term debt in pounds or dollars—so earning a rate of interest—confident that their future trading deficits can be financed by payment of these currencies or by their conversion into gold. These holdings are the *dollar* and *sterling balances* (see G7–8). Like gold, they can perform their function as international reserves only if there is confidence that they can be converted into other currencies and hence into goods and services at current exchange rates. There is one other form of international liquidity—drawing rights on the IMF (*see* G8). At the end of 1970 gold accounted for 47 per cent of total international liquidity, foreign exchange reserves for 41 per cent, the IMF for 8 per cent, and the newly created Special Drawing Rights (*see* G33) for 4 per cent.

In recent years two developments have undermined the present international monetary system. First, the growth of international trade has outstripped the growth of reserves with which to finance imbalances in this trade. Between 1952 and 1969 world trade, measured in dollars, rose by 220 per cent, whereas international liquidity, measured in dollars, rose by only 35 per cent. Gold reserves have been a declining proportion of international liquidity, partly because gold pro-

duction has been hampered by the fixed price in the face of rising costs of gold production, and also because an increasing proportion of newly-mined gold has found its way into private speculative hoards and not into official stocks. The other main source of new international liquidity was an increase in dollar balances. By the late 1960s dollar balances actually exceeded the United States gold reserves.

The second problem to have emerged is the weakness in the balance of payments of the reserve currency countries. Both Britain and the United States have had persistent deficits in recent years. As a result there have been periodic fears that the dollar or the pound would be devalued in terms of gold and other currencies; and this has resulted in speculation against the dollar and the pound (*see* G30). The inadequacy of international liquidity and the weakness of the reserve currencies produces a dangerous "deflationary bias" in the world economy (*see* G9).

(ii) The Gold Crisis 1968.

The United States has run a large and persistent payments deficit in the 1950s and 1960s. This was initially financed through the willingness of foreigners to run up dollar balances. However, distrust of the dollar has grown, and between 1960 and 1967 U.S. gold reserves were run down, from $19,500 million to $12,100 million. After the devaluation of sterling in November 1967, the interest of speculators transferred from the pound to the dollar. Since many speculators expected the devaluation of the dollar in terms of gold to be followed by a corresponding devaluation of other currencies, there was a growing demand for gold.

After 1961 the central banks of the major trading nations operated a *gold pool* in the London market, whereby they agreed to exchange gold for currencies at existing official exchange rates. But with the growing speculation against the dollar, the system could not be continued without endangering the U.S. gold reserves. The central bankers gathered for a crisis meeting in Washington on 17 March, and decided to terminate the gold pool. They introduced two markets for gold, with private transactions taking place in the free market at a price determined by supply and demand, and transactions among central banks taking place in the official market at the official gold price. The United States was now prepared to convert dollars into gold only for central banks, *i.e.*, to finance a deficit only on its current plus long-term capital account. In this way speculation against the dollar could be controlled; but the problem of the U.S. deficit on current and long-term capital account was still to be solved.

The further monetary crisis of November 1968, produced by speculation against the franc and towards the mark, the possibility that the incoming Nixon Administration would raise the dollar price of gold, and the limited sales on the free market by gold producers all helped to keep up the speculative demand for gold and its price in the free market. In the first year after the gold crisis the free market price averaged about $40 compared with the official price of $35 a fine ounce.

There was further currency speculation in 1969 in expectation of a realignment of European exchange rates. In August France, with a weak balance of payments, devalued the franc by 11·1 per cent, and in October West Germany, with a persistent surplus, revalued the deutschemark upwards by 9·29 per cent. Thereafter tension in the foreign exchange markets was relaxed, and dishoarding and a fall in speculative demand for gold coincided with large sales by producers, so that the free market price for gold fell to $35 a fine ounce. The IMF reached an agreement with South Africa to buy South African gold in certain circumstances, *e.g.*, when the gold price is $35 or below. This meant that newly-mined gold could now enter official reserves and that the free market price would be unlikely to fall below the official price.

(iii) The United States Deficit.

In 1970 the deficit in the United States balance of payments rose to a record level. This was financed by creditor countries increasing their dollar balances. They had little choice: a large scale conversion of dollar balances would force the United States to renounce its obligation to supply gold to central banks at $35 per ounce. It became increasingly clear that if the United States failed to reduce its deficit by restricting capital outflows or military expenditures abroad, the creditor countries would either have to go on financing American deficits by accumulating dollars or allow their currencies to appreciate in terms of the dollar. In 1971 the dollar appeared to be the weakest of the major currencies.

(iv) Reform of the International Monetary System.

There is an increasing shortage of international liquidity, which gives a deflationary twist to the world economy and threatens the continuation of free trade. What means are available to increase international liquidity? There are two main alternatives: a rise in the price of gold in terms of all currencies or the creation of an international paper money.

A rise in the gold price would increase international liquidity; first, by increasing the money value of existing and future gold reserves, and second, by encouraging gold production. However, there are certain disadvantages. It helps those countries most which need help least—those with large gold reserves; it represents a victory for the gold speculators and so acts as a stimulus to further hoarding and speculation in the future; it helps in particular the gold-producing countries Russia and South Africa; and finally, it represents a sheer waste of economic resources: gold has little value except as a means of international payment. The most likely method of securing a general rise in the price of gold would be a devaluation of the dollar. since most other currencies would be de-valued simultaneously. Therefore, devaluation could not cure the U.S. deficit. For these reasons the United States Government decided against devaluation of the dollar at the time of the gold crisis.

The domestic currency of the United Kingdom is not backed by gold: on a one pound note the Governor of the Bank of England promises to pay the bearer on demand the sum of one pound— another pound note! Yet, within Britain, there is complete confidence in the currency, because it is generally acceptable and so convertible into goods and services. Just as gold no longer backs the domestic currency, there is no need for gold in settlement of international payments. All we need is a generally acceptable international currency, *i.e.*, one in which all countries have confidence.

Such a currency could be created by an international authority constituted for this purpose; and it could be made available to deficit countries, which could then pay their creditors in the new currency. In this way the current shortage of international liquidity could be made good, and indeed gold—Keynes' " barbarous relic "—could be supplanted. There are various difficulties in such a scheme. It would involve some loss of national autonomy and the vesting of considerable power in the international authority issuing the paper currency. Decisions would have to be made as to which countries should receive the new currency, and in what quantities. And there is a fear that it would enable reckless governments to pursue inflationary policies without the discipline imposed by shortage of reserves, and that their inflation would be infectious. Many variations on this basic scheme have been devised in an attempt to surmount these—largely political— objections.

(v) Special Drawing Rights.

In the past the IMF has merely provided deficit countries with loans, to be repaid over a certain period (*see* G8). However, the amount of these credit facilities has been increased over time. In 1959 the quotas paid by members to the IMF were raised by 50 per cent, in 1964 by 25 per cent, and in 1970 by about 35 per cent. Moreover, in order to increase the resources available to neutralise the massive movements of short-term funds which had so disrupted balance of payments in 1960 and 1961, the IMF initiated a scheme for a " lenders' club ". In December 1961 the main trading countries— the *Group of Ten*—undertook (subject to some control by lending countries over the use of the funds) to make available loans totalling over £2,000 million to the IMF for relending to countries of the Group suffering an outflow of short-term funds.

In 1967 the members of the IMF agreed in principle to a scheme according *special drawing rights* (SDRs) to member countries, and in 1970 the scheme came into operation. SDRs are dis-tributed annually to all members in proportion to their quotas with the IMF. They have a fixed value in terms of gold, and like gold, are generally accepted as a means of payment. Thus a deficit country can use its SDRs to buy the currency of the countries with which it has a deficit, and the surplus countries, in accumulating SDRs, earn a rate of interest on them. This is a movement to-wards an international paper currency, since the SDRs, unlike IMF loans, do not have to be repaid: they are a permanent addition to international reserves. The first allocation—totalling $3,414 million, of which Britain received $410 million— was made in 1970, and further allocations were agreed for 1971 and 1972. The scheme was launched on a scale which is small in relation to the size of the problem; but it is a step in the right direction.

(vi) Sterling as a Reserve Currency.

The sterling balances (*see* G7 and 32) came under pressure from a new quarter in 1968. There were many sterling area holders of sterling balances, in-cluding most governments, who did not speculate against the pound in 1967 and suffered a capital loss when the pound was devalued. Anticipating further capital loss at the time of the gold crisis in 1968, they ran down their sterling balances, so endangering the British gold reserves. In September the central banks of the major indus-trial countries agreed at Basle to grant the United Kingdom new credit facilities of up to £800 million for ten years with which to finance such sales of sterling. Also the British Government guaranteed the value, in terms of US dollars, of most of the official sterling reserves held by these countries, in return for their holding at least a certain proportion of their reserves in sterling. These arrangements should help to protect sterling against the dangers of being a reserve currency.

(vii) The Eurodollar Market.

The Eurodollar market is a market for bank deposits which are denominated in foreign curren-cies. It derives its name from the fact that most of the banks which accept these foreign currency deposits are in Europe (including Britain) and most of the deposits are denominated in U.S. dollars. The Eurodollar market has grown at remarkable speed. A phenomenon of the 1960s, the market involved deposits of $9 billion in 1964 and $37 billion in 1969. The reason for that growth was the profitability of Eurodollar trans-actions. Banks found that, particularly if only large units of money were handled, they could profitably borrow funds in country A and lend in country B, while paying interest rates higher than those paid in country A and charging rates lower than those charged in country B. Its growth was helped by the continuous deficit in the United States balance of payments, since this meant that banks and institutions received dollars which they were willing to hold and lend. London is very important in the Eurodollar market: London banks accounted for no less than 57 per cent of the total external liabilities in U.S. dollars reported by European banks in 1968.

The Eurodollar market—involving great mobility of short-term funds—creates problems for the regulation of economic activity. The market affects the rates of interest and the availability of credit in different countries, and money movements can thwart both restrictive and expansionist monetary policies (*see* G22).

Trading Arrangements.

(i) First Application for Membership of the Common Market.

In mid-1961 it was announced that Britain would apply for full membership of the *European Economic Community*, otherwise known as the Common Market, set up by the Treaty of Rome which was ratified in 1958. The European Economic Community (EEC) consists of six full members —Belgium, France, Holland, Italy, Luxembourg, and Western Germany (*see* G9). Britain had participated in the negotiations which led up to its formation, and had argued in favour of a looser "free trade area" without a common external tariff, and excluding trade in agricultural products. No compromise acceptable to the Six was found, and Britain joined with six other European countries—Austria, Denmark, Norway, Portugal, Sweden, and Switzerland—in forming the *European Free Trade Area* (EFTA).

Later, however, when the Common Market proved to be highly successful in terms of the growth of production and trade, the British Government decided to apply for membership. There were three main problems to be solved in the negotiations. The first two—the trading links with Commonwealth countries, and the position of British agriculture—were those which had influenced the British attitude in the earlier negotiations. Now Britain also had obligations to her trading partners in EFTA. The Common Market countries welcomed the British application, but made it clear that renewed negotiations must take place within the framework of the Treaty.

(ii) The British Proposals.

The British delegation made the following proposals for the solution of Britain's special problems. For British *agriculture* there was to be a long "transition period"—that is to say, a period for adjustment before British agriculture became fully integrated into the Common Market agricultural arrangements—possibly 12 to 15 years from the date of joining the Common Market. By contrast, it was not proposed to negotiate for favourable conditions for British *industry*: on joining the Common Market, Britain was prepared to make a reduction in her tariffs equivalent to the reductions which had already been made by the Six.

Two lines of approach were suggested for protecting the trading positions of the under-developed countries of the Commonwealth. One involved granting those countries the status of "associated territories" which would give their products access to European markets on preferential terms. There was a precedent for this sort of arrangement, in that France had already negotiated associated status for some of her former colonies in Africa. But it was recognised that the Six might not be prepared to offer associated status to some of the larger under-developed countries of the Commonwealth—*e.g.*, India, and that some countries might wish to reject an offer of associated status for political reasons. As an alternative, therefore, it was suggested that the Common Market external tariff on some of the more important agricultural exports from these countries—*e.g.*, Indian tea—should be reduced or eliminated; and that arrangements should be made to ensure that the external tariff on manufactured goods exported from these countries—*e.g.*, textiles from Hong

Kong—did not lead to a reduction of such exports. For the more developed countries of the Commonwealth, there were proposals that the Common Market external tariff on raw material imports should be reduced or eliminated for certain Commonwealth produced materials, such as aluminium, zinc, and woodpulp. It was also proposed that certain arrangements should be made with respect to foodstuffs—chiefly wheat, meat, and dairy products—produced by developed members of the Commonwealth. The principle underlying these arrangements, it was suggested, should be that Commonwealth producers "be given in the future the opportunity for outlets for their products comparable to those they now enjoy."

(iii) The Negotiations.

In the course of prolonged negotiations, considerable progress towards a final agreement was gradually made: progress in reducing tariffs important in Commonwealth trade, in agreeing that Commonwealth countries in Africa and the West Indies should be offered associated status on the same terms as the ex-French territories, and in agreeing that the problems of India, Pakistan, and Ceylon could best be solved by trade treaties negotiated between the Common Market and these countries. The problem of temperate foodstuffs proved the most intractable. Britain wanted specific arrangements to ensure that Commonwealth-produced temperate foods would be able to find markets in Europe, at least in the short term. France made it clear that she envisaged a reduction of food imports into Common Market countries, to permit an expansion of her agricultural output: this point of view was clearly incompatible with the British proposal for "comparable outlets" for Commonwealth producers. Nor was there agreement on the transitional arrangements for British agriculture.

Nevertheless, it was the opinion of many observers that by January 1963 the stage had been set for a final round of bargaining, and that given goodwill on both sides Britain's entry could have been assured. It therefore came as a surprise when France decided that the negotiations should be broken off. Despite opposition from the other five, a French veto was imposed on the British application. Perhaps the fundamental reason for the breakdown can be inferred from a statement attributed to General de Gaulle: "The Europe I prefer is the Europe of the Six."

(iv) Britain's Second Application.

In 1967 the British Government again began discussing with the EEC countries the possibility of British membership. This move had the support of most British industrialists: a Confederation of British Industry Survey in March showed that 90 per cent of replying companies believe EEC membership would be to their advantage. Confidential discussions went on; but in December, France vetoed the opening of negotiations on Britain's entry. With the resignation of General de Gaulle in 1969 the Common Market issue became live again, and negotiations on the British application opened in 1970.

Although the negotiations were private, some facts became known, for instance on the important issue of the British contribution to the Common Market budget (mainly for supporting EEC farmers). The British delegation proposed that this be in the region of 13–15 per cent of the total budget but the Community proposed 20–25 per cent.

(v) The 1970 White Paper.

In February 1970 the British Government published a White Paper assessing the economic consequences of entry for the United Kingdom. The report recognised disadvantages as well as advantages. Britain would have to adopt the common agricultural policy and make a net contribution to the financing of that policy. Food prices would rise in Britain through the imposition of levies on imports from non-Community sources and the payment of Community prices for imports from other members. The maximum increase likely to

INDUSTRIAL PRODUCTION, EMPLOYMENT, AND PRODUCTIVITY, 1959–70

(Quarterly averages of seasonally adjusted index numbers, 1958 = 100)

Year	Quarter	Industrial production (1)	Employment in industry (2)	Productivity in industry $100 \times (1) \div (2)$
1959	I	102	100	102
1960	I	112	102	110
1961	I	114	104	109
1962	I	114	104	110
1963	I	113	101	112
1964	I	127	103	123
1965	I	132	105	125
1966	I	134	106	125
1967	I	132	103	128
1968	I	140	100	139
1969	I	145	100	144
1970	I	147	99	148
1970	IV	149	96	156

occur in retail food prices was estimated to be in the range 18–26 per cent spread over a period of years. The dismantling of tariffs on trade with the Community would reduce industrial prices.

The tariff cuts and the response of wages and prices to the increased cost of living would directly affect both industrial imports and exports: it being suggested that the balance of payments might be worsened by £125–275 million per annum on this account. But there would also be longer-run, dynamic and less predictable effects, through the stimulus to British industry of being in a market of 300 million inhabitants and growing more rapidly than our own. The White Paper concluded that the balance of economic advantage was uncertain and that the precise conditions negotiated for entry would be important.

Those economists who oppose British entry argue that the successful growth of the EEC countries since its formation probably would have occurred without it; that Britain will have to pay heavily to subsidise backward European agriculture; and they see a danger that Britain—having restricted in its economic policies by EEC rules—will become a depressed region of the Common Market.

(vi) The Werner Plan.

In 1970 the Commission of the European Economic Community published the Werner Plan, a report on the establishment of economic and monetary union of the EEC. The plan aimed at transferring within a decade the principal economic decisions from the national to the Community level, and at establishing within the Community complete freedom of movement of goods, services, persons and capital, with fixed and constant rates of exchange between national currencies or, preferably, a common currency. A centre of decision for economic policy would be established and made responsible to a European parliament. There was to be a common system of value-added taxation (see G42), and other taxes would be brought into line. The member countries have agreed to the initial stages of the Plan, e.g., to more co-operation in international currency arrangements.

These proposals have far-reaching economic and political implications, since they involve a considerable reduction of national sovereignty. For instance, the loss of power to correct balance of payments deficits by means of trade controls or variation in the exchange rate implies either that the deficit country's currency should be generally acceptable to its creditors (so that the country within the Community—like a region within a country—simply cannot have a balance of payments problem), or the country must resort to deflation. And even if there is a common currency, it is very likely that resources will concentrate in some regions of the Community to the neglect of other regions, possibly those far from the main centres of production and consumption. Complete mobility of resources is likely to produce a regional problem within the Community just as

it can produce a regional problem within a country. But the Community may not, to the same extent as a country, possess the political power and determination required to remedy the problem.

2. INTERNAL DEVELOPMENTS

Industrial Output and Employment.

In the fourth quarter of 1970, industrial production was 49 per cent higher than it had been in 1958. This expansion occurred largely in two spurts: during the twelve months between March 1959 and March 1960 industrial output increased by 11 per cent, and between March 1963 and March 1964 it rose by 14 per cent. The three years before March 1959, the three years between the booms and the three years after March 1964 were periods of industrial stagnation. Industrial production picked up again in 1967 and 1968, but growth (11 per cent in two years) was not as rapid as in the boom periods, and industrial employment actually fell. The table also indicates that numbers employed in industry were 4 per cent lower towards the end of 1970 (allowing for seasonal variation) than in 1958, so that productivity—output per person employed—rose by about 56 per cent over that period. Here again, a very high proportion of the increase was secured in the boom periods.

Restriction and De-restriction.

The 1960s have witnessed several changes in the emphasis of Government monetary and fiscal policies. In the first half of 1960 the emphasis was on restrictive policies, both because of the deterioration in the balance of payments position, and because it was apparent that the very rapid expansion of output had created shortages and inflation in the economy at home. No doubt there would have been a slowing down in the rate of growth of output even if restrictive measures had not been taken: an increase as rapid as that in 1959 was possible only because a substantial excess capacity had developed over the preceding years. But the measures taken to restrict demand reinforced this tendency, and growth in industrial output was halted.

A relaxation of restraints did help to stimulate some increase in output in the early months of 1961. But from July 1961—again primarily for balance of payments reasons—there was a phase of even sterner restrictions. The progressive relaxation of restrictions during the summer of 1962, coupled with measures designed to stimulate industrial output, had not had any major effect by the end of the year.

In some ways, the situation early in 1963 was analogous to that of early 1959. There was a substantial under-utilisation of capacity in many branches of industry, since some new investment had continued in 1960–62. Labour resources for expansion were available, in that unemployment —at over 3 per cent—was higher than in any period since the war. Consequently the expansionist policies of 1963 helped to produce a year of boom which saw a spurt of industrial output, and a substantial increase in productivity. This progress could not be maintained in 1964, when industrial production and productivity flattened out, and the balance of payments deteriorated. However, the 1960 remedy of deflation was not immediately repeated; it was now realised that "stop–go" policies were harmful to the growth of the economy, and that the balance of payments problem would have to be solved by other measures. Full employment was maintained between 1964 I and 1966 I, but industrial production per man rose by only 1·5 per cent per annum. Two reasons have been suggested for this slow growth of productivity: a decline in the average working week (output per man-hour increased more rapidly), and the tendency of employers to adjust their labour force to the level of production only with a considerable delay.

Balance of payments difficulties eventually led the Government to deflate the economy; and there was a fall in industrial production in the second half of 1966 as the July measures took effect. Employers now began to lay off workers, and unemployment rose from 1·2 per cent of the labour force in early 1966 to average 2·2 per cent in 1967. Despite the resumption of growth in 1967 and 1968, unemployment in the economy rose.

With industrial production stagnant in 1969 and 1970, and productivity continuing to rise, the rate of unemployment increased to 2·5 per cent in 1970 and to over 700,000 (2·7 per cent, seasonally adjusted) in early 1971. Industrial employment actually fell after the first quarter of 1969, and output per man rose as firms tried to "shake out" unneeded labour. The reasoning behind the government policy of prolonging the recession was no longer based on the balance of payments, since this was strongly in surplus. Rather, it was hoped that high unemployment would curb the rapid inflation.

Regional Planning.

Much publicity has been given in the 1960s to the varying degrees of prosperity and levels of unemployment in the United Kingdom (see G13). Government measures are necessary to reduce disparities and probably even to prevent them from growing.

There are essentially two ways of tackling the problem of regional imbalances: taking jobs to the people or bringing people to the jobs. In so far as the latter alternative is chosen, the Government should encourage the mobility of labour, e.g., through retraining schemes or a housing subsidy. However, the migration of population may damage community life in the denuded areas, and cause congestion, housing shortages, and overcrowding in the booming regions. The Government can create employment opportunities in the relatively depressed regions in various ways. It can try to induce expanding industries to set up new plants in these regions by offering tax incentives; it can authorise additional expenditure on public works —e.g., by accelerating road-building programmes —to provide additional employment; it can place orders for the goods it needs—e.g. defence contracts—where work is required.

On taking office in October 1964, the Labour Government made regional planning the responsibility of its Department of Economic Affairs. Britain was divided into eight regions, with the intention of producing a plan for each region. The Government also established two kinds of planning body: regional economic planning Councils and Boards to advise on and co-ordinate the planning of each region.

Recent Government policy to cure regional unemployment has taken the following forms. Various measures to defer public construction programmes have excluded the "Development Areas." Fiscal incentives to locate industry in the depressed regions have been given, e.g., the cash grants provided in 1966 for new plants and machinery in manufacturing were at twice the national rate in the Development Areas. By contrast, office building in the main conurbations, London and Birmingham, was strictly limited. To encourage the mobility of labour, the Government introduced redundancy compensation and

achieved some expansion in both public and private training facilities. In 1967 regional differentials in the selective employment tax were introduced (see G41). Under this scheme manufacturers in Development Areas were paid 30s. per week for each full-time adult male employee and lower amounts in respect of other workers; so giving the Development Areas a wage cost advantage in manufacturing of 5–10 per cent.

In 1964/5 special assistance to industry in the Development Areas was only £31 million. The estimate for the financial year 1968/9 was £265 million; taking the form mainly of the Regional Employment Premium and Investment grants.

In 1970 the incentive to invest in the Development Areas was affected by the Government's replacement of cash grants by a system of initial allowances against tax. Whereas cash grants were 40 per cent of investment in plant and machinery in Development Areas and 20 per cent in other areas, there was now to be free depreciation in Development Areas and 60 per cent initial allowances in other areas. The relative attractiveness of the Development Areas would be reduced by the halving of SET in 1971 and its abolition in 1972.

Planning for Faster Growth.

There has been an increasing dissatisfaction with the rate of growth achieved in this economy over the past decade or so. The economies of most Common Market countries have increased their industrial output at a much faster rate. Furthermore, there has been dissatisfaction with the way in which the economy has grown: the characteristic pattern has been one of sharp bursts of expansion interrupted by rather lengthy periods of stagnation.

(i) The National Economic Development Council.

To stimulate a more systematic study of the problems involved in securing a faster and more even rate of growth in the British economy, the Conservative Government established the *National Economic Development Council* (NEDC or "Neddy"). The two-tier organisation was similar to that of the corresponding planning council in France. The Council itself consisted of representatives from the T.U.C. and employers' organisations, Government ministers and independent members, and it was served by a group of experts. This group undertook research into the problems of securing a faster rate of growth, into the means of overcoming obstacles to growth, and into the economic policies which could be most conducive to faster growth.

In its first report, in 1963, the Council made a projection for the economy. It adopted a target rate of growth of output over the period 1961–66, equal to 4 per cent per annum, which was substantially faster than the rate of growth actually achieved in previous years. It attempted to predict how investment, exports, imports, consumption, and the output of each industry would have to grow if the target rate of growth was to be achieved. The merit of this exercise was twofold: it helped to focus Government attention on the long-term, by showing that policies designed to solve short-term difficulties might intensify the problem of raising long-term economic growth; and, by bolstering expectations, it encouraged firms to invest.

A particularly interesting feature of the work of the NEDC is its study of individual industries. Seventeen major industries were surveyed in detail to assess the changes in output, employment, productivity, investment, and exports which were feasible in each industry. Economic Development Committees (EDCs)—which have come to be known as "little Neddies"—were established as part of the NEDC machinery to report on the problems of individual industries. It is impossible for an individual firm or industry to make correct decisions on future expansion without knowing how the rest of the economy will behave; by relating planning at the national level and planning at the level of individual industries the NEDC did valuable work.

(ii) The Department of Economic Affairs.

In October 1964 the Labour Government established a new *Department of Economic Affairs* (DEA). While short-term measures to regulate the economy or the balance of payments remained the responsibility of the Treasury, the DEA took over from the Treasury the responsibility for long-term economic policy. The DEA was charged with the task of preparing and implementing a realistic plan for economic expansion, a prices and incomes policy and an industrial and regional policy. The NEDC, now reconstituted, became a consultative and advisory body; a link between the Government and the economic community. However, the EDC's continue to function and have produced a great many reports. The division between short- and long-term planning proved unsatisfactory, and in 1969 the DEA was abolished and its functions reverted to the Treasury.

(iii) The National Plan.

The National Plan for the British economy over the period 1964–70 was published by the Government in 1965. The Plan was based on the assumption that output would rise by 3·8 per cent per annum over the period. Since the labour force was expected to grow at 0·4 per cent per annum, this meant an annual growth in productivity of 3·5 per cent—considerably higher than the 2·7 per cent average over the period 1960–64. The Plan specified the changes in investment, consumption, and public expenditure required to achieve this target.

In many ways, the crucial assumptions were those concerned with the balance of payments. The Plan supposed that imports would increase by 4·0 per cent per annum, and that to achieve a "satisfactory" surplus of £250 million on the overall balance of payments in 1970, exports would have to rise by 5·6 per cent per annum. If such a rapid expansion of exports were not achieved—and in the period 1960–64 the annual increase averaged only 3·1 per cent—the whole Plan could be jeopardised, in that the balance of payments difficulties might, as in the past, appear to justify policies to restrict the growth in domestic output.

Indeed, this is precisely what happened. The tardy improvement in the balance of payments led the Government eventually in July 1966 to deflate the economy. The ensuing stagnation meant that the Plan's targets for 1970 could no longer be achieved. However, it should not be concluded that planning is necessarily an academic exercise: planning has a valuable sight-setting function; it can bolster firms' expectations and hence their investment; and it can help to co-ordinate their decisions. Rather, we should recognise that planning is worthless unless combined with Government policies which enable the planned targets to be reached.

(iv) " The Task Ahead ".

In the uncertain economic climate after the July measures there was little point in long-range planning. However, early in 1969 the Government published as a Green Paper a new planning document *The Task Ahead: an Economic Assess-ment to 1972.* It was neither a plan nor a forecast but " part of the consultative planning process ". Implementation was to take the form of consultation with the EDC or other representatives of each industry. The document was flexible in that new developments could be accommodated without requiring the whole assessment to be rewritten. There are three sets of projections—lower, " basic " and higher—on the assumptions of a growth rate in real output of 3, 3¼ and 4 per cent per annum respectively. These projections compare with an actual growth rate of 3·3 per cent per annum between 1960 and 1966.

In fact, the outcome again proved to be well below expectations. Between the first quarter of 1969 and the first quarter of 1971 real output rose by less than 2 per cent per annum. But this time the balance of payments could not be blamed for the shortfall. Instead it appeared that the stagnation was due to a loss of confidence by private investors, and to the monetary and fiscal policies of successive Governments concerned about the acceleration of inflation.

The Industrial Reorganisation Corporation.

The *Industrial Reorganisation Corporation* (IRC) was set up in December 1966 under Government auspices. Its functions were to promote industrial reorganisation in the interests of industrial efficiency, *e.g.*, by enabling industries to achieve economies of scale or by reorganising inefficiently managed firms. It assisted firms in agreed re-groupings and could intervene to encourage a particular takeover which, in its estimation, was in the public interest.

The IRC Act provided the Corporation with financial resources of up to £150 million. However, its objective in making loans was to "prod" and not to "prop" inefficient firms. It supported mergers in electronics, trawling, nuclear power, mechanical engineering, and other industries. In 1970 the incoming Conservative Government decided to wind up the IRC.

Inflation.

(i) Wages and Prices.

Retail prices continued to edge upwards in the 1960s (*see* G17–19). In 1968 they were 35 per cent higher than in 1958. Very little of this increase can be attributed to an increase in import prices. To explain the inflation we must look at the behaviour of labour costs. Between 1958 and 1968 the nationally negotiated weekly wage rates rose by 49 per cent, and weekly earnings—including overtime payments and payments negotiated on the factory floor—by 75 per cent. Since the increase in productivity during this period was slow, income from employment per unit of output (indicating labour costs per unit of output) rose by 38 per cent. These increased costs were passed on to the public in the form of increased prices, so that real earnings rose by only 29 per cent. The table shows annual average prices, earnings, real earnings, and also real disposable incomes (*i.e.*, the purchasing power of total personal incomes after income tax), all as indexes with 1963 = 100.

AVERAGE RETAIL PRICES, WEEKLY EARNINGS, REAL WEEKLY
EARNINGS AND REAL DISPOSABLE INCOMES 1963 = 100

	Retail prices	Weekly earnings	Real weekly earnings	Real disposable incomes
1958 . . .	89·6	78·4	87·5	81·5
1963 . . .	100·0	100·0	100·0	100·0
1964 . . .	103·3	107·1	103·7	104·2
1965 . . .	108·2	115·1	106·4	106·4
1966 . . .	112·5	122·5	108·9	108·5
1967 . . .	115·3	126·2	109·5	110·0
1968 . . .	120·7	136·8	113·3	112·1
1969 . . .	127·2	147·5	115·9	112·5
1970 . . .	135·3	165·2	122·1	116·5

(ii) The Growing Inflation.

A disturbing feature of the table is the growth in the rate of inflation in Britain after 1967. Between 1968 and 1969 retail prices rose by 5·5 per cent, between 1969 and 1970 by 6·5 per cent, and between January 1970 and January 1971 by 8·5 per cent. The increase in average weekly earnings rose also.

Why has there been this acceleration in the rate of inflation? In 1968 and 1969, it resulted partly from the increase in import prices consequent upon the devaluation of the pound in November 1967 (*see* G30), partly from the increase in indirect taxes introduced after devaluation in order to free resources for exports (*see* G41), and partly from the spurt in money wages when the Governments incomes policy weakened (*see* G39). But in 1970 the blame could be placed squarely on the " wage explosion ". Normally money wages rise more rapidly the greater the pressure of demand in the labour market. But with unemployment high in 1970, pressure of demand for labour could not be the explanation. Rather, the wage explosion appeared to reflect a general increase in militancy by trade unionists angered by the near-stagnation of real earnings and real disposable incomes after 1967 and possibly influenced by events in other countries (*see* below) Once begun it was maintained by the growth of expectations that prices would continue to rise rapidly.

In 1970 there was a sharp increase in real earnings (by 5 per cent), implying a decline in the share of profits. This share (gross trading profits as a proportion of domestic income) is normally low during a recession, but the share in 1970 dropped to 10 per cent, compared with 14 per cent in the recession of 1962. The implication was that the wage increases of 1970 would have a delayed effect on prices in 1971, and this might set off further wage demands. There was a grave danger that a vicious spiral of inflation would be maintained, or even accelerated, in 1971.

(iii) International Inflation.

The acceleration of inflation in Britain coincided with similar trends in other countries, including the United States, Japan, W. Germany, France, and Italy, as the table shows.

RISE IN CONSUMER PRICES

	1959–1969 *	1968–1969	1969–1970 **
United States .	2·3	5·4	5·7
Japan .	5·3	5·2	6·5
France .	3·9	6·4	5·9
Germany .	2·5	2·7	4·0
Italy .	3·6	2·6	4·7
United Kingdom	3·5	5·5	6·8

    * Annual average.
   ** Third quarter to third quarter.

Was this the result of a series of coincidences; did the inflations have a common cause; or were they " contagious "? Both France and Italy had major strikes and subsequent " wage explosions "; Britain's inflation too was " cost-push " not " demand pull " in character (*see* G4); Japan and W. Germany experienced strong demand pressures; and in the United States the price increases could be explained as a lagged reaction to the demand pressures of 1966–1969. Nevertheless, it is likely that inflation was to some extent transmitted from one country to another—particularly from the United States and particularly to small, trading countries—through its effects on the prices of imports and exports, and possibly through its effects on workers' expectations.

(iv) Effects of Inflation.

British Governments have been concerned about inflation mainly because of its effects on British competitiveness, and hence on the balance of payments. If our costs rise relative to competitors' costs, British exporters find it more difficult to compete in foreign markets if they raise their prices; and if they keep prices down in order to compete, this implies their having to accept lower profit margins on exports than on sales in the home market, and so discourages exporting.

But inflation can have other harmful consequences. It often produces a redistribution of income, with the strong gaining from the weak, *i.e.*, the poorly-organised workers and the pensioners. In inflationary conditions income gains can appear to result not so much from work or sacrifice as from ingenuity and the exercise of economic and political power. Inflation can breed uncertainty and industrial unrest. In 1970 the number of strikes was up by 60 per cent on the annual average for 1960–1966, and the number of working days lost was up by 260 per cent. This was both cause and effect of the inflation.

Incomes Policy.

Britain's competitive position in world trade has deteriorated relative to that of her main rivals the United States, West Germany, and France; hence her balance of payments difficulties. The British share in total world exports of manufactures fell from 17·7 per cent to 11·9 per cent between 1959 and 1967. There are essentially two methods of remedying this situation. We must secure either a relative fall in the external value of the pound, or a relative rise in its internal value. In other words, either there must be a devaluation of the pound in terms of other currencies, or we must have a policy to limit the increase in the British price-level. Up to 1967 the Government concentrated on the latter alternative; and attempts were made to introduce some form of *incomes policy*. In 1967 the Government opted for devaluation; but incomes policy was still necessary if the devaluation was to be successful.

(i) The Pay Pause.

In July 1961 the Chancellor of the Exchequer called for a " pause " in wages, salaries, and dividend payments. Exhortations for restraint have been a familiar feature of ministerial statements for many years, but on this occasion the Government soon made it clear that it intended to use such power as it has to influence the amount and timing of wage and salary awards. It has power to decide when the pay awards recommended by the Wages Councils—which fix minimum wages for 3½ million workers—shall be implemented. The Government's power is strongest over workers which it directly or indirectly employs, *e.g.*, civil servants, teachers, and Post Office workers. Their pay awards were cut back. The Government also had a limited influence on awards made in nationalised industries.

The " pay pause " came to an end in April 1962. It was envisaged as a temporary policy, and its effects are difficult to assess. It certainly postponed some wage awards which would otherwise have been made in that period, and it may have contributed to a stiffening of resistance to wage claims. But because the pause affected some groups of people more severely than others, this form of incomes policy was seen to be discriminatory.

(ii) The National Incomes Commission.

In February 1962 the Government issued a White Paper which outlined its incomes policy for the period after the pause. It stated that " the objective must be to keep the rate of increase in incomes within the long-term rate of growth of national production. . . . In recent years national production has risen by about 2 to 2½ per cent a year. . . . It is accordingly necessary that the increase of wages and salaries, as of other incomes, should be kept within this figure during the next phase." The Government stressed that most of the arguments which had in the past been advanced in justification of wage and salary claims—*e.g.*, increases in the cost of living, trends in productivity or profits in particular industries, and comparisons with levels or trends in other employments—should be given less weight; and that " general economic considerations "—*i.e.*, the increases which the economy can afford given the prospective rate of increase in national production —should be given more weight.

Late in 1962 the Government set up the *National Incomes Commission* (NIC). However, the powers of this body were limited. It could not participate in, nor comment upon, wage claims while negotiations were in progress unless the parties involved consented; and as the T.U.C. did not intend to co-operate with the Commission, such consent was unlikely. It could be asked to report on inflationary settlements which had been reached (unless the settlement was reached by arbitration); but it had no power to cancel or modify an agreement. NIC produced only 4 reports, and was wound up after the change in Government.

(iii) The National Board for Prices and Incomes.

In October 1964 the Labour Government's new Department of Economic Affairs was made responsible for achieving an incomes policy. The lessons of the past had been learned; the Government recognised that a successful incomes policy would require the support of both sides of industry. Its first objective was to achieve a " Joint Statement of Intent on Productivity, Prices and Incomes "; this was signed in December 1964. In this document the T.U.C. and the employers' organisations undertook to co-operate with the Government in producing an effective machinery for the implementing of an incomes policy.

It was Government policy that growth in earnings per employee should equal the planned growth in national output per employee of 3–3½ per cent per annum. Thus, in those industries (*e.g.*, engineering) in which productivity growth exceeds this " norm ", earnings should rise less rapidly than productivity, and in those industries (*e.g.*, railways) in which productivity growth falls short of the norm, earnings could rise more rapidly than productivity. Moreover, prices would be expected to fall in industries such as engineering, and permitted to rise in industries such as railways. Growth in earnings per employee should exceed the norm only in exceptional cases; *i.e.*, as a reward for increasing productivity by eliminating restrictive working practices; if necessary to transfer labour from one industry to another; if earnings are too low to maintain a reasonable standard of living; or if a group of workers have fallen seriously out of line with earnings for similar work.

To make specific recommendations on the basis of this policy, the Government set up a *National Board for Prices and Incomes*. It consists of an independent Chairman, a number of independent experts, a businessman and a trade unionist. The Prices Review Division of the Board can investigate the price of any goods in the economy, and the Incomes Review Division has power to investigate all claims and settlements relating to wages, salaries, and other incomes. In less than 5 years of operation the Board had produced over 150 reports on prices and earnings.

There was no statutory authority to enforce the recommendations of the Board: reliance was placed on voluntary methods and the power of persuasion and public opinion. However, in late 1965 the Government introduced a compulsory " Early Warning " system, whereby it is notified in advance of any intended increase in incomes or in certain prices. As a result, the Government and the Board have had time to consider increases before they are put into effect.

(iv) The Prices and Incomes Standstill.

A voluntary incomes policy is very difficult to implement, since it depends on co-operation among Government, workers, and employers; moreover, co-operation among representatives at the top may be undermined by " wage-drift " at the factory level. Thus the annual average of weekly wage-rates rose by no less than 6 percentage points between 1965 and 1966. In fact all of this increase took place in the period before July 1966. Clearly the voluntary incomes policy was meeting with little success.

Therefore, as part of the July measures taken to deal with the balance of payments problem, the Government introduced a " prices and incomes standstill." Increases in prices and incomes were as far as possible avoided altogether until the end of 1966. The only exceptions in the case of incomes were pay increases resulting directly from increases in output (*e.g.*, piece-work or over-time earnings) and from genuine promotion or regular increments on a predetermined scale. Increases already negotiated but not yet implemented were deferred for 6 months. The first half of 1967 was a period of " severe restraint." Any price increases were carefully examined, and the norm for income increases was zero. Any increase in earnings had to be justified by one of the four conditions for exception, referred to above. To enforce its " freeze " the Government took the unprecedented step of asking Parliament for reserve powers, which were to be used only if the need should arise. These powers—including penalties for offenders—were contained in the new Part IV of the Prices and Incomes Act. For the most part, there was a voluntary observation of the standstill; but from October 1966 the Government found it necessary to exercise its power of compulsion in a few cases, *e.g.*, laundry and dry cleaning charges, and a wage agreement in the electrical engineering industry. The power of compulsion lapsed in August 1967.

The period of compulsion was followed by a year in which there was to be a " nil norm " except where increases in incomes could be justified by one of the four criteria listed above. The Government could no longer legally enforce its policy, but it did retain the power to delay price and pay increases, through reference to the Board, by up to 7 months. Whereas the Government succeeded in almost stabilising wages and prices during the year in which it took compulsory powers, in the second half of 1967 weekly wage rates rose by 6 per cent. The advantage gained from the previous restraint was reduced but not entirely lost.

(v) Incomes Policy after Devaluation.

Incomes policy was made both more difficult and more important by the devaluation of the pound: more difficult in that devaluation involved a cut in the standard of living, and more important in that the trading benefit from devaluation should not be neutralised by inflation.

In April 1968 the Government published a White Paper outlining its policy for the period until the end of 1969. Wage increases must still be justified by the four criteria, and there is a " ceiling " to increases in income of 3½ per cent per annum except for " productivity agreements " and low-paid workers in certain cases. Price increases are permitted only as a result of unavoidable increases in cost per unit of output, and price reductions are required when costs fall. Dividend increases are also subject to the ceiling of 3½ per cent per annum, and home rent increases restricted. The Government intended to rely on the voluntary co-operation of unions and employers over pay; but it decided to lengthen its delaying powers for pay and price increases up to 12 months, and take powers to enforce price reductions recommended by the Board.

Between November 1967 and November 1968 the retail price index rose by 5·2 per cent, mainly due to the effect of devaluation on import prices. In the face of this rise in the cost of living the incomes policy met with firm resistance. In practice the nominal ceiling of 3½ per cent per annum rapidly became the normal increase. In the first year after devaluation basic wage rates rose by 6·0 per cent and average earnings by 7·5 per cent. Workers were able to protect themselves against the inflation and to increase slightly their real incomes.

During 1969 the process of wage and price inflation accelerated. Between November 1968 and November 1969 average earnings rose by 8·0 per cent and retail prices by 5·4 per cent. In December the Government published a White Paper on its incomes policy for the period after 1969. It laid down a norm for wage increases of 2·5 to 4·5 per cent per annum: increases should exceed the upper limit only in exceptional circumstances, *e.g.*, in productivity agreements, in cases where an inappropriate pay structure is rationalised *e.g.* by means of job evaluation, in the case of low-paid workers, and in the achievement of equal pay for women. Comparisons with other workers should not be used, except in the case of public servants (*e.g.*, teachers and nurses) whose productivity cannot be measured and whose pay tends to fall behind that of the private sector. The limit on the increase in company dividends of 3·5 per cent per annum was ended and the Government powers to delay the implementation of proposed wage and price increases were reduced. However, the incomes policy laid down in the White Paper was tempered by the imminence of a General Election and the recent cost of living increases; and it did not prevent a "wage explosion" occurring in 1970.

(vi) Conservative Policy.

On taking office in June 1970 the Conservative Government eschewed its predecessor's approach to incomes policy and disbanded the National Board for Prices and Incomes. To curb the inflation it maintained the economy in recession and squeezed company liquidity, hoping in this way to weaken wage pressures and strengthen the resistances of employers. In addition it attempted to resist demands for wage increases in the public sector, at the cost of prolonging strikes, *e.g.*, in electricity supply and postal services; and it intervened to curb price rises in the nationalised industries, *e.g.*, postal charges and steel prices. These measures were by no means a sure remedy for the inflation spiral. The Government placed its faith on its Bill for the reform of industrial relations to solve the problem of wage inflation in the long run.

Monetary and Fiscal Policies since 1960.

There is probably no country in the world which has made fuller use than Britain of budgetary policy as a means of stabilising the economy. Since 1941, almost all adjustments to the total level of taxation have been made with the object of reducing an excess in total demand or of repairing a deficit. Whereas in the United States there is still a public clamour for "balanced budgets," British Governments have accepted Keynesian principles—first laid down by Lord Keynes—for managing the economy by adjusting the level of taxation and private saving relative to public expenditure and private investment. This does not mean to say that British policies have always been successful. Apart from the difficulty of deciding when demand is excessive or deficient, there are the difficulties that data are available only with a serious time-lag, and may be inaccurate; that economic events cannot be predicted with any certainty; and that the quantitative effects of Government measures are not easy to estimate.

1960.

In the first half of 1960 there were a series of restrictive measures designed to curb the increase in home demand and to improve the balance of payments position. Bank Rate was raised to 6 per cent. To exert pressure on the banks' liquidity positions, and so help to curb bank advances, the banks were called upon to place special deposits (*see* **G21**) with the Bank of England. Restrictions on hire purchase transactions were also imposed. Furthermore, the Budget was restrictive: the Chancellor estimated an overall deficit (*see* **G24**) for 1960–61 of only £320 million.

1961.

The Budget was sternly anti-inflationary: profits tax and some indirect taxes were increased; but there was a major reduction in surtax. In addition, the Chancellor was granted powers to introduce, if he considered it necessary, an economic "regulator": a surcharge on, or rebate of, indirect taxes by up to 10 per cent. This power provides greater scope for using fiscal measures to influence the economy in the periods between Budgets. In July 1961 the Chancellor introduced a collection of restrictive measures. These measures were primarily intended to ease the critical foreign exchange situation but they were not without effect on the domestic economy. Bank Rate was raised to 7 per cent. To restrict

the growth in demand, the Chancellor imposed a 10 per cent surcharge in indirect taxation and called the banks to increase their special deposits at the Bank of England. Furthermore, the Chancellor announced that he aimed to restrict the increase in government spending. Not only was the outflow of funds stopped, but it was actually reversed. These measures were all too successful in restricting demand at home: there was a fall in industrial production in the second half of 1961.

1962.

The 1962 Budget was, however, no less restrictive in intention than the 1961 Budget. The estimated overall deficit, at £70 million, was virtually unchanged. There was a move towards uniformity of purchase tax rates. The main novelty of the 1962 Budget was a tax on certain speculative gains. From the summer of 1962 onwards, monetary and fiscal policies were designed to stimulate economic activity. Bank Rate was reduced to 4 per cent, all special deposits held by the Bank of England were released, qualitative restraints on bank lending were abolished, some post-war credits were released, investment allowances for industry were increased, and the purchase tax on cars reduced.

1963.

January 1963 saw further reduction in purchase taxes, and a very considerable increase in social payments. The estimated overall Budget deficit for 1963–64 was more than £600 million greater than that of the previous year. Tax reliefs were announced: the most important benefits to individuals were derived from increases in the allowances which can be charged against income before income tax is levied; in addition, Schedule A taxes were abolished for owner-occupiers. Other changes in taxation were designed to stimulate investment spending by companies: depreciation allowances were increased for tax purposes, and companies investing in areas of high unemployment were permitted to charge depreciation on their assets at a rate of their own choosing. The Budget was designed to provide a fiscal boost to the economy, and in this it succeeded: national output rose by more than 5 per cent over the year.

1964.

By 1964 the economy was beginning to show signs of strain, and the trade figures revealed a rapid deterioration in the balance of visible trade. The Chancellor's objective in his April budget was to slow down the rate of growth without producing deflation. He planned an overall deficit of £790 million, but provided for additional taxation by increasing the duties on tobacco and alcoholic drinks by about 10 per cent.

Both consumption expenditure and industrial production jumped sharply towards the end of 1964, and there were reports of a growing labour shortage. The balance of payments was heavily in deficit throughout the year. Nothing was done about it, however, until after the General Election in October. In November the Chancellor of the Exchequer presented a "little budget." An additional 6*d.* in the £ was placed on the standard rate of income tax, and there were increases in petrol duties, in National Insurance contributions and payments. But old-age pensions were increased. During the sterling crisis of November (*see* **G30**) Bank Rate was raised to 7 per cent to stem the outflow of funds, but this was not accompanied by a "credit squeeze" to restrict productive investments, as in the crisis of 1961. Unlike some of his predecessors, the Chancellor had not opted for deflation as the cure for the balance of payments deficit. Instead, reliance was placed on an import surcharge and an export rebate. However, the British policy came under fire from some European Governments, who called for a deflation of the British economy.

1965.

The Budget contained two major fiscal innovations, a corporation tax and a capital gains tax. Full employment was maintained in 1965. The

April Budget was not deflationary: the Government's overall deficit for 1965–66 was estimated at £720 million. In July, because the balance of payments had shown no sign of rapid improvement, the Chancellor found it necessary to introduce further measures: tighter controls on foreign exchange and on the terms of hire-purchase, and a postponement of public expenditure programmes. But this action was not sufficient to produce deflation, and at the end of the year unemployment was still very low.

1966.

The 1966 Budget was somewhat deflationary; but its impact was delayed until September when the new *selective employment tax* (SET) came into force. All employers were required to pay this tax at the weekly rate of 25s. for men, 12s. 6d. for women and boys and 8s. for girls. However, manufacturing industries received a refund of 130 per cent, the public sector 100 per cent, while other industries—*e.g.*, services and construction—receive no refund.

Up to mid-1966 the Labour Government's policy can be summarised as follows: to restrict the growth of demand somewhat but not as drastically as in the past, to take direct action on the immediate balance of payments, and to strengthen the long-run balance by means of productivity policy and incomes policy. However, in July, during yet another run on sterling, the Government embarked on a policy of deflation. In its "July measures" the Government raised indirect taxation 10 per cent by means of its "regulator," placed a 10 per cent surcharge on surtax, tightened building controls, cut public investment for 1967/8, increased hire-purchase restrictions, and raised Bank Rate to 7 per cent. As a result of these measures, the economy went into recession in the second half of 1966.

1967.

Despite unemployment of 2·4 per cent and predictions of a further rise during the year, the Chancellor produced a "no-change" April Budget, with an estimated surplus of £640 million. The balance of payments prevented him from taking reflationary measures. In mid-year the Government gave some stimulus to consumers' expenditure by relaxing hire purchase terms and increasing family allowances. But the balance of payments deteriorated, and, since further deflation was politically unacceptable, the Government devalued the pound. Devaluation was itself strongly reflationary—increasing demand for exports and for import-substitute goods—and had to be accompanied by measures to release resources for these industries. Bank Rate was raised to the unprecedented height of 8 per cent, bank advances were limited to all but priority borrowers, *e.g.*, exporters, hire purchase on cars was tightened, corporation tax was raised to 42½ per cent, and the SET premium was to be withdrawn except for Development Areas.

There were also to be cuts in defence, other public spending and nationalised industries' investment. Further cuts in government spending were announced in December, and again in January, when future defence spending was considerably reduced because of the decision to withdraw forces from East of Suez, and the planned rise in the school-leaving age from 15 to 16 was put off until 1972. Despite these several blows of the axe, public expenditure was still likely to rise in 1968/9 by nearly 4 per cent in real terms; but the rise in 1969/70 was estimated to be no more than 1 per cent.

1968.

The April budget was highly deflationary. The Chancellor increased taxation to yield an additional £920 million per annum. Most of this came from indirect taxation, with purchase tax and taxes on spirits, wines, and tobacco all raised. Motorists were particularly hit by the increased vehicle and petrol taxes—perhaps not unfairly in view of the heavy social costs caused by road congestion. SET was to be raised 50 per cent, and betting duties were put up. Partly to gain support for the incomes policy, the Chancellor raised family allowances and placed a heavy

"special levy" for one year on unearned income above £3,000 per annum. In deflating the economy the Chancellor was attempting to reduce private consumer demand so as to free resources for the export market and for replacing imports. Without such a transfer of resources the advantage gained from devaluation would be lost. His strategy was to produce an overall balance of payments surplus of the order of £500 million before resuming growth, and in this way to break the vicious circle of "stop-go".

There was a stronger recovery of consumer demand and output and a weaker improvement in the balance of payments in 1968 than the Chancellor had expected, and further restrictive measures were taken during the year. In May bank lending restrictions were tightened selectively, and in November hire purchase terms were tightened and the "regulator" used to raise indirect taxes by 10 per cent.

1969.

In February Bank Rate was raised to the record height of 8 per cent, partly to help reduce bank lending and partly to retain short-term funds in London; owing to the shortage of international liquidity (*see* G81) central banks compete for short-term capital by raising their discount rates.

The April Budget was somewhat restrictive; an additional £350 million per annum being raised in taxation. This was achieved mainly by increasing corporation tax to 45 per cent, and SET to 48 shillings a week for adult males. In an attempt to encourage saving the Chancellor introduced a contractual savings scheme offering attractive tax-free interest payments after a five- or seven-year period. Perhaps as a result of pressures from Britain's creditor, the IMF, the Chancellor emphasised the importance he would give to monetary policy (*see* G22). The Budget continued the strategy of improving the balance of payments at the expense of consumption.

In June the Chancellor published a Letter of Intent to the IMF stating his intention to limit the annual increase in real public expenditure to 1 per cent, and the increase in *domestic credit expansion* to £400 million. Domestic credit expansion is defined as the increase in the money supply adjusted for changes resulting from external transactions. In fact domestic credit expansion turned out to be negative in the financial year 1969/70: credit was extremely tight except for the manufacturing sector. The growth of the economy in 1969 was slight, output being about 2 per cent up on 1968. Investment and consumption stagnated, and the main impetus for expansion came from exports.

1970.

Early in the year there was some slack in the economy, which could be taken up by a policy of reflation. With the balance of payments improved and an election not far ahead, the Chancellor therefore reduced taxation by £220 million. Even then, because expenditure was to be restrained and income tax receipts rise with the inflation, he expected a Government budget surplus of £620 million. It could not be claimed that this was an electioneering budget: output was planned to rise by 3·5 per cent in the next year. But the period of severe restraint on private consumption was over, the expected increase being 3·9 per cent. Tax relief came largely in the form of increased personal allowances, but these were so arranged that people with lower incomes benefited most. Those over 65 benefited from increased tax exemption, and the minimum income for liability to surtax was raised because of the high cost of collecting surtax. Private investment was to be helped by the removal of quantitative controls on bank advances, and by increasing initial tax allowances on industrial building from 15 per cent to 30 per cent normally and 40 per cent in the Development Areas. The strength of the balance of payments enabled the Government to reduce Bank Rate from 8 per cent to 7½ per cent in March and again, to 7 per cent, in the Budget.

In October the new Government announced cuts in both public expenditure and taxation, taking effect from April 1971. There was to be a 6d. cut in the standard rate of income tax and a cut in corporation tax. Also investment grants were to be replaced by a system of 60 per cent initial allowances. Prescription charges and dental charges were increased, the subsidy on welfare milk was ended, the price of school meals was raised, and the system of import levies on farm produce was extended. These changes involved a redistribution of income away from the poor. However, a *family income supplement* (FIS) was introduced to provide a cash benefit for poor families with children.

Although real output grew by only 1½ per cent in 1970, the Chancellor did not take any measures which would have an immediate reflationary effect. Monetary restrictions, *e.g.*, requirements of increased *special deposits* (*see* G21), were applied during the year.

1971.

With business profits and liquidity down and business confidence weak, private investment was low and the economy continued to stagnate. There was a need for a reflationary policy in 1971. The April budget was somewhat reflationary with tax reductions of £550 million in the financial year 1971–72 and £680 million in a full year, inclusive of the reductions previously announced. The Chancellor claimed as his objective an increase in output of about 3 per cent per annum. The main budget changes for 1971 were a further cut in corporation tax to 40 per cent, a halving of SET, an increase by £40 per child in the tax allowances for children, a reduction in surtax particularly for very high income earners, and a general increase in national insurance benefits and contributions. The Chancellor also announced his intention to make far-reaching tax reforms in future years (*see* (v) below).

Tax Reforms.

(i) Capital Gains Tax.

The first move in this direction was the introduction of a tax on short term gains in 1962. But a more comprehensive innovation was the *capital gains tax* of 1965. This tax is levied on the gain realised on an asset between its purchase and sale, provided this does not exceed the gain between 6 April 1965 and sale. It applies to all assets, with limited exceptions: the most important being owner-occupied houses, and goods and chattels realised for less than £1,000. Gains realised by companies over any period are taxed at corporation tax rates. Gains by individuals on assets held for more than a year are taxed at a flat rate of 30 per cent. Gains realised within a period of one year were treated as ordinary income and taxed accordingly. However, in his 1971 Budget the Chancellor made these gains also subject to the 30 per cent flat rate. He also exempted individuals' capital gains where the assets sold during the year were valued at less than £500.

There are many administrative difficulties in implementing such a tax. Nevertheless, it is an important attempt to remedy the inequality in the taxation of earned and unearned incomes.

(ii) Corporation Tax.

In 1965 the Labour Government also introduced a *corporation tax*, to replace the existing company income tax and profits tax. This tax, at a rate of 40 per cent, was imposed on distributed as well as undistributed profits, so as to encourage the retention of profits for the financing of business expansion. The tax rate was subsequently raised to 42½ per cent and then to 45 per cent.

In 1970 the incoming Conservative Government reduced the rate of tax to 42½ per cent and in 1971 to 40 per cent. It was also announced that the Government intended to remove the discrimination in favour of retained and against distributed profits, by decreasing the rate on distributed profits so that the burden of corporation tax and income tax together would be equal to the corporation tax alone on retained profits. This would have the effects of reducing profit retentions, which would discourage investment, and of easing share issue, which would encourage investment.

(iii) Selective Employment Tax.

The *selective employment tax* (SET) was introduced in the 1966 Budget (*see* G41), became partly an instrument of regional policy in 1967, and was raised in both the 1968 and 1969 Budgets. In 1970 the Labour Chancellor announced that it would become related to earnings rather than to numbers employed as from 1972. However, the Conservative Chancellor announced that SET would be halved as from July 1971 and abolished in April 1972.

All employers are required to pay this tax, at different weekly rates for men, women and boys, and girls; but manufacturing firms and the public sector receive a refund. It is a selective tax on services and construction. The tax therefore discriminates against those industries which are labour-intensive, export little, and whose output bears little indirect taxation. The SET is therefore a rough and ready means of forcing employers to release hoarded labour, of subsidising exports, and of evening up the incidence of indirect taxation.

In 1970 Professor Reddaway, having been asked by the Treasury to investigate the effects of SET, produced the first of his Reports. This covered the distributive trades which account for no less than 2·8 million workers. The Report used statistical analysis to show that the growth in productivity in the distributive trades after 1965 was well above the rate expected in the absence of SET, and that profit margins and prices were lower than expected. The discrepancy could not be attributed entirely to SET, however, because other abnormal factors, *e.g.*, the progressive abolition of resale price maintenance (*see* G13), operated during that period. On the whole the Report was favourable to SET.

(iv) Value Added Tax.

In his 1971 Budget the Chancellor of the Exchequer announced that SET and purchase tax would be replaced by a *value added tax* in April 1973. A value added tax was seen to have certain advantages: it could be applied evenly to almost all goods and services unlike purchase tax which was imposed on only a limited range of goods; without infringing international rules exports could be exempted from the tax and so encouraged; and it would be in line with practice in the Common Market countries. The Chancellor proposed to exempt food, newspapers, periodicals and books, and also small traders. There might be a single rate or various rates of tax for different products.

The tax is levied as a certain percentage of *value added* at each stage of production (*see* G11). Here is a simple example on the assumption of a uniform 10 per cent rate. A producer imports raw materials valued at £100 and pays a tax of £10. He makes an intermediate product and sells it to a manufacturer for £200. The producer's value added is £100, so he pays another £10. The manufacturer makes a final product and sells it to a retailer for £500. His value added—accruing either as wages to his workers or as profits—is therefore £300, and he pays tax of £30. The retailer sells the product to domestic consumers for £700, his value added being £200 and his tax liability £20. The sum total of tax paid is £70, *i.e.*, 10 per cent of the final product price, but it is collected at each stage of production.

(v) Income Tax and Surtax.

In the 1971 Budget the Conservative Government proposed to replace the existing income tax and surtax with a single graduated personal tax in 1973. It would have the following four principal features. The existing pattern of personal allowances would be retained, there would be a basic rate covering a broad band of income and corresponding to the standard rate less earned income relief, there would be higher rates above the basic rate applicable to the higher incomes, and the distinction between earned and unearned income would be made by way of a surcharge on investment income above a certain level of such income. The purpose of the proposals was to simplify tax assessment and collection, to avoid misunderstanding as to the true marginal rates of tax, and to encourage saving.

GREEK MYTHS & LEGENDS

The ancient stories of Greece, woven into the fabric of our European culture by playwrights, artists and psychologists, are retold in the light of recent research. An index to the narratives ensures easy reference.

TABLE OF CONTENTS

GREEK MYTHS AND LEGENDS

PART I. INTRODUCTION

(a) The Significance of the Myths and Legends.

We all know how the stories and books that we knew in our youth have coloured our thought. So it is with the myths and legends of the Greeks. Their stories have entered the stream of consciousness of European men and women through the ages, affecting their literature and art, and even their ways of thinking.

The Origin of Myths. True myth has been defined by Robert Graves as "the reduction to narrative shorthand of ritual mime performed on public festivals, and in many cases recorded pictorially." These rituals were, says Graves, "archaic magic-makings that promoted the fertility or stability of a sacred queendom or kingdom—queendoms having, it seems, preceded kingdoms throughout the Greek-speaking area."

The immense diversity of these myths is partly due to geographical causes, for, in the widely differing districts of Greece, different conceptions of the divinity and varying rituals of propitiation were evolved. There are also historical causes, for the Mediterranean peoples worshipping an earth goddess were conquered by successive waves of Hellenes bringing with them some form of tribal sky god.

Legends. Interwoven with the religious myths were a host of legends, traditional stories, which though not authentic had, like the tales of Troy, a substratum of fact. There were, also, all kinds of fables and anecdotes, folk-tales such as that of Perseus, and allegories and romances, which fused with the myths and legends to make a fascinating complex of stories.

Their Preservation in Literary Form. These have been preserved for us largely by the Greek poets, especially by Homer in his *Iliad* and *Odyssey*, and by Hesiod in his *Theogony*, works which probably date from about the eighth century B.C. The Greek dramatists of the fifth century B.C.—Aeschylus, Sophocles, and Euripides —who relied on myth and legend for most of their plots, also handed on the ancient tales, though often in slightly altered form. Then about five centuries later Roman writers, such as Virgil, Ovid and Horace, modelling themselves on the Greeks, refashioned and embroidered their themes. It is not surprising that we have so many variants of the same tale.

This rich and complex treasure of Greek myth and legend has become increasingly familiar in Western Europe, at first in Latin versions, then after the Renaissance in the original Greek, and today in excellent modern translations.

Their Significance Today. Because of their extraordinary vitality and pervasiveness, some familiarity with Greek myth and legend is almost indispensable to a full appreciation of our European culture.

In Art and Literature. Great painters like Botticelli, Veronese and Rubens made the ancient stories the subject of their pictures, and writers from Shakespeare to James Joyce have enriched their work by constant reference. The French dramatists from Racine to Giraudoux are notable for relying on them for the basic plot of their dramas. Today when good and inexpensive translations enable us to go direct to Homer's *Iliad*, or to see Euripides' *Medea* on the stage, it is especially useful to have some general knowledge of the mythical background to the particular epic or play.

Psychology. Not only to those who love art and literature is the knowledge of Greek mythology rewarding. Psychologists have found here suggestive symbols for the profound mental processes they are endeavouring to elucidate. Through Freud the term "Œdipus complex" is now a commonplace, and Jung has found in the myths symbolic archetypes of human response.

Philosophy and Religion. Philosophers also have found it profitable to return to the myths. Bertrand Russell emphasises the influence of Greek religion on Greek philosophy, and, through such philosophers as Pythagoras and Plato, on Christianity itself.

Anthropology. Of recent years anthropologists scrutinising the myths have been able to discern something of the way of life of primitive societies. The two-volume Penguin *The Greek Myths*, by Robert Graves, incorporates some of their interpretations.

Archæology. Perhaps the most exciting of all recent investigations are those of the archæologists working on sites once considered only legendary. The German Schliemann, trusting to the fidelity of his Homer, actually unearthed the foundations of Priam's Troy and Agamemnon's Mycenæ, finding fabulous treasure and proving to the astonished world that these antique tales were indeed rooted in fact. Through Schliemann's trust in Homer we have added an early chapter to History, that of the Mycenæan culture of pre-classical Greek which flourished from about 1550 to 1200 B.C.

Another centre of ancient story, the island of Crete, was the field of Sir Arthur Evans' enquiries, and his excavation of the magnificent Palace of Cnossos not only pushed back the frontiers of history yet further to about 3000 B.C., but also showed how many Cretan legends had some factual basis.

More recent excavations at legendary Mycenæan sites on the mainland have led to the discovery of the Palace of Nestor at Pylos, and the House of Cadmus at Thebes.

Tablets found at Mycenæan towns and in Cnossos inscribed in an entirely unknown script, "Linear B," have challenged scholars with a fascinating puzzle. After years of study Michael Ventris and others have at last been able to decipher the script. Although so far only inventories are available, it is significant that the language used is archaic Greek. We now know therefore that the Greeks of the Mycenæan age could write, and that Homer's single reference to writing is once more a faithful record of fact. (See Book VI of the *Iliad* and the reference to Bellerophon's "folded tablet.")

(b) The Historical Background to the Myths and Legends.

Our knowledge of the earliest periods of Greek history is very recent. The great historian Grote, writing in 1846, said that we must consider the First Olympiad of 776 B.C. as the starting point. Anything earlier was matter for conjecture. It is largely due to the discoveries of archæologists that scholars are now able to push back the frontiers of history. From archæological evidence they can now reconstruct the probable course of events from as early a date as 3000 B.C.

3000 B.C. Early Bronze Age. It was about 3000 B.C., when the Neolithic Age was succeeded in the Eastern Mediterranean by the Early Bronze Age, that a bronze-using people, akin to those of early Crete and the Cyclades, entered Greece and fused with the Neolithic folk already there. These invaders were not Aryans, but of Mediterranean stock, and they worshipped the Great Goddess, a fertility goddess who appeared in many guises. She was unmarried, and in many instances her lover appeared to her in the form of a bird.

2000 B.C. Coming of Hellenes. A thousand years later, in the Middle Bronze Age a very different kind of people began to enter Greece. These were the Hellenes or Greeks, an Aryan people from the North, for whom transport and conquest were easy by reason of their horses and wheeled vehicles. Unlike their predecessors, they were patriarchal, and their chief divinity was a tribal sky-god, but as they fused with the pre-Hellenic stock already in the country, so their patriarchal worship mingled with the matriarchal and the sky-god married the earth-goddess.

Minyans and Ionians. Successive waves of these Hellenes invaded the country in three main groups beginning in about 2000 B.C. with Minyans and Ionians.

Minoan Culture. Penetrating far south to the islands, and to Sicily, Southern Italy, and Asia Minor, they became expert navigators. They were much influenced by a brilliant and sophisticated Minoan culture already flourishing in Cnossos in Crete, and this began to have considerable effect on the mainland of Greece from about 1580 B.C. onwards.

1400 B.C. Achæans. In about 1400 B.C., however, Cnossos fell, destroyed either by earthquakes or by invaders, for the Achæans, the second wave of Hellenes, had now begun to enter Greece and from about 1400 to 1100 B.C. Mycenæ on the mainland was probably the centre of civilisation in the Ægean world.

Mycenæan Culture. It is this Mycenæan culture of the Late Bronze Age which, seen through legend, is depicted in Homer's *Iliad* and *Odyssey*. Mycenæ is Agamemnon's own citadel, and other cities where archæological remains are now being found are named in the *Iliad's* "Catalogue of Ships." The Achæans as Homer shows them were a conquering feudal aristocracy and a concerted attempt probably made by them in the beginning of the twelfth century B.C. to seize the Black Sea trade may be reflected in the epic of the siege of Troy.

1200 B.C. Dorians. But the Achæans themselves were soon to be defeated, for at the end of the twelfth century B.C. the last influx of invading Hellenes, the Dorians, ancestors of the classical Greeks, entered the country. They practically destroyed the Mycenæan civilisation, and the Late Bronze Age now gave way to the Iron Age.

The Olympian Divinities. The close fusion between the early non-Aryan Mediterranean people, with their matriarchal culture, and the successive waves of patriarchal Hellenes was reflected in the Greek worship of Olympians. The ancient earth-goddess of fertility lived on in such guises as Aphrodite or Hera, and Zeus, sky-god of the Hellenes, appropriately took Hera to wife. Indeed, many deities, such as Demeter or Athene, combined, in the single divinity, both Mediterranean and Hellenic traits.

A third element in Greek Olympian religion derived from a Hittite culture flourishing in Asia Minor in about 1300 B.C. which had developed from a Hurrian culture of about 1500 B.C. Hesiod writing in about 750 B.C., incorporated some violent Hurrian myths of the cannibalism of the gods, in his *Theogony* or *Birth of the Gods.*

The "Epic Cycle." By the eighth century B.C. there was in existence a rich store of myth and legend known as the "Epic Cycle," which was drawn on by Homer and also by later poets and dramatists.

Homer's Picture. Homer, whose epics were probably completed at the end of the eighth or in the seventh century B.C. presents the composite myth and legend of Greece in highly civilised form, as the beliefs of a successful war-like aristocracy. The twelve deities dwelling on Olympus acknowledged the supremacy of Zeus, and Dionysus the god of wine and ecstasy who entered from Thrace in the eighth century B.C. was still an outsider, a god of the lower orders.

The Coming of Dionysus. But by the fifth century B.C. Dionysus had been accepted as an Olympian, taking the place of Hestia. The growing popularity of his worship which induced an ecstatic union with the god in a frenzy partly stimulated by wine, partly mystical, shows the need of the recently civilised Greeks for an impulsive religious expression which was not always satisfied by the prudent cults of the serene Olympians.

Orpheus. From the worship of Dionysus developed that of Orpheus, which aimed at mystic union with the god through enthusiasm wholly mystic, and through purification. The Orphics, believing in the transmigration of souls and an after life, had much influence on the Greek philosopher Pythagoras, and this influence was transmitted through Plato into Christianity itself.

The great influence of Greek religion on philosophy has only recently been recognised, and Bertrand Russell commends especially the study of John Burnet's *Early Greek Philosophy*, especially its second chapter, "Science and Religion."

(c) Bibliography.

There is no one book or Bible of Greek myths. Many versions exist, and in a short account it is not possible to record all variations. The reader is advised to consult the masterpieces of Greek literature now available in translation.

The Iliad. Homer, transl. E. V. Rieu. Penguin L14.
The Odyssey. Homer, transl. E. V. Rieu. Penguin L1.
The Theban Plays. Sophocles, transl. E. F. Watling. Penguin L3.
Electra and other plays. Sophocles, transl. E. F. Watling. Penguin L28.
Alcestis and other plays. Euripides, transl. P. Vellacott. Penguin L31.
Bacchae and other plays. Euripides, transl. P. Vellacott. Penguin L44.
Plays. Aeschylus, transl. G. M. Cookson. Everyman 62.
Dramas. Sophocles, transl. Sir George Young. Everyman 114.
Plays, 2 vols. Euripides, transl. A. S. Way. Everyman 63 and 271.
Greek Drama for Everyman. F. L. Lucas. J. M. Dent & Sons.

Men and Gods (Myths of Ovid). Rex Warner. Penguin 885.
Greeks and Trojans (Siege of Troy). Rex Warner. Penguin 942.
The Greek Myths, 2 vols. Robert Graves. Penguin.
The Golden Ass. Apuleius. transl. Robert Graves. Penguin L11.
The Greeks. H. D. F. Kitto. Pelican.
The Twelve Olympians. Charles Seltman. Pan.
Women in Antiquity. Charles Seltman. Pan.
The Bull of Minos. Leonard Cottrell. Pan.
Dr. Smith's Classical Dictionary. William Smith. John Murray.

A Smaller Classical Dictionary. Ed. Blakeney. J. M. Dent & Sons.

(d) **Guide to Pronunciation and Spelling.**

This Cyclopædia uses the long-established convention of spelling Greek names which is also used by such modern scholars as Robert Graves and E. V. Rieu.

It is helpful to remember that :—

" ch " and " c " are pronounced " k."

" œ " and " æ " are pronounced " ē," as in " see."

" eus " rhymes with " juice."

PART II. NARRATIVE OUTLINES

THE OLYMPIAN CREATION MYTHS, 1–22.

1. Uranus and Ge. The infinite and empty space which existed before creation was known as Chaos. The Earth, or Ge, sprang from Chaos, and herself gave birth to Uranus, the Heavens, and Pontus, the Sea. Ge then became, by Uranus, the mother of the hundred-handed giants, the Hecatoncheires or Centimani (Cottus, Briareus, also called Ægæon, and Gyes or Gyges) ; of the one-eyed Cyclopes (Brontes, Steropes and Arges) ; and of the twelve Titans. Greek writers give inconsistent lists of these Titans, but those most frequently mentioned are Cronus, Oceanus, Hyperion, and Iapetus, and the Titanesses Rhea, Themis, Tethys, and Mnemosyne.

2. Barbarous stories follow of Uranus' dealings with his descendants, and these have been influenced by myths from the Hittite culture which flourished in 1300 B.C. in Anatolia, or Asia Minor, and which probably embodied still earlier Babylonian material. These Hittite legends reached Greece through the Phœnicians, and Hesiod (eighth century B.C.), a poet whose family had recently come from Asia Minor incorporated them in his *Theogony*.

3. Revolt of Cronus. Uranus had thrown his rebellious sons the Cyclopes into Tartarus, in the Underworld, and Ge persuaded the Titans, with the exception of Oceanus, to rise against their father. She gave Cronus, the youngest, a flint sickle, and with this he unmanned Uranus. Drops from the wound falling upon Mother Earth, she bore the three Erinnyes or Eumenides, the furies Alecto, Tisiphone, and Megaera, and from drops that fell into the sea Aphrodite was born.

4. Uranus deposed, the Titans freed the Cyclopes, but Cronus, now supreme, consigned them again to Tartarus along with the Hundred-handed giants.

5. Cronus then married his sister Rhea, and mindful of the curse of Uranus and Ge, that he also would be deposed by his own son, he swallowed each of his children at birth.

6. Birth of Zeus. But when Zeus the youngest was born, Rhea gave Cronus a stone to swallow and saved Zeus, who, according to Minoan tradition, was brought up in the Dictæan cave in Crete. In 1900 the reputed " birth-cave " was explored by archæologists—probably the first men to enter for two thousand years, and there they found votive offerings to the god which may have been left there in the second millennium B.C. It was here that the Curetes, Rhea's priests, clashed their weapons to drown the cries of infant Zeus, while a goat, Amalthea, acted as his nurse, and was rewarded by being placed among the stars as Capricorn, while one of her horns became the Cornucopia or horn of plenty.

7. Zeus when of age was counselled by Metis, the daughter of Oceanus, and with Rhea's help gave to Cronus a potion which obliged him to disgorge first the stone and then his other children, Hestia, Demeter, Hera, Hades, and Poseidon. These now joined with Zeus in a contest against their father and the other Titans, who were led by Atlas.

8. War between Zeus and Titans. The war, known as the Titanomachia, was waged in Thessaly, and lasted ten years, until Ge promised Zeus victory if he would free the Cyclopes and the Hundred-handed giants from Tartarus.

9. The Cyclopes gave to Zeus a thunderbolt, to Hades a helmet of darkness, and to Poseidon a trident. Thus aided, the three brothers overcame Cronus, and the Hundred-handed giants stoned the other Titans, who were defeated and consigned either to an island in the West or to Tartarus, guarded by the Hundred-handed. Atlas was punished by being made to carry the sky on his shoulders, but the Titanesses were spared. The supersession of the old dynasty of Titans by the new order of gods is the theme of Keats' fine poem, *Hyperion.*

10. The Olympians. Zeus and his brothers now divided the government by lot. To Hades fell the Underworld, to Poseidon the sea, and to Zeus the sky, while the earth was common to all. Zeus, the greatest of the gods, lived on the lofty summit of Mt. Olympus between Macedonia and Thessaly, along with Poseidon and their sisters, Hestia, goddess of the hearth-fire, Demeter, goddess of agriculture, and Hera, who became the wife of Zeus. Seven other divinities, Aphrodite, Pallas Athene, Apollo, Artemis, Hephæstus, Ares, and Hermes were also numbered among the twelve great Olympians, and at a later date a new-comer, Dionysus, took the place of Hestia.

11. The Giants' Revolt. But the troubles of Zeus were not over. A post-Homeric story tells of the giants' revolt. Twenty-four giants with serpents' tails, sons of Ge, tried to avenge the imprisonment of their brothers the Titans by attacking Olympus. Led by Alcyoneus, they included Porphyrion, Ephialtes, Mimas, Pallas, Enceladus, and Polybutes. Only after terrible struggles in Olympus and on earth, were the giants defeated by the gods, who were helped by a magic herb of invulnerability found by Heracles, who always dealt the giants the final blow.

12. The story offered some explanation of huge bones found at Trapezus and volcanic fires at neighbouring Bathos and Cumæ, the reputed sites of the battles. The burial of Enceladus under Mt. Etna in Sicily, and of Polybutes under Nisyrus, likewise accounted for their volcanic nature. The inclusion of Heracles before his apotheosis indicates the late origin of the legend.

13. Ephialtes and Otus. Another version of the giants' revolt ascribes it to the gigantic Alœidæ, Ephialtes, and Otus, sons of Iphimedeia by Poseidon, but named after Alœus, whom their mother later married. At the age of nine Ephialtes and Otus first captured and imprisoned Ares, god of war, and then, vowing to outrage Hera and Artemis, they piled Mount Pelion on

Ossa in their attack on Heaven. Artemis induced them to go to the island of Naxos in the hope of meeting her, but disguised as a doe she leapt between them and they killed each other in error. Hermes then released Ares, and the spirits of the Aloeidæ were tied with vipers back to back to a pillar in Tartarus.

14. Typhon. After the destruction of the giants, Ge in revenge brought forth the gigantic monster Typhon, fathered on her by her own son Tartarus. His huge limbs ended in serpents' heads and his eyes breathed fire. When he approached Olympus the gods in terror fled to Egypt disguised as animals, Zeus as a ram, Apollo a crow, Dionysus a goat, Hera a white cow, Artemis a cat, Aphrodite a fish, Ares a boar and Hermes an ibis. Athene alone was undaunted and persuaded Zeus to attack Typhon. After a fearful struggle, in which Zeus was temporarily incapacitated and only rescued by Hermes and Pan, he destroyed Typhon with his thunderbolts and buried him under Mt. Ætna, which still breathes fire.

15. The flight of the gods to Egypt serves to explain the Egyptian worship of them in animal form.

16. Prometheus and Epimetheus. The creation of mankind is often ascribed to Prometheus, whose name signifies "forethought," as that of his brother, Epimetheus, means "afterthought." These two, unlike their brother Atlas, had supported Zeus during the war with the Titans. But Prometheus, the clever benefactor of mankind, by stealing fire from Olympus and giving it to humans, brought upon himself divine vengeance.

17. The infuriated Zeus ordered Hephæstus to make a lovely woman, Pandora, the Eve of Greek myth, who was endowed by the gods with baleful powers and taken by Hermes to Epimetheus. When he had married her, she opened a box from which escaped all ills which plague mankind.

18. Zeus punished Prometheus by chaining him to a crag in the Caucasus, where all day long an eagle tore at his liver, which grew whole again during the night. Only after many generations did Heracles, with the consent of Zeus, shoot the eagle and free the heroic rebel.

19. The agony of Prometheus is the theme of Æschylus' tragedy *Prometheus Bound*; the liberator is depicted in his lost drama, *Prometheus Unbound*. Shelley's dramatic poem of the same name takes Prometheus as a symbol of those who challenge tyranny for the sake of mankind.

20. Deucalion and Pyrrha. Deucalion, the son of Prometheus, is the Noah of Greek myth. When Zeus decided to wipe out mankind by releasing a great flood on earth, Deucalion, warned by his father, made an ark which saved both himself and his wife Pyrrha, daughter of Epimetheus. After nine days the flood subsided and the ark came to rest on Mt. Parnassus.

21. Deucalion and Pyrrha then earnestly prayed at the shrine of Themis that the earth might be re-peopled. Themis appeared and commanded them to throw the bones of their mother behind them. They interpreted this as meaning the rocks of mother earth and those flung by Deucalion became men, those thrown by Pyrrha women.

22. Their son, Hellen, was the mythical ancestor of all the Hellenes.

THE OLYMPIAN DEITIES, 23–128.

ZEUS, 23–28.

23. Zeus, identified with Jupiter by the Romans, was the greatest of the Olympian divinities, omni-potent king of gods, father of men, and possibly master even of fate. Legends of his origin and supremacy are told in para. 6–20.

24. Zeus was the bright god of the sky, whom the invading Achæans introduced into Greece in about 1200 B.C., together with his consort Dione. Her worship, however, did not penetrate south of Zeus' shrine at Dodona in Epirus, where the rustling of oak leaves was interpreted as the voice of the god, and Zeus found other wives. His Olympian consort was Hera, who was in origin the Great Goddess of the pre-Hellenic matriarchal society. This marriage symbolises the fusion of the Achæans with their predecessors.

25. He first married Metis, daughter of Oceanus and Tethys, but when she was pregnant with Athene he swallowed her and brought forth Athene from his head. His second wife was Themis, daughter of Uranus and Ge, a divinity representing order, and their children were the Horæ and the Mœræ, or Fates, though some say that the Fates were daughters of Erebus and Night, and that even Zeus was subject to them. To Zeus and Hera were born the deities Ares, Hebe, and Hephæstus, unless the latter was the parthenogenous son of Hera. Zeus was also the father of Persephone by his sister Demeter, of the Charities, or Graces, by Eurynome, and of the Muses by Mnemosyne.

26. By mortal women four Olympian deities were children of Zeus; Hermes the son of Maia, Apollo and Artemis the children of Leto, and Dionysus the son of Semele. Zeus loved many mortal women, and Hera was intensely jealous and revengeful towards them and their children.

27. Although Zeus' earliest oracle was at Dodona, he was said to dwell with his fellow divinities on the summit of Olympus in Thessaly, and was also worshipped at Olympia in Elis. The Greeks dated their era from the first festival of the Olympiad in 776 B.C.

28. Zeus alone used the thunderbolt and was called the thunderer. The oak, the eagle, and mountain summits were sacred to him, and his sacrifices were usually bulls, cows, and goats. His attributes were the sceptre thunderbolt, eagle, and a figure of Victory held in his hand. The Dodonean Zeus sometimes wore a wreath of oak leaves, the Olympian Zeus one of olive.

HERA, 29–35.

29. Hera, identified by the Romans with Juno, was the Great Goddess of the pre-Hellenic matriarchal society, whom Zeus, supreme god of the Achæans, appropriately took to wife.

30. She was said to be a daughter of Cronus and Rhea and reluctantly married her brother Zeus, who in the form of a cuckoo sought her out at Cnossos in Crete, or perhaps in Argos, and their wedding night was spent on Samos. Ge gave Hera the tree with the golden apples later guarded by the Hesperides.

31. Though Hera was treated with reverence by the gods, she was greatly inferior in power to Zeus and must obey him, her subordination reflecting the attitude of the Achæans towards women. Only in her power to bestow the gift of prophecy was Hera equal to her husband.

32. She was often rebellious and jealous of Zeus' intrigues and persecuted his children by mortal women. At one time, with Poseidon and Apollo, she led a conspiracy of all the Olympians save Hestia to put Zeus in chains. He was freed by Thetis and Briareus, and punished Hera by hanging her with wrists chained to the sky and an anvil on each ankle.

33. Hera bore Zeus Ares and Hebe and annually renewed her virginity by bathing in a spring near Argos. As properly speaking, the only married goddess among the Olympians, she was worshipped as goddess of marriage and the birth of children, the Ilithyiæ being her daughters.

34. Hera was of majestic stature, and her attributes were a diadem, veil, sceptre, and peacock. Samos and Argos were seats of her worship.

35. Because of the judgment of Paris she was relentlessly hostile to the Trojans.

HESTIA, 36–37.

36. Hestia, called Vesta by the Romans, and the eldest sister of Zeus, was a divinity brought to Greece by the invading Achæans. Though Poseidon and Apollo both sought her love, she swore by Zeus always to remain a virgin.

37. She was goddess of the fire on the hearth, supremely important in those days because so difficult to rekindle, and was naturally thought of as goddess of home life. Each town or city had its sacred hearth, which, like that of the home, was an asylum for suppliants. The first part of all sacrifices offered to the gods was due to Hestia, the most peaceable'and kindly of all the Olympians, but at a later date Dionysus took her place among the twelve Olympian gods.

ATHENE, 38–45.

38. Athene, whom the Romans identified with Minerva, was the embodiment of wisdom and power.

39. The Achæans brought with them a young warrior goddess, who bore the titles, Kore, Parthenos, Pallas, meaning girl, virgin, maiden, and she was in about 1700 B.C. identified with an older pre-Hellenic " Palace Goddess," worshipped in Crete. The " Palace Goddess " was one aspect of the Great Goddess, revered not for motherhood but for feminine intuition, and from pre-Hellenic times comes the name Athene.

40. The complex Pallas Athene was thus not only the patroness of women's arts such as weaving, protectress of agriculture, inventor of plough, rake, and ox-yoke, but also a warrior, a wise tactician, appearing in armour and wearing on her ægis or shield the head of Medusa, during the Trojan War the great protagonist of the Greeks. Legends of the birth of Pallas Athene reveal how the patriarchal Hellenes took over, and made their own a matriarchal divinity.

41. She was said to be a daughter of Zeus and Metis, but before her birth an oracle had foretold that she would be a girl, and that if Metis had another child it would be a son who would depose his father. Zeus therefore swallowed Metis, and later, suffered an agonising headache as he walked by Lake Triton. Hermes realising the cause, persuaded Hephæstus, or, according to some, Prometheus, to cleave open Zeus' skull, from which Athene sprang completely armed.

42. The centre of her cult was Attica and Athens, and legend said that when Athene and Poseidon contended for the possession of the city, the gods judged it should belong to Athene, who in planting the olive-tree had conferred the better gift.

43. Preferring to settle quarrels peaceably, Athene established here the court of the Areopagus, where if votes were equal, she herself gave a casting vote to free the accused, as in the trial of Orestes.

44. In 566 B.C. Pesistratus founded the great Panathenaic festival, celebrated every fourth year, and its magnificent procession was represented on the frieze of the Parthenon now in the British Museum, while the birth of Athene was represented in the gable at the east end of the Parthenon, and the contest with Poseidon at the west. Pesistratus also introduced a new coinage, with the head of Athene on one side, and the owl, her bird, upon the other.

45. Other pre-Hellenic acropolipses were sacred to Athene, and her worship flourished in Sparta, Corinth, Argos, and Thebes.

HEPHÆSTUS, 46–56.

46. Hephæstus, identified with Vulcan by the Romans, was the smith-god, a superb artist in metals.

47. He probably originated as a pre-Hellenic fire-god near the Mt. Olympus of Lycia in Asia Minor, where gaseous vapour, seeping through the soil, ignited. The Lycians emigrated to Lemnos, where they became known as Pelasgians, and again found fire issuing from the earth, and this fire became the symbol of their god Hephæstus.

48. The cult of Hephæstus spread to Athens, where his artistic genius was so venerated that in the frieze of the Parthenon where two pairs of gods are given positions of honour, Zeus appears with Hera, and Hephæstus with Athene.

49. In Homer's time Hephæstus was one of the twelve Olympians, his exalted position reflecting the importance of the smith in a Bronze Age society when weapons and tools had magical properties. He is, like other smith-gods, represented as lame, possibly because the tribe deliberately lamed their smith to prevent his running away, possibly because work at the forge developed muscular arms but feeble legs.

50. According to Homer, Hephæstus was the son of Zeus and Hera, though later tradition says that he was son of the goddess alone, just as his fire sprang mysteriously from the earth.

51. Born lame and weak, Hephæstus was so much disliked by Hera that she threw him from Olympus, when he fell into the sea and was cared for by the sea-goddesses Thetis and Eurynome in a grotto under the sea.

52. After nine years Hera took him back to Olympus, where he had a fire smithy, but on one occasion he enraged Zeus by taking Hera's part, so that he was again flung from Olympus, this time by Zeus. He was a day falling, and alighted in the evening on the island of Lemnos, as described in *Paradise Lost*, Book I, lines 740–746. Later writers diverge from Homer in making this second fall the cause of Hephæstus' lameness.

53. He again returned to Olympus and acted as mediator between Hera and Zeus, though the gods laughed at him as he hobbled about.

54. His workshop in Olympus was in his own palace, and all the palaces of the gods were made by him He also made the magnificent armour of Achilles, as is described in the eighteenth book of the *Iliad*, the necklace of Harmonia, and the bulls of Æëtes. Later accounts place his workshop on the volcanic island of Sicily, where the Cyclopes served him.

55. In the *Iliad*, Hephæstus' wife was Charis, but in the *Odyssey* she was Aphrodite, who was unfaithful to him with Ares. How Hephæstus caught the two together in an invisible net he had made, and exposed them to the ridicule of the gods, is told in a poem known as the " Lay of Demodocus," incorporated in the eighth book of the *Odyssey*.

56. Hephæstus' favourite spots on earth were Lemnos, and volcanic islands like Lipara, Hiera, Imbros, and Sicily. In Greek art he is represented as a vigorous man with a beard, carrying a hammer or similar instrument, and wearing an oval cap or chiton.

APHRODITE, 57–63.

57. Aphrodite, goddess of desire, identified by the Romans with Venus, was derived from the Great Goddess of pre-Hellenic times, her counterparts being the orgiastic Ishtar of Babylon and Astarte of Syria.

58. She was worshipped as a fertility goddess at Paphos in Cyprus, whence Phœnicians took her worship to Cythera, an island off Southern Peloponnesus. Probably as late as the eighth century B.C. her fertility cult was established on Acrocorinthus above Corinth. There was a similar sanctuary on Mt. Eryx in Western Sicily. In these places the goddess was served by young girls, but in other Greek states her worship was more that of protectress of the city.

59. According to Hesiod, Aphrodite sprang from the seed of Uranus and rose naked from the sea, as in Botticelli's picture "The Birth of Venus." Rising near the island of Cythera, she passed to Paphos in Cyprus.

60. Homer makes Aphrodite the daughter of Zeus and Dione, and represents her as wife to Hephæstus. She was, however, unfaithful to him and in love with Ares. The amusing situation when they were caught together is described in para. 55. Harmonia was one of their children.

61. Aphrodite also bore sons to Poseidon, and Priapus to Dionysus, and later stories tell that she bore Hermaphroditus to Hermes, and Eros to either Hermes, Ares, or Zeus.

62. Her love for the mortal Adonis is the theme of Shakespeare's *Venus and Adonis*, and one of the Homeric hymns tells of her passion for Anchises, cousin of Priam, to whom she bore Æneas, the hero of Virgil's *Epic*. Unfortunately Anchises, boasting of Aphrodite's love, was struck by Zeus with a thunderbolt.

63. Aphrodite possessed a magic girdle which made the wearer irresistibly lovely and desirable. Doves and sparrows were sacred to her. Her most beautiful statue was that of Praxiteles in the fourth century B.C., a copy of which is preserved in the Vatican. The Venus de Milo may be seen in the Louvre.

ARES, 64–67.

64. Ares, god of war, who was identified by the Romans with Mars, was a divinity of Thracian origin, whose worship spread through Macedonia to Thebes, Athens, and cities of the Peloponnesus, especially Sparta. Ares was, however, not popular with the Greeks, who disliked purposeless war and despised the Thracians for enjoying it, and their attitude is reflected in the myths of Ares.

65. He was the son of Zeus and Hera, and as he delighted in battle for its own sake he was hated by the other gods, except Eris, Hades, and Aphrodite, who was in love with Ares and he with her. The two were once trapped together in a net which Hephæstus had engineered, as is described in para. 55.

66. Ares was not always successful in battle. The Alceidæ conquered him and left him imprisoned in a brazen vessel for thirteen months, until he was released by Hermes. Athene twice vanquished him, and Heracles also defeated him and forced him to return to Olympus.

67. According to a late tradition, Ares once defended himself before the gods in a trial where he was accused of murdering Halirrhothius, son of Poseidon. Since he pleaded that he had saved his daughter, Alcippe, from being violated, Ares was acquitted, and the place of the trial became known as the Areopagus.

APOLLO, 68–80.

68. Apollo's worship probably derived from two sources, from the Dorians, who in about 1100 B.C. entered Greece and reached as far south as Crete, and from Ionians, living in the islands and mainland of Anatolia, or Asia Minor, who became acquainted with a Hittite divinity worshipped in Lycia, and hence called Lycius.

69. Apollo's Dorian shrine was at Delphi, near the Castalian spring on Mt. Parnassus, where he was called the Pythian, or Loxias, the Ambiguous. His Ionian shrine was at Delos, where he was called Lycius, and Phœbus, or Shining, and where he was more closely associated with his twin-sister, Artemis.

70. Legends said that Apollo and Artemis were the children of Zeus and Leto, but before their birth, jealous Hera caused Leto to wander from place to place till she gave birth to Artemis under a palm-tree at Ortygia, and to Apollo beside a palm in the isle of Delos.

71. This story is told in the Delian Homeric Hymn of 700 B.C., while the Delphic Hymn tells how Apollo, soon after his birth, sought out the she-dragon Python, on Mt. Parnassus, and there killed her, taking over the Oracle of Earth at Delphi, where his priestess the Pythoness became the mouthpiece of his oracles, which were imparted in hexameter verse. Apollo was commanded by Zeus to visit the Vale of Tempe for purification, and to preside over the Pythian games held in Python's honour.

72. Hera, still implacable, sent the giant Tityus to violate Leto, as she came with Artemis to Delphi, though some say that it was Artemis who was attacked, but the giant was killed by the arrows of Apollo and Artemis.

73. Apollo was not always subservient to Zeus. He once, with Hera, Poseidon, and other Olympians, bound Zeus with chains and was punished by being sent with Poseidon as bondman to King Laomedan, where by playing the lyre and tending the flocks he helped Poseidon to build the walls of Troy. On another occasion, furious that Zeus had slain his son Asclepius, Apollo retaliated by killing the Cyclopes. Zeus now sent him to serve King Admetus of Pheræ in Thessaly, and again he kept flocks. He also helped Admetus to win his bride Alcestis and even ensured that the king should be restored to life if one of his family would die in his stead.

74. Apollo loved many mortal women, including Cyrene, mother of Aristæus, Coronis, mother of Asclepius, the healer, and Aria, mother of Miletus. The nymph Dryope was also seduced by Apollo, but when he pursued the nymph Daphne she cried for help and was turned into a laurel, henceforth Apollo's tree; and the nymph Marpessa preferred his rival, Idas. Apollo loved Cassandra, daughter of Priam, and conferred on her the gift of prophecy, but, when she disappointed him, decreed that she should never be believed. Hyacinthus, a Spartan prince, in origin an earth deity, was beloved by Apollo, and when he was killed by the god's jealous rival, Zephyrus, the hyacinth flower sprang from his blood.

75. Apollo had varied characteristics. He was destroyer, as his arrows indicated, and sudden deaths were ascribed to him. It was he who sent plagues among the Greeks besieging Troy. But he was also protector, warding off evil, as his fatherhood of Asclepius indicated. He protected flocks and cattle, as his service to Laomedan and Admetus showed, and later writers particularly stressed this aspect.

76. As god of prophecy, Apollo could communicate the gift to gods and mortals, and of all the centres of his worship Delphi was the most famous. The shrine had probably been established by pre-Hellenic people, worshipping Mother Earth, and had been seized by invading Hellenes who killed Python the oracular serpent, took over the oracles in the name of their own Apollo, and held funeral games in honour of Python to placate the original inhabitants. The shrine was supposed to contain the Omphalos, or navel stone of earth, and a chasm which occasionally gave out intoxicating vapours. Over this Apollo's priestess, Pythia, sat on a tripod, and uttered his oracle after chewing intoxicating laurel leaf. She was regarded as the mystical bride of the god.

77. As god of song and music Apollo appears in the *Iliad* delighting immortals. He was said to have received the lyre from Hermes, and its seven strings were connected with the seven Greek vowels. In music none surpassed Apollo, not even Pan, nor Marsyas, the satyr who had found Athene's discarded flute which played by itself. Defeated in a contest, Marsyas was flayed alive by the victorious god. Apollo, as leader of the Muses, was called Musagetes. He valued order and moderation in all things, his favourite maxims being " Nothing in Excess," and " Know thyself."

78. Apollo also delighted in the foundation of towns, and his oracle was always consulted before a town was founded.

79. In later writers he was identified with the sun god, the result of Egyptian influence, for in Homer, Helios, god of the sun, is completely distinct from Apollo.

80. The worship of Apollo, typical of all that is most radiant in the Greek mind, has no counterpart in the religion of Rome. Not till the end of the third century B.C. did the Romans adopt his religion from the Greeks.

ARTEMIS, 81-89.

81. Artemis, whose Roman counterpart was Diana, had two chief aspects. One was as " Mistress of Animals," a goddess of the chase, worshipped in primitive matriarchal society, and probably owing something to the Britomartis and Dictynna, worshipped as huntresses in Crete. The other, originating in Asia Minor, was of the age-old mother-goddess, and is most clearly seen in Artemis Ephesia, who was worshipped as an orgiastic goddess.

82. Legends of the birth of Artemis are told in the story of Apollo, and as his sister she shared many of his characteristics. She carried bow and arrows, made for her by Hephæstus, and had power to send plague and sudden death, as when she and Apollo killed the children of Niobe. She was also protectress of children and young animals and goddess of the chase.

83. Like Apollo, Artemis was unmarried, and later writers stressed that she was a maiden goddess and severely punished any lapses. She changed Actæon to a stag to be torn to pieces by his own hounds, only because he had seen her bathing, and some traditions say that she killed Orion because of his unchastity. The nymph Callisto, who had been seduced by Zeus, was in the form of a bear hunted down by the hounds of Artemis.

84. When Apollo was identified with the Sun, Artemis was identified with Selene, the Moon.

85. The Arcadian Artemis, early worshipped in Arcadia as a huntress among the nymphs, was unconnected with Apollo.

86. Another aspect of the goddess was as the fierce Artemis of Tauris, to whom all strangers were sacrificed. Iphigeneia was once her priestess, and she and Orestes took her image to Brauron in Attica, whence the goddess was called Brauronia. This Brauronian Artemis was worshipped in Athens, and also in Sparta, where boys were scourged at her altar until they sprinkled it with their blood.

87. Artemis as an orgiastic goddess had her chief centre in Ephesus, with its immensely wealthy temple, and it was this Artemis that St. Paul encountered. (See Acts of the Apostles, Ch. XIX.)

88. Though usually regarded as a rural divinity, Artemis was supreme in three great cities, in Ephesus, in Marseilles, to which Ionian Greeks from Asia Minor took her cult between 600 and 540 B.C., and in Syracuse, where she was known as Artemis Arethusa.

89. The goddess was often portrayed as a huntress, as in the so-called Diana of Versailles, now in the Louvre. As huntress her chlamys reached only to the knees, and she carried a bow, quiver, and arrows, or a spear, and was accompanied with stags or dogs. As Selene, she wore a long robe and veil, and a crescent moon on her forehead.

HERMES, 90-98.

90. Hermes, whom the Romans called Mercurius, was originally one of the gods of the pre-Hellenic people, the divinity dwelling in the cairn, or " herma," set up by shepherds as a landmark in wild country, and so developing as a protector against predatory animals and a guide to travellers. This Hermes was identified with a similar divinity worshipped in Minoan Crete, a " Master of Animals," a son or lover of the Great Goddess, and therefore a god of fertility.

91. Legends said that Hermes was the son of Zeus and Maia, an embodiment of the Great Goddess, and a daughter of Atlas, whence Hermes' name Atlantiades.

92. The " Hymn to Hermes " of 600 B.C. tells that he was born in a cavern on Mt. Cyllene in Arcadia (from which he was sometimes called Cyllenius), and that he grew with amazing rapidity. When only a few hours old he went to Pieria and stole some of the oxen of Apollo, which he drove to Pylos, and then, returning to Cyllene, he invented the lyre by stringing a tortoise-shell with cow-gut. Apollo, on discovering the thief, accused him to Zeus, who ordered Hermes to restore the oxen. But when Apollo heard the lyre he was delighted, took it in exchange for the oxen, and became the friend of Hermes, leading him back to Zeus.

93. Zeus gave to Hermes supreme power over animals and appointed him his herald, Hermes also acted as herald to Hades, conducting shades to the underworld. (See Virgil's *Æneid*, Bk. IV, ll. 242 *sqq.*) As herald he was regarded as god of eloquence, whence St. Paul, " the chief speaker," was mistaken for him in Lystra of Asia Minor. (See Acts of the Apostles, Ch. XIV.) Heralds promote peace and therefore trade. Thus Hermes came to be looked on as god of peaceable commerce.

94. He was also god of prudence and cunning, and even of theft, and was said to have helped the Fates in composing the alphabet. Many inventions ascribed to Hermes, such as weights and measures, the musical scale, astronomy, olive-culture, and the arts of boxing and gymnastics, were pre-Hellenic, and the stories of his childhood may indicate how the Hellenes took over these arts in the name of their god Apollo. As a god of fertility and luck, Hermes presided over games of dice.

95. He played a part in such incidents as the rescue of Dionysus, the punishment of Ixion, the selling of Heracles to Omphale, the judgment of Paris, and the leading of Priam to Achilles, but his most famous exploit was perhaps the slaying of Argus, the hundred-eyed giant sent by Hera to watch Io.

96. Hermes had several sons, including Echion, herald to the Argonauts, Autolycus the thief, his son by Chione, and Daphnis.

97. His worship flourished in Arcadia, where he was to be found with Pan and the muses. It spread to Athens, and he became one of the best loved of the Olympians.

98. Hermes' attributes were the Petasus, a travelling-hat, in later time adorned with wings, the Alipes, or winged-sandals, and the Caduceus, or heralds' staff, whose white ribbons were later mistaken for serpents because he was herald to Hades. Sacred to Hermes were the tortoise, the palm-tree, the number four, and some kinds of fish, and his sacrifices were incense, honey, cakes, pigs, lambs, and kids.

POSEIDON, 99–109.

99. Poseidon, identified by the Romans with Neptune, derived from a god worshipped by the earliest Aryan invaders of Greece, the Minyans and Ionians, who entered the country in about 2000 B.C. It was with the aid of horses and wheeled vehicles that they quickly overcame any resistance, and their god Poseidon was often thought of as the horse whose hooves thunder on the earth. He is constantly spoken of in Homer as " earth-shaker," while many legends show him in equine guise. It is possible that he was originally thought of as a sky-god, a thunderer, and the mate of an earth-goddess who later developed as Demeter.

100. But when in about 1450 B.C., another wave of invading Aryans, the Achæans, entered Greece, they also brought their sky-god, a thunderer called Zeus, possibly in origin identical with Poseidon, and the latter, recognised as an older brother of Zeus, came to be revered as a sea-divinity, for the Minyans were, by now, expert in navigation.

101. According to legend, Poseidon was the eldest son of Cronus and Rhea, and when, after the deposition of Cronus, he and his brothers Zeus and Hades cast lots for sovereignty, the sea became Poseidon's share. He dwelt in an under-water palace near Ægæ in Eubœa, which is described in the beginning of the 13th book of the *Iliad*, and here he kept his horses with brazen hooves and golden manes, and when they drew his chariot over the sea it became tranquil.

102. He was said to have created the horse when disputing with Athene for the possession of Athens, and he taught men how to bridle horses. He was the protector of horse-races, and horse and chariot races were held in his honour on the Corinthian isthmus.

103. In the form of a horse he raped his sister Demeter, when she was disguised as a mare. Their offspring were the horse Arion and the nymph Despœna, and some say Persephone also, though according to another version Demeter was searching for Persephone, her daughter by Zeus, at the time of the rape.

104. Poseidon, though equal to Zeus in dignity, was less powerful and resented the pride of his younger brother. He once joined with Hera, Apollo, and other Olympians, to put Zeus in chains, and he and Apollo were punished by being sent as bondsmen to Laomedan. Here Poseidon built the walls of Troy, hence called Neptunia Pergama. When Laomedan refused the wages due, Poseidon sent a sea-monster, which would have devoured the king's daughter Hesione if she had not been rescued by Heracles. In the Trojan War, Poseidon naturally sided with the Greeks, though he became hostile to Odysseus after he had blinded Polyphemus, son of the god.

105. Poseidon desired earthly kingdoms, his attempts to take control possibly being political myths. He disputed with Athene for the possession of Athens, but she was awarded the city because her planting of the olive was judged the better gift. When these divinities, however, disputed the possession of Trœzen, Zeus judged they should share it equally. In his claim for Corinth, Poseidon received only the isthmus, where the quadrennial Isthmian games were held in his honour, while the Areopagus was awarded to Helios.

106. Poseidon first intended to marry Thetis, but when it was prophesied that her son would be greater than his father he paid court to Amphitrite, daughter of Nereus. Only after Delphinos had most eloquently pleaded his suit did Amphitrite accept Poseidon, who in gratitude placed Delphinos' image among the stars, as the Dolphin. Amphitrites' reluctance, paralleled by Hera's shrinking from Zeus, and Persephone's from Hades, probably represents the resistance of an early matriarchal society to a patriarchal system.

107. Poseidon's son by Amphitrite was Triton, but he had many more children by other divinities and mortals.

108. One of them, Scylla, was particularly hateful to Amphitrite, who is said to have turned her into a monster with six barking heads and twelve feet. Poseidon also loved the nymph Tyro, mother of his children Pelias and Neleus, and Æthra, the mother of Theseus. His offspring by Medusa were Chrysaor and Pegasus.

109. Sacrifices to Poseidon were usually black-and-white bulls. His symbol of power was the trident, possibly in origin a thunderbolt, by means of which he could shake the earth or subdue the waves, and which became in Hellenistic and Roman times a symbol of sea-power, as it is today. Poseidon's other attributes were the horse and the dolphin, and he was usually represented as accompanied by Amphitrite, Triton, Nereids, and dolphins.

DEMETER, 110–116.

110. Demeter, counterpart of the Roman Ceres, was probably in origin a divinity of the Minyans, who entered Greece in about 200 B.C., and who revered her as an earth-goddess, a mate to their sky-god, who later developed as Poseidon. Both these divinities could take the form of a horse. The worship of this earth-goddess then merged with that of the Great Goddess of the pre-Hellenic matriarchal society, and Demeter was worshipped as the corn-goddess.

111. She was daughter to Cronus and Rhea, and sister to Zeus, by whom she became the mother of Persephone, or Core, the maiden, herself another aspect of the goddess. According to the Homeric Hymn of the seventh century B.C., Hades asked Zeus' permission to marry Persephone, and as he received no downright refusal was emboldened to carry off the maiden as she was gathering flowers. Demeter wandered the earth searching for her daughter until Helios told her what Hades had done. She then shunned Olympus and wandered still on earth, which she forbad to bring forth fruit. Zeus finally told Demeter that her daughter might return, provided she had eaten nothing in the Underworld, and he sent Hermes to escort her back. Hades agreed to let Persephone go, but gave her a pomegranate to eat, and it was at last agreed that she should spend a third of the year with him in Hades, as Queen of the Underworld, and the rest of the year with Demeter, who once more allowed the earth to bear its fruit.

112. Inconsistent accounts are given of the place of the rape. Demeter's priests said it was Eleusis, about twelve miles from Athens, the Latin poets Enna in Sicily, where, according to Ovid, Persephone was gathering poppies. Some say it was Ascalaphus who saw Persephone take food in the Underworld and that because he revealed this, he was turned by Demeter into an owl.

113. It is said that during her wanderings, Demeter punished those, like Abas, son of Celeus, who were unkind to her, but showered blessings on those like Celeus himself and his son Triptolemus who received her hospitably in Eleusis and whom she taught the art of agriculture.

114. The Eleusinian Festival in honour of Demeter and Persephone was probably fully established in Athens by Pesistratus at the end of the sixth century B.C., probably about the time when the cult of Dionysus was instituted. There was an annual procession from Eleusis to Athens, and those who spoke Greek could be initiated into the final rite of the mysteries. The Thesmophoria, celebrating the foundation of laws, was also held in the goddesses' honour, in Athens and in other parts of Greece.

115. The myth originated in the most primitive rites of seed time and harvest at a time when only women practised the arts of agriculture. Persephone, representing the vegetation which dies down during the winter, had her counterpart in the primitive corn-puppet which was buried in winter to be dug up again sprouting in spring, and later writers saw the story as an expression of the death of the body and the immortality of the soul.

116. In art Demeter was represented with a garland of corn or a ribbon, and holding a sceptre, corn ears, or a poppy, and sometimes a torch and basket. Pigs were sacred to her. There is in the British Museum a fine statue of Demeter of about 330 B.C., which was found at Cnidos in Asia Minor.

DIONYSUS, 117–128.

117. Dionysus, god of wine, also called Bacchus by both Greeks and Romans, was not in Homer's time one of the aristocratic Olympian deities, but a god worshipped by humble folk whom wandering bands of ecstatic worshippers brought into Greece from Thrace in the eighth century B.C. The cult, which spread through Macedonia and Thessaly, to Bœotia, Delphi, Athens, and beyond, was characterised by a mystic frenzy when the worshippers, intoxicated with wine, believed themselves to be at one with Dionysus or Bacchus, sometimes called Bromius " the Boisterous." The men who followed him were known as Bacchoi, the women Bacchæ, or Bacchantes or Mænads, or in Athens and Delphi, Thyiads.

118. The immense popularity of the Dionysian cult, especially with women, indicates that among the recently civilised Greeks there was a longing for a more instinctive and impulsive life, valuing enthusiasm rather than prudence, and during the sixth century certain wise statesmen introduced the new cult among the other state religions. Dyonisiac festivals were established in Corinth, Sicyon, Delphi, and Athens. In Delphi the sepulchre of Bacchus was placed near the very tripod of Pythia, and his temple, a theatre, was at the highest point of the sacred precinct. In Athens Pesistratus founded the Dionysia and the Panathenaic Games at about the same time, and a theatre was set up where the worshippers of Bacchus enacted the first primitive drama. In the fifth century, when the Parthenon was finished, the new god had been accepted among the twelve Olympians taking the place of Hestia. This change incidentally secured a majority of gods over goddesses on Mt. Olympus, and is perhaps evidence of a society becoming increasingly patriarchal.

119. Legends said that Dionysus was the son of Semele by Zeus, who visited his beloved disguised as a mortal. When Semele was six months with child, jealous Hera, disguised as an old woman, persuaded her to ask her mysterious lover to appear in his true form. Unwillingly Zeus consented, " hapless Semele " was consumed by fire, and her unborn child sewn up in Zeus' thigh to be delivered three months later as Dionysus.

120. The child was first entrusted to Athamas and Ino of Bœotia, and reared in the women's quarters disguised as a girl, until Hera undeceived punished Athamas with madness so that he killed his own son. Hermes then took Dionysus to Mt. Nysa, where the nymphs cared for him, feeding him with honey, and where he first invented wine. Zeus later placed the images of the nymphs among the stars as Hyades.

121. When Dionysus had grown to manhood Hera drove him mad and he wandered through the world with his old tutor Silenus and a wild rout of Satyrs and Mænads. He went through Egypt, Syria, and Asia to India, overcoming military opposition, teaching the culture of the vine, founding cities and laws. He returned to Europe through Phrygia and then invaded Thrace.

122. Here Lycurgus, King of the Edones, opposed his worship, but, maddened by Rhea, he killed and mutilated his own son, and the Edones caused him to be torn to death by horses.

123. Dionysus now proceeded to Bœotia, and in Thebes was resisted by King Pentheus. But Pentheus was also driven mad and torn to pieces by the Mænads or Bacchæ, among whom were his own mother Agave and her two sisters, for in their frenzy they believed him to be a wild beast. This is the legend used by Euripides in his play, The Bacchæ.

124. Dionysus also visited the islands of the Adriatic. At Icaria he hired a ship bound for Naxos, but the sailors were Tyrrhenian pirates and steered towards Asia, intending to sell Dionysus into slavery. The god, however, turned himself into a lion and the oars into serpents. Ivy grew round the ship and flutes were heard. The terrified pirates, leaping overboard, were transformed to dolphins. Arrived at Naxos, Dionysus found Ariadne deserted by Theseus and at once married her. A Renaissance conception of this incident can be seen in Titian's picture " Bacchus and Ariadne " in the National Gallery, or in Tintoretto's picture in the Doge's Palace in Venice.

125. At Argos people refused at first to accept Dionysus, but when the women had been maddened by him, they admitted he was a god.

126. His worship established throughout the world, Dionysus was received into Olympus as one of the twelve great divinities, taking the place of Hestia. He brought Semele there from the Underworld, and she was henceforth known as Thyone.

127. Dionysus was worshipped as god of the vital and intoxicating powers of nature, and also, because of his close connection with tillage and early civilisation, as a law-giver. He was also god of tragic art. In art he was represented as young, handsome, and athletic, but later as slightly effeminate. He was accompanied with a wild crowd of Satyrs, and Mænads, the latter frenzied with wine and mystic exaltation, and carrying cymbals, swords, serpents, or the Thyrsus, a wand wreathed with ivy and crowned with a fir-cone. The worship of Dionysus appealed strongly to women, and many would spend the whole night on the mountain in ecstatic dancing and tearing wild animals to pieces. Sacred to the god were the ivy, laurel, and asphodel, and the dolphin, serpent, tiger, lynx, panther, and ass. His sacrifice was usually a goat or ass.

128. The myths of Dionysus are evidence that there was at first much opposition to the ritual use of wine, and the frenzy it engendered. The earlier drink of the Greeks had been a kind of beer flavoured with ivy and mead, and mead was the drink of Homer's Olympians. Wine was not invented by the Greeks, but probably first imported by them from Crete, whither vine culture had probably spread from Mt. Nysa in Libya. The use of wine spread from Thrace to Athens and other civilised cities. The story of Dionysus' wanderings in India represents the spread of vine culture there.

PERSEUS, 129–144.

129. The ancient folk-tale of Perseus, grandson of Acrisius, has been told by Kingsley in The Heroes.

130. Acrisius and Prœtus, the twin sons of Abas, King of Argos, eventually agreed, after much discussion, to divide their inheritance. Prœtus became ruler of Tiryns, whose massive walls he built by the aid of the Cyclopes, while Acrisius ruled uneasily in Argos, for an oracle had declared that he would be killed by a son born to his daughter Danaë.

131. To prevent this disaster, Acrisius had Danaë immured in a brazen dungeon or tower, with doors of brass, but all in vain, for Zeus visited her in a shower of gold, and she became the mother of Perseus.

132. Not daring to kill Danaë, Acrisius set mother and son adrift on the sea in a chest, which floated to the isle of Seriphos, one of the Cyclades. Here it was found by the sailor Dictys, and he took Danaë and her son to the king Polydectes, who received them hospitably.

133. When Perseus was grown to manhood, however, Polydectes sought to marry Danaë and

seized a pretext to send Perseus off to fetch the head of the Gorgon Medusa.

134. Medusa and her sister Gorgons, Stheno and Euryale, who were the daughters of Phorcys and Ceto, and dwelt in Libya, had once been beautiful. But Medusa lay with Poseidon in one of the temples of Athene, and the enraged goddess turned her into a winged monster with brazen claws and serpent hair, so hideous that she turned to stone all who looked upon her.

135. Athene, eager to help Perseus against her enemy, gave him a polished shield whereby he might see Medusa only in reflection. Hermes provided him with a sickle, and told him how to procure winged sandals, a magic wallet in which to carry the decapitated head, and Hades' helmet of invisibility.

136. On Hermes' advice Perseus visited the Gorgons' sisters, the Grææ, three old women grey from birth who had only one eye and one tooth between them, and these they passed from one to another. Perseus found them on Mt. Atlas, and, by snatching the eye and tooth, forced the Grææ to tell him where he could find the sandals, wallet, and helmet. They directed him to the Stygian nymphs, who gave him what he needed.

137. Flying westward to the land of the Hyperboreans, Perseus found the Gorgons asleep. He successfully beheaded Medusa and was astonished to see, springing fully grown from her body, the winged horse Pegasus and the warrior Chrysaor, both of whom had been begotten on her by Poseidon.

138. Though pursued by Stheno and Euryale, Perseus in Hades' helmet escaped to the south. Some say that he petrified the Titan Atlas by showing him the Gorgon's head and then flew over Æthiopia.

139. Here he saw, chained naked to a rock on the sea coast, the lovely Andromeda, and at once fell in love with her. He learned the cause of her plight from her parents, Cepheus, King of Æthiopia, and his wife Cassiopeia. The latter had rashly boasted that Andromeda was more beautiful than the Nereids, and when they had complained of this to Poseidon, the sea god had sent a monster to lay waste the country. Only by the sacrifice of Andromeda, said the oracle of Ammon, could the land be delivered.

140. Perseus promptly offered to rescue the maiden, provided she would become his wife, but, after he had slain the monster, Cepheus and Cassiopeia were reluctant to keep their promise, for they said Andromeda had already been contracted to another. Their protégé and his followers, arriving at the wedding, attempted to seize the bride, but were easily circumvented by Perseus, who showed them Medusa's head and turned them all to stone. Poseidon set the images of Cepheus and Cassiopeia among the stars, the latter in a humiliating position.

141. Perseus, with Andromeda, now hastened to Seriphos, where he found that Danaë and Dictys had been obliged to take refuge in a temple, but going to Polydectes' palace, he exposed the Gorgon's head and turned the king and all his followers to stone. He then gave the head to Athene, who set it in her ægis, and Hermes restored Perseus' accoutrements to the Stygian nymphs.

142. After making Dictys King of Seriphos, Perseus, taking with him Danaë and Andromeda, returned to Argos, and Acrisius, mindful of the oracle, fled to Larissa, in vain, however, for Perseus, visiting Larissa and taking part in public games, accidentally killed his grandfather by a throw of the discus.

143. Grieved by this mishap, Perseus arranged to exchange kingdoms with his cousin Megapenthes, the son of Prœtus, who now moved to Argos while Perseus became King of Tiryns. He

also founded Mycenæ, which, like Tiryns itself had mighty fortifications built by the Cyclopes.

144. The massive remains of both cities have been investigated by Schliemann and other archæologists, and remain as some of the most interesting antiquities in all Greece.

BELLEROPHON, 145–150.

145. The story of Bellerophon is told by William Morris in *The Earthly Paradise.*

146. Bellerophon, the son of Glaucus, King of Corinth, having killed one Bellerus, fled to Prœtus, King of Tiryns. Unfortunately Prœtus' wife, Anteia, fell in love with the young man, and when he refused her advances falsely accused him to her husband of trying to seduce her. Prœtus, reluctant to kill a guest, sent him instead to Anteia's father, Iobates, King of Lycia, carrying a letter which requested that the bearer be put to death.

147. Iobates also shrank from killing a guest and decided to send Bellerophon against the Chimæra, a fire-breathing monster with a lion's head, goat's body, and serpent's tail, said to be the offspring of Echidne and Typhon, which was now ravaging Lycia.

148. Bellerophon was advised to catch the winged horse Pegasus, sprung from Medusa. Pegasus, by striking his hoof on the earth of Mt. Helicon, had created the spring of Hippocrene, sacred to the Muses, and he was found by Bellerophon at another of his fountains, that of Pirene in the Acropolis of Corinth. The hero flung over the horse's head a golden bridle, which Athene had given him, and astride his flying steed he easily shot the Chimæra with his arrows.

149. The frustrated Iobates now sent Bellerophon against the Amazons, and, when the hero again returned victorious, planted an ambush of guards against his arrival. Bellerophon slew them all, and Iobates, convinced at last that there had been some mistake, produced Prœtus' letter and learned the truth. He gave his guest his daughter in marriage and made him his heir.

150. Later tradition records that Bellerophon presumptuously tried to soar to Olympus mounted on Pegasus, but that Zeus sent a gadfly which stung the horse and caused him to throw his rider to earth. Bellerophon ended his days in wretchedness, but Pegasus gained Olympus.

JASON AND THE ARGONAUTS, 151–163.

151. The story of Jason and the Argonauts was already popular in Homer's day, and has more recently been told by Kingsley in *The Heroes,* and by William Morris in *The Life and Death of Jason.*

152. Jason's father Æson, the rightful King of Iolcus, had been deprived of his kingdom by his two half-brothers, Pelias and Neleus. The mother of all three was Tyro, who, seduced by Poseidon, bore him the twins Pelias and Neleus. She exposed the twins, but they were reared by a horse-herd, and when Tyro later married Cretheus, founder and King of Iolcus, they were adopted by him.

153. Tyro's son by Cretheus was Æson, but on Cretheus' death Pelias imprisoned Æson, expelled Neleus, and made himself supreme. The life of Æson's infant son Jason was saved only because he was smuggled out of Iolcus and entrusted to the care of Cheiron, the Centaur.

154. When a young man, Jason returned to Iolcus, fearlessly demanding his kingdom, and

Pelias, to be rid of him, asked him to go to Colchis to fetch the golden fleece. This, the fleece of the ram on which Phrixus had escaped, and which he had given to King Æëtes of Colchis, was now hanging on an oak-tree in the grove of Ares, guarded night and day by a sleepless dragon.

155. Jason welcomed the enterprise and commanded Argus, the Thespian to build him a fifty-oared ship called the *Argo*, into whose prow Athene herself fitted an oracular beam. Most of the heroes of the day flocked to join Jason, and his crew included the Dioscuri, Castor and Polydeuces, Heracles, and Orpheus the musician.

156. They met many adventures on the way. After lingering too long with the women of Lemnos, they slipped through the Hellespont and reached Mysia. Here Hylas, the squire of Heracles, while fetching water was stolen away by the Naiads, leaving nothing but an empty pitcher, and Heracles left the *Argo* in a vain search for him.

157. On the island of Bebrycos the Argonauts were met by its king, Amycus, son of Poseidon, and a renowned boxer, who contrived to kill all strangers by challenging them to a boxing match, but Polydeuces met the challenge and killed the bully. In Thrace they freed the blind king and prophet Phineus from a plague of Harpies, and in gratitude he advised Jason how to navigate the Bosphorus. At its entrance were the perilous floating islands, the Symplegades. It is possible that rumours of icebergs gave rise to the fable of these islands, which clashed together and crushed any ship which attempted to pass between them. But Jason, following the advice of Phineus, released a dove, and the *Argo* slipped between the islands as they recoiled. Henceforth they remained fixed. After overcoming other dangers, the Argonauts at last reached the River Phasis and Colchis.

158. Here Æëtes promised that he would give Jason the fleece if he could yoke together two fire-breathing bulls with brazen feet, the work of Hephæstus, plough the field of Ares, and sow it with the dragon's teeth left over by Cadmus at Thebes. It was Medea who enabled Jason to perform this terrible task. This sorceress princess, the daughter of Æëtes by his first wife, fell instantly in love with Jason and promised to help him if he would swear by all the gods to marry her and be faithful. She gave him a fire-resisting lotion and he completed the task. Then when Æëtes failed to keep his promise Medea charmed the dragon to sleep while Jason took down the fleece and they fled together in the *Argo*.

159. The furious Æëtes pursued them, but Medea ruthlessly murdered the young half-brother Absyrtus she had brought with her, and cut him into pieces which she dropped one by one over the side of the boat. Æëtes, stopping to collect the fragments for burial, soon lost sight of the fugitives.

160. There are many conflicting accounts of the *Argo*'s return journey, but none of them is feasible, for the Greek knowledge of geography was at that time very limited. Tradition said that the ship reached the Western Mediterranean and visited the island of Circe, who purified Jason and Medea of murder.

161. On their return to Iolcus they found that Pelias had forced Æson to take his life, though one tradition mentioned by Ovid and by Shakespeare in *The Merchant of Venice*, says that he was renewed to youthful vigour by Medea. All agree that Medea took a terrible revenge on Pelias. She persuaded his daughters, with the exception of Alcestis, to cut their father up and boil him in a cauldron, promising falsely that this would rejuvenate him. Pelias' son Acastus, horrified at the murder, then expelled Jason and Medea and they repaired to Corinth.

162. For many years they lived happily until they were involved in the final tragedy, dramatised by Euripides in his *Medea*. Jason deserted Medea for Glauce, also called Creusa, daughter of Creon, and the sorceress sent the young bride a garment which consumed her in flames, set fire to the palace, and involved Creon also in death. Some say that Medea also killed her own children by Jason.

163. Medea then escaped in a chariot drawn by winged serpents and took refuge with Ægeus of Athens, who married her. But on Theseus' arrival in the city, Medea departed and after many wanderings became an immortal. Some say that Jason took his own life; others that he was mercifully killed when the poop of his own ship *Argo* fell upon him.

HERACLES, 164–202.

164. Heracles, the most famous of the Greek heroes, was the son of Alcmene by Zeus.

165. Alcmene's brothers having been killed by the Taphians, she would not consummate her marriage with her husband Amphitrion, son of Alcæus, until he had avenged their death. While Amphitrion was away from Thebes fighting the Taphians, Zeus visited Alcmene in her husband's likeness and told her how he had been victorious. The true Amphitrion returned the following day, and the ensuing confusion is the theme of comedies by Plautus, Molière, and Dryden.

166. Nine months later Zeus boasted that he was about to become the father of a son who would be called Heracles, or glory of Hera, and who would be ruler of the house of Perseus. The jealous Hera exacted from him a promise that any son born that day to the house of Perseus should be king. She then hastened the birth of Eurystheus, who was a grandson of Perseus, and delayed that of Heracles. Alcmene bore two children, Heracles, son of Zeus, and Iphicles, Amphitrion's son, who was a night younger. Alcmene, fearing Hera, exposed Heracles, but Hera in error nursed him, thus conferring on him immortality.

167. Returned to Alcmene, Heracles prospered, and when still in his cradle, strangled with either hand two terrible snakes which Hera had sent to destroy him. In his youth he was taught how to drive the chariot by Amphitrion, fighting by Castor, how to sing and play the lyre by Eumolpus, wrestling by Autolycus, and archery by Eurytus. Linus, who was once teaching him to play the lyre, censured him, and Heracles then promptly killed his teacher with his own lyre, so Amphitrion sent him away to keep cattle.

168. In his eighteenth year he set out to attack the lion of Mt. Cithæron which was destroying the herds of both Amphitrion and his neighbour Thespius. The chase lasted fifty days, and Thespius, who was Heracles' host all this time; rewarded him by giving up his fifty daughters to him. Heracles killed the lion with a wild-olive club and made himself a garment of the pelt, with the head as helmet, though some say that he wore the skin of the Nemean lion.

169. On his return to Thebes, Heracles challenged the Minyan heralds from Orchomenus, who had come to collect tribute of cattle, and then led a victorious campaign against the Minyans in which his foster-father Amphitrion was killed.

170. Heracles was rewarded by Creon King of Thebes, who gave him his eldest daughter, Megara or Megera, in marriage, and Heracles became by her the father of several children. Creon's youngest daughter was married to Iphicles.

171. But Hera now visited Heracles with madness, so that he killed his own children and two of Iphicles'. When he recovered his reason he went, after purification, to consult the oracle at Delphi. The Pythia, calling him, for the first time, Heracles, advised him to go to Tiryns and there serve Eurystheus King of Argos for twelve years, doing whatever he was commanded. At the end of that time immortality would be conferred on him.

172. Most reluctantly Heracles set out. The gods gave him gifts of armour, but he relied on his bow and arrows and on the olive clubs which he cut for himself. His nephew Iolaus, oldest son of Iphicles, accompanied him as his faithful charioteer and companion. Thus supported, Heracles embarked on the twelve gigantic tasks imposed on him by Eurystheus.

The Twelve Labours of Heracles.

173. The **First Labour** was to bring back the skin of the Nemean or Cleonæan lion, an enormous creature, said to be the offspring of Typhon and Echidne, which was devastating the valley of Nemea near Cleonæ. As the pelt could not be pierced by any weapon, Heracles strangled the lion with his hands. He rededicated the Nemean games to Zeus and took the lion's carcase back to Tiryns, where he flayed it with its own claws. Some say that he wore the pelt as his armour. Eurystheus was so terrified that he now took refuge in a brazen urn below the earth whenever Heracles approached.

174. The **Second Labour** was to kill the Lernean Hydra, another monster which was said to be the offspring of Echidne by Typhon, and which Hera brought up. It lived at the sevenfold source of the River Amymone and haunted the neighbouring swamp of Lerna. It had a dog-like body and nine snaky heads, one of them immortal. As soon as Heracles struck off one head with his club, two grew in its place, while an enormous crab seized the hero's foot. He crushed the crab and called on Iolaus to burn the necks of the eight heads as he crushed them. The immortal head was buried and Heracles poisoned his arrows in the monster's gall, so that henceforth any wound they caused was fatal. Hera placed the image of the crab among the signs of the zodiac.

175. The **Third Labour** was to capture alive the Ceryneian Hind. This creature had brazen feet and golden antlers, and was therefore often called a stag. Heracles pursued it tirelessly for a year, and eventually shot an arrow which pinned the forelegs together without causing bloodshed. He then carried the creature back on his shoulders.

176. The **Fourth Labour** was to capture alive the Erymanthian boar, which had come down from Mt. Erymanthus to ravage Psophis. During his journey Heracles was entertained by the Centaur Pholus, who had a cask of wine given by Dionysus. When this was opened, other Centaurs besieged the cave. Repulsed by Heracles, some of them fled to the Centaur Cheiron. Heracles accidentally wounded Cheiron, who was an old friend, with one of his poisoned arrows. Cheiron, an immortal, could not die, although he now longed to do so, and was relieved from pain only when he later surrendered his immortality to Prometheus. Heracles continued his pursuit of the boar, drove it into a snow-drift, bound it with chains, and carried it to Eurystheus, but when he heard that the Argonauts were gathering for Colchis he hastened to join them, accompanied by Hylas.

177. The **Fifth Labour** was to cleanse in one day the stables of Augeias, King of Elis, who had more cattle and sheep than any man on earth. The dung had not been cleared away for years. Heracles swore a bargain with Augeias that he would cleanse the stalls in one day in return for a tenth of the cattle, and Phyleus, son of Augeias, was a witness to their mutual oaths. Heracles then diverted the Rivers Peneius and Alpheus through the stalls, which were thus cleansed in a day. But Augeias now learned that Heracles had been under Eurystheus' orders, and therefore refused the reward and even denied the bargain. When Phyleus was loyal to the truth Augeias banished him. Heracles later avenged himself on Augeias.

178. The **Sixth Labour** was to free the marshy lake of Stymphalia in Arcadia of the Stymphalian birds which were sacred to Ares. These man-eating creatures had brazen beaks, claws, and wings, and used their feathers as arrows.

Heracles, helped by Athene, frightened the bird with a rattle and then shot them down, though some say that they flew off to the island of Aretiu in the Black Sea, where they were found later by the Argonauts.

179. The **Seventh Labour** was to capture the Cretan bull. Poseidon had sent the bull to Mino for a sacrifice, but he had substituted another, and it was now raging over the island. Heracles did not avail himself of Minos' offers of help, but captured the bull single-handed and took it to Eurystheus, who set it free again. It roamed through Greece to Marathon, where Theseu captured it and took it to Athens for sacrifice to Athene.

180. The **Eighth Labour** was to bring back the mares of Diomedes, a savage King of the Bistone in Thrace, who fed his horses on human flesh. On his way Heracles visited Admetus and free Alcestis from death. Then with a few companion he drove the mares down to the sea, and turnin to repel the attacking Bistones, he left them in th charge of his friend Abderus, who was soon eate by them. Heracles, however, killed Diomede and threw his body to the mares. He the founded the city of Abdera in honour of his frien and drove the mares back to Eurystheus, who set them free on Mt. Olympus, where they were eaten by wild beasts.

181. The **Ninth Labour** was to fetch for Admete daughter of Eurystheus, the golden girdle tha Hippolyte, Queen of the Amazons, had receive from Ares. After an eventful journey throug Europe and Asia, Heracles and his companion reached the land of the Amazons, where Hippolyte sister of Antiope, received him kindly and pro mised him the girdle. But Hera roused th Amazons, and they attacked Heracles. In th fight he killed their leaders and Hippolyte hersel from whom he took the girdle. On his way hom Heracles came to Troy, where he rescued Lao medan's daughter Hesione from a sea monste sent by Poseidon.

182. The **Tenth Labour** was to fetch the oxe of Geryon without either demand or payment Geryon, a powerful monster with three bodies lived on the island of Erythia. Its site was dis puted. Some said it was beyond the ocean stream Others identified it with Gades. Heracle travelled to the frontiers of Libya and Europe where he set up two pillars, Calpe and Abyla, o the two sides of the Straits of Gibraltar, henc called the "Pillars of Hercules." When Helio shone too brightly, Heracles shot at him with a arrow, and Helios, admiring such boldness, gav him a golden cup or boat in which he sailed t Erythia. Geryon's cattle were guarded by th two-headed dog Orthrus, said to be the offsprin of Typhon and Echidne, and the herdsme Eurytion, son of Ares. Heracles felled both o these with his club, and, after overcoming Geryor he sailed with the cattle to Tartessus in Spain where he returned the golden boat to Helios. O his adventurous journey back through Gaul, Italy Illyricum, and Thrace, he resisted many attempts such as that of Cacus, to steal the cattle and even tually handed them over to Eurystheus, wh sacrificed them to Hera.

183. The **Eleventh Labour** was to fetch th golden apples of the Hesperides. These grew o the tree which Hera had received from Ge at he wedding and which she had planted in a garde on Mt. Atlas. It was guarded by the Hesperide and the dragon Ladon, another offspring o Typhon and Echidne. Heracles first consulte Proteus, or as some say Prometheus, and, follow ing the advice he received, he persuaded Atlas t fetch the apples, while he himself upheld th celestial globe. According to some, he also sho Ladon. Atlas, returning with three apples, trie to avoid taking back the burden of the globe, bu Heracles, by a ruse, transferred the globe back t the giant's shoulders, took the apples, an hastened away. On his return journey he kille the giant Antæus, and also persuaded Zeus to fre Prometheus, the arrow with which Apollo sho the vulture being placed among the stars a

Sagitta. Eurystheus made Heracles a gift of the apples, but the hero dedicated them to Athene, who returned them to their rightful place.

184. The Twelfth Labour was to bring back the dog Cerberus from Tartarus, the most difficult task of all. Heracles descended from Tænarum in Laconia and was guided by Athene and Hermes. After he had crossed the Styx and freed his friend Theseus and Ascalaphus, he obtained Hades' permission to carry away Cerberus, provided he could do so without using any weapon. Heracles seized Cerberus by the throat and dragged him up to show Eurystheus. He then carried the monster back to Tartarus.

185. According to most writers Heracles now returned to Thebes and gave his wife Megara to his nephew Iolaus, but Euripides, in his play *Heracles*, uses a different version. He represents the hero first killing the tyrant of Thebes, who had attempted to kill Megara and her children, and then, driven insane by Hera, himself killing his wife and family.

186. Heracles now desired to marry Iole, daughter of his friend Eurytus, King of Œchalia. Eurytus had promised her to the man who could surpass him and his sons in shooting with the bow. Though Heracles surpassed them all, Eurytus still refused to give him Iole because he had murdered his own children, and in this Eurytus was supported by all his sons except Iphitus. Later when Iphitus appeared suspicious of him, Heracles in a frenzy of rage slew him. Though purified from this murder, he was still troubled in mind, and consulted the Delphic Oracle. He was advised to serve as a slave and to give the proceeds to the family of Iphitus.

187. Heracles was purchased by Omphale, Queen of Lydia, and widow of Tmolus, and he served her either for one or for three years. Later writers say that he lived effeminately at this time, and that he used to change garments with Omphale, but others say that he continued to perform heroic deeds.

188. His period of servitude to Omphale completed, Heracles sailed against Troy. On a previous occasion, probably when returning from the land of the Amazons, Heracles and his friend Telamon had come to Troy, where they had found Laomedan's daughter, Hesione, exposed naked to a sea-monster, sent by Poseidon (*see para.* 104). Heracles had freed Hesione and killed the monster, but Laomedan had refused to give him the reward he had promised, the white horses given by Zeus in exchange for Ganymede.

189. Heracles and Telamon therefore now sailed to Troy to take their revenge. How they sacked the city is described in para. 275. Hesione was given to Telamon and bore him the son Teucer. On his return, Heracles faced a terrible storm raised by Hera and perils on the island of Cos. He was then led by Athene to Phlegra, where he helped the gods in their battle with the giants.

190. Heracles now took his revenge on Augeias, who had refused him payment for cleansing the stables. He invaded Elis and eventually killed Augeias, his sons, and their allies, the Moliones, though some say that he spared Augeias. He then founded the Olympic Games, and fetched from the source of the Danube the wild-olive tree whose leaves should crown the victor. Heracles then destroyed the city of Pylus, which had helped Elis. He killed Neleus the king and all his sons except Nestor.

191. Heracles next marched against Hippocoon who had fought against him under Neleus. Hippocoon had driven out his brother Tyndareus and seized the kingdom of Sparta. Heracles killed him and all his sons, and restored Tyndareus. He was helped in this enterprise by Cepheus and his twenty sons, but Cepheus and seventeen sons were killed. It was about this time that Heracles seduced the priestess Auge, daughter of Aleus,

King of Tegea, and became by her the father of Telephus.

192. After four years in Arcadia, Heracles left for Ætolia, where Œneus was King of Calydonia and Pleuron. Heracles wished to marry Œneus' daughter Deianeira and won her by defeating Achelous, the mighty river-god, son of Oceanus and Tethys. He now sent Iolaus as leader of his sons by the daughters of Thespius to settle in Sardinia.

193. Three years later, while at a feast, Heracles accidentally killed the boy Eunomus, and went into voluntary exile, taking Deianeira and their son Hyllus.

194. They reached the River Evenus, across which the centaur Nessus carried travellers for a small fee. Heracles let Nessus carry Deianeira, while he himself swam, but the centaur galloped off with her and would have violated her if Heracles had not shot him through the breast. The dying centaur then told Deianeira to take his blood as a charm to keep Heracles' love.

195. Heracles now resided at Trachis, and from there invaded Œchalia with an army in order to avenge himself on Eurytus, who had refused to surrender his daughter Iole, even though Heracles had won her in the archery contest. The hero killed Eurytus and all his family, and sent Iole to Deianeira in Trachis while he visited Cenæum in Eubœa and prepared a thanksgiving sacrifice to Zeus.

196. He had sent Lichas to Deianeira to fetch a white shirt to wear at the ceremony. Deianeira, fearful that Iole might win Heracles' love, rubbed the shirt in Nessus' blood, not knowing that Heracles' arrow, steeped in the Hydra's blood, had poisoned it. When Heracles put the shirt on, it burned with excruciating agony into his body, and attempts to tear it off took his flesh with it. Heracles seized Lichas and flung him into the sea and then commanded his son Hyllus to take him to Trachis. Deianeira, aghast at what she had unintentionally done, hanged herself. Heracles asked Hyllus to promise to marry Iole and to build him a funeral pyre on Mt. Œta.

197. This tragic climax to Heracles' career has been dramatised by Sophocles in the *Women of Trachis*, or *Trachiniæ*, where Deianeiras' distress at Ioles' arrival and her ill-fated ruse to keep her husband's love are touchingly represented.

198. Heracles finally ascended his funeral pyre to be burned alive. To Philoctetes, who kindled the flame, he gratefully bequeathed his quiver, bow, and arrows. Thunderbolts demolished the pyre, and Heracles was carried by a cloud to Olympus. There he became immortal, Hera was persuaded by Zeus to adopt him as her son, and reconciled to her at last, he married her daughter Hebe.

The Children of Heracles,
or Heracleidæ.

199. Eurystheus now determined to expel from Greece Alcmene and all the children of Heracles. Only in Athens did they find protection, and when Eurystheus attacked the city he was resisted by Theseus (or by his son Demophon), Iolaus, and Hyllus. As an oracle had demanded the sacrifice of one of Heracles' children, his daughter Macaria killed herself. Eurystheus was then defeated, by either Iolaus or Hyllus, and despatched by Alcmene.

200. These events are the theme of Euripides' play, *The Children of Heracles* or *Heracleidæ*.

201. Hyllus later, endeavouring to enter Peloponnesus, was slain in single combat by Echemus, King of Tegea. Only Tleopolemus settled in Argos.

202. Some generations later, the descendants of of Heracles conquered Peloponnesus in conjunction with the Dorians. This legend indicates the conquest of the Achæans by the later invaders.

THESEUS, 203–218.

203. Theseus, the great hero of Attica, was the son of Æthra by Ægeus, King of Athens, though he was also reputed to be the son of Poseidon. Æthra was the daughter of Pittheus, King of Troezen and here she secretly brought up her young son.

204. When he was of age, Æthra showed him the sandals, and a sword which was an heirloom of Cecrops, that Ægeus had left for him under a great rock. Theseus was able to lift the rock, recover the tokens, and proceed to Athens.

205. He insisted on going not by sea, but by the dangerous land route, and, like Heracles, he freed the country of many terrors. He killed Periphetes, whose club he afterwards carried, Sinis, the the wild sow of Crommyum, Sciron, Cercyon, and Sinis' father Polypemon, who was surnamed Procrustes.

206. Meanwhile in Athens Ægeus had married Medea, who had fled for safety from Corinth. Medea recognised Theseus, and jealous for Medus, her son by Ægeus, she attempted to poison him. But Ægeus recognised Cecrops' sword in time and welcomed his son with great rejoicing. Medea fled, taking Medus, and Theseus then scattered other rivals, the fifty sons of Pallas, nephews of Ægeus, who had hoped to succeed him to the throne.

207. Theseus next captured and sacrificed to Athene, the Marathonian bull which Heracles had brought from Crete and which had been driven to Marathon.

208. He now, of his own free will, went as one of the seven youths who with seven maidens were chosen by lot to be sent to Crete as yearly tribute, to be devoured there by the Minotaur. But Ariadne, daughter of Minos, King of Crete, fell in love with Theseus, and gave him a sword and a clue of thread by which he might find his way out of the labyrinth where the Minotaur lived. Theseus slew the monster, released his fellow Athenians, and fled with them and Ariadne, but at Naxos he deserted her and she was consoled by Dionysus, to whom the island was sacred.

209. Theseus forgot on his return to hoist the white sail which was to have been a sign of victory, and Ægeus, seeing the black sail, threw himself in despair into the sea now called Ægean. Theseus then became the King of Athens.

210. He is said to have invaded the country of the Amazons either with Heracles or later, and here he carried off Antiope, who became his wife, though according to another tradition, Theseus took not Antiope but her sister Hippolyte. It is "Hippolyta" who appears as his bride in *The Midsummer Night's Dream*. In revenge the Amazons invaded Attica, and were eventually defeated by Theseus in the midst of Athens itself.

211. Later Theseus married Ariadne's sister Phædra, another daughter of Minos, who bore him the sons Acamas and Demophon. But Phædra fell desperately in love with her step-son Hippolytus (Theseus' son by either Antiope, or Hippolyte), and when the young man rejected her advances she killed herself, after leaving a letter falsely accusing him to Theseus. The enraged Theseus prayed to Poseidon that Hippolytus might die that very day, and the god sent a sea-monster which so terrified the chariot horses of Hippolytus that they dragged him to death. The story is the theme of Euripides' tragedy *Hippolytus*, and the *Phèdre* of Racine.

212. Theseus was a close friend of Pirithous, King of the Lapithae, and attended his wedding to Hippodameia, and when a drunken Centaur attempted to carry off the bride, Theseus joined with the Lapithæ in the famous fight against the Centaurs.

213. After Hippodameia's death, Pirithous and Theseus together carried off the girl Helen of Sparta, and she fell by lot to Theseus. As she was too young to marry, he concealed her in the village of Aphidnæ, where she was cared for by his mother Æthra.

214. Theseus then, full of misgiving, fulfilled his promise to Pirithous to help carry off another daughter of Zeus, by accompanying him to the Underworld to take away Persephone. But Hades chained them both to a rock, where they languished till Heracles came to the Underworld and released Theseus only (*see para.* 184).

215. Meanwhile Helen's brothers, the Dioscuri Castor and Polydeuces, invaded Attica, and being told by Academus where Helen was hidden, they rescued her, taking Æthra as her slave.

216. When Theseus returned from Tartarus he was unable to keep order among his people, who were being stirred up against him by Menestheus. He retired to the island of Scyros, where he was treacherously killed by King Lycomedes. He nevertheless returned in spirit to help the Athenians at the Battle of Marathon, and though Menestheus succeeded Theseus as king, the sons of Theseus were afterwards restored to the throne.

217. Theseus, like Heracles, took part in the heroic enterprises of his age. He joined in the Calydonian hunt and helped Adrastus at Thebes, and he may have been one of the Argonauts.

218. Although Athenians in later times looked on Theseus as an historical figure, ascribing political institutions to him, he was in fact a legendary hero.

CRETAN MYTHS, 219–239.

219. Recent archæological discoveries have indicated that many of the ancient legends concerned with Crete have a factual basis, and a very readable book on the subject is the "Pan" Book *Bull of Minos*, by Leonard Cottrell.

220. In 1899 Sir Arthur Evans began his excavations at Cnossos and soon unearthed the remains of the magnificent, unfortified and labyrinthine so-called "Palace of Minos" with its indications of an elegant and highly artistic civilisation.

221. From the architectural evidence available scholars now consider that there existed in Crete between 2500 and 1400 B.C., a "Minoan" pre-Hellenic culture which had affinities with that of Egypt. This maritime, commercial culture, its sea-power making fortification unnecessary, spread to the mainland of Greece, where it became known as Mycenæan. It is in fact possible that Crete may have exercised some kind of suzerainty over the mainland. The Cretans probably worshipped a goddess who was served by priestesses. The favourite sport was bull-fighting, in which men and women toreadors showed amazing skill. Cretan architects and engineers were exceptionally ingenious.

222. Discoveries such as these give special significance to such legends as that of Minos' sea power, and of Crete's exaction from Athens of a tribute of men and maidens for the Minotaur. Again the constant appearance of the bull in Cretan legend and Dædalus' building of the labyrinth appear to have foundation in historical fact.

223. It was to Crete that Zeus, in the form of a bull, brought Europa, said to be the daughter of Agenor, son of Poseidon and King of Phœnicia and of his wife Telephassa.

224. As the lovely Europa was playing on the sea-shore with her maidens, Zeus appeared as a white bull and she dared to climb on his back, an incident depicted in the masterly painting by

Paul Veronese in the Palace of the Doges in Venice. Suddenly Zeus, plunging into the sea, carried off Europa to Crete, where he fathered on her the three sons, Minos, Rhadamanthus, and Sarpedon. When the reigning king later married Europa he adopted her three sons as his heirs.

225. The brothers quarrelled, however, over the boy Miletus, son of Apollo. As Miletus preferred Sarpedon, they both fled from Minos to Asia Minor. Here Miletus founded the kingdom that bore his name, and Sarpedon, after aiding Cilix, King of Cilicia, against the Lycians, became king of the latter and was permitted by Zeus to live for three generations.

226. Rhadamanthus, though at first ruler of part of Crete, also found it wise to flee. He went to Bœotia, and on Amphitrion's death married Alcmene. So just a ruler did he prove, that he became one of the judges of the Underworld.

227. Minos, now sole ruler of Crete, was confirmed in his power by Poseidon, who sent him a magnificent white bull. This so delighted the king that he withheld it from sacrifice, and when it later ran savage it was captured by Heracles as his Seventh Labour, and eventually slain by Theseus.

228. Minos was the law-giver to Crete and was helped in the defence of the island by Talos, a bull-headed, brazen giant and by his powerful fleet.

229. Curious legends are told of Minos' loves. One was Procris, another Britomartis, a Cretan nymph whom he pursued for nine months, until she leaped into the sea and was deified by Artemis, sharing with her the epithet Dictynna.

230. Once when Minos was besieging Nisa, the fort of Megara, which belonged to King Nisus, Scylla, Nisus' daughter, fell in love with him, and killed her father by cutting off the hair on which his life depended. Although Scylla let him into the city, Minos was so horrified at her parricide that he left her, and she swam after his ship until her father's soul, changed to a sea-eagle, pounced on her, and she was turned to the bird Ciris. Others say that Minos drowned Scylla, and she was turned into the fish Ciris. She has sometimes been confused with Scylla the daughter of Phorcys.

231. The wife of Minos was Pasiphaë daughter of Helios and Persë and several of their children, as Glaucus, Androgeos, Ariadne, and Phædra were the subject of legend.

232. Glaucus when a boy was drowned in a cask of honey, and his body found by the seer Polyeidus. Unable to resuscitate Glaucus, Polyeidus was entombed with him, but here a serpent revealed a herb which restored Glaucus to life, and the seer and the boy were released.

233. Androgeos won every contest in the Pan-thenaic games and was slain at the instigation of Ægeus. Minos in revenge exacted from Athens a yearly tribute of seven youths and maidens to be devoured by the Minotaur.

234. This monster with bull's head and man's body, was the offspring of Pasiphaë and the white bull. Dædalus the craftsman had enabled her to satisfy her desire, and afterwards built the labyrinth in which her shameful offspring was housed.

235. When Ægeus' son Theseus voluntarily joined the youths destined for the Minotaur, Ariadne fell in love with him, and enabled him to kill the monster by giving him a sword and a clue of thread by means of which he found his way out of the labyrinth. Ariadne then escaped with Theseus, but was deserted by him on Naxos, where she was found by Dionysus, as depicted in Titian's " Bacchus and Ariadne " in the National Gallery. Tintoretto's picture in the Doge's Palace in Venice shows the marriage of Ariadne to the god.

236. Her sister Phædra was later married to Theseus, and her unrequited passion for her step-son Hippolytus and its tragic outcome has been described in para. 211.

237. The cunning Dædalus, whose craftsmanship was symbolic of the latest development in sculpture and architecture, had been welcomed by Minos after his flight from Athens. The legend runs that he had been so bitterly jealous of his nephew Talos, or Perdix, inventor of the saw, chisel, and compasses, that he threw him headlong from Athene's temple on the Acropolis. Athene changed Talos into the bird " perdix " or partridge, and the Areopagus banished Dædalus.

238. Welcomed to Crete, he found his skill greatly valued by Minos, until the king discovered how he had aided Pasiphaë. Minos then imprisoned Dædalus with his son Icarus in his own labyrinth. They were released by Pasiphaë, and Dædalus made wings fastened to the shoulders with wax on which they flew away. Icarus mounted too high, the sun melted the wax and he was drowned in the Icarian Sea, but Dædalus reached Cumæ near Naples, and fled thence to Sicily. Here Cocalus welcomed him, and when Minos pursued the craftsman, Cocalus' daughters enabled him ingeniously to kill the king.

239. After Minos' death, although his son succeeded him, Cretan civilisation collapsed. Minos himself became a judge in the Underworld.

THEBAN MYTHS, 240–271.

240. The legend concerning the origin of Thebes is that of Cadmus, who according to common tradition was the son of Agenor, son of Poseidon and the King of Phœnicia, and of his wife Telephassa.

241. The sister of Cadmus, Europa, was one day carried off by Zeus, who appeared to her in the form of a bull (as is described in para. 224) and Agenor sent Cadmus in search of his sister.

242. Unable to find her, Cadmus consulted the Delphic oracle, who advised him to relinquish his search but to follow a cow and build a town where she should sink down with fatigue. Cadmus followed the cow from Phocis to Bœotia, and where she rested he built Cadmea, later the citadel of Thebes.

243. Making sacrifice to Athene, he sent his men for water from a spring of Ares not knowing that it was guarded by a dragon which killed most of his men. When Cadmus had killed the dragon Athene advised him to sow its teeth, and immediately there sprang up, fully armed, the Sparti, or " Sown Men," who fought with each other till only five survived—Echion, Udæus, Chthonius, Hyperenor, and Pelorus. These five were the ancestors of Thebes, and with their help the Cadmea was built.

244. Zeus gave to Cadmus as wife Harmonia, daughter of Ares and Aphrodite, and the Olympian deities attended the wedding. Harmonia received as a gift from Aphrodite the famous necklace made by Hephæstus, which Zeus had originally given Europa, and which conferred irresistible loveliness upon its wearer. From Athene she received a magic robe which conferred divine dignity. The children of Cadmus and Harmonia were Autonoe, Ino, Semele the mother of Dionysus, Agave, Polydorus, and later Illyrius.

245. It is said that Cadmus introduced to Thebes from Phœnicia the use of letters.

246. In old age Cadmus resigned the throne to Pentheus, his grandson, the son of Agave and Echion. But Pentheus, resisting the worship of Dionysus, was destroyed by Agave and her sisters Autonoe and Ino, as is depicted in The Bacchæ of Euripides.

247. Cadmus and Harmonia then left Thebes and were later, in the form of serpents, received in the Islands of the Blessed.

248. Another legend concerning Thebes is that of Amphion and Zethus the twin sons of Antiope by Zeus.

249. Antiope was divorced by her husband Lycus of Thebes, and cruelly treated by his second wife, Dirce. Meanwhile Amphion and Zethus were brought up by cattle men on Mt. Cithæron. When they were old enough to know what had happened they took their revenge. They killed Lycus and Dirce, who was tied to the horns of a wild bull and her body thrown into a fountain which henceforth bore her name, and then took possession of Thebes.

250. Amphion and Zethus now built the lower fortifications below the Cadmea, and so skilfully did Amphion play on the lyre given him by Hermes that the stones moved into place of their own accord. The brothers ruled jointly, Zethus married Thebe, who gave her name to the city, and Niobe became the wife of Amphion.

251. Niobe, the proud daughter of Tantalus and sister of Pelops, had seven sons and seven daughters, and boasted that she was superior to Leto, who had only two children. As punishment to her, Apollo killed the boys with his arrows, and Artemis the girls, and Niobe "all tears" was turned by Zeus into a stone on Mt. Sipylus. The crag of Niobe, being snow-capped, appears to weep when the sun strikes the snow. It is said the Amphion also was either killed by Apollo or that he took his own life.

252. Most famous of Theban kings was Œdipus, who claimed direct descent from Cadmus through Polydorus, Labdacus, and Laius, and all three of the great Greek tragic dramatists were inspired by the fateful story of Œdipus and his children.

253. Œdipus the son of Laius, King of Thebes, and of his wife Jocasta, was as a new-born child exposed on Mt. Cithæron, his feet tied together and pierced with a nail, for Laius had learned from the oracle at Delphi that he would be killed by his own son. Found by a shepherd of Polybus, King of Corinth, the child was called from his swollen feet Œdipus, and was reared by Polybus as his own son.

254. When Œdipus grew to manhood, he was told by the Delphic oracle that he was destined to kill his own father and marry his mother, and he resolved never to return to Corinth. But going from Delphi, he met Laius riding in a chariot, and in a quarrel killed him.

255. Laius had been on his way to ask the Delphic oracle how he could rid Thebes of the Sphinx, a winged lion with the head and breast of a woman. This monster was said to be the off-spring of Typhon and Echidne, or of Orthrus and the Chimæra. Seated on a rock, she challenged each wayfarer with her riddle and strangled him when he failed to solve it.

256. Œdipus, arriving in Thebes, heard the Sphinx's riddle. "Which being, having only one voice, has sometimes two feet, sometimes three, and sometimes four and is weakest when it has most." Œdipus answered rightly that the being was man, who crawls in infancy and supports himself with a staff in old age, and the Sphinx thereupon flung herself to death.

257. As the Thebans had promised that whoever should vanquish the Sphinx should become king and marry Jocasta, Œdipus became King of Thebes and had four children by his own mother, Eteocles, Polyneices, Antigone, and Ismene.

258. Thebes, thus defiled by murder and incest, was visited by plague and the blind seer Teiresias said that the city would be saved when one of the "Sparti" (a title given also to descendants of the "Sown Men") should give his life. When he learned this, Menœceus, father of Jocasta, leapt from the walls to his death.

259. The plague still raging, Œdipus consulted Teiresias, and it is at this point that the famous

Œdipus Tyrannus of Sophocles begins. Œdipus was horrified when at last convinced of his unconscious guilt and, after Jocasta had hanged herself, he blinded himself with a pin taken from her garment and prayed her brother Creon to banish him.

260. Eventually Œdipus went into exile accompanied by Antigone, and followed later by Ismene. At Colonos in Attica he found refuge in a grove of the Eumenides and, protected by Theseus, was received at last by the gods. These last hours of Œdipus are most touchingly presented by Sophocles in his *Œdipus at Colonos.*

261. Angered by his sons' neglect, Œdipus had cursed them, saying that they should divide their inherited land by the sword. They therefore agreed to rule in turn, but when Eteocles' term had expired he refused to abdicate. Polyneices then sought the help of Adrastus, son of Talaus and King of Argos, whose daughter Argia he married while her sister Deipyle married Tydeus (son of Œneus of Calydon), who, on account of some murder he had committed, was also a fugitive.

262. When Adrastus prepared to restore Polyneices, his brother-in-law, the seer Amphiaraus prophesied death for all the leaders save Adrastus. Amphiaraus had married Adrastus' sister Eriphyle and Polyneices, following the advice of Tydeus bribed Eriphyle, giving her the famous necklace of Harmonia on the condition that she would persuade her husband to joint the expedition.

263. Adrastus, Amphiaraus, Polyneices, and Tydeus were joined by Capaneus, Hippomedon and Parthenopaeus, the son of Meleager and Atalanta, and these seven marched against Thebes. The war that followed was dramatised by both Æschylus, in his *Seven against Thebes* and by Euripides, in *The Phœnician Maidens.*

264. After Thebes had suffered initial reverses Teiresias prophesied that a royal prince must sacrifice himself, and a second Menœceus, the son of Creon, now took his own life.

265. The attackers were soon repelled. Capaneus, scaling the walls, was struck by Zeus with lightning. Tydeus, wounded by Melanippus might have been saved by Athene with an elixir given her by Zeus, but Amphiaraus, who bore him a grudge, persuaded him to drink the brains of the dead Melanippus. This so disgusted Athene that she left him to his fate. Hippomedon and Parthenopæus also having been killed, offered to settle the dispute in single combat with Eteocles, but both were mortally wounded. Amphiaraus fled in his chariot and the earth opened and swallowed him. As the seer had prophesied, Adrastus was the only one of the seven left alive.

266. Thebes was not unscathed. The *Antigone* of Sophocles opens at the point where Creon refused to allow burial to Polyneices. The courageous Antigone dared to disobey him and he ordered that she should be imprisoned alive in a cave. Here she hanged herself, and Creon's son Hæmon, to whom she was betrothed, took his own life in despair.

267. Euripides, in *The Suppliants*, dramatise the next phase of the story. Since the Theban had refused burial to their fallen enemies, Adrastus and the mothers of the slain went to Eleusis and secured the help of Theseus. He defeated the Thebans, and the bodies of the Argives receive burial rites, but Evadne, daughter of Iphis and wife of Capaneus threw herself on to the flaming pyre and perished.

268. Thebes was again attacked ten years later when Adrastus assembled the "Epigoni," the descendants of the "Seven." His own son Ægialeus made one, and also Diomedes, son of Tydeus, with his faithful companion Stheneleus son of Capaneus and Evadne.

269. Since Alcmæon, like his father Amphiaraus was unwilling to join the Epigoni, Thersande followed the example of his father Polyneices in once more bribing Eriphyle, this time with the magic robe of Harmonia. She then persuaded Alcmæon to join the expedition along with his brother the seer Amphilochus.

270. Ægialeus was killed before the walls of Thebes, and Teiresias then advised the Thebans to evacuate the city and himself accompanied them, though he died next dawn on drinking from the well of Tilphussa. That day Adrastus, hearing of Ægialeus' death, also died of grief, and in accordance with Teiresias' prophecy the Argives took the empty city.

271. Alcmæon, on return, slew his mother Eriphyle, in revenge for her vanity and deceit towards his father and himself. Pursued by the Erinnyes, he fled to Phlegeus, King of Psophis, who purified him and gave him his daughter Arsinoë in marriage. Alcmæon gave his wife Harmonia's necklace and robe, but was soon forced by the Erinnyes to flee once more. He was next purified by the river-god Achelous and married his daughter Callirrhoë, who soon demanded the necklace and robe. Alcmæon, daring to revisit Psophis, obtained them from Phlegeus on the pretext of taking them to Delphi, but when Phlegeus discovered that they were destined for Callirrhoë he ordered his sons to slay Alcmæon. Finally, Phlegeus himself sent the ill-fated treasures to Delphi.

LEGENDS OF TROY, 272-352.

272. One of the most romantic discoveries of modern times is that of the German Schliemann, who, trusting the descriptions of Homer, excavated a site on the coast of Asia Minor, near the entrance to the Dardanelles. Between 1871 and 1873 he unearthed the foundations not of one Troy but of seven, his most spectacular find being a hoard of exquisite gold ornaments. His work proved that Troy belonged not only to legend but also to history.

273. It is now considered that in the Bronze Age Troy was an important centre for trade. Frequently attacked, it was many times rebuilt, and Greeks, Cretans, and Phrygians all claimed to have had a hand in establishing it. In Homer's time, when the sixth Troy was standing, it had probably absorbed three small towns, Dardania, Tros or Troy, and Ilium, and was probably inhabited by three tribes, Dardanians, Trojans, and Ilians, whose names are all represented in the early legends of Troy's foundation.

274. One of these tells how Scamander of Crete founded a colony in Phrygia, and how, jumping into the River Xanthus, he changed its name to his own. The nymph Idæa bore him a son Teucer (whence the Trojans are called Teucri), and Teucer gave a piece of land to Dardanus, the son of Zeus by the Pleiad Electra, who built there the town of Dardania. The grandson of Dardanus was Tros, who became the father of Ilus and also of Ganymede, whom he relinquished to Zeus for a gift of horses. The son of Ilus was Laomedan.

275. It was to Laomedan that Zeus assigned Apollo and Poseidon as labourers. They built for him the walls of Troy, and when Laomedan refused payment, Poseidon sent the sea-monster, which would have devoured his daughter Hesione had not she been rescued by Heracles. But again Laomedan refused the agreed reward—the white horses given by Zeus in exchange for Ganymede—and Heracles returned later to sack Troy. He gave Hesione to his fellow-warrior Telamon, and killed Laomedan and all his sons save Podarces, who was ransomed by his sister Hesione, and his name changed to Priam, which means " redeemed."

276. After a few years Priam sent Antenor to demand that Telamon should send back Hesione, and the Greeks' scornful refusal was one of the causes of the Trojan War.

277. Priam had fifty sons, nineteen of them by his second wife Hecabe, or Hecuba, who bore him many famous children, including Hector, Paris, Deïphobus and the prophetic twins Helenus and Cassandra. Troilus may have been her son by Apollo.

278. Before the birth of her second son, Hecuba dreamed that she had brought forth a blazing firebrand, and the new-born child was therefore exposed on Mt. Ida. Brought up by a shepherd, he was called Paris, and later, by his courage earned the name Alexander or " defender of men." Paris was beloved by the nymph Œnone, but he deserted her as the result of a tempting suggestion of Aphrodite's.

279. The occasion of this was the famous " Judgment of Paris," of which a Renaissance version can be seen in Rubens' picture in the National Gallery.

280. The story goes that alone of all the gods, Eris was not invited to the marriage of Peleus and Thetis, and in revenge she flung in the golden apple of discord with " to the fairest " inscribed upon it. Immediately Hera, Athene, and Aphrodite disputed its possession, and Zeus commanded Hermes to lead the goddesses to Mt. Ida for Paris to judge the dispute.

281. Although Hera promised him rule in Asia, and Athene fame in war, Paris gave the apple to Aphrodite, who promised him as his wife the loveliest of all women.

282. Paris now discovered his parentage and was joyfully welcomed by Priam, and under Aphrodite's protection sailed to Sparta.

283. His sister Cassandra foretold doom, but was as usual unregarded. In her youth she had been loved by Apollo, who had taught her the art of prophecy on condition that she became his lover. But she had disappointed him, and Apollo had then ordained that her prophecy should never be believed.

284. Welcomed to Sparta by King Menelaus, Paris fell in love with his beautiful queen, Helen, and in Menelaus' absence he succeeded in carrying her off to Troy with much treasure, thus precipitating the Trojan War, now inevitable by reason of an oath sworn by the leading chieftains of Greece to defend Helen's husband.

285. Helen, the daughter of Leda by Zeus, had been brought up in the Court of Leda's husband, Tyndareus of Sparta. So lovely was she that even as a young girl she had been carried off by Theseus and Pirithous, to be rescued and brought back by her brothers, the Dioscuri. All the noblest in Greece then became rivals for her hand, and at the instigation of Tyndareus swore an oath to defend her chosen husband.

286. Helen married Menelaus, and when the Dioscuri were immortalised, he succeeded Tyndareus as King of Sparta.

287. After Helen had fled with Paris, leaving her husband and daughter Hermione, Menelaus summoned the chieftains to war. His powerful brother Agamemnon, King of Mycenæ, who had married Helen's half-sister, Clytemnestra, was leader, and from the Peloponnese came also old Nestor of Pylus, whose Palace has only recently been discovered. Nestor was the only one of Neleus' twelve sons spared by Heracles. Renowned for wisdom and eloquence, he had been a courageous fighter. He had defeated the Arcadians and Eleans and had taken part in the Calydonian hunt and the fight between Centaurs and Lapithæ. Although he had ruled over three generations, he gladly joined the expedition to Troy.

288. The courageous Diomedes, son of Tydeus, and King of Argos, also came from the Peloponnese with eighty ships. He had been one of the Epigoni who had taken Thebes, and two fellow Epigoni came with him—Sthenelus, son of Capaneus, and Euryalus, the Argonaut. Tleopolemus, son of Heracles, the Argive who had settled in Rhodes, brought nine ships, and Palamedes, son of Nauplius, joined the muster from Eubœa.

289. But Agamemnon needed more distant allies, and together with Menelaus and Palamedes, he went to Ithaca to persuade Odysseus to join them.

290. Odysseus was the son of Anticleia, a daughter of the wily thief Autolycus, and of Lærtes, King of Ithaca, though some say that his father was really Sisyphus. He had won his wife Penelope, daughter of King Icarius of Sparta, in a foot race, and when Icarius had tried to persuade Penelope to remain with him, Odysseus had told her she might do as she wished. Penelope had veiled her face to hide her blushes and had followed her husband to Ithaca.

291. An oracle had warned Odysseus not to join the expedition to Troy, and when the envoys arrived they found him ploughing and sowing salt. But the far-sighted Palmedes placed Odysseus' infant son Telemachus in front of the plough, and Odysseus was tricked into revealing his sanity and joining the expedition.

292. Agamemnon also welcomed allies from Salamis and Locris. From Salamis, bringing twelve ships, came Great Ajax, son of King Telamon, a courageous fighter, who boasted that he needed not the help of the gods. His half-brother, Teucer, son of Telamon by Hesione and the best archer in Greece, fought behind Great Ajax' shield. Little Ajax also fought with them. Son of Oileus, King of the Locrians, he was small in stature but swift of foot, and skilled in throwing the spear. He brought forty ships.

293. An important contingent from Southern Thessaly also sailed to Troy, for Calchas, a renegade prophet from Troy, foretold that the city could not be taken without the help of Achilles, son of Peleus, King of the Myrmidones at Phthia in Thessaly, and of the Nereid, Thetis.

294. By dipping her son into the Styx, Thetis had made him invulnerable, except for the heel which she was holding. Achilles had been taught by Cheiron and by his tutor Phœnix, and was renowned for strength, speed, and high courage.

295. Thetis, knowing that if Achilles went to Troy he would never return alive, sent him disguised as a girl to the Court of Lycomedes, King of Scyros, and here Lycomedes' daughter Deidamia bore him the son Neoptolemus, or Pyrrhus. When Odysseus, accompanied by Nestor and Ajax, visited Scyros, he left a spear and shield among a pile of gifts for the maidens, and Achilles, seizing these, revealed his identity.

296. Achilles joined the Greeks together with his tutor Phœnix and Patroclus, his cousin, who had come as a boy to Peleus' Court after an accidental murder and had become the inseparable friend of Achilles.

297. The Greeks were further strengthened by Idomeneus, King of Crete, who brought 100 ships and shared the command with Agamemnon. Meriones accompanied Idomeneus.

298. The fleet was fortunate in being abundantly supplied with provisions, by Anius, son and priest of Apollo in Delos, for his three daughters who had been dedicated to Dionysus received from the god power to produce at will corn, oil, and wine.

299. The expedition set out from Aulis, but first made a false landing and ravaged the country of Telephus, son of Heracles and Auge, and now King of Mysia. When he repelled the Greeks, Dionysus caused him to stumble over a vine, and he was wounded by Achilles. Told by an oracle that his wound could be cured only by him who had inflicted it, he visited the Greeks, who likewise knew through an oracle that they could not take

Troy without the aid of Telephus. Achilles therefore gladly cured him with rust from the spear which had injured him, and Telephus showed the Greeks the route they should take.

300. Assembled a second time at Aulis, the Greeks were delayed by unfavourable winds, for Agamemnon, by killing a hart, had vexed Artemis. Calchas foretold that only the sacrifice of Agamemnon's daughter Iphigenia would appease the goddess, and Agamemnon reluctantly gave his consent, though some say that Artemis snatched Iphigenia from the altar and bore her off to Tauris (*see para.* 396). Certainly the winds changed and the fleet set sail.

301. When they landed on the island of Tenedos, in sight of Troy, Achilles killed King Tenes and his father Cycnus, and here Philoctetes, son of Poeas suffered misfortune. Most famous of the Greek archers, he had been the friend of Heracles, and had received from him the famous bow and had poisoned arrows when he set fire to the hero's funeral pyre on Mt. Œta. He was now injured in the foot by one of these arrows or, as some say, by the bite of a snake, and the smell of the wound became so offensive that, on the advice of Odysseus, Philoctetes was left behind on the island of Lemnos.

302. It was probably from Tenedos that the envoys Menelaus, Odysseus and Palamedes were sent to Priam to request the return of Helen. They were courteously entertained by Antenor, the wisest of the Trojans, who advised that Helen should be sent back, but the Trojans were obdurate.

303. The Greeks then attacked the mainland, and Protesilaus of Thessaly, who was an uncle of Philoctetes, was the first to leap ashore, though he knew through an oracle that it meant death. Wordsworth, in his poem *Laodamia*, tells how Laodamia his wife, the daughter of Acastus, desolate with grief, begged the gods to let her husband return for only three hours. Hermes led Protesilaus to her, and when he died the second time she died with him.

304. Achilles, the second to land on Trojan soil, soon distinguished himself as the most courageous and formidable of all the Greeks.

305. It was against Achilles that Æneas entered the war. At first he took no part, although he was the son of Priam's cousin Anchises. But when Achilles raided his herds on Mt. Ida, he led his Dadanians against the Greeks, and distinguished himself in battle. His mother, Aphrodite, frequently helped him, and once carried him away when wounded by Diomedes, while the god Poseidon, though hostile to Troy, saved him from Achilles.

306. Many cities allied to Troy were raided by Achilles. In Thebes in Cilicia he killed King Eëtion, father of Hector's wife Andromache, while Great Ajax raided the Thracian Chersonesus and in Teuthrania killed the King Teuthras and took his daughter Tecmessa.

307. In the tenth year of the war the Greeks at last concentrated their armies before Troy itself, which was defended by the mighty Hector, by Æneas, and by many allies, including Sarpedon, a son of Zeus, who was in command of the Lycians.

308. The Greeks were hampered by rivalries between the chiefs. Odysseus took a cruel revenge on Palamedes, who had tricked him into joining the forces. He bribed one of Palamedes' servants to hide under his master's bed a letter written in the name of Priam, and then accused Palamedes of treachery. Palamedes' tent was searched, the letter was found, and he was stoned to death by the whole army. Thus perished the sage, who was said to have invented lighthouses, scales, measures, the discus, certain letters of the alphabet, and dice.

309. Then in the tenth year there broke out the notorious quarrel between Achilles and Agamemnon with which the *Iliad* opens. Chryseis, the daughter of the Trojan priest, Chryses had been taken prisoner and assigned to Agamemnon, and when Chryses came to ransom her, Agamemnon roughly repulsed him. Apollo, in revenge, sent a plague among the Greeks, and on Calchas' advice, Agamemnon unwillingly sent Chryseis back. He recompensed himself, however, by seizing Briseis, who had been given to Achilles, and Achilles then stubbornly refused to take any further part in the fighting, though some say that his motive in this was to curry favour with Priam, for he had fallen deeply in love with Priam's daughter Polyxena.

310. The Trojans quickly seized this opportunity to attack, and Agamemnon was glad to grant a truce so that Paris and Menelaus might settle the quarrel by a duel. But when Paris was losing, Aphrodite carried him away and fighting broke out again.

311. Diomedes wounded Æneas and Aphrodite and then strove with Glaucus, a Lycian prince second in command to Sarpedon, but when they remembered the friendship between their fore-fathers they desisted and exchanged gifts. Hector and Ajax fought in single combat till nightfall, when they also exchanged gifts, Hector giving Ajax a sword and receiving a purple baldric.

312. The Greeks, hard-pushed, were now forced to build a wall and trench, and when they were driven back even farther, Agamemnon in alarm offered to return Briseis to Achilles, but he courteously and firmly refused.

313. Diomedes and Odysseus then made a night-raid on the Trojan lines. After killing the spy, Dolon, they slew Rhesus the Thracian and drove off his snow-white horses, for an oracle had declared that once they had drunk of Scamander, and eaten the grass of the Trojan plain, the city would not be taken. The play *Rhesus*, attributed to Euripides, dramatises these incidents from the *Iliad*.

314. Next day, however, the Trojans victoriously set fire to the very ships, and Achilles went so far as to lend Patroclus his own armour and let him lead the Myrmidones. After killing Sarpedon, Patroclus drove the Trojans back to their very walls, until he was at last himself wounded by Euphorbus, son of Panthous, and slain by Hector, who at once stripped him of his borrowed armour, though Menelaus, who had killed Euphorbus, now joined with Ajax in rescuing the body.

315. Achilles was prostrate with grief, but Thetis visited him with new armour made by Hephæstus, and he made peace with Agamemnon, who at last sent Briseis back. Achilles then drove the terrified Trojans back to the city. The noble Hector alone withstood him, though Priam and Hecuba, implored him to come in. Thrice did Achilles chase Hector round the walls of Troy, and then finally killed him, stripped him of his armour, and, tying him by the ankles to his chariot, dragged him ignominiously back to the ship, though some say that Achilles dragged Hector three times round the walls of Troy by the purple baldric that Great Ajax had given him.

316. Each day at dawn Achilles, crazed with grief, pulled the corpse three times round the tomb of Patroclus until at last, in one of the most touching scenes of the *Iliad*, Priam, led by Hermes, went to Achilles' tent and begged to ransom his son's body for burial.

317. The lovely Penthesilea now came to the Trojans' aid. She was the daughter of Otrere and Ares, and Queen of the Amazons. But Achilles killed her, and as he mourned over her, he was ridiculed by Thersites, the ugliest and most scurrilous of the Greeks, and Achilles felled him with a blow. This angered Diomedes, a kinsman of Thersites, and he flung the body of Penthesilea into the Scamander, but it was rescued and honourably buried, some say by Achilles himself.

318. Memnon the black-skinned, handsome son of Eos and Priam's half-brother Tithonus, and King of Ethiopia, now reinforced the Trojans. He killed several Greeks, including Antilochus, the gallant son of Nestor, who, too young to sail from Aulis, joined his father later.

319. The vengeful Achilles then engaged Memnon in fierce single combat while Zeus weighed their fates in the balance. Memnon was slain and, at the request of Eos, Zeus honoured him by causing birds, called Memnonides, to rise from his funeral pyre and fight above it till they fell as a sacrifice. They were said to visit yearly the hero's tomb on the Hellespont.

320. Many great monuments, called Memnonia, were supposed by the Greeks to have been erected in Memnon's honour, the most famous being the colossal statue behind the temple of Egyptian Thebes, which gave forth each sunrise a sound like the breaking of a lyre-string.

321. Achilles' own course was now run, and in a battle near the Scæan gate Paris, aided by Apollo, shot him through the vulnerable ankle.

322. Great Ajax then killed Glaucus, and he and Odysseus rescued the body of Achilles. But they quarrelled violently over the possession of the armour. Homer, in the *Odyssey*, says that Odysseus killed Ajax, and that when he summoned the spirits of the dead, Ajax held sullenly aloof. Sophocles, however, in his tragedy *Ajax*, represents Ajax thrown into madness by defeat and slaying the sheep of the Greeks, believing them to be his rivals, and finally falling on the very sword that Hector had given him.

323. So many heroes dead, the Greeks lost heart, and Calchas said they must fetch the bow and arrows of Heracles. Odysseus and Diomedes therefore sailed to the island of Lemnos, where Philoctetes had been left to languish, and Sophocles, in his play *Philoctetes*, shows how he was persuaded to return.

324. Cured of his wound by one of the sons of Asclepius, either Machaon or Podalirius, Philoctetes challenged Paris to an archery contest. Mortally wounded, Paris besought his former lover Œnone to cure him, but she refused, and then in remorse at his death took her own life, events described by Tennyson in his *Death of Œnone*.

325. Helenus and Deiphobus now quarrelled for the possession of Helen, now homesick for Sparta, and when Deiphobus forcibly married her, Helenus, as some say, fled to Mt. Ida, where either he freely joined the Greeks, or was captured or ensnared by Odysseus, for Calchas had said that only Helenus knew the secret oracles which protected Troy. Helenus said it would fall that summer, if a bone of Pelops were brought to the Greeks, if Achilles' son Neoptolemus, or Pyrrhus, joined them, and if Athene's Palladium were stolen from the citadel.

326. Agamemnon at once sent for the shoulder-blade of Pelops, while Odysseus, Phœnix, and Diomedes went to Scyros and persuaded Lycomedes to let Neoptolemus join them. Odysseus then gave Neoptolemus his father's armour.

327. It is said that Priam now sent Antenor to Agamemnon to sue for peace, but Antenor, out of hatred for Deiphobus, conspired with the Greek leader as to how they might secure the Palladium. They arranged that Odysseus, disguised as a filthy runaway slave, should gain entrance to Troy. Recognised by Helen alone, he gained much useful information, including the confession that she longed to return home. It was either on this occasion that he stole the Palladium, or later when he was accompanied by Diomedes.

328. Odysseus is said to have devised the stratagem of the wooden horse. This was built by the cowardly Epeius, son of Panopeus, under the supervision of Athene, and it bore an inscription

saying that it was dedicated to the goddess. Then twenty-three or more of the bravest Greeks, including Neoptolemus, Odysseus, Sthenelus, and Thoas of Calydon, climbed into the hollow belly.

329. At nightfall, Agamemnon and the remaining Greeks burnt their camp and sailed to the island of Tenedos, leaving behind only Sinon, a cousin of Odysseus and grandson of the cunning Autolycus.

330. At dawn Priam and his sons found the wooden horse on the shore, and believing it to be sacred to Athene, had it hauled in spite of opposition up to the citadel. Cassandra declared that warriors were within it, and she was supported by Laocoön, son of Antenor, and priest to both Apollo and Poseidon, who flung a spear at the horse's flank and caused a clatter of arms. Their warning was, however, neglected, partly because Sinon, who had let himself be taken prisoner, said that the horse was the Greeks' atonement for stealing the Palladium, partly because the fate which now befell Laocoön was misinterpreted.

331. Laocoön had offended Apollo by marrying in spite of vows of celibacy, and the god now punished him by sending two enormous serpents, which crushed to death both the priest and his two sons—a disaster represented in the magnificent sculpture probably dating from the first century B.C. and now in the Vatican. Priam wrongly supposed this to be a punishment for smiting the horse, and it was now welcomed with feasting and revelry.

332. In the evening Helen with Deiphobus strolled round the horse and, imitating in turn the voice of each man's wife, she called to the heroes, who stifled their replies.

333. At night Agamemnon, warned by a beacon lit by Sinon, sailed to the shore, and as Antenor gave the word the warriors within the horse leapt down to slaughter and pillage.

334. Priam had been persuaded by Hecuba to take refuge with her and her daughters before an altar to Zeus, but their son Polites was slain before their very eyes by Neoptolemus, and when the old king feebly tried to attack the slayer, Neoptolemus butchered him also. Odysseus and Menelaus meanwhile killed and mangled Deiphobus, but Menelaus pardoned Helen, and led her safely to the ships.

335. Cassandra fled to the sanctuary of Athene, but Little Ajax roughly dragged her away, and she was claimed as booty by Agamemnon. Her sister Laodice, the wife of Helicaon, was mercifully swallowed up by the earth.

336. Hector's widow Andromache was given to Neoptolemus, and the Greeks, eager to exterminate the whole family of Priam, even killed her infant son Astyanax, by hurling him to death from the city walls, fearful lest he should one day avenge his parents.

337. At the demand of Achilles' ghost Polyxena was sacrificed to him by Neoptolemus, to ensure favourable winds. Some say this happened at Troy, others only when the Greek fleet had reached Thrace.

338. Hecuba fell to the share of Odysseus, who took her to the Thracian Chersonesus, and there she avenged the death of one of her sons. Polydorus, the youngest of Priam's sons, had, according to Homer, been slain by Achilles, but later accounts speak of another son of the same name. Just before the fall of Troy Priam had entrusted him, together with much gold, to Polymester, King of the Thracian Chersonesus, and when Troy fell Polymester murdered Polydorus for his gold and cast him into the sea. Hecuba discovered the body. She contrived to kill Polymestor and his two sons, and she then evaded the angry Thracians by turning herself into a bitch named Mæra.

339. Euripides combined this story of Hecuba's revenge with that of the sacrifice of her daughter Polyxena in his tragedy *Hecuba*.

340. Few of the inhabitants of Troy escaped death or slavery. The wise Antenor, his wife Theano, and their children were all spared, and were said to have sailed to the West Coast of the Adriatic and there to have founded Venice and Padua.

341. Æneas' carried on his back his blind father Anchises through the Dardanian gate and so to safety. The Romans said that he took with him the Palladium, that stolen by Odysseus being only a replica, and, after seven years' wandering, reached Latium, where he founded Lavinia, and became their ancestral hero.

342. Æthra, the mother of Theseus, who had served Helen as a slave, was rescued by her grandsons, Acamas and Demophon, the sons of Theseus and Phædra.

THE RETURNS FROM TROY.

343. Part of the ancient " Epic Cycle " of the Greeks was the cycle known as " The Returns," which was used both by Homer and Æschylus. It told of the adventures of the Greeks on their way home. Most suffered misfortune.

344. The fate of Agamemnon is described in para. 386–388, and that of Odysseus in para. 353–369.

345. Menelaus, who failed to sacrifice to Athene, took eight years, and only by seizing Proteus learned how to reach Sparta, where he married Hermione to Neoptolemus.

346. Neoptolemus had been accompanied by Andromache and by Helenus, who prophesied a safe route. He had abandoned his kingdom in Thessaly and settled in Epirus, part of which he gave to Helenus, who married Andromache. Neoptolemus then claimed Hermione, although her grandfather, Tyndareus, had betrothed her to Orestes, and as a result he was murdered, either by Orestes himself or at his instigation.

347. Many Greeks settled in Italy. Diomedes, hated by Aphrodite, finding on his return to Argos that his wife had been unfaithful, left for Ætolia to help his grandfather Œneus, and later settled in Daunia in Italy, where he married Euippe, daughter of King Daunus. He was buried in one of the islands since called Diomedeans, and his companions were turned into gentle birds. Philoctetes also settled in Italy.

348. Idomeneus, caught by tempest on his return to Crete, vowed to sacrifice to Poseidon the first person he met on return. As this was his own son, Crete was punished by pestilence, and Idomeneus exiled. He settled in Calabria in Italy.

349. Demophon, son of Theseus visited Thrace and gained the love of the king's daughter, Phyllis, but when he left her to visit Athens, she killed herself in despair of his return and was turned into a tree.

350. Many sailors were ship-wrecked on the dangerous promontory of Caphareus, where Nauplius, King of Eubœa, eager to avenge the death of his son Palamedes, lighted misleading fires.

351. The seer, Calchas, like Amphilochus, went safely overland to Colophon. Here he contended in prophecy with Mopsus, a son of Apollo and Manto, the daughter of Teiresias, and being surpassed, he died of grief. Amphilochus joined with Mopsus in founding the city of Mallus, but they killed each other in a fight for its possession.

352. Nestor alone returned home without mishap and enjoyed a happy old age.

THE WANDERINGS OF ODYSSEUS
353–369.

353. Odysseus' journey home, lasting ten years, and his final arrival in Ithaca are the theme of Homer's epic the *Odyssey*. E. V. Rieu says that this may be thought of as a novel, and Samuel Butler argued that it might well have been written by a woman! The incidents of the *Odyssey* form the background of reference to the *Ulysses* of James Joyce.

354. After leaving Troy, Odysseus and his men visited the Cicones, where he obtained several jars of sweet wine, and then they landed on the Libyan promontory of the Lotophagi. Here lived the Lotus-eaters, who gave his men some of the fruit, inducing the enervating dreaminess described by Tennyson in *The Lotus-eaters*.

355. Next, landing on the west coast of Sicily, Odysseus, with twelve companions, entered the cave of a giant, but when the owner, the one-eyed Cyclops, Polyphemus, son of Poseidon, came in with his flocks, he blocked the entrance with a gigantic stone, and devoured two of Odysseus' companions. Next evening, by which time only six of his men survived, Odysseus made Polyphemus drunk with his sweet wine and then blinded him. At dawn the Greeks escaped by clinging under the bodies of the sheep as they went out to graze, and so reached their ship, but henceforth they had to reckon with the vengeful hostility of Poseidon.

356. Odysseus was next entertained by Æolus, who gave him a bag of winds, but when his foolish crew untied this, they were blown back to Æolus, who now refused further help.

357. In Telepylos, city of Lamus, King of the cannibal Læstrygones, Odysseus lost all his ships except one, but in this he reached Æea, the island of the enchantress Circe, daughter of Helios and Perse. Men sent by Odysseus to explore were turned by her to swine, and only Eurylochus returned to tell the news. Odysseus, hastening to their rescue, was given, by Hermes, the plant Moly, which vanquished Circe's charms. She restored his companions and lavishly entertained them all for a year.

358. Then, on Circe's advice, Odysseus sought the counsel of the dead seer Teiresias. He sailed to the River Oceanus, and in the land of the Cimmerians summoned the spirits of the dead, who thronged to lap the blood of a libation he had prepared. First appeared Elpenor, one of his crew, who while drunk had fallen to death from Circe's roof. Later came Teiresias, who gave him prophetic advice, and then Anticleia, the mother of Odysseus, the men and women of antiquity, and his former comrades.

359. He again visited Circe, who advised him how to circumvent the Sirens and Scylla and Charybdis. Odysseus nullified the Sirens' spell by having himself lashed to the mast, and by filling the sailors' ears with wax, and he just avoided the whirlpool Charybdis, though Scylla's six mouths snatched and devoured as many of his seamen.

360. At the island of Thrinacia, against the warnings both of Teiresias and Circe, Odysseus' companions slaughtered the cattle of Helios, and when they put to sea Zeus destroyed all save Odysseus himself.

361. Clinging to wreckage, he drifted ten days until he reached the island of Ogygia. Here the nymph Calypso lovingly kept him for eight years, until at Athene's request Zeus sent Hermes to command his release.

362. On a raft that Calypso had taught him to make, Odysseus sailed for eighteen days, till it was wrecked by vengeful Poseidon. Then helped by Leucothea and Athene, Odysseus landed on the island of Scheria. Here he was led by the beautiful Nausicaa to the Court of her father

Alcinous, who was the prosperous ruler of the Phæacians. Alcinous gave Odysseus a ship, and after an absence of ten years he at last landed in Ithaca. Athene disguised him as a beggar and he was hospitably welcomed by his swineherd Eumæus.

363. Odysseus' mother Anticleia had died of grief, Lærtes his father had withdrawn to the country, and his wife Penelope had been keeping at bay a crowd of unruly suitors led by Antinous. She had promised to wed one of them when she had finished a robe for Lærtes, but each night she unpicked the work of the day, until her servants betrayed her ruse, and she was now hard-pressed. Her son Telemachus had gone in search of Odysseus, and after visiting Nestor and Menelaus, he now returned to Ithaca and also visited the hut of Eumæus.

364. Here Odysseus made himself known to Telemachus and they planned revenge. First the son set out for home, followed later by Odysseus still in beggar's disguise. He was recognised only by his aged hound Argus, which at once expired, and by his nurse Eurycleia.

365. Next day Penelope announced that she would accept the suitor who could shoot with the great bow of Eurytus which only Odysseus had been able to wield. No one could bend it till Odysseus seized it and shot Antinous. Supported by Telemachus, he killed the suitors, and at last made himself known to Penelope. He then visited Lærtes, but the kinsmen of the suitors rose against him and battle ensued until Athene, disguised as Mentor effected a reconciliation.

366. At this point the *Odyssey* ends, though Teiresias had prophesied that Odysseus must again set out on a journey and propitiate Poseidon and then return to an honourable old age till death came to him from the sea.

367. Tennyson, in his poem *Ulysses*, imagines him, even in age, hungry still for travel.

368. Another tradition says that Telegonus, son of Odysseus by Circe, while searching for his father, landed on Ithaca and began to plunder for food. When opposed by Odysseus and Telemachus, all unknowing he killed his father. He then took Telemachus and Penelope back to Æea, and there married Penelope, while Telemachus married Circe.

369. Although Homer represents Penelope as a faithful wife, other writers say that she became the mother of Pan, either by Hermes or by all the suitors. It is a tradition such as this that Joyce evidently follows in his *Ulysses*.

LEGENDS OF THE HOUSE OF PELOPS,
370–398.

370. Some of the most dramatic of all Greek stories have their setting in Mycenæ, city of the legendary hero Agamemnon. In 1876 Schliemann began excavation on this ancient site, and here he unearthed the famous shaft-graves with their precious treasures, which probably date from 1600 B.C., four centuries before the era of Agamemnon and the siege of Troy. Schliemann thus proved to the learned world that the city at all events was historical, and scholars now believe that it was the centre of a Late Bronze Age culture.

371. According to legend, Agamemnon was a descendant of Tantalus, son of Zeus and the nymph Pluto and father of Pelops, Broteas, and Niobe. Tantalus was said to be a wealthy king, but whether of Lydia, Argos or Corinth, is uncertain.

372. Highly favoured by his father Zeus, Tantalus was even invited to Olympian banquets, but he proved unworthy of such honours, divulging Zeus' secrets and stealing nectar and ambrosia from Olympus.

373. Tantalus was also said to have received from Pandareus a dog made of gold, and then to have sworn by Zeus that he had never seen or heard of it. As this dog was the one which Hephæstus had made for Rhea, and which she had set to watch the cradle of the infant Zeus, the gods were naturally incensed. Pandareus perished miserably, and his orphan daughters were carried off by Harpies, and Tantalus suffered agonising punishment for this and other crimes, the most ghastly of which was his murder of his son Pelops. Having invited the gods to a banquet, he cut Pelops into pieces and served them in a stew. Demeter, still grieving for Persephone, was the only divinity who did not notice what she was eating, and she consumed the shoulder.

374. Tantalus' punishment became proverbial. Tortured with thirst, he was placed in a lake whose waters receded whenever he attempted to drink, while above his head were laden fruit boughs which flew upwards as soon as he reached for them. Thus " tantalised," he also saw suspended above his head a huge rock which threatened to fall and crush him.

375. After punishing Tantalus, Zeus ordered Hermes to put the limbs of Pelops into a cauldron and boil them. Clotho took him from the cauldron, Demeter gave him an ivory shoulder, which became a kind of birthmark for his descendants, and Pelops was restored to life.

376. Pelops was later expelled from his kingdom of Phrygia and came with his followers to Pisa in Elis. Here Œnomaus, son of Ares, was king, and as an oracle had said that he would be killed by his son-in-law, he challenged to a chariot race all who came to woo his daughter, Hippodameia. If the young man won, he would marry Hippodameia, if not he would be killed by the spear of Œnomaus, which, like his wind-begotten horses, was a gift of his father Ares.

377. Many suitors had lost their lives when Pelops arrived in Pisa. He was already possessed of a winged golden chariot, the gift of Poseidon, but he also bribed Œnomaus' charioteer Myrtilus, the son of Hermes, with the promise of half the kingdom, to remove the lynch-pin from the chariot of his master and substitute one of wax. Œnomaus was flung out and killed, and Pelops married Hippodameia.

378. Pelops refused to keep faith with Myrtilus and flung him into the sea. Myrtilus, as he died, cursed the whole race of Pelops, and his image was set among the stars as the charioteer by his father Hermes. Pelops soon became master of Olympia and revived the Olympic Games. His wealth and power in the peninsula were so great that it was called the Peloponnesus, or " Island of Pelops."

379. The eldest sons of Pelops, Atreus and Thyestes, with the connivance of their mother, killed Chrysippus, their half-brother, and were obliged to flee their home.

380. They were kindly received at Mycenæ, and after the death of King Eurystheus, Atreus seized the kingdom in spite of the bitter rivalry of Thyestes, whom he forthwith banished.

381. Thyestes, however, who had already succeeded in seducing Atreus' second wife Ærope, now tricked his brother into killing Pleisthenes, his own son by his first wife. Atreus, planning grisly reprisals, lured Thyestes to Mycenæ by promising him half the kingdom. He then killed the sons of Thyestes and served him their flesh at a banquet. When the horror-stricken father realised what he had eaten, he laid a curse on the house of Atreus and fled once more.

382. Thyestes, seeking revenge, was advised by the Delphic Oracle to beget a son by his own daughter, and going to King Threspotus at Sicyon, where his daughter Pelopia was a priestess, he ravished her and fled.

383. Atreus now visited Sicyon, and, believing Pelopia to be a daughter of Threspotus, married her as his third wife. When she gave birth to Thyestes' son, Ægisthus, she exposed the baby, but Atreus, believing Ægisthus to be his own child, took him in and reared him.

384. When later Thyestes was seized and brought back to Mycenæ, Atreus commanded Ægisthus to slay him, but Thyestes disarmed the boy, and recognising him as his own son, ordered him to kill Atreus. Then, at last, Thyestes ruled in Mycenæ.

385. According to Homer, Atreus had two sons by Ærope, Agamemnon and Menelaus, and these two now took refuge with King Tyndareus of Sparta. Here Menelaus married Helen, daughter by Zeus of Tyndareus' wife, Leda, and some say that Agamemnon was helped by Tyndareus to expel Thyestes and gain his father's throne.

386. Agamemnon's wife was Clytemnestra (the daughter of Tyndareus and Leda), whom he forcibly married after killing her first husband in battle. But when his brother's wife, Helen, was stolen away by Paris, and the Trojan War broke out, Agamemnon was away fighting for ten years, and it was not difficult then for Ægisthus to seduce Clytemnestra.

387. Not only had Agamemnon forcibly married Clytemnestra, but he had also agreed to the sacrifice of their daughter, Iphigeneia at Aulis, and her cup of bitterness was full when she learned that he was returning from Troy, bringing with him Priam's daughter, the prophetess Cassandra, as his mistress.

388. It is at this point that Æschylus' great trilogy of the *Oresteia* begins. Clytemnestra conspired with Ægisthus to kill both Agamemnon and Cassandra. She welcomed her husband royally on his return, but while he was in his bath entangled him in a net, and after Ægisthus had twice struck him, she beheaded him with an axe. She then went out to kill Cassandra, who had refused to enter the palace because, in visionary trance, she was horrified to smell the ancient shedding of blood and the curse of Thyestes (*see para.* 381).

389. It was not difficult now for Clytemnestra to seize power, for Orestes, her young son, had been smuggled out of Mycenæ by his sister Electra, and for many years Clytemnestra and her paramour ruled in Mycenæ.

390. Ægisthus, however, lived in constant fear of vengeance. He would have killed Electra had Clytemnestra allowed, so he married her to a peasant, who was fearful of consummating their union. Orestes meanwhile had taken refuge with Strophius, King of Phocis, who had married Agamemnon's sister, and here he formed that friendship with the king's son, Pylades, which became proverbial.

391. The intensely dramatic situation at this point has inspired all three of the great Greek tragedians, and it is most interesting to compare the various interpretations given by Æschylus, in *The Libation Bearers*, the second play of his trilogy, by Sophocles, in *Electra*, and by Euripides, in *Electra*.

392. Electra, burning for revenge, sent constant messages to Orestes, and when he and Pylades were of age they came secretly to Mycenæ, and with Electra's help killed both Ægisthus and Clytemnestra.

393. The agonising punishment that Orestes now endured is portrayed in the *Eumenides*, the last play of Æschylus' trilogy, and in the *Orestes* of Euripides. Although the Delphic Oracle had encouraged Orestes to avenge his father, she was powerless to prevent his being pursued by the Erinnyes, the avengers of matricide, who drove him mad and hounded him from land to land. At length, on the further advice of the Pythian Priestess, he reached Athens and embraced the image of Athene in her temple on the Acropolis. The goddess then summoned the Areopagus to judge his case. Apollo defended him against the Erinnyes on the grounds that motherhood is less important than fatherhood, and he was acquitted by the casting vote of Athene, the verdict being a triumph for the patriarchal principle.

394. The furious Erinnyes were then pacified by Athene, who persuaded them to accept a grotto in Athens, where they would be offered sacrifices, libations, and first fruits. Their name henceforward was Eumenides, or the " well-meaning."

395. According to another tradition, followed by Euripides, in his *Iphigeneia Among the Taurians,* Orestes was told by Apollo that he would be freed from madness by fetching the statue of Artemis from the Tauric Chersonese.

396. When Orestes and Pylades reached Tauris they were seized by the barbarous natives, who sacrificed all strangers to Artemis, but they found to their amazement that the priestess was none other than Orestes' own sister Iphigeneia. Orestes believed that she had lost her life when sacrificed to Artemis at Aulis (as is described in para. 300), but she had in fact been rescued by the goddess and brought to Tauris as her priestess.

397. Iphigeneia, by her ready wit, rescued Orestes and Pylades from sacrifice, and all three returned to Greece, carrying with them the image of the goddess. Here they were reunited with Electra, and returned to Mycenæ, where Orestes, by killing Ægisthus' son and becoming king, finally ended the strife between the sons of Atreus.

398. Orestes, after killing his rival Neoptolemus, married his cousin Hermione, and Electra was married to Pylades.

THE UNDERWORLD, 399–409.

399. The Greeks expected to enter after death into the cheerless nether world, the domain of Hades, known to the Romans as Orcus, or Dis, but as Hades was possessor of all the rich metals and gems of the earth, the ancients usually preferred the euphemism " Pluto," " the wealth," when speaking of one so dreaded.

400. The word " Hades " was used too of his actual domain, which was also called Tartarus, although in the *Iliad,* the word " Tartarus " had been reserved for the very lowest region of the Underworld, where the rebel Titans had been thrust.

401. Hades, son of Cronus and Rhea, won the lordship of the nether world when his brother Zeus won the sky, and Poseidon the sea. His most treasured possessions were the helmet of darkness, given him by the Cyclopes, and the staff with which he drove the ghosts.

402. He ruled with his queen, Persephone, whom he had forcibly abducted from the upper world, but he was not always faithful to her, and she once changed the nymph Minthe, whom he was pursuing into the plant mint, and the nymph Leuce, whom he loved, was afterwards changed into the white poplar.

403. The companion to Persephone was Hecate, who had once aided Demeter in her search for the lost maiden. Hecate was a mysterious divinity, a triple goddess, mighty in heaven, on earth, and in the Underworld, honoured by Zeus and all the immortal gods. She came to be regarded by the Hellenes as primarily a dread divinity of the Underworld, as one who kept company with the dead and who fostered sorcery and witchcraft. She figures as such in *Macbeth.* Worshipped where three roads met, she was represented with three bodies and three heads.

404. Also dwelling in the Underworld were the Erinnyes, winged daughters of earth or of night, with serpent hair, who punished unnatural crime. They were later known euphemistically, as the " Eumenides," or " well-meaning," and this name was said to have been given them after the acquittal of Orestes, as is portrayed in the *Eumenides* of Æschylus. Late writers named three Erinnyes, Alecto, Megæra, and Tisiphone.

405. Ghosts conducted to Hades' realm by Hermes had first to cross the Styx, the " hated " river, and supplied by relatives with a coin laid under the tongue of the corpse, they paid the surly ferryman Charon. Without this coin they were unable to cross the Styx. Arrived on the farther bank, they propitiated Cerberus, represented by later writers as a fierce dog with three heads, said to be another of the monsters born to Echidne.

406. Styx was not the only river ghosts encountered. There was also Acheron, river of woe, Phlegethon, river of flames, Cocytus, river of wailing, and Lethe, the river of forgetfulness, where ghosts drank and forgot their past.

407. The three judges of the Underworld were Æacus, Rhadamanthus, and Minos. Wicked spirits were sent by them to the place of punishment, those who had led an indifferent life to the cheerless asphodel fields, and the virtuous to Elysium.

408. Although Elysium was said to be near the Underworld, it formed no part of Hades' dominion, and Homer placed it far away to the west of the earth, near Oceanus. It was a blessed abode, without cold or snow. Later writers also spoke of the " Fortunate Isles," located by Greek geographers as beyond the pillars of Heracles, and eventually identified with the Canary and Madeira islands.

409. In their picture of life after death the Greeks combined contradictory ideas. Broadly speaking, the figures of Persephone and Hecate represent the hopes of pre-Hellenic people for an after-life, while Hades personifies the Hellenic fear of the finality of death.

Part III. INDEX AND GLOSSARY

Note : The numbers in this part refer to the numbered paragraphs in Part II.

Abas. (1) Son of Celeus and Metanira, turned by Demeter into a lizard because he mocked her when she drank too eagerly. *See also* 113.
　(2) The grandson of Danaus and twelfth King of Argolis, was renowned for his sacred shield, the very sight of which subdued revolt. He was father of the twins Acrisius and Proetus.

Abderus, 180.

Absyrtus (or Apsyrtus), 159.

Abyla, 182.

Academus, 215.

Acamas, a son of Theseus and Phædra, went with Diomedes to Troy to demand the surrender of Helen. *See also* 211, 342.

Acastus was the son of Pelias, King of Iolcos. He joined the Argonauts, but after Medea had caused the death of Pelias, Acastus banished her and Jason. He later received Peleus kindly, but when he falsely suspected his guest of making love to his wife, he treacherously deserted him. Acastus and his wife were later slain by Peleus. The daughter of Acastus was Laodamia.

Apollo, 10, 14, 26, 32, 36, 68–80, 82–85, 92, 94, 104, 183, 251, 277 283, 298, 309, 321, 330, 331, 351, 393, 395.

Apple of Discord, 280.

Arachne, a Lydian maiden who challenged Athene to compete with her in weaving. When Athene found Arachne's work faultless, she angrily tore it up, and the terrified maiden hanged herself. Athene then turned her into a spider and the rope into a cobweb.

Arcadia, 85, 92, 97.

Arcas, son of Zeus and Callisto, who was supposed to have given his name to Arcadia.

Arctos, see Callisto.

Areopagus, 43, 67, 105.

Ares, see especially 64–67 and also 10, 13, 14, 25, 33, 55, 60, 61, 154, 158, 178, 243, 317, 376.

Arethusa, 88.

Arges, 1.

Argia, 261.

Argo, The, 155–160, 162.

Argonauts, 154–160.

Argos, 30, 33, 34, 45, 125, 130, 142, 143.

Argus. (1) The hound of Odysseus, 364.
(2) The hundred-eyed, 95.
(3) The builder of Argo, 155.

Aria, the mother of Miletus by Apollo.

Ariadne, 231, 235.

Arion. (1) An actual historical character was a lyric poet and player on the lyre, who lived at the Court of Periander of Corinth at about 625 B.C. The following curious fable is told of him, On one occasion Arion visited Sicily and won the prize in a musical contest. Laden with gifts, he took ship for Corinth, and the captain and crew decided to murder him for his treasure. They gave him permission to sing one last song. Arion then invoked the gods, and leapt into the sea. Here he was rescued by one of the music-loving dolphins that had gathered to hear his song, and taken on its back to Corinth, where he told Periander of his adventures. Later, when the ship arrived, the captain and crew swore that Arion had been detained in Sicily. Periander then confronted them with Arion himself and had them executed. The images of Arion and his lyre were set among the stars.
(2) A fabulous horse, 103.

Aristæus was the son of Apollo and Cyrene, born in Libya. He went to Thrace and fell in love with Eurydice, who, fleeing from him, perished by a snake bite. As a punishment Aristæus lost his bees, and how he raised a new swarm is told in Virgil's fourth Georgics. After death was worshipped as a god.

Arsinoë, 271.

Artemis, 10, 13, 14, 26, 69, 70, 72, 81–89, 251, 229, 300.

Ascalaphus, 112, 184.

Asclepius or Æsculapius was a son of Apollo by Coronis. He was brought up by Cheiron, who taught him healing. He once recalled a dead man to life and was killed by Zeus with a thunderbolt. At Apollo's request, however, he was placed among the stars. Another tradition says that Asclepius was a native of Epidaurus. In Homer he was not a god, but the " blameless physician," father of Machaon and Podalirius, physicians to the Greek Army. His supposed descendants were the Asclepiadæ, a caste of priests who transmitted from father to son the knowledge of medicine as a sacred secret. Epidaurus was the centre of Asclepius' worship. Cocks were sacrificed to him and serpents sacred.

Asopus, a river god, son of Oceanus and Tethys, and father of Evadne, Eubœa, and Ægina.

Astarte, 57.

Astræus, a Titan, was father, by Eos, of the beneficent winds and, some say, of the stars also.

Astyanax, 336.

Atalanta. (1) The Arcadian Atalanta, daughter of Iasus and Clymene, was exposed by her father and suckled by a bear. She always carried arms. She joined the Calydonian hunt and bore a son, Parthenopæus, to Meleager. Reconciled to her father, she refused to marry unless a suitor should conquer her in a foot race, those who failed in the attempt being killed by her. Eventually Milanion outstripped Atalanta by dropping in her way one after the other, three golden apples given him by Aphrodite. Atalanta stopped to gather these and lost the race. See also 263.
(2) The Bœotian Atalanta was said to be daughter of Schœneus and to have married Hippomenes, but the same tales are told of her. See Swinburne's play Atalanta in Calydon and the poem Atalanta's Race, by William Morris.

Athamas, was the son of Æolus and King of Orchomenus in Bœotia. At Hera's command he married Nephele, and had children Phrixus and Helle. But Athamas secretly loved Ino, daughter of Cadmus and Harmonia, who bore him Learchus and Melicertes. Deceived by Ino's intrigues, Athamas would have sacrificed Phrixus, had not a ram with a golden fleece, sent by Hermes, rescued the boy and flown through the air with him and his sister Helle. Between Europe and Asia, Helle fell into the straits since called Hellespont, but Phrixus reached Colchis, where he sacrificed the ram to Zeus and gave the fleece to Æëtes, from whom it was later carried off by Jason. Meanwhile Athamas, driven mad by Hera because he had sheltered Dionysus, killed his son Learchus, and Ino flung herself into the sea with Melicertes, where both were transformed into marine deities. Ino became Leucothea, and Melicertes changed to Palæmon. Athamas, forced to flee, settled in Thessaly. See also 120.

Athene, see especially 38–45 and also 14, 15, 48, 66, 77, 102, 105, 134, 135, 141, 148, 155, 178, 184, 189, 243, 244, 265, 280, 281, 325, 328, 330, 335, 345, 361, 362, 393, 394.

Athens, 42, 48, 86, 97, 102, 105, 112, 114, 117, 118, 128.

Atlantiades, 91.

Atlantis was a legendary island, west of the Pillars of Hercules. Its virtuous and powerful inhabitants, becoming degenerate, were defeated by the Athenians, and the island was swallowed up by the ocean in a day and night. See the Timæus of Plato.

Atlas, the son of Iapetus and Clymene, was father of the Pleiades, Hyades, and Hesperides. See also 7, 9, 16, 91, 138, 183.

Atlas, Mt., 136, 183.

Atreus, 379, 380, 381, 383, 384, 385, 397.

Atropos, one of the Fates.

Auge, 191.

Augeias, stables of, 177, 190.

Aulis, 299, 300, 318, 387.

Autolycus, 96, 167, 290, 329.

Autonoe, 244, 246.

Bacchæ, 117, 123. Also called Bacchantes, Mænads, or Thyiads.

"Bacchæ, The," 123, 246.

Bacchoi, 117.

Bacchus, a name for Dionysus, 117–128.

Bassareus was an epithet of Dionysus. " Bassaris " was a fox-skin which was worn by the god and also the Mænads in Thrace. Hence Bassaris means Mænad or Bacchante.

Bathos, 12

Baucis, see Philemon.

Bebrycos, 157.

Bellerophon, 145–150.

Bellerus, 146.

Belus, son of Poseidon and father of Ægyptus, Danaus, and Cepheus.

Bias, brother of Melampus.

Biton and Cleobis, sons of a priestess of Hera at Argos, in their filial devotion once dragged their mother's chariot to the temple. Their mother prayed Hera to grant them the best gift for mortals, and they both died while asleep in the temple.

Bœotia, 117, 120, 123.

Boreas, the North wind, was the son of Astræus and Eos, and brother to the other beneficent

Creon. (1) Of Corinth, 162.
    (2) Of Thebes, 259, 266.

Cretan Bull, 179, 227.

Crete, 68, 81, 90, 128, 219–239.

Cretheus, 152, 153.

Creusa. (1) Daughter of Creon of Corinth, 162.
    (2) Wife of Xuthus.

Crommyum, Sow of, 205.

Cronus, son of Uranus and Ge and father, by his sister Rhea, of Hestia, Demeter, Hera, Poseidon, Hades, and Zeus. *See also* 1–9.

Cumæ, 12.

Curetes, 6.

Cyclades, 132.

Cyclopes. Different accounts are given of the Cyclopes. Hesiod describes them as Titans (*see* 1, 3, 4, 8, 9). Homer speaks of them as one-eyed giant shepherds in Sicily, the Chief being Polyphemus (*see* 355). Later tradition describes them as helpers of Hephæstus living in Mt. Ætna (*see* 54). The walls of unhewn stone in Mycenæ and other ancient sites are known as Cyclopean (*see* 130, 143).

Cycnus, 301.

Cyllene, Mt., 92.

Cyllenius, 92.

Cynthus, a mountain in Delos where Leto bore Apollo and Artemis, hence called Cynthus, and Cynthia.

Cyprus, 58, 59.

Cyrene, daughter of Hypseus, was beloved by Apollo and became the mother of Aristæus. She was carried by Apollo from Mt. Pelion to Libya, where the city Cyrene was named after her.

Cythera, 58, 59.

Dactyli were beings who were supposed to have discovered iron and the art of working it by fire. Mt. Ida in Phrygia was their original abode.

Dædalus, 222, 234, 237, 238.

Danæ, 130, 131, 132, 133, 141, 142.

Danai, used in Homer of the Greeks.

Danaides were the fifty daughters of Danaus, son of Belus and King of Libya. Danaus' brother Ægyptus, the father of fifty sons, suggested a mass marriage, and Danaus in fear fled with his daughters to Argos, where he was elected king in place of Gelanor. The fifty sons of Ægyptus followed Danaus and asked for his daughters as wives. Danaus agreed, but gave each daughter a weapon with which to kill her bridegroom on the bridal night. All complied save Hypermnestra, who spared her husband Lynceus. Lynceus, after killing Danaus, became King of Argos. The story is the theme of Æschylus's play *The Suppliants.* In Hades the Danaides were condemned continually to carry water in sieves.

Danaus, *see* Danaides.

Daphne, a daughter of the river god Peneus in Thessaly, was pursued by Apollo in the vale of Tempe, but when she cried for help she was turned into a laurel-tree, which became the favourite tree of Apollo. The myth probably refers to the Hellenes' capture of Tempe, where the goddess Daphœne was worshipped by Mænads who chewed the laurel and thus intoxicated themselves. Afterwards only Apollo's Pythoness might chew laurel.

Daphnis was a son of Hermes and a nymph, who exposed him in a laurel grove. He was adopted by Sicilian shepherds, taught by Pan to play the pipes, and was looked on as the inventor of bucolic poetry. He was blinded by a nymph to whom he was faithless, and Hermes caused the fountain Daphnis at Syracuse to spring up in his honour.

Dardania, 273, 274.

Dardanus, 274.

Daulia or **Daulis** was an ancient town in Phocis It was the residence of Tereus and the scene of the story of Philomela and Procne, who are hence called Daulias.

Daunus, 347.

Deianeira, 192, 193, 194, 195, 196, 197.

Deidamia, 295.

Deiphobus, 277, 325, 327, 332, 334.

Deipyle, 261.

Delian Homeric Hymn, 71.

Delos, 69, 70.

Delphi, 69, 71, 72, 76, 117, 118, 171, 186, 242, 253, 254, 271, 382, 393.

Delphinos, 106.

Demeter, 7, 10, 25, 99, 103, 110–116, 373, 375.

Demodocus, 60.

Demophon. (1) Son of Celeus and Metaneira who received Demeter hospitably. In return the goddess tried to make their son immortal by holding him over the fire, but the scream of Metaneira broke the spell and Demophon died.
    (2) Son of Theseus, 199, 211, 342, 349.

Despœna, 103.

Deucalion, 20, 21.

Diana, 81, 89.

Dictæan Cave, 6.

Dicte, a mountain in the east of Crete, where Zeus was brought up, and hence called Dictæus.

Dictynna, 81, 229.

Dictys, 132, 141, 142.

Diomedes, Mares of, 180.

Diomedes, son of Tydeus, 268, 288, 305, 311, 313, 317, 323, 326, 327, 347.

Dione, 24, 60.

Dionysia, 118.

Dionysus, 10, 14, 26, 37, 61, 95, 114, 117–128, 298, 299.

Dioscuri were the twin heroes, Castor and Polydeuces (called by the Romans Pollux). According to Homer they were sons of Leda and King Tyndareus of Sparta, but some said that they were, like Helen, children of Leda and Zeus, and that all three were born at the same time out of an egg. Another tradition held that only Helen and Polydeuces were children of Zeus and that Castor was son to Tyndareus and therefore mortal. Polydeuces, famous as a boxer, and Castor, as tamer of horses, were inseparable. They were noted for their rescue of Helen from Aphidnæ (*see* 215), for their part in the Calydonian hunt and the expedition of the Argonauts (*see* 155, 157), and for their final battle with another pair of inseparable twins, their cousins and rivals, Idas and Lynceus, sons of Aphareus. Accounts of the battle vary, but it is usually said that Idas killed Castor, that Polydeuces killed Lynceus, and that Zeus intervened by slaying Idas with a thunderbolt. Polydeuces, the only survivor, implored Zeus to let him die with Castor, but Zeus decreed that the twins should spend their days alternately under the earth and among the gods. He also set their image among the stars as Gemini. The worship of the Dioscuri as divine spread from Sparta. Poseidon giving them power over wind and wave, they were worshipped especially as protectors of sailors. They were regarded as inventors of the war-dance and patrons of bards, and they presided at the Spartan Games. In art each is represented as mounted on a magnificent white horse, carrying a spear, and wearing an egg-shaped helmet crowned with a star.

Dirce, 249.

Dis, 399.

Dodona, 24, 27, 28.

Dolon, 313.

Dorians, 46.

Doris, daughter of Oceanus and Thetis, wife of her brother Nereus, and mother of the Nereides.

Dorus, son of Hellen, was the mythical ancestor of the Dorians.

Dryades were nymphs of trees.

Dryope, the daughter of King Dryops, was seduced by Apollo. She was afterwards carried away by the Hamadryads or tree-nymphs. *See also* 74.

Echemus, 201.

Echidne, a monster half woman, half serpent, said to be the mother of many monsters, such as:

Chimæra, 147; Nemean Lion, 173; Lernean Hydra, 174; Orthrus, 182; Ladon, 183; Sphinx, 255; Cerberus, 184, 405. Her mate was Typhon. She was killed by Argus.

Echion. (1) Son of Hermes, took part in the Calydonian hunt and was herald to the Argonauts.

(2) One of the Sparti, 243, 246.

Echo was a nymph who diverted Hera's attention with incessant talking while Zeus amused himself with the nymphs. When Hera discovered the trick she took from Echo all use of her voice except in repetition of another's speech. Echo then fell in love with Narcissus, a beautiful youth, who repulsed her, and she pined away in grief until only her voice remained. Artemis, in anger at Narcissus' coldness, caused him to fall in love with his own reflection in a fountain. In despair he took his own life and was turned into the flower.

Edones, 122.

Eëtion, 306.

Elatus, one of the Lapithæ, and father of Cæneus.

Electra. (1) The Pleiad, 274.

(2) Daughter of Agamemnon and Clytemnestra, 389, 390, 392, 397, 398.

"Electra" of Euripides, 391.

"Electra" of Sophocles, 391.

Electryon, King of Mycenæ, was the son of Perseus and Andromeda. His daughter Alcmene married Amphitryon.

Eleusis, in Attica, had a splendid temple of Demeter, 112, 113, 114.

Elpenor, 358.

Elysium, 407, 408.

Empusæ, daughters of Hecate, were horrible demons, with the haunches of asses and wearing brazen slippers. They could disguise themselves as bitches, cows, or maidens, and in the latter shape they would lie with men asleep and suck their strength till they died. The idea of Empusæ was probably brought from Palestine, where the Lilim, or daughters of Lilith, had similar characteristics.

Enceladus, 11, 12.

Endymion, King of Elis, was a beautiful Æolian youth, who, while sleeping in a cave on Carian Mt. Latmus, was seen by Selene the moon, who came down and kissed him. He afterwards returned to the cave and fell into a dreamless sleep. By his wife he had four sons, one of them being Ætolus, who conquered the land now called Ætolia. The myth probably indicates the fate of one who marries the moon Goddess. See Keats's *Endymion*.

Enipeus was the river god loved by Tyro.

Enna, 112.

Eos, in Latin Aurora, was the Dawn, daughter of Hyperion and Theia. She drove her chariot each morning to announce the approach of her brother Helios, and, as Hemera, accompanied his across the sky to arrive with him in the West in the evening as Hespera. Her husband was Astræus, said by some to be father by her of the stars and all winds save the East. Eos carried off several beautiful youths, including Orion, Cephalus, and Tithonus. Her son by Tithonus was Memnon. Eos asked Zeus to grant Tithonus immortality, but omitted to ask also for perpetual youth. Tithonus therefore shrank away until he became a cicada. Among Greeks in Asia Minor the golden cicada was an emblem of Apollo the sun god.

Epaphus, son of Zeus and Io, reigned over Egypt, and was rumoured to be the sacred bull, Apis.

Epeius, 328.

Ephesia (Artemis Ephesia), 81.

Ephesus, 87, 88.

Ephialtes, 11, 13.

Epigoni, 268, 269.

Epimetheus, 16, 17, 20.

Erato, the Muse of erotic poetry and mime, sometimes carries a lyre.

Erebus, or darkness, son of Chaos, begot Æther and Hemera by his sister Night. See also 25.

Erichthonius. (1) Son of Hephæstus. Athene entrusted to the daughters of King Cecrops of Athens a chest which they were forbidden to open. It concealed the infant Erichthonius. According to one version, the daughters (Agraulos, Pandrosos, and Herse) were overcome with curiosity and opened the chest. Seeing a serpent within it, they leapt in madness from the Acropolis to their death. Erichthonius succeeded Cecrops as King of Athens, and was himself succeeded by Padion.

(2) Erechtheus the second was grandson of Erechtheus, son of Hephæstus, and the son of Pandion, whom he succeeded as King of Athens. He was father by Praxithea of four sons, including Cecrops, and seven daughters, Protogonia, Pandora, Procris wife of Cephalus, Creusa, Oreithyia, Chthonia, and Otionia. When the Eleusinians under Eumolpus son of Poseidon attacked Athens, Erechtheus was told to sacrifice Otionia, whereupon her two eldest sisters, Protogonia and Pandora, also sacrificed themselves. Erechtheus slew Eumolpus, whereupon Poseidon demanded vengeance, and either he or Zeus slew Erechtheus.

Eridanus was a river god. Phæthon fell to his death here. Because amber was found here Eridanus was later supposed to be the Po.

Erigone, see Icarius.

Erinnyes or Eumenides, 3, 260, 271, 393, 394, 404.

Eriphyle, 262, 269, 271.

Eris, 65, 280.

Eros, who in Latin was named Amor or Cupid, was said to be the son of Aphrodite by either Ares, Hermes, or her own father Zeus. The early Greeks thought of him as a winged "sprite," but by the fifth century B.C. he was represented as a boy, irresponsible but lovely, flying on golden wings and carrying in his golden quiver arrows which could wound both men and gods, and torches. He was sometimes portrayed as blindfolded. He usually accompanied his mother Aphrodite. See also Psyche.

Erymanthian Boar, 176.

Erysichthon, son of Triopas, dared to cut down trees in a grove sacred to Demeter, and when he ignored protests she punished him with an insatiable hunger.

Eryx, Mt., 58.

Eteocles, 257, 261, 265.

Etna, Mt., 12.

Euippe. (1) The daughter of Cheiron, being with child by Æolus, son of Hellen, was changed into a horse. Their child was Melanippe.

(2) The daughter of Daunus, 347.

Eumæus, 362, 363.

Eumenides or Erinnyes, 3, 260, 271, 393, 394, 404.

"Eumenides," the play by Æschylus, 393, 404.

Eumolpus, "the good singer," was the son of Poseidon and Chione, the daughter of Boreas and Oreithyia. His mother threw him into the sea as soon as he was born, but his father Poseidon cared for him. He was brought up in Ethiopia, and lived later at the Court of King Tegyrius of Thrace, and then came to Eleusis in Attica. Here he became the priest of the mysteries of Demeter and Persephone. He initiated Heracles into the mysteries and taught him to sing and play the lyre. Eumolpus led an expedition against Erectheus of Athens, three of whose daughters sacrificed themselves to ensure victory. Eumolpus was killed by Erectheus, who was then himself slain by either Poseidon or Zeus. Eumolpus' descendants became hereditary priests of Demeter at Eleusis.

Eunomus, 193.

Euphorbus, 314.

Euphrosyne, one of the Charities or Graces.

Euridice, see Orpheus.

Euripides, 123, 161, 185, 200, 211, 246, 263, 267, 313, 339, 391, 393, 395.

Europa, 223–224, 244.

Eurus, son of Astræus and Eos, was the Southeast wind.

Euryale, 134, 138.

Euryalus, 288.

Eurycleia, 364.

Eurylochus, 357.

Eurynome, 25, 51.

Eurystheus, 166, 171–184, 199, 380.

Eurytion, 182.

Eurytus, 167, 186, 195, 365.

Euterpe, the Muse of lyric poetry, or of music, represented with a flute.

Evadne, 267, 268.

Evenus was father of Marpessa, who was carried off by Idas. Evenus then drowned himself in the river henceforth called after him.

Fates, or Mœræ, or Moiræ, known to the Romans as Parcæ, were the white-robed Clotho, Lachesis, and Atropos. Clotho spun the thread, Lachesis measured it, and Atropos cut it with her shears. At Delphi only Clotho and Atropos were worshipped. It has been suggested that the Fates originally represented phases of the moon. See also 25, 94.

Faunus, identified by the Romans with Pan.

Fortuna, Roman counterpart of Tyche.

" Fortunate Isles," 408.

Furies, see Eumenides and 3

Gæa, see Ge.

Galatea, a sea-nymph loved by Polyphemus; but Galatea loved Acis. See also Pygmalion.

Galinthias, daughter of Prœtus of Thebes and friend of Alcmene.

Ganymede, the most beautiful youth alive, was, according to the Homeric account, the son of King Tros and Callirrhoë. He was carried off by the gods to be cup bearer to Zeus, in place of Hebe. Later writers say that Zeus himself, in love with Ganymede, disguised himself as an eagle and carried him off. Zeus sent Tros as compensation a pair of horses. Other traditions do not agree as to Ganymede's parentage. The myth was very popular in Greece and Rome, as it gave a religious sanction to a man's passion for a youth (see Plato's Phædrus, 79). See also 274, 275.

Ge or Gæa, the Earth, 1, 3, 5, 8, 25, 30.

Geryon, 182.

Glauce, daughter of Creon, King of Corinth, also called Creusa, 162.

Glaucus. (1) King of Corinth, the son of Sisyphus and Merope, and father of Bellerophon, was torn to pieces by his own mares because he scorned the power of Aphrodite.
(2) Grandson of Bellerophon, 311, 322.
(3) Son of Minos, 231, 232.

Gordius, King of Phrygia, was originally a peasant. An oracle had informed the people of Phrygia that their new king would appear in a wagon, and when Gordius arrived riding in this way they acclaimed him king. He gratefully dedicated his cart to Zeus in the acropolis of Gordium. The pole was tied to the yoke by a curious knot and an oracle decreed that whoever should untie the knot should rule all Asia. Alexander severed it with his sword.

Gorge, daughter of Althæa, who with her sister Deianeira, kept her human form when their other sisters were changed by Artemis to birds. She was wife to Andræmon, mother of Thoas.

Gorgones, 134, 136, 138.

Greæ, 136.

Gyes or Gyges, one of Hecatoncheires, 1.

Hades. (1) The god, see especially 399–402, 409, and also 7, 9, 10, 65, 93, 98, 101, 106, 111, 135, 184, 214.
(2) The Underworld, 399–409.

Hæmon, 266.

Halirrhothius, 67.

Hamadryades were nymphs of trees.

Harmonia, 244, 247.

Harmonia, Necklace of, 244, 262, 271.

Harmonia, Robe of, 269, 271.

Harpy, a monster with a woman's head and a bird's wings and claws, used by the gods to torment mortals, 373.

Hebe was cup-bearer to the gods till Ganymede replaced her. Her Roman counterpart was Juventas. See also 25, 33, 198.

Hecabe, see Hecuba.

Hecale was a poor old woman who hospitably entertained Theseus when he was out hunting the Bull of Marathon.

Hecate, 403, 409.

Hecatoncheires, hundred-headed giants, 1.

Hector, 277, 307, 311, 314, 315, 322, 336.

Hecuba, 277, 278, 315, 334, 338, 339.

" Hecuba " of Euripides, 339.

Helen, 213, 215, 284, 285, 286, 287, 302, 325, 327, 332, 334, 385.

Helenus, son of Priam, 277, 325, 346.

Helicaon, 335.

Helicon, a range of lofty mountains in Bœotia sacred to Apollo and the Muses, hence called Heliconiades and Heliconides. The fountains of the Muses Aganippe and Hippocrene spring from Mt. Helicon. See also 148.

Helios or Helius, the Roman Sol, was the son of Hyperion and Theia, and brother of Selene and Eos. In Homer he was god of the sun. All-seeing, he reported such incidents as Aphrodite's faithlessness and the rape of Persephone, but failed to notice the theft of his own sacred cattle by Odysseus' companions. His wife Rhode bore him seven sons and one daughter, and his worship flourished in Rhodes, where the famous Colossus was an image of him. Sacred to Helios was the cock, and his sacrifices included white horses and rams, and honey. See also 79, 105, 111, 182, 231, 357, 360, and Phæthon.

Helle, daughter of Athamas and Nephele.

Hellen, the son of Deucalion and Pyrrha, was mythical ancestor of all the Hellenes. His sons were Æolus, who succeeded him, Dorus, and Xuthus.

Hellenes, 22, 40, 94.

Hellespont, 156.

Hephæstus, 10, 17, 25, 41, 46, 47, 48, 49, 50, 51, 52, 55, 56, 60, 65, 82, 158, 373.

Hera, see especially 29–35 and also 7, 10, 13, 14, 24, 25, 26, 48, 50–53, 65, 70, 72, 73, 104, 106, 119–121, 166, 167, 171, 174, 181, 189, 198, 280, 128.

Heracleidæ or Children of Heracles, 199–202.

Heracles, see especially 164–202 and also 11, 12, 18, 66, 95, 104, 155, 156, 323.

Hercules or Heracles, Pillars of, 182.

Hermaphroditus, 61.

Hermes, see especially 90–98 and also 13, 14, 17, 26, 41, 61, 66, 77, 111, 120, 135, 136, 141, 184, 250, 280, 303, 357, 361, 369, 375, 377, 378.

Hermione, 287, 345, 346, 398.

Hero, see Leander.

Herse, daughter of Cecrops, beloved by Hermes. To Herse and her sisters the infant Erichthonius was entrusted.

Hesiod, 2, 59.

Hesione, 188, 189, 275, 276.

Hesperides, 30, 183.

Hesperus, the evening star.

Hestia, 7, 10, 32, 36, 37, 118, 126.

Hiera, 56.

Hippocoon, 191.

Hippocrene, 148.

Hippodameia. (1) Daughter of Œnomaus, 376, 377.
(2) Wife of Pirithous, 212, 213.

Hippolyte, 181, 210, 211.

Hippolytus, 211.

" Hippolytus," 211.

Hippomedon, 263, 265.

Hippomenes, son of Megareus, married the Bœotian Atalanta.

Hippothous, grandson of Cercyon, who was slain by Theseus, and father of Æpytus, the King of Arcadia.

Hittites, 2, 68.

Homer, 49, 50, 52, 60, 79, 99, 117, 128, 151, 272, 273, 322, 338, 343, 353, 369, 385, 408.

Horæ, goddesses of the order of nature and the seasons (see 25). It is said that Zeus' fatherhood of the Horæ on Themis indicates that the Hellenes took over control of the calendar.

Hyacinthus, 74.

Hyades, 120.

Hydra of Lerna, 174, 196.

Hygeia, the goddess of health, was either the daughter or the wife of Asclepius. She is represented as dressed in a long robe and feeding a serpent from a cup.

Hylas, 156.

Hyllus, 193, 196, 199, 201.

Hyperboreans, 137.

Hyperenor, one of Sparti, 243.

Hyperion, a Titan and father of Helios, Selene, and Eos. 1, 9.

Hypermnestra, see Danaides.

Hypnus, the god of sleep.

Hypseus was the father of Cyrene beloved by Apollo.

Hypsipyle was the daughter of Thoas, King of Lemnos. When the women killed all the men in the island she saved her father. She welcomed Jason on the Argonauts' landing in Lemnos and bore him twins. Later the women of Lemnos discovered that she had spared Thoas and sold her as a slave to King Lycurgus of Nemea, who entrusted his son Opheltes to her care.

Iacchus, the name of Dionysus in the Eleusinian mysteries, where the god was regarded as the son of Zeus and Demeter.

Iapetus, a Titan and father of Atlas, Prometheus, and Epimetheus, 1.

Iasion, Iasius, or Iasus was the son of Zeus and Electra. Demeter loved him and bore him a son Pluton or Plutus, and Zeus, in anger, slew Iasion with a thunderbolt.

Icaria, 124.

Icarius. (1) Was an Athenian who received Dionysus hospitably and learned from him the cultivation of the vine. He gave some wine he had made to shepherds who, seeing double, believed they had been bewitched and killed Icarius. His daughter Erigone was led to his grave by his dog Mæra, and she hanged herself in despair from the tree under which her father had been buried.
(2) Of Sparta, 290.

Icarus, 238.

Ida, Mt., near Troy, 278, 280, 305, 325.

Idæa, 274.

Idas, the twin brother of Lynceus, was said to be son of Aphareus. He was in love with Marpessa, whom he carried off in a chariot given him by Poseidon, who was really his father. Idas' rival Apollo fought with him for Marpessa, but Zeus separated the combatants, and she chose Idas. With his devoted twin he took part in the Calydonian hunt, and the Argonauts' expedition, and both were finally killed in a battle with their rivals, the Dioscuri.

Idomeneus, 297, 348.

"Iliad," 77, 101, 309, 313, 316, 400.

Ilithyiæ, daughters of Hera, who in the Iliad and early poets are represented as helping women in childbirth. In the Odyssey and later poets only one goddess, Ilithyia, is represented. See also 33.

Illyrius, son of Cadmus, 244.

Ilus, 274.

Imbros, 56.

Inachus, son of Oceanus and Tethys, was first King of Argos, and gave his name to the river.

Ino, 120, 244, 246.

Io, daughter of Inachus was beloved by Zeus, who turned her into a white heifer through fear of Hera. The goddess Hera set Argus of the hundred eyes to watch the heifer, but Hermes, at Zeus' bidding, charmed Argus to sleep and cut off his head. Hera placed Argus' eyes in the tail of her favourite bird, the peacock, and sent a gadfly to torment Io, who fled from land to land till she came to the Nile. Here she recovered her human form and bore Zeus a son Epaphus. The Ionian Sea and the Bosphorus, (or cow's ford) were said to have derived their name from Io.

Iobates, 146–149.

Iolaus, 172, 174, 185, 192, 199.

Iolcus, 152, 153, 154, 161.

Iole, 186, 195, 196, 197.

Ion, see Xuthus.

Ionians, 68, 88, 99.

Iphicles. (1) Son of Amphitrion, 166, 170, 171, 172.
(2) One of the Argonauts.

Iphigeneia, 86, 300, 387, 395, 396, 397.

"Iphigeneia Among the Taurians" of Euripides, 395.

Iphimedeia, wife of Alcœus, 13.

Iphis, 267.

Iphitus, 186.

Irene, called Pax by the Romans, was goddess of peace and according to Hesiod one of the Horæ, daughters of Zeus and Themis. She was worshipped in Athens.

Iris, in the Iliad she appears as messenger of the gods, but in the Odyssey she is never mentioned. She was originally a personification of the rainbow.

Ishtar, 57.

Ismene, 257, 260.

Issa, daughter of Macareus, was loved by Apollo

Isthmian Games, 105.

Ithaca, 289, 290, 353, 362, 363, 368.

Itys was the son of Tereus and Procne.

Ixion, the son of Phlegyas, King of the Lapithæ, treacherously murdered his father-in-law. Though pardoned by Zeus, Ixion now tried to seduce Hera, but was deceived by a phantom, Nephele, who bore him a Centaur. Ixion was punished by being chained to a fiery wheel which rolled ceaselessly through the sky. His son was Pirithous. See Browning's Ixion.

Jason, 151–163.

Jocasta, 253, 257, 258, 259.

Juno, Roman counterpart of Hera, 29–35.

Jupiter, Roman counterpart of Zeus, 23–28.

Juventas, see Hebe.

Labdacus, 252.

Lachesis, one of the Fates.

Ladon, 183.

Lælaps, the swift dog which Procris gave to Cephalus.

Laërtes, 290, 363, 365.

Læstrygones, 357.

Laius, 252, 253, 254, 255, 258.

Lamia, daughter of Belus, loved by Zeus. She became one of the Empusæ.

Lamus, 357.

Laocoön, 330, 331.

Laodamia, wife of Protesilaus, 303.

Laodice. (1) Daughter of Priam, 335.
(2) Homeric name for Electra, daughter of Agamemnon.

Laomedan, 274, 275.

Lapithæ were a mythical people living in Thessaly and governed by Pirithous, who, being a son of Ixion, was half-brother to the Centaurs. Rivalry between the Centaurs and Lapithæ reached its climax at the celebrated struggle at the wedding of Pirithous. See also 212.

Larissa, 142.

Leander, a youth of Abydos, swam across the Hellespont every night to visit Hero, priestess of Aphrodite in Sestos. One night he was drowned, and Hero then flung herself into the

to the Underworld. Here his music delighted even Hades, so that he allowed Eurydice to follow her husband back to life, provided only that he did not look round. On the very threshold of life Orpheus anxiously looked back, and so lost Eurydice. He was so desolate with grief that the jealous Thracian women tore him to pieces in an orgy of Dionysus, a god whom he had neglected to honour. The Muses collected the fragments of his body, which were buried at the foot of Olympus, but his head, thrown into the River Hebrus, was carried still singing down to sea and on to Lesbos, whither his lyre also drifted, to be placed later as a constellation in the heavens at the intercession of Apollo and the Muses.

The Greeks considered Orpheus to be the greatest poet before Homer, and fragments of poetry extant were ascribed to him.

The religion " Orphism " was characterised by a sense of sin and the need for atonement, the idea of a suffering human god, and a belief in immortality. It had an influence on such philosophers as Pythagoras and Plato, and formed a link between the worship of Dionysus and Christianity.

Orthrus, 182, 255.

Ortygia, 70.

Ossa, 13.

Otrere, 317.

Otus, 13.

Ovid, 112, 161.

Palæmon, a sea-god, originally Melicertes, son of Athamas and Ino.

Palamedes, son of Nauplius, 288, 289, 291, 302, 350.

Palladium, 325, 327, 330, 341.

Pallas. (1) a giant, 11.
(2) a father of fifty sons, 206.
(3) a name for Athene, 39, 40.

Pan, the misshapen god with goat feet, horns, and tail, was said by some to be an ancient divinity coeval with Zeus, though most reported him to be the son of Hermes. He was the god of shepherds and flocks, living in rural Arcadia, hunting and dancing with the nymphs. He would also lurk in forests, startling travellers with a sudden shout and filling them with " panic." Pan loved many nymphs, including Syrinx, who fled in terror and was metamorphosed into a reed, from which Pan made the syrinx (or Pan's pipe) that he was said to have invented, for his love of music was well known. He was also said to have seduced Selene. The Olympians looked down on Pan as a rustic, uncontrolled divinity. He is the only god whose death was reported. The worship of Pan began in Arcadia, which was despised by the Greeks for its backwardness. It did not reach Athens till early in the fifth century B.C. The Romans later identified Pan with Faunus. *See also* 14, 77–97, 369.

Panathenaic, 44, 118, 233.

Pandareus, 373.

Pandion, King of Athens, was son of Erichthonius and father of Procne, and Philomela, and of Erechtheus, who succeeded him.

Pandora, 17.

Pandrosos, daughter of Cecrops. To her and her sisters, Erichthonius was entrusted.

Panopeus, 328.

Panthous, 314.

Paphos, 58, 59.

Parcæ, *see* Fates.

Paris, 35, 277–282, 284, 287, 310, 321, 324.

Parnassus, Mt., a lofty mountain range north-west of the Gulf of Corinth. The name was usually limited to the two-peaked summit north of Delphi, above which the Castalian spring issued. The mountain was one of the chief seats of Apollo and the Muses, and was also sacred to Dionysus. *See also* 20, 69, 7.

Parthenon, 44, 48, 118.

Partheno Pæus, 263, 265.

Parthenos, a name of Athene, 39.

Pasiphæ, 231, 234, 238.

Patroclus, 296, 314, 316.

Pegasus, 108, 137, 148, 150.

Pelasgians, 47.

Peleus, son of Æacus, King of Ægina, joined with his brother Telamon in killing their half-brother Phocus. Expelled by Æacus, he went to Phthia in Thessaly, where he was purified by the king's son Eurytion, but accompanying Eurytion to hunt the Calydonian Boar, he accidentally killed his benefactor. Peleus now fled to Acastus, King of Iolcos, who purified him, but here he was falsely accused by Acastus' wife. Acastus then took Peleus on a hunting expedition on Mt. Pelion, and while his guest was asleep secreted his sword and deserted him. Peleus would have been killed by Centaurs had not Cheiron rescued him. Zeus now decided to give to Peleus the Nereid Thetis as wife. Zeus himself would have married her had he not been warned by Themis that she would bear a son more illustrious then his father. Cheiron told Peleus how to master Thetis by holding her fast whatever form she might assume, and all the divinities save Eris came to the wedding. She in revenge cast in the golden apple, which caused, eventually, the Trojan War. Thetis bore to Peleus the hero Achilles, whose death he survived. *See also* 280, 293, 296.

Pelias, 108, 152, 153, 154, 161.

Pelides, the son of Peleus, that is Achilles.

Pelion, Mt., 13.

Pelopia, 382, 383.

Peloponnesus, 58, 378.

Pelops, 251, 325, 326, 371, 373, 375, 376, 377, 378, 379.

Pelorus, one of Sparti, 243.

Penelope, 290, 363, 365, 368, 369.

Peneus, a god of the River Peneus in Thessaly, son of Oceanus and Tethys and father of Daphne and Cyrene.

Penthesilea, 317.

Pentheus, 123, 246.

Perdix, nephew of Dædalus, 237.

Periclymenus, the Argonaut was the son of Neleus and brother of Nestor. Though he could assume what shape he chose, he was killed by Heracles.

Periphetes, a monster at Epidaurus who used to kill passers-by with an iron club. He was killed by Theseus.

Pero, daughter of Neleus and Chloris and wife of Bias.

Persë, daughter of Oceanus and wife of Helios, by whom she became the mother of Æëtes, Circe, Pasiphaë, and Perses.

Persephone, 25, 103, 106, 111–115, 214, 373, 402, 403, 409.

Perses, son of Helios and Persë and father of Hecate.

Perseus, 129–144, 166.

Pesistratus, 44, 114, 118.

Petasus, 98.

Phæacians, 362.

Phædra, 211.

Phæthon, " the shining," was a son of Helios by Clymene. He gained his father's permission to drive the chariot of the sun, but his incompetence provoked Zeus to kill him with a thunderbolt, and he fell into the River Po. His mourning sisters were turned into alder- or poplar-trees, which wept tears of amber. Phæthon's fate may represent the ritual death of the boy interrex for the sacred king, who ruled for one day and was then killed, usually by horses.

During the Bronze Age amber, sacred to the king, was carried from Baltic to Mediterranean via the Po valley.

Phalanthus, a mythical Spartan said to have founded Tarentum in Italy about 700 B.C.

Phasis, river, 157.

Pheræ was an ancient town in Thessaly, the home of Admetus.

Pheres, son of Cretheus and Tyro, was the father of Admetus and Lycurgus and the founder of Pheræ in Thessaly.

Philemon, an old man of Phrygia who, with his wife Baucis, hospitably received Zeus and Hermes.

Philoctetes, 198, 301, 303, 323, 324, 347.

"Philoctetes" of Sophocles, 323.

Philomela, see Tereus.

Phineus was the son of Agenor and ruled in Salmydessus in Thrace. He imprisoned his sons, by his first wife, Cleopatra, because of a false accusation made by their stepmother, Idæa, For this, or some other fault, he was punished with blindness, and two Harpies tormented him. When the Argonauts reached Thrace, Zetes and Calais, brothers of Cleopatra, killed the Harpies and were also said to have vindicated and freed their nephews, the sons of Phineus. In return, he advised Jason what course to take (see 157). Milton compares himself to Phineus (Paradise Lost, Book III, lines 35, 36).

Phlegethon, 406.

Phlegeus, 271.

Phocis, a country in Northern Greece, its chief mountain Parnassus and its chief river Cephissus, 390.

Phocus, son of Æacus, killed by his half-brothers Telamon and Peleus.

Phœbe, a name of Artemis as goddess of the moon.

Phœbus, 69.

"Phœnician Maidens, The," 263.

Phœnix, 294, 296, 361.

Pholus, a Centaur, 176.

Phorcys, a sea-deity, was, by Ceto, the father of Ladon, Echidne, the three Gorgons, and the three Greæ.

Phoroneus, son of Inachus and the nymph Melia, was an early mythical King of Argos.

Phrixus, son of Athamas and Nephele.

Phrygia, 121.

Phylachus, father of Iphiclus.

Phyleus, son of Augeias, 177.

Phyllis, beloved by Demophon, 349.

Pieria, on the south-east coast of Macedonia, was inhabited by Thracian people, who in early times worshipped the Muses, hence called Pierides. See also 92.

Pierides. (1) The Muses.
  (2) The nine daughters of Pierus, a king in Macedonia, named after the Muses. They were conquered in a contest with the Muses and turned into birds.

Pirene, 148.

Pirithous, the son of Ixion and Dia, was King of the Lapithæ in Thessaly. He became a close friend of Theseus. See also 212, 213, 214.

Pisa, in Elis, 376, 377.

Pittheus, King of Troezen, was son to Pelops and father of Æthra, 203.

Pleiades, daughters of Atlas and Pleione were companions of Artemis. They were changed into doves and placed among the stars.

Pleione, mother by Atlas of the Pleiades.

Pleisthenes, 381.

Pluto. (1) A name for Hades, 399.
  (2) The nymph, 371.

Podalirius, 324.

Podarces. (1) Original name of Priam, 275.
  (2) Son of Iphiclus, who led the Thessalians against Troy.

Pœas, 301.

Polites, 334.

Pollux, Roman name for Polydeuces.

Polybus, 253.

Polybutes, 11, 12.

Polydectes, 132, 133, 141.

Polydeuces, one of Dioscuri, 155, 157, 215, 285, 286.

Polydorus. (1) Son of Cadmus and Harmonia, 244, 252.
  (2) Son of Priam, 338.

Polyeidus, 232.

Polymester, 338.

Polymnia or Polyhymnia, the Muse of the sublime hymn.

Polyneices, 257, 261, 262, 263, 265, 266, 269.

Polypemon, see Procrustes and 205.

Polyphemus, 355. See also Galatea.

Polyxena, 309, 337, 339.

Pontus, 1.

Porphyrion, 11.

Poseidon, see especially 99–109 and also 7, 9, 10, 13, 32, 36, 42, 44, 60, 67, 73, 110, 134, 137, 139, 140, 152, 157, 211, 223, 227, 305, 330, 348, 362, 366, 377.

Praxiteles, 63.

Priam, 275, 276, 277, 282, 302, 309, 315, 316, 318, 327, 330, 331, 334, 336, 338.

Priapus, son of Dionysus and Aphrodite, a god of fruitfulness.

Procne, see Tereus.

Procris was the daughter of the second Erectheus to be King of Athens. She married Cephalus. See also 229.

Procrustes or the "Stretcher" was the surname given to the robber Polypemon. He used to tie travellers to a bed, and if they were too short he would rack them, and if too tall, he would hack off their legs. He was served in the same way by Theseus. See also 205.

Prœtus, son of Abas, King of Argolis, inherited the kingdom jointly with his twin brother Acrisius. Soon expelled, he fled to Iobates, King of Lydia, whose daughter Anteia, also called Sthenebœa, he married. Returning to Argolis, he forced his brother to divide the kingdom and became ruler of Tiryns, whose massive walls he built by aid of the Cyclopes. See also Melampus, Bellerophon.

Prometheus, 16–20, 41, 176, 183.

Protesilaus, 303.

Proteus was the prophetic old man of the sea, subject to Poseidon, whose flocks of seals he tended. By assuming any shape he chose, he could avoid the need of prophesying, unless gripped fast, when he would at last resume his usual shape and tell the truth. He could be found at midday in the island of Pharos. See also 183, 345.

Psamathe, see Linus (1).

Psyche appears in late Greek literature as a personification of the soul, purified by suffering to enjoy true love. The beauty of the maiden Psyche excited the envy of Aphrodite who sent Eros to persecute her, but he fell in love with her and secretly visited her nightly. When Psyche, urged by her two sisters, sought to discover his identity, he left her. Searching for Eros, she endured further persecution, but he secretly helped her, and she finally overcame Aphrodite's hatred, to become immortal and united with Eros for ever. The story is told in The Golden Ass of Apuleius.

Pygmalion of Cyprus is said to have fallen in love with the ivory image of a maiden that he himself had made, and to have prayed Aphrodite to breathe life into it. When she consented, Pygmalion married the maiden, whom he called Galatea. By her he became the father of Paphus and Metharme. It is probable that the story concerns a priest of Aphrodite at Paphus who kept the image of the goddess in order to retain power. See William Morris's version in The Earthly Paradise.

Pylades, 390, 392, 396, 397, 398.

Pylos, 92.

Pyrrha, 20, 21.

Pyrrhus, see Neoptolemus.

Pythia, 76, 118, 171.

Pythian or Pythius, 69.

Python, 71, 76.

also tore out Procne's tongue, but Procne wove a message for her sister into a robe. Philomela then released Procne, who, to avenge herself on her husband, killed and cooked their son Itys for Tereus to eat. When he realised what he had been eating, he pursued the sisters with an axe, but the gods changed all three into birds, Procne to a swallow, Philomela to a nightingale, and Tereus either to a hoopoe or hawk. Some say that Tereus tore out Philomela's tongue, that he told Procne that Philomela was dead, and that Procne became the nightingale, Philomela the swallow.

Terpsichore, the Muse of Choral Dance and Song, carries the lyre and plectrum.

Tethys, 1, 25.

Teucer. (1) Son of Scamander, 274.
(2) Son of Telamon, 189, 292.

Teucri, 274.

Teuthras, King of Mysia, married Auge. He was succeeded by Telephus, son of Auge by Heracles. See also 306.

Thalia. (1) One of the nine Muses, and in later times the Muse of Comedy, appearing with a comic mask, a shepherd's staff, or a wreath of ivy.
(2) One of the three Charities or Graces.

Theano, 340.

Thebe, 250.

Thebes, 240–271.

"Thebes, Seven against," of Æschylus, 263.

Themis, 1, 21, 25.

"Theogony," 2.

Thersander, 269.

Thersites, 317.

Theseus, 203–218, 260, 267.

Thesmophoria, 114.

Thespius, 168, 192.

Thessaly, 8, 10, 117.

Thetis was the kindly daughter of Nereus and Doris, who received in the sea depths both Hephæstus and Dionysus. Zeus and Poseidon both wished to marry her, but Themis foretold her son would be greater than his father, and she was given to Peleus. She became by him the mother of Achilles. See also 32, 51, 106, 280, 293, 294, 315.

Thoas, son of Andræmon, King of Calydon, sailed with forty ships against Troy. See also 328.

Thrace, 64, 117, 121, 128, 157.

Threspotus, 382, 383.

Thrinacia, 360.

Thyestes, 379, 380, 381, 382, 383, 384, 385, 388.

Thyia was said to be the first woman to have sacrificed to Dionysus. From her the Attic women who annually went to Parnassus to take part in Dionysus' orgies were called Thyiades, or Thyades. The word Thyades, however, means "raging women." They were the Bacchæ or Bacchantes.

Thyiades, 117.

Thyone, 126.

Thyrsus, 127.

Tilphussa, Well of, 270.

Tiresias, see Teiresias.

Tiryns, 130, 143, 144, 146, 171.

Tisphone, one of the Eumenides, 3, 404.

Titanesses, 9.

Titanomachia, 8.

Titans, 1, 3, 4, 7, 8, 9, 11, 16, 17, 400.

Tithonus, son of Laomedan and Strymo, was half-brother to Priam. By the prayers of his lover Eos he was granted by Zeus immortality, but as Eos had omitted to ask for perpetual yout..., he shrank away till he became a cicada. See Tennyson's poem Tithonus. See also 318.

Tityus, son of Gea (see 72). Tityus was sent to Tartarus. Here he was pegged on the ground covering nine acres, while two vultures, or two snakes, ate his liver.

Tleopolemus, 201, 288.

Tmolus, 187.

Trachiniæ, "Women of Trachis," 197.

Trachis, 195–197.

Trapezus, 12.

Triptolemus, 113.

Triton, son of Poseidon and Amphitrite. Sometimes writers spoke of Tritons in the plural, and they described them as having the upper part of the body in human form, the lower part that of a fish. Tritons carried a trumpet made of a shell (concha) which they blew to soothe the waves.

Triton Lake, 41.

Trœzen, the birthplace of Theseus, 105.

Troilus, 277, 304.

Trojan War, 276, 284–342.

Trophonius and Agamedes, sons of Erginus, built a temple for Apollo at Delphi. As a reward they lived merrily for six days, and on the seventh died in their sleep. Later Trophonius had an oracle of his own at Lebadeia in Bœotia.

Tros. (1) Grandson of Dardanus, 274.
(2) Part of Troy, 273.

Troy, 104, 272–342.

Tyche or Tuche, called by the Romans Fortuna and said to be daughter of Zeus, was a goddess more popular with the Romans than the Greeks. She was goddess of luck, conferring or denying gifts irresponsibly. She was portrayed sometimes juggling with a ball representing the instability of fortune, sometimes with a rudder as a guiding men's affairs, sometimes with Amalthea's horn or accompanied by Plutus.

Tydeus, 261, 262, 263, 265, 268.

Tyandreus, 191, 285, 286, 346, 385, 386.

Typhon, 14, 147, 173, 174, 182, 183, 255.

Tyro, 108, 152, 153.

Udæus, one of Sparti, 243.

Ulysses, see Odysseus.

Urania, the Muse of Astronomy appears with a staff pointing to a globe.

Uranus, 1, 2, 3, 4, 5, 25, 59.

Venus, a Roman goddess identified with Aphrodite, 57, 59, 62, 63.

Vesta, a Roman goddess identified with Æstia, 30.

Virgil, 62.

Xanthus, 274.

Xuthus, son of Hellen, married Creusa, daughter of Erectheus, King of Athens. Their sons were Ion and Achæus. After the death of Erectheus Xuthus judged that Creusa's eldest brother Cecrops should be king, and was expelled by his other brothers-in-law and settled in Achaia. Euripides, in his play Ion, represents Ion as son to Creusa and Apollo. Carried away as a baby to Delphi, he is at length recognised by Creusa and adopted by Xuthus.

Zagreus, in the Cretan legend, was a son of Zeus. The Titans tore him to pieces and ate him alive but Athene saved his heart. He was identified with Dionysus, and the ceremonies of his cult were designed to promote union with the god.

Zephyrus, son of Astræus and Eos, was the West wind, 74.

Zetes and Calais were winged beings, the twin sons of Boreas and Oreithyia. They accompanied the Argonauts and drove away the Harpies who had plagued the blind King Phineus, the husband of their sister Cleopatra (see 157). They also freed from prison the sons of Cleopatra, whom their own father Phineus had falsely suspected.

Zethus, 248, 249, 250.

Zeus, see especially 6–11, 14, 16, 17, 18, 20, 23–33 and also 36, 41, 48, 50, 52, 53, 60, 61, 65, 70, 71, 73, 83, 91, 92, 93, 100, 101, 103, 104, 105, 106, 111, 119, 120, 131, 150, 164, 165, 166, 198, 223, 224, 225, 244, 248, 251, 265, 274, 280, 285, 319, 334, 360, 361, 371, 372, 373, 375, 403.

THE CONTEMPORARY THEATRE

In recent years a new kind of theatre has been created under the influence of writers able to break with convention and experiment for themselves, making more imaginative use of stage and language. This section concerns the English theatre since 1950.

TABLE OF CONTENTS

IV. Directory of Dramatists

Arthur Adamov

Edward Albee

Jean Anouilh

Aleksei Arbuzov

John Arden

Fernando Arrabal

Isaac Babel

James Baldwin

Samuel Beckett

Brendan Behan

Robert Bolt

Edward Bond

John Bowen

Bertold Brecht

Peter Brook

Albert Camus

Paddy Chayevsky

Giles Cooper

Shelagh Delaney

Nigel Dennis

Marguerite Duras

Friedrich Dürrenmatt

Charles Dyer

T. S. Eliot

Jules Feiffer

Michael Frayn

Max Frisch

Christopher Fry

Athol Fugard

Jean Genet

Günter Grass

David Halliwell

Christopher Hampton

Michael Hastings

Rolf Hochhuth

Donald Howarth

Eugene Ionesco

Alfred Jarry

Ann Jellicoe

James Joyce

Heiner Kipphardt

Arthur L. Kopit

Bernard Kops

D. H. Lawrence

Henry Livings

Robert Lowell

Peter Luke

John McGrath

Frank Marcus

David Mercer

Arthur Miller

John Mortimer

Slawomir Mrozek

Peter Nichols

Eugene O'Neill

Joe Orton

John Osborne

Alexander Ostrovsky

Alun Owen

Harold Pinter

Terence Rattigan

David Rudkind

Jean-Paul Sartre

James Saunders

Peter Shaffer

N. F. Simpson

Wole Soyinka

Tom Stoppard

David Storey

Cecil P. Taylor

Peter Terson

Jose Triana

Boris Vian

Roger Vitrac

Frank Wedekind

Peter Weiss

Arnold Wesker

John Whiting

Tennessee Williams

Charles Wood

THE CONTEMPORARY THEATRE

This section concerns the English theatre since 1950 and is confined to plays produced before a live audience. It consists of four sections:

I. Introduction
II. Eminent Theatrical Groups
III. Glossary of Dramatic Terms
IV. Directory of Dramatists

I. INTRODUCTION

What significance can the modern audience be expected to find in such spectacles as squalid garrets and basements, characters most unrealistically bursting into song, old tramps changing hats, a young man trying to teach a set of weighing-machines to sing the Hallelujah Chorus, or three children continuously re-enacting the ritual murder of their parents?

These are some of the questions that trouble the playgoer, and since they are not always easy to answer it may be helpful first to consider what is the function of dramatic art, what are its constituents and background, and how to judge a play.

The Function of Dramatic Art.

It is not the function of art to make a statement but to induce an imaginative response, and the spectator receives not an answer to a question but an experience.

Drama, like the other arts, gives expression to that subtle and elusive life of feeling that defies logical definition. By feeling is to be understood the whole experience of what it feels like to be alive—physical sensations, emotions, and even what it feels like to think.

This flux of sensibility cannot be netted down in logical discourse, but can find expression in what Clive Bell, when discussing the visual arts, called " significant form."

The contemporary philosopher, Susanne Langer, in her book, Feeling and Form, has developed Clive Bell's concept, arguing that all artistic form is an indirect expression of feeling. The artist, be he painter, poet, or dramatist, creates an image, a form that gives shape to his feeling, and it is for the sensitive recipient to interpret its significance.

The especial province of drama, as was pointed out by Aristotle, is to create an image, an illusion of action, that action " which springs from the past but is directed towards the future and is always great with things to come." Both tragedy and comedy depict such action and the conflict which it normally entails.

The Therapeutic Effect of Drama.

One of the achievements of serious drama is to create an image that will objectify and help to resolve deep human conflicts.

Most people have at some time or another come away from a fine play feeling in some inexplicable way exhilarated and released, and it has long been recognised that drama can have a beneficial, even a therapeutic effect.

It is not difficult to understand the exhilarating effect of comedy, but more difficult to understand that of tragedy. In the 4th century B.C. Aristotle claimed that tragedy accomplishes a beneficial purgation of pity and terror and very recently Miss Bradbrook has attempted a psychological explanation of the effect of serious drama on the audience. She suggests that in watching a mature play we are encouraged to sympathise with many different characters at one and the same time, and it may be that the imaginative effort entailed has a corresponding movement in the unconscious mind. There, at the most primitive level, is an " internal society," the petrified infantile images of father, mother, and siblings, to which we are linked by inflexible attitudes. It may be that the sympathetic response to the playwright's images of these figures helps us to relax our rigid attitudes towards them so that the internal pattern of relationships shifts, and we experience a sense of release and a new access of energy.

It is noteworthy also that drama can be fully appreciated only in a public performance, a social event demanding the co-operation and understanding between author, players, and audience. Because it can flourish only in a community, normally a city, it has been called the metropolitan art.

The Constituents of Drama.

Drama is a complex art in that it uses two very different kinds of ingredient or material, one speech, the literary constituent, the other the gesture, movement, and confrontation of actors on an actual stage. Speech is man's most precise, subtle, and mature means of expression. Gesture and confrontation, which he shares to some degree with animals, is more primitive and some of the power of drama as an art form is its fusion of civilised speech and primitive gesture into one organic whole.

It is just possible to conduct brief scenes using only one of these media. The chorus in Shakespeare's Henry V is virtually confined to speech and there is in Galsworthy's Justice, revived in 1968, a remarkable wordless scene, showing a criminal in solitary confinement in his cell, that proved so moving that it is reputed to have led to an amendment of the penal code.

Perhaps the more primitive gesture has the greater emotional force, but it is the words made permanent in the literary script that up till now have constituted the commanding form of drama. Even the wordless mime is given permanence by the printed script.

The Ritual Element.

While speech and the confrontation of actors are essential to full drama, there is an element that has sometimes been neglected and that is ritual, perhaps the most primitive and evocative of all. The early tragedy of Greece was probably organically connected with the religious ritual of Dionysus and the matrix was song and dance. Similarly in England the origins of drama are to be found in church liturgy and ritual and civic occasion, both of which used procession, pageantry, costume, and symbolic insignia to great effect and also clowning which served as comic relief to the solemnity.

There have naturally been few dramatists who have been able to combine literary ability, a sense of stage situation and also skill in the use of ritual process. The enduring power of Shakespeare is due to his manifold genius in that he could deploy inimitable poetry, swift action, and such ritual enrichments as royal processions, crowning and dethroning, duelling and wrestling, masque and pageantry, song and dance.

The Background of Modern Drama.

The happy fusion of both literary and theatrical excellence which is to be found in Shakespeare's plays is extremely rare, for it demands not only a versatile genius but also a receptive audience and a suitable building. By the Restoration the delicate balance was already disturbed and by the middle decades of the 19th century popular taste had all but banished literature from the stage. The disorderly audiences of the time demanded only spectacular and sensational theatrical and musical effects, and in the vast monopoly theatres of Drury Lane and Covent Garden they could hardly hear, let alone appreciated, good dialogue. The managers discouraged men of genius, so that poets like Browning, who had no practical knowledge of the theatre, produced wordy " closet dramas," which were virtually un-actable, while the popular theatrical melodramas like *Maria Marten* or *Murder in the Red Barn*, are today unreadable.

With the gradual establishment of smaller theatres, catering for a sober middle-class audience, men of talent again began to write for the stage. It was the turn of literature to take command, and more popular and traditional techniques such as music and clowning were now banished to the music-hall and pantomime.

T. W. Robertson, Henry Arthur Jones and Pinero all furthered the trend towards realism but it was the genius of Ibsen, especially in such works as *Ghosts* and *The Wild Duck*, that set a high standard of excellence for the literary and realistic play of middle-class life. He expressed his profound insight into personal and social problems in finely constructed plays, written in naturalistic prose, the overtones of poetic uni-versality being conveyed in symbolism that was usually verbal.

Able writers, like Granville Barker and Gals-worthy, although they lacked the poetic power of Ibsen, firmly established in England a similar type of literary play, realistic, well-constructed, serious-minded, concerned with the middle class and almost exclusively verbal.

Some of the few exceptions to this preoccupation with the realistic and literary are to be found in Shaw. Like Shakespeare, he was not only a lit-erary genius. He was also well acquainted with stage-production and although much too wordy in old age, in his best comedies he combined some of the wittiest dialogue to be found in English drama along with the delightful shocks and surprises of total theatre. Androcles' engaging Lion belongs to the same family as Titania's Ass and Whitting-ton's Cat.

But Shaw in his prime was unique, and between the wars the verbal, realistic play was perpetuated by such writers as Maugham and Coward. Not over-concerned with psychological or social issues, they used it to portray the leisured classes.

By the 'forties the conventional West End play had with a few exceptions come to imitate not life but photography. Confined to the proscenium arch and realistic to the last trivial detail, it pre-sented a prosaic picture of middle- and upper-class life, with stereotyped situation, demanding only stock responses and lacking interest in ideas, poetic intensity, and genuine wit. With the star cast and the long commercial run, theatre-going had become not an artistic experience but a social occasion.

Apart from the novel comedies of such writers as Ustinov and Rattigan and the verse plays of T. S. Eliot and Fry, it was the revivals of the classics, English and European, that were bringing

genuine drama to the stage. Shakespeare could be enjoyed not only at Stratford and the Old Vic, but in the West End. It was largely due to Gielgud that Shakespeare was now a box-office draw.

Gielgud's fine histrionic sense, and his highly sensitive and poetic interpretation had earned him that rare distinction of being the Hamlet of his generation and as early as 1934 his production and performance at the New Theatre had broken all records since Irving.

As actor and producer, working with other fine artists, such as Edith Evans, Peggy Ashcroft, Olivier, Guinness and Scofield, Gielgud later con-firmed his success. Enthralling interpretations of plays by Shakespeare, Webster, Otway, Con-greve, Sheridan, Wilde and Chekhov demonstrated that the classics could have a wide popular appeal.

Other artists followed and in a successful season at the New Theatre, Sybil Thorndike, Olivier and Richardson played to crowded houses in *Oedipus*, *Henry IV*, *The Critic* and *Peer Gynt*.

Such achievements have reminded audience and aspiring playwright that there are many other dramatic styles than that of fashionable realism and so may even have helped to further the drama-tic revival that began in the 'fifties.

The Modern Revival.

Although artistic work overflows the tidy schemes of chronology, it is helpful to distinguish two main phases of contemporary drama, begin-ning with plays produced during the first sudden outburst of creativity.

The decade beginning 1955.

Many new playwrights first became known during an exciting decade. There were British premières of plays by continental writers such as Brecht, Ionesco, Genet, Dürrenmatt, Frisch, Vian, Hochhuth and Weiss and by the American Albee. British dramatists who soon established their reputation included Beckett, Osborne, Behan, Pinter, N. F. Simpson, Ann Jellicoe, Mortimer, Wesker, Arden, Shaffer, Saunders and Bolt. Most of these, fortunately, still continue to write.

It is never easy to identify causes of artistic renewal but one reason was that young men like Wesker injected new vigour into the jaded realistic mode by using it to express the vital stresses of the working people they knew. Hence the settings in shabby basements and attics (*see* **Neo-realism**). It was in such a setting in Osborne's *Look Back in Anger* (*q.v.*) that there suddenly exploded that blast of confused and impotent anger which expressed the frustration of so many of his con-temporaries.

More far-reaching was the general awareness among avant-garde playwrights that verbalism was not enough, and their readiness to experiment with the resources of " total theatre." Here the way had been shown by scholarly research into the history of the theatre which gave dramatists confidence to revive valid techniques such as song, music and clowning that the early 20th cent. had banished to the music-hall.

The most vital stimulus was the challenge of genius. Brecht's Epic Theatre (*q.v.*) offered a more free and fluid form than that of the " well-made play " (*q.v.*) and his novel uses of traditional theatrical devices (such as song, masks, extrava-gant costume and settings, direct address to the audience) were quickly adapted by dramatists like Arden, Bolt and Osborne.

Meanwhile Ionesco, whole-hearted devotee of the Theatre of the Absurd (*q.v.*), introduced mon-sters like the rhinoceros and exploited stage properties like empty chairs to satirise man's frightened and empty existence. He was soon followed by Saunders and by Simpson, whose weighing-machines symbolised the dominance of imagination by machinery. Devices recently restricted to pantomime were returning to the stage.

A pervasive and growing influence was that of Artaud's demand for a Theatre of Cruelty (q.v.). This is both the most novel and the most atavistic type of theatre, for it attempts to re-create in modern terms that primitive, even barbaric ritual from which drama evolved. It was clearly exemplified in 1964 in a play by Weiss (q.v.) and in England is still best known in translations.

Developments since 1965.

One of the most interesting aspects of recent theatre has been a fresh and topical approach to Shakespeare.

Some critics and producers have traced in his plays the bleak disenchantment of post-war Europe. As early as 1963 Peter Brook had said that his production of King Lear, with Paul Scofield as protagonist, owed much to the Polish critic, Jan Kott, whose book Shakespeare, our Contemporary, was published here in the following year.

Kott, who lived through the Nazi tyranny and the Stalinist occupation of Poland, urges that the power-politics, chicanery and violence of twentieth century Europe have their counterpart in the Wars of the Roses and the Tudor disturbances. He finds in Shakespeare's Histories and in the Tragedies, especially Macbeth, what he terms the " Grand Mechanism " of history, the blood-stained struggle for power with its terrible consequences, and he claims that Shakespeare " condemns war by showing up the Feudal butchery.

The series, " The Wars of the Roses," which was produced for the B.B.C. during 1965–6 by Peter Hall and John Barton with the Royal Shakespeare Company, vividly demonstrated the crime-ridden lust for power and the Feudal butchery. Meanwhile at Stratford and the Aldwych, the production of Henry V neglected the traditional, royal splendour and showed the king, grimy and battle-scarred, leading a tattered army, plagued by corrupt camp-followers. Played on a bare, gaunt stage, grey, metallic and cavernous, it was strikingly similar in tone and significance to Brecht's Mother Courage, running concurrently at the Old Vic.

Shakespearean comedy has also been approached afresh. In Clifford Williams's enchanting production for the National Theatre in 1967 of As You Like It, with an all-male cast, the women's parts were not being taken as in Shakespeare's time by boys with unbroken voices but by young men. Clifford Williams was aware of the unorthodox theories expressed by Kott in his The Bitter Arcadia. Kott observing the almost identical appearance of modern youths and girls was reminded of those Shakespearean comedies where the girl appears disguised as a youth. He argues that their theme is that of the sonnets—" the impossibility of choice between the youth and the woman, the fragile boundary between friendship and love . . . the universality of desire which cannot be contained or limited to one sex."

Notable recent re-interpretations of Shakespeare have included The Merchant of Venice in Victorian costume with Olivier as Shylock resembling a Rothschild financier, and Peter Brook's A Midsummer Night's Dream. Brilliantly original in setting, its magical effect was enhanced by the use of trapezes while the actors taking Theseus and Hippolyta also took the parts of Oberon and Titania.

Recent perspectives.

Meanwhile there have since 1965 been diverse influences from abroad through plays by Soyinka Duras, Jarry, Mrozek, Fugard, Feiffer, Lowell, Triana and Chayavsky. A new generation of British dramatists has become prominent including Mercer, Bond, McGrath, Storey, Terson, Nichols, Wood, Hampton and Stoppard. Some have experimented in fresh dramatic genres and techniques but generally speaking the most novel contribution of native authors and producers has been a new candour in the presentation of social problems.

Joe Orton, whose best play had been produced in 1964, popularised a peculiar brand of " black comedy " (q.v.).

A more serious innovation was the " theatre of fact." The Investigation of Peter Weiss set an example for plays which constitute a kind of " documentary " of the stage, the dramatist endeavouring to present objectively a selection and concentration of the actual events of contemporary history. But however detached, the author must by the very act of selection betray a certain bias, as indeed must the professional historian himself.

One of the most sober of such factual plays, Kipphardt's on Oppenheimer, followed Weiss in presenting a judicial enquiry, a trial scene being ripe with conflict, suspense and surprise. Hastings' Lee Harvey Oswald took the same pattern. Both were shown in 1966 during a season at Hampstead, the director, Roose-Evans, stressing its preoccupation with ethical problems demanding the live concern of the audience.

The R.S.C. has also carried out an experiment in a new genre, that of " Director's Theatre," and the involvement of the audience was certainly the purpose of US, directed by Peter Brook as a direct assault on our apathy concerning the war in Vietnam.

The avant-garde Living Theatre was well represented here in 1969 by Grotowski and by Julian Beck's dedicated and disciplined company which presented Paradise Now and their versions of Frankenstein and Antigone. In this new genre coherent narrative sequence is discarded in favour of a series of " happenings "—disparate theatrical images, involving movement, mime, inarticulate cries, rhythmic sound and music. These are frequently violent, sometimes in a talented company surprising and beautiful, but often unintelligible. Living Theatre is often imbued with the spirit of Artaud's " Theatre of Cruelty," stressing intense suffering to convey an anarchic message. Sometimes " audience participation " is invited, actors and spectators mingling with each other both on stage and in the auditorium.

A refreshing candour in the approach to social problems has been evident in plays involving biting criticism of the military mentality and recourse to war, notably McGrath's Bofors Gun, Vian's The Generals' Tea Party, and Charles Wood's Dingo and " H."

Meanwhile the pressing international problem of relations between black and white has been illuminated in plays by Fugard, Saunders, Robert Lowell and the Negro Le Roi Jones.

Illness both physical and mental is now frankly presented. Peter Nichols in 1967 used remarkable theatrical skill in revealing the effects on the parents of the incurable illness of a spastic child. His ironic The National Health (1969) was set in a grim hospital ward.

It is no longer unusual to see a play depicting the distressed mind. Storey's first play had as protagonist a young husband struggling through a nervous breakdown, and his touching work Home (1970) is set in the grounds of a mental hospital. Both he and Mercer have been concerned with the malaise of a generation educated beyond the parents, and playwrights as dissimilar as Mortimer and Triana have presented the disturbed personality.

There has steadily developed a sympathetic attitude towards sexual deviation. In 1965 A Patriot for Me, Osborne's uncompromising record of a homosexual, could be performed only privately, while Frank Marcus' The Killing of Sister George indicated a lesbian relationship only under cover of some obvious comic satire of B.B.C. serials and their credulous public. But by 1966 Charles Dyer's The Staircase, although serio-comic in tone, could give a direct and uncluttered picture of a homosexual partnership, and in 1968 Christopher Hampton's Total Eclipse was completely devoted to a sober, searching, and candid exploration of the historic relationship between Verlaine and Rimbaud.

The abolition in September 1968 of the Lord Chamberlain's powers of theatre censorship removed official taboos on the dramatist's freedom of expression, which will in future be conditioned by the public's response. There has been an increasing vogue for " permissiveness," in the use of four-letter words and in sexual reference. The revue *Oh! Calcutta!* (1970), sponsored by Tynan, included a representation of sexual intercourse and total nudity. The taboo on stage nakedness was broken.

The playgoer of today is in a curious dilemma. The avant-garde dramatist relies increasingly on theatrical device to the neglect of coherent speech while in the West End there has been a reaction towards the styles fashionable just before the modern revival. The " kitchen sink play " of Neo-realism (*q.v.*) is now seldom seen and a feature of 1970 has been a return to favour of the " well-made play," with revivals of Coward, Priestley and Maugham.

For those who enjoy both literature and exciting theatrical surprise one pleasure is the continuous stream of Shaw productions which has characterised the contemporary revival. The greatest sustenance of all is, of course, the abundant opportunity to enter imaginatively into the world of Shakespeare, the many-sided genius who reconciles the opposites. Here we are especially indebted to the exquisite ensemble playing of the National Theatre and the Royal Shakespeare Company.

Criteria of Judgment.

How can the value of novel and experimental plays be estimated? The ultimate test of time is obviously impossible and some of the critical principles by which traditional drama has been interpreted are no longer relevant to the revolutionary plays of Brecht and Ionesco.

The first canon of criticism is to remember that every art form determines the criteria by which it is judged, and the good dramatic critic does not approach any play with a pontifical set of rules but endeavours to keep an open mind, and so to discover its unique significance and value.

Since artistic form is an expression of human feeling, the first encounter with a work of art should be in a mood of extreme receptivity, so that by shedding preconceived notions, the recipient may be aware of the feeling implicit in the work, however novel or even bizarre the expression may be. The initial reaction to drama should be intuitive.

The nature and quality of the implicit feeling can then be considered. Is it an original and genuine response to experience, or perfunctory and stereotyped, is it intense or diffuse, profound or shallow, subtle or commonplace, reasoned or irrational?

Questioning its inherent feeling often reveals that a commercially successful piece, although " well-made," is valueless, while an unconventional work, like Pinter's *Dumb Waiter*, explores and reveals deep-seated anxieties and fears.

Drama is an especially complicated art, in that part of its material being words, it may also involve discussion of ideas. This discussion, however, should not be mistaken for a statement of the author's convictions. In a good play it is an expression of his characters' *feeling* about ideas, a very different thing.

Another enquiry concerns the appropriateness and beauty of the form in which the feeling is conveyed. Many consider that Beckett's *Waiting for Godot* conveys the same mood implicit in *King Lear*, and that each play is an image of man, disillusioned, adrift, assailed by despair in an alien universe. This recognised, the critic's task is to explore the form of the two plays. Apart from the fact that they both use a most improbable fable, they could hardly be more different. *King Lear* is a Renaissance verse tragedy of the fall of princes, with subtle presentation of character development and contrast, and with a coherent plot skilfully developed through arresting action up to the tragic climax. *Waiting for Godot* is a prose play about an abortive encounter, almost devoid of individual characterisation and story, with a static, circular structure and an ending as ambiguous and inconclusive as its beginning. Yet in either case the form of the play has artistic significance and appropriateness and repays analysis, and here again the critic needs to be a flexible interpreter of the artist's purpose.

The most searching question to be asked of a play is whether it is life-enhancing, whether, like the finest art, it gives delight or deepens understanding.

Most difficult to estimate are those plays like *Lear* or *Godot*, which express a mood of despair. But if man's honesty and endurance are ultimately affirmed, the play is not negative in import. Lear begs forgiveness and the tramps still wait. Similarly a biting satire may be positive if it helps to clear away old wood to make room for new growth. A facile optimism may be a betrayal.

Ideally the best way to know a play is first to see it on the stage, when its theatrical qualities can be enjoyed, and later to read it at leisure, when its literary value can be appreciated.

II. EMINENT THEATRICAL GROUPS

We are greatly indebted to a few enterprising and devoted groups—chiefly repertory companies and theatre clubs—which help to keep drama alive.

Foremost are the Royal Shakespeare Company and the National Theatre, which have earned an international reputation by their superb productions of both classics and new plays. Some groups, such as the English Stage Company and the Traverse Theatre, Edinburgh, have been particularly concerned in introducing new dramatists.

Many repertory theatres are doing exciting work and a comprehensive list of these can be found in the *Stage Year Book*.

Among commercial promoters H. M. Tennent can be relied on for the high quality of their revivals of period plays.

The Royal Shakespeare Company.

When Peter Hall was appointed managing director in January 1960 his enterprising work revolutionised the R.S.C. He decided to supple-

ment the annual season of Shakespeare at Stratford-on-Avon by a continuous repertory of classical and contemporary plays at the Aldwych, and in 1962 a special experimental season was also held at the Arts Theatre.

Under the directors, Peter Hall, Peter Brook, and Paul Scofield, a brilliant team of over 100 actors was gathered together and the imaginative direction and artistic perfection of the ensemble playing became world famous.

In the spring of 1968 there was a rearrangement among the artists and executives at the head of the R.S.C. Peter Hall gave up his post as managing director to become director with special responsibilities for R.S.C. films and for the design and building of the Company's new London theatre in the Barbican.

Each year at the Aldwych original Shakespearean productions from Stratford alternate with other classics and stimulating modern work. Between 1960 and 1965 there were productions of highly experimental plays by Beckett, Livings, Pinter, Saunders, and Whiting and by foreign writers such as Arrabal, Brecht, Dürrenmatt, Hochhuth, Tardieu, Vitrac, and Weiss.

The years 1966–7 saw new plays by Duras. Mrozek, Dürrenmatt, Triana, Feiffer, Mercer, and Dyer, and Peter Brook's much discussed *US*, as well as revivals of Gogol and Ibsen. A special American season was launched in the period 1968–9, with British premières from Albee. Chayavsky, Feiffer, and Kopit.

During the 1969–70 season there were premières of plays by Pinter, Albee, Mercer, and Günter Grass, as well as many most original interpretations of Shakespeare and a six weeks' festival in 1970 at the Roundhouse.

The annual World Theatre Season, dating from 1964, gives a unique opportunity for seeing ensembles from other countries, special apparatus for simultaneous translation having been installed.

An excellent innovation has been the mobile " Theatreground " for young people which since 1966 has worked in collaboration with educational and municipal authorities.

A thriving R.S.C. Theatre Club provides booking facilities and concessions, discussions and a quarterly magazine, *Flourish*.

The National Theatre.

Sixty years after Granville Barker and William Archer had formulated plans for a National Theatre, the inaugural production of *Hamlet* took place on 22 October 1963 at its temporary home, the Old Vic.

Laurence Olivier already appointed director, the nucleus of a distinguished company was formed and soon established its high reputation for exquisite ensemble playing, guest artists also appearing on occasion.

The intention has been to build up a large repertoire of classical and modern plays from all countries and the wide and varied list includes works by Shakespeare, Ben Jonson, Webster, Congreve, Farquhar, Pinero, Brighouse, Shaw, O'Casey, Maugham, Shaffer, Arden, Chekhov, Ostrovsky, Feydeau, Brecht, and Miller.

The imaginative quality of production and acting has been enthusiastically acclaimed by packed houses and the scenery has often been breathtaking, especially in the designs of the Czech, Svoboda, for Ostrovsky's *The Storm* and Chekhov's *The Three Sisters*.

Recently there has been added to the repertory a superb interpretation of Strindberg's *Dance of Death*, produced by Byam Shaw, with Olivier as Edgar. Gielgud has made his welcome début at The National in *Tartuffe* and Seneca's *Oedipus*. Clifford's fascinating production of *As You Like It* with an all-male cast has appeared, and contemporary pieces have included Stoppard's *Rosencrantz and Guildernstern Are Dead*, a work of great virtuosity, Charles Wood's " *H* ", *The Advertisement* by Natalia Ginzburg, and *The National Health* by Peter Nichols.

A most attractive booklet is issued for each production and is available to the audience at a trifling cost. This supplies authoritative information about the author, the play, its sources and inner references, notable productions and critical estimates, together with photographs, reproductions, and plans.

Productions of the National Theatre have appeared at the Chichester Festival Theatre, and have gone on provincial tours. In September 1965 the company made its first tour abroad, visiting the foremost Soviet theatre, the Kremljovesky, and the Freie Volksbühne in West Berlin.

In the autumn of 1967, there was a six-week tour of Canada. During the two-week continental tour of September 1968 the company played in Stockholm, Copenhagen, Belgrade and Venice.

A recent welcome development has been an experimental workshop season in the spring of 1969 when three different productions were staged during three weeks at the Jeannetta Cochrane Theatre.

In 1970 a new company, the Young Vic, was formed with its own auditorium in The Cut. It caters for the under-25s and has already offered a wide choice of playwrights, including Shakespeare, Beckett and Molière.

The English Stage Company.

Since 1956 the English Stage Company at the Royal Court has been tireless in its discovery and support of new talent. Formed to promote contemporary drama, the company acquired in 1956 a long lease of the Royal Court with George Devine (d. 1965) as director and Tony Richardson as assistant. Declaring themselves a Writers' Theatre, they were extraordinarily successful in discovering and sponsoring playwrights hitherto unknown, such as Osborne, N. F. Simpson, Ann Jellicoe, and John Arden, and in persuading the novelist Nigel Dennis to write for the stage.

An offshoot of the Company, the English Stage Society, initiated in May 1957 the inexpensive Sunday night " Productions without Decor ", which brought to light such successes as Wesker's *The Kitchen* and Owen's *Progress to the Park*.

Writers beginning to make their reputation elsewhere were welcomed. Beckett's *Endgame* and *Krapp's Last Tape* had their première here. Many distinguished foreign plays were seen in Britain for the first time at the Court, including Arthur Miller's *The Crucible*, Tennessee Williams' *Orpheus Descending*, Ionesco's *The Chairs* and *Rhinoceros*, Sartre's *Nekrassov* and *Altona*, Genet's *The Blacks*, and Brecht's *The Good Person of Szechwan*, the first Brecht ever staged in London.

In October 1965 William Gaskill succeeded Devine and the autumn season 1965 saw new plays, by Jellicoe, Simpson, and Bond. There have since been revivals of both classic and modern works and several British premières of unusual plays, including Wesker's *Golden City*, Orton's *Crimes of Passion*, Charles Wood's *Dingo*, and the Nigerian Wole Soyinka's *The Lion and the Jewel*. A most interesting departure has been to stage here plays from the past hitherto ignored, such as Jarry's seminal French play of 1896, *Ubu Roi*, the Russian Babel's *Marya* of 1933, and Wedekind's *Lulu*. The establishment of D. H. Lawrence as a dramatist, culminating in the special Lawrence season of 1968, was an event in theatrical history.

Similar seasons followed of three plays each by Osborne (1968), Bond (1969) and Storey (1969–70).

Lindsay Anderson and Anthony Page have become co-directors with Gaskill and the year 1970 has been extremely fruitful, with excellent revivals of the classics and five premières of plays by Howarth, Hampton, Wedekind and two by Storey, transferring to the West End. Theatre Upstairs, opened in 1969, still encourages the latest and most promising experimental work.

The Mermaid Theatre.

It was largely due to the efforts of Bernard Miles that in 1959 the City of London's first new theatre since Shakespeare's time was opened at Blackfriars. Commerce, industry, and the general public had generously given money, the City Corporation had granted the site at a peppercorn rent and the four-foot-thick surviving walls of a blitzed warehouse had been used as the shell for a delightful little theatre of 499 seats.

It has an open stage, based on that of Shakespeare's day, while an excellently raked auditorium, all on one tier, like a segment of a Greek amphitheatre, ensures perfect sight lines. The most modern lighting, revolving stage, and sound and film equipment are installed.

The Mermaid is now part of the City's artistic life with foyer exhibitions, films, concerts, and lectures. The enterprising " Molecule Club " for children uses ingenious theatrical means to demonstrate basic scientific principles.

The Mermaid has a fine, varied record of productions, including British premières of works by Brecht, Camus, and O'Casey. There have been revivals of Shakespeare, Ford, Dekker, Beaumont, and Fletcher and Shaw, and of foreign plays by Ibsen, Pirandello, Henry James, and Lessing.

The year 1967 was notable for an imaginatively planned cycle of four dramas by Euripides concerning the Trojan War, and by the English première of the fine verse play *Benito Cereno* (*q.v.*) by the distinguished poet, Robert Lowell.

In 1968 the theatre's special design was admirably used for the spectacular production of

Luke's *Hadrian the Seventh* (*q.v.*), and 1970 was marked by Pinter's moving production of James Joyce's long neglected *Exiles* (*q.v.*).

The National Youth Theatre.

Originating in Alleyn's School and the enterprise of Michael Croft, the N.Y.T. fosters in young people an appreciation of theatre, whether as audience or participants. Since 1959 it has performed annually in the West End. Constantly expanding it now has several companies and in its foreign tours has presented plays at the festivals in Paris and Berlin. Several members have become professional actors, including John Stride and Derek Jakobi of the National Theatre. Since 1967 it has been admirably served by plays specially commissioned from Terson.

Theatre Workshop.

Between 1953 and 1961 Joan Littlewood as director of Theatre Workshop at Stratford East introduced several new playwrights, including Behan and Delaney. Spontaneity, pseudo-

Brechtian techniques and social commitment rather than careful construction were the hallmarks of her work, her masterpiece being *Oh What a Lovely War* (M). This paradoxically used a period piece brilliantly to satirise the tragic futility of the first world war.

In 1967 Littlewood directed *MacBird* and *Mrs. Wilson's Diary.*

MacBird (P), by Barbara Garson, is an American parody on *Macbeth* in doggerel blank verse. Described by Brustein as " brutally provocative " and " grimly amusing," it attacks the American " Establishment," under Lyndon Johnson. Unfortunately Joan Littlewood made such alterations to the text that the satirical parallel with Shakespeare was blurred.

Mrs. Wilson's Diary (M), in form a jolly prewar musical, was described by its authors, Ingrams and Wells, as " an affectionate lampoon " on the Wilson administration.

In 1970 she returned to Stratford East, where she has produced Hill's *Forward Up Your End* and Wells' *The Projector*, set in Walpole's age but suggesting parallels with the collapse of flats at Ronan Point.

III. GLOSSARY OF DRAMATIC TERMS

Absurd Drama.

The Theatre of the Absurd, originating in Paris, was introduced here through the plays of Beckett and translations of Ionesco, Vian, and Vitrac. It has had considerable impact on Pinter, N. F. Simpson, Saunders, Stoppard, and Campton, while American absurdist plays by Albee, Gelber, and Kopit and by the Swiss, Frisch, have also been produced here.

The concept of the Absurd was first formulated by Camus to indicate the discrepancy between human reason and aspiration and an indifferent and hostile universe. But like Sartre he expressed his convictions through the traditional dramatic form.

Not every playwright of the Absurd is an existentialist and many are more concerned with an irrational human society than with the universe. What they have in common is a technique. All have discarded traditional realism and express absurdity through images that are themselves absurd, including bizarre situations and objects, both sad and comic, such as aged parents consigned to dustbins.

There is in the Absurd an element of Surrealism and Miss Bradbrook has suggested that a better term might be Theatre of Dream, for it is the unconscious dream mind that juxtaposes objects and incidents that in the waking state have no connection, such as a rhinoceros in a provincial street. Pinter seems to have an intuitive awareness of the hinterland of dream, while Simpson makes a conscious manipulation of Surrealism.

Frisch has ably demonstrated that the Absurd can be an effective vehicle for satire and many absurdist writers, such as Ionesco and Simpson, have satirised the modern prostitution of language corrupted by salesmen and politicians, and have used conversation of vapid emptiness to reveal its breakdown as a means of communication.

It is partly because of their distrust of language that they have had recourse to ludicrous objects and images, thus extending the range of total theatre.

The Aristotelian Play.

Brecht and Ionesco have disparagingly referred, somewhat inaccurately, to " Aristotelianism." Strictly speaking, this means the concept of tragedy which Aristotle first analysed in his *Poetics*, basing it primarily on the poetic tragedies of Sophocles, especially the *Oedipus Rex* (P), c. 425 B.C. The Aristotelian concept, revived since the Renaissance, has obviously been much modified, but certain basic principles can still be discerned.

Aristotle claims that poetry in general aims at that rational pleasure which is part of the good

life. He defines tragedy as the imitation of an action. By imitation he does not mean the description of an actual happening but of one that is possible. Hence the poetic licence whereby the dramatist may adapt historical material to his own theme.

Aristotle stresses that the action should be complete in itself and have inner coherence. Tragedy must have an intelligible beginning, a middle necessitated by the beginning and which itself necessitates the end. " The story . . . must represent one action, a complete whole, with its several incidents so closely connected that the transposal or withdrawal of any one will disjoint and dislocate the whole."

The action should be of some magnitude, with " incidents arousing pity and fear wherewith to accomplish the purgation of such emotions." Here is Aristotle's celebrated doctrine of purgation or " catharsis " which has been variously interpreted, some considering that something like a ceremonial purification is intended, with an ethical end in view, others that bodily or psychological relief from tension is meant.

Aristotle emphasised the paramount importance of action or plot, the characters being revealed in and through the action. The kind of plot recommended is one where the hero is an eminent man, neither inordinately good nor bad, whose misfortune is brought upon him by some error of judgment.

Here is the germ of the splendid Renaissance tragedy concerned with the fall of princes and also of the modern finely constructed play, such as Ibsen's *Ghosts*. Such a play has classical symmetry, the beginning, middle, and end, becoming in modern parlance the exposition, development, and climax or denouement. It has its own organic unity and inevitability. But although many writers, such as Sartre, still work within the classical disciplines many have discarded the traditional form.

Brecht and his followers have repudiated the whole pattern in favour of a sequence of self-contained episodes strung along a narrative thread, where ironic detachment supersedes the emotional involvement and catharsis of Greek tragedy.

In this day of the common man few are concerned with the fall of princes, and it is interesting to examine some of the more striking modern plays and to ask how far they stand up to the Aristotelian canon. Should a new concept of tragedy be evolved, that of potentiality unrealised, not a fall from greatness but a failure to rise?

Black Comedy.

Orton (*q.v.*) popularised a genre in which human suffering is presented as comic. The basic technique is the shock of violent juxtapositions both in language and incident. Death, mental illness, murder, sexual perversion, suddenly excite laughter because they are conveyed in deadpan jests and genteel terms, or are promptly succeeded by the bathos of farce. Like circus clowning, the style has some value, especially in satire, but it easily stifles compassion.

The Brechtian or Epic Play.

Many British dramatists have felt the pervasive influence of the Bavarian Brecht (*q.v.*), who developed a new kind of Epic or narrative play of debate, with a loose sequence of episodic scenes linked by commentary or songs. Discarding realism, Brecht attempted not to arouse the onlooker's emotions but to stimulate him to think about social issues and to take left-wing action. In the event his ambiguous central situation appealed to deeper levels of experience.

There have been several instances of the ambiguous protagonist, but English playwrights have tended to adopt not the political intentions but the style of the Epic genre. Esslin has said that Shaffer in *The Royal Hunt of the Sun* has joined " Bolt, Arden and John Whiting of *The Devils* in the select group of British dramatists who have genuinely benefited from the conception of epic . . . techniques in drama."

Theatre of Cruelty.

In 1938 Antonin Artaud published *The Theatre and its Double*, a collection of essays and letters, which forms the theoretic basis of the Theatre of Cruelty, his central purpose being a ritual of cruelty to exorcise fantasies.

Professor Brustein has described how Artaud hated industrial civilisation, believing, like Freud and D. H. Lawrence, that it stifled instinctual life. He claimed that the theatre, as the heart of a common culture, should enact a primitive ritual of cruelty, a sacrificial frenzy and exaltation. In this way it would bring to the surface and exorcise the spectator's latent anarchy, violence, and eroticism, serving as an " outlet for repressions."

Artaud's theories have yet to be proved. Anthropology has shown that a sacrificial blood ritual was long practised by primitive tribes without diminishing man's urge to cruelty, as is poetically conveyed in Edith Sitwell's *Gold Coast Customs* (see **M25**). A modern dramatic enactment can certainly make us aware of repressed violent impulses but does it clear them away?

As to technique, Artaud envisaged a total theatre appealing to total man, primarily visual, where the all-important director would deploy " music, dance, plastic art, pantomime, mimicry, gesticulation, intonation, architecture, scenery and lighting " to induce a state of trance. Attacking the inadequacy of a pallid conceptual language, Artaud demanded that dramatic language should have an emotional and incantatory effect.

Genet fulfils Artaud's demands and in England the specific Theatre of Cruelty has been best represented by his plays, the *Marat-Sade* of Weiss and Triana's *The Criminals*. Its influence can be seen also in *The Architect and the Emperor of Assyria* of Arrabal. But the methods of production advocated by Artaud have had a wide and pervasive influence on the movement towards total theatre.

Expressionism.

The genre flourished in Germany after the first world war, where its chief exponents were Kaiser and Toller, and in Czechoslovakia in the plays of Capek. O'Neill and O'Casey have also occasionally experimented with Expressionism.

Reacting from Realism with its insistence on individual psychology and the detailed representation of actual life, Kaiser, Toller, and Capek sought to express rather the general aspirations and fears of humanity, especially man grappling with the advent of machinery. Their characters are symbolic types, as the Nameless One, representing the mob in Toller's *Man and the Masses*. Their decor is stylised, the dialogue staccato, and the brief scenes are characterised by mass movement and swift action.

Wesker's *Chips* and Wood's *Dingo* employ Expressionism but in England generally it is the techniques rather than the aims of the genre that have been adopted.

Naturalism.

Naturalism in drama may be regarded as a special case of Realism, and it is not easy, nor perhaps always desirable, to make a sharp distinction between the two.

Naturalistic drama attempts to record as faithfully as possible the actual experiences of life, however banal, and to present life, undistorted by the playwright's theories or too much concern for artistic form. The virtues of Naturalism are fidelity and spontaneity. Its danger is that it may keep so close to life as to lose artistic form and tension, becoming the stage version of the tape recorder. *See* Slice-of-Life Play.

It was Zola in the 1870s who propounded the principles of Naturalism. Distrusting both the play of ideas and the well-constructed play as tending to impose on life a falsifying and artificial pattern, he urged that drama should record as objectively as possible the actual course of man's life, especially the way it is conditioned by environment.

Strindberg's *Miss Julie*, 1888, is an essay in Naturalism but the genre is found in its most accomplished form in the Russian theatre, especially in Stanislavsky's production at the Moscow Art Theatre of the plays of Chekhov and in 1902 of Gorky's *The Lower Depths*.

Neo-Realism.

There is nothing new in dramatic Realism (*q.v.*) as such. What is novel is the realistic presentation of the shabby lodgings and streets of the underprivileged. Gorky in *The Lower Depths* was perhaps the first dramatist to reveal the wretched condition of the destitute and this play influenced O'Neill's *The Iceman Cometh*. Their production in London, with a starkly realistic background, had some effect on those modern plays where the kitchen-sink and dustbin were as much in vogue as was formerly the fashionable drawing-room.

Any worth-while play has significance far beyond its milieu and modern neo-realistic plays vary greatly in theme and purpose. Wesker, Delaney, Livings, Owen, Osborne, Orton, Bond, Lawler, and Seymour have all used the style in differing ways.

Several of these playwrights have themselves been workers and their plays are an authentic interpretation of their own culture, once inaccessible to the middle-class audience. The fact that their work is occasionally loose in structure may be attributable to the influence of Naturalism (*q.v.*) or to the author's unacademic background. The advent of this fresh and vigorous drama from a group that has seldom been articulate is one of the most encouraging aspects of modern theatre.

Realism.

Writers of realistic drama, such as Galsworthy, attempt to create a stage illusion of actual life, usually through the medium of the well-constructed play. It is not always easy to distinguish between Realism and Naturalism—its extreme form—but one salient difference is that the latter tends to discard organised plot as imposing a false pattern on the flux of life.

Bolt, Cooper, Mortimer, Shaffer, and Porter have all written realistic plays, and since the 'fifties there has been a succession of competently constructed realistic plays associated with the novelists, Graham Greene, C. P. Snow, and Muriel Spark.

The Satirical Play.

Recent years have seen heartening revivals of plays by Shaw, triggered off by Stage Sixty's production of *Widowers' Houses*, with its topical relevance to Rachmanism. There followed a long succession of Shaw revivals.

Shaw has found few successors, for genuine satire is a most demanding art. Subjective hostility and negative criticism are not enough.

The motive power in Ibsen and Shaw was rational indignation, a most difficult fusion of strong emotion and objective reasoning, and their satire was constructive in that it implied and indicated positive values. It was also characterised by a precise aim at a specific target. Vague and wholesale denunciation diffuse a disagreeable tone which has a boomerang effect for it becomes associated not with the targets but with the playwright himself.

The graces of satire are detachment, irony, and wit and it flourishes apparently in a stable society such as that of the 18th century, which produced Swift and Voltaire. The European upheavals of the last half century have been unpropitious for satire and it is significant that the best plays in this genre, those of Frisch and Dürrenmatt, have come from neutral Switzerland.

The English playwright nearest to Shaw is Nigel Dennis, and Giles Cooper shared his ironic detachment.

The " Slice of Life " Play.

Here is an extreme kind of Naturalism, where the author has been so anxious to preserve fidelity to the natural spontaneity of living, that he has all but discarded form, as having a cramping and distorting effect.

One of the most typical examples is Henry Chapman's *You Won't Always Be On Top*, showing the disconnected minor incident and talk of men ostensibly " at work " on a building site. Shelagh Delaney's *The Lion in Love* is also in this vein.

Verse Drama.

During the 20th century several attempts have been made to revive drama in verse—the normal vehicle for the Renaissance playwright. Although the verse plays of Shakespeare and his contemporaries, kept alive in excellent revivals, still rise like the Himalayas above the contemporary scene, the dramatist today who tries to use verse has not the benefit of an unbroken tradition. Yeats, T. S. Eliot, and Christopher Fry all succeeded for a time in getting their verse plays on to the stage but at the moment the most successful poetic drama achieves its effect through poetic prose and the theatrical poetry of its situation and stage imagery. Dylan Thomas' *Under Milk Wood* successfully used these media. For many contemporary audiences it is Beckett, Arden, and Pinter who have captured the poetry inherent in drama.

The finest verse play seen on the English stage for many years is Robert Lowell's *Benito Cereno*.

The Well-made Play.

The term " well-made play " is most frequently used in a derogatory sense. Eric Bentley has pointed out that the " well-made play " is a form of classical tragedy, degenerate in that although the plot is ingeniously contrived, with arresting situation, intrigue, and suspense, the play is mechanical and devoid of feeling. The television series, *The World of Wooster*, is an example.

The expression was frequently used disparagingly of the French plays of Scribe and of Sardou, ridiculed by Shaw for his " Sardoodledum."

IV. INDIVIDUAL DRAMATISTS

This part, alphabetical in arrangement, includes dramatists whose work, whether English or in translation, has had its British première since 1950. Unless otherwise stated the quotation of date and actor refers to the British première.

Inexpensive paperback editions are referred to thus: F: Faber and Faber. M: Methuen. P: Penguin. Inexpensive acting editions can usually be obtained from French's Theatre Bookshop, 26 Southampton Street, W.C.2.

Arthur Adamov (b. 1908).

Adamov first wrote plays such as *Professor Taranne* (P), which translate his own personal neuroses into images of the absurd, until with the propagandist *Paolo Paoli* he adopted a Brechtian technique. His *Spring 1871*, an epic panorama of the Paris Commune, had its world première in London in 1962.

Edward Albee (b. 1928).

The American Albee is a brilliant satirist, master of the hostile dialogue of barbed intellectual wit, and an adept in utilising diverse styles. He was adopted by wealthy foster parents and his major plays express the claustrophobia, the introverted emotional involvements, the terrible emptiness that may lurk behind the deceptively secure façade of wealth.

His early plays include the absurdist *Zoo Story* (P) and *The American Dream* (P), and the realistic *The Death of Bessie Smith*.

Who's Afraid of Virginia Woolf? 1964. P.

A brilliant and scarifying satire on sterility in an American campus uses a ritual movement. George and Martha, named after the Washingtons, are an unsuccessful and childless middle-aged couple. They cherish a fantasy " son," whom George, to spite Martha, symbolically " murders " during a liquor-ridden night party, when they attack each other and their guests (a young couple also childless) with ferocious mental cruelty.

A Delicate Balance. 1969. P.

An icy surface glasses over treacherous depths in the well-to-do home of Tobias (Hordern) and Agnes (Peggy Ashcroft) and the play begins and

ends with her virtual monologue—phrased with the elegance of a Henry James—on how it will be if she goes mad.

Agnes holds the " delicate balance " of polite manners, while tolerant Tobias is now ineffectual and her alcoholic sister Claire persists in her sarcastic utterance of unwelcome truths. The most galling, obliquely hinted at, is that Tobias is more drawn to Claire than to Agnes.

Their son long since dead, and Tobias having then withdrawn from Agnes, their sole offspring is the neurotic Julia, who now returns home at the breakdown of her fourth marriage.

Suddenly their " oldest friends," Harry and Edna, arrive seeking asylum from some inexplicable terror of " nothing." Bewildered, but courteous, the hosts accept their guests, but after Julia has threatened to shoot the " intruders," Agnes forces Tobias to realise that they bring " the plague."

Tobias, unable to discard his last ideal of friendship, begs them to stay, while telling them this truth, but they depart, realising that they demand a sacrifice they themselves could not make.

Here is a microcosm of a society where love and friendship have died, humanism crumbles, and little but polite diplomacy survives, often a vehicle for fear and hostility. In tone it is a bitter inversion of the Apocryphal *Tobit*, with its touching pictures of religious faith, family love and neighbourliness, and the " entertaining of Angels unawares."

The literary provenance in subject and style is Eliot's *Family Reunion*, where another Harry, fleeing the furies, comes to a Wishwood, also dominated by a woman whose husband had loved her sister, like Clair also a visionary. But in Eliot the visionary is healer not destroyer, and Harry departs to " follow the bright angels."

With literary subtlety Albee exposes the " panic and emptiness " in a society losing its confidence and sense of values.

Tiny Alice. 1970.

A " metaphysical melodrama," of great emotional tension, possibly personal, is at surface level, like Dürrenmatt's *The Visit* (q.v.), a satire on materialism, with the victim sold to Mammon. It has another facet, the schema being primitive magic, the sexual initiation and ritual sacrifice of the victim. Here Albee draws on techniques of

K (80th Ed.)

the Theatre of Cruelty (q.v.). There are also echoes of T. S. Eliot's *The Cocktail Party* (q.v.) and of Lewis Carroll's *Alice*.

A brilliant first scene initiates a bargain between two astute and unsavoury men, literally " of the same school," who detest each other—the Cardinal, corrupt representative of the Church, and the Lawyer, emissary of Miss Alice, embodiment of Croesus. She is to confer immense wealth on the Church on condition that the lay brother Julian shall collect it.

With Julian, the gentle and compassionate protagonist, a deeper theme is developed, the distinction between actuality and symbol. His ideals being service, obedience and possible martyrdom, Julian has fought unremittingly against accepting illusion and a false god, the puppet made in man's image, instead of God the Creator.

But in Miss Alice's echoing castle he is confronted and confused by an extraordinary image, a huge model, an exact replica of the castle, and within it a tiny model of the model. Sometimes events within castle and model synchronise.

The play's sinister dimension now becomes clearer, as Miss Alice, her brutal lover, the lawyer, and the butler, a former lover, plan, with the acquiescence of the cardinal, to entrap Julian. Their purpose is consummated as Miss Alice by witchery and her appeal " Help me," seduces Julian, when she utters the cry " Alice." (On the satirical plane this may signify that only by orgasm can the millionairess realise her identity.)

Later, after Julian's marriage to Alice by the reluctant cardinal, the four participants in the plot circle round Julian drinking to " the ceremony " and " Alice." Julian is now told that Miss Alice is an illusion, a surrogate for the real Alice who is within the model. Refusing to accept this, he is callously shot by the lawyer and left to die alone, slumped against the model.

The disparate elements in this exciting and disturbing play are not perfectly fused. Although Miss Alice experiences conflict between her " awesome " rôle and genuine tenderness for Julian, the characters are, with the exception of the complex Julian, two-dimensional. He, in his shy integrity, is touchingly portrayed. But his problem of faith although clinically scrutinised is not penetrated. This is especially apparent in his ambiguous and over-long dying soliloquy.

The work is meticulously plotted and worded, motifs, gestures, and phrases poetically recurring with ironic and suggestive shifts of meaning.

Jean Anouilh (b. 1910).

Anouilh is a playwright of remarkable theatrical versatility and skill. Following Giraudoux, he has frequently employed classical themes, as in *Eurydice* (M), and *Antigone*, 1949 (M), with Olivier and Vivien Leigh. More recently he has treated historical figures, Saint Joan in *The Lark* (M), and Becket in the play of that name (M). The play within a play is a favourite expedient of his and he used it again in *The Fighting Cock* (M), produced at Chichester, 1966.

Anouilh's outlook is deeply pessimistic. A recurring theme is that purity is incompatible with experience of life and many of his protagonists say, " No." His plays fall into two categories—the fatalistic *pièces noires* and the romantic fantasies, *pièces roses*.

They have been extraordinarily popular on the London stage of the 'fifties and Anouilh's amoral attitude has been reflected in many West End successes.

Aleksei Arbuzov (b. 1908).

The Russian producer and playwright Arbuzov has been writing since 1930.

The Promise. 1966.

In the best tradition of naturalism *The Promise* is a moving and positive work free from both illusion and despair.

During the siege of Leningrad three adolescents, two boys and a girl, contrive to survive in a bombed house, and here in brief episodic scenes their hardship, gaiety, and the slow awakening of love are shown with a delicate and touching naturalism.

Four years later Lika must choose between the two men and although she loves the engineer Marat she chooses the dependent, poetic Leonidik. The decision brings fulfilment to no one and finally Leonidik courageously summons back Marat and leaves him and Lika together, a conclusion analogous to that of *The Caucasian Chalk Circle*.

John Arden (b. 1930).

Arden is a vigorous and gifted playwright, who has experimented with a variety of subjects and methods, sometimes too original and complex to find quick acceptance.

His characters are full-blooded and rich in human contradictions, and he has sympathetically brought to life even such bogeys as Herod and King John. He loves to dwell on some ambiguous personality, where generosity conflicts with violence, and to consider the problems of directing man's unruly vitality.

His favourite theme is the dispute between instinctual energy and good government and he pleads the case cogently for both sides, giving no facile judgment or direct " message," unless it be " the recognition of the fallibility of man." Thus although, like Brecht, he is deeply concerned with social and political dilemmas, he remains politically " uncommitted." He is above all the dramatist of the dilemma.

There has been a fruitful cross-fertilisation of Arden's interest in current events and his literary studies; and his historical plays, like Brecht's *Mother Courage*, combine a fine sense of period and a sharp relevance to some current issue.

Arden's plays are poetic in structure, depending in part on the recurrent image and metaphor and, like Arthur Miller in *The Crucible*, he has skilfully devised for each an appropriate dialect of time and place. At the same time he has a keen sense of theatre, and has successfully adapted techniques from Miracle plays, Elizabethan drama, music-hall, puppet stage, and Brechtian epic play.

Live Like Pigs. 1958. P.

Seventeen realistic scenes full of comic and frightening incident reveal how fatal conflicts develop between households at different social levels in a new housing estate. Street ballads in Brechtian style preface some scenes.

The Happy Haven. 1960. P.

Here, in a good-tempered satirical fable, enlivened by a dash of magic, Arden touches on problems of longevity.

Doctor Copperthwaite, the superintendent of the Happy Haven, an old people's home, is like a mediaeval alchemist, bent on producing an Elixir of Life and Youth, intending to use his five unsuspecting patients as guinea-pigs. But outwitted by them he is himself transformed into a small boy.

The theme is childishness. The egocentric demands of the very old are seen as amusing childish foibles, while Doctor Copperthwaite, so absorbed in his research as to forget ends for means, brings childishness on himself.

In form the play is an extended puppet show. The characters wear masks, the set is formalised, and there is even a dog, Hector, but unlike Dog Toby he is visible only to the dramatis personae.

Serjeant Musgrave's Dance. 1959. M.

For a fine play, which explores the ethical dilemma of war, Arden drew on two sources—contemporary events in Cyprus and a journal written by a deeply devout N.C.O. during the Crimean War. He has fused his material into vivid incidents, which he projects against the background of a fictitious colonial war of the 1880s.

In a frost-bound colliery town there arrive three private soldiers, led by the dominating Serjeant Musgrave. They claim to have come recruiting but are in fact deserters from a colonial war.

In spite of his rigid sense of military duty, Musgrave had been horrified by the terrible fivefold reprisals taken by the British for the assassination of a comrade, Billy Hicks. Believing himself to be God's agent, he has now come to

Billy's town, obsessed by one purpose, to expose war's horrors.

Exhibiting Billy's skeleton in the market-place, he at first wins sympathy in his denunciation of atrocities. Then bewildered by his own confused " logic," he demands twenty-five deaths in return for the five taken by the British and turns the gatling on the astonished crowd.

Suddenly, with the thaw, the Dragoons arrive and Musgrave finds himself awaiting execution, stunned that no one has learned the lesson he yearned to teach.

Fierce incident and macabre surprise are used for a play of ideas which enunciates no facile answer. It is typical of Arden's fair and non-doctrinaire approach that the dilemma of the religious man in face of war should be embodied in the fanatical and confused Musgrave. This has sometimes misled the audience, but the spirit of compassion implicit throughout the play is clearly revealed in the gentle, pacific Private Attercliffe, who is also to be executed with Musgrave. The women's parts are also significant, especially that of Mrs. Hitchcock, the owner of the inn, who visits Musgrave in prison and shows him how he had erred in trying to use war itself to end war. In his darkest despair she gives him hope, and it is symbolic that he accepts drink from her hand.

The complex play weaves together many tensions; harsh discord between colliery owner and strikers; contention between the three privates, each of whom is strongly individualised; the discrepancy between a woman's love and the careless soldier's life; Musgrave's own bitter inner struggle.

The dialogue has a wonderful period character and the soldiers' ballads and lyrical songs occur with complete naturalness.

The Workhouse Donkey. 1963. **M.**

Styled by Arden as a " vulgar melodrama, " this ample Brechtian play shows jockeying for power in a northern town between the Tory Alderman Sweetman, a wealthy brewer, and Alderman Butterthwaite (Frank Finlay), the Labour ex-mayor. Both attempt to manipulate the police and to enlist the support of the electorate, represented by the shifty turncoat Doctor Blomax, until all these four elements of the community are deeply corrupted.

Butterthwaite, called " the workhouse donkey " because born in the workhouse, is the dominating Rabelaisian character. A Dionysiac figure, he is drunken, lecherous, and amoral, yet devotedly loyal and generous. Finally in an attempt to help the treacherous Blomax he robs the Borough safe and brings disaster on himself and the town.

The personality of the late Mr. Joseph D'Arcy of Dublin inspired much of the play.

Armstrong's Last Goodnight. 1964. **M.**

The old " Ballad of Johnie Armstrang," *c.* 1603, forms the framework of a play concerning the dilemmas of government. Armstrong of Gilnockie, the Scots Border laird, freebooter and rebel, is invited to a meeting by the young Scottish King James V and then treacherously hanged. Arden has introduced into this stark story the historical character of the king's herald, Sir David Lindsay, poet and politician, and shows him at first striving by devious diplomatic expedients to persuade Armstrong (Albert Finney) to loyalty, before he finally advises force. The play is diversified by minor characters and incidents which overcomplicate the impressive ballad line.

The introduction of Lindsay was suggested to Arden by his reading of Conor Cruise O'Brien's book *To Katanga and Back*, for he was struck by " a basic similarity of moral " between 20th-century Africa and 16th-century Scotland, the rôle of O'Brien being similar to that which he invents for Lindsay.

Arden makes free use of Elizabethan pageantry and of Brechtian ballad-singing and the setting is the mediaeval convention of " simultaneous mansions," Gilnockie, the Border, and the Court all being formally represented on the stage at one and the same time.

Arden " constructed " a dialect to suggest place and period, but it is difficult to follow.

Left-handed Liberty. 1965. **M.**

Commissioned by the Corporation of the City of London to write a play to commemorate the 750th anniversary of Magna Carta, Arden presents the historical facts with very little transposition and addition.

He approaches his theme of liberty from an unusual angle, showing the aftermath of Runnymede in the apparent failure of the Charter, and demonstrating that the agreement had to take place in people's minds before it could become effective.

Arden does not present a clash of black and white. John is a rounded character, a slippery villain, but shrewd and energetic and gifted with the Plantagenet charm, while some of the barons are coarse and unscrupulous fighters.

The use of stylised scene emblems gives mediaeval colour to the simple staging and Arden has again invented a suitable dialect.

The Royal Pardon. 1967. **M.**

A play for young teenagers, that developed out of bedtime stories for the Arden children, was written in collaboration with Margaretta D'Arcy.

Squire Jonathan. 1968.

In a grim Gothic tower, centuries ago, threadbare old Jonathan, descended from kings, gloats over his treasure chest, suspicious of the Dark Men outside and desiring the White Woman. A foolish, clumsy blonde, she appears wearing a chastity belt and eventually refusing his jewels, goes to the Dark Men. The play, a dramatic metaphor, was interpreted on production as an image of Britain's current situation, Jonathan dressed as Wilson and the White Woman like a Britannia or Boadicea.

The Hero Rises Up. 1968. **M.**

Written with Margaretta d'Arcy, this parody of melodrama is a sardonic enquiry into the motivation of our national hero, Nelson.

Fernando Arrabal (b. 1932).

Born in Spanish Morocco, Arrabal was early involved in cruelty. He disowned his extraordinary mother who had abandoned her husband in the Franquist régime and says that in schooling and religion he was " brought up on sado-masochism." In 1955 he finally moved to France.

Even before reading Ionesco and Beckett he wrote plays considered as absurdist, characterised by Esslin as a " highly disturbing mixture of innocence and cruelty," and has been influenced by Kafka, Camus, Lewis Carroll, and Artaud's Theatre of Cruelty. From 1962 Arrabal developed his ritualistic Theatre as a Panic Ceremony, so called after the god Pan (*see* **H35**).

Disclaiming imagination Arrabal says, " What I do is to copy my memories or my dreams . . . almost exactly, without changing a word."

The Architect and the Emperor of Assyria. 1971.

After terrifying intensity of noise the lordly Emperor descends from the skies calmly announcing to a cowering man whom he later dubs his architect that he is the sole survivor.

The situation recalls *The Tempest*, the Emperor, like Prospero, an embodiment of civilisation, the Architect an amalgam of Caliban and Ariel, a primitive, at first ignorant even of language, yet retaining magical powers over nature.

These two, the sole inhabitants of a desert island, play out an unending repetition of sado-masochistic fantasies springing from infantile traumas. All but naked they circle each other in balletic movement and mime, instantaneously exchanging such rôles as master, persecutor, judge, lover, and mother.

In Act I the Emperor is usually dominant, though sometimes sobbing for comfort in the arms of his " mummy." In Act II he is judged by the Architect for murdering his own mother whom he gave to his dog to eat. He demands the same punishment and is killed and eaten by the Architect, who in his cannibalism sucks in the Emperor's civilisation but loses his former magical power.

Again come darkness and deafening noise, but this time the Architect descends, taking over the Emperor's rôle.

As in Triana's more disciplined *The Criminals*, the dramatic movement is cyclical, the remorseless, self-destroying recurrence of obsession, especially guilt-ridden hate and dependence on the mother. The play has some root in anthropology and recalls Artaud's theories, exposing man's most grisly unconscious motivation and deploying a most extensive range of theatrical devices. Garcia, the producer, uses brilliant lighting, baroque music, and even an electric fork-lift truck on which to mount a crucifixion sequence and the Emperor's slow giving birth to the Architect!

Tense and exciting in its assault on the senses and sensibilities, the work can yet have a shattering effect on the audience, which is implicitly called on to play the exhausting rôle of untrained psychiatrist, unable to further any resolution. The basic subject is that of Aeschylus' *The Eumenides* (*see* H30)—matricide pursued by guilt. But the Greek tragedy is in effect exhilarating, achieving that therapeutic catharsis described by Aristotle.

Isaac Babel (1894–1941).

Between 1937 and 1957 the work of Babel, the Russian Jewish short-story writer, was banned in Russia. He died in Siberia. *Sunset*, the first of his two extant plays, produced in Russia under Stanislavsky in 1928, appeared on B.B.C. television in 1964.

Marya. 1967. P.

Written in 1933 but not yet professionally produced in Russia, *Marya* is set in Petrograd in February 1920. It evokes a precise period in history—the flux and confusion just before the Bolsheviks consolidated their power in March 1920.

The organisation of the play is poetic, the balance and interplay between two social milieus. One is the decayed elegance of the liberal intelligentsia focused in the home of Mukovnin, a former General, where the men are well-disposed but impotent, the women unchaste. The other is the squalid house where Dymschitz, the Jewish merchant turned black-marketeer, lives with his hangers-on and crooks.

As in Chekhov, the characters are studied in psychological depth and the quiet naturalism of the style is sometimes startled by sudden violence as in the shootings after the rape of Ludmilla, Mukovnin's younger daughter, and the link between the two households.

James Baldwin (b. 1924). *See also* M8.

Baldwin is an American Negro novelist and essayist, and a champion of Civil Rights.

The Amen Corner. 1965.

Acted by a Negro cast including singers of Spirituals, the successful play gently probes the genuine and the self-deluded elements in religious experience.

Samuel Beckett (b. 1906). *See also* M9.

Beckett, an Anglo-Irishman, who has made his home in France, is both novelist and the most distinguished of the English dramatists of the Absurd. His world is drastically limited, peopled chiefly by old men awaiting their death, but it is the profoundly tragic world of Lear in the storm and it is conceived with the intensity and haunting power and suggestiveness of the true poet.

His work is poetic in its verbal imagery, sometimes as searching and macabre as that of Webster, and his dramatic prose has an underlying poetic rhythm often more flexible and effective than that of Eliot's verse. In structure his plays have a poetic symbolism, a latent significance, like that of the novels of James Joyce, Beckett's close friend, and their striking visual imagery has a kind of

theatrical poetry, as for instance the two tramps at the foot of a bare tree in *Waiting for Godot*. It is remarkable that so literary a playwright should also have succeeded with the wordless mime play.

Beckett's chief weakness as a dramatist is that the action and visual imagery are frequently too static, as in the motionless dustbins in *End Game*, much less effective theatrically than Ionesco's movable chairs.

Waiting for Godot. 1955. F.

This tantalising and compelling tragi-comedy, Beckett's masterpiece, originally written in French and produced in Paris in 1953, was later translated and performed in more than twenty countries.

Character and incident are pared to the bone and only a skeleton situation remains. At evening, on a desolate road, bare but for a single tree, two wretched tramps, Vladimir and Estragon, nicknamed Didi and Gogo, wait for a mysterious Mr. Godot. As they while away the time with desultory talk and clowning, a tragi-farcical diversion is provided by the entry of Pozzo and Lucky, bullying master and wretched slave, and a boy later brings a message that Mr. Godot cannot come but will arrive the next evening. After discussing whether or not they shall hang themselves from the tree, the tramps decide to go away for the night, but remain on the spot.

Act II presents "Next day, same place," the only difference being that the tree has sprouted a few leaves, and the basic pattern of Act I is repeated.

Although by the skilful use of music-hall techniques Beckett presents his tramps in the guise of amusing clowns, they are at the same time pathetically human as they waver between suicide and irrational hope. A fretful affection has kept them together over fifty years, and their dispositions are complementary, possibly even representing different aspects of the one personality.

Pozzo and Lucky, another pair of contrasting characters, are portrayed more farcically. The loud, confident Pozzo drives Lucky in as if he were a beast of burden. Lucky carries in his mouth the whip with which he is beaten and humbly obeys every insolent command. He dances for Pozzo and even thinks for him. In their second appearance Pozzo is blind and Lucky dumb.

They may be considered personifications respectively of master and slave, worldly materialism and higher values, the physical and the intellectual, body and soul, or the two aspects of a sado-masochistic relationship.

The play as a whole is a most complex dramatic symbol expressing man's anxiety and suffering as to his origin and destination.

The uncertainty is symbolised by the characters' confusion as to even the physical actualities of time and place, but the dominating symbol is the tramps' doubt as to Godot's identity and purpose.

Such an oversimplified interpretation as to equate Godot with God is inadequate, yet the play has undoubted Christian references. A tree is frequently used as an emblem of the Cross. Beckett, questioned about its theme, quoted a wonderful sentence in Saint Augustine, . . . "Do not despair; one of the thieves was saved. Do not presume; one of the thieves was damned."

Beckett neither affirms nor denies Saint Augustine's statement but inverts it into a question, more distressing than direct denial. Can we any longer accept the existence of divine grace and judgment? It is a question such as this that gives to the play its symbolic shape of doubt, and which is cogently expressed in the theatrical image of two outcasts at the foot of a tree, a tree of life which puts forth leaves, a tree of death which they contemplate using as a gallows.

Yet the significance of the play is even deeper than an exploration of religious doubt, its appeal wider and more contemporary. The anguished uncertainty of the 20th century is whether life has any meaning whatsoever and the play shows the suffering of man, lost and anxious in an apparently meaningless universe.

Some have considered it to be written from the point of view of existentialism: continuing vainly to hope for a supernatural revelation, the tramps lack the courage to come to terms with the nothingness of our existence and the need to choose and create our own destiny.

A Jungian psychologist, Eva Metman, has made a similar interpretation, remarking, "Godot's function seems to be to keep his dependents unconscious."

"Habit is a great deadener," says Vladimir. If Beckett's play enables the audience to escape the drug of habit and to face this image of anguish and so find some relief, then it may have the therapeutic value of that inner knowledge advocated by Freud and Jung.

It is not a play for those who cannot bear to suffer. When performed in San Francisco Gaol, the first play there for forty-four years, it held its audience of fourteen hundred convicts spellbound. They realised that each must find his own personal message. All knew that it spoke to those who must suffer and wait.

Endgame. 1958. F.

Also re-created from the French, this play again depicts a static situation. In a single, claustrophobic room, the selfish, materialistic Hamm, who keeps his senile and legless parents in dustbins, is now paralysed and blind and dependent on his servant Clov, who longs to leave him. But if Clov should leave, both would die, for Hamm owns the only store of food in a devastated and dead world. Finally Clov sees outside what may be a small boy, "a potential procreator," and he prepares for departure but remains immobile.

The play like poetry can be interpreted in several ways. Since Hamm and Clov are mutually dependent, it probably represents tension between complementary aspects of personality, Hamm sensation and emotion, and Clov intellect. As Clov has vision and sees the boy, the situation suggests the struggle of the mystic endeavouring to escape from a deadening materialism to a vital awakening of the spirit. It may also depict a period of traumatic depression when the whole external world seems dead and unreal. The play's overall impression is that of the dissolution of the personality in death, both personal and global.

Endgame lacks the wry humour of Waiting for Godot, and is less compelling than Ionesco's Exit the King, but is more potent in its latent imagery than is Ionesco's play.

Krapp's Last Tape. 1958. F.

In the briefest sketch, Krapp, a solitary, decrepit, unsuccessful old man listens to his own autobiographical tape-recording of thirty years ago, but the moment of miraculous insight it commemorates is now so meaningless to him that he switches off that section of the recording and broods on a description of his love-making.

Beckett employs a most effective stage device to pose contemporary queries as to the limitations of verbal communication and the continuity of personal identity.

Happy Days. 1962. F.

Here again the paralysis of later life is indicated. A woman talks ceaselessly, although progressively buried in a mound of earth until it reaches her neck.

Beckett's two "Mimeplays without Words" are in striking contrast to the plays in that all is conveyed in symbolic wordless action.

Brendan Behan (1923–64).

Behan, a Dubliner, uses personal experiences as substance for two unusual plays, considerably improved by Joan Littlewood (q.v.). Lacking structure and depth of characterisation, they are impressionistic, lively, and voluble and Behan's strong social convictions presented in comic terms are fully integrated.

The Quare Fellow. 1956. M.

The play was an effective plea for the abolition of capital punishment. Its claustrophobic scene is an Irish gaol during the twenty-four hours preceding the execution at 8 a.m. of "the quare fellow," a brutal fratricide. The murderer is never seen and the sombre theme is presented

obliquely, masked by the harsh irony of prison jests and the alternation of farcical and macabre incidents as the unnerving effects of impending death is shown on prisoners and warders. Although the play has little plot its structure was tautened by Joan Littlewood who also had to treble the length.

The film version is a distortion.

The Hostage. 1958. M.

Again the basic situation is waiting for an execution. The scene is a Dublin brothel. Here Irish patriots bring young Leslie, captured Cockney soldier, as hostage for an Irish political prisoner in Belfast who is to be executed next morning.

There is touching pathos as a little Irish maid tries to save Leslie, neither of these orphans realising what the strife is about, but in a raid on the house Leslie is shot. The mood is not consistent, for here the comedy is supplied by a host of irrelevant characters and the action is constantly held up by satirical songs and some mediocre backchat. This pseudo-Brechtian trimming detracts from the growing sense of alarm as Leslie gradually realises his fate. But the play does succeed in making the business of war seem extremely childish.

Robert Bolt (b. 1924).

Bolt has recently said, "I do like plays in which the people have ideas as well as predicaments" and he is one of the few dramatists who have scored West End successes with the play of ideas. He holds the balance of discussion so fairly that only in the outcome is it clear that he himself is committed. His earlier work, represented by The Flowering Cherry (1957), with Ralph Richardson, was in the realistic convention, but more recently he has experimented with other dramatic techniques, owing something to Brecht and to the Theatre of Cruelty and of the Absurd.

The Tiger and the Horse. 1960.

This play takes its title from Blake's "The Tygers of wrath are wiser than the horses of instruction." It is concerned with the inadequacy of detachment, the philosophy held by Jack Dean, (Michael Redgrave), the Master of an Oxbridge college, the well-balanced man who represents Blake's "horse," while his wife, Gwen, the "tiger," passionately concerned for the world's suffering, shows signs of neurosis. The action revolves round her wish to sign a petition for unconditional nuclear disarmament and Dean eventually, to save her from mental breakdown, bravely identifies himself with her and the cause, thereby deserting his philosophy and his career.

In its outcome the play stresses the value of social idealism, stifled as it may be by philosophic detachment and the pressures of conformity. It is typical of Bolt's dialectic that this value should be upheld by the disturbed Gwen and by Louis, an oddly irresponsible young man.

Bolt departs from the realistic style by trying to make his characters larger than life in being unusually articulate about what they stand for.

A Man for All Seasons. 1960. P.

Here Bolt attempts to give his characters heroic dimensions by striking back into history.

Believing that our need today is a sense of personal individuality or "self hood," he chooses as his hero of "self hood" Sir Thomas More. Bolt consciously uses the dramatist's privilege to adapt history to his own purpose, for the theory of conscience accepted by More was not subjective and existentialist but identical with that of Thomas Aquinas. Hence some inconsistency in his portrayal.

More was described by one of his contemporaries as "a man for all seasons" and Bolt presents More (Scofield) as not only flexibly adjusted to Renaissance society but also preserving an inner core of unassailable integrity. Suspected of a critical attitude to Henry VIII's divorce, he used his skill in "the thickets of the law," yet resolutely refused to swear the oath to the Act of Succession that would have released him from the

Tower and the block, because for him perjury meant the loss of the soul, the self. His constancy is thrown into relief by the growing corruption of Richard Rich, whose final perjury sends More to his death.

Bolt's More challenges comparison with Brecht's Galileo. He also is a man of supreme intelligence, whose inner certitude of truth is persecuted by an absolute power. He also skilfully avoids open clash until he must eventually make a final choice between astute temporising and commitment of his life to his belief. The difference is that More opts unequivocally for constancy.

Bolt uses what he calls a "bastardized version" of Brecht's style. Episodic scenes are strung along a strong thread of intellectual argument. There is also a commentator in the form of the Common Man, who with the aid of property box takes a swift succession of minor parts, changes of role which throw into relief the steadfast individuality of More.

Bolt, like Brecht, believing that beauty of language is a means of "alienation," matches fine passages from More himself with his own appropriate use of wit and imagery, using images of land to suggest society and its laws and those of water and sea the superhuman context.

The film version has been highly praised.

Gentle Jack. 1963.

Bolt depicts the conflict between the natural spontaneity of nature, represented by the magic figure of folk-lore, Jack-of-the-Green (Kenneth Williams) and the inhibitions of society in the person of Miss Lazara, a plutocrat (Edith Evans). Since Bolt believes that the modern doctrine of the return to nature may lead to violence, Jack finally contrives two murders. Bolt in dealing with this conflict could not, like Euripides in The Bacchae, draw on a familiar myth, and his allegorical plot proved puzzling, while the setting was too reminiscent of Dear Brutus. The play is too cerebral, the characters are more blueprints than flesh and blood.

The Thwarting of Baron Bolligrew. 1965.

A play for children over eight was much praised by the critics as inventive and entertaining.

Vivat! Vivat Regina! 1970.

A play with two 'heroines'—Elizabeth I and Mary Queen of Scots. In the same predicament, the conflict between royal statecraft and woman's desire for husband, child, and heir, they are in temperament sharply contrasted. Mary is shown as sophisticated, sensuous, passionate, and self-willed, ruthlessly conniving at plots to murder her rival. Elizabeth, listening to Cecil and Walsingham, foregoes her love for Leicester in the interest of the realm.

Since the period spanned is virtually that of Mary's return from France until her execution (with just a hint of England's coming victory over the Armada) she is the main dramatic focus, although Elizabeth's astute dialogues with her advisers are more interesting.

Bolt does not attempt the subtle complexity of A Man For All Seasons but he shows admirable expertise in the handling of space and time. Discarding realistic sets he employs emblematic properties, such as thrones, pulpits, desks, and heraldic blazons. Clever selective lighting serves to make viable even the exchange of letters. Thus the action shifts unhindered between places wide apart and moves swiftly through the years.

Edward Bond (b. 1935).

Most sensitive people share Bond's appalled dismay at contemporary violence and war, the drab monotony of industrialisation and the stifling of individuality, but it is not yet clear whether his obsessive images of violence, including infanticide, are objective or self-indulgent.

He is not yet in control of his material and is apparently animated by intense, subjective hostility to all authority. He attempts to rationalise this by a naïve anarchy, pontificating that "Society . . . makes men animals" unaware that he is tilting at an abstraction. Some statements are so solipsistic and perverse as to make his intellectual groundwork suspect.

Saved. 1965. M.

As a result of casual sexual intercourse with the promiscuous Pam, Len gets involved with her morose South London family, with Fred, the putative father of her baby, and with Fred's lewd gang, which murders the baby on the stage.

Since the play is largely in delinquents' argot, and is limited to a photographic study of inarticulate people, it is in itself somewhat inarticulate, but it constitutes a frank and compassionate social document.

Early Morning. 1968.

Esslin interprets this play as infantile fantasy. The archetypal authoritarian figures of mother, father, nurse, and grown-ups appear as Queen Victoria and the Consort at deadly enmity, Florence Nightingale, on whom Victoria has a Lesbian crush, and Gladstone and Dizzy waging civil war. The princes, Siamese twins, suggest sibling rivalry, and the final scene is a nightmare eternity of mutual cannibalism, whose psychoanalytic significance is oral eroticism and sadism. Esslin judges the play absurdist, innocuous as satire, but with an underlying substance "of great seriousness and poetic power."

Wardle says Bond is writing like a wrathful, "omnipotent baby" presenting a "solipsistic muddle," meriting case-book study rather than dramatic criticism.

Narrow Road to the Deep North. 1968. M.

The setting, visually very beautiful, is 17th-century Japan, where the War Lord, Shogo, is eventually overthrown by the Commodore, a "bragging mindless savage," representing Western civilisation, with the tambourine-banging Georgina, a somewhat outdated image of missionary zeal supporting imperialism.

Shogo maintains order by sheer atrocity, Georgina by inculcating also a puritan sense of sin, the "message" being that government is per se evil and our only hope the naked man, who finally rises from the river (recalling the Romantic myth of the "noble savage").

Bond's dubious dogma overlays the most moving aspect of the play, its latent plea for individualism.

Black Mass. 1970.

For the Sharpeville commemoration Bond wrote a bitter satire, showing a priest corrupted by the power of politician and police.

John Bowen.

Bowen first won recognition as a novelist.

After the Rain. 1967.

Bowen dramatises his own novel, where after a great deluge ill-assorted survivors drift on a raft and enact a version of history. Meanwhile the dictatorial Arthur imposes on them his authority, first as dictator and ultimately as god. Bowen dramatises this fantasy by setting it in a conventional framework: a history lecture given in A.D. 2197 on the origins of the new society descended from the party on the raft. Hypnotised criminals, guilty of such crimes as individuality, are used at intervals as teaching aids. They enact the story of the raft, until eventually Arthur (Alec McCowen) rebels, preferring death to his dramatic role.

The lecture serves as a conventional apologia to the enactment, which eschewing scenery and properties, makes use of the experimental techniques of Weiss's Marat Sade.

Little Boxes. 1968. M.

A double bill of realistic well-made plays again shows little communities in isolation. In this instance both groups have withdrawn deliberately from society.

In The Coffee Lace a pathetic vaudeville troupe, elderly and poverty-stricken, have refused to go out since their performance was cruelly ridiculed thirteen years previously.

Trevor shows a young Lesbian couple. One girl anticipating her parents' visit pays an actor to pose as boy friend. But both sets of parents arrive and lively farce develops as Trevor attempts simultaneously to attend two parties and to cook scones. All the parents depart refusing to admit the girls' relationship and the play ends on a sentimental note.

The Disorderly Woman. 1969. M.

Bowen follows Anouilh in his capable adaptation of a Greek play, Euripides's *The Bacchae* to a modern idiom.

Bertold Brecht (1898–1956).

Perhaps the most original and vigorous dramatist and producer of the century, the Bavarian Brecht was remarkable in his command of both literary and theatrical genius.

His practice and theory underwent constant modification. Early plays, like *Baal*, written to provide entertainment, reveal a satiric and anarchic attitude, and in 1928 the ironic *The Threepenny Opera* (P), made him famous. From 1930 onward his work became explicitly communistic, marked by the rejection of the individual in favour of a social ideal. But although Brecht always remained " committed " to Marxist ideology, most of his later plays, written after his withdrawal from Nazi Germany, are less didactic than humanist in spirit and it is by these mature works that he is best known in Britain.

After 1949 Brecht consolidated the famous Berliner Ensemble in East Berlin, where he developed his influential techniques of production. The most permanent feature of Brecht's mature drama are the Epic form and the *Verfremdung*, or " alienation " effect, both developed in reaction to the traditional dramatic form, which he dubbed " Aristotelian." He considered that the closely constructed Aristotelian play, which encourages the audience's emotional participation in the action, syphons off the spectator's emotion, leaving him a passive and acquiescent member of society.

According to Brecht, the drama should be not ritual but debate. The spectator should be a detached observer, calmly investigating the view of the world that confronts him, rationally considering arguments and stimulated to decisive social action. It is taken for granted that he will find the solution to problems in communism.

Brecht therefore developed his "Epic," or narrative play, loosely constructed with a sequence of individual scenes, functioning as independent dramatic illustrations or quotations to the narrative.

He uses a variety of techniques to establish the narrative tone, such as an actual story-teller on the stage, explanatory verses relayed before the scenes, and banner headlines which foretell the events to be portrayed. Although by throwing the action thus into the past tense, he discards the lure of suspense, his dramatic intelligence, vigour, and inventiveness excite lively interest and curiosity.

To break down the traditional identification of the spectator with the action, Brecht developed his celebrated " alienation " effect, devising techniques to keep him at a critical distance. This implies using an image that suddenly makes the familiar appear strange and novel to the onlooker, so that he is shocked into recognising its significance.

His productions were thus avowedly non-realistic and theatrical, sometimes appearing like an inspired charade. He used not only direct narration but direct address to the audience, formalised settings and properties, masks and stylised make-up, sometimes grotesque in character. His text, " scarcely more than a prompter's copy," was freely adapted during rehearsal, so that an acquaintance with the pattern of Brecht's mime and gesture is often necessary to the full understanding of his plays.

Few find in Brecht's mature work the plea for communism that he intended, and many of his protagonists, designed as exponents of capitalist villainy, appeal strongly to the sympathy. The compelling and fascinating central ambiguity can be ascribed, as Esslin has pointed out, to the tension between Brecht's conscious reason and the unconscious emotional experience on which every creative writer must intuitively draw. This profound tension is the major source of Brecht's power.

Brecht's influence has been pervasive, especially on the dramatists Arden, Bolt, Whiting, and Shaffer, and on the producer Joan Littlewood. Above all his iconoclastic attitude and his fertile experiment have been invaluable in encouraging a new and empirical approach to drama.

Esslin's book *Brecht: a Choice of Evils,* 1959, is authoritative.

Baal. Written 1918.

The amoral vagabond poet, Baal (O'Toole), driven by instinct and emotion, expresses the subjective experience of the youthful Brecht.

Galileo. Written 1938–9. M.

Brecht intended Galileo's recantation as an image of the scientist's allowing the State to assume authority over science. It has also been interpreted as Galileo's cunning expedient, allowing him to continue research.

Mother Courage. Written 1939. M.

In his panorama of war's futility, Brecht designed Mother Courage—a camp follower in the Thirty Years' War—as an epitome of the haggling profiteer. But his intuitive understanding of this dynamic, maternal figure, bereaved eventually of all three children, has endowed her with an ambiguous fascination.

The Good Person of Szechwan. Written 1938–40. M. P.

Shen Te (Peggy Ashcroft), the benevolent prostitute, has to disguise herself as Shui Ta, the harsh task-master, in order to survive in an unjust commercial society.

Puntila. Written 1940–1.

The drunken generosity of the mean landowner, Puntila, designed by Brecht to highlight his harshness when sober, has however given him an attractive inconsistency. The chauffeur who rejects Puntila's daughter, is a Schweikian character.

The Resistable Rise of Arturo Ui. Written 1941.

The late British première, 1967, of a minor play vividly illuminates Brecht's principles and method. The Chicago thug, Ui, and his cronies burlesque Hitler and his entourage and the horror of Nazism is offset by the brilliant clowning by Rossiter of Ui's abject cowardice and monstrous arrogance. The play successfully parodies Shakespeare's verse, especially in *Richard III*, but the picture of Chicago gangsters as vegetable dealers is unconvincing.

The Caucasian Chalk Circle. Written 1944–5. M. P.

The prologue to this delightful fairy-tale constitutes an overt plea for communism rare in Brecht's later work. The rascally judge Adzak, who takes bribes from the rich and gives judgment in favour of the poor, is one of Brecht's typical contradictory characters.

Peter Brook (b. 1925). Director.

US (or ambiguously *U.S.*). 1966.

US is a collaboration between director, actors, designers, musicians, and writers in an attempt to confront the Vietnam war and to involve the audience.

Brook admits anti-American bias.

The First Act is a violent theatrical assault on apathy. Brook re-employs techniques from Weiss's *Marat-Sade* and alternates utmost stillness, as in the initial mime of a Buddhist self-immolation, with loud music and noise. In the hideous uproar and confusion of a bombing raid at the climax a giant war-effigy from the proscenium crashes across the stage. Shattering assault is succeeded in Act Two by a penetration in depth, its centre being a dialogue between a white man about to burn himself alive and a girl whose cold, detached criticism gradually gives way to a bitter indictment of English parochial indifference. In an ambiguous poetic finale an actor silently releases butterflies, one of which he burns.

This daring and controversial use of theatre directly to involve the emotion of the audience in confrontation with contemporary political tragedy may mark a new departure.

Albert Camus (1913–60).

It was the French existentialist philosopher and novelist, Camus, who first enunciated the concept of the Absurd, describing it as whatever in human experience is incompatible with man's desire for reason, justice, happiness, and purpose.

Like Sartre, Camus expressed his views through the traditional dramatic form, and the plays most familiar here were those written before he had moved on to a more humanistic philosophy.

Caligula. French publication 1945. P.

The Roman Emperor, Caligula, suddenly decides to act in accordance with the absurdity of the universe and by his violent and perverse crimes forces on the Senators his own recognition of the absurd meaninglessness of existence.

Cross Purposes. French publication 1945. P.

Man's futile desire for happiness is dramatised in the legend of the mother and daughter who murder for gain the visitor to their inn, only to discover they have killed the son of the house. They then commit suicide.

Paddy Chayvesky (b. 1923).
The Latent Heterosexual. 1968.

This American play begins as a hilarious caricature of homosexuality and drug addiction as embodied in the outrageous poet, Morley. His novel has just earned him $72,000 and his accountant advises him to evade taxation by a token marriage and by turning himself into a Corporation.

The marriage, to an expensive prostitute, is a sensational success, but soon the Corporation usurps Morley's personal identity. Almost paralysed, he makes a frantic effort to liberate himself and can find his only resource in suicide.

The remorseless and impressive final scenes change the tone of the play and constitute a serious satire on the atrophy of the human personality by Big Business.

Giles Cooper (1918–66).
Everything in the Garden. 1962. P.

Cooper deftly uses sophisticated comedy for a sharp satire on the sacrifice of principle to money in an effeminate bourgeois society. Four bored middle-class wives become part-time employees in an exclusive brothel, while their complaisant husbands enjoy the tax-free profits. There is a sudden horrifying change of key when at a party a neighbour realises the position and the four men destroy this outsider in a kind of ritual murder. In Cooper's second version the play returns rather shakily to the comic vein.

Happy Family. 1966. P.

Cooper's last play, outwardly a light, witty comedy, is an incisive assured satire on arrested development and snobbish exclusiveness.

For the well-to-do Mark and his two sisters nobody exists outside the family trio, and they employ their leisure with nursery games, jingles, and punishments. When the elder sister introduces a fiancé he at first serves as catalyst, but he is retarded, a grocer's assistant posing as solicitor, a " nobody " to the sadistic Mark, who soon contrives that he shall be ousted from the family circle and the nursery prattle resumed.

The bizarre situation skilfully dramatises indifference to others and obsession with the clutter of the past that stifles natural growth.

It is illuminating to contrast Triana's use of the same family triangle.

Shelagh Delaney (b. 1939).

The young Salford girl attracted attention with *A Taste of Honey,* 1958 (M), and *The Lion in Love* 1960 (M), her last play. The artless candour of their portrayal of seedy workers and drifters wa: then a novelty and they owed much to the revision and production by Joan Littlewood (*q.v.*) Only *A Taste of Honey* now retains any signifi cance, its unconventional subject being the preg nancy of an adolescent expecting a black baby and befriended by a homosexual youth.

Nigel Dennis (b. 1912).

Dennis, also a novelist, is a satirist in the tradi tion of Voltaire. In a Shavian preface to hi first two plays he uses arguments sometime more sparkling than valid to attack his favourite targets—the doctrine of Original Sin and th assumptions of psychoanalysis (*see* **J42**). He urges that both undermine self-reliance and tene to delegate power over the mind to a hierarchy which may threaten personality.

Dennis adopts a Shavian dramatic style and hi vigorous first acts have strikingly novel situation and witty dialogue. Then satire tends to diver interest from from the characters, holding uj action and weakening structure, as in some o Shaw's later plays.

Cards of Identity. 1956.

The play was adapted from Dennis's novel An Identity Club exploits psychological technique to induce local people into accepting change names, memories, and identities and then use them as servants. Only in face of their Ban! Manager do the victims re-discover themselves Dennis infers that the basis of personality i memory, which the psychologist can so edit as to manipulate personality—a thesis not verified by any appeal to scientific evidence.

The Making of Moo. 1957.

A colonial civil servant has weakened the taboo on murder by unwittingly killing the river god He invents the new religion of Moo, complete with mythology, ritual, and ethics. In this bol satire Dennis exposes similarities between th efficacy of pagan ritual sacrifice and the doctrine o Atonement. In his preface he suggests that to conform to a religious sect is to belong to an Identity Club.

August for the People. 1961. P.

A satire on the tameness of the public whe admitted—at a fee—to " stately home," lack the pungency and inventiveness of Dennis's earl work.

Marguerite Duras (b. 1914).

The French novelist and script-writer of th film *Hiroshima Mon Amour,* has a sensitive fla for dialogue and for exploring the ebb and flow o feeling. Her naturalistic plays move subtl towards their climax, often the agony of parting as in the one-act *La Musica,* 1966 (P).

Days in the Trees. 1966.

The theme of the play, virtually a trio, is th love–hate relationship between mother (Pegg Ashcroft) and son. She had indulged her ow emotions by conniving at his playing truant fo " whole days in the trees," so that he is now in capable of love for anyone else. Finally, the ag ing woman admits to herself his callous egoisr and misery, as now a gambler and pimp he live contemptuously with the devoted girl for whor he procures.

Friedrich Dürrenmatt (b. 1921)

The German-Swiss Dürrenmatt acknowledges the Greek dramatists, Shakespeare, and Swift as major influences. He describes his work as "theatre of paradox," revealing "precisely the paradoxical effects of strict logic." He is an unsparing critic of contemporary society, whose dangerous tendencies he exposes in striking and bizarre fictions, reminiscent of the later Shaw.

The Marriage of Mr. Mississippi. 1959.

An extravaganza poses the opposition between two principles carried to their logical and farcical extreme. One is a passion for the law of Moses, interpreted as retributive justice. The other is pure Marxism. The two characters embodying these principles, together with a Quixotic lover, are manipulated and destroyed by an unscrupulous politician.

The Visit.

An old multi-millionairess revisits her birthplace and offers the inhabitants £1,000,000 to murder her former lover, who had denied her paternity order. Gradually persuading themselves that they are acting justly they comply.

Dürrenmatt cleverly maintains suspense in his withering satire on love of money, hypocrisy, and the sycophancy of press and radio.

The Physicists. 1963.

Dürrenmatt has said that this arresting play is not so much about the hydrogen bomb as about society itself and the impossibility of escaping the consequences of one's thinking.

The central character, attempting to suppress scientific discoveries that may lead to the hydrogen bomb, retires to a private asylum pretending to be in contact with King Solomon. There he is first in danger of two spies, pretending to the delusion that they are Einstein and Newton, and eventually of the mad proprietress whose use of his discoveries will lead to the destruction of the human race.

The Meteor. 1966.

Another play of paradox has as hero a man who wishes to die but cannot. Schwitter (Patrick Magee), famous dramatist and Nobel prizewinner, already proclaimed dead in hospital, returns to the garret of his youth to die. In vain. As the old egoist swaggers, drinks, makes love, one by one those who touch his orbit meet their death.

The symbolism is unclear. Is Schwitter the egoistic kind of artist who feeds on the lives of others? The most effective incident—his dialogue with an ancient tart—cynically suggests that his art also has been prostitution, for he too has supplied artificial emotion to meet public demand. The chief weakness of the play is that the surprise wears thin. An original idea adequate to a one-act play has been inflated too far.

Charles Dyer.

Dyer's first success was The Rattle of a Simple Man.

The Staircase. 1966. P.

One of the frankest plays concerning homosexuality is a dialogue between the middle-aged Charles Dyer (Scofield) and Harry C. Leeds (Magee) during a wretched Sunday night in their poky barber's shop in Brixton, the cage they have co-habited for twenty years.

Charlie is sardonic, aggressive, cruel; Harry, a messy talker" is softer, protective. Their endless squabbling in ribald argot, comic, and searing, vents their exacerbated irritation, but underneath is glimpsed the pain of social isolation, the mother fixation, the frustrated hankering for offspring, the fear of exposure.

T. S. Eliot (1888–1965). See also M24.

In his attempt to revive poetic drama the distinguished poet, T. S. Eliot, was moved by deeply religious and social aims, modestly regarding his work as experimental, "that of the first generation only." The verse he evolved was of a flowing poetic rhythm, "close to contemporary speech" and based on natural stress. Normally he used a line with three stresses and varying length.

In his two plays of the 'thirties Eliot had adopted the ritualistic themes and patterns of Greek drama and had achieved a certain tragic intensity. But the Cocktail Party inaugurated a new style, the theme still being Christian redemption and the plot deriving from Greek drama, but the idiom, that of the fashionable comedy of manners. In spite of subtle organisation the liaison has been an uneasy one.

It is curious that the creator of Prufrock should seem unable fully to animate his dramatis personae. This is partly because their inspiration is literary, partly because they are used to illustrate Anglican doctrine and to convey a message. Nor do they belong to the impeccable background against which they are so carefully placed.

The wealth and subtlety of reference of these plays and the beauty of the language make them a delight to the reader, but they are less compelling on the stage.

The Cocktail Party. 1949. F.

This play, revived in 1968, has its literary origin in Euripides' tragi-comedy Alcestis, the demi-god Hercules being replaced by Reilly, the psychiatrist, whose intervention breaks the back of the play, for it is not easy to sympathise with people who let their actions be so directed.

The Confidential Clerk. 1953.

Described as "high farce," this play derives from another tragi-comedy of Euripides, the Ion, whose theme of parents seeking their lost children reappears in Terence, Plautus, and Shakespeare.

The Elder Statesman. 1955.

Eliot here returns to a tragedy, the Oedipus at Colonus of Sophocles, but the youthful peccadilloes of Lord Claverton appear pallid compared with the patricide and incest of Sophocles' protagonist.

Jules Feiffer.

Feiffer, the New York strip-cartoonist of international fame, now writes plays.

Little Murders. 1967.

The blustering Newquist family of New York embody what Feiffer has called the "national paranoia" in face of "random violence," and when the daughter, Patsy, introduces her fiancé, Alfred, who is so strong that he never retaliates, they are incredulous. But Patsy is killed by some stray bullet, Alfred adopts the Newquist ethos, and the family is happily united sniping down harmless passers by.

The main theme is clear. "Man hates war but is fascinated by it. . . . Peace is a Sissy." The play began as a novel, which may account for the plethora of other stimulating ideas which are never fully integrated, and also for some highly entertaining satirical vignettes not entirely relevant.

God Bless. 1968.

This Shavian satire scintillates with dramatic and verbal paradox, epigram, and ironic understatement, and improves on reading.

It is timed in "the immediate future," with America waging war in three continents, and is set in the library of the Liberal Brackman (Dotrice), America's "oldest elder statesman."

On his 110th birthday he is cynically dictating the record of his shilly-shallying career, used by Feiffer as an image of the American Liberal compromise as a betrayal of principle, a "sellout." His narrative is punctuated by teletype and television presentations of mounting insurrection off-stage. Then two heavily armed agitators, for Peace and Civil Rights, formerly Brackman's Harvard students, enter, soon to be followed by the President himself.

As forty-six cities go up in flames, the President reveals that the agitators have actually been financed by him as a tactic to shake up Congress! But the " tactic has gotten out of hand " and while Civil War breaks out the four men settle down to effect yet another compromise. The revolutionaries insist on bombing ten cities, but the President is to decide which ten! The play operates as an urgent warning.

Michael Frayn.

The Two of Us. 1970.

A quartet of sketches, each involving only two actors (Richard Briers and Lynn Redgrave), ended with a hilarious playlet which had the genuine technical virtuosity of the Feydeau farce.

Max Frisch (b. 1911).

Frisch, a German-Swiss who has been influenced by Shaw and Brecht, dramatises current issues in ingenious, apt, and witty parables that have a lucid economy of outline.

The Fire-Raisers. 1961. M.

A delightful Absurdist satire on bourgeois self-delusion and ineptitude shows Biedermann (Alfred Marks) persuading himself that he can cajole the incendiaries about to set fire to his house by inviting them to a good dinner. The situation is analogous to that of Benes of Czechoslovakia who included communists in his government, and to that of the Germans who connived at Hitler.

Andorra. 1964. M.

An incisive and moving satire on the vicious pervasiveness of antisemitism shows the Andorrans' betrayal of the lad Andri, reputedly a Jewish foundling, to the invading totalitarian state. Andri is in fact a Gentile and his assumption of Jewish traits is an example of identity imposed from without by society.

Christopher Fry (b. 1907).

Fry, widely acclaimed in the 'forties for bringing verse back to the stage, has written comedies and religious plays, the latter culminating in *A Sleep of Prisoners*, 1951, commissioned for enactment in churches during the Festival of Britain.

Fry devises ingenious situations, often in terms of poetic fable, informed by implicit affirmation and hope, lightly and gaily conveyed. His special talent is the creation of a dramatic atmosphere, unique to each play. But like *Love's Labours Lost* they tend to be too static and are carried by the dynamic and magic of verse. His delightful early verse was sometimes too lavish and discursive and with *Curtmantle* he began to use a plainer style with brief, telling images.

His maturer work completes the quartet of the Seasons that had begun with the Spring comedy, *The Lady's Not for Burning*, 1948, O.U.P., and *Venus Observed*, 1950, O.U.P., an unusual and felicitous comedy of Autumn.

The Dark is Light Enough. 1954.

In a play of Winter an eccentric and saint-like old Countess (Edith Evans) gives asylum to men of both sides in the Hungarian rising of 1948. The theme of non-intervention is presented with an elegance that saves it from didacticism.

Curtmantle. 1962.

A vigorous play has as tragic protagonist Henry II, shown as an imperious autocrat, brilliant, generous, and headstrong. Redeeming England from anarchy by his firm foundation of Common Law, he yet makes the tragic error of promoting as Archbishop his tried friend, Becket, who then proves intransigent and inconsistent and triumphs by his martyrdom.

With remarkable skill Fry incorporates the truly tragic hero and emotional power of the Aristotelian play (*q.v.*) in a work modern in structure. The main themes interpenetrate: the progressive discovery of Henry's contradictory personality in his relations with Becket, his people, and the wife and sons who deserted him,

and the " interplay of different laws." The drama moves swiftly through the years 1158–89 the events successfully telescoped as in William Marshall's memory. Some prose is appropriately used and the poetry is disciplined and vivid.

A Yard of Sun. 1970.

It is July 1946 in Siena, time of the first post war Palio, that tense horse-race, which is also " galvanic liturgy of life." In war's aftermath two neighbouring families strive towards renewal. In one there are still brothers' conflicts to b resolved. Angelino's eldest son, the rebellious Roberto, ex-Partisan, now a devoted doctor, scathingly scornful of easy-going Luigi, faile politician and Blackshirt, and also of the long missing Edmondo, who suddenly turns up. war-profiteer, Edmondo is smugly eager to use hi financial expertise to contrive the families' for tunes.

Unwillingly Roberto is stirred by Edmondo' dazzling wife, embodiment of the passionate ex citement of the Palio. But her husband' machinations go comically awry and they soo depart.

Roberto now realises that he loves the simpl Grazia, daughter of the neighbour Giosetta whose putative husband has just returned from a concentration camp, and now believes in hi duty to return to his legal invalid wife. There i a hint of union between Giosetta and Angelino. Although the scheme of this quiet, humorou comedy is somewhat too neat and flat it is true t its theme of resurgence. The fruits of Autumn may come. The poetic imagery well expresse the differing personalities and the volatile Italia temperament.

Athol Fugard (b. 1932).

Fugard now has his own Theatre Group in hi home town, Port Elizabeth.

The Blood Knot. 1966. P.

Of two brothers belonging to the mixed race o " Cape Coloureds," one " tries for white." Th dialogue between them, both comic and naïve, an fraught with intense love and hate, is a microcosi of the terrible strains imposed by racial segrega tion.

People Are Living There. 1970. O.U.P.

In a shabby kitchen in Johannesburg, Milly, th slatternly, kindly landlady, who has just bee thrown over by her lover, her German lodger vainly tries to whip up a frenzied party for he fiftieth birthday. The only other participant are Shorty, a " retarded poor white," and th student Don, too immersed in Sartre's " anguish to do anything else.

They get down to the grim " rock bottom "; o mutual self-knowledge, of society's indifference t poverty, of the loss of youth and joy in the inevit able ageing process, measured by the frail chimin of a shaky grandfather clock. Only Milly' sense of humour at the ridiculous plight of th whole animal world preserves their precariou companionship.

This compassionate play recalls Sartre's *I Camera*, but has a more valid conclusion tha Sartre's dictum, " hell is other people."

Jean Genet (b. 1910).

The French Genet, abandoned as a child, ha lived as social outcast and criminal and, whil politically " uncommitted," has mirrored hi bitter repudiation of society in plays of frightening impact.

His dramatis personae have been the rejecte murderers (*Deathwatch* (F)), despised servants (*Th Maids* (F)), prostitutes (*The Balcony* (F) Negroes (*The Blacks* (F)), and Algerian peasant (*The Screens*). These have realised their fantasie of sex, power, violence, and revenge only by com pulsive ritual acts, so that sequences of arresting ceremonial, sometimes Absurdist, replace charac ter study and coherent plot.

In his destructive scorn of contemporary society, his recourse to rituals of violence, and his incantatory language, Genet satisfies the requirements of Artaud's Theatre of Cruelty.

The Maids. 1956. F.

Two sisters, maids to a fine lady, continually take it in turn to enact the rôle of mistress and maid so that each can vent her envy and rancour on the mistress. When their plot to murder the mistress misfires, one of them herself drinks the poisoned cup of tea.

Their compulsive charade, designed originally for a cast of young men, mirrors the obsessive and self-destroying conflict of envious love and hate in the mind of the outsider.

Triana's *The Criminals* has a similar theme and technique.

The Balcony. 1957. F.

This censored play had its world première at the Arts Theatre Club. It opens in a brothel, where the frequenters enact their fantasies of power by dressing up as bishop, judge, or general, until after an abortive revolution they are called upon by the Court to impersonate these authorities in actuality. Eventually the defeated revolutionary leader visits the brothel to enact the part of Chief of Police, who is then satisfied that his image also has been established in popular regard. The film gives a softened version of the play.

Günter Grass (b. 1927).

Grass, a notable German novelist and author of some early absurdist plays, has recently written propaganda for the Social Democratic Party of Federal Germany.

The Plebians Rehearse the Uprising. 1968.

Produced here first by amateurs in 1968, and then by the R.S.C. in 1970, *The Plebians* is set in a theatre in East Berlin. The date, 17 June 1953, is that of the spontaneous yet formidable rising of the workers in East Germany against the Ulbricht régime.

The play—not a documentary—imagines a situation in which the Boss, clearly a counterpart of Brecht the dramatist-producer, is rehearsing his Germanised version of *Coriolanus*, whose protagonist is the aristocrat, who, spurning the rebellious plebians, all but betrays his country.

Into the Boss's theatre intrude rebellious workers, asking him to write a manifesto which will give coherence to their inarticulate demands. But the dramatist who has indefatigably urged intelligent revolution, scorns their amateur incompetence. Despite the advice of his wife, he temporises, exploiting the workers' gestures and tape-recording their dialogue as material for his own play.

Finally, moved by the enthusiasm of a girl, herself inspired by Katrin in Brecht's *Mother Courage* (q.v.), the Boss resolves to support the uprising. But already the Russian tanks are moving in. Bitterly he realises that he has himself played the part of Coriolanus.

The play reflects not only Grass's disquiet about Brecht's rôle in a satellite dictatorship. It concerns the predicament of the modern artist—that of Grass himself—as to whether art or political commitment should take precedence. A significant minor incident in the play is that the response of the University to the workers' cry, ' Intellectuals. Solidarity," is merely to bar their windows. Grass clearly indicates that the lack of effective support of artists and intellectuals to the revolution they advocate results in a tragic cleavage in the nation—hence the sub-title, *A German Tragedy.*

David Halliwell.

Little Malcolm and His Struggle Against the Eunuchs. 1965. F.

A deliciously funny send-up of the angry young man cult is located in a Huddersfield garrett.

Here Malcolm, a beatnik ex-art student, compensates for his inadequacies—professional and sexual —by fantasies of Hitlerian power. He imposes on his three chums his farrago of " Dynamic Insurrection," which so distorts reality that they all finally beat up the nice girl who wants to help Malcolm.

The sources of disaffection and violence are scrutinised incisively but with sympathy.

K. D. Dufford. 1969. F.

Dufford, like Malcolm, a fantasy-ridden mediocrity, commits child-murder in order to hit the headlines. Too much interest is diverted from his fantasy to conflicting interpretations of his crime.

Christopher Hampton (b. 1946).

When Did You Last See My Mother? 1960. F.

Hampton frankly explores the predicament of the adolescent Ian, a bitterly alienated homosexual, in his triangular relationship with a former school friend, Jimmy, and with Jimmy's mother.

Total Eclipse. 1968. F.

The story of Verlaine's passionate infatuation for the younger poet Rimbaud (prototype of Brecht's Baal) is dispassionately and convincingly presented, almost like a chronicle, the opening and closing scenes being particularly skilful.

The Philanthropist. 1970. F.

An ingenious comedy, ironic parallel of Molière's *The Misanthropist* (M), is " set in the near future " in the room of a bachelor don, Philip, the " philanthropist."

In an arresting *coup de théâtre* an aspiring dramatist, trying to convince Philip and his friend Donald of the likelihood of his protagonist's suicide, unfortunately blows out his own brains.

Shortly afterwards a dinner party for six occasions some brilliantly precise and apt repartee. As in Molière, the characters are boldly delineated and effectively contrasted. Philip, a literal-minded philology don, disclaims critical judgment, but is fascinated by words in isolation, his lonely pastime devising anagrams. So anxious is he to please that he is terrified of hurting people, but his mumbling evasions give more offence than Don's trenchant criticisms.

The evening culminates in comic fiasco. Philip, too imperceptive to realise that his fiancée, Celia, wants to stay, lets her be " taken home " by an unscrupulous acquaintance, and out of pique she sleeps with him. Meanwhile Philip is too timid to refuse the nymphomaniac, Araminta, who stays the night " under conditions too appalling to relate."

Next day, Celia, having discovered Araminta at breakfast, returns again to break off her engagement with one too weak to control her. Philip, crestfallen, decides to approach Liz, only to find that she has spent the night with Don!

Harking back to Scene 1, Philip transposes " Imagine the theatre as real " into " I hate thee, sterile anagram." Then, taking a cigarette and a small pistol, he goes to join Don and Liz. Is this ambiguous finale a token suicide, Philip having previously given up smoking for fear of cancer, or does the anagram indicate a new fruitful involvement in life?

The significance of this " bourgeois comedy " is further appreciated by comparison with Molière's comedy of manners.

A common theme is the foibles of the age, in Molière courtly hypocrisy, in Hampton growing indifference to violence. Don's hilarious report of the news that an unhinged Tory disguised as a woman has mown down half the Cabinet is discussed with cool nonchalance. Only Philip is apalled.

Hampton's characters are of the same metal as their prototypes but the coin is reversed. The idealistic misanthropist, Alceste, rebukes flatterers, even his beloved, the coquettish Célimène, finally deciding to withdraw from society. The gentle Philip is in his privileged vocation already withdrawn, but lacking the courage of his own "lack of convictions," diffidently condones even the "frivolous" Celia.

But Hampton's focus has shifted from a man's passion for a woman to friendship between two men.

The play is too derivative to be entirely self-subsistent but Hampton skilfully incorporates a subjective penetration of Philip's complex nature into his meticulously structured comedy.

Michael Hastings (b. 1938).

Hastings' *Don't Destroy Me* was produced when he was 18. *Yes and After* (P) appeared in 1957.

The Silence of Lee Harvey Oswald. 1966. P.

The play, an example of "living theatre," begins with a straightforward narrative of the assassination of Kennedy, illustrated by film sequences and stills.

Then verbatim passages from the official interrogation briskly alternate with imaginative reconstructions of Oswald's domestic life—a technique which diffuses the sense of authenticity.

Rolf Hochhuth (b. 1931).

Hochhuth, like his predecessor Schiller, is specially interested in the historical play, using poetic licence to organise and adapt factual material to his own dramatic purpose.

The Representative. 1963. M. P.

Using some dramatis personae who represent historical personages, this play in verse exposes the failure of Pope Pius XII, Christ's "representative," to protest against the massacre of the Jews. Film sequences of the horrors of Auschwitz are used with harrowing effect.

Soldiers. 1968.

Hochhuth's inordinately long play had its genesis in his horror and protest at the bombing of non-combatants. It is set symbolically at Coventry Cathedral but contains a realistic play-within-the-play, the only part produced in 1968 and here discussed.

This is timed for the crucial months, May to July, 1943, and historical persons are assigned fictional parts. Hochhuth embodies his theme by presenting Cherwell as the "eminence grise" who advocates to Churchill (John Colicos), the commanding protagonist, a policy of ruthless saturation bombing. The theme is counterpointed by the suggestion that success in modern warfare demands not only barbarity but treachery. This is given personal urgency in Churchill's confrontation with his ally, the Polish General Sikorski, whose intransigent hostility to Russia was proving a threat to our precarious alliance with Stalin.

Hochhuth's sensational insinuation that Churchill connived at Sikorski's death is a striking and poignant dramatic image and is defended by some critics on the grounds that a play is an agreed fiction. Hochhuth himself, however, claims to have seen secret evidence and has by some been sharply criticised for traducing Churchill when he cannot produce this.

In the final Act, Bishop Bell is presented in a fictional impassioned protest to Churchill against civilian atrocities, but the arguments assigned to him do not unfortunately proceed to their logical conclusion that modern warfare is *per se* an atrocity and here the moral pressure of the play is dissipated.

Hochhuth boldly handles his dominant themes while organising the intricate political detail in a gripping and enthralling way. The presentation of historical characters is remarkably convincing and Churchill emerges as an idiosyncratic, massive, and tragic hero, fully aware of his moral dilemmas and ironically prescient of his role as the servant of history in winning a war that destroyed the balance of Europe.

Donald Howarth.

A Lily in Little India. 1965. P.

Two households are revealed simultaneously. Alvin nagged by his promiscuous mother finds some confidence in growing a lily bulb. This brings him into touch with Anna, an older spinsterish girl keeping house for her widowed father and eagerly corresponding with Maurice, her seaman brother. The hesitant friendship between Alvin and Anna is indicated with some charm and distinction.

Three Months Gone. 1970.

In a sequel Anna now orphaned is pregnant after a single sexual encounter with Alvin and tries to keep him at a distance. But the delicacy of their relationship is here swamped by extraneous incidents many of them phantasy involving the presence on stage of the virile Maurice and his encounter with Alvin's mother.

Eugene Ionesco (b. 1912).

Ionesco, one of the leading Parisian playwrights of the Absurd, differs from Camus and Sartre in that he expresses his conviction of life's absurdity, not rationally, but through images that are in themselves absurd.

In 1948, while learning English from a primer, Ionesco stumbled on his vocation, his shocked reaction to the platitudes he was memorising being dramatised in *The Bald Prima Donna*. Here he singled out aspects of contemporary life which remain as the chief targets of his ridicule.

One is the empty, myopic existence of the petit bourgeois, his lack of passion and thought, the yielding to conventional pressures, the urge to conform. Another is the desiccation of language which, stereotyped and inadequate, has become "nothing but clichés, empty formulas and slogans."

Ionesco's sense of life's absurdity has deep roots, for he is keenly aware of the anguish of the modern world, of the flight from reason, both tragic and absurd in its potentialities. He believes that by dramatising his own inner hurt he can best reveal a universal experience. In *The Shepherd's Chameleon* he has plainly stated that for him "the theatre is the projection on to the stage of the dark world within," the world of dream, anguish, dark desires, inner contradictions, and obsessions.

It follows naturally that he is little preoccupied with specific social problems. Regarding the human condition as wider and deeper than the social condition, he dislikes any kind of political message or conformism and deliberately repudiates the "committed" and didactic play.

Iconoclastic in both his principles and technique, Ionesco—as he indicated in *Victims of Duty*—has challenged most dramatic assumptions, including realism, the concept of the "Aristotelian play," consistent characterisation, motivation, plot, and the distinction between tragedy and comedy.

Discarding so much, Ionesco has evolved a new technique of shock tactic, using most ingenious theatrical devices to express his convictions. He attempts "to go right down to the very basis of the grotesque, the realm of caricature . . . to push everything to paroxysm, to the point where the sources of the tragic lie. To create a theatre of violence—violently comic, violently tragic."

In his plays, as in those of Pinter, the traditional dividing lines between tragedy and comedy melt away, for his amusing images are at the same time poignant, expressing as they do human disappointment and folly, so that his hilarious comedy may have a tragic import.

A characteristic technique is the use of proliferating material objects, which externalise the anxieties of his characters—an accumulation of chairs or eggs, for instance, or an expanding corpse. He hopes thus "to make the stage settings speak; to translate action into visual terms; to project visible images of fear, regret, remorse, alienation."

The discarding of proved theatrical techniques is risky. Shock tactics are successful only as long as they surprise by their novelty. It is a measure of Ionesco's talent that he continues to invent the novel and arresting.

In two of his most recent plays, *Rhinoceros* and *Exit the King*, the nihilism for which Ionesco has been criticised has been relieved by the assertion of the human value of fortitude.

Ionesco's plays were introduced into England in the 'fifties and they have had a marked and specific impact on English drama, especially on Simpson and Saunders. Although Pinter has a philosophy and style all his own, his work is based on similar presuppositions.

The Bald Prima Donna. Written 1948.

Characters from an English language manual come to life and pour out their clichés in a " parody of a play," which Ionesco first considered to be a " tragedy of language," but which proved theatrically very funny. The first dialogue between husband and wife is now a classic.

Thus Ionesco, almost by accident, wrote the first of many satirical exposures of the sterile language of those who live a merely mechanical existence.

The Lesson. Written 1950. P.

A nervous old professor coaches an eager young girl. Elaborately " proving " the impossibility of communicating by words, he arbitrarily decides what various words shall mean, until he rapidly gains assurance and eventually rapes and murders his pupil, the fortieth that day.

Ionesco illustrates the prostitution of language as a means to power, the sexual element in power, and the sadism lurking in the teacher–pupil relationship and indeed in all authority.

Jack. Written 1950.

Urged by his conventional family to settle down to married life, the Bohemian son, Jack, resists Roberte, the proposed bride, because having only two noses she is not ugly enough. He eventually succumbs to Roberte II with three noses. Ionesco parodies submission to bourgeois conformity.

The Chairs. Written 1951. P.

An ancient concierge and his wife prepare for a crowd of guests who are to hear his final message to posterity. As the totally invisible guests arrive the couple fetch more and more chairs for them, until, with the entry of the professional orator who is to pronounce the message, they jump into the sea. But the orator is deaf and dumb and his writing on the blackboard is a meaningless jumble.

The empty chairs constitute a most effective theatrical image for man's failure to communicate, and the dumb orator makes the record of a lifetime seem utterly futile. It may also suggest how meaningless can be the words of author and actor. Ionesco says, " The theme of the play is nothingness made concrete."

Victims of Duty. Written 1952.

By transforming a detective into a psychoanalyst, Ionesco argues that there is little difference between the psychological drama and the mere detective play.

Amédée. Written 1953. P.

A corpse in the flat of a married couple, constantly growing at a frightening rate, is a gruesome and appropriate image of their dead love.

Rhinoceros. Written 1958. P.

More and more rhinoceroses appear in a small provincial town. They are the inhabitants who, one after the other, want to be turned into these thick-skinned, aggressive animals. Finally only Bérenger (Olivier) resists the urge to conform. The terrifying lure of conformity is here skilfully and movingly illustrated.

Exit the King. Written 1963.

In an agnostic counterpart of the 15th-century Everyman, Ionesco shows King Bérenger (Alec Guinness), in his disintegrating palace, reluctantly submitting to the process of dying, his final resource being fortitude alone. This dramatic elegy, inspired by the final scenes of Richard II, is designed with bold simplicity, presenting man's mortal dissolution with unflinching honesty and a tenderness new in Ionesco.

Alfred Jarry (1873–1907).

Ubu Roi. 1966. M.

In 1896, Jarry, initiator of the " Pataphysics " movement, scandalised Paris with his startling Ubu Roi, precursor of Absurd drama.

The characters appear as grotesque puppets, shocking and comic. The shameless, greedy Ubu caricatures both Macbeth and bourgeois vulgarity and in his brutal conquest of Poland becomes a monstrous prototype of ruthless cruelty.

Ann Jellicoe (b. 1928).

Ann Jellicoe's initial work as producer has left its mark on her plays.

Discounting the concept of man as a rational creature and stressing that people are driven by emotions she concentrated in her early plays on people in a highly emotional and irrational condition. She deliberately tried to stir up in the audience the emotions portrayed on stage, employing violent stimuli—a barrage of visual action, rhythm, sound, and sheer noise. Words were reduced to a minimum and these few frequently incantatory and meaningless. Ann Jellicoe wanted the audience to yield unthinkingly to the emotional impact and to refrain from asking, " What does this mean? "

While these plays were often intense and exciting, they were severely limited in range and manner and to some degree obscurantist. The emotional is only one aspect of human experience, and it is inextricably entangled with intellectual experience which is just as valid. To dwell almost exclusively on the irrational to the neglect of coherent speech—man's hard-won tool of thought—is partial and misleading.

The function of the artistic image is so to reveal aspects of experience that they can be recognised and harmonised, and to elucidate the significance of the image intelligence is necessary.

In later work Ann Jellicoe appears to have discarded her theories.

The Sport of My Mad Mother. 1957 F.

A gang of Teddy boys, living in terror of another gang which never appears, is dominated by the fierce and enigmatic Greta. Exulting in their feelings of violence, they express themselves in inarticulate and disjointed words and phrases, staccato cries and incantatory songs. Flim, a commentator, emphasises these with a set of instruments, including a motor-horn, which makes sounds that are often discordant and a-rhythmic.

All this makes a receptive audience aware of what it may feel like to belong to an adolescent gang, but Greta is not easy to accept. A mother-schoolmistress figure, she finally gives birth to a child and is an embodiment of the Indian goddess, Kali. The epigraph of the play is " All creation is the sport of my Mad Mother, Kali." Ann Jellicoe explained that the play is based on myth and uses ritual, bodying forth " fear and rage and being rejected from the womb or tribe." Such symbolism demanding an interpretation of its significance is out of key with a play so deliberately " anti-intellect " and restricted to a direct emotional impact.

The Knack. 1961. F.

The knack in question is that of getting girls and three out of the four characters are frankly exposed in the irrational grip of sex. The inhibited Colin struggles with the over-experienced Tolen for the possession of Nancy (Rita Tushingham) and again the action is carried forward as much by improvisation as by coherent speech. The film version captures the play's spirit.

Shelley. 1965.

A lucid, well-documented chronicle play illustrates incidents in Shelley's life. But the simple straight-line structure is not suited to the complexity of poetic genius. The personality that emerges is that of the selfless social idealist and pamphleteer and the theme his theory of free love, involving Harriet and Mary in disaster. The predicament is viewed from the woman's angle and the initial germinal situation, that with Harriet, is so oversimplified as to be false.

The frequent change of brief scenes, effective in themselves, has a fragmented effect.

The Giveaway. 1969.

A would-be satire on commercial "free gift" competitions (and television stardom) is too painfully obvious and flimsy to carry any weight.

James Joyce (1882–1941). *See also* M6.

Exiles.

Joyce's only play, rejected by both Yeats and Shaw, was after some vicissitudes of production, wonderfully justified under Pinter's direction in 1970.

Its theme is the agony of mind and spirit engendered by a courageous attempt to live beyond the confines of law, convention, and habit. Richard Rowan returns to Dublin, a famous writer, after nine years' voluntary exile. He brings Bertha, his wife by common-law, who had devotedly left Ireland with him, and their little son, Archie.

Rowan again meets Beatrice, who has always loved him and with whom he has for years corresponded voluminously about his work. From complex motives, partly to assure himself that Bertha's union with him is still absolutely free of conventional ties, he encourages her growing intimacy with his old friend and disciple, Robert. But Bertha, who in her simplicity is envious of Beatrice's education and subtlety of mind, feels rejected and confused, Robert that he is acting in an underhand way, and Richard that he must be ever wounded by doubt as to their fidelity.

Only parental feeling for Archie and Bertha's profound tenderness for Richard save them. For Bertha, with "something wiser than wisdom in her heart," has an intuitive insight beyond Richard's probing manipulating intelligence. Since Richard is to some degree a self-portrait, Joyce's objective self-criticism is remarkable.

This taut and close-knit play in "three cat and mouse acts," where the past "is present here now," recalls Ibsen.

In its complexity of viewpoint and entanglement of personalities there is ample material for four plays such as Hopkins' television sequence, *Talking to a Stranger*, 1966 (P).

Heiner Kipphardt.

In the Matter of J. Robert Oppenheimer. 1966. M.

The play, already performed in 23 capitals, concerns Oppenheimer, "father of the A bomb." The source is documentary, the 3,000 pages of proceedings before the Personnel Security Board of the US Atomic Energy Commission in 1954.

A hearing taking over a month with 40 witnesses has been condensed and shaped so that evidence is represented by only 6 witnesses. Kipphardt's aim was to follow Hegel in stripping away the adventitious circumstances so that the essential situation clearly emerges. He has made a few additions, such as monologues and final statements, and all deviations from the literal documents are based on historical data.

The play therefore has an extraordinary authenticity and grip while the central dilemmas are lucidly presented. As *The New Scientist* pointed out, it is for the audience to answer the searching questions raised. Was Oppenheimer, with his communist connections, a security risk? Can a scientist work with state authorities and keep his integrity? Is he responsible for the use made of his discoveries?

Arthur L. Kopit (b. 1938).

Oh Dad, Poor Dad. 1961.

This play parodies the devouring American "Mom," who emasculates all her menfolk. She travels accompanied by her husband's corpse in a coffin and dresses and treats her son of 17 as a child. A gruesome Freudian fantasy is presented as a comic "tragifarce," but there is little latent content.

Indians. 1968.

The career of Buffalo Bill Cody exemplifies the sweeping theme of America's encroachment on the Redskins. It is focused in the spectacular device of Cody's famous Wild West Show, where imprisoned Indian Chiefs had been specially released to re-enact their former resistance. Cody, at the climax, faced by the accusing ghosts of Red Indians, voices America's compunction at their virtual extermination.

Bernard Kops (b. 1928).

Kops, who was born in Stepney, of Jewish working folk, left school at the age of thirteen.

His plays include *The Hamlet of Stepney Green*, 1958 (P), *Good-bye World*, 1959, *Change for the Angel*, 1960, *The Dream of Peter Mann*, 1960 (P), the one-act, *Stray Cats and Empty Bottles*, and *Enter Solly Gold*, 1962, chosen for performance in the provinces by Centre 42.

Kops is less successful with realism than with fantasy, enlivened with the gaiety of local colour and frequent Jewish folk-song.

Most of his plays are variations on a basic design—that of the idealistic dreamer-hero, with an uneasy relationship with his easy-going mother, who in some cases is courted by a suitor whom he dislikes. Eventually the hero realises that a devoted girl is his true mate. Kops' plays thus draw nourishment from a deep emotional source, that of the Oedipus-Hamlet myth, on to which he grafts the happy ending of the fairy tale.

Social criticism, especially of mass-produced goods is often a secondary theme.

The attraction of the plays is their fairy-tale charm and naiveté, their uninhibited joyousness and the easy way in which the rhythm of dialogue flows into verse, song, and dance. Kops is like a Jewish J. M. Barrie, with the significant difference that most of his heroes renounce their dream for reality.

The artistic tension between spontaneity of feeling and excellence of form has become so relaxed that dramatic intensity is often sacrificed. The plays are loosely constructed, and the dialogue sometimes so naturalistic as to be banal.

D. H. Lawrence (1885–1930). *See also* M7.

It is remarkable that the plays of Lawrence should have had to wait half a century before coming to the stage.

In 1965, at the Royal Court, Peter Gill directed Lawrence's first play, *A Collier's Friday Night* (P), written in 1906. He followed it in 1967 with *The Daughter-in-Law* (P) and in 1968 he restaged these two, together with *The Widowing of Mrs. Holroyd* (P) in a special Lawrence season acclaimed by the critics.

These plays, written before the First World War, depict Lawrence's Nottinghamshire mining community with faithful realism. The themes are the universals already familiar through the contemporary *Sons and Lovers*—sex antagonism, the wife who feels "superior" to her miner husband, her possessiveness of the gifted son and jealousy of his wife or sweetheart.

Events of hearth and home, with profound emotional implications, move forward with a leisurely naturalism that is undisturbed by a forced plot and that seems extraordinarily modern in its idiom.

Henry Livings (b. 1929).

The protagonist of Livings' frank and realistic comedies of working life is normally the little man, whose unforeseen reactions culminate in hilarious disaster which topples down the petty rulers. Farce and near fantasy are lightly used to suggest a plea for the disregarded people who support the social edifice.

Stop It, Whoever You Are. 1960. P.

The insignificant Perkin Warbeck, a lavatory attendant in a factory, is involved in a series of ludicrous mishaps, but indirectly gets his own back on his harsh and frigid wife and his mean, pompous landlord. The comedy, which is very funny indeed, culminates in a fantasy-like scene of Warbeck's death, a séance, and a gas explosion.

Big Soft Nellie or the Sacred Nit.

A farcical comedy has as protagonist a mother's boy who is the laughing stock of his mates.

Nil Carborundum. 1962. P.

The scene is the kitchen of an R.A.F. station and the action culminates in a riotously-funny mock commando raid, which exposes both the pilfering cook and service routines that are now an anachronism.

Eh? 1964. M.

In an ultra-modern factory the incompetent young boiler-man, Val (David Warner), brings his bride to sleep in the bottom bunk and gives most of his attention to growing giant mushrooms, and eventually blows the place to smithereens. Again a light-hearted farcical comedy shows the underdog confounding established authority. Incidently a fool's lapse starts the "mushroom cloud."

Honour and Offer. 1969. M.

The pompous lodger and mortgagee, Cash, secretly desires his "delicious" landlady and hates her needy and unscrupulous husband, a slick travelling salesman, who eventually fools him.

Robert Lowell (b. 1917). *See also* M28.

The first dramatic work of the distinguished American poet, Robert Lowell, is *The Old Glory*, a recent trilogy of plays in free verse based on stories of Hawthorne and Melville. Their unifying motif is the flag.

Benito Cereno. 1967.

The third and best play of Lowell's trilogy is based on a short story by Herman Melville, which had its origin in actual incident.

About the year 1800, while off Trinidad, Delano, Captain of an American trader, observes that a Spanish trader, the *San Domingo*, is in great difficulties and generously goes to her aid.

Captained ostensibly by Benito Cereno, the *San Domingo* is in fact in the hands of her cargo of revolted slaves who have spared his life only that he may navigate them back to Africa. The effete and exhausted Cereno lives at the knife point at the hands of Babu, the wily and insinuating Negro who is in actual command.

Delano fails to realise this, for Cereno dare not speak plainly, and the American is too opaque and self-assured to interpret ironic hints. Only when Babu openly defies him is he enlightened, but too late. The only safe course now left to him is open violence and without warning his seamen massacre all the Negroes.

In a final ominous incident the last survivor, Babu, cries out "The future is with us" before Delano empties his pistol into the Negro's body, crying, "This is your future."

This is one of the most truly poetic plays to be seen in London for many years, lucid in verse, rich in themes and suggestive power, austere in design, while the theatrical poetry of mimes, rituals, and masques is used with ironic significance. The Director, Jonathan Miller, envisaged it as a kind of inverted *Tempest*, the Spanish ship a black magic island and Cereno a drugged Prospero held captive by Babu, and he produced it in the formal and stylised manner of opera.

The play is also remarkable in its relevance to America's dilemma, domestic and foreign, including her ambiguous attitude to the contemporary Negro. Jonathan Miller points out that Lowell here shows "the penalties of uninformed generosity" and of the trilogy as a whole he says, "These plays are about the big-hearted blindness of the American nation and they show quite clearly how the country's cardinal virtues can . . . harden into the very vices which so disable the American pursuit."

In a world increasingly threatened by discord between white and coloured peoples *Benito Cereno* has an even wider implication.

Peter Luke.

Hadrian the Seventh. 1967. P.

The play derives from a novel by Rolfe (alias Corvo), an extraordinary, autobiographical fantasy of his own wish-fulfilment, where the oft-rejected hero, Rose, becomes Pope. Luke wisely identifies Rose with Rolfe and presents the elevation to the Papacy as a dream, astonishing, spectacular, and witty, within the shabby framework of Rolfe's own circumstances.

John McGrath (b. 1935).

Of Irish extraction, McGrath, who had wide experience in the army before reading English at Oxford, has now had several plays published.

Events while Guarding the Bofors Gun. 1966. M.

In situation, McGrath's masculine and disciplined play is a realistic counterpart of Giles Cooper's radio fantasy *Mathry Beacon*.

The futility of military routine is exposed with steely irony as, on a freezing night in Germany, during the Cold War, seven men guard the obsolete Bofors gun. The frustrating situation also engenders personal conflict. The uncontrollable desperado O'Rourke defies Lance Bombardier Evans. An insecure boy of 18, Evans is so obsessed by the hope that promotion may provide him a way of escape to England that he connives at insubordination. Finally O'Rourke's reckless suicide destroys them both.

Bakke's Night of Fame. 1968.

A play, faithfully based on the novel, *A Danish Gambit*, by William Butler, takes as subject the prisoner's last night in the condemned cell of an American prison.

Bakke, condemned for an apparently motiveless murder, enjoys being as provocative as possible, discomforting the well-meaning guard by first requesting then contemptuously rejecting the traditional routine of food and consolation. He entangles the priest with his contention that society is exercising not justice but revenge, his only constant demand being that he shall meet his "buddy," the executioner.

This granted, Bakke so needles and infuriates the executioner that the man is betrayed into a violent outburst, gloating over his imminent task. Bakke, gleeful and triumphant, has proved his point about revenge.

McGrath shows great ingenuity and expertise in manoeuvre and sudden surprise, but he has not quite achieved the tension and suspense nor the progression of the *Bofors Gun*. The significant encounter with the executioner comes too late and is treated too briefly.

Frank Marcus.

The best-known plays are *The Killing of Sister George*, 1965, and *Mrs. Mouse Are You Within?*, 1968. Both give a humorously sympathetic account of an unusual human relationship, offset by boisterous comedy coming from off-stage.

David Mercer (b. 1928).

Since 1961 Mercer has written television plays and also the film-script *Morgan or a Suitable Case for Treatment*. His first stage play, *Ride a Cock Horse*, was produced in 1965. He is concerned with the psychological predicament of today's able, educated young man of artisan origin (a reflection of his own situation as son of a Yorkshire engine-driver). He usually depicts him as estranged from his parents, disorientated, and childless.

Originally drawn to Marxism Mercer has recently said that whatever the society he is examining, "whether the Vatican or the Kremlin," he is most concerned with the individual "who's catching the muck that's flying off the ideological fan," but he has not yet successfully dramatised this concern on the stage.

Belcher's Luck. 1966.

The rickety English class structure is the framework of a complex play.

On his ramshackle country estate, contemptuously served by his former batman, Belcher, Sir Gerald is becoming senile, Helen, his icy, avaricious niece, persuades Belcher to goad her uncle to his death so that they may together inherit the property. She then scornfully dismisses Belcher in favour of Victor, his bastard son.

Victor, expensively educated by Sir Gerald, is mentally unstable and impotent, but this familiar Mercer figure is now on the periphery. The conflict between the chaste and physically timid Sir Gerald and the coarse and drunken Belcher has become the compelling focus.

After Haggerty. 1970. M.

Bernard Link, dejected after two unsuccessful marriages, suddenly finds his new flat invaded by the vociferous American Claire, deserted wife of the former tenant Haggerty. She brings her baby. Idiosyncratic " decorators " from " Rely-On " add to the comic confusion.

Meanwhile rather stereotyped flashbacks in the form of monologue reveal emotional stalemate; Bernard, international drama critic, addresses his parochial engine-driver father (invisible to the audience); and the adoring heiress, Claire, talks to the indifferent and anarchical Haggerty (also unseen).

Bernard's weary embarrassment is intensified by the unheralded arrival of his father, prejudiced and censorious, yet pathetic.

The play ends with two acts of cruelty. An empty coffin arrives from Haggerty, indicating his demise, and Bernard, exasperated by his father's mental atrophy, symbolically hangs the funeral wreath round his neck.

A latent topic is disillusion with communism and violent protest, but Mercer's favourite theme, the alienation of artisan father and educated son, finds no resolution. The dialogue is vigorous and inventive, especially in invective.

Flint. 1970. M.

The play presents the improbable situation of a kindly septuagerian Kensington vicar, Flint (Michael Hordern), agnostic since ordination, whose sexual obsessions and irregularities have long been the scandal of the diocese.

While conducting his latest affair in the vestry with the teen-age Dixie, a Liverpool Irish " scrubber " from Holloway gaol, already pregnant by another, Flint inadvertently sets the vestry on fire. Meanwhile his wife, hysterically crippled since her honeymoon, sets fire to the church. She is then murdered by her sister, formerly Flint's mistress, who promptly goes mad. Flint and Dixie escape abroad on his motor-bike and side-car. While she is in labour by the roadside, he helplessly crashes into an ammunition lorry and is killed.

Mercer has claimed that Flint's " humanity is more valuable and more deserving of our love and compassion than the institution to which he belongs." But to contrast the hero, presented as endearing, with some stagey clerics is unconvincing demonstration. Recent revivals of Shaw make *Flint* look paltry as a " play of ideas," especially as the individuals who " catch the muck " are the vicar's hapless women!

There is melodrama in plenty and some lively farcical comedy, but wordy meditations, virtually monologues, clog the action, so that the play lacks the pace and invention of the sparkling Feydeau farces recently translated by Mortimer.

Arthur Miller (b. 1915).

Arthur Miller, an admirer of Ibsen, shares his strong sense of moral purpose and of the individual's responsibility to the community. This is balanced by a sympathetic understanding of the insecurity of the individual in modern society.

Miller's characters, deeply felt and realised, are fallible men who suffer through their own errors of character or judgment in social conditions which are incomprehensible, indifferent, or even hostile to them.

A recurrent pattern is that of paternal responsibility within a patriarchal family unit, and the father's distress as he sees his errors hurting wife and sons. But the sense of responsibility flows

outwards to society as a whole, of which the family is but the growing point. Significantly—apart from the benign mother-figures—Miller's most balanced characters are lawyers.

His plays are well constructed, the dialogue economic and telling, and he has progressed from the realism of *All My Sons*, published 1947, to much freer experimental techniques, while the prose style has become more fluid and eloquent.

Death of a Salesman. Published 1949. P.

A compassionate and finely-balanced play exposes the impingement of hire-purchase commercialism on the ageing salesman, Willy Loman, a weak, foolish, and deeply affectionate man, and also reveals his overwhelming sense of guilt towards wife and sons. The play is worked out on two planes, the inexorable present and Willy's past which obsessively enacts itself within his mind. The film version with Frederick March, is excellent.

The Crucible. Published 1953. P.

In 1949 Marion Starkey's *The Devil in Massachusetts* dealt with a witch-hunt in Salem in 1692, and pointed out its relevance to our own age, also rent by " ideological intensities." In 1952 the activities of McCarthy gave it a special urgency.

In his powerful play Miller uses this historical incident to depict not an indifferent society but one in which positive evil is unleashed. The evils he explores are the persecution of a minority and the interference of the Establishment in the individual conscience.

Characteristically Miller focuses attention on the plain man, John Proctor, and he invents his former adultery with Abigail, so that the play is not a partisan manifesto but a study of the complex contradictions of actual life. The self-righteous fanaticism of the persecutors and Proctor's own growth in self-knowledge and courage are faithfully and poignantly portrayed.

A View From the Bridge. 1956. P.

Eddie Carbone, a Brooklyn docker, is so gripped by jealous possessiveness of his wife's niece, that he eventually betrays her two kinsmen, illegal immigrants, to the Authorities.

In a play of repressed sexual passion, with hints of incest and homosexuality, Miller shows mastery of a kind of situation new to him and the heightening tension is realised in taut and disciplined sequences.

A lawyer, Alfieri, acts as a Greek chorus but is powerless to intervene, for Eddie infringes something more primitive than the legal code and it is by the primitive vendetta that he is eventually killed.

Incident at Vichy. 1966. P.

Miller here turns to the responsibility of society for the individual in a play which exposes the latent racial hostility which even the best men may unconsciously harbour.

The example he takes is antisemitism, the place and time Vichy in 1942, the scene a bleak anteroom within sound of a railway, where sealed trucks are deporting Jews to the furnaces of Auschwitz. Here a group of men and a boy, Jewish suspects, await investigation. There is an atmosphere of chill horror and suspense as each tries to summon up his own pitiful defence against the premonition of the ghastly journey he must embark on, once he is summoned behind the closed door.

Eventually only two men remain, the two most aware and articulate, Doctor Leduc, a Jewish analyst (Anthony Quayle), and Von Berg (Alec Guinness), the only Gentile of the group, a cultured and humane Viennese Prince, who is horrified by the vulgarity and barbarism of the Nazis.

In their final dialogue Doctor Leduc convinces the Prince of his unconscious antisemitism and the Prince gives his safe-conduct to the doctor.

A subsidiary theme of the play is the way society imposes extrinsically an identity on the individual, in this instance, as in Frisch's *Andorra*, the rôle of victim on the Jewish people. Through

Leduc, Miller also criticises the Jews' acceptance of their rôle.

This disturbing play makes the greatest demands on the emotions, intelligence and humanity of the audience, who like the Prince to some degree undergo psycho-analysis. But the play is also characterised by a fine restraint. As in Æschylus' *Agamemnon* the violence takes place behind closed doors, with the significant difference that in Miller's play the chorus and victims are identical.

The Price. 1969.

Two brothers confront each other in an attic crowded with the heavy furniture of their dead father, a financier ruined in the Depression. Its imminent sale is the occasion of their first encounter in sixteen years.

Victor Franz, who had given up a scientific career to support his father, is now a policeman at retiring age but too immobilised by his past to begin a new career in spite of the hysterical pressure of his wife. Walter, a surgeon, in his slick pursuit of success has had a prolonged breakdown and a broken marriage. The " price," ostensibly that of the furniture, is the price each has paid for his decision in life and its inexorable results.

The brothers ruthlessly dissect and probe back to the motivation of their choice. Walter is forced to admit calculated callousness but drives Victor to realise that his sense of social responsibility was also flawed, for he had sentimentally sacrificed his potentiality to a disingenuous father too cowardly to work again.

But no reconciliation ensues. Victor angrily refusing the dubious job which Walter offers as a salve to conscience.

Miller describes his play as stripped to the skeletal structure of two lives, the home the dead husk from which they had developed. But the characters are complex and through the Ibsen-like situation runs a thread of delightful and significant comedy. Solomon, an ancient Jew, survivor of wildly differing professions and four marriages, is the furniture appraisor and embodies the resilience lacking in the Franz's. When he falls he bounces. He shrewdly decides to buy all the furniture at a fair price and at curtain fall sits gleefully in the chair of the beaten father, chuckling exuberantly at his decision to begin life afresh.

The play is realistic, but the muted significance of various remnants of bric-a-brac is symbolic in effect. Organised with meticulous artistry, it is lucid and profound, and rich in the wisdom of experience distilled. Acted without a break it holds the audience absorbed.

John Mortimer (b. 1923).

Mortimer, a barrister, first won success with his short plays, such as *The Dock Brief*, 1957, and *Lunch Hour*, 1960 (M)., originally written for radio and television.

Here his talents are seen at their best, especially his gift for seizing on an unusual encounter between " the lonely, the neglected, the unsuccessful," whom he envisages in realistic settings of shabby gentility, and he is particularly sympathetic to those who allow their fantasy to overlap or swamp actuality.

But the moment of insight that gives pathos to his short plays is not enough to illuminate those of full length, like *What Shall We Tell Caroline?* and *The Wrong Side of the Park*, which lack substance.

Two Stars for Comfort (1960, M.) is also unsatisfactory. In its basic situation it is an inflated version of *Collect Your Hand Baggage* (M), with little beyond sentiment and pseudo Laurentian special pleading to fill the gaps.

The Judge. 1967. M.

After 40 years' absence from his native city, the bachelor Mr. Justice Chard returns for his last assize. He seems to expect some unspecified accusation about Serena's Bohemian establishment, but when the judge finally confronts Serena there he demands condemnation of himself.

It is revealed that as a youth he had once had relations with her knowing her to be a minor, had subsequently paid for an abortion and that his whole life had been slowly undermined by a rankling sense of crime and inconsistency. When Serena tells him that there was no occasion for an abortion and that she got the money from him to go abroad with her lover, the bewildered and frustrated Chard goes berserk.

The plot is thus an inversion of Dürrenmatt's *The Trial.* The commanding themes of guilt and the difficult and exhausting process of judging are boldly focused in the complex compulsive personality of Chard. Balancing the themes of guilt and retribution is that of permissiveness, represented by Serena. She is unfortunately pictured in a superficial way as a shallow Bohemian, and her ménage is not unlike that satirised by Mrozek in *Tango*, and much of the potential tension of the play is therefore slackened. Is the author too indulgent to his off-beat characters?

In the scenes with the judge Mortimer returns to the milieu of *The Dock Brief* and much of the attraction of the play is in his wry attitude, fascinated, tolerant, and amused, to the ceremonies and quiddities of the legal process.

A Journey Round My Father. 1970.

An autobiographical play, affectionately centred on Mortimer's own father, also a barrister. Blinded by a minor accident, Father became increasingly eccentric, his oddities often proving very disconcerting to his small, rather isolated family circle.

It is now apparent that Mortimer's own boyhood and schooldays and his father's idiosyncracies and fascination with the law have all helped to give substance to the earlier plays. Chard in *The Judge* especially shares with Father several mannerisms and also a liking for young people.

Slawomir Mrozek (b. 1930).

Mrozek, a Pole, who began as journalist and cartoonist, has recently established a reputation for satirical short stories and short plays.

Tango. 1966. P.

Mrozek's first full-length play is like a satirical cartoon, an expressionistic exposure of the cultural and political vicissitudes of 20th-century Europe as liberalism, fascism, and communism succeed one another.

A slovenly household of ageing Bohemians sentimentally cherish their memories of youthful rebellion against social convention when just to dance the tango was an act of defiance.

The son, Arthur, detesting their sloppy anarchy of taste and morals, enlists his reactionary great-uncle Eugene in his own counter-revolution to restore the *status quo*. But he soon resorts to fascist rant and force, terrorising the family until he is himself cut down by his own henchman, the tough lout, Eddie. The curtain falls as Eddie forces Eugene to partner him in a tango.

To an English audience especially the flatness of characterisation incidental to the cartoon style may be a little unsatisfying, but the novel satire is exhilarating.

Peter Nichols.

A Day in the Death of Joe Egg. 1967. F.

Nichols has shown remarkable sensitivity and skill in developing his theme—the especial difficulties of monogamy when the only child, a ten-year-old girl, is hopelessly spastic. He uses comic techniques of revue as the parents re-enact their frustrating encounters with doctors and clergy. But below the jesting façade grows the realisation that the wife's compulsive maternity blinds her to her husband's needs and that his endurance is crumbling.

Nichols has a spastic child and says " It's a play about marriage. . . . Not autobiographical."

The National Health. 1969. F.

In a bleak men's ward in a decaying hospital the staff are normally competent but faceless. Interpolated are brief T.V. scenes of *Nurse Norton's*

Affair, a burlesque of the rosy view of the medical profession as seen on popular T.V.

The vignettes of the consultant, the chaplain, and the visitor, have the pungency of revue. The ward orderly acts as compère to the whole, and also as devil's advocate who maliciously destroys the beginning of a positive relationship between a neurotic but protective schoolmaster and the alcoholic he is helping.

The play has the sharp precision and comedy of partial truth.

Eugene O'Neill (1888–1953).

Although O'Neill's work belongs to the first half of the century, three of his later works had their delayed première here in the 'fifties, two of them making a great impression.

Recognised as the greatest and most influential of American playwrights, O'Neill at his best came to close grips with the serious issues of human life, showing man battling with a harsh environment and with his own inner passions. He was deeply involved with his characters, often the flotsam and jetsam of humanity, conceived with disillusioned compassion, and he could create the powerful theatrical situation which rivets the audience. On the stage these gifts went far to compensate for a looseness of structure and a dialogue which is singularly flat, poor in vocabulary, and lacking in rhythm. His plays are better acted than read.

O'Neill, lacking the advantage of an American dramatic tradition, experimented with many European techniques before finding his own most personal style—a faithful realism with suggestive overtones of emotion and reflection.

British playwrights like Wesker and Alun Owen resemble O'Neill. They also are committed to individuals, especially to working people living insecurely. Like him they reveal the subtle and inhibiting ties that bind members of a family or gang, subjects which lend themselves to a similar rather sprawling and diffuse structure and dialect style. So far they have not matched O'Neill's passionate and gripping intensity.

The Iceman Cometh. Published 1947.

In a naturalistic play, whose prototype is Gorky's *The Lower Depths*, down-and-outs await the arrival of the dionysiac Hickey. But Hickey has just murdered his wife and his abortive attempt to rouse them from "pipe dreams" to reality leaves them sunk even more deeply than before in drink and self-deceit. The pessimistic theme is that of Ibsen's *The Wild Duck* and the situation that of Beckett's *Waiting for Godot*.

Long Day's Journey Into Night. Published 1955.

An avowed autobiographical play depicts O'Neill's family on the day when his mother (Gwen Ffrangcon Davies) relapses into drug addiction and Eugene learns that he must leave there that he chose his vocation, this constitutes the one note of hope in a deeply mournful reverie. The Freudian love–hate relationships are unfolded with tender understanding.

Joe Orton (1933–67).

Orton was a successful commercial exponent of black comedy who also won praise from serious critics especially for his dialogue.

His range is narrow and he is preoccupied with crime, perverted sexuality, and violence portrayed without inhibition as hilariously comic, sometimes with satiric effect. The macabre plots give occasion for a flow of deadpan repartee, normally smutty, sometimes merely facetious, often very apt and funny indeed, always a parody of the would-be genteel. Nearly all Orton's characters speak alike and are as undifferentiated in their lingo as in their lack of morality.

The satire is in the form of caricature or parody and apart from its implications it is almost impossible to discover in Orton any expression of human value or aspiration. It is not always easy to discriminate between the unsavoury matter of his plays and the expertise and aplomb with which it is manipulated, and some feel that he defaces the image of life.

Entertaining Mr. Sloane. 1964. P.

The handsome young wastrel, Sloane, already a murderer, finds a cosy refuge with Kath. A slattern of forty, she smothers him with motherliness and, sexually insatiable, she seduces him from the first night. Her brother, Ed, a homosexual, soon employs Sloan as his "chauffeur." When Sloane tries to escape their possessiveness, his brutal murder of their father puts him into their power and they agree quite literally to share him, each having him for six months at a time.

The play scores by a skilfully handled plot, an ironic "poetic justice" and the sly and genteel euphemisms of the salacious dialogue, and it won the London Critics Variety Award as the best play of 1964.

Basically the plot is that of Pinter's *The Birthday Party*. In both cases a man on the run is sheltered by a slovenly older woman, but here Kath's sexuality vulgarises the situation and as she constantly refers to herself as Sloane's "mamma" and to their unborn child as his "brother" it is highly suggestive of incest. The kindly husband of Pinter's play has been replaced by the homosexual smart-Alec, Ed.

Loot. 1966. M. P.

Helped by his accomplice a young criminal secretes the loot from a burglary in his mother's coffin. This is the key situation in a macabre and complicated farce, which is also an exuberant caricature of funeral ritual, of a police which is represented as hamhanded and venal, and of cheap detective fiction. The characters are cardboard puppets manipulated by the plot and the play is notable for the fact that vice is completely triumphant.

Crimes of Passion. 1967. M.

A double bill consists of *The Ruffian on the Stair*, 1966, Orton's first play, and *The Erpingham Camp*, 1967. Frequent and fussy scene changes betray their origin in radio and television respectively.

The Ruffian on the Stair. 1967. M.

It is illuminating to see how Orton's first play, a grotesque and savage comedy, uses the plot but not the atmosphere of Pinter's first play, *The Room* (q.v.). Orton cuts any aura of mystery and makes all explicit. The occupants of the room are now Mike, a criminal living with an ex-prostitute, Joyce. The intruder is a boy ostensibly seeking revenge for his brother with whom he had lived in homosexual incest, and whom Mike had murdered. He is in fact seeking his own death and provokes Mike to murder him by pretending that he has seduced Joyce.

The Erpingham Camp. 1967. M.

A satire on holiday camps shows an uprising of the merrymakers who eventually kill Erpingham. The ebullient parody has some highly comic incidents.

It was first projected as a film script, a modern version of Euripides' *The Bacchae*, but was rejected by Lindsay Anderson. Euripides' great play with Freudian foresight shows Pentheus destroyed by revellers because he had repudiated the liberating worship of Dionysus. (*See* **H123**.) Orton's sketch completely lacks any such insight or complexity and Erpingham meets his fate simply because he is stupid and dictatorial.

What the Butler Saw. 1969. M.

A farce in a psychiatric clinic is typically Orton in its discrepancy between decorous speech and indecent behaviour, but pace and invention flag.

John Osborne (b. 1929).

Osborne has considerable theatrical talent, torrential eloquence and the journalist's flair for seizing the mood of his own generation.

All these gifts were evident in *Look Back in Anger*, 1956 (F), now well filmed and too familiar to need description. It was perfectly timed and its success immediate. The protagonist, Jimmy Porter, voiced the pent-up feelings of contemporary youth, especially of the classes newly educated, now baffled by the complacency of the privileged classes who had muddled through two wars and left them without sense of security or direction. The play's pervasive mood of self-pity and strident denunciation runs, with some variation, through much of Osborne's later work, although with the passing of years it seems increasingly subjective and irrelevant to the current situation.

In his major plays, *A Patriot for Me* excepted, Osborne keeps to the same basic pattern of characterisation and structure. In Jimmy Porter he created an unforgettable character, a myth. But Jimmy with some change of occupation and age is constantly reappearing, disaffected, disorganised by self-pity, articulate and dominating. Archie Rice and Bill Maitland are older but they also are Narcissus figures driven on by sado-masochistic urges to destroy themselves and their circle, and it is difficult to escape the impression that the typical Osborne protagonist is not presented with complete objectivity but serves in some degree as mouthpiece of the author. Osborne's minor characters are sketched in a perfunctory, rather stagey way, serving chiefly as audience or target to the protagonist, and there is little dramatic confrontation of equals.

Closely linked with the structure of the plays is the nature of the dialogue. Osborne's forte is rhetoric, the thinly disguised monologue, splendidly uninhibited, with some of the inebriation and excitement of the pub, and with the same coarse and bawdy jests. Sometimes it is a tirade of invective, sometimes shrill and hysterical, always commanding, always flowing exclusively from the protagonist. Minor characters are given little opportunity for repartee or discussion, their rôle being for the most part to act as " feed."

Osborne's plays cannot legitimately be defended as satire for in comparison with the masterpieces of Ibsen and Shaw they express merely negative hostility and are not based on any clear concept of the values that should be realised in a good society.

" There aren't any good, brave causes left," says Jimmy Porter. Neither here nor in any other play is there anything to suggest that Osborne does not endorse this destructive statement, one of the silliest of the century.

His invective is moreover too general, indiscriminate, and direct to be effective. His weapon is the bludgeon of sarcasm, seldom the rapier of irony. Some notable exceptions are to be found in *Luther* where the targets are limited and specific and the speech where Tetzel sells indulgences is finely ironic. In this play Osborne has learned from the intelligence of Luther and the process of history. He is too emotional and subjective a writer to excel in an art which demands disciplined thought and detachment.

The sameness in structure and tone in Osborne's work is cleverly mitigated by experiment in theatrical techniques. The realism of the garret scene in *Look Back in Anger* was in 1956 strikingly original. In *The Entertainer* and *Luther* he profited by the example of Brecht, and *Under Plain Cover* was influenced by Genet.

The Entertainer. 1957. F.

Osborne here attempts to use the Brechtian device of " endistancing," employing a framework of music-hall scenes, where Archie Rice (Olivier), a seedy comedian, tries to hold the stage with tawdry patter and songs in a dubious show with nudes called " Rock'n Roll New'd Look." These are intended to " endistance " realistic scenes of Archie's shabby home. But the " endistancing " device serves little purpose for the overall mood of unquestioned disillusion " whooped up " by drink and patter is in both planes unrelieved. Querulous complaint that England has lost the glory and glamour of Edwardian days is crystallised on the realistic plane by the report of the death of Archie's son at Suez and in the music-hall by the presentation of a nude Britannia, wearing only her helmet.

Osborne turns to the music-hall because he claims it to be a folk art with an immediate, direct contact. The film version is good.

Luther. 1961. F.

Luther, based on a recent biography, is a less subjective work, although Osborne again takes for his hero a rebel, the son of an unsympathetic mother, and emphasises the emotional and not the intellectual sources of Luther's protests.

The play is imitative of Brecht's *Galileo* both in its loose " epic " structure and also in the attempt to present the protagonist in an equivocal light. The first two acts give a sympathetic and leisurely portrayal of Luther's early conflicts of conscience and vigorous attack on superstition while in the third act he is hurriedly presented as having treacherously let down the peasants who had been encouraged to rise against the Emperor. But the political reasons for Luther's dilemma are not even hinted at and we are invited not to think, as in *Galileo*, but to condemn while ignorant of relevant facts. Structurally this sudden *volte face* is most damaging to the play.

The most effective scenes, such as Tetzel's selling of indulgences and Martin's sermon at Wittenberg are splendid rhetoric, without a word of dialogue and directed straight at the audience. Skilful period production and the acting of Albert Finney as Luther made the play theatrically effective.

Two Plays for England. 1962.

Two slight plays make a double bill.

The Blood of the Bambergs is a parody of a royal wedding. Monarchy is held up to ridicule along with its trappings of ceremonial and fulsome adulation by press and radio. The bridegroom having just been killed in his racing-car, an Australian press photographer is secretly passed off in his place. The final act is a film with an unctuous running commentary, the film device deriving from the German Expressionist theatre, where it was first used by Ernst Toller.

Under Plain Cover is intended as an attack on sensationalism in the press. The first part shows a pretty provincial couple dressing up in rôles symbolic of sex fantasy, their activities accompanied by a thin trickle of dialogue. In the second half dramatic presentation is abandoned in favour of a charade and commentary by a reporter who reveals that the couple were brother and sister, a feeble presentation of the compelling theme of incest. The first scene is a pallid imitation of the brothel scene in Genet's *The Balcony*, where the assuming of symbolic rôles has powerful sexual and political implications lacking in Osborne's play.

These sketches do not profess to offer convincing studies of character in action and unlike intelligent satire they do not imply positive standards nor use the mature techniques of irony and wit, but rely on parody and mimicry.

Inadmissible Evidence. 1964. F.

A play, which many have praised highly, has the ingredients of a commercial success. It provides the sensational spectacle of a middle-aged solicitor, Bill Maitland, obsessed with sex, and disintegrating under the influence of drink and drugs, and, thereby, such a rôle for the star actor (Nicol Williamson) as to constitute a stage *tour de force*.

The play opens with a dream sequence as Maitland is tried in the court of his own mind. What follows is his rancid outpouring of self-pity, as during forty-eight hours, he is progressively deserted by staff, clients, and mistress. Some of the minor characters are here reduced to unheard voices on the telephone and one actress serves to impersonate three faceless clients. Maitland's flagellation of himself and his circumstances is unrelieved and monotonous.

A Patriot for Me. 1965.

The protagonist of Osborne's best play, produced privately, is Redl, a distinguished army officer of the Austro-Hungarian Empire, who through his homosexuality is blackmailed into becoming a spy for Tsarist Russia.

Osborne is here finely objective and ironic. He uses a series of brief scenes with significant juxtaposition of characters and swift dialogue. The first act, showing Redl's gradual discovery of his nature, is extremely discriminating and adroit and the drag ball which opens Act Two is an astonishing *tour de force*.

Act Three shows a decline of tension as Redl, now a spy, himself declines, his fibre coarsened through a sequence of sordid infidelities by male lovers and prostitutes. His final unmasking and suicide is almost a foregone conclusion.

The play spans the years 1890–1913 and Osborne presents the ethos and atmosphere of the Imperial Army officer élite, undermined by espionage and treachery, in a vast and unforgettable panorama.

A Bond Honoured. 1966.

Osborne, in a free translation of *La Fianza Satisfecha*, is said to have distorted Lope de Vega's play and portrays yet another alienated, and narcissistic " hero."

Time Present. 1968. F.

The protagonist, Pamela, is a neurotic actress. Emotionally strangled by the familiar " Electra complex," an exaggerated devotion to her father, a once famous actor, now dying off-stage, she is unable to establish any satisfactory human relationship, in spite of love affairs and the friendship of the devoted Constance, a successful Labour M.P., in whose flat she is living.

Pamela's role is static and verbal; reiteration of her shallow scheme of values (a preference for style over vulgarity), sentimental reminiscences of her father and a relentless spate of contemptuous and indiscriminate derision. Phrased in modish argot some gibes have a bitter wit, especially pleasing to the prejudices of the illiberal.

A contrived plot is super-imposed. The exposition is clumsy, the climax, Pamela's decision to have an abortion to end her pregnancy by Constance's own lover.

Pamela's alienation which should arouse compassion, becomes tiresome rather than moving, largely because of the play's apparent assumption that her outpourings have objective value and interest.

The Hotel in Amsterdam. 1968. F.

United by fear and dislike of their employer, a film magnate, cryptically referred to as K.L., three couples retreat to a luxury hotel in Amsterdam as a hide-out from his encroachments.

They pass the weekend in denouncing K.L., drinking, and exchanging desultory jokes and complaints about homosexuals, mothers, and " the working class," until the unwelcome arrival of a relative and the news that K.L. has killed himself disturb the tenuous camaraderie.

Such a structure is perfunctory. Only the garrulous and petulant Laurie (Scofield) is individualised and the characters reveal and discover little of value about themselves or each other.

An interesting sidelight is that Laurie fancies himself as an authority on " the creative process," boasting, " What I do, I get out of the air." Is this Osborne's method? Great creative geniuses give a very different account.

Since the play indicates no positive norm, it cannot be defended as satire. Some critics praised it highly for its sense of mood. Others found it tedious.

Alexander Ostrovsky (1823–86).

The eminent Russian playwright is unfortunately little known in this country.

The Storm. 1966.

Written in 1859, Ostrovsky's fine realistic play portrays a social group unfamiliar to us, the petty tradesmen of an isolated township, who are avaricious, ignorant, and bigoted.

The widow, Kabanovna, is a warped and ruthless matriarch, who saps the vitality of her weak son and cruelly tyrannises over his hapless wife,

Katerina. The lonely, susceptible girl yields to the love of a young stranger from Moscow. Then sheltering in a church during a violent storm, she is overcome by superstitious dread and remorse. She confesses and later kills herself.

This perceptive tragedy is that of young and sensitive people striving to escape the yoke of rigid elders, but in the last resort succumbing to the harsh creed by which they have been indoctrinated.

Alun Owen (b. 1926).

Of Welsh stock but with an Irish mother, Alun Owen spent his youth in Liverpool.

His most characteristic style is the new naturalism nostalgically used to evoke the local colour of Liverpool. He seizes on its idiomatic dialects and the conflict implicit in the clash of race and religion while the ambition of the youngsters' ambition to get away to sea or to London gives a wider horizon to a parochial scene.

Progress to the Park. 1959. P.

This is a leisurely enquiry into the affinities and animosities of Liverpool working folk, especially of a group of four young men and a girl as they eddy about in street, pub, and park. The clash of race and religion is always just below the surface, and what thread of story there is concerns the crossing of young love by parental prejudice. The most lively character is the voluble Welsh Teifon, mouthpiece of Owen's views.

The Rough and Ready Lot. 1959.

A carefully constructed historical play concerns four mercenary officers in a revolutionary army in South America just after the American Civil War. In a different milieu religious strife is again the theme. The convictions of an Irish Catholic clash violently with those of a Welsh militant atheist as to whether they shall shell a Catholic monastery which blocks the pass. Eventually both men are killed, together with the vacillating English colonel, and it is the " simple and ordinary " man, Kelly, who takes command, the conflict of belief still unresolved.

There'll Be Some Changes Made. 1969.

In a lively first act, a Negress vigorously rouses the tearful Valerie, just betrayed by her first lover, to plan a tough revenge on the male sex. The play later loses momentum.

Harold Pinter (b. 1930).

Pinter, formerly an actor, is now considered as one of the leading playwrights of the " Theatre of the Absurd." He exerts an almost hypnotic power over his audience, for he has an assured theatrical expertise, an uncanny sense of the novel situation and the telling pause; and, as his plays find resolution in some final surprise, they are aesthetically satisfying.

His art has developed swiftly, and two main phases can now be distinguished. The early plays, culminating in *The Caretaker* in 1960, were concerned with the underprivileged and showed a growing sense of compassion and only a passing interest in sex. More recently Pinter has explored new ground. The plays have been much concerned with sexual experience; the background has usually been sophisticated; and the attitude detached, sometimes to the point of apparent indifference.

Whatever the subject, Pinter's plays have a certain poetic resonance, an imaginative absurdity. His power is probably due to his intuitive awareness of man's sub-conscious life and most of his plays present a dream-like sequence of events, half credible, half absurd. In the early plays the dream drifts into a familiar nightmare of the most primitive kind—that of the violent invasion of personal security—a fear that must have assailed man's stone-age ancestor as he lurked in the squalid shelter of his cave, terrified of wild beasts and the inexplicable catastrophes of nature. Many of Pinter's later plays are still dream-like, fantasies of sexual anxiety and gratification, especially as to marital fidelity.

The situation that first fascinated him was that of a room, a door, and two people. He has said, "Obviously they are scared of what is outside the room. The danger that breaks in on them is both comic and shocking, but bizarre as the predicament may be, the play is anchored in actual experience. "I think it is impossible," he says, "—and certainly for me—to start writing a play from any kind of abstract idea. . . . I start writing a play from an image of a situation and a couple of characters involved and these people always remain for me quite real."

But his basic situation is so novel and striking that, like poetry, it can be interpreted on more than one level, both as a revelation of those periods of intense private anxiety when the individual, all but distraught, holds on precariously to some tiny foothold, and also as an image of the predicament of the whole human race whose existence is threatened by ungovernable forces. Like Kafka, whom he admires, Pinter expresses vividly the feeling of inscrutable menace from some vague hinterland invading humdrum human existence. *The Birthday Party*, in particular, has much in common with Kafka's *The Trial*.

In his first three plays the threat is left deliberately unexplained, so that an aura of mystery surrounds the action and violence actually breaks through, but in *The Caretaker* there develops a more subtle menace from within, threatening the mind rather than the body and there is no overt violence.

The theme of uncertainty has persisted throughout. In his first play, *The Room*, 1957, he mystified his audience by contradictory information about insignificant details. This trick served perhaps to heighten the atmosphere of insecurity but some critics found it irritating, and in later plays, *The Collection*, for instance, we find instead a highly significant uncertainty as to people's veracity and motives. Pinter has explicitly stated that imprecision conveys a truer picture of our experience. "The desire for verification is understandable," he says, "but cannot always be satisfied," and he points out that it is particularly difficult to be precise about people's inner life and motives, especially if they are inarticulate. He consistently rejects the rôle of the omniscient playwright, like Ibsen, and looks at his characters through the eyes of the ordinary observer, frequently puzzled by human inconsistencies.

A related theme has been the ambiguous nature of personal identity, treated with increasing insight, from the puzzle as to who Riley may be in *The Room*, to the pathos of maimed personality in *The Caretaker*, and the possibility of divided personality in *The Lover*. Some of the disturbing fascination that Pinter exerts is due to the state of uncertainty in which he leaves his audience.

As a playwright of the Absurd Pinter is closest in feeling to Beckett, and he shares with Ionesco an awareness of the way that comedy interlocks with tragedy. "Everything is funny," says Pinter, "the greatest earnestness is funny; even tragedy is funny. And I think what I try to do in my plays is to get to this recognised reality of the absurdity of what we do and how we behave and how we speak." Occasionally, like Ionesco, he uses stage "furniture" to heighten the absurdity and both playwrights have a quick ear for the absurd clichés and *non-sequiturs* of everyday speech.

Pinter is a stylist in the use of stage dialogue, an expert in cockney dialect. It is talk rather than dialogue that he records, what Martin Buber has described as "monologue disguised as dialogue," for his characters talk at people rather than to them. They rarely listen or respond, each bolstering up his self-confidence in an intermittent "monologue" spiced with empty boasting. This is particularly appropriate to the confused and defeated people he portrays, who even in their defensive jargon shrink from human contact.

Although Pinter's dialogue appears on the surface to be little more than a tape-recording of casual talk, there is beneath the demotic prose a poetic rhythm more compelling than the carefully calculated verse rhythms of T. S. Eliot.

Esslin's study, *The Peopled Wound*, 1970, is recommended.

The Room. 1957. M.

Pinter's first play, written in four days for the drama department of Bristol University, is already characteristic. Rose, left alone at night, is nervously aware of the door of her dingy room, especially when a blind Negro, Riley, enters with a message from her father. Her husband on his return savagely kills Riley and Rose goes blind.

The murder of Riley, possibly a rather clumsy death symbol, is melodramatic, but the lit room is a vivid dramatic image of man's tiny area of comfort in an indifferent universe.

The Dumb Waiter, written 1957, produced 1960. M. and P.

In a one-acter Ben and Gus, hired assassins working for some mysterious "organisation," uneasily await their unknown victim in a basement room in Birmingham. The clattering descent of a mechanical Ionesco-like dumb-waiter increases their anxiety, until it is revealed that the victim is Gus himself. Situation and dialogue are both comic and taut with menace. The trite phraseology, as the killers mention "the senior partner," "the job," and "clearing up," ironically uses a business jargon. The tiny play is a microcosm of a treacherous world where violence can suddenly break up man's apparent alliances.

The Birthday Party. 1958. M.

In Pinter's first full-length play, the room is in a shabby boarding-house kept by the motherly Meg. Here Stanley, who claims to have been a concert pianist, has taken refuge, until he is suddenly unnerved by the arrival of a sinister pair, the specious Goldberg and the brutal McCann who like Gus and Ben are there "to do a job." They subject Stanley to a fantastic catechism, a parody of brain-washing, and during his phoney and ludicrous birthday party he is blindfolded and his glasses broken—symbolic of destructon of vision. Next morning the pair lead Stanley away, conventionally dressed in black jacket and striped trousers, incapable of speech, his personality disintegrated.

The menace here is economically sustained through indirect means, and the fact that the identity of the three main characters is never revealed adds to the terror. Some see Stanley as the political refugee; some, since he was a pianist, as the artist who is made to conform by the pressure of society. But by its deliberate lack of definiteness, the play has a wide reference to all who seek refuge from a strange and hostile world.

The Caretaker. 1960. M.

The play is set in a junk-filled room, where the kindly Aston lives in his brother's derelict house. He brings home an old tramp, Davies, who grudgingly agrees to stay as "caretaker" and then tries to encroach further by playing off one brother against the other, until finally rejected by both.

In a naturalistic background Pinter has created two unforgettable characters, presented in psychological depth with reference to their past, and has depicted their failure to come to terms with compassion and restraint.

Davies is one who bites the hand that feeds him. His very identity is suspect for he passes under an assumed name, having "left his papers" years ago "at Sidcup." But he never retrieves them, like Beckett's *Krapp* repressing part of his past. Aston haltingly tells Davies how he once had periods of unique lucidity, now destroyed by a terrifying shock-treatment he was subjected to in mental hospital, but Davies' only reaction is later to threaten him. It is remarkable that when Aston finally rejects Davies' last encroachment the plight of the tramp should seem as pitiful as Aston's own. Pinter having wisely rejected his first intention to end the play with the violent death of Davies.

This mature play shows a man actually opening the door to his fears and mastering them. Aston in his long speech faces the wrong done to him by "people." His unique vision destroyed, his only creative outlet has been tinkering with his hands, but as he tries to break out of his isolation by befriending another crippled human being, he unhappily meets a man so twisted by his own suffering and resentment that he cannot respond. Some find in Aston a moving image of the mystic and artist in man whose creative insight is destroyed by an imperceptive and mechanical society. The film is excellent.

A Slight Ache. 1961. M.

A short play, shows an elderly couple haunted by a match-seller, who stands speechless at their gate. Eventually the wife takes him into the home instead of the husband. Possibly the silent match-seller represents the unconscious desires of the wife and the anxieties of the husband.

A Night Out. 1961. M.

This compassionate and realistic brief play shows the clerk, Albert, trying one night to escape from the retarding domination of his nagging and self-righteous mother. After threatening her violently he finally finds himself in the room of a prostitute who proves equally peevish and would-be genteel. It is doubtful whether Albert's violent gestures have won him any independence.

The Collection. 1962. M.

In an assured comedy of manners, Pinter makes authentic use of mystification.

Did Stella in fact sleep with a stranger, Bill, in Leeds? She tells James, her husband, that she did so, but during the course of the friendship that develops between the two men, Bill gives three contradictory accounts of what is supposed to have occurred, while Harry, an older man who has given Bill a home, becomes increasingly jealous of James.

Ironically Stella's story, told perhaps to pique her husband, impels him away from her to male society and the changing of partners has the elegant formality and economy of a dance movement.

Pinterian violence is here only lightly indicated.

The Lover. 1963. M.

An arresting short play shows the husband (Alan Badel) and the wife (Vivien Merchant) as affectionate but distant partners, and then with provocative change of clothes as erotic lovers. The performance of symbolic rôles, including dressing up in fetish garments, had already been used by Genet. Pinter cleverly adapts the device to discriminate between the apparently incompatible strands in the marriage relationship, a distinction analogous to that between Aphrodite Urania and Aphrodite Pandēmus.

The Homecoming. 1965. M.

Teddy (Michael Bryant), a Doctor of Philosophy in an American University, brings his wife, Ruth (Vivien Merchant), on a surprise visit to his former home in North London, where Max (Paul Rogers), his widowed father, still lives with his two younger sons, Lenny and Joey. It is gradually revealed that Ruth before her marriage had been a "model" and the family decide to keep her as their common mistress, while Lenny, a pimp, arranges that she shall earn her keep as a prostitute. The plot is underlined by Lenny's bragging anecdotes of sexual brutality—a counterpart to the more undifferentiated violence of the earlier plays.

Because this is all presented with clinical detachment, the audience is induced to suspend emotion. Only at the last moment is this cool acceptance shattered by an outburst of human feeling when Max, aged 70, crawls sobbing to Ruth asking to be kissed and the audience is shocked into feeling the degradation involved.

On the surface the play is a disillusioned glance at life. "It would be ridiculous to maintain that what we know merits reverence," says Lenny. It may also be interpreted as a fantasy of sexual gratification, which in a dream state escapes the taboo of ethical and humane feeling and can be indulged in without demur. The use of some accepted sex symbols and the slow and trance-like acting, especially that of Ruth, is dream-like in

its effect and the final shock of degradation is analogous to waking up and realising what the dream has implied.

It is possible also to see in Teddy an acquiescent Hamlet. He returns home from a foreign university to find marital infidelity, for it is disclosed that his mother had been unfaithful with an uncle figure. Ruth is the counterpart of Ophelia, who was bidden by Hamlet, "Get thee to a nunnery"—(an Elizabethan cant term for brothel). Teddy is like Hamlet also in that he prefers "to operate on things and not in things."

The Homecoming is professionally brilliant, but it lacks the depth of reference and emotional power of Pinter's earlier plays.

Landscape and *Silence.* 1969. M.

Beckett's influence is apparent in two short plays, where inconclusive words and action are pared to the bone and whose theme is personal isolation. Both recall *Krapp's Last Tape* in their repetitive memories of past love.

Landscape, originally broadcast, is set in the kitchen of a country house, where the middle-aged caretaker appears to be telling his wife (Peggy Ashcroft) of the day's commonplace events and recalls an infidelity. She, absorbed in dreaming of a tender encounter on the sea-shore—possibly with him when younger—ignores him

Silence is even more spare and brief, although it took Pinter longer to write than any other play. Ellen sits between two men. Both have loved her in vain, although she has all but forgotten them. They are almost immobile, their only speech interlacing, fragmentary memories of love. These are redolent of the country, mostly at nightfall. The men are faintly characterised. Bates, the younger, remembers the market, a brothel; Rumsey his own house. Setting is discarded in favour of "three areas." In comparison with *Krapp's Last Tape, Silence* is like three simultaneous and hesitant tape-recordings running in a void.

The Tea Party and *The Basement.* 1970.

Two plays originally seen on television were perfectly suited to the medium of film, since both make swift transitions from objective happenings to subjective fantasies. They were however translated as faithfully as possible to the stage. Both involve the theme of encroachment on personal territory.

The Basement, written first, is like a chic version of *The Caretaker.* A fastidious bachelor, Law (Donald Pleasence), welcomes to his flat an old friend Stott, who brings his girl friend. Both promptly take possession, even of the host's bed. Law alternates between friendly chat and suppressed fantasies, such as romantic seduction of the girl and violent duelling with Stott. The play suddenly concludes with rôles reversed, Law being the visitor demanding admittance.

The Tea Party centres on Disson, a middle-aged plumbing tycoon. Just before his marriage to a young woman socially his superior, he engages a new secretary, Wendy (Vivien Merchant), teasingly seductive, with whom he is soon infatuated. His confusion increases when his patronising wife comes to the office as his secretary, and when he suspects an incestuous liaison between her and her parasite brother.

Since wife, secretary, and even he as husband have each a curious distorted double, Disson's vision, not surprisingly, becomes confused. A single table-tennis ball appears to him as two and he can only touch Wendy when blindfolded. His hysterical blindness culminates, at an office tea party, in complete loss of sight.

Poor Disson had, from the outset, been blind to his social position and his sexual needs.

Both in certain incidents and in the protagonist's paranoia the play has echoes of *The Birthday Party,* but now all on a fashionable level.

Terence Rattigan (b. 1911).

Rattigan, with his flair for light comedy, is an expert in the well-made play. His later, more serious work, includes *The Deep Blue Sea,* 1952, and *Ross,* 1962, about T. E. Lawrence.

A Bequest to the Nation. 1970.

A somewhat ornate historical play spans Nelson's final days in England. Like *Ross*, it sympathetically probes intimate problems of a national hero, its theme the conflict between Nelson's infatuation for Emma and his duty, to which finally she generously yields. Rattigan cleverly uses Nelson's ˉschoolboy nephew to emphasise duty to act as dramatic link with Lady Nelson and as the "juvenile sensibility," whereby Emma's tipsy decline is sharply focused.

David Rudkind.

Afore Night Come. 1962. P.

In a Worcestershire orchard the fruit pickers enact the ritual murder of a freakish old tramp whom they dread as a threat to their virility. A realistic working day world is infused with the primitive terror of *The Golden Bough.*

Jean-Paul Sartre (b. 1905).

The plays of the French philosopher, Sartre, can be fully interpreted only in the light of his atheistic existentialist philosophy. Discarding conventional morality, Sartre insists that the individual must evolve his own ethical code through daring freely to choose and act for himself. He must also will this freedom for others, and by seeking to establish an interdependence of freedoms he "engages," or "commits" himself in the political struggle.

Sartre himself is a communist and his best plays, like those of Brecht, are fully "committed" to left-wing ideology. They have sought to vindicate the inevitability of violence in the struggle for freedom and to decry the "bourgeois morality" which shrinks from such crime.

Sartre is also concerned with the "absurdity" of man's predicament as a rational creature in an illogical and indifferent universe, but unlike Ionesco he presents the situation, not through absurd images but through the medium of the traditional well-made play.

Sartre has had a considerable influence on the climate of ideas, encouraging an attitude of harsh disillusion and stimulating the current discussion as to whether or not drama should be a vehicle for social and political convictions. It is interesting to contrast the views of Wesker and Pinter on this issue.

Lucifer and the Lord. Published 1951. P.

The dilemma between non-violence and force is here given greater universality by being projected back into the time of the Peasants' Revolt in Germany. The brilliant General Goetz, having failed in a policy of Christian love, unflinchingly embraces a ruthless violence as the only possible "realist" social ethic.

Nekrassov. Published 1956. P.

A satirical farce ridicules the sensational anti-communism of a section of the popular French press.

Altona. Published 1956. P.

This play, showing a former Nazi officer going mad in an attempt to justify his own resort to torture, is an attack on "Western morality" in its own recourse to torture, used by French colonials in Algiers. The film version well reproduces the claustrophobic horror.

James Saunders (b. 1925).

In Saunders' early work the influence of Ionesco is apparent in the satirical use of a banal dialogue, in which the characters converse without communicating, and in the reference to some concrete symbol which represents their anxieties or predicament. His later work is reminiscent of Pirandello. Nevertheless Saunders' ingenious plays have a freshness and vigour all their own.

Alas Poor Fred.

In a one-act play a friend who had some time ago been cut in half is the symbol of a married couple's former passionate love life, long since sundered. The situation is like that of Ionesco's *Amédée.*

The Ark. 1959.

In a more direct style this full-length play of ideas re-interprets the Old Testament story.

Ends and Echoes. 1960.

This is the general title for three clever one-acters. In *Barnstable*, the most amusing one, a house is gradually collapsing around its unwitting inhabitants, a symbol of the disintegration of their conventional way of life.

Next Time I'll Sing to You. 1963.

Based on Raleigh Trevelyan's book on the hermit of Canfield, who died in 1942, this moving play uses the rehearsal style of Pirandello's *Six Characters.* Like an elegiac quintet is explores the theme of solitude.

A Scent of Flowers. 1964.

Like the previous play, this is a reconstruction of the past. It is gradually revealed that the character, Zoe, is in fact the spirit of a girl who has just committed suicide, because her love for a married man is incompatible with her religion. The play proceeds by her touching encounters with the circle of relatives and friends to whom she had turned in vain for help.

Neighbours. 1967.

Neighbours was presented with another short play, *Dutchman* (F), by Le Roi Jones. Both use an emotional encounter between a Negro and a white woman to focus the strain between the races.

A Negro invites himself into the flatlet of a young woman on the floor below. With some hesitation she entertains him. He then steadily challenges her enlightened liberalism as merely patronising and finally in what amounts to moral blackmail asks her to come and sleep with him. Confused and compassionate she yields.

The initial meeting is conveyed with much delicacy. Then as the Negro assumes the rôle of counsel for the prosecution, a logical pattern is unconvincingly forced on the naturalistic material.

Peter Shaffer (b. 1926).

Shaffer is an assured and ingenious dramatist whose first success was with the realistic well-made play and who has since moved on to freer modes of composition.

His plays operate successfully on two levels: they offer insight into the subtleties of personal relationships, especially into the difficulties of adjustment between people of different cultural background, and they also involve discussion of ideas. The aesthetic problem of distinguishing between genuine love of art and snobbish pretension is a recurring theme, often presented in a triangular situation.

Five Finger Exercise. 1958. P.

An alive, realistic play shows Clive, the young Cambridge student, growing away from his stifling mother, with her pretensions to modish culture, but failing to make contact with his honest philistine father. The advent of an enigmatic stranger, Walter, acts as a catalyst. Mother and son are both attracted to Walter, the father's fierce jealousy is aroused and Walter is narrowly saved from suicide.

Shaffer shows some of Ibsen's precision in his probing of a family situation where the members change and develop as they become painfully aware of their hidden drives.

The Private Ear and the Public Eye. 1962.

Two short and spare triangular plays both demonstrate the influence of artistic taste on the relationship between the sexes.

The Private Ear.

Bob, a shy music-lover, asks Ted to help him entertain a girl whom he has met at a concert. But the ignorant girl is won by the complacent Ted's vulgar patter and Bob, left alone, defaces his gramophone record and forces himself to listen to the broken music of love.

The Public Eye.

A witty, ironic comedy shows Charles, a correct and pompous dilettante, unwarrantably jealous, employing a private detective, Louis (Kenneth Williams) to spy on his wife. She becomes attracted to Louis because of their shared joy in things of beauty. With the entry of the iconoclastic Louis, a brilliant, comic invention, farce and tenderness go hand in hand with high comedy.

The Royal Hunt of the Sun. 1964.

A sweeping " epic " drama of Pizarro's fantastic conquest of Peru skilfully uses, as narrator, " old Martin," who watches his own boyhood as page to Pizarro. Shaffer deploys " total theatre " in dazzling ceremonial, processions and masks, in ritual dancing, mime and strange, metallic music.
There is rich thematic material in the clash of " two immense and joyless powers," in the conflict of Christianity and Sun worship. Personal tragedy develops in the mutual attraction felt by the grizzled Pizarro (Colin Blakeley) and the young Inca, Atahualpa (Robert Stephens). Captor and prisoner, they painfully seek for the god in each other and the Inca accepts death both as a sacrifice to friendship and the final test of his faith.

Black Comedy. 1965.

A highly successful brief comedy frankly uses an effective device of Chinese theatre. During a party the lights fail and the stage, although supposed to be in darkness, is still fully illuminated, so that the ludicrous behaviour of the dramatis personae is visible only to the audience.

The Battle of Shrivings. 1970.

The idealist Sir Gideon (Gielgud) whose home is " Shrivings " (suggestive of confession and penance) is an eminent philosopher. He is committed to belief in human perfectibility and pacifism, and lives a celibate life with his unselfish wife, Enid. With them resides David, son of Gideon's former pupil and friend Mark (Patrick Magee). Mark is a famous poet long expatriate, who now visits Gideon on the occasion of their both receiving an Oxford award.
The life and ideas of the robust and cynical Mark, who is now toying with Roman Catholicism, have become the antithesis of Gideon's and he maliciously challenges his host to an extraordinary contest. He will return to humanism if, whatever he may do, Gideon can endure his presence for the weekend!
Mark then disillusions Enid by revealing Gideon's homosexual past. He seduces the girl friend of his own son and cruelly pronounces him to be a bastard.
Both contestants win but both are broken. Gideon, bitterly taunted by Enid, is provoked to strike her and reduced to despair, while Mark is attacked and beaten down by his son.
The play, like Bolt's *The Tiger and the Horse* (*q.v.*), is an honourable attempt to dramatise philosophical and ethical problems, especially the discrepancy between man's idealistic convictions and his personal relationships. But lengthy exposition and discussion delay the final action and the characters and plot are too schematic for an organic development.
The fact that the play appeared soon after the death of Bertrand Russell and recalls his friendships with writers such as D. H. Lawrence, rather weakens its impact.

N. F. SIMPSON (b. 1919).

N. F. Simpson's plays of the Absurd are in the peculiarly English vein of Lewis Carroll and Edward Lear, a world of surrealist fantasy, *non-sequitur* and nonsense. It is almost a contradiction in terms to organise such material coherently and to do so in a full-length play is a *tour de force* which Simpson brought off in his *One Way Pendulum*. His best work ridicules the mechanical and conventional existence, the attenuation of feeling, of the little suburban home, his usual milieu.

The Resounding Tinkle. 1957. P. F.

A most unusual play, which pokes fun at suburban life, discards plot, progress, and characterisation, and the uniform dialogue is one continuous flow of clever verbal paradoxes and *non-sequiturs*. The apologetic " author " appears at intervals and in the final act there is a parody discussion of the play by a panel of " critics "—devices used by Ionesco in *The Shepherd's Chameleon*.
Simpson's verbal agility is exhilarating, but some find the play over-cerebral. It is certainly at the opposite end of the spectrum from Ann Jellicoe's *The Sport of My Mad Mother*.

One Way Pendulum. A Farce in a New Dimension. 1959. F.

Here Simpson has devised a framework built of whimsy and yet firm enough to carry its own logic and to be dramatically satisfying. The characters are drawn simply, but consistently, each with his own " humour," in the manner of Ben Jonson and the dialogue is a close parody of banal family interchange.
The play concerns a suburban family, the Groomkirby's, whose son, Kirby, is teaching a collection of weighing-machines to sing the Hallelujah Chorus. His ineffectual father is combining his two favourite hobbies of law and " do it yourself " carpentry, by building an enormous model of the Old Bailey in the living-room, where the phlegmatic mother pays a charwoman to eat up the " left-overs."
Finally a trial takes place in the Old Bailey and Kirby is convicted of murdering forty-three people in order that he may wear black, the weighing-machines being part of a complicated device to cause a holocaust of death.
The main theme of the play is the tyranny of things, which is exemplified by the absurd Ionesco-like objects. These are treated with the respect due to human beings while human beings are treated as things, and father and son are so obsessed by things that they cannot get into touch with one another.
The tyranny of mechanical routine and social custom is also indicated. Kirby will only eat when a cash-register rings and will only wear black when it is sanctioned by funeral convention.
The anxiety and guilt which result from a starved and mechanical existence are finally symbolised in the nightmare parody of a trial scene in the final act.
Although the stage objects are novel and intriguing and can be assigned a clear meaning they lack the suggestive power of Ionesco's chairs or rhinoceroses. Contrived rather than intuitive, they illustrate more than they illuminate the human condition. But the play is an original and successful experiment and the implied comment on the unconscious assumptions and compulsive habits of the Groomkirbys has a wide reference.
The film version is recommended.

The Cresta Run. 1965.

A play about counter-espionage proved disappointing, partly because its mockery is directed at a schoolboy dream rather than at a general malaise, partly because it lacks the bold structural outline of *One Way Pendulum*. Even the absurd objects—keys, codes, disguises—are trivial compared with the " Old Bailey." Simpson has also lost some of the claustrophobic compulsion of his earlier plays by his constant switching of the action from the home of the suburban couple to the Ministry and back again.

It is unfortunate that a promising latent theme —the compulsion felt by the Security man to divulge his secret information—is swamped by trivia, while the best jest is only a casual aside— the suggestion that in England Intelligence should logically be in the hands of private enterprise!

The Hole, 1957, and *The Form* are one-acters in the same style as the full-length plays.

Wole Soyinka (b. 1934).

Soyinka, a Nigerian and an English graduate, is an admirer of Brecht, Arden, and Dürrenmatt.

The Road. 1965.

The Road, set in a drivers' haven in Nigeria, successfully produced with a large cast of coloured actors, later won a Dakar award.

The Lion and the Jewel. 1966. O.U.P.

In a lively comedy, presented by the Ijinle Company of African actors, the jewel is Sidi, the belle of a Yoruba village. Elated at being photographed for a glossy magazine, she rejects both the native schoolmaster and the old chieftain, the Lion, until cunningly seduced by him she exultantly joins his harem.

Native culture, with vivid ritual dance and music, is presented as more alluring and virile than European, which is mocked both in amusing mimes and in the shabby, ineffective schoolmaster infatuated with Western gadgets.

Tom Stoppard (b. 1937).

Stoppard has written plays for radio, including the engaging *Albert's Bridge* (F), and for television.

Rosencrantz and Guildenstern are Dead. 1966. F.

Stoppard's diverting play is a gloss on *Hamlet* and he dovetails snatches of Shakespeare's tragedy with his own action or rather inaction, for his archtype is Beckett's *Waiting for Godot*.

He humorously chooses as protagonists the two nonentities, Rosencrantz and Guildenstern. Summoned inexplicably to Elsinore, they hang about, always on the fringe of great events they do not understand, passing the time, like Shakespearean jesters, in witty word play and fruitless speculation as to their situation and destiny.

Their predicament is a suggestive image of the bewilderment of the ordinary man faced with world events beyond his grasp and, at a deeper level, with the existential problem of man's very being on this earth, and the imminence of death.

The rehearsals of the Players, the counterpart of the enactments of Pozzo and Lucky in *Godot*, create a further film of unreality and illusion.

The play is too long, the second act not sufficiently contrasted, but it is remarkable that so derivative a play should be so delightfully fresh and original.

Enter a Free Man. 1968. F.

This comedy is an extended version of a television play of 1963. Reilly (Michael Hordern), a self-styled "inventor" of unworkable Heath Robinson gadgets, "leaves home" regularly every Saturday to spend in the pub the ten shillings pocket money allowed him by his working daughter, always to return home when his money has run out. His long-suffering wife (Megs Jenkins) has consoled herself with the hope that if he's to be "a failure anyhow, he might as well fail at something he'd like to succeed at"!

The situation, although genuinely funny and pathetic, is not adequate to a full-length play.

The Real Inspector Hound. 1968. F.

This crisp and intelligent burlesque, like Sheridan's *The Critic*, uses the device of the playwithin-the-play. It is a simultaneous parody of jaded theatrical convention and modish theatrical jargon.

Two critics are watching an absurd drawingroom whodunit, with a corpse ignored by all taking the centre of the stage. But the main focus of interest is the critics. Both are obsessed, the introverted Moon, only a "stand-in," by jealous hatred of his professional superior, the absent Higgs, while the eupeptic Birdfoot is always infatuated with the latest actress.

Then at the ringing of a stage telephone absurdity completely takes over. The call is from Birdfoot's suspicious wife! He is drawn on stage where he takes on the part of the fickle lover, soon to be followed by Moon, when told that the stage corpse is that of Higgs! In a few minutes both critics in consequence of their private obsessions have been shot dead, the sharp crack of retribution not unusual in Stoppard.

Beneath the glittering, zany surface of the play lies the concept of drama as the mirror, Hamlet's "mirror up to nature," wherein we see and identify ourselves with the dramatis personae.

The play formed part of a double bill with Sean Patrick Vincent's musical satire, *The Audition*. It appears that Stoppard's comic genius finds its best vehicle in the short play, which his dazzling virtuoso invention can sustain to the end.

David Storey (b. 1933).

Storey, also a novelist, is the son of a Yorkshire miner and helped to support himself at the Slade by playing professional Rugby for Leeds. He wrote the film-script for his own novel, *This Sporting Life*, and Lindsay Anderson, while directing it, encouraged him to revise his discarded play, *Arnold Middleton*.

Anderson has directed Storey's three subsequent plays and the imaginative rapport between producer and playwright has led to their being interpreted with singular insight and restraint.

One theme in Storey's work, as in Mercer's, is the stress felt by the educated offspring of working folk. His plays involve reference to mental trouble or instability and he is much interested in the theories of R. D. Laing.

The plays are grounded in every-day life, frequently in Storey's own experience. Yet they have become increasingly poetic in approach, in that their significance is consciously ambiguous, and "escapes and refuses definition." Storey deliberately leaves "all the options open." He also says that, if on reading something through, he "knows completely what it is all about, then it is dead," but if it mystifies him then it has "taken on an independent life of its own."

No two plays are alike and this versatility is most promising.

The Restoration of Arnold Middleton. 1967. P.

Arnold, a young schoolmaster (as Storey once was) is a jesting eccentric, his latest acquisition an outsize of armour introduced during the play's revision. But Arnold's clowning disguises the fact that he is going mad.

The theme is reminiscent of Mercer's *Morgan*, with the gorilla suit, but the exuberant comedy tends to blur the issue and the interpretation of the hero's instability and lightning recovery is inadequate.

In Celebration. 1969.

Three sons return home to celebrate the fortieth wedding anniversary of their parents, doting collier husband and complacent matriarch, who considers herself his social superior.

With first-hand realism Storey conveys the disorientation and embarrassed filial feeling of sons educated beyond their origins. The eldest brother, the iconoclastic Andrew, is hell-bent on tearing down the family façade and tries to force on stolid Colin and sensitive Steven his theory that their ambitious mother had distorted their lives into a false respectability to appease her own sense of guilt. When six months pregnant, she had felt obliged to marry the collier father and after the firstborn had died at the age of seven, she had tried to commit suicide.

After an extravagant dinner at the local hotel, Andrew lashes the bewildered father with his scorn and only the concerted efforts of Colin and Steven can help to reassure the old man and get Andrew away next morning before he can confront the mother.

The psychological motivation is not fully credible but this compassionate and close-knit play, with the past haunting the present, recalls Ibsen, especially since Andrew is an ignoble counterpart of Gregers Werle in *The Wild Duck*.

The Contractor. 1969.

Five men leisurely assemble and later dismantle a huge tent for the wedding of the contractor's daughter, while members of the family drift in and out. The workers' banter and taunts and the family casual talk hint at hidden hurts, but the focus of the play is the actual work on the tent—as in Ionesco a " thing "—presented here with no absurdity or phantasy but with almost the faithfulness of documentary, for Storey can draw on his own experience of the job.

The image is however metaphorical and because the play cannot " be confined to any one definition," Storey finds it one of his most satisfying works. He sometimes sees it as " somehow related to the decline and falling away of capitalist society " or " as a metaphor for artistic creation." Yet " it still continues to make sense—and complete sense—as the story of these men who put up this tent and that's that."

Home. 1970.

Sitting at a garden table, on the only two chairs available, two ageing gentlemen, Jack (Ralph Richardson) and Harry (Gielgud), gently and diffidently make conversation. Jack, slightly more dapper, and prone to pointless family anecdote, usually takes the initiative in their exchange of dated clichés and banalities. The broken phrases refer to wives now separated, ambitions unfulfilled, the clouds, but real communication can only be unspoken and there is sad irony in Jack's, " So rare these days nowadays to meet someone to whom one can actually talk."

When these leave, their places are taken by two rough, " Cor blimey " women, full of prurient innuendo and scandal, and when the gentlemen return and courteously escort " the ladies " to " corn beef hash," it has gradually become apparent that this is a mental " home." Act II begins with the entry of a leucotomised young man who aimlessly shifts the furniture about.

The play, heart-breaking in its naturalistic fidelity to human inadequacy, is handicapped by some monotony of incident and dialogue. But, like Beckett's *Godot*, also a strange quintet, it works through poetic suggestion. The ironic title and the furniture, inadequate for 2000 people, are significant as is the apparently irrelevant juxtaposition of phrases, which are in themselves ambiguous metaphors. (" This little island." " Shan't see its like." " Oh, no." " The sun has set." " Couple of hours.")

But the decline of hope and vitality (perhaps that of England herself) is most potently expressed by the unadorned shape of the play, the decline of the day from morning to evening, the sky overcast, the rain that of the old men's silent tears.

Cecil P. Taylor.

Taylor is quizzically interested in left-wing types, especially their inconsistencies and fallacies. He is very successful in a brisk, brief comedy like *Allergy*, 1966 (P). In *Bread and Butter*, 1966 (P) his naturalistic outline biography of two Jewish couples in the Gorbals between 1931 and 1965 is sympathetically done but too slight to sustain the full-length play.

Peter Terson (b. 1932).

Terson is a prolific writer, with a talent for fertile, fluent dialogue, which immediately establishes personalities and relationships. His most successful work has been done in active co-operation with two directors, Cheeseman and Croft.

In 1963, while working as a games master in the Vale of Evesham, Terson first contacted Cheeseman, director at Stoke-on-Trent, whose policy it is to find writers rather than plays, and through his encouragement and suggestions Terson wrote several plays located in the Vale. A recurrent theme of these is the mysterious power of nature as opposed to urban sophistication, and as in Rudkind's *Afore Night Come* (q.v.), a sinister theme often runs through them. Cheeseman considers Terson's greatest gift is " his capacity to write in a way that is both very funny and profoundly serious at the same time."

The Evesham plays include *A Night to Make the Angels Weep*, 1963, *The Mighty Reservoy*, 1964, P, *I'm in Charge of These Ruins*, 1966, *All Honour Mr. Todd*, 1966, and *Mooney and His Caravans*, 1967, P.

Terson became known nationally through his remarkable collaboration with Michael Croft, director of the N.Y.T. For *Zigger Zagger* (P) there was only a " fragmentary script " which was built up on stage by Terson, Croft, and the actors. Even *The Apprentices* (P), which began with a clear line of development, was considerably modified during rehearsal when Terson feels stimulated by the reactions of director and actors.

He writes about youngsters with affectionate zest and exuberant humour, vividly aware of the lack of opportunity offered by modern society to the younger school-leaver.

Zigger Zagger. 1967. P.

Dominating the play is a remarkable manipulation of a youthful football crowd which acts as a living backcloth to the scene. Harry, school-leaver and near-delinquent, is so possessed by its Dionysiac frenzy that he is opaque to all efforts of authoritative figures such as the youth officer and respectable relatives to gear him into a job. Eventually grudgingly accepting life's economic demands, he becomes an apprentice.

The Apprentices. 1968. P.

During mid-day breaks in a factory yard, crowded and animated as a Breughel, overalled apprentices play football, fight, flirt, and wrangle. The flurried foreman and older hands, caustic yet tolerant, act as foil.

The chief personalities are vividly presented in the round. In the centre is the derisive, irrepressible Bagley, priding himself on his " rebel's instinct," kindly at heart, yet an enthusiast for the barbarous " initiation " ritual. But the progress of events leaves him stranded. Led by the studious Geoff, his fellows, including Harry, are gaining qualifications and getting on and out. The factory, modernised, will need brains not muscle and all have lost interest in the " initiation." Bagley, a married man at 18, his wife already pregnant after a brief holiday encounter, ruefully drifts towards the older fitters he had despised.

Fuzz, 1969.

The crowd techniques of the N.Y.T. were again deployed in a lively dramatising of student protest movements, but students' own lack of a positive, unifying purpose became reflected in the play in itself.

Spring-Heeled Jack. 1970.

The setting for another N.Y.T. play, now directed by Barrie Rutter, is the rowdy yard of a crowded block of council flats. Lop, just back from prison for petty larceny, finds scant sympathy from the noisy, mixed population. He becomes suspected of murdering an old tramp and in the mounting hysteria he is identified with the mythical terrorist and voyeur, Spring-Heeled Jack. Only the intervention of a sympathetic Negro saves him.

The central momentum of the play tends to be dissipated in extraneous currents of action and farcical episodes.

Jose Triana (b. 1931).

Triana, born in Cuba, spent four years in Madrid but returned to Cuba after Castro's revolution and has now written several plays.

The Criminals. 1967.

The first Cuban play staged here depicts three adults, a brother and his two sisters, acting out fantasies of childhood, hatred of thwarting parents, and the tyranny of home, which culminate in a frenzied ritual of their murder of the parents at the end of Act One. The trial of the children in Act Two gradually develops into an enactment of the parents' mutual detestation. As the curtain falls the ritual begins afresh.

This intense play, in the genre of " Theatre of Cruelty " (*q.v.*), has less wealth of imagery than Weiss's *Marat-Sade* but a greater universality of reference than Genet's world of criminals and perverts. It may have been influenced by the work of Arrabal.

Triana shows great psychological insight; children's play is often a dramatic projection of their inner anxieties and conflicts and at all ages the sterile process of fantasy gives only temporary relief and must be endlessly and exhaustingly repeated. The most significant moment of the play is when the word " love " is timidly offered as an alternative only to be rejected.

An extremely apt parallel to Triana's vision was the contemporary Reith lecture (26 Nov. 1967), when Dr. Leach, the social anthropologist, criticised our unthinking acceptance of the inward turning type of family life, where " The parents fight: the children rebel." Of such a family Dr. Leach said, " The strain is greater than most of us can bear," and he considered it to be the source of our social discontents.

Triana's play effectively shows it as a potent source of man's aggression. Some critics have seen in it implications of Castro's resistance to the dominance of America.

Boris Vian (1920–59).

The French Vian was influenced by the Absurdist approach of Ionesco.

The Empire Builders. 1962.

Man's futile flight from death is imaged in a family trying to escape from a terrifying noise by moving up to a higher and higher floor and meaner quarters. Eventually the father alone reaches the attic, where he dies.

The Generals' Tea Party. 1966. P.

Written in 1951, Vian's biting, absurdist satire on the military mentality represents his general behaving like a small boy, afraid of Mama, and asking his playfellows—other generals—to tea. After deciding that war would be a nice idea, they then select the target—prophetically Algeria.

Roger Vitrac (1899–1952).

The French Vitrac, an associate of Artaud, attempted Surrealist plays which anticipate the Theatre of the Absurd.

Victor. 1964.

Victor is a boy of 9 but 7 foot tall and with a mature intelligence. He and his outsize girlfriend are the only rational beings in a farcical adult world.

Frank Wedekind (1864–1918).

The plays of the German Wedekind, a passionate amoralist, are preoccupied with the mysterious power of sex and in their intensity they sporadically break through the bounds of realism into fantasy and symbolism—techniques later to be deployed, although to different ends, in Expressionism (*q.v.*).

Spring Awakening. 1863.

Published in 1891, the play which concerns the lyrical rapture and the agony of puberty, is a fervid indictment of a disastrous and repressive "morality," of secretive or hypocrital parents and grotesquely tyrannical schoolmasters. Finally in a scene of nightmare fantasy, the

ruined adolescent, Melchior, searching for the grave of his sweetheart, dead through an abortion, is encountered by the ghost of his suicide friend and is himself only restrained from the same fate by the symbolic Man in the Mask.

Lulu. 1970.

Lulu is the title given by Peter Barnes to his adaptation of two plays, *Earth Spirit*, 1895, and its sequel *Pandora's Box*, 1903. Barnes's version keeps to the basic substance if not to the spirit of the original.

Wedekind's protagonist, Lulu, the incarnation of the instinctual life, symbolises sexual passion in its beauty, rapture, and terror. In her narcissism and uninhibited passion she destroys all who become hopelessly infatuated with her, unbridled erotic fantasy alternating with horror and the grotesque.

In Barnes's Act I, corresponsing to *Earth Spirit*, Lulu causes the death of her first husband by shock, the suicide of the second, and shoots the third, Schön.

In Act II, the sequel, she gradually degenerates to amateur prostitute, still adored by two ruined devotees, a lesbian countess and Schön's son. To him she has been successively foster-sister, stepmother, and mistress, the incarnation of a Freudian dream. These two also die and she is herself assassinated by a pervert casual client, Jack the Ripper.

Barnes's adaptation neglects the mystery and pathos of the original. The characters are presented flat. Only the countess and Schön's son are a little more than two-dimensional and so excite some sympathy. Fantasy and horror are abruptly succeeded by grotesque bathos in the modish spirit of black comedy (*q.v.*).

Peter Weiss (b. 1916).

The German-speaking Weiss has adopted Swedish nationality and Marxist doctrine.

The " Marat Sade." 1964.

The full title of this verse play, one of the most impressive exemplifications of Artaud's Theatre of Cruelty, is *The Persecution and Assassination of Jean-Paul Marat as Performed by the Inmates of the Asylum of Charenton under the Direction of the Marquis de Sade!* As the title indicates this complex work operates on receding planes of cruelty, thus exciting in the audience that vivid experience of violence which is the aim of Artaud.

Artaud's demand for primitive ritual which shall exorcise repressed fantasy is met by Corday's threefold visit and murder of Marat and also by the lunatics' frenzied miming of the ceremony of the guillotine—a background motif to the whole play. The use of pantomime and gesticulation on the open stage satisfy Artaud's demands for spectacle, for " poetry in space."

Peter Brook pointed out that these elements are not consistent with a Brechtian " alienation "—achieved by the device of a play within a play, the protesting comments of the director of the asylum, the intellectual debates between Sade and Marat and the ribald songs of a grotesque quartet of zanies. The effect is an inextricable blend ot the comic and the violent.

The Investigation. 1965.

A documentary of the Frankfurt War Crime Trials, edited by Weiss, had a multiple première in East and West Germany and at the Aldwych. Described by Weiss as an " Oratorio in 11 Cantos," after Dante's *Inferno*, it indicts the millions, including the German monoply capitalists, who tacitly supported the Nazi atrocities.

At the first impact the grisly facts leave an overwhelming impression of horror. It is remarkable that the author's restraint and dignity in presenting them and the formal austerity of his design have in retrospect the effect of **catharsis**.

The Song of the Lusitanian Bogey. 1969.

A passionate indictment of Portuguese colonial exploitation and oppression of Angola recalls in some of its techniques Peter Brook's *US*. It was splendidly acted by the New York Negro Ensemble.

Arnold Wesker (b. 1932).

Wesker, son of a Jewish-Hungarian father and a Russian mother, first became a chef, and worked in Norwich, London, and Paris, before taking a six months' course at the London School of Film Technique, where he wrote his first play.

He is known not only as a dramatist but also as a devoted socialist. Since 1962 much of his time has been given to his efforts to bring an enjoyment of good drama and art to people who would otherwise lack opportunity. To this end he has founded—under the aegis of the Trade Unions—the well-known Centre 42.

Wesker's early plays were in the naturalistic idiom, centred on the vivid portrayal of an East End Jewish family and a farm-labourer's family in Norfolk. He evidently found naturalism inadequate and there gradually appeared in his work strains of Expressionism, which in *Chips with Everything* became the dominant style. Wesker's hold on dramatic structure is erratic, but he has an exhilarating sense of movement on the stage.

His most individual characteristic is his passionate concern for his characters. They are presented in the round, living, aspiring, and erring, so that they achieve an independent existence, especially the women. Although male protagonists like Ronnie Kahn and Pip are seen both in their strength and weakness, Wesker does not entirely detach himself from them, somehow conveying his personal reactions to them—a conflict of love and exasperation. He has nevertheless gone much further than Osborne, for instance, in creating a truly objective image, as his more flexible dialogue indicates. He has a keen ear for social and personal idiosyncrasies, especially urban Jewish volubility and the fumbling speech of the country labourer.

Like Sartre, Wesker is deeply "committed." He is a convinced socialist but not a propagandist, for his plays explore the moral and practical difficulties of the socialist position and he shows unusual honesty in portraying Ronnie Kahn, the most vocal of socialists, as a weak if not renegade personality.

The Trilogy—The trilogy consists of three naturalistic plays in which a discursive history of the Jewish family, the Kahns, is fused with political debate on the course of socialism

Chicken Soup with Barley. 1958. P.

This is the springboard of the trilogy. It opens on October 4, 1936, the morning of Mosley's attempted march through the East End of London, when the curtain rises on the basement flat of the Kahns, a Jewish family dedicated to socialist activities. It is 1957 when the play ends with the disillusion of the son, Ronnie, at the Russian occupation of Hungary.

Each of the Kahns is a live human being, presented not for moral judgment but with sympathy. Especially commanding is the mother Sarah. What Jung might call an "extraverted feeling type," she is ignorant of events, contemptuous of books, a strenuous mother figure, and yet in her aggressive dynamic the most masculine person of the group, in contrast to her amiable but shiftless husband, Harry, and the vacillating Ronnie.

The central theme of the play is the conflict between attitudes of mind, "caring," or concern for the welfare of others, and indifference to it. The battle is fought on two fronts, in the home and politically, it being taken for granted that socialism is an expression of "caring." The stalwart Sarah is the centre of the two-fold conflict, for she attacks both social inertia and that of her husband and son.

Structurally the play is sprawling, but Wesker already shows his intuitive sense of theatrical movement. At the end of Scene I there is an exhilarating leap forward as the little band of fighters surges from the basement to the light. A more experienced dramatist might have placed

such a triumphal movement as the final climax, but the general pattern of the play is of recoil and listlessness, held only by Sarah's unshakeable faith in caring and in Ronnie's honesty with himself.

Roots. 1959. P.

There is here a skilful shift of scene to Norfolk, where Beatie Bryant (Joan Plowright), a farm-labourer's daughter on holiday from London, revisits her family. Beatie is engaged to Ronnie, who has for three years been trying to educate her, especially in the arts and in the intelligent use of words (the "bridges" of communication). She has ignored his advice but endlessly parrots his sayings to her phlegmatic family.

Preoccupied with the primal necessities of life the Bryants are the coarse "roots" from which Beatie has sprung. In spite of a rough friendliness they are ignorant, prejudiced, stubborn, and above all inarticulate.

When on the day appointed for his visit, Ronnie sends instead a letter saying their marriage would not work, Beatie is at last galvanised by shock into finding thoughts and words of her own. These folk she realises are without spiritual roots or standards. Then comes her ecstatic moment of self-realisation. She is at last thinking and speaking for herself.

Although he does not know it Ronnie has realised his ambition, "to save someone from the fire."

The play is well constructed, the characters and dialogue are convincing, Beatie delightful. The ideas discussed about "roots" and "bridges," develop organically from the situation.

I'm Talking about Jerusalem. 1960. P.

In 1946 the Kahns' daughter and her husband, Dave, settle in Norfolk to put into practice the theories of William Morris, but Dave, finding that his hand-made furniture cannot compete economically with the factory product, faces their failure and in 1959 they return to London.

The theme of disillusion is here fully analysed by the voluble Kahns, but the mood escapes despair and Dave's self-respect and sober appraisal of unpalatable facts is contrasted with the embittered cynicism of a friend.

The play is weak structurally. There is insufficient action and Dave is not a sufficiently commanding figure to hold things together. Then the intimate study of tender family relationships, suitable to a novel, is embarrassing, except for brief moments on the public stage.

Two symbolic moments in Act II indicate that Wesker was realising the limitations of realism. One is the miming of a simple ritual of reconciliation, the other a ritual enactment of the story of creation.

The Trilogy as a Whole—Wesker's trilogy throws up vital questions of good and evil, both personal and social, the chief perhaps being that of heredity. Must Ronnie and Beatie inherit their parents' limitations? Is Mrs. Bryant right when she says, "The apple don't fall far from the tree"? Is man foredoomed and his struggle vain? Ironically it is the undependable Harry who suggests that giving people some love may help them to change, while of socialism he says, "It'll purify itself." Who was right and in what degree?

The Kitchen. 1959. P.

In a two-acter, Wesker draws on his experience as a chef to give a vivid impression of a day in the kitchen of Marango's restaurant. The play is notable for its skilful contrasts in pace and movement. The quiet morning quickens to a frenzy of anxiety at lunch-time, and the doldrums of the afternoon are succeeded by the sudden outburst of a German who goes beserk.

The swirling vortex is an image of the blind activity of society, and, while avoiding the rigidity of allegory, Wesker clearly indicates that the kitchen is a microcosm of the world, where men with their casual contacts find themselves in a situation beyond their grasp. The play ends with the dramatic irony of Marango's failure to perceive that work and food alone cannot satisfy man's desires.

Although it destroyed the claustrophobic atmosphere the film version caught very well the movement of the play.

Chips with Everything. 1962. P.

In *R.U.R.* (*Rossum's Universal Robots*) the Expressionist playwright, Karel Capek, used robots as dramatis personae. In *Chips with Everything* Wesker brilliantly deploys Expressionism to illustrate the process whereby military discipline can reduce individuals to a robot-like uniformity, both the complacency of authority and the inertia of the ranks.

A squad of nine R.A.F. conscripts is subjected to a battery of bullying abuse from the corporal and psychological manipulation by the commissioned officers, until, their personal identity submerged, they learn to move as one mechanical unit and pass out to the blaring of a military band playing " God Save the Queen."

Expressionism is particularly appropriate to his purpose. He uses type characters to represent social forces—the best example being Corporal Hill—and the identity of the recruits is, with exceptions, indicated very lightly. The dialogue is for the most part staccato, while brief, stylised, symbolic scenes, such as the square bashing and bayonet practice, succeed one another rapidly, a triumphant instance of Wesker's innate command of stage movement.

As to the two recruits presented in greater detail: the plight of the gentle Smiler, broken and suffering, is sufficiently generalised to give pathos and depth to the play without disturbing its tone, but the predicament of Thompson is treated with too much psychological detail to be in key, especially as the portrait is not entirely convincing.

The son of a general, Thompson is at first resistant to authority and appears to be trying to assume leadership of the squad. But the habits of a class that can eat " chips with everything " are too distasteful for him, and accused by the recruits of " slumming " and assailed by the blandishments of the officers he suddenly capitulates and assumes officer's uniform.

The overall effect is tense and powerful, and scenes of moving comedy, such as the breathtaking mime of stealing coke, alternate with those where the audience, facing the same direction as the recruits themselves, cannot escape feeling the obliterating effects of the military machine.

The Four Seasons. 1965. P.

The course of love through the four seasons of the year is traced through the shared experience of a man and woman whose previous marriages had foundered. Wesker has unsuccessfully applied an Expressionist style to unsuitable material, a static situation without incident or plot.

Their Very Own and Golden City. 1966. P.

The driving power of an unusual play is probably Wesker's own struggle to realise a communal and artistic ideal in Centre 42.

He skilfully integrates a sweeping expressionistic panorama of social trends since 1926 with the creation of rounded, idiosyncratic characters. The inspired architect, Andrew Cobham, has a vision of the ideal city that shall set a pattern of living for the community, but its full achievement is thwarted by obscurantist Trade Unions and by his accepting the patronage of a Tory Minister and a capitalist industrialist. Andrew's emotional life is split between frustrated friendship with an aristocratic girl and estrangement form Jessie, his homely wife.

A vantage point is offered by recurring dreamlike scenes in Durham Cathedral. Acting as a flash forward they show Andrew the youth with his fellows and Jessie. Ecstatic with joy at the sublimity of the cathedral he envisages his own life-work. But the final scene, in keeping with the disillusion and compromise that have blighted his vision, serves as a sad, ironic flash-back.

The Friends. 1970.

Her brother, lover, and friends surround Esther's deathbed. Of Jewish working-class origin, they have become affluent and cultured but have lost direction. Disillusion as to the workers' capacity for culture is a theme adumbrated but not clarified. The situation is static and the dialogue often embarrassingly introverted and self-conscious.

John Whiting (1915–63).

John Whiting was an original playwright who was much preoccupied with the theme of self-destruction, but was slow to find his own style.

A Penny for a Song. 1951.

Written at a time of great personal happiness this is an agreeable whimsy, depicting two eccentric brothers in their Dorsetshire residence preparing to repel the armies of Napoleon. The appearance on the stage of a balloon and a home-made fire-engine give the authentic period touch of gentlemanly interest in scientific invention, and also impart to the farcical idyll a dash of panto-mime.

Whiting cleverly gives a comic perspective to the recent fear of foreign invasion and so takes the sting out of terror.

Saint's Day. 1951.

This play, written before *A Penny for a Song*, won the award in a Festival of Britain Play Competition.

It concerns self-destruction, its central figure being the octogenarian Paul Southman, once a famous revolutionary poet who had long ago gone into self-imposed exile because of popular outcry against his work.

The plays opens well. Southman is a striking figure, an embodiment of the angry artist at war with society, and like Swift in his aggressive scorn of compromise, his scurrilous style and final madness. His situation is at first sufficiently distanced to be convincing, but when the fashionable young writer Procathren introduces the glossy contemporary world it begins to seem implausible. Later Procathren accidentally kills Paul's grand-daughter, Stella, and then orders three deserting soldiers to hang Paul and Stella's husband, also an artist, and the initially powerful theme is swamped by melodrama.

The play generally is overloaded with half-developed symbolism and allusion.

Marching Song. 1954. P.

In a play much concerned with the existentialist stress on the inescapability of choice, Whiting returns to the theme of self-destruction.

The setting is generalised—a wealthy house " above a capital city in Europe." Rupert Forster, formerly a general, who seven years previously had inexplicably lost a decisive battle, here meets his dilemma. He must either face a trial, which might cause political unrest, or commit suicide. The choices are represented by two people.

In Act II Forster encounters Dido, a young woman who revives his sense of humanity and will to live. She represents the female side of personality, the Jungian anima and her name recalls the Dido of the Æneid, who by her love deflected Æneas from the path of military duty enjoined by fate.

In Act III he has a very different meeting with Captain Bruno, the embodiment of military ambition, who represents the male aspect of personality. To him Forster at last confesses the cause of his fatal defeat. He had been so overcome with compassion for children whom he had destroyed while they were impeding his tanks that he had been unable to follow up his advance. Bruno stigmatises the delay as military error and guilt and Forster commits suicide rather than face disgrace and imprisonment.

This is a strongly constructed play, its dominating theme worked out with single-minded austerity. But it lacks thrust and momentum. Forster's reversion to his original decision to commit suicide gives it a circular movement and it is more concerned to clarify judgment of the past than to affect the future. In its acknowledgment of the discrepancy between military code and humane ethic it is highly topical and stimulating.

The Devils. 1962. P.

Suggested to Whiting by Peter Brook, this intricate and distinguished play is based on Aldous Huxley's *The Devils of Loudun*, which treats of an actual case of suspected diabolism in France between 1623 and 1634.

Whiting employs two focal points. One is Grandier (Richard Johnson), again a man who invites his own destruction, a worldly and sensual priest who is yet gifted with a rare religious insight and compassion. The other is a hunchback prioress (Dorothy Tutin). Although she has not met Grandier, she becomes obsessed by fantasies of his amorous adventures and her resulting hysteria, which spreads throughout the convent, is suspected as diabolical possession, instigated by Grandier. Richelieu, for political reasons, uses this as a pretext to get rid of him. Grandier, in spite of excruciating torture and degradation, the prelude to his being burnt alive, struggles to retain his faith.

In its subject and theme *The Devils* is strikingly similar to Miller's *The Crucible*. Both plays show *l'homme moyen sensuel* accused of diabolism and beset by a woman's jealousy, fanatical superstition, and malignant spite, yet still keeping his integrity in the face of death.

There are significant differences. Whiting's intricate play is not realistic but Brechtian in style, with a series of brief episodes and a commentary by a sewerman, whose ironic and sceptical remarks counterpoint Grandier's eloquence. It lacks Miller's reference to the contemporary scene and its final note is one of harsh pessimism, as the sewerman tells the prioress that Grandier's bones are being prized by the crowd as superstitious " charms."

The final act presents an almost unbearable spectacle of a barbarous ritual of physical torture as the maimed and twitching Grandier is paraded in public procession through the streets.

Tennessee Williams (b. 1914).

The American Tennessee Williams is a playwright of great talent, whose freely flowing naturalistic plays combine violence and melodrama with haunting portrayal of personality, fluent dialogue, and original settings.

Of recent years the following major plays have been produced in Britain: *The Glass Menagerie*, 1948, revived 1965 (P); *A Street Car Named Desire* 1949 (P); *The Rose Tattoo* (P); *Cat on a Hot Tin Roof* (P); *Camino Real*, the least realistic play, 1957 (P); *Suddenly Last Summer* (P), *Period of Adjustment*, 1961, and *The Two-Character Play*, 1967.

Although his plays breathe the atmosphere of the Deep South—often decadent in tone—Williams, unlike the extravert Miller, is preoccupied not with social issues but with the inner life of his characters. Compelled by their own passions and obsessions and caught in the web of family relationships, they break away only at great cost and pain to themselves and others, so that a mood of determinism, sombre but not altogether despairing, broods over much of Williams' work.

He portrays the vulnerability of those who desire or love anything intensely, humanity's sense of guilt, defiant aggression and despair, all of which he claims to find within himself. The violence characterising so much of his work reaches its climax in *Suddenly Last Summer*.

Especially poignant are Williams' penetrating psychological studies of life's pathetic failures; the crippled Laura retreating to her glass menagerie, Blanche Dubois, of *Street Car*, and the alcoholic Brick and his childless wife in the *Cat*.

The Two Character Play. 1967.

Like the early *The Glass Menagerie*, the play treats of an ill-omened brother–sister relationship.

Believing them to be mad, the cast of a touring theatrical company have just deserted the two star actors, a brother and sister, Felice and Clare. Alone on the stage, the pair hysterically decide to put on Felice's own work, *The Two Character Play*. This play within the play is also about a brother and sister who stay immured in an overgrown house in their terror of facing the world outside. Their father had killed their mother and then committed suicide and people now suspect the brother–sister relationship. Whether it is the relationship of Felice and Clare or of the dramatic personae is left ambiguous in a Pirandello-like piece hovering on the confines of reality and illusion, sanity, and madness.

Charles Wood (b. 1932).

Ever since *Cockade*, 1963, Wood's plays have been chiefly concerned with military life. An exception was *Fill the Stage with Happy Hours*, 1967 (P).

Dingo. 1967. P.

Wood employs Expressionism to present a phantasmagoria of the last War, beginning in the desert and grinding through Stalag to the unconditional surrender of Germany. It is an assault on the emotions and sensations in a passionate attempt to bring home war's physical horror and spiritual attrition, but Wood's specific concern is to expose latent jingoism and political expediency and the futility of the heroism they demand.

The scurrilous words matter less than certain persistent images: the ranker, Dingo, epitome of bitter disillusion; Tanky, rendered simple-minded because he was powerless to release his mate, screaming to death in a flaming tank; an ENSA comedian who serves to parody Churchillian rhetoric, and breezy morale-boosting of High Command; a young subaltern, dressed as a blonde in a bikini for a concert party designed to cover an escape from Stalag, and now, with Tanky, lolling dead from the barbed wire.

The play is powerful but sprawling, cluttered, one-sided. It attacks the idea that Britain played a more disinterested rôle than in previous wars. It was fought, not for others, says Dingo, but " for all the usual reasons," an emotive statement that needs scrutiny.

" H ". 1969. M.

Wood's subject is the heroic march of the elderly General Havelock, or "H," during the Mutiny. His column vastly outnumbered and decimated by disease, he yet relieved Cawnpore and won twelve desperate battles before relieving Lucknow where he died of dysentery.

A devoted and chivalrous Christian and a disciplined commander, Havelock yet ordered some of the terrible reprisals then current, hanging mutinous sepoys or shooting them alive from the mouths of cannon. His equivocal behaviour helps to resolve and focus Wood's own conflicting impulses, his fascination with military discipline and his horror at the bestiality of war, so that the play is more unified than *Dingo*.

The core of the play is irony, centred in the action of the protagonist. But the irony proliferates, as in the contrast between the stylised Victorian language and the brutal deed, and in the many brief unconnected episodes, as, for instance, one recalling the mutual love and sacrifice between British and sepoys. These, demanding a constant reorientation of attitude, tend to distract and confuse.

The fact that Havelock's aide-de-camp is his own son suggests the tender perspective of home. Resolute in courage and obedience, the son differs from his father in opinion and faith and his eventual confession of Christianity at Havelock's death gives pathos to the scene.

The Brechtian epic style is well suited to the simple episodic structure. Brechtian devices are also used:—direct address to the audience, map titles and symbolic emblems, such as the simple blood-stained floor and awning, arrestingly conveying the Indian atrocities at Cawnpore. Brechtian in spirit too is the deliberate theatricality of short scenes projected within a little replica of the popular travelling stage.

Although Havelock on the surface resembles the Brechtian ambiguous protagonist, the chief weakness of the play is that he does not attain the commanding stature of a Galileo or a Mother Courage.

IDEAS & BELIEFS

This section explains many of the ideas and beliefs that have dominated men's minds during the centuries. The arrangement is alphabetical and the subjects fall broadly into three groups: religious, philosophical, and political.

IDEAS AND BELIEFS

THIS section explains many of the ideas and beliefs which people have held at different periods in history. Beliefs may be true or false, meaningful or totally meaningless, regardless of the degree of conviction with which they are held. Since man has been moved to action so often by his beliefs they are worth serious study. The section throws a vivid light on human history.

Man has always felt a deep need for emotional security, a sense of " belonging." This need has found expression in the framing of innumerable religious systems, nearly all of which have been concerned with man's relation to a divine ruling power. In the past people have been accustomed to think of their own religion as true and of all others as false. Latterly we have come to realise that in man's religious strivings there is common ground, for our need in the world today is a morality whereby human beings may live together in harmony.

There is also to be found in man an irresistible curiosity which demands an explanation of the world in which he finds himself. This urge to make the world intelligible takes him into the realm of science where the unknown is the constant challenge. Science is a creative process, always in the making, since the scientist's conjectures are constantly being submitted to severe critical tests. Basic scientific ideas are discussed in Section F.

In writing of beliefs, especially cherished beliefs, and of how they fit into the modern picture of the world, it is difficult to avoid causing some offence but the reader is assured that the writer has tried to be fair and helpful.

A

Abecedarians, name (derived from A B C) of a small German religious sect, founded by the Anabaptist Storch in 1522, who claimed that, as knowledge of the Scriptures was communicated directly by the Holy Spirit, it was wrong to learn to read. *See* Baptists.

Activists, those in a political movement who insist on taking active steps towards their objectives rather than merely putting forward a programme.

Acupuncture, a near-medical cult originating in China and based on the supposedly therapeutic effect of implanting fine gold needles in the spinal column. Practices of this kind, which are of arguable scientific status, seem to flourish in parts of the world where orthodox medicine has made little progress or where doctors and trained staff are scarce. Nevertheless, it is always worthwhile examining them, even if only to attempt to identify the presumably psychological basis of their effectiveness. In the case of acupuncture if any physical effect occurs it may be because the insertion of the needles has some anaesthetic effect on the nerves which have been prodded.

Adlerian Psychology. In 1911 the Viennese psychoanalyst Alfred Adler (1870–1937) together with his colleague Carl Gustav Jung broke with their friend Sigmund Freud over disputes concerning the latter's theoretic approach to psychoanalysis. Jung and Adler were themselves shortly also to part company, each to set up and develop his own " school " of psychoanalysis. Adler's system of psychotherapy is based on the idea, not of sex as a driving force as in the case of Freud, but on the concept of " compensation " or a drive for power in an attempt to overcome the " inferiority complex " which he held to be universal in human beings. The child naturally feels inferior to adults, but bullying, making him feel insignificant or guilty or contemptible, even spoiling, which makes him feel important within the family but relatively unimportant outside, increases this feeling. Or the child may have physical defects: he may be small or underweight, have to wear glasses, become lame, be constantly ill, or stupid at school. In these ways he develops a sense of inferiority which for the rest of his life he develops a technique to overcome.

This may be done in several ways: he may try to become capable in the very respects in which he feels incompetent—hence many great orators have originally had speech defects; many painters poor eyesight; many musicians have been partially deaf; like Nietzsche, the weakling, he may write about the superman, or like Sandow, the strong man, be born with poor health.

On the other hand he may overdo his attempt and overcompensate. Hence we have the bully who is really a coward, the small man who is self-assertive to an objectionable degree (Hitler, Napoleon, Stalin, and Mussolini were all small men) or the foreigner who like three of these men wanted to be the hero of their adopted country—Hitler the Austrian, Napoleon the Italian, Stalin the Georgian.

But what about the man who can do none of these things, who continues to fail to compensate? He, says Adler, becomes a neurotic because neurosis is an excuse which means " I could have done so-and-so but . . ." It is the unconscious flight into illness—the desire to be ill. Thus a man who used to have a good job lost it through no fault of his own and developed a " nervous break-down," one of the symptoms of which was a fear of crossing streets. Adler would have asked: " What purpose is served by this symptom? " " Why does he unconsciously not want to cross streets? " The answer was that he had only been offered inferior jobs, and although he felt for his family's sake that he ought to take them, something inside said: " No, I have been an important man and I cannot bear to do insignificant work —if I am unable to cross streets I am unable (through no fault of my own) to go out to work." Adler's treatment involves disclosing these subterfuges we play on ourselves so that we can deal with the real situation in a more realistic way. The criticism of Adler's theory is not that it is not true. It is. But it is not the whole truth, for people are much more subtle than Adler gave them credit for: Freud recognised this element of " secondary gain " in neurosis but he knew that there was more to it than that. Nevertheless Adler's method works well in some simpler cases. *See also* Psychoanalysis.

Adoptionism, in Christianity, a doctrine advanced at various times which holds that Jesus was not born divine but, in virtue of his human spiritual achievements, was designated by God as the Son of God at the moment of his baptism in the Jordan, as told in all the four Gospels. Among the sects who held this " heretical " doctrine were the Paulicians (*q.v.*). The " Adoptionist " view differs from the orthodox " Conceptionist " view only in regard to the moment in the life of Jesus when the incarnation took place.

Adventists, a group of American religious sects, the most familiar being the Seventh-Day Adventist Church, which observes Saturday as the true Sabbath. With more than a million members throughout the world, it shares with other Adventists a belief in the imminent second coming of Christ (a doctrine fairly widespread in the U.S.A. during the early decades of the 19th cent. when the end of the world was predicted by William Miller for 1843, then fo

1844). Modern Adventists content themselves with the conviction that the " signs " of the Advent are multiplying, the " blessed event " which will solve the world's ills. Believers will be saved, but the sects differ as to whether the unjust will be tortured in hell, annihilated, or merely remain asleep eternally.

Agnosticism. *See* **God and Man.**

Albigenses, also known as **Cathari.** French 12th cent. heretical sect (named after the town of Albi in Provence), who maintained that material things belonged to the realm of Satan and that salvation was to be achieved by crushing all animal instincts, particularly the sexual instinct; universal continence would end the domination of matter by the extinction of the human race. The eating of animal flesh was forbidden and vegetarianism enjoined in order to weaken the desires. Those who rigidly kept to these rules were initiated into the grade of the " Perfect "; those unable fully to comply were known as the " Believers ". Condemned as heretics by Pope Innocent III, the sect was finally exterminated in the Albigensian Crusade led by Simon de Montfort towards the end of the 12th cent. (In his thoroughness, de Montfort also succeeded in destroying the high culture of the Troubadours.) *See* **Manichaeism.**

Alchemy, ancient art associated with magic and astrology in which modern chemistry has its roots. The earliest mention of alchemy comes from ancient Egypt but its later practitioners attributed its origins to such varied sources as the fallen angels of the Bible, to Moses and Aaron, but most commonly to Hermes Trismegistus, often identified with the Egyptian god Thoth, whose knowledge of the divine art was handed down only to the sons of kings (cf. the phrase " hermetically sealed "). Its main object was the transmutation of metals. Egyptian speculation concerning this reached its height during the 6th cent. in the Alexandrian school. Brought to Western Europe by the Moslems, one of its most famous Arab exponents was Jabir (*c.* 760–*c.* 815), known to the Latins as Geber, who had a laboratory at Kufa on the Tigris. One school of early Greek philosophy held that there was ultimately only one elemental matter of which everything was composed. Such men as Albertus Magnus (1206–80) and Roger Bacon (1214–94) assumed that, by removing impurities, this *materia prima* could be obtained. Although Bacon's ideas were in many ways ahead of his time, he firmly believed in the philosopher's stone, which could turn base metals into gold, and in an elixir of life which would give eternal youth. Modern science has, of course, shown in its researches into radioactivity the possibility of transmutation of certain elements, but this phenomenon has little bearing on either the methods of the alchemist or the mysteries with which he surrounded them.

Anabaptists. *See* **Baptists.**

Analytical Psychology, the name given by Carl Gustav Jung (1875–1961) of Zürich to his system of psychology which, like Adler's (*see* **Adlerian psychology**), took its origin from Freud's psychoanalysis from which both diverged in 1911. Briefly, Jung differed from Freud: (1) in believing that the latter had laid too much emphasis on the sexual drive as the basic one in man and replacing it with the concept of *libido* or life energy of which sex forms a part; (2) in his theory of types: men are either extrovert or introvert (*i.e.* their interest is turned primarily outwards to the world or inwards to the self), and they apprehend experience in four main ways, one or other of which is predominant in any given individual—sensing, feeling, thinking, or intuiting; (3) in his belief that the individual's unconscious mind contains not only repressed material which, as Freud maintained, was too unpleasant to be allowed into awareness, but also faculties which had not been allowed to develop—*e.g.*, the emotional side of the too rational man, the feminine side of the too masculine one; (4) in the importance he attaches to the existence of a collective unconscious at a still deeper level which contains traces of ancient ways of thought which mankind has inherited over the centuries. These are the *archetypes* and include

vague primitive notions of magic, spirits and witches, birth and death, gods, virgin mothers, resurrection, etc. In the treatment of neuroses Jung believed in the importance of (*a*) the present situation which the patient refuses to face; (*b*) the bringing together of conscious and unconscious and integrating them.

In the 1940s and 50s interest in Jung's ideas waned, at least in academic circles, as the emphasis among experimental psychologists shifted closer and closer to the " hard " scientific line. This was also true in the field of psychoanalysis where the Jungian as opposed to the Freudian point of view became progressively less popular. At the present time this trend is beginning to reverse, and while Jung's offbeat views on astrology, telepathy, etc., are still unfashionable, a reappraisal of the significance of his views on the nature of the unconscious is taking place and many psychologists feel that his contribution to our understanding of the nature of human mental processes has been greatly underated. *See also* **Psychoanalysis.**

Anarchism, a political philosophy which holds, in the words of the American anarchist Josiah Warren (1798–1874), an early follower of Robert Owen, that " every man should be his own government, his own law, his own church." The idea that governmental interference or even the mere existence of authority is inherently bad is as old as Zeno, the Greek Stoic philosopher, who believed that compulsion perverts the normal nature of man. William Godwin's *Enquiry Concerning Political Justice* (1793) was the first systematic exposition of the doctrine. Godwin (father-in-law of Shelley) claimed that man is by nature sociable, co-operative, rational, and good when given the choice to act freely; that under such conditions men will form voluntary groups to work in complete social harmony. Such groups or communities would be based on equality of income, no state control, no property; this state of affairs would be brought about by rational discussion and persuasion rather than by revolution.

The French economist Proudhon (1809–65) was the first to bring anarchism to the status of a mass movement. In his book *What is Property?* he stated bluntly that " property is theft " and " governments are the scourge of God." He urged the formation of co-operative credit banks where money could be had without interest and goods could be exchanged at cost value at a rate representing the hours of work needed to produce each commodity. Like Godwin, he disapproved of violence but, unlike Marx, disapproved of trades unions as representing organised groups.

In communistic anarchism these ideas were combined with a revolutionary philosophy, primarily by the Russians Michael Bakunin (1814–76) and Peter Kropotkin (1842–1921) who favoured training workers in the technique of " direct action " to overthrow the state by all possible means, including political assassination. In 1868 anarchists joined the First International which broke up a few years later after a bitter struggle between Bakuninists and Marxists. Subsequently small anarchist groups murdered such political figures as Tsar Alexander II of Russia, King Humbert of Italy, Presidents Carnot of France and MacKinley of America, and the Empress Elizabeth of Austria.

Anarchism and communism differ in three main ways: (1) anarchism forms no political party, rejects all relationship with established authority, and regards democratic reform as a setback; (2) communism is against capitalism, anarchism against the state as such; (3) both have the final goal of a classless society, but anarchism rejects the idea of an intermediate period of socialist state control accepted by communism. Philosophical anarchists, such as the American writer Henry David Thoreau (1817–62), were primarily individualists who believed in a return to nature, the non-payment of taxes, and passive resistance to state control; in these respects Thoreau strongly influenced Gandhi as did the Christian anarchist Tolstoy. *See also* **Syndicalism.**

Anglicanism, adherence to the doctrine and

discipline of the Anglican, as the genuine representative of the Catholic Church. *See* Church of England.

Anglo-Catholicism. To Queen Elizabeth I the Church of England was that of the " middle way " in which human reason and commonsense took their place beside Scripture and Church authority. The extent to which these various factors are stressed creates the distinctions between " high " and " low " church. Anglo-Catholics tend to reject the term " Protestant " and stress the term " Catholic " and, although few accept the infallibility of the Pope, some Anglo-Catholic churches have introduced much or all of the Roman ritual and teach Roman dogmas. *See* Catholicism, Tractarianism.

Animism. To early man and in primitive societies the distinction between animate and inanimate objects was not always obvious—it is not enough to say that living things move and non-living things do not, for leaves blow about in the wind and streams flow down a hillside. In the religions of early societies, therefore, we find a tendency to believe that life exists in all objects from rocks and pools to seas and mountains. This belief is technically known as *animatism*, which differs from *animism*, a somewhat more sophisticated view which holds that natural objects have no life in themselves but may be the abode of dead people, spirits, or gods who occasionally give them the appearance of life. The classic example of this, of course, is the assumption that an erupting volcano is an expression of anger on the part of the god who resides in it. Such beliefs may seem absurd today, but it is worth realising that we are not entirely free of them ourselves when we ascribe " personalities " of a limited kind to motor cars, boats, dolls, or models which incur our pleasure or anger depending upon how well they " behave."

Anthropomorphism, the ascription of human physical and moral qualities to God or gods (in psychology to gods or animals). Psychologists use the term *Anthropopathy* for the ascription of such qualities specifically to the Deity.

Anthroposophy, a school of religious and philosophical thought based on the work of the German educationist and mystic Rudolf Steiner (1861–1925). Steiner was originally an adherent of Madame Blavatsky's theosophical movement (*see* Theosophy) but in 1913 broke away to form his own splinter group, the Anthroposophical Society, following ideological disputes over the alleged " divinity " of the Indian boy Krishnamurti. Steiner was much influenced by the German poet and scientist, Goethe, and believed that an appreciation and love for art was one of the keys to spiritual development. One of the first tasks of his new movement was the construction of a vast temple of arts and sciences, known as the Goetheanum, to act as the headquarters of the society. This structure, which was of striking and revolutionary architectural style, was unfortunately burnt down in 1922 to be replaced by an even more imaginative one which today is one of the most interesting buildings of its kind in the world. Anthroposophy, which ceased to expand greatly following its founder's death, is nevertheless well-established in various parts of the world with specialised, and often very well equipped, schools and clinics which propagate the educational and therapeutic theories of the movement. These, which include the allegedly beneficial powers of music, coloured lights, etc., have made little impact on modern educational ideas. but the schools have acquired a reputation for success in the training of mentally handicapped children, though one suspects that these successes are due to the patience and tolerance exercised in these establishments rather than to the curative value of colour or music " therapy " itself. Despite its apparent eccentricities, anthroposophy has made its mark on art and architecture, the outstanding modern painter Kandinsky, for example, being particularly influenced by Steiner's ideas and teachings.

Anticlericalism, resentment of priestly powers and privileges, traceable in England to Wyclif's insistence in the 14th cent. on the right of all men to have access to the Scriptures. The translation of the Bible into the common tongue was a great landmark in the history o the Bible and the English language. Wyclif principles were condemned by the Roma Church of his time but were readily accepte during the Reformation. Tudor anticlericalism arose from motives ranging from a greedy desir to plunder the riches of the Church to a genuine dislike of the powers of the priesthood whos spiritual courts still had the right to decide o points of doctrine or morals in an age when th layman felt he was well able to decide for him self. In innumerable ways the Church was per mitted to extort money from the laity. It i generally agreed, says Trevelyan, that the fina submission of church to state in England wa motivated quite as much by anticlericalism a by Protestantism. The rise of the Reforme churches in England satisfied the peopl generally and anticlericalism never became th fixed principle of permanent parties as hap pened in France and Italy from the time o Voltaire onwards.

Antisemitism, a term first applied about the middl of the last century to those who were anti Jewish in their outlook. Although thi attitude was prevalent for religious reason throughout the Middle Ages, modern anti semitism differed (*a*) in being largely motivate by economic or political conditions, and (*b*) i being doctrinaire with a pseudo-scientifi rationale presented by such men as Gobinea (1816–82) and Houston Stewart Chamberlai (1855–1927), and later by the Nazi and Fascis " philosophers." Beginning in Russia an Hungary with the pogroms of 1882 it graduall spread south and westwards where, in Franc the Dreyfus case provided an unsavour example in 1894. Thousands of Jews fro Eastern Europe fled to Britain and Americ during this period; for in these countries anti semitism has rarely been more than a persona eccentricity. During the last war the murde of six million Jews by the Nazis and thei accomplices led to a further exodus to variou parts of the world and finally to the creation o the state of Israel.

The individual Jew-hater makes unconsciou use of the psychological processes of projectio and displacement: his greed or sexual guilt i projected on to the Jew (or Negro or Catholic because he cannot bear to accept them as hi own emotions, and his sense of failure in life i blamed on his chosen scapegoat rather than o his own inadequacy.

But there are social causes too and politician in some lands are well versed in the techniqu of blaming unsatisfactory conditions (whic' they themselves may have in part produce upon minority groups and persuading others t do the same. Historically, the Jew is ideall suited for this role of scapegoat: (1) in th Middle Ages when usury was forbidden t Christians but not to Jews, the latter often be came moneylenders incurring the opprobriu generally associated with this trade (*e.g.*, to th simple-minded Russian peasant the Jew ofte represented, not only the " Christ-killer," bu also the moneylender or small shopkeeper t whom he owed money); (2) many trades bein closed to Jews, it was natural that they con centrated in others, thus arousing suspicions o " influence " (*i.e.* Jews are felt to occupy a plac in certain trades and professions which far ex ceeds their numerical proportion to the popula tion as a whole); (3) even with the ending o ghetto life, Jews often occupy *en masse* som parts of cities rather than others and this ma; lead to resentment on the part of the origina inhabitants who begin to feel themselves dis possessed; (4) Jews tend to form a closed societ; and incur the suspicions attached to all close societies within which social contacts are largel limited to members; marriage outside the grou is forbidden or strongly disapproved of, an the preservation, among the orthodox, o cultural and religious barriers tends to isolat them from their fellow citizens. Discrimina tion, hateful as it is, does not come from one sid only and it is such barriers as these that help t maintain an old and cruel folly. *See* Racism Zionism, Judaism.

Antivivisection, opposition to scientific experi mentation upon live animals based, according t its supporters, both on the moral grounds of the suffering imposed, and on the less secure claim that many doctors and scientists of repute have rejected the value of information gained in this way. It is true that the protagonists of the movement during its early days in the mid-19th cent. included a number of eminent physicians and surgeons, but few today—whatever their moral scruples—would deny the value of the results obtained. Without animal experiments we should be without vaccines, sera, or anti-toxins against smallpox, tetanus, typhoid, diphtheria, poliomyelitis, and a multitude of other diseases; we should have no detailed knowledge about vitamins, or about the effects of radioactive fallout; we would be unable to test out new drugs for safety before using them on human beings. There are in Britain two or three large national anti-vivisection societies and several smaller ones. Much of their work is co-ordinated through the British Council of Anti-Vivisection Societies. Animal experi-mentation is controlled by Act of Parliament which makes obligatory the possession of licences by experimenters, inspection of labora-tories by the Home Office, and the issue of annual returns of experiments. Many people would like the number of experiments on animals reduced and the law changed to pro-hibit any experiment in which there is any risk of inflicting suffering.

Apartheid, an Afrikaans word meaning "apart-ness," referred to by South African Government spokesmen as "separate development" or "self-development." To others it means the system of total racial discrimination between black and white South Africans—the per-manent inhabitants of the country—as enforced by the Nationalist Party since it came to power in 1948. Some degree of racial segregation has existed in South Africa since the earliest days of colonialism in the mid-17th cent. and the policy was continued by the United Party under Smuts and Hertzog from 1934 onwards though it was never a political issue. This changed when the Nationalist Party gained power and oppressive measures against the non-White segment of the population have grown steadily under Malan, Strydom, Verwoerd, and Vorster. *Apartheid* involves the beliefs in racial purity and *baaskap*, or white supremacy. It means keeping vast African populations in a condition of helotry. The official policy of the South African Government is to create separate self-governing black states in which the Africans would be guided to self-government and, it is claimed, eventually to independence. The first so-called bantu reserve was set up in the Transkei in 1962. But Africans with 70 per cent of the population would have only about 13 per cent of the land; cities and mineral areas would remain the reserve of the whites. Total *apartheid* or complete separation of the black and white races in South Africa remains un-likely to be realised since mining, the main industry of the country, is based on relatively low-paid African labour.

Afrikaner conservatism may be challenged by the recent split in the governing Nationalist Party—between the *verligtes* (enlightened) and the *verkramptes* (closed inwards)—a develop-ment which could lead to a more humanitarian outlook on race.

Apollinarianism, the heretical belief taught by Apollinaris (*c.* 313–*c.* 390), bishop of Laodicea, near Antioch, that in Jesus the human mind was replaced by the Divine Mind or Logos. The sect was later absorbed by the Monophysites (*q.v.*).

Arianism, formed the subject of the first great controversy within the Christian Church over the doctrine of Arius of Alexandria (d. 336) who denied the divinity of Christ. The doctrine, although at first influential, was condemned at the Council of Nicaea (325), called by the Emperor Constantine, at which Arius was opposed by Athanasius, also of Alexandria, who maintained the now orthodox view that the Son is of one substance with the Father. Arius was banished and the heresy had died out by the end of the 4th cent., but disbelief in the divinity of Christ has formed part of the doctrine of many minor sects since, notably in Uni-tarianism (*q.v.*).

Arminianism, the doctrine of Jacobus Arminius or Jakob Harmensen (1560–1609), the Dutch minister of a Protestant church in Amsterdam, who had trained in the universities of Leyden and Geneva where he learned the Calvinistic doctrine of predestination (*See* **Calvinism**). Later he became deeply convinced of the falsity of this belief which maintained that God had, by an eternal decree, predestined which people were to be saved and which eternally damned. In face of the bitter opposition of his opponent Franz Gomar and his party who held this view, Arminius asserted that God bestows for-giveness and eternal life on all who repent and believe in Christ. In England a modified Arminianism was later to become the theology of Wesleyan Methodism.

Assassins, a sect of Moslem Shi'ites, founded by the Persian Hasan i Sabbah (*c.* 1090), which for more than two centuries established a rule of terror all over Persia and Syria. The coming of the Mongols in 1256 destroyed them in Persia and the Syrian branch suffered a similar fate at the hands of the then Mamluk sultan of Egypt, *c.* 1270. It was a secret order, ruled over by a grand master, under whom the members were strictly organised into classes, according to the degree of initiation into the secrets of the order. The devotees, belonging to one of the lower groups, carried out the actual assassinations under strict laws of obedience, and total ignorance of the objects and ritual of the society. It is believed that the latter were given ecstatic visions under the influence of hashish, whence the term *hashshashin*, which became corrupted to " assassin."

Associationism. In psychology, the Association-ist school of the 19th cent. accepted the associa-tion of ideas as the fundamental principle in mental life. It was represented in Britain by the two Mills and Herbert Spencer, in Germany by J. F. Herbart (1776–1841). To these, mental activity was nothing but the association of " ideas " conceived of as units of both thought and feeling—the emotion of anger or the percep-tion of a chair were both " ideas "—and apart from them the self did not exist. Personality was simply a series of these units coming and going, adding to or cancelling each other out, in accord-ance with rigid and mechanistic scientific laws.

Assumption of the Virgin. The Roman Catholic belief, that the Blessed Virgin ascended bodily to heaven after her death, was proclaimed by Pope Pius XII towards the end of 1950. Protestants are liable to make the mistake of supposing that such dogmas are new additions to the faith invented by the pope of the moment. According to Catholic doctrine, no addition can be made to the " faith once de-livered to the saints," and every dogma is justified by reference to Bible texts and the traditions of the Church. Both Eastern and Western Churches have been permitted to be-lieve in the Assumption of the Virgin for over a thousand years, and the new dogma merely clarifies the old belief and makes it binding on the faithful.

Astrology, a pseudo-science bearing much the same historical relationship to astronomy as alchemy does to chemistry. Originally it was divided into the two branches of Natural Astrology which dealt with the movements of the heavenly bodies and their calculation, and Judicial Astrology which studied the alleged influence of the stars and planets on human life and fate. It was the former that developed into modern astronomy; the latter was, and remains, a primitive myth.

Astrology owes most to the early Babylonians (or Chaldeans) who, being largely nomadic in an environment which permitted an unobstructed view of the sky, readily accepted the idea that divine energy is manifested in the movements of the sun and planets. Gradually this concept became enlarged and the relative positions of the planets both in relation to each other and to the fixed stars became important together with the idea of omens—that, if a particular event occurred whilst the planets were in a particular position, the recurrence of that position heralded a recurrence of the same sort of event. Soon the planets became associated with almost every aspect of human life. They were bound up with the emotions, with parts of the body, so that astrology played quite a large part in medicine up to late mediaeval times. Not only was the position of the planet to be considered but also the particular sign of the zodiac (or house of heaven) it was occupying, and it was believed possible to foretell the destiny of an individual by calculating which star was in the ascendant (i.e. the sign of the zodiac nearest the eastern horizon and the star which arose at that precise moment) at the time of his birth. Astrology was popular among the Egyptians, the Romans (whose authorities found the Chaldean astrologers a nuisance and expelled them from time to time), and during the Middle Ages when astrologers were often highly respected.

Despite the apparent absurdity of astrological beliefs—for example, how could the pattern of light from stars billions of miles away possibly influence the temperament of single individuals on earth—a substantial number of intelligent and well-educated people take its study in all seriousness. The most interesting " convert " was the psychologist and philosopher, Carl Jung, who conducted a complex experiment in which he compared the " birth signs " of happily married and divorced couples and claimed to find that those most favourably matched in astrological terms were also those more likely to have permanent wedded bliss. Jung's otherwise world-shaking finding has been shown to be based on a simple statistical fallacy and is likely to be of little practical value to young people uncertain about their choice of marriage partner. However, Jung took his findings as evidence for his own theory of " synchronicity " (q.v.), an involved and near-metaphysical notion which holds that events in the universe may be significantly related in a " non-causal " fashion. For simpler souls astrology is still principally a source of entertainment, though human beings' natural inclination to peer into the future often draws them into astrology with at least semi-serious motives.

Atheism. See God and Man.

Atlantis, a mythical continent supposed to have lain somewhere between Europe and America and a centre of advanced civilisation before it was inundated by some great natural catastrophe in pre-Christian times. There is little, if any, serious historical or archaeological evidence for its existence, but the legend of the Golden Land destroyed when the waters of the Atlantic closed over it has remarkable staying power and is believed by large numbers of people. Plato wrote convincingly about the wonders of Atlantis in his dialogues Timaeus and Critias, while other writers gave suggested that the biblical story of the Flood is based on fragmentary accounts of the Atlantean deluge. The lost continent is also of occult significance, largely as the result of the writings of W. Scott-Elliott whose book, The Story of Atlantis (recently re-published by the Theosophical Society), alleged that by clairvoyance he had been able to contact the spirits of Atlanteans who had been destroyed because of their addiction to black magic. There even exists in Britain today a minor but ardent religious group, " The Atlanteans," who hold that Atlantis still exists today, but on a different metaphysical plane, and that it is possible to communicate with it via individuals with supposedly mediumistic powers (see Spiritualism). Members of the Atlanteans meet regularly to hear talks about the vanished continent and " trance addresses " by one of the high priests of Atlantis, Helio-Arconaphus. Such beliefs, though unusual, are essentially harmless and merely reflect the great variety of religious attitudes which human beings enjoy and to which they are entitled.

Atomism. (1) in philosophy, the atomists were a group of early Greek thinkers, the most important of whom were Leucippus (fl. c. 440 B.C.) and his younger contemporary Democritus (c. 460–370 B.C.). Prior to these men, although it had been agreed that matter must be composed of tiny ultimate particles and that change must be due to the manner in which these mingled or separated from each other, it was supposed that there existed different types of particle for each

material—e.g. for flesh, wood, hair, bone. The atomists taught that atoms were all made of a single substance and differed only in the connections (pictured as hooks, grooves, points, etc.) which enabled them to join each other in characteristic ways. Theirs was the first move towards modern atomic theory and a predecessor of the modern concept of chemical linkages. (2) in psychology, atomism refers to any theory which holds that mental states can be analysed without loss into elementary units, e.g. Associationism and Behaviourism (qq.v.).

Authoritarianism, a dictatorial form of government as contrasted with a democratic one based on popular sovereignty. Its alleged advantages are the avoidance of the delays and inefficiency said to be characteristic of the latter, but like " Bolshevism " the word is used today mainly as a form of abuse.

B

Baconian Method, the use of the inductive (as opposed to the deductive or Aristotelian) method of reasoning as proposed by Francis Bacon in the 17th cent. and J. S. Mill in the 19th cent. Deduction argues from supposedly certain first principles (such as the existence of God or Descartes's " I think, therefore I am ") what the nature of the universe and its laws must be, whereas the only means of obtaining true knowledge of the universe, in Bacon's view, was by the amassing of facts and observations so that when enough were obtained the certain truth would be known in the same way that a child's numbered dots in a playbook joined together by a pencilled line create a picture. However, this is not the way science progresses in practice (see **F3(1)**). Bacon underrated the importance of hypothesis and theory and overrated the reliability of the senses. In discussing the scientific tradition, Sir Karl Popper in his book, Conjectures and Refutations, says: " The most important function of observation and reasoning, and even of intuition and imagination, is to help us in the critical examination of those bold conjectures which are the means by which we probe into the unknown." Two of the greatest men who clearly saw that there was no such thing as an inductive procedure were Galileo and Einstein.

Baha'ism, faith teaching the unity of religions and the unity of mankind. It arose in Iran from the teachings of the Bab (Mirza Ali Mohammed, 1820–50) and the Baha'u'llah (Mirza Husain Ali, 1817–92), thought to be manifestations of God, who in his essence is unknowable. Emphasis is laid on service to others. It has communities in 300 states.

Baptists, a Christian denomination whose distinctive doctrines are that members can only be received by baptism " upon the confession of their faith and sins " and that " baptism in no wise appertaineth to infants." Baptism is therefore by total immersion of adults. Modern Baptists base their doctrines upon the teaching of the Apostles and some hold that the Albigenses (q.v.) maintained the true belief through what they regard as the corruption of the Roman Church in mediaeval times. On the other hand any connection with the Anabaptist movement during the Reformation is rejected and the beginning of the modern Church is traced to John Smyth, a minister of the Church of England who in Amsterdam came under the influence of the Arminians (q.v.) and Mennonites. Smyth died in 1612 when the first Baptist church in England was built at Newgate. This, the " General " Baptist Church, rejected Calvinistic beliefs and held the Arminian doctrine of redemption open to all, but some years later a split occurred with the formation of the " Particular " Baptist Church which was Calvinist in doctrine. In 1891 the two bodies were united in the Baptist Union and today the sect is spread throughout the world, notably in the U.S.A.

The Anabaptist movements of Germany, Switzerland, and Holland also practised adult baptism in addition to a primitive communism and demanded social reforms. Persecuted by both Catholics and Protestants, their leader, Thomas Münzer, and many others were burned at the stake (1525). However, this sect was noted for its violence under a religious guise, and its taking over of the state of Münster in 1533 was characterised by wild licentiousness, since, as Antinomians, they believed that the "elect" could do no wrong. A revival begun by Menno Simons (d. 1561), a Dutch religious reformer, led to the formation of the Mennonite sect which, whilst rejecting infant baptism, gave up the objectionable features of the Anabaptists. This reformed sect still exists as small agricultural groups in the original strongholds of the movement and in the United States.

Beat Generation, a term first used by the American writer Jack Kerouac (d. 1969), author of *The Town and the City* and *On The Road*, to define various groups spread across the face of the country, but notably New York and San Francisco, who, belonging to the post-war generation, represented a complex of attitudes. Briefly, these are: rejection of the values of the past and lack of conviction in the possibility of a future for humanity—hence an acceptance of nothing but the immediate present in terms of experience and sensations; rebellion against organised authority, not out of any political conviction (as in the case of anarchism), but rather from lack of any interest or desire to control events, nature, or people; contempt for the "Square"—the orthodox individual who, stuck firmly in his rut, "plays it safe" and remains confident of the rightness and decency of his moral values. The "Beatnik" has contracted out of what one of them describes as "an increasingly meaningless rat-race rigged up by and for Squares" which wastes effort and brutalises feeling. He loathes the pretences without which, he claims, the Square cannot succeed, and throwing off all masks is indifferent to the opinions of others, his dress, or the need to work, thus entering into "the inescapable truth and squalor of his own being." He "digs" (likes) everything, tries everything from drugs to sexual relationships, which have no significance outside the sensations of the moment to the advanced Beatnik or "hipster." All men are addressed as "man," all women as "chick." Of course, the above is an intellectualisation by such Beat writers as Kerouac, Allen Ginsberg, and Carl Solomon or Norman Mailer of a philosophy which for many Beatniks would be meaningless, being satisfied with any excuse for their own exhibitionism, sexual promiscuity, and psychopathic tendencies. Beards (in men), bare feet, sloppy clothes, and unwashed bodies were the familiar Beatnik uniform.

The Beat generation of the 1940s and 50s gave way to the Love generation or Flower people, with their flowers, beads, and cowbells. Their social philosophy was the same—living in the present, unconventionally, seeking personal freedom, believing drugs to be essential, claiming to be acting against the rat race, dissociating themselves from politics, taking a superficial interest in the religions of the East, borrowing much of their language, music, and ideas on dress from the American "hippy"; yet believing in the creation of a new and gentler society based on different forms and values.

Both the Beat and the Love generations have appealed largely to the younger segment of society who, disillusioned with orthodox religion and traditional politics, have sought outlets for their powerful, if poorly expressed, drives and emotions. Early group manifestations of the Beat and Drop-out variety had limited internal structure and no co-ordinated political motive and have thus constituted no threat to the established political forces and governments of the world. Quite recently, however, clear signs of coherent organisation in these numerically substantial groups have begun to emerge, giving rise to a powerful anti-establishment movement known as the "underground" (*q.v.*).

Behaviourism, a school of psychology founded in 1914 by J. B. Watson (1878–1958), an animal psychologist at Johns Hopkins University, Baltimore. Its main tenet was that the method of introspection and the study of mental states

were unscientific and should be replaced by the study of behaviour. When animals or human beings were exposed to specific stimuli and their responses objectively recorded, or when the development of a child, as seen in its changing behaviour, was noted, these alone were methods which were truly scientific. Watson contributed an important idea to psychology and did a great deal towards ridding it of the largely philosophical speculations of the past. But he also went to absurd extremes, as in his view that thought is nothing but subvocal speech, consisting of almost imperceptible movements of the tongue, throat, and larynx (*i.e.*, when we think, we are really talking to ourselves), and his further opinion that heredity is, except in grossly abnormal cases, of no importance. He claimed that by "conditioning," the ordinary individual could be made into any desired type, regardless of his or her inheritance.

The work of Ivan Pavlov had begun about 1901, but was unknown in America until about ten years later, and it was through another Russian, Vladimir Bekhterev, that the concept of "conditioning" was introduced into the country. Bekhterev's book *Objective Psychology,* describing his new science of "reflexology," was translated in 1913 and played a great part in the development of Behaviourist ideas. The conditioned reflex became central to Watson's theory of learning and habit formation (*e.g.*, he showed that a year-old child, at first unafraid of white rats, became afraid of them when they came to be associated with a loud noise behind the head). Finally all behaviour, including abnormal behaviour, came to be explained in terms of conditioned responses; these were built up by association on the infant's three innate emotions of fear, rage, and love, of which the original stimuli were, for the first, loud noises and the fear of falling; for the second, interference with freedom of movement; and for the third, patting and stroking.

Because of its considerable theoretical simplicity and its implicit suggestion that human behaviour could be easily described (and even modified or controlled), Pavlovian psychology appeared very attractive to the Communist regime in Russia, and before long it became the "official" dogma in universities and research laboratories. Whereas in America and Western Europe its severe limitations became gradually apparent, in Russia these were ignored or disguised for ideological reasons with the inevitable outcome that Soviet psychology failed to evolve and, at one stage, seemed to be no more than a pallid offshoot of physiology. The recent liberalisation which has been taking place throughout Soviet society has led to a considerable broadening of scientific horizons and Pavlovian ideas are no longer looked upon with such unquestioning reverence. In non-Communist countries simple Watsonian behaviourism has evolved into more sophisticated studies of animal learning, largely pioneered by the Harvard psychologist, Skinner. These techniques, which have shown that animals, from monkeys to rats, may be taught to solve a remarkable range of physical problems (such as pressing complex sequences of buttons or levers to escape from a cage) have themselves turned out to be rather disappointing in terms of advancing our general understanding of the workings of the human and animal brain. There is a growing feeling among psychologists that the real keys to the understanding of mankind will only be found through the study of man himself, and not of his simpler animal cousins. *See also* **Gestalt psychology.**

Benthamism. *See* Utilitarianism.

Black Power. The division of the world's population into races is now generally agreed by scientists to have arisen as the result of climatic and environmental pressures—the darker, more highly pigmented peoples tending to be better equipped to withstand higher solar output than the fairer, more northerly based types. For various reasons, again largely climatic and environmental, the first great advances in civilisation came from the temporary ascendancy over the black or near-black. Until quite recently—not much more than a century ago—the technological gulf between white and black was so vast that the negroid races were often held in slavery by the Europeans and while such a thought might be repugnant to most today, attitudes to coloured people still reflect a notion of inherent white " superiority " which it is easy to deny intellectually but difficult to shake-off emotionally. In the U.S.A., the most advanced and at the same time the most tormented multi-racial society in the world, the role of the substantial negroid population has changed dramatically in the last hundred years, shifting from that of slave to friendly servant, and then to near, or theoretical, equal. With this shift has come a corresponding change in the black community's view of itself, from relief at being no longer slaves, to gratitude at being allowed to do the menial jobs in the American society. More recently, with advances in educational opportunity and increasing political liberalisation, the attitude of the Negro in the U.S.A. has shifted yet again—from subservience to intellectual and physical equality, and even, perhaps, to inherent superiority. This new stand, rare at first, but spreading rapidly across America and other parts of the world throughout the 1960s, has crystallised in the concept and ideology of " Black Power," a movement of growing significance and importance in modern society. It is hard to trace the moment at which this formally emerged but one of its first expressions was the use by Negroes of the phrase " Black is beautiful," an apparent wakening of the belief that their colour, physique, features, hair, etc., were in no way aesthetically inferior to those of Europeans. Suddenly, in Negro communities it became no longer fashionable to artificially straighten hair, to bleach the skin, or even to copy white American clothing, social habits, speech, and mannerisms. Alongside this highly important psychological jump—a rejection of the white man's social patterns—came an increasing rejection of his political machinery as well, a belief that the black races should have political autonomy and power of their own and not as part of an integrationist evolution of Caucasian societies.

The Black Power movement at this moment has no formal political representation in the United States, largely because it spurns the normal democratic approach of offering up candidates for election, but its strength and growing potency is well understood by enlightened American politicians who take careful account of its views on current or proposed " racialist " legislation. Its present strategy is a declared one of attaining black supremacy and autonomy rapidly, by violence and revolution if necessary, and it has supporters in all sections of the Negro population—and among many of the younger whites as well. Whether open conflict between blacks and whites in America will ever break out on a large scale is at this time uncertain, but increasing liberalisation and better opportunities for educational and social advancement for Negroes must ultimately serve to ease tension, while an oppressive " white backlash " would inevitably provoke bloody conflict. The overt aggression and ruthlessness of the Black Power movement and its adherents is probably an understandable swing of the pendulum following centuries of abuse and suppression, but its latent strength and grim sense of purpose should not be underestimated. The famous incident at the Mexico Olympics, when American Negro athletes gave the " Black Power " salute as their national anthem was being played, brought the existence of the movement to the attention of millions of viewers across the world, and probably served as a salutary warning to white people to realise that the days of " inferior " and " superior " races are gone for ever.

Bolshevism, an alternative name for Communism (q.v.), usually used in the West in a derogatory sense. When the Russian Social Democratic Party at a conference held in London in 1903 split over the issue of radicalism or moderation, it was the radical faction headed by Lenin (who subsequently led the 1917 Revolution and became first Head of State of the Soviet Union) which polled the majority of votes. The Russian for majority is *bolshinstvo* and for minority *menshinstvo*; hence the radicals became known as Bolsheviki and the moderates as Mensheviki, anglicised as Bolsheviks and Mensheviks. *See* **Communism, Marxism.**

British Israelites, a religious group who hold the race-theory that the English-speaking peoples (of the White Race) are the lineal descendants of the " lost Ten Tribes " of Israel (deported by Sargon of Assyria on the fall of Samaria in 721 B.C.). They believe the Anglo-Saxons to be God's " Chosen People " in the literal sense of the term as it is used in the Old Testament by whom the world will be brought in readiness for the Millennium. The official organisation is the British–Israel World Federation of which the official journal is the *National Message.* Some British Israelites have the notion that the future can be foretold by the measurements of the Great Pyramid.

Buddhism, one of the great Oriental religions. It arose against the background of Hinduism in north India in the 6th cent. B.C., its founder (real or legendary) being the Hindu prince Siddhartha Gautama, known as the Buddha or " Enlightened One." Distressed by the problem of human suffering from which even death allowed no escape—since Buddha accepted the Hindu doctrine of a cycle of lives—he left his palace and his beloved wife and child to become a religious mendicant and ascetic, studying without success for six years the beliefs of Brahmin hermits and self-torturing recluses. After this fruitless search he sat down under a tree (the Bo-tree) and finally came to understand the cause and cure of suffering. The result of his meditations are enshrined in the " four noble truths " which are: (1) that existence is unhappiness; (2) that unhappiness is caused by selfish desire or craving; (3) that desire can be destroyed; (4) that it can be destroyed by following the " noble eightfold path " whose steps are: right views; right desires; right speech, plain and truthful; right conduct, including abstinence not only from immorality but also from taking life, whether human or animal; right livelihood, harming no one; right effort, always pressing on; right awareness of the past, the present, and the future; and lastly, right contemplation or meditation. The more man acquires merit by following these rules in his chain of lives, the sooner is *Nirvana* attained; he loses his individuality, not by annihilation, but " as the dewdrop slips into the shining sea," by merging with the universal life.

Buddhism teaches the way of salvation through ethics and discipline; it preaches the law of *karma*—that a man's actions control his destiny after death as inevitably as cause produces effect, so that his future is solely in his own keeping. A universal God plays no part in this religion, and in many Buddhist nations no word exists for the concept which was neither affirmed nor denied by Buddha himself but simply ignored. Nor did Buddha claim to be other than a man, although much superstition entered the religion at a later date; prayers were made to Buddha, ritual developed, sacred relics preserved under stupas, and the belief in a succession of Buddhas introduced; the sacred writings (*Tripitaka*) are divided into three parts: for the layman, the monks, the philosophers. They were produced by devotees at three councils—the first held immediately after the death of Buddha at the age of 80, the last at the order of King Asoka in 244 B.C. The founder himself wrote nothing.

Buddhism spread to Ceylon, Nepal, Tibet, Mongolia, Indo-China, Burma, Siam, China, and Japan, although on the whole losing influence in India. In Tibet, Buddhism developed into Lamaism (q.v.). In Ceylon and Burma it persisted in its pure form (the Hinayana), while in China and Japan it developed into the Mahayana with its bodhisattvas and avatars. Sects developed, one of the most important being the Chinese Ch'an (Japanese Zen) Buddhism (q.v.). Outside Asia there are active movements in many Western countries where the serenity and rational humanism of Buddhism appeals to intellectuals as diverse as staid humanists and eccentric beatniks.

Bushido, the traditional code of honour of the Samurai or Japanese military caste corresponding to the European concept of knighthood and chivalry with which it took its separate origin in the 12th cent. Even today it is a potent influence among the upper classes, being based on the principles of simplicity, honesty, courage, and justice which together form a man's idea of personal honour. *Bushido* was strongly influenced by Zen Buddhism (*q.v.*).

C

Calvinism, the branch of Protestantism founded basically (although preceded by Zwingli and others) by Jean Chauvin (1509–64), who was born in Noyon in Picardy. John Calvin, as he is usually called, from the Latin form of his name, Calvinius, provided in his *Institutions of the Christian Religion* the first logical definition and justification of Protestantism, thus becoming the intellectual leader of the Reformation as the older Martin Luther was its emotional instigator. The distinctive doctrine of Calvinism is its dogma of predestination which states that God has unalterably destined some souls to salvation to whom " efficacious grace and the gift of perseverance " is granted and others to eternal damnation. Calvinism, as defined in the Westminster Confession, is established in the Reformed or Presbyterian churches of France, Holland, Scotland, etc., as contrasted with the Lutheran churches, and its harsh but logical beliefs inspired the French Huguenots, the Dutch in their fight against Spanish Catholic domination, and the English Puritans. The rule set up under Calvin's influence in Geneva was marred by the burning at the stake of the anatomist Servetus for the heresy of " pantheism," or, as we should say, Unitarianism.

Perhaps its greatest single influence outside the Church was the result of Calvinist belief that to labour industriously was one of God's commands. This changed the mediaeval notions of the blessedness of poverty and the wickedness of usury, proclaimed that men should shun luxury and be thrifty, yet implied that financial success was a mark of God's favour. In this way it was related to the rise of capitalism either as cause or effect. Max Weber, the German sociologist, believed that Calvinism was a powerful incentive to, or even cause of, the rise of capitalism (*q.v.*); Marx, Sombart, and in England, Tawney, have asserted the reverse view—that Calvinism was a result of developing capitalism, being its ideological justification.

Capitalism is an economic system under which the means of production and distribution are owned by a relatively small section of society which runs them at its own discretion for private profit. There exists, on the other hand, a propertyless class of those who exist by the sale of their labour power. Capitalism arose towards the end of the 18th cent. in England where the early factory owners working with small-scale units naturally approved of free enterprise and free trade. But free enterprise has no necessary connection with capitalism; by the beginning of this century monopolies were developing and state protection against foreign competition was demanded. Capitalism is opposed by those who believe in socialism (*q.v.*), first, for the moral reasons that it leads to economic inequality and the exploitation of labour and the consuming public, and that public welfare rather than private profit should motivate the economic system; secondly, for the practical reason that capitalism leads to recurrent economic crises. Defenders of the system, however, maintain that it conduces to efficient production by providing the strongest incentive to enterprise and good service.

Catholicism. For those who are not Roman Catholics the term " Catholic " has two separate meanings. The more general refers to the whole body of Christians throughout the world, the more specific refers to a particular view of Christianity. In this latter sense the Church of England, the Orthodox Eastern Churches, and others consider themselves " Catholic " meaning that (*a*) they belong to Christ's Church as

organised on an accepted basis of faith and order; (*b*) they insist on the necessity of " liturgical " worship through established forms (*e.g.*, baptism, holy communion); (*c*) they emphasise the continuity of Christian tradition by the use of ancient creeds (*e.g.*, the Apostles' Creed, the Nicene Creed) and regard the ministry as a succession (Apostolic succession) deriving from early practice. In this sense there is thought to be no necessary contradiction between Catholicism and Protestantism regarded as a renewal of the Church in the 16th cent. by an appeal to the Scriptures as interpreted by the early Fathers of the Church. This definition obviously excludes Quakers, Christian Scientists, and many Nonconformist sects.

The **Roman Catholic Church** is the religious organisation of all those who acknowledge the bishop of Rome as head of the Christian Church, recognizing him as the lawful successor of St. Peter, who was the apostle appointed by Christ to be the head of the Church. Whereas in the Protestant Churches prayer and preaching play a central part (each individual soul seeking direct communication with God), in Roman Catholic worship the central service is the Mass, or Holy Eucharist, the seven sacraments (baptism, confirmation, eucharist, penance, extreme unction, orders, and marriage) being administered by a special priesthood. Church discipline and organisation are strong and authoritarian. *See* **Papal Infallibility.**

Catholic Apostolic Church, a body of Christians which originated in England *c.* 1831, founded on the teaching of Edward Irving (d. 1834). They disapprove of the term " Irvingites " by which they are sometimes known. The common doctrines of Christianity are accepted; symbolism and mystery characterise the elaborate liturgy, and lights and incense are used.

Characterology, the attempt made over many centuries to classify people into personality types on the basis of physical or psychological characteristics. The first attempt was made by Hippocrates in the 5th cent. B.C. who classified temperaments into the *sanguine* (or optimistic), the *melancholic*, the *choleric* (or aggressive), and the *phlegmatic* (or placid); these were supposed to result from the predominance of the following " humours " in the body: red blood, black bile, yellow bile, or phlegm respectively. Theophrastus, a pupil of Aristotle, described, with examples, thirty extreme types of personality (*e.g.* the talkative, the boorish, the miserly, etc.); these were basically literary and imaginative but about the same time " physiognomy " arose which attempted to interpret character from the face. Physiognomy became of importance again during the Renaissance and there are still those today who believe in it in spite of the fact that, broadly speaking, there is no connection whatever between facial features and personality (*i.e.* although it may be possible to tell from the features that a man is an idiot or some extreme abnormal type and some idea of character may be obtained from an individual's characteristic facial expressions, it is not possible to tell (as Johann Lavater, the best-known physiognomist of the late 18th cent. believed) from the shape of the nose, height of the brow, or dominance of the lower jaw, whether anyone is weak, intellectual, or determined). The contention of the 19th cent. Italian criminologist Cesare Lombroso that criminals show typical facial characteristics—prominent cheekbones and jaw, slanting eyes, receding brow, large ears of a particular shape—was disproved by Karl Pearson early this century when he found that 3,000 criminals showed no significant differences of features, carefully measured, from a similar number of students at Oxford and Cambridge.

It has, however, been noted that people in general tend to be intellectual or emotional, inward- or outward-looking, and this observation is reflected in the classifications of the Scottish psychologist, Alexander Bain (d. 1903), into intellectual, artistic, and practical; Nietzsche's Apollonian and Dionysian types; William James's " tender " and " toughminded "; and C. G. Jung's introvert and extrovert. Careful experiments have shown that these are not clear-cut and that most individuals fall in between the extremes.

Some connection has been found between temperament and body-build. The German psychiatrist Ernst Kretschmer (b. 1888) showed that manic-depressive patients and normal people who are extroverted and tend to alternate in mood (as do manic-depressives to an exaggerated degree) were usually short and stout or thick-set in build; schizophrenics and normal people, who both show shyness, serious or introverted reactions, were usually tall and slender. The former of " pyknic " body-build are " cyclothyme " in temperament, the latter with " schizothyme " temperament are of two bodily types—the tall and thin or " asthenic " and the muscularly well-proportioned or " athletic." The American Sheldon has confirmed these observations on the whole and gone into further details. According to him the basic body types are: (1) *endomorphic* (rounded build), corresponding to Kretschmer's pyknic, normally associated with the *viscerotonic* temperament (relaxed, sociable); (2) *mesomorphic* (squarish, athletic build), normally associated with the *somatotonic* temperament (energetic, assertive); and (3) *ectomorphic* (linear build) normally associated with the *cerebrotonic* temperament (anxious, submissive, restless). Glandular and metabolic factors have considerable effect on human personality and also, to some extent, on physique. It is not too surprising, therefore, to find an association between body build (or " somatotype " as Sheldon termed it) and general mood. However, Sheldon's original clear-cut and oversimplified categories of body-type are no longer looked upon as reliable indicators of personality.

Chartism, a socialistic movement in England (1837–55) which attempted to better the conditions of the working classes. Named after " The People's Charter " of Francis Place (1838), its programme demanded: (1) universal manhood suffrage; (2) vote by ballot; (3) equal electoral districts; (4) annual parliaments; (5) payment of members; (6) abolition of their property qualifications. Chartism was supported by the Christian socialists (*q.v.*), J. F. D. Maurice (1805–72), and Charles Kingsley (1819–75) with certain qualifications. The movement, while doomed to an early death, had considerable influence on the evolution of socialist ideas in England. It is worth noting that its demands—with the exception of the unworkable " annual parliament "—have largely been met today, though at the time they were thought by many to be both outrageous and impossible.

Chauvinism, a term applied to any excessive devotion to a cause, particularly a patriotic or military one. The word is derived from Nicholas Chauvin whose excessive devotion to Napoleon made him a laughing-stock.

Chirognomy, the attempt to read character from the lines in the hand (as contrasted with chiromancy or palmistry, in which an attempt is made to tell the future in the same way) is an ancient practice which, like astrology (*q.v.*) has no discernible scientific basis but a very considerable popular following. As with astrology, where it is hard to see what kind of link could exist between the constellations and human behaviour, so it is equally hard to see how the configuration of lines on the hand could be paralleled by psychological attributes. This argument might be thought of as irrelevant if palmistry, etc. actually had predictive power, but the plain fact is that when put to a scientific test, practitioners of these arts turn out to show no abilities beyond those with which a normally perceptive individual is equipped.

Chiropractice, the art of manipulation of the joints, in particular the spine, as a means of curing diseases, is a slightly fashionable quasi-medical practice. Few qualified doctors employ its questionable principles though, as with its near-neighbour osteopathy, it seems on occasions to be a useful complement to medical treatment. Much controversy surrounds the status of practitioners of fringe medicine of this kind. In America osteopathy (bone manipulation), which seems to be beneficial in many cases for the condition known as prolapsed or " slipped "

disc, is becoming gradually merged into orthodox medical practice.

Christadelphians, a religious denomination formed in the U.S.A. about 1848 at the time of the American Civil War by John Thomas, an Englishman from London. They claim to represent the simple apostolic faith of the 1st cent., and, in common with many other sects, hold that they alone interpret the Scriptures truly. None but those who share their beliefs will rise from the dead and enjoy immortal life when Christ returns after the battle at Armageddon when His kingdom will be established on earth with its capital in Jerusalem. The political events of our time are regarded as fulfilments of biblical prophecies preceding the millennial reign of Christ over the earth. For them heaven and hell do not exist. In social life Christadelphians keep to themselves and hold aloof from organisational activities, though they do take an interest in political events if only from the point of view of their belief in biblical prophecy.

Christianity, the religion founded by Jesus Christ whose teaching is found in the New Testament's four Gospels. Simple as His creed may seem it soon became complicated by the various ways in which Christians interpreted it, and the differences within the early Church are reflected in the numerous Councils held to define truth from heresy. The Eastern Church of the Byzantine Empire from the 5th cent. onwards had differed in various ways from the See of Rome and by 1054 the breach became permanent. The 16th cent. Reformation was the other great break in the unity of the Church and once Protestantism had given in effect the right to each man to interpret the Scriptures in his own way, the tendency to fragmentation increased so that, by 1650, there were no fewer than 180 sects, mostly dogmatic and intolerant towards each other. Today there are many more, some of which are mentioned in this section under the appropriate headings. Nevertheless there are signs today that the trend of disunity is being reversed. The modern ecumenical movement, which has its roots in the great missionary movement of the 19th cent., aims to bring about a reunion of Christendom by uniting Christians throughout the world on the simple basis of the acceptance of Jesus Christ as God and Saviour, *i.e.*, on the basis of Christian fellowship. The movement finds expression in the World Council of Churches (*q.v.*). The Christian life is expressed in the words of Christ: " Thou shalt love the Lord thy God with all thy heart and thy neighbour as thyself." For many it is the humanitarian side of Christianity that has meaning today: to accept responsibility for others, as well as for oneself. *See* chart, J11.

Christian Democrats, a term describing the members of moderate Roman Catholic political parties existing under various names in Belgium, France, the German Federal Republic (most German Protestants are in East Germany), Italy, and the Netherlands. In several of these countries they are the largest parliamentary party, their platform being based on a programme of moderate social reform advocated by members who in many cases have been active in wartime resistant movements. In spite of efforts of Dr. Adenauer of Germany and Sr. Fanfari of Italy in 1955 a Christian Democratic International has failed to develop.

Christian Science, a religious denomination founded by Mary Baker Eddy (1821–1910), an American lady who sought to organise a church which would reinstate primitive Christianity and its lost element of healing. The sacred books of the movement are the Bible and *Science and Health with Key to the Scriptures* (1891), a revision of *Science and Health*, first published by Mrs. Eddy in 1875. Its main tenets (quoting from an official Christian Science source) are " that nothing is real save God and His spiritual creation, including man in His image and likeness; that man's essential nature is spiritual and wholly good; that matter, evil, disease and sickness are unreal—illusions existing only through ignorance of God. Therefore Christian Scientists renounce for themselves medicine, surgery and drugs and rely on healing through prayer."

The name of the movement seems misleading

since it has nothing to do with any of the natural sciences of which Mrs. Eddy had no first-hand knowledge. In using the word, then, she meant that the teaching and acts of Jesus were rooted in unchanging divine law. Mrs. Eddy was at first interested in Spiritualism and afterwards, having been a patient of a faith-healer named Quimby, claimed to have been divinely healed. Some say she was indebted to him more than she cared to admit, others that there is no link with her teaching. There is also controversy about the efficacy of her methods. The denomination has a widespread membership; its newspaper, the *Christian Science Monitor*, read by many outside the movement, has well-written accounts of events going on in the world around us.

Christian Socialism, a movement launched in 1848, a year of revolutions throughout the continent, by a group in England designed to commit the Church to a programme of social reform. The leaders, notably J. F. D. Maurice, Charles Kingsley (both Anglican clergymen), and John Ludlow were deeply moved by the wretched conditions of the British working class and the two priests had, indeed, given active support to the Chartist movement (*q.v.*). However, all insisted that socialism in its existing forms ignored the spiritual needs of mankind and must be tempered with Christianity. Tracts were written to expose the sweated industries, the consequences of unrestrained competition, and the evils following the enclosure system; but, more concretely, Christian socialism fostered co-operative workshops and distributive societies based on those of the Rochdale pioneers, organised a working-man's college and set up elementary classes for education. It also supported the trade-union movement's right to organise and bargain for its members.

The traditions of Christian socialism have been carried on by the Fabian Society, by adherents of Guild Socialism, and by individuals who reject Marx's teaching of revolutionary change, and seek to bring it about by the methods of action through political parties, education, and encouragement of the unions. They believe that Christ's teachings can only be fully realised in a new society since Christianity implies social responsibility, and material factors are admitted to have an important bearing on the ability to lead a truly religious life. In the U.S.A. the eminent theologians Paul Tillich and Reinhold Niebuhr support these views. The factory-padre in Britain and the Catholic worker-priests of France bear evidence to the continuing influence of the early movement. In England the Christian Socialist Movement (CSM) was revived in 1960 by the coming together of organisations like the Socialist Christian League and the Society for Socialist Clergy and Ministers. *See also* Fabian Society, Guild Socialism.

Church of England. There is some evidence of possible continuity with the Christianity of Roman Britain, but in the main the Church derives from the fusion of the ancient Celtic church with the missionary church of St. Augustine, who founded the See of Canterbury in A.D. 597. To archbishop Theodore in 673 is ascribed its organisation in dioceses with settled boundaries, and in parishes. St. Augustine's church was in communion with Rome from the first, but the Church of England was not brought within papal jurisdiction until after the Norman conquest, and was at no time under the complete domination of Rome. It remains the Catholic Church of England without break of continuity, but during the Reformation the royal supremacy was accepted and that of the pope repudiated. It is the Established Church (*i.e.*, the official church of the realm), crowns the sovereign, and its archbishops and bishops in the House of Lords can act as a kind of " conscience of the state " at every stage of legislation. The policy of religious toleration has been accepted since the 16th cent. The Church is organised in two ecclesiastical provinces (Canterbury and York) and 43 dioceses. Its form of worship is embodied in the Book of Common Prayer.

The **Anglican Communion** comprises the churches in all parts of the world which are in communion with the Church of England. All the bishops of the Anglican Communion meet every ten years in the Lambeth Conference (first held in 1867), over which the Archbishop

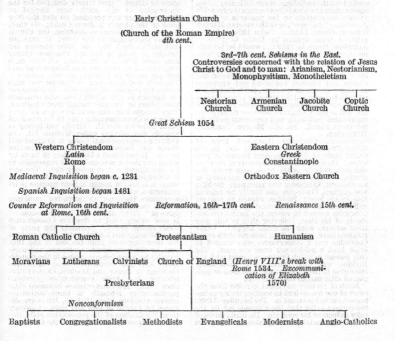

Early Christian Church

(Church of the Roman Empire)
4th cent.

3rd–7th cent. Schisms in the East.
Controversies concerned with the relation of Jesus
Christ to God and to man: Arianism, Nestorianism,
Monophysitism, Monotheletism

| Nestorian | Armenian | Jacobite | Coptic |
| Church | Church | Church | Church |

Great Schism 1054

Western Christendom   Eastern Christendom
Latin   *Greek*
Rome   Constantinople

Mediaeval Inquisition began c. 1231   Orthodox Eastern Church

Spanish Inquisition began 1481

Counter Reformation and Inquisition   *Reformation, 16th–17th cent.*   *Renaissance 15th cent.*
at Rome, 16th *cent.*

Roman Catholic Church   Protestantism   Humanism

Moravians   Lutherans   Calvinists   Church of England   (*Henry VIII's break with
                                                                                Rome* 1534.   *Excommuni-
                                                                                cation of Elizabeth*
                          Presbyterians   1570)

          Nonconformism

Baptists   Congregationalists   Methodists   Evangelicals   Modernists   Anglo-Catholics of Canterbury by custom presides as *primus inter pares*. The theme of the 1968 Conference was " The Renewal of the Church," and for the first time observers and laymen were admitted.

Church of Scotland, the established national church of Scotland, presbyterian in constitution, and governed by a hierarchy of courts—the kirk-sessions, the presbyteries, the synods, and the General Assembly. *See* Presbyterianism.

Clairvoyance. *See* Telepathy.

Communism. Communism, ideally refers to the type of society in which all property belongs to the community and social life is based on the principle " from each according to his ability, to each according to his needs." Since no such society as yet exists, the word in practice refers to the Communist Party's attempt to achieve such a society by initially overthrowing the capitalist system and establishing a dictatorship of the proletariat. The modern movement is based on Marxism as further developed by Lenin who applied Marx's analysis to the new conditions which had arisen in 20th cent. capitalist society. Noting the large trusts and combines which (according to the Marxian " theory of concentration ") with their large concentrations of capital were ousting the small producers of an earlier stage, Lenin concluded that the state (representing the ruling class) and these large capital interests which were collaborating in imperialist policies which would inevitably lead to recurrent wars; that the skilled worker would become more important and, receiving higher wages, would betray the proletariat by moving to the right; and that the poorer workers would continue to support revolutionary socialism. Communists believe that their first task is the establishment of socialism under which there remain class distinctions, private property to some extent, and differences between manual and brain workers. The state is regulated on the basis " from each according to his ability, to each according to his work." In time this gives place to communism as described above. Marxism–Leninism develops continuously with practice since failure to apply its basic principles to changed circumstances and times would result in errors of dogmatism. Mao Tse-tung worked out the techniques of revolutionary action appropriate to China; Che Guevara the guerrilla tactics appropriate to the peasants of Latin America. "Anyone", says the veteran Marxist thinker, Georg Lukács, "who thinks he can apply a book written by Lenin in 1920 to American youth in 1969 . . . would be terribly mistaken." Two fundamental principles of communism are (1) peaceful co-existence between countries of different social systems, and (2) the class struggle between oppressed and oppressing classes and between oppressed and oppressor nations. China, for example, holds that it is a mistake to lay one-sided stress on peaceful transition toward socialism otherwise the revolutionary will of the proletariat becomes passive and unprepared politically and organisationally for the tasks ahead. *See also* Maoism, Marxism, Trotskyism.

Confucianism. Confucius (Latinised form of K'ung-Fu-tzu) was born in 551 B.C. in the feudal state of Lu in modern Shantung province. He was thus a contemporary of Buddha, although nobody could have been more dissimilar. Where Buddha was metaphysical in his thought, Confucius was practical; Buddha was original, Confucius had hardly an original idea in his head; Buddha wanted to convert individuals to an other-worldly philosophy, Confucius wanted to reform the feudal governments of his time, believing that in this way their subjects would be made happier. Other religions have, in their time, been revolutionary; Confucius was a conservative who wanted to bring back a golden age from the past. The only respect in which Confucius agreed with the Buddha was that neither was particularly interested in the supernatural, and God or gods played little part in their religions.

Much of his time was spent in going from the court of one feudal lord to another trying to impress them by his example. For he suffered from the curious belief that the example set by the ruler influences his subjects. He made much of etiquette, trembling and speaking in low tones before princes, at ease and polite with his equals, and behaving with " lofty courtesy " to his inferiors. Promoting the idea of " the golden mean," he was not impressed by heroic deeds or unusual people, and was greatly displeased when he heard that a truthful son had reported that his father had stolen a sheep: "Those who are upright," he said, " are different from this; the father conceals the misconduct of the son, and the son conceals the misconduct of the father." One feels that Confucius would have felt not at all out of place in an English public school. Virtue brings its own reward in this world, ceremonial is important, politeness when universal would reduce jealousy and quarrels; "reverence the spirits but keep them far off." Destiny decides to what class a man shall belong, and as destiny is but another name for Nature prayer is unnecessary, for once having received his destiny, a man can demand and obtain from Nature what he chooses—his own will determines all things.

Although not very successful in his lifetime so far as the rulers were concerned, Confucius had numerous disciples who collected his teachings which are found, together with those of his later follower Mencius (372–289 B.C.), in the *Wu Ching* (five classics), and the *Shih Shu* (four books) which contain the Analects, The Great Learning, The Doctrine of the Mean, and the Book of Mencius. In time Confucianism became with Taoism and Buddhism one of the main religions in China. Unlike Buddhism it had little influence elsewhere.

Congregationalists, the oldest sect of Nonconformists who hold that each church should be independent of external ecclesiastical authority. They took their origin from the Brownists of Elizabeth's days. Robert Browne (*c.* 1550–*c.* 1633), an Anglican clergyman, who had come to reject bishops, was forced with his followers to seek refuge, first in Holland and then in Scotland where he was imprisoned by the Kirk. In later life he changed his views and is disowned by Congregationalists because of his reversion to Anglicanism. His former views were spread by Henry Barrow and John Greenwood who, under an Act passed in 1592 " for the punishment of persons obstinately refusing to come to church " (and largely designed for the suppression of this sect), were hanged at Tyburn. They had preached (*a*) that the only head of the church is Jesus Christ; (*b*) that, contrary to Elizabethan doctrine, the church had no relationship to the state; (*c*) that the only statute-book was the Bible whereas the Articles of Religion and the Common Prayer were mere Acts of Parliament; (*d*) that each congregation of believers was independent and had the power of choosing its own ministers. The body fled once more to Holland and were among the Pilgrims who set sail in the *Mayflower* for America in 1620 whilst those who remained were joined by Puritans fleeing from Charles I. They became free once more to live in England under the Commonwealth only to be repressed again under Charles II. Finally full liberty of worship was granted under William III. In 1833 the Congregational Union of England and Wales was formed which has no legislative power. It has issued a Declaration of Faith by which no minster is bound; he is responsible to his own church and to nobody else. The sect is widespread both in Britain and the U.S.A. where it is held in special honour because of its connection with the Pilgrim Fathers.

Conservatism. The name "Conservative" came into general use after 1834 in place of the older name of " Tory," although " Tory democracy " is now widely used to describe Conservative social reform policy. Originally the party of the aristocracy and landed gentry, Conservatism has been supported from the end of the 19th cent. by the large business interests, and more recently by lower-income groups in the population. Although originally based upon the teachings of Burke and Disraeli, Conservative doctrine has been considerably modified since 1945. The Conservatives increased their parliamentary strength in three successive general elections from 1951–59, but were defeated by Labour in 1964 and 1966. Contrary to all the findings of the pre-election polls, this trend was reversed in 1970 when the Conservatives regained power with a substantial majority. On the continent, Conservatism has generally been identified with fear of social progress, exaggerated respect for authority, and nationalism; such parties have more often than not been extremely reactionary and anti-democratic. *See also* Section **C**, Part **I**.

Coptic Church, the sect of Egyptian Christians who, holding " Monophysite " opinions (*i.e.*, refusing to grant the two natures, God and Man, of Christ), were declared heretical by the Council of Chalcedon in 451. They practise circumcision and have dietary laws. Their language is a direct descendant of ancient Egyptian. Like the Armenians, they are regarded as an heretical branch of Eastern Christianity. Their religious head is the patriarch of Alexandria.

Cynics, a school of philosophy founded in the time of Alexander the Great by Diogenes. Choosing to live like a dog by rejecting all conventions of religion, manners, or decency, and allegedly living in a tub, Diogenes unwittingly brought on his school the title " Cynic," meaning not " cynical," as the word is understood today, but " canine." His teacher, Antisthenes, who had been a disciple of Socrates, decided, afte the latter's death, that all philosophy was useless quibbling and man's sole aim should be simple goodness. He believed in a return to nature, despised luxury, wanted no government, no private property, and associated with working men and slaves. Far from being cynics in the modern sense, Diogenes and Antisthenes were virtuous anarchists rather like old Tolstoy (except that in the practice of their beliefs they were more consistent).

D

Darwinism. *See* Section **F**, Part **IV**. *See also* Vitalism.

Deism. *See* God and Man.

Demonism, Demons, and the Devil. Demons are ethereal beings of various degrees of significance and power which are believed to be implicated in men's good, but especially evil, fortune. They are common to most cultures. From the anthropological point of view the demon arose as a widespread concept in the following ways: (1) as a psychological projection into the outer world of man's own good or evil emotions and thoughts; (2) as a survival of primitive animism (*q.v.*), thus spirits are believed to haunt places, trees, stones, and other natural objects; (3) when by warlike invasion the gods of the vanquished become the devils of the conquerors (as when the Jews occupied Canaan); (4) as a primitive belief that spirits of the dead continue after death to hover near their former habitation, and not always entirely welcome to the living; (5) the conception of a supreme source of evil (the Devil or Satan) which took shape among the Jews during their sojourn in Babylon under the influence of Zoroastrianism (*q.v.*), a religion in which the struggle between the two spirits, Good and Evil, reached its height in the imagination of the ancient world. The Satan of the Old Testament was first regarded as one of God's servants (in the Book of Job he goes up and down the earth to see whether God's commands are obeyed), but when the Jews returned from their captivity he had become identified with Ahriman, the spirit of evil, who was in continual conflict with Ahura Mazda, the spirit of good. As Dr. Margaret Murray has pointed out, the primitive mind ascribed both good and evil to one power alone; the division into God and the Devil, priest and witch, belongs to a higher stage of civilisation. The worship of evil itself, or of its personification in Satan, is a curious practice which seems to have developed hand-in-hand with Christianity and to have received steady support from a small but measurable minority. Many of the ceremonies involved in Satanism or in the so-called Black Mass appear to have been no more than opportunities for sexual excesses of one kind or another—such indulgences being traditionally barred to devout Christians. The alleged power of sex as a form of magic was propagated by the talented but rather mad poet, Aleister Crowley (1875–1947) who scandalised pre-war Europe with his very well-publicised dabblings into Satanism. The self-styled " wickedest man in the world," Crowley was a pathetic rather than shocking figure and died a drug addict. He can hardly be said to have significantly advanced the cause of Demonology, though it has to be admitted that he tried very hard. *See also* Witchcraft, Magic.

Determinism and Free-will. The question of whether man is, or is not, free to mould his own destiny is one which has exercised the minds of philosophers since Greek mythology conceived of the Fates as weaving a web of destiny from which no man can free himself. Socrates emphasised that man could through knowledge influence his destiny whilst ignorance made him the plaything of fate; Plato went further in pointing out that man can, and does, defeat the purposes of the universe and its divine Creator. It is our duty to live a good life, but we can live a foolish and wicked one if we choose. Aristotle wrote " Virtue is a disposition or habit involving deliberate purpose or choice." If this were not so morality would be a sham.

The Problem for Theology. The last of the great philosophers of antiquity and one of the great influences in moulding Catholic theology was Plotinus (*c.* 204–270). Soul, he taught, is free, but once enmeshed in the body loses its freedom in the life of sense. Nevertheless, man is free to turn away from sensuality and towards God who is perfect freedom; for even when incarnated in matter the soul does not entirely lose the ability to rescue itself. This conception was carried over into the beliefs of the Early Christian Apologists because it appeared to be in line with the teaching of Jesus that He had come to save man from sin. Sin implies guilt, and guilt implies the freedom to act otherwise; furthermore ʾn all-good God cannot be responsible for the sin in the world which must be man's responsibility and this again implies freedom. Pelagius (*c.* 355–*c.* 425), a Welsh priest, not only believed in freewill but, questioning the doctrine of original sin, said that when men act righteously it is through their own moral effort, and God rewards them for their virtues in heaven. This belief became fairly widespread and was declared a heresy by the Church, being attacked notably by St. Augustine (354–430), a contemporary of Pelagius, who believed in predestination—that, since the sin of Adam, God had chosen who in all future history would be saved and who damned. This represents one tradition in Christianity: the determinism which leads to Calvinism (*q.v.*). St. Thomas Aquinas (1227–74), the greatest figure of scholasticism and one of the principal saints in the Roman Catholic Church, compromised between the two positions in the sense that, believing man to be free, he yet held that Adam's sin was transmitted to all mankind and only divine grace can bring salvation. But even when God wishes to bestow this salvation, the human will must co-operate. God foresees that some will not accept the offer of grace and predestines them to eternal punishment.

The Problem for Philosophy. With the Renaissance, thinkers began to free themselves from the domination of the Church and to study the world objectively and freely without preconceptions. But the more man turned to science, the more he discovered that the world was ruled by apparently inexorable laws and, since the scientist must believe that every event has a cause, he was led back to determinism. Man as part of the universe was subject to law too and all that existed was a vast machine. Francis Bacon (1561–1626) separated the fields of religion and science but left man subject completely to the will of God. Thomas Hobbes (1588–1679) was a rigid determinist and materialist although, having had trouble with the church in France whence, as a royalist, he had fled, he took care to announce that the Christian God is the Prime Mover.

Modern philosophy begins with René Descartes (1596–1650), a Frenchman who tried to reconcile the mechanical scientific universe of his time with the spiritual need for freedom.

He did this by separating completely mind and body; the former, he said, is free, the latter completely determined. But, by admitting that the will can produce states of body, he was left with the problem of how this could happen—a problem which the so-called Occasionalists solved to their own satisfaction by stating that the will is free and God so arranges the universe that what a person wills happens. Baruch Spinoza (1632–77), a Dutch Jew whose independence of thought had led to his excommunication from the Amsterdam Synagogue in 1656, was a complete determinist. He asserted that God and Nature are one, everything that happens is a manifestation of God's inscrutable nature, and it is logically impossible that things could be other than they are. Thus both Hobbes and Spinoza were determinists for entirely opposed reasons. The former as a materialist, the latter because he believed in the absolute perfection and universality of God. Yet the great religious mystic and mathematician Blaise Pascal (1623–62) held that, no matter what reason and cold logic may indicate, we *know* from direct religious experience that we are free. John Calvin (1509–64) and Martin Luther (1483–1546) were both determinists. *See* Calvinism, Lutheranism.

To the more practical British philosophers, John Locke (1632–1704) and David Hume (1711–76), free-will was related to personality. Locke believed that God had implanted in each individual certain desires and these determine the will; the desires are already there, but we use our will to satisfy them. Hume argued that a man's behaviour is the necessary result of his character and if he had a different character he would act otherwise. Accordingly, when a man's actions arise from his own nature and desires he is free. He is not free when external events compel him to act otherwise (*e.g.*, if he strikes another because his own nature is such he is free as he is not if he is compelled to do so against his desire). Leibnitz (1646–1716), although as a German metaphysical philosopher holding very different general views, said much the same thing—that choice is simply selecting the desire that is strongest. But most of the 18th cent. from Voltaire onwards, with the great exceptions of Rousseau and the later German philosophers Kant, Fichte, Schopenhauer, and Hegel, who were initially influenced by him, accepted determinism. Rousseau (1712–78) began to stem the tide by his declaration that man is a free soul striving to remain free and only prevented from being so by society and the cold science which stifles his feeling heart. Once again the will became important as Kant (1724–1804) asserted that belief in freedom is a moral necessity although it cannot be proved by reason; the moral nature of man shows that there is a " transcendental " world beyond the senses where freedom applies. Fichte and Schelling found freedom in the Absolute ego or God of whom each individual was part and thus also free. Hegel (1770–1831) saw the whole universe as evolving towards self-aware-ness and freedom in man although this could only be fully realised in a society that makes for freedom. Even God himself only attains full consciousness and self-realisation through the minds of such individuals as are free. This is the goal of the dialectical process. (*See* Dialectical Materialism.)

The Scientist's View. For the scientist the law of cause and effect is a useful hypothesis since, by and large, it is necessary for him to assume that all events are caused. Neverthe-less the modern tendency is to think in terms of statistical probability rather than relentless mechanistic causality, and, although the free-will problem does not concern the scientist as such, it is clear that freedom and determinism (assuming the terms to have any meaning at all) are not necessarily opposed. In sociology, for example, we *know* that certain actions will pro-duce certain results upon the behaviour of people in general, *e.g.*, that raising the bank rate will discourage business expansion. But this does not mean that Mr. Brown who decides in the circumstances not to add a new wing to his factory is not using his free-will. Even in the case of atoms, as Dr. Bronowski has pointed out, the observed results of allowing gas under pres-

sure in a cylinder to rush out occur because most of the atoms are " obeying " the scientific " law " relating to such situations. But this does not mean that some atoms are not busy rushing across the stream or even against it—they are, but the general tendency is outwards and that is what we note. Lastly, the modern philo-sophical school of Logical Analysis would probably ask, not whether Free-will or De-terminism is the true belief, but whether the question has any meaning. For what scientific experiment could we set up to prove one or the other true? The reader will note that some of the philosophers mentioned above are using the words to mean quite different concepts.

Dialectical Materialism, the combination of Hegel's dialectic method with a materialist philosophy produced by Karl Marx (1818–83) and his friend Friedrich Engels (1820–95). It is the philosophical basis of Marxism (*q.v.*) and Com-munism (*q.v.*). " Dialectic " to the ancient Greek philosophers meant a kind of dialogue or conversation, as used particularly by Socrates, in which philosophical disputes were resolved by a series of successive contradictions: a thesis is put forward and the opposing side holds its contradiction or antithesis until in the course of argument a synthesis is reached in which the conflicting ideas are resolved.

From Thesis through Antithesis to Synthesis. Hegel in the 19th cent. put forward the view that this process applies to the course of nature and history as they strive towards the perfect state. But to him, as to the Greeks, the conflict was in the field of ideas. The " universal reason " behind events works through the ideas held by a particular society until they are challenged by those of another which supersedes them and in turn, usually by war, becomes the agent of universal reason until the arrival of a new challenger. Hegel therefore regarded war as an instrument of progress and his Prussian compatriots found no difficulty in identifying their own state as the new agent of progress by universal conquest. Feuerbach, Lassalle, and other early socialists were im-pressed by some of Hegel's ideas: *e.g.*, that societies evolved (with the assumption that finally their own ideal society would be achieved) and that truth, morals, and concepts were relative so that a type of society that was " good " at one time was not necessarily so at another. But Marx and Engels in effect turned Hegel upside-down, accepted his dialectic but rejected his belief that ideas were the motive force. On the contrary, they said, ideas are determined by social and economic change as a result of materialistic forces. (*See* Calvinism, where it is pointed out that the Marxist view is not that Calvin changed men's economic ideas but rather that a developing capitalism un-consciously changed his.) The historical materialism of Marxism purports to show that the inexorable dialectic determines that feudalism is displaced by capitalism and capitalism by creating a proletariat (its anti-thesis) inevitably leads to socialism and a classless society. The state, as a tool of the dominant class, withers away. Dialectical materialism is applied in all spheres. As a philosophy there is little to be said for it save that it has shown us the close dependence of man's thoughts upon current material and social conditions. But as a battle-cry or a rational-isation of Marxism it wields immense power over the minds of men. *See* Marxism.

Dianetics. *See* Scientology.

Diggers, one of the many sects which flourished under the Commonwealth (others were the Muggletonians, the Levellers, the Millenarians, and the Fifth Monarchy Men), so-called because they attempted to dig (*i.e.* cultivate) untilled land. Gerrard Winstanley, a profoundly re-ligious man, and leader of the Diggers, believed in the economic and social equality of man and castigated the clergy for upholding the class structure of society. In his book *The True Leveller's Standard Advanced* (1649) he wrote: " Every day poor people are forced to work for fourpence a day, though corn is dear. And yet the tithing priest stops their mouth and tells them that ' inward satisfaction of mind ' was meant by the declaration ' the poor shall inherit the earth'. I tell you, the Scripture is to be really and materially fulfilled. You jeer at the name ' Leveller '; I tell you Jesus Christ is the Head Leveller.''

Disciples of Christ, a Protestant religious group founded in the United States early in the 19th century by Thomas Campbell, a Scot, his son Alexander, and Barton Warren Stone who had broken away from the Presbyterian church. The basis for faith and conduct is the Bible itself, each individual interpreting it for himself. The group has always had a liberal reputation and stands for racial equality and Christian unity. The Disciples of Christ Church is particularly strong in the central and western states of America.

Docetists, a Gnostic sect (q.v.) during the early centuries of Christianity who believed that, since it was unworthy that the Son of God should have died a humiliating death on the cross, the entity that was crucified was a mere phantom. Mohammed, who believed in Jesus as a prophet but not as divine, adopted these views. The heretical Albigenses were influenced by Docetism, Gnosticism, and Manichaeism (qq.v.).

Doukhobors, a religious sect of Russian origin, founded by a Prussian sergeant at Kharkov in the middle of the 18th cent., and now mainly settled in Canada. Like many other sects they belong to that type of Christianity which seeks direct communication with God and such bodies tend to have certain traits in common, such as belief in the " inner light," opposition to war and authority in general, and often ecstasies which show themselves in physical ways such as shaking, speaking in strange tongues (glossolalia), and other forms of what to the unbeliever seem mass hysteria. Liturgy, ritual, or ceremony is non-existent. The Doukhobors were persecuted in Tsarist Russia, but in 1898 Tolstoy used his influence to have them removed to Canada where the government granted them uninhabited land in what is now Saskatchewan and seven or eight thousand settled down in peace which they enjoyed for many years. Recently, however, their practices have caused difficulties once more; for even the most tolerant government which is prepared to accept pacifism, total dependence on communally-owned agriculture, refusal to engage in commerce, non-payment of taxes, rejection of the marriage ceremony and separation " when love ceases," finds it difficult to tolerate, as civilisation advances ever closer to Doukhobor communities, their proneness to " put off these troublesome disguises which we wear "—i.e., to walk about naked in the communities of their more orthodox neighbours. What the future of the Doukhobors in their various sects (for even they have their differences) will be it is impossible to say, but it is difficult to believe that these simple people can long resist the pressure of modern civilisation.

Dowsing. See Radiesthesia.

Druidism, the religion of Celtic Britain and Gaul of which Druids were the priesthood. They were finally wiped out by the Roman general Suetonius Paulinus about A.D. 58 in their last stronghold, the island of Anglesey There are two sources of our present beliefs in Druidism: (1) the brief and factual records of the Romans, notably Pliny and Julius Caesar, which tell us that they worshipped in sacred oak groves and presumably practised a religion doing reverence to the powers of nature which must have had its roots in early stone age times and had many cruel rites, e.g., human sacrifice; (2) the beliefs put forward by William Stukeley, an amateur antiquarian who from 1718 did valuable work by his studies of the stone circles at Stonehenge and Avebury. However, influenced by the Romantic movement, he later put forward the most extravagant theories which unfortunately are those popularly accepted by those without archaelogical knowledge today. Stonehenge and Avebury were depicted as the temples of the " white-haired Druid bard sublime " and an attempt was made to tie up Druidism with early Christianity, above all with the concept of the Trinity. In fact, these circles have no connection with the Druids. They may have made ceremonial use of them but recent evidence suggests that the megalithic stones at Stone-

henge (**L109**) belong to a Bronze Age culture (1860–1560 B.C.). Nor have Druidism and Christianity any relationship. Almost nothing is known of the religion. Yet such were its romantic associations that, even today, one hears of " Druidic " ceremonies practised at the appropriate time of year on Primrose Hill in the heart of London (though whether seriously or with tongue in cheek one does not know). In Wales the name Druid survives as the title for the semi-religious leaders of the annual festivals of Celtic poetry, drama, and music known as Eisteddfods. Lingering, but now tenuous, druidic connections are to be found in all Celtic parts including Cornwall and Brittany, where Eisteddfods are also held.

Dualism, any philosophical or theological theory which implies that the universe has a double nature, notably Plato's distinction between appearance and reality, soul and body, ideas and material objects, reason and the evidence of the senses, which infers that behind the world as we perceive it there lies an " ideal " world which is more " real " than that of mere appearance. In religions such as Zoroastrianism or the Gnostic and Manichaeism heresies (qq.v), it was believed that the universe was ruled by good and evil " principles "—in effect that there was a good God and a bad one. In psychology, dualism refers to the philosophical theories which believe mind and body to be separate entities. The opposite of dualism is monism which asserts the essential unity of the substance of the universe.

E

Ecumenism, a world movement which springs from the Christian belief that all men are brothers and that the Christian Church should be re-structured to give reality to the belief. Christ's church exists not to serve its own members, but for the service of the whole world. Some see the answer in a united church of a federal type (unity in diversity), others in an organic structure with one set of rules. The period since the convening of the Second Vatican Council by Pope John has been one of fervent discussion among Christian theologians with the aim of promoting Christian unity. See World Council of Churches.

Education. Education was no great problem to primitive man, but as societies became more complex people began to ask themselves such questions as: What should young people be taught? How should they be taught? Should the aim of their education be to bring out their individual qualities or rather to make them good servants of the state?

The first teachers were priests who knew most about the traditions, customs, and lore of their societies and thus the first schools were in religious meeting places. This was notably true of the Jews who learned from the rabbis in the synagogue, and throughout the Middle Ages in Christendom as will be seen later.

The Greeks. We begin, as always, with the Greeks whose city-states, based on slavery, educated men (not women) for the sort of life described in Plato's Dialogues—the leisured life of gentlemen arguing the problems of the universe at their banquets or in the market-place. This made it necessary to learn debate and oratory (or rhetoric) especially for those who proposed to take up politics. The Sophist philosophy taught the need to build up convincing arguments in a persuasive manner, to learn the rules of logic and master the laws and customs of the Athenians, and to know the literature of the past so that illustrations might be drawn from it. These strolling philosophers who taught for a fee were individualists showing the student how to advance himself at all costs within his community.

Socrates had a more ethical approach, believing that education was good in itself, made a man happier and a better citizen, and emphasised his position as a member of a group. His method of teaching, the dialectic or " Socratic " method, involved argument and discussion rather than overwhelming others by rhetoric and is briefly mentioned under **Dialectical Materialism** (*q.v.*). Today this method is increasingly used in adult education where a lecture is followed by a period of discussion in which both lecturer and audience participate; for psychologists have shown that people accept ideas more readily when conviction arises through their own arguments than when they are passively thrust down their throats.

Socrates' pupil Plato produced in his book *The Republic* one of the first comprehensive systems of education and vocational selection. Believing that men are of different and unequal abilities he considered that they should be put into social classes corresponding to these differences, and suggested the following method: (1) For the first 18 years of a boy's life he should be taught gymnastics and sports, playing and singing music, reading and writing, a knowledge of literature, and if he passed this course sent on to the next stage; those who failed were to become tradesmen and merchants. (2) From 18–20 those successful in the first course were to be given two years of cadet training, the ones thought incapable of further education being placed in the military class as soldiers. (3) The remainder, who were to become the leaders of society, proceeded with advanced studies in philosophy, mathematics, science, and art. Such education was to be a state concern, state supported and controlled, selecting men and training them for service in the state according to their abilities.

Plato's pupil Aristotle even suggested that the state should determine shortly after birth which children should be allowed to live and destroy the physically or mentally handicapped; that marriage should be state-controlled to ensure desirable offspring. However, in their time the leisured and individualistic Sophists held the field and few accepted the educational views of Plato or his pupil.

Rome. The Romans were not philosophers and most of their culture came from Greece. Administration was their chief aptitude and Quintilian (A.D. *c.* 35–*c.* 95) based his higher education on the earlier classical tuition in public speaking, but he is important for emphasising the training of character and for his humanistic approach to the method of teaching that caused his *Institutio oratoria* to be influential for centuries later—indeed one might almost say up to the time of the great Dr. Arnold of Rugby. Education, he believed, should begin early but one must "take care that the child not old enough to love his studies does not come to hate them" by premature forcing; studies must be made pleasant and interesting and students encouraged by praise rather than discouraged when they sometimes fail; play is to be approved of as a sign of a lively disposition and because gloomy, depressed children are not likely to be good students; corporal punishment should never be used because "it is an insult as you will realise if you imagine it yourself." The world became interested not in *what* he taught but *how* he taught it; he was the pioneer of humanistic education and character-training from Vittorino da Feltre (1378–1446) of Mantua, through Milton and Pope who commended his works, to the modern educationists who have studied their pupils as well as their books.

The Middle Ages: The Religious View. With the development of Christianity education once more became a religious problem. The earliest converts had to be taught Christian doctrine and were given instruction in " catechumenal " schools before admission to the group, but as the religion came increasingly into contact with other religions or heresies a more serious training was necessary, and from these newer " catechetical " schools, where the method used was the catechism (*i.e.*, question and answer as known to all Presbyterian children today), the Apologists arose among whom were Clement of Alexandria and the great Origen. From this time education became an instrument of the church and in 529 the Emperor Justinian ordered all pagan schools to be closed.

As typical of the best in mediaeval education whilst the lamp of civilisation burned low during the Dark Ages, after the fall of Roman power, and survived only in the monasteries, we may mention St. Benedict (*c.* 480–*c.* 547) of Monte Cassino. There, in southern Italy, a rule was established which became a part of monastic life in general. Monastic schools were originally intended for the training of would-be monks, but later others were admitted who simply wanted some education; thus two types of school developed, one for the *interni* and the other for *externi* or external pupils. Originally studies were merely reading in order to study the Bible, writing to copy the sacred books, and sufficient calculation to be able to work out the advent of holy days or festivals. But by the end of the 6th cent. the " seven liberal arts " (grammar, rhetoric, dialectic, arithmetic, geometry, music, and astronomy) were added.

The Renaissance. The close of the Middle Ages saw the development of two types of secular school. One came with the rise of the new merchant class and the skilled trader whose "guilds" or early trade unions established schools to train young men for their trades but ultimately gave rise to burgher or town schools; the other was the court school founded and supported by the wealthy rulers of the Italian cities—Vittorino da Feltre (mentioned above) presided over the most famous at Mantua.

These Renaissance developments are paralleled in northern Europe by the Protestant reformers who, having with Martin Luther held that everyone should know how to read his Bible in order to interpret it in his own way, were logically committed to popular education, compulsory and universal. In theory this was intended for biblical study, but writing, arithmetic, and other elementary subjects were taught and Luther said that, even if heaven and hell did not exist, education was important. Universal education is a Protestant conception.

Views of Philosophers. From this period onwards people were free to put forward any ideas about education, foolish or otherwise, and to create their own types of school. Of English philosophers who theorised about, but did not practise, education we may mention the rationalist Francis Bacon (1561–1626) who saw learning as the dissipation of all prejudices and the collection of concrete facts; the materialist and totalitarian Hobbes (1588–1679) who, as a royalist, believed that the right to determine the kind of education fit for his subjects is one of the absolute rights of the sovereign power or ruler; the gentlemanly Locke (1632–1704) whose ideal was a sound mind in a sound body to be attained by hard physical exercise, wide experience of the world, and enough knowledge to meet the requirements of the pupil's environment. The end result would be one able to get on with his fellows, pious but wise in the ways of the world, independent and able to look after himself, informed but reticent about his knowledge. Classics and religious study were not to be carried to excess, since Locke held that these subjects had been overrated in the past. Locke's pupil was the well-to-do, civilised young man of the 17th cent. who knew how to behave in society.

Jean-Jacques Rousseau (1712–78), a forerunner of the Romantic movement (*q.v.*), which despised society and its institutions, put emotion at a higher level than reason. His book *Emile* describes the education of a boy which is natural and spontaneous. Society, he holds, warps the growing mind and therefore the child should be protected from its influences until his development in accordance with his own nature is so complete that he cannot be harmed by it. During the first 4 years the body should be developed by physical training; from 5 to 12 the child would live in a state of nature such that he could develop his powers of observation and his senses; from 13 books would be used and intellectual training introduced, although only in line with the child's own interests, and he would be given instruction only as he came to ask for it. Moral training and contact with his fellows to learn the principles of sympathy, kindness, and helpfulness to mankind would be given between 15 and 20. Girls, however, should be educated to serve men in a spirit of modesty and restraint. His own five children he deposited in a foundling hospital.

Summary. Broadly speaking, then, there have been four main attitudes to education: (1) religious, with a view to a life beyond death; (2) state-controlled education, with a view to uniform subservience to authority; (3) " gentlemanly " education, with a view to social graces and easy congress in company; (4) the " childcentred " education, which attempts to follow the pupil's inner nature. It is unnecessary to mention the ordinary method of attempting to instil facts without any considerable degree of co-operation between pupil and teacher in order that the former may, with or without interest, follow some occupation in adult life; for this the philosophers did not consider. Today there remain the two fundamental principles: education for the advantage of the state and its ideology or education for individual development and freedom.

Four educationists of the modern period who have influenced us in the direction of freedom were Johann Pestalozzi of Switzerland (1746–1827) who, by trying to understand children, taught the " natural, progressive, and harmonious development of all the powers and capacities of the human being "; Friedrich Froebel (1782–1852) of Germany, the founder of the Kindergarten who, like Pestalozzi, was influenced by Rousseau but realised the need to combine complete personal development with social adjustment; Maria Montessori (1869–1952) whose free methods have revolutionised infant teaching; John Dewey (1859–1952) who held that the best interests of the group are served when the individual develops his own particular talents and nature.

Eleatics, the philosophers of Elea in ancient Greece who, at the time when Heraclitus (c. 535–475 B.C.) was teaching that change is all that exists and nothing is permanent, were asserting that change is an illusion. Of the three leaders of this school, Xenophanes asserted that the universe was a solid immovable mass forever the same; Parmenides explained away change as an inconceivable process, its appearance being due to the fact that what we see is unreal; and Zeno (the best-known today) illustrated the same thesis with his famous argument of the arrow which, at any given moment of its flight, must be where it is since it cannot be where it is not. But if it is where it is, it cannot move; this is based, of course, on the delusion that motion is discontinuous. The Eleatics were contemporaries of Socrates.

Empiricism. While not a single school of philosophy, empiricism is an approach to knowledge which holds that if a man wants to know what the universe is like the only correct way to do so is to go and look for himself, to collect facts which come to him through his senses. It is, in essence, the method of science as contrasted with rationalism (*q.v.*) which in philosophy implies that thinking or reasoning without necessarily referring to external observations can arrive at truth. Empiricism is typically an English attitude, for among the greatest empirical philosophers were John Locke, George Berkeley, and David Hume. *See* **Rationalism.**

Epicureanism. The two great schools of the Hellenistic period (*i.e.* the late Greek period beginning with the empire of Alexander the Great) were the Stoics and Epicureans, the former founded by Zeno of Citium (*not* to be confused with Zeno the Eleatic) (*q.v.*), the latter by Epicurus, born in Samos in 342 B.C. Both schools settled in Athens, where Epicurus taught that " pleasure is the beginning and end of a happy life." However, he was no sensualist and emphasised the importance of moderation in all things because excesses would lead to pain instead of pleasure and the best of all pleasures were mental ones. Pleasures could be active or passive but the former contain an element of pain since they are the process of satisfying desires not yet satiated. The latter involving the absence of desire are the more pleasant. In fact, Epicurus in his personal life was more stoical than many Stoics and wrote " when I live on bread and water I spit on luxurious pleasures." He disapproved of sexual enjoyment and thought friendship one of the highest of all joys. A materialist who

accepted the atomic theory of Democritus, he was not a determinist, and if he did not disbelieve in the gods he regarded religion and the fear of death as the two primary sources of unhappiness.

Epiphenomenalism. *See* **Mind and Body.**

Erastianism, the theory that the state has the right to decide the religion of its members, wrongly attributed to Erastus of Switzerland (1524–83) who was believed to have held this doctrine. The term has usually been made use of in a derogatory sense—*e.g.*, by the Scottish churches which held that the " call " of the congregation was the only way to elect ministers at a time when, about the turn of the 17th and 18th cent., they felt that Episcopalianism was being foisted on them. " Episcopalianism " (*i.e.* Anglicanism) with its state church, ecclesiastical hierarchy, and system of livings presented by patrons was to them " Erastian " in addition to its other " unscriptural practices."

Essenes, a Jewish sect which, during the oppressive rule of Herod (d. 4 B.C.), set up monastic communities in the region of the Dead Sea. They refused to be bound by the scriptural interpretations of the Pharisees and adhered rigorously to the letter of Holy Writ, although with additions of their own which cause them by orthodox Jews today to be regarded as a break-away from Judaism. Among their practices and beliefs were purification through baptism, renunciation of sexual pleasures, scrupulous cleanliness, strict observance of the Mosaic law, communal possession, asceticism. Akin in spirit, although not necessarily identical with them, were the writers of Apocalyptic literature preaching that the evils of the present would shortly be terminated by a new supernatural order heralded by a Messiah who would reign over a restored Israel. The casting out of demons and spiritual healing formed part of these general beliefs which were in the air at that time. The sect has an importance far beyond its size or what has been known about it in the past since the discovery from 1947 onwards of the Dead Sea Scrolls (*see* Section L) of the Qumran community occupying a monastery in the same area as the Essenes and holding the same type of belief. These scrolls with their references to a " Teacher of Righteousness " preceding the Messiah have obvious relevance to the sources of early Christianity and have given rise to speculations as to whether Jesus might have been influenced by views which, like His own, were unacceptable to orthodox Jews but in line with those of the Dead Sea communities. At the very least they seem to show that early Christianity was not a sudden development but a gradual one which had its predecessors.

Ethical Church, a movement typical of 19th cent. rationalism which attempted to combine atheism (or at any rate the absence of any belief in a God which was inconsistent with reason or based on revelation) with the inculcation of moral principles. Prayers were not used and ordinarily the service consisted in the singing of edifying compositions interspersed with readings from poems or prose of a similar nature by great writers holding appropriate views. It terminated in a talk on an ethical or scientific theme. There is an Ethical Church in London and the South Place Institution where Moncure Conway preached from 1864 to 1897 still exists.

Ethnocentrism, the exaggerated tendency to think the characteristics of one's own group or race superior to those of any others.

Evangelicanism, the belief of those Protestant sects which hold that the essence of the Gospel consists in the doctrine of salvation by faith in the atoning death of Christ and not by good works or the sacraments; that worship should be " free " rather than liturgical through established forms; that ritual is unacceptable and superstitious. Evangelicals are Low Churchmen.

Evangelism, the preaching of the Gospel, emphasising the necessity for a new birth or conversion. The evangelistic fervour of John Wesley and George Whitefield (*see* Methodism) aroused the great missionary spirit of the late 18th and 19th cent. George Fox, founder of the Society of Friends (q.v.), was also an evangelist. Evangelists can be Low, High, or Middle Churchmen.

Existentialism, a highly subjective philosophy which many people connect with such names as Jean-Paul Sartre (b. 1905) or Albert Camus (1913–60) and assume to be a post-war movement associated with disillusion and a sordid view of life. However, existentialism stems from Sören Kierkegaard (1813–55), the Danish " religious writer "—his own description of himself—in such works as *Either/Or, Fear and Trembling,* and *Concluding Unscientific Postscript.* Between the two wars translations of Kierkegaard into German influenced Martin Heidegger's (b. 1889) great work *Being and Time* and the other great existentialist Karl Jaspers (b. 1883); it has strongly influenced modern Protestant theology notably in Karl Barth, Reinhold Niebuhr, and Paul Tillich and beyond that field Gabriel Marcel (b. 1887), the Spanish writer Unamuno (1864–1936) in his well-known *The Tragic Sense of Life,* and Martin Buber of Israel (b. 1878) in his *I and Thou.* We have it on Heidegger's authority that " Sartre is no philosopher " even if it is to his works that modern existentialists often turn.

Existentialism is extremely difficult for the non-metaphysically-minded to understand; it deals, not with the nature of the universe or what are ordinarily thought of as philosophical problems but describes an attitude to life or God held by the individual. Briefly, its main essentials are: (1) it distinguishes between *essence,* i.e., that aspect of an entity which can be observed and known—and its *existence*—the fact of its having a place in a changing and dangerous world which is what really matters; (2) existence being basic, each self-aware individual can grasp his own existence on reflection in his own immediate experience of himself and his situation as a free being in the world; what he finds is not merely a knowing self but a self that fears, hopes, believes, wills, and is aware of its need to find a purpose, plan, and destiny in life; (3) but we cannot grasp our existence by thought alone; thus the fact " all men must die " relates to the essence of man but it is necessary to be involved, to draw the conclusion as a person that " I too must die " and experience its impact on our own individual existence; (4) because of the preceding, it is necessary to abandon our attitude of objectivity and theoretical detachment when faced by the problems relating to the ultimate purpose of our own life and the basis of our own conduct; life remains closed to those who take no part in it because it can have no significance; (5) it follows that the existentialist cannot be rationalist in his outlook for this is merely an escape into thought from the serious problems of existence; none of the important aspects of life—failure, evil, sin, folly—nor (in the view of Kierkegaard) even the existence of God or the truth of Christianity—can be proved by reason. " God does not exist; He is eternal," was how he expressed it; (6) life is short and limited in space and time, therefore it is foolish to discuss in a leisurely fashion matters of life or death as if there were all eternity to argue them in. It is necessary to make a leap into the unknown, e.g., accepting Christ (in the case of the Christian existentialist) by faith in the sense of giving and risking the self utterly. This means complete commitment, not a dependence on arguments as to whether certain historical events did, or did not, happen.

To summarise: existentialism of whatever type seems to the outsider to be an attitude to life concerning itself with the individual's ultimate problems (mine, not yours); to be anti-rationalist and anti-idealist (in the sense of being, as it seems to the believer, practical)—in effect it seems to say " life is too short to fool about with argument, you must dive in and become committed " to something. Sartre who calls himself an " atheist existentialist " is apparently committed to the belief that " hell is other people," but for most critics the main argument against existentialist philosophy is that it often rests on a highly specialised personal experience and, as such, is incommunicable.

Extra-sensory Perception. *See* Telepathy.

F

Fabian Society. In 1848 (the year of *The Communist Manifesto* by Marx and Engels) Europe was in revolt. In most countries the workers and intellectuals started bloody revolutions against the feudal ruling classes which were no less violently suppressed; hence on the continent socialism took on a Marxist tinge which to some extent it still retains. But at the same time England was undergoing a slow but non-violent transition in her political and industrial life which led the workers in general to look forward to progress through evolution. Marxism never became an important movement in England even though it took its origin here. There were many reasons for this: the agitation of the Chartists (q.v.); the writings of Mill, Ruskin, and Carlyle; the reforms of Robert Owen; the religious movement led by the Wesleys; the Co-operative societies; the Christian socialists. Furthermore legislation stimulated by these bodies had led to an extension of the franchise to include a considerable number of wage-earners, remedial measures to correct some of the worst abuses of the factory system, recognition of the trade unions, etc.

This was the background against which the Fabian Society was founded in 1884 with the conviction that social change could be brought about by gradual parliamentary means. (The name is derived from Quintus Fabius Maximus, the Roman general nicknamed "Cunctator," the delayer, who achieved his successes in defending Rome against Hannibal by refusing to give direct battle.) It was a movement of brilliant intellectuals, chief among whom were Sidney and Beatrice Webb, H. G. Wells, G. B. Shaw, Graham Wallas, Sidney Olivier, and Edward Pease. The Society itself was basically a research institution which furnished the intellectual information for social reform and supported all contributing to the gradual attainment by parliamentary means of socialism.

The Webbs' analysis of society emphasised that individualist enterprise in capitalism was a hang-over from early days and was bound to defeat itself since socialism is the inevitable accompaniment of modern industrialism; the necessary result of popular government is control of their economic system by the people themselves. Utopian schemes had been doomed to failure because they were based on the fallacy that society is static and that islands of utopias could be formed in the midst of an unchanging and antagonistic environment. On the contrary, it was pointed out, society develops: " The new becomes old, often before it is consciously regarded as new." Social reorganisation cannot usefully be hastened by violent means but only through methods consonant with this natural historical progression—gradual, peaceful, and democratic. The Fabians were convinced that men are rational enough to accept in their common interest developments which can be demonstrated as necessary; thus public opinion will come to see that socialisation of the land and industries is essential in the same way that they came to accept the already-existing acts in respect of housing, insurance, medical care, and conditions of work. Gradual " permeation " of the power groups—trade unions, political parties, managers, and enlightened employers—would speed the process.

The Society collaborated first in the formation of the Independent Labour Party and then with the more moderate Labour Party and the trade unions and Co-operative movement. But in general it disapproved of independent trade union action since change should come from the government and take political form. The class-war of Marx was rejected and so too was the idea of the exclusive role of the working class —reform must come from the enlightened co-operation of all classes—not from their opposition.

Faculty Psychology, a school of psychology, basically belonging to the early 19th cent. which sought to explain mental phenomena by referring them to the activity of certain agencies or faculties such as memory, imagination, will, etc., as if they were entities in their own right

J19

rather than merely general terms for various groups of mental phenomena. Its most extreme form was phrenology (q.v.) which found no less than thirty-seven so-called faculties.

Falangists. The Fascist Party of Spain founded in 1933 by José Antonio Primo de Rivera, son of the man who was dictator of the country from 1923 to 1930; he was shot by the Republicans. In 1937 the falangists who had shown unwelcome signs of social radicalism were merged with the other right-wing political groups to form the *Falange Española Tradicionalista y de las Juntas de Ofensive Nacional Sindicalistas* which replaced the Cortes (i.e. the Government) between 1939 and 1942 when the Cortes was reinstituted. The Falange is the only political party allowed in Spain. *See* **Fascism.**

Fascism. From the end of mediaeval times with the opening up of the world, the liberation of the mind and the release of business enterprise, a new spirit arose in Europe exemplified in such movements as the Renaissance, the Reformation, the struggle for democracy, the rise of capitalism, and the Industrial Revolution. With these movements there developed a certain tradition which, in spite of hindrances and disagreements or failures, was universally held both by right- and left-wing parties however strongly they might fail to agree on the best means of attaining what was felt to be a universal ideal. The hard core of this tradition involved: belief in reason and the possibility of human progress; the essential sanctity and dignity of human life; tolerance of widely different religious and political views; reliance on popular government and the responsibility of the rulers to the ruled; freedom of thought and criticism; the necessity of universal education; impartial justice and the rule of law; the desirability of universal peace. Fascism was the negation of every aspect of this tradition and took pride in being so. Emotion took the place of reason, the "immutable, beneficial, and fruitful inequality of classes" and the right of a self-constituted élite to rule them replaced universal suffrage because absolute authority "quick, sure, unanimous" led to action rather than talk. Contrary opinions are not allowed and justice is in the service of the state; war is desirable to advance the power of the state; and racial inequality made a dogma. Those who belong to the "wrong" religion, political party, or race are outside the law.

The attacks on liberalism and exaltation of the state derive largely from Hegel and his German followers; the mystical irrationalism from such 19th cent. philosophers as Schopenhauer, Nietzsche, and Bergson; from Sorel (*see* **Syndicalism**) came the idea of the "myth," and an image which would have the power to arouse the emotions of the masses and from Sorel also the rationale of violence and justification of force. But these philosophical justifications of fascism do not explain why it arose at all and why it arose where it did—in Italy, Germany, and Spain. These countries had one thing in common—disillusionment. Germany had lost the 1914–18 war, Italy had been on the winning side but was resentful about her small gains, Spain had sunk to the level of a third-rate power, and people were becoming increasingly restive under the reactionary powers of the Catholic Church, the landed aristocracy, and the army. In Marxist theory, fascism is the last fling of the ruling class and the bourgeoisie in their attempt to hold down the workers.

Italian Fascism. The corporate state set up by Benito Mussolini in Italy claimed to be neither capitalist nor socialist, and after its inception in 1922 the Fascist Party became the only recognised one. Its members wore black shirts, were organised in military formations, used the Roman greeting of the outstretched arm, and adopted as their slogan "Mussolini is always right." Membership of the Party was not allowed to exceed a number thought to be suited to the optimum size of a governing class and new candidates were drawn, after strict examinations, from the youth organisations. The Blackshirts, a fascist militia, existed separately from the army and were ruled by Fascist Headquarters.

At the head of government was Mussolini,

"Il Duce" himself, a cabinet of fourteen ministers selected by him and approved by the King to supervise the various functions of government, and the Grand Council or directorate of the Fascist Party, all the members of which were chosen by the Duce. Parliament, which was not allowed to initiate legislation but only to approve decrees from above, consisted of a Senate with life-membership and a Chamber of Fasci and Corporations composed of nominated members of the Party, the National Council of Corporations, and selected representatives of the employers' and employees' confederations. Private enterprise was encouraged and protected but rigidly controlled; strikes were forbidden, but a Charter of Labour enforced the collaboration of workers and employers whose disputes were settled in labour courts presided over by the Party. All decisions relating to industry were government-controlled (e.g., wages, prices, conditions of employment and dismissal, the expansion or limitation of production), and some industries such as mining, shipping, and armaments were largely state-owned.

Italian fascism served as a model in other countries, notably for the German National Socialist Party, in Spain and Japan, and most European nations between the wars had their small Fascist parties, the British version led by Sir Oswald Mosley being known as the British Union which relied on marches and violence. The Public Order Act of 1936 (see **D45**) was passed to deal with it. Although fascism in all countries has certain recognisable characteristics, it would be wrong to think of it as an international movement taking fixed forms and with a clearly thought-out rationale as in the case of communism. It is doubtful, for example, whether Japanese "fascism" was entitled to be described as such, and the Spanish Falange differs in many respects both in outlook and origins from the German or Italian varieties. In fact the word "fascist," like "bolshevik," is often used as a purely emotive term of abuse. *See* **Falange, Nazism.**

Fatalism. *See* **Determinism.**

Feedback Cult is the name given to a curious fad which began in America in 1970 and which is interesting because it incorporates complicated scientific equipment and experimental psychological methods into its practice. The basis of the cult is as follows: for nearly fifty years it has been known that the brain is the source of varied electrical signals of very low power which can be detected by attaching electrodes to the scalp and amplifying the pulses emitted. Much scientific controversy has surrounded these pulses, and their interpretation by skilled clinicians can lead to the detection of hidden cerebral disorders such as tumours, epileptic foci, etc. The presence of one particular rhythm the so-called alpha wave, which beats at 14 cycles per second—is believed to be dependent upon whether or not the individual is "attending" to something, particularly in the visual field. It is this alpha rhythm, or rather its control, that is the basis of the feedback cult.

Within the past decade it has been discovered that when some people are connected to an electroencephalograph (the device which records brain rhythms) and are shown the recorded tracings of their own brain waves as they actually occur, they find it possible to modify and control the nature of the waves—the alpha in particular. This, a scientific curiosity rather than a major discovery, soon caught the attention of followers of yoga and other systems seeking enhanced relaxation, "mental discipline," etc. The argument was advanced that for centuries man had been seeking to exercise control over his own mental activities, without however having much opportunity to assess his success—or lack of it. The use of the EEG with the individual's brain waves "fed back" to him for inspection would remedy this. The result has been a sudden surge of lay interest in electroencephalography and a boom in the sale of small, portable EEG machines. Followers of the cult, who may sit for hours inspecting the output from their own brains and attempting to modify it at will, claim that the activity promotes mental "relaxation" and a greater and deeper understanding of their own personal problems. It is probably hardly necessary to say that psychologists are extremely dubious about the reality of this as mental therapy, and the feedback cult will probably die away as soon as some new and equally attractive scientific toy is developed.

Fetichism, originally a practice of the natives of West Africa and elsewhere of attributing magical properties to an object which was used as an amulet, for putting spells on others, or regarded as possessing dangerous powers. In psychology the term refers to a sexual perversion in which objects such as shoes, brassières, hair, etc., arouse sexual excitement.

Feudalism. The feudal system took its origins from Saxon times and broadly speaking lasted until the end of the 13th cent. It was a military and political organisation based on land tenure, for, of course, society throughout this period was based almost entirely on agriculture. The activities of men divided them into three classes or estates. The First Estate was the clergy, responsible for man's spiritual needs; the Second was the nobility, including kings and emperor as well as the lesser nobles; the Third was composed of all those who had to do with the economic and mainly agricultural life of Europe. The praying men, the fighting men and administrators, and the toilers were all held to be dependent on each other in a web of mutual responsibilities.

The theory of feudalism, although it by no means always worked out in practice, was as follows: the earth was God's and therefore no man owned land in the modern sense of the word. God had given the pope spiritual charge of men, and secular power over them to the emperor from whom kings held their kingdoms, and in turn the dukes and counts received the land over which they held sway from the king. Members of the Second Estate held their lands on the condition of fulfilling certain obligations to their overlord and to the people living under them, so when a noble received a fief or piece of land he became the vassal of the man who bestowed it. To him he owed military service for a specified period of the year, attendance at court, and giving his lord counsel. He undertook to ransom his lord when he fell into enemy hands and to contribute to his daughter's dowry and at the knighting of his son. In return the lord offered his vassal protection and justice, received the vassal's sons into his household and educated them for knighthood.

The system was complicated by the fact that large fiefs might be subdivided and abbots often governed church lands held in fief from nobles. The serf or toiling man dwelt on the land of a feudal noble or churchman where he rendered service by tilling the soil or carrying out his craft for his manorial lord in return for protection, justice, and the security of his life and land. He was given a share in the common lands or pastures from which he provided for his own needs. In the modern sense he was not free (although at a later stage he could buy his freedom) since he was attached to the soil and could not leave without the lord's permission. On the other hand he could neither be deprived of his land nor lose his livelihood. Feudal tenures were abolished in England by statute in 1660, although they had for long been inoperative. In Japan a feudal system existed up to 1871, in Russia until 1917, and many relics of it still linger on (*e.g.* the *mezzadria* system of land tenure in parts of Italy).

Flying Saucers. In June 1947 an American private pilot, Kenneth Arnold, saw a series of wingless objects flying through the air at a speed which he estimated at thousands of miles an hour. He later told the press that the objects "flew as a saucer would if you skipped it across the water," and the phrase "flying saucers" was erroneously born. What Arnold actually saw has never been satisfactorily explained—it was probably a flight of jet fighters reflecting the sun's rays in a way that made them appear as discs—but since that date literally hundreds of thousands of people all over the world have reported the sighting of strange objects in the sky, coming in a bewildering range of shapes and sizes. Initially the American Air Force

launched an official enquiry—Project Bluebook —to attempt to solve the mystery of these "unidentified flying objects" or "U.F.Os," which finally folded in 1969 after concluding that the bulk of the sightings were probably misinterpretations of natural phenomena and that there was no evidence for the commonly held view that earth was being visited by spacecraft from some other planetary system. A rather similar conclusion was arrived at by the famous University of Colorado project—the Condon Committee—which published its findings in 1968. Despite this clear-cut official attitude, belief in the existence of flying saucers and their origin as alien space vehicles is exceedingly widespread and is held very strongly by people in all walks of life. In 1959 this striking social phenomenon attracted the attention of the psychologist, C. G. Jung. He noticed that the press were inclined to report statements that saucers existed when made by prominent people and not publish contrary statements made by equally prominent people. He concluded that flying saucers were in some way welcome phenomena and in his brilliant little book, *Flying Saucers—a modern myth,* he hypothesised that the U.F.Os were the modern equivalent of "signs in the skies." It was Jung's contention that the saucers were looked upon as the harbingers of advanced alien civilisations who had come to save the world from its descent into nuclear catastrophe— archangels in modern dress in fact.

Whatever the validity of this imaginative view of U.F.Os, it is undeniably true that they exercise a great fascination for millions of people, some of whom invest them with definite religious significance. The best example of the open incorporation of flying saucers into a religious belief system is to be found in the Aetherius Society, an international organisation with headquarters in Los Angeles but founded by a former London clerk, George King. Mr. King, who claims to be the mediumistic link between earth and the largely benevolent beings from outer space, regularly relays messages— notably from a Venusian known as Aetherius— to enthusiastic congregations at religious meetings. The sect, which is entirely sincere and dedicated in its beliefs, also makes pilgrimages to the tops of various mountains which have been "spiritually charged" with the aid of the spacebeings in their flying saucers.

Odd though such ideas may seem to most people, they can be readily understood within the context of the very marked decline in orthodox religious belief which we have seen in the past two decades. To an increasing number of people, many of whom feel a desperate need for spiritual guidance and enlightenment, the concepts of the traditionally Western religions seem somehow unsatisfactory. Many therefore turn to cults and splinter groups which use ideas and terminology which to them seem more at home in the twentieth century than those that sprung to life thousands of years ago. To members of the Aetherius Society, for example, the idea that Jesus Christ lives on Venus and rides around in a flying saucer is neither blasphemous nor ludicrous. As long as empty churches testify to the growing, if perhaps only temporary loss of contact between orthodox religions and the man-in-the-street, then one can expect such offbeat ideas as the cults surrounding flying saucers, and the science-fiction-like cult of Scientology (*q.v.*) to expand and flourish.

Fourierism. *See* Utopianism.

Freemasonry, a secret organisation with different systems in different countries. It shares with other secret societies the characteristics of being secret, having signs by which one fellow-member can recognise another, initiation ceremonies, peculiar regalia, and various grades of enlightenment. In England freemasonry was first organised in 1717 and in France and Germany in 1725 and 1737 respectively. Masons claim to be working for the good of mankind, and carry out various charitable works. Many notable people are in the movement. Whatever their beliefs there can be no doubt that on the continent freemasons have intervened in politics and the organisation is banned by the Roman Catholic Church. Absurd attempts have been made (and quite possibly are part of Masonic belief) to trace the society back to early and even Biblical times. Historically, of course, this is absurd, nor have freemasons any connection with the masons' guilds of the Middle Ages which were intended for masons in the ordinary sense of the word.

In its early days, and indeed until a decade or so ago, membership of the freemasons conferred definite business and social advantages, particularly in small communities where the leading middle-class figures were generally members. Recently this advantage has markedly declined and freemason lodges nowadays tend to be little more than worthy charitable organisations. The publication, by a number of disgruntled ex-masons, of the full details of rituals, initiation ceremonies, regalia, etc., has also tended to rob the movement of one of its greatest attractions —its role as an amiable secret society.

Freudian theory. *See* **Psychoanalysis.**

Friends, The Society of, or **Quakers,** a religious body founded in England in the 17th cent. by George Fox (1624–91). The essence of their faith is that every individual who believes has the power of direct communication with God who will guide him into the ways of truth. This power comes from the " inner light " of his own heart, the light of Christ. Quakers meet for worship avoiding all ritual, without ordained ministers or prepared sermons; there is complete silence until someone is moved by the Holy Spirit to utter his message.

In the early days Quakers gave vent to violent outbursts and disturbed church services. Friends had the habit of preaching at anyone who happened to be nearby, their denunciation of " steeple-houses " and references to the " inner light," their addressing everyone as " thee " and " thou," their refusal to go beyond " yea " and " nay " in making an assertion and refusing to go further in taking an oath, must have played some part in bringing about the savage persecutions they were forced to endure. Many emigrated to Pennsylvania, founded by William Penn in 1682, and missionaries were sent to many parts of the world. The former violence gave way to gentleness. Friends not only refused to take part in war but even refused to resist personal violence. They took the lead in abolishing slavery, worked for prison reform and better education. As we know them today Quakers are quiet, sincere, undemonstrative people, given to a somewhat serious turn of mind. The former peculiarities of custom and dress have been dropped and interpretation of the Scriptures is more liberal. Although Quakers refuse to take part in warfare, they are always ready to help the victims of war, by organising relief, helping refugees in distress, or sending their ambulance units into the heat of battle.

Fundamentalism is a term covering a number of religious movements which adhere with the utmost rigidity to orthodox tenets; for example the Old Testament statement that the earth was created by God in six days and six nights would be held to be factual rather than allegorical or symbolic. There is a strong minority undercurrent of support for various Fundamental religions, including such sects as Jehovah's Witnesses, the Seventh Day Adventists, etc. Although the holding of rigid beliefs in the literal truth of the Bible might seem to be frequently contrary to modern scientific findings, the fundamentalists at least do not have the problems of compromise and interpretation to face, and among many simple-minded and poorly educated people this is no doubt a great attraction.

G

Gestalt Psychology. In the latter half of the 19th cent. it became evident to psychologists that in principle there was no good reason why "mental" events should not be just as measurable and manageable as " physical ". ones. Intensive studies of learning, memory, perception, and so on were therefore undertaken and the begin-

nings of an empirical science of psychology were underway. In the early part of the 20th cent. the experiments of Pavlov (*see* **Behaviourism**) and his co-workers suggested that the behaviour of an animal, or even men, might ultimately be reduced to a descriptive account of the activities of nervous reflex loops—the so-called conditioned reflexes. With the publication of Watson's important book on Behaviourism in 1914 it looked as though the transfer of psychological studies from the field of philosophy to that of science could now take place. Actually the over-simplified picture of cerebral and mental pictures which Behaviourism offered was rather comparable to the billiard ball view of the universe so fashionable in Victorian science. Just as Behaviourism implied that there was a fundamental building block (the conditioned reflex) from which all mental events could be constructed, so Victorian physics assumed that the entire universe could be described in terms of a vast collection of atoms pushing each other around like billiard balls. The development of nuclear physics was to shatter the latter dream and at the same time a challenge to the naive " reflex psychology " came from the Gestalt experimental school.

The founders of this school were Max Wertheimer, Kurt Koffka and Wolfgang Kohler, three young psychologists who in 1912 were conducting experiments—notably in vision— which seemed to expose the inadequacies of the behaviourist position. The Pavlov–Watson view, as we have said, implied that complex sensory events were no more than a numerical sum of individual nervous impulses. Wertheimer's group proposed that certain facts of perceptual experiences (ruled out of court as subjective and therefore unreliable by Watson) implied that *the whole (Gestalt) was something more than simply the sum of its parts.* For example, the presentation of a number of photographs, each slightly different, in rapid series gives rise to cinematographic motion. In basic terms, the eye has received a number of discrete, " still " photographs, and yet " motion " is perceived. What, they asked, was the sensory input corresponding to this motion? Some processes within the brain clearly *added* something to the total input as defined in behaviourist terms. An obvious alternative—in a different sense modality—is that of the arrangement of musical notes. A cluster of notes played one way might be called a tune; played backwards they may form another tune, or may be meaningless. Yet in all cases the constituent parts are the same, and yet their relationship to one another is evidently vital. Once again the whole is something more than the simple sum of the parts.

The implications of all this appeared to be that the brain was equipped with the capacity to organise sensory input in certain well-defined ways, and that far from being misleading and scientifically unjustifiable, human subjective studies of visual experience might reveal the very principles of organisation which the brain employs. Take a field of dots, more or less randomly distributed; inspection of the field will soon reveal certain patterns or clusters standing out—the constellations in the night sky are a good illustration. There are many other examples, and Wertheimer and his colleagues in a famous series of experiments made some effort to catalogue them and reduce them to a finite number of " Laws of Perceptual Organisation " which are still much quoted today.

The rise of the Gestalt school came as an inevitable balance to the behaviourist viewpoint. But despite its undoubted descriptive merits and role in making psychology less simple if more realistic, Gestalt psychology never succeeded in the explanatory role for which much was hoped. Part of the difficulty, perhaps, was that its original theoretical slant seems to have been seriously off-key. Wolfgang Kohler, who was in fact a physicist as well as a psychologist, saw much in common between the forces of perceptual organisation in the brain and the constraining forces experienced in electromagnetic fields. It was known that the brain was a source of electrical energy, so why should it not be equipped with "fields" arising from the continuous basic neural activity? The search for permanent electrical fields in the brain continued unprofitably for decades, until the devastating experimental work of Lashley (1951) who inserted gold leaf in various parts of the rat brain and showed no effect on learning or the retention of maze problems. Today Gestalt psychology is of historical rather than immediate interest, though its significance in the development of modern psychology is undeniable.

Gnosticism. Among the many heresies of early Christianity, especially during its first two centuries, was a group which came under the heading of Gnosticism. This was a system or set of systems which attempted to combine Christian beliefs with others derived from Oriental and Greek sources, especially those which were of a mystical and metaphysical nature, such as the doctrines of Plato and Pythagoras. There were many Gnostic sects, the most celebrated being the Alexandrian school of Valentius (fl. c. 136–c. 160). "Gnosis" was understood not as meaning "knowledge" or "understanding" as we understand these words, but "revelation." As in other mystical religions, the ultimate object was individual salvation; sacraments took the most varied forms. Many who professed themselves Christians accepted Gnostic doctrines and even orthodox Christianity contains some elements of Gnostic mysticism. It was left to the bishops and theologians to decide at what point Gnosticism ceased to be orthodox and a difficult task this proved to be. Two of the greatest, Clement of Alexandria and his pupil Origen, unwittingly slipped into heresy when they tried to show that such men as Socrates and Plato, who were in quest of truth, were Christian in intention, and by their lives and works had prepared the way for Christ. Thus they contradicted Church doctrine which specifically said *Extra ecclesiam nulla salus*—outside the Church there is no salvation.

God and Man. The idea of gods came before the idea of God and even earlier in the evolution of religious thought there existed belief in spirits (*see* Animism). It was only as a result of a long period of development that the notion of a universal "God" arose, a development particularly well documented in the Old Testament. Here we are concerned only with the views of philosophers, the views of specific religious bodies being given under the appropriate headings. First, however, some definitions.

Atheism is the positive disbelief in the existence of a God. Agnosticism (a term coined by T. H. Huxley, the 19th cent. biologist and contemporary of Darwin) signifies that one cannot know whether God exists or not. Deism is the acceptance of the existence of God, not through revelation, but as a hypothesis required by reason. Theism also accepts the existence of God, but, unlike Deism, does not reject the evidence of revelation (*e.g.*, in the Bible or in the lives of the saints). Pantheism is the identification of God with all that exists (*i.e.*, with the whole universe). Monotheism is the belief in one God, Polytheism the belief in many (*see also* Dualism).

Early Greek Views. Among the early Greek philosophers, Thales (c. 624–565 B.C.) of Miletus, in Asia Minor, Anaximander (611–547 B.C.), his pupil, and Anaximenes (b. c. 570 B.C.), another Miletan, were men of scientific curiosity and their speculations about the origin of the universe were untouched by religious thought. They founded the scientific tradition of critical discussion. Heraclitus of Ephesus (c. 540–475 B.C.), was concerned with the problem of change. How does a thing change and yet remain itself? For him all things are flames—processes. "Everything is in flux, and nothing is at rest." Empedocles of Agrigentum in Sicily (c. 500–c. 430 B.C.) introduced the idea of opposition and affinity. All matter is composed of the so-called four elements—*earth, water, air,* and *fire*—which are in opposition or alliance with each other. All these were materialist philosophers who sought to explain the workings of the universe without recourse to the gods.

Socrates, Plato, and Aristotle. Socrates (470–

399 B.C.) was primarily concerned with ethical matters and conduct rather than the nature of the universe. For him goodness and virtue come from knowledge. He obeyed an "inner voice" and suffered death rather than give up his philosophy. He believed in the persistence of life after death and was essentially a monotheist. Plato (427–347 B.C.) was chiefly concerned with the nature of reality and thought in terms of absolute truths which were unchanging, logical, and mathematical. (*See* Mind and Matter.) Aristotle (384–322 B.C.) took his view of matter not from Democritus (atomic view) but from Empedocles (doctrine of four elements), a view which came to fit in well with orthodox mediaeval theology. Matter is conceived of as potentially alive and striving to attain its particular form, being moved by divine spirit or mind (*nous*). (An acorn, for example, is matter which contains the form "oak-tree" towards which it strives.) Thus there is a whole series from the simplest level of matter to the perfect living individual. But there must be a supreme source of all movement upon which the whole of Nature depends, a Being that Aristotle describes as the "Unmoved Mover," the ultimate cause of all becoming in the universe. This Being is pure intelligence, a philosopher's God, not a personal one. Unlike Plato, Aristotle did not believe in survival after death, holding that the divine, that is the immortal element in man, is mind.

Among the later Greek thinkers the Epicureans were polytheists whose gods, however, were denied supernatural powers. The Stoics built up a materialist theory of the universe, based on the Aristotelian model. To them God was an all-pervading force, related to the world as the soul is related to the body, but they conceived of it as material. They developed the mystical side of Plato's idealism and were much attracted by the astrology coming from Babylonia. They were pantheists. The Sceptics were agnostics.

From Pagan to Christian Thought. Philo, "the Jew of Alexandria," who was about 20 years older than Jesus, tried to show that the Jewish scriptures were in line with the best in Greek thought. He introduced the *Logos* as a bridge between the two systems. Philo's God is remote from the world, above and beyond all thought and being, and as His perfection does not permit direct contact with matter the divine *Logos* acts as intermediary between God and man. Plotinus (204–70), a Roman, and the founder of Neoplatonism, was the last of the great pagan philosophers. Like Philo, he believed that God had created the world indirectly through emanations—beings coming from Him but not of Him. The world needs God but God does not need the world. Creation is a fall from God, especially the human soul when enmeshed in the body and the world of the senses, yet (*see* Determinism) man has the ability to free himself from sense domination and turn towards God. Neoplatonism was the final stage of Greek thought drawing its inspiration from the mystical side of Plato's idealism and its ethics from Stoicism.

Christianity: The Fathers and the Schoolmen. It was mainly through St. Augustine (354–430), Bishop of Hippo in North Africa, that certain of the doctrines of Neoplatonism found their way into Christianity. Augustine also emphasised the concept of God as all good, all wise, all knowing, transcendent, the Creator of the universe out of nothing. But, he added, since God knows everything, everything is determined by Him forever. This is the doctrine of predestination and its subsequent history is discussed under Determinism.

In the early centuries of Christianity, as we have seen, some found it difficult to reconcile God's perfection with His creation of the universe and introduced the concept of the *Logos* which many identified with Christ. Further, it came to be held that a power of divine origin permeated the universe, namely the Holy Spirit or Holy Ghost. Some theory had to be worked out to explain the relationships of these three entities whence arose the conception of the Trinity. God is One; but He is also Three:

Father, Son (the *Logos* or Christ), and Holy Ghost.

This doctrine was argued by the Apologists and the Modalists. The former maintained that the *Logos* and the Holy Spirit were emanations from God and that Jesus was the *Logos* in the form of a man. The Modalists held that all three Persons of the Trinity were God in three forms or modes: the *Logos* as God creating, the Holy Spirit God reasoning, and God is God being. This led to a long discussion as to whether the *Logos* was an emanation from God or God in another form; was the *Logos* of like *nature* with God or of the same *substance*? This was resolved at the Council of Nicaea (325) when Athanasius formulated the orthodox doctrine against Arius (*q.v.*): that the one Godhead is a Trinity of the same substance, three Persons of the same nature—Father, Son, and Holy Ghost.

St. Thomas Aquinas (1227–74), influenced greatly by Aristotle's doctrines, set the pattern for all subsequent Catholic belief even to the present time. He produced rational arguments for God's existence: *e.g.*, Aristotle's argument that, since movement exists, there must be a prime mover, the Unmoved Mover or God; further, we can see that things in the universe are related in a scale from the less to the more complex, from the less to the more perfect, and this leads us to suppose that at the peak there must be a Being with absolute perfection. God is the first and final cause of the universe, absolutely perfect, the Creator of everything out of nothing. He reveals Himself in his Creation and rules the universe through His perfect will. How Aquinas dealt with the problem of predestination is told under Determinism.

Break with Mediaeval Thought. Renaissance thinkers, free to think for themselves, doubted the validity of the arguments of the Schoolmen but most were unwilling to give up the idea of God (nor would it have been safe to do so). Mystics (*see* Mysticism) or near-mystics such as Nicholas of Cusa (*c.* 1401–64) and Jacob Boehme (1575–1624) taught that God was not to be found by reason but was a fact of the immediate intuition of the mystical experience. Giordano Bruno held that God was immanent in the infinite universe. He is the unity of all opposites, a unity without opposites, which the human mind cannot grasp. Bruno was burned at the stake in 1600 at the instigation of the Inquisition (a body which, so we are told, never caused pain to anyone since it was the civil power, not the Inquisition, that carried out the unpleasant sentences) for his heresy.

Francis Bacon, who died in 1626, separated, as was the tendency of that time, science from religion. The latter he divided into the two categories of natural and revealed theology. The former, through the study of nature, may give convincing proof of the existence of a God but nothing more. Of revealed theology he said: "we must quit the small vessel of human reason . . . as we are obliged to obey the divine law, though our will murmurs against it, so we are obliged to believe in the word of God, though our reason is shocked at it." Hobbes (d. 1679) was a complete materialist and one feels that obeisance to the notion was politic rather than from conviction. However, he does mention God as starting the universe; in motion infers that God is corporeal, but denies that His nature can be known.

From Descartes Onwards. Descartes (1596–1650) separated mind and body as different entities but believed that the existence of God could be deduced by the fact that the idea of him existed in the mind. Whatever God puts into man, including his ideas, must be real. God is self-caused, omniscient, omnipotent, eternal, all goodness and truth. But Descartes neglected to explain how mind separate from body can influence body, or God separate from the world can influence matter.

Spinoza (1632–77) declared that all existence is embraced in one substance—God, the all-in-all. He was a pantheist and as such was rejected by his Jewish brethren. But Spinoza's God has neither personality nor consciousness, intelligence nor purpose, although all things follow in strict law from His nature. All the thought of everyone in the world, make up God's thoughts.

Bishop Berkeley (1685–1753) took the view that things exist only when they are perceived, and this naturally implies that a tree, for example, ceases to exist when nobody is looking at it. This problem was solved to his own satisfaction by assuming that God, seeing everything, prevented objects from disappearing when we were not present. The world is a creation of God but it is a spiritual or mental world, not a material one.

Hume (1711–76), who was a sceptic, held that human reason cannot demonstrate the existence of God and all past arguments to show that it could were fallacious. Yet we must believe in God since the basis of all hope, morality, and society is based upon the belief. Kant (1724–1804) held a theory similar to that of Hume. We cannot know by reason that God exists, nor can we prove on the basis of argument anything about God. But we can form an idea of the whole of the universe, the one Absolute Whole, and personify it. We need the idea of God on which to base our moral life, although this idea of God is transcendent, *i.e.*, goes beyond experience.

William James (1842–1910), the American philosopher (*see* Pragmatism), held much the same view: God cannot be proved to exist, but we have a will to believe which must be satisfied, and the idea works in practice. Hegel (1770–1831) thought of God as a developing process, beginning with "the Absolute" or First Cause and finding its highest expression in man's mind, or reason. It is in man that God most clearly becomes aware of Himself. Finally Comte (1798–1857), the positivist, held that religion belongs to a more primitive state of society and, like many modern philosophers, turned the problem over to believers as being none of the business of science.

Good and Evil.

Early Philosophers' Views. The early Greek philosophers were chiefly concerned with the laws of the universe, consequently it was common belief that knowledge of these laws, and living according to them, constituted the supreme good. Heraclitus, for example, who taught that all things carried with them their opposites, held that good and evil were like two notes in a harmony, necessary to each other. "It is the opposite which is good for us." Democritus, like Epicurus (*q.v.*), held that the main goal of life is happiness, but happiness in moderation. The good man is not merely the one who *does* good but who always *wants* to do so: "You can tell the good man not by his deeds alone but by his desires." Such goodness brings happiness, the ultimate goal. On the other hand, many of the wandering Sophist teachers taught that good was merely social convention, that there are no absolute principles of right and wrong, that each man should live according to his desires and make his own moral code. To Socrates knowledge was the highest good because doing wrong is the result of ignorance: "no man is voluntarily bad." Plato and Aristotle, differing in many other respects, drew attention to the fact that man is composed of three parts: his desires and appetites, his will, and his reason. A man whose reason rules his will and appetites is not only a good but a happy man; for happiness is not an aim in itself but a by-product of the good life. Aristotle, however, emphasised the goal of self-realisation, and thought that if the goal of life is (as Plato had said) a rational attitude towards the feelings and desires, it needs to be further defined. Aristotle defined it as the "Golden Mean"—the good man is one who does not go to extremes but balances one extreme against another. Thus courage is a mean between cowardice and foolhardiness. The later philosophers Philo and Plotinus held that evil was in the very nature of the body and its senses. Goodness could only be achieved by giving up the life of the senses and, freed from the domination of the body, turning to God, the source of goodness.

Christian Views. St. Augustine taught that everything in the universe is good. Even those things which appear evil are good in that they fit with the harmony of the universe like shadows in a painting. Man should turn his back on the pleasures of the world and turn to the love of God. Peter Abelard (1079–1142) made the more sophisticated distinction when he suggested that the wrongness of an act lies not in the act itself, but in the intention of the doer: " God considers not what is done but in what spirit it is done; and the merit or praise of the agent lies not in the deed but in the intention." If we do what we believe to be right, we may err, but we do not sin. The only sinful man is he who deliberately sets out to do what he knows to be wrong. St. Thomas Aquinas agreed with Aristotle in that he believed the highest good to be realisation of self as God has ordained, and he also agreed with Abelard that intention is important. Even a good act is not good unless the doer intended it to have good consequences. Intention will not make a bad act good, but it is the only thing that will make a good act genuinely good.

In general, Christianity has had difficulties in solving the problem of the existence of evil; for even when one accepts that the evil men do is somehow tied up with the body, it is still difficult to answer the question: how could an all-good God create evil? This is answered in one of two ways: (a) that Adam was given free-will and chose to sin (an answer which still does not explain how sin could exist anywhere in the universe of a God who created everything); (b) by denying the reality of evil as some Christians have chosen to do (e.g., Christian Science q.v.). The Eastern religions, on the other hand (see Zoroastrianism), solved the problem in a more realistic way by a dualism which denied that their gods were the creators of the whole universe and allowed the existence of at least two gods, one good and one evil. In Christianity there is, of course, a Devil, but it is not explained whence his evil nature came.

Later Philosophic Views. Hobbes equated good with pleasure, evil with pain. They are relative to the individual man in the sense that " one man's meat is another man's poison." Descartes believed that the power to distinguish between good and evil given by God to man is not complete, so that man does evil through ignorance. We act with insufficient knowledge and on inadequate evidence. Locke, believing that at birth the mind is a blank slate, held that men get their opinions of right and wrong from their parents. By and large, happiness is good and pain is evil. But men do not always agree over what is pleasurable and what not. Hence laws exist and these fall into three categories: (1) the divine law; (2) civil laws; (3) matters of opinion or reputation which are enforced by the fact that men do not like to incur the disapproval of their friends. We learn by experience that evil brings pain and good acts bring pleasure, and, basically, one is good because not to be so would bring discomfort.

Kant (see God and Man) found moral beliefs to be inherent in man whether or not they can be proved by reason. There is a categorical imperative which makes us realise the validity of two universal laws: (1) " always act in such a way that the maxim determining your conduct might well become a universal law; act so that you can will that everybody shall follow the principle of your action; (2) " always act so as to treat humanity, whether in thine own person or in that of another, in every case as an end and never as a means."

Schopenhauer (1788–1860) was influenced by Buddhism and saw the will as a blind impelling striving, and desire as the cause of all suffering. The remedy is to regard sympathy and pity as the basis of all morality and to deny one's individual will. This is made easier if we realise that everyone is part of the Universal Will and therefore the one against whom we are struggling is part of the same whole as ourselves.

John Stuart Mill and Jeremy Bentham were both representatives of the Utilitarian school, believing that good is the greatest good (happiness) of the greatest number (see Utilitarianism). Lastly, there is the view held mostly by political thinkers that good is what is good for the state or society in general (see State and Man).

Graphology, the study of the analysis of human handwriting. There are two approaches to this topic and it is important to separate them clearly. The first involves the attempt on the part of an expert to decide from looking at a signature (a) to whom it belongs, and (b) whether or not it is forgery. This art is a legitimate, though tricky area of study, and graphologists have been called in as expert witnesses in courts of law. The second approach involves attempts to detect such tenuous variables as character from a study of an individual's handwriting, and the facts here are altogether less clear. Psychologists find it difficult enough to assess character or personality in a face-to-face interview and even when they are equipped with a range of special tests. The general opinion here would seem to be that some slight information might be revealed by a careful study of handwriting, but that the overall effect would be too unreliable for this kind of graphology to be of practical value.

Guild Socialism, a British form of syndicalism (q.v.) created in 1906 by an architect, A. J. Penty, who was soon joined by A. R. Orage, S. G. Hobson, and G. D. H. Cole. The background to the movement was the situation that, although at that time the Labour Party had 29 members in the House of Commons, a period of severe economic crisis had shown the government unwilling and the Labourites unable to do anything about it; the workers were resorting again to direct action to secure their demands and the democratic and constitutional methods to which the Fabians had partly persuaded them seemed to have failed. The guild socialists advocated a restoration of the mediaeval guild system as was being recommended by the French syndicalists whose programme involved a return to direct economic action, a functional industrial structure, return of craftsmanship, and distrust of the state. Guild socialists believed that value was created by society as a whole rather than by individuals singly, and that capitalist economists had recommended the acquisition of wealth without emphasising the social responsibilities which wealth should bring. The trade unions were to be organised to take over and run their own industries after nationalisation. Thus guild socialists were not only against capitalism but also against state socialism in which the state took over the control of industry. Political authority was held to be uncongenial to human freedom and therefore nothing was to be gained by the substitution of state bureaucracy for capitalist control. The National Guilds League, formed in 1915, advocated the abolition of the wages system, self-government in industry, control by a system of national guilds acting in conjunction with other functional democratic organisations in the community. This body was dissolved in 1925, but the theories of guild socialism have undoubtedly influenced British socialism.

H

Heresy, originally meant a sect or school of thought holding views different from others (e.g., Pharisees and Sadducees within Judaism). Later it came to mean beliefs contrary to orthodox teaching (e.g., Arianism, Apollinarianism, Nestorianism).

Hinduism, the religion and social institutions of the great majority of the people of India. Hinduism has no fixed scriptural canon but its doctrines are to be found in certain ancient works, notably the *Veda*, the *Brahmanas*, the *Upanishads*, and the *Bhagavad-gita*. The dark-skinned Dravidians invaded India between about 3250 and 2750 B.C. and established a civilisation in the Indus valley. They were polytheists who worshipped a number of nature-gods; some elements of their beliefs persisted into Hinduism. They were subdued by a light-skinned Nordic people who invaded from Asia Minor and Iran about 1500 B.C. The language of these Aryan people was Vedic, parent of Sanskrit in which their religious literature (the Vedas) came to be written after many centuries of oral transmission.

The *Veda* or Sacred Lore has come down to us in the form of mantras or hymns of which there are four great collections, the best-known being the *Rig-Veda*. These Vedic Aryans worshipped nature-deities, their favourites being Indra (rain), Agni (fire), and Surya (the sun). Their religion contained no idolatry but became contaminated by the more primitive beliefs of the conquered Dravidians. Sacrifice and ritual became predominant in a ceremonial religion.

As a reaction a more philosophic form arose (c. 500 B.C.) with its scriptures in the *Upanishads*. At its highest level, known as Brahmanism, belief is in a subtle and sophisticated form of monotheism (*Brahma* is an impersonal, all-embracing spirit), but there is a tolerant acceptance of more primitive beliefs. Thus Vishnu (a conservative principle) and Siva (a destructive principle) grew out of Vedic conceptions. The two great doctrines of Hinduism are *karma* and transmigration. The universal desire to be reunited with the absolute (the *Atman* or *Brahma*) can be satisfied by following the path of knowledge. Life is a cycle of lives (*samsara*) in which man's destiny is determined by his deeds (*karma*) from which he may seek release (*moksa*) through ascetic practices or the discipline of Yoga (*q.v.*). Failure to achieve release means reincarnation—migration to a higher or lower form of life after death—until the ultimate goal of absorption in the absolute is reached.

In the great Sanskrit epic poems *Ramayana* and *Mahabharata* the deity takes three forms, represented by the divine personalities of Brahma, Vishnu, and Siva. There are also lower gods, demi-gods, supernatural beings, and members of the trinity may even become incarnate, as Vishnu became identified with Krishna, one of the heroes of the *Mahabharata* and the well-known *Bhagavad-gita*.

The ritual and legalistic side of Brahmanism is the caste system based on the elaborate codes of the *Law of Manu*, according to which God created distinct orders of men as He created distinct species of animals and plants. Men are born to be Brahmans, soldiers, agriculturists, or servants, but since a Brahman may marry a woman from any of these castes, an endless number of sub-castes arises.

Hinduism has always shown great tolerance for varieties of belief and practice. Ideas pleasant and unpleasant have been assimilated: fetichism, demon-cults, animal-worship, sexual-cults (such as the rites of *Kali* in Calcutta). Today, as would be expected in a country which is in the throes of vast social change, Hinduism itself is changing. Under the impact of modern conditions new ideas are destroying old beliefs and customs. *See also* Jainism, Sikhism.

Humanism, the term applied to (1) a system of education based on the Greek and Latin classics; and (2) the vigorous attitudes that accompanied the end of the Middle Ages and were represented at different periods by the Renaissance, the Reformation, the Industrial Revolution, and the struggle for democracy. These include: release from ecclesiastical authority, the liberation of the intellect, faith in progress, the belief that man himself can improve his own conditions without supernatural help and, indeed, has a duty to do so. " Man is the measure of all things " is the keynote of humanism. The humanist has faith in man's intellectual and spiritual resources not only to bring knowledge and understanding of the world but to solve the moral problems of how to use that knowledge. That man should show respect to man irrespective of class, race or creed is fundamental to the humanist attitude to life. Among the fundamental moral principles he would count those of freedom, justice and happiness.

Today the idea that people can live an honest, meaningful life without following a formal religious creed of some kind does not seem particularly shocking. It is an interesting gauge of the rapid change in social attitudes to religion that when, less than twenty years ago, the psychologist Margaret Knight tentatively advanced this thesis in a short B.B.C. talk, public opinion seemed to be outraged and both Mrs. Knight and the B.B.C. were openly attacked by the popular press for immoral and seditious teachings.

The British Humanist Association condemns the religious clauses of the 1944 Education Act and wants compulsory religious instruction in schools abolished.

Humanity, Religion of. *See* Positivism.

Hussites, the followers of John Hus, the most famous pupil of John Wyclif. He was the rector of Prague University and, although it is now by no means certain that his beliefs were heretical, he was condemned to death for heresy and burnt at the stake in 1415 at Constance whence he had come with a safe conduct issued by the Emperor Sigismund of Hungary. The latter based his action on the doctrine that no faith need be kept with heretics, but it is obvious that the main objection to Hus was his contempt for authority of any kind. After their leader's death, the Hussites became a formidable body in Bohemia and Moravia. They took up arms on behalf of their faith, their religion being strongly imbued with political feeling (hostility to Germanism and to the supremacy of the Roman Church). Their religious struggles for reform led to the Hussite Wars during which the movement splintered into several groups.

I

Iconoclast Heresy. In 726 the Byzantine Emperor Leo III forbade the use of images in worship by Imperial decree—a decree which was continued intermittently until 843 when the heresy was abandoned. This was the Iconoclast controversy in which Emperor and Papacy were violently opposed. In the end the image-worshippers triumphed and the sacred pictures (icons) have remained to this day. This ecclesiastical conflict between the Iconoclasts and the Papacy over a matter of ritual was the first of the crises which over three centuries were finally to bring about the schism between Orthodox Christendom and Western Christendom. Though temporary, the supremacy of the State over the Church was nevertheless of supreme importance. Although the Iconoclast heresy is often given as the reason for the absence of statues in the Eastern Churches there is no evidence that they existed to any extent even before the movement began.

Idealism, in a philosophical sense, the belief that there is no matter in the universe, that all that exists is mind or spirit. *See* Mind and Matter and Realism.

Immaculate Conception, one of the important dogmas concerning the Blessed Virgin Mary, as taught by the Roman Catholic Church, is that she was conceived and born without original sin (according to a bull of Pius IX, 1854). Christians in general believe in the immaculate conception of Jesus Christ.

Immortality. The belief in a life after death has been widely held since the earliest times. It has certainly not been universal, nor has it always taken a form which everyone would find satisfying. In the early stages of human history or prehistory everything contained a spirit (*see* Animism) and it is obvious from the objects left in early graves that the dead were expected to exist in some form after death. The experience of dreams, too, seemed to suggest to the unsophisticated that there was a part of man which could leave his body and wander elsewhere during sleep. In order to save space, it will be helpful to classify the various types of belief which have existed in philosophical thought regarding this problem: (1) There is the idea that, although *something* survives bodily death, it is not necessarily eternal. Thus most primitive peoples were prepared to believe that man's spirit haunted the place around his grave and that food and drink should be set out for it, but that this spirit did not go on forever and gradually faded away. (2) The ancient Greeks and Hebrews believed for the most part that the souls of the dead went to a place of shades there to pine for the world of men. Their whining ghosts spent eternity in a dark, uninviting region in misery and remorse. (3) Other people, and there were many more of these, believed in the transmigration of souls with the former life of the individual determining whether his next life would be at a higher or lower level. Sometimes this process seems to have been thought of as simply going on and on, by others (*e.g.*, in Hinduism and Buddhism) as terminating in either non-sentience or union with God but in any case in annihilation of the self as self. Believers in this theory were the Greek philosophers Pythagoras, Empedocles, Plato (who believed that soul comes from God and strives to return to God, according to his own rather confused notions of the deity. If it fails to free itself completely from the body it will sink lower and lower from one body to another.) Plotinus held similar views to Plato, and many other religious sects in addition to those mentioned have believed in transmigration. (4) The belief of Plato and Aristotle that if souls continue to exist after death there is no reason why they should not have existed before birth (this in part is covered by (3)), but some have pointed out that eternity does not mean " from now on," but the whole of time before and after " now "—nobody, however, so far as one knows, held that *individual* souls so exist. (5) The theory that the soul does not exist at all and therefore immortality is meaningless: this was held by Anaximenes in early Greek times; by Leucippus, Democritus, and the other Greek atomists; by the Epicureans from the Greek Epicurus to the Roman Lucretius; by the British Hobbes and Hume; by Comte of France; and William James and John Dewey of America. (6) The thesis, held notably by Locke and Kant, that although we cannot prove the reality of soul and immortality by pure reason, belief in them should be held for moral ends. (For the orthodox Christian view *see* God and Man, Determinism and Free-will.) From this summary we can see that many philosophies and religions (with the important exceptions of Islam and Christianity) without denying a future life do deny the permanence of the individual soul in anything resembling its earthly form (*see* Spiritualism, Psychic research).

Imperialism, the practice by a country, which has become a nation and embarked upon commercial and industrial expansion, of acquiring and administering territories, inhabited by peoples usually at a lower stage of development, as colonies or dependencies. Thus the " typical " imperialist powers of the 19th cent. and earlier were Britain, Belgium, Holland, Spain, and Portugal, whilst Germany, Italy, and Japan, which either did not have unity during this period or adequate industrial expansion, tried to make good their lacks in this direction by war in the 20th cent. The term " imperialism " is not easy to define today (although often enough used as a term of abuse). There is economic imperialism exerted, not through armies, but through economic penetration. There is what may be described as ideological imperialism, *e.g.*, the anti-communist crusade that led America (in the name of freedom) into acts of appalling inhumanity in Vietnam; the dogmatism that led the Soviet Union into the invasion of Czechoslovakia. The Afrikaners in South Africa pass laws to permit the exploitation of the black and coloured peoples in their midst. Israel, too, whatever one may think of its creation on humanitarian grounds, is surely a piece of land taken from the Arabs who formed 90 per cent of its population, by a people whose only rational claim is that their ancestors lived there two thousand years ago. Imperialism is a dangerous word and, before using it, we would do well to remember the retort of a British statesman who, when lecturing in America prior to Indian independence, was asked by an elderly matron: " What are you going to do about the Indians? " " Which Indians, madam —ours or yours? "

Irrationalism. An attitude that puts emotion and passion before reason.

Islam, the religion of which Mohammed (570–632) was the prophet, the word signifying submission to the will of God. It is one of the most widespread of religions. Its adherents are called Moslems or Muslims. Islam came later than the other great monotheistic religions (Judaism and Christianity) and may be regarded in some respects as a heresy. Mohammed accepted the inspiration of the Old Testament and claimed to be a successor to Moses, and although he did not recognise Jesus as God, he did recognise Him as a prophet (*see* Docetism).

The sacred book of Islam is the Koran, the most influential book in the world next to the Bible. According to Islamic belief the words were revealed to the prophet by God through the angel Gabriel at intervals over a period of 20 years, first at his native Mecca, and then at Medina. The book is divided into 114 *suras* or chapters: all but one begin with the words: " In the name of Allah, the Merciful, the Compassionate." It is written in classical Arabic, and Moslems memorise much or all of it. The Koran superseded the Gospel as Mohammed superseded Christ. Its ethical teachings are high.

The great advantage of Mohammedism is that, like orthodox Judaism, it is a literal-minded religion lived in everyday life. No Moslem is in any doubt as to exactly how he should carry on in the events of his day. He has five duties: (1) Once in his life he must say with absolute conviction: " There is no God but Allah, and Mohammed is His Prophet." (2) Prayer preceded by ablution must be five times daily—on rising, at noon, in mid-afternoon, after sunset, and before retiring. The face of the worshipper is turned in the direction of Mecca. (3) The giving of alms generously, including provisions for the poor. (4) The keeping of the fast of Ramadan, the holy month, during which believers in good health may neither eat nor drink nor indulge in worldly pleasures between sunrise and sunset. (5) Once in his life a Moslem, if he can, must make the pilgrimage to Mecca. In addition, drinking, gambling, and the eating of pork are forbidden and circumcision is practised. Polygamy is permitted, although decreasing; sexual relations outside marriage are disapproved of: marriage is only with the wife's consent; and divorce may be initiated by either husband or wife. A great advantage in the spread of Islam has been its lack of race prejudice.

Mohammed's main achievements were the destruction of idolatry, the welding of warring tribes into one community, the progress of a conquest which led after his death to the great and cultured empire which spread throughout the Middle East into north Africa, north India, and ultimately to Spain. That it did not spread all over Europe was due to the Muslim defeat by Charles Martel at Tours in 732 A.D.

J

Jainism. The Jains are a small Indian sect, largely in commerce and finance, numbering about 2 million. Their movement founded by Vardhamana, called Mahavira (the great hero), in the 6th cent. B.C. arose rather earlier than Buddhism in revolt against the ritualism and impersonality of Hinduism (*q.v.*). It rejects the authority of the early Hindu Vedas and does away with many of the Hindu deities whose place is largely taken by Jainism's twenty-four immortal saints; it despises caste distinctions and modifies the two great Hindu doctrines of *karma* and transmigration. Jain philosophy is based on *ahimsa*, the sacredness of all life, regarding even plants as the brethren of mankind, refusing to kill even the smallest insect.

Jansenism, the name given by the Roman Catholic Church to the heresy of Cornelius Jansen (1585–1638), a Dutch-born professor of theology at Louvain, derived from his work *Augustinus*, published after his death. This book set out to prove, by a study of the works of St. Augustine, that Augustine's teachings on grace, predestination and free-will (which, of course, Augustine denied) were opposed to Jesuit teaching. Already hostile to Jansen for forbidding them entry to Louvain university, the Jesuits were outraged and in 1653 Pope Innocent V condemned five of Jansen's propositions as heretical. This produced one of the most famous controversies in history in which the scholars and divines of the great convent of Port Royal in Paris defended the *Augustinus*, for which they were later expelled from their posts. Meanwhile the great Pascal (1623–62) had taken up his pen in their defence and exposed Jesuit hypocrisy in his *Lettres Provinciales*, one of the masterpieces of world literature for its brilliant phrasing, delicate irony, and deadly quotation from Jesuit writings. The Letters had given influence, filled the Jesuits with rage, but even Pascal could not stop the cruel persecution which followed. Another Jansenist text-book was published late in the century, Quesnel's *Moral Reflections on the New Testament*, which Pope Clement XI in his bull *Unigenitus* condemned as heretical in 1713. The French Church was split from top to bottom, the aged king Louis XIV supported the bull, and in 1720 it was made part of French law. Most Jansenists fled the country. Thus ended Jansenism in France but a small sect still exists in Holland, Catholic in everything except acceptance of the *Unigenitus*.

Jehovah's Witnesses, a religious body who consider themselves to be the present-day representatives of a religious movement which has existed since Abel " offered unto God a more excellent sacrifice than Cain, by which he obtained witness that he was righteous." Abel was the first " witness," and amongst others were Enoch, Noah, Abraham, Moses, Jeremiah, and John the Baptist. Pre-eminent among witnesses, of course, was Jesus Christ who is described in the Book of Revelation as " the faithful and true witness." Thus they see themselves as " the Lord's organisation," in the long line of those who through the ages have preserved on earth the true and pure worship of God or, as the Witnesses prefer to call Him, " Jehovah-God."

So far as other people are aware, the movement was founded by Charles Taze Russell (Pastor Russell) of Allegany, Pittsburgh, Pennsylvania, U.S.A. in 1881 under the name, adopted in 1896, of the Watch Tower Bible and Tract Society, which has continued as the controlling organisation of Jehovah's Witnesses. Its magazine, *The Watch Tower Announcing Jehovah's Kingdom*, first published in 1879, and other publications are distributed by the zealous members who carry out the house-to-house canvassing. The movement has a strong leadership.

Their teaching centres upon the early establishment of God's new world on earth, preceded by the second coming of Christ. Witnesses believe this has already happened, and that Armageddon " will come as soon as the Witness is completed." The millennial period will give sinners a second chance of salvation and " millions now living will never die " (the title of one of their pamphlets).

The dead will progressively be raised to the new earth until all the vacant places left after Armageddon are filled. There is, however, some doubt about the " goatish souls " who have made themselves unpleasant to the Witnesses, those who have accepted (or permitted to be accepted) a blood-transfusion contrary to the Scriptures, and others who have committed grave sins.

Every belief held by the movement, it is claimed can be upheld, chapter and verse, by reference to the Scriptures. Witnesses regard the doctrine of the Trinity as devised by Satan. In both wars Witnesses have been in trouble for their refusal to take part in war and it is only fair to add that six thousand suffered for the same reason in German concentration camps.

Judaism, the religion of the Jews, the oldest of the great monotheist religions, parent of Christianity and Islam, the development of which is presented in the Old Testament. The creed of Judaism is based on the concept of a transcendent and omnipotent One True God, the revelation of His will in the *Torah*, and the special relation between God and His " Chosen People." The idea of Incarnation is rejected, Jesus is not recognised as the Messiah. The *Torah* is the Hebrew name for the Law of Moses (the Pentateuch) which, Judaism holds, was divinely revealed to Moses on Mount Sinai soon after

the exodus of the Israelites from Egypt (1230 B.C.). Many critics deny the Mosaic authorship of the first five books of the Bible and believe them to be a compilation from four main sources known as J (Jahvist), E (Elohist), D (Deuteronomist) and P (Priestly Code), distinguished from each other by the name used for God, language, style, and internal evidence. From the historical point of view an important influence on Judaism may have been the monotheism of Ikhnaton, the " heretic " Pharaoh (note, for example, the derivation of Psalm 104 from Ikhnaton's " Hymn to the Sun ").

The Talmud is a book containing the civil and canonical laws of the Jews and includes the Mishna, a compilation from oral tradition written in Hebrew, and the Gemara, a collection of comments and criticisms by the Jewish rabbis, written in Aramaic. There are in fact two Talmuds: the one made in Palestine (the Jerusalem Talmud), finished at the beginning of the 5th cent., and the other made in Babylon, completed at the end of the 6th cent.

Judaism at the beginning of the Christian era had a number of sects: (1) the Pharisees (whose views include the first clear statement of the resurrection of the just to eternal life and the future punishment of the wicked) who held to the *Torah* and the universality of God; (2) the Sadducees, the upper class of priests and wealthy landowners, to whom God was essentially a national God and who placed the interests of the state before the *Torah*; they rejected ideas of resurrection and eternal life; (3) the Essenes (*q.v.*) who were regarded as a puritanical break-away movement by both parties. The views of the Pharisees prevailed.

Jewish writing continued through the years and some books were added to the *Torah*, among them the Three Major Prophets and certain books of the Twelve Minor Prophets. There were also the Apocalyptic writers who were unorthodox in their preaching of a divinely planned catastrophic end to the world with a " new Heaven and a new earth," preceded by a divine Messiah, and a future life—all of which beliefs influenced early Christianity. Judah Halevi of Toledo (c. 1085–c. 1140) and Moses Maimonides of Cordova (1135–1204) were the great Jewish philosophers.

Modern movements in Judaism stem from the Enlightenment, notably with Moses Mendelssohn in the 18th cent. who accepted, as was the tendency of the period, only that which could be proved by reason. He translated the Pentateuch into German thus encouraging German Jews to give up Yiddish and Hebrew for the language of the land and thereby preparing them for their vast contribution to Western civilisation. One of his disciples, David Friedländer (d. 1834) instituted " reform " Judaism behind which lay the desire for assimilation. He wanted to eliminate anything that would hamper the relationships of Jews with their neighbours or tend to call in doubt their loyalty to their adopted state. A similar movement in America (1885) called for the rejection of dietary laws, the inauguration of Sunday services, and the repudiation of Jewish nationalism. Between " reform " and orthodoxy there arose the conservative movement which, in England, includes prayers in English in the service, does not segregate men and women in the synagogue, and translates the Law in a more liberal way. (The fact is that it would be almost impossible for a strictly orthodox Jew to live in a modern industrialised community at all.)

Judaism is essentially a social and family religion which, more than almost any other, concerns itself with the observances of every aspect of daily life. As in Islam (*q.v.*) details are laid down in the most minute way for the behaviour of the orthodox.

The home is the main Jewish institution and Jews, like Catholics, cannot surrender their religion. Circumcision takes place eight days after birth, and a boy becomes a man for religious purposes at his Bar Mitzvah at the age of thirteen. Women are spared most of this because their place in the home is considered sufficiently sacred. Among festivals are Passover, recalling the Exodus; Rosh Hashanah (the Jewish New Year), the anniversary of the

Creation and the beginning of ten days of penitence ending with Yom Kippur (the Day of Atonement), a day of fasting spent in the synagogue; Purim, celebrating the deliverance of the Jews from Haman; and Chanukah, celebrating their victory against the Syrians under their leader Judas Maccabeus. A new and semi-religious festival is the Yom Haatzmaut, the anniversary of the birth of the new Jewish state of Israel.

K

Karma. See Buddhism, Hinduism.

Ku Klux Klan. After the American Civil War (1861–65) southern conservatives and ex-Confederate leaders began to fear (as they had every reason to do) both Negro and poor White rule. Taxes were rising owing to radical legislation and the tax-burdened and disenfranchised planters finally took to illegal means to achieve their ends by trying to effect an alliance with the poor White and small farmer through appealing to his anti-Negro prejudice.

Hence the Ku Klux Klan was formed in 1866 as a secret society by a small group of Confederate veterans in Tennessee with the intention of frightening Negroes by dressing in ghostly white robes in the guise of the spirits of dead soldiers. But the movement spread like wild-fire throughout the South encouraged by small farmers and planters alike. General Nathan Bedford Forrest was appointed " Grand Wizard " of the Klan " empire " and in every community armed Klansmen riding at night horsewhipped " uppity " Negroes, beat Union soldiers, and threatened carpet-bag politicians (i.e., fortune-hunters from the North). Soon several similar organisations arose, many of which did not stop at torture, burning property and murder. In fact, although claiming to be a " holy crusade " the Klan was a vicious and contemptible organisation in which former Southern leaders trying to regain control deliberately set poor and middle-class Whites against the Negroes by appeal to race-prejudice. Congress struck back with laws and intervention of Federal troops, and after a large number of convictions in South Carolina much of the violence stopped even if the feelings continued.

After the 1914–18 war the movement, dormant since 1900, revived as a sadistic anti-Negro, anti-Jewish, anti-Catholic society, spreading to the north as well as the south. By 1926, with its white-gowned hooligans and fiery crosses, the Klan began to subside once more. But it rose again after the second world war. After some cruel racial murders in Alabama during 1964–5 President Johnson denounced K-K-K terrorism and promised new criminal legislation to deal with the Klan.

Kuomintang, a Chinese Nationalist party founded in 1891 by Sun Yat Sen. It took part in the first Chinese revolution of 1911 and led the second the following year, dominating south China by 1930 and, under Chiang Kai-shek, who succeeded Sun Yat Sen on his death in 1925, conducted China's defence against Japanese invasion from 1937–45. Sun Yat Sen had attempted to found a democratic republic based on Western parliamentary democracy and in his famous *Testament* laid down the principles upon which the constitution of China should be based. In 1946, Sun Fo, the son of Sun Yat Sen, deplored the party's departure from the principles of social democracy and the welfare of the people in which his father had believed. Beginning as a movement largely inspired by Russia, the Kuomintang under Chiang Kai-shek degenerated into a reactionary and corrupt military oligarchy which, collapsing in 1949, was replaced by the Communist party, leaving Chiang and his followers to rule Formosa with American aid.

L

Lamaism, the religion of Tibet. Its beliefs and worship derive from the Mahayana form of Buddhism which was introduced into Tibet in 749 A.D. The emphasis laid by its founder on the necessity for self-discipline and conversion through meditation and the study of philosophy deteriorated into formal monasticism and ritualism. The Dalai Lama, as the reincarnated Buddha, was both king and high priest, a sort of pope and emperor rolled into one. Under him was a hierarchy of officials in which the lowest order was that of the monks who became as numerous as one man in every six or seven of the population. The main work carried out by this vast church-state was the collection of taxes to maintain the monasteries and other religious offices. Second in power to the Dalai Lama was the Panchen or Tashi Lama believed to be a reincarnation of Amitabha, another Buddha. The last Dalai Lama fled to India in 1959 when the Chinese entered his country. For a brief period following his departure, the Panchen Lama surprised the Western world by publicly welcoming the Communist invasion. How much of this was due to coercion at the time is not clear, but he later renounced the regime and the suppression of Lamaism in Tibet continued unchecked.

Latitudinarians, Anglican churchmen of exceedingly broad views (e.g., bishops who would admit dissenters—i.e., those rejecting the views or authority of the Established Church). Although still used today, the term applies especially to such eminent 17th cent. divines as Burnet, Hales, Tillotson, and Chillingworth.

Levellers, an English military-politico-religious party prominent in the Parliamentary Army about 1647 which stood for the rights of the people. See Diggers.

Liberalism. The Liberal Party is the successor to the Whigs (a nickname derived from *whigga-more* used in the 17th cent. for Scottish dissenters) of the 18th and 19th cent. Prior to the victory of the Labour Party in 1922, it was one of the two main British political parties. Liberals are moderately progressive in the sense that most appreciate the humanistic aspects of socialism while strongly disapproving of its policies of state control, and they dislike any form of monopoly, state-run or otherwise. In general, the Party advocates co-ownership in industry, electoral reform (proportional representation), protection of individual liberties, governmental reform, tax reform, strict measures against any form of monopoly, and separate parliaments for Scotland and Wales.

Logical Positivism, a school of philosophy founded in Vienna in the 1920s by a group known as " the Vienna circle ": their work was based on that of Ernst Mach, but dates in essentials as far back as Hume. Of the leaders of the group, Schlick was murdered by a student, Wittgenstein came to Britain, and Carnap went to America following the entry of the Nazis. Briefly the philosophy differs from all others in that, while most people have believed that a statement might be (a) true, or (b) false, logical positivists consider there to be a third category; a statement may be meaningless. There are only two types of statement which can be said to have meaning: (1) those which are tautological, i.e., those in which the statement is merely a definition of the subject, such as " a triangle is a three-sided plane figure " (" triangle " and " three-sided plane figure " are the same thing); and (2) those which can be tested by sense experience. This definition of meaningfulness excludes a great deal of what has previously been thought to be the field of philosophy; in particular it excludes the possibility of metaphysics. Thus the question as to whether there is a God or whether free-will exists is strictly meaningless, for it is neither a tautological statement nor can it be tested by sense-experience.

Lollards, a body of religious reformers and followers of Wyclif who were reviled and persecuted in the reign of Richard II. The name " Lollard " comes from the old English word meaning " mutterer "—a term of contempt used to describe the sect. Henry IV renewed his father's persecution of the group, even condemning one of his own personal friends, the Lollard leader Sir John Oldcastle, to be burnt at the stake.

Luddites, a group of peasants and working men

who deliberately destroyed spinning and farm machinery in England in the early part of the 19th cent., fearing that such devices would destroy their livelihood. Their name was taken from the eccentric Ned Lud who had done the same in a less organised way two or three decades earlier. The Luddites' worst fears were of course not realised, for far from putting human beings out of work the industrial revolution created jobs for a vastly increased population. Luddism, dormant for over a century, is beginning to appear again, if in muted form. Public anxiety about the rapid growth in computer technology is manifesting itself in the form of such groups as the Society for the Abolition of Data Processing Machines, which while not of course dedicated to the physical destruction of computers, urge for social and even governmental checks on the development of such things as " data banks." These are vast computer memory stores listing comprehensive records concerning all the people living in a city or country and able to cross-reference them in a way that has never previously been possible. The arguments for and against such data banks and other developments in computer technology are beyond the scope of this section, but the rise of this 20th cent. Luddism is of considerable historical and social significance.

Lutheranism. The Reformation had a long history before it became, under Luther and Calvin, an accepted fact. The mediaeval Church had held (as the Catholic Church holds today) that the sacraments were the indispensable means of salvation. Since these were exclusively administered by the clergy, any movement which attacked clerical abuses was forced by sheer necessity to deny the Church's exclusive control of the means of salvation, before it could become free from dependence on a corrupt priesthood. Hence the Albigenses and the Waldenses (qq.v.), the followers of John Hus and Wyclif (see Anticlericalism), were bound to deny the authority of the Church and emphasise that of the Bible. Luther began his movement primarily in order to reform the Church from its gross abuses and the famous ninety-five theses nailed to the door of the Church at Wittenberg in 1517 were not primarily theological but moral complaints dealing with the actual behaviour of the clergy rather than Church beliefs. But, unlike the earlier reformers, Luther had arrived at the right moment in history when economic individualism and the force of nationalism were bound, sooner or later, to cause the authorities in Germany to line up on his side. Thus he began with the support of the peasants who were genuinely shocked at the abuse of indulgences and other matters, but ended up by being supported by the noblemen who wanted to destroy the power of the pope over the German states and looked forward to confiscating the lands and property of the Church. When the peasants wanted the reform of actual economic abuses relating to the feudal system, Luther took the side of the nobles against them. The contemporary movement in Switzerland led by Ulrich Zwingli had no such secular support, and Zwingli was killed in 1531.

Martin Luther (1483–1546) was the son of a miner in Eisleben in Saxony, entered the order of Austin Friars in 1505, and later taught at the newly founded university of Wittenberg. After the publication of the theses the real issue so far as the Church was concerned was whether he was willing or not to submit to the authority of his superiors; Luther refused to compromise with his conscience in the famous words: " Here I stand; I can do no other." In a further statement Luther recommended the formation of a German national church, the abolition of indulgences and other means whereby Rome obtained money from Germany, and an end to the celibacy of the clergy. For this he was naturally excommunicated. His teaching was based on the German translation of the Bible, but he was by no means a fundamentalist: e.g., he denied that the Book of Hebrews was written by Paul, would have nothing to do with the Apocalypse, and regarded the letter of James as " an epistle of straw." The Scriptures were open to all and could be interpreted by private judgment enlightened by the Spirit of God.

Like Calvin, Luther was a predestinarian and determinist, but he was also a conservative and soon became alarmed about the position taken by many extremists once the Reformation was under way. He had really wanted the Church to reform itself, but when he alienated Rome he had perforce to rely more and more on the secular powers which finally resulted in the state-church form which became pronounced in Prussia and later elsewhere. Whereas Calvin wished the Church to be at least the equal of the State and in some respects its superior, Luther's rebellion resulted in the reverse, a state-controlled episcopalianism. See Calvinism, Presbyterianism.

M

McLuhanism. The name of Marshall McLuhan came into wide prominence in Britain about 1967. What is McLuhanism? Or rather, what are the aspects of the unusual explorations of this Canadian professor, whose three books appeared in this country at about the same time to make such an effective impact? The titles of the books are *The Mechanical Bride* (1951), *The Gutenberg Galaxy* (1962), and *Understanding Media* (1964). McLuhan pours out his ideas about the whole process of communication as it has extended mankind's horizons, and therefore mankind himself, from the invention of movable type up to and through the mechanical age. We are in the midst of a revolution right now, with vast sociological and technological changes; and we have not yet attained a language to match our need for communication in the new electronic age. It is the *form* of the new media—radio, television, films, and so on—which affects our patterns of human association rather than the *contents*. Hence the phrase " the medium is the message." It is therefore McLuhan's purpose to understand the social changes brought about by all these media which, outside the body and outside the brain, are extensions of oneself—the telephone, photography, record players, radio, T.V., computers, and so on. All these are wielding a power over us beyond our control and McLuhan turns his sardonic, witty, epigrammatic eye and pen on the new, cryptic, changing Electronic Man. McLuhan is a joker all right, but a very original one; and underneath the compelling and allusive wit are seams of sense still to be explored as time goes on. The ideas of *The Gutenberg Galaxy* are in essence that there have been two great turning points in human understanding since man learnt to read and write: the invention of the printed book and now the present electronic revolution. The old linear, logical method of thought and expression affected areas of our activity beyond what are normally associated with printing or even language; now, too, the present transformation is changing civilisation in a way still to be assessed, with profound and unsuspected changes in attitudes and thinking. We are being tightened up into a " global village," information flooding in to us from everywhere in unmanageable quantities, time and space being annihilated. There seems nothing which will not be affected: our personalities, the relations between individuals and between communities, war, crime, race, religion, literature, everything. Like a boxer McLuhan jabs this way and that, with an aphorism here and an epigram there, and allusions all the time. In a whirling attack on so many things about which we have grown comfortable and complacent, we are drawn in to construe the exciting messages from the frontier of a new and exciting age.

Magic, a form of belief originating in very early days and based on the primitive's inability to distinguish between similarity and identity. The simplest example would perhaps be the fertility rites in which it is believed that a ceremony involving sexual relations between men and women will bring about fertility in the harvest. Or the idea that sticking pins in an image of an individual will bring about harm or even death to the real person. Magic is regarded by some as a form of early science in that man in his efforts to control Nature had recourse to magical practices when the only methods he knew had failed to bring the desired results. It filled a gap. By others magic is regarded as an elementary stage in the evolution of religion. It can be said to have served a purpose there too. Yet magic differs from religion, however closely at times it may come to be related with it, in this important respect: religion depends upon a power *outside and beyond* human beings, whereas magic depends upon nothing but the casting of a spell or the performance of a ceremony—the result follows automatically. (We do well, as Dr. Margaret Murray reminds us, to keep in mind " that when anything regarded as out of the ordinary course of nature is brought about by human means it is called a miracle if the magician belongs to the beholder's own religion, but it is magic—often black magic—if the wizard belongs to another religion. In Grimm's words, ' Miracle is divine, Magic is devilish.' ")

The idea that " like produces like " is at the roots of imitative magic, and it is interesting to note that in some languages (*e.g.*, Hebrew and Arabic) there is no word for " resembles " or " similar to." Hence one says " All thy garments are myrrh " instead of " are *like* myrrh." It follows that an event can be compelled by imitating it. One engages in swinging, not for pleasure, but to produce a wind as the swing does; ball games are played to get rainy weather because the black ball represents dark rain-clouds; other ball games, in which one attempts to catch the ball in a cup or hit it with a stick, represent the sexual act (as some gentlemen at Lords may be distressed to hear) and bring about fertility; in medicine up till a few centuries ago herbs were chosen to cure a disease because in some respects their leaves or other parts looked like the part of the body affected (*e.g.*, the common wildflower still known as " eyebright " was used in bathing the eyes because the flower looks like a tiny eye).

Traces of these beliefs are still found today in children's games and the spells accompanying them have turned into nursery rhymes: dolls are the images of deposed gods or idols; tug-of-war was formerly a sex-conflict with men pulling one end and women the other to bring about fertility; skittles when knocked down by a ball produced the thunder-noise necessary to produce rain. There is reason to believe that the oldest words known in English, relics of our prehistoric language, are " Ena, mena, mina, mo " of the nursery rhyme.

Divination is another aspect of magic and no general of the past would have gone to war without consulting his diviners who referred to animals' livers, how the sacred chickens ate, or the way ceremonially shot arrows fell. Even Cicero wrote a book on divination discussing the significance of dreams, premonitions, and the flight of birds, which revealed the purposes of the gods. If we find it difficult to make any distinction between diviners, priests, medicine-men, rain-makers, shamans, and witch-doctors of early societies. we could perhaps say that they have crystallised out into priests, scientists, and humbugs of our own day. For it would appear that magic, like witchcraft, still exists today—not merely in the form of children's stories and fears, or grown-ups' enjoyment of creepy tales, belief in fortune-telling, omens, and amulets—but as cults attracting many who ought to have more sense. *See* Witchcraft, Demonism.

Malthusianism, the theory about population growth put forward by the Rev. Thomas Malthus (1766–1834) in *An Essay on Population* (1798). His three main propositions were: (1) " Population is necessarily limited by means of subsistence." (2) " Population invariably increases where means of subsistence increase, unless prevented by some very powerful and obvious checks." (3) " These checks, and the checks which repress the superior power of population, and keep its effects on a level with the means of subsistence, are all resolvable into moral restraint, vice and misery." In other words, no matter how great the food supply may

become, human reproductive power will always adjust itself so that food will always be scarce in relation to population; the only means to deal with this is by " moral restraint " (*i.e.*, chastity or not marrying), " vice " (*i.e.*, birth-control methods), or misery (*i.e.*, starvation). More specifically, Malthus claimed that while food increases by arithmetical progression, population increases by geometrical progression.

It is true that these gloomy predictions did not take place in Malthus's time largely owing to the opening up of new areas of land outside Europe, the development of new techniques in agriculture, the growth of international trade to poorer areas, the increased knowledge of birth-control, and developments in medical science which reduced the misery he had predicted. Furthermore, we now know that as a society becomes industrialised its birth-rate tends to fall. Nevertheless there are very few scientists who are not perturbed by the growth in the world's population which has increased from about 465 million in 1650 to over 3,000 million today.

Manichaeism. The early Christian apologists who had not yet acquired an adequate knowledge of philosophy had little intellectual trouble in dealing with the heathen; their trouble arose when confronted with religions which had a philosophical basis. Thus Gnosticism (*q.v.*) caused them a good deal of concern, Neoplatonism (*see* God and Man) rather less, since it could never appeal to the masses, and Manichaeism considerable anxiety. because it could appeal both to the philosopher and the masses. Mithraism (*q.v.*), the only other serious contendant, was troublesome for a different reason in that it was the religion of the Roman army and bore a close resemblance to Christianity itself.

Manichaeism was an Asiatic religion which developed from Zoroastrianism (*q.v.*) and shows the influence of Buddhism (*q.v.*) and Gnosticism (*q.v.*) being founded by Mani, a Persian, who was born in Babylonia, *c.* 216 A.D. Mani presented himself to Shapur I as the founder of a new religion which was to be to Babylonia what Buddhism was to India or Christianity to the West. His aspiration was to convert the East and he himself made no attempt to interfere directly with Christianity although he represented himself as the Paraclete (the Holy Ghost or " Comforter ") and, like Jesus, had twelve disciples. His success in Persia aroused the fury of the Zoroastrian priests who objected to his reforming zeal towards their religion and in 276 Mani was taken prisoner and crucified.

Of Mani's complicated system little can be said here, save that it is based on the struggle of two eternal conflicting principles, God and matter, or light and darkness. Like the Albigenses (who followed much of this heresy) Mani divided the faithful into two classes: the " Perfect " who were to practise the most rigid asceticism, and the " Hearers " whose discipline was much less severe. After death the former went to heaven immediately, the latter reached it only through a kind of purgatory, and the unbelievers were doomed to hell. Although its founder had no intention of interfering with the West, after his death his followers soon spread the religion from Persia and Mesopotamia to India and China. (Manichaeism flourished in China until the 11th cent.) It reached as far as Spain and Gaul and influenced many of the bishops in Alexandria and in Carthage where for a time St. Augustine accepted Manichaeism. Soon the toleration accorded it under Constantine ended and it was treated as a heresy and violently suppressed. Yet it later influenced many heresies, including, as we have seen, the Albigenses, and it even had some influence on orthodox Catholicism which had a genius for picking up elements in other religions which had been shown to appeal to worshippers provided they did not conflict unduly with fundamental beliefs.

Maoism is the branch of communism that reigns in China. It has been shaped by one of the most remarkable statesmen of modern times, Mao Tse-tung, who has set the pattern of revolution for poor peasant societies. The communist movement may be likened to a river

J31

with three principal streams: the left, represented by China, the right, represented by Yugoslavia, and the middle, represented by the Soviet Union. In Russia the civil war developed *after* the revolution; in China the communists fought their civil war *before* they seized power; the Yugoslav partisans won their own guerrilla war against the fascist powers—differences which had important political consequences. Russia suffered three decades of isolationism and totalitarian suppression (" an isolated and besieged fortress ") before the death of Stalin. Then came a marked, if zigzagging shift towards " liberalisation." Mao Tse-tung holds to the orthodox Leninist view about capitalism and communism, regards *détente* as a dangerous illusion and compromise and " revisionism " as a fatal error. The ideological dispute between these two great communist powers has developed since 1960 when Khrushchev ruthlessly withdrew economic aid and technical assistance and forced China into isolationism. It has been likened to the East–West schism in the Christian church. The solution is by no means predictable but having come through the " hundred flowers " campaign, the " great leap forward," and the " cultural revolution," China in foreign affairs is now reacting against isolationism. *See* **Section C, Part I.**

Maronites, a Roman Catholic community of Christians living in the Mount Lebanon region. Their secular clergy marry as in the Greek Church, but their bishops are celibate.

Marxism. The sociological theories founded by Karl Marx and Friedrich Engels on which modern communist thought is based. Marx and Engels lived in a period of unrestrained capitalism when exploitation and misery were the lot of the industrial working classes, and it was their humanitarianism and concern for social justice which inspired their work. They co-operated in 1848 in writing the *Communist Manifesto,* and in his great work, *Das Kapital* (1867), Marx worked out a new theory of society. He showed that all social systems are economically motivated and change as a result of technical and economic changes in methods of production. The driving force of social change Marx found to be in the struggle which the oppressed classes wage to secure a better future. Thus in his celebrated theory of historical materialism he interpreted history in terms of economics and explained the evolution of society in terms of class struggle. (*See* **Dialectical Materialism.**) " In the social production of their means of existence," he wrote, "men enter into definite and unavoidable relations which are independent of their will. These productive relationships correspond to the particular stage in the development of their material productive forces." Marx's theory of historical materialism implies that history is propelled by class struggle with communism and the classless society as the final stage when man will have emancipated himself from the productive process. Marx was the first to put socialism on a rational and scientific basis, and he foretold that socialism would inevitably replace capitalism and that in the transition period the revolutionary dictatorship of the proletariat would be necessary. His prophecy, however, came to realisation not in the advanced countries as he had envisaged but in backward Russia and China. *See also* **Communism.**

Mennonites. *See* **Baptists.**

Mensheviks. *See* **Bolshevism.**

Mesmerism, a rapidly vanishing name to denote the practice of hypnosis, which owes its popularity, though not its discovery, to the Frenchman Anton Mesmer (1733–1815). Mesmer's contribution was the realisation that a large number of what we would today call psychosomatic or hysterical conditions could be cured (or at least temporarily alleviated) by one or another form of suggestion. Mesmer himself relied on the idea of what he called " animal magnetism," a supposedly potent therapeutic force emanating from the living body which could be controlled by the trained individual. Mesmer used wands and impressive gadgetry to dispense the marvellous force and he effected a remarkable number of cures of complaints,

hitherto looked upon as incurable or totally mysterious in origin—the most typical of these being hysterical blindness, paralysis or deafness, nervous skin conditions, and so on. Hypnosis, which is a valid if very poorly understood psychological phenomenon even today, would probably have been developed much further had not efficient general anaesthetics such as ether, nitrous oxide, etc., been discovered, thus greatly diminishing its role as a pain reliever in surgery.

Mesmer, who was three parts charlatan, never really troubled to think deeply about the cause of his undoubted successes. The first man to treat hysteria as a formal class of illness and who made a scientific attempt to treat it with hypnosis was Ambrose Liébeault (1823–1904). He and his colleague Hippolyte Bernheim (1840–1919) believed: (*a*) that hysteria was produced by suggestion, and particularly by autosuggestion on the part of the patient, and (*b*) that suggestion was a normal trait found in varying degrees in everyone. These conclusions are true, but as Freud showed later are far from being the whole truth. *See* **Paris School of Psychotherapy.**

Methodism, the religious movement founded by John Wesley in 1738, at a time when the Anglican Church was in one of its periodic phases of spiritual torpor, with the simple aim of spreading " scriptural holiness " throughout the land. Up to that time Wesley had been a High Churchman but on a visit to Georgia in the United States he was much impressed by the group known as Moravians (*q.v.*), and on his return to this country was introduced by his brother Charles, who had already become an adherent, to Peter Böhler, a Moravian minister in England. Passing through a period of spiritual commotion following the meeting, he first saw the light at a small service in Aldersgate in May 1738 " where one was reading Luther's preface to the Epistle to the Romans " and from this time forth all Wesley's energies were devoted to the single object of saving souls. He did this for fifty years and at the end of his life confessed that he had wasted fifteen minutes in that time by reading a worthless book. Even when he was over eighty he still rose at 4 a.m. and toiled all day long.

Soon Whitefield, a follower with Calvinist views, was preaching throughout the country and Charles Wesley was composing his well-known hymns; John's abilities at this time were taken up in organising the movement described as " People called Methodists." They were to be arranged in " societies " which were united into " circuits " under a minister, the circuits into " districts " and all knit together into a single body under a conference of ministers which has met annually since 1744. Local lay preachers were also employed and to maintain interest the ministers were moved from circuit to circuit each year. These chapel services were not originally meant to conflict with the Church of England of which Wesley still considered himself a member. They were purely supplementary, and it used to be the custom (before the Methodists began to count themselves as Nonconformists) for Methodists to attend Church in the morning and Chapel in the evening.

The class-meeting was the unit of the organisation where members met regularly under a chosen leader to tell their " experiences " upon which they were often subjected to severe cross-examination. At the end of every quarter, provided their attendances were regular, they received a ticket of membership which entitled them to come to monthly sacramental services. If attendance was inadequate the name was removed from the list, without appearance on which nobody was deemed a member. The price of the ticket was " a penny a week and a shilling a quarter " but Wesley was not interested in receiving money from anyone who was not utterly devoted to the cause.

John Wesley introduced four other innovations, some of which were regarded by Churchmen who had previously been willing to commend his efforts in bringing religion to the poorer classes as dangerous: (1) He started the Sunday-school scheme and afterwards enthusiastically supported that of John Raikes, often regarded as the founder of the idea; this was of immense importance in the days before the Education Acts. (2) He reintroduced the Agapae or " love feasts " of the early Church which were fellowship meetings deepening the sense of brotherhood of the society. (3) He began to copy the open-air meetings of the eloquent Whitefield and soon unwittingly produced the most extraordinary results, finding that his sermons led to groans, tears, faintingfits, and all sorts of emotional expression. Even his open-air lay speakers produced like results and these came to be associated with Methodism and gave significance to the proud Anglican claim that *their* services would be " without enthusiasm." (4) After some hesitation he ventured to consecrate Dr. Thomas Coke, who was being sent as a missionary to America, as a bishop of his church. In addition to Wesley's religious work he was a great educator of the common man. Thus he introduced the cheap book and the church magazine, publishing books of any sort which he thought would edify and not harm even when the views expressed were different from his own—*e.g.*, Thomas à Kempis's *Imitation of Christ* and works of history biography, science, and medicine in some cases written by himself. In this way the movement with its cheap books and reading rooms had an influence far beyond its actual membership. Both the Anglican Church and the Evangelical movement of Wilberforce and others profited from Wesley's work. Some social historians, rightly or wrongly, have claimed that it was Wesley's influence among the working classes that spared England the revolutionary activity which characterised most other European countries during the first quarter of the 19th cent.

Methodism, especially after Wesley's death in 1791, began, like other movements, to develop schisms. There were the long-standing differences which the Baptist movement (*q.v.*) had shown too between Arminian and Calvinist sections—*i.e.*, between those who did and those who did not accept the doctrine of predestination. In the case of the Methodists, this led to a complete break in 1811. Then there were differences associated with the status of the laity, or the relationship of the movement with the Anglican Church. The " Methodist New Connection " of 1797 differed only in giving the laity equal representation with the ministers but the more important break of the Primitive Methodists in 1810 gave still more power to the laity and reintroduced the " camp-meeting " type of service. In 1815 the Bryanites or " Bible Christians " were formed, and a further schism which was even brought before the law courts was ostensibly over the foundation of a theological college. The real reason, of course, was that the ministers were becoming more Tory, whilst the laity were becoming more Radical. Finally in 1932, at a conference in the Albert Hall in London, the Wesleyan Methodists, the Primitive Methodists, and the United Methodists became one Church, the Methodist Church. Including America, where Methodism spread like wildfire, the Methodist is one of the largest Protestant Churches of today.

Mind and Matter.

Early Greek Views: Idealism and Dualism. Primitive peoples could see that there is a distinction between those things which move and do things by themselves and others, such as stones, which do not. Following the early state of Animism (*q.v.*), in which spirits were believed to have their abode in everything, they began to differentiate between matter or substance and a force which seems to move it and shape it into objects and things. Thus to the Greek Parmenides (fl. *c.* 475 B.C.), who was a philosopher of pure reason, thought or mind was the creator of what we observe and in some way not quite clear to himself it seemed that mind was the cause of everything. This is perhaps the first expression of the movement known as Idealism which says, in effect, that the whole universe is mental—a creation either of our own minds or the mind of God. But from Anaxagorus (488–428 B.C.) we have the clearer statement that mind or *nous* causes all movement but is distinct from the substance it moves.

He does not, however, think in terms of individual minds but rather of a kind of generalised mind throughout the universe which can be used as an explanation of anything which cannot be explained otherwise. This is the position known as Dualism (*q.v.*) which holds that both mind and matter exist and interact but are separate entities.

Most people in practice are dualists since, rightly or wrongly, mind and body are thought of as two different things; it is the " commonsense " (although not necessarily the true) point of view. Plato in a much more complex way was also a dualist although he held that the world of matter we observe is in some sense not the genuine world. The real world is the world of ideas and the tree we see is not real but simply matter upon which mind or soul has imprinted the idea of a tree. Everything that exists has its corresponding form in the world of ideas and imprints its pattern upon matter. Mind has always existed and, having become entangled with matter, is constantly seeking to free itself and return to God.

Plato's pupil Aristotle had a much more scientific outlook and held that, although it was mind which gave matter its form, mind is not *outside* matter, as Plato had thought, but *inside* it as its formative principle. Therefore there could be no mind without matter and no matter without mind; for even the lowest forms of matter have some degree of mind which increases in quantity and quality as we move up the scale to more complex things.

So far, nobody had explained how two such different substances as matter and mind could influence each other in any way, and this remains, in spite of attempts to be mentioned later, a basic problem in philosophy.

Two later ideas, one of them rather foolish and the other simply refusing to answer the question, are typified by the Stoics and some members of the Sceptic school. The first is that only matter exists and what we call mind is merely matter of a finer texture, a view which as an explanation is unlikely to satisfy anyone; the other, that of some Sceptics, is that we can know nothing except the fleeting images or thoughts that flicker through our consciousness. Of either mind or matter we know nothing.

Renaissance Attitude. Christian doctrines have already been dealt with (*see* God and Man, Determinism and Free-will), and the past and future of the soul is dealt with under Immortality. Nor need we mention the Renaissance philosophers who were really much more concerned about how to use mind than about its nature. When they did consider the subject they usually dealt with it, as did Francis Bacon, by separating the sphere of science from that of religion and giving the orthodox view of the latter because there were still good reasons for not wishing to annoy the Church.

17th-cent. Views: Hobbes, Descartes, Guelincx, Spinoza, Locke, Berkeley. Thomas Hobbes in the 17th cent. was really one of the first to attempt a modern explanation of mind and matter even if his attempt was crude. As a materialist he held that all that exists is matter and hence our thoughts, ideas, images, and actions are really a form of motion taking place within the brain and nerves. This is the materialist theory which states that mind does not exist.

Thus there are three basic theories of the nature of mind and body: idealism, dualism, and materialism, and we may accept any one of the three. But, if we accept dualism, we shall have to explain precisely the relationship between body and mind. In some of his later writings Hobbes seems to suggest that mental processes are the effects of motion rather than motion itself; *i.e.*, they exist, but only as a result of physical processes just as a flame does on a candle. This theory of the relationship is known as *epiphenomenalism.*

Descartes, the great French contemporary of Hobbes, was a dualist who believed that mind and matter both exist and are entirely different entities; therefore he had to ask himself how, for example, the desire to walk leads to the physical motion of walking. His unsatisfactory answer was that, although animals are pure automatons, man is different in that he has a soul which resides in the pineal gland (a tiny structure in the brain which today we know to be a relic of evolution with no present function whatever). In this gland the mind comes in contact with the " vital spirits " of the body and thus there is interaction between the two. This theory is known as *interactionism*, and since we do not accept its basis in the function of the pineal gland, we are simply left with the notion of interaction but without the explanation of how it takes place.

One of Descartes's successors, Arnold Guelincx, produced the even more improbable theory of *psychophysical parallelism*, sometimes known as the theory of the " two clocks." Imagine you have two clocks, each keeping perfect time, then supposing you saw one and heard the other, every time one points to the hour the other will strike, giving the impression that the first event causes the second, although in fact they are quite unrelated. So it is with the body and mind in Guelincx's view, each is " wound up " by God in the beginning in such a way as to keep time with the other so that when I have the desire to walk purely unrelated physical events in my legs cause them to move at the same time. A variety of this theory is *occasionism*, which says that whenever something happens in the physical world, God affects us so that we *think* we are being affected by the happening.

The trouble about all these theories is (*a*) that they really explain nothing, and (*b*) that they give us a very peculiar view of God as a celestial showman treating us as puppets when it would surely have been easier to create a world in which mind and matter simply interacted by their very nature. Spinoza, too, believed in a sort of psychophysical parallelism in that he did not think that mind and body interacted. But since in his theory everything is God, mind and matter are simply two sides of the same penny.

John Locke, another contemporary, thought of the mind as a blank slate upon which the world writes in the form of sensations, for we have no innate or inborn ideas and mind and matter do interact although he does not tell us how. All we know are sensations—*i.e.*, sense impressions. Bishop Berkeley carried this idea to its logical conclusion: if we know nothing but sensations, we have no reason to suppose that matter exists at all. He was, therefore, an idealist.

18th cent. Views: Hume, Kant. David Hume went further still and pointed out that, if all we know are sensations, we cannot prove the existence of matter but we cannot prove the existence of mind either. All we can ever know is that ideas, impressions, thoughts, follow each other. We do not even experience a self or personality because every time we look into our " minds " all we really experience are thoughts and impressions. Hume was quick to point out that this was not the same as saying that the self did not exist; it only proved that we cannot know that it does.

Kant made it clear that, although there is a world outside ourselves, we can never know what it is really like. The mind receives impressions and forms them into patterns which conform not to the thing-in-itself but to the nature of mind. Space and time, for example, are not realities but only the form into which our mind fits its sensations. In other words our mind shapes impressions which are no more like the thing-in-itself than the map of a battlefield with pins showing the position of various army groups at any given moment is like the battlefield. This, of course, is true. From physics and physiology we know that the sounds we hear are " really " waves in the air, the sights we see " really " electromagnetic waves. What guarantee do we have that the source is " really " like the impression received in our brain? Kant was the leader of the great German Idealist movement of the 18th cent. which in effect said: " why bother about matter when all we can ever know is mental? "

19th and 20th cent. Views. The Englishman Bradley, and the Frenchman Henri Bergson in the 19th and early 20th cent. both held in one form or another the belief that mind in some way creates matter and were, therefore, idealists, whereas Comte, the positivist (*q.v.*), and the Americans William James and John Dewey, held that mind is a form of behaviour. Certain acts (*e.g.*, reflexes) are " mindless " because they are deliberate; others which are intended may be described for the sake of convenience as " minded " (*i.e.*, purposeful). But like the majority of modern psychologists—insofar as they take any interest in the subject—they regarded mind as a process going on in the living body. Is there any reason, many now ask, why we should think of mind as being any different in nature from digestion? Both are processes going on in the body, the one in the brain, the other in the stomach and intestines. Why should we regard them as " things "?

Mithraism, a sun-religion which originated in Persia with the worship of the mythical Mithra, the god of light and of truth. It was for two centuries one of early Christianity's most formidable rivals, particularly in the West since the more philosophical Hellenic Christianity of the East had little to fear from it. (Arnold Toynbee has described Mithraism as " a pre-Zoroastrian Iranian paganism—in a Hellenic dress "; Manichaeism as " Zoroastrianism—in a Christian dress ".) Mithraism was a mystery-faith with secret rites known only to devotees. It appealed to the soldiers of the Roman Army which explains its spread to the farthest limits of the Roman empire and its decline as the Romans retreated. The religion resembled Zoroastrianism (*q.v.*) in that it laid stress on the constant struggle between good and evil and there are a number of parallels with Christianity, *e.g.*, a miraculous birth, death, and a glorious resurrection, a belief in heaven and hell and the immortality of the soul, a last judgment. Both religions held Sunday as the holy day of the week, celebrated 25 December (date of the pagan winter solstice festival) as the birthday of the founder; both celebrated Easter, and in their ceremonies made use of bell, holy water, and the candle. Mithraism reached its height about 275 A.D. and afterwards declined both for the reason given above and, perhaps, because it excluded women, was emotional rather than philosophical, and had no general organisation to direct its course. Yet even today, from the Euphrates to the Tyne, traces of the religion remain and antiquarians are familiar with the image of the sun-god and the inscription *Deo Soli Mithrae, Invicto, Seculari* (dedicated to the sun-god of Mithra, the unconquered). Mithraism enjoyed a brief revival of popular interest in the mid-1950s when workers excavating the foundations of the skyscraper, Bucklersbury House in the City of London, found the well-preserved remains of a Roman Mithraic temple. Despite a campaign to save the temple as a national monument, the skyscraper won and the London house of Mithras returned underground once more.

Mohammedanism. See Islam.

Monasticism. When in the 4th cent. A.D. Constantine in effect united state and church there were naturally many who hastened to become Christians for the worldly benefits they expected it to bring in view of the new situation. But there were others who, in their efforts to escape from worldly involvement, went into the deserts of North Africa and Syria to live as hermits and so in these regions there grew up large communities of monks whose lives of renunciation made a considerable impression on the Christian world. They were men of all types but the two main groups were those who preferred to live alone and those who preferred a community life. Among the first must be included St. Anthony, the earliest of the hermits, who was born in Egypt *c.* 250 and who lived alone in a hut near his home for fifteen years, and then in the desert for a further twenty. As his fame spread Anthony came forth to teach and advocate a life of extreme austerity, until by the end of his life the Thebaid (the desert around Thebes) was full of hermits following his example. (Not unnaturally, he was constantly assailed by lustful visions which he thoughtfully attributed to Satan.) In the Syrian desert St. Simeon

Stylites and others were stimulated to even greater austerities and Simeon himself spent many years on the top of a pillar in a space so small that it was only possible to sit or stand. With some of these men it is obvious that ascetic discipline had become perverted into an unpleasant form of exhibitionism.

The first monastery was founded by Pachomius of Egypt c. 315 and here the monks had a common life with communal meals, worship, and work mainly of an agricultural type. In the Eastern part of the Empire St. Basil (c. 360) tried to check the growth of the extreme and spectacular practices of the hermits by organising monasteries in which the ascetic disciplines of fasting, meditation, and prayer, would be balanced by useful and healthy activities. His monasteries had orphanages and schools for boys—not only those who were intended for a monkish life. But the Eastern Church in general continued to favour the hermit life and ascetic extremes. Originally a spontaneous movement, the monastic life was introduced to the West by St. Athanasius in 339 who obtained its recognition from the Church of Rome and St. Augustine introduced it into North Africa beyond Egypt. The movement was promoted also by St. Jerome, St. Martin of Tours, who introduced it into France, and St. Patrick into Ireland. The monastery of Iona was founded by St. Columba in 566. But it must be remembered that the Celtic Church had a life of its own which owed more to the Egyptian tradition than to Rome. Unlike the more elaborate monasteries of the continent those of the early Celtic Church were often little more than a cluster of stone bee-hive huts, an oratory, and a stone cross. It had its own religious ceremonies and its own art (notably its beautifully carved crosses and the illuminated manuscripts such as the Lindisfarne Gospel (c. 700) and the Irish Book of Kells dating from about the same time). The Scottish St. Ninian played a major part in introducing Egyptian texts and art to Britain where, mixed with Byzantine influences and the art of the Vikings, it produced a typical culture of its own. Strangely enough, it was the relatively primitive Celts who played almost as large a part in preserving civilisation in Europe during the Dark Ages as did the Italians since. It was St. Columbanus (c. 540–615) who founded the great monasteries of Annegray, Luxeuil, and Fontaine in the Vosges country, St. Gall in Switzerland, and Bobbio in the Apennines. So, too, it was the Anglo-Saxon Alcuin (c. 735–804) who was called from York by Charlemagne to set up a system of education throughout his empire; the most famous of the monastic schools he founded was at Tours. Among those influenced by him was the philosopher John Scotus Erigena.

Meanwhile from the south, as the disintegrating Roman empire became increasingly corrupt, St. Benedict of Nursia (c. 480–c. 543) fled the pleasures of Rome to lead a hermit's life near Subiaco. Here he founded some small monasteries, but c. 520 made a new settlement, the great monastery of Monte Cassino in southern Italy, where he established a " Rule " for the government of monks. This included both study and work and emphasised that education was necessary for the continuance of Christianity. As his influence spread his Rule was adopted by other monasteries, and schools became part of monastic life. It is not possible to describe the many different orders of monks and nuns formed since, nor the mendicant orders of friars (e.g., Franciscans, Dominicans, Carmelites, Augustinians). In many ways even those outside the Roman Catholic Church owe much to the monastic movement. Monasticism, of course, is not peculiar to Christianity and forms a major aspect of Buddhism, especially in the form of Lamaism in Tibet (q.v.).

Monophysitism, a heresy of the 5th cent. which grew out of a reaction against Nestorianism (q.v.). The majority of Egyptian Christians were Monophysites (Mono-physite = one nature)—i.e., they declared Christ's human and divine nature to be one and the same. This view was condemned at the Council of Chalcedon (A.D. 451) which pronounced that Jesus Christ, true God and true man, has two natures, at once

perfectly distinct and inseparably joined in one person and partaking of the one divine substance. However, many continued to hold Monophysite opinions, including the Coptic Church (q.v.), declaring the Council to be unoecumenical (i.e., not holding the views of the true and universal Christian Church).

Monopsychism, the theory of the intellect held by the Arab philosopher Averroës (1126–98) in his interpretation of Aristotle, maintaining that the individual intelligence has no existence in its own right but is part of the divine mind (nous) from which it emerges at birth and into which it is absorbed at death. He thus denied personal immortality, a view which was opposed by Christian philosophers.

Monothelites, a Christian sect of the 7th cent. which attempted to reconcile Monophysitism with orthodoxy. They admitted the orthodox view of Christ's two natures as God and man, but declared that He operated with one will. Monothelitism was condemned as heretical by the Council of Constantinople in 680 A.D.

Montanism, a Phrygian form of primitive Puritanism with many peculiar tenets into which the early Christian theologian Tertullian (c. 150–c. 230) was driven by his extremist views that the Christian should keep himself aloof from the world and hold no social intercourse whatever with pagans. The sect had immediate expectation of Christ's second coming and indulged in prophetic utterance which they held to be inspired by the Holy Ghost but which their enemies put down to prompting by the Devil. In seeking persecution and martyrdom they antagonised the Church and were suppressed.

Moral Re-Armament, a campaign launched in 1938 by an American evangelist of Lutheran background, Frank N. D. Buchman (1878–1961), founder of the Oxford Group Movement, and at first associated with the First Century Church Fellowship, a fundamentalist Protestant revivalist movement. On a visit to England in 1920 Buchman preached " world-changing through life-changing " to undergraduates at Oxford, hence the name Oxford Group. This revivalist movement was based on Buchman's conviction that world civilisation was breaking down and a change had to be effected in the minds of men.

Two of the Group's most typical practices were group confession of sins openly and the " quiet time " set aside during the day to receive messages from the Almighty as to behaviour and current problems. In the eyes of non-Groupers the confession (often of trivial sins) appeared to be exhibitionist and there was felt to be a certain snobbery about the movement which made it strongly conscious of the social status of its converts.

The Oxford Group gave way to Moral Re-Armament, the third phase of Buchmanism. M.R.A. men and women lay stress on the four moral absolutes of honesty, purity, love, and unselfishness. They believe they have the ideas to set the pattern for the changing world and, indeed, claim to have aided in solving many international disputes—political, industrial, and racial. Theologians complained of the Groups that their movement lacked doctrine and intellectual content; M.R.A. is no different in this respect.

Moravian Church, a revival of the Church of the " Bohemian Brethren " which originated (1457) among some of the followers of John Hus. It developed a kind of Quakerism that rejected the use of force, refused to take oaths, and had no hierarchy. It appears to have been sympathetic towards Calvinism but made unsuccessful approaches to Luther. As a Protestant sect it was ruthlessly persecuted by Ferdinand II and barely managed to survive. However, in the 18th cent. the body was re-established by Count Zinzendorf who offered it a place of safety in Saxony where a town called Herrnhut (God's protection) was built and this became the centre from which Moravian doctrine was spread by missionaries all over the world. Their chief belief (which had a fundamental influence on John Wesley—see Methodism) was that faith is a direct illumination from God which assures us beyond all possibility of doubt that we are saved, and that no goodness of behaviour, piety, or orthodoxy is of any use without this "sufficient sovereign, saving grace."

Mormons, or Latter-day Saints, one of the very numerous American religious sects; founded in 1830 by Joseph Smith, the son of a Vermont farmer, who, as a youth, had been influenced by a local religious revival though confused by the conflicting beliefs of the various denominations. He said that while praying for guidance he had been confronted by two heavenly messengers who forbade him to join any existing church but prepare to become the prophet of a new one. Soon, in a series of visions, he was told of a revelation written on golden plates concealed in a nearby hillside. These he unearthed in 1827 and with the help of " Urim and Thummim " translated the " reformed Egyptian " characters into English. Described as the *Book of Mormon*, this was published in 1830 and at the same time a little church of those few who accepted his testimony was founded in Fayette, N.Y. In addition the first of Joseph Smith's " miracles "—the casting out of a devil—was performed. The *Book of Mormon* purports to be a record of early American history and religion, the American Indians being identified as the ten Lost Tribes of Israel, whose fate has never failed to attract the attention of those who prefer myth to fact (cf. British Israelites). Jesus Christ is alleged to have appeared in America after His ascension. Yet Smith's eloquence was able to influence quite educated people, including Sidney Rigdon with whom he went into business for a time. *Doctrine and Covenants* is the title of another book dealing with the revelations Smith claimed to have received. Soon the sect was in trouble with the community both because its members insisted on describing themselves as the Chosen People and others as Gentiles and because they took part in politics, voting as Smith ordered them to. Smith was constantly in trouble with the police. Therefore they were turned out from one city after another until they found themselves a dwelling-place at Nauvoo, Illinois, on the Mississippi.

That would probably have been the end of the story had not Smith been murdered in 1844 and thereby made to appear a martyr, and had there not appeared Brigham Young, a quite extraordinary leader, who stamped out warring factions and drove out the recalcitrant. While persecutions continued Brigham Young announced that it had been revealed that he must lead the faithful to Salt Lake, then outside the area of the United States. There followed the famous trek of more than a thousand miles across desert country in which he led the way, reaching his journey's end in the forbidding valley of the Great Salt Lake on 24 July 1847. By 1851 30,000 Mormons had reached the Promised Land. Here they held their own in a hostile environment and under the practical genius of their leader carried through a vast irrigation scheme and built Salt Lake City which still serves as the headquarters of their sect. In 1850 their pioneer settlement was made Utah Territory, and in 1896 incorporated in the Union. The church was strictly ruled by its leader who also looked after affairs of state for thirty years until his death in 1877.

Polygamy, although opposed by some Mormons, and only sanctioned by Brigham Young when Salt Lake City had been built, is the best-known of Mormon doctrines. It brought the sect into much disrepute and was renounced in 1890. Mormons are millenarians, believing that some time Christ will appear and rule for a thousand years.

There are two orders of priests or leaders: the Melchizedeks, or higher order, include the apostles or ruling elders, and the high priest; the Aaronic priesthood, or lower order, attends to the temporal affairs of the church as the Melchizedeks attend to the spiritual. Members abstain from alcohol, tobacco, coffee, and tea. The church lays stress on the importance of revelation through visions, on education to meet the social, spiritual, and cultural needs of its members, and on community welfare. Members of the Church of Jesus Christ of Latter-day Saints now number over two million in congregations throughout the world.

The Reorganized Church of Jesus Christ of Latter-day Saints with its headquarters at Independence, Missouri, has been separate and distinct since 1852.

Muggletonians, one of the many sects which arose during the Commonwealth but, unlike most of the others (Levellers (*q.v.*), Diggers (*q.v.*), Fifth-Monarchy Men, and the Millenarians) which tended to have a strongly political aspect, this was purely religious. Founded by two journeymen tailors, Lodowick Muggleton and John Reeve, who interpreted the Book of Revelation in their own peculiar way, it was decided that Reeve represented Moses, and Muggleton, Aaron. They also believed that the Father, not the Son, had died on the cross (an ancient heresy) but added the strange statement that He left Elijah in control during His period on earth. Rejecting the doctrine of the Trinity, they also asserted that God has a human body. Nevertheless, for a time, they had a large number of followers.

Mysticism, a religious attitude which concerns itself with direct relationship with God, " reality " as contrasted with appearance, or the " ultimate " in one form or another. All the higher religions have had their mystics who have not always been regarded without suspicion by their more orthodox members, and, as Bertrand Russell points out, there has been a remarkable unity of opinion among mystics which almost transcends their religious differences. Thus, characteristic of the mystical experience in general, have been the following features: (1) a belief in insight as opposed to analytical knowledge which is accompanied in the actual experience by the sense of a mystery unveiled, a hidden wisdom become certain beyond the possibility of doubt; this is often preceded by a period of utter hopelessness and isolation described as " the dark night of the soul "; (2) a belief in unity and a refusal to admit opposition or division anywhere; this sometimes appears in the form of what seem to be contradictory statements: " the way up and the way down is one and the same " (Heraclitus). There is no distinction between subject and object, the act of perception and the thing perceived; (3) a denial of the reality of time, since if all is one the distinction of past and future must be illusory; (4) a denial of the reality of evil (which does not maintain, *e.g.*, that cruelty is good but that it does not exist in the world of reality, as opposed to the world of phantoms from which we are liberated by the insight of the vision). Among the great mystics have been Meister Eckhart and Jakob Boehme, the German religious mystics of the 13th and 16th cent. respectively, Acharya Sankara of India, and St. Theresa and St. John of the Cross of Spain. Mystical movements within the great religions have been: the Zen (*q.v.*) movement within Buddhism; Taoism in China; the Cabalists and Hasidim in Judaism; the Sufis within Islam; some of the Quakers within Christianity.

Mystery Religions. *See* Orphism.

N

Natural Law, the specifically Roman Catholic doctrine that there is a natural moral law, irrespective of time and place, which man can know through his own reason. Originally a product of early rational philosophy the Christian form of the doctrine is basically due to St. Thomas Aquinas who defined natural law in relation to eternal law, holding that the eternal law is God's reason which governs the relations of all things in the universe to each other. The natural law is that part of the eternal law which relates to man's behaviour. Catholic natural law assumes that the human reason is capable of deriving ultimate rules for right behaviour since there are in man and his institutions certain stable structures produced by God's reason which man's reason can know to be correct and true. Thus, the basis of marriage, property, the state, and the contents of justice are held to be available to man's natural reason. The rules of positive morality and civil law are held to be valid only insofar as they conform to the natural law, which man is not only capable of knowing but also of obeying.

Protestant theologians criticise this notion. Thus Karl Barth and many others hold that sinful and fallen man cannot have any direct knowledge of God or His reason or will without the aid of revelation. Another theologian Niebuhr points out that the principles of the doctrines are too inflexible and that although they are the product of a particular time and circumstance, they are regarded as if they were absolute and eternal. In fact, as most social scientists would also agree, there is no law which can be regarded as " natural " for all men at all times. Nor does it seem sensible to suppose that all or even many men possess either the reason to discern natural law or the ability to obey it; whether or not we accept man's free-will (and all Protestant sects do not), we know as a fact of science that people are not always fully responsible for their actions and some not at all.

Nazism, the term commonly used for the political and social ideology of the German National Socialist Party inspired and led by Hitler. The term *Nazi* was an abbreviation of National Socialist. Those in the Federal Republic today sympathetic to National Socialist aims are known as neo-Nazis. *See* Fascism.

Neoplatonism. *See* Determinism and Free-will and God and Man.

Nestorian heresy. The 5th cent. of the Christian Church saw a battle of personalities and opinions waged with fanatical fury between St. Cyril, the patriarch of Alexandria, and Nestorius, patriarch of Constantinople. Nestorius maintained that Mary should not be called the mother of God, as she was only the mother of the human and not of the divine nature of Jesus. This view was contradicted by Cyril (one of the most unpleasant saints who ever lived) who held the orthodox view. In addition to his utter destruction of Nestorius by stealthy and unremitting animosity Cyril was also responsible for the lynching of Hypatia, a distinguished mathematician and saintly woman, head of the Neoplatonist school at Alexandria. She was dragged from her chariot, stripped naked, butchered and torn to pieces in the church, and her remains burned. As if this were not enough Cyril took pains to stir up pogroms against the very large Jewish colony at Alexandria. At the Council of Ephesus (A.D. 431) the Western bishops quickly decided for Cyril. This Council (reinforced by the Council of Chalcedon in 451) clarified orthodox Catholic doctrine (*see* Monophysitism). Nestorius became a heretic, was banished to Antioch where he had a short respite of peace, but later, and in spite of his weakness and age, was dragged about from one place to another on the borders of Egypt. We are assured that his tongue was eaten by worms in punishment for the wicked words he had spoken, but later the Nestorian church flourished in Syria and Persia under the protection of the rulers of Persia and missions were sent to India and China.

Nihilism, the name commonly given to the earliest Russian form of revolutionary anarchism. It originated in the early years of Tsar Alexander II (1818–81), the liberator of the serfs, who, during his attempts to bring about a constitutional monarchy, was killed by a bomb. The term " nihilist," however, was first used in 1862 by Turgenev in his novel *Fathers and Children.* *See* Anarchism.

Nominalism. Early mediaeval thinkers were divided into two schools, those who regarded " universals " or abstract concepts as mere names without any corresponding realities (Nominalists), and those who held the opposite doctrine (Realism) that general concepts have an existence independent of individual things. The relation between universals and particulars was a subject of philosophical dispute all through the Middle Ages.

The first person to hold the nominalist doctrine was probably Roscelin or Roscellinus in the late 11th cent., but very little is known of him and none of his works remains except for a single letter to Peter Abelard who was his pupil.

Roscelin was born in France, accused twice of heresy but recanted and fled to England where he attacked the views of Anselm, according to whom Roscelin used the phrase that universals were a *flatus voci* or breath of the voice. The most important nominalist was the Englishman William of Occam in the 13th cent, who, once and for all, separated the two schools by saying in effect that science is about things (the nominalist view), whereas logic, philosophy, and religion are about terms or concepts (the Platonic tradition). Both are justified, but we must distinguish between them. The proposition " man is a species " is not a proposition of logic or philosophy but a scientific statement since we cannot say whether it is true or false without knowing about man. If we fail to realise that words are conventional signs and that it is important to decide whether or not they have a meaning and refer to something, then we shall fall into logical fallacies of the type: " Man is a species, Socrates is a man therefore Socrates is a species." This, in effect, is the beginning of the modern philosophy of logical analysis which, to oversimplify, tells us that a statement is not just true or untrue, it may also be meaningless. Therefore, in all the philosophical problems we have discussed elsewhere, there is the third possibility that the problem we are discussing has no meaning because the words refer to nothing and we must ask ourselves before going any further " what do we mean by God," has the word " free-will " any definite meaning?

Nonconformism, the attitude of all those Christian bodies which do not conform to the doctrines of the Church of England. Up to the passing of the Act of Uniformity in 1662 they were called " puritans " or " dissenters " and were often persecuted. The oldest bodies of nonconformists are the Baptists, Independents, and (in England) the Presbyterians; the Methodists, although dating from 1738, did not consider themselves nonconformists until some time later. The Presbyterians are, of course, the official Church of Scotland where it is the Anglicans (known as " Episcopalians ") who are the nonconformists, although not generally described as such.

O

Objectivism, a semi-political philosophy expounded by the American novelist, Ayn Rand, and interesting in as much as it was first propagated through two of her own best-selling novels. The thesis of Objectivism is the inherent suitability of the competitive capitalist system for the well-being and advancement of the human race. The seeds of man's destruction, Miss Rand believes, are to be found in the creeping menace of socialism, which by its tendency to encourage the individual to rely on the state rather than himself, undermines the dynamic power of human hard work and self-interest. In her first, and perhaps most significant novel, *The Fountainhead,* she tells the story of an unconventional and highly self-motivated architect, Howard Roark, who achieves world fame and success by a combination of hard work, talent, and refusal to compromise. Her second major novel, *Atlas Shrugged,* which is over 1100 pages long, pictures a world in which the " objectivists " (the hard-working, self-motivated, highly talented individuals in the human race) decide to pull out from society and set up a secret nation of their own. Left to its own devices, the world of socialist slackers and loafers slides into grey destruction. Objectivism seems to have arisen as a kind of counterblast to the growing tendency within some sections of the United States to decry capitalism as impersonal profiteering, and followers sport as their insignia a small badge depicting the dollar sign—the emblem incidentally of the secret states in *Atlas Shrugged.* The movement, which relies heavily on the talent and personality of its founder, has made little headway into formal American politics, but Miss Rand's books, which have sold literally by the millions, obviously touch a chord in many readers' minds.

Occam's Razor, the philosophical maxim by which William of Occam, the 13th cent. nominalist (*q.v.*), has become best-known. This states in the form which is most familiar: " Entities are not to be multiplied without necessity " and as such does not appear in his works. He did, however, say something much to the same effect: " It is vain to do with more what can be done with fewer." In other words, if everything in some science can be interpreted without assuming this or that hypothetical entity, there is no ground for assuming it. This is Bertrand Russell's version, and he adds: " I have myself found this a most fruitful principle in logical analysis."

Occultism. *See* Magic, Alchemy, Astrology, and Theosophy.

Orangemen, members of an Irish society formed in Ulster in 1795 to uphold Protestantism. Their name is taken from King William III, Prince of Orange, who defeated James II at the Battle of the Boyne (1690), hence the enormous banners depicting " King Billy on the Boyne " carried in procession on 12 July each year. Since 1921 the ruling political party of N. Ireland (the Unionist Party) has been largely maintained by the Orange Order. The Order has branches in many English-speaking countries but flourishes chiefly in Ulster.

Orgonomy, a pseudo-psychological theory advanced by the German psychiatrist Wilhelm Reich (1897–1957), a pupil of Freud, who was expelled from Germany for attacking the Nazis and who started life afresh in the U.S.A. like so many of his colleagues. Moving quickly away from orthodox psychoanalytic theories, Reich became increasingly obsessed with the view that all living things were permeated with a unique force or energy which he termed " orgone " and which he believed could be photographed and measured with a geiger counter. The key to the successful flow of orgone throughout the body was sexual intercourse and the resulting orgasm (hence " orgone "). Reich achieved a substantial following for his increasingly bizarre views and when he was sentenced to two-years' imprisonment in 1956 for alleged medical malpractice a " civil rights " controversy developed which has not died down to this date. There is a current strong revival of interest in Reich, orgonomy and some of his parallel ideas, particularly among the hippy and " underground " movements. His unfortunate and rather tragic death in prison has fanned the emotional issues and granted him the important role of martyr to his cause.

Origenists, a sect of early religionists led by the Christian Father Origen in the 3rd cent., who accepted in general the doctrines of Plotinus (*see* Neoplatonism). They believed that men's souls are created before their bodies and are striving to enter bodies as they are born. When the soul leaves the body it enters another body if it has been sinful since justice requires punishment; but the punishment happens naturally through the driving power of the sinner's own errors. The celestial bodies are believed also to have souls, and it is asserted that Christ was the Son of God only by adoption and grace. The Council of Constantinople in 553 condemned Origen's doctrines.

Orphism. The Greeks in general thought very little of their gods, regarding them as similar to human beings with human failings and virtues although on a larger scale. But there was another aspect of Greek religion which was passionate, ecstatic, and secret, dealing with the worship of various figures among whom were Bacchus or Dionysus, Orpheus, and Demeter and Persephone of the Eleusinian Mysteries. Dionysus (or Bacchus) was originally a god from Thrace where the people were primitive farmers naturally interested in fertility cults. Dionysus was the god of fertility who only later came to be associated with wine and the divine madness it produces. He assumed the form of a man or a bull and his worship by the time it arrived in Greece became associated with women (as was the case in most of the Mystery Religions) who spent nights on the hills dancing and possibly drinking wine in order to stimulate ecstasy; an

unpleasant aspect of the cult was the tearing to pieces of wild animals whose flesh was eaten raw. Although the cult was disapproved of by the orthodox and, needless to say, by husbands, it existed for a long time. This primitive and savage religion in time was modified by that attributed to Orpheus whose cult was more spiritualised, ascetic, and substituted mental for physical intoxication. Orpheus may have been a real person or a legendary hero and he, too, is supposed to have come from Thrace, but his name indicates that he, or the movement associated with him, came from Crete and originally from Egypt, which seems to have been the source of many of its doctrines. Crete, it must be remembered, was the island through which Egypt influenced Greece in other respects. Orpheus is said to have been a reformer who was torn to pieces by the Maenad worshippers of Dionysus. The Orphics believed in the transmigration of souls and that the soul after death might obtain either eternal bliss or temporary or permanent torment according to its way of life upon earth. They held ceremonies of purification and the more orthodox abstained from animal food except on special occasions when it was eaten ritually. Man is partly earthly, partly heavenly, and a good life increases the heavenly part so that, in the end, he may become one with Bacchus and be called a " Bacchus." The religion had an elaborate theology (*see* **Section H, 117–128**). As the Bacchic rites were reformed by Orpheus, so the Orphic rites were reformed by Pythagoras (*c.* 582–*c.* 507 B.C.) who introduced the mystical element into Greek philosophy which reached its heights in Plato. Other elements entered Greek life from Orphism. One of these was feminism which was notably lacking in Greek civilisation outside the Mystery Religions. The other was the drama which arose from the rites of Dionysus. The mysteries of Eleusis formed the most sacred part of the Athenian state religion, and it is clear that they had to do with fertility rites also, for they were in honour of Demeter and Persephone and all the myths speak of them as being associated with the supply of corn to the country (*see* **Section H, 110–116**). Without being provocative, it is accepted by most anthropologists and many theologians that Christianity, just as it accepted elements of Gnosticism and Mithraism, accepted elements from the Mystery Religions as they in turn must have done from earlier cults. The miraculous birth, the death and resurrection, the sacramental feast of bread and wine, symbolising the eating of the flesh and drinking of the blood of the god, all these are common elements in early religions and not just in one. None of this means that what we are told about Jesus is not true, but it surely does mean: (*a*) that Christianity was not a sudden development; (*b*) that the early Church absorbed many of the elements of other religions; (*c*) that perhaps Jesus Himself made use of certain symbols which He knew had a timeless significance for man and invested them with new meaning.

Orthodox Eastern Church. There are two groups of Eastern churches: (1) those forming the Orthodox Church dealt with here which include the ancient Byzantine patriarchates of Constantinople, Alexandria, Antioch, and Jerusalem, and the national churches of Russia, Greece, Yugoslavia, Bulgaria, Rumania, etc. (although Orthodox communities exist all over the world and are no longer confined to geographical areas); (2) the churches which rejected Byzantine orthodoxy during various controversies from the 5th to the 7th cent., notably the Coptic church (*q.v.*) and the Armenian church. Although all Orthodox churches share the same doctrine and traditions they are arranged as national independent bodies each with its own hierarchy. They do not recognise the pope, and the primacy of the patriarch of Constantinople is largely an honorary one. Although claiming to be the One Holy, Catholic, and Apostolic Church its alleged infallibility rests on universal agreement rather than on any one individual, and agreement over the faith comes from the Scriptures interpreted in the light of the Tradition. The latter includes dogmas relating to the Trinity,

Christology, Mariology, and Holy Icons; the testimony of the Fathers (St. Athanasius, St. Basil, St. John Chrysostom, St. Cyril of Alexandria, etc.); the canons or rules as formulated by the Councils and the Fathers. The Orthodox Church did not take part in the great Western controversies about the Bible, nor, of course, in the Reformation. Attempts have recently been made to improve relations between Rome and Constantinople: the two Churches agreed in 1965 to retract the excommunications cast on each other in A.D. 1054, which formalised the Great Schism.

Oxford Group. See Moral Re-Armament.

Oxford Movement. See Tractarianism.

P

Pantheism. See God and Man.

Papal Infallibility. The basis of papal infallibility is (a) that every question of morals and faith is not dealt with in the Bible so it is necessary that there should be a sure court of appeal in case of doubt, and this was provided by Christ when he established the Church as His Teaching Authority upon earth; (b) ultimately this idea of the teaching function of the Church shapes the idea of papal infallibility which asserts that the pope, when speaking officially on matters of faith or morals, is protected by God against the possibility of error. The doctrine was proclaimed in July 1870.

Infallibility is a strictly limited gift which does not mean that the pope has extraordinary intelligence, that God helps him to find the answer to every conceivable question, or that Catholics have to accept the pope's views on politics. He can make mistakes or fall into sin, his scientific or historical opinions may be quite wrong, he may write books that are full of errors. Only in two limited spheres is he infallible and in these only when he speaks officially as the supreme teacher and lawgiver of the Church, defining a doctrine that must be accepted by all its members. When, after studying a problem of faith or morals as carefully as possible, and with all available help from expert consultants, he emerges with the Church's answer—on these occasions it is not strictly an answer, it is *the* answer.

Historically speaking, the Roman Catholic Church of the early 19th cent. was at its lowest ebb of power. Pope Pius IX, in fear of Italian nationalism, revealed his reactionary attitude by the feverish declaration of new dogmas, the canonisation of new saints, the denunciation of all modern ideals in the Syllabus of Errors, and the unqualified defence of his temporal power against the threat of Garibaldi. It is not too much to say that everything regarded as important by freedom-loving and democratic people was opposed to the papacy at that time. In 1870, after a long and sordid struggle, the Vatican Council, convened by Pius IX, pronounced the definition of his infallibility. Döllinger, a German priest and famous historian of the Church, was excommunicated because, like many others, he refused to accept the new dogma. It is difficult not to doubt that there was some connection between the pronouncement of the pope's infallibility and his simultaneous loss of temporal power.

After the humanism of the Second Vatican Council (1962–5) the Pope's encyclical *Humanae Vitae* (1968), condemning birth control, came as a great disappointment to the many people (including theologians, priests, and laymen) who had expected there would be a change in the Church's teaching. The Church's moral guidance on this controversial issue, however, does not involve the doctrine of infallibility. (The Roman Catholic Church teaches that papal pronouncements are infallible only when they are specifically defined as such.)

Paris School of Psychotherapy. The Paris school is important because it was the school of the famous French neurologist Jean Charcot (1825–93), teacher of Sigmund Freud (1856–1939) and Pierre Janet (1859–1947). At a time when hypnosis and the neurosis known as hysteria were very much " in the air," and Liébeault and his colleagues (*see* **Mesmerism**) were regarding hysteria as a condition which was produced by autosuggestion, Charcot was maintaining the opposite view. Hypnosis, or the ability to be hypnotised, was, in his view, a symptom of a hysterical personality, and hysteria had a physiological basis.

Charcot was a highly controversial figure and his demonstrations were famous, if to some verging on the notorious; he aroused much antagonism among Roman Catholics by stating that faith cures at Lourdes were actually cases of hysteria and not, therefore, miraculous since they could equally well be cured by himself. His supposed words: " You will always find sex at the root of the trouble " and his pupil Janet's evidence that forgotten (or, as we should now say, repressed) traumatic events lay behind the symptoms which would go when the event was allowed expression, had a potent influence on the young Freud who made the uncovering of the past and the importance of sex the foundations of psychoanalysis. Modern belief is that Charcot was wrong about the physical basis of hysteria, wrong about the pathological significance of hypnosis, but right on the whole about the importance of sexual problems in neurosis.

Parapsychology, the name given to the study of psychical research (*q.v.*) as an academic discipline, and chosen to denote the topic's supposed status as a branch of psychology. The impetus behind parapsychology came from the psychologist William MacDougall who persuaded Duke University in North Carolina, U.S.A., to found a department of parapsychology under J. B. Rhine. Throughout the 1930s and 40s the work of Rhine and his colleagues, who claimed to have produced scientific evidence for the existence of E.S.P., attracted world-wide attention. Increasing reservations about the interpretation of Rhine's results and an apparent lack of any readily repeatable experiments, however, gradually eroded scientific confidence in the topic. Today there is a growing feeling in academic circles that parapsychology has failed to make its case and no longer merits much support as an independent scientific discipline. Rhine retired from university life in 1965 and the world-famous parapsychology laboratory at Duke was closed.

Parsees. See Zoroastrianism.

Paulicians, a Christian heretical sect which derives its name not from Paul the Apostle but from Paul of Samosata who was patriarch of Antioch, 260–72. His followers, the " Pauliani," were condemned for their "Adoptionist " (*q.v.*) attitude by the Council of Nicaea (325). Originally wide-spread in Anatolia, especially in Armenia from the 5th cent. onwards, they were cruelly persecuted by the Byzantine emperors and were deported (c. 755) to the Balkans to garrison that part of the East Roman empire. Elsewhere in this section the Albigenses or Cathari are mentioned; the Paulicians form part of their spiritual ancestry. It is debatable whether the "Adoptionist " doctrines professed by the Albigenses came from the Balkan Bogomils, through the Crusaders, or from the north of Spain, where there was an "Adoptionist " movement in the late part of the 8th cent. The evidence seems to be in favour of the Balkan influence but it should be noted that although the Bogomils were influenced by the Paulicians and the Manichaeans, the Paulicians themselves repudiated Manichaeanism. An authentic liturgical book of the Paulicians—*The Key of Truth*—was discovered in 1891 in Echmiadzin where the Armenian historical archives were kept. This manuscript throws new light on the heresy.

Pavlovian theory. See Behaviourism.

Phrenology, a psychological " school " founded in 1800 by two Germans, Franz Josef Gall and Johann Gaspar Spurzheim. Gall was an anatomist who believed there to be some correspondence between mental faculties and the shape of the head. He tested these ideas in prisons and mental hospitals and began to lecture on his findings, arousing a great deal of interest throughout both Europe and America, where his doctrines were widely accepted. Phrenology became fashionable, and people would go to "have their bumps read" as later men and women of fashion have gone to be psychoanalysed. Roughly speaking, Gall divided the mind into thirty-seven faculties such as destructiveness, suavity, self-esteem, conscientiousness, and so on, and claimed that each of these was located in a definite area of the brain. He further claimed that the areas in the brain corresponded to "bumps" on the skull which could be read by the expert, thus giving a complete account of the character of the subject. In fact, (a) no such faculties are located in the brain anywhere for this is simply not the way the brain works; (b) the faculties described by Gall are not pure traits which cannot be further analysed and are based on a long outdated psychology; (c) the shape of the brain bears no specific relationship to the shape of the skull. Phrenology is a pseudo-science; there is no truth in it whatever. But, even so, like astrology, it still has its practitioners.

Physiocrats. A French school of economic thought during the 18th cent., known at the time as Les Economistes but in later years named physiocrats by Du Pont de Nemours, a member of the School. Other members were Quesnay, Mirabeau, and the great financier Turgot. The physiocrats held the view, common to the 18th cent., and deriving ultimately from Rousseau, of the goodness and bounty of nature and the goodness of man " as he came from the bosom of nature." The aim of governments, therefore, should be to conform to nature; and so long as men do not interfere with each other's liberty and do not combine among themselves, governments should leave them free to find their own salvation. Criminals, madmen, and monopolists should be eliminated. Otherwise the duty of government is laissez-faire, laissez passer. From this follows the doctrine of free trade between nations on grounds of both justice and economy; for the greater the competition, the more will each one strive to economise the cost of his labour to the general advantage. Adam Smith, although not sharing their confidence in human nature, learned much from the physiocrats, eliminated their errors, and greatly developed their teaching.

Physiognomy. See Characterology.

Pietism, a movement in the Lutheran Church at the end of the 17th cent.—the reaction, after the sufferings of the thirty years' war, of a pious and humiliated people against learning, pomp and ceremony, and stressing the importance of man's personal relationship with God. The writings of Johann Georg Hamann (1730–88) who came from a Pietist family of Königsberg influenced Kierkegaard. The Pietist movement was the root of the great Romantic movement of the 18th cent.

Plymouth Brethren, a religious sect founded by John Nelson Darby, a minister of the Protestant Church of Ireland, and Edward Cronin, a former Roman Catholic, in 1827. Both were dissatisfied with the lack of spirituality in their own and other churches and joined together in small meetings in Dublin every Sunday for " the breaking of bread." Soon the movement began to spread through Darby's travels and writings and he finally settled in Plymouth, giving the popular name to the " Brethren." Beginning as a movement open to all who felt the need to " keep the unity of the Spirit," it soon exercised the right to exclude all who had unorthodox views and split up into smaller groups. Among these the main ones were the "Exclusives," the Kellyites, the Newtonites, and " Bethesda " whose main differences were over problems of church government or prophetical powers. Some of these are further split among themselves. Readers of Father and Son by Sir Edmund Gosse, which describes life with his father, the eminent naturalist Philip Gosse, who belonged to the Brethren, will recall how this basically kind, honest, and learned man was led through their teachings to acts of unkindness (e.g., in refusing to allow his son and other members of his household to celebrate Christmas and throwing out the small tokens they had secretly bought), and intellectual dishonesty (e.g., in refusing for religious reasons alone to accept Darwinism when all his evidence pointed towards it).

The original views of Darby which were perpetuated by the "Exclusive" Brethren were somewhat as follows: Christianity has fallen from New Testament purity and all Christendom and every Church is corrupt and has incurred God's displeasure, notably by establishing ministerial offices which hinder the believer's approach to God. Ministers should not be officials but possess special gifts (" Charismata ") granted from above and assigned by the Holy Ghost according to his will; these Charismata have no connection whatever with any official posts although in some cases they may coincide with them. The whole doctrine of the Brethren is based on the need for direct access to God and the rejection of any intermediate agency such as priests, ministers or presbyters. The Exclusive Brethren adopted new harsh rules in 1965 designed to prevent " Saints " (members) from having any contact with " Sinners " (non-members). Members sharing homes with non-members were to be expelled; members must declare their bank balances; unmarried members, single or widowed, must marry as soon as possible within the sect.

Today, the majority of Brethren belong to the " Open Brethren " assemblies and, unlike the " Exclusives," hold that the Lord's Supper (a commemorative act of " breaking the bread " observed once a week) is for all Christians who care to join them. Baptism is required and Brethren believe in the personal premillenial second coming of Christ.

Poltergeist, allegedly a noisy type of spirit which specialises in throwing things about, making loud thumpings and bangings, and occasionally bringing in " apports," i.e., objects from elsewhere. Most so-called poltergeist activities are plain frauds, but the others are almost invariably associated with the presence in the house of someone (often, but not always a child) who is suffering from severe mental conflicts usually of a sexual nature. The inference is that those activities which are not simply fraudulent are either due to some unknown influence exuded by such mentally abnormal people, or that they are actually carried out by ordinary physical means by such people when in a state of hysterical dissociation—i.e., unconsciously. The second hypothesis is much the more probable. See Psychic Research.

Polytheism. See God and Man.

Positivism, also known as the Religion of Humanity, was founded by Auguste Comte (1798–1857), a famous mathematician and philosopher born in Montpellier, France. His views up to the end of the century attracted many and it would have been impossible throughout that time to read a book on philosophy or sociology that did not mention them, but today his significance is purely of historical interest. In his Cours de Philosophie Positive (1830) he put forward the thesis that mankind had seen three great stages in human thought: (1) the theological, during which man seeks for supernatural causes to explain nature and invents gods and devils; (2) the metaphysical, through which he thinks in terms of philosophical and metaphysical abstractions; (3) the last positive or scientific stage when he will proceed by experiment and objective observation to reach in time " positive truth."

Broadly speaking, there is little to complain of in this analysis; for there does seem to have been some sort of general direction along these lines. However, Comte was not satisfied with having reached this point and felt that his system demanded a religion and, of course, one that was " scientific." This religion was to be the worship of Humanity in place of the personal Deity of earlier times, and for it he supplied not only a Positive Catechism but a treatise on Sociology in which he declared himself the High Priest of the cult. Since, as it stood, the religion was likely to appear somewhat abstract to many, Comte drew up a list of historical characters whom he regarded as worthy of the same sort of adoration as Catholics accord to their saints. The new Church attracted few members, even among those who had a high regard for Comte's scientific work, and its only significant adherents were a small group of Oxford scholars and some in his own country. Frederic Harrison was the best-known English adherent and throughout his life continued to preach Comtist doctrines in London to diminishing audiences.

Pragmatism, a typically American school of philosophy which comes under the heading of what Bertrand Russell describes as a "practical" as opposed to a "theoretical" philosophy. Whereas the latter, to which most of the great philosophical systems belong, seeks disinterested knowledge for its own sake, the former (a) regards action as the supreme good, (b) considers happiness an effect and knowledge a mere instrument of successful activity.

The originator of pragmatism is usually considered to have been the psychologist William James (1842–1910) although he himself attributed its basic principles to his life-long friend, the American philosopher, Charles Sanders Peirce (1839–1914). The other famous pragmatist is John Dewey, best-known in Europe for his works on education (for although American text-books on philosophy express opinions to the contrary, few educated people in Europe have taken the slightest interest in pragmatism and generally regard it as an eccentricity peculiar to Americans). James in his book *The Will to Believe* (1896) points out that we are often compelled to take a decision where no adequate theoretical grounds for a decision exist; for even to do nothing is to decide. Thus in religion we have a right to adopt a believing attitude although not intellectually fully convinced. We should believe truth and shun error, but the failing of the sceptical philosopher is that he adheres only to the latter rule and thus fails to believe various truths which a less cautious man will accept. If believing truth and avoiding error are equally important, then it is a good idea when we are presented with an alternative to believe one of the possibilities at will, since we then have an even chance of being right, whereas we have none if we suspend judgment. The function of philosophy, according to James, is to find out what difference it makes to the individual if a particular philosophy or world-system is true: "An idea is 'true' so long as to believe it is profitable to our lives," and, he adds, "the true is only the expedient in our way of thinking . . . in the long run and on the whole of course." Thus "if the hypothesis of God works satisfactorily in the widest sense of the word, it is true." Bertrand Russell's reply to this assertion is: "I have always found that the hypothesis of Santa Claus 'works satisfactorily in the widest sense of the word'; therefore 'Santa Claus exists' is true, although Santa Claus does not exist." Russell adds that James's concept of truth simply omits as unimportant the question whether God really *is* in His heaven; if He is a useful hypothesis that is enough. "God the Architect of the Cosmos is forgotten; all that is remembered is belief in God, and its effects upon the creatures inhabiting our petty planet. No wonder the Pope condemned the pragmatic defence of religion."

Predestination. *See* **Calvinism.**

Presbyterianism, a system of ecclesiastical government of the Protestant churches which look back to John Calvin as their Reformation leader. The ministry consists of presbyters who are all of equal rank. Its doctrinal standards are contained in the *Westminster Confession of Faith* (1647) which is, in general, accepted by English, Scottish, and American Presbyterians as the most thorough and logical statement in existence of the Calvinist creed. The Church of Scotland is the leading Presbyterian church in the British Isles.

The Reformation in Scotland was preceded by the same sort of awareness of the moral corruption of the Roman Church as had happened elsewhere, but for various political and emotional reasons, which need not be discussed here, the majority of the Scottish people (unlike the English who had been satisfied with the mere exchange of Crown for Pope) were determined on a fundamental change of doctrine, discipline, and worship, rather than a reform of manners. The church preachers had learned their Protestantism not from Luther but from Calvin and their leader John Knox had worked in Geneva with Calvin himself and was resolved

to introduce the system into Scotland. In 1557 the "Lords of the Congregation" signed the Common Band (*i.e.,* a bond or covenant) to maintain "the blessed Word of God and his congregation" against their enemies, and demanded the right to worship as they had chosen. However, the real date of the Scottish Reformation is August 1560 when Mary of Guise (the regent for Mary Queen of Scots who was not yet of age) died and the Estates met to settle their affairs without foreign pressure; the *Scots Confession* was drawn up and signed by Knox and adopted by the Estates.

The ideas on which the Reformed Kirk was based are found in the *Scots Confession,* the *Book of Discipline,* and the *Book of Common Order,* the so-called Knox's liturgy. Knox's liturgy, the same as that used in Geneva but translated into English, was used until Laud's attempt to force an Anglican liturgy on the Kirk led to an abandonment of both in favour of "free prayers."

The Presbyterian tradition includes uncompromising stress upon the Word of God contained in the Scriptures of the Old and New Testaments as the supreme rule of faith and life, and upon the value of a highly trained ministry, which has given the Church of Scotland a high reputation for scholarship and has in turn influenced the standard of education in Scotland. The unity of the Church is guaranteed by providing for democratic representation in a hierarchy of courts (unlike the Anglican Church, which is a hierarchy of persons). The local kirk-session consists of the minister and popularly elected elders (laymen). Ministers, elected by their flocks, are ordained by presbyters (ministers already ordained). Above the kirk-session is the court of the presbytery which has jurisdiction over a specified area; above that the court of synod which rules over many presbyteries; and finally the General Assembly which is the Supreme Court of the Church with both judicial and legislative powers, and over which the Moderator of the General Assembly presides. The function of the elders is to help the minister in the work and government of the kirk. The episcopacy set up by James VI and I, and maintained by Charles I was brought to an end by the Glasgow Assembly (1638), but General Assemblies were abolished by Oliver Cromwell and at the Restoration Charles II re-established episcopacy. The Covenanters who resisted were hunted down, imprisoned, transported, or executed over a period of nearly thirty years before William of Orange came to the throne and Presbyterianism was re-established (1690). Today Presbyterians no less than other Christian communities are looking at Christianity as a common world religion in the sense that the principles which unite them are greater than those which divide them. *See* **Church of Scotland, Calvinism.**

Protestant, the name first applied to those who favoured the cause of Martin Luther and who protested against the intolerant decisions of the Catholic majority at the second Diet of Speyer (1529), revoking earlier decisions of the first Diet of Speyer tolerating the Reformers in certain cases (1526). In general the name "Protestant" is applied to those Churches which severed connection with Rome at the time of the Reformation. The essence of Protestantism is the acceptance by the individual Christian of his direct responsibility to God rather than to the Church. *See* **Lutheranism, Presbyterianism, Calvinism.**

Psychedelism. For all his recorded history man has relied upon drugs of one kind or another to make his life more tolerable. These have generally been central nervous system depressants—*i.e.,* alcohol, hashish, etc.—and their use in most societies has been brought under careful government control. Most societies have also at some stage experimented with the use of certain drugs of another class—the hallucinogens. These, far from having the mentally tranquilising characteristics of small doses of alcohol, provoke striking changes in mental alertness, frequently coupled with visionary or hallucinatory experiences. The confusion and disorientation which accompany such states has led to social disapproval of their use in Western countries, and the favoured "legal" drug for centuries has been alcohol. In the 1950s the novelist Aldous Huxley in his essay *The Doors of Perception* wrote of his experiences with the drug mescalin, a derivative of the South American peyotl and a powerful hallucinogen. Huxley put forward the hypothesis that mescalin had given him not only an entirely original psychological experience but had also significantly "heightened" his perceptual ability—a development of the greatest possible interest to artists, writers, and poets. Huxley's book had considerable impact, stimulating other creative individuals into similar experiments, not always with such euphoric results. In England the author Richard Ward reported some frightening moments under the drug LSD in his *A Drug-taker's Notebook* and Huxley amplified the unpredictable nature of the drug-experience in *Heaven and Hell*, published in 1956. Although such experiments were technically illegal, public interest had been considerably aroused and in the 1960s, when it became easy to synthesise the most effective of the hallucinogens, LSD, its use began to be common among certain sections of society. In 1964 a sensational scandal rocked the great American university of Harvard when senior members of the teaching staff, including the psychologist Timothy Leary, were dismissed for using LSD and encouraging students in its use. Unrepentant, Dr. Leary set up a community near New York from whence the cult of psychedelism was propagated.

Psychedelism—which is not really an organised system of belief, but rather an attitude of mind—preaches that through the controlled use of drugs, particularly of the hallucinogenic variety, an individual may be made aware for the first time of the rich fields of experience which lie latent in the unconscious mind. The exploration of these territories will have both a liberating and an enriching effect, the outcome being to "turn on" the individual to the total reality of mind. So convinced do many of the proponents of psychedelia become of the significance of the experience of the so-called LSD "trip," that they are inclined to urge non-trippers to experiment with the drug. Herein, of course, lies one obvious danger, for the drug LSD is potentially a toxic substance which needs to be administered in minute doses if it is not to cause madness or even death. There is also much uncertainty about the possible long-term effects of "tripping," many psychologists and scientists believing that it leads to a progressive disorientation and destruction of the personality, a disintegration of which the individual drug-taker is seldom aware. If there is a credit side to psychedelism it may lie in the clear, if limited, evolution in popular music, art, and design and, to a lesser extent, literature which has been inspired by these excursions. By the beginning of 1970 there was some sign that the wave of interest in LSD and similar drugs was beginning to slacken off, possibly because of an increasing awareness of the possible grievous side-effects and of the largely illusory nature of the "insights" which the "trip" is supposed to provide. Dr Leary, the movement's leading figure, is also reported to be turning his interest elsewhere, notably into the more staid and traditional waters of Maoism (*q.v.*).

Psychic Research, the *scientific* study of so-called psychic phenomena as contrasted with Spiritualism (*q.v.*) which is the cult of those who already believe in their supernatural nature. It is obviously impossible here to summarise work that has been carried out (in Britain notably by the Society for Psychical Research, founded in 1882) on such subjects as mediumship, apparitions, telepathy and clairvoyance (discussed here separately under the heading of Telepathy), poltergeists (also discussed separately), levitation, and precognition.

But the point at which we must begin is the human mind and the nature of scientific evidence and so far as these are concerned the following points may be made.

(1) There is little use in discussing psychic phenomena until we realise that almost no human being—least of all one with strong convictions—is a completely trustworthy witness. A person may be utterly honest in every other respect except that in which his convictions are involved.

(2) This does not mean that a witness is either telling the whole truth or is simply lying; for the following possibilities exist: (*a*) he may be telling the truth: (*b*) he may be consciously lying for motives of his own; (*c*) his recollections may be incorrect in discussing something that happened in the past; (*d*) he may really believe that he saw or heard what he said he did and may be telling the truth *as he experienced it*—e.g., seeing a ghost—without realising that what he experienced is a product of his own unconscious mind; (*e*) there are various degrees of lying, for the mind has a natural tendency to add coherence and meaning to the only partly coherent events of the day, and it is a normal trait (consciously or unconsciously) to make a "good story" out of what originally were isolated and unconnected happenings; (*f*) even under the most favourable conditions the evidence of scientifically-trained people is not as good as it might be (cf. the psychological experiment in which a class of students is suddenly exposed to a deliberately contrived scene, e.g., two men eccentrically dressed rush into the lecture-room, exchange words, and have a quarrel—and the students are afterwards required to write down what they saw and heard, rarely 10 per cent. being even 70 per cent. correct as to what really happened).

(3) There are many aspects of "psychic" phenomena which are not "psychic" at all, but based on well-known scientific principles. How many people, for example, know: (*a*) that *every* physical illness has its psychological aspect, so that a person with chronic arthritis, let us say, may get up and walk for the first time in years after injection with a new drug which is later proved to be worthless or no better than aspirin (*e.g.*, cortisone), yet if a "spiritual healer" got the same results he would be acclaimed for his psychic powers; (*b*) that it is possible to be completely paralysed, totally blind or deaf, have total loss of sensation in some part of the body, have two or more personalities, *without any physical disease being present*, in the neurosis (cured daily by psychiatrists without mystery) known as hysteria.

(4) It is possible under hypnosis, or self-hypnosis, to produce stigmata—*e.g.*, marks resembling the nail-prints of the Crucifixion on hands and feet, to produce blisters at will, spontaneous bleeding, and many of the phenomena usually described as miraculous, in the consulting room and by scientific means.

(5) We all have more potent senses than we ordinarily realise. We may not consciously know the number of steps leading to our flat but can be made under hypnosis to tell. Furthermore, there are people who are hypersensitive in hearing and vision (often without being aware of it), so that in "thought-transference" experiments where they are sent to another room whilst others decide on some object or idea, they may subconsciously hear what is going on; or in card experiments in telepathy they may be able to read the face of the card reflected in the pupils of the "sender" opposite, or tell in a familiar pack which card is which from almost invisible differences on the backs of the cards.

(6) Most of us have no idea of the mathematical laws of probability and are therefore likely to misinterpret the "mysteriousness" of phenomena. Thus, suppose I have a "premonition" that someone has died and later find my feelings confirmed by the event, then I may not remember or know (*a*) that on many previous occasions I, in common with most other people, have had "premonitions" the vast majority of which did *not* come true; (*b*) that, on the last occasion I saw the person, or from things I may have heard, I may have unconsciously noted signs that all was not well and expected the event; (*c*) that the most "improbable" things happen quite normally (*e.g.*, during the last war a flying bomb fell through the roof of the British Museum and failed to explode, and some time later a second flying bomb fell *through the same hole* and likewise

failed to explode); (*d*) that the chance of a pack of cards being dealt so that each of four persons receives a complete suit is exactly the same as the chance that any other combination of cards may come up.

(7) That collective hallucinosis does occur (it would be invidious to mention in detail certain "miraculous happenings" which might hurt the religious susceptibilities of many, but we are entitled to ask how it is possible for the sun to stand still in the sky in the presence of thousands of people collected in a particular area when it is seen nowhere else in the world and has been noted by no astronomical laboratory?)

(8) Mediums have been proved to be prepared to do the most extraordinary things in order to deceive a suggestible audience seated in semi-darkness—*e.g.*, the so-called "ectoplasm" (a supposedly psychic substance or materialisation) which exudes from the medium's body has been found before the séance, as have "apports" or objects apparently appearing from nowhere, half-way down the medium's throat or in the stomach ready to be regurgitated, and even in other bodily apertures.

It is not maintained that psychic phenomena do not happen, but that we must be extremely cautious in accepting the evidence of our own, or even more, other people's, senses, and much less free in our interpretation of what has been observed really means. *See* Poltergeist, Telepathy, Spiritualism.

Psychoanalysis, an approach to the study of human personality involving the rigorous probing, with the assistance of a specially trained practitioner, of an individual's personal problems, motives, goals and attitudes to life in general. Often, and quite understandably, confused with psychology (of which it is merely a part), psychoanalysis has an interesting historical background and has attracted the interest of philosophers, scientists and medical experts since it emerged as a radical and controversial form of mental therapy at the turn of the century. The traditionally accepted founder is the great Austrian Sigmund Freud, but he never failed to acknowledge the impetus that had been given to his own ideas by his talented friend, the physiologist Joseph Breuer, who for most of his working life had been interested in the curious phenomena associated with hypnosis. Breuer had successfully cured the hysterical paralysis of a young woman patient and had noticed that under hypnosis the girl seemed to be recalling emotional experiences, hitherto forgotten, which bore some relationship to the symptoms of her illness. Developing this with other patients Breuer then found that the mere recalling and discussing of the emotional events under hypnosis seemed to produce a dramatic alleviation of the symptoms—a phenomenon which came to be known as *catharsis*. Breuer also noticed another curious side-effect, that his women patients fell embarrassingly and violently in love with him, and he gradually dropped the practice of "mental catharsis", possibly feeling that it was a bit too dangerous to handle. This left the field clear for Freud, whose brilliant mind began to search beyond the therapeutic aspects of the topic to see what light might be thrown on the nature of human personality and psychological mechanisms in general. The most important question concerned the "forgotten" emotional material which turned up, apparently out of the blue, during the hypnotic session. Freud rightly saw that this posed problems for the current theories of memory, for how could something once forgotten (a) continue to have an effect on the individual without him being aware of it, and (b) ultimately be brought back to conscious memory again. It must be remembered that at this time memory was considered to be a fairly simple process—information was stored in the brain and was gradually eroded or destroyed with the passage of time and the decay of brain cells. Once lost, it was believed, memories were gone for ever, or at best only partially and inaccurately reproducible. Furthermore, human beings were supposed to be rational (if frequently wilful) creatures who never did anything without thinking about it (if only briefly) beforehand and without being well aware of their reasons

for so doing. It was within this framework that Freud had his great insight, one which many people believe to be one of the most important ideas given to mankind. This was simply the realisation that the human mind was not a simple entity controlling the brain and body more or less at will, but a complex system made up of a number of integrated parts with at least two major subdivisions—the conscious and the unconscious. The former concerned itself with the normal round of human behaviour, including the larger part of rational thought, conversation, etc., and large areas of memory. The latter was principally devoted to the automatic control of bodily functions, such as respiration, cardiac activity, various types of emotional behaviour not subject to much conscious modification and a large storehouse of relevant "memories" again not normally accessible to the conscious mind. Occasionally, Freud proposed, an exceedingly unpleasant emotional or otherwise painful event might be so troublesome if held in the conscious mind's store, that it would get shoved down into the unconscious or "repressed" where it would cease to trouble the individual in his normal life. The advantages of this mechanism are obvious, but they also brought with them hazards. With certain kinds of memory, particularly those involving psychological rather than physical pain—as for example a severe sexual conflict or marital problem—repression might be used as a device to save the individual from facing his problem in the "real" world, where he might be able ultimately to solve it, by merely hiding it away in the unconscious and thus pretending it did not exist. Unfortunately, Freud believed, conflicts of this kind were not snuffed out when consigned to the basements of the mind, but rather tended to smoulder on, affecting the individual in various ways which he could not understand. Repressed marital conflicts might give rise to impotence, for example, or even to homosexual behaviour. Guilt at improper social actions similarly repressed might provoke nervous tics, local paralysis, etc, etc. Following this line of reasoning, Freud argued that if the unwisely repressed material could be dredged up and the individual forced to face the crisis instead of denying it, then dramatic alleviations of symptoms and full recovery should follow.

To the great psychologist and his growing band of followers the stage seemed to be set for a dramatic breakthrough not only in mental therapy but also in a general understanding of the nature of human personality. To his pleasure—for various reasons he was never too happy about hypnosis—Freud discovered that with due patience, skill and guidance an individual could be led to resurrect the material repressed in his unconscious mind in the normal, as opposed to the hypnotic, state. This technique, involving long sessions consisting of intimate discussions between patient and therapist became known as psychoanalysis, and it has steadily evolved from its experimental beginnings in the medical schools and universities of Vienna to being a major system of psychotherapy with a world-wide following and important theoretical connotations. Psychoanalysis, as practised today, consists of a number of meetings between doctor and patient in which the latter is slowly taught to approach and enter the territory of his subconscious mind, and examine the strange and "forgotten" material within. A successful analysis, it is claimed, gives the individual greater insight into his own personality and a fuller understanding of the potent unconscious forces which are at work within him and in part dictating his goals.

Freud's initial ideas were of course tentative, and meant to be so. He was however a didactic and forceful personality himself, unwilling to compromise on many points which became controversial as the technique and practice of psychoanalysis developed. The outcome was that some of his early followers, notably the equally brilliant Carl Jung and Alfred Adler, broke away to found their own "schools" or versions of psychoanalysis, with varying degrees of success. Today, psychoanalysis is coming under increasingly critical scrutiny, and its claims are being treated with a good deal of

J43

reservation. Notable antagonists include the English psychologist Professor H. J. Eysenck who points out that there is little if any solid experimental data indicating that psychoanalysis is a valid method of treating or curing mental illness. Analysists respond by saying that their system is closer to an art than a craft and not amenable to routine scientific experiment. The controversy will no doubt continue for some time to come, but whatever its validity as therapy, the basic ideas behind psychoanalysis—notably the reality and power of the unconscious mind—are beyond question and have given human beings definite and major insights into the greatest enigma of all—the workings of the human mind. *See also* **Section Q.**

Pyramidology, a curious belief that the dimensions of the Great Pyramid at Giza, if studied carefully, reveal principles of fundamental historical and religious significance. The perpetrator of this was a Victorian publisher, John Taylor, who discovered that if you divide the height of the pyramid into twice the side of its base you get a number very similar to *pi*—a number of considerable mathematical importance. Later discoveries in the same vein include the finding that the base of the pyramid (when divided by the width of a single casing stone) equals exactly 365—number of days in the year. Many books have been written on the interpretation of the dimensions of the pyramid, none of which has any scientific or archaeological validity. Pyramidology is simply a classic example of the well-known fact that hunting through even a random array of numbers will turn up sequences which appear to be " significant "—always provided that one carefully selects the numbers one wants and turns a blind eye to those that one doesn't!

Pyrrhonism, a sceptical philosophy which doubts everything.

Q

Quakers. *See* **Friends, The Society of.**

Quartodecimani, an early Christian community who celebrated the Easter festival on the 14th day of the month, when the Jews celebrated their Passover. In consequence of the confusion caused, the practice was condemned by the Council of Nicaea in 325.

Quietism, a doctrine of extreme asceticism and contemplative devotion, embodied in the works of Michael Molinos, a 17th cent. Spanish priest, and condemned by Rome. It taught that the chief duty of man is to be occupied in the continual contemplation of God, so as to become totally independent of outward circumstances and the influence of the senses. Quietists taught that when this stage of perfection is reached the soul has no further need for prayer and other external devotional practices. Similar doctrines have been taught in the Moslem and Hindu religions. *See* **Yoga.**

R

Racism, the doctrine that one race is inherently superior or inferior to others, one of the bases of racial prejudice. It has no connection whatever with the study of race as a concept, or the investigation of racial differences, which is a science practised by the physical anthropologist (who studies physical differences), or the social anthropologist (who studies cultural differences). Racism is simply a vulgar superstition believed in by the ignorant or mentally unbalanced, and it may be categorically stated as a scientific fact that racial superiority is a myth believed in by no scientist of repute. *See* **Sciences of Man, Section F, Part V.**

Radiesthesia, the detection, either by some " psychic " faculty or with special equipment, of radiations alleged to be given off by all living things and natural substances such as water, oil, metal, etc. The word radiesthesia is in fact a fancy modern name for the ancient practice of " dowsing," whereby an individual is supposed to be able to detect the presence of hidden underground water by following the movements of a hazel twig held in his hands. Dowsers, or water diviners, as they are sometimes called, claim also to be able to detect the presence of minerals and, hard though it may seem to believe, have actually been hired by major oil companies to prospect for desert wells—though without any notable successes. The theory of dowsing is that all things give off a unique radiation signal which the trained individual (via his twig, pendulum, or whatever) can " tune in " to, a theory which, while not backed up by any data known to orthodox sciences, is at least not too fantastically far-fetched. It is when radiesthesists claim to be able to detect the presence of oil, water, or precious metals by holding their pendulum *over a map* of the territory and declare that it is not necessary for them to visit the area in person to find the required spot that the topic moves from the remotely possible to the absurdly improbable. Some practitioners of this art state that they are able to perform even more marvellous feats such as determining the sex of chickens while still in the egg, or diagnosing illness by studying the movements of a pendulum held over a blood sample from the sick individual. Such claims when put to simple scientific test have almost invariably turned out as fiascos. Yet belief in dowsing, water-divining, and the like is still very widespread.

There is an important link between radiesthesia and the pseudo-science of *radionics*, which holds that the twig or pendulum can be superseded by complicated equipment built vaguely according to electronic principles. A typical radionic device consists of a box covered with knobs, dials, etc., by which the practitioner " tunes in " to the " vibration " given off by an object, such as a blood spot, a piece of hair, or even a signature. By the proper interpretation of the readings from the equipment the illness, or even the mental state, of the individual whose blood, hair, or signature is being tested, may be ascertained. The originator of radionics seems to have been a Dr. Albert Abrams who engaged in medical practice using radionic devices in America in the 1920s and 30s. The principal exponent in this country was the late George de la Warr who manufactured radionic boxes for diagnosis and treatment of illnesses, and even a " camera " which he believed to be capable of photographing thought. In a sensational court case in 1960 a woman who had purchased one of the diagnostic devices sued de la Warr for fraud. After a long trial the case was dismissed, the Judge commenting that while he had no good evidence that the device worked as claimed, he felt that de la Warr sincerely believed in its validity and thus was not guilty of fraud or misrepresentation. Some practitioners hold this as in some way justifying or accrediting the science of radionics but most observers feel that the case was more a triumph for British justice and the right of the individual to promote his beliefs whatever they may be—provided they are sincerely held and do no obvious social harm.

Ranters, a derisive term for the Primitive Methodists (*see* Methodism).

Rationalism is defined as " the treating of reason as the ultimate authority in religion and the rejection of doctrines not consonant with reason." In practice, rationalism has a double significance: (1) the doctrine as defined above, and (2) a 19th cent. movement which was given to what was then known as " free-thought," " secularism," or agnosticism—*i.e.*, it was in the positive sense anti-religious and was represented by various bodies such as the Secular Society, the National Secular Society and the Rationalist Press Association (founded in 1899).

In the first sense, which implies a particular philosophical attitude to the universe and life, rationalism is not easy to pin down although, at first sight, it would appear that nothing could be simpler. Does it mean the use of pure reason and logic or does it mean, on the other hand, the use of what is generally called the " scientific method " based on observation (*i.e.*, the evidence of our senses) and experiment? If we are thinking in terms of the use of pure reason and logic then the Roman Catholic Church throughout most of its history has maintained, not that the whole truth about religion can be discovered by reason, but as St. Thomas Aquinas held, the basis of religion—*e.g.*, the existence of God—can be rationally demonstrated. Nobody could have made more use of logic than the schoolmen of the Middle Ages, yet not many people today would accept their conclusions, nor would many non-Catholics accept St. Thomas's proofs of the existence of God even when they themselves are religious. The arguments of a first Cause or Prime Mover or the argument from Design on the whole leave us unmoved, partly because they do not lead us to the idea of a *personal God*, partly because we rightly distrust logic and pure reason divorced from facts and know that, if we begin from the wrong assumptions or premises, we can arrive at some very strange answers. If the existence of a Deity can be proved by reason, then one can also by the use of reason come to the conclusions, or rather paradoxes, such as the following: God is by definition all good, all knowing, all powerful—yet evil exists (because if it does not exist then it cannot be wrong to say " there is no God "). But if evil exists, then it must do so either because of God (in which case He is not all good) or in spite of God (in which case He is not all powerful).

Arguments of this sort do not appeal to the modern mind for two historical reasons: (1) many of us have been brought up in the Protestant tradition which—at least in one of its aspects—insists that we must believe in God by faith rather than by logic and in its extreme form insists on God as revealed by the " inner light "; (2) our increasing trust in the scientific method by direct observation and experiment. Thus, no matter what Aristotle or St. Thomas may say about a Prime Mover or a First Cause, we remain unconvinced since at least one scientific theory suggests that the universe did not have a beginning and if scientific investigation proved this to be so, then we should be entirely indifferent to what formal logic had to say.

The secularist and rationalist movements of the 19th cent. were anti-religious—and quite rightly so—because at that time there were serious disabilities imposed even in Britain by the Established Church on atheism or agnosticism and freedom of thought. They are of little significance now because very little is left, largely thanks to their efforts, of these disabilities.

Finally, although most people are likely to accept the scientific method as the main means of discovering truth, there are other factors which equally make us doubt the value of " pure " logic and reason unaided by observation. The first of these is the influence of Freud which shows that much of our reasoning is mere rationalising—*e.g.*, we are more likely to become atheists because we hated our father than because we can prove that there is no God. The second is the influence of a movement in philosophy which, in the form of logical positivism or logical analysis, makes us doubt whether metaphysical systems have any meaning at all. To-day, instead of asking ourselves whether Plato was right or wrong, we are much more likely to ask whether he did anything but make for the most part meaningless noises. Religion is in a sense much safer today than it ever was in the 19th cent. when it made foolish statements over matters of science that could be *proved* wrong; now we tend to see it as an emotional attitude to the universe or God (a " feeling of being at home in the universe," as William James put it) which can no more be proved or disproved than being in love.

Realism is a word which has so many meanings, and such contradictory ones, in various spheres, that it is difficult to define. We shall limit ourselves to its significance in philosophy. In philosophy, " realism " has two different meanings, diametrically opposed. (1) The most usual meaning is the one we should least expect from the everyday sense of the word— *i.e.*, it refers to all those philosophies from Plato onwards which maintained that the world of appearance is illusory and that ideas, forms, or universals are the only true realities, belonging to the world beyond matter and appearance— the world of God or mind. In early mediaeval times St. Thomas Aquinas was the chief exponent of this doctrine which was held by the scholastics as opposed to the Nominalists (*q.v.*). (2) In its modern everyday meaning " realism " is the belief that the universe is real and not a creation of mind, that although all we really experience is the evidence of our senses there is a reality that causes the appearance, the " thing-in-itself " as Kant described it. Material things may not really be what they appear to be (*e.g.*, a noise is not the " bang " we experience but a series of shock-waves passing through the atmosphere), yet, for all that, we can be sure that matter exists and it is very possible (some might add) that mind does not.

Reformation, the great religious movement of the 16th cent., which resulted in the establishment of Protestantism. John Wyclif (d. 1384), John Hus (d. 1415) and others had sounded the warning note, and when later on Luther took up the cause in Germany, and Zwingli in Switzerland, adherents soon became numerous. The wholesale vending of indulgences by the papal agents had incensed the people, and when Luther denounced these things he spoke to willing ears. After much controversy, the reformers boldly propounded the principles of the new doctrine, and the struggle for religious supremacy grew bitter. They claimed justification (salvation) by faith, and the use as well as the authority of the Scriptures, rejecting the doctrine of transubstantiation, the adoration of the Virgin and Saints, and the headship of the Pope. Luther was excommunicated. But the Reformation principles spread and ultimately a great part of Germany, as well as Switzerland, the Low Countries, Scandinavia, England, and Scotland were won over to the new faith. In England Henry VIII readily espoused the cause of the Reformation, his own personal quarrel with the Pope acting as an incentive. Under Mary there was a brief and sanguinary reaction, but Elizabeth gave completeness to the work which her father had initiated. *See* Lutheranism, Calvinism, Presbyterianism, Baptists, Methodism.

Reincarnation, the transmigration of souls. *See* Immortality, Hinduism, Buddhism.

Renaissance is defined in the *Oxford English Dictionary* as: " The revival of art and letters, under the influence of classical models, which began in Italy in the 14th century." It is a term which must be used with care for the following reasons: (1) Although it was first used in the form *rinascita* (re-birth) by Vasari in 1550 and people living at that time certainly were aware that something new was happening, the word had no wide currency until used by the Swiss historian Jacob Burchardt in his classic *The Civilization of the Renaissance in Italy* (1860). (2) The term as used today refers not only to art in its widest sense but to a total change in man's outlook on life which extended into philosophical, scientific, economic, and technical fields. (3) Spreading from Italy there were renaissance movements in France, Spain, Germany, and northern Europe, all widely different with varying delays in time. As the historian Edith Sichel says: " Out of the Italian Renaissance there issued a new-born art; out of the Northern Renaissance there came forth a new-born religion. There came forth also a great school of poetry, and a drama the greatest that the world had seen since the days of Greece. The religion was the offspring of Germany and the poetry that of England."

The real cause of the Renaissance was not the fall of Constantinople, the invention of printing, the discovery of America, though these were phases in the process; it was, quite simply, money. The rise of a new merchant class gave rise to individualist attitudes in economic affairs which prepared the way for individualism and humanism. The new wealthy class in time became patrons of the arts whereas previously the Church had been the sole patron and controller. Thus the artist became more free to express himself, more respected, and being more well-to-do could afford to ignore the Church and even, in time, the views of his patrons.

It is true that art continued to serve to a considerable extent the purposes of faith, but it was judged from the standpoint of art. Mediaeval art was meant to elevate and teach man; Renaissance art to delight his senses and enrich his life. From this free and questing spirit acquired from economic individualism came the rise of modern science and technology; here Italy learned much from the Arab scholars who had translated and commented upon the philosophical, medical, and mathematical texts of antiquity, while denying themselves any interest in Greek art and literature. Arabic-Latin versions of Aristotle were in use well into the 16th cent. The Byzantine culture, though it had preserved the Greek tradition and gave supremacy to Plato, had made no move forward. But the Greek scholars who fled to Italy after the fall of Constantinople brought with them an immense cargo of classical manuscripts. The recovery of these Greek masterpieces, their translation into the vernaculars, and the invention of printing, made possible a completer understanding of the Greek spirit. It was the bringing together of the two heritages, Greek science, and Greek literature, that gave birth to a new vision. But it was not only Aristotle and Plato who were being studied but Ovid, Catullus, Horace, Pliny and Lucretius. What interested Renaissance man was the humanism of the Latin writers, their attitude to science, their scepticism.

The period c. 1400–1500 is known as the Early Renaissance. During this time such painters as Masaccio, Uccello, Piero della Francesca, Botticelli, and Giovanni Bellini were laying the foundations of drawing and painting for all subsequent periods including our own. They concerned themselves with such problems as anatomy, composition, perspective, and representation of space, creating in effect a grammar or textbook of visual expression. The term High Renaissance is reserved for a very brief period when a pure, balanced, classical harmony was achieved and artists were in complete control of the techniques learned earlier. The High Renaissance lasted only from c. 1500 to 1527 (the date of the sack of Rome), yet that interval included the earlier works of Michelangelo, most of Leonardo's, and all the Roman works of Raphael.

Ritualism, a tendency which, during the 19th cent., developed in the High Church section of the Church of England to make use of those vestments, candles, incense, etc. which are usually regarded as features of the Church of Rome. Since some opposition was aroused, a Ritual Commission was appointed in 1904 to take evidence and try to find some common basis on which High and Low Church could agree with respect to ceremonial. The report of 1906 in effect recommended the giving of greater powers to bishops to suppress objectionable practices. Although they are often associated together, it is worth while pointing out that there was no special connection between the Oxford Movement or Tractarians (q.v.) and Ritualism because Pusey disliked ritual and even Newman, who eventually went over to Rome, held extremely simple services at his church of St. Mary's.

Roman Catholic Church, the Christian organisation which acknowledges the Pope as the lawful successor of St. Peter, the apostle appointed by Christ to be the head of His Church. The reforming impulse at the Second Vatican Council (1962–5) has set in train great movements towards religious unity and the reform and modernisation of the Roman Catholic Church.

Romantic Movement or Romanticism is the name given not so much to an individual way of thinking but to the gradual but radical transformation of basic human values that occurred in the Western world round about the latter part of the 18th cent. It was a great breakthrough in European consciousness and arose through the writings of certain men living during the half-century or more following, say, 1760. It arose then because both time and place were propitious for the birth of these new ideas. There was a revolution in basic values—in art, morals, politics, religion, etc. The new view was of a world transcending the old one, infinitely larger and more varied.

To understand the Romantic movement it is

necessary first to take note of the climate of thought preceding the great change; then to account for its beginning in Germany where it did (see Pietism) during the latter part of the 18th cent., and finally to appraise the writings of those men whose ideas fermented the new awakening. Briefly, the shift was away from French classicism and from belief in the all-pervasive power of human reason (the Enlightenment) towards the unfettered freedom that the new consciousness was able to engender. What mattered was to live a passionate and vigorous life, to dedicate oneself to an ideal, no matter what the cost (e.g., Byron).

The ideas of the Enlightenment (e.g., Fontenelle, Voltaire, Montesquieu) had been attacked by the Germans Hamann and Herder and by the ideas of the English philosopher Hume, but Kant, Schiller, and Fichte, Goethe's novel Wilhelm Meister, and the French Revolution all had profound effects on the aesthetic, moral, social, and political thought of the time. Friedrich Schlegel (1772–1829) said: " There is in man a terrible unsatisfied desire to soar into infinity; a feverish longing to break through the narrow bonds of individuality." Romanticism undermined the notion that in matters of value there are objective criteria which operate between men. Henceforth there was to be a resurgence of the human spirit, deep and profound, that is still going on.

Rotarianism. The Rotary Club is primarily an American association but has many members in Britain and presumably elsewhere since all Rotary Clubs are united in an international organisation. It consists of groups of business and professional men formed with the purpose of serving their community and humanity in general. The name is derived from the clubs entertaining in rotation.

S

Sabellian heresy. During the 4th cent. great controversies raged within the Christian Church over the divinity of Jesus Christ. Arius (see Arianism) denied Christ's divinity and maintained that the Father alone was truly divine. This doctrine was condemned at the Council of Nicaea (325), Arius being opposed by Athanasius who held the now orthodox view of the Trinity which was reaffirmed at the Council of Constantinople (381). The Sabellians, named after their founder Sabellius (fl. 215), a Libyan priest and theologian, held the view that God is indivisible but with three roles, appearing successively as the Father (the creator), as the Son (the redeemer), and as the Holy Spirit (the divine spirit within men). This view which makes the person of Jesus Christ ultimately an illusion, was condemned.

Salvation Army. The religious movement which in 1878 became known by this name arose from the Christian Mission meetings which the Rev. William Booth and his devoted wife had held in the East End of London for the previous thirteen years. Its primary aim was, and still is, to preach the gospel of Jesus Christ to men and women untouched by ordinary religious efforts. The founder devoted his life to the salvation of the submerged classes whose conditions at that time were unspeakably dreadful. Originally his aim had been to convert people and then send them on to the churches, but he soon found that few religious bodies would accept these " low-class " men and women. So it was that social work became part of their effort. Practical help, like the provision of soup-kitchens, accompanied spiritual ministration. Soon, in the interests of more effective " warfare " against social evils, a military form of organisation, with uniforms, brass bands, and religious songs, was introduced. Its magazine The War Cry gave as its aim " to carry the Blood of Christ and the Fire of the Holy Ghost into every part of the world." There were persecutions: mobs, sometimes encouraged by the police, assaulted the Salvationists who, although not the aggressors, were often punished by the magistrates. General Booth saw with blinding clarity that conversion must be accompanied by an improvement of external conditions. Various books had earlier described the terrible conditions of the slums, but in 1890 he produced a monumental survey entitled *In Darkest England and the Way Out*. From that time forward the Army was accepted and its facilities made use of by the authorities. To-day the Army's spiritual and social activities have spread to countries all over the world; every one no matter what class, colour, or creed he belongs to is a " brother for whom Christ died."

Sandemanians or Glassites, an obscure religious sect whose sole claim to fame is that one of its members was the great Michael Faraday, founder of the science of electromagnetism, who never failed to attend its Sunday services.

Sceptics. From Thales of Miletus (c. 624–565 B.C.) to the Stoics in the 4th cent. B.C. philosophers had been trying to explain the nature of the universe; each one produced a different theory and each could, apparently, prove that he was right. This diversity of views convinced the Sceptic school founded by Pyrrho (c. 360–270 B.C.) that man is unable to know the real nature of the world or how it came into being. In place of a futile search for what must be for ever unknowable, the Sceptics recommended that men should be practical, follow custom, and accept the evidence of their senses.

Schoolmen. From the time of Augustine to the middle of the 9th cent. philosophy, like science, was dead or merely a repetition of what had gone before. But about that time there arose a new interest in the subject, although (since by then Western Europe was entirely under the authority of the Catholic Church) the main form it took was an attempt to justify Church teaching in the light of Greek philosophy. Those who made this attempt to reconcile Christian beliefs with the best in Plato and Aristotle were known as " schoolmen " and the philosophies which they developed were known as " scholasticism." Among the most famous schoolmen must be counted John Scotus Erigena (c. 800–c. 877), born in Ireland and probably the earliest; St. Anselm, archbishop of Canterbury (1033–1109); the great Peter Abelard whose school was in Paris (1079–1142); Bernard of Chartres, his contemporary; and the best-known of all, St. Thomas Aquinas of Naples (1225–74), who was given the name of the " Angelic Doctor."

The philosophies of these men are discussed under various headings (God and Man, Determinism and Free-will), but being severely limited by the Church their doctrines differed from each other much less than those of later philosophical schools. However, one of the great arguments was between the orthodox Realists (q.v.) and the Nominalists (q.v.) and a second was between the Thomists (or followers of St. Thomas Aquinas) and the Scotists (followers of John Duns Scotus—not to be confused with John Scotus Erigena). The two latter schools were known as the Ancients, whilst the followers of William of Occam, the Nominalist, were known as the Terminalists. All became reconciled in 1482 in face of the threat from humanism of which the great exponent was Erasmus of Rotterdam (1466–1536) who hated scholasticism.

Scientology, an unusual quasi-philosophical system started by the American science-fiction writer L. Ron Hubbard, which claims to be able to effect dramatic improvement in the mental and physical well-being of its adherents. Originally developed in the United States as " Dianetics, the modern science of mental health," it was hailed in Hubbard's first book to be " a milestone for Man comparable to his discovery of fire and superior to his inventions of the wheel and the arch." Such extravagant statements exemplify the literature of the movement, which in the late 1950s began to expand in England when its founder came to live in East Grinstead. Followers of Dianetics and Scientology advance within the cult through a series of levels or grades, most reached by undertaking courses of training and tuition, payment for which may amount to hundreds and, in total, even thousands of pounds. These courses consist largely of specialised and complex mental exercises based on Hubbard's own variation of psychology and known as " processing " and " auditing." One of the principal goals of a Scientologist is the attainment of the state known as " Clear " (roughly speaking, one " cleared " of certain mental and physical handicaps) when it is believed he (she) will be a literally superior being, equipped with a higher intelligence and a greater command over the pattern of his (her) own life.

Orthodox psychologists tend to view both the practice and theory of Scientology with considerable misgivings and in the state of Victoria, Australia, the practice of Scientology is banned following a parliamentary inquiry under K. V. Anderson, Q.C., who described it as " a serious threat to the community, medically, morally and socially." In 1967 the Home Office announced that they would refuse Mr. Hubbard re-entry to Britain, that its centres would no longer be recognised as educational establishments, and foreigners arriving for its courses would not be granted student status.

Scientology has for some time been registered across the world as a Church, and its followers may attend religious services modelled on the movement's philosophy.

Shakers, members of a revivalist group, styled by themselves " The United Society of Believers in Christ's Second Appearing," who seceded from Quakerism in 1747 though adhering to many of the Quaker tenets. The community was joined in 1758 by Ann Lee, a young convert from Manchester, who had " revelations " that she was the female Christ; " Mother Ann " was accepted as their leader. Under the influence of her prophetic visions she set out with nine followers for " Immanuel's land " in America and the community settled near Albany, capital of New York state. They were known as the " Shakers " in ridicule because they were given to involuntary movements in moments of religious ecstasy.

Central to their faith was the belief in the dual role of God through the male and female Christ: the male principle came to earth in Jesus; the female principle, in " Mother Ann." The sexes were equal and women preached as often as men at their meetings which sometimes included sacred dances—nevertheless the two sexes, even in dancing, kept apart. Their communistic way of living brought them economic prosperity, the Shakers becoming known as good agriculturists and craftsmen, noted for their furniture and textiles. After 1860, however, the movement began to decline and few, if any, are active today.

Shamans, the medicine men found in all primitive societies who used their magical arts to work cures, and protect the group from evil influences. The *shaman* was a man apart and wore special garments to show his authority. Shamanism with its magical practices, incantations, trances, exhausting dances, and self-torture is practised even today by tribes that have survived in a primitive state of culture.

Shiites or Shia, a heretical Moslem sect in Persia, opposed by the orthodox Sunnites. The dispute, which came almost immediately after the death of the Prophet and led to bitter feuding, had little to do with matters of doctrine as such, but with the succession. After Mohammed's death, there were three possible claimants: Ali, the husband of his daughter Fatima, and two others, one of whom gave up his claim in favour of the other, Omar. The orthodox selected Omar, who was shortly assassinated, and the same happened to his successor as Ali was passed over again. The Shiites are those who maintain that Ali was the true vicar of the Prophet, and that the three orthodox predecessors were usurpers.

Shintoism, the native religion of Japan, primarily a system of nature and ancestor worship. After the defeat of Japan in the second world war Hirohito disavowed his divinity as ancestor of the Sun-goddess.

Sikhism. The Sikh community of the Punjab, which has played a significant part in the history of modern India, came into being during a period of religious revival in India in the 15th and 16th cent. It was originally founded as a religious sect by Guru (teacher) Nanak (1469–

1538) who emphasised the fundamental truth of all religions, and whose mission was to put an end to religious conflict. He condemned the formalism both of Hinduism and Islam, preaching the gospel of universal toleration, and the unity of the Godhead, whether He be called Allah, Vishnu, or God. His ideas were welcomed by the great Mogul Emperor Akbar (1542–1605). Thus a succession of Gurus were able to live in peace after Nanak's death; they established the great Sikh centre at Amritsar, compiled the sacred writings known as the *Adi Granth*, and improved their organisation as a sect. But the peace did not last long, for an emperor arose who was a fanatical Moslem, in face of whom the last Guru, Govind Singh (1666–1708), whose father was put to death for refusal to embrace Islam, had to make himself a warrior and instil into the Sikhs a more aggressive spirit. A number of ceremonies were instituted by Govind Singh; admission to the fraternity was by special rite; caste distinctions were abolished; hair was worn long; the word singh, meaning lion, was added to the original name. They were able to organise themselves into 12 *misls* or confederacies but divisions appeared with the disappearance of a common enemy and it was not until the rise of Ranjit Singh (1780–1839) that a single powerful Sikh kingdom was established, its influence only being checked by the English, with whom a treaty of friendship was drawn. After the death of Ranjit Singh two Anglo-Sikh wars followed, in 1845–46, and 1848–49, which resulted in British annexation of the Punjab and the end of Sikh independence. In the two world wars the Sikhs proved among the most loyal of Britain's Indian subjects. The partitioning of the continent of India in 1947 into two states, one predominantly Hindu and the other predominantly Moslem, presented a considerable problem in the Punjab, which was divided in such a way as to leave 2 million Sikhs in Pakistan, and a considerable number of Moslems in the Indian Punjab. Although numbering less than 2 per cent. of the population (c. 8 million) the Sikhs are a continuing factor in Indian political life. In 1966 the Punjab was divided on a linguistic basis—Punjabi-speaking Punjab and Hindi-speaking Hariana.

Socialism, a form of society in which men and women are not divided into opposing economic classes but live together under conditions of approximate social and economic equality, using in common the means that lie to their hands of promoting social welfare. The brotherhood of man inspires the aims of socialism in foreign, colonial, social, and economic policies alike. The word "socialism" first came into general use in England about 1834 in connection with Robert Owen's "village of co-operation" at New Lanark. About the middle of the 19th cent. Charles Kingsley and others established a form of Christian socialism, and William Morris, John Burns, and others founded a Socialist League in 1886. With the development of trade unions the socialist movement took a more practical trend. Fabianism (*q.v.*) associated in its early days with the names of Beatrice and Sidney Webb and George Bernard Shaw, aims at the gradual reorganisation of society by creating intelligent public opinion by education and legislation. The British Labour Party believes in peaceful and constitutional change to socialism by democratic methods based upon popular consent. A democratic programme of planned economy and public ownership of certain vital industries and services were features of socialist government from 1945–51 together with a comprehensive system of social security. Further radical reforms in the interest of social justice and industrial efficiency were initiated by the socialist government during its six years of office, 1964–70. *See also* Section C, Part I.

Southcottians, followers of Joanna Southcott, who died in 1814 shortly after announcing that (although over 50) she was about to give birth to a divine human being named Siloh. Miss Southcott certainly produced all the symptoms of pregnancy, and was even examined by the Royal physician who pronounced her unquestionably "with child." Although she even went "into labour," no child, divine or other-

wise, appeared and she seems to have died of something rather close to a broken heart. Her interesting symptoms would today be classed as "hysterical pregnancy"—a not uncommon condition which may mimic real pregnancy in a remarkable way. Joanna's followers remained loyal to her memory, however, and a tiny sect still survives to this day. Shortly before her death, incidentally, she handed to followers a number of locked and sealed boxes which she indicated contained, among other things, the secret of the universe. These were only to be opened 100 years after her death and then in the presence of 12 bishops. In 1927 one of these boxes unexpectedly turned up and it was ceremoniously opened at the Caxton Hall before a public audience. The organisers had to make do with only one bishop as most of the country's senior clerics pronounced themselves to be too busy to attend. Perhaps it was just as well for Miss Southcott's marvellous box was found to contain only a few rare coins, a horse pistol, a woman's embroidered nightcap, and a slightly improper novel, *The Surprises of Love*. One of the most endearing qualities of Joanna Southcott must have been her sense of humour. It is difficult to decide which is the stranger phenomenon, Joanna or her followers.

Spiritualism is a religion which requires to be distinguished from psychical research (*q.v.*) which is a scientific attempt carried on both by believers and non-believers to investigate psychic phenomena including those not necessarily connected with "spirits"—*e.g.*, telepathy or clairvoyance and precognition. As a religion (although for that matter the whole of history is filled with attempts to get in touch with the "spirit world") Spiritualism begins with the American Andrew Jackson Davis who in 1847 published *Nature's Divine Revelations*, a book which is still widely read. In this Davis states that on the death of the physical body, the human spirit remains alive and moves on to one or another of a considerable range of worlds or "spheres" where it commences yet another stage of existence. Since the spirit has not died, but exists with full (and possibly even expanded) consciousness, there should be no reason, Davis argues, why it should not make its presence known to the beings it has temporarily left behind on earth. In 1847, the year of the publication of Davis's book, two young girls, Margaret and Kate Fox, living in a farmhouse at Hydesville, New York began apparently to act as unwitting mediums for attempts at such between-worlds communication. The girls were the focus for strange rappings and bangs which it was alleged defied normal explanation and which spelt out, in the form of a simple alphabetical code, messages from the spirits of "the dead." The Fox sisters were later to confess that they had produced the raps by trickery, but by that time the fashion had spread across the world and before long "mediums" in all lands were issuing spirit communications (often in much more spectacular form). In the late 19th cent. Spiritualism went into a phase of great expansion and for various reasons attracted the attention of many scientists. Among these were Sir William Crookes, Sir Oliver Lodge, Professor Charles Richet, Alfred Russell Wallace, to say nothing of the brilliant and shrewd creator of Sherlock Holmes, Sir Arthur Conan Doyle. Today many people find it astonishing that people of such brilliance should find the phenomena of the seance room of more than passing interest, but the commitment of the Victorian scientists is understandable if we realise that Spiritualists, after all, claim to do no more than demonstrate as fact what all Christians are called on to believe—that the human personality survives bodily death. Furthermore, at the time of the late 19th cent. peak of Spiritualism, much less was known about human psychology and about the great limitations of sensory perception in typical seance conditions, when lights are dimmed or extinguished and an emotionally charged atmosphere generated. Today the most striking phenomena of the seance room—the alleged materialisation of spirit people and the production of such half-spiritual, half-physical substances as ectoplasm—are rarely if ever produced at Spiritualist meetings. Some say that the most probable explanation for this is that too many fraudulent mediums have been caught out and publicly exposed for the profession to be worth the risks. The movement today, which still has a large and often articulate following, now concentrates on the less controversial areas of "mental mediumship," clairvoyance and the like, or on the very widespread practice of "spirit healing." Where people are not deliberately deluded by bogus mediums acting for monetary reward (a practice which largely died out with the "death" of ectoplasm) Spiritualism probably has an important role to play in the life of many people whose happiness has been removed by the death of a much loved relative or spouse. It certainly does not deserve the violent attacks that are often made on it by orthodox clergy who allege that Spiritualists are communicating not with the souls of the departed but with the devil or his emissaries. To many people today belief in the devil would be looked upon as somewhat odder than belief in the survival of the individual spirit after death.

State and Man. Most of the early civilisations such as those of Egypt and Babylonia were theocratic, that is to say, they were arranged in a hierarchy with, at the peak, a king who was also an incarnation of the god. Needless to say, in such circumstances there was no room for philosophising about the nature of the state and the relationship which ought to exist between state and citizens. As usual, we have to turn to ancient Greece for the beginnings of thought about this problem. We do so as briefly as possible since in general it is only the later philosophers whose work has much contemporary interest and, in any case, most people today realise that the political philosophy of a particular time is bound to reflect the actual conditions prevailing then and as such is of mainly theoretical interest today.

The Greek Approach. The early pre-Socratic philosophers Democritus and the Pythagorean school for example, held that the individual should subordinate himself to the whole; they had no doubt that the citizen's first duty was to the state. The Greeks until the time of Plato were not really thinking in terms of individual rights, nor had they given much thought to what form the state should take—they simply accepted it. The first great attempt to describe the ideal state is to be found in Plato's *The Republic* which is referred to elsewhere (see Education). His pupil Aristotle did not try to form a utopia but made many comments on the nature of government. Thus, while agreeing that the state was more important than any individual person, he distinguished between good and bad states, and pointed out that to the extent that the state does not enable its citizens to lead virtuous and useful lives it is evil. A good constitution must recognise the inequalities between human beings and confer on them rights according to their abilities: among these inequalities are those of personal ability, property, birth, and status, as freeman or slave. The best forms of rule were monarchy, aristocracy, and democracy; the worst forms—tyranny, oligarchy (or rule of a powerful few), and ochlocracy (or mob-rule). The later Greek thinkers of Hellenistic times held two opposed points of view. The Epicureans (q.v.) taught that all social life is based upon self-interest and we become members of a group for our own convenience; therefore there are no absolute rights and laws—what is good is what members decide at that time to be good, and when they change their minds the law must change too. Injustice is not an evil in any god-given sense; we behave justly simply because if injustice became the general rule, we ourselves should suffer. The Stoics (q.v.), on the other hand, held that the state must dominate the individual completely and everyone must carry out, first and foremost, his social duties and be willing to sacrifice everything for it; but the state of the Stoics was no narrowly national one, but one that strove to become a universal brotherhood.

The Christian Approach. The orthodox Christian view is expressed in St. Augustine's book *The City of God*. Here it is held that the church, as the worldly incarnation of the City of God, is to be supreme over the state, and the head of the church is to be supreme over secular rulers. In addition it must be recognised that, whilst the secular ruler can make mistakes, the church does not, since it is the representative of God's kingdom on earth.

The Secular State. During the Renaissance (q.v.) people began to think for themselves and the results of their cogitations were not always pleasant; for it was during this time that many rulers, petty and otherwise, were seeking absolute authority. Two notable thinkers at this stage were Niccolo Machiavelli (1469–1527) in Italy and Thomas Hobbes (1588–1679) in England, where, of course, the Renaissance arrived later in history. Both supported absolute monarchy against the former domination of the church. The name of Machiavelli has become a by-word for any behaviour that is cunning and unscrupulous, but he was not really as bad as he is usually painted. It is, indeed, true that in his book *The Prince* he showed in the greatest detail the methods by which a ruler could gain absolute control and destroy civic freedom, but this despotism was intended as merely a necessary intermediate stage towards his real idea which was a free, united Italian nation wholly independent of the church. Hobbes was a materialist whose thesis was that man is naturally a ferocious animal whose basic impulse is war and pillage and the destruction of whatever stands in his way to gain his desires. But if he allowed himself to behave in this way his life would be "nasty, brutish, and short" so he creates a society in which he voluntarily gives up many of his rights and hands them over to a powerful ruler in his own interest. But having done this he must obey; even when the ruler is unjust, as he has no right to complain because anything is better than a return to his natural state. The religion of the king must be the religion of the people and the only things no ruler has the right to do is to cause a man to commit suicide or murder or to make him confess to a crime.

Views of Locke: Live and Let Live. John Locke (1632–1704) disagreed with these views. Man is naturally peaceful and co-operative and therefore social life comes readily to him. He sets up an authority in order to preserve the group and that is why laws are made; but the function of the state is strictly limited to maintaining the public good and beyond this men are to be left free. Therefore absolute power and the doctrine of the Divine Right of Kings were wrong because power ultimately rests with the people who have the right to make and break governments. It is also wrong that those who make the laws should be able to execute them. This is the important British doctrine of the separation of powers between the legislature and the executive which, in Britain and America, is regarded as one of the bases of democracy.

Rousseau's Social Doctrine. The only other views we need consider here are those of Jean-Jacques Rousseau (1712–78) and Herbert Spencer (1820–1903), since the views of the two important intervening figures, Hegel and Karl Marx, are dealt with elsewhere (see Dialectical Materialism) and after Spencer we come to a stage where political philosophy begins to merge with sociology and the social sciences. Rousseau is a puzzling figure. On the one hand he has been hailed as the prophet of freedom and on the other as the father of modern totalitarianism. His book *Social Contract* (1762) begins with the words: "Man is born free, and everywhere he is in chains." He says that he is in favour, not merely of democracy, but of direct democracy in which everyone has to give his assent to all measures as in the Greek city-states and in Geneva, of which city he was a citizen. (This method is still in force in respect of some measures in the Swiss cantons.) Natural society is based on a "social contract" or mutual agreement and Rousseau speaks of a "return to nature" which would ensure the sovereignty of the people at all times. Thus far, he seems to agree with Locke but soon we find that he is more akin to Hobbes, since (as we are learning in our own day) nothing is more tyrannical than the absolute rule of all the people. (Public opinion is more Hitlerian than Hitler.) As it turns out, then, the "social contract" consists in "the total alienation of each associate, together with all his rights, to the whole community" and "each of us puts his person and all his power in common under the supreme direction of the general will." Rousseau admired direct democracy in the small city-state, but if his doctrine is applied to large states, then the "general will" becomes absolute. It is in this sense that he is regarded as the forerunner of totalitarianism. Herbert Spencer is quoted only as an example of the inappropriate application of a biological theory to social issues. Influenced by Darwin's thesis of natural selection, he saw in society a struggle in which the fittest survived and the less fit perished. Each individual had the right to preserve himself, but in the case of human beings this depended upon group life in which, to some extent, each individual is limited by the rights of others. But this should not go too far, and he condemned the socialism of J. S. Mill which (a) would give over-much protection to the unfit, and (b) would give the state powers which it has no right to since the best government is the least government. In accordance with Darwinism free competition was essential. Stoics, the followers of Zeno, a Greek philosopher in the 4th cent. B.C., who received their name from the fact that they were taught in the Stoa Poikile or Painted Porch of Athens. They believed that since the world is the creation of divine wisdom and is governed by divine law, it is man's duty to accept his fate. Zeno conceived virtue to be the highest good and condemned the passions. (*See* **God and Man, State and Man, Determinism and Free-will** for a more detailed account of their beliefs.)

Subud, a cultish movement surrounding the Javanese mystic Pak Subuh which established its headquarters in England in 1958 and made newspaper headlines because of alleged "miracle" cures of both psychological and physical ills. The basis of Subud (which is a contraction of three Sanskrit words, Susila Budhi Dharma, meaning "the right living of the soul") is a single spiritual exercise, the *latihan*, in which the individual comes into contact with, or is overwhelmed by a metaphysical force of some kind which is supposed to produce great mental and physical changes. During the latihan people may make strange movements, some violent, and utter unusual cries or chants. Now better known in America than in Britain, Subud did not live up to the expectations of its early followers, many of whom were people of considerable intelligence and professional standing. It is of particular interest because it represents a unique incursion of a rather obscure Eastern cult into Western life, and suggests again that there is growing dissatisfaction in many quarters with orthodox religion and its contribution to the philosophy of the modern world.

Sunnites, the orthodox sect of Islam as contrasted with the Shiites or Shia (*q.v.*).

Swedenborgianism. The Church of the New Jerusalem, based on the writings of Emanuel Swedenborg (1688–1772), was founded by his followers eleven years after his death. The New Church is regarded by its members not as a sect but as a new dispensation bearing the same relationship to Christianity as Christianity does to Judaism.

Synchronicity, an attempt by the psychologist, Carl Gustav Jung, to explain the apparently significant relationship between certain events in the physical universe which seem to have no obvious "causal" link. This rather involved concept is easily understood if one realises that almost all scientific and philosophical beliefs are based on the notion that the continuous process of change which is taking place in ourselves and in the universe around us is dependent upon a principle known as causality. We can express this another way by saying that an object moves because it has been pushed or pulled by another. We see because light strikes the retina and signals pass up the nervous system to the brain. A stone falls to the ground because the earth's gravity is pulling it towards its centre, etc., etc. For all practical purposes every event can be looked upon as being "caused" by some other prior event and this is obviously one of the most important principles of the operation of the universe. Jung, however, felt that there is a sufficiently large body of evidence to suggest that events may be linked in a significant (*i.e.*, non-chance) way without there being any true causal relationship between them. The classic example he held to be the supposed predictive power of astrology by which there appears to be a relationship between the stellar configurations and the personality and life-pattern of individuals on earth. Jung was scientist enough to realise that there could be no causal connection between the aspect of the stars and the lives of people billions of miles from them, yet felt the evidence for astrology was strong enough to demand an alternative non-causal explanation. The trouble with synchronicity, which has not made much impact on the world of physics or of psychology, is that it is not really an explanation at all but merely a convenient word to describe some puzzling correspondences. The real question, of course, is whether there really are events occurring which are significantly but not *causally* linked, and most scientists today would hold that there were probably not. Still it was typical of the bold and imaginative mind of Jung to tackle head-on one of the principal mysteries of existence and come up with a hypothesis to attempt to meet it.

Syndicalism, a form of socialist doctrine which aims at the ownership and control of all industries by the workers, contrasted with the more conventional type of socialism which advocates ownership and control by the state. Since syndicalists have preferred to improve the conditions of the workers by direct action, *e.g.* strikes and working to rule, rather than through the usual parliamentary procedures, they have been closely related to anarchists (*q.v.*) and are sometimes described as anarcho-syndicalists. Under syndicalism there would be no state; for the state would be replaced by a federation of units based on functional economic organisation rather than on geographical representation. The movement had bodies in the United Kingdom, where guild socialism (*q.v.*) was strongly influenced by its doctrines, in France, Germany, Italy, Spain, Argentina, and Mexico, but these gradually declined after the first world war losing many members to the communists. Fascism (*q.v.*) was also strongly influenced by the revolutionary syndicalism of Georges Sorel in making use of his concept of the "myth of the general strike" as an emotional image or ideal goal to spur on the workers; with Mussolini the "myth" became that of the state. Mussolini was also influenced by Sorel's doctrine of violence and the justification of force. Syndicalism had a certain influence in the Labour Party in its early days, but was crushed by men like Ernest Bevin who began to fear that by involving the workers in direct responsibility for their industries, it would put them at a disadvantage when bargaining for wages.

T

Taoism, a religion which, although in a degenerate state, is still one of the great Eastern creeds. Its alleged founder, Lao-tze, is said to have been born in Honan about 604 B.C.; he is also said to be the author of the bible of Taoism, the *Tao-te-ching*, or in English *The Way of Life*, and to have disapproved of Confucius. This, if true, would hardly be surprising; for Taoism is eminently a mystical religion recommending doing nothing and resisting nothing, whereas Confucianism (*q.v.*) is eminently a practical code of living and its founder insisted on intervening in everything to do with social life. But the truth as revealed by modern scholarship is rather different. We are told that the poems of the *Tao-te-ching* are anonymous and probably originated among recluses in lonely valleys long before the time of Confucius; they were collected and given form at some time late in the 3rd cent. B.C. and their authorship attributed to Lao-tze. It is entirely possible that no such person ever existed (unlike Confucius, who certainly did), but if there were such a man he appears to have used a pseudonym since " Lao " is not a surname but an adjective meaning " old " and it was customary to attribute important works to old men on account of their supposed wisdom. Lao-tze simply means " the old philosopher," and although the *Tao-te-ching* is one of the most remarkable and instructive books ever written it is as anonymous as the Border Ballads.

It is apparent that the religion learned both from the ancient Chinese mystics and from Brahmanism: *Tao*, the Way, is impalpable, invisible, and incapable of being expressed in words. But it can be attained by virtue, by compassion, humility, and non-violence. Out of weakness comes true strength whereas violence is not only wrong but defeats its own ends. There is no personal God and such gods as men imagine are mere emanations of *Tao* which gives life to all things. *Tao* is Being. Works are worthless and internal renunciation is far better than anything that follows from the use of force because passive resistance convinces the other from within that he is in error, whereas violence only compels the external appearance of conviction whilst inwardly the individual is as before. " It is wealth to be content; it is wilful to force one's way on others."

Later Lao-tze became a divinity and indeed one of a Trinity each worshipped in the form of idols (which the founder had hated). Soon there was worship of the forces of nature: the stars, the tides, the sun and moon, and a thousand other deities among whom Confucius was one. The purest mysticism and wisdom had been utterly corrupted by contact with the world.

Telepathy and Clairvoyance. Telepathy is the alleged communication between one mind and another other than through the ordinary sense channels. Clairvoyance is the supposed faculty of " seeing " objects or events which, by reason of space and time or other causes, are not discernible through the ordinary sense of vision. Such claims have been made from time immemorial but it was not until this century that the phenomena were investigated scientifically. The first studies were undertaken by the Society for Psychical Research, which was founded in 1882 with Professor Henry Sidgwick as its first president. Since then it has carried out a scholarly programme of research without —in accordance with its constitution—coming to any corporate conclusions. In America the centre of this research was the Parapsychology Laboratory at Duke University (*see* Parapsychology) where at one time it was claimed clear scientific evidence for extra-sensory perception (ESP) had been obtained. These claims were treated with great reservation by the majority of scientists, and today there is a sharply decreasing scientific interest in the field.

Theism. *See* God and Man.

Theosophy (Sanskrit *Brahma Vidya* = divine wisdom), a system of thought that draws on the mystical teachings of those who assert the spiritual nature of the universe, and the divine nature of man. It insists that man is capable of intuitive insight into the nature of God. The way to wisdom, or self-knowledge, is through the practice of Yoga (*q.v.*). Theosophy has close connections with Indian thought through Vedic, Buddhist, and Brahmanist literature. The modern Theosophical Society was founded by Mme H. P. Blavatsky and others in 1875, and popularised by Mrs. Annie Besant.

Tractarianism, a Catholic revival movement, also known as the **Oxford Movement** (not to be confused with the so-called Oxford Group), which had its beginnings at Oxford in 1833. The leaders included the Oxford high churchmen E. B. Pusey, J. Keble and J. H. Newman. Through the *Tracts for the Times* (1833–41), a series of pamphlets which were sent to every parsonage in England, they sought to expose the dangers which they considered to be threatening the church from secular authority. The immediate cause of the movement was the

Reform Act (1832) which meant that the state was no longer in the safe keeping of Tories and Churchmen but that power was falling into the hands of Liberals and Dissenters. They advocated a higher degree of ceremonial in worship nearer the Roman communion. In *Tract 90* (the last) Newman showed how the Thirty-nine Articles themselves, which were regarded as the bulwark of Protestantism, could be made to square with Roman doctrine. It was obvious which direction the movement was taking and the romanizing tendency was widely resented. In 1845 Newman went over to Rome. Pusey and Keble persisted in their efforts to secure recognition of Catholic liturgy and doctrine in the Anglican Church. Catholicism of the Anglican type (*i.e.*, Catholic in ritual, ceremony, and everything save submission to the Pope) is termed Anglo-Catholicism (*q.v.*).

Transmigration of Souls. *See* Immortality, Buddhism, Hinduism.

Transubstantiation, the conversion in the Eucharist of the bread and wine into the body and blood of Christ—a doctrine of the Roman Catholic Church.

Trotskyism, a form of communism supporting the views of Leon Trotsky, the assumed name of Lev Bronstein (1879–1940) who, in 1924, was ousted from power by Stalin and later exiled and assassinated in Mexico. Trotsky held that excessive Russian nationalism was incompatible with genuine international communism and that Stalin was concentrating on the economic development of the Soviet Union to an extent which could only lead to a bureaucratic state with a purely nationalist outlook. After the Hungarian uprising in 1956, which was ruthlessly suppressed by the Soviet Armed Forces, a wave of resignations from Western Communist parties took place, many of the dissident elements taking to Trotskyism in its place.

U

Underground, the name given to an increasingly well-organised group, mainly composed of young people, university students, etc., which propagates anti-establishment and often highly controversial views. Its history, and to some extent its aims, are obscure, but it is a force of increasing power in Western society and its evolution is worth watching with care. The 1960s have been years of great metamorphosis in Europe and America with rapid changes taking place in our attitudes to war and peace, to sex and morals, to marriage and family, to church and state. For large sections of the population these changes have been too rapid and too radical by far, but for others they have been too slow. In particular, the liberalisation of the law on the so-called " soft drugs," notably marijuana, is advocated by a vocal and increasing minority of young people. The expression of their views has been finding outlet in magazines and newspapers, privately published and printed, which reach a wide circulation despite the disinclination of many newsagents to stock them. These publications, while frequently containing material of an obscene and, to many people, highly offensive nature, also contain articles, features, and poems by writers of repute, many of whom contribute regularly to more orthodox publications and yet are sympathetic to the " underground cause." The word underground here, incidentally, refers back to the " underground press " that published revolutionary material at great risk in Nazi occupied territories during the last war. With the exception of the risqué magazine *Private Eye*, which is largely concerned with acid political satire, the first of the genuine underground newsheets was the *International Times* (IT) which was followed in due course by *Oz* and *Rolling Stone*. All three papers are strongly anarchistic in flavour, uneven in literary merit, openly in favour of legalising marijuana (" pot "), and generally quite scandalous to the middle-class and middle-aged. This is not the place to argue the pros and cons of the underground arguments, nor to decide whether our "permissive society" has gone too far or not yet far enough. The important message that the appearance of the whole underground movement implies is that young people, because of greater financial independence, wider opportunities for travel, better education, and easier access to communication channels, such as printing presses, radio transmitters, etc., are beginning to make their admittedly controversial views more widely publicised. Furthermore, this is a trend which will inevitably develop rather than diminish and in the absence of authoritarian repression, these forces will have an increasing impact on our lives. *See also* Weathermen.

Unitarianism has no special doctrines, although clearly, as the name indicates, belief is in the single personality of God, *i.e.*, anti-trinitarian. This general statement, however, can be interpreted with varying degrees of subtlety. Thus unitarian belief may range from a sort of Arianism which accepts that, although Christ was not of divine nature, divine powers had been delegated to him by the Father, to the simple belief that Christ was a man like anyone else, and his goodness was of the same nature as that of many other great and good men. Indeed, today, many Unitarians deny belief in a personal God and interpret their religion in purely moral terms, putting their faith in the value of love and the brotherhood of man. The Toleration Act (1689) excluded Unitarians but from 1813 they were legally tolerated in England. Nevertheless attempts were made to turn them out of their chapels on the ground that the preachers did not hold the views of the original founders of the endowments. But this ended with the Dissenting Chapels Act of 1845. In America no such difficulties existed, and in the Boston of the 19th cent. many of the great literary figures were openly unitarian both in belief and name: *e.g.*, Emerson, Longfellow, Lowell, and Oliver Wendell Holmes.

Utilitarianism, a school of moral philosophy of which the main proponents were J. S. Mill (1806–73) and Jeremy Bentham (1748–1832). Bentham based his ethical theory upon the utilitarian principle that the greatest happiness of the greatest number is the criterion of morality. What is good is pleasure or happiness; what is bad is pain. If we act on this basis of self-interest (pursuing what we believe to be our own happiness), then what we do will automatically be for the general good. The serious failing of this thesis is (1) that it makes no distinction between the quality of one pleasure and another, and (2) that Bentham failed to see that the law might not be framed and administered by men as benevolent as himself. J. S. Mill accepted Bentham's position in general but seeing its failings emphasised (1) that self-interest was an inadequate basis for utilitarianism and suggested that we should take as the real criterion of good the social consequences of the act; (2) that some pleasures rank higher than others and held that those of the intellect are superior to those of the senses. Not only is the social factor emphasised, but emphasis is also placed on the nature of the act.

Utopias. The name "utopia" is taken from a Greek word meaning "nowhere" and was first used in 1516 by Sir Thomas More (1478–1535) as the title of his book referring to a mythical island in the south Pacific where he sited his ideal society. Since then it has been used of any ideal or fanciful society, and here a few will be mentioned. (The reader may recall that Samuel Butler's 19th cent. novel, describing an imaginary society in New Zealand where criminals were treated and the sick punished, was entitled *Erewhon* which is the word "nowhere" in reverse.) It should be noted that not all utopias were entirely fanciful—*e.g.*, Robert Owen's and François Fourier's beliefs, although found to be impractical, were, in fact, tried out.

Sir Thomas More. More wrote at a time when the rise of the wool-growing trade had resulted in farming land being turned over to pasture and there was a great wave of unemployment and a rise in crime among the dispossessed. More began to think in terms of the mediaeval

ideal of small co-operative communities in which class interests and personal gain played a decreasing part, a society which would have the welfare of the people at heart both from the physical and intellectual points of view. His utopia was one in which there was no private property, because the desire for acquisition and private possessions lay at the root of human misery. There was, therefore, only common ownership of land and resources. Each class of worker was equipped to carry out its proper function in the economic scheme and each was fairly rewarded for its share in production so that there was neither wealth nor poverty to inspire conflict. Nobody was allowed to be idle, until the time came for him to retire when he became free to enjoy whatever cultural pleasures he wished, but, since the system was devoid of the waste associated with competition, the working day would be only six hours. There was to be compulsory schooling and free medical care for everybody, full religious toleration, complete equality of the sexes, and a modern system of dealing with crime which was free from vindictiveness and cruelty. Government was to be simple and direct by democratically-elected officials whose powers would be strictly limited and the public expenditure kept under close scrutiny. It will be seen that More was far in advance of his age, and to most democratically-minded people in advance of an earlier utopia, Plato's *Republic*, which is described under the heading of Education.

James Harrington. James Harrington published his book *The Commonwealth of Oceana* in 1656 and offered it to Oliver Cromwell for his consideration but without tangible results. Better than any other man of his time Harrington understood the nature of the economic revolution which was then taking place, and, like More, saw the private ownership of land as the main cause of conflict. He put forward the theory that the control of property, particularly in the shape of land, determines the character of the political structure of the state; if property were universally distributed among the people the sentiment for its protection would naturally result in a republican form of government. The Commonwealth of Oceana was a society "of laws and not of men"—*i.e.*, it was to be legally based and structured so as to be independent of the good or ill-will of any individuals controlling it. Thus there must be a written constitution, a two-house legislature, frequent elections with a secret ballot, and separation of powers between legislature and executive—all today familiar features of parliamentary democracy, but unique in his time.

Saint-Simon. The utopias of the late 18th and 19th cent. come, of course, into the period of the industrial revolution and of laissez-faire capitalism. Individual enterprise and complete freedom of competition formed the outlook of the ruling class. Naturally the utopias of this period tended to have a strongly socialist tinge since such theories are obviously produced by those who are not satisfied with existing conditions. Saint-Simon's *New Christianity* (1825) is one such, and by many, Claude Henri, Comte de Saint-Simon (1760–1825) is regarded as the founder of French socialism. His book urged a dedication of society to the principle of human brotherhood and a community which would be led by men of science motivated by wholly spiritual aims. Production property was to be nationalised (or "socialised" as he describes the process) and employed to serve the public good rather than private gain; the worker was to produce according to his capacity and to be rewarded on the basis of individual merit; the principle of inheritance was to be abolished since it denied the principle of reward for accomplishment on which the society was to be founded. Saint-Simon's proposals were not directed towards the poorer classes alone, but to the conscience and intellect of all. He was deeply impressed with the productive power of the new machines and his scheme was, first and foremost, intended as a method of directing that power to the betterment of humanity as a whole.

Fourier. Francois Marie Charles Fourier (1772–1837), although by conviction a philosophical anarchist who held that human beings are naturally good if allowed to follow their natural desires, was the originator of what, on the face of it, one would suppose to be the most regimented of the utopias. It consisted of a system of "phalanxes" or co-operative communities each composed of a group of workers and technicians assured of a minimum income and sharing the surplus on an equitable basis. Agriculture was to be the chief occupation of each phalanx and industrial employment planned and so carefully assigned that work would become pleasant and creative rather than burdensome. One of his ideas was that necessary work should receive the highest pay, useful work the next, and pleasant work the least pay. The land was to be scientifically cultivated and natural resources carefully conserved. Most of the members' property was to be privately owned, but the ownership of each phalanx was to be widely diffused among members by the sale of shares. Such " parasitic and unproductive " occupations as stockbroker, soldier, economist, middle-man and philosopher would be eliminated and the education of children carried out along vocational lines to train them for their future employment.

The strange thing was that Fourier's suggestions appealed to many both in Europe and the U.S.A. and such men (admittedly no economic or technical experts) as Emerson, Thoreau, James Russell Lowell, and Nathaniel Hawthorne strongly supported them. An American Fourier colony known as Brook Farm was established and carried on for eight years when it was dissolved after a serious fire had destroyed most of its property.

Robert Owen. Robert Owen (1771–1858), a wealthy textile manufacturer and philanthropist, established communities founded on a kind of utopian socialism in Lanarkshire, Hampshire, and in America. Of his New Lanark community an American observer wrote: " There is not, I apprehend, to be found in any part of the world, a manufacturing community in which so much order, good government, tranquillity, and rational happiness prevail." The workers in Lanark were given better housing and education for their children, and it was administered as a co-operative self-supporting community in Scotland. Later in life Owen returned to sponsoring legislation that would remove some of the worst evils of industrial life in those days: reduction of the working day to twelve hours, prohibition of labour for children under the age of ten, public schools for elementary education, and so on. But he lived to see few of his reforms adopted. He also promoted the creation of co-operative societies, the formation of trades unions, labour banks and exchanges, the workers' educational movement, and even an Anglo-American federation. There can be no doubt that, if he saw little result himself, he left the imprint of his convictions to benefit future communities who may not even know his name.

V

Vitalism, the philosophical doctrine that the behaviour of the living organism is, at least in part, due to a vital principle which cannot possibly be explained wholly in terms of physics and chemistry. This belief was at one time held strongly by the late Professor C. E. M. Joad and is implicit in Henri Bergson's (1858–1941) theory of creative evolution. It was maintained by Bergson that evolution, like the work of an artist, is creative and therefore unpredictable; that a vague need exists beforehand within the animal or plant before the means of satisfying the need develops. Thus we might assume that sightless animals developed the need to become aware of objects before they were in physical contact with them and that this ultimately led to the origin of organs of sight. Earlier this century a form of vitalism described as "emergent evolution" was put forward. This theory maintains that when two or more simple entities come together there

may arise a new property which none of them previously possessed. Today biologists would say that it is the *arrangement* of atoms that counts, different arrangements exhibiting different properties, and that biological organisation is an essentially dynamic affair, involving the lapse of time.

W

Wahabis, members of an Arabian sect of Islam which originated in the teaching of Muhammad Ibn 'Abd-al-Wahab, born at the end of the 17th cent. He was deeply resentful of the Turkish rule which, in addition to its tyranny, had brought about innovations in the religion which Muhammad regarded as a perversion of its original form. He proceeded to reform Islam to its primitive conditions and impressed his beliefs on Mohammed Ibn Saud, a sheikh who spread them with the aid of his sword. Under the successors of Ibn Saud the power of the Wahabis spread over much of Arabia where it is dominant today in Saudi Arabia. Its particular characteristic is that it refuses to accept symbolic or mystical interpretations of the words of the Prophet and accepts quite literally the teaching of Islam. It is, in fact, a sort of Moslem fundamentalism. Although crushed by the Turks in 1811–15, the movement remains an important element in Mohammedanism.

Waldenses, a movement also known as " The Poor Men of Lyons," founded by Peter Waldo of that city about the same time, and in the same part of southern France, as the Albigenses (*q.v.*) with whom, however, they had nothing in common. Their main belief was a return to Apostolic simplicity, based on reading the Bible in their own language; their doctrines were somewhat similar to those of the Mennonites and the Quakers. However, they did not wish to separate themselves from the Church and were originally protected by several popes until the Lateran Council of 1215 excluded them mainly for the crime of preaching without ecclesiastical permission. From this time they were subjected to persecution, yet maintained some contact with the Church until the Reformation when they chose to take the side of the Protestants. Situated mainly on the sides of the Alps, half in Piedmont and half in France, they were persecuted or not according to the contemporary political convenience of the Dukes of Savoy, and the major attempt to destroy them called forth Oliver Cromwell's intervention and the famous sonnet of Milton. In spite of torture, murder, deportation, and even the kidnapping of their children, to have them brought up in the Roman Catholic faith, the sect survived, and still exists, having been granted full equality of rights with his Roman Catholic subjects by Charles Edward of Piedmont in 1848.

Weathermen, the rather incongruous name for the most radical and volatile of the many groups making up the so-called "underground" in the United States of America. Unlike most of the loosely-structured organisations involved in the growing anti-establishment front, the Weathermen appear to have direct rather than anarchistic political goals, taking a stand far to the left of traditional politics. Their avowed aim is the total overthrow of the current American political structure, with specific and carefully planned acts of violence as the tools of their trade and the civil police force as one of their prime targets. This has led to a series of bomb explosions, often cunningly planned, and brutal murders of police patrolmen which have deeply shocked the average American citizen. A particularly sinister and ominous feature, to most people's eyes, is the fact that the Weathermen appear to be largely drawn from the highly intelligent and well-educated strata, many of them with well-to-do and/or academic backgrounds. Members of this group make no secret of their contempt for the intellect and political attitudes of the American middle-class, and claim to demonstrate the impotence of Society by their ability to commit flagrant acts of violence with such ease and the equal ease with which they subsequently escape detection and arrest. In 1970 one of the leaders of the Weathermen, an attractive and dynamic woman university lecturer, was placed on the FBI's notorious "most wanted criminals" list. The elusive nature of the organisation and its uncertain background have led to a number of fantastic speculations about its true origins. One of the oddest of these is the notion, widely held in America, that the Weathermen are in reality financed and backed by the country's extreme *right*—as a means of discrediting in the public eye the slow but steady move towards socialism that seems to be developing there. Such speculations serve really to remind one that the political structure of the United States, remarkably stable for over a century, is entering a confused and tortured revolutionary phase.

Witchcraft. There are various interpretations and definitions of witchcraft from that of Pennethorne Hughes who states that " witchcraft, as it emerges into European history and literature, represents the old paleolithic fertility cult, plus the magical idea, plus various parodies of contemporary religions " to that of the fanatical Father Montague Summers who says that Spiritualism and witchcraft are the same thing. A leading authority on witchcraft, however, the late Dr. Margaret Murray, distinguishes between Operative Witchcraft (which is really Magic (*q.v.*)) and Ritual Witchcraft which, she says, " embraces the religious beliefs and ritual of the people known in late mediaeval times as ' witches.' " That there were such people we know from history and we know, too, that many of them—the great majority of them women—were tortured or executed or both. Many innocent people perished, especially after the promulgation of the bull *Summis desiderantes* by Pope Innocent VIII in 1484. Himself " a man of scandalous life ", according to a Catholic historian, he wrote to " his dear sons," the German professors of theology, Johann Sprenger and Heinrich Kraemer, " witches are hindering men from performing the sexual act and women from conceiving . . . " and delegated them as Inquisitors " of these heretical pravities." In 1494 they codified in the *Malleus Maleficarum* (Hammer of Witches) the ecclesiastical rules for detecting acts of witchcraft. Dr. Murray points out that there have ordinarily been two theories about witchcraft: (1) that there were such beings as witches, that they possessed supernatural powers and that the evidence given at their trials was substantially correct; (2) that the witches were simply poor silly creatures who either deluded themselves into believing that they had certain powers or, more frequently, were tortured into admitting things that they did not do. She herself accepts a third theory: that there were such beings as witches, that they really did what they admitted to doing, but that they did not possess supernatural powers. They were in fact believers in the old religion of pre-Christian times and the Church took centuries to root them out. That there existed " covens " of witches who carried out peculiar rites Dr. Murray has no doubt whatever. The first to show that witchcraft was a superstition and that the majority of so-called witches were people suffering from mental illness was the physician Johann Weyer of Cleves (1515–88). His views were denounced by the Catholic Church. Few people realise how deeply the notion of witchcraft is implanted in our minds and how seriously its power is still taken. For example, the Witchcraft Act was not repealed in this country until the 1950s. Furthermore, as recently as 1944, when the allied armies were invading Europe, the Spiritualist medium Mrs. Helen Duncan was charged with witchcraft and actually sent to prison—a prosecution which brought forth caustic comments from the then prime minister, Winston Churchill. *See also* Demonism.

Women's Liberation Movement, the name given to a loosely organised collection of women drawn from all ages and walks of life which appears to be emerging as a latter-day " super-suffragette " movement. Unlike the original suffragette movement, however, which advocated " Votes for Women," the 1970s' version seems to have less definite aims. The principal argument hinges on the fact that with the development of highly efficient methods of contraception (the " pill ") women need no longer be " slaves " to their family commitments and the traditional dominant and decision-making role of the male in our society must go. At the same time there should be no more wage or job discrimination against women. The movement is relatively strong in America and is acquiring some slight power in local and state politics.

World Congress of Faiths, an inter-religious movement which aims to break down barriers between faiths. The first step towards it was taken by the world's parliament of religions held in Chicago in 1893; and similar gatherings were held subsequently at intervals in Europe; but the actual organisation was formed in 1936 by Sir Francis Younghusband; and now an annual conference is held and educational activity carried on.

World Council of Churches, a union of Christian Churches from all over the world (including the Churches of the Protestant, Anglican, and Orthodox traditions, but excluding the Roman Catholic Church), engaged in extending Christian mission and unity throughout the world. All Churches which " accept our Lord Jesus Christ as God and Saviour " are eligible. This modern ecumenical movement stems from the great World Missionary Conference held at Edinburgh in 1910. The World Council was founded in 1948 and meets for consultation from time to time; the fourth assembly met at Uppsala in 1968 to discuss the theme "All Things New."

Y

Yoga, a Hindu discipline which teaches a technique for freeing the mind from attachment to the senses, so that once freed the soul may become fused with the universal spirit (*Atman* or *Brahman*), which is its natural goal. This is the sole function of the psychological and physical exercises which the Yogi undertakes, although few ever reach the final stage of *Samadhi* or union with *Brahman* which is said to take place in eight levels of attainment. These are: (1) *Yama,* which involves the extinction of desire and egotism and their replacement by charity and unselfishness; (2) *Niyama* during which certain rules of conduct must be adopted, such as cleanliness, the pursuit of devotional studies, and the carrying out of rituals of purification; (3) *Asana,* or the attainment of correct posture and the reduction to a minimum of all bodily movement (the usual posture of the concentrating Yogi is the " lotus position " familiar from pictures); (4)–(5) *Pranayama,* the right control of the life-force or breath in which there are two stages at which the practitioner hopes to arrive, the first being complete absorption in the act of breathing which empties the mind of any other thought, the second being the ability almost to cease to breathe which allegedly enables him to achieve marvellous feats of endurance; (6) *Pratyahara* or abstraction which means the mind's complete withdrawal from the world of sense; (7) *Dharana* in which an attempt is made to think of one thing only which finally becomes a repetition of the sacred syllable OM, and perhaps by a kind of self-hypnosis, leads (8) to *Samadhi* the trance state which is a sign of the complete unity of soul with reality.

Yoga is very old, and when the sage Patanjali (c. 300 B.C.) composed the book containing these instructions, the *Yoga Sutras,* he was probably collecting from many ancient traditions. Some of the claims made by Yogis seem, to the Western mind, frankly incredible; but in the West and especially in recent years Yoga methods have been used at the lower levels in order to gain improved self-control, better posture, and improved health. Whether it achieves these ends is another matter, but the genuine Yogi regards this as a perversion of the nature and purpose of the discipline.

Z

Zen Buddhism, a Buddhist sect which is believed to have arisen in 6th cent. China but has flourished chiefly in Japan; for some reason it has of recent years begun to attract attention in the West thanks to the voluminous writings of Dr. D. T. Suzuki and the less numerous but doubtless much-read books of Mr. Christmas Humphreys. But the fact that these writings exist does not explain their being read, nor why of all possible Eastern sects this particular one should be chosen in our times. What is Zen's attraction and why should anyone take the trouble to read about something (the word " something " is used for reasons that will become evident) that is not a religion, has no doctrine, knows no God and no after-life, no good and no evil, and possesses no scriptures but has to be taught by parables which seem to be purposely meaningless? One of the heroes of Zen is the fierce-looking Indian monk Boddhidharma (fl. *c.* 516–534) who brought Buddhism to China, of whom it is recounted that when the Emperor asked him how much merit he had acquired by supporting the new creed, the monk shouted at him: " None whatever! " The Emperor then wished to know what was the sacred doctrine of the creed, and again the monk shouted: " It is empty—there is nothing sacred! " Dr. Suzuki, having affirmed that there is no God in Zen, goes on to state that this does not mean that Zen denies the existence of God because " neither denial nor affirmation concerns Zen." The most concrete statement he is prepared to make is that the basic idea of Zen is to come in touch with the inner workings of our being, and to do this in the most direct way possible without resorting to anything external or superadded. Therefore anything that has the semblance of an external authority is rejected by Zen. Absolute faith is placed in a man's own inner being. Apparently the intention is that, so far from indulging in inward meditations or such practices as the Yogi uses, the student must learn to act spontaneously, without thinking, and without self-consciousness or hesitation. This is the main purpose of the *koan,* the logically insoluble riddle which the pupil must try to solve. One such is the question put by master to pupil: " A girl is walking down the street, is she the younger or the older sister? " The correct answer, it seems, is to say nothing but put on a mincing gait, to *become* the girl, thus showing that what matters is the experience of being and not its verbal description. Another *koan:* " What is the Buddha? " " Three pounds of flax " is attributed to T'ungshan in the 9th cent. and a later authority's comment is that " none can excel it as regards its irrationality which cuts off all passages to speculation." Zen, in effect, teaches the uselessness of trying to use words to discuss the Absolute.

Zen came to Japan in the 13th cent., more than five centuries after Confucianism or the orthodox forms of Buddhism, and immediately gained acceptance whilst becoming typically Japanese in the process. One of the reasons why it appealed must have been that its spontaneity and insistence on action without thought, its emphasis on the uselessness of mere words, and such categories as logical opposites, had an inevitable attraction for a people given to seriousness, formality, and logic to a degree which was almost stifling. Zen must have been to the Japanese what nonsense rhymes and nonsense books, like those of Edward Lear and Lewis Carroll, were to the English intellectuals. Lear's limericks, like some of the *koans,* end up with a line which, just at the time when one expects a point to be made, has no particular point at all, and *Alice in Wonderland* is the perfect example of a world, not without logic, but with a crazy logic of its own which has no relationship to that of everyday life. Therefore Zen began to impregnate every aspect of life in Japan, and one of the results of its emphasis on spontaneous action rather than reason was its acceptance by the Samurai, the ferocious warrior class, in

such activities as swordsmanship, archery Japanese wrestling, and later Judo and the Kamikaze dive-bombers. But much of Japanese art, especially landscape gardening and flower-arrangement, was influenced similarly, and Zen is even used in Japanese psychiatry. The very strict life of the Zen monks is based largely on doing things, learning through experience; the periods of meditation in the Zendo hall are punctuated by sharp slaps on the face administered by the abbot to those who are unsatisfactory pupils. Dr. Suzuki denies that Zen is nihilistic, but it is probably its appearance of nihilism and its appeal to the irrational and spontaneous which attracts the Western world at a time when to many the world seems without meaning and life over-regimented. However, it has influenced such various aspects o Western life as philosophy (Heidegger), psychi atry (Erich Fromm and Hubert Benoit) writing (Aldous Huxley), and painting (Di Zen Gruppe in Germany).

Zionism, a belief in the need to establish an autonomous Jewish home in Palestine which in its modern form, began with Theodor Herz (1860–1904), a Hungarian journalist working in Vienna. Although Herzl was a more or less assimilated Jew, he was forced by the Dreyfus case and the pogroms in Eastern Europe to conclude that there was no real safety for the Jewish people until they had a state of their own. The Jews, of course, had always in a religious sense thought of Palestine as a spiritual homeland and prayed " next year in Jerusalem," but the religious had thought of this in a philosophical way as affirming old loyalties not as recommending the formation of an actual state. Therefore Herzl was opposed both by many of the religious Jews and, at the other extreme, by those who felt themselves to be assimilated and in many cases without religious faith. Even after the Balfour Declaration of 1917, there was not a considerable flow of Jews to Palestine, which at that time was a pre dominantly Arab state. But the persecutions of Hitler changed all this and, after bitter struggles, the Jewish state was proclaimed in 1948. Today Zionism is supported by the vast majority of the Jewish communities everywhere (although strongly disapproved of in the Soviet Union as " Western imperialism ") and Zionism is now an active international force concerned with protecting the welfare and extending the influence of Israel.

Zoroastrianism, at one time one of the great world religions, competing in the 2nd cent. A.D. or almost equal terms from its Persian home with Hellenism and the Roman Imperial Government. Under the Achaemenidae (c. 550–330 B.C.) Zoroastrianism was the state religion o Persia. Alexander's conquest in 331 B.C brought disruption but the religion flourished again under the Sassanian dynasty (A.D. c. 226–640). With the advance of the Mohammedan Arabs in the 7th cent. Zoroastrianism finally gave way to Islam. A number of devotees fled to India there to become the Parsees. In Persia itself a few scattered societies remain

The name Zoroaster is the Greek rendering o Zarathustra, the prophet who came to purify the ancient religion of Persia. It is thought that he lived at the beginning of the 6th cent, B.C. He never claimed for himself divine powers but was given them by his followers. The basis of Zoroastrianism is the age-long war between good and evil, Ahura Mazda heading the good spirits and Ahriman the evil ones. Morality is very important since by doing right the worshipper is supporting Ahura Mazda against Ahriman, and the evil-doers will be punished in the last days when Ahura Mazda wins his inevitable victory.

The sacred book of this religion is the *Avesta.* If Zoroastrianism has little authority today, it had a very considerable influence in the past. Its doctrines penetrated into Judaism (q.v.) and, through Gnosticism, Christianity. The worship of Mithra by the Romans was an impure version of Zoroastrianism. Manichaeism (q.v.) was a Zoroastrian heresy and the Albigensianism of mediaeval times was the last relic of a belief which had impressed itself deeply in the minds of men.

GAZETTEER
OF THE
WORLD

A complete index to the maps with
up-to-date descriptive matter, together with a list of Commonwealth
countries with their land areas and
recent estimates of population.

GAZETTEER OF THE WORLD

An endeavour has been made to include all the more important places throughout the world. The small scale of the maps included in the Cyclopedia does not enable all places included in the gazetteer to be named on the maps.

In regard to the spelling of place names, the general principle followed has been to adopt national spellings. For those countries where the Latin Alphabet is not used, the principles for transliteration laid down by the " Permanent Committee on Geographical Names " of the Royal Geographical Society have been followed. Chinese entries are in the conventional English form. New official Chinese form, based on Chinese romanised alphabet adopted 1958, is in brackets. There may be a few instances where the spelling shown on the map does not conform to that used in the gazetteer.

ABBREVIATIONS USED IN THE GAZETTEER

GEOGRAPHICAL NAMES

Ala. = Alabama.
Ark. = Arkansas.
A.S.S.R. = Autonomous Soviet Socialist Republic.
Atl. Oc. = Atlantic Ocean.
B.C. = British Columbia.
Brit. = British.
Cal. = California.
Col. = Colorado.
Conn. = Connecticut.
CSSR = Czechoslovak Socialist Republic.
Del. = Delaware.
Eng. = England.
E.R. = East Riding.
Fla. = Florida.
Fr. = French.
Ga. = Georgia.
Ill. = Illinois.
Ind. = Indiana.
Kan. = Kansas.
Ky. = Kentucky.

La. = Louisiana.
Mass. = Massachusetts.
Md. = Maryland.
Me. = Maine.
Mich. = Michigan.
Minn. = Minnesota.
Miss. = Mississippi.
Mo. = Missouri.
Mont. = Montana.
N.B. = New Brunswick.
N.C. = North Carolina.
N.D. = North Dakota.
Neth. = Netherlands.
N.H. = New Hampshire.
N.J. = New Jersey.
N.M. = New Mexico.
N.R. = North Riding.
N.Y. = New York.
N.Z. = New Zealand.
O.F.S. = Orange Free State.
Okla. = Oklahoma.
Ore. = Oregon.

Pac. Oc. = Pacific Ocean.
Pa. = Pasadena.
Penns. = Pennsylvania.
R.I. = Rhode Island.
R.o.I. = Republic of Ireland.
R.S.F.S.R. = Russian Soviet Federal Socialist Republic.
S.C. = South Carolina.
Scot. = Scotland.
S.D. = South Dakota.
S.S.R. = Soviet Socialist Republic.
Tenn. = Tennessee.
U.A.R. = United Arab Republic.
U.S.S.R. = Union of Soviet Socialist Republics.
Va. = Virginia.
Vt. = Vermont.
Wash. = Washington
W.I. = West Indies.
Wis. = Wisconsin.
Wyo. = Wyoming.

Abbreviations of names of Counties in Gt. Britain and Rep. of Ireland are those recognised by the General Post Office.

OTHER ABBREVIATIONS

a. = area.
agr. = agriculture.
alt. = altitude.
approx. = approximate.
arch. = archaeological.
aut. rep. = autonomous republic.
ass. = associated.
bdy. = boundary.
bldg. = building.
bor. = borough.
C. = cape.
c. = city.
can. = canton.
cap. = capital.
cas. = castle.
cath. = cathedral.
ch. = chief.
co. = county.
co. bor. = county borough.
col. = colony.
colly. = colliery.
comm. = commercial.
cst. = coast.
ctr. = centre.
cty. = country.
dep. = department.
dist. = district.
div. = division.
E. = east or easterly.
elec. = electrical.
engin. = engineering.
estd. = estimated.
exp. = exports.

F. = firth.
fed. = federal.
fish. pt. = fishing port.
fortfd. = fortified.
ft. = feet.
G. = gulf.
gd. = good.
gen. = general.
gr. = great, group.
I. = island.
impt. = important.
inc. = including.
indep. = independent.
inds. = industries.
industl. = industrial.
Is. = islands.
L. = lake.
lge. = large.
lgst. = largest.
m. = miles.
machin. = machinery.
mftg. = manufacturing.
mkg. = making.
mkt. = market.
mnfs. = manufactures.
mng. = mining.
mt. = mount.
mtn. = mountain.
mun. = municipality.
mun. bor. = municipal borough.
N. = north or northerly.
nat. = national.
nr. = near.

p. = population.
par. = parish.
parlt. = parliament.
parly. = parliamentary.
prod. = products.
prot. = protectorate.
prov. = province.
pt. = port.
R. = river.
rep. = republic.
residtl. = residential.
rly. = railway.
rural dist. = rural district.
S. = south or southerly.
shipbldg. = shipbuilding.
sm. = small.
spt. = seaport.
sq. m. = square miles.
St. = Saint.
st. = state.
sta. = station.
sub. = suburb.
t. = town.
terr. = territory.
tr. = trade.
trib. = tributary.
univ. = university.
urb. dist. = urban district.
vil. = village.
W. = west or westerly.
wat. pl. = watering place.
wks. = works.
wkshps. = workshops.

Land = administrative division of W. Germany approx. corresponding to " province ".

A

Aabenraa, *spt.*, S.E. Jutland, Denmark; at head of Aabenraa fjord; cars, trailers, clothing; p. (1960) *14,219.*

Aachen, *t.*, N. Rhine–Westphalia, Germany; formerly Aix-la-Chapelle; one of the oldest cities in Germany, cath., famous baths; suffered badly from bombing in Second World War and was first large German town to be taken by the Allied Forces in 1944; non-ferrous metal inds. textiles, needles, footwear, elec. goods; p. (1968) *176,726.*

Aaiun, *cap.*, Saguia el Hamra region of Spanish Sahara.

Aalborg, *c.*, *spt.* Jutland, Denmark; shipbldg., cement, textiles, machin.; airport; p. (1965) *99,815.*

Aalen, *t.*, Baden-Württemberg, Germany; on R. Kocher; iron, textiles, lens mkg.; p. (1963) *33,700.*

Aalst, *see* Alost.

Aar, *R.*, Switzerland, flows through Brienz and Thun lakes, and thence into the Rhine, 181 m.; famous Aar gorges above Meiringen.

Aarau, *t.*, cap. Aargau can., Switzerland; precision tools and instruments, shoes, textiles; hydro-elec. plant; p. (estd.) *17,000.*

Aargau, *can.*, N. Switzerland; a. 542 sq. m.; extensive vineyards, cereals, orchards, metal prod., textiles, salt mining; p. (1961) *360,940.*

Aarhus, *c.*, principal spt. on E. coast of Jutland, Denmark; famous Gothic cath., univ.; iron, metals, shipbldg, marine engin., textiles, paper, chemicals; p. (1965) *187,342.*

Abaco, Gt., Bahama Is., W. Indies; p. (1953) *3,407.*

Abadan, *c.*, Iran; oil refineries; intern. airpt.; tech. coll.; p. (1967) *339,121.*

Abakan, *t.*, R.S.F.S.R., on R. Jenisei; sawmilling, food inds.; p. (1959) *56,000.*

Abbazia, *see* Opatija.

Abbeville, *mftg. c.*, on the R. Somme (N. France); connected with Paris and Belgium by canals; sugar-milling, carpets, biscuits, beer; p. (1962) *26,899.*

Abbeyleix, *t.*, *rural dist.*, Laoighis, Ireland; quarries; p. (rural dist. 1961) *11,813.*

Abbotsbury, *par.*, Dorset, Eng.; world-famous swannery.

Abbots-Langley, *par.*, Herts, Eng., birthplace of Nicholas Breakspeare (Pope Adrian IV); p. (1961) *18,157.*

Abeokuta, *t.*, Nigeria; N. of Lagos; palm oil, hard-woods; p. (1953) *84,000.*

Aberavon, *t.*, Glamorgan, Wales; on R. Avon, 8 m. E. of Swansea; harbour Port Talbot; lge. coal and iron inds., metals, tinplate, cables; p. (1961) *31,226.*

Aberayron, *urb. dist.*, Cardigan, S. Wales; p. (1961) *1,220.*

Abercarn, *urb. dist.*, Monmouth, Wales; coal and tron, tin-plate, knitting pins; p. (1961) *19,221.*

Aberchirder, *burgh*, Banff, Scot.; p. (1961) *755.*

Abercorn. *par.*, W. Lothian, Scot.; on the Forth; Roman wall built by Antoninus began here, and extended to Kirkpatrick on the Clyde; p. (1951) *806.*

Abercorn, *t.* Zambia; trading sta.; airfield; European p. (1959) *250.*

Aberdare, *urb. dist.*, Glamorgan, Wales, on the R. Cynon; wire cables; p. (1961) *39,044.*

Aberdeen, *co.*, Scot.; mtnous; agr., oats, barley, turnips, cattle; fisheries; granite, brewing, distilling, paper; a. 1,970 sq. m.; p. (1961) *298,503.*

Aberdeen, *c.*, Aberdeenshire and Kincardine, Scot.; at mouth of R. Dee, 100 m. N.E. of Edinburgh; univ.; sm. shipbldg., fishing, oats, whisky, paper mkg., granite, tourism; p. (1961) *185,379* of whom *23,254* S. of R. Dee are in Kincardine co.

Aberdeen, *t.*, S.D., U.S.A.; chemicals, foundry; p. (1960) *23,073.*

Aberdeen, *spt.*, Wash., U.S.A.; lumbering, salmon canning; p. (1960) *18,741.*

Aberdovey, *vat. pl.* Merioneth, Wales, on estuary of R. Dovey.

Aberfeldy, *burgh*, Perth, Scot., in Strath Tay, 4 m. below Loch Tay; mkt.; salmon and trout fishing resort; p. (1961) *1,469.* [(1951) *1,133.*

Aberfoyle, *par.*, Perth, Scot.; tourist resort; p.

Abergavenny, *mun. bor., t.*, Monmouth, on R. Usk; light engin., concrete prods.; p. (1961) *9,625.*

Abergele, *urb. dist.*, Denbigh, Wales; small wat. pl.; p. (1961) *7,982.*

Aberlour, Charlestown of, *burgh*, Banff, Scot.; on R. Spey, 12 m. S. of Elgin; p. (1961) *953.*

Abernethy, *burgh*, Perth, Scot.; on R. Tay once the cap. of the Pictish Kings; p. (1961) *601.*

Abersychan, *par.*, Monmouth, Wales; coal, iron, and steel; p. *25,748.*

Abertillery, *urb. dist.*, Monmouth.; coal, engin., leather goods; p. (1961) *25,160.*

Aberystwyth. *mun. bor., vat. pl.*, on Cardigan Bay at the mouth of the R. Ystwyth, Cardigan, Wales; univ. college; Nat. Library of Wales; p. (1961) *10,418.*

Abidjan, *cap.*, Ivory Coast, W. Africa; palm oil, cocoa, copra, hardwood, rubber; oil refining at Vridi nearby; p. (1963) *212,000.*

Abilene, *t.*, Kansas, U.S.A.; univ.; food prod., oilseeds, oil-refining, cotton; p. (1960) *90,368.*

Abingdon, *mun. bor.*, Berks, Eng., on R. Thames; cars, leather goods; p. (estd. 1967) *16,770.*

Abingdon, *t.*, Va., U.S.A.; lumbering, flour milling; mnfs. condensed milk, chemicals, tobacco; tourist resort; p. (1960) *4,758.*

Abington, *t.*, Mass., U.S.A.; shoes, textile machin.; p. (1960) *10,449.*

Abitibi, *R.* and *L.* R. flows into James Bay, Ontario, Canada; gold dist.

Abo, *see* Turku, Finland.

Abomey, *old cap.*, Dahomey, W. Africa; former slave mkt.; cotton; p. (estd. 1960) *18,900.*

Abovyan, *t.*, Armenian S.S.R.; 10 m. from Yerevan; new model t. founded 1963; planned p. *50,000.*

Aboyne and Glentanner, *par.*, Aberdeen. Scot.; hol. res. on R. Dee nr. Ballater; p. (1951) *1,651.*

Abraham, Plains of, nr. Quebec; Wolfe's victory over French under Montcalm, 1759.

Abram, *urb. dist.*, Lancs, Eng.; coal, engin., cotton mnfs.; p. (1961) *6,017.*

Abrantes, *t.*, Portugal, on the Tagus R.; French won battle here in Napoleonic Wars, 1807.

Abruzzi, *region* of Italy on the Adriatic, inc. provs. of Aquila, Chieti, Teramo; methane fields; p. (1961) *1,584,777.*

Abu, *mtn.*, Rajasthan, India, 5,653 ft.; Jain temples.

Abu Dhabi, *t.*, *emirate*, lgst of Trucial sts.; S.E. Arabian pen.; rich oil reserves; a. 80,000 sq. m.; p. (estd. 1968) *50,000.*

Abukir or Aboukir, *vil.* on Abukir Bay, U.A.R.; site of ancient Canopus; Battle of the Nile fought in the Bay, 1798; p. *7,086.*

Abu Simbel, Nile Valley, U.A.R.; famous anc. temples carved out of solid sandstone, one to Rameses II and the other to his Queen; saved from waters of Lake Nasser.

Abydos, *ruined c.*, Upper U.A.R.; celebrated for its temple of Osiris.

Abydos. *ruined castled t.*, Anatolia on the Dardanelles, which resisted Philip of Macedon; famous for the story of Leander and Hero.

Abyssinia, *see* Ethiopia.

Acajutla, *spt.*, Salvador, Central America; exp. coffee; cement, oil refining, fertilisers; p. (1960) *15,475.*

Acambaro, *t.*, Mexico; rly. junction; p. *17,643.*

Acapulco, *spt.*, Pacific coast, Mexico; tourism; exp. hides, cedar, fruit; p. (1960) *28,582.*

Accra, *spt.*, *cap.* Ghana, W. Africa; univ; airport (renamed Kotoka); pharmaceutics; p. (1960) *491,060* (inc. cap. dist, and rural a.).

Accrington, *mun. bor., mftg. t.*, Lancs, Eng.; 20 m. N. of Manchester; cotton ctr., coal, textile machin., engin., bricks; p. (estd. 1967) *37,470.*

Acerra, *t.*, S. Italy; destroyed by Hannibal 216 B.C.; restored 210 B.C.; olive oil, wine, hemp; p. *16,460.*

Achaia, *prov.*, Greece; a. 1,206 sq. m.; chief currant-producing dist.; spt., Patras; p. (1961) *236,770.*

Achalpur, *t.*, W. Madhya Pradesh, India; cotton.

Achill, *I.*, off the W. coast of Mayo, Ireland; agr., fishing.

Achill Head, *cape*, Mayo.

Achinsk, *industl. t.*, R.S.F.S.R., on R. Chulym; impt. rly. junction; manganese, cement; p. (1956) *42,400.*

Acireale, *spt.*, Sicily; sulphur baths; p. (1961) *43,752.*

Acklin, *island*, Bahamas, W. Indies; timber, sponges; p. (1953) *1,273.*

Aconcagua, *mtn.*, Andes, Argentine, S. America; highest peak of New World, alt. 22,835 ft.

Aconcagua, *prov.*, Chile; a. 3,939 sq. m.; cap. San Felipe; alfalfa and Mediterranean fruits; p. (1957) 154,075.

Aconquija, Sierra de, *mtn. range* N. Argentina, S. America; rises steeply from Chaco lowland to 18,000 ft.

Acqui, *ancient walled t.*, N. Italy, prov. Alessandria; famous cath., sulphur springs; p. 18,975.

Acre (Akka), *c., spt.*, Israel, famous for its sieges during Crusades and in 1799 withstanding Napoleon for 61 days; p. c. 18,000.

Acre, *st.*, Brazil; a. 59,139 sq. m., cap. Rio Branco; cattle, rubber, manioc; p. (estd. 1968) 204,081.

Acton, *former mun. bor.*, Middlesex, Eng.; now inc. in Ealing outer bor., Greater London. (*q.v.*), univ.

Ada, *t.*, Oklahoma, U.S.A.; p. (1960) 14,347.

Adamawa, *region*, W. Africa, divided between Nigeria and Cameroun; a. 70,000 sq. m.; ivory, groundnuts.

Adams, *mfg. t.* Mass., U.S.A.; paper, cottons, woollens, calcium quarrying; p. (1960) 11,949.

Adam's Bridge, chain of sandbanks, 22 m. long, in Palk Strait, between India and Ceylon. Construction of rail causeway mooted.

Adam's Peak, *sacred mtn.*, S. Ceylon, alt. 7,352 ft.

Adana, *t.*, Turkey; on R. Seihan; wool, cotton, grain, tobacco; p. (1965) 290,515.

Adapazari, *t.*, Turkey; rly. junction; agr. and tr. ctr., silk, linen; high grade concentrate from low grade iron ore deposits in Camdagi a.; p. (1965) 85,579.

Adda, *R.*, N. Italy, flows through L. Como to R. Po.

Addis Ababa, *cap.* Ethiopia; terminus of Jibuti rly.; p. (1960) 450,000.

Adelaide, *c., spt., cap.*, S. Australia; on R. Torrens, which flows into G. of St. Vincent; transcontinental rly. connections; univ.; cars, steel tubes, electrical appliances, chemicals, sugar and oil refining; p. (with subs) (1966) 726,930.

Adelboden, *t.*, Bern can., Switzerland; 19 m. S.W. of Interlaken; health resort, mineral springs.

Adélie Land, Antarctica; French terr. and dependency of Réunion.

Adelsburg, *t.*, Jugoslavia; 20 m. N.E. of Trieste; extensive grotto and stalactite cavern.

Aden, *spt.*, Southern Yemen (1967), S. Arabia, former Brit. col.; bay behind headlands of Aden t. and Little Aden, excellent anchorage. *See also* Yemen, Southern.

Aden, Gulf of, Arabian Sea; 48 m. l., 180 m. wide.

Aderno, *t.*, Sicily, Italy; at base of Mt. Etna, ancient ruins; p. 24,307.

Adige, *R.* in N. Italy; enters Adriatic N. of Po, length 240 m.

Adirondacks, *mtns.*, N.Y., U.S.A.; highest peak, Mt. Marcy, 5,345 ft.

Adiyaman, *t.*, Turkey; p. (1960) 17,021.

Adlington, *urb. dist.*, Lancs, Eng.; nr. Chorley; cotton, coal-mining; p. (1961) 4,281.

Admiralty G., N.W. of Western Australia.

Admiralty I., off Alaska mainland; belongs to U.S.A.; fishing, timber.

Admiralty Is., S.W. Pac. Oc. N. of New Guinea, comprise 40 sm. is.; Australian mandate; coconuts, copra; a. 663 sq. m.; p. 13,134.

Adonara, *I.*, one of Nusa Tenggara Is., Indonesia; p. (estd.) 25,000.

Adoni, *t.*, Andhra Pradesh, India; cotton market; p. (1961) 69,951.

Adour, *R.*, S.W. France; rises in Pyrenees, enters Bay of Biscay below Bayonne; length 207 m.

Adowa, *t., cap.*, Tigre prov., N. Ethiopia; alt. over 6000 ft., tr. and mkt. centre; p. c. 10,000.

Adra, *spt., t.*, Almeria, S. Spain; nr. Guardia Viejas salt beds and Berja lead-mines; sugar-cane, fish, fruit and veg. canning; p. (1957) 13,687.

Adrano, *t.*, Sicily, Italy; at S.W. foot of Etna; agr. mkt.; p. c. 29,000.

Adrar *oasis*, Sahara Desert, Algeria; salt, dates, grain; p. (1960) 44,116.

Adria, *mkt. t.*, Rovigo, Italy; formerly on cst., now 14 m. inland, old Etruscan c.

Adrian, *c.*, Michigan, U.S.A.; 73 m. W. of Detroit; p. (1960) 20,347.

Adrianople, *see* Edirne.

Adriatic Sea, branch of the Mediterranean, between Italy and Balkan Peninsula; forms G. of Venice on the N.; chief trading pts., Venice, Trieste, and Ancona on the N., Brindisi and

Dürres on the S.; a. 52,000 sq. m., length 450 m.

Adullam or **Aidelma**, Judean *c.* of Canaanite origin, S.W. Jerusalem, where David hid in cave from Saul.

Adwick le Street, *urb. dist.*, W.R. Yorks, Eng.; coal; p. (1961) 18,212.

Adzhar, *rep.*, Georgian S.S.R.; tea, citrus fruits, oil-refining, engin.; ch. t. Batumi; a. 1,100 sq. m.; p. (1959) 242,000.

Aegades, group of rocky Is. off W. coast of Sicily; ch. t. Favignana on I. of that name.

Aegean Is., between Greece and Turkey; called the Grecian Archipelago, inc. Crete, Cyclades, Sporades, and Dodecanese; a. 1,506 sq. m.; p. (1961) 477,476.

Aegean Sea, branch of the Mediterranean; studded with Is., between Greece and Turkey; connected through the Dardanelles with Sea of Marmara and thence through the Bosphorus Strait with the Black Sea. [fisheries.

Aegina, *I.*, Greece; in G. of same name, sponge

Aerö, *I.* in the Baltic off Denmark; p. (1960) 10,109.

Aetolia and Acarnania, *prov.*, N. Greece; cap. Missolonghi; p. (1961) 237,738.

Afam, S. Nigeria; oilfield; pipe-line E. to Pt. Harcourt.

Afars and Issas, French Territory of the, N.E. Africa, formerly French Somaliland (renamed 1967); extends inland from straits of Bab-el-Mandeb; plain, mainly below 600 ft.; hot, dry climate; shark and mother of pearl fisheries; salt, coffee, hides, oilseed; cap. Djibouti; a. 9,000 sq. m.; p. (estd.) 110,000.

Affric, Glen, Inverness, Scot.; 30 m. S.W. of Inverness; hydro-elec. scheme; opened 1952.

Afghanistan, *kingdom*, Asia; monarchy; cap. Kabul; comm. ctrs. Kabul, Kandahar; mtnous.; ch. Rs., Kabul and Helm; climate, intense summer heat, severe winter cold, scanty rainfall; races, Afghans, aboriginal hill-tribes; languages, official Persian, spoken Pushtu; religion, Islam; cereals, fruit, sheep, horses, camels; inds. carpets, woollens, silks; coalmining at Dara-i-Suf; natural gas at Shibarghan; rich copper, lead, iron resources undeveloped; a. 250,000 sq. m.; p. (est. 1968) 16,113,000.

Afragola, *t.*, Napoli prov., S. Italy; 5 m. N.E. of Naples; cereals, fruit, hemp; p. (1961) 45,881.

Africa, second largest *continent*; bounded on N. by Mediterranean, by Red Sea and Indian Ocean on E., by Atlantic Ocean on W.; adjoins Asia at Isthmus of Suez. Deserts in N., forests in centre, and lofty plateaux and veldts in S. Highest mtn., Kilimanjaro, 19,324 ft.; chief rivers, Nile, Congo, Niger, Zambesi; largest L. Victoria. Great Rift Valley (K69) in N. Africa. Rainfall heavy near equator, almost rainless in Sahara and Kalahari, elsewhere moderate. Agriculture: wine, olives, wheat, esparto grass in N.; cocoa, oil palm, groundnuts, coffee, cotton in centre; wheat maize, wool in S. Minerals: gold, diamonds, copper. Compared with only 4 at end of last war, 41 countries had achieved independence by 1970. Those still to become fully indep. are: the Spanish col. of Sahara; the Portuguese cols. of Angola, Port. Guinea, Mozambique; Afars and Issas (French Terr.); Rhodesia, and S.W. Africa; a. (approx.) 11,683,000 sq. m.; p. (estd. 1968) 336,000,000. [38,392.

Afyon Karahisar *t.*, Turkey; opium; p. (1960)

Agadir, *spt.*, S. cst. Morocco; wrecked by earthquake, 1960; new t. built S. of former c. in a. of greater geological stability; p. (estd. 1965) 30,000.

Agawam, *t.*, Mass., U.S.A.; engin.; p. (1960) 15,711.

Agder, E. and W., *two dists.*, Norway; (E.) a. 3,607 sq. m.; p. (1963) 77,639 (W.) a. 2,794 sq. m.; p. (1963) 112,012

Agen, *t., cap.* Lot-et-Garonne, France; 85 m. from Bordeaux; cath.; p. (1962) 35,120.

Agincourt, *vil.*, Pas-de-Calais, France; famed for battle in 1415 between English, led by Henry V, and French under d'Albert.

Agira, *t.*, Sicily, Italy; marble, cement, sulphur; p. 15,172.

Agra, *c.*, Uttar Pradesh, India; on Jumna R., 115 m. S.S.E. of Delhi; formerly cap. of Mogul Empire; famous Taj Mahal mausoleum; univ.; p. (1961) 508,680.

Agri, *t.*, Turkey, p. (1960) 19,786.

Agrigento, c., S. est. Sicily, Italy; grain, sulphur, salt; p. (1961) 47,094. Formerly Girgenti, founded Akragas, c. 580 B.C., famous for its temples; birthplace of Empedocles.

Agrinion, t., Greece; tobacco; p. (1951) 21,752.

Aguadilla, spt., Puerto Rico, Central America; exp. coffee and sugar; p. c. 16,000.

Aguascalientes, st., Mexico; cap. Aguascalientes; a. 2,499 sq. m.; p. (1960) 243,363.

Aguascalientes, t., cap., Aguascalientes, Mexico; alt. over 6000 ft.; 360 m. N.W. of Mexico City; wide range of local inds.; hot springs; p. (1960) 126,617.

Aguilar de la Frontera, t., S. Spain; wine, olives; Moorish castle, p. (1957) 15,224.

Aguilas, t. spt., Murcia, on E. cst. of Spain; exp. esparto, lead ores; p. c. 15,000.

Agulhas, O., 100 m. E. of C. of Good Hope, most southerly point of Africa.

Ahaggar, mtns., S. Algeria range 9,000–10,000 ft.

Ahlen, t., N. Rhine–Westphalia, Germany; on R. Werse; coal mining, metal and engin. wks.; p. (1963) 42,200.

Ahmedabad, temporary cap. Gujarat, India; Jain temple, splendid mosques, pottery, silk, gold, cotton; oilfield at Nawagam nearby; p. (1961) 1,149,918.

Ahmadnagar, c., Maharashtra, India; lge. trade in cotton and silk goods; p. (1961) 119,020.

Ahmedi, pt., Yemen; nr. Hodeida; oil storage.

Ahuachapán, dep., Salvador; cap. Ahuachapán; trade in coffee, sugar, tobacco. cereals; p. (1960) 130,710. [p. (1966) 21,401.

Ahvenanmaa (Åland), dep., Finland, a. 572 sq. m.;

Ahwaz, c., Iran, cap. Khuzestan prov.; airpt.; oil pipeline to Turkish pt. Iskenderun projected. p. (1967) 322,068.

Aigion, t., Greece; currants exported; p. 11,011.

Aigues-Mortes, t., Gard, France; on R. Rhône delta; canal centre, once spt. now 3 m. from Mediterranean; salt-works; p. (1962) 4,203.

Ailsa Craig, rocky I., off Ayrshire cst., Scot., alt. 1,114 ft.; gannetry.

Ain, dep., France; mainly agr., vines, grains, sheep, tobacco, silk; a. 2,248 sq. m.; p. (1968) 339,262.

Ain Sefra, terr., S. Algeria.

Aintab, t., Syria; military centre in the Middle Ages; hides, morocco leather; p. (1950) 72,743.

Aintree, vil., Lancs., Eng.; nr. Liverpool; nylon plant projected 1964.

Aïr, mtns., Niger, W. Africa; ch. t. Agades.

Airdrie, lge. burgh. mftg. t., N.E. Lanark, Scot.; 12 m. E. of Glasgow; coal-mng., iron inds., brick and concrete wks., steel tubes, pharmaceutics; p. (1961) 33,620.

Aire, R., W.R. Yorks, Eng.; trib. Ouse; l. 70 m.

Aireborough, urb. dist., W.R. Yorks., Eng.; p. (estd. 1967) 29,370.

Airolo, vil., Switzerland; at S. end of St. Gotthard tunnel.

Aisne, dep., France; agr.. timber, sugar, brewing, textiles; cap. Laon; a. 2,866 sq. m.; p. (1968) 526,346.

Aisne, R., N.E. France; trib. R. Oise; l. 150 m.

Aix, t., Bouches-du-Rhône, France; 18 m. N. of Marseilles; old cap. of Provence; thermal springs; p. (1962) 72,696.

Aix-la-Chapelle, see Aachen. [(1962) 18,270.

Aizu-Wakamatsu, t., N. Japan; lacquer ware, candles; p. (1965) 102,239.

Ajaccio, spt., cap. Corsica; timber, flour, olive oil, tobacco; p. (1962) 42,282. [p. (1961) 231,240.

Ajka, t., Hungary; industl.; aluminium, glass.

Ajman, emirate, one of seven Trucial sts.; p. (estd. 1968) 4,000.

Ajmer, t., Rajasthan, India; cotton, salt, opium;

Aksu (Aqsu), t., Sinkiang, China; walled town, impt. trading ctr. on caravan route; textiles, carpets, jade carving, tanning, metal wkg.; p. 50,000.

Akaroa, t., S. I. New Zealand; on Akaroa Harbour; scenic and historic interest.

Akershus, co., Norway; a. 2,064 sq. m.; p. (1968) 291,472; Akerhus fortress (14th cent.) at Oslo.

Akhisar, t., Turkey; ancient Thyatira; manganese, tobacco, olives, cotton, grain; p. (1965) 47,422.

Akhmim, t., Upper U.A.R.; linen and cotton goods; limestone quarries.

Akhtyirka, t., Ukrainian S.S.R.; metal wks.

Akimiski I., I., James Bay, Canada.

Akita, t., Japan; silk, metals, rice, oil-refining; p. (1964) 219,000.

Akmolinsk, see Tselinograd. [115,760.

Akola, t., Maharashtra, India; cotton; p. (1961)

Akosombo, pt., Ghana; pt. and new t. around L. Volta; textile factory being built; planned p. 50,000.

Akpatok I., I. in Ungava Bay, Labrador.

Akron, mftg. c., Ohio, U.S.A.; lge. rubber mftg. ctr.; maize mills, woollens, machin., chemicals, plastics, tools; p. (1960) 290,351.

Akrotiri, Cyprus; British sovereign a. within Rep.

Aksaray, t., Turkey; p. (1960) 20,046.

Aksehir, t., Turkey; p. (1965) 25,265.

Aktyubinsk, t. N.W. Kazakhstan S.S.R.; at S. end of Ural Mtns.; ferro-alloys, engin., lignite, elec. power, chemicals, copper; p. (1967) 131,000.

Akureyri, t., N. Iceland; herring fishery; p. (1962) 9,152. [exp. rice; p. c. 42,000.

Akyab, spt., Burma; at mouth of Kaladan R.;

Alabama, st., U.S.A.; cap. Montgomery, ch. pt. Mobile; minerals, cotton, cereals, sugar, fertilisers, chemicals, mng.; a. 51,609 sq. m.; p. (1970) 3,373,006.

Alagôas, maritime st., Brazil; cap. Macelo; cattle, sugar, cacao, cotton, rice, tobacco; a. 11,016 sq. m.; p. (estd. 1968) 1,400,258.

Alajuela, prov., Costa Rica, Central America; cap. Alajuela; coffee, sugar; p. (1963) 237,563.

Alameda, spt., Cal., U.S.A.; airport; fish mkts., shipbldg., fish-canning, resort; p. (1960) 61,316.

Alamosa, t., Col., U.S.A.; flour-milling, meat-packing, stockyards; p. (1960) 6,205.

Aland Is. (Ahvenanmaa), group belonging to Finland at entrance of G. of Bothnia; a. 572 sq. m.; p. (estd. 1958) 21,967.

Alasehir, t., Turkey; ancient Philadelphia; mineral springs, wheat, tobacco, raisins; p. (1960) 13,923.

Alaska, st., U.S.A.; in Arctic N. America; mtnous.; furs, timber, salmon fishing, mng., B.P. oil exploration; earthquake, 1964; a. 586,400 sq. m.; p. (1970) 294,607.

Alaska Highway, from Dawson Creek, B.C. to Fairbanks, Alaska, 1,527 m. long; built for Second World War programme; main supply base and H.Q. Edmonton, Alberta.

Alatau, mtns., bdy. of W. Turkestan and Sinkiang, China; group of 5 ranges, outliers of Tien-Shan; alt. up to 15,000 ft.; highest peak Khan Tengri, 22,800 ft.

Alava, Basque prov., N. Spain; ch. t. Vitoria; viticulture; a. 1,175 sq. m.; p. (1959) 130,887.

Alba, t., N. Italy; in Tanaro valley; mkt. for silk, cattle, grain, wine; p. (1936) 11,072.

Albacete, prov., S.E. Spain; cereals, fruit, sheep; a. 5,739 sq. m.; p. (1959) 384,849.

Albacete, t., cap., Albacete, Spain; agr. mkt., fruit, saffron; p. (1959) 74,807.

Alba-Iulia, t., Romania; on R. Mures, formerly Carlsburgh; union of Transylvania with Romania proclaimed here 1918; p. (1956) 14,776.

Alban Hills, volcanic group, 10 m. S.E. of Rome, Italy; circumference 35 m.; greatest alt. Monte Faete, 3,137 ft.; viticulture.

Albania, rep., S. Europe; lying along Adriatic, adjacent Jugoslavia and Greece; rugged mtnous. cty., fertile Adriatic littoral and Koritsa Basin; maize, wheat, olive oil, cheese, tobacco, wool, hides, horses, bitumen; cap. Tiranë; a. 10,629 sq. m.; p. (estd. 1968) 2,019,000.

Albany, st. cap., New York, U.S.A.; on R. Hudson; river pt., iron, brass, chemicals, textiles, paper, machin. tools, car equipment; p. (1960) 129,726.

Albany, spt., t., W. Australia; on King George Sound; agr. and pastoral; oil storage, wool, super-phosphates; p. (1966) 11,417.

Albay, t., Luzon I., Philippines, hemp, sugar, copra.

Albemarle I., lgst. of Galapagos in Pac. Oc.; alt. summit, 5,020 ft. above sea-level. [60 m.

Albemarle Sound, inlet, N. Carolina cst. U.S.A.

Albert, t., Somme, France; on R. Ancre; almost destroyed First World War and damaged again Second World War; aircraft, machin., hardware; p. (1962) 10,423.

Albert L., Africa; great reservoir of White Nile, extreme length 100 m., general breadth 20 m., alt. 2,100 ft.; greater part in Uganda.

Alberta, prov., W. Canada; Rockies, in W.; wheat, livestock, feed crops; coal less impt. with develop. of rich oil and gas resources; chemicals, timber; cap. Edmonton; a. 255,285 sq. m.; p. (est. 1969) 1,553,000.

Albertville, *t.*, Congo; on W. of L. Tanganyika; comm. ctr., rail-steamer transfer point; p. *c.* 30,000.

Albi, *cap.*, Tarn, France; cath.; industl. and comm. ctr. in coal mining dist.; p. (1962) 41,268.

Albigeois, *sub-region*, Basin of Aquitaine, France; centred on Albi; rich farming, cereals and vines; sm. coalfield and associated industries.

Albion, *t.*, Mich., U.S.A.; mnfs. iron goods; p. (1960) 12,749.

Albuquerque, *c.*, N. Mex., U.S.A.; on Rio Grande; wool, hides, timber, metals, cement; univ.; (1960) 201,189.

Albury, *t.*, N.S.W., Australia; on Murray R.; sheep farming, wool ctr.; p. (1966) 32,019 with Wondonga, Vic.

Alcalá de Henares, *t.*, Spain; 20 m. E. of Madrid; univ.; birthplace of Cervantes; p. (1957) 19,415.

Alcalá la Real, *t.*, Andalusia, Spain; p. (1957) 29,165.

Alcamo, *t.*, Sicily, Italy; 24 m. S.W. of Palermo; olives, oranges, lemons, wines; ruins of anc. Segesta nearby; p. *c.* 44,000.

Alcázar de San Juan, *t.*, nr. Ciudad Real, Spain; soap, gunpowder, wine; p. (1957) 25,139.

Alcázar Quivir (Al Kazral Kebir), *c.*, Morocco, N. Africa; 80 m. N.W. of Fez; p. (1960) 34,025.

Alcester, *t.*, *rural dist.*, Warwick, Eng.; needles and fish-hooks, agr. and mkt. gardening; p. (rural dist. 1961) 15,556.

Alcoy, *t.*, Spain; textiles, farm implements, mach., elec. engin., fine paper mkg.; p. (1959) 53,031.

Alcudia, *Roman walled t.*, Majorca I., Spain; 31 m. from Palma; site of Roman t. of Pollentia; p. (1957) 3,556.

Aldan, *navigable R.*, Siberia, U.S.S.R.; length 300 m.

Aldeburgh, *mun. bor.*, *spt.*, E. Suffolk, Eng.; 30 m. from Ipswich; fisheries; H.Q. of gr. of Eng. writers and musicians; p. (estd. 1967) 3,100.

Alderley Edge, *urb. dist.*, Cheshire, Eng.; p. (1961) 3,618.

Aldermaston, Berkshire, Eng.; Atomic Weapons Research Establishment.

Alderney, most N. of Channel Is.; agr. and hort. prods., dairying; sand, grit, gravel; tourism; t. St. Anne; airpt.; a. 1,962 acres; p. (1961) 1,472.

Aldershot, *mun. bor.*, Hants, Eng.; bricks; lge. military camp; p. (estd. 1967) 36,080.

Aldridge, *urb. dist.*, Staffs, Eng.; plastics, pack ing-cases; p. (1961) 50,981.

Aleksandrovsk, *see* Zaporozhe.　　　[(1962) 27,024.

Alençon, *t.*, *cap.*, Orne, France; textiles, lace; p.

Aleppo, *c.*, ch. tr. centre N. Syria; grain, textiles, carpets, dairying, cement, sugar, brewing; p. (1961) 496,231.

Alès, *t.*, Gard, France; trades in raw silk produced in region; coal mining, chemicals, iron-ore, pyrite, zinc; p. (1962) 43,370.

Alessandria, *c.*, N. Italy; 46 m. E. of Turin; linen, hats, macaroni; p. (1961) 92,291.

Alesund (Aalesund), *spt.*, W. coast Norway; fishing; p. (1968) 38,544.

Aletsch, *glacier*, Bernese Alps, Valais can., Switzerland; lgst. in Europe; length exceeds 15 m.

Aletschhorn, *mtn.*, Bernese Alps, Valais canton, Switzerland; alt. 13,763 ft.

Aleutian Is. (U.S.A.), N. Pac. Oc., chain of Is. stretching out 1,200 m. from the most S.W. point of Alaska towards Kamchatka.

Alexander City, *t.*, Ala., U.S.A.; formerly Young-ville; textiles; p. (1960) 13,140.

Alexandretta, *spt.*, *see* Iskenderun.

Alexandria, *ch. pt.*, U.A.R., N.E. Africa; founded by Alexander the Great, 332 B.C.; floating dock; exp. cotton, wheat, rice, gum; p. (1960) 1,513,000.

Alexandria, *t.*, Dunbartonshire, Scot.; on W. side of vale of Leven; cotton printing, bleaching, dyeing, torpedo wks.

Alexandria, *t.*, Louisiana, U.S.A.; rice, foundries; p. (1960) 40,279.

Alexandria, *c.*, *spt.*, N.E. Virginia, U.S.A.; on Chesapeake Bay; mnfs. foodstuffs, thread, cotton, leather goods; p. (1960) 91,023.

Alexandrina L., inlet, S. Australia; nr. Encounter Bay.

Alexandroupolis, *spt.*, Thrace, Greece; oak timber tr., many antiquities; p. (1961) 18,712.

Alford, *urb. dist.*, Lindsey, Lincoln, Eng.; agr. mkt., brewing, food-preserving; p. (1961) 2,134.

Alfortville, *t.*, Val-de-Marne, France; S.E. suburb of Paris, rubber, paper, glass, hosiery, metal wks.; p. (1954) 30,195.

Alfreton, *urb. dist.*, Derby, Eng.; coal, iron, stone, chemicals, textile, engin., hosiery, knitwear; p. (ested. 1967) 22,650.

Algeciras, *spt.*, Spain; on bay opposite Gibraltar; fishing, cork, oranges; winter health resort; oil refinery being built; p. (1959) 64,842.

Algeria, *indep. sov. st.* (3 July 1962), N. Africa; formerly under French rule; comprises 13 departments; fertile valleys, rugged mtns., barren plateaux; warm, moist winters, hot, dry summers; Berbers, Kabyles, Arabs, Tauregs; cap. Algiers; products: wine, fruit, olive oil, timber, tobacco, minerals; oil, natural gas and iron ore in Saharan regions; a. 856,000 sq. m.; p. (estd. 1968) 12,943,000.

Alghero, *spt.* on western coast of Sardinia; cath.; coral fisheries, fruit, wine.

Algiers, *cap. c.*, *pt.*, Algeria; old t. surmounted by 16th cent. Casbah (fortress); univ.; exp. wine, citrus fruit, iron ore; oil refining at Maison Carrée; airpt. at Maison Blanche, 10 m. E. of c.; p. (1963) 820,000.

Algoa Bay, about 425 m. E. of C. of Good Hope S. Africa.

Algonquin Park, Ontario, Canada; *park*, game reserve, tourist centre.

Alhama, *c.*, Granada, Spain; hot springs; p. (1957) 10,564.

Alhambra, *c.*, S. Cal., U.S.A.; oil refining equipment, felt, clay, aircraft, p. (1960) 54,807.

Alhaurin el Grande, *t.*, S. Spain; rly.; olive oil, marble quarries; p. (1957) 11,537.

Alicante, *prov.*, S.E. Spain; ch. t. Alicante; a. 2,267 sq. m.; p. (1959) 696,165.

Alicante, *spt.*, *t.*, E. Spain; tourism; wine, fruits, minerals; p. (1959) 117,204.

Alice, *t.*, Cape Prov., S. Africa; health resort; timber inds.; p. (1960) 3,536 inc. 746 whites.

Alice Springs, *t.*, N. Territory, Australia; ctr. vast pastoral holdings; tourism; Stuart highway (arterial road) to Darwin; p. (1966) 6,001.

Aligarh, *t.*, Uttar Pradesh, India; univ.; wheat, cotton, gold and silver work; p. (1961) 185,020.

Alingsås, *t.*, Sweden, E. of Gothenburg; clothing ind.; p. (1961) 17,546.

Aliwal North, *t.*, Cape Prov., S. Africa; sulphur springs, health resort; p. (1960) 10,706 inc. 2,629 Europeans.

Alkmaar, *c.*, Netherlands; world cheese mkt.; p. (1967) 49,561.

Allahabad, *t.*, Uttar Pradesh, India; univ.; Hindu pilgrimage ctr.; p. (1961) 411,955.

Allegan, *t.*, Mich., U.S.A.; mkt. for dairy and fruit products of the district; mnfs. drugs; p. (1960) 4,822.

Allegheny Mtns., U.S.A.; bold escarpment in the W. Section of the Appalachian system stretching from Pennsylvania to W. Virginia.

Allegheny, R., U.S.A.; joins the Ohio R., Pittsburgh, Penns.; length 350 m.

Allen, Bog of, *peat morass*, Ireland; a. 372 sq. m.

Allen, Lough, L., Ireland, length 5 m., breadth 3 m.; one source of R. Shannon.

Allenstein, *see* Olsztyn.

Allentown, *t.*, Penns., U.S.A.; on Lehigh R., furniture, silk, tobacco; lorries; p. (1960) 108,551.

Aller, *t.*, N.W. Spain; agr. mkt.; coal-, iron-, lead-mines; p. 23,600.

Alliance, *t.*, Ohio, U.S.A.; coal; p. (1960) 28,362.

Allier, *dep.*, France; coal- and iron-mining, mineral springs, wine, wheat; a. 2,848 sq. m.; p. (1968) 386,533.

Allier, R., Central Massif, France; rises in Cevennes; trib. of R. Loire.

Alloa, *spt.*, *burgh*, Clackmannan, Scot.; on N. bank of R. Forth 5 m. E. of Stirling; engin., brass, bricks, tiles, woollens, glass, distilling; p. (1961) 13,395.

Alma, R., Crimea, U.S.S.R.; great victory over Russia by Allies, 1854.

Alma-Ata, *cap.*, Kazakh S.S.R.; engin., textiles, leather, printing inds.; p. (1967) 636,000.

Almada, *t.*, Portugal; on R. Tagus opposite Lisbon; Salazar Bridge (opened 1966), links with Alcantara, sub. of L.; founded by English Crusaders; p. (1963) 30,688.

Almadén, *t.*, Sierra Morena, Spain; ancient Sisapon; quicksilver-mines; p. (1957) 12,375.

Almansa, *t.*, Spain; textiles, leather, shoes, soap, brandy; p. (1957) 15,990.

Almelo, t., Overijssel, Netherlands; 25 m. S.E. of Zwolle; cotton textile mnfs.; p. (1967) 57,722.

Almendralejo, t., Badajoz, Spain; wine, brandy; p. (1957) 21,394.

Almeria, prov., S. Spain; ch. t. Almeria; a. 3,338 sq. m.; p. (1959) 367,833.

Almeria, spt., t., S.E. Spain; cath.; exp. grapes, oranges, esparto grass, lead; p. (1959) 83,653.

Almondbury, t., W.R. Yorks, Eng.; joined to Huddersfield.

Aln, R., Northumberland, Eng.

Alnwick, urb. dist., Northumberland, Eng.; cas.; brewing, agr. machin.; p. (1961) 7,482.

Alor, I., one of Nusa Tenggara Is., Indonesia.

Alor Star, t., cap., Kedah st., Malaya; on main road and rly., N. airport; p. 32,424.

Alost (Aalst), t., Belgium; 14 m. N.W. of Brussels; rly.-junc.; weaving (linen, silk), brewing, rubber goods; p. (1968) 45,881.

Alpena, c., Thunder Bay, Mich., U.S.A.; cement, paper, tanneries, sawmills; p. (1960) 14,682.

Alpes-Maritimes, dep., S.E. France; ceded by Italy in 1860; ch. t. Nice; olives, wines, fruit; a. 1,443 sq. m.; p. (1962) 618,265.

Alphen on Rhine, t., S. Holland, Netherlands; on Old Rhine, 10 m. S.E. of Leiden; mkt. for dairy produce; p. (1967) 30,980.

Alps, highest mtns. in Europe; 600 m. long from G. of Genoa to near Vienna; 130 m. broad in Tyrol; principal peaks: Mont Blanc (15,784 ft.), Mont Rosa (15,217 ft.), Matterhorn (14,782 ft.).

Alps, Apuan, limestone range near Viareggio, Italy; source of Carrara marble.

Alps, Australian, mtn. range between E. Victoria and N.S.W.; highest peak, Mt. Kosciusko, 7,328 ft.

Alps, Southern, mtn. ridge between Westland and Canterbury, New Zealand, highest peak Mt. Cook 12,349 ft.

Als, I., Denmark, in the Little Belt, a. 130 sq. m.

Alsace-Lorraine, prov., France; industl., agr., wooded, minerals; total a. 5,601 sq. m. Taken from France, in 1871, retroceded 1919; now divided into deps. of Bas-Rhin (1,848 sq. m and p. (1962) 770,150; Haut-Rhin (1,354 sq. m. and p. (1962) 547,920; Moselle (2,403 sq. m. and p. (1962) 919,412.

Alsager, urb. dist., mkt. t., Cheshire, Eng.; motor vehicles; p. (1961) 7,800

Alsdorf, t., N. Rhine-Westphalia, Germany; 10 m. N.E. of Aachen; tar-distillation plant; p. (1963) 31,900.

Alston, t., Cumberland, Eng., on S. Tyne R. in N. Pennines; limestone quarrying, hosiery; p. (1961) 2,198.

Altai, mtns., S. boundary of Siberia; extend from sources of Obi to Gobi Desert more than 2,500 m. Bieluka Peak, alt. 13,644 ft.

Altamaha, R., Georgia, U.S.A.; flowing into Atlantic; length 150 m.

Altamira, caves, N. Spain; prehistoric shelters, paintings of animals (Magdalenian).

Altamura, t., Apulia, Italy; at foot of the Apennines; wines, wool; p. (1961) 43,735.

Altdorf, t., cap. Uri can., Switzerland; on R. Reuss; rubber goods, wood workings; p. (1961) 6,600.

Altena, t., N. Rhine-Westphalia, Germany; site of ancient cas. of Counts von der Marck; metals, wine; p. (1963) 24,100.

Altenburg, t., Leipzig, E. Germany; lignite mining, engin., metallurgy, mnfs. playing cards, textiles; p. (1963) 46,866. engin.; p. (1961) 9,158.

Alton, urb. dist., Hants, Eng.; breweries, light

Alton, t., Illinois, U.S.A.; machinery, glass, chemicals, flour; p. (1960) 43,047.

Altona, t., part of Hamburg, Germany; iron, textiles, breweries, glasswks., soap, leather, tobacco, fish canning; p. (estd. 1954) 250,000.

Altona, t., S. Victoria, Australia, 8 m. S.W. Melbourne; oil refinery, chemicals.

Altoona, c., Blair, Penns., U.S.A.; coal, rly. wks.; p. (1960) 69,083.

Altrincham, mun. bor., Cheshire, Eng.; heavy engin.; p. (estd. 1967) 41,017.

Altus, t., Okla., U.S.A.; cotton, livestock, grain mkt.; p. (1960) 21,225.

Altyn Tagh, part of Kunlun mtns., Tibet, 14,000 ft.

Alva, burgh, Clackmannan, Scot.; at S. foot of Ochil Hills, 3 m. N. of Alloa; woollens, printing, fruit and fish canning; p. (1961) 3,957.

Alvin, t., Texas, U.S.A.; grain mkt., oil wells; p. (1960) 5,643.

Alvsborg, co., Sweden; a. 4,919 sq. m.; p. (1961) 375,006.

Alyth, mftg. burgh, Perth., Scot.; in Strathmore, 17 m. N.E. of Perth; p. (1961) 1,862.

Amadeus, large salt L., N. Terr., Australia; 92 m. long.

Amadjuak Lake, Baffin I., Canada.

Amagasaki, t., Japan; sub. of Osaka; chemicals, polyethylene; iron and steel; oil refining; p. (1964) 485,000. [E. of Nagasaki.

Amakusa Bay, inlet, Kyushu, Japan; on W. cst.

Amakusa, I., Japan; kaolin.

Amalfi, spt., Italy; on G. of Salerno; tourist resort; fisheries. [p. 12,365.

Amalias, t., W. Greece; grapes, wine, currants; p. (1961) 15,000.

Amapá, Fed. terr., Brazil; a. 53,059 sq. m.; cap. Macapá; manganese ore; p. (estd. 1968) 109,076.

Amara, t., R. pt., Iraq; on left bank of R. Tigris 250 m. below Baghdad; Arab t. and agr. mkt. at R. crossing; p. 18,000.

Amarillo, t., Texas, U.S.A.; oil refining, creameries; p. (1960) 137,969.

Amasya, t., Turkey; on Yeshil-Irmak; fruit, salt, silk, wine; p. (1965) 33,539.

Amazon, R., S. America; lgst basin and extent of water of any river in the world; rises among the Andes as Alto Marañon, and flows 3,900 m. to the Atlantic. Ocean steamers penetrate to Iquitos, 1,935 m. from mouth. One of its affluents, the Madeira, has an extreme length of c. 2,000 m. Drains nearly 3 million sq. m.

Amazonas, st., Brazil; rubber, timber; a. 616,148 sq. m.; cap. Manáus (q.v.); p. (estd. 1968) 921,390.

Amazonas, dep., Peru; a. 13,943 sq. m.; cap. Chachapoyas; p. (1961) 117,525.

Amazonas, fed. terr., Venezuela; cap. Puerto Ayacucho on Orinoco R.; a. 70,000 sq. m.; p. (1961) 15,000. [(1961) 105,507.

Ambala, t., E. Punjab, India; cotton, flour; p.

Ambarchik, spt., Yakut rep., U.S.S.R.; air base, gold-mining; p. 10,000.

Ambato, c., Ecuador, S. America; S. of Quito, on slope of Mt. Chimborazo; alt. 8,859 ft.; textiles, canned fruits, leather gds.; p. (1950) 33,908.

Amberg, t., Bavaria, Germany; on R. Vils; iron, mining, engin., textiles; p. (1963) 42,300.

Ambes, Gironde, France; nr. Bordeaux; oil refining. [p. (1962) 7,600.

Ambert, t., Puy-de-Dôme, France; paper, cheese.

Amble, urb. dist., Northumberland, Eng.; exp. coal; p. (1961) 4,889.

Amblecote, urb. dist., Staffs., Eng.; glass, fireclay, iron wks.; p. (1961) 3 008.

Ambleside, sm. mkt. t., Westmorland, Eng.; nr. L. Windermere; tourist centre, slates.

Amboina, I., Moluccas, Indonesia; a. 314 sq. m.; spices; p. 66,321.

Amboina, t., cap., residency, Molucca Is., Indonesia; pt. on S. cst. of Amboina I.; shipyards; p. (estd.) 17,334.

Amboise, t., Indre-et-Loire, France; 15 m. E. of Tours; famous cas. and prison; p. (1962) 8,192.

Ambriz, spt., Angola; sugar-cane, coffee, copper.

Ameland, I., W. Frisian Is., Netherlands.

America, the lands of the Western hemisphere, comprising the continents of North and South America, separated by narrow Isthmus of Panama. Most N. point over 9,000 m. from C. Horn, the extreme S. point; p. (estd. 1967) 479,000,000. See also North, South, and Central America.

Amersfoort, c., Utrecht, Netherlands; on R. Eem; textiles, leather, tobacco, steam turbines; rly. junc.; p. (1967) 75,312.

Amersham, t., Bucks, Eng.; 17th-century mkt. hall; light inds.; radio chemical centre of U.K. Atomic Energy Authority; p. (of rural dist.) (1961) 56,565. [culture; p. (1960) 27,003.

Ames, t., Iowa, U.S.A.; State College of Agri-

Amesbury, t., Mass., U.S.A.; 40 m. N. Boston; cotton; p. (1960) 9,625.

Amesbury, t., rural dist., Wilts, Eng.; nr. ancient megalithic monuments of Stonehenge; p. (rural dist. 1961) 22,594.

Amherst, t., Mass., U.S.A.; machin.; Univ. of Mass.; p. (1960) 10,306. [p. (1961) 10,788.

Amherst, spt., Nova Scotia, Canada; shipbldg.;

Amiens, c., Somme, N. France; on R. Somme; fine cath.; velvet, linen, woollens, silks; p. (1968) 117,888. [of Seychelles.

Amirante Is., British group, Indian Ocean; S.W.

Amityville, *t.*, N.Y., U.S.A.; Long I. sub. of New York; seaside resort; p. (1960) *3,318*.

Amlwch, *urb. dist.*, *vat. pt.*, Wales; N. cst. of Anglesey; p. (1961) *2,910*.

Amman, *cap.*, Jordan; site of very ancient c.; aerodrome; p. (1962) *296,358*.

Ammanford, *urb. dist.*, Carmarthen, Wales; anthracite, brick mkg.; p. (1961) *6,264*.

Ammendorf, *t.*, Saxony–Anhalt, Germany; lignite mining, chemicals; p. (estd. 1954) *20,000*.

Ammer, R., Germany; joins Neckar nr. Tübingen.

Amorgos, *I.*, Grecian Archipelago; p. *3,069*.

Amoy (Xiamen) *c.*, former treaty-pt., Fukien, China; rail link to Yingtang, Kiansi; tea, fruit, bricks; p. (estd. 1953) *224,000*.

Amravati, *t.*, Maharashtra, India; textiles, timber; p. (1961) *137,875*.

Amritsar, *c.*, Punjab, India; holy Sikh city; univ.; shawls and carpets; p. (1961) *376,295*.

Amroha, *t.*, Uttar Pradesh, India; pilgrimage ctr.; p. (1961) *68,965*. [W. cst. of Schleswig.

Amrum, *I.*, one of N. Frisian Is., Germany; off

Amsterdam, *spt.*, *cap.* c., Netherlands; at junction of R. Amstel and the IJ; built on 96 Is. joined by 300 bridges, harbour can hold 1,000 ships; two univs., Royal Palace, Bourse; extensive tr.; exp. dairy prod., sugar, tobacco; shipbldg., diamond polishing, aeronautical, marine, elec. machin., oil refining; p. (1967) *866,421*.

Amsterdam, *t.*, N.Y., U.S.A.; woollens; p. (1960) *28,772*. [refining.

Amuay, *t.*, N. Venezuela, Paraguaná pen.; oil

Amu Darya (Oxus), R., U.S.S.R.; flows from the Pamir Mtns. to Aral Sea, length 1,350 m.

Amur, R., flows from Mongolia between Manchuria and E. Siberia into the Pacific, opposite Sakhalin I.; length 3,000 m.

Anaconda, *t.*, Montana, U.S.A.; copper, zinc, manganese; p. (1960) *12,054*.

Anadyr, R., U.S.S.R.; flows into Bering Sea.

Anaheim, *t.*, Cal., U.S.A.; p. (1960) *104,184*.

Anahuac, *depression*, central plateau, Mexico; average alt. 7,000 ft.; surr. by higher country inc. volcano Popocatapetl (17,887 ft.); contains Mexico City, a. approx. 1,500 sq. m.

Anaiza, *t.*, Nejd, Saudi Arabia; p. *25,000*.

Ancash, *dep.*, Peru; a. 14,700 sq. m.; ch. t. Huaraz; p. (1961) *586,889*. [joins the Humber.

Ancholme, R. Eng.; rises in Lincolnshire and

Anchorage, *t.*, Alaska, U.S.A.; timber, salmon fishing and canning; earthquake 28 Mar. 1964; p. (1960) *44,237*.

Ancona, *spt.*, Central Italy; on the Adriatic Sea; founded by Dorians, 1500 B.C.; sugar refineries, shipbldg.; p. (1961) *99,678*. [lead, copper.

Andalusia, *old div.*, S. Spain; citrus fruits, sherry.

Andalusian Mtns. (Baetic Mtns.), S. Spain; young Alpine fold mtns. stretching from Atl. Oc. (Cadiz) to Mediterranean (Alicante); inc. Sierra Nevada (highest peak, Mulhacén, 11,420 ft.); some minerals, esp. lead and silver.

Andaman and Nicobar Is., Bay of Bengal; constituted a Union Territory, India, 1 Nov. 1956; timber; a. 3,215 sq. m.; p. (1961) *63,548*.

Andenne. *t.*, Namur, Belgium; on the Meuse, mining, chalk quarrying, chemicals; p. (1962) *7,919*.

Anderlecht, *sub.* of Brussels, Belgium; spinning, weaving, dyeing; p. (1962) *96,454*.

Andermatt, *vil.*, Uri, Switzerland; at foot of Mt. St. Gotthard; tourist ctr., winter health resort.

Andernach, *t.*, Rhineland–Palatinate, Germany; on the Rhine, 70 m. N.W. of Coblenz; R. port; metallurgy; p. (1963) *21,200*. [(1960) *41,316*.

Anderson, *t.*, S.C., U.S.A.; cotton, lumber; p.

Anderson, *c.*, Indiana, U.S.A.; p. (1960) *49,061*.

Anderson, R., N.W. Terr., Canada; flows into Arctic Ocean.

Andes, *great mtn. system*, S. America; 4,500 m. long; from Panama to C. Horn, 40 m. broad; volcanic; several of the peaks are over 20,000 ft. high. Rich in minerals.

Andhra Pradesh, *state*, E. India; cap. Hyderabad; a. 106,286 sq. m.; p. (1961) *35,983,447*.

Andizhan, *t.*, Uzbekistan S.S.R.; formerly residence of Khans of Khokan; cotton, metals, petroleum, engin.; p. (1967) *164,000*.

Andoeukhep, *t.*, Cambodia; cotton ginning.

Andorra, *sm. st.*, E. Pyrenees, under joint suzerainty of Pres. of France and Bishop of Urgel (Spain), virtually indep.; livestock, wines, tobacco; a. 191 sq. m.; p. (estd. 1969) *18,000*.

Andover, *mun. bor.*, *mkt. t.*, Hants, Eng.; prehistoric earthwks.; p. (1961) *16,972*.

Andover, *t.*, Mass., U.S.A., on R. Merrimac; woollens, rubber; p. (estd. 1967) *21,880*.

Andria, *t.*, S. Italy; wine, olive oil, cotton textiles; p. (1961) *70,831*. [p. (1953) *70,136*

Andros, *largest I.*, Bahamas; sponges, sisal hemp;

Andros, *sm. spt.*, Andros I., Cyclades, Greek Archipelago; on E. cst.; p. (estd. 1960) *2,600*.

Andujar, *t.*, Spain; on Guadalquivir R.; mineral springs, pottery, soap, textiles, tanning, uranium plant; p. (1957) *23,499*.

Angara, R., Siberia, U.S.S.R.; trib. of Yenisei; navigable almost its entire length, rises nr. and flows through L. Baikal; length 1,300 m.

Angarsk, *t.*, E. Siberia; on R. Angara 20 m. N.W. Irkutsk; engin., saw milling; p. (1967) *179,000*.

Angel Falls, *waterfall*, Venezuela, nr. Ciudad Bolivar; 3,212-ft. drop. [Bothnia.

Angermanälven, R., Sweden; falls into G. of

Angermanland, *old div.*, Sweden; now mainly in prov. of Vasternoorland.

Angermünde, *t.*, Frankfurt, E. Germany; 40 m. N.E. Berlin; rly. ctr.; p. (1963) *12,784*.

Angers, *t.*, *cap.*, Maine-et-Loire, France; on R. Maine; mkt. t. for local produce, fruit, vegetables, Anjou wines, Cointreau; textiles; cath.; p. (1968) *128,533*.

Anglesey, *I.*, *co.*, N. Wales, separated from Caernarvon by Menai Straits; cattle rearing, farming; a. 276 sq. m.; p. (1966) *56,000*.

Angle Bay, Milford Haven, Pembroke; oil pipeline to Llandarcy.

Anglet, *t.*, Basses-Pyrénées, France; airport, woodworking, cellulose mftg.; p. (1962) *16,676*.

Angola (Port. W. Africa), Portuguese possession, W. Africa; cap. Luanda; ch. prod. palm oil, rubber, coffee, maize, sugar, wax, diamonds; newly discovered oilfields; a. 488,000 sq. m.; p. (estd. 1968) *5,362,000*.

Angoulême, *mftg. t.*, Charente, France; on R. Charente; cognac, paper; fine cath.; suffered during Huguenot wars; p. (1962) *51,223*.

Angra do Heroismo, *cap.*, Azores Is.; exp. wine, pineapples, flax; p. (1960) *102,365*.

Angren, *t.*, Uzbekistan S.S.R.; lgst. ctr. of lignite mng. in C. Asia; p. (1959) *55,000*.

Anguilla I., Leeward Is., W.I.; cap. The Valley; a. 35 sq. m.; p. (estd. 1967) *5,800*.

Angus, *co.*, Scot., formerly Forfar; agr. and mftg.; a. 875 sq. m.; p. (1961) *278,370*.

Anhalt, *dist.*, Saxony–Anhalt, Germany; former duchy; agr. and mining.

An Hoa, *t.*, S. Vietnam; industl., fertilisers.

Anholt, *I.*, Kattegat, Denmark; p. (1960) *239*.

Anhwei (Anhui), *prov.*, China; soya-beans, rice, tea, coal and iron; a. 54.319 sq. m.; cap. Hofei; p. (1953) *30,343,637*.

Anjou, *old div.*, France; on both sides of R. Loire within the Paris Basin; ch. t. Angers.

Ankara, *cap.*, Turkey; on the Sakarya R.; grain and fruit ctr.; mohair cloth; p. (1965) *902,218*.

Anking, *c.*, Anhwei prov., China; on Yangtze R.; rice, cotton, wheat, tanning; p. (1953) *105,000*.

Anklan, *t.*, Neubrandenburg, E. Germany; on Peene R.; p. (1963) *19,785*.

Ankleshwar, *t.*, Gujarat, India; natural gas, oil; gas pipelines to Ultaran and Barodi; p. (1961) *20,287*.

Annaba (Bône), *spt.*, Algeria; 280 m. E. of Algiers; fertile plain; phosphates, iron and steel wks.; p. (1963) *155,000*.

Annaberg, *t.*, Karl-Marx-Stadt, E. Germany; in Erz Mtns.; cobalt, tin, uranium mng.; p. (1963) *29,005*.

Annam, *region*, N. and S. Viet-Nam; formerly within French Union; divided by 17th parallel bdy. (1957); a. 56,973 sq. m. ch. t. Hué.

Annan, *burgh*, Dumfries, Scot.; on R. Annan, 2 m. from its mouth in Solway Firth; Chapelcross reactor sta.; p. (1961) *5,572*.

Annapolis, *cap.*, Maryland, U.S.A.; naval academy; p. (1960) *23,385*. [growing a.

Annapolis Valley, Nova Scotia; famous fruit

Ann Arbor, *c.*, Michigan, U.S.A.; on the Huron; University of Michigan; motor lorries, farm implements; p. (1960) *67,340*. [*48,251*.

An Nasiriya, *t.*, Iraq.; on Euphrates R.; p. (1950)

Annecy, *industl t.*, France, dep. of Haute-Savoie; at lower end of beautiful L. Annecy; p. (1962) *45,715*. [p. *17,822*.

Annen, *t.*, Germany; coal, steel, chemicals, glass;

Annonay, *t.*, Ardèche, France; mnfs. paper, woollens, silk, leather goods; p. (1965) *18,823*.

Ansbach, *t.*, Bavaria, Germany; machin., metallurgy, furniture inds.; rly. ctr.; p. (1963) *32,600*.

Anshan, *industl. c.*, Liaoning, N. China; at foot of Changpai Shan, 60 m. S.W. of Mukden; ctr. of ch. worked deposits of iron-ore in China; iron, steel, engin.; p. (1953) *549,000*.

Ansong, *t.*, Central Korea; 40 m. S.E. of Seoul; rice, silk cocoons; p. (estd. 1950) *20,000*.

Ansonia, *c.*, Conn., U.S.A.; machin., brass goods, cotton-braid inds.; p. (1960) *19,819*.

Antakya (Antioch), *ancient c.*, S. Turkey; on R. Orontes; tobacco, olives, maize, soap, silk; p. (1965) *57,584*.

Antalya, *t.*, Turkey; p. (1965) *71,632*.

Antarctica, *plateau continent* within Antarctic circle; 7,000–10,000 ft. high; volcanoes and several Is.; owned chiefly by Britain, Australia, New Zealand, France, Norway; penguins. *See also* Brit. Antarctic Terr.

Antarctic Ocean, lies approx. S. of 60° S.; contains Antarctica; whaling.

Antequera, *t.*, Spain; sugar, textiles; metallurgy, trade in olive oil, grain; p. (1957) *43,334*.

Antibes, *spt.*, France; Alpes-Maritimes; health resort; oranges, flowers for perfume mnfs.; p. (1962) *35,976*.

Anticosti, *barren I.*, N. of R. St. Lawrence, Canada; 140 m. by 28 m.; game preserve.

Antigua, *aut. st.*, in association with Gt. Britain; Leeward group, W.I.; sugar, molasses, pineapples; yacht harbour; oil refinery under construction; a. (inc. Barbuda and Redonda) 170 sq. m.; cap. St. Johns; p. (estd. 1970) *65,000*.

Anti-Lebanon, *mtn. range*, Syria; E. of Lebanon; length 60 m.; alt. 6,000–8,000 ft.

Antilles, Greater and Lesser, W. Indies, comprising the Archipelago enclosing the Caribbean Sea and G. of Mexico.

Antioquia, *dep.* Colombia, S. America; cap. Medellin; a. 25,402 sq. m.; maize, coffee, sugar, gold, silver, panama hats; p. (estd. 1962) *1,971,710.*   [inhabited.

Antipodes, *Is.*, New Zealand; in S. Pacific, un-

Antisana, *volcano*, Central Ecuador, S. America.

Antofagasta, *prov.*, Chile; exp. nitrates, copper; a. 47,502 sq. m.; p. (1960) *240,537*.

Antofagasta, *spt.*, Chile; cap. of prov.; nitrates, copper, lt. inds.; p. (1960) *91,400*.

Antony, *t.*, Hauts-de-Seine, France; brick wks., toys; p. (1962) *46,823*.

Antrim, *co.*, extreme N.E. of N. Ireland; co. t. Belfast; famous Giant's Causeway is on the N. coast; a. 1,098 sq. m.; p. (1966) *313,684*.

Antrim, *t.*, N. Ireland; on Six-Mile Water; linen, nylon; p. (1966) *5,468*.   [18,460.

Antsirabé, *t.*, Malagasy; thermal springs; p. (1957).

Antung (Andong), *c.*, Liaoning, China; on R. Yalu, 15 m. from mouth; Chinese frontier sta. main rly. from China into N. Korea; mkt. for agr. produce; lumbering; p. (1968) *657,435*.

Antwerp, *spt.*, Belgium; on R. Schelde; famous Gothic cath.; lge. refinery; great petroleum port; shpbldg., textiles, tobacco, distilling, diamond cutting, chemicals; p. incl. subs. (1968) *657,485*.

Antwerp, *prov.*, Belgium; grain, flax; a. 1,104 sq. m.; p. (1968) *1,518,464*.

Anyang, *c.*, Honan prov., China; coal, cotton ind.; p. (1953) *25,000*.

Anzhero-Sudzhensk, *t.*, W. Siberia, U.S.S.R.; nr. Tomsk; coal-mng., mng. equipment, pharmaceutics; p. (1967) *118,000*.

Anzin, *t.*, Nord, France; chief coal-mining centre of France; p. (1954) *15,658*.

Aomori, *spt.* Honshu, Japan; on bay of same name; salmon; chemicals; p. (1965) *224,433*.

Aosta, *t.*, *cap.*, Val d'Aosta, N. Italy; in valley of Dora Baltea at node of trans-Alpine routes; iron inds.; Mont Blanc road tunnel links to Martigny, Switzerland, opened 19 Mar. 64; p. (1951) *24,181*.

Apalachee Bay, Fla., U.S.A.; receives Apalachee R.

Apapa, *spt.*, sub. of Lagos, Nigeria; on mainland opposite I. on which Lagos is situated; modern pt. equipment, terminus of W. Nigerian rly. system; rly. wkshps.; exp. palm oil and kernels, hides and skins, ground-nuts, cocoa, rubber; imports cotton piece goods, machin.

Apeldoorn, *c.*, Gelderland, Netherlands; favourite holiday resort; precision instruments, metalware; p. (1967) *116,548*.

Apennines, mtn. "backbone" of Italy; length

800 m., width 70–80 m.; highest part is in Gran Sasso d'Italia.

Apia, *spt.*, Upolu, W. Samoa; p. *c. 10,000*.

Apiskigamish, *L.*, Labrador, Canada.

Apolda, *t.*, Erfurt, E. Germany; textiles, engin. chemicals; p. (1963) *29,313*.

Appalachian Mtns., parallel ranges between At. and Mississippi, stretching from Maine to Alabama. Highest peak, Mt. Mitchell, 6,684 ft.

Appenzell, *can.*, N.E. Switzerland; divided into the half-cantons, Appenzell Inner-Rhoden, a. 67 sq. m., cap. Appenzell; p. (1961) *12,943*; and Appenzell Ausser-Rhoden, a. 94 sq. m.. cap. Herisau; p. (1961) *48,920*.

Appenzell, *t.*, *cap.*, Appenzell, Switzerland; on R. Sitter; linen tr.; p. (1957) *5,001*.

Appleby, *mun. bor.*, *mkt. t.*, Westmorland, Eng.; on R. Eden; cas.; p. (estd. 1967) *1,501*.

Appleton, *c.*, Wis., U.S.A.; paper; p. (1960) *48,411*.

Appomattox, *R.*, Va. U.S.A.; joins James R.

Apsheron, *peninsula* on W. side of the Caspian; petroleum wells (nr. Baku) and mud volcanoes.

Apulia, *S.E. region*, Italy; pastoral plain; grain, fruits, livestock; wine, oil; a. 7,470 sq. m.; p. (1951) *3,214,854*.

Apurimac, *dep.*, Peru, S. America; ch. t. Abancay; a. 8,187 sq. m.; sugar; p. (1961) *275,910*.

Apurimac, *R.*, Peru; joins the Ucayali; l. 500 m.

Aqaba (Akaba), *pt.*, Jordan; loading of phosphates and discharging of oil; p. (1961) *9,223*.

Aqaba, *G.*, between Sinai Peninsula and Saudi Arabia. N.E. arm of the Red Sea.

Aquila degli Abruzzi, *t.*, *cap.*, Abruzzi prov., Italy; on R. terrace of R. Aterno; mkt. and sm. inds. associated with local farming; holiday resort; cath.; p. (1961) *56,314*.

Aquitaine, Basin of, *geographical region*, S.W. France; to W. and S.W. of Central Massif, to N of Pyrenees, bordered on W. by Atl. Oc.; warm, wet, oceanic climate; rich agric. lowland; inc. Landes, reclaimed sandy area; ch. ts. Bordeaux, Toulouse.

Arab Emirates, Federation of, comprises the 7 Trucial States, Bahrain and Qatar (30 March 1968).

Arabia, S.W. peninsula of Asia; mainly desert plateau; coffee, dates, gums, horses, camels; petroleum; divided between Saudi Arabia, Yemen, Southern Yemen, Muscat and Oman, Trucial States, Kuwait, Bahrain, and Qatar; a. c. 1,000,000 sq. m.; p. c. *8,000,000*.

Arabian Desert, U.A.R., N.E. Africa; between R. Nile and Red Sea; alt. approx. 1,200–6,000 ft.; a. c. 80,000 sq. m.

Arabian Sea, N.W. part of Indian Ocean, between Horn of Africa and India.

Aracaju, *spt.* *cap.* Sergipe st., Brazil; sugar, soap, textiles, tanneries; p. (estd. 1968) *156,243*.

Arad, *t.*, Israel; in Negev desert, E. of Beersheba; new t. inaugurated 21 Nov. 1962; ind. to be based on gasfields at Zohar and Kanaim; chemicals, fertilisers.

Arad, *t.*, Romania; on R. Maros, wine, corn, tobacco, textiles; p. (1963) *124,642*. [E. of Timor.

Arafura Sea, N. of Australia, S.W. of Papua, and Araguaia, *R.*, Brazil; trib. of Tocatins; length 1,000 m.

Araish (Laraish, Larache), *spt.*, Morocco, N. Africa; on Atlantic cst., 45 m. S.W. of Tangier; tr. in grain and fruit, cork; p. (1960) *30,763*.

Arak, *t.*, Iran; carpets; p. (1956) *53,929*.

Aral Sea, large salt *L.*, Kazakhstan Rep. (U.S.S.R.); a. 26,166 sq. m.; receiving the Amu and Syr Darya Rs.; no outlet.

Aran, *Is.* group in Galway Bay, Ireland; fishing.

Aranjuez, *t.*, Spain; on R. Tagus; mkt. gardens; strawberries, asparagus; p. (1957) *24,667*.

Ararat, *mtn.*, Turkey; supposed resting-place of Noah's Ark.

Ararat, *t.*, Victoria, Australia; on Hopteins R., 131 m. from Melbourne; p. (1961) *7,930*.

Aras R. (the ancient Araxes), rising in Armenia, flows through Transcaucasia to the Kur, 500 m.

Arauan, *trading t.*, Sahara desert, N. Timbuktu.

Arauco, *prov.*, S. Chile; a. 2,222 sq. m.; cereals, alfalfa, fruit; p. (1961) *94,079*.

Aravalli Mtns., Rajasthan, India; Mt. Abu, 5,650 ft.

Araxes R., rises in Armenia, flows through Transcaucasia to Caspian Sea; bdy. between Persia and U.S.S.R.

Arbroath, *royal burgh*, Angus cst., Scot.; engin., textiles (flax, jute, cotton, woollens), fishing; holiday resort; p. (1961) *19,533*.

Arcachon, *t.*, Gironde, S.W. France; on S. side of Bassin d'Arcachon (Bay of Biscay); fish. pt.; health resort; p. (1962) *15,820*.

Arcadia, *div.* of Peloponnesus, Greece; cap. Tripolis; p. (1951) *154,318*.

Archangel (Archangelsk), *t.*, *dist. ctr.*, U.S.S.R.; on E. side of Dvina estuary, White Sea; lge. harbour kept open in winter by ice-breakers; fishery headquarters; exp. and inds. connected with N. Russia's softwood resources; engin., hydro-elec.; p. (1967) *308,000*.

Arcos, *t.*, Cadiz, Spain; on R. Guadalete; famous Gothic church, ancient fortifications; cattle; cork trees; p. (1957) *21,120*.

Arcot, *t.*, India; 65 m. W. of Madras; taken by Clive 1751; p. (1961) *25,029*.

Arctic Ocean, seas in the N. polar area.

Arcueil, *sub.*, Paris, Val-de-Marne, France; on both sides of Brière valley S. of Paris; varied light inds. concerned with chemicals, clothing, foodstuffs; p. (1954) *18,067*.

Ardabil, *t.*, Azerbaijan, Iran; dried fruits, carpets; p. (1956) *65,720*.

Ardèche, *dep.*, S. France; Cévennes Mtns.; olives, wine silk, minerals; cap. Privas; a. 2,144 sq. m.; p. (1968) *256,927*.

Ardennes, *dep.*, N.E. France; farming, woollens, iron; cap. Mézières; a. 2,027 sq. m.; p. (1968) *309,380*.

Ardennes, *hilly wooded dist.*, Belgium, France, Luxembourg.

Ardmore, *t.*, Oklahoma, U.S.A.; coal, cotton, oil refineries; p. (1960) *20,184*.

Ardnacrusha, Clare, Ireland; power sta. on R. Shannon 3 miles N. of Limerick.

Ardnamurchan, most westerly point of mainland of Scotland, Argyll.

Ardres, *t.*, France; Pas de Calais; nr. site of "Field of the Cloth of Gold," where Henry VIII and Francis I met in 1520; p. (1962) *3,137*.

Ardrishaig, *t.*, *spt.*, Argyll, Scot.; on Loch Fyne; holiday resort.

Ardrossan, *burgh*, Ayr, Scot.; on Firth of Clyde, 25 m. S.W. of Glasgow; shipbldg., oil storage, road bitumen, engin.; p. (1961) *9,574*.

Arecibo, *c.*, *spt.*, N. coast of Puerto Rico; W. Indies; coffee, sugar; p. (1960) *28,460*.

Arendal, *spt.*, Norway; on Skagerrak; wood pulp, aluminium, shipping; p. (1960) *11,395*.

Arequipa, *dep.*, Peru; minerals, wool; cap. Arequipa; a. 21,947 sq m.; p. (1961) *392,352*.

Arequipa, *c.*, Peru; comm. ctr.; alpaca wool inds.; being developed as Peru's 1st prov. industl. a.; steel rolling mill, cement wks.; projected wks. for plastics, nylon, pharmaceutics, asbestos, car assembly; p. (1961) *221,900*.

Arezzo, *t.*, *cap.*, Arezzo prov., Tuscany, Central Italy; hill site in a basin within the Apennines at junction of valley routes; mkt. for silk, wine, olives; p. (1961) *74,245*.

Argentan, *t.*, Orne, France; gloves, lace; p. (1962) *13,411*.   [p. (1962) *82,458*.

Argenteuil, *t.*, Val-d'Oise, France; industl.;

Argentina, *rep.*, S. America, bounded by Atlantic, Andes, and Paraná, Uruguay, Paraguay and Pilcomayo Rs.; inc. Pampas and Patagonia; cap. Buenos Aires; agr. and pastoral; exp. meat, wool, wheat, maize, linseed, cotton; natural gas at Canadon Seco and Comodoro Rivadavia fields in S.; pipeline to Buenos Aires; a. 1,079,965 sq. m.; p. (estd 1968) *23,617,000*.

Argenton-sur-Creuse, *t.*, Indre, France; gloves, linen, lace; p. (1962) *6,906*.   [p. (1951) *85,389*.

Argolis, *prov.*, N.E. Morea, Greece; cap. Nauplion;

Argonne, *hill ridge*, S.E. Paris Basin, France; composed of greensand; wooded; alt. 1,000 ft.; a. approx. 250 sq. m.

Argos, *t.*, Greece; leading Dorian city prior to the 7th century B.C.; ancient acropolis, theatre; p. (1951) *14,706*.

Argostolion, *cap.*, Cephalonia I., Greece; shipbldg.; earthquake 1953; p. (1961) *8,205*.

Argun, *R.*, N.E. Asia; headstream of Amur; rises in Heilungkiang, China, and for 500 m. forms frontier between U.S.S.R. and China; length 1,000 m.

Argyll, *co.*, W. Scotland; mountainous, deer forests, pastoral, fishing, distilling; a. 3,165 sq. m.; p. (1961) *59,345*.

Ariano Irpino, *t.*, Italy; pottery; ancient Aequum Tuticum; p. *22,855*.

Arica, *t.*, *free spt.*, N. Chile; exp. sulphur, copper, silver; oil pipe-line connects to Sica-Sica (Bolivia); p. (1960) *46,542*.

Arichat, *spt.*, Madame I., off Cape Breton I., Nova Scotia, p. *675*.

Ariège, *dep.*, S. France; livestock, fruit, iron, copper; cap. Foix; a. 1,892 sq. m.; p. (1968) *138,478*.

Arima, *bor.*, Trinidad, W.I.; nr. Port of Spain; cacao industry; p. (1960) *10,900*.

Arish, El, *t.*, *cap.*, Sinai, Egypt; on Mediterranean at mouth of Wadi el Arish; p. (1947) *10,791*.

Arizona, *st.*, U.S.A.; bordering on Mexico; agr., stock-rearing, copper, silver, gold, cotton, oil; cap. Phoenix; a. 113,909 sq. m.; p. (1970) *1,752,122*.

Arjona, *t.*, Colombia, S. America; sugar; p. *10,410*.

Arkadelphia, *t.*, S.W. Ark., U.S.A.; cotton, lumber, flour mills; p. (1960) *8,041*.

Arkansas, *st.*, U.S.A.; cap. Little Rock; agr., bauxite, coal, petroleum, natural gas, timber; a. 53,102 sq. m.; p. (1970) *1,886,210*.

Arkansas, *R.*, U.S.A.; navigable 650 m.; length 1,450 m.

Arkansas City, *t.*, Kan., U.S.A.; oil, flour mills, packing plant; p. (1960) *14,262*.

Arklow, *urb. dist.*, *spt.*, Wicklow, Ireland; fisheries, copper, lead, bog iron, pottery; fertiliser plant under const.; p. (1966) *6,056*.

Arles, *ancient Roman c.*, Bouches-de-Rhône, France; on the Rhône; corn, wine, hats, silk; p. (1962) *42,353*.

Arlington, *t.*, Mass., U.S.A.; residtl. sub. of Boston; p. (1960) *49,953*.   [p. (1962) *13,373*.

Arlon, *t.*, cap. Luxembourg prvo., S.E. Belgium;

Armadale, *burgh*, West Lothian, Scot.; 10 m. S.W. Linlithgow; coal, iron, limestone, brick and fireclay wks., engin., hosiery; p. (1961) *6,193*.

Armagh, *co.*, Ulster, N. Ireland; a. 512 sq. m.; p. (1966) *125,031*.

Armagh, *urb. dist.*, Armagh, N. Ireland; cath.; linen, whisky; p. (1966) *11,000*.

Armavir, *old ruined cap.* of Armenia, U.S.S.R.; on the slope of the extinct volcano Algazhoz; grain, engin.; p. (1967) *134,000*.

Armenia, *const. rep.* U.S.S.R., former area divided between Turkey, Russia, Iran; rich mineral deposits; agr., cattle rearing, forestry; hydro-elec. stas. under constr.; cap. Yerevan; a. 11,900 sq. m.; p. (1970) *2,493,000*.

Armenia, *t.*, Colombia, S. America; coffee; p. (estd. 1959) *120,000*.

Armentières, *mftg. t.*, Nord, France; base of British operations against Lille in First World War; cloth, linen; p. (1962) *27,254*.

Armidale, *c.*, N.S.W. Australia; univ.; cath.; ctr. of wool industry; p. (1966) *14,990*.

Arnhem, *c.*, prov. cap., Gelderland, Netherlands; on R. Rhine; lge. tin smelter; light inds. using rubber and rayon; p. (1967) *134,921*.

Arnhem Land, N. part of N. Territory, Australia; with C. Arnhem.

Arno, *R.*, Central Italy; flows past Florence and Pisa into Mediterranean; Val d'Arno is the fruitful valley of the R..; length 75 m.

Arnold, *urb. dist.*, Sherwood Forest, Notts., Eng.; hosiery, brick mkg.; p. (estd. 1967) *30,640*.

Arnsberg, *t.*, N. Rhine–Westphalia, Germany; on R. Ruhr; metal and wood mftg.; spa; p. (1963) *21,700*.

Arnstadt, *t.*, Erfurt, E. Germany; on R. Gera, 10 m. S of Erfurt; artificial silk, leather goods, engin.; p. (1963) *26,929*.

Arosa, t. Grisons, Switzerland; resort.

Arpino, *t.*, Italy, textiles, paper, marble quarries, p. *10,564*.

Arrah, *t.*, Bihar, India; famous in the Mutiny; p. (1961) *76,766*.

Arran, *I.*, Bute, Scot.; in Firth of Clyde; contains many summer resorts; a. 165 sq. m.; p. (1961) *3,705*.

Arras, *t.*, *cap.*, Pas-de-Calais, France; famous for tapestry; grain; dyeing, brewing; battle, First World War (1917); p. (1962) *45,643*.

Arroux, *R.*, France; trib. of the Loire; flows past Autun; length 75 m.

Arrow Lakes, expansions of Columbia R., Brit. Columbia.   [*82,504*.

Arta, *prov.*, Epirus, Greece; on R. Arta; p. (1961)

Arta, *t.*, *cap.*, Arta, S. Epirus, Greece; on left bank of R. Arta, 10 m. N. of G. of Arta; purely agr. interests; p. (1961) *16,399*.

Arta, *G.*, between Albania and Greece; near which the Battle of Acitum was fought, 29 B.C.

Artem, *t.*, R.S.F.S.R.; 29 m. N.E. Vladivostok; ctr. of coal-mng. a.; p. (1959) 55,000.

Artemovsk, *t.*, Ukrainian S.S.R.; salt, coal, iron, mercury; p. (1959) 61,000.

Arth, *t.*, Schwyz, Switzerland; starting point of rly. up the Rigi; p. (1957) 2,904.

Arthur's Pass, pass running through the Southern Alps. S. Island, New Zealand, alt. 3,109 ft.

Arthur's Seat, famous hill, Edinburgh, Scot.; 822 ft.

Artois, *old div.*, France; now dept. Pas-de-Calais.

Aru, *Is.*, group, Indonesia, off coast New Guinea; pearl, tortoise-shell; a. 3,244 sq. m.; p. 13,139.

Aruba, *I.*, Leeward Is., Neth. Antilles; oil refining, shipping; a. 73 sq. m.; p. 57,213.

Arun, *R.*, Sussex, Eng.; flows into English Channel at Littlehampton; length 40 m.

Arundel, *mun. bor., mkt. t.*, W. Sussex, Eng.; on the Arun; Arundel Castle, seat of Duke of Norfolk; p. (estd. 1967) 2,710.

Aruppukkottai, *t.*, Tamil Nadu, India, 35 m. S. of Madura; p. (1961) 50,200.

Aruwimi, *R.*, Central Africa; trib. of Congo; route of Stanley's famous forest march in 1887; length 1,800 m.

Arve, *R.*, Haute-Savoie, France; falls into Rhône near Geneva; length 45 m.

Arvida, *t.*, S. Quebec, Canada; aluminium plant; nearby Shipshaw power development; p. (1961) 14,460.

Arvika, *t.*, N. of L. Vänern, Sweden; agr. machin. and implements, pianos, organs; p. (1961) 15,778.

As, *t.*, W. Bohemia, ČSSR.; 12 m. N.W. of Cheb; textile mnfs.; p. (1961) 9,640.

Asahigawa, *c.*, Hokkaido, Japan; industl. and transport ctr.; p. (1965) 245,246.

Asansol, *t.*, W. Bengal, India; rly. junction; coal-mng., iron, steel; p. (1961) 103.405.

Asbury Park, *t.*, N.J., U.S.A.; resort; elec. prod., seafood, trucks; p. (1960) 17,366.

Ascension I., part of Brit. col. St Helena, 760 m. N.W.; settlement Georgetown; nesting pl. of sooty tern; Brit. earth satellite stn. (1966); airstrip known as Miracle Mile. a. 34 sq. m.; p. (estd. 1968) 1,527.

Aschaffenburg, *t.*, Bavaria, Germany; on R. Main; cas.; inds. paper. textiles, engin.; transhipment pt.; p. (1963) 55,000.

Aschersleben, *t.*, Halle, E. Germany; potash and lignite mining, chemicals, textiles, engin., horticulture; p. (1963) 35,555.

Ascoli Piceno, *cath. c.*, Central Italy; cap. of prov. of same name; p. (1961) 49,070.

Ascot, *par.*, Berks, Eng.; famous racecourse at Ascot Heath.

Asenovgrad, *t.*, Bulgaria; S.E. of Plovdiv; p. (1956) 25,265.

Ashanti, *historic region*, Central Ghana; formerly powerful native state; timber, cocoa, goldmines; cap. Kumasi; a. 24,379 sq. m.; p. (1960) 1,108,548.

Ashbourne, *mkt. t.*, Derby, Eng.; near Dovedale; quarrying, milk processing, corsetry; p. (1961) 5,656.

Ashburton, *urb. dist.*, Devon, Eng.; old mkt. t. S. gateway to Dartmoor; p. (1961) 2,715.

Ashburton, *t.*, S. Island, New Zealand; ctr. of great wheat-growing dist.; p. (1966) 12.672.

Ashburton, *R.*, West Australia; flows into Indian Ocean at Onslow; length 400 m.

Ashby-de-la-Zouch, *urb. dist.*, Leicester, Eng.; hosiery, open-cast mining, soap mftg.; ruined cas. in which Mary Queen of Scots was imprisoned; p. (1961) 7,425.

Ashby Woulds, *urb. dist.*, Leicester, Eng.; coal and clay mining, pottery; p. (1961) 3,318.

Ashdod, *pt.*, Israel; new modern deep-water pt. on Med. cst., 20 m. S. of Jaffa (closed 1965).

Asheboro, *t.*, N.C., U.S.A.; chemicals, lumber, furniture, hosiery; p. (1960) 9,449.

Asheville, *c.*, *winter resort*, N. Carolina, U.S.A.; leather, textiles, furniture; p. (1960) 60,192.

Ashford, *urb. dist., mkt. t.*, Kent, Eng.; agr. implements, ironfounding; p. (estd. 1967) 34,070.

Ashikaga, *c.*, Honshu, Japan; cultural ctr.; old silk-weaving ctr.; anc. school with library of Chinese classics; p. (1964) 150,000.

Ashington, *urb. dist.*, Northumberland, Eng.; coal; p. (estd. 1967) 26,320.

Ashio, *t.*, Japan; 65 m. N. of Tokyo; copper; commerce; p. (1947) 20,997.

Ashland, *c.*, Kentucky, U.S.A.; on R. Ohio; iron, steel, lumber, leather; p. (1960) 31,283.

Ashland, *t.*, Penns., U.S.A.; coal-mining, knitwear, mine pumps; p. (1960) 5,237.

Ashland, *t.*, Wisconsin, U.S.A.; iron, steel; p. (1960) 10,132.

Ashtabula, *t.*, Ohio, U.S.A.; near L. Erie; farm implements, leather; p. (1960) 24,559.

Ashton-in-Makerfield, *urb. dist.*, Lancs.. Eng.; near Wigan; coal; p. (estd. 1967) 23,350.

Ashton-under-Lyne, *mun. bor., mftg. t.*, Lancs., Eng.; nr. Manchester; iron and steel, coalmining, textiles, light engin.; p. (estd. 1967) 49,050.

Ashuapmuchuan, *L.*, Quebec, Canada.

Asia, *largest continent*, extends over nearly onethird of the land surface of the earth. Chief mtn. ranges: Himalayas, Kunlun, Tien Shan, Altai; Tibetan plateau; chief Rs.: Ob, Yangtze, Yenisei, Lena, Amur, Hwang-ho, Mekong; deserts: Arabia, Thar, Takla Makan, Gobi; some very fertile valleys and plains. Climate very varied, extreme in N., monsoonal in S. and E. Gold, coal, oil, iron, manganese, antimony, tin. Principal countries, in Asia: Turkey in Asia, Israel, Jordan, Iran, Iraq, Afghanistan, India, Pakistan, Ceylon, Burma, China, Viet-Nam, Indonesia, Thailand, Malaysia, Korea, Japan and Soviet Asia. Industrialisation greatest in Japan, China, India, and Soviet Asia; a. c. 16,700,000 sq. m.; p. (estd. 1968) 2,006,000,000 (incl. Soviet Asia).

Asiago, *t.*, Vicenza, Italy; straw hats; site of Austro-Italian battle, 1916.

Asia Minor (Anatolia), Asiatic part of Turkey; chief c. Izmir, important spt. of Levant.

Asinara, *I.*, Mediterranean Sea; off N.W. coast Sardinia; 11 m. long; the ancient I. of Hercules.

Asir, part of Saudi Arabia, S. Arabia: cst. region between Yemen and Hejaz.   [Ireland.

Askeaton, *t.*, on estuary of R. Shannon, Limerick,

Asmara, *c.*, cap. Eritrea, N.E. Africa; alt. c. 7,300 ft.; on rly. which connects Massawa and Agordat; p. (estd. 1958) 120,000.

Asnières, *t.*, Hauts-de-Seine, France; dyes, perfumery; regattas; p. (1962) 82,201.

Asolo, *t.*, N.E. Italy; Roman remains.

Aspra Spitia, *t.*, Central Greece; new industl. t. close to Andikira Bay; aluminium wks.

Aspropotamos, *R.*, Greece; longest R. in the country; length 115 m.

Aspull, *urb. dist.*, Lancs, Eng.; near Wigan; coal, cotton; p. (1961) 6,753.

Assab, on Red Sea, Ethiopia; oil refinery.

Assam, *st.*, India; Brahmaputra R. flows through it; extensive tea plantations; rice, cotton, coal; oil development at Rudrasagar; cap. Shilong; a. 47,091 sq. m.; p. (1961) 11,872,772.

Assen, *t.*, prov. cap. Drenthe, Netherlands; p. (1967) 35,080.

Assens, *t.*, I. of Fyne, Denmark, on the Little Belt, p. (1960) 4,937.

Assiniboine, *R.*, Manitoba, Canada; joins Red R. at Winnipeg; length 1,500 m.

Assisi, *t.*, Umbria, Central Italy; 15 m. S.E. of Perugia; birthplace of St. Francis; fine cath. and old cas.; p. (1961) 5,353.

Assynt, *dist., L.*, Sutherland, Scot., 7 m.; agr. and creameries; p. (1961) 831.

Assyria, *heart of former empire*, N. plain of Mesopotamia (Iraq); drained by R. Tigris; now mainly pastoral farming a.; ruins of many ancient cas.; cap. Nineveh.

Astara, *pt.*, Azerbaydzahn, U.S.S.R., on Caspian Sea, at frontier with Iran; natural gas pipeline from Agha Jari and Marum fields nr. Persian Gulf, under constr.

Asterabad, *t.*, N. Iran; on S.E. shore of Caspian Sea; p. 28,000.

Asti, *t.*, Alessandria, Italy; fine cath.; wines; silk, motor cycles; p. (1961) 60,217.

Astipalaia, *I.*, Grecian Archipelago.

Astorga, *t.*, Spain, nr. Leon; cath.; p. (1957) 9,916.

Astoria, *t.*, Oregon, U.S.A.; salmon-canning; p. (1960) 11,239.

Astoria, N.Y., U.S.A.; industl. and residtl.; part of Queen's *bor.*, New York City; settled in 17th cent. as Hallett's Cove; renamed for J. J. Astor.

Astrakhan, *t.*, R.S.F.S.R.; on delta of R. Volga; univ.; fish, caviare, astrakhan wool, fruits, wheat, elec. power, engin.; p. (1967) 361,000.

Astrolabe Bay, on N.E. coast of New Guinea; arm of the Pacific Ocean.

Asturias, *old prov.*, N. Spain; now Oviedo, on Bay of Biscay.

Asunción, *cap. c.*, Paraguay; on junction of Rs. Paraguay and Pilcomayo; cath.; tobacco, sugar, leather; p. (estd. 1960) *305,000.*

Aswan, *administrative div.*, Upper U.A.R., N.E. Africa; a. 337 sq. m.; p. (1960) *385,000.*

Aswan, *t.*, Upper U.A.R.; on Nile at 1st cataract, ancient name Syene; near famous ruins, temples, catacombs; tourism; p. (1960) *48,000.*

Aswan Dam, Aswan, Upper U.A.R.; built 1902 to control Nile flood in U.A.R.; High Dam under constr. to provide cheap electric power and irrigation of 2 million acres in Lower U.A.R.

Asyut (Assiut), *prov.*, Upper U.A.R.; cap. Asyut; a. 787 sq. m.; p. (1960) *1,329,558.*

Asyut, *t.*, Upper U.A.R., N.E. Africa; pottery, ivory work; p. (1957) *121,000.*

Atacama, *prov.*, N. Chile; cap. Copiapó; rich in minerals, nitrates, borax, guano; a. 30,834 sq. m.; p. (1960) *104,266.*

Atacama Desert, Chile; arid coastal tract. rich in nitrates.

Ataléia, *t.*, Minas Gerais, Brazil; in mun. Teófilo Otoni; p. (estd. 1967) *118,112.*

Atami, *t.*, Honshu, Japan; on Sagami Bay; seaside hot-spring resort; p. (1965) *54,540.*

Atar, *t.*, Mauritania, W. Africa; rly. terminus, chief inland town; p. (1954) *4,200.*

Atbara, *t.*, Sudan; at confluence of Atbara R. with Nile; rly. wkshps., cement; p. (estd. 1951) *36,100.*

Atbara R., or Black Nile, Ethiopia and Sudan; trib. of Nile; length 790 m.

Ath, *t.*, Hainaut, Belgium; sugar refining, furniture, chemicals, silk; p. (1962) *10,973.*

Athabaska, *R.*, Alberta, Saskatchewan, Canada; navigable by steamers, save at Grand Rapids, near mouth of Clearwater R.; length 740 m.

Athabaska, *L.*, Alberta, Saskatchewan, Canada; a. 3,085 sq. m.

Athelney, hill formerly encircled by marsh near Taunton, Somerset, Eng.; between the Rs. Tone and Parret; King Alfred's hiding-place.

Athens, *cap. c.* Greece; most renowned c. in antiquity; ancient ctr. of Greek art and learning; Acropolis and many splendid temples; spinning, distilling, tanning, carpets; oil refinery nearby; p. of greater Athens (inc. Piraeus) (1961) *1,850,000,* of c. (1961) *628,000.*

Athens, *t.*, Georgia, U.S.A.; univ.; cotton goods, lumber; p. (1960) *31,355.*

Athens, *t.* Ohio U.S.A.; univ.; coal, light inds.; p. (1960) *16,470.*

Atherstone, *mkt. t., rural dist.*, Warwick., Eng.; N. of Coventry; hats, coalmng., footwear, granite quarrying; p. (rural dist. 1961) *24,394.*

Atherton, *urb. dist.*, Lancs., Eng.; 13 m. N.W. Manchester; coal, cotton, light engin.; p. (estd. 1967) *20,510.*   [*14,120.*

Athis-Mons, *t.*, Hauts-de-Seine, nr. Paris; p. (1954)

Athlone, *urb. dist., military sta.*, Westmeath, Ireland; on R. Shannon; p. (1966) *9,616.*

Atholl, *dist.*, N. Perth, Scot.; extensive deer forests and grouse moors; a. 450 sq. m.

Athos, *peninsula*, Chalkidike, N.E. Greece; Mt. Athos (6,000 ft.) at S. tip, known as Holy Mountain, home of monastic community; ch. t. Karyes.

Athy, *urb. dist.*, Kildare, Ireland; p. (1966) *4,055.*

Atikokan, *sm. t.*, Ontario, Canada; on Canadian National Rly. 110 m. W. of Fort William; ctr. of Steep Rock iron-ore mines.

Atiquizaya, *t.*, Ahuachapán, Salvador, Central America; p. *5,901.*

Atlanta, *c., st. cap.*, Georgia, U.S.A.; univ.; cotton, paper, farm implements, printing, clothing; p. (1960) *487,455.*

Atlantic City, *c.*, N.J., U.S.A., summer resort; p. (1960) *59,544.*

Atlantic Ocean, 2nd lgst ocean; a. (estd.) 31,830,000 sq. m.; conn. to Pac. Oc. by Panama Canal. Central ridge of volcanic activity runs S. from Iceland to Antarctic, some peaks emerging as Is. (*e.g.*, Azores, Ascension, Tristan da Cunha). Chief deeps: Milwaukee Deep (30,246 ft.) near Bahamas and Nares Deep (27,972 ft.) near Puerto Rico.

Atlántico, *dep.*, Colombia, S. America; cap. Barranquilla; a. 1,340 sq. m.; p. (estd. 1961) *612,170.*

Atlas, *great mtn. range*, N.W. Africa; extending 1,500 m. through Morocco and Algeria to Tunisia; highest peak Jebel Toubkal, 13,578 ft.

Atlit (Athlit), *t.*, Israel; S. of Haifa; site of Crusaders' pt.

Atmore, *t.*, Ala., U.S.A.; 35 m. N.E. of Mobile Bay; p. (1960) *8,173.*

Atoka, *t.*, Okla., U.S.A.; flour, lumber mills; p. (1960) *2,877.*

Atrato, *R.*, Colombia, S. America; flowing to G. of Darien, length 275 m.

Atrauli, *t.*, Uttar Pradesh, India; 16 m. from Aligarh; p. (1961) *17,936.*

Atrek, *R.*, Iran; enters Caspian Sea; length 250 m.

Atshan, *t.*, Fezzan, Libya, N. Africa; oil.

Attica, *dep.*, Greece; olives, grapes, figs; a. 1452 sq. m.; p. (1961) *2,057,994.*

Attica, *t.*, New York, U.S.A.; p. (1960) *2,758.*

Attleboro, *c.*, Bristol, S.E. Mass., U.S.A.; p. (1960) *27,118.*

Attock, *t.*, Pakistan; between Peshawar and Islamabad; oil wells; oil refining.

Atzcapotzalco, *t.*, Fed. Dist., Mexico; oil ref.; petro-chemicals.

Aubagne, *t.*, Bouches-du-Rhône, France; bricks, tiles, corks, meat processing; p. (1962) *21,889.*

Aube, *dep.*, N.E. France; cereals, fruit, livestock; cap. Troyes; a. 2,326 sq. m.; p. (1968) *270,325.*

Aube, *R.* France; trib. Seine; length 1,255 m.

Aubervilliers, *t.*, Seine, France; industl.; p. (1962) *70,836.*

Aubrac, *mtns.*, Auvergne, France.

Auburn, *t.*, Ind., U.S.A.; comm. ctr. for agr. area; light engin.; p. (1960) *6,350.*

Auburn, *c.*, Maine, U.S.A.; footwear; p. (1960) *24,449.*

Auburn, *t.*, N.Y., U.S.A.; shoes, woollens, farm implements; p. (1960) *35,249.*

Auch, *t.*, *cap.*, Gers, France; cottons, woollens poultry, wines; p. (1962) *20,384.*

Auchel, *t.*, Pas de Calais, F ance; coal; p. (1954) *14,825.*

Auchinleck, *par.*, Ayr., Scot.; coal; p. (1951) *6,808.*

Auchterarder, *burgh*, Scot.; 15 m. S.W. of Perth; health resort S. slopes of the vale of Strathearn; woollen inds.; p. (1961) *2,426.*

Auchterderran, *par.*, Fife., Scot.; coal; p. (1951) *17,599.*

Auchtermuchty, *burgh*, Fife., Scot.; at S. foot of Ochil Hills, 25 m. N.E. of Alloa; distilling, cotton spinning; p. (1961) *1,354.*

Auckland, *prov.*, N.I., New Zealand; farming, gold, Kauri gum, coal; a. 25,400 sq. m.; p. (1961) *996,281.*

Auckland, *spt. c.*, N.I., New Zealand; lgst. c. in N.Z.; seat of government 1845-64; extensive tr. and shipping; univ.; sawmills, sugar refinery, shipbldg., glass; steelwks projected 25 m. S. of A., in Waikato iron sand a.; p. (1966) *547,915;* of c. *149,989.*

Auckland Is., uninhabited group in Southern Ocean; 200 m. off New Zealand, discovered by British in 1806.

Aude, *maritime dep.*, S.E. France; grain, fruit, wine; slate, iron; cap. Carcassonne; a. 2,448 sq. m.; p. (1968) *278,323.*

Audenshaw, *urb. dist.*, Lancs., Eng.; metals, leather, pharmaceutics; p. (1961) *12,112.*

Audincourt, *t.*, Doubs, France; forges, automobile and textile plants; p. (1962) *12,527.*

Audubon, *t.*, W. Iowa, U.S.A.; canneries; p. (1960) *2,928.*

Aue, *t.*, Karl-Marx-Stadt, E. Germany; nr. Zwickau; uranium-mining, metallurgy, textiles; p. (1963) *31,740.*

Auerbach, *t.*, Karl-Marx-Stadt, E. Germany; textiles; p. (1963) *19,082.*

Augsburg, *c.*, Bavaria, Germany; at confluence of Rs. Lech and Wertach; cath; theological institute; textiles, aircraft and diesel engines; route ctr.; p. (1968) *211,733.*

Augusta, *t.*, Sicily, Italy; on sm. I. connected to E. cst.; good harbour used as naval base; fishing; lubricants; p. *25,437.*

Augusta, *spt.*, S.W. coast, W. Australia.

Augusta, *t.*, *cap.*, Me., U.S.A.; on Kennebec R.; footwear, cotton goods, paper; p. (1960) *21,680.*

Augusta, *c.*, Ga., U.S.A.; on Savannah R.; cotton, cotton-seed oil, chemicals, foundries; p. (1960) *70,626.*

Augustow, *t.*, Poland; on Suwalki canal.

Aulnay-sous-Bois, *t.*, Seine-St-Denis, France; p (1962) *47,686*.

Aunjetitz, *t.*, ČSSR.; site of early Bronze Age culture.

Aurangabad, *t.*, Maharashtra, India; textiles; p. (1961) *87,579*.

Auray, or Alrac, *t.*, Morbihan, Brittany, France; oysters, dairy produce; p. (1962) *8,354*.

Aurès, *mtn. massif*, Algeria, N. Africa; Berber stronghold.

Aurignac, *commune*, Haute-Garonne, France; caves, paleolithic remains; tanneries.

Aurillac, *t.*, *cap.*, Cantal, France; industl.; p. (1962) *27,056*.

Aurora, *t.*, Col., U.S.A.; residtl. sub. 5 m. E. of Denver; p. (1960) *48,548*.

Aurora, *t.*, E. Ind., U.S.A.; lumber, mnfs. coffins, furniture; p. (1960) *4,119*.

Aurora, *rly. c.* Ill., U.S.A.; textiles, foundries; p. (1960) *63,715*. [*4,683*.

Aurora, *t.*, Mo., U.S.A.; mining region; p. (1960)

Au Sable, *R.*, New York, U.S.A.; flows from the Adirondack Mtns. to L. Champlain.

Au Sable, *R.*, Mich., U.S.A., emptying into L. Huron.

Aussig, *see* Usti.

Austin, *t.*, Minn., U.S.A.; food prods.; p. (1960) *27,908*.

Austin, *c.*, *cap.*, Texas, U.S.A.; on R. Colorado; st. univ.; farming ctr.; bricks, furniture; p. (1960) *186,545*.

Austral and Rapa Is., French group in Pacific Ocean; largest I. Rurutu; a. 115 sq. m.; p. (1962) *4,371*.

Australasia, div. of Oceania including Australia, Tasmania, New Zealand, New Guinea and neighbouring archipelagos.

Australia, Commonwealth of, largest I. in world; Cook took possession for Britain 1770; Commonwealth proclaimed 1901, federation of N.S.W., Victoria, Queensland, S. Australia, W. Australia and Tasmania; includes also federal cap. terr., N. Territory; cap. Canberra (administered separately). Mtns. in E.; most salient feature great interior plains, mainly arid; chief rivers: Murray, Darling, Swan; saline lakes. Climate: interior extremely hot and dry, cst. more moderate, N. coast tropical. Agr.: wheat, hay, cane-sugar, fruit; sheep, cattle, dairying; timber; great mineral resources: iron, bauxite, tin, gold, lead, silver, copper, zinc, coal; offshore oil and natural gas; a. 2,967,909 sq. m.; p. (estd. 1968) *12,173,000*.

Australia, South, *st.* of the Australian Commonwealth, the "Desert State"; mainly undulating, interior forms part of central plateau of continent, mtns. in S. and S.E., 3,000 ft.; wheat crops, stock-raising, dairying, fruit, olives; lead, iron, uranium; exp. corn, wool, mutton; cap. Adelaide; a. 380,070 sq. m.; p. (estd. 1968) *1,136,400*

Australia, Western, *st.* Australia; lgst st., nearly a third of western part of continent; cap. Perth, on the Swan R.; wool, fruit, wheat, frozen meat; gold, bauxite, coal, high grade iron-ore, asbestos and ilmenite deposits; Kununurra Dam irrigation scheme for semi-arid northern regions; a. 975,920 sq. m.; p. (estd. 1968) *930,800*

Australian Alps, *see* Alps, Australian.

Australian Antarctic territory, part of Antarctica; between 45° E. and 160° E.; inc. Oates Land, King George V Land, Wilkes Land, Queen Mary Land, Kaiser Wilhelm II Land, Princess Elizabeth Land, MacRobertson Land, Kemp Land, Enderby Land, MacDonald Is., together with the research stas. of Mawson, Davis, and Wilkes; a. (estd.) 2,472,000 sq. m.

Australian Bight, Great, large indentation on Australian S. coast between C. Catastrophe and C. Arid (850 m.)

Australian Capital Territory, area surrounding Canberra, seat of Fed. Govt. of Australia; predominantly pastoral; a. 910 sq. m.; p. (estd. 1968) *117,200*.

Austria, *rep.*, Europe; forcibly incorporated into German Reich 1938, liberated 1945, recovered indep. 1955; mtnous., forested, drained by R. Danube; agr., forestry; tourism; lignite, anthracite, iron, textiles, pianos, brewing; hydroelec. and steam power plants; cap. Vienna; a. 32,376 sq. m.; p. (estd. 1968) *7,338,000*.

Austria, Lower, *st.*, Austria; cap. Vienna; a.

(excluding Vienna) 7,098 sq. m.; p. (excluding Vienna) (1961) *1,374,012*.

Austria, Upper, *st.*, Austria; cap. Linz; a. 4,625 sq. m.; p. (1961) *1,131,623*.

Autlán de Navarro, *t.*, Mexico; S.W. Jalisco state; p. *10,915*.

Autun, *c.*, Sâone-et-Loire, France; anc. Augustodunum; Roman remains: oil-shale refinery, leather, furniture, dyes, fertilisers; p. (1962) *17,165*.

Auvergne, old French prov. forming the present deps. of Puy-de-Dôme, Cantal and a small part of Haute-Loire.

Auvergne Mtns., *mtns.*, Central France; in N.W. of Central Plateau; highest peak, Mt. Dore, 6,188 ft.

Aux Cayes, *spt.* Haiti, W. Indies; on S. cst.; agr. exports; p. *25,000*.

Auxerre, *industl. c.*, *cap.*, Yonne, France; cath.; vines, bricks, iron and steel; p. (1962) *32,961*.

Auxonne, *fortfd. t.*, Côte d'Or, France; on R. Saône; mkt. gardening; p. (1962) *6,649*.

Ava, *c.*, Burma; on the Irrawaddy R.; former cap.; many pagodas, now ruins.

Avallon, *t.*, Yonne, France; on Cousin R.; ancient church; tourist ctr.; p. (1962) *6,371*.

Avebury (Abury), *par.*, *vil.*, Wilts., near Marlborough, Eng.; famous for its Megalithic remains.

Aveiro, *spt.*, *t.*, Portugal; wine; sardines; fruit; p. (1963) *16,011*.

Avellaneda, *industl. sub.* of Buenos Aires, Argentina; hides, wool; p. (1960) *170,000*.

Avellino, *t.*, *cap.*, Avellino prov., Italy; monastery; hazelnuts, linen, paper; p. (1961) *41,509*.

Averno, Alpine valley of Switzerland.

Aversa, *garrison t.* Italy; W. of Caserta; wine, hemp, soap and chemicals; p. (1961) *40,336*.

Aves (Bird Is.), group in the Caribbean Sea, W. Indies, belonging to Venezuela.

Avesta, *t.*, Kopparberg, Sweden; on Dal R.; iron, aluminium and charcoal wks.; p. (1961) *10,880*.

Aveyron, *dep.*, France; on rim of Central Plateau, watered by Rs. Lot, Aveyron, Tarn; extensive forests; grain, dairying, sheep; coal; cap. Rodez; a. 3,385 sq. m.; p. (1968) *281,568*.

Aviemore, *t.*, Inverness, Scot.; on R. Spey, 12 m. S.W. of Grantown; rly. junction; tourist resort.

Avigliano, *t.*, Lucania, Italy; 8. m. N.W. of Potenza; marble; p. *14,333*.

Avignon, *ch. t.*, Vaucluse, S.E. France; residence of Popes 1309–78, and anti-Popes 1378–1417; wines, silk-worm eggs, chemicals, leather; p. (1968) *86,096*.

Avila, *t.*, *cap.*, Avila prov.. Spain; univ., cath.; wool, pottery; p. (1957) *25,000*.

Aviles, *spt.*, Oviedo, Spain; exp. coal. lead, zinc, chemicals, fishing; p. (1957) *50,000*.

Avion, *t.*, Pas-de-Calais, France; coal-mining; p. (1954) *19,471*.

Avoca, *R.*, Ireland; drains Wicklow Mtns.

Avola, *t.*, Syracuse, Italy; almonds; p. (1936) *23,344*.

Avon, *R.*, Somerset, Eng.; enters Bristol Channel at Avonmouth; length 75 m.

Avon, *R.*, Warwick., Eng.; flows past Stratford to Severn at Tewkesbury; length 95 m.

Avon, *R.*, Wilts and Hants, Eng.; flows past Salisbury into English Channel at Christchurch; length 70 m.

Avonmouth, *spt.*, Gloucester, Eng.; outport of Bristol; at mouth of R. Avon; docks; seed crushing, petrol refinery, non-ferrous metal and chemical plants.

Avranches, *t.*, Manche, France; typical Normandy mkt. t. dealing in cider and dairy produce; p. (1962) *10,127*.

Awaji, *I.* at entry of Inland Sea, Japan; a. 219 sq. m.; highest peak, Yurimbayama, 1,998 ft.

Awe, Loch, Argyll, Scot.; 8 m. W. of Inveraray, bordered by Ben Cruachan (16 sq. m.); salmon and trout fishing; hydro-elec. sta. at Cruachan under construction.

Axar, *fiord*, N. Iceland.

Axbridge, *rural dist.*, Somerset, Eng.; p. (1961) *30,761*.

Axe, *R.*, Somerset, Eng.; rising in Mendip Hills and flowing to Severn.

Axholme, I. of N.W. Lincs, Eng.; formed by Rs. Trent. Don and Idle, and comprising seven parishes; rural dist. agr. and engin.; p. (estd. 1961) *14,110*.

Axminster, *rural dist.*, Devon, Eng.; brushes; flour and saw mills; carpet and press tool mftg.; p. (1961) *14,350*.

Axmouth, *t.*, E. Devon; fishing, holiday resort.

Ay, *t.*, Marne, France; Ay wine; p. (1954) *6,806*.

Ayacucho, *t.*, Peru; founded by Pizarro in 1539; univ.; cap. Ayacucho dept.; p. (1961) *22,000*.

Ayacucho, *dep.*, Peru, S. America; a. 18,185 sq. m.; p. (1961) *427,812*.

Ayamonte, *spt.* Spain; on Spanish–Portuguese frontier; p. (1957) *12,124*.   [*6,586*.

Ayaviri, *t.*, Puno, Peru; N.W. of L. Titicaca; p.

Aydin, *t.*, Turkey; ancient Tralles; rly.; cotton, grapes, olives, magnesite, lignite and arsenic; p. (1965) *43,289*.

Aylesbury, *mun. bor.*, *co. t.*, Bucks, Eng.; mkt. t.; dairying; p. (estd. 1967) *35,190*.

Aylesford, *t.*, Kent, Eng.; scene of battle between Britons and Saxons 445, death of Horsa; mkt. t., cement, paper mills; p. (1951) *3,644*.

Aylesham, *t.*, Kent, Eng.; N. of Dover; on Kent coalfield.

Ayr, *lge. burgh*, *spt.*, Ayr., Scot.; on Firth of Clyde, 30 m. S.W. of Glasgow; Burns born near by, 1759; racecourse; carpets, engin., footwear; p. (1961) *45,297*.

Ayrshire, *co.*, S.W. Scot.; dairy produce, early potatoes; coal, iron, woollens, cottons; civil nuclear power-sta. at Hunterston; a. 1,132 sq. m.; p. (1961) *342,855*.

Ayre, Point of, northernmost point, Isle of Man.

Aysen, *prov.*, Chile; a. 34,348 sq. m.; p. (1957) *31,518*.

Azamgarh, *t.*, Uttar Pradesh, India; p. (1961) *32,391*.

Azbest, *t.*, Sverdlovsk dist., U.S.S.R.; asbestos quarries; p. (1959) *60,000*.

Azerbaijan (East), *prov.*, N. Iran, bordering U.S.S.R.; agr.; cap. Tabriz; p. (1967) *2,598,022*.

Azerbaijan (West), *prov.*, N.W. Iran, bordering U.S.S.R. and Turkey; agr.; cap. Rezayeh; p. (1967) *1,087,702*.

Azerbaydzhan, Transcaucasia, constituent rep. of the U.S.S.R.; impt. oil industry; chemicals, farming, cattle, fishing; cap. Baku; a. 33,460 sq. m.; p. (1970) *5,111,000*.

Azogues, *t.*, cap. Canar prov., Ecuador; straw hats; p. (1950) *6,579*.

Azores, Portuguese group of islands in mid-Atlantic; abt. 900 m. W. of Lisbon; volcanic; fruit, wine; ch. seaports : Ponta Delgada on São Miguel I., Horta on Fayal I. and Angra do Heroismo on Terceira I.; a. 922 sq. m.; p. (1960) *337,000*.

Azov, *t. spt.*, R.S.F.S.R., on R. Don; fisheries; p. *27,500*.

Azov, sea, U.S.S.R.; joins Black Sea by Kerchenski Strait; fisheries, caviare.

Azpeitia, *t.*, N. Spain; nr. birthplace of St. Ignatius Loyola; mineral springs; p. (1957) *8,991*.

Azraq Desert Nat. Park, first Jordanian nat. park around oasis of Azraq. 60 m. E. of Amman; a. 1,500 sq. m.

Azuay, *S. prov.*, Ecuador, S. America; cap. Cuenca; Panama hats; a. 3,873 sq m.; p. (1950) *243,920*.

Azul, *t.*, Buenos Aires, Argentina; cattle and mkt. ctr.; p. (1960) *45,000*.

Azusa, *t. spt.*, Cal., U.S.A., exp. citrus fruit; p. (1960) *20,497*.

B

Baalbek, *c.*, Lebanon, S.W. Asia; old Heliopolis; ruins.   [p. (1967)*23,355*.

Baarn, *t.*, Utrecht, Netherlands; summer resort;

Bab-el-Mandeb, *strait* connecting Red Sea and Indian Ocean, 20 m. wide.   [(1967) *266,618*.

Babol, *c.*, Iran, Mazandaran prov.; airpt.; p.

Babushkin, *t.*, U.S.S.R.; residtl. and industl. sub. of Moscow; p. (1959) *112,000*.

Babuyan Is., group in Pac. Oc.; N. of Luzon in Philippines.

Babylon, *ancient cap.* of Babylonian Empire in Euphrates Valley about 60 m. S. of Baghdad, Iraq.

Bacacay, *t.*, Luzon, Philippines; hemp, copper deposits.

Bacau, *t.*, E. Romania; on R. Moldava; oil, sawmilling, textiles; p. (1963) *76,214*.

Back R., in N.W. Terr., Canada; falls into Arctic Ocean; length 360 m.

Bacolod, *t.*, *cap.* Negros I., Philippines; tr. ctr., sugar; p. (estd.) *147,000*.

Bacup, *mun. bor.*, *mftg. t.*, S.E. Lancs, Eng.; 20 m. Manchester; cotton, iron, brass, footwear; p. (estd. 1967) *16,420*.

Badagri, *t.*, W. of Lagos, Nigeria, W. Africa; on the Bight of Benin, formerly a great slave pt.

Badajoz, *prov.*, Spain; great reclamation scheme in progress; a. 8,349 sq. m.; p. (1959) *865,004*.

Badajoz, *forlfd.* *t.*, Badajoz prov., Spain; on Guardina R.; cath.; woollens, wax; p. (1959) *98,083*.

Badakshan, *prov.*, Afghanistan; drained by Oxus and trib.; salt, lapis lazuli; cap. Faizabad.

Badalona, *t.*, Barcelona prov., Spain; p. (1959) *87,665*.

Baden, *former Land*, W. Germany, now merged with Baden-Württemberg.

Baden, *t.*, Switzerland; health resort, mineral springs; p. (1960) *12,000*.

Baden-Baden, *t.*, Baden–Württemberg, Germany; fashionable spa; p. (1963) *40,200*.

Baden-bei-Wien, *wat. pl.*, Austria; 14 m. S.W. of Vienna; p. (1961) *22,484*.

Badenoch, *dist.*, Inverness, Scot.; mountainous, drained by Spey; deer forest.

Badenweiler, *wat. pl.*, Baden, W. Germany; W. part of Black Forest.

Baden-Württemberg, *Land*, S.W. Germany; mountainous and afforested (Black Forest) with much mineral wealth; salt; cap. Stuttgart; a. 13,808 sq. m.; p. (1968) *8,714,000*.

Bad Lands, S. Dakota, U.S.A.; stretches of infertile badly eroded soil.

Badrinath, *mtn.* and *t.*, Uttar Pradesh, India; pilgrim shrine of Vishnu.

Badulla, *t.*, Ceylon; tea; p. *13,387*.

Badwater, *salt pool*, California, U.S.A.; 280 ft. below sea-level, lowest point in N. America.

Baena, *t.*, Spain; olive oil; horse-breeding; p. (1957) *22,031*.

Baeza, *t.*, S. Spain; ancient Moorish city; olives, wine; p. (1957) *16,895*.

Baffin Bay, Canada; W. of Greenland, joined to the Atlantic by Davis Strait and to Arctic Oc. by Smith Sound; open 4 months a year.

Baffin I., Canada; a. 236,000 sq. m.; inhabited by scattered Eskimos; iron ore deposit.

Bagamoyo, *spt.*, *tr. ctr.*, Tanzania, E. Africa; p. *5,000*.

Bagé, *t.*, S. Brazil; tr. ctr.; p. (1960) *47,930*.

Bagenalstown, *t.*, Carlow, Ireland; milling, granite; p. (1956) *1,984*.

Baghdad, *prov.* or *liwa*, Iraq; between Persia and Syrian Desert; inc. some of the most fertile lands in the Tigris and Euphrates valleys; p. (estd. 1967) *2,270,639*.

Baghdad, *cap.*, Iraq; on R. Tigris; airport, term. Baghdad rly.; textiles, gum, bricks, tiles, metal inds.; p. (estd.) *656,399* (c.).

Bagheria, *t.*, Sicily, Italy; p. *19,000*.

Bagirmi, *dist.*, Central African Rep.; S. of L. Chad; cap. Messenya.

Bagnacavallo, *t.*, prov. Ravenna, Italy; p. *3,676*.

Bagnara, *t.*, prov. Reggio, Italy; wine, honey; p. (1936) *11,580*.

Bagnères de Bigorre, *t.*, Pyrenees, France; mineral springs; (1962) *11,254*.

Bagnes de Chable, *wat. pl.*, Valais, Switzerland.

Bagneux, *t.*, Hauts-de-Seine, France; p. (1954) *13,774*.

Bagni di Lucca, *t.*, Italy; 13 m. N. of Lucca; warm springs; p. *14,000*.

Bagni do San Guiliano, *t.*, Italy, nr. Pisa; warm, radioactive springs; p. (1936) *21,894*.

Bagnolet, *t.*, Seine, France; sub. of Paris; famous for " plaster of Paris " from local gypsum; textiles; p. (1954) *26,779*.

Bagolino, *t.*, prov. Brescia, Italy; sulphur spring; p. *3,613*.

Bagshot, *rural dist.*, Surrey, Eng., adjoining heath of same name; historically old postal town, 26 m. S.W. of London; p. (1961) *16,744*.

Baguio, *summer cap.* of Philippine Is.; Mtn. prov.; p. (1960) *50,436*.

Bahamas, *Is.*, self-gov. Br. col., W. Indies; first land in New World sighted by Columbus, extending 780 m. from Florida to Turks Is.; collective cap. Nassau, New Providence; salt, crawfish, agr. prod.; timber; tourism; a. 4,404 sq. m.; p. (estd. 1968) *170,000*.

Bahawalpur, *div.*, Punjab, West Pakistan; a. 15,918 sq. m.; p. (1961) *3,205,000*.

Bahia, *spt.*, Ecuador, S. America; p. *10.820*.

Bahia, *st.*, Brazil; cap. Salvador; a. 216,270 sq. m.; cattle, cacao, sugar, coffee, tobacco; oil, extensive mineral deposits; p. (estd. 1968) *6,914,658*.

Bahia Blanca, *spt.*, Argentina; industl. ctr., principle shipping point of S.; exports oil, grain, wool, hides; p. (1960) *150,000*

Bahia de Caraquez, *spt.*, Ecuador, S. America; p. *10,499*.

Bahrein Is., sheikhdom group in Persian G.; famous pearl fisheries; oil-wells; cap. Manamah; a. about 213 sq. m.; p. (1965) *182,203*.

Bahr El Benat Is., group in Persian G., off coast of Trucial Oman.

Bahr-el-Ghaza, *R.*, Sudan; trib. of White Nile R.

Bahr-el-Ghazal, *prov.*, Sudan, N.E. Africa; cap. Wau (*q.v.*); a. 77,820 sq. m.; p. (estd. 1951) *771,000*

Baia, *historic vil.*, Campania, Italy; beautifully situated on Bay of Naples; celebrated Roman pleasure resort.

Baia-Mare, *t.*, Romania; on Somes R.; gold, silver, lead, zinc, chemicals, uranium; p. (1963) *88,941*.

Baie-St. Paul, *t.*, Quebec, Canada; summer resort; hunting, fishing; p. (1961) *4,674*.

Baii, *t.*, on oil pipe-line, Iraq.

Baikal, *L.*, Siberia, U.S.S.R.; fresh-water; 6th lgst. in the world; frozen Nov.–May; skirted by Trans-Siberian Rly.; sturgeon, salmon; 40 m. wide; a. 13,700 sq. m.

Baildon, *urb. dist.*, W.R. Yorks, Eng.; nr. Bradford; p. (1961) *12,147*.

Baile Atha Cliath. *see* Dublin.

Bailen, *t.*, Spain; lead, ore; p. (1957) *10,129*.

Bailleul, *t.*, Nord, France; lace, linen; p. (1962) *12,926*.

Baillieston, *t.*, Lanark, Scot.; coal mining.

Baird, *t.*, Texas, U.S.A.; rly. junction; cotton, oil; p. *1,810*.

Bairnsdale, *t.*, Vic., Australia; on Mitchell R.; agr., timber, tourism; p. (1966) *7,785*.

Bakar, *pt.*, Jugoslavia; S. of Rijeka; new pt. and oil harbour.

Bakchisaray, *t.*, Crimea, U.S.S.R.; *old cap.* of Tartar Khans; p. (1956) *10,000*.

Baker I., Pacific Ocean.

Baker, *L.*, N.W. Terr., Canada.

Baker, *t.*, Ore., U.S.A.; gold, silver, lead, mineral springs; p. (1960) *9,986*.

Bakersfield, *c.*, S. Cal., U.S.A.; ctr. of oil-wells, refining; p. (1960) *56,848*.

Bakewell, *urb. dist.*, Derby, Eng.; tourist centre, Peak District; agr., mining, woollens; p. (1961) *3,603*.

Bakhchisarai, *t.*, Crimea, U.S.S.R.; leather, copper; p. *10,800*.

Bakony Wald, *mtns.*, forested, Hungary.

Baku, *cap.* Azerbaydzhan, S.S.R.; pt. of Caspian Sea; univ.; oil-wells; oil pipeline connects with Batumi; p. (1967) *1,164,000*.

Bala, *urb. dist.*, N. Wales; nr. Denbigh, Merioneth; light engin.; p. (1961) *1,603*.

Bala, *L.*, Merioneth, N. Wales; drained by the Dee.

Balaka, *t.*, S. Malawi; new t. 1966.

Balashov *t.*, Saratov area, R.S.F.S.R.; on Khoper R.; engin, aircraft plant; p. (1959) *64,000*.

Balasinor. former Gujarat st. now merged into Bombay st., India.

Balasore, *spt.*, Orissa, India; p. (1961) *33,931*.

Balaton, *L.*, lgst. in Hungary; 50 m. S.W. of Budapest; 50 m. long, 2–7 m. wide.

Balayan, *t.*, Luzon, Philippine Is.; at head of G. of Balayan; p. (1948) *18,305*.

Balboa, *dist.*, S.E. Canal Zone, Central America; p. (1960) *30,623*; *t.*, Pacific end of Panama Canal; p. (1960) *3,139*.

Balbriggan, *spt.*, Dublin, Ireland; hosiery; p. (1966) *3,249*.   [*3,928*.

Balclutha, *t.*, S.I., N.Z.; nr. Dunedin; p. (1961)

Bald Head Peak, Victoria, alt. 4,625 ft.; highest point in Dividing Range, Australia.

Bald Mtn., peak in Front Range, Col., U.S.A.; alt. 12,000 ft.

Baldock, *urb. dist.*, Herts., Eng.; on N. edge of Chiltern Hills and Gr. N. Road; hosiery, malting, light engin.; p. (1961) *6,764*.

Baldwin, *t.*, N.Y., U.S.A.; on S. Long I.; fisheries; p. (1960) *30,204*.

Baldwin, *t.*, Penns., U.S.A.; p. (1960) *24,489*.

Baldwinsville, *t.*, N.Y., U.S.A.; agr., livestock natural gas; p. (1960) *5,985*.

Balearic Is., Spain; include Majorca, Minorca, Iviza, Formentera; *ch.t.* Palma; fruit, fish, pigs; tourist ctr.; a. 1,936 sq. m.; p. (1959) *441,842*.

Baleswar, *R.*, one of the chief distributaries of the Ganges to Bay of Bengal.

Bali, off Java, Indonesia; mainly engaged in agr.; famous native dancers: a. (inc. Lombok) 3,937 sq. m.; p. (1961) *1,782,529*.

Balikesir, Turkey; p. (1965) *69,256*.

Balikpapan, *t.*, Kalimantan, Indonesia; oil; p. (1961) *91,706*.

Baliuag, *t.*, Luzon, Philippine Is.; rice, bamboo hats, mkt.; p. (1948) *30,670*.

Balkan Mtns., Bulgaria; highest peak, 7,780 ft.; Shipka Pass.

Balkan Peninsula, the easternmost of the three great southern peninsulas of Europe, between the Adriatic and Ionian seas on the W., and the Black Sea, Sea of Marmara and the Ægean Sea on the E., with an area of, roughly, 200,000 sq. m.; includes Jugoslavia, Bulgaria, Albania, Greece; chief mtns.: Rhodope, Pindus, Balkan; ch. rivers: Danube, Maritza, Vardar; ch. lakes: Scutari, Okhrida.

Balkh, *dist.*, Afghanistan; between the Kabul and the Oxus; corresponding to the ancient Bactria, rival of Nineveh and Babylon.

Balkh, *t.*, Afghanistan; associated with Zoroaster, called the " Mother of Cities "; destroyed by Jenghis Khan in 1221; silk; p. *12,466*.

Balkhash, *L.*, U.S.S.R.; fresh water, nr. frontier of W. Mongolia; receives the Ili R., but has no outlet, length 450 m., width 30–50 m.

Balkhash, *t.*, Kazakhstan S.S.R.; on N. shore of L.; copper, molybdenum; vermiculite discovered nearby; p. (1959) *53,000*.

Ballachulish, *vil.*, Argyll, Scot.; on S. shore of L. Leven, N.E. of Oban; tourism. [(1951) *1,359*.

Ballaghadorreen, *t.*, Roscommon, Ireland; p.

Ballantrae, *par.*, Ayr., Scot.; fishing; p. (1951) *886*.

Ballapali, forest reserve, Tamil Nadu, India.

Ballarat, *c.*, Victoria, Autralia; 73 m. N.W., Melbourne, former gold-field dist.; mkt. ctr.; engin., timber, brick and tiles; p. (1966) *56,304*.

Ballater, *burgh*, Aberdeen, Scot.; on R. Dee, 37 m. S.W. of Aberdeen; tourist resort, mineral wells; nr. the royal Highland residence of Balmoral; p. (1961) *1,132*.

Ballenas Bay, W. Coast, Lower California, Mexico.

Balleny Is., S. Ocean; volcanic isles.

Ballina, *urb. dist.*, *spt.*, Mayo, Ireland; agr. machin., flour mills; p. (1966) *6,187*.

Ballina, *t.*, N.S.W., Australia; at mouth of Richmond R.; resort, fishing; p. (1966) *4,924*.

Ballinasloe, *urb. dist.*, Galway and Roscommon, Ireland; large cattle fair; p. (1966) *5,326*.

Ballinger, *t.*, Texas, U.S.A.; grain, cattle, cotton-seed oil, flour; p. (1960), *5,043*.

Ballinrobe, *rural dist.*, Mayo, Ireland; E. of L. Mask; p. (1961) *13,492*.

Ballon d'Alsace, *mtns.* (4,101 ft.), Vosges, France; highest peak Ballon de Guebwiller, 4,690 ft.

Ballston Spa, *vat. pl.*, Saratoga, N.Y., U.S.A., p. (1960) *4,991*.

Bally L., Roscommon, Ireland, nr. Castlereagh.

Ballycastle, *spt.*, *mkt. t.*, *urb. dist.*, Antrim, N. Ireland; abbey and cas. ruins; seaside resort; p. (1966) *2,949*.

Ballyclare, *urb. dist.*, Antrim, N. Ireland; paper, linen, dyeing, asbestos-cement prod.; p. (1966) *4,583*.

Ballycottin Is., Ballycottin Bay, Cork, Ireland.

Ballymena, *mkt. t.*, *mun. bor.*, Antrim. N. Ireland; on R. Braid; linen and dyeing; p. (1966) *15,992*.

Ballymoney, *mkt t.*, *urb. dist.*, Antrim, N. Ireland; 40 m. N.W. of Belfast; linen, dairying; p. (1966) *3,520*.

Ballyness Bay, Donegal, Ireland.

Ballyshannon, *spt.*, Donegal, Ireland; at mouth of R. Erne; salmon fishery; p. (1966) *2,233*.

Balmain, *t.*, N.S.W., Australia; industl. sub. of Sydney; foundries, chemicals, glass, ship-bidg., lumber.

Balmoral Cas., Aberdeen, Scot.; royal residence, on R. Dee, 8 m. W. of Ballater.

Balotra, *t.*, Rajasthan, India; p. (1961) *12,110*.

Bairanald, *t.*, N.S.W., Australia; on R. Murrumbidgee, p. *1,249*.

Balsas, *R.*, Mexico; flows S. to Pacific Ocean through impt. sugar-cane growing valley of Morelos; length approx. 500 m.

Balta I., Shetland Is., Scot.

Baltic Is. (Fyn, Lolland, Nykobing, etc.); farming div. of Denmark; a. 5,123 sq. m.; p. *1,291,772*.

Baltic Sea, an arm of the Atlantic, opens into N. Sea by narrow channels between Denmark and Sweden; joined to White Sea and Arctic by White Sea Canal; surrounded by Sweden, Denmark, Germany, Finland and the Baltic Reps. of the U.S.S.R.; 900 m. long, greatest width 200 m., a. 160,000 sq. m.; partly frozen in winter.

Baltic–White Sea Canal, *see* Volga Baltic Waterway.

Baltimore, *c., spt.*, Maryland, U.S.A.; nr. head of Chesapeake Bay; fine harbour; sugar refining, steel, radios, aircraft, clothing, machin., ship-bldg., food canning; world's 1st nuclear-powered lighthouse; p. (1970) *895,222*; Greater B. *2,044,000*.

Baluchistan, *prov.* (revived 1970), West Pakistan; S. of Afghanistan; largely desert, rugged barren mtns.; cap. Quetta; a 52,900 sq. m.; cereals, potatoes, fruits, dates; p. (estd. 1951) *622,000*.

Baluchistan States, Kalat, Las Bela, Kharan and Mekran, incorporated in W. Pakistan, 1955.

Bamako, *c.*, Mali; p. (1963) *135,000*.

Bamangwato, *tr. dist.*, Botswana, S. Africa.

Bamberg, *c.* Bavaria, Germany; cath.; philosophical and theological institute; textiles, elec., leather and engin. inds.; p. (1963) *73,700*.

Bamberg, *t.*, S.C., U.S.A.; agr., lumbering, pine timber; p. (1960) *3,081*.   [and iron dist.

Bambuk or **Bambouk**, Mali; W. Africa; gold

Bamburgh, *t.*, Northumberland, Eng.; birthplace of Grace Darling, cas.

Bamian, *t.*, Afghanistan, N.W. of Kabul; rock-cut caves, colossal Buddhist statues.

Banam, *t.*, Cambodia; on Mekong R.; boat bldg., rice distilling; p. *28,000*.

Banana I., Brazil; length 220 m., width 50 m.

Banana Is., sm. group nr. Sierra Leone.

Banat, *dist.*, Romania; N. of R. Danube and E. of R. Tisza; p. (1963) *1,241,832*.

Banbridge, *t. urb. dist.*, Down, N. Ireland; on Bann R.; linen; p. (1966) *6,551*.

Banbury, *mun. bor., mkt. t.*, Oxford, Eng.; 80 m. from London; aluminium ind., furniture, printing, ladies wear; p. (estd. 1967) *26,540*.

Banchory, *burgh*, Kincardine, Scot.; on R. Dee, 17 m. S.W. of Aberdeen; p. (1961) *1,918*.

Banda, *t.*, Uttar Pradesh, India; cotton; p. (1961) *37,744*.

Banda Is., group in Moluccas, in Banda Sea, Indonesia; nutmegs and mace.

Bandar, *spt.*, Andhra Pradesh, India, on Coromandel cst.; cotton mftg., rice; p. (1961) *101,417*.

Bandar Abbas, *spt.*, S. Iran; airpt.; import and export ctr. p. (1967) *163,133*.

Bandar-e-Bushehr (Bushire), *spt.*, S.W. Iran, on Persian G., Iran's major pt.; p. *c. 30,000*.

Bandar-e-Pahlevi, *spt.*, N. Iran, on Caspian Sea. p. (1967) *59,737*.

Bandar-e-Shah, *spt.*, N. Iran, on Caspian Sea, on rly. from Tehran.

Bandar-e-Shahpur, *spt.*, Iran, on Persian G., term. of rly. from Tehran; petrochemical plant being built.

Bandawe, *mission sta.* on L. Malawi, Africa.

Bandjarmasin, *t.*, Kalimantan, Indonesia; rubber; p. (1961) *214,096*.

Bandoeng or **Bandung**, *t.*, W. Java; quinine, rubber, chemicals; radio sta.; p. (1961) *973,000*.

Banff, *burgh, cap.*, Banff, Scot.; on Moray Firth at mouth of R. Deveron; fisheries; tourism; p. (1961) *3,329*.

Banff, *co.*, Scot.; oats, barley, fisheries, distilling, woollen mnfs.; a. 630 sq. m.; p. (1961) *46,400*.

Bangalore, *c.*, Mysore st., India; former Brit. military sta. and administrative H.Q.; silks, cottons, carpets, aircraft, machine tools; p. (1961) *905,134*.

Bangka (Banka), *I.*, between Sumatra and Kalimantan, Indonesia; tin; a. 4,611 sq. m.; p. (1930) *205,363*.

Bangkok (Krung Thep), *spt., cap.*, Thailand; on Menam R.; 20 m. from the sea; royal palace, univ.; rice, tea, teak; p. (1963) *1,608,000*.

Bangor, *c., mun. bor.*, Caernarvon, Wales; on S. shore of Menai Strait; cath. univ. coll.; slate, light engin.; p. (1961) *13,977*.

Bangor, *wat. pl., mun. bor.*, Down, N. Ireland; on S. shore of Belfast Lough, 10 m. N.E. of Belfast; lt. inds.; carpets, hosiery; seaside resort; p. (1966) *26,885*.

Bangor, *pt.*, Maine, U.S.A.; on Penobscot R., lumber, boots, shoes, clothing, paper; p. (1960) *38,912*.

Bangor, *bor.*, E. Penns., U.S.A.; slate, agr., clothes; p. (1960) *5,766*.

Bangui, *cap.* of Ubangi-Shari terr., Central African Rep; on R. Ubangi; p. (1966) *237,971*.

Bangweulu, *L.*, Zambia; 150 m. long, 80 m. wide, contains 3 islands. Dr. Livingstone died at Illala, on S. shore of this L., in 1873.

Banias, *spt.*, Syria; terminus of oil pipe-line from Kirkuk, opened 1952.

Banjaluka, *t.*, Bosnia and Hercegovina, Jugoslavia; hot springs; tobacco; p. (1960) *45,000*.

Banka, *see* Bangka.

Banks I., Canada, Arctic Ocean; separated by Banks Strait from Melville I.

Banks Is., group of sm. Is. in S. Pacific; N.E. of New Hebrides.

Banks Peninsula, on E. coast of S.I., New Zealand.

Banks Strait, separating Furneaux Is. from Tasmania.

Bankura, *t.*, W. Bengal, India; on Hooghly R.; shellac, silk; p. (1961) *62,333*.

Bann, Upper and Lower R., N. Ireland; rises in co. Down, and flows through Lough Neagh to Atlantic nr. Coleraine; length 90 m.

Bannockburn, *vil.*, Stirling, Scot.; 3 m. S. of Stirling; Bruce's victory over Edward II, June 24th, 1314; coal; confectionery.

Bannu, *t.*, W. Pakistan; on Kurram R.; military sta.; sugar refining; p. *38,504*.

Banska Bystrica, *region*, Slovakia, ČSSR.; copper and silver mng., metal wks.; a. 3,564 sq. m.; p. (1961) *129,290*.

Banska Stiavnica, *t.*, ČSSR.; tr. ctr., gold, silver prod., lead, copper, zinc; p. (1947) (inc. Banska Bela) *11,870*.   [*41,950*.

Banstead, *urb. dist.*, Surrey, Eng.; p. (estd. 1967).

Bantam, *dist.*, W. Java; suffered severely from fever and volcanic eruption.

Bantry, *rural dist.* and *spt.*, Cork, Ireland; at head of Bantry Bay; fishing, farming; crude oil terminal on Whiddy Is.; p. (1961) *7,814*.

Banwy, *R.*, Montgomery, Wales.

Banzyville, *t.*, Congo; on R. Uele; p. *1,000*.

Ba'quba, *t.*, Iraq; on Diyala R., 32 m. N.E. of Baghdad; agr., rly.; p. *10,000*.

Bar, *spt.*, Dalmatian cst. Jugoslavia; p. *5,500*.

Bar Harbor, *t.*, S.E. Me., U.S.A.; holiday resort; p. (1960) *2,444*.   [*6,726*.

Baraboo, *t.*, Wis., U.S.A.; agr. tr. ctr.; p. (1960)

Baracaldo, *t.*, Biscay, Spain; ironwks.; p. *36,165*.

Baracoa, *spt.*, Cuba; bananas, coconuts; p. *10,395*.

Barada, *R.*, Syria; in plain of Damascus.

Barajas, *vil.*, Madrid, Spain; airport; p. *1,800*.

Baranovichi, *t.*, Byelorussian S.S.R.; 80 m. S.W. of Minsk; p. (1959) *58,000*.

Barauni, *t.*, N. Central Bihar, India; oil refining; oil pipelines to Gauhati, to Kanpur and from Haldia; p. (1961) *40,321*.

Barbacena, *t.*, E. Brazil; creameries; ceramics, glass; p. (1960) *41,931*.

Barbados, *I., indep. sov. st.*, within Brit. Commonwealth (1966); W.I.; sugar, molasses, rum, cotton; cap. Bridgetown; a. 166 sq. m.; p. (estd. 1969) *253,633*.

Barbary, *region*, N. Africa; includes Morocco, Algeria, Tunis, Tripoli, Barka and Fezzan.

Barbary Coast, general name applied to Mediterranean cst. of N. Africa between Strait of Gibraltar and C. Bon.

Barbastro, *t.*, Huesca, Spain; on R. Cinca; p. (1957) *9,331*.

Barberton, *t.*, Transvaal, S. Africa; citrus fruits, gold, asbestos, magnesite, talc, cotton; p. (1960) *11,016* inc. *2,705* whites.

Barberton, *t.*, Ohio, U.S.A., S.S.W. of Akron; tyre mftg.; p. (1960) *33,805*.

Barbizon, *vil.*, nr. forest of Fontainebleau; haunt of painters.

Barbuda and Redonda, *Is.*, Leeward Is., W.I.; dependencies of Antigua; sea-island cotton; a. 63 sq. m.; p. *1,000*.   [*1,780*]

Barcaldine, *t.*, Queensland, Australia; p. (1966.

Barcellona, *t.*, Sicily, Italy; silks; p. *25,580*.

Barcelona, *prov.*, N.E. Spain, Spain; cap. Barcelona; a. 2,942 sq. m.; p. (1967) *3,495,021*.

Barcelona, *c., spt., cap.*, Barcelona prov., Spain; "Manchester of Spain"; cottons, paper, leather, glass, soap; exp. olives, wines, cork; p. (1965) *1,656,000*.

Barcelona, *t.*, N. Venezuela; *cap.* of Azoátegui st.; agr. tr.; brewing; p. (1961) 44,773.

Barcoo R., see Cooper's Creek.   [9,175.

Bardejov, *t.*, ČSSR.; hot springs; p. (1961)

Bardera, *t.*, Somalia; head of navigation on Juba R.; p. 1,500.

Bardsey, I., Irish Sea; off coast of Wales nr. N. point of Cardigan Bay; lighthouse.

Bareilly, *c.*, Uttar Pradesh, India; bamboo, furniture; p. (1961) 272,828.

Barents Sea, part of Arctic Ocean E. of Spitzbergen to N. Cape; cod, haddock.

Bari, *spt.*, S. Italy; on Adriatic, 69 m. N.W. of Brindisi; cath.; olive oil, wines, fruit, soap; p. (1965) 335,000.

Barinas, *t.*, cap. Barinas st., Venezuela; cattle, oil; p. (1961) 25,707.

Barisal, *t.*, East Pakistan; nr. Tetulia at mouth of Ganges; river pt.; great damage and loss of lives due to cyclone 1965; p. (1961) 59,900.

Barka, *dist.*, Libya, N. Africa.

Barking, *outer bor.*, E. London, Eng.; on R. Roding; inc. Dagenham; metal refining and smelting, insulation, cellulose; lge. power sta. and largest gaswks. in Europe; p. (1966) 171,000.

Barkly Tableland, N. Terr., Australia.

Barkly West, *t.*, Cape Province, S. Africa; diamonds.

Barkul, *t.*, Shensi, W. China; p. (estd. 1947) 19,097.

Barlad, *t.*, Romania, Moldavia; soap, textiles; p. (1963) 48,191.

Bar-le-Duc, *t.*, *cap.* Meuse, France; cotton, hosiery; p. (1962) 20,168.

Barlee, L., W. Australia.

Barletta, *t.*, *spt.*, Italy; wine; p. (1961) 68,035.

Barlin, *t.*, Pas de Calais, France; coal-mines, lime, cement; p. (1954) 9,186.

Barmouth, *t.*, *urb. dist.*, Merioneth, Wales; on cst. of Cardigan Bay; chemicals; p. (1961) 2,348.

Barnack, *rural dist.*, Huntingdon and Peterborough, Eng.; p. (1961) 4,420.

Barnard Castle, *mkt. t.*, *urb. dist.*, Durham, Eng.; health resort; woollens, penicillin; p. (1961) 4,969.

Barnaul, *t.*, W. Siberia, R.S.F.S.R.; chemicals, engin., textiles, sawmilling; p. (1967) 395,000.

Barnes, see Richmond upon Thames.

Barnesville, *t.*, Ga., U.S.A.; cotton mills; p. (1960) 4,919.

Barnesville, *t.*, Ohio U.S.A.; coal, natural gas, glass, paper, evaporatde milk; p. (1960) 4,425.

Barnet, *former urb. dist.*, Herts, Eng.; now outer bor., Greater London; comprising former bors. of Finchley and Hendon, and urb. dists. of Barnet, East Barnet and Friern Barnet; p. (1966) 317,000.   [27,800.

Barneveld, *t.*, Gelderland, Netherlands; p. (1967)

Barnoldswick, *urb. dist.*, W.R. Yorks, Eng.; p. (1961) 10,267.   [p. 1,663.

Barnsdall, *t.*, N. Okla., U.S.A.; oil, gas, agr.;

Barnsley, *mftg. t.*, *co. bor.*, W.R. Yorks, Eng.; machin., plastics; former coalmng. ctr.; p. (estd. 1967) 75,910.

Barnstable, *t.*, Mass., U.S.A.; summer resort; fisheries; p. (1950) 10,480.

Barnstaple, *mkt. t.*, *mun. bor.*, Devon, Eng.; on R. Taw; seaside resort; concrete, glove mkg.; p. (estd. 1967) 16,340.

Baroda, *former st.*, India; now part of Gujarat st.; cereals, cotton, sugar, tobacco, opium; a. 2,961 sq. m.; p. (1961) 1,527,326.

Baroda, *t.*, Gujarat, India; univ.; palaces, Hindu temples; natural gas pipeline from Ankleshwar; oil refining nearby at Jawaharnagar; p. (1961) 295,326.

Barotseland, *prov.*, Zambia; savannah grasslands; livestock, grain, teak; a. 63,000 sq. m.; p. (1964) 378,000.

Barquisimeto, *t.*, Venezuela; sugar, coffee, cacao, cereals, cattle, copper, textiles; p. (1961) 196,557.

Barra Is., southerly groups, Outer Hebrides, Scot.; a. 348 sq. m.; lighthouse on Barra Head; p. 2,250.   [N. of Cairo.

Barrage, *vil.*, U.A.R., N.E. Africa; on Nile, 35 m.

Barranca Bermeja, *t.*, Colombia, S. America; oilfield, oil-refining, paper mkg., petro-chemicals; p. (estd. 1959) 65,000.

Barranqueras, *t.*, Chaco terr., N. Argentina; on Parana R.; exp. hardwoods, cotton.

Barranquilla, *pt.*, Colombia, S. America, on left bank nr. mouth of R. Magdalena; textiles, perfumes, saw mills, cement, pharmaceutics, river craft; p. (estd. 1962) 452,140.

Barre, *c.*, Vt., U.S.A.; granite; p. (1960) 10,387.

Barren L., volcano in Bay of Bengal.

Barren R., Ky. U.S.A.; length 120 m.

Barrhead, *mftg. burgh*, Renfrew, Scot.; 7 m. S.W. of Gasgow; iron and cotton; p. (1961) 14,422.

Barrie, *c.*, Ontario, Canada; light inds., boat bldg.; p. (1956) 16,573.

Barrier Ranges, *mns.*, on boundary of S. Australia and N.S.W., Australia; alt. 2,000 ft.

Barrier Reef, Great, *coral reef*, Pac. Oc.; extending for 1,200 m., 10–150 m. from coast of Australia.

Barrington, *t.* R.I., U.S.A.; shipbuilding, fish, residtl. resort; p. (1960) 13,826.

Barron, *t.*, Wis., U.S.A.; dairy products, lumber; p. (1960) 2,338.

Barrow, O., Mackenzie, Canada.

Barrow Falls, nr. Keswick, Cumberland, Eng.

Barrowford, *urb. dist.*, Lancs., Eng.; p. (1961) 4,531.

Barrow, R., Leinster, Ireland; rises in Slieve Bloom Mtns., and flows to Waterford Harbour.

Barrow-in-Furness, *spt.*, *co. bor.*, N. Lancs, Eng.; iron and steel, paper, shipbldg., engin.; p. (estd. 1967) 64,650.

Barrow-on-Soar, *rural dist.* and *t.*, Leicester, Eng.; p. (rural dist. 1961) 57,131.

Barrow Point, most northerly headland in Alaska, N. America.

Barry, *mun. bor.*, Glamorgan, Wales; "outport" of Cardiff; coal, tin-plate, chemicals, plastics; p. (1961) 42,039.

Barsac, *t.*, Gironde, France; Sauterne wine; p. (1954) 2,320.

Barsi, *t.*, Maharashtra, India; cotton, oil-seeds; p. (1961) 50,389.

Barstow, *t.*, Cal., U.S.A.; early silver mining and frontier town; p. (1960) 11,644.

Bar-sur-Aube, *t.*, Aube, France; wine, brandy; furniture; p. (1954) 4,387.

Bar-sur-Seine, *t.*, Aube, France; p. (1962) 2,763.

Barth, *spt.*, Rostock, E. Germany; shipyd. engin., furniture, sugar; p. (1963) 12,406.

Bartholomew Bayou, R., Ark., U.S.A., l. 275 m.

Bartin, *t.*, N. Turkey; p. (1960) 11,655.

Bartlesville, *t.*, Okla., U.S.A.; oil refining, zinc smelting, metal prod., leather goods; p. (1960) 27,893.

Barton-upon-Humber, *urb. dist.*, Lindsey, Lincs, Eng.; cycles, rope-making, bricks, tiles, chemical manure; p. (1961) 6,584.

Bartow, *t.*, Fla., U.S.A.; phosphates, citrus canneries, cigar-mkg.; p. (1960) 12,849.

Barvas, *par.*, Lewis, Scot.; p. 5,876.

Basel, *can.*, Switzerland; divided into the halfcantons, Basel-Stadt, a. 14 sq. m., cap. Basel; p. (1961) 225,588, and Baselland, a. 165 sq. m., cap. Liestal; farming, vines, forests; p. (1961) 148,282.

Basel, *c.*, *cap.*, Basel, Switzerland; head of barge navigation on Rhine; chemicals, ribbons; p. (1961) 205,800.

Bashee R., Cape Province, S. Africa.

Bashi L., gr. in Pac. Oc.; N. of Luzon in the Philippines.

Bashkir, *Rep.* R.S.F.S.R., U.S.S.R.; farming, gold, copper, coal, oil, engin., chemicals, textiles; cap. Ufa; p. (1959) 3,335,000.

Basildon, *t.*, Essex, Eng.; in lower Thames valley, 8 m. S.E. of Brentwood; one of "New Towns" designated 1949 to relieve population congestion in London; incorporated S. part of Billericay urb. dist. and N. part of Thurrock urb. dist; gen. and elec. engin., cars, clothing, tobacco, photographic apparatus; p. (estd. 1965) 66,488.

Basilicata, *dep.*, Italy; wheat, maize, vines, olive, oil; a. 3,855 sq. m.; p. (1961) 602,661.

Basingstoke, *mftg. and mkt. t.*, *mun. bor.*, N. Hants Eng.; 50 m. W. London; vehicles, farm implements, pharmaceutics; p. (estd. 1967) 33,230.

Basle, see Basel.

Basque Prov., Spain; comprising three provs., Alava, Guipuzcoa, Vizcaya, where Basque language is spoken and also N. of Pyrenees in France.

Basra, *prov.* or *liwa* on Euphrates, Iraq; 60 m. from the sea; p. (1956) 404,303.

Basra, *t.*, *river pt.*, Iraq; dates; p. (1956) 159,355.

Bass Rock, in firth of Forth, opposite Tantallon Castle, E. Lothian, Scot.; gannetry.

Bass Strait, between Victoria and Tasmania; offshore oilfields.

Bassano, *t.*, Italy; on R. Brenia; vines, olives, majolica; p. *20,527*.

Bassein, *t.*, Burma; on mouth of Irrawaddy R., univ.; exp rice; airfield.

Bassein, *R.*, Burma.

Bassenthwaite, *L.*, Cumberland, Eng.; length 4 m., breadth 1 m.; fishing.

Basses-Alpes, *frontier dep.*, S.E. France; olives, wines; cap. Digne; a. 2,697 sq. m.; p. (1954) *84,335*.

Basses-Pyrénées, *see* Pyrénées-Atlantique.

Basse-Terre. *ch. t.*, Guadeloupe Fr. W. Indies; p. (estd. 1965) *12,000*.

Basseterre, *cap.* St. Kitts I. Leeward group; W.I.; new tourist development at nearby Frigate Bay; p. (1957) *35,878*.

Båstad, *summer resort*, Sweden; international tennis; p. *2,300*.

Bastia, *t.*, *spt.*, Corsica, France; p. (1962) *50,580*.

Bastogne, *t.*, Belgium, nr. Luxembourg; p. (1962) *5,893*.

Bastrop, *t.*, N. La., U.S.A.; on Colorado R. mills; p. (1960) *15,193*.

Bastrop, *t.*, Texas, U.S.A.; on Colorado R.; lignite; p. (1960) *3,001*.

Basoutoland, *see* Lesotho.

Bata, *ch.t.* Equatorial Guinea, W. Africa; p. *5,000*

Bataan, *t.*, Philippine Is; plywoods and veneer, pulp, paper; oil refining nearby.

Batabanó, *t.*, Cuba; sponges; p. (1953) *5,075*.

Batangas, *prov.*, Philippine Is., oil refining; p. (1960) *681,414*.

Batavia, *see* Djakarta.

Batavia, *c.*, N.Y., U.S.A.; farm implements; p. (1960) *18,210*.

Bataysk, *t.*, Rostov region, R.S.F.S.R.; rly. junction; grain and cattle, engin., p. (1959) *52,000*.

Batesar, *t.*, Agra dist., India; on the R. Jumna; comm. ctr.

Batesville, *t.*, Ark., U.S.A.; marble, manganese; p. (1960) *6,109*.

Batesville, *t.*, Ind., U.S.A.; furniture; p. (1960) *3,349*.

Bath, *t.*, Maine, U.S.A.; on R. Kennebec; p. (1960) *10,717*.

Bath, *c.*, *co. bor.*, Somerset, Eng.; Roman baths, hot springs, medicinal waters; fine Regency architecture; univ.; elect. engin., metals and limestone; p. (estd. 1967) *85,870*.

Bathgate, *burgh*, West Lothian, Scot.; 6 m. S. of Linlithgow; coal-mng., quarrying, metal, elec., hosiery, cars; p. (1961) *12,686*.

Bathurst, *I.*, off coast of N. Terr., Australia; 30 m. long; Aborigines reserve; cypress pine milling.

Bathurst, *t.*, N.S.W., Australia; ctr. of pastoral, agr., fruit district; brewing, boots and shoes, lt. engin., cement pipes; p. (1966) *17,220*.

Bathurst, *sp.*, *cap.*, Gambia, W. Africa; at mouth of Gambia R.; airport; groundnuts; p. (1963) *27,809*.

Batina, fertile coastal plain, Oman, Arabia; produces early-ripening dates famous for flavour.

Batley, *industl. t.*, *mun. bor.*, W.R. Yorks, Eng.; heavy woollens, shoddy; p. (estd. 1967) *41,160*.

Batna, *commune*, Algeria; N. Africa; rly. to Biskra; p. *10,622*.

Baton Rouge, *cap.*, Louisiana, U.S.A.; on Mississippi R.; cotton seed, oil-refining; p. (1960) *152,491*.

Battambang, *prov.*, Cambodia; 180 m. N.E. of Pnom-Penh; cotton mill; p. (1962) *551,860*.

Battam I., Malay Arch.; 20 m. S. of Singapore.

Battersea, *see* Wandsworth.

Batticaloa, *t.*, *cap.*, E. Prov., Ceylon; p. *12,984*.

Battle, *t.*, *rural dist.*, Sussex, Eng.; battle of Hastings fought here 1066; p. (rural dist. 1961) *30,558*.

Battle Creek, *c.*, Michigan, U.S.A.; on Kalamazoo R.; engin., cereal prod.; p. (1960) *44,169*.

Battleford, *t.*, N., Canada; at junction of Battle R. with Saskatchewan R.; mixed farming; p. (1951) *7,489*.

Battle Harbour, nr. Strait of Belle I., Labrador.

Battle Mountain, *t.*, Nev., U.S.A.; copper-mines.

Batu Gajah, *t.*, Malaya; in valley Kinta R.; tin-mines; residtl.; p. (1947) *7,480*.

Batu, L. E. Indies, Indonesia.

Batumi, *t.*, *spt.*, Georgian S.S.R.; oil, engin., citrus fruits, tea; oil pipeline connects with Baku; p. (1959) *82,000*.

Bauchi, *t.*, central Nigeria; ctr. of impt. tin-mining a.; p. *10,000*.

Baud, *t.*, Orissa, India; on R. Mahanadi.

Bauld, *C.*, northernmost part of Newfoundland, N. America.

Baures, *R.*, E. Bolivia; flowing from L. Guazamire to R. Guapore; length 300 m.

Buaru, *t.*, São Paulo st., Brazil; comm. ctr., food inds; p. (estd. 1968) *110,961*.

Bautzen, *t.*, Dresden, E. Germany; on R. Spree; textiles, engin., iron inds.; p. (1963) *42,431*.

Bauya, *t.*, Sierra Leone, W. Africa; rly. junction.

Bavaria, *Land*, Germany; hilly, forested; ch. rivers; Danube, Main, Isar, Inn; ch. inds.; agr., dairying, rye, oats, hops, sugar-beet. brewing, glass, sugar, toys, chemicals, jewellery; cap. Munich (*q.v.*); a. 27,112 sq. m.; p. (1968) *10,406,000*.

Bavarian Alps, *mtns.*, Germany.

Bawdwin, *t.*, Burma; wolfram, lead, zinc, silver, rubies.

Baxley, *t.*, S.E. Ga., U.S.A.; pecan nuts, tobacco; p. (1950) *3,234*.

Baxter Springs, *t.*, S.E. Kan., U.S.A.; lead- and zinc-mines; p. (1960) *4,498*.

Bayamon, *t.*, Puerto Rico, W. Indies; fruit, tobacco, sugar, coffee; p. (1960) *72,134*.

Baybay, *t.*, Leyte, Philippine Is.; impt. comm. pt.; p. (1948) *50,725*.

Bayburt, *t.*, Turkey, p. (1960) *11,968*.

Bay City, *mftg. t.*, Mich., U.S.A.; on Saginaw R., 108 m. N.W. of Detroit; fishing, chemicals beet-sugar; p. (1960) *53,604*.

Bay City, *t.*, Texas, U.S.A.; sulphur, oil; p. (1960) *11,656*.

Bayeux, *t.*, Calvados, France; cath., museum, Bayeux tapestry; p. (1962) *10,641*.

Bay Is., group G. of Honduras, Central America; lgst., Ruatan; coconuts, bananas; p. (1961) *8,863*.

Bay of Islands, inlet and harbour on N.I., New Zealand.

Bayombong, *t.*, Philippine Is.; p. (1948) *14,079*.

Bayonne, *fortfd. t.*, Basses-Pyrénées, S.W. France; cath.; noted for fine hams, invention of bayonet; aircraft; p. (1968) *42,743*

Bayonne, *t.*, N.J., U.S.A.; 6 m from New York; chemicals, oil-refining; p. (1960) *74,215*.

Bayport, *t.*, Minn., U.S.A.; on St. Croix R.; state prison; p. (1960) *3,205*.

Bayreuth, *c.*, Bavaria, S. Germany; home of Wagner; famous for musical festivals in magnificent national theatre; textiles, porcelain, engin.; p. (1963) *61,700*.

Baytown, *t.*, S.E. Texas, U.S.A.; oil-wells, toluene factory; p. (1960) *28,159*.

Baza, *t.*, S. Spain; W. of Lorca; lead, iron, mercury, sugar; p. (1957) *23,450*.

Beachy Head, 575 ft. high, on Sussex cst., loftiest headland in S. Eng.

Beaconsfield, *t.*, Tasmania, Australia; on W. of estuary of Tamar R.; tin mining.

Beaconsfield, *urb. dist.*, Bucks., Eng.; residtl.; p. (1961) *10,019*.

Beaconsfield, *t.*, Cape Province, S. Africa; diamonds.

Bear I., Arctic Ocean; 130 m. S. of Spitzbergen.

Bear L., on border of Idaho and Utah, U.S.A.

Bear L., Great, N.W. Terr., Canada; outlet to Mackenzie R. through Great Bear R.; a. 14,000 sq. m.

Béarn, *old prov.* now Basses-Pyrénées, France.

Bearsden, *burgh*, Dunbarton, Scot.; p. (1961) *17,022*.

Beas (Bias), R., Punjab, India; trib. of Sutlej R.; one of the "five rivers."

Beas de Segura, *t.*, Spain; wine, oil, fruits, flax; p. *14,953*.

Beatrice, Neb., U.S.A.; health resort on Big Blue R.; p. (1960) *12,132*.

Beattock, *pass*, S. Uplands, Scot.; gives access from valley of R. Clyde to R. Annan; used by main W. cst. rly. route from Carlisle to Glasgow and Edinburgh; alt. 1,014 ft.

Beaucaire, *t.*, Gard, France; noted fair; p. (1962) *11,211*.

Beauce, *natural division* ("*pays*"), Central France; low, level, plateau of limestone S.W. of Paris and R. Seine; arid, few surface streams; thin layer of loam (limon) permits agr.; impt. wheat-growing area; population mainly grouped in lge. vils.

Beaufort, *t.,* S.C., U.S.A.; S.W. of Charleston; canning and shipping point for farming and fishing region; tourist ctr.; p. (1960) *6,298.*

Beaufort West, *t.,* Cape Province, S. Africa; sheep, karakul; p. (1960) *16,323* inc. *5,297* whites.

Beaujolais, France; wine-growing dist.

Beaulieu, *par.,* Hants. Eng.; on Beaulieu R.; abbey; car museum; p. *1,201.*

Beauly, *R.,* Inverness, Scot.; flows to Beauly Loch.

Beauly, *t.,* Inverness, Scot.; on Beauly R.; p. *890.*

Beaumaris, *mun. bor., wat. pl.,* cap. Anglesey, N. Wales; on Menai Strait; cas., ruins; light engin.; p. (1961) *1,960.*

Beaumont, *c.,* E. Texas, U.S.A.; lumbering, petroleum; p. (1960) *119,175.*

Beaune, *t.,* Côte d'Or, France; wines, casks, farm implements; p. (1962) *15,382.*

Beausoleil, *t.,* Alpes-Maritime, France; p. (1962) *12,833.*

Beauvais, *t., cap.,* Oise, France; cath.; Gobelin tapestry; p. (1962) *36,533.*

Beaver, *R.,* Penns., Ohio, U.S.A.; rises in Allegheny Plateau, flows N. towards L. Erie, turns S.E. into R. Ohio just below Pittsburgh; valley provides easiest route from Pittsburgh to L. Erie pts., contains many steel-mkg. ts., Youngstown, Newcastle, Warren; length 130 m.

Beaver Dam, *c.,* Wisconsin, U.S.A.; summer resort on L.; p. (1960) *13,118.*

Beaver Falls, *t.,* Penns., U.S.A.; machin., pottery, coal, natural gas; p. (1960) *16,240.*

Beaver Meadows, *bor.,* E. Penns., U.S.A.; anthracite, textiles; p. (1960) *1,392.*

Beawar, *t.,* Rajasthan, India; cotton; p. (1961) *53,931.*

Bebington, *mun. bor.,* Cheshire, Eng.; soap, chemicals, engin.; p. (estd. 1967) *55,520.*

Becancourt, *t.,* Quebec, Canada; on S. bank of St. Lawrence; integrated steel mill projected.

Beccles, *mun. bor.,* Suffolk, Eng.; printing, engin., malting; p. (estd. 1967) *7,850.*

Béchar (Colom-Béchar), *t.,* N.W. Algeria; terminus of rly. through Oran dep.; p. (1960) *45,539.*

Bechuanaland, *see* Botswana.

Beckenham, *former mun. bor.,* Kent, Eng., now inc. in Bromley outer London bor. (*q.v.*); p. (1961) *77,265.*

Beckley, *c.,* S.W. Va., U.S.A.; coal; p. (1960) *18,642.*

Beckum, *t.,* N. Rhine–Westphalia, Germany; cement, chalk, engin. wks.; p. (1963) *21,200.*

Bedale, *mkt. t., rural dist.,* N.R. Yorks, Eng.; at N. end of Vale of York; tent mkg.; p. (rural dist. 1961) *8,215.*

Beddgelert, *par.,* Caernarvon, Wales; resort; slate.

Beddington and Wallington, *mun. bor.,* Surrey, Eng. nr. Croydon; p. (1961) *32,588.*

Bedford, *mun. bor.,* Beds, Eng.; on R. Ouse, 50 m. N. of London; general engin. inc. marine and elect., bricks, ironfounding, aero research; p. (estd. 1967) *67,300.*

Bedfordshire, S. Midland co., Eng.; co. t. Bedford (*q.v.*); agr., mkt. gardening, brickmkg., cement, vehicles, engin.; a. 473 sq. m.; p. (1966) *428,000.*

Bedford, *t.,* Indiana, U.S.A.; p. (1960) *13,024.*

Bedford, *t.,* Ohio, U.S.A.; p. (1960) *15,223.*

Bedford Level, once over 400,000 acres of peat marsh in S. Fenland; first successful draining initiated by Earl of Bedford in 1634.

Bedlington, *urb. dist.,* Northumberland, Eng.; iron, coal; p. (estd. 1967) *30,810.*

Bedloe's I., or Liberty I., N.Y. harbour, U.S.A.; on which statue of Liberty stands.

Bedminster, *t.,* Somerset, Eng.; sub. of Bristol.

Bedourie, *t.,* Queensland, Australia.

Bedrashem, *t.,* U.A.R., N.E. Africa; on R. Nile.

Bedwas and Machen, *urb. dist.,* Mon., Wales; gas, coal and coke by-prods.; p. (1961) *10,231.*

Bedwellty, *urb. dist.,* Mon., Wales; coal, iron, elec. goods, car upholstery; p. (1961) *27,336.*

Bedworth, *urb. dist.,* Warwick., Eng.; coal-mng., limestone quarrying, engin., textiles; p. (estd. 1967) *39,100.*

Bedzin, *t.,* S. Poland; coal, zinc, metals, chemicals bricks, sugar-beet; p. (1965) *42,000.*

Beechworth, *t.,* Victoria, Australia; gold, pastoral and agr.

Beechy Point, *C.,* N.E. cst. Alaska, U.S.A.

Beemaning Mtn., highest peak Blue Mtns., N.S.W., Australia; alt. 4,100 ft.

Beenleigh, *t.,* Queensland, Australia; 24 m. S. Brisbane.

Beerberg, *highest mtn.,* Thüringer Wald, Germany; alt. 3,266 ft.

Beernem, *t.,* W. Flanders, Belgium; p. (1962) *5,829.*

Beersheba, *t.,* Israel; ctr. for development of the Negev; p. (1953) over *20,000.*

Beeskow, *t.,* Germany; on R. Spree.

Beeston and Stapleford, *urb. dist.,* Nottingham, Eng.; engin., drugs, telephones; p. (estd. 1967) *62,070.*

Beeville, *c.,* Texas, U.S.A.; mnfs. oilfield equipment; oil-wells; p. (1960) *13,811.*

Beg, *L.,* Antrim, N. Ireland.

Bega, *R.,* S. Hungary; canalised trib. to R. Tisza.

Bègles, *t.,* Gironde, France; mftg.; p. (1954) *23,176.*

Beheira, *prov.,* Lower U.A.R., N.E. Africa; in delta of Nile R.; cotton; a. 1,639 sq. m.; p. (1960) *1,685,679.*

Behistun, *t.,* Iraq; in ruins; monuments of Darius the Great.

Beilan, *t., mtn. pass,* Syria-S.W. Asia; E. of G. of Iskenderun; ancient Amanus of "Syrian Gates."

Beilngries, *t.,* Bavaria, Germany; on Ludwig's canal.

Beilstein, *t.,* Germany; on R. Moselle.

Beira, *spt., cap.,* prov. Manica and Sofala, Mozambique; airport; rly. runs inland to Salisbury (Rhodesia) and Blantyre (Malawi); exp. sugar, maize, cotton; oil pipeline to Umtali; p. (1960) *64,600* inc. *16,000* Europeans.

Beirut, *cap.* Lebanon, S.W. Asia; most impt. *spt.* Syria and Lebanon; ancient historic t., now busy shipping and mercantile ctr.; silk, wool, fruits; p. (estd 1964) *700,000.*

Beisan, *t.,* Israel, in Jordan valley, *c.* 300 ft. below sea level; archaeological finds date from *c.* 1500 B.C.; rebuilt since 1948 by Israelis.

Beit el Faki, *t.,* Yemen, Arabia; coffee.

Beit Jala, *t.,* Jordan.

Beit Jibrin, *t.,* Israel, in Judæan Hills.

Beja, *dist.,* Portugal; pig-breeding dist.; olive oil, pottery; cath.; airfield under construction for training of German pilots; p. (1960) *283,152.*

Bejaia (Bougie), *spt.,* Algeria; impt. tr. ctr.; exp. wood, hides; oil pipe-line connection to Hassi-Messoud; p. (1954) *43,934.*

Bejar, *t.,* Spain; cloth; p. *c. 13,000.*

Bekes, *t.,* Hungary; wheat; p. (1962) *24,100.*

Békéscsaba, *t.,* Hungary; milling; rly. junction; poultry processing plant; p. (1962) *50,664.*

Belaya Tserkov, *t.,* N. Ukrainian S.S.R.; agr. and comm. ctr.; p. (1959) *71,000.*

Belbeis, *t.,* U.A.R., N.E. Africa; agr. ctr. on W. edge of cultivated Nile delta.

Belcher Is., two sm. groups in Hudson Bay, N.W. Terr., Canada.

Belding, *c.,* Mich., U.S.A.; silk mills; p. (1960) *4,387.*

Belem, *sub.* of Lisbon, Portugal; fine church, monastery.

Belém, *spt.,* cap. Pará st., Brazil; comm. ctr., ch. pt. of Amazon basin (rubber, Brazil nuts, cacao, timber); univ.; p. (estd. 1968) *563,996.*

Belen, *t.,* Catamarca, Argentina.

Béiep Arch., about 7 m. N.E. of New Caledonia.

Belfast, *spt., co. bor., cap.* N. Ireland; Antrim (and partly Down), at head of Belfast Lough; Britain's lgst single shipyard; linen mnf., rope, tobacco, distilling, aircraft, fertilisers, computers; oil refinery on E. side of harbour; univ.; Houses of Parliament, Stormont Cas.; p. (estd. 1968) *391,000.*

Belfast, *t.,* Maine, U.S.A.; p. (1960) *6,140.*

Belfodio, *t.,* Ethiopia; nr. border with Sudan.

Belford, *rural dist.,* Northumberland, Eng.; agr., whinstone quarrying; p. (1961) *4,994.*

Belfort, *fortress t.,* Belfort, France; between Jura and the Vosges; heavy inds., rly. wks., sm. cotton ind.; p. (1962) *51,280.*

Belfort, *dep.,* France; ch. t., Belfort; a. 235 sq. m.; p. (1968) *118.450.*

Belgaum, *t.,* Mysore, India; cotton; p. (1961) *126,727.*

Belgian Congo. *See* Congo.

Belgium, *cty.*, W. Europe; climate temperate; ch. rivers: Scheldt, Meuse; races: Flemish, Walloon; languages: Flemish, French; religion: Roman Catholic; ch. inds.: agr., cereals, sugar-beet, potatoes, cattle, pigs, horses; minerals: coal; mnfs.: iron and steel machin., engin., metals, shipbldg., textiles, brewing, distilling; exp. mnf. goods; communications: rail, road, canal; cap. Brussels; ch. port, Antwerp; univ. at Brussels, Ghent, Liége, Louvain; a. 11,755 sq. m.; p. (1968) *9,660,000.*

Belgorod, *t.*, Kursk, R.S.F.S.R.: chalk, slate, lumber, soap, leather, engin.; p. (1959) *71,000.*

Belgorod-Dnestrovski, *t.*, Ukraine, U.S.S.R.: mouth of Dniester R.; wine, wool, fruit; p. (1956) *21,600.*

Belgrade (Beograd), *cap. c.*, Jugoslavia: at junc. of Save and Danube; univ.; mnfs. tobacco, woollens, aircraft; p. (1964) *678,000.*

Belhaven, *t.*, N.C., U.S.A.; on Pamlico Sound; fishing, lumbering; p. (1960) *2,386.*

Belitung or Billiton, *I.* Between Sumatra and Kalimantan, Indonesia; tin; a. 1,866 sq. m.; p. *102,375.*

Belize, *R.*, Brit. Honduras, Central America; 150 m. long; rises in N.E. Guatemala and flows E. into G. of Honduras at B.

Belize, *t.*, *cap.*, British Honduras, Central America; mahogany, dyewoods, bananas; almost devastated by hurricane 31 Oct. 1961; cap. to be moved to new site 50 m. further inland; p. (1960) *32,824.*

Bell, *I.*, Newfoundland, E. Canada; in Conception Bay, 20 m. N.W. of St. Johns; impt. Wabana iron-ore deposits outcrop on N.W. cst., smelted on Pictou coalfield, Nova Scotia; a. 12 sq. m.; p. of Wabana (1956) *7,373.*   Bay.

Bell, *R.*, Quebec, Canada; flows N. into James Bell, *t.*, Cal., U.S.A.; residtl. c. 5 m. S. of Los Angeles; p. (1960) *19,371.*

Bell Bay, *pt.*, Tasmania, Australia; on right bank of Tamar R.; modern pt. and site of aluminium refinery.

Bell Rock, Scot.; famous rock and lighthouse 12 m. S.E. of Arbroath.

Bellagio, *t.*, Italy; on L. Como; resort.

Bellaire, *mftg. t.*, Ohio, U.S.A.; on Ohio R.; coal, limestone, glass, enamelware; p. (1960) *11,502.*

Bellary, *fortfd. c.*, Mysore, India; cotton; p. (1961) *85,673.*

Belleek, *par.* and *vil.*, Fermanagh, N. Ireland; on Erne R.; china; p. *1,300.*

Bellefontaine, *t.*, Ohio, U.S.A.; agr. ctr., light mnfs.; holiday resort; p. (1960) *11,424.*

Bellefonte, *bor.*, Penns., U.S.A.; limestone quarries; p. (1960) *6,083.*

Belle Fourche, *t.*, S.D., U.S.A.; on Belle Fourche R.; beet sugar, flour, bricks, dairy produce; p. (1960) *4,087.*   land, near Geneva.

Bellegarde, *fort* on frontier of France and Switzer-

Belle Ile, *I.* off S. coast of Brittany, France.

Belle Isle Strait, N. America; between Newfoundland and Labrador, on N. shipping route to Canada from Europe.   Australia.

Bellenden Ker Hills, *mtn. range*, N. Queensland,

Belleville, *c.*, Ontario, Canada; dairying, fruit; deposit of white marble nearby; p. (1961) *30,655.*

Belleville, *t.*, Ill., U.S.A.; brewing, iron founding, shoes, flour; p. (1960) *37,264.*

Belleville, *t.*, N.J., U.S.A.; p. (1960) *35,005.*

Bellevue, *c.*, Ohio, U.S.A.; limestone, farm implements, car parts; p. (1960) *8,282.*

Bellevue, *t.*, Penns., U.S.A.; p. (1960) *11,412.*

Bellevue, *t.*, Queensland, Australia; goldfields.

Belley, *t.*, Ain, France; p. (1962) *6,442.*

Bellflower, *t.*, Cal., U.S.A.; p. (1960) *44,846.*

Bellingham, *rural dist.*, Hexham, Northumberland, Eng.; coal; p. (1961) *5,285.*

Bellingham, *t.*, *spt.*, Wash., U.S.A.; saw-mills, paper-mills, salmon canning; p. (1960) *34,688.*

Bellingshausen, *sea*, S. Antarctic; lying W. of Graham Land.

Bellinzona, *t.*, Switzerland; on R. Ticino; 14 m. N. of Lugano; three castles built on hills dominating t.; p. (1957) *12,060.*

Bellot Strait, channel on Arctic coast, N. America; separates Boothia and N. Somerset.

Bellows Falls, *t.*, Vt., U.S.A., on Connecticut, R.; paper, farm implements; p. (1960) *3,831.*

Belluno, *c.*, Venetia, N. Italy; fine cath.; silk; p. (1961) *31,224.*

Belluno, *prov.* Venetia, N. Italy; a. 1,276 sq. m.; p. (1961) *205,700.*

Belmar, *t.*, N.J., U.S.A.; seaside resort, fishing; p. (1960) *5,190.*

Belmez, *t.*, Córdoba prov., S. Spain; on. N. flank of Sierra Morena, 38 m. N.W. of Córdoba; ctr. of sm. coalfield; p. (1959) *9,672.*

Belmont, *t.*, Cape Province, S. Africa; 56 m. S. of Kimberley.

Belmont, *t.*, Mass., U.S.A.; p. (1960) *28,715.*

Belmont, *t.*, N.C., U.S.A.; p. (1960) *5,007.*

Belo Horizonte, *t.*, cap. Minas Gerais, Brazil; impt. inland c.; ctr. rich agr. and mng. region; steel mills, food inds., textiles, diamond cutting; oil pipeline from Guanabara; p. (estd. 1968); *1,167,026.*

Beloit, *c.*, Wisconsin, U.S.A.; on Rock R., diesel engines, farm implements; p. (1960) *32,846.*

Beloit, *c.*, Kan., U.S.A.; on Solomon R.; tr. ctr. for agr. region; p. (1960) *3,837.*

Beloretsk, *t.*, Bashkir A.S.S.R.; iron, metal inds.; p. (1959) *59,000.*

Belovo, *t.*, W. Siberia, R.S.F.S.R.; coal mng., zinc, engin.; p. (1967) *115,000.*

Beloyarsk, R.S.F.S.R.; atomic power sta. in Urals.

Belper, *urb. dist.*, Derby, Eng.; hosiery, textiles, paint, oil wks., iron foundries; p. (1961) *15,563.*

Belt, Great, *strait*, Denmark; separates Fyn I. from Själland I.; deep-water channel too winding for easy navigation; crossed by train ferry at its narrowest point (16 m.) between Nyborg and Korsor; approx. length 37 m.

Belt, Little, *strait*, Denmark; separates Fyn I. from Jutland; too shallow for large ships; bridged by road-railway bridge nr. Fredericia; approx. length 30 m.

Belterra, *dist.*, Pará st., N.E. Brazil; on R. Tapajoz, 30 m. S. of confluence with R. Amazon at Santarem; a. 950 sq. m.; known as Fordlandia.

Beltsy, *t.*, Moldavian S.S.R.; on trib. of Dniester R.; p. (1959) *67,000.*

Belturbet, *t.*, *urb. dist.*, Cavan, Ireland; on R. Erne; distilling; p. (1951) *1,152.*

Bembridge, *vil.*, I. of Wight, Eng.; resort, yachting; p. *1,975* (par.).

Bemfica, Angola, W. Africa; oilfields.

Bemidji, *t.*, Minn., U.S.A.; lumber, cement, bricks, woollen goods; resort; p. (1960) *9,958.*

Ben Alder, *mtn.*, Grampian Range, Scot.; nr. Loch Erich; alt. 3,757 ft.

Ben Arthur, *mtn.*, Argyll, Scot.; alt. 2,891 ft.

Ben Attow, *mtn.*, Ross and Inverness, Scot.; alt. 3,383 ft.

Ben Avon, *mtn.*, Aberdeen, Scot.; alt. 3,834 ft.

Ben Cruachan, *mtn.*, Argyll, Scot.; alt. 3,689 ft.

Ben Doran or Doireann, *mtn.*, Argyll, Scot.; alt. 3,523 ft.

Ben Hope, *mtn.*, Sutherland, Scot.; alt. 3,040 ft.

Ben Lawers, *mtn.*, Perth, Scot.; by Loch Tay; alt. 3,984 ft.

Ben Ledi, *mtn.*, Perth, Scot.; N.W. of Callander; alt. 2,875 ft.

Ben Lomond, *mtn.*, Stirling, Scot.; E. side of L. Lomond; alt. 3,192 ft.

Ben Lomond, *mtn.*, New England range, N.S.W., Australia; alt. 5,000 ft.

Ben Lomond. *mtn.*, Tasmania, Australia; alt. 5,010 ft.; tin and wolfram mined on S.E. slopes.

Ben Macdhui, *mtn.*, S.W. Aberdeen, Scot.; Cairngorm gr; second highest peak in Brit. Is.; alt. 4,296 ft.

Ben More, *mtn.*, S.W. Perth, Scot.; 10 m. W. of Loch Earn; alt. 3,843 ft.; also mtns. in Sutherland, Hebrides and I. of Mull.

Ben Nevis, *mtn.*, Inverness, Scot.; at Lochiel; highest peak in Brit. Isles, alt. 4,406 ft.

Ben Nevis, *mtn.*, Otago, New Zealand; alt. 9,125 ft.

Ben Nevis, *mtn.*, Cornwall, Tasmania, Australia; alt. 3,910 ft.

Ben Venue, *mtn.*, nr. Loch Katrine, Perth, Scot.; alt. 2,393 ft.

Ben Vorlich, *mtn.*, Perth, Scot.; alt. 3,224 ft.

Ben Wyvis, *mtn.*, Ross, Scot.; nr. Dingwall; alt. 3,429 ft.

Benalla, *t.*, *dist.*, Victoria, Australia; pastoral and agr.; p. (1961) *8,433.*

Benares, *see* Varanasi.

Benbecula I., Outer Hebrides, Inverness, Scot.; a. 36 sq. m.

Benbecula Sound, passage between the I. and S. Uist, Outer Hebrides.

Bendery, *t.*, Moldavian S.S.R.; textiles, p. (estd. 1961) *63,000*.

Bendigo, *c.*, Victoria, Australia; former gold-mining dist., engin., brickwks., wool, eucalyptus oil and hardboard mftg., food processing; p. (1966) *42,191*.

Benevento, *prov.*, Italy; a. 819 sq. m., containing many Roman remains; p. (1961) *297,153*.

Benevento, *c.*, Italy; cath.; leather; p. (1961) *54,744*.

Benfleet, *urb. dist.*, Essex, Eng.; saw mills, joinery wks., light inds.; p. (estd. 1967) *43,890*.

Bengal, West, *st.*, India; a. 33,928 sq. m.; p. (1961) *34,926,279*; rice, oilseeds, sugar cane, tobacco, jute, silk, tea, coal, mesta, potatoes; served by 3 st. rlys.; Ganges alluvial plains and delta; ch. c. Calcutta which adjoins jute manuf. ctr. Howrah. (Former prov. of Bengal split 1947—W. Bengal to India, E. Bengal to Pakistan).

Bengal, Bay of, part of Indian Ocean washing E. shores of India and W. shores of the Indo-Chinese Peninsula; receives waters of Rs. Krishna, Ganges, Brahmaputra, Irrawaddy.

Benghazi, *spt.*, Libya, N. Africa; on the G. of Sidra; joint cap. with Tripoli; former starting-point for caravans to Egypt and the interior; cereals; p. (estd. 1954) *71,000*.

Bongore Head, *C.*, Antrim, N. coast Ireland; E. of Giant's Causeway.

Benguela, *c.*, Angola, S.W. Africa; rly. runs inland to Congo and Zambia; beeswax, maize, cattle, sugar; p. (1960) *52,300* inc. *11,500* whites.

Benha, *t.*, U.A.R.; impt. mkt. t., rail and road ctr. in heart of cultivated a. of Nile delta.

Benholm, *par.*, Kincardine, Scot.; ancient cas.; p. (1951) *1,028*.

Beni, *dep.*, N.E. Bolivia, S. America; cap. Trinidad; a. 93,354 sq. m.; p. (1962) *161,800*.

Benicarlo, *spt.*, Valencia, Spain; on Mediterranean cst.; wines; p. (1957) *9,385*.

Benin, W. Africa; between Niger delta and Dahomey; traversed by Benin R.; former African kingdom and slaving ctr., now dist. incorporated in Nigeria; palm prod. and foodstuffs; famous African bronze ctr.; ch. t. Benin.

Benin, *t.*, Nigeria; ·W. Africa; cap. Mid-West region; palm oil, mahogany; p. (1953) *54,000*.   [Africa.

Benin, Bight of, part of G. of Guinea, W.

Beni Suef, *t.*, U.A.R.; on Nile, 60 m. S. of Cairo; carpets, cotton; p. (1960) *79,000*.

Benkulen, *spt.*, Sumatra, Indonesia; p. *13,418*.

Benmore, *O.*, Antrim, N.E. point of N. Ireland; alt. 636 ft.

Bennettsville, *t.*, S.C., U.S.A.; yarn, tyre linings, lumber; p. (1960) *6,963*.

Bennington, *t.*, Vt., U.S.A.; p. (1960) *8,023*.

Benoni, *t.*, Transvaal, S. Africa; engin.; p. (1960) *135,467* (inc. *41,305* whites).

Benrath, *i.*, Germany; on Rhine R.; R. pt. and industl. t.; chemicals, machin.; p. *25,929*.

Bensberg, *t.*, N. Rhine–Westphalia, Germany; 10 m. from Cologne; iron-mining, foundries; p. (1963) *33,400*.

Bensheim, *t.*, Hessen, Germany; ctr. of fruit and wine dist.; textiles, paper, metallurgy; p. (1963) *24,800*.

Bentang (Bintang), *t.*, Kalimantan, Indonesia.

Bentley with Arksey, *urb. dist.*, W.R. Yorks, Eng.; p. (estd. 1967) *23,650*.

Benton, *t.*, Ark., U.S.A.; p. (1960) *10,399*.

Benton, *t.*, Ill., U.S.A.; p. (1960) *7,023*.

Benton Harbor, *t.*, Mich., U.S.A.; midway along E. cst. L. Michigan; p. (1960) *19,136*.

Benue, *R.*, W. Africa; chief trib. of Niger.

Benwell, *t.*, Northumberland, Eng.; sub. of Newcastle.

Ben-y-Gloe, *mtn.*, Glen Tilt, Perth, Scot.; alt. 3,671 ft.

Beograd, *see* Belgrade.

Beppu, *t.*, Kyushu, Japan; hot spring resort; p. (1965) *118,938*.

Berat, *c.*, Albania; p. (1945) *11,872*.

Berbera, *pt.*, Somalia, N.E. Africa; on G. of Aden; former winter cap. of Br. Somaliland Prot.; exports livestock from pastoral hinterland; new deep-sea pt. completed 1969; airpt.

Berbice, *co.*, Guyana, S. America; bauxite; p. (1946) *96,623*.

Berchem, *industl. sub.*, Antwerp, Belgium; metal, chemical inds.; p. (1968) *50,333*.

Berdichev (Ossipevsk), *t.*, Ukrainian S.S.R.; ctr. of sugar a.; engin., lt. inds.; p. (1959) *53,000*.

Berck-Plage, *wat. pl.*, France, on Eng. Channel; p. (1962) *15,543*.

Berdyansk (Osipenko), *spt.*, Ukrainian S.S.R.; on Sea of Azov; a ctr. of the salt ind.; exp. grain, hemp, wool, agr. machin.; engin., oil refining; p. (1959) *65,000*.

Berea, *t.*, N. Ohio, U.S.A.; sandstone quarries, building blocks; p. (1960) *16,592*.

Bere Regis, *mkt. t.*, Dorset, Eng.

Berezina, *R.*, U.S.S.R.; trib. Dnieper; French disaster on the retreat from Moscow; length 350 m.

Berezniki, *t.*, R.S.F.S.R., salt, chemicals, paper; p. (1967) *134,000*.

Berga, *t.*, Spain; medieval cas.; p. (1957) *8,023*.

Bergama, *t.*, Turkey; ancient Pergamos, ruins; p. (1960) *21,797*.

Bergamo, *c.*, Lombardy, Italy; 34 m. N.E. Milan; fine cath. and academy; silk industry; p. (1961) *113,512*.

Bergedorf, *t.*, Germany; sub. of Hamburg; on R. Elbe; glass, leather; p. *19,962*.

Bergen, *spt.*, W. coast Norway; univ.; most impt. comm. pt. in kingdom; shipping, fishing; mftg. inds.; p. (1968) *116,794*.

Bergenfield, *t.*, N.J., U.S.A.; clothing, light mnfs., pianos; p. (1960) *27,203*.

Bergen op Zoom, *c.*, N. Brabant, Netherlands; sugar-beet; p. (1967) *38,155*.

Bergerac, *t.*, Dordogne, France; on R. Dordogne; grain, wine; ancient Huguenot stronghold; p. (1962) *25,971*.

Bergisch-Gladbach, *t.*, N. Rhine–Westphalia, Germany; E. of Cologne; paper, metallurgy, textiles; p. (1963) *44,500*.

Bering I., most W. of the Aleutian Is., N. America.

Bering Sea, part of N. Pac. Oc. between Aleutian Is. and Bering Strait, upwards of 1,600 sq. m.; fishing.

Bering Strait, *narrow sea* which separates Asia from N. America; 36 m. wide at narrowest part.

Bering Current (Okhotsk Current, or Oyashio), *ocean current*, N. Pac. Oc.; flows through Bering Strait from Arctic, along E. cst. of Kamchatka and Japanese Is. Hokkaido, Honshu; relatively cold; moderate summer temperatures along cst. causes fogs.

Berja, *t.*, Almeria, Spain; wine and fruit; p. (1957) *11,011*.

Berkeley, *parish*, Gloucester, Eng.; nr. R. Severn, 2 m. S. of Sharpness; civil nuclear power-sta.

Berkeley, *c.*, Cal., U.S.A.; univ.; p. (1960) *111,268*.

Berkeley Canal, Gloucester, Eng.; connects Sharpness on S. side Severn estuary with Gloucester; navigable only for small coasting vessels; opened 1827; length 15 m., depth 11 ft.

Berkhampstead (Berkhamsted), *urb. dist.*, Herts, Eng.; chemicals, wooden ware; p. (1961) *13,051*.

Berkley, *t.*, Mich., U.S.A.; sub. of Detroit; p. (1960) *23,275*.

Berkshire, *co.*, Eng.; downland including Inkpen Beacon, White Horse Hills, drained by Thames and tribs., Kennet, Cole, Pang; wooded; agr.; oats, dairying; biscuits; co. t. Reading; a. 725 sq. m.; p. (1966) *586,000*.

Berlin, *c.*, former cap. of Germany; on R. Spree; fourth c. on continent of Europe for population; enclave within East Germany; divided 1945 into 4 occupation zones: Soviet (East Berlin, p. *1,082,349*), British, American and French (West Berlin, p. *2,141,441*); total a. 890 sq. km.; inds. include elec. goods, optical and chemical prod., furniture, paper, foodstuffs, textiles, machin., publishing and printing; gr. route ctr. (each occupying force has an airfield).

Berlin, *t.*, New Hampshire, U.S.A.; p. (1960) *17,821*.

Bermejo, *t.*, Tarija dep., Bolivia; oil.

Bermejo R., *trib.* R. Parana, Argentina.

Bermeo, *spt.*, Spain; nr. Bilbao, Bay of Biscay; fishing; p. (1957) *12,517*.

Bermondsey, *see* Southwark.

Bermuda, Brit. group coral islands (360 in number of which 20 are inhabited) N. Atlantic; about 600 miles E. of S. Carolina, U.S.A.; total area 21 sq. m.; Hamilton, on Long Island is the ch. t.; British and U.S. air and naval stations; favourite winter resort for Americans;

potatoes, onions, lily bulbs; bananas; p. (of. gr) (estd. 1968) *51,000*.

Bermudez, asphalt lake, Venezuela, S. America; a. 2 sq. m.

Bernard, Great St., one of the Alps in the S. of the Valais, Switzerland; highest point 11,116 ft.; height of mtn. pass between Italy and Switzerland, 8,120 ft.; famous hospice for travellers in monastery on mtn. Great St. Bernard road tunnel, *see* K146.

Bernard, Little St., one of Graian Alps, Savoy S. of Mt. Blanc, France; pass traversed by Hannibal 218 B.C.

Bernay, *t.*, Eure, France; horse fair; dairying, clothing mftg., soap; p. (1962) *10,112*.

Bernburg, *t.*, Halle, E. Germany; cas.; chemicals, machin.; p. (1963) *44,738*.

Berne, *c.*, *cap.* can. Berne and *fed. cap.* Switzerland; on Aar R.; cath., univ.; textiles; p. (1961) *166,100*.

Berne, *can.*, Switzerland; fertile valleys, dairying; watches; tourist district; a. 2,657 sq. m.; p. (1961) *883,523*.

Bernese Oberland, Switzerland; Alpine region; ch. peaks; Finsteraarhorn, Jungfrau; resorts: Interlaken, Grindelwald; summer and winter ctrs.

Bernina, *pass* and *mtn.*, Switzerland; alt. 13,300 ft.

Beroun, *t.*, Bohemia, ČSSR.; textiles, sugar ref., cement, coal, iron, limestone; p. (1961) *15,597*.

Berri, *t.*, S. Australia; ctr. of irrigated fruit-growing a., on Murray R.

Berri, *oilfield*, Saudi Arabia; 45 m. N.W. of Ras Tannura, between Qatif and Khursaniyah; the field extends offshore.

Bertinoro, *t.*, Forli, Italy; famous wines.

Berwick, *maritime co.*, S.E. of Scot.; co. t. Duns; hilly; agr.; sheep, cattle; woollens, fishing, paper; a. 457 sq. m.; p. (1961) *22,441*.

Berwick-upon-Tweed, *spt.*, *mun. bor.*, Northumberland, Eng.; fishing, light engin., tweeds, knitwear; p. (including Tweedmouth and Spittall) (estd. 1967) *11,650*.

Berwyn, *t.*, Ill., U.S.A.; p. (1960) *54,224*.

Berwyn Mtns., range mid-Wales; alt. of highest peak 2,716 ft.

Besançon, *t.*, Doubs, France; observatory; univ.; farm implements, textiles; watch- and clock-making; p. (1968) *113,214*.

Besiktas, now Beşiktaş, *dist. and sub.*, Istanbul, Turkey; p. (1950) *63,611*.

Beskids, W. and E., *min. range*, Poland, Czechoslovakia, E. Europe; northern range of Carpathian mtn. system, seldom exceeds alt. 4,000 ft., many passes; forested; length 200 m.

Bessarabia, *terr.*, ceded to U.S.S.R. by Romania, 1940, now part of Moldavian S.S.R.; agr.

Bessbrooke, *t.*, Armagh, N. Ireland; on Newry Canal; p. (1966) *3,325*.

Bességes, *t.*, Gard, France; coal-mining, steel, silk; p. (1954) *5,823*.

Bessemer, *t.*, Ala., U.S.A.; iron and steel; p. (1960) *33,054*.

Bessemer, *t.*, Mich., U.S.A.; iron; p. (1960) *3,304*.

Besshi, *see* Niihama.

Besuki, *mountainous prov.* E. Java, Indonesia.

Betanzos, *t.*, Spain; wine; p. (1957) *10,824*.

Bethany, *vil.* on Mt. of Olives 2 m. Jerusalem, now Eizariya.

Bethany, *missionary sta.*, S.W. Africa; p. *544*.

Bethel, *anc. c.*, the modern Beitin, Jordan; 10 m. N. Jerusalem.

Bethel, *t.*, Cape Province, S. Africa; rich farming a.; p. (1960) *11,952* inc. *4,003* whites.

Bethesda, *t.*, Maryland, U.S.A.; p. (1960) *56,527*.

Bethesda, *urb. dist.*, Caernarvon, Wales; slate, light engin.; p. (1961) *4,151*.

Bethlehem, *t.*, Jordan; 5½ m. S.W. Jerusalem; birthplace of Christ; p. (1961) *15,777*.

Bethlehem, *t.*, Penns., U.S.A.; 50 m. N. of Philadelphia; iron-wks.; p. (1960) *75,408*.

Bethnal Green, *see* Tower Hamlets.

Bethphage, former vil. on Mt. of Olives, above Bethany, Israel, S.W. Asia.

Bethsaida, ancient vil. on W. side of Sea of Galilee, Israel, S.W. Asia.

Bethshemesh, *t.*, Israel, S.W. Asia; 24 m. W. of Jerusalem; archaeological site.

Béthune, *t.*, Pas de Calais, France; oil, salt, coal; p. (1968) *27,154*.

Bettendorf, *t.*, Iowa, U.S.A.; steel, oil burners; p. (1960) *11,534*.

Betteshanger, *mining vil.*, Kent, Eng.; on N. flank of N. Downs, 4 m. W. of Deal.

Betws-y-Coed, *urb. dist.*, Caernarvon, Wales tourist and artists' resort; p. (1961) *773*.

Betul, *t.*, Madhya Pradesh, India; p. (1961) *19,360*.

Betwa. *R.*, of Bhopal, India, trib. of Jumna R.; length 360 m.

Beuel, *t.*, N. Rhine–Westphalia, Germany; on R. Rhine opposite Bonn; chemicals, furniture; p. (1963) *33,000*.

Beuthen, *see* Bytom.

Beuzeval, *t.*, Calvados, France; on Eng. Channel; seaside resort; p. (1962) *2,363*.

Beveland, *I.*, S. Netherlands; between the old Maas and Hollands Diep.

Beverley, *mkt. t.*, *mun. bor.*, E.R. Yorks, Eng.; fine minster; p. (estd. 1967) *17,220*.

Beverly, *c.*, Mass., U.S.A.; boots, shoes, machin.; p. (1960) *36,108*.

Beverly Hills, *t.*, California, U.S.A.; p. (1960) *30,817*.

Beverwijk, *t.*, nr. Haarlem, N. Holland, Netherlands; p. (1967) *41,956*.

Bewdley, *mun. bor.*, Worcester, Eng.; p. (estd. 1967) *5,610*.

Bexhill, *mun. bor.*, Sussex, Eng.; resort; p. (estd. 1967) *32,350*.

Bexley, *former bor.* W. Kent; now outer bor., Greater London, Eng., inc. Chislehurst and Sidcup (N. of the A.20) Crayford and Erith; p. (1966) *215,000*.

Bexley, *t.*, Ohio, U.S.A.; p. (1960) *14,319*.

Beykoz, *t.*, Turkey; on Bosporus Strait; p. (estd. 1960) *40,000*.

Beyoglu, *div.* of Istanbul, Turkey; residtl. quarter of Europeans; p. (1945) *234,750*.

Beypazari, *t.* Turkey; 65 m. W. of Ankara; rice, fruit, cotton; p. (1960) *3,866*.

Beysehir, *L.*, Turkey; 25 m. long; alt. 7,068 ft.

Bezhitsa, *t.*, R.S.F.S.R.; fused with Bryansk (*q.v.*) in 1956.

Béziers, *t.*, Hérault, France; wines, brandy; chemicals; p. (1962) *75,541*.

Bezons, *sub.* of Paris, France; on Seine R.; light mnfs; p. (1954) *16,993*.

Bezwade, *see* Vijayawada.

Bhadravati, *t.*, Mysore, India; steel; p. (1961) *65,776*; of new town *41,281*.

Bhagalpur, *t.*, Patna, Bihar, India; rice, maize; p. (1961) *143,850*.

Bhamo, *t.*, Upper Burma; on R. Irrawaddy; market ctr.; ruby mines; teak; p. *c. 10,000*.

Bhandara, *dist.*, Maharashtra, India, a. 3,582 sq. m.; rice, oilseeds, wheat, bamboo, tobacco; p. (1961) *1,263,286*.

Bhandara, *cap.* of Bhandara dist., Maharashtra, India; 30 m. E. of Nagpur; cotton cloth, brass mftg.; p. (1961) *27,710*.

Bharatpur, *t.*, Rajasthan, India; cloth; p. (1961) *49,776*.

Bhatpara, *t.*, W. Bengal, India; on R. Hooghly; p. (1961) *147,630*.

Bhavnagar, *dist.*, Gujarat, India; a. 4,652 sq. m.; p. (1961) *1,119,435*.

Bhavnagar, *t.*, *spt.*, Gujarat, India; cotton, silk and gold embroidery; p. (1961) *176,473*.

Bhilai, Madhya Pradesh, India; steel plant; rails and rly. sleepers; p. (1961) of industl. t. *86,116*; of Durg *47,114*.

Bhim-Gora, sacred pool, place of Hindu pilgrimage, Uttar Pradesh, India.

Bhir, *dist.*, Maharashtra, India; a. 4,268 sq. m.; wheat, cotton, linseed, sugar; cap. Bhir, 190 m. E. of Bombay; p. (1961) *1,001,466*.

Bhiwani, *t.*, India; cottons; p. (1961) *58,194*.

Bhopal, *c.*, st. cap., Madhya Pradesh, India; impt. trade ctr.; p. (1961) *185,374*.

Bhuj, *ch. t.*, Kutch, Gujarat, Bombay, India; p. (1961) *38,953*.

Bhutan, *indep. st.*, E. Himalayas; cap. Thimphu; ch. prod.: Indian corn, millet, lac, rice, cloth; valuable forests; a. (approx.) 18,000 sq. m.; first motor road link with India constr. 1960–2; p. scattered and nomadic, *c. 750,000*.

Bhuvaneshwar, *cap.*, Orissa, India; 18 m. from Cuttack; p. (1961) *38,211*.

Biafra, Bight of, W. Africa; bay lying E. of the G. of Guinea between the Niger and Cape Lopez.

Biala-Krakowska, *commune*, Krakow dep., Poland; agr., tr. ctr., cattle, textiles.

Bialogard, *c.*, N.W. Poland; formerly in Germany; industl. and transport ctr.

Bialystok, *prov.*, E. Poland; cap. Bialystok; a. 9,021 sq. m.; p. (1965) *1,160,000*.

Bialystok, *t.*, Poland; *cap.* of Bialystok prov., nr. Grodno; engin., textiles, chemicals, saw-milling; p. (1965) *133,000.*

Biancavilla, *t.*, Sicily, Italy; oranges.

Biarritz, *t.*, Basses-Pyrénées, France; on Bay of Biscay; seaside resort; p. (1962) *25,514.*

Biba-El-Kubra, *t.*, U.A.R., N.E. Africa; on Nile; p. *1,000.*

Biberach, *t.*, Baden-Württemberg, Germany; on R. Riss; spa; wood, metal and engin. inds.; p. (1963) *23,100.*

Bicester, *urb. dist.*, Oxford, Eng.; rly. junction; lace; p. (1961) *5,513.*

Bida, *t.*, N. Nigeria, W. Africa; p. *10,000.*

Bidassoa, *R.*, on Spanish–French frontier.

Biddeford, *c.*, Maine, U.S.A.; cotton mnf.; re-sort; p. (1960) *19,255.*

Biddulph, *urb. dist.*, Stafford, Eng.; nr. Leek; coal mng., machin., textiles, furniture; p. (1961) *14,060.*

Bideford, *mun. bor.*, N. Devon, Eng.; on R. Torridge; ropes, sails, boat bldg., glove mkg.; p. (estd. 1967) *10,850.*

Biebrich, *t.*, Germany; on Rhine; dyes; p. *19,504.*

Biel (Bienne), *t.*, Berne, Switzerland; watches; p. (1961) *61,200.*

Bielawa, *t.*, Wroclaw prov., S.W. Poland; tex-tiles; p. (1965) *31,000.*

Bielaya-Tserkov, *t.*, Ukraine, U.S.S.R.; on trib. of Dnieper R.; fairs, tr. in cattle, beer, grain; p. *54,000.*

Bielefeld, *t.*, Rhine–Westphalia, Germany; ch. ctr. of linen industry; machin., bicycles; p. (1968) *168,783.*

Biella, *t.*, Novara, Italy; textiles; p. (1961) *50,209.*

Bielsko-Biala, *t.*, Katowice prov., Poland; wool-lens, linen, metal, chem.; p. (1965) *82,000.*

Bien-hoa, *t.*, nr. Saigon, S. Viet-Nam; sugar refin-ing; cotton mills.

Bienne, *L.*, N.E. Neuchâtel, Switzerland.

Bierley, *par.*, W. Riding, Yorks, Eng.; coal, iron; p. *16,000.*

Bies-Bosch, reclaimed fenland area between N. Brabant and S.W. Netherlands; sugar refining, dairying; a. 55 sq. m.

Big Black, *R.*, trib. of Mississippi, U.S.A.

Big Bone Lick, *locality*, N. Ky., U.S.A.; E. of Ohio R.; deposit of fossil mammoth.

Biggar, *burgh*, Lanark, Scot.; in S. Uplands, 10 m. S.E. of Lanark; p. (1961) *1,403.*

Biggarsberg, *mtns.*, Natal, S. Africa; branch of the Drakensberg, highest point, Indumeni, 7,200 ft.

Biggleswade, *urb. dist.*, Beds, Eng.; in valley of R. Ouse, 9 m. S.E. of Bedford; ctr. of fruit-growing and mkt. gardening dist.; hydraulic machin. tools, hosiery, caravans; p. (1961) *8,047.*

Big Horn Mtns, Wyo. and Mont., U.S.A.; Rockies; highest alt., 12,000 ft.

Big Horn, *R.*, Wyo., U.S.A.; trib. of Yellow-stone R.

Bihač, *t.*, Jugoslavia; on R. Una; p. (1959) *14,000.*

Bihar, *state*, Indian Union; a. 67,196 sq. m.; cap. Patna (*q.v.*); ch. R., Ganges; agr.: rice, wheat, maize, sugar-cane, tobacco, oil-seeds; minerals: coal, iron, mica; ind.: iron and steel, oil refining at Barauni; p. (1961) *46,455,610.*

Bihé, *dist.*, Angola (Port. W. Africa).

Bihor Mtns., Romania.

Bilsk, *c.*, Siberia, U.S.S.R.; p. (1967) *176,000.*

Bijapur, *t.*, Mysore, India; cotton; ruins; p. (1961) *78,854.*

Bijeljina, *t.*, Jugoslavia; p. (1959) *18,000.*

Bijnore, *t.*, Uttar Pradesh, India; p. (1961) *33,610.*

Bikaner, *t.*, Rajasthan, India; p. (1961) *150,634.*

Bikini, *atoll*, Pacific Ocean; scene of atomic-bomb tests.

Bilaspur, *t.*, Madhya Pradesh, India; silks, cot-tons; p. (1961) *86,706.*

Bilbao, *spt.*, N. Spain; cap. Basque prov. of Viscaya; formerly famous for rapier making; iron ore, smelting; pipeline from Ayoluengo oilfield under construction; p. (1965) *356,000.*

Biecik, *t.*, Turkey; p. (1960) *7,535.*

Bilina, *c.*, Bohemia, ČSSR.; wat. pl., mineral springs; p. (1961) *10,394.*

Bilabong, *R.*, N.S.W., Australia.

Billericay, *mun. bor.*, Essex, Eng.; lost land and individuality to Basildon.

Billinge and Winstanley, *urb. dist.*, Lancs, Eng.; coal bricks; p. (1961) *6,941.*

Billingham, *t.*, *urb. dist.*, Durham, Eng.; on N. of Tees estuary; chemicals, shipbldg. and re-pairing, iron and steel, plastics, fertilisers; oil refinery; p. (1961) *32,130.*

Billings, *t.*, Montana, U.S.A.; cattle-raising. wool; p. (1960) *52,851.*

Billingsgate, London, Eng.; old river-gate and wharf, now chief fish mkt. of England.

Billiton (Belitung) I., Indonesia; tin.

Bilma, *oasis*, Niger, W. Africa; p. *1,000.*

Biloxi, *t.*, Miss., U.S.A.; fishing, tourist ctr.. U.S. Air Force base; p. (1960) *44,053.*

Bilsen, *t.*, Belgium; mkt. ctr. for fruit growing area; p. (1962) *6,517.*

Bilston, *former mun. bor.*, Stafford, Eng.; absorbed in Wolverhampton co. bor. (1966); mkt.; p. (1961) *33,077.*

Bima, *t.*, Sumbawa, Indonesia.

Binab, *t.*, Azerbaijan, Persia; nr. L. Urmia.

Binalbagan, *t.*, Negros I., Philippine Is.; sugar.

Binan, *t.*, Luzon, Philippine Is.

Binangonan, *t.*, Luzon, Philippine Is.

Binche, *t.*, Belgium; lace, clothing; p. (1962) *10,426.*   [cattle.

Bingara, *t.*, N.S.W., Australia; wool, wheat,

Bingen, *t.*, Rhineland Palatinate, Germany; on Rhine R.; at S. entrance to Rhine gorge; wine; beautiful scenery; p. (1963) *20,500.*

Bingerville, *spt.*, Ivory Coast, Africa.

Bingham, *rural dist.*; Notts., agr.; p. (1961) *25,145.*

Bingham Canyon, *t.*, N. Utah, U.S.A.; copper. silver, gold, lead; p. (1960) *1,516.*

Binghamton, N.Y., U.S.A.; on Susquehanna R.; boot factories; p. (1960) *75,941.*

Bingley, *urb. dist.*, *mkt. t.*, W.R. Yorks, Eng.; on R. Aire, 16 m. N.W. of Leeds; textiles, engin., agr.; p. (estd. 1967) *24,590.*

Bingol-dag, *mtns.*, Turkey; S. of Erzurum; highest peak 12,310 ft.

Bintang I., largest island of the Riouw Archi-pelago, Indonesia; bauxite.

Bio-Bio, *R.*, Chile; rises in Andes, flows N.W. to Pac. Oc. at Talcahuano; length 300 m.

Bio-Bio, *prov.*, Chile; cap. Los Angeles; a. 4,342 sq. m.; p. (1960) *179,934.*

Biratnagar, *t.*, S.E. Nepal, in the Terai; jute, sugar, cotton milling, stainless steel; p. (1961) *33,293.*

Birbhum, *dist.*, W. Bengal, India; cap. Suri; healthy climate; rice, sugar; mnfs. silk, cotton; a. 1,757 sq. m.; p. (1961) *1,446,158.*

Birchington, *t.*, Kent, Eng.

Birdsboro, *bor.*, Penns., U.S.A.; on Schuylkill R.; coal, steel; p. (1960) *3,025.*

Birjand, *t.*, Iran; p. *25,000.*

Birkenhead, *co. bor.*, Cheshire, Eng.; on R. Mersey, opp. Liverpool; docks, shipbldg., engin., clothing, metal, wood, glass; p. (estd. 1967) *143,550.*

Birket El Qarun, "Lake of the Horns," Fayum, Egypt, N.E. Africa.

Birmingham, *c., co. bor.*, Warwick, Eng.; industl. cap. Midlands, second lgst. c. Gt. Britain; motor vehicles, components and accessories; univ., cath., town hall; p. (estd. 1969) *1,086,400.*

Birmingham, *t.*, *cap.*, Ala., U.S.A.; coal, iron, limestone, steel, aircraft, chemicals, textiles; p. (1960), *340,839.*

Birmingham, *t.*, Mich., U.S.A.; p. (1960) *25,525.*

Birnam, *vil.*, Perth, Scot.; location of Birnam Wood—Macbeth; former royal forest.

Birni, *t.*, Dahomey, W. Africa; p. *1,000.*

Birobidzhan, *t.*, U.S.S.R.; admin. ctr.; lt. and wood inds.; p. (1959) *41,000.*

Birr, *mkt. t.*, *urb. dist.*, Offaly, Ireland; on Little Brosna R.; farming; observatory; p. (1966) *3,266.*

Bir Tlacsin, Libya, Africa; 120 m. S.W. Tripoli; oilfields.

Bisbee, *t.*, Arizona, U.S.A.; very rich copper deposits, gold, silver, lead; p. (1960) *9,850.*

Biscarosse, Landes, France; 45 m. S.W. Bordeaux; rocket and missle testing range projected; p. (1962) *3,336.*

Biscay, *see* Vizcaya.

Biscay, Bay of, stormy a. of the Atl. W. of France and N. of Spain, from Ushant to C. Ortegal; the Roman Sinus Aquitanicus; heavy seas.

Bisceglie, *t.*, *spt.*; Apulia, Italy; on E. cst. 22 m. N.W. of Bari; fishing; p. (1961) *41,451.*

Bischheim, *t.*, Bas-Rhin, France; N.W. sub. of Strasbourg, furniture, porcelain; p. (1954) *11,430*.

Bischoff, Mt., *t.*, Tasmania, Australia; tin.

Bischofswerda, *t.*, Dresden, E. Germany; quarrying, glass and iron inds.; rly. ctr.; p. (1963) *11,285*.

Bishop, *t.*, Cal., U.S.A.; cattle, tungsten; p. (1960) *2,875*.

Bishop Auckland, *urb. dist.*, Durham, Eng.; contains palace of Bishop of Durham; coal, iron, light engin.; p. (estd. 1967) *34,650*.

Bishop Rock, *isolated rock, lighthouse*, Scilly Is., 36 m. S.W. of Land's End, Cornwall; recognised internationally as E. end of trans-Atlantic ocean crossing.

Bishop's Stortford, *mkt. t., urb. dist.*, Herts., Eng.; on Stort R.; grain; p. (estd. 1967) *21,010*.

Bishop's Waltham, *par.*, Hants, Eng.; bricks.

Bishop Wearmouth, *t.*, pt. of Sunderland, Co. Durham.

Biskra, *c.*, Algeria, N. Africa; admin. ctr., winter resort; oasis nearby produces dates; p. *c. 53,000*.

Bisley, *t.*, Gloucester, Eng.; nr. Stroud.

Bismarck, *cap. c.*, N. Dakota, U.S.A.; on Missouri R.; p. (1960) *27,670*.

Bismarck Arch., 3 large and several small islands off New Guinea, formerly German, now Australian Trust Terr.; total native p. (estd. 1962) *174,115*.

Bissagos Is., off W. Africa, Port Guinea; ch. t. Bolama.

Bissao, *t., spt.*, Port Guinea; p. *5,000*.

Bistrita, *t.*, Romania; p. (1963) *23,346*.

Bitetto, *t., sm. spt.*, Apulia, Italy; on E. cst. 5. m. N.W. of Bari; fishing; p. *5,991*.

Bitlis, *I.*, Turkey; p. (1945) *74,449*.

Bitlis, *t.*, Turkey; minerals, Armenian massacre; p. (1960) *16,562*.

Bitolj (Monastir), *t.*, Macedonia, Jugoslavia; many mosques, military H.Q., great tr. in corn, grain, flour, hides and woollen stuffs; tanning, carpets; p. (1959) *43,000*.

Bitonto, *t.*, Apulia, on E. cst. 7 m. N.W. of Bari; Italy; olive oil, wine; fine cath.; p. *29,731*.

Bitterfeld, *t.*, Halle, E. Germany; lignite mining; engin., chemicals; p. (1963) *30,900*.

Bitterfontein, *t.*, Cape Province, S. Africa.

Bitter Lakes, Isthmus of Suez, U.A.R., utilised by Suez Canal.

Bitterroot, *mtns.*, U.S.A.; range of the Rockies, highest point Ajax Mtn., 10,900 ft.; rly. tunnel 2 m. long.

Bitton, *t.*, Gloucester, Eng.; mining.

Biwa, *L.*, Japan; a. 180 sq. m.; 330 ft. above sea-level; 300 ft. deep; connected by canal with Osaka.

Biyala, *t.*, Gharbīya prov.; Lower U.A.R.; N.E. Africa; rice, millet, cotton; p. (1947) *17,731*.

Biysk, *t.*, W. Siberia, R.S.F.S.R.; engin., textiles; p. (1959) *146,000*.

Bizerta, *spt.*, Tunisia, N. Africa; international dockyard; the ancient Hippo Zaritus; fishing; oil refining; steelwks, tyres; p. (1956) *46,681*.

Bizot, *commune*, N.E. Algeria; p. *10,845*.

Bjelovar, *t.*, Croatia, Jugoslavia; p. (1959) *12,000*.

Björnborg, *see* Pori.

Blaauw B. Mtns., Transvaal, S. Africa.

Blaavands Huk, Denmark; nr. Esbjerg.

Black Belt, *area* on coastlands of Miss. and Ala., U.S.A.; black soil prairie land, good for cotton.

Black Bluff, *min.*, N. Tasmania, Australia.

Blackburn, *co. bor.*, Lancs, Eng.; textiles, engin., light inds.; p. (estd. 1967) *100,910*.

Black Country, Eng., Midlands; formerly impt. iron-working and coal-mining district round the Birmingham area.

Blackdown Hills, Devon, Eng.

Black Forest (Schwarzwald), *mtns.*, Germany; resort, forests, a. 1,844 sq. m.; highest peak Feldberg, alt. 4,696 ft.

Black Gang Chine, picturesque ravine on S. Coast, Isle of Wight, Eng.

Black Hawk, *mining t.*, Rocky Mtns., Colorado, U.S.A.

Black Head, *C.*, Galway Bay, Clare, Ireland.

Blackhead, *C.*, on N. entrance to Belfast Lough, N. Ireland; lighthouse.

Blackheath, *open common*, S.E. London, Eng.; a. 267 acres.

Black Hills, *mtns.*, between S.D. and Wyo., U.S.A.; highest, Horney Peak, alt. 7,240 ft.

Black Isle, *peninsula*, between Cromarty and Beauly Firths, Ross and Cromarty, Scot.; agr., fisheries, quarrying; a. 240 sq. m.

Black Lake, *t.*, S. Quebec, Canada; asbestos mines; p. (1961) *4,180*.

Blackley, *t.*, S.W. Lancs, Eng.; N. sub. of Manchester; dye wks.

Black Mountain, *t.*, N.C., U.S.A.; resort.

Black Mtns., range of Appalachians, U.S.A.; Mt. Mitchell, alt. 6,684 ft.

Black Mtns., *range*, Brecknock, S. Wales; highest peak, Brecknock Van, alt. 2,631 ft.

Blackpool, *co. bor.*, Lancs, Eng., on cst. of Fylde dist.; Britain's most popular holiday resort; p. (estd. 1967) *151,510*.

Black Prairie, *region*, Texas, U.S.A.; extends 350 m. S.W. from Ouochita Mtns. to Austin; contains very fertile Black Waxy and Grande Prairie sub-regions devoted almost entirely to cotton growing; ch. ts., Dallas, Fort Worth, Austin; a. 30,000 sq. m.

Black River Falls, *t.*, Wis., U.S.A.; lumber, flour, dairying, poultry; p. (1960) *3,195*.

Blackrock, *t.*, Ireland; sub. 4 m. from Dublin.

Blackrod, *urb. dist.*, Lancs, Eng.; nr. Chorley; weaving; p. (1961) *3,609*.

Black Sea, *inland sea* between Russia and Turkey; 740 m. long, 390 m. broad; receives waters of Danube, Dnieper, Dniester, Don, Bug and other rivers; communicates with Mediterranean by Strait of Bosporus, Sea of Marmara and Dardanelles.

Blacksod Bay, coast of Mayo, Ireland.

Blackstone, *t.*, Mass., U.S.A.; textiles; p. (1950) *4,968*.   [(1960) *3,659*.

Blackstone, *t.*, Va., U.S.A.; tobacco mkt.; p.

Black Volta, *R.*, Upper Volta and Ghana; rises in Futa Jallon Plateau, flows E., S. and E. into R. Volta; length, over 800 m.

Black Warrior, *R.*, Ala., U.S.A.; flows through coalfields; navigable; water power.

Blackwater, *R.*, Hants and Essex, Eng.

Blackwater, *R.*, Ireland; three of this name.

Blackwater, *R.*, U.S.A. (Mont., Fla., and Va.).

Black Waxy, *see* Black Prairie.

Blackwell, *c.*, Okla., U.S.A.; gas, oil, wells, refining, zinc smelting; meat packing; p. (1960) *9,588*.

Blaenau Ffestiniog, *see* Ffestiniog.

Blaenavon, *t., urb. dist.*, Monmouth, Wales; mining; p. (1961) *8,424*.

Blagoevgrad, *t.*, formerly Gorna Dzhumaya, ch. t. Bulgarian Macedonia; p. (1956) *21,833*.

Blagoveshchensk, *t.*, E. Siberia, R.S.F.S.R. on R. Amur; wat. p.; engin., sawmilling; p. (1967) *118,000*.

Blair Atholl, *par.*, Perth, Scot.; tourist resort; p. (1951) *1,368*.

Blairgowrie and Rattray, *burgh*, Perth, Scot.; at foot of Scot. Highlands, 18 m. N.E. of Perth; fruit; linen; agr. machin., canning inds.; p. (1961) *5,168*.

Blairmore, *t.*, Alberta, W. Canada; on Canadian Pacific Rly., 160 m. S.W. of Medicine Hat, at approach to Crow's Nest Pass; coal-mining ctr. on Alberta Coalfield; p. (1961) *1,980*.

Blairsville, *t.*, Penns., U.S.A.; p. (1960) *4,930*.

Blakely, *t.*, Ga., U.S.A.; peanuts, lumber, turpentine; p. (1960) *3,580*.

Blanc-Mesnil (Le), *t.*, Hauts-de-Seine, nr. Paris; p. (1954) *25,363*.

Blanc, Mt., France; highest peak of Alps; alt. 15,782 ft.

Blanca Pk., Col., U.S.A.; alt. 14,390 ft.

Blanche Bay, on N.E. coast of New Britain, Bismarck Arch.; inner part site of Rabaul.

Blanchester, *t.*, Ohio, U.S.A.; textiles, pumps; p. (1960) *2,944*.

Blanco, *t.*, Cape Province, S. Africa.

Blandford, or Blandford Forum, *mkt. t., mun. bor.*, Dorset, Eng.; lime and stone, agr. implements; p. (estd. 1967) *3,640*.

Blanes, *spt.*, Spain; N.E. of Barcelona; holiday resort; p. (1957) *7,039*.

Blankenberge, *spt.*, N. Belgium; seaside resort; p. (1962) *10,252*.

Blantyre, *c.*, Malawi; in Shire Highlands; linked by rail to Beira; comm. ctr.; tobacco; p. (1966) *109,795*.

Blantyre, *par.*, Lanark, Scot.; birthplace of Dr. Livingstone; aero engines; p. (1951) *17,766*.

Blarney, *vil.*, 4 m. N.W. Cork, Ireland; cas. and Blarney stone; woollen mftg.

Blaydon, *urb. dist.*, Durham, Eng.; coal-mining; p. (estd. 1967) *31,880.*

Blekinge, *co.*, Sweden; a. 1,173 sq. m.; p. (1961) *144,468.*

Blenheim, *t.*, S.I., New Zealand; fruit; p. (1966) *13,242.*

Bletchley, *urb. dist.*, Bucks, Eng.; rly. junction, bricks, brushes; p. (estd. 1967) *24,980.*

Blida, *t.*, Algeria, N. Africa; flour, citrus fruits; p. (1954) *67,000.*

Bloemfontein, *t.*, *cap.*, O.F.S., S. Africa; cattle ctr.; engin., glass, bricks, meat canning; p. (1960) *140,924* inc. *61,213* Whites.

Blois, *co.*, Loire-et-Cher, France; on Loire; 30 m. S.W. of Orleans; château; wines; p. (1962) *36,426.*

Blood R., Natal, S. Africa.

Bloody-Foreland, *C.*, Donegal, N.W. Ireland.

Bloomfield, *t.*, Ind., U.S.A.; p. (1960) *2,224.*

Bloomfield, *t.*, N.J., U.S.A.; p. (1960) *51,867.*

Bloomington, *t.*, Ill., U.S.A.; coal, motor cars; p. (1960) *36,271.*

Bloomington, *t.*, Ind., U.S.A.; wheat, corn, alfalfa; furniture, structural glass, radios; p. (1960) *31,357.*

Bloomsburg, *t.*, Penns. U.S.A.; iron; p. (1960) *10,655.*

Blorca, *t.*, Java, Indonesia; teak; p. *18,451.*

Bludenz, *t.*, Austria; cotton, watches; p. (1961) *11,127.*

Bluefield, *t.*, W. Va., U.S.A.; coal, iron, limestone, steel foundries, silica, lumber; p. (1960) *19,256.*

Bluefields, *R.* in Nicaragua, Central America.

Bluefields, *t.*, Nicaragua; on E. cst.; bananas, timber; p. (1960) *11,376.*

Blue Grass, *dist.*, Ky., U.S.A., area where blue grass abundant; horse breeding.

Blue Mountains, chain in N.S.W., Australia; highest peak, 4,100 ft.

Blue Mountains, *t.*, N.S.W., Australia; tourist centre; p. (1961) *28,070.*

Blue Mountains, Jamaica, W. Indies.

Blue Nile (Bahr-el-Azrek), *R.*, rising in tablelands of Ethiopia, joins the White Nile at Khartoum; its seasonal flooding provides the bulk of water for irrigation in Sudan and U.A.R.

Blue Nile, *prov.*, Sudan; a. 54,577 sq. m.; cap. Wad Medani (*q.v.*); p. (estd. 1951) *1,840,600.*

Blue Point, Long I., U.S.A.; oysters.

Blue Ridge Mtns., U.S.A.; most E. ridge of Appalachian Mtns. in Virginia and North Carolina.

Bluff Harbour, S.I., New Zealand; 18 m. from Invercargill; spt. for Southland prov.

Bluffton, *t.*, Ind., U.S.A.; farm implements, lumber; p. (1960) *6,238.*

Blumenau, *t.*, Santa Catarina st., Brazil; butter, sugar; p. (estd. 1968) *84,139.*

Blyth, *spt. mun. bor.*, Northumberland, Eng.; exp. coal; shipbldg.; p. (estd. 1967) *36,120.*

Blytheville, *t.*, Ark., U.S.A.; tr. ctr. for agr. region; p. (1960) *20,797.*

Blythswood, *t.*, Cape Province, S. Africa.

Bo, *t.*, Sierra Leone, W. Africa; gold; adm. headquarters.; p. (1963) of dist. *209,000.*

Boa Vista, *t.*, *R. pt.*, cap. Roraima st., Brazil; p. (estd. 1967) *34,659.*

Bobadilla, *t.*, S. Spain; N. of Málaga.

Bobbili, *t.*, Andhra Pradesh, India; tr. ctr. in agr. a.; p. (1961) *25,592.*

Bobbio, *t.*, Emilia-Rogmagna, Italy, in northern Apennines; ctr. European cultural life, 9th–12th cent.; St. Columban founded monastery, 612.

Bobigny, *t.*, Seine, France; p. (1954) *18,521.*

Bobrawa, *R.*, Lower Silesia; W. Poland; trib. of R. Oder; length 158 m.

Bobrek Karb, *t.*, Silesia, Poland; German before 1945; coal, coke, steel, ammonia.

Bobrinets, *t.*, Ukrainian S.S.R.; tobacco factories; p. *10,000.*

Bobruisk, *fortress, t.*, Byelorussian S.S.R., on R. Berezina; engin., sawmilling; p. (1967) *117,000.*

Bocas del Toro, *prov.*, Panama; cap. B. del T.; p. (1960) *32,600.*

Bochetta, La, *pass*, Liguria, Italy; used by main routes across Ligurian Apennines from Genoa to Lombardy Plain.

Bocholt, *t.*, N. Rhine-Westphalia, Germany; machin., textiles, elect. goods; p. (1968) *46,100.*

Bochum, *t.*, N. Rhine-Westphalia, Germany; 11 m.

W. of Dortmund; ctr. of iron and steel ind.; chemicals, foodstuffs; p. (1968) *345,320.*

Bockum-Hövel, *t.*, N. Rhine-Westphalia, Germany; N.W. of Hamm; coal-mining; p. (1963) *24,700.*

Bodaibo, *t.*, R.S.F.S.R.; N.E. of L. Baikal; gold, engin.; p. (1956) *14,600.*

Bodega Bay, Cal., U.S.A.; 20 m. W. of Santa Rosa; nuclear power sta.

Bodele, *area*, Chad, W. Africa; cotton, tobacco, forage grasses.

Boden, *t.*, Sweden; on Lulea R.; mil. ctr.; comm. ctr.; p. (1961) *13,719.*

Bodensee, *see* Constance, L.

Bodmin, *mun. bor.*, *co. t.*, Cornwall, Eng.; on S.W. flank of Bodmin Moor; china clay, lt. engin.; p. (estd. 1967) *7,370.*

Bodmin Moor, *upland*, N.E. Cornwall, Eng.; granite quarries, kaolin; lower slopes cultivated, higher slopes used for sheep pastures; average alt. 1,000 ft., highest point, Brown Willy, alt. 1,375 ft.

Bodö, *spt.*, Norway; within Arctic Circle at entrance to Salten Fjord, fishing, woollen goods; p. (1968) *27,542.*

Boeleleng, *s t.*, Bali, Indonesia; rice; harbour unsafe during monsoon. [*114,474.*

Boeotia, *prov.*, Greece; a. 1221 sq. m.; p. (1961)

Bogalusa, *t.*, La., U.S.A.; p. (1960) *21,423.*

Bognor Regis, *t.*, *urb. dist.*, Sussex, Eng.; seaside resort; p. (estd. 1967) *30,840.*

Bogor, *t.*, Java, Indonesia; p. (1961) *154,092.*

Bogotá, *cap.*, Colombia, S. America in E. Cordileras, 9,000 ft. above sea level; cath., museum, univ.; textiles, cement and brick mkg., leather, glassware, tyres, oil refining; p. (estd. 1965) *1,488,000.*

Bogovodsk, *see* Noginsk.

Bohemia, former W. prov. of Czechoslovakia; abolished 1948; plateau girdled by mountains; drained by R. Elbe; agr.: wheat, rye, hops, flax, sugar-beet; minerals: lignite, graphite; mnfs. textiles, sugar, pottery, machin., boots; p. inc. Moravia (1962) *9,566,753.*

Böhmerwald (Bohemian Forest) Mtns., forested range between Czechoslovakia and Bavaria; 150 m. long; highest points; Aber, alt. 4,848 ft., Rachelberg, alt. 4,743 ft.

Bohol, *I.*, Philippines; 1,492 sq. m.; p. (1960) *529,200.*

Boiro, *commune*, La Coruña, Spain; cattle, fishing, sardine canning; p. *11,668.*

Bois-Colombes, *t.*, Seine, France; p. (1954) *27,899.*

Boise City, *t.*, *cap.*, Idaho, U.S.A.; silver, hot springs; p. (1960) *34,481.*

Boise, *R.*, Idaho, U.S.A.

Bojador, *C.*, Rio de Oro, Africa.

Bokaro, *t.*, Bihar, India; 150 m. N.W. of Calcutta; steel plant.

Bokn Fjord, Norway; N. of Stavanger, 35 m. long, 10–15 m. wide.

Boksburg, *t.*, Transvaal, S. Africa; gold, coal; p. (1960) *70,933* inc. *27,806* whites.

Bolama, *spt.*, Port. Guinea; p. *4,000.*

Bolan Pass, Baluchistan, Pakistan; pass from Pakistan to Afghanistan; summit 5,900 ft.

Bolbec, *t.*, Seine-Maritime, France; 12 m. E. of Le Havre; p. (1962) *12,492.* [*22,760.*

Boldon, *urb. dist.*, Durham, Eng.; p. (estd. 1967)

Boleslawiec (Bunzlau), *t.*, Lower Silesia, Poland, German before 1945; on the Bobrawa R., pottery; p. (1965) *27,000.*

Bolgrad, *t.*, Ukrainian S.S.R.; corn; p. *10,000.*

Bolivar, *t.*, Argentina; p. (1947) *13,773.*

Bolivar, *dep.*, Colombia, S. America, cap. Cartagena; a. 22,981 sq. m.; p. (estd. 1959) *780,650.*

Bolivar, *prov.*, Ecuador, S. America; cap. Guarando; a. 1,150 sq. m.; p. (1950) *109,305.*

Bolivar, *st.*, Venezuela; ch. t., Cuidad Bolivar; a. 91,868 sq. m.; p. (1961) *213,543.*

Bolivia, *inland rep.*, S. America, bounded by Brazil, Paraguay, Argentina, Chile and Peru; cap. nominally Sucre, actual administrative H.Q. La Paz; plateau, mountains; Boliv. Andes; volcanoes; L. Titicaca, Poope, drained by tribs. of Amazon; climate varies with elevation; monkeys, jaguars; forests; savannahs; agr. in backward condition; rubber, quinine, cattle, hides; ch. exp. tin; petroleum; lead and zinc at Matilde; language, Spanish; a. 415,000 sq. m.; p. (estd. 1970) *4,658,000.*

Bolkhov, *t.*, Ukrainian S.S.R. monastery; impt. inds.; p. *10,000.*

Bollington, *t.*, *urb. dist.*, Cheshire, Eng.; nr.

Macclesfield, cotton, calico printing and dye wks.; p. (1961) 5,642.

Bolobo, t., Congo, Africa, on R. Congo.

Bologna, ancient c., Emilia, N. Italy; on N. flank of Apennines; impt. route ctr. commanding road (over Futa Pass) and rly. (through Apennine Tunnel) across Apennines to Florence; mnfs. sugar, macaroni; nuclear research ctr.; p. (1965) 481,000.

Bologna, prov., Italy; a. 1,465 sq. m.; p. (1961) 843,440.

Bologoye, t., R.S.F.S.R.; depot and impt. junction on the Leningrad and Moscow Rly.; p. 10,000.

Bolonchen, t., Campeche, Mexico.

Bololondron, mun. t., Matanzas, W. Cuba; p. (estd.) (of mun.) 11,823 (of t.) 3,710.

Bolsa Island, Cal., U.S.A.; nuclear power and desalination project in progress.

Bolsena, L., Latium region, Italy; occupies lge. extinct volcanic crater in S. of Tuscan Hills; a. (approx.) 50 sq. m.

Bolshoya Volga, t., R.S.F.S.R.; 80 m. N. of Moscow, at junct. of Volga and Moscow Volga Canal; Soviet Institute of Nuclear Studies.

Bolsover, urb. dist., Derby, Eng.; limestone, coal, textiles; p. (1961) 11,770.

Bolsward, c., Friesland, Netherlands; dairying, linseed, bricks; p. (1947) 7,389.

Bolt Hd., headland, Devon, Eng.; alt. 430 ft.

Bolton, co. bor., Lancs, Eng.; cotton and manmade fibres, iron, coal, chemicals; p. (estd. 1967) 156,400.

Bolton, Abbey, W.R. Yorks, Eng.; famous ruined abbey.

Bolu, t., Turkey; in ancient state of Bithynia; at Hija, S. of the t., are warm medicinal springs; p. (1960) 13,743.

Bolus Head, O., Kerry, Ireland.

Bolzano, t., Venetia Tridentina, Italy; on R. Isarco at S. approach to Brenner Pass; resort; p. (1961) 89,070

Boma, t., Congo, Africa, on Congo estuary; exports timber, cocoa, palm prods., bananas; p. c. 32,000.

Bomarsund, strait, Ahvenanmaa Is., Gulf of Bothnia.

Bombay, former st., India; divided into sts. of Maharashtra and Gujarat 1 May 1960.

Bombay, Greater, spt., cap. Maharashtra, India; harbour, docks, rly. ctr.; univ.; greatest cotton ctr. in India; pt. handles nearly half of cty's foreign tr.; p. (1961) 4,152,056.

Bomnak, t., Chita Region, U.S.S.R.; on S. slopes of Stanovoi Mtns., in valley of R. Zeya; centre of alluvial gold workings.

Bonaca I., Honduras, Central America; in Caribbean Sea.

Bonaire I., Netherlands W. Indies; off N. cst. of Venezuela; goat rearing; scantily populated.

Bonavista Bay, Newfoundland, Canada.

Bonduku, t., E. Ivory Cst., nr. Ghana; impt. trading sta.

Bondy, commune, France; N.E. sub. of Paris; brewing, chemicals; p. (1954) 22,411.

Bône, see Annaba.

Bo'ness, spt., burgh, W. Lothian, Scot.; on Firth of Forth, 4 m. E. of Grangemouth; light foundries, timber yds.; p. (1961) 10,194.

Bonham, t., Texas, U.S.A.; cotton; p. (1960) 7,357.

Bonhill, par., Dunbarton, Scot.; dyeing; p. (1951) 16,333.

Bonifacio, spt., fort., Corsica, France; opposite Sardinia, on Strait of Bonifacio; cork, olive-oil, oyster tr.; p. (1954) 2,157.

Bonin Is., Pac. Oc., Japan; 15 islands, volcanic; 600 m. S. of Tokyo.

Bonn, t., federal cap. W. Germany; at confluence of Rs. Sieg and Rhine; univ.; seat of W. German parliament; birthplace of Beethoven; metal, paper and elect. goods; p. (1968) 137,986.

Bonne Terre, c., E. Mo., U.S.A.; lead mines; p. (1960) 3,219.

Bonneville Dam, Ore., Wash., U.S.A.; across R. Columbia 40 m. above Portland (Ore.); provides irrigation to valleys in Columbia-Snake Plateau; lge. hydro-electric power-sta.; locks permit navigation from Portland up middle courses of Columbia and Snake Rs.

Bonneville Salt Flats, Utah, U.S.A.; remains of ancient lake; world automobile speed tests, 1937–47.

Bonny, t., S. Nigeria, W. Africa; at mouth of R. Bonny, Bight of Biafra; oil terminal.

Bonnyrigg and Lasswade, burgh, Midlothian Scot.; 7 m. S.E. of Edinburgh; paper, carpets; p. (1961) 6,331.

Bonthe, t., Sierra Leone, W. Africa; rutile production; p. (1963) of dist. 80,000.

Boom, t., Antwerp, Belgium; bricks, tanning, brewing; p. (1962) 17,431.

Boone, t., Iowa, U.S.A.; coal; p. (1960) 12,468.

Booneville, c., W. Ark., U.S.A.; lumber and cotton mills; tuberculosis sanatorium; p. (1960) 2,690.

Boonton, t., N.J., U.S.A.; agr. and industl. ctr.; p. (1960) 7,981.

Boothia, peninsula (a. 13,100 sq. m.) and G. on Arctic coast; Franklin dist. Canada.

Bootle, co. bor., Lancs, Eng.; on E. side of entrance to Mersey estuary; shipping, engin., timber, flour; p. (estd. 1967) 81,290.

Boppard, t., Rhineland Palatinate, Germany; p. (1946) 7,189.

Borås, t., S. Sweden; on R. Wiske, nr. Göteborg; cotton spinning and weaving textiles, hosiery, tyres; p. (1961) 67,069.

Bordeaux, spt., Gironde, France; nr. mouth of R. Garonne; cath., univ.; exp. wines, liqueurs, sugar, potatoes, pit props; oil refining nearby; p. (1968) 270,996.

Bordentown, c., N.J., U.S.A.; on Delaware R.; formerly impt. pt.; p. (1960) 4,974.

Bordeyri, t., Iceland; on Rumaflot inlet.

Bordighera, t., Italy; Riviera winter resort.

Boreham Wood, t., Herts, Eng.; light engin., computors, film studios.

Borger, c., N.W. Texas, U.S.A.; gas and petroleum; p. (1960) 20,911.

Borgerhout, sub. of Antwerp, Belgium; candle and tobacco factories; p. (1968) 50,012.

Borgo, San Donnino, t., Italy; cath.; p. 17,154.

Borgo, San Lorenzo, t., Italy; olives and wine.

Borgosesia, commune, N.W. Italy; on Sesia R.; textiles; p. 13,716.

Borgo Val di Taro, commune, N. Italy; lignite; p. 15,209.

Borinage, dist. round Mons, Belgium; coal.

Borislav, c., Ukrainian S.S.R., formerly Polish; oilfield, natural gas, engin.; p. (1956) 29,600.

Borisoglebsk, t., R.S.F.S.R.; p. (1959) 54,000.

Borisokova, t., Kursk, U.S.S.R.; metals.

Borisov, t., Byelorussian S.S.R.; scene of defeat of Napoleon, 1812; chemicals, saw mills, hardware; p. (1959) 59,000.

Borispool, t., Ukrainian S.S.R.; p. 25,000.

Borlänge, t., Sweden; iron, paper, engin. and chemical wks.; p. (1961) 26,685.

Bormio, vil., Lombardy, Italy; alpine resort; mineral springs; p. 1,910.

Borna, t., Leipzig, E. Germany; lignite, machin.; p. (1963) 19,331.

Bornem, t., Antwerp, Belgium; chemicals, elec. goods; p. (1961) 9,896.

Borneo, lgst. island Malay Arch.; a. 285,000 sq. m., length 830 m., breadth 600 m.; Kinibalu Range, alt. 13,700 ft.; forests, jungle, swamps; rice, sago, spices, coconuts, rubber, hardwood; politically divided into Indonesian Borneo (Kalimantan) and Sabah.

Borneo, N., part of Fed. of Malaysia, see Sabah.

Bornholm, Danish I., Baltic; a. 210 sq. m.; agr.; fishing; porcelain, clay; cap. Rönne; p. (1960) 48,373.

Bornu, cty., Nigeria, Africa; S.W. Lake Chad; formerly a Negro kingdom, 51,000 sq. m.; p. (estd.) 5,000,000.

Boroboedoer, Java, Indonesia; gr. Buddhist temple, once ruined, now restored under government care.

Boronga Is., in Bay of Bengal.

Borongan, t., Philippine Is.; on cst., 36 m. E. of Catbalogan; coconut plantations; p. (estd.) 21,340.

Borovichi, t., R.S.F.S.R.; on Msta R., 160 m. S.E. of Leningrad; p. (estd.) 28,500.

Borrolooia, N. Terr., Australia; sheep.

Borromean Is., four sm. islets in L. Maggiore; incl. Isola Bella, site of Stresa Conf., 1935.

Borrowdale, valley, Cumberland, Eng.; tourist resort; blacklead mines.

Borthwick, par., Midlothian, Scot.; with old cas.; p. (1951) 3,153.

Borzhom, vat. pl., Georgian S.S.R.; hot mineral springs; p. (1966) 15,600.

Boscastle, sm. spt., Cornwall, Eng.; resort; pilchard fishing.

Bosham, *vil.*, Sussex, Eng.; 4 m. W. of Chichester; Saxon church; resort, yachting, fishing.

Boskoop, *vil.*, S. Holland, Netherlands; flowering-shrub nurseries; p. (1967) *10,641.*

Bosnia and Hercegovino, *fed. unit*, Jugoslavia; formerly part of Austria; cap. Sarajevo; mountainous, forested, fertile valleys; agr.; tobacco, cereals, fruit; cattle, sheep pigs; a. 19,768 sq. m.; p. (1960) *3,377,000.*

Bosporus or Strait of Constantinople, between Black Sea and Sea of Marmara; suspension bridge, first to link Europe and S.W. Asia. due for completion 1973.

Bossier City, *t.*, La., U.S.A.; p. (1960) *32,776.*

Boston, *t.*, *mun. bor.*, *spt.*, Holland, Lincs, Eng.; on R. Witham, 4 m. from the Wash; shipping, agr. mkt.; timber, fruit and vegetable canning; p. (estd. 1967) *24,990.*

Boston, *spt. c.*, *cap.* Mass., U.S.A.; univ., museum; fine harbour; 2nd Atlantic pt.; comm. fisheries; metal, leather, rubber and elec. goods, textiles, shoes; rly. ctr.; p. (1970) *628,215;* Greater Boston *2,730,000.*

Bosworth or Market Bosworth, *t.*, *rural dist.*, Leics., Eng.; battle between Richard III and Henry VII, 1485; p. (rural dist. 1961) *27,493.*

Botany Bay, N.S.W., Australia; on E. cst., 10 m. S. of Sydney; resort; first settled by British in 1787; old penal colony.

Bothnia, G. of, N. of Baltic; between Finland and Sweden, breadth about 100 m.

Bothwell, *par.*, Lanark, Scot.; coal, iron; p. (1951) *63,185.*

Botosani, *t.*, N. Moldavia, Romania; rich pastoral cty.; flour milling, tanning; p. (1963) *47,319.*

Botswana, Rep. of, *indep. sov. st.* within Brit. Commonwealth (Sept. 1966), S.W. Africa; stretches from Orange R. to Zambesi R., and merges W. into Kalahari desert; Bamangwato ch. tribe; cap. Gaberones; cattle-rearing; lge. potential copper and nickel ores; a. 222,000 sq. m.; p. (estd.) *611,000.*

Bottrop, *t.*, N. Rhine-Westphalia, Germany; N.W. of Essen; coal, coke, chemicals; p. (1968) *108,703.*

Botucatu, *t.*, Brazil; p. (1960) *33,878.*

Bouches-du-Rhône, *dep.*, S. France; cap. Marseilles; cereals, olives, vines; pottery, silk; a. 2,035 sq. m.; p. (1968) *1,470,271.*

Bougainville I., Solomon Is., Pac. Oc.; a. 4,100 sq. m.; p (1959) *53,130.*

Bougainville, C., jutting into Timor Sea, W. Australia.

Bougie, *see* Bejaia.

Bouillon, *t.*, Ardennes, Belgium; p. (1962) *3,042.*

Boulder, *t.*, West Australia; incl. in Kalgoorlie mun.; p. (1966) *19,892* (joint p.).

Boulder, *t.*, Col., U.S.A.; gold- and silver-mining dist.; univ.; p. (1960) *37,718.*

Boulder City, *t.*, Nevada, U.S.A.; nr. Great Boulder Dam, gr. engin. project; p. (1960) *4,059.*

Boulogne-Billancourt, S.W. sub. of Paris, France; p. (1962) *107,074.*

Boulogne-sur-Mer, *spt.*, Pas-de-Calais, France; resort; fishing; cement; chocolates; channel ferry; p. (1962) *50,036.*

Boundary, *t.*, Yukon, Canada.

Bound Brook, *bor.*, N.J., U.S.A.; paints, chemicals, asbestos, clothing; p. (1960) *10,263.*

Bountiful, *t.*, Utah, U.S.A.; mkt. gardens, fruit, especially cherries; irrigation necessary; p. (1960) *17,039.*

Bounty I., New Zealand, S. Pac. Oc.

Bourbonne-es-Bains, *t.*, France; mineral springs.

Bourg-en-Bresse, *t.*, *cap.*, Ain dep., France; copper goods, pottery; p. (1962) *35,640.*

Bourges, *t.*, *cap.*, Cher dep., France; cath.; brewing, cutlery, machin., aircraft; p. (1962) *63,479.*

Bourget, L., Savoy, France.

Bourg-la-Reine, *t.*, Seine, France; p. (1962) *17,908.*

Bourg-Madame, *vil.*, France; on Franco-Spanish border; international bridge.

Bourgoin, *t.*, Isère, France; industl.

Bourke, *t.*, N.S.W., Australia; on R. Darling nr. head of intermittent navigation, terminus of rly. running inland from Sydney and Newcastle; collects wool from sheep farms and despatches by R. to Adelaide (S. Australia) and by rail to Sydney; p. (1947) *2,205.*

Bourne, *urb. dist.*, Kesteven, Lincs., Eng.; agr. machin.; p. (1961) *5,339*

Bournemouth, *co. bor.*, Hants, Eng.; on S. cst.,

E. of Poole Harbour; seaside resort; p. (estd. 1967) *150,000.*

Bournville, *model industl. t.*, Warwick., Eng.; 4 m. S.W. of Birmingham; initiated by Mr. Geo. Cadbury; chocolate and cocoa wks.

Bourtange, *t.*, Netherlands; nr. German frontier.

Boussu, *commune*, Belgium; coal, industl.; p. (1962) *11,483.*

Bouvet I., uninhabited island in S. Atlantic belonging to Norway, a. about 22 sq. m.

Boves, *t.*, Sommes dep., France; S.E. Amiens.

Bovino, *t.*, Apulia Italy.

Bow, *par.*, E. London, Eng.; industl.; properly Stratford-at-Bow.

Bow, *R.*, Alberta, N.W. Canada; head of Saskatchewan R.

Bow Fell, *mtn.*, W. Cumberland, at head of Borrowdale, 4 m. N.W. of Wast Water, alt. 2,960 ft.

Bowden, *urb. dist.*, Cheshire, Eng.; p. (1961) *4,478.*

Bowen, *spt.*, N. Queensland; on Port Denison, 725 m. N.W. of Brisbane; meat wks.; coke plant; p. (1966) *5,134.*

Bowes, *t.*, N.R., Yorks, Eng.; on R. Greta, S.W. of Barnard Castle; mkt. t. for Stainmore dist. of Pennines.

Bowesdorp, *t.*, Cape Prov., S. Africa.

Bowie, *t.*, N. Texas, U.S.A.; oil, gas, coal, clay mining; p. (1960) *4,566.*

Bowland Fells, W. offshoot of mid-Pennines, W.R. Yorks., between Rs. Lune and Ribble; mountain limestone and millstone grit.

Bowland, Forest of, *hills*, Lancs, Eng.; millstone grit moors; many reservoirs supply water to industl. S. Lancs.

Bowling, *vil.*, Dumbarton, Scot.; on N. bank of R. Clyde, 10 m. N.W. of Glasgow; large oil refinery.

Bowling Green, *t.*, Ky., U.S.A.; tr. ctr. for agr. a.; limestone; p. (1960) *28,338.*   [7,397.

Bowmanville, *pt.* L. Ontario, Canada; p. (1961)

Bowness, *t.*, Westmorland, Eng.; on L. Windermere; tourist ctr.

Bowness, *par.*, Cumberland, Eng.; p. *1,050.*

Box Hill, nr. Dorking, Surrey, Eng.; E. of R. Mole gap through N. Downs; chalk; wooded, fine views.

Boyacá, *dep.*, Colombia, S. America; cap. Tunja; a. 24,928 sq. m.; p. (1962) *849,390.*

Boyle, *mkt. t.*, Roscommon, Ireland; on R. Boyle; dairying; p. (1966) *1,789.*

Boyne, *R.*, Leinster, Ireland; length 80 m.

Bozrah, *ancient c.*, S. Damascus, Syria, S.W. Asia; modern Busra; many arch. remains.

Bra, *t.*, Piedmont, Italy; 28 m. S. of Turin.

Brabant, *cent. prov.*, Belgium; fertile and wooded; many breweries; mnfs. linen, cloth, paper, lace; cap. Brussels (*q.v.*); a. 1,267 sq. m.; p. (1968) *2,148,513.*

Brabant, North, *prov.*, Netherlands; S. of Gelderland; N. half of former Duchy; cattle rearing; gram. hops, beetroot, etc.; cap. 's-Hertogenbosch; a. 1920 sq. m.; p. (estd. 1960) *1,512,787.*

Brac, *I.*, Adriatic Sea, Jugoslavia.

Bracadale, *vil.* and *L.*, Skye. Scotland.

Brackley, *mun. bor.*, Northants, Eng.; p. (estd. 1967) *4,040.*

Bracknell, *t.*, Berkshire, Eng.; on Thames Valley terrace, 10 m. S. of Windsor; one of "New Towns" designated 1949 to relieve population congestion in London; extends N. and W. of old vil. of Bracknell; engin., sealing compounds, plastics; central weather forecast sta.; p. (estd. 1965) *25,448.*

Brackwede, *t.*, N. Rhine-Westphalia, Germany; S.W. of Bielefeld; iron and machin.; p. (1963) *26,300.*

Brad, *t.*, Romania, on R. Muresul; p. (1956) *9,963.*

Braddock, *t.*, Penns., U.S.A.; iron and steel; p. (1960) *12,337.*

Bradford, *t.*, Penns., U.S.A.; oil; p. (1966) *15,061.*

Bradford, *co. bor.*, *c.*, W.R. Yorks, Eng.; 9 m. W. of Leeds; univ.; ctr. wool-textile inds.; engin., and chemical inds.; p. (estd. 1969) *293,210.*

Bradford-on-Avon, *t.*, *urb. dist.*, Wilts, Eng.; on R. Avon on E. flank of Cotswolds; mnfs. rubber goods, elect. instruments; p. (1961) *5,757.*

Brading, *par.*, Isle of Wight, Eng.; commands gap through central chalk ridge.

Bradwell, *par.*, Essex, mouth of R. Blackwater; civil nuclear power-sta.; p. (1961) *1,116.*

Brady, *t.*, Texas, U.S.A.; p. (1960) *5,338.*

Braemar, *par.*, in the Grampians, Aberdeen, Scot.; containing Balmoral estate; p. (1951 with Crathie) *1,291.*

Braeriach, *mtn.*, Scot.; Inverness and Aberdeen; alt. 4,248 ft.

Braga, *prov.*, N. Portugal; fruit growing, cattle, textiles; p. (1963) *615,500.*

Braga, *c.*, *cap.* B. prov., N. Portugal, nr. Oporto; cath; steel; p. (1960) *40,977.*

Braganza, *dist.*, Tras-os-Montes, Portugal; silk; p. (1960) *238,588.*

Braganza, *t.*, Portugal; mediæval cas.; p. (1960) *8,075.* [length 1,800 m.

Brahmaputra, *R.*, India, Tsangpo in Tibet;

Braich-y-Pwll, S.W. point of Caernarvon, Wales.

Braila, *t.*, Romania; on Danube, nr. Galati; grain ctr.; p. (1963) *123,132.*

Braintree, *t.*, Mass., U.S.A.; p. (1960) *31,069.*

Braintree and Bocking, *urb. dist.*, Essex, Eng.; on Blackwater; rayon mftg., metal windows, engin.; p. (estd. 1967) *22,310.*

Brakpan, *t.*, Transvaal, S. Africa; p. (1960) *78,788.*

Brampton, *t.*, Ontario, Canada; flower growing ctr., tanning, timber; p. (1961) *18,467.*

Branco, *C.*, Brazil, Pernambuco st.

Brandenburg, *see* Neubrandenburg.

Brandenburg, *t.*, Potsdam, E. Germany; on R. Havel; steel, tractors, bicycles, textiles, machin.; p. (1963) *89,243.*

Brandon, *c.*, Manitoba, Canada; p. (1961) *28,166.*

Brandon and Byshottles, *urb. dist.*, Durham, Eng.; coal-mining; p. (1961) *19,531.*

Brandywine Creek, *R.*, Penns, U.S.A.; Americans defeated by British, 1777.

Branford, *t.*, Conn., U.S.A.; light mnfs., fishing, oysters; resort; p. (1960) *16,567.*

Brantford, *c.*, Ontario, Canada; farm implements, cycles, bus and truck parts; p. (1961) *55,201.*

Brasilia, *fed. cap.*, Brazil, Goiás st.; inaugurated 21 April 1960; 600 m. N.W. Rio de Janeiro; designed for pop. 500,000; p. (estd. 1968) *379,699.*

Brasov, *t.*, Romania; at foot of Transylvanian Alps; cloth, leather; p. (1963) *228,299.*

Brass, *t.*, Nigeria, W. Africa; at mouth of Brass R.; trading settlement.

Bratislava, *t.*, ČSSR.; on R. Danube 30 m. below Vienna; univ.; 2 palaces; rly. ctr.; textiles, chemicals, engin., oil refining; linked to Mozyr', U.S.S.R. by "Friendship Oil Pipeline"; p. (1968) *266,000.*

Bratsk, *t.*, central Irkutsk Oblast, R.S.F.S.R. on Angara R., at mouth of Oka R., 115 m. N.N.E. of Tulun; ship repair yards, lumber, iron-ore, wood processing, chemicals; large hydro-electric sta.; p. (1959) *51,000.*

Brattleboro, *t.*, Vt., U.S.A.; p. (1960) *9,315.*

Brava, *spt.*, Somalia; p. *4,000.*

Bray, *urb. dist.*, Wicklow, Ireland; on Irish Sea cst., 11 m. S. of Dublin; popular wat. pl.; p. (1966) *12,657.* [Dublin.

Bray Head, point on E. cst. of Ireland, S. of

Brazil, United States of, *rep.*, S. America; a. 3,289,000 sq. m.; 4th lgst cty in world, exceeded in size only by U.S.S.R., China and Canada; covers variety of land and climate; in S., great Brazilian plateau, in N., Amazon R. basin (thickly forested); leading industl. nation of Latin America; agr.; coffee, cotton, sugar, cocoa, rubber, fruits, hardwoods; cattle-raising; manganese, iron, gold, diamonds; adm. through 22 sts., 4 terrs., and Fed. Dist.; cap. Brasilia; lgst industl. ctr. São Paulo; pop. mainly White, Negro, Indian, Mestizo; Portuguese official language; p. (estd. 1968) *89,574,572.*

Brazil, *t.*, Ind., U.S.A.; coal, clay, bricks, china; p. (1960) *8,853.*

Brazil Current, *ocean current*; flows S. along E. cst. of Brazil; relatively warm.

Brazos, *R.*, Texas, U.S.A.; length 950 m.

Brazzaville, *cap.*, Congo (ex French), Equat. Africa; connected by rly. with the Atlantic at Pointe-Noire; R. pt. under construction; airport; p. (1962) *135,632.*

Breadalbane, *mountainous dist.*, W. Perth, Scot.

Brechin, *royal burgh*, Angus, Scot.; on S. Esk; cath.; p. (1961) *7,114.*

Breckenridge, *t.*, N. Texas, U.S.A.; oil, gas wells; exp. cattle, grain; p. (1960) *6,273.*

Breckland, *geographical region*, S.W. Norfolk,

N.W. Suffolk, Eng.; chalk, overlain by sand, gives dry soils; much heathland; sm. fertile valleys cultivated, wheat, rye, sugar-beet; ch. ts. Brandon, Lakenheath; a. 200 sq. m.

Brecknock, *co.*, Wales; mountainous; rs. Wye, Usk; cereals, dairy produce; timber; coal, iron; a. 744 sq. m.; p. (1966) *55,000.*

Brecon, (Brecknock), *mun. bor.*, Wales; agr.; p. (1961) *5,797.*

Brecon Beacons, *mtns.*, S. Wales 5 m. S. of Brecon; highest peak, 2,910 ft.; National Park.

Breda, *c.*, N. Brabant, Netherlands; rayon, linen carpets, soap, brewing; p. (1967) *119,239.*

Bredbury and Romiley, *urb. dist.*, Cheshire, Eng.; iron, steel, paper; p. (estd. 1967) *27,620.*

Bregenz, *cap.*, Vorarlberg, Austria; at E. end of L. Constance; the Roman Brigantium; resort; p. (1961) *21,423.*

Breidha Fjord, large inlet, W. coast, Iceland.

Bremen, *t.*, *spt.*, cap. of *Land* Bremen, Germany; on R. Weser 40 m. from N. Sea; ocean liner, tr. and trans-shipment pt.; imports cotton, cereals, tobacco; inds.: cars, machin., textiles, tobacco. shipbldg., oil refining, steel mill; p. (1968) *604,997.*

Bremen, *Land*. W. Germany; cattle rearing, mkt. gardening; a. 156 sq. m.; p. (1968) *754,000.*

Bremerhaven, *spt.*, Germany; "outport" of Bremen at mouth of Weser R.; docks; impt. fish. pt., shipbldg.; p. (1968) *149,196.*

Bremersdorp, *see* Manzini.

Bremerton, *t.*, Wash., U.S.A.; on Puget Sound; naval dockyard; elec. equipment, machin.; p. (1960) *28,922.*

Brenham, *t.*, Texas, U.S.A.; oil, cotton, dairy produce; p. (1960) *7,740.*

Brenner Pass, Italy; famous pass leading from Italy into Austria, over Alps.

Brent, *outer bor.*, Greater London, Eng.; comprising the former mun. bors. of Wembley and Willesden; p. (1966) *295,000.*

Brentford and Chiswick, *former mun. bor.*, Middx., Eng. now inc. in Hounslow (*q.v.*); brewing, soap, coal gas, light engin.; p. (1961) *54,332.*

Brentwood, *urb. dist.*, *mkt. t.* Essex, Eng.; films, agr. implements, steel-tubing; p. (estd. 1967) *57,000.*

Brentwood, *sub.* of St. Louis, Mo., U.S.A.; residtl.; p. (1960) *12,250.*

Brescia, *t.*, Italy; cath.; palace; silks, woollens, iron and steel; p. (1961) *174,116.*

Breslau, *see* Wrocław.

Bressanone, *t.*, N.E. Italy; ceded to Italy 1919 by Austria; cath., health resort; p. *9,503.*

Bressay I., Shetland Is., Scotland.

Brest, *t.*, *spt.*, Finistère dep., N.W. France; naval sta., arsenal; metal inds.; fishing, ropes, soap; oil refining nearby; p. (1968) *159,857.*

Brest (Brest Litovsk), *t.*, Byelorussian S.S.R., on Polish frontier; Treaty of Brest Litovsk, March, 1918; route ctr. and agr. mkt.; textiles; p. (1959) *73,000.*

Bretton Woods, N.H., U.S.A.; resort; site of U.S. monetary and financial conference, 1944.

Brevik, *t.*, *pt.*, Norway; p. (1961) *12,338.*

Brewer, *t.*, Me., U.S.A.; on Penobscot R.; wood pulp, paper, bricks; p. (1960) *9,009.*

Briançon, *t.*, France; p. (1962) *10,105.*

Bridgend, *urb. dist.*, *mkt. t.*, Glamorgan, S. Wales; industl. trading estate; iron, coal, stone, paper; p. (1961) *15,156.*

Bridge of Allan, *burgh*. Stirling, Scot.; 2 m. N. of Stirling; mineral springs; glass; p. (1961) *3,312.*

Bridgeport, *t.*, Conn., U.S.A.; sewing machines, typewriters, valves, hardware, machin., rubber and elec. goods, chemicals, plastics; p. (1960) *156,748.*

Bridgeport, *t.*, Ohio, U.S.A.; on Ohio R.; glass, tin, sheet metal, boat bldg.; p. (1960) *3,324.*

Bridgeport, *bor.*, Penns., U.S.A.; iron and steel, woollens, quarrying; p (1960) *5,306.*

Bridgeton, *t.*, N.J., U.S.A.; founded by Quakers; glasswks., fruit; p. (1960) *20,966.*

Bridgetown, *t.*, Barbados, W.I.; deep water harbour; p. (1960) *95,000.*

Bridgewater, *mftg. t.*, Mass., U.S.A.; nr. Boston; p. (1960) *10,263.*

Bridgewater Canal, Manchester–Runcorn–Leigh; crosses ship canal by means of Barton swing bridge, length 38 m.

Bridgnorth, *rural bor.*, Salop. Eng.; cas.; carpets, radio equipment; p. of t. (1961) *7,552.*

Bridgwater, *mun. bor., pt.*, Somerset, Eng.; on R. Parrett, 10 m. from Bristol Channel; bricks and tiles, engin., wire rope, fibre fabrics, cellophane; p. (estd. 1967) *26,580.*

Bridlington *mun. bor.*, E. Riding, Yorks, Eng.; on Bridlington Bay, S. of Flamborough Head; impt. fishing; seaside resort; p. (estd. 1967) *26,370.*

Bridport, *mun. bor., mkt. t.*, Dorset, Eng.; rope, line and twine, engin., concrete prods.; sm. seaside resort; p. (estd. 1967) *6,510.*

Brie, *natural division (" pays ")*, Central France; low, level, plateau of limestones and clays, S.E. of Paris; loam (limon) cover and plentiful water supply encourage agr.; grains, sugar-beet, fruit, dairy cattle; densely populated.

Brieg, *see* Brzeg.

Brielle, *spt.*, R. Maas, S. Holland, Netherlands; on Voorn I.

Brienz, *t.*, Switzerland; resort; wood carving; on L. Brienz; p. *2,637.*

Brierfield, *urb. dist.*, Lancs, Eng.; cotton weaving; p. (1961) *6,958.*

Brierley Hill, *urb. dist.*, Staffs., Eng.; on R. Stour; cut glass, castable metal goods, firebricks, roofing and tilling; p. (1961) *56,377.*

Brigg, *mkt. t., urb. dist.*, Lindsey, Lincs, Eng.; ctr. of agr. dist. between Lincoln Heights and Wolds; sugar-beet, jam, seed crushing, hosiery; p. (1961) *4,906.*

Brigham, *t.*, Utah, U.S.A.; sugar-beet, peaches, canning, woollens; p. (1960) *11,728.*

Brighouse, *industl. t., mun. bor.*, W.R., Yorkshire, Eng.; on R. Calder, 3 m. S.E. of Halifax; textiles and engin.; p. (estd. 1967) *32,710.*

Brightlingsea, *urb. dist.*, Essex, Eng.; on R. Colne; oysters, boat bldg.; p. (1961) *4,801.*

Brighton, *co. bor.*, E. Sussex, Eng.; 50 m. S. of London; lge. seaside resort and residtl t.; univ.; light inds.; p. (estd. 1967) *162,160.*

Brindisi, *spt.*, Apulia, S. Italy; on Adriatic cst. sea and air connections to Middle East; cath.; cas.; wine, olive oil, silk, petrochemicals; oil refining; p. (1961) *70,084.*

Brinkley, *t.*, Ark., U.S.A.; cotton, lumber; p. (1960) *4,636.*

Brioude, *t.*, Haute-Loire, France; tr. ctr. for agr. a.; p. (1962) *6,928.*

Brisbane, *t., pt., cap.,* Queensland, Australia; univ.; docks; shipbldg.; meats, wool, hides and skins; oil refining, fertilisers; p. (1966) *719,140.*

Bristol, *t.*, Conn., U.S.A.; foundries, ball bearings, clocks, bells; p. (1960) *45,499.*

Bristol, *c.. co., co. bor., spt.*, Gloucester-Somerset border, Eng.; on R. Avon 9 m. from Bristol Channel; "outport" at Avonmouth; cath.; univ.; docks; aircraft engin., tobacco, paint, printing and light inds.; p. (estd. 1969) *427,230.*

Bristol, *t.*, Penns., U.S.A.; cottons, woollens; p. (1960) *12,364.*

Bristol, *c.*, Va., U.S.A.; dairy produce, tobacco; (p, (1960) *17,144.*

Bristol, *t.*, R.I., U.S.A.; fish, textiles, rubber goods, shoes, wire, yacht wks., yachting; p. (1960) *14,570.*

Bristol, *t.*, Tenn., U.S.A.; rayon, paper, leather goods, furniture, mining equipment, transport ctr., especially for cattle; p. (1960) *17,582.*

Bristol Channel, arm of the Atlantic between S. cst. of Wales and Somerset and Devon; noted tidal bores.

British Antarctic Territory, *Brit. col.*, created 3 March 1962; consists of all land and Is. S. of lat. 60° S. and between 20° and 80° W. longitude; comprising Graham Land peninsula, S. Shetlands, S. Orkneys and smaller Is., excluding S. Georgia and S. Sandwich Is. *See* K190.

British Columbia, *prov.*, Canada; diversified topography and landscape; rich mineral and forest resources; principal Rs.: Columbia, Fraser, Kootenay, Peace; lumbering, farming, dairying and livestock; fruit growing, canning, salmon fisheries; coal, copper, gold, lead, silver, iron ore, molybdenum, gas, oil in N.E.; cap, Victoria; a. 366,255 sq. m.; p. (estd. 1969) *2,000,000.*

British East Africa, formerly comprised Kenya, Tanganyika, Uganda, together with the islands of Zanzibar and Pemba. *See* under their respective headings.

British Guiana, *see* Guyana.

British Honduras, *self-gov. Br. col.*, Central America; heavy rainfall; tropical forests; mahogany, logwood, bananas; poor communications; cap. Belize; subject to tropical hurricanes; a. 8,866 sq. m.; p. (estd.) *116,000.*

British Indian Ocean Terr., *Brit. col.*, created Nov. 1965; consists of the Chagos Archipelago (of which Diego Garcia is lgst. I.) 1200 m. N.E. of Mauritius, and Is. of Aldabra, Farquhar, and Desroches in the W. Indian Oc.; p. (1965) *1,400.*

British Is., *archipelago*, N.W. Europe, comprising 2 large islands: Great Britain, Ireland; and 5,000 small islands; a. 121,633 sq. m.

British Solomon Is., *prot.*, W. Pacific; coconuts, rubber, pineapples, bananas; a. 11,500 sq. m.; p. (estd.) *148,000.*

British Virgin Islands, *see* Virgin Islands.

British West Africa, formerly comprised Gambia, Sierra Leone, Gold Coast (Ghana), Nigeria, and parts of Togoland and Cameroons. *See* under their separate headings.

Briton Ferry, *t., pt.*, Glam., S. Wales; at mouth of R. Neath; steel wks., engin., ship-breaking.

Brittany, *prov.*, France; farming; fishing; a. 13,643 sq. m.; p. *3,000,000.*

Brittle, *L.*, Skye, Scot.

Brive, *t.*, Corrèze dep., France; vegetables, wines; truffles, straw; p. (1962) *43,683.*

Brixham, S. Devon, Eng.; incorporated in Torbay co. bor.; fishing; resort; p. (1961) *10,679.*

Brixton, *dist.*, S.W. London, Eng.

Brno, *t.*, ČSSR.; brewing, cloth. engin.; cath., univ.; p. (1965) *327,000.*

Broad Haven, *t.*, New Town planned on St. Brides Bay, Wales.

Broad Law, *mtn.*, Peebles, Scot.

Broads, The, Norfolk, Eng.; yachting, fishing and fowling centre.

Broadstairs, *urb. dist.*, Kent, Eng.; seaside resort; 3 m. N.E. of Ramsgate; p. (estd. 1967) *20,300.*

Broadway, *par.*, Worcester, Eng.; tourist ctr., Cotswolds; p. *1,860.*

Brocken, Harz Mtns., Germany; highest point (3,745 ft.).

Brockport, *t.*, N.Y., U.S.A.; dairying, mkt. gardens; N.Y. St. Teachers' College; p. (1960) *5,256.*   [(1960) *72,813.*

Brockton, *c.*, Mass., U.S.A.; shoes, machin.; p.

Brockville, *c.*, Ont., Canada; entry pt. on R. St. Lawrence; farm implements; marine engin.; p. (1961) *17,744.*

Brody, *t.*, Ukranian S.S.R.; oil, linked to Czechoslovakia by " Friendship Oil Pipeline ".

Broken Hill, *c.*, N.S.W., Australia; silver, lead, zinc; p. (1966) *30,001.*

Broken Hill, Zambia. *see* Kabwe.

Brokopondo, Surinam, S. America; aluminium smelter under construction 1966.

Bromberg, *see* Bydgoszcz.

Bromborough, *see* Bebington and Bromborough.

Bromley, *former mun. bor.*, Kent, Eng.; now outer bor., Greater London, inc. Beckenham, Chislehurst, and Sidcup (S. of the A.20) Orpington, Penge; p. (1966) *302,000.*

Bromsgrove, *urb. dist., old mkt. t.* Worcs., Eng.; 13 m. S.W. Birmingham; wrought ironwk., lt. engin.; p. (estd. 1967) *38,480.*

Bromyard, *urb. dist., mkt. t.*, Hereford, Eng.; hops, glove mkg., engin., floor-tiles; p. (1961) *1,681.*

Bron, *t.*, Rhône, France; airport; p. estd. *15,000.*

Bronx, one of the five boroughs of N.Y. City, U.S.A.; and connected by bridges with bor. of Manhattan; p. (1960) *1,424,815.*   [town.

Bron y Mor, *t.*, Cardigan Bay, Wales; new seaside

Brookline, sub. of Boston, Mass., U.S.A.; resdtl.; p. (1960) *54,044.*

Brooklyn, *bor.*, N.Y. City, linked with Manhattan bor. by Brooklyn, Manhattan and Williamsburgh suspension bridges across East R.; and with Staten I. by Verrazano-Narrows bridge (longest in world); mainly residtl. with numerous mftg. and comm. interests; p. (1960) *2,627,319.*

Broom, *loch* on N.W. cst. of Ross and Cromarty, Scot.

Brora, *t.*, Sutherland, Scot.; on E. cst., 12 m. N.E. of Dornoch Firth; ctr. of sm. coalfield; Harris Tweed ind.

Brotton, *t.*, N.R. Yorks, Eng., nr. Guisborough; iron and steel mftg.

Brough, *mkt. t.*, Westmorland, Eng.; in upper Vale of Eden, 4 m. N. of Kirkby-Stephen.

Broughshane, *vil.*, Antrim, N. Ireland.

Brownhills, *urb. dist.*, Staffs, coal-mining; p. (1961) 26,392.

Brownsville, *t.*, Texas, U.S.A.; livestock, sugar-cane; p. (1960) 48,040.

Brown Willy, *mtn.*, Cornwall, Eng.; alt. 1,375 ft.

Brownwood, *t.*, Texas, U.S.A.; exp. cotton, grain, wool, poultry, dairy prod.; p. (1960) 16,974.

Broxbourne, *t.*, Hertford, Eng.; on gravel terrace to W. of R. Lea about 20 m. N.E. of London; ctr. of very intensively cultivated district, mkt.-garden and glasshouse crops; light inds.; "dormitory" t. linked with London; p. (1961) 3,839.

Bruay-en-Artois, *t.*, Pas de Calais, France; p. (1968) 28,628.

Bruchsal, *t.*, Baden-Württemberg, Germany; tobacco, paper, machin.; p. (1963) 23,600.

Bruck, *t.*, Austria; p. (1961) 16,087.

Brue, *R.*, Somerset, Eng.

Bruges (Brugge), *t.*, *inland pt.*, Belgium; mkt.-hall with 13th-century belfry; univ.; impt. mkt. for grain, cattle, horses, engin., elec. goods; glass, textiles, lace; p. incl. subs. (1968) 105,715.

Brühl, *t.*, N. Rhine-Westphalia, Germany; 8 m. S. of Cologne; cas.; lignite, iron, sugar refining; p. (1963) 37,200.

Brunei, *Br. prot. st.*, N. Borneo; oilfields; cutch, rubber, sago, pepper. timber; a. 2,226 sq. m.; p. (est. 1969) 130,000.

Brünn, *see* Brno.

Brunsbüttelkoog, *t.*, mouth of Elbe, canal opposite Cuxhaven, Germany; p. (estd. 1954) 10,100.

Brunswick (Braunschweig), *c.*, Lower Saxony, Germany; on R. Oker; medieval bldgs.; canning, tinplate mftg., optics, pianos, drugs, vehicles; p. (1968) 226,305.

Brunswick, *t.*, Me., U.S.A.; p. (1960) 9,444.

Brussels, *c.*, *cap.* Belgium; town hall, palace, parliament houses, univ., museum; mnfs., lace, carpets, silk, cottons, rayon; p. (1968) 1,079,181 (inc. subs.)

Bryan, *t.*, Texas, U.S.A.; mkt. ctr.; cotton gins, compresses; oil mills; p. (1960) 27,542.

Bryansk, *t.*, R.S.F.S.R.; sawmilling, engin. textiles, chemicals, phosphates, steel; oil pipeline from Kuybyshev; p. (1967) 276,000.

Brynmawr, *urb. dist.*, Brecon, Wales; iron, coal, steel, rubber goods; p. (1961) 6,471.

Brzeg (Brieg), *t.*, Silesia, Poland; German before 1945; on R. Oder; chemicals; p. (1965) 28,000.

Bua, *t.*, Fiji Islands, Pacific.

Bucaramanga, *t.*, *cap.* Santander. Colombia; coffee; cigar and cigarette mkg.; p. (estd. 1962) 221,779.

Buchan Ness, *C.*, nr. Peterhead, E. Scot.

Bucharest, *c.*, *cap.*, Romania; cath.; palace, univ.; textiles, grain, chemicals, pharmaceutics, oil refinery engin.; glass; p. (1963) 1,366,794.

Buckfast, S. Devon, Eng.; famous Abbey.

Buckfastleigh, *urb. dist.*, S. Devon, Eng.; wool, quarrying; p. (1961) 2,550.

Buckhannon, *t.*, W. Va., U.S.A.; agr. and pastoral ctr.; coal, gas, lumber, leather; p. (1960) 6,386.

Buckhaven, and Methil, *burgh*, Fife, Scot.; on N. side of Firth of Forth, 8 m. N.E. of Kirkcaldy; coal, oilsilk, brickmkg. inds; p. (1961) 21,104.

Buckie, *burgh*, Banff, Scot.; boat- and yacht-bldg.; fisheries; p. (1961) 7,666.

Buckingham, *co.*, England; wooded, beeches; includes Vale of Aylesbury; farming, dairy produce, ducks, sheep; mnfs., chairs, lace, paper; a. 749 sq. m.; p. (1966) 542,000.

Buckingham, *mun. bor.*, Bucks, Eng.; on Ouse R.; agr. bricks; p. (estd. 1967) 4,810.

Buckley, *urb. dist.*, Flint, Wales; small castings; (1961) 7,658.

Bucyrus, *t.*, Ohio, U.S.A.; machine-mnfs.; p. (1960) 12,276.

Budsfoc, *sub.* of Budapest, Hungary; wine cellars.

Budapest, *twin-cap.*, Hungary; Buda on right bank and Pest on left bank of Danube; parlt., univ.; steel, textiles, chemicals, engin., motor-buses, oil refining; mineral springs; p. (1965) 1,935,000.

Budaun, *t.*, Uttar Pradesh, India; sugar-cane, rice; ruins; p. (1961) 58,770.

Bude, *see* Stratton and Bude, Cornwall.

Budejovice, *t.*, ČSSR.; pencils, beet, porcelain, anthracite, domestic woodware; p. (1961) 63,949.

Budge-Budge, *t.*, W. Bengal, India; hemp, rice; p. (1961) 39,824.

Budleigh Salterton, *urb. dist.*, E. Devon; resort; p. (1961) 3,871.

Buena Park, *t.*, Cal., U.S.A.; citrus fruits, truck farms, oilfields; p. (1960) 46,401.

Buenaventura, *spt.*, Colombia; lumber yards, tanning, fish canning; p. (estd. 1962) 60,220.

Buenos Aires, *c.*, *cap.* Argentina; on Rio de la Plata, fine buildings, lgst. c. in S. hemisphere; univ.; tr. ctr.; carpets, cloth, cigars, boots and shoes, iron-ore; p. (estd. 1966) 3,876,000.

Buenos Aires, *prov.*, Argentina; a. 118,467 sq. m.; treeless plain; sheep and cattle; cereals, fruit, tobacco; p. (1960) 6,735,000.

Buffalo, *c.*, *pt.*, N.Y., U.S.A.; on L. Erie; univ.; iron, steel, oil refining, aircraft, car parts, elec. goods, textiles, meat packing, brewing; p. (1960) 532,759.

Bug, *R.*, in Ukraine, flows into Black Sea; length 348 m.

Bug, *R.*, Poland; trib. of Vistula R.; since 1939 frontier between Poland and Ukraine S.S.R.

Buga, *c.*, Colombia, S. America; tr. ctr. for sugar, coffee, cacao, rice, cotton; p. (estd. 1959) 75,220.

Buganda, *prov.*, Uganda, E. Africa; located W. of L. Victoria largely at alt. between 4,500 and 6,000 ft.; intensive cultivation, cotton (ch. comm. crop), plantains, millets; *cap.* Kampala.

Bugisu, *dist.*, Uganda; coffee.

Bugulma, *t.*, Tatar A.S.S.R., R.S.F.S.R.; oil ctr.; p. (1959) 61,000.

Builth Wells, *urb. dist.*, N. Brecknock, Wales; on upper course, R. Wye; medicinal springs; p. (1961) 1,602.

Buitenzorg, *see* Bogor.   [12,796.

Bujalance, *c.*, Spain; E. of Cordova; p. (1957)

Bujumbura, *cap.* Burundi; p. (estd. 1965) 70,000.

Bukhara (Bokhara), *t.*, Uzbek S.S.R., U.S.S.R.; in Amu Darya valley at W. foot of Tien Shan; mkt. for cotton, sunflower seed, wheat grown in irrigated Bukhara Oasis; impt. tr. ctr. at W. terminus of ancient caravan route from China; linked by Trans-Caspian rly. to Krasnovodsk, by Turk-Sib. rly to Novo Sibivsk; natural gas nearby; pipeline to Urals; textiles; p. (1959) 69,000.

Bukittinggi, *t.*, Sumatra, Indonesia; p. (1957) 53,700.

Bukoba, *t.*, *pt.*, Tanzania, E. Africa; located midway along W. shore of L. Victoria; exp. coffee, rice, plantains and other foodstuffs to L. pts. in Kenya and Uganda.

Bukovina, Northern, formerly Romania, ceded to U.S.S.R. in 1940; now part of Ukraine; a. about 6,000 sq. km.; ch. t. Chernovitsy; Carparthian Mtns., forested; farming, cereals; cattle.

Bulawayo, *t.*, Rhodesia; impt. rly. and indus. ctr.; airpt.; agr. mnfs.; p. (1965) 237,000.

Buldan, *t.*, Turkey; p. (1960) 10,431.

Bulgaria, *rep.*, Eastern Europe; mountainous; Balkan Mtns., R. Danube N. boundary; climate: hot summer, cold winter, milder in S.; heavy summer rainfall; 5 lge. dams; hydro-electric stas.; religion: Greek Orthodox; communications: main rail from Central Europe passes through to Istanbul; grain, wines, rose-oil, pigs, iron, manganese, copper, lead, zinc. pyrites, salt, chemicals, oil, tobacco, clothing; a. 42,796 sq. m.; p. (1967) 8,334,000.

Bultfontein, *t.*, Cape Province, S. Africa; diamonds; p. (1960) 3,491 inc. 1,380 whites.

Bunbury, *t.*, *spt.*, W. Australia; on cst. 112 m. S. of Fremantle; pt. and comm. ctr. of lge. pastoral, agr. fruit growing and timber dist., wool, phosphates, oil; p. (1966) 15,453.

Buncrana, *urb. dist.*, Donegal Ireland; salmon; p. (1966) 3,120.

Bundaberg, *t.*, Queensland, Australia; on Burnett R.; sugar factories, timber, butter, iron; p. (1966) 25,404.

Bungay, *urb. dist.*, Suffolk, Eng.; on R. Waveney; printing, malting; p. (1961) 3,581.

Bunker Hill, Charlestown, now part of Boston, Mass., U.S.A.; battle between Americans and British, 1775.

Buntingford, *par.*, Herts, Eng.; on E. Anglian Heights, 10 m. N.W. of Bishop's Stortford; p. (1961) 1,559.

Bunzlau, *see* Boleslawiec.

Buraida, *t.*, Nejd, Saudi Arabia; p. (estd.) 50,000.

Burbank, *c.*, Cal., U.S.A.; airport, aeroplanes; p. (1960) 90,155.

Burdur, *t.*, Turkey; p. (1965) *28,960.*

Bure, *R.*, Norfolk, Eng.

Burg, *t.*, Magdeburg, E. Germany; on Ihle Canal; leather goods, iron, furniture, machin.; p. (1963) *30,026.*

Burgas *spt.*, Bulgaria; on Black Sea; copper, engin., chemicals, textiles; oil refining; pt. for oil tankers under construction; p. (1956). *72,795*

Burgenland, *prov.*, Austria; a. 1.526 sq. m.; p. (1961) *271,001.* [tiles; p. (1961) *13,990.*

Burgess Hill, *urb. dist.*, Sussex, Eng.; bricks,

Burghausen, *t.*, W. Germany; oil refining; pipeline to Munich.

Burgos, *c.*, Spain; cath.; hosiery, leather cloth, tyres; p. (1959) *87,520.*

Burgos, *prov.*, Old Castile, Spain; ch. t., Burgos; oil; a. 5,425 sq. m.; p. (1959) *401,891.*

Burgstädt, *t.*, Karl-Marx-Stadt, E. Germany; textiles, machin.; p. (1963) *17,167.*

Burgundy, *old prov.*, N.E. France; composed largely of upper valley of R. Saône; famous vineyards; strategic position on route leading between plateau of Vosges and Jura Mtns. from Rhône valley to Rhine valley.

Burhanpur, *t.*, Madhya Pradesh, India; ancient walled Mogul city; textiles, brocades; p. (1961) *82,090.*

Burlington, *t.*, S. Ont., Canada, on L. Ontario, N.E. of Hamilton; in fruit-growing a.; industl. development; tourism; p. (estd.) *47,000.*

Burlington, *c.*, Iowa, U.S.A.; on bluffs of Mississippi R.; machin., furniture; p. (1960) *32,430.*

Burlington, *pt.*, Vt., U.S.A.; E. side of L. Champlain; state univ.; timber; p. (1960) *35,531.*

Burma (Union of), *rep.* 1948; ch. mtns.: Arakan Yoma, Pegu Yoma; chief rivers: Irrawaddy, Salween; forested; agr.: rice, fruit, tobacco; timber, teak; minerals; petroleum, precious stones, rubies, sapphires; textile, sugar and jute mills projected; cap. Rangoon; a. 261,789 sq. m., p. (estd. 1969) *27,000,000.*

Burnham-on-sea, *t.*, *urb. dist.*, Somerset, Eng.; on Bridgwater Bay, 10 m. S. of Weston-super-Mare; resort; p. (1961) *9,850.*

Burnham-on-Crouch, *urb. dist.*, Essex, Eng.; yacht sailing, oysters, boat bldg.; p. (1961) *4,167.*

Burnie, *spt.*, Tasmania, Australia; pastoral and agr., paper pulp mftg; chemicals; oil terminal; p. (1966) *18,028.*

Burnley, *industl. t.*, *co. bor.*, Lancs, Eng.; cotton, weaving, coal; p. (estd. 1967) *78,060.*

Burntisland, *royal burgh*, East Fife, Scot.; on F. of Forth, nr. Kirkcaldy; shipbldg., aluminium inds.; p. (1961) *6,036.*

Burra, E. and W., two Shetland Is., Scot.

Burray, one of the Orkney Is., Scot.

Burriana, *t.*, *spt.*, Spain; oranges, wine; p. (1957) *17,697.*

Burrinjuck, *t.*, N.S.W. Australia; on Murrumbidgee R., N. of Canberra; site of impt. dam providing irrigation in Riverina dist.

Burry Port, *urb. dist.*, Carmarthen, Wales; p. (1961) *5,671.*

Bursa, *c.*, Turkey; 60 m. S. Istanbul; fruits, carpets, tapestry; cap. of Bithynia prior to the Christian Era, and later of the Ottoman Empire; p. (1965) *212,518.*

Burslem, *t.*, part of Stoke-on-Trent, Staffs.

Burton Latimer, *urb. dist.*, Northants., Eng.; p. (1961) *4,401.*

Burton-on-Trent, *industl. t.*, *co. bor.*, Staffs, Eng.; brewing, malting, rubber goods, engin., steel, footwear, chemicals; p. (estd. 1967) *50,220.*

Buru, *I.*, Indonesia; W. of Serang.

Burujird, *t.*, Iran; cotton, carpets; p. (1956) *49,228.*

Burundi, *indep. kingdom* (1 July 1962), formerly Urundi, part of U.N. trust terr. of Ruanda-Urundi under Belgian adm.; cap. Bujumbura; coffee; a. 10,747 sq. m.; p. (estd. 1967) *3,340,000.*

Bury, *industl. t.*, *co. bor.*, S.E. Lancs.; on R. Irwell to S. of Rossendale Fells; cotton, textiles, engin., paper makg.; p. (estd. 1967) *64,540.*

Bury St. Edmunds, *mun. bor.*, W. Suffolk; monastic remains; farm implements, brewing, sugar-beet processing; p. (estd. 1967) *24,260.*

Buryat, *rep.*, R.S.F.S.R., U.S.S.R.; lge. deposit of graphite; ch. t. Ulan Ude; a. 135,500 sq. m.; p. (1959) *671,000.*

Bushey, *t.*, *urb. dist.*, Herts., Eng.; p. (estd. 1967) *24,310.*

Bushire, *see* Bandar-e-Bushehr.

Buskerud, *co.*, Norway; a. 5,738 sq. m.; p. (1968) *192,752.*

Busto Arsizio, *t.*, Varese prov., N. Italy; 19 m. N.W. of Milan; cotton milling ctr., iron, steel, rayon, textile machin.; p. (1961) *64,367.*

Bute, *I.*, *co.*, Firth of Clyde, Scotland; 16 m. long and 3–5 m. broad; ch. t., Rothesay; a. 218 sq. m.; p. (1961) *15,129.* [Argyll.

Bute, Kyles of, *strait*, 6 m. between isles of Bute and

Butt of Lewis, *promontory* with lighthouse; Lewis, Hebrides, Scot.

Butte, *c.*, Montana, U.S.A.; copper, lead, silver; p. (1960) *27,377.*

Buttermere, *L.*, Cumberland, Eng.

Buxton, *mun. bor.*, Derby, Eng.; wat. p. nr. High Peak dist.; spa t.; lime quarrying nearby; p. (estd. 1967) *19,730.*

Buzau, *t.*, Romania; rly. ctr.; cath.; wheat, timber, petroleum; p. (1963) *79,588.*

Buzuluk, *t.*, R.S.F.S.R.; in Urals; engin.; ctr. of agr. a.; p. (1959) *55,000.*

Bydgoszcz, *t.*, N. Central Poland; on R. Brda; R. pt., rly. ctr.; elec. equip., machine tools, chemicals; p. (1965) *255,000.*

Bydgoszcz, *prov.*, Poland; cap. B.; drained by Rs. Vistula, Brda and Notec; a. 8,031 sq. m.; p. *c. 1,704,000.*

Byelorussia (White Russia), *constituent rep.*, U.S.S.R.; cap. Minsk; oil at Rechitsk; salt at Mozyr; a. 81,090 sq. m.; p. (1970) *9,003,000.*

Byron C., most easterly point of Australia, Pacific coast of N.S.W.

Bytom (Beuthen), *t.*, Upper Silesia, Poland; German before 1945; coal, zinc, lead and iron mining; iron inds.; p. (1965) *192,000.*

C

Cabinda, *Port. enclave*, Atl. cst., W. Africa; separated from Angola by Congo R. est.; hardwoods, coffee, cocoa, palm oil prods.; recent oil find; a. 2,794 sq. m.; p. *c. 50,000.*

Cabot Strait, entrance of Gulf of St. Lawrence between C. Breton I. and Newfoundland.

Cabra, *t.*, Spain; 30 m. S.E. of Córdova; college; p. (1957) *22,174.*

Cáceres, *prov.*, W. Spain; pastoral; a. 7,705 sq. m.; p. (1959) *566,202.*

Cáceres, *t.*, Spain; largest bull-ring in Spain; ancient Castra Caecilia; p. (1957) *52,000.*

Cachan *t.*, Seine, France; p. (1954) *16,965.*

Cachar, *dist.*, Assam, India; tea-growing ctr.; a. 2,688 sq. m.; p. (1961) *1,378,476.*

Cachoeira, *t.*, Bahia, Brazil; historic c.; p. (estd. 1968) *32,432.*

Cachoeira do Sul, *t.*, Rio Grade do Sul, Brazil; p. (estd. 1968) *98,927.*

Cadarache, *t.*, S. France; nr. Aix-en-Provence; nuclear research centre.

Cader Idris, *mtn.*, Merioneth, Wales; alt. 2,929 ft.

Cadillac, *t.*, Mich., U.S.A.; rubber tyres, wood and metal prod.; p. (1960) *10,112.*

Cadiz, *maritime prov.*, S. Spain; cap. Cadiz; a. 2,827 sq. m.; p. (1959) *811,581.*

Cadiz, *fortress t.*, *spt.*, Andalusia, S. Spain; sherry, cork, fruit, olive oil, tunny fish; naval base; univ.; one of most ancient ts. in Europe, built by Phoenicians, c. 1100 B.C.; p. (1959) *113,325.*

Caen, *c. cap.*, Calvados, France; church and abbey, tomb of William the Conqueror; univ.; iron ore, lace, gloves exported; severely damaged in Second World War; p. (1968) *110,762*

Caerleon, *urb. dist.*, Monmouth, Wales; on R. Usk, 3 m. N.E. of Newport; Roman remains; agr. machin. tools, bricks; p. (1961) *4,184.*

Caernarvon, *royal bor.*, *cap.* Caernarvonshire, N. Wales; on S. shore of Menai Strait; cas. where first Prince of Wales (Edward II) was christened; slate, bricks, plastics; p. (1961) *8,993.*

Caernarvonshire, *mtnous. marit. co.*, N. Wales; slate and stone quarries, lead-mines; oats, barley, sheep, cattle; highest peak, Snowdon (3,560 ft.); a. 569 sq. m.; p. (1966) *120,000.*

Caerphilly, *urb. dist.*, Glamorgan, S. Wales; cas.; coal, iron, light inds.; p. (1961) *36,008.*

Caesar Mazaca, *anc. c.*, Asia Minor; residence of the Cappadocian Kings; the modern Kayeri, Turkey.

Caesarea Palestina, *old c.*, Israel, 20 m. S. Mt. Carmel; cap. of Herod the Great.

Caeté, *t.*, Minas Geraes st., Brazil; at foot of Serra do Espinhaço, 50 m. E. of Belo Horizonte; lge. iron and steel wks.

Cagayan, *prov.*, Luzon, Philippine Is.; p. (1960) 555,819.

Cagliari, Italian *prov.*, comprising S. half of Sardinia; a. 5,179 sq. m.; p. (1961) 733,489.

Cagliari, *spt.*, *cap.* Sardinia, on S. cst.; cath. and univ.; exp. lead, zinc; p. (1964) 200,000.

Cagnes-sur-Mer, *t.*, Alpes-Maritimes dep., France; Riviera resort; p. (1954) 11,066.

Caha, *mtns.*, on boundary of Cork and Kerry, Ireland; cas.; highest point 2,249 ft.

Cahir, *t.*, Tipperary, Ireland; on R. Suir; ancient cas. and abbey; p. (1966) 1,740.

Cahirciveen, *t.*, Kerry, Ireland; p. (1966) 1,649.

Cahors, *t.*, *cap.*, Lot, France; cath.; distilleries, shoe factories; p. (1954) 15,384.

Caibarien, *t.*, Cuba; sugar pt.; p. (1953) 22,657.

Caicos Is., *see* Turks and Caicos Is.

Cairngorm, *mtn.*, Inverness and Banff Scot.; alt. 4,084 ft.; national nature reserve.

Cairns, *spt.*, Queensland, Australia; on Trinity Bay; bulk sugar pt.; tourist ctr.; p. (1966) 25,555. [alt. 4,241 ft.

Cairntoul, *mtn.*, Inverness and Aberdeen, Scot.;

Cairo, *c.*, *cap.* U.A.R.; on R. bank of Nile at head of Nile delta; univ.; tourist ctr.; mnfs. cotton, paper, silk; p. (1960) 3,346,000.

Cairo, Ill., U.S.A.; confluence of Mississippi and Ohio; extensive traffic; p. (1960) 9,348.

Caister, *vil.*, N. of Yarmouth, Norfolk, Eng.; ruined cas.; holiday resort.

Caithness, *co.*, Scot.; most N. part of mainland; flat, with much moorland; herring fishery; poor agr.; quarrying; ch. ts. Wick, Thurso; a. 686 sq. m.; p. (1961) 27,345.

Caivano, *industl. t.*, Italy; N.E. of Naples.

Cajalco Reservoir, S. Cal., U.S.A.; hill-top location nr. Riverside, 55 m. S.E. of Los Angeles; stores water brought 242 m. by aqueduct from Parker Res. on R. Colorado, for distribution throughout Los Angeles plain.

Cajamarca, *dep.* N. Peru; mining and agr.; gold and silver deposits found 1965; a. 12,538 sq. m.; p. (1961) 543,090.

Cajamarca, *t.*, *cap.* Cajamarca prov., Peru; mng. ctr., dairying, cloth, leather, straw hats; thermal springs; p. (1961) 37,000.

Calabar, *spt.*, S.E. Nigeria, W. Africa; exp. palm oil, kernals, rubber, ivory, cement; p. c. 47,000.

Calabozo, *t.*, N. Venezuela, S. America; cattle, agr., tr. ctr.; p. 7,123.

Calabria, *region*, extreme S.W. Italy; mountainous and fertile; highest point Mt. Pollino 7,325 ft.; ch. R. Crati; cereals, wine, olives, fruit; copper, marble; tunny fish; a. 5,830 sq. m.; p. (1961) 2,045,215.

Calafat, *t.*, Romania; on Bulgarian frontier, opp. Vidin; p. (1956) 8,069.

Calahorra, *t.*, Logrono, Spain; cath.; pimentoes, wine; on R. Ebro; p. (1957) 13,524.

Calais, *spt.*, Pas de Calais, N.E. France; cross-channel ferry pt. opposite to and 21 m. distant from Dover; lace, fishing; p. (1962) 70,707.

Calama, *oasis*, Antofagasta prov., N. Chile; in Atacama desert at foot of Andean Cordillera, 130 m. N.E. of Antofagasta on main rly. to La Paz; water from R. Loa supplies Antofagasta and used for irrigation locally.

Calamar, *t.*, Bolivar dep., Colombia; on R. Magdalena 60 m. from mouth, connected by rail to Cartagena; handles traffic between Cartagena and Magdalena valley; p. (estd. 1959) 21,000.

Calamianes Is., Philippine Is.; between Mindoro and Palawan Is. [p. 11,285.

Calanas, *commune*, S. Spain; pyrites, olives;

Calarasi, *t.*, S.E. Romania; on the Danube; comm. ctr.; p. (1963) 29,474.

Calasiao, *t.*, Luzon, Philippines; hats; p. (1948) 23,269.

Calatafimi, *commune*, Sicily; Garibaldi defeated Neapolitans, May 1860; p. 11,484.

Calatayud, *t.*, Spain; 55 m. S.W. Saragossa; cas.; weapons; flour milling; p. (1957) 18,762.

Calbayog, *t.*, Samar, Philippine Is.; hemp trade, fisheries; p. (1960) 77,532.

Calbe, *t.*, Magdeburg, E. Germany; on R. Saale; iron smelting. lignite mng., machin., chemicals; p. (1963) 16,859.

Calcutta, *c.*, *spt.*, W. Bengal, India; on R. Hooghli; vast tr. from Ganges plain; univ.; jute-mills; exp. jute, cotton, sugar-cane, rice, tea, silk, coal; p. (1961) corporation a. 2,927,289; metropolitan a. 5,500,195.

Caldas, *dep.*, Colombia, S. America; cap. Manizales; a. 5,160 sq. m.; p. (1962) 1,399,590.

Calder, *t.*, S.W. Midlothian; shale mines, oilwks.; p. 3,200.

Calder, R., Lancs, Eng.; joins the Ribble.

Calder, R., W.R. Yorks, Eng.; trib. of Aire R.

Calder Hall, Cumberland; first full-scale nuclear power sta. in world (1956) owned and operated by U.K. Atomic Energy Authority; electricity and plutonium prod.

Caldwell, t., Idaho, U.S.A.; p. (1960) 12,230.

Caldy I., off Pembroke coast, Wales; lighthouse; Trappist monastery.

Caledonian Canal, from Moray Firth to Loch Linnhe, Scot., connecting North Sea with Atlantic; 62½ m. long; opened in 1822.

Calf of Man, *sm. I.*, S.W. I. of Man, Eng.; a. 620 acres.

Calgary, *ch. t.*, Alberta, Canada; ctr. of ranching country; lumber-mills, tanneries, oil refining; p. (1966) 330,575.

Cali, *t.*, *cap.*, Valle del Cauca, Colombia; on Cauca R.; comm. ctr.; in rich agr. a.; coal mined nearby; textiles, tyres, paper, plastics; p. (estd. 1962) 693,120. [spices; p. (1961) 192,521.

Calicut, *spt.*, *mfg. t.*, Kerala, India; exp. coffee,

California, most impt. of Pacific States U.S.A.; mountainous and forested but fertile valleys; salubrious climate; rich in minerals oil, natural gas, gold, silver, copper, steel; oil refining; films; fruit; cap. Sacramento; ch. pt. San Francisco; lgst. c. Los Angeles; has 279 incorporated cities; a. 158,693 sq. m.; p. (1970) 19,696,840.

California Current, E. Pac. Oc.; flows N. to S. along cst. of Ore., and Cal., U.S.A.; relatively cold water; reduces summer temp. and causes fog in cst. a. especially nr. San Francisco.

California, G. of, Mexico; 700 m.l.; inlet of Pac. Oc.

California, Lower, *terr.*, Mexico; between Gulf of C. and Pacific; cap. La Paz; chiefly a sterile region; some mineral wealth; a. 55,654 sq. m.; p. (1950) 287,366. [Coast, India.

Calimere Point, most S. point of Coromandel

Calistoga, t., Cal., U.S.A.; tr. ctr., wine, grapes; hot springs; p. (1960) 1,514.

Callan, *rural dist.*, *mkt. t.*, Kilkenny, Ireland; on the King's R.; p. (1961) 5,963.

Callander, *mkt. t.*, *burgh*, Perth, Scot.; on R. Teith, 15 m. N.W. of Stirling; "the gate of the Highlands," tourist resort; p. (1961) 1,654.

Callao, *dep.*, Peru; cap. C.; a. 14 sq. m.; p. (1961) 213,206.

Callao, *t.*, *spt.*, cap. Callao dep., Peru; linked by rly. to Lima; exp. sugar, cotton; oil refining; p. (estd. 1963) 214,186.

Calne, *mkt. t.*, *mun. bor.*, Wilts, Eng.; on Marden R.; lge bacon factory; p. (estd. 1967) 9,290

Calonne-Ricouart, *commune*, Pas-de-Calais dep., France; coal; p. (1954) 10,897.

Calota, gold-field dist., Colombia, S. America.

Calstock, t., E. Cornwall, Eng.; on Tamar estuary.

Caltagirone, *c.*, Catania, Sicily; cath.; local mkt.; p. (1961) 44,212.

Caltanissetta, *t.*, *cap.*, Caltanissetta prov., Sicily, Italy; cath.; sulphur; p. (1961) 62,115.

Caluire-et-Clare, t., Rhône, France, on Saône R.; coal; p. (1954) 19,886.

Calumet, t., Mich., U.S.A.; on peninsula in L. Superior; copper-mining; p. (1960) 1,139.

Calvados, *dep.*, N.W. France; cap. Caen; livestock, dairying, fisheries, textiles, liqueur brandy; a. 2,197 sq. m.; p. (1968) 519,695.

Calvinia, t., Cape Province, S. Africa; p. 3,627.

Cam, R., Cambridge, Eng.; trib. of Ouse; length 40 m. [m.; p. (1953) 618.258.

Camagüey, *prov.*, Cuba, W. Indies; a. 10,169 sq.

Camagüey, *t.*, *cap.*, Camagüey, Central Cuba; p. (1953) 110,388.

Camajore, *t.*, Central Italy; foot of Apuan Alps, in prov. of Lucca; old church.

Camargue, *delta dist.*, Bouches-du-Rhône, France; at mouth of R. Rhône; famous col. of flamingoes; a. 300 sq. m.

Camarihos Norte, *prov.*, Luzon, Philippine Is.; mtns. and fertile land; agr., minerals; cap. Daet; a. 829 sq. m.; p. (1960) 188,091.

Camas, t., Wash., U.S.A.; agr., pulp, paper, fruit canning; p. (1960) 5,666.

Cambay, G., separates Kathiawar peninsula from Gujerat st., India.

Camberwell, see Southwark.

Cambodia, *kingdom* (until 1969), proclaimed Khen

Republic (1970), S.E. Asia, between Thailand and S. Vietnam; former associate st. of Fr. Union; cap. Phnom-Penh on Mekong R.; mainly agr.; rice, rubber, maize, pepper, kapok, livestock; Great L., or Tonle Sap., impt. for fisheries; car assembly, cigarette makg., textiles, plywood, paper, tyres, cement; oil refinery nr. Kompong Som. a. 70,000 sq. m.; p. (estd. 1969) 7,000,000.

Camborne, t., Cornwall, Eng.; 11 m. S.W. Truro; old tin- and copper-mines; engin., radio-television assembly, textiles and chemicals; p. (Camborne-Redruth urb. dist.) (estd. 1967) 37,600.

Cambrai, t., Nord dep., France; on Schelde R.; linen, brewing, soap; p. (1954) 29,567.

Cambridge and Isle of Ely, co., Eng.; Rs. Ouse, Nen, Cam; wheat, oats, potatoes, fruit, dairying, light engin., light indus.; p. (1966) 294,000.

Cambridge, mun. bor., univ. c., co. t., Cambridge, Eng.; on Cam R.; famous univ. with residtl colleges; leading ctr. of research-based ind.; p. (estd 1969) 100,200.

Cambridge, c., Mass., U.S.A., 3 m. from Boston; seat of Harvard Univ.; mnftg.; impt. research ctr.; p. (1960) 107,716.

Cambuslang, par., Lanark, Scot.; turkey red dyeworks, hosiery, engin, plate mill; on Clyde R.; p. (1951) 26,861.

Camden, inner bor., N. London, Eng.; incorporating former bors. of Hampstead, Holborn and St. Pancras; p. (1966) 240,000.

Camden, mftg. and residtl. c. N.J., U.S.A.; on Delaware R., suburban and opposite Philadelphia; iron foundries, chemicals, glass, wireless sets, shipbldg.; p. (1960) 117,159.

Camden Town, industl. and residtl. dist., London, Eng.; N.E. of Regent's Park.

Camel, R., E. Cornwall, Eng.; length 30 m.

Camerino, c., Macerata, Central Italy, in Apennines; the ancient Camerium annexed to Papal States in 16th century; univ. cath.

Cameron, c., Texas, U.S.A.; p. (1960) 5,640.

Cameron Bay, t., N.W. Terr., Canada; by Gr. Bear Lake; radium.

Cameroons, British (North and South), former U.N. trust terrs. under British adm. (Northern part achieved independence as part of Nigeria (Sardauna prov.), and Southern part as part of Cameroun (Western prov.) (1961); a. 34,081 sq. m.; p. (estd 1960) 1,621,000.

Cameroun, Fed. Rep. of, ind. sovereign st. (Jan. 1960); comprises Eastern Cameroun (former U.N. trust terr. under French adm.) and Western Cameroun (former U.N. trust terr. under British adm.). Fed. cap. Yaoundé; timber, cocoa, palm kernels, palm oil, groundnuts, bananas, coffee; a. 183,000 sq. m.; p. (estd. 1968) 5,562,000.

Camiguin, I., Philippines; in Mindanao Sea; mtns.; sugar, rice, tobacco; a. 96 sq. m.; p. (1960) 11,000.

Campagna, Italy; malarial coastal plain round Rome; now being drained; new commune of Latina founded 1932.

Campania, region, S. Italy; ch. t. Naples; a. 5,250 sq. m.; p. (1961) 4,756,094.

Campaspe, R., Victoria, Australia; rises in Grampian Mtns., flows N. into R. Murray at Echuca; supplies water for irrigated area between Rochester and Echuca; length, 140 m.

Campbellton, t., spt., New Brunswick, Canada; lumbering, fishing; (1961) 9,873.

Campbelltown, t., N.S.W., Australia; dairy and poultry ctr.; proposed as satellite t. for Sydney; p. (1966) 22,812.

Campbeltown, burgh, spt., Argyll, Scot.; on Firth of Clyde cst. of peninsula of Kintyre; distilling, fishing; p. (1961) 6,525.

Campeche, st., Yucatan, Mexico; hot, flat and unhealthy; rice, cotton, logwood, chicle, sisal; a. 19,670 sq. m.; p. (1960) 168,219.

Campeche, cap. t. of st., spt., Mexico; on G. of Mexico; exp. logwood, sisal, hemp; p. (1960) 31,272. [lands; battle 1797.

Camperdown, vil. on dunes, N. Holland, Netherlands.

Campina Grande, t., Paraíba, Brazil; agr.; textiles, veg. oils; p. (estd. 1968) 157,149.

Campinas, t., Brazil; 55 m. N. of São Paulo; coffee; machin.; rubber gds.; p. (estd. 1968) 252,145.

Campine or Kempenland, dist., provs. Limburg and Antwerp, Belgium; coalfield.

Campo Belo, t., Minas Gerais st., Brazil; impt. cattle ctr.; p. (estd. 1968) 30,810.

Campobasso, prov., Italy; in Appenines; a. 1,692 sq. m.; p. (1961) 332,121.

Campobasso, fortfd. t., cap. t. 50 m. N.E. Naples, Italy; famous for cutlery and arms; p. (1961) 34,314.

Campobello di Licata, t., Sicily; sulphur-mines.

Campobello di Massara, t., Sicily; quarrying.

Campos, t., agr. ctr.; Rio de Janeiro, Brazil; sugar, cement; p. (estd. 1968) 389,045.

Campos do Jordão, t., Brazil; alt. 5,570 ft.; health resort, known as the Switzerland of Brazil; p. (estd. 1968) 19,676.

Campsie Fells, range of hills, Stirling, Scot.; highest point, 1,894 ft.

Campulung, t., Muscel, Romania; N.W. of Bucharest.; summer resort; p. (1963) 22,696.

Canada, Dominion of, N. America; dominion founded 1867, inc. twelve provinces; Nova Scotia, New Brunswick, Prince Edward I., Quebec, Ontario, Manitoba, Saskatchewan, Alberta, Brit. Columbia, Newfoundland with Labrador, Yukon and Northwest Territories (Franklin, Keewatin, Mackenzie); cap. Ottawa; Great Lakes; Rocky Mtns.; Great Plains; St. Lawrence, Saskatchewan, and Mackenzie Rs.; Trans-Canada Highway 4860 m. long runs from St. John's (Newfoundland) to Victoria (B.C.) opened 1962; extreme climate, Pacific seaboard mild; conniferous forest belt except for Central grass-lands, tundra in N.; agr.: wheat, oats, dairying; pulp, paper; coal, gold, copper, nickel, zinc, lead, radium, uranium; oil, natural gas; fisheries; furs; hydro-electric power; impt. mnfs.; a. 3,851,809 sq. m.; p. (estd. 1969) 21,007,000.

Canada Dam, Bihar, Indian Union; on R. Mayurakshi, 160 m. from Calcutta.

Canadian Coast Range, mtns., B.C., W. Canada; extend N.W. to S.E. along cst.; penetrated by deep inlets (fjords) with very little cst. plain; drained by short, swift Rs., crossed only by R. Skeena in N., R. Fraser in S., which give access to interior; marked climatic barrier, to W. equable climate with heavy all-year rain, to E. more extreme semi-arid climate, especially on valley floors.

Canadian R., trib. (flowing from New Mexico) of Arkansas R., U.S.A.; length 900 m.

Canal du Centre, canal, Saône-et-Loire dep., France; links Rhône-Saône valley at Chalonsur-Saône with R. Loire at Digoin; serves Le Creusot Coalfield; length 60 m.

Canal Zone, Panama; strip of land leased to U.S.A. for Panama Canal; a. 648 sq. m. (276 sq. m. water); p. (1960) 42,122.

Cananea, t., Mexico; cattle, copper, silver, lead, zinc; p. 11,006.

Cañar, prov., Ecuador; cap. Azogues; Inca remains; agr., Panama hats; a. 1,521 sq. m.; p. (estd. 1962) 112,618.

Canaries Current, ocean current; flows S. along N.W. cst. of Africa from Casablanca to C. Verde; relatively cold and has very marked cooling effect on Saharan coastlands.

Canary Is., or Canaries, N. Atl. Oc.; group of 7 Is. belonging to Spain, 60 m. off cst. Africa and 700 m. S. of Gibraltar; compr. Tenerife I., the lgst. (cap. Santa Cruz), Gran Canaria (cap. Las Palmas), Palma, Gomera, Hierro, Fuerteventura, Lanzarote; tropical produce: ch. exp. bananas, oranges, tomatoes, vegetables and tobacco; wine, cochineal; a. 4,685 sq. m.; p. (1962) 967.177.

Canastota, t., N.Y., U.S.A.; engin., furniture, plastics; p. (1960) 4,896.

Canberra, Australian Capital Territory, Australia; on Gr. Dividing Range (alt. c. 6,000 ft.) 200 m. S.W. of Sydney; seat of govt. of Commonwealth; univ.; 911 sq. m.; p. (of t. 1966) 92,199.

Cancale, t., Ille-et-Vilaine dep., N. France; St. Michael's Bay; oysters; p. (1954) 5,463.

Candia (Herakleion), c., Crete; midway along N. cst.; olive oil, raisins; p. (1961) 64,492.

Canea, see Khania.

Canelones, dep., Uruguay; wine; a. 1,834 sq. m.; p. (1953) 201,359.

Cañete, sm. spt., Lima dep., Peru, S. America; 75 m. S.E. of Callao; exp. cotton grown under irrigation in Canete valley.

Cangas de Onis, commune, Spain; agr., cattle; coal, copper, tanning; p. (1957) 10,713.

Cangas de Tineo, t., Oviedo, Spain; nr. N. cst., 35 m. E. of Oviedo; woollens, linens; p. (1957) 21,500.

Canicatti, *t.*, Sicily; sulphur; in fruit-growing dist.; p. *27,860.*

Canna, *sm. I.*, Hebrides, Scot.; basaltic pillars.

Cannanore, *t.*, Kerala, India; exp. timber, coconuts; p. (1961) *48,960.*

Cannet (Le), *t.*, Alpes-Maritimes, France; p. (1954) *11,601.*

Cannes, *spt..* dep. Alpes-Maritimes, France; 20 m. S.W. Nice; famous winter resort; perfumes; p. (1968) *67,152.*

Cannock and Hednesford, *urb. dist.*, Staffs, Eng., on S.W. flank of Cannock Chase, 7 m. N.E. of Wolverhampton; coal-mng., engin., bricks, tiles, tools, elec. goods, car parts; p. (estd. 1967) *52,030.*

Canonsburg, *bor.*, Penns., U.S.A.; coal, gas, oil; p. (1960) *11,877.*

Canopus, *anc. c.*, Lower U.A.R.; gr. temple to Serapis.

Canosa, *t.* Apulia, S. Italy; cath.; the Roman Canusium; ctr. of olive-growing dist.; p. *27,341.*

Cantabrians, *mtns.*, N. Spain, from Pyrenees to Cape Finisterre, hgst. pk. Peña Vieja (8,736 ft.).

Cantal, *mountainous dep.*, Central France; mineral springs, grain, dairying; coal, marble; cap. Aurillac; a. 2,229 sq. m.; p. (1968) *169,330.*

Canterbury, *c.*, *co. bor.*, Kent, Eng.; at foot of N. Downs on R. Stour; famous cath. founded A.D. 597 by St. Augustine; shrine of the murdered Thomas à Becket, a place of pilgrimage for centuries; univ.; fruit growing, tanning; p. (estd. 1969) *33,140.*

Canterbury, *prov.*, S.I., N.Z.; cap. Christchurch; a. 13,940 sq. m.; p. (1961) *339,883.*

Canterbury Plains, rich grazing and wheatgrowing dist. S.I., N.Z.; along E. cst., famous for " Canterbury Lamb "; ch. t. Christchurch; ch. pt. Lyttelton.

Can Tho, *t.*, S. Vietnam; on Mekong R.; rice, fish; tr. ctr.; p. *27,000.*

Canton (Guangzhou) *ch. c.*, Kwantung, S. China; on bank of Chu-kiang (Pearl R.); former treaty pt; impt. tr. ctr.; thermal power stas; machin. bldg. plant; p. (1957) *1,840,000.*

Canton, *t.*, Ill., U.S.A.; mnfs.; p. (1960) *13,588.*

Canton, *industl. and agr. c.*, Ohio, U.S.A.; coal, farm machin., engin.; p. (1960) *113,631.*

Canton R., *see* Chukiang.

Canvey I., *urb. dist.*, Essex; fronting the Thames; resort; radio components, bookbinding, iron and wire wk., oil storage; oil refinery projected; liquid gas terminal; p. (estd. 1967) *22,170.*

Cap-de-la-Madeleine, *t.*, Que., Canada; p. (1961) *26,925.*

Cap Haitien, *spt.*, Rep. of Haiti; on N. cst.; bombarded by British 1865; p. (1961) *24,959.*

Capannori, *t.*, Lucca, Italy; silk ind.; p. *39,527.*

Cape Breton I., Nova Scotia, E. Canada; farming, timber, fishing; ch. t. Sydney; a. 3,120 sq. m.

Cape Chidley, *I.* off N. point of Labrador.

Cape Coast, *t.*, Ghana; on cst. 60 m. S.W. of Accra; palm oil; p. (1960) *41,143.*

Cape Girardeau, *t.*, Mo., U.S.A.; p. (1960) *47,924.*

Cape Kennedy, E. Fla., U.S.A., on Atl. Oc., seaward extremity of barrier is. sheltering Bahama R. Lagoon; mil. base for testing missiles.

C. of Good Hope, S. Africa; famous headland, S. of Cape Town, 1,000 ft. high.

Cape Province (formerly **Cape of Good Hope Colony**), *prov.*, Rep. of S. Africa; physical features: Drakensberg Mtns., Orange and Caledon R., Gr. Karroo, Lit. Karroo; scanty rain except S. and E. cst.; sheep raising; wheat, citrus fruits, grapes, tobacco; fisheries; diamond and copper mng. in Namaqualand; automobile assembly, textiles, food canning; includes Transkeian terrs. in east.; a. 278,465 sq. m.; p. (1960) *5,362,853* incl. *1,003,207* whites.

Cape Town, *c.*, *spt.*, cap. of Cape Province, and legislative cap. of Rep. of S. Africa; on Table Bay, 30 m. N. of C. of Good Hope; communication by rail direct with Rhodesia, Transvaal, Orange and Natal; docks; cath.; univ.; exp. wool, gold, diamonds; oil refinery under construction at Milnerton 6 m. N.E., p. (1960) *745,942* (inc. *286,418* Whites).

C. Verde Islands, Portuguese Is., in Atlantic, 350 m. W. of C. Verde, Africa; divided into two groups, Barlavento (Windward) and Sotavento (Leeward); 15 Is. and islets; a. 1,516 sq. m.; agr., sugar, and fruit-growing; cap. Praia; São Vicente coaling sta. for all navigation to S. America; p. (estd. 1968) *245,000.*

Capernaum, in time of Christ impt. place in Palestine, on the N. shore of the L. of Galilee; the modern **Tell Hum** (Israel).

Capo d'Istria, *see* Koper.

Cappoquin, *t.*, Waterford, R.o.I, on Blackwater R.

Capraja, Italian I. in the Mediterranean, 16 m. E. Corsica; anciently called Capraria.

Caprera, Italian I. off N.E. Sardinia, where Garibaldi lived.

Caprese, *commune*, Tuscany, Italy; birthplace of Michelangelo; p. *3,195.*

Capri, *I.* and *t.*, in Bay of Naples; tourist resort; residence of Augustus and Tiberius; the ancient Caprae; famous Blue Grotto; fine wines; p. (*t.*) *4,500*; (*I.*) *8,050.*

Capua, *ancient fort. c.*, Campania, Italy; 20 m. N. of Naples; founded by the Etruscans, came under Roman rule, sacked by the Saracens; modern t. 2 m. N. of site of ancient Casilinum; fireworks-mkg.; cath.; p. *14,375.*

Carácas, *cap.*, Venezuela; 8 m. inland from its pt., La Guaira; alt. about 3,000 ft.; cath.; univ.; coffee, cacao, textiles, soaps, detergents, steel, car assembly; underground rly. projected; p. (1961) *739,255.*

Caravaca, *t.*, Murcia, Spain; iron, tanning; p. (1957) *21,700.*   [(1957) *20,965.*

Carballo, *t.*, Corunna, Spain; industl.; fishing; p.

Carbon County, N. Utah, U.S.A.; contains immense reserves of good coking coal suitable for blast furnaces; not yet developed.

Carbondale, *t.*, Penns., U.S.A.; anthracite; p. (1960) *13,595.*

Carbonia, *t.*, Sardinia; built 1937–38 nr. lignite and barite area; p. *12,000.*

Carcagente, *t.*, W. of Cullera, Valencia, Spain; oranges; p. (1955) *18,002.*

Carcar, *t.*, Cebu, Philippine Is.; sugar ind.; p. (1948) *32,318.*

Carcassonne, *t.*, Aude, France; on Aude R.; historic citadel guarding impt. routeway from Aquitaine to Rhône valley; farm implements; wines, cloth; p. (1962) *43,709.*

Carchi, *prov.*, Ecuador; cap. Tulcan; a. 1,495 sq. m.; p. (1962) *93,824.*

Cardamon Hills, Travancore, S. India; forms extreme S.W. edge of Deccan plateau; drained W. by R. Periyan, E. by R. Vaigai; rainfall less seasonal than over most of India; "China" tea plantations on middle slopes; rise to over 8,000 ft. alt.

Cárdenas, *t.*, Matanzas, Cuba; sugar, rice, rum; p. (1953) *47,750.*

Cardiff, *cap. c.*, *spt.*, *co. bor.*, Glamorgan, Wales; univ.; docks, coal, iron, steel, engin., elect. goods, brewing, paper; p. (estd. 1968) *287,000.*

Cardigan, *mun. bor.*, *co. t.*, Cardigan, S. Wales; on Teifi R.; p. (1961) *3,730.*   [N. and S.

Cardigan Bay, *lge. bay*, W. Wales, 70 m. extent

Cardiganshire, *maritime co.*, S. Wales; mountainous; mainly agr., mines and quarries; a. 692 sq. m.; p. (1966) *53,000.* [oil refining.

Cardón, *t.*, N. Venezuela, Paraguaná peninsula;

Cardross, *industl. vil.*, Dunbarton, Scot.; on R. Clyde; Robert Bruce d. 1329 in Cardross Castle.

Cardwell, *t.*, Queensland, Australia; harbour; gold-mining dist.   [(1960) *3,722.*

Carey, *t.*, Ohio, U.S.A.; mkt. gardening; p.

Cargenbridge, *t.*, Kirkcudbright, Scot.; chemicals, plastics.

Caribbean Sea, between W. Indies and Central and S. America; a. 7,500 sq. m.

Caribou Range, *mtns.*, B.C., W. Canada; mass of ancient crystalline rocks inside the gr. bend of R. Frazer; widespread occurrence of lode and alluvial gold; mainly above 5,000 ft.

Caribou, *t.*, Maine, U.S.A.; p. (1960) *8,305.*

Carlbrod, *t.*, Jugoslavia; on Nisava R.; p. *4,000.*

Carimata I., off S.W. Borneo, Indonesia.

Carinthia, *prov.*, Austria; cap. Klagenfurt; mtnous.; mineral springs; rye, oats; lead, iron; a. 3,681 sq. m.; p. (1961) *495,226.*

Carisbrooke, *t.*, I. of Wight, Eng.; cas. prison of Charles I (1647–8); p. (1951) *5,232.*

Carlingford, *t.*, *spt.*, Louth, Ireland; on Carlingford Bay; oysters.   [Louth. Ireland.

Carlingford, Lough, *inlet* of sea between Down and

Carlinville, *t.*, Ill., U.S.A.; bricks and tiles, agr. machin.; p. (1960) *5,440.*

Carlisle, *t.*, *co. bor.*, Cumberland, Eng.; on Eden R.; 8 m. from Solway Firth; impt. route ctr.; ancient cas. and cath.; textiles, biscuits, metal boxes; p. (estd. 1967) *70,950.*

Carlisle, *bor.*, Penns., U.S.A.; boots and shoes; p. (1960) *16,623*.

Carlow, *co.*, Leinster, Ireland; co. t., Carlow; a. 346 sq. m.; p. (1966) *33,479*.

Carlsbad, *see* Karlovy Vary.

Carlsbad, *t.*, N.M., U.S.A.; p. (1960) *25,541*.

Carlsbad Cavern, N.M., U.S.A.; gr. cave in limestone through which flows R. Pecos; stalactites, stalagmites; tourist attraction; length 4,000 ft., width 600 ft., height of roof 300 ft.

Carlsruhe, *see* Karlsruhe. [p. (1960) *6,042*.

Carlstadt, *bor.*, N.J., U.S.A.; brass, marble;

Carlton, *urb. dist.*, Notts. Eng.; 2 m. N.E. of Nottingham; lace, hosiery; p. (estd. 1967) *41,660*.

Carluke, *t.*, *par.*, Lanark, Scot.; engin., mng., fruit growing and preserving; p. (1951) *11,415*.

Carmagnola, *mftg. t.*, N. Italy; on Melba R.; p. *12,241*.

Carmarthen, *mun. bor.*, *co. t.*, Carmarthenshire, Wales; on Towy R.; anthracite, limestone quarrying; p. (1961) *13,249*.

Carmarthen Bay, Carmarthen, Wales; 18 m. across.

Carmarthenshire, *co.*, S. Wales; co. t., Carmarthen; mountainous; mining; mainly pastoral land; a. 920 sq. m.; p. (1966) *166,000*.

Carmaux, *t.*, Tarn, France; glass mftg.; p. (1954) *11,485*.

Carmel, Mt., *mtn.*, N.W. Israel; extends 12 m. to Med.; hgst. peak, 1,818 ft.; in biblical times ass. with prophets Elijah and Elisha.

Carmen de Bolivar, *spt.*, Campeche Bay, Mexico.

Carmiel *c.*, N. Israel; new t. built between Acre and Safad, in the Galilean hills; planned for p. *50,000*. [(1957) *27,115*.

Carmona. *t.*, Spain; olives, wine, fruit; p.

Carnac, *vil.*, Morbihan, N.W. France; S.E. of Lorient; prehistoric stone monuments and circles.

Carnarvon, *t.*, W. Australia; on R. Gascoyne; NASA tracking sta.; p. *4,000*.

Carnatic, *region*, S.E. India, between E. Ghats and Coromandel cst. where earliest European settlements were established. [(1960) *11,387*.

Carnegie, *bor.*, Penns., U.S.A.; steel, iron; p.

Carnew, *vil.*, Wicklow, Ireland; granite, slate.

Carnforth, *t.*, *urb. dist.*, Lancs, Eng.; rly. ctr.; p. (1961) *4,113*.

Carnoustie, *burgh*, Angus, Scot., on N. Sea; 6 m. S.W. of Arbroath; resort; p. (1961) *5,511*.

Carnsore Point, S. Wexford, Ireland.

Carntogher Mtns., *range of mtns.*, Londonderry, N. Ireland.

Carnwath, *vil.*, Lanark, Scot.; coal, shale, iron.

Caro, *t.*, Mich., U.S.A.; sugar-beet refining; p. (1960) *3,534*.

Carolina, *see* N. and S. Carolina.

Caroline Is., *archipelago* in W. Pac. Oc.; 549 in number, lying between the Philippines and the Marshall Gr., former Japanese mandate now part of U.S. Pac. Trust Terr.; ch. exp. copra.

Caroni R., Venezuela, S. America; hydro-elec. complex at confluence Orinoco R. under constr.

Carpathian Mtns., *range* separating Czechoslovakia and Hungary from Galicia, and Transylvania from Moldavia, 805 m. long; highest point, Tatra 8,740 ft.

Carpentaria, G. of, North Australia; between C. Arnhem and C. York.

Carpentras, *c.*, Vaucluse, France; on R. Auzon; many antiquities; p. (1954) *15,076*.

Carpi, *industl. t.*, Modena, Central Italy; cath.; p. (1961) *45,208*.

Carrantuohill Mtn., Kerry, Ireland; loftiest in Magillicuddy's Reeks and all Ireland, alt. 3,414 ft.

Carrara, *t.*, Massa-e-Carrara, Central Italy; famed for white marble; p. (1961) *64,901*.

Carrickfergus, *spt.*, *mun. bor.*, Antrim, N. Ireland; on N. shore of Belfast Lough; textiles, nylon fibres, tobacco inds.; p. (1966) *10,926*.

Carrickmacross, *mkt. t.*, *urb. dist.*, Monaghan, Ireland; hand made lace; p. (1966) *2,094*.

Carrick-on-Shannon, *co. t.*, *rural dist.*, Leitrim, Ireland; p. (of t.) (1966) *1,636*.

Carrick-on-Suir, *mkt. t.*, *urb. dist.*, Tipperary, Ireland; coal, timber; p. (1966) *4,830*.

Carrizal-Bajo, *t.*, Atacama prov., Chile; port for Carrizal-Alto, 25 m. E. [10,973.

Carrollton, *t.*, Ga., U.S.A.; textiles; p. (1960)

Carron, *vil.*, Stirling, Scot.; nr. Falkirk; famous ironwks.

Carron, Loch, *inlet*, W. cst., Ross and Cromarty, Scot.; followed by rly. from Dingwall to Kyle and Lochalsh.

Carse of Gowrie, Perth, Scot.; fertile cstl. dist. between Perth and Dundee, S. of Sidlaw Hills; sm. fruits, especially raspberries.

Carshalton, *see* Sutton.

Carson City, *st. cap.*, Nevada, U.S.A.; silver- and gold-mining dist.; p. (1960) *5,163*.

Cartagena, *spi.*, *cap.*, dep. Bolivar, Colombia, S. America; shares with Barranquilla tr. brought down Magdalena R.; platinum, coffee, chemicals, textiles, fertilisers; oil pipe terminal; p. (estd. 1962) *185,160*.

Cartagena, *spt.*, Murcia, E. Spain; fine wharves and harbour; naval arsenal; cath.; shipbldg., metal-wkg.; p. (1959) *123,301*.

Cartago, *t.*, Cauca, Colombia, S. America; coffee, tobacco, cattle; p. (estd. 1959) *64,830*.

Cartago, *prov.*, Costa Rica, Central America; cap. C.; coffee, fruits; p. (1963) *154,500*.

Carteret, *bor.*, N.J., U.S.A.; metal and oil refining, chemicals, tobacco; p. (1960) *20,502*.

Carter Fell, *mtn.*, a summit of the Cheviot hills, on the Eng./Scot. border, 1,815 ft.

Carthage, *c.*, N.E. Tunis, N. Africa; ruins of ancient Carthage, destroyed by Romans 146 B.C.

Carthage, *t.*, Mo., U.S.A.; coal; p. (1960) *11,264*.

Cartmel, *par.*, Lancs, Eng.; near Ulverston.

Carupano, *spt.*, Venezuela, S. America; exp. coffee, cacao; airport; p. (1961) *30,000*.

Carvine, *t.*, Pas-de-Calais, France; p. (1954) *15,780*.

Casablanca, autonomous c., Morocco, N. Africa; motor plant; p. (1960) *965,277*.

Casablanca, *t.*, Valparaiso, Chile.

Casa Branca, *t.*, S.E. of Lisbon, Portugal.

Casale, *t.*, Piedmont, Italy; cath.; cement; p. (1961) *40,827*.

Casalmaggiore, *t.*, Italy; on R. Po, near Parma.

Casas Grandes, *t.*, N.W. Chihuahua st., Mexico; Aztec ruins; p. *2,000*.

Cascade Range, N. America; extends N. and S. through Brit. Columbia, Washington and Oregon between Rocky Mtns. and Pacific cst. Highest peak, Mt. Rainier, 14,408 ft.

Cascade Tunnel, longest rly. tunnel in N. America, Wash., U.S.A.; carries trunk rly. from Spokane to Seattle through Cascade Mtns.; length 7¾ m.

Cascina, *t.*, Pisa, Italy; on R. Arno; silk mnfs.

Caserta, *t.*, Italy; on N. edge of Plain of Naples; royal palace; cath.; silks; p. (1961) *50,810*.

Cashel, *c.*, *urb. dist.*, Tipperary, Ireland; cath. (ruined) on Rock of Cashel; p. (1966) *2,682*.

Casino, *t.*, N.S.W., Australia; ctr. for mkt., forestry and meat processing; p. (1966) *8,498*.

Casiquiare, R., Venezuela, joins Orinoco to the Rio Negro, a trib. of the Amazon.

Caspe, *t.*, Spain; on R. Guadalupe; p. *9,033*.

Casper, *t.*, Wyo., U.S.A.; petroleum; p. (1960) *38,930*.

Caspian Sea, *salt lake*, U.S.S.R. and Iran; a. 163,800 sq. m.; between Europe and Asia; lgst inland sea in world; 92 ft. below sea surface; max. depth 3,200 ft. in S.; fisheries; pts. Astrakan (mouth of Volga), Baku (oil ctr.), Derbent.

Casquets, *dangerous rocks*, 7 m. W. of Alderney. Channel Is.; lighthouse.

Cassaba (Kassaba), *see* Turgutlu.

Cassel, *t.*, *see* Kassel.

Cassilis, *t.*, N.S.W., Australia; 115 m. N.W. of Newcastle in impt. gap in Gr. Dividing Range between Hunter and Liverpool Ranges, giving access from Newcastle to interior.

Cassino, *t.*, Campania, Italy; formerly San Germano; the ancient Casinum nr. famous monastery.

Castelbuono, *t.*, Sicily; mineral springs.

Castelfiorentino, *t.*, Tuscany, nr. Florence, Italy; light inds.

Castelfranco, *t.*, Treviso, Italy; fine church and paintings; silk; p. *4,240*.

Castel Gandolfo, *t.*, Central Italy, in Alban Hills; papal summer residence; p. (estd.) *5,000*.

Castellamare, *dockyard t.*, Italy; on Bay of Naples at foot of Vesuvius; mineral springs; wat. pl.; p. (1961) *64,618*.

Castellamare del Golfo, *spt.*, N.W. Sicily; wat. pl., tuna fishing; p. *18,032*.

Castellón de la Plana, *prov.*, Spain; on Mediterranean, part of ancient Valencia, mainly mtns., a. 2,579 sq. m.; cap. Castellón; p. (1959) *334,472*.

Castellón de la Plana, *t.*, Spain; porcelain, oranges, carob-wood, onions, wines; oil refining; p. (1959) *57,780.*

Castelnaudary, *t.*, Aude, France, on Languedoc canal, burned by Black Prince, 1355; p. (1954) *8,760.*

Castelo Branco, *c.*, Portugal; *cap.* of dist. same name; p. of dist. (1960) *325,800.*

Castelvetrano, *t.*, Sicily, Italy; industl.; wine; p. *24,746.*

Castiglione, *t.*, Sicily, Italy; near Catania; sulphur refining.

Castiglione Fiorentino, *t.*, Italy; nr. Arezzo; sericulture.

Castile, formerly a kingdom of Spain; now div. into Old and New Castile.

Castine, *t.*, Me., U.S.A.; on Penobscot Bay; resort; fishing.

Castlebar, *urb. dist., cap.*, Mayo, Ireland; " Race of Castlebar " battle fought here in 1798 Rebellion; bacon curing, hat-mkg.; p. (1966) *5,630.*

Castleblayney, *urb. dist.*, Monaghan, Ireland; nr. Dundalk; p. (1961) *2,125.*

Castle Cary, *mkt. t.*, Somerset, Eng.; N.E. of Yeovil; dairying; p. (1951) *1,664.*

Castlecary, *vil.*, Stirlingshire, Scot.; sta. on Roman wall; silica, fire-clay deposits.

Castlecomer, *rural dist.*, N. Kilkenny, Ireland; p. (1961) *7,328.*

Castle Donington, *t.*, *rural dist.*, Leics. Eng.; p. (of dist. 1961) *9,809.*

Castle Douglas, *burgh*, Kirkcudbright, Scot.; 15 m. S.W. of Dumfries; cattle fairs; p. (1961) *3,253.*

Castleford, *mun. bor.*, W.R. Yorks, Eng.; 10 m. S.E. of Leeds at confluence of Rs. Aire and Calder; coal-mng., chemical, glass and clothing mnfs., flour-milling, brick-mkg.; p. (estd. 1967) *39,630.*

Castleisland, *t.*, Kerry, Ireland; agr. ctr.; p. (1966) *1,673.*

Castlemaine, *t.*, Victoria, Australia; at foot of Gr. Dividing Range, 25 m. S. of Bendigo; dairying, sheep; engin; wool; p. (1966) *7,082.*

Castlerea, *rural dist.*, Roscommon, Ireland; p. (of dist.) (1961) *13,337.*

Castletown, *t.*, Isle of Man; former cap.; p. (1956) *1,755.*

Castletown Berehaven, *spt.*, Cork, Ireland; on Bantry Bay.

Castres, *t.*, Tarn, France; on R. Agoût; former Huguenot stronghold; cath.; textiles, soap, earthenware; p. (1962) *40,005.*

Castries, *cap., spt.*, St. Lucia, Windward Is., W.I.; greatly damaged by fire June 1948; fine harbour; p. (1957) *25,000.*

Castro del Río, *t.*, Andalusia, Spain; on R. Guadjo; industl.; p. (1957) *14,126.*

Castrogiovanni, see Enna.

Castrop-Rauxel or **Kastrop Rauxel**, *t.*, N. Rhine-Westphalia, Germany; industl.; coal, cement, tar prod., tiles, brandy; p. (1963) *88,500.*

Castro Urdiales, *spt.*, Santander, N. Spain; sardines, iron ore; p. (1957) *11,646.*

Castrovillari, *hill t.*, S. Italy; built on cliff above R. Coscile; mkt. ctr. for local cereals, wine, oil and silkworms; p. (estd.) *10,000.*

Cat I. (or **Guanahani**), Bahamas, W. Indies; a. 340 sq. m.; p. (1953) *3,201.*

Catacaos, *t.*, Piura dep., Peru; Panama hats.

Catalonia, *old prov.*, N.E. Spain; mountainous; wooded; cereals; mnfs.; cottons, woollens, silks; rich in minerals; cap. Barcelona; nuclear power sta. projected; a. 12,427 sq. m.; p. (1957) *3,240,000.*

Catamarca, *prov.*, N.W. Argentina; cap. C.; farming; gold, silver, copper mng.; a. 40,942 sq. m.; p. (1960) *172,000.*

Catamarca, *t., cap.*, Catamarca prov., N.W. Argentina; located in Andean foot-hills 80 m. S. of Tucuman; ctr. of irrigated oasis producing vines, apricots, cherries, cotton; thermal springs; p. (1960) *29,000.*

Catanduanes, *I.*, off Luzon, Philippines; hilly, fertile; rice, corn, cotton, hemp, coconuts; a. 552 sq. m.; p. (1960) *1,563,000.*

Catania, *prov.*, Sicily; ch. t.. Catania; a. 1907 sq. m.; p. (1961) *884,447.*

Catania, *c.*, Sicily; on E. cst. at foot of Mt. Etna; city several times rebuilt in consequence of earthquakes; cath.; univ.; textiles, dyeing; p. (1965) *396,000.*

Catanzaro, *c.*, S. Italy; univ.; silks, velvets; p. 961) *72,723.*

Catasauqua, *bor.*, Penns., U.S.A.; industl.; flour, cement, textiles; p. (1960) *5,062.*

Catastrophe, *C.*, S. extremity of Eyre Peninsula, S. Australia.

Catawba, *R.*, N.C., U.S.A.; rising in Blue Ridge Range; length 300 m.

Caterham and **Warlingham**, *urb. dist.*, Surrey, Eng.; on N. Downs; residtl.; p. (estd. 1967) *36,910.*

Cathay, ancient name for China and E. Tartary.

Catoche, *C.*, N.E. point of Yucatan, Mexico.

Catrine, *t.*, Ayr, Scot.; mftg.

Catskill Mtns., N.Y., U.S.A.; gr. in Appalachians, W. of Hudson R.; holiday resort.

Cauca, *I.*, Colombia; trib. of Magdalena; length 600 m.

Cauca, *dep.*, Colombia Rep.; cap. Popayán; a. 11,657 sq. m.; p. (1962) *529,040.*

Caucasia, region between Black Sea and Caspian, divided by Caucasus Mtns. into N. or Cis-Caucasia and Trans-Caucasia.

Caucasus, *lofty mtn. range* between Caspian and Black Sea; highest summits Mt. Elbruz (18,463 ft.) and Kasbek (16,546 ft.); length of system about 950 m., greatest width 120 m.; many lofty passages and lge. glaciers.

Caudebec, *ancient t.*, Seine-Maritime, France; oil refinery nearby; p. (1962) *9,270.*

Cauderan, *commune*, Gironde, France; sub. of Bordeaux; p. (1954) *26,548.*

Caudete, *t.*, Albacete, Spain; p. (1957) *7,862.*

Caudry, *t.*, Nord, France; lace and tulle; p. (1962) *13,475.*   [12,987.

Cauquenes, *t.*, Chile; cap. of Maule prov.; p.

Causses, Les, *limestone plateau*, Aveyron, Tarn deps., S. France; on S.W. flank of Central Plateau; caverns, gorges of Rs. Lot and Tarn; sheep provide milk for Roquefort cheese; alt. 3,000–5,000 ft.

Cauterets, *vil.*, dep. Hautes-Pyrénées, France; mineral springs.

Cautin, *prov.*, S. Chile; cap. Temuco; a. 6,705 sq. m.; p. (1960) *475,121.*

Cauvery, *R.*, S. India; rises in the W. Ghats, flows into Bay of Bengal through Mysore and Madras; length 400 m.

Cava or **La Cava**, *t.*, Salerno, Italy; summer resort; textiles; p. (1961) *42,235.*

Cavaillon, *commune*, Vaucluse, France; cath.; p. (1962) *17,218.*

Cavan, *inland co.*, Ulster, Ireland; a. 746 sq. m.; agr.; distilling; p. (1966) *53,815.*

Cavan, *urb. dist., co. t.*, Cavan, Ireland; 72 m. S.W. Belfast; p. (1966) *4,165.*

Cavarzere, *t.*, Venice, N. Italy; on R. Adige; industl.; p. *22,821.*

Cavite, *spt.*, Luzon, Philippines; oil refining nearby; p. (1960) *54,891.*

Cavour Canal, *irrigation canal*, Piedmont and Lombardy regions, N. Italy; links R. Po nr. Chivassa with R. Ticino 10 m. N.E. of Novara; provides water for 250,000 acres of rice-fields and meadow-land; length 80 m.

Cawnpore (Kanpur), *cap.*, Cawnpore dist., Uttar Pradesh. India; on the Ganges; 130 m. N.W of Allahabad; grain, cotton, woollens, aircraft mftg.; p. (1961) *947,793.*

Caxias, *t.*, Maranhão, Brazil; on Itapecuru R.; cotton, rice; p. (1960) *60,607.*

Cayambe, *mtn.*, Andes, Ecuador; alt. 19,535 ft.

Cayenne, *spt., cap.*, Fr. Guiana, S. America; famous for pepper; p. (estd. 1965) *19,000.*

Cayey, *t.*, S.E. Puerto Rico; tobacco, coffee, sugar; p. *5,622.*

Cayman Is., West Indies, a. 100 sq. m.; p. (estd.) *10,000*; consists of Grand Cayman, cap. George-town; Little Cayman; and Cayman Brac; turtle and shark fishing.

Cazalla de la Sierra, S.W. Spain; iron and lead; aniseed; p. (1957) *11,347.*

Ceará, *st.*, N. Brazil; sugar, cotton, coffee, fishing, handicrafts; cap. Fortaleza; uranium and copper deposits; 57,173 sq. m.; p. (estd. 1968) *3,838,329.*

Cebu, *I.*, Philippines; mtnous, forested; copper, cement; a. 1,702 sq. m.; p. (1960) *1,185,600.*

Cebu, *ch. t.*, Cebu I., trade ctr. of Visayan Is.; p. (estd.) *310,000.*

Cedar or **Red Cedar**, *R.*, Iowa, U.S.A.; trib. of Mississippi R., length 400 m.

Cedar Falls, *t.*, Iowa, U.S.A.; p. (1960) *21,195.*

Cedar Mountain, *hill*, Va., U.S.A.; here Stonewall Jackson defeated Banks 1862.

Cedar Rapids, c., Iowa, U.S.A.; rly. ctr.; farm machin., lumber; p. (1960) 92,035.

Cedartown, t., Ga., U.S.A.; textiles, rubber tyres; cottonseed oil; p. (1960) 9,340.

Cedros, I., off W. coast, Lower Cal., Mexico.

Cefalù, spt., Palermo, N. Sicily; famous Norman cath. with mosaics; vines, oranges; fishing; p. c. 13,000.

Ceglie, c., Lecce, S. Italy; wine. olive oil, building stone; p. c. 21,000.

Cehegin, t., Murcia. Spain; on R. Quipar; p. (1957) 15,330.

Celaya, t., Guanajuato, Mexico; ctr. rich farming a.; many inds.; p. c. 35,000.

Celebes, see Sulawesi.

Celina, t., W. Ohio, U.S.A.; resort; furniture, canning; p. (1960) 7,659.

Celje, t., Slovenia, Jugoslavia; lignite, zinc smelting; p. (1960) 29,000.

Celle, t., Lower Saxony, Germany; on R. Aller; former residence of the Dukes of Brunswick-Lüneburg; cas.; metal, leather, paints, textiles, oil; p. (1963) 59,000.

Cenis, Mont, see Mont Cenis.

Cento, t., Ferrara, Italy; industl.; p. 4,942.

Central African Republic, ind. sov. st. within French Community, Equatorial Africa; cap. Bangui; a. 234,000 sq. m.; p. (1968) 2,256,000.

Central America, between Mexico and S. America, from the Isthmus of Tehuantepec to that of Panama; includes Guatemala, Honduras, Nicaragua, Salvador, Costa Rica, Panama, Brit. Honduras; tropical climate; forests, savannahs p. (estd. 1965) 30,000,0 0.

Central Asia, usually applied to regions between 30° and 40° N. lat. and 55° and 85° E. long.; Russian C.A. is the land between China and Afghanistan and the Caspian, now consisting of various Soviet Reps.

Central Falls, c., Rhode Is., U.S.A.; nr. Pawtucket; cotton goods; p. (1960) 19,858.

Central Greece and Euboea, geographical div., Greece; contains the cap. Athens; a. 9,704 sq. m.; p. (1961) 2,823,658.

Central Province, prov., Iran, cap. Tehran; p. (1967) 4,950,394.

Centralia, t., Ill., U.S.A.; p. (1960) 13,904.

Cephalonia, see Kephallenia.

Ceram (Serang), I., Moluccas, Indonesia; a. c. 7,191 sq. m.; copra, resin, sago, fish; p. (incl. offshore Is.) 720,000.

Ceres, t., Cape Province, S. Africa; on R. Hex; health resort; p. (1960) 6,173.

Cerignola, t., Foggia, Italy; Spanish victory over French 1503; p. (1961) 49,287.

Cerigo, see Kythera.

Cernauti, see Chernovtsy.

Cernavoda, t., Dobruja, Romania; on R. Danube, 70 m. S. of Braila; p. (1956) 3,302.

Cerro de Pasco, t., dep. Junin, Peru; silver, coal, lead; copper smelting; large vanadium mines W. of t.; p. (1961) 19,354.

Cerro Rico, mtn., Bolivia; in Andes, W. of Potosí; alt. 15,680 ft.; v. rich silver, tin, tungsten ores.

Certaldo, commune, Firenze, Italy; anc. cas.; home of Boccaccio; p. 12,094.

Cesena, old industl., t., Forli, Italy; cath.; antiquities; sulphur-mines, wines; p. (1961) 79,704.

Ceská Lipa, t., ČSSR.; on R. Plouenice N. of Prague; industl.; p. (1961) 14,038.

Ceská Trebová, old t., ČSSR.; W. of Pardubice; engin., textiles; p. (1961) 13,031.

Ceské Budejovice, t., ČSSR.; on R. Vltava 80 m. S. of Prague; pencils, porcelain, brewing, anthracite; p. (1961) 63,949.

Cesky Tesin, (Teschen), Silesia, ČSSR., (divided between Poland and Czechoslovakia); coal and ironwks.; p. (1961) 15,508.

Cessnock, t., N.S.W., Australia; coal-mining declining 1968; clothing wks.; p. (1966) 15,329 inc. Bellbird.

Cette, see Sète.

Ceuta, spt., Morocco; opposite to and 16 m. from Gibraltar; cath.; the ancient Abyla, one of the Pillars of Hercules; p. (1950) 59,936.

Cévennes, mtns., S. France; separating basins of Rhône, Loire and Tarn; highest point Mt. Mézenc, alt. 5,794 ft.

Ceylon, I., indep. sov. st. within Br. Commonwealth (1948); in Indian Ocean, S.E. of India; fertile plains, mountainous interior; principal prod.: rice, rubber, tea, coconuts, fruits and spices; rubber tyres and tubes, hardware, tiles;

cap. and ch. spt. Colombo; steel mill at Oruwala; a. 25,332 sq. m.; p. (estd.) 11,964,000.

Chacaburo, t., E. Argentina; agr. ctr.; p. 15,000.

Chachapoyas, t., cap. of Amazonas dep., N. Peru; agr., forest prod.; p. (1946) 5,494.

Chaco, terr., N. of Argentina; part of Gran Chaco; farming and prairie land; cap. Resistencia; a. 38,468 sq. m.; p. (1960) 535,000.

Chad, L., lge sheet of water of N. Central Africa; a. 50,000 sq. m. when in flood, varies in extent with season, and is drying up, shallow, many Is., lies between the wooded region of the Sudan and the steppes leading to the Sahara desert.

Chad, ind. sov. st. within French Community, Equatorial Africa; cap. Fort Lamy; a. 488,000 sq. m.; p. (estd. 1968) 3,460,000.

Chadderton, urb. dist., Lancs. Eng.; cotton and chemical mftg.; p. (estd. 1967) 31,880.

Chagford, par., Devon, Eng.; stone circles.

Chagos, Is., Indian Ocean; administered from Mauritius; fine harbour in Diego Garcia.

Chagres, spt., Panama, S. America; on N. side of Isthmus of Panama; p. 1,300.

Chaguaramas, Trinidad, W.I., part of naval base leased to U.S.A. since 1941.

Chahar Mahal Bakhtiiyari, region, Iran; W. of Isfahan; mainly mtnous.; cap. Sharkord; a. 6,072 sq. m.; p. (1967) 209,057.

Chakray-Ting, t., Cambodia; cement plant.

Chalcidice, see Khalkidhiki.

Chalcis, t., Euboea, Greece; p. (1961) 24,745.

Chaleur Bay, Canada; between N. Brunswick and Gaspé Peninsula, Quebec.

Chalon-sur-Saône, ancient industl. c., Saône-et-Loire, E. France; glass, iron; p. (1962) 45,993.

Châlons-sur-Marne, c., Marne, N.E. France; 20 m. E. of Epernay; cath.; military ctr.; brewery ind.; p. (1962) 45,348. [11,473.

Chamalières, t., Puy-de-Dôme, France; p. (1954)

Chaman, t., Baluchistan, Pakistan; on Afghan frontier; terminus of rly. through Quetta.

Chamba, t., Himachal Pradesh, India; 100 m. N.E. of Amritsar; p. (1961) 3,609.

Chambal, R., trib. of R. Jumna rising in Vindhya hills; length 650 m.

Chambersburg, bor., Penns., U.S.A.; foundries, brewing; p. (1960) 17,670.

Chambéry, t., cap., Savoie, S.E. France; silk, leather; p. (1962) 47,447. [wines.

Chambolle-Musigny, commune, Côte d'Or, France;

Chambon-Feugerolles, t., Loire, France; coal, iron, steel mftg.; p. (1954) 17,695.

Chamonix, t., Haute-Savoie, France; at foot of Mont Blanc, in valley of R. Arve; winter sports ctr.; road tunnel links to Aosta; p. (1954) 5,699.

Champagne, old prov., N.E. France; famous for its wine; wheat, sheep, impt. tr. fairs in Middle Ages.

Champagne Humide, natural division (" pays "), Central France; clay vale, runs 100 m. N.E. from Auxerre to Bar-le-Duc; drained by Seine, Aube, Marne, Aisne and many tribs.; heavily wooded, marshy; where cleared and drained, grain cultivation.

Champagne Pouilleuse, natural division (" pays "), Central France; barren chalk plateau, extends 80 m. N.E. from Sens to Reims; drained by Aisne, Vesle, Seine, Aube, Marne; dusty downland pastures; sheep; vine growing on S.-facing valley sides and S.E.-facing escarpment of Falaise de l'Ile de France favours production of Champagne wines, ch. producing ctrs.; Châlons-sur-Marne, Reims, Epernay.

Champaign, t., Ill., U.S.A.; foundries; p. (1960) 49,583.

Champerico, spt., S.W. Guatemala; coffee.

Champigny-sur-Marne, t., Seine, France; embroidery; piano keys; p. (1962) 57,925.

Champlain, L., U.S.A.; N. frontier of N.Y., state; discharges by Richelieu R. into St. Lawrence; flanked by trunk route from New York to Montreal; a. 600 sq. m.

Champlain Canal, N.Y. U.S.A.; follows gap between Adirondack Mtns. and Green Mtns. occupied by Hudson R.; links Albany with L. Champlain and allows through barge traffic between New York and St. Lawrence valley.

Chanaral, spt., N. Atacama, Chile; lies in gold and copper mng. ctr.; p. (1960) 21,098.

Chancelade, commune, Dordogne, France; arch. type-site of Chancelade culture (late paleolithic).

Chanda, *t.*, Nagpur, Maharashtra, India; ancient temples; p. (1961) *51,484*.

Chanda, *dist.*, Maharashtra, India; teak forests, coal, iron; a. 9,200 sq. m.; p. (1961) *1,238,070*.

Chandausi, *t.*, Uttar Pradesh, India; cotton, hemp; rly. ctr.; p. (1961) *48,557*.

Chandernagore, *t.*, W. Bengal, India; on Hooghly R.; French 1816–1949; cotton; p. (1961) *67,105*.

Chandigarh, *Union terr.*, E. Punjab, India; situated on plateau at foot of Himalaya, S.W. of Simla; built 1951–3 by Le Corbusier; univ.; cap. of Punjab st., p. (1961) *89,321*.

Changchow (Changzhou), *c.*, Kiangsu, China; in valley of Yangtze R., on Grand Canal 70 m. S.E. of Nanking; mkt. for intensively cultivated dist.; silk; p. (1953) *297,000*. [*855,000.*

Changchun, *c.*, Kirin, China; rly. ctr.; p. (1953)

Changnacheri, *t.*, Kerala, S. India; tea, cotton spinning, silk; p. (1961) *42,376*.

Changpai Shan, *mtns.*, form bdy. between China and N. Korea; drained by Rs. Yalu, Ertao, Tumen; highest point, Peiktusan, alt. 8,005 ft.

Changsha, *c.*, *cap.*, Hunan prov., China; tea, rice, antimony; p. (1953) *651,000*.

Changshu, *c.*, Kiangsu, China; in valley of Yangtze R. 65 m. N.W. of Shanghai; mkt. for local agr. produce; p. (1953) *101,000*.

Channel Islands, gr. of self-governing Is. belonging to the British Crown off N.W. cst. France, of which the lgst. are Jersey, Guernsey, Alderney and Sark; part of the old Duchy of Normandy; vegetables, flowers, fruit, granite; two famous breeds of dairy cattle; tourist resort; German occupation, 1940–45; ch. t. St. Helier, Jersey; total a. 75 sq. m.; p. (1961) *110,503*.

Chantaburi, *t.*, *spt.*, Thailand, rubies and other precious stones.

Chantada, *commune*, N.W. Spain; cattle, leather, soap, bricks, linen; p. (1957) *14,467*.

Chantilly, *t.*, Oise, France; famous race-course; p. (1946) *5,105*.

Chanute, *mkt. t.*, Kan., U.S.A.; oil, gas; refineries, cement; p. (1960) *10,849*.

Chaochow (Chaozhou), *c.*, Kwangtung, S. China; on Han R. 20 m. N. of Swatow; ctr. of cultivated plain; rice, sugar, tea; linked to Swatow by rly.; p. (1953) *101,000*.

Chapala, *L.*, Mexico; chiefly in Jalisco st.; a. 1,300 sq. m.

Chapayev, *see* Gurev.

Chapayevsk, *t.*, Kuibyshev Region, R.S.F.S.R.; chemicals, agr. machin.; p. (1959) *83,000*.

Chapelcross, nr. Annan, Dumfriesshire, Scot.; nuclear reactor sta.; power and plutonium prod.

Chapel-en-le-Frith, *mkt. t.*, *rural dist.*, Derby, Eng.; p. (1961 rural dist.) *18,366*.

Chapelizod, *sub.* of Dublin, Ireland; on R. Liffey.

Chapra, *t.*, Bihar; on Ganges R.; ctr. of saltpetre and indigo tr.; p. (1961) *75,580*.

Chard, *mun. bor.*, Somerset, Eng.; lace, iron, engin., shirt and cotton mftg.; p. (estd. 1967) *6,910*.

Chardzhou, *t.*, Turkmen S.S.R.; on the Central Asia Rly.; textiles, chemicals; p. (1959) *66,000*.

Charente, *dep.*, W. France; cap. Angoulême; ctr. of distilling tr., cognac; a. 2,305 sq. m.; p. (1968) *331,016*.

Charente, R., W. France; flows into Bay of Biscay below Rochefort.

Charente-Maritime, *dep.*, S.W. France; cap. La Rochelle; wine, wheat; oysters, pilchards; a. 2,791 sq. m.; p. (1968) *483,622*.

Charenton-le-Pont, *commune*, Seine dep., France; N.E. sub. of Paris; boats, pottery, rubber; p. (1954) *22,079*.

Charleroi, *t.*, Hainaut, Belgium; on R. Sambre; coal-mng.; glass; p. (1968) *233,426* (inc. subs.).

Charleroi, *t.*, Penns., U.S.A.; steel, glass; p. (1960) *8,148*. [(1960) *9,964*.

Charles City, *c.*, Iowa, U.S.A.; on Cedar R.; p.

Charleston, *t.*, Ill., U.S.A.; dairy produce, flour, shoes; p. (1960) *10.505*.

Charleston, *c. spt.*, S. Carolina, U.S.A.; lumber, metal, concrete, fertilisers, chemicals, plastics, cigars, fabrics; p. (1960) *60,182*.

Charleston, *t.*, *cap.*, W. Virginia, U.S.A.; on Kanawha R.; in bituminous coal dist.; chemicals, glass, tools, oil, natural gas, lumber, coal processing; p. (1960) *85,796*.

Charlestown, *ch. t.*, Nevis I., Leeward Group; p. (1957) *15,446*.

Charleville, *see* Rathluirc.

Charleville-Mézières, *t.*, Ardennes dep., N.E. France; on Meuse R.; iron, bricks, nails, hardware; p. (1962) *50,229*.

Charleville, *t.*, Queensland, Australia; on Warrego R., 400 m. W. of Brisbane; pastoral dist.; p. (1966) *4,799*. [(1960) *2,751.*

Charlevoix, *pt.*, *t.*, L. Michigan, U.S.A.; p.

Charlotte, *c.*, N.C., U.S.A.; key rly. junction; machin., chemicals, textiles; p. (1960) *201,564*.

Charlotte, *t.*, S. Mich., U.S.A.; furniture, car parts; p. (1960) *7,657*.

Charlottenburg, *t.*, Germany; on R. Spree; sub. of Berlin; palace; china, beer, machin.

Charlottesville, *t.*, Va., U.S.A.; on Rivanna R.; univ.; Monticello—home of Thomas Jefferson; p. (1960) *29,427*.

Charlottetown, *spt.*, *cap.*, Prince Edward I., Canada; Parliament buildings; iron foundry, shipyards, fisheries; p. (1961) *18,318*.

Charlton Kings, *urb. dist.*, Gloucester, Eng.; at foot of Cotswolds nr. Cheltenham; p. (1961) *7,744*.

Charnwood Forest, *upland district*, Leicester, Eng.; to W. of Soar valley, 12 m. N.W. of Leicester; composed of ancient rocks; stone-crushing; largely forests; used for recreation by industl. ts. of E. Midlands; alt. 600–900 ft.

Charters Towers, *t.*, N. Queensland, Australia; 925 m. by rail from Brisbane; pastoral ctr.; p. (1966) *7,533*.

Chartres, *c.*, *cap.*, dep. Eure-et-Loir, France; fine Gothic cath.; milling, brewing, distilling; p. (1954) *28,750*. [near Grenoble.

Chartreuse, La Grande, France, famous monastery

Chateaubriant, *t.*, Loire-Inférieure, France; rly. ctr.; p. (1946) *7,965*. [p. (1946) *7,283.*

Château Thierry, *t.*, Aisne, France; on R. Marne;

Châteauroux, *t.*, Indre, France; 60 m. S.E. of Tours on R. Indre; woollens, machin.; p. (1962) *46,772*.

Châtelet, *t.*, Hainaut, Belgium; on R. Sambre; coal, pottery; p. (1962) *15,483*. [20,095.

Châtelineau, *t.*, Hainaut, Belgium; p. (1962)

Châtellerault, *t.*, Vienne, France; 40 m. S. of Tours; cutlery, small arms; p. (1954) *23,583*.

Châtenay-Malabry, *t.*, Seine, France; p. (1954) *14,269*.

Chatham, *mun. bor.*, *dockyard*, (*former naval arsenal*), Kent, Eng.; on estuary of R. Medway; light inds.; p. (estd. 1967) *53,560*.

Chatham, *t.*, *spt.*, New Brunswick, Canada; lumbering, fish exporting; p. (1961) *7,109*.

Chatham, *c.*, Ontario, Canada; farming, fruit, machin., canned vegetables; p. (1961) *29,826*.

Chatham, Is., New Zealand dependency; a. 372 sq. m.; lgst. I., Wharekauri; (1961) *487*.

Châtillon-sur-Seine, *t.*, Côte d'Or, France; on R. Seine, 45 m. S.E. of Troyes; p. (1954) *12,526*.

Chatou, *t.*, Hauts-de-Seine, France; p. (1954) *15,338*.

Chatsworth, *par.*, Derby, Eng.; on R. Derwent; seat of Duke of Devonshire.

Chattanooga, *c.*, Tenn., U.S.A.; on Tennessee R.; univ.; rly. ctr.; cottons; iron, steel, chemicals, paper, metals; p. (1960) *130,009*.

Chatteris, *urb. dist.*, Cambridge and Isle of Ely, Eng.; mkt. t.; p. (1961) *5,490*.

Chaudière Falls, on Ottawa R., above Ottawa, Canada; hydro-electric power-sta.

Chauk, *t.*, Burma; on Irrawaddy R.; chemical fertiliser plant being built, due for completion 1970.

Chaumont, *t.*, Haute-Marne, France; gloves, leather; p. (1954) *19,346*.

Chauny, *t.*, Aisne, France; on R. Oise; chemicals, glass; p. (1954) *10,544*.

Chautauqua, *L.*, N.Y. st., U.S.A.; summer resort.

Chaux-de-Fonds, La, *t. can.*, Neuchâtel, Switzerland; ctr. of watchmkg. ind.; p. (1957) *33,300*.

Chaves, *t.*, N. Portugal; cath.; hot salt springs; linen silk; p. (1960) *13,156*.

Chaville, *t.*, Seine-et-Oise, France, p. (1954) *14,508*.

Cheadle, *rural dist.*, Staffs, Eng.; coal pits, metal mnfs.; p. (1961) *33,153*.

Cheadle and Gatley, *urb. dist.*, Cheshire, Eng.; textile finishing and bleaching; p. (estd. 1967) *54,920*.

Cheb, *t.*, ČSSR.; nr. Bavarian frontier; industl. ctr.; motor cycles, machin., textiles; p. (1961) *20,590*.

Cheboksary, *t.*, cap. R.S.F.S.R.; textiles, hydroelec., engin., wood-working; p. (1967) *170,000*.

Cheboygan, *t.*, Mich., U.S.A.; on L. Huron; sawmills; p. (1960) *5,859*.

Cheddar, *vil.*, Somerset, Eng.; famous limestone caves in Mendips; cheese, strawberries.

Cheduba I., Bay of Bengal, Burma; fertile, well-wooded; a. 240 sq. m.

Chefoo (Yantai), *c.*, *former treaty pt.*, Shantung, China; on N. cst. of peninsula; p. (1953) *116,000*.

Chekiang (Zhijiang), *maritime prov.*, S.E. China; cap. Hangchow; exp. silk, cotton, etc.; a. 39,486 sq. m.; p. (1953) *22,865,747*.

Cheling Pass, on bdy. between Kwangtung, Hunan, S. China; historic route across Nanling mtns., now followed by Hankow to Canton trunk rly.; alt. 984 ft.   [*19,539*.

Chelles, *t.*, Seine-et-Marne, France; p. (1954)

Chelm, *t.*, E. Poland; nr. Lublin; cath.; 1944 Manifesto of Poland's Liberation issued here; p. (1965) *35,000*.   [Maldon.

Chelmer, *R.*, Essex, Eng.; joins R. Blackwater at

Chelmno (Kulm), *t.*, Poland; on R. Vistula; ancient wells; large oil mills, engin., impt. tr.; p. (1946) *11,634*.

Chelmsford, *co. t.*, *mun. bor.*, Essex, Eng.; 30 m. N.E. London; cath.; agr. mkt.; radio, elec. engin., brewing; p. (estd. 1967) *55,210*.

Chelsea, *see* Kensington and Chelsea.

Chelsea, *t.*, Mass., U.S.A.; rubber goods, shoes, paper; p. (1960) *33,749*.

Cheltenham, *t.*, *mun. bor.*, Gloucester Eng.; spa; educational ctr.; aircraft mfftg. and repair, precision instruments; p. (estd. 1967) *75,640*.

Chelyabinsk, *t.*, R.S.F.S.R.; on Mijas R. W. Siberian lowlands; metallurgy and machin.; pipeline to natural gas field Gazli opened Nov. 1963; p. (1967) *820,000*.

Chelyuskin C., most N. point of Asia.

Chemnitz, *see* Karl-Marx-Stadt.

Chemulpo, *see* Inchon.

Chenab, *R.*, W. Punjab, Pakistan; one of " five rivers " of Punjab; rises in Himalayas, flows S.W. into R. Sutlej; dams at Merala and Khanki provide water for Upper and Lower Chenab Irrigation Canal Systems; length approx. 900 m.

Chengchow (Zhengzhou), *c.*, *cap.* Honan prov., China; 15 m. S. of Hwang-Ho, where it emerges on to N. China Plain; impt. route ctr. and rly. junction where Peking to Hankow rly. crosses Sian to Tunghai rly.; p. (1953) *595,000*.

Chengtu (Chengdu), *c.*, *cap.* Szechwan prov., China; silk, rice; p. (1957) *1,107,000*.

Chepstow, *mkt. t.*, *urb. dist.*, Monmouth, Eng.; on R. Wye 2 m. above confluence with R. Severn; Severn Bridge links to Aust (Glos.); fine ruined cas.; light engin., brush mkg., asphalt, limestone; p. (1961) *6,041*.

Chequers, *seat*, Bucks, Eng.; official residence of Prime Minister.

Cher, *central dep.*, France; cap. Bourges; grain, wines, iron, porcelain; a. 2,819 sq. m.; p. (1968) *304,601*.   [Auvergne Mtns.

Cher, *R.*, France. trib. of R. Loire, flowing from

Cherbourg, *spt.*, Manche, France; N. cst. of Contentin Peninsula; opposite to and 80 m. dist. from Portsmouth; naval arsenal, shipbldg.; metals, ropes, fishing; p. (1962) *40,013*.

Cheremkhovo, *t.*, R.S.F.S.R.; N.W. of Irkutsk; coal, engin., chemicals; p. (1967) *111,000*.

Cherepovets, *c.*, R.S.F.S.R.; steel, engin., sawmills; p. (1967) *159,000*.

Cheribon, *spt.*, Java, Indonesia; N. cst., 120 m. E. of Jakarta; rice, tea, coffee; p. *54,079*.

Cherkassy, *t.*, Ukrainian S.S.R.; nr. Kiev, on Dnieper R.; sugar, engin.; p. (1959) *83,000*.

Chernigov, *t.*, Ukrainian S.S.R.; on Desna R.; caths.; univ.; flour, textiles, chemicals; p. (1967) *132,000*.

Chernogorsk, *t.*, R.S.F.S.R.; 10 m. N. of Abakan; ctr. of Minusinsk coal-mng. basin; p. (1959) *51,000*.

Chernovtsy, *t.*, Ukrainian S.S.R.; univ.; Greek cath.; wheat, dairy produce, textiles, engin., chemicals; p. (1967) *175,000*.

Chernyakovsk (Insterburg), *t.*, Lithuanian S.S.R.; chemicals, textiles; p. (1959) approx. *50,000*.

Cherokee, *t.*, Iowa, U.S.A.; p. (1960) *7,724*.

Cherrapunji, *t.*, Assam, India; in Khasi Hills; reputed wettest place in world, av. annual rainfall 500 in.

Chertsey, *urb. dist.*, Surrey, Eng.; on S. bank of R. Thames, 4 m. below Staines; residtl; aircraft components, cement; p. (estd. 1967) *44,710*.

Cherwell, *R.*, trib. of Thames, nr. Oxford; l. 30 m

Chesapeake Bay, *inlet* on Atlantic coast, U.S.A.; extending 200 m. from mouth of Susquehanna R. to C. Charles; shellfish ind.; bridge-tunnel (opened 1964) spans entrance to Bay.

Chesham, *residtl. t.*, *urb. dist.*, Bucks, Eng.; in heart of Chiltern Hills; printing, textiles, light engin.; p. (1961) *16,236*.

Cheshire, *co.*, Eng.; cap. Chester; plain; Rs. Mersey and Dee; dairying, mkt. gardening; salt, coal; mnfs.; textiles, chemicals, shipbldg.; a. 1,056 sq. m.; p. (1966) *1,472,000*.

Cheshire, *t.*, Conn., U.S.A.; agr., formerly copper, and barytes mined; p. (estd. 1967) *42,900*.

Cheshunt, *urb. dist.*, Herts, Eng.; in Lea valley, 7 m. S. of Hertford; bricks, mkt. gardening, horticulture; p. (1961) *35,371*.

Chesil Bank, Dorset, Eng.; shingle ridge from Portland to Bridport.

Chester, *c.*, *co. bor.*, Cheshire, Eng.; at head of estuary of R. Dee; cath., ancient walls and old timbered houses; engin., metal goods; p. (estd. 1967) *60,360*.

Chester, *t.*, S.C., U.S.A.; cotton mnfs.; flour; granite; p. (1960) *6,906*.   [p. (1960) *63,658*.

Chester, *t.*, Penns., U.S.A.; large inds., textiles.

Chesterfield, *mkt. t.*, *mun. bor.*, colly. dist., Derby, Eng.; on Rother R.; 8 m. S. of Sheffield; iron, steel, engin., coal-mng., glass, elec. lamps, galvanised goods, chemicals; 14th-cent. church with crooked spire; p. (estd. 1967) *70,020*.

Chesterfield Inlet, arm of Hudson Bay, Canada; 250 m. by 25 m.

Chesterfield Is., *dep.*, New Caledonia, Pac. Oc.; French; about 342 m. W. of N.C.

Chester-le-Street, *urb. dist.*, Durham, Eng.; clothing, confectionery; p. (estd. 1967) *20,300*.

Chesterton, *sub.* of Cambridge, Eng.; p. *35,950*.

Cheviot, *t.*, S.W. Ohio, U.S.A.; clothes, leather goods; flour; p. (1960) *10,701*.

Cheviot Hills, between Scot. and Northumberland, Britain; highest point The Cheviot, 2,676 ft.

Cheyenne, *R.*, S.D., U.S.A.; trib. of Missouri; length 500 m.

Cheyenne, *cap.*, Wyo., U.S.A.; cattle-ranching dist.; rly. ctr.; p. (1960) *43,505*.

Chiana, Val de, *valley*, central Italy; longitudinal depression separating Tuscan Hills from Central Apennines; occupied by upper course of R. Arno, middle course of R. Tiber; followed by main route from Florence to Rome.

Chiangmai, *prov.*, N.W. Thailand; cap. Chiangmai; a. 8,839 sq. m.; p. (1960) *798,483*.

Chiangmai, *c.*, Chiangmai prov., N.W. Thailand; on Ping R.; tr. ctr., teak; p. (1960) *65,736*.

Chiapas, *Pacific st.*, Mexico; cap. Tuxtla-Gutierrez; mountainous, forested; coffee, tobacco, sugar and cocoa, cattle; a. 28,729 sq. m.; p. (1960) *1,210,870*.

Chiatura, *t.*, Georgian S.S.R.; manganese; p. (1956) *19,200*.

Chiavari, *t.*, Liguria, Italy; on the Riviera; shrine of the Madonna; p. *17,588*.

Chiba, *cap.* of Chiba prefecture, Japan; on E. Tokyo Bay; impt. tr. ctr.; giant shipyard; oil refining; aluminium, chemicals; new airpt. projected 1972; p. (1964) *301,000*.

Chicago, *c.*, Ill., U.S.A.; on S. shore of L. Michigan; second lgst. U.S. c.; economic heart of Mid-West; comm. ctr. called " The Loop "; immense tr. by rail and Great Lakes, flourishing univ.; grain mkt., pork, beef canning, agr. implements, iron and steel, machin., clothing, furs, electronic equipment, metals, chemicals, petrol, coal; lgst. airpt. in world; p. (1970) *3,325,263*; Greater Chicago (1970) *6,894,000*.

Chichester, *c.*, *mun. bor.*, W. Sussex, Eng.; on S. cst. plain, 11 m. W. of Arundel; fine cath.; agr.; p. (estd. 1967) *20,640*.

Chickamauga Creek, U.S.A.; branch of the Tennessee R. above Chattanooga; Civil War battles; site of National Park.

Chickasha, *t.*, Okla., U.S.A.; maize, cotton; p. (1960) *14,866*.

Chickerell, E. Dorset, Eng.; 3 m. N.W. of Weymouth; site for nuclear power sta.; on shores of East Fleet R.

Chiclana, *mftg. t.*, Spain; nr. Cadiz; p. (1957) *18,262*.

Chiclayo, *ch. t.*, Lambayeque dep., Peru; rice, sugar, wheat, coffee; p. (1961) *54,400*.

Chico, *t.*, N. Cal., U.S.A.; food processing, lumber, cement; p. (1960) *14,757*.

Chicopee, t., Mass., U.S.A.; on Connecticut R.; hardware, carpets, cars; p. (1960) 61,553.

Chicoutimi, t., Quebec, Canada; on Chicoutimi R.; hydro-elec. power-sta.; lumber, pulp, paper; p. (1961) 31,657.

Chidambaram, t., Tamil Nadu, India; nr. Cuddalore; p. (1961) 40,694.

Chidley C., most N. point of Labrador, Hudson Strait, Canada.   [ft. above sea-level.

Chiem, L., large lake nr. Munich, Germany, 1,500

Chieri, t., Piedmont, Italy; nr. Turin; was mediæval republic; Gothic church; silks, cottons; p. 14,747.   [347,824.

Chieti, prov., S. Italy; a. 1,142 sq. m.; p. (1961)

Chieti, t. cap., prov. Chieti, S. Italy; the ancient Teate Marrucinorum; Europe's lgst. glass plant, using methane from Abruzzi field; p. (1961) 48,011.

Chigirik, t., Uzbek S.S.R.; new town being built (1963), 21 m. S. of Tashkent.

Chignecto Bay, inlet of Bay of Fundy, Canada.

Chigwell, urb. dist., Essex, Eng.; on borders of Epping Forest; Hainault Estate, now incorporated in Redbridge, Greater London; residtl.; p. (estd. 1967) 56,040.

Chihli, see Hopei.

Chihli, G. of, see Pohai, Gulf of.

Chihuahua, st., Mexico; adjoining the U.S.A.; mining, stock-raising and agr.; a. 94,822 sq. m.; p. (1960) 1,226,793.

Chihuahua, c., cap., Chihuahua st., Mexico; fine cath.; on Mexican Central Rly.; silver, cottons, woollens; p. (1960) 150,430.

Chikchi, pen., R.S.F.S.R.; world's first Arctic nuclear power sta. being built.

Chikuho, t., N. Kyushu, Japan; largest coalmines in the country.   [Valley.

Chilcoot, R., pass., Alaska, leading into Yukon

Chile, rep., S. America, independent of Spain since 1818; Pacific coastal strip rising sharply to Andes; Atacama Desert in N., fertile valleys in ctr., heavy rains in S.; Spanish language; Roman Catholic; forested in S.; dairying, sheep, wool; gr. nitrate output, copper, iron ore, coal, iodine, paper, petroleum; cap. Santiago; ch. pt. Valparaiso; length 2,660 m., breadth 69–270 m., a. 285,133 sq. m.; p. (estd. 1968) 9,351,000.

Chilka, L., inlet, E. coast, Orissa, India.

Chillán, c., cap. Nuble prov., Chile; destroyed 1939 by one of world's worst recorded earthquakes; since rebuilt; agr. and comm. ctr.; p. (1961) 82,947.

Chillicothe, c., Ohio, U.S.A.; on Scioto R., mftg.; furniture, leather; p. (1960) 24,957.

Chilliwack, t., B.C., Canada; on Fraser R.; dairy produce, fruit, lumber; p. (1961) 8,259.

Chiloé, I. and S. prov. Chile; cap. San Carlos, suffered earthquakes 1939 and 1960; ch. pt. Ancúd destroyed 1960: a. 9,058 sq. m.; p. (1960) 98,662.   [p. (1960) 12,673.

Chilpaneingo, c., cap., Guerrero st., Mexico;

Chiltern Hills, chalk hills, Oxon., Bucks., Beds, and Herts., Eng.; highest point 904 ft. nr. Wendover.

Chimborazo, min., Ecuador, Andes; extinct volcano, alt. 20,610 ft.

Chimborazo, prov., Ecuador; cap. Riobamba; a. 2,089 sq. m.; p. (estd. 1962) 279,607.

Chimbote, spt. Peru; steel, iron-ore, coal; tinned fish, fish-meal; p. (1961) 90,000.

Chimkent, t., Kazakh S.S.R.; chemicals, engin., textiles; lead smelting; p. (1967) 209,000.

China, People's Republic of, Asia, consists of 27 provs. (inc. Taiwan, the aut. regions of Kwangsi Chuang, Ningsia, Inner Mongolia, Sinkiang Uighur, and Tibet). Total a. 4,300,000 sq. m.; mtnous. in N. and W., fertile valleys and plains in E.; Rs.: Yangtze, Si, Yellow, Canton, Yalu, Sungari; climate, extreme in N.; monsoon in S.; wheat, barley, maize, millet in N.; rice (staple food), sugar in S.; cotton, tea, hemp, jute, flax; livestock; cotton, woollen and silk mnfs.; flour- and rice-milling; great mineral wealth; coal, iron, tin, antimony, wolfram, bismuth, molybdenum; oil; rural electrification; p. (estd.) 730,000,000.

China Sea, part of W. Pacific between Korea and Philippines; divided by the narrow Formosa Strait into two areas; N. China Sea, including Yellow Sea, and S. China Sea.

Chinandega, t., Nicaragua, Central America; cotton, sugar, bananas; iron wks.; p. (1960) 19,025.

Chincha Is., gr. off cst. of Peru; p. (of ch. t.) 14,763.

Chinchow (Jinzhou), c., Liaoning prov., China; cement, glass, bricks, tiles, paper and wood pulp, oil; p. (1953) 352,000.

Chincoteague, t., and I., E. Va., U.S.A.; fisheries, poultry; p. (1960) 2,131.

Chindwin, R., Burma; ch. trib. of Irrawaddy; rising in Patkoi Hills, navigable in rainy season.

Chindwin, Upper and Lower, provs., Burma; fertile plains and extensive teak forests, rice.

Chingford, see Waltham Forest.

Chingleput, t., India; S. of Madras; cotton weaving, salt mnfs.; p. (1961) 25,977.

Chingola, t., Zambia, copper-mng.

Chinju or Shinshu, t., S. Korea; cotton; p. 30,269.

Chinkiang (Zhenjiang), c., Kiangsu, China; former treaty pt. Yangtse-kiang, 48 m. below Nanking; tr. ctr.; p. (1953) 201,000.

Chinkolobwe, mines, Congo; uranium.

Chinon, t., Indre-et-Loire, Central France; on R. Vienne, industl.; ruined cas., once a royal residency; nuclear power sta.; p. (1954) 6,743.

Chinquinquira, t., Boyaca, Colombia; pilgrimage ctr.; comm. ctr.; coffee, cattle; p. (estd. 1959) 24,150.

Chinwangtao (Qinhuangdao), c., spt., former treaty pt., Hopeh, N. China; on Yellow Sea cst., 150 m. N.E. of Tientsin; only good natural harbour on N. China cst.; exp. coal from Kailan mines; p. (1953) 187,000.

Chioggia, spt., cath. c., N. Italy; on I. in G. of Venice; fishing; p. (1961) 47,151.

Chios, see Khios.

Chippenham, t., mun. bor., Wilts, Eng.; mkt. t. on R. Avon; rly. signal and brake equipment, bacon curing, tanning; p. (estd. 1967) 18,640.

Chippewa Falls, c., Wis., U.S.A.; flour, lumber; p. (1960) 11,708.

Chipping Campden, vil., Gloucester, Eng.; in Cotswold Hills; formerly impt. for woollens.

Chipping Norton, mun. bor., mkt. t., Oxford, Eng., nr. Banbury; p. (estd. 1967) 4,420.

Chipping Sodbury, mkt. t., Gloucester, Eng.; 8 m. N.E. of Bristol.

Chirchik, t., Uzbekistan S.S.R.; 20 m. N.E. of Tashkent; engin., chemicals; hydro-elec. stas.; p. (1959) 65,000.   [188,350.

Chiriqui, prov., Panama; cap. David; p. (1960)

Chirk, t., Denbigh, Wales; on R. Cleriog, S. of Wrexham; slate, coal.

Chisinau, see Kishinev.

Chislehurst and Sidcup, see Bexley and Bromley.

Chistyakovo, see Thorez.

Chita, t., rly. junct. Siberia, R.S.F.S.R.; on upper Amur R., 400 m. E. of L. Baikal; coal, engin., chemicals, sawmilling; p. (1967) 201,000.

Chitral, st., Pakistan; N.W. Frontier Provs.

Chittagong, dist., East Pakistan; ch. t., Chittagong; p. (estd. 1951) 11,783,000.

Chittagong, c., spt., East Pakistan; on E. cst. of Bay of Bengal; exp. jute, tea; oil-refining; steel mill; suffered severe damage by cyclone May 1963; p. (1961) 364,205.

Chittaranjan, t., W. Bengal, India; new t. on Barakhar R., in steel ctr. of Asasol and Tatanagan; rly. locomotive wks.; p. (1961) 28,957.

Chobrum, see Godwin-Austen Mt.

Choctawhatchee, R., Ala. and Fla., U.S.A.; length 180 m.

Choisy-le-Roi, t., Seine, France; cloth factories; p. (1962) 41,269.

Cholet, t., Maine-et-Loire, France; cotton, linen, flannel mnfs.; p. (1962) 37,557.

Cholon, t., S. Viet-Nam; 10 m. S.W. of Saigon; rice; p. inc. with Saigon (1964) 1,371,000.

Cholula, ancient c. of Puebla, prov., Mexico; Aztec temple, pyramid of Cholula, and other remains.

Chomutov, mftg. t., ČSSR.; p. (1961) 33,152.

Chonos Archipelago, Chile, about 120 islands on W. coast of Patagonia.

Chooz, t., Ardennes, France; pressurized water reactor; nuclear power sta. linked with Belgian grid.

Chorley, industl. t., mun. bor., N. Lancs, Eng.; on W. flank of Rossendale Fells, 7 m. S.E. of Preston; cotton, engin.; proposals for expansion as "New Town" with Leyland (50,000 acres); p. (estd. 1967) 31,170.

Chorley Wood, urb. dist., Herts, Eng.; p. (1961) 6,964.

Chorrilos Pass, Argentina; in E. cordillera of Andes at alt. 14,655 ft.; used by rly. from Tucuman to Antofagasta.

Chorzow (Królewska Huta), *t.*, Upper Silesia, Poland; coal, iron and steel, chemicals, engin.; p. (1965) *154,000.*

Choukoutien, *vil.*, Hopeh prov., N.E. China; site of discovery of bones of extinct Pekin man.

Chowtsun, *t.*, *former treaty pt.*, Shantung, N.E. China; silk; rly.; p. *46,200.*

Christchurch, *t.*, *mun. bor.*, Hants, Eng.; on S. cst. 5 m. E. of Bournemouth; holiday resort, aircraft, light inds.; p. (estd. 1967) *30,270.*

Christchurch, *c.*, *cap.*, Canterbury, S.I., N.Z.; univ.; cath., mus.; comm. ctr. of lamb, wool and grain prov.; airpt.; p. (1966) *246,773* or *c. 161,566.*

Christiansand, *see* Kristiansand.

Christianshaab, Danish settlement on Disco Bay, W. Greenland; meteorological sta.

Christianstad, *see* Kristianstad.

Christiansund, *see* Kristiansund.

Christmas I., in Indian Oc., Australian terr. since Oct. 1, 1958; a. 52 sq. m., healthy climate, phosphate deposits; p. (estd.) *3,653.*

Christmas I., lge. coral atoll in Pacific, one of Line Is.; discovered by Cook 1777; 100 m. in circum.; U.K. nuclear test site, 1957–64.   [*15,514.*

Chrudim, *t.*, ČSSR.; horse mkt., mnfs.; p. (1961)

Chrzanow, *commune*, S. Poland; 27 m. from Krakow; coal, locomotives, leather, bricks; p. (1965) *23,000.*

Chu, *R.*, Kazakh S.S.R., U.S.S.R.; rises in Tien Shan, flows N.W. for 500 m. into inland drainage basin; Chumysh Dam provides hydro-electricity and water for intensive cultivation under irrigation of cotton, sugar-beet, citrus fruits.

Chuanchow (Quanzhou), *c.*, Fukien prov.; China; rice, wheat, sugar cane; p. (1953) *108,000.*

Chuchow (Zhuzhou), *c.*, Hunan prov., China; p. (1953) *127,000.*

Chu Kiang (Canton R. or Pearl R.), Kwangtung, S. China; one of most impt. waterways of China; fertile delta known as " land of fish, rice and fruit "; around Canton network of elec. drainage and irrigation stas., built since 1959.

Chubut, *prov.*, Argentine; cap. Rawson; a. 87,152 sq. m.; agr.; p. (1960) *142,000.*

Chudleigh, *mkt. t.*, Devon, Eng.; on R. Teign; stone quarrying; p. (1951) *1,944.*

Chudskoye, *L.*, between R.S.F.S.R. and Estonia S.S.R.; 70 m. long.   [gold deposit.

Chukotkaa, *pen.*, U.S.S.R.; extreme N.E.; rich

Chula Vista, *t.*, Cal., U.S.A.; agr., aircraft; p. (1960) *42,034.*

Chungking (Zhongqing), *t.*, *former treaty pt.*, Szechwan, China; on Yangtze-Kiang; comm. ctr., S.W. China; exp. silk, soya-beans, sugar; p. (1957) *2,121,000.*

Chuquibamba Mtns. (alt. 21,000 ft.), Peru.

Chuquicamata, *part* of Calama *commune*, N. Chile; lgst. copper-mines in the world; p. (1960) *30,476.*

Chuquisaca, *dep.*, Bolivia; cap. Sucre; a. 36,132 sq. m.; p. (1962) *307,600.*

Chur (Coire), *t.*, cap. Grisons can., Switzerland; Upper Rhine Valley; cath. and hist. bldgs.; fruit and wine; p. (1960) *20,000.*

Church, *urb. dist.*, *sub.* Accrington, Lancs, Eng.; cotton weaving and engin.; p. (1961) *5,880.*

Church Stretton, *urb. dist.*, Salop, Eng.; p. (1961) *2,712.*

Churchill, *R.*, Canada; enters Hudson Bay at Churchill; 925 m.; fine harbour.

Churchill, *R.*, formerly Hamilton R. flows into H. inlet, cst. of Labrador, Canada; magnificent waterfall, Churchill Falls.

Churchill, *t.*, Manitoba, Canada; terminus of Hudson Bay rly.; summer wheat route from prairie provs.   [tea, rice.

Chusan I., off E. cst. of China; cap. Tinghai;

Chusovoy, *t.*, R.S.F.S.R.; in Urals; iron and steel; p. (1959) *60,000.*

Chuvash, *rep.*, A.S.S.R., U.S.S.R.; a. 7,107 sq. m.; p. (1959) *1,098,000.*

Cibao, *lowland area*, Dominican Republic, Central America; extends along N. side of Cordillera de Cibao for approx. 100 m.; cacao, tobacco, maize; densely populated, ch. t. Santiago.

Cicero, *t.*, Ill., U.S.A.; p. (1960) *69,130.*

Ciechanów, *t.*, Poland; 49 m. N.W. of Warsaw; agr. inds.; p. (1965) *21,000.*

Cienaga, *spt.*, N. Colombia; exp. cotton, bananas, cacao; p. (estd. 1962) *69,900.*

Cienfuegos, *t.*, *spt.*, Cuba; sugar, tobacco; p. (1960) *100,000.*

Cieszyn, *t.*, Katowice, Poland; p. (1965) *24,000.*

Cieza, *t.*, Murcia, Spain; in fertile raisin and orange-growing dist.; p. (1957) *23,328.*

Cilicia, *ancient prov.*, S.E. Anatolia, Turkey.

Cincinnati, *c.*, Ohio, U.S.A.; on Ohio R.; " the Queen City "; univ.; pork-packing, machin., tools, soap, electrotypes, seed processing, chemicals; p. (1960) *502,550.*

Cinderford, *lge. vil.*, Gloucester, Eng.; in Forest of Dean, 12 m. S.W. of Gloucester; ch. mining ctr. on sm. F. of D. coalfield.

Cinque Ports, ancient English pts. on cst. of Kent and Sussex; original 5: Sandwich, Dover, Hythe, Romney, Hastings; Winchelsea and Rye added later. *See* L.23.

Cintra, *see* Sintra.

Circleville, *t.*, Ohio, U.S.A.; agr. ctr., maize; wheat; p. (1960) *11,059.*

Cirencester, *t.*, *urb. dist.*, Gloucester, Eng.; the Roman Corineum; p. (1961) *11,836.*

Citlaltépetl (Aztec name for Orizaba), *mtn.*, volcanic peak, Veracruz st., Mexico, highest point in Mexico; 18,701 ft.

Cittadella, *t.*, Venetia, Italy; nr. Padua; mediæval walls and towers; p. *12,679.*

Cittanova, *t.*, Reggio, Italy; built on ruins of Casalnuovo; olive-oil ind.

Citta Vecchia, *c.*, Central Malta; former cap.

Ciudad Bolivar, *spt.*, Bolivar st., Venezuela; on R. Orinoco; (formerly called Angostura); great comm. ctr.; coffee; cattle; p. (1961) *56,032.*

Ciudad Juarez, *t.*, Mexico; p. (1960) *261,683.*

Ciudad Madero, *t.*, Mexico; styrene and detergent plants.

Ciudad Real, *prov.*, S. Central Spain; grazing grounds, forest and quicksilver mines; cap. Ciudad Real; a. 7,622 sq. m.; p. (1959) *583,930.*

Ciudad Rodrigo, *c.*, Salamanca, Spain; captured by French 1707 and 1710, by the English 1706, stormed by Wellington in 1812; fine cath.; p. (1957) *12,600.*

Ciudad Trujillo, *see* Santo Domingo.

Civitavecchia, *spt.*, Latium, Italy; on W. cst., 30 m. N. of mouth of R. Tiber; sulphur springs; p. *34,400.*

Clackmannan, *smallest co.*, Scot.; flat in Carse, and hilly elsewhere; co. t. Alloa; coal, textiles (esp. woollens), metal work, brewing, distilling, agr.; a. 544 sq. m.; p. (1961) *41,391.*

Clacton-on-Sea, *t.*, *urb. dist.*, Essex, Eng.; on E. cst., 12 m. S.E. of Colchester; seaside resort; light inds.; residtl.; p. (estd. 1967) *34,250.*

Clairton, *t.*, S.W. Penns., U.S.A.; coal, iron, steel, chemicals; p. (1960) *18,389.*

Clairvaux, *vil.*, Aube, France; famous Cistercian Abbey.

Clamart, *t.*, Seine, France; p. (1962) *48,290.*

Clanwilliam, *t.*, Cape Province, Rep. of S. Africa, on Oliphant R.; p. *1,468.*

Clare, *co.*, Munster, Ireland; co. t. Ennis; oats, potatoes; sheep, cattle; oysters, salmon; a. 1,294 sq. m.; p. (1966) *73,539.*

Clare, *t.*, S. Australia; on W. flank of Flinders Mtns., 70 m. N.E. of Adelaide; ctr. of wine-producing dist.; p. (1966) *1,534.*

Clare I., Clew Bay, Mayo, Ireland.

Clarence Strait, between Melville I. and P. Darwin, N. Terr., Australia.

Clarence, *R.*, N.S.W., Australia; length 240 m.

Clarksburg, *t.*, W. Virginia, U.S.A., machin., glass. pottery; p. (1960) *28,112.*

Clarksdale, *t.*, Miss., U.S.A.; p. (1960) *21,105.*

Clarksville, *t.*, Tenn., U.S.A.; on Cumberland R.; tobacco mkt.; p. (1960) *22,021.*

Clausthal-Zellerfeld, *t.*, Lower Saxony, Hanover, Germany; iron, lead, copper, silver, zinc; tourist ctr.; p. (estd. 1954) *17,200.*

Clawson, *t.*, Mich., U.S.A.; p. (1960) *14,795.*

Clay Cross, *urb. dist.*, Derby, Eng.; coal and iron; p. (1961) *9,173.*

Clayton-le-Moors, *urb. dist.*, Lancs, Eng.; nr. Blackburn; textile machin., cotton and blanket weaving, bristles, soap; p. (1961) *6,421.*

Clear, Alaska; site of American ballistic missile early warning station.   [off S.W. cst.

Clear, C. (southernmost point of Ireland), Clear I.,

Clearwater, *t.*, Fla., U.S.A.; citrus fruit, flowers, fish; resort; p. (1960) *34,653.*

Cleator Moor, *colly. t.*, Cumberland, Eng.; p. *8,291.*

Cleburne, *t.*, Texas, U.S.A.; rly wks., flour; p. (1960) *15,381.*

Cleckheaton, *mftg. t.*, Yorks, Eng.; nr. Bradford; woollens, blankets.

Clee Hills, Salop, Eng.; between Rs. Severn and Teme; alt. 1,800 ft.

Cleethorpes, *t., mun. bor.*, Lindsey, Lincs, Eng.; on E. cst. 3 m. S. of Grimsby; resort; p. (estd. 1967) *33,970.*

Clent, *hills*, N.E. Worcester, Eng.; about 10 m. S.W. of Birmingham, on S. edge of S. Staffordshire coalfield, overlooking valley of R. Stour; well wooded; used for recreation by industl. ts. around Birmingham; maximum alt. 1,036 ft.

Clerkenwell, *industl. dist.*, London, Eng.; immediately N. of the City.

Clermont-Ferrand, *t.*, Puy-de-Dome, France; fine Gothic cath.; former cap. of Auvergne; rubber; chemicals; food ind.; p. (1968) *154,110.*

Clevedon, *urb. dist.*, Somerset, Eng.; at mouth of R. Severn; seaside resort; quarrying, bricks, footwear; p. (1961) *10,642.*

Cleveland, *hilly agr. dist.*, N.R. Yorks, Eng.; between R. Tees and Whitby.

Cleveland, *c., port*, Ohio, U.S.A.; on L. Erie; rly. ctr.; steamboat mnfs.; machin., iron foundries, lumber, coal, oil-refining, meat canning, steel, metals, aircraft, refrigerators, chemicals; p. (1970) *738,956*; Greater C. *2,043,000.*

Clevees, *see* Kleve.

Clew Bay, Mayo, Ireland; 10 m. by 7 m.

Clichy, *t.*, Seine, France; p. (1962) *56,495.*

Clifton, *sub.*, Bristol, Eng.; on R. Avon; mineral springs; famous suspension bridge.

Clifton, *t.*, New Jersey, U.S.A.; nr. Passaic; p. (1960) *82,084.*

Clinton, *c.*, Iowa, U.S.A.; on Mississippi R.; iron and steel; p. (1960) *33,589.*

Clinton, *t.*, Mass., U.S.A.; on Nashua R.; machin., carpets; p. (1960) *12,848.*

Clinton Golden Lake, *L.*, Mackenzie, N.W. Terr., Canada.

Clipperton I., Pacific Oc., S.W. of Mexico; belongs to France (since 1931).

Clitheroe, *t., mun. bor.*, Lancs, Eng.; on R. Ribble; cotton weaving, limestone quarrying; p. (estd. 1967) *12,640.*

Clonakilty, *urb. dist.*, Cork, Ireland; nr. Bandon; corn, farming; p. (1966) *2,341.*

Cloncurry, *t.*, Queensland, Australia; in pastoral and copper-producing dist. S. of the G. of Carpentaria; p. (1966) *2,174.*

Clones, *mkt. t., urb. dist.*, nr. Dundalk, Monaghan, Ireland; rly. ctr.; p. (1961) *2,107.*

Clonfert, *c.*, Galway, Ireland; famous monastery.

Clonmel, *t., urb. dist.*, Tipperary, Ireland; on R. Suir; agr. ctr.; fairs; cider, footwear; p. (1966) *11,026.*

Clovelly, *par.*, Devon, Eng.; seaside resort, picturesque fishing vil.

Clovis, *t.*, N.M., U.S.A.; rly. junction, tr. ctr., wheat, cattle; p. (1960) *23,713.*

Cloyne, *mkt. t.*, nr. Middleton, Cork, Ireland.

Cluj, *c.*, Romania; textiles, uranium, engin.; p. (1963) *204,400.*

Clunes, *gold-mining t.*, Victoria, Australia, nr. Ballarat.

Clutha R., S.I., New Zealand.

Clwyd, *R.*, Denbigh, N. Wales; flows into Irish Sea at Rhyl; length 30 m.

Clydach, *t.*, Glamorgan, Wales; on R. Tawe, 5 m. N.E. of Swansea; steel wks., nickel refineries.

Clyde, *R.*, Lanark, S.W. Scot.; navigable to Glasgow; greatest shipbldg. ctr. in world; length 96 m.; twin-road tunnel under R. in Glasgow (Whiteinch–Linthouse) completed 1963.

Clyde, Firth of, Scot.

Clydebank, *burgh*, Dunbarton, Scot.; on the Clyde adjoining Glasgow; shipbldg., sewing machin., tyres, biscuits; p. (estd. 1968) *50,211.*

Clydesdale, *valley* of R. Clyde, S.W. Scot., agr.; fine horses.

Coachella Valley, Cal., U.S.A.; part of old bottom of G. of Cal. which lies N.W. of Stalon Sea; arid; dates and citrus fruits under irrigation from Imperial Valley irrigation system.

Coahuila, *st.*, Mexico; cap. Saltillo; maize, cotton; silver, coppn, coal, gold; a. 55,062 sq. m.; p. (1960) *907,734.*

Coalbrookdale, *vil.*, Salop, Eng.; old coal- and iron-mines.

Coalville, *t., urb. dist.*, Leics. Eng.; nr. Ashby-de-

la-Zouch; coal-mining, engin., elastic webbing; p. (estd. 1967) *28,150.*

Coanza, R., Angola; length 660 m.

Coast Range, *mtns.*, U.S.A.; along Pacific cst.

Coatbridge, *burgh*, Lanark, Scot.; 10 m. E. of Glasgow; coal, iron and steel, prefabricated houses, tubes, engin.; p. (1961) *53,946.*

Coatesville, *t.*, Penns., U.S.A.; iron, steel, brass, textiles; p. (1960) *12,971.*

Coats I., S. of Southampton I., Hudson Bay, Canada.

Coatzacoalcos (Puerto México), *spt.*, Mexico; on G. of Campeche; oil refinery; chemicals, fertilisers; p. *13,740.*

Cobalt, *t.*, Ontario, Canada; silver, cobalt, arsenic, nickel; p. (1961) *2,209.*

Coban, *t.*, Guatemala, Central America; coffee and Peruvian bark tr.; p. (estd. 1960) *42,300.*

Cobar, *t.*, N.S.W., Australia; copper; sawmills; p. (1966) *2,343.*

Cobh (Queenstown), *spt., urb. dist.*, Cork, Ireland; fine harbour and docks; p. (1966) *5,608.*

Cobija, *cap.* of Pando dep., N.W. Bolivia; rubber; p. (1962) *2,537.*

Cobourg, *t.*, Ontario, Canada; on L. Ontario; dairying, fruit, woollens; p. (1961) *10,646.*

Coburg, *t.*, Bavaria, Germany; old cas.; wickerwork, furniture, metal, machines, toy inds.; p. (1963) *43,100.*

Cochabamba, *dep.*, Bolivia; a. 25,288 sq. m.; p. (1962) *550,300.*

Cochabamba, *t., cap.* dep. Cochabamba, Bolivia; cath.; oil refining, shoes, rubber tyres, fruit, canning; modern milk plant; hydro-elec. plant projected; p. (1962) *92,008.*

Cochin, *spt.*, Kerala, India; Malabar cst.; exp. coconut oil, tea; oil refining; p. (1961) *35,076.*

Cochin China, *historic region*, formerly part of French Indo-China, bounded by Cambodia on N., China Sea on E., and G. of Siam on W.; drained by Mekong R.; one of world's great rice-growing regions; since 1954, when Vietnam was partitioned, became heartland of S. Vietnam; ch. c. Saigon; a. c. 26,500 sq. m.

Cockburn Land, N. of Baffin I., Arctic Canada.

Cockermouth, *t., urb. dist.*, Cumberland, Eng.; coal, agr., shoe mfg.; p. (1961) *5,823.*

Cocle, *prov.*, Panama, Central America; cap., Penonomé; p. (1960) *93,156.*

Cocos or Keeling Is., *2 coral atolls*, Indian Ocean; since 1955 terr. of Australia; ch. prod. coconuts; strategic psn. S.E. of Ceylon, 530 m. W. of Christmas I., N.E. of Mauritius; radio and cable sta.; civil aviation marine base; German cruiser *Emden* destroyed by Australian cruiser *Sydney* on N. Keeling I. in 1914; a. 5 sq. m.; p. (estd.) *1,000.*

Cod, C., S.E. point of Mass. Bay, U.S.A.; summer resort; fishing, boat bldg.; p. (estd. 1960) *55,000.*

Coesfeld, *t.*, N. Rhine–Westphalia, Germany; textiles, machin.; p. (1963) *20,700.*

Coeur d'Alene, *t.*, Idaho, U.S.A.; lead, silver lumber; p. (1960) *14,291.*

Coffeyville, *t.*, Kan., U.S.A.; p. (1950) *17,133.*

Cognac, *t.*, Charente, France; cognac, bottles; p. (1954) *19,026.*

Cohoes, *c.*, N.Y., U.S.A.; on Hudson R.; hosiery, paper, foundries; p. (1960) *20,129.*

Coimbatore, *t.*, Tamil Nadu, India; coffee, sugar, cotton spinning; p. (1961) *286,305.*

Coimbra, *c.*, Portugal; univ., cath., wine-growing, earthenware mnfs.; p. (1960) *46,313.*

Coin, *commune* Malaga, Spain; soap, paper, textiles, oil, wine, marble; p. (1957) *20,000.*

Cojutepeque, *t.*, El Salvador, Central America; cigars; rice, sugar, coffee in a.; p. (1960) *18,536.*

Colac, *t.*, Victoria, Australia; nr. Melbourne; farming and dairying dist; flax, engin., and brickmaking; p. (1966) *9,497.*

Colchagua, *prov.*, Chile; cap. San Fernando; stock raising; a. 3,422 sq. m.; p. (1961) *181,593.*

Colchester, *mun. bor.*, Essex, Eng.; on R. Colne; univ.; light inds., engin., oyster fisheries; p. (estd. 1967) *72,600.*

Cold Harbour, *vil.*, Va., U.S.A.; battles between Grant and Lee, 1864.

Coldstream, *burgh*, Berwick, Scot.; on R. Tweed; agr. engin., and knitwear; p. (1961) *1,227.*

Coldwater, *t.*, Mich., U.S.A.; engin.; flour, cement, leather goods; p. (1960) *8,850.*

Coleford, *t.*, Gloucester, Eng.; in Forest of Dean; ctr. of sm. coal-mining dist.; p. *2,300.*

Colenso, *t.*, Natal, S. Africa; on R. Tugela; battle 1899; p. *2,145.*

Coleraine, *urb. dist. spt.*, Londonderry, N. Ireland; on R. Bann, 4 m. from sea; univ.: linen, acrilan mftg., distilling; p. (1966) *13,578.*

Coleshill, *t.*, Warwick, Eng.: lurgi gasification plant projected; new colliery 1965; p. *3,177.*

Colima, *volcano* (30 m. N.E. of c.), Mexico, alt. 12,685 ft.

Colima, *st.*, Mexico: on Pacific cst.; cap. Colima; a. 2,009 sq. m.; p. (1960) *164,450.*

Colima, *c.*, Mexico; on Colima R. in fertile valley; p. (estd.) *25,000.*   [ster fishing ind.

Coll, *I.*, off coast of Mull, Argyll, Scot.: agr., lobColle di Val d'Elsa, *commune,* Siena, Italy: cath.: metal mftg.; p. *11,052.*   [p. (1966) *7,616.*

Collie, *t.*, Western Australia; sub-bituminous coal;

Collingswood, *t.*, N.J., U.S.A.; p. (1960) *17,370.*

Collingwood, *t.*, Ontario, Canada; on L. Huron: shipbldg., steel; p. (1961) *8,385.*

Collinsville, *t.*, Ill., U.S.A.; coal, zinc smelting, canning; women's clothes; p. (1960) *14,217.*

Colmar, *t.*, cap. Haut-Rhin dep., France; vines, textiles, rayon, brewing; p. (1962) *54,264.*

Colne, *t.*, *mun. bor.*, E. Lancs, Eng.: cotton mnfs.; p. (estd. 1967) *18,850.*

Colne, *R.*, Essex, Eng.; oysters.

Colne Valley, *urb. dist.* W.R. Yorks; woollens; p. (estd. 1967) *20,760.*

Cologne, (Köln), *c. Land* N. Rhine–Westphalia, Germany; on R. Rhine at N. end of Rhine gorge; cath.; univ.; eau-de-Cologne, electrotechnical ind., machin., metallurgy, paper, wood, chemicals, cars, oil refining, textiles; impt. R. pt. and route ctr.; p. (1968) *856,011.*

Colomb-Béchar, *see* Béchar.   [p. (1962) *77,090.*

Colombes, *t.*, Seine, France; mftg. sub. of Paris;

Colombia, *rep.*, S. America, mountainous in W. (Cordilleras), swampy, llanos in E.; climate mainly tropical. Rs.: Magdalena, Cauca and tribs. of Amazon: Spanish language: Roman Catholic: coffee, tobacco, cocoa, cattle ; gold, platinum, oil, emeralds: oilfield in Amazon a.; cap. Bogotá; a. 439,997 sq. m.; p. (estd. 1968) *19,829,000.*

Colombo, *cap.*, *pt,* Ceylon; exp. tea, rubber, coconuts; p. (1963) *510,947.*

Colón, *c.*, Panama, Central America: at Atlantic end of Panama Canal; comm. ctr., oil refining nearby; p. (1960) *59,598.*

Colonia, *dep.* Uruguay; cap. Colonia; a. 2,193 sq. m.; p. (1953) *135,038.*

Colonsay, *I.*, Inner Hebrides, Scot.: 8 m. long; ecclesiastical antiquities; p. (inc. Oronsay) *238.*

Colorado, *st.*, U.S.A.: in Rocky Mtns.; agr. with irrigation; pastoral; gold, copper, silver, coal, petroleum, uranium: cap. Denver (*q.v.*); a. 104,247 sq. m; p. (1970) *2,195,887.*

Colorado, *R.*, W. of N. America, formed by union of Grand and Green Rs. (2,000 m. long, navigable for 600 m.), with cañon (6,000 ft. deep).

Colorado, *R.*, flows into Blanca Bay, Argentina.

Colorado, *R.*, Texas, U.S.A.; length 900 m.

Colorado Springs, *wat. pl.*, *health resort*, Col., U.S.A.; 64 m. S. Denver: smelting; p. (1960) *70,194.*

Colton, *t.*, S.E. Cal., U.S.A.; fruit and vegetable canning; mkt. gardening; p. (1960) *18,666.*

Columbia, *c.*, Mo., U.S.A.: st. univ.: flour, lumber; p. (1960) *36,650.*

Columbia, *t.*, Penns., U.S.A.; mnfs.; p. (1960) *12.075.*

Columbia, *cap.*, S.C., U.S.A.: burned 1865; univ.: cotton mills; ironwks.; p. (1960) *97,433.*

Columbia, *t.*, Tenn., U.S.A.; mftg.; livestock mkt.; p. (1960) *17,624.*

Columbia, *R.*, on Pacific slope of N. America; rises in Brit. Columbia, flows through Wash., U.S.A.; salmon fishing; length 1,400 m.

Columbia, Dist. of, U.S.A.; on left bank of Potomac R.; contains Washington, the federal cap. of U.S.A.; a. 69 sq. m.; p. (1960) *763,956.*

Columbia, Mt., Alberta, Canada (alt. 12,294 ft.).

Columbus, *st, cap.*, Ohio, U.S.A.; rly. ctr.; st. univ.; machin., paper, aircraft machin., chemicals; p. (1970) *533,418.*

Columbus, *t.*, Ga., U.S.A.; cotton goods, machin.; p. (1960) *116,779.*

Columbus, *t.*, Ind., U.S.A.; engin.; leather goods; p. (1960) *20,778.*   [p. (1960) *24,771.*

Columbus, *t.*, Miss., U.S.A.; cotton, dairying;

Colwyn Bay, *t.*, *mun. bor.*, on cst., 6 m. E. of Llandudno; Denbigh, N. Wales; seaside resort; diamond tools; p. (1961) *23,090.*

Comacchio, *c.*, Italy; nr. the Adriatic, 20 m. N. Ravenna; p. *12,609.*

Comayagua, *c.*, Honduras Rep., Central America; cath.; univ.; p. (1961) *5,192.*

Combe Capelle, *rock shelter*, nr. Dordogne, France; discovery of race type of Aurignacian period, 1909.

Combe Martin, *vil.*, Devon, Eng.; 5 m. E. of Ilfracombe; popular seaside resort; p. (1951) *1,920.*

Comber, *t.*, Down, N. Ireland; linen; p. (1966) *3,925.*

Comiso, *t.*, Sicily, Italy; medicinal spring, porcelain mnfs.; p. *29,555.*

Commentary, *t.*, Allier, France; nr. Moulins; mining; p. (1954) *9,259.*

Como, *c.*, N. Italy; at foot of Alps, on L. Como; silk ind.; oranges, olives; p. (1961) *82,070.*

Como, *L.*, N. Italy (35 m. long), tourist resort.

Comodoro Rivadavia, *spt.*, Chubut prov. Argentina; on San Jorge Gulf, 550 m. S.W. of Bahia Blanca; military zone; ch. source of oil in Argentine; p. (1960) *40,000.*

Comorin, *C.*, most S. point of India.

Comoro Is., unit of French Community with full intern. aut.; Mozambique channel, midway between Africa and Malagasy; cap. Dzaoudzi on Mayotte I.; total a. about 838 sq. m.; turtle fishing; vanilla, copra, sisal, timber, perfume plants; p. (estd. 1968) *244,000.*

Compiègne, *t.*, Oise, France; sugar-mills, rope; Armistice signed between Allies and Germany 1918; French surrendered to Hitler in 1940; p. (1954) *22,325.*

Compton, *t.*, Cal., U.S.A.; heavy engin., glass, oil refining; p. (1960) *71,812.*

Conakry, *cap.*, Guinea; experimental fruit gardens; textiles; airfields; p. (estd. 1965) *113,000.*

Concarneau, *t.*, Finistère, France; on I. nr. Quimper; salted fish and preserve tr.; p. (1954) *10,341.*

Concepción, *prov.*, Chile; cap. Concepción; Lota-Coronel coalfield, lgst in Chile; a. 2,201 sq. m.; p. (1961) *535,633.*

Concepción, *c. prov. cap.*, Chile; shipping ctr. through its pt. Talcahuano; univ.; comm. and cultural t.; severe earthquakes 1939 and 1960; p. (1961) *186,700.*

Concepción, *t.*, Paraguay; trade ctr.; p. (estd. 1960) *34,000.*

Concepción C., on cst. of California, U.S.A.

Conception Bay, Newfoundland, Canada; N.W. of St. Johns.

Conchos, *R.*, Chihuahua prov., Mexico, Central America; flows N.E. from Sierra Tarahumare to Rio Grande; cotton under irrigation in upper valley.

Concón, *t.*, Chile; on N.E. point of Valparaiso Bay; oil refining.

Concord, *t.*, Mass., U.S.A.; literary ctr.; textiles; p. (1960) *12,275.*

Concord, *t.*, N.C., U.S.A.; cotton, textiles; p. (1960) *17,799.*

Concord, *t.*, *cap.*, N.H., U.S.A.; on Merrimore R.; granite, machin., textiles; p. (1960) *28,991.*

Concordia, *t.*, Argentina; on Uruguay R.; p. (1960) *56,000.*

Condamine, *R.*, Queensland, Australia; trib. of R. Darling.

Conegliano, *commune*, N. Italy; silks, wines, light mftg.; p. *15,434.*

Coney I., *t.*, N.Y., U.S.A.; on Long I., 5 m. long, comprises Manhattan Beach, Brighton Beach, W. Brighton and W. End; seaside resort.

Congleton, *t.*, *mun. bor.*, E. Cheshire, Eng.; on S.W. margin of Pennines; agr., salt, clothing, textiles; p. (estd. 1967) *18,650.*

Congo, Rep. of the, *ind. sov. st. within French Community*, Equatorial Africa; cap. Brazzaville; a. 130,000 sq. m.; p. (1968) 870,000.

Congo, Rep. of the, *ind. sov. st.* (ex-Belgian); Central Africa; div. into 8 provs.: Bandundu, Central Congo, East Kasai, Eastern Province, Equator, Katanga, Kivu, West Kasai; climate: uniformly hot, heavy rains; tropical forests; agr., palm oil, cotton, rice, copal, coffee, ivory, rubber; minerals: copper, gold, diamonds, tin, uranium; communications mainly river, some rail; cap. Kinshasha; ch. ts. Buma, Kinsangani, Lubumbashi; a. 906,000 sq. m.; p. (estd. 1968) *16,730,000.*

Congo, *R.*, greatest R. in Africa, numerous tribs.; estd. length 3,000 m.; drains 1,500,000 sq. m., navigable from sea to Matadi for ocean steamers.

from Matadi to Stanley Pool interrupted by rapids and falls, again navigable to Stanley Falls: estuary, 7–10 m. wide.

Conisborough, *t.*, *urb. dist.*, W.R., Eng.; limestone, bricks, tiles; p. (1961) *17,596*.

Coniston, *t.*, Ontario, Canada; on rly. 8 m. E. of Sudbury; nickel smelting; town built by and for nickel-mining company.

Coniston Old Man, *mtn.*, nr. L. Coniston, Lancs, Eng. (alt. 2,575 ft.).

Coniston Water, *L.*, N. Lancs. Eng.; length 5½ m.; tourist resort.

Conjeeveram (Kancheepuram), *t.*, Tamil Nadu, S. India; pilgrimage ctr.; silk, cotton, weaving; p. (1961) *92,714*.

Connacht, *prov.*, Ireland; (includes cos. Galway, Mayo, Sligo, Leitrim, Roscommon); mntnous. in W.; farming, fishing; a. 6,863 sq. m.; p. (1966) *401,518*.

Connah's Quay, *urb. dist.*, Flint, Wales; p. (1961) *8,355*.

Connaught, *see* Connacht.

Connaught Tunnel (Can. Pac. Rly.), B.C., Canada; longest in N. America (5 m.), 5,000 ft. under Mt. Sir Donald (Selkirk Mtns.).

Connecticut, *st.*, New England, U.S.A.; cereals, tobacco, dairying; fishing; watches and clocks, firearms, aircraft, engin., copper, brass, machin.; cap. Hartford; lgst. c. New Haven; a. 5,009 sq. m.; p. (1970) *2,987,950*.

Connecticut, *R.*, flows S. to Long I. Sound, U.S.A.; length 450 m.

Connellsville, *t.*, Penns., U.S.A.; coke, machin., motor cars; p. (1960) *12,814*.

Connemara, *mtns.*, *dist.*, W. of Ireland, Galway; many lakes and bogs; tourist resort.

Conowingo Dam, Penns., U.S.A.; situated on lower Susquehanna R.; hydro-electric power-sta. supplies power to inds. in Philadelphia.

Conroe, *t.*, Texas, U.S.A.; oil, timber; p. (1960) *9,192*.

Consett, *urb. dist.*, Durham, Eng.; on edge of Pennines, 10 m. S.W. of Newcastle; iron, steel, coke, coal; p. (estd. 1967) *37,500*.

Conshohocken, *bor.*, Penns., U.S.A.; iron, steel, surgical instruments, textiles; p. (1960) *10,259*.

Constance (Konstanz), *c.*, Baden-Württemberg, Germany; on L. Constance; cath.; textiles, machin., chemicals, elect. inds.; route ctr.; p. (1963) *55,100*.

Constance, L., or Bodensee, between Switzerland and Germany; 45 m. long, 9 m. broad; a. 207 sq. m.; R. Rhine flows through.

Constanța, *spt.*, Romania; on the Black Sea; exp. petroleum, wheat; p. (1963) *153,871*.

Constantina, *t.*, Andalusia, Spain; p. (1957) *14,619*.

Constantine, *dep.*, N. Algeria; cap. Constantine; p. (1960) *1,411,000*.

Constantine, *t.*, N. Algeria; wheat, woollens, leather; stands 2,130 ft. high upon a rock; p. (1960) *223,000*.

Constantinople, *see* Istanbul.

Conversano, *c.*, Bari, S. Italy; cath.; olives, citrus fruits; mnfs.

Conway, *t.*, S.C., U.S.A.; river pt.; cotton, tobacco, lumber; p. (1960) *8,563*.

Conway, *mun. bor.*, *spt.*, Caernarvon, N. Wales; at mouth of R. Conway; sm. seaside resort; cas.; quarrying, light engin.; p. (1961) *11,392*.

Cooch Behar, *dist.*, W. Bengal, India; a. 1,289 sq. m.; rice, jute, tobacco; p. (1961) *1,019,806*.

Cooch Behar, *t.*, Cooch Behar, India; on Torsha R.; p. (1961) *41,922*.

Cook, *mtn.*, alt. 12,349 ft.; highest point in S. Alps, New Zealand.

Cook Inlet, S. cst., Alaska; U.S.A. (200 m. long); oil; pipeline connects oilfields of Granite Point with marine terminal at Drift R.

Cook Is., British group (Rarotonga, lgst.) in S. Pacific, annexed to New Zealand, 1901; internal self govt. 1965; bananas, oranges, copra; p. (estd. 1965) *20,000*.

Cook Strait, *channel* between N. and S. Is. of N.Z.; 15–18 m. wide; undersea cable completed 1965.

Cookham, *t.*, *rural dist.*, Berks., Eng.; on R. Thames nr. Maidenhead; p. (rural dist. 1961) *17,169*.

Cookstown, *mkt. t.*, *urb. dist.*, Tyrone, Ireland; cement wks.; p. (1966) *5,542*.

Coolin Mtns., *see* Cuillin Hills.

Cooma, *t.*, N.S.W., Australia; mkt. t. and pastoral ctr.; tourism; H.Q. of Snowy Mts. Authority; p. (1966) *9,101*.

Coonoor, *t.*, Tamil Nadu, India; sanatorium 6,000 ft. above sea-level; p. (1961) *30,690*.

Cooper's Creek (Barcoo), R., Central Australia; rises in Warrego Range, Gr. Dividing Range; flows S.W. into marshes of L. Eyre; provides water for livestock in semi-arid region; 900 m.

Coorg, *former st.*, now inc. in Mysore, India; mtnous., forests; coffee, rice, rubber, tea; cap. Mercara; a. 1,587 sq. m.; p. (1961) *322,829*.

Coorong, The, S. Australia; lagoon and long tongue of land on cst.

Coosa, R., Ala., U.S.A.; length 350 m.

Cootamundra, *t.*, N.S.W., Australia; agr. and mftg.; p. (1966) *6,207*.

Cootehill, *mkt. t.*, *urb. dist.*, Cavan, Ireland; Bellamont forest; p. (1951) *1,439*.

Copeland Is., gr. off N.W. coast of Down, N. Ireland, at entrance to Belfast Lough.

Copenhagen, *ch. spt.*, *cap.*, Denmark; on E. cst of Själland I.; royal palace, univ., library naval sta.; steel, metal, textiles, clothing breweries; airport; p. (1965) *1,377,605*.

Copiapo, *cap.*, Atacama prov., Chile; impt. copper and iron mng. ctr.; p. (1960) *37,224*.

Copparo, *commune*, Ferrara, N. Italy; drainer agr. land, in R. Po delta; p. *23,777*.

Coppercliff, *t.*, E. Ontario, Canada; mining, nickel-copper smelting; p. (1961) *3,600*.

Coppermine, R., N.W. Terr., Canada; flows N into Arctic Ocean; length 300 m.

Coquet I., off cst. Northumberland, Eng.

Coquilhatville *see* Mbandaka.

Coquimbo, *prov.*, Chile, on Argentine border copper-mining dist.; cap. La Serena; a 15,397 sq. m.; p. (1960) *393,664*.

Coquimbo, *spt.*, Chile; prin. exps: iron, copper, and manganese ores; p. (1962) *52,250*.

Coracora, *t.*, S. Peru; mining; pt. Chala p. *8,000*.

Coral Sea, Pacific Ocean, extending from the New Hebrides to Australia.

Coral Sea Islands Territory, *Fed. terr.*, Australia; scattered Is., E. of Gt. Barrier Reef, off Queensland cst; possibility of oil exploration.

Coraopolis, *bor.*, S.W. Penns., U.S.A.; iron, steel glass; p. (1960) *9,643*.

Corato, *t.*, Apulia, Italy; farming ctr., olive oil wine; p. *44,139*.

Corbeil-Essonnes, *t.*, Essonne, France; on R Seine, 12 m. S.E. of Paris; flour mills, printing paper; p. (1962) *27,033*.

Corbridge, *t.*, Northumberland, Eng.; on R. Tyne nr. Hexham; p. *2,415*.

Corby, *t.*, Northants, Eng.; 7 m. N. of Kettering steel wks.; one of " New Towns," designated 1950; steel wks., shoes, clothing, lamps; p. (estd. 1967) *46,630*.

Cordeli, *t.*, S.W. Ga., U.S.A.; tr. ctr.; peanuts cotton mills, sawmills; p. (1960) *10,609*.

Córdoba, *agr. prov.*, Argentina; cap. Córdoba a. 65,195 sq. m.; p. (1960) *1,760,000*.

Córdoba, *c.*, Argentina; univ.; wheat, flour, wool shoes; car and aircraft prod.; p. (1960 *600,000*.

Córdoba, *dep.*, Colombia, S. America; cap Monteria; p. (estd. 1959) *377,690*.

Córdoba, *t.*, Veracruz, Mexico; cottons, woollens coffee; p. (1960) *32,883*.

Córdova, *prov.*, Andalusia, Spain; cap. Córdova agr., olives, vines, livestock; a. 5,299 sq. m. p. (1959) *805,150*.

Córdova, *t.*, Andalusia, Spain; cap. of C. prov. on Guadalquivir R.; cath.—formerly a sacre mosque of Mohammedans; textiles, leather distilling; p. (1965) *215,000*.

Corentyne, R., forms bdy. between Brit. an Netherland Guiana; length 400 m.

Corfe Castle, *par.*, Dorset, Eng.; cas. ruins mkt., potter's clay.

Corfu, *see* Kerkyra.

Corigliano, *t.*, S. Italy; 4 m. from E. cst. o Calabria; agr.; p. *15,206*.

Coringa, *t.*, Madras, India; at mouth of Godavari R

Corinth, Isthmus of, divides the Saronic G. from G. of Corinth, Greece; cut across by Ship Canal.

Corinth Canal, *ship canal*, S. Greece; traverses Isthmus of Corinth, links G. of Corinth and Ionian Sea with Saronic G. and Ægean Sea opened 1893; length 3½ m., depth 26 ft.

Corinthia, *prov.*, Greece; p. (1961) *112,491*.

Corinto (Corinth), *c.*, Greece; at W. end of Isth of Corinth; occupies a site 3 m. distant from the ancient classic c. destroyed by earthquake. 1858; currants, olive oil, silk; p. (1961) *15,892*.

Corinto, *ch. spt.*, N.W. Nicaragua; exp. hides, sugar, coffee; p. (1960) *7,096*.

Cork, *co*, S. Ireland; lgst. and most S.; mtns.; dairying, brewing, agr., fisheries; cap. Cork; a. 2,890 sq. m.; p. (1966) *339,525*.

Cork, *spt., co. bor.*, Cork, Ireland; at mouth of R. Lee; univ.; woollens, butter, cattle, brewing, cars, rubber; p. (1966) *122,066*.

Cork Harbour, pt. of call (Cobh) for Atlantic steamers.

Corleone, *t.*, Palermo, Sicily, Italy; mineral springs; p. *13,704*.

Coriu, *t.*, Turkey in Europe; grain mkt.: p. (1965) *27,156*.

Cormeilles-en-Parisis, Hauts-de-Seine, France; p. (1954) *10,638*.

Corner Brook, *c.*, W. Newfoundland; gd. harbour; pulp, paper; p. of E. and W. (1961) *25,185*.

Corning, *t.*, N.Y., U.S.A.; dairying, tobacco; p. (1960) *17,085*.

Cornwall, *co.*, S.W. Eng.; mkt. gardening, oats, cattle, fishing, minerals, kaolin, granite, tin, lt. engin.; extreme point Land's End; co. to. Bodmin; a. 1,357 sq. m.; ⅞p. (1966) *353,000*.

Cornwall, *c.*, Ontario, Canada; on St. Lawrence R.; H.Q. of Seaway Authority; textiles, pulp, paper, flour; p. (1961) *43,639*.

Cornwallis Is., Arctic Ocean, Canada.

Coro, *t.*, Venezuela; agr.; p. (1950) *28,307*.

Corocoro, *sm. t.*, La Paz dep., Bolivia; at alt. 13,000 ft. in Central Andes, 50 m. S. of La Paz; impt. copper-mining ctr.; p. (1946) *4,500*.

Coromandel Cst., cst. of S.E. Tamil Nadu, India.

Coronado, Cal., U.S.A.; fashionable seaside resort; p. (1960) *18,039*.

Coronation Gulf, arm of Arctic Ocean; extreme point N. Canada; discovered by Franklin.

Coronel, *spt.*, Chile; p. *23,027*.

Coronel Oviedo, *t.*, Paraguay; p. (1945) *33,098*.

Corpus Christi, *c.*, Texas, U.S.A.; cotton; p. (1960) *167,690*.

Corrèze, *minous. dep.*, S. Central France; cap. Tulle; cereals, wines, cattle, timber, coal, granite, iron; a. 2,272 sq. m.; p. (1968) *237,858*.

Corrib, Lough, *L.*, Galway and Mayo, R.o.I.; a. 68 sq. m.; R. Corrib flows from it into Atl.

Corrientes, *prov.*, Argentina; cap. Corrientes; a. 34,325 sq. m.; p. (1960) *543,000*.

Corrientes, *t.*, Argentina; on Paraná R.; univ.; cattle, sugar, rice, cotton; p. (1960) *104,000*.

Corrientes, C., Mozambique, Port. E. Africa.

Corry, *t.*, Penns., U.S.A.; oil, engin., metal wks., furniture; p. (1960) *7,744*.

Corsham, *mkt. t.*, Wilts, Eng.

Corsica (Corse), French I. and prov. in Mediterranean; forested, mtns.; agr., olives, lemons, chestnuts, vine growing; cap. Ajaccio; a. 3,367 sq. m.; p. (1962) *275,465*, excluding Bastia.

Corsicana, *t.*, Texas, U.S.A.; p. (1960) *20,344*.

Corso, C., N. point of Corsica.

Cortland, *t.*, N.Y., U.S.A.; stoves, wine; p. (1960) *19,181*.

Cortona, *t.*, Tuscany, Italy; nr. Perugia; silk factories; p. *30,222*.

Coruh, *prov.*, N.E. Turkey, a. 3,408 sq. m.; p. (1960) *193,684, spt.*, the *cap.* p. *13,361*.

Corum, *prov.*, N. Central Turkey in Asia, a. 4,339 sq. m.; p. (1955) *485,847. t.* its *cap.* p. (1965) *41,200*.

Corumba, *port*, Mata Grosso, Brazil; on R. Paraguay; p. (1960) *36,744*.

Corunna, *see* La Coruña.

Corvallis, Ore., U.S.A.; rich farming section, canning, lumber; p. (1960) *20,669*.

Coryton, *t.*, Essex, Eng.; on Thames, oil refining; oil pipeline to Stanlow refinery under constr.

Coseley, *t.*, Staffs., Eng.; partly absorbed in Wolverhampton (1966); p. (1961) *39,557*.

Cosenza, *c.*, S. Italy; ctr. for figs, oranges, olive oil, wine, silk; cath., cas.; p. (1961) *77,590*.

Cosenza, *prov.*, Calabria, Italy; a. 2,566 sq. m.; p. (1951) *685,572*.

Coshocton, *t.*, Ohio, U.S.A.; coal, gas, oil; pottery, enamelware; p. (1960) *13,106*.

Cosne, *t.*, Nièvre, France; on R. Loire; pottery.

Costa Brava, *reg.*, Catalonia, Spain; tourism.

Costa del Sol, *reg.*, Malaga cst., Spain; tourism.

Costa Rica, *rep.*, Central America; cap. San José; volcanic mtns.; agr., coffee, bananas, rubber, gold; a. 19,300 sq. m.; p. (estd. 1969) *1,706,000*.

Costa Smerelda, N.E. Sardinia, Italy; deserted cst. being developed

Côte d'Or Mtns., N.E. part of Central Massif; max. alt. 1,968 ft.

Côte d'Or, *dep.*, E. France; traversed by R. Saône; cap. Dijon; wines, live-stock, iron and steel; a. 3,391 sq. m.; p. (1968) *421,192*.

Cotentin, *peninsula*, N. France; 50 m. long; Cherbourg, at its extremity, 80 m. from Portsmouth.

Côtes-du-Nord, *agr. dep.*, Brittany, W. France; cap. St. Brieuc; wheat, flax, iron, slate, fishing, linen-mkg.; a. 2,787 sq. m.; p. (1968) *506,102*.

Cotopaxi, *vol.*, (alt. 19,613 ft.) in the Andes of Ecuador, nr. Quito; loftiest active volcano in the world; recent eruptions have caused great damage to Ecuador.

Cotopaxi, *prov.*, Ecuador, S. America; cap. Latacunga; a. 2,595 sq. m.; p. (estd. 1962) *193,929*.

Cotrone, *spt.*, Catanzaro, S. Italy; good tr. in wine, olive oil, etc.; p. *21,496*.

Cotswold Hills, W. Eng., between Lower Severn and Upper Thames; highest point, Cleeve Cloud, 1,031 ft.; fine sheep pastures.

Cottbus, *t.*, Cottbus, Germany; on R. Spree; textiles, metallurgy; rly. ctr.; p. (1963) *71,390*.

Coudekerque-Branche, S. E. sub. of Dunkerque, Nord dep., France; tar and lubricant refinery, textiles; p. (1954) *15,334*.   [*11,092*.

Coueron, *t.*, Loire Atlantique, France; p. (1954)

Coulsdon and Purley, *former urb. dist.*, Surrey, Eng., now inc. in Croydon outer bor. Greater London; in dry valley of N. Downs, 4 m. S. of Croydon; residtl.; chalk quarries; p. (1961) *74,738*.

Council Bluffs, *c.*, Iowa, U.S.A.; on Missouri R.; rly. ctr., farm implements, paper, machin.; p. (1960) *54,361*.

Courbevoie, *t.*, industl. sub. of Paris, France; on R. Seine; p. (1962) *59,941*.

Courcelles, *t.*, Hainaut, Belgium; coal, linen, factories; p. (1962) *17,331*.

Courneuve (La), *t.*, Seine, France; p. (1954) *18,349*.

Courtrai, *see* Kortrijk.

Cove and Kilcreggan, *burgh*, Dunbarton, Scot.; at junction of Loch Long and R. Clyde; p. (1961) *877*.

Coventry, *mfg. c., co. bor.*, N. Warwick, Eng.; 18 m. E.S.E. of Birmingham; ctr. of cycle, motor-cycle, motor-car ind.; aircraft, tools; chemicals; projectiles, textiles; cath.; univ.; p. (estd. 1969) *335,650*.   [*23,091*.

Covilha, *t.*, Portugal; cloth factories; (1960)

Covington, *industl. c.*, Ky., U.S.A.; on R. Ohio, opp. Cincinnati; machin., leather, furniture; p. (1960) *60,376*.

Covington, *t.*, Va., U.S.A.; X-ray equipment, paper, rayon, textiles; p. (1960) *11,062*.

Cowbridge, *mun. bor.*, Glamorgan, S. Wales; nr. Cardiff; p. (1961) *1,065*.

Cowdenbeath, *burgh*, Fife, Scot.; 5 m. N.E. of Dunfermline; coal; p. (1961) *11,918*.

Cowes, *t.*, *urb. dist.*, I. of Wight. Eng.; on both sides of estuary of R. Medina; home of the Royal Yacht Squadron; regattas and yacht bldg.; aircraft, p. (1961) *16,974*.

Cowley, *sub.*, Oxford, Oxfordshire, Eng.; 3 m. S.E. of Oxford; mnfs. motor vehicles.

Cowra, *t.*, N.S.W., Australia; famous wheat dist. and site of state experimental farm; sm. mfg ctr.; p. (1966) *7,082*.

Cozenza, *t.*, *cap.*, prov. Cozenza, Italy; iron and steel; p. *40,032*.

Cozumel I., E. of Yucatan Peninsula; Mexico.

Cracow, *see* Kraków.

Cradle, Mt., *mtn.*, Tasmania, alt. 5,069 ft.

Cradock, *t.*, Cape Province; wool tr.; p. (1960) *19,476* inc. *5,200* whites.

Craigavon, *c.*, Armagh, N. Ireland; new "city in a garden" under constr., 10 m. long, merging Portadown and Lurgan, linked by motorway, to provide major base for ind.

Crail, *burgh*, Fife, Scot.; p. (1961) *1,066*.

Craiova, *cap.*, Oltenia, Romania; p. (1963) *140,526*.

Cramlington, *t.*, Northumberland, Eng; 8 m. N. of Newcastle; "New Town" designated 1964 (local authorities and private enterprise); proposed p. *48,000*; major industl. estate to be established.

Cranbrook, *rural dist., mkt. t.*, Kent, Eng.; hops and grain; p. (rural dist. 1961) *14,158*.

Cranford, *t.,* N.J., U.S.A.; iron. chemicals; p. (1960) *26,424.* [*66,766.*

Cranston, *c.,* Rhode I., U.S.A.; mnfs.; p. (1960)

Crater L., Ore., U.S.A.; in National Park, is a gr. body of water 2,000 ft. deep and 6 m. across, set in a crater of an extinct gigantic volcano, 8,000 ft. high.

Crathie and Braemar, *pars.,* Aberdeenshire, Scot.; adjoining Balmoral Cas. and Abergeldie Cas. estates; p. (1951) *1,291.*

Crato, *t.,* Ceara st., Brazil; at foot of Chapados de Araripe, approx. 300 m. by rail S. of Fortaleza; ctr. of irrigated area producing cotton, sugar, rice; p. (1960) *27,649.*

Crau, La, *region,* Bouches-du-Rhône dep., S.E. France; dry, pebbly area E. of Rhône delta; winter pasture for sheep.

Craven, *dist.,* Central Pennines, Eng.; relatively low limestone plateau, alt. mainly below 800 ft. except where capped by grits in N. Craven; typical limestone features, caves, stalactites and stalagmites, steep-sided valleys (dales); drained by R. Ribble to S.W., R. Aire to S.E.; largely moorland, sheep rearing in valleys, rearing of cattle for fattening elsewhere, cultivation of root and fodder crops; R. valleys give the only easy routes across Central Pennines, Leeds to Preston, Leeds to Carlisle; ch. mkt. ts. and route ctrs., Skipton, Settle.

Crawfordsville, *t.,* Ind., U.S.A.; p. (1960) *14,231.*

Crawley, *t.,* Sussex, Eng.; on N.W. flank of the Weald 9 m. S. of Reigate; one of " New Towns " designated 1947 to relieve population congestion in London; extends from vil. of Crawley N. towards Horley; engin., pharmaceutics, metal, leather, wooden goods; p. (estd. (1967) *62,200.*

Crayford, *former urb. dist.,* Kent, Eng.; now inc. in Bexley, Greater London; engin., fabric printing, oil and resin ref. [*4,422.*

Crediton, *mkt. t., urb. dist.,* Devon, Eng.; p. (1961)

Creil, *t.,* Oise, France; on R. Oise, 30 m. N. of Paris; machin. mnf.; p. (1954) *13,500.*

Crema, *commune,* Cremona, N. Italy; cath.; wine, silk, linen, lace, hats; p. *25,163.*

Cremona, *c.,* N. Italy; on R. Po; silk, cotton, stringed instruments; birthplace of Stradivari; p. (1961) *74,242.*

Crete, *I.,* E. Mediterranean; 60 m. from Greek mainland; cap. Khania (Canea), Heraklion (Candia) lgst. c.; incorporated into Greece after Balkan Wars (1913); exp. fruit, oil, etc.; a. 3,235 sq. m.; p. (1961) *483,258.*

Créteil, *t.,* Seine, France; p. (1954) *13,793.*

Creus, C., juts out into Mediterranean Sea, Spain, nr. French border.

Creuse, *dep.,* Central France; agr., etc.; cap. Gueret; a. 2,164 sq. m.; p. (1968) *156,876.*

Creusot, Le, *t.,* Saône-et-Loire, France; lge. ordnance works; p. (1954) *28,663.*

Creutzwald-la-Croix, *t.,* Moselle dep., N.E. France; coal, iron foundries; p. (1954) *10,183.*

Crevillente, *t.,* Spain; wine, wheat and fruit; p. (1957) *12,636.*

Crewe, *t., mun. bor.,* Cheshire, Eng.; 20 m. S.E. of Chester; lge. rly. wks.; impt. rly. junction; aircraft and refrigerator wks., clothing, engin., motor vehicles; p. (estd. 1967) *52,400.*

Crewkerne, *mkt. t., urb. dist.,* Somerset, Eng.; 8 m. S.W. of Yeovil; sailcloth, twine, webbing, gloves, concrete prod.; p. (1961) *4,215.*

Criccieth, *t., urb. dist.,* Caernarvon, N. Wales; on N. shore of Cardigan Bay; sm. seaside resort; p. (1961) *1,671.*

Crickhowell, *rural dist., mkt. t.,* Brecon, S. Wales; on R. Usk; paper; p. (rural dist. 1961) *7,483.*

Cricklade, *t., rural dist.,* N. Wilts., Eng.; on R. Thames, 8 m. N.W. of Swindon; p. (rural dist. 1961) *17,869.*

Crieff, *burgh, summer resort,* Perth, Scot.; on R. Earn, 15 m. W. of Perth; egg hatchery, preserve wks.; p. (1961) *5,773.*

Crimea Peninsula, jutting into Black Sea, U.S.S.R.; wheat, tobacco, fruit; campaign 1854-55 between Russia and the Allied Force of Turkey, Britain, France and Sardinia was chiefly fought out here (Alma, Balaclava and Sevastopol).

Crimmitschau, *t.,* Karl-Marx-Stadt, E. Germany, nr. Zwickau; woollen-cloth. machin.; p. (1963) *30,891.*

Crinan Canal, across peninsula of Kintyre, S.W. Scot.; connecting Loch Gilp with the Atlantic; length 6 m.

Cristóbal, *dist.,* Panama Canal Zone, Central America; adjoins Colón at N. entrance to Canal; p. (1960) *11,499;* of t. (1960) *817.*

Croaghpatrick, *mtns.,* Mayo, Ireland. 2,510 ft.

Croatia, *fed. unit,* Jugoslavia; formerly part of Austria; mtns.; cereals, potatoes, tobacco timber, pigs, sheep, cattle; cap. Zagreb; a. 16,418 sq. m.; p. (estd. 1960) *4,207,000.*

Crockett, *t.,* E. Texas, U.S.A.; lumber, cotton-seed oil, pecan nuts; p. (1960) *5,356.*

Crocodile R., *see* Limpopo.

Croix, *t.,* Nord, France; p. (1954) *18,702.*

Cromarty, *burgh,* Ross and Cromarty, Scot.; off N.E. cst. of Black Isle; p. (1961) *605.*

Cromer, *t., urb. dist.,* Norfolk, Eng.; on N. cst. of E. Anglia; seaside resort; p. (1961) *4,895.*

Crompton, *mfg. t., urb. dist.,* Lancs, Eng.; 2 m. S. of Rochdale; cotton, engin., elec. lamps; p. (1961) *12,707.*

Crooked I., Bahama Is., W. Indies; p. (1953) *836.*

Crosby or Great Crosby, *mun. bor.,* S. Lancs. Eng.; on Liverpool Bay, 3 m. N. of Bootle; residtl.; seaside resort; p. (estd. 1967) *59,650*

Cross, *R.,* S.E. Nigeria; rises in Cameroon Highlands, flows W. and S. into G. of Guinea at Calabar; useful inland waterway; length approx. 400 m.

Cross Fell, *mtn.,* Cumberland, Eng.; on E. border of co.; alt. 2,930 ft.

Crow Head, *O.,* Kerry, Ireland.

Crowley, *t.,* S. La., U.S.A.; rice mills, rice experiment sta.; p. (1960) *15,617.*

Crows Nest Pass, B.C., Alberta, Canada; southernmost pass across Canadian Rocky Mtns.; used by rly. from Medicine Hat to Spokane (U.S.A.); alt. summit 4,459 ft.

Croydon, *residtl. t., former co. bor.,* Surrey, Eng. now outer bor. Greater London; inc. Coulsdon and Purley; lt. inds.; formerly airpt. (closed 1959); p. (1966) *327,000.*

Crozet Is., mountainous uninhabited group in S. Indian Ocean; French.

Cruzeiro, *t.,* São Paulo st., Brazil; p. (estd. 1968) *37,273.*

Csepel, *sub.,* Budapest, Hungary; iron and steel oil refining, leather, paper; p. (1965) *60,000*

Csongrad, *mkt. t., agr. dist.,* Hungary; at junction of Rs. Theiss and Koros; p. (1962) *20,399.*

Cuba, *I.,* W. Indies; taken from Spain by the U.S.A., but later constituted an independent rep.; climate, insular tropical, plentiful rainfall; tropical forest; agr., sugar-cane, tobacco, maize, fruits, mahogany and cedar, hardwoods, iron, copper, rayon, cement; cap. Havana; a. 44,206 sq. m.; p. (estd. 1968) *8,074,000.*

Cubango, *R.,* S. Africa, enters L. Ngami.

Cuckfield, *mkt. t., urb. dist.,* Sussex, Eng.; p. (estd. 1967) *23,800.*

Cuckmere, *R.,* Sussex, Eng.; rises in High Weald and flows S. into English Channel 4 m. W. of Beachy Head; passes through S. Downs in very beautiful gap; length 23 m.

Cucuta, *t.,* cap. Santander del Norte, Colombia, S. America; coffee, tobacco, cattle; p. (estd. 1959) *131,410.*

Cudahy, *t.,* Wis., U.S.A.; p. (1960) *17,975.*

Cuddalore, *spt.,* Tamil Nadu, India; nr. Pondicherry; exp. oil-seeds, cottons; p. (1961) *79,163.*

Cuddapah, *t.,* Andhra Pradesh, India; cotton cloth factories, millet, rice; p. (1961) *49,027.*

Cudillero, *commune,* Oviedo, N.W. Spain; manganese; p. *10,630.* [*9,042.*

Cudworth, *urb. dist.,* W.R Yorks, Eng.; p. (1961)

Cue, *t.,* W. Australia; goldfields.

Cuenca, *c.,* Cuenca, Spain; on R. Jucar; p. (1949) *25,215.*

Cuenca, *agr. and mining prov.,* Central Spain; furniture, leather, paper; a. 6,588 sq. m.; p. (1959) *326,753.*

Cuenca, *cap.,* Azuay, Ecuador; univ.; cath.; sugar, tyres, flour mills; p. (1962) *63,000.*

Cuernavaca, *cap.,* Morelos St., Mexico; ancient Indian t. captured by Cortes; p. *30,567.*

Cuesmes, *coal mng. t.,* adjoining Mons, Belgium; p. (1962) *10,799.*

Cuiabá, *c., cap.,* Mato Grosso, Brazil; ctr. pastoral a.; gold and diamonds produced; galena deposit nearby; p. (estd. 1968) *87,316.*

Cuidadela, *t.,* Balearic Is., Spain; W. cst. of Minorca; cath.; ancient ruins; cheese mnfs.; p. *10,716.* [Sgurr Alasdair; alt. 3,251 ft.

Cuillin Hills, I. of Skye, Scot.; highest peak

Culebra, *valley and mtns.*, N. New Mexico.

Culebra, *spt. and I.*, Puerto Rico; W. Indies.

Culgoa, *R.*, trib. of Darling R., Queensland and N.S.W., Australia.

Culiacán, *c.*, cap. Sinaloa, Mexico; tropical fruits, sugar, cotton; pt., at Altata p. (estd.) *49,000*.

Cullera, *spt.*, Valencia, Spain; on R. Jucar; p. (1957) *14,831*. [mining ind.

Cullinan, *t.*, Transvaal, S. Africa; ctr. of diamond-

Culloden Moor, 6 m. E. of Inverness, Scot.; defeat of Bonnie Prince Charlie, 1746.

Culver City, Cal., U.S.A.; large motion-picture plant; p. (1960) *32,163*.

Cumaná, *spt., c.*, Sucre, Venezuela; coffee, cacao; sardine canning; airport; p. (1961) *73,400*.

Cumaná, *G.*, N. Venezuela.

Cumberland, *co.*, Eng.; S.E. part of Lake Dist., ch. mtns.: Scafell, Helvellyn, Skiddaw; ch. Ls.: Ullswater, Derwentwater, Thirlmere; oats, sheep rearing, dairying, fishing, coal, iron ore, iron and steel, shipbldg.; 2 nuclear power stas.; a. 1,516 sq. m.; p. (1966) *296,000*.

Cumberland, *industl. t.*, Md., U.S.A.; on Potomac R.; iron and steel; p. (1960) *33,450*.

Cumberland, *t.*, R.I., U.S.A.; iron, cotton, silk, granite; p. (1960) *18,763*. [700 m.

Cumberland, *R.*, Ky., U.S.A.; trib. of Ohio;

Cumberland Gap, Ky., U.S.A.; ch. break in high E. wall of Cumberland Plateau; gives access from upper Tennessee valley to Cumberland and Ohio valleys; very impt. routeway in colonisation of Ky.

Cumberland Is., off coast of Queensland, Australia.

Cumberland Plateau, *mtn. region*, Ky., Tenn., Ala., U.S.A.; forms S.W. zone of Appalachian mtn. system terminating abruptly towards Tennessee valley to E., Cumberland valley to W.; drained W. by tribs. of Cumberland and Ohio Rs.; composed of horizontal sandstones overlying coal; thinly populated by backward farming communities except where mining ts. occur in valleys cut down to coal; mainly between 1,200 and 3,000 ft.

Cumbernauld, Dunbarton, Scot.; designated "New Town" 1955; to accommodate 50,000 "over-spill" from Glasgow; adding machines; p. (estd. 1965) *16,448*.

Cumbrae, *Is.*, in F. of Clyde, off est. of Ayr, Scot.

Cumbrian Mtns., Lake District, Cumberland, Westmorland and Lancashire, Eng.

Cumnock and Holmhead, *sm. burgh, mng. dist.*, Ayr, Scot.; p. (1961) *5,403*.

Cundinamarca, *dep.*, Colombia, S. America; contains the fed. cap. Bogotá; a. 9,106 sq. m.; p. (1962) *2,121,680*.

Cunene, see Kunene, R. [*529,963*.

Cuneo, *prov.*, Italy; a. 2,870 sq. m.; p. (1961)

Cuneo, *cap.*, Cuneo prov., Italy; cath.; cotton, paper; p. (1961) *45,709*.

Cupar, *burgh*, Fife, Scot.; on R. Eden, W. of St. Andrews; linen; sugar beet; p. (1961) *5,495*.

Curaçao I. (Netherlands Antilles), in the Caribbean, off N. est. of Venezuela; oil refining, phosphates, salt, aloes, resin, hides, skins; a. 210 sq. m.; p. (1963) *127,164*.

Curanilahua, *commune*, Aranco, Chile; coal-mining; p. *13,026*.

Curepipe, *t.*, Central Mauritius; health resort; p. (estd. 1968) *50,000*. [*116,391*.

Curico, *prov.*, Chile; a. 2,214 sq. m.; p. (1961)

Curico, *t.*, Chile; agr. and comn. ctr.; flour milling, brewing, wines; p. (1961) *32,600*.

Curitiba, *t.*, cap. Paraná st., Brazil; industl. and comm. ctr.; coffee, maté, chemical, pharmaceutical, and forest prods., foodstuffs; univ.; p. (estd. 1968) *616,548*.

Curtea de Arges, *t.*, Romania; on S. slopes of the Transylvanian Alps; p. (1956) *10,764*.

Curwensville, *bor.*, Penns., U.S.A.; firebrick, leather, clay, clothing; p. (1950) *3,332*.

Curzola or Korcula, I., *i.*, Dalmatia, Jugoslavia; in the Adriatic; fishing, seafaring, agr.

Cushing, *t.*, Okla., U.S.A.; oil, gas, refineries, industl. ctr.; p. (1960) *8,619*.

Cuttack, *t.*, Orissa st., India; on Mahanadi R.; long famous for gold and silver filigree work; p. (1961) *146,308*.

Cuxhaven, *spt.*, Lower Saxony, Germany; outport of Hamburg at the mouth of R. Elbe; fine harbour, docks, fishing; p. (1968) *44,900*.

Cuyahoga, *R.*, in N. Ohio, U.S.A., flowing into L. Erie at Cleveland; length 85 m.

Cuyahoga Falls, *t.*, Ohio, U.S.A.; p. (1960) *47,922*.

Cuyapo, *mun.*, Luzon, Philippines; rice, sugar, tobacco, hemp; p. *24,570*.

Cayuri, *R.*, Venezuela, enters sea Brit. Guiana.

Cuzco, *ancient t.*, Peru; in the Andes at alt. 11,400 ft. in valley of Urubamba R.; once cap. of the Incas; temple and fortress; besieged and sacked by Manco Inca in 1536; cath.; cottons, woollens; p. (1961) *68,000*.

Cuzco, *dep.*, Peru; a. 55,716 sq. m.; p. (1961) *590,958*.

Cwmamman, *urb. dist.*, Carmarthen, Wales; on R. Loughor, 12 m. N.E. of Llanelly; p. (1961) *4,272*.

Cwmbran, *t.*, Monmouth, Wales; in valley of Avon-Lwyd, 5 m. N. of Newport; one of "New Towns" designated 1949 comprises bulk of Cwmbran urb. dist. and extends N. towards Pontypool; iron, motor accessories, wire, elec. goods, bricks, tiles, pipes; p. (estd. 1965) *35,560*.

Cyclades, group of about 220 Is. Grecian arch.; ch. t. Hermopolis (Syros); a. 1,023 sq. m.; p. (1961) *99,931*.

Cyprus, Republic of, *I.*, *indep. sov. st.* within Brit. Commonwealth (1960), E. Mediterranean; 40 m. from Turkey, 60 m. from Syria; cap. Nicosia; prin. pt. Famagusta; exports carobs, potatoes, tobacco, vegs., grapes, citrus fruits; copper-mng. in decline; tourism; a. 3,572 sq. m.; p. (estd.) *631,000*.

Cyrenaica, see Libya.

Czechoslovak Socialist Republic (ČSSR.), *fed. two-rep. st.*, Central Europe; former provs. of Bohemia, Moravia, Slovakia of geographical significance only; mtnous.; fertile valleys; agr.: potatoes, sugar-beet, cereals, hops, lumbering; coal, iron, sugar, textiles, glass, stoneware, machin., chemicals, footwear, cars, cycles; cap. Praha (Prague); a. 49,331 sq. m.; p. (1968) *14,445,000*.

Czeladz, *t.*, S.W. Poland; coal; p. (1965) *31,000*.

Czernowitz, see Chernovtsy.

Czestochowa, *c.*, Katowice prov., S. Poland; on Warta R.; old pilgrimage monastery; rly. and industrl. ctr.; iron and steel, textiles; p. (1965) *175,000*.

Czirknitzer (Zirknitzer), *L.*, with I. in Carniola, Jugoslavia, S. of Ljubljana, 6 m. long; extraordinary variations in depth.

D

Daanbantayan, *mun.*, N. Cebu, Philippine Is.; rice, sugar; p. *24,198*.

Dabhoi, *t.*, Gujarat, India; architectural remains; p. (1961) *30,841*.

Dabrowa Gornicza *t.*, Poland; 38 m. N.W. of Kraków; coal, zinc, iron ore; p. (1965) *60,000*.

Dacca, *ch. c.*, E. Pakistan; univ.; on Buriganga R., old channel of Ganges; jute, muslin; medical radioisotope ctr.; p. (1961) *556,712*.

Dachau, *t.*, Bavaria, Germany; paper, elec. goods, brewing; concentration camp during last war; p. (1963) *30,000*.

Dachstein, *mtn.*, Salzkammergut, Austria; alt. 9,830 ft.

Dade City, *t.*, Fla., U.S.A.; ctr. of mkt. gardening and citrus region; kaolin; p. (1960) *4,759*.

Dadra and Nagar Haveli, Union Terr., India; admin. ctr. Silvassa; a. 189 sq. m.; p. (1962) *57,963*.

Dagenham, *former mun. bor.*, Essex, Eng.; on N. bank of R. Thames, 10 m. E. of London; now inc. in Barking outer London bor. (except N. Chadwell Heath Ward inc. in Redbridge); motor cars, drugs, chemicals; p. (1961) *108,363*.

Dagestan, Caucasian prov. of R.S.F.S.R., U.S.S.R.; one of the most mountainous dists. in the world; cap. Makhachkala; cotton, orchards and vineyards; machin., engin, oil; a. 19,400 sq. m.; p. (1959) *1,063,000*. [Finland.

Dago (Hiiumaa), *I.*, Estonia, at entrance G. of

Dagupan, *t.*, Pangasinan, Luzon, Philippines; on Lingayen Bay; comm. ctr.; p. (1960) *63,191*.

Daharki Mari *t.*, Pakistan; 350 m. N.E. of Karachi; fertiliser plant projected.

Dahlak Archipelago, gr. of Is. in Red Sea, nr. Massawa; pearl fishing.

Dahomey, *ind. sov. st. within French Community*, W. Africa; forests, palm-oil; cap. Porto Novo; a. 47,000 sq. m.; p. (1968) *2,571,000*.

Daimiel, *mkt. t.*, Ciudad Real, Spain; cheeses, oil, wine; p. (1957) *20,204*.

Dairen, *see* Talien.

Dakar, *spt., air and naval base.* Senegal, W. Africa, S.E. of Cape Verde behind Gorée I., impt. adm. ctr.; airpt. for S. America: groundnuts; p. (1960) *383,000*.

Dakhla, *oasis,* Libyan Desert, U.A.R.; 170 m. S.W. of Asyut; dates, olives; stage on caravan route from Cyrenaica to Upper U.A.R.

Dakota, *R.,* trib. of Missouri R., U.S.A.

Dakovica, *t.,* Jugoslavia; 80 m. E. of Cetinje; p. (1959) *20,000*.

Dalälven, *R.,* S. Central Sweden; length 325 m.

Dalaguete, *t.,* Cebu, Philippines; sugar, maize; p. *30,000*.   [nuclear reactor (1963).

Dalat, *t.,* S. Viet-Nam; 140 m. N.E. Saigon;

Dalbeattie, *burgh,* Kircudbright, Scot.; granite, dairy prod. gloves; p. (1961) *3,104.*

Dalby, *t.,* Queensland, Australia; likely to increase with devel. of Moonie oilfield; dairying, timber; p. (1966) *8,870.*   [posed p. *10,000*.

Dalgety, *t.,* on Fife cst., Scotland; New t. pro-

Dalhousie, *health resort,* Chamba, Himachal Pradesh, India; 7,687 ft. above sea-level.

Dalhousie, *spt.,* N.B., Canada; lumber, lobsters, salmon; resort; p. (1961) *5,856.*

Dalkeith, *burgh,* Midlothian, Scot.; 6 m. S.E. of Edinburgh; coal; ironwks.; p. (1961) *5,864.*

Dalkey, *t.,* Dublin, Ireland; on E. cst.; 4 m. N. of Wicklow border; seaside resort; residtl.; p. (1956) *5,526.*

Dallas, *c.,* Texas, U.S.A.; in cotton and grain-growing region; machin., aeroplanes; p. (1970) *836,121;* Greater D. *1,539,000.*

Dalmatia, *dist.,* N.E. Adriatic cst., Jugoslavia; limestone (Karst) plateau; olive oil, wine; a. 4,916 sq. m.; p. *622,000.*   [p. (1960) *17,868.*

Dalton, *t.,* N. Ga., U.S.A.; cotton and sawmills;

Daltonganj, *t.,* Bihar, India; on R. Koël; shellac, cement; p. (1961) *25,270.*

Dalton-in-Furness, *t., urb. dist.,* N. Lancs, Eng.; limestone quarrying, woollens, felt mftg.; abbey ruins; p. (1961) *10,317.*   [Bay.

Daly, *R.,* N. Terr., Australia; flowing into Anson

Daman (Damao), *spt.,* India; 100 m. N. Bombay; fishing, ship-bldg., cotton; p. (1960) *22,388.*

Damanhur, *t.,* U.A.R.; on E. margin of Nile delta, 25 m. S.E. of Alexandria; mkt. for local agr. produce; p. (1960) *126,000.*

Damaraland, formerly part of German S.W. Africa now administered by Union of S. Africa; only pt., Walvis Bay; cattle rearing.

Damascus (Arabic Esh-Sham), *cap.,* Syria; 57 m. S.E. of its pt. Beirut; claims to be oldest continuously inhabited c. in world; metal-wk., glass, cement; p. (1961) *507,503.*

Dambovitta, *R.,* Romania; rises in Mt. Omul (Transylvanian Alps), flows S. through Bucharest to R. Danube; flows through impt. oilfields; length 150 m.

Damghan, *t.,* Iran; nr. Caspian Sea; p. *16,500.*

Damietta, *t.,* Nile Delta, U.A.R.; cotton; p. (1960) *72,000.* [ctr. and mkt.; p. (1961) *44,678.*

Damoh, *t.,* N. Madhya Pradesh, India; agr.

Dampier, *spt.,* W. Australia; mouth of Fitzroy R.; new pt. (1965) for shipping of iron ore; solar salt evaporation plants projected.

Dampier Archipelago, *gr. of sm. Is.,* off N.W. Australia.

Dampier Strait, *channel* between N.W. of New Guinea and Waigeu I.

Dampier Strait, Bismarck archipelago, between Umboi and New Britain. [p. (1962) *10,012.*

Dampremy, *commune,* Hainaut, Belgium; coal;

Danakil or Dankali Country, Eritrea; cst. land between Red Sea and Ethiopia; potash being exploited; sm. pt. and road projected.

Danao, *t.,* Cebu, Philippines; rice and sugar dist.; p. (1960) *32,326.*

Danbury, *t.,* Conn., U.S.A.; hat-mkg. ind. since 1780; p (1960) *22,928.*

Dandenong, *c.,* Victoria, Australia; 19 m. E. of Melbourne; growing industl. ctr.; p. (estd. 1968) *23,700.*

Dannemora, *t.,* Sweden; 25 m. N.E. of Uppsala; iron ore worked since 1579; p. *1,062.*

Dannevirke, *t.,* N.I., N.Z.; p. (1961) *5,517.*

Dansalan, *chartered c.,* cap. of Lanao prov., Philippine Is.; resort; p. (1948) *19,657.*

Danube, *R.* second longest R. in Europe; rises in Black Forest, Germany, and flows E. into Black Sea; navigation for steamers from Ulm to the sea; Vienna, Budapest, Belgrade and other large cs. on its banks; length 1,750 m.

Danvers, *t.,* Mass., U.S.A.; p. (1960) *21,926.*

Danville, *c.,* Ill., U.S.A.; coal; p. (1960) *41,856.*

Danville, *t.,* Ky., U.S.A.; mkt. for tobacco, hemp; horses; p. (1960) *9,010.*

Danville, *c.,* Va.; cotton, tobacco; p. (1960) *46,577.*

Danzig, *see* Gdansk.

Darbhanga, *t.,* Bihar, India; rice, oil-seeds, grain, sugar; p. (1961) *103,016.*

Dardanelles, *strait* between Europe and Turkey, connecting Ægean Sea with Sea of Marmara; (the ancient Hellespont), 40 m. long.

Dar-es-Salaam, *spt., cap.,* Tanzania, E. Africa; univ. coll.; textile mill projected; oil refining; pipeline to Ndola, Zambia; naval base and Tanzania-Zambia rly. being built with Chinese aid; p. (1967) *272,515.*   [6 881.

Darveld, *urb. dist.,* W.R. Yorks, Eng.; p. (1961)

Darfur, *prov.,* Sudan, N.E. Africa; between Kordofan and Wadai; inhabited by Arabs and Negroes; cap. El Fasher; a. 138,150 sq. m.; p. (1947) *832,800.*   [p. (1960) *19,715.*

Darien, *region,* Panama; tortoiseshell, pearls, gold;

Darjeeling, *hill t.,* West Bengal, India; tea, quinine; has suffered from earthquake and landslips; p. (1961) *40,651.*

Darkhan, *new t.,* Mongolia; on R. Hara; industl.

Darlaston, *former urb. dist.,* Staffs, Eng.; partly absorbed in Wolverhampton (1966); nuts, bolts, fabricated steel mnfs., drop forgings, car components; p. (1961) *21,732.*

Darling, *R.,* N.S.W., Australia; rises in Gr. Dividing Range, flows S.W. into Murray R. at Wentworth; length 1,702 m.

Darling Downs, *plateau,* S.E. Queensland, Australia; grazing cty.; ch. t. Toowomba.

Darling Range, *mtns.;* granite range; gt. grazing cty. of W. Australia; parallel with cst., highest peak, 3,500 ft.

Darlington, *t., co. bor.,* Durham, Eng.; locomotive, wagon and bridge bldg., woollen yarn mnf.; engin.; p. (estd. 1967) *84,720.*

Darmstadt, *t.,* Hesse, W. Germany; cas.; comm. ctr.; metallurgy, paper, machin., radio, chemicals, plastics; p. (1968) *139,558.*

Dart, *R.,* Devon, Eng.; rises in Dartmoor, flows S. into English Channel at Dartmouth; l. 46 m.

Dartford, *mkt. t., mun. bor.,* Kent, Eng.; nr. S. cst. of Thames Est. 15 m. E. of London; Dartford–Purfleet road tunnel (1963); engin., chemicals, quarrying, paper; p. (estd. 1967) *46,520.*

Dartmoor, *high stony plateau,* S.W. Devon, Eng.; granite; kaolin; sheep and ponies; a. 220 sq. m.; highest point, High Willhays, 2,039 ft.

Dartmouth, *spt., mun. bor.,* S. Devon, Eng.; on W. of estuary of R. Dart; Royal Naval College; pottery; p. (estd. 1967) *7,190.*

Dartmouth, *t.,* Nova Scotia; p. (1961) *46,966.*

Dartmouth, *t.,* Mass., U.S.A.; p. (1960) *14,464.*

Dartmouth, *pt.,* Richmond Bay, Prince Edward I., Canada.   [coal; p. (1961) *14,111.*

Darton, *urb. dist.,* W.R. York., Eng.; nr. Barnsley;

Darvel, *burgh,* Ayr, Scot.; on R. Irvine, 8 m. E. Kilmarnock; curtains, carpet; p. (1961) *3,255.*

Darwen, *t., mun. bor.,* N.E. Lancs, Eng.; on flank of Rossendale Fells, 3 m. S. of Blackburn; cottons, tile and glaze brick, paint and paper, mftg.; p. (estd. 1967) *28,810.*

Darwin, *c., spt.,* N. Terr., Australia; landing place of world airlines—England to Australia; p. (1966) *20,261.*

Dashava, settlement in Lvov Oblast, W. Ukraine, U.S.S.R.; ctr. of rich natural gas field and starting point of gas pipe-line to Kiev and Moscow, built after 2nd World War.

Datia, *t.,* Madhya-Pradesh, India; stone-walled, palaces; p. (1961) *29,430.*

Datteln, *t.,* N. Rhine-Westphalia, Germany; coal, leather, iron; p. (1963) *31,200.*

Daugavpils, *t.,* Latvian S.S.R. on Dvina R.; textiles, engin., rly. repair wks.; p. (1959) *65,000.*

Daura, *t.,* nr. Baghdad, Iraq; oil refining.

Davão, *t.,* Mindanao, Philippines; p. (estd.) *279,000.*

Davenport, *c.,* Iowa, U.S.A.; at foot of Rock I.; rapids; on Mississippi R.; flour mills; p. (1960) *88,981.*

Daventry, *t., mun. bor.,* Northampton, England.; 9 m. S.E. of Rugby; boot-mkg., light engin.; wireless-transmission sta.; p. (estd. 1967) *6,560.*

David, *t.,* cap. Chiriqui prov., Panama; timber, coffee, cacao, sugar; p. (1960) *22,924.*

Davis Strait, *channel* between Greenland and

Baffin Land, N.W. Terr., Canada; connects Atlantic with Baffin Bay.

Davos-Platz, *Alpine winter resort*, Grisons, Switzerland; alt. 4,845 ft.; p. *9,259.*

Dawley, *t., urb. dist.*, Shropshire, Eng.; on S.E. flank of The Wrekin; ironwks., pipe, cement, roadstone, asphalt and brick wks., engin.; new t. with Wellington and Oakengates forms new t. of Telford; p. (estd. 1966) *21,240.*

Dawlish, *t., urb. dist.*, S. Devon, Eng.; on S. cst. between estuaries of Rs. Exe and Teign; seaside resort; p. (1961) *7,507.*

Dawson, *t.*, Yukon Terr., Canada; on Yukon R., nr. the Klondyke goldfields; asbestos mng. projected 1968; p. (1961) *846.*

Dax, *t.* Landes, S.W. France; on Adour R.; hot sulphur spring; horse mart; p. (1962) *18,422.*

Dayton, *c.*, Ohio, U.S.A.; on Great Miami R.; univ.; aeroplanes, elec. machin., rubber goods; p. (1960) *262,332.*

Daytona Beach, *t.*, Fla., U.S.A.; resort, tr. and shipping, ctr.; p. (1960) *37,395.*

De Aar, *t., rly. junction*, Cape Province, S. Africa; 500 m. from Cape Town; rlys. from N.W. (Luderitz, Walvis Bay) and S.E. (Pt. Elizabeth, E. London) join Cape Town to Johannesburg trunk rly.; p. *9,137.*

Dead Sea, *salt-water L.* between Israel and Jordan; surface 1,286 ft. below level of the Mediterranean; a. 340 sq. m., length 47½ m., greatest width 9½ m., greatest depth 1,309 ft.; receives waters of Jordan; high mineral content.

Deal, *mun. bor., ancient spt.*, E. Kent, Eng.; on S.E. cst. 7 m. N.E. of Dover; opposite Goodwin Sands; seaside resort; Julius Cæsar is said to have first landed nr.; p. (estd. 1967) *26,780.*

Dean, Forest of, Gloucester, Eng.; between Wye and Severn Rs.; coal-mining.

Dearborn, *t.* Mich., U.S.A.; p. (1960) *112,007.*

Dearne, *urb. dist.*, W.R. Yorks, Eng.; p. (estd. 1967), *26,720.*

Death Valley, *depression*, Cal., U.S.A.; in Mohave Desert, 150 m. N.E. of Los Angeles; completely arid; floor covered with saline deposits; tourist attraction; depth of valley floor 276 ft. below sea-level.

Debar, *t.*, Jugoslavia; nr. Drin R.; tr. ctr., cattle breeding, sulphur springs; p. *6,913.*

Debra Markos, *cap.*, Gojjam prov., Ethiopia; p. approx. *5,000.*

Debrecen, *t.*, Hungary; 114 m. E. of Budapest; univ.; ctr. of pastoral dist.; fairs; pharmaceutics, medical instruments; p. (1965) *146,000.*

Decatur, *t.*, Ala., U.S.A.; steel, textiles; p. (1960) *29,217.*

Decatur, *t.*, Ga.. U.S.A.; p. (1960) *22,026.*

Decatur, *c.*, Ill., U.S.A.; mnfs., coal; p. (1960) *78,004.*

Decazeville, *t.*, Aveyron, S. France; coalmine (due for closure); p. (1962) *12,032.*

Deccan, The, gr. upland of S. India, bounded by the Narbada and Kistna Rs.

Dedham, *t.*, Mass., U.S.A.; p. (1960) *23,869.*

Dedza, *t.*, S. Malawi, new t.; p. (1966) *2,261.*

Dee, *R.*, N. Wales and Cheshire; length 90 m.

Dee, *R.*, Aberdeen and Kincardine, Scot.; length 87 m.

Dee, *R.*, Kirkcudbright, Scot.; length 38 m.

Dee, *R.*, Louth, Ireland; flowing to Dundalk Bay; length 20 m.

Defiance, *t.*, N.W. Ohio, U.S.A.; light mftg., trade and agr. ctr.; p. (1960) *14,553.*

De Funiak Springs, *t.*, Fla., U.S.A.; in agr. region; turpentine; p. (1960) *5,282.*

Dehdasht, *c.*, Iran; cap. Kuhgilvieh and Boer Ahmadi dist.; p. (1967) *112,544.* [*111,013.*

Dehiwala (Mt. Lavinia), *t.*, Ceylon; p. (1963)

Dehra Dun, *t.*, Uttar Pradesh, India; p. (1961) *156,341.*

Deir-ez-Zor, *t.*, Syria; on Euphrates R.; on motor route between Damascus and Baghdad; p. (1961) *59,757.*

Dej, *t.*, on Szamos R., Romania; lge. distillery; p. (1963) *22,327.*

Delabole, *vil.*, Cornwall, Eng.; on N.W. flank of Bodmin Moor; lge. slate quarries.

Delagoa Bay, *natural harbour*, Mozambique; Port E. Africa; ch. pt. Lourenço Marques.

Delaware, *Atlantic st.*, U.S.A.; agr., lumber, fertilisers, minerals, leather, chemicals, machin.; cap. Dover; ch. pt. Wilmington; a. 2,057 sq. m.; p. (1970) *542,979.*

Delaware, *R.*, flows from New York State along the Pennsylvania border, through New Jersey to Delaware Bay; length 350 m.

Delaware Bay, *inlet*, Atlantic cst., U.S.A.; drowned estuary of R. Delaware, extends 80 m. inland from C. May into heart of highly industl. a. of Philadelphia.

Delaware, *c.*, Ohio, U.S.A.; p. (1960) *13,282.*

Delemont, *t.*, Berne, Switzerland; watchmkg.; p. (1960) *8,000.*

Delft, *c., pt.*, S. Holland, Netherlands; on Schie R., nr. Rotterdam; famous techn. univ.; ceramics (delftware), tool mftg., precision instruments; 13th cent. Old church and 15th cent. New church; p. (1967) *79,805.*

Delhi, *union terr.*, India; hot and arid region between Indus valley and alluvial plain of Ganges; irrigation to support agr.; New Delhi (*q.v.*) and Old Delhi chief ctrs.; a. 573 sq. m.; p. (1961) *2,658,612.*

Delitzsch, *t.*, Leipzig, E. Germany; 16 m. E. of Halle; sugar, chemicals; p. (1963) *23,614.*

Delmenhorst, *t.*, Lower Saxony, Germany; nr. Bremen; jute, woollens, linoleum, foodstuffs; p. (1963) *59,300.*

Delphi, in ancient Phocis, Central Greece, north of Gulf of Corinth; famous for Delphic oracle on Mt. Parnassus.

Del Rio, *spt.*, Texas, U.S.A.; mkt. for agr a., grapes; exp. wool, sheep; p. (1960) *18,612.*

Demavend, *mtn.*, 17,604 ft.; highest peak, Elburz Mtns., N. Persia, extinct volcano.

Demerara, *co.*, Guyana; between Essequibo and Demerara Rs.; exp. sugar, molasses, rum; p. (1946) *220,639.*

Demirkapu, "The Iron Gate," rocky defile, through which the Danube rushes, in the Transylvanian Alps.

Demirtas, *t.*, Turkey; nr. Bursa; car wks.

Demmin, *t.*, Neubrandenburg, E. Germany; sugar ind.; p. (1963) *16,735.* [p. (1968) *27,973.*

Denain, *t.*, Nord, N. France; nr. Douai; coal;

Denbigh, *co.*, Wales; sheep, dairying, coal, slate, quarrying; a. 669 sq. m.; p. (1966) *176,000.*

Denbigh, *mun. bor., co. t.*, Denbigh, N. Wales; dairying, slate; in Vale of Clwyd, 10 m. S. of Rhyl; p. (1961) *8,044.*

Denby Dale, *urb. dist.*, W.R. Yorks, Eng.; 8 m. W. of Barnsley; coal-mining, woollen textiles; p. (1961) *9,304.*

Dendermonde or Termonde, *t.*, E. Flanders, Belgium; nr. Ghent; p. (1962) *9,740.*

Den Haag, *See* Hague, The

Denham, *vil.*, Bucks., Eng.; 1 m. E. of Gerrards Cross; former ctr. of Brit. film industry.

Den Helder, *see* Helder.

Denholme, *t., urb. dist.*, W.R. Yorks, Eng.; nr. Bradford; dairying, textiles; p. (1961) *2,596.*

Denia, *spt.*, Spain; 45 m. N.E. of Alicante; oranges, raisins, grapes, onions; toy mkg.; p. (1957) *11,859.*

Denison, *t.*, Iowa, U.S.A.; ctr. of agr. region; p. (1960) *4,930.*

Denison, *c.*, Texas, U.S.A.; on Red R.; cotton, lumber; p. (1960) *22,748.*

Denizli, *t.*, Anatolia, Turkey; 47 m. S.W. of Izmir; gardens—" the Damascus of Anatolia "; nr. site of Laodicea; p. (1965) *61,320.*

Denmark, *kingdom*, N.W. Europe; consisting of peninsula of Jutland and islands in Baltic; agr. and associated inds.; coastal fisheries; shipbldg., diesel engines; cap. Copenhagen; a. 16,576 sq. m.; p. (1968) *4,855,300.*

Denny and Dunipace, *burgh*, Stirling, Scot.; 6 m. W. of Falkirk; steel castings, precast concrete; p. (1961) *7,761.*

Dent Blanche, *mtn.*, in Pennine Alps, S. Switzerland; height 14,318 ft.

Dent du Midi, *mtn.*, Valais Alps, Switzerland; alt. 10,778 ft.

Denton, *urb. dist.*, Lancs, Eng.; nr. Manchester; felt-hat mkg.; p. (estd. 1967) *37,900.*

D'Entrecasteaux Is., gr. off S.E. New Guinea, administered by Australia.

D'Entrecasteaux Point, *C.*, S.W. extremity of Australia.

Denver, *c., cap.*, Col., U.S.A.; on the E. slope of Rocky Mtns., on South Platte R.; univ.; oil, electronic equipment, mng. machin., livestock, canning; tourism; p. (1970) *512,691.*

Deoband, *t.*, Uttar Pradesh, India; nr. Meerut; p. (1961) *29,930.*

Deogarh, *t.*, Santal Pargans dist., Bihar, India;

numerous temples, place of pilgrimage; p. (1961) *30,813*. [p. (1961) *9,383*.

Deori, *t.*, Madhya Pradesh, India; nr. Sagar;

De Pere, *t.*, Wis., U.S.A.; agr. ctr.; mftg.; boots, paper, chemicals, bricks; p. (1960) *10,045*.

Deptford, *see* Lewisham.

De Quincy, *t.*, La., U.S.A.; oil, gas, lumber, rice, sugar; p. (1960) *3,923*.

Dera Ghazi Khan, *cap.*, West Punjab, Pakistan; W. side of R. Indus; silk, brass, ivory goods, handsome mosques; p. *25,000*.

Dera Ismail Kahn, *div.*, W. Pakistan; p. (1961) *2,085,000*.

Dera Ismail Khan, *t.*, W. Pakistan; on Indus R.; adm. ctr., caravan ctr.; p. (1961) *46,100*.

Derbent, *t.*, *spt.*, R.S.F.S.R.; on W. side of Caspian Sea; textiles, petrol; p. (1956) *41,800*.

Derby, *co. bor.*, *co. t.*, Derbyshire, Eng.; on R. Derwent; rly. wks., pottery, aircraft engine mnf. and repair, vehicles, textiles; natural gas beneath Calow vil; p. (estd. 1967) *127,910*.

Derby, *t.* Conn., U.S.A.; rubber, metal, hardware mftg.; p. (1960) *12,132*.

Derby, *sm. spt.*, W. Australia; on natural harbour of King Sound on N.W. cst. of Australia; hinterland little developed but potential gold and cattle-ranching within a. of artesian basin.

Derbyshire, *co.*, Eng.; hilly and rich in minerals; lge. part of N. and W. scheduled as Nat. Park; E. part highly industl.; *co. t.*, Derby; a. 1,041 sq. m.; p. (1966) *912,000*.

Dereham, East, *t.*, *urb. dist.*, Norfolk, Eng.; 14 m. W. Norwich; agr. implements; p. (1961) *7,197*.

Derg, Lough, in basin of R. Shannon, Ireland, separating Galway and Clare from Tipperary.

Derg, *L.*, Donegal, with cave on I. much visited by R.C. pilgrims and known as " St. Patrick's Purgatory."

Derna, *spt.*, Libya, N. Africa; p. (estd. 1951) *15,600*.

Derry, *t.*, N.H., U.S.A.; boots, shoes; p. (1960) *6,987*.

Derwent, *R.*, Cumberland, Eng.; length 33 m.

Derwent, *R.*, Derby, Eng.; length 60 m.

Derwent, *R.*, Yorks, Eng.; length 57 m.

Derwent, *R.*, trib. of the Tyne R., Eng.; length 30 m.   [Bay; length 30 m.

Derwent, *lgst. R.*, Tasmania; flowing to Storm

Derwentwater, *L.*, Cumberland, Eng.; nr. Keswick; 3 m. long.   [L. Titicaca.

Desaguadero, *R.*, Bolivia, S. America; outlet of

Desaguadero, *plateau*, S. Peru and W. Bolivia between the Andes ranges, the second highest in the world.

Desborough, *t.*, *urb. dist.*, Northants, Eng.; boot and shoe mnfs., iron; p. (1961) *4,555*.

Désirade, *I.*, Fr. W. Indies; nr. Guadeloupe; a. 10 sq. m.; p. *1,581*.

Des Moines, *R.*, Iowa, U.S.A.; trib. of Mississippi rising in Minnesota; length 550 m.

Des Moines, *c.*, *cap.* Iowa State, U.S.A.; rly. and mftg. ctr.; p. (1960) *208,982*.

Des Plaines, *t.*, Ill., U.S.A.; p. (1960) *34,886*.

Desna, *R.*, trib. of Dnieper R., U.S.S.R.; length 550 m.

Despoto Dagh, *mtn. range*, Balkans; alt. 7,800 ft.

Dessau, *t.*, Halle, E. Germany; at confluence of Mulde and Elbe Rs.; cas.; machin., rly. carriages, paper, sugar, chemicals; route ctr.; p. (1963) *95,730*.

Detmold, *t.*, N. Rhine–Westphalia, Germany; cas.; paints, wood inds.; p. (1963) *30,600*.

Detroit, *ch. c.*, *pt.*, Mich., U.S.A.; busy comm. and industl. ctr.; univ.; gt. grain mart; and ctr. of the " Ford " motor-car wks., aeroplanes, military tanks, synthetic diamonds, pharmaceutics, tools, chemicals, steel; lgst. exporting t. on Great Lakes; p. (1970) *1,492,914*; Greater Detroit (1970) *4,162,000*.

Detroit, *R.*, channel between L. St. Clair and L. Erie (25 m.), separates st. of Michigan from Ontario, Canada; carries more shipping than any other inland waterway in the world.

Deurne, *t.*, Belgium; nr. Antwerp; p. (1962) *69,498*.

Deventer, *c.*, Overijssel, Netherlands; on IJssel R.; industl. ctr., machin., textile and carpet inds.; Hanse t. in Middle Ages; p. (1967) *61,623*.

Deveron, *R.*, Aberdeen and Banff, Scot.; flows into Moray Firth; length 61 m.

Devizes, *mkt. t.*, *mun. bor.*, N. Wilts, Eng.; on Kennet Avon Canal at N. foot of Marlborough Downs; tobacco and snuff, bricks, tiles, bacon curing; p. (estd. 1967) *9,000*.

Devon, *R.*, trib. of Forth, Scot.; length 34 m.

Devonport, *fortfd. spt.*, S. Devon, Eng.; adjoins Plymouth on Tamar estuary; royal dockyards and naval sta.; road bridge to Saltash across Tamar; p. included with Plymouth.

Devonport, *spt.*, Tasmania Australia; 82 m. from Launceston; agr. dist.; canning, foundry inds.; p. (1966) *14,848*.

Devenport, *bor.*, Auckland, N.Z.; naval base and dockyard; p. (1966) *11,092*.

Devonshire, *maritime co.*, S.W. Eng.; between English and Bristol Channels; famous for cream and cider; ch. ts. Exeter and Plymouth; a. 2,611 sq. m.; p (1966) *865,000*.

Dewsbury, *t.*, *co. bor.*, W.R. Yorks, Eng.; on R. Calder, 8 m. from Leeds; heavy woollens, coal-mining, dyewks.; p. (estd. 1967) *52,730*.

Dexter, *t.*, Mo., U.S.A.; cotton, flour, poultry; p. (1960) *5,519*.

Deyeth, *t.*, Cambodia; plywooods.

Dez Dam, Iran, over Dez R., Khurzistan prov., opened 16 Mar. 1963.

Dhahran, *spt.*, Saudi-Arabia; oil.

Dhanbad, *t.*, Bihar, India; lead, zinc, tools, radio assembly; p. (1961) *46,756*.

Dhanushkodi, *t.*, Tamil Nadu, India; on I. Palk Strait; ferry pt. for passenger traffic from India to Ceylon.

Dhar, *t.*, Madhya Pradesh, India; cultural and tr. ctr.; p. (1961) *28,325*.

Dharmsala, *hill sta.*, E. Punjab, India; 100 m. N.E. of Amritsar; sanatorium; alt. 6,000 ft.; imposing mtn. scenery; p. (1961) *10,255*.

Dharwar, *t.*, Mysore, India; 70 m. E. of Goa, Carnatic; univ.; cotton mnf.; p. (1961) *77,163*.

Dhaulagiri, *mtn.*, Himalayas, Nepal; alt. 26,810 ft.

Dhekelia, Cyprus; Brit. sovereign a. within Rep.; p. (1960) *3,602*.

Dholpur, *t.*, Rajasthan, India; p. (1961) *27,412*.

Dhrangadhra, Saurashtra, India; 75 m. W. of Ahmedabad; chemicals, salt, cotton, bldg. stone, brass vessels, pottery; p. (1961) *32,197*.

Dhufar, *fertile prov.*, Oman, Arabia; sugar-cane, cattle; ch.t.Salalah; ch.pt.Mirbat.

Dhulia, *t.*, Khandesh dist., Maharashtra, India; cotton ind., p. (1961) *98,893*.

Diamante, *t.*, E. Argentina; on Paraná R.; grain, cattle; p. *11,518*.

Diamante, *R.*, Mendoza prov., Argentina; rises in Andes, flows E. to R. Salado; irrigates oasis of San Rafael; length 200 m.

Diamantina, *t.*, Minas Gerais, Brazil; ctr. of diamond dist.; p. (estd. 1968) *34,267*.

Diber, *prefecture*, Albania; p. (estd.) *83,491*.

Dibrugarh, *t.*, Assam, India; terminus of rail and river communications along Brahmaputra from Calcutta; coal, tea; p. (1961) *58,480*.

Dickson L., Kara Sea, Arctic Ocean, U.S.S.R.

Didymoteikhon, *t.*, Thrace, Greece; on R. Maritza; p. *10,150*.

Diego Garcia, *I.*, Brit. Indian Oc. Terr.; coaling sta.; 12½ m. long, 6½ m. wide; ch. exp. coconut oil, tortoise-shell; p. (1962) *660*.

Diego Suarez, *t.*, *Bay*, extreme N. of Madagascar, French Naval Base; p. (1957) *38,212*.

Dieppe, *cross-Channel pt.*, Seine-Maritime, France; 35 m. N. of Rouen; fisheries, shipbldg., machin.; p. (1962) *30,327*.

Differdange, *t.*, S.W. Luxembourg; iron ore, cattle; p. (1960) *17,637*.   [p. (1961) *35,028*.

Digbol, N.E. Assam, India; oil fields and refinery;

Digne, *t.*, Basses-Alpes, France; nr. Aix; cath.; p. (1962) *13,660*.

Dijon, *t.*, Côte-d'Or, E. France; the Roman *Divonense castrum*; cath.; bathing; casino; gt. wine tr., tobacco, brewery, textiles; p. (1968) *150,791*.   [p. (1962) *3,867*.

Diksmuide, *t.*, W. Flanders, Belgium; on Yser R.;

Dillingen, *t.*, Bavaria, Germany; on R. Danube, 20 m. downstream from Ulm; p. *6,500*.

Dilolo, *L.*, Angola; nr. source of Zambesi R.

Dimitrovgrad, *t.*, Bulgaria; founded 1947; fertilisers, chemicals, super phosphate plant, iron, thermo-electric sta.; p. (1956) *34,162*.

Dimitrovo, *t.*, Bulgaria, formerly Pernik; steel blast furnaces; p. (1956) *59,721*.

Dinan, *t.*, Côtes-du-Nord, France; nr. St. Brieux; medieval houses and ramparts; mineral water; p. (1962) *16,438*.

Dinant, *fortfd. t.*, Namur, Belgium; on R. Meuse; brass, copperware, summer resort; p. (1962) *6,803*.

Dinapore, *military t.,* Bihar, India; on Ganges R., nr. Patna; p. (1961) *70,766.*

Dinard, *hol. res.,* Ille-et-Vilaine, France; op. St. Malo; ch. wat. pl. of Brittany; p. (1962) *9,432.*

Dinaric Alps, *mtn. range,* Jugoslavia; highest peak, Dinara, alt. 6,007 ft.

Dindigul, *t.,* Tamil Nadu, India; 25 m. S. of Trichinopoly; cigars, tobacco; p. (1961) *92,947.*

Dingras, *mun.,* Luzon, Philippine Is.; rice, hemp, tobacco; p. *22,434.*

Dingwall, *burgh,* Ross and Cromarty, Scot.; at head of Cromarty Firth; p. (1961) *3,752*

Dinslaken, *t.,* N. Rhine-Westphalia, Germany, N. of Duisburg; coal, steel, iron, footwear, timber; oil pipeline from Wesseling under construction; p. (1963) *46,400.*

Diomede Is., two barren granitic islets in Behring Strait between Alaska and Siberia; accepted bdy. between Soviet and U.S. territory.

Diourbel, *t.,* Senegal, W. Africa; hides, groundnuts; p. *18,006.*

Diredawa, *t.,* Ethiopia; 25 m. N. of Harar, rly. wks.; p. (estd. 1960) *40,000.*

Dirk Hartog I., off Shark Bay, W. Australia.

Disko I., off W. cst. of Greenland in Baffin Bay; contains harbour of Godhavn, cap. N. Greenland; rendezvous for whalers; a. 3,200 sq. m.

Dismal Swamp, *morass,* S. Virginia and N. Carolina, U.S.A.; contains L. Drummond and extends 30–40 m. S. from nr Norfolk.

Diss, *mkt. t., urb. dist.,* Norfolk, Eng.; on R. Waveney 28 m. S.W. of Norwich; agr. implements; p. (1961) *3,682.*

Ditchling Beacon, nr. Brighton, Sussex, Eng.; alt. 813 ft.   [p. *14,916.*

Dittersbach, *commune,* S.W. Poland; coal, drugs;

Diu, *spt., I.,* off S. coast of Bombay, India; oil nearby at Kayakoy; a. 20 sq. m.; p. (1960) *14,271.*   [p. (1954) *11,187.*

Divion, *commune,* Pas de Calais France; coal;

Divnogorsk, *t.,* R.S.F.S.R.; 25 m. W. of Krasnoyarsk on R. Yenisei; dam builders' t.; p. (1963) *25,000.*

Dixon Entrance, *channel* between Queen Charlotte I. and Alaska.

Diyarbakir, *t.,* Anatolia, Turkey; on Tigris R.; head of navigation: ancient Amida, old walls, gates, citadel; morocco leather, filigree work; p. (1965) *102,624.*   [p. (1956) *52,153.*

Dizful, *t.,* Persia ; 32 m. N.W. of Shushtar: indigo;

Djajapura (Sukarnapura), *cap. c.,* West Irian, Indonesia.

Djakarta (Batavia), *cap. c.,* Java, Indonesia; comm. ctr.; textiles; p. (1961) *2,973,052.*

Djambi, *dist.* and *t.,* Sumatra, Indonesia; on E. cst. plain 100 m. N.W. of Palembang; productive oil-field; a. (dist.) 17,345 sq. m.; p. (1961) of dist. *744,331* of t. *113,080.*

Djapara-Rembang, *prov.,* N.E. Java; petroleum, sugar, rice; a. 2,339 sq. m.; p. *1,885,548.*

Dneprodzerzhinsk, *t.,* Ukrainian S.S.R.; W. of Dnepropetrovsk on Dnieper R.; iron and steel, engin., chemicals; hydro-elec. sta. nearby; p. (1967) *219,000.*

Dnepropetrovsk, *t.,* Ukrainian S.S.R.; on Dnieper R.; univ.; coal, iron, steel, manganese, engin., chemicals, sawmilling, tyres; p. (1967) *790,000.*

Dneprorudnyy, *t.,* Ukrainian S.S.R.; new t. on S. shore of Kakhovta reservoir, tentatively called Dneprograd, now renamed; p. (1964) *6,000.*

Dneprostroy, *see* Zaporozhe.

Dnieper, R., S.E. Europe; rises in U.S.S.R., flows into the Black Sea; connected by canals with Baltic, etc.; the Dneprostroy dam, a barrage erected across the R. at Kichkas by the Soviet Government, feeds the lgst. power-sta. in the world; length 1,400 m.

Dniester, R., S.E. Europe; rises in Carpathians and flows into the Black Sea; length 700 m.

Doab, *dist.,* between "two rivers" Jumna and Ganges, Uttar Pradesh, India.

Döbeln, *t.,* Leipzig, E. Germany; machin., metallurgy, wood, cigar and sugar inds.; p. (1963) *29,327.*

Dobrich, *t., see* Tolbukhin.

Dobruja, *dist.,* E. Romania; a. 6,102 sq. m., ch. pt. Constanta, traversed by ancient wall of Trajan; p. (1963) *517,016.*

Dobsina, *t.,* CSSR.; cave containing ice-field of 2 acres: asbestos, iron ore; p. *5,300.*

Doce, R., Brazil; flows to Atlantic; length 400 m.

Dodecanese, gr. of 12 Greek Is. in Ægean Sea, to S. of Greek Archipelago; Italian 1912–46; a. 1,055 sq. m.; p. (1961) *122,346.*

Dodge City, *t.,* Kan., U.S.A.; p. (1960) *13,520.*

Dodoma, *mkt. t.,* Tanzania, E. Africa; 250 m. W. of Dar-es-Salaam on central Tanganyika rly. from Dar-es-Salaam to Kigoma; also on main N. to S. motor road.

Dodworth, *urb. dist.,* W.R. Yorks, Eng.; nr. Barnsley; coal; p. (1961) *4,139.*

Dogger Bank, *sandbank* in N. Sea, between England and Denmark; depth varies from 6 to 20 fathoms; valuable fishing ground; action between British fleet under Beatty and German fleet under Hipper; *Blücher* sunk Jan. 1915.

Dogs, I. of, *riverside dist.,* formed by bend in the R. Thames off Greenwich, London, Eng.; Millwall docks and shipbldg. yards.

Dokai Bay, *inlet,* N. Kyushu, Japan; landlocked bay on S. side of Shimonoseki Straits; flanked by highly industl. zone inc. Yawata, Wakamatsu, Tobata cs.; requires constant dredging; length 4 m., width ¼–1½ m.

Dokkum, *t.,* Friesland, Netherlands; p. *5,073.*

Dôle, *t.,* Jura, E. France; on R. Doubs, nr. Dijon; ancient cap. of Franche-Comté, ceded to France in 1678; birthplace of Pasteur; p. (1954) *22,022.*

Dolgarrog, *sm. t.,* N.E. Caernarvon, Wales; aluminium, milling; p. (1951) *572.*

Dolgelly, *urb. dist., ch. t.,* Merioneth, N. Wales; agr., quarrying, timber; p. (1961) *2,267.*

Dollar, *burgh,* Clackmannan, Scot.; at foot of Ochil Hills, 6 m. N.E. of Alloa; p. (1961) *1,955.*

Dollar Law, *min.,* nr. Peebles, Scot.; alt. 2,680 ft.

Dolomites, *gr. of limestone mtns.,* S. Tyrolese Alps, N.E. Italy; tourist district; peaks assume fantastic forms; principal peak, Marmolata 11,000 ft.

Dolon-Nor, *t.,* Mongolia, China; Buddhist temples; brass idols; p. *30,000.*

Dom, *mtn.,* Valais, Switzerland; alt. 14,942 ft.

Dominica, *aut. st.* in association with Gt. Britain; Windward Is., W.I.; limejuice, sugar, cacao, fruits, spices; extremely beautiful; cap. Roseau; a. 290 sq. m.; p.(estd. 1968) *72,000.*

Dominican Rep, indep. Spanish-speaking E. part of I. of Hispaniola, Antilles; cap. Santo Domingo; sugar, coffee, cacao, bananas, tobacco, bauxite, iron ore, cement; a. 19,332 sq. m.; p. (estd. 1968) *4,029,000.*

Domodossola, *frontier t.,* Piedmont, N. Italy, nr. Simplon; tourist ctr.; p. *10,550.*

Don, R., Aberdeen, Scot.; flows into N. Sea; salmon; length 82 m.

Don, R., W.R. Yorks, Eng.; trib. of R. Ouse length 70 m.

Don, R., Maine-et-Loire, France; length 40 m.

Don, lge. R., W. Russia; falls into Sea of Azov below Rostov; navigable to Voronezh; access to the Volga by the Don–Volga Canal.

Donaghadee, *spt., urb. dist.,* Down, N. Ireland; nearest point to Scot.; carpets; seaside resort; p. (1966) *3,649.*

Donaueschingen, *t.,* Baden-Württemberg, Germany; at confluence of Rs. Brigach and Breg forming R. Danube; cas.; textiles; p. (estd. 1954) *8,900.*

Donawitz, *commune,* Styria prov., Austria; lignite, iron and steel; p. *17,623.*

Donbas, *industl. region,* Ukraine, U.S.S.R.; in valleys of Rs. Donetz and lower Dnieper; about 9,000 sq. m.; produces 60% Russia's coal; adjoins Krivoi Rog ironfields; many lge. industl. ts.   [wine, fruit; p. *21,095.*

Don Benito, *t.,* Badajoz, Spain; tr. in wheat,

Doncaster, *t., co. bor.,* W.R. Yorks, Eng., on Don R. 17 m. N.E. of Sheffield; tractors, nylon mnftg.; coal mines; racecourse; p. (estd. 1967) *85,910.*

Donchery, *ancient t.,* Ardennes, France, on R. Meuse, nr. Sedan; scene of gr. battle 1870.

Donegal (Tirconnail), *co.,* N.W. Ireland; ch. t. Donegal, a. 1,865 sq. m.; p. (1966) *108,486.*

Donegal, *spt., cap.,* Co. Donegal, Ireland; on W. cst. of Donegal Bay; homespun tweeds, carpets; p. (1966) *1,507.*

Donets, R., Ukraine S.S.R., U.S.S.R.; rises in uplands of central Russia, flows S.E. 400 m. into R. Don; crosses impt. Donets coalfield. *See* Donbas.

Donetsk (Stalino), *t.,* Ukraine S.S.R.; coal, iron, steel, engin., chemicals; p. (1967) *823,000.*

Donges, Loire Atlantique, France; nr. St. Nazaire; oil refinery.

Dongola, New, *t.,* Sudan; left bank of R. Nile above 3rd Cataract; Old D., in ruins; p. *15,000.*

Donna, *t.*, S. Texas, U.S.A.; sugar refining, fruit and vegetables; p. (1960) 7,522.

Donzère-Mondragon, Provence, France; site of gr. barrage on Rhône supplying hydro-elec. power, completed 1952.

Doon, *R.*, Ayr, Scot.; flows from Loch Doon to Firth of Clyde; length 26 m.

Dora Baltea, *R.*, N. Italy; rises in Mt. Blanc, flows E. and S. through Val d'Aosta to R. Po at Chivasso; impt. routeway from N. Italy to Switzerland (through Gr. St. Bernard Pass) and France (through Little St. Bernard Pass); length 95 m.

Dora Riparia, *R.*, Italy; trib. of R. Po, flowing from Cottian Alps past Turin; length 60 m.

Dorchester, *mun. bor. co. t.* Dorset, Eng.; on R. Frome; Roman remains: lime, agr., engin., tent mkg.; p. (estd. 1967) 13,570.

Dorchester, *pt. of entry*, N.B., Canada; on Penticodiac R.; p. 1,000.

Dordogne, *dep.*, S.W. France; a. 3,550 sq. m.; cap. Périgueux; p. (1968) 374,073.

Dordogne, *R.*, France; joins Garonne to form the Gironde; length 290 m.

Dordrecht, *c.*, nr. Rotterdam, Netherlands, on R. Merwede; timber, shipbldg., seaplanes; p. (1967) 88,475.

Dorking, *mkt. t.*, *urb. dist.*, Surrey, Eng.; on R. Mole to S. of gap through N. Downs; residtl.; light inds.; p. (estd. 1967) 23,010.

Dornoch, *burgh*, Sutherland, Scot.; on N. side of Dornoch Firth; health resort; p. (1961) 933.

Dorohoi, *t.*, Moldavia, Romania; 33 m. S.E. of Chernovtsy; gr. annual fair; p. (1956) 14,771.

Dorp, *t.*, Germany; on R. Wupper, nr. Cologne; mnfs.; p. 14,000.

Dorset, *co.*, S. Eng.; mainly agr.; sheep; Purbeck marble, Portland stone; co. t. Dorchester; a. 988 sq. m.; p. (1966) 333,000.

Dorset Heights, *hills*, extend E. to W. across Central Dorset, Eng.; chalk, smooth slopes, few streams; short, dry, grass; pastoral farming, sheep; some cultivation where soil is deep enough; rise to 800–900 ft.

Dorsten, *t.*, N. Rhine–Westphalia, Germany; on R. Lippe; coal, iron, elec., chemical inds.; p. (1963) 37,600.

Dortmund, *t.*, N. Rhine–Westphalia, Germany; impt. Ruhr comm. ctr.; coal, iron, steel, machin., brewing; p. (1968) 645,728.

Dortmund–Ems Canal, N. Rhine–Westphalia, Germany; links Dortmund on Ruhr Coalfield with R. Ems 5 m. above Lingen; impt. coal, iron-ore traffic; length 90 m.

Dorval, *t.*, Quebec, Canada; p. (1961) 18,592.

Dothan, *t.*, Ala., U.S.A.; p. (1960) 31,440.

Douai, *t.*, Nord, France; nr. Lille on Scarpe R.; coal, iron and engin. wks.; bell founding, arsenal; p. (1968) 49,187.

Douarnenez, *spt.*, Finistère, N.W. France; on D. Bay; sardine fisheries; p. (1962) 20,304.

Doubs, *dep.*, E. France; traversed by the Jura range and the R. Doubs; chiefly agr.; watch-mkg. ind.; cap. Besançon; a. 2,052 sq. m.; p. (1968) 426,363.

Douglas, *cap.*, I. of Man; 75 m. W. of Liverpool, Eng.; seaside resort; p. (1956) 20,361.

Douglas Point, on shore of L. Huron, Ont., Canada; nuclear power sta.   [reactor.

Dounreay, Caithness, Scot.; fast-breeder nuclear

Douro, *R.*, Portugal and Spain; enters Atlantic below Oporto; known as Duero R. in Spain; length 485 m.

Douro Littoral, *prov.*, Portugal; textiles, wine, fruit, cattle; cap. Oporto; a. 1,314 sq. m.; p. (1950) 1,237,170.

Dove, *R.*, Derby and Staffs, Eng.; trib. of Trent; flows through beautiful dales; length 45 m.

Dover, *packet pt.*, *mun. bor.*, Kent, Eng.; one of old Cinque pts.; nearest spt. to France, the Strait of D. being only 21 m. wide; chief pt. for passenger and mail traffic with Continent; p. (estd. 1967) 36,060.

Dover, *cap.*, Del., U.S.A.; p. (1960) 7,250.

Dover, *t.*, N.H., U.S.A.; p. (1960) 19,131.

Dover, *t.*, N.J., U.S.A.; iron, munitions, explosives; knitwear, silk; p. (1960) 13,034.

Dovercourt, *sub.*, Harwich, Essex, Eng.; seaside resort.

Dowlais, *mining dist.*, Merthyr Tydfil, S. Wales; fertilisers, nylon.

Down, *maritime co.*, N. Ireland; agr. and fisheries; industl. round Belfast; cap. Downpatrick; a. 957 sq. m.; p. (1966) 286,930.

Downers Grove, *t.*, N.E. Ill., U.S.A.; dairy produce; tools, furniture; p. (1960) 21,194.

Downey, *t.*, Cal., U.S.A.; agr.; aircraft, cement, asbestos prod., machin., soap.; p. (1960) 82,505.

Downham Market, *t.*, *urb. dist.*, Norfolk, Eng.; on R. Ouse; flour-milling, malting, sheet-metal wks.; p. (1961). 2,650

Downpatrick, *urb. dist.*, *co. t.*, Down, N. Ireland; on R. Quoile; linen; p. (1966) 4,291.

Downs, *roadstead*, natural harbour of refuge for shipping between Kent coast and Goodwin Sands in the English Channel.

Downs, North and South, two chiefly pastoral broad chalk ridges in S.E. Eng.; N. Downs ending at Dover, and S. Downs at Beachy Head and enclosing the Weald; fine grazing ground for sheep.

Downton, *t.*, S. Wilts, Eng.; nr. Salisbury; on R. Avon; agr. college.

Drachenfels, *mtn.* peak on the Rhine, the steepest of the Siebengebirge range, nr. Königswinter; alt. 1,065 ft.; ascended by light rly.; famous cave of legendary dragon.

Draguignan, *cap.*, Var. dep., S.E. France; nr. Toulon; p. (1962) 16,085.

Drakensberg, *mtn. chain* between Natal and Orange Free State, S. Africa; extending 500 m. from Gt. Fish R. to Olifants R.; highest peak Mont-aux-Sources 10,763 ft.; rly. crosses range by Van Reenen Pass.

Drama, *pref.* Macedonia, Greece; cap. Drama; p. (1961) 120,936.

Drammen, *spt.*, Norway; nr. Oslo, on the Drammen R.; shipyard; exp. timber, wood-pulp, paper; p. (1968) 47,527.

Drancy, *t.*, Seine, France; p. (1962) 65,940.

Drava, *R.*, Jugoslavia; trib. of Danube, flows from the Tyrol across Carinthia and Styria, joining D. nr. t. of Osijek; length 450 m.

Drenthe, *E. prov.*, Netherlands; on German frontier; cap. Assen; a. 1,028 sq. m.; p. (1967) 348,001.

Dresden, *t.*, Dresden, E. Germany; on R. Elbe 50 m. E. of Leipzig; fine art collections; cigarette, engin., chem., brewing, gen. inds., optical and photographic apparatus, porcelain, glass, impt. route ctr.; oil pipeline from Schwedt under construction; p. (1963) 499,014.

Dreux, *t.*, Eure-et-Loir, France; nr. Chartres; hardware, heavy iron mnfs.; p. (1954) 16,818.

Driffield, *urb. dist.*, E.R. Yorks, Eng.; on Yorks. Wolds 13 m. N. of Beverley; oil-cake wks.; p. (1961) 6,890.

Drina, *R.*, trib. Sava, Jugoslavia, separating Serbia from Bosnia; length 300 m.

Dröbak, *spt.*, S.E. Norway; winter pt. for Oslo; summer resort; p. (1961) 2,735.

Drogheda, *spt.*, Louth, Ireland; considerable tr. in agr. produce, salmon, etc.; stormed by Cromwell in 1649; p. (1966) 17,823.

Drogobych, *t.*, Ukrainian S.S.R.; petroleum, engin.; p. (1959) 42,000.

Drohobycz, *t.*, Ukraine, U.S.S.R.; 40 m. S.W. of Lwow; ctr. of lge. oilfields, refineries; p. 32,622.

Droitwich, *t.*, *mun. bor.*, Worcester, Eng.; brine baths, salt wks., wireless-transmission sta.; light inds.; p. (estd. 1967) 8,970.

Drôme, *dep.*, S.E. France; traversed by Alps and watered by Rs. Rhône, Drôme and Isère; cap. Valence; agr., forestry, sericulture, textile ind.; a. 2,533 sq. m.; p. (1968) 342,891.

Dromore, *mkt. t.*, *urb. dist.*, Down, N. Ireland; on Lagan R.; linen; p. (1966) 2,081.

Dronfield, *t.*, *urb. dist.*, Derby, Eng.; between Chesterfield and Sheffield; iron, coal, edged tools, engin. and agr. implements; p. (1961) 11,294.

Droylsden, *urb. dist.*, Lancs., Eng.; sub. of Manchester; cotton spinning; chemicals; p. (estd. 1967) 25,340.

Drummondville, *t.*, Quebec, Canada; 45 m. N.E. of Montreal; woollens; p. (1961) 27,909.

Drummoyne, *c.*, N.S.W., Australia; sub. of Sydney, on Parramatta R.

Drumochter Pass, Grampian Mtns., Scot.; carries main Perth to Inverness rly. from Glen Garry into valley of R. Spey; highest alt. reached by any main rly. in Gr. Britain, 1,484 ft.

Duala, *spt.*, Cameroun Rep., W. Africa; rly. to Yaoundé; p. *18,000.*

Dubai, *ch. t. and pt.*, Trucial States, Arabia; entrepôt tr.; deep-water harbour and airpt. projected; p. (estd.) *60,000.*

Dubbo, *t.*, N.S.W., Australia; on Macquarie R., 180 m. N.W. of Sydney; in extensive pastoral and agr. dist.; p. (1966) *15,563.*

Dublin, *co.*, Ireland; co. t. Dublin; a. (inc. c. of Dublin) 356 sq. m.; p. (1966) *793,790.*

Dublin (Baile Atha Cliath), *co. bor., cap.* Rep. of Ireland; at mouth of R. Liffey; cath., univ., cas.; spirit and chemical produce, stout, glass, etc.; p. (1966) *568,271.*

Dubois, *c.*, Penns., U.S.A.; 75 m. N.E. of Pittsburgh; coal; p. (1960) *10,667.*

Dubrovnik (Ragusa), *c.*, W. coast of Jugoslavia; oil, silk, leather inds.; p. (1960) *21,000.*

Dubuque, *c.*, Iowa, U.S.A., on Mississippi R.; clothing, carriage wks.; p. (1960) *56,606.*

Duchov, *t.*, N.W. Bohemia, ČSSR.; 5 m. S.W. of Teplice; glass, pottery; p. *15,000.* [nickel.

Dudinka, Arctic *spt.* on R. Yenisei, R.S.F.S.R.;

Dudley, *t., co. bor.*, Worcester, Eng.; 8 m. N.W. Birmingham; engin., clothing, leather goods, firebricks, chains, cables; p. (estd. 1967) *177,760* inc. p. of a. in Staffs. added to bor. 1966.

Dudweiler, *t.*, nr. Saarbrücken, Saarland; coal-mines and ironwks.; p. (1963) *29,700.*

Dueñas, *mun.*, Panay, Philippine Is.; rice, hemp; p. *16,310.*

Duffel, *commune*, Antwerp, Belgium; foundries, distilleries, paper, coarse woollen cloth; p. (1962) *13,365.*

Duisburg, *t., R. pt.*, N. Rhine–Westphalia, Germany; on E. bank of R. Rhine at confluence with R. Ruhr, 10 m. N. of Düsseldorf; extensive iron and steel inds., machin., textiles, chemicals, impt. route and R. tr. ctr.; p. (1968) *462,334.*

Dukeries, *dist.*, Sherwood Forest, Notts, Eng.; so called from ducal mansions in dist.

Dukinfield, *t., mun. bor.*, Cheshire, Eng.; 6 m. S.E. of Manchester; textiles, engin., rope and twine; p. (estd. 1967) *17,120.*

Dukla, *pass*, Carpathian Mtns., Central Europe; easy route N. from Hungarian Plain to Poland; alt. 1,650 ft. [rice, cotton, sugar; p. *28,69*

Dulag, *mun.*, Leyte I., Philippine Is.; hemp,

Dulcigno (Ulcinj), *ancient c.*, Montenegro, Jugoslavia; tobacco, olive oil; p. *5,000.*

Dülken, *t.*, N. Rhine–Westphalia, Germany; nr. Krefeld, machin., textiles, leather goods; p. (1963) *21,300.*

Duluth, *pt.*, Minn., U.S.A.; at W. end of L. Superior; gr. tr. in grain, timber and iron ore; natural gas pipeline into the Mesabi Iron Range; p. (1960) *106,884.*

Dumbarton, *burgh., co. t.*, Dunbarton, Scot.; on N. bank of R. Clyde, 12 m. below Glasgow; shipbldg, valve and tube-mkg., iron and brass-ware; p. (1961) *26,335.*

Dum-Dum, South, *t.*, W. Bengal, India; ammunition; p. (1961) *111,284.*

Dumfries, *maritime co.*, S. Scot.; on Solway Firth; N. parts mtns., much of the remainder pastoral; lead ore, coal, sandstone; a. 1,068 sq. m.; p. (1961) *88,423.*

Dumfries, *co. burgh*, Dumfries, Scot.; on R. Nith, 10 m. from Solway Firth; p. (1961) *27,275.*

Dunaujváros, *t.*, Hungary; New Town built from vil. of Dunapentele; iron and steel wks., paper inds., engin.; p. (1962) *34,998.*

Dunbar, *spt., burgh*, E. Lothian, Scot.; 25 m. E. of Edinburgh; potatoes; p. (1961) *4,003.*

Dunbarton, *co.*, W. Scot;. agr., stock-raising, shipbldg., chemicals, dyeing, paper-mkg., mining, quarrying, lt. engin.; a. 246 sq. m.; p. (1961) *184,546.*

Dunblane, *mkt. burgh*, Perth, Scot.; on Allan Water, 5 m. from Stirling; ancient cath.; woollen ind., light engin.; p. (1961) *2,922.*

Duncan, *c.*, Okla., U.S.A.; oil; oilwell machin.; asphalt, cottonseed oil; p. (1960) *20,009.*

Duncan Bay, *t.*, Vancouver I., B.C.; newsprint.

Duncansby Head, *promontory*, Caithness, N.E. Scot.

Dundalk, *spt., urb. dist., cap.*, Louth, Ireland; impt. rly. ctr.; engin., footwear, tobacco, brewing; p. (1966) *19,834.*

Dundas, *t.*, Ontario, Canada; at W. end of L. Ontario; leather, paper; p. (1961) *12,912*

Dundee, *c., spt.*, Angus, Scot.; on Firth of Tay, 50 m. N. Edinburgh; jute mnf., shipbldg.,

engin., computers, refrigerators, clocks, watches, preserves, linoleum; univ.; p. (1961) *182,959.*

Dundonald, *vil.*, coast of Ayr, 5 m. S.W. of Kilmarnock; coal; p. (par.) *18,400.*

Dunedin, *cap.*, Otago, S.I., N.Z.; named after the old name of Edinburgh; univ.; wool and dairy produce; p. (1966) *108,680.* of c. *77,149.*

Dunfermline, *burgh*, Fife, Scot.; at foot of Leven Hills, 14 m. E. of Alloa; damask linen tr., rubber; p. (inc. Rosyth) (1961) *47,159.*

Dungannon, *t.*, Tyrone, N. Ireland; p. (1966) *7,335.*

Dungarvan, *spt., urb. dist.*, Waterford, Ireland; brewing, woollens; p. (1966) *5,376*

Dungeness, *headland of shingle*, Kent, Eng.; 10 m. S.E. of Rye; civil nuclear power-sta. (1964); a second (due 1972); linked by power cable to France 1961.

Dunkeld, *t., par.*, Perth, Scot.; on R. Tay at entrance to Strathmore; cath.; tourist resort; p. (1951) *833.*

Dunkirk or Dunkerque, *spt.*, Nord, France; strong fort; gd. harbour and tr.; fisheries, shipbldg., oil refining; steel mill; scene of evacuation of B.E.F. 1940; p. (1968) *27,504.*

Dunkirk, *pt.*, N.Y., U.S.A.; on L. Erie; p. (1960) *18,205.*

Dun Laoghaire (Kingstown), *spt., co. bor.*, Dublin, Ireland; mail packet sta., fishing; p. (1966) *55,885.*

Dunloe, Gap of, *mtn. pass*, nr. L. of Killarney, Kerry, Ireland.

Dunmanway, *t.*, Cork, Ireland; on R. Brandon; tweeds, blankets; p. (1951) *1,439.*

Dunmore, *t.*, Penns., U.S.A.; nr. Scranton; anthracite; p. (1960) *18,917.*

Dunmow, Gr., *mkt. t.*, Essex Eng.; on R. Chelmer; 10 m. N.W. of Chelmsford; p. (par.) (1961) *3,827.*

Dunmow, Little, *vil.*, 2 m. E. of Gr. Dunmow; "Dunmow Flitch" trial here annually; p. (1961) *359.*

Dunnet Head, *promontory*, Caithness, N.E. Scot.

Dunnottar, *par.*, Kincardine, Scot.; nr. Stonehaven; ruined cas.; p. (1951) *1,514.*

Dunoon, *burgh, wat. pl.*, Argyll, Scot.; on N. side of Firth of Clyde, nearly op. Greenock, ancient cas.; holiday resort; p. (1961) *9,211.*

Duns, *burgh*, Berwick, Scot.; agr. and allied inds.; p. (1961) *1,838.*

Dunsinane, *hill*, Sidlaws, Scot.; nr. Perth; alt. 1,012 ft.; referred to by Shakespeare in "Macbeth."

Dunsmuir, *t.*, N. Cal., U.S.A.; summer resort; hunting, fishing; p. (1960) *2,873.*

Dunstable, *t., mun. bor.*, Beds, Eng.; on N. edge of Chiltern Hills, 4 m. W. of Luton; motor vehicles, sparking-plugs, car components, engin., cement, rubber and plastic goods; p. (estd. 1967) *23,940.*

Duque de Caxias, *t.*, Rio de Janeiro st., Brazil; oil refining; p. (estd. 1968) *324,261.*

Duquesne, *c.*, Penns., U.S.A.; 9 m. S.E. of Pittsburgh; steelwks.; p. (1960) *15,019.*

Du Quoin, *c.*, Ill., U.S.A.; meat packing, flour, leather goods, shoes; p. (1960) *6,558.*

Durance, *R.*, S.E. France; trib. of Rhône; rapid current; length 217 m.

Durango, *inland st.*, N.W. Mexico; mining, agr., stock-raising; a. 42,272 sq. m.; p. (1960) *760,836.*

Durango, *cap.*, D. state, Mexico; cath.; silver, gold, copper, iron-ore; p. (1960) *70,000.*

Durant, *c.*, S. Okla., U.S.A.; cotton gins and compresses, cottonseed oil; p. (1960) *10,467.*

Durban, *spt.*, Natal, Rep. of S. Africa; ch. comm. t. in S.E. Africa; maize, wool, hides, oil and sugar refining, chemicals, textiles, engin.; oil pipeline to Johannesburg; p. (1960) *655,370* (inc. *194,276* Whites).

Düren, *t.*, N. Rhine–Westphalia, Germany; on R. Ruhr, 23 m. S.W. of Cologne; textiles, leather, machin., rly ctr.; p. (1963) *52,600.*

Durgapur, *t.*, W. Bengal; steel plant, coke oven plant; p. (1961) *41,696.*

Durham, *cath. c., mun. bor., co. t.*, Durham, N.E. Eng.; univ.; carpet, organ, confectionery mftg.; p. (estd. 1967) *24,410.*

Durham Co., N.E. Eng.; fertile valleys, moorland; coal, limestone; cattle; shipbldg., iron, steel, chemicals; a. 1,015 sq. m.; p. (1968) *1,542,000.*

Durham, *c.*, N.C., U.S.A.; tobacco factories; p. (1960) *78,302.*

Durlach, *t.*, Baden–Württemberg, Germany;

2½ m. E. Karlsruhe; cas.; cycles, machin.; p. (estd. 1954) *25,000.*

Dürrës (Durazzo), *spt.* Albania, on Adriatic; pt. for Tirana; tobacco ind.; p. (1960) *32,000.*

Dursley, *t.*, Glos., Eng.; 13 m. S. by W. of Gloucester; engin. inds., agr. mach.; p. *5,355.*

Duryea, *bor.*, Penns., U.S.A.; anthracite; silk; p. (1960) *5,626.*

Dushanbe (former Stalinabad), *t.* cap. Tadzhik S.S.R.; univ.; engin., textiles; p. (1967) *323,000.*

Düsseldorf, *cap.*, N. Rhine–Westphalia, Germany; on R. Rhine, 20 m. N. of Cologne; admin. and cultural ctr., art and medical academies; iron, steel, machin., soap, cars, paper, chemical inds.; impt. trans-shipment pt.; p. (1968) *683,303.*

Dust Bowl, *region*, U.S.A.; name applied to Great Plains on E. flank of Rocky Mtns.; subject to severe soil erosion by wind, particularly in drought years (1933, 1936) due to destruction of natural vegetation by excessive ploughing.

Dutch Guiana, *see* Surinam.

Dutch Harbour, *t.*, Unalaska I., Aleutian gr., N. Pac. Oc.; strategic American naval base.

Dvina, *R.*, (N.) flows to White Sea at Arkhangelsk, and is formed by the junction of the Rs. Sukhona and Vychgeda, U.S.S.R.; connected by canal with Neva and Volga; length 1,000 m.

Dvina, *R.*, Latvia, U.S.S.R.; rises near sources of Volga and Dnieper, flows to G. of Riga; l. 65 m.

Dysart, *spt.*, *mun. bor.*, Fife, on F. of Forth, Scot.; linen, coal; p. *9,068.*

Dzaudzhikau, *see* Ordzhonikidze.

Dzerzhinsk, *industl. t.*, R.S.F.S.R.; W. of Gorki; chemicals (fertilisers, explosives); p. (1967) *196,000.*

Dzhalil, *t.*, R.S.F.S.R.; new t. 30 m. N.E. of Almetyevsk to serve new A. oilfield.

Dzhambul, *t.*, Kazakhstan S.S.R.; on R. Talis and Turksib rly.; chemicals; p. (1967) *152,000.*

Dzhezkazgan, *t.*, Kazakh S.S.R.; 350 m. W. of L. Balkhash; copper-mines; manganese ore near-by; p. (1956) *29,100.*

Dzierzoniow, *t.*, S.W. Poland, formerly Germany; ceded to Poland at Potsdam conference; tex-tiles, machin.; cattle, grain mkt.; p. (1965) *31,000.*

Dzungaria, *region*, Sinkiang prov., N.W. China; lies between Tien-Shan highlands of Soviet-Chinese frontier and Altai mtns.; former historic kingdom of Zungaria.

E

Eagle Grove, *c.*, N. Iowa, U.S.A.; gypsum, agr.; p. (1960) *4,381.*

Ealing, *outer bor.*, Greater London; comprising former bors. of Acton, Ealing and Southall; p. (1966) *304,000.*

Earby, *urb. dist.*, W.R. Yorks, Eng.; cotton, plastic, cloths, agr. machin.; p. (1961) *4,983.*

Earlestown, *mftg. t.*, S. Lancs., Eng.; included in Newton le Willows urb. dist.; engin., glass.

Earn, *R.*, Perth, Scot.; issues from Loch Earn (6½ m. long) and flows into the Tay R.; length 46 m.

Earnslaw, *mtns.*, S. I., N.Z.; highest peak, 9,165 ft.

Easdale, *I.*, off W. Argyll, Scot.; nr. Oban; slate quarries. [gas terminal.

Easington, *t.*, E.R. Yorks.; nr. Hull; natural

East C., extreme N.E. point of Asia.

East C., extreme E. point of New Zealand, named by Capt. Cook on his first voyage in 1769.

East Anglia, comprises Norfolk and Suffolk, Eng.; former Anglo-Saxon kingdom; one of Britain's most productive agr. regions.

East Anglian Heights, *hills*, extend S.W. to N.E. across N.E. Hertfordshire, N. Essex and S.W. Suffolk, Eng.; chalk overlain by glacial clays and sands; smooth, rolling surface; region of lge. farms and lge. fields, mixed farms mainly grain; rarely exceed 600 ft. alt.

East Barnet, *former urb. dist.*, Herts, Eng., now inc. in Barnet outer bor., Greater London (*q.v.*); residtl.; p. (1961) *40,641.*

East Bengal, E. *div.* of Pakistan; includes part of former Bengal Presidency; rice, jute, cotton; a. 5,091 sq. m.; p. (estd. 1951) *42,119,000.*

East Chicago, *c.*, Ind., U.S.A.; L. Michigan; iron and steel wks., oil refining; p. (1960) *57,669.*

East Cleveland, *t.*, Ohio, U.S.A.; residtl.; p. (1960) *37,991.*

East Coast Bays, *bor.*, N.Z., p. (1966) *12,357.*

East Greenwich, *t.*, Rhode I., U.S.A.; light mftg.; shellfish; summer resort; p. (1960) *6,100.*

East Grinstead, *t.*, *urb. dist.*, E. Sussex, Eng.; in ctr. of the Weald, 9 m. W. of Tunbridge Wells; agr. mkt.; famous hospital for plastic surgery; p. (1961) *15,421.*

East Ham, *former co. bor.*, Essex, Eng.; mftg. sub. E. of London, docks; chemicals; now inc. in Newham bor., Greater London.

East Indies (Malay Archipelago), gr. of Is. be-tween Asia and Australia, inc. Borneo, Sulawesi, New Guinea, Sumatra, Java, Bali, Timor (see under Kalimantan and Indonesia); sugar, coffee, spices, fruits, rubber, tobacco, sago, tapioca, canes.

East Kilbride, *t.*, N. Lanark, Scot., 7 m. S.S.E. of Glasgow; designated "New Town" 1947; lge. agr. machin., aero engines, engin., elec. goods; seawater distillation plant; knitwear, clothing; p. (estd. 1965) *45,933.*

East Liverpool, *c.*, Ohio, U.S.A.; pottery mnfs.; p. (1960) *22,306.*

East London, *spt.*, C. Prov., S. Africa; at mouth of Buffalo R.; holiday resort; trading ctr.; inds. inc. car assembly, textiles, engin.; p. (1960) *114,584* (inc. *48,725* Whites).

East Lothian (Haddington), *co.*, S.E. Scot.; cereals, potatoes, sheep, coal; *co. t.*, Hadding-ton, a. 267 sq. m.; p. (1961) *52,653.*

East Main R., Labrador, Newfoundland, Canada; flowing into James Bay.

East Moline, *t.*, Ill., U.S.A.; p. (1960) *16,732.*

East Orange, *t.*, N.J., U.S.A.; residtl. sub., New York; p. (1960) *77,259.*

East Pakistan, *prov.*, Pakistan; comprises E. terrs. of prov. of Bengal and former Assam dist. of Sylhet; cap. Dacca; severe flooding 1970; a. 55,126 sq. m.; p. (1961) *50,844,000.*

East Palestine, *t.*, Ohio, U.S.A.; clay, coal, oil, pottery; p. (1960) *5,232.* [*41,955.*

East Providence, *t.*, Rhode I., U.S.A.; p. (1960)

East Retford, *mun. bor.*, Notts, Eng.; on R. Idle, 6 m. E. of Worksop; rubber, wire ropes, engin.; p. (estd 1967) *18,770.*

East Riding, Yorkshire, *see* Yorkshire, East Riding.

East River, *tidal strait* about 16 m. long and from 600 to 4,000 ft. wide; the R. separates the bors. of Manhattan and Bronx from the bors. of Queens and Brooklyn.

East St. Louis, *c.*, R. *pt.*, Ill., U.S.A.; on Missis-sippi R.; large stockyards; meat packing; p. (1960) *81,712.*

East Stonehouse, *t.*, Devon, Eng.; adjoining Plymouth and Devonport.

Eastbourne, *t.*, *co. bor.*, E. Sussex, Eng.; on S. cst. to E. of Beachy Head; seaside resort; p. (estd. 1967) *66,800.* [images, ruins; p. *250.*

Easter I., E. Pac. Oc., W. of Chile; stone

Eastern Province, Zambia; groundnuts, maize, tobacco; prov. ctr. Fort Jameson; a. 22,350 sq. m.; p. (1964) *507,000.*

Eastham, *vil.*, Cheshire, Eng.; on S. of Mersey estuary, nr. entrance to Manchester Ship Canal.

Easthampton, *t.*, Mass., U.S.A.; p. (1950) *10,694.*

Eastleigh, *t.*, *mun. bor.*, Hants, Eng.; locomotives; p. (estd. 1967) *43,070.*

Easton, *t.*, Mass., U.S.A.; p. (1960) *9,069.*

Easton, *c.*, Penns., U.S.A.; on Delaware R.; rly. ctr., coal, steel, machin., furniture; p. (1960) *31,955.*

Eastview, *t.*, Ontario, Canada; p. (1961) *24,555.*

Eastwood, *t.*, *urb. dist.*, Notts, Eng.; coal; p. (1961) *10,585.*

Eau Claire, *c.*, Wis., U.S.A.; on Chippewa R.; timber, paper, furniture; p. (1960) *37,987.*

Eaux Bonnes, Les, *wat. pl.*, Pyrenees, S. France.

Eaux Chaudes, *wat. pl.*, Pyrenees, S. France.

Ebal, Mt., Israel; opposite Gerizim; alt. 2,986 ft.

Ebbw Vale, *t.*, *urb. dist.*, Monmouth, Wales; 17 m. N.W. of Newport; coal, iron, steel, tinplate, bricks, pipes, precast concrete; p. (1961) *28,631.*

Eberswalde, *t.*, Frankfurt, E. Germany; N.E. of Berlin; iron, wood and cardboard wks.; p. (1963) *32,906.*

Ebingen, *c.*, Württemberg, Germany; knitwear, velvet, precision tools; p. (1963) *21,400.*

Eboli, *t.*, Campagna, Italy; E. of Salerno.

Ebro, *R.*, N.E. Spain; flows to Mediterranean from Cantabrian Mtns.; length 440 m.

Ebury, *R.*, Monmouth, Wales; trib. of Usk R.

Eccles, *mun. bor.*, Lancs, Eng.; 4 m. W. of Man-chester; iron and steel, cotton, textiles, leather, chemicals, coal-mining; p. (estd. 1967) *41,400.*

Ecclesfield, *t.*, W.R. Yorks, Eng.; N. of Sheffield; cutlery. [Stafford; p. *3,630*.

Eccleshall, *mkt. t.*, Staffs, Eng.; 6 m. N.W. of

Echague, *t.*, Philippine Is.; tobacco ctr.

Echternach, *t.*, Luxembourg; famous abbey; Whitsun dancing-procession; p. (1960) *9,820*.

Echuca, *t.*, Victoria, Australia; on R. Murray; 50 m. N.E. of Bendigo; rly. ctr.; irrigation wks.; diary prods., timber; p. (1966) *8,014*.

Ecija, *t.*, Seville, Spain; olive oil, wine, pottery; the Roman Astigi; p. *34,944*.

Eck, Loch, *L.*, Argyll, Scot.; 6 m. long.

Eckernförde, *spt.*, Schleswig-Holstein, Germany; on Baltic N.W. of Kiel; fishing; resort; p. (1963) *20,400*.

Eckington, *t.* Derby, Eng.; S.E of Sheffield; coal, agr. implements; p. *14,614*.

Ecorse, *t.*, Mich., U.S.A.; p. (1960) *17,328*.

Ecuador, *rep.*, S. America; on Equatorial Pacific cst.; Andes mtns.; Chimborazo, 20,600 ft.; climate: lowlands tropical, uplands cool and dry; race chiefly Indian speaking the Quechua language; poor communications; cocoa, sugar, coffee, cereals, fruits, gold, copper, silver, Panama hats; cap. Quito; a. 106,508 sq. m.; p. (estd. 1968) *5,695,000*.

Edam, *t.*, S. Holland, Netherlands; on cst. IJsselmeer; cheese, tool mftg.; p. (1967) *16,553*.

Eday, *I.*, Orkney Is., Scot.; the Ocelli of Ptolemy. [(estd. 1949) *8,000*.

Ed Damar, *cap.*, Northern Prov., Sudan; p. 15 m. S.W. of Khartum.

Eddystone, *rock with lighthouse*, Eng. Channel; 15 m. S.W. of Plymouth.

Ede, *t.*, Gelderland, Netherlands; livestock; pianos; p. (1967) *67,558*.

Ede, *t.*, W. Prov., Nigeria; p. *57,500*.

Eden, *R.*, Westmorland, Eng.; rises in Pennines, flows N.W. to Solway Firth below Carlisle; length 65 m.

Edenton, *t.*, N.C., U.S.A.; groundnuts, cotton, herring fisheries; p. (1960) *4,458*.

Edessa (Edhessa), *t.*, *cap.*, Pella prefecture, Macedonia, Greece; p. (1961) *15,534*.

Edgbaston, *residtl. dist.*, Birmingham, Eng.

Edgehill, *ridge*, 15 m. S. Warwick, Eng.; first battle in Civil War, 1642.

Edgewater, *t.*, N.J., U.S.A.; sub., connected by ferry with New York; p. (1960) *4,113*.

Edgware, *t.*, Middlesex, Eng.; N. sub. of London; residtl.; p. (1961) *20,127*.

Edina, *t.*, Minn., U.S.A.; p. (1960) *28,501*.

Edinburgh, *c.*, Midlothian; cap. Scot.; royal burgh on F. of Forth; univ., cas.; palace (Holyrood); printing, publishing, brewing, electronics equipment; Edinburgh Festival in August; Leith, with docks is joined to E.; p. (estd. 1968) *466,000*.

Edirne, *c.*, Turkey; on left bank of the Marica R.; greatly developed by Hadrian 125; residence of the Sultans 1366–1453; wine, tobacco, silk, perfume; p. (1965) *46,264*.

Edjelé, *t.*, Algeria,; oilfields; pipeline to La Skhirra, Tunisia.

Edmonton, *c.*, cap. Alberta, Canada; fast-growing c. (46 sq. m.) on both sides of N. Saskatchewan R.; high-level bridge links Strathcona; immense war-time activity ("invasion"), now major Canadian military ctr.; univ.; international air ctr.; oilfields and farming; oil and chemical inds.; p. (1966) *401,299*.

Edmonton, *former mun. bor.*, Middlx., Eng.; now inc. in Enfield outer bor., Greater London (*q.v.*); residtl.; light inds.; p. (1961) *91,956*.

Edremit, *t.*, Balikesir, N.W. Turkey; cereals, opium; silverwk.; p. (1960) *22,246*.

Edward, *L.*, on frontier of Uganda and the Congo (ex-Belgian), one of the sources of R. Nile; alt. 3,000 ft., length 44 m., breadth 32 m

Edwardsville, *t.*, Ill., U.S.A.; p. (1960) *9,996*.

Eekloo, *t.*, E. Flanders, Belgium; textiles; p. (1962) *18,571*. [*35,832*.

Eger, *c.*, Hungary; wine, soap; cath.; p. (1962)

Egersund, *spt.*, S. cst., Norway; pottery, china, engin.; fishing; p. (1960) *3,868*.

Eggan, *R. pt.*, Ilorin, Nigeria; p. *10,000*.

Egham, *urb. dist.*, Surrey, Eng.; on R. Thames, nr. Staines; contains field of Runnymede, where King John signed Magna Carta; residtl.; p. (estd. 1967) *31,670*.

Egmont, *mtn.*, N.I., N.Z.; volcanic; alt. 8,200 ft.

Egremont, *mkt. t.*, Cumberland, Eng.; S. of Whitehaven; limestone, iron ore; p. (1961) *6,943*.

Egypt, *see* United Arab Republic.

Ehen, *R.*, Cumberland, Eng.; issues from Ennerdale Water to Irish Sea; length 12 m.

Ehrenbreitstein, *t.*, *fort.*, Germany; on R. Rhine opposite Koblenz.

Eibar, *c.*, Guipuzcoa, N. Spain; iron, steel mftg., ordnance wks.; p. (1957) *16,318*.

Eibenstock, *t.*, Saxony, Germany; p. *7,760*.

Eider, *R.*, Germany; connected with Kiel canal; length 90 m.

Eifel, *plateau of ancient rocks*, W. Germany; lies N. of R. Moselle, terminates in steep slope forming W. edge of Rhine gorge between Koblenz and Bonn; drained by Kyll, Ahr, Rur; formerly cultivated, now largely woodland and moorland; farming in valleys; rises to just over 2,000 ft.

Eiger, *mtn.*, one of the highest peaks of the Bernese Oberland, Switzerland; alt. 13,042 ft.

Eigg, *I.*, Inner Hebrides, Scot.; 15 m. S.W. of Mallaig; basaltic rocks on cst.; rises to 1,289 ft.

Eilat, *new spt.*, Negev, Israel; on Gulf of Akaba; oil; copper at Timna; p. (estd. 1953) *400*.

Eildon Hills, Roxburgh, Scot.; S. of Melrose; highest point 1,385 ft.

Eilenburg, *t.*, Leipzig, E. Germany; rly. junction; machin., chemicals; p. (1963) *21,050*.

Eindhoven, *c.*, N. Brabant, Netherlands; electronic equipment, motor vehicles, tobacco and textile inds.; techn. univ.; p. (1967) *183,637*.

Einsiedeln, *t.*, Schwyz, Switzerland; monastery, pilgrim ctr.

Eire, *see* Ireland, Republic of.

Eisenach, *t.*, Erfurt, E. Germany; on R. Hörsel, at foot of Thuringian forest; ctr. of Werra potash field; cars, machin., textiles; birthplace of J. S. Bach; p. (1963) *47,854*.

Eisenberg, *t.*, Gera, E. Germany; pianos, porcelain, cement, machin.; p. (1963) *13,666*.

Eisenerz Alps, *mtn. range*, Austria; most northerly range of Alps, overlooking Danube valley between Linz and Vienna; impt. iron-ore deposits; alt. from 6,000 to 9,000 ft.

Eisenhüttenstadt, *t.*, Frankfurt, E. Germany; iron smelting; p. (1963) *35,671*.

Eisleben, *t.*, Halle, E. Germany; birthplace of Luther; machin., copper- and silver-mining ctr.; p. (1963) *33,589*.

Ekibastuz, *t.*, Kazakhstan S.S.R.; 75 m. S.W. of Pavlodar; ctr. of rapidly developing mng. a. coal, gold, metals; coal-fed generating plant projected, to supply power to European Russia; p. (1956) *15,000*.

El Alamein, *vil.*, U.A.R.; in Libyan Desert 60 m. S.W. of Alexandria, scene of gr. Allied victory, Second World War; oilfield nearby; terminal nr. Sidi Abd el-Rahman.

El Callao, *t.*, Bolivar, st., Venezuela; in ctr. of Guiana Highlands, 125 m. S.E. of Ciudad Bolivar; ctr. of impt. gold-mining region.

El Centro, Cal., U.S.A.; rich agr. a. reclaimed from the desert; p. (1960) *16,811*.

El Dorado, *t.*, Ark., U.S.A.; oil; p. (1960) *25,292*.

El Dorado, *t.*, Kan., U.S.A.; p. (1960) *12,523*.

El Faiyûm or El Fayum, *oasis t.*, *cap.* of Faiyûm prov., U.A.R.; nr. L. Moeris; predynastic arch. finds; lgst. cultivated a. of U.A.R. outside Nile flood plain; uranium; p. (1960) *102,000*.

El Fasher, *cap.*, Darfur Prov., Sudan; p. (estd. 1961) *28,462*. [ch. t. Hofuf.

El Hasa, *dist.*, Saudi Arabia; on Persian Gulf.

El Jadida (Mazagan), *spt.*, Morocco; grain and wool tr.; p. (1960) *40,302*.

El Khârga, *oasis*, Libyan desert, U.A.R.; 85 m. S.W of Asyut; p. *5,000*.

El Misti, *volcano*, Peru, S. America; N.E. of Arequipa; alt. 19,170 ft.

El Obeid, *cap.*, Kordofan, Sudan; 200 m. S.W. of Khartoum; ivory, gums, ostrich feathers; p. (estd. 1961) *56,970*.

El Oro, *prov.*, Ecuador; cap. Machala; a. 2,238 sq. m.; p. (estd. 1962) *162,591*.

El Paso, *c.*, Texas, U.S.A.; on Rio Grande; natural gas distribution, ore refining; p. (1960) *276,687*.

El Quantara (El Kantara), *t.*, U.A.R.; on E. bank of Suez Canal, 21 m. S. of Pt. Said; terminus of Palestine Rly. system; linked by ferry across canal (and temporary swing bridge) to El Quantara (W.) on Egyptian Rly. systems.

El Teniente, *t.*, central Chile; copper-mines; p. *11,761*.

Elan, t., Radnor, Wales; rises on S.E. sides of Plynlimon, flows S.E. then N.E. into R. Wye at Rhayader; lower valley contains series of 4 lge. reservoirs, length 4 m., capacity 10,000 million gall.; ch. source of water for Birmingham.

Elâzig, t., E. Turkey; dam and hydro-elec. project planned at Keban, 30 m. to N.W. at confluence of E. and W. branches of Euphrates; p. (1965) 78,899.

Elba, i., off Tuscan cst., Italy; iron ore, wine, marble, salt; Napoleon's first exile here; ch. t. Porto Ferrajo; a. 140 sq. m.; p. (1960) 26,000.

Elbasan, prefecture, Albania; cap. Elbasan; p. (1958) 430,000.

Elbe, R., Czechoslovakia, Germany; the Roman "Albis"; rises in Bohemia and flows into N. Sea at Cuxhaven, 65 m. below Hamburg; navigable for 500 m. of total length 725 m.

Elbert, mtn., Col., U.S.A.; alt. 14,420 ft.

Elbeuf, t., Seine-Maritime, France; woollens; p. (1954) 17,293.

Elblag (Elbing), spt., N. Poland (since 1945), formerly in E. Prussia; shipbldg., machin., vehicles; p. (1965) 85,000.

Elbruz Mt., Caucasus, highest in Europe (18,480 ft.), over-topping Mont Blanc by 2,698 ft.

Elburz, mtn. range, N. Iran; bordering on Caspian Sea; highest peak, Demavend, 18,500 ft.

Elche, t., Alicante, Spain; 15 m. S.W. of Alicante; palm groves; oil, soap; p. (1959) 72,706.

Eldorado, radium mine, N.W. Terr., N. Canada; situated on E. shore of Gr. Bear Lake nr. Arctic Circle; produces 40% of world's radium, sent to Pt. Hope, Ontario, for refining.

Electra, t., N. Texas, U.S.A.; oil; drilling tools and equipment; p. (1960) 4,759.

Electrona, Tasmania, Australia; carbide wks. based on local limestone and hydroelec. power; unique in S. hemisphere.

Elektrenai, t., Lithuanian S.S.R.; new township nr. Vievis, at site of thermal power stn.

Elektrostal, t., R.S.F.S.R.; 35 m. E. of Moscow; steel, engin.; p. (1967) 116,000.

Elephant Butte Dam, N.M., U.S.A.; on Rio Grande, 125 m. above El Paso; built to control flood water; lake, a. 60 sq. m., supplies irrigation water to 780 sq. m. in N.M. and Texas, water also supplied to Mexico.

Elephanta, I., Bombay Harbour, India; cave sculptures.

Elephantine, I., in Nile, Upper U.A.R.; site of nilometer. [engin. wks.

Eleusis, t., Greece; nr. Athens; ship repair yard;

Eleuthera, I., Bahamas, T.W.I.; p. (1953) 6,070.

Elgin, t., Ill., U.S.A.; watches, elec. goods, machin. chemicals, wood prod.; p. (1960) 49,447.

Elgin, co. t., burgh, Moray, Scot.; ancient ruined cath.; woollens; p. (1961) 11,971.

Elgon Mt., extinct volcano, on bdy. of Kenya and Uganda; 40 m. in diam.; alt. 14,100 ft.; cave dwellings on slopes.

Elie and Earlsferry, burgh, Fife, Scot.; summer resort; p. (1961) 1,128.

Elisabethville, see Lubumbashi.

Elizabeth, mftg. t., N.J., U.S.A.; univ.; sewing machines, iron, oil-ref.; p. (1960) 107,698.

Elizabeth, satellite t. 17 m. N. of Adelaide, S. Australia; p. (1966) 47,000; proposed p. 60,000.

Elizabeth, t., N.C., U.S.A.; timber ind.; p. (1960) 14,062.

Elizabethton, t., Tenn., U.S.A.; manganese; rayon; p. (1960) 10,896.

Elkhart, t., Ind., U.S.A.; E. of Chicago; paper, machin.; p. (1960) 40,274.

Elk Mtns., lofty range, W. Col., U.S.A.; highest point Castle Peak, alt. 14,115 ft.

Elland, t., urb. dist., W.R. Yorks, Eng.; on R. Calder, 3 m. S.E. of Halifax; woollens; p. (1961) 18,353.

Ellesmere, t., Shropshire, Eng.; 8 m. N.W. of Wem; mkt. agr.; p. (1961) 2,254.

Ellesmere, agr. dist., S.I., N.Z.; on Canterbury Plain nr. Christchurch.

Ellesmere I., lge. I. extreme north of Arctic Canada; barren, uninhabited; a. 41,000 sq. m.

Ellesmere Port, t., mun. bor., N.W. Cheshire, Eng.; on Manchester Ship Canal and 9 m. S.S.E. of Liverpool; impt. petrol docks and refinery; metal mftg., paper, engin.; p. (estd. 1967) 52,950.

Elliot Lake, t., N. Ontario; ctr. of uranium mines; p. 25,000.

Ellis I., New York harbour, U.S.A.; served as ch. immigration ctr., 1892-1943.

Ellon, burgh, Aberdeen, Scot.; on R. Ythan; p. (1961) 1,456.

Ellwood, t., Penns., U.S.A.; p. (1960) 12,413.

Elmhurst, t., Ill., U.S.A.; p. (1960) 36,991.

Elmina, t., Ghana, W. Africa; fortress; tr. in palm oil, ivory, gold; p. 15,200.

Elmira, mftg. t., N.Y., U.S.A.; rly. goods, farm implements; burial place of Mark Twain; p. (1960) 46,517.

Elmshorn, t., Germany; N.W. of Hamburg; p. (1963) 35,400. [p. (1960) 26,658.

Elsinore (Helsingor), t., spt., Denmark; shipbldg.;

Elstree, t., Herts., Eng.; 4 m. W. of Barnet; residential; films, light engin., silk hosiery; p. (1961) 24,782. [London.

Eltham, residtl. dist., Kent, Eng.; S. sub. of

Eluru, t., Andra Pradesh, India; cotton; carpets, hosiery, oil; p. (1961) 108,321.

Elvas, c. (fortfd.), Portugal; on Guadiana R.; plums, olives; p. (1960) 11,742.

Elwood, industl. t., Ind., U.S.A.; on Duck Creek; grain, tinplate; p. (1960) 11,793.

Ely, c., Cambridge and I. of Ely, Eng.; on S. fringe of the Fens; mkt., cath.; agr. ctr. (fruit, roots); p. (1961) 9,815.

Ely, I. of, see Cambridge and Isle of Ely.

Elyria, t., Ohio, U.S.A.; mftg.; p. (1960) 43,782.

Emba, R., Kazakh S.S.R.; rises in S. end of Ural Mtns., flows S.W. to Caspian Sea; crosses productive Ural-Emba oilfield.

Emden, spt., Lower Saxony, Germany; nr. mouth of R. Ems; freighting, shipbldg., cars; fishing prod., imports iron ore, corn; exp. coal and iron from Ruhr; p. (1963) 46,100.

Emilia-Romagna, region, N. Italy; S. of Po R.; agr. (grain, wine, fruits); a. 8,542 sq. m.; p. (1961) 3,646,507.

Emmaus, bor., Penns., U.S.A.; textiles, rubber prod.; p. (1960) 10,262.

Emmen, t., Drenthe, Netherlands; 30 m. S.E. of Groningen; elec. machin., ball bearings, tinplate, iron wks.; p. (1967) 75,660.

Empedrado, t., Argentina; oranges, rice in a.; p. (1960) 21,000.

Empoli, t., Florence, Italy; textile mnfs., straw plaiting, leather goods, pottery; p. 21,000.

Emporia, t., Kan., U.S.A.; stock-raising; p. (1960) 18,190. [p. 7,070.

Ems, t., Germany; on Lahn R.; spa, silver, lead;

Ems, R., N. Germany; rises in Teutoburger Wald, flows N. to N. Sea at Emden; length 205 m.

Emscher, R., W. Germany; rises in Sauerland, flows W. through heart of Ruhr coalfield to enter R. Rhine at Hamborn; canalised for most of its course; length 55 m.

Emsdetten, t., Germany; on R. Ems; textiles; p. (1963) 26,000.

Encarnación, pt., cap., Ipatua dep., S.E. Paraguay; on Paraná R.; exp. timber, maté, tobacco, cotton, hides; p. (estd. 1960) 35,000.

Encounter Bay, S. Australia, receives Murray R.

Enderby Land, terr., Antarctica; S. of C. of Good Hope. [18,775.

Endicott, t., N.Y., U.S.A.; shoe mftg.; p. (1960)

Endrick, R., Stirling, Scot.; flows to Loch Lomond; length 29 m. [(1960) 1,485.

Enez, t., S. Turkey-in-Europe; nr. Gallipoli; p.

Enfield, former mun. bor.; Middlesex Eng.; now outer bor. Greater London; comprising former bors. of Edmonton, Enfield and Southgate; p. (1966) 263,000.

Engadine, Switzerland; upper valley of Inn R.; health resort; chief t. St. Moritz.

Engaño, c., S. extremity of Luzon, Philippine Is.

Engelberg, t., Unterwalden, Switzerland; tourists; old monastery; p. 2,409.

Engels, t., R.S.F.S.R.; on Volgar R. opposite Saratov; textiles, chemicals, petroleum refining; p. (1967) 120,000.

Enghien-les-Bains, t., Seine-et-Oise, France; p. (1962) 12,504.

England (with Wales), forms S. and lgst. div. Gr. Britain; length 420 m., greatest breadth 360 m.; ch. mtns.: Cheviot Hills, Pennine Chain, Cumbrian Gr., Cambrian Mtns., Dartmoor, Exmoor; ch. Rs.: Thames, Severn, Trent, Mersey, Gr. Ouse, Yorkshire Ouse; climate: temperate maritime; vegetation: woods, moor, heath, grassland; ch. inds.: agr.: arable, pastoral, dairying; ch. crops: wheat, barley, oats, sugar-beet, potatoes, hops, fruit.

livestock; cod, haddock; coal, iron; iron and steel mnfs., machinery, machine tools, engin., prods., road vehicles and aircraft, ships, textiles, pottery; good road and rail comm.; cap. London; a. 50,333 sq. m.; p. (estd. 1969) *46,102,870*

Englewood, *t.,* N.J., U.S.A.; p. (1960) *26,057.*

English Channel (La Manche), *narrow sea* separating England from France; extends from Strait of Dover to Land's End in Cornwall; length 300 m., greatest width 155 m.

Enham-Alamein, Hants.; rehabilitation ctr. for disabled ex-service men; 2½ m. N. of Andover; light inds.   [ments; p. (1960) *38,859.*

Enid, *t.,* Okla., U.S.A.; ironwks., farm immp

Enkhuizen, *c., spt.,* N. Holland, Netherlands; on W. cst. IJsselmeer; picturesque c.. p. (1967) *11,231.*

Enna (Castrogiovanni), *t.,* Sicily; rock salt, sulphur-mines; famous for its connection with the Proserpine legend; p. (1961) *28,145.*

En Nahud, *t.,* central Sudan; tr. in cattle, ivory, cotton, ostrich feathers; p. *19,300.*

Ennepetal, *t.,* N. Rhine-Westphalia, Germany; on R. Ennepe; t. created 1949 with merging of Milspe and Voerde; iron, machin.; p. (1963) *32,000.*

Ennerdale Water, *L.,* Cumberland, Eng.

Ennis, *mkt. t., urb. dist.,* Clare, Ireland; farming, flour; p. (1966) *5,831.*

Enniscorthy, *mkt. t., urb. dist.,* Wexford, Ireland; brewing, tanning; p. (1966) *5,762.*

Enniskillen, *co. t., mun. bor.,* Fermanagh, N. Ireland; brewing, nylon mftg., meat processing; p. (1966) *7,154.*

Enns, *R.,* Austria; S. trib. of Danube; 112 m.

Enschede, *c.,* Overijssel, Netherlands; cotton-spinning, weaving, textile mach., engin.; techn. univ.; p. (1960) *123,799.*

Entebbe, *t.* Uganda, E. Africa; on L. Victoria; univ.; cotton ginning; p. (estd.) *11,000.*

Enterprise, *c.,* Ala., U.S.A.; peanuts; p. (1960) *11,410.*

Entre Rios, *prov.,* Argentina; between Paraná and Uruguay Rs.; wheat, linseed, livestock; cap. Paraná; a. 29,427 sq. m.; p. (1960) *804,000.*

Entrocamiento, *t.,* Central Portugal, on Tagus R.

Enugu, *cap.* E. prov., Nigeria; coal; p. (1953) *63,000.*   [(1962) *22,799.*

Epernay, *t.,* Marne, France; champagne; p.

Ephesus, *ruined c.,* Turkey, S. of Izmir.

Ephrata, *t.,* S.E. Penns., U.S.A.; cattle rearing, printing; p. (1960) *7,688.*

Epinal, *cap.,* Vosges dep., France; on Moselle R.; textiles, printing; p. (1962) *37,308.*

Epirus, *dist.,* N.W. Greece; a. 3,688 sq. m.; p. (1961) *352,604.*   [dairying; p. (1961) *10,001.*

Epping, *t., urb. dist.,* Essex, Eng.; mkt. gardening,

Epping, *forest,* Essex, Eng.

Epsom and Ewell, *mun. bor.,* Surrey, Eng.; 18 m. S.W. of London; residtl., racecourse; drain pipes, brick tiles; p. (estd. 1967) *72,320.*

Equatoria, *prov.,* Sudan; a. 76,995 sq. m.; cap. Juba; p. (estd. 1951) *632,900.*

Equatorial Guinea, *rep.,* W. Africa; (formerly Span. overseas prov.) consists of mainland terr. of Rio Muni and Is. of Fernando Po, Annobon, Corisco, Elobey Grande and Elobey Chico; total a. 10,832 sq. m.; total p. (1968) *281,000*; cap. Santa Isabel.

Erandio, *t.,* N. sub. of Bilbao, Spain; iron ore, paper, tobacco, wine; p. *11,268.*   [Antarctica.

Erebus, *mtn.,* active volcano, Victoria Land,

Eregli, *spt.,* Black Sea, Turkey; rly. to Zonguldak coal-mines; steel wks.; p. (1960) *8,815.*

Erfurt, *c., cap.,* Erfurt, E. Germany; cath., ctr. of mkt. gardening and seed-growing dist.; textiles, machin., foodstuffs, footwear, radios, heavy engin.; p. (1963) *189,817.*

Ericht, *loch,* Perth, Inverness, Scot.; in central Grampians; 15¼ m. long; hydro-elec. scheme.

Erie, *lake,* N. America; separating Canada from U.S.A.; polluted waters; a. 9,940 sq. m.; 241 m. long, 57 m. broad.

Erie, *industl. c., lake pt.,* Penns., U.S.A.; iron and steel ind.. engin.; p. (1960) *138,440.*

Erie Canal, *see* New York State Barge Canal.

Eriskay, I., Outer Hebrides, Scot.

Erith, *former mun. bor.,* Kent, Eng.; on S. bank of Thames estuary 5 m. below London; engin., oil refining, cables, plastics, paints and varnishes, timber, concrete prods.; p. (1961) *45,043*; now inc. in Bexley bor., Greater London.

Eritrea, *prov.,* Ethiopia; fed. within Ethioipa 1952; former Italian col., N.E. Africa; tobacco. cereals, pearl fishing; cap. Asmara, a. *45,754* sq. m.; p. (estd. 1960) *1,000,000.*

Erivan, *cap.* Armenian S.S.R., U.S.S.R.; situated in deep valley in Caucasus Mtns.; woollen mnfs., fruit canning, machine tools; p. (1939) *200,000.*

Erlangen, *t.,* Bavaria, Germany; univ.; textiles, elec. and precision engin., gloves; p. (1963) *73,200.*   [hides; p. (1961) *117,253*

Earnakulam, *t.,* Kerala, India; cotton, coffee.

Erne, *R.,* (72 m.) and *L.,* N. Ireland, flows to Donegal Bay.   [*73,762.*

Erode, *t.,* S. Tamil Nadu, India; cotton; p. (1961)

Erskine, *t.,* Renfrewshire, Scot.; new satellite t.

Erzgebirge (Ore Mns.), *mtn. range,* Germany; highest peak, 4,122 ft.

Erzurum, *t.,* Turkey; agr. ctr. on fertile plateau 6,200 ft. a.s.l.; formerly of gr. strategic impt.; p. (1965) *106,301.*

Esbjerg, *spt.,* Denmark; W. cst. of Jutland; export harbour on N. Sea cst.; exp. agr. prod.; fishing; airport; p. (1965) *55,582.*

Escanaba, *t.,* Mich., U.S.A.; iron, shipping, lumber, chemicals; p. (1960) *15,391.*

Escatrón, *t.,* Spain; on Ebro R.

Esch-sur-Alzette, *t.,* Luxembourg; mining ctr.; p. (1960) *27,954.*

Eschwege, *t.,* Hessen, Germany; cas.; machin., textiles, leather, cigars, chemicals; p. (1963) *24,000.*

Eschweiler, *t.,* N. Rhine-Westphalia, Germany; N.W. of Aachen; lignite mng., steel, iron, metal-lurgy, leather, textiles; p. (1963) *40,000.*

Escondido, *t.,* Cal., U.S.A.; p. (1960) *16,377.*

Esdraelon, *plain,* Israel; S.W. Asia; between Carmel and Gilboa Mtns.

Esfahan. *See* Isfahan.

Esher, *urb. dist.,* Surrey, Eng.; on R. Mole. residtl.; Sandown Park racecourse; p. (estd. 1967) *62,980.*

Eshowe, *health resort,* Natal, S. Africa; 40 m. from Tugela R.; p. (1960) *4,919* inc. *1,945* whites.

Esk, *R.,* Dumfries, Scot., rises in S. Uplands, flows S. into Solway Firth; length 50 m.

Esk, *R.,* N.R. Yorks., Eng.; flows E. into N. Sea at Whitby; length 28 m.

Eskilstuna, *t.,* Sweden; on R. of same name; iron, steel, machin.; p. (1961) *59,072.*

Eskisehir, *t.,* Turkey; W. of Ankara, anc. Dory-laeum; rly. ctr.; meerschaum; p. (1965) *174,451.*

Esmeralda, *t.,* Venezuela, S. America; on Orinoco R

Esmeraldas, *prov.,* Ecuador, S. America; cap. E. on R. of same name; cacao, tobacco; a. 5,464 sq. m.; p. (estd. 1962) *124,742.*

Esmeraldas, *pt.,* Ecuador; bananas, timber, tobacco, cacao, rubber; gold mines nearby; p. (1962) *13,169.*

Espírito Santo, *maritime st.,* Brazil; sugar, cotton, coffee, fruits, forests, thorium; cap. Vitória; a. 15,785 sq. m.; p. (estd. 1968) *1,921,352.*

Essaouira (Mogador) *spt.,* Morocco, N. Africa; cereals, almonds, gum-arabic, crude oil; p. (1960) *26,392*

Essen, *t.,* N. Rhine-Westphalia, Germany; ch. t., in W. Ruhr; coal-mng., steel (Krupp), elec. and light engin.; p. (1968) *699,562.*

Essendon, *sub.,* Melbourne, Victoria, Australia; racecouse, air-port.

Essentuki, *t.,* Stavropol, U.S.S.R.; light mnfs., medicinal springs; p. *23,000.*

Essequibo, *R.,* Guyana; length 620 m.

Essex, *co.,* Eng.; bounded on S. by Thames, on E. by North Sea; co. t. Chelmsford; lies mainly on London Clay and chalk; agr.: wheat, barley, sugar-beet; market gd.; S.W. part of Greater London with manf. subs.; motor wks. at Dagenham; oil refs. at Shell Haven; civil nuclear power-stn. at Bradwell; univ. at Colchester; a. 1,528 sq. m.; p. (1966) *1,244,000.*

Esslingen, *t.,* Baden-Württemberg, Germany; on R. Neckar; mach. and rly. shops; textiles, chemicals, leather goods; Liebfrauen church (1440); p. (1963) *83,900.*

Este, *t.,* N.E. Italy; ancient fortress; iron, pottery, chemicals; p. *14,438.*   [*53,372.*

Estelí, *dep.,* W. Nicaragua; a. 772 sq. m.; p.

Estepona, *spt.,* Malaga, Spain; wine, olives, citrus fruit, sardines; p. (1957) *12,913.*

Eston, *t., urb. dist.,* N.R. Yorks, Eng.; 3 m. E. of Middlesbrough; iron and steel, shipbldg. and repairing; p. (1961) *37,160.*

Estonia, *constituent rep.*, U.S.S.R.; formerly independent st.; climate: severe winter, mild summer, moderate rainfall; farming and dairying, textiles, matches, leather: a. 17,610 sq. m.; cap. Tallin; p. (1970) *1,357,000.*

Estoril, watering-place and thermal spa, Portugal; N. side of Tagus estuary. [peak 7,524 ft.

Estrela, Serra da, *mtn. range.* Portugal; highest

Estremadura, *prov.*, Portugal; cap. Lisbon; a. 2,064 sq. m.; p. (1950) *1,595,067.*

Esztergom, *t.*, Hungary; weaving; mineral springs; cath.; p. (1962) *23,716.*

Etampes, *t.*, Seine-et-Oise; France; 30 m. S. of Paris; commerce; p. (1962) *13,658.*

Etang de Berre, *lagoon*, Bouches-du-Rhône, S.E. France; lies E. of Rhône delta, separated from Gulf of Lions by low Chaîne de l'Estaque; traversed by Rhône–Marseille Canal; salt pans; oil refineries in a.; approx. a. 100 sq. m.

Etaples, *t.*, Pas de Calais, France; seaside resort; p. (1962) *8,647.*

Etawney, *L.*, Manitoba, Canada.

Ethiopia (Abyssinia), *indep. sovereign st.*, Africa; under Italian domination 1936–41; federated with Eritrea 1952; tableland with average height 3,000 ft. intersected deep valleys; Samen Mtns. 15,000 ft.; summer rains; pastoral, farming, coffee; cap. Addis Ababa. a. 400,000 sq. m.; p. (estd. 1969) *24,769,000.*

Etna, *volcano*, N.E. Sicily, Italy; recent eruptions have raised height from 10,768 ft. to 11,121 ft.

Etna, *t.*, Penns., U.S.A.; p. (1960) *5,519.*

Eton, *t.*, *urb. dist.*, Bucks, Eng.; on N. bank of R. Thames opposite Windsor; famous public school, founded by Henry VI, p. (1961) *3,901.*

Etowah, *R.*, Ga., U.S.A.; trib. of Coosa R.

Etruria, *t.*, Staffs, Eng.; potteries, ironwks.

Ettelbrück, *t.*, Luxembourg; p. *4,373.*

Etterbeek, *commune*, sub. Brussels, Belgium; carpets, brewing; p. (1962) *53,091.*

Ettrick, *R.*, Selkirk, Scot.; length 32 m.

Eucla, *t.*, W. Australia; close to bdy. of S. Australia on Transcontinental rly.; artesian wells.

Euclid, *t.*, Ohio, U.S.A.; p. (1960) *62,998.*

Eucumbene Dam and L., N.S.W., Australia, major storage of Snowy Mtns. hydroelec. scheme; will hold eight times as much water as Sydney Harbour when completed.

Eugene, *t.*, Ore., U.S.A.; univ.; ironwks.; p. (1960) *50,977.* [11,326.

Eunice, *t.*, La., U.S.A.; cotton, rice; p. (1960)

Euphrates, *lgst. R.* in S.W. Asia; rises in Armenian uplands and joined by the Tigris, enters Persian G. at Shatt-et-Arab; length 1,780 m.

Eure, *dep.*, Normandy, France; agr., fruit, livestock, textiles; cap. Evreux; a. 2,331 sq. m.; p. (1968) *383,385.*

Eure-et-Loir, *dep.*, N. France; flour, textiles, iron, paper; cap. Chartres; a. 2,291 sq. m.; p. (1968) *302,207.*

Eureka, *c.*, Cal., U.S.A.; timber; p. (1960) *28,137.*

Europe, *continent*; a. 3,900,000 sq. m.; greatest length N. to S. 2,400 m. breadth E. to W. 3,300 m.; ch. mtns.: Alps, Pyrenees, Carpathians, Balkans, Apennines, Sierra Nevada, Urals, Caucasus; ch. Rs.: Volga, Danube, Rhine, Dnieper, Ural, Don; ch. lakes: Ladoga, Onega, Peipus, Vänern, Vättern; climate: Arctic border, long cold winter, short cool summer, snow; W. seaboard, cool summer, mild winter, abundant rainfall; Continental, warm summer, cold winter; Mediterranean, hot dry summers, warm wet winters; vegetation: N. tundra; Scandinavia and N. Russia, coniferous forests; European plain, woodlands; Mediterranean, drought-resisting evergreens; S. Russia, steppe; Caspian shores, desert; ch. inds.: agr., cereals, fruits, sugar-beet, potatoes, flax, hemp; pastoral, cattle-rearing, dairying, fishing; forestry; wood pulp, paper; mining, iron, coal, petroleum; hydro-elec. power; mountainous regions. Politically divided into reps., kingdoms, principalities and a grand duchy; p. (estd.) *633,000,000.* (incl. European U.S.S.R.)

Europort, name of the latest expansion of the Rotterdam docks; capable of handling 100,000-ton oil-tankers; oil refining.

Euros, *prefecture*, Thrace, Greece; cap. Alexandroupolis; p. (1961) *157,901.*

Euskirchen, *t.*, N. Rhine–Westphalia, Germany; W. of Bonn; cloth, glass, wood, paper wks.; p. (1963) *21,000.*

Evanston, *t.*, Ill., U.S.A.; on L. Michigan; sub. of Chicago, seat of N.W. Univ.; p. (1960) *79,283.*

Evanston, *t.*, Wyo., U.S.A.; coal, oil, iron; dairying, agr.; p. (1960) *4,901.*

Evans Strait, divides Southampton Land from Coats I., Hudson Bay, Canada.

Evansville, *mftg. c.*, Ind., U.S.A.; on Ohio R.; hardwood tr., coal, farm implements; p. (1960) *141,543.*

Everest, Mt. (Chomolungma = Goddess Mother of the Earth), Himalaya, on frontier of Nepal and Tibet; alt. 29,028 ft.; highest mtn. in the world; Hillary and Tenzing first to reach summit in 1953.

Everett, *mftg. t.*, Mass., U.S.A., nr. Boston; iron and steel; p. (1960) *43,544.*

Everett, *t.*, Wash., U.S.A.; timber, salmon, fruit; p. (1960) *40,304.*

Everglades, Fla., U.S.A.; extensive marshes.

Evesham, *mkt. t.*, *mun. bor.*, Worcester, Eng.; on R. Avon, in Vale of Evesham, 15 m. S.E. of Worcester; fruit ctr.; p. (estd. 1967) *13,140.*

Evora, *cap.*, Evora prov., Portugal; iron, cork; famous for its mules; p. (1960) *24,144.*

Evreux, *t.*, *cap.*, Eure, France; iron, glass, textiles; p. (1962) *40,158.*

Evvoia (Euboea), *Greek I.*, Aegean Sea; 115 m. long; wheat, olive oil, wine; cap. Khalkis; p. (1951) *163,720.*

Ewing, *t.*, N.J., U.S.A.; p. (1960) *26,628.*

Exe, *R.*, Somerset and Devon, rises on Exmoor, flows S. to English Channel at Exmouth; length 44 m.

Exeter, *c.*, co. bor., co. t., mkt. t., Devon, Eng.; E. of Dartmoor on R. Exe 8 m. from the sea; univ.; cath.; aircraft components, leather goods; p. (estd. 1967) *92,550.* [(1950) *5,130.*

Exeter, *bor.*, Penns., U.S.A.; coal, timber; p.

Exmoor, *moorland tract*, Somerset, Devon, Eng.; highest point, Dunkery Beacon, 1,707 ft.

Exmouth, *t.*, *urb. dist.*, Devon, Eng.; on E. side of estuary of R. Exe; holiday resort; p. (estd. 1967) *22,420.* [p. *3,000.*

Exmouth, *t.*, W. Australia; new t. opened 1967;

Exploits, *R.*, Newfoundland, Canada; length 150 m.

Extremadura, *old prov.*, S.W. Spain; largely plateau, alt. 1,500–3,000 ft.; heathy moorland; sheep; less arid conditions than in remainder of central Spain allow olives, vines, cereals; irrigation in valleys of Tagus, Guadiana; gov. project to develop a. in progress.

Exuma, *gr. sm. Is.*, Bahamas, W.I.; p. (1953) *2,919.*

Eye, *mkt. t.*, *mun. bor.*, Suffolk, Eng.; 18 m. N. of Ipswich; anc. church; p. (estd. 1967) *1,640.*

Eyemouth, *burgh*, Berwick, Scot.; on E. cst., 9 m. N. of Berwick; fishing; p. (1961) *2,160.*

Eyre, *L.* (salt), N. part of S. Australia; a. 4,000 sq. m., 38 ft. below sea-level; practically dried up.

Eyre Peninsula, S. Australia; between G. of St. Vincent and Spencer G.

Eyzies, Les, *commune*, Dordogne dep., France; caves, arch. interests, Paleolithic paintings, Cromagnon type site.

F

Faaborg, *spt.*, Fyn I., Denmark; p. (1960) *5,135.*

Fabriano, *mftg. i.*, Marches, Italy; 30 m. S.W. of Ancona; fine cath.; paper; p. *26,625.*

Fabrizia, *t.*, nr. Monteleone, Italy; p. *4,150.*

Facone, *sacred I.*, Honshu, Japan; 57 m. from Tokyo.

Faenza, *t.*, Ravenna, Italy; at foot of Apennines 15 m. S.W. of Ravenna; pottery (faience), silk; p. (1961) *51,085.*

Fagersta, *t.*, Vastmanland, Sweden; iron, steel smelting; p. (1961) *15,527.*

Failsworth, *t.*, *urb. dist.*, Lancs, Eng.; N.E. of Manchester; textiles, elec. goods; p. (estd. 1967) *22,520.*

Fair I., midway between Shetland and Orkney, Scot.; bird sanctuary; famous for brightly patterned, hand-knitted articles.

Fairbanks, *t.*, Alaska, U.S.A.; p. (1960) *13,311.*

Fairfield, *t.*, Ala., U.S.A.; p. (1960) *15,816.*

Fairhaven, *t.*, Mass., U.S.A.; p. (1960) *14,233.*

Fairhead, *C.*, N.W. Antrim, N. Ireland.

Fair Lawn, *t.*, N.J., U.S.A.; p. (1960) *26,628.*

Fairmont, *t.*, W. Va., U.S.A.; p. (1960) *27,477.*

Fairweather, *mtn.*, Alaska, N. America; alt. 14,872 ft.

Faiyum, *see* El Faiyum.

Faizabad, *ch. t.*, Badakhshan, N.E. Afghanistan.

Fakenham, *t.*, Norfolk, Eng.; on R. Wensum.

Fal, *R.*, Cornwall, Eng.; flows to the English Channel; length 23 m.

Falaise, *t.*, Calvados, France; birthplace of William the Conqueror; scene of rout of a German Army, 1944; p. (1962) *6,711.*

Falaise de l'Ile de France, *low S.E.-facing escarpment*, 50 m. S.E. and E. of Paris, France; overlooks " pays " of Champagne Pouilleuse; ch. vine-growing dist. for champagne-wine ind. of Rheims, Epernay.

Falcón, *st.*, Venezuela; bordering Caribbean Sea; cap. Coro; p. (1961) *340,450.*

Falkirk, *burgh*, Stirling, Scot.; 10 m. S.E. of Stirling; foundries, bricks, chemical, aluminium wks., concrete, timber yards; battles 1298 and 1746; p. (1961) *38,043.*

Falkland, *burgh*, Fife, Scot.; 3 m. S. of Auchtermuchty; mkt.; p. (1961) *1,032.*

Falkland Is., *Brit. Crown col.*, S. Atlantic, comprises E. and W. Falkland and adjacent Is.; sheep rearing (for wool); cap. Port Stanley on E. Falkland I.; a. 4,700 sq. m.; p. (estd.) *2,098.*

Falkland Is. Dependencies, comprise S. Georgia (ctr. of whaling ind.) and S. Sandwich Is. (S. Shetland, S. Orkney Is., and Graham's Land were constituted a separate col. in 1962 and now form British Antarctic Territory (*q.v.*)).

Fall River *industl. c.*, Mass., U.S.A.; cottons, dyeing, brewing, iron; p. (1960) *99,942.*

Falmouth, *spt., mun. bor.*, Cornwall, Eng.; on W. side of estuary of R. Fal, 10 m. S. of Truro; fine sheltered harbourage; seaside resort; fisheries, ship repairing, mng., quarrying, lt. engin.; p. (estd. 1967) *17,350.* [peninsula.

False Bay, *inlet* on E. side of C. of Good Hope

Falster, *I.* in the Baltic, Denmark; cap. Nyköbing; p. (1960) *46,662.* [*13,305.*

Falticeni, *t.*, N.E. Romania; timber; p. (1956)

Falun, *t.*, Kopparberg, Sweden; iron, paper, pyrites, zinc and lead ore; p. (1961) *18,313.*

Famagusta, *t., spt.*, Cyprus; on E. cst., 2½ m. S. of ruins of ancient Salamis; p. (1960) *34,774.*

Famatina, *t.*, La Rioja prov., Argentina; in foothills of Andes, 360 m. N.W. of Cordoba; copper-mines.

Fannich, *loch*, Ross, Scot.; (6½ m. long), drains to Cromarty F.

Fanning, *Brit. I.*, Gilbert and Ellice Is. col.; N. Pac. Oc.; a. 15 sq. m.; guano, mother-of-pearl; p. 196.

Fano, *t.*, Italy; on Adriatic cst., N. of Ancona; resort; p. (1961) *41,033.*

Fanö, *I.*, Denmark; off W. cst. of Jutland, opposite Esbjerg; a. 20 sq. m.; p. (1960) *2,675.*

Farafra, *oasis*, Libyan Desert, U.A.R.; 200 m. W. of Asyut; dates; stage on caravan route from Cyrenaica to Upper U.A.R.

Farciennes, *commune*, S.W. Belgium; coal, mftg.; p. (1962) *11,359.*

Fareham, *t., urb. dist.*, Hants., Eng.; at N.W. corner of Portsmouth Harbour; sm. boats, ceramics; p. (estd. 1967) *75,330.*

Farewell, *C.*, southernmost tip of Greenland.

Farewell, *C.*, most northerly point S.I., N.Z.

Fargo, *c.*, N.D., U.S.A.; on Red R.; grain, farm-machin.; p. (1960) *46,662.*

Faribalut, *t.*, Minn., U.S.A.; flour, factories; p. (1960) *16,928.*

Faridpur, *t.*, E. Bengal, Pakistan; cloth, carpets; p. (1961) *28,300.*

Faringdon, *mkt. t.*, Berks, Eng.; on N. edge of Vale of White Horse; p. *11,450.*

Farmington, *t.*, N.M., U.S.A.; p. (1960) *23,786.*

Farmington, *t.*, N. Conn., U.S.A.; residtl. and industl.; p. (1960) *10,798.*

Farnborough, *t., urb. dist.*, Hants, Eng.; 3 m. N. of Aldershot military camp; Royal Aircraft Establishment; p. (estd. 1967) *40,020.*

Farne Is., off Northumberland cst., Eng.; a. 80 acres; since 1923 bird sanctuaries.

Farnham, *mkt. t., urb. dist.*, Surrey, Eng.; at N. Foot of N. Downs, 10 m. W. of Guildford; pottery, engin., coach mkg.; p. (estd. 1967) *29,840.*

Farnworth, *mftg. t., mun. bor.*, Lancs, Eng., nr. Bolton, cotton mnfs.; p. (estd. 1967) *26,700.*

Faro, *prov.*, Portugal, cap. Faro; fruit, fishing, wines, salt; a. 2,028 sq. m.; p. (1963) *314,900.*

Faro, *spt. cap.*, Faro prov., Portugal; wine, fruit, cork; p. (1963) *18,909.*

Faro, *C.*, N. point of Sicily, nearest to Italy.

Faroe Is., 200 m. N.W. of the Shetlands, Scot.; cap. Thórshavn (Strömó I.); Danish possession; fishing, agr.; a. 540 sq. m.; p. (1968) *38,000.*

Farrell, *t.*, Penns., U.S.A.; p. (1960) *13,793.*

Farrukhabad, *t.*, Uttar Pradesh, India; on Ganges R.; gold, lace, brass wk.; p. (1961) *94,591.*

Fars, *prov.*, S. Iran; agr.; cap. Shiraz; p. (1967) *1,499,472.*

Fasa, *t.*, Fars Prov., Iran; silk, wool; p. 10,000.

Fasano, *t.*, Bari, Italy; industl.; p. over *20,000.*

Fastnet, *lighthouse* in Atlantic, 4½ m. S.W. C. Clear, Irish cst.

Fatehpur, *t.*, Uttar Pradesh, India; hides, grain; p. (1961) *28,323.* [pilgrimage ctr.

Fatima, *hamlet*, W. Portugal, near Leiria; R.C.

Fatshan (Foshan), *c.*, Kwangtung, China; S.W. of Canton; iron and steel, textiles; p. (1953) *123,000.*

Faucilles, Les Monts, *range of hills*, connecting Vosges and Langres plateau, E. France; highest point about 1,600 ft.

Favara, *t.*, Sicily, Italy; sulphur, marble.

Faversham, *old mkt. t., mun. bor.*, Kent, Eng.; 10 m. W. Canterbury; fruit, hops, bricks, brushes, engin.; p. (estd. 1967) *14,260.*

Fawley, *t.*, Hants, Eng.; on W. shore Southampton Water; lge oil refinery; p. (1951) *6,515.*

Fayal I., Azores; orange growing; cap. Horta.

Fayetteville, *t.*, Ark., U.S.A.; univ.; rly. and tr. ctr., agr. implements, resort; p. (1960) *20,274.*

Fayetteville, *t.*, N.C., U.S.A.; p. (1960) *47,106.*

Fear, *C.*, point of the N. Carolina cst. U.S.A.

Feather, *R.*, Cal., U.S.A.; trib. of Sacramento R.

Featherstone, *t., urb. dist.*, W.R. Yorks, Eng.; coal; p. (1961) *14,633.*

Fécamp, *sm. spt., wat. pl.*, Seine-Maritime, France; 12th cent. abbey; fishing; p. (1962) *19,851.*

Fedchenko, *glacier*, lgst in U.S.S.R.; in Pamir-Altai mtns of central Asia; 50 m.l.

Federal Dist., *st.*, Mexico; a. 431 sq. m.; p. (1960) *4,871,000.*

Fehmarn, *I.*, off Schleswig-Holstein, W. Germany; a. 72 sq. m.; p. *12,000.*

Feira de Santana, *t.*, Bahia, Brazil; cattle, tobacco, beans, manioc; p. (estd. 1968) *133,396.*

Feldberg, *mtn. peak*, Black Forest, Germany; alt. 4,900 ft.

Feidkirch, *t.*, Vorarlberg, Austria; on Swiss frontier; p. (1961) *17,343.*

Felixstowe, *pt., urb. dist.*, E. Suffolk, Eng.; 12 m. S.E. Ipswich; seaside resort, fertilisers; dock development; container facilities; p. (1961) *17,254.*

Felling, *urb. dist.*, Durham, Eng.; Tyneside mftg. and colly. dist.; p. (estd. 1967) *38,870.*

Feltham, *see* Hounslow. [*19,000.*

Feltre, *t.*, Venetia, Italy; cath.; silk, wine; p.

Fenny Stratford, *mkt. t.*, Bucks, Eng.; 2 m. E. of Bletchley; straw-plaiting; p. *4,300.*

Fens, The, *low-lying dist.* round Wash; protected by high embankments against flooding by spring tides; includes parts of 6 English cos.

Fenton, *t.*, Staffs, Eng.; nr. Stoke-on-Trent; earthenware wks.

Feodosiya, *spt.*, Crimea, U.S.S.R.; harbour; tobacco, hosiery; p. (1956) *42,600.*

Ferbane, *vil.*, Co. Offaly, Ireland; milled peat elec. generating sta. [cath.; p. *14,625.*

Ferentino, *t.*, prov. Rome, Italy; wine, olive oil;

Ferghana, *region*, Uzbek S.S.R., U.S.S.R.; deep basin at W. end of Tien Shan Mtns.; drained W. by R. Syr Darya; semi-arid but extensive irrigation system allows intensive cultivation of cotton, citrus fruits, silk, rice; ch. ts., Kokand, Namangan.

Ferghana, *t.*, Uzbekistan S.S.R.; hydro-elec., petroleum refining, textiles; deposits of ozo-cerite located nearby; p. (1959) *80,000.*

Fergus Falls, *t.*, Minn., U.S.A.; flour, dairy produce; p. (1960) *13,733.*

Fermanagh, *inland co.*, N. Ireland; bisected by R. Erne and lakes; cap. Enniskillen; stock-raising, dairying, stone; a. 714 sq. m.; p. (1966) *49,876.*

Fermo, *c.*, Ascoli, Italy; p. *25,000.*

Fermoy, *t.*, Cork, Ireland; on R. Blackwater; p. (1966) *3,207.*

Fernando de Noronha, *I., terr.*, N.E. cst. Brazil; penal settlement and met. sta.; cap. Vila dos Remédios; p. (estd. 1968) *2,400.*

Fernando Po, *I.*, Equatorial Guinea, W. Africa; in Bight of Biafra; mtnous; coffee, cocoa, bananas, timber; p. (1968) *61,000* inc. *4,900* Europeans.

Ferndale, *t.,* Mich., U.S.A.; p. (1960) *31,347.*

Fernie, *t.,* Brit. Columbia, Canada; in Rockies, nr. Crows Nest Pass; coal.

Ferozepore, *t.,* Punjab, India; wheat; p. (1961) *97,932.*

Ferrara, *prov.,* N. Italy; cap. Ferrara; a. 1,019 sq. m.; p. (1961) *398,663.*

Ferrara, *fortfd. c.,* N. Italy; nr. head of delta of R. Po; cath., univ.; mnfs. silk, hemp, wine; mkt. for fertile plain; oil refinery nearby; petrochemicals; p. (1961) *151,145.*

Ferro, *most S.W. I.,* Canary Is.; a. 106 sq. m.; was chosen by Fr. scientists (1630) as first meridian; cap. Valverde.

Ferrol, *spt., naval arsenal,* Spain; on N.W. cst. nr. Corunna; p. (1950) *77,030.*

Ferryhill, *vil.,* Durham, Eng.; 5 m. S. of Durham, in gap through limestone ridge which separates Wear valley from Tees valley; commands main N. to S. route along lowland E. of Pennines.

Fertile Crescent, an arc of fertile land from the Mediterranean Sea, N. of the Arabian Desert, to Persian Gulf; home of some very early civilisations and migrations.

Festiniog, *see* Ffestiniog.

Fethiye, *spt.,* Turkey; opp. Rhodes; p. (1960) *7,652.*

Fetlar I., Shetland Is., Scot.; 6½ m. long by 2¾ m. wide.

Feuerbach, *industl. c.,* Baden–Württemberg, Germany; N.W. sub. of Stuttgart; sandstone; p. (1963) *27,000.*

Fez, *c.,* Morocco, N. Africa; lies inland 100 m. E. of Rabat; one of the sacred cities of Islam; univ. attached to mosque (one of lgst. in Africa); impt. comm. ctr.; p. (1960) *216,133.*

Fezzan, *prov.,* Libya, N. Africa; numerous wells and inhabited oases.

Ffestiniog (Festiniog), *urb. dist.,* Merioneth, N. Wales; at head of Vale of Ffestiniog 9 m. E. of Portmadoc; contains vils. of Ffestiniog and Blaenau Ffestiniog; impt. slate quarries; world's lgst pumped-storage hydroelec. sta. (1963); cement; p. (1961) *6,677.*

Fianarantsoa, *t.,* Malagasy; p. (1957) *34,845.*

Fichtelgebirge (Fir Mtns.), *mtn. range,* N.E. Bavaria, Germany; highest peak, Schneeberg; alt. 3,454 ft.

Fife, *peninsula, co.,* E. Scot.; between the F. of Tay and Forth; *co. t.* Cupar; a. 492 sq. m.; p. (1961) *320,541.*

Fife Ness, extreme E. point, Fife, Scot.

Figuéira da Foz, *t.,* Portugal; resort at mouth of R. Mondego; corn, wine; p. (1960) *10,855.*

Figuéras, *fortfd. t.,* Gerona, Spain; nr. French frontier; glass, cork, leather; p. (1957) *16,589.*

Fiji, *indep. st.* within Commonwealth (1970); group of 322 coral Is. (106 inhabited) in S. Pac.; forests, bananas, coconuts, sugar-cane; cap. Suva on Viti Levu I.; a. 7,095 sq. m.; p. (estd.) *505,000.*

Filey, *t., urb. dist.,* E.R. Yorks, Eng.; on E. cst. 5 m. S.E. of Scarborough; seaside resort; p. (1961) *4,705.*

Filton, Bristol, Glos., Eng.; aircraft wks.

Finchley, *former mun. bor.,* Middx., Eng., now inc. in Barnet outer bor., Greater London, (*q.v.*); residtl.; p. (1961) *69,370.*

Findhorn, *fishing vil.,* Moray, Scot.; resort.

Findlay, *mftg. t.,* Ohio, U.S.A.; on Blanchard R.; p. (1960) *30,344.*

Findochty, *sm. burgh.,* Banff, Scot.; p. (1961) *1,331.*

Findon or Finnan, *fishing vil.,* Kincardine, Scot.

Fingal's Cave, Staffa I., Inner Hebrides, W. Scot.; basaltic columns.

Finistère, *dep.,* N.W. France; cap. Quimper; cereals fruit, livestock; coal, granite; fishing; a. 2,730 sq. m.; p. (1968) *768,929.*

Finisterre, *C.,* extreme N.W. point of Spain.

Finland, *rep.,* Europe, low-lying tableland, glaciated, innumerable lakes; forested; oats, rye, barley, potatoes; timber, wood-pulp, textiles; iron mining; official languages, Finnish and Swedish (Swedish names mainly as alternatives on W. cst.); mainly agr.; cap. Helsinki; a. 117,975 sq. m.; p. (1966) *4,626,956.*

Finland, G. of, E. arm of Baltic Sea, 250 m.

Finnart, Dunbartonshire, Scot.; oil terminal situated in Loch Long, N.W. Glasgow; pipeline to Grangemouth.

Finnmark, *most northerly co.,* Norway; inhabited by Lapps; whale fisheries; lge. copper deposits discovered nr. Reppan fjord; a. 18,581 sq. m.; p. (1968) *76,367.*

Finsbury, *see* Islington.

Finsteraarhorn, *min.,* Switzerland, (14,023 ft.) highest peak in Bernese Oberland.

Finsterwalde, *t.,* Cottbus, E. Germany; textiles, furniture, metallurgy, glass; p. (1963) *21,117.*

Finucane I., *pt.,* W. Australia; deepwater pt. to ship iron ore and new t. projected.

Fir Mountains, *see* Fichtelgebirge.

Firenze, *see* Florence.

Firminy, *mfto. t.,* Loire, France; S.E. of St. Etienne; p. (1954) *21,161.*

Fishguard and Goodwick, *spt., urb. dist.,* N. Pembroke, Wales; on S. of Cardigan Bay; steamer connection to Cork and Rosslare (Ireland); p. (1961) *4,898.* [machin.; p. (1960) *43,021.*

Fitchburg, *c.,* Mass., U.S.A.; woollens, paper,

Fitzroy, *R.,* W. Australia; flows into King Sound.

Fiume, *see* Rijeka. [p. *17,550.*

Fivizzano, *t.,* Tuscany, Italy; mineral springs;

Flagstaff, *t.,* Arizona, U.S.A.; seat of Lowell Univ.; p. (1960) *18,214.*

Flamborough Head, *C.,* Yorks cst., Eng.; chalk cliffs, alt. 500 ft.; lighthouse.

Fläming, *heathland,* Potsdam, E. Germany; occupies low sandy ridge, alt. below 800 ft., 50 m. S.W. of Berlin; heathland, coniferous woodland; former military training a.

Flanders, *dist.,* Belgium. divided into two provs. of W. (1,248 sq. m., p. (1968) *1,042,586.*) and E. (1,147 sq. m., p. (1968) *1,305,717*; caps. Bruges and Ghent. [*4,515.*

Flat River, *c.,* Mo., U.S.A.; lead mines; p. (1960)

Flattery Cape, on Pacific cst., Wash., U.S.A.

Flèche, La, *t.,* Sarthe, France; nr. Le Mans; p. (1962) *14,392.*

Fleet, *t., urb. dist.,* Hants, Eng.; 4 m. N.W. of Aldershot; p. (estd. 1967) *20,650.*

Fleetwood, *spt., mun. bor.,* Lancs, Eng.; at mouth of Wyre; fishing; lge. chemical plant projected nearby; p. (estd. 1967) *28,630.*

Flémalle, 2 *communes,* Liége prov., Belgium; glass; p. (1962) *13,857.*

Flensburg, *spt.,* Schleswig-Holstein, Germany; on Baltic cst.; coal; shipbldg., machin., iron, chemicals, fishing; p. (1963) *97,000*

Flevosted, *t.,* Netherlands; administrative ctr. of new S.E. Polder. [G. of Carpentaria.

Flinders, *R.,* Queensland, Australia; flowing to

Flinders Range, *mtns.,* S. Australia; extend 250 m. N.E. from head of Spencer G.; alt. 3,900 ft.

Flin Flon, *t.,* Manitoba, Canada; 90 m. by rly. N. of The Pas; ctr. of gold-mining a.; p. (1961) *11,104.*

Flint, *c.,* Mich., U.S.A.; motor cars, lumber, woollens, aeroplane engines; p. (1960) *196,940.*

Flint, *mun. bor., co. t.,* Flintshire, Wales; viscose textile yarn, pulp; p. (1961) *13,690.*

Flint I., (Brit.), Pac. Oc.; uninhabited.

Flintshire, *co.,* Wales; stock-raising; coal, iron, steel, textiles, chemicals; a. 257 sq. m.; p. (1966) *161,000.*

Flodden, *vil.,* Northumberland, Eng.; on R. Till; famous battle 1513, James IV of Scotland defeated by the Earl of Surrey.

Flora, *c.,* Sogn og Fjordane, Norway; new c. 85 m. N. of Bergen; p. (1965) *7,700.*

Florange, *t.,* Moselle, France; p. (1962) *14,270.*

Florence (Firenze), *c.,* Tuscany, Italy; on R. Arno; leather-work; famous for art treasures, cath. and churches; ruled by Medici 1421–1737; birthplace of Dante and Michelangelo; severely affected by heavy floods Nov. 1966; p. (1965) *454,000.*

Florence, *c.,* N.W. Ala., U.S.A.; iron, textiles, lumber, food; airport; p. (1960) *31,649.*

Florence, *t.,* S.C., U.S.A.; p. (1960) *24,722.*

Flores, *I..* most north-westerly of the Azores gr.; Portuguese; cap. Santa Cruz; French to set up ballistic missiles tracking sta.

Flores, *I.,* Indonesia; W. of Timor, one of Lesser Sunda Is.; mtnous., densely forested; a. *c.* 6,627 sq. m.; p. (incl. offshore Is.) *194,000.*

Flores, *dep.,* Uruguay; cap. Trinidad; a. 1,744 sq. m.; p. (1953) *35,565.* [nesia.

Flores Sea, between Sulawesi and Flores, Indo-

Florianópolis, *spt.,* cap. Santa Catarina st., Brazil; comm. ctr., fishing; p. (estd. 1968) *130,012.*

Florida, *st.,* U.S.A.; between Atlantic and G. of Mexico; resort a.; tourism; lumber, paper, minerals; fruit, vegetables, sugar, cotton; cattle raising; cap. Tallahassee; a. 58,560 sq. m.; p. (1970) *6,671,162.*

Florida, *dep.,* Uruguay; cap. Florida; a. 4,673 sq. m.; p. (1953) *106,284.*

ATLAS OF THE WORLD

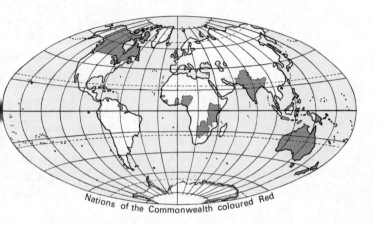

Nations of the Commonwealth coloured Red

CONTENTS

©

PRINTED BY JOHN BARTHOLOMEW AND SON, LTD.,
AT THE GEOGRAPHICAL INSTITUTE, EDINBURGH

4388

2

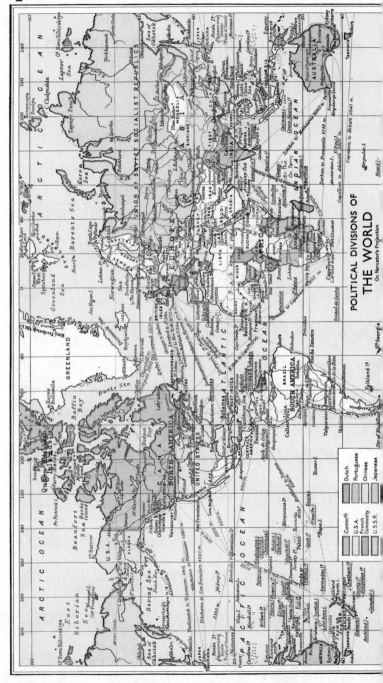

POLITICAL DIVISIONS OF
THE WORLD
On Mercator's Projection

Commlth	Dutch
U.S.A.	Portuguese
French Community	Chinese
U.S.S.R.	Japanese

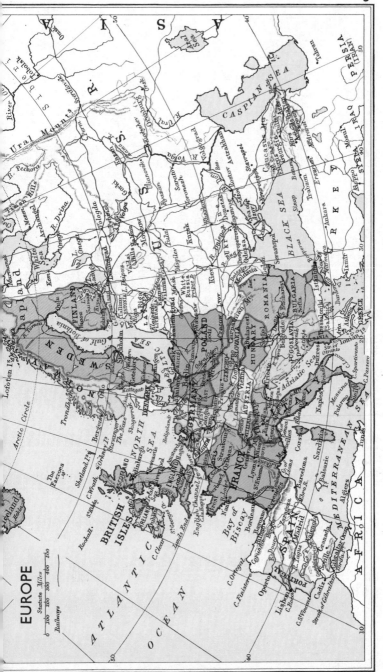

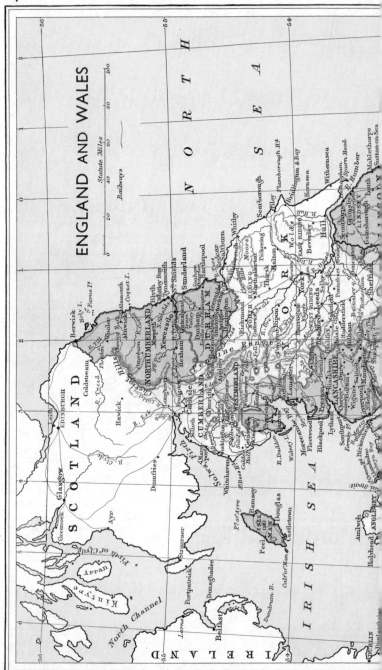

ENGLAND AND WALES

Statute Miles

Railways

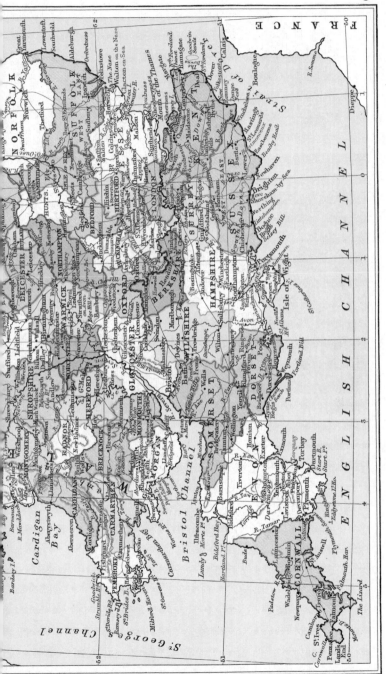

6

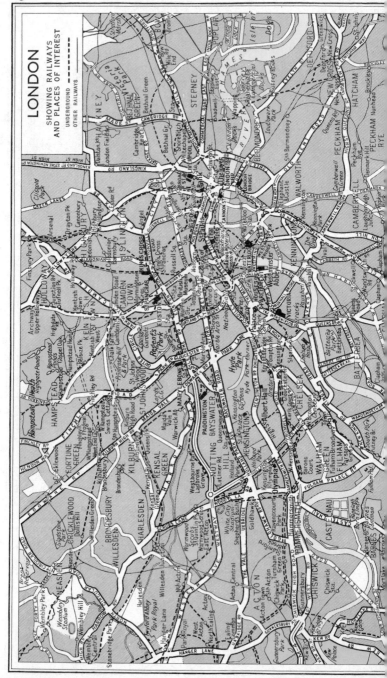

LONDON

SHOWING RAILWAYS AND PLACES OF INTEREST

UNDERGROUND ————
OTHER RAILWAYS ————

LONDON DISTRICT

Main Roads	0	5	10	15 Miles

Main Roads
Other Roads
Secondary Roads
Railways

SCOTLAND

Statute Miles

0   10   20   30   40

Railways

ZETLAND

Same Scale

Yell
Unst
Fetlar
Whalsey
Sandness
Lerwick
Bressay
Fitful Hd.
Sumburgh Hd.

Nth. Rona
Sula Sgeir

ORKNEY

Westray
Nth. Ronaldsay
Rousay
Sanday
Eday
Stronsay
Shapinsay
Skara Brae
Kirkwall
Stromness
Hoy
Sth. Ronaldsay

Pentland Firth

C.Wrath
L. Eriboll
Kyle of Tongue
Strathy Pt.
Dunnet Hd.
Scrabster
John O'Groats Ho.
Duncansby Hd.
Thurso

CAITHNESS
Wick
Noss Hd.

L. Laxford
Eddrachillis
Pt. of Stoer

SUTHERLAND

L. Naver

Morven

NORT...

SEA

L. Shin
L. More
Assynt
L. Assynt
Lairg
Brora
L. Enard
Helmsdale
Golspie

LEWIS
Stornoway
North Minch

58

Harris
Tarbert
Little Minch
Loch Broom
L. Ew
L. Gruinard
Ullapool
Dornoch Firth
Dornoch
Tarbat Ness
Ben Dearg
Tain

St. Kilda
Lochmaddy
North Uist
Benbecula
Loch Maree
L. Torridon
Cairn Gorm
Fannich
Ben Wyvis

ROSS & CROMARTY
Dingwall
Strathpeffer
Conon
Beauly
Cromarty
Forres
Nairn
Elgin
Fochabers
Banff
Portsoy
Buckie
Cullen
Macduff

MORAY

NAIRN

BANFF

ABERDEE...

South Uist
Eriskay
Barra
Barra Hd.

Skye
Portree
L. Bracadale
Cuillin Hills
Kyle of Lochalsh
Glenelg
Ben Attow
Inverness
Beauly
Loch Ness
Fort Augustus
Crowmarty
Inverurie
Aberdeen
Huntly
Keith
Pe...
R. Don
Aviemore

INVERNESS

Kingussie
Ben Macdui
L. Oich
Cairn Gorm
Ballater
Aboyne
Banchory

KINCARDINE
Inverbervie

Canna
Rum
Eigg
Muck
Ardnamurchan Pt.
Coll
Tiree
Staffa
Iona
Mull

Sound of Mull
Tobermory
Ben More

L. Arkaig
Mallaig
L. Shiel
L. Eil
Loch Lochy
L. Loyne
L. Eil
Fort William
Ben Nevis
4406
Kinlochleven
Loch Leven
Glencoe
Ballachulish
Linnhe
L. Eil
L. Ericht
L. Rannoch
Schiehallion
Ben Lawers
L. Tay

Grampian Mountains

Blair Atholl
Killiecrankie Pass
Pitlochry
Dunkeld
Aberfeldy

ANGUS
Clova
Brechin
Mont...
Forfar
Coupar Angus
Carnoustie
Arbroath
Dundee
Broughty Ferry

Skerryvore L.H.

ATLANTIC
OCEAN

56

Colonsay
Oronsay
Jura

Firth of Lorn
Oban
Kerrera
Loch Awe
Inveraray
Loch Fyne
Loch Long

ARGYLL

Ben Cruachan
Ben More
L. Earn
Ben Vorlich
Crieff
L. Tay
Ben Lawers
Ben Ledi
Callander
Doune
Dunblane
Scone
Perth

PERTH

Kinross
Loch Leven

Cupar
St. Andrews

FIFE

Islay
Bowmore
Port Ellen
Mull of Oa
Gigha

Kintyre
Campbeltown
Machrihanish
Mull of Kintyre
Sanda

Loch Lomond
Ben Lomond
R. Forth
Stirling
Alloa
Alva
Dunfermline
Kirkcaldy
Burntisland
Firth of Forth

STIRLING

Strait of Gigha
Sound of Jura
Ardrossan
Bute
Arran
Goat Fell
Brodick
Holy I.
Lamlash

Kilbrennan Sound

Dumbarton
Paisley
Renfrew
Greenock
Glasgow

RENFREW

Hamilton
Airdrie
Coatbridge
Motherwell
Wishaw

MIDLOTHIAN

Edinburgh
Leith
Dalkeith
Musselburgh
Haddington

E. LOTHIAN

Dunbar

Berwick

BERWICK
Dun...
Greenlaw
Coldstream

LANARK

Lanark
Kilmarnock
Irvine

AYR

Prestwick
Ayr
Maybole
Girvan
Turnberry
Ailsa Craig
Ballantrae

PEEBLES
Peebles

Tinto
Leadhills
Sanquhar
Moffat

SELKIRK
Galashiels
Melrose
Selkirk
Broad Law
Hawick

ROXBURGH
Kelso
Jedburgh
Cheviot Hills

DUMFRIES

L. Doon
R. Nith
L. Ken
Merrick
R. Dee
Dumfries
Lockerbie
Langholm
Annan
Carlisle

KIRKCUDBRIGHT
Newton Stewart
Castle Douglas
Kirkcudbright

WIGTOWN
Stranraer
Portpatrick
Wigtown

Luce Bay
Burrow Hd.
Wigtown Bay
Mull of Galloway

Solway Firth

ENGLAN...

IRELAND
Londonderry
Larne
Belfast

North Channel

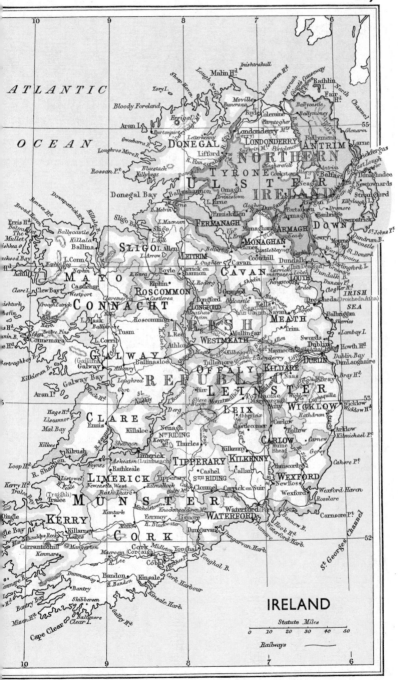

IRELAND

Statute Miles
0 10 20 30 40 50

Railways

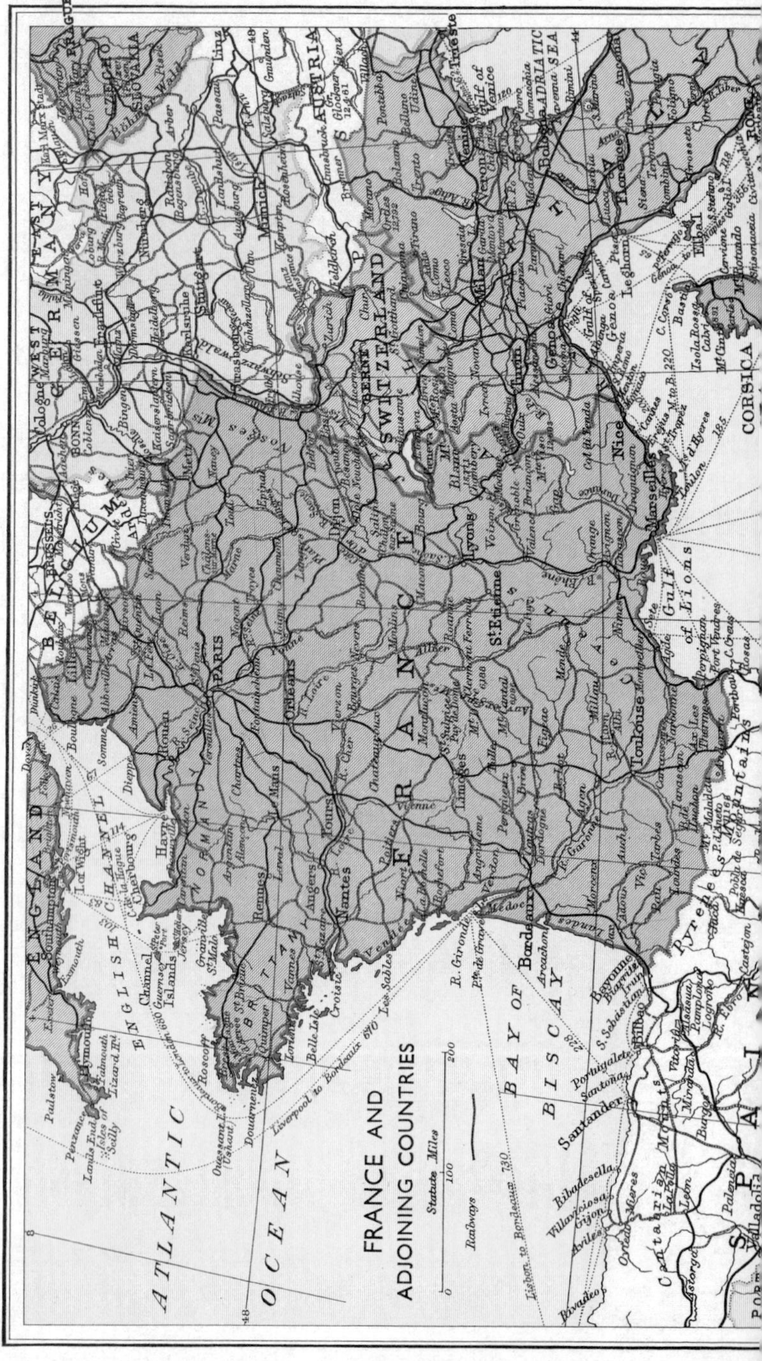
FRANCE AND
ADJOINING COUNTRIES
Statute Miles
0
100
200
Railways
ATLANTIC
OCEAN
BAY OF
BISCAY
ENGLISH
CHANNEL
GULF of LIONS
ADRIATIC SEA
FRANCE
SWITZERLAND
BELGIUM
AUSTRIA
CORSICA
PARIS
Bordeaux
Lyons
Marseilles
Toulouse
Nantes
Orleans
Nice
Turin
Milan
Genoa
BERNE
Munich
Stuttgart
Frankfurt
Trieste
PRAGUE
Florence
ROME
Santander
Bilbao
Bayonne

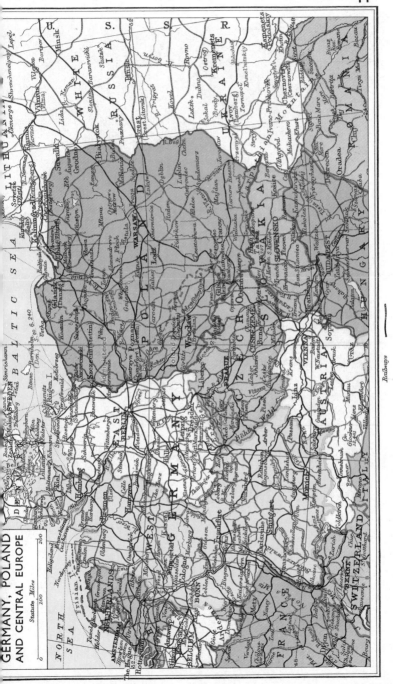

GERMANY, POLAND AND CENTRAL EUROPE

Statute Miles
0   100   200

Railways

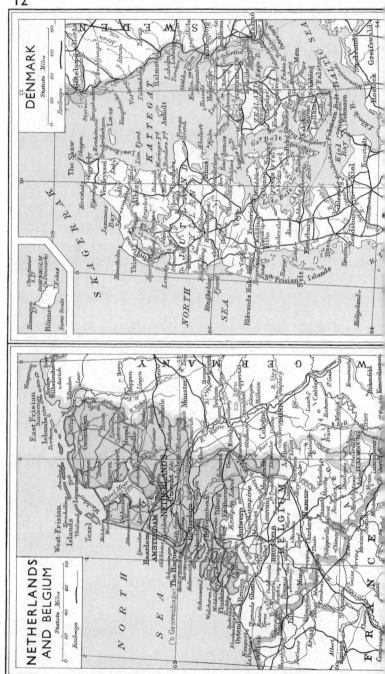

DENMARK

Statute Miles

0 20 40 60 80

Railways

BORNHOLM
(to Denmark)
Same Scale

Hammern
Römer
Neksö
Christiansö

SKAGERRAK

KATTEGAT

BALTIC SEA

NORTH SEA

JUTLAND

ZEALAND

LOLLAND

FALSTER

The Skaw

Nth. Frisian Islands

Heligoland

NETHERLANDS AND BELGIUM

Statute Miles

0 20 40 60 80

Railways

NORTH SEA

NETHERLANDS

BELGIUM

GERMANY

FRANCE

LUXEMBURG

West Frisian Islands

East Frisian Islands

Texel

AMSTERDAM
Haarlem
The Hague ('s Gravenhage)

BRUSSELS

Antwerp

Cologne

BONN

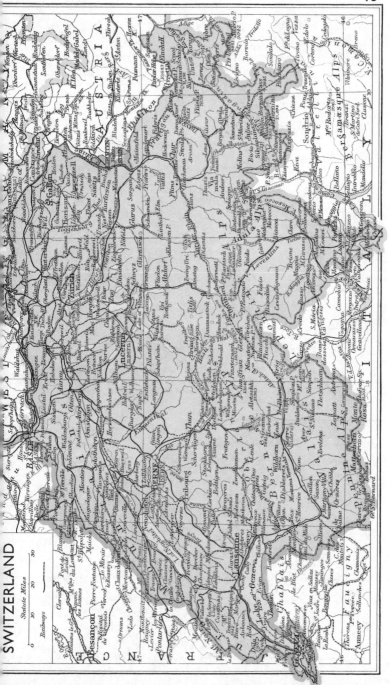

SWITZERLAND

Statute Miles

0   10   20   30

Railways

14

SCANDINAVIA AND BALTIC LANDS

West of Greenwich

On the same scale

East of Greenwich

Statute Miles
0   50   100   200   300

Railways

ICELAND

Horn (North C.)   Sudhavsfjordur   Langanes
Isafjordur   Akureyri
Breidha fd.   Bordeyri   Seydisfjordur
Faxafloi   Vatna Jökull   Djupivogur
REYKJAVIK   Öraefa J. 6290
Hafnarfjördhr   Helda
Vestmannaeyjar
Surtsey

North Cape Nordkyn
Hammerfest   Nordkyn   Vardö
                  Tana Vadsö Varanger Fd.
                  Kirkenes Pechenga Kola
Tromsö   Alta Lake Inari Polyarny Murmansk
Senja   Kola
Lofoten   Narvik   Imandra
Islands   Torne Tisk

NORWAY SWEDEN LAPLAND FINLAND
KARELIA ESTONIA LATVIA LITHUANIA
DENMARK GERMANY POLAND WHITE RUSSIA

NORTH SEA BALTIC SEA Gulf of Bothnia Gulf of Finland Gulf of Riga

Arctic Circle

Reykjavik Copenhagen Stockholm Helsinki Tallinn Riga Warsaw Berlin

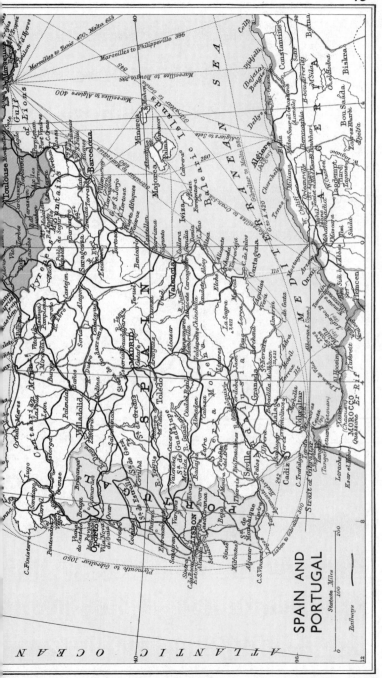

SPAIN AND
PORTUGAL

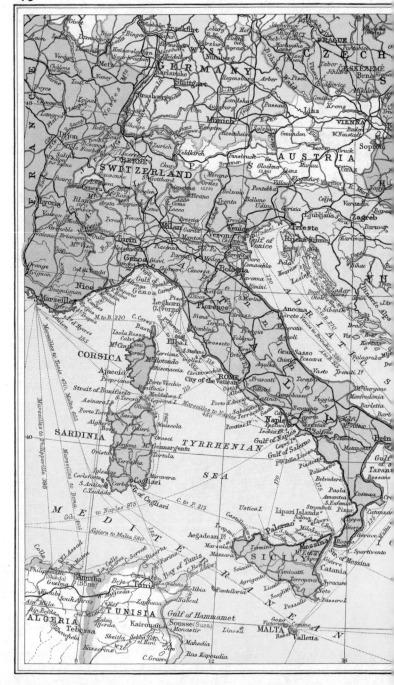

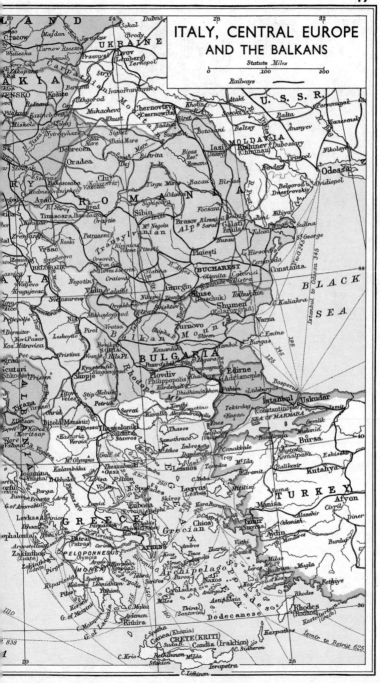

ITALY, CENTRAL EUROPE
AND THE BALKANS

Statute Miles

0   100   200

Railways

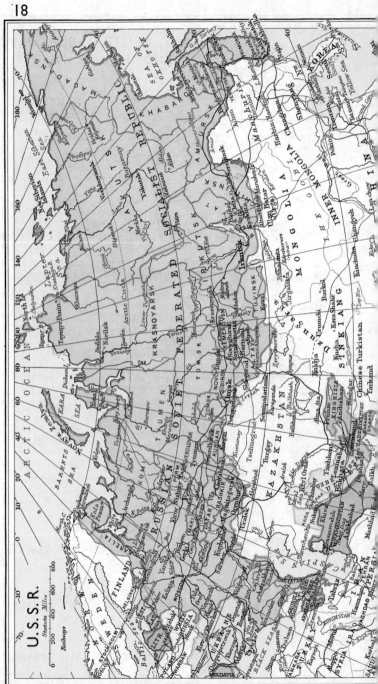

U.S.S.R.

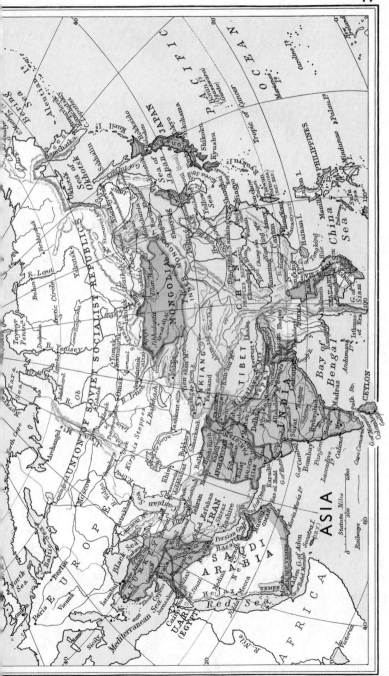

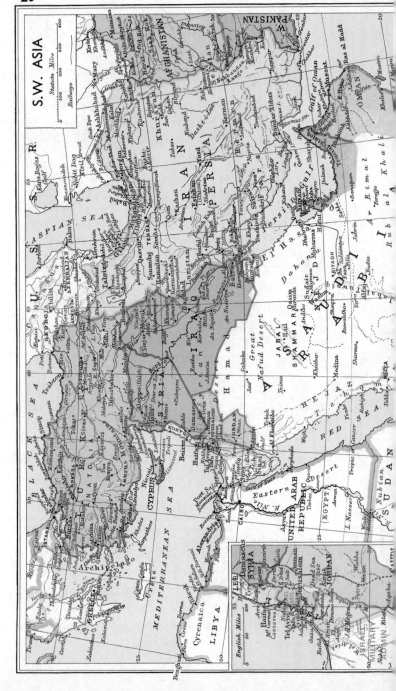

S.W. ASIA

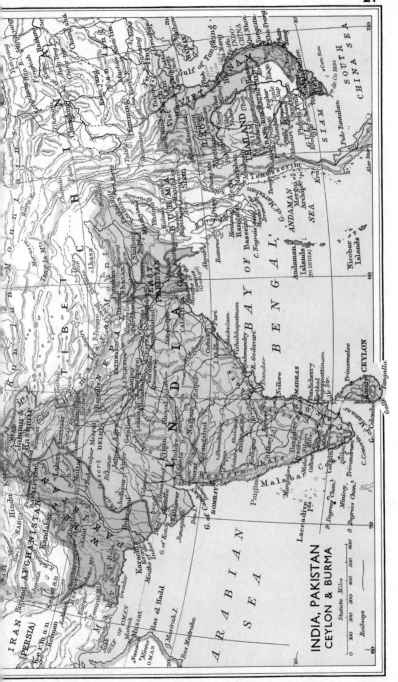

INDIA, PAKISTAN
CEYLON & BURMA

Statute Miles

0   100   200   300   400   500   600

Railways

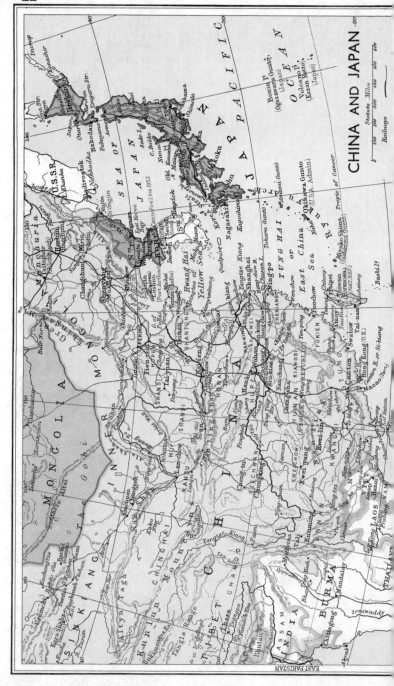

CHINA AND JAPAN

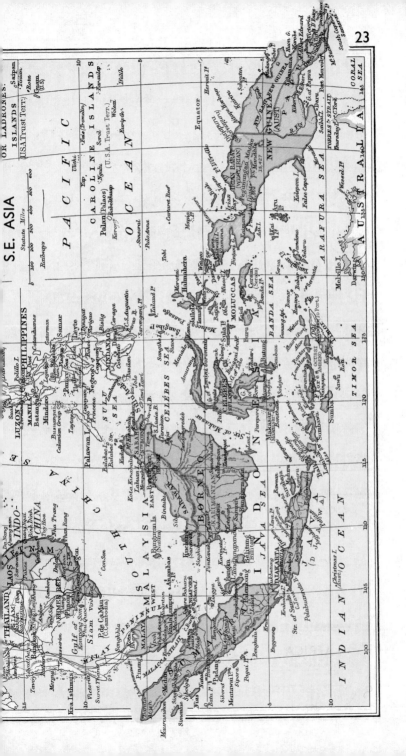

S.E. ASIA

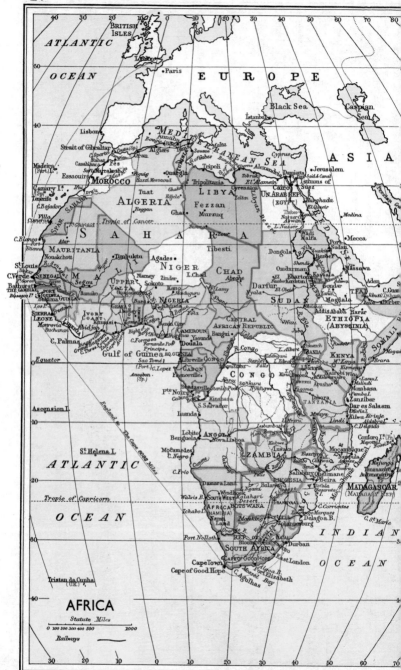

AFRICA

Statute Miles

0 100 200 300 400 500   1000

Railways

T.F.A.I.—Territoire Français des Afars et des Issas.

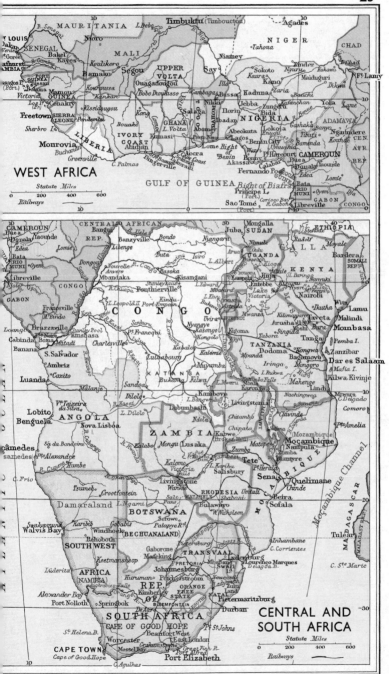

WEST AFRICA

Statute Miles

0   200   400   600

Railways

10

GULF OF GUINEA

CENTRAL AND SOUTH AFRICA

Statute Miles

0   200   400   600

Railways

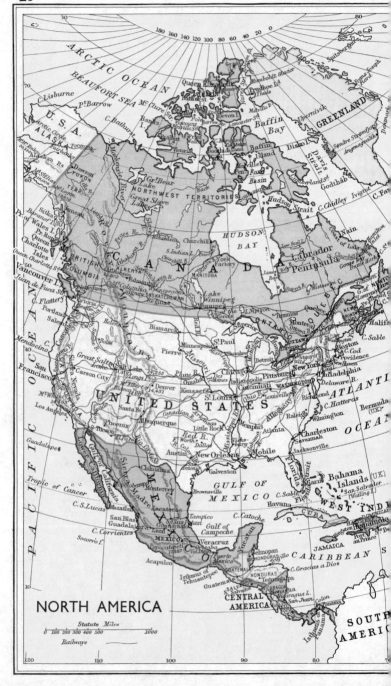

NORTH AMERICA

Statute Miles

0 100 200 300 400 500   1000

Railways

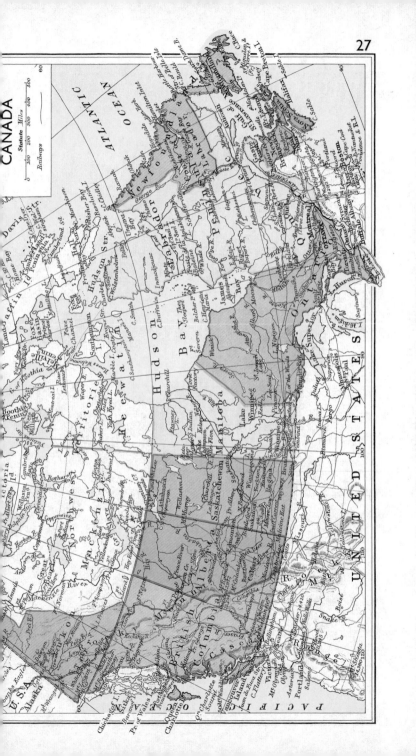

CANADA

Statute Miles
100   200   300   400   500

Railways

ATLANTIC OCEAN

Davis Str.

Baffin Id

Hudson Str.

Labrador

Newfoundland

Quebec

Hudson Bay

Keewatin

Ontario

Mackenzie

Northwest Territories

Saskatchewan

Manitoba

Alberta

British Columbia

Yukon

U.S.A.
Alaska

UNITED STATES

PACIFIC

UNITED STATES

Statute Miles

0 100 200 300 400 500

29

MEXICO,
CENTRAL AMERICA
AND WEST INDIES

Statute Miles
0   100 200 300 400 500 600
Railways ——
Rio

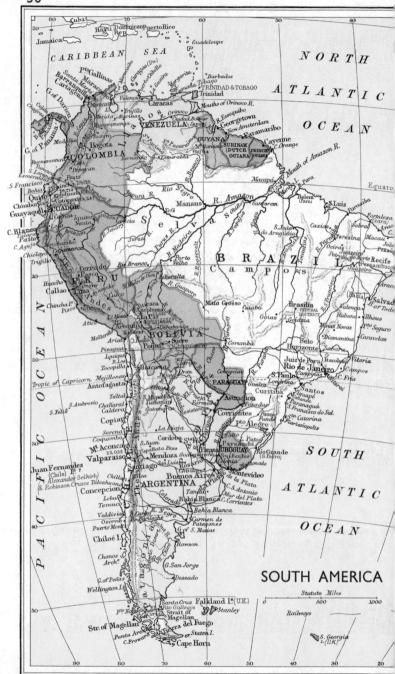

SOUTH AMERICA

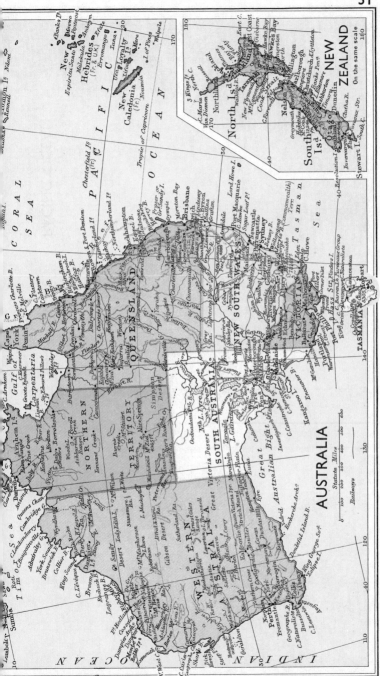

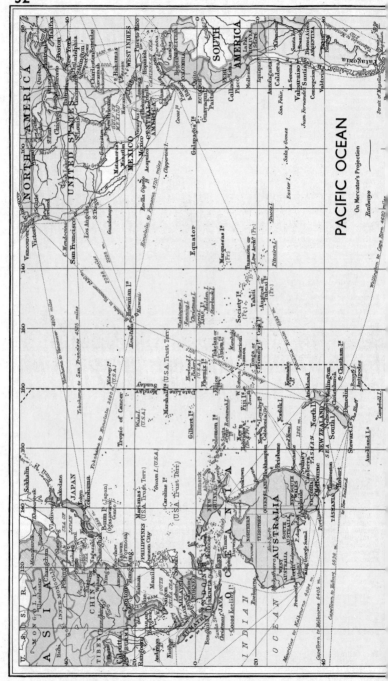

PACIFIC OCEAN

On Mercator's Projection

Railways

Floridabanca, *t.,* Luzon. Philippine Is.; sugar, rice; p. *17,521.*

Florida Strait, between Florida and Bahama Is.; course of " Gulf Stream " from Gulf of Mexico.

Florina, *see* Phlorina.

Flume, The, picturesque gorge, Franconia Mtns., N.H., U.S.A.

Flushing, *see* Vlissingen.

Flushing Meadow, *t.,* Flushing Bay, Long Island, N.Y., U.S.A.; U.N.O. meeting place.

Fly, *R.,* New Guinea; flows S.E. to G. of Papua.

Fochabers, *vil.,* Moray, Scot.; nr. mouth of Spey; tourist resort; food canning ind.

Focsani, *t.,* Putna dist., Romania; on R. Milkov; soap, petroleum (1963) *36,854.*

Foggia, *prov.,* Apulia, S. Italy; a. 2,683 sq. m.; p. (1961) *632,332.*

Foggia, *t.,* S. Italy, Apulia; cath.; industl.; p. (1961) *117,485.*

Fogo, *I.,* Atl. Oc.; in Cape Verde gr.; volcanic.

Folda Fjord, W. coast, Norway.

Foligno, *t.,* Perugia, Italy; remarkable grotto; numerous factories; p. (1961) *48,069.*

Folkestone, *packet pt., mun. bor.,* Kent, Eng.; seaside resort. pt. for Folkestone–Boulogne route to France 29 m.; p. (estd. 1967) *43,880.*

Fond du Lac, *mfg. t.,* Winnebago Lake, Wis., U.S.A.; cath.; p. (1960) *32,719.*

Fonsagrada, *industl. t.,* Lugo, Spain; p. (1957) *13,925.*

Fonseca Bay, *inlet* on Pacific cst. of C. America, bordering on Nicaragua; U.S.A. naval base; (U.S.A. have acquired the option for a canal route through Nicaragua).

Fontainebleau, *t.,* Seine-et-Marne, France; on R. Seine, 35 m. S.E. of Paris; magnificent forest (a. 42,500 acres) and palace; porcelain; Ecole d'Artillerie; p. (1962) *22,704.*

Fontenay-le-Comte, *industl. t.,* Vendée, France; p. (1962) *12,104.* [Paris; p. (1954) *36,739.*

Fontenay-sous-Bois, *t.,* Seine, France; sub. of

Fontenoy, *vil.,* Belgium; nr. Tournai; battle, 1745; Marshall Saxe defeated the Allies under Duke of Cumberland; p. (1962) *639.*

Fontevrault, *t.,* dep. Maine-et-Loire, France.

Foochow (Fuzhou), *c.,* Fukien, China; former treaty pt.; gr. tea-exporting ctr.; p. (1953) *553,000.*

Foots Cray, *sm. t.,* Kent, Eng.; paper-mills.

Forbach, *t.,* Moselle, France; p. (1962) *22,106*

Forbes, *t.,* N.S.W., Australia; mkt. ctr.; sm. mnfg.; p. (1966) *7,370.*

Fordingbridge, *mkt. t.,* Hants, Eng.; on R. Avon, sail-cloth; p. *3,394.*

Fordlandia, *t.,* Pará, N.E. Brazil; on Tapajoz R.; one of the Ford rubber plantations.

Foreland, N. and S., two headlands, on E. cst. of Kent, Eng.; lighthouse.

Forest Hill, *t.,* Ontario, Canada; p. (1961) *20,489.*

Forest Hills, *residtl. a.,* part of Queen's bor., N.Y., U.S.A.; on Long I.; p. *21,400.*

Forest Park, *t.,* Georgia, U.S.A.; p. (1961) *14,201.*

Forfar, *burgh,* Angus, Scot.; in Strathmore, 17 m. S.W. of Montrose; linen, jute; p. (1961) *10,252.*

Forli, *ancient c.,* Emilia Italy; silk factories, ironwks.; felt; p. (1961) *91,146.*

Formby, *t. urb. dist.,* Lancs, Eng.; on W. cst., 6 m. S.W. of Southport; p. (1961) *11,730.*

Formentera, *I.,* Balearic Is., S. of Ibiza; 13 m. long; cereals, wine, tunny fishing; p. (1957) *2,657.*

Formia, *t.,* Caserta, Italy; the ancient Formiæ.

Formigine, *t.,* Modena prov., N. Italy; silk, leather; p. *10,985.*

Formosa, *see* Taiwan.

Formosa, *prov.,* N. Argentina; bordering on Paraguay; timber; cap. Formosa; a. 27,825 sq. m.; p. (1960) *178,000.*

Fornaes, *c.,* extreme E. point of Jutland.

Forres, *burgh,* Moray, Scot.; nr. mouth of R. Findhorn, 25 m. E. of Inverness; distilling, oat and woollen mills; p. (1961) *4,780.*

Forst, *t.,* Cottbus, E. Germany; on R. Neisse; E. section of t. Polish since 1945; textiles; p. (1963) *28,931.*

Fort Augustus, *vil.,* Inverness, Scot.; at S.W. end of Loch Ness; on Caledonian Canal; Fort now Abbey.

Fort Collins, *c.,* Col., U.S.A.; ctr. of rich farming a.; grain, sugarbeet, livestock; site of Colorado State Univ.; p. (1960) *25,027.*

Fort de France (formerly Fort Royal), *cap.,* Martinique, W. Indies; has a land-locked harbour of some 16 sq. m.; exp. rum, sugar; p. (estd. 1960) *60,648.*

Fort Dodge, *t.,* Iowa, U.S.A.; on Des Moines R., in rich agr. cty.; grain, pottery, coal; p. (1960) *28,399.*

Fort Frances, *t.,* Ontario, Canada; pulp, lumbering; p. (1961) *9,481.*

Fort George, *R.,* Labrador, Canada; flowing into James Bay.

Fort Johnson, *t.,* S. Malawi, on L. Malombe; new t., 1966; tobacco; airpt.

Fort Lamy, *t., cap.,* Chad, Africa; p. (1965) *92,000.*

Fort Landerdale, *t.,* Fla., U.S.A.; prefab. bldg. mftg., concrete prod., fertilisers; p. (1960) *83,648.*

Fort Madison, *c.,* Iowa, U.S.A.; meat packing; p. (1960) *15,247.*

Fort Myers, *t.,* Fla., U.S.A.; p. (1960) *22,523.*

Fort Pierce, *t.,* Fla., U.S.A.; p. (1960) *25,256.*

Fort St. John, *t.,* B.C., Canada; on Peace R.; oilfield; p. (1961) *3,619*

Fort Scott, *t.,* Kan., U.S.A.; maize, wheat, cattle; p. (1960) *9,410.*

Fort Smith, *c.,* Ark., U.S.A.; on Arkansas R.; rly. ctr., cotton, maize, wagons, furniture; p. (1960) *52,991.*

Fort Victoria, *t.,* Rhodesia; agr. and mining ctr., cattle; historic ruins in Zimbabwe Nat. Park; p. (1958) *10,700* (incl. *1,700* Europeans).

Fort Wayne, *c.,* Ind., U.S.A.; rly.-carriage bldg. and machine shops; p. (1960) *161,776.*

Fort William, *c.,* Ontario, Canada; on L. Superior; grain pt.; p. (1961) *45,214.*

Fort William, *burgh,* Inverness, Scot.; nr. head of Loch Linnhe, at base of Ben Nevis; aluminium factory; pulp- and paper-mill at Corpach; p. (1961) *2,715.*

Fort Worth, *c.,* Texas, U.S.A.; rly. and comm. ctr. on Trinity R.; livestock and grain mkt.; petroleum, meat packing, aeroplanes, oilfield equipment; site of Texas Christian Univ.; p. (1960) *356,268.*

Fort Yukon, Alaska, U.S.A.; trading sta. on Yukon R.; p. *274.*

Fortaleza, *cap.,* Ceará st., Brazil; exp. sugar, cotton, hides, carnauba wax; p. (estd. 1968) *846,069.*

Fortescue, *R.,* W. Australia.

Forth, *R.,* Scot.; rises on Ben Lomond, and flows E. into F. of Forth nr. Alloa; length 65 m.

Forth Bridge, *rly. bridge,* Scot.; spans F. of Forth between N. and S. Queensferry; length 1½ m. Forth road bridge (suspension) just upstream opened 1964; length 5,980 ft.

Forth, Firth of, *lge. inlet,* E. cst. of Scot.; submerged estuary of R. Forth; navigable by lge. vessels for 40 m. inland to Grangemouth; other pts., Leith, Rosyth (naval), Bo'ness; length (to Alloa) 50 m., width varies from 1 to 13 m.

Forth and Clyde Canal, Scot.; links F. of Forth at Grangemouth, and F. of Clyde at Glasgow; length 38 m.

Fortrose, *t., burgh,* Ross and Cromarty, Scot.; on S. cst. of Black Isle, on Moray Firth; p. (1961) *902.*

Fortune Bay, *inlet,* S. cst. of Newfoundland, Canada.

Fossano, *t.,* Italy; nr. Turin; cath.; paper, silk; p. *21,850.*

Fos-sur-mer, *t.,* Bouches-du-Rhône, S. France; nr. Marseilles; deepwater pt.; oil refinery.

Fostoria, *t.,* Ohio, U.S.A.; glass, quarries, stockyards; p. (1960) *15,732.*

Fotheringhay, *vil.,* on R. Nene, Northampton, Eng.; Mary Queen of Scots beheaded in F. Castle, 1587.

Fougères, *t.,* Ille-et-Vilaine, France; cas.; p. (1962) *25,171.* [*4,234.*

Fougerolles, *t.,* Haute-Saône, France; p. (1962)

Foula, I., Shetland Is., Scot.; westward of main gr.

Foulness Island, Essex, Eng.

Foulweather, *C.,* Ore., U.S.A.

Fountains Abbey, fine ruin, Cistercian, founded 1132, W.R. Yorks, Eng.; nr. Ripon.

Fourmies, *t.,* Nord, France; nr. Valenciennes; p. (1954) *13,414.*

Foveaux Strait, N.Z.; separates S.I. from Stewart I.

Fowey, *spt., mun. bor.,* Cornwall, Eng.; on W. of Fowey estuary, 22 m. W. of Plymouth; seaside resort, fishing; exp. kaolin; p. (1961) *2,237.*

Fox Is., one of the Aleutian Is. gr.

Foxe Basin and Channel, to N. of Hudson Bay, between Baffin I. and Southampton I.

Foxe Peninsula, Baffin I., Franklin, Canada.

Foyers, *falls*, Inverness, Scot.; E. of Loch Ness, nr. Fort Augustus; aluminium wks., hydro-elec. scheme.

Foyle, Lough, estuary of Foyle R., between Donegal and Londonderry, N. Ireland.

Foynes Is., R.o.I.; oil terminal on N. side, E. of Battery Point.

Foz do Iguaçu, *t.*, Paraná, Brazil; highway (coffee road) under constr. from Paranaguá.

Framingham, *industl. t.*, Mass., U.S.A.; 10 m. W. of Boston; p. (1960) 44,526.

Framlingham, *mkt. t.*, E. Suffolk, Eng.; 15 m. N.E. of Ipswich.

Franca, *c.*, São Paulo st., Brazil; 160 m. N. of Campinas; p. (1960) 47,244.

Francavilla, *t.*, Lecce, Italy; wine, oil, leather; p. 21,375.

France, *rep. (former monarchy and empire)*, W. Europe, bounded N. by Belgium and English Channel, W. by the Bay of Biscay, S. by the Pyrenees and the Mediterranean, E. by Italy. Switzerland and Germany. Greatest length about 600 m., greatest breadth 540 m.; a. 212,600 sq. m., or 3½ times size of England and Wales; F. is divided into 90 metropolitan deps.; ch. ts. are Paris (the cap., the fifth lgst. c. in Europe), Bordeaux, Marseilles, Lyons, Lille, Nice and Toulouse: 19 univs.; ch. mtns.: Cevennes, Jura, Vosges, Pyrenees; ch. Rs.: Seine, Loire, Rhône, Garonne; climate, temperate; agr.: wheat, oats, potatoes, sugar-beet, vine, fruits, silk, cattle, sheep, dairying; minerals; coal, iron, bauxite, potash; mnfs.: iron and steel, machin., textiles; communications excellent; p. of the Rep. (1969) 50,545,000. The French Community was set up in 1959 as successor to the French Union.

Franceville, *t.*, Gabon, Equatorial Africa; on R. Ogowe; manganese mines opened 1962.

Francisco Morazán, *dep.* central Honduras; a. 3,870 sq. m.; p. (1961) 284,540.

Francis Lake, *L.*, Yukon Canada. [p. 10.000.

Francistown, *gold-mining t.*, Botswana, Africa;

Frankental, *t.*, Rhineland Palatinate, Germany; N.W. of Mannheim; engin., farm implements, metallurgy, cork; p. (1963) 35,800.

Frankfort, *t.*, Ky., U.S.A.; mining, horsebreeding; p. (1960) 18,365.

Frankfort, *t.*, Ind., U.S.A.; p. (1960) 15,302.

Frankfurt-on-Main, *c.*, Hessen, W. Germany; restored cath.; univ.; birthplace of Goethe; machin., cars, chemicals, publishing, elec. engin., transhipment pt., airfield; p. (1968) 660,377.

Frankfurt-on-Oder, *t.*, E. Germany; 50 m. from Berlin; gr. route ctr.; machin., iron; E. section of t. (Slubice) Polish since 1945; p. (1963) 58,339.

Frankischer (Franconian) Jura, *plateau with steep N.-facing edge*, S.W. Germany; runs 80 m. S.W. from Fichtelgebirge; drained by Regnitz and Altmühl Rs.

Franklin, *t.*, N.H., U.S.A.; p. (1960) 6,742.

Franklin, *bor.*, N.J., U.S.A.; ctr. of U.S. zinc ind.; p. (1960) 3,624.

Franklin, *c.*, Penns., U.S.A.; petroleum, oil-well tools, rolling stock; p. (1960) 9,586.

Franklin, *t.*, Tasmania, Australia; 20 m. from Hobart; principal fruit-growing dist. in I.

Franklin, *dist.*, N.W. Terr., Canada; comprising the Is. of Arctic Canada from Banks I. to Baffin I., including Boothia Peninsula and Melville Peninsula; sparsely populated; furs; a. 554,032 sq. m.

Frantiskové Lázne (Franzensbad), *t.*, W. Bohemia; famous spa ČSSR

Franz Josef Land, U.S.S.R., *archipelago* in Arctic Ocean; N. of Novaya Zemlya; a. 7,050 sq. m.; mainly ice-covered.

Frascati, *t.*, Italy; 12 m. S.E. of Rome; summer resort; famous villas and arch. remains; nuclear research ctr.; p. 11,425.

Fraser, *R.*, B.C., Canada; rises at 6,000 ft. on W. slopes Rocky Mtns.; famous salmon fisheries; lenth 850 m.

Fraserburg, *agr. t.*, Cape Province, S. Africa; supply sta. for stock-raisers between Calvinia and Carnarvon.

Fraserburgh, *cst. burgh*, N.E. Aberdeen, Scot.; extreme N.E. of Buchan peninsula; impt. herring

fishery; tool factory; p. (1961) 10,462.

Fraserville, *t.*, Quebec, Canada; on St. Lawrence R.

Fratta Maggiore, *t.*, Italy; 6 m. from Naples; p. 18,100.

Frauenfeld, *cap.*, Thurgau, Switzerland; cas.; cotton; p. (1957) 10,048.

Fray Bentos, *t.*, *cap.*, Rio Negro, Uruguay; on R. Uruguay 50 m. from its mouth; meat canning and salting, meat extracts; p. (1963) 14,000.

Frechen, *t.*, N. Rhine–Westphalia, Germany; W. of Cologne; lignite, pottery; p. (1963) 28,000.

Fredericia, *spt.*, *t.*, Veile, Jutland, Denmark; traffic ctr., barracks; new bridge over Little Belt; textiles, silver and plates wks., art. fertilisers; oil refinery projected; p. (1960) 29,870.

Frederick, *c.*, Md., U.S.A.; canning, tanning; p. (1960) 21,744.

Fredericksburg, *t.*, Va., U.S.A.; scene of severe Federal rebuff, Civil War; p. (1960) 13,639.

Fredericton, *t.*, *cap.*, N.B., Canada; on St. John R.; univ., cath.; lumbering; p. (1961) 19,683.

Frederiksberg, *sub.*, Copenhagen, Denmark; p. (1965) 110,847.

Frederikshaab, *sm. spt.* on W. cst. of Greenland.

Frederikshavn, *spt.*, *fishing t.*, N. cst. of Jutland; iron wks., canneries; p. (1960) 22,522.

Frederikstad, *t.*, Norway; at mouth of Glommen R.; tr. ctr.; pulp, paper, electrotechnical inds., shipbldg., whale oil refining; p. (1968) 30,089.

Fredonia, *t.*, N.Y., U.S.A.; p. (1960) 8,477.

Freehold, *t.*, N.J., U.S.A.; p. (1960) 9,140.

Free Port, *mftg. t.*, Ill., U.S.A., on the Pecatonica R.; p. (1960) 26,628. [(1960) 34,419.

Free Port, *t.*, Long Island, N.Y.; U.S.A.; p.

Freeport, *spt.*, Texas; sulphur, chemicals, magnesium from sea; p. (1960) 11,619.

Freetown, *cap.*, Sierra Leone, W. Africa; univ.; coaling sta.; exp. palm oil; diesel power plant; oil refinery being built; p. (1963) 128,000.

Fregenal de la Sierra, *t.*, Spain; nr. Badajoz; p. (1957) 11,716.

Freiberg, *c.*, Karl-Marx-Stadt, Germany; cath.; cas.; metallurgy, textiles, glass, porcelain; p. (1963) 48,062.

Freiburg (Fribourg), *can.*, Switzerland; much forest and unproductive land; a. 645 sq. m.; p. (1961) 159,194.

Freiburg, *cap.*, Freiburg, Switzerland; between Berne and Lausanne; fine viaduct and bridges; univ.; machin., chocolate; p. (1957) 29.005.

Freiburg im Breisgau, *t.*, Baden-Württemberg, Germany; in Black Forest; cath., univ.; textiles, paper, metallurgy; p. (1968) 161,455.

Freising, *c.*, Bavaria, Germany; cath.; agr. machin., textiles, brewing; p. (1963) 28,800.

Freital, *t.*, Dresden, E. Germany; coal-mining, iron, leather, glass, uranium ore processing; p. (1963) 35,895.

Fréjus, *cst. t.*, Var. France; p. (1962) 20,318.

Fréjus, Col de, the Alpine pass under which the Mont Cenis tunnel runs.

Fremantle, *c.*, *spt.*, W. Australia; at mouth of Swan R., 12 m. S.W. from Perth, principal pt. of commerce in W. Australia and first Australian pt. of call for mail steamers; oil refining; wheat, wool; p. (1966) 32,134.

Fremont, *t.*, Cal., U.S.A.; p. (1960) 43,790.

Fremont, *t.*, Nebraska, U.S.A.; on Platte R.; 33 m. from Omaha; flourmills, canneries; p. (1960) 19,698.

Fremont, *c.*, Ohio, U.S.A.; on Sandusky R.; petroleum field; p. (1960) 17,573.

Fremont's Peak, highest peak of Wind River Range, Wyoming St., U.S.A.; alt. 13,570 ft.

French Equatorial Africa, formerly comprised the French African cols. Gabon (cap. Libreville), Middle Congo (cap. Brazzaville), Ubangi-Shari (cap. Bangui), and Chad (cap. Fort Lamy); timber, ivory; a. 953,740 sq. m.; p. (1957) 4,879,000. These sts. are now indep. within Fr. Community. See under separate headings: Gabon, Congo, Central African Rep., Chad.

French Guiana, *col.*, S. America; forests; cocoa, gold, phosphates; lge. deposits of bauxite at Kaw Mt. to be exploited; poor communications; cap. Cayenne; a. 34,740 sq. m.; p. (estd. 1968) 46,000.

French, *R.*, Ontario, Canada; the outlet of L. Nipissing into L. Huron.

French Somaliland, *see* Afars and Issas.

French Soudan. *See* Mali.

French West Africa, comprised former French cols. of Dahomey, Ivory Coast, Mauritania, Niger,

French Guinea, Upper Volta, Senegal, French Soudan.

Freshwater, *sm. t., bathing resort,* I. of Wight, Eng.; at W. end of I., 8 m. W. of Newport.

Fresnillo, *t.,* Zacatecas St., Mexico; p. *25,000.*

Fresno, *c.,* Cal., U.S.A.; ctr. of impt. irrigated fruit-growing dist.; dairying, copper, petroleum; p. (1960) *133,929.*

Friedrichshafen, *t., L. pt.,* Germany; on L. Constance; machin., boat bldg., motors; p. (1963) *39,300.*

Friedrichstal, *t.,* Saar; coal-mining, steel wks.; p. (estd. 1954) *16,400.*

Friendly Is., *see* Tonga.

Friern Barnet, *former urb. dist.,* Middx., Eng.; now inc. in Barnet outer bor., Greater London (*q.v.*); residtl.; p. (1961) *28,813.*

Friesland. *prov.,* Netherlands; dairying, horses, cattle; natural gas on Ameland I.; a. 1,325 sq. m.; p. (1967) *506,311.*

Frimley and Camberley, *urb. dist.,* Surrey. Eng.; 3 m. N. of Farnborough (Hants); light engin., plastics; p. (estd. 1967) *40,660.*

Frinton and Walton, *urb. dist.,* Essex, Eng.; on E. cst., 5 m. N.E. of Clacton; seaside resort; p. (1961) *9,576.* [linen; p. *10,667.*

Friol, *commune,* Lugo, N.W. Spain; leather,

Frisches Haff, *shallow freshwater lagoon,* Baltic cst. of Poland; 53 m. long, 4–11 m. broad.

Frische Nehrung, *sandspit,* G. of Gdansk, Baltic Sea; astride bdy. between Poland, U.S.S.R.; almost separates Frisches Haff (Zalew Wislany) from G. of Gdansk; length 36 m.

Frisian Islands, *chain of Is.* stretching from Zuyder Zee and N. to Jutland, along the csts. of the Netherlands and N. Germany; ch. Is. are Texel, Vlieland and Ameland.

Friuli-Venezia Giulia, *aut. reg.* (created 1963), N.E. Italy; comprising 3 provs. Udine (p. *800,000*), Gorizia (p. *140,000*), and Trieste (p. *300,000*); cap. Trieste.

Frobisher Bay, *inlet* in S. Baffin I., N. Canada, extending 200 m. between Cumberland Sound and Hudson Strait.

Frodingham, *t.,* Lincoln, Eng.; on W. flank of limestone ridge, Lincoln Edge; impt. iron-ore open-cast mines; mnfs. iron and steel; p. (1961) *67,257* (with Scunthorpe).

Frodsham, *mkt. t.,* Cheshire, Eng.; 10 m. N.E. Chester; chemicals.

Fromo, *mkt. t., urb. dist.,* Somerset, Eng.; on R. Frome, 11 m. S. of Bath; p. (1961) *11,440.*

Frontignan, *t.,* Herault, S. France; oil refining; oil pipeline under sea from Sete; p. (1962) *8,309.*

Frosinone, *industl. t.,* Lazio, Italy; on R. Cosa; p. (1961) *30,796.*

Froward, *C.,* Magallanes prov., Southern Chile.

Frunze, *cap.,* Kirgiz S.S.R.; univ.; meat packing, engin., textiles; p. (1967) *370,000.*

Fthiotis and Focis, *pref.,* Greece; cap. Lamia; p. (1951) *199,794.*

Fucino, *L.* (*now drained*), Aquila, Central Italy; old volcanic crater.

Fuente de Cantos, *industl. t.,* Badajoz, Spain; p. (1957) *10,027.*

Fuente-Ovejuna, *t.,* Córdoba, Spain; ctr. of lead-mining dist., honey prod.; p. (1957) *17,000.*

Fuerteventura, *I.,* Canary gr.; a. 663 sq. m.; p. (1962) *18,333.*

Fujeira, *emirate,* one of seven Trucial sts., Persian Gulf; p. (estd. 1968) *10,000.*

Fujisawa, *t.,* Honshu, Japan; bearings machin.; p. (1965) *175,183.*

Fujiyama, extinct volcano, Japan, 60 m. S.W. of Tokyo; pilgrim resort; alt. 12,395 ft.

Fukien (Fujian) *prov.,* China; cap. Foochow (Fuzhou); tea, rice, cotton, sugar, tobacco; paper, coal, gold, silver; a. 45,845 sq. m.; p. (1953) *13,142,721.*

Fukui, *t.,* Honshu, Japan; silk, paper; p. (1965) *169,636.*

Fukuoka, *t.,* Kyushu, Japan; comm. ctr.; silk, fabrics, dolls; p. (1965) *749,808.*

Fukushima, *c.,* N. Japan; chemicals, coal, iron prod.; pears, cherries; p. (1965) *173,678.*

Fukuyama, *t.,* S. Hokkaido, Japan; p. (1964) *161,000.*

Fulda, *c.,* Hesse, W. Germany; nr. Cassel; on R. Fulda; palace, abbey; textiles, metallurgy, rubber; route ctr.; p. (1963) *44,900.*

Fulda, *R.,* Central Germany; with the Werra forms the R. Weser.

Fulham, *see* Hammersmith.

Fullerton, *t.,* Cal. U.S.A.; p. (1950) *56,180.*

Fulton, *t.,* Mo., U.S.A.; firebrick and shoe factories; p. (1960) *11,131.*

Fulton, *c.,* N.Y., U.S.A.; woollens, cutlery, paper; p. (1960) *14,261.*

Fulwood, *urb. dist.,* Lancs, Eng.; 2 m. N.E. of Preston; p. (1961) *15,966.*

Funchal, *t., spt., cap.,* Madeira; winter resort; wine; p. (1960) *43,301.*

Fundy, Bay of, *inlet* between Nova Scotia and New Brunswick, Canada.

Furneaux, *Is.,* gr. in Bass Strait, belonging to Tasmania.

Furness, *dist.,* N.W. Lancs, Eng.; between Morecambe Bay and the Irish Sea; haematite iron ore.

Fürstenwalde, *industl. t.,* Frankfurt, E. Germany; on R. Spree; metallurgy, leather; p. (1963) *31,881.*

Fürth, *t.,* Bavaria, Germany; nr. Nürnberg; furniture mftg., toys, metallurgy, glass, paper, radio, footwear; p. (1963) *98,300.*

Fusan, *see* Pusan.

Fushiki, *t., spt.,* Honshu, Japan; on Toyama Bay to E. of Noto Peninsula; lge. coastwise tr. in rice from Koga and Toyama plains; exp. chemicals, lumber, metals; imports metals, coal, bean-cake, flax.

Fushun, *c.,* Liaoning, N. China; at foot of Changpai Shan, 22 m. S.E. of Mukden; most impt. coal-mines in Far East; possesses world's thickest bituminous coal seam (417 ft.) worked by deep and open-cast mines; p. (1953) *679,000.*

Fushimi, *c.* Honshu, Japan; sub. of Kyoto; p. (1965) *128,281.*

Fusin (Fuxin), *c.,* Liaoning prov., China; coal mng.; agr.; p. (1953) *105,000.*

Futa, La, *pass,* Tusco-Emilian Apennines, N. Italy; used by main road from Bologna to Florence; alt. 2,962 ft.

Futa Jalon, *upland dist.,* mostly in Guinea, W. Africa, with outliers in Liberia and Sierra Leone.

Futuna and Alofi, *Is.,* S. of Wallis Is., dependency of Fr. col. of New Caledonia; p. about 2,000.

Fylde, *rural dist., geographical sub-region,* W. Lancs., Eng.; extends along W. cst. between estuaries of Ribble and Wyre; low, flat plain behind coastal sand dunes, covered by fertile glacial deposits; cultivated where drained, grain, vegetables; impt. pig and poultry rearing dist.; ch. t., Blackpool, famous holiday resort; p. (rural dist., 1961) *16,928.*

Fylingdales, ballistic missile early warning station on Yorkshire moors.

Fyn, *I.,* Denmark; in the Baltic Sea; a. 1,320 sq. m.; cap. Odense; p. (1960) *376,872.*

Fyne, *loch* on Argyll cst. W. Scot.; an arm of F. of Clyde; length 40 m.

Fyzabad, *t.,* Uttar Pradesh, India; sugar; p. (1961) *88,296.*

G

Gabes, *spt.,* Tunisia; on G. of Gabes, 200 m. S. of Tunis; dates, henna, wool; p. (1961) *24,400.*

Gaberone, *cap.,* Botswana, S.W. Africa; cattle, sorghum, maize; manganese mng.; p. (estd. 1965) *12,000.*

Gabon, *ind. sovereign st.,* within Fr. Community, Equatorial Africa; cap. Libreville; ivory, ebony. palm-oil; a. 101,400 sq. m.; p. (estd. 1970) *630,000.*

Gadag-Betgeri, *t.,* Mysore, India; cotton and silk weaving; p. (1961) *76,614.*

Gadsen, *industl., t.,* Ala., U.S.A.; cotton, cars, coal, iron, steel; p. (1960) *58,088.*

Gaeta, *spt., fort,* Caserta, Italy; 40 m. N.W. of Naples; the ancient Caietae Portus; cath.; p. *22,882.*

Gaffney, *t.,* S.C., U.S.A.; limestone, textiles; p. (1960) *10,435.*

Gafsa, *t.,* Tunisia; phosphates; p. (1961) *24,300.*

Gaillac, *t.,* Tarn, France; wines; p. (1962) *9,058.*

Gaillard Cut, *excavated channel,* Panama Canal Zone; carries Panama Canal through Culebra Mtn. from L. Gatun to Pac. Oc.; length 7 m.

Gainesville, *t.,* Fla., U.S.A.; p. (1960) *29,701.*

Gainesville, *t.,* Ga., U.S.A.; p. (1960) *16,523.*

Gainesville, *t.,* Texas, U.S.A.; p. (1960) *13,093.*

Gainsborough, *mkt. t., urb. dist.*, Lincs., Eng.; on R. Trent, 15 m. N.W. of Lincoln; shipping, agr. implements, engin., milling, malting, timber; p. (1961) *17,276*. [broad.

Gairdner, *L.*, S. Australia; 130 m. long, 23 m.

Galápagos, *volcanic Is.*, Pac. Oc.; 600 m. W. Ecuador; consists of 12 lge. and several 100 sm. Is.; only 5 inhabited; administered by Ecuador; peculiar fauna and flora; guano; a. 2,868 sq. m.; p. (1962) *2,412*.

Galashiels, *burgh*, Selkirk, Scot.; on Gala Water, 2 m. above confluence with R. Tweed; tweeds, woollens; p. (1961) *12,374*.

Galati, *Black Sea pt.*, Romania, on Danube R.; naval base; engin., steel; p. (1963) *111,906*.

Galatina, *t.*, Apulia, Italy; p. *20,300*.

Galena, *t.*, Ill., U.S.A.; lead, zinc, marble, granite; p. (1960) *4,410*.

Galesburg, *t.*, Ill., U.S.A.; engin.; p. (1960) *37,243*.

Galicia, *former Austrian prov.*, Polish 1918–39, since 1939 E. part transferred to Ukrainian S.S.R. and W. remaining Polish (provs. Kraków and Rzeszów).

Galicia, *old prov.*, N.W. Spain; now forming provs. of La Coruña, Lugo, Orense and Pontevedra; mountainous; dairying; mining, lead, copper, iron; p. (1957) *2,600,000*.

Galilee, *N. div.* of Palestine in Roman period, containing Capernaum, Nazareth.

Galilee, Sea of (Lake Tiberias), also known as L. Gennesaret; 13 m. l., 6 m. wide, 150 ft. deep, 680 ft. below level of Med.; Israel plans to draw water from L. to irrigate Negev.

Galion, *t.*, Ohio, U.S.A.; mftg.; rly. ctr.; p. (1960) *12,650*.

Galla and Sidamo, *prov.*, Ethiopia.

Galle, *spt.*, Ceylon; on S.W. cst.; extensive tr. in tea, coconut oil, cement; p. (1963) *64,942*.

Galleana, *mkt. t.*, León Prov., Mexico; at foot of Sierra Madre Oriental, 120 m. S. of Monterrey; focus of tr. between tropical lowlands and high plateau.

Gallego, R., N.E. Spain; rises in Pyrenees, flows S. to R. Ebro at Zaragoza; R. provides water for irrigation around Zaragoza; valley used by main rly. across Pyrenees from Pau (France) to Zaragoza; length 110 m.

Gallegos, *t., cap.*, Santa Cruz terr., Argentina; p. *7,003*. [p. *12,200*.

Gallipoli, *spt.*, Italy; on E. shore G. of Taranto;

Gallipoli, *see* Gelibolu.

Gallipolis, *t.*, Ohio U.S.A.; p. (1950) *7 871*.

Gällivare, *dist.*, N. Sweden; inside Arctic Circle, 120 m. N.W. of Lulea; iron ore; p. *26,200*.

Galloway, *dist.*, S.W. Scot.; inc. the cos. of Wigtown and Kirkcudbright.

Galloway, Mull of, extreme S.W. point of Scot.

Gallup, *t.*, N.M., U.S.A.; coal, wool, sheep, cattle rearing; p. (1960) *14,089*.

Galston, *burgh*, Ayr, Scot.; on R. Irvine, nr. Kilmarnock; hosiery, lace; p. (1961) *4,023*.

Galt, *t.*, Ontario, Canada; mnfs.; p. (1961) *27,830*.

Galty Mtns., Tipperary, Ireland; alt. 3,000 ft.

Galveston, *c., spt.*, Texas, U.S.A.; on I. in G. of Mexico; gr. cotton pt.; mills, foundries; p. (1960) *67,175*.

Galway, *co.*, Galway Bay, Connacht, Ireland; fishery, cattle, marble quarrying; a. 2,452 sq. m.; p. (1966) *148,190*.

Galway, *t. cap.*, Galway, Ireland; univ.; p. (1966) *24,495*.

Gambela, *tr. sta.*, leased to Sudan by Ethiopia.

Gambia, *indep. sov. st.* within Brit. Commonwealth (1965), W. Africa; narrow terr., average 20 m. wide, extends 200 m. inland astride R. Gambia; hot all year, summer rain; savannah grassland; ground-nuts, palm-kernals, beeswax, hides; cap. Bathurst; a. 4,000 sq. m.; p. (estd. 1969) *357,000*.

Gambia, R., Fr. W. Africa and Gambia, rises in Futa Jallon Plateau, flows N. and W. into Atl. Oc. at Bathurst; forms main means of communication through Gambia. [(1961) *5,725*.

Gander, *airport*, Newfoundland, Canada; p.

Gandhinagar, *new cap.*, Gujarat, India; on Sabarmati R. 13 m. N. of Ahmedabad; under construction; planned initial p. *75,000* rising to *200,000*.

Gandia, *t. spt.*, Valencia, Spain; fruit exp.; silk spinning p. (1957) *20,160*.

Ganges (Ganga), *gr. sacred R.*, India; rises in Himalayas and flows to Bay of Bengal, by several delta mouths, one one of which stands Calcutta. Delta very fertile and densely populated. Navigable for lge. ships from Allahabad; length 1,500 m.

Gangtok, *t.*, cap. Sikkim, E. Himalayas; trade ctr., carpets; p. (1965) *12,000*. [(1961) *1,872 530*.

Ganjam, *dist.*, Orissa, India; a. 4,324 sq. m.; p.

Gap, *c.*, Hautes Alpes, S.E. France; silk and other textiles; p. (1962) *21,935*.

Gard, *Mediterranean dep.*, France; cap., Nîmes; vines, olives, sericulture; a. 2,270 sq. m.; p. (1968) *487,544*.

Garda, L., between Lombardy and Venezia, Italy; a. 143 sq. m.; greatest depth, 1,135 ft.

Garden City, *t.*, Mich., U.S.A.; p. (1960) *38,017*.

Garden City, *t.*, N.Y., U.S.A.; p. (1960) *23,948*.

Garden Grove, *t.*, Cal., U.S.A.; p. (1960) *84,238*.

Gardena, *t.*, S.W. Cal., U.S.A.; mkt.-gardening; p. (1960) *35,943*.

Gardiner, *t.*, Me., U.S.A.; p. (1960) *6,897*.

Gardner, *t.*, Mass., U.S.A.; chair mftg.; p. (1960) *19,038*.

Garfield, *t.*, N.J., U.S.A., p. (1960) *29,253*.

Garfield Heights, *t.*, Ohio, U.S.A.; iron, steel, oil refineries, abrasives; p. (1960) *38,455*.

Garforth, *urb. dist.*, W.R. Yorks, Eng.; p. (1961) *14,641*

Garigliano, Italy; nuclear power plant projected.

Garland, *t.*, Texas, U.S.A.; p. *38,501*.

Garmisch-Partenkirchen, *t.*, Bavaria, Germany; winter sports; p. (1963) *26,600*.

Garo Hills, *mountainous dist.*, Assam, India; a. 3,119 sq. m.; dense forests; p. (1961) *307,228*.

Garonne, *R.*, S.W. France; rises at foot of Mt. Maladetta (Pyrenees), and enters the Gironde estuary 20 m. below Bordeaux; length 350 m.

Garonne, Haute, *dep.*, S. France; a. 2,458 sq. m.; p. (1968) *690,712*.

Garrigue, *region*, Languedoc, S. France; low limestone hills, run N.E. to S.W., W. of Rhône delta; semi-arid; scanty vegetation; winter pasture for sheep, olives; Montpellier, Nîmes located on S. flank.

Garston, *spt.*, southern end Bootle and Liverpool docks; Lancs, Eng.; docks; p. *28,000*.

Garut, *t.*, W. Java, Indonesia; mtn. resort; p. *24,219*.

Gary, *c.*, Ind., U.S.A.; at S. end of L. Michigan; steel, tin-plate, cement, soap, chemicals, oil refining; p. (1960) *178,321*.

Gascony, *ancient prov., duchy*, S.W. France.

Gaspé, *peninsula*, Quebec, Canada; on S. side of St. Lawrence.

Gateshead, *t., co. bor.*, Durham, Eng.; on R. Tyne, opp. Newcastle; engin.; p. (estd. 1967) *100,780*.

Gatineau, *R.*, Canada; trib. of Ottawa R., which it joins nr. Ottawa; length 300 m.

Gatooma, *t.*, Rhodesia; farming, mining and cotton mnfs., gold, mineral deposits; p. (1958) *10,000* (incl. *2,000* Europeans).

Gatun, *artificial L.*, Panama Canal Zone, Central America; passed through by Panama Canal; alt. 40 ft. above Caribbean Sea; a. 250 sq. m.

Gatwick, Surrey–Sussex border; 25 m. S. London; 1st airport in world where trunk road, main rly. line and air facilities combined in one unit.

Gauhati, *t.*, Assam, India; univ.; silk, cotton, lace, oil refinery; oil pipeline from Barauni; p. (1961) *100,702*.

Gauri-Sankar, *mtn.* in Himalayas; 35 m. W. of Mt. Everest; alt. 23,440 ft.

Gävle, *spt.*, Sweden; timber, textiles, steel, porcelain; p. (1961) *54,768*.

Gävleborg, *co.*, Sweden; ch. t., Gävle; a. 7,610 sq. m.; p. (1961) *293,070*.

Gaya, *t.*, Bihar, India; famous Buddhist pilgrim ctr.; cottons, silks; p. (1961) *151,105*.

Gayyarah, Mosul, Iraq; bitumen refinery.

Gaza, *spt.*, U.A.R.; exp. cereals, wool; p. *c. 100,000*.

Gaza Strip, *cstl. a.* under Egyptian admin. since 1949; occupied by Israeli troops, Nov. 1956–March 1957, and since June 1967.

Gazientep, *t.*, Turkey; S.W. of Malatya; p. (1965) *153,367*.

Gazli, Uzbekistan S.S.R.; 60 m. N.W. of Bukhara; natural gas field discovered mid-1950's; pipeline to Chelyabinsk opened Nov. 1963.

Gdansk *prov. (voivodship)*, Poland; ch. t. Gdansk (Danzig); a. 4,290 sq. m.; p. (1965) *1,353,000*.

Gdansk (Danzig), *spt.*, Poland; on R. Vistula; impt. Baltic pt.; Prussian, 1814–1919; free city under Treaty of Versailles; annexed to Germany, 1939; restored to Poland, 1945; industr. and comm. ctr.; shipbldg., machin., chemicals, metals; p. (1965) *319,000*.

Gdynia, *spt.,* Poland; built by Poland as pt. after 1924 when Danzig was a free city; impt. comm. pt.; rly. ctr.; metal, machin., food inds.; p. (1965) *165,000*.

Géant, Aiguille du, *mtn.* in Savoy Alps, France; alt. 13,170 ft.; nearby Col du Géant, pass from Chamonix to Italy, alt. 11,145 ft.

Geel, *t.,* Belgium; 30 m. E. of Antwerp; nuclear power plant projected.

Geelong, *spt.,* Port Phillip, Victoria, Australia; fine harbour; tr. in flour, wool; oil refining; aluminium, agr. machin.; superphosphates; cars, carpets; p. (1966) *104,974*.

Geislingen, *t.,* Wurttemberg, Germany; p. (1963)

Gela, *t.,* S. Sicily, Italy; in cotton growing a.; petro chemicals; p. (1961) *54,774*.

Gelderland, *prov.,* Netherlands; E. and S. of Utrecht prov., a. 1,939 sq. m.; cap. Arnhem; cereals, tobacco; cattle rearing; p. (1967) *1,434,439*.

Gelibolu, (Gallipoli), *t.* and *peninsula* on the Dardanelles, Turkey; vines, sericulture; scene of unsuccessful landing by British and Anzac troops 1915; p. (1960) *12,956*.

Gelligaer, *t., urb. dist.,* Glamorgan, Wales; 4 m. N.E. of Pontypridd; mining; p. rural dist. (1961) *34,572*.

Gelsenkirchen, *t.,* N. Rhine–Westphalia, Germany; nr. Dortmund; collys., ironwks., glass, chemicals, oil refining; p. (1968) *352,350*.

Gemmi, *mtn. pass* across Swiss Alps, Valais to Berne; alt. 7,600 ft.   [cattle; p. *14,500*.

General Pico, *t.,* S. central Argentina; grain,

Geneva, *c.. cap. can.* Geneva, Switzerland; at W. end of L. Geneva, R. Rhône flows through c.; cath., univ.; former H.Q. of League of Nations, H.Q. of I.L.O., W.H.O., I.T.U., International Red Cross; watch-mkg., jewellery, elec. goods, chocolate; tourist resort; p. (1961) *179,400*.

Geneva, *can.,* Switzerland; a. 109 sq. m.; p. (1961) *259,234*.

Geneva, *L.,* S.W. corner of Switzerland; 45 m. E.-W. in form of crescent; a. 224 sq. m.

Geneva, *t., N.Y., U.S.A.*; engin.; p. (1960) *17,286*.

Génissiat, France; site of gr. barrage and hydro-elec. power sta. on Rhône below Geneva; completed 1950.

Genk, *t.,* Limburg, Belgium; stainless steel wks.; p. (1968) *56,031*.

Gennevilliers, *t.,* Seine, France; p. (1962) *42,611*.

Genoa, *maritime prov.,* Liguria, N. Italy; a. 1,582 sq. m.; p. (1961) *1,044,633*.

Genoa (Genova), *spt., comm. c.,* on G. of Genoa; fine palaces, cath., univ.; shipbldg., engin., tanning, sugar, textiles; p. (1965) *848,000*.

Gentilly, *t.,* Seine, France; p. (1954) *17,497*.

Gentilly, Quebec, Canada; nuclear power sta. being built.

George, *t.,* Cape Province, S. Africa; footwear, sawmilling, hops; p. (1960) *14,505* inc. *8,635* whites.

Georgetown, *cap.,* Guyana, S. America; on Demerara R.; exp. sugar, cocoa, coffee, timber, gold, diamonds, bauxite; p. (1962) *93,350*.

Georgetown, *t., S.C., U.S.A.*; fish, lumber, cotton; p. (1960) *12,261*.

Georgetown, *t.,* Washington D.C., U.S.A.; on R. Potomac; univ., cath.

Georgetown, *c., spt.* Penang, Malaya; p. *189,068*.

Georgia, *st., U.S.A.*; on Atlantic cst.; forested, agr.; cotton, tobacco, corn, peanuts, fruit; textiles, lumber, chemicals, steel; chief ts.; Atlanta (cap.) and Savannah; a. 58,876 sq. m.; p. (1970) *4,492,038*.

Georgia, *constituent rep.,* U.S.S.R.; maize, tobacco, wheat; engin., metallurgy, manganese mng., oil, gold deposit discovered nr. R. Inguri in a. of new h.e.p. project 1965; cap. Tbilisi; a. 27,000 sq. m.; p. (1970) *4,688,000*.

Georgian Bay, *lge. inlet,* Ontario, Canada; E. shore of L. Huron; many impt. lake pts. (Owen Sound, Parry Sound) where Prairie wheat is transhipped to rly. for despatch to Montreal; a. approx. 4,500 sq. m.

Gera, *t.,* Gera, E. Germany; lignite, woollens, printing; p. (1963) *104,198*.

Geraldton, *spt.,* W. Australia; 306 m. from Perth; in agr. and pastoral dist.; exp. gold, copper, wool; natural gas nearby; p. (1961) *10,878*.

Germany, after defeat in Second World War divided into E. and W. Germany. W. Germany is Federal st. (declared sovereign May 5, 1955) of 9 Länder, Schleswig-Holstein, Hamburg, Lower Saxony, Bremen, North Rhine–Westphalia, Hesse, Rhineland Palatinate, Baden-Württemberg, Bavaria, and Saarland (incorporated 1957); previously divided into British, American, and French zones; a. 96,000 sq. m.; admin. ctr. Bonn; p. (1969) *59,060,000* excl. W. Berlin: E. Germany comprises 14 dists., Rostock, Schwerin, Neubrandenburg, Magdeburg, Potsdam, Frankfurt, Erfurt, Halle, Leipzig, Cottbus, Suhl, Gera, Karl-Marx-Stadt, Dresden; previously the Soviet zone, became sovereign st., March 25, 1954; a. 41,571 sq. m.; p. (1968) *16,002,000*. Berlin under four-Power control; ch. German inds.: agr.; rye, oats, wheat, potatoes, sugar-beet, wines; pastoral; cattle, pigs, sheep; forests, timber; minerals; coal, lignite, iron, potash, copper, zinc, salt; mnfs., machine., shpbldg., textiles, chemicals, dyes, printing, etc.; commerce; communications very good.

Germiston, *t.,* Transvaal, S. Africa; nr. Johannesburg; gold mng.; rly. wkshps., engin., machin., chemicals; gas pipeline from Sasolburg, O.F.S.; p. (1960) *204,605* (inc. *84,419* Whites).

Gerona, *maritime prov.,* N.E. Spain; cap. G.; textiles, coal, paper; a. 2,264 sq. m.; p. (1959) *345,320*.

Gerrards Cross, *t.,* S.E. Bucks, Eng.; 9 m. E. of High Wycombe; residtl.; p. (1951) *2,942*.

Gers, *dep.,* S.W. France; cap. Auch; grain, vines, brandy; a. 2,429 sq. m.; p. (1962) *181,577*.

Gers, *R.,* rising in the Pyrenees, flows to the Garonne; length 75 m.

Gettysburg, *t.,* Penns., U.S.A.; Federal victory 1863; granite; p. (1960) *7,960*.

Gevelsberg, *c.,* Westphalia, Germany; iron stoves; p. (1963) *32,100*.

Gezira, *dist.,* Sudan, N.E. Africa; situated between Blue and White Niles above confluence at Khartoum; approx 4,700 sq. m. capable of irrigation by water drawn from Blue Nile at Sennar Dam; large-scale growing of high-quality cotton; total a. approx. 7,800 sq. m.

Ghadames, *oasis,* Sahara Desert, Libya; N. Africa; at point where Tunis, Algeria, Libya converge 300 m. S.W. of Tripoli.

Ghaghara (Gogra), *sacred R.,* India; rising in Tibet, flows through Uttar Pradesh; trib. of Ganges; length 300 m.

Ghana, Rep. of, W. Africa; sovereign and ind. st. within British Commonwealth since 6 March 1957; agr.; cocoa, palm-oil, groundnuts; mahogany, manganese, gold, diamonds; cap. Accra; harbours at Takoradi and Tema; total a. 91,843 sq. m.; p. (estd. 1970) *8,545,561*.

Ghardaia, *t.,* S. Algeria; p. (1960) *58,327*.

Ghats, E. and W., *two mtn. ranges* bordering the triangular upland of S. India, the Deccan; alt. of ch. summits, 4,700–7,000 ft.

Ghazipur, *t.,* N. India; on Ganges R., E. of Varanasi; agr. school; p. (1961) *37,147*.

Ghazni, *fortfd. mtn. t.,* Afghanistan; 78 m. S.W. of Kabul; gr. tr. ctr.; cap. of the Empire of Mahmud, c. A.D. 1000; p. *10,500*.

Ghazvin, *c.* and *dist.,* Central Prov., Iran; agr.; irrigation plant.

Ghent, *c.,* Belgium; cap. of E. Flanders, on R. Scheldt; cath. univ.; extensive cotton, woollen, sugar inds.; plastics, photographic materials; oil refinery under construction; p. (1968) *232,915*, inc. subs.

Giant's Causeway, *famous basaltic columns,* on promontory of N. cst. of Antrim, Ireland.

Giarre, *t.,* Sicily, Italy; nr. Mt. Etna; industl.; p. *20,050*.

Gibare, *t.,* Oriente prov., Cuba, W. Indies; exp. bananas; p. *8,045*.

Gibraltar, City of, *Brit. terr.,* W. end of Mediterranean; on rocky peninsula (1,396 ft.) extreme S. of Spain; naval base of great strategic importance; free pt.; captured by British in 1704; a. 2¼ sq. m.; civilian p. (estd.) *27,000*.

Gibraltar, Strait of, connects Atlantic and Mediterranean; its narrowest breadth is 9 m.

Gibson Desert, centre of W. Australia.

Gibson Island, *t.,* Queensland, Australia; nr. N. bank of Brisbane R.; fertiliser wks.

Giessen, *t.,* Hesse, Germany; on R. Lahn; univ.; tobacco, engin., textiles; p. (1963) *69,800*.

Gifu, t., Central Honshu, Japan; silk; paper; cormorant fishing; p. (1965) *358,190*.

Gigha, I., Argyll, Scot.; off W. cst.; 6 m. long, 2 m. wide; p. (with Cara) *243*.

Gijón, spt.. Oviedo. Spain; on Bay of Biscay; gd. harbour; tobacco, petroleum, coal, earthenware; steel wks. nearby; p. (1959) *121,692*.

Gila, R., New Mexico and Arizona, U.S.A.; trib. of Rio Colorado; water used for irrigation in Imperial Valley; length 650 m.

Gilan, prov., N.W. Iran, on Caspian Sea, bounded by U.S.S.R.; sub-tropical climate; agr., inc. cotton and rice; cap. Rasht; p. (1967) *1,754,650*.

Gilbert and Ellice Islands Colony, gr. of coral Is. (Brit.), Micronesia, Pac. Oc.; ch. crops: pandanas fruit and coconuts; exp. phosphates and copra; a. 369 sq. m.; p. (estd.) *55,000*.

Gilgit, cap., Gt. extreme N.W. dist. of Kashmir.

Gilgit, R., of the Punjab rising in Chitral, trib. of the Indus, flowing along the Gilgit valley into Kashmir.

Gill, Lough, L., on borders of cos. Sligo and Leitrim, Ireland.

Gillespie, t., Ill., U.S.A.; coal; p. (1960) *3,569*.

Gillingham, t., mun. bor., Kent, Eng.; 2 m. E. of Chatham; cherry orchards, cement, light inds.; p. (estd. 1967) *83,930*.

Gilly, t., Hainaut, Belgium, nr. Charleroi; coal; p. (1962) *23,878*.

Giiolo I., see Halmahera I.

Gilp Loch, Argyll, Scot.; inlet of Loch Fyne, at head of Crinan Canal.

Gioja del Colle, c., Bari, S. Italy; olive oil, wine, wool; p. *24,000*.

Giovinazzo, spt., S. Italy; on the Adriatic, N. of Bari; p. *12,150*.

Gippsland, dist., S.E. Victoria, Australia; a. 13,900 sq. m.; mntous.; farming, grazing; coal.

Girardot, t., Colombia, S. America; impt. R. pt. and airport on upper course of R. Magdalena, 685 m. upstream from Caribbean Sea; linked by rly. (70 m.) to Bogotá; coffee, hides, ceramics; p. (estd. 1959) *50,000*.

Giresun, spt., Black Sea, Turkey, W. of Trabzon; p. (1960) *19,946*.

Girga, t., Upper U.A.R.; on R. Nile; p. *1,000*.

Girga, admin. div., Upper U.A.R., N.E. Africa; a. 595 sq. m.; p. (1960) *1,574,000*.

Girgenti, (same as Agrigento, q.v.), t., S. Sicily, Italy; famous for its Greek temples.

Girishk, t., Afghanistan; on Helmand R.; ctr. of agr. dist.

Gironde, dep., France; vineyards, grain, fruit, wines; cap. Bordeaux; a. 4,140 sq. m.; p. (1968) *1,009,390*.

Gironde, R., estuary, S.W. France; formed by junction of Rs. Garonne and Dordogne; navigable to Pauillac.

Girton, par., nr. Cambridge, Eng.; women's college.

Girvan, burgh, Ayr, Scot.; on F. of Clyde, 18 m. S.W. of Ayr; summer resort; p. (1961) *6,159*.

Gisborne, c., spt., N.I., N.Z.; on Poverty Bay, 60 m. N.E. of Napier; freezing-wks.; p. (1966) *24,939*.

Gisburn, t., W.R. Yorks; on R. Ribble, nr. Clitheroe.

Giugliano, t., Italy; N.W. of Naples; mnfs.; p. *20,500*. [*20,000*.

Giulianova, t., Teramo, Italy; fruit, grain; p.

Giurgiu, pt., Romania; on R. Danube; opposite Ruse; good tr.; timber; p. (1963) *51,520*.

Givet, t., Ardennes, N.E. France; on R. Meuse; tanneries; p. (1962) *7,925*.

Givors, t., Rhône dep., France; on Rhône R.. 10 m. S. of Lyons; mnfs.; oil refining nearby at Feyzin; p. (1962) *17,232*.

Giza, admin div., U.A.R.; cap. Giza; a. 392 sq. m.; p. (1960) *1,337,000*.

Giza, t., Lower U.A.R.; on the Nile, 3 m. S.W. of Cairo; nr. pyramids of Khafra (Chephren), Khufu (Cheops) and Men-ka-va; also the Sphinx; contains Museum of Egyptian antiquities; film ind.; p. (1960) *250,000*.

Gjinokastër (Argyrocastro), prefecture, Albania; cap Q.; p. (estd.) *159,695*.

Gjövik, t., S. Norway; on L. Mjosa; furniture, footwear, light inds.; p. (1968) *24,517*.

Gjuhëzës, C. (Glossa C.), Albania, Strait of Otranto.

Glace Bay, t., Nova Scotia, Canada; coal; p. (1961) *24,186*.

Gladbeck, t., N. Rhine–Westphalia, Germany; N. of Essen; coal-mining, chemicals, rly. junction; p. (1963) *83,700*.

Gladewater, t. N.E. Texas, U.S.A.; oil, lumber; p. (1960) *5,742*.

Gladstone, t., Queensland, Australia; alumina refining, oil, chemicals; p. (1966) *12,372*.

Gladstone, t., S. Mich., U.S.A.; harbour; mnfs. sports equipment; p. (1960) *5,267*.

Glamorgan, co., S. Wales; immense coal and iron deposits; copper and tin smelting; machin.; chemicals; co. t. Cardiff; a. 813 sq. m.; p. (1966) *1,252,000*.

Glamorgan, Vale of, see Gwent, Plain of.

Glarus, can., Switzerland; E. of Schwyz; a. 264 sq. m.; sheep, cheese, cottons; p. (1961) *40,148*.

Glarus, c., cap., can. G., Switzerland; on R. Linth, nr. Weesen; p. (1957) *5,724*.

Glasgow, c. burgh, Lanark, Scot.; on R. Clyde; third lgst. c. in Gr. Britain; many thriving mnfs; shipbldg., heavy and light engin., electronics equipment, printing; ctr. of great industrial belt; univ. and famous cath.; p. (estd. 1968) *949,000*.

Glasport, bor., Penns., U.S.A.; tools, steel, hoops, glass; p. (1960) *8,418*.

Glastonbury, t., mun. bor., Somerset, Eng.; at foot of Mendip Hills, 5 m. S.W. of Wells; noted 8th-century abbey with legend of thorn planted by Joseph of Arimathea, also adjacent to Avalon, burial I. of King Arthur; gloves, sheepskin rug and slipper mnfs.; p. (estd 1967) *6,220*.

Glatz, see Klodzko.

Glauchau, t., Karl-Marx-Stadt, E. Germany; on R. Mulde; woollens, calicoes, dyes, machin.; p. (1963) *33,370*.

Glazov, t., R.S.F.S.R., in Urals; saw-milling, metal inds.; p. (1959) *59,000*.

Gleiwitz, see Gliwice.

Glen, The, beautiful valley and resort in White Mountain dist. of New Hampshire, U.S.A.

Glen Affric, Inverness, Scot.; drained E. to Moray Firth; hydro-elec. scheme.

Glen Garry, Inverness, Scot.; used by Perth to Inverness rly. on S. approach to Drumochter Pass.

Glen Innes, hill t., N.S.W., Australia; alt. 3,518 ft.; pastoral and agr. dist.; p. (1966) *5,754*.

Glen More. Scottish valley traversed by Caledonian canal, from Fort William to Inverness; cattle-ranching being attempted.

Glen Roy, Inverness, Scot.; 15 m. N.E. of Fort William; remarkable terraces, remains of series of glacial lakes.

Glen Spean, Inverness, Scot.; used by Glasgow to Fort William rly.

Glencoe, Argyll, Scot.; S.E. of Ballachulish; scene of massacre of MacDonalds, 1692.

Glendale, t., Cal., U.S.A.; p. (1960) *119,442*.

Glendalough, valley, Wicklow, Ireland; scenic beauty; ecclesiastical ruins; tourists.

Glendora, t., Cal., U.S.A.; p. (1960) *20,752*.

Glenelg, R., S.W. Victoria, Australia; 200 m.

Glenelg, t., S. Australia; on Holdfast Bay; now incl. in met. a. of Adelaide; 1st settlement on mainland.

Glenoldon, bor., Penns., U.S.A.; surgical instruments; p. (1960) *7,249*.

Glenrothes, t., Fifeshire, Scot.; one of the "New Towns" designated 1948; coal, transistor factory, mng. machin.; photo precision ind.; p. (estd. 1965) *17,443*.

Glens Falls, t., N.Y., U.S.A.; on Hudson R.; lime kilns and many mnfs.; lumber, paper; p. (1960) *18,580*.

Glenside, t., S.E. Penns., U.S.A.; mnfs. rubber and wood prod.; paints, toys; p. (1950) *9,654*.

Glittertind, mtn., Opland co., S. Norway; highest peak in Scandinavia; alt. 8,140 ft.

Gliwice, (Gleiwitz), t., Upper Silesia, Poland; German before 1945; nr. Katowice; chemicals, iron and steel; p. (1965) *164,000*.

Globe, t., Ariz., U.S.A.; copper, manganese, gold, silver, vanadium, tungsten mining; p. (1960) *6,141*.

Glogow (Glogau), c., Poland, German before 1945; on R. Odra; cath.; sugar, wood, iron inds.; rly. junction; p. (1946) *1,681*.

Glommen R., Norway; lgst. Norwegian R.. flows S. in Skaggerak. [Albania.

Glossa, C. (see Gjhuëzës, C), strait, Otranto,

Glossop, mkt. t., mun. bor., Derby, Eng.; at W. foot of Pennines, 12 m. S.E. of Manchester; cotton, paper, food canning; p. (estd 1967) *19,480*.

Gloucestor, *co.*, W. of Eng.; fertile valleys, Cotswold Hills; dairying, cheese, sheep, coal machin., textiles, glass, broadcloth; a. 1,257 sq. m.; p. (1966) *1,054,000*.

Gloucester, *cath. c., co. bor.*, on R. Severn; aircraft mftg. and repair, wagon wks., engin., matches, nylon; p. (estd. 1967) *88,050*.

Gloucester, *t.*, Mass., U.S.A.; fishing; granite; p. (1960) *25,789*. [*21,741*.

Gloversville, *c.*, N.Y., U.S.A.; gloves; p. (1960)

Glyder Fach, *mtn.*, Caernarvonsh., N. Wales; alt. 3,262 ft. [3,279 ft.

Glyder Fawr, *mtn.*, Caernarvonsh., N. Wales; alt.

Glyncorrwg, *urb. dist.*, Glamorgan, Wales; 4 m. N. of Maesteg; coal, iron; p. (1961) *9,902*.

Gmünd, *t.*, Baden-Württemberg, Germany; on R. Rems, nr. Stuttgart; clocks, metallurgy, glass, costume jewellery; p. (estd. 1954) *34,100*.

Gniezno (Gnesen), *mftg. t.*, Poland; E. of Poznan cath.; linen; p. (1965) *47,000*.

Gôa, Daman and Diu, Union Terr. of, India, former Port. India; p. (1960) *626,978*.

Goajira, *peninsula* on G. of Maracaibo, N. cst. of S. America; crossed by bdy. of Venezuela and Colombia.

Goalunda, *pt.*, Pakistan; at junction of Rs. Ganges and Brahmaputra. [2,866 ft.

Goat Fell, *mtn.*, I. of Arran, Bute, Scot.; alt.

Gobi, steppes and stony or sandy desert in Central Asia; divided into two principal divs.; Shamo in Central Mongolia, and the basins of the Tarim, E. Turkestan; length about 1,500 m. (E. to W.), breadth 500–700 m.; average elevation 4,000 ft.; crossed by Kalgan–Ulan Bator highway.

Godalming, *t.*, *mun. bor.*, Surrey, Eng.; 4 m. S.W. of Guildford; 1st public supply of elec. 1881; tanning, timber yards, corn mills, knitwear; Charterhouse School; p. (estd. 1967) *17,810*.

Godavari, *R.*, India; flows E. across Deccan to Bay of Bengal; forms large delta; length 900 m.

Goderich, *pt.*, Ont., Canada; on S.E. cst. L. Huron; transh. wheat from prairies; p. (1961) *6,411*.

Godesberg, Bad, N. Rhine–Westphalia, Germany; nr. Bonn; famous Spa; chalybeate springs; p. (estd. 1954) *46,700*.

Godhavn, Danish settlement, Disco I., W. of Greenland; whaling; scientific sta.

Godhra, *t.*, Gujarat, India; timber tr.; tanneries; p. (1961) *52,167*.

Godstone, *vil.*, *rural dist.*, Surrey, Eng.; nr. Reigate; p. (1961) rural dist. *40,068*.

Godthaab, *t.*, Greenland; first Danish col. 1721.

Godwin Austen (K²), Mt., Himalaya, second highest in the world; alt. 28,250 ft. Summit reached by Prof. Desio in July 1954. Mt. named Chobrum. [(1961) *5,472*.

Gogo, *spt.*, Gujarat, India; on G. of Cambay; p.

Gogra, *see* Ghaghara R. [*47,631*.

Goiana, *t.*, Pernambuco st., Brazil; p. (estd. 1968)

Goiânia, *t.*, cap. Goiás st., Brazil; comm. and industl. ctr.; p. (estd. 1968) *345,085*.

Goiás, *st.*, Central Brazil; mountainous, forested; stock raising; tobacco; gold, diamonds; cap. Goiânia, on Vermelho R.; a. 247,900 sq. m.; p. (estd. 1968) *2,745,711*.

Golborne, *t.*, *urb. dist.*, Lancs, Eng.; man-made fibres; p. (1961) *26,100*.

Golconda, *fort and ruined c.*, nr. Hyderabad, S. India; famous for its legendary diamond troves.

Gold River, *t.*, B.C., Canada; on W. cst. of Vancouver I. at junct. of Heber and Gold Rs. new t. 1967.

Golden Gate, entrance of Bay of San Francisco, California, U.S.A.; famed Golden Gate Bridge, opened 1937. [the harbour of Istanbul.

Golden Horn, *peninsula* on the Bosporus, forming

Golden Triangle, the area of Britain and the continent roughly bounded by Birmingham, Frankfurt, and Paris, which incl. London and south-east England, northern France, the Ruhr, Belgium and Luxembourg, and the southern half of Holland.

Golden Vale, *dist.*, Limerick, Tipperary, Ireland; lies between Slieve Bloom Mtns. and Galtee Mtns., drained W. to Shannon and E. to Suir; rich farming a., beef and dairy cattle, pigs.

Golden Valley, *t.*, Minn., U.S.A.; p. (1960) *14,559*.

Goldsboro, *t.*, N.C., U.S.A.; on Neuse R.; cotton, tobacco; p. (1960) *28,873*.

Golspie, *co.t.*, Sutherland, Scot.; fishing pt.

Gomal Pass, from Afghanistan to W. Punjab, Pakistan over Sulaiman mtns.

Gomel, *t.*, Byelorussia S.S.R.; on R. Sozh; engin., chemicals, clothing inds.; p. (1959) *166,000*.

Gomera, *I.*, Canaries; 13 m. S.W. Tenerife; cap. San Sebastian; p. (1962) *30,747*.

Gometray I., Hebrides, included in co. Argyll, Scot.; fishing, sta., and harbour. [*21,000*.

Gonaives, *spt.*, Haiti, W. Indies; on W. cst.; p.

Gonda, *t.*, Uttar Pradesh, India; p. (1961) *43,496*.

Gondar, *t.*, Amhara prov., Ethiopia; p. *22,000*.

Good Hope, *t.*, N.W. Terr., Canada; on Mackenzie R.

Good Hope, C. of, *see* C. of Good Hope.

Goodenough Bay, *inlet*, N. coast of Papua, New Guinea.

Goodwin Sands, *dangerous sand-banks* off E. cst. of Kent, Eng.; shielding the Down roadstead.

Goole, *t. mun. bor.*, W.R. Yorks, Eng.; second pt. to Hull on Humber est.; iron, shipbldg., flour milling, fertilisers, alum and dextrine mftg.; p. (estd. 1967) *18,570*.

Goonhilly, Cornwall Eng.; space communications sta. of G.P.O.. likely to be one of most advanced satellite communication stas. in world.

Goose Bay, *t.*, Labrador, Canada; on Hamilton R.

Göppingen, *t.*, Baden–Württemberg, Germany; between Ulm and Stuttgart; machin., iron, wood, chemicals; p. (1963) *48,600*.

Gorakhpur, *t.*, Uttar Pradesh, India; on the Rapti R., 100 m. N. of Varanasi; grain, timber; fertilisers; Govt. agr. school; p. (1961) *180,255*.

Gore, *bor.*, Southland, S.I., N.Z.; p. (1966) *8,105*.

Gorgan, *c.*, Iran, Mazandaran prov.; p. (1967) *309,878*.

Gorgonzola, *t.*, N. Italy; 12 m. N.E. of Milan, famous for its cheese.

Gori, *t.*, Georgia, U.S.S.R.; grain, timber; p. (1961) *33,100*.

Gorinchem, *t.*, S. Holland, Netherlands; p. (1967) *24,786*.

Gorki (formerly Nizhni-Novgorod), *t.*, R.S.F.S.R.; at confluence of Rs. Oka and Volga; gr. comm. ctr.; engin., chemicals, petroleum refining, steel, textiles, cars, glass; p. (1967) *1,100,000*.

Gorleston, Norfolk. Eng.; at mouth of R. Yare; seaside resort; inc. in co. bor. of Gt. Yarmouth.

Görlitz, *t.*, Dresden, E. Germany; on W. Neisse R.; iron, wood, metallurgy, machin.; p. (1963) *89,578*.

Gorlovka, *t.*, Ukrainian S.S.R.; in Donets Basin; coal, chemicals, engin.; oil pipeline connects with Grozny oilfields; p. (1967) *348,000*.

Gorno-Altaysk, *t.*, R.S.F.S.R.; 60 m. S.E. of Biysk, nr. Chuya highway to Mongolia; p. (1959) *27,000*.

Gornyy Snezhnogorsk, *t.*, R.S.F.R.S.; new town in Siberian Arctic on R. Hantaiki, 35 m. W.N.W. Komsomolsk; tin mng.

Gorseinon, *vil.*, Glamorgan, S. Wales; nr. Loughour estuary, 4 m. N.W. of Swansea; steel-wks., zinc refineries.

Gort, *rural dist.*, Galway, Ireland; p. (1961) *8,187*.

Gorizia (Görz), *c.*, cap. Gorizia prov., N.E. Italy, cas.; agr. mkt., fruit, wine; cotton mills, textile mach.; p. (1961) *41,854*.

Göschenen, *vil.*, Switzerland; at W. end of St. Gotthard tunnel.

Gosford, *t.*, N.S.W., Australia: 50 m. N. of Sydney; resort and commuter t.; food processing, bldg. materials; p. (1966) *11,312*.

Gosforth, *t.*, *urb. dist.*, sub. to Newcastle-on-Tyne, Eng.; coal; p. (estd. 1967) *27,540*.

Goshen, *c.*, Ind., U.S.A.; p. (1960) *13,718*.

Goslar, *t.*, Lower Saxony, Germany; at foot of Harz Mtns.; clothing mnfs., wood inds.; rly junction; p. (1963) *41,000*.

Gosport, *mun. bor.*, *spt.*, Naval depot, Hants, Eng.; W. side of Portsmouth harbour; shipbldg., engin.; p. (estd. 1967) *75,320*.

Gossau, *vil.*, St. Gallen, Switzerland; embroidery, lace; agr. ctr.; butter and cheese wks,; p. *7,914*.

Göta, R., Sweden; flows from L. Vänern to the Kattegat; also canal connecting L. Vänern with the Baltic; the G. Canal provides a popular tourist trip from Stockholm to Göteborg.

Götaland, southernmost of 3 old provs. of Sweden; a. 39,000 sq. m.; name used only in weather forecasts.

Göteborg and Bohus, *prov.*, Sweden; on cst. of Kattegat; a. 1,989 sq. m.; p. (1961) *624,762*.

Göteborg, *c.*, *cap.*, Göteborg and Bohus, Sweden; at mouth of R. Göta; second c. in Sweden for commerce and ind.; shipbldg., oil refining; deepwater tanker terminal; p. (1960) *404,758*.

Gotha, *t.*, Erfurt, E. Germany; iron, machin. porcelain, printing, cartography; p. (1963) 56,611.

Gotland I., *fertile Swedish I.* in the Baltic; cap. Visby; a. 1,225 sq. m.; p. (1961) 54,322.

Gottesberg, *t.*, S.W. Poland; coal, mftg.; assigned to Poland at Potsdam conference; p. 8,000.

Göttingen, *t.*, Lower Saxony, Germany; univ.; scientific instruments, pharmaceutics, film studios; p. (1968) 112,560.

Gottwaldov (Zlin), *industl. t.*, ČSSR.; 40 m. E. of Brno; footwear, leather and domestic woodware inds.; p. (1961) 54,189.

Gouda, *t.*, S. Holland, Netherlands; on R. Hollandse IJssel, 11 m. from Rotterdam; cheese, candle mnfg.; ceramics, pipes; p. (1967) 46,823.

Gough I., Atl. Oc. dependency of St. Helena; breeding ground of the great shearwater.

Goulburn, *c.*, N.S.W., Australia; commands route across Gr. Dividing Range; in agr. dist. W. of Sydney; cath.; wool, shoes; p. (1966) 20,849.

Goulburn R., Victoria, Australia.

Gourock, *burgh*, Renfrew, Scot.; on Firth of Clyde, 2 m. W. of Greenock; p. (1961) 9,609.

Gouverneur, *t.*, N. N.Y., U.S.A.; mines talc, lead, zinc; mnfs. wood pulp, silk; p. (1960) 4,946.

Govan, *par.*, Lanark, Scot.; on the Clyde, part of Glasgow; shipbldg.; p. (1951) 312,911.

Governor's I., *fort*, Boston Harbour; also fortfd. islet in harbour of N.Y., U.S.A.

Govindpura, *t.*, Madhya Pradesh, India; nr. Bhopal; heavy elec. goods; p. (1961) 20,747.

Gower, *peninsula*, W. Glamorgan, Wales.

Gowerton, *vil.*, Glamorgan, S. Wales; 4 m. W. of Swansea; steel-wks.

Gowrie, Carse of, fertile tract N. side Firth of Tay, Scot.; includes Dundee, Kinnoul, Perth.

Goya, *t.*, Argentina; on R. Paraná; cattle; p. (1960) 40,000.

Gozo, *Br. I.* in Mediterranean, nr. Malta; the ancient Gaulos; surrounded by perpendicular cliffs; a. 26 sq. m.; p. 27,612.

Graaff-Reinet, *t.*, Cape Province, S. Africa; fruit growing, wool; p. (1960) 16,703 inc. 5,565 whites.

Graciosa, *I.*, Azores gr., N.W. of Terceira.

Grado, *commune*, Oviedo, N.W. Spain; iron foundries; p .(1957) 17,585.

Grado-Aquileia, N. Adriatic, prov. Gorizia, Italy; pleasure resort and former Roman spt.; rich in early Christian mosaics and other antiquities; p. (est.) 3,000.

Graengesberg, *dist.*, Kopparberg co., Sweden; on S. fringe of Scandinavian mtns.; iron ore deposits.

Grafton, *t.* N.S.W., Australia; on Clarence R.; dairy prod., timber; p. (1966) 15,944.

Graham, *t.*, N. Texas, U.S.A.; oil refining, flour milling; p. (1960) 8,505.

Graham I., the lgst. of the Queen Charlotte gr. in the Pacific; off cst. of Brit. Co umbia.

Graham Land, Falkland Is. Dependencies, Antarctica; mtnous, icebound; discovered 1832.

Grahamstown, *c.*, Cape Province, S. Africa; univ.; cath.; p. (1960) 32,611 inc. 10,668 Europeans.

Graian Alps, *mtns.* between Savoy and Piedmont; highest point Gran Paradiso; alt. 13,320 ft.

Grain Coast, general name formerly applied to cst. of Liberia, W. Africa; "grain" refers to pepper, spices, etc.

Grammichele, *t.*, E. Sicily, Italy; 23 m. S.W. of Catania; marble; p. 14,014.

Grammont, *t.*, E. Flanders, Belgium; nr. Ghent, on Dender R.; mftg; p. (1962) 9,585.

Grampians, *highest mtns.* of Scot.; highest point Ben Nevis; alt. 4,406 ft.; includes Cairngorms, high granitic mtns.

Granada, *prov.*, S. Spain; traversed by Sierra Nevada; wheat, olives, textiles, liqueurs, paper; a. 4,838 sq. m.; p. (1959) 779,434.

Granada, *ancient c.*, Granada, S. Spain; at foot of Sierra Nevada; formerly cap. of the Moorish Kingdom of G., now cap. of fertile maritime prov.; famous 14th-century Alhambra; p. (1959) 145,169.

Granada, *c.*, Nicaragua, Central America; distilling, soap, furniture; p. 38,918.

Granby, *c.*, Quebec, Canada; on Yamaska R.; sawmills, leather; p. (1961) 31,463.

Gran Chaco, *extensive dist.*, N. Argentina and Paraguay; flat with lge. areas of forest; quebracho.

Grand Bank, *submarine plateau*, extending S.E. from Newfoundland, Canada; a. 500,000 sq. m.; impt. cod fisheries.

Grand Bassam, *t.*, *spt.*, Ivory Cst., W. Africa; exp. bananas, palm-kernels; p. 5,743.

Grand Bahama, one of the Bahama Is., W. Indies; p. (1953) 4,095.

Grand Canal, *canal*, N. China; about 1,000 m. long from Tientsin to Hangchow; built between A.D. 605-18 and 1282-92; now silted up and cst. or rail transport more impt.

Grand Canal, main water thoroughfare through Venice, Italy. [(1962) 404,581.

Grand Canary, *I.*, Canaries; cap. Las Palmas; p.

Grand Canyon, Arizona, U.S.A.; narrow gorge, 3,000 to over 5,000 ft. deep of Colorado R.

Grand Cayman I., T.W.I.; a. 85 sq. m.; coconuts; cap. Georgetown; p. (estd. 1957) 6,636.

Grand Combin, *mtn.* in the Alps, N. of Aosta, Italy; alt. 14,141 ft. [14,458.

Grand-Comme (La.), *t.*, Gard, France; p. (1962)

Grand Coulée Dam, Wash., U.S.A.; across R. Columbia 110 m. below Spokane; world's lgst. dam; reservoir formed 151 m. long, a. 130 sq. m. supplies irrigation water to 1,900 sq. m. between Rs. Columbia and Snake; hydro-elec. power sta. when complete will generate 2,700,000 h.p.

Grande Chartreuse, La, *monastery*, Isère, France; 15 m. N. of Grenoble; famous for its liqueur.

Grande Prairie, *t.*, Alberta, Canada; wheat; p. 8,000.

Grand Forks, *t.*, N.D., U.S.A.; on Red R.; in wheat region; p. (1960) 34,451.

Grand Island, *c.*, Nebraska, U.S.A.; cattle and grain t.; p. (1960) 25,742.

Grand Junction, *t.*, Col., U.S.A.; p. (1960) 18,694.

Grand Lake, *lgst. L.*, Newfoundland; a. about 200 sq. m.

Grand Lahou, *t.*, Ivory Cst., W. Africa; p. 1,000.

Grand' Mère, *t.*, Quebec, Canada; pulp and paper mills; p. (1961) 15,806.

Grand Prairie, see Black Prairie.

Grand Rapids, *c.*, Mich., U.S.A.; on Grand R.; furniture mkg., car and aircraft parts, chemicals, paper; p. (1960) 177,313.

Grand R., Mich., U.S.A.; enters L. Mich. at Grand Haven, navigable to Grand Rapids; length 250 m.

Grand R., W. Colorado and E. Utah, U.S.A.; trib. of the Colorado R.; length 350 m.

Grand Turk I., *seat of government*, Turks and Caicos Is.; p. 1,693.

Grange, *t.*, *urb. dist.*, N. Lancs, Eng.; on N. cst. of Morecambe Bay; sm. summer resort; p. (1961) 3,117.

Grangemouth, *burgh*, Stirling, Scot.; on F. of Forth, 20 m. W. of Leith; shipbldg. and repair, marine engin., oil refining, petroleum prods., chemicals, pharmaceutics; electronics and elec. ind; oil pipeline to Finnart; p. (1961) 18,860.

Granite City, Ill., U.S.A.; p. (1960) 40,073.

Gran Sasso d'Italia, *rugged limestone highlands*, Abruzzi, Central Italy; highest part of Apennines, Monte Corno alt. 9,584 ft.; winter sports ctr., Aquila.

Grantham, *t.*, *mun. bor.*, Lincoln, Eng.; on Witham R.; tanning, agr. machin., engin., brewing, malting, basket mkg.; p. (estd. 1967) 26,350.

Grant Land, *region*, N. of Ellesmere I., Arctic Canada.

Grantown-on-Spey, *burgh*, Moray, Scot.; on R. Spey; health resort; p. (1961) 1,581.

Grants Pass, *t.*, S.W. Ore., U.S.A.; fruit growing; lumber, mining, fishing; p. (1960) 10,118.

Granville, *spt.*, *wat. pl.*, Manche, France; at mouth of the Bosq; fisheries; p. (1962) 11,482.

Granville, *sub.*, Sydney, N.S.W., Australia.

Grasmere, *vil.*, Westmorland, Eng.; at head of Grasmere L.; home of Wordsworth.

Grasse, *t.*, *health resort*, Alpes-Maritimes, S.E. France; perfumes; p. (1962) 27,226.

Graubünden (Grisons), *can.*, Switzerland; cap. Chur; a. 2,746 sq. m.; p. (1961) 147,458.

Graudenz, see Grudziadz.

's-Gravenhage, see Hague.

Graves, Pointe de, N. point of Médoc Peninsula, France; in famous wine dist.

Gravesend, *spt.*, *mun. bor.*, Kent, Eng.; S. bank R. Thames facing Tilbury; shipping, paper, cement, tyres, engin.; p. (estd. 1967) 54,930.

Gravina, *industl. c.*, Apulia, Italy; p. 20,775.

Gray's Peak, Rocky Mtns., Col., U.S.A.; alt. 14,341 ft.

Grays Thurrock, *urb. dist.*, Essex, Eng.; on the

Thames, nr. Tilbury Fort; oil refining, metal refining, cement, paper board, margarine, soap mftg.; p. (estd. 1967) *121,670*.

Graz, *t.*, Austria; on R. Mur; machin., iron and steel, rly. wks.; p. (1964) *249,000*.

Great Altai, *range of mtns.*, lying mainly in outer Mongolia but also in Western Siberia.

Great Atlas, *mtns.*, N.W. Africa; alt. 7,000 ft.

Great Australian Basin, *artesian basin*, Australia; underlies plains of S.W. Queensland, N.W. New South Wales, N.E. of S. Australia; water supply used on sheep-farms, cattle-ranches, in a. from Normanton in N. to Renmark in S., Ooodnadatta in W. to Roma in E.; a. 570,000 sq. m.

Great Australian Bight, *wide inlet*, S. of Australia, between C. Arid and Port Whidbey; 850 m.

Great Barrier Reef, *coral reef barrier*, off N.E. cst. of Australia; 1,000 m. long. 75–100 m. from cst; currently being eaten away by the starfish, *Acanthaster planci*.

Great Basin, *high plateau region* between the Wasatch and Sierra Nevada Mtns., U.S.A., inc. most of Nev., parts of Utah, Cal., Idaho, Ore., Wyo.; inland drainage ctr. Great Salt Lake; a. 210,000 sq. m.; much desert; sparse p.

Great Bear Lake, Arctic Circle, in N.W. Terr., Canada, over 150 m. long; a. 14,000 sq. m.; outlet through Great Bear R. to Mackenzie R.

Great Belt, *strait*, separating I. of Fyn from Sjaelland, Denmark.

Great Britain, *see* England, Scotland, Wales, British Isles.

Great Dividing Range, *mtn. system*, E. Australia; extends, under different local names, from Queensland to Victoria and separates E. cst. plains from interior; reaches max. alt. in Mt. Koskiusko (7,328 ft.), in Australian Alps, on bdy. between Victoria and New South Wales.

Great Falls, *t.*, Mont., U.S.A.; on Missouri R.; wool; gold, silver; lead and copper smelting; p. (1960) *55,357*.

Great Fish R., Cape Province, S. Africa.

Great Fisher Bank, *submarine sandbank* in N. Sea; 200 m. E. of Aberdeen, 100 m. S.W. of Stavanger; valuable fishing-ground; depth of water, from 25 to 40 fathoms.

Great Gable, *mtn.*, Cumberland, Eng.; alt. 2,949 ft.

Great Harwood, *t.*, *urb. dist.*, Lancs. Eng.; 5 m. N.E. of Blackburn; cotton weaving, textiles, engin.; p. (1961) *10,718*.

Great Karroo, Cape Province, S. Africa; high plateau; ostrich farming.

Great Lakes, N. America; comprising 5 fresh-water Ls.: Superior, Michigan, Huron, Erie, Ontario; frozen 4 to 5 months in winter; enormous L. traffic in cereals, iron, coal, etc.; a. 96,000 sq. m. *See* St. Lawrence Seaway. [pan.

Great Makarikari, Botswana, South Africa; salt

Great Namaqualand, S. region of S.W. Africa.

Great Ormes Head, *promontory*, N. Wales; nr. Llandudno.

Great Plains, *lowland area* of central N. America, extending E. from Rocky Mtns. and S. from Mackenzie to S. Texas.

Great Rift Valley, geological fault extending from S.W. Asia to E. Africa, 3,000 m. in length; includes L. Tiberias, Jordan Valley, Dead Sea, Gulf of Aqaba, Red Sea, and chain of Ls. from Rudolf to Nyasa; a branch runs through Ls. Tanganyika, Edward and Albert.

Great St. Bernard, *pass*, Switzerland. *See* K146.

Great Salt Lake, Utah, U.S.A.; in the Great Basin plateau of N. America; 90 m. long; a. over 2,000 sq. m.; alt. 4,218 ft.; receives Bear, Jordan and Beaver Rs.; no outlet.

Great Sandy Desert, N. part, W. Australia.

Great Slave Lake, N.W. Terr., Canada; length 300 m.; greatest breadth 50 m., outlet Mackenzie R.

Great Slave R., Canada, flowing between L. Athabaska and the Great Slave L.

Great Smoky Mtns., Tenn., U.S.A.; with Blue Ridge Mtns. form E. Zone of Appalachian Mtn. system; rise to alt. over 6,000 ft.; largely preserved as National Park.

Great Victoria Desert, W. and S. Australia, lies north of Nullarbor Plain.

Greater Antilles Is., W. Indies.

Greece, *kingdom*, S. part of Balkan Peninsula, bounded on N. by Albania, Jugoslavia and Bulgaria, on W. and S. by the Mediterranean, and on the E. by the Ægean Sea, and inc. Is. in the Mediterranean, Ægean and Ionian Seas;

cap. Athens; agr.: cereals, tobacco, currants, vines, fruit; sheep, goats, cattle; minerals: iron, lead, magnesite, lignite; mnfs.: olive oil, wine, textiles, chemicals, shipyds., oil refining; a. 51,182 sq. m.; p. (estd. 1965) *8,550,000*.

Greeley, *t.*, Col., U.S.A.; nr. Denver, site of st. college of education; lumber, flour; p. (1960) *26,314*.

Green Bay, *c.*, Wis., U.S.A.; tr. in timber, flour, etc., paper, coal; p. (1960) *62,888*.

Greenfield, *t.*, Mass., U.S.A.; p. (1960) *14,389*.

Greenhithe, Thames-side, nr. Dartford, Kent, Eng.

Greenland, *I.*, between Arctic Ocean and Baffin Bay; lofty ice-capped plateau; peopled by coastal settlements of Eskimos; whale oil, seal skins; some coal, lead, zinc; U.S. base at Thule; part of Danish kingdom; cap. Godthaab; a. 840,000 sq. m., of which 708,000 sq. m. are under a permanent ice-cap; p. (estd.) 33,000.

Greenlaw, *t.*, Berwick, Scot.

Green Mtns., Vermont section of Appalachian mtns; highest peak, alt. 4,430 ft.

Greenock, *spt.*, *burgh*, Renfrew, Scot.; on S. shore of Firth of Clyde, 20 m. W. of Glasgow; container facilities; shipbldg., sugar-refining, woollens, chemicals, aluminium casting, tin plate inds.; p. (1961) *74,578*.

Greenore, *cape*, Louth, Ireland; separating Dundalk Bay from Carlingford, Lough.

Green R., trib. of Grand R., Utah, U.S.A.; length 750 m. [p. (1960) *119,574*.

Greensboro', *c.*, N.C., U.S.A.; cotton, tobacco;

Greensburg, *t.*, Penns., U.S.A.; iron and glass factories; p. (1960) *17,383*.

Greenville, *t.*, Miss., U.S.A.; on Miss. R.; cotton tr.; p. (1960) *41,502*.

Greenville, *c.*, S.C., U.S.A.; in the cotton belt; p. (1960) *66,188*.

Greenville, Texas, U.S.A.; cotton, rayon, shipping; p. (1960) *19,087*.

Greenwich, *inner bor.*, London, Eng.; inc. most of former bor. of Woolwich on S. bank of R. Thames; famous for its Royal Observatory (now moved to Herstmonceux), Royal Naval College and National Maritime Museum; p. (1966) *232,000*.

Greenwood, *t.*, Miss., U.S.A.; p. (1960) *20,436*.

Greenwood, *t.*, S.C., U.S.A.; p. (1960) *16,644*.

Greifswald, *spt.*, Rostock, E. Germany; on Baltic inlet; shipbldg., textiles, wood inds.; p. (1963) *47,563*.

Greiz, *t.*, Gera, E. Germany; paper, textiles, chemicals; p. (1963) *38,470*.

Grenaa, *t.*, Randers, Jutland, Denmark; textiles, furniture, engin.; p. (1960) *9,088*.

Grenada, *I.*, *aut. st.* in association with Gt. Britain; W.I.; cap. St. George's; fruit, cocoa, spices a. (inc. the Grenadines) 133 sq. m.; p. (estd.) *102,000* (inc. some of the Grenadines).

Grenadines, *Brit. gr. of sma. Is.*, between Grenada and St. Vincent, Windward Is.; sea-island cotton.

Grenoble, *fortfd. c.*, Isère, S.E. France; on R. Isère; 60 m. from Lyons; gloves, buttons, machin., liqueurs, cement; joint Franco-German nuclear research reactor; p. (1968) 161,616. [(1960) *21,967*.

Gretna, *t.*, La., U.S.A.; on the Mississippi R.; p.

Gretna Green, *vil.*, Dumfriesshire, Scot., on Eng. border; famous as place of runaway marriages, 1754–1856.

Grey Range, *mtns.*, S.W. Queensland, Australia; extends S.W. from Gr. Dividing Range towards Flinders Range and Spencer G.; forms divide between streams draining E. to R. Darling and those draining W. to L. Eyre.

Greymouth, *spt.*, S.I., N.Z.; on W. cst. at mouth of Grey R.; ch. t. prov. of Westland; coal; p. (1966) *8,654*.

Griffin, *c.*, Ga., U.S.A.; cotton factories and tr.; p. (1960) *21,735*.

Grim, *C.*, N.W. Tasmania.

Grimaldi, *caves*, N.W. Italy; remains of prehistoric man, late Paleolithic, found there.

Grimsby, *spt.*, *co. bor.*, Lincoln, Eng.; on S. bank of R. Humber; Britain's major fishing pt., food processing; chemical ind. at nearby Immingham; p. (estd. 1967) *95,110*.

Grimsel Pass, Bernese Alps, Switzerland; alt. 7,100 ft.

Grindelwald, *vil.*, Bernese Oberland, Switzerland; tourist ctr.

Griqualand East, *dist.*, Cape Province, S. Africa;

pastures, wool; ch. t. Kokstad; a. 6,602 sq. m.; p. 265,000.

Griqualand W., dist., Cape Province, S. Africa; diamonds; ch. t., Kimberley; a. 15,197 sq. m.; p. 160,793. [French cst. to Dover.

Gris-Nez, C., N.E. France; nearest point on

Grisons (Graubünden), can., Switzerland; one-half only productive, many glaciers, contains the mtn. health resorts of Davos-Platz (alt. 5,115 ft.), St. Moritz (alt. 6,089 ft.), Arosa (alt. 6,108 ft.); a. 2,746 sq. m.; p. (1960) 145,600.

Grivegnee, t., Belgium; nr. Liége; ironwks.; p. (1962) 23,340.

Grodno, t., W. Byelorussia (Polish until 1939); agr.; engin., textiles, chemicals; p. (1959) 72,000.

Grodziaz Mazowiecki, commune, Poland; 12 m. S.W. of Warsaw; p. 18,737.

Gronau, t., N. Rhine–Westphalia, Germany; nr. Dutch frontier; textiles, rly. junction; p. (1963) 26,000.

Grong,spt.,Norway,on Falda Fjord; p. (1961) 2,052.

Groningen, c., cap. Groningen, Netherlands; comm. ctr.; univ.; woollens, glucose, shipbldg.; p. (1967) 156,208.

Groningen, prov., N.E. Netherlands; agr. and dairying; natural gas deposits at Slochteren; a. 883 sq m.; p. (1967) 508,173.

Groote Eylandt. I., G. of Carpentaria; off cst. of N. Terr., Australia; manganese ore mng.

Grootfontein, t., S.W. Africa; copper- and lead-mining; world's lgst. known meteorite on nearby farm; p. (1960) 3,722 inc. 1,195 whites.

Grosseto, prov., central Italy; ch. t. Grosseto, a. 1,735 sq. m.; p. (1963) 216,704.

Grosseto, t., cap. Grosseto prov., Central Italy; severely affected by heavy floods Nov. 1966; p. (1961) 51,004.

Groton, industl. t., Conn., U.S.A.; opp. New London at mouth of Thames R.; p. (1960) 10,111.

Grottaglie, t., Lecce, Apulia, Italy; nr. Brindisi; white glaze pottery; p. 14,850.

Grove City, bor., Penns., U.S.A.; engines, carriages; p. (1960) 8,368.

Groznyy, t., N. Caucasia, R.S.F.S.R.; on R. Terek; naphtha wells, refinery, engin.; starting point of oil pipelines to Makhachkala Tuapse and Gorlovka; p. (1967) 319,000.

Grudziadz (Graudenz), t., on R. Vistula, Polish Pomerania; sawmilling; p. (1965) 71,000.

Grünberg, see Zielona Gora.

Gruyère, dist., can. Fribourg, Switzerland; cheese.

Gstaad, fashionable summer and winter res., Bernese Oberland, Switzerland.

Guadalajara, c., Mexico; cap. of Jalisco st.; cotton and wool mnfs.; cath.; gas pipe-line from Salamanca; p. (1960) 736,800.

Guadalajara, prov., Spain; agr. and salt mines; a. 4,709 sq. m.; p. (1959) 195,637.

Guadalajara, mfg. t., G. prov., Spain; woollens, leather; p. (1957) 15,700.

Guadalaviar, R., E. Spain; flows into Mediterranean, nr. Valencia; length 130 m.

Guadalcanal, I., Brit. Solomon Is., Pac. Oc.

Guadalquivir, R., Spain; flows through Andalusia to Atlantic; length 375 m.

Guadalupe Hidalgo, t., Mexico; treaty signed 1848 ending Mexican–U.S. war; p. (estd.) 29,000.

Guadeloupe and Dependencies, Leeward gr.; a. 722 sq. m.; sugar produce; ch. pt. Pointe à Pitre; p. (1967) 320,000. French Overseas Dept.; Leeward gr. consists of Guadeloupe (p. 113,412, ch. t. Basse-Terre), Grande Terre p. (113,545, ch. t. Pointe à Pitre); united a. of Is., 583 sq. m.; and 5 smaller Is., Marie Galante, Désirade, St. Barthelemy and St. Martin (total p. 304,000) still inhabited by white descendants of French emigrants of 300 years ago; mountainous; rum, sugar, coffee, bananas.

Guadiana, R., forms part of Spanish and Portuguese frontier; flows into Bay of Cadiz; length 510 m.; Extremadura valley reclamation scheme in progress.

Guadiana del Caudillo, new t., nr. Badajoz, Spain; linen, hemp goods, cattle foods.

Guadix, c., Granada, S. Spain; cath.; hats, hemp, brandy, pottery, mats, carpets; p. (1957) 30,088.

Guaira, La, spt., Venezuela; motor road to Carácas; exp. hides, cocoa, coffee; p. (1961) 20,275.

Gualdo Tadino, commune, central Italy; cath.; pottery; p. 12,791.

Gualeguaychu, t., Entre Rios, Argentina; cattle and agr. ctr.; p. (1960) 43,000.

Guam, I., most S. and lgst. of Marianas Archipelago, N. Pacific; naval sta. of the U.S.A.; Polaris submarine base at Apra harbour; ch. t. Agaña and spt. is Piti; maize, sweet potatoes, bananas; a. 209 sq. m.; p. (1960) 67,044.

Guanabacoa, industl. t., nr. Havana, Cuba; p. 21,999.

Guanabara, st., Brazil; cap. Rio de Janeiro; p. (estd. 1968) 4,207,322. [p. (1963) 141, 523.

Guanacasta, prov., Costa Rica, Central America;

Guanajuato, st., Central Mexico; very fertile, productive and prosperous; a. 11,804 sq. m.; p. (1960) 1,735,490.

Guanajuato, ch. t., G. st., Mexico; 250 m. from Mexico c.; cotton, silver, lead; p. (1960) 23,379.

Guanta, spt., Anzoategui st., Venezuela, S. America; on Caribbean Sea, linked by road to Barcelona (10 m.); exp. oil.

Guantanamo, t., Cuba; sugar, coffee, bananas, cacao; p. (1965) 123,000.

Guapore, R., Brazil, S. America; joins the Mamore; length 900 m. [9,094.

Guarda, t., Portugal; alt. over 3,000 ft.; p. (1960)

Guarda, vine-growing dist., Portugal; between Rs. Tagus and Douro; p. (1963) 279,100.

Guardafui, C., most E. point of Africa.

Guatemala, republican st., Central America; adjoins Mexico, Br. Honduras and El Salvador, coffee, bananas, chicle; lead, zinc, and cadmium mined in sm. quantities; a. 45,452 sq. m.; p. (estd. 1968) 4,864,000.

Guatemala City, cap. c., Guatemala; cath.; univ.; minerals: gold, silver, copper, lead; p. (estd. (1965) 573,000.

Guayaquil, ch. pt., Ecuador, S. America; on Guayas R., 30 m. above its entrance to the Bay of Guayaquil; devastated by fire in 1896 and 1899; univ.; cath.; sawmills, foundries, machin., brewing; p. (1963) 506,000.

Guayas, prov., Ecuador; cap. Guayaquil; a. 8,331 sq. m.; p. (1960) 525,600.

Guaynabo, t., Puerto Rico W.I.; p. (1960) 40,257.

Gubat, mun., Luzon, Philippine Is.; hemp, coconuts, sugar-cane region; p. 22,850.

Gubbio, t., Perugia Italy; lustre ware; p. 30,850.

Gubin (Guben), t., R. pt., on R. Neisse between E. Germany and Poland; formerly in Prussian prov. of Brandenburg; comm. ctr.; textiles, machin., leather, synthetic fibre; p. (estd. 1939) 45,800.

Gudbrandsdal, gr. valley, S. Norway; leads S.E. from Dovre Fjeld towards Oslo; drained by R. Logan; used by main road Oslo to Trondheim; provides relatively lge. a. of cultivable land; hay, oats, barley, dairy cattle.

Gudiyatam, t., Tamil Nadu, India; p. (1961) 50,384.

Guebwiller, t., Haut-Rhin, France; cottons; p. (1962) 10,864.

Guelph, c., Ontario, Canada; cloth, yarn, pottery, agr. and veterinary colleges; p. (1961) 39,838.

Guernsey, Channel Is., between cst. of France and England; tomatoes, grapes (under glass), flowers, cattle; tourist res.; t. and ch. spt. St. Peter Port; a. 15,654 acres; p. (1961) (inc. Herm and Jethou) 45,126.

Guerrero, Pacific st., Mexico; cereals, cotton, coffee, tobacco; cap. Chilpancingo; ch. pt. Acapulco; a. 24,885 sq. m.; p. (1960) 1,186,716.

Guiana, region, S. America; a. 179,000 sq. m.; comprises Guyana and Fr. Guiana and Surinam.

Guiana Highlands, plateau, S. America; extend approx. 900 m. from E. to W. across S. parts of Venezuela, Guyana, Surinam, Fr. Guiana; steep sides, rounded tops approx. 3,000 ft. alt. but rise to 9,350 ft. in Mt. Roraima; chiefly composed crystalline rocks rich in minerals.

Guienne, old French prov., separated by R. Garonne from Gascony.

Guildford, c., co. t., mun. bor., Surrey, Eng.; 30 m. S.W. London; on gap cut by R. Wey through N. Downs; cath.; univ.; vehicles, agr. implements, light inds.; residl., p. (estd. 1967) 55,470.

Guinea, ind. rep. (Oct. 1958), formerly Fr. Guinea; member of Union of African States; iron-ore, bauxite, diamonds, groundnuts, palm oil; cap. Conakry; a. 97,000 sq. m.; p. (1963) 3,795,000.

Guinea, general name for W. African coastlands round the greatest bend of G. of G. from the Gambia to the Congo.

Guinea, Portuguese. See Portuguese Guinea.

Guinea, Spanish. See Equatorial Guinea.

Guinea Current, *ocean current*, flows W. to E. along Guinea Cst., diverted away from cst. in Bight of Benin by C. Three Points. [22,669.

Güines, *t.*, Havana, Cuba, W. Indies; sugar; p.

Guinobatan, *mun.*, Luzon, Philippine Is.; hemp; lime deposits; p. *26,419.*

Guipuzcoa, *Basque prov.*, Spain; mftg., minerals. agr.; cap. San Sebastian; tourism; a. 728 sq. m.; p. (1959) *455,388.*

Guisborough, *t.*, *urb. dist.*, N.R. Yorks, Eng.; in Cleveland iron-mng.; a. S.E. of Middlesbrough; steel, sawmilling, clothing; p. (1961) *12,079.*

Gujarat, *st.*, India; formerly part of Bombay st.; cap. temporarily Ahmedabad; new cap. Gandhinager, 13 m. N. of A. under construction; oil development in Cambay area; fertiliser plant projected; a. 72,245 sq. m.; p. (1961) *20,633,350.*

Gujranwala, *c.*, W. Pakistan; N. of Lahore; power plant projected; p. (1951) *120,860.*

Gujrat, *t.*, W. Pakistan; on Chenab R.; pottery and furniture; p. (1941) *22,000.* [*53,000.*

Gukhovo, *t.*, N. Caucasus, R.S.F.S.R.; p. (1959)

Gulbarga, *t.*, Gulbarga dist., Mysore, India; oil, cotton, flour, paint; p. (1961) *97,069.*

Gulf Basin, W. Australia; artesian well basin.

Gulfport, *t.*, Miss., U.S.A.; p. (1960) *30,204.*

Gulf Stream, current of the Atlantic, issuing from Gulf of Mexico by Florida Strait.

Gulf Stream Drift, *see* North Atlantic Drift.

Gummersbach, *t.*, N. Rhine–Westphalia, Germany; textiles, leather, metallurgy, paper, machin.; p. (1963) *32,400.*

Gumti, *R.*, trib. of Ganges, India; flows past Lucknow. [p. (1961) *187,122.*

Guntur, *t.*, Andhra Pradesh, India; cotton mftg.;

Gurgan (Asterabad), *t.*, N. Persia; nr. S.E. end of Caspian Sea; carpets, cotton, rice.

Guryev, *t.* Kazakh S.S.R.; on mouth of R. Ural, entrance to Caspian Sea; petrol refining, engin.; oil pipeline to Orsk; p. (1959) *78,000.*

Gus-Khrustalnyy, *t.*, R.S.F.S.R., 40 m. S. of Vladimir; impt. ctr. of glass ind.; p. (1959) *53,000.*

Güstrow, *t.*, Schwerin, E. Germany; S. of Rostock; cas.; steel and wood inds.; rly. junction; p. (1963) *38,897.*

Gütersloh, *t.*, N. Rhine–Westphalia, Germany; nr. Bielefeld; silk and cotton inds.; famous for its Pumpernickel (Westphalian rye bread); machin., furniture, publishing, metallurgy; p. (1963) *53,300.*

Guyana, *indep. sov. st.* within Brit. Commonwealth (1966), S. America; flat, swampy cst., interior highlands; climate, very hot, heavy rainfall along cst.; tropical forests; agr.; sugar, rice, coffee; cattle; hardwoods; minerals; bauxite, diamonds, gold, manganese; copper in Cuyuni and Groete Creek areas; iron ore nr. Essequibo estuary; molybdenum at Eagle Mt.; fisheries; poor communications; cap. Georgetown; a. 83,000 sq. m.; p. (estd.) *730,000*; became a co-operative republic in 1970.

Gwadar, *t.*, W. Pakistan; p. *15,000.*

Gwalior, *dist.*, Madhya Pradesh, India; a. 2,002 sq. m.; p. (1961) *657,576.*

Gwalior, *t.*, Madhya Pradesh, India, formerly Lashkar, 76 m. S. of Agra; cotton spinning, muslin, carpets, cereals, sugar-cane; bauxite; p. (1961) *300,587* inc. Morar. [Pakistan.

Gwatar, *spt.* on G. of Oman, Persia; by border of

Gwelo, *t.*, Rhodesia; impt. indust. ctr.; p. (1961) *37,590* inc. *8,590* Europeans.

Gwent, Plain of (Vale of Glamorgan), *lowland dist.*, Glamorgan, S. Wales; lies S. of moorland of S. Wales Coalfield, extends E. into Monmouth; fertile soils; mixed farming except in industl. areas of Cardiff. Barry.

Gympie, *t.*, Queensland, Australia; on Mary R., 106 m. from Brisbane; former goldfield; now dairying and pastoral dist., tropical fruits, especially pineapples; p. (1966) *11,277*

Györ, *c.*, Hungary; at junction of R. Raab with arm of R. Danube; cath.; horses, textiles. chemicals, engin., rolling stock, bridge parts, p. (1962) *72,319.*

H

Haarlem, *t.*, cap. N. Holland prov., Netherlands; textiles, printing, brewing, bulb growing; cath.; p. (1967) *172,263.*

Habab, *dist.*, W. coast Red Sea, Ethiopia.

Hachioji, *c.*, Honshu, Japan; weaving, silk-cotton mixtures; p. (1964) *178,000.*

Hackensack, *t.*, N.J., U.S.A.; iron foundries, silk, jewellery, paper; p. (1960) *30,521.*

Hackney, *inner bor.*, N.E. London, Eng.; incorporates former bors. of Shoreditch and Stoke Newington; furniture, clothing, footwear; p. (1966) *251,000.*

Haddington, *burgh, cap.*, E. Lothian, Scot.; on R. Tyne 16 m. E. of Edinburgh; woollen mnf.; grain mkt., corn mills, lt. engin., hosiery; p. (1961) *5,506.*

Haderslev, *t.*, Denmark; tobacco, clothing, knitted goods p. (1960) *19,735.*

Hadhramaut, *dist.*, Southern Yemen; ch. pt. and c. Mukalla; fertile coastal valley; frankincense, aloes, tobacco, shawls, carpets; p. *150,000* (estd.).

Hadsund, *t.*, Jutland, Denmark; p. (1960) *3,424.*

Hafnarfjördur, *t.*, S. of Reykjavik, Iceland; p. (1962) *7,490.*

Hagen, *t.*, N. Rhine–Westphalia, Germany, N.E. of Wuppertal; iron, steel, chemicals, textiles, paper; p. (1968) *200,266.*

Hagenau, *t.*, Bas-Rhin, France; textiles, porcelain, soap, beer; p. (1962) *21,841.*

Hagerstown, *c.*, Md., U.S.A.; machin., furniture, chemicals; p. (1960) *36,660.*

Hagonoy, *mun.*, Luzon, Philippine Is.; maize, rice, sugar.

Hague, C. de La, Cotentin Peninsula, France; French fleet defeated by British 1692.

Hague, The, or 's-Gravenhage or Den Haag, *t.*, S. Holland, Netherlands; seat of government; permanent court of international justice; adm. ctr.; urban inds., mach. and metal wares; engin., printing; p. (1967) *586,187.*

Haifa, *ch. spt.*, Israel; on Bay of Acre at foot of Mt. Carmel; terminus of Iraq oil pipeline; inds. include oil refining, car assembly, steel, chemical wks, petro-chemicals; Technion univ.; p. (estd. 1951) *190,000.*

Hail, *t.*, Neid, Saudi Arabia; p. over *10,000.*

Hailsham, *mkt. t.*, *rural dist.*, Sussex, Eng.; 5 m. N. of Eastbourne; mats, rope and twine; p. (rural dist. 1961) *42,372.*

Hainan, *I.*, S. coast of China; ch. t. Kiungchow; densely wooded, camphor, mahogany, rosewood; a. 13,974 sq. m.

Hainaut, *prov.*, Belgium, adjoining N.E. border of France; industl. and agr.; coal- and iron-mines; a. 1,436 sq. m.; p. (1968) *1,336,677.*

Hainburg, *t.*, Austria; on R. Danube; tobacco; Roman remains; p. (1961) *6,437.*

Haine, *R.*, Belgium and Nord, France; trib. of R. Scheldt; length 40 m.

Haiphong, *t.*, *ch. port*, N. Viet-Nam; thriving tr.; cotton, thread, soap, glass, enamel ware, fish canning; p. (1960) *369,000.*

Haiti, *rep.* (the "Black Republic"), W. Indies; consists of W. portion of I. of Hispaniola; cap. Port au Prince; language French; coffee, sisal, sugar, textiles, soap, cement, rum; a. 10,204 sq. m.; p. (estd. 1969) *4,768,000.*

Hakodate, *spt.*, Hokkaido, Japan; fishing ctr., sulpher, dried fish, timber; p. (1965) *243,413.*

Hal, *t.*, central Belgium; flax; p. (1962) *19,508.*

Halberstadt, *c.*, Magdeburg, E. Germany; cath.; metallurgy, rubber inds., engin.; rly. junction; p. (1963) *46,355.*

Halden, *t.*, S.E. Norway; wood-pulp, paper, footwear, cotton spinning; nuclear research reactor; p. (1960) *10,006.*

Haldensleben, *t.*, Magdeburg, E. Germany; leather, stoneware; p. (1963) *21,254.*

Haldia, *pt.*, W. Bengal, India; nr. mouth of R. Hooghli; satellite pt. for Calcutta to handle coal, ore, crude; oil pipeline to Barauni; refinery.

Halesowen, *industl. t.*, *mun. bor.*, S.W. of Birmingham, Worc., Eng.; coal, weldless tubes, elec. gds., stainless steel forgings, engin.; p. (estd. 1967) *50,390.*

Halesworth, *t.*, *urb. dist.*, E. Suffolk, Eng.; on R. Blyth 7 m. S. of Beccles; farming, corn mills, malting, engin.; p. (1961) *2,252.*

Halifax, *spt.*, *cap.*, Nova Scotia, Canada; gr. tr.; univ.; naval sta. and dockyard, open in winter; machin., iron foundries, boots and shoes, oil refining; p. (1961) *183,946.*

Halifax, *t.*, *co. bor.*, W.R. Yorks, Eng.; E. flanks Pennines, 8 m. S.W. of Bradford; carpets, textiles and machine tools; p. (estd. 1967) *94,770.*

Hall Peninsula, S.E. Baffin Land, Canada; between Cumberland Sound and Frobisher Bay.

Halland, *co.*, Sweden: a. 1,901 sq. m.; p. (1961) 170,060.

Halle, *t.*, Halle, E. Germany; on R. Saale: univ.; lignite, potash, engin., chemicals; p. (1963) 278,729.

Hallein, *t.*, Salzburg, Austria; on Austro-German frontier, 13 m. S. of Salzburg; impt. salt-mines; p. (1961) 13,329.   [culture type site.

Hallstatt, *vil.*, Upper Austria; early Iron Age

Halluin, *frontier industl. t.*, Nord, France; on R. Lys; p.   (2) 14,138.

Halmahera, *I.*, Indonesia; mountainous, active volcanoes, tropical forests; spices, pearl fisheries; grows sago and rice; a. 6,648 sq. m.

Halmstad, *spt.*, Kattegat, Sweden; iron and steel wks., machin. engin., cycles, textiles, leather, jute, wood-pulp; p. (1961) 39,032.

Hals, *t.*, Jutland, Denmark; on Lim Fjord.

Halstead, *t.*, *urb. dist.*, Essex, Eng.; on R. Colne, 12 m. N.W. of Colchester; rayon weaving, farming; p. (1961) 6,465.   [p. (estd. 1967) 50,660.

Haltemprice, *t.*, *urb. dist.*, E. Riding, Yorks, Eng.;

Haltom City, *t.*, Texas, U.S.A.; p. (1960) 23,133.

Haltwhistle, *mkt. t.*, *rural dist.*, Northumberland, Eng.; on R. Tyne; coal, paint wks., agr.; p. (rural dist. 1961) 6,884.

Hama, *c.*, Upper Syria; on R. Orontes; the ancient Hamath, cap. of a kingdom in time of Kings David and Solomon; cement wks.; p. (1961) 116,362.

Hamadan, *dist.*, W. Iran; cap. Hamadan; p. (1967) 888,663.

Hamadan, *(anc. Ecbatana)*, *c.* Iran, cap. prov.; carpets, pottery; airpt.; tomb of Avicenna; p. (1967) 553,598.

Hamamatsu, *t.*, S. Honshu, Japan; on cst. plain 60 m. S.E. of Nagoya; ctr. of rich agr. mftg. region; textiles, dyeing, musical instruments, motor cycles; p. (1964) 370,000.

Hamar, *t.*, Norway; on L. Mjösa; ctr. of rich agr. dist.; tr. and mftg. inds.; p. (estd. 1960) 13,000.

Hamburg, *Land*, W. Germany; cap. Hamburg; a. 299 sq. m.

Hamburg, *gr. spt.*, *industl. and comm. t.*, *Land* Hamburg, N. Germany; astride R. Elbe, 85 m. upstream from N. Sea; second lgst. German t.; and ch. pt.; univ. and hydrographic institute; handles vast tr., inc. liner traffic and barge traffic down Elbe from Saxony and Bohemia (Czechoslovakia), also much trans-shipment of goods; imports fuel, raw materials for inds., foodstuffs; exports textiles, leather goods, chemicals, light-engin. prod.; ch. inds., shipbldg., fishing, food processing, leather, brewing, tobacco, textiles, rubber, oil, wood; impt. airport; p. (1968) 1,823,000.

Hamburg, *t.*, N.Y., U.S.A.; optical goods: mkt. gardening; p. (1960) 9,145.

Hamburg, *bor.*, S.E. Penns., U.S.A.; coal, mnfs.; p. (1950) 3,805.

Hame (Tavastehus), *dep.*, Finland; a. 7,118 sq. m.; p. (1966) 608,091.

Hamelin (Hameln), *t.*, Lower Saxony, Germany; on R. Weser; iron, textiles; legend of " The Pied Piper "; p. (1963) 49,500.

Hamilton, *t.*, *pt.*, Bermuda I.; cap. Bermudas; tourism; p. (estd. 1957) 3,000.

Hamilton, *t.*, W. Victoria, Australia; mkt. ctr. for dairying and grazing a.; p. (1966) 10,052.

Hamilton, *c.* and *L. pt.*, S.E. Ontario, Canada; at W. end of L. Ontario; varied metallurgical mnfs.; fruit ctr.; univ.; p. (1966) 449,116.

Hamilton, *c.*, N.I., N.Z., on Waikato R.; univ.; p. (1966) 63,000.

Hamilton, *burgh*, Lanark, Scot.; in Clyde valley, 10 m. S.E. of Glasgow; co. admin. hdqtrs.; elec. goods, iron and steel foundries, carpet mftg., cotton, woollen and knit-wear goods; p. (1961) 41,928.

Hamilton, *c.*, Ohio, U.S.A.; on the Gr. Maine R., thriving ind. and tr.; p. (1960) 72,354.

Hamilton, *R.*, *see* Churchill R.

Hamm, *t.*, N. Rhine–Westphalia, Germany; on R. Lippe, nr. Dortmund; rly. marshalling yards, iron inds.; p. (1963) 71,300.

Hamme, *t.*, E. Flanders, Belgium; rope, linen and lace factories; p. (1962) 16,880.

Hammerfest, *spt.*, Norway; world's most northerly t.; fishing; p. (1961) 5,604.

Hammersmith, *Thames-side inner bor.*, London, Eng.; inc. former bor. of Fulham; industl., residtl.; elec. and car accessories, synthetic rubber; p. (1966) 214,000.

Hammond, *c.*, Ind., U.S.A.; ironwks., pork packing; p. (1960) 111,698.

Hammond, *t.*, La., U.S.A.; strawberry culture; p. (1960) 10,563.

Hamoaze, estuary of R. Tamar, Plymouth, Eng.

Hampshire, *co.*, Eng.; ch. town Southampton: farming; shipbldg., brewing, tanning; a. 1,503 sq. m.; p. (1966) 1,483,000.

Hampstead, *see* Camden.

Hampton, *Thames-side t.*, inc. in Richmond upon Thames, outer London bor., Eng.; Hampton Court Palace in the par.; Hampton Wick is a mile E. of H. Court.

Hampton, *t.*, S.E. Va., U.S.A.; oldest English community in the U.S.; fishing, oyster and crab packing; p. (1960) 89,258.

Hamtramck, *t.*, Mich., U.S.A.; p. (1960) 34,137.

Han, *R.*, Hupeh, China; rises in S.W. Shensi prov., flows E. between Tsingling mtns. and Tapa range of N. Szechwan into Yangtze R. at Wuhan; ch. trib. of Yangtze; length *c.* 800 m.

Han, *R.*, S. China; forms rich agr. delta nr. Swatow; length *c.* 250m.

Hanau, *t.*, Hessen, Germany, on R. Main; rubber and non-ferrous metals inds., jewellery; p. (1963) 48,500.

Hanchung, *c.*, S.W. Shensi prov., China; on Han R.; nr. Szechwan border; agr. and tr. ctr.; former Nancheng; p. 85,000.

Hancock, *t.*, Mich., U.S.A.; copper-mines; iron and brass mnfs.; p. (1960) 5,022.

Hangchow (Hangzhou), *c.*, *cap.*, Chekiang, China; head of H. Bay; former treaty pt.; extensive tr.; ctr. of silk-weaving ind.; p. (1953) 697,000.

Hanko, *t.*, on S. point, Finland; p. (1966) 9,414.

Hankow, *c.*, *former treaty pt.*, Hupeh, China; 700 m. from mouth of Yangtze R.; great tea mart, iron and steel wks., textiles, flour. *See* also Wuhan.

Hanley, *industl. t.* (now inc. in co. bor. of Stoke-on-Trent), Staffs, Eng.; pottery, china.

Hannibal, *c.*, Mo, U.S.A.; on R. Mississippi; timber and wagon bldg.; p. (1960) 20,028.

Hanoi, *c.*, *cap.*, N. Viet-Nam; ancient " Ke-Sho " or " great market " on the Red R.; old Annamese fort, now modern comm. ctr.; univ.; cotton, silks, tobacco, pottery; superphosphate and magnesium phosphate nearby; bricks, concrete, rubber; p. (1960) 644,000.

Hanover, *t.*, *cap.*, Lower Saxony, Germany; W. of Brunswick; iron, textiles, machin., paper, biscuits, cigarettes, cars, rubber processing, chemicals; gr. route ctr.; p. (1968) 521,904.

Hanover, *bor.*, Penns., U.S.A.; mnfs. shoes, jute, wire cloth; p. (1960) 15,538.

Hanwell, *t.*, Middlx., Eng.; on R. Brent; p. (1961) 24,991.

Hanyang, *industl. c.*, China; opp. Hankow, on Yangtze R; lge. iron wks. *See also* Wuhan.

Haparanda, *spt.*, N. Sweden; salmon fishing; exp., timber, and prod. of the Lapps; p. (1961) 3,394.

Hapur, *t.*, W. Uttar Pradesh, India; tr. in sugar, timber, cotton, brassware; p. (1961) 55,248.

Harar, *cap.* Harar prov., Ethiopia; hides and skins, ivory, cattle; p. approx. 25,000.

Harbin, *c.*, Heilungkiang, China; former treaty pt.; rly. junction; soya-beans, flour, tanning, distilling; machin.; p. (1953) 1,163,000.

Harbour Grace, *t.*, *pt.*, Conception Bay, Newfoundland, Canada; p. (1961) 2,650.

Harburg, *spt.*, Hanover, Germany; on R. Elbe, nr. Hamburg; linseed-crushing, india-rubber ind., etc.

Hardanger Fjord, W. cst. Norway; 75 m. long.

Hardt Mtns., W. Germany; northward continuation of Vosges on W. of Rhine rift valley; formerly forested, now lgely cleared for pasture; highest points reach just over 2,000 ft.

Hardwar, *t.*, Uttar Pradesh, India; on R. Ganges; gr. annual fair and pilgrimage; p. (1961) 58,513.

Harelbeke, *t.*, N.W. Belgium; p. (1962) 16,998.

Hargeisa, *t.*, Somalia; comm. ctr. of livestock-raising region; airpt.

Hariana, *st.*, India, formed 1966 when Punjab st. was partitioned on linguistic basis; Hindu speaking; joint cap. with Punjab st. Chandigarh until its own cap. is built; p. (estd. 1966) 7,000,000.

Haringey, *outer bor.*, Greater London, Eng.; comprising former bors. of Hornsey, Tottenham and Wood Green; p. (1966) 255,000.

Hari-Rud, *R.*, N. Afghanistan and Iran; the ancient " Arius "; length 650 m.; (*Rud* = river).

Harlech, *t.*, Merioneth, Wales; on Cardigan Bay, 10 m. N. of Barmouth; famous cas.; farming.

Harlen, *R.*, N.Y., U.S.A.; and Spuyten Duyvil Creek together form a waterway *c.* 8 m. long, extending from the East R. to Hudson R., and separates the bors. Manhattan and Bronx.

Harlingen, *spt.*, Friesland, Netherlands; margarine, mixed farming, fish; natural gas; p. 10,400.

Harlow, *t.*, Essex, Eng.; in valley of R. Stort, 22 m. N.E. of London; one of "New Towns" designated 1947; spreads S.W. from nucleus of old mkt. t. of Harlow; engin., glass, furniture mkg., metallurgy; p. (estd. 1967) 71,370.

Harnosand, *t.*, Sweden; on G. of Bothnia; engin., saw-mills, pulp, graphite prod.; p. (1961) 17,163.

Harpenden, *t.*, *urb. dist.*, Herts, Eng.; in Chiltern Hills, 5 m. N. of St. Albans; Rothamsted agr. experimental sta.; rubber, hosiery, basket mftg., engin.; p. (estd. 1967) 22,020.

Harringay, *see* Haringey.

Harris, *par.*, Lewis I., Outer Hebrides, Scot.; inc. several sm. islets; tweeds, fishing; p. 4,467.

Harrisburg, *c.*, *cap.*, Penns., U.S.A.; iron, steel factories, machin., cigarettes, cotton goods; p. (1960) 79,697.

Harrisburg, *t.*, Ill., U.S.A.; p. (1960) 9,171.

Harrison or East Newark, *industl. t.*, N.J., U.S.A.; p. (1960) 11,743.

Harrogate, *t.*, *mun. bor.*, *spa*, W.R. Yorks, Eng.; in valley of R. Nidd, 14 m. N. of Leeds; numerous chalybeate springs; p. (estd. 1967) 60,720.

Harrow, *outer bor.*, Greater London, Eng.; famous public school; camera mftg.; p. (1966) 209,000.

Harstad, *ch. t.*, Lofoten Is., N.W. Norway; herring ind., woollen goods; p. (1960) 4,023.

Hart Fells, *mtn.*, between Peebles and Dumfries, Scot.; alt. 2,651 ft.

Hartebeestpoort Dam, Transvaal, Rep. of S. Africa; on R. Crocodile (Limpopo), 25 m. W. of Pretoria; supplies water for cultivation, under irrigation, of cotton, maize, tobacco.

Hartford, *cap.*, Conn., U.S.A.; lge. comm. ctr., seat of Trinity College; small arms, typewriters, elec. machin., aircraft engin., ceramics, plastics; p. (1960) 162,178.

Hartford City, Ind., U.S.A.; p. (1960) 8,053.

Hartland Point, Barnstaple Bay, N. Devon, Eng.

Hartlepool, *spt.*, *co. bor.*, Durham, Eng.; on E. cst., 3 m. N. of estuary of R. Tees; iron inds., shipbldg., light inds., timber; good sands for holiday-makers to the S.; p. (estd. 1967) 98,040.

Hartsville, *t.*, S.C., U.S.A.; cotton, rayon, silk, textiles; nuclear power plant being built; p. (1960) 6,392.

Harvey, *t.*, N.E. Ill., U.S.A.; rolling stock, diesel engines, heavy machin.; p. (1960) 29,071.

Harwell, *vil.*, Berkshire, Eng.; 12 m. S. of Oxford; Atomic Energy Research Estab.; nuclear power research and prod. of radioisotopes.

Harwich, *spt.*, *mun. bor.*, Essex, Eng.; on S. cst. of estuary of R. Stour; packet sta. for Belgium, Netherlands, Denmark; docks, container facilities, naval base; p. (estd. 1967) 14,400.

Harz Mtns., *range* in Hanover and Brunswick, Germany; highest peak the Brocken; 1,142 m. forested slopes rich in minerals; length 57 m.

Haslemere, *mkt. t.*, *urb. dist.*, Surrey, Eng.; 13 m. S.W. of Guildford, on hills of Hindhead and Blackdown; residtl.; lt. inds.; p. (1961) 12,528.

Haslingden, *t.*, *mun. bor.*, Lancs, Eng.; on Rossendale Fells, 3 m. S. of Accrington; cotton, stone quarrying, engin.; p. (estd. 1967) 14,150.

Hasselt, *t.*, prov. Limbourg, Belgium; gin distilleries; p. (1962) 37,198.

Hassi Messoud, *t.*, Algeria, Africa; lge. oilfield; 24 inch pipe-line to Bejaia.

Hassi R'Mel, *t.*, Algeria, Africa; natural gas.

Hastings, *t.*, *co. bor.*, E. Sussex, Eng.; on S. cst., midway between Beachy Head and Dungeness; seaside resort; one of the Cinque Ports; p. (estd. 1967) 66,850.

Hastings, *t.*, N.I., N.Z.; on Hawke's Bay, nr. Napier; p. (1966) 26,867.

Hastings, *t.*, Nebraska, U.S.A.; p. (1960) 21,412.

Hastings-on-Hudson, *t.*, N.Y., U.S.A.; residtl.; copper wire; p. (1960) 8,979.

Hatay (formerly Sanjak of Alexandretta), ceded to Turkey by France 1939; p. (1960) 441,209.

Hatfield, *t.*, Herts, Eng.; on Great North Road, 19 m. N. of London; one of "New Towns"

designated 1948 growing around old t. of Bishops Hatfield; light engin., aircraft; p. (estd. 1965) 23,635.

Hathras, *t.*, Aligarh dist., W. Uttar Pradesh, India; sugar, cotton, carved work; p. (1961) 64,045.

Hatteras. *C.*, N.C., U.S.A.; stormy region.

Hattiesburg, *t.*, Miss., U.S.A.; p. (1960) 34,989.

Hattingen, *t.*, N. Rhine-Westphalia, Germany; S.E. of Essen; machin., textiles; p. (1963) 30,700.

Hatvan, *mkt. t.*, Hungary; E. of Budapest; sugar refining; canning; p. (1962) 20,080.

Haugesund, *spt.*, S. Norway; on S.W. coast, 35 m. N. of Stavanger; ch. ctr. of herring fishery; canning inds.; p. (1968) 27,294.

Hauraki, *G.*, E. cst. N.I., N.Z.

Hautmont, *t.*, Nord France; p. (1954) 15,978.

Haut-Rhin, *see* Rhin-Haut.

Haute-Garonne, *see* Garonne-Haute.

Haute-Loire, *see* Loire-Haute.

Haute-Marne, *see* Marne-Haute.

Haute-Saône, *see* Saône-Haute.

Haute-Savoie, *see* Savoie-Haute.

Haute-Vienne, *see* Vienne-Haute.

Hantes-Pyrénées, *see* Pyrénées, Hautes.

Hauts-de-Seine, *dep.*, France, Paris region; p. (1968) 1,461,619.

Havana, *spt.*, *cap.*, Cuba; ch. c. of the W. Indies; cigars, tobacco, sugar, rum, coffee, woollens, straw hats, iron-ore; oil refining on outskirts of t.; p. (estd. 1965) 983,000.

Havant and Waterloo, *urb. dist.*, Hants, Eng.; at foot of Portsdown Hill, 6 m. N.E. of Portsmouth; computer mnf. plant and programming work; p. (estd. 1967) 99,830.

Havel, *R.*, Germany; flowing to R. Elbe (221 m.).

Haverfordwest, *co. t.*, *mun. bor.*, Pembrokeshire, Wales; 6 m. N.E. of Milford Haven; agr. mkt.; Norman cas.; p. (1961) 8,872.

Haverhill, *t.*, *urb. dist.*, Suffolk, E. Eng.; p. (1961) 5,446.   [(1960) 46,346.

Haverhill, *t.*, Mass. U.S.A.; boot factories; p.

Havering, *outer bor.*, E. London, Eng.; inc. Hornchurch and Romford (*q.v.*); p. (1966) 250,000.

Haverstraw, *t.*, N.Y., U.S.A.; brick-mkg.; p. (1960) 5,771.

Havre, Le, *spt.*, Seine-Maritime, France; on English Channel at mouth of R. Seine; fine boulevards; ship-bldg., engin., chemicals, ropes, cottons, oil refining; pipeline to Grandpuits; p. (1968) 199,509.

Havre de Grace, *t.*, Md., U.S.A.; resort; duck shooting; p. (1950) 7,809.

Hawaii, *I.*, lgst. of Hawaiian gr.; three great volcanic mtns., Mauna Kea (13,796 ft., highest island mtn. in world, dormant), Mauna Loa (13,680 ft., world's most active volcano), Hualalī (last erupted, 1801); ch. pt. Hilo (devastated by tidal wave, 1946); lava deserts, bamboo forests; sugar-cane, cattle, coffee; tourism; deep-sea fishing; p. (1960) 61,332.

Hawaiian Is. (Sandwich Is.), *st.*, Pac. Oc., admitted 1959 as 50th st. of U.S.A.; chain of coral and volcanic Is.; a. 6,424 sq. m.; cap. Honolulu on S.E. cst. of Oahu I.; p. (1970) 748,575.

Hawarden, *t.*, *rural dist.*, Flint, N. Wales; steel plant; p. (rural dist. 1961) 36,299.

Hawash, *R.*, Ethiopia, flows E. of Shoa frontier; length 500 m.

Hawera, *bor.*, N.I., N.Z.; p. (1966) 8,142.

Hawes Water, *L.*, Westmorland, Eng. (2½ m.).

Hawick, *burgh*, Roxburgh, Scot.; on R. Teviot, 18 m. S.W of Kelso; hosiery, tweed and woollens; p. (1961) 16,204.

Hawke's Bay, *prov. dist.*, N.I., N.Z.; on E. cst.; cap. Napier; a. 4,260 sq. m.; p. (1961) 114,516.

Hawkesbury, *R.*, N.S.W., Australia; length 330 m.

Hawkesbury, *t.*, Ontario, Canada; p. (1956) 7,874.

Haworth, *t.*, W.R. Yorks, Eng.; nr. Keighley; home of the Brontës.

Hawthorne, *t.*, S.W. Cal., U.S.A.; residtl.; in gasand oil-producing area; p. (1960) 33,035.

Hawthorne, *bor.*, N.J., U.S.A.; paint, glass textiles, dyewks.; p. (1960) 17,735.

Hay, *R.*, Alberta, Canada; flows into G. Slave Lake.   [p. (1961) 1,321.

Hay, *urb. dist.*, Brecknock, Wales; on R. Wye;

Hay, *t.*, N.S.W., Australia; situated on R. Murrumbidgee on N. edge of Riverina dist.; collecting ctr. for fruit and wheat grown under irrigation, for despatch by rail E. to Narandera and Sydney, or by river W. to Adelaide.

Hayange, t., Moselle, France; ironwks.; p. (1954) 11,060.

Hayden, Mt., or Grand Teton peak, Rockies, Wyo., U.S.A.; alt. 13,600 ft.

Haydock, t., urb. dist., Lancs, Eng.; coal-mining; p. (1961) 12,070.

Hayes and Harlington, former urb. dist., Middx., Eng.; now inc. in Hillingdon outer bor., Greater London (q.v.); residtl.; elec. goods, gramophones, aeroplane mftg.; p. (1961) 67,912.

Hayle, t., Cornwall, Eng.; nr. St. Ives; engin.; p. 5,800.

Hayling Island, resort, Hants, Eng.; E. of Portsmouth.

Haystack, summit of the Adirondacks, Vt., U.S.A.; alt. 4,919 ft.

Hayward, t., Cal., U.S.A.; p. (1960) 72,700.

Hayward's Heath, mkt. t., Sussex, Eng.; nr. Cuckfield; cattle mkt.; p. 5,400.

Hazard, t., Ky., U.S.A.; gas, coal, sawmills, steel mills; p. (1960) 5,958.   [40,958.

Hazaribagh, t., Bihar, India; coal, mica; p. (1961)

Hazebrouck, t., France, Nord; rly. ctr., textiles, grain, livestock; p. (1954) 15,525.

Hazel Grove and Bramhall, urb. dist., Cheshire, Eng.; p. (estd. 1967) 34,800.

Hazleton, c., Penns., U.S.A.; anthracite region; coal, iron, textiles, iron and steel mnfs.; p. (1960) 32,056.   [residtl.

Headingley, sub., Leeds, Yorks, Eng.; mainly

Healdtown, mission sta., nr. Fort Beaufort, Cape Province, S. Africa.

Heanor, t., urb. dist., Derby, Eng.; 7 m. N.E. of Derby; coal, hosiery, rly. wagons, pottery, prefabricated timber bldgs. mftg.; p. (estd. 1967) 24,270.

Heard, I., S. Indian Ocean; 280 m. S.E. of Kerguelen I.; Australian possession.

Heathrow, vil., Middx, Eng.; on W. margin of built-up area of London; site of London Airport; arterial road link with London.

Hebburn, t., urb. dist., Durham, Eng.; on R. Tyne, 4 m. below Gateshead; shipbldg., engin., and colliery inds.; p. (estd. 1967) 24,940.

Hebden Royd, urb. dist., W.R. Yorks, Eng.; cotton factories, dyewks., heavy engin.; p. (1961) 9,409.

Hebrides or Western Is., Scot., grouped as Outer and Inner Hebrides; ch. t. Stornoway, Lewis; a. 2,850 sq. m.

Hebron, t., Jordan; 16 m. S.W. of Jerusalem; p. (1961) 37,911.

Heckmondwike, t., urb. dist., W.R. Yorks, Eng.; p. (1961) 8,420.

Hedmark, co., Norway; on Swedish border; a. 10,621 sq. m.; p. (1968) 177,882.

Heerenveen, commune, Friesland prov., N. Netherlands; livestock; p. (1967) 29,758.

Heerlen, t., Limburg, Neth.; 14 m. E. of Maastricht; traces of Roman occupation; coal mng.; p. (1967) 76,940.

Heide, t., Schleswig-Holstein, Germany; ctr. of petroleum dist.; machin., food preserving; p. (1963) 20,100.

Heidelberg, famous univ. t., Baden-Württemberg, Germany; on R. Neckar, nr. Mannheim; cas.; tobacco, wood, leather, rly. carriages; rly. junction; nylon plant projected; p. (1968) 121,466.

Heidenheim, t., Baden-Württemberg, Germany; N.E. of Ulm; textiles, machin., metallurgy, furniture; p. (1968) 50,000.

Heilbronn, t., r. pt., Baden-Württemberg, Germany; engin., vehicles, foodstuffs; p. (1963) 92,400.

Heilungkiang (Heilungjiang), prov., N. China; a. c. 180,000 sq. m.; tractor farming, lumbering, coal, gold; cap. Harbin; p. (1953) 11,897,309.

Hejaz, region, Saudi Arabia; mainly desert; very poor communications; ch. t. Mecca; a. 150,000 sq. m.; p. 1,000,000 (estimated).

Hekla, volcano, Iceland; alt. 5,095 ft.

Helder (Den Helder), t., N. Holland, Netherlands; on strait between peninsula and I. of Texel; naval base; on cst. 50 m. N. of Amsterdam; p. (1967) 55,727.

Helena, t., Ark., U.S.A.; on Mississippi R.; shipping ctr. for cotton; p. (1960) 11,500.

Helena, cap., Mont., U.S.A.; gold, silver, iron, smelting; p. (1960) 20,227.

Helensburgh, residtl. burgh, Dunbarton, Scot.; on N. side of Firth of Clyde at entrance to Gare Loch; metal goods; p. (1961) 9,605.

Heletz, Negev, Israel; oilwells.

Heligoland, German I., N. Sea, off mouth of Elbe; formerly British.

Helikon, mtn., Greece; between G. of Corinth and L. Kopais; alt. 5,736 ft.

Hell Gate R., Mont., U.S.A.; trib. of Bitter Root R.

Hellendoorn, commune Overijssel, Netherlands; textiles; p. (1967) 28,252.

Hellespont, see Dardanelles.

Hellin, t., Albacete, Spain; sulphur-mines; p. (1957) 30,026.

Helmond, t., N. Brabant, Netherlands; on the Zuid-Willemsvaart (canal); textiles; p. (1967) 46,834.

Helmsley, mkt. t., ctr. of rural dist., N.R. Yorks. See also Pickering, Vale of.

Helmstedt, t., Lower Saxony, Germany; E. of Brunswick; coal and potassium mining, textiles, machin.; p. (1963) 29,100.

Helmund, R., Afghanistan; falls into L. Hamun; length 650 m.

Helsingborg or Hälsingborg, spt., Sweden; on the Sound, opposite Helsingör, Denmark; shipyd., engin., textiles, rubber goods, chemicals; p. (1961) 76,574.

Helsingör, t., Själland, Denmark; shipyds, textiles, rubber boots; p. (1960) 26,653.

Helsinki (Helsingfors), spt., cap. Finland; on G. of Finland, harbour ice-bound Jan. to April except for channel opened by ice-breaker; univ.; timber prod., textiles, carpets, etc.; p. (1966) 508,353.

Helston, mkt. t., mun. bor., Cornwall, Eng.; on R. Cober, 8 m. W. of Falmouth; tourist ctr. famous for its festival of the Furry or Floral Dance (8 May); p. (estd. 1967) 9,240.

Helvellyn, mtn., Cumberland, Eng.; 9 m. S.E. Keswick; alt. 3,118 ft.

Helwan, t., U.A.R.; 15 m. S. of Cairo; iron and steel complex projected.

Hemel Hempstead, t., Herts, Eng.; on S. slopes of Chilterns, 9 m. N. of Watford; one of "New Towns" designated 1947; consists of bulk of mun. bor. of Hemel Hempstead with new growth to E. and S.E.; mun. bor. exists as separate entity; scientific glass, elec. engin., cars; p. (estd. 1967) 64,100.

Hempstead, t., Long I., N.Y., U.S.A.; p. (1960) 34,641.

Hemsworth, urb. dist., W.R. Yorks, Eng.; 6 m. S.E. of Wakefield; p. (1961) 14,401.

Henderson, c., Ky., U.S.A.; tobacco, cotton, coal; p. (1960) 16,892.

Henderson, t., N.C., U.S.A.; cotton, tobacco, mkt. and mnfs.; p. (1950) 10,996.

Hendon, former mun. bor., Middx., Eng.; now inc. in Barnet outer bor. Greater London, (q.v.); many light inds.; p. (1961) 115,843.

Hengelo, t., Overijssel, Neth.; industl. ctr., metals; cattle mkt.; lace mkg., textiles; p. (1967) 68,007.

Hengyang, c., Hunan, China; on Siang R. in foot-hills to S. of Yangtze plain; nr. impt. lead- and zinc-mng. dist.; p. (1953) 235,000.

Hénin-Liétard, t., Pas-de-Calais, France; p. (1962) 25,660.

Henley-on-Thames, mun. bor., Oxford, Eng.; 5 m. N.E. of Reading; mkt. gardening, brewing; p. (estd. 1967) 10,550.   [p. (1962) 11,899.

Hennebont, t., Morbihan, France; on R. Blavet;

Henrietta Maria, C., Ontario, Canada; on Hudson Bay.

Henry, C., Va., U.S.A.; at S.entrance to Chesapeake Bay.

Hensbarrow, upland a., Cornwall, Eng.; granite; impt. kaolin-mining dist., kaolin exported by sea from Fowey; rises to over 1,000 ft.; a. 30 sq. m.

Henzada, t., Burma, on R. Irrawaddy; p. 28,542.

Herat, cap. c. of prov. same name, Afghanistan; on Hari Rud; strongly fortified; has been called "the key of India"; crude petroleum and chrome ore in a.; p. (1948) (of prov.) 1,142,343; (of t.) (1964) 62,000.

Hérault, dep., S. France; wines, fruit, olives, cheese, sheep-rearing; cap. Montpellier; a. 2,402 sq. m.; p. (1968) 591,397.

Herculaneum, buried c., Italy; 7 m. E.S.E. Naples; re-discovered in 1709.

Heredia, prov., Costa Rica, Central America; cap. Heredia; p. (1963) 83,878.

Hereford, co., Eng.; on Welsh border; fertile;

fruit, cereals, hops, cattle, sheep, cider, salmon, limestone; a. 842 sq. m.; p. (1966) 140,000.

Hereford, c., mun. bor., co. t., Hereford, Eng.; on R. Wye; cath.; steel for turbines and aircraft rockets, tiles, engin., timber, cider and preserves, p. (estd. 1967) 46,120.   [(1962) 17,697.

Herenthals, commune, N. Belgium; mftg.; p.

Herford, t., N. Rhine–Westphalia, Germany; on R. Werra; cotton, flax, furniture, cigars, confectionery, metallurgy; p. (1963) 55,700.

Herisau, t., cap. can. Appenzell Ausser-Rhoden, Switzerland; muslin mftg., embroidery, dyeing; p. (1957) 13,407.

Herm, sm. 1. of Channel Is., English Channel; 4 m. N.W. Sark and N.E. of Guernsey; remarkable shell-beach; a. 320 acres; p. 90.

Hermon, mtn., on Syria-Lebanon bdy., nr. Israel; alt. 9,835 ft.

Hermosillo, t., cap., Sonora, Mexico; on Sonora R.; univ.; impt. tr.; distilling, silver; p. (1961) 14,402. 50,000.

Hermoupolis, spt., cap., Cyclades, Greece; p.

Herne, t., N. Rhine–Westphalia, Germany; nr. Dortmund; coal, iron, machin., chemicals; p. (1968) 101,955.

Herne Bay, t., urb. dist., Kent, Eng.; on cst., 62 m. from London; p. (estd. 1967) 24,100.

Herning, t., Jutland, Denmark; knitting ind.; p. (1960) 24,790.

Heröya, S. Norway; nuclear power plant projected.   [61,672.

Herrera, prov., Panama, cap. Chitré; p. (1960)

Hersfeld, c., Hessen, Germany; textiles; machin., wood, iron, leather, mineral baths; p. (estd. 1954) 22,800.

Herstal, t., Belgium; nr. Liége; repeating rifle wks., aero-engines; p. (1962) 29,693.

Herstmonceux, vil., nr. Hastings, Sussex, Eng.; cas.; site of Royal Greenwich Observatory.

Herten, t., N. Rhine–Westphalia, Germany; coal, machin.; p. (1963) 52,300.

Hertford, co., Eng.; undulating parks, woods, wheat, fruit; light inds., elec. engin., pharmaceutics; a. 632 sq. m.; p. (1966) 872,000.

Hertford, co. t., mun. bor., Hertford, Eng.; on R. Lea, 20 m. N. of London; pharmaceutics, flour milling, rolling stock, diesels, brewing; p. (estd. 1967) 18,660.

's-Hertogenbosch, t., Netherlands; on Rs. Dommel and Aa; cap. of N. Brabant prov.; famous cath.; cattle mkt.; industl. development; p. (1967) 79,151.

Hesse, Land, W. Germany; hilly and wooded; grain, fruit, cattle; inds. Frankfurt, Kassel, Darmstadt; wines prod. along Rhine valley; cap. Wiesbaden; a. 8,150 sq. m.; p. (1968) 5,333,000.

Hesse-Nassau, former Prussian prov., now part of Hesse.

Heston and Isleworth, see Hounslow.

Hetch Hetchy Dam, Cal., U.S.A.; on R. Tuolumne 100 m. upstream from St. Joaquin R.; ch. source of irrigation for middle St. Joaquin valley; supplies water and hydro-elec. to San Francisco; height 430 ft., capacity 1,466,000 million gallons.

Hetton, t., urb. dist., Durham, Eng.; 5 m. N.E. of Durham; coal; p. (1961) 17,463.

Héverlé, commune, central Belgium; mkt. gardens; p. (1962) 16,495.

Hex, R., Cape Province, Rep. of S. Africa; rises in Lange Berge, flows S.W. to Gr. Berg R. at Worcester; valley gives access to Gr. Karroo and Central African tableland, is used by trunk rly. from Cape Town to Johannesburg.

Hexham, mkt. t., urb. dist., Northumberland, Eng.; on R. Tyne, 20 m. W. of Newcastle; p. (1961) 9,397.

Heysham, see Morecambe and Heysham.

Heywood, t., mun. bor. Lancs, Eng.; 3 m. E. Bury; coal, cotton, chemicals; p. (estd. 1967) 30,400.

Hiawassee, R., Tenn., U.S.A.; trib. Tenn. R.

Hibbing, t., Minn., U.S.A.; iron ore; p. (1960) 17,731.

Hickory, t., N.C., U.S.A.; p. (1960) 19,328.

Hidalgo, st., Mexico; cap. Pachuca; mng., coffee, sugar, tobacco; a. 8,057 sq. m.; p. (1960) 994,598.   [62,063.

High Point, c., N.C., U.S.A.; textiles; p. (1960)

High Wycombe, t., mun. bor., Bucks, Eng.; 15 m. N.W. of Windsor; furniture, paper mkg.; freeze dry egg processing; p. (estd. 1967) 55,980.

Higham Ferrers, mkt. t., mun. bor., Northants, Eng.; 3 m. E. of Wellingborough; footwear and leather dressing; p. (estd. 1967) 4,380.

Highgate, residtl. dist., London, Eng.; on hill N. of Camden bor.; p. (1961) 15,580.

Highland, Park, t., Mich., U.S.A.; motor cars; p. (1960) 38,064.

Highland Park, bor., N.I., U.S.A.; non-metallic sta. of U.S. Bureau of Mines; p. (1960) 11,049.

Hilden, t., N. Rhine–Westphalia, Germany; S.E. of Düsseldorf; textiles, iron, chemicals; p. (1963) 39,900.

Hildesheim, c., Lower Saxony, Germany; at foot of Harz Mtns.; cath.; machin., farm implements, textiles, ceramics; p. (1963) 98,800.

Hilla, liwa, Iraq; on R. Euphrates; nr. ancient Babylon; p. (1956) 274,567.

Hilleröd, t., N.E. Själland, Denmark; agr. implements; p. (1960) 11,605.

Hillingdon, outer bor., Greater London, Eng.; comprising former urb. dists. of Hayes and Harlington, Ruislip and Northwood, Yiewsley and W. Drayton and mun. bor. of Uxbridge; p. (1968) 233,000.

Hillside, t., N.J., U.S.A.; engines; speed boats; drugs; lumber; p. (1960) 22,304.

Hilo, c., Hawaii; nr. lgst. active volcano in the world, Mauna Loa; alt. 13,600 ft.

Hilversum, t., Netherlands; nr. Utrecht; outstanding modern architecture; floorcloth factories, wireless equipment; broadcasting sta.; p. (1967) 102,756.

Himachal Pradesh, Union terr., India; cap. Simla; p. (estd. 1966) 2,855,000.

Himalayas, vast chain of mtns. along N. border of India; 1,600 m. long; highest peak, Mt. Everest, 29,028 ft.

Himeji, industl. t., S. Honshu, Japan; on shore of Inland Sea, 30 m. W. of Kobe; iron and steel ind., heavy engin.; oil refining; p. (1964) 359,000.

Hinckley, mkt. t., urb. dist., on border of Leicester and Warwick, Eng.; hosiery, boots, carboard boxes, dye wks., engin.; p. (estd. 1967) 43,910.

Hinckley Point, Somerset, Eng.; civil nuclear power-sta.; 2nd sta. now being built.

Hindenburg, see Zabrze.   [nr. Haslemere, Eng.

Hindhead, hilly common and health resort, Surrey,

Hindiya Barrage, dam, Iraq; across R. Euphrates, 30 m. above Hilla; provides flood control and irrigation in a. between Shatt el Hilla and R. Euphrates.

Hindley, t., urb. dist., Lancs, Eng.; 2 m. S.E. of Wigan; cotton, paint, knitwear, asbestos; p. (estd. 1967) 21,900.

Hindu Kush, mtn. range, mainly in N.E. Afghanistan; highest peak Tirich Mir (25,426 ft.) in Chitral dist., W. Pakistan; Salang tunnel (opened 1964) with 2-lane motor highway cuts H.K. at height of 11,000 ft., runs 800 ft. below mtn. top, 1½ m.

Hindustan, former name of part of N. India between Himalayas and Vindhya ranges.

Hinojosa del Duque, commune, S. Spain; copper; agr.; textiles; p. (1957) 15,629.

Hirado, I., off W. cst. Japan; nr. Sasebo; famous for blue and white porcelain.

Hirfanli Dam, project on R. Kizilirmak 90 m. S.E. Ankara, Turkey, 1961.

Hirosaki, t., Honshu, Japan; castle; lacquer ware; p. (1965) 151,624.

Hiroshima, spt., c., central Honshu, Japan; close to the "Island of Light" with its famous Shinto temple; first city to be destroyed by atomic bomb (6 Aug. 1945); now rebuilt; p. (1965) 504,245.

Hirschberg, see Jelenia Gora.

Hispaniola, Greater Antilles, W. Indies; lge. I., divided between the Haiti and Dominican Reps; a. 29,536 sq. m.

Hispar, glacier, Karakoram mtns., length 38 m.

Hitchin, mkt. t., urb. dist., Herts, Eng.; in gap through Chiltern Hills, 35 m. N. of London; light engin., tanning, chemicals, distilling; p. (estd. 1967) 26,240.   [185 sq. m.

Hjälmaren Lake, Sweden; S.W. of L. Malar; a.

Hjorring, t., Jutland, N. Denmark; biscuit and clothing wks.; p. (1960) 15,038.   [Martaban.

Hlaing (Rangoon), R., Burma; flows to G. of

Hobart, spt., cap., Tasmania, Australia; on R. Derwent; univ.; gr. fruit exp.; zinc, cadmium, superphosphates, textiles; p. (1966) 119,415.

Hobbs, t., N.M., U.S.A.; oil-well area; supply ctr.; p. (1960) 26,275.

Hoboken, *t.*, Antwerp, Belgium: shipbldg.; refractory metals; p. (estd. 1957) *30,552.*

Hoboken, *c.*, N.J., U.S.A.; lge. ocean commerce; p. (1960) *48,441.*

Hobro, *spt.* Jutland, Denmark; at W. end of Mariager Fjord; cattle feed factory; p. (1960) *8,208.*   [*15,791.*

Höchst, *t.*, Hessen, Germany; on R. Main; p.

Hochstetter, *mtn.*, S.I., N.Z.; in Southern Alps; alt. 11,200 ft.

Hoddesdon, *t.*, *urb. dist.*, Herts, Eng.; in Lea valley, 4 m. S. of Ware; nursery trade, tomatoes, etc.; p. (estd. 1967) *20,640.*

Hodeida, *spt.*, Yemen, Arabia; on Red Sea; naval base; p. *50,000.*

Hodmezovasarhely, *t.*, S.E. Hungary; wheat, fruit, tobacco, cattle; natural gas pipeline from Szeged; p. (1962) *53,223*

Hof, *t.*, Bavaria, Germany; on R. Saale; textiles, iron, machin., porcelain, glass, brewing; p. (1963) *56,200.*

Hofei (Hefei), *c.*, *cap.* Anhwei prov., China; rice growing a.; cotton and silk; p. (1953) *184,000.*

Hoffman, *mtn. peak* of the Sierra Nevada, California; alt. 8,108 ft.   [*100,000.*

Hofuf, *t.*, Hasa, Saudi Arabia; p. (estd. 1956)

Hog's Back, Surrey Eng.; chalk ridge; alt. 505 ft.

Hohe Tauern, *Alpine range*, Tyrol, Austria; rugged crystalline rocks; highest point, Grau Glockner, alt. 12,461 ft.

Hohenlimburg, *t.*, N. Rhine–Westphalia, Germany; nr. Dortmund; cas.; textiles, iron, steel; p. (1963) *26,800.*

Hohenstein-Ernstal *t.*, Karl-Marx-Stadt, E. Germany; textiles, metal goods; p. (1963) *17,136.*

Hohenzollern, *former prov.*, Germany; Upper Danube; a. 441 sq. m.

Hoihow (Haikou), *c.*, Kwangtung prov., China; comm. ctr.; p. (1953) *135,000.*

Hokitika, *t.*, S.I., N.Z.; on W. cst., 20 m. S. of Greymouth; p. (1961) *3,005.*

Hokkaido, *lge. I.*, Japan, N. of Honshu; a. 34,276 sq. m.; p. (1962) *5,000,000.*

Holbaek, *t.*, Sjaelland, Denmark; W. of Copenhagen; engin. and motor wks.; p. (1960) *15,475.*

Holbeach, *mkt. t.*, S. Lincoln, Eng.; in Fens, 7 m. E. of Spalding; agr., brewing; p. (1948) *5,382.*

Holderness, *div.*, E.R. Yorks, Eng.; between R. Humber and N. Sea; agr. and pastoral.

Holguin, *t.*, E. Cuba, W. Indies; exp. cattle, maize, tobacco, hardwoods; p. (1960) *227,000.*

Holland, *see* Netherlands.

Holland, Parts of, *admin. div.* of Lincoln, Eng.; adjoining the Wash; ch. ts. Boston, Spalding; a. 419 sq. m.; p. (1961) *103,327.*

Holland, *t.*, Mich., U.S.A.; p. (1960) *24,777.*

Holland, N., *prov.*, Netherlands; a. 1,051 sq. m.; p. (1967) *2,200,602.*   [p. (1967) *2,902,572.*

Holland, S., *prov.*, Netherlands; a. 1,130 sq. m.;

Hollandia, former name of cap. W. New Guinea, renamed Kota Baru by Indonesia, then Sukarnapura, now Djajapura.

Holidaysburg, *bor.*, Penns., U.S.A.; coal, iron ore, limestone; foundries, machine shops; p. (1960) *6,475.*

Hollywood, *sub.* Los Angeles, Cal., U.S.A.; ctr. of film industry.

Holmesdale, Vale of, *geographical sub-region*, Kent, E. Surrey, Eng.; extends along foot of N. Downs escarpment E. from Dorking; drained by Rs. Mole, Darent, Medway, Len, Stour; heavy clay soils; woodland or rich meadowland; dairy farming; some cultivation along N. and S. fringe; ch. ts., Dorking, Reigate, Sevenoaks, Maidstone, Ashford have grown up on gaps through hills to N. and S. of the Vale; length 60 m., average width 1 m.

Holmfirth, *t.*, *urb. dist.*, W.R. Yorks, Eng.; 5 m. S. of Huddersfield; textiles, engin.; p. (1961) *18,391.*

Holroyd, *t.*, N.S.W., Australia; sub. of Sydney.

Holstein, former Danish Duchy, now inc. in Schleswig-Holstein *Land* of Germany.

Holston, *R.*, U.S.A.; head of Tenn. R.; flows through Va. and Tenn.; length 300 m.

Holsworthy, *rural dist.*, *mkt. t.*, N. Devon, Eng.; p. (1961) rural dist. *5,795*; t. *1,619.*

Holt, *t.*, Denbigh, Wales; on R. Dee, 7 m. S. of Chester.   [Sheringham.

Holt, *mkt. t.*, N. Norfolk, Eng.; 5. m. S.W. of

Holyhead, *spt.*, *urb. dist.*, Anglesey, Wales; on Holyhead I.; mail packet sta. for Ireland; light engin., woodwkg., clocks; site for aluminium smelter; I. is 7½ m. long, width ¼ m. to 4 m.; p. (1961) *10,408.*

Holy I., off cst. of Anglesey, Wales.

Holy I., Scot., in F. of Clyde, nr. I. of Arran.

Holy I. (Lindisfarne), off cst. of Northumberland. Eng.

Holyoke, *c.*, Mass., U.S.A.; impt. mftg. ctr., paper, machin.; on Connecticut R.; seat of Mount Holyoke College for women; p. (1960) *52,689.*

Holytown, *t.*, Lanark, Scot.; nr. Glasgow; coal, steel; p. *20,669.*

Holywell, *mkt. t.*, *urb. dist.*, Flint, N. Wales; woollen, rayon and paper inds.; p. (1961) *8,459.*

Holywood, *spt.*, *urb. dist.*, Down, N. Ireland; on S. shore of Belfast Lough; seaside resort; p. (1966) *7,795.*

Holzminden, *t.*, Lower Saxony, Germany; on R. Weser; chemicals, machin., lumber; p. (1963) *22,900.*

Homberg, *t.*, N. Rhine–Westphalia, Germany; on R. Rhine opposite Duisburg; coal-mining, machin., chemicals; p. (estd. 1954) *32,200.*

Homburg, *t.*, Hessen, Germany; spa, cas.; iron, machin., dyes, leatherwk.; p. (1963) *35,500.*

Homburg, *t.*, Saar; univ.; iron, wood, glass, brewing; p. (1963) *31,000.*

Home Counties, term applied to the geographical counties adjoining London, *i.e.*, Middlesex, Surrey, Essex, and Kent; sometimes Hertfordshire, Buckinghamshire, and Berkshire are included, and occasionally Sussex.

Homs, *t.*, W. Syria; on R. Orontes; ancient Emesa; silk, textiles, cement; oil refinery; pipeline from Karachok fields; p. (1961) *164,362.*

Honan (Henan), *fertile prov.*, N.E. China; traversed by Yellow R.; cap. Kaifeng; cereals, coal; a. 64,545 sq. m.; p. (estd. 1957) *48,670,000.*

Honda, *t.*, Tolima dep., Colombia; coffee; p. (estd. 1959) *21,000.*

Honduras, *rep.*, Central America; mtnous.; bananas, coconuts, coffee, hardwoods; panama hat mkg.; silver and lead mng.; cap. Tegucigalpa; a. 43,227 sq. m.; p. (estd. 1969) *2,535,000.*

Honduras, British, *see* British Honduras.

Honesdale, *bor.*, Penns., U.S.A.; coal, textiles, shoes, glass; p. (1960) *5,569.*

Honfleur, *spt.*, Calvados, France; fine harbour; p. (1962) *9,132.*

Hong Kong, *Brit. I.* and *Crown Col.*, China; at mouth of R. Canton; inc. peninsula of Kowloon and Is.; cap. c. Victoria; total a. 398 sq. m.; univ.; free pt.; irregular coastline; entrepôt trade; textiles (50 per cent of total exports), plastics, electrical goods, metal products, electronics, toy inds.; p. (estd. 1969) *4,000,000* (mainly Chinese).

Honiton, *t.*, *mun. bor.*, E. Devon, Eng.; on R. Otter, 16 m. E. of Exeter; trout fishing; p. (estd. 1967) *5,260.*

Honolulu, *c.*, *cap.*, Hawaiian Is.; on the I. of Oahu; gd. harbour, fruit, canning, sugar; p. (1960) *294,179.*

Honshu, *lgst. I.* of Japan; oil; a. 88,919 sq. m.

Hood Mt., highest peak Cascade range, Ore., U.S.A.; alt. 11,225 ft.

Hoogeven, *t.*, Drenthe, Netherlands; canned fruits and vegetables; p. (1967) *33,730.*

Hooghli or Hughli, *R.*, W. branch of R. Ganges, India; flows into Bay of Bengal; Calcutta on its banks.

Hook of Holland, *spt.*, Netherlands; packet sta. with steamer connections to Harwich, Eng.

Hooker Mt., Rockies, Brit. Columbia, Canada.

Hoole, *t.*, *urb. dist.*, Cheshire, Eng.; 2 m. N.E. of Chester; mnfs.; p. (1951) *9,054.*   [Vet R.

Hoopstad, *t.*, Orange Free State, S. Africa; on

Hoorn, *old fishing t.*, N. Holland, Netherlands; on IJsselmeer, 20 m. N. of Amsterdam; cheese and cattle mkts.; birthplace Tasman, discoverer of Tasmania and New Zealand, founder of Batavia; p. (1967) *17,072.*   [U.S.A.

Hoosack, *mtns.*, part of Green Mtn. range, Mass.,

Hoosick Falls, *t.*, N.Y., U.S.A.; paper, elec. goods; agr. implements; p. (1960) *4,023.*

Hopedale, *t.*, Labrador cst., Newfoundland, Canada.

Hopeh (Hebei), *prov.*, N.E. China; cap. Tientsin; cereals, cotton, iron ore; a. c. 75,000 sq. m.; p. (estd. 1957) *44,720,000.*

Hopetown, *t.*, Cape Province, S. Africa; on Orange R.; p. (1960) *2,631.*

Hopewell, t., Va., U.S.A.; synthetic textiles, chemicals, pottery; p. (1960) 17,895.

Hopkinsville, c., Ky., U.S.A.; p. (1960) 19,465.

Hoquiam, spt., Wash., U.S.A.; lumber, salmon, tuna fishing, oysters, canning; p. (1960) 10,762.

Hor, unlocated biblical mtn. between Dead Sea and G. of Aqaba, the place of Aaron's death.

Horbury, urb. dist., W.R. Yorks, Eng.; nr. Wakefield; p (1961) 8,642.

Hordaland, co., Norway; a. 6,043 sq. m.; ch. t. Bergen; p. (1968) 247,327.   [steel; p. 35,000.

Horde, t., Germany; nr. Dortmund; coal, iron.

Horeb, mtn., another name for Mt. Sinai.

Horley, sm. t., Surrey, Eng.; on R. Mole. 7 m. S.E. of Dorking.   [in Hormuz Strait.

Hormuz, I., off S. cst. of Iran and nr. Qishm I.;

Horn, C., most S. point of S. America; noted for severe gales encountered there.

Horn (North C.), N. point of Iceland.

Horncastle, mkt. t., urb. dist., Lindsey, Lincoln, Eng.; at confluence of Rs. Bain and Waring at foot of Lincoln Wolds; impt. cattle fairs, malting, corn. horse fairs; p. (1961) 3,768.

Hornchurch, former urb. dist., Essex, Eng.; nr. Romford; residtl.; general engin.; now inc. in Havering bor., Greater London; p. (1961) 131,014.   [13,907.

Hornell, c., N.Y., U.S.A.; rly. car wks.; p. (1960).

Hornsea, t., urb. dist., E.R. Yorks, Eng.; on E. cst.. 13 m. N.E. of Hull; seaside resort; p. (1961) 5,949.

Hornsey, see Haringey.

Horsens, spt.. Jutland, Denmark; brewing, diesel engines, weaving, etc. goods; p. (1965) 37,106.

Horsforth, t., urb. dist., W.R. Yorks, Eng.; in Aire valley 4 m. N.W. of Leeds; cloth, tanning, light engin.; p. (1961) 15,351.

Horsham, t., urb. dist., W. Sussex, Eng.; on R. Arun at W. end of forested dist. of the High Weald; agr.. timber, engin., and chemicals; p. (estd. 1967) 24,690.

Horsham, t., Victoria, Australia; on R. Wimmera; pastoral, dairying and agr. dist.; agr. machin.; p. (1966) 10,557.

Horta, ch. spt., Fayal I., Azores, Atl. Oc.; cap. of dist.; fruit, wine, winter resort; p. of dist. (1960) 49,735, of t. 7,109.

Horten, spt., Norway; nr. Oslo; naval base; shipbldg., mftg. inds.; p. (1960) 13,289.   [Ocean.

Horton, R., N.W. Terr., Canada; flows into Arctic

Horwich, t., urb. dist., S. Lancs. Eng.; on W. edge of Rossendale Fells, 4 m. N.W. of Bolton; bleaching and cotton spinning, calico printing, paper, coal, stone; p. (1961) 16,067.

Hoshangabad, t., Madhya Pradesh, India; on Narbada R.; p. (1961) 19,284.

Hoshiarpur, t., Punjab, India; lacquer wks., inlaid goods; p. (1961) 50,739.

Hospitalet, t., Spain; p. (1965) 176,000.

Hot Springs, c., Ark., U.S.A.; health resort; p. (1960) 28,337.

Houdeng-Goegnies, commune, S.W. Belgium; coal, smelting, glasswks.; p. (1962) 8,769.

Houghton-le-Spring, t., urb. dist., Durham. Eng.; 5 m. S.W. of Sunderland; coal; p. (estd. 1967) 31,610.   [22,974.

Houilles, t., Hauts-de-Seine, France; p. (1954

Hounslow, outer bor., Greater London, Eng.; inc. former bors. of Brentford and Chiswick, Heston and Isleworth, Feltham and Hounslow; p. (1966) 207,000.

Housatonic, R., Conn. and Mass., U.S.A.; empties into Long Island Sound; length 150 m.

Houston, t., Renfrewshire, Scot.; new satellite t.

Houston, c., spt., S. Texas, U.S.A., N.W. Galveston B.; gr. pt., lgst c. of S.; oil refineries, oilfield machin., steel, chemicals, paper, processing, milling and assembling plants; NASA's manned space flight ctr. and lunar science institute; p. (1970) 1,213,064; Greater Houston 1,958,000.

Houston Ship Canal, Texas, U.S.A.; links Houston to head of shallow Galveston Bay and continues through bay to deep water; provides site for heavy inds.; opened 1915; total length 45 m.

Hove, t., mun. bor., E. Sussex, Eng.; on S. cst., continuous with Brighton; residtl.; holiday resort; p. (estd. 1967) 72,140.

Howe, C., Victoria; S.E. extremity of Australia.

Howell, t., S.E. Mich., U.S.A.; p. (1960) 4,861.

Howrah, c., W. Bengal, India; faces Calcutta across Hooghli R.; jute, cotton, shipbldg.; p. (1961) t. 512,598, dist. 2,038,477.

Howth, hill, nr. Dublin; alt. 563 ft.

Hoy, I., Orkneys. Scot.

Hoylake, t., urb. dist., Cheshire, Eng.; on N. cst. of Wirral peninsula; residtl; p. (estd. 1967) 32,400.

Hoyland Nether, urb. dist., W.R. Yorks, Eng.; p. (1961) 15,707.

Hradec Králové, t., ČSSR.; p. (1961) 55,147.

Hron, R., ČSSR.; trib. of R. Danube.

Huacho, spt., Peru, S. America; pt. for cotton and sugar, cottonseed oil; p. (1963) 27,219.

Huancavelica, dep., Central Peru; a. 8,297 sq. m.; cap. H.; p. (1961) 298,892.

Huancayo, cap., Junin, Peru; woollen mills, artificial silk; p. (1961) 20,000.

Huanuco, dep., Central Peru; a. 15,426 sq. m.; ch. t. Huanco; p. (1961) 339,888.

Huaras, ch. t., Ancash, Peru; mineral springs, copper, silver, coal; p. (1961) 11,628.

Hubli, t., Mysore, India; E. of Goa; cotton, silkweaving; p. (1961) 171.326.

Hucknall, industl. t., urb. dist., Nottingham, Eng.; 5 m. N. of Nottingham; hosiery, coal; p. (estd. 1967) 25,720.

Huddersfield, mftg. t., co. bor., W.R. Yorks, Eng.; on edge of Pennines, 10 m. S. of Bradford; wool textiles, chemicals, engin.; p. (estd. 1967) 132,120.

Hudiksvall, spt., Sweden; on inlet of G. of Bothnia; salting and engin. wks., sawmills; p. (1961) 11,979.

Hudson, t., N.Y., U.S.A.; cement, textiles, machin.; p. (1960) 11,075.

Hudson, R., N.Y., U.S.A.; flows from the Adirondacks to New York Harbour; with valley of Mohawk R. makes gr. highway of tr. between Gr. Lakes and New York; length 350 m.

Hudson Bay, inland sea, Canada; communicating by Hudson's Strait (400 m. long) with Davis Strait: salmon, cod; a. 540,000 sq. m.

Hué, c., S. Viet-Nam; nr. mth. of Hué R.; royal palace; glass factories; impt. tr.; p. (1960) 103,870.

Huelva, maritime prov., S.W. Spain; copper-mining, vine and olive growing, stock-raising, fisheries, brandy distillery, etc.; a. 3,906 sq. m.; p. (1959) 403,090.

Huelva, spt., cap. Huelva, Spain; on G. of Cadiz; oil refining; chemicals; p. (1959) 76,845.

Huercal Overa, t., Almeria, S.E. Spain; silver-lead- and copper-mining; p. (1957) 13,968.

Huesca, frontier prov., N.E. Spain; mtnous.; forested; a. 5,849 sq. m.; p. (1959) 242,332.

Huesca, t., cap., Huesca prov., Spain; on R. Isuela; cath.; gr. wine and timber tr. with France, pottery, leather, cereals; p. (1957) 25,500.

Hugh Town, cap., St. Mary's I. Scilly Isles.

Huhehot, c., Inner Mongolia; China; p. (1953) 148,000.

Huila, dep., Colombia, S. America; a. 7,990 sq. m.; cap. Neiva; p. (estd. 1959) 353,090.

Huizen, commune, Netherlands, prov. N. Holland; radio sta.; fishing; plastics; p. (1967) 19,502.

Hulan, t., N. China; 20 m. N. of Harbin; tr. ctr.; on Harbin-Aigun rly.

Hull or Kingston-upon-Hull, c., spt., co. bor., E.R. Yorks, Eng.; third pt. of U.K.; at influx of R. Hull, in estuary of the Humber; univ.; impt. mnfs. and gr. shipping tr.; docks, fishing, ship repairing, rope, machin., chemicals, tanning, veg. oils, flour milling, seed crushing, paint, cement; p. (estd. 1969) 292,600.

Hull, c., Quebec. Canada; faces Ottawa across R. Ottawa; sawmills, paper; p. (1961) 56,929.

Humber, estuary of Rs. Ouse and Trent, separating Yorks and Lincoln, Eng.; fine waterway; 1–7 m. wide, length 38 m.

Humboldt Bay, inlet, Cal., U.S.A.; nuclear experimental breeder reactor.

Humboldt, mtn. range. E. Nevada, U.S.A.

Humboldt Current, see Peru Current.

Hume Lake, artificial lake, N.S.W., Australia; formed by dam where R. Murray leaves Gr. Dividing Range, just below confluence with R. Mitta Mitta; supplies water for irrigation in upper Riverina dist.; approx. capacity 4,000 million cu. ft.

Hunan, inland prov., China; coal, zinc, tea, wheat, rice. tung oil; cap. Changsha; a. 79,378 sq. m.; p. (1953) 33,226,954.

Hungary, rep., Central Europe; ch. physical features; central plain of treeless steppes; R. Danube. R. Tisza, Carpathian mtns., L.

Balaton; hot, dry summer, rainfall moderate; race, Magyar; agr., wheat, maize, potatoes, sugar-beet; livestock, poultry; mach., textiles, metal prods., chemicals; coal, lignite, bauxite, oil; communications good; cap. Budapest; a. 35,912 sq. m.; p. (1965) *10,160,000.*

Hungerford, *mkt. t., rural dist.*, Berks, Eng.; on R. Kennet, p. (rural dist. 1951) *9,411.*

Hunmanby, *t.*, E.R. Yorks. Eng.; S. of Scarborough; bricks and tiles.

Hunsrück, *mtn. a.*, Rhineland-Palatinate. Germany; highest point, 2,677 ft.

Hunstanton, *urb. dist.*, Norfolk, Eng.; S.E. shore of Wash; seaside resort; p. (1961) *4,843.*

Hunter, R., N.S.W., Australia; rises in Liverpool Range, Gr. Dividing Range, flows S. and E. into Tasman Sea at Newcastle; valley of Hunter and ch. trib. Goulburn lead from Newcastle up to Cassilis Gate through Gr. Dividing Range to interior; length, approx. 250 m.

Hunterston, Ayrshire, Scot.; civil nuclear power station.

Huntingdon and Peterborough, *inland co.,* Eng; mkt. gardening, fruit-growing, agr.; p. (1966) *184,000.*

Huntingdon, *co. t.*, Hunts, Eng.; on R. Ouse, 6 m. above St. Ives; birthplace of Oliver Cromwell; canning, engin., processed rubber, confectionery; Huntingdon and Godmanchester, *mun. bor.*, p. (estd. 1967) *14,760.*

Huntington, *t.*, Ind., U.S.A.; on Little R.; rly. and wool wks .; p. (1960) *16,185.*

Huntington, *c.*, W. Va., U.S.A.; on Ohio R.; machine wks., lumbering; p. (1960) *83,627.*

Huntly, *mkt. burgh*, Aberdeen, Scot.; at confluence of Rs. Bogie and Deveron; farming, woollens; p. (1961) *3,952.*

Huntly, *t.*, N.I., N.Z.; on Waikato R.; 65 m. S. of Auckland; coal; p. (1961) *4,617.*

Huntsville, *t.*, Ala., U.S.A.; cotton-mills; p. (1960) *72,365.*

Huon, I., 170 m. N. of and *dep.* of New Caledonia, Pacific; very barren group.

Hupeh (Hubei), *prov.*, China; N. of the Yangtze-Kiang; cap Wuhan; tea, cotton, wheat, coal, paper; a. 71,955 sq. m.; p. (1953) *27,789,693.*

Hurlford and Crookedholme, *ts.*, Ayr, Scot.; nr. Kilmarnock; iron, fireclay, worsteds, coal-mng.

Huron, L., between Canada and U.S.A.; one of the Gr. Lakes of the St. Lawrence basin; a. 23,610 sq. m.; 280 m. long. [*14,180.*

Huron, *t.*, S.D., U.S.A.; meat prod.; p. (1960) *18,155.*

Hurstville, *sub.*, S. of Sydney, N.S.W., Australia; p. *22,667.*

Hürth, *t.*, N. Rhine–Westphalia, Germany; S.W. of Cologne; lignite-mining, machin., chemicals; impt. elec. power sta.; p. (1963) *47,500.*

Husi, *mftg. t.*, Romania; tobacco, wine; p. (1956) *18,155.*

Huskvarna, *t.*, Sweden; S. extremity of L. Vättern; lt. inds.; p. (1961) *13.763.*

Husum, *spt.*, Schleswig-Holstein, Germany; rly. junction; p. (1963) *24,600.*

Hutchinson, *c.*, Kan., U.S.A.; p. (1960) *37,574.*

Hutt, *urb. a.*, N.I., N.Z.; p. (1966) *114,739.*

Huy, *t.*, Belgium; on R. Meuse; nr. Liége; vine-growing dist.; p. (1962) *13,493.*

Huyton with Roby, *urb. dist.*, Lancs. Eng.; sub. of Liverpool; p. (estd. 1967) *69,180.*

Hwai Ho (Yellow Sea), arm of the Pac. Oc. between Korea and China; branches into the Gs. of Pohai and Liaotung; greatest width 400 m., length 600 m.

Hwang Ho (Yellow R.), China; rises nr. source of Yangtze-Kiang, Tibet, flows through N.W. China into G. of Pohai; l. 2,600 m.

Hwangshih (Huangshi), *c.*, Hupeh prov., China; cement and lime wks.; p. (1953) *111,000.*

Hyde, *industl. mkt. t., mun. bor.*, Cheshire, Eng.; on R. Tame, 5 m. S.E. of Manchester; textiles, clothing, engin., leathercloth, rubber, paper prod.; p. (estd. 1967) *38,760.*

Hyderabad, *dist.*, Andhra Pradesh, India; rice, cotton, wheat; a. 1,957 sq. m.; p. (1961) *2,062,995.*

Hyderabad, *ch. t.*, of Andhra Pradesh, India; on R. Musi; walled t. and impt. comm. ctr.; univ.; p. (1961) *1,251,119.*

Hyderabad, *t.*, W. Pakistan; on R. Indus; arsenal; univ.; silks, gold and silver wk.; pottery, cement; heavy elec. plant; p. (1961) *434,537.*

Hyderabad, *dist.*, W. Pakistan; p. (1961) *2,542,000.*

Hydra, I., Greece; off Morea; a. 26 sq. m.; p. *3,693.*

Hyères, *winter health resort*, Var, France; vines, oranges, flowers, fruit; p. (1962) *33,693.*

Hyères, Iles d', *sm. archipelago of Is.*, off French Riviera cst. [rubber plant.

Hythe, nr. Southampton, Hants., Eng.; synthetic

Hythe, *t., mun. bor.*, Kent, Eng.; on S. cst., 3 m. W. of Folkestone; one of the Cinque Ports; Royal school of musketry; p. (estd. 1967) *11,180.*

I

Iasi, *see* Jassy.

Iba, *spt., mun.*, cap. of Zambales prov., Luzon, Philippine Is.; uranium, lumbering; p. *8,299.*

Ibadan, *t.*, cap. Western prov., Nigeria; 60 m. N. of Lagos; silk, tobacco, cotton; univ.; p. *600,000.*

Ibagué, *cap.*, Tolima, Colombia, S. America; cotton, tobacco, sugar, leather gds.; p. (estd. 1959) *133,380.*

Ibarra, *t.*, Ecuador, S. America; at foot of Volcano of Imbabura; p. (1962) *14,031.*

Iberian Peninsula, S.W. peninsula of Europe; containing sts. of Spain and Portugal; derived from the Iberian people who lived along the R. Ebro (Iberus); a. 229,054 sq. m.; p. *35.470,953.* [*7,588.*

Iberville, *t.*, Quebec, Canada; lt. engin.; p. (1961)

Ibicui, *t.*, S. Paraguay; iron ore; p. *14,350.*

Ica, *cst. dep.*, Peru; cap. Ica; a. 9,796 sq. m.; p. (1961) *243,617.*

Iceland, I., N. Atl. Oc.; 130 m. E. Greenland; independent rep.; barren and mtnous., with ice-covered plateaus and volcanoes; glacier fields cover 5,000 sq. m.; highest peak, Oraéfa Jökull, alt. 6,950 ft.; main ind. fishing; cap. Reykjavik; a. 39,709 sq. m.; p. (1969) *203,000.*

Ichang, *pt.*, Hupeh, China; on Yangtze R.; cotton, rice, oil; large tr.; p. *107,940.*

Ichinomiya, *t.*, S.E. Honshu, Japan; ancient Shinto shrine; textiles, pottery; p. (1964) *192,000.*

Ichow, *c.*, Shantung, China; at foot of Shantung highlands, 80 m. N.E. of Tungshan (Suchow); silk ind.; p. (estd.) *100,000.*

Icknield Way, *ancient highway* in S. Eng.; from nr. Bury St. Edmunds, through Wantage to Cirencester and Gloucester.

Icod, *commune*, N.W. Tenerife, Canary Is.; agr., silk; p. *13,263.*

Ida, *mtn.*, Central Crete, Greece; famous in Greek mythology; 8,058 ft.

Idaho, *mtn. st.*, U.S.A.; part of Rocky Mtns. in st.; rich mineral region; cap. Boise City; a. 83,557 sq. m.; p. (1970) *698,275.*

Idaho Falls, *t.*, Idaho, U.S.A.; food processing, lumbering; silver, lead, and gold mines near by; nuclear experimental breeder reactor; p. (1960) *33,161.*

Idar-Obestein, *t.*, Rhineland-Palatinate, Germany; gem cutting, jewellery; p. (1963) *30,400.*

Idle, *mftg. t.*, W.R. Yorks, Eng.; in Aire valley, 3 m. N. of Bradford; woollens, motor cars.

Idle, R., Notts, Eng.; trib. to R. Trent.

Idrija, *t.*, N.W. Jugoslavia; ancient cas.; mercury mines; cinnabar; p. *10,317.*

Ifni, *enclave*, S. Morocco; ceded by Spain to Morocco 1969; cap. Sidi Ifni; a. 700 sq. m.; p. (1963) *54,000.*

Igarka, *sm. t.*, Siberia, R.S.F.S.R.; on R. Yenesei, 400 m. from its mouth; graphite plant, nickel-mines, lumber-mills; p. (1956) *15,200.*

Iglesias, *t.*, Sardinia, Italy; N.W. of Cagliara.

Igualada, *t.*, Barcelona, Spain; leather, textiles; ctr. of wine-producing dist.; p. (1957) *16,945.*

Iguassu, R., S. Brazil; famous falls. [*6,983*

Iisalmi, *t.*, Finland; E. of Kokkola; p. (1966)

IJ, *inlet*, IJsselmeer, now separated by locks, forming part of canal system of Amsterdam.

IJmuiden, *t.*, N. Holland, Netherlands; on cst. at mouth of N. Sea Canal; fishing; gasification plant, steel-mill; p. (1968) *135,334* (incl. Velzen and Beverwijk).

IJsselmeer (Lake IJssel). Netherlands; shallow expanse of water. formerly Zuider Zee; separated from N. Sea by Wieringen–Friesland Barrage (length 19 m.) constructed 1932; active land reclamation in progress, lgst. a. being Northeast Polder (185 sq. m.); chief c. on inlet (IJ) is Amsterdam; when reclamation complete, water a. will be reduced to 408 sq. m.

Ilagan, t. Mindanao, Philippines; integrated steel mill; p. (1960) 58,433.

Ilam, dist., W. Iran; p. (1967) 170,567; cap. Ilam, p. (1967) 91,545.

Ilchester, t., Somerset, Eng.; on R. Yeo; N.W. of Yeovil; birthplace of Roger Bacon.

Ile-Ife, t., Nigeria, W. Africa; 54 m. from Ibadan.

Iletsk, t., Kazakh. S.S.R., on R. Ilek, trib. of R. Ural; S. of Chkalov; rock salt; p. 13,010.

Ilford, former mun. bor., Essex, Eng.; E. sub. of London on R. Roding; bordering on Hainault Forest, now inc. in Redbridge Outer London bor. (q.v.); paper-mills, elec. and radio equipment, films and photoplate wks.; p. (1961) 178,024.

Ilfracombe, t., urb. dist., N. Devon, Eng.; on cst. of Bristol Channel; seaside resort; p. (1961) 8,701.

Ilhéus, spt., Bahia, Brazil; exp. cacao, timber; p. (estd. 1968) 100,687.

Ili, R., Central Asia, rises in Tien Shan and flows into L. Balkhash; length 850 m.

Ilia (Ælis), prefecture, S. Greece; cap. Pyrgos; p. (1951) 188,274.

Ilion, t., N.Y., U.S.A.; firearms; office equipment; p. (1960) 10,199.

Ilkeston, t., mun. bor., Derby, Eng.; 7½ m. W. of Nottingham; coal, iron, engin., locknit fabrics, needles, plastics; p. (estd. 1967) 35,340.

Ilkley, t., urb. dist., spa, W.R. Yorks, Eng.; on R. Wharfe 15 m. N.W. of Leeds; local mkt.; p. (1961) 18,519.

Ill, R., E. France; rises in Jura Mtns., flows N. through Mulhouse, Colmar, Strasbourg, enters Rhine 12 m. below Strasbourg; length 135 m.

Illawara, dist., N.S.W., Australia; forming belt of land between S. tableland and cst.; very fertile; dairy farming; coal seams; ch. ts., Kiama, Wollongong, Bulli, Geringong.

Ille-et-Vilaine, dep., N.W. France; on English Channel; a. 2,699 sq. m.; agr.; cap. Rennes; p. (1968) 652,722.

Illimani, Mt., nr. La Paz, Bolivia; 21,184 ft.

Illinois, st., U.S.A.; named after its principal R.; a large trib. (360 m.) of Mississippi R.; cap. Springfield; lgst. t. Chicago; iron and steel, coal and oil; agr.; a. 56,400 sq. m.; p. (1970) 10,973,986.

Illogan, vil., Cornwall, Eng.; N.W. of Redruth; tin, copper; p. (par.) 8,300.

Illyria, region, mainly Jugoslavia, stretching along Adriatic Sea from Trieste in N. to Albania in the S. and inland as far as Rs. Danube and Morava.

Ilmen, L., S. of Novgorod, Russia; a. 360 sq. m.; fisheries.

Ilmenau, t., Suhl, E. Germany; at N. base of Thüringer Wald, S.S.E. of Gotha; porcelain, toys, glass; p. (1963) 19,115.

Ilminster, t., urb. dist., Somerset, Eng.; 10 m. S.E. of Taunton; cutstone, concrete, collars, radio valves; p. (1961) 2,784.

Ilobasco, c., Salvador, Central America; cattle, coffee, sugar, indigo; p. 21,225.

Iloilo, cap., prov of Iloilo, Panay Philippines; coconut oil, fishing ind.; p. (estd.) 187,000.

Ilorin, t., N. Nigeria, W. Africa; on Lagos–Kano rly.; agr. and caravan ctr.; govt. sugar growing scheme at Bacita; p. 54,636.

Imabari, t., spt., N.W. Shikoku, Japan; on shore of Inland Sea; mnfs. cotton textiles, paper, canned fruits; p. (1965) 104,470.

Imbabura, prov., Ecuador; a. 2,414 sq. m.; cap. Ibarra; p. (1960) 182,700.

Imbros, Turkish I., Ægean Sea; fruit-growing.

Immingham, pt., Lindsey, Lincoln Eng.; on S. cst. of Humber, 8 m. N.W. of Grimsby; lge. docks; new deep-sea oil and coal terminals, chemicals, engin., refinery nearby at Killingholme.

Imola, t., Italy; S.E. of Bologna; cath.; glass, pottery; p. (1961) 51,289.

Imperial Valley, S. Cal., U.S.A.; extends 30 m. S.E. from Salton Sea to Mexican bdy.; mainly below sea-level; hot, arid climate; cotton, dates, wheat under irrigation; water brought

from Colorado R. by Imperial Canal (Laguna Dam) and All-American Canal (Imperial Dam) nr. Yuma; total irrigated a. (1938) 700 sq. m.

Imphal, ch. t., Manipur, India; p. (1961) 67,717.

Inari L., extensive L., Lappi, Finland; outlet into Barents Sea; a. 685 sq. m.

Inca, t., I. of Majorca, Spain; p. (1957) 12,522.

Ince-in-Makerfield, urb. dist., Lancs., Eng.; nr. Wigan; coal, cotton, engin., wagon-bldg.; p. (1961) 18,027.

Inchgarvie, islet, F. of Forth, Scot.; forms central support of the Forth rail bridge.

Inchkeith, fortfd. I., F. of Forth, Fife, Scot.

Inchon, spt., S. Korea; on W. cst.; soya beans, rice; glass; diesel engines; p. (1962) 430,000.

Indan, mun., Luzon, Philippine Is.; rice; p. 11,240.

Independence, t., Mo., U.S.A.; on prairie, S. of Missouri R.; p. (1960) 62,328.

Independence, t., Iowa, U.S.A.; p. (1960) 7,069.

Independence, t., Kan., U.S.A.; p. (1960) 11,222.

India, peninsula subcontinent, Asia; comprises India, Pakistan, and Ceylon; ch. mtns.: Himalayas (Everest 29,028 ft.), E. and W. Ghats, Sulaimain range, Hindu Kush, Karakoram; Ganges Plain, Thar desert; ch. Rs.: Indus, Ganges, Brahmaputra; climate: monsoonal; vegetation: dense forests in region of high rainfall; sal, teak; elsewhere savannah or jungle, bamboo; coconuts on cst.; variety of races; inds.: agr., rice, wheat, millet, sugarcane, cotton, jute, tea, rubber, linseed, cattle, sheep, goats; forests, timber; minerals: coal petroleum, manganese, lead, gold, silver; mnfs.: cottons, jute, milling, engin., machin., brass, carpets; communications: good rail and sea; total a. 1,606,742 sq. m.; total p. (1961) approx. 542,851,695.

India, Republic of (Indian Union), indep. sov. st. within Br. Commonwealth (1947), consists of 17 states and 10 centrally adm. terrs.; cap. New Delhi; mainly agr.; ch. crops, rice wheat, sugar-cane, millet, maize, barley; prin. expts. tea, cottons, fabrics, raw cotton, leather, fruits, nuts, iron and other metal ores; industl. expansion; intern. airpts., New Delhi, Calcutta, Bombay; a. 1,262,000 sq. m.; p. (estd. 1969) 519,749,000

Indian Harbour, Labrador cst., nr. Hamilton Inlet, Canada.

Indian Ocean extends from S. of Asia and E. of Africa to the C. of Good Hope and C. Leeuwin in Australia, separated from the Pacific by the Malay Archipelago and Australia; a. 29,340,000 sq. m.

Indian Territory, since 1907 part of the st. of Okla., U.S.A.

Indiana, st., between Kentucky and Michigan, Illinois and Ohio, U.S.A.; agr., coal, limestone, clay, petroleum, cement, glass; cap. Indianapolis; a. 36,291 sq. m.; p. (1970) 5,143,422.

Indianapolis, cap., Ind., U.S.A.; on White R.; impt. rly. ctr.; meat packing, jet engines, aircraft parts, chemicals, pharmaceutics; p. (1970) 742,613.

Indigirka R., Yakut, U.S.S.R.; flows into Laptev Sea; length 1,100 m.

Indo-China, S.E. Asia; federation in French Union until end of hostilities July 1954. Consisted of the three sts. of Viet-Nam, Cambodia and Laos.

Indonesia, Republic of, S.E. Asia (comprising Java, Sumatra, Kalimantan, Sulawesi, West Irian, 15 minor Is., thousands of smaller ones); climate: tropical, abundant rainfall; equatorial forest; race: Malay; agr.: rice, maize, sweet potatoes, sugar-cane, coffee, tea, tobacco, oil palms, cinchona, spices, rubber; petroleum, tin, coal, bauxite; mineral wealth; cap. Djakarta (Batavia); p. (1969) 118,000,000.

Indore, t., Madhya Pradesh, Indian Union; in valley of R. Narbada; cotton-mills; p. (1961) 394,941.

Indre, dep., Central France; agr. and industl.; cap. Châteauroux; a. 2,666 sq. m.; p. (1968) 247,178.

Indre-et-Loire, dep., Central France; to the N.W. of Indre; agr., vines, silk factories; cap. Tours; a. 2,377 sq. m.; p. (1968) 437,870.

Indus, R., W. Pakistan; rises in Tibet, and flows through Kashmir, Punjab, Sind, to the Arabian Sea; length 1,800 m.; 5 tribs.: Jhelum, Chenab, Ravi, Beas, Sutlej, one of world's major R. systems; Indus Waters irrigation scheme under development.

Inebolu, *spt.*, Anatolia, Turkey; on cst. of Black Sea; tr. in mohair and wool; p. (1960) *5,886.*

Ingersoll, *t.*, Ontario, Canada; N.E. of Hamilton; p. (1961) *6,874.*

Ingleborough, *mtn.*, near Settle, Yorks, Eng.; limestone; underground caves, stalactites, stalagmites; alt. 2,373 ft.

Inglewood, *c.*, S.W. Cal., U.S.A.; chinchilla farms; furniture; light engin.; p. (1960) *63,390.*

Ingolstadt, *t.*, Bavaria, Germany; on Danube, nr. Munich; cas.; machin., cars, tobacco, oil refining; oil pipeline from Genoa; transalpine pipeline under construction from Trieste, through N.E. Italy and Austria to Ingolstadt.; p. (1963) *64,600.*

Inhambane, *spt.*, Mozambique; sugar, copra, oil-seeds, bricks, soap, tiles; p. (1960) *67,265.*

Inishmore, *lgst. of Aran Is.*, Galway, Ireland; 30 m. S.W. of Galway; fishing; p. *1,500.*

Inkerman, *t.*, Crimea, U.S.S.R.; nr. E. extremity of Sevastopol harbour; battle 1854.

Inkpen Beacon, *hill*, Berks. Eng.; W. end of N. Downs, 7 m. S.W. of Newbury; highest point reached by chalk hills in Eng.; alt. 975 ft.

Inkster, *t.*, S.E. Mich., U.S.A.; residtl.; p. (1960) *39,097.*

Inland Sea, Japan; length 250 m., breadth 10–40 m.; ch. spts.: Hiroshima, Okayama, Kobe.

Inn, *R.*, traversing Switzerland, the Austrian Tyrol and Bavaria; enters R. Danube at Passau; the ancient Œnus; length 320 m.

Innerleithen, *burgh and health resort*, Peebles, Scot.; on R. Tweed, 5 m. S.E. of Peebles; woollen cloth and knitwear; p. (1961) *2,299.*

Inner Mongolia, *aut. region*, N. China; stretches along S. border of Mongolian People's Rep.; cap. Huhehot; p. (1957) *9,200,000.*

Innisfail, *t.*, Queensland, Australia; ch. sugar-producing ctr. of Australia; p. (1966) *7,419.*

Innsbruck, *cap.*, the Tyrol, Austria; on R. Inn; commands N. approach to Brenner Pass; univ.; military stronghold; p. (1963) *108,000.*

Inowroclaw, *t.*, N. Poland; nr. Bydgoszcz; rock-salt, iron pyrites; agr. prod.; p. (1960) *47,000.*

Insterburg, *see* Chernyakovsk.

Interlaken, *t.*, Bernese Oberland, Berne, Switzerland; on R. Aar, between Ls. Thun and Brienz; tourist resort; p. (1957) *4,368.*

Inuvik, *t.*, Canadian Arctic; built above the permanent frost.

Inveraray, *burgh*, Argyll, Scot.; nr. head of Loch Fyne; herring fishing; p. (1961) *501.*

Inverbervie, *burgh*, Kincardine, Scot.; on E. cst., 8 m. S. of Stonehaven; linen, rayon inds.; p. (1961) *921.*

Invercargill, *c.*, S.I., N.Z.; on S.E. cst.; sawmills, freezing wks.; aluminium smelter; served by Bluff Harb.; p. (1966) *43,572.*

Inverell, *t.*, N.S.W., Australia; 383 m. N. of Sydney; wheat and lamb cty.; tin; p. (1966) *8,411.*

Invergordon, *burgh, spt.*, Ross and Cromarty, Scot.; on N. side of Cromarty Firth, 12 m. N.E. of Dingwall; naval pt.; lge. chemical ind. and aluminium smelter projected; p. (1961) *1,640.*

Inverkeithing, *burgh*, Fife, Scot.; on F. of Forth, nr. Dunfermline; shipbreaking, paper mkg., quarrying; p. (1961) *4,069.*

Inverkip, *par., vil.*, Renfrew, Scot.; 6 m. S.W. of Greenock; par. contains Gourock; wat. pl.; p. (1951) *17,288.*

Inverness, *co.*, Scot.; mountainous and well wooded; rising to Ben Nevis 4,406 ft.; Caledonian Canal crosses co.; little cultivation; deer forests and grouse moors, fishing, sheep breeding, distilleries; hydroelec. schemes at Foyers, Glen Cannich, and Lochaber; a. 4,351 aq. m.; p. (1961) *83,425.*

Inverness, *burgh, co. t.*, Inverness, Scot.; on Moray Firth nr. N.E. end of Caledonian Canal; distilleries, light engin., tweeds; fisheries and agr.; p. (1961) *29,773.*

Inverurie, *burgh*, Aberdeen, Scot.; on R. Don, 14 m. N.W. of Aberdeen; rly. ctr., wool fair; tourism; p. (1961) *5,152.* [tralia.

Investigator I., off cst. of Eyre Peninsula, S. Aus-inyokern, *t.*, E. Cal., U.S.A.; naval ordnance research sta.; p. (1960) *11,684.*

Ioannina (Janina), *prefecture*, Epirus, Greece; ch. t. Ioannina; p. (1961) *154,201.*

Ioannina (Janina), *t.*, Epirus, Greece; nr. Albanian frontier; embroidery; p. (1961) *34,997.*

Iona, *I.*, off cst. of Mull, Argyll, Scot.; early Scottish Christian ctr.; restored abbey; St. Columba's burial place; ancient burial place of Scottish kings.

Ionian Is., gr. in Mediterranean, belonging to Greece, formerly under British protection; comprising Kerkyra, (Corfu), Kephallenia, Zákynthos, Levkás, Ithake, Paxos and Kytherá; suffered from severe earthquakes in Aug. 1953; total a. 752 sq. m.; p. (1961) *212,573.*

Ionian Sea, Mediterranean; between Greece on E; Italy and Sicily on W.

Iowa, *st.*, U.S.A.; prairie cty; over 1,000 ft. above sea-level; watered by Mississippi and Missouri; farming, dairying, maize, wheat, oats, potatoes; coal; cars, chemicals; cap. Des Moines; a 56,290 sq. m.; p. (1970) *2,789,893.*

Iowa City, Iowa, U.S.A.; farming, stockbreeding; p. (1960) *33,443.*

Ipin (Yibin), *c.*, Szechwan prov., China; cereals, match mfg.; p. (1953) *176,000.* [*80,874.*

Ipoh, *t.*, Perak, Malaya; tin; textiles; p.

Ipswich, *co. t., co. bor.*, Suffolk, Eng.; at head of estuary of R. Orwell; diesel engines, general engin.; p. (estd. 1967) *121,670.*

Ipswich, *c.* S.E. Queensland, Australia; coal, woollens; rly. wks.; bricks, earthenware, hardboard; p. (1966) *53,396*

Iquique, *c.*, N. Chile, a pt. on Pacific; exports nitrates and iodine from Atacama desert; fish canning; p. (1960) *53,800.*

Iquitos, *ch. t.*, Loreto, Peru; shipyards, docks; rubber, cotton, saw-mills, oil refining; p. (1961) *54,300.*

Iraklion (Heraklion), *prefecture*, Crete; cap. Iraklion; p. (1961) *207,437.*

Iraklion (Candia), *cap.*, Crete; central position on N. cst. at foot of terraced hill slopes; wine, olive oil, fishing; p. (1961) *63,458.*

Iran (Persia), *kingdom*, S.W. Asia; central table-land 3,000–5,000 ft.; ch. range Elburz mtns., (Demavend 18,500 ft.); Rs. few; centre mainly arid, N. cst. and parts of W. very fertile; climate varies widely; agr.: rice, cotton, tobacco, fruits, nuts; impt. oil ind., carpet mnfg.; heavy ind. and mng. developing; exp. of natural gas to U.S.S.R. projected; cap. Tehran; a. 628,000 sq. m.; p. (1970) *28,150,000.*

Irapuata, *c.*, central Mexico; agr. ctr.; p. *60,000.*

Iraq, *rep.* (since July 1958), S.W. Asia; approx. co-extensive with ancient Mesopotamia; ch. Rs.: Tigris, Euphrates; climate: hot, rainless, in summer, cool in winter, scanty rainfall; agr. depends on irrigation; ch. crops, dates, cotton, wheat, maize, barley; impt. oilfields; lgst. pt. Basra; cap. Baghdad; dam and power sta. on Euphrates projected; a. 116,600 sq. m.; p. (estd., 1970) *8,634,000.*

Irbit, *t.*, Sverdlovsk region, U.S.S.R.; engin., motor cycles, wood-wkgs., pharmaceutics; mkt., famous fair; p. (1956) *41,200.*

Ireland, I., W. of Great Britain; ch. physical features; L. Neagh in N.E., Rs. Shannon, Boyne, Blackwater, Barrow, Nore, Suir, Liffey; ch. mtn. groups—all near cst.—Mourne Mtns., Wicklow Mtns., Mtns. of Kerry; climate, mild and damp; called "the emerald isle" because of its grasslands; a. 32,000 sq. m.; p. (1961) *4,321,411.*

Ireland, Republic of (Eire), *sov. ind. st.* covering 26 of the 32 cos. of Ireland inc. the 3 provs. of Leinster, Munster and Connaught (Cannacht) together with 3 of the cos. (Cavan, Monaghan and Donegal), of the former prov. of Ulster. Ceased to be member of Brit. Commonwealth in 1949; mainly agr.: root crops, oats, barley; livestock; fisheries; main industl. development around cap. Dublin; a. 26,600 sq. m.; p. (1966) *2,880,752.*

Irish Sea, Brit. Is.; between Gt. Britain and Ireland, connecting N. and S. with Atl. Oc.; 200 m. long; 50–140 m. wide; greatest depth 140 fathoms; a. 7,000 sq. m.

Irkutsk, *t.*, R.S.F.S.R.; on R. Angara; on Trans-Siberian Rly.; univ.; engin., sawmilling, petro-leum refining, chemicals; hydro-elec. power stn.; p. (1967) *409,000.*

Irlam, *t., urb. dist.*, Lancs, Eng.; steel, engin., tar, soap, glycerine, margarine; p. (1961) *15,365.*

Iron Country, Utah, U.S.A.; vast reserves of iron ore; undeveloped due to inaccessibility.

Iron Gate, Romania; famous rapids in R. Danube; Romanian-Yugoslavian hydro-elect. and navigation project, 1964–71.

Iron Mountain, *t.*, Mich., U.S.A.; former iron mining ctr.; p. (1960) *9,299.*

Ironton, *c.*, Ohio, U.S.A.; machin.; coal, iron, fireclay; p. (1960) *15,745.*

Ironwood, *t.*, Mich., U.S.A.; iron-mining, lumbering; p. (1950) *11,466.*

Irrawaddy, *R.*, Burma; flows S. to Bay of Bengal; navigable for lge. steamers 900 m.; irrigation wks.; length 1,300 m.

Irthlingborough, *t.*, *urb. dist.*, Northants., Eng.; p. (1961) *5,125.*

Irtysh, *R.*, Siberia, U.S.S.R.; trib. of R. Ob; two-thirds navigable; crossed by Trans-Siberian Rly. at Omsk; length 2,500 m.

Irun, *t.*, N.E. frontier, Spain; nr. San Sebastian; tanning and brandy distillery; paper mills, iron; Roman remains; p. (1957) *19,956.*

Irvine. *royal burgh. spt.*, Ayr. Scot.; nr. mouth of R. Irvine, 7 m. W. of Kilmarnock; "New t" designated 1966; hosiery, lt. engin., bottle, chemical wks.; p. (1961) *16,910*, estd. final p. *80,000.*

Irvington, *t.*, N.J., U.S.A.; p. (1960) *59,379.*

Irvington, *t.*, N.Y., U.S.A.; residtl.; light engin.; p. (1960) *5,494.*

Irwell, *R.*, S. Lancs, Eng.; flows past Manchester to the Mersey; length 30 m.

Isa Town, *new t.*, Bahrain; 4 m. from Manamah; proposed p. *35,000.*

Isarco, *R.*, N. Italy; rises nr. Brenner Pass, flows S. into R. Adige at Bolzano; used by main rail and road routes from N. Italy to Austria; length 50 m.

Ischia, *I.*, in G. of Naples, Italy; saline baths; cap. I.; a. 26 sq. m.; p. *30,000.*

Ischl, *t.*, Austria; wat. pl., saline baths; p. (1961) *12,703.* [S. of Jaffa.

Isdud (Ashdod), *ancient Philistine c.*, Israel; 20 m.

Ise Bay, *inlet*, S. Honshu, Japan; flanked by ch. textile mftg. a. of Japan with 5 million people ctred. on Nagoya; length 40 m. width 15–20 m.

Iselle, *t.*, N.W. Italy; S. terminal of Simplon Pass and tunnel.

Isère, *dep.*, S.E. France; drained by Rs. Isère and Rhône; cap. Grenoble; mtnous.; cereals; wine, butter cheese; iron, coal, lead, silver copper; gloves, silks; a. 3,178 sq. m.; p. (1968) *768,000.*

Isère, R., S.E. France; rises in W. Alps (Grande Sassière), flows W. into R. Rhône nr. Valence; used to generate hydro-elec.; used with trib. R. Arc, by main rly. from France to N. Italy through Mt. Cenis (Fréjus) Tunnel.

Iserlohn, *t.*, N. Rhine-Westphalia, Germany; iron, steel, metalwks.; needles; p. (1963) *56,300.*

Iseyin, *t.*, Lagos st., Nigeria, W. Africa.

Isfahan (anc Aspadana), *c.*, central Iran; prov. cap.; historical and picturesque c., noted for its carpets and metalware; steel mill under constr.; tourism; airpt.; p. (1967) *862,454.*

Ishikari, *t.*, Hokkaido, Japan; on cst. of Otaru Bay, 10 m. N. of Sapporo; ctr. of second lgst. coalfield in Japan; sm. petroleum production.

Ishimbay, *t.*, Bashkir A.S.S.R., R.S.F.S.R.; on R. Belaya; ctr. of Ishimbay oilfields; p. (1956) *44,400.*

Ishpeming, *c.*, Mich., U.S.A.; machin., gold, silver, iron, marble; p. (1960) *8,857.*

Isiro (Paulis), *t.*, N.E. Congo; admin. offices; cotton ginneries; rly. repair shops.

Isis, *R.*, head stream of R. Thames, Eng.; so named until its confluence with Thames at Dorchester, Oxfordshire.

Iskenderun, *spt.* Hatay, Turkey; pt. and rly. terminus; oil; fertilisers; oil pipeline from Ahwaz (Iran) projected; p. (1965) *69,259.*

Islamabad, proposed new *fed. cap.*, Pakistan; outside Rawalpindi below Himalayas; nuclear power sta.

Islay, *I.*, Inner Hebrides; Argyll, Scot.; 13 m. W. Kintyre; a. 235 sq. m.

Isle of Grain, *rural a.*, Kent; flat promontory once separated from mainland by a tidal estuary; lge. oil refinery.

Isle Royale, *I.*, in L. Superior, Mich., U.S.A.

Isleworth, *see* Hounslow.

Islington, *inner bor.*, London, Eng.; N. of City; incorporates former bor. of Finsbury; univ.; industl. and residtl.; p. (1966) *255,000.*

Ismailia, *t.*, U.A.R., at mid-point of Suez Canal on L. Timsah, 45 m. N.N.W. of Suez; has rail connections with Cairo, Suez and Port Said; p. (1960) *25,194.*

Isna (Esneh), *t.*, Upper U.A.R.; caravan ctr.; barrage; p. (1947) *18,458.*

Isonzo, *R.*, Illyria, Italy; flows into Adriatic Sea.

Isparta, *t.*, Turkey; N. of Antalya; p. (1965) *42,968.* [research ctr.

Ispra, *t.*, Varese, Italy, nr. L. Maggiore; nuclear

Israel, *indep. Jewish rep.*, since 1948; part of former Palestine mandate; cap. Jerusalem, impt. ts. Tel Aviv, Haifa; mainly agr.: grains, vegs., olives, citrus-fruit prod.; processed foods, textiles, wearing apparel, pharmaceuticals; little mineral wealth except for potash and other chemicals from Sea of Galilee and Dead Sea; a. 8,050 sq. m.; p. (estd. 1969) *2,853,000.*

Issoudun, *t.*, Indre. France; leather, parchment, woollens, farm implements; p. (1962) *14,483.*

Issy, *t.*, France; on R. Seine; sub. of Paris; p. (1962) *53,293.*

Issyk-kul, *L.*, Kirgizia, U.S.S.R.; alt. 4,476 ft.; a. 250 sq. m.; drained by R. Chu.

Istanbul (Constantinople), *ch. spt.*, former cap., Turkey; on Golden Horn pen. on European cst. at entry of Bosporus into Sea of Marmara; div. into old "Stamboul" on S. side and dists. of Galata and Beyoglu (Pera) on N.; the ancient Byzantium; magnificent mosque of Sta Sophia; comm. and finan. ctr.; bridge across Bosporus due for completion 1973; p. (1965) *1,750,642.*

Istria, *peninsula*, N. Adriatic Sea; formerly Italian. now divided between Jugoslavia and Italy; agr., olives, vines, oranges, maize; rural p. mainly Slavs, ts. mainly Italian.

Ita, *c.*, S. Paraguay; cattle, agr.; leather; p. *16,892.*

Itabira, *t.*, Minas Geraes st., Brazil; on Brazilian Plateau, 60 m. N.E. of Belo Horizonte; lgst. deposits of iron ore in Brazil. [*54,268.*

Itabuna, *c.*, E. Brazil; coffee, tobacco; p. (1960)

Itajai, *t.*, at mouth of Itajaí R., S. Brazil; exp. lumber, tobacco, starch, sassafras oil; p. (1960) *55,000.*

Italy, *rep.*, S. Europe; peninsula 750 m. long and 100–120 m. broad; many Is. (ch. Sardinia, Sicily); mtns. in N. (Alps) and in ctr. and S. (Apennines); ch. R. Po; wheat and other cereals, vines, olives, fruit; cattle, sheep; sulphur, iron and iron pyrites, mercury, lead zinc; Carrara marble; hydro-elec. power, natural gas; mnfs.; cottons, silks, sugar, glass, furniture, olive oil; gen. engin., cars; fisheries; cap. Rome; urban and industl. N. contrasts with underdeveloped Mezzogiorno (*q.v.*); a. 116,235 sq. m.; p. (estd. 1968) *53,000,000.*

Itasca, *L.*, a source of Mississippi R. Minn., U.S.A.; alt. 1,575 ft.

Itatiaia, *mtn.*, highest mtn. in Brazil; 9,255 ft.

Itaugua, *t.*, S.W. Paraguay; lace mkg.; p. *11,300.*

Ithaca, *t.*, N.Y., U.S.A.; on Cayuga L.; seat of Cornell Univ.; elec. clocks; p. (1960) *28,799.*

Ithake, *one of the Ionian Is.*, Greece; a. 37 sq. m.; ch. t. Ithake; severe earthquake, 1953.

Ito, *t.*, Honshu, Japan; on E. cst. of Izu pen.; hot-spring resort; p. (1965) *59,404.*

Itzehoe, *t.*, Schleswig-Holstein, Germany; on Stor R.; wood, cement, machin.; p. (1963) *36,900.* [(1959) *66,000.*

Ivano-Frankovsk, *t.*, Ukrainian S.S.R.; oil; p.

Ivanovo, *t.*, R.S.F.S.R.; N.E. of Moscow; textiles, iron and chemical wks.; peat-fed power stas.; p. (1967) *398,000.* [cryolite.

Ivigtut, *Danish stllement*, S.W. Greenland;

Iviza, *I.*, Balearic gr. in the W. Mediterranean; Spanish; cath.; tourism.

Ivory Coast, *ind. sov. st.*, within French Community, W. Africa; climate, tropical; maize, coffee, rubber, mahogany; dense forests; cap. Abidjan; a. 189,000 sq. m.; p. (1968) *4,100,000.*

Ivrea, *t.*, Italy; on the Dora Baltea, nr. Turin; silks, cotton mnfs.; p. *14,473.*

Ivry-sur-Seine, *t.*, France; on R. Seine, sub. of Paris; organs, chemicals, iron and steel; p. (1962) *53,646.*

Iwamizawa, *t.*, W. Hokkaido, Japan; rly. junction; coalfield; p. (1965) *65,508.*

Iwanai, *spt.*, S.W. Hokkaido, Japan; copper, coal, sulphur; fisheries; p. (1947) *20,394.*

Iwo, *t.*, Nigeria, W. Africa; nr. Ibadan; p. (1953) *100,000.*

Izegem, *commune*, N.W. Belgium; linen, tobacco; p. (1962) *17,157.*

Izhevsk, *t.*, R.S.F.S.R.; steel, engin.; p. (1967) *360,000.*

Izieux, *t.*, Loire, France; nr. St. Etienne.

Izmail, *former prov.* of Bessarabia, Romania; ceded to U.S.S.R. in 1940, and now part of Ukrainian S.S.R.

Izmail, *t.*, Ukrainian S.S.R.; on R. Danube; food inds.; p. (1956) *43,400.*

Izmir (Smyrna), *c.*, Turkey; at head of G. of Smyrna, Anatolia; exp. figs, raisins, tobacco, carpets, rugs; anc. and historic c.; ch. comm. ctr. of the Levant; p. (1965) *417,413.*

Izmit, *t.*, Turkey; E. end of Sea of Marmara; cereals, tobacco, oil refinery and polythene plant under construction; p. (1965) *90,061.*

Izúcar, *t.*, Puebla, Mexico; nr. Popocatepetl; p. *7,065.*

J

Jabbok, *R.*, Syria, trib. of R. Jordan; length 45 m.
Jablonec, *t.*, ČSSR.; on R. Neisse; artificial jewellery; p. (1961) *27,266.*
Jaboatoa, *c.*, E. Brazil; sub. of Recife; p. (1960) *33,963.*
Jaca, *fortfd. t.*, N. Spain; at foot of Pyrenees; p. (1957) *9,035.*
Jachymov, *t.*, ČSSR.; spa; uranium-mines, pitchblende, lead, silver, nickel, cobalt; p. *6,896.*
Jackson, *c.*, Mich., U.S.A.; on Grand R.; locomotives, motor-car accessories; p. (1960) *50,720.*
Jackson, *t.*, cap. Miss., U.S.A.; cotton tr.; p. (1960) *144,422.*
Jackson, *t.*, Tenn., U.S.A.; univ.; cotton, cottonseed oil, engines, sewing-machines; p. (1960) *33,849.*
Jackson, *t.*, Ohio, U.S.A.; foundries, gas wells; p. (1960) *6,980.*
Jacksonville, *t.*, Ark., U.S.A.; p. (1960) *14,488.*
Jacksonville, *c.*, *pt.* Fla., U.S.A.; univ.; on St. John's R.; chemicals, shipbldg. and repair, printing, lumber, cigar mftg.; p. (1970) *513,439.*
Jacksonville, *t.*, Texas, U.S.A.; rly., ctr.; fruit, vegetables, cotton; p. (1960) *9,540.*
Jacksonville, *c.*, Ill., U.S.A.; woollens, rly. wks.; p. (1960) *21,690.*
Jacobabad, *frontier sta.*, Sind, Pakistan; one of hottest places in the Indian sub-continent; p. (1961) *35,200.*
Jacobina, *t.*, Baia, Brazil; on R. Itapicura; p. *4,389.*
Jacobsdal, *t.*, Orange Free State, S. Africa; on Riet R.
Jacobstadt, *see* Yekabpils.
Jacques-Cartier, *R.*, Quebec, Canada; trib. of St. Lawrence.
Jacques-Cartier, *t.*, Quebec, Canada; p. (1961) *40,807.*
Jacuhy, *R.*, S. Brazil; rises in S. edge of Brazilian Plateau, enters Atl. Oc., through lagoon, Lagoa dos Patos; length 350 m.
Jade, or Jahde, *estuary*, N. Sea, Germany; fine harbour and entrance to pt. of Wilhelmshaven.
Jaduguda, Bihar, India; uranium plant.
Jaen, *prov.*, S. Spain; mines, wine, garden produce, leather, weaving; a. 5,209 sq. m.; p. (1959) *773,563.*
Jaen, *t.*, *cap.*, Jaen, S. Spain; N. of Granada; p. (1959) *60,395.*
Jaffa-Tel Aviv, *t.*, Israel; orange-growing dist.; spt. closed 1965; p. (estd. 1956) *364,000.*
Jaffna, *t.*, *spt.*, N. Ceylon; p. (1963) *94,248.*
Jagdalpur. *t.*, Madhya Pradesh, India; p. (1961) *20,412.*
Jagersfontein, *t.*, O.F.S., S. Africa; most impt. diamond mine; p. (1960) *3,885* inc. 785 whites.
Jahrom, *t.*, Fars, Iran; tobacco, dates; p. *15,000.*
Jakarta, *see* Djakarta.
Jaipur, *cap. c.*, Rajasthan, India; comm. ctr.; univ.; p. (1961) *403,444.*
Jalalabad, *t.*, S. of Kabul R., Afghanistan; cane sugar; p. (estd. 1964) *44,000.*
Jalapa, *dep.*, S.E. Guatemala; maize, beans; cap. Jalapa; a. 797 sq. m.; p. (1964) *97,996.*
Jalapa, *cap.*, Veracruz st., Mexico; p. (1960) *60,000.*
Jalgaon, *t.*, *dist.*, Maharashtra, India; cotton, linseed; p. (1961) of t. *80,351;* of dist. *1,765,047.*
Jalisco, *Pacific st.*, Mexico; well timbered, agr., mining; cap. Guadalajara; a. 31,149 sq. m.; p. (1960) *2,443,261.*
Jallieu, *commune*, Isère, S.E. France; light mnfs.; p. (1954) *5,241.*

Jalna, *t.*, Maharashtra, India; E. of Aurangabad; p. (1961) *67,158.*
Jalon, *R.*, Spain; rises in Iberian Mtns., flows N.E. into R. Ebro nr. Zaragoza; valley forms main rly., road route from Madrid to Ebro Valley.
Jaluit, *I.*, Marshall Is., Pa.. Oc.
Jamaica, *I.*, *indep. sov. st.* within Br. Commonwealth (1962); W.I., divided into three cos., Middlesex, Surrey and Cornwall; mountainous, highest peak (in Blue Mtns.) 7,420 ft.; cap. Kingston; univ.; bauxite, alumina, cement, sugar, rum, molasses, coffee, bananas, cocoa; tourism; a. 4,411 sq. m.; p. (estd.) *1,972,000.*
Jamalpur, *t.*, N.E. Bihar, Indian Union; p. (1961) *57,039.*
Jambes, *commune*, S. Belgium; sub. of Namur; glass, engin.; p. (1962) *13,426.*
James (or Powhattan), *R.*, Va., U.S.A.; flows from Blue Ridge to Chesapeake Bay; length 450 m.
James Bay, S. part of Hudson Bay, Canada; length about 1,250 m.
Jamestown, *c.*, N.D., U.S.A.; cattle; food processing; p. (1960) *15,163.*
Jamestown, *spt.*, *cap.*, St. Helena I.; flax; p. (1961) *1,700.*
Jamestown, *c.*, N.Y., U.S.A.; summer resort and mftg.; p. (1960) *41,818.*
Jamestown, *t.*, *dist.*, Va., U.S.A.; nr. mouth of James R., where first English permanent settlement was founded 1607.
Jammer Bay, *bay*, W. cst. of Vendsyssel, Jutland, Denmark.
Jammu and Kashmir, *st.*, N.W. India and N.E. Pakistan; divided along cease-fire line; traversed by ranges of the Himalayas; in Jhelum valley is the celebrated vale of Kashmir, producing abundant crops of wheat and rice; cap. Srinagar; winter cap. Jammu; a. 92,780 sq. m.; p. (1961) *3,560,976.*
Jamshedpur, *t.*, Bihar, India; W. of Calcutta; Tata iron and steel wks.; p. (1961) *328,044.*
Jämtland, *co.*, Sweden; a. 19,967 sq. m.; p. (estd. 1963) *134,200.*
Janesville, *t.*, Wis., U.S.A.; in agr. region; textiles, machin.; p. (1960) *35,164.*
Janina, *see* Ioannina.
Janiuay, *t.*, Panay, Philippines; fine woven fabrics.
Jan Mayen I., between Spitzbergen and Iceland, Arctic Ocean; belongs to Norway; seal and whale fisheries; government weather-forecast sta.; a. about 144 sq. m.
Japan, *cty.*, E. Asia; ch. Is. Shikoku, Hokkaido, Honshu, Kyushu; mtnous.; 18 active volcanoes; subject to earthquakes; industl., comm. and financ. nation; 25 per cent agr.; climate varies according to latitude, in N. temperate, in S. sub-tropical, warm summers, abundant rainfall; vegetation, broad-leaved forest and meadows, coniferous forest; fine harbours, good communications; ch. inds.; agr., rice, cereals, mulberry and silk, tobacco, cotton, tea; coal, iron, copper; lumber; fisheries; textiles, silks, cottons, woollens; shipbldg., engin., machin., chemicals, electronics, metal mnfs., paper; oil from Honshu; cap. Tokio; a. 143,000 sq. m.; p. (1970) *104,649,017.*
Japan, Sea of, portion of Pac. Oc. between Korea, U.S.S.R. and Japan.
Japan Current, *see* Kuroshio.
Japen I., Irian Bay, West Irian, Indonesia.
Japura, *R.*, Colombia, Brazil. S. America; rising in the Andes of Colombia, and flowing through Brazil to R. Amazon; length 1,300 m.
Jarocin, *t.*, Poland; S. of Poznan; p. *11,818.*
Jaroslaw, *mftg. t.*, Rzeszow, Poland; on R. San; garrison; p. (1965) *27,000.*
Jarrahi, *R.*, S.W. Iran; flows into Persian G.
Jarrow, *t.*, *mun. bor.*, Durham, Eng.; on S. bank of R. Tyne, 7 m. below Gateshead; ship repairing and engin.; steel and tube wks.; oil storage; birthplace of Venerable Bede; diecastings and knitting wool mkg. at Bede Trading Estate; p. (estd. 1967) *29,120.*
Jasper, *t.*, E. Texas, U.S.A.; cattle, agr., lumber; p. (1960) *4,880.*
Jasper Place, *t.*, Alberta, Canada; p. (1961) *30,530;*
Jassy (Lasi), *t.*, Romania; former cap. Moldavia. in vineyard dist.; textiles, chemicals; p. (1963) *159,541.*
Jászbereny, *t.*, Hungary; on R. Zagyva; engin.; p. (1962) *30,454.*

Jativa, *t.*, Valencia, Spain; wine, oil, fruit; p. (1957) *18,092.* [*18,655.*

Jau, *c.*, São Paulo st., S.E. Brazil; coffee; p.

Jauf, *t.*, Nejd, Saudi Arabia; p. exceeds 10,000. [p. *8,276.*

Jauja, *t.*, Junin, Central Peru; E. of Lima;

Jaunpur, *t.*, Uttar Pradesh, India; on R. Gumti; perfumes; p. (1961) *61,851.*

Java, *ch. I.*, Indonesia; mtns. (many volcanic); loftiest peak, 12,057 ft.; agr., rubber, tobacco, sugar, coffee, tea; oil palms, cinchona, spices; coal, tin, gold, silver; teak forests; petroleum; steel plant in W. densely populated; cap. Djakarta; a. 50,390 sq. m.; p. (inc. Madura) (1967) *72,600,000.*

Javari (Yavari), *R.*, forms bdy. between Peru and Brazil; trib. of R. Amazon.

Java Sea, part of the Pac. Oc. between N. cst. Java, Borneo and Sumatra.

Jaworzno, *industl. t.*, Poland; nr. Cracow; coal; p. (1965) *59,000.*

Jaxartes R., *see* Syr Darya.

Jayuya, *mun.*, central Puerto Rico, W. Indies; sugar, tobacco, cotton; p. *14,589.*

Jeanerette, *t.*, S. La., U.S.A.; sugar, pecan nuts, rice; p. (1960) *5,568.*

Jeanette, *bor.*, Penns., U.S.A.; natural-gas region; p. (1960) *16,565.*

Jebba, *t.*, Nigeria, W. Africa; on R. Niger.

Jebel Aulia, *vil.*, Sudan; S. of Khartoum; proposed site for dam across White Nile R. Es Suweida. [6,000 ft.

Jebel ed Druz, *terr.*, S.E of Hauran, Syria; ch. t.

Jebel-Hauran, high tableland of Syria; alt.

Jebel Musa or Mt. Sinai. *See* Sinai.

Jebl-us-Siraj, *t.*, Afghanistan; cement wks.

Jedburgh, *burgh*, Roxburgh, Scot.; on R. Jed, 12 m. S.W. of Kelso; abbey ruins, tweeds, woollens, rayon; p. (1961) *3,647.*

Jefferson, *t.*, Texas, U.S.A.; near oilfield; cattle, grain; p. (1960) *3,082.*

Jefferson City, *cap.*, Mo., U.S.A.; on R. Missouri, 100 m. W. of St. Louis; shoes, tiles, farm implements; p. (1960) *28,228.*

Jeffersonville, *mftg.*, Ind., U.S.A.; on Ohio R.; p. (1960) *19,522.*

Jehol, former *prov.*, China; divided 1955 among Hopei and Liaoning provinces and Inner Mongolian Region; p. (1953) *5,160,822.*

Jelenia Góra (Hirschberg), *t.*, Lower Silesia, Poland; German before 1945; spa, rly. junction; p. (1965) *54,000.*

Jelep-la, *high pass*, leading from Sikkim, N. India, to Tibet; alt. 14,390 ft.

Jelgava (Mitau), *t.*, Latvia U.S.S.R.; on R. Aa; textiles, sugar; p. (1956) *31,600.*

Jemappes, *industl. t.*, Hainaut, Belgium; on the Haine R.; coal, iron; French victory over Austria 1792; p. (1962) *12,950.*

Jena, *t.*, Gera, E. Germany; on R. Saale; univ.; observatory; glass, books, pianos, optical mftg. (Zeiss); p. (1963) *83,451.*

Jennings, *t.*, La., U.S.A.; agr.; oil wells; p. (1960) *11,387.*

Jenolan Caves, N.S.W., Australia; in Blue Mtns., 20 m. S.W. of Katoomba; lge. natural caves in limestone, stalactites, stalagmites.

Jeremie, *spt.*, S.W. Haiti; p. *6,000.*

Jerez de la Frontera, *t.*, Andalusia, Spain; 14 m. N.E. of Cadiz; sherry; p. (1959) *137,194.*

Jerez de los Caballeros, *commune*, S.W. Spain; marble, cork, tr. ctr. for agr. region; p. *16,154.*

Jericho, *vil.*, Jordan Valley, Jordan; estd. through recent excavations as oldest t. in the world (6000 B.C.); p. (1961) *10,284.*

Jersey, *I.*, lgst. of Channel Is., 13 m. W. of Fr. cst; potatoes, tomatoes, cauliflowers, flowers, fruit, cattle; tourist resort; t. St. Helier; a. 45 sq. m.; p. (1961) *63,345.*

Jersey City, *spt.*, N.J., U.S.A.; opp. New York on Hudson R.; canning, iron, steel, tobacco, chemicals; rly. ctr.; p. (1960) *276.101.*

Jerusalem, *c.*, Holy Land; 2,660 ft. above sea-level, between Dead Sea and Mediterranean; The " Holy City " of the Jews and sacred c. of Christians and Mohammedans; before the annexation by Israel in 1967 of the Old City (under Arab admin.) divided between Israel and Jordan; now under Israeli control; adopted by Israel as cap. in 1950, though not recognised by U.N.; p. (estd. 1967) *266,300.*

Jervis Bay, *Commonwealth terr.*, acquired as site for

port for Canberra by Federal Government of Australia 1909; a. 28 sq. m.; p. *360.*

Jesi, *t.*, Ancona, Italy; cath.; p. *23,600.*

Jesselton, *see* Kota Kinabalu.

Jhansi, *t.*, Uttar Pradesh, India; p. (1961) *169,712.*

Jharia, *t.*, Bihar, India; firebricks; p. (1961) *33,683.*

Jhelum. *R.*, W. Punjab, Pakistan; most W. of the five Rs. of the Punjab; Mangla Dam, under Indus Waters Treaty, completed 1967.

Jibuti (Djibouti), *pt.* on G. of Aden, cap. French Somaliland; rly. link with Addis Ababa; impt. transit trade; p. (estd. 1965) *41,000.*

Jičín, *t.*, N.E. Bohemia, ČSSR.; mkt.; p. (1961) *12,970.*

Jidda, *spt.*, *t.*, Hejaz, nr. Mecca, Saudi Arabia; steel mill projected; p. (estd.) *150,000.*

Jihlava, *t.*, Moravia, ČSSR.; timber, grain, textiles; p. (1961) *34,744.*

Jimena de la Frontera, *t.*, Spain; nr. Cadiz; p. *10,123.*

Jimma, *t.*, *prov. cap.*, Ethiopia; coffee ctr.; connected by road with Addis Ababa.

Jinja, *t.*, Uganda, E. Africa; on N. shore of L. Victoria where R. Nile drains from L. over Ripon Falls; hydro-elec. power scheme; cotton mnfs., copper smelting, flour and maize milling; rly. to Kampala; p. (1960) *29,741.*

Jinotega, *t.*, Nicaragua; coffee; p. (1961) *50.325.*

João Pessoa, *t.*, cap. Paraíba st., Brazil; through its pt. Cabedelo expts cotton, sugar, minerals; p. (estd. 1968) *189,096.*

Joban, *dist.*, N.E. Honshu, Japan; third lgst. coalfield in Japan; ch. t. Fukushima.

Joda, Orissa, India; ferromanganese plant.

Jodhpur, *t.*, Rajasthan, Indian Union; p. (1961) *224,760.*

Joensuu, *t.*, on chain of Ls., S.E. Finland; p. (1966) *32,677.* [*11,034.*

Joeuf, *t.*, Meurthe-et-Moselle, France; p. (1954)

Jogjakarta, *c.*, Java; 40 m. S. of Semarang; connected with Jakarta by rail; citadel, with palace; p. (1961) *313,000.*

Johanna, *I.*, of the Comoro gr. in Mozambique Channel; p. *12,870.*

Johannesburg, *c.*, Transvaal, S. Africa; univ.; gold-mining ctr. of Witwatersrand; diamond cutting, engin., textiles, chemicals; oil pipeline from Durban; p. (1960) *1,110,905* (inc. *398,517* whites).

John o' Groat's House, *place* nr. Duncansby Head, Caithness, Scot.

Johnsonburg, *bor.*, Penns., U.S.A.; chemicals, paper, iron and steel; p. (1950) *4,567.*

Johnson City, *t.*, N.Y., U.S.A.; leather, chemicals, paper; p. (1960) *19,113.*

Johnson City, N.E. Tenn., U.S.A.; mkt., iron, textiles; p. (1960) *29,892.*

Johnston, *t.*, Providence, Rhode I., U.S.A.; p. (1960) *16,898.*

Johnstone, *mftg. burgh*, Renfrew, Scot.; on R. Black Cart, nr. Paisley; iron, brass, machine tools, textile ind.; p. (1961) *18,369.*

Johnstown, *t.*, N.Y., U.S.A.; glove mftg.; p. (1960) *10,390.*

Johnstown, *c.*, Penns., U.S.A.; on Connemaugh R.; immense steel wks.; p. (1960) *53,949.*

Johore, *st.*, Malaysia, at S. end of Malaya; forested; rubber, rice, copra, tin, iron, bauxite; a. 7,330 sq. m.; p. (estd. 1966) *1,278,289.*

Johore Bharu, *t.*, cap Johore, Malaya; across the Strait from Singapore; p. (1957) *126,099.*

Joina Falls, Mali; dam projected for hydro-elec. and irrigation purposes, under auspices of Organisation of Riparian States of R. Senegal (Guinea, Mali, Mauritania, Senegal).

Joinville, *t.*, Santa Catarina, Brazil; exp. timber, matté tea; textiles, machin., car parts, plastics; p. (1960) *45,500.*

Jökulsa, *R.*, flowing into Axar Fjord, Iceland.

Joliet, *t.*, Ill., U.S.A.; rly. and mftg. ctr.; p. (1960) *66,780.*

Joliette, *t.*, Quebec, Canada; woollens, paper, tobacco; p. (1961) *18,088.*

Jonesborough, *t.*, Ark., U.S.A.; p. (1960) *21,418.*

Jönköping, *co.*, Sweden; cap. Jönköping; a. 4,447 sq. m.; p. (1961) *285,271.*

Jönköping, *t.*, cap. Jönköping, Sweden; paper matches, textiles, footwear; p. (1961) *50,652.*

Jonquière, *t.*, S. Quebec, Canada; lumber, rly. shops; p. (1961) *28,588*.

Joplin, *t.*, Mo., U.S.A.; lead-mng; p. (1960) *38,958*.

Jordan, *kingdom*, bounded by Israel, Syria, Saudi Arabia and Iraq; agr. but lge. areas of desert; phosphate deposits and potash; cap. Amman; West Bank of R. Jordan occupied by Israeli forces since June 1967; a. 39,050 sq. m.; p. (estd. 1969) *2,200,000*.

Jordan, *R.*, famous in Bible history; flowing S. from Anti-Lebanon along a sinuous course, mostly below sea-level to the Dead Sea, its rapidity and variant depth render it unnavigable, and no t. of any importance has ever been built on its banks; length 120 m.

Jorullo, *volcano*, Michoacan st., Mexico, 4,265 ft.

Jos, *t.*, central Nigeria; on Bauchi Plateau. 60 m. S.W. of Bauchi; impt. tin-mines.

Jotunheimen, *mtn. region*, central Norway; Goldhopiggen, 8,097 ft., Glittertind, 8,048 ft.

Joyce's Country, *mtnous. dist.*, Galway, Ireland.

Juan de Fuca Strait, between Vancouver I. and Washington st., U.S.A.

Juan Fernandez, *rocky I.*, S. Pac. Oc.; belonging to Chile; a. 38 sq. m.; famous for Alex. Selkirk (Robinson Crusoe), 1704–9. [Equator.

Juba, *R.*, E. Africa; flows to Indian Ocean. nr. the Juba, *cap.*, Equatorial Prov., Sudan; p. *10,000*.

Jubbulpore, *t.*, Madhya Pradesh, India; carpets, cottons; oil mills, ordnance wks.; p. (1961) *367,215*.

Juby, *C.*, Rio de Oro., N.W. Africa.

Jucar, *R.*, E. Spain; rises in Serrania de Cuenca, flows S.E. to G. of Valencia, Mediterranean Sea; length 250 m.

Juchitan, *t.*, S.E. Mexico; mkt. for rich agr. region; p. (1950) *14,550*.

Judaea, *div.* of Palestine in the Roman period.

Judenburg, *t.*, Styria, Austria; on R. Mur; p. (1961) *9,869*.

Juggernaut, *see* Puri.

Jugoslavia, *Federal People's Rep.*, comprising former terrs. of Serbia, Montenegro, Croatia, Dalmatia, Bosnia, Herzegovina and Slavonia; farming, wheat, maize, barley, rye, oats, fruits, plums; sheep, cattle, pigs, goats; timber, coal, iron, copper, lead, cement, chromium, salt, bauxite; cap. Belgrade; a. 98,386 sq. m.; p. (1968) *20,186,000*.

Juiz de Fora, *t.*, Minas Gerais, Brazil; impt. textile ctr.; p. (estd. 1968) *194,135*.

Jujuy, *prov.*, Argentina; cap. San Salvador de Jujuy; a. 16,859 sq. m.; p. (1960) *240,000*.

Julfa, *c.*, N. Iran; on frontier with U.S.S.R., impt. customs and transit ctr. on overland route from Europe.

Julian Alps, *mtn. range*, Venetia, Carinthia, Carniola and Croatia; highest peak, Triglav. 9,394 ft. [well.

Julianehaab, *sta.*, Greenland; N.W. of C. Farewell.

Jülich, *t.*, Germany; nr. Aachen; "pebble bed" nuclear reactor projected.

Jullundur, *t.*, Punjab, India; cotton and silk mnfs.; p. (1961) *222,569*.

Jumet, *t.*, Belgium; nr. Charleroi; mftg. and mining; p. (1962) *28,653*.

Jumilla, *t.*, Murcia, Spain; exp. fabrics; p. (1957) *20,851*.

Jumna, *R.*, N. India; ch. trib. of R. Ganges; rises in the Himalayas and flows past Delhi and Agra to Allahabad; length 860 m.

Junction City, Kan., U.S.A.; p. (1960) *18,700*.

Jundai, *t.*, São Paulo st., Brazil; industl. ctr.; p. (estd. 1968) *124,368*.

Juneau, *c.*, cap., Alaska, U.S.A.; at foot of Chilkoot mtns.; lumbering; fisheries; gold settlement (1881); p. (1960) *6,797*.

Jungfrau, *peak*, Bernese Oberland, Switzerland; height 13,642 ft.; electric rly. from Kleine Scheidegg to Jungfraujoch.

Juniata, *R.*, Penns., U.S.A.; flows to the Susquehanna at Petersburg.

Junin, *inland dep.*, Peru; traversed by the Andes; copper, silver, lead; ch. t. Huancayo; a. 22,814 sq. m.; p. (1961) *507,908*.

Jura, *mtns.*, Switzerland and France; highest peak Crête de la Neige; alt. 5,654 ft.; length 180 m., width up to 30 m.

Jura, *dep.*, E. France; named from the mtns.; many vineyards; forests. cereals, watches, toys; a. 1,951 sq. m.; p. (1968) *233,547*.

Jura, *I.*, Argyll, Scot.; off W. cst.; a. 146 sq. m.

Jurua R., trib. of R. Amazon.

Jutland, *peninsula*, Denmark; intensive agr. and poultry farming; a. 11,411 sq. m.; p. (1960) *2,018,168*.

Jyväskylä, *t.*, central Finland; mkt.; pulp and paper; p. (1966) *53,004*.

K

Kabankalan, *mun.*, Negros Occidental, Philippine Is.; agr.; p. *29,315*.

Kabansk, *t.*, E. Siberia, U.S.S.R.; nr. L. Baikal; agr. and industl.

Kabarda-Balkar, A.S.S.R., Transcaucasia, U.S.S.R.; non-ferrous metals, gold, platinum, iron ore, coal, arsenic; a. 4,800 sq. m.; p. (1959) *420,000*.

Kabinda, *t.*, Angola, W. Africa; on W. cst., 30 m. N. of Congo estuary; p. *1,000*.

Kabul, *c.*, *cap.*, Afghanistan; on R. Kabul, S. of the Hindu Kush; 6,900 ft. above sea level; univ.; excellent climate; wool, leather wks.; p. (estd. 1964) *400,000*.

Kabul, *R.*, flowing through Afghanistan to the R. Indus at Peshawar, Pakistan; length 270 m.

Kabwe (Broken Hill before 1969) *t.*, Zambia; comm. and mng. ctr.; lead, zinc, vanadium; p. (1964) *43,000*.

Kachin State, *div.*, Burma; comprising former Myitkyina and Bhamo dists: 29.500 sq. m.

Kadiyevka, *t.*, Ukrainian S.S.R.; coal, iron and steel, synthetic rubber; p. (1967) *138,000*.

Kaduna, *t.*, N. Nigeria; cap. of Northern Provs.; impt. rly. junction with main rlys. to Lagos, Pt. Harcourt; aluminium wks.; p. c. *45,000*.

Kaffraria, *extensive dist.*, Cape Province, S. Africa; comprising Griqualand E., Tembuland, Transkei, and Pondoland.

Kafue, *R.*, Zambia; famous gorge.

Kafue, *t.*, Zambia; 28 m. S. of Lusaka; iron and steel mill being built.

Kagoshima, *spt.*, at S. end of Kyushu I., Japan; rocket launching site nearby at Uchinoura; p. (1965) *328,446*. [inhabited.

Kahoolawe, *I.*, Hawaiian Is.; a. 45 sq. m.; un-

Kai Islands, *Is.*, Indonesia; between New Guinea and Timor; timber; a. 680 sq. m.; p. *51,000*.

Kaiapoi, *t.*, S.I., N.Z.; on the Waimakariri R.; woollens; p. (1961) *3,109*.

Kaieteur Falls, Guyana, S. America; located where R. Potaro leaves Guiana Highlands; among world's highest falls (741 ft.).

Kaifeng, *c.*, *cap.*, Honan, China; on Hwang-Ho R.; one of the most ancient cities in China; cottons; p. (1953) *299,000*.

Kaikoura, *t.*, S.I., N.Z.; on E. cst., 80 m. N.E. of Lyttelton; in this region are the Kaikoura ranges, in which the highest peaks are Tapuaenuku (9,465 ft.) and Alarm (9,400 ft.).

Kainji Dam, Nigeria; power sta. transmission system and river transportation on R. Niger, projected.

Kaiping, *t.*, Hopeh, N. China; 80 m. N.E. of Tientsin; second lgst. coal-mining a. (Kailan mines) in China; coal exported through Chinwangtao.

Kairouan, *holy c.* of the Moslems, Tunisia, N. Africa; 80 m. S.S.E. of Tunis; founded *c.* A.D. 670; mosque; p. (1961) *34,000*.

Kaiserslautern, *t.*, Rhineland Palatinate, Germany; nr. Mannheim; iron, textiles, machin., tobacco, wood; p. (1968) *100,000*.

Kaiser Wilhelm's Land, *Australian dependency*, Antarctica.

Kaishu, *cap.* of Kokai prov., W. Korea; p. *29,688*.

Kajaani, *t.*, on Oulu L., Finland; p. (1966) *17,780*.

Kakamega, *t.*, Kenya, E. Africa; 30 m. N. of Kisumu; ctr. of gold-mining dist.

Kakhovka, *t.*, Ukrainian S.S.R.; on R. Dnieper; hydro-elec. sta.; p. (1956) *19,200*.

Kakinada, *t.*, *spt.*, Andhra Pradesh, India; cotton, oil seeds; p. (1961) *122,865*.

Kalahari Desert, *t.*, *or. infertile tract* of S. Central Africa, between the R. Orange and the Zambesi; mainly in Botswana; alt. 3,700 ft.; a. 20,000 sq. m.; inhabited chiefly by Bushmen.

Kalamata, *t.*, Peloponnese, Greece; nr. Sparta; silk ind., figs, currants, olive oil exp.; p. (1961) *38,211*.

Kalamazoo, *c.*, Mich., U.S.A.; rly. ctr., engin.; college; p. (1960) *82,089*.

Kalat, *div.*, W. Pakistan; a. 53,995 sq. m.; p. (1961) *589,000*.

Kalgan (Zhangjiakou), c., Hopeh prov., China; nr. Gt. Wall 110 m. N.W. of Peking; tea, wool, hides; p. (1953) *229,000*.

Kalgoorlie, t., W. Australia; on transcontinental rly. route 350 m. E. of Perth; semi-desert conditions; gold-mng. a.; p. (1966) *19,892* incl. Boulder.

Kalimantan (Indonesian Borneo); oil, rubber, rice, hardwood; a. 208,286 sq. m.; quartzites discovered in S.E.; p. (1961) *4,101,475*.

Kalinin, t., R.S.F.S.R.; on trib. of R. Volga; cath.; engin., textiles, chemicals; p. (1967) *311,000*.

Kaliningrad, prov., R.S.F.S.R., U.S.S.R.; cap. K., oil discovered in a.

Kaliningrad (formerly Königsberg), t., formerly E. Prussia, now U.S.S.R.; on R. Pregel; cath.; fine bldgs; shipbldg., machin., wood-pulp, chemicals, sugar-beet; tea ctr.; p. (1967) *261,000*.

Kalisz, t., Poland; on R. Prosna; industl. ctr., textiles; oldest Polish t., mentioned in 2nd century A.D. by Ptolemy; p. (1965) *75,000*.

Kalmar, co., S. Sweden; cap. Kalmar; a. 4,485 sq. m.; p. (1961) *235,770*.

Kalmar, spt., Sweden; on E. cst.; matches, shipbldg., food inds.; p. (1961) *30,839*.

Kalna, vil., on Mt. Trara Planina, Yugoslavia; uranium mine and plant; nuclear power sta.

Kalocsa, t., Hungary; on R. Danube; cath., palace; wine; p. (1962) *13,786*.

Kalpakkam, nr. Madras, India; nuclear power sta. being built.

Kaluga, t., R.S.F.S.R.; on R. Oka; chemicals, engin., hydro-elec.; p. (1967) *176,000*. [*73,482.*

Kalyan, spt., Thana, Maharashtra, India; p. (1961)

Kama, R., U.S.S.R.; trib. of R. Volga, which it joins S. of Kazan; length 1,400 m.

Kamaishi, t., spt., N.E. Honshu, Japan; serves Kamaishi–Sennin iron-ore field, lgst. worked deposits and reserves in Japan; impt. iron and steel ind.; p. (1947) *26,200*.

Kamakura, t., Honshu, Japan; on shore of Sagami Bay; tourism; p. (1965) *113,329*.

Kamaran I., Red Sea; Southern Yemen, formerly under Brit. occupation, 1915–67; a. 22 sq. m.; p. c. *2,200*.

Kamchatka, peninsula, E. Siberia, U.S.S.R.; mtns. with volcanoes (Klyuchevsk, alt. 16,512 ft.); mineral wealth, fisheries on cst., climate cold, wet and foggy; cap. Petropavlovsk.

Kamenets Podolski, t., Ukrainian S.S.R.; brewing, tobacco; p. (1956) *33,000*.

Kamensk-Shakhtinskiy, t., R.S.F.S.R.; on R. Severskiy Donets; coal-mng., engin., artificial fibres; p. (1959) *58,500*.

Kamensk Uralsk, t., R.S.F.S.R.; aluminium, iron, steel, engin.; p. (1967) *159,000*.

Kamet, mtn., N. Garhwal dist., Himalayas; alt. 25,477 ft.; until 1953 (Everest) highest mtn. climbed (Smythe, 1931).

Kamloops, c., B.C., Canada; on Thompson R.; formerly Fort Thompson; in " Wild West " area; on transcontinental rlys.; supply ctr. for mining and grazing dist.; p. (1961) *10,076*.

Kampala, cap., Uganda, E. Africa; univ. coll.; ch. comm. ctr.; lt. inds.; coffee processing; p. (1959) *46,780*.

Kampar, t., Perak, Malaysia; p. *17,449*.

Kampen, t., Overijssel, Netherlands; on R. IJssel; cigar mkg.; p. (1967) *28,942*.

Kamp-Lintfort, t., N. Rhine–Westphalia, Germany; abbey; coal-mng.; p. (1963) *35,900*.

Kampot, prov.; Cambodia; pepper; cement plant at Chakrey Ting; p. (1962) *337,879*.

Kamyshin, mftg. t., R.S.F.S.R.; on R. Volga; textiles; mkt. gardening, grain; p. (1959) *55,000*.

Kan, R., S. China; rises in Nan Shan, flows N. into L. Poyang; valley provides route for main road from Kiangsi prov. to Kwangtung prov. over Meiling Pass.

Kanawha, R., W. Va., U.S.A.; rises in Allegheny Mtns., flows S.W. to Hinton, then turns N.W. across Allegheny Plateau into R. Ohio; lower course runs through ch. mining a. of W. Va. coalfield nr. Charleston; length 350 m. approx.

Kanazawa, t., Kaga, Honshu, Japan; silks, ceramics, lacquer ware; p. (1965) *335,528*.

Kanchenjunga, mtn., on Nepal–Sikkim bdy., N.E. India; 3rd highest mtn. in world; alt. 28,146 ft.

Kandahar, prov., S. Afghanistan; mountainous; cap. K.; p. (1948) *1,063,496*.

Kandahar, c., former cap., Afghanistan; alt. 3,400 ft.; 370 m. from Herat; linked by road to Kushka (Turkmenia) via Herat; fruit pre-

serving and canning; textiles; p. (estd. 1964) *115,000*.

Kandy, t., Ceylon; in ctr. of I., 75 m. from Colombo at alt. 3,000 ft.; resort in hot season; tea and cocoa; p. (1963) *67,768*.

Kangaroo I., S. Australia; eucalyptus; p. (1966) *3,380*. [machin.; p. (1960) *27,666*.

Kankakee, t., Ill., U.S.A.; farm implements;

Kano, c., N. Nigeria, W. Africa; gr. emporium for region; impt. airport and rly. terminus; p. (estd.) *295,432*.

Kanpur, t., Uttar Pradesh, India; fertilisers.

Kansas, st., U.S.A.; called the " Sunflower State "; prairie; farming, maize, wheat; cattle, dairying, pigs; coal, petroleum, natural gas, lead, meat-packing, flour-milling, aircraft, chemicals, machin.; cap. Topeka; a. 82,276 sq. m.; p. (1970) *2,222,173*.

Kansas City, Mo., U.S.A.; on right bank of R. Missouri; univ.; gr. livestock mart., car and aircraft assembly, steel, metal; meat pkg., food processing; p. (1960) *475,539*, adjoins Kansas City, Kansas; p. (1960) *121,901*.

Kansk, t., R.S.F.S.R., on Trans-Siberian rly.; ctr. of industl. a.; textiles, wood-working; p. (1959) *74,000*.

Kansu (Gansu), prov., N. China; bordering Inner Mongolia; cap. Lanchow; wheat, cotton, tobacco; livestock; mineral resources; a. 151,161 sq. m.; p. (1953) *12,928,102*.

Kant, t., Kirgiz S.S.R.; 12 m. E. of Frunze; to be expanded to industl. c.; proposed p. *100,000*.

Kaohsiung, spt., Taiwan; on S.W. cst.; exp. rice, sugar; oil refining, aviation spirit, diesel oil; p. (1962) *276,000*.

Kapfenberg, commune, Austria; iron, chemicals, paper; resort; p. (1961) *23,859*.

Kaposvar, t., Hungary; textiles; p. (1962) *45,054*.

Kara-Bogaz, lge. G. on E. cst. of Caspian Sea, Turkmen S.S.R.; very high salinity, impt. deposits of Glauber's salt used in local chemical ind.; a. 7,000 sq. m. [p. (1965) *47,660*.

Karabük, t., Turkey; N. of Ankara; steel wks.;

Karachi, Fed. Terr. of, div., Sind, W. Pakistan, on the Indus delta; univ.; spt., air ctr.; oil refining; industl. gases; steel mill; natural gas from Sui; nuclear power sta. under construction; a. 8,400 sq. m. p. (1961) *2,153,000*.

Karaganda, t., Kazakh S.S.R.; on impt coalfield; engin.; iron and steel wks.; p. (1967) *489,000*.

Karakorum Mtns., Kashmir, India; on border with China; hgst peak Godwin-Austen.

Kara-Kum, sand desert, Turkmen S.S.R.; canal 510 m. long across desert completed 1962.

Kara Sea, Arctic Ocean; E. of Novaya Zemlya; navigation open July–Sept.

Karbala, t., Iraq; N.W. of Hilla; ctr. of pilgrimage; sacred c. of Shiites; p. (1961) *219,015*.

Karcag, t., E. Hungary; tortoiseshell goods; p. (1962) *25,787*.

Karelia A.S.S.R., U.S.S.R., incorporated into R.S.F.S.R. July '56; cap. Petrozavodsk; rich in timber, minerals, precious metals; a. 69,720 sq. m.; p. (1959) *649,000*.

Kariba Dam, in Kariba gorge of Zambezi R., on Rhodesia–Zambia border; operated jointly by the two govts.; one of lgst dams in world with vast artificial lake supplying hydroelec. power to Rhodesia, Malawi, and the Copperbelt of Zambia; completed 1960.

Karikal, former Fr. prov., united with India 1954; on E. cst.; p. (1961) *22,252*.

Karkonosze (Riesengebirge), mtn. range, between Polish Silesia and Bohemia; highest peak Sniezka (Schneekoppe), 5,275 ft.

Karl-Marx-Stadt, t., Karl-Marx-Stadt, E. Germany; cottons, woollens, machin., cars, furniture, chemicals, engin.; p. (1963) *288,597*.

Karlovac, t., Croatia, Jugoslavia; S.W. of Zagreb; chemicals; p. (1959) *30,000*.

Karlovy Vary, t., vat. pl., ČSSR.; on R. Ohre; health resort; porcelain; p. (1961) *42,819*.

Karlshamn, t., Sweden; oil refining, demagnetising sta.; p. (1961) *11,657*.

Karlskoga, mkt. t., Sweden; E. of L. Vänern; armaments, iron and steel; p. (1961) *35,606*.

Karlskrona, ch. naval sta., Sweden; on the S. cst.; lighting fixtures, china; p. (1961) *32,977*.

Karlsruhe, t., Baden-Württemberg, Germany; chemicals, engin., elec., tobacco ind, oil refining; rly. junction; outport on Rhine; nuclear reactor projected (1957); oil pipeline to Lavera, nr. Marseilles, opened 1963; p. (1968) *255,762*.

Karlstad, *t.*, Sweden; on N. shore L. Vänern; ironwks. hy. engin., machin.; p. (1961) *43,064.*

Karnak, *vil.* Upper U.A.R.; on Nile, the site of ancient Thebes; ruined temples.

Karpathos, *I.*, Dodecanese, Greece; Mediterranean Sea; between Rhodes and Crete, p. *3,747.*

Karoos, **Gr.** and **Little**, extensive treeless plateau between mtn. ranges covered by scrub, W. Cape Prov., S. Africa.

Kars, *c.*, Turkey; woollens, carpets; p. (1965) *41,236.* [(1961) *46,842.*

Karvina, *t.*, ČSSR.; coal, iron, chemicals; p.

Kasai, *R.*, Angola and Congo, Central Africa; rises in Bihé Plateau (Angola) and flows over 1,200 m. into R. Congo 120 m. above Kinshasa.

Kasanlik, *t.*, Central Bulgaria; captured from Turks at surrender of Sipka Pass 1878; famous for attar of roses; p. (1956) *30,934.*

Kashan, *c.*, Iran; Isfahan prov.; carpets, velvet; p. (1967) *153,986.* [R. Yarkand.

Kashgar, *R.*, E. Turkestan; flowing 500 m. to the

Kashing, *t.*, N. Chekiang, E. China; on Grand Canal; mkt. and tr. ctr.; p. *c. 86,000.*

Kashmir, *see* Jammu and Kashmir.

Kassala, *prov.*, Sudan; a. 134,450 sq. m.; p. (estd. 1951) *788,200.*

Kassel, *t.*, Hesse, W. Germany; on R. Fulda; cas.; iron. machin., cars, wood; route ctr.; p. (1968) *212,920.*

Kastamonu, *t.*, Karasu, Turkey; cap. of Turkish I. same name; great comm. ctr.; fruit, cotton, mohair; p. (1960) *19,450.* [*10,162.*

Kastoria, *t.*, N. Greece; E. of Vérroia; p. (1961)

Katanga, *prov.*, Congo; cap. Lubumbashi; copper, radium, uranium; cattle; a. 180,000 sq. m.; p. *1,178,029.*

Katmandu, *cap.*, Nepal; on Vishnumati R., 75 m. from Indian frontier; highway to Kodari; hydro-elec. sta.; brick and tile wks.; p. (1961) *195,260.*

Kathiawar, *peninsula*, Gujarat, India.

Katoomba, *t.*, N.S.W., Australia; holiday resort; alt. 3,300 ft.; p. (1966) *10,513.*

Katowice, *prov.*, S. Poland; cap. K.; mng. and industl. a., drained by upper Vistula and upper Warta Rs.; a. 3,674 sq. m.; p. *3,253,000.*

Katowice, *c.*, S. Poland; ch. mng. and industl. ctr.; heavy machin., chemicals; p. (1965) *286,000.*

Katrine, Loch, S.W. Perth, Scot.; on R. Teith, 8 m. long; principal source of Glasgow water supply; beautiful scenery.

Kattegat, arm of North Sea linked with Baltic; separates Denmark (Jutland) from Sweden; 40–70 m. wide.

Katwijk, *t.*, Neth., S. Holland; on N. Sea, 15 m. from the Hague; resort; synthetic resins; p. (1967) *33,666.* [*28,176.*

Kauai, *I.*, Hawaiian Is.; a. 555 sq. m.; p. (1960)

Kaunas (Kovno), *t.*, Lithuanian S.S.R.; on R. Niemen; old-time cap.; univ.; metal goods, chemicals, textiles; hydro-elec. sta. under construction; p. (1967) *276,000.*

Kavalla, *prefecture*, Macedonia, Greece; ch. t. Kavalla; p. (1961) *140,445.*

Kavalla, *t.*, Kavalla, Greece; on Bay of Kavalla; gr. tobacco ctr.; p. (1961) *44,517.*

Kavaratti, *I.*, Laccadive, Minicoy and Amindivi Is., India; admin. ctr. of Union terr.; p. (1961) *2,828.*

Kawasaki, *c.*, Honshu, Japan; S. sub. of Tokyo; pilgrims; engin.; steel plate, petro-chemicals, synthetic resins, rubber; p. (1964) *789,000.*

Kawerau, *t.*, N.I., N.Z.; pulp and paper mill; p. (1961) *4,413.*

Kawthoolei, *div.*, Burma; former Karen st. extended to include areas in Tenasserim and Irrawaddy, inhabited by Karens. [*126,913.*

Kayseri, *t.*, Turkey; S.E. of Ankara; p. (1965)

Kazakhstan, *constituent rep.*, U.S.S.R.; cap. Alma-Ata; steppe with stock-raising; lge. desert areas, being made fertile by irrigation; grain in N.; coal at Karaganda; asbestos at Dzhetygara; metaborite (richest boron mineral); minerals, oil; atomic power sta. being built in W., on Caspian Sea; a. 1,072,797 sq. m.; p. (1970) *12,850,000.*

Kazan, *t.*, R.S.F.S.R.; impt. tr. ctr. for E. U.S.S.R., Turkestan Bokhara and Iran; cath.; univ.; engin., chemicals, synthetic rubber, textiles, oil refining, paper; natural gas pipeline to Minnibayevo (Tatar A.S.S.R.); p. (1967) *804,000.*

Kazan Retto (Volcano Is.), *gr. of Is.*, Pac. Oc.; S. of Ogasawara Is. and of Japan.

Kazerun, *t.*, S.W. Iran; oranges, cotton, opium; p. (1956) *30,659.* [*17,417.*

Kazincbarcika, *t.*, Hungary; chemicals; p. (1962)

Kazvin, *t.*, Navistain, Iran; good transit tr.; p. (estd. 1950) *80,000.*

Kearny, *t.*, N.J., U.S.A.; mnfs.; p. (1960) *37,472.*

Kearsley, *urb. dist.*, Lancs, Eng.; chemicals and paper, cotton; p. (1961) *10,302.*

Keban Dam, S.E. Turkey; at confluence of the E. and W. branches of Euphrates; projected.

Kecskemet, *t.*, Hungary; nr. Budapest; fruit canning, wine distilling; p. (1962) *63,327.*

Kedah, *st.*, Malaysia, N.W. Malaya; rice, rubber, coconuts; a. 3,660 sq. m.; cap. Alor Star; p. (estd. 1966) *913,595.*

Kedzierzyn, *t.*, Opole, Poland; p. (1965) *26,000.*

Keeling Is., *see* Cocos Is.

Keelung, *c.*, N. Taiwan; naval base and prin. pt.; chemicals; gold, sulphur and copper mng.; p. (estd.) *226,400.*

Keene, *c.*, N.H., U.S.A.; mnfs.; p. (1960) *17,562.*

Keeper, *mtn.*, Tipperary, Ireland; alt. 2,265 ft.

Keewatin, *dist.*, Northwest Terr., Canada; chiefly "barren lands "; a. 228,160 sq. m.

Kei (Kai) Is., *gr.* off cst. of W. Irian, Indonesia, in Banda Sea; densely forested; p. *50,648.*

Keighley, *t.*, *mun. bor.*, W.R. Yorks., Eng.; in Aire valley, 15 m. N.W. of Leeds; engin., textiles; p. (estd. 1967) *55,710.*

Keith, *burgh*, Banff, Scot.; on Isla R.; mftg. inds.; in agr. dist.; p. (1961) *4,208.*

Kelaniya, *t.*, Ceylon; tyre factory.

Kelantan, *st.*, Malaysia; N.E. Malaya; rice, coconuts, rubber; a. 5,720 sq. m.; cap. Kota Bharu; p. (estd. 1966) *665,711.* [(1960) *5,061.*

Kellogg, *c.*, N.E. Idaho. U.S.A.; lead-mines; p.

Kelso, *burgh*, Roxburgh, Scot.; at confluence of Rs. Teviot and Tweed; p. (1961) *3,964.*

Kelvin, *R.*, Scotland, flows S.W. to Clyde at Partick; length 21 m.

Kemerovo, *t.*, R.S.F.S.R.; S.E. of Tomsk; iron, chemicals, coal, textiles; p. (1967) *358,000.*

Kemi (Kymmene), *dep.*, Finland; a. 3,537 sq. m.; cap. K.; p. (1966) *347,696.*

Kempsey, *t.*, N.S.W., Australia; dairy prod. timber; p. (1966) *8,173.*

Kempston, *urb. dist.*, Bedford, Eng.; on R. Ouse, 3 m. S.W. of Bedford; p. (1961) *9,173.*

Kempten, *t.*, Bavaria, Germany; nr. L. Constance; Benedictine Abbey; textiles, furniture, paper; rly. junction; p. (1963) *44,500.*

Ken, *R.*, N. India, flows to the Jumna; length 230 m.

Kena, *see* Qena.

Kendal, *mkt. t.*, *mun. bor.*, Westmorland, Eng.; engin., footwear, woollens; p. (estd. 1967) *19,140.*

Kenilworth, *mkt. t.*, *urb. dist.*, Warwick, Eng.; 4 m. S.W. of Coventry; ruined cas.; lt. engin., agr. repair wk.; p. (estd. 1967) *20,450.*

Kenitra. *See* Mina Hassan Tani. [*6,982.*

Kenmare, *rurl dist.*, *t.*, Kerry, Ireland; p. (1961)

Kenmore, *t.*, N.Y., U.S.A.; p. (1960) *21,261.*

Kennebec, *R.*, Maine, U.S.A.; flows to Atlantic; length 200 m.

Kennet, *R.*, Wilts and Berks, Eng.; trib. of R. Thames; followed by main rly. London to W. of England; length 44 m.

Kenosha, *c.*, Wis., U.S.A., on W. shore of L. Michigan; mnfs.; p. (1960) *67,899.* [London.

Kensal Green, *dist.*, Middx, Eng.; sub. N.W.

Kensington and Chelsea, Royal Borough of, *inner bor.*, W. London, Eng.; mainly residtl.; contains K. Palace and Gardens; p. (1966) *215,000.*

Kent, *maritme co.*, S.E. Eng.; agr., stock-raising, hops and cherries; co. t. Maidstone; a. 1,525 sq. m.; p. (1966) *1,325,000.*

Kentucky, *E. central st.*, Mississippi basin, U.S.A.; agr., coal, fluorspar, petroleum, natural gas; tobacco, chemicals, machin., metal, steel, hemp, asphalt; tobacco, hay, corn; cattle and horse raising; cap. Frankfort; lgst. c. Louisville, at falls of Ohio R.; a. 40,395 sq. m.; p. (1970) *3,160,555.*

Kentucky, *R.*, U.S.A.; flows from Cumberland Mtns. to the Ohio R.; length 350 m.

Kenya, Rep. of, *indep. sov. st.* within Brit. Commonwealth (1963), E. Africa; cst. strip flat, interior elevated; climate varies according to elevation; vegetation tropical; forests on cstal. belt, semi-desert and grasslands on uplands, hydroelec. stns. at Wanjii, Tana, and Kinda; ruma (under constr.); mainly agr.; maize-sugar, coconuts, sisal, cotton, coffee, pyrethrum; cattle, sheep; bamboo, pencil cedar, hardwoods; gold; oil refining at Changamwe; cap. Nairobi; a. 224,960 sq. m.; p. (estd.) *10,890,000*

Kenya, Mt., *volcanic pk.,* Kenya; 17,040 ft.

Keokuk, *industl., c.,* S.E. Iowa, U.S.A.; on Mississippi at foot of Des Moines rapids; p. (1960) *16,316.* ([1961) *62,090.*

Keos (Chios), Ægean Is., Greece; cap. Keos; p.

Kephallenia (Cephalonia), one of the Ionian Is., Greece; currants, olive oil; cap. Argostolion; devastated by earthquake 1953; a. 315 sq. m.; p. (1961) *46,302.*

Kerala, *st.,* India; cap. Trivandrum; plantations producing rubber, tea, pepper; zircon; a. 15,002 sq. m.; p. (1961) *26,903,715.*

Kerch, *spt.,* Ukrainian S.S.R.; iron and steel, manganese, vanadium and phosphorus; shipbldg.; fisheries; p. (1967) *115,000.*

Kerguelen, *French archipelago,* dependency of Madagascar, S. of Indian Ocean; whaling and fishing sta.; a. 1,400 sq. m.

Kerkrade, *t.,* Limburg, Neth.; anc. Abbey; music ctr.; p. (1967) *50,566.*

Kérkyra (Corfu), most N. of Ionian Is., Greece; a. 274 sq. m.; mtnous.; p. (1961) *101,555.*

Kérkyra, *spt., cap.,* Kérkyra I., Greece; wine, fruits, olives; p. (1961) *26,991.*

Kermadec Is., S. Pac. Oc., gr. belonging to New Zealand, 600 m. N.N.E. of New Zealand; a. 13 sq. m.; meteorological sta. on Sunday I. (lgst. of gr.); p. (1961) *10.*

Kerman, *prov.,* S. Iran; mtnous, much desert land; agr.; carpets; coal and iron ore mng. being developed; recent copper find; major irrigation scheme projected; p. (1967) *243,770.*

Kerman, *c.,* S. Central Iran; prov. cap.; airpt.; p. (1967) *163,689.* [airpt.; p. (1967) *424,978.*

Kermanshah, *c.,* Iran; cap. Kermanshahan prov.;

Kermanshahan, *prov.,* Iran; frontier Iraq; oilfields; p. (1967) *779,336.*

Kern, *R.,* E. Cal., U.S.A.; one of most impt. power-generating Rs. in st.

Kerry, *maritime co.,* Munster, Ireland; a. 1,816 sq. m.; cap. Tralee; p. (1966) *112,642.*

Keski Soumen, *dep.,* Finland; p. (1966) *248,282.*

Kesteven, *administrative div.,* Lincoln, Eng.; ch. ts. Grantham, Stamford and Sleaford; a. 724 sq. m.; p. (1961) *49,946.*

Keswick, *mkt. t., urb. dist.,* Cumberland, Eng.; on Greta R.; at N. end of L. Derwentwater; tourist ctr.; pencils; p. (1961) *4.752.*

Ketchikan, *t.,* Alaska, U.S.A.; halibut, salmon; pulp, lead, zinc; p. (1960) *6,483.*

Kettering, *mkt. t., mun. bor.,* Northants, Eng.; nr. Wellingborough; iron, steel, boots, shoes; p. (estd. 1967) *39,270.*

Kettering, *t.,* Ohio, U.S.A.; p. (1960) *54,462.*

Kew, *sub.* London, Surrey, Eng.; on R. Thames opp. Brentford; contains Kew Gardens. (Kew Observatory is in Old Deer Park, Richmond.)

Kewanec, *t.,* N.W. Ill., U.S.A.; agr.; coal, engin.; p. (1960) *16,324.* [15,144.

Keynsham, *t., urb. dist.,* Somerset, Eng.; p; coal,

Key West, *c.,* Fla., U.S.A.; on sm. I. same name about 100 m. from the mainland; naval sta., and cigar factories; nearest U.S.A. pt. to the Panama Canal; p. (1960) *33,956.*

Khabarovsk, *t.,* R.S.F.S.R.; on Amur R.; cath.; oil refining, aircraft engin., sawmilling; oil pipeline connects with oilfields in N. Sakhalin; cellulose, cardboard; p. (1967) *420,000.*

Khairpur, *div.,* W. Pakistan; a. 6,050 sq. m.; p. (1961) *2,586,000.*

Khalkidhiki (Chalcidice), *prefecture,* Macedonia, Greece; cap. Poliyicos; p. (1961) *79,838.*

Khamgaon, *t.,* Maharashtra, India; cotton; p. (1961) *44,432.* [refinery; p. *5,000.*

Khanaqin, *t.,* Iraq; nr. E. frontier; oil-fields,

Khandwa, *t.,* Madhya Pradesh, India; S. of Indore; cotton, oil-pressing; p. (1961) *63,505.*

Khania (Canea), *prefecture* I. of Crete; cap. Khania; p. (1961) *130,898.*

Khania (Canea), *cap.* Crete; in sheltered bay on N.W. cst.; p. (1961) *38,467.*

Khanka Lake, *L.,* on Manchurian border, U.S.S.R.

Kharan, *dist.,* W. Pakistan; a. 18,508 sq. m.; p. (estd. 1951) *54,000.*

Kharkov, *c.,* Ukrainian S.S R.; on R. Donets; univ., cath.; rly. ctr. farm implements, engin., paper, chemicals; p. (1967) *1,092,000.*

Khartoum, *prov.,* Sudan; a. 5,700 sq. m.; p. with Omdurman (1956) *275,000.*

Khartoum cap. Sudan; at confluence of White and Blue Niles; univ.; ivory, gum. ostrich feathers, brewing; p. (estd. 1956) *87,000.*

Khartoum North, *t.,* Sudan; lge. textile mill; p. (1961) *39,081.*

Khashm el Girba, *t.,* Sudan; new t. on Atbara R., between Khartoum and Ethiopian border; for p. of Wadi Halfa which will be inundated by Aswan Lake; sugar refinery.

Khasi Hills, Assam, N.E. India; form abrupt S. edge to middle Brahmaputra valley; very heavy monsoon rains on S.-facing slopes; lower slopes forested; middle slopes constitute impt. tea-growing region; rise to over 6,000 ft.

Khaskovo, *t.,* Bulgaria; woollens, carpets, silk, tobacco; p. *27,294.*

Kherson, *t.,* Ukrainian S.S R.; 10 m. up R. Dnieper from Black Sea; grain, oil refining, engin., textiles, shipbldg.; p. (1967) *222,000.*

Khingan, Gr. and Little, *mtn. ranges,* Inner Mongolia and Heilungkiang prov., N.E. China; rich timber resources.

Khios, *I.,* Ægean Is., Greece; wines, figs, fruits, marble; cap. Khios; p. (1961) *62,090.*

Khiva, *originally vassal st.* of Russia; now part of Uzbekistan, U.S.S.R.

Khiva, *t.,* Uzbekistan, U.S.S.R.; silks, cottons, carpets; p. (estd.) *25,000.*

Khmelnitskiy (Proskurov), *t.,* Ukrainian S.S.R.; on R. Bug; machin. tools, textiles, food inds.; p. (1959) *62,000.*

Khor Abdulla, Iraq; in Persian G. nr. Basra; deep water oil loading island terminal inaugurated 1963.

Khorramshahr, *spt.,* S.W. Iran; leading pt. on Persian G.; import and export ctr.; p. (1967) *156,323.*

Khotin, *c.,* Ukrainian S.S.R., in Bessarabia, on Dniester R.; food processing plants.

Khovu-Aksy, *t.,* Tuva A.S.S.R.; on R. Elegest, 50 m. S.W. of Kyzyl; new town 1956; cobalt deposit being developed.

Khurasan, *prov.,* Iran; W. of Afghanistan; ch. prod. wool; cap. Meshed; p. (estd. 1956) *1,300,000.* [p. (1961) *41,491.*

Khurja, *t.,* Uttar Pradesh, India; cotton, pottery;

Khorasan, *prov.,* N.E. Iran; bounded by U.S.S.R. and Afghanistan; agr.; wool; turquoise; cap. Mashhad; p. (1967) *2,494,283.*

Khuzestan, *prov.,* W. Iran; frontier Iraq; leading petroleum ctr.; large dams; cap. Ahwaz; p. (1967) *1,614,576.*

Khyber, *difficult mtn. pass,* between W. Punjab, Pakistan and Afghanistan; followed by route from Peshawar to Kabul, traversed by Alexander the Great and by two British expeditions.

Kiamusze (Jiamusi) *c.,* Heilungkiang prov. China; p. (1953) *146,000.*

Kiang-si (Jiangxi), *inland prov.,* China; S. of the Yangtze-Kiang; cap. Nanchang; rice, wheat, tea, silk, cotton; a. 66,600 sq. m.; p. (1953) *16,772,865.*

Kiangsu (Jiangsu), *maritime prov.,* China; exp. much silk; a. 42,085 sq. m.; cap. Chinkiang; p. (1953) *41,252,192.* [Peninsula, China.

Kiaochow Bay, *inlet* on S. side of Shantung

Kicking Horse Pass, *mtn. pass,* over Rocky Mtns., B.C., Canada; used by Canadian Pac. Rly.

Kidderminster, *t., mun. bor.,* Worcester, Eng.; on R. Stour 4 m. above its confluence with R. Severn; carpets, engin., sugar-beet refining, textile machin., elec. vehicles, drop forgings; p. (estd. 1967) *45,510.*

Kidsgrove, *mfftg. t., urb. dist.,* "Potteries," Staffs., Eng.; 3 m. N.W. of Stoke-on-Trent; chemicals, metal wks., rayon, silk and nylon spinning, precast concrete, ceramics; p. (estd. 1967) *21,790.*

Kiel, *spt.,* cap. Schleswig-Holstein, Germany; univ.; Baltic naval pt.; shipbldg. and allied inds., elec. goods, textiles, fishing; p. (1968) *269,327.*

Kiel Canal (Kaiser-Wilhelm-Kanal), Germany; 61 m. long, connects N. Sea with the Baltic; opened in 1895, reconstructed 1914.

Kielce, *co.,* Central Poland; minerals, agr.; cap. K.; a. 17,000 sq. m.; p. (1965) *1,899,000.*

Kielce, *t.,* Central Poland; tr. ctr., metal inds., sawmills, glass and food processing factories; dates from 12th cent.; p. (1965) *102,000.*

Kiev, *c., cap.,* Ukraine, U.S.S.R.; on R. Dnieper; once cap. of Muscovite Empire; cath.; univ.; machin., grain, in a. of rich mineral deposits engin.; natural gas pipeline runs from Dashava; p. (1967) *1,371,000*.

Kigoma, *impt. tr. t.*, Tanzania, Africa; W. terminus of the Central Rly. on L. Tanganyika; p. (1957) *3,970*. [*31,000*

Kikinda, *t.*, Vojvodina, Jugoslavia; p. (1959)

Kilauea, *crater*, 3,646 ft. high, on S.E. slope of Mauna Loa, Hawaii, one of lgst. active craters in world; over 2 miles in diameter.

Kildare, *inland co.*, Leinster, Ireland; a. 654 sq. m.; p. (1966) *66,486*.

Kildare, *mkt. t., cap.*, Kildare, Ireland; cath.; close by is the famous racecourse, the Curragh of Kildare; p. (1966) *2,731*.

Kilimanjaro, *volcanic mtn.*, Tanzania, E. Africa; highest peak in the continent; alt. 19,321 ft.

Kilindini, *spt.*, Kenya; adjoins Mombasa; the finest harbour on E. cst. of Africa.

Kilkenny, *inland co.*, Leinster, Ireland; cap. Kilkenny; pastoral farming, coal, black marble; a. 796 sq. m.; p. (1966) *60,472*.

Kilkenny, *t.*, cap. Kilkenny, Ireland; on R. Nore; local mkt.; p. (1966) *10,057*. [Ireland.

Killcieran Bay, *lge. intricate indentation*, Galway,

Kilkis, *prefecture*, Macedonia, Greece; cap. Kilkis; p. (1961) *102,847*.

Killarney, *t., urb. dist.*, Kerry, Ireland; local mkt. and tourist ctr.; p. (1966) *6,870*.

Killarney, Is. of, Lower, Middle and Upper, celebrated for their beauty; tourist resorts.

Killiecrankie, Pass of, Scot.; on R. Garry; at S. approach to Drumochter Pass; used by main rly. Perth to Inverness.

Kill van Kull, channel between N.J. and Staten I., N.Y., c., U.S.A.

Killybegs, *t.*, Donegal, Ireland; on Donegal Bay.

Killyleagh, *t.*, on Stangford L., Down, N. Ireland; p. (1966) *2,169*.

Kilmarnock, *rly. ctr., lge. burgh*, Ayr, Scot.; on R. Irvine, 11 m. N.E. of Ayr; carpet factories, textile and ironwks.; p. (1961) *47,509*.

Kilmore, *t.*, Victoria, Australia; 30 m. N. of Melbourne; in impt. gap between Grampian Mtns. and Australian Alps.

Kilo-Moto, *goldfield*, Congo, Central Africa; in N.E. of st., 50 m. W. of L. Albert; linked by motor road to R. Congo (Stanleyville) and L. Albert (Kasenyi).

Kilpatrick, New, *par.*, Dunbarton, Scot.; north of R. Clyde; p. (1951) *54,931*.

Kilpatrick, Old, *par.*, Dunbarton, Scot.; on bank of R. Clyde, 9 m. N.W. of Glasgow; lowest ferry across Clyde; p. (1951) *49,248*.

Kilrenny and Anstruther, *burgh*, Fife, Scot.; at entrance to Firth of Forth; fishing, hosiery, oilskin mnfs.; p. (1961) *2,588*.

Kilrush, *spt., urb. dist.*, S.W. Clare, Ireland; on R. Shannon; p. (1966) *2,734*.

Kilsyth, *burgh*, Stirling, Scot.; at S. foot of Campsie Fells, 10 m. W. of Falkirk; whinstone quarries, coal-mining; p. (1961) *9,331*.

Kilwinning, *burgh*, N. Ayr, Scot.; 5 m. E. of Ardrossan; p. (1961) *7,287*; to be incorporated in new t. Irvine.

Kimberley, *c.*, Cape Province, S. Africa; 20 m. from R. Vaal; diamond-mng. dist.; asbestos, manganese, iron, cement, engin.; p. (1960) *91,816* inc. *27,460* Europeans.

Kimberley, *goldfield dist.*, W. Australia; big deposits of bauxite discovered 1965.

Kimberly, *t.*, B.C., Canada; on R. Kootenay in valley between Selkirk Range and Rocky Mtns.; site of Sullivan Mine; lg. lead- zinc mine; ores smelted at Trail; p. (1956) *5,730*.

Kincardine, *maritime co.*, E. Scot., between Angus and Aberdeen; agr. and fishing; co. t. Stonehaven; a. 383 sq. m.; p. (1961) *48,810*.

Kinder Scout, *mtn.*, N. Derby, Eng.; highest point of the Peak dist.; alt. 2,088 ft.

Kindu, *t.*, Congo, Central Africa; on R. Congo; p. *10,628*.

Kineshna, *t.*, U.S.S.R.; N.W. of Gorki; pt. for Ivanovo industl. a.; textiles; p. (1959) *84,000*.

Kineton, *mkt. t.*, Warwick, Eng.; nr. Stratford-on-Avon.

King George's Sound, W. Australia; nr. Albany; fine harbour and bay.

Kinghorn, *burgh*, Fife, Scot.; on Firth of Forth, 3 m. S. of Kirkcaldy; p. (1961) *2,112*.

Kingsbridge, *mkt. t., urb. dist.*, S. Devon, Eng.; at head of Kingsbridge estuary, 10 m. S.W. of Dartmouth; p. (1961) *3,283*.

Kingsclere and Whitchurch, *mkt. t., rural dist.*, N.

Hants, Eng.; on R. Test, 10 m. S.W. of Basingstoke; p. (rural dist. 1961) *23,264*.

Kings Langley, *t.*, Herts, Eng.; 5 m. N. of Watford; paper, light engin.; p. (1961) *4,255*.

King's Lynn, *spt., mun. bor.*, Norfolk, Eng.; on R. Ouse, 3 m. above its mouth; docks; fishing, agr. machin., canning, chemical fertilisers, shoes; p. (estd. 1967) *28,370*.

King's River, Cal., U.S.A.; flows from Sierra Nevada to L. Tulare. [p. (1960) *26,314*.

Kingsport, *t.*, N.E. Tenn., U.S.A.; varied mnfs.;

Kingston, *c.*, Ont., Canada; E. end of L. Ontario; cap. of United Canada, 1841-4; univ., military college; lge inds; p. (1961) *53,926*.

Kingston, *cap.*, Jamaica, W. Indies; oil refining; p. (estd. 1962) *180,000*. [(1960) *29,260*.

Kingston, *t.*, N.Y., U.S.A.; tobacco mftg.; p.

Kingston, *t.*, Penns., U.S.A.; p. (1960) *20,261*.

Kingston-upon-Hull, *see* Hull.

Kingston-upon-Thames, *former co. t., mun. bor.*, Surrey, Eng.; now The Royal Borough of Kingston-upon-Thames, *outer bor.*, Greater London; inc. bors. of Malden and Coombe and Surbiton; residtl.; with Royal Park; aircraft parts; p. (1964) *145,977*.

Kingstown, *see* Dun Laoghaire.

Kingstown, *spt., cap.*, St. Vincent, W.I.; cath. botanic gardens; p. (1956) *6,500*.

Kingsville, *t.*, Texas, U.S.A.; in ranching area; agr., light inds.; p. (1960) *25,297*.

Kingswood, *urb. dist.*, Gloucester, Eng.; nr. Bristol; elec. vehicles, motor cycles, boots, brushes, tools; p. (estd. 1967) *28,710*.

Kington, *mkt. t., urb. dist.*, N.W. Hereford, Eng.; 12 m. W. of Leominster; p. (1961) *1,861*.

Kingussie, *burgh*, Inverness, Scot.; between Cairngorm Mtns. and Monadhliath Mtns., on R. Spey; summer resort; p. (1961) *1,079*.

King William I., off Boothia peninsula in Arctic Ocean, Canada.

King William's Town, *t.*, Cape Prov., S. Africa; on Buffalo R.; industl. ctr.; p. (1960) *14,328* inc. *6,873* whites.

Kinhwa, *c.*, Chekiang, China; in fertile, intensively cultivated basin, 85 m. S.W. of Hangchow p. (estd. 1947) *211,140*.

Kinibalu, *mtn.*, Sabah; alt. 13,455 ft.

Kinlochleven, *vil.*, Argyll, Scot.; at head of Loch Leven; hydro-elec. power sta., aluminium smelting. [N.E. Aberdeen cst., Scot.

Kinnaird Head, *promontory*, nr. Fraserburgh, or N.E. Aberdeen cst., Scot.

Kinross, *sm. inland co.*, Scot.; between Fife and Perth; hilly; oats, potatoes, sheep, cattle; a. 78 sq. m.; p. (1961) *6,704*.

Kinross, *co. burgh*, Kinross, Scot.; on Loch Leven, 16 m. N.E. of Alloa; coal, linen mnfs.; p. (1961) *2,365*.

Kinsale, *spt., urb. dist.*, on K. Harbour, Cork, Ireland; p. (urb. dist. 1961) *7,993*.

Kinshasa (Leopoldville), *cap.*, Congo; above the cataracts on R. Congo; founded by Stanley; p. (1964) *403,000*. [deposits of alluvial tin.

Kinta Valley, S.E. Perak, Malaya; very impt.

Kintyre, *peninsula*, Argyll, Scot.; length 40 m.; greatest breadth 11 m.; S. point the Mull of Kintyre.

Kioga, *L.*, Uganda, E. Africa; on R. Nile midway between L. Victoria and L. Albert; very shallow, fringed with marsh; land reclamation.

Kiölen or Kjölen, *mtn. range*, Scandinavia; highest point Mt. Sulitelma; alt. 6,150 ft.

Kirgiz Steppes, *gr. plains and uplands*, Kirghizia S.S.R., U.S.S.R.; N. of the Caspian and Aral Seas, inhabited by the wandering Mongolian Tatar race numbering nearly *3,000,000*.

Kirghizia, *constituent rep.*, U.S.S.R.; S.W. of Siberia; livestock breeding, mineral resources; a. 77,000 sq. m.; cap. Frunze; p. (1970) *2,933,000*. [iron ore mng.

Kiriburn, *t.* on border of Bihar and Orissa, India

Kirin (Jilin), *prov.*, China; S. of the Sungari R. and N. of Korea and the Liaotung Peninsula; fertile; soyabeans; timber; good rly. services; cap. Kirin, a. 34,616 sq. m.; p. (1953) *11,290,073*

Kirin (Jilin), *c., cap.*, Kirin, N.E. China; on Sungari R. at outlet of Sungari reservoir; impt. position on rly. from Changchun to coastal ports, p. (1953) *435,000*.

Kirkburton, *urb. dist.*, W.R. Yorks, Eng.; S.E. of Huddersfield; woollens; p. (1961) *18,066*.

Kirkby, *urb. dist.*, Lancs., Eng.; p. (estd. 1967) *63 800*.

Kirkby in Ashfield, *t.*, *urb. dist.*, Notts, Eng.; 10 m. N.W. of Nottingham; coal; p. (estd. 1967) 22,450.

Kirkby Moorside, *mkt. t.*, *rural dist.*, N.R. Yorks, Eng.; sailplanes, gliders; p. (1961) 4,402.

Kirkcaldy, *spt. t.*, *burgh*, Fife, Scot.; on N. side of F. of Forth; shipping; linoleum, potteries, linen bleaching, engin.; p. (1961) 52,371.

Kirkcudbright, *maritime co.*, S.W. Scot.; abutting on Irish Sea and Solway Firth; chiefly agr.; a. 909 sq. m.; p. (1961) 28,877.

Kirkcudbright, *co. burgh*, Kirkcudbright, Scot.; on Kirkcudbright Bay, Solway Firth, 25 m. S.W. of Dumfries; agr., hosiery; p. (1961) 2,448.

Kirkenes, *t.*, Finnmark, N. Norway; on S. arm of Varanger Fjord, nr. Norway–U.S.S.R. bdy.; iron-ore mines. [weaving; p. (1961) 4,760.

Kirkham, *t.*, *urb. dist.*, Lancs., Eng.; cotton

Kirkintilloch,*burgh*,Dunbarton,Scot.; on Forth and Clyde Canal; iron, coal-mng; p. (1961) 2,448.

Kirkland Lake, *t.*, Ontario, Canada; on rly. nr. Quebec–Ontario bdy., 45 m. N. of Cobalt; ctr. of impt. gold-mng. dist.; p. (estd. 1956) 19,000.

Kirkstone Pass, *min. pass*, Westmorland, Eng.; used by main road between Ullswater and Windermere Lakes.

Kirksville,*industl. t.*,Mo.,U.S.A.; p.(1960) 13,123.

Kirkuk, *t.*, Iraq; mart for Arab horses; lge. oilfield with pipelines to Tripoli, Haifa and Banias: p. (1956) 89,917.

Kirkwall, *burgh*, Pomona I., Orkneys, Scot.; off the N.E. Scottish cst.; p. (1961) 4 315. [29,421.

Kirkwood, *sub.*, St. Louis, Mo., U.S.A.; p. 1960)

Kirov, *t.*, R.S.F.S.R.; on trans-Siberian Rly.; engin., sawmilling, chemicals, leather inds.; p. (1967) 302,000.

Kirovabad, *t.*, W. Azerbaydzhan S.S.R.; copper, manganese mines; textiles, petroleum, aluminium plant under construction; p. (1967) 170,000.

Kirovgrad, *t.*, Urals; copper; p. (1954) 50,000.

Kirovograd, *t.*, Ukrainian S.S.R.; engin.; p. (1967) 161,000.

Kirovsk, *t.* R.S.F.S.R.; on Kola peninsula; apatite, nephelite, chemicals; p. (1954) 50,000.

Kirriemuir, *burgh*, Angus, Scot.; on N. margin of Strathmore, 5 m. W. of Forfar; jute weaving, oat milling; p. (1961) 3,485.

Kiruna, *t.*, N. Sweden; inside Arctic Circle, N.W. of Lulea; linked by rly. to Narvik (Norway); impt. deposits of iron ore; p. (1961) 26,804.

Kisangani (Stanleyville), *t.*, Congo, Africa; on R. Congo nr. Stanley Falls.

Kiselevsk, *t.*, W. Siberia, R.S.F.S.R.; coalmng., engin.; p. (1967) 139,000.

Kishinev, *cap.* Moldavian S.S.R., U.S.S.R.; univ.; agr., engin.; vineyards; p. (1963) 254,000.

Kislovodsk, *t.*, R.S.F.S.R.; spa; p. (1959) 79,000.

Kismayu, *pt.*, Somalia; new deep-water harbour; airpt. [length 90 m.

Kissimee R., Fla., U.S.A.; flows to L. Okeechobee;

Kisumu,*spt.,cap.*,Nyanza prov., Kenya, E. Africa; at head of Kavirondo G. on L. Victoria; original W. terminus of rly. from Mombasa; still handles bulk of cotton from Buganda and coffee from N. Tanzania for transhipment E. by rail; p. (1962) 23,200.

Kitakyushu City, *c.*, N. Kyushu, Japan; one of Japan's largest municipalities on merging (1963) of ts. Moji, Kokura, Tobata, Yawata and Waka-matsu; sixth c. to enjoy special aut. rights; p. (1970) 1,042,319.

Kitchener, *c.*, Ontario, Canada; agr. machin., tyres, hardware; p. (1961) 74,485.

Kittatinny Mtns. or Blue Mtns., Penns. and N.J., U.S.A.; ridge of Appalachian system.

Kitwe, *t.*, Zambia; contiguous to mine township of Nkana, ctr. of copperbelt; p. (1966) 146,000.

Kiukiang, *c.*, *former treaty pt.*, Kiangsi, China; Yangtze-Kiang; p. (1948) 180,897.

Kiungchow, *c.*, *cap.*, Hainan Is., China; on N. cst.; former treaty pt.

Kivu, L., Central Africa; N. of L. Tanganyika by which it is joined by Russisi R.; length 55 m.; a. 1 100 sq. m.

Kizel, *t.*, R.S.F.S.R., in Urals; ctr. of coal mng. a.; mng. equipment; p. (1959) 60,000.

Kizilirmak (or Red River), the lgst. R. of Turkey in Asia; rises in Kisil Dagh, flows to Black Sea via Sivas; l. 600 m.

Kladno, *mng. t.*, ČSSR.; 10 m. N.W. of Prague; coal, iron, steel, engin.; p. (1961) 49,561.

Klagenfurt, *t.*, *cap.*, Carinthia, Austria; winter sports ctr.; varied mnfs.; p. (1961) 69,218.

Klaipeda (Memel), *spt.*, Lithuanian S.S.R.; nr. N. extremity Kurisches Haff; exp. timber, textiles, chemicals, paper; p. (1967) 125,000.

Klamath, *L.*, Cal. and Ore., U.S.A., discharges by K. R. (275 m.) to Pacific.

Klamath Falls, *t.*, Ore., U.S.A.; p. (1960) 16,949.

Klamono, *t.*, New Guinea, nr. Klasafet R.; oil pipe-line to Sorong harbour.

Klang, *t.*, Selangor, Malaya; designated future st. cap.; coffee, rubber; p. 33,506.

Klatovy, *t.*, S.W. Bohemia, ČSSR.; mkt.; rose-growing a., textiles; p. (1961) 14,004.

Klerksdorp, *t.*, S. Transvaal, S. Africa; gold, dia-monds: p. (1962) 48,500 inc. 22,000 whites.

Kleve (Cleves) *t.*, N. Rhine–Westphalia, Germany; nr. Netherlands bdy; foodstuffs, leather, machin., tobacco; p. (1963) 22,100.

Klin, *t.*, R.S.F.S.R., 45 m. from Moscow; glass, textiles; p. (1959) 53,000.

Klondyke, *R.*, Yukon, Canada; small trib. of Yukon in gold-mine region.

Klodzko (Glatz), *t.*, Lower Silesia, Poland, German before 1945; on R. Nisa (Neisse); rly. junction: p. (1965) 25,000.

Knaresborough, *mkt. t.*, *urb. dist.*, W.R. Yorks., Eng.; 3 m. N.E. of Harrogate; p. (1961) 9,311.

Knighton, *mkt. t.*, *urb. dist.*, Radnor, Wales; on R. Teme; p. (1961) 1,817.

Knockmealdown Mtns., cos. Waterford and Tipperary, Ireland; highest point 2,609 ft.

Knossos, *ruined c.*, *cap.* of ancient Crete; S.E. of Candia; ctr. of Cretan Bronze Age culture, *c.* 1800 B.C.

Knottingley, *t.*, *urb. dist.*, W.R. Yorks, Eng.; on R. Aire, 12 m. S.E. of Leeds; engin., glass, tar distilling, chemicals, shipbldg.; p. (1961) 11,153.

Knoxville, *c.*, Tenn., U.S.A.; univ.; textiles; marble, plastics, chemicals, aluminium; agr. tobacco; p. (1960) 111,827.

Knutsford, *mkt. t.*, *urb. dist.*, Cheshire, Eng.; 6 m. N.E. of Northwich; p. (1961) 9,389.

Kobe, *t.*, *spt.*, Honshu, Japan; at E. end of Inland Sea; shipbldg., silk-weaving; steel wks.; gr. tr.; p. (1970) 1,288,754.

Koblenz (Coblenz) *t.*, Rhineland Palatinate, Ger-many; at confluence of Rs. Rhine and Moselle; fine buildings, wine, paper, machin., leather, ceramics; p. (1968) 105,434.

Kocaeli, *prov.*, Turkey; on G. of Sea of Marmara.

Kochi, *c.*, Shikoku, Japan; industl.; fishing; p. (1965) 217,889.

Kodiak I., N. Pac. Oc.; the lgst. I. of W. Alaska; (90 m. long); fur-trading, extensive salmon fishing, canning; ch. settlement St. Paul, on Chiniak R.; suffered earthquake damage 28 Mar. 1964; p. (1960) 2,628.

Kofu, *c.*, Honshu, Japan; silk, vegetables, grapes; p. (1964) 172,000.

Kohat, *t.*, N.W. Pakistan; on trib. of Indus; military t.; cement wks.; p. (1961) 49,800.

Koh-I-Baba Mtns., Afghanistan, spur of the Hindu Kush; highest point 17,640 ft.

Kohima, *dist.*, Nagaland, India; a. 2,374 sq. m.; p. (1961) 168,924. [engin.; p. (1967) 128,000.

Kokand, *t.*, Uzbek S.S.R.; textiles, chemicals,

Kokiu (Gejiu), *c.*, Yunnan prov., China, tin-mng.; p. (1953) 160,000.

Kokkola (Gamla Karleby), *t.*, Finland; on cst. G. of Bothnia; p. (1961) 16,153.

Kokomo, *c.*, Ind., U.S.A.; on Wild Cat R.; steel, glass, agr. region; p. (1960) 47,197.

Koko Nor (Ching Hai), *salt L.*, Tsinghai prov., China; alt. 10,000 ft. in Tibetan highlands; a. *c.* 2,300 sq. m.

Kokura, *c.*, N. Kyushu, Japan: 40 m. N.E. of Fukuoka; steel, chemicals, porcelain ware, tex-tiles, p. (1960) 286,000.

Kola, *peninsula*, R.S.F.S.R.; extension of Lapland.

Kola, *t.*, R.S.F.S.R.; nr. Murmansk, on Kola Peninsular. [146,811.

Kolar Gold Fields, Mysore, India; p. (1961)

Kolding, *mkt. t.*, Vejle, Denmark; good harbour; engin., lt. inds.; p. (1960) 35,101.

Kolguev, *I.*, Arctic Oc.; at entrance of Cheshsk G., N.E. of Arkhangelsk. [(1961) 187,442.

Kolhapur, *t.*, Maharashtra, India; bauxite; p.

Kolo, *t.*, Poland; on l. of the Warta; pottery.

Kolobrzeg (Kolberg), *c.*, *spt.* W. Pomerania, Poland, German before 1945; cath.; resort; fishing: p. (1965) 22,000.

Kolomna, *t.*, R.S.F.S.R., 72 m. S.E. of Moscow; engin., locomotives, machin.; p. (1967) 131,000.

Kolyma R., flows into E. Siberian Sea, R.S.F.S.R.

Komárno, *industl. t.*, ČSSR.; on R. Danube; textiles; p. (1961) *24,009*. [p. (1962) *25,832*.

Komlo, *t.*, Hungary; new mng. t.; coking coal;

Komotene, *cap.*, Rhodope, Thrace, Greece; p. (1961) *28,335*. [mill; textiles.

Kompong Cham, *t.*, Cambodia cotton ginning

Kompong Som (Sihanoukville), *t.*, Cambodia; tractors, oil refining.

Komsomolsk, *c.*, R.S.F.S.R.; built by volunteer youth labour after 1932; heavy industl. development; oil refining; pipeline connects with oilfield in N. Sakhalin; p. (1967) *207,000*.

Komsomoloskiy, *c.*, Mordvinian A.S.S.R.; on site of present workers' settlement; planned p. *50,000*.

Königshütte, *see* Chorzow.

Konotop, *t.*, Ukrainian S.S.R.; rly. junct. on Moscow–Kiev line; engin., metals; p. (1959) *53,000*.

Konstantinovka, *industl. t.*, Ukraine, S.S.R. U.S.S.R.; in heart of Donbas industl. region, 38 m. N. of Donetsk; heavy engin., iron and steel, zinc smelting; p. (1959) *89,000*.

Konya, *l.*, Turkey; well wooded; opium; ch. t. K. (the ancient Iconium); impt. tr.; p. (1965) *157,801*.

Koolyanobbing, *t.*, W. Australia; mng. t.; high-grade haematite and limonite ores; linked to rly. between Kwinana and Kalgoorlie 1968.

Kootenay R. (Flat Bow R.), trib. of the Columbia R. flowing in Mont.. U.S.A., and B.C.; length 450 m.

Koper (Capo d'Istria), *spt.*, Jugoslavia; cath., old fort; Austro-Italian disputes over ownership since very early days; p. (1960) *10,100*.

Kopeysk, *t.*, R.S.F.S.R.; in Urals; lignite mng., agr. and mng. machin.; p. (1967) *167,000*.

Köping, *t.*, Sweden; W. of L. Malaren; iron ore and minerals; p. (1961) *17,592*. [(1961) *285,862*.

Kopparberg, *co.*, Sweden; a. 11,649 sq. m.; p.

Korangi, *t.*, W. Pakistan; oil refinery.

Korba, *t.*, Madyha Pradesh, India; mng. a.; fertilisers; p. (1961) *12,424*.

Korce (Koritza), *t.*, S.E. Albania; sugar refining, brewing; p. (1960) *34,000*.

Kordofan, *prov.*, Sudan, Africa; a. 146,930 sq. m.; cap. El-Obeid; p. (estd. 1951) *1,671,600*.

Korea, *rep., peninsula*, E. Asia; extending between Yellow Sea and Sea of Japan; annexed by Japan in 1910; after Second World War separated into 2 zones along 38th parallel, N. under Russian influence, the S. under American. **Korea, N.:** a. 46,814 sq. m.; mainly agr.; iron ore, steel ingots, oilwells; ch. t. Pyongyang; p. (estd.) *12,000,000*. **Korea S.:** a. 38,452 sq. m.; mainly agr., forestry, fisheries; tungsten, salt; oil refining at Ulsan; cap. Seoul; p. (estd.) *30,000,000*.

Korkino, *t.*, R.S.F.S.R.; in Urals; coal mng.; p. (1959) *85,000*.

Korsör, *spt.*, Sjaelland I., Denmark; fine harbour; glass wks.; p. (1960) *14,276*.

Kortrijk (Courtrai), *t.*, W. Flanders, Belgium; linen, lace; p. (1968) *45,170*.

Kos (Cos), *I.*, Dodecanese Is.. Greece.

Kosciusko, *peak*, Australian Alps, N.S.W., Australia; highest peak in Gr. Dividing Range; alt. 7,328 ft.

Kosi, *barrage*, Bhimnagar, nr. Nepalese–Indian frontier below foothills of Himalayas, inaugurated 1965; hydroelec. plant. projected.

Kosiće, *c.*, ČSSR.; Gothic cath.; univ.; magnesite, chemicals, textiles. sheet steel; p. (1962) *79,581*.

Kosova-Metohija, *aut. reg.*, Yugoslavia; p. (1959) *950,000*.

Kostroma, *c.*, R.S.F.S.R.; at confluence of Rs. Volga and Kastromo; textiles, engin.; p. (1967) *205,000*.

Koszalin (Köslin), *t.*, Poland; N.E. of Szczecin; paper mftg., engin., textiles; p. (1965) *52,000*.

Koszalin, *prov.*, N.W. Poland; cap. K.; mainly agr.; a. 6,930 sq. m.; p. *680,400*.

Kota Kinabalu, *spt.*, *cap.*, Sabah, Malaysia; on W. cst.; rubber; p. (1960) *21,719*.

Kotah, *t.*, Rajasthan, India; on R. Chambal; muslins; p. (1961) *120,345*.

Köthen, *t.*, Halle, E. Germany; N. of Halle; cas.; metallurgy, sugar, machin., chemicals; rly. junction; p. (1963) *33,773*. [(1966) *32,859*.

Kotka, *spt.*, on Gulf of Finland; wood pulp; p.

Kotri, *t.*, W. Pakistan; on R. Indus, opposite Hyderabad; barrage 4½ m. N. of the t., started to help irrigate Sind; p. *7,617*.

Kottayam, *t.*, Kerala, India; p. (1961) *52,625*.

Koulikoro, *t.*, Mali, W. Africa; on upper course of R. Niger; mkt. for ground-nuts, gum-

arabic, sisal; linked by R. to Timbuktu and Gao; rly. terminus, 760 m. from Dakar.

Kovrov, *t.*, R.S.F.S.R.; on Gorki rly. line and R. Klyazma; imst. agr. exp. ctr.; engin., textiles; p. (1967) *114,000*.

Kowloon, *spt.*, S.E. China; on mainland opp. Hong Kong I.; tr. ctr.; p. (1961) *726,976*.

Koyali, *nr.* Baroda, Gujarat, India; oil refining.

Kozani, *prefecture*, Macedonia, Greece; cap. Kozani; p. (1961) *190,607*.

Kragerö, *spt.*, Telemark, Norway; exp. ice, timber, wood-pulp, etc.; p. (1961) *4,329*.

Kragujevac, *t.*, central Serbia, Jugoslavia; cath., college, arsenal, garrison; p. (1960) *46,000*.

Kra, Isthmus of, between G. of Siam and Indian Oc.; connects Malaya with Asian mainland.

Krakatao, *volcanic I.*, Strait of Sunda, Indonesia; greater part destroyed by eruption, 1883.

Kraków, *prov.*, Poland; cap. Kraków; a. 6,367 sq. m.; p. (1965) *2,127,000*.

Kraków, *t.*, Poland; machin., chemicals. farm implements; univ.; p. (1965) *520,000*.

Kramatorsk, *c.*, E. Ukraine, U.S.S.R.; heavy engin., metallurgy; p. (1967) *136,000*.

Kramfors, Sweden; on G. of Bothnia; paper mill and sulphite pulp wks. projected.

Krasnodar, *t.*, R.S.F.S.R.; on R. Kuban; oil refining, engin., textiles; p. (1967) *395,000*.

Krasnoturinsk, *t.*, R.S.F.S.R.; in Urals, 6 m. N.W. of Serov; aluminium, coal; p. (1959) *62,000*.

Krasnovodsk, *t.*, Turkmen S.S.R.; oil refining, engin.; p. (1956) *38,000*.

Krasnoyarsk, *t.*, R.S.F.S.R.; on Trans-Siberian Rly. at crossing of R. Yenesei; oil refining, engin., synthetic rubber; copper deposits nearby; polyester fibre plant projected; chemical plants; iron ore deposits to be developed; p. (1967) *557,000*.

Krasnyy Luch, *t.*, Ukrainian S.S.R.; coal mng.; Shterovka power sta. nearby; p. (1959) *94,000*.

Krefeld, *t.*, N. Rhine–Westphalia, Germany; ctr. of German silk ind.; steel. machin., chemicals, soap; rly. junction; p. (1968) *225,681*.

Kremenchug, *t.*, Ukrainian S.S.R.; on R. Dnieper; timber, engin., textiles; hydro-elec. sta.; oil refining; p. (1967) *129,000*.

Krems, *industl. t.*, Austria; on R. Danube; vinegar, white lead; p. (1961) *21,046*.

Kreuznach, *t.*, N. Rhine–Westphalia, Germany; on R. Nahe; metallurgy, leather, optical and chemical inds.; viticulture; mineral baths; p. (estd. 1954) *31,800*.

Krishna, *R.*, S. India; rises in W. Ghats, flows E. across Deccan plateau into Bay of Bengal; lower valley and delta under intensive rice cultivation; densely populated; length 850 m.

Kristiansand, *spt.*, Norway; 160 m. S.W. of Oslo; cath.; tr., inds., shipping; p. (1968) *53,736*.

Kristianstad, *co.*, Sweden; a. 2,485 sq. m.; p. (1961) *256,475*.

Kristianstad, *t.*, Sweden; 10 m. from the Baltic; clothing, machin.; p. (1961) *25,813*.

Kristinehamn, *L.*, *pt.*, Sweden; on L. Vänern; egin., machin.; p. (1961) *21,547*.

Krivoi Rog, *t.*, Ukrainian S.S.R.; on R. Ingulats; rich coal and iron dist.; p. (1967) *498,000*.

Krkonose (Riesengebirge), range between Polish Silesia and Bohemia; highest peak Snežka (Schneekoppe) 5,275 ft.

Kroměříž, *t.*, Moravia, ČSSR.; mnfs., engin.; p. (1961) *20,583*. [(1961) *158,977*.

Kronoberg, *co.*, Sweden; a. 3,828 sq. m.; p.

Kronstadt, *spt.* (*strongly fortfd.*), on I. in G. of Finland; Baltic pt. and naval sta., R.S.F.S.R.; scene of naval mutiny which precipitated the Russian Revolution; p. (1954) *50,000*.

Kroonstad, *t.*, O.F.S., S. Africa; on R. Valseh; agr. and rly. ctr.; engin., milling; p. (1960) *42,438* inc. *13,068* whites.

Kropotkin, *t.*, E. Krasnodar terr. R.S.F.S.R.; grain; engin.; p. (1959) *54,000*.

Krugersdorp, *t.*, Transvaal, S. Africa; named after President Kruger; gold-mining, uranium, manganese; p. (1960) *89,493* inc. *30,241* whites.

Krumlov, *t.*, Bohemia, ČSSR.; on N. slopes of Böhmer Wald; graphite-mines; p. (1961) *8,931*.

Krusevac, *t.*, Jugoslavia; mkt.; munitions; p. (1959) *25,000*.

Kuala Lumpur, *c.*, West Malaysia; cap. of Fed. of of Malaysia and of Selangor st.; univ.; p. (1959) *477,238*.

Kubango (Okovango), *R.,* flows from Angola into L. Ngami, Botswana.

Kuching, *cap.,* Sarawak, Malaysia; gold discovered nearby at Bau; p. (1960) *50,579.*

Kuchinoerabu, *I.,* Japan; S. of Kyushu; mtns.

Kuçovë, nr. Berat, Albania; oil prod. and refining; pipe-line connects to Vlonë.

Kufra, *oasis,* Libya.

Kuhgilvieh and Boer Ahmad, *dist.,* W. Iran; cap. Dehdasht; p. (1967) *165,112.*

Kuibyshev, *t.,* R.S.F.S.R.; on R Volga; at head of central Asian and Siberian rlys.; comm. ctr.; engin., sulphur, paper, oil refining; p. (1967) *969,000.* [mines; p. (1953) *108,000.*

Kuldja (Yining), *c.,* Sinkiang, China; iron, coal

Kulmbach, *t.,* Bavaria, Germany; textiles, cars, brewing; p. (1963) *23,100.* [*407,052.*

Kumamoto, *spt.,* W. Kyushu, Japan; p. (1965)

Kumasi, *ch. t.,* Ashanti, Ghana; univ.; aerodrome; p. (1960) *190,323.*

Kumbakonam, *t., sacred c.,* Tamil Nadu, India; Cauvery delta; silks, cottons; p. (1961) *92,581.*

Kumta, *t.,* Mysore, India; on sea cst.; sandalwood; carving; p. (1961) *16,223.*

Kunene (Cunene), *R.,* Angola; lower course forms bdy. between Angola and South-West Africa; *c.* 750 m.

Kungur, *t.,* R.S.F.S.R., S.E. Perm.; agr.; leather; kaolin; oil ind. equip.; p. (1959) *65,000.*

Kun Lun (Kwen Lun), *mtns.,* Tibet; extend 1,800 m. E. from Pamirs along N. edge of high plateau of Tibet; drained N. into inland drainage basin of Lop Nor; alt. frequently exceeds 18,000 ft. [industl.; p. (1953) *699,000.*

Kunming, *c.,* Yunnan, China; univ.; comm. ctr.;

Kununurra Dam, Ord R., W. Australia; opened 1963; to irrigate 200,000 acres of semi-arid land for cotton, rice, and cattle.

Kuopio, *dep.,* Finland; p. (1966) *267,353.*

Kuopio, *t.,* Finland; on L. Kalki; p. (1966) *52,097.*

Kur, *R.,* Transcaucasia, U.S.S.R.; flows to Caspian S.; length 520 m.

Kurdistan (Country of the Kurds), includes parts of E. Turkey, Soviet Armenia, N.E. Iraq, and N.W. Iran.

Kure, *c.,* S.W. Honshu, Japan; spt. and naval base; engin.; mnfs.; p. (1965) *225,013.*

Kurgan, *t.,* R.S.F.S.R.; on the Trans-Siberian Rly. nr. Tobolsk; tr. in cattle and foodstuffs, agr. engin.; p. (1967) *205,000.*

Kuria Muria Is., Muscat and Oman, off cst. of Oman, consisting of 5 barren islands.

Kuril Is., *chain of sm. Is.,* N. Pacific, U.S.S.R.; extending from Kamchatka to Hokkaido; mainly mtns.

Kurisches Haff (Kurštu Martos), *shallow lagoon,* Baltic cst. of Lithuanian S.S.R., U.S.S.R.; receives water of R. Niemen; narrow entrance to Baltic Sea at N. end of lagoon commanded by pt. of Klaipeda (Memel); length, 60 m., maximum width, 20 m.

Kurische Nehrung, *sandspit,* Baltic Sea; almost cuts off Kurisches Haff from Baltic Sea; length, 55 m.

Kuroshio (Japan Current), *ocean current,* flows N.E. along Pacific cst. of Kyushu, Shikoku and S. Honshu, relatively warm water, exerts slight warming influence on this cst. in winter.

Kushiro, *spt.,* S.E. Hokkaido, Japan; exp. lumber; p. (1965) *174,105.*

Kursk, *region,* adj. N. Ukraine, R.S.F.S.R.

Kursk, *t.,* R.S.F.S.R.; in fruit-growing dist., gr. annual fair; engin., textiles, synthetic rubber; p. (1967) *249,000.* [inds.; p. (1967) *114,000.*

Kustanay, *t.,* Kazakh S.S.R.; on R. Tobol; light

Kustendil, *t.,* Bulgaria; on trib. of R. Struma; fruit-growing dist; p. (1956) *25,025.*

Kütahya, *t.,* W. Central Turkey; agr. market ctr., ceramics; p. (1965) *49,227.*

Kutaisi, *c.,* Georgian S.S.R.; on R. Rion; chemicals, textiles, barium, engin.; big coal deposits being mined; p. (1967) *156,000.* [*20,976.*

Kutaradja, *t.,* N. Sumatra, Indonesia; p. (1958)

Kutch, *peninsula,* N.W. cst., India, Gujarat st., largely barren except for fertile strip along Arabian Sea; p. (1961) *696,440.*

Kutch, Rann of, *desert region* covered with salt, but flooded during monsoons; nine-tenths belongs to India; one-tenth to Pakistan.

Kutchan, *t.,* S.W. Hokkaido, Japan; 45 m. N.W. of Muroran; ctr. of second lgst. iron-ore field in Japan; ore smelted at Muroran.

Kutno, *t.,* Lodz, Poland; p. (1965) *27,000.*

Kuwait, *indep. sov. st.,* Arabia; on N.W. cst of Persian G.; undulating desert; lgst oil producing cty in Middle East; p. (1969) *733,000.* (most of whom live in c. of Kuwait).

Kuzbas (Kuznetsk Basin), *industl. reg,* Siberia, U.S.S.R.; lies S. of Trans-Siberian Rly. in upper valleys of Rs. Ob and Tom; second lgst. coal output in U.S.S.R., iron and steel mftg., heavy metallurgical ind.; ch. ts., Novosibirsk, Novokuznetsk, Kemerovo, Leninsk-Kuznetsky.

Kwangsi Chuang (Guang Zhuang), *aut. reg.,* China; cap. Nanning; sugar, tobacco, rice, indigo, silk; a. 85,452 sq. m.; p. (1953) *19,560,822.*

Kwangtung (Guangdong), *prov.,* China; cap. Canton; rice, tea, sugar, silk; a. 85,447 sq. m.; p. (1953) *34,770,059.*

Kwanto Plain, S.E. Honshu, Japan; lgst. a. of continuous lowland in Japan, extends 80 m. inland from Tokyo; composed of: (1) low, badly-drained alluvial plain devoted to intensive rice cultivation; (2) higher, drier terraces under mulberry, vegetables, tea, tobacco; very dense rural p., especially on lower ground; lge. number of urban ctrs., inc. Tokyo, Yokohama; a. 5,000 sq. m.

Kwan Tong, *t.,* Hong Kong; new industl. t. on E. of Kowloon Bay.

Kwanza (Cuanza), *R.,* Angola, W. Africa; rises in Bihé and flows to Atlantic; length 700 m.

Kweichow (Guizhou), *prov.,* S.W. China; cap. Kweiyang; cereals, silk, timber, gold, silver, mercury; a. 68,139 sq. m.; p. (1953) *15,037,310.*

Kweilin (Guilin), *c.,* Kwangai Chuang, China; univ.; textiles, sugar refining, timber; p. (1953) *145,000.*

Kweiyang (Guiyang), *c.,* Kweichow prov., China; univ.; comm. and industl.; p. (1953) *271,000.*

Kwidzyn (Marienwerder), *c.,* Poland, German before 1945; cath.; cas.; p. (1965) *22,000.*

Kwinana, *t.,* W. Australia; 12 m. from Fremantle on shores of Cockburn Sound; oil refinery and steel plant, alumina reduction, blast furnace; integrated steelwks. by 1978.

Kyle of Lochalsh, *vil., sm. spt.,* Ross and Cromarty, Scot.; at entrance to Loch Alsh, facing S. end of I. of Skye; terminus of rly. across Highlands from Dingwall; ch. pt. for steamers to N.W. cst., I. of Skye, Outer Hebrides; p. (1951) *1,525.*

Kyles of Bute, *sound,* between Argyll cst. and N. Bute, Scot.

Kymore, *t.,* Madhya Pradesh, India; nr. Katni; cement wks.; p. (1961) *12,319.*

Kyoto, *c., cap.* Kyoto *prefecture,* Honshu, Japan; univ.. temples; former cap. of Japan; p. (1970) *1,418,933.*

Kyrenia, *t.,* Cyprus; on N. cst.; p. (1960) *3,498.*

Kythera (Cerigo), *I.,* S. of Peloponnesos, Greece; a. 107 sq. m.

Kyushu, one of the lge. Is. of Japan; W. of Shikoku; mtns.; rice, wheat, tea, hemp, coal, copper; ch. t. Nagasaki; a. 16,247 sq. m.

Kyustendil, *t.,* Bulgaria; in foothills of Osogovo Mts.; lge lead and zinc deposits; combined plant for mng. and ore dressing projected.

Kzyl Orda, *R.,* Kazakh S.S.R.; large dam being constructed to irrigate rice plantations.

L

La Ceiba, *spt.,* Honduras; on Atlantic cst.; exp. bananas; p. (1961) *24,868.*

La Coruña, *prov.,* N.W. Spain; cap. La Coruña; oil refinery; a. 3,051 sq. m.; p. (1959) *1,010,695.*

La Coruña, *spt.,* cap. La Coruña prov., N.W. Spain; fishing; import. tr.; p. (1965) *182,000.*

La Crosse, *t.,* W. Wis., U.S.A.; mkt., agr.; light mnfs.; rubber; p. (1960) *47,575.*

La Estrada, *c.,* N.W. Spain; mineral springs; agr., cattle; p. *27,240.*

La Grange, *t.,* Ga., U.S.A.; p. (1960) *23,632.*

La Grange, *t.,* Ill., U.S.A.; p. (1960) *15,285.*

La Guaira, see Guaira, La.

La Libertad, *dep.,* Peru; a. 10,206 sq. m.; ch. t. Trujillo; p. (1961) *586,681.* [p. (1959) *61,119.*

La Linia, *t.,* Spain, nr. Gibraltar; vegetables, fruit;

La Madeleine, *t.,* Nord, France; p. (1954) *22,331.*

La Mancha, see Mancha, La.

La Paz, *dep.,* Bolivia; traversed by the Andes; cap. La Paz; cocoa, coffee, rubber, minerals; tin mng. at Catari; a. 40,686 sq. m.; p. (1962) *1,140,300.*

La Paz, *t.*, Bolivia, seat of govt., Sucre is legal cap.; impt. comm. ctr.; copper, alpaca wool, cinchona, textiles; p. (1960) *347,394*.

La Plata, *c.*, *spt.*, Argentina; cap. Buenos Aires prov.; univ.; refrigerated meat prods.; oil refining; p. (1960) *340,000*.

La Plata, Rio de (R. Plate), *lge. estuary*, between Argentina, Uruguay, S. America; receives water of Rs. Parana, Uruguay; est. provides sites for lge. spts. Buenos Aires, La Plata, Montevideo; length 200 m., max. width 50 m.

La Porte, *t.*, Ind., U.S.A.; flour, iron and steel, woollens; p. (1960) *21,157*.

La Puebla, *t.*, Majorca. Balearic Is.; p. *10,147*.

La Rioja, *prov.*, Argentina; a. 33,394 sq. m.; cap. La R.; p. (1960) *128,000*.

La Rochelle, *t.*, *spt.*, *cap.*, Charente-Maritime, France; locomotives, glass, sugar, fish; cath.; p. (1962) *68,445*.

La Salle, *c.*, Ill., U.S.A.; coal; p. (1960) *11,897*.

La Salle, *t.*, Quebec, Canada; p. (1961) *30,904*.

La Serena, *cap.* Coquimbo prov., Chile; cath.; p. (1962) *61,500*.

La Skhirra, *pt.*, on G. of Gabes, Tunisia; oil; pipe-line to Edjelé under construction.

Le Tuque, *t.*, S. Quebec, Canada; R. pt.; lumbering; resort; p. (1961) *13,023*.

La Unión, *t.*, Spain; nr. Cartagena; iron, manganese, sulphur; p. (1957) *10,131*.

Laaland, *I.*, Danish, Baltic Sea; a. 462 sq. m.; forests; cap. Maribo.

Labrador, *mainland a.*, prov. Newfoundland, Canada, separated from I. by Strait of Belle I.; barren, severe climate; rich iron ore reserves nr. Quebec bdy.; Churchill R. power project; cap. Battle Harbour; a. 112,826 sq. m.; p. (1966) *21,157*.

Labrador City, *t.*, Newfoundland, Canada; new t. built 1965, nr. Wabush L. to house workers of iron ore mines.

Labuan, *I.*, Sabah, Malaysia; rubber, rice, coconuts; cap. Victoria; a. 35 sq. m.; p. (1960) *14,904*.

Laccadive, *Is.*, Arabian Sea; about 200 m. off Malabar cst. joined with Minicoy and Amindivi Is. to form Union Territory, India; coir, coconuts; cap., Kavaratti; p. of Territory (1961) *24,108*.

Lachine, *t.*, Quebec, Canada; at head of L. rapids; summer resort, timber, bridge-bldg., wire, rope; p. (1961) *33,630*.

Lachine Canals, Quebec, E. Canada; skirt Lachine Rapids on St. Lawrence R. immediately above Montreal; give access to Montreal from Gr. Lakes for steamers of 14 ft. draught; length 9 m.

Lachlan, *R.*, N.S.W., Australia; trib. R. Murrumbidgee; length 700 m.

Lackawanna, *t.*, N.Y., U.S.A.; on L. Erie; iron and steel; p. (1960) *29,564*.

Laconia, div. of Peloponnesus, Greece; cap. Sparta; p. (1961) *118,449*.

Laconia, *G.*, S. Peloponnesus, Greece.

Laconia, *c.*, N.H., U.S.A.; hosiery, rly. wks.; p. (1960) *15,288*.

Lacq, *t.*, S.W. Aquitaine, France; 15 m. N.W. Paris; oil, natural gas, sulphur. [monastery.

Lacroma, *I.*, Jugoslavia; holiday resort, château.

Lacrosse, *c.*, Wis., U.S.A.; rly. ctr., flour, timber; p. (1960) *47,575*.

Ladakh, *dist.*, of the Upper Indus, bordering Tibet; ch. t. Leh; p. (1961) *88,651*.

Ladoga, *L.*, nr. Leningrad, U.S.S.R. (lgst. in Europe); a. 7,100 sq. m.; drained to G. of Finland by R. Neva.

Ladybank, *burgh*, Fife, Scot.; 5 m. S.W. of Cupar; rly. wks., malt, linen; p. (1961) *1,207*.

Ladysmith, *t.*, Natal, S. Africa; rly. wks., coal, cotton mills; besieged by Boers 1899-1900; p. (1960) *22,997* inc. *7,260* Europeans.

Lafayette, *c.*, Ind., U.S.A.; univ.; timber, farm implements; p. (1960) *42,330*.

Lafayette, *t.*, La., U.S.A.; timber, cottonseed oil; p. (1960) *40,400*. [alt. 5,259 ft.

Lafayette, *peak*, White mtns. range, N.H., U.S.A.;

Lagan, *R.*, N. Ireland; flows into Belfast Lough; length 35 m.

Lagoa dos Patos, *L.*, Brazil; drained by Rio Grande do Sul; length 140 m.

Lagoa Mirim, *L.*, on bdy. between Brazil and Uruguay; drains N.; length 110 m.

Lagos, *spt.*, *cap.*, Nigeria; good natural harbour; univ.; exp. palm oil and kernels, cocoa, ground-nuts, hides; imports machin., cotton piece goods; rly. wks.; p. (1963) *675,352*.

Laguna, *dist.*, Durango st., Mexico; former L. bed irrigated by R. Nazas and Aguanaval; ch. cotton-growing region in Mexico; ch. t., Torréon; a. 100,000 sq. m.

Laguna Dam, *see* Imperial Valley.

Laguna de Terminos, *inlet*, Campeche, Mexico; 70 m. by 40 m. [14 m.

Laguna Madre, *lagoon*, Texas, U.S.A.; 110 m. by

Lahn, *R.*, Germany; enters R. Rhine at Koblenz; length 135 m.

Lahore, *div.*, W. Pakistan; ch. t. Lahore; p. (estd. 1951) *5,340,000*.

Lahore, *ch. c.*, W. Pakistan; univ., cath., temples, mosques; textiles, pottery, carpets, industl. gases; atomic research ctr.; p. (1961) *1,296,477*.

Lahr, *t.*, Baden-Württemberg, Germany; at W. edge of Black Forest; tobacco, cardboard, leather, precision mechanics; p. (1963) *22,800*.

Lahti, *t.*, S. Finland; p. (1966) *81,652*.

Lajes, *t.*, Santa Catarina, Brazil; p. (estd. 1968) *96,889*.

Lake Charles, *t.*, La., U.S.A.; oil, rice, timber; holiday resort; p. (1960) *63,392*.

Lake District, *mountainous dist.*, Cumberland and Westmorland, Eng.; tourist resort, beautiful scenery, inc. Ls. Windermere, Ullswater, Derwentwater, etc.

Lake Forest, *t.*, Ill., U.S.A.; on L. Michigan; p. (1960) *10,687*.

Lake of the Woods, *L.*, E. of Winnipeg, Ontario, on bdy. between Canada and U.S.A.

Lake Success, *vil.*, N.Y., U.S.A.; temporary H.Q. of U.N.O. since 1946; p. (1960) *2,954*.

Lakeland, *t.*, Fla., U.S.A.; agr., fruit ctr., phosphates; holiday resort; p. (1960) *41,350*.

Lakeview, *t.*, Ont., Canada; thermal elec. power plant projected; to be lgst. in world.

Lakeview, Ore., U.S.A., uranium mill; p. *3,262*.

Lakewood, *t.*, N.J., U.S.A.; winter resort; p. (1960) *13,004*.

Lakewood, *t.*, Ohio, U.S.A.; sub. of Cleveland; grapes; p. (1960) *66,145*. [p. *18,620*.

Lalin, *t.*, N.W. Spain; agr. ctr., paper, tanning;

Lambay, *I.*, off cst. Dublin co., Ireland.

Lambayeque, *dep.*, N. Peru; sugar, cotton, tobacco; cap. Chiclayo; a. 4,613 sq. m.; p. (1961) *363,297*.

Lambersart, *commune*, Nord, France; sub. Lille; spinning; p. (1954) *19,092*.

Lambeth, *inner bor.*, London, Eng.; inc. part of former bor. of Wandsworth (Clapham and Streatham); L. Palace, residence of Archbishop of Canterbury; p. (1966) *339,000*.

Lambezellec, *t.*, Finistère, France; tr. ctr.; p. (1946) *19,227*.

Lamesa, *t.*, N.W. Texas, U.S.A.; cotton, maize, cattle; p. (1960) *12,438*.

Lamia, *cap.*, Phthiotis prefecture, Greece; p. (1961) *21,509*.

Lammermuir Hills, E. Lothian, Scot.; highest peak Lammer Law, alt. 1,733 ft.

Lampedusa, *I.*, Mediterranean; S. of Malta.

Lampeter, *mkt. t.*, *mun. bor.*; Cardigan, S. Wales; on R. Teifi; St. David's College; p. (1961) *1,853*.

Lamu, *I.*, off cst. of Kenya; p. *3,576* (non-African).

Lanai, one of the Hawaiian Is.; fruit, sugar, cotton, livestock; a. 141 sq. m.; p. *3,360*.

Lanark, *co.*, Scot.; coal, iron, steel, textiles; co. t. Lanark; a. 897 sq. m.; p. (1961) *1,626,317*.

Lanark, *royal burgh*, *co. t.*, Lanark, Scot.; in Clyde valley 22 m. S.E. of Glasgow; hosiery, chenille fabrics, tanning; p. (1961) *8,436*.

Lancashire, *mftg. dist.*, *industl. co.*, N.W. Eng.; Liverpool most impt. spt.; Manchester gr. comm. ctr.; Preston adm. hdqrs.; mnfs. inc. textiles, engin. prod., chemicals, foodstuffs; coal-mining; co. t. Lancaster; a. 1,875 sq. m.; p. (1966) *5,189,000*.

Lancaster, *c.*, *mun.*, *bor.*, *co. t.*, Lancs, Eng.; 6 m. up R. Lune; cas.; univ.; linoleum, cotton, artificial silk inds.; p. (estd. 1967) *47,060*.

Lancaster, *t.*, Ohio, U.S.A.; in natural-gas region; agr.; flour, machin., glass; p. (1960) *29,916*.

Lancaster, *bor.*, Penns., U.S.A.; agr. ctr.; mnfs. light and heavy iron and steel prod.; p. (1960) *61,055*. [wide.

Lancaster, *sound*, N.W. Terrs., Canada; 50 m.

Lanchow (Lanzhou), *c.*, *cap.*, Kansu, China; on R. Hwang-Ho; silk, tobacco, grain tea-tr. ctr.; oil refining; gaseous diffusion plant; p. (1953) *397,000*.

Lanciano, *t.*, Abruzzi e Molise, Italy; wine, fruit, oil, silk, linen; p. *22,450*.

Lancing, *vil.*, Sussex, Eng.; on S. cst., 2 m. E. of Worthing; seaside resort; college; light inds.; p. *13,000*.

Landau, *t.*, Rhineland-Palatinate, Germany; on R. Queich; cigar mfg., wine, iron ind.; here the carriages called Landaus were first made; p. *(1963) 30,000*.

Landes, *dep.*, S.W. France; on Atlantic cst.; agr., vineyards, resin; cap. Mont-de-Marson; a. 3,604 sq. m.; p. *(1968) 277,381*.

Landes, Les, *coastal sub-region*, Aquitaine, S.W. France; fringes Bay of Biscay from Pointe de Grave to Biarritz; coastal sand dunes and lagoons backed by low, flat plain of alternate sandy tracts and marsh; reclaimed by drainage and afforestation, now over half a. covered by pine forests; turpentine, timber; oilfield; length 150 m., maximum width of dune belt 7 m., of plain 40 m.

Landrecies, *t.*, Nord, France; on R. Sambre.

Land's End, extreme S.W. point of Eng. on Cornish cst.

Landshut, *t.*, Bavaria, Germany; on R. Isar; cas.; elec. inds., glass, metallurgy, textiles, coal; rly. junction; p. *(1963) 50,600*.

Landskrona, *spt.*, Sweden; shipping and tr. ctr.; hy. machin., lt. inds.; p. *(1961) 28,826*.

Lanett, *t.*, E. Ala., U.S.A.; textiles; p. *(1960) 7,674*.

Langanes, *C.*, N.E. cst., Iceland.

Langebergen, *mtns.*, Cape Province, Rep. of S. Africa; extend 150 m. E. to W. parallel to S. cst. of Africa; form barrier to access from cst. plain to Little Karroo, broken across by valley of R. Gouritz; max. alt. exceeds 4,500 ft.

Langefjell, *mtn. gr.*, Romsdal, Norway; highest peak 8,101 ft.

Langeland, *I.*, Gr. Belt, Denmark; a. 111 sq. m.; p. *(1960) 18,692*.

Langholm, *mkt. burgh*, Dumfries, Scot.; on R. Esk; 18 m. N. of Carlisle; woollen mills, tanning; p. *(1961) 2,369*.   [Eng.

Langley, *industl. dist.*, nr. Birmingham, Worcs.,

Langnau, *t.*, Switzerland; ch. t. of the Emmental; cheese, cloth mills, pottery; p. *8,300*.

Langreo, *t.*, Asturias, Spain; hilly, agr. and fruit-growing dist., colly. and iron-wks.; p. *(1959) 64,347*.

Langres, *fortfd. t.*, Haute-Marne, France; the ancient Andematunnum; cath.; grain, livestock, cutlery, wine; p. *(1962) 10,493*.

Languedoc, *prov.*, S. France; wine.

Languedoc, *canal*, S. France; unites Mediterranean with R. Garonne at Toulouse, France.

Lannemazan, *sub-region*, Aquitaine, S.W. France; belt 50 m. wide stretches over 100 m. along foot of Pyrenees W. of Toulouse; consists of immense deltas of glacial gravel deeply cut by tribs. of Rs. Garonne and Adour; valleys liable to severe floods in summer, intervening plateau dry, bare; scantily populated.

Lansdowne, *t.*, *sub.*, Philadelphia, S.E. Penns., U.S.A.; p. *(1960) 12,612*.

Lansford, *bor.*, Penns., U.S.A.; p. *(1950) 1,487*.

Lansing, *cap.*, Mich., U.S.A.; tr., mnfs. iron goods; cars; chemicals; p. *(1960) 107,807*.

Lanzarote, *I.*, Canary Is.; volcanic, mountainous; grapes, cochineal; cap. Arrecife; p. *(1962) 36,519*.

Laoag, *t.*, N. Luzon I., Philippines; cereals, tobacco, cotton, sugar; p. *40,800*.

Laoighis or Leix Co., Leinster, Ireland; mtns. and bog; inland pasture and tillage; cap. Port Laoighise (Maryborough); a. 664 sq. m.; p. *(1966) 44,662*.

Laon, *cap.*, Aisne, France; fort, cath.; metal, linen mftg.; p. *(1962) 27,261*.

Laos, *kingdom*, former associate st. of Fr. Union; mtnous. and densely forested; a. 89,320 sq. m.; cereals, sugar, cotton, cattle, some minerals but only tin mined in sm. quantities; cement; modern saw and rice mills; admin. cap. Vientiane; p. *(estd. 1969) 2,893,000*.

Lapeer, *t.*, E. Mich., U.S.A.; wooden prod.; p. *(1960) 6,160*.

Lapland, *terr.*, N. Europe, in Norway, Sweden, Finland and U.S.S.R.; extending from the Norwegian cst. to the White Sea; mainly mtn. and moorland, with many lakes; a. 130,000 sq. m.; p. *100,000*.

Lappi (Lappland), *dep.*, N. Finland; a. 36,308 sq. m.; p. *(1966) 220,008*.

Laptev Sea (Nordenskiöld Sea), *inlet* of Arctic Ocean; between Severnaya Zemlya and N. Siberian Is., R.S.F.S.R.

Larache, *spt.*, Morocco; on Atl. cst. 40 m. S. of Tangier; cork; p. *(1960) 30,763*.

Laramie, *c.*, Wyo., U.S.A.; univ., cattle; p. *(1960) 17,520*.

Larbert, *par.*, Stirling, Scot.; brass and copper wares, chemicals, confectionery; p. *13,763*.

Laredo, *c.*, Texas, U.S.A.; frontier c. on Rio Grande; iron, steel, oil, bricks, hides, wool; p. *(1960) 60,678*.

Largo, *par.*, Fife, Scot.; fishing, holiday resort; p. *(1951) 2,499*.

Largs, *burgh*, Ayr, Scot.; on F. of Clyde opposite Is. of Bute and Cumbrae; seaside resort, fishing; battle 1263; p. *(1961) 9,100*.

Larissa, *prefecture*, Thessaly, Greece; cap. Larissa; p. *(1961) 237,653*.

Larissa, *t.*, cap. Thessaly, Greece; agr. tr. ctr.; p. *(1961) 55,391*.

Laristan, *prov.*, S. Iran; on Persian G.; mainly mtns., camels, silk; cap. Lar.

Lark, *R.*, Cambridge, Eng.; trib. of R. Ouse; length 26 m.

Larkhall, *t.*, Lanark, Scot.; Industl. Estate; foundry, hosiery, silk dye wks.; p. *14,055*.

Larnaka, *spt.*, Cyprus; the ancient Citium; grain, cotton, fruit; oil refinery projected; p. *(1960) 19,824*.

Larne, *svt.*, *mun. bor.*, Antrim, N. Ireland; at entrance to Larne Lough, 18 m. N. of Belfast; cross channel service to Stranraer; p. *(1966) 17,278*.

Larvik, *spt.*, Norway; S.W. of Oslo; seaside resort; engin., pulp, stone; p. *(1961) 10,479*.

Las Bela, *dist.*, Baluchistan, W. Pakistan; a. 7,132 sq. m.; p. *(estd. 1951) 76,000*.

Las Cruces, *t.*, N.M., U.S.A.; agr. with irrigation; lead, fluorspar mining; p. *(1960) 29,367*.

Las Palmas, *Spanish prov.*, Canary Is.; comprising Gran Canaria, Lanzarote, Fuerteventura and smaller Is.; bananas, potatoes, tomatoes, fishing; a. 1,565 sq. m.; p. *(1962) 459,433*.

Las Palmas, *t.*, Gran Canaria, Canary Is.; cap. of Las Palmas prov.; p. *(1965) 239,000*.

Las Tres Marias, *Is.*, off W. cst. Mexico.

Las Vegas, *t.*, Nevada, U.S.A.; resort; p. *(1960) 64,405*.

Las Vegas, *t.*, N. Mexico, U.S.A.; E. of Santa Fé; p. *(1960) 6,023*.

Las Villas, *prov.*, Cuba; a. 8,264 sq. m.; p. *(1953) 1,030,162*.

Lashio, *t.*, Burma; on R. Salween; end of the Burma Road to China; p. *4,638*.

Lashkar, *see* Gwalior.

Lasithi, *prefecture*, Crete; cap. Ayios Nikolaos; p.   [(1961) 73,843.

Lasswade, *see* Bonnyrigg and Lasswade.

Latacunga, *cap.*, Cotopaxi prov., Ecuador; tr. ctr., paper, malt; p. *(1960) 29,423*.

Latakia, *spt.*, Syria; tobacco, olive oil, sponges; p. *(1961) 68,498*.

Latin America, the Spanish-, Portuguese- and French-speaking countries of N. America, S. America, Central America and the West Indies, incl. the reps. of Argentina, Bolivia, Brazil, Chile, Colombia, Costa Rica, Cuba, Dominican Republic, Ecuador, El Salvador, Guatemala, Haiti, Honduras, Mexico, Nicaragua, Panama, Paraguay, Peru, Uruguay and Venezuela; sometimes Puerto Rico, French West Indies, and other Is. of the West Indies are included, and occasionally Brit. Honduras, Guyana, French Guiana, and Surinam.

Latina, *see* Littoria.

Latium, *see* Lazio.

Latrobe, *t.*, S.E. Penns., U.S.A.; p. *(1960) 11,932*.

Latronico, *t.*, Potenza, Italy; p. *5,175*.

Latvia, *constituent S.S. rep.*, U.S.S.R., on the Baltic Sea; former independent st.; mainly agr.; cap. Riga; principal spts. Ventspils, Liepaya; a. 24,800 sq. m.; p. *(1970) 2,365,000*.

Lauenburg, *see* Lebork.

Launceston, *t.*, *mun. bor.*, Cornwall, Eng.; agr. mkt.; mng., quarrying, lt. engin.; p. *(estd. 1967) 4,600*.

Launceston, *c.*, Tasmania, Australia; wool, textiles, fruit; cars; p. *(1966) 60,453*.

Laurel, *t.*, Miss., U.S.A.; p. *(1960) 27,889*.

Laurens, *t.*, S.C., U.S.A.; cotton, glass; p. *(1960) 9,598*.

Laurentide, *escarpment* of Laurentian plateau, E. Canada.

Laurium, *hills, dist.,* Greece; silver and lead.

Laurium (formerly **Calumet**), *vil.,* Mich., U.S.A.; copper; p. (1950) *3,211.*

Lausanne, *cap.,* Vaud, Switzerland; nr. L. Geneva; cath., univ.; rly. junction, iron, chocolate, paper; p. (1961) *130,500.*

Lauterbrunnen, *vil.,* Bern can., Switzerland; highest and most famous of its waterfalls (Staubbach 980 ft.); tourist ctr.; p. *2,958.*

Lautoka, *spt.,* Viti Levu, Fiji Is.; sugar ctr.

Lauven, *R.,* Norway; length 200 m.

Lavagna, *t.,* Genoa, Italy; shipbldg., marble; p. *8,100.*

Laval, *t., cap.,* Mayenne, France; cotton, paper, machin., marble; cas.; p. (1962) *43,196.*

Lavera, *pt.,* nr. Marseilles, commencement of 470 m. oil pipeline to Karlsruhe, W. Germany, operated April 1963; oil refining.

Laverton, *t.,* W. Australia; 200 m. N. Kalgoorlie.

Lawndale, *t.,* Cal., U.S.A.; p. (1960) *21,740.*

Lawrence, *c.,* Kan., U.S.A.; st. univ., paper, machin.; p. (1960) *32,858.*

Lawrence, *c.,* Mass., U.S.A.; on Merrimac R., N.W. of Boston; textiles paper, footwear, engin.; p. (1960) *70,933.*

Lawrenceburg, *t.,* Tenn., U.S.A.; textiles, cheese, phosphates; p. (1950) *5,442.*

Lawton, *t.,* Okla., U.S.A.; p. (1959) *61,697.*

Laxey, *vil.,* I. of Man; flour-milling, woollen mills, meerschaum pipes.

Lazio, *region,* Italy; a. 6,634 sq. m.; p. inc. Vatican City and Rome; p. (1961) *3,922,783.*

Le Bouscat, *t.,* Gironde, France; p. (1954) *19,558.*

Le Havre, see Havre, Le.

Le Maire, *strait,* between Staten I. and Tierra del Fuego, S. America.

Le Mans, *cap.,* Sarthe, France; cath.; linen, ironmongery, chemicals, motor cars, aeroplanes; motor-racing; p. (1968) *143,246.*

Le Puy, *t.,* Haute-Loire, France; p. (1962) *28,648.*

Lea, *R.,* Eng.; rises in Chiltern Hills nr. Luton, flows E. and S. into R. Thames; length 46 m.

Lead, *t.,* S.D., U.S.A.; gold, mnfs. jewellery, mng. equipment; resort; p. (1960) *6,211.*

Leader Water, *R.,* Scot.; trib. of R. Tweed, which it joins nr. Melrose; length 21 m.

Leadgate, *t.,* Durham, Eng.; 2 m. N.E. of Consett; coal, mftg.

Leadhills, *mng. vil.,* S.W. Lanark, Scot.; lead.

Leadville, *c.,* Col., U.S.A.; in Arkansas valley; mining ctr.; p. (1960) *4,008.*

Leaf, *R.,* flowing into Ungava Bay, Labrador, Canada.

Leam, *R.,* Warwick, Eng.; trib. R. Avon; 25 m.

Leamington, *t.,* Ont., Canada; tobacco, canned vegetables; p. (1961) *9,030.*

Leamington (Royal Leamington Spa), *t., mun. bor.,* Warwick, Eng.; on R. Leam, 24 m. S.E. of Birmingham; fashionable spa; gen. (engin.) inds.; p. (estd. 1967) *44,860.*

Leaside, *t.,* Ontario, Canada; p. (1961) *18,579.*

Leatherhead, *t., urb. dist.,* Surrey, Eng.; on R. Mole to N. of gap through N. Downs; boiler mftg., engin.; p. (estd. 1967) *38,090.*

Leavenworth, *c.,* Kan., U.S.A.; on Missouri; rly. ctr. and military post, furniture, machin., bricks, coal; p. (1960) *22,052.*

Lebanon, *rep.,* S.W. Asia; mountainous; mainly agr.; textiles, garments, wooden, metal goods; cap. Beirut; a. 4,300 sq. m.; p. (estd. 1968) *2,600,000.*

Lebanon, *mtn. range,* Lebanon st. and N. Israel; highest peaks Dahr-el-Khadeb (10,052 ft.) and Timarum (10,539 ft.).

Lebanon, *t.,* Penns., U.S.A.; coal, iron, steel, mnfs.; rubber, food, tobacco; p. (1960) *30,045.*

Lebork (former German **Lauenburg**), *t.,* Poland; p. (1965) *23,000.*   [(1961) *12,560.*

Lebu, *spt., cap.,* Arauco prov., Chile; coal; p.

Lecce, *t.,* Apulia, Italy; cas.; p. (1961) *74,123.*

Lecco, *t.,* Italy; on L. Como; silk, cotton, copper, iron; p. (1961) *48,230.*

Lech, *R.,* Germany; trib. of Danube; 177 m.

Leczyca, *t.,* Poland; p. *20,996.*

Ledbury, *t., urb. dist.,* Hereford, Eng.; at W. foot of Malvern Hills; mkt., fruit preserving, tanning; p. (1961) *3,632.*

Ledeberg, *t.,* Belgium; nr. Ghent; industl.; p. (1962) *11,127.*

Lee, *R.,* Cork, Ireland; flows past Cork c. to Cork harbour; length 50 m.

Lee-on-Solent, *t.,* Hants, Eng.; on Southampton Water; p. *4,000.*

Leeds, *c., co. bor.,* W.R. Yorks, Eng.; on R. Aire; at E. margin of Pennines; univ.; lge. clothing ind., varied engin. mnfs., furniture, tanning; p. (estd. 1969) *503,720.*

Leek, *mkt. t., urb. dist.,* Staffs, Eng.; 11 m. N.E. of Stoke-on-Trent; silk mnfs.; p. (1961) *19,173.*

Leer, *pt.,* Lower Saxony, Germany; nr. confluence of Leda and Ems; iron, machin., textiles; harbour and route ctr.; p. (1963) *20,200.*

Lees, *urb. dist.,* Lancs, Eng.; cotton; p. (1961) *3,729.*

Leeston, *t.,* S.I., N.Z.; on Canterbury Plain, nr. Christchurch; agr. ctr.; p. (1951) *738.*

Leete's I., Conn., U.S.A.; on Long I. sound.

Leeton, *t.,* N.S.W., Australia; New t., ctr. of fruit and rice farming as part of Murrumbidgee Irrigation A.; p. (1966) *5,814.*

Leeuwarden, *prov. cap.,* Friesland, Netherlands; agr.; iron, metal goods, bicycles; p. (1967) *86,805.*

Leeuwin, *C.,* S.W. point of Australia.

Leeward Is., W.I.; inc. Antigua, Barbuda, Redonda, Montserrat, Virgin Is., St. Kitts, Nevis, Anguilla, Sombrero; ch. prod., sugar, fruit; Is. cap. St. John's, Antigua; total a. 423 sq. m.; p. (1952) *119,700.*

Leeward Is. (Dutch), part of Neth. Antilles, consisting of St. Maarten (a. 34 sq. m.; p. *1,697*), St. Eustatius (a. 31 sq. m.; p. *945*), Saba (a. 9 sq. m.; p. *1,150*).

Leeward Is. (French), E. Pacific, inc. Huahiné Raiatéa, Tahaa, Bora-Bora-Maupiti; p. (1962) *16,177.*

Leghorn or **Livorno,** *prov.,* Italy; a. 133 sq. m.; p. (1961) *313,599.*

Leghorn or **Livorno,** *spt., prov. cap.,* Italy; on W. cst.. 10 m. S. of mouth of R. Arno; shipbldg., glass, wire, olive oil, hats, marble; p (1961) *159,973.*   [p. (1965) *20,000.*

Legionowa, *t.,* Warsaw, Poland; new town (1951);

Legnago, *t.,* Lombardy, Italy; on R. Adige; fort, sugar, cereals; p. *20,175.*

Legnano, *t.,* Lombardy, Italy; N.W. of Milan; cotton, silk, machin.; p. (1961) *42,460.*

Leh, *ch. t.,* Ladakh, Kashmir, India; on R. Indus; caravan ctr; p. (1961) *3,720.*

Lehigh, *R.,* Penns., U.S.A.; trib. of Delaware R.; length 120 m.   p. (1960) *6,318.*

Lehighton, *bor.,* Penns., U.S.A.; anthracite;

Leicester, *c., co. t., co. bor.,* Leics., Eng.; on R. Soar; univ.; footwear, hosiery, knitwear, engin., and elec. goods, chemicals; p. (estd. 1969) *278,470.*

Leicestershire, *co.,* Eng.; mainly agr.; co. t. Leicester; a. 832 sq. m.; p. (1966) *716,000.*

Leichhardt, W., *sub.* of Sydney, N.S.W., Australia; p. *31.500.*

Leiden (Leyden), *t.,* S. Holland, Neth.; printing, textiles, medical apparatus; univ.; p. (1967) *102,425.*

Leigh, *t., mun. bor.,* S.W. Lancs, Eng.; 5 m. S.E. of Wigan; mkt.; coal-mining; silks, cottons, brass, iron; p. (estd. 1967) *46,600.*

Leigh-on-Sea, *t.,* Essex, Eng.; on N. cst. of Thames estuary, 2 m. W. of Southend; holiday resort, fishing; p. (1961) *10,059.*

Leigh's L. Wyo., U.S.A.; links with Snake R.

Leighton Buzzard, *t.,* Bedford, Eng.; at N.E. end of Vale of Aylesbury; tiles, engin., sand quarrying; p. (1961) *11,649.*

Leine, *R.,* N.W. Germany; trib. of R. Aller; length 130 m.

Leinster, *S.E. prov.,* Ireland; a. 7,620 sq. m.; agr.; p. (1966) *1,412,465.*

Leipzig, *c.,* Leipzig, E. Germany; at junction of Rs. Pleisse, Elster and Parthe; univ., cath.; comm., publishing, metal, textile, chemical, steel, paper, machin. and elec. inds., vehicles; birthplace of Wagner; p. (1963) *588,135.*

Leiston-cum-Sizewell, *t., urb. dist.,* E. Suffolk, Eng.; on cst., 4 m. E. of Saxmundham; agr. implements; p. (1961) *4,119.*

Leith, *spt.,* Midlothian, Scot.; Edinburgh sub.; shipbldg., timber, whisky; p. *81,613.*

Leith Hill, Surrey, Eng.; nr. Dorking; alt. 993 ft.; Lower Greensand crest.

Leitmeritz, see Litoměřice.

Leitrim, *Co.,* Connacht, Ireland; agr.; cap. Carrick-on-Shannon; a. 613 sq. m.; p. (1966) *30,532.*

Leix, *co.,* see Laoighis.

Leixões, *spt.,* Portugal; at mouth of R. Douro.

Lek, *R.*, Netherlands; one of the branches of the Neder Rijn; from Wijk-bij-Duurstede to Krimpen nr. Rotterdam; length 40 m.

Leland, *t.*, Miss., U.S.A.; cotton, vegetables, nuts; p. (1960) 6,295.

Lema, *Is.*, Sea of Hong Kong in China Sea.

Lemgo, *t.*, N. Rhine–Westphalia, Germany; E. of Bielefeld; furniture, ttexiles; p. (1963) 21,700.

Lemnos, *I.* (Greek), Ægean Sea; 20 m. long; fertile valleys; tobacco, fruit, sheep, goats; cap. Kastron; p. 4,000.

Lemvig, *spt.*, Jutland, Denmark; fishing, agr. machin.; p. (1960) 5,783.

Lena, *gr. R.*, Siberia, R.S.F.S.R.; rising in mtns. W. of Lake Baikal and flowing N. to the Arctic Ocean; length 2,800 m.

Lenin Dam (Dnieper Dam), *see* Zaporozhe.

Leninabad, *t.*, Tadzhik S.S.R.; on R. Syr Darya, S. of Tashkent; cottons, silks, fruit-preserving; hydro-elec. sta.; p. (1959) 77,000.

Leninakan, *t.*, Armenian S.S.R.; silk, textiles, engin.; p. (1967) 130,000.

Leningrad, *c.*, R.S.F.S.R.; at mouth of R. Neva; cath., palaces, univs.; engin., oil ref., chemicals, textiles, synthetic rubber, steel, paper; founded by Peter the Gr. as St. Petersburg; p. (1970) 3,950,000.

Leninogorsk, *t.*, Kazakh S.S.R.; lead, zinc, silver, copper, gold; p. (1959) 67,000.

Leninsk-Kuznetski (Charjui), *t.*, R.S.F.S.R.; heavy engin., power-sta., coal, gold; p. (1967) 140,000.

Lenkoran, *spt.*, Azerbaydzhan S.S.R.; on Caspian Sea; ctr. of rice, citrous fruits, tea a.; p. (1956) 30,800.

Lennox, *ancient Scottish div.*, comprising Dunbarton, parts of Stirling, Perth and Renfrew.

Lennox Hills, *mtn. range*, between Dunbarton and Stirling, Scot.

Lennoxtown, *t.*, Stirling, Scot.; coal-mining, bleaching, print and alum wks.; p. 2,590.

Lennoxville, *t.*, Quebec, Canada; on St. Francis R.; univ.; p. 1,927.

Lens, *t.*, Pas de Calais, France; on canal of same name; ironwks., soap, sugar; p. (1968) 41,874.

Lentini or Leontini, *t.*, Sicily, Italy; on plain of Catania; cereal, oil, wine; p. 23,150.

Leoben, *old mining t.*, Styria, Austria; walls and tower; p. (1961) 36,257.

Leominster, *t., mun. bor.*, Hereford, Eng.; 13 m. N. of Hereford; rly. junction, mkt., cider, cattle, agr. tools, glove mkg.; p. (estd. 1967) 6,930.

Leominster, *c.*, Mass., U.S.A.; wood prod., light mnfs.; p. (1960) 27,929.

León, *t.*, Nicaragua; cath., univ.; footwear, textiles; p. (1960) 46,000.

León, *t.*, Mexico; textiles, leather, gold, silver; p. (1960) 209,469.

León, *prov.*, Spain; agr., livestock, coal, iron; cap. León; a. 5,937 sq. m.; p. (1959) 591,231.

Leonforte, *t.*, Sicily, Italy; sulphur-mines, cattle, oil, wine; p. 19,400.

Leonidion, *t.*, Greece; on G. of Nauplia; p. 3,452.

Leonora, *sm. t.*, W. Australia; 140 m. N. of Kalgoorlie; gold-mines.

Léopoldville. *See* Kinshasa.

Lercara, *t.*, Sicily, Italy; macaroni mftg., sulphur-mines; p. 11,000.

Lerici, *coastal t.*, Italy; nr. Spezia; macaroni mftg.; old cas.

Lérida, *prov.*, Spain; wine, olive oil, livestock, wool, timber; a. 4,656 sq. m.; p. (1959) 334,807.

Lérida, *t., cap.* of L. prov., Spain; on R. Segre; 2 caths.; textiles, leather, glass; p. (1959) 59,040.

Lerins, *Is.* (French), in Mediterranean; nr. Cannes.

Leros, *Is.*, Dodecanese, Greece.

Lerwick, *cap.*, Shetland Is., Scot.; on Mainland; fishing; p. (1961) 5,906.

Les Baux, *commune*, Bouches-du-Rhône, France; bauxite first discovered here; not impt. now.

Les Causses, *see* Causses, Les.

Les Landes, *see* Landes, Les.

Les Lilas, *commune*, Seine, France; glass, chemicals, metallurgy; p. (1954) 18,590.

Les Sables d'Olonne, *commune*, Vendée, France; shipbldg.; fish, canning; p. (1962) 19,256.

Lesbos, *see* Mytilene I.

Leskovac, *t.*, Serbia, Jugoslavia; on R. Morava; hemp, flax, tobacco; p. (1959) 29,000.

Leslie, *burgh*, Fife, Scot.; 7 m. N. of Kirkcaldy; paper, flax, bleaching; p. (1961) 3,421.

Lesotho (Basutoland), *indep. sov. st.*, S. Africa; at head of Orange R., and enclosed on S. by Drakensberg Mtns.; mtnous plateau; univ. at Roma; mainly agr., maize, wool. mohair; cap. Maseru; a. 11,716 sq. m.; p. (1966) 969,634.

Lesser Antilles, *see* Antilles.

Lesser Slave. *L.*, Central Alberta, Canada.

Lesvos (Lesbos), *Greek prefecture* and *I.* in Ægean Sea; cap. Mitilini (Mytilene); p. (1961) 140,144.

Leszno, *t.*, Poznan, W. Poland; engin., distilling, tobacco; p. (1965) 31,000.

Letchworth (Garden City), *t., urb. dist.*, Herts, Eng.; at foot of Chiltern Hills, 2 m. N.E. of Hitchin; first garden c., founded by Sir Ebenezer Howard 1903; engin., office equipment; p. (estd. 1967) 28,110.

Lethbridge, *t.*, Alberta, Canada; coal, oil; p. (1961) 35,454.

Letterkenny, *t.*, Donegal, Ireland; on Lough Swilly; tourist ctr., flax; p. (1966) 4,513.

Leuna, *t.*, Halle, E. Germany; 3 m. S. of Merseburg; chemicals; oil pipeline from Schwedt; p. (1963) 12,702.

Levanger, *spt.*, Norway; at N. end of Trondheim Fjord; p. (1961) 1,711.

Levant, French and Italian name for E. cst. of Mediterranean.

Leven, *burgh*, Fife, Scot.; on N. side of F. of Forth, 10 m. N.E. of Kirkcaldy; linen, coal; p. (1961) 8,872.

Leven, *L.*, Kinross, Scot.; associated with escape of Mary Queen of Scots from Castle I., 1568.

Leven, *salt-water L.*, Argyll, Inverness, Scot.

Levenshulme, *industl. t.*, Lancs, Eng.; sub. of Manchester.

Leverkusen, *t.*, N., Rhine–Westphalia, Germany; on R. Rhine, N. of Cologne; iron. machin., textiles, chemicals; p. (1968) 107,886.

Levin, *bor.*, N.I., N.Z.; p. (1966) 11,402.

Levis, *t.*, Quebec, Canada; on St. Lawrence R., opposite Quebec; rly. terminus, landing place for Transatlantic passengers; p. (1961) 15,112.

Levkas (Santa Maura), Ionian Is., Greece; ch. t. and spt., L.; mtns.; grapes, currants; a. 110 sq. m.; p. (1961) 23,969 of t. 6,552.

Levoča, *t.*, ČSSR.; N.W. of Kosice; industl.; p. (1961) 13,768.

Lewes, *co. t., mun. bor.*, E. Sussex, Eng.; on R. Ouse at N. entrance to gap through S. Downs; mkt., agr. ctr.; old buildings; iron wks.; p. (estd. 1967) 14,080.

Lewis, *I.*, Outer Hebrides, Scot.; fishing, tweeds; ch. t. Stornoway; a. 770 sq. m.; p. 31,687.

Lewisham, *inner bor.*, London, Eng.; inc. former bor. of Deptford; residtl.; industl.; p. (1966) 289,000.

Lewiston, *t.*, Idaho, U.S.A.; gold, silver, lead; agr., lumber; p. (1960) 12,691.

Lewiston, *c.*, Maine, U.S.A.; textiles, machin., timber; p. (1960), 40,804.

Lexington, *c.* Ky., U.S.A.; univ.; tobacco, horse-rearing; p. (1960) 62,810.

Lexington, *t.*, Mass., U.S.A.; nr. Boston; mftg.; first battle in American War of Independence, 1775; p. (1960) 27,961.

Leyburn, *t.*, N.R. Yorks, Eng.; in lower Wensley-dale; mkt.; lead, lime; p. 1,440.

Leyden, *see* Leiden.

Leyland, *t., urb. dist.*, Lancs, Eng.; 5 m. S. of Preston; motors, cotton, paint and varnish, rubber goods; p. (1961) 19,241.

Leyre, *R.*, S.W. France; length 40 m.

Leyte, *I.*, Philippines; a. 2,785 sq. m.; p. (1960) 1,072,600.

Leytha (Leitha), *R.*, Austria; flowing to the Danube below Vienna.

Leyton, *see* Waltham Forest.

Leytonstone, part of Waltham Forest, Eng.; p. (1961) 12,254.

Lhasa (Lasa), *c., cap.*, Tibet, China; "forbidden" c.; Buddhist ctr., temple, monasteries, shrines; caravan tr. in carpets, silk, lace, gold, tea; p. (1953) 50,000.

Liao-ho, *R.*, Liaoning, N.E. China, flows into G. of Liaotung, Yellow Sea; navigable for last 400 m. of course; length approx. 1,000 m.

Liaoning, *prov.*, N.E. China; incl. lower course and delta of Liao-ho; extremely fertile; gr. mineral resources; cap. Mukden; p. (1953) 18,545,147.

Liaotung, *peninsula*, N.E. China; nr. G. of same name

Liaoyang, *c.*, Liaoning, N.E. China; in fertile valley of Liao-ho; p. (1953) 102,000.

Liaoyuan, c., Kirin, China; p. (1953) *120,000*.

Liberal, t., S.W. Kan., U.S.A.; natural gas, flour, machin.; p. (1960) *13,813*.

Liberec, t., ČSSR.; on R. Neisse; univ.; textiles, chemicals, tr. ctr.; p. (1962) *65,267*.

Liberia, *rep.*, W. Africa; rubber, palm kernels, palm oil, cocoa, timber; rich iron ore deposits, diamond mng.; cap. Monrovia; a. 43,000 sq. m.; p. (estd. 1969) *1,200,000*.

Libmanan, *mun.*, Luzon, Philippine Is.; hemp, rice; p. *23,000*.

Libourne, t., Gironde, France; on R. Dordogne; vineyards, brandy, sugar, woollens; p. (1954) *19,474*.

Libreville, c., *cap.* Gabon; pt. on G. of Guinea; exp. tropical hardwoods, rubber, cacao; p. c. *31,000*.

Libya, *indep. sov. st.* (1951), Mediterranean cst., N. Africa; consists of 3 former provs. Tripolitania, Cyrenaica and Fezzan; joint caps. Tripoli and Benghazi; one of the world's lgst. producers of crude oil; agr. in cstl. regions; renamed Libyan Arab Republic after 1969 *coup d'état*; a. 810,000 sq.m.; p. (estd. 1968) *1,803,000*.

Libyan Desert, part of the Sahara, Africa.

Lichfield, c., *mun. bor.*, Staffs, Eng.; 7 m. N.W. of Tamworth; cath.; agr. and light inds.; p. (estd. 1967) *22,100*.

Lichtenstein, t., Karl-Marx-Stadt, E. Germany; textiles; p. (1963) *13,978*.

Lick Observatory, on Mt. Hamilton, Cal., U.S.A.

Lickey Hills, Worcester, Eng.; 4 m. S.W. of Birmingham; sm. l. of ancient rocks; largely wooded; rise to 956 ft.

Licking, R., Ky., U.S.A.; trib. of Ohio R.; 220 m.

Licosa, C., Italy; S. side of G. of Salerno.

Liddel, R., Roxburgh, Dumfries, Scot.; trib. of R. Esk.; valley used by "Waverley Route" rly. from Carlisle to Edinburgh.

Lidköping, t., Sweden; on L. Vänern; iron, porcelain inds.; p. (1961) *16,353*.

Liechtenstein, *sm. principality*, Europe; between Austria and Switzerland; agr., cattle, cotton weaving and spinning, leather goods; cap. Vaduz; a. 62 sq. m.; p. estd. (1968) *21,2000*.

Liège, *prov.*, Belgium; minerals; cap. Liége; a. 1,525 sq. m.; p. (1968) *1,019,105*.

Liége (Luik), c., *prov. cap.*, Belgium; at junction of Rs. Meuse and Ourthe; cath., univ.; textiles, machin., coal, iron, glassware, fire-arms; p. (1968) *152,488*; inc. subs. *452,713*.

Lier, t., Belgium; textiles, mnfs.; p. (1962) *28,887*.

Liepaja, *spt.*, Latvian S.S.R.; fishing inds.; engin, steel, chemicals; p. (1959) *71,000*.

Liestal, *cap.* of the half-can. Baselland, Switzerland; p. *7,211*.

Liévin, *mftg. t.*, Pas-de-Calais, France; adjoining Lens; coal-mining; p. (1954) *31,808*.

Liévres, R., Quebec, Canada; trib. of St. Lawrence R.

Liffey, R., Ireland; flows from Wicklow to Dublin Bay; length 50 m.

Lifu, I. (French); Loyalty Is., Pacific.

Ligao, t., Luzon, Philippine Is.; sugar, rice.

Lightning Ridge, N.S.W., Australia; black opal field.

Lignice (Liegnitz), t., Silesia, Poland; German before 1945; cas.; foodstuffs, textiles, rly. junction; p. (1965) *72,000*.

Liguria, *region*, N.W. Italy; inc. provs. of Genoa and Porto Maurizio; a. 2,089 sq. m.; p. (1961) *1,717,630*.

Ligurian Sea, Mediterranean; N. of Corsica.

Lika, R., Jugoslavia; partly underground; length 30 m.

Lille, *cap.*, Nord, France; on R. Deule; univ.; linens, cottons, rayons, iron, sugar, chemicals; p. (1968) *190,546*.

Lillehammer, t., Norway; in R. Lagen valley; tourist ctr.; agr., lumbering; p. (1968) *20,023*.

Lilongwe, t., main ctr. of Central Region, Malawi; site for new cap.; p. (1966) *19,176*.

Lim Fjord, *shallow strait*, Jutland, Denmark; connects N. Sea with Kattegat; length 100 m.

Lima, *dep.*, Peru; a. 15,048 sq. m.; p. (1961) *2,321,198*.

Lima, *cap.*, Peru; univ.; comm. ctr., textiles, leather, furniture, iron-ore; spt. Callao; p. (1963) *1,700,000*.

Lima, c., Ohio, U.S.A.; on Ottawa R.; rly. wks., oil, car bodies, refrigerators; p. (1960) *51,037*.

Limassol, *spt.*, Cyprus; wine, grapes, raisins; p. (estd. 1959) *37,000*.

Limavady, t., *urb. dist.*, Londonderry, N. Ireland; mkt.; linen; p. (1966) *4,811*.

Limbach, t., Karl-Marx-Stadt, E. Germany; hosiery, textiles, machines; p. (1963) *26,287*.

Limbe, t., Malawi, Africa; merged with Blantyre (*q.v.*); elec. and power plants; p. *7,140*.

Limburg, *prov.*, Belgium; agr., livestock, gin, sugar-beet. mftg.; cap. Hasselt; a. 930 sq. m.; p. (1968) *638,593*.

Limburg, *prov.*, Neth.; drained by R. Maas (Meuse); cap. Maastricht; agr., cattle, coal, iron; a. 846 sq. m.; p. (1967) *980,276*.

Limburg, c., Hessen, Germany; on R. Lahn; cath.; iron, machin., glass, paper; rly. junction; p. (estd. 1954) *15,800*.

Limehouse, *par.*, Tower Hamlets, E. London, Eng.; on R. Thames; p. (1961) *7,582*.

Limeira, t., São Paulo, Brazil; ctr. of orange cultivation; hats, matches; p. (1960) *54,000*.

Limerick, co., Munster, Ireland; agr., livestock, fishing; a. 1,307 sq. m.; p. (1966) *137,276*.

Limerick, co. bor., *spt.. cap.*, Limerick, Ireland; at head of Shannon estuary; bacon, tanning, shipbldg.; p. (1966) *55,885*.

Limmat, R., Switzerland; trib. of R. Aar; flows through c. of Zurich; length 80 m.

Limoges, ch. t., Haute-Vienne France; porcelain, kaolin paste; p. (1968) *132,935*.

Limón, *prov.*, Costa Rica, Central America; p. (1963) *68,263*.

Limón, *prov. cap.*, *spt.*, Costa Rica, Central America; comm. ctr.; oil refining nearby; p. (1963) *22,505*.

Limousin, *old prov.*, and *natural division* ("pays"), Central France; located W. of Auvergne; plateau, average alt. 1,000 ft., composed of old crystalline rocks; exposed, damp climate; rich pasture favours raising of dairy cattle, horses; kaolin deposits; ch. t., Limoges.

Limpopo, or Crocodile R., S. Africa.

Linares, *prov.*, Chile; a. 3,790 sq. m.; cap. L.; p. (1961) *190,350*.

Linares, t., Chile; wine, fruit, cereals, vegetables; p. (1961) *51,481*.   [(1959) *58,327*.

Linares, t., Spain; lead-mining and mftg.; p.

Lincoln, *agr. co.*, Eng; a. 2,665 sq. m.; divided into 3 administrative dists.; Holland, p. (1966) *105,000*; Kesteven, p. (1966) *226,000*; Lindsey, engin., agr. machin.; p. (1966) *453,000*.

Lincoln, c., co. bor., co. t., Lincoln, Eng.; on R. Witham in gap through Lincoln Edge; cath.; heavy engin., iron foundries, bricks, lime, seed milling, malting; p. (estd. 1967) *77,320*.

Lincoln, c., Ill., U.S.A.; coal, agr.; pottery; p. (1960) *16,890*.

Lincoln, *cap.*, Nebraska, U.S.A.; rly. ctr., flour; agr. machin., watches, cars, chemicals, rubber goods; p. (1960) *128,521*.

Lincoln, t., R.I., U.S.A.; limestone, textiles; p. (1960) *13,545*.

Lincoln Edge, *hill ridge*, Lincoln, Eng.; runs N. from Ancaster through Lincoln to Humber; narrow ridge with steep scarp slope to W., broken across by R. Witham at Lincoln; composed of limestone, little surface drainage; iron-ore deposits worked in N. nr. Scunthorpe; sheep, barley; rarely exceeds 300 ft. alt.

Lincoln Park, *sub.* of Detroit, Mich., U.S.A.; residtl.; p. (1960) *53,933*.

Lincoln Wolds, *low plateau*, Lindsey, Lincoln, Eng.; runs N. 45 m. from Wash to Humber; chalk covered with glacial deposits; mixed farming, grains, roots, sheep; lge. farm units; scantily populated; rise to approx. 450 ft.

Lindau, t., Bavaria, Germany; situated on I. in L. Constance; foodstuffs, machin., elec. goods; route ctr.; p. (1963) *25,500*.

Linden, t., N.J., U.S.A.; p. (1960) *39,931*.

Lindsey, N. div., Lincoln, Eng.; ch. ts. Lincoln, Grimsby; a. 1,520 sq. m.; p. (1961) *504,678*.

Lingen, t., Lower Saxony, Germany; on Dortmund–Ems Canal; oil refining, textiles, cheese, cellulose; route ctr.; p. (1963) *25,400*.

Linköping, t., S E. Sweden; hy. engin., aero-engin., pianos, furniture; p. (1961) *65,237*.

Linlithgow, *burgh*, co. t., W. Lothian, Scot.; 15 m. W. of Edinburgh; paper, glue, chemicals, distilling, brewing; p. (1961) *4,327*.

Linnhe, L., Argyll, Scot.; 21 m. long; entrance to Caledonian canal.

Linosa, I. (Italian), Mediterranean, W. of Malta.

Linslade, t., *urb. dist.*, Bucks, Eng.; 1 m. N.W. of Leighton Buzzard; p. (1961) *4,127*.

Linwood, t., N.E. Renfrew, Scotland; 3 m. W. of Paisley; cars.

Linz, c., cap., Upper Austria; on Danube; boats, brewing, printing, iron, steel, textiles; cath.; p. (1964) 202,000.

Lions, G. of, Mediterranean, S. France.

Lipa, t., Luzon, Philippine Is.; sugar, tobacco, cocoa, maize; p. (1960) 69,036.

Lipari Is., Italy; volcanic, Stromboli 3,155 ft.; a. 45 sq. m.; olives, grapes, wine, sulphur; lgst. I. and cap. L.; p. 19,500.

Lipetsk, industl t., R.S.F.S.R.; on the R. Voronezh; iron, engin., ferro-alloys; p. (1967) 237,000.

Lippe, R. Germany; trib. of Rhine; length 110 m.

Lippstadt, t., N. Rhine–Westphalia, Germany; on R. Lippe; metallurgy, textiles, rly. ctr.; p. (1963) 38,500.

Liri, R., Central Italy; rises in Alban Hills, flows S.E. to Cassino and then S.W. to G. of Gaeta; valley followed by main road from Rome to Naples; length 105 m.

Lisbon, spt., cap., Portugal; on R. Tagus; cas. cath.; univ.; cotton, silk, gold, silver, chemicals; p. (1960) 818,000.

Lisburn, t., urb. dist., Antrim, N. Ireland; on R. Lagan, 6 m. S.W. of Belfast; tyre valves; p. (1966) 21,538.

Lisieux, t., Calvados, France; cath.; flannel, dairying, footwear, machin.; p. (1962) 22,472.

Liskeard, mkt. t., mun. bor., Cornwall, Eng.; on R. Looe at S. edge of Bodmin Moor; mining, tanning, chemicals; p. (estd. 1967) 4,700.

Lisle, t., Tasmania; gold.

Lismore, mkt. t., rural dist., on R. Blackwater, Waterford, Ireland; p. (1961) 8,027.

Lismore, Scot., I., 12 m. long in Loch Linnhe near Oban; p. 200.

Lismore, t., N.S.W., Australia; dairying, sugar-refining, maize, potatoes, textiles, engin.; p. (1966) 19,740.

Lissa, I., Jugoslavia; wine.

Listowel, urb. dist., Kerry, Ireland; on R. Feale; cas. ruins; p. (1961) 2,858.   [(1960) 7,330.

Litchfield, c., Ill., U.S.A.; natural gas, oil; p.

Litherland, t., urb. dist., Lancs, Eng.; N. sub. of Liverpool; tanning, rubber processing, tar distilling, tin smelting; p. (estd. 1967) 24,820.

Lithgow, t., N.S.W., Australia; coal-mining, ironwks., potteries; p. (1961) 14,222.

Lithuania, constituent rep., U.S.S.R.; former independent st.; agr., livestock, timber; cap. Vilnius; a. 25,174 sq. m.; p. (1970) 3,129,000.

Litomerice, t., CSSR.; on R. Elbe; brewing, agr. ctr.; p. (1961) 16,884.

Little Bahama, one of the Bahama Is., W.I.

Little Belt, strait, separating Jutland from I. of Fyn, Denmark.

Little Cayman, I., see Cayman Is.

Little Colorado, R., Arizona, U.S.A.; trib. of Colorado R.   [timber; p. (1960) 7,551.

Little Falls, c., Minn., U.S.A.; on R. Mississippi;

Little Falls, t., N.Y., U.S.A.; on Mohawk R.; paper, leather, bicycles, knitted goods; p. (1960) 8,935.

Little Lever, urb. dist., Lancs, Eng.; residtl. and industl.; p. (1961) 5,088.

Little Rock, c., Ark., U.S.A.; on Arkansas R.; oil, cotton-seed cakes, cotton, machin., and many diversified inds.; livestock; p. (1960) 107,813.   [length 300 m.

Little Sioux, R., Iowa, U.S.A.; trib. of Missouri;

Littleborough, t., urb. dist., Lancs, Eng.; 3 m. N.E. of Rochdale; cotton, woollens, dyeing; p. (1961) 10,514.

Littlehampton, t., urb. dist., W. Sussex, Eng.; on S. cst. at mouth of R. Arun; holiday resort, sm. spt.; p. (1961) 15,647.

Littleport, mkt. t., Cambs, Eng.; N. of Ely; agr.

Littleton, t., N.H., U.S.A.; mftg.; p. (1960) 3,355.

Littoria (Latina), t., Lazio, Italy; in ctr. of re-claimed area of Pontine Marshes, 38 m. S.E. of Rome; mkt. ctr., on which planned road system converges; built since 1932; nuclear power sta. nearby; p. (1961) 48,395.

Liverpool, c., spt., co. bor., Lancs, Eng.; 2nd lgst. pt. in Gr. Britain; on N. bank at entrance to Mersey estuary; deep-sea container berths at Seaforth; shipping and ship-repairing; elec. mnfs. and engin., flour milling, sugar refining, seed and rubber processing, cars; cath., univ.; p. (estd. 1969) 677,450.

Liverpool, t., N.S.W., Australia; within met. a. of Sydney; mkt. and processing ctr. for dairy prod.; elec. goods, woollens; p. (1966) 60,552.

Liversedge, t., W.R. Yorks, Eng.; woollens, chemicals, machin.; p. 15,000.   [8,229.

Livingston, t., Mont., U.S.A.; industl.; p. (1960)

Livingston, "new town" (designated 1962), on bdy. of W. Lothian and Midlothian, Scot.; p. (estd. 1968) 6,500.

Livingstone Falls, cataracts on R. Congo, Africa.

Livingstone, t., Zambia; on Zambesi R. where the rly. bridges the r., stands at 3,000 ft.; former cap.; impt. saw-mills ctr.; p. (1962) 31,560 inc. 4,000 Europeans.   [9,600 ft.

Livingstone, mtns., Tanzania, highest point,

Livorno, see Leghorn.

Livry-Gargain, t., Seine-St-Denis, France; p. (1962) 29,683.

Lizard, The, C., Cornwall. Eng.; S. point of Eng.

Ljubljana, cap., Slovenia, Jugoslavia; on Laibach R.; textiles, chemicals, bell mftg, engin.; p. (estd. 1964) 178,000.

Llanberis, t., Caernarvon, Wales; tourist ctr. at base of Snowdon; p. 2,370.

Llanberis, pass, Caernarvon, N. Wales; between mtns. Snowdon and Clyder Fawr; road carries heavy tourist traffic; summit alt. 1,168 ft.

Llandaff, c., Glamorgan, S. Wales; part of Cardiff; cath.; p. 13,227.

Llandarcy, vil., Glamorgan, S. Wales; on cst. Swansea Bay, Bristol Channel; lge. oil-refinery; pipe-line to Angle Bay, Pembroke.

Llandilo, t., urb. dist., E. Carmarthen, Wales; on R. Towy, 10 m. E. of Carmarthen; agr. mkt.; p. (1961) 1,906.

Llandovery, t., mun. bor., N.E. Carmarthen, Wales; on R. Towy, 11 m. N.E. of Llandilo; agr., forestry; fertilisers, cattlefood, bricks, tourist ctr.; p. (1961) 1,896.

Llandrindod Wells, t., urb. dist., mid-Radnor, Wales; medicinal waters; p. (1961) 3,248.

Llandudno, t., urb. dist., Caernarvon, Wales; between Gr. and Little Orme's Head; resort; elec. domestic goods; p. (1961) 17,852.

Llandysul, t., S. Cardigan, Wales, on R. Teifi; woollen milling; p. (1951) 2,590.

Llanelli, spt., mun. bor., Carmarthen, Wales; on N. cst. of Loughor estuary; coal-mng., steel and tin-plate wks., mng. machin.; p. (1961) 29,994.

Llanera, commune, N.W. Spain; horticulture; coal; p. 11,424.

Llanfairfechan, t., N. Caernarvon, Wales; under Penmaenmawr Mt.; seaside resort; granite quarrying; p. (1961) 2,861.

Llanfair Caereinion, t., Montgomery, Wales; mkt., flannel; p. 1,665.

Llanfyllin, t., mun. bor., Montgomery, Wales; 11 m. S.W. of Oswestry; brewing, malting; Roman remains; p. (1961) 1,251.

Llangefni, t., urb. dist., Anglesey, Wales; in ctr. of the I.; mkt. and agr. t.; p. (1961) 3,209.

Llangollen, t., urb. dist., Denbigh, Wales; on R. Dee; mkt., tourist ctr., flannel mftg., light engin., slate quarrying; p. (1961) 3,050.

Llanidloes, t., mun. bor., Montgomery, Wales; on R. Severn; leather, ironfoundry, engin. wks.; p. (1961) 2,375.

Llanos, lowland region, Venezuela and Colombia, S. America; drained by R. Orinoco and tribs.; high temperatures throughout year, but rain chiefly in summer; ch. vegetation, coarse grass which withers during dry season (Dec. to May); little developed, some cattle-rearing.

Llanos de Urgel, upland region, Lérida, N.E. Spain; semi-arid; formerly steppe-land, now irrigated by R. Segre; vine, olive, maize, to-bacco.   [(1960) 182,181.

Llanquihue, prov., Chile; a. 7,005 sq. m.; p.

Llanrwst, t., urb. dist., Denbigh, Wales; on R. Conway; 10 m. S. of Conway; mkt., tourist ctr.; p. (1961) 2,571.

Llanstephan, vil., Carmarthen, Wales; cas.

Llantrisant, rural dist., Glamorgan, Wales; iron, coal, quarrying; Royal Mint; p. (rural dist. 1961) 27,125.

Llanwrtyd Wells, t., urb. dist., Brecknock, Wales; iron, farming; p. (1961) 536.

Lleyn, peninsula, rural dist., Caernarvon, N. Wales; extends W. from Snowdonia to Bardsey I., separates Cardigan Bay from Caer-narvon Bay; crystalline rocks form hills in E., otherwise low, undulating; pastoral farming, sheep, cattle; settlements mainly on cst., fishing vils. and sm. seaside resorts; ch. t.,

Pwllheli; a. 180 sq. m.; p. rural dist. (1961) 16,521. [24,903.

Llwchwr, *urb. dist.*, Glam., S. Wales; p. (1961)

Loa, *R.*, N. Chile.

Loango, *spt.*, Congo (ex-French), Eq. Africa; N. of mouth of R. Congo; rubber, palm-oil exp.

Loanhead, *burgh*, Midlothian, Scot.; 5 m. S.E. of Edinburgh; coal, iron ore, engin.; p. (1961) 5,023. [16,805.

Lōbau, *industl. t.* Dresden, E. Germany; p. (1963)

Lobaye, *R.*, Congo rep., Eq. Africa.

Lobito, *spt.*, Angola, Africa; N. of Benguela; exp. copper, maize; rly. terminus; p. (1960) 79,600 (inc. 15,000 whites). [Talara; oil-wells.

Lobitos, *t.*, Piura dep., Peru; on cst. 20 m. N. of Locarno, *t.*, Switzerland; on L. Maggiore; tourist ctr.; L. treaty 1925; figs, olives, pomegranates; p. 7,700 (inc. subs. 12,000).

Lochaber, *mountainous dist.*, S. Inverness, Scot.; contains Ben Nevis.

Lochalsh, *see* Kyle of Lochalsh.

Lochgelly, *burgh*, Fife, Scot.; nr. Dunfermline coal-mining: p. (1961) 9,114.

Lochgilphead, *co. t.*, Argyll, Scot.; at head of Loch Gilp, 2 m. N. of Ardrishaig; tourist ctr.; p. (1961) 1,208.

Lochmaben, *burgh*, Dumfries, Scot.; in Annandale, 7 m. N.E. of Dumfries; p. (1961) 1,279.

Lochy, Loch, Inverness, Scot.; used by Caledonian Canal; 10 m. long; R. Lochy flows 8 m. to Fort William from S. end of the loch.

Lockerbie, *burgh*, Dumfries, Scot.; in Annandale 10 m. E. of Dumfries; sheep mkt.; p. (1961) 2,826. [agr.; p. (1960) 6,084.

Lockhart, *t.*, Texas, U.S.A.; cotton, petroleum,

Lock Haven, *c.*, Penns., U.S.A.; on Susquehanna R.; timber; p. (1960) 11,748. [7,560.

Lockport, *t.*, Ill., U.S.A.; rly. ctr.; p. (1960)

Lockport, *c.*, N.Y., U.S.A.; on Erie canal; machin., paper pulp, fruit; p. (1960) 26,443.

Loddon, *R.*, Victoria, Australia; rises in Grampian Mtns., flows N. into R. Murray at Swan Hill; water used for irrigation in N. Victoria; length approx. 200 m. [p. (1962) 7,234.

Lodève, *t.*, Hérault, France; cloth mftg.; cath.;

Lodi, *c.*, Italy; on R. Adda; cheese, majolica ware; cath.; p. 29,000.

Lodi, *t.*, Cal., U.S.A.; in San Joaquin valley; agr., especially grapes; packing plants; p. (1960) 22,229.

Lodi, *t.*, N.J., U.S.A.; p. (1960) 23,502.

Lodore, *waterfall*, nr. Keswick, Cumberland, Eng.

Lodz, *prov.*, Central Poland; a. 7,904 sq. m.; p. (1965) 1,665,000.

Lodz, *t.*, Central Poland; the "Manchester of Poland"; textiles, paper, engin.; p. (1965) 744,000.

Lofoten Is., *storm-swept gr.*, off N.W. cst. Norway; stretching 175 m.; mainly mtns.; cod and herring fishing.

Loftus, *t.*, *urb. dist.*, N.R. Yorks, Eng.; on N.E. flank of Cleveland Hills; stone, iron and steel; p. (1961) 8,111.

Logan, *c.*, Utah, U.S.A.; p. (1960) 18,731.

Logan, *t.*, Ohio, U.S.A.; coal, natural gas, oil; leather, wool mnfs.; p. (1960) 6,417.

Logan, *mtn.*, S.E. Yukon, Canada; alt. 19,850 ft.

Logansport, *c.*, Ind., U.S.A.; on Wabash and Erie canal; timber, fruit, grain, machin., woollens; p. (1960) 21,106.

Logroño, *prov.*, N. Spain; cap. Logroño; a. 1,946 sq. m.; p. (1959) 232,386.

Logroño, *c.*, N. Spain, ctr. of wine growing a.; comm. and agr. mkt. t.; p. (1957) 55,465.

Loir, *R.*, France; trib. of R. Sarthe; length 150 m.

Loire, *R.*, France; lgst. in cty., flows from Cévennes Mtns. to Atlantic; length 625 m.

Loire, *dep.*, France; agr. (potatoes vineyards), mining, mftg.; cap. St. Etienne; a. 1,853 sq. m.; p. (1968) 722,383.

Loire, Atlantique, *dep.*, W. France; cap. Nantes; a. 2,695 sq. m.; p. (1968) 861,452.

Loire, Haute, *dep.*, France; cap. Le Puy; a. 1,930 sq. m.; p. (1968) 263,337

Loiret, *dep.*, France; agr., vineyards, distilling, mftg.; cap. Orléans; a. 2,630 sq. m.; p. (1968) 430,629.

Loir-et-Cher, *dep.*, Central France; cap. Blois; a. 2,479 sq. m.; p. (1968) 267,896.

Loja, *prov.*, Ecuador; cap. Loja; a. 3,705 sq. m.; p. (estd. 1962) 285,351.

Lokeren, *t.*, Belgium; textiles, chemicals, tobacco; p. (1962) 25,975.

Lokoja, *t.*, Nigeria; at confluence of Rs. Niger and Benue; military sta.; importance decreased since rlys. opened; p. 2,122.

Lolland, *I.*, Danish Baltic Sea; a. 462 sq. m.; forests; cap. Maribo; p. (1960) 83,170.

Lombardy, *region*, N. Italy: in R. Po Valley; a. 9,190 sq. m.; p. (1961) 7,390,492.

Lombardy, Plain of, N. Italy; extensive lowland flanked by Alps, Apennines, Adriatic Sea; built up by alluvium from R. Po, its tribs. and R. Adige; zone bounding main Rs. liable to floods, elsewhere irrigation necessary on account of hot summers; intensively cultivated, rice, maize, flax, clover, lucerne, wheat, apples, dairy cattle, mulberry; densely populated; many industl. ts.. Milan, Novara, Pavia, etc.; length 250 m., width from 50 to 120 m.

Lombok, one of the lesser Sunda Is., Indonesia; mtnous volcanic terrain; Wallace's Line passes between Lombok and Bali; ch. t. Mataram; p. 1,300,000.

Lomé, *spt.*, *cap.*, Togo, W. Africa; on G. of Guinea; deep water pt. exp. cacao, cotton, palm prods.; phosphates; p. (estd. 1964) 80,000.

Lomme, *commune*, Nord, France; spinning, hats; p. (1954) 23,488.

Lomond, *L.*, between Dunbarton and Stirling cos., Scot.; contains 30 Is.; lgst. loch in Scot.; length 20 m.; a. 27 sq. m.

Lomond Hills, Kinross and Fife, Scot.; alt. 1,713 ft. and 1,471 ft. [p. (1965) 22,000.

Lomza, *t.*, Poland; on Narew R.; grain, timber;

London, *cap. c.*, Eng.; lies at head of ocean navigation on Thames est.; inc. 12 inner and 20 outer bors.; main communication, financial and cultural ctr.; Port of London with 92 m. of waterway and c. 400 acres of dock estate, inc. 36 m. of quayage, is with New York and Rotterdam one of 3 lgst pts in world; univ.; many historic bldgs.; p. (estd. 1968) 7,764,000. (Greater London); (1966) 4,600 (c.).

London, *t.*, Ontario, Canada; on R. Thames, 65 m. W. of Hamilton; industl. ctr.; univ.; p. (1966) 207,396.

Londonderry, *co.*, N. Ireland; a. 816 sq. m.; p. (1966) 118,664.

Londonderry (or Derry), *co.* Derry, N. Ireland; on left bank of R. Foyle, 4 m. upstream from Lough Foyle; shirt mftg.; textiles; acetylene from naphtha; training ctr. for ind.; p. (1966) 55,681.

Londonderry, *O.*, Timor Sea, W. Australia.

Londrina, *t.*, Paraná, Brazil; agr. and industl. ctr.; p. (estd. 1968) 226,332.

Long Beach, *c.*, Cal., U.S.A.; tourism; petrol, shipbldg., fishing, canning, aircraft, chemicals; p. (1960) 344,168.

Long Beach, *t.*, Long I., N.Y., U.S.A.; holiday resort; p. (1960) 26,473.

Longbenton, *t.*, *urb. dist.*, Northumberland, Eng.; 3 m. N.E. of Newcastle; coal-mng.; p. (estd. 1967) 43,480. [p. (1960) 26,223.

Long Branch, *c.*, N.J., U.S.A.; seaside resort;

Long Eaton, *t.*, *urb. dist.*, Derby, Eng.; on R. Trent. 5 m. S.W. of Nottingham; rly. wks., lace mftg., elec. cables, flexible tubing, hosiery; p. (estd. 1967) 32,430.

Longford, *co.*, Leinster, Ireland; peat bogs; dairy farming; co. t. Longford; a. 421 sq. m.; p. (1966) 28,943.

Long Forties Bank, *submarine sandbank*, N. Sea; 80 m. E. of Aberdeen; valuable fishing-grounds; depth of water, from 25 to 40 fathoms.

Long I., part of N.Y., U.S.A.; separated from mainland by East R.; contains Queens and Brooklyn, bors. of New York City; mkt. gardening, fisheries, oysters, holiday resorts; a. 1,682 sq. m.

Long I., Bahamas Is., W.I.; p. (1953) 3,755.

Long, Loch, *arm of sea*, between Dunbarton and Argyll, Scot.; length 17 m.

Longmeadow, *t.*, S.W. Mass., U.S.A.; residtl.; p. (1960) 10,547.

Longreach, *t.*, Queensland, Australia; in ctr. of Gr. Australian (artesian) basin, 400 m. W. of Rockhampton; where rly. from cst. crosses R. Thompson; collecting and forwarding ctr. for cattle and wool; p. (1966) 3,864.

Longridge, *t.*, *urb. dist.*, Lancs, Eng.; 6 m. N.E. of Preston; cotton, nails; p. (1961) 4,677.

Long's Peak, *mtn.*, Col., U.S.A.; alt. 14,271 ft.

Longueuil, *t.*, Quebec, Canada; p. (1961) 24,131

Longview, *t.*, Texas, U.S.A.; p. (1960) 40,050.

Longview, *t.*, Wash., U.S.A.; p. (1960) 23,349.

Longwy, *t.*, Meurthe-et-Moselle, France; fortfd.; iron, porcelain; p. (1962) 22,214.

Long Xuyen, *mkt. t.*, S. Vietnam; p. 148,000.

Lons-le-Saunier, *cap.*, Jura, France; salt springs; wine, agr.; livestock; p. (1962) 19,041.

Loce, *urb. dist.*, Cornwall, Eng.; on Looe estuary; holiday resort; p. (1961) 3,878.

Lookland, *t.*, S.W. Ohio, U.S.A.; chemicals, paper, light mnfs.; p. (1960) 5,292. [p. (1954) 14,582.

Loos, *t.*, Pas-de-Calais, France; coal-mining;

Lop Nor, *marsh*, Sinkiang, W. China; in Tarim Basin at foot of Altyn Tagh; ctr. of inland drainage, receives water from R. Tarim; former atomic testing grounds.

Lorain, *c.*, Ohio, U.S.A.; on L. Erie; shipbldg., steelwks., fisheries; p. (1960) 68,932.

Lorca, *t.*, Murcia, Spain; agr. prod., woollens, chemicals; bishop's palace; p. (1959) 61,657.

Lord Howe I., Australian I., S. Pac. Oc., length 7 m., width 1½ m.; *c.* 436 m. N.E. of Sydney; palm seed ind.; p. (1958) 223.

Lorena, *t.*, São Paulo st., Brazil; p. (1968) 39,263.

Lorestan, *see* Luristan.

Loreto, *t.*, Ancona, Italy; pilgrim ctr.; p. 6,700.

Loreto, *dep.*, Peru; rubber; cap. Iquitos; a. 119,270 sq. m.; p. (1961) 330,335.

Lorient, *spt.*, Morbihan, France; on Bay of Biscay; govt. dockyds. and arsenal; metals, fishing; p. (1968) 66,444.

Lörrach, *t.*, Baden-Württemberg, Germany; N.E. of Basle; textiles, tobacco, chocolate mnfs., machin.; p. (1963) 31,200.

Lorraine, *prov.*, France: agr.: wine, iron.

Los Angeles, *c.*, S. Cal., U.S.A., booming modern c. (" the city of angels "), busiest pt. in Cal.; fine harbour; one of world's lgst. urban areas; 400 m. of freeway (1,500 m. planned by 1980); many prosperous inds., inc. aircraft, missiles, chemicals, machin., electronic equipment, food processing; film ctr.; fine climate; p. (1970) 2,782,400; of Greater Los Angeles c. 6,962,000.

Los Angeles, *c.*, cap. Bio Bio, Chile; wine fruit, timber; p. (1960) 79,000.

Losinj, *I.*, Jugoslavia; summer resort, tr.

Los Rios, *prov.*, Ecuador, S. America; a. 2,295 sq. m.; cap. Babahoyo; p. (estd. 1962) 244,651.

Los Santos, *prov.*, Panama, Central America; cap. Las Tablas; p. (1960) 70,554.

Lossiemouth, *burgh*, Moray, Scot.; on Moray F., 5 m. N. of Elgin; fishing; p. (1961) 5 855.

Lot, *R.*, S. France; trib. of Garonne R.; length 272 m.

Lot, *dep.*, S.W. France; livestock, wine, cereals, coal, iron; a. 2,018 sq. m.; cap. Cahors; p. (1968) 151,198. [(1961) 51,679.

Lota, *pt.*, Chile; coal-mng. ctr.; ceramics; p.

Lot-et-Garonne, *dep.*, S.W. France; agr. (cereals, vines, fruit); cap. Agen; a. 2,079 sq. m.; p. (1968) 290,592.

Lothians, *Scottish dist.*, S. of F. of Forth, cos. Mid Lothian, W. Lothian and E. Lothian.

Lötschental, *picturesque valley*, can. Valais, Switzerland; ch. vil., Kippel.

Loughborough, *t.*, *mun. bor.*, Leicester, Eng.; on R. Soar 10 m. N. of Leicester; engin., elec. gds., chemicals, textiles; univ.; p. (estd. 1967) 39,580.

Loughor, *R.*, Glamorgan, S. Wales; rises in Black Mtns., flows S.W. into Bristol Channel; lower valley submerged to form estuary, length 8 m., width 4 m., around which cluster steel-wks. and zinc refineries of Llanelly, Bynea, Gorseinon, Gowerton, etc.

Loughton, *t.*, Essex, Eng.; on border of Epping Forest; residtl.; p. (1961) 33,864.

Louisiana, *st.*, U.S.A.; agr., tobacco, cotton, sugar, timber, minerals and mfftg., oil, gas; cap. Baton Rouge; ch. spt. New Orleans; a. 48,523 sq. m.; p. (1970) 3,564,310.

Louisville, *c.*, Ky., U.S.A.; on Ohio R.; univ.; lgst. tobacco mkt. in world; chemicals, paints, cars, machin., elec. goods, synthetic rubber; p. (1960) 390,639.

Loulé, *t.*, Portugal; esparto-grass ctr.; porcelain, leather; p. 23,000.

Lourdes, *t.*, France; on R. Pau; great pilgrim ctr.; slate, marble; p. (1962) 16,376.

Lourenço Marques, *spt.*, *cap. c.*, Mozambique, Port. E. Africa; rly. terminus, coaling-sta., oil refining; lge. deposits of bentonite being worked in a. p. (estd. 1967) 441,363.

Louth, *t.*, *mun. bor.*, Lindsey. Lincoln, Eng.; on E. edge of Lincoln Wolds; abbey ruins; cattle mkt., farm implements, rope mkg., lime, malting, canning; p. (estd. 1967) 11,470.

Louth, *maritime co.*, Leinster, Ireland; mtns., bog and barren land; salmon fishing; cap. Dundalk; a. 316 sq. m.; p. (1966) 69,162.

Louvain, *t.*, Belgium; univ.; lace, brewing, tobacco mftg.; p. (1962) 32 474.

Louviers, *t.*, Eure, France; on R. Eure; cloth mftg.; p. (1962) 13,668.

Loveland, *t.*, N. Col. U.S.A.; beet-sugar refined, vegetables, fruit canning; p. (1960) 9,734.

Low Archipelago, *see* Tuamotu Is.

Low Countries. Name applied to Belgium and The Netherlands. *See under separate headings.*

Lowell, *c.*, Mass., U.S.A.; at junction of Merrimac and Concord Rs.; 30 m. N. of Boston; textiles, machin., chemicals, carpets; James Whistler, the artist, born here; p. (1960) 92,107.

Lower Austria, *prov.*, Austria; industl., agr.; ch. t. Vienna; a. 7,098 sq. m.; p. (1961) 1,374,012.

Lower Hutt, *c.*, N.I., New Zealand; p. (1966) 57,524. [p. (1968) 7,039,000.

Lower Saxony, *Land*, Germany; a. 18,226 sq. m.

Lowestoft, *fishing pt.*, *mun. bor.*, Suffolk, Eng.; on E. Anglian cst. 9 m. S. of Gr. Yarmouth; holiday resort, fish processing plants; base for North Sea gas; p. (estd. 1967) 49,160.

Lowther Hills, *mtns.*, between Dumfries and Lanark, Scot.; highest point 2,403 ft.

Loyalty Is., S. Pac. Oc.; included in French administration of New Caledonia; copra; lgst. Is., Maré, Lifou, Uvéa; a. about 800 sq. m.

Loyang, *c.*, Honan prov., China; industl.; ball bearing and mng. machin.; p. (1958) 500,000.

Lozère, *dep.*, S.E. France; traversed by Cévennes Mtns.; agr., silkworm-rearing, stock-raising; cap. Mende; a. 1,996 sq. m.; p. (1968) 77,258.

Lualaba, *R.*, Congo, Central Africa; rises nr. Elisabethville in Katanga prov., flows N. approx. 500 m. to Kikondja, where joined by R. Lufira to form R. Congo; name also applied to main stream of R. Congo as far downstream as Ponthierville.

Luanda, *pt.*, *cap. c.*, Angola; oil refining; hydroelec. wks; p. (1962) 220,000 inc. 55,000 whites.

Luang Prabang, *c.*, Laos, on Mekong R.; silk, ivory, rubber; pagoda; (1962) 8,000.

Lubbock, *c.*, N. Texas, U.S.A.; p. (1960) 128,691.

Lübeck, *c.*, *spt.*, cap. Schleswig-Holstein, Germany; on R. Trave; cath.; shipbldg., machin., chemicals, textiles, iron, foodstuffs; pt. and rly. junction; p. (1968) 243,138. [(1965) 1,901,000.

Lublin, *prov.* E. Poland; agr.; a. 10,834 sq. in. p.

Lublin, *t.*, *prov. cap.*, Poland; textiles, engin., agr. tr.; cath., 2 univs.; p. (1965) 203,000.

Lubnaig, *Loch*, Perth, Scot.; drains to R. Teith by the R. Leny. [engin., chemicals; p. 23,332.

Lubny, *t.*, Ukrainian S.S.R.; on rly. E. of Kiev;

Lubumbashi (Elizabethville), *t.*, Katanga, Congo; copper mng. ctr.; p. (1959) 183,808 inc. 13,808 whites.

Lucca, *c.*, cap. Lucca, Tuscany, Italy; nr. Pisa; cath., churches; jute mftg., tobacco, silk, cotton, and oil-refining inds.; p. (1961) 85,940.

Lucena, *t.*, Córdoba, Spain; olive oil, ceramics, gilt metals; p. (1957) 35,530.

Lucenec, *t.*, ČSSR.; on Hungarian border; magnesite, textiles, sawmilling; p. (1961) 16,102.

Lucera, *t.*, Apulia, Italy; 8 m. W. of Foggia; cas., cath.; silk mftg.; p. 17,000.

Lucerne (Luzern), *can.*, Switzerland; agr., pastoral, vineyards; oil refinery projected at Schötz/Ettiswil; cap. Lucerne; a. 576 sq. m.; p. (1961) 253,446.

Lucerne (Luzern), *t.*, *cap.*, Lucerne can., Switzerland; at W. end of L. Lucerne; light inds.; impt. tourist ctr.; p. (1961) 70,600.

Lucerne, *L.*, Switzerland; also known as Lake of the Four Cantons; length 23 m.

Luchow (Luzhou), *c.*, Szechwan, China; coal, iron, kaolin; synthetic ammonia plant; p. (1953) 289,000.

Luckenwalde, *t.*, Potsdam, E. Germany; on R. Nuthe; textiles, footwear, machin., wood and metals, chemicals; p. (1963) 28,741.

Lucknow, *c.*, cap. Uttar Pradesh India; on R. Gumti; rly. ctr., muslin embroidery, brocade mftg.; famous defence of L. in Indian Mutiny 1857; univ.; p. (1961) 655,673.

Lüdenscheid, *t.*, Rhine- N.Westphalia, Germany; S.E. of Barmen; hardware; p. (1963) 58,500.

Lüderitz, *t.,* S.W. Africa; on cst. of Kalahari desert; linked by rly. to S. African rly. system at De Aar; diamonds; p. (1960) *3,604.*

Ludhiana, *t.,* Punjab, India; nr. R. Sutlej, W. of Simla; p. (1961) *244,032.*

Ludington, *t.,* Mich., U.S.A.; on Lake M.; wood-wkg.; p. (1960) *9,421.*

Ludlow, *rural bor.,* Salop., Eng.; at foot of Clee Hills on R. Teme; agr. mkt.; agr. implements, meters, gauges; p. of t. (1961) *6,774.*

Ludvika, *t.,* Sweden; elec. goods; p. (1961) *12,253.*

Ludwigsburg, *t.,* Baden-Württemberg, Germany; N. of Stuttgart; cas.; textiles, foodstuffs, machin., toys; p. (1963) *75,500.*

Ludwig's Canal, Germany; unites Rs. Danube and Main; length 110 m.

Ludwigshafen, *t.,* Rhine-Palatinate, Germany; on R. Rhine, opposite Mannheim; chemicals, marine diesel engines, metallurgy, glass; R. pt. and rly. junction; oil pipeline from Rotterdam under construction; p. (1968) *172,981.*

Lufkin, *c.,* Texas, U.S.A.; lumber, engin.; food prod.; p. (1960) *17,641.*

Lugano, *t.,* Ticino, Switzerland; on L. Lugano; tourist ctr., silk, paper; p. (1957) *19,112.*

Lugano, *L.,* Italy–Switzerland; length 16 m.

Lugansk, *industl. t.,* Ukraine S.S.R.; S. of R. Donets in Donbas region; impt. rly. eng. factories; textiles; p. (1967) *339,000.*

Lugnaquilla, *mtn.,* Wicklow, Ireland; highest point in Wicklow Mtns., alt. 3,039 ft.

Lugo, *prov.,* N.W. Spain; fisheries, leather; cap. Lugo; a. 3,815 sq. m.; p. (1959) *500,648.*

Lugo, *t., prov. cap.,* Spain; on R. Minho; tanning, textiles; p. (1959) *50,137.*

Luichow (Luizhou), *c.,* Kwangsi Chuang, China; comm. ctr.; p. (1953) *159,000.*

Lukuga, intermittent outlet of L. Tanganyika, Africa, linking with R. Congo.

Luleå, *spt.,* N. Sweden; on Lule R. at head of G. of Bothnia; iron ore, timber, engin.; p. (1961) *65,237.*

Lulworth Cove, *sm. inlet,* Dorset, Eng.; on S. cst., 9 m. E. of Weymouth; formed by sea breaching hard coastal rocks and eroding softer rocks behind; tourism.

Lumbira, *t.,* on N. shore of L. Nyasa, Tanzania.

Lund, *t.,* Sweden; nr. Malmö; univ.; packaging ind.; steam boilers; p. (1961) *40,380.*

Lundy I., Bristol Channel; 12 m. N.W. of Hartland Point, N. Devon, Eng.; 2½ m. long by 1 m. wide. [45 m. to Irish Sea.

Lune, *R.,* Lancs. and Westmorland, Eng.; flows

Lüneburg, *t.,* Lower Saxony, Germany; S.E. of Hamburg, on Ilmenau R.; chemicals, wood, iron, paper; rly. junct.; p. (1963) *60,900.*

Lünen, *t.,* N. Rhine–Westphalia, Germany; N.E. of Dortmund; coal, metallurgy, glass, wood; R. pt. and rly. ctr.; p. (1963) *72,200.*

Lunéville, *t.,* Meurthe-et-Moselle, France; S.E. of Nancy, on R. Meurthe; cottons, woollens, hosiery, porcelain; p. (1962) *24,463.*

Lungchow, *t.,* Kwangsi, China; nr. Vietnam frontier; military sta.; p. *13,600.*

Lungi, *t.,* Sierra Leone, W. Africa; nr. Freetown; only civil airport in st.

Lupata Gorge, Mozambique, Port. E. Africa; narrow pass occupied by R. Zambesi.

Lurgan, *t., mun. bor.,* Armagh, N. Ireland; textiles, tobacco mftg.; to merge with Portadown to form c. of Craigavon; p. (1966) *20,677.*

Luristan (Lorestan), *dist.,* W. Iran; mainly mtnous; cap. Khorramabad; p. (1967) *683,139.*

Lusaka, *cap. c.,* Zambia, in Central prov.; comm. and admin. ctr. of agr. region; p. (estd. 1966) *151,400.*

Lushun, *see* Port Arthur.

Luta, *special mun.,* S. Liaoning prov., China; comprising Port Arthur Naval Base District and the pts. of Port Arthur and Talien (Dairen).

Luton, *t., co. bor.,* Beds., Eng.; in Chiltern Hills nr. source of R. Lea; motor vehicles, engin., hat mkg., aircraft, gear instruments, chemicals; p. (estd. 1967) *153,320.*

Lutong, *pt.,* N. Sarawak, Malaysia; oil refining.

Lutsk, *t.,* Ukrainian S.S.R.; comm. ctr., mnfs.; p. (1959) *49,000.*

Luxembourg, *prov.,* S.E. Belgium; on French border; wooded and hilly; a. 1,705 sq. m.; cap. Arlon; p. (1968) *219,368.*

Luxembourg, *grand duchy,* Europe; on borders of France, Germany, Belgium; upland, much over 1,000 ft.; very impt. deposits of iron ore;

cap. Luxembourg; a. 999 sq. m.; p. (1968) *336,500.*

Luxembourg, *t., cap.,* Luxembourg; in S. of Grand Duchy; iron and steel, heavy engin., leather, paper inds.; p. (1965) *79,000.*

Luxor, *vil.,* Upper U.A.R.; on E. bank of R. Nile; site of Thebes; ruined temples; p. *5,000.*

Luzon, *I.,* lgst. in Philippines; mtns.; cotton, coffee, sugar, cereals, coal, copper; cap. Manila; a. 40,420 sq. m.; p. (1960) *12,875,100.*

Lvov, (Pol. Lwów, Ger. Lemberg), *c.,* Ukraine, U.S.S.R.; ceded by Poland 1939; univ., 3 caths.; engin., textiles, chemicals oil-refining, sawmilling; p. (1967) *502,000.*

Lyallpur, *t.,* Punjab, W. Pakistan; univ.; cotton, chemicals, fertilisers; p. (1961) *425,200.*

Lydd, *mkt. t., mun. bor.,* Kent, Eng.; on Romney Marsh, 4 m. S.W. of New Romney; "lyddite" shells, concrete; airport; p. (estd. 1967) *4,170*

Lydda, *c.,* Israel; rly. junction, airport; mentioned in the Bible, and the reputed birthplace of St. George; p. (estd.) *20,000.*

Lydenburg, *t.,* Transvaal, S. Africa; gold, cotton, wheat, sheep; p. (1960) *7,393* inc. *3,306* whites.

Lydney, *par.,* Gloucester, Eng.; in Forest of Dean; iron, coal; p. *4,158.* [alt. 2,000 ft.

Lyell, *mtn.,* Stanley Range, N.S.W., Australia;

Lyell, *mtn.,* Cal., U.S.A.; in Sierra Nevada; alt. 13,190 ft.

Lyme Regis, *spt., mun. bor.,* Dorset, Eng.; on bdy. between Devon and Dorset; holiday resort, p. (estd. 1967) *3,300.*

Lymington, *t., mun. bor.,* Hants, Eng.; on The Solent at mouth of R. Lymington; small spt., yachting; p. (estd. 1967) *32,580.*

Lymm, *t., urb. dist.,* Cheshire, Eng.; 5 m. W. of Altrincham; salt mftg.; mainly residtl.; p. (1961) *7,330.*

Lynbrook, *t.,* Long I., N.Y., U.S.A.; p. (1960) *19,881.*

Lynchburg, *c.,* Va., U.S.A.; footwear, agr. implements, tobacco; p. (1960) *54,790.*

Lyndhurst, *t.,* N.J., U.S.A.; synthetic perfumery; p. (1960) *21,867.*

Lynemouth, nr. Blyth, Northumberland, Eng.; aluminium smelter projected.

Lynher, *R.,* Cornwall, Eng.; length 26 m.

Lynn, *spt.,* Mass., U.S.A.; footwear, elec. appliances; p. (1960) *944,78.* [of Chatham strait.

Lynn Canal, *fiord,* Alaska, U.S.A.; continuation

Lynton, *t., urb. dist.,* N. Devon, Eng.; 17 m. W. of Minehead on Bristol Channel; seaside tourist ctr. of Exmoor; p. (1961) *1,918.*

Lynwood, *t.,* S.W. Cal., U.S.A.; engin.; p. (1960) *31,614.*

Lyon, *c.,* Iowa, U.S.A., on Mississippi R.; p. (1960) *14,468.* [38 m.

Lyon, *R.,* Perth, Scot.; trib. of R. Tay; length

Lyonnais, *mtns.,* France; W. of Lyons.

Lyons, *c. cap.,* Rhône dep., France; at confluence of Rs. Saône and Rhône; comm. ctr., silk, rayon, chemicals, engin.; heavy lorries; univ.; oil refinery nearby; world ctr. for cancer research; p. (1968) *527,800.*

Lys, *R.,* Belgium and France, trib. of R. Scheldt; length 100 m.

Lysterfiord, N.E. arm of the Sogne fiord, Norway; length 25 m.

Lytham St. Annes, *t., mun. bor.,* N. Lancs, Eng.; on N. cst. of Ribble estuary, 4. m. S. of Blackpool; holiday ctr., shipbldg.; p. (estd. 1967) *36,620.*

Lyttelton, *spt.,* S.I., N.Z.; on N. cst. of Banks Peninsula; ch. pt. of Canterbury Plain; exp. mutton wool, wheat; p. (1961) *3,403.*

Lyubertsy, *t.,* R.S.F.S.R.; industl. sub. on Moscow-Kazan rly.; agr. engin.; p. (1967) *115,000.*

M

Ma'an *t.,* S. Jordan, term of rly. through Amman to Beirut; Hijaz rail line to Medina restored and extension to Saudi Arabia planned; p. (1961) *6,899.*

Maas, *R.,* Dutch name for the R. Meuse after it has entered the Netherlands.

Maasin, *mun.,* S.W. Leyte, Philippine Is.; cst. tr.; hemp; p. *29,264.*

Maastricht, *t., cap.,* Limburg, Neth.; on R. Meuse; pottery, glass, textiles, brewing; p. (1967) *95,393.* [Europort.

Maasvlakte, seaward extension of Rotterdam's

Mablethorpe and Sutton, *t.*, *urb. dist.*, Lindsey, Lincs, Eng.; holiday resort; p. (1961) *5,389.*

Macao, *Port. terr.*, S. China; consists of peninsula and 2 sm. Is. (Taipa and Colôane) to S. of estuary of Canton R.; a. 6 sq. m.; oldest European col. in Asia (1557); p. (estd. 1965) *280,290.*

Macao, *c.*, Macao terr., S. China; occupies peninsula section of the terr.; impt. fisheries.

Macapá, *cap.*, Amapá st., Brazil; at mouth of R. Amazon; p. (estd. 1968) *74,464.*

Macassar, *ch. t., pt.*, Sulawesi, *see* Makasar.

Macassar, *strait*, Indonesia, *see* Makasar.

Macau, *spt.*, Rio Grande do Norte, Brazil; p. (estd. 1965) *280,000.*

Macclesfield, *t., mun. bor.*, Cheshire, Eng.; at foot of Pennines, 10 m. S. of Stockport; on R. Bollin; mkt., textiles, clothing, paper prods., engin.; p. (estd. 1967) *40,900.*

Macdonald Is., *terr.* of Australia, Antarctica.

Macdonnell Range, *mtns.*, Northern Terr., Australia; highest part of desert tableland, centrally situated within the continent; some gold and mica mines, but development hampered by aridity and isolation; highest alt. 4,482 ft.

Macduff, *spt. burgh*, Banff, Scot.; 2 m. E. of Banff; fishing; p. (1961) *3,479.*

Macedonia, *dist.*, Greece; cereals tobacco, fruit, opium, fishing; p. (1961) *1,890,654.*

Macedonia, *fed. unit*, Jugoslavia; cap. Skopje; a. 10,598 sq. m.; p. (1960) *1,387,000.*

Maceió, *spt., cap.*, Alagoas st., Brazil; cotton, sugar, tobacco, soap, sawmills, distilleries; p. (estd. 1968) *221,250.*

Macerata, *prov. cap.*, Italy; cath., univ.; terra-cotta, glass, chemicals; p. (1961) *37,464.*

Macgillicuddy's Reeks, *mtns.*, Kerry, Ireland; highest peak, Carrantuohill, alt. 3,414 ft.

Machala, *t.*, S.W. Ecuador; cocoa, coffee, leather, gold; p. (1962) *22,730.*

Machynlleth, *t., urb. dist.*, Montgomery, Wales, on R. Dovey; tourist ctr., clothing mftg.; p. (1961) *1,903.*

Macintyre, *R.*, N.S.W., Australia; forms border between Queensland and N.S.W.; trib. of R. Darling; length 350 m.

Mackay, *spt.*, Queensland, Australia; on R. Pioneer; sugar, dairying and banana ctr.; p. (1966) *24,566.*

Mackenzie, *township*, Guyana; bauxite; p. approx. *15,000* mostly Negro.

Mackenzie, *dist.*, N.W. Terrs., Canada; a. 527,490 sq. m.; forests and tundra; oil, radium, uranium; furs and timber.

Mackenzie, *R.*, Northwest Terrs., Canada; rises in Rocky Mtns. as Athabaska R. and flows into L. Athabaska, leaves as Slave R. and thence into Gr. Slave L., which it leaves as M. R. into Beaufort Sea; length 2,350 m.

Mackinac Sound, connects Ls. Michigan and Huron, N. America.

Mackinney, *c.*, N.E. Texas. U.S.A.; cotton ctr.; (1960) *13,763.*   [Yukon R.

Macmillan, *R.*, N.W. Terrs., Canada; trib. of

Macnean, *L.*, cos. Leitrim and Fermanagh, Ireland.

Macomb, *c.*, Ill., U.S.A.; industl.; p. (1960) *12,135.*

Mâcon, *t., cap.*, Saône-et-Loire, France; on R. Saône; ruined cath.; agr. implements, wines, copper; rope; p. (1962) *30,671.*

Macon, *c.*, Ga., U.S.A.; on Ocmulgee R.; univ.; rly. junction, ironwks., cotton mftg.; p. (1960) *69,764.*

Macon, *i.*, E. Miss., U.S.A.; cotton, dairying, lumbering; p. (1960) *2,432.*

Macquarie, I., *Australian I.*, S. Pacific; 900 m. S.E. of Tasmania, Australia; 21 m. long, 2 m. wide; uninhabited except for meteorological and research base.

Macquarie, *R.*, N.S.W., Australia; trib. of R. Darling; length 350 m.

Macroom, *t.*, Cork, Ireland; on R. Sullane; agr. tr., fishing; p. (1961) *2,169.*

Mactan, *I.*, off Cebu, Philippine Is.; mangroves, coconuts; a. 24 sq. m.; p. *40,103.*

Madagascar, *see* Malagasy Republic.

Madang, *t.*, Papua–New Guinea; copra ctr.; p. *500.*

Madawaska, *t.*, Me., U.S.A.; spt.; lumber, pulp, paper-mills; p. (1960) *4,035.*

Madawaska, *R.*, Ontario, Canada; trib. of Ottawa R.; length 230 m.

Maddalena, *I.*, off N.E. cst. of Sardinia, Italy.

Maddaloni, *t.*, Naples, Italy; p. *21,975.*

Madeira, *Portuguese I.*, Atl Oc.; wine, sugar, fruits; holiday resort; cap. Funchal; a. 315 sq. m.; p. (1963) *268,700.*

Madeira, *R.*, Brazil; trib. of R. Amazon; together with Mamoré R.; l. 2,000 m.

Madeley, *t.*, Salop, Eng.; on R. Severn; mkt., coal- and iron-mining; p. *7,300.*

Madera, *t.*, central Cal., U.S.A.; agr., lumber, wines; p. (1960) *14,430.*

Madhya Bharat, formerly a st., absorbed by Madhya Pradesh, 1 Nov. 1956.

Madhya Pradesh, *st.*, Indian Union; absorbed the sts. of Bhopal, Uindhya Pradesh, and Madhya Bharat 1 Nov. 1956; rice, jute, pulses, oilseeds, cotton; forests; manganese, coal, marble, limestone; cotton textiles; cap. Bhopal; a. *171,217* sq. m.; p. (1961) *32,372,408.*

Madinat Al Shaab, *cap.*, South Yemen People's Rep.

Madison, *c.*, Ind., U.S.A.; on Ohio R.; mftg.; p. (1960) *10,097.*

Madison, *t.*, Ill., U.S.A.; heavy engin. wks.; p. (1960) *6,861.*

Madison, *cap.*, Wis., U.S.A.; univ.; agr. tools, machin., footwear; p. (1960) *126,706.*

Madison Heights, *t.*, Mich., U.S.A.; p. (1960) *33,343.*

Madisonville, *t.*, Ky., U.S.A.; p. (1960) *13,110.*

Madras, *see* Tamil Nadu.

Madras, *c., spt., cap.*, Tamil Nadu, S. India; on S.E. (Coromandel) cst.; cath., univ.; comm. ctr., cottons, tanning, brewing, potteries, rly. coaches; oil refinery; p. (1961) *1,729,141.*

Madre de Dios, *dep.*, E. Peru; ch. t. Maldonado; forested; gold, silver; a. 58,827 sq. m.; p. (1961) *13,437.*

Madre de Dios, *R.*, Bolivia; trib. of R. Madeira; rises in Peru.

Madrid, *cap.*, Spain; on R. Manzanares; univ., cath., palace; Prado; gold and silver work; leather goods; chemicals, furniture mftg.; p. (estd. 1967) *3,000,000.*

Madrid, *prov.*, Spain; agr., freestone, granite, gypsum quarried; a. 3,089 sq. m.; cap. M.; p. (1967) *3,270,000.*

Madura, *I.*, Indonesia; off N.E. of Java; cereals, coconuts, fishing, cattle rearing, salt; a. 1,770 sq. m.; p. (1930) *1,962,462.*

Madurai, *c.*, Tamil Nadu, India; univ.; coffee, muslin, brasswk., wood carving; p. (1961) *424,810.*

Maebashi, *c.*, Honshu, Japan; mulberry trees, silk production; p. (1964) *190,000.*

Maelstrom, *whirlpool*, N.W. cst., Norway.

Maentwrog, *vil.*, Merioneth, N. Wales; in Vale of Festiniog, 2 m. E. of Festiniog; ch. hydro-elec. power-sta. in N. Wales.

Maesteg, *t., urb. dist.*, Glamorgan, Wales; dorm. t. for steel wks. at Pt. Talbot; coal-mining, cosmetics; p. (1961) *21,652.*

Mafeking, *t.*, C. Prov., S. Africa; famous siege, 1899–1900; p. (1960) *8,279 inc. 4,159* whites.

Magadan, *spt.* R.S.F.S.R.; on N. side of Sea of Okhotsk; engin.; p. (1959) *62,000.*

Magallanes, *prov.*, Chile; sheep-rearing; cap. Punta Arenas; fox breeding; petroleum; a. 52,271 sq. m.; p. (1960) *73,037.*

Magdalen, Is., G. of St. Lawrence, Canada.

Magdalena, *dep.*, Colombia; coffee, cotton, rubber; cap. Santa Marta; a. 20,813 sq. m.; p. (estd. 1961) *500,640.*

Magdalena, *R.*, Colombia; length 1,000 m.

Magdeburg, *c.*, Magdeburg, E. Germany; on R. Elbe; cath.; beet-sugar, chemicals, iron, steel, mng. machin., heavy engin.; route ctr. and R. pt.; p. (1963) *267,733*

Magelang, *t.*, Java, Indonesia; tr. ctr.; p. (1961) *96,454.*

Magellan, *strait*, between Tierra del Fuego and Chile, S. America.

Magenta, *t.*, N. Italy; nr. Milan; silk, matches; p. *12,650.*

Magenwil, Aargau, Switzerland; oil refinery projected.

Maggiore, *L.*, N. Italy–Switzerland; a. 82 sq. m.; contains Borromean Is.; tourist resort.

Maghreb, collective name given to Arabic speaking countries bordering Mediterranean in N. Africa (Morocco to Libya).

Magnet Mtn., S. Urals, R.S.F.S.R.; very rich

deposit of magnetite iron ore; smelted at Magnitogorsk, and in Kuzbas region.

Magnitogorsk, *t.*, R.S.F.S.R.; at S. end of Ural Mtns.; iron, steel, engin., iron ore, chemicals; term. of oil pipeline from Shkapovo in Bashkiria; p. (1967) *352,000*.   [p. (1961) *13,139*.

Magog, *t.*, S. Quebec, Canada; textiles, mnfs.;

Mahad Al-Dhahab, *t.*, Hejaz, Saudi-Arabia; between Mecca and Medina; gold-mining.

Mahalla El Kubra, *t.*, Lower U.A.R.; cotton textile ctr.; p. (1960) *63,000*.

Mahanadi, *R.*, India; flows from Orissa to Bay of Bengal; length 520 m.   [p. (1960) *8,536*.

Mahanoy City, *t.*, Penns., U.S.A.; anthracite;

Maharashtra, *st.*, India; ch. ts.: Greater Bombay (cap.), Poona, Nagpur, Sholapur, Kolhapur, Amravati, Nasik, Malegaon, Nagar, Akola, Ulhasuagar, Thana; a. 118,717 sq. m.; p. (1961) *39,553,718*.

Mahé, *former Fr. prov.*, S. India; united with India 1954: cap. Mahé.   [cheese; p. *18,220*.

Mahón, *spt. cap.*, Minorca, Balearic Is., Spain;

Maidenhead, *t.*, *mun. bor.*, Berks. Eng.; on R. Thames, 9 m. above Windsor; light engin., printing, jam mkg.; p. (estd. 1967) *43,700*.

Maidens, The, *gr. of dangerous rocks*, nr. Larne, off Antrim cst., N. Ireland.

Maidstone, *co. t.*, *mun. bor.*, Kent, Eng.; on R. Medway; hops, fruit ctr.; brewing, paper, agr. tools, confectionery; p. (estd. 1967) *65,790*.

Maikop, *t.*, Adygeysk, U.S.S.R.; oil-refineries; woodwkg., food inds.; p. (1959) *82,000*.

Main, *R.*, Germany; trib. of R. Rhine; l. 304 m.

Main, *Hudson Bay Co's.* fort, at mouth E. Main R., Labrador, Canada.

Maine, *st.*, New England, U.S.A.; mtns., with much forest; potatoes, paper pulp, metals, woollens, shoes, processed foods; cap. Augusta; ch. spt. Portland; a. 33,215 sq. m.; p. (1970) *977,260*.

Maine, *R.*, France; formed by junction of Sarthe and Mayenne, flows 7 m. to R. Loire at Angers.

Maine-et-Loire, *dep.*, France; agr.. vineyards; cap. Angers; a. 2,811 sq. m.; p. (1968) *584,709*.

Mainland. (1) *I.*, lgst. of Shetlands, Scot. (2) *I.*, lgst. of Orkneys, *see* Pomona.

Mainz, *c.*, *cap.* Rhineland-Palatinate, Germany; at confluence of Rs. Rhine and Main; R. pt; cath., univ., cas.; cement, engin., optical glass, food processing; p. (1968) *171,582*.

Maioli, *t.*, Taiwan; fertilisers.

Maison-Carrée, *commune*, N. Algeria; 5 m. E. of Algiers; p. *24,341*.

Maisons-Alfort, *t.*, Seine, France; p. (1962) *51,689*.

Maisons-Laffitte, *t.*, Yvelines, France; p. (1962) *19,385*.

Maitland, *t.*, N.S.W., Australia; on R. Hunter, nr. Newcastle; agr., pastoral ctr., coal-mining, textiles; p. (1966) *23,105*.

Maizuru, *c.*, *spt.*, Honshu, Japan; naval base; sheet glass; p. (1960) *99,615*.

Majorca *or* **Mallorca**, *see* Balearic Is.

Majunga, *spt.*, Madagascar; at mouth of R. Ikopa; cement factory; p. *50,000*.   [*384,000*.

Makasar, *ch. t.*, *pt.*, Sulawesi, Indonesia; p. (1961)

Makasar, *strait*, Indonesia; separates Kalimantan from Sulawesi; 240 m. wide.

Makeyevka, *t.*, Ukrainian S.S.R.; iron and steel, engin. coal; p. (1967) *410,000*.

Makhachkala, *spt.*, R.S.F.S.R.; oil-refining, chemicals, textiles, engin.; p. (1967) *158,000*.

Makó, *t.*, Hungary; agr.; flour milling; p. (1962) *29,541*.   [m.; p. (estd. 1951) *143,000*.

Makran, *reg.*, W. Pakistan–Iran; a. 26,000 sq.

Makurdi, *t.*, Nigeria, W. Africa; on R. Benue, 150 m. upstream from confluence with R. Niger at Lokoja; mkt. for palm prod., ground-nuts; site of rly. bridge across R. Benue on E. main rly. from Pt. Harcourt to Kaduna.

Makwar, *vil.*, Sudan, N.E. Africa; on R. Blue Nile, 200 m. upstream from Khartoum; site of Sennar Dam.

Malabar Coast, India; name applied to W. cst. of India from Goa to southern tip of peninsula at Cape Comorin; sand dunes backed by lagoons; coastlands intensively cultivated, rice, spices, rubber, coconuts; ch. pt. Cochin.

Malacca, *st.*, S.W. Western Malaysia; originally part of Brit. Straits Settlements (*q.v.*); cap. M.; a. 640 sq. m.; p. (1968) *404,275*. [Peninsula.

Malacca, *strait*, separates Sumatra from Malay

Maladetta, with Pic d' Anéto, highest point in the Pyrenees; alt. 11,174 ft.

Málaga, *Mediterranean prov.*, S. Spain; agr.,

exp. wine, fruits, olive oil; a. 2,813 sq. m.; p. (1959) *772,517*.

Málaga, *spt.*, *cap.*, Málaga, Spain; red oxide, olive oil, wine and fruit; oil pipeline from Puertollano refinery; p. (1965) *322,000*.

Malagasy Republic, *I.*, *indep. sov. st.*, E. African cst.; within Fr. Community; cap. Tananarive; ch. spt. Tamatave; a. 227,800 sq. m.; p. (estd. 1969) *7,199,000*.

Malakal, *cap.*, Upper Nile, Sudan; p. (1956) *9,630*.

Malakoff, *t.*, S.W. Paris, France; residtl.; p. (1954) *28,876*.

Malang, *t.*, Java, Indonesia; p. (1961) *342,000*.

Mälar, L., S.E. Sweden; connected with the Baltic by Södertelge canal, has 1,260 Is.; length 80 m.; a. 477 sq. m.   [(1965) *105,207*.

Malatya, *t.*, central Turkey; fruit, opium; p.

Malawi, **Rep.** of, *indep. sov. st.* within Brit. Commonwealth (1964), Central Africa; along W. cst. L. Malawi; hot wet summers, cool dry winters; savannah vegetation, subtropical forest; tea, tobacco, groundnuts, cotton, coffee, ivory; cap. Zomba (Lilongwe site of new cap.); a. *45,411* sq. m.; p. (1966) *4,039,583*.

Malawi, *L.*, Central Africa, southward extension of the Great Rift Valley; 1,500 ft. above sea-level; length 350 m., breadth 40 m.; drains by R. Shire into R. Zambesi.

Malay Archipelago, *lge. gr. of tropical Is.* extending 4,800 m. from the Nicobar Is. in Bay of Bengal to the Solomon Is. in the Pacific; inc. Sumatra, Java, Borneo, Celebes, Philippines, New Guinea, Bismarck Archipelago.

Malaysia, East, name given in 1966 to Sarawak and Sabah (the two Borneo terrs. forming part of Fed. of Malaysia), separated from West Malaysia by South China Sea.; p. (estd.) *1,544,000*.

Malaysia, Federation of, *indep. fed.* within Brit. Commonwealth (1963), comprising West Malaysia and East Malaysia; plantation inds., mineral wealth; fed. cap. Kuala Lumpur; a. 129,000 sq. m.; p. (estd.) *10,384,000*.

Malaysia, West, name given in 1966 to mainland Malaya (9 Malay sts., Penang and Malacca); rubber, tin, iron ore, timber, palm oil prods., fruit; cap. Kuala Lumpur; a. 50,840 sq. m.; p. (estd.) *8,840,000*.

Malbork (Marienburg), *t.*, Poland; on R. Nogat; cas.; rly. junction; p. (1965) *28,000*.

Malden, *c.*, Mass., U.S.A.; mftg. sub. of Boston; rubber gds., hosiery furniture; p. (1960) *57,676*.

Malden I., Line Is., Central Pac. Oc.; a. 35 sq. m.; guano, uninhabited. British, discovered 1825.

Malden and Coombe, *former mun. bor.*, Surrey, Eng.; now inc. in *Royal Borough* of Kingston-upon-Thames; light inds.; p. (1961) *46,637*.

Maldive Is., *indep. sultanate* (1965), 2,000 low-lying coral Is., under Brit. prot. 1887–1965; 400 m. S. W. of Ceylon, about 215 of which are inhabited; cap. Malé; Britain retains facilities on Addu Atoll (incl. airfield on Gan I.) until 1986; coconuts, millet, fruit, fishing, coir and lace-mkg.; p. (estd.) *106,000*.

Maldon, *t.*, *mun. bor.*, Essex, Eng.; at head of Blackwater estuary; agr. machin., steel window-frames, flour milling; p. (estd. 1967) *12,010*.

Maldonado, *dep.*, Uruguay; a. 1,587 sq. m.; p. (1953) *67,933*.

Malham Cove, W. R. Yorks, Eng.; in Craven dist. of N. Pennines, 10 m. N.W. of Skipton; semicircular amphitheatre surrounded by limestone cliffs from base of which emerges R. Aire.

Malin Head, Donegal, Ireland; most N. point.

Mali, Republic of, *ind. sovereign st.*, W. Africa; millet, sorghum, rice, maize, groundnuts, cotton; cap. Bamako; a. 465,000 sq. m.; p. (1968) *4,787,000*.   [p. *15,089*.

Malinao, *mun.*, Luzon, Philippine Is.; hemp;

Malines (Mechelen), *c.*, Belgium; on R. Dyle; cath.; rly. ctr., furniture, textiles, leather, car assembly, detergents, paint; p. (1968) *65,823*.

Malita, *t.*, Mindanao, Philippines; p. *30,755*.

Mallaig, *vil.*, S.W. Inverness, Scot.; on Sound of Sleat; rly. terminus; fish; p. *1,000*.

Malleco, *prov.*, S. Chile; cap. Angol; a. 5,511 sq. m.; p. (1960) *207,477*.

Malling, *t.*, *rural dist.*, Kent, Eng.; 3 m. W. of Maidstone; mkt., fruit ctr., chemicals; p. (rural dist. 1961) *40,680*.

Mallow, *mkt. t.*, Cork, Ireland; on R. Blackwater; agr., fishing, flour mills, tanneries, condensed milk, dehydrated foods; p. (1966) *5,539*.

Malmédy, *t.*, Belgium; transferred to Belgium from Germany after the First World War; tanning, dyeing, paper-wks.; p. (1962) *6,387*.

Malmesbury, *t.*, *mun. bor.*, Wilts, Eng.; on R. Avon, 8 m. N. of Chippenham; mkt.; abbey; elec. eng. ind.; p. (estd. 1967) *2,680*.

Malmesbury, *t.*, Victoria, Australia; on R. Campaspe, 20 m. S.E. of Bendigo; dam across R. provides water for domestic and mining purposes to Bendigo.

Malmesbury, *t.*, S.W. Cape Prov., S. Africa; mineral springs; p. *5,731*.

Malmö, *spt.*, S. Sweden; on The Sound; docks; shipbldg., textiles, cement; p. (1961) *229,388*.

Malmöhus, *co.*, Sweden; a. 1,872 sq. m.; p. (1961) *625,667*.

Malo-les-Bains, *sub.* of Dunkerque, Nord, France; seaside resort; p. (1954) *12,101*.

Malone, *t.*, N.Y., U.S.A.; iron-mining; p. (1960) *8,737*.

Malta, *I.*, *indep. sov. st.* within Brit. Commonwealth (1964); in Mediterranean, 60 m. S. of Sicily; cap. Valetta; received George Cross for heroism in Second World War; deep water quay; dry docks; no raw materials; textiles; tourism; a. (inc. Gozo and Comino) 122 sq. m.; p. (1968) *314,175* [(1961) *13,691*.

Maltby, *urb. dist.*, W. Riding. Yorks, Eng.; p.

Malton, *mkt. t.*, *urb. dist.*, N.R. Yorks, Eng.; on R. Derwent, in S.W. of Vale of Pickering; brewing, ironwks.; p. (1961) *4,430*.

Maluti, *mtn. range*, Lesotho, S. Africa; highest peak Machacha, alt. 10,990.

Malvern or Great Malvern, *t.*, *urb. dist.*, Worcester, Eng.; at E. foot of Malvern Hills; spa; annual dramatic festival; stone quarrying, agr. machin., motor-cars, electronics wks., plastics; p. (estd. 1967) *28,630*.

Malvern Hills, *narrow ridge* forming bdy. between Worcester and Hereford, Eng.; rises very abruptly from Severn Valley to over 1,000 ft. between Malvern and Bromsberrow; moorland, woodland on lower slopes; length 8 m., width, under 1 m., maximum alt., 1,395 ft.

Malverne, *t.*, N.Y., U.S.A., on Long I.; residtl. sub. of New York; p. (1960) *9,968*.

Mamaroneck, *t.*, N.Y., U.S.A.; textiles, mnfs. oils; p. (1960) *17,673*.

Mammola, *t.*, Reggio, S. Italy; p. *9,925*.

Mammoth Caves, Ky., U.S.A.; Green K.; stalactite formations in avenues aggregating 150 m. long.

Mamore or Rio Grande, *R.*, Bolivia; trib. of R. Beni; length 500 m. [3,862 ft.

Mam Soul, *mtn.*, Ross and Inverness, Scot.; alt.

Man, I. of, in Irish Sea; 30 m. from England (Cumberland) and N. Ireland (Down) 20 m. from Scotland (Wigtown); ch. t. Douglas; old cap. Castletown; administered according to own laws; tourism; refinery on N.W. cst. between Rue Point and Point of Ayre under construction; a. 227 sq. m.; p. (1961) *48,151*.

Mana, *R.*, Fr. Guiana, S. America; 175 m.

Manabi, *prov.*, Ecuador; on W. slope of the Andes; cap. Puertoviejo; cacao, sugar; a. 7,891 sq. m.; p. (estd. 1962) *614,803*.

Manacor, *t.*, Majorca, Spain; 30 m. from Palma; artificial pearls, wine; 7 m. from its spt. Porto Cristo; stalactite caves of Drach and Hams; p. (1957) *18,956*.

Managua, *cap.*, Nicaragua; nr. Lake M.; 30 m. from pt. Puerto Somoza; rebuilt after 1931 earthquake; p. (1960) *207,000*.

Manakau, *c.*, N.I., N.Z.; p. (1966) *73,218*.

Manamah, *cap.*, Bahrein Is., Persian Gulf; (1965) *62,000*. [5,000.

Mananjary, *t.*, E. Malagasy, sugar, coffee; p.

Manaqil Canal, fed by waters from Blue Nile released through Semnar dam; helps cultivate 600,000 acres of Gezira desert. [Ceylon.

Manar, *G.*, with Palk Strait separates India from

Manasarowar, *sacred L.*, Tibet.

Manatee, *t.*, Fla., U.S.A.; lumber, fruit and vegetable canning; p. (1950) *3,582*.

Manáus (Manaos), *c.*, *cap.*, Amazonas st., N.W. Brazil; on Rio Negro nr. confluence with Amazon; impt. R. pt., airpt.; oil ref.; former rubber ctr.; in free zone (4,000 sq. m.) recently set up to encourage development in Amazonas; p. (estd. 1968) *249,797*.

Mancha, La, *plain*, Cuidad-Real prov., S. Spain; in shallow depression on central plateau, average alt. between 1,500 and 3,000 ft., drained by headstreams of R. Guadiana; semi-arid climate with hot summers, cold winters; widespread salt deposits; Merino sheep, esparto grass; Spain's lgst. grape-growing region.

Manche, *maritime dep.*, N.W. France; on English Channel; agr. and dairying; cap. Saint Lo; ch. port Cherbourg; a. 2,475 sq. m.; p. (1968) *451,939*.

Manchester, *c.*, *spt.*, *co. bor.*, S. Lancs, Eng.; on R. Irwell (which separates it from Salford): inland terminus of Manchester Ship Canal; ct r of cotton and man-made fibre textile inds.; engin. heavy, light and elec., machine tools, petro- chemicals, dyestuffs, pharmaceutical goods; univ.; comm., cultural and recreational cap. of N.W. England; p. (estd. 1969) *593,770*.

Manchester, *t.*, E. Iowa, U.S.A.; tr. ctr.; flour milling; woollen goods; p. (1960) *4,402*.

Manchester, *c.*, N.H., U.S.A.; at Amoskeag Falls, on the Merrimac R.; textiles, footwear, machin.; p. (1960) *88,282*.

Manchester, *t.*, Conn., U.S.A.; textiles (silk); p. (1960) *41,906*.

Manchester Ship Canal, *ship canal*, S. Lancs, Ches., Eng.; joining Manchester to Mersey estuary at Eastham; can be used by ocean steamers; length 35½ m.

Manchuria, *former Chinese outer terr.*, no longer exists as administrative unit, comprised nine provs.—Liaoning, Kirin, Heilungkiang, Liaopeh, Nunkiang, Hsingan, Sunkiang, Hokiang and Antung; mountainous, N.W. and E.; drained to N. by Sungari and S. by Liao Rs.; forested; soya-beans, wheat, coal, iron, gold, silver.

Mandal, *t.*, Norway; p. (1961) *5,156*.

Mandalay, *c.*, Upper Burma; on the R. Irrawaddy, 400 m. N. of Rangoon; formerly cap. of kingdom; silk, old carved wooden palace and many pagodas; p. (1955) *182,367*.

Manduria, *t.*, Italy; tr. ctr.; p. *17,675*.

Mandvi, *spt.*, Kutch, India; p. (1961) *26,609*.

Manfredonia, *spt.*, Foggia, Italy; cath.; p. *18,600*.

Mangalore, *spt.*, Mysore, India; exp. coffee, coconuts, rice, spices, fertilisers; p. (1961) *142,669*.

Mangere, N.I., N.Z., 13 m. S. of Auckland; international airport (opened 1965).

Mangerton, *mtn.*, Kerry, Ireland.

Mangla Dam, W. Pakistan, world's lgst. earthfilled dam, on Jhelum R., part of Indus Basin irrigation scheme.

Mangotsfield, *urb. dist.*, Gloucester, Eng.; p. (1961) *24,092*.

Manhattan, I., N.Y., U.S.A.; at mouth of Hudson R.; a. 22 sq. m. forms major part of bor. of Manhattan (p. (1960) *1,698,281*) of N.Y. City.

Manica and Sofala, *prov.*, Mozambique; comprises dists. of Beira and Tete; cap. Beira; p. (1962) *779,462*.

Manicouagan, *R.*, Canada; flows S. from Quebec prov. to St. Lawrence, S.W. of Baie Comeau where there is dam and hydroelec. plant; length 300 m.

Manila, *c.* cap. Philippines, S.W. Luzon; ch. pt. of Is.; univ.. cath.; general tr.; fishing ind.; p. (estd.) *1,402,000*.

Manipur, Union Terr., India; rice, cotton, fruits; cap. Imphal; a. 8,628 sq. m.; p. (1961) *780,037*.

Manisa, *t.*, Turkey; comm. ctr., cotton, silk; p. (1965) *69,394*.

Manistee, *c.*, Mich., U.S.A.; on L. Michigan; timber, salt, fruit; p. (1960) *8,324*.

Manitoba, *prov.*, Canada; wheat, rich mineral deposits, fisheries; diverse inds.; cap. Winnipeg; a. 251,000 sq. m.; p. (estd. 1969) *977,000*.

Manitowoc, *c.*, Wis., U.S.A.; on L. Michigan; shipbldg., iron, aluminium goods, flour; p. (1960) *32,275*.

Manizales, *cap.*, Caldas, Colombia; coffee, textiles, leather gds., chemicals; p. (estd. 1962) *176,080*.

Manjil Dam, Iran; on Sefid Rud (white river), Gilan prov.; 352 ft. high.

Mankato, *c.*, Minn., U.S.A.; agr. tools, flour, brewing; p. (1960) *23,747*.

Mannheim, *t.*, Baden-Württemberg, Germany; gr. R. pt. at confluence of Rs. Neckar and Rhine; cas.; machin., vehicles, cellulose, steel, elec., foodstuffs. tobacco. wood, textiles, chemicals; p. (1968) *326,302*.

Manningtree, *par.*, Essex, Eng.; head of Stour estuary; fishing, yachting; p. (1961) *524*.

Manorhamilton, *t.*, Leitrim, Ireland; rly. wks.

Manresa, *t.*, Spain; textiles, paper, chemicals, ironwks.; p. (1957) *40,452*.

Mans, Le, see Le Mans.　　　　　　　[Coats I.

Mansel I., Hudson Bay, Canada; S.E. of

Mansfield, t., mun. bor., Notts, Eng.; on E. flank of Pennines, 12 m. N. of Nottingham; iron, coal, hosiery, footwear mftg., sand-quarrying, metal box wks., textiles, lt. engin.; p. (estd. 1967) 55,540.

Mansfield, t., Mass., U.S.A.; textiles, engin.; confectionery; p. (1960) 4,674.

Mansfield, c., Ohio, U.S.A.; machin., farm tools, paper, rubber goods; p. (1960) 47,325.

Mansfield Woodhouse, t., urb. dist., Notts, Eng.; 2 m. N. of Mansfield; stone quarries; Roman remains; p. (estd. 1967) 23,600.

Mansura, t., Lower U.A.R.; cotton mftg.; p. (1960) 152,000.　　　　　　　　[(1962) 19,228.

Manta, t., Ecuador; coffee panama hats.; p.

Mantanzas, t., Venezuela; on S. bank of R. Orinoco; steel wks.

Mantes-la-Jolie, t., Yvelines, France; on R. Seine; cath., agr. prod., hosiery, musical instruments; p. (1962) 19,227.

Mantiqueira, mtn. range, Brazil; N.W. of Rio de Janeiro; highest peak Itatiaia 9,255 ft.

Mantua, prov., Italy; a. 903 sq. m.; p. (1961) 382,515.　　　　　　　　[p. (1961) 61,580.

Mantua, t., N. Italy; on R. Mincio; ironwks.;

Manukau, new t., N.I., N.Z., in subs. of Auckland; comprising former co. of Manukau; p. (1966) 73,218

Manukau Harbour, N.I. N.Z.; lge shallow inlet on W. cst. of Auckland pen.; provides additional harbour facilities for spt. of Auckland but shallow water limits usefulness; mainly used for recreational sailing.

Manyen, R., U.S.S.R.; trib. of R. Don; length 300 m.; canal is being built through R. to the Caspian to provide through connection with Black Sea.

Manzala (Menzala), lagoon, Mediterranean cst., Egypt, N.E. Africa; extends E. from Damietta mouth of Nile to Pt. Said; fringed by salt marsh; a. 800 sq. m.

Manzanares, R., Spain; trib. of R. Jarama.

Manzanares, t., Spain; 30 m. E. of Ciudad Real; soap, bricks, pottery mftg., agr. prod.; p. (1957) 18,204.　　　　　　　　[42,252.

Manzanillo, spt., Cuba; sugar, rice; p. (1960)

Manzanillo, spt., Colima, Mexico; Mexico's chief inlet and outlet on Pac. Oc.; p. (1961) 13,030.

Manzini (Bremersdorp), t., Swaziland, S. Africa.

Mar, ancient dist., Aberdeen, Scot.; between Rs. Don and Dee.

Maracaibo, spt., cap., Zulia st., Venezuela; on W. of narrow entrance to L. Maracaibo; univ.; oil, coffee, cocoa, and hide exp.; shipbldg.; p. (1961) 432,902.

Maracaibo, G., and L., Zulia st., Venezuela, S. America; brackish lake, 120 m. long, 60 m. wide; oil-wells on fringes and drilled into lake floor.

Maracay, t., W. Venezuela; mftg. and military ctr.; p. (1961) 134,120.　　　[(1956) 36,556.

Maragheh, t., Iran; on N. end of L. Urmia; p.

Marajó, I., at mouth of the Rs. Amazon and Pará, Brazil; a. 173 sq. m.

Maralinga, S. Australia; 200 m. N.E. Eucla; joint U.K.–Australian atomic testing ground; first weapon exploded here 27 Sept. 1956.

Maranhão, st., N.E. Brazil; rice, cotton, sugar, tobacco, coffee, cattle, gold, copper; oil in the Barreirinhas a.; cap. São Luiz; a. 129,271 sq. m.; p. (estd. 1968) 3,497,890.

Marañon, R., see Amazon, R.　　　[p. (1962) 3,836.

Marans, t., Charente-Maritime, France; industl.;

Maras, t., S. central Turkey; tr. in Kurdish carpets; p. (1965) 63,315.

Marathon, plain, Greece; battle between Greeks and Persians 490 B.C.

Marazion, mkt. t., Cornwall, Eng.; on Mount's Bay; pilchard fisheries; p. 1,100.

Marbella, spt., Malaga, Spain; cas.; iron mines; oranges, sugar cane, cotton; p. (1957) 9,921.

Marble, I., Keewatin, N.W. Terrs., Canada.

Marble Bar, t., W. Australia; located 85 m. inland by rail from Pt. Hedland; ctr. of Pilbara goldfields.

Marblehead, spt., Mass., U.S.A.; holiday resort, footwear; p. (1960) 18,521.

Marburg, t., Hesse, W. Germany; univ., cas.; instruments, pharmaceuticals, wall-paper mftg.; p. (1963) 47,590.

Marcaria, t., Italy; on R. Oglio; industl.; p. 10,475.

March, mkt. t., urb. dist., I. of Ely, Eng.; in Fens. 12 m. N.W. of Ely; impt. rly. junction; mkt., farm tools; p. (1961) 13,119.

Marchena, t., Spain; on R. Guadalquivir; mftg.; p. (1957) 20,326.

Marches, The, region, central Italy; extending from eastern slopes of Apennines to Adriatic cst.; embracing provs. of Macerata, Ascoli-Piceno, Acona, and Pesaro e Urbino; maize, wine, tobacco, silk, paper; a. 3,744 sq. m.; p. (1961) 1,347,234.

Marchienne-au-Pont, t., Belgium; on R. Sambre; tr. ctr.; p. (1962) 19,870.

Marcq-en-Barœul, commune, sub. Lille, Nord, France; textiles, foundries; p. (1954) 24,564.

Marcus Hook, t., Del., U.S.A.; on right bank of R. Del. 15 m. below Philadelphia.

Mar del Plata, t., Argentina; on C. Corrientes; seaside resort; p. (1960) 300,000.

Mardin, t., Turkey; agr., textiles; p. (1965) 31,123.

Maree, L., Ross and Cromarty, Scot.; length 12½ m., breadth 2½ m.; contains many Is.

Mareotis or Birket-et-Mariut, L., Lower Egypt; separated from Mediterranean by ridge of sand on which stands Alexandria; length 50 m., width 20 m.

Margam, t. in Pt. Talbot mun. bor., W. central Glamorgan, S. Wales; on cst. of Swansea Bay; lge. new steel-wks., lgst. steel-rolling mill in Europe; p. (estd. 1955) 18,300.

Margarita, I., Venezuela; in the Caribbean S.; pearl fisheries, fishing, fibre wks.; cap. Asuncion, a. 450 sq. m.; p. (1961) 87,500.

Margate, t., mun. bor., Kent, Eng.; W. of N. Foreland, in the Isle of Thanet; seaside resort; p. (estd. 1967) 49,060.

Margelan, t., E. Uzbek S.S.R.; agr. ctr., tr. especially cotton and silk; p. (1959) 68,000.

Mari, autonomous Soviet Socialist rep., U.S.S.R.; cap. Ioshkar Ola; p. (1959) 647,000.

Mariana, t., Minas Gerais. Brazil; tr. ctr.; gold mng.; p. (estd. 1968) 26,671.

Mariana Is., chain of Is., W. Pacific; U.S. Trust Terr.; most impt. are Guam, Saipan and Tinian; a. c. 370 sq. m.; p. c. 75,000.

Marianské Lázne (Marienbad), t., ČSSR.; spa; antimony; p. (1961) 12,597.

Maribor, t., Slovenia, Jugoslavia; fruit ctr., leather goods, wine, rly. wks.; p. (1960) 84,000.

Marie Galante, I., Lesser Antilles gr.; Fr. possession; sugar-cane; p. (1960) 16,037.

Marienburg, see Malbork.

Marienwerder, see Kwidzyn.

Marietta, t., Ohio, U.S.A.; at confluence of Muskingum R. with Ohio R.; timber, ironwks., coal, oil, natural gas; p. (1960) 16,847.

Marigliano, t., Campagna, Italy; p. 14,155.

Mariinsk Canal, see Volga Baltic Waterway.

Marília, t., São Paulo st., Brazil; coffee, cotton, oil, peanuts; p. (estd. 1968) 107,305.

Marin, spt., N.W. Spain; fishing; textiles; naval school; p. (1957) 17,592.

Marinette, t., Wis., U.S.A.; on L. Michigan; paper, pulp, timber; p. (1960) 13,329.

Marino, t., Sicily, Italy; p. 6,625.

Marion, c., Ind., U.S.A.; natural gas, iron, paper, glass, wireless sets; p. (1960) 37,854.

Marion, t., Ohio, U.S.A.; agr. implements, steam shovels, tractors; p. (1960) 37,079.

Marion, c., S. Ill., U.S.A.; fruit; coal; engin.; p. (1960) 11,274.

Maritime Alps, mtn. ranges, S. France–Italy.

Maritime Provinces, embraces Canadian provs. of Nova Scotia, New Brunswick, Pr. Edward I.

Maritsa, R., Bulgaria and Greece; length 260 m.

Maritzburg, see Pietermaritzburg.

Mariupol, see Zhdanov.

Marken, I., nr. Amsterdam, Neth.; tourism.

Market Deeping, t., Lincoln, Eng.; on R. Welland; brewing, rope; p. 876.

Market Drayton, t., urb. dist., Salop, Eng.; on R. Tern, 5 m. S. of Newcastle-under-Lyme; agr. implements, nylon mftg.; p. of t. (1961) 5,853; of urb. dist. (estd. 1966) 16,000.

Market Harborough, t., urb. dist., Leicester, Eng.; on R. Welland, 8 m. N.W. of Kettering; elec. engin., foodstuffs, corsetry; p. (1961) 11,556.

Market Rasen, t., urb. dist., Lindsey, Lincoln, Eng.; 14 m. N.E. of Lincoln; agr. ctr.; p. (1961) 2,257.

Market Weighton, *t.*, E.R. Yorks, Eng.; malting, iron; p. *1,735.*

Markinch, *burgh*, Fife, Scot.; 8 m. N. of Kirkcaldy; paper mftg., whisky blending and bottling; p. (1961) *2,446.*

Marl, *t.*, N. Rhine–Westphalia, Germany; in the Ruhr; coal-mining and chemicals; p. (1963) 73,300. [(1960) *18,819.*

Marlboro, *c.*, Mass., U.S.A.; boot mftg.; p.

Marlborough, *t., mun. bor.*, Wilts, Eng.; on R. Kennet in heart of Marlborough Downs; agr., tanning, brewing; public school; p. (estd. 1967) *5,910.*

Marlborough, *prov. dist.*, S.I., N.Z.; pastoral; a. 4,220 sq. m.; cap. Blenheim; p. (1961) *27,740.*

Marlborough Downs, *hills*, Wilts, Eng.; chalk; highest point, Milk Hill, 976 ft.

Marlin, *t.*, Texas, U.S.A.; hot artesian water; oil; cotton; dairying; p. (1950) *7,099.*

Marlow, *t., urb. dist.*, Bucks, Eng.; on R. Thames; mkt., tourist ctr.; brewing and chair mkg.; p. (1961) *8,704.*

Marmande, *t.*, Lot-et-Garonne, France; on R. Garonne; brandy, liqueur, woollens, iron; p. (1962) *14,004.*

Marmara, *sea*, separates Europe from Anatolia.

Marmolata, highest point of Dolomite Alps, S. Tyrol, Italy; alt. 11,045 ft.

Marne, *R.*, Central France; rises in Plateau de Langres, flows N.W. and W. across Champagne Humide, Champagne Pouilleuse and Beauce, joins R. Seine just above Paris; with Marne–Rhine and Marne–Saône Canals it forms impt. inland waterway linking Seine with Rhine and Rhône valleys; length (approx.) 325 m.

Marne, *dep.*, N.E. France; agr. wines, textiles, minerals; cap. Châlons-sur-Marne; a. 3,168 sq. m.; p. (1968) *485,388.*

Marne, Haute, *dep.*, France; a. 2,420 sq. m.; cap. Chaumont; p. (1968) *214,336.*

Maros, *R.*, Hungary; trib. of R. Theiss; length 400 m.

Marple, *t., urb. dist.*, Cheshire, Eng.; 3 m. E. of Stockport; textiles; p. (estd. 1967) *23,300.*

Marquesas, *I. gr.* (Fr.), Pac. Oc.; a. 480 sq. m.; lgst. Is. Nukuhiva and Hivaoa; bananas, sugarcane, copra; p. (1962) *4,837.*

Marquette, *c.*, Mich., U.S.A.; on L. Superior; iron-ore deposits, timber, rly. wks.; p. (1960) *19,824.*

Marradi, *t.*, Italy; p. *8,275.*

Marrakesh, *c.*, Morocco; tourist ctr., leather goods; p. (1960) *243,134.*

Marree, *sm. t.*, S. Australia; on rly. from Pt. Augusta to Alice Springs; terminus of overland stock route from Queensland.

Marsa el-Brega, *new pt.*, Gulf of Sirte, Libya; oil pipeline from Zelten; one projected from Raguba oilfield; refinery projected.

Marsala, *spt.*, Sicily, Italy; wine ctr.; p. (1961) 81,327. [(1960) *4,347.*

Marseilles, *t.*, N. Ill., U.S.A.; paper, bricks; p.

Marseilles, *c., spt.*, cap. Bouches-du-Rhône, S. France; cath., univ., palace; comm. pt., coal, iron, bauxite, marine engin., aircraft, glass, agr. prod., wines, oil refining; oil pipeline to Karlsruhe (1963); p. (1968) *889,029.*

Marshall, *c.*, Mo., U.S.A.; p. (1960) *9,572.*

Marshall, *c.*, Texas, U.S.A.; rly. wks., canning, foundries; p. (1960) *23,846.*

Marshall, *spt.*, W. Liberia, W. Africa; exp. rubber; p. *1,000.*

Marshall, *I. gr.*, N. Pac. Oc.; U.S. Pac. Trust Terr., formerly Japanese mandate; total a. 150 sq. m.; sugar-cane, copra; ch. I. Jaluit; p. (1958) *13,928.*

Marshalltown, *t.*, Iowa, U.S.A.; on I. R.; iron, steel, machin., food canning; p. (1960) *22,521.*

Marshfield, *spt.*, Ore., U.S.A.; fishing, lumber, mining; p. (1950) *5,218.*

Marshfield, *t.*, Wis., U.S.A.; mftg. ctr. in timber region; p. (1960) *14,153.*

Martaban, *t.*, Burma; on R. Salween.

Martha's Vineyard, *I.*, Mass., U.S.A.; holiday resort, ch. ts. Vineyard Haven, Oak Bluffs, Edgartown; 21 m. long.

Marti, *t.*, Cuba; sugar, sisal; p. *5,060.*

Martigny, *t.*, Valais, Switzerland; peaches, tourist resort; linked by road tunnel to Aosta, Italy; p. (1957) *6,572.*

Martigues, *t.*, Bouches-du-Rhône, France; nr. Marseilles; p. (1962) *21,526.*

Martinao, *t.*, Italy; industl., tr. ctr.; p. *38,325.*

Martinez, *c.*, W. Cal., U.S.A.; industl., oil refineries, copper smelting; p. (1960) *9,604.*

Martinique, *I.*, (Fr.) W. Indies; cap. Fort-de-France; sugar, rum; a. 400 sq. m.; p. (estd. 1967) *333,000.*

Martinsburg, *c.*, W. Va., U.S.A.; in Shenandoah valley; rly. wks., cider. textiles; p. (1960) *15,179.*

Martin's Ferry, *t.*, Ohio, U.S.A.; on O. R., iron and steel mftg., coal-mining; p. (1960) *11,919.*

Marton, *t.*, N.I., N.Z., p. *2,810.*

Martos, *t.*, Andalusia, Spain; agr. ctr., wines, sulphur springs; p. (1957) *30,404.*

Mary, *t.*, Turkmen. S.S.R.; cereals, fruit, textiles; p. (1959) *48,000.*

Maryborough, *t., pt.*, Queensland, Australia; fruit ctr., mng. and sugar mill machin., cars, ships, sawmills; p. (1966) *20,381.*

Maryborough, *t.*, Victoria, Australia; rly. ctr.; agr., pastoral, wool. engin.; p. (1966) *7,694.*

Maryborough, *see* Port Laoighise, Ireland.

Mary Kathleen, *t.*, Queensland, Australia; new t., nr. uranium field in Cloncurry a.

Maryland, *st.*, U.S.A.; steel, copper, smelting and refining, coal, asbestos, potash, salts, aircraft, chemicals; agr., livestock; cap. Annapolis; lgst. c. Baltimore; a. 10,577 sq. m.; p. (1970) *3,874,642.*

Maryport, *mkt. t., urb. dist.*, Cumberland, Eng.; on the Irish Sea; coal, iron, plastics, footwear; p. (1961) *12,334.*

Marysville, *t.*, Cal., U.S.A.; fruit; p. (1960) *9,553.*

Marysville, *t.*, Kan., U.S.A.; rly. ctr. in rich agr. region; p. (1960) *4,143.*

Marysville, *t.*, Ohio, U.S.A.; mkt., grass seed, livestock; p. (1960) *4,952.*

Maryville, *c.*, E. Tenn., U.S.A.; lumber; clothes; quarries; p. (1960) *10,348.*

Masai Land, *dist.*, S. Kenya, Africa.

Masaya, *cap. c.* of M. dep. S.W. Nicaragua; agr., tobacco; p. (1959) *99,573.*

Masbate, *I.*, Philippines; a. 1,262 sq. m.; p. (1960) *280,300.*

Mascara, *t.*, Algeria; wine, oil, cereals; p. (1948) *35,078.*

Mascarene Is., collective name of Mauritius, Rodriguez and Réunion, in Indian Ocean.

Masham, *t.*, N.R. Yorks, Eng.; on R. Ure; 9 m. N.W. of Ripon; mkt., sheep fair; p. *1,702.*

Mashhad (Meshed), *c.*, N.E. Iran; prov. cap. Khorassan; pilgrimage ctr.; shrine *(meshed)* of Imam Riza; agr.; carpets; turquoise; p. (1967) *707,884.* [cultivation.

Mashonaland, *prov.*, Rhodesia; tobacco and maize

Masira, I., off est. of Oman, Arabia.

Mask, *L.*, Mayo and Galway, Ireland; length 12 m., width 2–4 m.

Mason City, *t.*, Iowa, U.S.A.; on the Sheel Rock R.; cement, bricks, sugar-beet; p. (1960) *30,642.*

Massa or Massa Carrara, *t.*, Italy; olive oil, paper, tobacco, marble; p. (1961) *55,331.*

Massachusetts, *st.*, New England, U.S.A.; fisheries, agr., textiles, footwear, iron and steel goods, elec. machin., rubber goods, leather, paper, wood pulp; cap. Boston; a. 8,257 sq. m.; p. (1970) *5,630,224.*

Massafra, *t.*, Italy; industl.; p. *12,275.*

Massarosa, *commune*, Tuscany, Italy; agr.; p. *12,546.*

Massawa, *spt.*, Eritrea; pt. for Ethiopia, on Red Sea; fine harbour; pearl fishing; p. *c.* 25,000.

Massena, *t.*, N.Y., U.S.A.; p. (1960) *15,478.*

Messenya, *t.*, Central African Rep., nr. L. Chad; cap. of Bagirmi.

Massillon, *c.*, Ohio, U.S.A.; coal, machin., glass, aluminium ware; p. (1960) *31,236.*

Masterton, *t.*, N.I., N.Z.; p. (1966) *17,596.*

Matabeleland, *dist.*, Rhodesia; cereals, sugar, cotton, gold. [23,000.

Matadi, *pt.*, Congo; nr. mouth of R. Congo; p.

Matagalpa, *t.*, Nicaragua; coffee, cattle; gold mng. in a.; p. (1961) *14,090.* [(1941) *14,090.*

Matale. *t.*, Ceylon; Buddhist monastery; p.

Matamoros, *t.*, Mexico, on Rio Grande; livestock tr. ctr.; p. (1960) *93,334.*

Matanzas, *prov.*, Cuba; sugar, tobacco, rice; a. 3,259 sq. m.; p. (1953) *395,780.*

Matanzas, *spt., prov. cap.*, Cuba; exp. sugar, cigars; rayon plant; p. (1953) *63,916.*

Matapan, *O.*, W. side of G. of Laconia, Greece.

Matara, *spt.*, S. Ceylon; p. *22,908.*

Matarani, S. Peru; oil refinery being built.

Mataro, *spt.*, Spain; nr. Barcelona; fisheries, textiles, chemicals, paper; p. (1957) *31,642.*

Matera, t.. Italy; N.W. of Taranto; tr. ctr.. leather, oil; p. (1961) 38,233.

Matlock, t., urb. dist., Derby, Eng.; on R. Derwent; 15 m. N. of Derby; health resort, tourist ctr., quarrying, light inds.; p. (1961) 18,486.

Mato Grosso, st., Brazil; cap. Cuiabá; a. 475,707 sq. m.; p. (estd. 1968) 1,363,980.

Mato Grosso, plateau, Mato Grosso st., Brazil; average alt. 3,000 ft., acts as divide between Amazon and Parona–Paraguay R. systems; reserves of gold, diamonds, manganese but largely undeveloped.

Matrah, t., Muscat and Oman, Arabia.

Matsue, t., Honshu, Japan; p. 1965) 110,534.

Matsumoto, t., Japan; silkworm tr.; p. c. (1964) 150,000.

Matsuyama, c., Japan; p. (1965) 282,651.

Matterhorn, German name for (Fr.) Mt. Cervin, (It.) Monte Cervino; Pennine Alps, Switzerland; alt. 14,678 ft, (see Zermatt).

Mattoon, c., Ill.. U.S.A.; ironwks., flour, bricks, agr. tr.; p. (1960) 19,088.

Maturin, t., Venezuela; comm. ctr.; airport; p. (1961) 53,445.

Matyásföld, sub. Budapest, Hungary; lge bus wks., refrigerator vans.

Matzen, vil., E. Lower Austria; 4m. N. of Gänserndorf; oil.

Maua, t., São Paulo st., Brazil; porcelain; p. (estd. 1968) 34,150.

Mauban, spt., Luzon, Philippine Is.; p. 14,832.

Mauchline, par., Ayr, Scot.; associated with Robert Burns; p. 4,000.   [42,576.

Maui, I., Hawaiian Is.; a. 728 sq. m.; p. (1960)

Maule, prov., Chile; a. 2,172 sq. m.; p. (1961) 93,942.   [180 m.

Maumee, R., Ind., U.S.A.; flows to L. Erie;

Mauna Kea, volcano, Hawaii; alt. 13,823 ft.

Mauna Loa, volcano, Hawaii; alt. 13,675 ft.

Mauritania, Islamic Republic of, ind. sov. st. within French Community, W. Africa; livestock, gum, salt; cap. Nouakchott; a. 419,000 sq. m.; p. (estd. 1968) 1,120,000.

Mauritius, I., indep. sov. st. within Brit. Commonwealth (1968); Indian Ocean; 500 m. E. of Malagasy; volcanic mtns.; bounded by coral reefs; sugar, rum; cap. Port Louis; a. 805 sq. m.; p. (estd.) 810,000.

Mawddach, R., estuary, Merioneth. Wales; 19 m.

Mawson, Australian national research base, Antarctica.   [textiles, timber.

Maxwelltown, t., Dumfries. Scot.; on R. Nith;

May, I., Firth of Forth, Fife, Scot.

Mayagüez, c., spt., Puerto Rico; sugar, coffee, tobacco; p. (estd.) 84,000.

Maybole, burgh, Ayr, Scot.; 8 m. S. of Ayr; footwear, agr. implements; p. (1961) 4,677.

Mayen, c., Rhine prov., Germany; mftg., brewing; leather; quarries; p. 14,327.

Mayenne, dep., N.W. France; pastoral and agr.; cap. Laval; a. 1,987 sq. m.; p. (1968) 252,762.

Mayenne, R., France; trib. of R. Sarthe; 125 m.

Mayfield, t., S.W. Ky., U.S.A.; tobacco; dairy prod.; clothing; p. (1960) 10,762.

Mayo, maritime co., Connacht, Ireland; broken cst.. much barren mtn. land, many large lakes; agr., fishery; co. t. Castlebar. a. 2,126 sq. m.; p. (1966) 115,588.

Mayotte, ch. I., Fr. col., Comoro Archipelago, Mozambique Channel; sugar-cane, vanilla, cacao, a. 140 sq. m.; p. 18,000.

Maywood, t. Ill., U.S.A.; adjoining Chicago; residtl., some mnfs.; p. (1960) 27,330.

Mazagan, see El Jadida.

Mazamet, t.. Tarn, France; tanning, leather wks.; p. (1962) 17,891.

Mazandaran, prov., N.E. Iran; Caspian Sea, frontier U.S.S.R.; subtropical climate; agr.; cap. Sari; p. (1967) 1,843,388.

Mazar, t., Afghanistan; 200 m. N. of Kabul; chemical fertilisers from natural gas and thermal elec. plant projected; p. (estd. 1964) 40,000.

Mazarrón, t., Murcia, Spain; metal wks., flour, soap; p. (1957) 15,225.

Mazatenango, t., S.W. Guatemala; coffee, cacao, sugar, fruit; p. (1960) 26,120.

Mazatepec, t., Puebla, Mexico; hydro-elec. plant.

Mazatlán, spt., W. cst. Mexico; hides, minerals, fruit; oil refinery being built; p. (1960) 50,000.

Mazingarbe, t., Pas-de-Calais, France; p. (1954) 10,311.

Mazzara, t., Sicily, Italy; cath., ruined cas.; agr. prod.; p. 24,250.

Mazzarino, t., Sicily, Italy; mftg.; p. 21,580.

M'babane, t., Swaziland; alt. 3,800 ft.; administrative ctr.; European p. (1960) 1,092.

Mbandaka (Coquilhatville), t., Congo; at confluence of Rs. Congo and Ruki.   [refinery.

M'Bao, Senegal, W. Africa; 11 m. from Dakar; oil

McAlester, t., Okla., U.S.A.; coal-mining ctr., rly. wks.; p. (1950) 17,878.

McClintock Channel, strait, between Prince of Wales's land and Victoria I., Arctic Canada.

McComb, t., Miss., U.S.A.; p. (1960) 12,020.

McKeesport, c., Penns., U.S.A., on Monongahela R.; coal, iron and steel; p. (1960) 45,489.

McKees Rocks, t., Penns., U.S.A.; on Ohio R.; iron, glass; p. (1960) 13,185.   [I., Canada.

M'Clure, strait, between Banks I. and Melville

McPherson, t., Yukon, Canada; on Peel R.

McPherson, t., Kan., U.S.A.; in oil-field region; refining plants; p. (1950) 8,689.

Mead, L., Cal., U.S.A.; on R. Colorado behind Boulder (Hoover) Dam; world's lgst. reservoir; stores water for irrigation in Imperial Valley and Yuma dist; length 115 m.

Meadowfield, Durham, nr. Brandon; major industl. estate proposed.

Meadville, c., Penns., U.S.A.; on French Creek; univ.; rly. wks., rayon yarn; p. (1960) 16,671.

Mealfuarvonie, mtn., on side of L. Ness, Scot.; alt. 2,284 ft.

Meath, maritime co., Leinster, Ireland; pastoral; co. t., Trim; a. 906 sq. m.; p. (1966) 67,279.

Meathus Truim, see Edgeworthstown.

Meaux, t., Seine-et-Marne, France; on R. Marne; cath.; dairying; p. (1962) 23,305.

Mecca, holy c., Saudi Arabia; Mohammedan pilgrim ctr.; p. (estd.) 200,000.

Mechanicsburg, bor., S. Penns., U.S.A.; steel; clothes; p. (1950) 6,786.

Mechelen, see Malines.

Mecklenburg, former Land, Soviet Zone, Germany; bordering on Baltic Sea; abolished as admin. unit, 1952; Schwerin was the cap.; a. 8,856 sq. m.

Medan, cap., E. Sumatra, Indonesia; rubber, tobacco; p. (1961) 479,000.

Medellin c., Colombia, S. America; univ.; textiles, tobacco, coffee, cement, glass, steel; hydroelec. plant; p. (estd. 1962) 690,710.

Medford, t., Mass., U.S.A.; sub. of Boston; residtl.; chemicals, machin., textiles; p. (1960) 64,971.   [leather; p. 14,903.

Medicina, commune, N. Italy; textiles, agr.;

Medicine Bow, mtns., Col. and Wyo., U.S.A.

Medicine Hat, t., Alberta, Canada; on S. Saskatchewan R.; rly. junction; coal, natural gas, flour; p. (1961) 24,484.

Medina, t., W. Australia; oil refinery.

Medina, t., N. Ohio, U.S.A.; bees, honey, beeswax; p. (1960) 8,235.

Medina, c., Saudi Arabia; tomb of Mohammed; rail line to Ma'an restored (1964–7); harbour at Yenbo (Yanbu); fruit, dates; p. (estd.) 50,000.   [14,889.

Medinia-Sidonia, t., Spain; agr. prod.; p. (1957)

Mediterranean, gr. inland sea, almost tideless, dividing Europe from Africa; and communicating with the Atlantic by the Strait of Gibraltar and Black Sea by the Dardanelles, Sea of Marmara and Bosporus, E. part touches Asia in the Levant; total length W. to E. 2,200 m.; greatest width of sea proper about 700 m.; water a. 900,000 sq. m.; greatest depth 14,695 ft.; ch. Is.: Corsica, Sardinia, Sicily, Crete, Cyprus, and the Balearic, Lipari, Maltese, Ionian grs., also Grecian Archipelago.

Médoc, old dist., Gironde, France, extending for about 48 m. along Garonne R.; noted for wines.

Medveditsa, R., U.S.S.R.; trib. of R. Don; 330 m.

Medway, R., Kent, Eng.; length 70 m.; Medway Bridge (part of London–Dover motorway) completed 1962.

Meekatharra, t., Murchison goldfields, W. Australia.

Meerane, t., Karl-Marx-Stadt, E. Germany; textiles, machin., chemicals; p. (1963) 24,170.

Meerut, c., Uttar Pradesh, India; scene of outbreak of Indian Mutiny, 1857; p. (1961) 283,997.

Megara, t., Greece; p. (1951) 14,118.

Mehsana, t., Gujarat, India; rice, cotton, toabcco; p. (1961) 32,577.

Meiktila, dist., Upper Burma; teak forests; cap. M.; paper mill; p. (of t.) 8,830.

Meiling Pass, on bdy. between Kwangtung, Kiangsi, S. China; provides historic routeway across Nanling mtns., followed by old imperial highway from Nanking to Canton; alt. approx. 1,000 ft.

Meiningen, *t.*, Suhl, E. Germany; on R. Werra; cas.; machin., chemicals; p. (1963) *24,379.*

Meiringen, *t.*, Switzerland; nr. to Aar Gorge; resort, wood carving, hand weaving; p. *3,285.*

Meissen, *c.*, Dresden, E. Germany; on R. Elbe; cath.; famous porcelain wks., textiles, iron, furniture, elec. machine.; p. (1963) *47,676.*

Meknès, *c.*, Morocco, N. Africa; agr. ctr., olives; p. (1960) *175,943.*

Mekong, *R.*, S.E. Asia; rises in Tibet and separates Laos and Thailand, descends to Cambodian plain, joins Tonle Sap nr. Phnom Penh, divides to flow S.E. through S. Viet-Nam to form vast delta at entrance to S. China Sea; length 2,800 m.

Melanesia, *chain of I. grs.*, S. Pacific; New Britain, Solomon, Santa Cruz, New Hebrides, New Caledonia, Loyalty and other archipelagos

Melbourne, *spt. cap.*, Victoria, Australia; at mouth of Yarra R.; comm. ctr.; textile and knitting mills, machin. mftg., cars; botanical gardens; univ., caths.; p. (1966) *2,108,499.*

Meld, *t.*, Potenza, Italy; cath.; p. *14,300.*

Melilla, *spt.*, Morocco, N. Africa; exp. iron ore; convict settlement; p. (1950) *85,010.*

Melipilla, *t.*, central Chile; agr., dairy prod.

Melitopol, *t.*, Ukrainian S.S.R.; engin.; ctr. of rich fruit growing a.; p. (1967) *115,000.*

Melksham, *t., urb. dist.*, Wilts, Eng.; on R. Avon, 5 m. N.E. of Bradford-on-Avon; rubber wks., heavy engin., flour mills, creameries, rope and matting; p. (1961) *8,279.*

Mělník, *t.*, ČSSR.; p. (1961) *13,100.*

Melrose, *burgh*, Roxburgh, Scot.; on R. Tweed; 4 m. E. of Galashiels; ruined abbey, dist. ass. with Sir Walter Scott; p. (1961) *2,133.*

Meltham, *t., urb. dist.*, W.R. Yorks, Eng.; 4 m. S.W. of Huddersfield; woollen textiles; p. (1961) *5,413.*

Melton Mowbray, *t., urb. dist.*, Leicester, Eng.; on Lincoln Heights, 15 m. N.E. of Leicester; mkt., hunting dist.; famous pork pies; footwear, wool spinning mills; p. (1961) *15,913.*

Melun, *t.*, cap. Seine-et-Marne, France; on R. Seine; agr. tools and prod.; p. (1962) *28,796.*

Melville I., off N. cst., Arnhem Land, Australia.

Melville I., N.W. Terrs., Arctic Canada.

Memaliaj, *t.*, Albania; new mng. t. on banks of R. Vjosa.

Memmingen, *t.*, Bavaria, Germany; rly. junction; machin., textiles; p. (1963) *31,300.*

Memphis, *ancient c.*, Egypt; on R. Nile; 10 m. S. of Cairo; near by are Sakkara ruins.

Memphis, *c.*, Tenn., U.S.A.; on R. Mississippi; rly. ctr., timber, cotton seed, ironwks., oil; textiles, chemicals; p. (1970) *620,873.*

Mena, *t.*, W. Ark., U.S.A.; lumber, bricks, cotton, flour; tourist resort; p. (1960) *4,383.*

Menado, *t.*, Sulawesi, Indonesia; p. (1961) *129,912.*

Menai Bridge, *urb. dist.*, Anglesey, Wales; p. (1961) *2,337.*

Menai Strait, separates Isle of Anglesey from Caernarvon, Wales; crossed by Britannia rly. and Menai suspension bridges; 14 m. long, ½ m. to 2 m. wide.

Menam, *R.*, W. Thailand, length 750 m.

Menasha, *t.*, Wis., U.S.A.; on L. Winnebago; mnfs.; p. (1960) *14,647.*

Mende, *t.*, cap. Lozère, France; on R. Lot; serge mftg.; p. (1962) *10,061.*

Menden, *t.*, N. Rhine–Westphalia, Germany; metallurgy, elec. prod.; p. (1963) *28,400.*

Mendip Hills, Somerset, Eng.; limestone range containing many karst features inc. Cheddar Gorge and Wookey Hole; length 20 m.; highest point 1,067 ft.

Mendoza, *prov.*, W. Argentina; alfalfa, vines, olives, fruit, peppermint; cap. Mendoza; a. 57,445 sq. m.; p. (1960) *826,000.*

Mendoza, *t.*, cap. Mendoza prov., Argentina; on Transandine Rly.; wine-producing dist.; petroleum; p. (1960) of c. *110,000* greater M. *250,000.*

Menen, *t.*, W. Flanders, Belgium; tobacco tr., textiles, rubber gds., soap; p. (1962) *22,620.*

Menfi, *t.*, Sicily, Italy; industl.; p. *10,225.*

Mengtsz, *c.*, Yunnan, China; ruined in Tai-ping rebellion; tin, cotton ginning ctr.; p. *193,004.*

Menominee, Mich., U.S.A.; on M. R.; industl. ctr. for lumber, sugar beets, dairy prod.; p. (1960) *11,289.*

Menomonie, *c.*, Wis., U.S.A.; on Red Cedar R.; farm ctr. and dairy prod.; p. (1960) *13,276.*

Menteith, L., of, S.W. Perth, Scot.; between Rs. Forth and Teith; a. 2½ sq. m.

Menton, *t.*, Alpes-Maritimes, S. France; on Mediterranean cst.; health resort, olive oil, wines, perfumes; p. (1962) *20,069.*

Meppel, *t.*, Drenthe, Netherlands, 13 m. N. of Zwolle; shipbldg.; p. (1967) *19,192.*

Merano, *t.*, Tyrol, N. Italy; health resort; p. *30,350.*

Merced, *t.*, Cal., U.S.A.; p. (1960) *20,068.*

Mercedes, *cap.*, Soriano dep., Uruguay; livestock ctr.; resort; p. (1963) *34,000.*

Mercedes, *t.*, S. Texas, U.S.A.; cotton, oil, fruit; veg. canning; p. (1960) *10,943.*

Merchantville, *bor.*, N.J., U.S.A.; paper, lead mnfs.; p. (1960) *4,075.* [fishing.

Mergui, *archipelago*, Burma; teak, rice, pearl

Mergui, *t.*, Tenasserim, Lower Burma; on Bay of Bengal; pearl fishing; p. *20,405.*

Mérida, *t.*, Badajoz, Spain; on R. Guadiana; agr. dist., textiles; p. *23,886.*

Mérida, *cap.*, Yucatán, Mexico; univ.; sisal-hemp, ropes, cigars, brandy; p. (1960) *170,834.*

Mérida, *t.*, cap. Mérida st., Venezuelan Andes; univ., cath; tourist ctr.; world's highest cable rly. to Espejo peak (15,380 ft.); p. (1961) *40,404.*

Meriden, *c.*, Conn., U.S.A.; hardware mftg.; p. (1960) *51,850.*

Meridian, *t.*, Miss., U.S.A.; in cotton-growing region; p. (1960) *49,374.*

Merioneth, *maritime co.*, N. Wales; pastoral and mining; nuclear power-sta. at Trawsfynydd; co. t., Dolgellau; a. 600 sq. m.; p. (1966) *38,000.*

Meriti, *c.*, S.E. Brazil; 10 m. N. Rio de Janeiro; p. (1947) *38,645.* [Galilee, Israel.

Merom, Waters of, *L.*, modern Hule L., Upper

Merrick, *mtn.*, Kirkcudbright, Scot.; highest peak in S. Uplands of Scot.; alt. 2,764 ft.

Merrill, *t.*, N. Wis., U.S.A.; wooden goods, paper, knitwear; p. (1960) *9,451.*

Merrimac, *R.*, N.H. and Mass., U.S.A.

Merse, *geographical sub-region*, S.E. Scot.; comprises lower valleys of Rs. Tweed and Teviot below Melrose and Hawick; glacial deposits form low hillocks *en échelon*, which largely influence the pattern of streams, roads, settlements, etc.; most favoured part of Scot. for crop growing, wheat, barley, root crops (for feeding to cattle, sheep); ch. ts. Hawick, Kelso, Berwick-on-Tweed (Eng.); a. approx. 220 sq. m.

Mersea, *I.*, at mouth of R. Colne, Essex, Eng.; oysters; holiday resort; length 5 m., width 2 m.

Merseburg, *c.*, Halle, E. Germany; on R. Saale; cath., cas.; paper, machin., tobacco, chemicals; p. (1963) *52,545.*

Mersey, *R.*, between Lancs and Cheshire, Eng.; enters Irish Sea by fine estuary at Liverpool; length 68 m.

Merseyside, *lge. conurbation*, S.W. Lancs. and N. Cheshire, Eng.; comprises: (1) spt. and industl. a. either side of lower Mersey estuary; (2) residtl. a. of W Wirral Peninsula; a. 150 sq. m.; p. (estd. 1968) *1,351,000.. See also under* Bebington, Birkenhead, Bootle, Crosby, Ellesmere Pt., Hoylake, Huyton, Litherland, Liverpool, Neston, Wallasey, Wirral. Oil pipeline links with Thames estuary refineries.

Mersey Tunnel biggest underwater tunnel in world, linking Liverpool and Birkenhead; opened 1934; main tunnel 2 m. l., with branch bores, 3 m.; second tunnel (two-way) planned.

Mersin, *spt.*, Turkey; oil refining; textiles, fruit, cereals, timber; p. (1965) *87,267.*

Mertert-Grevenmacher, *R. pt..* on Moselle, Luxembourg.

Merthyr Tydfil, *t., co. bor.*, Glamorgan, S. Wales; in narrow valley of R. Taff, 22 m. N.W. of Cardiff; coalmng. ctr.; hosiery, aircraft, bricks, elec. domestic goods; p. (1961) *59,003.*

Merton, *outer bor.*, Greater London, Eng.; inc. former bors. of Mitcham, Wimbledon, and Merton and Morden; p. (1966) *184,000.*

Meru, *mtn.*, Tanzania, E. Africa; extinct volcano overlooking E. arm of Gr. Rift valley; coffee plantations at alt. 5,000–6,000 ft., some rubber below 4,000 ft.; alt. summit 14,953 ft.

Merv, *see* Mary.

Mesa, *t.*, Arizona, U.S.A.; agr. and cotton ginning ctr.; helicopter mftg.; p. (1960) *33,772.*

Mesabi Range, *hills*, N.E. Minn., U.S.A.; about

100 m. long, alt. 200–500 ft.; vast iron-ore deposits.

Mesagna, *t.,* S. Italy; mnfs.; p. *17,300.*

Meshed, *see* Mashhad.

Messina, *c., spt.,* Sicily, Italy; opposite Reggio; univ.; exp. fruit, wine, silk, oil; silk mnf.; p. (1965) *265,000.*

Messina, *strait,* between Sicily and Italian mainland; length 22 m. minimum width 3 m.

Messinia, *prefecture,* Peloponnese, Greece; cap. Kalamai; p. *210,728.*

Mesta, *R.,* Bulgaria, Greece; rises in Rhodope Mtns., flows S.E. into Ægean Sea 15 m. E. of Kaválla; valley famous for tobacco; known in Greece as Nestos; approx. length 175 m.

Mestre, *t.,* Italy; on lagoon at landward end of causeway linking Venice to mainland; p. *11,750.*

Mesurado, *R.,* Liberia, Africa; 300 m. long.

Meta, *R.,* Colombia and Venezuela; navigable for 400 m.; trib. of R. Orinoco; length 750 m.

Metemma, *t.,* Sudan; opposite Shendi, on R. Nile.

Methil, *t.,* Fife, Scot.; on F. of Forth; united with Buckhaven.

Methuen, *t.,* Mass., U.S.A.; textiles, footwear; p. (1960) *28,114.* 　　　　　　[(1960) *7,339.*

Metropolis, *c.,* Ill., U.S.A.; on R. Ohio; p.

Mettmann, *t.,* N. Rhine–Westphalia, Germany; nr. Düsseldorf; iron, machin.; p. (1963) *25,800.*

Metuchen, *bor.,* N.J., U.S.A.; residtl., chemicals, needles, rubber; p. (1960) *14,041.*

Metz, *c.,* cap. Moselle, France; on R. Moselle 25 m. N. of Nancy; cath.; metals, wines, leather goods, preserved fruits; p. (1968) *107,537.*

Meudon, *t.,* Hauts-de-Seine, France; nr. Versailles; observatory; glass, linen, ammunition; p. (1962) *35,824.*

Meurthe, *R.,* France; length 70 m.

Meurthe-et-Moselle, *dep.,* E. France; agr., vineyards, mining; cap. Nancy; a. 2,037 sq. m.; p. (1968) *705,413.*

Meuse, *dep.,* N.E. France; livestock, mining, wine; cap. Bar-le-Duc; a. 2,408 sq. m.; p. (1968) *209,513.*

Meuse (Maas), *R.,* France; rises in Haute-Marne, flows past Verdun into Belgium past Namur and Liége into the Netherlands and joins the Waal, left arm of the Rhine; length 570 m.

Mexborough, *t., urb. dist.,* W.R. Yorks, Eng.; on R. Don, 10 m. above Doncaster; potteries, iron; p. (1961) *17,095.* 　　　　　　[500 m.

Mexcala, *R.,* S. Mexico; flows into Pacific; length

Mexia, *t.,* Texas, U.S.A.; rly. ctr.; cotton, oil, engin.; p. (1960) *6,121.* 　　　[p. (1960) *174,540.*

Mexicali, *cap.,* N. Terr., Lower California, Mexico;

Mexico, *fed. rep.,* S. of N. America; contains much forest, fertile land and mtn. dists.; rich in minerals, silver, copper, arsenic, oil, zinc, lead; stock-raising and agr. are the ch. occupations in the N States; cap. Mexico City; a. 758,000 sq. m.; p (estd. 1970) *50,000,000.*

Mexico City, *cap. c.,* Mexico; in plain, alt. 7,460 ft. above sea-level; many noteworthy bldgs.; extensive tr. and inds.; p. (estd. 1968) *7,100,000.*

Mexico, *st.,* Mexico; a. 8,267 sq. m.; cap. Toluca; p. (1960) *1,897,851.*

Mexico, *c.,* Mo., U.S.A.; firebrick and shoe factories; p. (1960) *12,889.*

Mexico, G. of, *lge. inlet* of the Atlantic (1,000 m. E. to W. by 800 m. N. to S.) lying S. of U.S.A. and E. of Mexico. Communicates by Florida Strait with the Atlantic and by Channel of Yucatán with the Caribbean Sea.

Meycauayan, *mun.,* Luzon, Philippines; rice, sugar, maize; p. *16,082.*

Mezhdurechensk, *t.,* R.S.F.S.R.; W. Siberia, on R. Tom'; new coalmng. ctr.; p. (1959) *55,000.*

Mézières, *see* Charleville-Mézières.

Mezőkovesd, *t.,* Hungary; agr. and industl.; p. (1962) *18,640.* 　　　　　[(1962) *23,329.*

Mezőtur, *t.,* Hungary; mkt., flour, pottery; p.

Mezzogiorno, *lge underdeveloped region,* Southern Italy; comprising Abruzzo and Molise, Campania, Basilicata, Apulia, Calabria and the Is. of Sicily and Sardinia; mtnous., fertile cstl. a.; citrus, vines, olives, wheat, beans; p. (estd. 1969) *19,000,000.*

Mhow, *t.,* Madhya Pradesh, India; cotton; p. (1961) *48,032.*

Miagao, *t.,* Panay, Philippines; tr. ctr., mnfs.

Miami, *c.,* Fla., U.S.A.; on Biscayne Bay, at mouth of Miami R.; famous resort and recreational ctr.; varied inds.; intern. airpt.; p. (1960) *291,688.*

Miami, *t.,* Okla., U.S.A.; tr. ctr., agr., cattle; packing, mining; p. (1960) *12,869.*

Miamisburg, *t.,* Ohio, U.S.A.; p. (1960) *9,893.*

Miani, *t.* N.W. Punjab, Pakistan; salt; p. about *6,000.* 　　　　　　　　[(1951) *550,000.*

Mianwali, *dist.,* W. Punjab, Pakistan; p. (estd.

Miass, *t.,* R.S.F.S.R. in Urals, 56 m. S.W. Chelyabinsk; gold mng. ctr.; cars; p. (1967) *119,000.*

Michigan, *st.,* U.S.A.; in valley of Gr. Lakes; industl.; cars, iron and steel goods, petroleum, minerals; some agr.; cap. Lansing; a. 58,216 sq. m.; p. (1970) *8,776,873.*

Michigan, L., N. America; in basin of St. Lawrence R., enclosed by two peninsulas of the st. of M. and by Wis., Ill. and Ind.; a. 23,900 sq. m.; discharges by Straits of Mackinac to L. Huron.

Michigan City, *t.,* Ind., U.S.A.; on L. M.; rly. wks., furniture, hosiery; (1960) *36,653.*

Michipicoten, *R.,* Ontario, Canada; flows 125 m. to L. Superior.

Michoacan, *st.,* Mexico; on the Pacific; mtnous. and rich in minerals; cap. Morelia; a. 23,200 sq. m.; p. (1960) *1,851,876.*

Michurinsk, *t.,* R.S.F.S.R.; N.W. of Tambov; engin., textiles, food inds.; agr. exp. ctr.; p. (1959) *80,000.*

Micronesia, *Is.,* S. Pacific; inc. the Carolines, Marshalls, Marianas, and Gilbert Is.

Middleburg, *t.,* cap. Zeeland, Neth.; on Walcheren I. nr. Flushing; margarine, timber, optical instruments; p. (1967) *27,996.*

Middelburg, *t.,* Transvaal, S. Africa; coal, iron, copper, cobalt; p. (1960) *12,907* inc. *4,886* Europeans.

Middelfart, *t.,* Fyn, Denmark; off Fredericia; p. (1960) *8,801.*

Middleboro, *t.,* Mass., U.S.A.; agr. ctr.; p. (1960) *6,003.*

Middlesboro, *t.,* Ky., U.S.A.; p. (1960) *12,607.*

Middlesbrough, *spt.,* Cleveland dist., N.R. Yorks., Eng.; enlarged M. now forms co. bor. of Teeside; on S. side of Tees estuary; impt. iron and steel ind., heavy engin., shipbldg. and coal exp.; oil refinery projected; p. (1961) *157,308.*

Middlesex, *former co.,* S.E. Eng.; N. of R. Thames; absorbed in Greater London 1964; a. 232 sq. m.; p. (1961) *2,230,093.*

Middleton, *mkt. t.,* Durham, Eng.; civil airport projected; on R. Tees.

Middleton, *t., mun. bor.,* S.E. Lancs, Eng.; mkt.; textiles, engin.. chemicals; p. (estd. 1967) *58,140.*

Middletown, *c.,* Conn., U.S.A.; on C. R.; univ.; p. (1960) *33,250.*

Middletown, *c.,* N.Y., U.S.A.; on Walkill R.; ironwks.; p. (1960) *23,475.*

Middletown, *c.,* Ohio, U.S.A.; in Miami and Erie canal; p. (1960) *42,115.*

Middletown, *bor.,* Penns., U.S.A.; on Susquehanna R.; p. (1960) *11,182.*

Middlewich, *t., urb. dist.,* Cheshire, Eng.; on Rs. Dane, Wheelock, and Croco, 5 m. N. of Crewe; salt, chemicals, silk, clothing; p. (1961) *6,833.*

Midhurst, *t.,* Sussex, Eng.; on R. Rother; mkt., agr. ctr.; brick, timber, lime wks.; p. *1,812.*

Midland, *t.,* Mich., U.S.A.; chemicals, salt, oil; p. (1960) *27,779.*

Midland, *t.,* Texas, U.S.A.; oilfield ctr., cotton ginning, natural gas; p. (1960) *62,625.*

Midleton, *urb. dist.,* Cork, Ireland; mkt.; p. (1966) *4,173.*

Midlothian, *co.,* Scot.; dairying, coal-mining, paper, brewing, fishing; a. 362 sq. m.; p. (1961) *580,332.* 　　　　　　[(1961) *59,532.*

Midnapore, *t.,* W. Bengal, India; silkworm tr.; p.

Midway, *Is.,* Pac. Oc.; calling-place on air-routes between San Francisco and Asia, mid-way between Asia and U.S.A. (to which it belongs).

Miechowice, *t.,* S.W. Poland; coal, iron foundries; p. *14,608.* 　　　　　　　　[leather; p. *16,837.*

Miedzyrzecz (Meseritz), *t.,* E. Poland; agr.,

Mieres, *t.,* Spain; on R. Leno, nr. Oviedo; minerals, agr. prod.; p. (1959) *69,623.*

Mihama, Fukui, Japan; nuclear reactor under construction 1968.

Mihoro, Gifu. Japan; power plant under construction.

Mikkeli (St. Michel), *dep.,* Finland; a. 6,750 sq. m.; p. (1966) *230,144.*

Milan, *c.,* N. Italy; on R. Olona; cath., univ.; textiles, machin., motors, chemicals, por cultural, comm. and industl. ctr.; p. (1965) *1,673,000.*

Milas, *t.*, S.W. Turkey in Asia; agr., fruit; carpets; p. (1960) *11,676.*

Mildenhall, *t.*, W. Suffolk, Eng.; on R. Lark; 10 m. N.W. of Bury St. Edmunds; mkt., flour; p. *3,235.*

Mildura, *c.*, Victoria, Australia; on R. Murray; irrigation ctr., fruit, canning, food processing; p. (1966) *12,931.*

Miles City, *c.*, Mont., U.S.A.; on Yellowstone R.; cattle; p. (1960) *9,665.*

Milford, *t.*, Conn., U.S.A.; residtl., resort; fish; light engin.; p. (1960) *41,662.*   [*13,722.*

Milford, *t.*, Mass., U.S.A.; boot mnfs.; p. (1960)

Milford Haven, *spt.*, *urb. dist.*, Milford Haven, Pembroke, Wales; major oil pt., providing access and anchorage for 100,000-ton oil tankers; 2 refineries, fishing, trawlers built and repaired, net mkg., beryllium; p. (1961) *12.802.*

Milford Sound, *inlet*, at S. extremity of S.I. N.Z., tourist restort; noted for grandeur of scenery, and rare birds.

Milianah, *t.*, Algeria; tr. ctr.; p. *5,000.*

Militello, *t.* Sicily, Italy; agr.; p. *10,770.*

Milk, *R.*, Mont., U.S.A.; trib. of Missouri R.; length 500 m.

Millau, *t.*, Aveyron, France; on R. Tarn; glove mnfs.; p. (1962) *22,174.*

Millbrook, *t.*, Hants, Eng.; at mouth of R. Test, nr. Southampton.

Millersburg, *bor.*, Penns., U.S.A.; machin., shoes; p. (1950) *2,861.*   [*7,318.*

Millinocket, *t.*, Me., U.S.A.; paper; p. (1960)

Millom, *t.*, Cumberland, Eng.; on N.W. cst. of Duddon estuary; ironwks. (closed 1968 after 100 years); p. *8,708.*

Millport, *burgh*, Bute, Scot.; on Gr. Cumbrae I., in F. of Clyde; resort; cath.; quarries; p. (1961) *1,592.*

Millville, *c.*, N.J., U.S.A.; on Maurice R.; glass, iron, cotton; p. (1960) *19,096.*

Milnerton, *t.*, S. Africa; nitrogenous fertiliser plant.

Milngavie, *burgh*, Dunbarton, Scot.; 5 m. N.W. of Glasgow; textiles; p. (1961) *8,594.*

Milnrow, *t.*, *urb. dist.*, S.E. Lancs, Eng.; sub. of Rochdale; cotton and waste spinning, engin., brick mkg., paper and tube mftg.; p. (1961) *7,819.*

Milos, *I.*, Cyclades, Greece; volcanic; length 13 m.; fruits, gypsum, sulphur; famous statue of Venus found here in 1820.   [p. *11,291.*

Milspe, *commune*, Westphalia, Germany; ironwks.;

Milstin, *peak*, Atlas Mtns., Morocco. N. Africa; alt. 11,400 ft.

Milton, *t.*, Mass., U.S.A.; sub. of Boston; p. (1960) *26,375.*

Milton, *t.*, Penns., U.S.A.; on Susquehanna R.; ironwks.; p. (1960) *7,972.*

Milton Keynes, *vil.* Bucks; a. 3 sq. m.; site and name of new c. for London overspill to comprise Bletchley, Wolverton and Stoney Stratford; a. 34 sq. m.   [mkt.

Milverton, *t.*, Somerset, Eng.; 6 m. W. of Taunton.

Milwaukee, *c.*, Wis., U.S.A.; on L. Michigan, 70 m. N. of Chicago; univ.; rly. ctr., cars, meat canning, agr. tools, machin., iron and steel castings, generators; dairying; p. (1970) *709,537*: Greater M. *1,393,000.*

Mimico, *t.*, Ontario, Canada; p. (1961) *18,212.*

Minab, *t.*, Iran; orchards; p. about *10,000.*

Mina Hassan Tani (Kenitra), *t.*, Morocco; 18 m. N. of Rabat; developed since 1912; exp. grain; p. (1960) *86,775.*   [Canada.

Minas Basin, *E. arm*, Bay of Fundy, Nova Scotia.

Minas Gerais, *st.*, Brazil; world's biggest iron ore reserve; gold, diamonds, manganese, aluminium; cotton, coffee; hydroelec. power sta.; cap. Belo Horizonte; a. 226,051 sq. m.; p. (estd. 1968) *11,776,817.*

Minas Novas, *t.*, Minas Gerais, Brazil; p. (estd. 1968) *24,003.*

Minatitlán, *t.*, E. Mexico; petroleum refineries; petrochemicals; p. (1940) *18,539.*

Minch, The, *channel* between the Outer and Inner Hebrides; 24 m. to 40 m. wide.

Minchinhampton, *t.*, Gloucester, Eng.; in Cotswold Hills, 4 m. S.E. of Stroud; mkt., woollens, brewing; p. *3,500.*

Mincio, *R.*, Italy; trib. of R. Po; drains L. Garda; length 38 m.

Mindanao, 2nd lgst. I. of Philippines; pineapples,
O (80th Ed.)

hemp, coconuts, coffee; iron, gold, coal, copper, plywoods and veneer; paper, pulp; ch- ts. Zamboanga, Davao; off N.E. cst. is Mindanao Deep (c. 35,000 ft), one of greatest known ocean depths; a. 36,536 sq. m.; p. (1960) *5,358,900.*

Minden, *c.*, N. Rhine-Westphalia, Germany; on R. Weser at crossing of Mittelland Canal; cath.; glass, tobacco, metal, wood, leather, meat prod.; p. (1963) *48,900.*

Minden, *t.*, La., U.S.A.; exp. cotton; petroleum, natural gas; p. (1960) *12,785.*

Mindoro, *I.*, Philippines, S. of Luzon; a. 3,759 sq. m.; p. (1960) *291,100.*

Minehead, *t.*, *urb. dist.*, Somerset, Eng.; at N foot of Exmoor, on Bristol Channel cst.; mkt., holiday resort; p. (1961) *7,674.*

Mineo, *t.*, Sicily, Italy; mftg.; p. *11,400.*

Mineola, *t.*, N.Y., U.S.A.; sub. N.Y. c.; glass, packing; p. (1960) *20,519.*

Minersville, *bor.*, Penns., U.S.A.; on Schuylkill R.; p. (1960) *6,606.*

Minervino, *t.*, S. Italy; industl.; p. *18,375.*

Minho, *R.*, separates Portugal from Spain in N.W.; length 170 m.

Minia, *t.*, U.A.R.; on R. Nile; cotton, tr. ctr; p. (1960) *94,000.*

Minicoy Is., Arabian Sea, joined with Laccadive and Amindivi Is. to form *Union terr.* (India).

Minneapolis, *c.*, Minn., U.S.A.; on Mississippi R., at Falls of St. Anthony; univ.; flour, timber, agr. machin., linseed oil; chemicals, textiles, paper; p. (1960) *482,827.*

Minnesota, *st.*, U.S.A.; iron-ore, agr., flour, timber, meat; cap. St. Paul; a. 84,068 sq. m.; p. (1970) *3,767,975.*

Minnick, Water of, R., Ayr and Kirkcudbright, Scot.; trib. of R. Cree; length 15 m.

Minorca (Menorca), Spanish I., Balearic Is., Mediterranean Sea; fruits, olives, cereals, cattle, minerals; cap. Mahón; a. 283 sq. m.; p. (1957) *42,478.*

Minot, *t.*, N.D., U.S.A.; p. (1960) *30,604.*

Minsk, *cap.*, Byelorussian S.S.R.; univ.; engin., textiles, elec. power; p. (1967) *717,000.*

Minya Konka, *mtn.*, Szechwan, China; at E. end of Plateau of Tibet; highest mtn. in China; alt. approx. 23,000 ft.

Miosnavo, *t.*, Norway; length 24 m.

Miquelon, *I.*, French, off S. cst. Newfoundland, Canada; fisheries.

Mira, *t.*, Italy; on Brenta Morta; p. *19,600.*

Miranda, *st.*, N. Venezuela; pastoral and agr.; cap. Los Teques; p. (1961) *492,349.*

Miranda, *t.*, N.E. Spain; on R. Ebro; p. (1957) *18,094.*

Mirandola, *t.*, Modena, Italy; p. *20,875.*

Mirano, *t.*, N. Italy; p. *14,600.*

Mirfield, *urb. dist.*, W.R. Yorks, Eng.; on R. Calder, 3 m. S.W. of Dewsbury; woollens; p. (1961) *12,289.*

Miri, *t.*, Sarawak; oil ctr.; p. (1960) *13,350.*

Mirim, *L.*, Brazil and Uruguay; 115 m. long, 20 m. wide.

Mirzapur, *t.*, Uttar Pradesh, India; on R. Ganges; carpets, brassware; p. (1961) *100,097.*

Misburg, *vil.*, Lower Saxony, Germany; on Weser-Elbe Canal, 5 m. E. of Hanover; oil refining; p. (estd.) *8,530.*

Mishawaka, *c.*, Ind., U.S.A.; on St. Joseph R.; agr. implements; p. (1960) *33,361.*

Misilmeri, *t.*, Sicily, Italy; p. *11,420.*

Misiones, *terr.*, Argentina; farming and stock-raising; cap. Posadas; a. 11,749 sq. m.; p. (1960) *391,000.*

Miskolcz, *t.*, Hungary; univ.; porcelain, textiles, iron and steel, cement, bricks, refrigeration plants; p. (1965) *167,000.*

Misoöl, *I.*, N. of Ceram, Indonesia.

Mission, *t.*, S. Texas, U.S.A.; fruit, cotton, vegetables; engin.; p. (1960) *14,081.*

Mississinewa, *R.*, Ind., U.S.A.; trib. of Wabash R.; length 140 m.

Mississippi, *st.*, U.S.A.; cotton, sweet potatoes, pecan nuts, rice, sugar cane, sorghum cane; cable; petroleum, natural gas, chemicals, shipbldg.; cap. Jackson; a. 47,776 sq. m.; p. (1970) *2,158,872.*   [length 100 m.

Mississippi, *R.*, Canada; trib. of Ottawa R.

Mississippi, *R.*, U.S.A.; length c. 2,350 m. (Mississippi-Missouri-Red Rock, c. 3,860 m.).

Missolonghi, *c.*, *spt.*, *cap.*, Aetolia and Acarnania, Greece; currants; p. (1961) *11,266.*

Missoula, c., Mont.,'U.S.A.; on Klark R.; univ.; rly. wks., agr., fruit, oil ref.; p. (1960) 27,090.

Missouri, st., U.S.A.; livestock, maize, coal, iron, tobacco; cap. Jefferson City; ch. t. St. Louis; a. 69,674 sq. m.; p. (1970) 4,636,247.

Missouri, R., U.S.A.; trib. of Mississippi R.; length (including the Madison) 3,047 m., navigable 2,400 m.

Missouri Coteau, hill ridge, N. America; runs N.W. to S.E. across prairies of Saskatchewan (Canada), N. and S. Dakota (U.S.A.); rises abruptly from 1,600 to 2,000 ft.

Missouri, Little, R., U.S.A.; trib. of M. R.; length 450 m.

Mistassini, L., Quebec, Canada; 100 m. long.

Mistretta, t., Sicily, Italy; mnfs.; p. 10,800.

Misurata, t., Tripolitania, Libya, N. Africa; on cst. of Mediterranean, 110 m. E. of Tripoli; mkt. for local agr. produce; p. (1954) 66,735.

Mitau, see Jelgava.

Mitcham, former mun. bor., Surrey, Eng.; now inc. in Merton outer London bor.(q.v.); calico printing, elec. engin.; p. (1961) 63,653.

Mitchell, R., Queensland, Australia; flows into G. of Carpentaria.

Mitchell, t., S. Dakota, U.S.A.; univ.; farming; p. (1960) 12,555.

Mitchell, mtn. pk., Black Mtns., N. Carolina, U.S.A.; alt. 6,684 ft.

Mitchelstown, t., Cork, Ireland; nr. Fermoy; p. (1966) 2,617.

Mitidja, plain, Algeria, N. Africa; borders Mediterranean 25 m. E. and W. of Algiers; intensive cultivation of vine; ch. ts. Algiers, Blida.

Mito, c., N. Japan; lime tree growing; p. (1965) 154,983.

Mitrovica, t., Jugoslavia; on R. Sava; livestock, mkt.; p. (1959) 22,000.

Mittelland Canal, inland waterway system, N. Germany; system of canals and canalised Rs.; links Dortmund–Ems Canal nr. Rheine through Minden, Hanover, Magdeburg, Berlin to R. Oder at Frankfurt-on-Oder; makes use of natural E.–W. troughs across the N. German Plain.

Mittweida, t., Karl-Marx-Stadt, E. Germany; metallurgy, textiles; p. (1963) 20,592.

Miyazaki, c., Kyushu, Japan; famous shrine; chemicals, lumbering; p. (1965) 182,870.

Mizen Head, C., S. Ireland; W. of C. Clear.

Mjösa, lqst. L., Norway; 55 m. long.

Mlada Boleslav (Jungbunzlau), t., Bohemia, ČSSR.; chemicals; p. (1961) 25,694.

Mljet, I., Adriatic Sea; part of Jugoslavia.

Moanda, Leopoldville, Congo; oil refinery.

Moate, t., W. Meath Ireland; p. (1951) 1,274.

Moberly, c., Mo., U.S.A.; rly. wks., grain, iron, hosiery, footwear; p. (1960) 13,170.

Mobile, c., spt., Ala., U.S.A.; on R. M.; shipbldg., cotton exp.; p. (1960) 202,779.

Moçâmedes, pt., Angola, W. Africa; ore pier; linked by rail to Cassinga mines.

Mocha, fortfd. spt., Yemen, Arabia; on Red Sea; coffee; p. 5,000.

Modane, t., S.E. Savoie, France; commands routes via Mont Cenis Pass and tunnel; p. (1962) 5,137.

Modder, R., C. Prov., S. Africa; trib. of Orange R.

Modena, t., prov. cap., Italy; cath., univ.; textiles, fruit, grain, leather; p. (1961) 139,496.

Modesto, t., Cal., U.S.A.; fruit, vegetables; p. (1960) 36,585.

Modica, t., Sicily, Italy; cheese, macaroni, grain, wines; p. (1961) 44,050.

Modjokerto, t., E. Java, Indonesia; sugar; fossil man discovered 1934; p. 23,600.

Mödling, t., Austria; on R. Brühl, metalwks., sulphur-baths; p. (1961) 17,274.

Moers, t., N. Rhine–Westphalia, Germany; N.E. of Krefeld; cas.; coal-mining, metal ind.; p. (estd. 1954) 36,300.

Moffat, burgh, Dumfries, Scot.; in Annandale, 15 m. N.W. of Lockerbie; health resort; p. (1961) 1,917.

Moffat Tunnel, Col., U.S.A.; carries trunk rly. from Chicago to San Francisco under Rocky Mtns. between Denver and Salt Lake City; length 6¼ m.

Mogadishu, pt., cap. c., Somalia, N.E. Africa; fish canning, hides; airpt.; deep-sea pt. projected; p. (1958) 86,643.

Mogador, see Essaouira.

Mogi das Cruzes, t., São Paulo st., Brazil; p. (estd. 1968) 111,554.

Mogilev, c., Byelorussian S.S.R.; on R. Dnieper; engin., textiles, chemicals; p. (1967) 164,000.

Mogilev Podolski, t., Ukrainian S.S.R.; on Dniester R.; tr., flour, sugar refining; p. (1939) 22,271.

Mohác, t., Hungary; on R. Danube; R. pt.; flour, brewing; p. (1962) 18,100.

Mohammedia, t., Morocco, N. Africa; oil refining; p. (1960) 35,010.

Mohawk, R., N.Y., U.S.A.; trib. of Hudson R.; followed by impt. road, rly. and canal routes across Appalachian Mtns.; length 175 m.

Moidart, L., cst. dist., S.W. Inverness, Scot.

Moisie, R., Labrador, Canada, flows S. into G. of St. Lawrence.

Moissac, t., France; on R. Tarn; abbey; p. 7,435.

Mojave, desert, Cal., U.S.A.

Moji, spt., Kyushu, Japan; now part of Kitak-yushu City newly formed 1963 (q.v.); exp. coal, cement, timber, sugar, cotton, thread; p. (1960) 152,081.

Mokau, R., S.I., N.Z.

Mokpo, spt., W. cst. S. Korea; ctr. of food-processing and cotton-ginning; p. (1955) 113,492.   [ctr.; p. (1962) 25,404.

Mol, t., N.E. Belgium; nuclear energy research

Mola di Bari, spt., Apulia, Italy; grain, livestock, olives, wine; p. 18,775.

Mola di Gaeta, t., Italy; p. 15,950.

Mold, co. t., urb. dist., Flint, N. Wales; on R. Alyn; chemicals, roadstone; p. (1961) 6,857.

Moldau, see Vltava.

Moldavian S.S.R., const. rep., U.S.S.R.; viniculture, fruit-growing, mkt. gard.; cap. Kishinev; a. 13,200 sq. m.; p. (1970) 3,572,000.

Moldavia, prov. Romania; a. 14,660 sq. m.; wine; ch. t. Jassy; p. 2,850,068.

Mole, R., Surrey, Eng.; rises in central Weald, flows N. into R. Thames nr. Molesey; cuts impt. gap through N. Downs between Dorking and Leatherhead; length approx. 50 m.

Molenbeek-Saint-Jean, t., Belgium; nr. Brussels; large mftg. ctr.; p. (1962) 63,488.

Molesey, E. and W. t., Surrey, Eng.; at junction of Rs. Mole and Thames; residtl.; p. 8,500.

Molfetta, spt., Apulia, Italy; olive oil, macaroni, wine; p. (1961) 61,684.

Molina de Segura, commune, S.E. Spain; tinned food and jams; salt wks; p. (1957) 14,683.

Moline, c., Ill., U.S.A.; on Mississippi R.; agr. implements, ironwks., flour; p. (1960) 42,705.

Molise, region, S. Central Italy, on Adriatic; cap. Campobasso.   [18,000.

Mollendo, spt., Peru; bricks, fishing; p. (1961)

Mölndal, c., S.W. Sweden; paper, textiles; margarine; p. (1961) 26,502.

Molokai, I., Hawaiian Is.; a. 260 sq. m.; p. 5,258.

Molotov, see Perm.

Molsheim, t., Bas-Rhin, France; W. of Strasbourg; sword and bayonet mkg; p. (1962) 5,197.

Molucca or Spice Is., Indonesia; between Sulawesi and West Irian; spices, sago, timber, pearls, rice, copra; ch. t. Ternate; a. 191,681 sq. m.; p. (1961) 789,534.

Mombasa, spt., Kenya; ch. harbour, Killindini; rly. terminus; oil refinery; exp. tropical produce (ivory, hides, rubber, etc.); p. (1962) 178,400.

Mön, I., off cst. of Själland, Denmark; a. 90 sq. m.; cap. Stege; p. (1960) 13,107.

Mona Passage, strait, Caribbean Sea; separates Hispaniola from Puerto Rico.

Monaca, bor., Penns., U.S.A.; glass, light engin.; p. (1960) 8,394.

Monaco, principality, S. France; divided into 3 sections, Monaco Ville, La Condamine and Monte Carlo (famous Casino); tourism; olive oil, perfumes; a. 360 acres; p. (estd.) 23,000.

Monadhliath Mtns., Inverness, Scot.; on W. side Strathspey; highest peak Carn Mairg, 3,087 ft.

Monaghan, inland co., Ireland; mainly pastoral and agr.; a. 500 sq. m.; p. (1966) 45,726.

Monaghan, co. t., Monaghan, Ireland; on the Ulster Canal; cath.; p. (1966) 4,019.

Monaro, mtn. plateau, N.S.W., Australia; a. 8,335 sq. m.

Monastir, see Bitolj.

Moncalieri, commune, Piedmont, N.W. Italy; on R. Po; industl.; p. 21,181.

Mönch or "The Monk", mtn., Bernese Alps, Switzerland; alt. 13,468 ft.

Mönchen-Gladbach, t., Land, North Rhine-Westphalia, Germany; 16 m. W. of Düsseldorf; rly. ctr., cotton and wool; p. (1968) 151,890.

Monchique, *t.*, Algarve, Portugal; spa; wine, oil, chestnuts; p. *10,000.*

Monclova, *t.*, N.E. Mexico; coffee; copper, silver, zinc, lead-mines; p. (1941) *7,181.*

Moncton, *t.*, N.B., Canada; rly. ctr., textiles; oil near by; p. (1961) *43,840.*

Mondego, *R.*, Portugal; length 130 m.

Mondovi, *t.*, Cuneo, Italy; porcelain, paper, silk; p. *20,900.*   [wire; p. (1960) *18,428.*

Monessen, *t.*, Penns., U.S.A.; steel, tinplate,

Monfalcone, *commune*, N.E. Italy; chemicals, shipbldg., cotton mills; p. (1948) *19,634*

Monferrato, *low hills*, Piedmont, N. Italy; S. and S.E. of Turin between valleys of R. Po and R. Tanaro; celebrated vineyards, produce Asti Spumante wines; alt. never exceeds 1,500 ft.

Monforte, *t.*, Galicia, Spain; soap, linen; p. (1957) *21,682.*

Monghyr, *dist.*, Bihar, India; a. 3,975 sq. m.; agr.; mica; p. (1961) *3,387,082.*

Mongla, *pt.*, E. Pakistan; on Pussur R.; shipping pt. under construction.

Mongol-Buryat, A.S.S.R., U.S.S.R.; E. of L. Baikal; cattle breeding.

Mongolia, *vast elevated plateau*, in heart of Asia between China and U.S.S.R. *See* Mongolian People's Republic and Inner Mongolia.

Mongolia, Inner, *see* Inner Mongolia.

Mongolian People's Republic (Outer Mongolia), *indep. st.*, Asia; bordered by China on W., S. and E. and by U.S.S.R. on N.; mainly plateau 5,000–10,000 ft. with Altai mtns. in N.W. and Gobi Desert in S.; watered by numerous Rs.; many Ls.; cap. Ulan Bator; livestock, wool, hides, skins; gold, coal; close links with U.S.S.R.; a. 604,000 sq. m.,; p. (estd. 1970) *1,227,000.*

Monmouthshire, *co.*, S. Wales; coal, iron, steel, agr.; a. 546 sq. m.; p. (1966) *436,000.*

Monmouth, *co. t., mun. bor.*, Monmouthshire, at confluence of Rs. Wye and Monnow; mkt. ctr.; tinplate, timber, crushed limestone, wrought ironwk.; p. (estd. 1967) *6,010.*

Monmouth, *t.*, Ill., U.S.A.; mnfs., coal; p. (1960) *10,372.*

Monnow, *R.*, Monmouth and Hereford, Eng.; trib. of R. Wye; length 28 m.

Monongahela, *R.*, W. Va., U.S.A.; joins Allegheny R. at Pittsburgh to form Ohio R.

Monongahela City, Penns., U.S.A.; mining, natural gas; p. (1960) *8,388.*

Monopoli, *spt.*, Apulia, Italy; oil, wine, fruit, flour tr.; p. *26,725.*   [p. *18,625.*

Monreale, *t.*, Sicily, Italy; cath.; fruit, almonds;

Monroe, *c.*, La., U.S.A.; cotton ctr., natural gas, paper, printing ink; p. (1960) *52,219.*

Monroe, *t.*, Mich., U.S.A.; paper, machin.; p. (1960) *22,963.*   [p. (1960) *10,882.*

Monroe, *t.*, N.C., U.S.A.; marble quarries; mftg.;

Monrovia, *cap., spt.*, Liberia, Africa; at mouth of R. St. Paul; exp. rubber, palm oil; p. estd. (1965) *81,000.*

Mons, *t.*, Belgium; on R. Trouville; cath.; coal, cotton, rayon, iron, engin., glass, brewing, radios, aluminium ware; H.Q. of NATO (SHAPE) nearby at Casteau; p. (1962) *27,062.*

Monserrat or Montserrat, *mtn.*, Spain; alt. 4,000 ft.

Monsummano, *t.*, Italy; N.W. of Florence; health resort; some mnfs.; p. *9,125.*

Montagnana, *t.*, Italy; p. *12,100.*

Mont Blanc, *mtn.*, Alps; on confines of Italy and France; alt. 15,782 ft.; longest road tunnel in world (opened to traffic 1965) linking Courmayeur (Italy) and Chamonix (France), length 7½ m.

Mont Cenis Pass, W. Alps; on bdy. between France and Italy; approached from W. by Isère–Arc valleys, from E. by Dora Riparia; alt. 6,876 ft.

Mont Cenis Tunnel, W. Alps; on bdy. between France and Italy; carries main rly. from Lyons to Turin under Col de Fréjus; approached from W. by Isère–Arc valleys, from E. by Dora Riparia; opened 1871; length 7½ m.

Mont-d'Or, *mtns.*, France; highest peak, 6,188 ft.

Mont Genèvre, *mtn.*, Cottian Alps, France; alt. 6,100 ft.   [power project.

Mont St. Michel, *I.*, N. France; tourist ctr; tidal

Montalcino, *t.*, Italy; industl.; p. *9,925.*

Montana, *st.*, U.S.A.; cap. Helena; Rocky Mtns.; copper, silver, gold, lead; pastoral, agr.; a. 147,138 sq. m.; p. (1970) *682,133.*

Montargis, *t.*, Loiret, France; hosiery, chemicals, rubber; p. (1962) *17,645.*

Montauban, *t.*, Tarn-et-Garonne, France; on R. Tarn; cath.; silk, agr. produce, wines; p. (1962) *43,401.*

Montbéliard, *t.*, Doubs, France; S. of Belfort; watch, textiles, mngs., agr. tr.; p. (1968) *23,908.*

Montceau-les-Mines, *t.*, Saône-et-Loire, France; coal, textiles, metal-working; p. (1962) *29,364.*

Montclair, *t.*, N.J., U.S.A.; residtl. suburb of New York; paper goods mnfs.; p. (1960) *43,129.*

Mont-de-Marsan, *t.*, Landes, France; p. (1962) *23,254.*

Monte Bello Is., *gr.*, off N.W. cst., Australia; about 85 m. N. of pt. of Onslow; first British atomic weapon exploded here 3 Oct. 1952.

Monte Carlo, *t.*, Monaco; tourist resort, casino; p. (1961) *9,516.*

Monte Corno, *mtn.*, Italy; in Central Apennines; alt. 9,583 ft.

Monte Gargano, *peninsula*, S. Italy; projects into Adriatic Sea nr. plain of Foggia; formed by limestone plateau, alt. over 3,000 ft.; pasture on upper slopes, woodland on lower slopes; a. approx. 400 sq. m.   [p. *5,575.*

Monte Maggiore, *t.*, Sicily, Italy; agr. interests;

Monte Perdu, *mtn.*, Pyrenees, Spain; alt. 10,997 ft.

Monte Rosa, *gr.*, Pennine Alps, on border of Italy and Switzerland; highest peak 15,203 ft.

Monte Rotondo, *highest min.*, Corsica; alt. 9,071 ft.

Monte Sant-Angelo, *t.*, Italy; pilgrim ctr.; p. *24,550.*

Monte Viso, *mtn.*, Cottian Alps, Italy; alt. 12,605 ft.

Montecristi, *t.*, W. Ecuador; Panama hats; copra mkt.; p. (estd. 1962) *4,000.*

Montefrio, *t.*, Spain; W. of Granada; cas.; alcohol, soap, cotton mnfs.; p. *12,000.*

Montégnée, *commune*, Liége prov., E. Belgium; mftg. sub. Liége; p. (1962) *11,503.*

Montego Bay, *spt.*, Jamaica; famous for its beauty; p. (1947) *11,547.*

Monteleone di Calabria, *t.*, Italy; cas.; p. *15,675.*

Montélimar, *t.*, Drôme, France; nr. R. Rhône; bricks, tiles, "nougat," coal-mining; p. (1954) *16,632.*

Montenegro, *dist.*, Jugoslavia; agr., pastoral; cap. Cetinje; a. 13,837 sq. m.; p. (1960) *489,000.*

Montereau-faut-Yonne, *t.*, Seine-et-Marne, France; on R. Seine; agr. tools, footwear, brick mftg.; p. (1962) *14,121.*

Monterey, *c.*, Cal., S. of San Francisco; resort of artists and writers; impt. sardine indus., fruit, and veg. canneries; p. (1960) *22,618.*

Monteria, *t.*, cap. Cordoba, Colombia, S. America; tobacco, cacao, cotton, sugar; p. (1959) *96,150.*

Monterrey, *t., cap.*, Nuevo León, Mexico; cath.; textiles, brewing, ironwks., minerals; thermoelec. plant; sheet metal; p. (1960) *596,993.*

Montespertoli, *mkt. t.*, Italy; S.W. Florence; p. *11,850.*   [p. *15,300.*

Montevarchi, *t.*, Italy; on R. Arno; industl.;

Montevideo, *spt., cap.*, Uruguay; on N. cst. of La Plata estuary; univ.; livestock prod. mnfs. and exp.; p. (estd. 1956) *922,885.*

Montezuma, *t.*, Ga., U.S.A.; mkt. for winter mkt. garden produce, cottonseed oil; p. (1950) *2,921.*

Montgomery, *co.*, N.E. Wales; cap. Montgomery; a. 797 sq. m.; p. (1966) *44,000.*

Montgomery, *co. t., mun. bor.*, Montgomery, N.E. Wales; in upper Severn valley, 8 m. N.E. of Newtown; agr. mkt.; p. (1961) *970.*

Montgomery, *c., cap.*, Ala., U.S.A.; cotton, timber, fertilisers; comm. ctr.; rly. wks.; p. (1960) *134,393.*

Montgomery, *t.*, W. Punjab, Pakistan; livestock; leather, cotton; p. (1961) *25,100.*

Montichiari, *commune*, Lombardy, N. Italy; mftg.; p. *11,650.*

Montignies-sur-Sambre, *t.*, Belgium; coal, ironwks.; p. (1962) *24,092.*

Montigny-lès-Metz, *commune*, Moselle, France; residtl. sub. Metz; botanic gardens; p. (1954) *19,271.*

Montilla, *commune*, S. Spain; agr., wines; textiles, pottery, soap; p. (1957) *24,002.*

Montluçon, *t.*, Allier, France; on R. Cher; agr. ctr.; machin., cutlery, chemicals, mirrors; p. (1962) *58,855.*   [*16,682.*

Montmorency, *t.*, Val d'Oise, France; p. (1962)

Montoro, *c.*, S.W. Spain; on R. Guadalquivir; agr. prod., olive oil; p. (1957) *15,396.*

Montpelier, *c.*, cap. Vt., U.S.A., on Winooski R.; varied inds.; p. *8,000.*

Montpellier, *t.*, cap. Hérault, France; univ., wines, fruit, silk, chemicals, agr.; p. (1968) *161,910.*

Montreal, c., spt., Quebec, Canada; at confluence of Ottawa and St. Lawrence Rs.; caths., univ.; major industr., comm. and fin. ctr.; extensive harbour installations; diverse mnfs.; lgst. c. and spt. in Canada; p. (1966), 2,436,817.

Montreuil-sous-Bois, t., Seine, France; mnfs., fruit; p. (1962) 92,316.

Montreux, t., Switzerland; on L. Geneva; health resort; p. 19,000.

Montrose, spt., burgh, Angus, Scot.; on E. cst. at mouth of S. Esk R.; chemicals, and rope wks., linen, fisheries; p. (1961), 10,702.

Montrouge, t., Seine, France; paper, perfumes precision tools; p. (1962) 45,324.

Montserrat, I., Leeward Is., W.I.; limes, fruits, carrots and onions; ch. t. Plymouth; a. 39 sq. m.; p. (estd. 1967) 14,500. [p. (1960) 1,060.

Montville, t., S.E. Conn., U.S.A.; paper, textiles.

Monza. t., Lombardy, Italy; cath.; comm., textiles, leather, hats; p. (1961) 84,445.

Moonie, t., Queensland, Australia; 200 m. W. of Brisbane; oilfields; pipeline to Lytton, at mouth of Brisbane R.

Moorea, one of the ch. Is., the Society gr., Pac. Oc.; a. 50 sq. m.; p. (1962) 4,147.

Moorfoot Hills, range, Peebles and Midlothian, Scot.; alt. 2,136 ft.

Moorhead, t., W. Minn., U.S.A.; potatoes, dairying, poultry; p. (1960) 22,934. [Bay.

Moose R., Ontario, Canada; flows to James

Moosehead, L., Me., U.S.A.; source of Kennebec R.; 35 m. long, 10 m. wide.

Moose Jaw, c., Saskatchewan, Canada; rly. junction; agr. ctr.; agr. implements, oil refining; p. (1961) 33,206.

Moquegua, dep., S. Peru; cotton, maize, fruit; cap. M.; a. 5,549 sq. m.; p. (1961) 51,315.

Moquegua, t., Peru; wines; p. (1961) 3,385.

Mora, t., Spain; industl.; p. (1957) 10,844.

Moratalla, t., Spain; N.W. of Murcia; cloth, alcohol, wines; p. 14,536.

Moratuwa, t., Ceylon; p. (1946) 50,700.

Morava, R., Czechoslovakia and Austria; trib. of R. Danube; length 212 m.

Morava, R., Jugoslavia; rises in Crna Gora (S. of Dinaric Alps), flows N. into R. Danube 50 m. below Belgrade; valley used by trunk rly. from Belgrade to Thessaloniki (Salonika) and Athens, Sofia and Istanbul (Constantinople); length approx. 350 m.

Moravia, old prov., Czechoslovakia; agr., forestry, coal, textiles; p. inc. Bohemia (1962) 9,566,753.

Moray, co., N.E. Scot.; cereals, fisheries, distilling, woollens; co. burgh, Elgin; a. 482 sq. m.; p. (1961) 49,156.

Moray Firth, arm of N. Sea; on Scottish E. cst., between Ross and Cromarty, and Nairn, Moray cos.

Morbihan, dep., France; on Bay of Biscay; agr. (apples), mining, fishing; cap. Vannes; a. 2,739 sq. m.; p. (1968) 540,474.

Morceux, t., Landes, France; p. (1962) 4,166.

Mordov A.S.S.R., U.S.S.R.; between Rs. Oka and Volga; agr.; a. 9,843 sq. m.; p. (1959) 1,000,000.

Morea, see Peloponnisos.

Morecambe and Heysham, t., mun. bor., N. Lancs. Eng.; on S. shore of Morecambe Bay; Morecambe, holiday resort; Heysham, port for N. Ireland and oil refinery; nuclear power sta. to be built on cst. S. of Morecambe; p. (estd. 1967) 40,810.

Moree, t., N.S.W., Australia; in agr. and grazing region; mkt.; p. (1966) 7,774.

Morelia, c., cap., Michoatán, Mexico; cath.; textiles, sugar; p. (1960) 100,828.

Morelos, inland st., Mexico; mtns., forested; cap. Cuernavaca; a. 1,916 sq. m.; p. (1960) 386,264. [(1968) 221,173.

Möre Og Romsdal, co., Norway; a. 5,812 sq. m.;

Moret-sur-Loing (Moret les Sablons), t., 40 m. S. of Paris on picturesque R. Loing.

Morez, t., S.E. Jura, France; precision instruments, optical equipment, winter sports.

Morgan, t., R. pt., S. Australia; on R. Murray, where it suddenly turns S. approx. 150 m. from its mouth; handles transhipment of Murray and Darling R. traffic to rail for despatch to Adelaide.

Morgantown, t., W. Va., U.S.A.; coal, oil, gas fields; chemicals, heavy ind.; p. (1960) 22,487.

Morioka, c., N. Honshu, Japan; textiles, ironwks.; p. (1964) 171,000.

Morlaix, spt., Finistère, France; tobacco, paper, brewing, agr.; p. (1962) 20,248.

Morley, t., mun. bor., W.R. Yorks, Eng.; 3 m. S.W. of Leeds; woollens, coal-mining, stone quarrying, tanning; p. (estd. 1967) 43,790.

Morocco, ind. sovereign st., since March 1956 (formerly French and Spanish prots.) N.W. Africa; cap. Rabat; chief ts. Casablanca, Marrakesh, Tangier, Fez, Meknès, Tetuan, Oujda, Safi, Mina Hassan Tani; agr., forest, and animal prod.; fruits; phosphates, manganese, iron ore, lead, zinc; coal, petroleum. sugar refining; a. 180,000 sq. m.; p. (estd. 1968) 14,580,000.

Morogoro, t., Tanzania, E. Africa; on E. edge of Central African plateau, alt. approx. 3,000 ft., 110 m. by rail W. of Dar-es-Salaam; ctr. of sisal- and cotton-growing a.

Morón, t., Venezuela; on Caribbean cst. nr. Puerto Cabello; industl.; natural gas.

Morón de la Frontera, commune, S.W. Spain; olives; iron ore; marble; p. (1957) 30,137.

Morotai I., N. of Molucca, Indonesia.

Morpeth, mun. bor., Northumberland, Eng.; nr. Newcastle; coal-mining, iron; p. (estd. 1967) 14,340.

Morrinsville, t., N.I. N.Z.; agr. ctr.; p. (1961) 4,111.

Morriston, vil., Glamorgan, S. Wales; on R. Tawe, 2 m. N.E. of Swansea; zinc smelting and refining steel.

Morristown, t., N.J., U.S.A.; holiday ctr., fruit; p. (1960) 17,712.

Morrisville, bor., Penns., U.S.A.; on Delaware R.; rubber prod.; p. (1960) 7,790.

Morro Velho, mng-dist., Minas Geraes, Brazil; in Serra do Espinhaço, 10 m. S. of Belo Horizonte; deep rich gold-mines; ch. t. Nova Lima.

Mors, I., N. Jutland, Denmark; a. 138 sq. m.; p. (1960) 26,766.

Morven, mtn., Aberdeen, Scot.; nr Ballater; alt. 2,862 ft. [alt. 2,313 ft.

Morven, mtn., Caithness, Scot.; nr. Berriedale;

Morwell, t., Victoria, Australia; industl.; coal mng.; p. (1966) 16,578.

Moscow, c., R.S.F.S.R.; cap., U.S.S.R.; on R. Moskva; caths., univ., Kremlin, palaces; leading cultural, political and comm. ctr.; textiles, steel. engin., oil refining, chemicals; p. (1970) 7,061,000.

Moscow Sea (Ucha Reservoir), artificial L., R.S.F.S.R.; created behind dam on R. Volga at Ivankovo; supplies water to Moscow, maintains level on Moscow-Volga Canal, and supplies water to 8 hydro-elec. power-stas.; a. 127 sq. m.

Moscow-Volga Canal, R.S.F.S.R.; links R. Volga at Ivankovo with Khimki suburb of Moscow; forms part of Leningrad-Moscow inland waterway; opened 1937; length 80 m.

Moselle, dep., N.E. France; cap. Metz; a. 2,403 sq. m.; p. (1968) 971,314.

Moselle. R., France and Germany; trib. of R. Rhine; length 328 m.; canalised between Thionville and Coblenz (168 m.).

Moshi, t., Tanzania, E. Africa; on S.E. flank of Mt. Kilimanjaro; ctr. of coffee-growing dist. at alt. approx. 5,500 ft.; despatches coffee by rail to Tanga or Mombasa. [249 m.

Moskva, R., U.S.S.R.; trib. of R. Oka; length

Mosonmagyaróvár, t., Hungary; aluminium wks.; agr. machin.

Moss, spt., Norway; pulp, paper, machin., textile inds.; p. (1968) 23,693.

Mossamedes, spt., Angola, Africa; exp. rubber; fishing, fertilisers; p. 8,977.

Mossel Bay, spt., C. Prov., S. Africa; oysters, whaling; wool, cereals; p. (1960) 12,178 inc. 4,333 whites. [steel; p. 6,000.

Mossend, t., Lanark, Scot.; nr. Glasgow; iron and

Mossgiel, t., S.I., N.Z.; woollens; p. (1961) 6,463.

Mossley, mun. bor., Lancs, Eng.; 3 m. E. of Oldham; mkt. t., textiles, iron and steel; p. (estd. 1967) 9,630.

Most, t., ČSSR.; lignite, chemicals; Druzhba crude oil pipeline extended to chemical wks.; p (1961) 44,490.

Mostar, t., Herzegovina, Jugoslavia; on R. Naretva; bauxite, lignite, aluminium plant; p. (1960) 43,000.

Mosul, t., Iraq; on R. Tigris; comm. ctr., impt. during crusades; agr. prod., livestock, textiles; p. (1960) 341,000.

Motala, t., on L. Vättern, Sweden; radio sta.; engin., woollen goods; p. (1961) 27,148.

Motherwell and Wishaw, *burgh*, Lanark, Scot.; in Clyde valley, 15 m. S.E. of Glasgow; coal, iron, steel, machin., engin., silk, nylon; p. (1961) 72,799. [p. (1957) 23,420.

Motril, *spt.*, Spain; minerals, cotton, sugar, fruits;

Mottarone, Monte, *mtn.*, Italy, between L. Maggiore and L. Orta; alt. 4,892 ft.

Moulins, *t.*, cap. Allier, France; on R. Allier; cath., ruined château; timber wks., brewing; p. (1954) 24,437. [timber; p. (1955) 101,720.

Moulmein, *spt.*, Burma on R. Salween; rice,

Moundsville. *c.*, W. Va., U.S.A.; on Ohio R.; coal, glass, zinc; p. (1960) 15,163.

Mount Adams, *peak*, White Mtns., N.H., U.S.A.; alt. 5,679 ft.

Mount Albert, *bor.*, Auckland, N.Z.; p. (1966) 25,721. [fruit.

Mount Barker, *t.*, extreme S.W. of W. Australia;

Mount Carmel, *bor.*, Penns., U.S.A.; on Wabash R.; coal-mng., clothing mftg.; p. (1960) 10,760.

Mount Clemens, *t.*, Mich., U.S.A.; on Clinton R.; mineral springs; p. (1960) 21,016.

Mount Desert, *I.*, Me., U.S.A.; a. 100 sq. m.: mtns.: summer resort. [18,392.

Mount Eden, *bor.*, Auckland, N.Z.; p. (1966)

Mount Goldsworthy *t.*, W. Australia; new t. being developed in iron ore mng. a.

Mount Gambier, *t.*, S. Australia; pastoral, agr. ctr.; timber, dairy prod. processing; p. (1966) 17,146.

Mount Holly, *t.*, N.J., U.S.A.; textiles, clothes, leather; p. (1960) 13,271.

Mount Isa, *t.*, W. Queensland, Australia; in Selwyn Range 80 m. W. of Cloncurry; copper mng.; p. (1966) 16,713.

Mount Kennedy, *mtn.*, Yukon, 3 m. E. of Mt. Hubbard on Alaskan border; alt. 14,000 ft.

Mount Lofty Range, *mtn. range*, S. Australia; lies immediately E. of Adelaide approx. 5 m. from St. Vincent G.; forms barrier to routes leaving Adelaide N.E. and E.; lower slopes support vineyards and outer suburbs of Adelaide; rises to over 3,000 ft.

Mount McKinley, highest in N. America (20,300 ft.) in Alaskan national park.

Mount Pleasant, *t.*, Mich., U.S.A.; oil, lumber, sugar-beet, dairy prod.; p. (1960) 14,875.

Mount Prospect, *t.*, Ill., U.S.A.; p. (1960) 18,906.

Mount Roskill, *bor.*, Auckland, N.Z.; p. (1966) 33,472.

Mount Tom Price *t.*, W. Australia; new t., being developed in iron ore mng. a.

Mount Vernon, *c.*, Ill., U.S.A.; timber, flour, woollens, coal; p. (1960) 15,566.

Mount Vernon, *c.*, N.Y., U.S.A.; on Bronx R.; sub. of N.Y.; residtl.; p. (1960) 76,010. Takes its name from George Washington's house on the Potomac. in Virginia, 15 m. S. of Washington, D.C.; varied inds., incl electronic equipment.

Mount Vernon, *c.*, Ohio, U.S.A.; on Kokosing R.; timber goods, mnfs.; p. (1960) 13,284.

Mount Wellington, *bor.*, Auckland, N.Z.; p. (1966) 18,357.

Mountain Ash, *urb. dist.*, Glamorgan, Wales; in narrow valley 3 m. S.E. of Aberdare; coal; p. (1961) 29,590.

Mountain Province, *prov.*, N. Luzon, Philippines; rice, metal working; copper; h.e.p. at Ivogon; a. 5,458 sq. m.; p. 296,874.

Mountain View, *t.*, Cal., U.S.A.; p. (1960) 30,889.

Mountmellick, *t.*, *rural dist.*, Laoighis, Ireland; mkt. tanning, malting; p. (rural dist. 1961) 22,596. [wide; fishery grounds.

Mount's Bay, *inlet*, S. cst. Cornwall, Eng.; 20 m.

Mourenx, *t.*, S.W. Aquitaine, France; nr. Lacq; new town in oil dist.; p. (1966) 8,660. [2,796 ft.

Mourne Mtns., Down, N. Ireland; highest peak,

Mouscron, *t.*, Belgium; cotton- and wool-weaving; p. (1962) 36,595.

Mouse or Souris, R. Canada and U.S.A.; trib. of Assiniboine R.; length 500 m.

Moy, R., Mayo and Sligo, Ireland; length 35 m.

Mozambique, *Portuguese col.*, E. Africa; sugar, oil-nuts, cotton, maize; oil refining, cement; rich deposits of coal, iron ore, and semi-precious stones near Namapa; cap. Lourenço Marques; a. 298,000 sq. m.; p. (estd. 1968) 7,274,000.

Mozambique Channel, *strait*, Indian Ocean; separates Malagasy from mainland of Africa; length 1,000 m., width from 250 to 600 m.

Mozambique Current, *ocean current*, flows N. to S. along E. cst. of Mozambique and Natal, E. Africa; relatively warm water.

Mozdok, *t.*, R.S.F.S.R.; on Rostov–Baku rly.; oil pipe-lines; p. 14,008.

Much Hoole, Lancs.; S.W. Preston, Eng.; site for nuclear power sta.

Muck, *I.*, Inner Hebrides, Scot.; S. of Eigg.

Mühlhausen, *t.*, Erfurt, E. Germany; on R. Unstrut; textiles, machin., tobacco; p. (1963) 45,362.

Mukachevo (Munkács), *t.*, Ukrainian S.S.R.: furniture, textiles, tobacco; p. (1956) 44,000.

Mukden (Shenyang), *c.*, *cap.*, Liaoning, N.E. China; on Hun-Ho in narrowest part of lowland with hilly country on both sides; impt. rly. junction with main routes N. to Harbin and Trans-Siberian Rly., S. to Peking, Luta and into Korea; gr. comm. and educational ctr.; machin, bldg. plant; p. (1956) 2,290,000.

Mula, *t.*, Spain; tr. ctr.; p. (1957) 15,127.

Mulde, *R.*, Germany; trib. of R. Elbe; length 130 m.

Mulhacén, *mtn.*, Sierra Nevada range, Spain; alt. 11,420 ft. (highest peak Europe, outside Alps).

Mülheim-an-der-Ruhr, *t.*, N. Rhine–Westphalia, Germany; on R. Ruhr; cas.; coal-mining, iron, steel, tobacco, engin., elec., oil refining; airport; p. (1968) 189,919.

Mulhouse, *t.*, Haut-Rhin, France; textiles, machin.; p. (1968) 116,336.

Mull, *I.*, Argyll, Scot., included in Hebrides; a. 357 sq. m.; granite, pastoral farming; ch. t. Tobermory.

Mull of Galloway, S. point of Wigtown, Scot.

Mullet, The, *peninsula*, W. cst. Mayo, Ireland.

Mullingar, *co. t.*, Westmeath, Ireland; on Brosna R.; mkt.; agr. ctr., tanning; p. (1966) 6,453.

Multan, *div.*, W. Punjab, Pakistan; ch. t., Multan; p. (1961) 6,953,000.

Multan, *t.*, W. Punjab, Pakistan; on R. Chenab; carpets, silks, pottery; steel, thermal sta.; gas pipeline to Lyallpur; p. (1961) 358,000.

Muncie, *t.*, Ind., U.S.A.; on White R.; iron, steel, glass and paper; p. (1960) 68,603.

Münden, *t.*, Germany; on R. Weser; picturesque medieval t.; cas.; leather and rubber goods tobacco fact.; p. 22,000.

Munhall, *t.*, Penns., U.S.A.; p. (1960) 17,312.

Munich (München), *c.*, cap. Bavaria, Germany; on R. Isar; univ., cath., palace, museum, " English Garden "; comm. ctr.; scientific instruments; machin., brewing, textiles, tobacco, chemicals. elec. engin.; film studios; route ctr.; p. (1968) 1,279,405.

Münster, *c.*, N. Rhine–Westphalia, Germany; cath., univ., cas.; leather, metal machin., rly. junction; p. (1968) 203,461.

Munster, *prov.*, S.W. Ireland; includes cos. Waterford, Kerry, Cork, Limerick, Clare Tipperary; a. 9,475 sq. m.; p. (1966) 969,902.

Muonio, *R.*, part of boundary between Finland and Sweden; flows into G. of Bothnia.

Mur, *R.*, Austria; trib. of R. Drava; length 250 m. [Canada.

Murchison, *C.*, Hall Peninsula, Baffin I.,

Murchison, *R.*, W. Australia; length 800 m.

Murchison, *peak*, Rocky Mtns., B.C., Canada; alt. 13,500 ft.

Murchison Falls, on Victoria Nile, Uganda.

Murcia, *prov.*, S.E. Spain; former kingdom; minerals, cereals, fruit; cap. Murcia; a. 4,369 sq. m.; p (1959) 808,610.

Murcia, *c.*, *cap.*, Murcia, Spain; on R. Segura; cath., univ.; p. (1965) 259,000.

Murfreesboro, *t.*, Tenn., U.S.A.; p. (1960) 18,991.

Murg, *R.*, Germany; trib. of R. Rhine; length 40 m. [m. to desert swamps.

Murgab or Murghab, *R.*, Afghanistan; flows 250

Murmansk, *spt.*, R.S.F.S.R., U.S.S.R.; on Kola-peninsula; ice-free throughout year; engin., elec. power; fishing, shipbldg.; marine power sta. utilising tidal energy projected; p. (1967) 279,000.

Muron, *t.*, R.S.F.S.R.; mkt. gardening; textiles, engin.; p. (1959) 73,000.

Muroran, *spt.*, Hokkaido, Japan; on W. cst.; industl.; iron ore; p. (1965) 161,252.

Murray, *R.*, separates N.S.W. and Victoria, Australia; major R. of continent, length 1,600 m.

Murray, *t.*, N. Utah, U.S.A.; sub. Salt Lake City; lead smelting; p. (1960) 16,806.

Murrumbidgee, *R.*, N.S.W., Australia; trib. of R. Murray; length 1,350 m.

Murshidabad, *t.*, W. Bengal, India; silk, weaving,

ivory carving, gold and silver embroidery; p. (1961) *16,990*.

Murwillumbah, *t.*, N.S.W., Australia; sugar, butter processing ctr.; p. (1966) *7,304*.

Murzuk, *t.*, Libya, N. Africa; in Fezzan Oasis; tr. ctr.; p. *1,000*.

Mus, *t.*, Turkey; W. of L. Van; p. (1960) *12,015*.

Muscat and Oman. *See* Oman.

Muscat, *t.*, *cap.*, Oman, Arabia; on S. cst. of G. of Oman; good harbour; dates, mother-of-pearl; p. (estd. 1962) *6,200*.

Muscatine, *c.*, Iowa, U.S.A.; on Mississippi R.; meat packing, timber ind.; p. (1960) *20,997*.

Muscle Shoals, *rapids*, in Tennessee R., U.S.A.; site of Wilson dam.

Musgrave Range, *mtns.*, on bdy. between S. Australia and N. Terr., Australia; isolated highland in ctr. of continent; arid; rise to over 3,000 ft.

Muskegon, *c.*, Mich., U.S.A.; engin., motor cars, accessories, aeroplane engines; p. (1960) *46,485*.

Muskingum, *R.*, Ohio, U.S.A.; trib. of Ohio R.; length 240 m.

Muskogee, *t.*, Okla., U.S.A.; rly. wks., oil refining, cotton, flour; p. (1960) *38,059*.

Musselburgh, *anc. burgh*, Midlothian, Scot.; on S. Firth of Forth at mouth of R. Esk; wire, cables, nets, twine; paper mkg.; golf course; p. (1961) *17,273*.

Mussel Shell, *R.*, Mont., U.S.A., trib. of Missouri R.

Mussomeli, *t.*, Sicily; agr. interests; p. *12,500*.

Mutankiang (Mudanjiang), *c.*, Heilungkiang prov., China; pulp, paper, machin., flour milling; p. (1953) *151,000*.

Muttra or Mathura, *t.*, Uttar Pradesh, India; on R. Jumna; Hindu ctr.; p. (1961) *125,258*.

Muz Tagh, *mtn. pass*, Karakoram Mtns., E. Turkestan; alt. 18,980 ft.

Muzaffarpur, *t.*, Bihar, India; univ.; p. (1961) *109,480*.

Muzo, *mun.*, central Colombia; emerald-mining; p. (1959) *5,000*.

Muzuntan, *t.*, U.S.S.R.; goldfields nearby.

Mwanza, *t.*, N. Tanzania, E. Africa; pt. on L. Victoria; rly. terminus; shirt-mkg.; p. *6,000*.

Mweelrea, *mtn.*, Mayo, Ireland; alt. 2,688 ft.

Mweru, *L.*, between Congo and Zambia; alt. 3,000 ft.; a. 2,700 sq.m.; lge. fisheries.

Myaungmya, *dist.*, Lower Burma; ch. t. Patanawa; p. *7,773*.

Mycenae, *ancient c.*, N. Argolis, Greece; ruins.

Mykonos, *I.*, N. Cyclades, Greece; p. *4,188*.

Mymensingh. *t.*, Bengal, Pakistan; rice, jute; p. (1961) *53,200*.

Mynyddislwyn, *t.*, *urb. dist.*, Monmouth, Eng.; in narrow valley of W. Ebbw R., 7 m. N.W. of Newport; coal-mng., elec. goods, kerb- and flagstones; p. (1961) *15,433*.

Mynydd-Mawr, *mtn.*, N. Wales; alt. 2,293 ft.

Myslowice, *t.*, Poland; nr. Katowice; rly. junc.; coal, flax mills, bricks; p. (1965) *44,000*.

Mysore, *st.*, S. India; hydro. elec. power; gold, iron and steel, manganese; coffee, tea, cotton; cap. Bangalore; a. 74,210 sq. m.; p. (1961) *23,586,772*.

Mysore, *t.*, Mysore, India; univ.; carpets, comm. ctr.; p. (1961) *253,524*.

Mytishchi, *t.*, R.S.F.S.R., 12 m. N.E. Moscow; lorries, coaches; p. (1967) *110,000*.

Mytilene (Lesbos), *I.*, Greece; in Aegean Sea; highest point 3,080 ft.; olives, figs, lemons, oranges, grapes; antimony and marbles; ch. t. Mytilene; a. 618 sq. m.; p. (1951) *154,683*.

Mzombe, *R.*, Kenya; trib. of Ruaha R.; length 110 m.

Mzymta, *R.*, U.S.S.R.; flows to Black Sea.

N

Naab, *R.*, Bavaria, Germany; joins R. Danube nr. Ratisbon; length 90 m.

Naarden, *c.*, N. Holland, Neth.; nr. Hilversum; arboriculture; ceramics; p. (1967) *17,003*.

Naas, *mkt. t.*, *cap.*, Kildare, Ireland; former cap. Leinster; p. (1966) *4,528*. [*15,000*.

Nabeul, *t.*, Tunisia, N. Africa; winter resort; p.

Nabi Saleh, *I.*, forming part of st. of Bahrein, Arabia; about 2 m. in circumference.

Nablus, *c.*, Jordan; N. of Jerusalem; nr. Old Testament c. of Shechem (Sichem, Sychem), the first Palestinian site mentioned in Genesis; Jacob's Well and Mt. Gerizim adjacent; p. (1961) *45,658*.

Nachod, *t.*, ČSSR.; on R. Mettaj at entrance to Lewin Nachod Pass; Prussian victory over Austrians 1866; cotton spinning, dyeing; p. (1961) *17,848*. [mftg.; p. (1960) *12,674*.

Nacogdoches, *t.*, Texas, U.S.A.; lignite; mkt.;

Naestved, *mkt. t.*, Själland, Denmark; paper, iron, footwear; p. (1960) *19,617*.

Nagaland, *st.*, India (1963); incorporates Naga Hills and Tuengsang; tribal a., formerly parts of Assam; adm. ctr. Kohima; a. 6,366 sq. m.; p. (1961) *369,000*.

Nagano, *c.*, central Honshu, Japan; on R. Sinanogawa, 100 m. S.W. of Niigata; cultural ctr.; silk mftg., reed organs, computers; p. (1965) *172,836*.

Nagaoka, *t.*, N.W. Honshu, Japan; lge. oil production ctr.; p. (1960) *148,254*.

Nagapatinam, *t.*, Tamil Nadu, India; at mouth of R. Vettar; rly. terminus; cotton, tobacco, groundnuts; p. (1961) *59,063*.

Nagasaki, *c.*, *spt.*, Kyushu, Japan; engin., shipbldg., enamelled and lacquer ware; 2nd c. to be destroyed by atomic bomb in Second World War; since rebuilt; p. (1965) *405,479*.

Nagh Hamadi (Nag' Hammâdi), *t.*, Upper U.A.R., N. Africa; on R. Nile 160 m. above Asyût; site of barrage (opened 1930) to regulate Nile flood and ensure irrigation of Girga prov.; barrage carries Cairo–Shellal rly. across Nile; junction for light rly. to Kharga Oasis.

Nagina, *t.*, Uttar Pradesh, India; sugar; p. (1961) *30,427*.

Nagoya, *t.*, Owari, Honshu, Japan; thriving cap.; gr. tr., ch. ceramic ind. ctr., cotton and silk wks.; oil refining; p. (1970) *2,034,022*.

Nagpur, *t.*, Maharashtra, India; univ.; Hindu temples; salt, grain, cotton; p. (1961) *643,659*.

Nagy Banya, *mining t.*, Romania; gold, silver, lead. Bega.

Nagyenyed, *t.*, Transylvania, Romania; on R. Maros; wood carving, educational ctr., famous for wine in Middle Ages.

Nagykanizsa, *t.*, Hungary; distilling, milling; glasswks., machin.; p. (1962) *34,491*.

Nagykikinda, *t.*, Torontál, Jugoslavia; flour and fruit ctr. [*25,250*.

Nagykoros, *mkt. t.*, Hungary; wine; p. (1962)

Naha, *spt.*, Ryuku Is., Japan; U.S.A. control; mkt., textiles; U.S.A. air base; p. (1950) *44,779*.

Nahe, *R.*, Germany, flows 69 m. to R. Rhine, nr. Bingen. [fertilisers; p. (1961) *8,877*.

Nahorkatiya, N.E. Assam, India; oil-fields;

Nailsworth, *t.*, *urb. dist.*, Gloucester, Eng.; in Cotswold Hills, 4 m. S. of Stroud; woollens; p. (1961) *3,613*.

Nain, *c.*, Iran; noted for very fine carpets; p. (1967) *40,289*.

Nairn, *mar. co.*, Scot., on Moray F. between Moray and Inverness; much moorland; farming, quarries, fishing; a. 200 sq. m.; p. (1961) *8,421*.

Nairobi, *c.*, *cap.*, Kenya. E. Africa; 327 m. from Mombasa; univ.; Uganda Rly. ctr.; lt. inds.; big-game shooting; p. (1962) *266,700*.

Naivasha, *L.*, Kenya; located on floor of Gr. African Rift Valley; alt. 6,000 ft.

Najibabad, *t.*, Uttar Pradesh, India; tr. in timber, sugar, metal mnfs.; p. (1961) *34,310*.

Nakhichevan, *t.*, Azerbaydzhan S.S.R.; salt mines in a.; food and wine inds.; p. (1959) *25,000*.

Nakhodka, *t.*, R.S.F.S.R.; pt. on Sea of Japan, 45 m. E. of Vladivostok; pt. of call for foreign ships; new town 1950; p. (1959) *63,000*.

Nakhon Ratchasima, *t.*, Thailand; copper mkt.; p. (1960) *42,218*.

Nakhornsri-Ayuthaya, *t.*, Thailand; 42 m. N. of Bankok; temples; p. (1960) *32,368*.

Nakuru, *t.*, Kenya rift valley (6,024 ft.), E. Africa; protected bird sanctuary (flamingoes) on L. Nakuru; wool processing, fertilisers; p. (1962) *37,900*.

Nakshov, *spt.*, Laaland I., Denmark; sugar refining; p. (1960) *16,639*.

Nalchik, *t.*, R.S.F.S.R.; N. Caucasus; p. (1967) *114,000*.

Namaqualand, *region*, south west cst. of Africa; divided by Orange R. into Great N. in S.W. Africa, and Little N. in Cape Province, Rep of, S. Africa; semi-arid; a. 100,000 sq. m.; copper. diamonds.

Namangan, *industl. t.*, Uzbekistan, S.S.R.; on the Syr Daria; textiles, leather; p. (1967) *154,000*.

Nam Dinh, *impt. tr. t.*, N. Vietnam, nr. mouth of Red R.; p. *25,000.*

Namibia. *See* South-West Africa.

Nam Ngum, in Mekong R. a.; hydro-electric power plant projected.

Namrup, *t.*, Assam, India; fertilisers.

Namoi, *R.*, in N.S.W., Australia; trib. of Darling R.; 270 m. [p. *5,000.*

Nampula, *ch. t.*, Mozambique, Port. E. Africa:

Namsos, *spt.*, central Norway; on Folda Fjord lumber, fish canning; textiles; copper; p. (1961) *5,269.*

Namur, *prov.*, Belgium; bordering on France; collieries, iron ore, woodland; a. 1,413 sq. m.; p. (1968) *381,578.*

Namur, *fortfd. c.*, Belgium; at confluence of Meuse and Sambre Rs.; p. (1962) *32,396.*

Nanaimo, *c.*, *pt.*, B.C., Canada; on Vancouver I.; timber and allied inds.; fisheries; harbour; boating and yachting; tourism; p. (1966) *15,188*; Greater N., *38,000.*

Nanchang, *c.*, Kiangsi, China; on Kan R.; major transportation and industl. ctr.; textiles, machin., chemicals, paper; dates from Sung dynasty (12th cent.); p. (1963) *398,000.*

Nancheng, *see* Hanchung.

Nancy, *ch. t.*, Meurthe-et-Moselle, France; old cap. Lorraine; gr. industl. activity, metals, cottons, woollens, chemicals, embroidery; p. (1968) *123,428.*

Nanda Devi, *mtn.*, Uttar Pradesh, India; alt. 25,645 ft.; first climbed by British team, 1936.

Nanded, *t.*, Maharashtra, India; on R. Godovari; muslins and tr. ctr.; p. (1961) *81,087.*

Nanga Parbat, *mtn.*, N.W. Kashmir, India, in W. Himalayas; alt. 26,660 ft.

Nanking (Nanjing), *gr. c.*, Kiangsu, China; on Yangtze R.; cap. during Kuomintang régime, 1928–49; famous seat of learning; cotton cloth, silk, ink; contains tombs of founders of the Ming dynasty; road–rail bdge. over lowest reaches of Yangtse R. opened 1.10.1969; p. (estd. 1952) *1,020,000.*

Nanling (Nanshan), *mtns.*, S. China; form divide between Rs. flowing N. to Yangtze R. and S. to Si R.; crossed by historic Cheling and Meiling Passes; alt. mainly below 6,000 ft.

Nanning, *c.*, cap. Kwangsi, China; on Yu R.; ch. mkt. on S. frontier; p. (1953) *195,000.*

Nan Shan, *mtns.*, Central China; branch range of Kunlun; between Yangtze and Si R. basins.

Nanterre, *t.*, Seine, France; nr. Paris; noted for cakes; aluminium mftg.; p. (1962) *83,528.*

Nantes, *t.*, cap. Loire-Atlantique, France; on R. Loire; univ.; locomotives, biscuit mftg., wood pulp, bell foundries, machine wks., chemicals, sugar, oil, textiles. stained glass, nursery gardens; p. (1968) *259,208.*

Nanticoke, *t.*, Penns., U.S.A.; on Susquehanna R.; anthracite, canning; p. (1960) *15,601.*

Nantucket, *I.*, Mass., U.S.A.; official W. end of trans-Atlantic sea-crossing; summer resort; fishing; p. (1960) *2,804.*

Nantung (Nantong), *c.*, Kiangsu, China; on N. bank of Yangtze R. estuary 20 m. N.W. of Haimen; cotton; p. (1953) *260,000.*

Nantwich, *mkt. t.*, *urb. dist.*, Cheshire, Eng.; on R. Weaver, 3 m. S.W. of Crewe; brine baths, fox-hunting ctr.; clothing, food prodn.; p. (1961) *10,454.*

Nantyglo and Blaina, *urb. dist.*, Monmouth, Wales; in narrow valley 2 m. N. of Abertillery; coal, iron, footwear, rubber prods.; p. (1961) *10,950.*

Nao, *C.*, E. cst. Spain; opposite Balearic Is.

Napier, *c.*, *cap.*, Hawke's Bay, N.I. N.Z.; exp. frozen meat; p. (1966) *35,072.*

Naples, (Napoli), *c.*, *spt.*, Campania, S. Italy; on Bay of N., at foot of Vesuvius, opposite site of ancient Pompeii; sanctuary of Madonna di Pompeii; grotto of Pozzuoli, Castel del Ovo, grand cath.; votive church of San Francesco di Paola; monastery of San Martino; subject to earthquakes and volcanic eruptions; impt. shipping; mnfs.; macaroni, vermicelli, wine, olive-oil, shipbldg.; p. (1965) *1,236,000.*

Napo, *R.*, Ecuador; trib. of Amazon; length 800 m.

Napoleon, *t.*, N.W. Ohio, U.S.A.; light mnfs.; p. (1960) *6,739.*

Nara, *t.*, Honshu, Japan; S. of Kyoto; shrines and temples, colossal image of Buddha; old cap. of Japan; lacquer ware; p. (1965) *134,577.*

Narbada, *see* Narmada.

Narbeth, *mkt. t.*, *urb. dist.*, Pembroke, Wales; nr. head of Milford Haven; p. (1961) *960.*

Narbonne, *t.*, Aude, France; wines, sulphur. tiles; p. (1962) *35,899.*

Nardo, *t.*, Lecce, Italy; textiles; p. *20,558.*

Narenta, *R.*, Jugoslavia; flowing 140 m. to Adriatic. [length 200 m.

Narew, *R.*, Poland; flows to R. Bug, nr. Warsaw;

Narino, *dep.*, Colombia, S. America; a. 11,545 sq. m.; cap. Pasto; p. (estd. 1959) *628,840.*

Narmada, *R.*, Central India; flowing W. through Madhya Pradesh and Gujarat to G. of Cambay; length 800 m.

Narni, *t.*, Perugia, Italy; linoleum.

Narrabri, *t.*, N.S.W., Australia; 300 m. N. of Sydney; observatory with stellar interferometer (1964); p. (1966) *5,953.* [Rhode I., U.S.A.

Narragansett Bay, *inlet* of the Atlantic off cst. of

Narrandera, *t.*, N.S.W., Australia; on R. Murrumbidgee on N. margin of Riverina dist.; collecting ctr. for wool, mutton, wheat, fruits produced in irrigated a. fringing Murrumbidgee from Narrandera to Hay; p. (1966) *4,897.*

Narrogin, *t.*, W. Australia; p. (1966) *4,864.*

Narva, *t.*, Estonian S.S.R.; founded in 1223 by the Danes; cath.; textile factories, engin.; hydro-elec.; p. (1956) *21,000.*

Narvik, *t.*, N.W. Norway; opposite Lofoten Is.; ice-free throughout year, linked by rly. to impt. iron-ore fields in N. Sweden; exp. iron ore; p. (1960) *13,311.*

Nashua, *c.*, N.H., U.S.A.; cotton, paper, carpets, ironwks.; p. (1960) *39,096.*

Nashville, *c.*, *cap.*, Tenn., U.S.A.; on Cumberland R.; river pt., rly. ctr; fine capitol and other public bldgs.; impt. comm. and educat. ctr.; univs. and colleges; cellophane, rayon, food and tobacco prods., shoes, printing and publishing; p. (1960) *170,874.*

Nasik, *t.*, Maharashtra, India; on R. Godavari; Hindu pilgrim ctr.; metal work, cotton weaving; p. (1961) *131,103.*

Nasirabad, *t.*, Ajmer dist., Rajasthan, India; p. (1961) *24,148.*

Naso, *t.*, nr. Messina, Sicily; industl.; p. *8,000.*

Nassau, *I.*, Cook Is., S. Pac. Oc.; New Zealand terr.; uninhabited.

Nassau, *t.*, cap. Bahamas, W. Indies; all impt. Is. of the Bahamas connected with N. by radio telegraphy; resort; pearls, sponges, fruit; p. (estd. 1965) *55,000.*

Nasser City, rural development at Kom Ombo, N. of Aswan, for resettlement of 50,000 Nubians before formation of Lake Nasser behind the High Dam. [p. *18,400.*

Nässjö, *t.*, S. Sweden; rly ctr.; furniture, textiles;

Natal, *cap.*, Rio Grande do Norte, Brazil; sugar, cotton, salt, carnauba wax, hides; p. (1960) *162,537.*

Natal, *prov.*, Rep. of S. Africa; sub-tropical coastal climate; sugar-cane, tea, cereals; minerals (especially coal); oil discovered at Dannhauser; cap. Pietermaritzburg; a. 33,578 sq. m.; p. (1968) *239,590.*

Natanz, *prov.*, Iran; in hill cty. between Kashan and Isfahan; pears and other fruits.

Natchez, *c.*, Miss., U.S.A.; in rich cotton-growing dist.; p. (1960) *23,791.*

Natchitoches, *t.*, La., U.S.A.; on Red R.; p. (1960) *13,924.* [*28,831.*

Natick, *t.*, Mass., U.S.A.; boots, shoes; p. (1960)

Natick, *t.*, R.I., U.S.A.; cotton, light mnfs.; p. *3,560.*

Naturaliste, C., N.E. Tasmania.

Naturaliste, C., S. of Geographe Bay, W. Australia.

Naucratis, *ancient c.*, between Cairo and Alexandria; excavated by Flinders Petrie and Gardiner.

Naugatuck, *industl. t.*, Conn., U.S.A.; mnfs. rubber, iron castings; p. (1960) *19,511.*

Naumburg, *c.*, Halle, E. Germany; at confluence of Rs. Unstrut and Saale; annual Hussite feast; cath.; textiles, leather, toys, chemicals; p. (1963) *37,905.*

Nauplia, *see* Navplion.

Nauru, *I.*, *indep. sov. st.* (1968); phosphate ind.; world's smallest indep. st.; a. 8 sq. m.; p. (1966) *6,056.*

Nauta, *t.*, Peru; on confluence of Rs. Maranon and Ucayali.

Navan (An Uamh), *urb. dist.*, Meath, Ireland; p. (1961) *3,996.*

Navanagar, *see* Bhavnagar.

Navarino or Neocastro, *spt.*, Greece; on W. cst.

Morea; Turkish–Egyptian fleet destroyed in the harbour by allied English, French and Russians in 1827.

Navarra, *prov.*, *old kingdom*, N. Spain; bounded by the Pyrenees; cap. Pamplona; grain, fruits, olives, wines, cattle-rearing, copper, silver, lead; a. 4,055 sq. m.; p. (1959) *399,033.*

Navasota, *t.*, E. Texas, U.S.A.; mkt., cotton processing mills; p. (1960) *4,937.*

Navsari, *t.*, Gujarat, India; cotton, leather, metalwork; p. (1961) *51,400.*

Naxos, *I.*, Greece; lgst. of the Cyclades; a. 164 sq. m.; famous for wine and fruit.

Nayarit, *st.*, Mexico; a. 10,444 sq. m.; cap. Tepia; p. (1960) *389,929.*

Nazareth, *t.*, Israel; 21 m. S.E. Acre; associations with early life of Christ; p. (1963) *26,400.*

Naze, The, *c.*, S. point of Norway.

Nazilli, *t.*, S.W. Turkey; on R. Menderes; agr., esp. olives; p. (1965) *41,121.*

Ndola, *t.*, Zambia, Central Africa; nr. bdy. with Katanga prov., Congo, 110 m. by rail N. of Kabwe; ctr. of rich copper-mng. a., less impt. lead- and zinc-mng; minerals despatched by rail E. to Beira and W. to Lobito Bay; p. (1964) *108,000.*

Neagh, Lough, *L.*, N. Ireland; lgst freshwater L. in Brit. Is.; a. 153 sq. m.; drained by R. Bann.

Neath, *t.*, *mun. bor.*, Glamorgan, Wales; 6 m. up R. Neath from Swansea Bay; coal, aluminium inds., oil ref.; p. (1961) *30,884.*

Nebit-Dag, *t.*, Turkmen S.S.R.; 95 m. S.E. of Krasnovodsk; ctr. of oil and ozokerite a.; p. (1956) *30,400.*

Nebraska, *st.*, U.S.A.; mainly prairie; cap. Lincoln; farming, meat-packing, oats, wheat, maize, hay, potatoes, sugar-beet, apples, wool, livestock, petroleum, cement, mng., minerals; a. 77,227 sq. m.; p. (1970) *1,468,101.*

Nebraska, *R.*, trib. of Missouri R., U.S.A.

Neckar, *R.*, Germany; rising between the Swabian Jura, nr. Schwenningen, and the Black Forest; through Württemberg–Baden to the Rhine at Mannheim; length 240 m.

Neder Rijn, *R.*, Netherlands; more northerly of two branches of main Rijn; length 40 m.

Needham, *t.*, Mass., U.S.A.; nr. Boston; mnfs.; p. (1960) *25,793.*   p. *1,349.*

Needham Market, *t.*, Suffolk, Eng.; on R. Gipping;

Needles, *gr. of rocks*, jutting out at W. extrem. I. of Wight, Eng.

Neemuch, *t.*, Madhya Pradesh, India; p. (1961) *36,287.*

Neenah, *c.*, Wis., U.S.A.; timber yards, flour and paper mills; summer resort; p. (1960) *18,057.*

Neftyne Kamni, *t.*, built on piles over Caspian Sea for Russian oil workers.

Negapatam, *see* Nagapattinam.

Negev, *reg.*, S. Israel, pioneering a.; natural gas.

Negoiul, *mtn.*, Transylvanian Romania: 8,346 ft.

Negombo, *spt.*, *urb. dist.*, N.W. prov., Ceylon; metal and leather work; p. (1963) *47,028.*

Negotin, *t.*, E. Jugoslavia; on Romanian border; p. *6,633.*

Negril Beach, Jamaica; 25 m. W. of Montego Bay; new resort to further Jamaica's tourist tr.

Negri Sembilan, *st.*, Malaysia; S.W. Malaya; a. 2,580 sq. m.; cap. Seremban; p. (estd. 1966) *503,323.*

Negritos, *t.*, Piura dep., Peru; on cst., 15 m. S. of Talara; impt. oil-field.

Negro, Rio, *prov.*, Argentina; a. 77,610 sq. m.; cap. Viedma; p. (estd. 1960) *204,200.*

Negro Rio, *R.*, Argentina; flows into G. of St. Mathias.

Negro, Rio, Brazil, Colombia, S. America; one of the ch. tribs. of R. Amazon; rises in Colombia, joins the Amazon in N. Brazil.

Negros, *I.*, Philippines; S. of Mindanao; copper, a. 4,905 sq. m.; p. (1960) *1,862,500.*

Nehbandan Range, *mtns.*, E. Persia.

Neheim-Hüsten, *t.*, N. Rhine–Westphalia, Germany; at confluence of Rs. Möhne and Ruhr; lamps, metals, chemicals; p. (1963) *34,700.*

Neikiang (Neijiang), *c.*, Szechwan prov., China; agr. ctr.; p. (1953) *190,000.*

Neilston, *par.*, nr. Glasgow, Renfrew, Scot.; bleachfields, cotton, coal.

Neisse or Nisa, *R.*, tribs. of R. Oder, (1) Western Neisse, now frontier between Poland and Germany to Czechoslovak frontier, (2) Eastern Neisse in E. Silesia.

Neiva, *t.*, Colombia, S. America; on R. Magdalena;

cattle, coffee, panama hats; p. (estd. 1959) *71,170.*

Nejd, *dist.*, Central Arabia; with Hejaz, forms kingdom of Saudi Arabia; mainly desert; impt. oil wells, horses, camels, dates, various fruits; cap. Riyadh: p. *4,000,000* (estimated).

Nellore, *t.*, Andhra Pradesh, India; dyeing; rice; p. (1961) 106,797.

Nelson, *mftg. t.*, *mun. bor.*, Lancs, Eng.; on N. flank of Rossendale 3 m. N.E. of Burnley; cotton, rayon, iron and brick wks., light engin.; p. (estd. 1967) *30,630.*

Nelson, *prov.*, S.I. N.Z.; cap. Nelson; a. 10,870 sq. m.; p. (1961) *74,281.*

Nelson, *c.*, S.I. N.Z.; nr. head of Tasman Bay; fruit packing, timber, cath.; p. (1966) *26,218.*

Nelson, *R.*, Canada; drains L. Winnipeg to Hudson Bay; length (with its gr. trib. the Saskatchewan) 1,450 m.

Nemunas, *R.*, U.S.S.R.; flowing to the Kurisches Haff, S.E. Kaliningrad; length 50 m.

Nenagh, *mkt. t.*, *urb. dist.*, Tipperary, N. Riding, Ireland; p. (1966) *4,542.*

Nene, *R.*, Northants, Eng., rises nr. Naseby and flows 90 m. to the Wash.   [length 450 m.

Neosho. *R.*, Kan., U.S.A.; trib. of Arkansas R.;

Neosho, *t.*, S.W. Mo., U.S.A.; mkt., lumber, agr., lead-mining; p. (1960) *7,452.*

Nepal, *ind. kingdom*, Himalayas; bounded on N. by Tibet, on E. by Sikkim, on S. and W. by India; exp. cattle, hides and skins, opium and other drugs, timber; cigarette and sugar factories at Janakpur and Brijung; cap. Katmandu; a. 54,362 sq. m.; p. (estd. 1969) *10,845,000.*

Nepalgant, *t.*, S.W. Nepal; in the Terai; tr. ctr.; cereals, oilseeds, hides; p. (1961) *15,817.*

Nephin, *mtn.*, Mayo, Ireland; alt, 2,646 ft.

Nepanagar, *t.*, E. Nimar, Madhya Pradesh, India; India's only newsprint plant; p. (1961) *8,780.*

Nerbudda, *see* Narbada.

Nerchinsk, *t.*, R.S.F.S.R.; on Nertcha R., S.E. Siberia; gold, non-ferrous metals; p. (1956) *11,600.*

Ness, Loch, *L.*, Inverness, Scot.; occupies N.E. end of Glenmore; forms link in Caledonian Canal; very deep; 22¾ m. long.

Neston, *t.*, *urb. dist.*, Cheshire, Eng., on N. side of Dee estuary; residtl.; p. (1961) *11,836.*

Nestos, *R.*, see Mesta.

Nesvizh, *t.*, W. Byelorussia, U.S.S.R.; p. *10,000.*

Netherlands, *kingdom*, W. Europe; divided into 11 provinces; bounded by the N. Sea, Germany, and Belgium; ch. cs.: Amsterdam (cap.), Rotterdam (ch. pt.), The Hague (seat of Government), Utrecht, Eindhoven, Haarlem, Groningen; country low-lying, cst. protected by dykes; fertile and productive; agr., butter- and cheese-mkg., mkt. gardening, distilling and various mnfs., shipbldg., machin., tobacco, sugar, diamond-cutting, electronic equipment, electric lamps, motor cars, lorries; Delta plan, lgst. of its kind in world, for sealing off Rhine and Scheldt estuaries of Zeeland and S. Holland by series of great dykes and sea walls, due for completion late 1970s; a. 12,868 sq. m.; p. (estd. 1967) *12,535,307.*

Netherlands Antilles (Curaçao), grs. of Is., Caribbean Sea; off N. cst. Venezuela; consist of Neth. Windward and Leeward Is.; a. 394 sq. m.; cap. Willemstad; p. (1967) *215,000.*

Netze, *see* Notec.

Neubrandenburg, *dist.* E. Germany; mng. and agr.; p. (1963) *650,877.*

Neubrandenburg, *t.*, Neubrandenburg, E. Germany; fibreglass, machin., chemicals; p. (1963) *38,762.*

Neuchâtel, *can.*, Switzerland; mountainous dist., Jura Mtns.; cattle, cheese, chocolate, watches, cutlery, cottons, hosiery; a. 309 sq. m.; p. (1961) *147,633.*

Neuchâtel, *t.*, *cap.*, Neuchâtel, Switzerland; on N.W. shore of Lake N.; watchmkg., jewellery, condensed milk; oil refinery projected nearby; p. (1964) *35,600.*

Neuchâtel, *L.*, Switzerland; at S.E. foot of Jura Mtns. at the W. end of the central Swiss plateau; drains N.E. to R. Aar; length 36 m., width 3–5 m.

Neugersdorf, *t.*, Dresden, E. Germany; ironwks., textiles; p. (1963) *12,083.*

Neuhausen, *commune*, N. Switzerland; aluminium wks. ; p. (1941) *6,355.*

Neuilly-sur-Seine, *sub.*, W. of Paris, France; fine bridge and cas.; p. (1962) *73,315.*

Neumünster, *t.*, Schleswig-Holstein, Germany; N. of Hamburg; tanning, cloth, machin., chemicals; p. (1963) *75,000*.

Neunkirchen, *t.*, Saar, Germany; iron, coal; p. (1963) *46,100*.

Neuquén, *prov.*, Argentina; agr. and stock-raising; a. 37,245 sq. m.; cap. Neuquén; p. (1960) *111,000*.

Neuquen, *t.*, cap. Neuquen Prov., Argentina; fruit farming; p. (1960) *17,500*.

Neu-Ruppin, *t.*, Potsdam, Germany; on L. Ruppin; fire extinguishers, chemicals; p. (1963) *22,102*.

Neusalz, *see* Nowa Sól.

Neusandetz, *see* Nowy Sacz.

Neusatz (Novi Sad), *t.*, Jugoslavia; on R. Danube; formerly a royal free c.; almost destroyed by the Austrians in 1849; literary and comm. ctr.; coal; p. (estd. 1959) *97,000*.

Neuse, *R.*, N.C., U.S.A.; flows to Pamlico Sound; length 300 m.

Neuss, *c.*, N. Rhine–Westphalia, Germany; mnfs. iron goods, textiles, paper; rly. junction; p. (1968) *115,079*.

Neustadt, *see* Wiener-Neustadt.

Neustadt, *t.*, Rhineland-Palatinate, Germany; on R. Haardt; metal, paper, textiles; p. (1963) *30,800*.

Neustrelitz, *t.*, Neubrandenburg, E. Germany; machin.; p. (1963) *28,334*.

Neutitschein, *see* Novy Jičin.

Neutra, *see* Nitra.

Neuwied, *t.*, Rhineland-Palatinate, Germany; on R. Rhine; cas.; ironwk., wood, pumice stone; p. (1963) *26,600*.

Neva, *R.*, R.S.F.S.R.; drains L. Ladoga S.W. via Leningrad to G. of Finland; 40 m. long.

Nevada, *mtn. st.*, U.S.A.; between Utah, Oregon and Idaho, and bounded S. and W. by California; mining: gold, silver, copper, tungsten, gypsum, iron, lead; livestock, agr., timber; tourism; cap. Carson City; a. 110,540 sq. m.; p. (1970) *481,893*.

Nevada, *c.*, Mo., U.S.A.; zinc-mining and smelting; p. (1960) *8,416*.

Nevers, *c.*, cap. Nièvre, France; on R. Loire; cath.; the Roman Noviodunum; porcelain and faience industry; iron goods; farm implements; aircraft; p. (1962) *41,051*.

Neves, *t.*, Rio de Janeiro st., S.E. Brazil; sugar, coffee; p. (1960) *85,741*.

Nevis, *I.*, Leeward Is., W.I.; ch. prod. cotton; ch. t. Charlestown; a. 50 sq. m.; p. *13,000*.

Nevis, Loch, *arm of sea*, off cst. of Inverness, Scot.; 14 m. long.

New Albany, *c.*, Ind., U.S.A.; on R. Ohio; glass, furniture, leather, iron and steel, car bodies; p. (1960) *37,812*.

New Amsterdam, *t.*, Guyana; on Berbice R.; p. (1962) *15,000*.

New Amsterdam, *t.*, Manhattan I., U.S.A., taken by English from Dutch, 1664, and renamed New York.

New Antwerp, *t.*, on Congo R., Congo.

New Bedford, *c.*, *spt.*, Mass., U.S.A.; on estuary of R. Acushnet; whale-fishery ctr.; mnfs. cottons, cordage, glass, shoes; p. (1960) *102,477*.

New Bern, N.C., U.S.A.; tr. in timber, tobacco, cotton; p. (1960) *15,717*.

New Braunfels, *c.*, Texas, U.S.A.; cotton goods, leather; lime; beauty spot; p. (1960) *15,631*.

New Brighton, *t.*, Cheshire, Eng.; at entrance to Mersey estuary; residtl.; resort.

New Brighton, *bor.*, Penns., U.S.A.; coal-mining; p. (1960), *8,397*.

New Brighton, *t.*, S.I., *seaside resort*, nr. Christchurch, New Zealand; p. (1961) *10,219*.

New Britain, *lgst. I.*, Bismarck Archipelago, Papua–New Guinea; a. (with adjacent Is.) 14,600 sq. m.; p. (1957) *100,375* (inc. approx. *3,856* non-indigenous).

New Britain, *c.*, Conn., U.S.A.; iron and brass mnfs.; p. (1960) *82,201*.

New Brunswick, *prov.*, Canada; forest-clad, mtns., many Ls.; lumber, pulp, paper, agr., fishing, canning; lead, zinc, barytes, natural gas; mnfs.; cap. Federiction; combined road and rail tunnel, bridge and causeway link with Prince Edward I. projected (1966–70); a. 28,354 sq. m.; p. (estd. 1969) *626,000*.

New Brunswick, *c.*, N.J., U.S.A.; on Raritan R.; chemicals, motor lorries, motor parts, leather, hosiery and hardware; p. (1960) *40,139*.

New Caledonia, *I.*, *Fr. Col.*, S. Pacific; coffee copra, chrome ore, nickel, iron, manganese; cap Nouméa; a. 8,548 sq. m.; p. (estd. 1965) *89,000*.

New Castle, *t.*, Ind., U.S.A.; steel mnfs., motor parts; p. (1960) *20,349*.

New Castle, *t.*, Penns., U.S.A.; tinplate, glass, steel wire, iron, coal; p. (1960) *44,700*.

New Cumberland, *bor.*, Penns., U.S.A.; tobacco, clothes; p. (1960) *9,257*.

New Delhi, *c.*, cap. India; on Jumna R.; adm. and trade ctr.; textile mills, printing, light inds.; univ.; government house; adjoining is Old Delhi, anc. cap. of Mogul empire; p. *260,272* (incl. Old Delhi, *292,429*). *See* Delhi for p. of Union terr.

New Dongola or Maraka, *t.*, Nubia, Sudan; on R. Nile; p. *10,000*.

New England, the six N.E. Atlantic sts. of U.S.A.: Me., N.H., Vt., Mass., R.I., Conn.

New Forest, *woodland region*, Hants, Eng.; a. 93,000 acres; ch. t. Lyndhurst. [*57,451*.

New Forest, *rural dist.*, Hants, Eng.; p. (1961)

New Galloway, *burgh*, Kirkcudbright, Scot.; on R. Dee; p. (1961) *327*.

New Glasgow, *spt.*, Nova Scotia, Canada; p. (1961) *9,782*.

New Guinea (Australian), *see* Papua–New Guinea.

New Guinea, West, *see* West Irian.

New Hampshire, *st.*, New England, U.S.A., touching the Canadian border; forested and mountainous; agr. and fruit-growing extensively pursued; paper and forest products, textiles, shoes; granite; cap. Concord; ch. t. Portsmouth; principal mftg. ctr. Manchester; a. 9,304 sq. m.; p. (1970) *722,753*.

New Haven, *c.*, *pt.*, Conn., U.S.A.; on New Haven Harbour, inlet of Long I. Sound; Yale Univ.; firearms, clocks, hardware, radiators, rubber goods; meat-packing; p. (1960) *152,048*.

New Hebrides Condominium, *I.*, Pac. Oc.; roughly 500 m. W. of Fiji and 250 m. N.E. of New Caledonia; administered jointly by France and Britain; 3 active volcanoes, on Tanna, Ambrym and Lopevi; earth tremors frequent; forested: meat canning, soap; a. 5,700 sq. m.; p. (estd.) *80,000*.

New Holland, *vil.*, rly. term., ferry pt. for crossing to Hull; on R. Humber, Lincoln, Eng.

New Iberia, *sm. pt.*, La., U.S.A.; fishing, sugar, cotton, rice; timber tr.; p. (1960) *29,062*.

New Ireland, *I.*, Bismarck Archipelago, Papua–New Guinea; a. (with adjacent Is.) 3,800 sq. m.; p. (1957) *36,512* (native), (1954) *713* (non-indigenous).

New Jersey, *Atlantic st.*, U.S.A.; adjoining New York; mixed farming, petroleum-refining, smelting, chemicals, sanitary ware, motor vehicles; glass sand, zinc, iron ore, clay; cap. Trenton; ch. cs.; Newark and Jersey City; a. 7,836 sq. m.; p. (1970) *7,091,995*.

New Kensington, *t.*, Penns., U.S.A.; aluminium ind.; p. (1960) *23,485*.

New Lexington, *t.*, Ohio, U.S.A.; coal, oil and natural gas; p. (1960) *4,514*.

New London, *c.*, *pt.*, Conn., U.S.A.; at mouth of R. Thames; harbour; fishing, engin., machin., silk and woollen wks.; p. (1960) *34,182*.

New Mexico, *st.*, U.S.A.; N. of the Mexican Rep., and S. of Colorado st.; traversed by the Rocky Mtns.; uranium, potash salts, pumice, beryllium, copper, petroleum; agr.: cereals, fruit, vegetables, cotton, livestock; cap. Santa Fé; a. 121,666 sq. m.; p. (1970) *998,257*.

New Milford, *t.*, Milford Haven, Pembroke, Wales.

New Milford, *t.*, N.W. Conn., U.S.A.; dairy prods., tobacco, foundries, textiles, chemicals; p. (1960) *3,023*.

New Mills, *industl. t.*, *urb. dist.*, Derby, Eng.; at W. foot of Pennines 6 m. S.E. of Stockport; textile printing, bleaching and dyeing, rayon, paper, emery and glass-cloth mftg., iron and brass mnfs.; p. (1961) *8,510*.

New Mirpir, *t.*, W. Pakistan; new t. 2 m. from old Mirpur submerged by Mangla Lake on 29 Aug. 1967; planned p. *40,000*.

New Norfolk, *t.*, Tasmania, Australia; hops, apples; p. (1966) *5,775*.

New Orleans, *c.*, *spt.*, La., U.S.A.; on delta of Mississippi R.; the gr. cotton mart of America, and a busy comm. and mftg. ctr.; univ., cult. tr.; p. (1970) *585,787*.

New Philadelphia, *c.*, Ohio, U.S.A.; impt. rly. and canal ctr.; p. (1960) *14,241*.

New Plymouth, *c., spt.*, N.I., N.Z.; on W. cst. at N. foot of Mt. Egmont; sm. oil deposits; ctr. of dairy-farming dist.; p. (1966) *31,843*.

New Providence, *I.*, Bahama Is., W. Indies; contains cap., Nassau; p. (1953) *46,125*.

New Quay, *t., urb. dist.*, Cardigan, Wales; on cst. of Cardigan Bay, 18 m. S.W. of Aberystwyth; p. (1961) *951*.

New Radnor, *rural dist., co. t.*, Radnor, Wales; on slope of Radnor Forest, 6 m. S.W. of Presteign; p. (of dist. 1961) *2,050*.

New River, *artificial aqueduct*, Herts to Islington, London, Eng.; length 36 m.

New Rochelle, *c.*, N.Y., U.S.A.; on Long I. Sound; residtl.; p. (1960) *76,812*.

New Romney, *t., mun. bor.*, Kent, Eng.; nr. S. cst. to E. of Dungeness; one of the Cinque Ports, in the rich agr. dist. Romney Marsh; old harbour silted up by shingle, and now a mile from sea; p. (estd. 1967) *3,620*.

New Ross, *mkt. t., urb. dist.*, Wexford, Ireland; brewing and malting; p. (1966) *4,568*.

New South Wales, *st.*, S.E. Australia; much mineral wealth in tablelands and mtns.; silver, lead, coal, zinc, iron and steel; agr., corn, potatoes, fruit-growing, sheep, wool, cattle, meat; Snowy Mtns. hydroelec. scheme; cap. Sydney; a. 309,433 sq. m. (exclusive of Capital Terr. of Canberra); p. (estd. 1968) *4,430,200*.

New Waterway (Nieuwe Waterweg), *ship canal*, S. Holland, Neth.; connects R. Lek 7 m. below Rotterdam with N. Sea cst. at Hook of Holland.

New Westminster, *t.*, B.C., Canada; at mouth of R. Fraser; former cap. col.; exp. timber, canned salmon; p. (1961) *33,654*.

New York, *st.*, U.S.A.; one of the original sts.; touching Canada on the N., and reaching the Atlantic on the S.; known as the "Empire State"; inc. Long I. and Staten I.; mixed agr., Portland cement, iron ore, stone, sand and gravel, zinc, petroleum, gypsum, titanium concentrate, steel; Albany is the state cap. a. 49,576 sq. m.; p. (1970) *17,979,712*.

New York, *c., spt.*, N.Y., U.S.A.; ch. comm. ctr. of U.S.A. and W. hemisphere; originally founded by Dutch settlers as New Amsterdam on Manhattan I.; gr. portion situated on Long I.; fine parks and bridges, skyscrapers, gd. harbour; world's longest bridge (Verrazano) spans mouth of N.Y. harbour opened 1964; univ.; ch. inds.; cloth textiles, printing and publishing, iron and steel wks., machin., sugarrefining, meat packing, chemicals, leather; p. (1970) *7,771,730*; of Greater N.Y. (1970) *11,410,000*.

New York State Barge Canal (Erie Canal), N.Y. st., U.S.A.; links Tonawanda on Niagara R. with Hudson R. via the Mohawk gap through Appalachian Mtns.; provides through water route from N.Y. to Gr. Lakes; opened as Erie Canal 1825, improved 1918; length 339 m. (with branches 525 m.), depth 12 ft.

New Zealand, *Brit. Dominion*, S. Pac. Oc.; E. of S.E. Australia and Tasmania, just over 1,200 m. from Sydney, N.S.W.; it consists of two main Is., N.I. and S.I. (a. 102,375 sq. m.), Stewart I. (670 sq. m.), Chatham Is. (372 sq. m.), Cook I. and several smaller Is.; the Is. are mountainous and contain numerous Ls., thermal springs and geysers; the scenery being varied and beautiful, and the climate everywhere healthy; there are active and dormant volcanoes in N.I.; cap. Wellington; principal exp.; wool, butter, frozen meat, cheese, hides. skins and pelts; p. (estd. 1969) *2,780,839* (Maori *220,718*) excluding Cook, Niue and Tokelau Is.

Newark, *t.*, Del., U.S.A.; univ.; p. (1960) *11,404*.

Newark, *mkt. t., mun. bor.*, Notts, Eng.; on R. Trent 17 m. N.E. of Nottingham; ball bearings, brewing and malting; p. (estd. 1967) *25,030*.

Newark, *c.*, N.J., U.S.A.; meat packing, printing, elec. goods, paints, chemicals, cars, aircraft, leather; p. (1960) *405,220*.

Newark, *c.*, Ohio, U.S.A.; on R. Licking; rly. carriage wks., mnfs.; p. (1960) *41,790*.

Newark, *t.*, N.Y., U.S.A.; horticulture, glass, light mnfs.; p. (1960) *12,868*.

Newbiggin-by-the-Sea, *t., urb. dist.*, on E. cst., 4 m. N. of Blyth; sm. seaside resort; coal-mining; Northumberland; Eng.; p. (1961) *10,066*.

Newburgh, *burgh*, Fife, Scot.; on S. side of Firth of Tay, 8 m. E. of Perth; p. (1961) *2,079*.

Newburgh, *c.*, N.Y., U.S.A.; on Hudson R.; clothing and machin. mftg.; p. (1960) *30,979*.

Newburn, *t., urb. dist.*, Northumberland, on R. Tyne, 3 m. W. of Newcastle; Eng.; pure graphite for nuclear reactors; p. (1961) *27,879*.

Newbury, *mkt. t., mun. bor.*, Berks, Eng.; on R. Kennet, 17 m. S.W. of Reading; engin., furniture, paper, cardboard boxmaking; p. (estd. 1967) *21,980*.

Newburyport, *c., spt.*, Mass., U.S.A.; on Merrimac R.; boot and shoe factories, comm. and fisheries; p. (1960) *14,004*.

Newcastle, *spt., urb. dist.*, on Dundrum Bay; Down, N. Ireland; resort; p. (1966) *4,336*.

Newcastle, *t.*, W. Natal, S. Africa; coal, iron, steel, wood, grain, hemp; p. (1960) *17,539* inc. *3,212* whites.

Newcastle, Greater, *c.*, N.S.W., Australia; at mouth of R. Hunter; 2nd c. of st.; gr. coal depot of S. hemisphere and leading provincial industl. ctr.; iron and steel, engin., shipbldg., chemicals; p. (1966) *233,967*.

Newcastle Emlyn, *urb. dist.*, Carmarthen, Wales; on R. Teifi; p. (1961) *648*.

Newcastle-under-Lyme, *t., mun. bor.*, Staffs., Eng.; 2 m. W. of Stoke-on-Trent, on Lyme Brook; iron and steel, mng., quarrying, textiles, nonferrous metals, bricks, tiles; p. (estd. 1967) *77,950*.

Newcastle upon Tyne, *c., spt., co. bor.*, Northumberland, Eng.; on N. bank of R. Tyne, 10 m. from the N. Sea; connected by bridges with Gateshead, Durham; great shipbldg. and colly. pt.; univ. cath. many fine public bldgs.; coal-mining, heavy engin., iron and steel, heavy chemicals; p. (estd. 1969) *240,340*.

Newcomerstown, *t.*, E. Ohio, U.S.A.; coal, steel, tinplate, bricks; p. (1960) *4,273*.

Newent, *mkt. t., rural dist.*, Gloucester, Eng.; 8 m. S. of Ledbury; p. (rural dist. 1961) *3,724*.

Newfoundland, *I.*, with Labrador, *prov.* Canada; E. of the G. of St. Lawrence; in E. low. in W. rugged mtns., many Ls.; coniferous forest; fishing, cod, salmon, halibut, lobster, seal; lumber, wood-pulp, paper; iron ore, lead, zinc, copper, asbestos; hydro-elec. power; climate is severe; cap. St. John's; a. prov. 156,185 sq. m. (I. 43,359 sq. m., Labrador 112,826 sq. m.); p. (1966) *493,396* (I. *472,239*; Labrador *21,157*).

Newham, *outer bor.* Greater London, Eng.; comprising the former co. bors. of East and West Ham, part of Barking, (W. of Barking Creek), Woolwich (N. of Thames); p. (1966) *259,000*.

Newhaven, *packet pt., urb. dist.*, E. Sussex, Eng.; on S. cst. at mouth of R. Ouse, 9 m. E. of Brighton; passenger pt. for Dieppe; boat bldg. and light inds.; p. (1961) *8,325*.

Newlyn, *picturesque vil.*, Cornwall, Eng.; on Mount's Bay, 1 m. W. of Penzance; fishing and fish canning; p. *3,902*.

Newmarket, *t., urb. dist.*, Suffolk, Eng.; at foot of E. Anglian Heights, 11 m. N.E. of Cambridge; horse-racing ctr.; famous Heath (partly in Cambridgeshire); mkt. gardening, agr. and agr. engin.; p. (1961) *11,207*. [p. (1961) *8,932*.

Newmarket, *t.*, S.E. Ont. Canada; leather mnfs.;

Newmilns and Greenholm, *burgh*, Ayr, Scot.; on R. Irvine, 12 m. E. of Kilmarnock; muslin and lace curtain mnf.; p. (1961) *3,541*.

Newport, *t., mun. bor., cap. of I.*, I. of Wight, Eng.; on R. Medina, in gap through central Chalk ridge; mkt.; brewing, joinery and coach wks., bait mnfs.; p. (estd. 1967) *19,690*.

Newport, *t., co. bor.*, Monmouth, Wales; on R. Usk, 5 m. from its mouth; timber terminal and deepwater berth; shipbldg., engin., iron and steel, aluminium, coal, paper-board, confectionery, chemicals, plastics; p. (1961) *108,107*.

Newport, *mkt. t., urb. dist.*, Salop,Eng.; 8 m. N. E. of Wellington; p. (1961) *4,370*.

Newport, *burgh*, Fife, Scot.; on S. side of Firth of Tay, opp. Dundee; p. (1961) *3,326*.

Newport, *c.*, Ky., U.S.A.; on Ohio R.; a. residtl. sub. of Cincinnati, with impt. local inds.; p. (1960) *30,070*.

Newport, *c.*, R.I., U.S.A.; on Narragansett Bay; seaside resort; permanent p. (1960) *47,049*.

Newport, *spt.*, S. Vietnam; on N. outskirts of Saigon; lge pt. inaugurated 1967.

Newport News, *c., spt.*, Va., U.S.A.; on north shore of estuary of James R. on Hampton Roads; lge. harbour; shipbldg.; outlet for Virginian tobacco and Appalachian coal; p. (1960) *113,662*.

Newport Pagnell, *mkt. t., urb. dist.*, Bucks, Eng.; on R. Ouse, 11 m. S.W. of Bedford; p. (1961) *4,722.*

Newquay, *t., urb. dist.*, Cornwall, Eng.; on N. Cornish cst.; seaside resort; p. (1961) *11,377.*

Newry, *t., urb. dist.*, Down, N. Ireland; at head of Carlingford Lough; machin., rope, brewing, granite; p. (1966) *12,214.*

Newton, *c.*, Kan., U.S.A.; silks, worsted; p. (1960) *14,877.*

Newton, *c.*, Mass., U.S.A.; on R. Charles; mnfs.; p. (1960) *92,384.* [(1966) *47,194.*

Newtonabbey, *urb. dist.*, Antrim, N. Ireland; p.

Newton Abbot, *mkt. t., urb. dist.*, Devon, Eng.; at head of Teign estuary; rly. junction; pottery, lt. engin.; p. (1961) *18,066.*

Newton Aycliffe, *t.*, Durham, Eng.; 6 m. N.W. of Darlington; one of " New Towns " designated 1947; engin. prod., textiles, plastics, paints; p. (estd. 1965) *16,040.*

Newton-le-Willows, *t., urb. dist.*, Lancs., Eng.; famous Vulcan locomotive wks. founded by George Stephenson (now being closed down); paper, textiles; p. (estd. 1967) *22,300.*

Newton-Stewart, *burgh*, Wigtown, Scot.; on R. Cree, 5 m. N. of Wigtown; wool, creameries and agr. inds.; p. (1961) *1,980.*

Newtown, *c.*, N.S.W., Australia; S. sub. Sydney; ironwks., paint; p. (1947) *25,293.*

Newtown and Llanllwchaiarn, *mkt. t., urb. dist.*, Montgomery, Wales; on R. Severn, 8 m. S.W. of Montgomery; precision instruments, machin. tools; p. (1961) *5,512*; plan for expansion, p. *11,000.*

Newtownards, *spt., mkt. industl. t., mun. bor.*, Down, N. Ireland; 7 m. E. of Belfast; hosiery; p. (1966) *12,928.*

Neyland, *t., urb. dist.*, Pembroke, Wales; on Milford Haven; rly. terminus; p. (1961) *2,149.*

Nezhin, *t.*, Ukrainian S.S.R.; rly. junction on Kiev–Moscow line; p. (1954) *50,000.*

Ngami, *L.*, Botswana, S. W. Africa; swamp, the remnant of a much larger L. [alt. 7,515 ft.

Ngauruhoe, *mtn.*, N.I., N.Z.; an active volcano;

Niagara, *R.*, forming part of boundary between Canada and U.S.A.; flows from L. Erie to L. Ontario; has rapids and the famous falls (167 ft.); gr. hydro-elec. power-sta.; length 35 m.

Niagara Falls, *t.*, Ontario, Canada; opp. the falls; carborundum, canning, silverware, castings; p. (1961) *22,351.*

Niagara Falls, *c.*, N.Y., U.S.A.; extending along the summit of cliff for 3 miles; paper, flour, aluminium; p. (1960) *102,394.*

Niamey, *t.*, Niger rep., W. Africa; one of the termini (the other is Zinder) of the trans-Sahara motor routes; p. (estd. 1963) *42,000.*

Nias, *I.*, W. of Sumatra, Indonesia; 95 m. long.

Niassa, *prov.*, Mozambique, Port. E. Africa; ch. t. Nampula; p. (1962) *276,795.*

Nicaragua, *rep.*, Central America; tropical forest; heavy rain in summer; uniformly hot; coffee, cocoa, sugar, bananas; gold and silver; cap. Managua; a. 57,145 sq. m.; p. (estd. 1969) *1,915,000.*

Nicastro, *mfg. t.*, Calabria, Italy; W. of the Apennines; olives, wine; p. *24,869.*

Nice, *c., spt., cap.*, Alpes Maritimes, France; on Mediterranean cst., at the foot of the Alps; beautiful climate and surroundings; joins ancient t. of Cimiez; ceded to France in 1860 by Sardinia; winter health resort; fruit and flower exp., perfume mftg.; p. (1968) *322,442.*

Nicobar Is., *see* Andaman and Nicobar Is.

Nicosia, *c., cap.*, Cyprus; agr. trade ctr.; textiles, cigarettes, leather, pottery mnfs.; remains of Venetian fortifications; mosques; airpt.; cap. of admin. dist. same name; p. (1965) *103,000.*

Nicoya, G. of, *inlet*, Costa Rica.

Nidd, *R.*, trib. of R. Ouse, W.R. Yorks, Eng.

Nidwalden, *can.*, Switzerland; a. 106 sq. m.; p. (1961) *22,188.*

Niederherrnsdorf, *t.*, S.W. Poland; formerly Germany; coal, explosives; p. *11,706.*

Niederwald, *hill*, opposite Bingen-on-the-Rhine, Germany; national monument commemorating German triumph over France 1870–71, and formation of the G. Empire.

Niemen or Memel, *R.*, Poland and U.S.S.R.; flowing to the Kurisches Haff; length 500 m.

Nienburg, *t.*, Lower Saxony, Germany; on R. Weser; glass, metal, wood, chemicals; p. (1963) *23,300.*

Nieuwveld Range, *mtns.*, C. of Gd. Hope, Union of

S. Africa; part of S. terminal escarpment of African tableland; overlooks Gr. Karroo to its S.; forms impenetrable barrier to routes; mainly over 5,000 ft., max. alt. 6,276 ft.

Nièvre, *central dep.*, France; traversed by Morvan Mtns.; forests, livestock, coal, iron, steel; cap. Nevers; a. 2,659 sq. m.; p. (1968) *247,702.*

Nigde, *t.*, Turkey; p. (1960) *18,010*

Nigel, *t.*, Transvaal, S. Africa; gold mng.; industl.; p. (1960) *33,896* inc. 7,880 whites.

Niger, *gr. R.*, W. Africa; rises nr. sea in outer mtn. zone of W. Africa, as R. Tembi, and sweeps round by Timbuktu to a delta in the G. of Guinea, on a circuitous course of 2,600 m., receiving its gr. trib. the R. Benue, about 250 m. from the mouth; navigable for 1,000 m.

Niger, *indep. sovereign st.*, W. Africa; millet, groundnuts, rice; sheep, goats; cap. Niamey; a. 484,000 sq. m.; p. (1968) *3,806,000.* [1964.

Niger Dam, Nigeria; at Kainji I.; dam projected

Nigeria, Republic of, *indep. sovereign st.*, within Br. Commonwealth (Oct. 1, 1960), West Africa; occupying lower basin of R. Niger, with region adj. up to Lake Chad; exp. world's lgst. supply of palm kernels and palm oil; groundnuts, cocoa, rubber, cotton, bananas; tin, asbestos, coalmng.; natural gas pipeline from fields at Owaza to Aba, E. Nigeria; oil in the Niger delta a.; cap. Lagos, lgst. c. Ibadan; fed. divided into 12 sts. in lieu of regions May 1967; total a. 356,669 sq. m.; p. (estd. 1968) *62,650,000.*

Nightingale, *I.*, most S. of Tristan da Cunha gr., S. Atlantic.

Niigata, *c., port*, Honshu, Japan; coal, petroleum; gas pipeline to Tokio under constr.; p. (1964) *345,000.*

Niihama, *c.*, N. Shikoku, Japan; on cst. of Inland Sea 20 m. S.E. of Imabari; refines copper obtained from Besshi Mines 12 m. to the S.; petrochemicals; p. (1966) *125,155.*

Niitakayama, *mtn.*, Taiwan I., China; highest mtn. of Niitaka Chain; alt. 12,939 ft.

Nijar, *t.*, Almeria, Spain; fruit, nuts, grain; textiles, porcelain; lead, manganese, iron ore; p. *10,107.*

Nijmegen, *c.*, E. Neth.; on R. Waal, nr. Arnhem; univ.; mnfs. ale, Prussian blue, cigars, pottery, metal-work; p. (1967) *144,004.*

Nijni-Novgorod, *see* Gorki.

Nikaria, *I.*, Dodecanese Archipelago, Greece.

Nikko, *t.*, Honshu, Japan; famous temples and shrines; beautiful tourist resort; p. (1966) *32,031.*

Nikolayev, *fortfd. t.*, Ukrainian S.S.R.; nr. Kherson, at head of estuary R. Bug; 2nd lgst. shipbldg. ctr. in U.S.S.R.; engin., petroleum refining; p. (1967) *289,000.*

Nikolayevsk, *t., pt.*, R.S.F.S.R.; on R. Amur; iron ore, engin., oil refining; p. (1954) *50,000.*

Nikopol, *t.*, Ukrainian S.S.R.; on R. Dnieper; manganese prod.; engin., steel; p. (1959) *81,000.*

Nikšić, *t.*, Montenegro, Jugoslavia; N. of Cetinje; p. (1960) *16,000.*

Nile, *the longest R.* in the world (*see* **White Nile** (Bahr-el-Abiad) and **Blue Nile** (Bahr-el-Azrek)); flows through a longer stretch of basin (over 2,450 m. in a direct line) than any other R. in the world, and along all its windings measures 4,145 m.; on Upper Nile navigation is hindered by sudd (floating vegetation); R. rises April, overflows Sept.; formerly cultivation entirely dependent on annual floods, but now assisted by dams, at Asyût, Aswan, Sennar, for regulating flow and navigation; first stage of Aswan High Dam completed 1964 when Nile waters were diverted.

Niles, *t.*, Ohio, U.S.A.; p. (1960) *19,545.*

Nilgiri Hills, Tamil Nadu, S. India.

Nîmes, *t.*, Gard, France; Roman antiquities, educational institutions; silk, cottons, carpets, machin., wine tr.; p. (1968) *123,292.*

Nineveh, *celebrated ancient c.*, Iraq, stood on E. bank of upper R. Tigris, opp. modern Mosul.

Ningpo (Ningbo), *c., spt.*, Chekiang, China; 100 m. from Shanghai; leading fishing pt., comm. and mnf. ctr. p. (1953) *238,000.*

Ningsia, *aut. reg.*, N.W. China; bounded on N. by Inner Mongolia; cap. Yinchwan; p. (estd. 1957) *1,810,000.*

Ninh Binh, *t.*, N. Viet-Nam; p. *25,000.*

Ninove, *t.*, Belgium; on R. Dender; industl.; p. (1962) *11,898.*

Niobrara, *R.*, U.S.A.; trib. of Missouri R.; flows from Wyoming to Nebraska; length 450 m.

Niort, *t.*, Deux-Sèvres, France; noted for its mkt. gardens, and leather mnf. (gloves); p. (1962) 44,630.

Nipigon. L., in Thunder Bay dist., Ontario, Canada; 70 m. long, 50 m. wide, 1,000 ls.; discharges by N. R. to Lake Superior; 30 m.

Nipissing, *L.*, Ontario, Canada; 50 m. long, 35 m. wide.

Niriz, *t.*, Fars prov., S.W. Iran; on old caravan route from Kerman to Shiraz; p. 9,000.

Niš, *t.*, Jugoslavia; on R. Nishava; p. (1960) 75,000.

Nišava, *R.*, Jugoslavia; rises in Stara Planina, flows N.W. into R. Morava nr. Niš; valley used by trunk rly. from Belgrade to Sofia and Istanbul (Constantinople); length over 100 m.

Niscemic, *commune*, Caltanissetta prov., Sicily; sulphur, agr.; p. 20,281.

Nishapur, *mkt. t.*, N.E. Iran; Khurasan,; in fertile a.; cotton, fruits; famous turquoise mines nearby; birthplace of Omar Khayyám; impt. archaeological finds dating 9th and 10th cent.; p. *c.* 30,000.

Nishinomiya, *c.*, S. Honshu, Japan; brewing, vegetable oils; p. (1964) 317,000.

Niterói, *t.*, cap. Rio de Janeiro st., Brazil; mftg. and residtl.; p. (estd. 1968) 303,575.

Nith, *R.*, S.W. Scot.; flows to Solway Firth, S. of Dumfries; followed by main rly. from Carlisle to Kilmarnock and Glasgow; length 71 m.

Nitra (Neutra), *R.*, ČSSR.; trib. of R. Waag; length 100 m.

Nitra, *t.*, ČSSR.; on R. Nitra; p. (1961) 34,242.

Niue or Savage I., Pac. Oc.; one of Cook Is., but under separate admin.; belongs to New Zealand; ch. pt. Alofi; copra, plaited basketware, sweet potatoes; a. 100 sq. m.; p. (1968) 5,302.

Nivelles, *t.*, Brabant, Belgium; rly. wkshps., paper; p. (1962) 14,483.

Nivernais, *old prov.*, France, now forming Nièvre prov. and part of Cher.

Nizampatam, *t.*, *spt.*, Tamil Nadu, India; formerly called Pettipollee after the neighbouring village of Pedapalle; first trg. estab. made by the Brit. in the Madras presidency in 1611.

Nizheudinsk, *t.*, W. Irkutsk, R.S.F.S.R.; new mftg. t.; p. 10,342.

Nizhniy Tagil, *t.*, R.S.F.S.R.; in Ural mtns.; iron ore, iron and steel, railway cars, engin., chemicals; p. (1967) 375,000. [Ogowe.

Njole, *t.*, Congo Rep., Equatorial Africa; on R.

No, *L.*, Bahr-el-Ghazal prov., Sudan, N.E. Africa; vast swamp a. 350 m. S.W. of Khartoum receiving Rs. Bahr-el-Jebel and Bahr-el-Ghazal (to form White Nile); flow of water blocked by papyrus reed and floating weed (sudd); gr. loss of water by evaporation.

Noakhali, *dist.*, and *t.*, Chittagong div., Pakistan; p. (of t.) 13,063.

Nobi Plain, S. Honshu, Japan; located at head of Ise Bay; composed of : (1) low, badly drained alluvial plain on W. under intensive rice cultivation, (2) higher, drier, terraces on E. under mulberry, vegetables, pine-woods; very dense urban and rural p.; ch. textiles and pottery mftg. a. in Japan; inc. cities Nagoya, Gifu, Yokkaichi; a. 720 sq. m.

Noblesville, *t.*, Ind., U.S.A.; agr., horse breeding; p. (1960) 7,664.

Nocera Inferiore, *t.*, Italy; nr. Naples; the ancient Nuceria Alfaterna; p. (1961) 43,050.

Nogent-sur-Marne, *t.*, Seine, France; S.E. sub. Paris; chemicals, knives; p. (1954) 23,581.

Noginsk, *t.*, R.S.F.S.R.; nr. Moscow; textiles, metals; natural gas pipeline from Central Asia projected; p. (1959) 93,000.

Noisy-le-Sec, *t.*, Seine, France; p. (1954) 22,337.

Nola, *t.*, Italy; at foot of Vesuvius, 12 m. N.E. of Naples; was an ancient c. of Campania, noted for its vases; p. 20,253.

Nome, *cst. t.*, Alaska, U.S.A.; gold; (1960) 2,316.

Noordoostpolder, Overijssel, Neth.; land reclaimed from Zuider Zee, 1942; a. 185 sq. m.; p. (1967) 31,016.

Noordwijk, *resort*, W. cst., Neth.; p. (1967) 20,563.

Noranda, *t.*, Quebec, Canada; 12 m N.E. of Rouyn; goldmines; p. (1961) 11,477.

Norcia, *t.*, Italy; old walls, cath.; famous for pork and terra-cotta.

Nord, *N. dep.*, France; on Belgian frontier and N. Sea; flourishing agr., mining, iron and coal, textile and chemical mnfs.; cap. Lille; a. 2,229 sq. m.; p. (1968) 2,417,899.

Nordenham, *pt.*, Lower Saxony, Germany; on Lower Weser; cables, textiles, metals, shipbldg., fishing pt.; p. (1963) 27,100.

Norderney, *I.*, Frisian Is., Germany; resort.

Nordhausen, *c.*, Erfurt, E. Germany; in Harz Mtns.; cath.; engin., agr. machin., clothing inds.; rly. junction; p. (1963) 41,401.

Nordhorn, *t.*, Lower Saxony, Germany; nr. Neth. frontier; textiles; p. (1963) 40,200.

Nordkapp or N. Cape, *most N. point*, Europe; on Magerö I., Norway.

Nordkyn, *most N. point*, with N. Cape, of the European mainland, Norway, opposite N. Cape.

Nordland, *co.*, Norway; a. 14,728 sq. m.; p. (1968) 244,636.

Nordlingen, *t.*, Bavaria, Germany; carpet factories; p. 8,800.

Nore, The, *sandbank, lightship*, Thames estuary, Eng.

Nore, *R.*, Ireland; trib. of R. Barrow; length 70 m.

Norfolk, *co.*, E. Eng.; noted for shallow lake expanses known as the Broads, popular yachting region; farming, corn, potatoes, cattle, fisheries (Yarmouth), brewing, boots, mustard, farm machin.; cap. Norwich; a. 2,055 sq. m.; p. (1966) 586,000.

Norfolk, *c.*, Nebraska, U.S.A.; on Elkhorn R.; in farming country; p. (1960) 13,111.

Norfolk, *c.*, Va., U.S.A.; impt. naval sta.; spt.; shipbldg. and repair, car assembly, food processing, lumber, fertilisers; p. (1960) 305,872.

Norfolk I., *fertile Australian I.*, Pac. Oc.; 800 m. E. of N.S.W. partial autonomy 1957; formerly a penal settlement; discovered by Captain Cook, 10 Oct. 1774; bean seed, whaling; a. 13 sq. m.; p. (resident-1969) 1,232.

Noric Alps, *mountainous region*, Styria, S. Austria.

Norilsk, *t.*, E. Siberia, R.S.F.S.R.; most N. t. in Russia; coal mng. uranium, nickel, copper; natural gas pipeline from W. Siberia; p. (1967) 127,000.

Normal, *t.*, Ill., U.S.A.; mkt. gardening, fruit, plants; univ.; p. (1960) 13,357.

Norman, *t.*, Okla., U.S.A.; oil-field; cotton processing; agr.; univ. of Okla.; p. (1960) 33,412.

Norman Wells, *t.*, N.W. Terr., Canada; at confluence of R. Mackenzie and G. Bear R., 70 m. W. of G. Bear L.; ctr. of rich oil-field.

Normandy, *old French prov.*, on Eng. Channel; mainly agr.; now divided into deps. Manche, Calvados, Eure, Seine-Maritime and part of Orne; Rouen was cap.; the Roman Lugdunensis; later a powerful Dukedom; conquered England, 1066.

Normanton, *t.*, *urb. dist.*, W.R. Yorks, Eng.; on R. Calder 2 m. E. of Wakefield; coal-mining, rly. wks.; p. (1961) 18,307.

Norrbotten, *co.*, N. Sweden; a. 40,754 sq. m.; cap. Piteå; p. (1961) 261,672.

Norris Dam, Tenn., U.S.A.; across R. Clinch at confluence with R. Tenn., N.W. of Knoxville; lgst. dam Tenn. Valley Authority (TVA); built for flood control and hydro-elec.

Norristown, *bor.*, Penns., U.S.A.; textiles, hosiery, carpets; p. (1960) 38,925.

Norrköping, *pt.*, *t.*, Sweden; N.E. of Linköping; textiles, margarine, paper; agr. machin.; ocean-going shipping through Lindö Canal; p. (1960) 91,661.

Norte de Santander, *dep.*, Colombia, S. America; a. 8,295 sq. m.; cap. Cucuta; p. (estd. 1959) 412,440.

North Adams, *c.*, Mass., U.S.A.; on R. Hoosac; textiles, boots, and shoes; p. (1960) 19,905.

North America, *northern continent*, of Western hemisphere, comprising Mexico, U.S.A., Canada, Greenland and excl. Central America and the W. Indies; cst. much indented; on W. high chain of mtns., lower range in E., and central plain. Climate varies considerably owing to wide range of latitude and altitude; great extremes of temperature; abundant rainfall on E. cst. and N. of W. cst.; S. of W. cst. Mediterranean; Mexico, sub-tropical and tropical. Vegetation diverse, varying with alt., latitude and climate; coniferous forests in N.; originally deciduous forests from E. cst. to approx. 100° W., then grassland to mtn. vegetation of W. range: semi-desert in S.W. Prairies once home of bison. Agr.: temperate and tropical prod., cereals, cotton, tobacco, sugar-beet, potatoes, etc.; lumbering; rich in minerals, coal, petroleum iron, manganese, etc. Gen. inds., comm., shipbldg. Formerly inhabited by Red Indians; now mainly occupied by white races, with many negroes in S.; p. (estd. 1968) 222,000,000.

North Atlantic Drift, drift of surface waters of Atl. Oc. N.E. from Gulf Stream towards Europe; relatively warm; supplies prevailing S.W. winds with warmth and moisture to modify climate of Brit. Is. and countries on N.W. margin of European Continent. *See* Gulf Stream, Section L.

North Attleboro, *t.,* Mass., U.S.A.; jewellery mnfs.; p. (1960) 14,704.

North Bay, *c.,* Ontario, Canada; p. (1961) 23,781.

North Berwick, *burgh,* E. Lothian, Scot.; on S. of F. of Forth, 20 m. E .of Edinburgh; seaside resort; golf course; p. (1961) 4,161.

North Brabant, *prov.,* Neth.; cap. 's-Hertogenbosch; a. 1,920 sq. m.; p. (estd. 1967) 1,700,866.

North Braddock, *t.,* Penns., U.S.A.; p. (1960) 13,204.

North Cape, *see* Nordkapp.

North Cape, *most northerly point,* N.I., N.Z.

North Carolina, *S. Atlantic st.,* U.S.A., E. of Tennessee and S. of Virginia; agr., maize, cotton-growing and mftg., tobacco culture and mftg., timber, scrap mica, textiles; cap. Raleigh; ch. pt., Wilmington; a. 52,712 sq. m.; p. (1970) 4,961,832.

North Channel, Brit. Is.; gives access from Atl. Oc. to Irish Sea between S.W. Scotland (Galloway) and N.E. Ireland (Antrim); length 60 m.; narrowest width 15 m.

North Chicago, *t.* Ill., U.S.A.; chemicals, metallurgy, elec. goods; p. (1960) 20,517.

North Crimean Canal, *canal,* U.S.S.R.; linking R. Dnieper with Black Sea and Sea of Azov, crossing steppes of S. Ukraine and the Crimea, terminating at Kerch; 1st section (77 m. long) opened Oct. 1963; when completed will be 220 m. long, 125 m. of which will be navigable.

North Dakota, *N.W. st.,* U.S.A.; mainly rolling prairie; agr., wheat, maize, oats, barley, flax, cattle, horses, sheep; coal, petroleum; cap. Bismarck; a. 70,665 sq. m.; p. (1970) 610,648.

North Downs, range of low chalk hills across S. Eng., forming cliffs at Dover; alt. about 800 ft.

North Eastern New Guinea, part of New Guinea under Australian administration as Trusteeship terr. under United Nations; a. 69,700 sq. m.

North East Passage, along N. cst. Europe and Asia between Atlantic and Pacific. *See* Gen. Inf.

North Holland, *prov.,* Neth.; a. 1,051 sq. m.; cap. Haarlem; natural gas in Schermer Polder nr. Alkmaar; p. (1967) 2,200,602.

North Island, *lge I.,* New Zealand; dairy prod.; lge. clay deposits at Matauri Bay; processing at Kaeo; a. 44,281 sq. m.; p. (1964) 1,820,118.

North Little Rock, *t.,* Ark., U.S.A.; p. (1960) 58,032.

North Osetian, A.S.S.R., U.S.S.R.; a. 3,100 sq. m.; cereals, livestock, petroleum; p. (1959) 449,000.

North Platte, *c.,* Nebraska, U.S.A., on N. Platte R.; in irrigated reg. of the Great Plains; grain, livestock, processed meat; p. (1960) 17,184.

North Platte, *R.,* rises in N. Colorado, flows 680 m. through Wyoming, across W. Nebraska to join S. Platte at c. of North Platte; extensive power and irrigation developments.

North Providence, *see* Nassau.

North Rhine–Westphalia, *Land,* Germany; a. 13,153 sq. m.; p. (1968) 16,951,000.

North River, Kwangtung, S. China; rises in Nan Ling mtns., flows S. into Canton delta; length 300 m.

North Sea, arm of the Atlantic, E. of Gr. Brit., W. of Norway, Sweden and N. Germany, and N. of Holland, Belgium and France; length 600 m., width 400 m.; good fisheries.

North Sea Canal, *ship canal,* N. Holland, Neth.; connects Amsterdam to N. Sea at IJmuiden; depth 46 ft., length 16 m.

North Shields, *mkt. t.,* Northumberland, Eng.; Tyne pt. and part of the borough Tynemouth; marine engines, chain cables, anchors, rope.

North Sydney, *spt.,* C. Breton I., Nova Scotia; Canada; docks, coal; p. (1961) 8,657.

North Tonawanda, *c.,* N.Y., U.S.A.; on Niagara R.; mnfs.; p. (1960) 34,757.

North Walsham, *mkt. t., urb. dist.,* Norfolk, Eng.; 13 m. N.E. of Norwich; p. (1961) 5,010.

North-West Frontier Province, *prov.* (revived 1970), W. Pakistan; mtnous, fertile valleys; bounded by Hindu Kush and Afghanistan on N., and on S. by Baluchistan and Punjab; ch. c. Peshawar; wheat, barley, sugar cane, tobacco, cotton; iron, copper, marble quarrying; irrigation wks.; a. 14,263 sq. m.; p. (estd. 1951) 3,239,000.

North-West Passage, between Atl. and Pac. along Arctic cst. of Canada. *See* Section L.

North-West Staging Route, a daisy chain of airfields built during last war linking Edmonton, Alberta, with Whitehorse, Yukon.

Northwest Territories, Canada; N.W. region of Canada, north of 60° Lat. N., between Yukon on W., Hudson Bay on E.; divided into 3 dists., Franklin, Mackenzie and Keewatin; cap. Yellowknife; gold- and silver-mng., petroleum, furs, fisheries; a. 1,304,903 sq. m.; p. (estd. 1969) 31,000.

North York. Moors, *limestone plateau,* N.R., Yorkshire; lies S. of estuary of R. Tees; drained N. to R. Tees, S. to R. Derwent and to N. Sea by R. Esk; heather moorland; some pastoral farming on lower slopes; impt. iron-ore quarrying along N. edge in Cleveland dist.; alt. varies from 1,000 to 1,500 ft.

Northallerton, *t., urb. dist.,* N.R. Yorks, Eng.; in broad gap between Cleveland Hills and Pennines; dairy farming and agr. dist.; car and agr. engin., leather; p. (1961) 6,720.

Northam, *t.,* W. Australia; on R. Avon. 66 m. from Perth, Australia; timber, metal wks.; p. (1966) 7,392.

Northampton, *S. Midland co.,* Eng.; chiefly agr.; iron, mining and mftg.; footwear, lace, leather, flax, light engin.; co. t., Northampton; a. 998 sq. m.; p. (1966) 428,000.

Northampton, *t., co. bor.,* Northampton, Eng.; on R. Nene; footwear mftg., leather goods, light engin.; p. (estd. 1967) 121,890.

Northampton, *c.,* Mass., U.S.A.; textiles, paper; univ.; p. (1960) 30,058.

Northampton, *t.,* Penns., U.S.A.; cement; beer; clothes; quarrying; p. (1960) 8,866. [10,476.

Northbridge, *industl. t.,* Mass., U.S.A.; p. (1950).

Northern Ireland, consists of the administrative cos. of Antrim, Armagh, Down, Fermanagh, Londonderry and Tyrone, and administrative bors. of Belfast and Londonderry. Has its own parliament and executive Government under a Governor appointed by the Crown. Returns 12 members to British House of Commons; agr., oats, potatoes; textiles, chemicals, tobacco ind., electronic equip.; shipbldg; tourism; univs.; cap. Belfast; a. 5,452 sq. m.; p. (estd. 1969) 1,513,000.

Northern Territory, a large tract of land N. of S. Australia; stock-raising, copper, gold, uranium, manganese, salt, bauxite; silver, mica, tin, tungsten; lead-zinc; rice at Humpty Doo, 30 m. S. of Darwin; a. 520,280 sq. m.; ch. t. Darwin; p. (estd. 1968) 64,000. [(1960) 8,707.

Northfield, *c.,* S. Minn., U.S.A.; agr., dairying; p.

Northfleet, *t., urb. dist.,* Kent, Eng.; on S. bank of R. Thames, adjoining Gravesend; cement, paper, rubber, tyres, cables; p. (estd. 1967) 24,660.

Northumberland, *N. maritime co.,* Eng.; on border of Scot.; pastoral, mining, coal and lead, mftg.; chemicals, glass, engin., and shipbldg. on Tyneside; cap. Newcastle-upon-Tyne; a. 2,019 sq. m.; p. (1961) 818,988.

Northumberland Straits, separates Prince Edward I. from Nova Scotia and New Brunswick; 9 m. combined road and rail tunnel, bridge and causeway to link provs. projected.

Northwich, *mkt. t., urb. dist.,* Cheshire, Eng.; on R. Weaver, 10 m. S.E. of Runcorn; chemicals, salt, engin.; p. (1961) 19,374. [(1950) 4,315.

Norton, *t.,* S.W. Va., U.S.A.; coal, mftg.; p.

Norton, *t., urb. dist.,* E.R. Yorks, Eng.; on R. Derwent opposite Malton; p. (1961) 4,773.

Norton Sound, *inlet,* W. cst. Alaska, Behring Sea; 200 m. long.

Norwalk, *t.,* Conn., U.S.A.; on Long I. Sound; good harbour, oysters, iron foundries, clothing; p. (1960) 67,775. [88,739.

Norwalk, *t.,* Cal., U.S.A.; oil refining; p. (1960)

Norwalk, *bor.,* Ohio, U.S.A.; mftg. ctr. of farming dist.; p. (1960) 12,900.

Norway, *kingdom*, N. Europe; fjord cst., mtnous; climate influenced by prevailing winds, heavy rain and snowfall cstal regions; barley, forest prod., aluminium, pyrites; fisheries; hydro-elec. power; cap. Oslo; a. 124,556 sq. m.; p. (1968) *3,802,243*.

Norwich, *c.*, *co. bor.*, *co. t.*, Norfolk, Eng.; on R. Wensum just above confluence with R. Yare; univ.; cath., old cas., cult. ctr., agr. ctr.; footwear, food mnf.; p. (estd. (1969) *118,800*.

Norwich, *c.*, Conn., U.S.A.; firearms, cutlery and machin., textiles; p. (1960) *38,506*.

Norwood, S., *sub. div.*, Lambeth, Surrey, Eng.; mainly residtl.

Norwood, Ohio, U.S.A.; *sub.*, Cincinnati; p. (1960) *24,580*.

Norwood, *t.*, Mass., U.S.A.: p. (1960) *24,898*.

Nossi bé, *Is.*, Indian Ocean; off W. cst of Madagascar; a. 130 sq. m.; sugar; tourist resort.

Notec (Netze), *R.*, Poland; trib. R. Warta; 140 m.

Noto, *c.*, Sicily; W. of Syracuse; cath.; wine, olive oil, mnfs.; p. *32,575*.

Notodden, *t.*, S. Norway; hydro-elec. power; iron smelting; nitrates; p. (1961) *7,383*.

Notre Dame Bay, N. cst., Newfoundland, Canada.

Nottingham, *midland co.*, Eng.; wheat, oats, barley, cattle, coal, oil; co. t. Nottingham; a. 844 sq. m.; p. (1961) *902,966*.

Nottingham, *c.*, *co. bor.*, *co. t.*, Nottingham, Eng.; on R. Trent, at S.E. end of Pennines; ctr. of English lace ind.; univ., R.O. cath., fine buildings, cas., museum, mkt. square; hosiery, cycles, engin., pharmaceutical ind., chemicals tobacco; p. (estd. 1969) *303,000*.

Nouakchott, *cap.*, Mauritania, W. Africa; p. (estd. 1962) *6,000*.

Nouméa or Port de France, *cap.*, New Caledonia; p. (1962) *35,000*.

Nova Friburgo, *t.*, Rio de Janeiro, Brazil; health resort; p. (1968) *93,364*.

Nova Iguaçú, *t.*, Rio de Janeiro, Brazil; steel, tyres, chemicals; p. (estd. 1968) *473,319*.

Nova Lima, *t.*, Minas Gerais st., Brazil; in Serra do Espinhaço, 10 m. S. of Belo Horizonte; adjacent to impt. gold-mines of Morro Velho; p. (estd. 1968) *32,336*.

Nova Lisboa (Huambo), *t.*, Angola, Africa; E. of Benguela; rly. repair shops; p. (1960) *60,800* (inc. *14,000* whites).

Novara, *Alpine prov.*, N. Italy; a. 2,548 sq. m.; p. *458,905*.

Novara, *mftg. t.*, nr. Milan; p (1961) *86,190*.

Nova Scotia, *maritime prov.*, Canada; mainly fertile uplands and rich valleys, but with mtns. along the cst. nr. Bay of Fundy; agr., fruit, livestock, dairying, much mineral wealth, coal and gypsum, and very valuable fisheries; cap. Halifax; a. 21,068 sq. m.; p. (1969) *764,000*.

Nova Zembla (Novaya Zemlya), *ipc. Is.*, Arctic Ocean, U.S.S.R.; furs, walrus, whale, seal fisheries, lead, zinc and copper; nuclear testing a. [mftg.; p. (1961) *22,041*.

Nove Zamky, *t.*, Slovakia, ČSSR.; mkt. and Novgorod, *t.*, R.S.F.S.R.; sawmills, engin., p. (1959) *61,000*.

Novi Ligure, *t.*, Alessandria, Italy; nr. Genoa; noted for silk mftg.; p. *21,575*.

Novi Pazar, *t.*, Serbia, Jugoslavia; on R. Rashka; p. (1959) *17,000*.

Novi Sad (Neusatz), *t.*, Jugoslavia; on R. Danube; opposite Petrovaradin; formerly royal free c., almost destroyed by Austrians 1849; tr. in fruit, wine, vegetables, corn; p. (1961) *112,000*.

Novocherkask, *t.*, R.S.F.S.R.; 20 m. N.E. of Rostov; engin., chemicals; p. (1967) *116,000*.

Novokuybyshevsk, *t.*, R.S.F.S.R.; Volga region; lge. oil processing plant; p. (1959) *63,000*.

Novokuznetsk (Stalinsk) *t.*, R.S.F.S.R.; Kuznets; coal, iron, steel, engin., chemicals, aluminium; p. (1967) *484,000*.

Novomoskovsk (Stalinogorsk), *t.*, R.S.F.S.R.; on R. Don; lignite, fertilisers, chemicals; p. (1967) *124,000*.

Novorossiisk, *spt.*, R.S.F.S.R.; on N.E. cst. of Black Sea; engin., textiles; lgst. cement producer in U.S.S.R.; p. (1967) *120,000*.

Novoshakhtinsk, *t.*, R.S.F.S.R.; on Rostov-Kharkov highway; coalmng., chemicals; p. (1967) *108,000*.

Novosibirsk, *t.*, R.S.F.S.R.; on R. Ob; hydro-elec., steel, tin smelting, engin., textiles, chemicals, sawmilling; p. (1967) *1,049,000*.

Novo Troitsk, *t.*, R.S.F.S.R.; in Urals, 11 m. S.W.

of Orsk; cement, iron and steel; p. (1959) *57,000*. [power sta.

Novovoronezh, U.S.S.R., on R. Don; nuclear

Nòvý Jicín (Neutitschein), *t.*, Moravia, ČSSR.; farm machin. and engin.; p. (1961) *16,560*.

Nowa Huta, *t.*, Poland; S.E. Kraków, on R. Vistula; newly developed metallurgical ctr.; p. (1954) *50,000*.

Nowa Sól (Neusalz), *t.*, Lower Silesia, Poland; on R. Oder; chemicals; p. (1965) *29,000*.

Nowata, *t.*, N.E. Okla., U.S.A.; agr., natural gas, oil-field gear; p. (1950) *3,965*.

Nowawes, *c.*, Brandenburg, Germany; textiles, engin., chemicals; p. *26,975*.

Nowra-Bomaderry, *t.*, N.S.W., Australia; on E. cst. at mouth of Shoalhaven R.; collecting ctr. for agr. and pastoral prod. of coastal plain; at S. terminus of rly. along E. cst. of Australia; paper mill; p. (1966) *9,642*.

Nowy Sacz, *industl. t.*, Krakow, S. Poland; on R. Dunajec; lignite; p. (1965) *37,000*.

Nsanje (Port Herald), *t.*, Malawi, Africa; pt. on Shire R.

Nubia, *region*, Africa, extending on both sides of Nile from Aswan, U.A.R., southwards to Khartoum, Sudan.

Nubian Desert, Sudan, N.E. Africa; between R. Nile and Red Sea; alt. 1,200–9,000 ft.; a. approx. 90,000 sq. m.

Nuble, *prov.*, Chile; bordering on Argentina; a. 5,484 sq. m.; cap. Chillan; p. (1961) *327,105*.

Nueces, *R.*, Texas, U.S.A.; flows to G. of Mexico; length 400 m. [p. (1961) *89,492*.

Nueva Esparta, *st.*, Venezuela; cap. La Asuncion;

Nuevo Laredo, *c.*, E. Mexico; agr., cotton, maize, cattle rearing; p. (1960) *107,473*.

Nuevo León, *st.*, Mexico; agr. and stock raising, sugar; cap. Monterrey; a. 25,134 sq. m.; p. (1960) *1,078,848*.

Nukualofa, *cap.* of Polynesian kingdom of Tonga.

Nukus, *t.*, Uzbek S.S.R.; in Khorezm oasis; p. (1959) *39,000*.

Nullarbor Plain, S. Australia; low, level, limestone plateau fringing Gr. Australian Bight; arid; treeless, salt-bush scrub; crossed by Transcontinental Rly. between Naretha (W. Australia) and Ooldea; rly. is dead straight dead level for 298 m.

Nun, *ch.* mouth of R. Niger, Africa.

Nun, *R.*, Inner Mongolia, Heilungkiang, N. China; trib. of Sungari; length 500 m.

Nun, *R.*, on S. frontier of Morocco, N. Africa; with t. thereon; length 130 m.

Nuneaton, *mkt. t.*, *mun. bor.*, Warwick, Eng.; on R. Anker, 18 m. S. of Birmingham; coal-mining, quarrying, textiles, engin., tit. inds.; p. (estd. 1967) *63,420*.

Nuremberg (Nürnberg), *t.*, Bavaria, Germany; cas., museum, cultural academy and many historic bldgs.; elec. mnfs., machin., heavy vehicles, toys, pencils and crayons; rly. junction; p. (1968) *470,778*.

Nusa Tenggara, *Is.*, Indonesia; p. (1961) *3,775,127* inc. Bali *5,557,656*.

Nutley, *t.*, N.J., U.S.A.; p. (1960) *29,513*.

Nyasa, *L.*, see Malawi, L.

Nyasaland, *see* Malawi.

Nyborg, *t.*, Denmark; on Fyn I.; p. (1960) *11,667*.

Nyeri, *t.*, Kenya; p. (1962) *7,400*.

Nyiregyháza, *mftg. t.*, Hungary; wine, farming; implements; p. (estd. 1957) *55,000*.

Nykobing, spt., Falster I.,Denmark; light engin., food-packing, margarine, sugar-refining, tobacco ind.; p. (1960) *17,850*.

Nyköping, *spt.*, Sweden; at head of inlet on cst., comm. and industr.; cars; p. (1961) *24,250*.

Nystad (Uusikaupunki), *spt.*, Abo-Björneborg, Finland; on G. of Bothnia; p. (1966) *5,074*.

O

Oadby, *urb. dist.*, Leics, Eng.; 3 m. S.E. of Leic.; boots and shoes; p. (1961) *12,266*.

Oahu, *I.*, Hawaiian Is., Pac. Oc.; sugar, pine-apples; tourist ctr.; cap. Honolulu; a. 604 sq. m.; p. (1960) *500,409*.

Oak Park Village, *t.*, Ill., U.S.A.; now included in Chicago; p. (1960) *61,093*.

Oakengates, *t.*, urb. dist., Salop, Eng.; 15 m. N.W. of Wolverhampton; iron and steel, precast concrete, engin.; expansion of t. projected; p. (1961) *12,158*.

Oakham, *co. t., urb. dist.*, Rutland, Eng.; 9 m. S.E. of Melton Mowbray; mkt.; hosiery; p. (1961) *4,571.*

Oakland, *c.*, Cal., U.S.A.; on San Francisco Bay; residtl. sub.; cars, shipbldg., fruit canning, elec. machin., clothing, tanneries, chemicals; p. (1960) *367,548.* [p. (1966) *13,186.*

Oamaru, *bor., spt.*, S.I., N.Z.; wool, frozen meat;

Oaxaca, *st.*, Pacific cst., Mexico; cereals, rubber, coffee, mining; cap. Oaxaca; a. 36,371 sq. m.; p. (1960) *1,727,266.*

Oaxaca, *c., cap.*, Oaxaca st., Mexico; alt. 4,800 ft.; ctr. of cochineal tr.; table linen weaving, wool zarapes; coffee; silver, gold; cattle; p. (1960) *60,000.*

Ob, *G.*, U.S.S.R.; inlet of Arctic Oc.; length 600 m.

Ob, *R.*, W. Siberia, U.S.S.R.; flows from the Altai Mtns. to the G. of Ob; length (with trib. R. Irtish) 2,600 m.

Oban, *spt., burgh*, Argyll, Scot.; on F. of Lorne; summer resort of Highland tourists; terminus of rly. from Stirling; ctr. for local shipping; woollens, tartans; p. (1961) *6,859.*

Obed, Alberta, Canada; 150 m. W. of Edmonton; major natural gas a.

Oberlahnstein, *t.*, Germany; at junction of Rs. Rhine and Lahn; cas., ancient walls; mng.

Oberammergau, *vil.*, Upper Bavaria, Germany; scene of decennial Passion Play; p. *1,500.*

Oberhausen, *t.*, N. Rhine-Westphalia, Germany; nr. Duisburg; cas.; coal, iron, steel, zinc, chemicals, rly. junction; p. (1968) *249,941.*

Obi I., *sm. I.*, between Halmahera and Serang, Indonesia.

Obidos, *t., R. pt.*, Brazil; 500 m. up R. Amazon; cacao, cotton; p. (1960) *3,500.*

Obihiro, *t.*, Hokkaido, Japan; p. (1947) *36,555.*

Obninsk, *t.*, R.S.F.S.R.; 60 m. S.W. of Moscow; atomic power sta.

Obok, *spt.*, Fr. Terr. of Afars and Issas, N.E. Africa; on Red Sea; coaling sta.; p. *1,000.*

Obuasi, *t.*, Ghana, W. Africa; p. (1960) *23,000.*

Obwalden, *can.*, Switzerland; a. 190 sq. m.; p. (1961) *23,135.*

Ocaña, *ancient t.*, Toledo, Spain; on Ocaña plateau; cas.; pottery, wine; p. (1957) *6,840.*

Ocaña, *t.*, Magdalena st., Colombia; coffee, hides; p. (estd. 1959) *21,200.*

Ocean I., Brit. col., Gilbert and Ellice Is., Pac. Oc.; high-grade phosphate; p. (1956) *2,446.*

Oceania, name given to the Is. of the Pacific; comprising Australasia, Polynesia, Melanesia, Micronesia; copra, sugar, fruit, timber; pearl fishing; gold, minerals, phosphates; a. 3,286,000 sq. m.; p. (estd. 1968) *13,500,000.*

Ochil Hills, Scottish range reaching from the F. of Tay to nr. Stirling; highest peak, Ben Cleugh, 2,363 ft.

Ockmulgee, *R.*, Ga., U.S.A.; trib. of Altamaha R.; length 280 m. [length 250 m.

Oconee, *R.*, Ga., U.S.A.; joins the Ockmulgee;

Odawara, *t.*, Japan; nr. Tokyo; gr. tr.; p. (1965) *143,377.*

Odda, *t.*, S. Norway; on Haugesund; electro-chem. and metallurgic inds.; p. (1961) *7,383.*

Odemiş, *t.*, Asiatic Turkey; N.E. of Aydin; tobacco, cereals, silk, cotton, flax, olives, raisins, figs; minerals; p. (1965) *30,621.*

Odendaalsrust, *t.*, O.F.S., S. Africa; gold ctr.; p. (1960) *15,047* inc. *6,070* whites.

Odense, *co.*, Denmark; now includes all N.W. Fyn; a. 699 sq. m.; p. (1965) *218,667.*

Odense, *spt.*, cap. of Fyn, Denmark; ancient c. said to have been founded by Odin; birthplace of Hans Andersen; elec. motors, shipyd., engin., textiles, footwear; p. (1965) *132,978.*

Odenwald, *mtns.*, Hessen, Germany; wooded; highest point Katzenbuckel, 2,057 ft.

Oder or **Odra**, *R.*, Central Europe; flowing from Moravia to Baltic through Polish Silesia, forming (since 1945) frontier between Poland and Germany, flows past Wroclaw (Breslau), Frankfurt and Szczecin (Stettin); length 560 m.

Odessa, *t.*, Texas, U.S.A.; impt. oil ctr., chemicals, foundry prod.; p. (1960) *80,338.*

Odessa, *spt.*, Ukrainain S.S.R.; on Black Sea; cath., univ.; gr. grain exp.; engin., oil-refining, chemicals; ice-bound for a few weeks in winter; bombarded by English and French 1845; p. (1967) *753,000.*

Offaly, *co.* (late King's co.), prov. Leinster, Ireland; much marshy land (inc. Bog of Allen),

---

barren uplands (Slieve Bloom and other mtns.); fertilising factory for ammonium nitrate from peat in Blackwater Bog; ch. t. Tullamore; a. 772 sq. m.; p. (1966) *51,707.*

Offenbach, *t.*, Hesse, W. Germany; on R. Main; cas., leather museum; machin., chemicals, leather goods, metals; p. (1968) *116,746.*

Offenburg, *t.*, Baden-Württemberg, Germany; on R. Kinzig; textiles, glass, rly. junction; p. (1963) *28,600.*

Ogbomosho, *t.*, Nigeria; p. (1953) *140,000.*

Ogden, *c.*, Utah, U.S.A.; nr. the Great Salt L.; rly. ctr.; beet sugar, meat packing, flour milling; p. (1960) *70,197.*

Ogdensburg, *c., pt.*, N.Y., U.S.A.; on St. Lawrence R., opp. Prescott; gd. tr.; p. (1960) *16,122*

Ogeechee, *R.*, Ga., U.S.A.; flows to Atlantic, S. of Savannah; length 200 m.

Oglio, *R.*, Italy; traverses L. Iseo; flows to the Po; length 135 m.

Ogmore and **Garw**, *t., urb. dist.*, Glamorgan, Wales; in narrow valley, 6 m. N. of Bridgend; industl.; p. (1961) *20,955.*

Ogowe, *R.*, Gaboon, Africa; length 750 m.

Ohau, *L.*, Mt. Cook dist., S.I., N.Z.; fed by glaciers; 12 m. by 22 m.; hydroelec. plant projected.

O'Higgins, *prov.*, Chile; a. 2,745 sq. m.; p. (1961) *292,296.*

Ohio, *R.*, U.S.A.; trib. of Mississippi R.; formed in Penns., by the junction of the Monongahela and Allegheny Rs. at Pittsburgh, thence navigable for 975 m. to Cairo in Kentucky, 1,200 m. from the mouth of the Mississippi R.

Ohio, *st.*, U.S.A.; drained by Ohio R. and tribs.; gr. agr. and industl. region; maize, wheat, oats, cattle; lime, sand and gravel, salt, coal, petroleum, gas, iron and steel wks., machin., timber; cap. Columbus; lgst. cs. Cleveland and Cincinnati; a. 41,122 sq. m.; p. (1970) *10,542,630.*

Ohre (Eger), *R.*, Bohemia, Czechoslovakia; rises in Fichtelgebirge, flows N.E. into Labe (Elbe) at Litoměrice; flows through several sm. lignite fields, spas of Karlovy Vary (Karlsbad); length 140 m   [(1959) *15,000.*

Ohrid, *t.*, S. Jugoslavia; nr. Albanian border; p.

Oich, Loch, *L.*, Great Glen, Inverness, Scot.; 6 m. long, 1 m. wide.

Oil City, Penns., U.S.A.; on Allegheny R.; oil, machin.; p. (1960) *17,692.*

Oise, *dep.*, N. France; traversed by R. Oise; forests, cereals, fruits, iron, textiles; cap. Beauvais; a. 2,272 sq. m.; p. (1968) 540,988

Oise, *R.*, trib. of R. Seine, France; canalised, navigable to Chauny; length 186 m.

Oita, *spt.*, Japan; exp. coal; cattle; p. (1964) *229,000.*

Ojos del Salado, *mtn.*, N.W. Argentina; alt. 22,572 ft.

Oka, *R.*, U.S.S.R.; trib. of R. Volga at Gorki; length 929 m.   [length 500 m.

Oka, *R.*, Siberia, U.S.S.R.; trib. of R. Angora;

Okanagan, *R.* and *L.*, B.C., Canada; fruit-growing dist.   [industl.; p. (1965) 194.409.

Okasaki, *t.*, Honshu, Japan; nr. G. of Ovari;

Okayama, *t.*, Honshu, Japan; exp. paper, minerals, firebricks; shipbldg.; rly. ctr.; cattle rearing; p. (1965) *291,825.*

Okehampton, *mkt. t., mun. bor.*, Devon, Eng.; on N. flank of Dartmoor; stone; p. (estd. 1967) *3,810.*

Okha, *spt.*, E. cst. Sakhalin I., R.S.F.S.R.; exp. petroleum; lge. refinery projected; p. (1954) *50,000.*

Okhotsk, Sea of, N.E. Asia; 1,000 m. by 500 m.; enclosed by the Siberian mainland, Kamchatka, the Kurils and Sakhalin I.

Oki Is., off cst. of Honshu, Japan; a. 135 sq. m.

Okinawa, *I.*, Ryuku Is., Japan, under U.S. control until 1972; lgst. and most impt. of Ryuku Is., cap. Naha; 2 lgst. U.S. air bases Kadena and Naha; a. 579 sq. m.; p. (1956) *665,315.*

Oklahoma, *st.*, U.S.A.; prairie, plains and mtns.; cereals, cotton, stock-raising, petroleum, gas, zinc, coal, gypsum, lead; ch. ind. petroleum refining; cap. Oklahoma City; a. 69,919 sq. m.; p. (1970) *2,498,378.*

Oklahoma, *c.*, Okla., U.S.A.; univ.; oil and by-prod., oil processing, field machin., iron, steel, flour mills, meat pkg.; p. (1960) *324,253.*

Okmulgee, *t.*, Okla., U.S.A.; p. (1960) *15,951.*

Oktyabrsky, *t.*, Bashkir, A.S.S.R.; on R. Ik; in new oil-mng. dist., the "New Baku"; p. (1959) *65,000.*

Öland, I., Baltic Sea; off E. cst. Sweden; separated from mainland by Kalmar Sound; a. 533 sq. m.; ch. t. Borgholm, a seaside resort.

Old Castile, *historical div.*, Spain; now divided into Santander, Soria, Segovia, Logrono, Avila, Valladolid, Palencia and Burgos provs.

Old Fletton, *urb. dist.*, Hunts, Eng.; on R. Nene opposite Peterborough; bricks. gen. and elec. engin., beet sugar, fruit and vegetable canning, tar distilling; p. (1961) *11,673.*

Old Forge, *bor.*, Penns., U.S.A.; anthracite coal; p. (1960) *8,923.*

Old Kilpatrick, *see* Kilpatrick, Old.

Oldbury, *mun. bor.*, Worcs., Eng.; nr. Birmingham; iron, steel, chemical, brick, glass inds.; p. (1961) *53,935.*

Oldbury-on-Severn, Glos., Eng.; nuclear power sta.

Oldenburg, *t.*, Lower Saxony, Germany; on R. Hunte; grand-ducal palace; impt. horse fair; food processing, lt. inds.; rly. junction; natural gas nr. to cst.; p. (1968) *131,197.*

Oldham, *mftg. t., co. bor.*, Lancs, Eng.; on R. Medlock, 4 m. N.E. of Manchester; cotton, textile, and machin. mftg.; p. (estd. 1967) *109,840.*

Oldmeldrum, *burgh*, Aberdeen, Scot.; 4 m. N.E. of Inverurie; p. (1961) *1,083.*

Olean, *t.*, N.Y., U.S.A.; on Allegheny R.; oil region; p. (1960) *21,868.*

Olenek, *R.*, Ukrainian S.S.R.; flows W. of the Lena, into Laptev Sea, Arctic Ocean; length 800 m.

Oléron, Ile d', *I.*, Bay of Biscay; lies off estuary of R. Charente, Aquitaine, France; vine, oysters, salt; length 18 m., maximum width 7 m.

Olga, *spt.*, R.S.F.S.R.; on cst. of Japan Sea; iron ore; p. *1,000.* [*16,017.*

Olhão, *t.*, Faro, Portugal; fisheries; p. (1960)

Olifant, *R.*, Transvaal, S. Africa; trib. of Limpopo.

Olinda, *c.*, Pernambuco st., Brazil; seaside resort; phosphates; p. (1960) *100,545.*

Oliobiri, S. Nigeria; oilfields; pipe-line to Pt. Harcourt, 80 m. W.

Oliva, *t.*, Valencia, Spain; nr. Alicante; wine dist., ducal palace; p. (1957) *13,343.*

Olivenza, *t.*, Spain; nr. Portuguese frontier; p. (1957) *13,334.* [p. (estd. 1960) *160,000.*

Olivos, *sub.*, Buenos Aires, Argentina, S. America;

Olkhon, I., L. Baykal, R.S.F.S.R.; manganese.

Oimutz, *see* Olomouc.

Olney, *t.*, N. Bucks, Eng.; 11 m. S.E. Northampton; boots, shoes, lace; dairying; p. *2,651.*

Olomouc (Olmütz), *c.*, ČSSR.; formerly one of the ch. fortresses of Austria; cath., univ.; iron and steel engin., textiles; p. (1962) *70,116.*

Oloron, *t.*, Basses-Pyrénées, France; on Gave d'Oloron; cath.; p. (1962) *13,598.*

Olsnitz, *t.*, Saxony, Germany; on Weisse Elster; carpet mnfs.

Olsztyn (Allenstein), *t.*, N.W. Poland, cap. Olsztyn prov.; on R. Alle, 100 m. N. of Warsaw; cas.; machin., wood inds.; p. (1965) *75,000.*

Olt, *R.*, Romania; joins R. Danube at Nikopol.

Olten, *t.*, Switzerland; on R. Aare; rly. junction; motor, cement, machin. wks.; p. (1957) *16,485.*

Oltenita, *t.*, Romania; on R. Danube, nr. Bulgarian border; p. (1956) *14,111.*

Olvarria, *t.*, E. Argentina; 200 m. S.W. Buenos Aires; rly. ctr.; p. *24,326.*

Olvera, *t.*, Spain; nr. Cadiz; on R. Guadalete; p. (1957) *10,232.*

Olympia, *plain*, Peloponnesus, Greece, on R. Ellis where the Olympic Games were held.

Olympia, *cap.*, Washington st., U.S.A.; timber, machin., farm prod.; p. (1960) *18,273.*

Olympus, *mtn.*, Thessaly, Greece; W. of G. of Thessalonika; alt. 9,753 ft.; home of ancient Greek Gods.

Olympus, *mtn.*, Turkey; nr. Troy.

Olympus, Mt., Wash., U.S.A.; alt. 8,150 ft.

Om, *R.*, Siberia, R.S.F.S.R.; trib. of R. Irtish; length 330 m.

Omagh, *t., urb. dist.*, Tyrone, N. Ireland; on R. Strule 28 m. S. of Londonderry; corn, tanning; shirt factories; tourist ctr.; p. (1966) *9,857.*

Omaha, *c.*, Nebraska, U.S.A.; on Missouri R.; gr. tr., ctr., one of the lgst. livestock and meat-packing ctrs. in the U.S., gold and silver smelting and refining, steel fabrication, industl. alcohol prod.; p. (1960) *301,598.*

Oman, *sultanate*, S.E. Arabia; agr., fruit (dates), oil; cap, Muscat; a. 82,000 sq. m.; p. (estd. 1970) *750,000.*

Oman, G. of, Arabian Sea; connected through strait of Hormuz to Persian G.; length 300 m., width 130 m.

Omaruru, *t.*, S.W. Africa; creamery, aerodrome; p. (1960) *2,639* inc. *743* whites.

Ombai Is., Indonesia; N. of Timor.

Omdurman, *c.*, Sudan on R. Nile, opp. Khartoum; built by the Mahdi; old Dervish cap.; here Kitchener defeated the Dervishes, 1898; tr. in ivory, gum arabic, cattle, camels; p. (estd. 1956) *130,000.*

Ometepe, *I.*, L. Nicaragua, Central America, with volcano; alt. 5,747 ft.

Omine, *t.*, Japan; anthracite coal-mines.

Omsk, *t.*, W. Siberia, R.S.F.S.R.; on the R. Irtish; on Trans-Siberian Rly., caravan ctr.; cath.; engin., chemicals, textiles, oil refining; p. (1967) *746,000.*

Omuta, *t.*, Kyushu, Japan; coal; p. (1964) *221,000.*

Onahama, *pt.*, N.E. Japan; copper refinery under construction. [p. (1957) *7,225.*

Onate, *t.*, Guipuzcoa, Spain; nr. Bilbao; industl;

One Tree Hill, *bor.*, Auckland, N.Z., p. (1966) *12,905.*

Onega, *L.*, R.S.F.S.R.; 85 m. from L. Ladoga; a. 3,765 sq. m.; connection with R. Volga by canal.

Onega, *R.*, R.S.F.S.R.; flows to G. of Onega; length 400 m.

Oneglia, *spt.*, Italy; on G. of Genoa. nr. Nice, Italy; olive-oil tr. [p. (1968) *16,238.*

Onehunga, *spt., bor.*, N.I., N.Z.; nr. Auckland;

Oneida, *L.*, N.Y., U.S.A.; nr. Syracuse; 20 m. by 6 m.; discharges via Oneida R. to Seneca R.

Oneonta, *t.*, N.Y., U.S.A.; on Susquehanna R.; rly. wagon wks.; p. (1960) *13,412.*

Onomichi, *t.*, Honshu, Japan; p. (1947) *48.726.*

Onstwedde, *t.*, Groningen, Neth.; mnfs.; p. (1967) *27,666.*

Ontario, *L.*, N. America; smallest of the Gr. Lakes of the St. Lawrence basin, separating the Canadian prov. of O. from N.Y., U.S.A.; polluted waters; a. 7,500 sq. m.; depth 740 ft.

Ontario, *prov.*, Canada; formerly called Upper Canada; St. Lawrence and Ottawa Rs., Gr. Lakes; extreme climate, milder in peninsula in S.; coniferous forest; good communications; hydro-elec. power; nuclear power sta. at Chalk R.; wheat, oats, fruit, dairying, cattle, lumbering, gold, silver, copper, lead, uranium, nickel, oil, farm implements, rly. rolling stock, motor vehicles, machin., textiles, furs, wood pulp, newsprint, cap. Toronto; contains Ottawa; a. 412,582 sq. m.; p. (estd. 1969) *7,425,000.*

Onteniente, *t.*, Valencia, Spain; on R. Clariano; woollen gds., paper mills; p. (1957) *14,689.*

Oodnadatta, *t.*, S. Australia; on uncompleted N. to S. trans-continental rly.; p. *100.*

O'okiep, *t.*, Cape Province, S. Africa; copper-mining dist.; p. (with neighbouring villages—whites and non-whites) *5,000.*

Oosterhout, *t.*, N. Brabant, Netherlands; nr. Breda; mnfs.; p. (1967) *23,677.*

Ootacamund, *t.*, Tamil Nadu, India; ch. t. in Nilgiri Hills; summer headquarters of Tamil Nadu Govt.; sanatorium; p. (1961) *50,140.*

Opala, *t.*, Congo; on Lomami R.; palm-nuts, gum copal.

Opalton, *t.*, Queensland, Australia; opals.

Opatija, (former It. Abbazia), *t.*, Jugoslavia, tourist resort known as the "Nice" of the Adriatic.

Opava, (former Troppau), *t.*, ČSSR.; textiles, paper, sugar; p. (1961) *42,523.* [gold.

Ophir, *dist.*, N.S.W., Australia; nr. Bathurst;

Ophir, *mtn.*, S. Malaya, alt. 4,186 ft.

Ophir, *mtn.*, N.I., N.Z.; nr. Dunedin.

Opladen, *t.*, N. Rhine-Westphalia, Germany; on R. Wupper; metals, textiles, chemicals; p. (1963) *36,300.*

Opobo, *spt.* Nigeria; exp. palm-oil and kernels.

Opole (Oppeln), *t.*, S. Poland, cap. Opole prov.; on R. Oder; R. pt., rly. junc.; trade ctr.; cement, metals, furniture; former cap. Prussian prov. of Upper Silesia (1919–45); p. (1965) *75,000.*

Oporto, *spt.*, Portugal; on R. Douro; second c. in Portugal; comm.; royal palace of Torre de Marca; cath.; univ.; ctr. of port-wine tr., sardine fisheries, cottons, woollens, silks, distilling, sugar refineries; fruit; oil refinery projected; p. (1960) *310,000.*

Opotiki, *t.*, N.I., N.Z.; ctr. of maize dist.; p. (1961) *2,559.*

Oppeln, *see* Opole.

Oppland, *co.*, Norway; a. 9,608 sq. m.; p. (1968) *168,888.*

Oradea, (former Nagyvarad), *t.*, Romania; nr. Hungarian border; rly. junction, farming pottery, engin.; p. (1963) *122,535.*

Öraefa Jokull, *highest mtn.*, Iceland; alt. 6,409 ft.

Oran *dep.*, N. Algeria; p. (1948) *1,990,729.*

Oran, *c.*, *spt.*, N. Algeria; tr. in wines, wool, cereals, meat, skins; founded by Moors; occupied by French 1831–1962; fine roadstead Mers-el-Kebir; former French naval and military sta.; p. (1960) *393,000.*

Orange, *t.*, N.S.W., Australia; fruit packing, meat, wool, bricks, elec. machin.; p. (1966) *22,200.*

Orange, *ancient t.*, Vaucluse, France; silks, sugar, fruit; p. (1954) *17,473.*

Orange, *t.*, Mass., U.S.A.; p. (1960) *3,689.*

Orange, *c.*, N.J., U.S.A.; adj. Newark; calculating machines, radio, textiles, drugs; p. (1960) *35,789.*

Orange, *C.*, N. Brazil, S. America.

Orange, *R.*, Cape Province, S. Africa; flows from Basutoland to the Atlantic; part forms S. bdy. between Cape Province and Orange Free State; length 1,300 m.

Orange Free State, *prov.*, Rep. of S. Africa; plateau land, Drakensberg to N.E., Rs Orange, Vaal and Caledon; sheep, cattle, horses, wheat, maize, fruit, tobacco, coal, diamonds; cap. Bloemfontein; a. 49,647 sq. m.; p. (1960) *1,386,547* (inc. *276,745* whites).

Oranienburg, *t.*, Potsdam, E. Germany, on R. Havel; industl.; chemicals, metals, machin.; p. (1963) *21,075.*

Oras, *t.*, Samar, Philippines; p. *20,962.*

Orastie, *t.*, Romania; on R. Muresul; p. (1956) *10,488.*

Orbetello, *t.*, Tuscany, Italy; cath.; p. *10,631.*

Ord of Caithness, *hill, headland*, nr. Helmsdale, Scot.; alt. 1,200 ft.

Ordos, *desert region*, Inner Mongolia; lies S. and E. of Yellow R.; mean alt. 3,300 ft.

Ordu, *spt.*, Turkey; on Black Sea; gd. tr.; exp. manganese; p. (1965) *27,307.*

Ordzhonikidze, *t.*, Caucasia, R.S.F.S.R.; on R. Terek; hydro-elec., lead, silver, zinc smelting; nat. gas pipeline to Tbilisi; p. (1967) *212,000.*

Örebro, *co.*, Sweden; timber, machin., matches; cap. Örebro; a. 3,650 sq. m.; p. (1961) *262,239.*

Örebro, *t.*, *cap.*, Örebro, Sweden; footwear, textiles, paper; p. (1961) *75,434.*

Oregon, *Pacific st.*, U.S.A.; Cascade, Cst. and Blue Mtns.; Colombia R. and tribs.; L. valleys; rainy cst., drier interior (agr with irrigation); cereals, sugar-beet, fruit, cattle, gold, silver, copper, coal, uranium; fisheries, canning, meat-packing, timber, milling; cap. Salem; a. 96,891 sq. m.; p. (1970) *2,056,171.*

Oregon City, Ore., U.S.A.; on Willamette R. at the falls; p. (1950) *7,682.*

Orekhovo-Zuyevo, R.S.F.S.R.; E. of Moscow, on R. Klyazma; cottons, woollens, silk, linen and knitted goods; p. (1967) *117,000.*

Orel, *t.*, R.S.F.S.R.; on R. Oka; univ.; iron, engin.; p. (1967) *202,000.*

Orenburg, *c.*, R.S.F.S.R.; on Ural R.; engin., leather, silk; p. (1967) *316,000.*

Orense, *inland prov.*, N.W. Spain; timber and fruit-growing, agr.; cap. Orense; a. 2,694 sq. m.; p. (1959) *468,242.*

Orense, *t.*, cap. Orense, Spain; on R. Minho; flour, leather, iron; p. (1959) *64,747.*

Ore Sound, *str.*, between Sjaelland and S. Sweden; freezes occasionally.

Orford Ness, *cst. prom.*, Suffolk, Eng.; 2¼ m. long.

Oriente, *prov.*, Cuba; a. 14,128 sq. m.; p. (1953) *1,797,606.*

Oriente, *terr.*, S. America; in dispute between Peru and Ecuador; situated E. of Andes, between R. Putumayo and R. Marañon; mainly dense forest, reputedly rich in minerals.

Orihuela, *t.*, Alicante, Spain; on R. Segura; leather, silks, textiles, wine, cereals, fruit; p. (1957) *15,345.*   [p. (1969) *15,345.*

Orillia, *t.*, Ont., Canada; wood-working, metal;

Orinoco, *R.*, Venezuela; rises Parima mtns., flows circuitously to Atlantic opposite Trinidad; its trib., the Cassiquiare, connects it with the Rio Negro and the Amazon; length 1,480 m.

Orissa, *st.*, India; agr. with few ts.; Hirakud dam across Mahanadi R.; Paradeep being devel. as pt.; rice; cap. Bhuvaneshwar; a. 60,164 sq. m.; p. (1961) *17,548,346.*

Orizaba, *t.*, Veracruz, Mexico; textiles, paper mills, breweries; p. (1960) *70,000.*

Orizaba, *mtn.*, Veracruz, Mexico; volcanic; called Citlatépetl in Aztec times; alt. 18,701 ft.

Orkney, *co.*, Scot.; a gr. of 68 Is. in the N. Sea, 29 being inhabited; principal Is. Pomona, Sanday, Westray; antiquarian remains, stone circles; farming, fishing; cap. Kirkwall; total a. about 360 sq. m.; p. (1961) *18,743.*

Orlando, *c.*, Fla., U.S.A.; winter resort; citrus fruit; industl.; p. (1960) *88,135.*

Orléanais, *old prov.* France, corresponding mainly to deps. Loire-et-Cher, Eure-et-Loire Loiret.

Orléans, *c.*, Loiret, France; on R. Loire; cap. of Orléanais; cath.; univ.; gr. tr. in wine, brandy, textiles, chemicals; farm implements; statue of Joan of Arc; p. (1968) *95,828.*

Orleans, I. of, Quebec, Canada; in St. Lawrence R., nr. Quebec; a. 70 sq. m.

Ormes Head, Great and Little, promontories on cst. Caernarvon, N. Wales.

Ormoc, *t.*, Leyte, Philippines; p. (1960) *62,764.*

Ormskirk, *t.*, *urb. dist.*, Lancs., Eng.; 14 m. N.E. of Liverpool; light engin., clothing, timber, agr.; p. (estd. 1967) *25,440.*

Orne, *dep.*, Normandy, France; agr., dairying, stock-keeping, fruit-growing, cider, mineral springs, iron; cap. Alençon; a. 2,372 sq. m.; p. (1962) *280,549.*   [dustl. ctr.; p. *8,400.*

Örnsköldsvik, *t.*, Sweden; on G. of Bothnia; in-

Oronsay, *sm. I.*, S. Colonsay, Argyll, Scot.

Orontes, *R.*, Lebanon, Syria, Turkey; rises in Lebanon Mtns., flows N. in deep trench between Lebanon and Anti-Lebanon Mtns. to Plain of Antioch (Antakya), then turns W. and breaks through mtns. to Mediterranean Sea; upper valley above Hama forms cultivated belt, width 10 m., used by Aleppo–Beirut rly.; middle valley is marshy; lower valley and Plain of Antioch intensively cultivated, mulberry, citrus and hard fruits, grain; length over 400 m.

Oroquieta, *t.*, Mindanao, Philippines; p. *26,640.*

Oroshaza, *mkt. t.*, S.E. Hungary; in agr. and pig-keeping dist.; p. (1962) *31,867.*

Orosziany, *t.*, Hungary; coalmng.; p. (1967) *16,700.*

Orotava, *t.*, Tenerife, Canary Is.

Oroya, *t.*, Peru, S. America; copper smelting; lead refining; p. (1961) *15,000.*

Orpington, *see* Bromley.   [p. (1961) *10,663.*

Orrell, *t.*, *urb. dist.*, Lancs., Eng.; W. of Wigan;

Orsha, *t.*, Byelorussian S.S.R.; on R. Dnieper; textiles, metal workings; p. (1959) *64,000.*

Orsk, *t.*, R.S.F.S.R.; on R. Ural; growing industl. t. of the Ural industl. region; iron and steel, locomotives, iron–chrome–nickel ores; term. of oil pipeline; p. (1959) *176,000.*

Orsova, *mkt. t.*, Romania; on R. Danube, nr. the Iron Gates Pass; oil-refining; p. (1965) *6,527.*

Orta, *L.*, Italy; W. of Lago Maggiore; a. 7 sq. m.

Orta, *t.*, Foggia prov., Italy; on shore of L. Orta.

Ortegal, *C.*, N. cst. Spain.

Orthez, *t.*, Basses-Pyrénées, France; scene of Wellington's victory over Soult (1814); leather, hams, chocolate; p. (1962) *8,829.*

Ortona, *t.*, Abruzzi Molise, Italy; cap. of ancient Frentani; on Adriatic; cath.; wines; p. *19,104.*

Oruro, *dep.*, Bolivia; a. 20,657 sq. m.; cap. Oruro; p. (1962) *265,400* (large proportion Indians).

Oruro, *t.*, Bolivia; alt. 12,160 ft.; gold, silver, copper, tin; p. (1962) *86,835.*

Oruwala, *t.*, Ceylon; steel rolling mill.

Orvieto, *t.*, Umbria, Italy; on R. Paglia; cath., Etruscan antiquities; wines, olive oil, cereals; pottery, lace; p. *20,352.*

Orwell, *R.*, Suffolk, Eng.; estuary of R. Gipping; runs from Ipswich to Harwich.

Osasco, *t.*, São Paulo st., Brazil; industl. ctr.; p. (estd. 1968) *135,576.*

Osaka, *lge. spt.*, *c.*, *comm. ctr.*, Honshu I., Japan; gr. tr.; silk, cotton, rayon cloth, tea, iron, glass, shipbldg., sugar-refining, arsenal; Shinto and Buddhist temples; p. (1970) *2,980,409.*

Oschersleben, *t.*, Magdeburg, E. Germany; sugar, chemicals, engin.; p. (1963) *19,128.*

Ösel I. (Saaremaa), Baltic, Estonian S.S.R.; ch. t. Kuressare.   [*65,000.*

Osh, *t.*, Kirghiz, S.S.R.; silk, food inds.; p. (1959)

Oshawa, *c.*, Ontario, Canada; motors; p. (estd. 1965) *69,000.*

Oshima, *I.*, Tokyo Bay, Japan; lgst and most

northerly of Izu-shichito gr.; site of volcanic Mt. Mihara (2,477 ft.).

Oshkosh, c., Wis., U.S.A.; on Fox R.; meat pkg., farming, flour, motors; p. (1960) *45,110.*

Oshogbo, t., Nigeria; p. (1953) *123,000.*

Osijek (Esseg), t., Croatia, Jugoslavia; nr. Hungarian front.; cottons, silks, beet-sugar, glass, oil refining; p. (1959) *75,000.*

Osinniki, t., R.S.F.S.R.; W. Siberia; new ctr. of coal mng.; thermal power sta.; p. (1959) *68,000.*

Osipenko, *see* Berdyansk.

Oskaloosa, t., Iowa, U.S.A.; in agr. and colly. region; p. (1960) *11,053.*

Oskarshamn, *spt.*, Sweden; on Kalmar Sound; seldom icebound; shipbldg.; p. *12,900.*

Oslo (formerly Christiania), c., *cap.*, *ch. spt.*, Norway; on fjord of same name; cath., univ.; woollens, cottons, condensed milk, paper; exp. timber, fish, matches; p. (1968) *484,275.*

Osnabrück, c., Lower Saxony, W. Germany; on R. Hase, linked by canal with Ems–Weser Canal; inland pt. and industl. ctr.; iron and steel mills; mach., textile and paper mnfs.; p. (1968) *139,861.*

Osorno, t., Chile; agr. ctr.; in beautiful, forested cty.; Germanic atmosphere; p. (estd.) *93,686.*

Osorno, *mtn.*, Chile; volcanic peak, 8,790 ft.

Osorno, *prov.*, S. Chile; p. (1960) *160,156.*

Ossa (Kissavos), *mtn.*, Thessaly; N. of Vale of Tempe and Olympus; alt. 6,194 ft.

Ossett, *mun. bor.*, W.R. Yorks, Eng.; 3 m. W. of Wakefield; woollens, coal-mining, engin.; p. (estd. 1967) *16,460.*

Ossining, t. N.Y., U.S.A.; on Hudson R.; famous "Sing-Sing" prison; p. (1960) *18,662.*

Ostend, *spt.*, Belgium; passenger route between Britain and continent of Europe; popular resort; casino, fisheries, shipbldg., textiles, tobacco; p. (1968) *57,765.*

Östergötland, *co.*, Sweden; on Baltic cst.; a. 4,266 sq. m.; cap. Linköping; p. (1961) *357,693.*

Östersund, t., Jämtland, Sweden; on Stor L.; mil. ctr.; rly. wkshps., bricks; p. (1961) *24,866.*   *[214,410.*

Östfold, *co.*, Norway; a. 1,613 sq. m.; p. (1968)

Ostia, *ancient pt.*, Italy; at mouth of R. Tiber; marshy situation; arch. remains, cath.

Östra Kvarken, *channel*, Gulf of Bothnia, between Sweden and Finland.

Ostrava, t., ČSSR.; univ.; coal, iron, steel, chemicals, oil-refining; p. (1965) *259,000.*

Ostróg, t., on Horyn R., W. part of Ukrainian S.S.R. (Volhynia), U.S.S.R.

Ostrogochsk, t., R.S.F.S.R.; nr. R. Don; tallow and cattle tr., tanneries; p. *10,000.*

Ostrów Wielkopolski, t., Poznan, Poland; agr. machin.; perfume; p. (1965) *46,000.*

Ostrowiec Swietokrzyski (Ostrovets), t., Kielce, Poland; on trib. Oder; lignite, iron ore, iron; cattle mkt.; p.(1965) *43,000.*

Ostuni, t., Lecce, Italy; mnfs. and tr.; p. *27,602*

Osuna, t., Seville, Spain; p. (1957) *23,250.*

Oswaldtwistle, t., *urb. dist.*, Lancs, Eng.; at N. foot of Rossendale Fells, 3 m. E. of Blackburn; cotton weaving, spinning and dyeing; chemicals; p. (1961) *11,915.*

Oswego, c., N.Y., U.S.A.; on L. Ontario; taken by Montcalm 1756, and the British 1814; waterpower; hosiery, matches, textiles, engines; p. (1960) *22,155.*

Oswestry, *rural bor.*, Salop, Eng.; at foot of Welsh mtns., 18 m. N.W. of Shrewsbury; cas.; rly. engine wks.; p. (of t. 1961) *11,193.*

Oswiecim, t., Krakow, Poland; p. (1965) *36,000.*

Otago, *dist.*, S.I., N.Z.; mtnous., afforested, rich in gold; farming, sheep, fruit; lge. deposit of jade found at head of L. Wakatipu; cap. Dunedin (*q.v.*); a, 25,220 sq. m.; p. (1961) inc. Southland *270,067.*

Otago Harbour, Otago dist., S.I., N.Z.; Dunedin and Port Chalmers are ports on this harbour.

Otanmäki, Finland; rich deposit of magnetite-ilmenite ore found 1953.

Otaru, *spt.* Hokkaido, Japan; herring fisheries; coal-mining, lumbering; p. (1965) *196,771.*

Otira Tunnel, S.I., N.Z.; carries rly. from Christchurch to Greymouth through S. Alps nr. Arthur's Pass; length 5¼ m.

Otley, t., *urb. dist.*, W.R. Yorks, Eng.; on R. Wharfe, 10 m. N.W. of Leeds; printing, machin., wool, paper mkg., leather, furnishings; p. (1961) *11,930.*

Otranto, *fishing t.*, S. Italy; on Strait O.; cas.;

submarine cable sta.; once a flourishing c.; cath., fine mosaic pavement; bauxite exp.

Ottawa, c., Ontario, Canada; cap. of Dominion of Canada; on R. Ottawa, 100 m. W. of Montreal; univ., caths., parliament bldgs.; hydro-elec. power, lumbering, sawmills, paper, flour, leather, matches, machin., ironware; p. (1966) *494,535.*

Ottawa, R., Canada; trib. of St. Lawrence, forming boundary between Ontario and Quebec; length 625 m.

Ottawa, t., Ill., U.S.A.; at mouth of Fox R.; grain, glass; p. (1960) *19,408.*

Ottawa, t., Kan., U.S.A.; on Osago R.; rly. wks.; p. (1960) *10,673.*

Ottery St. Mary, *mkt. t.*, *urb. dist.*, Devon, Eng.; 10 m. E. of Exeter; silk, rope, brushes; birthplace of S. T. Coleridge; p. (1961) *4,121.*

Ottoshoop, t., Transvaal, S. Africa; gold, fluor-spar.

Ottumwa, c., Iowa, U.S.A.; on Des Moines R.; in midst of great coalfield and agr. dist.; iron and steel, meat packing; p. (1960) *33,871.*

Otway, *hills*, S.W. Victoria, Australia; sheep.

Otwock, t., Warsaw, Poland; (1965) *38,000.*

Ouachita or Washita, R., Arkansas, U.S.A.; trib. of Red R.; length 550 m.

Oudenaarde (Audenarde), t., Belgium; Allies defeated French 1708; textiles; p. (1962) *6,906.*

Oudtshoorn, t., Cape Province, S. Africa; on Olifants R.; ostrich farms, tobacco, fruit; tourism; caves; p. (1960) *22,186* inc. *8,921* whites.

Oued Gueterini, t., Algeria, 70 m. S.E. Algiers; oil.

Ougadougou, t., *cap* , Voltaic Rep., W. Africa; p. *18,000.*

Oughter, L., *lough*, Cavan, Ireland.

Oughterard, t., Galway, Ireland; marble quarries, farming, fishing; p. (1951) *498.*

Oujda, t., Morocco; phosphate dist.; p. (1960) *128,645.*

Oullins, t., dep. Rhône, France; nr. Lyons; locomotive repair shops; textiles, glass, leather; p. (1954) *19,224.*

Oulton Broad, L., Suffolk, Eng.; nr. Lowestoft.

Oulu (Uleåborg), *co.*, N. Finland; partly forest and partly agr.; cap. Oulu; a. 21,887 sq. m.; p. (1966) *419,889.*

Oulu (Uleåborg), t., *cap.*, Oulu, Finland; on G. of Bothnia (Baltic Sea) at mouth of R. Oulu; lumbering; p. (1966) *78,950.*

Oulu, L., Finland; 40 m. long.

Oundle, *mkt. t.*, *urb. dist.*, Northants, Eng.; on R. Nene, 7 m. S.W. of Peterborough; public school; p. (1961) *2,546.*

Ouro Preto, t., Brazil; former cap. of Minas Gerais st.; iron, manganese, gold; textiles; p. (1960) *31,400.*

Ourthe, R., Belgium; trib. of R. Meuse; l. 90 m.

Ouse or Great Ouse, R., Norfolk, Eng.; flows N.E. to the Wash; length 156 m.

Ouse, R., Yorks, Eng.; formed by Rs. Swale and Ure, flows to Humber estuary; length 130 m.

Ouse, R., Sussex, Eng.; flows to English Channel at Newhaven; length 30 m.

Outremont, t., Quebec, Canada; p. (1961) *30,753.*

Ovalle, t., Coquimbo prov., Chile; fruit, wool; manganese, mng.; p. (1960) *46,553.*

Ovar, t., Beira Litoral, Portugal; on Avera lagoon; onions and other vegetables, sardines, wine, wheat; p. *12,729.*

Overijssel, *prov.*, Neth.; dairying, fishing, cottons; a. 1,299 sq. m.; p. (1967) *887,261.*

Overton, t., *rural dist.*, Flint, N. Wales; 5 m. S.E. of Wrexham; p. (rural dist. 1951) *6,760.*

Oviedo, *maritime prov.*, N. Spain; agr., fruit, sardine, and other fisheries; cap. O.; a. 4,204 sq. m.; p. (1960) *995,233.*

Oviedo, t., *cap.*, Oviedo, Spain; on R. Nalon; Gothic cath., univ.; coal; textiles, leather, matches; gr. mkt.; p. (1959) *128,766.*

Owatonna, t., Minn., U.S.A.; p. (1960) *13,409.*

Owends, *pt.*, Liberia; deep water pt. being built to serve iron-ore mines at Belinga.

Owen Falls Dam, Uganda; inaugurated 1 Apr. 1954; converts L. Victoria into reservoir for irrigation of U.A.R. and Sudan; also to supply Uganda industries with hydro-elec. power.

Owen Sound, t., L. pt., Ontario, Canada; on S.W. cst. of Georgian Bay, L. Huron; E. terminus of lgst. wheat-carrying L. steamers; linked by rly. to Toronto (125 m.) and Montreal; p. (1961) *17,421.*

Owen Stanley, *range*, Papua, New Guinea; highest peak Mt. Victoria; alt. 13,121 ft.

Owens, L., S. Cal., U.S.A.; on E. flank of Sierra Nevada 20 m. S.E. of Mt. Whitney; water taken by 225-m.-long aqueduct to Los Angeles; a. 120 sq. m.

Owensboro', *t.*, Ky., U.S.A.; petroleum, farming, stock-raising, tobacco; p. (1960) *42,471.*

Owosso, *c.*, Mich., U.S.A.; on Shiawassee R.; timber tr.; p. (1960) *17,006.* [length 350 m.

Owyhee, *R.*, Ore., U.S.A.; trib. of Snake R.;

Oxelösund, Sweden; on Baltic cst., S. of Stockholm; steelwks., tarcoke, glass; p. (1961) *10,007.*

Oxford, *co.*, S. Midlands, Eng.; mainly agr.; cereals, paper, gloves, blankets, agr. implements, motor cars; cap. O.; a. 749 sq. m.; p. (1966) *349,000.*

Oxford, *co. bor., univ. c., co. t.*, Oxford, Eng.; between Thames and its trib. Cherwell, 63 m. from London by rail; famous univ. with residtl. colleges, printing, steel wks., motor wks. at Cowley; p. (estd. 1968) *109,720.*

Oxnard, *t.*, Cal., U.S.A.; citrus fruits, sugar beet, oil refining; p. (1960) *40,265.*

Oxus R., *see* Amu Darya.

Oyashio, *see* Bering Current.

Oyo, *t.*, Nigeria; p. (1953) *72,000.*

Oyster Bay, *t.. cst. resort*, N.Y., U.S.A.; on Long I.; home of Theodore Roosevelt; p. (1950) *5,215.* [ch. *t.* Joplin.

Ozark Mtns., Okla. and Ark., U.S.A.; lead, zinc;

Ozd, *t.*, Hungary; iron and steel; p. (1962) *35,959.*

P

Paarl, *t.*, Cape Province, S. Africa; summer resort; wines, fruit, tobacco; flour, saw and textile mills; p. (1960) *41,540,*(inc. *14,123* whites).

Pabianice, *t.*, Poland; nr. Lodz; textiles, farming implements, paper; p. (1965) *59,000.*

Pabna, *t.*, Bengal, E. Pakistan; oil, carpets; p. (1961) *40,700.*

Pacasmayo, *spt.*, Peru, S. America; exp. rice, sugar, cotton, cacao, hides, copper, lead, zinc, silver; p. (1961) *6,000.*

Pachitea, *R.*, Peru, S. America; rises in Andes, flows N. to R. Ucayali; sm. German immigrant colonies in upper valley; length 320 m.

Pachmarhi, Madhya Pradesh, India; summer cap., tourist ctr.; p. (1961) *6,142.*

Pachuca, *cap.*, Hidalgo st., Mexico; silver; p. (1960) *70,000.*

Pacific Ocean; a. 68,000,000 sq. m.; lgst. ocean in the world; extends from W. cst. of America to E. cst. of Asia and Australia and the S. Ocean in the S.; enters Arctic Ocean via Bering Strait; greatest length N. to S. 8,000 m.; breadth, 10,000 m.; mean depth 12,560 ft., greatest depth 37,800 ft. in the Marianas Trench (1960 dive).

Padang, *spt.*, Sumatra, Indonesia; coffee, spices, rubber, tobacco, copra; p. (1961) *143,699.*

Paddington, *see* Westminster, City of.

Paderborn, *c.*, N. Rhine–Westphalia, Germany; cath., other historic bldgs.; foodstuffs, textiles, metals; p. (1963) *56,600.*

Padiham, *urb. dist.*, Lancs, Eng.; at N. foot of Rossendale Fells, 4 m. S.W. of Nelson; textiles; p. (1961) *9,893.*

Padstow, *t., spt., urb. dist.*, Cornwall, Eng.; on W. side of Camel estuary 4 m. N.W. of Wadebridge; light inds.; sm. seaside resort; p. (1961) *2,457.*

Padua, *t.*, Italy; cath., arcades, ancient bridges; machin., chemicals, silks, cloth, distilling; p. (1964) *212,000.*

Paducah, *c.*, Ky., U.S.A.; on Ohio R.; saw-mills, tobacco, railway wks.; p. (1960) *34,479.*

Paeroa, *bor.*, N.I., N.Z.; p. (1961) *2,896.*

Pag, *I.* and *spt.*, Jugoslavia; timber, salt; cath.; p. (of I.) *4,349.*

Pagan, *t.*, Burma; ruins; lacquer work.

Pago-Pago, *spt.*, Samoan Is., Pac. Oc.; U.S. naval sta.; p. (1950) *1,586.*

Pahang, *st.*, Malaysia; central Malaya; cap. Kuala Lipis; forested; a. 13,280 sq. m.; p. (estd. 1966) *418,720.*

Pahiatua, *bor.*, N.I., N.Z.; dairying; p. (1961) *2,577*

Pahlevi, *t.*, Iran; nr. Resht, on Caspian Sea; rice, hides, skins, fruit; p. (estd.) *33,000.*

Pai, *R.*, Hopeh, China; unites with Yungting R., Huto R., and flows to G. of Chihli; length 300 m.

Paignton, *t.*, S. Devon, Eng.; incorporated in Torbay co. bor.; resort; farming, cider; p. (1961) *30,289.*

Paimpont, *fishing pt.*, Cotes du Nord, N.W. France; on N. cst. of Brittany, 20 m. N.W. of St. Brieuc; lobster fishing; p. (1962) *1,791.*

Painted Desert, area of bare, multi-coloured rocks, Arizona, U.S.A.

Paisley, *burgh*, Renfrew, Scot.; 5 m. W. of Glasgow; ancient abbey; thread and rope spinning, shipbldg., chemicals, engin., preserves, car bodies; p. (1961) *95,753.*

Paita, *pt.*, Peru, S. America; exp. cotton, wool, flax, panama hats; lge. whaling sta. to S.; p. (1961) *6,958.*

Pakhoi, *former treaty pt.*, Kwangtung prov., China; indigo, groundnuts, hides, leather, sugar, fish; p. (1931) *36,000.*

Pakistan, Islamic Republic of, *indep. sov. st.* within Br. Commonwealth (1947), forming part of sub-continent of India; consists of West Pakistan (cap. Lahore), and East Pakistan (cap. Dacca); prin. expts. raw jute, cotton, hides and skins, oilseeds, tea; cap. Rawalpindi (till new fed. cap. Islamabad is built); a. 365,529 sq. m.; p. (estd. 1969) *111,830,000. See* East Pakistan, West Pakistan.

Paknampoh, *t.*, Thailand; on R. Meinam, at upper limit of steam navigation.

Pakokku, *t.*, Burma; comm. ctr.; sugar, rice, tobacco, oil-fields, teak; p. *23,115.*

Palagruz, *I.*, Adriatic Sea; formerly Italian; ceded to Jugoslavia by peace treaty 1947.

Palanpur, *t.*, Gujarat, India; p. (1961) *29,139.*

Palau Is., *group of Is.*, in Pac. Oc.; p. (1958) *8,845.*

Palawan, *I.*, Philippines; coffee, resin, timber; a. 4,550 sq. m.; p. (1960) *104,500.*

Palayamcottai, *t.*, Tamil Nadu, India; rice, coffee, cotton, tobacco; p. (1961) *51,002.*

Palembang, *t.*, Sumatra, Indonesia; cap. P. residtl.; cotton, rubber, coffee; fertilisers; tyres; p. (1961) *475,000.*

Palencia, *inland prov.*, Old Castile, Spain; partly fertile plain, partly wooded and mntainous; cap., Palencia; a. 3,093 sq. m.; p. (1959) *239,041.*

Palencia, *t., cap.*, Palencia, Spain; N. of Valladolid; ctr. of rich wheat-growing dist.; ironfounding and weaving; p. (1957) *50,000.*

Palermo, *spt.*, Sicily, Italy; cath., univ.; machin., chemicals, wines, fruit, tobacco; p. (1965) *633,000.*

Palestine or The Holy Land, historic region, bounded by Syria and Lebanon on the N., Jordan on the E., the Egyptian prov. of Sinai on the S., and the Mediterranean on the W.; a. when under British mandate 10,429 sq. m.; p. (estd. 1948) *782,000. See* Israel.

Palestine, *t.*, Texas, U.S.A.; agr. and forest region; p. (1960) *13,974.*

Palghat, *t.*, Kerala, India; p. (1961) *77,620.*

Palitana, *t.*, Gujarat, India; a. c. of Jain temples inhabited by priests and their servants; p. (1961) *24,581.*

Palk Strait, India; separating India from Ceylon.

Palm Beach, *t.*, Fla., U.S.A.; Atl. coastal resort.

Palm Beach, *t.*, N.S.W., Australia; N. of Sydney; tourist resort.

Palma, *spt.*, Majorca I., Spain; cath., palaces; wine, fruit, silk; cap. Balearic Is.; p. (1965) *171,000.*

Palmarola I., Pontine Is., Italy; vineyards.

Palmerston North, *c.*, N.I., N.Z.; dairying, sheep; univ; rly. junction; p. (1966) *47,667.*

Palmira, *t.*, Colombia; tobacco, coffee, rice, cocoa, sugar, grain; p. (estd. 1959) *124,000.*

Palmyra (ancient Tadmor), *c.*, in Syrian desert, 120 m. N.E. of Damascus; extensive ruins; p. *10,000.*

Palmyra Is., Pac. Oc., U.S.A.; coral islets; coconuts; p. *32.*

Palni Hills, *range*, between E. and W. Ghats, S. Deccan, India; highest peak 7,050 ft.

Palos, *spt.*, Huelva, S. Spain; on Rio Tinto; starting point for Columbus in 1492.

Palos, C. de., Mediterranean, S.E. cst. of Spain.

Palua, *pt.*, Venezuela; pt. of shipment for iron mines at El Pao; nearby Caroni hydro-elec. plant built to serve steel wks. and aluminium plant.

Pamiers, *t.*, Ariège, France; elec. steel furnaces; wine; leather; p. (1962) *13,953.*

Pamir Mtns., *high mtn. plateau* ("roof of the world"), Tadzik S.S.R., Central Asia; Mt.

Communism (24,590 ft.) climbed by Russo British team 1962.

Pamlico Sound, *lge. lagoon*, on E. cst. of N.C., U.S.A.; length 75 m., width 25 m.

Pampa, La, *terr.*, Central Argentina; stock-rearing; cap. Santa Rosa; a. 55,669 sq. m.; p. (1947) *166,929.*

Pampas, Argentina; vast plains stretching from the Rio Negro on the S. to the Gran Chaco in the N., and E. from the Andes to the Atlantic; woodless, level country; rich pastures in E., supporting countless numbers of sheep and cattle, W. mostly barren.

Pampilla, *t.*, Peru; on cst. N. of Callao; oil refinery under construction.

Pamplona, *t.*, Colombia; coal, gold, coffee, cocoa, wheat, brewing, textiles; p. (estd. 1959) *22,800.*

Pamplona, *t.*, Spain; cath., fortress, univ.; textiles, leather, paper, flour, soap, earthenware; p. (1959) *88,410.*

Panama, *rep.*, Central America; mountainous; climate hot throughout year, abundant rains; languages Spanish; religion R.C.; communications poor; cattle-raising, farming; pearls, bananas, cocoa, coconuts, rubber, sugar, coffee, timber, shrimps; cap. Panama City; a. 28,575 sq. m.; p. (estd. 1969) *1,415,000.*

Panama, *canal zone*, Panama; strip of land 47 m. long by 10 m. wide, extending 5 m. on either side Panama Canal, under U.S. jurisdiction; p. (estd. 1969) *56,000.*

Panama Canal, Canal Zone, Panama; length 51 m. ranging in width from 300 to 1,000 ft., minimum depth 41 ft.; time of transit through canal 7–8 hours; canal starts at Cristobal (Atlantic), to Gatun locks, through Gatun Lake, Culebra cut, Pedro Miguel locks, Miraflores locks to Balboa (Pacific). *See also* Section L.

Panama City, *c.*, *spt.*, cap. Panama; harbour at S. entrance to Canal; cath.; oil refining, steel rolling mill, cement plant, lt. inds.; p. (1967) *412,000.*

Panarukan, *spt.*, Java, Indonesia; exp. tobacco, sugar; p. *7,455.*

Panay, *I.*, Philippines; between Negros I. and Mindoro I.; a. 4,446 sq. m.; cotton, rice, sugar, coffee; p. (1960) *1,746,600.*

Pancevo, *t.*, Voivodina, Jugoslavia; wheat, maize, timber, glass, textiles, ironwks., oil refining; (1959) *40,000.* [on R. Damodar.

Panchet Hill Dam and power sta.; Bihar, India;

Pandharpur, *t.*, Maharashtra, India; on R. Bhima; temple, pilgrimages; p. (1961) *45,421.*

Pando, *dep.*, Bolivia; p. *18,600*; cap. Cobija; p. (1962) *24,400.*

Panevezys, *t.*, Lithuanian S.S.R.; textiles; p. (1954) *60,000.*

Pangalanes Canal (Canal Des Pangalanes), Malagasy; follows E. cst. from Farafangana to Tamatave, through series of lagoons; 300 m.

Pangani, *spt.*, Tanzania, E. Africa; copra, sisal hemp, maize; p. *3,000.*

Pangkalanbrandan, *spt.*, Sumatra, Indonesia; oil-refining and exp.

Panipat, *t.*, E. Punjab, India; silver and brass, cotton goods, blankets, carpets, pottery; p. (1961) *67,026.*

Panjsher Valley, Afghanistan; silver-mines, unexploited; mica-mine.

Pantar I., Lesser Sunda Is., Indonesia; mtns.;

Pantelleria, *volcanic I.*, Mediterranean, Italy; midway between W. Sicily and Tunisia; a. 58 sq. m.; ch. t. P. on N.W. cst.; figs, raisins, vines, capers, cereals; fishing; p. *10,000.*

Pantin, *sub.*, Paris, France; glasswork, sugar ref., tobacco factories, chemicals, leather, tallow; p. (1962) *46,401.*

Paoki (Baoji), *c.*, Shensi prov., China; cotton weaving; millet, wheat; p. (1953) *130,000.*

Paoting (Baoding), *c.*, Hopeh prov., China; on the Yungting R.; gr. tr.; p. (1953) *197,000.*

Paotow (Baotou), *c.*, Inner Mongolia; on left bank of Yellow R., on road and rly. routes to E. China; airfield; terminus of caravan routes through Gobi desert and Tarim basin to Turkestan; gr. tr. and industl. ctr.; steelwks.; p. (1958) *650,000.*

Papakura, *bor.*, N.I., N.Z.; p. (1966) *11,278.*

Papatoetoe, *c.*, N.I., N.Z.; p. (1966) *20,576.*

Papeete, *t.*, *pt.*, Tahiti I. Pac. Oc.; cap. Tahiti and of French Settlements in Oceania; exp. copra, vanilla, phosphates and mother-of-pearl; p. (1962) *19,903.*

Paphos, *admin. dist.*, W. cst. Cyprus; ancient c.; Old P. dates from 3000 B.C., New P. impt. seapt.; rich deposits of copper and iron pyrites, sulphur in Vretsia a.; p. (1960) of dist. *58,159* of t. *9,083.*

Papua–New Guinea, *terr.*, Eastern New Guinea; admin. by Australia; cap. Port Moresby; gold, copra, rubber, timber; oil 30 m. offshore; Surinubu Dam (*q.v.*) opened 1963; no rlys.; total a. 183,540 sq. m.; p. (estd. 1969) *2,307,064* (incl. *43,391* non-indigenous, mainly Australian).

Pará, *st.*, Brazil; densely forested; rubber, fruits, cacao, Brazil nuts; cap. Bélem; a. 474,155 (estd. 1968) *1,959,756.*

Paraguay, *rep.*, S. America; undulating cty., swamps, forests; Rs., Paraguay, Pilcomayo, Paraná; climate, hot summers, warm winters, moderate rainfall; religion, R.C.; communications poor; fertile; cattle, yerba maté, oranges, sugar, maize, cotton, tobacco, lumber, quebracho extract; iron, manganese, copper; meat packing; oil refining at Villa Elisa; cap. Asinción; a. 157,006 sq. m.; p. (estd. 1968) *2,350,000.*

Paraguay, R., S. America; rises in plateau of Mato Grosso, flows S. and joins R. Paraná nr. Corrientes; forms bdy. between Brazil and Bolivia, Brazil and Paraguay; approx. length 1,200 m.

Paraíba, *st.*, N.E. Brazil; livestock, cotton, sugar cane; tin, scheelite; cap. João Pessoa; a. 21,800 sq. m.; p. (estd. 1968) *2,252,636.*

Paraíba, R., S. Brazil; rises in São Paulo st., and flows between Rio de Janeiro and Minas Gerais to the Atlantic N.E. of Rio de J.; length 650 m.

Paramaribo, *spt.*, *cap.*, Neth. Guiana; (Surinam); on R. Surinam; ch. exp., bauxite, timber. rubber, rice, fruit; p. (1959) *113,478.*

Paraná, *cap.*, Éntre Rios prov., Argentina; pt. for grain, cattle, sheep; road tunnel to Santa Fé under construction; p. (1960) *109,600.*

Paraná, *st.*, S. Brazil, between Paraná R. and Atl. Oc.; extensively forested; maté, timber, coffee; cap. Curitiba; a. 77,717 sq. m.; p. (estd. 1968) *7,216,582.*

Paraná, R., Brazil; formed by junction of Rs. Rio Grande and Parnaíba; flows W. between Paraguay and Argentina; flows into Rio de la Plata; navigable to Brazil frontier nr. Iguaçu Falls; length 2,000 m.

Paranaguá, *spt.*, Paraná st., Brazil; ch. pt. for Paraná; in lagoon harbour; modern highway links with Asuncion (Paraguay); p. (1960) *27,723.*

Pardubice, *t.*, ČSSR.; univ.; saw-milling; brewing, distilling; p. (1961) *52,655.*

Parentis, *t.*, Landes, France; nr. L. Biscarosse 40 m. S.S.W. Bordeaux; oil: lignite mined nearby; p. (1962) *2,493.*

Parenzo, *spt.*, Italy; cath.; fishing; Roman remains.

Pariñas, *C.*, Peru, S. America.

Paris, *c.*, *cap.*, France, on R. Seine, 110 m. from mth.; cultural ctr.; 12 boulevards radiate from Arc de Triomphe; Notre Dame, Louvre, Tuileries, Palais Royal; oldest bridge Pont Neuf (1578–1604); royal forests and palaces nearby, *e.g.*, Fontainebleau, Rambouillet, Chantilly; univ. (founded 12th cent.); German siege 1870–71; German occupation 1940–44; luxury inds., publishing, furniture, food, clothing; heavy inds. in northern subs.; admin. a. called " Ville de Paris "; oil refineries at Grandpuits, 25 m. S.E., and Porcheville in W.; p. (1968) *2,590,771*; of Greater Paris (1968) *8,196,746.*

Paris, *t.*, Texas, U.S.A.; cotton, fruit, canned goods; p. (1960) *20,977.*

Parkersburg, *c.*, W. Va., U.S.A.; on Ohio R.; iron- and steel-wks., oil and natural gas, coal, glassware, rayon, porcelain; p. (1960) *44,797.*

Parkes, *t.*, N.S.W., Australia; mkt.; rly. junction; p. (1966) *8,431.*

Parma, *prov.*, Emilia, Italy; a. 1,258 sq. m.; p. (1961) *381,624.*

Parma, *t.*, N. Italy; between Apennines and R. Po; univ., cath.; tr. ctr.; food processing, wine, cheese; precision instruments; agr. machin., footwear, felt hats; p. (1961) *140,844.*

Parnaíba, R., rises in Brazil, flows into N. Atlantic Ocean, forms bdy. between Maranhão and Piaui; length 750 m.

Farnaiba, *spt.*, Piaui, Brazil; cotton, cattle; p. (1960) *39,951.*

Parnassos, *min. ridge*, Greece; 83 m. N.W. of Athens, nr. the ancient Delphi, the modern Liak- hura; highest summit, Licoreia, alt. 8,068 ft.

Parnu, *t.*, Estonian S.S.R.; on G. of Riga; resort; flax, timber, wood pulp, woollens; p. (1956) *33,600.*

Páros, *I.*, Grecian Archipelago; W. of Naxos; a. 63 sq. m.; cap. P.

Parramatta, *c.*, N.S.W., Australia; pt. near head of Parramatta R. (spanned by lgst concrete bridge in world) in met. a. of Sydney; expts. woollen and leather goods; p. (1966) *107,006.*

Parrett, *R.*, Somerset, Eng.; flows to Bristol Channel, nr. Bridgwater; length 35 m.

Parry (Mauke), *I.*, Pac. Oc.; part Cook Is., N.Z.; p. 773.

Parry Sound, *t.*, Ont., Canada; lumbering; p. (1961) *6,004.*

Parsons, *t.*, Kan., U.S.A.; coal, natural gas, machin.; p. (1960) *13,929.*

Partinico, *t.*, Sicily, Italy; silk; p. *22,080.*

Pasadena, *c.*, Cal., U.S.A.; N. of Los Angeles; in fruit-growing region, base of San Gabriel Mtns.; 200-in. telescope on Mt. Palomar; famous for its carnival; p. (1960) *116,401.*

Pasco, *t.*, Wash., U.S.A.; on Snake R.; p. (1960) *14,522.*

Pasco, *see* Cerro de Pasco.

Pas-de-Calais, *dep.*, N. France; coal, iron; farming, sugar distilling, paper, pottery; cap. Arras; a. 2,606 sq. m.; p. (1968) *1,397,159.*

Pasig, *t.*, Luzon, Philippines; comm. ctr. of the L. region; p. *29.170.*

Pasir Mas, *t.*, Kelantan, Malaysia; rly. junction.

Passage West, *urb. dist., spt.*, Cork, Ireland; shipping, fishing; p. (1951) *2,658.*

Passaic, *c.*, N.J., U.S.A.; silk, chemicals, dyes, rubber goods, mill machin., springs, steel cabinets, tin cans; p. (1960) *53,963.*

Passaic, *R.*, N.J., U.S.A.; flows 100 m. to Newark Bay.

Passau, *t.*, Germany, at confluence of Rs. Danube, Inn and Ilz; near Austrian frontier; trans- shipment base, inds. inc. leather, porcelain, tobacco and brewing; p. (1963) *31,200.*

Passchendaele, *t.*, Belgium; impt. strategic point in First World War; p. (1962) *3,115.*

Passero I., Mediterranean Sea; off S.E. cst. of Sicily, Italy.

Pasto, *t.*, *cap.*, Narino dep., Colombia; on flank of Pasto volcano; univ.; gold near by; p. (estd. 1959) *110,790.*

Pasuruan, *spt.*, Java, Indonesia; exp. sugar, tapioca; p. *36,973.*

Patagonia, Argentina; extensive region, E. of Andes; elevated plateau, arid, sterile; princi- pal Rs., Colorado, Rio Negro and Chubut; oil and minerals, unworked; lge. tracts of grazing for sheep, horses and cattle.

Patan, Gujarat, India; swords, silk and cotton goods; p. (1961) *50,264.*

Patan, *valley t.*, Nepal; p. (1961) *135,230.*

Patani, *spt.*, Thailand; tin exp., fishing; p. *109,252.*

Paterno, *t.*, Sicily, Italy; N.W. of Catania; mineral springs, wines; p. (1961) *42,935.*

Pater Noster Is., Indonesia; coconuts.

Paterson, *c.*, N.J., U.S.A.; principal ctr. silk mftg.; aeroplane engines; textiles; machin.; p. (1960) *143,663.*

Pathankot, *t.*, E. Punjab, India; fruit preserving; p. (1961) *46,330.*

Patia R., Colombia; gold, platinum found.

Patiala, *t.*, Punjab, India; iron and steel mftg.; flour; p. (1961) *125,234.*

Patino Mines, *see* Uncia.

Patkai, *hills*, India; Chaukan; alt. 9,020 ft.

Patmos, *I.*, one of the Dodecanese, Aegean Sea; a. 13 sq. m.; p. (estd.) *3,000.* (According to Rev. 1. 9. the exiled St. John wrote the Revela- tion here.)

Patna, *cap.*, Bihar, India; univ.; rice, indigo, cotton, salt.; p. (1961) *364,594.*

Patras, *spt.* " Peloponnese ", Greece; citadel and cas.; currants, raisins, figs, olives, wine, skins, etc.; p. (1961) *95,364.*

Pau, *t.*, Pyrénées-Atlantique, France; on Gave du Pau; cas.; health resort; linen, chocolate, hams, wine; natural gas nearby; p. (1968) *74,005.*

Pauillac, *t*, Gironde, France; oil refining; natural gas; p. (1962) *5,725.*

Paulis, *see* Isiro.

Paulo Affonso, *falls*, São Francisco R., Brazil; 260 ft.; Tres Marias dam and power sta. inau- gurated 1960.

Pavia, *t.*, Italy; cath., univ.; walled city; battle site 1525; olives, silk, wine; Parmesan cheese; oil refining at Spineto; p. (1961) *73,503.*

Pavlodar, *pt.*, Kazakh, S.S.R.; on R. Irtysh; chemicals, sulphates, agr. machin., locomotives, aluminium, oil processing; p. (1967) *145,000.*

Pavlovo, *t.*, R.S.F.S.R.; on R. Oka; iron and steel, engin.; p. (1956) *42,600.*

Pawtucket, *c.*, R.I., U.S.A.; on P. R. used for water-power, woollen, cotton and silk goods; machin.; chemicals; first cotton-spinning factory established in the U.S.A. 1790; p. (1960) *81,001.*

Paysandu, *dep.*, Uruguay; p. (1953) *92,417.*

Paysandu, *t.*, Uruguay; meat, cattle, sheep, wool; footwear, soap; p. (estd. 1956) *60,000.*

Pazardzhik, *t.*, Bulgaria; on main rly. line to Istanbul; p. (1956) *39,499.*

Paz de Rio, *t.*, Boyaca, Colombia; steel; iron ore, coal, limestone nearby; hydro-elec. sta. pro- jected.

Peace, *R.*, Canada; rises in Rocky Mtns., and flows to L. Athabaska; length 1,000 m.

Peak, The, *Pennine hill dist.*, mid-Eng.; extending from Chesterfield to Buxton, and Ashbourne to Glossop; mainly composed of limestone with typical Karst features; tourists; highest point Kinder Scout, alt. 2,080 ft.

Pearl, *R.*, *see* Chu Kiang.

Pearl Harbour, *landlocked harbour*, Oahu I., Hawaiian Is., one of finest natural harbours in E. Pacific; U.S. Naval base. Attacked by Japanese without warning on 7 Dec. 1941.

Peary Land, Greenland.

Peč, *t.*, Jugoslavia; nr. Albanian border; tobacco, fruit; p. (1959) *25,000.*

Pechelbronn, Alsace, France; oilfields.

Pechenga (Petsamo), *spt.*, R.S.F.S.R., U.S.S.R.; on left bank of R. Petsamon 10 m. upstream from Barents Sea; formerly Finnish, ceded to U.S.S.R. Sept. 1944; ice-free throughout year, thanks to influence of N. Atlantic Drift; exp. nickel, timber, cobalt.

Pechora, *R.*, flowing into Arctic Ocean, R.S.F.S.R. 1,000 m. long, 700 m. navigable.

Pecos, *R.*, N.M. and Texas, U.S.A.; trib. of Rio Grande; length 764 m.

Pécs, *t.*, Hungary; cath., univ., airport; coal, chemicals, majolica; p. (1965) *134,000.*

Peebles, *bor.*, *co. t.*, Peebles, Scot.; on upper course of R. Tweed; hydro. woollen cloth knitwear; p. (1961) *5,545.*

Peebles, *co.*, Scot.; hilly, Broad Law, 2,754 ft.; sheep, woollen cloth, knitwear; a. 346 sq. m.; p. (1961) *14,117.*

Peekshill, *t.*, N.Y., U.S.A.; on Hudson R.; iron- wks.; p. (1960) *18,737.*

Peel, *t.*, I. of Man, Eng.; midway along W. cst.; cas., cath., ruins; resort; fisheries; p. *2,612.*

Peel Fell, *mtn.*, Northumberland, Eng.; 1,964 ft.

Pegasus, *Bay*, S.I., N.Z.

Pegu, *dist.*, Lower Burma; annexed by Brit. 1852; teak forests; industl. a.; p. *2,961,249.*

Pegu, *c.*, Pegu prov., S. Burma; R. pt., rly. junc.; founded *c.* 825 A.D.; many temples, inc. Shwe May Daw Pagoda; bronze statuettes mnfd.; p. *c. 48,000.*

Pegu Yoma, *mtns.*, Burma; separate valleys of Rs. Irrawadi and Sittang.

Pei Kiang, *see* North River

Peine, *t.*, Lower Saxony, Germany; N.W. of Brunswick; iron, furniture, textiles; p. (1963) *30,300.*

Peipus, *see* Chudskoye.

Peiraieus, *spt.*, Greece; pt. of Athens; principal pt. of Greece; arsenal; wines, brandy, cur- rants, vinegar; marble; machin.; p. (1961) *1,853,000* inc. Athens.

Pekalongan, *t.*, N. cst. Java, Indonesia; exp. sugar, rubber; p. (1961) *102,380.*

Pekan, *t.*, Pahang, Malaya; p. *5,000.*

Pekin, *t.*, Ill., U.S.A.; cereal prods., distilling, leather, metal goods; p (1960) *28,146.*

Peking (Beijing), *c.*, *cap.*, China; cultural ctr. and c. of gr. arch. beauty; for hundreds of years seat of the Chinese emperors (Mongol, Ming and Manchu régimes); surrounded by 22 m. of towering walls broken by 16 gates; p. (estd. 1958) *5,420,000.*

Pelée, *mtn.*, Martinique; active volcano, devastated town of St. Pierre 1902, loss of over 30,000 lives, later eruption caused further 2,000 deaths; alt. 4,400 ft.

Pelew Is., Caroline Is., Pac. Oc.; coral, primitive agr.; bauxite; p. *12,798*.

Pella, *prefecture*, Macedonia, Greece; cap. Edessa; p. (1961) *133,128*.

Pelly, *R.*, trib. of R. Yukon, N.W. Terr., Canada.

Peloponnesos, *peninsula*, S. part of Greece, separated from mainland proper by G. of Corinth; a. 8,356 sq. m.; p. (1961) *1,096,390*.

Pelotas, *t.*, Rio Grande do Sul, Brazil; pt. on lagoon S.S.W. Pôrto Aleque; meat-packing and industl. ctr.; p. (estd. 1968) *208,672*.

Pelvoux, *min.*, France; between Isère and Hautes Alpes; alt. 12,920 ft.

Pemba, *I.*, part of indep. st. of Zanzibar; E. Africa; a. 380 sq. m.; cloves and copra, coconuts, exp. mangrove bark for tannin; p. (1958) *133,858*.

Pembroke, *t.*, Ont., Canada; lumbering; p. (1961) *16,791*.

Pembroke, *co.*, Wales; fertile; stock-raising, steel, fishing, shipbldg.; a. 617 sq. m.; p. (1966) *97,000*.

Pembroke, *mkt. t.*, *mun. bor.*, Pembroke, Wales; on S. side of Milford Haven; cas., ruins of Monkton Priory; naval dockyard, light engin.. metal ind., woollens; p. (1961) *12,737*.

Pembroke Dock, Pembroke, Wales.

Penang, *I.*, *st.* West Malaysia; cap. Georgetown, pt. for N. Malaya handling rubber and tin; paper mill; the first Brit. Straits Settlement (*q.v.*); a. 400 sq. m.; p. (estd. 1966) *743,833*.

Penarth, *urb. dist.*, Glamorgan, Wales; on Severn estuary 2 m. S. of Cardiff; ship repairing, wood, cement, bricks; p. (1961) *20,897*.

Pendleton, *t.*, Ore., U.S.A.; p. (1960) *14,434*.

Penge, *see* Bromley.

Pengpu (Bengbu), *c.*, Anhwei, China; on Hwai Ho 105 m. N.W. of Nanking; on Tientsin–Nanking rly.; p. (1953) *253,000*.

Penicuik, *burgh*, Midlothian, Scot.; on N. R. Esk, 7 m. S. of Edinburgh; paper, iron; p. (1961) *5,824*.

Penistone, *mkt. t.*, *urb. dist.*, W.R. Yorks., Eng.; on R. Don; steel; p. (1961) *7,071*.

Penki (Benqi), *c.*, Liaoning prov., China; metallurgical ctr.; p. (1953) *449,000*.

Penmaenmawr, *t.*, *urb. dist.*, Caernarvon, Wales; 4 m. W. of Conway; resort; p. (1961) *3,754*.

Pennine Alps, Switzerland; division of Alpine system; ch. peaks; Matterhorn (14,782 ft.), Weisshorn (14,804 ft.). Mischabelhörner (14,942 ft.); includes Zermatt; winter sports.

Pennine Range, *mtn. range*, running N. to S. from Cheviot Hills to Derby, Eng.; length 140 m.

Pennsylvania, *st.*, U.S.A.; originally proprietary colony of Penn family, and later one of the 13 original sts. in the Union; traversed N.E. to S.W. by Appalachians; ch. Rs.: Delaware, Susquehanna, Allegheny and Monongahela; iron and steel, coal (bituminous and anthracite), natural gas, petroleum; maize, wheat, oats, rye; textiles, machin., motor cars, tobacco; cap. Harrisburg; ch. ts.; Pittsburgh, Philadelphia; a. 45,333 sq. m.; p. (1970) *11,663,301*.

Penrhyn, *dist.*, Caernarvon, Wales; nr. Bethesda; slate quarries.

Penrith, *mkt. t.*, *urb. dist.*, Cumberland, Eng.; at N. foot of Shap Fell, 18 m. S.E. of Carlisle; ruined cas.; agr. mkt.; agr. implements, egg-packing sta.; tourist ctr.; p. (1961) *10,931*.

Penrith, *t.*, N.S.W., Australia; in Sydney met. a.; ctr. for mkt. gardening; p. (1966) *35,970*.

Penryn, *t.*, *mun. bor.*, Cornwall, Eng.; on estuary of R. Fal, 2 m. N.W. of Falmouth; fishing; granite quarries; p. (estd. 1967) *4,990*.

Pensacola, *spt.*, Fla., U.S.A.; safest land-locked harbour in G. of Mexico; naval sta.; fish, naval requisites, wool, hides, cotton and lumber mills; p. (1960) *56,752*.

Penticton, *t.*, B.C., Canada; fruit farming, canning; p. (1961) *13,859*.

Pentire Point, headland, Cornwall, Eng.

Pentland Firth, strait between Orkney and the Caithness cst., N. Scot.

Pentland Hills, *range*, Scot.; running from Lanark–Edinburgh–Peebles; highest point Scald Law, 1,896 ft.

Pentland Skerries, *small Is.*; Pentland Firth, Scot.

Penybont, *rural dist.*, Glamorgan, Wales; coal-mining; p. (1961) *41,992*.

Pen-y-Ghent, peak in Pennine Range, W.R. Yorks, Eng.; 2,231 ft.

Penza, *t.*, R.S.F.S.R.; between Penza and Kuibyshev; grain, sawmills, paper, soap and candles, engin.; " Druzhba " oil pipeline from Mozyr; p. (1967) *324,000*.

Penzance, *t.*, *mun. bor.*, Cornwall, Eng.; on Mounts Bay; seaside resort, good harbour; pilchard fishing, copper, tin. and china clay, textiles, lt. engin.; p. (estd. 1967) *18,900*.

Peoria, *c.*, Ill., U.S.A.; river pt.; farming implements, grain; distilling, brewing, mng.; p. (1960) *103,162*.

Perak, *st.*, Malaysia; N.W. Malaya; cap. Ipoh; tin; a. 8,030 sq. m.; p. (estd. 1966) *1,613,728*.

Pereira, *t.*, Caldas, Colombia; cath.; coffee, brewing, thread mkg.; p. (estd. 1959) *183,730*.

Perekop, Isthmus of, connects Crimea with Ukraine, and rail focus in ctr. of maize-growing a.

Pergamino, *t.*, Buenos Aires prov., Argentina; on Pampas 60 m. S. of Rosario; impt. road and rail focus in ctr. of maize-growing a.

Périgueux, *t.*, *cap.*, Dordogne, France; on R. L'Isle; cath.; china, iron, woollens, figs. truffles; pâté de foie gras; marshalling yards; rly. repair shops; p. (1962) *41,134*.

Perim, *I.*, Straits of Bab-el-Mandeb at southern entrance to Red Sea; Southern Yemen; formerly part of Brit. col. of Aden; a. 5 sq. m.; p. (1946) *360*.

Perlis, *st.*, Malaysia; N. Malaya; cap. Kangar; rice, tin, coconuts; a. 310 sq. m.; p. (estd. 1966) *116,393*.

Perm, *formerly* Molotov, *t.*, R.S.F.S.R.; on R. Kama, N.W. of Sverdlovsk; hydro-elec., oil, textiles, engin., chemicals, copper; p. (1967) *785,000*.

Pernambuco, *st.*, N.E. Brazil; mntnous interior, cst. fertile; cap. Recife; sugar, cotton, manioc, tobacco, fruits; a. 37,962 sq. m.; p. (estd. 1968) *4,728,830*.

Pernis, *t.*, opp. Rotterdam, Netherlands; lge oil refinery; oil pipeline to Wesserling (nr. Cologne); pipeline to carry ethylene to Terneuzen.

Perovo, *t.*, R.S.F.S.R.; nr. Moscow; engin., chemicals, agr. research institutes; p. (1959) *143,000*.

Perpignan, *fortfd. t.*, Pyrénées-Orientales, France; cath.; wine, brandy, silk, wool; p. (1968) *102,191*. [27,900.

Perreux-sur-Marne, *t.*, Seine, France; p. (1962)

Persepolis, *ruins*, ancient cap. of Persia.

Pershore, *mkt. t.*, *rural dist.*, Worcs. Eng.; on R. Avon, 8 m. S.E. of Worcester; abbey church; preserves, machin.; p. (1961) *17,599*.

Persia. *See* Iran.

Persian G., arm of Indian Oc., through G. of Oman and Strait of Ormuz, between Iran and Arabia; ch. pts. Bandar-e-Bushehr (Bushire), Abadan, Kuwait; Bahrein, lgst. I.

Perth, *co.*, Scot.; Trossachs and P. of Killiecrankie; noted for beautiful scenery; crossed by Grampians in N. and W.; ch. peaks, Ben More, Ben Lowers, Schiehallion; ch. Rs.: Tay, with tribs. Isla, Garry, Tummel, Sarn; pastoral; fruit; distilling; textiles; a. 2,493 sq. m.; p. (1961) *127,018*.

Perth, *burgh*, Perth, Scot.; on R. Tay, in gap between Sidlaw and Ochil Hills; cap. of Scot. till assassination of James I in 1437; near by is Scone Palace; cath.; linen, winceyettes, brewing, rope, dyeing; p. (1961) *41,199*.

Perth, *c.*, cap. W. Australia; 12 m. above pt. of Fremantle; univ., observatory, race-courses; lge. bauxite deposit nearby; p. (1966) inc. subs. *449,494*.

Perth Amboy, *spt.*, N.J., U.S.A.; terracotta wks.; shipyards and dry docks; p. (1960) *38,007*.

Peru, *rep.*, S. America; traversed N. to S. by the Andes, attaining 22,000 ft.; ch. Rs., Marañon, Ucayali; in S.E., L. Titicaca (12,450 ft.) lgst. L. in S. America; climate, eastern, very hot, drenching rains, central or mountain zone, sun intensely hot, but shade temperatures low; W. and Pacific cst., heat not excessive, scanty rainfall; religion R.C.; poor communications; sugar, cotton, coffee, wool, hides, timber, cocoa. wheat, tobacco, petroleum, silver, copper, iron ore, fertilisers; cap. Lima; a. 482,258 sq. m.; p. (estd. 1968) *12,772,000*. (Indians 46 per cent., *mestizos* and whites 53 per cent).

Peru (Humboldt), Current, *ocean current*, S. Pac. Oc.; flows N. along cst. of N. Chile and Peru;

relatively cold water causes lower air temperatures and produces cloud and fog.

Perugia, *spt.*, Umbria, Italy; on R. Tiber; univ., observatory; woollens, silks, lace; foodstuffs, furniture, pottery, chemicals, agr. machin.; p. (1961) *109,596*.

Pervouralsk, *t.*, R.S.F.S.R.; in Urals, 25 m. W. of Sverdlovsk; pipe rolling mill; p. (1967) *109,000*.

Pesaro, *Adriatic spt.*, Italy; N.W. of Ancona; resort; figs, wines, oil, silks; majolica ware; sulphur; sugar-refining; p. (1961) *65,601*.

Pescadores Is., *group of Is.*, 30 m. W. of Formosa; total a. about 51 sq. m.; since 1945 Chinese, formerly Japanese.

Pescara, *t.*, Italy; at estuary of R. Aterno, E. cst.; olive oil, soap, pasta, pottery; fishing; p. (1961) *87,076*.

Peshawar, *t.*, W. Pakistan; on rly. to Khyber Pass commanding route Afghanistan–India; military sta.; univ; coal, fruit, sugar; cottons, ambroidery, wood carving, copper ware, boat bldg., marble; p. (1961) *218,691*.

Peshawar, *div.*, W. Pakistan; p. (1961) *5,088,000*.

Pesquilerto, *R.*, trib. of Rio Grande del Norte, Mexico.

Pest, *c.*, Hungary; on left bank of R. Danube, opposite Buda, and connected therewith by suspension bridge, the two cs. forming the Hungarian cap. of Buda-Pest (*see* Budapest).

Petah Tiqva, *t.*, Israel; agr. ctr.; oranges; textiles, chemicals, metal goods, tanning; p. (1960) *62,700*.

Petaling Jaya, *t.*, West Malaysia; industl. estate nr. Kuala Lumpur.

Peter I., *uninhabited I.*, Antarctic Ocean; belonging to Norway; a. about 94 sq. m.

Peterborough., *t.*, Ont., Canada; flour milling, elec. machin., trailers, agr. equipment, plastics, textiles, paper; p. (1961) *47,185*.

Peterborough, Soke of, *see* Huntingdon and Peterborough.

Peterborough, *c.*, *mun. bor.*, Huntingdon and Peterborough, Eng.; on R. Nene at the margin of The Fens; cath.; rly. ctr.; diesel engines; general engin.; p. (estd. 1967) *66,100*.

Peterhead, *spt.*, *burgh*, E. Aberdeen, Scot.; on E. cst., 27 m. N.E. of Aberdeen; herring fisheries, tweed; granite quarries; p. (1961) *12,497*.

Peterlee, *t.*, Durham, Eng.; on plateau of E. Durham, 11 m. E. of Durham; one of "New Towns" designated 1948; ctr. of coal-mng. dist.; mohair and worsted spinning; clothing and wood-wool mftg.; p. (estd. 1965) *17,963*.

Petermann Peak, Greenland; alt. 9,175 ft.

Petersburg, *c.*, Va., U.S.A.; tobacco, meat-canning, cotton; optical goods; p. (1960) *36,750*.

Petersfield, *t.*, Hants. Eng.; on R. Rother, 12 m. N.W. of Chichester; p. (1961) *7,379*.

Petit Morin. *R.*. France; trib. of R. Marne.

Petone, *sub.* Wellington, N.I., N.Z., p. (1966) *10,143*.

Petra, *ancient t.*, Jordan; temples. rock tombs and Roman ruins.   [San Francisco.

Petra. *t.*, Majorca, Spain; birthplace of founder of

Petropavlovsk, *spt.*, Kamchatka Pen., U.S.S.R.; fishing; p. (1967) *119,000*.

Petropavlovsk, *t.*, Kazakh. S.S.R.; on R. Ishim; flour, leather, meat canneries; furs, engin.; p. (1967) *162,000*.

Petrópolis, *t.*, Rio de Janeiro, Brazil; health resort, 2,300 ft. above sea-level; p. (estd. 1960) *200,052*.

Petrosani, *t.*, Romania; S. of Deva; coal; p. (1963) *134,245*.

Petrovgrad, *t.*, N.W. Jugoslavia; p. *32,833*.

Petrovsk, *t.*, S.E. Siberia, R.S.F.S.R.; iron and steel, non-ferrous metallurgy; p. (1954) *50,000*.

Petrozvodsk, *t.*, R.S.F.S.R.; L. Onega; univ.; mica, paper, engin.; p. (1967) *164,000*.

Petsamo, *see* Pechenga.

Petten, *t.*, Netherlands; 30m. N.W. of Amsterdam, on cst.; atomic research ctr.

Petworth, *mkt. t.*, *rural dist.*, W. Sussex, Eng.; in Rother valley, 12 m. N.E. of Chichester; building stone; p. (rural dist. 1961) *9,463*.

Pevensey Levels, *marshy area*, E. Sussex, Eng.; lie behind coastal sand-bars between Eastbourne and Bexhill, extend 5 m. inland to Hailsham; now largely drained, cattle pastures; a. 24 sq. m.

Pewsey, *vil.*, *rur. dist..* Wilts. Eng.; in Vale of Pewsey, 7 m. E. of Devizes; farming, iron, bricks, tiles; p. (rural dist. 1961) *16,971*.

Pforzheim, *t.*, Baden-Württemberg, Germany;

S.E. of Karlsruhe; gold, silver, metal wks. jewellery; p. (1963) *86,100*

Phan Rang, ctr. of irrigation scheme, S. Viet-Nam.   [fish; p. *5,000*.

Phan Thiet, *spt.*, S. Viet-Nam; exp. dried and salt

Pharsala, *c.*, Thessaly, Greece; S. of Larissa; Cæsar's triumphs over Pompey.

Philadelphia, *c.*, *pt.*, Penns., U.S.A.; univ., R.C. cath., masonic temple; mint, academy of fine arts; shipbldg., locomotives, machin., surgical instruments, carpets, woollens, cottons, worsteds; sugar, and petroleum refining; ctr. of War of Independence, from 1790 to 1809; fed. cap. founded by Wm. Penn 1682; p. (1970) *1,926,529*;   Greater   Philadelphia   (1970) *4,774,000*.

Philae, *I.*, Upper U.A.R.; in Nile above Aswan Dam; temples dating from late Egyptian and classical times incl. famous temple to Isis; submerged by dam waters.

Philippeville, *t.*, *spt.*, Algeria; wine, sheep, cattle, cereals, cork, cigarettes, mineral water, macaroni, fish canning; p. (1954) *70,000*.   [1,554.

Philippeville, *t.*, Namur, S. Belgium; p. (1962)

Philippine Is., *rep.*, Asia; comprising over 7,000 Is., lgst. being Luzon, Mindanao, Mindoro and Palawan; mountainous, many volcanoes, highest Apo, 10,312 ft.; coal, iron, copper, gold; dye-woods, rice. maize, tobacco, coffee, cotton, Manila hemp; coconuts, cigars, pearl fisheries; cap. Quezon City; p. (estd. 1970) *37,933,000*.

Philippopolis, *see* Plovdiv.

Philipstown, *see* Daingean.

Phillipsburg, *c.*, N.J., U.S.A.; on Delaware R.; water-power, machin., rly. wks.; silk and pulp; p. (1960) *18,502*.   [ing; p. (1960) *30,364*.

Phitsnulok, *t.*, central Thailand; temples; weav-

Phlorina (Florina), *pref.*, Greece; occupied by Bulgaria, April 1941, restored to Greece by peace treaty of 1947; cap. Phlorina; p. (1961) *67,233*.

Phlorina (Florina), *t.*, Phlorina, Greece; in basin at alt. 3,000 ft., 10 m. from Jugoslav border, 15 m. from Albanian border. purely agr. interests; p. (1961) *11,933*.

Phnom-Penh. *t.*, *R. pt.*, cap. Cambodia, on Mekong R.; univ., airpt.; rice, cotton; hydroelec. and storage dam project being built to W.; p. (1965) *404,000*.   [bricks; abattoir.

Phnom Sar, *t.*, Cambodia; brewing, fertilisers,

Phoenix, *c.*, Arizona, U.S.A.; winter resort; iron. steel, aircraft, electronics, clothing; p. (1970) *580,275*.

Phoenix Group, *Is.*, Pac. Oc.; part of Gilbert and Ellice I. colony; a. 16 sq. m.; U.S. now have some rights over Canton and Enderbury; Canton used as international airport; p. (1958) *1,257*.

Phthiotis, *pref.*, Greece; cap. Lamia; p. (1961) *159,373*.

Phuket, *t.*, S. Thailand; tin smelting plant projected; p. (1960) *28,033*.

Piacenza, *prov.*, Emilia, Italy; a. 965 sq. m.; p. (1961) *282,813*

Piacenza, *t.*, Italy; cath., palaces, arsenal; motor cars, chemicals, cement; p. (1961) *87,930*.

Pianosa I., Italy; penal settlement; cereals, vineyards, olives; p. *1,000*.

Pias, *t.*. Alentejo Baixo. S. Portugal; E. of Beja.

Piatra-Neamt, *t.*, Moldavia, Romania; timber, pharmaceuticals, soap; p. (1963) *48,572*.

Piaui, *st.*, Brazil; cattle, cotton, sugar, tobacco, rubber; silver, iron and lead; a. 96.262 sq. m.; cap. Teresina; p. (estd.1968) *1,432,634*.

Piave, *R.*, N.E. Italy; flows to Adriatic; length 125 m.

Piazza Armerina, Sicily, Italy; oil, wines and nuts; remarkable Roman mosaics (recently discovered); p. *28,420*.

Picardy, *old prov.*, France; which included all the Somme dep. and parts of Pas de Calais, Aisne and Oise; old battle sites, Agincourt and Crécy.

Pichincha, *prov.*, Ecuador; cap. Quito—the cap. of Ecuador; a. 6,218 sq. m.; p. (1950) *386,520*.

Pickering, *mkt. t.*, *urb. dist.*, N.R. Yorks, Eng.; on N. margin of Vale of Pickering, 6 m. N. of Malton; church with murals; iron, bricks; p. (1961) *4,193*.

Pickering, Vale of, E.R. Yorks, Eng.; wide, flat-floored vale, once occupied by glacial lake; bounded to N. by N. York Moors, to S. by York Wolds; drained W. by R. Derwent, which leaves Vale through Kirkham gap; alluvial soils, marshy in ctr.; crop-farming along margins, grain, fodder crops; cattle grazing on damper meadows in ctr.; ch. ts. Pickering, Malton, Helmsley.

Pico da Bandeira, *mtn.*, Brazil; alt. 9,462 ft.

Picton, *t.*, S.I., N.Z.; freezing wks.; tourist and fishing ctr.; p. (1961) *2,320.*

Pidurutalagala, *mtn.*, Ceylon; alt. 8,295 ft.; highest peak in Ceylon.

Piedmont, *region*, N. Italy; rice, wheat, vines, fruits; silk, cottons, woollens; a. 9,813 sq. m.; p. (1961) *3,889,962.*

Piedras Negras, *frontier t.*, Mexico; cattle mkt., coal, silver, zinc and copper; p. *15,663.*

Pierre, *t., cap..* S.D., U.S.A.; on Missouri R.; p. (1960) *10,088.*

Pietermaritzburg, *t., cap.*, Natal, S. Africa; 30 m. N.W. of Durban; named after Piet Retief and Gerhardus Maritz, two Boer leaders; lt. inds.; tanning; iron-ore mng. in a.; p. (1960) *95,124* inc. *39,472* Europeans.

Pietersburg, *t.*, Transvaal, S. Africa; gold, asbestos, tin; cereals, tobacco, cotton, oranges, lemons; p. (1962) *28,000* inc. *11,000* whites.

Piet Retief, *t.*, Transvaal, S. Africa; tobacco, fruit, mealies, wattle gr. in dist.; p. (1960) *8,604* inc. *2,745* whites.

Pikes Peak, *mtn.*, Col., U.S.A.; alt. 14,109 ft.

Pila (Schneidemühl), *t.*, N.W. Poland (since 1945); formerly in Prussian prov. of Pomerania; trade ctr., lignite mines nearby; p.(1965) *33,000.*

Pilar, *t.*, Paraguay; cotton, timber, hides, oranges; p. (estd. 1960) *10,000.*

Pilatus, *mtn.*, Switzerland; alt. 6,988 ft.

Pilawa (Pilau), *t., spt.*, R.S.F.S.R.; shipbldg., fishing.

Pilbara, *dist.*, W. Australia; metal ores inc. gold, copper, tin; iron ore; ch. mining ctr., Marble Bar.

Pilbara, *new t.*, W. Australia; iron ore mng.

Pilcomayo, *R.*, rising in S. Bolivia, and flowing through the Gran Chaco, separates W. Paraguay from Argentina; trib. of the Paraguay; length 1,400 m.

Pilibhit, *t.*, Uttar Pradesh, India; rice, pepper, sugar; p. (1961) *57,527.*

Pilion, *celebrated mtn.*, S. of Mt. Ossa, Thessaly, Greece; alt. 5,310 ft.

Pillon Pass, Switzerland; alt. 5,092 ft.

Pimlico, *dist.*, Westminster, London, Eng.

Pinar del Rio, *prov.*, W. Cuba, W. Indies; tobacco, asphalt; a. 5,211 sq. m.; p. (1953) *448,422.*

Pinar del Rio, *t.*, Cuba, W. Indies; tobacco; p. (1953) *38,885.*

Pinawa, *t.*, Manitoba, Canada; 55 N.E. of Winnipeg; nuclear research; p. (1965) *8,000.*

Pind Dadan Khan, *t.*, W. Pakistan; coal; p. *11,445.*

Pindus. *mtn. chain*, between Thessaly and Albania, Greece; highest peak 8,050 ft.

Pine Bluff, *c.*, Ark., U.S.A.; cotton, motor-cars; p. (1960) *44,037.*

Pine Creek, *t.*, Arnhem Land, N. Terr., Australia; gold; p. *115.*

Pinerolo, *t.*, Italy; S.W. of Turin; cath.; silk, cotton, woollens; p. *22,390.*

Pines, Is. of, *dependency* of Fr. col. New Caledonia; a. 58 sq. m.; convict settlement.

Pinetown, *t.*, Natal; residtl., industl.; p. (1960) *12,799* inc. *6,965* Europeans.

Pinios R., Greece; flows into G. of Thessaloniki.

Pinjarra, *t.*, W. Australia; rly. junction; timber and stock-raising dist.

Pinneberg, *t.*, Schleswig-Holstein, Germany; N.W. of Hamburg; rose cultivation, metals, leather; p. (1963) *29,900* [a. 1,180 sq. m.

Pinos I. (I. of Pines), Caribbean Sea; S. of Cuba; working inds.; p. (1956) *36,500.*

Pinsk, *t.*, Byelorussia, U.S.S.R.; paper, woodworking inds.; p. (1956) *36,500.*

Piombino, *t.*, Italy; port for Elba I.; steel wks.; p. *26,238.*

Piotrkow Trybunalski, *industrl. t.*, Poland; S. of Lodz; p. (1965) *57,000.*

Pique, *t.*, Ohio, U.S.A.; N. of Dayton; ironwks., woollens; nuclear reactor; p. (1960) *19,219.*

Piraeus, *see* Peiraieus.   [olives; p. *14,875.*

Piran, *spt.*, Istria, Jugoslavia; salt, wines,

Piracicaba, *t.*, São Paulo, Brazil; sugar, cattle, coffee, oranges; p. (1960) *80,670.*

Pirmasens, *t.*, Rhineland–Palatinate, Germany; S.W. of Mannheim; footwear, leather goods; p. (1963) *53,100.*

Pirna, *t.*, Dresden, E. Germany; on R. Elbe; textiles, paper, glass; p. (1969) *41,076.*

Pirot, *t.*, Jugoslavia; nr. Bulgarian border; Jugoslavia; p. *13,033.*   [*365,582.*

Pisa, *prov.*, Italy; a. 1,180 sq. m.; p. (1961)

Pisa, *c.*, Italy; at head of Arno delta, 12 m. N.E. of Leghorn; famous leaning tower, cath., univ.; mineral baths, cotton, silk; p. (1961) *91,108.*

Pisco, *spt.*, Peru, S. America; cotton; lead, zinc; whaling; p. (1961) *17,000.*

Pisco, *dep.*, Peru, S. America; p. (1961) *123,917.*

Pisek, *t.*, CSSR.; brewing, iron foundries, textiles; p. (1961) *19,542.*

Pistoia, *t.*, Tuscany, Italy; on Arno plain, N.W. of Florence; iron and steel goods, silk, macaroni; p. (1961) *82,401.*

Pitcairn I., E. Pacific; British col.; incs. Henderson, Ducie, and Oeno Is.; sweet potatoes, bananas, oranges, coconuts; a. 2 sq. m.; p. (1965) *186*, mostly descendants of the mutineers of the *Bounty.*

Pitch Lake, Trinidad I., W.I.; located in the S. of the I., 10 m. S.W. of San Fernando; natural deposit of asphalt; tourism; a. 212 acres.

Pitea, *spt.*, N. Sweden; on G. of Bothnia; saw mills; p. (1961) *7,426.*

Pitesti, *t.*, Romania; on Arges R.; petroleum, fruit, grain; lge. automobile plant; oil refinery under construction; p. (1963) *67,236.*

Pitlochry, *burgh*, Perth, Scot.; on R. Tummel, 4 m. S. of Pass of Killiecrankie; summer resort; distilleries, hydros; p. (1961) *2,051.*

Pittenweem, *burgh*, Fife, Scot.; at entrance to Firth of Forth; fisheries; p. (1961) *1,576.*

Pittsburgh, *c.*, Penns., U.S.A.; univ.; R.C. cath., coll., Carnegie Library and Institute; port on Ohio R.; ctr. of richest American coalfield; natural gas, petroleum, iron and steel, machin., metal goods, meat packing, glass, aluminium, chemicals; p. (1970) *512,676*; Greater P. *2,382,000.*

Pittsfield, *c.*, Mass., U.S.A.; textiles, paper, plastics, elec. machin., hol. resort; p. (1960), *57,879.*

Pittston, *t.*, Penns., U.S.A.; anthracite, coal, machin.; p. (1960) *12,407.*   [*716,337.*

Piura, *N. dep.*, Peru; a. 15,190 sq. m.; p. (1961)

Piura, *t.*, Peru; p. (1961) *32,100.*

Pladju, *t.*, S. Sumatra, Indonesia; oil refining; linked by pipe-line with Tempino and Bejubang.

Plainfield, *c.*, N.J., U.S.A.; sub. New York City; printing, motor lorries, machin., chemicals, hosiery; p. (1960) *45,330.*

Plaistow, *dist.*, E. London, Eng.; p. (1961) *10,424.*

Planitz, *t.*, Saxony, Germany; S.W. of Zwickau; textiles, tobacco; p. (estd. 1954) *25,100.*

Plate R. or Rio de la Plata, estuary of the Rs. Paraná and Uruguay flowing to the Atlantic between Argentina and Uruguay, length 170 m.; width at head 25 m., at mouth 138 m.

Plattsburg, N.Y., U.S.A.; pt. of L. Champlain; tourist ctr.; military post; p. (1960) *20,172.*

Plauen, *t.*, Karl-Marx-Stadt, E. Germany; textiles, machin., cable, leather, paper, radios; rly. junction; p. (1963) *79,111.*

Plenty, Bay of, N.I., N.Z.; on E. cst.; 130 m. wide.

Plettenberg, *t.*, N. Rhine–Westphalia, Germany; on R. Lenne; iron wks.; p. (1963) *29,000.*

Pleven, *forlfd. t.*, Bulgaria; many mosques; famous siege 1877; woollens, silks, wines; p. (1956) *57,758.*

Plock, *t.*, Poland; on R. Vistula, nr. Warsaw agr.; oil refinery and petrochemical plant; p. (1965) *54,000.*

Ploesti, *t.*, Prahova dist., Romania; petroleum, engin.; p. (1963) *170,894.*

Plovdiv (Philippopolis), *c.*, Bulgaria; on R. Marica; univ., Greek cath.; wheat, fruit, silks, woollens, tobacco, leather, attar of roses, cars; p. (1956) *162,518.*

Plumstead, *dist.*, S.E. London, Eng.

Plymouth, *c., spt., co. bor.*, S. Devon, Eng.; on Plymouth Sound; comprises the "three towns" of Plymouth, Devonport and Stonehouse; R.C. cath., guildhall, museum; shipbldg.; seaside resort; fishing and fish canning, light inds.; p. (estd. 1969) *248,470.*

Plymouth, *spt.*, Mass., U.S.A.; Pilgrim Hall, Pilgrim Fathers landed in 1620 from *Mayflower*, established first English colony; textiles, cordage, machin., cottons, woollens; p. (1950, *10,540.*   [*2,500*)

Plymouth, *ch. t.*, Montserrat I., T.W.I.; p. (1957)

Plymouth, *t.*, Pen ns., U.S.A.; coal; p. (1960) *10,401.*

Plynlimmon, *mtn.*, Montgomery and Cardigan, Wales; alt. 2,469 ft.

Plzen (Pilsen), *t.*, ČSSR.; coal, iron ore, steel, engin., chemicals; p. (1965) *142,000.*

Po, *R.*, Italy; flows from Monte Viso, through Piedmont and Lombardy to the Adriatic; length, 340 m.; natural gas deposits Po valley.

Pocatello, *t.*, Idaho, U.S.A.; rly. wks.; livestock; cheese; p. (1960) *28,534.*

Pocklington, *mkt. t.*, *rural dist.*, E.R. Yorks, Eng.; at foot of York Wolds, 12 m. E. of York; milling, malting, bricks, tiles, agr.; p. (rural dist. 1961) *13,933.*

Pocos de Caldas, *t.*, Minas Gerais, Brazil; bauxite; tourism; p. (estd. 1968) *44,504.*

Podolsk, *t.*, R.S.F.S.R.; S. of Moscow; engin., tin smelting, cement; p. (1967) *160,000.*

Podrinye, *dist.*, W. Serbia, Jugoslavia; antimony.

Pohai (Chihli), G. of, N. China; together with G. of Liaotung forms shallow expanse of water almost cut off from Yellow Sea by Liaotung and Shantung peninsulas; receives water and silt of Hwang Ho; a. approx. 15,000 sq. m.

Pohjois Karjalan, *dep.*, Finland; p. (1966) *198,063.*

Point Clairette, Equatorial Africa; oilfield.

Point-à-Pierre, Trinidad; oil refinery; natural gas pipeline from Forest Reserve field.

Pointe-à-Pitre, *ch. t.*, Grande Terre I., Guadeloupe, Lesser Antilles; p. (1960) *26,160.*

Point-Claire, *t.*, Quebec, Canada; p. (1961) *22,709.*

Pointe-des-Galets, *ch. pt.*, Ile de la Réunion, Indian Ocean (Fr.).

Pointe-Noire, *impt. spt.*, Congo Rep. (ex-French), Equatorial Africa; aerodrome; copper ore, potash, timber, groundnuts; p. (1962) *54,643.*

Point Fortin, Trinidad; oil field and refinery.

Poitiers, *t.*, Vienne, France; chemical, dairy, metalwkg. inds.; univ.; Black Prince defeated French (1356); p. (1962) *62,222.*

Poland, *rep.*, Europe; bounded by Germany, the Baltic Sea, Russia, and Czechoslovakia; largely lowland, rising from Baltic to Carpathians on S. border; ch. Rs.; Vistula and tribs.; climate: hot summers, very cold winters, moderate rainfall; good communications; agr.: cereals, potatoes, sugar-beet, forests, cattle, sheep, horses, pigs; minerals: coal, iron, steel, petroleum, natural gas, potash: cap. Warsaw; a. 121,131 sq. m.; p. (1969) *32,676,000.*

Pollokshields, *S.W. sub.*, Glasgow, Scot.; industl. and residtl.

Polotsk, *t.*, Byelorussian S.S.R.; cath.; gasoline prod., oil refining; oil pipeline to Latvian pt. of Ventspils; p. (1965) *38,100.*

Polotskiy, *t.*, Byelorussian S.S.R.; 8 m. W. of Polotsk; new oil workers' t. 1963.

Poltava, *industl. t.*, Ukrainian S.S.R.; horses, cattle, grain, engin., textiles; synthetic diamond plant; p. (1967) *177,000.*

Polynesia, *sub-div.*, Oceania; I. groups in Pacific within 30° N. and S. of the equator; between 135° E. and W. longitude.

Pomerania, *former prov.*, N. Germany; in post-war redivision part E. of R. Oder to Poland; part W. of R. Oder incorporated in Land Mecklenburg, E. Germany; farming, shipbldg. fishing.

Pomona or Mainland, lgst. of the Orkney Is., Scot. Kirkwall (cap.) and Stromness on I.

Pomona, *c.*, Cal., U.S.A.; fruit-culture; p. (1960) *67,157.*   [8,012 sq. m.

Pomorze, *prov.*, Poland; cap. Bydgoszcz; a.

Pompeii, *ruined c.*, Italy; stood 13 m. S.E. of Naples, at foot of Vesuvius; destroyed A.D. 79 by volcanic eruption, site re-discovered in 1748; many most interesting excavations; also modern c. near by; fine church with famous collection of silver and gold plate.

Ponape I., Caroline Is., Pac. Oc.; copra, ivory, nuts, starch, bauxite; a. 134 sq. m.; p. (1958) *14,335.*

Ponca City, *t.*, Okla., U.S.A.; p. (1960) *24,411.*

Ponce, *c.*, Puerto Rico, W. Indies; coffee, sugar, rum; p. (1960) *114,965.*

Pondicherry, *cap.*, former Fr. Settlements in India; united with India 1954; cotton, rice; a. of dist. 185 sq. m.; p. (1961) *369,079;* of c. *40,421.*

Pont-à-Mousson, *t.*, Meurthe-et-Moselle, France; R. Moselle; ironwks., paper, velvet, cement wks.; p. (1962) *13,037.*

Ponta Delgada, *c.*, *t.*, *spt.*, São Miguel I., Azores; p. (1960) *22,316.*

Pouta Grossa, *t.*, Paraná, Brazil; rly. junction;

maté, rice, timber, tobacco, bananas, cattle, jerked beef; p. (estd.1968) *152,581.*

Pontardawe, *vil.*, Glamorgan. S. Wales; on R. Tawe, 9 m. N.E. of Swansea; zinc smelting and refining, steel wks.

Pontchartrain, Lake, *shallow lake,* lower Mississippi flood plain, U.S.A., connected by canal to New Orleans which lies 6 m. to the south, and by deltaic channels to the gulf of Mexico.

Pontefract, *t.*, *mun. bor.*, W.R. Yorks, Eng.; 7 m. E. of Wakefield; cas. ruins; coal, furniture, confectionery; p. (estd. 1967) *29,630.*

Pontevedra, *prov.*, Spain, on Atl. cst., bordering Portugal; agr., livestock, fisheries; cap. Pontevedra; a. 1,695 sq. m.; p. (1959) *736,069.*

Pontevedra, *spt.*, cap. Pontevedra prov.; Spain; fishing; p. (1949) *46,168.*

Ponthierville, *t.*, Congo, Africa; nr. Stanley Falls, Congo R.; p. *1,000.*

Pontiac, *c.*, Mich., U.S.A.; on Clinton R.; fishing and shooting, motor cars, rubber goods, machin., varnish; p. (1960) *82,233.*

Pontianak, *t.*, *cap.*, Kalimantan, Indonesia; exp. rubber, copra; p. (1961) *150,220.*

Pontine Is., off W. cst. of Italy; in Tyrrhenian Sea; a. 4½ sq. m.; p. *6,000.*

Pontine Marshes, *region.* Latium, S. Italy; coastal zone S.E. of Rome extending from Velletri to Terracina; formerly highly malarial fens, largely drained and colonised 1930–35; 3,200 new farms, 4 new ts.; ch. t. Littoria; a. c. 250 sq. m.   [Moritz; tourist resort.

Pontresina, *t.*, Grisons, Switzerland; E. of St.

Pont-y-mister, *vil.*, Monmouth, Eng.; in valley of R. Ebbw, 6 m. N.W. of Newport; lge. steel-wks., zinc refineries.

Pontypool, *t.*, *urb. dist.*, Monmouth, Eng.; coal, iron, steel, glass, bricks, tin galvanising, nylon at Manhilad; p. (1961) *39,879.*

Pontypridd, *t.*, *urb. dist.*, Glamorgan, Wales; on R. Taff, 12 m. N.W. of Cardiff; coal, iron; p. (1961) *35,536.*

Ponza I., Pontine Is., Italy; wine, wheat, flax; fishing; bentonite-mining; a. 3 sq. m.

Poole, *mkt. t.*, *spt.*, *mun. bor.*, E. Dorset, Eng.; on Poole Harbour, 4 m. W. of Bournemouth; seaplane base; yachting; marine engin. tent mkg., bricks, chemicals; p. (estd. 1967) *97,520.*

Poona, *t.*, Maharashtra, India; univ.; cotton, sugar, rice; p. (1961) *737,426.*

Poopo, *L.*, Oruro dep., Bolivia; S. America; situated in Andes at alt. 12,120 ft.; very shallow; fed from L. Titicaca by R. Desaguadero, which flows over saline beds; no outlet, therefore salt-water; max. length 50 m., width 30 m.

Popayan, *cap.*, Cauca Dep., Columbia; cath., univ.; gold, silver, platinum, copper near by; p. (estd. 1959) *57,770.*

Poperinghe, *t.*, W. Flanders, Belgium.; woollens linens, hops; p. (1962) *12,409.*

Poplar, *see* Tower Hamlets.   [17,887 ft.

Popocatepetl, *volcano,* nr. Pueble, Mexico; alt.

Porbandor, *spt.*, Gujarat, India; cement, silk, cotton; imports coal, dates, timber, manchin; petroleum; birthplace of Mahatma Gandhi; p. (1961) *75,081.*

Porcupine Hills, *t.*, Ont., Canada; on rly. 40 m. S. of Cochrane; ctr. of impt. gold-mng dist.

Pordenone, *dist.*, *t.*, within Friuli-Venezia Giulia reg.; Italy; cath; cottons, silks, pottery.

Pori (Björneborg), *spt.*, S. Finland; at mouth of R. Kokemäen; copper refinery, rolling mills, match, paper and pulp wks.; p. (1966) *60,205.*

Porirua, *c.*, Wellington, N.I., N.Z.; p. (1966) *22,190.*

Porjus, *t.*, Norrbotten, N. Sweden; on R. Lulea, where it leaves Stora Lulevatten; impt. hydro-elec. power-sta. supplies power to iron-ore mining dists. of Gällivare and Kiruna, also to Narvik rly.

Porsgrunn, *spt.*, Norway; timber, shipping, engin., porcelain, explosives; p. (1968) *31,765.*

Port Alfred, *t.*, Canada; Upper St. Lawrence R.; imports bauxite for smelting at Arvida (lgst. smelter in world, 1959).

Port Alfred, *t.*, Cape Province, S. Africa; resort; p. (1960) *6,171* (inc. 1,412 whites).

Port Amelia, *spt.*, Mozambique; sisal, coconuts, cotton, maize, groundnuts; p. (1960) *55,902.*

Port Antonio, *t.*, Jamaica, W. Indies; p. *5,482.*

Port Arthur, *c.*, S.W. Liaoning prov., China; naval base at entrance to Pohai R.; p. (estd.) *200,000.* *See* Luta.

Port Arthur, *L. pt.,* Ontario, Canada; on N.W. cst. of L. Superior; lumbering, mining, grain-milling, exp. ctr.; p. (1961) *45,276.*

Port Arthur, *t.,* Texas, U.S.A.; p. (1960) *66,676.*

Port Arzew, *pt.,* Algeria; world's 1st comm. plant to liquefy natural gas for exp. opened 1964; oil pipeline from Haoud el Hamra projected; oil refinery being built.

Port Assab, *t.,* Ethiopia; oil refining.

Port au Prince, *spt., cap.,* Haiti, W. Indies; coffee, cacao; p. (1960) *240,000.*

Port Augusta, *t., spt.,* S. Australia; at head of Spencer G.; fine harbour; salt field; exp. wheat, fruit; p. (1966) *10,123.*

Port Blair, *spt. cap.,* Andaman and Nicobar Is. p. (estd.) *16,000.*

Port Chalmers, *t., bor.,* S.I., N.Z.; docks, ship-yards; p. (1961) *3,120.*

Port Chester, *t.,* N.Y., U.S.A.; on Long I. Sound; summer resort, cottons and woollens; p. (1960) *24,960.*

Port Colborne, *t.,* Ont., Canada; port on L. Erie; iron smelting; nickel, copper refining; p. (1961) *14,886.*

Port Elizabeth, *spt.,* Cape Province, S. Africa; on Algoa Bay; bilingual univ.; exp. skins, wool, ostrich feathers, mohair; foundries, soap, chemicals, car assembly, food preservation, sawmills; p. (1960) *270,815* (inc. *94,085* whites).

Port Erin, *vil.,* I. of Man, Eng.; on S.E. cst.; seaside resort, fisheries.

Port Essington, *N. point.* of Coburg Peninsula, N. Terr., Australia; pearl culture experiments.

Port Francqui, *t.,* Congo; present terminus of Congo rly. on Kasai R.; p. *5,000.* [p. *1,000.*

Port Fuad, *t.,* U.A.R.; N. entrance to Suez Canal;

Port Gentil, *spt.,* Gabon, Eq. Africa; exp. palm oil, mahogany, ebony; sawmills, fishing; oil refining; p. *5,000.*

Port Glasgow, *burgh. spt.,* Renfrew, Scot.; on S. bank of R. Clyde, 17 m. below Glasgow; ship-bldg. and repairing, textiles, rope, canvas mftg.; p. (1961) *22,551.*

Port Harcourt, *spt.,* Nigeria; 30 m. from sea on E. branch of Niger delta; terminus of E. Nigerian rly. system; tin, palm oil, groundnuts; bitumen plant, tyres; oil refining; p. (1953) *72,000.*

Port Hedland, *sm. spt.,* W. Australia; on N.W. cst. 285 m. S.W. of Broome; exp. gold and other metals from Pilbarra gold-field; imports food and machin.; linked to Marble Bar by narrow-gauge rly.; new t. being built 5 m. inland to absorb impact of Mt. Newman iron ore project; twin ts. to be linked by industl. belt.

Port Hope, *t.,* Ont., Canada; midway along N. shore of L. Ontario, fruit, dairying, radium refining; p. (1961) *8,091.* [castle.

Port Hunter, N.S.W., Australia; port for New-

Port Huron, *t.,* Mich., U.S.A.; on L. Huron; summer resort, mineral springs, dry docks, grain elevators; motor-car parts; p. (1960) *36,084.* [for Sydney.

Port Jackson, N.S.W., Australia; *natural harbour*

Port Kembla, *spt.,* N.S.W., Australia; S. of Wollongong; iron and steel wks., gold refining, textiles. [mills; p. (1966) *3,435.*

Port Laoighise, *mkt. t.,* Laoighis, Ireland; corn-

Port Lincoln, *spt.,* S. Australia; exp. wheat, frozen meat, tallow, wool; fertilisers; p. (1966) *8,367.*

Port Louis, *c. cap., pt.,* Mauritius, Indian Ocean; ch. comm. ctr.; p. (estd. 1968) *135,000.*

Port Lyautey (Kenitra), *see* Mina Hassan Tani.

Port Macquarie, *t.,* N.S.W., Australia; on Has-tings R.; resort; p. (1966) *7,090.*

Port Mahon, *see* Mahon.

Port Moody, *terminus,* Canadian Pacific Rly., Van-couver, Brit. Columbia; p. *1,512.*

Port Moresby, *spt., ch. t.,* Papua, New Guinea; promising copper deposits; exp. copra, sandal-wood, coffee, rubber, shell; univ.; p. (estd. 1963) *14,000.*

Port Natal, *see* Durban.

Port Nelson, *spt.,* Manitoba, Canada; on cst. of Hudson Bay at mouth of R. Nelson; linked by rly. to trans-continental systems via The Pas; exp. wheat, minerals; closed by ice for 7 months each year.

Port Nolloth, *spt.,* Cape Province, Rep. of S. Africa; pt. serving copper- and diamond-mining dists.

Port of Spain, *cap.,* Trinidad, W.I.; cocoa, sugar, asphalt; natural gas pipeline from Penal; p. (estd. 1963) *94,000.*

Port Phillip, *lge. inlet,* Victoria, Australia; land locked bay, Melbourne on N., Geelong on W.

Port Pirie, *c., spt.,* S. Australia; smelting ores, gold refining; exp. wheat, minerals; p. (1966) *15,549.*

Port Radium, *t.,* N.W. Terr., Canada; on Gr. Bear L.; pitchblende deposits; p. *300.*

Port Said, *spt.* U.A.R.; N. end Suez Canal; Free Trade a.; coaling sta.; p. (1960) *246,000.*

Port St. Mary, *vil.,* I. of Man, Eng.; on S.E. cst.; resort; fisheries, boat-bldg.

Port Shepstone, *t.,* Natal, S. Africa; sugar, bark, fibre, maize, fruit. dairying, poultry; cement; p. (1960) *4,238* inc. *1,775* whites.

Port Stanvac, S. Australia; 15 m. S. of Adelaide; oil refining.

Port Sudan, *spt.,* Sudan; 30 m. N. of Suakin; linked by rail to Atbara and Khartoum; oil refining; p. (1960) *51,790.*

Port Sunlight, Cheshire, Eng.; modern garden village founded 1888 by Lord Leverhulme for the employees of Lever Brothers' Port Sunlight factories; p. *6,000.*

Port Swettenham, *spt.,* Selangor, Malaysia; exp. tin. rubber, copra, pineapples; p. *11,300.*

Port Talbot, *pt., mun. bor.,* Glamorgan, S. Wales; on E. side of Swansea Bay; impt. iron and steel ind., copper, coal; new deep-water harbour serves as ore terminal; p. (1961) *50,223.*

Port Taufiq, *spt.,* U.A.R.; S. end of the Suez canal; p. *1,000.*

Port Vendres, *spt.,* Pyrénées-Orientales, France; nr. Perpignan; p. (1962) *5,085.*

Portadown, *t., mun. bor.,* Armagh, N. Ireland; on R. Bann, 25 m. S.W. of Belfast; linen, lace, farming; to merge with Lurgan to form c. of Craigavon; p. (1966) *20,710.*

Portaferry, *spt.,* Down, N. Ireland; shipping fisheries; p. (1966) *1,426.*

Portage, *t.,* Wis., U.S.A.; iron; p. (1960) *7,822.*

Portage la Prairie, *spt.,* Manitoba, Canada; grain exp.; p. (1961) *12,383.* [*11,017.*

Portalegre. *t.,* Portugal · cath.; mkt.; p. (1960)

Portarlington, *t.,* Offaly, Ireland; farming; first place to have elec. power-sta. using local peat fuel; p. (1966) *2,804.*

Portbou, *t.,* on Fr. side of Franco-Spanish border, opposite Rosas on Mediterranean cst.

Porthcawl, *t., urb. dist.,* Glam., Wales; on cst. 10 m. S.E. of Pt. Talbot; resort; p. (1961) *11,082.*

Portici, *spt.,* Campania, S. Italy; on Bay of Naples 5 m. S.E. of Naples; dockland sub. of Naples; p. (1961) *50,373.*

Portishead, *t., urb. dist.,* Somerset, Eng.; on Severn estuary 3 m. S.W. of Avonmouth; shipping; p. (1961) *6,440.*

Portknockie, *burgh,* Banff, Scot.; on N. Buchan cst., 5 m. E. of Buckie; sm. fishing pt.; p. (1961) *1,245.*

Portland, *urb. dist.,* Dorset, Eng.; 4 m. S. of Weymouth on sheltered N.E. side of I. of Port-land; lge. artificial harbour; p. (1961) *11,542.*

Portland, *t., spt.,* Me., U.S.A.; comm. cap. of Me.; lge. fisheries; paper, pulp, lumber, processed food, clothing; p. (1960) *72,566.*

Portland, *c.,* Ore., U.S.A.; gr. wheat and wool tr.; flour milling, shipbldg., fishing and canning, aluminium, lumber; p. (1960) *372,676.*

Portland Canal, *fjord,* N.W. cst. of America, form-ing boundary between Alaska and B.C.

Portland, I. of, *peninsula,* Dorset, Eng.; limestone mass, linked to mainland by shingle spit, Chesil Bank, terminates S. in Portland Bill; naval base, prison, Borstal inst.; limestone quarry-ing; masonry wks.

Portmadoc, *spt., urb. dist.,* Caernarvon, Wales; on Tremadoc Bay; linked by light rly. to Ffestiniog; copper and slate exp.; p. (1961) *3,419.*

Porto, *see* Oporto.

Pôrto Alegre, *c., cap.,* Rio Grande do Sul st., Brazil; exp. lard, preserved meats, rice, timber, tobacco; textiles, chemicals, furniture, brew-ing, metallurgy; oil refinery under construc-tion; pipeline connects with Rio Grande do Sol; p. (estd. 1968) *932,801.*

Porto Empedocle, *spt.,* Sicily, Italy; sulphur refin-ing, flour, furniture, lime, gypsum; p. *14,764.*

Porto Marghera, *spt.,* Venezia, N. Italy; extends along cst. S. from landward end of the causeway linking Venice to the mainland; the modern pt. of Venice, reached by ship canal dredged through shallow lagoon; oil-refineries.

Porto Novo, *t., cap.*, Dahomey, W. Africa; nr. Bight of Benin; p. (1965) 65,000.

Porto Vecchio, *t.*, Corsica; on E. cst.; p. 5,304.

Pôrto Velho. *cap.*, Rondônia st., Brazil; p. (estd. 1968) 83,178.

Portobello, *resort*, Midlothian, Scot.; on Firth of Forth, 3 m. E. of Edinburgh; bricks, pottery, paper.

Porto Torres, *spt.*, Sardinia, Italy; exp. iron ore; p. 7,251.

Portree, *t., par.*, I. of Skye, Scot.; on sound of Raasay; fishing, tweed mill; p. 2,120.

Portrush, *spt., urb. dist.*, Antrim, N. Ireland; 5 m. N. of Coleraine; tourism; p. (1966) 4,357.

Ports and Isles of Persian Gulf, *dist.*, Iran; along E. cst. Persian Gulf; extensive oil ind.; very hot; cap. Bandar-e-Bushehr; p. (1967) 346,784.

Ports and Isles of Oman Sea, *dist.*, S. Iran; arid, very hot; cap. Bandar Abbas; p. (1967) 336,784.

Portsdown Hill, *chalk ridge*, Hants, Eng.; extends E. to W. behind Portsmouth from Havant to Fareham; water-storage reservoirs supply Portsmouth; lined with early 19th-century fortifications for defence of Portsmouth; length 6 m., alt. 400 ft.

Portsea Is., *fortfd. I.*, between Portsmouth and Langston Harbours.

Portslade-by-Sea, *urb. dist.*, E. Sussex, Eng.; 1 m. W. of Hove; p. (1961) 15,750.

Portsmouth, *c., co. bor., naval pt.*, Hants, Eng.; opposite I. of Wight; has lgst. naval establishment in the world; Portsmouth is the garrison t.; Portsea has the naval dockyards, Landport is residtl., and Southsea is a popular wat. pl. within the bor. a.; across the harbour is Gosport; shipbldg.; general mnfs.; p. (estd. 1969) 214,800

Portsmouth, *t.*, N.H., U.S.A.; summer resort, naval dockyard, cotton; the 1905 Peace Treaty between Japan and Russia was negotiated here; p. (1960) 25,833.

Portsmouth, *c.*, Ohio, U.S.A.; iron and steel goods, aircraft, boots, shoes, bricks; p. (1960) 33,637.

Portsmouth, *spt.*, Va., U.S.A.; naval dockyard; farm produce, cotton, rly. wks.; p. (1960) 114,775.

Portsoy, *spt., burgh*, Banff, Scot.; 5 m. W. of Banff; fisheries, meal milling; p. (1961) 1,690.

Portugal, *rep.*, Iberian peninsula, S.W. Europe; interior mountainous, with wide, fertile valleys; mild winter, hot summers; agr.: cereals, fruit, etc.; livestock; cork, pine and other timbers; copper; fisheries; textiles, pottery, tanning, wine, olive oil; cap. Lisbon; a. 35,404 sq. m.; p. (1969) 9,526,000 (inc. Azores and Madeira).

Portugalete, *spt.*, Biscay prov., Spain; nr. Bilbao; p. (1957) 12,211.

Portuguesa, *st.*, Venezuela; cap. Guanare; p. (1961) 203,707.   [length 200 m.

Portuguesa, *R.*, Venezuela, trib. of R. Apure;

Portuguese Guinea, Portuguese col., W. Africa; on Atlantic cst.; cap. Bissau; palm nuts, groundnuts, rubber, wax; a. 13,900 sq. m.; p. (estd. 1968) 529,000.

Portuguese Timor, *col.*, E. Indies; mtns.: copra, coffee, cocoa beans, maize, rice, hides, wax, timber; cap. Deli; a. 7,330 sq. m.; p. (estd. 1967) 566,000.

Porvenir, *spt.*, Chile; chief t. Tierra del Fuego; wool; p. mainly Jugoslav.   [(1966) 13,687.

Porvoo, *spt.*, Finland; engin. forest inds.; p.

Porz, *t.*, N. Rhine-Westphalia, Germany; on R. Rhine, S.E. of Cologne; glass, metals, paper; p. (1963) 51,000.

Posadas, *t.*, Spain; on R. Guadalquivir, nr. Cordova; p. (1957) 7,491.

Posados, *cap.*, Misiones Terr., Argentina; on Alto Paraná R., on border of Paraguay; yerba-maté, tobacco; p. (1960) 44,000.

Posen, *see* Poznan.

Pössneck, *t.*, Gera, E. Germany; S.E. of Weimar; porcelain, textiles, leather; p. (1963) 19,455.

Postillon Is., Lesser Sunda Is., Indonesia; coco-nuts.

Potcheístroom, *t.*, Transvaal, S. Africa; on the Mooi R.; univ.; agr.; malt, timber, engin.; p. (1962) 44,000 inc. 21,000 whites.

Potenza, *t.*, Italy, cap. of prov. Potenza; situated on hill above R. Basento 2,700 ft. above sea-level; agr. and ind. ctr.; p. (1961) 42,659.

Potgietersrust, *t.*, Transvaal, S. Africa; agr. ctr.; cattle; citrus fruits; p. (1961) 11,000 (inc. 5,400 whites).

Poti, *spt.*, Georgian S.S.R.; manganese, saw-mills, engin.; p. (1956) 42,500.

Potomac, *R.*, U.S.A.; dividing Virginia from Maryland; flowing past Washington to Chesa-peake Bay; length 400 m.

Potosi, *dep.*, Bolivia, adjoining Chile and Argentina; famous for silver- and tin-mines; cap. Potosi; a. 45,031 sq. m.; p. (1962) 619,600.

Potosi, *c.*, Bolivia; on slope of Cerro Gordo de Potosi, 13,350 ft. above sea-level; tin, silver, copper, lead; p. (1962) 55,233.

Potsdam, *cap.*, Potsdam, E. Germany; lies on R. Havel 18 m. S.E. of Berlin; beautiful parks and gardens, and many palaces, inc. former Imperial residence; scene of conference between Allies on boundary questions, 1945; motor and locomotive wks., engin.; p. (1963) 115,093.

Potteries, The, *dist.*, N. Staffs, Eng.; ctr. of earthenware ind., comprising ts. Burslem, Hanley, Fenton, Tunstall, Stoke, and Longton.

Potters Bar, *t., urb. dist.*, Herts., Eng.; residtl.; p. (estd. 1967) 24,730.

Pottstown, *t.*, Penns., U.S.A.; iron and steel, farm implements, silk; p. (1960) 26,144.

Pottsville, *c.*, Penns., U.S.A.; iron and steel, rly. wks.; p. (1960) 21,659.

Poughkeepsie, *c.*, N.Y., U.S.A.; on Hudson R.; clothing and iron factories; agr. implements; oil clarifiers; p. (1960) 38,330.

Poulton-le-Fylde, *urb. dist.*, Lancs, Eng.; 4 m. N.E. of Blackpool; farming; p. (1961) 12,767.

Povenets, *t.*, R.S.F.S.R.; on L. Onega; cellulose, paper; p. 2,000.

Powis, Vale of, Montgomery, Wales; runs 12 m. N.E. from Montgomery between Welsh Mtns. and Long Mtn.; drained by R. Severn; cattle-rearing; ch. t. Welshpool; av. width 2 m.

Poyang Hu, *lge. l.*, Kiangsi, China; on S. margin of Yangtze-Kiang plain; receives water of Kan Kiang and tribs., drains N. into Yangtze-Kiang; surrounded by flat, intensively cultivated land, rice, sugar, mulberry; size varies greatly with season, max. a. (in late summer) 1,800 sq. m.

Poznan, *prov.*, W. Poland; stock-raising, mining, mnfs. inc. locomotives; a. 15,152 sq. m.; p. (1965) 2,126,000.

Poznan, *t., cap. of prov.*, oldest cap. of Poland; on R. Warta: cath., univ.; engin., iron founding, chemicals; p. (1965) 438,000.

Pozoblanco, *t.*, Spain; cattle fairs, lead-mines; p. (1957) 14,703.

Pozzuoli, *t.*, Italy; 2 m. W. of Naples; ancient Puteoli; mineral baths, ordnance wks.; notable Roman ruins; p. (1961) 51,308. [p. (1960) 1,528.

Praest, *t.*, Sjalland, Denmark; on Fakse fjord;

Prague (Praha), *c., cap.*, ČSSR.; picturesque, anc. c. on R. Vltava; comm. and cultural ctr.; univ. (founded 1348); extensive mnfs.; machin., sugar, leather, milling, chemicals; p. (1965) 1,020,000.

Prahova, *R.*, Walachia, Romania; rises in Transylvanian Alps, flows S. through impt. Ploesti oilfield into R. Ialomita; length approx. 110 m.

Prato, *t.*, Italy; 8 m. N.W. of Florence; cath., medieval cas. and fortifications; straw plaiting, cottons, woollens, machin.; p. (1961) 111,285.

Prebalkhash (Balkhash), *t.*, Kazakh. S.S.R.; copper; p. (1954) 50,000.

Predeal Pass, Romania; carries main road and rly. across Transylvanian Alps from Bucharest to Brasov; alt. over 4,000 ft.

Preesall, *urb. dist.*, Lancs, Eng.; N. of Blackpool; p. (1961) 2,356.

Pregel, *R.*, Poland; flows to Frisches Haff, nr. Kaliningrad; length 125 m.

Prek Ihnot, Cambodia; power and irrigation development project on Lower Megong R.

Prenzlau, *t.*, Neubrandenburg, E. Germany; p. (1963) 19,955.

Prerov, *t.*, ČSSR.; S.E. of Olomouc; hardware, textiles; p. (1961) 30,511.

Prescelli Myndd, *mtns.*, N.E. Pembroke, Wales.

Prescot, *mfg. t., urb. dist.* S.W. Lancs, Eng.; 4 m. S.W. of St. Helens; mkt., elec. cable ind.; p. (1961) 13,077.

Prescott, *pt.*, Ontario, Canada; on R. St. Lawrence; p. (1961) 5,366.

Presidio St. Vicente, *t.*, N.M., U.S.A.; on Rio Grande del Norte.

Prešov, *t.*, ČSSR.; linen mnfs.; p. (1961) 35,121.

Prestatyn, *t.*, *urb. dist.*, Flint, Wales; on N. cst., 3 m. E. of Rhyl; seaside resort; p. (1961) *10,771*.

Prestea, *t.*, Ghana; gold-mining region.

Presteign, *mkt. t.*, *urb. dist.*, Radnor, Wales; on R. Lugg, 10 m. N.W. of Leominster; p. (1961) *1,190*. *[11,577.*

Preston, *t.*, Ont., Canada; furniture; p. (1961)

Preston, *t.*, *pt.*, *co. bor.*, Lancs, Eng.; on R. Ribble; textiles, engin., aircraft wks.; p. (estd. 1967) *106,010*.

Prestonpans, *burgh*, E. Lothian, Scot.; on S. side of Firth of Forth, 9 m. E. of Edinburgh; " Bonnie Prince Charlie " defeated British here in 1745; bricks, soap, brewing; p. (1961) *3,104*.

Prestwich, *industl. t.*, *mun. bor.*, Lancs, Eng.; in valley of R. Irwell, 3 m. N.W. of Manchester; cotton bleaching and dyeing, soap, furnishings; p. (estd. 1967) *33,480*.

Prestwick, *burgh*, Ayr, Scot.; on Firth of Clyde, 3 m. N. of Ayr; impt. golfing ctr. and trans-Atlantic airport; resort; p. (1961) *12,564*.

Pretoria, *c.*, Transvaal, admin, cap of Rep. of S. Africa; fine admin. bldgs., univ.; impt. tr. ctr.; inds. inc. engin., chemicals, iron and steel; p. (1960) *422,590* inc. *207,202* whites.

Préveza, *prefecture*, Greece; cap. Préveza; p. (1961) *62,387*.

Préveza, *fortfd. t.*, Préveza, Greece; on G. of Arta; gd. shipping tr.; p. (1961) *11,172*.

Pribalkhash, *see* Balkhash.

Pribram, *t.*, Bohemia, ČSSR.; lead-, silver-mng, zinc, barium, antimony; p. (1961) *25,729*.

Prichard, *t.*, Ala., U.S.A.; meat packing, canning, fertilisers, wood and paper prod.; p. (1960) *47,371*.

Prieska, *t.*, Cape Prov., S. Africa; on Orange R.; sheep, cattle, horses; blue asbestos; p. (1960) *6,464* inc. *1,738* whites.

Prijedor, *t.*, Croatia, Jugoslavia; on E. flank of Dinaric Alps, 65 m. S.E. of Zagreb; iron-ore mines.

Prilep, *t.*, Macedonia, Jugoslavia; p. (1959) *36,000*.

Prince Albert, *t.*, Saskatchewan, Canada; lumbering, furs; p. (1961) *24,168*.

Prince Albert Peninsula, *dist.*, Victoria I., Arctic Canada.

Prince Albert Sound, *inlet*, Victoria I., Arctic Canada.

Prince Edward I., *prov.*, Canada; dairying, fishing, agr.; bridge-tunnel link with New Brunswick projected; cap. Charlottetown; a. 2,184 sq. m.; p. (estd. 1969) *110,000*.

Prince George, *t.*, B.C., Canada; oil refining; p. (1961) *13,877*.

Prince of Wales I., off cst. of C. York Peninsula, Queensland, Australia.

Prince of Wales, *C.*, Bering Strait, Alaska.

Prince Rupert, *c.*, B.C., Canada; Pacific pt. of Canadian National Rly.; p. (1961) *11,987*.

Princes Risborough, *mkt. t.*, Bucks, Eng.; at N. foot of Chiltern Hills, in gap used by main rly.; chairs, brewing; p. *2,438*.

Princeton, *bor.*, N.J., U.S.A.; seat of Princeton Univ.; p. (1960) *11,890*. *[son.*

Princetown, *vil.*, Devon, Eng.; nr. Dartmoor pri-

Principe and S. Tomé, *Portuguese Is.*, G. of Guinea, Africa; products, cacao, coffee, coconuts, etc.; a. 372 sq. m.; p. (1968) *65,000*.

Pripet (Pripyat), *R.*, Byelorussian S.S.R.; trib. of R. Dnieper; length 350 m.

Pripet Marshes, Byelorussian S.S.R.; a. 30,000 sq. m.; greater part reclaimed.

Priština, *t.*, *cap.*, Kosmet, Jugoslavia; on R. Sitnic; many mosques; sugar and coffee; p. (1959) *32,000*.

Progreso, *spt.*, Yucatan, Mexico; sisal; warehousing; p. (1960) *14,000*.

Prokopevsk, *t.*, S.W. Siberia, R.S.F.S.R.; nr. Novokuznetsk; metallurgy, coal; p. (1967) *291,000*.

Frome, *t.*, Burma; on R. Irrawaddy; silk, rice, cotton, tobacco; p. *28,295*.

Proskurov, *see* Khmelnitskiy. *[m.*

Prosna, *R.*, Poland; trib. of R. Warta; length 120

Prostějov, *t.*, ČSSR.; match-mkg., brewing, malt and sugar; geese-breeding; p. (1961) *35,519*.

Provence, *old maritime prov.*, S.E. France; now deps. Var, Basses-Alpes, Bouches-du-Rhône, and part of Vaucluse.

Providence, *c.*, R.I., U.S.A.; at head of Narragansett Bay; univ.; jewellery, textiles, silverware, rubber goods, machin., oil, coal; p. (1960) *207,498*.

Provo, *c.*, Utah, U.S.A.; at base of Wasatch mtns., nr. shore of Utah Lake; flour, bricks, blast furnaces; p. (1960) *36,047*.

Prudhoe, *urb. dist.*, Northumberland, Eng.; coal; p. (1961) *9,959*.

Prudhoe Bay, N. Alaska; recent oil finds.

Prussia, *old st.*, former kingdom, Germany; E. Prussia partitioned between Russia and Poland.

Pruszkow, *t.*, Poland; nr. Warsaw; elec. plant; engin; p. (1965) *39,000*.

Prut, *R.*, flows between Romania and Bessarabia from the Carpathian Mtns. to the Black Sea; length 360 m.

Przemysl, *frontier t.*, Poland; on bdy. between Poland and Ukrainian S.S.R.; timber, leather, corn, chemicals; p. (1965) *50,000*.

Psel, *R.*, U.S.S.R.; flows to the R. Dnieper at Kremenchug; length 300 m.

Pskov, *t.*, R.S.F.S.R., U.S.S.R.; on R. Velykaya; flax tr., leather, sawmills, flour mills, cordage; p. (1959) *81,000*.

Pucalpa, *R. pt.*, Peru; on R. Ucayali; sawmills, rosewood oil; p. (1961) *20,000*.

Pudsey, *t.*, *mun. bor.*, W.R. Yorks, Eng.; between Leeds and Bradford; mnfs., woollens; p. (estd. 1967) *37,380*. *[50,488.*

Pudukkottai, *t.*, Tamil Nadu, S. India; p. (1961)

Puebla, *st.*, Mexico; agr.; coffee and sugar growing; a. 13,124 sq. m.; p. (1960) *1,973,837*.

Puebla, *c.*, Mexico; one of the oldest and most impt. cs.; alt. 7,137 ft.; cath.; cottons, onyx, glazed tiles; p. (1960) *289,049*.

Pueblo, *c.*, Col., U.S.A.; on R. Arkansas; coal; iron- and steel-wks.; copper, gold and silver smelted; p. (1960) *91,181*.

Puentearéas, *t.*, Spain; nr. Vigo; vine growing, porcelain; p. (1957) *14,987*.

Puente Genil, *t.*, Córdoba, Spain; olive oil, quince pulp; p. (1957) *30,465*.

Puerto Barrios, *pt.*, Guatamala; rly. term.; oil refining; p. (estd. 1960) *30,980*.

Puerto Berrio, *R. pt.*, Colombia; on R. Magdalena; serves Medellin; p. (1959) *12,500*.

Puerto Cabello, *spt.*, Venezuela; on the Caribbean S., nr. Valencia; lge. exp.; asbestos, vegetable oils, soap, candles; p. (1961) *48,000*.

Puerto Colombia, *t.*, Colombia; resort; former ocean pt. for Barranquilla; p. (1947) *4,896*.

Puerto Cortes, *spt.*, Honduras rep., Central America; p. (1961) *17,412*.

Puerto de Santa Maria, *spt.*, Cadiz, Spain; wine, glass; p. (1957) *28,300*.

Puerto la Cruz, *t.*, Venezuela; 10 m. from Barcelona; oil refining; p. (1961) *45,000*.

Puerto Limon, Costa Rica; oil refinery under construction.

Puerto México, *see* Coatzacoalcos.

Puerto Montt, *spt.*, Chile; in sheep-farming dist.; S. term. of rlys.; devastated by earthquake, May 1960; lumber, cattle, potatoes; p. (1961) *45,400*.   [p. (1961) *11,705*.

Puerto Natales, *spt.*, Chile; wool, frozen meat;

Puerto Ordaz. *See* Santo Tomé de la Guayana.

Puerto Plata, *t.*, Dominican rep. Central America; p. (1960) *26,139*.

Puerto Real, *spt.*, Andalusia, Spain; summer resort; wine and oil tr.; p. (1957) *13,061*.

Puerto Rico, *W. Indian I.*, Greater Antilles; ceded by Spain to U.S.A. in 1898 (since 1952 free cmwlth. ass. with U.S.A.); nuclear reactor at Punta Higuera; sugar, tobacco, rum, textiles, iron ore, salt, marble, white clay; cap. San Juan; a. 3.423 sq. m.; p. (estd. 1970) *2.777,000* mainly natives of mixed Spanish and aboriginal descent.

Puerto Salinas, *spt.*, Venezuela; oil-transhipment.

Puerto Saurez, *R. pt.*, Bolivia; on R. Paraguay; collecting ctr. for rubber, coffee, Brazil nuts.

Puerto Varas, *t.*, Chile; tourist ctr. in Chilean " Switzerland "; p. (1961) *26,615*.

Pugoda, *t.*, Ceylon; cloth mill.

Puget Sound, Washington, U.S.A.

Puket, *I.*, ch. Thailand pt. on Malay Peninsula; tin-mines; p. *30,000*.

Pula, *spt.*, Croatia, Jugoslavia; arsenal, naval base; cement; ship-breaking; footwear, tar, flour, tobacco, fishing; p. (1959) *35,000*.

Pulacayo, *t.*, Bolivia; alt. 13,600 ft.; silvermines; p. *8,000*.

Pulo Tantalam, strip of land connecting Burma with Malay Peninsula, Thailand.

Pulo Wai I., Sumatra, Indonesia; hilly, forests; ch. pt. Sabang.

Pumpherston, *vil.*, nr. Edinburgh, Scot.; oil refining.

Puna, bleak, uninhabited plateau of Peru and Bolivia; alt. 12,000–18,000 ft.

Punjab, *geographical region*, comprising N.W. of Indus plains, Indian sub-continent; extensive irrigation from the " five rivers "—Jhelum, Chenab, Ravi, Bias, Sutlej; cotton, sugar, cereals; now divided politically between India and Pakistan.

Punjab (East), *former st.*, India; partitioned on linguistic basis 1966; Punjab-speaking Punjab st. (a. 21,630 sq. m.; p. *12,000,000*, incl. 55 per cent Sikh); and Hindi-speaking Hariana st. (a. 17,010 sq. m.; p. *7,600,000*); certain hill areas transferred to Himachal Pradesh; joint cap. Chandigarh (until Hariana's own cap. is built).

Punjab (West), *prov.* (revived 1970), W. Pakistan.

Puno, *dep.*, Peru, S. America; p. (1961) *637,077*.

Puno, *t.*, Peru; p. (1961) *15,880*.

Punta Arenas, *t., free pt.*, Magallanes prov., Chile; most S. c. in the world; mutton, wool; whaling; coal nearby; natural gas pipeline from Kimiri-Aike; p. (1961) *46,872*.

Puntarenas, *prov.*, Costa Rica; p. (1963) *155,599*.

Puntarenas, *spt.*, Costa Rica, Central America; one of the ch. comm. pts. of the country, stands on Gulf of Nicoya; p. (1963) *33,878*.

Purbeck, I. of, *dist.*, Dorset, Eng.; Corfe cas. in ctr.; limestone (Purbeck " marble ") quarries.

Puri, *dist.*, Orissa, India; cap. P. famous for its temple and festival of the god Vishnu and his monster car, Juggernaut; p. (1961) *1,865,439*.

Purley, *former urb. dist.*, Surrey, Eng.; now inc. in Croydon outer bor. Greater London.

Purnea, *t.*, Bihar, Indian Union; tobacco; p. (1961) *40,602*.

Pursat, *mkt. t.*, Cambodia, Indo-China; between Pnompenh and Thailand frontier; p. *96,000*.

Purús, *R.*, Peru; trib R. Amazon; 1,400 m.

Pusan (Fusan), *pt.*, S. Korea; on S.E. cst.; silk, hides, rice; elec. apparatus, cars; steel mill at Pohang nearby; p. (1962) *1,271,000*.

Puteaux, *sub.*, Paris, France; woollens, dyes; p. (1962) *39,637*.   [London.

Putney, *S.W. residtl. and industl.* Thames-side sub.,

Putrid Sea, *see* Sivash.

Putumayo, *R.*, Ecuador; trib. of R. Amazon; length 700 m.   [alt. 4,806 ft.

Puy-de-Dôme, *peak*, Auvergne Mtns., France;

Puy-de-Dôme, *dep.*, France; drained by R. Allier; generally mountainous; agr., vineyards; coal, silver, lead; cap. Clermont-Ferrand; a. 3,090 sq. m.; p. (1968) *547,743*.

Puy, Le, *cap.*, Haute-Loire, France; lace-mkg.; p. (1962) *28,648*.

Puymorens Tunnel, Pyrenees, on bdy. between France and Spain; carries main rly. between Toulouse and Barcelona.

Pwllheli, *spt., mun. bor.*, Caernarvon, N. Wales; on S. cst. of Lleyn peninsula; seaside resort; inshore fishing, boat bldg.; p. (1961) *3,642*.

Pyatigorsk, *t.*, Caucasus, R.S.F.S.R.; spa, sulphur springs; engin., radio equip.; p. (1959) *69,000*.

Pyinmana, *t.*, Burma; rly. junction; sugar mills projected; p. *17,656*.

Pylos, *t.*, S.W. Peleponnese, Greece; shipblbg. and repair yard and heavy metalworking factory projected.

Pyongyang, *cap. c.*, N. Korea; located 40 m up Taedong R.; coal and iron ore deposits; silk, textiles; p. (1960) *940,000*.

Pyrenees, *range of mtns.*, S.W. Europe; dividing France from Iberian Peninsula; 270 m. long; hgst. peak Pic d'Anéto (Maladetta) 11,174 ft.

Pyrénées-Atlantique, *dep.*, S. W. France; mainly agr., livestock; cap. Pau; a. 2,978 sq. m.; p. (1968) *508,734*.

Pyrénées, Hautes, *dep.*, S. France; agr., vines, nuts, livestock, marble quarries; cap. Tarbes; a. 1,750 sq. m.; p. (1968) *225,730*.

Pyrénées-Orientales, *dep.*, S. France; on Mediterranean; wheat, wine, silk-worm culture, stock-rearing; cap. Perpignan; a. 1, 599 sq. m.; p. (1968) *281,976*.

Pyrgos, *t.*, Elis, Greece; prov. Elis, nr. Patras; has suffered from earthquakes; p. (1961) *20,553*.

Q

Qaiyara, Al, *t.*, Iraq; route ctr.; oil resources undeveloped.

Qalyub, *t.*, U.A.R.; rly. junction; p. *5,000*.

Qalyûblya, *administrative div.*, Egypt; a. 364 sq. m.; p. (1947) *690,156*.

Qara Dagh, *t.*, Iraq; gum.

Qarun (Karun), *see* Birket el Qarun.

Qasr el Azraq, *t.*, Jordan; oasis; rice.

Qasvin, *c.*, Iran; p. (1956) *66,386*.

Qatar, *sheikdom*, Arabia; includes Q. Peninsula, Persian G.; oil-mining; a. 4,000 sq. m.; p. (estd. 1970) *130,000*.

Qatif, *fortfd. t.*, El Hasa, Saudi Arabia.

Qatlava Depression, N. Egypt; a. 7,000 sq. m.

Qena, *t.*, Egypt; on R. Nile; water jars and bottles; p. (1960) *58 000*.

Qishm, *I.*, Southern Yemen, at entrance of Persian G.; hilly; cereals, vegs., fruit, salt; p. *15,000*.

Qisil-Qum, *desert region*, central Asia; covering dried-up a. of extended Pleistocene Aral Sea.

Qizan, *spt.*, Saudi Arabia; cereals, pearl-fishing, salt.

Quantock Hills, Somerset, Eng.; S. of Bridgwater Bay; highest pt., 1,262 ft., officially designated (1957) as a place of " outstanding natural beauty."

Quaregnon, *t.*, Hainaut prov., Belgium; Mons colly. dist.; ironwks. and tobacco factories; p. (1962) *18,063*.

Quarnero, *G.*, Adriatic Sea; between Croatian cst. and Istria.

Quarto, *G.* of, *arm.* G. of Cagliari, Sardinia.

Quatre Bras, *nr.* Waterloo, S. Brabant, Belgium.

Queanbeyan, *t.*, N.S.W., Australia; pastoral, dairying and mixed farming dist.; mkt. and service ctr.; bldg. materials; p. (1966) *12,489*.

Quebec, *prov.*, Canada; pulp, paper, textiles; metal smelting, chemicals; agr., forestry, rich mineral reserves: copper, gold, zinc, iron ores, molybdenum; elec. power; cap. Quebec, lgst. c. Montreal; a. 594,860 sq. m.; p. (estd. 1968) *5,976,000*.

Quebec, *c. cap.*, Quebec, Canada; on St. Lawrence R.; univ.; fine harbour, handsome gov. bldgs.; furs, textiles, leather, paper; oil refinery at St. Romauld under construction; p. (1966) *413,397*.

Quebec-Labrador Trough, Canada; geological formation extending through central Quebec prov. to Ungava Bay, Hudson Strait; immense reserves of iron-ore (locally " red gold ").

Quedlinburg, *c.*, Halle, E. Germany; at foot of Hartz Mtns.; cas. cath.; cheese; aniline dyes, metals, engin.; p. (1963) *31,251*.

Queen Alexandra Ra., Antarctica; highest pk., Mt. Kirkpatrick, 14,600 ft.

Queenborough, *t., mun. bor.*, Kent, Eng.; on R. Swale, I. of Sheppey; chemicals, glass, pottery, glue, iron; p. (1961) *3,044*.

Queen Carola Harbour, W. cst. Buka Is., Solomon Is., Pac. Oc.

Queen Charlotte's Is., *group*, N. of Vancouver I., off cst. of Brit. Columbia; ch. Is.: Graham I., Moresby I.; valuable halibut fishing ind.

Queen Charlotte Sound, *strait* separating Vancouver I. from Brit. Columbia mainland, a continuation of Johnstone Strait.

Queen Maud Land, Antarctica; claimed by Norway; ice crystal mtns., 10,000 ft. high for 100 m. along cst.

Queens, *bor.*, N.Y. City, U.S.A.; p. (1960) *1,809,578*.

Queensferry, *burgh*. W. Lothian, Scot.; on S. side of Firth of Forth; ferry across Firth; p. (1961) *2,929*.

Queensferry N., *vil.*, Fife, Scotland.

Queensland, *st.*, N.E. Australia; great grassy plains and cst. highlands; agr.: maize, wheat, sugar-cane, cotton, pineapples, bananas; dairying; cattle, sheep, wool; timber; coal, copper. gold, uranium; oil at Moonie and Alton; cap. Brisbane: a. 667,700 sq. m.; p. (estd. 1968) *1,751,800*.

Queenstown, *see* Cobh.

Queenstown, *t.*, Cape Province, S. Africa; in the Great Kei R. valley; prosperous agr. region; p. (1960) *33,126* (inc. 9,743 whites).

Queenstown, *t.*, Tasmania, Australia; mng.; p. (1966) *4,292*.

Quelimane, *pt.*, Mozambique; rly. term; rubber, almonds, copra, coffee, cotton, sisal, tea, tobacco, sugar, wax, ivory; notorious in 18th and 19th cent. as slave mkt.; p. (1960) *156,887*.

Quelpart (Cheju Do), *I.*, Yellow Sea; 60 m. S. of Korea (40 m. by 17 m.) belonging to S. Korea.

Quemoy, *gr. of Is.*, off Chinese mainland near Amoy, held by Nationalist forces; p. (estd.) *50,000* (plus garrison of *40,000*).

Que Que, *t.*, Rhodesia; alt. 3,979 ft.; gold-mining, farming, ranching dist. ctr.; iron and steel; tobacco, vegs., citrus fruit; p. (1958) *11,200* (incl. *2,200* Europeans).

Quequen, *t.*, E. Argentina; seaside resort.

Querétaro, *st.*, central Mexico; agr.; minerals, famous for opals; a. 4,432 sq. m.; p. (1960) *355,045*.

Querétaro, cap. Q., Mexico; at alt. 6,346 ft., cotton mills; an Aztec c., Emperor Maximilian executed here (1867); p. (1960) *60,000*.

Querimba Is., off Mozambique.

Quesnel, *t.*, B.C., Canada; on R. Frazer, 360 m. N. of Vancouver; impt. alluvial gold workings.

Quetta, *t.*, W. Pakistan; at end of Bolan Pass, on road to Kandahar; tr. and military ctr.; thermal sta. under construction; lge. coal reserves nearby; iron ore deposits; p. (1961) *106,633*.

Quetta, *div.*, W. Pakistan; coloured marble in the Chagai a.; p. (1961) *585,000*.

Quezaltenango, *c.*, Guatemala, Central America; on slopes of Cerro Quemado volcano; ctr. of tr. for W. part of the rep.; textiles; p. *50,750*.

Quezon City, *cap.*, Philippines; N. E. of Manila; nuclear reactor; p. (estd.) *502,000*.

Quibdo, *t.*, Colombia, S. America; on R. Atrato; p. (estd. 1959) *41,350*.

Quiberon, *t.*, Morbihan, France; on Quiberon Bay, nr. Lorient; p. (1962) *4,540*.

Quibor, *t.*, Venezuela; 40 m. S.S.W. Barquisimeto; blankets from local wool.

Quicamao, *t.*, st. Rio de Janeiro, Brazil; nr. Camos; industl.

Quillota, *comm. t.*, Valparaiso, Chile; nr. Santiago; p. *17,232*.

Quilmes, *industl. sub.*, Buenos Aires, Argentina; brewing, textiles, ironware, glass; Eng. public school; p. (estd. 1960) *120,000*.

Quilon, *t.*, Kerala, India; on Malabar cst., gd. tr.; coconuts, pepper, timber; p. (1961) *91,018*.

Quilpie, *t.*, Queensland, Australia; rly. connects interior with Brisbane.

Quimper, *fortfd. t.*, Finistère, France; nr. Brest; pilchards, pottery, paper, leather, brewing; p. (1962) *50,670*.

Quimperlé, *t.*, Finistère, France; 34 m. E.N.E. Quimper; industl.; p. (1962) *11,163*.

Quincy, *t.*, Ill., U.S.A.; milling, tobacco, iron-ware, machin.; p. (1960) *43,793*.

Quincy, *c.*, Mass., U.S.A.; granite, foundries, ship-bldg.; p. (1960) *87,409*.

Quindio, *pass*, Colombia; provides impt. route-way through Cordillera Central; 11,099 ft.

Qui Nhon, *t.*, S. Viet-Nam; rice, coconut oil, copra, dried fish, groundnuts; p. *10,000*.

Quintana Roo, *terr.*, Mexico; cap. Chetumal; a. 19,438 sq. m.; p. (1960) *50,169*.

Quintero, *t.*, Chile; naval air sta.; copper refining.

Quintin, *t.*, dep Côtes-du-Nord, France; nr. St. Brieuc.

Quinto, *R.*, Argentina; flows S.E. from the Sierra de San Luis and becomes lost in a morass; length 250 m.

Quiringua, *ruined ancient t.*, nr. Isabel, Guatemala, Central America; on R. Mohtagua.

Quistello, *t.*, Mantua, Italy; on R. Secchia; p. *9,450*.

Quito, *c.*, *cap.*, Ecuador; in the Andes, 15 m. S. of the Equator; alt. 9,350 ft.; textiles, shoes, soap, pharmaceutics; p. (1963) *368,000*.

Qum (Qom), *c.*, Iran, pilgrimage ctr.; shrine of Fatima (daughter of Mohammed and sister of Imam Riza); rly. junc.; p. (1967) *179,434*.

Quorndon, or Quorn, *sm. t.*, Leicester, Eng.; on R. Soar, 3 m. S. of Loughborough; ctr. of fox-hunting dist.

Quorra, *R.*, Africa; one of the names given to the R. Niger; below Timbuktu.

Quseir, *t.*, U.A.R.; on Red Sea cst.; caravan tr. ctr.; uranium; p. *1,000*.

Quyquyo, *t.*, S. Paraguay; copper, manganese; p. *6,590*.

R

Raab, *see* Györ.

Raalte, *til.*, Overijssel, Neth.; nr Zwolle; industl.; p. (1967) *18,306*.

Raasay, *I.*, E. of Skye, Inverness, Scot.; 13 m. long, 3½ m. wide.

Rab I., at head of Adriatic, Jugoslavia; marble. silk mnfs.; resort; a. 74 sq. m.; p. *6,354*.

Rabat or New Salle, *c.*, *spt.*, Morocco; at mouth of Bu Regreg; cath., univ.; leather and carpet mnfs.; p. (1960) *227,445*.

Rabaul, *spt.*, New Britain, Papua-New Guinea; copra ctr.; p. *4,500*.

Rabot, *t.*, Malta; on Gozo I.

Racalmuto, *t.*, Girgenti, Sicily; agr.; p. *13,825*.

Race, *C.*, S.E. Newfoundland, Canada.

Racibórz (Ratibor), *t.*, Upper Silesia, Poland; German before 1945; on R. Oder; textiles, metals, wood, engin.; p. (1965) *36,000*.

Racine, *c.*, Wis., U.S.A.; on L. Michigan, 10 m., S. of Milwaukee; motor cars, farm implements; p. (1960) *89,144*.

Radauti, *t.*, Bukovina, Romania; paper, glass, engin.; p. (1956) *15,949*.

Radcliffe, *mun. bor.*, Lancs, Eng.; nr. Manchester; paper-mkg., cotton weaving, engin.; p. (estd. 1967) *27,610*.

Radebeul, *t.*, Dresden, E. Germany; on R. Elbe; machin.; p. (1963) *40,177*.

Radford, *t.*, Va., U.S.A.; iron smelting, lumbering; p. (1960) *9,371*.

Radnorshire, *inland co.*, S. Wales; oats, wheat; sheep rearing, breeding Welsh ponies, mineral springs; cap. Presteign; a. 471 sq. m.; p. (1966) *18,000*.

Radom, *industl. t.*, Kielce, Poland; nr. Warsaw; engin.; p. (1965) *143,000*. [*29,000*.

Radomsko, *t.*, Poland; S. of Lodz; p. (1965)

Radomsyl, *t.*, Ukrainian S.S.R.; textiles.

Radstock (Norton Radstock), *t.*, *urb. dist.*, Somerset, Eng.; 10 m. S.E. of Bristol; collieries; p. (1961) *12.782*.

Radzionkow, *t.*, Katowice, Poland; New Town (1951) p. (1965) *27,000*.

Rafah, *t.*, U.A.R., on Israel bdy.

Raffadali, *t.*, Girgenti, Sicily, Italy; agr.; p. *10,825*.

Ragaz, Bad, *t.*, *resort*, St. Gall, Switzerland; on R. Tamina; hot springs; ancient Abbey of Pfäfers, 2,697 ft. above sea-level.

Ragusa, *c.*, Syracuse, Italy; cheese factories; oil; p. (1961) *55,274*.

Ragusa, *see* Dubrovnik.

Rahad, *R.*, Sudan; trib. of Blue Nile.

Rahmánfya, El, *t.*, Lower U.A.R.; nr. Rosetta; on R. Nile.

Rahway, *c.*, N.J., U.S.A.; on R. Rahway; residtl. for New York business men; p. (1960) *27,699*.

Raiatéa, *I.*, Society Is., Pac. Oc.; lgst. of Fr. Leeward gr. 130 m. N.W. Tahiti; p. (1962) *6,210*.

Raichur, *t.*, Mysore, India; pottery; p. (1961) *63,329*.

Raigarh, *t.*, cap. Raigarh *dist.*, Madhya Pradesh, India; silk mnfs.; rice; p. (1961) *36,933*.

Rainford, *urb. dist.*, Lancs, Eng.; nr. St. Helens; coal; p. (1961) *5,385*.

Rainier, *mtn.*, Washington, U.S.A.; 14,530 ft.

Rainton, E. and W., *colly. dists.*, nr. Durham, Eng.

Rainy, *L.*, on border of Canada and Minn., U.S.A., drained by Rainy R. to Lake of the Woods.

Raipur, *t.*, Madhya Pradesh, India; p. (1961) *139,792*.

Raismes, *t.*, Nord, France; nr. Valenciennes; lace ind.; p. (1954) *14,577*.

Rajahmundry, *t.*, Andhra Pradesh, India; on the delta of the Godivari R.; p. (1961) *130,030*.

Rajasthan, *st.*, India; farming, millet, cotton, pulses, textiles, ivory; ch. towns, Jaipur, (cap.), Udaipur, Alwar, Jodhpur; section of canal scheme inaugurated 1961 at Hanumangarh, 200 m. N.W. of New Delhi; nuclear power sta. projected; copper mines and ore processing at Khetri; a. 132,077 sq. m.; p. (1961) *20,155,602*.

Rajkot, *t.*, Gujarat, India; p. (1961) *194 510*.

Rajshahi, *t.*, Rajshahi dist., E. Pakistan; on R. Ganges; univ.; silk inds.

Raki-Ura I., *see* Stewart I.

Rakka, *t.*, Nigeria, W. Africa; on Lower Niger R.

Rakos Palota, *sub.* Budapest, Hungary.

Rakovnik, *t.*, Bohemia, ČSSR.; mkt., mining; p. (1961) *11,979*.

Raleigh, *c.*, N.C. U.S.A.; educational ctr.; rly. wks., cotton-mills; p. (1960) *93,931*.

Ralick, *chain of Is.*, Marshall gr., Pac. Oc.; parallel with Ratack chain.

Ramacca, *commune*. E. Sicily; marble; linen; agr.; p. *12,521*.

Rambervilliers, *t.*, Vosges, France; nr. Nancy; p. (1962) *7,060*.

Rambouillet, ., Yvelines, France; nr. Versailles; ancient château; p. (1962) *12,593*.

Rameswaram, *t.*, S. India; on Rameswaram I., Palk Strait; contains a great Dravidian temple, one of the Hindu holy places of pilgrimage; p. (1961) *6,801*.

Ramgunga, *R.*, India; trib. of R. Ganges, which it joins nr. Cawnpore; length 300 m.

Ramle, *t.*, Israel; S. of Lydda; p. (1946) *16,380*.

Ramleh, *t.*, U.A.R.; E. of Alexandria; p. *52,000*.

Ramme, *t.*, Ringkjobing, Jutland, Denmark.

Ramnad, *t.*, Tamil Nadu, India; on peninsula projecting towards Rameswaram I.

Râmnicu-Sărat, *t.*, Romania; scene of several battles; petroleum; p. *19,267*.

Râmnicu-Vâlcea, *c.*, Romania; on R. Olt; cath., monasteries; salt-mining; hot springs; p. *15,162*.

Rampur, *t.*, Uttar Pradesh, India; N.W. of Bareilly; damask, sugar, pottery; p. (1961) *135,407*.

Ramree I., Bay of Bengal, Indian Ocean; off cst. Arakan, Lower Burma; 50 m. long.

Ramsbottom, *t.*, *urb. dist.*, Lancs, Eng.; on R. Irwell, 4 m. N. of Bury; cottons, bleaching, dyeing, engin., paper mftg., p. (1961) *13,813*.

Ramsey, *mkt. t.*, *urb. dist.*, Hunts, Eng.; on edge of The Fens, 7 m. N. of St. Ives; engin., agr.; p. (1961) *5,697*.

Ramsey, *t.*, *spt.*, I. of Man; on N.E. cst.; holiday resort; p. (1956) *4,621*.

Ramsey, *residtl. bor.*, N.J., U.S.A.; ctr. of dairying region; p. (1960) *9,527*.

Ramsey I., off cst. of Pembroke, Wales.

Ramsgate, *t.*, *mun. bor.*, Kent, Eng.; on S. cst. of I. of Thanet; resort; p. (estd. 1967) *38,810*.

Rana Pratap Sagar, Rajasthan, India; nuclear power sta.

Rancagua, *c.*, Colchagua prov., Chile; agr. tractors; p. (1961) *61,832*.

Rance, *R.*, Brittany, France; world's first major tidal hydro-elec. sta. (opened 1966).

Ranchi, *t.*, Bihar, India; admin. ctr.; rice, tea, shellac; p. (1961) *140,253*

Rand, *gold-mining dist.*, Transvaal, S. Africa (*see* Witwatersrand).

Randazzo, *t.*, Catania, Sicily; on S. slopes of Mt. Etna; 2,474 ft. above sea-level; p. *16,325*.

Randers, *t.*, Denmark; medieval monastery; machin., foundries; exp. dairy produce; p. (1965) *42,923*.

Randstad, the dispersed conurbation that comprises Rotterdam, Amsterdam and The Hague.

Ranenburg, *t.*, U.S.S.R.; on R. Voronezh.

Rangiora, *t.*, S.I., N.Z.; 20 m. N.W. of Christchurch; ctr. of lge. agr. dist.; p. (1961) *3,540*.

Rangitaiki R., N.I., N.Z.; flows N. into Bay of Plenty.

Rangoon, *c.*, *cap.*, Burma; on E. arm of Irrawaddy delta; 2 caths., many mosques, temples and pagodas; gr. tr., and many impt. mnfs.; rice, oil, lumber; ivory and wood carving; textiles; p. (estd. 1965) *1,530,000*.

Rangpur. *t.*, E. Pakistan; on R. Ghaghat; jute; p. (1961) *40,600*. [p. (1961) *30,113*.

Raniganj, *t.*, W. Bengal, India; iron, coal-mines;

Rani-Nur, *famous rock-cave*, Khandgiri Hill, Puri dist., Orissa, India.

Rannoch, *Loch*, Perth, Scot.; 9 m. long, 1 m. wide; drained to R. Tay.

Rapallo, *t.*, *vat. pl.*, Liguria, N.W. Italy; on G. of Genoa, 22 m. E. of Genoa; most celebrated resort on Italian Riviera di Levante; p. (1946) *14,675*.

Rapanui or Easter I., *I.*, Pac. Oc.; W. of Chile.

Raphoe, *par.*, co. Donegal, Ireland; cath.; mkt.; woollens. esp. tweeds; p. *2,600*.

Rapid City, *t.*, S.D., U.S.A.; p. (1960) *42,399*.

Rappollsweiler, *t.*, Bas Rhin, France; nr. Selestat; walled; known as "the pipers' town."

Raqqa, *t.*, Syria; on R. Euphrates; p. *2,000*.

Raritan, *t.*, N.J., U.S.A.; p. (1960) *15,334*.

Rarotonga, *volcanic I.*, Pac. Oc.; cap. of Cook Is.; fruit canning; ch. t. and pt. Avarua; p. *7,363*.

Ras-al-Had, *O. E.* extremity Arabia.

Rasgrad, *t.*, Bulgaria; nr. Ruschuk, on R. Ak-Lom.

Ras Lanuf, *oil terminal*, on G. of Sidra, Libya; pipeline from Hofra oilfield.

Ras Mohammed, *S. point*, Sinai Peninsula.

Ras Tannura, *spt.*, Nejd. Saudi Arabia; lge. oil-refinery.

Rashin, *t.*, N. Korea; nr. U.S.S.R. frontier.

Rasskazovo, *t.*, Tambov reg., U.S.S.R.; ironwks.; wheat; p. *25,168*.

Rastrick, *industl. t.*, W.R. Yorks, Eng.; on R. Calder, nr. Halifax.

Rat Is., *group of Is.*, Aleutian Archipelago.

Ratack, *chain of Is.*, Marshall Gr., Pac. Oc., parallel with Ralick chain.

Rathenow, *t.*, Potsdam, E. Germany; on R. Havel; optical glass; p. (1963) *29,491*.

Rathkeale, *mkt. t.*, *rural dist.*, Ireland; nr. Limerick; p. (rural dist. 1961) *11,726*.

Rathlin, *I.*, off Fair Head, N. Antrim, N. Ireland; 5 m. by 1 m.

Rathven, *par.*, Banff, Scot.; farming, sandstone, limestone, slate; p. *15,404*.

Ratibor, *see* Raciborz.

Ratingen, *t.*, N. Rhine–Westphalia, Germany; N.E. of Düsseldorf; textiles, machin., glass; p. (1963) *37,200*.

Ratisbon, *see* Regensburg.

Ratnagiri, *pt.*, Maharashtra, India; all weather pt.; p. (1961) *31,091*.

Ratnapura, *t.*, Ceylon; graphite; p. *12,441*.

Rattray Head, Aberdeen, Scot. [(1966) *23,952*.

Rauma, *spt.*, Finland; on G. of Bothnia; p.

Raunds, *t.*, *urb. dist.*, Northants, Eng.; 5 m. N.E. of Wellingborough; p. (1961) *4,593*.

Raurkela, *t.*, Orissa, India; steel, tinplate, iron, fertilisers; p. (1961) *90,287*.

Rava Ruskaya, *t.*, Ukrainian S.S.R.; oil processing; quarrying; lignite; p. *12,000*.

Ravenglass, *t.*, Cumberland, Eng.; nr. mouth of R. Esk.

Ravenna, *region*, Emilia, Italy; a. 715 sq. m.; p. (1961) *323,969*.

Ravenna, *c.*, Emilia, N. Italy; on marshy plain, nr. the Adriatic, 45 m. E. of Bologna; cath., archiepiscopal palace, famous mosaics; agr. mkt. and ctr. for sugar-beet and beet sugar; sericulture; oil refining, petrol chemicals; p. (1961) *115,205*. [p. (1960) *10,913*.

Ravenna, *t.*, N.E. Ohio. U.S.A.; engin., rubber;

Ravensburg, *t.*, Baden–Württemberg, Germany; nr. Konstanz; p. (1963) *31,800*.

Ravenscraig, *t.*, nr. Motherwell, Lanark., Scot.; hot strip steelmill; cold reduction mill at Gartcosh 8 m. away. [Dewsbury.

Ravensthorpe, *industl. t.*, W.R. Yorks, Eng.; nr.

Ravi, *R.*, Punjab, India; trib. of the Chenab; used for irrigation; length 450 m.

Rawalpindi, *div.*, W. Pakistan; between Lahore and Peshawar; p. (1961) *3,879,000*.

Rawalpindi, *t.*, Pakistan; on R. Leh, W. Pakistan; fortfd.; admin., comm. and rly. ctr.; rly. wks., brewing, foundries, oil refining, industl. gases; p. (1961) *340,175*.

Rawlins, *t.*, S. Wyo., U.S.A.; mkt., coal, oilfields, ranching; p. (1950) *7,415*.

Rawmarsh, *t.*, *urb. dist.*, W.R. Yorks, Eng.; 2 m. N.E. of Rotherham; engin.; p. (1961) *19,603*.

Rawson, *spt.*, *cap.*, Chubut terr., Argentina; S. of Valdes Peninsula; fish, fruit, livestock; p. *2,500*.

Rawson, *industl. t.*, nr. Leeds, Yorks, Eng.

Rawtenstall, *t.*, *mun. bor.*, Lancs, Eng.; on R. Irwell in ctr. of Rossendale Fells; cotton weaving; p. (estd. 1967) *22,630*.

Ray, *C.*, S.W. Newfoundland, Canada; beginning of Long Range, of which the highest peak is 2,673 ft.

Rayleigh, *t.*, *urb. dist.*, Essex, Eng.; 5 m. N.W. of Southend; light inds.; p. (estd. 1967) *24,850*.

Raynham, *t.*, S.E. Mass., U.S.A.; mkt. ctr. for agr. products, poultry, eggs; p. *2,141*.

Razeim, *L.*, Dobrodea, Romania; 25 m. long.

Ré or Rhe, *I.*, W. cst. Charente-Inférieure, France; opp. a. Rochelle; salt mftg.; ch. t. St. Martin.

Reading, *t.*, *co. bor.*, Berks, Eng.; at confluence of Rs. Thames and Kennet; univ.; biscuits, engin., electronics, seed-growing and mkt. gardening, tin-box mftg., printing; p. (estd. 1967) *126,380*.

Reading, *t.*, Mass., U.S.A.; nr. Boston; p. (1960)

Reading, *c.*, Penns., U.S.A.; on Schuylkill R.; ironwks.; p. (1960) *98,177*.

Recanati, *t.*, Macerata, Italy; industl.; p. *16.325*.

Recife, *spt.*, *cap.*, Pernambuco, Brazil; univ.; exports sugar, cotton, coffee; called the Brazilian Venice; fine natural harbour; p. (estd. 1968) *1,100,464*.

Recklinghausen, *t.*, N. Rhine–Westphalia, W. Germany; nr. Dortmund; collieries, iron, machin., textiles, chemicals; p. (1968) *125,801*.

Recôncavo, *dist.*, Bahia st., N.E. Brazil; surrounds bay at mouth of R. Paraguassu; intensive cultivation of sugar-cane, cotton, tobacco, rice, by Negro farmers; ch. ts. São Salvador, Cachoeira.

Red Basin, *see* Szechwan.

Red Bay, Antrim, N. Ireland.

Red Deer R., trib. of Saskatchewan, R., Alberta, Canada.

Red Lake, *t.*, Ontario, Canada; nr. L. Winnipeg; gold.

Red R. (China), *see* Song-koi.

Red R., U.S.A.; trib. Mississippi, flows from New Mexico through the Staked Plain; length, 1,600 m.

Red R. of the North, U.S.A.; rises in Minnesota and thence N., separating N. Dakota and Minnesota, U.S.A., and thence into Manitoba, Canada, to join Assiniboine R.; length 650 m.

Red Sea, *arm of the sea* separating Arabia from Africa; connects with the Indian Ocean by the Straits of Bab-el-Mandeb; length 1,400 m., greatest width 230 m.

Red Wing, *c.*, Minn., U.S.A.; on the Mississippi R., at head of L. Pepin; flour mills, grain tr.; p. (1960) *10,528.*

Redbank, *t.*, N.J., U.S.A.; summer resort, fishing, mkt. gardens, light mnfs.; p. (1960) *12,482.*

Redbridge, *outer bor.*, E. London, Eng.; incorporating former bors. of Ilford, Wanstead and Woodford, Chigwell (Hainault Estate), Dagenham (N. Chadwell Heath ward); mainly residtl.; p. (1966) *247,000.*

Redcar, *t.*, *mun. bor.*, N.R. Yorks, Eng.; on E. cst., nr. mouth of R. Tees; seaside resort; steel wks., engin., slag bricks, toys: p. (1961) *31,460.* [p. (1966) *26,999.*

Redcliffe, *t.*, Queensland, Australia; holiday t.

Redding, *c.*, N. Cal., U.S.A.; lumber, mining, agr.; tourists; p. (1960) *12,773.*

Redditch, *t.*, *urb. dist.*, Worcester, Eng.; 12 m. S. of Birmingham; needles, fish tackle, cycles, springs, aluminium alloys, chromium and cadmium plating; designated "New Town" 1964; p. (estd. 1967) *36,900.*

Rede, *R.*, Northumberland, Eng.; trib. of R. Tyne.

Redhill, *t.*, Surrey, Eng.; at foot of N. Downs, adjoining Reigate; residt.; refractory sands.

Redlands, *t.*, Cal., U.S.A.; p. (1960) *26,829.*

Redonda, *I.*, Leeward group, Caribbean Sea; between Montserrat and Nevis.

Redondela, *t.*, Pontevedra, Spain; on Vigo estuary; old feudal castles; p. (1957) *17,024.*

Redruth, *t.*, part of Camborne–Redruth urb. dist., Cornwall, Eng.; tin-mine dist., chemicals, engin., textiles; p. (1961) (with Camborne) *36,090.*

Redwood City, *c.*, W. Cal., U.S.A.; shipbldg., saltwks.; exp. sequoia; p. (1960) *46,290.*

Ree, Lough, *L.*, Ireland; between Roscommon, Longford and Westmeath, an extension of R. Shannon; 17 m. long. [*14,250.*

Regello, *t.*, Val d'Arno, Italy; nr. Florence; p.

Regensburg (Ratisbon), *c.*, Bavaria, Germany; N.E. of Munich on R. Danube; cath.; brewing, machin., wood, chemicals; p. (1968) *125,966.*

Reggio di Calabria, *t.*, Calabria, Italy; on Strait of Messina; cath.; perfumes, silks, terracotta; train ferry to Messina (Sicily); has suffered from earthquakes; p. (1961) *150,334.*

Reggio nell' Emilia, *c.*, *cap.*, Emilia–Romagna, N. Italy; at N. foot of Apennines, 40 m. N.W. of Bologna; locomotives, aircraft; fine church of the Madonna della Ghiara; sericulture, cheese-mkg.; p. (1961) *116,515.*

Regina, *t., cap.*, Saskatchewan, Canada; foundries, oil-wks., sawmills; helium gas exp.; p. (1966) *131,127.*

Region Oriental, Ecuador; a. 219,095 sq. m.; p. *295,200*; consists of provs.—Napo Pastaza and Santiago Zamora; about 110,000 sq. m. of region inhabited.

Regla, *t.*, Cuba, W. Indies; nr. Havana; p. *23,037.*

Rehoboth, *t.*, S.W Africa; salt. mining, cattle; p. *9,727.* [p. *c. 10,500.*

Rehovoth, Israel; agr. (citrus) and scientific ctr.

Reichenbach, *t.*, Karl-Marx-Stadt, E. Germany; paper, metals; p. (1963) *29,189.*

Reichenberg, *see* Liberec.

Reidsville, *t.*, N.C., U.S.A.; tobacco mkt., mnfs., textiles, turpentine; p. (1960) *14,267.*

Reigate, *mkt. t., mun. bor.*, Surrey, Eng.; at foot of N. Downs, 5 m. E. of Dorking; residtl.; fuller's earth, freestone; p. (estd. 1967) *56,340.*

Reims, *t.*, Marne, France; on R. Vesle; famous Gothic cath.; univ.; champagne ctr., cloth

factories, woollen inds. and tr., dye wks.; p. (1968) *152,967.*

Reindeer L., Saskatchewan, Canada.

Rembang, *t.*, Java; oil, teak, rubber; p. *13,791.*

Remscheid, *t.*, N. Rhine–Westphalia, Germany; nr. Düsseldorf; cutlery, machin., textiles; p. (1968) *135,197.*

Renaix (Ronse), *t.*, Belgium; nr. Ghent; linen, woollens; dyeing, bleaching; p. (1962) *25,122.*

Rendsburg, *t.*, Schleswig-Holstein, Germany; on N. Sea–Baltic Canal; metals, elec. goods, shipbldg.; p. (1963) *35,100.*

Renfrew, *maritime co.*, W. Scot.; S. of R. Clyde; agr., mftg., and comm., coal, iron, shipbldg., machin., printing; ch. industl. ctrs. Paisley and Greenock; a. 245 sq. m.; p. (1961) *338,815.*

Renfrew, *co. t., burgh*, Renfrew, Scot.; nr. R. Clyde, 5 m. W. of Glasgow; p. (1961) *17,946.*

Renfrew, *t.*, Ontario, Canada; p. (1961) *8,935.*

Rennes, *c.*, *cap.*, Ille-et-Vilaine, France; 40 m. S. of St. Malo; univ.; dairying and agr. dist.; farm implements, sail-cloth, oil refining nearby; p. (1968) *180,943*

Reno, *lgst. c.*, Nevada, U.S.A.; seat of Univ. of Nevada; st. agr. college; famous for easy divorce procedure; p. (1960) *51,470.*

Rensselaer, *t.*, N.Y., U.S.A.; on R. Hudson facing Albany; p. (1960) *10,506.*

Repton, *rural dist.*, Derbyshire, Eng.; agr., clay, coal-mining, sanitary ware; p. *29,780.*

Republican Fork or **Pawnee**, *R.*, trib. of Kansas R., Col., U.S.A.; length 550 m.

Repulse Bay, on S. side of Melville Peninsula, N. Canada.

Requeña, *t.*, Valencia, Spain; sulphur springs of Fuentepodida: p. (1957) *20.253*

Resende, *t.*, Rio de Janeiro, Brazil; chemicals, rly. junc.; univ.; p. (estd. 1968) *64,950.*

Resht (Rasht), *c.*, Iran; prov. cap. Gilan, in a. producing rice, cotton, silk; carpets; nearby Pahlevi serves as pt.; p. (1967) *358,172.*

Resina, *t.*, S. Italy; on Bay of Naples at W. foot of Vesuvius; p. (1961) *45,148.*

Resistencia, *t.*, *cap.*, Chaco, Argentina; cotton, quebracho, cattle; p. (1960) *94,000.*

Resolution, *t.*, N.W. Terr., Canada; on S. shore of Gr. Slave L.

Resolution I., off S.W. cst. of S.I., New Zealand.

Resolution Is. (Brit.), N. of Labrador, at entrance Hudson Strait, Franklin, Canada.

Resolven, *t.*, N. Glamorgan, Wales, on R. Neath 6 m. N.E. of Neath; aluminium; p. (1951) *4,353.*

Retalhulen, *t.*, *cap.*, R. dep., Guatemala, Central America; coffee, sugar; p. (1960) *29,361.*

Rethymnon, *prefecture*, I. of Crete; cap. Rethymnon; p. (1961) *69,843.*

Rethymnon, *cap.*, Rethymnon, Crete; p. (1961) *14,999.*

Réunion. Ile de la (formerly Bourbon), *Fr. I.*, Indian Ocean; between Mauritius and Malagasy; sugar growing; cap. St. Denis; a. 970 sq. m.; p. (estd. 1968) *426,000.*

Reus, *t.*, Tarragona, Spain; textiles, leather, soap; p. (1957) *35,950.*

Reuss, *R.*, Switzerland; flows N. from the St. Gotthard Pass through L. Lucerne, joining Aar R. near Brugg; length 98 m.

Reutlingen, *t.*, Baden-Württemberg, Germany; S. of Stuttgart; textiles, metals, machin., leather; p. (1963) *70,600.*

Reval, *see* Tallin.

Revda, *t.*, R.S.F.S.R.; in Urals, 29 m. W. of Sverdlovsk; iron, copper, chemicals; p. (1959) *55,000.*

Revere, *t.*, Mass., U.S.A.; sub. of Boston; resort; p. (1960) *40,080.*

Revilla Gigedo Is., *gr. of Is.*, belonging to Mexico, Pac. Oc.; ch. Is., Socorro, San Benito.

Rewa, *t.*, Madhya Pradesh, India; rice, coal; p. (1961) *43,065.*

Rewari, *t.*, Punjab, India; S.W. of Delhi; turban and brass-ware mnfs.; p. (1961) *36,994.*

Reykjavik, *c.*, *cap.*, Iceland; on S.W. cst.; univ., cath.; exp. fish, skins, wool; aluminium smelting at Straumsvik nearby; p. (1964) *87,000.*

Reynella-Port Noarlunga, *t.*, S. Australia; abattoirs, wine mkg.; p. (1966) *11,775.*

Rezayeh, *c.*, Iran; prov. cap. W. Azerbaijan; p. (1967) *291,369.*

Rezé, *t.*, Loire Atlantique, France; p.(1954) *19,000.*

Rheine, *t.*, N. Rhine–Westphalia, Germany; on R. Ems; textiles, machin.; p. (1963) *46,400.*

Rheinhausen, *t.*, N. Rhine–Westphalia, Germany; on R. Rhine; S. of Duisburg; coal-mining, iron, textiles; p. (1963) *70,500*.

Rheinkamp (Repelen-Baerl before 1950), *t.*, N. Rhine–Westphalia, Germany; on R. Rhine, N.W. of Duisberg; coal-mng.; p. (1963) *38,900*.

Rheydt, *t.*, N. Rhine–Westphalia, Germany; W. of Düsseldorf; textiles, machin., rly. junction; p. (1968) *100,070*.

Rhin (Bas), *dep.*, N.E. France; cap. Strasbourg; a. 1,848 sq. m.; p. (1968) *827,367*.

Rhin (Haut), *dep.*, N.E. France; cap. Colmar; a. 1,354 sq. m.; p. (1968) *585,018*.

Rhine, *R.*, rises in Switzerland, can. Grisons, passes through L. Constance, skirts Baden, traverses Hesse, Rhineland, and the Neth., flowing to N. Sea by two arms, Oude Rijn and the Waal (the latter discharging finally by the Maas); famous for its beauty, especially between Bonn and Bingen; ch. falls at Schaffhausen; once a natural barrier between E. and W. Europe, the Rhine is now spanned by 30 rly. bridges, and its navigation declared free in 1868; length 800 m.

Rhineland Palatinate (Rheinland-Pfalz), *Land*, Germany; a. 7,665 sq. m.; cap. Mainz; p. (1968) *3,645,000*.

Rhinns (Rins), *peninsula*, on W. cst. Islay I., Inner Hebrides, Scot.; lighthouse.

Rhio-Lingga Archipelago, *gr. of Is.*, Indonesia; mainly in Malacca Strait; a. 12,235 sq. m.

Rhode Island, *st.*, New England, U.S.A.; washed by the Atlantic, and surrounded by Massachusetts and Connecticut; divided by Narragansett Bay, with many islands, lgst. being that from which the st. takes its name; jewellery, silver-ware, textiles, rubber, granite; agr., fisheries; cap. Providence; a. 1,214 sq. m.; p. (1970) *922,461*.

Rhodes (Rhodos), *I.*, Dodecanese Is.; off S.W. cst., Anatolia, belonging to Greece; cap. R.; figs, oranges, grapes; p. (1940) *61,791*.

Rhodes, *t.*, *cap.*, I. of Rhodes, Greece; on N.E. cst.; p. (1951) *24,186*.

Rhodesia, *self-gov. Brit. col.* (illegal rep. declared 1969) central Africa; tobacco, maize, fruit, cattle; gold, coal, asbestos, chrome ore, magnesite; crystalline graphite ore deposits being developed; cap. Salisbury; a. 150,333 sq. m.; p. (estd. 1969) *4,817,950* African; *252,450* non-African.

Rhodope Mtns., *range*, S. Bulgaria; rise to 10,200 ft. [tini; p. (1961) *109,194*.

Rhodopi, *prefecture*, Thrace, Greece; cap. Komo-

Rhöngebirge, *mtn. gr.*, Thuringia, Germany; highest peak 3,100 ft.

Rhondda, *t.*, *urb. dist.*, Glamorgan, Wales; in narrow Rhondda valley, 7 m. N.W. of Pontypridd; coal-mining ctr.; p. (1961) *100,314*.

Rhône, *R.*, Switzerland and France; rising in the Rhône glacier of the St. Gotthard mtn. gr., and flowing through the L. of Geneva and E. France to the G. of Lyons in the Mediterranean; length 507 m.; power stas. at Sion and Geneva; canals, dams, locks and power stas. form part of French Rhône Valley project (1937–72).

Rhône, *dep.*, S.E. France; drained by R. Rhône, and its trib. R. Saône, which unite at Lyons; agr., grain, potatoes, wine; vine-growing, many mnfs., silks, textiles; cap. Lyons; a. 1,104 sq. m.; p. (1968) *1,325,611*.

Rhyl, *t.*, *urb. dist.*, Flint, N. Wales; between Bangor and Chester, at entrance Vale of Clwyd; resort; furniture mkg.; p. (1961) *21,825*.

Rhymney, *t.*, *urb. dist.*, Monmouth, Eng.; on R. Rhymney, 4 m. E. of Merthyr Tydfil; mining; p. (1961) *8,859*. [of comm.

Rialto, *I.* and *dist.*, on Grand Canal, Venice; ctr.

Ribadesella, *spt.*, Spain; W. of Santander; iron mines; p. (1957) *7,692*.

Ribatejo, *prov.*, Portugal; a. 2,794 sq. m.; p. (1950) *459,853*.

Ribe, *mkt. t.*, Jutland, S. Denmark; on W. cst.; iron wks.; p. (1960) *7,809*.

Ribble, *R.*, Yorks and Lancs, Eng.; followed by main rly. route Leeds to Carlisle; length 75 m.

Ribeira, *t.*, Galicia, Spain; on peninsula of Arosa estuary; agr., cattle-rearing, fishing.

Ribeirão Preto, *t.*, São Paulo st., Brazil; mkt. in rich agr. a. esp. coffee, cotton, sugar; p. (estd. 1968) *169,845*.

Riberalta, *R. pt.*, Colonia Terr., Bolivia, S. America; on R. Beni above rapids which limit navigation to upper course; collecting ctr. for wild rubber.

Richborough, *pt.*, Kent, Eng.; at mouth of R. Stour; pt. was derelict but now being developed as a private pt.; chemicals, antibiotics.

Richelieu or **Chambly**, *R.*, Quebec, Canada; flows from L. Champlain to the St. Lawrence R. at L. St. Peter; length 80 m.

Richmond-upon-Thames, *outer bor.*, Greater London, Eng.; inc. former bors. of Barnes, Richmond and Twickenham; industl. and residtl.; beautiful park and riverside scenery; p (1966) *180,000*.

Richmond, *t.*, *mun. bor.*, N.R. Yorks, Eng.; at E. foot of Pennines on R. Swale; p. (estd. 1967) *7,300*. [*71,854*.

Richmond, *t.*, Cal., U.S.A.; oil refining; p. (1960)

Richmond, *c.*, Ind., U.S.A.; on R. Whitewater; mnfs.; p. (1960) *44,149*.

Richmond, *c.*, Ky., U.S.A.; in tobacco-growing and horse-rearing region; p. (1960) *12,168*.

Richmond, one of the five bors. of New York City, U.S.A.; p. (1957) *210,146*.

Richmond, *c.*, *cap.*, Va., U.S.A.; on falls on R. James; agr. tobacco mftg. ctr. and mart; chemicals, iron and steel, lumber; p. (1960) *219,958*.

Rickmansworth, *mkt. t.*, *urb. dist.*, Herts, Eng.; at confluence of Rs. Colne and Chess, 3 m. S.W. of Watford; paper, brewing; residtl.; p. (estd. 1967) *30,290*.

Rideau Canal, Canada; from Ottawa R., to Kingston on L. Ontario; length 132 m.

Ridgefield, *t.*, N.J., U.S.A.; p. (1960) *10,788*.

Ridgewood, *t.*, N.J., U.S.A.; p. (1960) *25,391*.

Riesa, *t.*, Dresden, E. Germany; on R. Elbe, nr. Meissen; steel wks., sawmills; p. (1963) *38,929*.

Riesengebirge, *mtns.*, Germany; (Czech **Krkonose**, Polish **Karkonósze**).

Riesi, *t.*, Sicily, Italy; industl.; p. *20,200*.

Rieti, *t.*, Perugia, Italy; an ancient Sabine t. in famous fertile dist.; mnfs.; p. (1961) *34,580*.

Riff (Er Rif), *mtns.*, Morocco, N.W. Africa; extend E. along N. African cst. for 200 m. from Straits of Gibraltar; inaccessible and economically unattractive, terr. of semi-nomadic tribes; rises to over 7,000 ft. in many places.

Riga, *cap.*, Latvian S.S.R.; at head of G. of Riga; gr. industl. activity; machin., glass, paper, cottons; rly. and shipbldg., exp. wheat, flax, hemp, dairy produce; p. (1967) *666,000*.

Rigi, *mtn.*, nr. L. Lucerne, Switzerland; alt. 5,905 ft.

Rijeka-Susak, *t.*, Jugoslavia; formerly Fiume; belonged to Austria-Hungary before First World War, then to Italy; ceded to Jugoslavia by Italy after Second World War; rival pt. to Trieste; petrol refining, tobacco, chemicals, hydro-elec., shipbldg.; p. (1961) *101,000*.

Rimac, *R.*, Lima dep., Peru; S. America; rises in W. cordillera of Andes and flows W. to Pac. Oc.; provides water for irrigation and for c. of Lima; length 75 m.

Rimini, *t.*, Emilia, Italy; on the Adriatic cst.; mineral springs, sea-bathing, thriving inds.; p. (1961) *92,912*.

Rimnic, *t.*, Romania; on R. Rimnic, nr. Bucharest; industl; p. (1963) *22,242*.

Rimouski, *t.*, Quebec, Canada; on S. bank St. Lawrence R.; lumber; tourists; p. (1961) *17,739*.

Ringerike, *c.*, Buskerud, Norway; new c. 25 m. N.W. of Oslo and inc. former t. of Hönefoss; p. (1968) *28,779*.

Ringköbing Fjord, *inlet*, W. cst. Jutland, Denmark.

Ringwood and Fordingbridge, *mkt. t.*, *rural dist.*, Hants, Eng.; on R. Avon, nr. Christchurch; p. (rural dist. 1951) *23,908*.

Rio Branco, *R.*, flows c. 350 m. from Guiana Highlands through Brazil to join Rio Negro.

Rio Branco, *t.*, cap. of Acre st., Brazil; p. (estd. 1968) *70,730*.

Rio Cuarto, *t.*, Cordoba prov., Argentina; agr. ctr.; p. (1960) *70,000*. [length 500 m.

Rio das Mortes, *R.*, Brazil; trib. of the Araguay;

Rio de Janeiro, *st.*, S.E. Brazil, on Atl. Oc.; coffee, sugar, fruit; ctr. of heavy ind.; cement, textiles; sugar refineries at Campos, steel wks. at Volta Retonda; cap. Niterói; a. 16,500 sq. m.; p. (estd. 1968) *4,505,938*.

Rio de Janeiro, *c.*, *spt.*, former fed. cap. Brazil; on Bay of Rio de Janeiro; many fine bdgs., flourishing tr. and inds.; rly. wks.; shipyards; mnfs. iron, steel, cement, textiles, sugar, tyres, pharmaceutics, china, sheet glass; p. (1968) *4,207,322*.

Rio de la Plata, *see* Plate R.

Río de San Juan, *R.*, Utah, New Mexico and Colorado, U.S.A.; length 350 m.

Río Dulce. *R.*, Santiago st., Argentina; length 400 m.

Rio Grande, *headstream* of the R. Paraná, Brazil; Furnas dam at Passos, Minas Gerais.

Rio Grande, *R.*, flows from st. of Colorado through New Mexico to the G. of Mexico; forms bdy. between Texas, U.S.A. and Mexico; Elephant Butte, Caballo, and Falcon dams; known also as Rio Grande do Norte and Río Bravo; length *c.* 1,885 m.

Rio Grande, *spt.*, Rio Grande do Sul, Brazil; impt. pt. and comm. ctr.; meat-pkg., fish-canning, textile mills; p. (estd. 1968) *117,500.*

Rio Grande City, *t.*, U.S.A., on Rio Grande R.; oil, natural gas; p. (1960) *5,835.*

Rio Grande do Norte, *st.*, N.E. Brazil; cotton, sugar, salt, scheelite; cap. Natal; a. 20,478 sq. m.; p. (estd. 1968) *1,291,195.*

Rio Grande do Sul, *st.*, S. Brazil; stock-raising, meat-processing, wheat, wine, wool; lge coal deposits at São Jeronimo; cap. Pôrto Alegre; a. 103,353 sq. m.; p. (estd. 1968) *6,560,504.*

Rio Muni, Equatorial Guinea, W. Africa, on cst. between Cameroun and Congo; with Fernando Po and other Is. forms Equatorial Guinea; ch. t. Bata; cacao, coffee, bananas, timber; a. 10,040 sq. m.; p. (1968) *183,000* inc. *3,000* Europeans.

Rio Negro, *R.*, Argentina; rises in the Andes, and flows through the terr. of Rio Negro to the Atlantic; length 650 m.

Rio Negro, *prov.*, Argentina; S. of Pampa; cap. Viedma; cattle-rearing region; a. 77,610 sq. m.; p. (1960) *193,000.*

Rio Negro, *dep.*, Uruguay; cap. Fray Bentos; a. 3,269 sq. m.; p. (1953) *51,954.*

Río Piedras, *t.*, Puerto Rico, W. Indies; univ.; merged with San Juan 1951.

Rio Salada, *R.*, Argentina; rises in the Andes, and flows S.E. to R. Paraná, at Buenos Aires; length 1,000 m.

Rio Tinto, *t.*, Spain; at W. end of Sierra Morena, 40 m. N.E. of Huelva; lead- and copper-mines; p. (1957) *10,000.*

Riobamba, *c.*, Chimborazo, Ecuador; on R. St. Juan; woollens, cotton gds., cement, ceramics; Inca palace ruins; p. (estd. 1960) *35,099.*

Rioja, *region*, N. Spain, Upper Ebro; famous for wines, orange groves; ch. ctr. Logroño.

Rioja, La, *prov.*, Argentina; gold- and copper-mines; cap. La Rioja; a. 33,394 sq. m.; p. (1960) *128,000.*

Riom, *t.*, Puy-de-Dôme, France; nr. Clermont Ferrand; p. (1962) *15,416.*

Rion, *R.*, Georgian S.S.R.; flows from Caucasus to Black Sea; lower half navig.; hydro-elec. sta. at Kutais. (In Greek mythology the R. Phasis of the Argonauts.)

Rionero, *t.*, Potenza prov., S. Italy; nr. Melfi; industl.; p. *12,025.*

Ripley, *mkt. t.*, *urb. dist.*, Derby, Eng.; 7 m. N.E. of Derby; coal, iron, heavy engin., bricks, agr. implements; p. (1961) *17,601.*

Ripley, *t.*, W. Tenn., U.S.A.; lumbering; veneer; cottonseed processing; p. (1960) *3,782.*

Ripon, *c.*, *mun. bor.*, W.R. Yorks, Eng.; on R. Ure; cath.; paint, varnish, prefabricated concrete structures; p. (estd. 1967) *11,520.*

Ripon, *t.*, Wis., U.S.A., on Green L., p. (1950) *5,619.*

Riposto, *t.*, Sicily, Italy; on E. cst. nr. Taormina; wine export; p. *10,725.*

Ripponden, *urb. dist.*, W.R. Yorks, Eng.; nr. Halifax; p. (1961) *5,765.*

Risca, *t.*, *urb. dist.*, Monmouth, Eng.; on R. Ebbw, 5 m. N.W. of Newport; coal, iron and steel, bricks, tiles, plastics; p. (1961) *14,008.*

Rishton, *t.*, *urb. dist.*, Lancs, Eng.; at N. foot of Rossendale Fells, 4 m. N.E. of Blackburn; p. (1961) *5,431.*

Risley, nr. Warrington, Lancs., Eng.; headquarters of Engineering Group of U.K. Atomic Energy Authority; site of Manchester's New t.; proposed p. *50,000.*

Riva, *t.*, Trentino, Italy; battle zone in First World War, Nov.–Dec. 1915; p. *12,950.*

Rivas, *spt.*, Nicaragua, Central America; p. (1960) *19,159.*

Rive-de-Gier, *t.*, Loire, France; on R. Gier, nr. Lyons; mining ctr.; p. (1962) *16,677.*

Rivera, *dep.*, Uruguay; cap. Rivera; a. 3,793 sq. m.; p. (1953) *91,740.*

Riverina, *pastoral cty.*, N.S.W., Australia; between Lachlan-Murrumbidgee and Murray Rs.; sheep, agr. with irrigation; gold, coal; ch. ts., Wagga Wagga, Albury; a. 26,600 sq. m.

River Rouge, *t.*, Mich., U.S.A.; p. (1960) *18,147.*

Riverside, *t.*, Cal., U.S.A.; p. (1960) *84,332.*

Riverside, *t.*, N.J., U.S.A.; p. (1960) *8,474.*

Riverside, *t.*, Ontario, Canada; p. (1961) *18,089.*

Riviera, the belt of cst. between the mtns. of the shore of the G. of Genoa, N. Italy, from Spezia to Nice; picturesque scenery, sheltered, mild climate; fashionable health resort.

Riyadh, *t.*, *cap.*, Saudi Arabia; 230 m. inland from Persian G.; palace; univ.; p. (estd.) *300,000.*

Rizal, *prov.*, *t.*, central Luzon, Philippine Is.; chiefly agr.; food processing, steel mill, cement; a. 791 sq. m.; p. of t. (1960) *132,673.*

Rize, *t.*, Turkey; nr. Trabzon, on Black Sea; p. (1965) *27,069.*

Rjukan, *t.*, Telemark, S. Norway; 35 m. N.W. of Notodden, impt. nitrate factories; p. (1961) *5,637.*

Road Town, *spt.*, Tortola; *cap.* Virgin Is.; p. (1960) *900.*

Roanne, *t.*, Loire, France; nr. St. Etienne; textile, cottons, woollens, silk; p. (1962) *53,203.*

Roanoke, *1.*, off cst. N.C., U.S.A.; 13 m. long.

Roanoke, *R.*, Va., and N.C., U.S.A.; flows into Albemarle Sound; length 230 m.

Roanoke, *t.*, Ala. U.S.A.; cotton mnfs., clothes; p. (1960) *5,288.*

Roanoke, *c.*, S.W. Va., U.S.A.; on R. R.; ironwks.; p. (1960) *97,110.*

Roaring Creek, Brit. Honduras, C. America; site of new cap. 50 m. inland, at junction of W. Highway with Hummingbird Highway.

Roatan Is., Honduras, in G. of H.

Robin Hood's Bay, *picturesque inlet with fishing vil. on cst.*, N.R. Yorks, Eng.; nr. Whitby.

Robson, Mt., Alberta, Canada, 12,972 ft.

Roca, C. da, most W. point of estuary of R. Tagus, Portugal.

Roch, *R.*, Lancs, Eng.; rises in E. of Rossendale Fells, central Pennines, flows S.W. into R. Irwell nr. Bury; with R. Calder provides relatively easy route across Pennines from Leeds to Manchester; used by rail, road, canal; length approx. 20 m.

Rocha, *dep.*, Uruguay; a. 4,280 sq. m.; cap. Rocha; p. (1953) *86,334.*

Rochdale, *t.*, *co. bor.*, Lancs, Eng.; at S. foot of Rossendale Fells, on R. Roch; textiles, textile engin., rayon spinning, elec. engin.; co-operative movement started here, 1844; p. (estd. 1967) *86,960.*

Rochefort, *t.*, S. Belgium; p. (1962) *3,996.*

Rochefort, *c.*, Charente-Maritime, France; fishing pt.; former impt. naval base; p. (1962) *33,584.*

Rochelle, La, *c.*, cap. Charente-Maritime, France; on Bay of Biscay; impt. fishing pt.; shipbldg.; p. (1962) *68,445.*

Roches Point, E. side of Cork harbour, Ireland.

Rochester, *c.*, *mun. bor.*, Kent, Eng.; on R. Medway, adjoining Chatham; cath., cas.; aeronautical, elec. and mechanical engin., paint, varnish; p. (estd. 1967) *55,100.*

Rochester, *c.*, Minn., U.S.A.; in grain-growing dist.; p. (1960) *40,663.*

Rochester, *t.*, N.H., U.S.A.; on Cocheco R.; shoes, textiles; p. (1960) *15,927.*

Rochester, *c.*, N.Y., U.S.A.; on Genesee R.; univ.; hydro-elec. power; cameras, films, optical instruments, thermometers, electronic equipment; p. (1960) *318,611.*

Roche-sur-Yon, La, *t.*, Vendée, France; on R. Yon; cas.; called formerly Bourbon Napoleonville; p. (1962) *25,456.*

Rochford, *t.*, *rural dist.*, Essex, Eng.; 3 m. N. of Southend; timber wharves, boat bldg., brick mkg.; p. (rural dist. 1961) *30,306.*

Rockall, *sm. I.*, N. Atl. Oc.; lies 200 m. W. of Outer Hebrides; forms highest part of submarine bank which forms good fishing-ground; uninhabited. Annexed by Britain, 1955.

Rockall Deep, *submarine trench*, N. Atl. Oc.; between N.W. Ireland and Rockall I.; depth exceeds 1,600 fathoms.

Rockaway, *bor.*, N.J., U.S.A.; iron founding and products; textiles, lumber; p. (1960) *5,413.*

Rockaway Beach, *summer resort*, on sandbar of Long I.; now incorporated with Queens, one of the 5 bors. of New York City, U.S.A.

Rockford, c., Ill., U.S.A.; machin. and furniture mftg.; p. (1960) 126,706.

Rockhampton, c., pt., Queensland, Australia; on R. Fitzroy; comm. cap. of Central Queensland; meat-preserving; fruit canning; cotton ginning; rly. wks.; p. (1966) 45,349.

Rock Hill, c. S.C., U.S.A.; industl.; p. (1960) 29,404.

Rockingham, t., N.C., U.S.A.; cotton mnfs., paper, lumbering, peaches; p. (1950) 3,356.

Rock Island, c., Ill., U.S.A.; on R. Mississippi; lumbering, flour mills, glass, farm implements; elec. equipment; p. (1960) 51,863.

Rockland, c., spt., Ma., U.S.A.; on Penobscot Bay; shipbldg., granite quarrying; p. (1950) 9,234.

Rockland, t., Mass., U.S.A.; shoemkg., engin.; p. (1960) 13,080.

Rock River, Wis., U.S.A.; trib. of the Mississippi; length 375 m.

Rockville, c., Conn., U.S.A.; on Hockanum R.; silks, woollens; p. (1960) 9,478.

Rocky Mount, t., N.C., U.S.A.; p. (1960) 32,147.

Rocky Mountains, extensive chain, N. America; extending along the W. portions of Canada and the U.S.A. from Alaska to Mexico; the highest accurately measured point in the U.S.A. system is Mt. Massive (14,418 ft.); other high peaks are Mt. Elbert (14,431 ft.), Blanca Peak (14,390 ft.), Mt. Harvard (14,399 ft.), La Plata Peak (14,340 ft.), and Mt. Uncompahgre (14,306 ft.). Mt. St. Elias, in Alaska, is computed to be 18,008 ft. high, and was long held to be the highest peak in N. America, but is now known to be surpassed by Mt. McKinley (20,300 ft.) in the Alaska range, and by Mt. Logan (19,850 ft.), the highest peak in Canada.

Rodas, mun., Cuba; sugar; p. 21,288.

Rödby, t., Denmark; on S. cst. of Lolland; p. (1960) 3,551.

Rodewisch, t., Karl-Marx-Stadt, E. Germany; engin., textiles; p. (1963) 12,458.

Rodez, t., cap., Aveyron, France; on R. Aveyron; cath.; woollens; p. (1962) 24,352.

Rodosto, see Tekirdag.

Rodriguez, I., British dependency of Mauritius, Indian Ocean; 350 m. N.E. of Mauritius; principal exp., cattle, beans, salt, fish and goats; 42 sq. m.; p. (estd. 1968) 20,000.

Roebling, t., N.J., U.S.A.; established by steel-cable mkg. company; p. (1960) 3,272.

Roermond, t., Limburg, Neth.; on R. Maas; minster; paper, beer, cloth; p. (1967) 36,842.

Roeselare, t., W. Flanders, Belgium; on R. Lys, nr. Courtrai, cotton, linen, lace; p. (1968) 40,091.

Roes Welcome, channel between Southampton I. and N.W. Terr. Canada.

Rogaland, co., Norway; a. 3,546 sq. m.; p. (1968) 259,969.

Rogers, t., Ark., U.S.A.; fruit, vegs.; tourists; p. (1960) 5,700.

Rogerstone, t., S. Monmouth, Eng., on R. Ebbw 3 m. W. of Newport; aluminium; p. (1951) 4,453.

Rohtak, t., Punjab, India; mkt., cotton textiles; fortifications; p. (1961) 88,193.

Rokko, C., Honshu, Japan; jutting into Sea of Japan.

Rolphton, Ontario, Canada; nuclear power plant.

Roma, t., Queensland, Australia; in agr. dist. nr. Mt. Horrible; natural gas (pipeline to Brisbane); oil; p. (1966) 6,000.

Roman, t., Romania; on R. Moldava; cath.; p. (1963) 45,930.

Romania, rep., E. Europe; bounded by U.S.S.R., Hungary, Jugoslavia and Bulgaria, consisting of 39 counties and 3 cities of regional status (Bucharest, Constanta, and Petrosani); plain drained by Danube and tribs. Prut, Siret, Dambovita, Oit Jiu; except Transylvania, mountainous: Carpathians, Transylvanian Alps; very warm summers, severe winters, rainfall moderate, chiefly, in summer; agr., maize, wheat, barley, oats; grape vines, fruit; sheep, cattle, pigs, horses; forests, timber; minerals, petroleum, natural gas, lignite, copper, salt; flour-milling, brewing, distilling, oil-refining, chemicals; cap, Bucharest; a, 91,671 sq. m.; p. (estd. 1968) 19,721,000.

Romans, t., Drôme, France; on R. Isère; formerly seat of ancient abbey; p. (1962) 27,662.

Romblon Is., prov., of Philippine Is.; low, fertile;

ch. crops, abaca and copra; gold, marble; a. 512 sq. m.; p. (1960) 16,700.

Rome, c., cap., Italy; on R. Tiber, 15 m. from the sea; one of the most famous cities in the world; ctr. of the Roman Catholic Church and former cap. of the greatest st. in the ancient world; situated on the original " seven hills " of the old Roman metropolis, and in the valleys between, along the R.; contains the celebrated cath. ch. of St. Peter, in the Vatican City, many historical monuments, a univ. and several institutions devoted to art and learning; created cap. of mod. United Italy in 1871; mnfs. and tr.; p. (1965) 2,514,000.

Rome, c., Ga., U.S.A.; on Coosa R.; in cotton region; p. (1960) 32,226.

Rome, c., N.Y., U.S.A.; on the Mohawk R.; dairying ctr.; p. (1960) 51,646.

Romford, former mkt. t., mun. bor., Essex, Eng.; 12 m. E. of London; now inc. in Havering bor. Greater London; brewing, light inds.; p. (1961) 114,584.

Romilly-sur-Seine, t., Aube, France; nr. Troyes; textile factories; p. (1962) 15,966.

Romney, see New Romney.

Romney Marsh, coastal marsh, Kent, Eng.; formed by blocking of R. Rother by shingle spit of Dungeness which extends from Rye to Hythe; now largely drained; pastures for special Romney Marsh breed of sheep; a. 50 sq. m.

Romsdal, Möre Og, dist. Norway; cap. Molde; a. 5,812 sq. m.; p. (1961) 212,020.

Romsey, mun. bor., Hants, Eng.; on R. Test, 8½ m. N.W. of Southampton; mkt. ctr.; p. (estd. 1967) 7,660; rural dist. with Stockbridge (1961) 21,615.

Ronaldshay, N. and S., Is. of the Orkneys.

Roncesvalles, mtn. pass., in the Pyrenees, Spain; 20 m. N.E. of Pamplona, Navarra; Charlemagne's army under Roland, who was slain, defeated here, 778.

Ronda, t., Malaga, Spain; ancient Moorish t. 42 m. N. of Gibraltar; mnfs. chocolate, leather, fruit, wines; p. (1957) 30,962.

Rondônia st., Brazil; on Bolivian border; cap. Pôrto Velho; p. (estd. 1968) 115,233.

Rongotai, Wellington, N.Z.; international airport.

Rönne, t., Denmark; on W. cst. of Bornholm; granite; p. (estd.) 13,000.

Ronse, see Renaix.

Roodepoort-Maraisburg, t., Transvaal, S. Africa; mng. and industl.; p. (1960) 94,740 (inc. 40,711 whites).

Rooppur, nr. Ishurdi, East Pakistan; nuclear power plant projected 1964.

Roorkee, t., Uttar Pradesh, India; univ.; p. (1961) 45,801.

Roosendaal, industl. t., S.W. of N. Brabant, Neth.; nr. Breda; p. (1967) 44,102.

Roosevelt, R., trib. of Madeirj R., Brazil.

Roosevelt Dam, Arizona, U.S.A.; on R. Salt 130 m. above Phoenix on edge of Colorado Plateau; supplies irrigation for cultivation of 360 sq. m. in lower valley of R. Salt and upper valley of R. Gila; hydro-elec. power-sta.

Roper R., N.E. Northern Terr., Australia; navigable for about 90 m. inland.

Roquefort-sur-Soulzon, t., S.E. Aveyron, France; caves in limestone cliffs used for ripening cheese.

Roraima, mtn., at junc. of boundaries of Brazil, Guyana, and Venezuela; 9,350 ft.

Roraima, terr., Brazil; cap. Boa Vista; a. 82,749 sq. m.; p. (estd. 1968) 41,344.

Rorschach, t., Switzerland; lace; p. (1957) 11,325.

Rosa Monte, highest pk., Pennine Alps, Italy; alt. 15,217 ft.

Rosario, t., Santa Fé, Argentina; on R. Paraná; rly. terminus; univ.; chemicals, metals, leather, bricks, milling; p. (1960) 760,000.

Rosas. t., Spain; on Franco-Spanish border, opp. Portbou on the Mediterranean cst; fishing pt.; p. (1957) 2,720.

Roscommon, inland co., Connaught, Ireland; a. 949 sq. m.; p. (1966) 56,130.

Roscrea, mkt. t., Tipperary and Offaly, Ireland; on Little Brosna R.; p. (1966) 3,510.

Roseau, t., Dominica, Windward Is.; p. (1957) 13,500.

Roseburg, t., S.W. Ore., U.S.A.; roses, fruit, poultry; canning, sawmills; p. (1950) 8,390.

Roselle, t., N.J., U.S.A.; p. (1960) 21,032.

Rosenheim, t., Bavaria, Germany; on R. Inn 35 m. S.E. of Munich; sulphur springs; impt

K144

brine wks., machin., wood, iron, textiles, brewing; rly. junction; p. (1963) 32,000.

Rosetta (Rashid), t., Lower U.A.R.; on W. distributary of R. Nile, 43 m. N.E. Alexandria.

Roseville, t., E. Cal., U.S.A.; exp. fruit, wines; p. (1960) 13,421.

Roskilde, mkt. t., Denmark; 20 m. W. of Copenhagen; fine cath. containing tombs of Kings and Queens of D.; royal palace; dairy prod.; leather; p. (1960) 31,928.

Ross, mkt. t., urb. dist., Hereford, Eng.; on R. Wye, cider; p. (1961) 5,643.

Ross and Cromarty, cst. and Highland co., Scot.; total a. 3,202 sq. m.; ch. t. Dingwall; p. (1961) 57,607.

Ross Dependency, Antarctica, N.Z.; p. (1961) 198.

Ross I., Victoria Land, Antarctica.

Ross Sea, sea extending to 85° S. in the Antarctic.

Rossan Pt., headland, N. side of Donegal Bay, Ireland.

Rossano, c., Cosenza, S. Italy; nr. G. of Taranto; old t. under the Byzantine Empire; alabaster and marble quarries; silk, olive oil; p. 17,425.

Rossendale Fells (Rossendale Forest), upland region, S.E. Lancs, Eng.; forms W. extension of Pennines between Mersey and Ribble valleys; composed of hard, impervious millstone grit; covered by boggy moorland; many reservoirs store soft water for cotton-spinning ts. along S. edge (Bolton, Bury, Rochdale), cotton-weaving ts. along N. edge (Blackburn, Accrington, Burnley) and sm. industl. ts. in Irwell valley within Rossendale; alt. mainly above 1,200 ft.

Rosslare, spt., Wexford, Ireland; on extreme S.E. of Ireland; steamer connections to Fishguard (Wales).

Rostock, spt., Rostock, E. Germany; nr. mouth of R. Warnow; univ.; shipbldg., ship repair ind., fisheries; deep-water harbour; oil pt.; p. (1964) 170,000.

Rostov, t., pt., R.S.F.S.R.; on R. Don, 10 m. up from Sea of Azov (Black Sea); a gr. grain mart and comm. and industl. ctr.; engin., elec. power, paper; p. (1967) 737,000.

Roswell, t., N.M., U.S.A.; p. (1960) 39,593.

Rosyth, t., Fife, Scot.; naval dockyard.

Rothamsted, hamlet, Herts, Eng.; in Chiltern Hills, 1 m. S. of Harpenden; lge. agr. experimental sta.

Rother, R., Sussex and Kent, Eng.; rises in the Weald, flows S.E. into English Channel at Rye; length 31 m.

Rother, R., Hants and Sussex, Eng.; trib. of R. Arun; length 24 m.

Rother, R., Derby and Yorks, Eng.; flows to R. Don at Rotherham; length 21 m.

Rotherham, t., co. bor., W.R. Yorks; on R. Don, 4 m. N.E. of Sheffield; iron, steel, coal, glass; p. (estd. 1967) 86,670.

Rotherhithe, S.E. Thames-side-dist., London, Eng.

Rothes, burgh, Moray, Scot.; on R. Spey 12 m. S.E of Elgin; p. (1961) 1.105.

Rothesay, burgh, Bute, Scot.; on E. cst. of I. of Bute in Firth of Clyde; tourism; p. (1961) 7,656.

Rothwell, t., urb. dist., Northants, Eng.; 3 m. N.W. of Kettering; boots, shoes; p. (1961) 4,766.

Rothwell, t., urb. dist., W.R. Yorks, Eng.; on R. Aire, 3 m. S.E. of Leeds; mining; chemicals, bricks, tiles, copper tubes, stone and sand quarrying; p. (estd. 1967) 27,130.

Rotondo, mtn., Corsica, France.

Rotorua, c., N.I., N.Z.; health resort; hot springs; p. (1966) 25.978.

Rotterdam, spt., wealthy comm. c., Neth.; on R. Nieuwe Maas; linked to N. Sea at Hook of Holland by "New Waterway" ship canal; Europe's lgst. pt., second in world; breweries, sugar-ref., oil-ref., shipbldg., chemicals, clocks; p. (1967) 723,955.

Rotti, I. (50 m. by 20 m.) off cst. of Timor, Malay Archipelago, Indonesia; p. 59,221.

Roubaix, t., Nord, France; nr. Lille; on the Roubaix canal 1 m. from the Belgian frontier; woollen mnfs., grape and tomato forcing; gr. tr., many educational institutions and fine bldgs.; p. (1962) 113,163.

Rouen, c., Seine-Maritime, France; over 50 m. up R. Seine; textiles, chemicals, oil refining; magnificent cath. and church; badly damaged Second World War; p. (1968) 120,471.

Roumania. see Romania.

Roukela, see Raukela.

Rousay, Orkney Is., Scotland.

Roussillon, old prov., S. France; lies in depression at E. end of Pyrenees, in dep. of Pyrénées Orientales; largely irrigated by many sm. streams; olive, vine, wheat.

Rouyn, mining t., Quebec, Canada; at end of L. Abitibi; gold, copper, zinc; p. (1961) 18,716.

Rovereto, c., S. Tyrol, Italy; on R. Adige; silk, leather, paper, cottons; p. 20,575.

Rovigo, prov., Venetia, Italy; cap. Rovigo; a. 684 sq. m.; p. (1961) 270,983.

Rovigo, t., cap., Rovigo prov., Italy; on R. Adige, 20 m. S. of Padua; agr. mkt.; p. (1961) 45,271.

Rovno, t., Ukrainian S.S.R.; 110 m. N.E. of Lvov; comm. ctr.; p. (1959) 57,000.

Rowley Regis, industl. t., mun. bor., Staffs, Eng.; adjoins Dudley; p. (1961) 48,166.

Roxboro', t., N.C., U.S.A.; cotton, tobacco, mnfs.; p. (1950) 4,321.

Roxburgh, inland co., S. Scot.; stretching halfway along the Eng. border; hilly; sheep-rearing; woollens, tweed; cap. Jedburgh; a. 670 sq. m.; p. (1961) 43,171.

Royal Leamington Spa, see Leamington.

Royal Oak, t., Mich., U.S.A.; p (1960) 80,612.

Royan, t., Charente-Maritime, France; S. of Rochelle; fishery, tr.,industl.; p. (1962) 17,232.

Royersford, bor., S.E. Penns., U.S.A.; light iron and steel mnfs.; glass; p. (1950) 3,862.

Royston, mkt. t., urb. dist., Herts, Eng.; at N. foot of E. Anglian Heights, 7 m. N.E. of Baldock; p. (1961) 6,166.

Royston, urb. dist., W.R. Yorks, Eng.; coal-mining; p. (1961) 8,490.

Royton, t., urb. dist., Lancs. Eng.; 4 m. N.E. of Manchester; cotton spinning; p. (1961) 14,476.

Roznava, t., ČSSR.; W. of Košice; antimony; p. (1961) 10,227.

Ruabon, par., Denbigh, N. Wales; on Salop border; coal, iron, tile wks., chemicals; p. 3,333.

Ruanda-Urundi, see Rwanda and Burundi.

Ruapehu, highest mtn., N.I., N.Z.; volcanic peak at S. extremity of central volcanic dist.; alt.9,175ft.

Rubicon, R. of Central Italy, flowing to the Adriatic, crossed by Julius Cæsar and his armies in 49 B.C. Has been identified with the Fiumicino or the Uso. There is a R. Rubicon (It. Rubico) a few m. N. of Rimini and S. of Cervia.

Rubtsovsk, t., W. Siberia, R.S.F.S.R.; agr. engin.; p. (1967) 140,000.

Ruby Mines, dist., Mandalay, Upper Burma; hilly region of the Shan plateau, rich in precious stones; H.Q. t. Mogôk, in ctr. of the mining dist.

Ruda Slaska, t., Katowice, Poland; industl; p. (1965) inc. Nowy Bytom 141,000.

Rudnyy, t., Kazakh S.S.R.; new town 30 m. S.W. of Kustanay; iron ore mining and dressing plant supplying Magnitogorsk; p. (1958) c. 40.000

Rudolf, L., N.W. Kenya, in Great Rift Valley; a. 3,500 sq. m.

Rudolph I., of Franz Josef Land, Arctic Ocean; Russian naval base; met. sta.

Rudolstadt, t., Gera, E. Germany; on R. Saale; cas.; porcelain, metals; p. (1963) 23,474.

Rueil Malmaison, t., Hauts-de-Seine; nr. Paris; p. (1962) 56,024.

Rufiji, R., Tanzania; E. Africa; flows to the Indian Ocean; length 450 m.

Rugby, mkt. t., mun. bor., Warwick, Eng.; on R. Avon, 11 m. E. of Coventry; famous Public school; elec. and gen. engin., motor and aircraft patterns; p. (estd. 1967) 56,450.

Rugeley, mkt. t., urb. dist., Staffs, Eng.; on R. Trent, 9 m. S.E. of Stafford; coal, iron, tanning; p. (1961) 13,012.

Ruhr, industl. dist., W. Germany; lies to E. of R. Rhine, on either side of R. Ruhr; rich coalfield; impt. iron and steel, heavy engin. inds. based on local coal and iron ore from Luxembourg, Spain, Sweden; water communications to N. Sea along R. Rhine and Dortmund–Ems Canal; ch. ts. Essen,Duisburg,Düsseldorf,Dortmund,Bochum.

Ruislip-Northwood, former urb. dist., Middlesex, Eng.; now inc. in Hillingdon bor. Greater London (q.v.); residtl.; p. (1961) 72,791.

Rukwa, L., E. Africa; between L. Tanganyika and L. Malawi in the rift valley; 30 m. by 12 m., a. increasing.

Rum, I., Inner Hebrides, Argyll, Scot.; 8½ m. by 8 m.

Rumaila, Iraq; oilfield; pipe-line links to the Zubair–Fao system.

Rumania, see Romania.

Rum Jungle, N. Terr., Australia; 70 m. S.E. of Darwin; uranium mng.; silver, lead and copper deposits.

Runcorn, *industl. t., urb. dist.*, Cheshire, Eng.; on S. side of Mersey estuary; new Runcorn-Widnes bridge over Mersey and Manchester Ship canal opened 1961 (lgst. span arch in Europe); designated " New Town " 1964; chemicals; p. (estd. 1967) *30,650.*

Rupert, *R.*, Canada; flows from L. Mistassini to James Bay; length 300 m.

Ruse, *t.*, Bulgaria; on R. Danube, opp. Giurgiu in Romania; univ., arsenal, barracks; beer, sugar, tobacco; p. (1956) *53,523.*

Rushden, *t., urb. dist.*, Northants, Eng.; 3 m. E. of Wellingborough; shoes; p. (1961) *17,370.*

Rusholme, *t.*, E. of Manchester, S.E. Lancs. Eng.; industl. and residtl.

Russell *t.*, Kan., U.S.A.; mkt. in agr. and cattle region, oil and gas fields; p. (1960) *6,113.*

Rüsselsheim, *t.*, Hessen, Germany; on R. Main, E. of Mainz; car mftg. (Opel); p. (1963) *44,100.*

Russian Soviet Federal Socialist Republic (R.S.F.S.R.) *ch. constituent rep.*, U.S.S.R.; ch. inds. : wheat, rye, oats, barley, potatoes, sugarbeet, fruits, sunflower, cotton, hemp, tobacco; sheep, cattle, dairying, pigs, horses; lumbering, timber, wood-pulp; coal, petroleum, iron, manganese, etc.; machin., textiles, oil-refining, cement, bricks a. 6,310,594 sq. m.; cap. Moscow; p. (1970) *130,090,000.*

Rustavi, *t.*, Georgian S.S.R., new *t.* 20 m. S.E. Tbilisi; metallurgical plant; p. (1959) *62,000.*

Rustenburg, *t.*, Transvaal, Rep. of S. Africa; on N.W. edge of High Veld, 60 m. W. of Pretoria; local mkt. for agr. produce, sorghum, maize, cotton; p. (1960) *20,866* (inc. *10,648* whites).

Rutbah, *t.*, Iraq; on oil pipe-line from Iraq to Haifa.

Rute, *t.*, Cordova, Spain; nr. Lucerna; industl.; p. *18,903.*

Ruthenia, *dist.*, U.S.S.R.; formerly part of Romania, ceded to U.S.S.R. in 1945, now part of Ukrainian S.S.R.

Rutherford, *t.*, N.J., U.S.A.; p. (1960) *20,473.*

Rutheriordton, *t.*, N.C., U.S.A.; gold, lumber, textiles; agr.; p. (1950) *3,146.*

Rutherglen, *burgh*, Lanark, Scot.; on R. Clyde, S.E. of Glasgow; industl., chemicals, tubes, paper, wire ropes, bolts, chenilles, webbing; p. (1961) *25,067.*

Ruthin, *t., mun. bor.*, Denbigh, Wales; Vale of Clwyd, 8 m. S.E. of Denbigh; p. (1961) *3,502.*

Rutigliano, *t.*, Bari, Italy; agr.; p. *10,650.*

Rutland, *midland co.*, Eng.; smallest in cty.; agr. farming, livestock; cheese, stone, iron; a. 152 sq. m.; cap. Oakham; p. (1966) *28,000.*

Rutland, *t.*, Vt., U.S.A.; marble quarries, machin. and furniture; p. (1960) *18,353.* [p. *25,225.*

Ruvo, *t.*, Bari, Italy; cath.; olive-oil presses;

Ruwenzori, *mtn. range*, on Uganda-Congo border, overlooking W. arm of Gr. Rift Valley, midway between L. Albert and L. Edward; hgst peaks, Mt. Margherita (16,798 ft.), Mt. Alexandra (16,750 ft.); lower slopes covered in equatorial rain forest, coffee plantations on middle slopes above 5,000 ft.

Rwanda, *indep. rep.*, (1 July 1962), formerly kingdom of Ruanda, part of U.N. trust terr, of Ruanda-Urundi under Belgian adm.; coffee; cap. Kigali; a. 10,169 sq. m.; p. (estd. 1968) *3,405,000.*

Ryan Loch, *arm of sea*, on cst. Wigtown, Scot.; 8 m. by 2 m.

Ryazan, *t.*, R.S.F.S.R.; S.E. of Moscow; distilling, leather, engin.; p. (1967) *297,000.*

Rybinsk, *t., R. pt.*, R.S.F.S.R.; on R. Volga; engin., textiles, hydro-elec.; p. (1967) *209,000.*

Rybinsk Sea (Rybinsk Reservoir), R.S.F.S.R.; artificial L.; created behind dams on R. Volga and R. Sheksna at Rybinsk; part of scheme to regulate flow of R. Volga and to incorporate it in a vast inland waterway system; opened 1945; approx. a. 1,500 sq. m.

Rybnik, *t.*, S.W. Poland; engin., brewing, furniture-mkg.; p. (1965) *38,000.*

Rydal Water, *L.*, nr. Ambleside, Westmorland, Eng.; vil. adjacent contains Rydal Mount, where Wordsworth lived.

Ryde, *t., mun. bor.*, I. of Wight, Eng.; on N.E. cst.; yachting ctr. and seaside resort; boat and yacht bldg.; steamer connection across Spithead to Portsmouth; p. (estd. 1967) *21,200.*

Rye, *t., mun. bor.*, *Cinque Pt.*, E. Sussex, Eng.;

at mouth of R. Rother to W. of Dungeness; shipbldg. and fishing; p. (estd. 1967) *4,400.*

Ryton, *t., urb. dist.*, Durham, Eng.; on R. Tyne W. of Newcastle; ironwks.; p. (1961) *13,485.*

Ryuku Archipelago, *chain of Is.*, 650 m. long, between Taiwan and Kyushi I., Japan; total a. 1,803 sq. m.; incl. Amami-gunto, Okinawa and Sakishima; ch. t. Naha on Okinawa.; mtnous., volcanic; sugar, pineapple, tobacco; steel bars, chemical adhesives; under U.S. control since end of war; self-gov. since 1962; p. (1956) *807,400.*

Rzeszow, *prov.*, S.E. Poland; a. 7,110 sq. m.; agr.; p. (1965) *1,693,000.*

Rzeszow, *t.*, S.E. Poland; industl. development since 1950; p. (1965) *69,000.*

Rzhev, *t.*, R.S.F.S.R.; on R. Volga; industl. and comm. engin.; p. (1956) *42,000.*

S

Saale, *R.*, Halle and Gera, Germany; trib. of R. Elbe; length 225 m.

Saalfeld, *t.*, Gera, E. Germany; on R. Saale; famous cas. and grottos; machin., chocolate mftg.; p. (1963) *29,635.*

Saane, *R.*, Switzerland; flows to R. Aar, nr. Berne; length 65 m.

Saar, *R.*, Lorraine, Saarland, Palatinate; rises in the Vosges and flows N.W. to R. Moselle, nr. Trier; length 153 m.

Saar, *st.*, W. Europe; in valley of Saar; administered by League of Nations 1919–35 and returned to Germany after plebiscite; economic attachment of Saar to France agreed upon by Allied powers after Second World War; reunited politically with German Federal Republic 1 Jan. 1957 as a *Land.* Impt. coalfields iron; ch. t. Saarbrucken; p. (1968) *1,129,000.*

Saarbrücken, *cap.*, Saarland, on R. Saar, opp. Sanct, Johann; cas.; rich coalfield; iron and steel wks., textiles, leather, paper, oil refining at Klarenthal nearby; p. (1968) *131,937.*

Saarebourg, *t.*, Moselle, France; on R. Saar, 30 m. N.W. of Strasbourg; mnfs. gloves, watch springs; p. (1962) *13,280.*

Saare Maa (Ösel), *I.*, Baltic Sea; at entrance to G. of Riga, Estonian S.S.R., U.S.S.R.; consists of low plateau, bleak and barren; ch. t., Kuresaare; a. approx. 900 sq. m.

Saarlouis, *t.*, Saarland, Germany; on R. Saar; coal-mng., wood, metals; p. (1963) *36,800.*

Sabac, *t.*, Jugoslavia; on R. Sava; old cas.; fruit, cattle, pigs, coal, zinc; p. (1959) *22,000.*

Sabadell, *t.*, Spain; N.W. of Barcelona; linen and cloth mills, flour, paper, distilling, iron founding; p. (1959) *86,417.*

Sabah, East Malaysia, *formerly* N. Borneo; tropical climate but equable, heavy rainfall; largely forested; hardwoods, rubber, tobacco, copra, cutch, hemp; cap. Kota Kinabalu; a. 29,387 sq. m.; p. (estd. 1966) *577,812.*

Sabahiyah, *t.*, Kuwait; new t. being built between Ahmadi and Fahahil.

Sabang, *spt.*, Sumatra, Indonesia; bunkering sta.; p. *8,855.*

Sabará, *t.*, Minas Gerais, Brazil; historic *c.*, museum of gold; p. (estd. 1968) *26,464.*

Sabine, *R.*, Texas and La., U.S.A.; flows through S. Lake (an expansion of the R. 18 m. long) to Gulf of Mexico; length 500 m.

Sable Cape, *S. point*, Fla., U.S.A.

Sable I., off S.E. cst., Nova Scotia; 45 m. long.

Saclay, France; ENEA Neutron Data Compilation Centre.

Saco, *c.*, Me., U.S.A.; cotton mnfs.; p. (1960) *10,515.*

Saco, *R.*, U.S.A.; flows from White Mtns. in New Hampshire to Saco B., Mne.; 160 m. long.

Sacramento, *c., cap.*, Cal., U.S.A.; on the R. Sacramento; Capitol and R.C. cath.; rail wkshps., smelting, meat and fruit packing, flour, lumber, metal prods., rocket and missiles ind.; p. (1960) *191.667.*

Saddleback (Blencathara), *mtn.*, Cumberland, Eng.; nr. Keswick; alt. 2,847 ft.

Saddleworth, *t., urb. dist.*, W.R. Yorks, Eng.; in Pennines, 5 m. N.E. of Oldham; woollen, paper mkg., engin.; p. (1961) *17,010.*

Sado, *I.*, off cst. of Honshu, Japan; gold and silver mines; rice, fishing; a. 331 sq. m.

Sadon, *t.*, R.S.F.S.R.; zinc, lead, lead smelting.

Safad, *t.*, N. of Sea of Galilee, Israel; p. *11,300.*

Saffron Walden, *mkt. t., mun. bor.*, Essex, Eng.; on E. Anglian Heights 12 m. N. of Bishops Stortford; agr.; hort. and engin.; p. (estd. 1967) *9,410*.

Safi, *spt.*, W. cst. Morocco; resort; poor harbour, gr. grain and wool tr.; lge. phosphate plant; fishing; p. (1960) *81,072*.   [p. (1955) *126,432*.

Saga, *t.*, Kyushu, Japan; coal-mining, fishing:

Sagaing, *div.*, Upper Burma; mtn. ridges, fertile plains; rice, wheat, peas, cotton; a. 50,086 sq. m.; p. *2,322,675*.

Sagaing, *t.*, Upper Burma; on R. Irrawaddy; pagodas; groundnuts. cotton, millets, tobacco, cattle; textile mill projected; p. *c. 15,000*.

Saganoseki, *sm. t.*, N.E. Kyushu, Japan; on Bungo Strait, 15 m. E. of Oita; impt. gold-, copper-, silver-mines.   [*104,676*.

Sagar, *t.*, Madhya Pradesh, India; univ.; p. (1961)

Sagastyr, *I.*, at mouth of R. Lena, R.S.F.S.R.

Saginaw, *c.*, Mich., U.S.A.; on R. Saginaw; in agr. and timber region; machin., railwks., beet-sugar; p. (1960) *98,265*.

Sagua la Grande, *t.*, Cuba; on R. of same name; machin., chemicals, bricks, tiles, salt; p. (1953) *26,187*.

Saguenay, *R.*, Quebec, Canada; length from L. St. John to St. Lawrence R. about 100 m.; of gr. depth, beautiful scenery; hydro-elec. power developed.

Sagunto, *t.*, Spain; nr. Valencia; p. (1957) *26,932*.

Sahara, the gr. N. African desert between the Sudan and the Barbary sts., extending from the Atlantic to the Nile, inc. Tripoli and Fezzan; a. 3,500,000 sq. m.; the E. portion is known as the Libyan desert, that part E. of the R. Nile, being often called the Nubian Desert; numerous oases with ts. and tr. ctrs.; oil pipe lines to Algerian and Tunisian csts.; p. (estd. *2,500,000*), nomadic Arab and Berber tribes.

Saharan Atlas, S. range of Atlas mtns. in Algeria which reach 7,080 ft. in Aurès and 4,693 ft. in " Tunisian backbone."

Saharan Oases, *terr.*, S. Algeria; p. *39,575*.

Saharanpur, *c.*, Uttar Pradesh, India; rly. wks., wood carving; furniture, paper, tobacco, mnfs.; p. (1961) *185,213*.   [(1961) *31,409*.

Sahibganj, *t.*, Bihar, India; on R. Ganges; p.

Saida, *see* Sidon.

Saidabad or Sirdjan, *t.*, Laristan, Iran; S.W. of Kerman, nr. Kuh-i-Lalehzar mtn.; p. *10,000*.

Saigon, *c.*, *spt.*, S. Viet-Nam; on R. Saigon, to E. of Mekong delta, 60 m. from sea; lge. comm. ctr.; cath.; citadel, arsenal and naval yd.; spices rice; paper mill; p. (1965) *1,485,000*. (with Cholon).

Saih-El-Maleh, *pt.*, Oman; oil terminal.

Saimaa, *L.*, Finland; a. of water which forms basin of R. Vuoksi; total expanse of water 390 sq. m.; canal connects with G. of Finland and runs partly through Soviet terr.

St. Abb's Head, *rocky promontory*, Berwick, Scot.

St. Agnes Head, Cornwall, Eng.

St. Albans, *c.*, *mun. bor.*, Herts, Eng.; on N. margin of Vale of St. Albans, 20 m. N.W. of London; faces remains of Roman Verulamium across R. Ver; light inds., electronics, instrument mkg.; cath.; residtl.; p. (estd. 1967) *52,470*.

St. Albans, *t.*, Vt., U.S.A.; dairy farming; p. (1960) *8,806*.   [industl.; p. (1954) *10,765*.

St. Amand, *t.*, Cher., France; on R. Cher;

St. Andrews, *burgh*, Fife, Scot.; on N.E. cst. of Fife; seaside resort; univ.; famous golf course; p. (1961) *9,888*.

St. Anne, *t.*, Alderney, Channel Is.; church designed by Sir George Gilbert Scott.

St. Anthony, *waterfalls*, on R. Mississippi; U.S.A. predominant factor in site of Minneapolis (Minn.).

St. Asaph, *c.*, *rural dist.*, Flint, N. Wales; on R. Clwyd, 4 m. N. of Denbigh; cath.; optical glass mkg.; p. (rural dist. 1961) *9,478*.

St. Augustine, *t.*, Fla., U.S.A.; resort; p. (1960) *14,734*.

St. Austell, *mkt. t., urb. dist.*, Cornwall, Eng.; on S. flank of Hensbarrow, 14 m. N.E. of Truro; holiday resort; china clay, stone quarrying. engin., wood and cork; p. (estd. 1967) *23,990*.

St. Barthélemy, *French I.*, W. Indies; dependency of Guadeloupe; p. (1960) *2,079*.

St. Bees Head, *promontory*, 2½ m. N.W. of St. Bees, Cumberland, Eng.; freestone quarries, tin.

St. Benoît, *t.*, Ile de la Réunion, Indian Ocean; connected by rail with ch. port, Pointe-des-Galets.

St. Bernard Pass, Great, on Italian–Swiss bdy., W. Alps; carries main road from W. Switzerland to Plain of Lombardy; approached from N. by trib. of upper Rhône, from S. by Val d'Aosta; 8,120 ft. above sea level. The Great St. Bernard road tunnel (3½ m.) constr. 1958–62 links Cantine de Proz (Valais can., Switzerland) and St. Rhémy (Italy); under tunnel will run projected 260 m. pipeline from Genoa to Aigle.

St. Bernard Pass, Little, on French–Italian bdy., W. Alps.; links Isère valley with Val d'Aosta; alt. approx. 5,000 ft.

St. Boniface, *t.*, Manitoba, Canada; sub. of Winnipeg; p. (1961) *37,600*.

St. Bride's Bay, Pembroke, Wales.

St. Brieuc, *t.*, Côtes-du-Nord, France; college, cath.; ironwks., textiles, timber and cst. tr.; p. (1962) *47,307*.

St. Catharines, *c.*, Ont., Canada; on Welland Canal; mkt. for Niagara fruit-growing reg.; agr. implement wks., timber mills, flour mills, tanneries and varied inds.; (1961) *48,472*.

St. Chamond, *t.*, Loire, France; nr. St. Etienne; silk, ribbons, rayon; rly. wks.; coal-mining; p. (1962) *36,589*.

St. Charles, *c.*, Mo., U.S.A.; nr. St. Louis; tobacco and flour; p. (1960) *21,189*.

St. Clair, *L.*, Canada–U.S.A.; part of link between L. Huron and L. Erie.

St. Clair, *R.*, N. America; flows from L. Huron through L. of St. Clair into L. Erie; forms bdy. between Michigan (U.S.A.) and Ontario (Canada); impt. link in Gr. Lakes waterway; length 85 m., depth dredged to 20 ft.

St. Clair Shores, *t.*, Mich., U.S.A.; residtl. sub. of Detroit; p. (1960) *76,657*.

St. Claude, *t.*, Jura, France; at confluence of Rs. Tacon and Bienne; cath.; fancy shell, horn and ivory mnfs.; p. (1962) *12,649*.

St. Cloud, *t.*, Hauts-de-Seine, France; 6 m. from ctr. of Paris; fine park, château; residtl.; porcelain; p. (1962) *26,746*.

St. Cloud, *t.*, Minn., U.S.A.; on R. Mississippi; timber yds., dairying, farming; p. (1960) *33,815*.

St. Croix, *I.*, Virgin Is., gr., U.S.A.; ch. inds. sugar cultivation, stock raising, vegetable growing, rum mnf.; a. 82 sq. m.; p. (1950) *12,096*.

St. Croix, *R.*, Wis., U.S.A.; trib. of the Mississippi; length 200 m.

St. Davids, *c.*, Pembroke, Wales; 15 m. S.W. of Fishguard; cath., ruins of Bishop's Palace; p. *1,595*.

St. Davids Head, *prom.*, on cst. of Pembroke, Wales.

St. Denis, *t., N. sub.*, Paris, France; industl. and residtl.; abbey, burial pl. of Kings of France; chemicals, machin., spirits, soap; p. (1962) *95,072*.

St. Denis, *spt.*, *cap.*, Ile de la Réunion (French), Indian Ocean; p. (estd. 1965) *65,000*.

St. Dié, *t.*, Vosges, France; on R. Meurthe; cath.; iron, copper, machin., hosiery; p. (1962) *24,373*.

St. Dizier, *t.*, Haute-Marne, France; on R. Marne; iron, steel, copper, boats; p. (1962) *36,361*.

St. Elias, *mtn.*, Alaska, U.S.A.; alt. 18,024 ft.

St. Etienne, *t.*, *cap.*, Loire, France; nr. Lyons; ribbon-weaving, boot-lace, silk, velvet, engin., armaments, motor-cycles, cycles, chemicals, and iron mftg. ctr., in coal-field dist.; p. (1968) *213,468*.

St. Eustatius, one of the Neth. Antilles, W. Indies; a. 31 sq. m.; p. (1963) *1,103*.

St. Francis R., Quebec, Canada; hydro-elec. power.

St. Francis, *R.*, Mo., U.S.A.; trib. of R. Mississippi; forms bdy. of Ark.; length 450 m.

St. Gall (St. Gallen), *can.*, Switzerland; mountainous; forest; vineyards; cattle raising; cotton spinning, lace; cap. St. G.; a. 777 sq. m.; p. (1961) *339,489*.

St. Gall, *t.*, Switzerland; on R. Steinach; cath.; cottons and embroidery; p. (1961) *76,700*.

St. George, *bay*, W. cst. Newfoundland, Canada.

St. George, *I.*, Grenada Is., Brit. W. Indies; wireless sta.   [quarried; p. *1,169*.

St. George, *spt.*, N.B., Canada; various granites

St. George's Channel, Brit. Isles; part of Irish Sea separating Wales from Ireland.

St. George's I., Fla., U.S.A.

St. Germain-en-Laye, *t.*, Yvelines, France; on R.

Seine; former royal château; cottons, woollens; p. (1962) *37,391.*

St. Germans, *mkt. t., rural dist.,* Cornwall, Eng.; 4 m. W. of Saltash; p. (rural dist. 1961) *14,775.*

Saint Gotthard, *mtn. gr.,* Alps, S. central Switzerland, crossed by St. Gotthard Pass (6,935 ft.). St. Gotthard Rly. passes through St. Gotthard tunnel (9¼ m., max. alt. 3,786 ft.). Road tunnel (10 m.) under pass Göschenen to Airolo under constr.; motorways linking pass with Zurich, Basle and Lugano being built.

St. Gowan's Head, *promontory,* Pembroke, Wales.

St. Helena, *I., Brit. col.,* Atl. Oc.; 1,200 m. from W. cst. Africa; spt. and only t. Jamestown; Napoleon imprisoned 1815–21, and Boer captives 1900; famous for its wirebird, species of plover peculiar to I.; a. 47 sq. m.; p. (estd.) *5,000.*

St. Helens, *t., co. bor.,* Lancs, Eng.; 12 m. E. of Liverpool; connected by canal with R. Mersey; coal, iron, alkali; copper smelting, glass, fibreglass, plastics; p. (estd. 1967) *103,320.*

St. Helier, *spt.,* Jersey, Channel Is.; p. *26,484.*

St. Hyacinthe, *c., spt.,* Quebec, Canada; on Yamaska R.; cath.; farm machin., woollens, leather; p. (1961) *22,354.*

St. Ives, *t., mun. bor.,* Cornwall, Eng.; at entrance to St. Ives Bay; fishing, holiday resort; p. (estd. 1967) *8,780.*

St. Ives, *mkt. t.,* Huntingdon, Eng.; on R. Ouse, 4 m. E. of Huntingdon; timber, gravel, concrete prod., engin., canning, agr. machin.; p. (1961) *4,076.*

St. James, *t.,* Man., Canada; p. (1961) *33,977.*

St. Jean, *t.,* Quebec, Canada; rly. junction; porcelain, pottery, tiles; p. (1961) *26,988.*

St. Jérôme, *t.,* Quebec, Canada; pulp, paper, knitted goods, woollens, rubber goods, cement, bricks; p. (1961) *24,546.*

St. John, *c., spt.,* N.B., Canada; cottons, woollens, machin., paper, lumbering, sugar refinery; fisheries (corn tr.; p. (1961) *95,563.*

St. John, *I.,* U.S. Virgin Is. gr.; a. 19 sq. m.; ch. inds. charcoal, stock-raising, tourists; was noted for bay leaf oil, but ind. now dormant.

St. John, *L.,* Quebec, Canada; on Saguenay R.

St. John, *R.,* N.B., Canada; flows to Bay of Fundy; length 450 m. [*12,000.*

St. John, *t., cap.,* Antigua, W. Indies; p. (1957)

St. John's Point, *C.,* Down, Northern Ireland; forming N. side of Dundrum Bay.

St. Johns R., Fla., U.S.A.; flows to Atlantic; length 350 m.

St. John's, *spt., c., cap.,* Newfoundland, Canada; on E. cst.; first Eng. settlement in America; univ.; gr. tr. in fish, cod, oil, etc.; p. (1961) *90,838.*

St. John's Wood, *residtl. dist.,* N.W. London, Eng.; contains Lord's Cricket Ground.

St. Joseph, *t.,* Mich., U.S.A.; on L. Mich.; resort; industl.; p. (1960) *11,755.*

St. Joseph, *c.,* Mo., U.S.A., on M. R.; rly. ctr.; meat packing, clothing, farm implements; p. (1960) *79,673.* [paper; p. *6,449.*

St. Joseph d'Alma, *t.,* Quebec, Canada; pulp,

St. Joseph Lake, Ontario, Canada.

St. Junien, *t.,* Haute Vienne, France; on R. Vienne; fine churches, shrine; gloves, leather; porcelain wks.; p. (1962) *11,424.*

St. Just, *t., urb. dist.,* Cornwall, Eng.; nr. Lands End, 6 m. W. of Penzance; dairying; tin-mining; p. (1961) *3,636.*

St. Kilda, *rocky I.,* most W. of the Hebrides, Scot.; 3 m. long; bird sanctuary, famous for its wren, a sub-species.

St. Kilda, *wat. pl.,* Victoria, Australia; nr. Melbourne; p. *26,000.*

St. Kitts-Nevis-Anguilla, Leeward gr. of Is., W.I.; *aut. st.* in assocn. with Britain (Anguilla unilaterally seceded from union 1967); sugar, sea island cotton, molasses; a. 136 sq. m.; cap. Basse-Terre; p. (estd. 1967) *58,000.*

St. Laurent, *t.,* Quebec, Canada; p. (1961) *49,805.*

St. Laurent des Eaux, *t.,* Loir-et-Cher, France; 15 m. S.W. Orleans; nuclear power sta.; p. (1962) *992.*

St. Laurent du Maroni, *t.,* Fr. Guiana; penal admin. ctr.; p. *2,000.*

St. Lawrence, G. of, Canada; arm of Atlantic, partly enclosed by Newfoundland and Nova Scotia; impt. fisheries. [100 m. long.

St. Lawrence I., Alaska, U.S.A.; in Bering Sea;

St. Lawrence, *gr. R.,* of N. America; length from the source of its headstream, the St. Louis, 2,100 m.; forms the outlet of the great lakes (Superior, Michigan, Huron, Erie and Ontario and the bdy. between the st. of N.Y., U.S.A., and Ontario, Canada; ch. tribs.: Ottawa, Richelieu, St. Maurice, Saguenay.

St. Lawrence Seaway, N. America; joint Canada-U.S.A. project links head of the Gr. Lakes with Atl. Oc., providing channel 27 ft. min. depth enabling lge. ocean-going vessels to reach American continent; provides major source of hydroelectric power to industl. areas; opened 1959.

St. Lawrence Ship Canal, Canada. Channel deepened to provide safe navigation for ocean-going vessels from deep water to Montreal; depth 35 ft. at low water; links St. Lawrence Seaway at Montreal. [seaside resort.

St. Leonards, *t.,* Sussex, Eng.; W. of Hastings;

St. Lô, *t.,* Manche, France; on R. Vire; cath.; cloth mnfs.; p. (1962) *17,035.*

St. Louis, *t.,* Senegal, W. Africa; at mouth of R. Senegal; cath., pal.; rly. and road ctr.; airport; exp. oilseeds and skins; p. (1948) *51,000.*

St. Louis, *t.,* Ile de la Réunion, Indian Ocean; p. (1960) *25,220.*

St. Louis, *c.,* Mo., U.S.A.; on R. Mississippi 10 m. below confluence of Rs. Miss. and Mo.; two univs., impt. rly. and river junction; mkt. for furs, livestock, grain, farm prod.; banking and fin. ctr.; varied mnfs.; mach., cars, aircraft, leather goods, beer, chemicals; p. (1970) *607,718*; Greater St. L. *2,340,000*

St. Louis Park, *t.,* Minn., U.S.A.; tools, dental supplies; p. (1960) *43,310.*

St. Lucia Bay, *inlet* of the Indian Oc. at mouth of R. Umvolozi, S. of St. Lucia L., Natal, S. Africa.

St. Lucia I., *aut. st.* in association with Gt. Britain; Windward Is., W.I.; mtnous, forested, fertile valleys; exp. bananas and other tropical agr. prod.; a. 238 sq. m.; cap. Castries; p. (estd. 1968) *108,000.*

St. Malo, *spt.,* Ille-et-Vilaine, France; cas. and church (formerly a cath.); agr. prod., shipping, fishing, and tourist inds.; p. (1962) *17,800.*

St. Maria di Leuca, *C.,* S. Italy.

St. Marie, *C.,* S. point of Malagasy.

St. Martin, *French I.,* W. Indies; dependency of Guadeloupe; p. (1946) *6,786.*

St. Martin, *I.,* Neth. Antilles, W. Indies; a. 13 sq. m.; p. (1948) *1,697.*

St. Marylebone, *see* Westminster, City of.

St. Mary's I., Scilly Is., Brit. Isles.

St. Matthew I., Alaska; U.S.A.; in Bering Sea.

St. Maur-des-Fosses, *sub.,* Paris, Seine, France; garden city; p. (1962) *70,681.*

St. Maurice, *vil.,* Valais, Switzerland; nr. Martigny; 6th cent. abbey; once a leading Burgundian t.

St. Maurice, *R.,* Quebec, Canada; trib. of St. Lawrence R.; hydro-elec. power developed; length 400 m.

St. Mawes, *vil.,* Cornwall, Eng.; on E. cst. of estuary of R. Fal; holiday resort, fishing.

St. Michael's Mt., *castled rock,* Cornwall, Eng.; the ancient Ictis; alt. 230 ft.

St. Michel, *t.,* Que., Canada; p. (1956) *24,540.*

St. Mihiel, *t.,* Meuse, France; on R. Meuse, nr. Bar-le-Duc; industl.; Benedictine abbey; lace; p. (1962) *5,366.*

St. Monance, *burgh,* Fife, Scot.; p. (1961) *1,406.*

St. Moritz, *picturesque t., health resort,* Switzerland; in the Upper Engadine; winter sports; alt. 6,090 ft.; spa; p. *4,000.*

St. Nazaire, *t.,* Loire-Atlantique, France; at mouth of R. Loire, nr. Nantes; docks and shipping; steelwks., aircraft; exp. wine, sardines, silk, oil refining nearby; p. (1968) *63,289.*

St. Neots, *mkt. t., urb. dist.,* Hunts, Eng.; on R. Ouse, 10 m. N.E. of Bedford; shoes, brewing, milling, paper mkg., sports equipment, plastics; (1961) *5,570.*

St. Niklaas, *mftg. t.,* E. Flanders, Belgium; nr. Antwerp; cottons, woollens, lace, rayon, carpets; p. (1968) *48,873.* [p. *14,662.*

St. Ninians, *par.,* Stirling, Scot.; woollens, nails;

St. Omer, *t.,* Pas-de-Calais, France; cath., abbey ruins; brewing, distilleries, soap, linen; p. (1962) *20,911.*

St. Ouen, *t., sub.,* Paris, France; on R. Seine; light inds., copper, aluminium goods, furniture, gloves; power sta.; p. (1962) *52,103.*

St. Pancras, *see* Camden.

St. Paul, *c., cap.,* Minn., U.S.A.; faces Minneapolis across the R. Mississippi; cath.; univ.; meatpacking, foundries, cars, electronics, industl. abrasives; p. (1960) *313,411.*

St. Paul, *spt.*, Ile de la Réunion (French), Indian Ocean; p. (1960) *28,681.*

St. Paul, *R.*, Liberia; flows to the Atlantic nr. Monrovia; length 300 m.

St. Paul de Loanda, *t.*, Angola; exp. rubber, ivory, palm oil, coffee, coconuts, rum.

St. Peter, *L.*, Canada; expansion of St. Lawrence R. above Three Rivers; 20 m. by 9 m.

St. Peter Port, *seaport, cap.*, Guernsey, Channel Is.; wat. pl.; fruit, flowers, vegetables; p. *15,706.*

St. Petersburg, *c.*, Fla., U.S.A.; resort; p. (1960) *181,298.*

St. Pierre, *t.*, Martinique I., Fr. W. Indies; ch. t. in Fr. W. Indies; completely destroyed by eruption of Mt. Pelée, 1902.

St. Pierre and Miquelon, *French terr.*, consisting of 8 sm. Is. off S. cst. of Newfoundland : a. of St. Pierre gr., 10 sq. m.; a. of Miquelon gr., 93 sq. m.; ch. t. St. Pierre, fisheries; p. of St. P. and M. (1967) *5,000.*

St. Pierre-des-Corps, *t.*, Indre-et-Loire, France; p. (1954) *10,656.* [*27,573.*

St. Pierre, *t.*, Réunion, Indian Ocean; p. (1960)

St. Pölten, *t.*, Lower Austria; nr. Vienna; cotton spinning and hardware mftg.; p. (1961) *40,112.*

St. Quentin, *t.*, Aisne, France; on R. Somme; lace, tulle, woollens, chemicals, ironwks.; p. (1962) *62,579.* [antiquities.

St. Rémy, *t.*, Bouches-du-Rhône, France; Roman

St. Servan, *spt.*, Ille-et-Vilaine, France; opp. St. Malo; p. (1954) *13,763.*

St. Thomas, *see* São Tomé.

St. Thomas, *I.*, Virgin Is. gr., Atl. Oc.; belongs to U.S.A.; rum and bay rum, sugar, truck-farming, cattle, deep-sea fishing; bunkering of ships, handicrafts, tourism; a. 32 sq. m.; p. (1950) *14,559* (with St. John).

St. Thomas, *t.*, Ontario, Canada; rly. wkshps., flour, flax; p. (1961) *22,469.*

St. Trond, *t.*, Limbourg, Belgium; brewing, distilling; p. (1962) *20,976.*

St. Valéry-sur-Somme, *spt.*, Somme, France; resort of pilgrims; here William the Conqueror embarked for Eng. 1066; fishing; p. *3,071.*

St. Vincent, *C.*, S.W. Portugal; Spanish fleet defeated by British 1797.

St. Vincent, Gulf of, *lge. inlet*, S. Australia; penetrates 100 m. inland, max. width 35 m.; Pt. Adelaide located on E. side.

St. Vincent, *I.*, *aut. st.* in association with Gt. Britain; one of Windward gr.; W.I.; sugar, arrowroot, cotton, peanuts; cap. Kingstown; a. 150 sq. m.; p. (estd. 1967) *85,000.*

Sainte Agathe des Monts, *t.*, Quebec, Canada; tourist resort; p. (1961) *5,725*

Sainte Croix, Virgin Is., W. Indies; former possession of Denmark, now U.S.A.

Saintes, *t.*, Charente-Maritime, France; cath.; Roman antiquities; suffered in Huguenot wars; agr. implements; earthenware; p. (1954) *23,768.*

Saipan I., Marianas, Pac. Oc., U.S.A. trusteeship; sugar, coffee , fruit; a. 71 sq. m.; p. (1958) *7,250.*

Sakai, *spt.*, Japan; local import ctr.; iron machin., vinyl pipe plant; oil refining; p. (1964) *439,000.*

Sakania, *t.*, Congo; frontier sta. on rly. between Lubumbashi and Zambia.

Sakata, *t.*, Honshu, Japan; p. (1965) *95,982.*

Sakhalin, *I.*, off E. cst. Asia; S. half ceded by Japan to U.S.S.R., 1945; a. about 13,930 sq. m.; herring fisheries, coal, naphtha, alluvial gold, oil, timber, natural gas; oil pipeline connects to Komsomolsk and Khabarovsk refineries; p. (1959) *651,000* inc. Kurile Is.

Sakishima, *Is.*, E. of Formosa.

Sakmara, *R.*, R.S.F.S.R.; rises in Ural Mtns., trib. of R. Ural; length 350 m.

Sala, *t.*, Västmanland, Sweden; silver-mine worked for over 400 years, now to limited extent; lime, bricks; p. (1961) *11,015.*

Saladillo, *R.*, N. Argentina; upper course of R. Dulce.

Salado Rio, *R.*, Argentina; trib. of the R. Paraná; length 1,000 m. [Norte.

Salado, Rio, *R.*, Mexico; trib. of Rio Grande del Salamanca, *t.*, Guanajuato st., Mexico; oil refining; ammonia plant; natural gas pipeline to Guadalajara.

Salamanca, *prov.*, Leon, W. Spain; cap. Salamanca; a. 4,756 sq. m.; p. (1959) *422,114.*

Salamanca, *t.*, *cap.*, Salamanca prov., Spain; on R. Tormes; oldest Spanish univ., 2 caths., many convents; p. (1959) *88,316.* [Terr.; gold.

Salamaua, *t.*, *pt.*, New Guinea, Australian Trust.

Salamis, *I.*, Greece; opposite harbour of Athens; famous naval battle, 480 B.C.

Salamis, *spt.*, Greece; naval base; p. *17,312.*

Salar de Uyumi, windswept, dry, salt flat, S.W. Bolivia.

Salavat, *t.*, R.S.F.S.R.; in Bashkiria, 90 m. S. of Ufa; ctr. of oilfield; glass factory; became t. in 1954; p. (1959) *60,000.* [lgst., 180 sq. m.

Salayer Is., *gr.*, S. of Celebes, Indonesia; a. of

Sala-y-Gomez I., Pac. Oc.; Chilean; uninhabited.

Salazar, Mexico, nr. Mexico City; at alt. 9,500 ft.; nuclear reactor for radioisotopes for] medical, industl. and agr. purposes.

Salcombe, *t.*, *urb. dist.*, S. Devon, Eng.; 4 m. S. of Kingsbridge; resort; fishing; p. (1961) *2,558.*

Saldanha B., *inlet* on W. cst. C. of Good Hope, S. Africa; whaling, fishing; granite, quarrying; length 17 m.

Sale, *t.*, *mun. bor.*, Cheshire, Eng.; on R. Mersey, 2 m. S. of Stretford; p. (estd. 1967) *55,140.*

Sale, *t.*, Victoria, Australia; 128 m. from Melbourne; ctr. of lge. agr. and pastoral dist.; plastics, engin.; p. (1966) *8,648.*

Salé or Salch, *spt* , Fez, Morocco; formerly pirate headquarters; p. (1960) *75,799.*

Salekhard, *t.*, *R. pt.*, N.W. Siberia, R.S.F.S.R.; on R. Ob; fisheries, collecting ctr. for furs; exp. timber; p. (1956) *16,000.*

Salem, *t.*, Tamil Nadu, India; carpets, weaving, farming ctr.; p. (1961) *249,145.*

Salem, *c.*, Mass., U.S.A.; 15 m. from Boston; cottons, lumber products, leather goods, machin. wireless valves; p. (1960) *39,211.*

Salem, *t.*, N.J., U.S.A.; in fruit-growing dist.; p. (1960) *8,941.*

Salem, *c.*, Ohio, U.S.A.; steel; p. (1960) *13,854.*

Salem, *c.*, *cap.*, Ore., U.S.A.; on Williamette R.; univ.; fruit-packing, flour milling and canning; p. (1960) *49,142.* [p. *19,100.*

Salemi, *t.*, Sicily, Italy; the ancient Halicyæ:

Salerno, *spt.*, Campania, Italy; on G. of Salerno, 30 m. S.E. of Naples; cottons, silks, printing, leather; vine-growing dist.; p. (1961) *118,171.*

Salford, *c.*, *co. bor.*, Lancs. Eng.; on R. Irwell, adjoining Manchester; engin., clothing mftg.; p. (estd. 1967) *143,430.*

Salgótarján, *t.*, N. Hungary; coalmng., agr. machin., tools, glass; p (1962) *30,000.*

Salima, *t.*, Malawi, S. Africa; alt. 1,672 ft.; term. of rly. from Beira on L. Malawi; p. (1966) *2,301.*

Salina, *c.*, Kan., U.S.A.; on Smoky Hill R.; univ.; flour milling, cattle mkt., farm implements; p. (1960) *43,202.*

Salina, *I.*, Lipari Is., Italy; in the Mediterranean, 6 m. long; 2 volcanic cones.

Salina Cruz, *t.*, *spt.*, Oaxaca, Mexico; terminal pt. of Tehuantepec rly.; shallow harbour; dyewoods, coffee, hemp, hides and skins; p. *8,243.*

Salinas, *t.*, Ecuador; cable sta.; holiday resort; 118 m. from Guayaquil.

Salinas, *R.*, Cal., U.S.A.; rises in U.S. Coast Range, flows N.W. into Bay of Monterey, Pac. Oc.; fertile valley floor irrigated to produce hard and stone fruits, mkt.-garden produce (especially lettuce), alfalfa; length, 140 m.

Salinas-Grandes, *gr. marsh a.*, Argentina; N. of Córdoba.

Salisbury, *cath. c.*, *mun. bor.*, Wilts, Eng.; at S. foot of Salisbury Plain at confluence of Rs. Avon and Wily; cath.; pure Early English with tallest spire in Eng. (404 ft.); mkt. t.; eng. inds.; p. (estd. 1967) *35,990.*

Salisbury, *c.*, *cap.* Rhodesia; airways ctr.; univ.; ctr. gold mng. a.; inds. inc. fertilisers, tobacco, machin.; p. (1965) *327,000.*

Salisbury, *t.*, Md., U.S.A.; iron and steel goods, woodwork, canning; p. (1960) *16,302.*

Salisbury, *t.*, N.C., U.S.A.; cotton, grain, timber, textiles, refrigerators; p. (1960) *21,297.*

Salisbury Plain, Wilts Eng.; undulating upland N. of Salisbury; Stonehenge; army training-ground. [*14,541.*

Sallaumines, *t.*, Pas-de-Calais, France; p. (1954)

Salmon, *R.*, Idaho, U.S.A.; trib. of Snake R.; length 450 m.

Salon, *t.*, Bouches-du-Rhône, France; on Canal de Craponne; soap and oil wks.; p. (1962) *22,629.*

Salpau Selka, Finland; most southerly gravel ridge; forested; winter sports.

Salsette I., N. of Bombay, India; a. 241 sq. m.; connected by bridge and causeway with Bombay; cave antiquities and temples.

Salt, *R.,* Arizona, U.S.A.; rises in Colorado Plateau, flows W. into Gila R. 20 m. below Phoenix; length 240 m. *See also* Roosevelt Dam.

Salt Fork, *R.,* Okla., U.S.A.; trib. of Arkansas R.

Salt Lake City, *c., cap.,* Utah, U.S.A.; nr. Gr. Salt Lake, H.Q. of Mormonism; temple and univ.; mng.; agr.; steel, oil, textiles, meat pkg.; livestock; p. (1960) *189,454.*

Salta, *N. prov.,* Argentina; sugar, vines, oranges, oil; cap. Salta; a. 62,511 sq. m.; p. (1960) *413,000.*

Salta, *c.,* Argentina; on R. Salta; sugar, vines, oranges, tobacco, oil. minerals; cath., college; p. (1960) *120,000.*

Saltash, *mkt. t., mun. bor.,* Cornwall, Eng.; on W. side of Tamar estuary; lowest bridge (rly.) and road bridge to Devonport across Tamar; farming, fishing, malting; p. (estd. 1967) *8,410.*

Saltburn, *t., urb. dist.* (with Marske), N.R. Yorks, Eng.; on E. cst. 3 m. S.E. of Redcar; seaside resort; p. (1961) *12,482.*

Saltcoats, *sm. burgh,* Ayr, Scot.; on Firth of Clyde, 2 m. S. of Ardrossan; chemicals, shipyards and rly. sheds; p. (1961) *14,187.*

Saltillo, *cap.,* Coahuila st., Mexico; cottons, flour, woollens, cereals, gold, silver, lead, copper, iron, zinc, coal; p. (1960) *99,101.*

Saltney, *t.,* Flint, Wales; on R. Dee, 2 m. S.W. of Chester; oil and fat refining; p. (1951) *2,642.*   [p. (1953) *108,030.*

Salto, *dept.,* Uruguay; cap. Salto; a. 4,865 sq. m.;

Salto, *cap.,* S. dep., Uruguay; leather, salted meats, sugar cane and beet; p. (estd. 1956) *60,000.*

Salton Sea, *L.,* S. Cal., U.S.A.; 263 ft. below sea-level in depression which extends N.W. from head of G. of Cal.; ctr. of inland drainage; a. 270 sq. m. *See also* Imperial Valley.

Salton Sink, Cal., U.S.A.; inland depression 287 ft. below sea-level.

Saluggia, *t.,* Piedmont; N. Italy; nuclear reactor.

Saluzzo, *t.,* Italy; nr. Cunei; cath., cas.; leather, silks, hats; p. *17,000.*

Salvador, El, *rep.,* Central America; on Pacific cst.; very hot, abundant summer rain but dry winter; coffee, sugar, rubber, tobacco, gold, silver, iron, mercury, ginned cotton; h.e.p. sta. at Guayabo Rapids; smallest and most densely populated of Central American States; cap. San Salvador; a. 7,722 sq. m.; p. (estd. 1968) *3,266,000.*

Salvador, *spt.,* cap. Bahia, Brazil; coffee, cocoa, tobacco, hides, castor seed, sisal; oil field and refinery at Matanipe; p. (estd. 1968) *892,392.*

Salween, *R.,* Burma; rises in Tibet, flows S. to G. of Martaban; many rapids; length 1,800 m.

Salzach, *R.,* Austria; trib. of R. Inn; length 130 m.

Salzburg, *prov.,* Austria, adjoining Bavaria and the Tyrol; on N. slope of E. Alps; many L., thermal springs; much mineral wealth; cap. Salzburg; a. 2,762 sq. m.; p. (1961) *347,292.*

Salzburg, *c.,* Austria; on R. Salzach; cath., cas.; birthplace of Mozart; tourist resort; salt, dairying, musical instruments; annual musical festival; p. (1964) *115,000.*

Salzgitter, *t.,* Lower Saxony, Germany; S.W. of Brunswick; steel, engin., wagon bldg., fertilisers; p. (1968) *117,013.*   [mines.

Salzkammergut, *lake dist.,* Upper Austria; salt-

Salzwedel, *t.,* Magdeburg, E. Germany; on R. Jeetze; chemicals, sugar, metals; p. (1963) *20,567.*   [tion.

Samakh, *t.,* Israel; on Sea of Galilee; rly. junc-

Samar, *I.,* Philippines; S. of Luzon; 147 m. long, 50 m. wide; a. 5,050 sq. m.; copper; p. (1960) *735,700.*

Samara, *see* Kuibyshev.

Samaria, *ancient c.,* Jordan, now Sabastye.

Samarinda, *t.,* Borneo, Indonesia; on E. cst.; p. *11,046.*

Samarkand, *c.,* Uzbek S.S.R.; E. of Bukhara; mosques and ancient ruins; univ.; textiles, engin.; p. (1967) *240,000.*

Samarra, *t.,* Iraq; on R. Tigris; Moslem holy c.; p. *8,000.*

Samawa, *t.,* Iraq; on R. Euphrates; cereals, carpets; p. *10,000.*

Sambalpur, *t.,* Orissa, India; on R. Mahanadi; ruined fort, old temples; cottons, silks; p. (1961) *38,915.*

Sambar, *C.,* S.W. Kalimantan, Indonesia.

Sambhal, *t.,* Uttar Pradesh, India; p. (1961) *68,940.*

Sambhar, *t.,* Rajasthan, India; p. (1961) *14,139.*

Sambre, *R.,* Belgium and N.E. France; trib. R. Meuse at Namur; length 110 m.

Samburu, *t.,* Kenya; rly. sta.

Samnan, *t.,* Iran; iron, sulphur ores, petroleum.

Samoa, Western, *indep. sov. st.* (1962), member of Commonwealth (1970); former UN trusteeship terr. under N.Z.; gr. of 9 Pacific Is.; lgst. Savaii; Apia, on Opulu, cap. and ch. pt.; exp. copra, cacao beans, bananas; a. 1,097 sq. m.; p. (estd. 1969) *141,000.*

Samoa Is., Samoan gr. Pac. Oc.; E. of 171° long., W. of Greenwich; belong to U.S.A.; a. 76 sq. m.; lgst. I. Tutuila; ch. pt. Pago Pago; admin. ctr. Fagatogo; American naval sta.; p. (1960) *20,051.*

Samokov, *t.,* Bulgaria; S. of Sofia; industl.; p. (1956) *16,748.*

Samos, *I.,* Ægean Sea; Greek terr.; off W. cst. Anatolia; fine wine, silk, tobacco, cotton; cap. Vathéos; a. 180 sq. m.; p. (1961) *52,034.*

Samothrake, *rugged I.,* Ægean Sea; alt. 5,248 ft.; the "Thracian Samos"; sulphur springs, sponges; a. 71 sq. m.; p. mainly Greeks.

Samshui, *t., former treaty pt.,* Kwangtung, China; good tr. with Hong Kong; p. (1931) *9,160.*

Samsö, *I.,* Kattegat, Denmark; a. 42 sq. m.; p. (1960) *6,429.*

Samsun, *spt.,* Trabzon, Turkey; on Black Sea cst.; exp. tobacco, grain. timber. wax. wool, skins, copper goods, antimony; p. (1965) *106,921.*

San, *R.,* S.E. Poland; trib. of R. Vistula, bdy. between Poland and Ukraine.

San Ambrosia, *I.,* off cst. Chile.

San Angelo, *t.,* Texas, U.S.A.; on R. Concho; cattle, wool, mohair mkt.; dairy produce, petroleum, machine-shop prod.; p. (1960) *58,815.*

San Antonio, *sm. coastal t.,* Angola, Africa; at mouth of R. Congo; serves as occasional pt. of embarkation for travellers from lower regions of Congo (ex-Belgian).

San Antonio, *spt.,* Chile; nearest pt. for Santiago; holiday resort; exp. copper; p. (1961) *64,722.*

San Antonio, *c., winter resort,* Texas, U.S.A.; at mouth of San Pedro R.; cath., fort., arsenal, univ.; producing, refining and mnftg. oil prod. and equipment, textiles, machin; meat pkg., food processing; p. (1970) *650,188.*

San Antonio, *C.,* most westerly point of Cuba.

San Benito, *spt.,* G. of Tehuantepec, Mexico.

San Bernardino, *t.,* Paraguay; holiday resort.

San Bernardino, *c.,* Cal., U.S.A.; railroad ctr.; citrus-fruit packing and shipping ctr.; p. (1960) *91,922.*   [*154,000.*

San Carlos, *t.,* Luzon, Philippines; p. (estd.)

San Carlos de Bariloche, *t.,* Argentina; on S. shore of L. Nahuel Huapi; tourist ctr.; p. (1960) *18,000.*   [p. *14,325.*

San Casciano, *t.,* Italy; nr. Florence; industl.;

San Cataldo, *t.,* Sicily; Italy; good tr.; p. *22,700.*

San Cristóbal, (formerly Cuidal Real), *t.,* Chiapas, Mexico; cath.; textiles; p. (1940) *11,768.*

San Cristóbal, *c., cap.,* Táchira st., Venezuela; cath.; cement; wireless sta.; p. (1961) *96,102.*

San Diego, *t.,* Cal., U.S.A.; on Pacific cst., 10 m. N. of Mexican border; naval installation; fine harbour, winter health resort; fish-canning, aircraft, marble, onyx. missiles. electronics; p. (1970) *675,788;* Greater San D. *1,311,000.*

San Felipe, *cap.,* Yaracuy st., Venezuela; sugar, cacao, cotton, maize, fruits, rice, hides; p. (1961) *29,274.*

San Felipe de Aconcagua, *t.,* Chile; nr. Valparaiso; agr. ctr., copper and gold mng.; p. (1961) *27,149.*

San Fernando, *t.,* Chile; agr. ctr.; p. (1961) *37,834.*

San Fernando, *t.,* B. of Cadiz, S. Spain; pt. has naval arsenal; salt mftg.; much of surrounding marshland now reclaimed; p. (1957) *41,196.*

San Fernando, *t.,* Venezuela; at confluence of Apuré and Portuguesa Rs.; ctr. cattle ranching region of upper Llanos; oil concessions not yet developed; p. (1961) *21,544.*

San Fernando, *spt.,* Trinidad I., W.I.; on W. cst. of Trinidad, 25 m. S. of Port of Spain; exp. sugar, asphalt, petrol; p. (estd. 1957) *38,850.*

San Francisco, *t.,* Argentina; on rly. between Córdoba and Santa Fé.

San Francisco, *c.*, *spt.*, Cal., U.S.A.; on the San F. bay; entrance spanned by Golden Gate Bridge, second longest single-span bridge in the world; univ.; engin., canning, lumber mills, printing, publishing, chemicals, machin., petrol; p. (1970) *704,209*; Greater San F. *3,068,000*.

San Francisco Pass, Argentina–Chile; across Andes at alt. 15,505 ft.

San Francisco de Macoris, *t.*, Dominican rep., W. Indies; p. (1964) *128,657*.

San Geronimo, *t.*, Oaxacast., Mexico; rly. junction.

San Giovanni a Teduccio, *t.*, S. Italy; at foot of Vesuvius; iron mines, rly. wkshps.; p. *27,475*.

San Giovanni in Persiceto, *t.*, N. Italy; nr. Bologna; p. *20,450*.

San Isidro, *t.*, E. Argentina; N. sub. Buenos Aires; resort; p. (1960) *80,000*.

San José, *prov.*, Costa Rica, Central America; cap. San J.; bauxite mng. nr. San Isidro del General projected and road connecting S.I. del G. with Punta Uvita where sm. pt. will be built.

San José, *t.*, *cap.*, Costa Rica; cath., univ., observ.; coffee tr.; p. (1963) *267,454*.

San José, *c.*, Cal., U.S.A.; in Santa Clara valley; nr. is Lick Observatory; resort; fruit and vegetable canning; lumber prod., woollens, leather; p. (1960) *204,196*.

San José, *dep.*, Uruguay; a. 2,688 sq. m.; cap. San J.; p. (1953) *96,848*.

San José, *t.*, *cap.*, San José, Uruguay; grain, flour milling; p. (1963) *20,000*.

San Juan, *prov.*, Argentina; at foot of the Andes; a. 34,432 sq. m.; cap. San Juan; gold, copper; p. (1960) *352,000*.

San Juan, *t.*, cap. San Juan, Argentina; wine, fruit, cattle; p. *112,286*.

San Juan, *c.*, *cap.*, Puerto Rico, Central America; cath.; univ.; naval sta., airport; distilleries, sugar; p. (1960) *431,705*.

San Juan R., Central America; divides Nicaragua and Costa Rica; plans made for its canalisation, which would give both countries a clear waterway from Caribbean to Pacific; length 90 m.

San Juan, R., Mexico; trib. of Rio Grande; length 160 m.

San Juan del Norte (Greytown), *spt.*, S.E. pt. of Nicaragua on Caribbean Sea.

San Juan del Rio, *t.*, Durango, Mexico; p. *6,694*.

San Juan del Sur, *spt.*, Nicaragua, Central America; coffee, timber, sugar; p. (1960) *4,223*.

San Juaquin, *spt.*, Lower Cal., Mexico; on W. cst.

San Lorenzo, *min.*, S. Argentina; alt. 12,000 ft.

San Lorenzo, *t.*, Argentina, 14 m. N. Rosario; lge. chemical wks.

San Lucas, *C.*, point of Lower Cal., Mexico.

San Luis, *prov.*, Argentina; oranges, grapes; a. 29,700 sq. m.; cap. S.L.; p. (1960) *174,000*.

San Luis, *t.*, *cap.*, St. Luis, Argentina; cattle, grain, wines; onyx quarrying; p. (1960) *33,000*.

San Luis Obispo, *t.*, Cal., U.S.A.; p. (1960) *20,437*.

San Luis Potosí, *st.*, Mexico; agr. and mining; cap. San Luis Potosí; a. 24,415 sq. m.; p. (1960) *1,048,297*.

San Luis Potosí, *t.*, *cap.*, San Luis Potosí st., Mexico; arsenic plant, clothing, cottons, rly. wks., lead-, silver- and gold-refining; sulphur fields; wool hides, cattle; p. (1960) *159,980*.

San Marco in Lanis, *t.*, Foggia, Italy; p. *19,275*.

San Marino, *small republic*; on spurs of Apennines, Italy; ch. exp.: wine, woollen goods, hides, building stone; farming, cattle-raising; wine; a. 23·8 sq. m.; cap. San Marino; p. (estd. 1968) *18,470*.

San Marino, *t.*, *cap.*, San Marino; on hill-top, alt. over 1,200 ft., 12 m. S.W. of Rimini; tourists; wine, curios for sale to tourists; p. *2,200*.

San Martin, *dep.*, Peru; ch. t. Moyobamba; a. 17,448 sq. m.; p. (1961) *162,592*.

San Mateo, *t.*, Cal., U.S.A.; residtl. sub. San Francisco; p. (1960) *69,870*.

San Miguel, *c.*, El Salvador, Central America; on Rio Grande; nr. malarial swamps; cotton, sisal, coffee, cattle; p. (1960) *80,769*.

San Nicolas, *R. pt.*, Argentina; on Paraná R.; cattle, flour, agr. produce, distillery; steel plant; p. (1960) *55,000*.

San Pedro, *spt.*, Cal., U.S.A.; sub. Los Angeles; naval base; p. (1950) *36,527*.

San Pedro de Macoris, *t.*, Dominican Rep., W. Indies; p. (1948) *24,200*.

San Pedro Sula, *t.*, Honduras, Central America;

ctr. for banana and sugar inds.; rice mill; p. (1961) *58,931*.

San Quintin Bay, *spt.*, Lower Cal., Mexico.

San Rafael, *t.*, W. Argentina; agr., cattle, fruit.

San Remo, *sm. pt.*, Italy; famous winter seaside resort on Italian riviera; flower mkt., olive oil, lemons, wine; 12th cent. church; p. *31,625*.

San Roque, *C.*, E. Brazil.

San Roque, *t.*, Andalusia, Spain; nr. Gibraltar; p. (1957) *15,333*.

San Salvador or Watling's I., Bahama Is., W. Indies; discovered by Christopher Columbus, 1492; p. (1953) *694*.

San Salvador, *cap.*, El Salvador; univ., observatory; silks, cottons, cigars; p. (1965) *253,000*.

San Salvador de Jujuy, *t.*, Argentina; wheat, maize, sugar; minerals, timber; p. (1960) *52,000*.

San Sebastian, *c.*, *spt.*, *cap.*, Guipuzcoa, Spain; captured by Wellington 1813; gd. tr. and fisheries; sailcloth, cottons, paper, glass; p. (1959) *129,395*.

San Severo, *mkt. t.*, S. Italy; hill-top site, 15 m. N.W. of Foggia, Apulia; cath.; wine ctr., cream of tartar, bricks; p. (1961) *48,443*.

San'a, *cap.*, Yemen, Arabia; walled c. 7,270 ft. above sea-level; tr. in silk, cottons and china; jewellery, arms, fruit; p. (estd. 1965) *100,000*.

Sanandaj, *c.*, Iran; prov. cap. Kordestan; p. (1967) *204,676*.

Sanchez, *spt.*, Dominican Rep., W. Indies; situated on the Bahia de Sumana, at E. end of Cibao lowland dist.; linked to Santiago by rail; exp. cacao, tobacco.

Sancti Spiritus, *c.*, Santa Clara, Cuba; in grazing dist.; sugar, tobacco; p. (1953) *37,740*.

Sandakan, *impt. tr. c.*, Sabah, E. Indies; N.E. cst.; fine natural harbour; exp. timber, rubber, copra, hemp, salt fish; p. (1960) *28,806*.

Sandalwood (Sumba), *I.*, in Malay Archipelago, S. of Flores, Indonesia; very fertile; horse-breeding; rice, maize, tobacco, timber, cinnamon; cap. Waingapu; a. 4,305 sq m.; p. *251,126*.

Sanday, *I.*, Barra Is., Orkney, Scot.

Sandbach, *t.*, *urb. dist.*, Cheshire, Eng.; 5 m. S.E. of Middlewich; salt, chemicals, motor vehicles; p. (1961) *9,856*.

Sandoa, *t.*, Congo; on upper Lulua R.

Sandown-Shanklin, *t.*, *urb. dist.*, I. of Wight, Eng.; on Sandown Bay; resort; p. (1961) *14,257*.

Sandringham, *par.*, Norfolk, Eng.; Royal residence; farming. [p. *5,529*.

Sandur, *t.*, Mysore st., India; manganese, iron;

Sandusky, *c.*, Ohio, U.S.A.; on S. cst., L. Erie; tr. in coal, fruit, and foodstuffs; paper, farm implements, chemicals; p. (1960) *31,989*.

Sandwich, *t.*, *mun. bor.*, *Cinque pt.*, Kent, Eng.; at mouth of Stour R.; mkt., light inds., chemicals nearby; p. (estd. 1967) *4,590*.

Sandwich Is., *dependency* of Falkland Is., Brit. Crown Col. S. Atlantic.

Sandy, *t.*, *urb. dist.*, Beds, Eng.; 3 m. N.W. of Biggleswade; mkt. gardening; p. (1961) *3,892*.

Sandy Hook, *peninsula*, N.J., U.S.A.; projecting into lower bay of N.Y.; yachting ctr.

Sanford, *t.*, Fla., U.S.A.; p. (1960) *19,175*.

Sanga, R., trib. of Congo R., Equatorial Africa.

Sangir (Sangihe), *Is.*, Indonesia; between Philippines and Celebes; eruption of volcano on ch. I. killed 12,000 inhabitants, 1856.

Sankt Ingbert, *t.*, Saarland, N.E. of Saarbrücken; coal-mining, iron, glass, machin., textiles, leather; p. (1963) *28,700*.

Sankuru, R., trib. of Kasai R., Congo.

Sanlucar, *t.*, Cadiz, Spain; nr. mouth R. Guadalquivir; wines and agr. produce; ruined cas.; p. (1957) *35,363*.

Sanniya Hor, L., Iraq; linked to R. Tigris; shallow, acts as flood control reservoir.

Sannois, *t.*, Seine-et-Oise, France; p. (1954) *13,644*.

Sanok, *t.*, Poland; nr. Rzeszów; metallurgy; p. *11,176*.

Sansanding, *t.*, Mali, W. Africa; lge. barrage across R. Niger.

Santa Ana, *c.*, El Salvador, Central America; municipal palace, barracks; coffee, sugar; p. (1959) *130,976*.

Santa Ana, *t.*, Cal., U.S.A.; fruit farming, oilfields, mnfs. farm implements, preserved fruits; p. (1960) *100,350*.

Santa Bárbara, *dist.*, Honduras; Panama hats; p. (1962) *145,100*.

Santa Barbara, *t.*, *winter resort*, Cal., U.S.A.; at foot of Santa Inez mtns.; fruit, oil; p. (1960) *58,259*.

Santa Catarina, *st.*, Brazil; a. 37,000 sq. m.; coal; tobacco, manioc, fruit; pine reserves; p. (1968) *2,705,394*.

Santa Clara, *t.*, Cuba; at alt. over 1,200 ft.; sugar, tobacco, cattle; p. (1965) *127,000*.

Santa Clara Valley, Cal., U.S.A.; extends S. from San Francisco Bay; intensive fruit-growing under irrigation, prunes; ch. t. San José.

Santa Cruz, *spt.*, Patagonia, Argentina; sheep.

Santa Cruz, *prov.*, S. Argentina; sheep, horses; cap. Gallegos; a. 93,952 sq. m.; p. (1960) *53,000*.

Santa Cruz, *t.*, Bolivia; alt. 1,500 ft.; univ.; sugar, coffee, rice, cattle; oil refining; Japanese settlement nearby; p. (1962) *72,708*.

Santa Cruz, *dep.*, Bolivia; cap. S. C.; p. (1962) *326,900*.

Santa Cruz, *c.*, Cal., U.S.A.; on Monterey Bay; popular seaside resort, fruit, and vegetable canning; fishing; p. (1960) *25,596*.

Santa Cruz, *t.*, cap. Tenerife I., Canary Is.; p. (1962) *133,100*.

Santa Cruz Is., Pac. Oc.; Brit. Solomon Is.

Santa Cruz de la Sierra, *t.*, Bolivia; on R. Piray; sugar, flour; distilling; p. *33,000*.

Santa Cruz de Tenerife, *prov.* (Spanish), Canary Is., Atl. Oc.; inc. Is. of Tenerife, Palma, Gomera, Hierro; a. 1,329 sq. m.; p. (1962) *507,744*.

Santa Fé, *prov.*, Argentina; agr. and stock farming; cap. Santa Fé; a. 52,056 sq. m.; p. (1960) *1,866,000*.

Santa Fé, *t.*, Argentina; on I. in R. Salado; cath., univ.; dairy prod.; zinc and copper smelting; road tunnel to Panama under construction; p. (1960) *203,900*.

Santa Fé, *t.*, N.M., U.S.A.; at base of Sangre de Cristo range; oldest capital in U.S. founded by Spaniards 1610; p. (1960) *34,676*.

Santa Isabel, *cap.*, Equatorial Guinea, W. Africa; harbour; p. (estd. 1965) *37,000*.

Santa Maria, *t.*, Rio Grande do Sul, Brazil; p. (estd. 1968) *141,610*.

Santa Maria, *t.*, Campania, Italy; on site of ancient Capua; cath.; glass, leather; p. *36,637*.

Santa Maria de Gerona, Spain; nr. Burgos; nuclear power plant being built.

Santa Marta, *spt.*, *cap.*, Magdalena dep., Colombia, S. America; cath.; bananas; p. (1960) *64,400*.

Santa Maura, *see* Levkás.

Santa Monica, *c.*, Cal., U.S.A.; sub. Los Angeles; residtl.; p. (1960) *83,249*.

Santa Rosa, *t.*, *cap.*, La Pampa terr., Argentina; p. (1960) *17,000*.

Santa Rosa, *t.*, Cal., U.S.A.; fruit, grain, dairying; p. (1960) *31,027*.

Santa Rosalia, *t.*, peninsula of Lower Cal., Mexico; located E. cst. on G. of Cal.; impt. copper-mines.

Santander, *dep.*, Colombia, S. America; E. of the Magdalena R.; cap. Bucaramanga; a. 12,379 sq. m.; p. (estd. 1959) *838,430*.

Santander, *prov.*, Spain; agr., grape growing, fisheries; cap. Santander; a. 2,108 sq. m.; p. (1959) *427,235*.

Santander, *spt.*, *cap.*, Santander prov., Spain; former summer resort of the Court; cath.; exp. iron and zinc ore; p. (1959) *113,116*.

Santarém, *t.*, Pará, Brazil; rubber, cacao, Brazil nuts, sugar; p. (estd. 1968) *111,706*.

Santarém, *dist.*, *t.*, Portugal; in fertile valley of R. Tagus; cap. S.; p. (1960) of dist. *480,038*, of t. *16,449*.

Santiago, *prov.*, Chile; cap. Santiago; a. 5,557 sq. m.; p. (1961) *2,283,977*.

Santiago de Chile, *c.*, *cap.*, Chile; on R. Mapocho; most populous t. on Pacific side of S. America; cath., univ.; national library; leather, textiles, chemicals, cars; p. (1961) *2,114,000*.

Santiago de Compostella, *c.*, Corunna, Spain; on R. Sar; cath. (with tomb of St. James); univ.; beer, spirits, paper, linen; p. (1950) *55,553*.

Santiago de Cuba, *c.*, *spt.*, Cuba, W. Indies; on S. cst.; former cap. of I.; cath; univ.; expts. minerals, agr. prod., woods; Spanish fleet destroyed by U.S. warships 1898; p. (1965) *241,000*.

Santiago de los Caballeros, *t.*, Dominican Rep., W. Indies; p. (1967) *330,000*.

Santiago del Estero, *t.*, Argentina; on R. Dulce; p. (1960) *92,000*.

Santiago del Estero, *prov.*, Argentina; cap. S. del E.; a. 52,511 sq. m.; p. (1960) *477,000*.

Santiago-Zamora, *prov.*, Ecuador; p. (1950) *21,046*.

Säntis, *mtn.*, on bdr. Swiss cans. St. Gallen and Appenzell, alt. 8,216 ft., Europe's highest television transmitter on summit.

Santo Domingo, *spt.*, *cap.*, Dominican Rep.; cath. univ.; p. (1967) *577,000*.

Santoña, *spt.*, Spain; on No. cst., E. of Santander.

Santorene, *see* Thera.

Santos, *c.*, *spt.*, São Paulo, Brazil; world's ch. coffee pt.; also exp. oranges, bananas, cotton, and industl. prod.; tog. with São Vicente and nearby Guarujá resort ctr.; p. (estd. 1968) *313,771*.

Santo Tomé de la Guayana, *c.*, S.E. Venezuela; new industl. c. nr. confluence of Orinoco and Caroni Rs.; iron mines, steel, hydroelec. power and aluminium plants in a.; vast industl. complex projected.

São Carlos, *t.*, São Paulo st., Brazil; 120 m. N.W. of São Paulo; ctr. of coffee-growing a.; textiles, refrigerators, furniture; p. (estd. 1968) *73,256*.

São Francisco, *R.*, Brazil; flows from Minas Gerais prov., to Atlantic; navigable for 150 m. below cataract of Paulo Afonso; length 1,600 m.

São Goncalo, *t.*, Rio de Janeiro, Brazil; fast-growing c.; p. (estd. 1968) *329,764*.

São Jeronimo, *t.*, Rio Grande do Sul, Brazil, low-grade coal; p. (estd. 1968) *36,531*.

São João do Meriti, *t.*, Rio de Janeiro, Brazil; industl. and comm. ctr.; p. (estd. 1968) *255,201*.

São José dos Campos, *t.*, São Paulo, Brazil; industl. ctr.; cattle; p. (estd. 1968) *91,542*.

São Leopoldo, *t.*, Rio Grande do Sui st.. S. Brazil; 20 m. N. of Porto Alegre. mkt. t; (1960) *41,023*.

São Luis, *pt.*, cap. Maranhão st., Brazil; on São Luis I.; noted cultural ctr. in 19th cent.; p. (estd. 1968) *218,783*.

São Miguel, *I.*, Azores; ch. c. Ponta Delgada; pineapples, oranges, tea; tourism.

São Paulo, *st.*, Brazil, on Atlantic cst.; major industl. a. of S. America; coffee, cotton, sugar, rice, maize; vehicles, elec. gds., chemicals, textiles, telecomm. equipment, metal-wkg. plants; cap. São Paulo, Santos lgst pt. in Brazil; a. 95,454 sq. m.; p. (estd. 1968) *16,631,060*.

São Paulo, *c.*, *cap.* São Paulo st., Brazil; fast-growing c., comm. and industl. ctr. of Brazil and leading c. of S. America; vehicles, machin., elec. gds., textiles, pharmaceutics; aluminium refinery projected; nearby pt. Santos ships rich agr. prod. from hinterland; p. (estd. 1968 *5,684,706* (mun. a.); of Greater São Paulo (estd. 1968) *6,206,544* (inc. Santo André (p. *289,442*); São Bernardo do Campo (p. *97,301*); São Caetano do Sul (p. *135,095*).

São Roque, *c.*, Rio Grande do Norte st., N.E. Brazil; most N.E. point of S. America.

São Tomé with Principe Is. in the G. of Guinea; Portuguese; p. (1965) *64,000*.

Saône, *R.*, France; rises in Vosges, and flows to R. Rhône at Lyons; length 282 m.

Saône-et-Loire, *dep.*, France; mtnous; noted vineyards; cap. Mâcon; a. 3,331 sq. m. p. (1968) *550,362*.

Saône-Haute, *dep.*, France; mainly agr.; cap. Vesoul; a. 2,074 sq. m.; p. (1968) *214,716*.

Sapporo, *c.*, Hokkaido, Japan; industl., admin., educational ctr.; oil, iron, non-ferrous metals; p. (1970) *1,010,102*.

Saqqära, *t.*, U.A.R.; tombs and pyramids; nr. site of Memphis.

Saragossa. *see* Zaragoza.

Sarajevo, *t.*, *cap.*, Bosnia and Herzegovina, Jugoslavia; indust. and rly. ctr.; mnfs.; univ.; (estd. 1964) *213,000*.

Saransk, *t.*, R.S.F.S.R.; Mordov A.S.S.R. 145 m. S.E. of Gorkiy; univ.; elec. equipment; engin.; p. (1967) *146,000*.

Sarapul, *R. pt.*, R.S.F.S.R., on R. Kama; boots, shoes, gloves, engin.; p. (1959) *68,000*.

Saratoga Springs, N.Y., U.S.A.; summer resort at foot of Adirondack mtns., mineral springs; p. (1960) *16,630*.

Saratov, *t.*, *pt.*, R.S.F.S.R.; on R. Volga; univ engm., ball-bearings, textiles, oil-refining, saw-milling; p. (1967) *699,000*.

Sarawak, *st.* East Malaysia; exp. sago. rubber, oil, pepper; cap. Kuching; a. 47,071 sq. m.; p. (estd. 1966) *886,312*.

Sardinia, *I.*, *aut. region*, Italy; Mediterranean; mtnous.; sheep, cattle, fishing, wheat, barley, fruit, wine; oil refining at Sarroch on S. cst.; cap. Cagliari; part of former kingdom of Sardina belonging to house of Savoy; a. 9,302 sq. m.; p. (1961) *1,413,289*.

Sargasso Sea, *zone*, situated in S.W. of North Atlantic; relatively still sea within swirl of warm ocean currents. Noted for abundance of gulf-weed on its surface, rich in marine life. Named by Columbus.

Sari, *c.*, Iran, prov. cap. Mazandaran; p. (1967) *206,463*

Sark, *I.*, Channel Is.; 6 m. E. of Guernsey; picturesque scenery; farming; fishing; tourist ctr.; a. 1,274 acres; p. inc. Brechou *560*.

Sark, *R.*, forms extreme W. bdy. between Scot. and Eng.

Sarnia, *t.*, Ontario, Canada; on St. Clair R.; car parts, machin., oil refineries, petro-chemical inds.; p. (1961) *50,976*.

Sarpsborg, *t.*, Norway; on R. Glommen; mftg. inds.; lgst. pulp and paper concern in kingdom; p. (estd. 1960) *13,500*.

Sarreguemines, *t.*, Moselle, France; 7 m. S.E. of Saarbrücken; porcelain, plush leather, matches; p. (1962) *23,248*.

Sarria, *t.*, Lugo, Spain; p. (1957) *16,142*.

Sarthe, *dep.*, N.W. France; undulating surface; farming, apples, livestock; coal, linen, potteries; cap. Le Mans; a. 2,412 sq. m.; p. (1968) *461,839*.

Sarthe, *R.*, France; trib. of R. Loire; l. 165 m.

Sârzana, *t.*, Liguria, Italy; nr. Spezia; cath.; silks; p. *13,650*.

Sasebo, *spt.*, Kyushu, Japan; p. (1965) *247,069*.

Saseno I., Adriatic Sea; off cst. of Albania.

Saskatchewan, *prov.*, Canada; coniferous forests and plains; Rs. Saskatchewan and Churchill; many lge. Ls.; extreme climate; hydro-elec. power; gr. wheat prov.; livestock, dairying; oil, coal, copper, zinc, potash, uranium, helium plants, furs, fisheries; cap. Regina; a. 251,700 sq. m.; p. (estd. 1969) *961,000*.

Saskatchewan, *R.*, Canada; flows from Rocky mtns. through L. Winnipeg and thence by R. Nelson to Hudson Bay; length 1,450 m.

Saskatoon, *c.*, Saskatchewan, Canada; univ.; flour, cement, oil refining; p. (1966) *115,892*.

Sasolburg, *t.*, O.F.S., S. Africa; oil from coal production; gas pipeline to Germiston a. p. (1960) *12,557* (inc. *6,723* whites).

Sasovo, *t.*, R.S.F.S.R.; wood inds.; p. *10,000*.

Sassari, *t.*, Sardinia, Italy; nr. G. of Asinara; cath., univ., palaces; tobacco and macaroni wks.; oil, grain; p. (1961) *89,482*.

Satara, *t.*, Maharashtra, India; p. (1961) *48,709*.

Sattahip, *pt.*, Thailand; new pt. inaugurated 1967.

Satu-Mare, *t.*, N.W. Romania; pottery, textiles; p. (1963) *63,656*.

Saudi Arabia, *lgst. kingdom*, pen. of Arabia; cap. Riyadh; formerly kingdom of Hejaz (cap. Mecca) and Nejd (cap. Riyadh); mainly desert; nomadic pop; Moslem; dates, wheat, barley; impt. oil concessions; oil refining at Jeddah; a. 1,500,000 sq. m.; p. (estd) *7,100,000*.

Sauerland, *dist.*, *Land*, N. Rhine–Westphalia, W. Germany; plateau, alt. from 500 to 1,500 ft., E. of Rhine and between valleys of Sieg and Ruhr; agriculturally poor, largely forested; crossed by R. Wupper, with which are associated industl. ts. Wuppertal (textiles), Solingen and Remscheid (cutlery and special steel).

Sault Ste. Marie, *c.*, Mich., U.S.A.; on L. Superior at rapids; flour, woollens, locomotives; p. (1960) *18,722*.

Sault Ste. Marie, *c.*, Ontario, Canada; on L. Superior at rapids; pulp, paper, iron, steel; p. (1961) *43,088*.

Saulte Ste. Marie Canals ("Soo"), Canada and U.S.A.; twin canals on Canadian and American side of shallow channel linking L. Superior and L. Huron; traversed by all wheat and iron-ore traffic from L. Superior pts.; length (Canadian) 1 m.; depth 18 ft.

Saumur, *t.*, Maine-et-Loire, France; on R. Loire, 30 m. S.W. of Tours; wines, enamels, tinware; p. (1962) *22,876*.

Savage or Niue, Cook Is., Pac. Oc.; under N.Z.; ch. exp. native plaited ware, bananas, copra, and sweet potatoes; ch. pt. Alofi; a. 100 sq. m.

Savaii I., *lgst. of Samoan gr.*, Western Samoa, Pac. Oc.; a. 703 sq. m.

Savannah, *c.*, *spt.*, Ga., U.S.A.; Kraft paper, sugar refining, ship bldg. and repair, fertilisers, paint; p. (1960) *149,245*.

Savannah, *R.*, U.S.A.; flows between Ga. and S.C. to Atl. Oc.; length 450 m.

Save, *R.*, France; trib. of R. Garonne; 65 m. l.

Saverne, Col de, *low pass*, N.E. France; carries trunk rly. from Paris to Strasbourg and the Orient between Vosges and Hardt Mtns.; gradual approach from W., steep descent to E. into Rhine valley.

Savigliano, *t.*, Piedmont, Italy; silk; p. *18,725*.

Savoie or Savoy, *dep.*, S.E. France; on Italian border; mountainous; mineral springs, pastoral, dairying; cap. Chambéry; Vanoise Park (1st French nat. park); a. 2,389 sq. m.; p. (1968) *233,921*.

Savoie (Haute), *dep.*, France; mountainous; farming, wine, cheese; cap. Annecy; a. 1,774 sq. m.; p. (1968) *378,550*.

Savona, *spt.*, Genoa, Italy; cath.; iron, shipbldg., glass and tinplate wks.; exp. preserved fruits and tomatoes; p. (1961) *71,007*.

Sawbridgeworth, *t.*, *urb. dist.*, Herts, Eng.; on R. Stort, 4 m. S. of Bishops Stortford; malting, fruit preserving; p. (1961) *4,633*.

Saxmundham, *mkt. t.*, *urb. dist.*, Suffolk, Eng.; 18 m. N.E. of Ipswich; p. (1961) *1,538*.

Saxony, *former Land*, E. Germany; farming, printing, type-founding, toys, textiles, lace, spirits, beer, coal, iron, mineral springs; ch. ts. Dresden, Leipzig, Karl-Marx-Stadt.

Sayan Mtns., *range of mtns.*, between Rs. Yenisei and Angra, R.S.F.S.R.

Scafell Pike, *mtn.*, Cumberland, Eng.; in N. Pennines; highest in Eng.; alt. 3,210 ft.

Scalby, *t.*, *urb. dist.*, N.R. Yorks, Eng.; 3 m. N.W. of Scarborough; p. (1961) *7,251*.

Scalpay, *I.*, off E. cst. of Skye, Scot.

Scalpay, Harris, Outer Hebrides, Scot.

Scalloway, Shetlands, on W. cst. of Mainland; the anc. cap.; ruined castle.

Scapa Flow, *strait*, N. Scot.; between Pomona and Hoy, Orkney Is.; surrendered German fleet scuttled, 1919.

Scarba, *I.*, Argyll, Scot.; off N. end of Jura.

Scarborough, *t.*, *mun. bor.*, N.R. Yorks, Eng.; on E. cst. 18 m. N.W. of Flamborough Head; seaside resort; p. (estd. 1967) *42 200*.

Scarpanto, *I.*, Dodecanese, Greece; E. Mediterranean; between Rhodes and Crete,; p. *8,747*.

Schaan-Vaduz, *t.*, Liechtenstein; point where Arlberg Express (Paris–Vienna) passes through the principality.

Schaffhausen, *most N. can.*, Switzerland; on R. Rhine; pastoral and afforested; cap. Schaffhausen; p. (1961) *65,931*.

Schaffhausen, *t.*, cap. Schaffhausen can., Switzerland; on the Rhine; cath., cas.; famous falls, iron, steel, aluminium, cottons, brewing, distilling; p. (1957) *25,371*.

Schaumburg-Lippe, *former st.*, between provs. of Hanover and Westphalia, Germany, now part of Lower Saxony; farming; coal-mining.

Schefferville, *t.*, Canada; 360 m. N. of St. Lawrence estuary and connected to it (at Seven Islands) by rly.; ctr. of iron-ore mines of Quebec-Labrador trough; p. (estd.) *3,500*.

Schelde (Scheldt), *R.*, France, Neth. and Belgium; rises in Aisne, France, flows to N. Sea; 248 m.

Schenectady, *c.*, N.Y. U.S.A.; foundries, wireless-transmitting apparatus, locomotive; synthetic diamonds; p. (1960) *81,682*.

Scheveningen, *seaside resort*, Neth.; 2 m. N.W. of The Hague; fishing.

Schiedam, *t.*, Neth.; W. of Rotterdam; distilleries, gin; shipyds., mnfs., chemicals, machin.; p. (1967) *82,222*.

Schiehallion, *mtn.*, Perth, Scot.; alt. 3,547 ft.

Schiltigheim, *t.*, Bas-Rhin, France; machin., factory equipment; p. (1954) *22,798*.

Schlei, *narrow inlet* of Baltic, Schleswig-Holstein, Germany; 25 m. long.

Schleswig, *c.*, *pt.*, Schleswig-Holstein, Germany; cath., cas.; rope wks., tanning, freighting; p. (1963) *33,600*.

Schleswig-Holstein, *Land*, N. Germany; retroceded from Denmark 1920; cap. Kiel; moors and plain farming, livestock; textiles, tobacco, oil; a. 6,048 sq. m.; p (1968) *2,529,000*.

Schlettstadt, see Sélestat.

Schneidemühl, see Pila.

Schönebeck, *t.*, Magdeburg, E. Germany; on

R. Elbe; metals, chemicals, brewing; p. (1963) *45,035.*

Schoonebeek, *vil.*, Drente, Neth.; S. of Emmen; lge. oilfield; p. (1967) *7,473.*

Schouten I., West Irian, Indonesia; in Irian Bay; p. *26,487.*

Schouwen I., Zeeland, Neth.; in N. Sea.

Schuylkill R., Penns., U.S.A.; flows into Delaware R.; length 130 m.

Schwabach, *t.*, Bavaria, Germany; S. of Nürnberg; metal inds.; p. (1963) *23,900.*

Schwäbisch-Gmünd, *c.*, Baden-Württemberg, Germany; E. of Stuttgart; cath.; clocks, glass, optical, precious metal and jewellery inds.; p. (1963) *40,500.*

Schwarzwald (Black Forest), *forest belt*, Land Baden-Württemberg, W. Germany; a. 1,844 sq. m.; highest peak Feldberg, alt. 4,900 ft.

Schwechat, *t.*, Austria; nr. Vienna; oil refining; oil pipeline to Trieste; p. (1961) *13,403.*

Schwedt, *t.*, Frankfurt, E. Germany; on R. Oder; lge. oil refinery; oil pipeline from Mozyr; p. (1963) *14,775.*

Schweinfurt, *t.*, Bavaria, Germany; on R. Main, N.E. of Würzburg; metals, machin., ball bearings, dyes, brewing; p. (1963) *57,800.*

Schwelm, *t.*, N. Rhine–Westphalia, Germany; E. of Wuppertal; metals machin., textiles, paper; p. (1963) *34,200.*

Schwenningen, *t.*, Baden-Württemberg, Germany; clocks, metals, footwear; p. (1963) *32,600.*

Schwerin, *cap.*, Schwerin, E. Germany; indust. and educational; cath., palace; p. (1963) *94,786.*

Schwyz. *forest can.*, Switzerland; cap. Schwyz; a. 350 sq. m.; p. (1961) *78,048.* [(1957) *12,464.*

Schwyz, *t.*, Switzerland; nr. L. of Lucerne; p.

Sciacca, *spt.*, Sicily, Italy; nr. Agrigento; cath.; H.Q. of Mediterranean coral fishery; sardines, olives; mineral springs; p. approx. *25,000.*

Scilla, *promontory*, Strait of Messina, Calabria,Italy.

Scilly Is., *gr.*, 30 m. S.W. of Land's End, Cornwall, Eng.; total a. 10 sq. m.; lgst. I., St. Marys; cap. Hugh Town; flowers. vegetables; p. (1961) *2,273.* [mouth; length 250 m.

Scioto, *R.*, Ohio, U.S.A.; joins Ohio at Portsmouth.

Scone, *par.*, Perth, Scot.; place ot residence and coronation of early Scottish kings; from here Edward I. removed the Stone of Destiny to Westminster Abbey in 1297; tourist ctr.; civil aerodrome.

Scotland, Brit. Is.; N. part of Gr. Britain; contains 33 cos.; home affairs administered by Dep. of Secretary of State for Scot.; physically divided into Highlands (many islands on W.), Middle Lowlands and S. Uplands; highest peaks, Ben Nevis 4,406 ft. and Ben Macdhui 4,296 ft.; ch. Ls., L. Lomond, L. Ness; ch. Rs., Clyde, Tweed, Tay, Spey, Dee. Forth; climate, maritime; agr. in E., grazing in W.; oats, barley, wheat, potatoes, fruit; coal, iron, oil-shale, granite; fisheries; mnfs., textiles, shipbldg.; machin., distilling, sugar-refining, printing; hydroelectric development in Highlands; cap. Edinburgh; Glasgow, ch. comm. and industl. t.; a. 30,414 sq. m.; p. (1969) *5,195,000.*

Scranton, *c.*, Penns., U.S.A.; on R. Susquehanna; anthracite, iron foundries, steel wks., locomotives, and silk mnfs.; p. (1960) *111.443.*

Scunthorpe, *t.*, *mun. bor.*, Lindsey, Lincs, Eng., on Lincoln Edge, 6 m. S. of the Humber; iron-mng. and smelting, steel girders, engin., chemicals, tar distillation, hosiery, lt. inds.; p. (estd. 1967) *71,010.*

Scutari (Albania), *see* Shkodra.

Scutari (Turkey), *see* Usküdar.

Seaford, *t.*, *urb. dist.*, E. Sussex, Eng.; 3 m. E. of Newhaven; seaside resort; p. (1961) *10,994.*

Seaforth Loch, Lewis, Outer Hebrides, Scot.; 14 m. long.

Seaham, *spt.*, *urb. dist.*, Durham. Eng.; Seaham Harbour, on E. cst. 4 m. S. of Sunderland; modern colly. workings, extending under sea; p. (estd. 1967) *25,200.*

Seathwaite, *vil.*, Cumberland, Eng.; 7 m. from Keswick, close to Styhead (1,430 ft.); exceptionally heavy annual rainfall (above 150 in.).

Seaton, *t.*, *urb. dist.*, S. Devon, Eng.; on Lyme Bay at mouth of R. Axe; seaside resort; freestone quarries; p. (1961) *3,410.*

Seaton Carew, Durham, Eng.; within Hartlepool co. bor.; proposed site for nuclear power sta. nr. mouth of R. Tees.

Seaton Valley, *t.*, *urb. dist.*, Northumberland, Eng.; nr. Blythe; coal-mining; p. (estd. 1967) *28,410.*

Seattle, *spt.*, Wash., U.S.A.; univ.. cath.; shipbldg., aeroplanes, glass, fish-canning, fishing, packing, lumbering. chemicals, trucks, buses; p. (1970) *524,263;* Greater S. *1,404,000.*

Sebnitz, *t.*, Dresden, E. Germany; p. (1963) *14,520.*

Secunderabad, Andhra Pradesh, India; military sta.; p. (1961) *78,412.*

Sedalia, *c.*, Mo., U.S.A.; farming, meat-packing; machin., textiles, coal; rly. ctr. and wks.; p. (1960) *23,874.*

Sedan, *t.*, Ardennes, France; on R. Meuse; weaving; machin., metal ware, woollens, flour; battle 1870; p. (1962) *22,284.*

Sedgley, *t.*, Staffs, Eng.; partly absorbed in Wolverhampton (1966); metal wks., bricks, engin., fireclay goods; p. (1961) *21,927.*

Segezha, *t.*, R.S.F.S.R.; on L. Vyg; cellulose, paper, sawmilling.

Sego, *L.*, R.S.F.S.R.; 20 by 20 m.; N.W. of L. Onega; outlet into White Sea.

Ségou, *t.*, *R. pt.*, Mali, W. Africa; on R. Niger; ctr. of irrigation scheme; cotton, hides, cattle, wax, salt; p. (1957) *21,000.*

Ségou Canal, W. Africa; leaves R. Niger 4 m. below Bamako, extends 130 m. N.E. to Ségou; irrigates 3,000 sq. m. on right bank of Niger and assists navigation.

Segovia, *prov.*, Old Castile, Spain; agr.. stock-keeping, and mftg.; cap. Segovia; a. 2,682 sq. m.; p. (1959) *204,484.*

Segovia, *c.*, Spain; nr. R. Eresma; cath.; iron-ware, cloth, earthenware, paper, flour.

Segre, *R.*, Lérida, N.E. Spain; rises in E. Pyrenees, flows S.W. into R. Ebro; water irrigates the a. around Lérida, the lgst. block of irrigated land in Spain; length approx. 170 m.

Segura, *R.*, Spain, flows to Mediterranean at Guardamar; 180 m.

Seibersdorf, Austria; ENEA experimental food irradiation project.

Seikan Tunnel, links main Japanese I. of Honshu with northern I. of Hokkaido under Tsugaru Straits; length 23 m. (14 m. under seabed).

Seim, *R.*, Ukrainian S.S.R.; trib. of R. Desna; length 300 m.

Seine, *R.*, France; rising in Côte d'Or dep., and flowing past Paris and Rouen to English Channel at Havre; length 473 m.

Seine-et-Marne, *dep.*, N. France; agr.. stock-raising, dairying; " Brie " cheese; porcelain, gypsum, flagstone; cap. Melun; a. 2,275 sq. m.; p. (1968) *604,340.*

Seine-Maritime, *dep.*, N. France; undulating and fertile; grain, dairying, textiles, iron, shipbldg., flax, chemicals; fisheries; cap. Rouen; a. 2,448 sq. m.; p. (1968) *1,113,977.*

Seine-Saint-Denis, *dep.*, N.E. Paris, France; mkt. gardens; p. (1968) *1,251,792.*

Seistan and Baluchistan, *twin prov.*, Iran; co. ts. Zabol, Zahedan (rly. term. Pakistan rly. from Quetta through Mirjaveh, the customs post on Iranian frontier).

Sekondi, *spt.*, Ghana, W. Africa; connected with and largely superseded as a pt. by Takoradi harbour; p. (1965) *104,000* (inc. Takoradi).

Selangor, *st.*, W. Malaysia; central Malaya; cap. Kuala Lumpur (to relieve congestion, Kajang designated future cap.); chemicals; a. 3,150 sq. m.; p. (estd. 1966) *1,386,251.*

Selby, *mkt. and industl. t.*, *urb. dist.*, W.R. Yorks, Eng.; on R. Ouse, 13 m. S. of York; ancient abbey church; flour-milling, flax, oil-cake; p. (1961) *9,869.*

Sele, *R.*, S. Italy; rises in S. Apennines, flows W. into G. of Salerno; headwaters now carried E. through gr. Apennine tunnel (7 m.) to irrigate plateau of Apulia in S.E. Italy.

Selenga, *R.*, Mongolia and Siberia; flows into L. Baikal; length 750 m.

Selkirk, *co.*, Scot.; mountainous (Broad Law 2,723 ft.); sheep, oats, woollens; cap. Selkirk; a. 267 sq. m.; p. (1961) *21,055.*

Selkirk, *bor.*, *co. t.*, Selkirk, Scot.; on Ettrick Water; 4 m. S. of Galashiels; tartans, tweeds; p. (1961) *5,634.*

Selkirk Mtns., B.C., Canada; run N.W. to S.E. parallel with Rocky Mtns. and occupy inside of the great bend of R. Columbia; ancient rocks, highly mineralised; pierced by Connaught Tunnel on Canadian Pacific Rly. route through

Kicking Horse Pass to Vancouver; rise to over 9,000 ft.

Selma, *c.*, Ala., U.S.A.; on Alabama R.; in cotton-growing dist.; also dairying, lumbering, ironwks., fertilisers; p. (1960) *28,385.*

Selsey, *t.*, Sussex, Eng.; on Selsey Bill, 7 m. S. of Chichester; coastal resort; fishing.

Selsey Bill, *peninsula*, between Bognor Regis and Portsmouth, Sussex, Eng.

Selukwe, *t.*, Rhodesia; alt. 4,734 ft.; goldmng., chrome ore, molybdenum; ranching, agr.

Selwyn Range, *mtns.*, Queensland, Australia; extends 350 m. W. from Gr. Dividing Range; forms divide between Rs. flowing N. to G. of Carpentaria and Rs. flowing S. to Darling; gold, copper; alt. mainly below 1,500 ft.

Semarang, *spt.*, Java, Indonesia; exp. sugar, tobacco, tapioca, kapok; shipbldg., rly. repairs, cement, sawmills; p. (1961) *503,000.*

Seminole, *t.*, Okla., U.S.A.; p. (1960) *11,464.*

Semipalatinsk, *t.*, Kazakh. S.S.R.; on R. Irtysh; lge meat-packing plant; textiles, sawmilling, engin.; rich gold deposit found in a. 1965; p. (1967) *197,000.*

Semlin, see Zemun.

Semmering Pass, *low pass*, Austria; provides route across E. Alps for rly. from Vienna to Venice · alt. below 3,000 ft.

Semnan, *dist.*, N. Iran; much desert land; cap. Semnan; p. (1967) *59,152.*

Sena, *t.*, Mozambique; on R. Zambesi.

Sendai, *t.*, Honshu, Japan; salt, fish; p. (1964) *480,000.*

Senegal, *R.*, W. Africa; flowing from Kong mtns. W. and N.W. to Atlantic at St. Louis, above Cape Verde; length 1,000 m.

Senegal, *indep. sovereign st.*, within Fr. Community; N. of R. Gambia; groundnuts; chromium 375 m. E. of D.; cap. Dakar; a. 78,000 sq. m.; p. (estd. 1968) *3,685,000.*

Senekal, *t.*, O.F.S., S. Africa; tr. ctr.; wool, wheat; p. (1960) *7,409* (inc. *1,984* whites).

Senigallia, *t.*, Italy, N.W. of Ancona; p. *26,345.*

Sennar, *t.*, Sudan; on Blue Nile, on rly. route to Khartoum, Suakin, Pt. Sudan; dam for irrigation and control of Nile floods; hydro elec. power sta.; p. *1,000.*

Sennin, see Kamaishi.

Sens, *t.*, Yonne, France; on R. Yonne; cath., the ancient Agedincum; farm implements, boots, chemicals, cutlery; p. (1962) *21,742.*

Sensuntepeque, *t.*, E. Salvador, Central America; pottery, distilling; p. (1960) *27,070.*

Senta, *t.*, Jugoslavia; on R. Tisa; flour, leather, sugar, wine. agr., machin., chemicals, paper; p. (1959) *20,000.*

Seoul, *cap.*, S. Korea; brassware, pottery, silk; processing clinker into cement; p. (1963) *3,376,000.*

Septimer, *mtn. pass*, Swiss Alps, can. Grisons; alt. 7,611 ft.

Seraing, *t.*, Liége, Belgium; extensive ironwks.; engin.; p. (1968) *40,850.*

Serampore, *t.*, W. Bengal, India; former Danish settlement; cotton and silk weaving, pottery, jute- and paper-mills; p. (1961) *91,521.*

Serang, *I.*, Indonesia. See Ceram.

Serbia, *fed. unit*, Jugoslavia; former independent kingdom; a. 33,930 sq. m.; cap. Belgrade; p. (1960) *7,593,000.*

Seremban, *t.*, cap., Negri Sembilan, Malaya; p. *25,000.*

Seres, see Sérrai.   [290 m.

Sereth, *R.*, Romania; trib. of R. Danube; length

Sergipe, *cst. st.*, Brazil; forested; tobacco, maize, sugar, cotton; oil deposits; cap. Aracaju; a. 8,129 sq. m.; p. (estd. 1968) *850,603.*

Sergo, see Kadiyevka.

Seria, *t.*, Brunei; oil ctr.; linked by pipe-line with Lutong.   [Ægean Sea.

Sériphos, *I.*, Cyclades gr., Grecian Archipelago,

Serov, *t.*, R.S.F.S.R., in Urals; iron and steel; natural gas pipeline from Ingrim; p. (1967) *105,000.*

Serowe, *c.*, Botswana, S.W. Africa; p. (1964) *34,000.*

Serpukhov, *t.*, R. pt., R.S.F.S.R.; on R. Oka, S. of Moscow; engin., textiles; p. (1967) *120,000.*

Serra da Mantiqueira, *mtn. range*, highest in Brazil;

Serra do Espinhaço, *mtns.*, Brazil; highest peak, Itambe, 6,705 ft.; iron-ore deposits.

Serra do Mar, *mtns.*, Brazil; form steep E. edge of Brazilian Plateau S. from Rio de Janeiro.

Sérrai (Seres), *prefecture* Macedonia, Greece; cap. Sérrai; p. (1961) *248,045.*

Sérrai (Seres), *t.*, Macedonia, Greece; on Struma R.; woollens, cottons, carpets; p. (1961) *40,063.*

Sesto San Giovanni, *sub.*, Milan, Italy; machin., glass, chemicals, plastics; p. (1961) *71,384.*

Sète (formerly Cette), *spt.*, Hérault, France; on Mediterranean cst.; chemicals, fisheries; exp. oysters, brandy, wine; oil pipeline under the sea to Frontignan; p. (1962) *36,816.*

Setif, *mkt. t.*, E. Algeria; alt. 3,596 ft.; cereals, horses; p. (1948) *51,674.*

Setouchi, *coastal region*, S.W. Honshu, N. Shikoku, Japan; flanks shores of Inland Sea; sm. plains backed by terraced hillsides; intensive agr., rice, mulberry, tea, citrus fruits; many sm. ts. engaged in fishing, local tr. and varied inds. inc. textiles, salt-extraction from brine.

Setté Cama, *spt.*, Gaboon, Equat. Africa; open roadstead, landing difficult owing to swell; exp. timber; oil nearby.

Settle, *mkt. t.*, *rural dist.*, W.R. Yorks, Eng.; on R. Ribble in heart of Craven dist.; caves with remains of extinct fauna; thread, cotton; p. (rural dist 1961) *13,782.*

Settsu Plain, S. Honshu, Japan; located at head of Osaka Bay at E. end of Inland Sea; intensively cultivated alluvial lowlands, ch. crops, rice, vegetables, oranges; gr. industl. belt extends along cst. through Kobe, Osaka, Kishiwada; engin., chemicals, textiles; a. 500 sq. m.

Setubal, *c.*, *spt.*, Lisbon, Portugal; on R. Sado; boatbldg., fishing, sardine-curing, lace, salt, fertilizers etc.; p. (1960) *44,435.*

Seul Lac, *L.*, S. of St. Joseph L., Ont., Canada.

Sevan (Gokcha), *lge. L.*, Armenian S.S.R.; alt. 6,340 ft.; never freezes; surrounded by high, barren mtns.

Sevan, *t.*, Armenian S.S.R.; underground hydro-elec. power sta.

Sevastopol, *spt.*, Ukrainian S.S.R.; built on ruins left after famous siege 1855; Black Sea resort; naval arsenals; leather, tiles, machin.; exp. grain; p. (1967) *200,000.*

Seven Islands, *pt.*, on St. Lawrence, Quebec, Canada; iron brought by rail from Schefferville; airline service but no highway.

Sevenoaks, *mkt. t.*, *rural dist.*, Kent, Eng.; in Vale of Holmesdale, 5 m. N.W. of Tonbridge; residtl; agr., light inds.; Knole Park; p. (1961) *17,604.*

Severn, *R.*, W. of Eng. and N. Wales; rises in Montgomery and flows to Bristol Channel; length 215 m.; suspension bridge at estuary opened 1966.

Severn, *R.*, Ontario, Canada; flows to Hudson Bay; length 350 m.

Severn Tunnel, Eng.; under estuary of R. Severn between Pilning (Glos.) and Severn Tunnel Junction (Mon.); carries main rly. from London to S. Wales; longest main-line rly tunnel in Brit. Is.; length nearly 4½ m.

Severodvinsk, *t.*, R.S.F.S.R.; on Dvina Bay, White Sea; metals, bldg. materials; p. (1959) *79,000.*

Seville, *prov.*, Spain; agr., mining; cap. Seville; a. 5,430 sq. m.; p. (1959) *1,226,730.*

Seville, *pt.*, *cap.*, Seville, Spain; on R. Guadalquivir; Gothic cath.; palace, univ.; ironware, machin., cigars, silks, porcelain, brewery, cotton and wool mills, aircraft; exp. lead, iron, mercury, cork, oranges. lemons, wine; birthplace of Velasquez and Murillo; p. (1965) *549,000.*

Sèvres, *t.*, Hauts-de-Seine, France; on R. Seine; celebrated porcelain mnfs.; p. (1962) *20,290.*

Sèvres (Deux), *dep.*, N. France; p. (1968) *326,462.*

Seychelles Is., *Brit. col.*, Indian Ocean; consisting of 92 Is., lgst I. Mahé; cap. Victoria; exports prods. of coconut palm, phosphate, essential oils and spices; famous for species of nut; total a. 156 sq. m.; p. (estd.) *49,981.*

Seyne or La Seyne-sur-Mer, *t.*, Var, France; nr. Toulon; shipbldg.; p. (1962) *34,270.*

Sfax, *spt.*, Tunisia; admin. ctr.; exp. phosphate, olive oil, salt, esparto grass, cereals, dates, hides; imports food, coal, textiles. soap; sponges; fishing; natural gas found in a. p. (1966) *250,000.*

Sgurr Mor, *mtn.*, Ross and Cromarty, Scot.; alt. 3,483 ft.

Shabani, *t.*, Rhodesia; asbestos; p. (1958) *7,930* (incl. *1,700* Europeans).

Shadrinsk, *t.*, R.S.F.S.R.; W. Siberia, 160 m. S.E. of Sverdlovsk; car parts, printing presses; p. (1959) *52,000.*

Shaftesbury, *mkt. t., mun. bor.*, Dorset, Eng.; 10 m. N. of Blandford; p. (estd. 1967) *3,434.*

Shahjahanpur, *c.*, Uttar Pradesh, India; on Deoha R.; sugar; p. (1961) *117,702.*

Shahpur, *t.*, W. Punjab, Pakistan; cotton; p. *8,545.*

Shaker Heights, *t.*, Ohio, U.S.A.; p. (1960) *36,460.*

Shakhty (Alexandrovsk Grushevski), *t.*, R.S.F.S.R.; coal, engin., elec. power; p. (1967) *208,000.*

Shamaldy-Say, *t.*, Kirghiz S.S.R.; new town on site of Uch-Kurgan hydroelec. sta.

Shamokin, *bor.*, Penns., U.S.A.; iron mftg., anthracite; p. (1960) *13,674.*

Shan State, *div.*, Burma; a. 57,500 sq. m.; p. *2,500,000*; elevated plateau through which flows R. Salween; iron, lead, silver, zinc; former Federated Shan States and Wa States, E. Burma.

Shandakan Tunnel, N.Y. st., U.S.A.; carries water under Catskill Mtns. to augment water supply of c. of N.Y.; length 18 m.

Shanghai, *c., pt.*, Kiangsu, China; on Whangpoo trib. of Yangtze-Kiang; most impt. of the former Chinese treaty pts., considerable exp. silk and tea; mnfs. paper, cigarettes, cotton; shipbldg., engin., machin., chemicals, plastics, nylon, synthetic fibres; p. (estd. 1957) *7,100,000.*

Shangkiu (Shangqiu), *c.*, Honan prov., China; agr. ctr.; silk weaving; p. (1953) *134,000.*

Shanklin, *see* Sandown-Shanklin.

Shannon Airport, Clare, Ireland; N.W. of Limerick; on main transatlantic air route; ctr. of industl. estate.

Shannon, *R.*, Ireland; separating Connaught from provs. of Leinster and Munster, and flowing to Atlantic at Loop Head; length 224 m.

Shansi (Shanxi), *inland and hilly prov.*, N. China, bounded W. and S. by the Hwang-Ho; coal, iron ore, petroleum, salt; cap. Taiyuan; a. 60,394 sq. m.; p. (1953) *14,314,485.*

Shantung (Shandong), *maritime prov.*, China, on the G. of Chihli and the Yellow Sea; fertile plain; grain, silk, fruit; coal, iron, lead, copper; cap. Tsinan; a. 56,447 sq. m.; p. (1953) *48,876,548.*

Shaohing (Shaoxing), *c.*, Chekiang prov., China; rice, wheat, cotton; p. (1953) *131,000*

Shaoyang, *c.*, Hunan prov., China; coal and iron mng.; timber; p. (1953) *127,000.*

Shap, *par.*, Westmorland, Eng.; near by is Shap Summit 914 ft., an impt. pass traversed by rly. and by a main road; granite.

Shapinsay, Orkney Is., Scot.

Shari, *R.*, Mali, W. Africa; flows from the S. to L. Chad; navigable for greater part ot course; length 70 m.

Sharjah, *emirate*, one of seven Trucial sts., Persian G.; p. (estd. 1968) *40,000.*

Sharkord, *c.*, prov. cap. Chahar Mahal Bakhtiyari, Iran; p. (1967) *178,607.*

Sharon, *plain*, Israel; citrus fruits, vines, poultry.

Sharon, *c.*, Penns., U.S.A.; ironwks., bricks, elec. goods; p. (1960) *25,267.*　　　[estuary.

Sharpness, *vil.*, Glos., Eng.; on S. shore, Severn

Shasta, *mtn.*, Cal., U.S.A.; 14,380 ft.

Shatt-al-Arab, *R.*, Iraq; formed by union of Tigris and Euphrates, flows thence to head of Persian G.; length 120 m.

Shatura, *t.*, R.S.F.S.R.; E. of Moscow; elec. power-plant; p. (1954) *50,000.*

Shawinigan Falls, *c.*, Quebec, Canada; pulp and paper; p. (1961) *32,169.*

Shawnee, *c.*, Okla., U.S.A.; cottons, meat-preserving; p. (1960) *24,326.*

Sheaf, *R.*, W.R., Yorks, Eng.; rises in S.E. Pennines, flows N.E. to join R. Don at Sheffield; for last 2 m. narrow valley crowded with smaller factories of Sheffield; valley provides main route to S. (Chesterfield) and S.W. (Manchester via Totley); length 11 m.

Shebelinka, natural gas fields nr. Kharkov, Ukraine; pipelines to Kharkov-Bryansk and Dnepropetrovsk–Odessa.

Sheboygan, *c.*, Wis., U.S.A.; on L. Michigan; furniture mftg., pianos, gloves, enamelled ware; p. (1960) *45,747.*

Shechem, *see* Nablus.

Sheerness, *spt., urb. dist.*, Kent, Eng.; on I. of Sheppey at entrance to estuary of R. Medway; former royal dockyard and garrison; deepwater comm. pt.; electronics, furniture, coach bldg.; p. (1961) *14,123.*

Sheffield, *c., co. bor.*, W.R. Yorks, Eng.; on cramped site at confluence of Rs. Sheaf and Don; univ.; heavy engin. ctr., famous for high quality steels, cutlery, tools; p. (estd. 1969) *528,860.*

Shelbyville, *t.*, Ind., U.S.A.; on Big. Blue R.; mftg. ctr. in colly. and agr. region; p. (1960) *14 317.*

Shellhaven, *oil refineries*, Essex, Eng.; on N. side of Thames estuary, nr. Stanford-le-Hope.

Shelton, *t.*, Conn., U.S.A.; old vil. of Huntingdon, has 18th-century houses; p. (1960) *18,190.*

Shenandoah, *t.*, Penns., U.S.A.; anthracite; p. (1960) *11,075.*

Shenandoah, *R.*, Va., U.S.A.; trib. of Potomac R.

Shenao, Taiwan; E. of Keelung; oil refinery being built.

Shendi, *t.*, Sudan; on R. Nile; p. *14,300.*

Shensi (Shenxi), *prov.*, China; W. of Hwang-Ho; wheat, cotton; coal, petroleum; cap. Sian; a. 72,919 sq. m.; p. (1953) *15,881,281.*

Shenyang, *see* Mukden.

Shepparton, *t.*, Victoria, Australia; ctr. of veg. and orchard a.; fruit canning, metal, brick wks.; p. (1966) *17,523.*

Sheppey, I. of, Kent, Eng.; in Thames estuary E. of mouth of R. Medway; 9 m. long, 5 m. wide; cereals, sheep-raising.

Shepshed, *t., urb. dist.*, Leicester, Eng.; 3 m. W. of Loughborough; gloves, boots, shoes, needles; p. (1961) *7,179.*

Shepton Mallet, *mkt. t., urb. dist.*, Somerset, Eng.; at foot of Mendip Hills, 5 m. S.E. of Wells; shoes cider; p. (1961) *5,518.*

Sherborne, *mkt. t., urb. dist.*, Dorset, Eng.; 4 m. E. of Yeovil; famous abbey and school; p. (1961) *6,062.*

Sherbrooke, *c.*, Quebec, Canada; at confluence of Rs. St. Francis and Magog; woollens, cottons, carpets, machin., sawmills; p. (1961) *66,554.*

Shercheil, *sm. spt.*, Algeria; mkt.; p. *12,650.*

Sheridan, *t.*, Wyo., U.S.A.; p. (1960) *11,551.*

Sheringham, *t., urb. dist.*, Norfolk, Eng.; on E. cst. 4 m. W. of Cromer; seaside resort; fishing; p. (1961) *4,836.*

Sherman, *t.*, Texas, U.S.A.; tr. in cotton and corn; p. (1960) *24,988.*

Sherwood Forest, *ancient royal woodland*, Notts., Eng.

Shetland Is., Scot.; in Zetland co., 50 m. N.E. of the Orkneys; about 100 in gr.. ch. I., Mainland; textile, fishing; cattle, sheep, ponies; potatoes; ch. t. Lerwick; a. 551 sq. m.; p. (1961) *17,809.*

Sheyenne, *R.*, Dakota, U.S.A.; trib. of Red R.; length 325 m.

Shifnal, *mkt. t., rural dist.*, Shropshire, Eng.; 5 m. S.E. of Wellington; malting, coal, iron; p. (rural dist., 1961) *14,234.*

Shigatze, *t.*, Tibet; on R. Tsangpo; tr. ctr. on main caravan routes; p. *9,000.*

Shihkiachwang (Shijiazhuang), *c.*, Hopeh prov., China; cotton milling, glass mftg.; p. (1953) *373,000.*

Shikarpur, *t.*, N. Sind, Pakistan; tr. ctr., gems and silk; p. over *62,000.*

Shikoku, *one of the lge. Is.* Japan; S. of Honshu; rice, salt, paper, fish, lumber; a. 7,248 sq. m.

Shildon, *t., urb. dist.*, Durham, Eng.; 3 m. S of Bishop Auckland; rly. wks.; p. (1961) *14,372.*

Shilka, *R.*, E. Siberia; R.S.F.S.R.; trib. of R. Amur; length 760 m.

Shillong, *cap.*, Assam, India; at alt. 4,500 ft. in Khasi Hills; ctr. of impt. tea-growing dist.; p. (1961) *102,398.*

Shimabara, *t.*, Japan; holiday resort; p. (1966) *44,175.*

Shimizu, *spt.*, Japan; tea ctr.; oranges, paper, tinned fruit and fish; p. (1965) *219,000.*

Shimoda, *spt.*, Honshu, Japan; between Nagoya and Yokohama; p. (1965) *63,493.*

Shimonoseki, *spt.*, Honshu I., Japan; at extreme S.W. of I.; tunnel links island of Kyushu; impt. rail and steamer ctr.; p. (1965) *254,376.*

Shin, *Loch*, Sutherland, Scot.; 16½ m. long; drained by R. Shin to the R. Oykell.

Shipka Pass, Bulgaria; over the Balkan Mtns., 47 m. N.E. of Plovdiv.

Shipley, *t., urb. dist.*, W.R. Yorks, Eng.; on R. Aire, 8 m. N.W. of Leeds; worsted mnfs.; p. (estd. 1967) *29,480.*

Shiraz, *c., cap.*, Fars, Iran; beautifully sited in vine-growing dist.; textiles, rugs, metalwk., light elec. ind.; tourist ctr.; tombs of Saadi and Hafez (brothers of Imam Riza); known as "city of roses and nightingales"; pleasant winter climate; airpt.; p. (1963) *230,000*.

Shiré, *R.*, flows out of L. Malawi south through Malawi and Mozambique to Zambesi R.; length *c.* 370 m.

Shirwa or Chilwah, *shallow L.*, nr. Malawi, Africa; 40 m. long, 14 m. wide; has 4 Is.

Shizuoka, *spt.*, Honshu, Japan; tea refining, blending, packing; oranges, fruit tinning; woodwork; textiles; p. (1965) *367,705*.

Shkodra (Scutari), *L.*, 29 m. long; on borders of Montenegro and Albania; outlet via R. Bojana into Adriatic.

Shkodra (Scutari), *t.*, Albania; stands at foot of S. L. (ancient cap. Illyria); cas. cath.; tobacco ind., cement; p. (1960) *41,000*.

Shoa, *st.*, Ethiopia; SE. Amhara.

Shoalhaven, *t.* and *R.*, N.S.W., Australia; tourism.

Shoeburyness, *t.*, Essex, Eng.; on N. side of Thames estuary, 3 m. E. of Southend; barracks, gunnery school, bricks; p. (1961) *10,855*.

Sholapur, *c.*, Maharashtra, India; between Hyderabad and Poona; lge. bazaar, temples, etc., silk, cotton cloth; p. (1961) *337,583*.

Shoreditch, *see* Hackney.

Shoreham-by-Sea, *t.*, *urb. dist.*, W. Sussex, Eng.; at mouth of R. Adur, 4 m. E. of Worthing; old spt. and mkt. t.; oil jetty; boat bldg., chemicals, soap, preserves; p. (1961) *17,391*.

Shoshone Falls, on Snake R., Idaho, U.S.A.; height 200 ft.

Shott esh Shergui, lgst. saline L., Algeria.

Shotts, *plateau*, N. Africa; upland region with salt Ls., within Atlas mtns.

Shreveport, *c.*, La.. U.S.A.; industl. ctr. in cotton-growing dist.; petroleum; p. (1960) *164,372*.

Shrewsbury, *co. t.*, *mun. bor.*, Salop, Eng.; on R. Severn 12 m. above Ironbridge gorge between The Wrekin and Wenlock Edge; agr. and dairy equipment, machin., elec. goods; impt. cattle and sheep mkt.; famous public school; fine churches, Shire Hall, Guildhall; p. (estd. 1967) *53,870*.

Shropshire (Salop), *N.W. midland co.*, Eng.; bordering on Wales; fine pastoral country with hills and woodland, agr. and dairying; iron; mnfs.; cap. Shrewsbury; a. 1.347 sq. m.; p. (1966) *322,000*.

Shumen (Kolarovgrad) *t.* Bulgaria; S.E. of Ruse; cloth; occupied by Russians, 1878; p. (1956) *41,670*.

Shurma, *t.*, Hejaz, Saudi Arabia; S. of Medina.

Shusha, *t.*, Azerbaydzhan S.S.R.; spa; p. massacred by Moslems 1926; p. (1956) *5,700*.

Shustar, *t.*, Iran; carpets, woollens, pottery, etc.; shallow-draught boats can reach Shallili, nr. S. by R. Karun; p. *20,000*.

Shuya, *t.*, R.S.F.S.R.; engin., textiles; p. (1959) *64,000*.

Shwebo, *t.*, Central Burma; on R. Irrawaddy.

Si Kiang, *ch. R.*, S. China; headstreams rise in Yunnan plateau, form main R. nr. Sunchow; R. then flows E., enters S. China Sea through lge. delta nr. Hong Kong; lower valley intensively cultivated, rice, sugar-cane, tea; tropical climate permits continuous cultivation of most crops throughout year; valley very densely populated.

Sialkot, *t.*, W. Pakistan; N.E. of Lahore; sports goods, musical and surgical instruments, paper; p. (1961) *164,346*.

Siam. *See* Thailand.   [N.W. to S.E.

Siam, G. of, *lge. inlet*, S. China Sea; 385 m. from

Sian (Xian), *c.*, *cap.*, Shensi, China; mkt.; oil- and saw-mills; p. (estd. 1957) *1,500,000*.

Siangtan (Xiangtan), *c.*, Hunan prov., China; tea ctr.; rice, cotton, hemp; coal-mng. in a.; p. (1953) *184,000*.

Siauliai, *t.*, Lithuanian S.S.R.; 115 m. N.W. of Vilnius; impt. rly junction; food inds.; p. (1959) *60,000*.

Šibenik, *t.*, Jugoslavia; naval base; fishing, weaving, woollens, chemicals; bauxite; p. (1959) *23,000*.

Siberia, *terr.*, U.S.S.R.; from the Ural Mtns. to Sea of Okhotsk and Bering Strait, bounded by the Arctic on the N., and on the S. by Mongolia and Turkestan; climate mostly severe; ch. ts. Novosibirsk (cap. W.S.) and Irkutsk (cap. E.S.); rich in coal, iron, minerals; oil and gas in W. Siberian lowland; resources not yet fully known; a. 4,210,420 sq. m.; p. (1959) *18,228,000*.

Siberut, *I.*, S. of Sumatra, Indonesia.

Sibi, *t.*, W. Pakistan; gypsum mng.

Sibiu, *t.*, Central Romania; linen, leather, brewing; p. (1963) *100,659*.

Sibu, *t.*, Sarawak, E. Malaysia; 80 m. up R. Rejang; p. (1960) *29,630*.

Sicily, *the lgst. I.*, Mediterranean Sea; former kingdom and now an aut. region of Italy; produces corn, oranges, olives, silk, almonds, sardines, sulphur and salt; oil in dist. of Ragusa, Gela Fontasarossa; pleasant climate; mountainous, highest point the volcano Mt. Etna; ch. ts. Palermo, Catania, Messina; severe earth tremors, 1968; a. 9,926 sq. m.; p. (1961) *4,711,783*.

Sicuani, *t.*, S. Peru, S. America; alt. 11,650 ft.; agr. and pastoral dist. ctr.; p. *15,000*.

Sidamo, *see* Galla and Sidamo.

Sidi-bel-Abbès, *t.*, W. Algeria; wheat, barley, tobacco, olives, vines; cattle, wool; footwear, bricks, furniture, cheese, macaroni; p. (1960) *105,000*.

Sidi-Kacem (Petit Jean) *t.*, Morocco, N.W Africa; oilfield and refinery; p. (1960) *19,478*.

Sidlaw Hills, *low mtn. range*, Angus, Perth, Scot.

Sidmouth, *mkt. t.*, *urb. dist.*, Devon, Eng.; on S. cst., 15 m. S.E. of Exeter; seaside resort; Honiton lace, gloves; p. (1961) *11,139*.

Sidon, *cst. t.*, Lebanon; on Mediterranean, S. of Beirut; terminal of oil pipe-line from Saudi Arabia; refinery; p. *17,695*.

Siedlce, *t.*, Poland; E. of Warsaw; p. (1965) *36,000*.

Siegburg, *t.*, N. Rhine–Westphalia, Germany; on R. Sieg; Benedictine abbey; dyes, iron, ceramics.; p. (1963) *34,100*.

Siegen, *t.*, N. Rhine–Westphalia, Germany; on R. Sieg; 2 cas.; iron-mining and smelting, machin., leather; p. (1963) *49,600*.

Siemianowice Slaskie, *t.*, Poland; nr. Katowice; (1965) *66,000*.

Siena, *hill-town*, Tuscany, Italy; 32 m. S. of Florence; spreads over three hilltops with Piazza del Campo in between where celebrated Palio festival (horse-races) are held; 13th- and 14th-cent. arch., cath.; agr. mkt., tanning, glass, textiles, bricks; *panforte* confectionery; tourist ctr.; p. (1961) *62,215*.

Siero, *t.*, Oviedo, Spain; on R. Nora; agr., livestock-raising, coal-mining; p. *30,931*.

Sierra da Estrella, *see* Estrella, Sierra da.

Sierra de Baudo, *mtn. range*, Columbia, S. America.

Sierra de Gata, *mtn. range*, Portugal–Spain.

Sierra de Gredos, *mtn. range*, Central Spain.

Sierra de Guadarrama, *mtn. range*, Central Spain.

Sierra Leone, *ind. sov. st.* within British Commonwealth (1961), W. Africa situated between Guinea and Liberia; covered with ranges of hills; ch. prod., palm kernels, ginger, piassava, kolas; iron ore, diamonds, chromite, gold; cap. Freetown; a. 27,925 sq. m.; p. (estd.) *2,475,000*.

Sierra Madre, *mtn. range*, W. cst., Mexico and Guatemala.

Sierra Mojada, *mtn. range*, Central Mexico.

Sierra Morena, *mtn. range*, Spain; between Guadalquivir and Guadiana basins, highest point 5,500 ft.

Sierra Nevada, *mtn. range*, Granada, Spain; highest summit, Mulhacen.

Sierra Nevada, *mtn. chain*, Cal., U.S.A.; highest peak Mt. Whitney, alt. 14,898 ft.

Sierra Nevada de Mérida, *mtn. range*, W. Venezuela; S. America; extends N.E. from San Cristóbal to Barquisimeto; extension of E. range of Andes, alt. over 16,000 ft.; impt. coffee plantations from 3,000 to 6,000 ft. on slopes.

Sierra Nevada de Santa Marta, *mtns.*, Colombia, S. America; summits over 19,000 ft.

Sighet, *t.*, N. Romania on U.S.S.R. frontier; p. (1963) *27,528*.

Siglufjörd, *spt.* N. Iceland; herrings; p. (1962) *2,625*.

Siguiri, *t.*, Guinea, W. Africa; on R. Niger; gold; p. *11,000*.

Sihanoukville, *see* Kompong Som.

Siirt, *t.*, Turkey; S. of Bitlis; p. (1965) *25,397*.

Sikasso, *t.*, Mali, W. Africa; mkt., route ctr.

Sikkim, *st.* E. Himalayas, adjoining Tibet, Nepal and Bhutan; dense forests, with rich flora and orchidaceae, but rice and corn grown in clearings; India–Tibet tr. routes run through st.; cap. Gangtok; lge. copper deposits nr. Ranikhola, Gangtok; a. 2,745 sq. m.; p. (1961) *161,080*.

Sila La, *min. massif*, Calabria, S. Italy; granite mass occupying full width of peninsula; alt. over 3,500 ft., max. 6,327 ft.

Silchester, *par.*, Hants, Eng.; between Basingstoke and Reading; impt. ctr. of the Roman road system; many Roman remains.

Silesia (Polish Śląsk, Czech Slezsko), *geographical region*, Europe; extends on both sides of Oder R.; rich in coal, zinc, iron, arsenic; farming, sugar-beet, cereals, fruit, general ind.; has frequently changed hands, in 1919 was divided between Germany (70%), Poland (25%), and Czechoslovakia (5%); in 1945 the former German part became Polish, now forms 2 provs., caps. Katowice and Wroclaw; p. *4,764,500*; the Czechoslovakian part is united with Moravia; p. *200,000*.

Silistra, *t.*, Bulgaria; on N.E. Romanian border, on Danube R.; cloth. distilleries, sawmills, grapes; p. (1956) *20,350*.

Silkeborg, *t.*, Jutland, Denmark; W. of Aarhus; paper, textiles; (1960) *24,465*. [coal, grain.

Silksworth, *t.*, Durham, Eng.; adjoining Sunderland bor.; new t. projected.

Silloth, *resort*, on Solway Firth, Cumberland, Eng.; Silver City, *t.*, N.M., U.S.A.; gold, iron, silver; cattle; health resort; p. (1960) *6,972*.

Silvermines, *vil.*, Co. Tipperary, R.o.I.; 5 m. S.W. of Nenagh; lead and zinc.

Silver Spring, *t.*, Md., U.S.A.; sub. to Wash.; p. *43,294*.

Simalur, *I.*, S. of Sumatra, Indonesia.

Simcoe, L., N. of L. Ontario, Canada; 30 m. by 18 m.

Simeto, R., Sicily, Italy; rises in central Sicily, flows E. across plain of Catania into Mediterranean; lower course bordered by malarial marshes; length 54 m.

Simferopol, *t.*, Ukrainian S.S.R.; on R. Salghir nr. Sevastopol; soap, candles, fruits, engin.; p. (1967) *217,000*.

Simla, *t.*, Punjab, India; alt. 7,075 ft. above sea, with sanatorium; p. (1961) *42,597*.

Simonstown, W. Cape Prov., S. Africa; naval sta., docks; p. (estd. 1963) *10,220* inc. *5,120* Europeans.

Simplon, *mtn.*, Switzerland; alt. 11,695 ft.; the pass over the Simplon (alt. 6,594 ft.) from Domodossola, Italy, to Brig in the Rhône valley, Switzerland, was originally made by Napoleon I. The Simplon rly. tunnel leads from Brig on the Swiss side to Iselle in the Val di Vedro on the Italian and is the longest in the world, 12½ m.

Simpson Desert, S.E. of Alice Springs, Northern Terr.. extending into S. Australia.

Sinai, *peninsula*, easternmost part of Egypt, between Gs. of Aqaba and Suez, at head of Red Sea; a. 11,055 sq. m., mainly desert in N., granitic ridges in S. rising to 8,500 ft. at Jebel Katrun; Jebel Musa or Mt. Sinai (7,359 ft.) is one of numerous peaks; mineral resources; coal-mine at Maghâra; occupied by Israeli troops, Nov. 1956–March 1957, and since June 1967.

Sinaloa, *st.*, Mexico; on G. of Cal.; agr. and mining, rich in gold, silver, copper, iron and lead; cap. Culiacán; a. 22,580 sq. m.; p. (1960) *838,404*.

Sind, *prov.* (revived 1970), W. Pakistan; lower Indus valley; agr. depends on irrigation; Gudda barrage (1963) to irrigate large a.; adm. ctr Karachi; cereals, hemp, cotton, indigo; a. 50,443 sq. m.; p. (1951) *4,619,000*.

Sindara, *t.*, Gabon, Africa; admin. ctr.

Sindri, *t.*, Bihar, India; fertiliser plant; p. (1961) *41,315*.

Singapore, *I.* and *c.*, S. E. Asia; at tip of Malay pen.; Republic within Brit. Commonwealth on secession from Malaysian Fed. 1965; Brit. Govt. retained right to maintain military base; univ.; vast *entrepôt* tr.; chemicals; a. 225 sq. m.; p. (estd. 1969) *2,033,500*.

Singen, *t.*, Baden-Württemberg, Germany; N.W. of L. Constance; foodstuffs, metals; p. (1963) *35,500*.

Singhbhum, *dist.*, Bihar, India; iron- and steel-wks; a. 5,191 sq. m.; p. (1961) *2,049,911*.

Sinhailien (Xinhailien), *c.*, Kiangsu, China; formed by merger of Sinpu, Tunghai and Lien-yienkang; p. (1953) *208,000*.

Sining (Xining), *c.*, Tsinghai prov., China; wool, salt, timber; p. (1953) *94,000*.

Sinkiang-Uighur (Xinjiang), *aut. region*, China, bordering on Soviet Union and Kashmir; cereals, cotton, wool, silk; cap. Urumchi; a. 705,962 sq. m.; p. (1953) *4,873,608*.

Sinneh, *t.*, Iran; carpets; p. *32,000*.

Sinop, *Turkish t.*, on Black Sea; timber, silk; p. (1960) *9,899*.

Sinsiang (Xinxiang), *c.*, Honan prov., China; cotton weaving, flour milling; p. (1953) *171,000*.

Sintra (Cintra), *t.*, Portugal; summer resort, 18 m. from Lisbon; convention of S., 1808.

Sion, *cap.*, Valais, Switzerland; on R. Rhône; built on two castled hills; cath.; hydroelec. plant nearby; p. (1957) *10,904*.

Sioux City, Iowa, U.S.A.; on R. Missouri; meat-packing, foundries, elec. goods, cement; p. (1960) *89,159*.

Sioux Falls, *t.*, S.D., U.S.A.; on Big. Sioux R.; in rich wheat region; machin., cars, farming implements; nuclear reactor; p. (1960) *65,466*.

Sir Edward Pellew, *gr. of Is.*, N. Australia; in G. of Carpentaria.

Sistan and Baluchestan, *twin prov.*, Iran; bounded by Afghanistan and Pakistan; cap. Zahedan; much desert land; arid, very hot; p. (1967) *456,435*. [53,834.

Sitapur, *t.*, Uttar Pradesh, India; p. (1961) Sitka (formerly Novo Archangelsk), *t.*, S.E. Alaska, U.S.A.; on Baranof I., in Sitka Sound; was ch. pt. of former Russian America; gold-mines; lumbering, canning; naval and coaling sta.; p. (1960) *3,237*.

Sitra, *I.*, Persia G.; forming part of st. of Bahrain, Arabia, 3 m. long and 1 m. wide; oil pipeline and causeway carrying road extends out to sea for 3 m. to deep-water anchorage.

Sittang, R., Burma; rises in Pegu Yoma, flows S., enters G. of Martaban, Andaman Sea through delta; valley intensively cultivated; rice; delta forested;; length 610 m.

Sittang Bridge, *t.*, Burma; lge. paper mills.

Sittingbourne and Milton, *mkt. t.*, *urb. dist.*, Kent, Eng.; on Milton Creek, 9 m. E. of Chatham; paper-mills, brick-wks.; cement; insecticides; ctr. of fruit-growing dist.; p. (estd. 1967) *28,470*.

Sivas, *prov.*, Turkey; rich in minerals, has mineral springs with fertile grain-growing soil, fine orchards and vineyards, besides timber forests; cap. Sivas; p. (1965) *705,077*.

Sivas, *t.*, Turkey; in the Kizil Irmak valley; mnfs. woollens; p. (1965) *109,165*. [U.S.S.R.

Sivash or Putrid Sea, lagoon on E. side of Crimea, Siwa, *oasis*, Egypt; in Libyan Desert, 300 m. S.W. of Alexandria; dates, olives, remains of temple of Ammon and the fountain of the Sun; 20 m. long, 1 m. wide; p. *1,000*.

Sizewell, Suffolk, Eng.; nuclear power sta.

Sjælland, I., Denmark; lgst. I.; agr., fishing, mnfs.; ch. t. Copenhagen; a. 2,840 sq. m.; p. (1960) *1,771,557*.

Skagen, *t.*, N. Denmark; on cst. of the Skagerrak; fishing, tourism; p. (1960) *10,390*.

Skagerrak, arm of N. Sea, giving access to the Kattegat, between Norway and Denmark, 70–90 m. wide.

Skagway, *sm. spt.*, Alaska, U.S.A.; at head of Lynn Canal inlet, 400 m. N.W. of Prince Rupert; linked by rly. to Whitehorse on Upper R. Yukon; boomed in gold rush (in 1898, p. *15,000*), subsequently declined; p. (1960) *659*.

Skåne (Scania), *peninsula*, extreme S. of Sweden; corresponds approx. to cos. Malmöhus, Kristian-stad; most favoured part of Sweden in relief, soil, climate; intensive farming, wheat, barley, sugar-beet, fodder crops, dairy cattle; ch. ts. Malmo, Lund, Hälsingborg; a. approx. 4,000 sq. m. [250,180.

Skaraborg, *co.*, Sweden; a. 3,269 sq. m.; p. (1961) Skarzysko-Kamienna, *t.*, Kielce, Poland; p. (1965) *37,000*. [mark.

Skaw, The (Grenen), *C.*, at extreme N. of Den-Skeena, R., B.C., Canada; rises in N. Rocky Mtns., flows S.W. to Pac. Oc. at Prince Rupert; lower valley used by Canadian National Rly. from Edmonton (Alberta) to Prince Rupert via Yellowhead Pass; length approx. 400 m.

Skegness, *t.*, *urb. dist.*, Lindsey, Lincoln, Eng.; on E. cst.; farming, vegetables; resort; light engin.; p. (1961) *12,843*.

Skellefteå, *t.*, N. Sweden; on Bothnia G., mng., chiefly copper, gold,; p. (1961) *22,730*.

Skelmersdale, *t.*, *urb. dist.* Lancs. Eng.; coal, bricks, drainpipes; designated "New Town" 1961; spun yarn; p. (estd. 1965) *8,695*.

Skelton and Brotton, *t.*, *urb. dist.*, N.R. Yorks, Eng.; at N. foot of Cleveland Hills, 10 m. E. of Middlesbrough; steel flooring; p. (1961) *13,186*.

Skiddaw, *mtn.*, Cumberland, Eng.; E. of Bassenthwaite L.; alt. 3,054 ft.

Skien, *spt.*, Bratsberg, Norway; on R. Skien; saw-mills, ice, and timber tr.; p. (1968) 44,213.

Skierniewice, *t.*, Lodz, Poland; S.W. of Warsaw; p. (1965) 24,000.

Skipton, *t.*, *urb. dist.*, W.R. Yorks, Eng.; on R. Aire, 6 m. N.W. of Keighley; cotton and rayon; cas.; p. (1961) 12,933.

Skive, *t.*, N. Jutland, Denmark; fishing; rly. ctr.; p. (1960) 15,558.   [engin.; p. 16,740.

Skopin, *t.*, R.S.F.S.R.; S.E. of Moscow; lignite.

Skopje, *t.*, *cap.*, Macedonia, Jugoslavia; the ancient Scupi, one of oldest ts. in Balkans; almost completely destroyed by earthquake 26 July 1963 (over 1,000 deaths); chrome mines in neighbourhood; iron and steelplate wks.; p. (estd. 1964) 212,000.

Skövde, *t.*, Sweden; between Ls. Vänern and Vättern; garrison t., cars, cement; p. (1961) 23,946.

Skowhegan, *t.*, Me., U.S.A.; p. (1950) 6,183.

Skye, *I.*, lgst. of the Inner Hebrides, Inverness, Scot.; mountainous; sheep-farming and fisheries; only town, Portree; a. 547 sq. m.

Skyros, *I.*, Grecian Archipelago, E. of Evvoia (Euboea).

Slagelse, *old t.*, Sjaelland, Denmark; food inds.; iron and silver wks.; p. (1960) 20,562.

Slanic, *t.*, Wallachia, Romania; on S. flank of Carpathian Mtns., 22 m. N. of Ploesti; impt. salt deposits; p. (1956) 6,842.

Slask, see Silesia.

Slatina, *t.*, Romania; on R. Olt, 87 m. W. of Bucharest; ancient churches; p. (1956) 13,331.

Slave, *R.*, N.W. Terr., Canada; flows into Gr. Slave L.

Slave Coast, portions of Guinea cst., W. Africa, embracing Dahomey and Nigeria.

Slavonia, former Crown land (with Croatia) of Hungary; now Jugoslavia.

Slavyansk, *t.*, Ukrainian S.S.R.; coal, chemicals, salt, engin.; p. (1959) 83,000.

Sleaford, *mkt. t.*, *urb. dist.*, Kesteven, Lincoln, Eng.; 12 m. N.E. of Grantham; agr. and agr. implements, malting, seeds; p. (1961) 7,834.

Sleepers, The, *gr. of Is.*, Hudson Bay, Canada.

Slezsko, see Silesia.

Slieve Bloom, *hill range*, Offaly and Laoghis cos., Ireland; highest point 1,733 ft.

Slieve Donard, *mtn.*, N. Ireland; highest of the Mourne Mtns., co. Down; alt. 2,796 ft.

Sligo, *cst. co.*, Connacht, Ireland; pasture, tillage, barren mtn., and turf; livestock, fishing; a. 737 sq. m.; p. (1966) 51,073.

Sligo, *t.*, Sligo, Ireland; on Sligo Bay; distilling, flour, fisheries; p. (1966) 13,297.

Slioch, *mtn.*, Ross and Cromarty, Scot.; 3,217 ft.

Sliven, *t.*, E. Roumelia, Bulgaria; famous for black wine; p. (1956) 46,383.

Slough, *t.*, *mun. bor.*, Bucks, Eng.; on river terrace N. of R. Thames, 23 m. W. of London; many light inds.; p. (estd. 1967) 86,860.

Slovakia, *old prov.*, ČSSR.; consists largely of Carpathian Mtns.; ch. t. Košice; a. 18,902 sq. m.; p. (1961) 4,175,017.

Slovenia, *fed. unit*, Jugoslavia; cap. Ljubljana (Laibach); a. 6,266 sq. m.; p. (1959) 1,589,000.

Slupsk (Stolp), *t.*, Pomerania, Poland; German before 1945; cas.; machin., agr. implements; p. (1965) 59,000.

Småland, *dist.*, S. Sweden; barren upland area S. of L. Vättern; moorland, deciduous forest; contrasts greatly with remainder of S. Sweden.

Smederevo, *t.*, Serbia, Jugoslavia; nr. Belgrade; p. (1959) 22,000.

Smethwick, *co. bor.*, Staffs, Eng.; N.W. sub. of Birmingham; machin., engin., iron, glass; p. (1961) 68,372.

Smichov, *t.*, ČSSR.; on R. Vltava; connected by bridge with Prague; mnfs.; p. 54,370.

Smith Sound, Arctic Canada; connects Kane Bay with Baffin Bay.

Smoky Hill, *R.*, Col., Kan., U.S.A.; trib. of Kansas R.; length 400 m.

Smolensk, *c.*, R.S.F.S.R.; on both banks of the R. Dnieper; tallow, linen, iron and copper smelting, engin.; p. (1967) 189,000.

Smyrna, see Izmir.

Snaefell, *highest mtn.*, I. of Man; alt. 2,034 ft.

Snake R. or Lewis Fork, trib. of Columbia R., flows from Wyo. to Wash., U.S.A.; length 1,050 m.

Sneek, *c.*, Friesland, Neth.; nr. Leeuwarden; yachting ctr.; mnfs.; p. (1967) 24,464.

Sneeuwbergen, *mtn. range*, Cape Prov., S. Africa.

Snizort, Loch, *arm of sea* (14 m. long), N. of I. of Skye, Scot.

Snohetten, *mtn.*, highest in Dovrefjeld range Norway; alt. 7,565 ft.

Snowdon, *mtn.*, nr. Caernarvon, Wales; (highest in Eng. and Wales); alt. 3,571 ft.

Snowy, *R.*, N.S.W. and Victoria, Australia; rises in Mt. Kosciusko, flows S. into Bass Strait 80 m. W. of C. Howe; length 270 m. Snowy Mtns. project (1950–75) to provide hydroelec. power and irrigation.

Soar, *R.*, Leicester, Nottingham, Eng.; rises in uplands of S. Leics, flows N.W. through Leicester, Loughborough, into R. Trent nr. Long Eaton; hosiery and knitwear inds. in lower valley; 43 m. long.

Sobat, *R.*, Sudan, N.E. Africa; rises in S.W. of Abyssinian Highlands, flows N.W. into R. Nile 80 m. below L. No; one of ch. sources of Nile flood-water; Abyssinia receives monsoon rains April to Oct., max. discharge into White Nile, Nov. and Dec.; length over 500 m.

Soche, see Yarkand.

Sochi, *t.*, R.S.F.S.R.; on Black Sea at foot of main Caucasian range; health resort with subtropical climate and sulphur springs; developed since 1933; p. (1967) 182,000.

Society Is., *archipelago*, S. Pac. Oc.; between the Tuamotu Archipelago and Friendly Is., under Fr. protection; ch. I. Tahiti; ch. prod. phosphate and copper; cap. Papeete ; p. 37,303.

Socotra, Southern Yemen, G. of Aden, Indian Ocean; formerly British; livestock; exp. "Dragon's Blood", myrrh, frankincense, aloes; a. 1,382 sq. m.; p. c. 9,000.

Sodbury, *rural dist.*, Glos, Eng.; aircraft, bricks, quarrying, coal-mining; p. (1961) 44,826.

Söderhamn, *spt.*, Sweden; on G. of Bothnia, N. of Gavle; timber, wood-pulp, iron, engin.; p. (1961) 13,010.

Södermanland, *co.*, Sweden; S.W. of Stockholm; a. 2,634 sq. m.; p. (1961) 227,615.

Södertälje, *t.*, Sweden; on L. Malar; engin., tools, machin., cars, aluminium; p. (1961) 33,152.

Soerabaya or Surabaya, *spt.*, Java, Indonesia; dockyards and arsenal; oil; coffee, rice, cotton, sugar, tapioca; glass; p. (1961) 1,007,000.

Soerakarta, or Solo, *t.*, Java, Indonesia; p. (1961) 368,000.

Soest, *c.*, N. Rhine–Westphalia, Germany; cath.; iron ind.; p. (1963) 34,200.

Soest, *t.*, Utrecht, Neth.; artistic earthenware, toys; p. (1967) 32,958.

Sofala and Manica, *prov.*, Mozambique; N. of Inhambane; by some identified with the "Land of Ophir" of the Bible; cap. Beira.

Sofia, *t.*, *cap.*, Bulgaria; the ancient Sardica, and the Triaditza of the Byzantine Greeks; on Golem Isker R.; univ.; sugar, beer, flour, leather, silk, tobacco, maize, linen, engin., chemicals; p. (1967) 855,876.

Sogn og Fjordane, *co.*, Norway; a. 7,135 sq. m.; p. (1968) 227,031.

Sogne Fjord, longest in Norway.

Sohâg, *t.*, U.A.R.; on R. Nile; p. (1960) 62,000.

Soignies, *t.*, Belgium; on R. Senne; granite, flax; p. (1962) 10,946.

Soissons, *t.*, Aisne, France; iron, copper, farm implements, glass, sugar; p. (1954) 20,484.

Söke, *t.*, Turkey; liquorice, fruits, cereals, livestock; emery, lead; p. (1965) 27,140.

Sokoto, *t.*, Nigeria, W. Africa; groundnuts, rice, cotton, cattle, hides and skins. Founded 1809 as cap. of native st. of S., pop. mainly Hausa and Fulani; p. 48,000.

Sol Iletsk, *t.*, R.S.F.S.R.; near Kazakhstan border; potash; p. 10,000.

Soleftea, *t.*, Västernorrland, Sweden; on G. of Bothnia; p. (1961) 9,888.

Solent, The, *strait* separating the I. of Wight from the mainland; extends from Hurst Castle to Calshot.

Soleure (Solothurn), *can.*, N. Switzerland; arable, pastoral, and afforested; a. 306 sq. m.; p. (1961) 200,816.

Solihull, *co. bor.*, Warwick, Eng.; 5 m. S.W. of Birmingham; motor wks., drawing office equipment, stellite alloys mftg.; p. (estd. 1967) 105,890.

Solikamsk, *t.*, R.S.F.S.R.; on R. Kama; potash

and magnesium salts; chemicals, fertilisers, paper; p. (1956) *41,200*.

Solingen, *t.*, N. Rhine–Westphalia, Germany; 15 m. E. of Düsseldorf; cutlery ctr.; p. (1968) *174,353*.

Sóller, *t.*, Majorca, Spain; p. (1957) *9,377*.

Solna, *t.*, nr. Stockholm, Sweden; p. (1961) *51,094*.

Solnechnyy, *see* Gornyy Snezhnogorsk.

Solomon Is., *Brit. prot.*, S. Pac.; inc. all Is. in 900-m. archipelago, S. and S.E. of large I. of Bougainville; copra, trochus shell, timber; bauxite, nickel; volcanic soil; a. 11,500 sq. m.; (estd.) *149,000*.

Solor I., Lesser Sunda Is., Indonesia; a. 114 sq. m.

Solothurn, *can.*, N.W. Switzerland; crossed by Jura mtns. and R. Aar; agr., pastoral, industl.; a. 306 sq. m.; p. (1961) *200,816*.

Solothurn (Soleure), *t.*, *cap.*, can. Solothurn, Switzerland; on R. Aar; watches, jewellery, cottons, motor production; p. (1957) *16,744*.

Sölvesborg, *spt.*, Sweden; tanneries; p. *4,246*.

Solway Firth, *arm* of Irish Sea, between Dumfries, Kirkcudbright, Scot., and Cumberland; length 40 m.

Somaliland, French. *See* Afars and Issas.

Somali Republic, *ind. sovereign st.* since 1 July 1960, comprising former U.N. trust terr. under Italian adm. (cap. Mogadishu) and former British Somaliland Prot. (cap. Hargeisa) which achieved ind. June 26, 1960; consists of torrid coastal strip from bdy. of Kenya N. along Indian Oc. up to 300 m. inland and strip along G. of Aden. up to 150 m. inland; hot, dry climate (tempered inland by alt.); livestock, maize, food-crops, hides, bananas; cap. Mogadishu; total a. 246,200 sq. m.; p. (1968) *2,745,000*.

Sombor, *t.*, Serbia, Jugoslavia; cattle, grain; p. (1962) *37,800*.

Sombrero I., Brit. Leeward Is., W.I.; phosphate of lime; Board of Trade lighthouse.

Somerset, *S.W. co.*, Eng.; bounded inland by Glos, Devon, Wilts and Dorset; pasture, arable, orchard and woodland, with mines, quarries and mnfs.; impt. fisheries; co. t. Taunton; a. 1,620 sq. m.; p. (1966) *638,000*.

Somerset West, *t.*, Cape Province, S. Africa; wine, fruit, veg.; explosives, fertilisers, chemicals; p. (1960) *3,234* inc. *4,225* whites.

Somersworth, *t.*, N.H., U.S.A.; on Salmon Falls R.; mnfs.; p. (1960) *8,529*.

Somerville, *c.*, Mass., U.S.A.; sub. of Boston; varied mnfs.; p. (1960) *94,697*.

Somme, *dep.*, N. France; mainly agr. with thriving textile inds.; cap. Amiens; a. 2,443 sq. m.; p. (1968) *512,113*.

Somme, R., France; flows in deps. Aisne and Somme to English Channel; length 116 m.

Sommen, L., Sweden (25 m. by 8 m.) 15 m. E. of L. Vättern.

Somport Tunnel, on bdy. France–Spain; carries main rly. from Pau to Zaragoza under Central Pyrenees; length 5 m.

Sönderborg, *spt.*, S. Jutland, Denmark; resort; cas. (military barracks); p. (1960) *20,653*.

Sondrio, *prov.*, Lombardy, Italy; silk; a. 1,233 sq. m.; cap. Sondrio; p. (1961) *13,717*.

Songea, *t.*, Tanzania, E. Africa; admin. ctr.; wheat, coffee, tobacco.

Song-koi (Red R.), *R.*, rises in Yunnan plateau, S.W. China, flows S.E. through N. Vietnam, enters G. of Tongking; Hanoi is nr. head of delta; Haiphong nr. one of R. mouths; lower valley densely populated and intensively cultivated; length approx. 800 m. [(1963) *29,231*.

Sonneberg, *t.*, Suhl, E. Germany; toys; p.

Sonora, *st.*, Mexico; on G. of Cal.; silver-mines, stock-raising, grain, cotton, sugar, fruit, tobacco growing; cap. Hermosillo; a. 70,477 sq. m.; p. (1960) *783,378*.

" Soo " Canals, *see* Saulte Ste. Marie Canals.

Soochow (Suzhou), *c.*, Kiangsu, China; nr. Shanghai; former treaty pt.; silk, weaving and exp.; cotton, rice; p. (1953) *474,000*.

Sopot, *spa, seaside resort*, Poland; on W. shore of Gdańsk B.; p. (1965) *45,000*.

Sopron, *t.*, N.W. Hungary; on R. Hunte; holiday resort; viticulture; p. (1962) *42,333*.

Sorata, *t.*, Bolivia; 57 m. W. La Paz; nr. Andes peak of Ancohuma (Illampu).

Sorau, *see* Zary.

Sorel, *t.*, Quebec, Canada; sawmills, foundries, engin.; p. (1961) *17,147*.

Soria, *prov.*, Old Castile, Spain; agr. and cattle-rearing, with cheese, timber, wool and salt exp.; cap. Soria; a. 2,977 sq. m.; p. (1959) *154,987*.

Soria, *t. ... cap.*, Soria, Spain; on R. Douro; p. (1957) *21,500*.

Soriano, *dep.*, Uruguay; a. 3,561 sq. m.; cap. Mercedes; p. (1953) *99,927*.

Sormova, *industl. sub.*; 6 m. W. of Gorkiy on R. Volga; Byelorussian S.S.R.; machin., diesel motors, boilers, ships, tanks.

Soro, *t.*, Själland, Denmark; p. *3,191*.

Sorocaba, *t.*, São Paulo st., Brazil; rly. wks.; textiles, cement, footwear, wines, fertilisers; p. (estd. 1968) *142,835*.

Sorrento, *cst. t.*, S. Italy; nr. S. extremity G. of Naples; popular resort, anciently celebrated for its fine wines; p. *26,325*.

Sör-Tröndelag, *see* Tröndelag.

Sosnowiec, *t.*, S.W. Poland; rly. junction; coal, iron, textiles; p. (1965) *140,000*.

Sotteville-lès-Rouen, *t.*, Seine-Maritime, France; rly. wks.; p. (1954) *25,626*.

Soufrière, *mtn.*, Basse-Terre I., Lesser Antilles Gr. W. Indies; volcanic; highest peak in Lesser Antilles; alt. 4,869 ft.

Sound, The, *channel* between the Kattegat and the Baltic, 3 m. across at narrowest part.

Sousse (Susa), *spt.*, Tunisia; p. (1956) *48,172*.

South Africa, Republic of, *ind. rep.* (withdrew from Br. Commonwealth May 31, 1961), compr. provs. Cape Province, Natal, Transvaal and O.F.S.; climate, Mediterranean to tropical; vegetation, evergreens in C. region, grassland (veld) in E.; cereals, cotton, sugar, vines, citrus fruit, sheep and cattle, ostriches, gold, diamonds, coal, copper, tin, various mnfs.; admin. cap. Pretoria, legislative cap. Cape Town; a. (inc. Walvis Bay) 472,685 sq. m.; p. (estd. 1968) *19,167,000* (inc. *3,639,000* whites).

South America, southern continent of Western hemisphere incl. Argentina, Bolivia, Brazil, Chile, Colombia, Ecuador, Paraguay, Peru, Uruguay, Venezuela and Guyana; physical features, cst. regular except in S.W., Andes Mtns. along whole of W. cst., Brazilian Highlands on E. cst., rolling plains in ctr.; climate, diverse, varying with latitude and alt.; equatorial, hot and wet; Atacama, a rainless desert on middle W. cst. In S. temperate; vegetation, varying with latitude, alt., climate, from coniferous, deciduous and tropical forest to tropical and temperate grasslands and deserts; ch. inds.; temperate and tropical agr.; cocoa, coffee, sugar-cane, rubber, cereals; cattle, sheep; minerals; gold, silver, copper, tin, diamonds, nitrates; factory inds. developing gradually; races: Europeans, mainly of Spanish and Portuguese descent, Indians, Negroes, mulattoes and mestizos (mixed races); a. 7,300,000 sq. m.; p. (estd. 1965) *164,000,000*.

South Arabia, Federation of. *See* Yemen, Southern.

South Bend, *c.*, Ind., U.S.A.; carriage and wagon wks., iron foundries, paper- and flour-mills, farming implements, aeroplanes; seat of Notre Dame University; p. (1960) *132,445*.

South Carolina, *st.*, U.S.A.; level in E., and mtns. in W.; cereals, cotton, tobacco; textiles, chemicals, lumber; cap. Columbia; ch. pt., Charleston; a. 31,055 sq. m.; p. (1970) *2,522,881*.

South Coast, *t.*, Queensland, Australia; p. (1957) *22,800*.

South Dakota, *st.*, U.S.A.; mixed farming, wheat; gold, silver, gypsum, lumbering, flourmilling, butter, cheese, meat-packing; cap. Pierre; a. 77,047 sq. m.; p. (1970) *661,406*.

South Downs, *range chalk hills*, Sussex and Hants, Eng.

Southern Arabia, Protectorate of, the name adopted by Aden on accession to Federation (Jan. 1963).

South Gate, *industl. t.*, Cal., U.S.A.; paint, chemicals, tiles, furniture, tires, machin.; p. (1960) *53,831*.

South Georgia, Brit. I., S. Atl. Oc.; a. 1,450 sq. m.; mtns., whaling ctr.

South Holland, *prov.*, Neth.; flat, intersected by Rs. and dykes; cap. The Hague; a. 1,130 sq. m.; p. (1960) *2,706,810*.

South I., *lge. I.*, N.Z.; contains S. Alps (highest Mt. Cook, 12,349 ft.), Canterbury Plains; wool, mutton, dairy prod., fruit; Benmore hydroelec. sta., on Waitiki R.; a. 58,093 sq. m.; p. (1964) *770,669*.

South Kensington, *dist.*, in W. London; contains Victoria and Albert Museum, Geological and Science Museums, British Museum of Natural History, Commonwealth Institute, Albert Hall.

South Molton, *mkt. t., mun. bor.*, Devon, Eng.; at S. foot of Exmoor, 10 m. S.E. of Barnstaple; textiles, cosmetics; p. (1961) *2,994*.

South Orange, *c.*, N.J., U.S.A.; p. (1960) *16,175*.

South Orkney Is., Antarctica; whaling; met. sta.

South Portland, *c.*, Me., U.S.A.; on Portland harbour; p. (1960) *22,788*.

South Sandwich Is., Antarctica; whaling.

South Shetland, *Brit. archipelago*, S. Atlantic; 400 m. S. C. Horn.

South Shields, *t., co. bor.*, Durham, Eng.; on S. bank at mouth of R. Tyne; coming holiday resort; coal, engin., lingerie; p. (estd. 1967) *107,760*.

Southall, *t., former mun. bor.*, Middlesex, Eng., now inc. in Ealing outer bor. Greater London (*q.v.*); residtl.; many varied light inds.; p. (1961) *52,983*.

Southam, *mkt. t., rural dist.*, Warwick, Eng.; 5 m. S.E. of Leamington; lime, cement, mineral spring; p. (1961) *15,457*.

Southampton, *c., spt., co. bor.*, Hants, Eng.; at head of Southampton Water on peninsula between estuaries of Rs. Test and Itchen; univ.; extensive docks for passenger-liners; container facilities; ship repairing, oil refining, cable mkg., electronics, synthetic rubber; p. (estd. 1967) *207,790*.

Southampton, *c.*, S. pt. of Coates I., Hudson Bay, Canada.

Southampton Water, *inlet*, Hants, Eng.; comprises drowned estuaries of Rs. Itchen and Test; gives access from Solent and Spithead to spt. of Southampton; length 9 m., width 1–1½ m.

Southborough, *t., urb. dist.*, Kent, Eng.; in ctr. of The Weald, 2 m. N. of Tunbridge Wells; residtl.; chalybeate spring; p. (1961) *9,770*.

Southbridge, *t.*, Mass., U.S.A.; optical instruments and cutlery; p. (1960) *15,889*.

Southend-on-Sea *t., co. bor.*, Essex, Eng.; on N. side of Thames estuary; wireless factory, varied light inds.; air ferry terminal; p. (estd. 1967) *165,760*.

Southern Alps, *range of mtns.*, S.I., N.Z.

Southern Cross, *t., rly. junction*, W. Australia; on main Transcontinental Rly. 220 m. E. of Perth; gold-mines, now declining.

Southern Ocean, surrounds Antarctica; pack ice.

Southern Rhodesia, *see* Rhodesia.

Southgate, *former mun. bor.*, Middlesex, Eng.; now inc. in Enfield outer bor. Greater London (*q.v.*); residtl.; p. (1961) *72,359*.

Southland, *prov.*; S.I., N.Z.; cap. Invercargill; big agr. a.; wheat, meat, wool; a. 11,170 sq. m.; p. (1961) *93,697*.

Southport, *t., co. bor.*, Lancs, Eng.; on S. side of Ribble estuary; 18 m. N. of Liverpool; seaside resort; residtl.; p. (estd. 1967) *79,710*.

Southport, *wat. pl.*, Queensland, Australia; 50 m. S. of Brisbane; pastoral, dairying, fruit-growing and timber dist.; p. (1947) *8,432*.

Southsea, *dist.*, Portsmouth, Hants, Eng.; seaside resort.

Southwark, *inner bor.*, London, Eng.; incorporating former bors. of Bermondsey and Camberwell; p. (1966) *304,000*.

Southwell, *mkt. t., rural dist.*, Notts, Eng.; cath.; coal-mining, agr.; p. (rural dist. 1961) *45,818*.

South-West Africa (Namibia), *terr.*, under U.N. responsibility (still being admin. by S. Africa despite U.N. termination of mandate, Oct. 1966); mostly desert, scanty rainfall; cattle, ostriches; diamonds, tin, copper; cap, Windhoek; a. 318,261 sq. m.; p. (estd. 1966) *610,100*.

Southwold, *spt., mun. bor.*, E. Suffolk, Eng.; on E. cst. 8 m. S. of Lowestoft; fishing; resort; p. (estd. 1967) *2,140*.

Soviet Harbour, *spt.*, G. of Tartary, R.S.F.S.R.; sawmilling; p. (1954) *75,000*.

Sowerby Bridge, *t., urb. dist.*, W.R. Yorks, Eng.; on R. Calder, 3 m. W. of Halifax; woollens; p. (1961) *16,224*.

Sowjetsk (Tilsit), *t.*, R.S.F.S.R.; German before 1945; on R. Memel; cas.; foodstuffs. machin., wood; p. (1956) *34,100*.

Sozh, *R.*, Ukrainian S.S.R.; trib. of R. Dnieper; length 240 m.

Spa, *t.*, Liége, Belgium; mineral springs, resort; [p. (1962 *9,040*.

Spain, *kingdom* (without a sovereign), S.W. Europe; interior plateau; climate varied, very hot summers, warm rainy winters, N.W. mild, and wet, central plateau extremes of heat and cold; evergreen trees and shrubs; cereals, vines, citrus fruits, olives, nuts; sheep, goats, pigs; coal, copper, iron, lead, zinc, mercury, colophony, turpentine, cork; mnfs. wine, sugar, silk, brewing; oil refining; leading ind. tourism; cap. Madrid; a. 196,700 sq. m.; p. (1969) *33,500,000*.

Spalding, *mkt. t., urb. dist.*, Holland, Lincoln, Eng.; in The Fens, 10 m. up the R. Welland from The Wash; agr.; bulb mkt., agr. machin., sugarbeet, fruit canning; p. (1961) *14,821*.

Spandau, *t.*, Potsdam, E. Germany; firearms, gunpowder; previously gr. military ctr.

Spanish Guinea, *see* Equatorial Guinea.

Spanish Sahara, *Spanish col.*, N.W. African cst.; comprising Rio de Oro and Saguia el Hamra; lge. reserves of phosphate at El Aiun being exploited; a. 125,000 sq. m.; p. (estd. 1967) *48,000*.

Spanish Wells, *I.*, Bahamas, W. Indies; p. (1953) *665*.

Sparrows Point, *t.*, Md., U.S.A.; situated on Chesapeake Bay at entrance to Bear Creek; impt. iron and steel ind.

Sparta, *famous ancient c.*, the Morea, Greece; on the R. Eurotas; passed under Roman rule, 146 B.C.; p. (1961) *10,412*.

Spartanburg, *t.*, S.C., U.S.A.; cotton; p. (1960) *44,352*.

Spartel, *C.*, International Zone, N.E. Africa.

Spartivento, *C.*, Italy; most S. point of Italian mainland.

Spenborough, *mun. bor.*, W.R. Yorks, Eng.; textiles, plastics, wire; p. (estd. 1967) *38,440*.

Spencer Gulf, *lge. inlet*, S. Australia; penetrates 240 m. inland, max. width 75 m.

Spennymoor, *t., urb. dist.*, Durham, Eng.; 5 m. S. of Durham; mnfs.; p. (1961) *19,104*.

Sperrin Mtns.,Tyrone and Londonderry, N.Ireland.

Spey, *R.*, Inverness, Moray, and Banff, the most rapid in Scot., flows N.E. to Moray Firth; length 107 m.

Speyer, *c.*, Rhineland-Palatinate, Germany; cas.; its famous Diet of 1529 condemning the Reformation gave rise to the term "Protestant"; textiles, tobacco, machin., footwear, beer, sugar, paper; oil refining; p. (1963) *39,800*.

Spezia, La, *spt.*, Liguria, Italy; on Bay of Spezia; arsenal, docks, maritime inds., elec. machin., and olive oil; p. (1961) *121,191*.

Spice Is., *see* Moluccas.

Spitalfields, *par.*, E. London, Eng.; former silk-weaving dist., introduced by Huguenots, 17th. cent.

Spithead, *roadstead*, between Portsmouth and the I. of Wight, Eng.; used by ships of Royal Navy.

Spitsbergen (Svalbard), *I. gr.*, belonging to Norway; well within Arctic Circle; mountainous; sealing and whaling; coal-mining; asbestos, copper, gypsum, iron, marble, mica, zinc and phosphate deposits; a. 24,294 sq. m.; p. (1956) Norwegian *1,530*, Russian *2,746*.

Split (Spalato), *c.*, Jugoslavia; wine, olive oil, bauxite, shipping; p. (1959) *84,000*.

Splügen Pass, Rhaetian Alps; between Lombardy and Grisons, Switzerland; alt. 6,939 ft.

Spokane, *R.*, Idaho, U.S.A.; flows to the R. Columbia at Washington; length 120 m.

Spokane, *t.*, Wash., U.S.A.; on R. Spokane, at the fall which is used for hydro-elec. power; gr. timber tr., flour and sawmills, mng.; cement, elec. goods; p. (1960) *181,603*.

Spoleto, *t.*, Perugia, Italy; truffles; p. *32,600*.

Spondon, *t.*, Derby, Eng.; on R. Derwent, 3 m. E. of Derby; textiles; nylon plant projected 1964.

Sporades, *I.*, Grecian Archipelago in the Ægean and neighbouring seas; belonging to Greece, includes Samos, Kos. etc.

Spree, *R.*, E. Germany; flowing W. past Berlin to the Havel at Spandau; length 227 m.

Spremberg, *t.*, Cottbus, Germany; on R. Spree; lignite, mining, glass, elec., metals, cloth, bicycles, machin.; p. (1963) *22,931*.

Springbok, *t., cap.*, Namaqualand, Cape Prov., S. Africa; copper-mining; p. (1960) *3,111*.

Springfield, *c.*, *cap.*, Ill., U.S.A.; gr. rly. ctr.; iron, watches, etc.; p. (1960) *83,271.*

Springfield, *c.*, Mass., U.S.A.; mnfs. cars, elec. apparatus and paper; p. (1960) *174,463.*

Springfield, *c.*, Mo., U.S.A.; flour milling; Congregational college; p. (1960) *95,865.*

Springfield, *c.*, Ohio, U.S.A.; agr. implements. motor lorries; p. (1960) *82,723.*

Springfontein, *t.*, O.F.S., S. Africa; rly. ctr.; p. (1960) *2,850* inc. *758* whites.

Springs, *t.*, Transvaal, Rep. of S. Africa; E. of Johannesburg; gold mng., engin., machin., cars, elec. goods; uranium plant; p. (1960) *135,231* inc. *36,445* whites.

Spurn Head, *C.*, E. Yorks, Eng.; at mouth of Humber estuary.

Sretensk, *t.*, R.S.F.S.R.; coal, machin., leather, woodworking.

Srinagar, *t.*, *cap.*, Kashmir, India; on R. Jhelum in W. Himalayas; 5,263 ft. above sea-level; silver and copper wares, carpet weaving, paper; univ.; p. (1961) *285,257.*

Sriracha, *t.*, Thailand; sawmills; oil refinery; (p. 1960) *10,472.*

Stade, *t.*, Lower-Saxony, Germany; nr. Hamburg; leather, wood, textiles; p. (1963) *31,400.*

Staffa, *I.*, the Inner Hebrides, W. Scot.; 6 m. N. Iona, off W. cst. Mull; Fingal's Cave, 227 ft. long, with other basaltic caves.

Stafford, *co. t.*, *mun. bor.*, Staffs, Eng.; on R. Sow, 15 m. N. of Wolverhampton; heavy elec. and other engin. works; p. (estd. 1967) *52,560.*

Staffordshire, *W. midland co.*, Eng.; rich in iron and coal, the " Black Country " being famous; also lge. Potteries dist., famous breweries, and many thriving mnfs.; co. t. Stafford; a. 1,153 sq. m.; p. (1966) *1,802,000.*

Staines, *mkt. t.*, *urb. dist.*, Surrey, Eng.; on R Thames, 4 m. S.E. of Windsor; linoleum, machin., petrol engines; p. (estd. 1967) *55,190.*

Stainmore, *pass*, N.E. Yorks, Eng.; crosses N. Pennines from Greta valley into upper Eden valley; used by main road but only minor rly.; alt. 1,370 ft

Staithes, N.R. Yorks., Eng.; 9 m. N.W. of Whitby; potash mng.

Stalin, *see* Brasov.

Stalin Canal, *see* Volga Baltic Waterway.

Stalinabad *see* Dushanbe.

Stalingrad, *see* Volgograd.

Stalino *see* Varna.

Stalino, *see* Donetsk.

Stalinogorsk, *see* Novomoskovsk.

Stalinsk, *see* Novokuznetsk.

Stalybridge, *t.*, *mun. bor.*, Cheshire, Eng.; on R. Tame, 5 m. E. of Manchester; cotton and wool, engin., plastics, rubber goods, elec. cables; p. (estd. 1967) *21,770.*

Stamboul, *see* Istanbul.

Stamford, *c.*, Conn., U.S.A.; on shore of Long I. Sound; p. (1960) *92,713.*

Stamford, *mkt. t.*, *mun. bor.*, Kesteven, Lincoln. Eng.; 10 m. N.W. of Peterborough; agr. inds., elec. goods, plastics; p. (estd. 1967) *13,120.*

Standerton, *t.*, Transvaal, S. Africa; on R. Vaal; livestock, oats; p. (1960) *16,863* inc. *6,698* Europeans.

Standish-with-Langtree, *urb. dist.*, Lancs, Eng.; 4 m. N.W. of Wigan; coal-mining, silk mftg.; p. (1961) *9,689.*

Stanger, *t.*, Natal, S. Africa; tea, sugar, maize, wattle; p. (1960) *9,557* inc. *1,740* whites.

Stanimaka *see* Asenovgrad.

Stanislaus, *R.*, Cal., U.S.A.; trib. of the San Joaquin R.; length 200 m.

Stanislav, *see* Ivano-Frankovsk.

Stanley, *t.*, *urb. dist.*, Durham, Eng.; 10 m. N.W. of Durham; mnfs.; p. (estd. 1967) *44,690.*

Stanley, *spt.*, *cap.*, Falkland Is.; whaling; p. (estd. 1958) *1,135.*

Stanley, *urb. dist.*, W.R. Yorks, Eng.; p. (1961) *16,749.*

Stanley Falls, on the Upper Congo R., Congo, Africa; nr. the Equator, named after the explorer, Sir H. M. Stanley.

Stanley Pool, an expansion of the Lower Congo, Africa; 25 m. long. 16 m. wide.

Stanleyville, *see* Kisangani.

Stanlow, inc. in Ellesmere Port, urb. dist., Cheshire; petrol ref., oil-storage dks. and terminal; chemicals.

Stanovoi Mtns., *range of mtns.*, U.S.S.R.; extends from N. of R. Amur to nr. Sea of Okhotsk.

Stans, *cap.*, half-can. Nidwalden, Switzerland; mkt. t., orchards; p. *4,200.*

Star of the Congo, *t.*, Katanga, Congo, Africa; copper-mining.

Stara Planina (Balkan Mtns.), Bulgaria; highest peak, 7,780 ft.

Stara Zagora, *t.*, Central Bulgaria; copper smelting, mineral springs; nitrogen fertiliser plant; p. (1956) *55,322.*

Stargard Szczecinski, *t.*, Poland; prev. in Prussia; woollens, machin., cottons, spirits; p. (1965) *38,000.*

Start Point, *C.*, nr. Dartmouth, Devon, Eng.

Stassfurt, *t.*, Magdeburg, E. Germany; potash salts, chemicals, machin., metals; p. (1963) *26,166.*

Staten I., the most S. point N.Y. st., U.S.A.; shipyards; linked with Brooklyn by Verrazano-Narrows bridge (opened 1964); also island off Tierra del Fuego, S. America, 45 m. long.

States of the Church or Papal States, former indep. terr. under the temporal rule of the popes, prior to 1870; comprised Latium, Umbria, the Marches, E. Emiglia-Romagna.

Stavanger, *spt.*, Rogaland, Norway; margarine and preserved-food, woollen mills, fish curing and canning, shipbldg.; oil refinery at Sola under construction; p. (1968) *80,781.*

Staveley, *t.*, *urb. dist.*, Derby, Eng.; 3 m. N.E. of Chesterfield; coal, iron, chemicals; p. (1961) *18,071.*

Stávnice, *t.*, ČSSR.; impt. mining ctr., producing silver, copper, lead.

Stavropol, *see* Togliatti.

Stawell, *t.*, Victoria, Australia; 150 m. N.W. of Melbourne; agr. pastoral, viticulture ctr.; p. (1966) *5,904.*

Steelton, *bor.*, Penns., U.S.A.; steel foundries; p. (1960) *11,266.*

Steep Holm I., Bristol Channel, Eng.

Steep Rock, *see* Atikokan.

Stellenbosch, *t.*, C. Prov., Rep. of S. Africa; 25 m. E. of Cape Town; univ.; wines, sawmilling, brick and tile mkg.; p. (1960) *22,233* inc. *10,673* Europeans.

Stendal, *c.*, Magdeburg, E. Germany; cath.; iron, sugar wks.; p. (1963) *37,204.*

Stepney, *see* Tower Hamlets.

Sterlitamak, *t.*, Bashkir, R.S.F.S.R.; on S.W. flank of Ural Mtns., 120 m. N.E. of Chkalov (Orenburg); impt. oil-refineries on " Second Baku " oilfield; linked by pipeline to Stavropol; p. (1967) *156,000.*

Sternberk, *t.*, Moravia, ČSSR.; N. of Olomouc; textile mftg.; p. (1961) *11,215.*

Stettin, *see* Szczecin.

Steubenville, *c.*, Ohio, U.S.A.; iron, steel, paper, glass, coal, natural gas; p. (1960) *32,495.*

Stevenage, *t.*, Herts, Eng.; 4 m. S.E. of Hitchin; one of " New Towns " designated 1946; agr., light engin., school furniture, elec. goods, chemicals, aircraft parts; p. (estd. 1967) *58,690.*

Stevenston, *sm. burgh*, Ayr, Scot.; p. (1961) *10,174.*

Stewart, *R.*, trib. of R. Yukon, N.W. Terr., Canada.

Stewart I., S. or S.I., N.Z.; a. 670 sq. m.; oysters.

Stewarton, *burgh*, Ayr, Scot.; 5 m. N. of Kilmarnock; woollens, carpets; p. (1961) *3,387.*

Steyning, *vil.*, E. Sussex, Eng.; on R. Adur, 4 m. N. of Shoreham at entrance to gap through S. Downs; residtl.; p. *1,875.*

Steyr, *t.*, Austria; on R. Enns nr. Linz; bicycles, lorries, small-arms factories; p. (1961) *38,306.*

Stilton, *vil.*, Huntingdon, Eng.; 6 m. S.W. Peterborough; famous for cheese.

Stinchar, *R.*, Ayr, Scot.; flows W. to sea at Ballantrae; length 30 m.

Stirling, *ancient burgh*, Stirling, Scot.; on R. Forth in gap between Campsie Fells and Ochil Hills; cas.; univ.; coal-mng., engin., concrete, rock, wool, rubber gds; p. (1961) *27,553.*

Stirling, *midland co.*, Scot., borders Firth of Forth; coal-mining, agr., textiles; a. 466 sq. m.; p. (1961) *194,858.*

Stockerau, *t.*, Austria; machin., chemicals; p. (1961) *11,853.*

Stockholm, *c.*, *cap.*, Sweden; on Is. at outlet of L. Malar; called the " Queen of the Baltic " for the beauty of its surroundings; comm. ctr.; machin., textiles, leather, sugar, chemicals; many academic institutions; p. (1961) *808,484.*

Stockport, *t.*, *co. bor.*, Cheshire, Eng.; on R. Mersey, 5 m. S.E. of Manchester; cotton, man-made fibres, engin.; p. (estd. 1967) *141,030*.

Stocksbridge, *urb. dist.*, W. R. Yorks; p. (1961) *11,137*.

Stockton, *t.*, Cal., U.S.A.; farm implements, flour, lumber; p. (1960) *86,321*.

Stockton-on-Tees, *mkt. t.*, *mun. bor.*, Durham, Eng.; 4 m. W. of Middlesbrough; impt. iron and steel inds., plywood; first rly. for passenger traffic opened in 1825 between Stockton and Darlington; 18th cent. town hall; racecourse; p. (1961) *81,198*.

Stoke-on-Trent, *c.*, *co. bor.*, Staffs, Eng.; at S.W. foot of the Pennines; formed in 1910 by union of the "five towns" of Arnold Bennett's novels, Hanley, Burslem, Tunstall, Longton, and Fenton (with Stoke-upon-Trent); ceramics, coal, iron and steel, engin., brick and tile wks.; precast concrete; p. (estd. 1969) *272,260*.

Stoke Newington, *see* Hackney.

Stokesley, *mkt. t.*, *rural dist.*, N.R. Yorks, Eng.; 7 m. S of Middlesbrough; agr.; p. (rural dist. 1961) *25,571*.

Stolberg, *t.*, N. Rhine–Westphalia, Germany; E. of Aachen; metals, glass, wood, chemicals; p. (1963) *33,200*.

Stolp, *see* Slupsk.

Stone, *mkt. t.*, *urb. dist.*, Staffs, Eng.; on R. Trent, 7 m. S. of Stoke-on-Trent; footwear, tiles, porcelain, scientific glassware; p. (1961) *8,791*.

Stoneham, *t.*, Mass., U.S.A.; boots and shoes; p. (1960) *17,821*.

Stonehaven, *fishing t.*, *burgh*, Kincardine, Scot.; on E. cst., 14 m. S. of Aberdeen; distilling, net mftg.; p. (1961) *4,500*.

Stonehenge, *prehistoric gr. of monumental stones*, on Salisbury Plain, Wilts, Eng.; date of erection estd. between 1860–1500 B.C.

Stonehouse, *par.*, Lanark, Scot.; coal, linen; p. *4,204*.

Stony Stratford, *mkt. t.*, Bucks, Eng.; on R. Ouse, nr. Buckingham; engin., lace.

Stornoway, *spt.*, *burgh*, Ross and Cromarty, Scot.; on E. cst. of I. of Lewis, Outer Hebrides; ctr. Harris Tweed ind.; fishing ctr.; p. (1961) *5,221*.

Stour, R., Kent, Eng.; flows past Canterbury to Pegwell Bay; length 40 m.

Stour, R., Somerset, Dorset, and Hants, Eng.; trib. of R. Avon; length 55 m.

Stour, R., Suffolk and Essex, Eng.; flows E. to sea at Harwich; length 42 m.

Stour, R., Worcs. and Staffs, Eng.; trib. of R. Severn; length 20 m.

Stourbridge, *t.*, *mun. bor.*, Worcs, Eng.; on R. Stour, 9 m. W. of Birmingham; coal, iron and steel, brick and glass wks.; p. (estd. 1967) *51,300*.

Stourport-on-Severn, *urb. dist.*, *mkt. t.*, Worcs, Eng.; at confluence of Rs. Stour and Severn; carpets, iron and steel goods, porcelain, ceramics; p. (1961) *11,751*.

Stowmarket, *t.*, *urb. dist.*, Suffolk, Eng.; on R. Gipping, 11 m. N.W. of Ipswich; I.C.I. paint factory ctr.; p. (1961) *7,790*.

Strabane, *t.*, *urb. dist.*, Tyrone, N. Ireland; salmon fishing, agr. ctr.; p. (1966) *8,513*.

Straits Settlements, *former Brit. crown col.*, Malay Peninsula; comprised Penang, Malacca, and Singapore, estbl. 1867, dissolved 1946; Christmas I., the Cocos Is. and Labuan were at various times part of the col. *See* West Malaysia.

Stralsund, *spt.*, Rostock, E. Germany; opposite Rügen I.; grain tr., machin., metals, fish smoking, shipbldg.; p. (1963) *68,791*.

Strand, *t.*, Cape Province, S. Africa; resort; p. (1960) *13,313* inc. *7,067* whites.

Strangford Lough, *arm of sea*, Down, N. Ireland; 18 m. long, 6 m. wide at entrance.

Stranraer, *burgh*, Wigtown, Scot.; at head of Loch Ryan; steamer service to Larne, Antrim, N. Ireland; creameries, brewing, knitwear; p. (1961) *9,249*.

Strasbourg, *fortfd. c.*, *cap.*, Bas-Rhin, France; on R. Ill just above confluence with R. Rhine; captured 1870, regained 1918; fine cath., univ., imperial palace, many handsome new public bldgs.; extensive tr.; oil refining; machin., textiles, chemicals; p. (1968) *249,396*.

Stratford, *dist.*, E. London, Eng.; in bor. Newham; mftg.

Stratford, *c.*, Ontario, Canada; woollens, farm machin., flour, sawmills, engine wks.; p. (1961) *20,467*.

Stratford, *t.*, on R. Housatonic, Conn., U.S.A.; aircraft; p. (1960) *44,712*.

Stratford-on-Avon, *c.*, *mun. bor.*, Warwick, Eng.; on R. Avon, 11 m. S.W. of Leamington; birthplace of Shakespeare; memorial theatre, library. tourist ctr.; light inds.; p. (estd. 1969) *19,110*.

Strathaven, *t.*, Lanark, Scot.; cas.; knitwear, agr. engin., fibre glass; p. *4,207*.

Strathmore, *lowland belt.*, central Scot.; extends from Crieff N.E. to Montrose; flanked to N. by Scot. Highlands, to S. by Sidlaw, and Ochil Hills; drained by Rs. Earn, Tay, Isla, S. Esk; famous for cereals and small fruits; length 60 m., width 7–10 m.

Strathpeffer, *wat. pl.*, Ross and Cromarty, Scot.; 5 m. W. of Dingwall; spa.

Strathspey, *valley of the Spey*, Scot.; 70 m. long.

Stratton and Bude, *resort*, N. Cornwall, Eng.; 12 m. S. of Hartland Point; p. (1961) *5,095*.

Straubing, *t.*, Bavaria, Germany; on R. Danube; cas.; brewing, tiles, chemicals, machin.; p. (1963) *36,700*.

Strawberry, R., Utah, U.S.A.; on E. slopes of Wasatch Mtns. 80 m. S.E. of Salt Lake City; dammed to supply irrigation water, led through 3½ m. tunnel under Wasatch Mtns. to 100 sq. m. cultivable land round L. Utah.

Streator, *c.*, Ill., U.S.A.; bricks, glass, hardware, farm implements; p. (1960) *16,864*.

Street, *t.*, *urb. dist.*, Somerset, Eng.; at foot of Polden Hills, 7 m. S.W. of Wells; footwear, leather, vehicle wks.; p. (1961) *6,660*.

Stresa, *vil.*, Piedmont, Italy; favourite health resort on L. Maggiore; p. (estd.) *4,500*.

Stretford, *mun. bor.*, S.E. Lancs, Eng.; sub. of Manchester; engin., chemicals; p. (estd. 1967) *60,010*.

Stromboli, I., Lipari Is., N. of Sicily. Tyrrhenian Sea; active volcano, alt. 3,038 ft.; p. *853*.

Stromness, *mkt. burgh*, *pl.*, Mainland, Orkney Is., Scot.; 13 mm. W. Kirkwall; p. (1961) *1,477*.

Stromstad, *spt.*, Sweden; on Skagerrak; seaside resort; shipbldg.; fishing; p. (1961) *4,039*.

Stronsay, Orkney Is., Scot.

Stroud, *mkt. t.*, *urb. dist.*, Eng.; in Cotswold Hills, on R. Frome; cloth, carpets, plastics, engin.; p. (1961) *17,461*.

Strumble Head, *promontory*, N. Pembroke, Wales.

Stryj, R., Poland; trib. of R. Dniester.

Stryj, *t.*, Poland; sawmills, matches; p. *25,000*.

Stungmeanchy, *t.*, Cambodia; glass plant.

Sturminster Newton, *mkt. t.*, *rural dist.*, Dorset, Eng.; on R. Stour, 6 m. N.W. of Blandford; creameries; p. (rural dist. 1961) *9,566*.

Sturt Desert, area N.E. of S. Australia.

Stuttgart, *c. cap.*, Baden-Württemberg, Germany; on R. Neckar; cas., cath.; cars, machin., elec. engin., hosiery, knitwear; route ctr.; oil refinery nearby; p. (1968) *617,472*.

Styr, R., Poland; trib. of R. Prypei (Pripet); length 250 m.

Styria, *prov.*, Austria; grain, wine and fruit; stock-rearing, tourist tr.; a. 6,326 sq. m.; p. (1961) *1,137,865*.

Styrian Alps, that portion of the Alpine mtn. system E. of the Hohe Tauern.

Suakin, *former pt.*, Sudan, N.E. Africa; on Red Sea; now used only for pilgrim traffic to Jeddah.

Suanhwa (Xuanhua), *c.*, Hopeh prov., China; iron mng.; p. (1953) *114,000*.

Subotica, *t.*, Serbia, Jugoslavia; boots, rly. material, farming, stock-raising; tri-phosphate wks.; p. (estd.) *80,000*.

Suceava, *t.*, S. Bukovina, Romania; former residence of Moldavian princes; fancy leather; p. (1963) *62,557*.

Suchan, *t.*, R.S.F.S.R.; coal; p. (1956) *48,900*.

Süchow (Suzhou), *c.*, Kiangsu, China; on Tai-Hu, 40 m. W. of Shanghai; gr. comm. and industl. ctr., silks, cottons, rice; p. (1953) *c. 373,000*.

Sucre, *cap.*, Chuquisaca dep. and legal cap. of Bolivia; univ. and cath.; cement plant.; p. (1962) *54,270*.

Sucre, *st.*, Venezuela; cap. Cumana; p. (1961) *401,992*.

Sudan, The, *ind. sovereign st.* since Jan. 1956, N.E. Africa; formerly Anglo-Egyptian condominium; bounded by Egypt, Libya, Chad, Central African Rep., Congo, Uganda, Ethiopia, and Red Sea; cotton, gum arabic, hides, ground nuts, sugar; iron ore mng.; cap. Khartoum; a. 977,000. sq. m.; p. (1968) *14,770,000*. danese Republic. *See* Mali.

Sudbury, *t., mun. bor.,* W. Suffolk, Eng.; on R. Stour, 12 m. N.W. of Colchester; p. (estd. 1967) *7,060*. [(1956) *46,025*.

Sudbury, *t.,* Ontario, Canada; nickel, copper; p.

Sudeten Mtns., *range.* Poland, Czechoslovakia; separating Bohemia and Moravia from Silesia.

Suez, *spt.,* U.A.R., N.E. Africa; at head of G. of Suez (arm of Red Sea) and S. entrance of Suez Canal, which crosses the Isthmus of Suez to the Mediterranean at Port Said and is of very gr. value to shipping; the ancient Arsinoë; Port Tewfiq adjoining has quay and docks; p. (1960) *203,000*.

Suez, *G.,* Red Sea; N.W. arm of Red Sea between Arabian Desert and Sinai Peninsula, Egypt; southern approach to Suez Canal; length 190 m., width varies from 12 to 25 m.

Suez Canal, *ship canal,* U.A.R., N.E. Africa; connects Mediterranean Sea (Pt. Said) with Red Sea (Suez) through Is. Manzala, Timsah and Bitter; saves over 4,000 m. on journey N.W. Europe to India, 1,000 m. to Australia; opened 1869; length, 101 statue m.; closed since June 1967.

Suffolk, *most E. maritime co.,* Eng.; bounded by Essex, Norfolk, Cambridge and the N. Sea; mixed agr., dairying; fisheries; mnf. of agr. implements; civil nuclear power-sta. at Sizewell (1966); co. t. Ipswich; a. 1,482 sq. m. divided for admin. purposes into Suffolk E. p. (1966) *371,000* and Suffolk W. p. (1966) *148,000*.

Suhl, *t.,* Suhl, E. Germany; toys, armaments; p. (1963) *26,907*. [pipeline to Karachi.

Sui, Baluchistan, W. Pakistan; natural gas;

Suir, *R.,* Ireland; flows E. to Waterford Harbour.

Sukarnapura, *see* Djajapura.

Sukhumi, *spt.,* Georgian S.S.R.; resort; sawmilling; p. (1959) *64,000*.

Sukkur, *t.,* Pakistan; on. R. Indus, 230 m. N.E. of Karachi; gr. dam for irrigation; thermal sta. under construction; p. (1961) *103,000*.

Sulaiman, *mtns.,* Asia; range bounding the Punjab and Baluchistan. [272,442.

Sulaimaniya, *liwa,* Iraq; a. 4,554 sq. m.; p. (1956).

Sulawesi (Celebes), I., Indonesia; mtnous., forested; copra, coffee, bauxite; ch. pt. Menado, Makasar; a. 73,160 sq. m.; p. (1961) *7,079,349*.

Sulina, *t.,* Romania; at mouth of Sulina branch of Danube R.; considerable grain tr.; p. *3,622*.

Sullana, *t.,* N. Peru; rly. ctr.; maize, cotton, cinchona bark, fishing, whaling; p. (1961) *23,000*.

Sultanabad, *t.,* Persia; carpet mftg.; p. *55,000*.

Sulu Is., Philippines; archipelago between Borneo and the Philippines; incl. over 400 volcanic Is. and coral islets; a. 950 sq. m.; under U.S. control 1899–1940.

Sumatra, *I.,* Malay Archipelago, Indonesia; coffee, sugar, rice, pepper; gold, tin, petroleum, coal; a. 161,612 sq. m.; p. (1967) *13,300,000*.

Sumba, *I.,* Indonesia; part of Timor Archipelago.

Sumbawa, one of the Nusa Tenggara Is., Indonesia; in E. Indian Archipelago, E. of Lombok; a. (inc. nearby Is.) 5,240 sq. m.; p. *314,343*.

Sumgait, *t.,* Azerbaydzhan S.S.R.; on Caspian Sea; 25 m. N.W. of Baku; metallurgical ind.; chemicals; p. (1959) *52,000*.

Sumy, *t.,* Ukrainian S.S.R.; engin., chemicals, textiles; p. (1967) *135,000*. [m. long.

Sunart, Loch *sea arm,* Argyll cst., W. Scot.; 19½

Sunbury-on-Thames, *urb. dist.,* Middx., Eng.; W. of London; residtl., water wks., gravel pits; petrol research establishment; p. (1961) *33,437*.

Sunda Strait, between Java and Sumatra, Indonesia; 13 m. wide, contains the volcanic I. of Krakatao.

Sundarbans, The, *tract of forest and swamps,* fringing the delta of the Ganges, E. Pakistan; 165 m. long, 81 m. wide; rice grown in N.; tigers and crocodiles found in S.

Sunday I., lgst. of Kermadec Is., N.Z.; 20 m. in circuit and with a p. of *10* is the only one of the Kermadec Is. that is inhabited; met. and radio sta. established on I. [Algoa Bay; 200 m. long.

Sunday, *R.,* Cape Prov., S. Africa; flows into

Sunderland, *spt., co. bor.,* Durham, Eng.; at mouth of R. Wear; gr. shipbldg. and coal-exp. ctr. (inc. Monkwearmouth and parts of Bishopwearmouth), best gas coal, also engin., glass, paper and rope; fine harbour, piers and docks; p. (estd. 1967) *219,270*.

Sundsvall, *spt.,* Västernorrland, Sweden; on a wide bay of the Baltic nr. Hernösand; timber and wood-pulp inds.; p. (1961) *29,493*.

Sungari, *R.,* N. China; trib. of R. Amur; inc. the Nonni; length over 1,000 m.

Sungpan, *t.,* Szechwan, China; silver, gold, lead; linseed oil, paper; smelting, engin.

Superior, *c.,* Wis., U.S.A.; at head of L. Superior; gr. tr. in grain, timber, coal, shipbldg. and flour mills; oil refining; p. (1960) *33,563*.

Superior, *L.,* N. America; lgst. sheet of fresh water in the world; lies between Canada and the U.S.A.; one of the chain of gr. Ls. in the St. Lawrence system; outlet to L. Huron by the St. Mary's R., receives the waters of the St. Louis, Pigeon and Nipigon; a. 32,000 sq. m.

Surat, *c.,* Gujarat, India; on R. Tapti; cotton, silk, embroidery; p. (1961) *288,026*.

Surbiton, *former mun. bor.,* Surrey, Eng., on R. Thames, nr. Kingston; now inc. in Royal Borough of Kingston-upon-Thames (*q.v.*); residtl.; light engin., bricks, tiles, elec. components; p. (1961) *62,940*.

Suresnes, *t.,* Seine, France; p. (1962) *40,151*.

Surinam, *R.,* Neth. Guiana, S. America; flows N. to Atl. Oc. nr. Paramaribo; length 300 m.

Surinam (Neth. Guiana), *Dutch col.,* S. America; ch. exp. bauxite, timber, rubber, rice, fruit; cap. Paramaribo; a. 55,000 sq. m.; p. (estd.) *375,000*.

Surinumu Dam, 30 m. from Port Moresby, Papua; part of hydro-elec. scheme; opened 1963.

Surrey, *S. co.,* Eng.; S. of R. Thames; cereals, livestock, vegetables; residtl.; a. 722 sq. m.; p. (1966) *977,000*.

Surry, Va., U.S.A.; nuclear power sta. being built on James R.

Sus, *R.,* S. prov. Morocco, N. Africa; flowing to the Atlantic nr. Agadir; length 130 m.

Susa, *see* Sousse.

Susquehanna, *R.,* N.Y., Penns., and Md., U.S.A.; flows to Chesapeake Bay through highly industl. a.; routeway, W. from Philadelphia and Baltimore across Appalachian Mtns.; length 422 m.

Sussex, *maritime co.,* S.E. Eng.; adjoining Surrey, Kent and Hants, and washed by Eng. Channel; traversed E. to W. by the S. Downs; co. t. Lewes; a. 1,457 sq. m.; divided administratively into Sussex E. p. (1966) *710,000* and Sussex W. p. (1966) *450,000*.

Susten Pass, *modern alpine road,* alt. 7,296 ft., between Haslital and Reuss valley, links Bernese Oberland with Gotthard road.

Sutherland, *N. co.,* Scot.; N.W. Moray Firth, washed by Atlantic and N. Sea; grazing and forest land, most sparsely pop. in Scot.; mountainous, with many lochs; co. t. Dornoch; a. 2,102 sq. m.; p. (1961) *13,442*.

Sutlej, *R.,* West Pakistan; rises in the Himalayas and flows to the R. Indus; used for lge.-scale irrigation; length 1,000 m.

Sutton, *outer bor.,* Greater London, Eng.; inc. former bors. of Beddington and Wallington, Sutton and Cheam, and Carshalton; p. (1966) *166,000*.

Sutton Coldfield, *t., mun. bor.,* Warwick, Eng.; 6 m. N.E. of Birmingham; hardware, plastics; television transmitter; p. (estd. 1967) *81,630*.

Sutton-in-Ashfield, *t., urb. dist.,* Notts, Eng.; 3 m. S.W. of Mansfield; coal, light engin.; hosiery; p. (estd. 1967) *40,630*.

Suva, *c., cap.,* Fiji Is.; on Viti Levu I., fine harbour; p. (estd. 1965) *38,000*.

Suwalki, *t.,* N.E. Poland; nr. Lithuanian S.S.R. bdy.; timber, grain, woollens; p. (1965) *22,000*.

Suwannee, *R.,* Fla., and Ga., U.S.A.; flows to G. of Mexico; known as "Swanee River." length 250 m.

Svendborg, *spt.,* Fyn, Denmark; mnfs., earthenware, tobacco, exp. butter; p. (1960) *23,892*.

Sverdlovsk, *t.,* R.S.F.S.R.; on R. Iset, at E. base of the Ural Mtns.; steel, engin., chemicals, textiles; p. (1967) *940,000*. [of White Sea.

Sviatoi Nos, *C.,* Arctic cst., U.S.S.R.; nr. entrance

Svir, *R.,* U.S.S.R.; flowing between L. Onega and L. Ladoga; length 125 m.

Svistov, *t.,* Bulgaria; on R. Danube, Romanian border; p. (1956) *18,448*.

Svobodnyy, *t.,* R.S.F.S.R.; on R. Zeya, 105 m. N. of Blagoveshchensk; agr. equipment, sawmilling; p. (1959) *57,000*.

Svolær, *spt.,* Norway; ch. t. Lofoten Is.; fishing; p. (1961) *3,321*.

Swabia, *dist.,* Bavaria, Germany; a. 3,807 sq. m.; cap. Augsburg.

Swabian Alps, *mtns.*, Württemberg, Germany; inc. the Swabian Jura range between valleys of Neckar and Danube.

Swadlincote, *t.*, *urb. dist.*, Derby, Eng.; 3 m. E. of Burton-on-Trent; collys., potteries, engin., clothing; p. (1961) *19,222*.

Swaffham, *mkt. t.*, *urb. dist.*, Norfolk, Eng.; forestry; p. (1961) *3,210*. [R. Ouse; length 60 m.

Swale, *R.*, N.R. Yorks, Eng.; joins R. Ure to form

Swale, *channel*, between I. of Sheppey and Kentish mainland, Eng.; 16 m. long.   [nr. Perth.

Swan, *R.*, W. Australia; flows to Indian Ocean,

Swan Hill, *t.*, Victoria, Australia; fruit growing and dairying under irrigation; canning; p. (1966) *7,376*.

Swanage, *mkt. t.*, *urb. dist.*, Dorset, Eng.; on bay, E. cst. I. of Purbeck; seaside resort; stone quarries; p. (1961) *8,112*.

Swanland, *region*, W. Australia; consists of extreme S.W. corner of W. Australia; hot, dry summers and mild winter with adequate rain; forests of Karri and Jarrah; agr. vines, citrus and deciduous fruits, wheat; highest pop. density in W. Australia; ch. ts. Perth, Fremantle, Bunbury.

Swansea, *c.*, *spt.*, Glamorgan, Wales; on Swansea Bay, Bristol Channel; univ. coll.; coal and iron, copper, steel, zinc, chemicals; lge. exp. anthracite, aluminium wire and cable, refrigerators; p. (1961) *166,740*.

Swat, *dist.*, Malakand, N.W. Frontier, W. Pakistan.

Swatow (Shantou), *c.*, *spt.*, Kwangtung, S. China; on S.E. cst. nr. mouth of Han Kiang, 200 m. N.E. of Hong Kong; gd. harbour; fishing; sm. coastal tr., mainly with Hong Kong; exp. tangerines; p. (1953) *280,000*.

Swaziland, *indep. kingdom* within Brit. Commonwealth (Sept. 1968), S. Africa; S.E. of the Transvaal; agr., sugar, citrus, cotton, rice; iron ore and coal-mng., hydroelectr. power; timber and pulp ind.; asbestos, gold, tin, barytes; cap. Mbabane; a. 6,704 sq. m.; p. (estd.) *395,000*.

Sweden, *kingdom*, N. Europe; forming E. (and larger) part Scandinavian Peninsula; mountainous W., but otherwise flat and dissected by Rs. and many Ls., while one-fourth of the land is forest; gr. timber exp. and mining of iron ore, lead, silver, arsenic; cereals, root crops, hay, livestock, paper, pulp, steel, shipbldg., textiles, matches, machin., glass, chemicals, ceramics, furniture, cap. Stockholm; a. 173,426 sq. m.; p. (1968) *7,893,704*.

Swidnica (Schweidnitz), *t.*, Lower Silesia, Poland; German before 1945; textiles, machin.; p. (1965) *44,000*.

Swift Current, *t.*, Saskatchewan, Canada; p. (1961) *12,186*

Swilly, Lough, *arm of the Atlantic*, cst. of Donegal, Ireland; 25 m. long.

Swindon, *t.*, *mun. bor.*, Wilts, Eng.; in upper Thames Valley (Vale of White Horse), 27 m. S.W. of Oxford; gr. rly. wks.; impt. riy. junction; mkt. for local dist.; heavy engin., textiles, tobacco, cars; p. (estd. 1967) *97,920*.

Swinoujscie (Swinemünde), *spt.*, Pomerania, Poland, German before 1945; on I. of Usedom (Uznam), Baltic Sea; spt. for Szczecin; spa and summer resort; p. (1965) *22,000*.

Swinton, *t.*, *urb. dist.*, W.R. Yorks, Eng.; in Don valley, 3 m. N.E. of Rotherham; coal, iron, potteries, bricks and tiles; p. (1961) *13,420*.

Swinton and Pendlebury, *mun. bor.*, Lancs, Eng.; 5 m. W. of Manchester; cotton spinning, coal, engin., accumulator mftg.; p. (estd. 1967) *40,760*.

Switzerland, *fed. rep.*, Cen. Europe; upland region, with Jura Mtns. on N. and Alps to S.; dairying, butter, cheese, chocolate, etc., wine; watches and clocks, elec. machin.; very dependent on lge. tourist tr.; 4 national languages; cap. Bern; a. 15,944 sq. m.; p. (1968) *6,115,000*.

Sydenham, *S.E.*, *sub.*, London, Eng.; residtl.; site of the Crystal Palace, burnt down 1936.

Sydney, *c.*, *cap.*, N.S.W., Australia; principal spt. on shore of Pt. Jackson Bay; many beautiful bdlgs. and parks, stretching S. to Botany Bay; univ.; lge. comm. and active inds.; magnificent bridge, harbour and docks; six-lane highway bridge under construct. oil refinery under construction; p. (1966) *2,444,735*.

Sidney or S. Sydney, *spt.*, C. Breton I., Nova Scotia; iron and steelwks., coal, chemicals; p. (1956) *32,162*.

Sydney Mines, *t.*, Nova Scotia, Canada; coal; p. [(1961) *9,122*.

Syktyvkar, *t.*, R.S.F.S.R.; on Vychegda R.; sawmilling, engin.; p. (1959) *64,000*.

Syra, *I.* of the Cyclades, Ægean Sea; part of Greece; p. (1951) *33,775*.

Syracusa, *t.*, Sicily, Italy; on I. of Ortygia, off E. cst.; cath.; exp. olive oil, oranges, lemons, locust beans, almonds, wine, chemicals, pottery, etc; chemicals at Priolo; p. (1961) *90,333*.

Syracuse, *c.*, N.Y., U.S.A.; air conditioners, electronic equipment, jet engines; chemicals, salt, machin., cars, seat of Syracuse Univ.; p. (1960) *216,038*.   [into Aral sea.

Syr Darya, *R.*, Kazakhstan, U.S.S.R.; flowing

Syrian Arab Republic, *rep.*, S.W. Asia; seceded from United Arab Rep. 28 Sept. 1961; stretches along E. shore of Mediterranean and E. to the R. Euphrates; chiefly agr.; cereals, olives, fruit, goats, sheep; silk, wool, cement, soap; oil; pipeline from Karachok fields to Homs and Tartus; phosphate deposits; cap. Damascus; a. 70,800 sq. m.; p. (estd. 1970) *6,294,000*.

Syzran, *t.*, R.S.F.S.R.; on R. Volga; petroleum refining, engin.; p. (1967) *167,000*.

Szarvas, *t.*, Hungary, S. of Mezőtur; industl.; p. (1962 *18,950*.   [sq. m.; p. (1965) *848,000*.

Szczecin, *prov.*, Poland; cap. Szczecin; a. 12,100

Szazhalombatta, *t.*, Hungary, on R. Danube, 15 m. S. of Budapest; lgst. oil refinery in Hungary; oil supplied through Druzhba pipeline.

Szczecin (Stettin), *spt.*, Pomerania, Poland, German before 1945; at mouth of R. Odra (Oder); cas.; engin., iron, textiles, paper; p. (1965) *310,000*.

Szczecinek (formerly German Neustettin), *t.*, W. Polish Pomerania; p. (1965) *26,000*.

Szechwan (Sichuan), *prov.*, China; cereals, sugar, tea, cotton, silk, coal, iron, salt, petrol; cap. Chengtu; a. 144,996 sq. m.; p. (1953) *62,303,999*.

Szeged, *t.*, Hungary; on Theiss R., 100 m. S.E. of Budapest; univ.; cath.; gr. comm. and industl. ctr.; leather, breweries, textiles; oil nearby at Tape; natural gas pipeline from deposit under oilfield; p. (1965) *113,000*.

Székesfehérvár, *t.*, Hungary; nr. Budapest; aluminium and metal processing; radios, cycles; p. (1962) *57,757*.

Szentes, *t.*, Hungary; p. (1962) *30,979*.

Szeping (Siping), *c.*, Kirin prov., China; agr. distributing ctr.; cement; p. (1953) *126,000*.

Szolonok, *t.*, Hungary; on R. Tisza, E. of Budapest; machin., paper ind., cellulose, chemicals; p. (1962) *47,919*.

Szombathely, *t.*, Hungary; cath.; rly. ctr.; textiles, tanning, shoe mkg.; p. (1962) *55,849*.

Szőny, *t.*, Hungary; oil refining, linked to U.S.S.R. by " Friendship Oil Pipeline; " p. (1962) *4,600*.

T

Taasinge, *I.*, Denmark; S. of Fyn; 9 m. long; p. (1960) *4,866*.   [charcoal; fishing; p. *1,500*.

Tabarka, *spt.*, Tunisia; mkt. exp. cork, tanning,

Tabasco, *maritime st.*, Mexico; on Bay of Campeche, adjoining Guatemala; cacao, sugarcane, tobacco, rubber, pepper, maize, rice and hard-woods; cap. Villa Hermosa; a. 9,782 sq. m.; p. (1960) *496,340*.   [and Amazon.

Tabatinga, *t.*, Brazil; on junction of Rs. Javari

Table Bay, *inlet of Atlantic*, cst. of C. of Gd. Hope, S. Africa; site of Cape Town.

Table Mountain, Cape Prov., S. Africa, nr. Cape Town; alt. 3,549 ft.

Tabor, *t.*, ČSSR.; S. of Prague, on R. Luznice; cigars, beer; p. (1961) *19,561*.

Tábor, Mt., N. Palestine; S.E. of Nazareth.

Tabora, *t.*, Central Tanzania; E. Africa; at junction of rlys. from Dar es Salaam and L. Victoria; agr.; p. (1960) *15,350*.

Tabriz, *c.*, Iran, cap. E. Azerbaijan; metal inds., machine tool complex projected; famous blue mosque; airpt.; p. (1967) *806,631*.

Tachira, *st.*, Venezuela, S. America; cap. San Cristobal; p. (1961) *399 163*.

Tacna, *dep.*, Peru; terr. transferred by treaty from Chile, 1929; mainly desert; nitrate of soda, silver, copper; subject to earthquakes; a. 4,930 sq. m.; ch. t. T.; p. (1961) *69,176*.

Tacna, *t.*, Peru, airport.; p. (1961) *18,000*.

Tacoma, *spt.*, Wash., U.S.A.; on Puget Sound;

shipping, fishing, iron, steel, copper, electro-chemicals, aluminium; p. (1960) *147,979*.

Tacuarembó, *dep.* Uruguay, S. America; a. 8,112 sq. m.; cap. Tacuarembó; p. (1963) *19,658*.

Tadcaster, *rural dist.*, *mkt. t.*, on R. Wharfe, W.R. Yorks, Eng.; brewing, stone, paper board; p. (rural dist. 1961) *26,725*.

Tadmor, *see* Palmyra.

Tadoussac, *t.*, Quebec, Canada; on R. Saguenay where it enters St. Lawrence R.; tourist ctr.; oldest settlement in Canada (1599).

Tadzhik, *constituent rep.*, U.S.S.R., cereals, cotton, fruit, horticulture, cattle breeding; minerals, gold, petroleum, coal; magnetic iron ore prospecting in the Kara Mazar mtns.; cap. Dushanbe; a. 55,700 sq. m.; p. (1970) *2,900,000*.

Taegu, *c.*, S. Korea; silk-spinning and cotton-ginning mills; nylon yarn; p. (1962) *717,000*.

Taejon, *t.*, S. Korea; S. of Seoul; fish, petroleum, cereals; p. (1962) *269,000*.

Taff, *R.*, Glamorgan, Brecknock, Wales; rises in Brecon Beacons, flows S.E. across coalfield to Bristol Channel at Cardiff; length 40 m.

Tafilalet, Morocco, N. Africa; oasis of the Sahara, E. of Atlas; ch. t. Abuam; dates.

Taganrog, *spt.*, R.S.F.S.R.; on Sea of Azov; steel, engin.; p. (1959) *201,000*.

Tagliamento, *R.*, N.E. Italy; rises in Carnic Alps, flows S. into Adriatic Sea (G. of Venice); valley used by rly. from Venice to Vienna via Semmering Pass; length 100 m.

Tagus, *R.*, Spain and Portugal; flows W. across Meseta to Atlantic at Lisbon; length 540 m.

Tahiti, *principal I.*, of Society gr, French Polynesia; Pac. Oc.; fertile cst. land, picturesque; a. 402 sq. m.; cap. Papeete; p. (1962) *45,430*.

Tahoe, *L.*, Cal, Nevada, U.S.A.; in Yosemite National Park, Sierra Nevada, at alt. 6,225 ft., surrounded by summer resorts; a. 200 sq. m.

Taichow (Taizhou), *c.*, Kiangsu prov., China; rice ctr.; p. (1953) *160,000*.

Taif, *t.*, Hejaz, Saudi Arabia; 75 m. E. of Mecca; on plateau 5,000 ft. high; walled t.; gardens, vineyards; summer admin. ctr. of the Hejaz; p. *25,000*.

Taihape, *t.*, N.I., N.Z.; 161 m. N.E. of Wellington; in the King Country, on Hautapu R.; sheep and dairy farming, saw-milling; p. (1961) *2,684*.

Tai Hu, *L.*, Kiangsu, China; focus of intensive system of sm. canals and waterways 60 m. N. of Shanghai; a. approx. 100 sq. m.

Taima, *t.*, Saudi Arabia; cereals, dates, fruit, tobacco, rock salt.

Taimyr Peninsula, N. cst., Siberia. U.S.S.R.; terminates with C. Chelyuskin.

Tainan, *t.*, Taiwan, China; sugar, rice; p. (1957) *229,500*.

Taipeh (Taipei), *c.*, cap. Taiwan; admin., cultural and industl. ctr. of I.; p. (1968) *1,608,213*.

Taiping, *t.*, Perak, W. Malaya; resort; p. *48,000*.

Taiwan (Formosa), *I.*, China, 100 m. E. of mainland; U.S.A. protection; fishing, rice, tea, sugar, coal, gold, oil, natural gas, textiles; cap. Taipeh; a. 13,890 sq. m.; p. (1970) *14,312,000*.

Taiyuan, *c.*, Shansi, China; on Fuen-Ho; p. (1953) *721,000*.   [p. (1965) *243,444*.

Takamatsu, *t.*, Japan; N. cst. Shikoku; gr. tr.;

Takaoka, *t.*, Honshu, Japan; ctr. of rice tr.; lacquer wk.; cars; p. (1965) *140,000*.

Takapuna, *c.*, N.I., N.Z.; p. (1966) *23,098*.

Takasaki, *t.*, Honshu, Japan; coal mines, raw silk; radiation chemistry research ctr.; p. (1965) *174,000*.

Takhnan, *t.*, Cambodia; tyres.

Takoradi, *spt.* Ghana, West Africa; as spt. has superseded Sekondi; rly. to Kumasi thence to Accra; exp. cocoa, palm-oil, rubber, bauxite, gold, manganese, industl. gases; p. (1960) *41,000*.

Talara, *t.*, N. Peru, S. America; on C. Pariñas; oil refining; p. (1961) *40,000*.

Talavera, *c.*, Spain; on Tagus R.; cloth, leather, wine; p. (1957) *22,152*.

Talca, *prov.*, Chile; cap. Talca; a. 3,721 sq. m.; p. (1961) *226,052*.

Talca, *t.*, cap. Talca prov., Chile; S. of Santiago; lge. mftg. ctr.; matches, footwear, paper and flour mills, foundries; p. (1961) *80,277*.

Talcahuano, *spt.*, Chile, nr. Concepción; naval sta.; grain and exp. ctr.; steel plant at Huachipato; p. (1961) *99,231*.

Talence, *t.*, Gironde, France; p. (1962) *26,911*.

Talien (Dairen), *c.*, *spt.*, S. Liaoning prov., China; on Liaotung pen., Bay of Korea; together with

Port Arthur adm. as part of special mun. of Luta *(q.v.)*; p. (estd. 1957) *1,508,000*.

Tallahassee, *c.*, Fla., U.S.A.; cigars; p. (1960) *48,174*.

Tallahatchee, *R.*, trib. of Miss., U.S.A.; flows S.W. and becomes R. Yazoo; length 240 m.

Tallin, *spt.*, *cap.*, Estonian S.S.R., U.S.S.R.; timber, shipbldg., textiles; p. (1967) *335,000*.

Taltal, *spt.*, Chile; S. of Antofagasta; exp. nitrates and silver; p. (1961) *5,897*.

Tamale, *ch. t.*, Northern Terr., Ghana, W. Africa; aerodrome; p. (1960) *49,223*.

Tamar, *R.*, Devon and Cornwall, Eng.; flows S. to Plymouth Sound; length 45 m.

Tamar, *R.*, Tasmania, Australia; formed at confluence of North Esk and South Esk at Launceston, flows into Bass Strait nr. Georgetown.

Tamatave, *ch. pt.* Madagascar, on Indian Oc.; exp. graphite, rice, chromite ore; oil refinery; p. (1959) *48,627*.

Tamil Nadu *(formerly* Madras*)*, *st.*, India; rice, millet, oilseeds, cotton, indigo. spices, tobacco, tea; fertilisers; ch. ts. Madras, Madurai, Tiruchirapalli; a. 50,331 sq. m.; p. (1961) *33,686,953*.

Tamaulipas, *st.*, Mexico; on G. of Mexico, S. of Texas; nitrates, cereals, sugar, coffee, cattle, petroleum; cap. Ciudad Victoria; a. 30,731 sq. m.; p. (1960) *1,024,182*.

Tambov, *t.*, R.S.F.S.R.; on R. Oka; synthetic rubber, engin. chemicals; p. (1959) *170,000*.

Tampa, bay on W. cst. Fla., U.S.A.; 40 m. long.

Tampa, *c.*, Fla., U.S.A.; popular winter resort, cigar factories, phosphates, electronics; fruit growing and canning; p. (1960) *274,970*.

Tampere (Tammerfors), *t.*, S. Finland; on rly. between Helsinki and Vaasa; textiles, leather, paper; p. (1966) *144,175*.

Tampico, *spt.*, Mexico; on the R. Panuco, 9 m. from the G. of Mexico; fruits, sugar. maize; p. (1960) *122,197*.   [length 200 m.

Tampico, *R.*, Mexico, flows to G. of Mexico;

Tamworth, *t.*, N.S.W., Australia; on R. Peel; milling; ch. comm. ctr. of Northern Table land; bldg. inds., agr. engin.; p. (1966) *21,682*.

Tamworth, *t.*, *mun. bor.*, Staffs, Eng.; on R. Tame, 5 m. S.E. of Lichfield; ancient cas.; coal, light engin.; p. (estd. 1967) *34,600*.

Tana, *lge. L.*, N. Ethiopia, nr. Gondar, source of Blue Nile, 45 m. long, 40 m. wide; surrounded by marsh, papyrus swamp.

Tana, *R.*, forming part of bdy. between Finland and Norway, flows into Arctic Ocean.

Tana R., *ch. R.*, Kenya, E. Africa.

Tananarive, *c.*, *cap.*, Madagascar; ctr. of commerce, communications and tourism; univ.; p. (1965) *254,000*.

Tanaro, *R.*, N. Italy; trib. of R. Po; 125 m. long.

Tandil, *t.*, Argentina; resort; granite quarried nearby; p. (1960) *70,000*.

Tandjoengbalai, *spt.*, Sumatra, Indonesia; exp. tobacco, copra, shipyards.

Tanga, *spt.*, Tanzania, E. Africa; rly. terminus; on plateau overlooking Tanga Bay; hydroelec. sta; p. *38,000*.

Tanganyika, *gr. L.*, E. Central Africa; 400 m. long, greatest width 45 m. ; a. about 12,700 sq. m.; 2,800 ft. above sea; discovered by Burton and Speke in 1868, and later explored by Livingstone, Stanley and others.

Tanimbal Is., S. Moluccas, Indonesia; gr. of 66 islands; forests, swamps; maize, rice, coconuts, sago; p. *31,847*.

Tangier, *free pt.*, Morocco, N. Africa; on Strait of Gibraltar; no longer internationalised zone but integral part of kingdom of Morocco; summer cap.; shipyd.; cigarettes, fishing; p. of t. (1960) *141,714*.

Tangshan, *c.*, Hopeh prov., China; mun. limits incl. whole Kailan coal mng. a.; p. (1953) *693,000*.

Tanta, *t.*, Lower U.A.R.; 55 m. N. of Cairo; impt. rly. junction; religious fairs; p. (1960) *184,000*.

Tanzania, United Rep. of, *indep. sov. st.*, E. Africa; within Brit. Commonwealth; comprising former sts. of Tanganyika and Zanzibar; climate tropical, varies with elevation; ch. prod., sisal, coffee, cotton, groundnuts, pyrethrum, copra, cloves, ebony, hardwoods; sugar mill and refinery projected in Kilombero Valley; diamond deposits discovered nr. Kahama, 80 m. N. of Tabora; cap. Dar es Salaam; a. 362,870 sq. m.; p. (1967) *12,311,991*.

Tapachula, *ch. t.,* S. Mexico; coffee, cattle, tobacco, sugar refineries, sawmills; p. (1940) *43,032.*

Tapajóz, *R.,* trib. of R. Amazon.

Tapti, *R.,* W. India; flows W. to G. of Cambay at Surat from Betul dist., Madhya Pradesh; length 450 m.

Tapungato. *mtn.,* W. Argentina; alt. 22,300 ft.

Taquari, *R.,* Brazil; trib. of R. Paraguay; length 400 m.   [length 200 m.

Tara, *R.,* Siberia, R.S.F.S.R.; trib. of R. Irtysh.

Tarakan, *spt.,* Borneo, Indonesia; on Tarakan I.; oil; p. (of I.) *12,000.*

Taranaki, *prov.,* N.I., N.Z.; a. 3,750 sq. m.; [p. (1961) *99,721.*

Taranto, *t.,* Lecce, Italy; on G. of Taranto, inlet of Ionian Sea; maritime arsenal with gr. comm. and industl. interests; strong cas.; cottons, velvets, soap, oil; steel wks.; cement; oil refinery; famous for its oyster and mussel fisheries; p. (1964) *205,000.*

Tarapaca, *prov.,* N. Chile; nitrates, silver; cap. Iquique; a. 21,340 sq. m.; p. (1960) *133,775.*

Tarapore, *t.,* Maharashtra, India; 62 m. N. of Bombay; atomic power sta.

Tarascon, *t.,* Bouches-du-Rhône, France; connected by bridges with Beaucaire on opposite bank of R. Rhône; old cas. famous festival; silk and fruit; p. (1962) *8,910.*

Tarawera Mtn., *volcanic peak,* N.I., N.Z.; c. 1,000 ft.; in Hot Springs dist.; eruption in 1866 destroyed L. Rotomahana (water later returned to form bigger and deeper L.).

Tarbat Ness, *promontory,* N. Side of Moray Firth, Ross and Cromarty, Scot.

Tarbela Dam, W. Pakistan; on R. Indus 30 m. upstream from Attack and 40 m. N.W. of Rawalpindi; projected.

Tarbes, *t., cap.,* Hautes-Pyrénées, France; on R. Adour; cath., paper, flax, woollens, machin., metals, aircraft, leather; p. (1962) *50,715.*

Taree, *t.,* N.S.W., Australia; dairying, agr., fishing, timber and fibre-boards; p. (1966) *10,559.*

Târgu-Jiu, *t.,* Romania; coal, petroleum, timber; p. *17,698.*

Târgul-Mures, *t.,* Romania; on R. Maros; famous old fort, with Gothic Calvinist cath., where in 1571 religious liberty was promulgated for the first time in Europe; gd. tr.; p. (1945) *41,118.*

Tarifa, *c.,* Spain; on Gibraltar Strait; most S. point of mainland of Europe; fish tr., cereals, oranges, wines; p. (1957) *18,098.*

Tarija, *prov.,* Bolivia; cap. Tarija; a. 24,786 sq. m.; p. (1962) *142,600.*

Tarija, *t., cap.,* Tarija prov., Bolivia; S.E. of Potosi; maize, wheat, vines; p. (1962) *20,851.*

Tarma, *t.,* Peru, S. America; alt. 9,980 ft.; maize, cotton, oranges, bananas; p. (1961) *7,860.*

Tarn, *R.,* France; trib. of R. Garonne; has famous rocky gorge 31 m. long in its upper course; length 235 m.

Tarn, *dep.,* S. France, watered by Tarn and its tribs.; wheat and wine; cap. Albi; a. 2,232 sq. m.; p. (1968) *332,011.*

Tarn-et-Garonne, *dep.,* W. France; corn, wine, woollens, paper, silk; cap. Montauban; a. 1,440 sq. m.; p. (1968) *183,572.*

Tarnow, *t.,* Poland; E. of Kraków; agr.; farm implements, glass; industl. development since 1950; p. (1965) *77,000.*

Tarragona, *prov.,* Spain; on the Mediterranean; vineyards and agr.; cap. Tarragona; a. 2,426 sq. m.; p. (1959) *364,075.*

Tarragona, *fortfd. spt.,* cap. Tarragona, Spain; at mouth of R. Franconi; mnfs. alcohol, liqueurs, chocolate, paper, silk, fish-salting; p. (1957) *42,000.*

Tarrasa, *t.,* Barcelona, Spain; in fruit and vine-growing dist.; royal college; thriving inds.; p. (1959) *86,469.*

Tarsus, *ancient c.,* Turkey; nr. Adana, opposite Cilician Gates; orange and citron groves; ruined Roman temple; birthplace of Apostle Paul; exp. cotton, wool, hides; p. (1965) *57,035.*

Tartary or **Tatary,** *region,* Central Asia; now divided into Chinese or E. Turkestan, and W. Turkestan, U.S.S.R.

Tartary, Gulf of, *arm of the Sea of Japan,* separating Sakhalin from the Siberian mainland.

Tartu (formerly **Dorpat**), *t.,* Estonian S.S.R.; univ.; saw milling, engin.; p. (1959) *74,000.*

Tarudant, *t.,* Morocco, N. Africa; mkt., orange water, leather, pottery, copper, brass; p. *12,877.*

Tashkent, *cap.,* Uzbek. S.S.R. on Syr Darya R.; univ.; extensive silk mnfs.; engin; pipeline from Gazil natural gas field; p. (1967) *1,127,000.*

Tasman Bay, *lge. inlet,* S.I., N.Z.; penetrates N. cst., between Separation Point and D'Urville I.; enclosed by mtns., sheltered, fertile, coastal fringe; ch. ts. Nelson, Motueka.   [the world.

Tasman Glacier, S.I., N.Z.; one of the lgst. in

Tasmania (formerly Van Diemen's Land), *I., st.,* Australia; plateau with fertile valleys; temperate climate; forest and grasslands, grain, fruit, cattle-raising; aluminium, copper, zinc, lead, tin, silver; electro-metallurgical inds.; cap. Hobart: a. 26,383 sq. m.; p. (estd. 1968) *386,000.*

Tatar, A.S.S.R., U.S.S.R.; oil, natural gas; ch. t. Kazan on R. Volga; p. (1956) *2,847,000.*

Tatra Mtns. (High Tatra), highest Carpathian gr., Czechoslovakia, alt. 8,743 ft.

Tatung (Datong), *c.,* Shansi prov., China: impt. coalfield; p. (1953) *229,000.*

Taubaté, *t.,* São Paulo st., Brazil; industl. ctr.; p. (1960) *64,863.*

Tauber, *R.,* Germany; trib. of R. Main; l. 74 m.

Taunton, *co. t., mun. bor.,* Somerset, Eng.; on R. Tone at W. end of Vale of Taunton; old cas.; apples, cider, clothing tr., engin., plastics; p. (estd. 1967) *37,180.*   [ries; p. (1960) *41,132.*

Taunton. *c.,* Mass., U.S.A.; cotton, iron found-

Taunus, *mtn. range,* Hessen, Germany; between the R. Lahn and the Rs. Rhine and Main.

Taupo, *L.,* N.I., N.Z.; lgst. L. in N.Z.; geysers, hot springs in vicinity; 25 m. by 17 m.

Tauranga, *c.,* N.I., N.Z.; p. (1966) *23,390.*

Taurida or **Krim,** *dist.,* Crimean Peninsula, U.S.S.R., separated from Ukraine by Perekop Peninsula, divided by R. Salgir; a. 24,540 sq. m.; wheat, tobacco, fruit.

Taurus Mtns., *range,* S. Turkey.

Tavastehus (Häme), *dep.,* Finland; cap. Tavastehus; a. 7,118 sq. m.; p. (1958) *573,444.*

Tavistock, *mkt. t., urb. dist.,* Devon, Eng.; on R. Tavy, 12 m. N. of Plymouth; p. (1961) *6,086.*

Tavoy, *t.,* Burma; between Thailand and the Bay of Bengal, W. of Bangkok; rice, tin-mining.

Tavy, *R.,* Devon, Eng.; trib. of R. Tamar; length 20 m.

Taw, *R.,* Devon, Eng.; flows from Dartmoor to Barnstaple Bay; length 50 m.

Taxco, *t.,* Mexico; alt. 5,600 ft.; gold- and silver-mining; tourist ctr.; p. (1960) *10,076.* [jected.

Taxila, *t.,* W. Pakistan; heavy machin. wks. pro-

Tay, *R.,* Scot.; flows S.E. from Loch Tay in Perth to the Firth of Tay; longest R. in Scotland.

Tay Bridge, *rly. bridge,* E. Scot.; spans Firth of Tay from Wormit (Fife) to Dundee (Angus); carries main E. cst. rly. from Edinburgh to Aberdeen; length 2 m.; road bridge (longest in Britain) spanning R. at Dundee, opened 1966.

Tay, Firth of, *lge. inlet,* E. cst. Scot.; extends inland almost to Perth; length 27 m., max. width 3 m.

Tayabas, *t.,* Luzon, Philippines; on slope of extinct volcano Banajao; in rice- and coconut-growing dist.

Tayeh, *industl. t.,* Hupeh, China; lies to S. of Yangtze-Kiang, 42 m. S.E. of Wuhan; ctr. of very impt. iron-ore deposits; iron and steel inds., heavy engin.

Tayport, *burgh,* Fife, Scot.; at entrance to Firth of Tay; opposite Broughty Ferry; linen, jute; p. (1961) *3,151.*

Taz, *R.,* Siberia, R.S.F.S.R.; flows to Bay of Tazovsk in Gulf of Obi; length 300 m.

Tbilisi (Tiflis), *cap.,* Georgian S.S.R.; petroleum refining, engin., textiles; natural gas pipeline to Ordzhonikidze; p. (1965) *823,000.*

Tczew (Dirschau), *t.,* Pomerania, Poland; on R. Vistula; rly. wks., sugar, agr. implements; p. (1965) *37,000.*

Team Valley, Durham, Eng.; impt. trading estate has been developed here.

Te Aroha, *t.,* N.I., N.Z.; between Hamilton and Thames; one of the ch. resorts in the thermal springs dist.; p. (1961) *3,058.*

Te Awamutu, *t.,* N.I., N.Z.; S. of Hamilton agr. and dairying dist.; p. (1961) *5,423.*

Tebessa, *t.,* Algeria; alt. 2,789 ft.; mkt.; embroidery, carpets; phosphate deposits near by.

Tecuci, *t.,* Romania; N.W. of Galati; battle, 1476 (between Stephen the Great and the Turks); p. (1963) *27,326.*

Teddington, *S.W. sub.* of London, inc. in Greater London outer bor. of Richmond-upon-Thames; National Physical Laboratory; p. (1961) *13,455.*

Tedzhen, *R.*, Turkmenistan and N. Iran; flowing into Hari-Rud.

Tees, *R.*, N. Eng.; flows E. from Pennines to N. Sea between Yorks and Durham; length 70 m.

Teeside, *co. bor.*, N.R., Yorks. Eng.; formed by enlarged Middlesborough; p. (estd. 1968) *392,500.*

Teesport, *oil refinery*, between Redcar and Middlesbrough.

Tegal, *spt.*, Java, Indonesia; sugar; p. (1961) *89,016.*

Tegucigalpa, *c., cap.*, Honduras, central America; lies on R. Choluteca; alt. 3,200 ft. above sealevel; univ.; inter-ocean highway, connecting the t. with both Caribbean Sea and Pacific constructed; bananas, p. (1965) *154,000.*

Tehran, *cap. c.*, Iran, 70 m. due S. of Caspian Sea; mftg. and comm. ctr., incl. car assembly; modern bldgs. and hotels; gas pipeline to U.S.S.R. projected; nuclear ctr. for CENTO; intern. airpt.; p. of t. and dist. (1966) *2,695,000.*

Tehuantepec, *t.*, Mexico; on the Tehuantepec R., nr. the Pacific cst. of the Isthmus; once an Indian cap.; cath.; p. *10,087.*

Tehuantepec, Isthmus of, separates G. of Mexico from the Pacific at narrowest point of Mexico; width 130 m.

Teifi, *R.*, S.W. Wales; rises in Cambrian Mtns. nr. Strata Florida, flows S.W. and W. into Cardigan Bay 14 m. N.E. of Fishguard; forms bdy. between Cardigan and Carmarthen, Cardigan and Pembroke; sm. flannel ind. in ts. and vils. in lower valley; length 94 m.

Teign, *R.*, Devon, Eng.; flows to sea at Teignmouth from Dartmoor; length 30 m.

Teignmouth, *t., urb. dist.*, Devon, Eng.; at mouth of R. Teign, 13 m. S. of Exeter; resort; yacht-bldg.; p. (1961) *11,576.*

Tekirdag, *t.*, Turkey in Europe; on Sea of Marmara, W. of Istanbul; grain; p. (1965) *26,964.*

Tela, *spt.*, Honduras Central America; on Atlantic cst.; p. (1961) *13,408.*

Tel Aviv, *c.*, Israel, founded by Zionists, 1909; finan. ctr.; tourist resort; many mnfs.; p. with Jaffa (1960) *387,000.*

Telemark, *co.*, Norway; a. 5,837 sq. m.; p. (1968) *156,466.*

Telford, *new t.* (1963), Shropshire, 20 m. W. Wolverhampton; p. (estd. 1969) *70,000*; eventual p. *222,000.*

Tellicherry, *t., spt.*, Kerala, India; exp. coffee, cardamoms, sandalwood, and coconuts p.; (1961) *44,763.*

Telok Betong, *spt.*, Sumatra, Indonesia; exp. pepper, agr. products; p. *25,170.*

Tema, *new pt., t.* nr. Accra, Ghana, opened 1962; big industr. devel., incl. aluminium smelter, deep-water harbour, oil refinery.

Teme, *R.*, on border of Wales and Worcester, Eng.; trib. of R. Severn; length 70 m.

Temes, *R.*, S.W. Romania; flows to R. Danube, nr. Belgrade; length 180 m.

Temir-Tau, *t.*, Kazakh S.S.R.; iron, steel, synthetic rubber, soda; lge thermal power sta.; p. (1967) *147,000.*

Temperley, *t.*, nr Buenos Aires, Argentina; impt. rly. junction; p. (1960) *105,000.*

Temple, *rly. t.*, Texas, U.S.A.; in cotton-growing dist.; p. (1960) *30,419.*

Templemore, *mkt. t., urb. dist.*, Tipperary, Ireland; on R. Suir; p. (1966) *2,031.*

Temuco, *c., cap.* Cautin prov., Chile; cath.; cereals, apples, timber; p. (1961) *117,115.*

Tenasserim, *div.*, lower Burma; on Thailand border; tin rice; p. *2,110,420.*

Tenasserim, *t.*, lower Burma; on cst. at mouth of R. Tenasserim; length 250 m.; p. *10,000.*

Tenby, *mkt. t., mun. bor.*, Pembroke, Wales; on W. side of Carmarthen Bay, Bristol Channel; seaside resort; p. (1961) *4,752.*

Tenedos, *I.*, Ægean Sea; off W. cst. Turkey; 7 m. long; Turkish possession.

Tenerife, *I.*, Canary Is.; tourist resort; wheat, fruits, wines, oil refining; contains extinct volcanic peak of Tenerife; alt. 12,182 ft.; cap. Santa Cruz; a. 782 sq. m.; p. (1962) *394,466.*

Tengri-Nor, *L.*, Tibet; N.W. Lhasa; 80 m. long.

Tennessee. *R.*, Tenn., Ky.. U.S.A.; lgst. and most impt. branch of the Ohio; its valley once liable to flooding, now controlled by dams, and land improved by the Tennessee Valley Authority; length 782 m.

Tennessee. *S. central st.*, U.S.A.; between Mississippi R. and the Appalachian Mtns.; agr.:

cotton, pecans, sorghum, maize; oil, natural gas, lignite, cement, salt; inds.: chemicals, synthetic rubber, primary magnesium (from sea-water), steel wks.; cap. Nashville; ch. pt. Memphis; a. 42,244 sq. m.; p. (1970) *3,833,777.*

Tenos, *I.*, Greek Archipelago, Ægean Sea; one of the Cyclades.

Tenterden, *mkt., t. mun. bor.*, Kent, Eng.; 8 m. N. of Rye; church with famous 140 ft. tower.; p. (estd. 1967) *5,620.*

Teófilo Otoni, *t.*, Minas Gerais, Brazil; cattle; semi-precious stone polishing; p. (estd. 1968) *134,476.*

Tepic, *cap.*, Nayarit st., Mexico, p. *54,000.*

Teplice, *vat. pl.*, ČSSR., N.W. of Prague; textile and hardware inds.; p. (1961) *42,893.*

Teramo, *prov.*, Abruzzi, Italy; a. 1,067 sq. m.; cap. Teramo; p. (1961) *238,303.*

Teramo, *t.*, Italy; pottery and silks; ancient Interamnium; p. (1961) *41,629.*

Terek, *R.*, N. Caucasia, R.S.F.S.R.; flows to Caspian Sea; length 350 m.

Teresina, *t., cap.*, Piaui st., Brazil; comm. ctr.; light inds.; p. (estd. 1968) *184,836.*

Terezopólis, *t.*, Rio de Janeiro, Brazil; health resort; textiles; p. (estd. 1968) *69,636.*

Termini, *spt.*, Sicily, Italy; S.E. of Palermo; tunny fishing, macaroni, olive oil; wine, sulphur; p. *19,050.* [p. (estd.) *9,000.*

Ternate. Moluccas Is.. Indonesia; sago, spices;

Terneuzen, *t.*, Neth.; on W. Schelde R.; pipeline to be constructed to carry ethylene from Pernis; p. (1967) *20,029.*

Terni, *t.*, Perugia, Italy; amongst the Apennines; iron and steelwks., arms factory, jute; p. (1961) *94,015.*

Ternopil (Tarnopol), *t.*, Ukrainian S.S.R.; E. of Lvov; engin.; p. (1959) *52,000.*

Terranova, *t.*, Sardinia, Italy; on N.E. cst.; textiles, fishing; p. *10,157.*

Terre Adélie, name given to Fr. terr. and I. in Antarctic; estd. a. 160,000 sq. m.

Terre Haute, *c.*, Ind., U.S.A.; coal, natural gas, flour, paper, glass, foundries; p. (1960) *72,500.*

Terschelling, *I.*, Frisian Is., Neth.; at entrance to Zuyder Zee.

Teruel, *prov.*, S. Aragon, Spain; timber forests, coal, weaving, etc.; cap. Teruel; a. 5,721 sq. m.; p. (1959) *225,434.* [p. (1949) *19,047.*

Teruel, *t., cap.*, Teruel prov., on R. Turia; cath.;

Teslin Lake, S. of Yukon, N.W. Terr., Canada; source of R. Lewes. [Southampton Water.

Test or Anton, *R.*. Hants, Eng.; flows to head of

Tettenhall, *former urb. dist.*, Staffs, Eng.; absorbed in Wolverhampton (1966); p. (1961) *14,800.*

Tetuan, *ch. spt.*, Morocco, N. Africa; p. (1960) *101,352.*

Tetyukhe, *t.*, R.S.F.S.R.; on cst N.E. of Vladivostock; cadmium refinery; p. *5,000.*

Teutoburger Wald, *mtn. range*, Germany.

Teviot, *R.*, Roxburgh, Scot.; trib. of R. Tweed; length 37 m.

Tewkesbury, *mkt. t., mun. bor.*, Glos, Eng.; on R. Avon. 1 m. above confluence with R. Severn; milling, light engin.; p. (estd. 1967) *8,250.*

Texarkana, *c.*, Texas and Ark., U.S.A.; bdy. passes down middle of main street, timber and cotton region; rly. wkshps.; total p. (1960) *50,006.*

Texas, *st.*, S.W. U.S.A.; a. 263,644 sq. m.; prairie, mtns. in W.; chemicals, oil, gas, wood and leather products; meat pkg., fishing, mng.; agr. cotton; cap. Austin; ch. pt. Galveston; a. 267,339 sq. m.; p. (1970) *10,989,123.*

Texel, *I.*, W. Frisian Is., Neth.; a. 83 sq. m.; scene of several naval battles; p. (1967) *11,003.*

Tezcuco or Texocco, *L.*, Mexico; a. 77 sq. m.; less than 2 ft. deep; contains no fish.

Thailand (Siam), *kingdom*, S.E. Asia much jungle; hot, abundant summer rainfall; mainly agr.; rice, rubber, teak-wood, jute, maize; cotton, tobacco, iron ore, copper, tin, chem. fertilisers; cap. Bangkok; a. 200,418 sq. m. p. (1969) *34,738,000.* [steel plant.

Thai Nyuyen, *t.*, N. Vietnam, S.E. Asia; iron and

Thame, *mkt. t., urb. dist.*, Oxford, Eng.; on R. Thame, 7 m. S.W. of Aylesbury, p. (1961) *4,197.*

Thame, *R.*, trib. of R. Thames, Eng.; length 35 m.

Thames, *R.*, Eng.; rises in the Cotswold Hills, Glos. and flows past Oxford, Reading, Windsor and London to the Nore; length 210 m.

Thames, *R.*, Ontario, Canada; flows into L. St. Clair; length 160 m. [length 86 m.

Thames, *R.*, N.Z., flows N. to G. of Hauraki;

Thameshaven, *lge. oil refinery*, Essex, Eng.; on N. cst. of Thames estuary 8 m. below Tilbury.

Thanet, I. of, *lge. promontory*, N.E. extremity, Kent, Eng.; formed by bifurcation of R. Stour; contains Margate, Ramsgate and Broadstairs, with other seaside resorts.

Thanjavur, *t.*, Tamil Nadu, India; silks, carpets, jewellery, inlaid metals; impt. Brahman ctr.; p. (1961) *111,099*.

Thar Desert, on bdy. between India and W. Pakistan; covers slopes between N.W. Deccan and irrigated valley of R. Indus; completely barren, lack of Rs. or level land prevents irrigation; crossed only by caravan routes.

Tharawaddy, *dist.*, Pegu, Lower Burma; mainly forest, with rice fields in the clearings; a. 2,815 sq. m.; p. of *dist. 508,319*; of *t. 7,131*.

Thaton, *dist.*, Tennasserim div., Burma; rice and tobacco.

Thaya, *R.*, Austria; trib. of the R. March; length 130 m.

Thebes, *ruined ancient cap.*, Upper U.A.R.; on both banks of R. Nile; site now partly occupied by vils. Karnak and Luxor; impt. arch. discoveries in Valley of the Kings in 1923.

Theiss, *see* Tisa.

The Pas, *t.*, Manitoba, Canada; on R. Saskatchewan 80 m. upstream from L. Winnipegosis; rly. junction on line from Prairie Provs. to Churchill on Hudson Bay; branch line to Flin Flon.

Thera, *volcanic I.*, Greek archipelago, Ægean Sea; 10 m. long; cap. Thera.

Thermopylæ or Pylæ, celebrated pass between Mt. Æta and the sea, N.E. Greece; battle between Persians and Spartans, 480 B.C.

Thesprotia, *prefecture*, Epirus, Greece; cap. Hegoumenitsa; p. (1961) *52,075*.

Thessaloniki (Salonika), *prefecture*, Greece; p. (1961) *542,880*.

Thessaloniki, *t.*, Greece; at head of G. of Thessaloniki; woollens, soap, cottons, brewing, import and exp. tr.; oil refining; contains fiscal free zone; p. (1961) *250,920*.

Thessaly, *dist.*, Central Greece; containing two main prefectures, Larisa and Trikkala; horse-breeding; a. 5,208 sq. m.; p. (1961) *695,385*.

Thetford, *t.*, *mun. bor.*, Norfolk, Eng.; on Little R. Ouse; industl. estate for London overspill projected; fruit and vegetable canning, pulp mfg., engin.; p. (estd. 1967) *10,400*.

Thetford Mines, *t.*, Quebec, Canada; asbestos mining ctr.; p. (1956) *19,316*.

Thibodaux, *t.*, S.E. La., U.S.A.; comm. and mkt. ctr. for agr. dist.; petroleum; p. (1960) *13,043*.

Thielt, *t.*, Belgium; 17 m. W. of Ghent; lace, wool, cotton, linen; p. (1962) *3,732*.

Thiers, *t.*, Puy-de-Dôme, France; cutlery; p. (1962) *17,442*.

Thiès, *t.*, Senegal, W. Africa; rly. ctr. and wkshps.; groundnuts; p. (1957) *39,100*.

Thika, *t.*, Kenya, E. Africa; nylon processing.

Thimphu, *cap.*, Bhutan; hydro-elec. plant; 110 m. road-link to Phuntsholing (Sikkim), 1968.

Thionville, *t.*, Moselle, N. France; nr. Luxembourg border; fruit, vegetables, tanning, brewing; p. (1968) *37,079*.

Thirlmere, *L.*, Cumberland, Eng.; 3 m. long; furnishes part of the water supply of Manchester by a conduit of 96 m.

Thirsk, *mkt. t.*, *rural dist.*, N.R. Yorks, Eng.; in wide gap between Pennines and Cleveland Hills, 7 m. S.E. of Northallerton; flour; p. (rural dist. 1961) *13,060*.

Thisted, *t.*, Thyland, Denmark; on Lim Fjord; p. dairy prod., brewing; p. (1960) *8,768*.

Tholen, *I.*, S.W. Netherlands; a. 46 sq. m.; p. *15,000*.

Thok-Jalung, *t.*, Tibet; in Aling Kangri Mtns.; gold-mining ctr.

Thomar, *t.*, Portugal; paper, cheese; route ctr.; *11,333*.

Thomasville, *c.*, Ga., U.S.A.; cotton region; p. (1960) *18,246*.

Thompson, *R.*, B.C., Canada; rises in Monashee Mtns. flows S.W. into R. Frazer 140 m. upstream from Vancouver; valley forms impt. routeway used by trunk rlys. from Vancouver E. towards Yellowhead Pass (Canadian National Rly.) and Kicking Horse Pass (Canadian Pacific Rly.); length approx. 280 m.

Thompson, *t.*, Manitoba, Canada; nickel producing a.

Thonburi, *c.*, Thailand; industl. ctr.; rice and saw mills, fertilisers, tyres; p. (1964) *460,000*.

Thonon-les-Bains, *t.*, Haute Savoie, France; resort on L. Geneva; p. (1962) *18,501*.

Thorez, *t.*, Ukrainian S.S.R.; formerly Chistyakovo; coalmng.; p. (1959) *92,000*.

Thornaby-on-Tees, *t.*, *mun. bor.*, N.R. Yorks; opposite Stockton-on-Tees; iron and steel mnf., heavy engin., wire ropery, flour and sugar milling; p. (1961) *22,786*.

Thornbury, *mkt. t.*, *rural dist.*, Glos, Eng.; 10 m. N. of Bristol; aircraft mftg.; p. (rural dist. 1961) *30,685*.

Thornton Cleveleys, *t.*, *urb. dist.*, Lancs, Eng.; 4 m. N.E. of Blackpool; p. (estd. 1967) *24,430*.

Thórshavn, *cap.*, *pt.*, Faroe Is.; p. (1960) *7,447*.

Thousand Isles, *L.*, at outfall of L. Ontario; the islets really number 1,500–1,800, and are partly situated in N.Y. State and partly in Canada.

Thrace, ancient name of terr. in S.E. Europe, part of which has been added to Greece; successively under Macedonian, Roman, Byzantine and Turkish rule, before passing to Greece; tobacco; a. 3,315 sq. m.; p. (1961) *356,555*.

Three Kings, *gr. of Is.*, N. of N.Z.; plants and shrubs of extreme rarity. [of Benin.

Three Points, *c.*, Ghana; W. extremity of Bight

Three Rivers (Trois Rivières), *c.*, *pt.*, Quebec, Canada; at confluence of St. Maurice and St. Lawrence Rs.; wood-pulp mnf.; exp. grain, cattle; p. (1956) *50,483*.

Thule, N.W. Greenland; 1,000 m. from N. Pole; American air base and site of ballistic missile early warning sta.; spt. open 2–3 mths. p.a.

Thumba, Kerala, India; space science and technological ctr.

Thun, *L.*, Berne can., Switzerland; occupies valleys of R. Aar where it leaves Alpine region; separated from L. Brienz by deltaic neck of land on which is Interlaken; a. 38 sq. m.

Thun, *t.*, Berne, Switzerland; on N.W. end of L. Thun, 16 m. S.E. of Berne; mil. training ctr.; cas. on hill above t.; p. (1957) *24,157*.

Thur, *R.*, Switzerland; flows to R. Rhine, nr. Schaffhausen; length 70 m.

Thurgau, *can.*, N.E. Switzerland, on L. Constance, dairying, fruit, textiles; cap. Frauenfeld; a. 388 sq. m.; p. (1961) *166,420*.

Thuringia, *former Land*, E. Germany, bordered on Bavaria to S., Saxony-Anhalt, Lower Saxony and Hesse to N. and E.; drained by Rs. Saale and Werra; crossed by Thuringer Wald and extending to Harz mtns.; cap. Weimar; now dists. of Erfurt, Suhl and Gera.

Thuringian Forest or Thüringer Wald, *wild, wooded hill range*, Central Germany; 95 m. long; famous for romantic scenery and legends.

Thurles, *mkt. t.*, Tipperary (N. Riding), Ireland; on R. Suir; horse fair; p. (1966) *6,743*.

Thursday, *I.*, Torres Strait, Queensland; pearl and trochus fishery ctr.; p. (1966) *2,549*.

Thurso, *burgh*, Caithness, Scot.; on Thurso Bay; most N. t. on Scottish mainland; ancient stronghold of the Northmen; p. (1961) *8,038*.

Tiaret, *t.*, W. Algeria, N. Africa; in strategic pass; walled; agr. mkt.; cereals, wool, cattle; p. *22,344*.

Tiber, *R.*, Italy; flows from Apennines to Mediterranean, passing through Rome; l. 220 m.

Tiberias, *t.*, Israel; on Sea of Galilee (Lake Tiberias); gypsum quarried near by; inland pt.; p. (1946) *11,810*.

Tibesti, *mtns.*, on bdy. between Libya and Chad, Equatorial Africa; barren in spite of slight rainfall; mainly above 6,000 ft., maximum alt. 11,155 ft.

Tibet, *aut. reg.*, China; lofty plateau, called "the roof of the world", its lowest plains being 12,000 ft. above sea-level; semi-desert; Chinese suzerainty restored, 1951; network of roads being built, inc. one across Himalayas to Katmandu.; exp. wool, musk, gold, skins, and drugs; cap. Lhasa; a. 70,003 sq. m.; p. c. *6,000,000*.

Ticino or Tessin, *can.*, Switzerland; forests, vineyards, olives, agr.; contains parts of Ls. Maggiore and Lugano; cap. Bellinzona; lgst. t. Lugano; a. 1,086 sq. m.; p. (1961) *195,566*.

Ticino, *R.*, Switzerland and Italy; trib. of Po; forms S. approach to St. Gotthard Pass; length 150 m.

Tickhill, *urb. dist.*, W.R. Yorks., Eng.; cas.; p. (1961) *2,584*. [fruit; a. 30 sq. m.; p. *19,126*.

Tidore I., Moluccas, Indonesia; coffee, tobacco.

Tien Shan or Celestial Mtns., *lofty chain*, N. frontier China, Sinkiang-Kirghizia; hgst. peak 24,000 ft.

Tientsin (Tianjing), *c., former treaty pt., mun. prov.*, Hopei, China; 70 m. S.E. Peking; cottons silks; exp. wool, skins, soya-beans; tractor plant; p. (1953) *2,693,831*.

Tierra del Fuego, *archipelago*, extreme S. America, separated from Patagonia by Strait of Magellan, divided politically between Chile and Argentina; a. (Argentine part) 8,344 sq. m.; p. *7,500*; oil field at Rio Grande.

Tiffin, *c.*, Ohio, U.S.A.; milling, brewing, foundries; p. (1960) *21,478*. [dom ; cap. Adua.

Tigre, *st.*, Ethiopia, formerly an independent kingdom.

Tigre, *R.*, S. America; rises in Ecuador and flows mainly through Peru to the R. Marañon (Amazon); length 400 m.

Tigris, *R.*, Turkey; rising in mtns. of Armenia and Turkestan, flowing S.E. to join the Euphrates 40 m. N.W. of Basra; length 1,100 m.; dam projected 35 m. N. of Mosul

Tikhvin, *t.*, R.S.F.S.R.; on R. Syas; aluminium ores; p. (1954) *50,000*.

Tilburg, *c.*, N. Brabant, Neth.; nr. Breda; woollens, textiles, tobacco, leather; p. (1967) *148,497*.

Tilbury, *pt.*, Essex, Eng.; on N. bank of R. Thame 20 m. E. of London; within Port of London; major container terminal; p. (1961) *13,387*.

Tillicoultry, *burgh*, Clackmannan, Scot.; on Devon R.; woollen, worsted, paper mkg.; p. (1961) *3,963*.

Tilmanstone, *mining vil.*, Kent, Eng.; on N. flank of N. Downs, 4 m. S.W of Deal; on Kent coalfield, coal despatched by overhead cable to Dover.

Timaru, *c.*, S.I., N.Z.; wool, milling, skins; p. (1966) *27,314*.

Timbuktu, Mali, Africa; 8 m. N. of the N. bend of R. Niger, on border of the Sahara desert; agr. tr. ctr.; p. (1957) *7,000*; flourished as comm. mart, and Moslem ctr., 14–16th cent.

Timisoara, *t.*, W. Romania; impt. comm. and industl. ctr., tobacco, petroleum, paper; fortress, cas., cath.; p. (1963) *167,907*.

Timmins, *t.*, Ontario, Canada; gold running out; vast deposits of copper, zinc, silver, discovered 1964; p. (1961) *29,270*.

Timor, I., lgst. of Lesser Sundas; W. part belongs to Indonesia (a. c. 5,765 sq. m.; p. c. *425,000*; cap. Kupang; sandalwood, copra, cattle, hides) and E. part to Portugal (a. 7,333 sq. m.; p. c. *566,000*; cap. and ch. pt. Dili; sandalwood, coffee, copra, tobacco, wax).

Timor Archipelago, *gr. of Is.*, Indonesia; of which the lgst. is Timor (E. part Portuguese; remainder Indonesian); total a. 24,450 sq. m.; fishing, exp. copra; p. *1,657,376*.

Timor Sea, that part of the Indian Ocean N.W. of W. Australia, and S. of Timor I.

Timsah, *L.*, U.A.R., N.E. Africa; sm. L. midway along Suez Canal; formerly used for recreational purposes by Brit. garrison in Canal zone.

Tinogasta, *t.*, Catamarca prov., Argentina; in E. foot-hills of Andes 120 m. N.W. of Catamarca; impt. copper-mines.

Tintagel, *vil.*, Cornwall, Eng.; ruined cas.; reputed birthplace of King Arthur; tourists.

Tinto, *R.*, Huelva, Spain; flows W. to the Atlantic; length 65 m.

Tinto Hills, Lanark, Scot.; highest peak 2,300 ft.

Tipperary, *inland co.*, Munster, Ireland; a. 1,659 sq. m.; divided into Tipperary co. (N.R.), p. (1966) *53,832*; and Tipperary co. (S.R.), p. (1966) *68,946*.

Tipperary, *t.*, Tipperary, Ireland; 29 m. S.E. Limerick; mftg., butter, lace; p. (1966) *4,507*.

Tipton, *t., mun. bor.*, Staffs. Eng'; 2 m. W. of Bromwich; metals, engin.; p. (1961) *38,091*.

Tiranë, *t., cap.*, Albania; univ.; textiles, metallurgy; p. (1966) *153,000*.

Tiraspol, *t.*, Moldavian S.S.R.; on R. Dniester; heat and power-sta. recently constructed; milling tobacco; p. (1959) *62,000*.

Tire, *t.*, Aydin, Turkey; raisins, tobacco, cotton; p. (1965) *27,245*.

Tiree, *I.*, Inner Hebrides, Scot.; off cst. of Mull; sm. fresh-water lochs and Scandinavian forts.

Tirlemont (Flemish Thienen), *t.*, ctr. of Belgian sugar-refining; Brabant, Belgium; machin.,

woollens, leather; captured by Marlborough, 1705; p. (1962) *22,766*.

Tiruchirapalli, *formerly* Trichinopoly, *t.*, Tamil Nadu, India; on R. Cauvery; cigars, goldsmith's wk.; boiler plant; p. (1961) *249,862*.

Tisa (Tisza), *R.*, U.S.S.R., Hungary, Jugoslavia; rises in E. Carpathians, flows N.W. to Cop, thence S. across flat, agr. plain of Gr. Arföld into R. Danube 45 m. below Novi Sad; approx. length 600 m.; navigable in part.

Tiszapalkonya, *t.*, Hungary; new town; chemical ctr.

Titicaca, *L.*, Bolivia, Peru, S. America; between 2 ranges of the Andes, on borders of Bolivia and Peru; 12,645 ft. above the sea; a. 3,200 sq. m.; average width 27 m. length 101 m.; almost cut in two by peninsula of Copacabana; nearly 700 ft. deep on E. side, shallow W. and S.; contains numerous Is., lgst. Titicaca; it is drained on the S. side by the R. Desaguadero.

Titograd (Podgorica), *t.*, Montenegro, Jugoslavia; nr. Albanian frontier; p. (1959) *22,000*.

Titov Veles, *t.*, Jugoslavia; on R. Vardar, and main rly. to Belgrade; maize, silk; p. (1960) *25,100*.

Tiverton, *mkt. t., mun. bor.*, Devon, Eng.; 14 m. N. Exeter; lace and silk mftg.; p. (estd. 1967) *14,370*.

Tivoli, *t.*, Rome, Italy; sulphur baths.

Tjirebon, *t.*, Java, Indonesia; oil refining; p. (1961) *158,299*.

Tlaxcala, *st.*, Mexico; adjoining Puebla; a. 1,555 sq. m.; cap. Tlaxcala; p. (1960) *346,699*.

Tlemcen, *t.*, Algeria, N. Africa; exp. textiles, carpets, ostrich feathers, olive oil, grain and onyx; p. (1954) *73,000*.

Tobago, *I.*, with Trinidad *indep. st.* within Brit. Commonwealth (1962); exp. sugar, rum, rubber, cotton, tobacco, coffee, etc.; cap. Scarborough on S. side; a. 116 sq. m.; p. (1960) *33,200*, nearly all Negroes.

Tobata, *c., spt.*, N. Kyushu, Japan; now part of Kitakyushu City newly formed 1963 (*q.v.*) on S. shore of Shimonoseki Strait at ent. to Tokai Bay; iron and steel ind., engin., sugar-refining, glass, bricks; lge. mod. coal docks.

Tobermory, *burgh*, Argyll, Scot.; on I. of Mull at N. entrance to Sound of Mull; p. (1961) *668*.

Tobol, *R.*, W. Siberia, R.S.F.S.R.; trib. of R. Irtysh; length 500 m.

Tobolsk, *t.*, W. Siberia. R.S.F.S.R.; on R. Irtysh; shipbldg., sawmilling, fishing; p. (1956) *35,300*

Tobruk, *spt.*, Libya, N. Africa; on cst. 220 m. E. of Benghazi; p. (estd. 1951) *2,500*.

Tocantins, *R.*, provs. Pará and Goiaz, Brazil; flows N. through the Pará estuary to the Atlantic; navigation interrupted by rapids 200 m. above Pará; length, 1,700 m.

Toce, *R.*, N. Italy; rises in Lepontine Alps, flows S. and S.E. into L. Maggiore; valley used by trunk rly. from Milan to Berne as S. approach to Simplon Tunnel; length, 54 m.

Tocopilla, *spt.*, Chile; exp. nitrate, copper ore, sulphates, iodine; p. (1960) *22,244*.

Todmorden, *mkt. t., mun. bor.*, W.R. Yorks, Eng.; nr. source of R. Calder, 6 m. N.E. of Rochdale; cottons, machin.; p. (estd. 1967) *16,100*.

Togliatti, *t.*, R.S.F.S.R., U.S.S.R.; formerly Stavropol; on R. Volga, 35 m. W.N.W. of Kuybyshev; engin., motor wks., natural gas; (1967) *171,000*.

Togo Republic of, *indep. sov. st.* (April 1960), W. Africa, formerly U.N. trust terr. under French adm.; cap. Lomé; mainly agr.; yams, sweet potatoes, green peppers, beans, millet, sorghum, coffee cocoa; phosphate plant; a. 21,220 sq. m.; p. (1968) *1,769,000*. (Br. Togoland integrated in Ghana on achieving independence 1957.)

Tokaimura, *vil.*, Ibaraki, Japan; nuclear reactor and lge. nuclear power sta.

Tokat, *t.*, Turkey; on Tokat I., N. of Sivas; copper and yellow leather mftg.; Armenian massacre 1895; p. (1965) *33,006*.

Tokelau or Union Isles, gr. of 3 Is., Brit. col., Pac. Oc.; 300 m. N. of W. Samoa administered by N.Z.; a. 4 sq. m.; p. (1968) *1,832*.

Tokio, *c., spt., cap.*, Japan; on Tokio Bay, S.E. cst. of Honshu; univ. imperial palace; gr. comm. ctr; silks, machin., lacquer, pottery, "chlorela" artificial food production, metal tableware, chemicals; p. (1970) *8,832,647*; of Greater Tokio *11,353,724*.

Tokoroa, *co. t.*, N.I., N.Z.; kraft paper, pulp, and sawn timber; p. (1966) *11,229*.

Tokushima, *t.*, E. cst. Shikoku, Japan; cottons, reed organs; p. (1965) *193,233*. [*42,815*.

Tolbukhin, *t.*, Bulgaria, former Dobrich; p. (1956)

Toledo, *prov.*, Spain; mtnous.; agr., vineyards, stock-raising; a. 5,925 sq. m.; p. (1959) *531,824*.

Toledo, *ancient c., cap.*, Toledo, Spain; on R. Tagus; with cath., and many specimens of Gothic, Moorish and Castilian architecture in its picturesque narrow streets; famous Alcázar palace citadel; sword-mkg. still flourishes; p. (1957) *46,465*.

Toledo, *c.*, Ohio, U.S.A.; on Maumee R.; gr. rly. ctr. covering 28½ sq. m.; glass, car parts, oil refining; p. (1960) *438,000*. [alt. 18,143 ft.

Tolima, *volcano*, Andes, Columbia, S. America;

Tolima, *dep.*, Colombia, S. America; a. 8,874 sq. m.; cap. Ibague; p. (estd. 1961) *875,650*.

Tolna, *t.*, Hungary; on R. Danube; nuclear power sta. projected.

Toluca, *t.*, Mexico; brewing, flour, cottons; p. (1960) *60,000*. [length 400 m.

Tom, *R.*, Siberia, R.S.F.S.R.; trib. of R. Obi;

Tomaszow Mazowiecki, *c.*, Lodz prov., Poland; woollens, synthetic fibres, agr. tools; p. (1965) *52,000*. [the Mobile; length 500 m.

Tombigbee, *R.*, Miss., U.S.A.; flows S. to form

Tomsk, *region*, Siberia, R.S.F.S.R.; adjoining Chinese frontier; agr., dairying, stock-raising, fisheries, mining, mftg.

Tomsk, *c.*, Siberia, U.S.S.R.; on R. Tom, and branch of Trans-Siberian rly.; univ., cath.; engin., chemicals; p. (1967) *311,000*.

Tonawanda, *t.*, N.Y., U.S.A.; on Niagara R.; mnfs.; p. (1960) *21,561*.

Tonbridge, *mkt. t., urb. dist.*, Kent, Eng.; on R.; Medway, 13 m. S.W. of Maidstone; rly. wks., light inds.; castle (orig. Norman), public school; p. (estd. 1967) *28,550*.

Tönder, *t.*, Denmark; old houses; cattle-breeding; lace; p. (1960) *7,192*.

Tonga, *indep. sov. st.* within Br. Commonwealth (1970); *c.* 150 Is. Pac. Oc., 400 m. S.E. Fiji; Polynesian kingdom; ch. I. Tongatapu; cap. Nukualofa; fishing, agr., bananas, coconuts; oil discovered 1969; a. 270 sq.m.; p. (estd.) *81,000*.

Tongariro, *volcanic peak*, N.I., N.Z.; in ctr. of volcanic dist.; alt. 6,458 ft.; hydroelec. plant projected. [mineral springs; p. (1962) *16,240*.

Tongeren (Tongres), *episcopal c.*, Belgium;

Tongking, *region*, N. Viet-Nam; formerly within French Union; rice, sugar-cane, tobacco, coffee, cotton, silk, coal, tin, limestone; a. 40,530 sq. m.; ch. t. Hanoi; ch. pt. Haiphong.

Tonk, *t.*, Rajasthan, India; mica; p. (1961) *43,413*.

Tonlé Sap, *L.*, Cambodia, Indo-China; one of world's lgst. fishing ctrs.

Tönsberg, *t.*, Norway; on Bay nr. entrance to Oslo fjord; tr. ctr.; shipping; H.Q. of sealing- and whaling-fleet, oil mills; p. (estd. 1960) *12,500*.

Toowoomba, *c.*, Queensland, Australia; wheat, pastoral and dairying dist., flour-milling, wine, engin., agr. machin.; p. (1966) *52,120*.

Topeka, *t., cap.*, Kan., U.S.A.; on Kansas R.; flour-milling, engin., machin., ige. tr.; p. (1960) *119,484*.

Torbay, *co. bor.*, S. Devon, Eng.; formed by amalgamation of Torquay, Paignton and Brixham; p. (estd. 1968) *98,657*.

Torcello, *I.*, with ancient Byzantine cath., on lagoon nr. Venice, Italy. [(1962) *13,599*.

Torhout, *t.*, W. Flanders, Belgium; textiles; p.

Tormes, *R.*, Spain; trib. of Douro; length 150 m.

Toronto, *c., pt., metrop. a., cap.* Ontario, Canada; on Bay of Toronto, L. Ontario; spacious harbour; univ.; extensive tr. and mnfs.; oil refining; fine parliament bldgs., parks; a. 240 sq. m.; p. (1966) of met. a. *2,158,496*.

Torontoy, *gorge*, Cuzco dep., Peru; located on R. Urubamba 50 m. N.W. of Cuzco.

Torpoint, *urb. dist.*, Cornwall, Eng.; on Plymouth Sound; p. (1961) *4,260*.

Torquay, *t.*, S. Devon, Eng.; incorporated in Torbay co. bor.; on N. Side of Tor Bay; seaside resort with all-year season.

Torre Annunziata, *t., spt.*, Italy; on Bay of Naples; arms factory, macaroni mftg., sericulture; p. (1961) *58,400*.

Torre del Greco, *spt.*, Italy; on Bay of Naples; at foot of Mt. Vesuvius; seaside resort; lava quarries, shipbldg; p. (1961) *77,576*. [p. *16,069*.

Torredonjimeno, *t.*, Jaen, Spain; wine, wheat, fruit;

Torremolinos, cst. resort Spain; S. of Malaga.

Torrens, *L.*, S. Australia; 130 m. long, 20 m. wide; varies from brackish lake to salt marsh.

Terreón, *t.*, Coahuila, Mexico; ctr. of comm. agr.; oil pipe-line connects to Chihuahua; thermo-elec. plant; p. (1960) *179,955*.

Torres Strait, between C. York, Queensland, Australia, and New Guinea; 90 m. wide, dangerous navigation.

Torridge, *R.*, Devon, Eng.; flows from Hartland Dist. to Bideford Bay; length 53 m.

Torrington, *t.*, Conn., U.S.A.; metal-plate wk., woollens; p. (1960) *30,045*.

Torrington, *t., mun. bor.*, Devon, Eng.; on R. Torridge, 4 m. S.E. of Bideford; ball clay; glass wks.; p. (estd. 1967) *2,920*.

Tortona, *t.*, N. Italy; the Roman Dertona: cath.

Tortosa, *fortfd. t.*, Spain; on R. Ebro; wine, oil, fruit, paper, leather; p. (1957) *45,672*.

Tortuga, *I.*, Caribbean Sea; off N.W. cst. of Hispaniola; provides shelter from N.E. trade winds for Port de Paix; 25 m. by 10 m.

Torun (Thorn), *t.*, S. Pomerania, Poland; on R. Vistula; univ.; grain, timber; p. (1965) *114,000*.

Tosya, *t.*, Turkey; grapes, rice, cotton, wool, mohair, weaving; p. (1960) *13,690*.

Totnes, *t., mun. bor.*, Devon, Eng.; on R. Dart, 6 m. N.W. of Dartmouth; cider; p. (estd. 1967) *5,630*.

Totonicapan, *t.*, Guatemala, Central America; hot springs, gardens; pottery, furniture, textiles; p. (estd. 1960) *40,100*.

Tottenham, *former mun. bor.*, Middx., Eng.; now, inc. in Haringey outer bor., Greater London (*q.v.*); industl. and resdtl.; p. (1961) *113,249*.

Tottington, *urb. dist.*, Lancs. Eng.; cotton and artificial silk goods; p. (1961) *6,133*.

Touggourt or Tuggurt, *t.*, S. Algeria; edge of Sahara; rly. terminus; dates; p. (1960) *107,661*.

Toul, *t.*, Meurthe-et-Moselle, France; on R. Moselle; wines, brandy, earthenware, lace; p. (1962) *15,031*.

Toulon, *c., spt., naval sta.*, Var, France; on Mediterranean cst.; arsenal, fine bldgs., shipbldg, lace-mkg., vines, olive oil, fisheries; Port-Cros nat. park nearby; p. (1968) *174,746*.

Toulouse, *t.*, Haute-Garonne, S. France; on R. Garonne; cath.; paper, leather, stained glass, aircraft engin.; projected aeronautical and space research ctr.; p. (1968) *370,796*.

Tourane, *t.*, S. Vietnam; weaving wks., elec. plant, cotton mills.

Tourcoing, *t.*, Nord France; 10 m. N.E. of Lille; textiles, carpets, cement; p. (1962) *90,105*.

Tournai, *t.*, Hainaut, Belgium; on R. Scheldt; nr. Mons; famous cath.; textiles, carpet mftg.; p. (1962) *33,346*.

Tours, *t.*, Indre-et-Loire, France; cath.; iron, steel, wines, leather, textiles; p. (1968) *128,120*.

Towcester, *mkt. t., rural dist.*, Northants, Eng.; 9 m. S.W. of Northampton; boot-mkg.; p. (rural dist. 1961) *15,198*.

Tower Hamlets, *inner bor.*, E. London, Eng., inc. former bors. of Bethnal Green, Stepney and Poplar; industl.; p. (1966) *203,000*.

Tow Law, *urb. dist.*, Durham, Eng.; in Wear Dale, 10 m. N.W. of Bishop Auckland; p. (1961) *2,920*.

Townsville, *spt.*, Queensland, Australia; on E. cst., 2nd pt. of st.; exp. prods. of rich dairying, pastoral, and mining terr.; copper refining; gen. inds.; p. (1966) *56,687*. [Bay; length 65 m.

Towy, *R.*, S. Wales; flows S.W. to Carmarthen

Towyn, *mkt. t., urb. dist.*, Merioneth, Wales; on cst. of Cardigan Bay, 3 m. N.W. of Aberdovey; p. (1981) *4,466*.

Toyama, *c.*, Honshu, Japan; located centrally on Etchu plain to E. of Noto Peninsula; administrative and comm. ctr. of region; aluminum smelting; p. (1964) *218,000*.

Trabzon, *spt.*, Turkey; on Black Sea cst.; caravan ctr.; exp. tobacco, carpets, hides; reputed to be the ancient Trapezus; p. (1965) *65,598*.

Trafalgar, *C.*, S.W. cst., Cadiz, Spain; Nelson's famous victory, 1805.

Trail, *t.*, B.C., Canada; lgst. metallurgical smelter in Brit. Commonwealth; p. (1961) *11,580*.

Tralee, *cst.*, *t.*, Kerry, Ireland; on R. Lee; exp. grain, butter; p. (1966) *11,211*.

Tranent, *burgh* E. Lothian. Scot.; 10 m. E. of Edinburgh; coal; p. (1961) *6,317*.

Trani, *spt.*, Apulia, Italy; on the Adriatic; 12th-century cath.; p. *30,551*.

Transbaikal, *dist.*, Siberia, R.S.F.S.R.; E. of L. Baikal; mineral wealth; ch. t., Chita.

Transcaucasia, name given to region of U.S.S.R. which comprises the constituent reps. of Georgia, Armenia, and Azerbaydzhan; ch. t., Tbilisi.

Transkei, *Bantu reserve*, E. Cape, S. Africa; cereals, fruits, cattle, sheep; limited Bantu self-gov., pop. mainly employed in mines in Transvaal and Orange Free State; cap. Umtata; a. 16,544 sq. m.; p. (1963) 1,300,000.

Transvaal, *prov.*, Rep. of S. Africa; hot summers, temperate winters; grassland, agr., maize, tobacco, sheep, wool, cattle, gold, diamonds; coal, copper, tea, engin., brewing, pottery; a. 110,450 sq. m.; cap. Pretoria; nuclear reactor in the N.; p. (1960) 6,273,477 (inc. 1,468,305 whites).

Transylvania, *former prov.*, Hungary, now in Romania; cereals, tobacco, sheep, cattle, horses; surrounded and traversed by the Carpathians.

Transylvanian Alps, *range of high mtns.*, Romania.

Trapani, *fortfd. spt.*, W. Sicily, Italy; salt, wine, olive oil, fish, alabaster, coral, mother-of-pearl; exp.; p. (1961) 75,537.

Traralgon, *t.*, Vic., Australia; paper, cement, clothing; p. (1966) 14,080.

Trasimeno, *L.*, Umbria, central Italy; occupies lge. extinct volcanic crater; drained S. to R. Tiber; a. approx. 60 sq. m.

Trás-os-Montes e Alto-Douro, *prov.*, N. Portugal; ch. t. Tua; a. 47,340 sq. m.; p. (1950) 636,322.

Traun, *R.*, Austria; trib. of R. Danube; enters L. known as Traun See; length 100 m.

Travancore-Cochin, *former st.*, S. India; included in Kerala st. 1 Nov., 1956; rice, coconuts, pepper, tapioca, hardwoods; univ.

Traverse City, *t.*, Mich., U.S.A.; timber inds., tr.; p. (1960) 18,432.

Trawsfynydd, Merioneth, Wales; within N. Wales Nat. Pk.; atomic power sta.

Trebizond, *see* Trabzon.

Tredegar, *mining t., urb. dist.*, Monmouth, Eng.; in narrow valley 3 m. W. of Ebbw Vale; p. (1961) 19,792.

Treforest, *t.*, Glam., Wales; on R. Taff; lge. trading estate established in 1930s to alleviate unemployment in primary inds. of S. Wales; aircraft accessories, electronics, chemical, pharmaceutical, rayon, metal wks.

Treinta y Tres, *dep.*, Uruguay; a. 3,682 sq. m.; cap. Treinta y Tres; p. (1953) 72,063.

Trelew, *t.*, Patagonia, Argentina; ch. comm. t.; sheep; p. (1960) 11,500.

Trelleborg, *spt.*, S. Sweden; most impt. rubber fact. in cty.; p. (1961) 19,209.

Tremadoc Bay, N. Wales; N. part of Cardigan Bay between Lleyn pen. and Merioneth cst.

Trengganu, *st.*, Malaysia; N. E. Malaya; rice, rubber, coconuts; tin, iron; cap. Kuala Trengganu; a. 5,050 sq. m.; p. (estd. 1966) 371,370.

Trent, *R.*, Eng.; rises in N. Staffs, and flows to join the Ouse in forming the estuary of the Humber; length 170 m.

Trentino-Alto Adige, *aut. region*, N. Italy; a. 5,252 sq. m.; p. (1961) 785,491.

Trento, *t., cap.*, Venezia Tridentina, N. Italy; on R. Adige; p. (1961) 74,766.

Trenton, *c., cap.*, N.J., U.S.A.; on Delaware R.; ironwks., pottery, rubber, and other mnfs.; p. (1960) 114,167.

Tres Arroyos, *t.*, E. Argentina; agr. and livestock ctr.; p. (1960) 40,000.

Treves (or Trèves), *see* Trier.

Treviglio, *t.*, Lombardy, Italy; E. of Milan; silk mftg.; p. 19,615.

Treviso, *t.*, Lombardy, Italy; cath.; majolica ware, silks, woollens; p. (1961) 75,217.

Trichinopoly, (*see* Tiruchirapalli).

Trier, *c.*, Rhineland-Palatinate, Germany; on R. Moselle; cath.; Roman antiquities (Porta Nigra); wine cellars, tobacco, leather, textiles, machin., brewing; p. (1968) 104,470.

Trieste Free Territory, *former free st.*, on the Adriatic; constituted by Peace Treaty with Italy, 1947, as compromise between conflicting Jugoslav and Italian claims; a. 287 sq. m.; Zone A handed over to Italy, Zone B to Yugoslavia, 1954.

Trieste, *spt., cap.* Friuli-Venezia Giulia, N. E. Italy; shipbldg., fishing; cath., cas., Roman antiquities; oil pipeline to Schwechat, nr. Vienna; p. (1964) 280,000.

Trikkala, *prefecture*, Thessaly, Greece; cap Trikkala; p. (1961) 142,450.

Trikkala (the ancient Trikal), *t.*, Thessaly, Greece; nr. Larissa; mosques; grain p. (1961) 27,876.

Trincomalee, *t., naval sta.*, N.E. cst., Ceylon; gd. harbour; tobacco, rice, palms; p. 32,507.

Tring, *mkt. t., urb. dist.*, Herts, Eng.; in gap through Chiltern Hills, 9 m. N.W. of Hemel Hempstead; dairy farming; p. (1961) 6,051.

Trinidad, *I.*, with Tobago, *indep. st.*, within Brit. Commonwealth (1962); W.I.; oil, natural gas, asphalt, sugar, rum, coconut oil, molasses, cocoa, citrus fruits; tourism; cap. Pt. of Spain; a. 1,980 sq. m.; p. (estd.) 1,030,000.

Trinidad, *cap.* Beni, Bolivia; p. (1962) 14,505.

Trinidad, *t.*, Cuba, W.I.; exp. honey; p. 16,756.

Trinity, *R.* Texas, U.S.A.; flows S.E. to Galveston Bay; length 500 m.

Trino, Piedmont, N. Italy; 11 m. S.S.W. of Vercelli; nuclear power sta.

Tripoli, *pt.*, Lebanon; terminus on Mediterranean of oil pipe-line from Iraq; p. (estd.) 210,000.

Tripoli, *c., pt.* on Mediterranean, one of caps. of Libya; stands on edge of palm-oasis, site of ancient Oea; tourist, comm, and mnf. ctr.; good harbour; p. (estd.) 231,995.

Tripolis, *cap.*, Arcadia, Peloponnese, Greece; tapestries, leather; p. (1961) 13,500.

Tripura, Union Terr., India; hilly; rice, jute, cotton, sugar cane; cap. Agartala; a. 4,036 sq. m.; p. (1961) 1,142,005.

Tristan da Cunha, *sm. gr. of Brit. Is.*, S. Atl. Oc.; ch. I. Tristan; evacuated 1961 (volcanic eruption) but resettled 1963; p. (estd.) 280.

Trivandrum, *t.*, Kerala, S. India; univ.; woodcarving; p. (1961) 239,815.

Trnava, *t.*, ČSSR.; on R. Vah; cloth, sugar; p. (1961) 31,732. [16,182.

Trnovo (Tirnovo), *t.*, Bulgaria; copper wk.; p.

Troitsk, *t.*, S. Urals, R.S.F.S.R.; leather, knitwear; lge. thermal power sta.; p. (1959) 76,000.

Trollhättan, *t.*, Sweden; famous waterfalls, with generating-sta.; cars; p. (1961) 32,051.

Trombay, *I.*, off Bombay, India; oil refining; atomic reactor; zirconium metal produced; fertilisers.

Troms, *co.*, Norway; a. 10,006 sq. m.; p. (1968) 135,104.

Tromsö, *spt.*, Troms, Norway; on sm. I. of Tromsö, in Tromsö Sound; seal and walrus fishing; canning; p. (1968) 36,340.

Tronador, *volcano*, Andes, S. America; on Argentine-Chilean bdy.; alt. 11 352 ft.

Tröndelag, N., *co.*, Norway; a. 8,659 sq. m.; p. (1963) 116,469

Tröndelag, S., *co.*, Norway; a. 7,241 sq. m.; p. (1963) 215,274.

Trondheim, *spt.*, Norway; on W. cst. on S. side of Trondheim Fjord; shipbldg., engin.; exp. timber and wood-pulp, butter, fish, copper; contains ancient cath., burial place of early Norwegian kings and place of coronation of recent sovereigns; p. (1968) 120,818.

Troon, *burgh*, Ayr, Scot.; on Firth of Clyde, 6 m. N. of Ayr; gd. harbour and graving docks; shipbldg., hosiery; seawater distillation research ctr. projected; p. (1961) 9,932.

Troppau, *see* Opava.

Troste, nr. Llanelly, Wales; steel strip mill, tin plate; newly developed 1952.

Trossachs, *mtn. defile*, Perth, Scot.; tourist resort.

Trowbridge, *mkt. t., urb. dist.*, Wilts, Eng.; 3 m. S.E. of Bradford-on-Avon; cloth wks., bacon curing, dairying, engin.; p. (1961) 15,833.

Troy, *c.*, N.Y., U.S.A.; at confluence of Rs. Hudson and Mohawk; great shirt-mftg. ctr.; p. (1960) 67,492.

Troyes, *c.*, Aube, France; on R. Seine; former cap. Champagne; magnificent cath., hosiery, iron, looms, mnfs.; p. (1968) 74,898.

Trucial States (or Emirates), *seven sts.*, E. Arabia, along Persian G. (Abu Dhabi, Ras-al Khaima, Sharjah, Ajman, Fujeira, Umm-al-Ghuwain); ch. t. Dubai; Brit. prot. to be withdrawn by end 1971; a. 32,000 sq. m.; p. (estd. 1968) 180,000.

Trujillo, *spt.*, Honduras, Central America; on Atlantic cst.; p. (1958) 3,016.

Trujillo, *ch. t.*, La Libertad, Peru; univ.; cath.; cocaine mftg., sugar, brewing, tanneries, rice mills; p. (1961) 122,000.

Trujillo, *old t.*, Spain; N.E. Badajoz; wheat. wine, fruit; birthplace of Pizarro; p. (1957) 14,587. [coffee; cap. T.; p. (1961) 326,634.

Trujillo, *st.*, Venezuela, S. America: cocoa.

Truk Is., Caroline Is., Pac. Oc., U.S.A. Trusteeship; coral, copra, dried fish; a. 50 sq. m.; p. (1958) 19,307.

Truro, *c., mun. bor.*, Cornwall, Eng.; at confluence of Rs. Kenwyn and Allen; cath.; tin smelting, jam wks., light engin. textiles; p. (estd. 1967) 14,430.

Truro, *t.*, Nova Scotia, Canada; on Salmon R.; hosiery; p. (1961) 12,421.

Trutnov, *t.*, ČSSR.; at foot of Riesengebirge; coal, linen; p. (1961) 22,961.

Tsamkong (Zhanjiang), *c.*, Kwangtung prov., China; cotton milling, leather mnfs.; p. (1953) 166,000.

Tsangpo, *R.*, Tibet; one of the headstreams of the R. Brahmaputra; length 850 m.

Tschenstokov, *see* Czestochowa.

Tselinograd, *t.*, Kazakhstan, S.S.R.; nr. Karaganda coalfield; engin.; p. (1967) 171,000.

Tsinan (Jinan), *c.*, Shantung, China; on the south bank of the Hwang Ho, 100 m. from the G. of Chihli; mnfs. glass, textiles, precious stones; p. (1953) 680,000.

Tsinghai (Qinghai), *prov.*, China; between Nan Shan and Kunlun mtns.; cap. Sining; a. 269,187 sq. m.; p. (1953) 11,676,534.

Tsingtao (Qingdao), *c.*, Shantung, China; salt, silk; former treaty pt.; p. (1953) 917,000.

Tsitsihar (Qiqihar), *c.*, Heilungkiang, N. China; on the Vladivostock portion of the Trans-Siberian rly.; p. (1953) 345,000.

Tsugaru Strait, Japan; separates Is. Hokkaido and Honshu; links Sea of Japan with Pac. Oc.; length 45 m., width 15–20 m.

Tsumeb, *t.*, S.W. Africa; rly. terminus; copper, lead, zinc; p. (1960) 7,769 inc. 2,987 whites.

Tsuruga, *spt.*, Japan; on W. cst. Honshu; rayon textiles, cotton, atomic power plant projected; p. (1965) 32,343.

Tuam, *mkt. t., rural dist.*, Galway, Ireland; p. (1961) (of dist.) 25,676 (of t. 1966) 3,621.

Tuamotu, *coral archipelago*, S. Pac. Oc.; belonging to France; a. of gr. 330 sq. m.; pearl fisheries; p. of gr. (1962) 7,097.

Tuapse, *spt.*, R.S.F.S.R., U.S.S.R.; at foot of Caucasus Mtns. on N. cst. of Black Sea; at W. end of oil pipe-line from Baku and Makhach Kala; impt. oil refineries; p. (1954) 50,000.

Tubarao, *t.*, Santa Catarina st., S. Brazil; on E. cst., 175 m. N. W. of Pôrto Alegre; coal-mines; p. (1960) 29,615.

Tübingen, *t.*, Baden-Württemberg, Germany; on R. Neckar; univ., cas.; machin., paper, textiles; p. (1963) 53,300.

Tucson, *c.*, Arizona, U.S.A.; on Santa Cruz R.; founded in 1560 by a Jesuit mission, and from 1867 to 1877 was the cap. of Arizona; seat of Univ. of Arizona; winter resort; aircraft, electronics, clothing; p. (1960) 212,892.

Tucumán, *prov.*, Argentina; agr. and stock-raising; cap. Tucumán; a. 8,817 sq. m.; p. (1960) 780,000.

Tucumán, San Miguel de, *c.*, cap. Tucumán prov., Argentina; on R. Salí; univ.; breweries, saw-mills, flourmills, sugar; p. (1960) 290,000.

Tugela, *R.*, Natal, S. Africa; rises in Drakensberg Mtns. and flows to Indian O.; length 300 m.

Tula, *region*, R.S.F.S.R., U.S.S.R.; S. of Moscow; pasturage, stock-keeping, iron and coal.

Tula, *t.*, R.S.F.S.R., U.S.S.R.; on both banks R. Upa; engin., iron ore nearby; p. (1967) 371,000.

Tulare, L., S. Cal., U.S.A.; ctr. of inland drainage 40 m. S. of Fresno; streams feeding it used for irrigation; in drought years L. dries up completely; a. 90 sq. m.

Tulbagh, *t.*, Cape Prov., Rep. of S. Africa; on Gr. Berg R., 65 m. N.E. of Cape Town.

Tulcea, *t.*, Dobroja, Romania; on Danube; chemicals, copper; p. (1963) 29,932.

Tulenovo, Balchik dist., on Black Sea, Bulgaria; oil production.

Tulkarm, *t.*, Jordan; agr. ctr.; rly. junction; p. (1961) 19,343.

Tullamore, *mkt. t., urb. dist.*, Offaly, Ireland; on Grand Canal; farming, distilling, brewing; p. (1966) 6,650.

Tulle, *t., cap.*, Corrèze, France; cath.; p. (1962) [20,790.

Tulsa, *c.*, Okla., U.S.A.; 2nd lgst. c. in st.; oil-well machin., aeroplanes; p. (1960) 261,685.

Tumbes, *dep.*, Peru, S. America; cap. Tumbes; a. 1,590 sq. m.; p. (1961) 52,403.

Tummel, *R.*, Perth, Scot.; trib. of R. Tay; used by Perth to Inverness rly. as S. approach to Drumochter Pass.

Tunbridge Wells, *mkt. t., Royal mun. bor.*, Kent, Eng.; on border of Sussex, 5 m. S. of Tonbridge; chalybeate waters; p. (estd. 1967) 43,490.

Tung Hai or Eastern China Sea, name of part of the Pac. Oc. bordering S. China.

Tunghwa (Tonghua), *c.*, Kirin prov., China; p. (1953) 129,000.

Tungting Hu, *lge. L.*, Hunan, China; on S. margin of Yangtze-Kiang plain; receives waters of Yuan Kiang and Siang Kiang, drains N. to Yangtze-Kiang; surrounded by flat, intensively cultivated land, rice, sugar, mulberry; size varies greatly with season; maximum a. (in late summer) 2,500 sq. m.

Tunguska, Upper, Stony and Lower, *Rs.*, Siberia, U.S.S.R.; all rise in Sayan Mtns. nr. L. Baikal and flow N.W. through forested country into R. Yenesei.

Tunis, *ch. t.*, Tunisia, N. Africa; spt. on bay off G. of Tunis; univ., notable mosques; tourist ctr.; many inds., much tr.; the ruins of ancient Carthage are to the N.E.; p. (1956) 680,000.

Tunisia, *ind. sovereign st.* since March 1956, formerly French prot., N. Africa; agr., stock-rearing, mineral and phosphate wkg., silk and carpet weaving, pottery mftg., fishing (inc. sponges), also fruit- and flower-growing and perfume distillation; lge. steelwks. at Menzel-Bourguiba projected; oil deposits in El Borma a.; cap. Tunis; a. 45,000 sq. m.; p. (1968) 4,660,000. [63,500

Tunja, *t.*, cap. Boyaca, Colombia; p. (estd. 1959)

Turda, *t.*, Transylvania, Romania; salt-mines; p. (1963) 63 421.

Turfan (Tulufan), *c.*, Sinkiang, China; below sea-level on the S. side of the Tian-Shan Mtns.

Turgai, *dist.*, U.S.S.R.; N. of Sea of Aral, forms part of Kazakh. rep.; a. 175,219 sq. m.; agr. and cattle-breeding; antimony p. 500,000 (largely nomadic Kirghiz).

Turgutlu (Kassaba), *t.*, Manisa prov., Turkey; 30 m. E.N.E. of Izmir; lignite, cotton, melons; p. (1965) 35,079.

Turin (Torino), *c.*, N. Italy; on Rs. Po and Dora; former cap. Piedmont and Sardinian sts.; cath., univ., royal palace and cas., and Palazzo Carignano; leather, textiles, engin.; extensive tr.; p. (1969) 1,107,000.

Turkestan E., *terr.* included in Sinkiang, China; separated from W. or former Russian Turkestan by Pamir plateau; mainly desert.

Turkey, *rep.*, Europe and Asia; has lost much of 19th-century terrs.; evergreen trees, shrubs, livestock, cereals, tobacco, figs, fruits, copper, silver, coal, carpets, silk, wine, olive oil, handi-crafts, oil nr. Iskenderun and along shores of Marmara Sea; cap. Ankara; lgst. t. Istanbul; a. 294,200 sq. m.; p (estd. 1969) 33,627,000.

Turkmenistan, *const. rep.*, U.S.S.R.; agr. based on irrigation, fruit, cotton, wool; sulphates, petroleum, mnfs., carpets; cap. Ashkhabad; a. 189,603 sq. m.; p. (1970) 2,158,000.

Turks and Caicos, *Is.*, Caribbean Sea; West Indies; about 30 sm. Is.; geographically the S.E. continuation of the Bahamas; Caicos Is. separated by narrow channel from Turks Is.; ch. prod., salt, conches, sisal, sponges. Total a. 166 sq. m.; p. (estd. 1965) 6,272.

Turku (Abo), *spt.*, S. Finland; Swedish and Finnish univs., archiepiscopal see; p. (1966) 140,139

Turku-Pori (Abo-Björneborg), *dep.*, Finland; a. 8,500 sq. m.; p. (1966) 674,073.

Turner Valley, *dist.*, Alberta, Canada; oilfield; natural gas.

Turnhout, *t.*, Belgium; nr. Antwerp; textiles, lace, playing-card mnf.; p. (1962) 36,701.

Turnu Severin, *t.*, Romania; below the Iron Gate cataracts of R. Danube; grain, salt, petroleum; p. (1963) 36,831.

Turriff, *burgh*, Aberdeen, Scot.; nr. R. Deveron; p. (1961) 2,686.

Turton, *t., urb. dist.*, Lancs, Eng.; 4 m. N. of Bolton; mnfs.; p. (1961) 13,673.

Tuscaloosa, *t.* Ala., U.S.A.; st. univ.; p. (1960) 63,370.

Tuscany, *region, former grand duchy*, Italy; includes provs. Arezzo, Florence, Leghorn, Siena, Grosseto, Lucca, Pisa, and Massa and Carrara;

cereals, olive oil, wine, copper, lead, mercury, marble, textiles, porcelain; a. 8,876 sq. m.; p. (1961) *3,267,374*.

Tuticorin, *spt.*, Tamil Nadu, India; cotton-spinning, salt, pearls; p. (1961) *124,273*.

Tuttlingen, *t.*, Baden-Württemberg, Germany; on R. Danube; musical instruments, tanning, footwear, steel, textiles; p. (1963) *25,200*.

Tuva, *aut. rep.*, U.S.S.R.; formerly Tannu Tuva rep., bounded on E., W., and N. by Siberia, and on S. by Mongolia; cap. Kyzyl; pastoral; asbestos ctr. at Ak-Tovurak, a. about 64,000 sq. m.; p. (1959) *172,000*.

Tuy Hoa, *t.*, S. Vietnam; fertilisers, tyres, sugar mill.

Tuxtla Gutierrez, *t.*, Chiapas, Mexico; alt. 1,500 ft.; ctr. for sisal, tobacco, coffee, cattle; p. (1960) *23,262*.

Tuzla, *t.*, Jugoslavia; salt-springs, coal, timber, livestock, grain, fruit; p. (1959) *49,000*.

Tweed, *R.*, S.E. Scot.; rises in Peebles, and reaches sea at Berwick; dividing Berwick from the Eng. co. Northumberland; famous for its salmon fisheries; length 97 m.

Twelve Pins, star-shaped *mtn. range*, Galway, Ireland; Benbaum, alt. 2,395 ft.

Twickenham, *former mun. bor.*, Middx., Eng.; now inc. in Richmond upon Thames (*q.v.*); Rugby Football Union ground; p. (1961) *100,822*.

Tychy, *t.*, Katowice, Poland; p. (1965) *63,000*.

Tyldesley, *t.*, *urb. dist.*, Lancs, Eng.; 4 m. S. of Bolton; mnfs.; p. (1961) *16,813*

Tyler, *c.*, Texas, U.S.A.; fruit, livestock, cotton; p. (1960) *51,230*.   [zinc, copper.

Tynagh, *mine* on Longhrea, Galway, R.O.I.; lead.

Tyne, *R.*, Durham and Northumberland, Eng.; formed by junction of N. and S. Tyne at Hexham; flows E. to sea at Tynemouth and S. Shields; valley gives easy route across mtns. from Newcastle to Carlisle; forms a continuous harbour (with shipbldg. and other wks.) from Newcastle to Tynemouth; length 80 m.; road tunnel between Wallsend and Jarrow under constr.

Tynemouth, *t., spt. co. bor.*, Northumberland, Eng.; at mouth of R. Tyne, on its N. bank; inc. in its a. the townships of Tynemouth, N. Shields, Cullercoats, Chirton, Preston, Percy Main, E. Howden and New York; favourite wat. pl. with old priory and cas.; gd. harbour; fishing, ship repairing, coal bunkering, laminated plastics; oil storage; p. (estd. 1967) *72,440*.

Tyneside, *lge. conurbation*, S.E. Northumberland, N.E. Durham, Eng.; comprises highly industl. built-up a. astride R. Tyne for 14 m. from its mouth to Scotswood Bridge; huge exp. of coal, abroad and round Brit. csts.; shipbldg., heavy engin.; a. 90 sq. m.; p. (estd. 1968) *843,000*. *See also under* Gateshead, Newcastle upon Tyne, S. Shields, Tynemouth, Jarrow, Wallsend, Felling, Hebburn, Gosforth, Longbenton, Newburn, Wickham, **Whitley Bay.**

Tyrol, *mountainous region*, Alps, Europe; falls within Austria and Italy; between Munich and Verona, which are linked by the Brenner Pass; the Tyrol embraces all the highest peaks of the Austrian Alps, culminating in the Ortler Spitz; two-fifths forest; cap. Innsbruck; mtn. pasture, vineyards, silk inds.; a. 4,884 sq. m.; p. of Austrian T. (1961) *462,899*.

Tyrone, *inland co.*, N. Ireland; agr. and dairying; cap. Omagh; a. 1,260 sq. m.; p. (1966) *135,634*.

Tyrrhenian Sea, part of Mediterranean between Italy and Corsica, Sardinia and Sicily.

Tyumen, *t.*, R.S.F.S.R.; on R. Tura, engin.; textiles; natural gas nearby in Berezovo vil.; oil pipeline connects with Shaim; p. (1967) *218,000*.

Tzekung (Zigong), *c.*, Szechwan, China; petroleum, natural gas, salt wks.; p. (1953) *291,000*.

Tzepo (Zibo), *c.*, Shantung, China; formed by merging 1950 coal mng. ts. of Tzechwan and Poshan and 1954 addition of Changchow; p. (estd.) *284,000*.

U

Uanapú or Anapú, *R.*, Brazil; trib. of R. Pará; length 400 m.

Ubangi, *R.*, central Africa; trib. of R. Congo; with R. Congo forms W. bdy. between Central African Rep. and Congo; length 1,400 m.

Ubangi-Shari, *see* **Central African Republic.**

Ube, *spt.*, S. Honshu, Japan; chemical cement machin., coal; p. (1965) *159,000*.

Ubeda, *t.*, Jaen, Spain; on R. Guadalquivir; in vineyard and fruit-growing dist.; old walls; p. (1957) *30,249*.

Uberaba, *t.*, Minas Gerais, Brazil; cattle, maize, manioc, rice, sugar; p. (1960) *72,053*.

Ucayali *R.*, Peru, S. America; head-stream of R. Amazon; over 1,400 m. long navigable for 1,000 m.   [(1962) *73,159*.

Uccle, *t.*, Belgium; nr. Brussels; industl.; p.

Uckfield, *mkt. t.*, *rural dist.*, E. Sussex, Eng.; 8 m. N.E. of Lewes; p. (rural dist. 1951) *43,132*.

Udaipur, *t.*, Rajasthan, India; 2,469 ft. above sealevel; marble palace of the Maharajah; temple of Siva; embroidery, cotton cloth; p. (1961) *111,139*.

Uddevalla, *spt.*, S. Sweden; N. Göteborg; prefab. houses, timber, granite quarrying, textiles; p. (1961) *34,290*.

Udi, *t.*, S. Nigeria, W. Africa; 100 m. N. of Pt. Harcourt; impt. mining ctr. on Enugu coal-field; linked by rail to Kaduna and Pt. Harcourt.

Udine, *t.*, N.E. Italy; between Alps and G. of Venice; old cas. (now barracks); silk, velvet, and cotton inds.; p. (1961) *85,205*.

Udmurt, *autonomous Soviet Socialist Rep.*, part of R.S.F.S.R., U.S.S.R., cap. Izhevsk.

Uelzen, *t.*, Lower Saxony, Germany; on Lüneberger Heath; machin. chemicals, sugar; p. (1963) *24,500*.

Ufa, *t.*, R.S.F.S.R.; in W. Urals at confluence of Rs. Ural and Belaia; iron and copper foundries and machin. wks., saw-mills, textiles, oil; p. (1967) *683,000*.

Uganda, *indep. sov. st.* within Br. Commonwealth (1962); E. Central Africa; ch. R. Nile; Ruwenzori Range, Mt. Elgon on Kenya border; Ls. inc. parts of Victoria, Edward, Albert, and whole of Kioga; moderate rainfall; cotton, coffee, tea, oilseeds, tobacco, groundnuts, maize; copper, beryl, tin; timber; Owen Falls hydroelec. power plant; cap. Kampala; a. 93,981 sq. m. inc. 13,680 sq. m. swamp and water; p. (estd.) *8,133,000*.

Ughelli, *t.*, Nigeria; glass wks.

Uinta, *mtn. range* Utah, U.S.A.; its highest points are Emmons (13,694 ft.), Gilbert Peak (13,687 ft.), and Wilson (13,300 ft.).

Uist, N. *I.*, Outer Hebrides, Inverness, Scot.; separated from I. of Skye by Little Minch; length, 17 m., width 3–13 m.

Uist, S., *I.*, Outer Hebrides, Inverness, Scot.; most S. lge. I. of Outer Hebrides gr.; length 22 m., width 8 m.

Uitenhage, *t.*, Cape Prov., S. Africa; summer resort, fruit, wool, rly. wks., tyres, car assembly, textiles; p. (1960) *48,755* inc. 17,531 whites.

Ujiji, *t.*, in sm. terr. same name (a. 920 sq. m.) on E. shore L. Tanganyika, E. Africa; where Stanley found Livingstone 1871; p. (1957) *12,149*.   [p. (1947) *63,093*.

Ujiyamada, *t.*, Japan; sacred c. of Shintoism;

Ujjain, *t.*, Madhya Pradesh, India; sacred c.; univ.; p. (1961) *144,161*.

Ujpest, *t.*, Hungary; nr. Budapest; elec. engin.; leather, shoes, textiles, furniture, pharmaceutics; p. *76,000*.

Ukerewe, *I.*, on L. Victoria, Central Africa.

Ukpilla, *t.*, Nigeria; cement wks.

Ukraine, *constituent rep.*, U.S.S.R.; fertile "black earth" region; agr., wheat, maize, barley; tobacco, sheep, pigs; coal, iron-ore, manganese; mnfs., flour, sugar brewing, chemicals, smelting, hydro-elec. oil; cap. Kiev; a. 225,000 sq. m.; p. (1970) *47,136,000*.

Ulan Bator, *t.*, *cap.*, Mongolian People's Republic; in stock-raising region; comm. ctr.; iron, metals, machin.; woollen inds., furniture; p. (1962) *218,000*.

Ulan-Ude (Verkhneudinsk), *t.*, Siberia, R.S.F.S.R.; on L. Baikal; engin., textiles, glass, leather; p. (1967) *220,000*.

Ulcinj, *ancient c.*, Montenegro, Jugoslavia; tobacco olive oil; p. *5,000*.

Uleåborg (Oulu), *spt.*, Finland; on G. of Bothnia; shipbldg exp. pitch, timber, hides, butter; p. (1961) *59,163*.

Ulhasnagar, *c.*, Maharashtra, India; new c. built for refugees from Pakistan; p. (1961) *107,760*.

Ullswater, *L.*, on border Cumberland and Westmorland, Eng.; 8 m long; outlet by R. Eamont to the Eden.

Ulm, c., Baden-Württemberg, W. Germany; on R. Danube; cath.; machin., textiles, cars, radios; rly junction; p. (1963) 94,400.

Ulsan, t., S. Korea; oil refining, fertilisers.

Ulster, anc. Irish prov.; comprised nine counties: six of these (Down, Antrim, Armagh, Fermanagh, Londonderry and Tyrone) now form Northern Ireland. a. 5,238 sq. m.; p. (1961) 1,423,127; three counties (Cavan, Monaghan, Donegal) are in the Rep. of Ireland; largely agr. tourism; gr. industl. expansion; a. 3,123 sq. m.; p. (1966) 208,027.

Ulva, I., Argyll, Scot.; off W. cst. of Mull; 5 m. long.

Ulverston, t. urb. dist., N.W. Lancs, Eng.; nr. Morecambe Bay; paper-mills, hardware mftg.; iron, corn, brewing; p. (1961) 10,515.

Ulyanovsk, t., R.S.F.S.R.; on R Volga; engin., textiles; p. (1967) 275,000. [50,000.

Uman, t., Ukrainian S.S.R.; iron; p. (1954) 55,534,000.

Umbria, region, Italy; between Tuscany and the Marches, and Rome and the Abruzzi; comprising the prov. of Perugia; mtnous., fertile valleys; a. 3,271 sq. m.; p. (1961) 788,546.

Ume älv, R., Sweden; flows S.E. to the G. of Bothnia; length 250 m.

Umeå, t., Sweden; at mouth of Ume älv; woodpulp; cultural ctr.; p. (1961) 22,623.

Umm-al-Ghuwain, emirate, one of seven Trucial sts., p. (estd. 1968) 8,000.

Umtali, t., Rhodesia; impt. distr. ctr., timber, fruit, veg., car assembly, engin., textiles; oil refinery at Feruka; pipeline to Beira p. (1961) 41,900 inc. 8,410 whites.

Umtata, t., E. Cape Prov., S. Africa; admin. ctr. of Transkeian terrs; cath; p. (1960) 12,287, inc. 3,439 whites.

Una, R., N. Jugoslavia; trib. of R. Sava.

Unalaska, lge. I., Alaska, U.S.A.; in Aleutian gr.; mtnous., treeless; ch. pt. of Bering Strait.

Uncia, t., Oruro dep., Bolivia; alt. 13,000 ft. in E. Cordillera of Andes, 60 m. S.E. of Oruro; site of impt. Patino tin-mines.

Ungava Bay, arm of Hudson Strait, projecting into Labrador, N.E. Canada; lge. forests in the S., minerals abundant, recent exploitation of impt. medium and low-grade iron deposits.

Union, t., Murcia prov., Spain, E. of Cartagena; ctr. of rich lead, silver, iron and zinc mines; p. c. 13,000.

Union of Soviet Socialist Republics, cty., Europe, Asia; stretches across two continents from the Baltic Sea to the N. Pac. Oc. and from the Arctic to the Black Sea, bounded on the W. by Finland, Poland, Hungary and Romania, on the S. by Turkey, Persia, Afghanistan, and China; The Union consists of 15 Union Republics; R.S.F.S.R., Ukrainian, Byelorussian, Azerbaydzhan, Georgian, Armenian, Turkmen, Uzbek, Tadzik, Kazakh, Kirghiz, Moldavian, Estonian, Lithuanian and Latvian S.S.R.'s. These reps. are divided into 126 terrs. and regions which include 18 autonomous reps., 10 autononomous regions and 10 national areas. European portion, separated in the E. from Asia by Ural Mtns., is a vast low plain with Caucasus Mtns. in the S. In Asia the ctr. and N. is occupied by the vast plain of Siberia, rising in the S. to lofty mtn. ranges, Pamirs, Tien Shan, Sayan, Yablonovy, Stanovoi, etc. Rs. are impt.: Dnieper, Volga, Ural and Don in Europe flowing southwards; Ob, Yenisei and Lena in Asia flowing northwards into Arctic Ocean; and Amur into Pac. Oc. N. and central regions—long, cold winters; short, cool summers, S. regions—temperate and sub-tropical; desert and semi-desert E. of Caspian Sea. In N. tundra and immense forests with lumbering and associated inds.; agr., wheat, oats, barley, rye, flax, potatoes, sugar-beet, tobacco, cotton, silk, rubber, vines, tea, rice; rich fisheries; impt. minerals; coal, oil, lignite, iron ore, manganese, chrome ore, platinum, copper, lead, zinc, nickel, uranium, asbestos, mica, apatite, nepheline, bauxite; many hydro-elect. plants inc. lgst. in Europe; nuclear power stas.; good rly. and canal systems; highly developed inds. inc. metallurgical prods., textiles, chemicals, cellulose-paper and lumbering, leather goods, foodstuffs preparation. Ch. spts. Leningrad, Murmansk, Arkhangelsk, Vladivostok (kept open by icebreakers), Odessa, Sevastopol, Novorossik, Batumi; cap. Moscow; a. 8,649,000 sq. m.; p. (1970) 241,748,000.

Union City, t., N.J., U.S.A.; many small firms do embroidery work; p. (1960) 52,180.

Union Islands. See Tokelau.

United Arab Republic (Egypt), indep. sov. st. (1958). N.E. corner Africa; desert, except fertile Nile valley; agr. depends on annual rise of Nile waters and irrigation (Aswan High Dam); cotton, rice, sugar cane, wheat, barley, maize, onions, fruit; cotton yarn and textiles; phosphates; oilfield in Israeli-occupied Sinai and recent finds offshore in G. of Suez and in Western Desert; cap. Cairo; ch. spts. Alexandria, Port Said, Suez; a. 386,000 sq. m.; p. (1969) 33,000,000.

United Kingdom, cty., N.W. Europe; separated from continent of Europe by Eng. Channel; consists of Gr. Britain (Eng., Wales, Scot.) and N. Ireland; a. 94,214 sq. m.; p. (estd. 1969) 55,534,000.

United States, federal rep., N. America; ch. physical features: Great Ls., lgst. freshwater a. in the world; ch. Rs.: Mississippi-Missouri, Rio Grande del Norte, Colorado, Hudson, Susquehanna, Savannah, Columbia; ch. mtns.: Rocky Mtns., Coast Range, Sierra Nevada, Appalachian Mtns.; Great Basin, great plains, Piedmont plateau, coastal plains; climate in N.E.—cool, temperate, rainfall all year round, warm summers, cold winters; in central plains and Gr. Basin—continental climate of extremes; in N.W.—cool temperate with abundant rainfall warm summers, cold winters; in S.W. on Pacific cst.—Mediterranean climate of very warm summers and drought, mild winters with rainfall, dense fogs off Pacific cst.; in S. and S.E. sub-tropical, hot summers, mild winters with abundant rainfall in the S.E. decreasing towards the W.; ch. inds.: agr., maize, wheat, oats, etc., fruit, potatoes, hay, alfalfa, cane- and beet-sugar, cotton, tobacco; pastoral farming, ranching, dairying, sheep, wool, cattle, pigs, horses; lumbering, timber, wood-pulp; fishing off Grand Bank, Newfoundland, for cod, etc., and in W. for salmon; minerals: coal, petroleum, natural gas, phosphate, iron ore, copper, lead, gold, silver, zinc, aluminium, mercury; mftg. of all kinds; commerce; comprises 50 sts. and Dist. of Columbia; cap. Washington; lgst. ts. New York, Chicago, Los Angeles, Philadelphia; total a. (inc. possessions) 3,553,898 sq. m.; p. (estd. 1970) 200,263,721.

University City, t., Mo., U.S.A.; p. (1960) 51,249.

Unna, t., N. Rhine–Westphalia, Germany; coalmng., machin., iron; p. (1963) 31,000.

Unst, I., Shetlands; most N. of gr.; length 12½ m.

Unstrut, R., Saxony, Germany; trib. of R. Saale, length 110 m.

Untersee, W. portion of L. of Constance.

Unterwalden, old can., Switzerland; now subdivided into Obwalden and Nidwalden; dairying, fruit and livestock; ch. ts. are Sarnen and Stans.

Upholland, t., urb. dist., Lancs., Eng.; 4 m. W. of Wigan; bricks; p. (1961) 7,451.

Upper Austria, prov., Austria; cap. Linz; a. 4,625 sq. m.; p. (1961) 1,131,623.

Upper Hutt, c., N.I., N.Z.; p. (1966) 19,084.

Upper Nile, prov., Sudan. N.E. Africa; cap. Malakal; a. 92,270 sq. m.; p. (1964) 1,037,736.

Upper Seal Lake, Labrador, Newfoundland, Canada.

Upper Volta, see Voltaic Republic.

Uppsala, co., E. Sweden; N. of L. Mälar; cap. Uppsala; a. 2,056 sq. m.; p. (1961) 167,735.

Uppsala, t., cap. Uppsala, Sweden; on R. Sala; 45 m. from Stockholm; univ., cath.; lt. inds.; p. (1961) 77,518.

Ur, ancient Chaldean c. Iraq; 130 m. W.N.W. of Basra; ruins; flourished about 3,000 B.C.

Ural Mtns., R.S.F.S.R.; mtns. separating Asia from Europe; 2,050 m. long; highest summit, Tolposis Mtn., 5,430 ft.

Ural, R., R.S.F.S.R.; flows S.W. and S. to the Caspian Sea; length 1,500 m.

Uralsk, t., Kazakh S.S.R.; on R. Ural; grain-trading and cattle-mart. ctr.; flour, leather, woollens, iron-ware; p. (1967) 119,000.

Uranium City, N. Saskatchewan, Canada; nr. N. shore of L. Athabasca, ctr. of Beaverlodge uranium-mining a.; founded 1951; p. (1953) approx. 500. [of st. univ.; p. (1960) 27,294.

Urbana, c., Ill., U.S.A.; on Embarrass R.; seat **Urbino**, t., N. Marche, Italy; cath., univ.; silk, cheese, olive oil; p. 20,375.

Ure, *R.*, N.R. Yorks., Eng.; flows E. and S.E. to the Swale to form the Ouse; length 50 m.

Urfa, *t.*, Turkey; nr. Syrian border; gd. local tr.; p. (1965) *72,873.*

Uri, *can.*, Switzerland; S. of L. of Lucerne; forest and mtn.; traversed by St. Gotthard Rly. and R. Reuss; cap. Altdorf; a. 415 sq. m.; p. (1961) *32,021.*

Urmia (Rizaieh), *t.*, Azerbaijan, Iran; birth-place of Zoroaster; p. *64,000.*

Urmia, L. of, nr. Tabriz, N.W. Iran; 85 m. by 30 m.; salt and shallow.　　　　[*43,300.*

Urmston, *urb. dist.*, Lancs., Eng.; p. (estd. 1967)

Urubamba, *R.*, Peru, S. America; rises in E. Cordillera of Andes; forms one of head streams of R. Amazon; length 350 m.

Urubupunga, *t.*, Brazil; new t. for 10,000 at site of hydro-elec. sta.

Uruguaiana, *t.* Brazil; on R. Uruguay; cattle ctr.; jerked beef, soap, candles; p. (1960) *48,358.*

Uruguay, *rep.*, S. America; climate, temperate; moderate rainfall; vegetation temperate and sub-tropical grasslands; language, Spanish; religion, R. C.; cattle- and sheep-rearing, wheat, olives, grapes, gold, textiles; cap. Monte-video; a. 72,153 sq. m.; p. (1968) *2,818,000.*

Uruguay, *R*, S. America; rises in S. Brazil, and flows between Argentina and Brazil and Uruguay to Rio de la Plata; length 850 m.

Urumchi (Wulumuchi), *c.*, Sinkiang, China; p. (1953) *141,000.*　　　　　　　　　　　　[wide.

Urup, *I.*, Kurile gr., Pac. Oc.; 50 m. long; 12 m.

Usa, *R.*, U.S.S.R.; flows E. from the Urals to the Pechora; length 220 m.

Usak, *t.*, Turkey; connected by rail with Izmir; noted for pile carpet-weaving; p. (1965) *38,815.*

Usedom (Uznam), *I.*, Baltic Sea; off mouth of R. Oder; since 1945 the E. part belongs to Poland, the W. (the larger part) to Germany; I. is 30 m. long and 14 m. wide.

Ushant, *I.*, off cst. of Finisterre, France; at entrance to Eng. Channel; it was off Ushant that Lord Howe gained his great naval victory on the "glorious first of June," 1794.

Ushuaia, *t.*, Argentina; most southerly t. in world; sheep farming, timber, furs; freezing plant; p. *6,000.*

Usk, *R.*, S. Wales; flows S. to Bristol Channel; length 57 m.

Usküdar (Scutari), *t.*, Turkey; on Bosporus, op-posite Istanbul; mkt. ctr.; various mnfs.; bridge under constr. to European side of Bosporus; p. (estd. 1960) *85,000.*

Uspallata Pass, Andes, Argentina; used by the Mendoza–Valparaiso Transandine rly.

Ussuri, *R.*, N. China; rises in Maritime prov. of R.S.F.S.R., flowing *c.* 500 m. to R. Amur; final 300 m. forms Sino-Soviet boundary.

Ussuriysk (Voroshilov), *t.*, R.S.F.S.R.; 70 m. N. of Vladivostok; rly. junction; soya oil, sugar; p. (1967) *123,000.*

Ust Kamenogorsk, *t.*, Kazakhstan, U.S.S.R.; lead refining; hydro-elec. power sta. nearby on R. Irtish; p. (1967) *207,000.*

Ustica, *I.*, Italy; hilly; fruit, olives, grain, osiers; fishing; a. 3 sq. m.

Usti Nad Labem, *t.*, ČSSR.; on the Elbe; chemicals, coal; p. (1962) *63,819.*

Usumacinta, *R.*, Mexico and Guatemala, Central America; trib. of R. Tabasco; length 400 m.

Usumbura, *t.*, Burundi, Africa; cotton ginnery, soapwks.; exp. cotton, coffee, hides; p. (estd. 1949) *17,188.*

Utah, *W. st.*, U.S.A.; farming, wheat, maize, barley, rye, livestock, sugar-beet, fruits; copper, silver, lead, gold, coal, uranium, vanadium; petroleum; fruit-canning; cap. Salt Lake City; a. 84,916 sq. m.; p. (1970) *1,060,631.*

Utah, *L.*, U.S.A., drains by R. Jordan to Gr. Salt L., 23 m. by 8 m.

Utica, *c.*, N.Y., U.S.A.; on Mohawk R.; clothing and other mnfs.; p. (1960) *100,410.*

Utiel, *t.*, Spain; W. of Valencia; brandies, wines; p. (1957) *13,365.*

Utrecht, *prov.*, Neth.; between Gelderland and N. and S. Holland; fertile agr., cattle rearing, horticulture; a. 526 sq. m.; p. (1967) *758,007.*

Utrecht, *c.*, Neth.; on Old R. Rhine; univ., cath.; chemical and cigar factories; printing, machin., woollens, silks, velvets; p. (1967) *274,485.*

Utrera, *t.*, Spain; S.E. of Seville; industl.; p. (1957) *34,893.*

Uttar Pradesh, *st.*, India; Himalayas on N. bdy.,

drained by Ganges and Jumna; splendid irriga-tion; wheat, rice, millet, barley, maize, cotton, sugar, oil-seeds; ch. ts. Allahabad, Lucknow (cap.), Varanasi, Cawnpore, Agra, Meerut; a. 113,410 sq. m.; p. (1961) *73,746,401.*

Uttoxeter, *t.*, *urb. dist.*, Staffs, Eng.; on R. Dove, 10 m. N.W. of Burton-on-Trent; machin., biscuit mftg.; p. (1961) *8,168.*

Uusimaa, *dep.*, Finland; a. 4,435 sq. m.; cap. Helsinki; p. (1966) *942,947.*

Uvira, *pt.*, Congo, Central Africa; on N.W. cst. of L. Tanganyika; exp. coffee, cotton, hides; bricks, cotton ginning.

Uxbridge, *mkt. t.*, *former mun. bor.*; Middx. Eng.; on R. Colne; now inc. in Hillingdon outer bor., Greater London; residtl.; light inds., film studio; p. (1961) *63,941.*

Uzbekistan, *constituent rep.*, U.S.S.R.; intensive farming based on irrigation; rice, cotton, fruits, silk, cattle, sheep; cap. Tashkent; alluvial gold deposits and bauxite in Kyzyl-Kum desert; a. 159,170 sq. m.; p. (1970) *11,963,000.*

Uzen, (Gr. and Little), *Rs.*, U.S.S.R., flowing 250 m. to the Caspian Sea.

Uzgen, *region*, Kirghiz, S.S.R., U.S.S.R.; coal cotton. engin.

Uzhgorod, *t.*, Ukrainian S.S.R.; univ.; wood-workings, food inds.; engin.; p. (1959) *47,000.*

Uzhoi Cape, *promontory*, on Ob. Bay, N. Siberia, U.S.S.R.

Uzlovaya, *t.*, R.S.F.S.R.; 30 m. S.E. of Tula; coal mng.; impt. rly. junction; p. (1959) *54,000.*

V

Vaal, *R.*, S. Africa; rises in Drakensberg Mtns., and flows between the Transvaal and Orange Free State to join the Orange R. nr. Kimberley; length 560 m.

Vaasa (Vasa), *dep.*, Finland; cap. Vaasa; p. (1966) *448,509.*

Vaasa, *t.*, *pt.*, *cap.*, Vaasa, Finland; on G. of Bothnia; oats, butter, cattle exp.; p. (1966) *47,528.*

Vác, *t.*, Hungary; on R. Danube; chemicals, textiles, cement. boat-mkg.; p. (1962) *26,679.*

Vaduz, *t.*, *cap.*, Liechtenstein; p. (1960) *3,398.*

Váh, *R.*, Czechoslovakia; trib. of R. Danube; length 200 m.

Valais, *can.*, Switzerland; comprising upper valley of R. Rhône; surrounded by high mtns.; cap. Sion; a. 2,021 sq. m.; p. (1961) *177,783.*

Valdai Hills, U.S.S.R.; N.W. of Moscow; highest summit 1,100 ft.

Val d'Aosta, *aut. reg.*, N. Italy;　　　[power sta.

Valdecañas, Spain, 120 m. S.W. Madrid; dam and

Val-de-Marne, *dep.*, France, Paris reg.; p. (1968) *1,121,340.*

Valdepeñas, *t.*, Central Spain; mineral springs, wine; p. *26,000.*

Valdivia, *prov.*, S. Chile; cap. Valdivia; a. 7,721 sq. m.; p. (1960) *302,779.*

Valdivia, *t.*, cap. Valdivia, S. Chile; on R. Calle-calle nr. the sea (pt. Corral); damaged by earth-quake and tidal wave, May 1960; univ.; metal, wood and leather goods; paper, flour, brewing; p. (1961) *85,000.*

Val d'Oise, *dep.*, France, Paris reg.; p. (1968) *693,269.*

Valdosta, *t.*, Ga., U.S.A.; rly. ctr., cotton mills, light engin.; p. (1960) *30,652.*

Valence, *t.*, cap. Drôme, France; on left bank of R. Rhône; metal-founding, silks, hosiery, vineyards; p. (1962) *55,023.*

Valencia, *prov.*, Spain; on Mediterranean; agr., vineyards, olive-, fig-, and orange-growing, stock-rearing, silk, tapestry carpet mftg.; cap. Valencia; a. 4,239 sq. m.; p. (1959) *1,451,037.*

Valencia, *t.*, cap. Valencia, Spain; on R. Turia, 3 m. from the Mediterranean; univ., museum, cath.; active industl. and comm. ctr.; mnfs., linen, leather, cigars, silks, exp. wine, fruits, corn, etc.; p. (1965) *585,000.*

Valencia, *I.*, S.W Kerry, Ireland; 6 m. by 2 m.

Valencia, *t*, Venezuela, S. America; univ.; ctr. of agr. a.; most industrialised town in rep.; p. (1961) *161,410.*

Valencia, *L.*, Venezuela; a. 216 sq. m.; sur-rounded by swampy flats used for cattle-grazing.

Valenciennes, *t.*, Nord, France; on R. Escaut; tex-tiles, machin.; oil ref.; famous for lace ind.; (1968) *46,626.*　　　　　　　　　　　　[*44,820.*

Valera, *t.*, Trujillo, Venezuela; airport; p. (1961)

Valladolid, *prov.*, Central Spain; agr., vineyards, livestock, mnfs.; cap. Valladolid; a. 3,155 sq. m.; p. (1959) *368,049.*

Valladolid, *t.*, cap. Valladolid, Spain; on R. Pisuerga; seat of army corps, univ. cath.; thriving inds. and tr.; p. (1965) *172,000.*

Vallecas, *sub.* Madrid, Spain.

Valle d'Aosta, *aut. region*, N.W. Italy; a. 1,260 sq. m.; p. (1961) *99,754.*

Valle del Cauca, *dep.*, Colombia, S. America; cap. Cali.; a. 8,083 sq. m.; p. (estd. 1959) *1,596,650.*

Vallejo, *c.*, Cal., U.S.A.; exp. fruit and corn, milling; p. (1960) *60,977.*

Vallenar, *t.*, Atacama prov., Chile; agr. ctr.; dried fruit, wines; iron ore nearby; p. (1960) *30,793.*

Valletta, *spt.*, *cap. c.*, Malta; on N.E. cst. of I.; strongly fortfd., fine harbour; univ.; cath.; p. (1967) *15,254.* (paper; p. (1961) *27,297.*

Valleyfield, *t.*, Quebec Canada; textiles, glazed

Valona, *see* Vlonë.

Valparaiso, *prov.*, Chile; cap. Valparaiso; a. 1,860 sq. m.; p. (1961) *648,449.*

Valparaiso, *c.*, *spt.*, cap. Valparaiso, Chile; the most impt. pt. on the Pacific cst. of S. America; and the ch. mftg. comm. and industl. ctr. of the Rep. of Chile; locomotives. rolling-stock, sugar-refining, textiles, chemicals, tanneries; p. (1961) *259,241.*

Van, *fortfd.*, *c.*, Turkey; on E. side of L. Van, S. of Erzurum; p. (1965) *31,010.*

Van, *prov.*, Turkey; mtnous., pastoral; sulphur springs, petroleum wells; p. (1965) *267,111.*

Vancouver, *spt.*, B.C., Canada; international airport and terminus of trans-continental rly.; univ.; lumbering, shipblds., fishing; oil- and sugar-refining; p. (1966) *892,286.*

Vancouver, *t.*, Wash., U.S.A.; dairying, milling, fruit, lumbering, canning; p. (1960) *32,464.*

Vancouver, *I.*, B.C., Canada; off W. cst.; mtnous., forests; woodpulp, paper; tourism; cap. Victoria; a. 13,049 sq. m.; p. (1956) *361,952.*

Vandellos, Tarragona, Spain; nuclear power sta.

Vanderbijlpark, *t.*, Transvaal, S. Africa; on Vaal R.; ctr. for steel wks.; p. (1960) *41,318* (inc. 21,857 whites).

Van Diemen Gulf, between Darwin and Coburg Peninsula, N. Terr., Australia.

Vänern, *lge. L.* Sweden; W.N.W. of L. Vättern, with which it is connected by canal (and thence with the Baltic); a. 2,149 sq. m.

Vänersborg, *L. pt.*, Sweden; on a tongue of land between the R. Göta and the Vasobotten (the southernmost bay of L. Vänern); footwear, wood and sulphite pulp; p. (1961) *18,491.*

Vannes, *ch. t.*, Morbihan, France; on S. cst. Brittany; shipbldg., ironwks., breweries, ropes, leather, oysters; p. (1962) *34,107.*

Var, *R.*, Alpes-Maritimes, France; flows S. to the Mediterranean Sea; length 60 m.

Var, *dep.*, S. France; on the Mediterranean; pasture, vineyards, sericulture, wines, olives, paper; cap. Draguignan. Toulon lgst. c.; a. 2,333 sq. m.; p. (1968) *555,926.*

Varanasi (formerly Benares) *t.*, India; on Ganges, Hindu holy city; annual pilgrimage; temples, mosques, palaces, univ.; brocade, gold, silver, lacquer, locomotives; p. (1961) *489,864.*

Varanger Fjord, an inlet of the Arctic Ocean into Finnmark, Norway's most N. prov

Varazdin, *t.*, Croatia, Jugoslavia; on R. Drava; woollens, coal; p. (1959) *23,000.*

Varberg, *spt.*, Halland, Sweden; resort; granite quarries; p. *11,874.*

Vardar, *R.*, Jugoslavia, Greece; flows S. into G. of Thessalonika; length 280 m.

Varde, *t.*, W. Jutland, Denmark; agr. and route ctr.; food processing; steelwks.; p. (1960) *9,577.*

Varese, *t.*, N. Italy; silk-spinning, wine, paper, leather, aircraft; p. (1961) *64,977.*

Värmland, *co.*, Sweden; a. 7,427 sq. m.; p. (1961) *291,085.*

Varna, *fortfd. spt.*, Bulgaria; on Black Sea; univ.; shipbldg., textiles, grain; trading ctr.; p. (1956) *119,769.*

Varpalota, *t.*, Hungary; lignite mines; aluminium, fertilisers, oil; p. (1962) *22,853.*

Vásárhely or Hódmezö Vásárhely, *t.*, Hungary; wine, tobacco.

Västerås, *t.*, *cap.*, Västmanland, Sweden; on N. bay of L. Malar; Gothic cath. (with episcopal library), 16th-century cas.; impt. elec. inds.; ower sta.; p. (1961) *77,946.*

Västerbotten, *co.*. Sweden; a. 22,839 sq. m.; p. (1961) *239,625.*

Västernorrland, *co.*, Sweden; a. 9,925 sq. m.; p. (1959) *283,231.*

Västervik, *t.*, Sweden; on Baltic cst.; engin., iron, wire, nails, chemicals, paper; p. (1961) *18,193.*

Västmanland, *co.*, Sweden; N. of L. Malar; cap. Västeras; a. 2,611 sq. m.; p. (1961) *232,589.*

Vathéos, *spt.*, Samos I., Greece; exp. wine, olive oil, leather, tobacco, raisins.

Vatican City, the Papal st. of Italy; a. 108·7 acres; p. (estd.) *1,000.*

Vatna Jökull, *mtn.*, Iceland; elevated snowfield.

Vättern, *L.*, Sweden; 25 m. S.E. L. Vänern; a. 733 sq. m.

Vaucluse, *dep.*, S.E. France; ag.., wines, sericulture, linen, silks, pottery; cap. Avignon; a. 1,381 sq. m.; p. (1968) *353,966.*

Vaud, or Pays de Vaud, *can.*, W. Switzerland; N. of L. of Geneva; timber, forests and vineyards; cap. Lausanne; a. 1,239 sq. m.; p. (1961) *429,512.*

Växjö, *t.*, Sweden; engin., timber wks., hosiery; p. (1961) *24,041.*

Vecht, R., Neth.; branch of Rhine, flows into IJsselmeer.

Vecses, *t.*, Hungary; p. (1962) *15,540.*

Véjer de la Frontera, *t.*, Spain; nr. C. Trafalgar; agr. and stock-rearing; p. (1957) *12,569.*

Vejle, *spt.*, Jutland, Denmark; gd. harbour and tr.; textiles, iron ind., leather, soap; p. (1960) *31,362.*

Velbert, *t.*. N. Rhine–Westphalia, Germany; N.W. of Wuppertal; metal ind. locks and keys; p. (1963) *53,000.*

Veleki Bečkerek, *see* Zrenjanin.

Veles, *see* Titov Veles.

Velez Málaga, *c.*, Malaga, Spain; famous for wine, raisins, sugar, olive oil; p. (1957) *31,610.*

Veliki Ustyug, *t.*, R.S.F.S.R.; on R. Sukhona; shipbldg., silver craft; p. (1956) *35,800.*

Velletri, *t.*, Italy; foot of the Alban Hills overlooking Pontine Marshes; gd. wine; at this spot Garibaldi gained a victory over the King of Naples, 1849; p. (1961) *40,053.*

Vellore, *t.*, Tamil Nadu, India; perfumes, etc.; p. (1961) *113,742.*

Veluwe, *dist.*, Gelderland, Neth.; between Arnhem and IJselmeer; low hills of glacial sands and sand-dunes; heathland and pinewoods; relatively low p. density.

Vendée or La Vendée, *dep.*, W. France; on Bay of Biscay; agr., fishing; cap. La Roche-sur-Yon; a. 2,692 sq. m.; p. (1968) *421,250.*

Vendôme, *t.*, Loir-et-Cher, France; on R. Loire; leather goods, cottons; p. (1962) *14,176.*

Venetia (Veneto or Venetia Euganea), *div.* N.E. Italy; between the Alps and the Adriatic; embraces provs. Vicenza, Verona, Venice, Udine, Treviso, Padua, Belluno and Rovigo; cap. Venice; a. 7,098 sq. m.; p. (1961) *3,833,837.*

Venetia Tridentina, *div.*, N. Italy; mountainous, lying between Austrian and Swiss frontiers and L. Garda; embraces provs. Trento and Bolzano; cap. Trento; a. 5,250 sq. m.; p. (1961) *747,221.*

Venezia Giulia, *see* Friuli-Venezia Giulia.

Venezuela, *rep.*, S. America; on Caribbean cst.; climate tropical, with temperate uplands, wet summers, dry winters, tropical forests, and grasslands (llanos); petroleum (one of the lgst. oil producing ctys. of the world), gold, copper, iron ore, coal, asphalt; new inds. in petrol a. inc. aluminium, cars, textiles, glass, agr. implements; pearl fishing, coffee, cocoa, sugar, maize, cotton, indigo, balata, tobacco; cap. Carácas; a. 352,143 sq. m.; p. (estd. 1968) *9,859,174.*

Venice, *maritime c.*, Italy; built on group of islets within a lagoon in G. of Venice, at head of the Adriatic; splendid architecture; rich in art treasures and historic associations; glassware, gold, silver, embroidery, lace, damask, shipbldg.; p. (1965) *364,000.*

Venlo, *t.*, Neth.; on the Maas; brewing, leather, ceramics, needles, tobacco; p. (1967) *60,773.*

Vennachar, *Loch*, Perth. Scot.; expansion of R. Teith.

Ventimiglia, *t.*, *cst. resort*, Italy; on Mediterranean cst. nr. Fr. border; cath.; p. *17,081.*

Ventnor, *t.*, *urb. dist.*, I. of Wight, Eng.; on S. cst., 11 m. S. of Ryde; mild climate, tourist and health resort; p. (1961) *6,410.*

Ventolene I., Pontine Is., Italy; vineyards, fruit.

Veracruz, c., pt., Veracruz, Mexico; on G. of Mexico; exp. ores, precious metals, textiles, raw cotton and petrol; p. (1960) 144,232.

Veracruz, prov., Mexico; contains volcano Orizaba; cap. Jalapa; a. 27,736 sq. m.; p. (1960) 2,727,899. [Santiago; p. (1968) 157,400.

Veraguas, prov., Panama, central America; cap.

Vercelli, c., Piedmont, Italy; cath.; cottons, woollens, machin., aircraft parts; exp. rice; p. (1961) 50,197.

Verde, C., most W. point, Africa, Senegal.

Verden, c., Lower Saxony, Germany; S.E. of Bremen; cath.; machin., glass, tobacco; p. (estd. 1954) 19,900.

Verdun, t., Quebec, Canada; p. (1961) 78,317.

Verdun, fortfd. t., Meuse, France; on R. Meuse; 12th-century cath.; confectionery, liqueur, hardware factories; scene of famous battle in First World War; p. (1962) 25,238.

Vereeniging, t., Transvaal, S. Africa; coal, iron and steel, bricks; Treaty of Vereeniging (31 May 1902) ended Boer War; p. (1962) 88,008 inc. 26,234 whites.

Verkhneudinsk, see Ulan-Ude.

Verkhneuralsk, t., R.S.F.S.R.; on Upper Ural R.; tanneries, distilleries; p. (1956) 11,000.

Verkhoyansk, t., Yakutsk A.S.S.R., R.S.F.S.R.; in N.E. Siberia; coldest place in world; mean January temp. of −59° F.; ctr. of fur trapping a.; p. (1956) 1,800.

Vermont, st., New England, U.S.A.; adjoining Quebec prov., Canada; traversed by the Green Mtns.; farming, dairying, stock-raising, lumbering, quarrying, machin. tool and textile mnftg.; cap. Montpelier; a. 9,609 sq. m.; p. (1970) 437,744.

Vern, Ille-et-Vilaine, France; nr. Rennes; oil refining. [p. (1961) 10,250.

Vernon, t., B.C., Canada; fruit, farming, canning;

Verona, fortfd. c., Venetia, Italy; on R. Adige; beautiful cath.; Roman antiquities; active tr. and inds.; iron goods, machin., paper, silk; p. (1964) 240,000.

Verona, prov. of Venetia region, Italy; a. 1,188 sq. m.; p. (1961) 665,053.

Verroia, t., N. Greece; S.E. of Thessaloniki; ancient Berea; p. (1961) 25,765.

Versailles, pref., Yvelines, France; 12 m. W.S.W. of Paris; famous royal palace; mkt. gardening, distilleries, etc.; Treaty of Versailles 1919; p. (1962) 95,149.

Verulamium, site of ancient Roman t., Herts, Eng.; on R. Ver, opposite St. Albans.

Verviers, t., Belgium; nr. Liége; cloth mnfs., glass, polystyrene mftg.; p. (1962) 35,125.

Vest Fjord, strait, separates Lofoten Is., from mainland, Norway. [169,779.

Vestfold, co., Norway; a. 96,359 sq. m.; p. (1968)

Vesuvius, famous active volcano, S. Italy; on side of Bay of Naples; alt. 3,984 ft.; its eruption in A.D. 79 destroyed Pompeii and Herculaneum.

Veszprem, t., Hungary; in Bakony; univ. for chemical ind.

Veurne (Furnes), t., W. Flanders, Belgium; sugar-refining; warehouses; p. (1962) 7,315.

Vevey, t., Vaud, Switzerland; on N.E. shore of L. of Geneva; chocolate, watches, machin.; p. (1957) 14,264.

Veyangoda, t., Ceylon; textiles.

Viacha, t., Bolivia, S. America; rly. junction nr. La Paz; cement; p. 2,000.

Viana do Castello, dist., Portugal; cap. Viana do Castello; a. 814 sq. m.; p. (1960) 280,100.

Viana do Castello, t., Portugal; at mouth of R. Lima, nr. Oporto; p. (1960) 14,371.

Viareggio, spt., resort, Italy; on Mediterranean, nr. Pisa; monument to the poet Shelley; p. (1961) 47,323.

Viazma, t., R.S.F.S.R.; N.E. of Smolensk, industrial.

Viborg, t., Jutland, Denmark; comm. and admin. ctr., knitted goods; cath.; p. (1960) 23,265.

Viborg (Viipuri), spt., R.S.F.S.R., U.S.S.R.; on G. of Finland; impt. industl. and transport ctr.; agr. machin., timber; p. (1959) 51,000.

Vicenza, c., Italy; woollens, cottons, silks, pottery, furniture mkg.; p. (1961) 97,617.

Vich (Vique), c., Spain; nr. Barcelona; cath.; mnfs.; p. (1957) 16,975.

Vichuga, t., R.S.F.S.R., N.E. of Ivanovo; ctr. of cotton ind.; p. (1959) 51,000.

Vichy, t., wat. pl., Allier, France; 35 m., S. of Moulins; mineral springs, lge. exp. of waters; seat of Gov. during German occupation. p. (1962) 32,178.

Vicksburg, c., Miss., U.S.A.; on cliffs above a "cut-off" L. on R. Mississippi; furniture, machin.; mftg. ctr. in cotton and timber region; prominent in American Civil War, Confederate surrender 1863; p. (1960) 29,130.

Victoria, st, Australian Commonwealth; mixed farming, grapes, mnfs., machin., hardware, textiles, wine, gold, coal, tin; oil refining at Crib Point, 45 m. from Melbourne; natural gas off E. cst.; cap. Melbourne; a. 87,884 sq. m.; p. (estd. 1968) 3,356,900.

Victoria, c., cap., B.C., Canada; on Vancouver I., sawmills, cement, chemicals, fish-canning; tourism; p. (1966) 57,453. [p. 42,873.

Victoria, spt., cap., Espirito Santo st., Brazil;

Victoria, t., cap., Seychelles, Ind., Oc.; gd. harb.

Victoria, t., cap., Labuan I., Sabah; fine harbour; p. (estd. 1957) 2,526.

Victoria, t., cap., Hong Kong; built on reclaimed land; p. (estd. 1965) 675,000.

Victoria Falls, on the R. Zambesi, Zambia, discovered by Livingstone in 1855; falls are 1,860 yd. wide and broken by islands and rocks.

Victoria, L., Kenya, Uganda, Tanzania, E. Africa; lgst. L. of Africa; lies on the Equator; a. 25,000–26,000 sq. m.; discharges to the N. by R. Nile; 3,705 ft. above sea; discovered by Captain Speke in 1858.

Victoria, L., on Gr. Pamir, Central Asia; 13,870 ft. above sea-level; supposed to be ch. source of the R. Oxus.

Victoria, R., flows into Queens Channel, N.W. cst. of Northern Terr. Australia.

Victoria Land, terr., N. Canada; S.E. of Prince Albert Land. [Ross in 1841.

Victoria Land, region, Antarctica; discovered by

Victoria Nile, R., Uganda, E. Africa; name of R. Nile from its source at L. Victoria until it enters L. Albert.

Victoria Strait, separates Victoria I. from King William I., Arctic Canada.

Victoria West, t., Cape Province, S. Africa; p. 2,535.

Victoriaville, t., Quebec, Canada; woodworking; p. (1961), 18,720.

Vidin, fortfd. t., Bulgaria; on R. Danube; ruined mosque and palace; p. (1956) 23,932. [7,000.

Viedma, t., cap., Rio Negro Argentina; p. (1960)

Vienna (Wien), cap., Austria; on branch of R. Danube; ranks also as prov.; univ., gothic cath. (St. Stephen's Church), Rathaus, Parliament bldgs., magnificent Prater park; thriving comm. and mnfs., silks, iron, steel, breweries, etc.; p. (1964) 1,639,000.

Vienne, R., France; trib. of the Loire; l. 220 m.

Vienne, dep., W. France; grain, wine, cutlery, arms; cap. Poitiers; a. 2,711 sq. m.; p. (1968) 340,256.

Vienne, t., Isère, France; nr. Grenoble, on R. Rhône; textiles, gloves; p. (1962) 23,163.

Vienne, Haute (Haute-Vienne), dep., France; fruits, cereals, livestock, porcelain; cap. Limoges; a. 2,119 sq. m.; p. (1968) 341,589.

Vientiane, cap., Laos; p. (estd. 1962) 100,000.

Viersen, t., N. Rhine-Westphalia, Germany; S.W. of Krefeld; textiles, machin., furniture, paper ind.; p. (1963) 42,200.

Vierzon, t., Cher, France; nr. Bourges; mnfs.; p. (1962) 31,951.

Viet-Nam, S.E. Asia; formerly within the French Union, covering 3 countries of Tongking, Annam and Cochin-China. Since 1954 div. into 2 zones. S. zone (Rep. of Vietnam) a. 66,300 sq. m., p. (estd. 1968) 17,414,000; cap. Saigon; rice, rubber. N. zone (Dem. Rep. of Vietnam) a. 63,000 sq. m., p. (1968) 20,700,000; cap. Hanoi; rice, coal, cement, apatite (phosphate).

Viet-Tri, t., N. Vietnam; 80 m. N.W. of Hanoi; chemicals, paper mill, sugar refining.

Vigevano, t., Lombardy, Italy; on R. Ticino; cath.; silks; p. (1961) 57,069.

Vigo, fortfd. t.; Galicia, Spain; on Rio de Vigo; impt. fishery and shipping inds.; flour, sugar, petroleum, leather; p. (1965) 166,000.

Vijayavada, t., Andhra Prad., India; irrigation dam, Kistna R., rice; p. (1961) 230,397.

Vila de João Belo (Chai Chai), t., Mozambique, Port. E. Africa; on R. Limpopo; exp. sugar, rice, timber, maize.

Vila Nova de Gala, t., Portugal; sub. of Oporto;

on R. Douro; pottery, wine-casks, tobacco and glass factories; p. (1960) 45,739.

Vila Real, dist., Portugal; a. 1,636 sq. m.; p. (1960) 333,156 of t. 10,263.

Villa Hermosa, cap., Tabasco, Mexico; p. (1960) 33,587.

Villa María, t., Argentina; rly. junction; grain, timber, dairying; p. (1960) 50,000.

Villach, t., Austria; iron, timber, leather, beer; tourist ctr.; p. (1961) 32,971.

Villanueva de la Serena, t., prov., Badajoz, Spain; wine, wheat, hemp and fruit; p. (1957) 18,391.

Villanueva y Geltrú, spt., Spain; nr. Barcelona; cotton ind., tyres; p. (1957) 19,483.

Villarrica, t., Paraguay; cath.; tobacco cotton, sugar, yerba-maté, hides, wines; p. (estd. 1960) 30,700.

Villavicencio, t., cap. Meta, Colombia, S. America, cattle raising; p. (estd. 1962) 48,355.

Villaviciosa, spt., Spain; on N. cst. 10 m. E. of Gijon; p. (1957) 20,348.

Villefranche, t., Rhône, France; on R. Rhône, nr. Lyons; cottons, wines; p. (1962) 24,957.

Villejuif, t., Seine, France; p. (1962) 46,130.

Villena, t., Alicante, Spain; silk, salt, brandy; p. (1957) 19,994.

Villeneuve St. Georges, t., Val-de-Marne, France; marshalling yards; p. (1962) 28,231.

Villeurbanne, t., Rhône, France; sub. Lyons; silk, rayon, metallurgy, chemicals, leather, glass; p. (1962) 107,630.

Villingen, t., Baden-Württemberg, Germany; in the Black Forest; clocks, elec., metals; p. (1963) 34,000.

Vilnius (Wilno, Vilna), cap., Lithuanian S.S.R.; Polish from 1919 to 1939; univ., cath.; timber, chemicals, engin.; p. (1967) 305,000.

Vilvorde, t., Brabant, Belgium; on R. Senne; oil and chemical factories; p. (1962) 32,133.

Viña del Mar, t., Chile; social resort; textiles, sugar; p. (1960) 126,441.

Vincennes, t., Ind., U.S.A.; milling, glass, steelwks.; p. (1960) 18,046.

Vincennes, sub., Paris, France; p. (1962) 50,499.

Vindhya, mtn. range, Madhya Prad., India; separating the Deccan from the Ganges basin

Vindhya Pradesh, former st., Indian Union; now absorbed into Madhya Pradesh 1 Nov. 1956; cereals, oil seeds; coal, iron, copper, bauxite.

Vinnitsa, t., Ukrainian S.S.R.; on R. Bug, 120 m. S.W. of Kiev; agr. mkt. t.; engin., chemicals, textiles; p. (1967) 154,000.

Virginia, st., U.S.A.; S. of Md.; tobacco culture; famous for natural bridge in Rockbridge County and mineral springs; " Virginia Leaf " tobacco is the finest the U.S. produces; rayon, shipbldg., iron, coal, chemicals; cap. Richmond; a. 40,815 sq. m.; p. (1970) 4,543,249. See also W. Virginia. [Eng.

Virginia Water, artificial L., nr. Windsor, Berks,

Virgin Is. (Brit.), part of Leeward Is. gr., W. Indies, a. 59 sq. m.; lgst. I. Tortola; fruit, vegetables, charcoal, rum, sugar, tobacco; p. (estd.) 10,500.

Virgin Isles (U.S.A.), gr. in the W. Indies; E. of Puerto Rico; purchased by U.S.A. from Denmark 1917, comprising the Is. of St. Croix, St. Thomas and St. John, and about 50 sm. Is.; total a. 133 sq. m.; oil refinery projected at St. Croix, p. (estd. 1969) 70,000.

Visby, old spt., Sweden; on Gotland I. in Baltic Sea; rich in historic interest; Gothic churches; resort; p. (1961) 15,604.

Viscaya, Basque prov., Spain; on Bay of Biscay; mineral inds., shipping, etc.; cap. Bilbao; a. 836 sq. m.; p. (1959) 722,030.

Vistula, R., Poland; rising in Silesia, and flowing past Krakow and through Poland to the Baltic nr. Gdańsk; navigable from Krakow to the sea; length 693 m.

Vitebsk, t., Byelorussian S.S.R.; on R. Dvina, 354 m. W. of Moscow; textile, machin. tools, food inds.; rly. junction; p. (1967) 194,000.

Viterbo, c., Italy; N. of Rome; alum mines, matches; p. (1961) 49,543.

Vitim, R., E., Siberia, R.S.F.S.R.; flows to R. Lena; length 900 m.

Vitória, spt., Espírito Santo, Brazil; exp. coffee, cocoa, fruit, iron ore; sugar refining, boots, shoes, textiles, cement; p. (estd. 1968) 121,843.

Vitoria, cap., Alava, Spain; wine, hardware, mules, horses; p. (1959) 60,148.

Vittoria. t., Sicily, Italy; silk mftg.; p. (1961) 38,628.

Vittorio Veneto, t., Italy; N. of Venice; resort; mineral springs; silk; p. 24,234.

Vizagapatam, impt. spt., E. cst. India; Andhra Prad.; exp. manganese and other mineral ores, tobacco, oil-seed, myrabalams and coir; sm. shipyard; oil-refining; fertilisers; p. (1961) 182,004.

Vizcaíno Bay, Lower Cal., Mexico.

Vizcaya, prov., N. Spain; cap. Bilbao; a. 836 sq. m.; p. (1950) 569,188.

Vizeu, dist., Portugal; cap. Vizeu; a. 1,955 sq. m.; p. (1960) 498,292. [76,808.

Vizianagram, t., Andhra Prad., India; p. (1961)

Vlaardingen, fishing t., S. Holland, Neth.; on R. Nieuwe Maas; p. (1967) 74,582.

Vladimir, c., R.S.F.S.R.; between Gorki and Moscow; cath.; farm produce, fruit, tobacco, engin., chemicals; p. (1967) 203,000.

Vladivostok, t., ch. spt., Siberia, U.S.S.R.; univ., H.Q. Army of the Far East; terminus of the Trans-Siberian rly. and airline from Moscow; oil-refining; p. (1967) 379,000. [Neth.

Vlieland, Friesian I., at entrance to IJsselmeer,

Vlissingen, spt., wat. pl.; Walcheren I., Zeeland, Neth.; summer resort, fishing and shipbldg. ctr.; p. (1967) 38,564.

Vionë, spt., Albania; on Strait of Otranto, Adriatic Sea; salt; oil pipe-line connects from Kuçovë; p. (1960) 33,000.

Vltava, R., Bohemia, Czechoslovakia; flows to R. Elbe, below Prague; length 262 m.

Voghera, t., Italy; silks; p. 30,422.

Voi, t., impt. rly. junction, Kenya, E. Africa; 90 m. N.W. of Mombasa on rly. to Nairobi; branch connection with Tanzania rly. system allows agr. produce from Arusha and Moshi dists. to pass through Mombasa as alternative to Tanga.

Voiron, t., Isère, France; on R. Isère nr. Grenoble; p. (1962) 15,585.

Volga, R., U.S.S.R.; rises on Vladai plateau, flows in a serpentine course to the Caspian at Astrakhan; frozen in winter; 2,325 m. long.

Volga Baltic Waterway (Mariinsk Waterway), R.S.F.S.R.; inland deep water navigation network linking Black Sea and Caspian Sea in S. with Baltic Sea and White Sea in N.

Volgograd (former Stalingrad), c., R.S.F.S.R.; on R. Volga, S. of Saratov; steel, engin., chemicals, oil-refining, hydro-elec. sta.; fierce siege and successful defence Sept. to Nov. 1942 turning point of the last war; p. (1967) 720,000.

Volhynia, dist., part of Ukraine S.S.R., U.S.S.R.; on Polish frontier (Polish 1919–39); a. 13,750 sq. m.; now prov. of Lutsk and Rovno.

Volkhov, R., R.S.F.S.R.; flows from L. Ilmen to L. Ladoga; length 130 m.

Völklingen, t., Saarland; on R. Saar; coal-mining, metallurgy. p. (1963) 42,900.

Volksrust, t., Transvaal, S. Africa; dairying; rly. wkshps.; p. (1960) 8,096 inc. 3,776 Europeans.

Vologda, t., R.S.F.S.R., U.S.S.R.; engin., textiles, sawmilling; p. (1967) 166,000. [(1951) 51,134.

Vólos, spt., Greece; at head of G. of Vólos; p.

Volpiano, nr. Turin, Italy; oil refinery under construction; pipeline to Geneva projected.

Volsk, t., R.S.F.S.R.; on R. Volga; gd. tr.; ironwks., tanneries, milling; p. (1959) 62,000.

Volta Redonda, t., Rio de Janeiro, Brazil; stateowned steel plants; p. (estd. 1968) 118,114.

Volta (White Volta), R., drains extensive terr. in Niger Bend, flows S. through Ghana to delta on Guinea cst. 70 m. E. of Accra; forms main means of communication; rapids make through navigation impossible; length 950 m. Volta R. project for industrialisation of Ghana: dam and power plant at Akosombo, aluminium smelter at Tema. See also Black Volta.

Voltaic Republic (former Upper Volta), ind. sov. st., W. Africa; cap. Ouagadougou; a. 100,000 sq. m.; p. (estd. 1968) 5,155,000.

Volterra, hill t., Tuscany, Italy; Etruscan and mediaeval walls; alabaster; p. 19,054. [10,000.

Voltri, t., Italy; shrine, shipbldg., ironwks.; p.

Volzhskiy, t., R.S.F.S.R.; new town 10 m. E. of Volgagrad; p. (1959) 67,000.

Vorarlberg, prov., Austria; cap. Bregenz (q.v.); a. 1,004 sq. m.; p. (1961) 226,323. [11,780.

Vordingborg, S., t., Zealand, Denmark; p. (1960)

Vorkuta, dist., Siberia, R.S.F.S.R.; about 120 m. W. of mouth of R. Ob; new coal-mining ctr. which supplies entire European north U.S.S.R.; p. of Vorkuta t. (1959) 55,000.

Voronezh, region, R.S.F.S.R., U.S.S.R.; agr.

stock-rearing, woodwork and domestic mnfs.; cap. Voronezh.

Voronezh, *t.*, R.S.F.S.R., U.S.S.R.; on R. Voronezh nr. its junction with R. Don; univ.; impt. comm. ctr.; synthetic rubber, engin.: p. (1967) 592,000.

Voroshilovgrad *see* Lugansk.

Voroshilovsk, *t.*, Ukrainian S.S.R.; 25 m. S.W. of Lugansk; ctr. of iron, steel and coking inds.; p. (1956) 98,000.

Vosges, *mtn. chain*, E. France; 190 m. long; highest summit, the Ballon de Guebwiller (4,672 ft.).

Vosges, *E. frontier dep.*, France; agr., dairying, vineyards, textiles, coal, stone; cap. Epinal; a. 2,305 sq. m.; p. (1968) 388,201.

Voskresensk, *t.*, R.S.F.S.R.; S.E. Moscow; lignite, chemicals, fertilisers; p. (1954) 50,000.

Votkinsk, *t.*, R.S.F.S.R.; 38 m. N.E. of Izhevsk; lge. engin. plant; p. (1959) 59,000.

Voyusa, *R.*, rises in Greece, flows N.W. through Albania into Strait of Otranto.

Vranja, *t.*, Jugoslavia; flax and hemp culture and mnf.; nr. is health resort of Vranyskas Banya; p. (1959) 15,000.

Vratca, *t.*, Bulgaria; on R. Vratcanska; jewellery, wine, silk, tanning; p. (1956) 26,582.

Vrede, *t.*, O.F S., S. Africa; agr. ctr.; horse-breeding; p. (1960) 6,770 (inc. 2,106 whites).

Vrsac, *t.*, Jugoslavia; milling, wine, brandy; p. (1959) 30,000.

Vryburg, *t.*, Cape Province, S. Africa; gold field in a.; stock-raising; p. (1960) 14,597 (inc. 4,309 whites).

Vryheid, *t.*, Natal, S. Africa; coal, iron, copper, gold, silver, lead mines; p. (1960) 10,783 (inc. 4,920 whites).   [Romania and Transylvania.

Vulcan Pass, in the Carpathian Mtns. between

Vulcano, *I.*, Lipari gr., Tyrrhenian Sea; located 12 m. off N.E. cst., Sicily; active volcano; gave its name as generic title for this type of mtn.

Vychegda, *R.*, Komi A.S.S.R., R.S.F.S.R.; flows W. to N. Dvina R.; length 700 m.

Vyrnwy, *L.*, *artificial reservoir*, Montgomery, Wales; with a dam 1,180 ft. long furnishing water for Liverpool; 5 m. long; a. 1,121 acres

Vyshni-Volochek, *t.*, R.S.F.S.R., U.S.S.R.; 74 m. N.W. of Kalinin; flour-milling, textiles, glass inds.; p. (1959) 66,000.

W

Waag. *see* Vah.

Waal, *R.*, Neth.; S. arm of R. Rhine.

Wabana, *see* Bell I.   [12,621.

Wabash, *c.*, Ind., U.S.A.; rly. ctr.; p. (1960)

Wabash, *R.*, Ohio and Ind., U.S.A.; trib. of R. Ohio; length 550 m.

Wabash and Erie, *canal*, Ind., U.S.A., longest canal in U.S.A.; 476 m. long.

Wabush, *t.*, Labrador, Canada; iron ore mines; p. (1965) 2,700.

Waco, *c.*, Texas, U.S.A.; on Brazos R.; univ.; cotton ctr., woollens grain, iron, leather; p. (1960) 97,807.

Wadai, *dist.*, Equatorial Africa; nr. L. Chad; desert and oases; pastoral; ivory, ostrich feathers; a. 17,000 sq. m.; p. (1947) 1,000,000.

Wadden Zee, *G.*, between W. Frisian Is. and N. Neth.

Waddington, *mtn.*, B.C., Canada; alt. 13,260 ft.

Wadebridge, *spt.*, *rural dist.*, Cornwall; at head of Camel estuary 6 m. N.W. of Bodmin; china clay; p. (rural dist. 1961) 14,907.

Wädenswil, *t.*, Zürich, Switzerland; on L. Zürich; silk, wool, textiles; wine, fruit; p. 10,000

Wadi Halfa, *t.*, Sudan, N.E. Africa; on R. Nile; at 2nd cataract; rly. terminus of Sudan rlys.; inundated by Aswan L.; new t. Khashm el Girba for inhabitants.

Wad Medani, *t.*, *cap.*, Blue Nile Prov., Sudan, Africa; grain, oil, soap; p. (1956) 57,000.

Wadsworth, *t.*, Ohio, U S.A.; matches, valves, engin.; p. (1960) 10,635.

Wagadugu, *see* Ouagadougou.   [Canada.

Wager Bay, *inlet*, of Hudson Bay, N.W. Terr.,

Wagga Wagga, *c.*, N.S.W., Australia; on R. Murrumbidgee; wheat, agr. pastoral ctr., dairying; large stock mkt., timber, rubber; p. (1966) 25,939.

Wahiawa, *t.*, Oahu I., Hawaii; pineapples; p. (1960) 15,512.   [Indonesia.

Waigeo, *I.*, off N. cst., Dutch New Guinea,

Waihi, *t.*, N.I., N.Z.; gold-mining; p. (1961) 3,164.

Waikaremoana, *L.*, N.I., N.Z.; hydro-elec. power plant.

Waikato, *R.*, N.I., N.Z.; the longest in N.Z.; length 220 m.

Wainuiomata, *co. t.*, on Wainuiomata R., N.I., N.Z.; p. (1966) 13,948.

Wairakei, *t.*, N.I., N.Z.; on L. Taupo; health resort; geothermal power sta.

Waitaki, *t.*, Otago, S.I., N.Z.; Benmore hydro-elec. power plant projected; p. (1961) 11,018.

Waitzen. *t.* Hungary; on R. Danube.

Wakamatsu, *t.*, Kyushu, Japan; now part of Kitakyushu City newly formed (1963) (*q.v.*); lacquer ware, mnfs.; p. (1960) 106,975.

Wakatipu, *L.*, Otago, S.I., N.Z.; 52 m. long, 3 m. wide; 1,200 ft. deep; 1,070 ft. above sea-level.

Wakayama, *spt.*, Honshu, Japan; cotton; p. (1964) 318,000.

Wake I., Pac. Oc.; between Marianas and Hawaii; calling-place on trans-Pacific air-routes; belongs to U.S.A.

Wakefield, *p.c., co. bor.*, W.R. Yorks, Eng.; on R. Calder; 8 m. S. of Leeds; cath.; worsted and woollens, coal, iron, boiler mkg., chemicals, glass, engin.; p. (estd. 1967) 60,200.

Wakefield, *t.*, Va., U.S.A.; George Washington's birthplace; p. 657.

Walachia, *dist.*, S. Romania; cereals, fruits; ch. t. Bucharest; a. 29,561 sq. m.; p. 5,029,212.

Walbrzych (Waldenburg), *t.*, Silesia, Poland; German before 1945; textiles, coal, porcelain, iron ware; p. (1965) 125,000.

Walcheren, *I.*, Zeeland, Neth.; 12 m. long, low-lying, agr.; was flooded to stop German advance in Second World War.

Waldeck, *see* Hessen-Nassau.

Waldenburg, *see* Walbrzych.

Wales, *principality*, S.W. of Gt. Britain; flanked by Irish Sea, St. George's Channel and Bristol Channel; mtns.; coal, slate, oats, barley, good pasturage, smelting tin, copper. iron; cap. Cardiff; a. 8,016 sq. m.; p. (estd. 1969) 2,724,540 (incl. Monmouthshire).

Walker, *t.*, Northumberland, Eng.; on R. Tyne; industl. sub. of Newcastle.

Wallaceburg, *t.*, Ontario, Canada; glass, brass, iron; sugar, flour; p. (1961) 7,881.

Wallaroo, *spt.*, S. Australia; clothing, fertilisers; p. (1966) 2,093.

Wallasey, *co. bor.*, on Mersey estuary, adjoining Birkenhead. Cheshire. Eng.; residtl., seaside resort (New Brighton); p. (estd. 1967) 102,470.

Walla Walla, *t.*, Wash., U.S.A.; on Mill Creek; cereal and fruit ctr., agr. tools, flour. leather; p. (1960) 24,536.

Wallensee, *L.*, Switzerland; 11 m. long.

Wallhamn, *pt.*, Sweden; on Tjörn I., 20 m. N.W. of Göteborg.

Wallingford, *t.*, *mun. bor.*, Berks, Eng.; on R. Thames, to N. of its gap between Chiltern Hills and Lambourn Downs; p. (estd. 1967) 5,870.

Wallingford, *t.*, Conn., U.S.A.; steel, brass, silver and nickel ware; tools, wire; p. (1960) 29,920.

Wallington, *t.*, N.J., U.S.A.; curtains, paints; p. (1960) 9,261.

Wallis Archipelago, *I. gr.*, S. Pacific; a. 40 sq. m.; status as overseas terr. Fr. Community (1962); p. (1959) 6,000.

Wallsend, *t.*, *mun. bor.*, Northumberland, Eng.; on N. bank of R. Tyne; 4 m. below Newcastle; coal-mining, shipbldg., engin., iron, plywood, plastics and quartz glass; p. (estd. 1967) 48,290.

Walmer, *t.*, Kent, Eng.; 2 m. S. of Deal; holiday resort; cas., residence of Warden of Cinque Ports; p. 5,335.

Walney, *I.*, off cst. of Lancs., Eng.; opposite Barrow.

Walpole, *t.*, Mass., U.S.A.; nr. Boston; p. (1960) 14,053.

Walpole, *I.*, dep. of New Caledonia; Pac. Oc.; Fr. possession, lies S.E. of Maré (Loyalty Is.).

Walsall, *t.*, *co. bor.*, Staffs, Eng.; 5 m. E. of Wolverhampton; leather and iron goods, engin., steel tubes; p. (estd. 1967) 183,680.

Walsham, N., *see* North Walsham.

Walsingham, *G.*, on Cumberland Peninsula, Baffin I., Canada.

Walsum, *t.*, N. Rhine–Westphalia, Germany; at confluence of Emscher and Rhine; coal-mining, paper, cellulose; p. (1963) 46,400.

Waltham, *c.*, Mass., U.S.A.; nr. Boston; watchmkg., textiles, motors, furniture, shoes, paper; p. (1960) *55,413*.

Waltham Abbey (Waltham Holy Cross), *t.*, Essex, Eng.; 13 m. N.E. London, on edge of Epping Forest; glasshouses (tomatoes); Norman nave of abbey part of parish church; gunpowder factories S. of *t.*; p. (1961) *11,655*.

Waltham Forest, *outer bor.*, E. London, Eng.; incorporating former bors. of Chingford, Leyton, Walthamstow; industl. and residtl.; p. (1966) *240,000*.

Walthamstow, *see* **Waltham Forest**.

Walton and Weybridge, *urb. dist.*, Surrey, Eng.; on R. Thames, 17 m. S.W. of London; engin., aircraft; p. (estd. 1967) *51,190*.

Walton-le-Dale, *t.*, *urb. dist.*, N.E. Lancs, Eng.; on R. Ribble, 2 m. E. of Preston; mkt. gardening, cottons, timber; p. (estd. 1967) *24,350*.

Walvis Bay, *dist.* and *spt.*, administered by S.W. Africa; a. 374 sq. m.; fishing, whaling; p. (1961) *16,490* (inc. *5,067* Europeans).

Wandsbeck, *t.*, Germany; sub. of Hamburg; beer, brandy, tobacco; p. *40,000*.

Wandsworth, *inner bor.*, S.W. London, Eng.; inc. Battersea; on R. Wandle at influx into Thames; oil-mills, metal-wks., paper, brewing; p. (1966) *332,000*.

Wanganui, *c.*, N.I., N.Z.; on R. Wanganui; wool, grain, meat, dairy prod.; p. (1966) *36,045*.

Wanganui, *R.*, N.I., N.Z.; l. 160 m., famous for its beauty.

Wangaratta, *c.*, Victoria, Australia; 145 m. from Melbourne; agr. dist.; nylon and woollen wks.; p. (1966) *15,167*.

Wankie, *t.*, Rhodesia; site of coalmng. ind.; 215 m. N.W. Bulawayo; p. (1958) *19,610* (incl. 2,460 Europeans).   [Hills; lead-mines.

Wanlockhead, *vil.*, Dumfries, Scot.; in Lowther

Wanne-Eickel, *t.*, N. Rhine–Westphalia, Germany; N.W of Bochum; coal-mining, chemicals; p. (1968) *100,510*.

Wansbeck, *R.*, Northumberland, Eng.; flows E. from Pennines into N. Sea 3 m. N. of Blyth; length 23 m.

Wanstead and Woodford, *see* **Redbridge**.

Wantage, *mkt. t.*, *urb. dist.*, Berks, Eng.; in Vale of the White Horse; hempen cloth, brass; p. (1961), *5,940*.

Wapping, *Thames-side dist.*, London, Eng.; contains the London Docks; industl.; p. *3,200*.

Warangal, *t.*, Andhra Prad., India; p. (1961) *156,106*.

Waratah, *t.*, N. Tasmania, Australia; tin-mining ctr.; magnetite ore on R. Savage, 25 m. W.S.W.

Warburg, *t.*, Germany; on R. Diemel; industl.

Wardha, *R.*, Madhya Pradesh, India; trib. of R. Wainganga; length 254 m.

Ware, *mkt. t.*, *urb. dist.*, Herts, Eng.; on R. Lea; 2 m. N.E. of Hertford; malting, bricks; p. (1961) *9,987*.

Wareham, *mkt. t.*, *mun. bor.* Dorset, Eng.; on R. Frome, on N. of I. of Purbeck, 8 m S.W. of Poole; agr. engin., pipes; p. (estd. 1967) *3,490*.

Waremme (Borgworm), *t.*, Belgium; p. (1962) *6,818*.   [dairying, iron; p. (1963) *19,693*.

Waren, *t.*, Neubrandenburg, E. Germany; timber,

Warley, *t.*, *co. bor.*, Worc., Eng.; p. (estd. 1967) *169,440*.

Warminster, *t.*, *urb. dist.*, Wilts, Eng.; on Wylye watershed at edge of Salisbury Plain; agr. mkt., gloves, silk; p. (1961) *9,855*.

Warnemünde, *spt.*, Germany; ferry pt. for rail traffic between Berlin and Copenhagen; shipbldg., resort; p. *6,374*.

Warragamba Dam, 40 m. W. Sydney, New S. Wales, Australia; 450 ft. high, opened Oct. 14, 1960; when in full operation a 36-mile lake will be formed behind dam, impounding 460,000 millions gallons of water.

Warrego, *R.*, Queensland, N.S.W., Australia; trib. of R. Darling; length 400 m.

Warren, *c.*, Ohio, U.S.A.; on Mahoning R.; coal and iron-mining, iron and steel mftg.; p. (1960) *59,648*.

Warren, *bor.*, Penns., U.S.A.; on Allegheny R.; natural gas, petroleum, oil-refining; furniture, tools; p. (1960) *14,505*.

Warrenpoint, *spt.*, *urb. dist.*, Down, N. Ireland; at head of Carlingford Lough; holiday resort; p. (1966) *3,579*.

Warrenton, *t.*, Cape Province, S. Africa; cheese-mkg.; p. (1960) *5,980* (inc. *1,559* whites).

Warrington, *t.*, *co. bor.*, Lancs., Eng.; on R. Mersey, 18 m. E. of Liverpool; aluminium rolling and drawing, soap, chemicals, brewing, iron and steel; to be expanded as New Town with p. *205,000* by 1991; p. (estd. 1967) *73,880*.

Warrnambool, *c.*, *spt.*, Victoria, Australia; mkt., agr. dairying, wood, timber, plastics, engin.; p. (1966) *17,497*.

Warsak Dam, W. Pakistan; on Kabul R., 15 m. N. of Peshawar, nr. Khyber Pass; hydroelec. power and irrigation project.

Warsaw or Warszawa, *prov.*, Poland; on Vistula and Bug Rs.; a 10,900 sq. m.; p. (1965) *2,453,000*.

Warsaw or Warszawa, *cap.*, Poland; on R. Vistula; cath., univ.; rly. ctr.; iron and steel, engin., textiles, chemicals; p. (1965) *1,253,000*.

Warsop, *t.*, *urb. dist.*, Notts, Eng.; 4 m. N.E. of Mansfield; limestone, gravel; p. (1961) *11,596*.

Warta, *R.*, Poland; trib. of R. Oder; length 450 m.

Warwick, *t.*, Queensland, Australia; coal, agr., sawmilling; p. (1962) *9,813*.

Warwick, *co.*, Eng.; coal, iron, limestone, fruit livestock, motors, metal goods; co. t. Warwick; a. 976 sq. m.; p. (1966) *2,095,000*.

Warwick, *co. t.*, *mun. bor.*, Warwick, Eng.; on R. Avon, 8 m S.W. of Coventry; cas.; agr. implements, brewing, malting, rope, iron; p. (estd. 1967) *17,700*.

Warwick, *c.*, R.I., U.S.A.; on Narragansett Bay; cotton mnfs.; p. (1960) *68,504*.

Wasatch Mtns., *range*, Utah and Idaho, U.S.A.

Wash, The, *bay*, N. Sea between Lincs and Norfolk, Eng.; 22 m. long, 15 m. wide; partly reclaimed.

Washa, *L.*, La., U.S.A.; 14 m. long.

Washburne, *mtn range*. Yellowstone National Park, U.S.A.; highest summit 10,345 ft.

Washington, *t.*, *urb. dist.*, Durham, Eng.; 5 m. S.E. of Gateshead; coal, iron and steel, stone quarrying, chemicals; designated "New Town" 1964; p. (estd. 1965) *20,000*.

Washington, *st.*, U.S.A.; coal, iron, minerals, forests, agr.; cap. Olympia; ch. ts. Seattle and Tacoma; a. 68,192 sq. m.; p. (1970) *3,352 892*.

Washington, *c.*, *cap.*, U.S.A.; in Dist. of Columbia, on Potomac R.; White House, Capitol, univs., govt. bldgs, parks; world's first weather ctr. 1965; p. (1970) *764,000*; Greater W. *2,875,000*.

Washington, *t.*, Penns., U.S.A.; coal, petroleum, steel, glass, chemicals; p. (1960) *23,540*.

Washington I., Pac. Oc. (Gilbert and Ellice Is. col.); a. 6 sq. m., coral atolls; copra; p. *56*.

Washita, *R.*, Ark. and La., U.S.A.; trib. of Red R.; length 400 m.   [(1962) *13,923*.

Wasmes, *t.*, Belgium; nr. Mons; coal-mining; p.

Wasquehal, *t.*, Nord, France; textiles, chemicals, oil-refineries; p. (1954) *12,363*.

Wast Water, *L.*, Cumberland, Eng.; 3 m. long.

Watchet, *t.*, *urb. dist.*, Somerset, Eng.; on cst. of Bristol Channel; 5 m. E. of Minehead; paper mkg., fishing; p. (1961) *2,596*.

Waterbury, *c.*, Conn., U.S.A.; on Naugatuck R.; watches, pins, brass goods, elec. and photographic goods, chemicals; p. (1960) *107,130*.

Waterford, *co.*, Munster, Ireland; agr., livestock, fisheries; co. t. Waterford; a. 721 sq. m.; p. (1966) *72,986*.

Waterford, *co. t.*, *spt.*, Waterford, Ireland; on R. Suir; cath.; brewing, fishing; p. (1966) *29,642*.

Waterloo, *vil.*, Belgium; battle, 1815; p. (1962) *12,261*.

Waterloo, *c.*, Iowa, U.S.A.; on Cedar R.; agr. produce and tools; p. (1960) *71,755*.

Waterloo, *t.*, Ontario, Canada; p. (1961) *21,366*.

Waterloo-(with-Seaforth), *urb. dist.*, Lancs, Eng.; at mouth of R. Mersey; N. sub. of Liverpool; residtl.; p. *15,447*.   [cattle; agr. ctr.

Waterpoort, *t.*, Transvaal, S. Africa; on R. Sand;

Watertown, *t.*, Conn., U.S.A.; plastics, textiles, hardware, wire prods.; p. (1960) *14,812*.

Watertown, *t.*, Mass., U.S.A.; on Charles R.; arsenal; p. (1960) *39,092*.

Watertown, *c.*, N.Y., U.S.A.; on Black R.; carriage wks., steam-engines, silk, agr. tools; p. (1960) *33,306*.   [packing; p. (1960) *14,077*.

Watertown, *t.*, S.D., U.S.A.; machin., meat-

Watertown, *c.*, Wis., U.S.A.; on Rock R.; univ.; mnfs.; p. (1960) *13,943*.

Waterville, *c.*, Me., U.S.A.; on Kennebec R.; univ.; cotton mnfs. rly. wks.; p. (1960) *18,695*.

Watervliet, *c.*, N.Y., U.S.A.; on Hudson R.;

arsenal; iron goods, woollens, asbestos goods; p. (1960) *13,917.*

Watford. *t., mun. bor.*, Herts, Eng.; on R. Colne, 16 m. N.W. of London; mkt.; many varied inds., inc. light and elec. engin., paper, printing; p. (estd. 1967) *76,310.*

Wath, *t., urb. dist.*, W.R. Yorks, Eng.; 4 m. N. of Rotherham; coal, quarrying; p. (1961) *15,191.*

Watling, *Brit. I.*, Bahamas, W. Indies; reputed landing place of Columbus.

Watlington, *t.*, Oxford, Eng.; at N. foot of Chiltern Hills, 5 m. S.W. of Princes Risborough; lace; p. *1,386.* [holiday resort.

Watson's Bay, N.S.W., Australia; nr. Sydney;

Wattenscheid, *t.*, N. Rhine–Westphalia, Germany; E. of Essen; coal metals, footwear; p. (1963) *79,700.*

Wattrelos, *t.*, Nord, France; nr. Lille; textiles, mnfs.; p. (1962) *41,319.*

Watu Bella Is., Moluccas, Indonesia; coconuts, sago.

Wau, *cap.*, Bahr-el-Ghazal, Sudan, N.E. Africa; p. *6,000.*

Waukegan, *c.*, Ill., U.S.A.; on L Michigan; summer resort; steel, brass, motors, sugar refining; livestock, agr. ctr.; p. (1960) *55,719.*

Waukesha, *t.*, Wis., U.S.A.; health resort; p. (1960) *30,004.*

Wausau, *c.*, Wis., U.S.A.; on Wisconsin R.; timber, paper, machin., leather, silver-fox farms; p. (1960) *31,943.*

Wauwatosa. *c.*, Wis., U.S.A.; sub. of Milwaukee; p. (1960) *56,923.* [50 m.

Waveney, *R.*, Norfolk and Suffolk, Eng.; length

Waverly, *t.*, N.Y., U.S.A.; dairying, tr. ctr.; p. (1960) *5,950.* [(1960) *12,749.*

Waxahachie, *t.*, Texas, U.S.A.; rly. ctr.; p.

Wayatinah, Tasmania, Australia; hydro-elec. commission vil. (1956), dam, lagoon and power sta.; at confluence of Nive and Derwent Rs.

Waycross, *t.*, Ga., U.S.A.; rly. wks., timber, naval stores, machin., agr. prods.; p. (1960) *20,944.*

Waynesboro, *t.*, Penns. U.S.A.; industl.; p. (1960) *10,427.* [(1960) *26,203.*

Wazan or Ouezzan, *sacred c.*, Morocco; p.

Waziristan, *dist.*, N.W. frontier, Pakistan; mtns.; a. 5,000 sq. m.; p. (1951) *264,000.*

Weald, The, wooded and pastoral tracts S.E. Eng., extending from Folkestone, Kent, through Surrey, Hants and Sussex to the sea about Beachy Head.

Wear, *R.*, Durham, Eng.; rises in the Pennines, flows through Durham to N. Sea at Sunderland; length 60 m. [length 45 m.

Weaver, *R.*, Cheshire, Eng.; trib. of R. Mersey;

Weaver Hills, Staffs, Eng.; alt. 1,300 ft.

Webb City, *c.*, Mo., U.S.A.; lead, zinc mining; p. (1960) *6,740.*

Webster, *t.*, Mass., U.S.A.; on French R.; textiles, footwear; p. (1960) *12,072.*

Webster Grove, *t.*, Mo., U.S.A.; p. (1960) *28,990.*

Weddell Sea, arm of S. Atl. Oc., Antarctica; whaling and sealing.

Wednesbury, *t., mun. bor.*, Staffs, Eng.; 8 m. N.W. of Birmingham; iron, aluminium, metal inds.; rly. carriages, elec. goods; p. (1961) *34,511.*

Wednesfield, *former urb. dist.*, Staffs, Eng.; absorbed in Wolverhampton (1966); mkt.; metal tubes, materials handling engin.; p. (1961) *32,986.*

Wed Zem, *t.*, Morocco; phosphate; p. *12,223.*

Weehawken, *t.*, N.J., U.S.A.; coal depot. rly. ctr.; mnfs.; p. (1960) *13,504.* [*34,308.*

Weert, *t.*, Limburg, Neth.; industl.; p. (1967)

Wei *R.*, Shensi, China; rises in highlands of Kansu, flows E. between highlands of Shansi and Tsinling Shan to join Yellow River nr. Tungkwan; valley contains very fertile loess soils; formed cradle of Chinese civilisation; length approx. 500 m.

Weiden, *t.*, Bavaria, Germany; porcelain glass, textiles; p. (1963) *42,200.*

Weifang, *c.*, Shantung, China; coal-mng. ctr.; tobacco processing; p. (1953) *149,000.*

Weihai *spt.*, Shantung, China; cotton, silk, oil-seed; summer resort; p. *222,000.*

Weimar, *t.*, Erfurt, E. Germany; on R. Ilm; 2 cas., Goethe and Schiller houses; cultural institutes; elec. metal footwear, textiles, machin.; p. (1963) *64,406.*

Weinheim, *t.*, Baden–Württemberg, Germany; cas.; leather, machin. rubber; p. (1963) *28,800.*

Weipa, Queensland, Australia; new t., pt., and alumina plant; bauxite.

Weissenfels, *t.*, Halle, E. Germany; on R. Saale; cas.; footwear, paper, metals; p. (1963) *46,600.*

Weisshorn, *mtn. peak*, Switzerland; alt. 14,770 ft.

Weisskirchen, *see* Bela Crkva.

Wejh, *spt.*, Hejaz, Saudi Arabia.

Welkom, *t.*, O.F.S., S. Africa; ctr. of O.F.S. goldfields; p. (1964) *128,000.*

Welland, *t.*, Ont., Canada; on Welland Canal; farm machin., steel tubing, castings, rope; p. (1956) *15,935.*

Welland, *R.*, Northants and Lincs, Eng.; rises in Northampton Heights, flows N.E., enters The Wash 10 m. below Spalding; length 70 m.

Welland Ship Canal, Ontario, Canada; connects Ls. Erie and Ontario; length 27 m.; 2-lane waterway projected. 1963. [*26,071.*

Wellesley, *t.*, Mass., U.S.A.; residtl.; p. (1960)

Wellesley Is., *gr.*, in the Gulf of Carpentaria, belonging to Queensland, Australia.

Wellingborough, *t., urb. dist.*, Northants, Eng.; on R. Nene, 9 m. N.E of Northampton; mkt. footwear, diverse inds.; p. (estd. 1967) *33,820.*

Wellington, *mkt. t., urb. dist.*, Shropshire, Eng.; 12 m. E. of Shrewsbury; steel wks., brewing, toys, storage tanks, timber yds., agr.; its ancient name was Watling Town, because it stood on the line of Watling Street: with Dawley and Oakengates forms new t. of Telford. p. (1961) *13,630.*

Wellington, *mkt. t.*, Somerset, Eng.; 6 m. S.W. Taunton, anc. woollen ind. still survives; dairy prod.; p. (1961) *7,523.*

Wellington, *c., spt.*, N.I., cap. N.Z.; univ.; foundries, cold storage, soap, candles, footwear; p. (1966) *167,844;* of *c. 131,655.*

Wellington, *prov.*, N.I., N.Z.; a. 10,870 sq. m.; p. (1961) *473,621.*

Wellington, *t.*, Cape Prov., S. Africa; tanning, dried fruits, wine, jam, textiles; p. (1960) *10,330* (inc. *3,736* whites).

Wellington, *L.*, Gippsland, Victoria. Australia; shallow; fishing.

Wells, *c., mun. bor.*, Somerset, Eng.; at W. foot of Mendip Hills; cath., bishop's palace; paper, brushes, textiles, scientific inst.; p. (estd. 1967) *7,620.*

Wells-next-the-Sea, *t. urb. dist.*, Norfolk, Eng.; ancient pt. on N. cst. of E. Anglia, 14 m. W. of Sheringham; whelks, cockles and mussels; p. (1961) *2,490.*

Wellston, *c.*, Ohio U.S.A.; rly. ctr.; furniture; p. (1960) *5,728.*

Wellsville, *c.*, Ohio, U.S.A.; on Ohio R.; coal-mining, agr.; p. (1960) *7,117.*

Wels, *t.*, Austria; machin., leather, paper; natural gas; p. (1961) *41,060.*

Welshpool, *mkt. t., mun. bor.*, Montgomery, Wales; on R. Severn, 7 m. N. of Montgomery; nr. is Powis Castle; lt. inds. based on agr., hosiery; p. (1961) *6,332.*

Welwyn Garden City, *urb. dist.*, Herts, Eng.; 21 m. N. of London. Founded by Sir Ebenezer Howard in 1920 as the first of the satellite ts. of London; one of the "New Towns" designated 1948, inc. Hatfield, Hertford, and Welwyn rural dist.; pharmaceutics, plastics, radio, and electronics, light inds.; p. (estd. 1967) *41,460.*

Wem, *t.*, Salop, Eng.; nr. Shrewsbury; mkt., flour, tanning, malting; p. (1961) *2,603.*

Wembley, *former mun. bor.*, Middx., Eng.; now inc. in Brent outer bor. Greater London, (*q.v.*); light ind., sports ctr.; p. (1961) *124,892.*

Wemyss, *par.*, Fife, Scot.; fishing pt., coal-mining; p. *26,619.*

Wemyss Bay, *t.*, Renfrew, Scot.; holiday resort, residtl.; impt. ctr. for Clyde steamers.

Wenatchee. *t.*, Wash., U.S.A.; fruit (apple) ctr. and inds.; p. (1960) *16,726.*

Wenchow (Wenzhou), *c., spt.*, Chekiang, China; nr. mouth of Wu Kiang 230 m. S.W. of Shanghai; textile, silk inds.; exp. wood, tea, agr. prod.; fishing; coastal tr.; p. (1953) *202,000.*

Wendover, *t.*, Bucks, Eng.; at N. foot of Chiltern Hills, 4 m. S.E. of Aylesbury, at entrance to wind gap; agr. mkt.; p. (1961) *6,151.*

Wengen, *vil.*, Bernese Oberland, Switzerland; alt. 4,200 ft.; resort; p. *1,230.*

Wenlock or Much Wenlock, *t. mun. bor.*, Salop, Eng.; on N.E. end of Wenlock Edge, 11 m. S.E. of Shrewsbury; iron and coal; p. (1961) *14,929.*

Wenlock Edge, *narrow ridge*, Shropshire, Eng.; extends 18 m. S.W from Much Wenlock to Craven Arms; limestone; moorland, woodland on margins, particularly steep N.W. flank; width 1–1½ m., mainly above 950 ft. alt.

Wensleydale, N.R. Yorks, Eng.; valley in N. Pennines drained E. by R. Ure; cattle reared for fattening on lowland farms; some dairying (cheese); length 35 m.

Wentworth, *t.*, *R. pt.*, N.S.W. Australia; at confluence of Rs. Murray and Darling; ships wool downstream to Morgan and round to Adelaide.

Werdau, *t.*, Karl-Marx-Stadt, E. Germany; on R. Pleisse; textiles, machin., tools; p. (1963) 24,634.

Werdohl, *t.*, N. Rhine-Westphalia, Germany; metal goods, glass; p. (1963) 22,800.

Wermelskirchen, *t.*, N. Rhine-Westphalia, Germany; S.E. of Remscheid; footwear, iron, textiles; p. (1963) 25,200.

Wernigerode, *t.*, Magdeburg, E. Germany; cas.; elec., glass, wood, metals, sugar; p. (1963) 33,161. [tories; p. (1962) 12,384.

Wervicq, *t.*, Belgium; nr. Ypres; tobacco fac-

Wesel, *c.*, N. Rhine-Westphalia, Germany; confluence of Rs. Lippe and Rhine; cath.; machin., potteries; p. (1963) 32,100.

Weser, *R.*, Germany; flows N. to N. Sea at Bremerhaven; navigable for 270 m.; total length 440 m.

Wesermünde, *t.*, Bremen, Germany; nr. mouth of R. Weser; adjoins Bremerhaven; brewing, bricks; p. (1946) 77,491.

Wesseling, *t.*, N. Rhine-Westphalia, Germany; on R. Rhine, S. of Cologne; oil refining, petrochemicals; p. (1963) 21,200.

Wessex, *ancient kingdom*, S. Eng.; inc. Berks, Hants, Wilts, Dorset, Somerset and Devon.

West Allis, *t.*, Wis., U.S.A.; iron and steel goods; p. (1960) 68,157.

West Bengal, *st.*, India; delta of Ganges; rice, jute, oilseeds; cap. Calcutta; a. 33,945 sq. m.; p. (1961) 34,967,634.

West Bridgford, *t.*, *urb. dist.*, Notts, Eng.; at junction of Grantham canal with R. Trent; p. (estd. 1967) 28,030.

West Bromwich, *t.*, *co. bor.*, Staffs, Eng.; on R. Thame, 5 m. N.W. of Birmingham; heavy engin. and allied inds., chemicals, springs, oil red.; p. (estd. 1967) 172,650.

West Chester, *bor.*, Penns., U.S.A.; residtl. sub. Philadelphia; mkt. gardening, dairying, agr. tools; p. (1960) 15,705.

West Dean, *rural dist.*, Gloucester, Eng.; coal-mining, forestry; p. (1961) 17,472.

West Ham *former co. bor.*, Essex, Eng.; sub. to E. of London; bordered by Rs. Thames and Lea; now inc. in Newham bor., Greater London; residtl.; extensive docks, rubber, soap, jute-wks., engin., smelting, chemicals; p. (1961) 157,367.

West Hartford, *t.*, Conn., U.S.A.; residtl. sub. of Hartford; metal goods, ctr. for dairying, tobacco-growing dist.; p. (1960) 62,210.

West Hartlepool, *see* Hartlepool, W.

West Haven, *bor.*, Conn., U.S.A.; sub. of New Haven; p. (1960) 42,567.

West Indies *or Antilles*, *I. grs.*, Atl. Oc.; extend between the csts. of Florida and Venezuela, separating the Caribbean Sea and the G. of Mexico from the Atlantic; sugar, tobacco, fruits, cotton, coffee, cocoa; inc. Cuba, Haiti, Dominican Rep., Bahamas, Barbados, Jamaica, Leeward Is., Trinidad and Tobago, Windward Is., Guadeloupe, Martinique, Curacao, Puerto Rico, Virgin Is.

West Irian, *prov.*, Indonesia; formerly West New Guinea and Dutch col.; came under Indonesian adm. 1963; inaugurated as prov. 1969; cap. Djajapura (formerly Sukarnapura).; a. (inc. Ternate) 115,861 sq. m.; p. (1969) 896,000.

West Lothian, *co.*, Scot.; agr., coal, iron, bricks, engin., hosiery; co. t. Linlithgow; a. 120 sq. m.; p. (1961) 92,764.

West New York, *t.*, N.J., U.S.A ; on Hudson R.; grain elevators, silks rubber goods, cotton-seed oil; p. (1960) 35,547. [39,895.

West Orange, *t.*, N.J., U.S.A.; industl.; p. (1960)

West Pakistan, *prov.*, Pakistan; separated from E. Pakistan by 1,100 m. of Indian terr.; comprises 4 provs. (revived 1970): The Punjab, Sind, Baluchistan, North-West Frontier Province; cap. Lahore, ch. pt. Karachi; 5 gt. Rs.

Indus with tribs. Jhelum, Chenab, Ravi, and Sutlej; wheat, cotton, rice, oilseeds, rocksalt; a. 310,403 sq. m.; p. (1961) 43,000,000 (excl. Fed. terr. of Karachi).

West Point, *military sta.*, N.Y., U.S.A.; on Hudson R.; Military Academy.

West Springfield, *t.*, Mass., U.S.A.; industl.; p. (1960) 25,385.

West Virginia, *st.*, U.S.A.; coal, salt, petroleum, agr. (cereals, tobacco), pastoral; cap. Charleston; a. 24,181 sq. m.; p. (1970) 1,701,913.

West Warwick, *t.*, R.I., U.S.A.; p. (1960) 21,414.

Westbrook, *c.*, Me., U.S.A.; paper, cottons, silks; p. (1960) 13,820.

Westbury, *t.*, *urb. dist.*, Wilts, Eng.; at N. foot of Salisbury Plain; rly. junction; woollens, bricks, glove mnfs.; p. (1961) 5,409.

Western Samoa. *See* Samoa, Western.

Westerwald, *plateau of old volcanic rocks*, W. Germany, ending in steep slope E. of R. Rhine between Koblenz and Bonn; drained to Rhine by R. Lahn and R. Sieg; fertile soil; pasture-land or deciduous woodland; sm. quantities of iron ore in Siegerland.

Westfield, *t.*, Fife, Scot.; Lurgi gas plant.

Westfield, *c.*, Mass., U.S.A.; cigars, paper. machin., bicycles, radiators; p. (1960) 26,302.

Westfield, *t.*, N.J., U.S.A.; p. (1960) 31,447.

Westgate-on-Sea, *t.*, Kent, Eng.; nr. Margate; agr., seaside resort; p. 4,554.

Westhoughton, *urb. dist.*, S.E. Lancs, Eng.; coal-mining, cottons; p. (1961) 16,254.

Westland, *prov.*, S.I. N.Z.; coal, timber, gold; cap. Hokitika; a. 4,880 sq. m.; p. (1961) 17,954.

Westmeath, *co.*, Leinster, Ireland; pasture, agr., dairying; with much bog; co. t. Mullingar; a. 708 sq. m.; p. (1966) 52,849.

Westminster, City of, *inner bor.*, London, Eng.; on N. bank of R. Thames; W. of City of London; incorporates former bors. of Paddington and St. Marylebone; contains Houses of Parliament, Westminster Abbey, Government offices, Royal Palaces (Buckingham Palace and St. James's); p. (1966) 263,000.

Westmorland, *co.*, N.W. Eng.; covering part of the Lake Dist. (Windermere, Ullswater, Grasmere, etc.); sheep, oats, bldg.-stone, tourist ind.; cap. Appleby; most populous t., Kendal; a. 789 sq. m.; p. (1966) 67,000.

Westmount, *t.*, Que. Canada; p. (1961) 25,012.

Weston-super-Mare, *t.*, *mun. bor.*, Somerset, Eng.; on Bristol Channel, 20 m. S.W of Bristol; holiday resort; p. (estd. 1967) 44,170.

Westphalia, *see* N. Rhine-Westphalia.

Westport, *spt.*, *urb. dist.*, Mayo, Ireland; on Westport Bay; mkt., cereals; p. (1961) 2,883.

Westport, *spt.*, S.I., N.Z.; on R. Buller; cst. shipping; coal; p. (1961) 5,464.

Westport, *t.*, Conn., U.S.A.; residtl.; woollens, twine, soap, disinfectants; p. (1950) 11,667.

Westray, *I.*, Orkney Is., Scot.; 10 m. long; p. 1,270. [Bay; seaside resort.

Westward Ho!, *vil.*, N. Devon, Eng.; on Bideford

Westwood, *t.*, Queensland, Australia; coal-mining.

Wetherby, *t.*, W.R. Yorks, Eng.; on R. Wharfe; mkt., malting, brewing; p. 2,126.

Wethersfield, *t.*, Conn., U.S.A.; oldest regular settlement in C.; lge. st. prison; agr. implements, seeds; p. (1960) 20,526.

Wetteren, *t.*, Belgium; on R. Schelde; textiles; p. (1962) 20,250.

Wetterhorn, *mtn.*, Switzerland; alt. 12,165 ft.

Wetzlar, *c.*, Hessen, Germany; on R. Lahn; cath.; optical instruments, metals, radios, textiles, footwear; p. (1963) 37,800.

Wewoka, *t.*, Okla., U.S.A.; oil wells; agr., bricks, petrol; p. (1960) 5,954.

Wexford, *maritime co.*, Leinster, S.E. Ireland; pasture agr., dairying, fishing; cap. Wexford; a. 901 sq. m.; p. (1966) 83,355.

Wexford, *t.*, *cap.*, Wexford; Leinster, S.E. Ireland; on R. Slaney; p. (1966) 11,533.

Wey, *R.*, Hants, Surrey, Eng.; rises in W. Weald, flows N. into R. Thames nr. Weybridge; cuts impt. gap through N. Downs at Guildford; length 35 m.

Weybridge, *see* Walton and Weybridge.

Weymouth and Melcombe Regis, *t.*, *mun. bor.*, Dorset, Eng.; on Weymouth Bay, 8 m. S. of Dorchester; torpedo and boatbldg., bricks, tiles, engin.; holiday resort; p. (estd. 1967) 42,160. [(1960) 48,177.

Weymouth, *t.*, Mass., U.S.A.; footwear mnf.; p.

Whakatane, *t.*, N.I., N.Z.; on Bay of Plenty; board mills; p. (1961) 7,169.

Whales. Bay of, *inlet* in Ross Dep. Antarctica; exploration base.

Whangarei, *t.*, N.I., N.Z.; agr., fruit; oil refining; natural gas pipelines from Kapuni; p. (1966) 27,573.

Whangpoo, *R.*, Kiangsu, China; tidal creek upon which Shanghai is situated; runs 14 m. inland from Yangtze-Kiang estuary nr. Woosung.

Wharfe, *R.*, W.R. Yorks, Eng.; trib. of R. Ouse; length 60 m.

Wheeling, *c.*, W. Va., U.S.A.; on Ohio R.; rly. and comm. ctr., iron and steel, pottery; p. (1960) 53,400.

Whernside, *mtn.*, W.R. Yorks, Eng.; alt. 2,414 ft.

Whickham, *t.*, *urb. dist.*, Durham, Eng.; nr. Gateshead; coal-mining, iron and steel, chemicals, rope mnf.; p. (estd. 1967) 27,890.

Whitburn, *burgh*, W Lothian Scot.; 20 m. S.W. of Edinburgh; coal, limestone; p. (1961) 5,902.

Whitby, *spt.*, *urb. dist.*, N.R. Yorks, Eng.; at mouth of R. Esk. 17 m. N.W. of Scarborough; abbey; holiday resort; fisheries; potash to be mined nearby; p. (1961) 11,662.

Whitby (formerly Windsor), *t.* Canada; on L. Ontario; p. (1961) 14,685.

Whitchurch, *t.*, Salop, Eng.; 13 m. S.W. of Crewe; mkt., malting, cheese; p. (1961) 7,159. [length 350 m.

White, *R.*, Ark., U.S.A.; trib. of Mississippi R.;

White, *R.*, Ind., U.S.A.; trib. of Wabash R.; length 330 m.

White, *R.*, Ark., Mo., U.S.A.; trib. of Mississippi R.; 300 m. navigable; length 800 m.

White Mtns., part of Appalachian system. N.H., U.S.A.; highest summit, Mt. Washington, 6,288 ft.

White Nile (Bahr-ei-Abiad), *R.*, Sudan, N.E. Africa; strictly, name applied to stretch of R. Nile between L. No and Khartoum; distance over 500 m.

White Plains, *t.*, N.Y., U.S.A.; on Bronx R.; residtl.; battle 1776; p. (1960) 50,485.

White Russia, *see* Byelorussia.

White Sea or G. of Arkangelsk, *inlet* of the Arctic Ocean, R.S.F.S.R.; a. 47,346 sq. m.

Whiteadder, *R.* Berwick, Scot.; trib. of R. Tweed; length 34 m. [p. (1961) 14,370.

Whitefield, *urb. dist.*, Lancs, Eng.; cotton mnf.;

Whitehall, *t.*, N.Y., U.S.A.; at head of L. Champlain; timber tr.; p. (1960) 4,016.

Whitehaven, *spt.*, *mun. bor.*, Cumberland, Eng.; on Solway Firth. 3 m. N. of St. Bees Head; coal, methane gas, tanning. chemicals, flour and silk mills; p. (estd. 1967) 27,050.

Whitehead, *t.*, *urb. dist.*, Antrim, N. Ireland; at entrance to Belfast Lough; seaside resort; p. (1966) 2,740.

Whithorn, *royal burgh*, Wigtown, Scot.; 9 m. S. of Wigtown; cath.; p. (1961) 986.

Whitehorse, *c.*, cap. Yukon Terr., Canada; ctr. coal and copper mng., hunting and fur trapping; once a gold " boom town "; H.Q. Royal Canadian Mounted Police; end of Alaska highway linking Edmonton, Alberta; p. (1961) 5,031.

Whitley Bay, *mun. bor.*, Northumberland. Eng.; 3 m. N. of Tynemouth; seaside resort; plastics; p. (estd. 1967) 38,380.

Whitney, *mtn.*, Sierra Nevada, Cal., U.S.A.; alt. 14,898 ft.

Whitstable, *spt.*, *urb. dist.*, Kent Eng.; on Thames estuary. 6 m. N. of Canterbury; holiday resort, oysters; p. (estd. 1967) 22,510.

Whittington or Whittington Moor, *par.*, Derby, Eng.; nr. Chesterfield; coal-mining. iron, steel; p. 8,317.

Whittlesey, *t.*, *urb. dist.*, I. of Ely, Eng.; in The Fens, 8 m. W. of March; bricks, mkt. gardening; p. (1961) 9,324

Whitworth, *urb. dist.*, S.E. Lancs, Eng; cottons. coal, slate; p. (1961) 7,031.

Whyalla, *c.*, *spt.*, S. Australia; impt. steel and shipbldg. inds.; ironstone, pig-iron, steel; p. (1966) 22,126.

Wichita, *c.*, Kan., U.S.A.; in Arkansas valley; rly. wks.; oil refineries and equipment; meat-packing ctr. in agr. and stock-raising region; p. (1960) 254,698.

Wichita, *R.*, Texas, U.S.A.; trib. of Red R.; length 225 m.

Wichita Falls, *c.*, Texas, U.S.A.; oil-refining; p. (1960) 101,724.

Wick, *spt.*, *burgh*, Caithness, Scot.; on E. cst. 14 m. S. of John O'Groats; herring-fisheries ctr.; p. (1961) 7,397.

Wicklow, *maritime co.*, Leinster, Ireland; pastoral and agr.; cap. Wicklow: a. 781 sq. m ; p. (1966) 60,281.

Wicklow, *t.*, cap., Wicklow, Leinster, Ireland; on S.E. cst.. 35 m. S. of Dublin; mkt.; sm. seaside resort; p. (1966) 3,340.

Wicklow, *mtns.*, Wicklow, Ireland; highest summit, Lugnaquillia, 3,039 ft.

Widnes, *t.*, *mun. bor.*, Lancs, Eng.; on R. Mersey. 12 m. E of Liverpool; anhydrite acid, asbestos, cement, wire cables, chemicals, explosives, fertilisers, copper and zinc; p. (estd. 1967) 54,600.

Wiener Neustadt, *t.*, Lower Austria; 20 m. S. of Vienna; machin., pottery; p. (1961) 33,845.

Wieringermeer Polder, *reclaimed a.*, N. Holland, Neth.; located in N.W. of IJsselmeer; reclaimed in 1930, maliciously flooded by Germans but drained again 1945; largely meadowland; a. 78 sq. m.

Wiesbaden, *t.*, cap. Hesse, W. Germany; at S. edge of the Taunus; spa; cas.; p. (1968) 259,076.

Wigan, *t.*, *co. bor.*, S.W. Lancs. Eng.; 16 m. N.E. of Liverpool; coal, cotton. engin., chemicals, cement; p. (estd. 1967) 79,720.

Wight, I. of, *co.*, Eng.; Eng. Channel, separated from Hants by Spithead and The Solent; wheat, sheep, cement; holiday resort; ch. ts.: Newport, Cowes. Ryde; a. 147 sq. m.; p. (1966) 97,000.

Wigston, *t.*, *urb. dist.*, Leic., Eng.; 4 m. S. of Leicester; rly. wks., engin., hosiery; p. (estd. 1967) 26,630.

Wigtown, *maritime co.*, S.W. Scot.; agr., mainly dairying, creameries; agr. implements; cap. W.; a. 485 sq. m.; p. (1961) 29,107.

Wigtown, *burgh*, Wigtown Scot.; on Wigtown Bay, Solway Firth; fishery; creamery, distillery; p. (1961) 1,201.

Wilcannia, *t.*, *R. pt.*, N.S.W., Australia; on R. Darling, 350 m. upstream from Wentworth; sends wool and minerals downstream to Morgan, Murray Bridge, Echuca for transhipment by rail to Adelaide or Melbourne.

Wilhelmshaven, *spt.*, Lower Saxony, Germany; 40 m. N.W. of Bremen; shipbldg., machin., textiles, furniture, elect., wood, leather; harbour; oil pipeline; p. (1968) 102,484.

Wilkes-Barre, *c.* Penns., U.S.A.; on Susquehanna R.; anthracite-mining, machin., locomotives, iron and steel, textiles; p. (1960) 63,551.

Wilkes Land, Antarctica; featureless plateau, alt. 9,500 ft.; immense glaciers; U.S. base taken over by Australia in 1959.

Wilkinsburg, *bor.*, Penns., U.S.A.; Pittsburgh sub.; residtl.; timber wks.; p. (1960) 30,066.

Willamette, *R.*, Ore., U.S.A.; rises in Cascade Mtns., flows N. into Columbia R. below Portland; valley gives rich agr. land, wheat, root-crops, dairy produce, hard and soft fruits; ch. ts. Portland, Salem; length approx. 300 m.

Willemstad, *pt.*, *cap.*, Neth. Antilles; on Curaçao I.; oil refining; p. (estd. 1963) 60,000.

Willenhall, *former urb. dist.*, Staffs, Eng.; partly absorbed in Wolverhampton (1966); locks and keys, drop forgings; p. (1961) 32,317.

Willesden, *former mun. bor.*, Middx., Eng.; now inc. in Brent outer bor., Greater London, (*q.v.*); on impt. rly. junction; residtl. and industl.; p. (1961) 171,001.

Williamsburg, *c.*, Va., U.S.A.; oldest incorporated c. in America; p. (1960) 6,832.

Williamsport, *c.*, Penns.. U.S.A.; on Susquehanna R.; rly. ctr., timber, machin., silks; summer resort; p. (1960) 41,967.

Williamstown, *spt.*, *sub.*, Melbourne, Victoria, Australia; at mouth of Yarra R.; naval dockyds., shipbldg., railway wks., rifle range; p. (1958) 30,388.

Willimantic, *c.*, Conn., U.S.A.; on Willimantic R.; textiles, thread; p. (1960) 13,881.

Wilmette, *t.*, Ill., U.S.A.; residtl. sub. Chicago; p. (1960) 28,268.

Wilmington, *c.*, *spt.*, Del., U.S.A.; on Delaware R.; shipbldg., gunpowder, machin., iron- and steel-wks.; chemicals; leather, cork, rubber goods; p. (1960) 95,827.

Wilmington, *spt.*, N.C., U.S.A.; exp. cotton, tobacco, timber, fertilizers; shipbldg., textiles, chemicals; p. (1950) 45,043.

Wilmslow, *t.*, *urb dist.*, Cheshire, Eng.; on R. Bollen, 6 m. S.W. of Stockport; residtl., cotton mnfs.; p. (estd. 1967) *23,160*.

Wilsden, W.R. Yorks, Eng.; nr. Bradford; worsted mnfs.; p. *2,500*.

Wilson, *t.* N.C., U.S.A.; tobacco, cotton, timber; p. (1950) *23,010*. [Victoria, Australia.

Wilson's Promontory, juts into Bass Strait,

Wilton, *t.*, *mun. bor.*, Wilts, Eng.; on R. Wylye, 3 m. W. of Salisbury; agr. mkt., carpets, felt; p. (estd. 1967) *4,240*.

Wilton, *industl. estate*, Cleveland, Yorks.; S. side of Tees estuary; heavy organic- and petro-chemicals; nylon polymer plant projected 1964.

Wiltshire, *S.W. inland co.*, Eng.; agr. and pastoral; cap. Salisbury; a. 1,345 sq. m.; p. (1966) *471,000*.

Wimbledon, *former mun. bor.*, Surrey, Eng.; now inc. in Merton outer London bor.; residtl.; famous common and internationally famous tennis tournament; p. (1961) *56,994*.

Wimborne Minster, *t.*, Dorset, Eng.; on R. Stour; agr. machin., car body bldg.; p. (1961) *4,156*.

Wimmera, *N.W. dist.*, Victoria, Australia; a. 24,000 sq. m.; pastoral areas of fruit-growing under irrigation.

Winburg, *t.*, O.F.S., S. Africa; was the first cap. of O.F.S.; tr. ctr.; p. (1960) *1,454* whites.

Wincanton, *t.*, Somerset, Eng.; at N.W. foot of Salisbury Plain; mkt., agr., cheese; p. *2,047*.

Winchcomb, *t.*, Gloucester, Eng.; nr. Cheltenham; silk, flour, tanning; cas.; p. *2,546*.

Winchelsea, *ancient t.*, Sussex, Eng.; 2 m. S.W. of Rye; formerly an impt. walled spt., now 2 m. inland; p. *693*.

Winchester, *c.*, *mun. bor.*, Hants, Eng.; on R. Itchen, 12 m. N. of Southampton; ancient cap. of the Saxons; cath., famous Public School, barracks; brewing, malting, agr. produce; p. (estd. 1969) *31,070*.

Winchester, *t.*, Ky., U.S.A.; agr. livestock; p. (1960) *10,187*.

Winchester, *t.*, Mass., U.S.A.; sub. of Boston; p. 1960) *19,376*.

Winchester, *c.*, Va., U.S.A.; in Shenandoah valley; p. (1960) *15,110*.

Windermere, *lgst. Eng. L.*, in Westmorland and Lancs; outlet to Morecambe Bay; 10 m. long, 1 m. wide.

Windermere, *urb. dist.*, Westmorland, Eng.; on E. shore of L.; tourist ctr.; p. (1961) *6,556*.

Windhoek, *cap.*, S.W. Africa; fruit, silver, copper, lead; p. (1962) *43,000* inc. *25,200* Europeans.

Windorah, *t.*, Queensland, Australia; pastoral, sheep and cattle.

Wind River Mtns., Wyo., U.S.A.; range of Rockies; Fremont's Peak, 13,576 ft.

Windrush, *R.*, Oxford, Gloucester, Eng.; trib. of R. Thames.

Windscale, Cumberland, Eng.; nuclear reactors for defence purposes.

Windsor, *t.*, N.S.W., Australia; farming ctr.; p. (1961) *12,015*.

Windsor, *c.*, *pt.*, Ontario, Canada; linked to Detroit, U.S.A., by tunnel bridge and ferry; cars, tyres, paint, drugs, salt; p. (1966) *211,697*.

Windsor, *t.*, Conn., U.S.A. on Connecticut R.; p. (1960) *19,346*.

Windsor, New, *t.*, *mun. bor.*, Berks, Eng.; on R. Thames, 20 m. W. of London; famous royal cas. (founded by William the Conqueror) and park, St. George's Chapel and the Royal Mausoleum; p. (estd. 1967) *29,920*.

Windward, Is., W.I., consisting of Grenada, St. Vincent, St. Lucia and Dominica; a. 826 sq. m.; p. *336,000*.

Windward Is., (Neth.) part of Neth. Antilles, W. Indies: consisting of 3 Is.; Curaçao, Aruba, and Bonaire.

Windward Passage, *channel*, 60 m. wide, between Cuba and Haiti.

Winfield, *c.*, Kan., U.S.A.; on Walnut R.; educational and comm. ctr., agr.; p. (1960) *11,117*.

Winfrith Heath, Dorset, Eng.; UKAEA Atomic Energy Establishment (ENEA *Dragon* project inaugurated 1964).

Winneba, *t.*, Ghana, W. Africa; p. (1960) *25,000*.

Winnebago, *L.*, Wis. U.S.A.; 27 m. long.

Winnipeg, *c.*, *cap.*, Manitoba, Canada; at junction of Red and Assiniboine Rs; caths., univ.; rly. ctr.; ch. world wheat mkt.; meat packing and food processing plants; lgst. garment mnf. ctr. in Canada; oil ref.; p. (1966) *508,759*.

Winnipeg, *L.*, Manitoba, Canada; 40 m. N. of Winnipeg; 260 m. long, 25–60 m. wide; contains several lge. Is. (Reindeer, 70 sq. m.; Big I., 60 sq. m.).

Winnipegosis, *L.*, Manitoba and Saskatchewan, Canada; a. (exclusive of Is.) 2,000 sq. m.; 50 m. W. of L. Winnipeg, into which it drains.

Winnispesaukee, *L.*, N.H., U.S.A.; 24 m. long.

Winona, *c.*, Minn., U.S.A.; on R. Mississippi; rly. ctr., timber, grain tr., medicines, shoes, furs.; p. (1960) *24,895*.

Winooski or **Onion**, *R.*, Vt., U.S.A.; length 90 m.

Winsford, *urb. dist.*, Cheshire, Eng.; on R. Weaver; 4 m. S. of Northwich; only rock salt mine still working in Brit. Is.; p. (1961) *12,733*.

Winslow, *t.*, Bucks, Eng.; mkt., agr. ctr.; p. *1,539*.

Winston-Salem, *c.*, N.C., U.S.A.; tobacco and cotton mnfs.; p. (1960) *111,135*.

Winterswijk, *t.*, Gelderland, Neth.; industl.; p. (1967) *26,243*.

Winterthur, *t.*, Zurich, Switzerland; on Eulach R.; rly. ctr., locomotives, machines, cottons, wine; p. (1961) *84,300*.

Winthrop, *cst. t.*, Mass., U.S.A.; residtl. sub. of Boston, summer resort; p. (1960) *20,303*.

Wipper, *R.*, Germany, trib. of R. Rhine; length 50 m.

Wiri, *t.*, New Zealand, 15 m. S. of Auckland; aluminium fabricating mill.

Wirksworth, *t.*, *urb. dist.*, Derby, Eng.; in Pennines, 5 m. S. of Matlock; lead-mng., limestone, fluorspar wks.; p. (1961) *4,930*.

Wirral, *urb. dist.*, W. Cheshire, Eng.; between estuaries of Dee and Mersey; residtl.; p. (estd. 1967) *25,650*.

Wisbech, *t.*, *mun. bor.*, of Ely, Cambs., Eng.; on R. Nene, 11 m. from its mouth in the Wash; mkt. gardening, fruit growing and canning, agr. implements; p. (estd. 1967) *17,410*.

Wisconsin, *st.*, U.S.A.; leading dairy st. of Union; timber, iron ore, lead, zinc, stone, sand, and gravel; agr. machin., cars, engin.; cap. Madison; ch. t. Milwaukee; a. 56,154 sq. m.; p. (1970) *4,366,766*.

Wisconsin, *R.*, Wis., U.S.A.; trib. of R. Mississippi; length 600 m.

Wishaw, *burgh*, Lanark, Scot.; joined with Motherwell; rly. wks., engin., coal, iron, steel.

Wiske, *R.*, N.R. Yorks, Eng.; trib. of R. Swale; length 24 m.

Wismar, *spt.*, Rostock, E. Germany; on Baltic Sea, N. of Schwerin; metals, sugar, canning, shipbldg.; p. (1963) *57,277*.

Witbank, *t.*, Transvaal. S. Africa; power sta.; coal-mng.; carbide, cyanide, steel; p. (1960) *24,510* (inc. *8,482* whites).

Witham, *R.*, Rutland and Lincs. Eng.; flows into The Wash; length 80 m.

Witham, *t.*, *urb. dist.*, Essex. Eng.; 9 m. N.E. of Chelmsford; agr., mkt. gardening; malting. metal windows; p. (1961) *9,459*.

Withernsea, *t.*, *urb. dist.*, E.R. Yorks, Eng.; on E. cst. 15 m. E. of Hull; holiday resort; agr., fishing; p. (1961) *4,963*.

Withnell, *t.*, *urb. dist.*, Lancs, Eng.; at N. foot of Rossendale Fells, 3 m. S.W. of Blackburn; textiles, stone, paper; p. (1961) *2,840*.

Witney, *t.*, Oxford, Eng.; on R. Windrush, 10 m. W. of Oxford; woollens, blankets, gloves; p. (1961) *9,217*.

Witten, *t.*, N. Rhine–Westphalia, Germany; on R. Ruhr; glass, machin., metals, chemicals, optical inds.; p. (1963) *97,400*.

Wittenberg, *t.*, Halle, E. Germany; on R. Elbe; cas.; ctr. of Reformation and burial place of Luther; he burnt Papal bull against him here in 1520; iron, machin., textiles; p. (1963) *46,544*.

Wittenberge, *t.*, Schwerin, E. Germany; on R. Elbe; woollens, machin., rly. junction; p. (1963) *32,328*. [mining.

Witwatersrand, *dist.*, Transvaal, S. Africa; gold-

Wivenhoe, *t.*, *urb. dist.*, Essex, Eng.; on R. Colne; boatbldg., oysters, lt. inds.; p. (1961) *2,729*.

Wloclawek, *t.*, *pt.*, N. Poland; on R. Vistula; brewing, iron-wks., pottery, nitrate fertilising; p. (1965) *63,000*.

Woburn, *t.*, Bedford, Eng.; 5 m. N.E. of Leighton Buzzard; Woburn Abbey (seat of Dukes of Bedford). [p. (1960) *31,214*.

Woburn, *c.*, Mass., U.S.A.; chemicals, footwear;

Woking, *t.*, *urb dist.*, Surrey, Eng.; 4 m. N. of

Guildford; wireless parts, aeroplane equipment; mkt., residtl.; p. (estd. 1967) *78,840.*

Wokingham, *t., mun. bor.,* Berks, Eng.; 5 m. S.E. of Reading; mkt., agr. and agr. machin., bricks; p. (estd. 1967) *17,980.*

Wolds, The, *chalk hill range,* Lincoln, E.R. Yorks, Eng.; pastoral; 45 m. long.

Wolf Rock, *isolated rock, lighthouse*; at approach to Eng. Channel from Bay of Biscay; 9 m. S.W. of Lands End, Cornwall.   [Canada.

Wolfe, *I.,* in L. of 1,000 Is., St. Lawrence R.,

Wolfenbüttel, *t.,* Lower-Saxony Germany; S. of Brunswick; cas., Lessing museum; textiles, machin., canning; p. (1963) *39,700.*

Wolfsburg, *t.,* Lower Saxony, Germany; on R. Aller N.E. of Brunswick; Volkswagen wks.; p. (1963) *74,100.*

Wollaston, L. N.W. Terr., Canada; 50 m. long.

Wollongong, Greater, *c.,* N.S.W., Australia; coal-mining, iron- and steel-wks., fertilisers, chemicals, bricks; dairying; p. (1966) *162,835.*

Wolmaransstad, *t.,* Transvaal, S. Africa; diamonds; p. (1960) *6,041* inc. *2,474* whites.

Wolsingham, *t.,* Durham, Eng.; on R. Wear; woollens, coal, agr. tools, marble; p. *3,535.*

Wolverhampton, *t., co. bor.* (incl. Bilston, Wednesfield, and Tettenhall), Staffs, Eng.; heavy and light engin., tyres and rubber, boilers, rayon, elec. engin. and apparatus, iron wks., aircraft and motor components, hollow-ware, tools, strongrooms and safes, paints; p. (estd. 1969) *264,520.*

Wolverton, *t., urb. dist.,* Bucks, Eng.; on R. Ouse, 15 m. S.W. of Bedford; rly.-carriage wks.; p. (1961) *13,116.*

Wolyn (*former Wollin*), *I.,* Baltic Sea; off mouth of R. Oder; Polish; a. 133 sq. m.; p. *21,000.*

Wombwell, *urb. dist.,* W.R. Yorks, Eng.; at E. foot of Pennines, 7 m. N. of Sheffield; coal-mining, bricks; p. (1961) *18,701.*

Wonokromo, *sub.* of Soerabaya, Indonesia; oil refining.

Wonsan, *spt.,* N. Korea; exp. rice, cattle, hides, fish; p. (estd. 1942) *122,185.*

Wonthaggi, *t.,* Victoria, Australia; clothing, engin.; p. (1966) *4,672.*

Woodbridge, *t., urb. dist.,* E. Suffolk, Eng.; on R. Deben; engin., brush mkg.; p. (1961) *5,927.*

Woodbridge, *t.,* N.J., U.S.A.; tiles, bricks, terra-cotta; p. (1960) *78,846.*

Woodbury, *t.,* N.J., U.S.A.; nr. Philadelphia; (1960) *12,453.*

Wood Green, *former mun. bor.,* Middx., Eng.; now inc. in Haringey outer bor., Greater London, (*q.v.*); p. (1961) *47,945.*

Woodhall Spa, *t., urb. dist.,* Lindsey, Lincs, Eng.; 4 m. S.W. of Horncastle; health resort; p. (1961) *1,990.*

Woodside, *burgh* Aberdeen, Scot.; on R. Don; paper; p. *7,698.*

Woodstock, *t.* Ontario, Canada; on R. Thames; dairying, woollens, agr. tools; p. (1961) *20,486.*

Woodstock, *t., mun. bor.,* Oxford, Eng.; on Glynne R. 7 m. N.W. of Oxford; glove mnfs.; Blenheim Palace; p. (estd. 1967) *2,260.*

Wookey Hole, *cave,* Mendip Hills, Somerset, Eng.; at foot of limestone hills, 2 m. N.W. of Wells; R. Axe emerges from the cave.

Woolgar, *t.,* Queensland, Australia; gold.

Woolwich, *former met. bor.,* London, Eng.; a. S. of R. Thames incorporated in Greenwich; a. N. of Thames incorporated in Newham; Royal Ordnance Factory (Woolwich Arsenal) closed 1966; of total Defence Department estate of 1,193 acres, 500 acres being developed by GLC for housing purposes; free ferry across Thames; p. (1961) *146,603.*

Woomera, S. Australia; about 270 m. N.W. of Adelaide; base for joint U.K.–Australian guided-weapon testing range extending N.W. across the continent; established 1947.

Woonsocket, *c.,* R.I., U.S.A.; on Blackstone R.; textiles, rubber goods; p. (1960) *47,080.*

Wooster, *c.,* Ohio, U.S.A.; univ.; agr. ctr.; p. (1960) *17,046.*   [Bassett.

Wootton Basset, *see* Cricklade and Wootton

Worcestershire, *midland co.,* Eng.; W. of Warwick; agr.; pasturage, hops, orchards, minerals, mnfs.; co. t. Worcester; a. 699 sq. m; p. (1966) *663,000.*

Worcester, *c., co. bor.,* Worcester, Eng.; on R. Severn, 24 m. N. of Gloucester; cath.; machin., porcelain, glove mkg.; p. (estd. 1967) *70,230.*

Worcester, *t.,* C. Prov., S. Africa; viticultural and industrl. ctr., Goudini spa nearby; p. (1960) *32,301* inc. *10,858* Europeans.

Worcester, *c.,* Mass. U.S.A.; univ.; iron, footwear, tools; p. (1960) *186,587.*

Workington, *spt., mun. bor.,* Cumberland, Eng.; on Solway Firth, at mouth of Derwent R.; coal. iron, steel, shipbldg., cycles, motors; p. (estd. 1967) *29,900.*

Worksop, *t., mun. bor.,* Notts, Eng.; 15 m. S.E. of Sheffield; coal-mining, timber, glasswks., knitwear, refractory bricks; quarrying; p. (estd. 1967) *35,580.*

Worms, *c.,* Rhineland-Palatinate, Germany; on R. Rhine, cath.; "Nibelungen city"; wine ctr.; chemicals, leather textiles, machin., metals; p. (1963) *63,100.*

Worms Head, *promontory,* on Glamorgan cst., Gower Peninsula, Wales.

Worsborough, *urb. dist.,* W.R. Yorks, Eng.; coalmng., timber, gunpowder; p. (1961) *14,577.*

Worsley, *urb. dist,* S.E. Lancs, Eng.; cottons, iron, coal; p. (estd. 1967) *48,750.*

Worthing, *t., mun. bor.,* W. Sussex, Eng.; on S. cst., 10 m. W. of Brighton; holiday resort, mkt. gardening, horticulture; p. (estd. 1967) *81,200.*

Wotton-under-Edge, *t.,* Gloucester, Eng., nr. Stroud; mkt., agr. ctr., woollens; p. *3,121.*

Wowoni I., Celebes, Indonesia.

Wrangel I., Arctic Ocean; off N. cst., R.S.F.S.R.

Wrangel, *t.,* Alaska, U.S.A.; p. (1960) *1,315.*

Wrangell, *min.,* Alaska, U.S.A.; alt. 17,500 ft.

Wrath, *C.,* N.W. Sutherland, Scot.

Wrekin, *hill,* Salop, Eng.; alt. 1,320 ft.

Wrexham, *t., mun. bor.,* Denbigh, Wales; 11 m. S.W. Chester; steel, engin., textiles, brick wks., chemicals, tanning; tyres; p. (1961) *35,427.*

Wroclaw (Breslau), *prov.,* Poland–Lower Silesia; industl., coal, ironwks., agr.; cap. Wroclaw; a. 9,552 sq. m.; p. (1965) *1,967,000.*

Wroclaw (Breslau), *c.,* Silesia, Poland; German before 1945; on R. Oder; univ., cath.; metals, textiles, machin., foodstuffs; p. (1965) *474,000.*

Wroxeter, *vil.,* Salop, Eng.; on R. Severn, 5 m. S.E. Shrewsbury; site of Roman *c.* of Uriconium.

Wuchang, *c.,* Hupeh, China; on R. Yangtze, opp. Hankow; cottons, tea; comm. ctr. *See* Wuhan.

Wuchow (Wuzhou), *R. pt.,* Kwangsi, China; on R. Si; tr. ctr.; exp. tung oil, hides, aniseed; p. (1953) *111,000.*

Wuhan, *industl. c.,* Hupeh, China; at head of navigation by ocean-going steamers of R. Yangtze; formed by amalgamation of Hankow, Hanyang, Wuchang; combined p. (1953) *1,427,000. See also under separate headings.*

Wuhu, *c.,* Anhwei, China; on R. Yangtze; tea, silk, coal; p. (1953) *242,000.*

Wupper, *R.,* Germany; trib. of R. Rhine; length 40 m.

Wuppertal, *c.,* N. Rhine–Westphalia, Germany; formed by amalgamation of Barmen and Elberfeld; textiles, rubber goods, paper, metals, pharmaceuticals; p. (1968) *411,974.*

Württemberg-Hohenzollern, *Land,* Germany; now merged with Baden-Württemberg.

Würzburg, *c.,* Bavaria, Germany; on R. Main; univ.; machin., metals, chemicals, printing, engin.; route ctr.; p. (1968) *120,463.*

Wurzen, *c.,* Leipzig, E. Germany; on R. Mulde; cath., cas.; machin., furniture, leather, foodstuffs; p. (1963) *23,824.*

Wusih (Wuxi), *c.,* Kiangsu, China; on N. shore of Tai Hu, 75 m. W. of Shanghai; silk, cottonweaving; p. (1953) *582,000.*

Wutungkiao (Wutongqiao), *c.,* Szechwan prov., China; 15 m. S.E. of Loshan; p. (1953) *199,000.*

Wyalong, N.S.W., *see* West Wyalong.

Wyandotte, *c.,* Mich., U.S.A.; on Detroit R.; chemicals; p. (1960) *43,519.*

Wye, *R.,* Bucks, Eng.; rises in Chiltern Hills above High Wycombe, flows S.E. to R. Thames at Cookham.   [length 20 m.

Wye, *R.,* Derby, Eng.; trib. of R. Derwent

Wye, *R.,* Eng. and Wales; rises in Plynlimmon, flows S.E. into R. Severn at Chepstow; length 130 m.   [sta. projected.

Wylfa Head, Anglesey, N. Wales; nuclear power

Wymondham, *t.,* Norfolk, Eng.; 9 m. S.W. of Norwich; mkt.; brush-making; Benedictine abbey, founded 1107; p. (1961) *5,896.*

Wyoming, *st.,* U.S.A.; livestock, agr., coal-mining, minerals, petroleum; cap. Cheyenne; a. 97,914 sq. m.; p. (1970) *332,591.*

Wyoming, *valley,* N.E. Penns., U.S.A., on Susquehanna R.; coal; length 30 m.

Wyre. R., Lancs, Eng.; rises in Pennines, flows W. into Lancaster Bay at Fleetwood; length 28 m.

Wyvis, Ben, *mtn.,* Scot., *see* Ben Wyvis.

X

Xanthi, *t.,* Thrace, Greece; on R. Mesta; tobacco; p. (1961) *26,377.*

Xanthus, *ruined c.,* Turkey; on R. Xanthus.

Xauen, *t.,* Morocco, N. Africa; p. *14,473.*

Xenia, *c.,* Ohio, U.S.A.; in Miami valley; twine, footwear, agr. ctr.; p. (1960) *20,445.*

Xeres, *see* Jerez de la Frontera.

Xingu, *R.,* Brazil; trib. of the Amazon; navigable in its lower course; length 1,200 m.

Xochicalco, *ruins,* Mexico.

Xochimilco, *L.,* Mexico; formerly contiguous with L. Tezcuco.

Xochimilco, *sub.,* Mexico City; famous for flower-lined canals; on L. Xochimilco; p. *14,370.*

Xois, *ancient c.,* Lower U.A.R.; cap. Ancient Egypt in 17th century B.C.

Y

Yablonovy, *mtn. range,* Siberia, Asiatic R.S.F.S.R.; E. of L. Baikal; highest peak, Sokhondo, *c.* 8,230 ft.; crossed by Trans-Siberian rly.

Yaila Mtns., Ukrainian S.S.R., U.S.S.R.; form S.E. margin of Crimea Peninsula, extend from Sevastopol to Kerch; forested on middle slopes, pasture on upper slopes; forms marked climate barrier between mild winters of Mediterranean cst. to the S. and cold winters to the N.

Yakima, *t.,* Wash., U.S.A.; agr., livestock; p. (1960) *43,284.*

Yakima, *R.,* Wash., U.S.A.; trib. of Columbia R.; length 208 m

Yakova, *t.,* Albania; nr. Shkodra.

Yakushima, *I.,* Osumi Gr., Japan; S. of Kyushu; mtns., forest.

Yakut, A.S.S.R., U.S.S.R.; gold-mining; a. 1,530,253 sq. m.; p. (1959) *247,000.*

Yakutsk, *t.,* R.S.F.S.R.; on R. Lena; p. (1959) *74,000.*

Yala, *t.,* S. Thailand; tin-mining.

Yalta, *spt.,* Ukrainian S.S.R.; on Black Sea; p. (1956) *34,100.*

Yalu, *R.,* forms bdy. between Manchuria and N. Korea; flows into Yellow Sea.

Yamagata, *t.,* Honshu, Japan; mnfs.; p. (1966) *193,737.*

Yamaguchi, *t.,* Honshu, Japan; p. (1966) *98,977.*

Yamal, *peninsula,* R.S.F.S.R.; jutting into Arctic Ocean; lge oil and gas deposits nearby.

Yambol, t., Bulgaria; on R. Tunja; ruined mosque; corn tr.; p. (1956) *42,038.*

Yamethin, *dist.,* Upper Burma; teak forests, rice; ch. t. Yamethin; p. *9,291.*

Yamina, *t.,* Gambia, W. Africa; p. *6,700.*

Yamina or Nyamina, *t.* Nigeria, W. Africa; on R. Niger; tr. ctr.

Yana, *R.,* Siberia, U.S.S.R.; length 1,000 m.

Yanago, *t.,* Japan; business ctr.; cotton textiles; p. (1947) *50,027.*

Yanaon or Yanam, *prov.,* *t.* formerly Fr. Orissa, united with India 1954; p. (1961) *7,032.*

Yanbu, *spt.,* Arabia; on E. cst. of Red Sea; pt. for Medina.

Yangchow (Yangzhou), *c.,* Kiangsu, China; on Grand Canal; comm. ctr.; p. (1953) *180,000.*

Yangchuan (Yangqan), *c.,* Shansi prov., China; ironworking ctr.; p. (1953) *177,000.*

Yangi-yer, *t.,* Uzbek S.S.R., founded 1957 as ctr. for new irrigated cotton lands of the Hunger steppe.

Yangtze River, China; rises in plateau of Tibet, flows E. to E. China Sea, Pac. Oc. nr. Shanghai; traverses " Red Basin " of Szechwan, a deep gorge above Ichang, and finally a broad, level plain; many lge. cs. on its banks, Chungking, Ichang, Wuhan (Hankow, Hayang, Wuchang), Nanking, Chinkiang; navigable by ocean-going vessels 1,800 m. to Ichang; total length 3,500 m.

Yannina, *see* Ioánnina.

Yaoundé, *cap.,* Cameroun Rep., W. Africa; p. (estd. 1965) *93,000.*

Yap, I., Carolines, Pac. Oc., U.S.A. trusteeship; a. 79 sq. m.; cable sta.; p. (1958) *5,459.*

Yapura, *R.,* Brazil and Colombia, S. America; trib. of R. Amazon; navigable for 600 m.; length 1,500 m.

Yaracuy, *st.,* Venezuela; cap. San Felipe; p. (1961) *175,291.*

Yare, *R.,* Norfolk, Eng.; flows E. to N. Sea at Gorleston; length 50 m.

Yaritagua, *t.,* Venezuela; tobacco, coffee, cocoa, sugar; p. *5,399.*

Yarkand (Soche), *c.,* Sinkiang, China; tr. ctr.; wheat, rice, beans, fruit, carpets, textiles; p. (estd.) *60,000.*

Yarkand, *R.,* Sinkiang, China; trib. of Tarim R.; length 500 m.

Yarmouth, *spt.,* Nova Scotia, Canada; shipbldg., fisheries; p. (1961) *8,636.*

Yarmouth *par.,* I. of Wight, Eng.; on N.W. cst.; 8 m. W of Newport; holiday resort; p. *893.*

Yarmouth, Great, *fishing pt., co. bor.,* Norfolk, Eng.; at mouth of R. Yare; holiday resort; fish processing plants; base for North Sea gas; p. (estd. 1967) *51,910.*

Yaroslavl, *t.,* R.S.F.S.R.; on R. V lga; cath.; synthetic rubber, engin., textiles, chemicals, sawmilling; p. (1967) *486,000.*

Yarra, *t.,* Victoria, Australia; length 100 m.

Yasan, N. Bulgaria; nr. Pleven and oil reservoir Dolni Dubnik; lge. refinery under construction.

Yatschushiro, *t.,* Kyushu, Japan; p. (1965) *103,000.*

Yavary, *R.,* S. America; on Brazilian–Peruvian frontier; trib. of R. Marañon; length 450 m.

Yawata, *t.,* Kyushu, Japan; now part of Kitak-yushu City newly formed 1963 (*q.v.*); chemicals, iron and steel; p. (1960) *332,000.*

Yazd, *c.,* Iran, Isfahan prov.; carpets, textiles; p. (1967) *280,442.*

Yazoo, *c.,* Miss., U.S.A.; on Yazoo R.; agr. tr.; p. (1960) *11,236.* [length 280 m.

Yazoo, *R.,* Miss., U.S.A.; trib. of R. Mississippi;

Yazoo, *dist.,* Miss., U.S.A.; very flat, low-lying flood plain of R. Mississippi and R. Yazoo, extends 220 m. along R. from Memphis to Vicksburg; very fertile alluvial soil, but subject to disastrous floods; one of ch. cotton-growing dists. in U.S.A.

Yecla, *t.,* Spain; mkt.; p. (1957) *24,046.*

Yeddo, old name of Tokio, Japan.

Yegoryevsk, *t.,* R.S.F.S.R.; 72 m. S.E. of Moscow; lge. textile ind.; p. (1959) *59,000.* [Dvina.

Yekabpils, *t.,* Kurland, Latvian S.S.R.; on R.

Yeletz, *t.,* R.S.F.S.R.; on R. Sosna; grain and cattle tr.; p. (1959) *78,000.*

Yell, *I.,* Shetlands, Scot.; 17 m. long; p. *1,883.*

Yellow R., *see* Hwang Ho.

Yellow Sea (Hwang-hai), *arm* of Pacific Ocean, between China and Korea; length 600 m., greatest width 400 m.; max. depth 500 ft.

Yellowhead Pass, B.C., Alberta, Canada; most N. and lowest of main passes across Rocky Mtns.; carries Canadian National Rly. on route from Edmonton to Vancouver and Prince Rupert; summit alt. 3,700 ft.

Yellowknife *t.,* N.W. Terr., Canada; on N. shore of Gr. Slave L.; ctr. of impt. gold-mining dist.; linked by air to Edmonton, Alberta.

Yellowstone, *t.,* Wyo., U.S.A.; 20 m. long, 15 m. wide; alt. 7,740 ft.; in Y. National Park.

Yemen, *republic,* S.W. Arabia; bounded by Saudi Arabia on N., Southern Yemen on S.; prin. c. Sana; barley, wheat, millet, coffee, hides; a. 75,000 sq. m.; p. *c. 5,000,000.*

Yemen, Southern, People's Republic of, *indep. sov. st.* (1967), S.W. Arabia, on G. of Aden; mtnous., desert; exp. long-staple cotton; former Brit. Aden col. and prot.; incl. Is. of Perim, Kamaran and Socotra; cap. Madinat al Shaab; a. 117,000 sq. m.; p. (estd. 1969) *1,195,000.*

Yenakievo, *t.,* Ukrainian S.S.R.; coal, iron and steel; p. (1959) *92,000.*

Yenangyaung, *t., R. pt.,* Burma; on left bank of R. Irrawaddy, 280 m. N. of Rangoon; ctr. of Burma oilfields.

Yenesei, *R.,* Siberia, R.S.F.S.R.; rises in Sayan Mtns., flows N. into Arctic Ocean; ch. tribs. Upper, Stony and Lower Tunguska Rs.; length 3,300 m.

Yentai, *see* Chefoo.

Yeo or Ivel, *R.,* Dorset, Somerset, Eng.; trib. of R. Parrett; length 24 m.

Yeovil, *t., mun. bor.*, Somerset, Eng.; on R. Yeo; 22 m. S.E. of Taunton; glove mnf., aeroplane wks. engin.; dairying; p. (estd. 1967) 25,450.

Yerevan, *cap.*, Armenian S.S.R.; engin., chemicals, synthetic rubber, textiles, aluminium; p. (1967) 643,000.

Yeshil-Irmak, *R.*, Turkey; flows N. to Black Sea; length 200 m.

Yeshil Kul, *L.*, Chinese Turkestan (Sinkiang).

Yes Tor, *2nd highest summit*, Dartmoor, Devon, Eng.; alt. 2,028 ft.

Yevpatoriya (Eupatoria), *spt.* Ukrainian S.S.R.; chemicals, leather, locks, dried fish; new port being built 1963; p. (1959), 57,000.

Yeysk, *t.*, R.S.F.S.R.; N. Caucasus, pt. on Taganrog Bay; resort; engin.; p. (1959) 55,000.

Yezd, *t., prov. cap.*, Iran; caravan ctr.; p. (estd. 1949) 56,000.

Yezo, *see* Hokkaido.

Yiewsley and West Drayton, *former urb. dist.*, Middx., Eng.; now inc. in Hillingdon outer bor. Greater London; varied light inds.; p. (1961) 23,723.

Yingkow (Yingkou), *c.*, Liaoning prov., China: 20 m. up R. from mouth of Liao-ho; soyabean prods.; p. (1953) 131,000.

Ykspihlaja, *sub.* of Kokkola, W. Finland; foundries, chemicals.

Yokkaichi, *industl. c., spt.*, S. Honshu, Japan; on W. cst. of Ise Bay, 23 m. S.W. of Nagoya; silk, cotton and woollen goods, petro chemicals, synthetic rubber; p. (1964) 221,000.

Yokohama, *ch. spt.*, Honshu, Japan; W. side of Tokio Bay; silks, tea, cars; p. (1970) 2,237,513.

Yokosuka, *spt.*, Honshu, Japan; S. of Tokio; holiday resort; thermal power sta.; p. (1965) 317,411.

Yola, *t.*, N Nigeria Africa; nr. R. Benue; agr. tr.; p. 5,310.

Yonkers, *c.*, N.Y., U.S.A.; on Hudson R.; light inds.; p. (1960) 190,634.

Yonne, *dep.*, France; agr., wines, minerals; cap. Auxerre; a. 2,894 sq. m.; p. (1968) 283,376.

York, *c., co. bor., co. t.*, Yorks, Eng.; on R. Ouse; in central position in Vale of York; cath., cas., univ.; mkt., confectionery; rly. workshops; p. (estd. 1969) 107,940.

York, *I. gr.*, Torres Strait (between New Guinea and Australia).

York, *R.*, tidal estuary of Chesapeake Bay, U.S.A.

York, *c.*, Nebraska, U.S.A.; rly. ctr.; p. (1960) 6,173.

York, *c.*, Penns., U.S.A.; agr. tools, confectionery, tobacco; p. (1960) 54,504.

York, *C.*, Hayes Peninsula. Greenland

York, *C.*, Queensland, Australia; most N. point on mainland of Australia.

York Factory, *t.*, on Nelson R. Hudson Bay, Manitoba, Canada.

York, Vale of, *broad lowland*, Yorks, Eng.; extends N. to S. between Pennines to W. and N. Yorks Moors and Yorks Wolds to E.; drained to Humber by R. Ouse and tribs. from N. by Rs. Don and Trent from S.; flar apart from low transverse ridge Stamford Bridge to Harrogate; glacial and alluvial soils have required draining; crop farming, wheat, barley, root-crops, associated with fattening of beef cattle; settlement mainly marginal; ch. t. York; length 60 m.; width varies from 10 m. in N. to 30 m. in S.

Yorke, *peninsula*, S Australia; separates Spencer G. and G. of St. Vincent; 100 m. long, 30 m. wide.

Yorkshire, *lgst. co.*, Eng.; divided into 3 Ridings, N., E. and W.; cap. York; a. 6,081 sq. m ; p. (1961) 4,722,661.

Yorkshire, East Riding, *admin. co.*, Yorks, Eng.; farming, pastoral on Wolds, arable elsewhere; ch. t. Hull; a. 1,172 sq. m.; p. (1966) 543,000.

Yorkshire, North Riding, *admin. co.*, Yorks, Eng; farming, pastoral on Moors, mixed elsewhere; iron-ore mng. in Cleveland Hills; heavy inds. around Middlesbrough; ch. t. Middlesbrough; a. 2,128 sq. m.; p. (1966) 584,000.

Yorkshire, West Riding, *admin. co.*, Yorks, Eng.; pastoral farming on Pennines, but highly industl. on coalfield at foot of Pennines; woollens steel, engin.; ch. ts. Leeds (in N.), Sheffield (in S.); a. 2,780 sq. m.; p. (1966) 3,736,000.

Yorkshire Moors, *hills*, N.R. Yorks, Eng.; inc. North Yorks Moors, Cleveland Hills and

Hambleton Hills; bounded to N. by Tees Valley, S. by Vale of Pickering, W. by Swale Valley, E. by sea; composed of oolitic limestone; good sheep pastures; impt. iron-ore deposits worked in Cleveland Hills; maximum alt. 1,489 ft.

Yorkshire Wolds, *hills*, E.R., Yorks, Eng.; extend N.E. from Humber and terminate in Flamborough Head; composed of chalk; smooth slopes and short grass give gd. sheep pasture; average alt. 600 ft.

Yorkton, *t.*, Saskatchewan, Canada; agr. ctr.; p. (1961) 9,995.

Yoruba, *dist.*, Nigeria; ch. ts., Oyo, Ibadan, Abeokuta and Illorin.

Yosemite Falls, 3 cataracts, of Yosemite Creek, Cal., U.S.A.

Yoshkar-Ola, *t.*, Mariy A.S.S.R.; R.S.F.S.R.; 80 m. N.W. of Kazan; wood processing, food inds.; p. (1967) 133,000.

Youghal, *spt., urb. dist.*, Cork, Ireland; on estuary of the Blackwater; p. (1966) 5,098.

Youngstown, *industl. c.*, Ohio, U.S.A.; on Beaver R., 60 m. N.W. of Pittsburgh; iron- and steel-mkg., heavy engin.; p. (1960) 166,689.

Yoyang, *c.*, Hunan, China; at outlet of Tung Ting L. on the bank of the R. Yangtze; p. 4,800.

Yozgat, *t.*, Turkey; p. (1960) 18,263.

Ypres (Ieper), *t.*, Belgium; automatic textile loom mkg.; 2 battles, First World War; p. (1962) 18,213.

Ypsilanti, *c.*, Mich., U.S.A.; on Huron R.; agr. mkt., mnfs.; p. (1960) 20,957.

Yssingeaux, *t.*, Haute-Loire, France; nr. Le Puy; mnfs.; p. (1962) 5,889.

Ystad, *spt.*, S. Sweden; on Baltic Sea; agr. machin., soap; p. (1961) 13,711.

Yuba, *R.*, Cal., U.S.A.; trib. of Feather-Sacramento R.

Yucatan *st.*, Mexico; cereals, cotton; cap. Merida; a. 23,926 sq. m.; p. (1960) 614,049.

Yucatan, *strait*, connects G. of Mexico with Caribbean Sea.

Yuan Kiang, *R.*, Hunan, China; length 400 m.

Yugoslavia, *see* Jugoslavia.

Yukon, *R.*, Canada–Alaska; flows N.W. and W. into Bering Strait; navigable for 1,200 m.; length 2,000 m.

Yukon Territory, *prov.*, Canada; ntnous. (Mt. Logan 19,850 ft.); gold, silver, lead, zinc, cadmium, coal; Alaska Highway links with Brit. Columbia and Alberta; chief ts. Dawson, and Whitehorse (cap.); a. 207,076 sq. m.; p. (estd. 1969) 15,000.

Yuma, *t.*, Arizona, U.S.A.; at confluence of Rs. Gila and Colorado nr. Mexican–U.S.A. bdy.; ctr. of irrigated agr., obtaining water from Laguna and Imperial Dams; cotton, citrus fruits, alfalfa; p. (1960) 23,974.

Yunnan, *S.W. prov.*, China; adjoining Burma; mountainous; agr., minerals; cap. Kunming; a. 162,342 sq. m.; p. (1953) 17,472,737.

Yuzhno-Sakhalinsk, *t.*, R.S.F.S.R.; at S. end of Sakhalin I; paper, light inds.; p. (1959) 86,000.

Yvelines, *dep.* France, Paris region; p. (1968) 853,386.

Yverdon, *t.*, Switzerland; cas.; tourist ctr.

Z

Zaandam, *t.*, N. Holland, Neth.; paper, oil, timber, cement; p. (1967) 57,099.

Zabrze (Hindenburg), *t.*, Upper Silesia, Poland; German before 1945: steel, coal, engin., chemicals; p. (1965) 200,000.

Zacapa, *t.*, Guatemala, Central America; sulphur springs; tobacco; p. (estd. 1960) 35,300.

Zacatecas, *st.*, Mexico; silver-mines; cereals, fruit, sugar; a. 28,122 sq. m.; p. (1960) 817,331.

Zacatecas, *t., cap.*, Zacatecas, Mexico; silver, pottery, comm. ctr.; p. (1960) 24,454.

Zacatecoluca, *t.*, El Salvador, Central America; cigar mkg., hand looms; coffee, cotton, sugar, vanilla in a.; p. (1960) 30,810.

Zadar (Zara), *spt.*, Jugoslavia; formerly Italian; cath.; maraschino, flour, glass; p. (1959) 22,000.

Zagan (Sagan), *t.*, Silesia, Poland; German before 1945: on R. Bober; cas.; textiles, paper, lignite; p. (1965) 21,000.

Zagazig, *t.*, Egypt; on Nile Delta; cotton, grain tr.; p. (1960) 124,000.

Zagorsk, *t.*, R.S.F.S.R.; 44 m. N.E. of Moscow; woodcarving, toy mkg.; p. (1959) 73,000.

Zagreb, *t.*, Jugoslavia; on R. Sava; cath., univ.; engin., textiles, chemicals, paper, asbestos; p. (1964) *491,000*.

Zagros, *mtns.*, Persia; highest, Zardeh Kuh, 14,921 ft.

Zahedan, *c.*, Iran, prov. cap. Sistan and Baluchestan; airpt.; term. of rly. from Pakistan; p. (1967) *79,257*.

Zahle, *t.*, Lebanon, S.W. Asia; on slopes of L. mtn.; p. (estd 1950) *78,031*.

Zakopane, *t.*, Poland; in High Tatra mtns.; tourist resort; p. (1965) *26,000*.

Zakynthos, *Ionian I.* Greece; cap. Zante; currants; devastated by severe earthquake, 1953; a. 277 sq. m.; p. (1961) *35,451*.

Zalaegerszeg, *t.*, Hungary; in Göcsej dist.; oilfields.

Zambesi, *R.*, S.E. Africa; flows E. to Mozambique Channel, Indian Ocean; navigable for 1,700 m.; length 2,200 m. [p. (1962) *1,369,961*.

Zambesia, *prov.*, Mozambique; ch. t., Quelimane;

Zambia, *indep. sov. st.* within Brit. Commonwealth (1964), Central Africa; landlocked, bordering Congo, Angola, South-West Africa, Rhodesia, and Botswana (50-yd. frontier across Zambesi); tropical climate, moderate rains; savannah vegetation; maize, tobacco, wheat, coffee; zinc, copper, vanadium, gold, ivory; fishing ind.; irrigation system under development on Kafue Flats; mica in the Lundazi a.; cap. Lusaka; a. 291,000 sq. m.; p. (estd.) *4,100,000*.

Zamboanga, *t.*, Mindanao, Philippines; rice, sugar, tobacco, timber, copper; p. (estd.) *164,000*. [sq. m.; p. (1959) *320,335*.

Zamora, *prov.*, Spain; cap. Zamora; a. 40,835

Zamora, *t., cap.*, Zamora, Spain; on R. Duero; olive oil, wines; p. (1957) *45,000*.

Zamosc, *old t.*, Poland; bentwood furniture mnf.; p. (1965) *30,000*.

Zanesville, *t.*, Ohio, U.S.A.; textiles, pottery, machin.; p. (1960) *39,077*.

Zanjan, *c.*, Iran, prov. cap. Gilan; p. (1967) *461,588*.

Zante, *t.*, Zakynthos, Greece; p. (1961) *9,506*.

Zanzibar, *I.*, E. Africa; joined with former st. of Tanganyika to form Tanzania; cloves, coconuts, copra; cap. Zanzibar; a. 1,020 sq. m.; p. (1967) *354,360* (inc. Pemba).

Zapala, *t.*, W. Argentina; in Andes; rly. term.; oilfield.

Zaporozhe (Dneprostroy), *industl. t.*, Ukrainian S.S.R.; on R. Dnieper, 45 m. S.E. of Dnieperpetrovsk; nr. Lenin (Dnieper) Dam and hydroelec. power-sta. (558,000 kW.); iron- and steelwks., ferro-alloys, engin., aluminium, chemicals, cars, elec. equipment; p. (1967) *571,000*.

Zaragoza, *prov.*, Spain; cap. Zaragoza; a. 6,611 sq. m.; p. (1959) *643,825*.

Zaragoza, *t.*, Spain; on R. Ebro; 2 caths., univ., citadel; captured by Moors 8th century, once cap. of Aragon; beer, spirits, woollens, iron ware; p. (1965) *393,000*.

Zarate, *t.*, Entre Rios, Argentina; paper wks.; p. (1960) *52,000*.

Zaria, *t.*, N. Nigeria, Africa; univ.; cotton ctr.; p. (1953) *54,000*.

Zary (Sorau), *t.*, Brandenburg, Poland; German before 1945; textiles, pottery; p. (1965) *23,000*.

Zastron, *t.*, O.F.S., S. Africa; alt. 5,507 ft.; agr. ctr.; p. (1960) *4,440* inc. *1,625* whites.

Zawiercie, *t.*, Poland; industr. ctr.; coal, iron, textiles, glass; p. (1965) *37,000*.

Zdunska Wola, *t.*, Poland; nr. Lodz; p. (1965) *27,000*.

Zealand (Sjaelland), *I.*, Denmark; between Kattegat and Baltic; a. (with Is. attached) 2,709 sq. m.; ch. t. Copenhagen; p. *1,771,557*.

Zeebrugge, *spt.*, Belgium; connected with Bruges by ship canal; glass ind.; petrol storage and conditioning depot; oil refinery; rolling mill equip.; p. (1947) *3,450*.

Zeeland, *prov.*, S.E. Neth.; fishing; cap. Middelburg; a. 690 sq. m.; p. (estd. 1967) *295,374*.

Zeilah, *t.*, Somali Rep., E. Africa; on G. of Aden; p. *1,000*.

Zeist, *t.*, Utrecht, Neth.; metalware, Meccano toys, silverware; p. (1967) *55,501*.

Zelenodolsk, *t.*, R.S.F.S.R., on R. Volga 25 m. W. of Kazan; rly. junction; sawmills; p. (1959) *60,000*.

Zelten, Libya, N. Africa; 200 m. S. of Benghazi; oil field; pipeline Mersa al-Brega.

Zenica, *t.*, Jugoslavia; lge. iron and steel wks; p. (1959) *47,000*.

Zerbst, *t.*, Magdeburg, E. Germany; on R. Nuthe, S.E. of Magdeburg; cas.; machin.; p. (1963) *18,862*.

Zermatt, *vil.*, Valais, Switzerland; at foot of Matterhorn; tourist ctr. [*39,000*.

Zgierz, *t.*, Poland; nr. Lodz; linens; p. (1965)

Zhdanov (Mariupol), *spt.*, Ukrainian S.S.R.; on Azov Sea; iron and steel, zirconium, chemicals; p. (1967) *373,000*.

Zhitomir, *t.*, Ukrainian S.S.R.; engin.; p. (1967) *133,000*.

Zielona Gora (Grünberg), *t.*, Silesia, Poland; German before 1945; lignite mining, viticulture; p. (1965) *62,000*. [(1965) *26,152*.

Zile, *t.*, Turkey; cereals, fruit, wool, rugs; p.

Zillertal, *valley*, Tyrol, Austria; drained by R. Ziller, trib. of R. Inn; length 50 m.

Zillertal Alps, *mtns.*, Austria; in Tyrol.

Zinder, *t.*, Niger, W. Africa; terminus of transSaharan motor route; tr. ctr.

Zipaquira, *t.*, Colombia; 30 m. N. of Bogota; cattle farming; salt mines; p. (estd 1959) *29,880*.

Zistersdorf, *t.*, N.E. Austria; recently developed oilfields.

Zittau, *t.*, Dresden, E. Germany; on R. Mandau; woollens, linens, machin., cars, chemicals; p. (1963) *42,863*.

Žižkov, *t.*, ČSSR.; sub. of Prague; p. *91,082*.

Zlatoust, *t.*, R.S.F.S.R.; in the Ural Mtns.; steel, chemicals, sawmilling; p. (1959) *161,000*.

Zlin, *see* Gottwaldov.

Znojmo or Znaim, *t.*, ČSSR.; pottery, textiles, mkt. gardening; p. (1961) *23,956*.

Zomba, *cap. c.*, Malawi, 2,900 ft. above sea level on slopes of Zomba mtn., 42 m. N.E. Blantyre; univ.; p. (1966) *19,616*.

Zonguldak, *t.*, Turkey; p. (1965) *60,865*.

Zorita De Los Canos, Guadalajara, Spain; on R. Tagus; nuclear power plant.

Zorritos, *t.*, Tumbes dep., Peru, S. America; on cst., 10 m. from Ecuador bdy.; oilfield.

Zoutpansberg, *dist.*, N.E. Transvaal, S. Africa; goldfields, mtns.

Zrenjanin (Veliki Bečkerek), *t.*, Vojvodina, Jugoslavia; on R. Begej; flour, leather, timber, sugar, wine, paper, agr., machin.; p. (1960) *52,100*.

Zug, *can.*, Switzerland; cap. Zug; a. 93 sq. m.; p. (1961) *52,489*.

Zugspitze, *mtn.*, Bavarian Alps, highest peak in Germany, 9.722 ft.

Zuider Zee, *see* IJselmeer.

Zulia, *st.*, Venezuela, S. America; cap. Maracaibo; p. (1963) *1,044,000*.

Zululand, *prov.*, Natal; livestock, cereals, fruit, sugar, coffee, tea, gold, coal; a. 10,427 sq. m.

Zungeru, *t.*, Nigeria, Africa; on Lagos–Kano rly.

Zurich, *can.*, Switzerland; cottons, silks; a. 668 sq. m.; p. (1961) *952,304*.

Zurich (Zürich), *c.*, Switzerland; on L. Zurich and R. Limmat, lgst. t.; cap. of Z. prov.; cath., univ.; paper, silks, cottons, machin.; p. (1961) *439,600*.

Zutphen, *c.*, Gelderland, Neth.; on R. IJssel; paper, tanning, engin.; p. (1967) *27,017*.

Zveitina, Libya; new oil terminal 1968; pipeline from Idris field.

Zwartebergen, *mtns.*, Cape Province, Rep. of S. Africa; extending 200 m. E. to W. flanked by Gr. Karroo to N. Little Karroo to S.; form impenetrable barrier except where broken across by headstreams of R. Gouritz; rise to over 7,000 ft.

Zwartsluis, *t.*, Neth.; nr. Zwolle; p. *3,348*.

Zweibrücken, *t.*, Rhineland-Palatinate, Germany; nr. Saarbrücken; cas.; machin., footwear, textiles; p. (1963) *33,300*.

Zwickau, *t.*, Karl-Marx-Stadt, E. Germany; on R. Zwickhauser Mulde; cas.; coal, motors, machin., textiles; p. (1963) *129,389*.

Zwolle, *c.*, Overijssel, Neth.; canal ctr.; cattle mkt., cottons, ironwks.; p. (1967) *59,877*.

Zyrardow, *t.*, Poland; nr. Warsaw; mnfs.; p. (1965) *31,000*.

Zyryanovsk, *t.*, Kazakhstan S.S.R.; lead, zinc; p. (1959) *54,000*.

THE COMMONWEALTH

The Commonwealth is a free association of independent member nations together with their dependencies at various stages of political advance. Member nations include Britain, Canada, Australia, New Zealand whose membership of the Commonwealth dates from the Statute of Westminster, 1931, India (1947), Pakistan (1947), Ceylon (1948), Ghana (1957), the Federation of Malaya (1957), which in 1963 became Malaysia, the Federation (now the Federal Republic) of Nigeria (1960), Cyprus (1960)., Sierra Leone (1961), Tanganyika (1961), which in 1964 united with Zanzibar (1963) to become Tanzania, Jamaica (1962), Trinidad and Tobago (1962), Uganda (1962), Kenya (1963), Malawi (1964), Malta (1964), Zambia (1964), the Gambia (1965), Singapore, which seceded from the Malaysian Federation (1965), Botswana (1966), Guyana (1966), Lesotho (1966), Barbados (1966), Mauritius (1968), Swaziland (1968), Western Samoa (1970), Fiji (1970) and Tonga (1970). Nauru, which became independent in 1968, has the status of "special membership" of the Commonwealth. *See also* Section C, Part II.

I.—MEMBERS OF THE COMMONWEALTH
(including territories for which members other than the U.K. are responsible).

Country	Land Area (sq. miles)	Recent Population Estimates
United Kingdom	94,214	55,534,000
Canada (incl. Newfoundland and Labrador)	3,851,809	21,007,000
Australia (Commonwealth of)	2,967,909	12,173,000
Cocos Islands	5	1,000
Christmas Island	52	3,653
Norfolk Island	13½	1,232
Papua and New Guinea	183,540	2,350,455
Antarctic territory	5,000,000	—
New Zealand	103,736	2,781,000
Island Territories (Cook Is. self-gov. st.)	194	24,478
Ross Dependency	160,000 (estimated)	262
India (Republic of)	1,262,000	519,749,000
Pakistan (Republic of)	365,529	111,830,000
Ceylon	25,332	11,964,000
Ghana (Republic of)	91,843	8,545,561
Nigeria (Federal Republic of)	356,669	62,650,000
*Cyprus (Republic of)	3,572	631,000
Sierra Leone	27,925	2,475,000
Tanzania (United Republic of)	362,820	12,311,991
Uganda	93,981	8,133,000
Jamaica	4,411	1,972,000
Trinidad and Tobago	1,980	1,030,000
Kenya (Republic of)	224,960	10,890,000
Malaysia (Federation of)	129,000	10,384,000
Malawi (Republic of)	45,411	4,039,583
Malta and Gozo	122	314,175
Zambia (Republic of)	291,000	4,100,000
Gambia (Republic of)	4,060	357,000
Singapore (Republic of)	225	2,033,500
Botswana (Republic of)	222,000	611,000
Guyana (Republic of)	83,000	730,000
Lesotho	11,716	969,634
Barbados	166	253,633
Mauritius	805	810,000
Swaziland	6,704	395,000
Western Samoa	1,097	141,000
Fiji	7,095	505,000
Tonga	270	81,000

* The United Kingdom retains sovereignty over areas totalling about 99 sq. m.

The West Indian Associated States (Antigua, St. Kitts–Nevis–Anguilla, Dominica, St. Lucia, St. Vincent and Grenada) enjoy a special relationship with Britain. They are fully self-governing but Britain retains general responsibility for their defence and external relations. This relationship can be terminated either by the island territory concerned or by the British Government. Anguilla unilaterally seceded from the St. Kitts union in 1967.

II.—TERRITORIES FOR WHICH THE U.K. IS RESPONSIBLE AND WHICH ARE ADMINISTERED THROUGH THE FOREIGN AND COMMONWEALTH OFFICE.

(Some of the very small, or practically uninhabited, islands have been omitted.)

Region and Territory	Status	Land Area (sq. miles)	Recent Population Estimates
Central Africa:			
Rhodesia	Colony (self-gov.)	150,333	5,070,400
Far East:			
Brunei	Protected state (self-gov.)	2,226	130,000
Hong Kong	Colony	398	3,988,000
Mediterranean:			
*Gibraltar	City (non-self-gov. terr.)	2½	27,000
Caribbean:			
Montserrat	Colony	39	14,500
Cayman Is.	Colony	100	10,000
British Honduras	Colony (intern. self-gov.)	8,866	116,000
Virgin Islands	Colony	59	10,500
Western Pacific:			
Pitcairn	Colony	2	186
Western Pacific High Commission Territories:			
British Solomon Islands Protectorate .	Protectorate	11,500	148,000
Gilbert and Ellice Islands Colony . .	Colony	369	55,000
New Hebrides	Anglo-French Condominium	5,700	80,000
Atlantic Ocean:			
Falkland Islands	Colony	4,700	2,098
Dependencies:			
S. Georgia	Dependency of Falkland Islands	1,450	531
S. Sandwich Is..	Dependency of Falkland Islands		Uninhabited
British Antarctic Territory:			
S. Shetlands, S. Orkneys, Graham's Land	Colony	500,000	No permanent inhabitants
Bahamas	Colony (intern. self-gov.)	4,404	170,000
Turks and Caicos Is.	Colony	166	6,272
Bermuda	Colony	21	51,000
St. Helena	Colony	47	5,000
Ascension	Dependency of St. Helena	34	1,527
Tristan da Cunha	Dependency of St. Helena	38	280
Indian Ocean:			
Seychelles	Colony	156	49,981
†British Indian Ocean Territory . . .			1,400

Note.—An illegal declaration of independence was declared in Rhodesia on 11 November 1965. *See* Section C, Part II.

* Under the new Constitution, which came into effect in 1969, Gibraltar became known as the City of Gibraltar. It is no longer a colony, but "part of Her Majesty's dominions."

† This territory consists of the Chagos Archipelago (formerly part of Mauritius) and Aldabra, Farquhar and Desroches Islands (formerly part of Seychelles).

GENERAL INFORMATION

Some three thousand entries, including a number of scientific terms and explanations. Cross references direct the reader to fuller information elsewhere in the book. A list of Nobel Prize Winners will be found at the end of the section.

GENERAL INFORMATION

A

Aard-vark (Dutch *aarde* = earth + *vark* = pig), name given by the Boers to a genus of ant-eating mammals peculiar to Africa. They are nocturnal and burrowing, with an arched back, and usually grow to a length of 5 ft.

Abacus, a device for making arithmetical calculations, consisting of parallel bars on which are strung movable coloured beads. The earliest form of this instrument was used in Mesopotamia about 3000 B.C., and its use spread westwards throughout the Græco–Roman world and eastwards to China. An efficient form of the abacus is still used today in parts of Asia.

Abdication. The term usually refers to the renunciation of the royal office by a reigning monarch. Both Edward II (1327) and Richard II (1399) were forced to abdicate, James II left the throne vacant without waiting for a formal deposition, and the abdication of Edward VIII was effected by the Declaration of Abdication Act, 1936. Since 1688 when Parliament declared James II to have abdicated by reason of desertion and subversion of the constitution, no British monarch can abdicate without the consent of Parliament.

Aberration, in astronomy, is the apparent displacement of a star due to the speed of the observer with the earth (see Parallax). In optics (i) spherical aberration is when there is blurring of the image and fringes of colour at its edges, due to failure of lens to bring light to a single focus; (ii) chromatic aberration is due to the refractive index of glass being different for light of different colours. For instance, violet light is bent more than red.

Abiogenesis, or spontaneous generation: the origination of living from non-living matter. The term is applied to such discredited ideas as that frogs could be generated spontaneously by the action of sunlight on mud, or maggots arise spontaneously in dead meat without any eggs from which the maggots hatch being present. Spallanzani (1729–99) upset the hypothesis of spontaneous generation; Pasteur dealt it a death-blow.

Abominable Snowman. *See* Yeti.

Aborigines, a term first applied to an ancient mythical people of central Italy, derives from the Latin *ab origine* = from the beginning. It now signifies the original inhabitants of any country, in particular the aboriginal tribes of Australia. In contrast to their highly complex social and religious customs, the material culture of Australian aborigines is very low and ill adapted to stand up to contact with European civilisation. Originally estimated at 300,000, their number has dropped in the last 200 years to some 40,000. A referendum held in 1967 showed that the majority of Australians wished to give the Aborigines citizen rights and thus end the discrimination against them.

Absolute Temperature, Absolute Zero. This is a refined notion requiring some study of thermodynamics for its full understanding. For setting up an absolute temperature scale one must first assign a numerical value to one fixed temperature. For this, the triple point of water has been chosen, *i.e.*, the temperature at which solid, liquid, and gaseous water are all in equilibrium. The triple point is defined to be 273·16 K where K is read for kelvin (after Lord Kelvin). This temperature is 0·01 °C on the Celsius scale (*q.v.*) and is thus very close to the melting point of ice. Suppose the pressure and volume of a mass of gas are measured (i) at the triple point of water, giving $(pV)_{tr}$ as the product of the pressure and volume; and (ii) at any unknown temperature T K, giving (pV) as the product. Then the absolute temperature, T K, is defined by

$$T\,\mathrm{K} = 273 \cdot 16\,\frac{(pV)}{(pV)_{tr}}$$

It is to be understood that the gas pressure is very low. The nature of the gas is immaterial. More subtly, it can be shown that the temperature so defined is identical with that derived in a rather abstract way in the science of thermodynamics. The absolute scale is therefore also called the thermodynamic scale. Absolute temperatures can be obtained from Celsius temperatures by adding 273·15; thus the absolute temperature of melting ice is 273·15 K. Conversely, absolute zero is a temperature 273·15 K below the temperature of melting ice, *i.e.*, −273·15 °C. Theory shows that absolute zero is unattainable, but it has been approached to within about 1 millionth of a degree. Within ten or so degrees of absolute zero, matter develops some remarkable properties. *See* Kelvin, Cryogenics, Superconductor, Helium.

Absolution, an ecclesiastical term denoting the liberation of a person guilty of sin from its consequences by the act or intercession of religious authority.

Abstract Art, a term applied to 20th cent. plastic arts in which form and colour possess aesthetic value apart from the subject. Usually represented as a modern movement beginning with Cézanne. The idea is ancient, abstract design being found in the Neolithic period, in folk-art, and particularly in Moslem art (which forbids naturalistic representations especially of the human figure). Among those in the tradition are Kandinsky, Braque, Mondrian, Calder.

Acetic Acid, an organic acid produced when ordinary (ethyl) alcohol is fermented by the organism called *Acetobacter aceti*. The same oxidation process yields vinegar; this is a weak and crude solution of acetic acid obtained by trickling dilute alcoholic liquor over beech-wood shavings at 35 °C. The souring of wine is due to the same process. Acetic acid is used as a food preservative and flavouring material, and in the manufacture of cellulose acetate and white lead.

Acetylene, a compound of carbon and hydrogen prepared from calcium carbide and water. A very reactive gas, it is used industrially on a large scale to prepare acetaldehyde, chlorohydrocarbon solvents, and many intermediates for plastics manufacture. Burns in air with a highly luminous flame, formerly used for lighting purposes, but is now widely used, with oxygen, in welding. For safe storage and transportation it is dissolved in acetone.

Acids, substances having a tendency to lose a positive ion (a proton). This general definition overcomes difficulties of earlier views which merely described their properties and asserted that they are chemically opposite to bases. As a whole acids contain ionisable hydrogen, replaceable by a metal, to form a salt. Inorganic acids are compounds of non-metals or metalloids, *e.g.*, sulphuric, phosphoric acid. Carboxylic acids contain the group –COOH. F22.

Acolyte, one who assists the priest at Mass by saying the responses and by waiting on him.

Act of God, a natural catastrophe that could not be foreseen or averted.

Advent, a period devoted to religious preparation for the coming celebration of the Nativity (Christmas). It comprises four Sundays, and commences on the one nearest to St. Andrew's Day (Nov. 30). Advent was not observed before the 4th cent.

Advocatus Diaboli ("the devil's advocate"), a Roman Catholic functionary who presents opposing evidence in regard to the life of any deceased person it may be proposed to canonise.

Aeolian Harp, a musical instrument once very popular. It consists of catgut stretched over a wooden sound-box which, when placed out of doors in the wind, can be made to emit many pleasing harmonies.

Aerenchyma. Plant tissue which is spongy because there are large air spaces between the cells in which gases can circulate. This aerating tissue is characteristic of marsh and water-plants.

Aerodynamics, the science of gases (especially air) in motion, particularly in relation to aircraft (aeronautics). The idea of imitating the birds by the use of wings is of ancient origin. Leonardo da Vinci first carried out experiments in a scientific manner. The invention of the balloon in 1783 and the researches of scientists and engineers in the 19th cent. ultimately led to the development of the aeroplane.

Aerolites, the name given to the class of meteorites composed chiefly of heavy silicates. The other two main classes are *siderolites* (nickel–iron and silicates) and *siderites* (nickel–iron).

Aerosol, a suspension of a liquid in a gas; for example, a fog is very small drops of water suspended in air. Formed by spraying the liquid in air, aerosols are used to disperse liquids over a wide area in crop spraying, air freshening, and pest control.

Afrikander, type of cattle bred in South Africa.

Afrikaner, an Afrikaans-speaking South African, usually of Dutch descent.

After-damp occurs in a mine after an explosion causing suffocation. It is composed mainly of carbon dioxide and nitrogen and contains water vapour and carbon monoxide (produced by the burning, in a restricted supply of air, of fine coal dust).

Agape, a " love-feast " held by the early Christians in commemoration of the Lord's Supper. *See* J32 (1).

Agar-agar, a vegetable jelly obtained from seaweeds, widely used in jellies, canned meat and poultry, and as a constituent in medicinal and cosmetic preparations. Used by bacteriologists to solidify broth and blood upon which bacteria are cultivated. Chief sources of supply: Far East and California.

Agaric, large fungi of the family *Agaricaceae*, which includes the mushroom and what are popularly called " toadstools," though the idea that these two lay terms sharply differentiate between edible and poisonous fungi is an incorrect one. Characteristic of the agarics is the presence of a cap or *pileus* (bearing underneath the spore-shedding gills) and a stalk or *stipe*.

Agate, a variety of chalcedony. Parallel bands of colour are often characteristic. Germany, Brazil, and India furnish the main supplies, and Scotland has a species of agate called Scotch pebble.

Agave, the American aloe or Century Plant which sometimes does not attain to flowering maturity under sixty or seventy years, and then dies. The flower spray may reach a height of 20 feet and in its development the rush of sap is so great that the Mexicans collect for brewing the strong spirit called mescal. 1,000 litres of sap can be obtained from a single plant. Some species of agave yield sisal used for making cord and rope.

Agnus Dei (Lamb of God), a short anthem said or sung at a certain point of the Roman Catholic Mass or Anglican communion service. (John i. 29.)

Air is a mixture of gases forming the atmosphere we breathe. Nitrogen, oxygen, and argon are always present in air; a typical sample of dry air might contain these gases in the following proportions (by volume): nitrogen, 78·06%; oxygen, 21%; argon, 0·94%. A small quantity of carbon dioxide is present, about 3 parts in 10,000 parts of air. This carbon dioxide is the source of carbon compounds built up by green plants in photosynthesis (**F28**); in the process carbon dioxide is absorbed from the air and oxygen returned, the reverse of the respiratory process of animals. Air also contains a quantity of water vapour, and traces of ammonia, nitrogen oxides, hydrogen, sulphur dioxide, hydrogen sulphide, ozone and of the rare gases helium, krypton, neon, and xenon. In a city smoke and dust particles may be as abundant as 100,000 particles per cc. A litre of air at 0 °C. and 700 mm pressure weighs 1·2932 grams. *See also* Atmosphere, Pollution.

Alabaster, a soft crystalline form of sulphate of lime, or granulated gypsum, easily worked for statuary and other ornamental articles, and capable of being highly polished. Volterra, in Tuscany, yields the finest; that in highest ancient repute came from Alabastron in Egypt, near to the modern Antinoë.

Alb, white vestment reaching to the feet, worn by priests in religious ceremonies.

Albatross, a large sea-bird of almost pure white, black and white, or brown plumage. It nests in colonies on remote islands, but at other times rarely approaches land. Of the thirteen species, nine are found in the southern oceans, one in the tropics, and the three others in the North Pacific.

Albert Memorial, a large Gothic monument designed by Sir George Gilbert Scott, and embellished with sculptures by eminent artists. Erected in memory of Prince Albert in Kensington Gardens at a cost of £120,000.

Alcázar, the palace at Seville, famed for the beauty of its halls and gardens, in ancient days the residence of the Moorish kings.

Alcohols. A class of organic compounds of general formula R–OH, where R is an aliphatic radical. " Alcohol " is the name used for ethyl alcohol (ethanol); this is produced by distilling fermented liquors, and synthetically from ethylene, a product of petroleum cracking. Industrially ethyl alcohol is used in the manufacture of chloroform, ether, perfumes, etc. Diluted with wood alcohol or other denaturants ethyl alcohol is called " methylated spirits "; the denaturants are varied according to the industrial purposes for which it is required, the methylated spirits then being largely exempt from duty. Wood alcohol (methyl alcohol or methanol) can be obtained by distilling wood, or synthetically from water gas. *See* F24(1).

Alcoholic Strength. In Great Britain the standard is the proof gallon which is an imperial gallon of spirits containing 49·28 per cent. of alcohol by weight or 57·1 per cent. by volume at 60 °F. In Europe the strength of spirits is usually measured by the Guy-Lussac hydrometer. In the U.S.A., because of the smaller gallon, 1·37 U.S. proof gallons = 1 British proof gallon. In Britain the alcoholic content of spirits and liqueurs appears on the bottle in degrees proof. Whisky, for example, at 70° proof (or 30° under proof) contains 70/100 × 57·1 alcohol, or about 40 per cent. The alcoholic content of wines is not shown on the label.

Aldehyde, the generic term for a class of chemical compounds of general formula R–CHO, where R is an organic radical. Except for formaldehyde, which is a gas, aldehydes are volatile liquids. They are produced by oxidation of primary alcohols. Most important aldehyde is formaldehyde used in making the plastics described as formaldehyde resins. Formalin (formaldehyde solution in water) is much used for preserving zoological specimens.

Alder, a river-side tree of the genus *Alnus*, including some 30 species and found in north temperate regions and the Andes. The only species native to Britain is *A. glutinosa*, which has been described as " guardian of river-banks " because of the way its roots bind together the sand and stones, and so slow down erosion. The wood is used for furniture and charcoal.

Aldine Editions are the beautiful books printed in Venice by the Renaissance printer Aldo Pio Manuzio and his family between 1490 and 1597. Italics were first introduced in these books.

Algae, flowerless plants living mostly in water. Seaweeds and the green pond scums are the best known algae. The green powder found on trees is composed of a microscopic alga (*Protococcus*).

Algebra, a branch of mathematics in which symbols are used in place of numbers. Sir Isaac Newton styled it the " universal arithmetic." The Chinese were able to solve the quadratic equation before the Christian era but it was Al-Khowa-rizmi, an Arab mathematician of the early 9th cent., who introduced algebra to Europe.

Alhambra, the ancient palace of the Moorish kings at Granada in Spain, built in the 13th and 14th cent. Though part of the castle was turned into a modern palace under Charles V., the most beautiful parts of the interior are still preserved—the graceful halls and dwelling-rooms grouped round the Court of Alberca and the Court of Lions, with their fountains, arcades, and lovely gardens.

Aliphatic describes derivatives of hydrocarbons having chains of carbon atoms, as distinct from rings of carbon atoms as in benzene (*see* Aromatic). The gas butane is aliphatic.

Alkali, the general name given to a number of

chemicals which are bases (*q.v.*). The term should be limited to the hydroxides of metals in the first and second group of the periodic table and of ammonia, *e.g.*, NaOH, KOH. They are used commercially in the manufacture of paper, glass, soap, and artificial silk. The word comes from the Arabic *al-kali* meaning calcined wood ashes. Alkalis are extremely soluble in water and neutralise acids to form salts and water.

Alkaloids, a large group of natural products which contain nitrogen; they are usually basic. Isolated from plants and animals, they include some hormones, vitamins, and drugs. Examples are nicotine, adrenalin, and cocaine. Many alkaloids are made synthetically for medicinal use, *e.g.*, morphine, quinine. Their function in plants is not well understood. *See* Belladonna.

Alligator, the crocodile of America, common in the lower Mississippi and adjacent lakes and marshes, varying in length from 2 to 20 feet.

Alloys are combinations of metals. They are made because of their valuable special properties, *e.g.*, durability, strength, lightness, magnetism, rust-resistance, etc. Some well-known ones are brass (zinc + copper), coinage bronze (copper + zinc + tin), steels (iron + carbon + various other materials), soft solder (tin + lead), dental fillings (mercury + various ingredients).

All Saints' Day (Nov. 1) is common to both the English and Roman Catholic Churches, and is in commemoration of the saints generally, or such as have no special day set apart for them. Instituted by Pope Boniface IV., early in the 7th cent., this ecclesiastical festival was formerly called " All Hallows."

All Souls' Day (Nov. 2) is a festival of the Roman Church, intended for the mitigation by prayer of the sufferings of souls in purgatory. The commemoration was enjoined by Abbot Odilo of Cluny during the 11th cent. upon the monastic order over which he presided, and was afterwards adopted generally throughout the Roman Communion.

Allspice, a flavouring obtained from a West Indian tree of the myrtle family, *Pimenta officinalis.* The essential oil of its unripe fruit is a powerful irritant, and the bruised berries are carminative.

Alluvium, accumulations of sand, mud, gravel, etc., washed down by rivers and forming distinct deposits.

Almond, the fruit of the *Amygdalus communis,* originally indigenous to Persia, Asia Minor, and N. Africa; now cultivated in Italy, Spain, France, the U.S.A., and Australia. It yields both bitter and sweet oil. Bitter almond oil is obtained by macerating and distilling the ripe seeds; it is used for flavouring and scenting purposes, its fragrant odour being due to the presence of benzaldehyde and hydrogen cyanide. When the seeds are pressed sweet almond oil results: this is used in perfumery, and also as a lubricant for very delicate machinery.

Almuce, a fur stole worn by certain canons.

Aloe, large plants of the lily family, with about 180 species found mainly in the S. African veldt and Karroo. The bitter purgative drug (aloes) is prepared by evaporating the plant's sap. *See* Agave.

Alpaca, a South American ruminant related to the llama whose long, fine wool is woven into a soft dress fabric known by the same name. Sir Titus Salt first manufactured alpaca cloth (1836). Saltaire, near Bradford, remains to evidence the success which for many years attended the enterprise.

Alpha Particle, or alpha-ray, fast-moving helium nucleus ejected by some radioactive atoms, *e.g.*, polonium. It is a combination of 2 neutrons and 2 protons. *See* **F11** (1).

Alphabet (so called from the first two letters of the Greek alphabet—alpha, beta) is the term applied to the collection of letters from which the words of a language are made up. It grew out of the knowledge that all words can be expressed by a limited number of sounds arranged in various combinations. The Phoenicians were the first to make use of an alphabetic script derived from an earlier Semitic alphabet (earliest known inscriptions *c.* 1500–950 B.C.) from which all other alphabets have sprung. The stages in the development of the alphabet were mnemonic

(memory aids), pictorial (actual pictures), ideographic (symbols), and lastly phonetic. All the ideographic systems died out, with the exception of that of the Chinese.

Altimeter, an instrument used in aircraft to estimate altitude; its usual essential feature is an aneroid barometer which registers the decrease of pressure with height. Roughly 1 millibar corresponds to 30 ft. To read an aircraft altimeter correct for its destination, the zero setting must be adjusted for difference of ground height and difference of surface pressure, especially when pressure is falling or when flying towards low pressure.

Altitude, an astronomical term used to signify the angular elevation of a heavenly body; this is measured with a quadrant or sextant. In aeronautics it is the height (in feet or metres) above sea-level.

Alto-Relievo, a term applied to sculptured designs which are depicted in prominent relief on a flat surface, technically signifying that the projection exceeds one-half the true proportions of the objects represented. Basso-relievo is carving kept lower than one-half such projection.

Alum is a compound salt used in various industrial processes, especially dyeing, its constituents being the sulphate of one univalent metal or radical (*e.g.*, potassium, sodium, ammonium, rubidium, caesium, silver, thallium) and the sulphate of a tervalent metal (*e.g.*, aluminium, iron, chromium, manganese), and water of crystallisation.

Alumina is the oxide of aluminium. Very valuable as a refractory material. The ruby is almost 100 per cent. alumina; so also are the emerald, oriental amethyst, etc. An hydrated aluminium oxide is bauxite, chief ore of aluminium from which the metal is extracted electrolytically.

Aluminium is a light metal which conducts electricity well. Its specific gravity at 20 °C is 2·705. Melting point of aluminium is 660·2 °C. It is made commercially by electrolysing bauxite dissolved in cryolite (double fluoride of aluminium and sodium). Aluminium alloys because of their strength and lightness are being increasingly used for the construction of railway coaches, automobiles, aeroplanes, etc.

Amadavat, a popular cage bird of the weaver family, mainly crimson with white spots, so named because the first specimens came from Ahmadabad in India about 1700.

Amalgam is the term applied to any alloy of which mercury forms a part.

Amber, a brittle resinous substance; in origin, fossilised resin. Obtained mostly from the Baltic coasts, and used for ornaments, pipe mouth-pieces, etc.

Ambergris is a waxy substance produced in the intestines of the sperm whale, and generally found floating on the sea. It is a valuable perfumery material.

Amblyopsis, a species of fish, practically sightless, and with inoperative organs of hearing and feeling, that inhabit the Mammoth Cave of Kentucky. A remarkable illustration of the failure of senses not brought into use.

America's Cup, a prize trophy first offered in 1851 by the Royal Yacht Squadron and open to yachts of all nations. It was won in the first year by the " America," a New York yacht, and has remained on that side of the ocean ever since, despite attempts to recapture it by Lord Dunraven, Sir Thomas Lipton, Mr. T. O. M. Sopwith, and others. The last attempt by Great Britain was in 1964, when *Sovereign* was beaten by the American *Constellation.* Another attempt is to be made in 1973. Australia challenged in 1962 with *Gretel*, and in 1967 with *Dame Pattie*, but unsuccessfully. *See also* U32(2).

Amethyst, the violet variety of quartz, used as a precious stone, containing traces of manganese, titanium, and iron. The finest coloured specimens come from Brazil and the Urals.

Amice, a linen vestment worn about the neck by Roman and many Anglican priests over the alb when officiating at Mass or Holy Eucharist. Formerly worn on the head by priests and pilgrims.

Amines, organic chemicals composed of carbon, hydrogen, and nitrogen. They are derived from ammonia, which they resemble in smell and chemical characteristics. The smell of bad fish is due to the presence of amines. Important industrially as intermediates in a wide variety of products, for example, the synthesis of dye-stuffs and man-made fibres such as nylon.

Amino acids, organic compounds containing an amine group and an acid group. They are the " building bricks " of proteins (*q.v.*). *See* **F27**(1), 29.

Ammeter, an instrument for measuring the current flowing in an electric circuit. A contraction of ampere-meter. *See* **Ampere.**

Ammonia, a colourless gaseous compound comprising three atoms of hydrogen to one of nitrogen. Formerly it was made by heating the horns and hoofs of deer, acquiring the name of spirits of hartshorn. The ammonia of commerce is now procured by coal decomposition in the course of gas-making and by direct synthesis. In the very important Haber process of ammonia production by fixation of atmospheric nitrogen, the nitrogen is made to combine with hydrogen and the ammonia so prepared is converted into nitric acid, ammonium nitrate or ammonium sulphate. The Haber process made Germany self-sufficient in nitrates in the first world war, and was afterwards exploited all over the world.

Ammonites, extinct animals related to the Nautilus. The chambered shell is coiled, usually in a plane spiral, and they are confined to Mesozoic rocks.

Ammonium, the basic radical of ammonium salts. Composed of one atom of nitrogen and four of hydrogen, it behaves chemically like an ion of a monovalent alkali metal. Ammonium chloride is known as " sal ammoniac." " Sal volatile " is ammonium carbonate.

Amnesty, an act of grace by which a ruler or governing power pardons political offenders.

Amorphous, a term used to indicate the absence of crystalline form in any body or substance.

Ampere, unit of electric current in the SI system of units; named after André Marie Ampère, who in the 1820s helped to lay the foundations of modern electromagnetism. Defined as that constant current which, if maintained in two parallel rectilinear conductors of infinite length, of negligible circular cross section, and placed at a distance of one metre apart in a vacuum, would produce between these conductors a force equal to 2×10^{-7} newton per metre length.

Amphibia. *See* **F33**(2).

Amphioxus *or* **Lancelet,** a primitive chordate occurring in sand-banks around British shores and elsewhere.

Ana, a collection of criticisms, observations, or opinions about a particular person, place or subject. Used as a suffix especially applies to a person's memorable sayings, anecdotes about or publications bearing on, as in *Johnsoniana, Alexandriana, Victoriana.*

Anabolism. *See* **Catabolism.**

Anarchism. *See* **J3.**

Anchor, an instrument used for keeping ships stationary. Great improvements have been introduced in recent years, stockless anchors being now chiefly used, consisting of a shank and a loose fluke. Lloyds' rules prescribe the number and weight of anchors which must be carried by merchant ships.

Anchorite is a religious person who retires into solitude to employ himself with holy thoughts. Among the early Christians, anchorites were numerous, but in the Western Church they have been few. Their reputation for wisdom and prescience was high, and kings and rulers in olden days would visit their cells for counsel. An anchorite or " ankret " was in mediæval times a source of fame and profit to the monastic house within which he was voluntarily immured.

Anchovy, a fish of the herring family, distinguished by its large mouth and projecting snout, plentiful in the Mediterranean; and much esteemed when cured.

Ancient Lights are rights of light enjoyed by a property owner over adjoining land. Such a right is obtained either by uninterrupted enjoyment for twenty years, or by written authority, and once legally established cannot be upset, no building being permissible that would seriously interfere with the privilege.

Anemometer, an instrument for measuring the strength of the wind. In the most widely used

pattern the rotation, about a vertical axis, of a group of hemispherical or conical cups gives a measure of the total flow of air past the cups, various registering devices being employed. The Dines anemograph provides a continuous record of the variation in both velocity and direction; changes of pressure produced in a horizontal tube, kept pointing into the wind by a vane, cause a float, to which a pen is attached, to rise and fall in sympathy with the gusts and lulls. The recently devised hot-wire anemometer, depending upon the change of electrical resistance experienced by a heated wire when cooled, enables very gentle air currents to be investigated.

Aneroid is the kind of barometer which does not depend upon atmospheric support of a mercury (or other liquid) column. It consists of a metallic box, partially exhausted of air, with a corrugated lid which moves with atmospheric changes. A lever system magnifies the lid movements about 200 times and atmospheric pressure is read from a dial. The construction of the vacuum chamber provides automatic compensation for temperature changes. An aneroid barometer is the basic component of an altimeter.

Angelica, an aromatic plant of the Umbelliferae order, *Angelica officinalis,* valuable as a flavouring and possessing medicinal properties. In olden times supposed to protect against poison.

Angelus, a church bell rung in Roman Catholic countries, at morn, noon, and sunset, to remind the faithful to say their Angelic Salutation.

Angevin Dynasty includes the Plantagenet kings from Henry II. to Richard II. The name was derived from Henry II.'s father, Geoffrey, Count of Anjou.

Angles, a northern tribe originally settled in Schleswig, who with the Saxons and Jutes invaded Britain in the 5th cent.

Angstrom, a unit of wavelength, named after the Swedish physicist A. J. Angstrom (1814-74), equal to one hundred-millionth of a centimetre (10^{-8} cm). It is used to measure wavelengths of light, X-rays, etc.

Aniline, a simple aromatic compound related to benzene and ammonia. It is obtained from coal-tar. The name recalls the fact that it was first prepared by distilling indigo (*anil* is Portuguese for indigo). In 1856 W. H. Perkin (1838-1907) discovered the first aniline or coal-tar dye, mauve, and thus founded the modern dyestuff industry.

Animal Kingdom. *See* **F32.**

Anise, an umbelliferous plant (*Pimpinella anisum*) found in Egypt and the Levant, and valued for its fruit, aniseed, possessing certain medicinal properties and yielding an aromatic, volatile oil. Also used in cooking. The anise of the Bible is *Anethum graveolens, i.e.,* dill.

Annates were acknowledgments formerly paid to the popes by way of fee or tax in respect of ecclesiastical preferment, and consisted usually of a proportion of the income (" first-fruits ") of the office. Introduced into England in the 13th cent.; annexed to the Crown under Henry VIII.; transferred to a perpetual fund for the benefit of the poorer clergy in 1704. *See* **Queen Anne's Bounty.**

" **Annual Register,**" a yearly record of political and literary events, founded by Edmund Burke (as editor) in 1759 and Robert Dorsley, the bookseller.

Annunciation, Feast of the (March 25), is a church festival commemorating the message of the incarnation of Christ brought by the angel Gabriel to the Virgin Mary, hence the title Lady Day.

Anointing is the pouring of consecrated oil upon the body as a mark of supreme honour. In England it is restricted chiefly to the ceremony of the monarch's coronation, and the spoon with which the oil is applied forms part of the English regalia. In the Roman Catholic Church anointing represents the sacrament of extreme unction.

Ant. There are about 6,000 species of ants, which belong to the same order (Hymenoptera) as the bees, wasps, and ichneumon flies. They are social in habit, living in communities of varying size and development. There are three basic castes in ants—the females or *queens,* the *males,* and the *workers* (the last-named being neuter), although specialised forms of workers are sometimes found, *e.g.*, the *soldiers* of the harvesting ants. In the communities of those species of ants which evolved most recently there is a highly complex social life and well-developed division of labour. Some species of these ants make slaves of other species, stealing the cocoons before the adult forms emerge. Many ants "milk" greenflies, which they protect for their honey-like secretion, and most ants' nests contain many "guests," such as beetles and silver fish. Some ants harvest grains of corn, and others, from S. America, live on fungi which they cultivate in underground "mushroom beds."

Antarctic Exploration. In earlier centuries it was thought that a great continent must exist in the southern hemisphere, around the South Pole, to balance the known land masses in the north. Its supposed extent was greatly reduced in the 18th cent., particularly when Capt. Cook sailed for the first time south of the Antarctic Circle and reached the edge of the ice pack. A portion of the ice-covered continent—the coast of Graham Land—was first sighted by Lieut. Edward Bransfield in 1820. Explorers of several other nations sighted portions of the coast-line in other quarters, but the first extensive exploration was made by Capt. James Clarke Ross, who with the *Erebus* and *Terror* penetrated into the Ross Sea in 1841, and discovered the great Ross Ice Barrier in 78° South lat. Interest in the Antarctic did not revive until after 1890, when an international scheme of research was drawn up. A Norwegian, C. E. Borchgrevink, in 1898–1900, was the first to winter in the Antarctic and to travel on the ice barrier. The British share in this work was carried out by Capt. R. F. Scott's expedition in the *Discovery*, 1901–4. Scott's party sledged across the barrier to 82° 17' South, then a record "farthest south." A little later, Ernest Shackleton beat this by travelling to within 100 miles of the South Pole. In 1910 Scott organised his second expedition of the *Terra Nova*, and became engaged against his will in a "race for the Pole," when, after his departure, the Norwegian Arctic explorer, Roald Amundsen, suddenly announced that he was sailing for the Antarctic. Amundsen set up his base at the eastern end of the Barrier, and, relying on dog teams for hauling his sledges, reached the Pole on December 14, 1911. Meanwhile Scott and his party, their start delayed by adverse weather, were marching southwards, man-hauling their sledges, for Scott was against the use of dogs. After an arduous journey they reached the Pole one month after Amundsen. The return was a struggle against the weather and increasing weakness, probably due to scurvy, until at last they perished within a few miles of their base. After the First World War the development of the whaling industry greatly stimulated further exploration. Outstanding expeditions included that of Admiral R. E. Byrd, 1929, when he flew over the South Pole; The British Graham Land expedition, 1934, which carried out the first extensive mapping of any part of the Antarctic continent; and the U.S. Navy's Antarctic Expedition of 1940, when the whole continent was circumnavigated and great areas photographed from the air. In recent years valuable work has been done by the first International expedition, the Norwegian–British–Swedish Expedition to Queen Maud Land, and by the French in Adélie Land. The Falkland Island Dependencies Survey, set up during the war, has continued the scientific exploration of Graham Land. The Antarctic was the scene of high adventure during the International Geophysical Year (1957–58), when scientists from many countries participated in the explorations. The Commonwealth Trans-Antarctic Expedition set out from opposite sides of the continent and met at the South Pole, the U.K. party, led by Sir Vivian Fuchs, from the Falklands, and Sir Edmund Hillary and his party from New Zealand. The U.K. party accomplished the first crossing of the White Continent in 99 days. Their scientific work included the making of seismic and complementary gravimetric studies at frequent intervals along the 2,200-mile traverse. Since the Antarctic is becoming important for many reasons, in weather forecasting, in the whaling industry, and as a possible centre for world air routes, the tempo of exploration and research will become even faster in the future.

Anteater. There are two unrelated families of anteaters, the Myrmecophagidae and the Manidae. Among the former the Great Anteater (*Myrmecophaga jubita*) is the largest species, over 6 ft. in length, occurring in Central and S. America. Only half its size is the lesser Anteater (*Tamandua tetradactyla*); this is found in forests of tropical America and Trinidad. The Two-toed Anteater (*Cyclopes didactylus*) belongs to South America and Trinidad. These three animals live mostly on termites; they are adapted to this diet, having large claws for digging out ants, and a tubular mouth with a long sticky tongue. The Manidae are the Scaly Anteaters or Pangolins, widely distributed over Africa and the Orient. The difference between the two families is that the first has hair covering the body, the latter has horny scales instead.

Antennae, paired feelers of insects and crustacea.

Anthem, a choral composition, with or without instrumental accompaniment, usually sung after the third collect in the Church of England service. The words are from the Scriptures, and the composition may be for solo voices only, for full choir, or for both. Among the chief British composers of anthems are Tallis, Purcell, Croft, Boyce, Goss, and Stainer.

Anthracite is a black coal with a brilliant lustre. It contains 92% and over of carbon and burns slowly, without smoke or flame. *See* Coal.

Anthropoid, meaning "resembling man," a suborder of the primate mammals including man and also the gibbon, chimpanzee, orang-utan, and gorilla.

Antibiotics. *See* Index to Section P.

Anticyclone, a region where barometric pressure is greater than that of its surroundings. Such a system is distinguished on weather charts by a pattern of isobars, usually circular or oval-shaped, enclosing the centre of high pressure where the air is calm. In the remaining areas light or moderately strong winds blow spirally outwards, in a clockwise direction in the Northern Hemisphere (and in the reverse direction in the Southern Hemisphere), in accordance with Buys Ballot's law (an observer with back to wind in Northern Hemisphere has lower pressure to left; in Southern to right). Over the British Isles anticyclonic weather is generally quiet and settled, being fair, warm, and sunny in summer and either very cold and often foggy or overcast and gloomy in winter. These systems move slowly and sometimes remain practically stationary for days at a time, that over Siberia being particularly well defined. Extensive belts of almost permanent anticyclones occur in latitudes 30° N. and 30° S. Persistent anticyclonic weather with easterly winds during the months December to March, 1962–3, brought the coldest and hardest winter to Britain since 1740 (taking the Midlands as representative).

Antimony. Metal element, symbol Sb. In group V of the periodic table. Exists in various forms, the stable form being a grey brittle metal with a layer structure. The other forms are non-conductors. On being burned, it gives off dense fumes of oxide of antimony. By itself it is not of special utility; but as an alloy for hardening other metals, it is much used. As an alloy with lead for type-metal, and with tin and copper or zinc for Britannia-metal, it is of great value. Most important antimony ore is stibnite (antimony sulphide).

Anti-Pope, one elected in opposition to one held to be canonically chosen; commonly applied to the popes Urban VI. and Clement VII., who resided at Avignon during the Great Schism (1378–1417).

Anti-proton, the "negative proton," an atomic particle created in high energy collisions of nuclear particles. Its existence was confirmed in Oct. 1955. *See* **F14.**

Antisemitism. *See* **J4.**

Antlers are the branched horns of deer, the branches being called tines. Antlers originate as outgrowths of the frontal bone, and are usually shed once a year. Except in the reindeer and caribou they are restricted to the male.

Apartheid. *See* J5.

Ape, a term applied to the gorilla, chimpanzee, orang-utan, and gibbon—the anthropoid apes.

Aphelion, the point in the orbit of a planet farthest from the sun; the opposite of perihelion.

Aphids. *See* T29 (2).

Apis, the sacred bull worshipped by the ancient Egyptians; also the scientific name for the bee.

Apocalyptic writings are those which deal with revelation and prophecy, more especially the Revelation of St. John.

Apocrypha (hidden writings), the books which were included in the Septuagint (Greek) and Vulgate (Latin) versions of the Old Testament but excluded from the sacred canon at the Reformation by the Protestants on the grounds that they were not originally written in Hebrew nor regarded as genuine by the Jews. The books include: 1 and 2 Esdras, Tobit, Judith, additions to Esther, Wisdom of Solomon, Ecclesiasticus, Baruch. Song of the Three Holy Children, History of Susannah, Bel and the Dragon, Prayer of Manasses, 1 and 2 Maccabees. The term is usually applied to the additions to the old Testament, but there are also numerous Christian writings of the same character. *The New English Bible* with the Apocrypha was published in 1970.

Apogee, that point in the orbit of a heavenly body which is farthest from the earth; used in relation to the sun, moon, and artificial satellites. The sun's apogee corresponds to the earth's aphelion. *See* Perigee.

Apostasy is a revolt, by an individual or party, from one form of opinions or doctrine to another. Julian, the Roman Emperor (331–63), brought up as a Christian, became converted to paganism and on coming to the throne (361), proclaimed religious toleration. Hence his name, Julian the Apostate.

Apostles. The twelve apostles who were disciples of Jesus were: Simon Peter and Andrew (his brother), James and John (sons of Zebedee), Philip, Bartholomew, Thomas, Matthew, James, Thaddaeus, Simon, and Judas Iscariot. After the Ascension Matthias was chosen to take the place of Judas. St. Paul is always referred to as the chief apostle, though he is not one of the twelve. St. Barnabas has also been called an apostle.

Apostles' Creed, applied to the most ancient of the Church's statements of its belief: " I believe in God the Father Almighty; and in Jesus Christ his only Son our Lord, who was born of the Holy Ghost and the Virgin Mary. . . ." A later version is used in the Church of England at morning and evening prayer.

Apostolic Fathers were the immediate disciples or followers of the Apostles, especially such as left writings behind. They included Barnabas, Clement of Rome, Ignatius of Antioch, Hermas, Papias of Hieropolis, and Polycarp.

Appeasement Policy. The name of the policy during 1937 and 1938 of yielding to the demands of Hitler and Mussolini in the hope that a point would be reached when the dictators would co-operate in the maintenance of peace. The policy culminated in the Munich Agreement (which was the subject of much criticism) after a series of concessions including the recognition of the Italian conquest of Abyssinia and the German annexation of Austria. The policy was finally demonstrated as futile when Hitler seized Czechoslovakia in March 1939.

Appian Way, the oldest and finest of the Roman roads originally laid by Appius Claudius (312 B.C.) from Rome to Capua and thence to Brundisium (Brindisi).

Approved Schools were residential schools, subject to Home Office inspection, for the training of young persons under 17 who, because of disturbed behaviour as a result of unfavourable influences such as bad environment or parental neglect, were guilty of offences or in need of care and protection and had been sent to them by magistrates from juvenile or other courts. The approved school order was abolished by the Children and Young Persons Act 1969. Such young people may now be committed to the care of a local authority and accommodated in a system of community homes ranging from children's homes to borstal type institutions.

April, the fourth month of the year, from the

Roman *Aprilis* derived from *aperire* " to open " —the period when the buds begin to open.

Apse is a semicircular recess, arched or dome-roofed, at the end of the choir, aisles, or nave of a church.

Aqueducts are conduits in which water flows or is conveyed from its source to the place where it is to be used. Most famous builders were the Romans and the oldest Roman aqueduct was the Aqua Appia, which dates from about 310 B.C. Among modern aqueducts may be mentioned that of Glasgow, which brings water to that city from Loch Katrine; that of Manchester, which taps Thirlmere; that of Liverpool, with Lake Vyrnwy in North Wales as its source, and the Fron Aqueduct, Radnorshire, which carries water from the Elan Valley to Birmingham.

Arabesque, the term applied to the elaborate decoration based on flowing lines used in Moorish art.

Arabian Nights, a collection of fascinating tales of the Orient, of mixed Indian, Persian, Arabic, and Egyptian origination, and first made known in Europe by Antoine Galland, a French Oriental scholar whose original translation was called *The Thousand and One Nights*.

Arabic Numerals. The modern system of numbering 0, 1, 2, 3, 4, 5, 6, 7, 8, 9, in which the digits depend on their position for their value, is called the Arabic numerical notation. The method is, in fact, of Indian origin. By the 9th cent. Hindu science was available in Arabic, and the Persian mathematician Al-Kwarizimi (*c.* 830) in his *Arithmetic* used the so-called " Arabic " system of numbering. Gradually the method spread to Europe, taking the place of the Roman system which was useless for calculation. The West is indebted to the Arabs for the zero symbol, the lack of which had been a serious drawback to Greek mathematics. It made the invention of decimal fractions possible.

Aragonite, the unstable form of calcium carbonate found as a mineral in some young deposits. It crystallises in the orthorhombic system but tends to revert to calcite (*q.v.*).

Aramaic Languages, the Semitic dialects current in Mesopotamia and the regions extending southwest from the Euphrates to Palestine from about the 12th cent. B.C. until after the rise of Islam, when Aramaic was superseded by Arabic. Both Aramaic and Greek were spoken in Palestine during the time of Christ.

Archaeopteryx, a fossil bird providing a connecting link between reptiles and birds. It had feathers, jaws with teeth, no bill, reptilian bones and skull, a long tail, and it probably used its fore-limbs for gliding flight. The first specimen, found in 1861, in the Solenhofen limestone of Bavaria, is in London's Natural History Museum.

Archbishop, the chief of the bishops of an ecclesiastical province in the Greek, Roman, and Anglican churches. In the Church of England there are two archbishops, the Archbishop of Canterbury, called the Primate of *all* England, and the Archbishop of York, styled the Primate of England.

Archimedes' Principle. When a body is weighed in air and then in any fluid, the apparent loss in weight is equal to the weight of fluid displaced. This scientific fact was noted by the Syracusan philosopher Archimedes (287–212 B.C.) and is frequently used as a basis for density measurements.

Architecture, the art and science of building. The provision of shelter for mankind by the orderly arrangement of materials in a manner which expresses man's attitude to living. The forms which buildings take are the outcome of the function for which they are to be used, of the architect's aesthetic sensibility and of the structural method adopted. Until the last hundred years structural methods were limited to timber frames, and columns, lintels, load-bearing walls, arches, vaults, and domes in brick or stone. From these few basic elements have evolved the great variety of historic styles of building to be found throughout the world. To give but one example, the Greeks created those systems of decorated columns and beams, known as the Orders, which were adapted by the Romans, revived decoratively rather than structurally during the Renaissance and are still used in debased form on the more presumptuous type of modern building. In recent years, however, architecture has taken on a new meaning. Once confined to the rich, in the form of Church, State, or Commerce, it is now, with the coming of democracy, recognised as an essential social service for all. This, and the development of new structural techniques and materials (steel, aluminium, sheet glass, reinforced concrete, plastics, and plywoods, to name a few), have made the interest in historic styles, the mainstay of the older architect, of secondary importance. Modern architecture is the creation of buildings with the highest possible standards of functional performance in terms of efficient planning and structure, good artificial and natural lighting, adequate heating or cooling, and proper acoustic conditions consistent with the price the client can afford to pay. At the same time the architect's task is to design a structure, and the spaces the structure delimits, internally and externally, which are aesthetically stimulating and satisfying, and well related to the land and buildings around.

Arctic Exploration. Modern exploration of the Arctic begins in the 16th cent., when men sought to reach the East Indies by sailing through the Arctic to the Pacific Ocean. The Northeast Passage, via the shores of northern Asia, was the first attempted. In 1553 and 1554 the English navigators Sir Richard Chancellor and Stephen Burrough sailed into the White Sea, but were prevented by storms and ice from advancing farther eastwards. The project was later revived by the Dutch: Barendts in 1594 discovered Spitsbergen, but also failed to get beyond Novaya Zemlya. It was not, in fact, until 1879 that the Swede, A. E. Nordenskiöld, in the *Vega*, succeeded in reaching the Pacific. The attempts to find a North-west Passage were more numerous and determined. In 1585 John Davis penetrated Davis Strait and coasted along Baffin Island. Hopes ran high when Henry Hudson discovered Hudson Bay in 1610, but a practicable passage continued to elude explorers. The problem was to find a navigable route through the maze of channels in the short summer season, and to avoid being frozen in with supplies exhausted. After the Napoleonic Wars the Admiralty sent out many naval expeditions which culminated in Sir John Franklin's expedition with the *Erebus* and *Terror* in 1845. The ships were beset by ice in Victoria Channel and, after Franklin's death, were abandoned by their crews, who perished from scurvy and starvation on their march southwards. To ascertain their fate, several further expeditions were despatched, and the crew of the *Investigator*, commanded by R. J. M'Clure, sailing eastwards from Bering Strait, were the first to make the Passage, though in doing so they were obliged to abandon their ship. It was thirty years before the Norwegian, Roald Amundsen, succeeded in sailing the *Gjoa* from east to west. In the meantime, the North Pole had become the goal of explorers. Nansen, in 1893, put the *Fram* into the ice-pack to drift across the Polar basin, and himself made an unsuccessful attempt on the Pole across the pack. This was eventually achieved by the American explorer Robert E. Peary, who after several expeditions in the North Greenland region, sledged to the Pole with Eskimo companions in 1909. The next phase was the employment of airships and aeroplanes in Arctic exploration. In 1926 Admiral Byrd made the first flight over the Pole, and in the same year Amundsen and Lincoln Ellsworth flew the airship *Norge* from Spitsbergen to Point Barrow, Alaska. Two years later, the *Italia*, commanded by the Italian, Nobile, was wrecked on a return flight from the Pole, and Amundsen lost his life in an attempt to rescue the survivors. With modern developments in aircraft and navigation, flights over the Polar basin are almost a routine matter, and passenger flights between Europe and America via northern Greenland are being pioneered. The first voyage under the North Pole was made in August 1958 by the American nuclear-powered submarine *Nautilus*.

Arenaceous Rocks, the rocks composed of grains of sand, chiefly sandstones; quartz is the most abundant mineral in these rocks.

Argillaceous Rocks are a sedimentary group, including the shales and clays.

Argon, chemical element, symbol A. This was the first of the inert gases (*q.v.*) to be isolated from air by Rayleigh and Ramsay in 1894. Argon is used for filling gas-filled metal filament electric lamps. In gas discharge tube it gives a blue glow.

Arithmetic, the branch of mathematics that deals with numerical calculations as in counting, measuring, weighing. The early civilisations used simple arithmetic for commercial purposes, employing symbols and later letters of the alphabet as numerals. When Hindu-Arabic numerals replaced Roman numerals in the Middle Ages it meant a great step forward and led to rapid developments—the invention of logarithms, slide-rule, calculating machines.

Ark of the Covenant was the sacred chest of the Hebrews and symbolised God's presence. It was overlaid with gold inside and outside. It accompanied the Israelites into battle and was once captured by the Philistines. Eventually it found a resting-place in Solomon's Temple.

Armada, Spanish, the naval expedition fitted out by Phillip II. of Spain in 1588 against England, commanded by the Duke of Medina Sidonia. It comprised 129 ships, was manned by 8,000 sailors and carried 19,000 soldiers and more than 2,000 cannon. Against this formidable force Elizabeth had only 80 ships, manned by 9,000 sailors, under Lord Howard of Effingham, under whom served Drake, Hawkins, and Frobisher. The British Fleet awaited the Armada off Plymouth, and at Tilbury there was a considerable defensive land force under the command of the Earl of Leicester. On July 19 the ships of the Armada were sighted off the Lizard, disposed in a crescent seven miles long from horn to horn. The excellent manoeuvring of the English, their fire-ships, and a gale from the N.W. combined so effectively to cripple the Spanish ships that the Armada was scattered in confusion, a very small remnant contriving to reach home via the North of Scotland. It was impossible to embark the army of Parma waiting in the Netherlands. Elizabeth had a medal struck bearing in Latin the inscription, " God blew, and they were scattered."

Armadillo, a genus of animals related to the sloths and anteaters, belonging to South America, and carrying a hard bony covering over the back, under which one species (*Tolypeutes*) can completely conceal itself when attacked, rolling itself up like a hedgehog.

Armageddon, according to the Revelation of St. John, the great battle in which the last conflict between good and evil is to be fought.

Armillary Sphere, an early form of astronomical apparatus with a number of circles representing equator, meridian, ecliptic, etc. Used by Hipparchus and Ptolemy and up to the time of Tycho Brahe for determining the position of the stars.

Aromatic. A term used by chemists, originally to describe compounds like benzene, having a characteristic smell. It is a term which implies a collection of chemical characteristics, the salient features being a flat ring structure and a general similarity to benzene.

Arsenic, a metalloid element, symbol As, in group V of the periodic table usually met with as a constituent of other minerals, sometimes by itself. Its compounds are very poisonous. Lead arsenate is a powerful insecticide used for spraying fruit trees. The more stable allotropic form (grey) has a layer structure, and conducts electricity.

Artesian Wells take their name from Artois in France, where the first wells of this kind were constructed in 1126. They are to be found only when a water-bearing bed is sandwiched between two impervious beds. When a boring is made to the lower part of the bed, the pressure of water is sufficient to cause the water to overflow at the surface. Artesian wells were known to ancient Egypt and China, and have existed in the Sahara since the earliest times. The fountains in Trafalgar Square are fed by artesian wells sunk through the London clay into the chalk about 400 ft.

Arthur's Seat, a hill of volcanic origin, 823 ft. high,

dominating Holyrood Park, to the south-east of Edinburgh.

Articles. The *Six Articles* are those contained in an Act of Henry VIII, and were of Roman Catholic origin. The *Thirty-nine Articles* were drawn up for the English church at the Reformation. They are printed at the back of the Prayer Book. Candidates for holy orders in the Church of England are required to subscribe to them, though the form of assent has recently been modified.

Art Nouveau, a term applied to the "new art" which spread across Europe and the U.S.A. during the 1890s. It was mainly a style of architecture and interior decoration which attempted to break with the old traditions of darkness and "heaviness" by the use of the new materials of cement, steel, and glass from which it created patterns characterised by: (a) over-elaboration; (b) relatively naturalistic but tortuous representations of plants, etc.; (c) a ubiquity which left no surface undecorated. Typical of the extravagances of Art Nouveau are the cast-iron lilies with copper tendrils, the cupboard doors and chair-backs with heart-shaped holes, and the furniture shaped like animals, examples of which are still with us. In Britain the movement was basically a continuation of the Arts and Crafts movement of William Morris; Aubrey Beardsley represented this essentially fin-de-siècle school in his drawings.

Arts and Crafts Movement, the English revival of decorative art which began about 1875 as a revolt against the existing vulgarity of internal decoration and furnishings and the pettiness of academic art. Inspired by William Morris and Burne-Jones together with Rossetti, it was strongly influenced by the former's mediaevalism, his hatred of industrialism, and his own version of socialism which included the regeneration of man by handicrafts. His firm of Morris & Co. produced wallpapers, tapestries, furniture, stained-glass windows, carpets, and fabrics in a style totally different from that of contemporary Victorian decoration. Morris's Kelmscott Press did much to raise the standards of book design and printing. *See* Art Nouveau.

Arum, a genus of plants of the Araceae family, of which there is but one British species, the wake-robin or cuckoo-pint, sometimes also styled "Lords and Ladies." Its pointed leaves and spikes of scarlet poisonous berries are familiar in the hedgerows.

Arundel Marbles, a collection of ancient Greek sculptures formed by Thomas Howard, Earl of Arundel in the 17th cent. and presented to Oxford University by his grandson, Henry Howard, who became Duke of Norfolk.

Aryans, nomadic peoples who made their way in successive waves from the Eurasian steppes to the Indus and the Nile during the first half of the 2nd millennium B.C. They crossed the Hindu Kush into N.W. India and settled in the valleys of the Indus and Ganges, where an earlier Indus civilisation had flourished, c. 3250-2750 B.C. Their religious ideas are reflected in the Veda (oldest Hindu scriptures, written down many centuries later in Vedic, parent language of Sanskrit). Those who made their way to Syria and Egypt founded the Hyksos empire (c. 1680-1580 B.C.). The Aryans introduced the horse-drawn chariot and spoke a language from which the great Indo-European family of languages is derived, with one group in India and Iran, and another in Europe.

Asafoetida, an acrid, strong-smelling gum resin exuded from the stem of an umbelliferous plant, *Ferula foetida,* found in Persia and Afghanistan. Formerly used medicinally to treat hysteria; still used in cooking in India, Iran, and France.

Ascension Day, or Holy Thursday, is the 40th day after Easter.

Ascot Races are an annual fashionable function dating from 1711 and taking place on Ascot Heath, only six miles from Windsor, in June. These races have always had royal patronage. The course is nearly two miles long.

Ash, a familiar deciduous tree of the genus *Fraxinus,* of over 60 species, native to North-temperate regions. The ash held an important place in Norse mythology, as it was supposed to support the heavens with its roots in Hell. The species native to Britain, and to Europe,

is *F. excelsior,* a tall tree with compound leaves, greenish flowers, winged seeds, and black buds in winter. It is a valuable timber tree, tough and elastic, and largely used for wheels and handles. The rowan, or mountain ash, *Sorbus aucuparia,* with similar leaves and orange berries, belongs to a different family. *F. pendula* or weeping ash is a weeping strain which makes an ideal natural summer house.

Ashes, The, the symbol which distinguishes the winning cricket team in the Australian Test Matches. In 1882 the Australians won at the Oval by 7 runs. After the match the following epitaph appeared in the *Sporting Times:* "In affectionate remembrance of English Cricket which died at the Oval on Aug. 29, 1882, deeply lamented by a large circle of sorrowing friends and acquaintances. R.I.P. NB. The body will be cremated and the ashes taken to Australia." When the English Eleven went to Australia the same winter it was said that they had come to recover the "ashes." England won two out of three matches, and after the third match the ashes of what is now generally believed to have been a stump were presented in an urn to Ivo Bligh, later Lord Darnley. He bequeathed the urn to the M.C.C., and it now stands in the Memorial Gallery at Lord's.

Ash Wednesday, first day of Lent, the seventh Wednesday before Easter.

Assassination, treacherous murder for political ends, usually of a ruler or distinguished person. Among the most notable: Julius Caesar, 44 B.C.; Thomas Becket, 1170; David Rizzio, 1566; William the Silent, 1584; Henry IV. of France 1610; Jean Paul Marat, 1793; Abraham Lincoln, 1865; Alexander II. of Russia, 1881; Archduke Francis Ferdinand of Austria, 1914; Dr. Dollfuss, 1934; King Alexander of Yugoslavia, 1934; Mahatma Gandhi, 1948; King Abdullah of Jordan, 1951; Liaquat Ali Khan, 1951; King Feisal of Iraq, 1958; Mr. Bandaranaike, 1959; President Kennedy, 1963; Malcolm X, 1965; Dr. Verwoerd, 1966; Dr. Martin Luther King, 1968; Senator Robert Kennedy, 1968; Mr. Tom Mboya, 1969.

Asteroids are minor planets most of whose orbits lie between those of Mars and Jupiter; they were unknown until the discovery of Ceres by Piazzi in 1801. More than a thousand have been named and many thousands are believed to exist. After 1891 they were identified by their paths on exposed photographic plates. Most of them have a diameter of well under 50 miles. Ceres, with a diameter of c. 480 m., is the largest, then there are Pallas (c. 304 m.), Juno (120 m.), Vesta (240 m.), Astraea, Adonis, Hermes, Hidalgo, Eros, Amor, Apollo, and the Trojan group which all take their names from Homer's *Iliad*—Achilles, Patroclus, Hector, Nestor, Priam, Agamemnon, Ulysses, Aeneas, Anchises, Troilus, Ajax, and Diomede. The asteroid Icarus (diameter c. ½ mile) makes the closest approach to the Sun, and was within a few miles of the Earth on June 14, 1968. A full list of asteroids has been issued by the Spanish astronomical historian, Prof. A. Paluzie-Borrell.

Astrolabe, a mediaeval scientific instrument for taking altitudes, observing the sun by day and the stars by night, and used for telling the time and finding the latitude. Used by the ancient Greeks, later by the Arabs and Persians, and introduced into Europe by way of Spain in the 14th cent. Chaucer is said to have sent his son Lois, a ten-year-old student at Oxford, an astrolabe with a treatise on its use in 1391.

Astronomical unit, the mean distance from the centre of the earth to the centre of the sun, or half the major axis of the earth's elliptical orbit. It has been known for some 300 years that the earth–sun distance is roughly 93 million miles, but over the past 60-odd years astronomers have attempted to determine it with ever-greater accuracy, using various methods of computation. Spencer Jones (1931) deduced a value of 93,004,000 miles; the American astronomer E. K. Rabe (1950) obtained a value of 92,914,800 miles; and data from the *Pioneer V* space probe gave a value of 92,925,100 miles. There are two basic ways of determining the unit: one is based on observations of the minor planet Eros, the other is the radar method, based on the time taken for a radio signal bounced off the planet Venus to return to earth. The earth–sun distance is a fundamental value in astronomy.

Astrology. *See* J5.

Astronomy. The Pythagoreans believed the stars and planets moved with uniform circular velocity in crystalline spheres, centred round the earth (the "harmony of the spheres"). Hipparchus (190–120 B.C.) made the first star catalogue, discovered the precession of the equinoxes and introduced the idea of epicyclic motion. His planetary system, in the form it was presented by Ptolemy 200 years later, held until the Renaissance when Copernicus revived the heretical view first put forward by Aristarchus of Samos (310–230 B.C.) that the sun and not the earth was at the centre. Galileo, accurate observer and experimenter, went beyond Copernicus; helped by the contributions of Tycho Brahe, Giordano Bruno, Kepler and others, he was able to overthrow the Ptolemaic system of the heavenly spheres and Aristotelian philosophy, and pave the way for Newton and modern astronomy. To Galileo we owe the conception of acceleration; to Newton the theory of universal gravitation; they showed that the same laws govern both celestial and terrestrial physics. Three landmarks in more recent times were the discovery of Uranus by Herschel in 1781 which extended the solar system as then recognised; the estimation by Hubble in 1924 of the distance of Andromeda, which showed that our Galaxy was just one of many; and Einstein's theory of relativity which improved on Newton's theory of the solar system by bringing gravitation into the domain of space-time. Today radiotelescopes and space probes are advancing astronomical knowledge and making it possible to explore regions beyond the scope of optical telescopes. The following have held the position of Astronomer Royal (period of office in brackets): John Flamsteed (1675–1719), Edmund Halley (1719–42), James Bradley (1742–62), Nathaniel Bliss (1762–65), Nevil Maskelyne (1765–1811), John Pond (1811–35), Sir George Airy (1835–81), Sir William Christie (1881–1910), Sir Frank Dyson (1910–33), Sir Harold Spencer Jones (1933–55), Sir Richard Woolley (1956–   ). *See* F5–7.

Astrophysics, a branch of astronomy concerned with the physical nature and constitution of celestial bodies. Developments in space research technology have contributed to the great advance in this branch of science.

Athanasian Creed, one of the three ancient creeds of the Christian Church, often referred to as the *Quicunque Vult,* is a statement of the doctrine of the Trinity and the Incarnation, and though named after St. Athanasius, the view is now widely held that it is the work of St. Ambrose (339–97).

Athodyd, also called "Ramjet" or "Propulsive Duct." This can be considered as an extremely simple gas-turbine engine, without any rotating parts. A power plant with great possibilities for high-speed aerial flight, it consists of a diffuser, combustion chamber, and exhaust chamber; its thrust results from the fact that the gases leaving the athodyd have a higher velocity than the gases entering it.

Atmosphere is the gaseous envelope of the earth, and consists of a mixture of gases (*see* Air) and water vapour, the variability of the latter being of great importance meteorologically. The ozone layer, which absorbs ultra-violet radiation which would be lethal to plant life if it reached the ground, is concentrated at about 20 miles above the earth but extends to about twice that height. The lower level of the atmosphere up to a height of about 7 miles (6 miles at the Poles and 10 miles at the Equator) is known as the *troposphere,* and it is in this region that nearly all weather phenomena occur. This is the region of most interest to the forecaster studying temperature, humidity, windspeeds, and the movement of air masses. Temperature falls with height by about 1° C. per 500 ft. in this layer. The *tropopause* is the boundary between the troposphere and the *stratosphere.* Temperature varies little in the lower levels of this region: it is mainly cloudless, and has no vertical currents. Strangely enough, the lowest temperatures of the atmos-

phere are to be found not at the Poles, but at about 11 miles above the Equator, where a temperature as low as −80 °C. has been recorded! Temperatures begin to rise about 20 miles from the earth's surface at about the same rate as they fall in the troposphere, owing to the absorption of solar radiation by the concentration of ozone. The stratospheric air is extremely dry. Near the 60-mile level a number of important atmospheric phenomena occur. Above this level the oxygen becomes predominantly monatomic in contrast to the normal diatomic form at lower altitudes. This is the *ionosphere,* extending to heights over 500 miles from the earth's surface. This layer acts as an electrical radio mirror which makes long-distance radio transmission possible. The auroras are most frequently observed at altitudes near 60 miles but do extend at times far higher. *See also* **Ionosphere.**

Atmospherics are electrical impulses which are believed to originate in atmospheric electrical discharges such as lightning. They give rise to crashing background noises in the loudspeakers of radio sets, interfering with reception at distances of up to 4,000 miles from the centre of the disturbance. The location of atmospherics with the aid of radio direction-finding methods gives warning of the approach of thunder storms.

Atom. *See* F9–14, F20.

Atomic Pile, an apparatus containing a fissionable element and a moderator, such as heavy water or graphite, in which a self-sustaining fission process proceeds at a controllable rate. The first atomic pile, constructed on a squash court at Chicago, was operated for the first time on December 2, 1942, under the direction of Dr. Enrico Fermi. The pile contained 12,400 lb. of uranium. *See* **Nuclear Reactors.**

Augsburg Confession, name given to the doctrine of faith of the Lutheran churches, drawn up by Melanchthon and endorsed by Luther for the Diet of Augsburg (1530).

August, named after the Emperor Augustus, because it was his "lucky" month.

Auks, duck-like sea-birds, black and white, with short, narrow wings, compact bodies, and legs set well back. Breed in colonies on rocky coasts of N. Europe (incl. British Isles) and spend most time in coastal waters. Migrate south in winter. The Auk family includes the Razorbill, Little Auk, Guillemot, and Puffin. The Great Auk became extinct in the 19th cent. after ruthless hunting for the sake of its feathers. Except for the Black Guillemot, they lay only one egg a year.

Aulic Council, a supreme court of the Holy Roman Empire, established by Maximilian I., in 1501.

Aurora polaris. This wonderful phenomenon of the night sky is a common sight in some high latitudes, north and south. It is visible less often in temperate latitudes, and only very seldom in the tropics. As seen in the northern hemisphere it is called the aurora borealis or northern lights, and in the south, the aurora australis or southern lights. The zone of maximum frequency surrounds the north magnetic pole and includes Greenland, northern Canada, and the north coast of Alaska. Auroral displays may take several forms, *e.g.,* a faint glow, a diffuse ribbon of light crossing the heavens, great folded waving curtains like draperies; the whole sky may be a grand panoply of light. Both the aurora and the magnetic storm associated with it are ascribed to the envelopment of the earth in a great cloud or stream of solar gas shot out from stormy areas on the sun (sunspots) that has travelled to the earth at a speed of over a thousand miles a second. The gas is mainly atomic hydrogen, but the atoms are broken up into their two parts, protons and electrons. These are both electrically charged. This renders them subject to the influence of the earth's magnetic field, which deflects many of them to the high latitudes where the aurora is most commonly seen. The aurora is a kind of light essentially different from that of the rainbow which is a partly subjective phenomenon. Each beholder sees his own rainbow, whose light is sunlight refracted and reflected by many raindrops. The raindrops that produce his rainbow depend on his position as well as on the direction of the sun. The aurora, on the contrary, is a light as objective as that of a candle, though produced differently. It is a self-luminescence of the air in particular regions of the atmosphere that lie far above the clouds. By simultaneous observation from stations twenty or more miles apart it is possible to locate the position of the luminous air, *i.e.*, to determine the height of the aurora, its location in plan, and its form and volume.

Austerlitz, Battle of, was fought near Brünn, in Moravia, on December 2, 1805, when Napoleon defeated the Russians and Austrians under Kutuzon.

Auto-da-Fé, or Act of Faith, was the ceremony connected with the sentencing of heretics under the Inquisition of Spain and Portugal, the persons found guilty being imprisoned or burned alive. The ceremony took place in some public square, sometimes in the presence of the king and court.

Automation is a recently coined word, used to designate the adoption of methods of automatic control either of manufacturing processes or of any business process involving a large mass of routine work. The word is used in broader and narrower senses. In its broadest sense it covers any form of mechanisation which largely replaces human labour by the work of automatic or semi-automatic machines, such as has been in progress continuously since the Industrial Revolution; but it is better kept to a narrower meaning, in which it is confined to the recent development of electronic or similar devices, involving feedback (automatic detection and correction of malfunction). Human labour is eliminated save for that needed for watching and maintaining the elaborate machines used. In this sense, automation has been spreading rapidly in advanced countries. *See* G12(1).

Autumn, the third season of the year, begins with the autumnal equinox, and ends with the winter solstice, but the term is generally understood as covering the period from mid-August to mid-November.

Auxins, "plant hormones," organic substances produced by plants to regulate growth. Synthetic auxins are now widely used, *e.g.*, for promotion of root formation in cuttings, differential weed control, prevention of premature dropping of fruit, in storage of potatoes and hard fruit, and to overcome frost damage to fruit buds.

Average is a single number designed to give a typical example of a set of numbers, *e.g.*, a cricketer's batting average for a season gives an idea of his typical score. There are several kinds of average and their uses are studied in the science of statistics (*q.v.*). A statement that "so and so is the average value" can be misleading if one does not know which average is meant. Three common averages are: the arithmetic average (or mean), the mode, and the median. The arithmetic average of *n* numbers is found by adding them together and dividing by *n*; this is a very common method of averaging. The mode of *n* numbers is the most frequently occurring number. The median is the middle number, *i.e.*, the number which is smaller than just as many of the other numbers as it exceeds. Of the numbers 1, 2, 2, 2, 2, 3, 4, 5, 6, 8, 9, the arithmetic mean is 4, the mode is 2, the median is 3.

Avocet, a graceful wading bird related to the stilts, of black-and-white plumage, bluish legs, and slender upturned bill. There are four species. Avocets nest in colonies and there is one in the sanctuary on Havergate Island, Suffolk.

Avogadro's Hypothesis. This is a fundamental concept of chemistry. Equal volumes of all gases under the same conditions of temperature and pressure contain the same number of molecules. This law was instrumental in assigning the formulæ of molecules. The hypothesis was put forward in 1811, but was not generally accepted until 1860. *See* F21(2).

Aztecs, the name of a native and powerful race found in Mexico when the Spaniards first discovered that country, and with difficulty subdued.

B

Babiroussa, a ferocious, long-legged wild pig, native of the Celebes, sometimes called the horned-hog, because of the long upper tusks in the male, which are developments of the canine teeth which grow upwards, piercing the upper lip, and curving backwards, often broken in fighting.

Baboon, monkeys belonging to the African genus *Papio*. They are considered the lowest of the Old World (Catarrhine) monkeys, and walk on all fours. In the main terrestrial, but take to trees after food. The mandrill is closely related.

Babylonian Captivity, the period spent by the Jews in Babylon after Jerusalem was captured by Nebuchadnezzar, the Babylonian emperor, in 586 B.C. Traditionally the captivity lasted 70 years, but when Babylon was in turn taken by Cyrus in 538 B.C., the exiles were permitted to return to Jerusalem. The term is also applied in church history to the period 1309–78 when the papacy moved to Avignon, into the control of the French monarchy.

Badger, a carnivorous mammal related to the weasel, of nocturnal and burrowing habits, inoffensive, subsisting chiefly on roots and insects, though sometimes mice, young rabbits, and eggs form part of its diet. Badger-baiting was a favourite sport in Britain until it was prohibited in the middle of 19th cent. The badger does little harm and quite a lot of good; badger digging is to be condemned as a cruel sport.

Bagpipe. Once popular all over Europe, this instrument is still played in Scotland, Ireland, Brittany, and elsewhere. The bag acts as a reservoir of air and, when squeezed by the player's arm, forces air through the pipes. One of these, the Chanter pipe, provides the tune and is played by the fingers as in a flageolet. The remainder, the Drone pipes, give a continuous, unvarying note.

Bailey Bridge, invented by Sir Donald Bailey and first used in N. African campaign 1942–3. Built up of pre-fabricated girders, it can be easily transported and erected.

Bailie, is a Scottish term for the magistrate of a municipal corporation or royal burgh.

Bailiwick, a feudal term denoting the limits of a bailiff's jurisdiction. The term has survived in the Channel Islands, where Jersey and Guernsey are Bailiwicks.

Bakelite. A plastic material made from phenol, formaldehyde, and urea. It is used in the manufacture of electrical fittings because of its insulating properties.

Balance of Power was the doctrine in British policy whereby European groups should be so balanced as to prevent the emergence of a dominating Power. Thus the balance was maintained between the Triple Alliance (Germany, Austria and Italy) and the Triple Entente (Great Britain, France and Russia) and preserved peace from 1871 to 1914. After the first world war there was tentative support of Germany's recovery to counterweight a possible French hegemony; but when Germany's power grew under Hitler culminating in the second world war, Britain, France and Russia again became allies. By the end of the war the old system of a balance of power centred upon Europe collapsed to give way to a thermonuclear balance of power between the super-Powers, the Soviet Union (Warsaw Pact) and the United States (Nato alliance).

Baldachin (It. *Baldachino*), a canopy usually supported by four pillars over throne, altar, or other sacred object. The name is also applied to the silken canopy used in processions and borne by the priest who carries the Host.

Balearic Crane, the crowned crane of the Balearic Islands and the North African mainland, distinguished by its yellowish, black-tipped occipital tuft and by its trumpet note.

Baleen or "whalebone" the name given to a series of horny plates growing from the roof of the mouth in those whales classified as Whale-bone or Baleen Whales (Mystacoceti) There are 300–400 or so plates on each side, and their inner edges are frayed, the whole system constituting a filter for collecting minute organisms used for food. The Baleen Whales include the Right-Whales, the Pacific Grey-Whale, and the Rorquals. *See* Whales.

Ballet is a combination of four arts; dancing, music, painting, and drama, each of which is ideally of equal importance. The movement of the individual dancers and the "orchestration" of the whole group is in the hands of the choreographer. The dancer's training follows certain basic rules but save in classical ballet there is considerable freedom of movement. Ballet as we know it today developed professionally at the Court of King Louis XIV. of France, though it owes its origins to Italy and in the earliest times to Greece and Rome. Its movements were made up from the dances of courtiers, country folk and tumblers. Technique grew more complex as costume became modified, the body gaining complete freedom with the invention of tights. A succession of great dancers—French, Italian and latterly Russian left their imprint on the art. Contemporary ballet reflects the aesthetic of the Russian, Sergei Diaghilev. In England Dame Ninette de Valois has laid the foundation of a national ballet, at Sadler's Wells and Covent Garden, with a personality that reflects the national character. A Royal Charter was granted in 1957 setting up the Royal Ballet to co-ordinate the activities of the Sadler's Wells group.

Ballistics, the science dealing with the motion of projectiles, especially shells, bombs, and rockets. Great advances have been made in this science in recent years.

Balloon, the modern balloon consists of a bag of plastic material inflated with a gas lighter than air. The first ascent by man in a hot-air balloon was made on Nov. 21, 1783, and in a hydrogen balloon on Dec. 1, 1783. The most famous of the early scientific flights by manned balloons were those of the Englishmen Coxwell and Glaisher, in 1862, when a height of 7 miles was reached. The first aerial crossing of the English Channel by Blanchard and Jeffries was made on 7 Jan. 1785. Piccard's ascent to 10 miles, in 1931, marked the conquest of the stratosphere. Four years later the huge American balloon Explorer II, inflated with nearly 4 million cubic feet of helium, carried a team of scientists with their floating laboratory to an altitude of 14 miles. In 1957 a pressurised balloon carrying an American doctor rose 19 miles above the Earth. Captive kite-balloons were widely used in the war as defensive measures against air attack. Meteorologists send their instruments up in balloons to collect data about the upper atmosphere, and of recent years physicists have learned much about cosmic radiation from the study of photographic plates sent to the upper regions in balloons. The American balloon satellites *Echo I* and *II* move round the Earth in orbits several hundred miles high, and, as the brightest of the earth satellites, can be seen with the naked eye as brilliant points moving across the sky. Ballooning as a hobby is carried on by a number of enthusiasts.

Balsam, a big genus (140 species) of flowering plants. Many species are cultivated for their showy flowers, *e.g. Impatiens noli-me-tangere,* the yellow balsam or "touch-me-not," so called because the fruit explodes when touched, slinging out the seeds. Balsam fir is a conifer (*Abies balsamea*) from which Canada balsam gum is obtained.

Baltimore Bird, a lively black-and-orange bird of the oriole sub-family extending from Brazil to Canada; builds a well-constructed hanging nest, and has a fine voice.

Bamboo, a genus of strong grasses, some species growing to over 120 ft. in height; much used by oriental peoples for all kinds of purposes. The young shoots of some species are tender and esculent. *See* **T5** (2).

Banana (family *Musaceae*), a large herbaceous plant cultivated in moist regions of the tropics, and one of the most productive plants known. The main areas of commercial cultivation are in tropical America, the Canary Islands, and West Africa. World production is estimated at 20 million tons, of which only 3 million are for trade.

Bandicoots, Australasian marsupial mammals, of the size of a large rat or rabbit. They are burrowing animals living largely on insects. The rabbit-eared bandicoot, restricted to Australia, has shrew-like snout, long ears like a rabbit, long crested tail, and a silky coat. The long-nosed bandicoot has a spiny coat and comes from E. Australia. The pig-footed bandicoot has two functional toes on the foot, like a pig.

Bantu (native word = people), term loosely used for large family of Negro races of Southern Africa.

Baobab, a tropical African tree. The species *Adansonia digitata* is one of the largest trees known, though not the tallest; the trunk can reach 30 ft. in thickness. The fruit is woody, but its juice provides a cooling beverage. The bark yields a fibre used for making rope and cloth.

Barbary Ape, a large monkey belonging to the genus *Macaca.* It is the only monkey living in relative freedom in Europe, a small colony being found on the Rock of Gibraltar. It has no tail.

Barberry, a genus of berry-producing shrubs containing a hundred species. Several species are cultivated for their flowers and bright berries. Has an interesting pollination mechanism; the base of each stamen is sensitive to touch, and insects probing for nectar cause top of stamen to spring inwards, so dusting visitor's head with pollen which can then be carried to the next flower visited. The common barberry (*Berberis communis*) harbours one stage of the fungus that causes rust of wheat.

Barbican, a fortified entrance to a castle or city, with projecting towers. In the London street called Barbican there was formerly a barbican in front of the city gates.

Barbiturates. A group of drugs derived from a parent compound called barbituric acid: phenobarbitone is the best-known example. They induce sleep and are used in the manufacture of sleeping pills and sometimes as anaesthetics, but they have the disadvantage of being habit forming. *See also* **P23** (2).

Barbizon School, a school of mid-19th-cent. landscape painters whose main tenet was a return to nature with an exact rendering of peasant life and country scenery painted on the spot. It was named after the village of that name in the Forest of Fontainebleau, where its chief members—Millet, Theodore Rousseau, Daubigny, and Diaz—made their home. Their practice of painting direct from nature, which was far from universal at that time, made them the precursors of **Impressionism** (*q.v.*).

Barcarolle, a Venetian gondolier's song applied to instrumental as well as vocal compositions.

Bard, among the ancient Celts a poet or minstrel whose mission was to sing of heroic deeds. He was supposed to have the gift of prophecy, and was exempt from taxes and military service.

Barilla, soda carbonate or soda ash obtained by burning certain salt-marsh plants (*e.g.* the saltwort, *Salsola kali*). It used to be in great demand, until the product of the Leblanc and then the Solvay ammonia-soda process was made available by the chemical industry.

Barium, metal element, symbol Ba. In group II of the periodic table. The metal is soft and easily cut. It occurs as the sulphate and carbonate in nature. It was first prepared by Sir Humphry Davy in 1808, as an amalgam, by electrolysis of barium chloride. The pure metal was not isolated until 1901.

Barium meal. Barium sulphate is opaque to X-rays and before taking X-ray pictures of the alimentary canal radiologists give a "barium meal" to the patients so that the alimentary canal shows up more clearly.

Barnacles constitute a sub-class (*Cirripedia*) of the Crustacea. The barnacle fouling the bottom of ships is the Goose Barnacle, which has a long muscular stalk and a shell composed of five plates. The Acorn Barnacles, which cover rocks, breakwaters, etc., just below high-water mark are similarly constructed, but have no stalk. The manner of feeding of barnacles was vividly described by T. H. Huxley, who said the barnacle is "a crustacean fixed by its head kicking the food into its mouth with its legs." It was a naval surgeon, J. Vaughan Thompson, who discovered in 1830 that barnacles have a free-swimming larva (or nauplius). In the Middle Ages a curious myth grew up to the effect that the Barnacle changed into a sea-bird called, for that reason, the Barnacle Goose.

Barometer is an instrument for measuring atmospheric pressure, invented at Florence by Torricelli, pupil of Galileo, in 1644. The standard method consists of balancing the air column against a column of mercury, used on account of its high density. The mercury is contained in a long glass tube, closed at one end, and inverted in a cistern also containing mercury. The height of the mercury column, supporting the air column, is taken as the pressure at the time, and can be read off very accurately by means of a vernier scale. Present-day tendency is to express the readings in units of pressure instead of length, the millibar being adopted (1 mb = 1000 dynes per sq. cm.; 1000 mb ≡ 29·53 inches of mercury approx.). The standard instrument is correct for pressures at 0°C in Lat. 45°, so that corrections have to be applied for temperatures and latitudes other than these. Also a correction has to be made for reducing the pressure to mean sea level. *See* Aneroid.

Baron, title given in feudal England to a man who held his land directly from the king by military or other honourable service. The first baron created by letters patent was John Beauchamp de Holt, Baron of Kidderminster, in 1387. A baron is a member of the fifth and last grade of the peerage of the United Kingdom and is addressed as " Lord." Life peers and life peeresses rank with hereditary barons and baronesses according to the date of their creation. In Scotland the term baron is used of the possessor of a fuedal fief, or the representative by descent of such a fief. The equivalent of the English baron, as a rank of the Scottish peerage, is Lord of Parliament.

Baronet, the lowest hereditary title, instituted by James I. to provide funds for the colonisation of Ulster. The first baronet was Sir Nicholas Bacon. Since 1964 no recommendations for hereditary honours have been made.

Baroque, a term used for the art style of the period *c.* 1600–1720 which was the artistic accompaniment of the Jesuit counter-Reformation. Its most obvious characteristics are: (*a*) its emotional appeal and dramatic intensity both related to its deliberate intention as propaganda (" a good picture makes better religious propaganda than a sermon " said one of its exponents); (*b*) in architecture, a style which is heavily and sometimes almost grotesquely ornate, plentifully covered with voluptuous sculpture on which draperies float rather than hang, with twisted and spiral instead of plain or fluted columns, and unnecessary windows or recesses added for ornament rather than use; (*c*) its emphasis on the whole at the expense of the parts such that a building's sculpture merges into its architecture and both into its painting (Baroque paintings are as closely knit as a jigsaw puzzle so that one cannot isolate individual figures as would be possible in a Renaissance one). Baroque architecture owing to its origin is found mainly in the Catholic countries: Italy, France, Austria, Bavaria, *e.g.*, the Barberini Palace, Rome, designed by its greatest exponent Bernini and others; the Church of the Invalides, Paris. Baroque artists include Caravaggio, Guido Reni, Murillo and Rubens, the greatest Northern Baroque painter. The Baroque style merges gradually into Rococo (*q.v.*).

Barque, a small sailing vessel with three or four masts. A three-masted barque has fore- and mainmasts square-rigged, the mizzenmast fore-and aft-rigged.

Barrow is an ancient artificial mound of earth or stone raised over the site of a burial. In Britain barrows were built from 2500 B.C. until the late Saxon period, but the Egyptian ones the earliest barrows known, the great pyramids being a spectacular development of the custom of ceremonial burial. Silbury Hill, south of Avebury, is the biggest artificial mound in Europe, 1680 ft. in circuit at the base, 315 ft. at top, and 135 ft. high.

Bartholomew, Massacre of St., occurred in Paris on the night of Aug. 24, 1572, when over two thousand Huguenots were massacred by order of the Catholic French Court.

Basalt Rocks are fine-grained, dark coloured, of igneous origin and occur either as lava flows as in Mull and Staffa, or as intrusive sheets, like the Edinburgh Castle Rock and Salisbury Craig. One of the most noted examples of columnar basalt is that of the Giant's Causeway in Ireland.

Basanite. A smooth black siliceous mineral, or flinty jasper; a crypto-crystalline quartz

used as a touchstone for testing the purity of gold, etc., by means of the mark left after rubbing the metal with it. Sometimes styled the Lydian stone.

Base, a substance having a tendency to accept a proton (H⁺). This is a wide definition and covers unconventional types of compounds. In aqueous solution bases dissolve with formation of hydroxyl ions, and will neutralise an acid to form a salt. In non-aqueous solvents, like liquid ammonia or hydrogen fluoride, compounds classically regarded as salts can be bases. *e.g.*, sodium fluoride is a base in hydrogen fluoride solution. *See* F22.

Basilisk, is a lizard of aquatic habits, with an elevated crest (which it can erect or depress at will) down the centre of its back.

Basques, people of N. Spain and S.W. France, oldest surviving racial group in Europe, who have preserved their ancient language which is unrelated to any other tongue.

Bas-Relief (" low relief "), a term used in sculpture to denote a class of sculptures the figures of which are only slightly raised from the surface of the stone or clay upon which the design is wrought.

Bastille, a castle or fortress in Paris, built in the 14th cent., and used as a state prison, especially for political offenders. Its bad repute as an instrument of despotism excited the hatred of the populace, who stormed and demolished it on July 14, 1789, at the beginning of the Revolution.

Bastinado, an oriental punishment, by beating with a pliable cane on the soles of the feet.

Bats. These mammals fly by means of a membrane stretched between each of the long fingers of the hand and between the fifth finger and the body. Another membrane stretches between the legs and the tail. There are twelve British species; namely, the Noctule, Leisler's B., Serotine, Pipistrelle, Long-eared B., Daubenton's B., Natterer's B., Whiskered B., Bechstein's B., Barbastelle, Greater Horseshoe, and Lesser Horseshoe Bats. Bats avoid obstacles and locate their prey by emitting pulses of very high frequency sound, inaudible to the human ear (unless a bat detector is used). Blindness does not affect this ability but deafness leaves them comparatively helpless. Bats are mostly insectivorous, catching the insects in their open mouths while flying; some eat fruit. During the winter they survive on their stored fat. The Vampire Bats, feeding exclusively on blood, are confined to tropical America. *See* Ultrasonics.

Bath, Order of the, believed to have been established by Henry IV. at his coronation in 1399; remodelled in 1725 as a military order; formally instituted in three classes in 1815; civil division added in 1847. In the Order are three classes: G.C.B., or Knight Grand Cross of the Bath; K.C.B., or Knight Commander of the Bath; C.B., or Companion of the Bath. Companionship of the Bath does not carry knighthood nor entitle the holder to the prefix " Sir." The motto of the order is *Tria juncta in uno* (Three joined in one). The insignia for civil and military and the three classes vary. *See* Knighthood.

Battery, Electric, the common term for an electric cell but really meaning a combination of two or more cells. A cell is a device for converting stored chemical energy into electricity which can then be used for heat, light, traction, or any desired purpose. A *primary* cell will do this until the chemical action is completed and the cell is then useless. In a *secondary* cell, the chemical actions are reversible and the cell can be returned to its initial condition and used again. This is done by passing an electric current through—a process called recharging. A common primary cell is the Leclanché dry cell used in torches. This works by the action of sal-ammoniac on electrodes made of zinc and carbon. About a century after it came into common use it is still the chief source of power for portable equipment in armed forces. A common secondary cell is the lead and sulphuric acid accumulator used in cars. Many other types of cell are known and some are under development because the demands of space travel, medicine, warfare, etc., call for batteries of lighter weight, greater reliability, or special properties. *See* Fuel Cell, Energy Conversion.

Bauhaus, a German institution for the training of architects, artists, and industrial designers, founded in 1919 at Weimar by Walter Gropius, (d. 1969). It was closed by Hitler in 1933 and re-opened at Chicago. The Bauhaus doctrine held that there should be no separation between architecture and the fine and applied arts; that art, science, and technology should co-operate to create " the compositely inseparable work of art, the great building." Thus it was an organisation with a social purpose. The original institution, at the instigation of Gropius, included on its teaching staff not only architects and technicians but also such noted artists as Paul Klee and Wassily Kandinsky.

Bauxite, the chief ore of aluminium. Chemically it is aluminium oxide. Aluminium metal is made industrially by electrolysing purified bauxite dissolved in fused cryolite. Chief producing areas: Surinam, Guyana, U.S.A., France, Hungary, Indonesia, U.S.S.R., Yugoslavia, Italy.

Bayeux Tapestry, a famous tapestry representing the conquest of England by William the Conqueror. It is embroidered on a band of linen 231 ft. long and 20 in. wide in blue, green, red, and yellow, divided into 72 scenes ranging over the whole story of the conquest. The accepted view is that the tapestry was commissioned for Bayeux Cathedral, but a new interpretation is that it is an Anglo-Norman secular work of art, much influenced by the contemporary *chansons de geste* (songs of deeds), executed by English embroiderers for a Norman patron. A representation can be seen in the Victoria and Albert Museum in London.

Beagle, a small hound that tracks by scent, and formerly used for hare hunting.

Bears belong to the Ursidae family of the Carnivora. They are plantigrade mammals, walking (like man) on the soles of their feet. Found in most parts of the world except Australia. The common Brown Bear was once spread over the whole of Europe; it became extinct in England about the 11th cent.; 7–8 ft. in length, and stands 3 ft. or more at the shoulder. The Grizzly Bear of N. America is larger, and the coat is shorter and greyer. The Polar Bear is remarkable in having a white coat all the year round; it spends much time in water, and unlike the other bears it is entirely carnivorous. Bear-baiting was made illegal in England in 1835.

Beaufort Scale of wind force is used to specify numerically the strength of the wind. Since the introduction of anemometers to measure the actual velocity, equivalent values of the ranges in miles per hour at a standard height in the open have been assigned to the Beaufort numbers. *See* N10.

Beaver, a genus of mammals of the Rodentia order, with short, scaly ears, webbed hind feet, and a long broad scaly tail. They grow up to 4 ft. long, and live in communities, constructing dams and lodges where they breed. Found in N. America, Russia, and Poland. Hunted mercilessly by trappers for its valuable pelt before protective laws were passed.

Bedford Level comprises parts of Norfolk, Suffolk, Huntingdon, Northampton, Lincoln, and Cambridge, generally called the Fens, 70 miles long and 20 to 40 miles broad. It was reclaimed and drained in the 17th cent. by the Earl of Bedford and the Dutch engineer Cornelius Vermuyden.

Bedlam (a corruption of Bethlehem) was a priory in Bishopsgate, afterwards converted into a hospital for lunatics. The asylum was transferred to St. George's Fields, Lambeth, in 1815. The term " bedlamite " came to be applied to any person behaving like a madman.

Beech, a deciduous tree belonging to the genus *Fagus* of some eight or nine species found in north temperate regions. The common beech, *F. sylvatica*, is believed to be native to Britain and is one of our finest trees, with massive trunk, long, pointed winter buds, and smooth, grey bark. There is little undergrowth under its dense shade. It is shorter lived than the oak, taking about 200 years to reach full size and then declining. The timber of beech has a variety of uses, *e.g.*, spoons, handles, tools, and chairs.

Bee-eater, name of a family of brilliantly coloured birds closely related to the rollers and kingfishers inhabiting the tropical and sub-tropical parts of Africa, Asia and Europe. The European species successfully nested in Britain for the first time in 1955 and a pair nested in Alderney in 1956. With their long curved beaks they catch insects on the wing, especially bees and butterflies, and lay their eggs in dark nest tunnels.

Beefeater. *See* Yeomen of the Guard.

Beeswax, the secretion of the bee, used for the formation of the cells or honey-comb of the hive; when melted it is what is commercially known as yellow wax, white wax being made by bleaching. Being impervious to water, it acts as a good resistant and is an article of much utility.

Beetles (Coleoptera) constitute one of the biggest orders of insects, numbering over 200,000 species. There are two pairs of wings; the hind pair are used for flight, while the front pair are hardened to form a pair of protective covers (elytra). Some beetles have lost the power of flight and then the elytra are joined together.

Bel and the Dragon is the title of certain supplementary chapters to the " Book of Daniel " of an apocryphal character. First appeared in the Septuagint, but the Jewish Church did not accept it as inspired. In 1546 the Council of Trent declared it to be canonical.

Bell, a hollow body of metal used for making sounds. Bells are usually made from bell-metal, an alloy of copper and tin. Small bells used for interior functions are often made of silver, gold, or brass. Ordinary hand-bells are of brass. From the 7th cent. large bells have been used in England in cathedrals, churches, and monasteries. The greatest bell in the world is the " King of Bells " in the Kremlin at Moscow which weighs about 198 tons, is 20 ft. 7 in. high and 22 ft. 8 in. in diameter. It was cast in 1733, but cracked in the furnace (the broken part weighed 11 tons) and is now preserved as a national treasure. Other large bells in Russia, include the 171-ton one at Krasnogvardersk, near Leningrad, and the one of 110 tons at Moscow. The Great Bell (Great Paul) at St. Paul's, cast in 1881, weighs 16¾ tons, and is the largest in the United Kingdom. Other gigantic bells are the Great Bell at Peking (53 tons); Nanking (22 tons); Cologne Cathedral (25 tons); Big Ben, Westminster (13½ tons); Great Peter, York Minster (10 tons). The Curfew bell is rung in some parts of England to this day, notably at Ripon. The number of changes that can be rung on a peal of bells is the *factorial* of the number of bells. Thus four bells allow 24 and eight bells 40,320.

Belladonna *or* Deadly Nightshade (*Atropa belladonna*) a well-known poisonous wild plant found in Southern Europe and Western Asia. The alkaloid atropine it contains is valuable in medicine, although a large dose is poisonous.

Bell, Book, and Candle. To curse by " bell, book, and candle " was a form of excommunication in the Roman Church ending with the words: " Do to the book, quench the candle, ring the bell."

Benedicite, the canticle in the Book of Common Prayer, known also as " The Song of the Three Holy Children."

Benedictines are monks and nuns of the Benedictine Order who live under the rule of St. Benedict—the monastic code whose influence on the religious and cultural life of the West has been so powerful. The rule is marked by an absence of extravagant asceticism. The greatest of the early Benedictines was Pope Gregory I (590–604) who sent St. Augustine of Canterbury to Anglo-Saxon England. Gregorian plainsong is named after him. *See also* J34(1).

Benedictus, a canticle used in the morning service of the English Church, and deriving its name from the first word of the Latin verse, *Benedictus*, blessed.

Benzene. An aromatic hydrocarbon obtained from coal tar and some petroleum fractions. It is a volatile inflammable liquid with a characteristic smell. The molecule consists of a flat ring of six carbon atoms, each bound to one hydrogen atom. Benzene is the parent member of many aromatic organic compounds and is widely used in industry to synthesise intermediates for fibres, dyestuffs, explosives, and pharmaceutical chemicals.

Beryl, a mineral, of which the emerald is a grass-green variety. Composed of beryllium and aluminium silicates. The pure mineral is colourless; the colour of most beryl comes from traces of impurities, notably iron and chromium. Otherwise it is yellowish, greenish-yellow, or blue, and is found in veins which traverse granite or gneiss, or embedded in granite, and sometimes in alluvial soil formed from such rocks.

Beryllium. Metallic element, symbol Be. Very similar to aluminium, it is stronger than steel and only one-quarter its weight. It is not very abundant, its main source is the mineral, beryl. Copper containing 2% beryllium is used for making springs. Because of its special properties the metal is used as a component in spacecraft, missiles and nuclear reactors. This accounts for its recent development on a technical scale. The metal powder is toxic.

Bessemer Process, for making steel depends on the forcing of atmospheric air into molten pig iron to burn out the impurities. *See* **Steel.**

Betel, the leaf of an Indian climbing plant, of pungent, narcotic properties. It is destructive to the teeth, and reddens the gums and lips.

Bhang, the Indian name for the hemp plant *Cannabis sativa,* the leaves and seed-capsules of which are chewed or smoked. The potent drug which comes from flowers of the female plant is called hashish in Arabia and marihuana in the United States and Mexico. *See* **P23(2).**

Bible (Greek *biblion* = scroll of paper; pl. *biblia* = writings) includes the Hebrew sacred Scriptures (Old Testament) and those held sacred by the Christians (New Testament). The Old Testament—the prehistoric portion—consists of 39 books, and is divided into three parts: (1) the Law, (2) the Prophets, (3) Miscellaneous Writings. The Old Testament was written in Hebrew except for parts of Ezra and Daniel, which were in Aramaic. It was not until the 9th cent. A.D. that a complete Hebrew text was made, the so-called Massoretic text. Before that the main versions were the Alexandrian Greek translation (Septuagint) made in the 2nd cent. B.C. and St. Jerome's Latin Vulgate of the 4th cent. A.D. (It was Jerome who used the Latin word "testament" (formed from *testis* = a witness)). Portions were translated into the Anglo-Saxon in the 8th cent. and the Venerable Bede put the greater part of St. John's gospel into English, but it was not until 1535 that a complete printed English version appeared—the Coverdale Translation. The Authorised Version dates from 1611 in the reign of James I., and because of its beautiful phraseology it has had a lasting appeal. The Revised Version dates from 1885. *The New English Bible,* with the Apocrypha, was published in 1970. It is a new translation in plain English prose of the earliest Hebrew, Aramaic, and Greek manuscripts. The finding of the Dead Sea Scrolls (since 1947) has added to our knowledge of Scripture.

Billion, in English usage, a million million, or 10^{12}; in American and French usage, a thousand million, or 10^9.

Bill of Rights, or Declaration of Rights, was the document setting forth the conditions upon which the British throne was offered to William and Mary in 1688. This was accepted and ultimately became an Act of Parliament.

Binary Notation, for numbers, is a way of representing numbers using only two digits, 0 and 1. Electronic digital computers handle numbers in this form and many people these days are having to learn it. Many school children find it both easy and fascinating—as did the great philosopher and mathematician Leibniz. The ordinary, or decimal numbers, 0, 1, 2, 3, 4, 5, 6, 7, 8, 9, 10 are written in binary notation as follows: 0, 1, 10, 11, 100, 101, 110, 111, 1000, 1001, 1010. The reader might divine the rules from this. The point is that you "carry 1," *i.e.,* move the digit 1 a place to the left, when you reach 2. In decimal notation you move 1 a place left when you reach 10. In other words, instead of columns for units, tens, hundreds, thousands, etc., the columns are for units, twos, fours, eights, etc. In binary notation: "1 + = 0 with 1 to carry." Since every digit in binary notation is either 0 or 1 it requires one bit of information to specify a binary digit. *See* **Bit.**

Biological Warfare, is the use for warlike purposes of bacteria, viruses, fungi, or other biological agents. These can be used to spread distress, incapacity, disease, or death among the enemy's people or livestock. One of the strange uses to which mankind puts its science is to make naturally infective organisms even more virulent for military use. This sort of research can be done in many countries; it is much cheaper and easier to hide than nuclear weapons development. Secret attack by biological agents is supposed to be easy and it may affect the populations without damaging buildings or bridges. However, the true effectiveness of biological warfare is largely unknown—meteorological conditions alone might render an attack completely unreliable.

Birch, a genus of deciduous trees including about 40 species and found only in northern regions. Birches native to Britain, and to Europe generally, are of two species—the silver birch, *Betula pendula,* with its graceful, drooping branches and triangular leaves, and the white birch, *Betula pubescens,* which has erect branches and soft oval leaves. Birch timber is an important plywood timber, the bark is used for tanning leather, and wintergreen oil comes from the bark of black birch, *Betula lenta,* a North American species. The birch is not a long-lived tree, few standing for more than a hundred years. The tallest recorded is at Woburn in Bedfordshire, 102 ft. high.

Birds, or Aves, are, next to mammals, the highest class of animal life. There are two kinds of modern birds—*Carinatae,* possessing keeled breast-bones and having power of flight; *Ratitae,* having raft-like breast-bones, and incapable of flight; and a sub-class of fossil birds, Archaeornithes, including *Archaeopteryx.* It is estimated that there are about 120 million land birds breeding in Great Britain, including 10 million each of the chaffinch and blackbird, 7 million each of the starling and robin and about 2 million sparrows.

The wheatear is usually the first of the migratory birds to return, often reaching Britain at the end of February and always before the middle of March; the sand martin is the first of the "early swallows" to return, followed by the house martin. The first cuckoo arrives about the middle of April, and the whinchat, garden warbler, and sedge warbler during the last week in April. The nightjar, spotted flycatcher, and red-backed shrike are not seen until the first week in May. The swift is among the last to return from Africa and the earliest to depart. Bird-nesting is illegal in Britain. *See also* **F33, Z21.**

Birds of Paradise, over 40 species of tropical birds inhabiting the dense forests of New Guinea and neighbouring islands. The male birds are remarkable for their brilliant plumage, long tail feathers, and ruffs on wings and neck, which are displayed to advantage during courtship. Related to the Bower Birds of Australia, and crows.

Biretta, a four-cornered head-covering worn by ecclesiastics of the Roman Church and varying in colour according to the rank of the wearer. A cardinal's biretta is red, a bishop's purple, a priest's black.

Bise, a keen dry north wind prevalent in Switzerland and South France.

Bishop is a Christian ecclesiastic, a person consecrated for the spiritual government of an area, a diocese or province, to the spiritual oversight of which he has been appointed (diocesan bishops), or to aid a bishop so appointed (suffragan bishops). In the Church of England there are forty-three diocesan bishops, all nominated by the Crown. Two, Canterbury and York, are archbishops having primacy in the respective provinces. The archbishops of Canterbury and York and the bishops of London, Durham, and Winchester and twenty-one other diocesan bishops in the order of seniority are spiritual peers, and sit in the House of Lords. The (Disestablished) Church of Ireland has two archbishops and twelve bishops; the (Disestablished) Church of Wales an archbishop and five bishops and the Episcopal Church in Scotland seven bishops. *See also* Cardinal.

Bismuth, metallic element, symbol Bi, in group V of the periodic table. Like antimony, its stable form is a grey, brittle, layer structure; electrical conductor. It is readily fusible, melting at 264° C and boiling at about 1420° C. Wood's metal, an alloy with one of the lowest melting points (under 150° F, so that a spoon made of it will melt when placed in a cup of hot tea), contains four parts bismuth, two parts lead, one part tin, one part cadmium.

Bison, a genus of wild cattle, distinguished from the ox by its shorter, wider skull, beard under the chin, high forequarters, and, in winter, a great mane of woolly hair covering head and forequarters. There are two species, the European and the American bison, both now protected in game preserves.

Bit, formerly the word often referred to the metal piece in the mouth of a bridled horse, now more likely to be a technical expression in the mouth of a computer expert. A bit is a unit of information; it is the information that can be conveyed by indicating which of two possibilities obtains. Any object that can be either of two states can therefore store one bit of information. In a technical device, the two states could be the presence or the absence of a magnetic field, or of an electric voltage. Since all numbers can be represented in the binary system (*see* Binary Notation) by a row of digits which are *either* 0 *or* 1, it takes one bit of information to specify a binary digit. Bit is short for binary digit.

Bittern, a bird of the heron genus, with long, loose plumage on the front and sides of the neck. It is a solitary bird inhabiting marshes, but rare in Britain.

Bivalves, shell-fish whose shell consists of two hinged valves, lying one on each side of the body, such as mussels, oysters, and cockles.

Blackbird, or Merle, a member of the Thrush family, a familiar song bird in Britain. Male is all-black with orange bill; female is mottled brown with brown bill; the young are spotted brown.

Blackcock and Greyhen (as the female is called) are closely related to the Capercaillies but smaller. They nest on the ground and prefer wooded country to open moors. Found in northern half of northern hemisphere. Polygamous, they perform excited courtship dances; the male is a handsome blue-black bird with white undertail, the female dark brown mottled.

Black Death, the plague which swept across Europe in the years 1848–50, beginning in the ports of Italy, brought in by merchant ships from Black Sea ports. It was the worst scourge man has ever known; at least a quarter of the European population was wiped out in the first epidemic of 1348. It reached England in the winter of that year. The disease was transmitted to man by fleas from black rats, though this was not known at the time, the specific organism being *Bacillus pestis*. The disease continued to ravage Europe in recurrent outbreaks up to the late 17th cent. The epidemic which raged in England in 1665 wiped out whole villages and one-tenth of London's population of 460,000. Samuel Pepys wrote a grim account of it in his *Diary*. *See also* Labourers, English Statute of.

Black Hole of Calcutta, the name given to the place where a captured British garrison was confined in 1756, during the struggle for India between the French and British. Into a noisome space, about 20 ft. square, 146 persons were driven and only 23 were found alive the next morning. The authenticity of the story has been called into question, but after sifting the evidence Professor H. H. Dodwell, in the *Cambridge History of the British Empire*, believes it to be substantially true.

Black-letter, the Old English or Gothic type first used in printing blocks.

Black Woodpecker (*Dryocopus martius*), a large, black bird about the size of a rook, with slightly crested scarlet crown, found in many parts of Europe.

Blenny, a group of marine fishes with spiny rays part of the fin running along the back. Several species are found around the British coast.

Blood Groups. *See* Index to Section P, *also* F50.

Bloody Assizes, the assizes, conducted in 1685 by George Jeffreys, Lord Chief Justice, at which participants in the Duke of Monmouth's rebellion against King James II. were tried. They were marked by relentless cruelty.

Bluebird, a migratory bird of North America, deriving its name from its deep blue plumage. It is one of the few song birds of America, and familiar in the woods from early spring to November. In India and Malaya there is the Fairy Blue-bird; the male is black with shiny blue upper parts. The bluebird was used as the symbol of happiness by Maeterlinck in his play *The Blue Bird*.

Blue Peter, a blue flag with a white square in the centre, is hoisted 24 hours before a ship leaves harbour (the letter P in the alphabet of the International Code of Signals).

Blue Ribbon, a term in general use to denote the highest honour or prize attainable in any field or competition. Thus the Derby is the blue ribbon of the turf. The expression is derived from the highest Order of Knighthood in the gift of the British Crown, the insignia of which is a garter of blue velvet.

Blue Stocking, a term used to describe a learned or literary woman, particularly if pedantic and undomesticated. It is said that the term derives from the Bas-Bleu club of Paris, which was attended by the literary savantes of the 17th cent. In England a similar literary club was formed about 1780, whose members were distinguished by their blue stockings.

"Blue" Sun, Moon, etc., a phenomenon caused by the scattering of sunlight by transparent particles suspended in the atmosphere, the effect being that blue light is transmitted and red light extinguished to direct vision. The dust from the Krakatoa eruption in 1883 and the drifting layer of smoke from the forest fires in Alberta, Canada, in September 1950 gave rise to "blue" moons and suns, phenomena sufficiently rare to be described as occurring "once in a blue moon." In the cold climatic conditions of the Pamirs and the far north, vegetation is said to look "blue" on account of the rays of high calorific value (red, yellow, green) being absorbed, while only the blue and violet are transmitted. It was Tyndall who first explained the blue colour of the sky.

Boa, a term applied to a family of snakes of large size, some attaining a length of 30 ft. They are not poisonous, but kill their prey by crushing —constriction—hence the name "boa constrictor." They occur both in the Old World and the New, but are more abundant in the latter. Most Boas retain the eggs within the body until young are fully developed, whereas the Pythons almost all lay leather-shelled eggs.

Boar, or Wild Hog, an animal largely distributed over the forest regions of Europe, Asia, Africa, and South America. It has a longer snout and shorter ears than its descendant the domestic hog, and is provided with tusks. Having to forage for itself, it is a more active and intelligent animal than the pig of the sty, and offers good sport to the hunter.

Boat, an open vessel, propelled by oars or sails, or both. The boats of a ship of war are the launch, barge, pinnace, yawl, cutters, jolly boat, and gig; of a merchant vessel, the launch, skiff, jolly boat or yawl, stern boat, quarter-boat, and captain's gig. Every ship is compelled to carry adequate, fully provisioned and equipped lifeboats.

Bode's Law, a numerical relationship formulated by Bode in 1772, which states that the relative mean distances of the planets from the sun are found by adding 4 to each of the terms 0, 3, 6, 12, 24, 48, 96. The actual mean distances (in millions of miles) are: Mercury, 36; Venus, 67·2; Earth, 92·9; Mars, 141·6; Jupiter, 483·3; Saturn, 886·0; Uranus, 1782·8. The gap between Mars and Jupiter caused Bode to predict the existence of a planet there, which was later confirmed by the discovery of Ceres and other minor planets. The law breaks down, however, for Neptune and Pluto.

Boer War, lasted from Oct. 11, 1899, when the Boers invaded Natal, to May 31, 1902, when the Treaty of Vereeniging ended hostilities. At first the operations of the British troops in

Cape Colony were unsuccessful and disastrous reverses were sustained. Lord Roberts was then sent out as Commander-in-Chief, with Lord Kitchener as Chief-of-Staff, and from February, 1900 when Kimberley was relieved and Cronje was compelled to surrender and Ladysmith and Mafeking were relieved, the struggle was practically over.

Boiling-point is the temperature at which a liquid boils. At that point the pressure of the vapour is equal to the pressure of the atmosphere. Under increased pressure the b. p. rises and under less pressure, as on the top of a mountain, it is lower. At standard atmospheric pressure (760 mm of mercury) the b.p. of water is 100°C; alcohol 78·4°C; ether 35·6°C.

Books, Sizes of. See Section N.

Books, Classification of. All libraries are classified to facilitate reference, but the favourite system is the Dewey Decimal System, which divides the whole field of knowledge into ten Main Classes: General Works; Philosophy; Religion; Sociology; Philology; Natural Science; Useful Arts and Applied Science; Fine Arts; Literature; History (including geography and travel and biography). Each of these Main Classes is again subdivided into ten main divisions. As an example: the main class of Sociology receives the number 300. This range 300 to 400 (the next main class) is graduated into tens, and Economics is 330. The range 330 to 340 is again graduated, and the subject of Labour and Capital is 331. This process is carried on by decimals so that 331·2 deals with Remuneration for Work, 331·22 with Wage Scales, and 331·225 with Extra Pay.

Borax (Sodium Pyroborate) is a white, soluble, crystalline salt. It is widely and diversely used, e.g., as a mild antiseptic, in glazing pottery, in soldering, in the making of pyrex glass, as a cleansing agent and sometimes as a food preservative. Borax occurs naturally in the salt lakes of Tibet, where it is called tincal, in California (Borax Lake, Death Valley), and elsewhere

Bore. In physical geography, an almost vertical wall of water which passes upstream along certain estuaries. Its formation requires special conditions of river flow, incoming high tide, and shape of river channel. It can be spectacular and dangerous on some rivers. In Britain the best known is the Severn bore which can be a few feet high and move at 10 or 12 m.p.h. In some parts of Britain the bore is called an eagre.

Boron. A metalloid element, symbol B. There are two forms, one crystalline, the other amorphous. It is not very abundant in nature but occurs in concentrated deposits. It is best known in boric acid, which is used as a mild antiseptic (called boracic acid) and borax (q.v.). Boron compounds are essential to some plants, e.g., beans. Used in the preparation of various special-purpose alloys, such as impact resistant steel. Compounds of boron and hydrogen are used as rocket fuels.

Borstal, an institution where young offenders between 15 and 21 on conviction may be sent for detention and reform. Emphasis is placed on vocational training in skilled trades. The Children and Young Persons Act 1969 makes provision for the minimum age to be raised to 17, if and when the Home Secretary makes an order to that effect. The first was opened in 1902 at the village of Borstal, near Rochester in Kent.

Boston Tea Party, an incident which occurred on Dec. 17, 1773, on board some tea-ships in Boston Harbour. High taxation imposed by the British Parliament under George III. had caused bitter feelings, and instigated by popular meetings, a party of citizens, disguised as Indians, boarded the tea-ships and threw the tea overboard. This incident was a prelude to the American War of Independence (1775–83).

Bounds Beating, an old Anglo-Saxon custom. The parish clergyman and officials go round the parish boundaries accompanied by boys who beat the boundary stones with long sticks of willow. The ceremony takes place on the Rogation days preceding Ascension Day.

Bourgeoisie, a term used by Marxists to indicate those who do not, like the proletariat, live by the sale of their labour. They include, on the one hand, industrialists and financiers or mem-

bers of the liberal professions and, on the other, small artisans and shop-keepers who, although their standard of living may not be appreciably higher (and today is often lower) than that of the proletariat, are described as the "petty bourgeoisie." According to the Marxist view of history, the bourgeoisie arose with modern industrialism after it had overthrown the old feudal aristocracy and replaced it as ruling class.

Bow, an instrument for propelling arrows, and, in the days when it was a weapon of war, was usually made of yew or ash, and was about 6 ft. long, with an arrow 3 ft. long. It was the weapon with which Crécy, Poitiers, and Agincourt were won. The cross-bow was Italian and was adopted in France, but did not become popular in Britain.

Bow Bells is the peal of the London church of St. Mary-le-Bow, Cheapside, within sound of which one must be born to be entitled to be called a "cockney." Bow Bells had not been heard since 1939, but they once again rang out over the City of London on Dec. 20, 1961.

Bowdlerize, to expurgate a book. Derived from Thomas Bowdler (1754–1825), the editor of the Family Shakespeare, in which "those words and expressions are omitted which cannot with propriety be read aloud in a family." He treated Gibbon's History of the Decline and Fall of the Roman Empire in the same way, omitting "all passages of an irreligious and immoral tendency." Such prudery met with ridicule and hence the words "bowdlerism," "bowdlerist," etc.

Power Bird, native to Australia and New Guinea and related to the Bird of Paradise, though often less striking in appearance. In the mating season the male builds a "bower" of sticks and grasses for courtship displays and as a playground. The Gardener Bower Bird of Papua makes a lawn in front of his bower and adorns it with bright coloured pebbles and flowers which are replaced as they wither. The female builds her nest away from the bower.

Boycott, a term used in connection with a person that the general body of people, or a party or society, refuse to have dealings with. Originally used when Captain Boycott (1832–97) was made the victim of a conspiracy by the Irish Land League which prevented him making any purchases or holding any social intercourse in his district. He had incurred the League's hostility by a number of evictions.

Brass, an exceedingly useful alloy of copper and zinc. Much brass is about two-thirds copper, but different proportions give different properties. It is harder than copper and easily worked. Brass in the Bible (Matt. x, 9) probably refers to bronze.

Breadfruit Tree (Artocarpus altilis), a native of the South Sea Islands; the fruits are a brownish green, about the size of a melon, and contain a white pulpy substance which is roasted before being eaten. The tree grows 40 ft. or more. Captain Bligh's ship Bounty was on a voyage to Jamaica carrying a cargo of 1,000 breadfruit trees when the mutiny occurred.

Breeder Reactor, a kind of nuclear reactor (q.v.) which besides producing energy by the fission process also produces (" breeds ") more nuclear fuel at the same time. A typical reaction is: a neutron induces fission of a U-235 nucleus which breaks up into two medium-sized nuclei and some neutrons; one of the latter then enters a U-238 nucleus turning it into U-239 which then decays radioactively via neptunium into plutonium which is useful fuel. There are technical problems in breeder reactors which have delayed their practical use but the "breeding" principle is so valuable that experiments have gone on for many years in, e.g., Scotland and Idaho, and breeder reactors will no doubt increase in importance the more the supply of natural nuclear fuel appears to become depleted.

Breviary (Lat. breviarium=abridgment), the short prayer-book of the Roman Catholic Church which gives the Divine Office, i.e., the canonical hours or services. The directions for Mass are in the Missal. The modern Roman breviary is a reformed version of the 11th-cent. breviary and was produced by Pope Pius V. in 1568 in response to a decree of the Council of Trent. All Roman Catholic priests are required to recite the whole of the breviary services allotted for each day. *See also* **Matins.**

Bridges are structures for continuing a road, railway, or canal across a river, valley, ravine, or a road or railway at a lower level. From early times bridges were made of timber, stone, or brick, and it was not until the 19th cent. that wrought- and cast-iron were used. Today the materials mostly used are steel and reinforced concrete. Among the most famous of ancient bridges is that of S. Angelo at Rome, built by Hadrian as the Pons Aelius, A.D. 134. The Rialto bridge at Venice dates from 1588. The Ponte Santa Trinita at Florence, one of the finest Renaissance bridges and deemed the most beautiful in the world, was destroyed by German mines in 1944 but has now been reconstructed just as it was before. The first stone bridge across the Thames was begun in 1176. It had 19 arches and was lined with houses and stood until 1831 when it was replaced by the granite bridge designed by Sir John Rennie. By 1972 this will have been replaced by a new three-span concrete bridge with a six-lane carriageway and two footways. The first cast-iron bridge was at Ironbridge, Madeley, Shropshire, built in 1779 and now in need of repair. Telford's Menai suspension bridge (1825) has since been enlarged but the original design has been maintained. Another example of Britain's supremacy in constructional iron-work was Robert Stephenson's tubular bridge across the Menai Straits (1850), the prototype of all modern plate girder railway bridges. Other famous bridges are the Niagara (suspension), Forth railway bridge (cantilever), London Tower bridge (suspension), Tay railway bridge, Victoria Jubilee bridge across the St. Lawrence at Montreal (an open steel structure), Sydney Harbour bridge, Lower Zambesi bridge, Storstrom bridge in Denmark, Howrah bridge at Calcutta, with the third largest cantilever span in the world, the Volta bridge of Ghana and the Auckland Harbour bridge, both built in recent years, the Verrazano-Narrows bridge spanning New York's harbour from Brooklyn to Staten I., exceeding by 60 ft. the centre span of San Francisco's Golden Gate bridge. Britain is engaged in the largest bridge building programme for over a century. The road suspension bridge across the Firth of Forth, completed in 1964, has the largest single span in Europe (3,300 ft.). The Medway bridge, completed in 1963, is one of the largest pre-stressed concrete structures in the world. The Severn suspension bridge (from which the design principles for the new bridge across the Bosphorus were taken) and the Tay road bridge were completed in 1966, the Tinsley viaduct, near Sheffield, was opened in 1986.

Britannia Metal, an alloy of tin, antimony, and copper, harder than pure tin, corrosion-resistant, used for teapots, and jugs (often electroplated).

British Association for the Advancement of Science, The, was founded in 1831 by a group of British scientists under the leadership of Charles Babbage (1792–1871) to stimulate scientific inquiry and promote research in the interest of the nation. Its meetings are held annually in different cities of the United Kingdom. It is divided into sections which include the chief physical and biological sciences, economics, anthropology and archaeology, psychology and education, engineering, forestry, agriculture, and there is also a division for studying the social and international relations of science. The 1971 meeting was to take place in Leicester under the presidency of Sir Alexander Cairncross.

British Museum, was created by an Act of Parliament in 1753, when the Sir Hans Sloane collection, which the British Government had acquired for £20,000, was added to the Cottonian Library and the Harleian Manuscripts. It was opened to the public in 1759 at Montagu House, Bloomsbury. The acquisition of the library of George III. (now known as the King's Library) in 1823 made larger premises necessary, and the present building in Great Russell Street was completed in 1847 from designs by Sir Robert Smirke. The great domed Reading Room was opened in 1857, and the Natural History Department was transferred to South Kensington in the eighties. As a museum it is perhaps the

most famous in the world, since, apart from its colossal library of books and manuscripts, it has many priceless collections of sculptures, antiquities, prints and drawings, coins and medals. *See also* **Libraries.**

British Railways. The name under which the railways of Britain were unified on January 1, 1948. Instead of the former four main railway systems six regions were formed: London Midland region (former L.M.S.R.) Western (former G.W.R.), Southern (formerly S.R.), Eastern (southern area of former L.N.E.R.), N.E. region (N.E. of former L.N.E.R.), Scottish region (Scottish system of the former L.M.S.R. and L.N.E.R.). The most far-reaching change in the modernisation and re-equipment programme since 1955 has been the replacement of steam traction by electric and diesel locomotives. Under the chairmanship of Lord (then Dr.) Richard Beeching the British Railways Board planned a viable railway system by closing uneconomic branch lines, by developing new services on the liner train principle, and by utilising a more limited trunk route system. Under the Labour Government an integrated system of transport was worked out, embracing rail, road, canals, shipping, etc., itself integrated in the pattern of the country's social and economic needs. A 11,000-mile basic network was fixed (8,000 route miles previously proposed), with a further 2,500 miles under review. Unremunerative services necessary on social grounds were to receive a Government subsidy. The name was changed to British Rail in 1964.

British Standard Time, The British Standard Time Act of 1968 put Britain an hour ahead of Greenwich Mean Time (GMT) throughout the year for an experimental 3 years. This brought Britain into line with countries in Western Europe where Central European Time is observed. In 1970 Parliament called for the restoration of the previous position—BST in the summer months and GMT in the winter months—as from 31 Oct. 1971.

Brocken-spectre or **Glory.** The series of coloured rings which an observer sees around the shadow of his own head (or an aeroplane in which he is travelling) as cast upon a bank of mist or thin cloud. This effect is produced by reflection and refraction of sunlight in minute water-droplets in the air just as in a rainbow.

Bromine. A non-metal element, symbol Br, member of the halogen family (*q.v.*). It is a red, evil-smelling liquid (Greek *bromos*, a stink). It is an abundant element. In the U.S.A. bromide is extracted from sea-water on a large scale. It unites readily with many other elements, the products being termed bromides. Its derivatives with organic compounds are used in synthetic chemistry. Bromoform is a liquid resembling chloroform. Bromides are used in medicine to calm excitement.

Bronze is primarily an alloy of copper and tin, and was one of the earliest alloys known, the Bronze Age in the evolution of tool-using man coming between the Stone Age and the Iron Age. Some modern bronzes contain zinc or lead also, and a trace of phosphorus is present in " phosphor-bronze."

Bubble Chamber. An instrument used by physicists to reveal the tracks of fast fundamental particles (*e.g.*, those produced in large accelerating machines) in a form suitable for photography; closely related to the Wilson cloud chamber (*q.v.*), but the particles leave trails of small bubbles in a superheated liquid (often liquid hydrogen) instead of droplets of liquid in a supersaturated gas; invented in 1952 by the American physicist, Dr. D. Glaser, Nobel Prizeman, 1960, and developed by Prof. L. W. Alvarez, Univ. of California, Nobel Prizeman, 1968.

Buckingham Palace, London residence of British sovereigns since 1837. Originally built for the Duke of Buckingham (1703); bought by George III. in 1762 and remodelled by Nash 1825–36.

Buddhism. *See* **J8.**

Bulk Purchase. Arrangements for bulk purchase involve undertakings by a country, or by some agency within it, to buy from another country specified quantities of its products, either at prices fixed in advance or with provision for adjusting the prices at specified intervals to take account of general price movements. Such long-term arrangements may be, but need not be, combined with undertakings by the seller to buy specified quantities, or specified values, of the products of the purchasing country in exchange. The purpose of bulk-purchase arrangements is, on the one hand, to provide the seller of the goods in question with assured markets and, on the other, to assure the buyers of needed supplies of their goods.

Buntings, name of a group of finches, seed-eating birds, usually found in open country. The Yellowhammer, Reed Bunting, Corn Bunting, and Cirl Bunting are resident in Britain; the Snow Bunting (which breeds in small numbers in Scotland) and Lapland Bunting are regular winter visitors, and the Ortolan is among the rare visitors.

Butane, a colourless inflammable gas made of carbon and hydrogen; formula C_4H_{10}. Found in natural gas and made as a by-product of oil refining. Butane, like propane (q.v.), can easily be liquefied and moved safely in cans and tanks. It is thus useful as a "portable gas supply"; also used in internal combustion fuels.

Byzantine Art developed in the eastern part of the Roman empire after Constantine founded the city of Constantinople (A.D. 330). It has many sources—Greek, Syrian, Egyptian, and Islamic —and reached its zenith in the reign of Justinian (527–65). The major art form was ecclesiastical architecture, the basic plan of which was Roman—either basilican (symmetrical about an axis) or centralised (symmetrical about a point). Arched construction was developed, and the dome became the most typical feature, although, unlike the Roman dome which was placed on a round apartment, the Byzantine dome was placed on a square one on independent pendentives. Frequently small domes were clustered round a large one as in the case of the great church of Santa Sophia (537), the climax of Byzantine architecture. Usually the churches were small and include those of SS. Sergius and Bacchus, Sta. Irene (in Constantinople), S. Vitale in Ravenna, and the much later and larger St. Mark's in Venice. Byzantine art also took the form of miniatures, enamels, jewels, and textiles, but mosaics, frescos, and icons (q.v.) are its greatest treasures.

C

Cacao, *Theobroma cacao,* is an evergreen tree, from 15 to 20 ft. high, growing abundantly in tropical America, West Africa, the West Indies, Ceylon, etc., yielding seeds, called cocoa beans, from which cocoa and chocolate are manufactured. The fruit is 7–10 in. long, hard and ridged; inside are the beans, covered with a reddish-brown skin, which are first fermented, then dried. The trees mature at five to eight years and produce two crops a year.

Cactus, a family of flowering plants numbering about a thousand species adapted to living in very dry situations. The stem is usually fleshy, being composed of succulent tissue, remarkably retentive of water; commonly equipped with sharp thorns which deter animals from eating them. The roots are generally very long, tapping soil water over large area; a "prickly pear" cactus may have roots covering a circular area 25 ft. or more in diameter. The leaves are commonly insignificant or absent, and the stem takes over the photosynthetic leaf function and becomes accordingly flattened to expose greater area to sunlight and air. In some kinds of cactus (e.g. *Echinocactus*) the stem is shaped almost like a sea-urchin.

Cadmium. A metallic element, symbol Cd, chemically similar to zinc and mercury. Used in alloys to lower the melting point, as in Wood's metal with bismuth and tin. Alloyed with copper to make electric cables. Like zinc, it is a protective metal and is used in electro-plating. The cadmium-vapour lamp gives a characteristic frequency used in measuring wavelength.

Caesium, also spelt Cesium, is an alkali metal element, symbol Cs, in first group of the periodic table. It resembles rubidium and potassium and was discovered by Bunsen and Kirchhoff in 1860. It was the first element whose existence was discovered spectroscopically. The caesium atom consists of a heavy nucleus surrounded by 55 electrons, 54 of which are arranged in stable orbits, and one of which, known as the valency electron, is in a less stable orbit surrounding them. Used in the construction of photo-electric cells and as an accurate time standard (atomic clock).

Calcium, a silvery-white metallic element, symbol Ca. It melts at 810° C. and is very reactive. It was discovered by Sir Humphry Davy in 1808, but not until 1898 was it obtained pure, by Moissan. Does not occur as metal in nature, but calcium compounds make up a large part of the earth's crust. Most important calcium sources are marble, limestone, chalk (all three are, chemically, calcium carbonate); dolomite, which is the double carbonate of calcium and magnesium; gypsum, a hydrated calcium sulphate; calcium phosphate and calcium fluoride. Igneous rocks contain much calcium silicate. Calcium compounds are essential to plants and are used in fertilisers. Animals require calcium and phosphorus for bone and teeth formation; deficiency is treated by administration of calcium phosphate. Strontium is chemically similar to calcium, and the radio-active strontium 90 from atomic "fall-out" is therefore easily assimilated by the body.

Calendar, a collection of tables showing the days and months of the year, its astronomical recurrences, chronological references, etc. The Julian Calendar, with its leap year, introduced by Julius Cæsar, fixed the average length of the year at 365¼ days, which was about 11 minutes too long (the earth completes its orbit in 365 days 5 hours 48 minutes 46 seconds of mean solar time). The cumulative error was rectified by the Gregorian Calendar, introduced in Italy in 1582, whereby century years do not count as leap years unless divisible by 400. This is the rule we now follow. England did not adopt the reformed calendar until 1752, when she found herself 11 days behind the Continent.

Calends, the first day of the month in the Roman calendar, when interest fell due, and proclamations as to the order of days were made.

Calorie. Unit of quantity of heat. The "small" or fundamental calorie is the amount of heat required to raise the temperature of 1 gram of water from 14·5 to 15·5 °C. This is the gram-calorie used in physics and chemistry. The large Calorie (written with a capital C), commonly used in nutritional connotations, is equal to 1000 small calories and is called the kilogram-calorie.

Calvinism. *See* **J9.**

Calypso, West Indian song in the form of a doggerel lampoon composed spontaneously and sung to a guitar.

Cambridge University had a sufficiently good teaching reputation to attract Oxford students in 1209, when lectures at their own university were suspended. In 1226 it had a Chancellor who was recognised by King and Pope. The first college to be founded was Peterhouse in 1284. The university was reorganised and granted a Charter of Incorporation by an act of Elizabeth in 1571. The colleges with their dates of foundation are Christ's (1505), Churchill (1960), Clare (1326), Clare Hall (1966), Corpus Christi (1352), Darwin (1964), Downing (1800), Emmanuel (1584), Fitzwilliam (1966), Gonville and Caius (1348), Jesus (1496), King's (1441), Magdalene (1542), Pembroke (1347), Peterhouse (1284), Queens' (1448), St. Catharine's (1473), St. Edmund's House (1896), St. John's (1511), Selwyn (1882), Sidney Sussex (1596), Trinity (1546), Trinity Hall (1350), University (1966). The women's colleges are: Girton (1869), Newnham (1875), New Hall (1954), Hughes Hall (formerly Cambridge T.C.) (1885), and Lucy Cavendish Collegiate Society (1965) (for women research students and other graduates). Women were admitted to degrees (though not allowed to sit for examination) in 1920, and to full membership of the University in 1948.

Camel, a large ruminant quadruped, inhabiting Asia and Africa, where it is largely used as a beast of burden. There are two species—the Arabian camel or dromedary, with only one hump; and the Bactrian, or double-humped camel. There are no wild dromedaries, and the only wild bactrians occur in the Gobi Desert. The camel is able to go for long periods without water, not, as was formerly believed, because it stored water in its hump, but because of the unique mechanism of its physiology which enables it to conserve water at the expense of not sweating until 104° F. is reached.

Campanile, or bell-tower, is separate from but usually adjoining its parent church. The most famous are in Italy. Giotto's tower at Florence, adjoining the cathedral of Santa Maria dei Fiore, is architecturally the finest in the world. Others are at Cremona, the loftiest in Italy (364 ft.) and Pisa (the leaning tower). The magnificent pointed campanile of St. Mark's, Venice, which collapsed in 1902 and has since been rebuilt in its original form, was begun in 902.

Canal, an artificial watercourse used for navigation which changes its level by means of locks. The completion of the Bridgewater Canal in 1761 to take coal from Worsley to Manchester marked the beginning of canal building in industrial Britain. There are some 2,500 miles of navigable inland waterways in Great Britain today, 1,850 miles of which are under the control of the British Waterways Board set up by the Transport Act, 1962. The English network is based on the four great estuaries Mersey, Humber, Severn, and Thames. Under the Transport Act, 1968, the Board is enabled to maintain an extensive network of amenity waterways.

Canary, a light, sweet wine from the Canaries and chief export until the grape blight of 1853. Much consumed in Britain from Tudor to Georgian times. Also, a cage bird. *See* Z22.

Candela, unit of luminous intensity, symbol cd (N8). An idea of the value which this unit represents may be gained from the fact that light obtained from a 40 W filament-type electric lamp or bulb is approximately the same as would be given by a point source of luminous intensity 30 cd.

Candlemas, an English and Roman Church festival in celebration of the Purification of the Virgin Mary. The date is February 2.

Canon, a term applied to signify a recognised rule for the guide of conduct in matters legal, ecclesiastical, and artistic, or an authoritative ordinance: thus we have Canonical Scriptures, Canon Law, etc. A Canon is also a dignitary of the Church, usually a member of a cathedral chapter in the Anglican communion, or in the Roman Church a member of an order standing between regular monks and secular clergy.

Canonical Hours were seven in number in the Western Church; Matins and Lauds, before dawn; Prime, early morning service; Terce, 9 a.m.; Sext, noon; Nones 3 p.m.; Vespers, 4 p.m.; Compline, bed-time.

Canonisation, the entering of one of the faithful departed on the list of saints of the Roman Catholic Church. The rules governing canonisation were simplified by papal decree in 1969. The forty English martyrs, of whom Edmund Campion was one, executed between 1535 and 1679 and beatified long ago, were canonised in 1970. Beatification, by which a person is called blessed, is usually followed by canonisation, but not necessarily.

Canticles, the name given to the scriptural passages from the Bible sung by the congregation in the various Christian liturgies. They are the *Benedicite*, *Benedictus*, *Magnificat*, *Nunc Dimittis*.

Capercaillie, the largest of the grouse family, found in the Scottish highlands and the pine forests and mountainous regions of Northern and Central Europe and Asia.

Capet, the family name of the royal house of France, founded by Hugh Capet in 987, with its collateral branches. The main line of the dynasty came to an end in 1328 with the death of Charles IV when the throne passed to the related house of Valois. The direct Valois line ended in 1498 with the death of Charles VIII. The first of the Bourbon line was Henry IV whose descendants ruled France (except during the French Revolution and the Napoleonic era) until 1848.

Capitalism. *See* J9.

Capuchins are members of a mendicant order of Franciscans, founded in the 16th cent. with the aim of restoring the primitive and stricter observance of the rule of St. Francis, so called

from the capuce or pointed cowl worn by them.

Carat, a term used in assessing the value of gold and precious stones. In connection with gold, it represents the proportion of pure gold contained in any gold alloy, and for this purpose the metal is divided into 24 parts. Thus 24-carat indicates pure gold, and any lesser number of carats shows the proportion of gold contained in the alloy. The carat as a measure of weight is now obsolete, having been replaced by the *metric carat* of 0·2 grams.

Caravan, a band of travellers or traders journeying together for safety across the Eastern deserts, sometimes numbering many hundreds. There are several allusions to caravans in the Old Testament. The great caravan routes of this period from Egypt to Babylon and from Palestine to Yemen linked up with the Syrian ports and so with western sea commerce. Many wars have been fought in the past over their control.

Carbohydrates. *See* P40, F23.

Carbon, a non-metallic chemical element which occurs in crystalline form as diamonds and graphite; amorphous forms of carbon include charcoal and soot, while coke consists mainly of elementary carbon. The biochemistry of plants and animals largely hinges upon carbon compounds. The study of carbon compounds is called Organic Chemistry. **Carbon 14.** A radioactive isotope of carbon, with a half-life c. 6,000 years, used in following the path of compounds and their assimilation in the body. Also used in determination of the age of carbon-containing materials such as trees, fossils, and very old documents. *See* F24.

Carbonari, members of a secret political society originated in Naples, and at one time very numerous. Their chief aim was to free Italy from foreign rule, and they exerted considerable influence in the various revolutionary movements in the first half of the 19th cent. Their name was adopted from the charcoal-burners (*carbonari*), and their passwords, signs, etc., were all in the phraseology of the fraternity.

Carbon dioxide. Commonest of the oxides of carbon. It is formed when carbon and its compounds are burnt with abundant supply of air, and when carbon compounds are oxidised in the respiration process of animals. The atmosphere contains carbon dioxide to the extent of about three parts in 10,000; this figure remains more or less constant because, while carbon dioxide is always being added by animal respiration and the burning of fuels, such as coal and oil by man, plants are constantly removing it in the process known as photosynthesis (F28) or carbon assimilation.

Carbon monoxide is a colourless gas with no taste or smell. It is formed when coal and coke are burnt with a restricted supply of air; the blue flame to be seen in a coke brazier, for instance, is the flame of carbon monoxide. This gas is very poisonous, forming with the haemoglobin of the blood a compound which is useless for respiration and cherry red in colour which gives a visible symptom of poisoning by carbon monoxide. With nickel it forms a volatile compound, called nickel carbonyl, and this reaction is the basis of the Mond process for extracting nickel.

Cardinal, one of the chief dignitaries of the Roman Catholic Church who constitute the Pope's council, or Sacred College, and when the papal chair is vacant elect a Pope from among themselves. There are three orders: cardinal bishops, members of the Roman Curia (the central administration of the Church) and bishops of sees near Rome; cardinal deacons, also members of the Curia, holding titular bishoprics; and cardinal priests who exercise pastoral duties over sees removed from Rome, though some are members of the Curia. Their numbers were fixed by Pope Sixtus V in 1586 at 6, 14, and 50 respectively. Both Pope John XXIII and Pope Paul VI increased the number and since 1969 there have been 136, the highest number in the history of the Church. Their insignia was trimmed of embellishment by papal decree in 1969 with the abolition of the famous red hat (the galero) and the shoes with buckles. Cardinals must now retire at 80.

Cardinal Virtues, according to Plato these were justice, prudence, temperance, fortitude—

natural virtues as distinct from the *theological* virtues of the Roman Catholic Church, faith, hope, charity. The phrase " seven cardinal virtues," combining the two, figures in mediæval literature. *See* Sins, Seven Deadly.

Carmelites, a body of mendicant friars taking their name from Mount Carmel, where the order was first established in the 12th cent. The original rule of the order required absolute poverty, abstinence from meat and a hermit life. The rigidity of the rule of the order was mitigated by Innocent IV. They wear a brown habit with white mantle, hence their name of White Friars. The order of Carmelite nuns was instituted in the 15th cent.

Carolingians, dynasty of Frankish rulers founded in the 7th cent. The family was at its height when represented by Charlemagne. It ruled, with interruptions, until 987 when the Capetian dynasty succeeded.

Carp, a well-known fresh-water fish, found in plenty in most European and Asiatic still waters; reaches a length of about 2 ft., and under favourable conditions lives for about 40 years. Familiar British members of the family are the roach, rudd, dace, chub, gudgeon, tench, minnow, barbel, bream and bleak. The goldfish, popular in ornamental ponds, is the domesticated variety of a Far Eastern member of the carp family.

Carthusians, an order of monks founded in 1084 by St. Bruno at the Grande Chartreuse near Grenoble, and introduced into England about a century later. They built the Charterhouse (corruption of Chartreuse) in London in 1371. The chief characteristics of the order are a separate dwelling-house in the precincts of the charterhouse for each monk, and the general assembly in the Church twice in the day and once at night. They wear a white habit, with white scapular and hood. The liqueur *Chartreuse* was invented by the order and is still their secret. For many years they have derived large revenues from its sale. The order of Carthusian nuns was founded in the 12th cent.

Casein, the chief protein in milk and cheese. It is coagulated by the action of rennet or acid. An important class of plastics (" casein plastics ") are produced from it, and these plastics are converted into buttons, knitting-needles, etc. 8000 gallons of milk yield about a ton of casein.

Cassowary, a genus of ostrich-like birds which, together with the emu, form a separate order found only in Australasia. All species are black, with brightly coloured necks, and with a horny crest on the head. Noted for fleetness.

Castor-oil Plant (*Ricinus communis*), an African shrub now cultivated in most tropical countries. It has broad palmate leaves and bears a spiny fruit containing seeds which when pressed yield the well-known oil.

Cat, the general name for all members of the class *Felidae* of the carnivorous order, from the lion down to the domestic cat. The latter is believed to be descended from the European and African wild cats. Egypt is credited with having been the first country in which the cat was domesticated. *See* Z9–12.

Catabolism, Anabolism, are the terms used to describe the two types of metabolic pathway. Catabolic pathways are routes by which large organic molecules are broken up by enzymes into their simpler constituents *e.g.*, starch into glucose. The anabolic pathways are the routes by which complex molecules are synthesised from simple sub-units, *e.g.*, proteins from amino acids.

Catalyst. A substance which speeds up a chemical reaction without being changed itself. Various aluminium and titanium compounds are catalysts in the formation of polythene from ethylene. Palladium catalyses the reaction of hydrogen with oxygen (hence its use in gas lighters). Enzymes in the body hasten the breakdown of carbohydrates and proteins by catalytic action. *See* F24(2).

Cataracts are gigantic waterfalls. The most famous are those of Niagara in North America, the Orinoco in South America, the Victoria Falls on the Zambesi in Africa, the Falls of the Rhine at Schaffhausen, and the Cascade of Gavarni in the Pyrenees.

Catechism, an elementary book of principles in any

science or art, but more particularly in religion, in the form of questions and answers. There is a great variety of these, including the Lutheran, prepared by Luther in 1529, Calvin's Geneva (in 1536), and the Anglican, in the Book of Common Prayer.

Catenary, the name of the curve taken up by a flexible uniform chain or clothes line supported at its two ends.

Caterpillar, the larva of a butterfly or moth, worm-like in its segmented body, with 3 pairs of jointed true legs often curiously marked and coloured, and frequently more or less hairy.

Cathedral, the chief church of a diocese, so called from its containing a Bishop's seat, or episcopal chair. The town in which it is situated is a cathedral city. Some celebrated cathedrals are St. John Lateran of Rome, Notre Dame of Paris, the cathedrals of Cologne and Milan, St. Paul's in London, Canterbury Cathedral, York Minster, and the cathedrals of Durham, Bristol, Gloucester, Peterborough, Exeter, Liverpool, and Coventry (destroyed by bombs, now rebuilt).

Catholicism. *See* J9.

Cat's-eye, a kind of quartz, much valued as a gem, opalescent, and of various shades.

Cavalier, a name adopted during the troubles of the Civil War to designate the Royalist party; it is also used generally in reference to a knightly, gallant, or imperious personage.

Caves, natural hollow places in the earth, frequently found in Carboniferous limestone areas. The underground caves are formed by the action of rainwater carrying carbon dioxide, a dilute acid which slowly attacks the limestone rocks. The main caves in the British Isles are in the Mendips, Derbyshire, Yorkshire, S. Wales, and in County Clare. The floods of Sept. 1968 moved masses of debris in some of the British caves, redistributing it in a major way; new routes were blocked and old passages reopened. The scientific study of caves is known as speleology.

Cedar, a dark-leaved, cone-bearing, horizontal-branched evergreen tree that grows to a considerable height and girth, the best known species in Britain being the Cedar of Lebanon, which was introduced in the 17th cent.

Celluloid, one of the first synthetic thermoplastic materials, discovered by Alexander Parkes in 1865 when he was attempting to produce synthetic horn. It is made by treating cellulose nitrate with camphor and alcohol. Photographic film is made of a similar, but less-inflammable material, formed by the use of cellulose acetate instead of the nitrate.

Cellulose, a carbohydrate, and a constituent of nearly all plants. Cellulose occurs in an almost pure state in the fibres of linen (flax), absorbent cotton, jute, and filter-paper (used in laboratories).

Celsius was an 18th cent. Swedish scientist (B13) after whom the modern Celsius temperature scale is named. Since 1954, $^{\circ}C$ stands for " degree Celsius " instead of " degree Centigrade " but this is only a change in name. Both symbols refer to the temperature scale which calls the melting point of ice $0^{\circ}C$ and the boiling point of water at one atmosphere pressure $100^{\circ}C$. *See* Absolute Temperature.

Celts, an ancient race of W. Europe, originally from southern Germany (2nd millennium B.C.), united by a common language and culture, who spread westward into Spain, northward into Britain, eastward to the Black Sea, reaching Galicia in Asia Minor. The " La Tène " iron age Celts invaded Britain 250 B.C. After Britain was conquered by the Romans and invaded by the Angles and Saxons there remained as areas of Celtic speech only Wales (Brythonic speakers), Ireland, Scotland, Isle of Man (Gaelic speakers). The late Celtic period in Britain produced a distinctive Christian art (*e.g.*, the Lindisfarne Gospel *c.* 700, and the Irish Book of Kells, dating from about the same time).

Centrifuge, a machine which produces large accelerations by utilising the radial force caused by rotating a body about a fixed centre. Centrifuges have found extensive application in modern science. They can be used for the separation of one size of particle from another (for this use in biochemistry see F20) or in the training of astronauts where the accelerations occurring during rocket lift-off can be simulated in a centrifuge on the ground.

Ceramics, are substances in which a combination of one or more metals with oxygen confers special and valuable properties. These include hardness, and resistance to heat and chemicals. Ceramic comes from the Greek word for pottery, and pottery materials of mud and clay were probably the first man-made ceramics. Nowadays the range is enormous and growing; apart from all the pottery materials, there are fire-bricks, gems, glasses, concretes, nuclear reactor fuel elements, special materials for electronic devices, coloured pigments, electrical insulators, abrasives, and many other things. The scientific study of ceramics is part of materials science (*see* Materials Science). The need to design ceramic objects has inspired great art, and the production of ceramics is a major industry.

Cerium, a scarce metallic element discovered by Berzelius in 1803. A mixture of cerium and thorium nitrates is used in the manufacture of gas mantles, which owe their incandescent property to the deposit of cerium and thorium oxide with which they are coated.

Chain reaction. *See* F12(1).

Chalcedony, a mixture of crystalline silica and amorphous hydrated silica, *i.e.,* of quartz and opal. It has a waxy lustre, and is much used by jewellers for necklaces, bracelets, etc. Commonly it is white or creamy. Its bright orange-red variety is called carnelian; its brown variety, sard. Chrysoprase, plasma, bloodstone are varieties which are respectively pale apple-green dark leek-green, green with red spots.

Chalk, a white limestone, calcium carbonate, found in the Upper Cretaceous deposits (formed from the shells of minute marine organisms). In southern England the chalk is a soft rock, but in Yorkshire, Scotland, and Ireland it is solid limestone. French chalk is hydrated magnesium silicate, a variety of talc.

Chamberlain, Lord, the senior officer of The Royal Household who is responsible for all ceremonial within the palace (levées, courts, garden parties, entertainment of foreign royalties and heads of state) but not the coronation or state opening of parliament. He is also in charge of appointments to The Royal Household. His office as censor of plays was abolished in 1968.

Chamberlain, Lord Great, one of the great officers of state whose duties are now mainly ceremonial. He attends the monarch at the state opening of parliament and at the coronation and is custodian of the Palace of Westminster (Houses of Parliament). The office is hereditary, dating from Norman times, and is held for one reign in turn by the descendants of the De Veres, Earls of Oxford.

Chameleon, a family of lizards with numerous species. Their ability to change colour is well known, but exaggerated, and is due to the movement of pigment cells beneath the skin. They are slow in movement, arboreal, and mainly insectivorous. Found in Africa, India, Ceylon, Madagascar, and Arabia.

Chamois, a species of antelope, native of Western Europe and Asia. About the size of a goat, it lives in mountainous regions, and possesses wonderful leaping power, so that it is very difficult to capture. Its flesh is much esteemed, and from its skin chamois leather is made, although to-day sheep and goat skins are usually substituted. The mating season is Oct.–Nov. and the fawns are born in May or June. Live to be 20–25 years old.

Channel Tunnel, a scheme to bore a tunnel through 20–30 miles of chalk under the sea between Dover and Calais has been a subject for discussion ever since Albert Mathieu first conceived the idea as a practical possibility in 1802. In the 1830s proposals for a bridge were made. Investigations have been undertaken from time to time, the most recent being that of the Channel Tunnel Group, composed of British, French, and American interests, which was set up in 1957. In 1964 it was announced that the British and French Governments had decided in principle to go ahead with a rail tunnel, thus accepting the recommendations of the Anglo-French study group published in 1963. In 1968 the Minister of Transport said that if studies confirmed the case for the tunnel, it should be possible to complete it by 1976. It is to be financed by private capital but operated by a Franco-British public authority. Estimated cost (1968) £300 million. The ferry terminal is expected to be at Cheriton, the passenger terminal near Saltwood, both near Folkestone, and the freight terminal at Stanford or Sevington, both situated between Folkestone and Ashford.

Chapel Royal, the church dedicated to the use of the Sovereign and Court. There are, among others, chapels royal at St. James's Palace, Buckingham Palace, Windsor, Hampton Court, the Tower, and Holyrood. *See also* E4(2).

Characterology. *See* J9.

Charcoal, a term applied to wood that has been subjected to a process of slow smothered combustion. More generally it refers to the carbonaceous remains of vegetable, animal, or combustible mineral substances submitted to a similar process. Charcoal from special woods (in particular buckthorn) is used in making gunpowder. Bone charcoal finds use in sugar refining, as it removes dark colouring matter present in the crude syrup.

Chasuble, a sleeveless vestment worn by ecclesiastics over the alb during the celebration of Mass. It is supposed to symbolise the seamless coat of Christ.

Cheese, an article of food made from the curd of milk, which is separated from the whey and pressed in moulds and gradually dried. There are about 500 varieties differing with method of preparation and quality of milk. They used to be made in the regions after which they are named but nowadays many of them are mass-produced, *e.g.,* Cheddar is made not only in all parts of Britain but in Canada, New Zealand, Australia, Holland, and the U.S.A. Cheeses may be divided into 3 main classes: (1) soft, *e.g.,* Camembert, Cambridge, Port l'Evêque; (2) blue-veined, *e.g.,* Stilton, Gorgonzola, Roquefort (made from ewe's milk), (3) hard-pressed, *e.g.,* Cheddar, Cheshire, Gruyère, Parmesan, Gouda.

Cheetah or "hunting leopard," the large spotted cat of Africa and Southern Asia whose ability to run at 45 m.p.h. for 500 yards makes it the swiftest four-footed animal alive.

Chemistry is the science of the elements and their compounds. It is concerned with the laws of their combination and behaviour under various conditions. It had its rise in alchemy (J2) and has gradually developed into a science of vast magnitude and importance. Organic chemistry deals with the chemistry of the compounds of carbon; inorganic chemistry is concerned with the chemistry of the elements; physical chemistry is concerned with the study of chemical reactions and with the theories and laws of chemistry. *See* F20–6.

Chestnut, the fruit of the chestnut tree; those of the Spanish chestnut, *Castanea vesca,* furnish a favourite esculent. The wood is used in carpentry; while the horse-chestnut (*Æsculus hippocastanum*) is much employed in brush-mounting and in cabinet work.

Chiaroscuro, a term used in painting to denote the arrangement of light and shade in a picture.

Chiltern Hundreds, three hundreds—Stoke, Burnham, and Desborough—the stewardship of which is now a nominal office under the Chancellor of the Exchequer. Since about 1751 the nomination to it has been used as a method of enabling a member of Parliament to resign his seat on the plea that he holds an office of honour and profit under the crown. (This has been a disqualification for Parliament since 1707.)

Chimpanzee, a large anthropoid ape, a native of tropical West Africa, of a dark brown colour, with arms reaching to the knee, and capable of walking upright. Its brain is about a third of the weight of the human brain, but is anatomically similar. The animal has considerable intelligence and powers of learning. A suitable subject for space flight experiments.

China Lobby, the name applied to the body of opinion and pressure in American politics which strenuously opposes recognition of Communist China, and advocates support of Chiang Kai-shek.

Chinchilla, a South American burrowing rodent.

Grey in colour, and white underneath. It is greatly esteemed for its beautiful fur.

Chippendale Furniture was introduced in the reign of George I. by Thomas Chippendale, a cabinet-maker from Yorkshire who migrated to London and set up for himself in St. Martin's Lane, Charing Cross. He was fonder of inventing designs for furniture than of making it, and in 1752 published a book of patterns; the London furniture-makers of the day soon began to model their work upon it.

Chivalry, an international brotherhood of knights formed primarily during the 13th cent. to fight against the infidels in the Crusades. For the French the major battle was against the Moslems in the Holy Land and North Africa, the Spaniards fought the same enemy in their own country, and the Germans were concerned with the heathen of Baltic lands, but Chaucer's "very perfect gentle knight" had fought in all these areas. One did not easily become a knight who had to be of noble birth and then pass through a period of probation, beginning as a boy page in the castle of some great lord, serving his elders and betters humbly while he was taught good manners, singing, playing musical instruments, and the composition of verse. Probably he learned Latin, but he certainly learned French, which was the international language of knights as Latin was of scholars. At fourteen he became a squire and learned to fight with sword, battle-axe, and lance, and to endure conditions of hard living while carrying out his duties of waiting on his lord, looking after his horses, and in time accompanying him in battle. Only if he showed himself suitable was he finally knighted by a stroke of the hand or sword on the shoulder from the king or lord. Knighthood was an international order and had its special code of behaviour: to honour one's sworn word, to protect the weak, to respect women, and defend the Faith. To some extent it had a civilising effect on the conduct of war (e.g., knights of opposing sides might slaughter each other in battle but feast together after), but, since war was regarded as the supreme form of sport, it cannot be said to have contributed to peace.

Chlorine, a gaseous element of the halogen family, first isolated in 1774 by Scheele by the action of manganese dioxide on hydrochloric acid. It unites easily with many other elements, the compounds resulting being termed chlorides. The gaseous element is greenish-yellow, with a pungent odour. It is a suffocating gas, injuring the lungs at a concentration as low as 1 part in 50,000, and was used during the first world war as a poison gas. Has a powerful bleaching action, usually being used in form of bleaching powder, made by combining lime and chlorine. Also a valuable disinfectant; used, for instance, in rendering water of swimming baths sterile.

Chloroform, a volatile colourless liquid, compounded of carbon, hydrogen, and chlorine. It is a powerful solvent, not naturally occurring but synthesised on a large scale. When the vapour is inhaled it produces unconsciousness and insensibility to pain. It owes its discovery to Liebig, and its first application for medical purposes to Sir James Young Simpson (P5(2)).

Chlorophyll, the green pigment contained in the leaves of plants, first discovered by P. J. Pelletier (1788-1829) and J. B Caventou (1795-1877) in 1818. Enables the plant to absorb sunlight and so to build up sugar. The total synthesis of chlorophyll was reported in 1960 by Prof. R. B. Woodward. This is an outstanding achievement in the field of organic chemistry. See Photosynthesis, F28.

Chouans, the name given to the band of peasants, mainly smugglers and dealers in contraband salt, who rose in revolt in the west of France in 1793 and joined the royalists of La Vendée. Balzac gives a picture of the people and the country in which they operated in his novel Les Chouans. They used the hoot of an owl as a signal—hence the name.

Chough, a member of the crow family, of glossy blue-green-black plumage, whose long curved bill and legs are coral red. It used to be abundant on the cliffs of Cornwall, but its haunts are now restricted to the rocky outcrops of the western coasts and in the mountains near by. It nests in cleft rocks and caves. The Alpine chough with yellow bill inhabits the mountainous districts of Europe and Asia and is not found in Britain. It was found at 27,000 ft. on Everest.

Christmas means "mass of Christ" from the old English Cristes maesse, which is celebrated by the Western church on December 25. The actual day on which Christ was born is not known and there is some uncertainty about the year. December 25 as the day of Nativity was not generally observed until the 5th cent. A.D., though, as the winter solstice, it had long been observed as a pagan festival of sol invictus (unconquered sun). The first Christmas card dates from about 1843 and the Christmas tree, of pagan origin, was introduced into England from Germany where it had been a tradition since the Middle Ages. Santa Claus is a corruption of Santa Nikolaus (St. Nicholas) patron saint of children, whose feast day properly falls on December 6.

Chromatic Scale, a scale proceeding in intervals of one semitone. E.g., chromatic scale in C: C–D♭–D–E♭–E–F–G♭–G–A♭–A–B♭–B–C.

Chromium, a very hard, bluish-white metal element, symbol Cr, melting at a very high temperature (above 1900° C.). Its chief ore is chromite or chrome iron-ore (ferrous chromite). "Ferro-chrome" is produced by heating chromite and anthracite in an electric furnace, and chrome steels are prepared by adding the pre-calculated amount of ferro-chrome to melted steel. Best known chrome steel is stainless steel first made by Brearley in 1912 and since then developed greatly at Sheffield. A typical formula is 18 per cent. chromium, 8 per cent. nickel, 74 per cent. iron. Equally important are Stellite alloys, containing chromium, cobalt, tungsten (or molybdenum), which have made possible modern high-speed cutting tools. Dies used in manufacture of plastics are commonly of chrome steel. The elementary metal finds little use alone except in chromium-plating for motor cars, etc.

Chromosomes, the structures contained within the nucleus of every animal and plant cell by which genetic information is transmitted. The chromosome number in somatic (body) cells is constant for each species of plant and animal, e.g., man (46), cat (38), mouse (40), honey bee (16), fruit fly Drosophila (8), potato (48). Chromosomes are long molecules composed of deoxyribonucleoproteins (i.e., proteins and DNA). Human chromosomes have been the subject of much recent research since it has been found that certain disorders are associated with chromosomal aberration, e.g., in Mongolism an extra chromosome is present. See also Genes, Cell Division, F30(2).

Church Commissioners. The Church Commissioners were established in 1948 by the amalgamation of Queen Anne's Bounty (established 1704) and the Ecclesiastical Commissioners (established 1836) to administer Church revenues and to manage Church property generally. The Commissioners own in investments and real estate a total of over £400 million.

Church of England. See J11.

Cid, The, a famous Spanish hero of the 11th cent. Don Rodrigo Diaz de Vivar, who, before he was twenty, led a Spanish force against the Moors, and drove them out of Spain. He is celebrated in poem, play, and romance.

Cilia, minute hair-like projections on the surface of some cells, which beat together in wavelike movements like the wind over a corn-field. These movements can be used as a means of locomotion as in the aquatic organism paramecium. Cilia are also found on the outer layers of the human trachea where they waft particles upwards to the throat, thus protecting the lungs. See F34, P31, also Flagella.

Cinchona, the tree native to the Andes which is famous for its bark, source of the drug quinine. It was introduced into Ceylon, India, and Java, the latter becoming the main supplier of quinine.

Cinque Ports, a number of seaport towns on the coast of Kent and Sussex, originally five: Hastings, Romney, Hythe, Dover, and Sandwich. Winchelsea and Rye were added later. These ports were required to furnish a certain number of ships, ready for service, and in return they were granted many privileges. The official residence of the Lord Warden (Sir Robert Menzies) is Walmer Castle, near Dover.

Cistercians, an order of monks and nuns taking their names from Citeaux, near Dijon, where their first monastery was established in 1098. The order was noted for the severity of its rule. They were famous agriculturists. The habit is white, with a black cowl or hood. The order declined, and in the 17th cent. there was a reform movement instituted by the Trappists, who were later organised into a separate order.

Citron, a species of citrus (*Citrus medica*) related to the lemon, whose fruit has thick rind used for candied peel.

Civil List is the annual sum payable to the Sovereign to maintain the Royal Household and to uphold the dignity of the Crown. The amount is granted by Parliament upon the recommendation of a Select Committee and has to be settled afresh in the first six months of a new reign. The Civil List of Queen Victoria was £385,000; Edward VII. and George V., £470,000; Edward VIII. and George VI., £410,000; Elizabeth II., £475,000. The annuities payable to members of the Royal Family do not form part of the Civil List but are a charge on the Consolidated Fund; Queen Mother, £70,000; Duke of Edinburgh, £40,000; Duke of Gloucester, £35,000; Princess Margaret, £15,000. Prince Charles has his own income from the Duchy of Cornwall (£220,000 a year) half of which he passes to the Exchequer. The other royal children will receive state allowances when they are 21. Apart from the Civil List, the Consolidated Fund grants, and revenue from the Duchy of Cornwall, the official income of the monarchy includes the sums which Parliament votes to Government departments every year and revenue from the Duchy of Lancaster. The royal finances are being reviewed in 1971.

Cleopatra's Needle on the Thames Embankment is of the time of Tuthmosis III. (1500–1450 B.C.). The monolith had nothing to do with Cleopatra, as it only came to Alexandria after her death. It was first erected at the Biblical On (Greek Heliopolis), sacred City of the Sun. It was presented to the British Government by Mehemet Ali in 1819, but not brought to this country until 1878. Weight, 180 tons; height, 68½ ft.

Climate is a generalised representation of the day-to-day weather conditions throughout the year, the combination of all weathers thus determining the climate of a place. Averages and extremes of temperature, variation of humidity, duration of sunshine and cloud cover, amount of rainfall and frequency of snow, frost, gales, etc., are amongst the data normally investigated. The interiors of great land masses are characterised by large ranges of temperature and low rainfall (continental climate), while proximity to oceans has an ameliorating effect with increase in rainfall (oceanic climate). Presence of mountain ranges and lakes and configuration generally produce local modifications of climate, also apparent between the centre and the outlying suburbs of a city. There is evidence that vast changes of climate have occurred during geological time. Since the mid-19th cent. most of the world has shown a tendency to be warmer; the rise in annual mean temperature is now over 1° C. But this trend now seems to be easing off. Latitude introduces zones of climate, *e.g.*, tropical rain, subtropical steppe and desert, temperate rain and polar.

Clock, a device for measuring the passage of time. The earliest timekeeper was the shadow-clock, a primitive form of sundial, used in Ancient Egypt about 1500 B.C. To find the time at night the water-clock or clepsydra was used. The sand-glass dates from the 15th cent. No one knows when the first mechanical clocks were invented, but it is known that a complicated mechanical clock driven by water and controlled by a weighbridge escapement was built in Peking in 1090. The Dover Clock in the Science Museum is not the earliest surviving clock in England, as was once believed, but early 17th cent. The Salisbury Cathedral clock dates from 1386 and that of Wells Cathedral from 1392. The pendulum clock was invented

by the Dutch scientist Christiaan Huygens(1625–95). The first watches were made in Nuremberg shortly after 1500. The marine chronometer is a high-precision timepiece used at sea for giving Greenwich mean time. The quartz-crystal clocks are accurate to one thousandth of a second a day, and the improved atomic clock, recently developed at the British National Physical Laboratory, which makes use of the natural vibrations of the caesium atom, is said to be an almost absolute measure of time (accurate to 1 sec. in 300 years, *i.e.*, one part in 10^{10}).

Cloisonné, a kind of fine pottery with enamelled surface, decorated with elaborate designs, the outlines of which are formed by small bands or fillets of metal. The Byzantines excelled in this work, but in the 20th cent. Japan and China led in Cloisonné-ware.

Cloud chamber, an apparatus invented by C. T. R. Wilson in which the tracks of atomic particles can be made visible. Just as the vapour trails tell of the track of an invisible aircraft high up in the air, so the vapour trails of an unseeable particle can tell of its behaviour. The rays under investigation pass through a chamber containing a gas, *e.g.*, air thoroughly cleansed of dust, supersaturated with water- or alcohol-vapour. As the particle passes through it forms a track of tiny water droplets which can be photographed. After a long and honourable history this wonderful instrument is now virtually obsolete. A later ingenious device for tracking fast fundamental particles is the Bubble chamber (*q.v.*).

Clouds are formed by the ascent of moist air, the type depending on the way the air ascends and the height at which condensation occurs. There are three main classes: (1) high cloud (above 20,000 ft.)—cirrus (delicate and fibrous), cirrostratus (thin white veil), and cirrocumulus (delicately rippled) consisting of ice crystals; (2) medium cloud (above 7,000 ft.)—altostratus (dense, greyish veil) and altocumulus (broken flattened cloudlets)—chiefly water particles, often supercooled; (3) low cloud (from near ground to 7,000 ft.)—cumulus (fair weather, broken, dome-topped), cumulonimbus (heavy, towering to great heights), stratocumulus (layer of globular masses or rolls), stratus (like fog but off the ground), nimbostratus (low, rainy cloud). The highest clouds of all, and the rarest, are the noctilucent, seen only on summer nights in high latitudes. They form at about 50 miles above the earth and consist of ice-coated dust from meteors.

Clover, plants of the *Trifolium* genus, family *Leguminosae,* with about 250 species. These are "nitrogen fixing" plants and include red clover, white clover, alsike clover, and crimson clover. They are of great importance in agriculture because in a good pasture they supply directly or indirectly most of the protein available to the animals. Seed of "wild white" clover has been accepted since about 1939 as the indispensable plant of good United Kingdom grassland, largely through the efforts of pioneers like D. A. Gilchrist (1859–1927).

Cloves are the dried flower-buds of a species of myrtle (*Eugenia caryophyllata*) grown principally in Zanzibar and Madagascar.

Coal. Until recently the most important single fuel has been coal. It is a mineral of organic origin, formed from the remains of vegetation which over millions of years has changed to coal by the effects of heat and pressure from over-lying rock or water. All coal contains moisture, inflammable volatiles, mineral impurities (some of which remain as coal ash after the coal is burnt), and fixed carbon (the coke that is left after the volatiles have been driven off). The relative proportions vary—from Anthracite, a hard coal containing the highest proportion of fixed carbon, to Lignite or brown coal which is little more than a hard peat. World reserves of bituminous coal have been estimated at 7.5×10^{12} tons. If one adds the reserves of brown coal and lignite, this figure is increased by about 15 per cent. The proportion of the reserves that could be economically recovered varies from country to country and estimates vary from 50 to 100 per cent of the reserves. The reserves are highly localised—over half being located in the Soviet Union. In the United Kingdom coal has formed the basis of past industrial prosperity. Peak output occurred in 1913 when 287 million tons were mined, one third of which was exported. At the end of the Second World War (1946) production had fallen to 183 million tons and was far below demand. During the next ten years great efforts were made to increase coal output but, quite suddenly in 1956, demand for coal fell as oil became a popular fuel and since then the problem has been to cut back the coal industry without causing undue social problems. A future market of about 170 to 180 million tons is envisaged beyond 1970. In 1947 the British coal industry was brought under public ownership and all its assets were vested in the National Coal Board.

Coat of Arms, in heraldry, is a device containing a family's armorial bearings. In mediæval times it was an actual coat upon which such device was embroidered, and knights wore it over their armour.

Cobalt, a white metal melting at 1490 °C. Two main ores are *cobalt glance* (in which the element is combined with arsenic and sulphur) and *smaltite* (cobalt arsenide). The principal sources are Ontario and the Congo. Various cobalt alloys are important, *e.g.*, stellite, ferrocobalt and carboloy. Its monoxide is an important colouring medium, and is used for colouring glass and porcelain-blue.

Cobra, hooded and very venomous snakes. The best known species are the Indian Cobra, the Egyptian Cobra, and the Black-necked Cobra. Their food consists chiefly of small rodents. The King Cobra is almost exclusively a snake-eater. "Spitting" Cobras (or Ringhals) of S. Africa are a related genus, capable of spitting their venom several yards.

Coca, a S. American shrub, *Erythroxylon coca*, also cultivated in Java. The leaves yield cocaine, classified as a dangerous drug; used medicinally as a local anaesthetic, especially on the eyes and in dentistry. When the natives chew the leaves they are enabled to withstand astonishing amounts of hunger and fatigue, as cocaine acts both as a mental stimulant and as an anaesthetic on the mucous lining of the stomach.

Cochineal *or* **Carmine**, a dyestuff consisting of the dried bodies of the female scale insect (*Dactylopius coccus*) which feeds on cacti. Of ancient origin, the dye was well known to the Aztecs, and was used widely in the Middle Ages. The famous scarlet tunics worn by the English during the Napoleonic wars owed their colour to carmine. To-day it is almost entirely replaced by aniline dyes.

Cockatoo, a member of the parrot family, bearing a crest of feathers on the head, native to Australia and adjacent regions. Predominant colour is white tinged with yellow or scarlet while some species have dark plumage. The great black cockatoo of New Guinea is slaty black with pale red cheeks and can crack Kanary nuts which usually require a hammer to break them open.

Cockchafer (*Melolontha*), one of the most destructive of beetles, the larvae feeding on roots. It is about 1 inch in length, of a brownish colour, and emits a loud whirring sound when flying.

Cockle, the popular name of the bi-valve shell-fish of the genus *Cardium*, found plentifully in sandy bays near low-water line; there are numerous British species.

Cockroach, inaccurately called the "black beetle"; a pest of bakeries and kitchens. In Britain two species are commonly found: the Common Cockroach (*Blatta orientalis*), resident since the time of Elizabeth I, dark brown, about an inch long, with the wing covers long in the male and short in the female; and the German Cockroach (*Blatta germanica*), now the most common, half the size, dark yellow, with both sexes fully winged. All species have long antennae and flattened, leathery, shiny bodies. They are nocturnal and omnivorous.

Cocoa. *See* Cacao.

Coconut Palm (*Cocos nucifera*), a tropical tree, growing to a height of 100 ft., with a slender, leaning trunk surmounted by giant feather-like leaves. One of the most important sources of food and raw material for people living in the tropics. The juice of the fruit, or coconut, is drunk; the kernel is eaten fresh or dried to form copra, which yields animal feeding stuffs and oil, used in the manufacture of soap, margarine, cosmetics, synthetic rubber, etc.; leaves are used for thatching; leaf stalks for canes, fence posts, needles, etc., and the trunk for houses and bridges. Main producing areas: Indonesia, Philippines, Malaysia, Ceylon, and S. India.

Codes, a term used to designate a system of laws properly classified. The Code of Hammurabi, king of Babylon, *c.* 1700 B.C., had extensive influence over a long period. The Romans formulated several codes of historic importance including the Theodosian Code which summarised the Roman laws from the time of Constantine to 438 A.D. The final codification was made under order of the Emperor Justinian by his chief minister Tribonian and published in 529 with a new edition in 534. The most important of modern codes is the *Code Napoléon*, compiled between 1803 and 1810, and still in force. It has been used as an example for the codification of the laws of a number of countries from America to Japan. Under Frederick the Great the law of Prussia was codified. English law has never been codified, although the law on certain subjects has been gathered up into a single statute. The Law Commission Act, 1965, was passed to consolidate and codify the law wherever possible. *See* D8(2).

Codex, a manuscript volume of the Scriptures comprising the Sinaitic codex of the 4th cent., the Vatican codex of the same period, the Alexandrine codex of the 5th cent., and others. The British Museum, in 1933, purchased the *Codex Sinaiticus* from the Soviet Government for £100,000.

Coffee, a shrub found originally in Arabia and Abyssinia, but now extensively grown in the West Indies, Brazil, India, and Central America. It yields a seed or berry which, after undergoing the necessary preparation, is ground and largely used in most countries as a popular breakfast beverage. The best coffee is the Mocha, an Arabian variety. The stimulating effect of coffee is due to the caffeine, which is also present in tea. The beverage was introduced into Europe in the 16th cent., and the first London coffee shop was opened in 1682.

Coke is the solid residue remaining when coal is carbonised and nearly all the volatile constituents have been driven off. Used as fuel, and as an agent for reducing metallic oxides to metals, *e.g.*, iron ore to iron, in the manufacture of steel.

Colorado Beetle, a serious pest of potato crops. Both adults and larvae feed on the foliage where the orange eggs are laid. The grub is reddish, with two rows of small black spots on each side. The adults are about ½ in. long with yellow and black striped wing cases. The beetle is avoided by birds because of its nasty taste, and is controlled by arsenical sprays.

Colosseum, the name of the Flavian amphitheatre at Rome, begun by Vespasian and finished by Titus A.D. 80. In general outline it still remains one of the most magnificent ruins in the world. In the arena of this great building the famous gladiatorial displays and mimic naval battles used to be given, and about 50,000 spectators could be accommodated.

Colossus is the name which the ancients gave to any statue of gigantic size. The Colossus at Rhodes, which was a bronze statue of the sun god, Helios, was the most famous, and reckoned among the seven wonders of the world. It stood over 100 ft. high at the mouth of the harbour. There is no truth in the legend that ships could pass between its legs. It fell in an earthquake in 224 B.C.

Coluga, also known as "flying lemur", caguan or kubuk, a remarkable mammal which may be regarded as an aberrant insectivore or an aberrant form of the earliest ancestor of the bats. It has nothing to do with lemurs. There are two genera, one inhabiting the Philippines and one inhabiting Malaya. They have a parachute-like membrane which covers them from the neck to the tip of the tail, by means of which they can glide from treetop to ground a distance of up to 70 yards.

Column, in architecture, is an upright solid body serving as a support or decoration to a building.

Columns consist of a pedestal, a shaft, and a capital, over which the supported entablature rises. They are named according to the styles of architecture of which they form part, being Doric, Tuscan, Ionic, Corinthian, or Composite as the case may be.

Comets are celestial bodies which move about the solar system in elliptical or hyperbolic orbits. Usually these star-like bodies are accompanied by a long shining tail. The hyperbolic comets are seen once only, and do not reappear; the elliptical comets are periodic, and their recurrence can be calculated with accuracy. The head of a comet is believed to consist of small lumps of solid matter accompanied by dust particles and gases such as carbon dioxide and methane. It used to be thought that the tail was produced by the pressure of sunlight on the cometary material but a modern explanation is that it is produced by the combined action of the solar wind (a continuous stream of ionised hydrogen originating in the sun) and the interplanetary magnetic field. When they run parallel the effect is to produce a long streaming tail pointing away from the sun. Chief among the periodic comets is Edmund Halley's, the first to return as predicted in 1757. It reappears about every 76 years and is next due in 1985. The most spectacular comet of the 19th cent. was that found by Donati in 1858.

Common Law. *See* **D7.**

Commons are the remnants of the mediaeval open fields round villages in which the villagers had rights in common, *e.g.*, (i) estover—the right of taking wood for house building or firewood; (ii) pasture—the right of grazing beasts; (iii) turbary—the right of digging turf; (iv) piscary—the right to fish. Many of these common lands were enclosed during the agrarian revolution which went on steadily in England from the 15th cent. onwards, and with their enclosure common rights vanished. A Royal Commission on Common Land described the commons in 1965 as the "last reservoir of uncommitted land" which provide, as far as the public is concerned, by far the largest part of the accessible open spaces of the country. Under the Commons Registration Act, 1965, it was the duty of County Councils and County Borough Councils to make a register of all common land and all town and village greens in their areas.

Commons, House of, the Lower House of the British Parliament. *See* **Section C, Part II.**

Commune of Paris has twice played a dramatic part in the history of France. In 1792 it was able, through its control of the administrative organisation of Paris, to override the National Assembly. In 1871, after the withdrawal of the Prussian troops, it tried to assert its authority. Public buildings were destroyed by members of the Commune and civil war raged during April and half May, but Government troops suppressed the rising.

Communism. *See* **J12.**

Compass *or* **Mariner's Compass** is an instrument by which the magnetic meridian is indicated, and comprises a horizontal bowl containing alcohol and water, a card upon which the thirty-two points of the compass are marked, and the steel needle which always points to the meridian. Although the discovery of the directive property of a magnet is credited to the Chinese, the first practical use of this property in a compass was made in western Europe in the 12th cent. Aircraft and ships now largely employ gyrostatic compasses which are not affected by electrical and magnetic disturbances. Sperry, Brown, and Anschutz are three important types of gyroscopic compass.

Computer, a technical device for accepting an input of information, processing this information according to some prescribed programme of operations and supplying an output of processed information. Many types of operation can be performed on many types of information and computers are now indispensable in science, business, warfare, government, and other activities. Early thinkers in this field were Pascal (17th cent.), Babbage (19th cent.) and Turing (1930s), but electronic computers as we know them appeared during the Second World War and the first commercial machine was on sale in 1950. Computers are millions of times faster than human beings at computing; and the introduction of computers into an organisation does more than just speed up the calculations, it tends to transform the whole nature of the organisation. The possibilities for future developments seem enormous. Analogue computers and digital computers are two different kinds stemming from the difference between *measuring* and *counting*. Analogue types handle data that is represented by physical quantities of continuously variable size such as voltages or lengths. These quantities can be made to vary like the quantities in a problem which the computer is set to solve; the problem is thus solved by analogy. A slide rule is a rudimentary analogue computer in which numbers are represented by lengths of rule. Digital computers handle actual numbers expressed in digits and the quantities in the problem are represented by discrete numbers. These can all be expressed in binary form and thus stored or handled in bits. *See* **Bit, Binary Notation.**

Conclave, an assembly of Roman Catholic cardinals met together to elect a pope. The last Conclave was held in the Vatican in June 1963 when Cardinal Montini, archbishop of Milan, was elected Pope Paul VI.

Concordat, an agreement or convention between the pope and a secular government regarding ecclesiastical matters. The Concordat of Worms in 1122 between Calixtus II. and the Emperor Henry V. was famous as deciding a long struggle in regard to investiture. In 1801 Napoleon concluded a concordat with Pius VII. defining the restored relations between the head of the Church and the French Roman Catholics.

Condor, a large eagle of brilliant black plumage with a circlet of white feathers round its neck. It is a native of the Andes.

Confederation is a free association of sovereign states united for some common purpose. It is to be distinguished from a **Federation,** which is a union of states with one central government, each state relinquishing its sovereignty, though retaining some independence in internal affairs.

Confucianism. *See* **J12.**

Coniferae are cone-bearing trees, including firs, pines, cedars, cypresses, junipers, yews, etc., and are widely distributed in temperate regions.

Conservatism. *See* **J12.**

Consistory, a council or meeting of councillors; also the higher ecclesiastical courts and senates of the Anglican and Roman Churches.

Constitution, the fundamental organic law or principles of government of a nation, state, society, or other organised body, embodied in written documents, or implied in the institutions and customs of the country or society. The government of the U.S.A., unlike Great Britain, works upon a written Constitution. It was framed when the U.S.A. came into existence as a sovereign body, when the Constitution built a republic out of a federation of thirteen states, based on representative government. The constitution was adopted in 1789, and its strength has been tested by the fact that, substantially unchanged, it is now the groundwork for a federation which now comprises fifty states.

Continent, a word used in physical geography to denote the larger continuous land masses in contrast to the great oceans of the earth. They are: Eurasia (conventionally regarded as 2 continents, Europe and Asia), Africa, North America, South America, Australia and Antarctica.

Continental Drift. The hypothesis of drifting continents is due to F. B. Taylor, an American geologist who published his theory in 1908, and to the Austrian meteorologist Alfred Wegener in 1910. The latter was impressed by the matching coasts of South America and Africa, which seemed to him to fit together like the pieces of a jigsaw puzzle. Since then many other people have taken up and developed the idea. According to Wegener, at one time there were two primary super-continents, Laurasia and Gondwanaland. The one in the northern hemisphere consisted of North America, Europe, and the northern part of Asia. Its southern counterpart included Antarctica, Australia, India, Africa and South America. These super-continents broke up, and their various bits moved apart. In particular, the southern hemisphere continents drifted radially northwards away from the south pole, and the two Americas shifted westwards from Europe and Africa. What would have been the leading edges of the land masses on this hypothesis, are now heavily buckled up into mountain belts, such as the Cordillera and the Alpine-Himalayan chain. The resistance afforded to drifting by the strong ocean floors may well have been the cause of such structures. Despite the wealth of geological facts which have a bearing on the problem of continental drift, none of these has been able to decide the issue in a conclusive manner. Further studies of rock magnetism (*q.v.*) and of fossil climates should ultimately establish the concept of continental drift on a firm basis. *See also* **Earth, F8.**

Conurbation, a term which has been defined as " an area occupied by a continuous series of dwellings, factories, and other buildings, harbours, and docks, urban parks and playing fields, etc., which are not separated from each other by rural land; though in many cases in this country such an urban area includes enclaves of rural land which is still in agricultural occupation." The term has been widely adopted for the contiguous densely populated areas which form continuous urban areas. The seven officially recognised in Britain are: Greater London, West Midlands, S.E. Lancashire, West Yorkshire, Merseyside, Tyneside, Clydeside.

Convention is an assembly of delegates, representatives, members of a party met to accomplish some specific civil, social, political, ecclesiastical or other important object.

Convocation, an assembly called together to deliberate ecclesiastical affairs. In the Church of England the provinces of Canterbury and York each have their convocation. The term is also applied to assemblies of the graduates of certain universities.

Coot. A very widely distributed bird of the rail family and a common resident of the British Isles. The adult is black with a conspicuous white bald shield on the forehead and a white bill. The juvenile is brownish grey with whitish breast and throat. The coot flies heavily, but swims well. It dives frequently and can remain submerged for a considerable time. It is pugnacious and in winter gregarious. The food is chiefly vegetable. The large nest is usually built among aquatic vegetation and the young are fed by both parents. Another species, the Crested Coot, occurs in S. Europe.

Copper, one of the most familiar of metals, symbol Cu, used in ancient times as an alloy with tin in producing bronze, and preceding iron as an industrial material. Copper ores are most abundant in the U.S.A., Chile, Canada, Zambia, and the Congo. All copper compounds are poisonous. Copper sulphate is largely used in calico-printing and in the production of blue and green pigments.

Copyright. Under the Copyright Act, 1956, copyright subsists in every original literary, dramatic, musical, and artistic work if the author is a British subject or a citizen of the Republic of Ireland or resident in the United Kingdom, or if the work is first published in the United Kingdom. The Act provides that, except in certain special cases, the author of the work shall be the first owner of the copyright, and there are no formalities, such as registration or payment of fees, to be accomplished. Copyright includes the right to reproduce the work in any material form, to perform the work in public, or, if the work is unpublished, to publish the work. The Act also protects sound recordings, films, and television and sound broadcasts. Literary, dramatic, musical, and artistic works which enjoy the protection of the Act are automatically protected in those countries which are parties to the Berne Copyright Convention or the Universal Copyright Convention. In general, copyright in literary, dramatic, musical, and artistic works is vested in the author for the period of his lifetime and 50 years following, after which it passes into the public domain and becomes freely available to any who wish to make use of it. The Copyright Libraries, entitled to receive copies of books published in the United Kingdom are given under **Libraries.** A new copyright convention was signed in Stockholm in 1967 which gives " under-developed " countries the right to reproduce, without payment if they choose, any books to be used for teaching, study, or research. The Government Department responsible for matters in connection with copyright is the Industrial Property Department, Board of Trade, 25, Southampton Buildings, London, W.C.2.

Coral, an order of small marine animals closely related to the sea-anemone, but differing from it in their ability to develop a limy skeleton. They multiply sexually and by budding. The structure of the coral secretions assumes a variety of forms, fan-like, tree-like, mushroom shape, and so forth. Red coral (the skeleton of *Corallium rubrum*) is mainly obtained from the Mediterranean. The coral reefs of the Pacific and Indian Oceans are often many miles in extent. Living corals occur only in warm seas at about 23 °C. *See also* **Gt. Barrier Reef, K69.**

Cordite, a smokeless explosive adopted for small arms and heavy artillery by the British Government in the naval and military services in 1889, and composed of 58 parts of nitro-glycerine, 37 of gun-cotton, and 5 of vaseline. It is a jelly or plastic dough, and used in the form of sticks.

Cork, the bark of a species of oak, *Quercus suber,* grown largely in the South of Europe and North America. The cork tree is said to yield bark every six to ten years for 150 years, and grows to a height of from 20 to 40 ft. Its lightness, impermeability, and elasticity enable it to be used for a variety of commercial purposes, especially for stoppers of bottles.

Cormorant, a large, long-billed water-bird which captures fish by diving. It has bronze-black plumage with white cheeks and sides and is found around the sea coasts of most parts of the world, including the British Isles. It nests in colonies on sea cliffs and rocky ledges. The Shag or Green Cormorant is a smaller bird with green-black plumage and a crest.

Corncrake. *See* **Landrail.**

Corn Laws were statutes intended for the benefit of British agriculture, and restricted import and export of grain. From the 14th to the mid-19th cent. such laws were in force, and were often of a stringent nature. They became so oppressive and caused corn to reach so high a price that the poorer classes were plunged into distress. A powerful anti-corn law agitation was organised, of which Cobden, Bright, and Villiers were the leaders, and Sir Robert Peel, in 1846, at the time of the Irish potato famine, carried through free trade. The repeal of the Corn Laws marked an important phase in the transformation of an agricultural to an industrial Britain.

Coronae, series of luminous rings surrounding sun or moon produced by the diffraction of light by water droplets in the atmosphere. Usually seen when sun shines through altostratus clouds. The outside of the ring is red and the inside bluish. *See* **Halo.**

Corpus Christi Festival is one of the great celebrations of the Roman Catholic Church, and takes place on the Thursday after Trinity. It was instituted by Pope Urban IV. in 1264.

Cortes, the name of the Parliamentary assemblies of Spain and Portugal.

Cosmic Rays, a form of radiation coming from outer space, of deep penetrating power and of great scientific interest. The rays are believed to consist chiefly of fast protons, with a few α-particles and other positive nuclei. By interacting with the gas of the atmosphere, these rays initiate a complex series of events, in the course of which other particles (" secondary radiations ") are generated. The secondary rays contain virtually all the particles listed on **F14;** indeed, several particles were first discovered as secondary cosmic rays. Cosmic rays are investigated at and below sea-level, on mountains, in mines, in balloons, rockets, and satellites. Origin still uncertain. *See* **F3(2).**

Cosmology is the science which studies the whole universe, its origin, its nature, its size, and evolution. At present it is a very active science partly because new techniques such as radioastronomy are revealing more facts about distant parts of the universe and partly because of fruitful clashes between theoretical ideas. *See* **F3-7.**

Cotton, the name of a plant of several species,

bearing large yellow flowers with purple centres. These centres expand into pods, which at maturity burst and yield the white fibrous substance known as cotton. The raw cotton contains a large proportion of seeds which are removed by " ginning." Long before the Christian era, cotton had been grown and used with great skill in India to make fabrics. The industry was not introduced into England until the middle of the 17th cent. when Protestant refugees from Flanders came to settle in the wool textile districts of East Anglia and Lancashire. With improvements in machinery and expansion of overseas trade in the 18th and 19th cent., Lancashire became the centre of the world's cotton industry. Since the second world war man-made fibres have taken the place of cotton. Cotton reacts with nitric acid to form gun cotton, which is combined with more sensitive explosives to give a more safely handled substance.

Coulomb, a unit of electric charge, named after the French naval engineer, Charles Augustin de Coulomb (1736–1806), equal to the quantity of electricity transferred in one second by a current of one ampere.

County. The word county was introduced after the Norman conquest as an equivalent of the old English " shire." England has 41 geographical counties, Wales 13, Scotland 33, and Ireland 32. The number of administrative counties differs from the number of geographical counties because the division for Local Government purposes is made on grounds of convenience. Under the London Government Act, 1963, the county of Middlesex was absorbed in Greater London.

Coup d'Etat, a violent change in the government of a state carried out by force or illegally. Examples are the overthrow of the French Republic in 1851 by Louis Napoleon, who then became Emperor, and more recently the military *coups* in the Middle East which brought about the abdication of Farouk of Egypt in 1952 and the assassination of Feisal of Iraq in 1958.

Court Leet, a court of record held annually before the steward of any particular manor or lordship; originally there was only one court for a manor, but in the time of Edward I. it branched into two, the court baron and the court leet.

Coypu or **Nutria rat,** a large beaver-like rodent found in S. America; now wild in E. Anglia, where it is causing damage to dykes, reeds, and crops, having escaped from farms where it is bred for its fur.

Crane, a large, graceful wading-bird with elegant long legs and neck, greyish plumage, superficially resembling the heron and related to the bustard. They migrate in **V** or **W** formation and have trumpet-like voices. There are several species, found in all continents except S. America, including the Crowned Crane with golden coronet and the Demoiselle with tuftlike crest of white feathers. The Common Crane nested in East Anglia in mediaeval times but now comes only as a rare visitor from the Continent.

Credit is an advance of money or of goods or services in consideration of a promise of payment later. Trade credit is such an advance from trader to customer; bank credit is an advance of money by a bank to a client, whether a business firm or a private person, in consideration of an interest payment by the borrower.

Creed, (Latin *credo* = I believe), a formal statement of belief. The three orthodox Christian creeds are the Apostles' Creed (a summary of their teaching), the Nicene Creed (drawn up by the Church Council at Nicaea in A.D. 325 to define its theological doctrines), and the Athanasian Creed (concerning the nature and divinity of Christ). *See also* under individual headings.

Cremation, the ancient custom, revived in modern times, of burning the dead. Cremation was first legalised in Great Britain in 1885 and the first crematorium opened at Woking in that year. Application for cremation must be accompanied by two medical certificates.

Cricket, a genus of insects of the grasshopper order which move by leaps. The male produces a chirping noise by rubbing its wing-covers together.

Crimean War (1853–56). This war between Russia and the allied powers of Turkey, England, France, and Sardinia, was connected with the Eastern Question (*q.v.*) and the desire of Russia for a port on the Mediterranean. Chief engagements were the Alma, Balaclava, and Inkerman. Fighting virtually ceased with fall of Sevastopol in Sept. 1855. Treaty of Paris signed March 30, 1856.

Crocodile, the name of the largest existing reptile, and classed with the alligator and the gavial. The crocodile inhabits the Nile region, the alligator the lower Mississippi, and the gavial is found in many Indian rivers.

Crow, a family of birds including many well-known species such as the rook, raven, jackdaw, carrion crow, hooded crow, magpie, nutcracker, jay, and chough.

Crusades were military expeditions undertaken by some of the Christian nations of Europe with the object of ensuring the safety of pilgrims visiting the Holy Sepulchre and to retain in Christian hands the Holy Places. For two centuries nine crusades were undertaken: First, 1095–99, under Godfrey of Bouillon, which succeeded in capturing Jerusalem; Second, 1147–49, led by Louis VII. of France, a dismal failure, which ended with the fall of Jerusalem; Third, 1189–92, in which Richard I. of England took part, making a truce with Saladin; Fourth, 1202–4, led by French and Flemish nobles, a shameful expedition, resulting in the founding of a Latin empire in Constantinople; Fifth, 1217–21, led by John of Brienne; Sixth, 1228–29, under the Emperor Frederick II.; Seventh, 1248–54, under St. Louis of France; Eighth, 1270, under the same leadership, but cut short by his death on an ill-judged expedition to Tunis; Ninth, 1271–72, led by Prince Edward of England, which accomplished nothing. Millions of lives and an enormous amount of treasure were sacrificed in these enterprises and Jerusalem remained in the possession of the " infidels." The chief material beneficiaries were the Italian maritime cities; the chief spiritual beneficiary was the pope; but in literature and the arts both Europe and the Levant benefited enormously from the bringing together of the different cultures.

Cryogenics (Greek roots: productive of cold) is the science dealing with the production of very low temperatures and the study of their physical and technological consequences. " Very low " is often taken to mean below about $-150°C$. The growth of cryogenics (essentially a 20th-cent. science) is connected with the discovery of how to liquefy all gases including even helium which resisted liquefaction until 1908. Scientifically, cryogenics is important partly because special phenomena (*e.g.*, superconductivity (*q.v.*)) appear at low temperatures and partly because more can be learned about ordinary properties by studying them in the absence of heat. Technologically, cryogenics is becoming more and more significant, for example, liquefied gases are rocket propellants, superconductors make valuable magnets, tissue-freezing techniques (using very cold liquids) have been introduced into surgery. *See* Absolute Temperature.

Crystal, in everyday usage, a solid chemical substance bounded by plane surfaces which show a regular geometrical arrangement as, *e.g.*, quartz crystals, rock salt, snow flakes. In physics the term means any solid whose atoms are arranged in a regular three-dimensional array. This includes most solids, even those not particularly crystalline in appearance, *e.g.*, a lump of lead. Common *non*-crystalline substances are liquids, jellies, glass.

Cubism, the name of a revolutionary movement in art created in the years 1907–9 by the two painters Picasso and Braque. Rejecting purely visual effects, they approached nature from an intellectual point of view, reducing it to mathematical orderliness. Its respectable grandparent was Cézanne who had once written: " you must see in nature the cylinder, the sphere, and the cone "—a concept which, together with the contemporary interest in Negro sculpture, moved the two founders of the movement to experiment with the reduction of natural forms to their basic geometrical shapes. In practice, this meant combining several views of the object all more or less superimposed in order to express the idea of the object rather than any one view of it. The name Cubism was derisive and the movement aroused the same opposition as Impressionism, Fauvism, and the later Futurism. Picasso's *Young Ladies of Avignon* was the first Cubist painting and his "Head" (1909) the first Cubist sculpture. Three phases are recognised: (1) Cubism under the influence of Cézanne; (2) high or analytical Cubism (c. 1909–12) concentrating on the breaking-down of form to the exclusion of interest in colour; (3) synthetic Cubism (c. 1913) making use of *collage* in which pieces of pasted-on paper (illustrations, wallpaper, newspaper) and other materials were used in addition to paint. Amongst other early cubist painters were Metzinger, Gleizes, Gris, and Léger.

Cuckoo, a well-known migratory bird which is found in Great Britain from April to July, hawk-like in shape, with a very characteristic note, uttered during the mating season only by the male. The hen has a soft bubbling call. It lays its eggs in the nests of other birds, *e.g.*, the meadow pipit and hedge sparrow, but only one egg in each nest. Feeds mainly on insects, particularly hairy caterpillars.

Cuneiform, (Latin = *wedge-shaped*), an ancient method of writing by impressing wedge-like strokes into tablets of damp clay which when dried and hardened formed a permanent script. Cuneiform writing developed from its original pictographic form into a phonetic writing and can be traced back to the non-Semitic Sumerians of ancient Mesopotamia, the earliest civilisation known to us. It passed to the Semitic Accadians of Babylonia in the 3rd millennium B.C. who adapted it to their own language. Decipherment by Sir Henry Rawlinson, 1835.

Curfew (Old Fr. *covre-feu* = cover fire), a regulation common throughout Europe in mediæval times by which, at a fixed hour in the evening, the church bell was rung as a signal that fires were to be put out and the people were to go to bed. The custom originated in the fear of fire when buildings were built of timber. Nowadays a curfew is imposed by the military in areas where riots or disturbances are expected, compelling the civilian population to remain indoors after nightfall.

Curia, the central government of the Roman Catholic Church. By the reform which came into force on Jan 1, 1968, its twelve Sacred Congregations or "ministries" were reorganised and reduced to nine. The aim of the reform was to streamline the Curial offices so that the Church's machinery can cope with modern problems, so favouring the desires expressed by the Ecumenical Council convened by Pope John.

Curie, a measure of the rate at which radioactive material emits radiation. One curie is a disintegration rate of $3 \cdot 7 \times 10^{10}$ disintegrations per second.

Curlew, a wading-bird of which there are several species. It frequents marshy places, feeds on worms, insects, molluscs, and berries and possesses a very long, down-curved bill.

Currency is the name given to the types of cash money—metal or paper—in use in an area (*e.g.* pound, sterling, dollar, franc). It also designates the actual coins or notes issued. Its amount is usually subject to regulation by the Government, or by a Central Bank acting on the Government's behalf. Britain changed over to a £-based decimal currency in Feb. 1971. *See also* **Foreign Currencies, N9.**

Cybernetics, the science concerned with the automatic control and communication processes in both animals and machines. Thus it is concerned with brain function, information theory, electronic computers, and automation.

Cyclone, a term usually applied to a tropical revolving storm. Cyclones often occur towards the end of the hot seasons and are mainly confined to tracks in the western areas of the oceans, being known as hurricanes (Caribbean and Pacific), cyclones (Indian Ocean), and typhoons (China Seas). The circulation of air in a cyclone is similar to that in the *depression* of temperate latitudes, but the region of low pressure is much more localised and the pressure gradients steeper. Winds of hurricane strength and torrential rain occur generally, although at the centre of the storm there is a small area, known as the "eye," where fair, calm weather prevails.

Cyclotron, a machine for accelerating charged particles such as protons to very high energies. Devised by E. O. Lawrence in California in 1930, it uses a magnetic field to make the particles traverse nearly circular paths and an electric field to give them an additional pulse of energy each time round. The accelerated particles impinge on targets, and the resulting events are a basic source of information for nuclear physicists. The cyclotron is obsolescent and has led to the development of other machines, *e.g.*, betatrons, synchrotrons. Britain has two major national high-energy machines: *Nimrod* (7,000 MeV proton synchroton) and *Nina* (4,000 MeV) electron accelerator).

D

Dactylopterus, a fish of the gurnard family, with wing-like pectoral fins; sometimes known as the flying fish, though that appellation is more generally given to *Exocaetus exiliens*.

Dadaism (French *Dada* = hobby-horse) was a hysterical and nihilistic precursor of Surrealism (*q.v.*) resulting from the shock produced by the first world war. Beginning in Zurich about 1915, it spread to other continental cities, such as Berlin and Paris, dying out in 1922. The movement was deliberately anti-art, destructive, and without meaning; it intended to scandalise by such tricks as "compositions" made out of anything that came to hand—buttons, bus tickets, pieces of wire, bits of tin, etc. Other excesses included incoherent poetry, Dada night-clubs, plays, and short-lived newspapers. Many Dadaist painters became Surrealists at a later stage, but where Surrealism is a deliberate attempt to present subconscious and dream-like images, Dadaism was sheer anarchism. Among its chief exponents were Hans Arp, Marcel Duchamp, André Breton, Guillaume Apollinaire, and Max Ernst, all of whom subsequently became noted in more reputable ways.

Daddy Longlegs, or Crane-fly, a slender long-legged fly of the family Tipulidae. The larvae which do damage to lawns and plants are called leather-jackets. The Americans call Harvestmen (*q.v.*) daddy longlegs.

Daguerreotype, a first practical photographic process, invented in Paris by M. Daguerre during the years 1824–39. The light-sensitive plate was prepared by bringing iodine in contact with a plate of silver. After exposure a positive image came by development of the plate in mercury vapour. Even for open-air scenes the first daguerreotypes involved exposure of 5–10 minutes. The wet collodion process (1851) rendered the technique obsolete.

Dail Eireann, the name of the national parliament of the Irish Republic.

Damaskeening, the art of inlaying one metal upon another, largely practised in the East in mediæval times, especially in the decoration of sword blades.

Dandies, the name given to a class of exquisites prominent in early Victorian days, and who attracted attention by excessive regard for dress. Their feminine counterparts were the dandizettes.

Danegeld, a tax imposed in England in Anglo-Saxon times to raise funds for resisting the Danes or to buy them off. Edward the Confessor abolished the tax, but it was revived by the Conqueror and subsequently retained, under another name, after the danger from the Danes was past. It is the basis of all taxation in this country. Domesday Book (*q.v.*) was originally drawn up for the purpose of teaching the State how to levy the tax.

Danelaw, the law enforced by the Danes in the kingdoms of Northumbria, East Anglia, and in the districts of the five (Danish) boroughs—lands grouped round Leicester, Nottingham, Derby, Stamford, and Lincoln—which they occupied during the Viking invasions of the 9th and 10th cent. The country occupied was also called the Danelaw or Danelagh.

Darter, 1. Snakebirds, a genus of the pelican family, with long, pointed bill and serpent-like neck and resembling cormorants in appearance. There are 5 species. 2. Numerous species of small freshwater fish belonging to the Perch family, found in N. America.

Date Palm, *Phoenix dactylifera*, one of the oldest known food plants widely cultivated in N. Africa and W. Asia. It grows to 100 ft. and continues to bear for 2 or 3 centuries, its fruit being of great value as a food. From the leaves the Africans make roofs for their huts; ropes are made from the fibrous parts of the stalks; and the sap furnishes a stimulating beverage.

Dauphin, the title borne by the eldest sons of the Kings of France from 1349 to the Revolution of 1830.

Day is the most natural unit of time and may be defined as the period of rotation of the earth relative to any selected heavenly body. Relative to the sun it is called the *solar day*. Relative to a fixed star it is called the *sidereal day*. Owing to irregularities in the earth's movements, the time taken for the earth to rotate through 360° relative to the sun is variable, and so the *mean solar day* of 24 hours has been introduced. which is the average throughout the year. The *mean solar day* is our standard, used for purposes of the calendar. and astronomers use *sidereal* clocks to check mean solar time. In practice, for convenience, the sidereal day is determined by the earth's rotation relative to the vernal equinox or first point of Aries, and is equal to 23 hours 56 minutes and 4·091 seconds of mean solar time (*i.e.*, about 4 minutes shorter than a solar day). *See* **Time.**

DDT, (dichloro-diphenyl-trichloroethane). A very powerful insecticide which has had wide success in the control of diseases, such as malaria and typhus, which is carried by insects. Mosquito swamps are sprayed with DDT to kill the carriers. Because this toxic chemical breaks down very slowly it builds up in birds and animals and its use is now banned in Britain. Its detection in Antarctic wild life confirmed that DDT pollution was virtually world-wide.

Deacon, an ecclesiastical official, who assists in some of the smaller ministerial duties in church or chapel; in the Anglican Church he ranks below a priest.

Dead Languages are such as the ancient Greek and Roman tongues, which are no longer spoken but are preserved in literature.

Dead Sea Scrolls, a group of ancient Jewish documents, consisting of scrolls and fragments which have been recovered since 1947 in the vicinity of Qumran near the Dead Sea and which represent one of the most important finds ever made in the field of biblical archæology and Christian origins. The scrolls, written in Hebrew or Aramaic, were found in caves, the first by chance by an Arab shepherd in 1947. These consisted of biblical texts older by a thousand years than the earliest Hebrew manuscript of the Old Testament (A.D. 895). Many fragments have since been discovered, comprising the whole of the Old Testament with the exception of Esther. In addition there are commentaries and other non-biblical writings, including one called " The War of the Sons of Light with the Sons of Darkness." The writing on the scrolls indicates that they were written over a period of two centuries, the greater proportion before the birth of Christ. A nearby ruin is believed to have been the home of a religious sect called the Essenes (J17), to whom the scrolls belonged. By the aid of the latest scientific techniques, including radiocarbon tests, the age of the scrolls is being accurately determined. An account of the scrolls and their implications is given in Edmund Wilson's *The Dead Sea Scrolls: 1947–1969.*

Dean, a Church of England dignitary, ranking below a bishop, and the head of the chapter of a cathedral. A rural Dean supervises a *deanery* or group of parishes. There are also Deans of Faculties in some universities, and at Oxford and Cambridge the *Dean* is in charge of chapel services and disciplinary arrangements.

Death Watch Beetle (*Xestobium rufovillosum*), a wood-boring beetle, larger than the common furniture beetle, found chiefly in the old oak beams of churches and other historic buildings. The grub bores from 4–12 years. The name " death watch " comes from the superstition

that the ticking sound, made by the beetle striking its head against the wood, is a sign of approaching death. The death watch beetle in the roof of Westminister Hall is being smoked out by means of an insecticide called gamma benzine hexachloride. *See also* **Furniture Beetle, Woodworm.**

Decalogue, name given to the Ten Commandments of the Old Testament. There are two versions of them, differing in detail: Exodus xx. 2–17 and Deuteronomy v. 6–21. They are of Hebrew origin and are recognised by Jews and Christians as the divine law given by God to Moses on Mt. Sinai. Most of them are prohibitions in contrast to the beatitudes (pronounced by Christ in the Sermon on the Mount) which are positive, *e.g.*, Blessed are the merciful.

December, the last month of the year in our calendar, and the tenth in the old Roman.

Deciduous Trees are such as shed their leaves at certain seasons as distinguished from evergreens or permanent foliaged trees or shrubs.

Decimal System is based on the unit of 10. Duodecimal System is based on the unit of 12. Fractional numbers are expressed as divisions of 10 and 12 respectively. Thus:

Fraction	Decimal	Duodecimal
½	0·5	0:6
⅓	0·3333	0:4
¼	0·25	0:3
⅕	0·2	0:2497
⅙	0·1666	0:2
⅛	0·125	0:16
1/12	0·0833	0:1
1/24	0·04166	0:06

Decimal currency was imposed on France in 1795. The United Kingdom changed over to decimal currency on 15 February 1971. The six new coins are:

Denomination	Value	Metal
½ new penny	1·2d.	bronze
1 new penny	2·4d.	bronze
2 new pence	4·8d.	bronze
5 new pence	1s.	cupro-nickel
10 new pence	2s.	cupro-nickel
50 new pence	10s.	cupro-nickel

Declaration of Independence was an Act by which the American Congress, on July 4, 1776, declared the American colonies to be independent of Great Britain. " Independence Day " is a holiday in the United States.

Defender of the Faith (*Defensor Fidei*), a title conferred upon Henry VIII. by Pope Leo X. in 1521 for entering the lists against Luther with his book on *The Assertion of the Seven Sacraments.* In 1554 the title was confirmed by Parliament and has been used ever since by English sovereigns.

Deflation is a policy designed to bring down costs by reducing the supply of means of payment. It is usually advocated as a remedy for inflation, and in this connection is often referred to as Disinflation. It usually results in a fall in employment. The " credit squeezes " of the 1950s in Great Britain were designed to have a disinflationary effect.

Dehydrate, to eliminate the water from a substance. The process of dehydration is now used in the food industry, as a result of wartime research, in making such things as dried egg and packet soups. Most vegetables contain over 90% of water, and much of this can be removed under vacuum at low temperatures without appreciably impairing the flavour. The lightness of the dehydrated products is an advantage when supplies have to be transported.

Deliquescence, the process of dissolving by the absorption of moisture from the atmosphere. For instance, chromic acid crystals on exposure to the air quickly deliquesce.

Delta, a triangular tract of land between diverging branches of a river at its mouth, and so called from its general resemblance to the Greek letter Δ *delta.* The best-known examples are the deltas of the Nile, the Ganges, the Niger, and the Mississippi.

Deluge, a flood, commonly applied to the story of the Deluge in the Bible, in which Noah and the Ark figure. A similar tradition lingers in the mythologies of all ancient peoples.

Democratic Party, one of the two great American political parties, originated about 1787, advocating restrictions on the federal governments and in opposition to the federalists. It was in 1825 that a group who were in favour of high tariffs seceded, later to become the Republican Party. The Democratic Party was split again over slavery before the Civil War (1861–65), and in the main the southern states have been supporters of the Democrats. The economic depression helped the Democrats to power in 1932 (*see* New Deal) and they held office until 1953 when Eisenhower became President. In 1960 Kennedy narrowly won the Presidency and in 1964 Lyndon Johnson swept in with a landslide victory over the Republican candidate. In 1964 Humphrey was beaten by Nixon, the Republican candidate. The symbol of the party is a donkey, invented, like the Republican's elephant, by the cartoonist Nash.

Demoiselle, the Numidian crane, a wading-bird. Also, a sub-order of dragon flies which close their wings over their backs when at rest.

Dendrite, a stone or mineral on or in which tree-like tracery appears, the result of the action of the hydrous oxide of manganese.

Density, a measure of the mass per unit volume of a material, usually expressed in grams per cubic centimetre. *Specific gravity* is the ratio of the density of a material at the temperature under consideration to that of water at the temperature of its maximum density (4 ° C). In grams per cubic centimetre the density of gold is 19·3, silver 10·5, lead 11·3, water 0·99997, air 0·00129.

Depreciation of a currency is a fall in its relative value in terms of gold or of other currencies. The term is most often used to indicate a fall in the value of one country's money in relation to others.

Depression, a region where barometric pressure is lower than that of its surroundings. These areas of low pressure enclosed by the isobars are usually less extensive than anticyclones and may vary from 100 to 1,000 miles in diameter. The winds, often of gale force when the depression is deep, blow round the system in an anticlockwise direction in the Northern Hemisphere (in the reverse direction in the Southern Hemisphere) and inwards across the isobars. The majority of depressions which cross the British Isles travel from the Atlantic, sometimes in series or families, at rates of between a few miles and 700 miles in a day, bringing their generally unsettled weather with them.

De Profundis (out of the depths), the first two words of the Latin version of the 130th Psalm, and commonly used to designate this psalm.

Deserts, vast, barren, stone or sandy wastes where there is almost no rainfall and little or no vegetation. These regions are found in the interior of the continents Africa, Asia, and America between 20° north and 30° north and south of the equator. Europe is the only continent without deserts. The most famous are the Sahara, the largest in the world, the Gobi desert of central Asia, the Kalahari desert of south-west Africa, and the great Australian desert.

Detention Centres in Britain are for young people (boys and girls) over 14 but under 21 who have been found guilty of an offence for which an adult could be sent to prison. Controlled by the Home Office.

Determinism and Free-will. *See* Section J.

Deuterium or "heavy hydrogen." The second isotope of hydrogen; the third is called tritium. Deuterium atoms have in their nuclei a neutron as well as a proton; tritium nuclei have two neutrons and one proton. In ordinary hydrogen gas about one out of every 5,000 atoms is a deuterium atom. Deuterium was discovered in 1932 by Professor Harold Urey. The oxide of deuterium corresponding to water is called " heavy water." The nucleus of the deuterium atom is called a deuteron. An anti-deuteron consisting of an anti-proton and an anti-neutron was produced at Brookhaven in 1965, the first compound anti-nucleus ever to be produced.

Devaluation is a definite, official downward valuation of a country's currency in terms of its exchange value with other currencies. The £ was devalued in 1949, when an official exchange rate of £1 = \$2.8 was established, and again in 1967, to a rate of £1 = \$2.4.

Devonian System in geology refers to the strata between the Silurian and the Carboniferous Formations. It includes the Old Red Sandstone Formation. The fauna of the Devonian include the group of fishes known as the Rhipidistra (on the evolutionary route towards the amphibians), Actinistia (cœlacanth), and the Dipnoi or lung fishes. *See* F44.

Dew, moisture deposited by condensation of water vapour on exposed objects especially during calm, cloudless nights. The loss of heat from the ground after sunset, by radiation, causes the layer of atmosphere close to the surface to be chilled below the temperature, known as the dew-point, at which the air is saturated with vapour. Part of the vapour condensed may be transpired from blades of grass and foliage of plants.

Dew Pond is a shallow artificial pond which is on high ground and rarely dries up, even during prolonged droughts, despite being used by cattle and sheep as a drinking source. The name arose from the belief that dew deposits at night provided the moisture for replenishment. Drainage of rain-water and mist condensed on neighbouring trees and shrubs are probably more important factors.

Dialectical Materialism. *See* J14.

Diamond, a mineral, one of the two crystalline forms of the element carbon (the other is graphite), the hardest known substance, used as a gem and in industry. India was the first country to mine diamonds (the Koh-i-noor, known since 1304, came from Golconda near Hyderabad). The celebrated diamond mines of South Africa were discovered in the 1870s. Other important diamond producing countries are Angola, Sierra Leone, Congo, Tanzania, Guyana, and the Soviet Union. Diamonds can be made artificially by subjecting carbon to very high temperatures and pressures; many industrial diamonds are made this way. Antwerp is the main diamond centre of the world, London the main marketing centre, Amsterdam the main diamond cutting centre.

Diatoms. One-celled algae, common in fresh and salt water. Distinctive feature is the siliceous wall which is in two halves, one fitting over the other like the lid of a box. These walls are often very finely and beautifully sculptured. The diatoms constitute a class of the plant kingdom known as the Bacillariophyta. *Diatom ooze* is a deep-sea deposit made up of diatom shells. *Diatomite* or *diatomaceous earth* is the mineral form that such diatom oozes assume (sometimes known as kieselguhr which mixed with nitroglycerine yields dynamite).

Diatonic Scale. The ordinary major and minor scales on which most European music is built, *e.g.*,

C major   C – D – E – F – G – A – B – C
Tone intervals   1 – 1 – ½ – 1 – 1 – 1 – ½
C minor   C – D – E♭ – F – G – A♭ – B♭ – C
Tone intervals   1 – ½ – 1 – 1 – ½ – 1 – ½

Dies Irae (the Day of Wrath), a famous 13th-cent. Latin hymn of the Roman Catholic Church, part of the Requiem Mass.

Diesel Engine. A compression-ignition engine. The air in the cylinder is compressed to over 500 lb. per sq. in. and its temperature is about 800° F.; oil injected into the hot compressed air ignites immediately. The modern oil engine has been evolved mainly from the principles enunciated by Herbert Akroyd-Stuart in his patent of 1890 and, like the steam and other inventions, represents the improvements achieved by many men, including those by Rudolf Diesel of Germany, in respect of high compression pressures and greater fuel economy.

Diet, in German history, an assembly of dignitaries or delegates called together to debate upon and decide important political or ecclesiastical questions. The most famous imperial Diets were those held at Worms (1521), Speyer (1529), and Augsburg (1530), all of which dealt with matters of religious conflict arising from the Reformation.

Diffusion is the process of mixing which occurs when two liquids or gases are in contact. It is most rapid between gases, and, as laid down by Graham's law, "the rates of diffusion of different gases are in the inverse proportion to the square roots of their relative densities."

Diffusion arises through the continual movement of molecules. Even in solids diffusion can occur. If a block of gold and a block of silver are welded together, after some time particles of gold are found in the silver, and *vice versa*.

Dimensions in common speech are the magnitudes of length, breadth, and thickness giving, the size of an object, thus a line has only one dimension: length; a plane surface two: length and breadth; and a solid three: length, breadth, and thickness. In mathematics, hypothetical objects with any number of dimensions are considered. In physics and mechanics, dimensions are numbers which relate the units in which any quantity is measured to the so-called fundamental units. The latter are usually but not necessarily those of length, mass, and time. " Dimensional analysis " is an important technique of scientific reasoning.

Dimorphism, the quality of assuming two distinct forms. For instance, carbon, which is graphite in one form, is the diamond in another.

Dinosaur, the name given to a group of extinct reptiles of the Mesozoic period, some of which were of immense size—much larger than crocodiles. *See* Diplodocus.

Diorite, an igneous rock of crystalline structure composed of felspar and hornblende. It used to be classed as greenstone.

Dip Needle. Instrument for measuring the *dip* or inclination of the earth's magnetic field.

Diplodocus, one of the best known of the extinct mammoth dinosaurs. Fossil remains have been discovered in the Jurassic rocks of the United States. Some reached a length of over 80 ft.

Dipnoi *or* Lung Fishes. These have the air bladder adapted to function as a lung, and they can remain alive when the stream or marsh in which they live dries up. Species of lung fish occur in Australia, Africa, and S. America.

Diptera, an order of insects. Their main characteristic is that they are two-winged, and the common house-fly is the best-known example. There are at least 50,000 species of these insects, including gnats, blow-flies, mosquitoes, tsetses.

Diptych was a folding two-leaved tablet of wood, ivory, or metal, with polished inner surfaces, utilised for writing with the style by the ancient Greeks and Romans. The same term was applied to the tablets on which the names of the persons to be commemorated were inscribed in the early Church. In art any pair of pictures hinged together is styled a diptych.

Discus, a circular piece of metal or stone about 12 in. in diameter, used in athletic contests by the ancient Greeks and Romans. Throwing the discus was a very favourite game, which was deemed worthy of celebration in Myron's famous *Discobolus* (c. 460 B.C.–450 B.C.), the best copy of which is in Rome.

Disk, an astronomical term denoting the seemingly flat surface of celestial bodies as seen by the eye.

Distillation, a process used to separate liquids of different boiling points. This is effected by placing the mixture in a distillation apparatus and heating. The liquid with the lower boiling point distils over first, the vapour being condensed and collected, forming the first *fraction*. With continued heating the second liquid reaches its boiling point, distils over and the mixture is said to be *fractionated*. Mixtures of liquids with close very high boiling points require more elaborate apparatus. Fractional distillation is a common process in the chemical industry, particularly in the refining of petroleum.

DNA (Deoxyribonucleic acid), a polymer molecule in the form of a double-strand helix containing many thousands of sub-units. Contains the genetic information coded in sequences of sub-units called bases. The Nobel Prize for medicine was awarded in 1962 for the discovery of the structure of DNA; that for 1968 for interpreting the genetic code and its function in protein synthesis. *See* Nucleic Acids, *also* L128.

Docks are enclosed water spaces where ships rest while being loaded or unloaded, repaired, or waiting for cargo. There are three main types: the wet dock in which water is maintained at the level of high tide so that vessels remain afloat while loading and unloading; and the tidal

dock, with open entrance to permit free ebb and flow of tide (*e.g.*, Glasgow, Southampton (which has double tides)); and the dry dock, or graving dock, for overhauling and repairing vessels, so constructed that, after a ship has been docked, the water can be drawn off (*e.g.*, Southampton, Tilbury). The floating dock is a type of dry dock. The Port of London Authority operates four main groups of docks. With the closing of some of the older up-river docks, down-river docks, notably at Tilbury, have being extensively developed.

Dodo, an extinct bird, giant and flightless, which lived on the island of Mauritius up until 250 years ago. Another species, the white dodo, lived on Réunion. Some reached exceptional sizes. By the end of the 17th cent. Mauritius, Rodriguez, and Réunion had all been colonised, and the dodo along with many other birds vanished forever because of their inability to stand up to man and the animals imported into the islands.

Dog-days, a period of 40 days (3 July–11 Aug.) when Sirius rises and sets with the sun. The ancient superstition, which can be traced back in Greek literature to Hesiod (8th cent. B.C.), was that this star exercised direct influence over the canine race.

Doge, the chief magistrate in the former republics of Venice (697–1797) and Genoa (1339–1797, 1802–5).

Dogfish, a large family of small sharks, seldom more than 3 ft. in length. The flesh is sold as "rock salmon." The eggs are contained in horny cases called "mermaid's purses." The commonest of the British dogfishes are the spur-dogs.

Doldrums, a nautical term applied to those areas of the Atlantic and Pacific towards which the trade winds blow and where the weather is calm, hot, and sultry but liable to change suddenly to squall, rendering navigation difficult.

Dolomite, a name applied to a limestone containing appreciable magnesium; also the mineral dolomite, a double carbonate of magnesium and calcium.

Dolphin, an ocean mammal of the whale order, from 6 to 8 ft. long, with a long, sharp snout, and of an active disposition. They abound in most temperate seas and swim in shoals. A few species live in large rivers (Ganges and Amazon). They can cruise for long periods at around 15 knots and produce bursts of speed in the region of 20 knots, the water apparently flowing smoothly past their bodies. Dolphins are some of the most intelligent of mammals and are currently the subject of scientific experiments in communication.

Dome, a large cupola, hemispherical in form, rising over the main building of a cathedral or other prominent structure. The finest existing dome, that of the Pantheon at Rome, is also the oldest, dating from the time of the Emperor Hadrian. It is 142 ft. in diameter and about the same in height. The dome of St. Peter's, in the same city, has a double shell, is 330 ft. high and 140 ft. in diameter. The dome of the cathedral at Florence is 139 ft. in diameter and 310 ft. high, and that of St. Paul's, London, has 3 shells and is 112 ft. in diameter and 215 ft. high. The circular reading-room of the British Museum has a dome 140 ft. in diameter and is 106 ft. high. Malta's Mosta dome is also famous.

Domesday Book is the famous register of the lands of England framed by order of William the Conqueror. According to Stowe, the name was derived from *Domus dei*, the name of the place where the book was deposited in Winchester Cathedral; though by others it is connected with doom in the sense of judgment. Its compilation was determined upon in 1084, in order that William might compute what he considered to be due to him in the way of tax from his subjects. William sent into each county commissioners to make survey. They were to inquire the name of each place, the possessor, how many hides of land were in the manor, how many ploughs were in demesne, how many homagers, villeins, cottars, serving men, free tenants, and tenants in soccage; how much wood, meadow, and pasture; the number of mills and fish ponds; what had been added to or taken away from the place; what was the gross value at the time of Edward the Confessor. So minute was the survey that the Saxon chronicler of the time reports " there was not a single hide, nor one vintage of land, nor even, it is shame to tell, though it seemed no shame to do, an ox, nor a cow, nor a swine was left that was not set down." The record, which did not take in Northumberland, Cumberland, Durham, and parts of Lancashire and Westmorland, was completed on Nov. 15, 1085, and was comprised in two volumes—one a large folio, sometimes called the Little Domesday, which deals with Essex, Norfolk, and Suffolk, the other a quarto, sometimes called the Great Domesday. The first is written on 384 double pages of vellum in one and the same hand, and in a small but plain character, each page having a double column. The quarto is written on 450 pages of vellum, but in a single column and in a large, fair character. The original is preserved in the Public Record Office. *See also* **Danegeld.**

Dominicans, an order of mendicant preaching friars founded by St. Dominic in Languedoc in 1215 and confirmed by the Pope in 1216. The rule of the order was rigorous. The dress was a white habit and scapular with a long black mantle. This gave them the name of Black Friars. Their official name is Friars Preachers.

Donjon, the keep, or inner tower of a castle, and the strongest and most secure portion of the structure. This was the last refuge of the garrison, and there was usually a prison on the lower floor, hence the name *dungeon.*

Don Juan, the legendary hero of many famous works, supposedly based on the life and character of the unscrupulous gallant Don Juan Tenorio of 14th-cent. Seville. The first dramatisation of the legend and the most famous is Tirso de Molina's *El Burlador de Sevilla.* Don Juan was also the subject of Molière's *Le Festin de Pierre,* Mozart's *Don Giovanni,* Byron's *Don Juan,* and José Zorilla's *Don Juan Tenorio.* The latter is played on All Saints' Day throughout Spanish-speaking countries.

Don Quixote, the " knight of the doleful countenance," the hero and title of Cervantes' classic novel of 16th-cent. Spain. Don Quijote de la Mancha, a gentle country gentleman of lofty but unpractical ideals, having read many chivalric romances, believes he is called upon to redress the wrongs of the world. Mounted on his nag Rosinante and accompanied by his companion Sancho Panza, a hard-headed and practical peasant, he sets out on his journeys of knight-errantry

Dormouse, a family of small, squirrel-like rodents widely distributed throughout Europe and Asia, and living mainly on fruit and nuts. It is of nocturnal habits and sleeps through the winter.

Dot, a French term indicating the property which a wife brings to her husband on marriage and is usually settled on the woman, being her separate property, though the income from it may go towards the general household expenses.

Dotterel, a handsome bird of the plover family found in northern Europe and Siberia. Nests in the Cairngorms, the Grampians, and E. Ross. Very tame.

Doukhobors. *See* **J15.**

Drachm (or **Drachma**), an ancient Greek silver coin and weight. One drachma was equivalent to six obols. The word has survived as the name of a weight: Avoirdupois, one-sixteenth part of an ounce; Apothecaries' Weight, one-eighth part of an ounce.

Drag. Term used in mechanics for resistance offered by a fluid to the passage of a body moving through it. When speed of sound is reached drag increases abruptly. The lift/drag ratio gives the aeroplane designer his measure of aerodynamic efficiency.

Dragon, a fabulous monster common to folk-lore in most countries; generally represented as a winged reptile with fiery eyes and breath of flame. A dragon guarded the garden of the Hesperides; in the New Testament there is mention of the "dragon, that old serpent, which is the devil "; St. George, England's patron saint, is supposed to have overcome the dragon; mediaeval legend abounds in dragons; in heraldry the dragon has also a conspicuous place; and in China it was the imperial emblem.

Dragonade, the term given to the series of perse-

cutions of Huguenots in France in the reign of Louis XIV., just before and after the revocation of the edict of Nantes, dragoons being chiefly employed in the work. Since then the term has been used in reference to any onslaught on the people by soldiers.

Dragonet, the name of the fish of the *Callionymus* genus, beautifully coloured, and about a foot in length. They are common on the British coast and in the Mediterranean.

Dragon Fly, the common name of a well-known order of insects having two pairs of membraneous wings, and often of very brilliant colours. They are swift of flight and may be seen hovering over sheets of water in the sunshine all through the summer. Their chief food is mosquitoes.

Dragon's Blood, a dark-red resinous substance obtained from the fruit of a Malay palm, and possessing medicinal virtues. In a special technique used for making line blocks in printing, dragon's blood is used.

Drama. *See* **M40; Contemporary Theatre, I1–40.**

Drawbridge, a bridge that can be lifted up so that no passage can be made across it. It was a usual feature of a fortified castle in the Middle Ages, and was raised or lowered by chains and levers. It spanned the fosse, and on the approach of an attacking party was raised and formed a special barricade to the gate. Modern drawbridges are such as are raised to allow of the passage of boats up and down a river or estuary. The Tower Bridge is a famous London bridge of this type.

Drongo. The King Crow or Indian Black Drongo is frequently seen in India perched on branches or telegraph wires, darting suddenly to catch insects and to attack crows and hawks. Other members of the family are found in Asia, Africa, and Australia. Its plumage is black with steel-blue gloss.

Drosophila *or* **Fruit Fly. More** has been learnt by geneticists from breeding experiments with this insect than with any other.

Dross, the name generally applied to the refuse of molten metal, composed of slag, scales, and cinders.

Drought, a period of dry weather, is a normal and recurring condition in many warm climates, and is frequently provided against by irrigation. In the British Isles really long rainless spells are somewhat rare, and an " absolute drought " is defined officially as a period of at least fifteen days on each of which the rainfall is less than $\frac{1}{100}$ inch. The summer of 1959 was wholly without precedent in all parts of Britain for lack of rainfall, abundant sunshine, and warm weather. In South Yorkshire an absolute drought lasted 59 days, the longest period in British records.

Drupe is the scientific term for stone fruit. The stone forms the inner part (endocarp) of the fruit, and encloses a seed or kernel which is liberated after the fleshy part (pericarp) has rotted.

Dry-rot, the term was first used about 1775 to describe the fungal decay of timber in buildings. Creosote distilled from coal tar is the standard material for preservation of timber, and pentachlorophenol and copper naphthenate are two compounds now extensively used. Dry wood always escapes dry-rot. Chief fungi causing dry-rot are *Merulius* and *Poria.*

Duck, water bird smaller than the related goose and swan, which together form the family Antidae. Duck refers to the female, drake to the male. The duck family falls into two separate groups: the river or freshwater (surface feeding) ducks, such as the mallard, pintail, wigeon, shoveler, mandarin, teal, garganey; and the sea (diving) ducks, such as the goldeneye, pochard, scoter, eider, and the fish-eating mergansers or "sawbills." The ancestor of all domestic breeds, with the exception of the muscovy, is the mallard.

Duckbill, *Ornithorhynchus anatinus,* also duckbilled platypus, a fur-covered, egg-laying, nest-building mammal inhabiting Australia and Tasmania. It has webbed feet and a muzzle like a duck's bill and is about 20 in. long.

Ductility is a property possessed by most metals which renders them capable of being stretched without breaking. Gold is the most, and lead the least ductile of metals, the order being gold, silver, platinum, iron, copper, palladium, aluminium, zinc, tin, lead. In animated nature the spider and the silkworm produce secretions of notable ductility.

Dugong. A marine mammal, belonging to the order Sirenia (sea-cows). Inhabits Red Sea and Indian Ocean; also found as far East as the Philippines and Australia. Lives on seaweed. Related to the Manatee.

Duke, the highest rank in the British peerage next to that of a royal prince. Edward, the Black Prince, eldest son of Edward III., who died before his father, was the first English duke, being created Duke of Cornwall in 1337. Since then all Princes of Wales have held that title.

Dukeries, a range of English woodland and park country, mainly in Nottinghamshire, comprising the adjacent demesnes of several English dukes and nobles. The Dukeries include Sherwood Forest and the estates of Welbeck Abbey, Clumber Park, Worksop Manor, and Thoresby Hall.

Dunes. Sand dunes are elliptical or crescent-shaped mounds of loose sand produced by wind action. The dune has a gentle slope on windward side; a steep slope on the leeward side.

Dunlin, very common small wading-bird of the Sandpiper family nesting in Britain. Its range extends to other areas where it also breeds.

Dunmow Flitch, a custom which originated in the parish of Little Dunmow, Essex, in the reign of Henry III., which was that the husband who was prepared to swear before the prior, convent, and townsfolk of Dunmow that he had not repented of marriage or quarrelled with his wife for a year and a day, should be rewarded with the gift of a flitch of bacon. The custom has frequently been revived.

Dunnock (*Prunella modularis*), a small bird of rich brown and dark grey plumage common in gardens and hedgerows. Sings a cheerful song all the year round. Called hedge-sparrow in southern England. Another member of the same family, the larger Alpine Accentor (*Prunella collaris*), is found on rocky mountain slopes of Europe and Asia.

Duodecimo, a sheet of paper folded into twelve leaves, written " 12mo."

Durbar, a term used in India from the Persian word *darbár* meaning " court " or " audience." It may be either a council for administering affairs of state, or a purely ceremonial gathering. The word was applied to great ceremonial gatherings like Lord Lytton's durbar for the proclamation of the Queen-Empress in 1877 and the Delhi durbar of 1911.

Dust, solid particles of matter floating in the atmosphere, produced chiefly by volcanic eruptions, sand-storms in desert regions, and industrial and domestic smoke. When the island of Krakatoa erupted in 1883, more than 1 cubic mile of dust was thrown into the air and carried three times round the earth by the explosion wave. The particles in dust-storms are much finer than those in sand-storms and are swept up to far greater heights. The local whirlwinds which form over loose dry soils are termed dust-devils.

Dyke. A wall-like intrusion of igneous rock which cuts across the bedding or other layered structure of the country rock; the word also signifies in alternative usage, a sea-wall and an open drain.

Dynamite, a powerful explosive whose chief element is nitro-glycerine. It was discovered by Nobel in 1867, who absorbed nitro-glycerine in kieselguhr; has a disruptive force of about eight times that of gunpowder.

Dynamo. Machine for transforming mechanical energy into electrical energy. Depends on principle of electromagnetic induction whereby a current is produced in a conductor (*e.g.*, copper wire) traversing a magnetic field. The two essential parts of a dynamo are the conductors or *armature* and the *field magnets*.

Dynasty, a succession of monarchs of the same family, as the Carlovingian dynasty, the Bourbon dynasty, the Plantagenet dynasty, etc.

E

Eagle, large bird of prey with huge hooked bill, related to the buzzard, kite, hawk, harrier, falcon, and vulture, together forming the family Falconidae. There are many species to be found throughout the world, the Golden, Imperial, Tawny, Spotted, and Lesser Spotted being found in Europe. The Golden Eagle, a magnificent-looking bird, nests in the Scottish Highlands, and the White-tailed Sea Eagle, which used to breed in Britain, is now only an occasional visitor. The eagle has been the symbol of royal power since the earliest times, and the American or Bald Eagle is the emblem of the United States.

Earl, a British title of nobility of the third rank, duke and marquis coming first and second. The title dates from Saxon times, and until 1337 ranked highest in our peerage.

Earl-Marshal, in England ranks as the eighth of the great officers of state, is head of the College of Arms, attends the sovereign in opening and closing the session of Parliament, arranges state processions (especially coronations) and assists in introducing newly created peers in the House of Lords. The office is hereditary in the family of the Dukes of Norfolk.

Earth, our habitable globe, is the third of the planets of the solar system in order from the sun, and on an average throughout the year takes 24 hours to turn completely round relative to the sun, the whole earth revolving round the sun in a slightly elliptical orbit once in a year of 365·2564 days. The mean distance of the earth from the sun is 93,004,000 miles. The shape of the earth is that of an oblate spheroid, its equatorial and polar axes measuring 7,926 miles and 7,900 miles respectively. Earth satellite studies have shown that it is also slightly pear-shaped, with the stalk towards the north pole. The scale of this effect is such that the south pole is 50 ft. nearer the centre of the earth than the north pole. The crust consists of an outer layer of surface soil of varying thickness, beneath which there is a mass of hard rock several miles deep, the percentage (by weight) of the principal elements present being oxygen 47, silicon 28, aluminium 8, sodium and potassium 5, iron 4·5, calcium 3·5, magnesium 2·2, titanium 0·5, hydrogen 0·2, carbon 0·2, phosphorus and sulphur 0·2. Mass of the earth is estimated to be 6,000 million million million tons. Two-thirds of the earth's surface is covered with water. It has only one satellite, the moon. The earth receives more light from the sun in 13 seconds than it does from the moon in one year. Weather changes are independent of the moon. A recent estimate of the age of the earth's crust is 5,000 million years. Recent discoveries suggest that the earth is embedded in the atmosphere of the sun and that some of the heat that reaches us from the sun gets here by direct conduction through interplanetary space. *See* F8-9.

Earthquake, a sudden violent disturbance of the earth's crust; the region of the surface immediately above the " focus," or source where the earthquake originates, is termed the " epicentre." On account of their destructive power earthquakes have attracted attention from the earliest times, but accurate study dates only from the last century and the development of a world-wide network of recording stations from the present one. The majority of severe earthquakes result from fractures, usually along existing faults, in underlying rock strata subjected to great strains, the shearing movement sometimes extending to the surface. These dislocations set up vibrations which are propagated as waves throughout the bulk of the earth or round the crust. Frequently the main shock is followed by a series of smaller aftershocks. Minor local earthquakes may be attributed to the effects of volcanic activity, but most of the larger ones originate in non-volcanic regions along well-marked lines of weakness in the earth's crust. Generally the ground is felt to tremble, undergoing oscillations which may gradually or suddenly increase to a maximum and accompanied by sounds. Where there is movement of the sea-bed a tidal wave may result. One of the greatest of historic times was that which destroyed and flooded Lisbon in 1755. Among the notable shocks of the present century rank those of San Francisco (1906), Messina, Italy (1908), China (1920), Japan (1923). Napier, New Zealand (1931), N.E. Assam (1950), Ionian Is. (1953), Agadir, Morocco (1960), Chile (1960), Iran (1962), Yugoslavia (1963), E. Turkey (1966), W. Sicily (1968), Peru (1970).

Earthworm, of which there are several species, has a cylindrical body, tapering at both ends, and segmented into rings. It moves by contraction of its rings, aided by retractive bristles; is eyeless, but has a mouth, gullet, and stomach. Earthworms exist in immense numbers, and perform an important part in the scheme of nature by loosening the soil and rendering it more amenable to tillage. They also form a valuable food for birds and many mammals, and are unequalled as bait for certain kinds of fish.

Earwig, a genus of insects possessing two pairs of wings and anal forceps. It is nocturnal, lives on vegetable matter, and hides by day under stones or in flowers, *e.g.*, dahlias. The old belief that it deliberately creeps into people's ears is altogether unfounded. *See* **T30**(2).

Easter, the annual Christian festival in commemoration of the resurrection of Christ, the English name being derived from Eostre, goddess of Spring. The date cannot fall earlier than March 22 nor later than April 25. Many disputes arose among the early Christians as to the proper time to celebrate this day which governs all other movable feasts. It was eventually ruled at the Council of Nicaea in 325 that Easter Day should be the first Sunday after the full moon following the vernal equinox. If this happens to be a Sunday, then Easter Day is the Sunday after. It should be remembered, however, that this moon is a hypothetical moon of the ecclesiastical calendar, quite imaginary, and generally one or two days later than the real moon we see in the heavens. In fact the reverend fathers at Nicaea did us a bad turn in having anything to do with the moon but then they had no Astronomer Royal to advise them of the complications. *See also* **Section N**.

Eastern Question, a term formerly applied to the problems arising from the instability of the Mohammedan power of Turkey and its relations with the other nations of Europe. Later connected with other problems of the Near East, such as the possession of Constantinople and the position of the Balkan states.

East India Company was incorporated by Elizabeth in 1600. In 1613 the Company set up a factory at Surat, India, and in 1662 Bombay came under the Company's influence and developed into an important trading port. Dupleix wanted to establish French power in India and a struggle for supremacy took place. Clive gained the victory for England and thenceforward British dominion in India remained undisputed except by native princes. In 1772 Warren Hastings was appointed the first Governor-General and in 1784 Pitt's India Act established a Board of Control for the India Company. A great increase of trade resulted, and this rule continued down to 1858, when, as a result of the mutiny, the Crown assumed the sovereignty. With the passing of the Indian Independence Act of 1947, British dominion ended and India was handed back to the Indians.

Eau-de-Cologne, a popular distilled perfume first manufactured at Cologne in the 18th cent. by Johann Maria Farina, an Italian, and since made in large quantities in Cologne and elsewhere.

Ebony, a name applied to various hard black woods, the best of which are grown in Mauritius and Ceylon. There are also Indian and American varieties. Only the inner portions, the heartwood, of the trees are of the necessary hardness and blackness. Ebony is largely used in ornamental cabinet work, for piano keys, canes, etc.

Ecce Homo ("Behold the Man!"), used in reference to the pictures and sculptures representing Christ crowned with thorns.

Ecclesiastical Courts, courts for administering ecclesiastical law and maintaining the discipline of the Church of England. Introduced by the Normans. Originally they had jurisdiction over both clergy and laity. *See also* **D28**(1).

Eclipse, the partial or complete obscuring of one heavenly body by another. An eclipse of the sun occurs when the moon, which is 1/400th of the diameter of the sun and about 1/390th as far away, obscures some portion of the sun as seen by an observer on the earth. A total eclipse occurs when the whole of the sun's disc is covered by the moon. Astronomers travel many thousands of miles to observe the outer layers of the sun and its corona, which is only possible when the light from the sun is totally obscured by the moon during the few minutes of an eclipse. The total solar eclipse of 7 March 1970, as seen from Mexico, was watched by millions on their television screens. Total solar eclipses have occurred over parts of the British Isles in the years 1424, 1433, 1598, 1652, 1715, 1724, 1927, 1954 (visible from the Shetland Is.), and the next will be seen only from near Land's End on 11 August, 1999.

Ecliptic is the sun's apparent path in the sky: the great circle described by the sun from west to east in the course of a year. The sun is exactly on the equator on approx. March 21, and Sept. 23, and the points where the celestial equator and ecliptic intersect on these days are called the *equinoctial points*. On approx. June 21 and Dec. 22 the sun reaches its greatest and least midday elevation and its greatest distance north and south of the equator, and the points on the ecliptic on these days are called the *solstices* (*see* Seasons, **N10**). These four points are equidistant from each other by 90°. The equinoctial points are not fixed. The angle of inclination of the ecliptic to the equator is called the obliquity of the ecliptic, which is also variable, being influenced by the gravitational action of the other planets on the earth. At present the angle is 23½°.

Ecumenical Council, a general council of the Christian Church summoned when important questions of Church doctrine and policy are to be decided. The early councils were predominantly Greek and convoked by the emperor. Those summoned by the pope when they meet at the Lateran Palace in Rome are called Lateran Councils; others have met at Constance, Florence, Trent, and the Vatican. Their decisions are not binding on the rest of Christendom. Only 21 Ecumenical Councils have been held in the history of Christendom. The first was held at Nicaea in 325 when the mystery of the Trinity was defined. The 21st (known as the 2nd Vatican Council), convened by Pope John, opened in Oct. 1962 in St. Peter's Rome, and ended in Dec. 1965. Two of the principal themes were the reunion of all Christians with the Church of Rome and the Church's place in the modern world. At the last session of the Council the Pope announced his decision to establish for the first time an international synod of bishops in Rome for consultation and collaboration in the government of the Roman Church. This Senate of Bishops will provide the balancing factor alongside the Curia, which represents the Papacy and not the episcopasy.

Edda, the name given to two important collections of early Icelandic literature—*the Elder or Poetic Edda*, poems handed down from the 9th and 10th cent., probably Norwegian in origin, and the *Younger* or *Prose Edda* of Snorri Sturluson compiled about 1230. They treat of mythical and religious legends of an early Scandinavian civilisation.

Eddystone Lighthouse, 13 miles south of Plymouth, is one of the most isolated in the world. The tower is 168 ft. high, and its light can be seen for 17½ miles. The present structure is the fourth that has occupied this dangerous position. The first was of wood, completed by Winstanley in 1698, but it was destroyed by storm in 1703. In 1708 a second and stronger lighthouse was built by Rudyerd. This lasted until 1755, when it was destroyed by fire. Smeaton built the third lighthouse of granite and this withstood storm and tempest for over a hundred years, 1759–1881. The present lighthouse, also of granite, was built 1879–81 on a nearby rock by Sir James Douglass.

Edelweiss, a white perennial flower of the daisy order, common in Alpine regions.

Education, History of. *See* **J15**.

Eels, edible fishes of the order Apodes, with snakelike body covered with minute scales embedded in the skin. The common or freshwater eel *Anguilla anguilla* is found in the Atlantic coastal areas of N. America and Europe and in the Mediterranean, and breeds S.E. of Bermuda. The electric eel of S. America is a variety of great interest, being able to cause electric shocks.

Egret, a slender, graceful bird of the heron family, of pure white plumage, famed for its beautiful silky plumes (aigrettes), which appear in the breeding season, and for which it was ruthlessly hunted and would have been exterminated had not international action been taken to protect it. The Little Egret with black bill, black legs, and yellow feet breeds in Mediterranean lands.

Eider, a large diving duck, found along the rocky coasts of northern latitudes, well known for the beautifully warm soft down, called "eider down," which the female bird plucks from her breast to line her nest. In Norway and Iceland the haunts of the eider are preserved and the birds protected by law on account of the much prized "eider down," which is collected from the nests just before the breeding season. "Eider down" is so elastic that a pound or two of it will fill an ordinary bed covering.

Eiffel Tower, built by the French engineer Alexandre Gustave Eiffel (1832–1923) for the Paris Exhibition of 1889. The tower which is made of iron is 985 ft. high and weighs about 7,000 tons.

Eisteddfod (a sitting) was originally a congress of Welsh bards and minstrels, and dates from before the 12th cent. These assemblies, discontinued for a long period, were resumed in 1819, and have been held yearly since, each lasting three or four days. Their object is to foster the Welsh patriotic spirit; they are devoted to orations and competitions in poetry, singing, and harp-playing, prizes being awarded to the successful contestants.

Eland, largest species of antelope, native of Africa; large pointed horns, stands 5 feet high at the withers, and weighs several hundred pounds.

Elder, small trees of the *Sambucus* genus, with pinnate leaves, and clusters of white flowers and, later, small purplish-black berries. The black elder, the best known, is common in most parts of Europe, and thrives in Britain. A wine is made from its berries.

El Dorado, a "golden land," was an idea much favoured in the days of the early Spanish explorers. It was believed that somewhere on the South American continent there was a country abounding in gold and precious stones. Many expeditions were fitted out to discover it. Sir Walter Raleigh also went forth on this illusive quest. The term is still used in regard to any place of rich promise.

Electret, a piece of solid matter which retains a permanent electric polarisation analogous to the magnetic polarisation of a permanent magnet. There are various recipes for making them; carnauba wax is a common constituent.

Electricity. *See* F18, *also* Energy Conversion.

Electric Light is produced in several ways, commonly by causing a tungsten wire to heat up to incandescence by passing a current through it. Current may also be forced through ionised gases, causing them to glow. Such discharges include neon lights, sodium and mercury-vapour street-lamps, and various intense electric arcs used for technical purposes. In fluorescent lights an electric discharge causes ultra-violet (invisible) light, which then excites luminosity in certain chemical substances called luminescent materials. Other forms of electric lighting are being investigated.

Electric Telegraph may be said to date from 1836, when Sir Charles Wheatstone and his co-inventor Cooke introduced their Single-Needle instrument, which was soon followed by the Double-Needle apparatus. Morse, in 1837, invented his famous recording instrument. The first electric cable was between Dover and France, and was laid in 1850. The first Atlantic cable was laid in 1858, and the second in 1866. It was in 1899 that the first Marconi wireless telegraph messages were sent between England and France.

Electroencephalograph, an instrument which records the minute voltages produced by the electrical activity of the brain by means of electrodes taped to the scalp. The record of brain waves, known as EEG, shows that there is a general cycle of activity in the brain that underlies both sleep and wakefulness.

Electrolysis is the condition established when an electric current passes through a conducting substance, between electrodes, resulting in decomposition and separation into constituents. Water thus becomes decomposed into hydrogen and oxygen.

Electromagnetic waves. *See* F13.

Electrometer, an instrument for measuring differences of electrical potential. The moving part, perhaps a needle, is affected by electrostatic forces and no current flows through the instrument. High sensitivity can be obtained.

Electron. *See* F10, 14.

Electron Microscope. A microscope in which beams of electrons are focused by magnetic lenses in a manner analogous to the focusing of light beams in the ordinary optical microscope. Modern electron microscopes have very high resolving power and can magnify up to 1,500,000 times, making it possible to explore the cell and the virus. A development of the electron microscope is the scanning electron microscope (stereoscan), recently developed at Cambridge, which can examine an essentially thick object, giving a very large depth of focus. *See* F27(2).

Electronvolt, unit of energy used in nuclear physics. It is the amount of energy required to move one electronic charge through a potential difference of one volt. It is very small—1.6×10^{-12} ergs—and therefore suited to atomic physics. 1 MeV = a million electronvolts and this larger unit is used in nuclear energy physics.

Electronics. The science which deals with the behaviour and control of free electrons. It started with the discovery of the electron by Sir J. J. Thomson in 1897. The practical applications, constituting electronic engineering, have given us radio, radar, photo-electric cells, cathode-ray oscillographs, electron microscopes, television. Nowadays electronics uses devices like transistors such that the electrons move inside solid matter instead of *in vacuo*. This is sometimes referred to as "solid state electronics."

Electrophorus, a simple device for producing static electricity, consisting of a smooth disc of resin or ebonite mounted on a metal base and with a metal cover carrying an insulated handle. The disc is first electrified (negatively) by rubbing it with a dry catskin or flannel and the cover replaced, the upper surface receiving a positive charge and the lower a negative. On lifting off the cover, after having touched it with the finger, the negative charge leaks away to earth and the positive charge is isolated on the cover. The action may be repeated a number of times before it is necessary to replenish the original charge on the disc. Of historical interest only.

Elements. In chemistry, an element is a substance in the simplest form to which it has been reduced. Ninety elements are found naturally on the earth, one is observed spectroscopically in the stars, and a further twelve have been made artificially. Between them these elements can appear in some 1,200 different isotopes, of which 317 occur in Nature. (There are 274 stable isotopes among 81 stable elements.) *See* F20, *also* F66.

Elephant, a proboscidian mammal of which only two species survive—the Asiatic, in India, and the African elephant. No other animals possess a trunk. Both males and females have large ivory tusks, of considerable commercial value. The Indian elephant is usually about 9 ft. high and weighs about 3 tons; African elephants are larger, weigh about 6 tons, and are usually much fiercer. Several fossil elephants of still larger bulk have been discovered, including the mammoth and the mastodon. The Indian elephant is domesticated and used as a beast of burden, and may live 70 years.

Eleusinian Mysteries, festivals common throughout ancient Greece, agricultural in their symbolism.

Elgin Marbles, a collection of ancient Greek sculptures and architectural fragments got together by the 7th Earl of Elgin and brought to England between 1802 and 1812. These celebrated treasures had originally formed part of the Parthenon at Athens, and were probably carved by pupils of the sculptor Phidias. Lord Elgin expended over £70,000 upon them, and they were purchased for £35,000 for the British Museum, where they can now be seen displayed.

Elk, the largest animal of the deer family, possessing enormous antlers, and standing, when mature, about seven feet high. The American moose is of the same family.

Elm, a stately, wide-spreading tree having some 20 species spread over north-temperate regions, several of which are native and peculiar to Britain. The grandest of the field elms is the English elm, *Ulmus procera*, which may reach a height of 140 ft. and a girth of 25 ft. The wych elm, *U. glabra*, or Scots elm, is a valuable hardwood and used in boat-building.

Elzevir, the name of a celebrated family of Dutch printers, who produced editions of Latin, French, and German classics, which were highly valued for their beauty of type and accuracy of printing. They flourished in the 17th cent.

Embalming, the process by which dead bodies are preserved from decay by means of spices and drugs. The art reached perfection in ancient Egypt, as the mummies which still exist so powerfully testify. In modern times many experiments in embalming have been tried, with various degrees of success.

Ember-days are set apart for fasting and prayer in the Western Church, at the periods appointed for ordination, viz., the Wednesday, Friday, and Saturday after the first Sunday in Lent, Whit-Sunday, Sept. 14 (Holy Cross Day), and Dec. 13 (St. Lucia's Day). They are of very ancient origin.

Embossing, the art of stamping in relief letters or designs upon pliant substances.

Embryology, that branch of biology which deals with embryos, tracing their development from fertilisation of the germ or seed to birth.

Emerald. The rich green variety of beryl (beryllium aluminium silicate). The colour is due to the presence of chromium oxide.

Emery, a granular substance of the corundum order, generally mixed with other metallic substances, and used in a powdered state for polishing and grinding purposes. Emery is mined in Asia Minor and the Grecian archipelago.

Enamel, a vitrified substance applied as a coating to pottery and porcelain. The art was practised by the Assyrians and Egyptians, and was introduced into Europe by way of Greece. Enamels are all either of the transparent or opaque kind, and are susceptible to an immense variety of colouring, according to the metallic oxides introduced.

Encaenia, a festival commemorating a dedication; at Oxford University the annual commemoration of benefactors, accompanied by the conferring of honorary degrees, is held in June.

Encyclical Letters, a term used in reference to letters addressed by the Pope to his bishops upon matters of doctrine or discipline.

Encyclopaedists, a term first applied to the eminent writers who collaborated in the French *Encyclopédie* (1751–65). They included Diderot, D'Alembert, Voltaire, Helvetius; their writings generally were sceptical as to religion, destructive as to politics, and had great influence in popularising the social ideas which afterwards resulted in the French Revolution.

Energy. One of the most fundamental concepts of science. A body in motion possesses *kinetic energy* as a result of the *work* done by the forces creating the motion. But a force which does work to stretch a spring does not create motion. Instead, the work is stored up in the spring and is one example of *potential energy*. A raised body also possesses potential energy which turns into kinetic when the body falls. The *heat energy* contained in a body is the sum of the kinetic and potential energy of the constituent atoms which are vibrating all the time. Heat and motion are obtainable from electrical, magnetic, chemical, atomic, and other sources, and physicists therefore define corresponding forms of energy. The vital point is that all forms of energy are transferable into one another *without loss or gain*. This is the Law of Conservation of Energy. It is one of the most fundamental laws of science, and its general validity is the reason why energy is an important idea. Since Einstein, it has been recognised that mass also is interchangeable with energy. *See* F15, *also* Nuclear Energy.

Energy Conversion. For practical purposes it is frequently necessary to change energy from one into another of its many forms; indeed

almost every activity does this in one way or another. The primary sources of energy are the sun, uranium and other elements from which nuclear energy can be drawn, and the tides. The sun is not much used *directly* because its heat is intermittent and not very intense, but solar cookers and solar batteries (*q.v.*) are used in spacecraft. The sun can be used *indirectly* because it has produced, *via* living processes, fossil fuels like coal and oil and still continues to generate winds, rain, and rivers and hence hydroelectric and wind power. Commonly both fossil fuels and the energy of river or tidal waters are converted into electricity. Windmill type electricity generators are also quite common. The bulk of electricity production is a two-stage process: first fossil or nuclear fuel is used to create heat (*see* Nuclear Reactors); then the heat is used to raise steam and drive generators. Efforts are being made to convert heat into electricity more directly, *e.g.*, by using thermoelectric or thermionic effects (*q.v.*), but these have not been used for large-scale production. Once electrical energy is available, factories can make chemical batteries in great numbers and these can then be used as portable energy sources, as can petrol and other refined forms of fossil fuel. *See* Battery, Fuel Cell.

English Language. *See* M44.

Engraving is the art of cutting or otherwise forming designs of pictures on wood, stone, or metal surfaces for reproduction by some method of printing. Wood-engraving was the earliest in the field, dating from the 15th cent. Later, engraving on steel and copper plates was introduced, and mezzotint, lithography, stipple, aquatint, etc. Most modern methods of reproduction are based on photography.

Ensilage, a method of storing and preserving fodder, vegetables, etc., in pits dug in the ground and excluded from air or light. The system was practised in ancient Rome and revived in England in the 19th cent.

Entablature, that portion of a building which surmounts the columns and extends to the roof of the tympana of the pediments; it comprises the architrave, the frieze, and the cornice.

Entomology is the study of insects. *See* Insects.

Entrepreneur. An entrepreneur or undertaker, is a firm which brings together the factors of production needed for producing goods or services, undertaking the risks and uncertainties involved—though it may transfer some of them by insurance or by other methods. The entrepreneur may be either an individual or a company or corporation, private or public.

Enzymes. Organic catalysts which accelerate chemical processes occurring in living organisms. There are a large number present in the cell, and most have a high degree of specificity. Enzyme mechanisms are the key to basic biological processes. *See* F25(1), 30(1).

Epaulette, a shoulder badge fringed with cord, worn by English army officers until 1855; now confined to naval officers, and varying in form and richness according to the rank of the wearers.

Ephemoptera *or* **May-flies,** an order of insects. In the larval condition they exist from two to three years aquatically, but no sooner do they arrive at maturity than their lives are hurried to a close. They rise up in pyramids on warm summer nights, take no food, propagate, and perish. The Latin name expresses the fact that the adults have an ephemeral existence.

Ephod, a vestment worn by a Jewish high priest, and sometimes by priests of lower rank. In olden times it was of rich texture and set with gems.

Epiphany, a church festival celebrated on January 6, Twelfth Day.

Equator, the imaginary great circle of the earth, every point of which is 90 degrees from the earth's poles, and dividing the northern from the southern hemisphere. It is from this circle that the latitude of places north and south is reckoned. The celestial equator is the circle in which the plane of the earth's equator meets the celestial sphere (the imaginary sphere, in which the observer is at the centre, used for representing the apparent positions of the heavenly bodies).

Equinox, the time when the sun crosses the plane

of the earth's equator, making day and night of equal length.

Eras are distinctive periods of time associated with some remarkable historical event or personage. *The Christian era* is computed according to a 6th-cent. reckoning to begin with Jesus's birth, A.D. 1. The date is placed some years too late. Scholars now believe that Jesus was born *c.* 6 B.C. The *Jewish era* dates from 3761 B.C.; the *Julian era* from the alteration of the calendar by Julius Caesar 45 B.C.; the *Mohammedan era* from the date of the *Hejira*, or the flight of Mohammed from Mecca to Medina, which is A.D. 622, July 16, in the Gregorian Calendar.

Erbium, belongs to the group of rare-earth metals discovered by Mosander in 1842.

Erg, the unit of work and energy in the centimetre-gram-second system; the energy involved when a force of 1 dyne moves its point of application through a distance of 1 cm.

Erl-King, a forest fiend of German mythology, who lured children from their homes and carried them off. In Goethe's ballad the " Erlkönig " it is a traveller's child who is lured to destruction.

Ermine. *See* Stoat.

Ernie, the name given to the " electronic random number indicator equipment ", the electronic machine which selected the prizewinning numbers in the first Premium Bond draw held June 1–2, 1957.

Eros. This asteroid is 15–20 miles in diameter. It comes closer to the earth than any other member of the solar system with the exception of the moon and several very small asteroids. Determination of solar parallax based on observations of Eros in 1930–31 yielded the most accurate estimate of the distance of the sun from the earth (93,004,000 miles).

Erse, a term used by Lowland Scottish, and English writers for the Gaelic language spoken in the Highlands of Scotland. Sometimes erroneously applied to Irish, the Gaelic language as spoken in Ireland and revived as an official language in recent times. Dr. Johnson, Sir Walter Scott, and other writers used " Erse " to signify Scottish Gaelic. The language of the Scottish Lowlands (that used by Robert Burns) is related to the English language and not to Gaelic and is variously termed Scots, Braid Scots, the Doric, the Scottish vernacular, and, fashionably of late, Lallans.

Escurial or **Escorial**, Spanish monastery built in the mountains near Madrid by Philip II to commemorate the victory over the French at Saint-Quentin (1557). A palace was added later and it also includes a church, library and royal mausoleum. Built in granite in sombre style, it is one of the finest buildings in Europe.

Escutcheon, a shield-shaped surface called a field, upon which a man's armorial bearings are represented. A woman's is lozenge-shaped.

Esparto Grass grows in great abundance in Spain and North Africa, and the pulp is largely used for paper-making as well as for other purposes.

Esperanto, an artificial international language created by L. Zamenhof of Warsaw and first published in 1887. It does not seek to replace national languages but to serve as a second language for international communication. It is based on the internationality of many words in the principal modern languages, and is entirely phonetic in spelling and pronunciation.

Esquire, formerly a title applied to a young man of noble birth who attended on a knight and carried his shield. The title ranked next below that of knight and was applied to the eldest sons of knights and the younger sons of peers. Later it became a courtesy title and given to any man as a mark of respect.

Essential Oils are oils derived from plants by distillation or expression, and much used in perfumery as well as to some extent in medicine.

Estate Duty is the duty payable upon the value of all property passing on the death of any person. The charge to duty is not limited to property owned by the deceased but may extend to other property, *e.g.*, to trust funds from which the deceased received income in his lifetime and to gifts made by the deceased within seven years of his death (one year in the case of a gift for public or charitable purposes). For deaths occurring after 30 March 1971 estates not over £12,500 are exempt from duty. On estates of a higher value duty is chargeable by reference to rates ranging from 25 per cent to 85 per cent on successive slices of the estate.

Estates of the Realm in Great Britain are the Lords Spiritual, the Lords Temporal, and the Commons. They are the great classes invested with distinct political powers, and whose concurrence is necessary to legislation.

Esters. Organic chemicals formed by combining an alcohol with an acid. They have a pleasant smell, and occur naturally in plants as the scent of flowers. Manufactured for use in the perfumery industry, and as flavourings in food. Some esters are used as solvents, notably amyl-acetate (" pear drops ") in quick-drying paints. The polymeric fibre " Terylene " consists of chains of molecules containing many ester groups, formed by reacting an alcohol having two alcoholic (OH) groups with an acid having two acid (COOH) groups.

Etching, a process of engraving, on copper usually, the design being drawn with a steel needle, and the lines produced by the action of an acid.

Ether, in chemistry, is a volatile inflammable liquid composed of carbon, hydrogen, and oxygen. It is a valuable anaesthetic obtained by heating alcohol with sulphuric acid. In physics, in the 19th cent., all space was supposed to be filled with a substance called ether, the chief property of which was to carry light waves, *i.e.*, light was supposed to be waves in this all-pervading medium known as the ether. Speculation and experiment concerned with the ether were very fruitful in advancing physics. Ultimately the attempts by Michelson and Morley to detect the motion of the earth through the ether were unsuccessful in this respect but profoundly successful in stimulating the theory of relativity. The ether concept has now been abandoned. *See also* F15(1).

Ethylene. A gas compounded of carbon and hydrogen, it is related to acetylene and ethane. Industrially it is obtained as a by-product in petroleum refining. It has wide uses as a starting material in the industrial manufacture of intermediates, especially alcohol. Its most important application is in the production of polythene (poly-ethylene). *See* Catalyst.

Etruscans, people believed to have come from Asia Minor who colonised Italy about 900 B.C., settled in what is now Tuscany and part of Umbria, reached the height of their civilisation about 500 B.C., and were ultimately absorbed by the Romans. They were skilled technicians in bronze, silver, and goldwork, and excelled in the art of granular decoration.

Etymology treats of the science and structure of words, including classification and derivation.

Eucalyptus. This genus includes 300 species of evergreen, leathery-leaved trees native to Australia. The oils yielded by different species vary a great deal in their scent and other properties and are chiefly used in pharmacy and perfumery; about 30 species produce oils suitable for medicinal purposes. Various species produce timber.

Euro-dollar Market. An international financial market, located mainly in Britain and Europe, for lending and borrowing dollars, *i.e.*, titles to dollar deposits in United States banks. *See* Section G, Part IV.

Europium, element discovered by Demarcay in 1906. A member of the rare-earth metal group.

Evaporation is the process by which a solid or liquid is resolved into vapour by heat. The opposite process is condensation. Wherever a liquid or solid surface is exposed, evaporation takes place into the space above. If the vapour is continually removed the solid or liquid vanishes into vapour; the higher the temperature the quicker the process. If the vapour is confined, then it collects, getting more concentrated until as many atoms of vapour are condensing as are evaporating. The vapour is then said to be saturated. Evaporation of water from sea, soil, plants, skin, etc., is continuously in progress, so it is a process of fundamental importance to meteorology, botany, physiology, industry, not to speak of human comfort and homely activities such as laundering.

Everest Expeditions. For many years after Mt. Everest had been shown to be the highest mountain in the world, political conditions in Nepal, lying south of the summit, and in Tibet, to the north, prevented mountaineers from attempting an ascent. At last in 1921 the Tibetan authorities gave permission, and the first expedition, organised, as were all subsequent British expeditions, by a joint committee of the Royal Geographical Society and the Alpine Club, and led by Col. C. K. Howard-Bury, was sent out. This was primarily a reconnaissance; besides mapping the northern flanks, it found a practicable route up the mountain. By 1939, six further expeditions had climbed on the northern face. Some were baulked by bad weather, others by problems previously little known, such as the effect of high altitudes on the human body and spirit. Nevertheless, notable climbs were accomplished. In 1924, for example, Col. E. F. Norton reached 28,163 ft., and it was on this expedition that G. L. Mallory and Andrew Irvine were seen going well at about the same height. They never returned, however, and what disaster befell them is not known. After the war, political conditions again closed the Tibet route; permission was eventually obtained from the Nepalese Government to make the attempt from the south. In 1951 a reconnaissance expedition under Eric Shipton reached the ice-fall at the exit of the Western Cwm (a high valley lying south-west of the massif), and reported favourably on the prospects for an ascent. The first attempt from this side was made the following year by a Swiss expedition led by Dr. E. Wyss-Dunant, two members of which made an attempt on the summit, but were stopped at approx. 28,200 ft. by the intense cold and the very strong winds. When the British 1953 Expedition, led by Col. John Hunt (now Lord Hunt), was being organised, stress was laid on three main points; proper acclimatisation of the climbers; use of oxygen for the final stages; and the establishment of very high altitude camps, so that the final assault parties would set out fresh and unencumbered. Great attention was also paid to recent developments in diet, clothing, and equipment. In all these matters the 1953 expedition was able to draw on the accumulated experience of their predecessors. By the end of April, a base camp had been established below the ice-fall, and with the aid of thirty-four Sherpa porters supplies had been carried up into the Western Cwm. The next critical stage was the ascent of the steep head of the cwm, the Lhotse face, with the threat of avalanches always present. By most strenuous efforts, a camp was established on the South Col (25,800 ft.) on May 21. From this camp on May 26, T. D. Bourdillon and R. C. Evans climbed the South Peak of Everest (28,720 ft.), then the highest altitude ever attained. On May 28, Edmund Hillary and the Sherpa leader, Tenzing Norkey, spent the night at the highest camp (27,900 ft.) and on the following day, May 29, climbed to the South Summit, negotiated the difficult final ridge, and reached the summit of Everest—the climax of a long, arduous, and stirring endeavour.

Evolution, in the words of Sir Julian Huxley, " a natural process of irreversible change which generates novelty, variety, and increase of organisation." The theory, as laid down by Darwin, is that all existing species, genera, and classes of animals and plants have developed from a few simple forms by processes of change and selection. Up to the time of Darwin a large part of the civilised world believed that life had been created suddenly at the beginning of the world which God had created, according to Archbishop Usher, on 22 Oct. 4004 B.C. The evidence of the rocks, however, has given a more convincing theory of creation, and by studying the fossils preserved in the various layers of the earth's crust the past history of the earth's life has been pieced together. Darwin has been called the Newton of biology. *See* **F46.**

Excommunication, exclusion from the rights and privileges of the Church. It is of two kinds—the major, which means a total cutting off, and the minor, which shuts out only from participation in the Eucharist. In mediæval times, major excommunications were often launched against rulers and leaders.

Exchequer, which derives its name from the checkered tablecloth on which accounts were calculated in early Norman times, is a term connected with the revenues of the Crown. In former times it had jurisdiction in all revenue matters. The term Exchequer is now applied to the Governmental department which deals with the public revenues, the working head of which is the Chancellor of the Exchequer.

Existentialism. *See* **J18.**

Exploration. Modern exploration began in the second half of the 15th cent. with the voyages of the great Portuguese and Spanish discoverers. They were followed by sailors of other European nations, who profited from their developments in navigation and from their charts, and in less than one hundred years the coast-lines of much of the Americas, Africa, and south-west Asia had been revealed and the globe circumnavigated. The motives of these early explorers were mixed: they were seeking adventure, trade, plunder, national power, and the conversion of the heathen. Few if any were directly interested in advancing scientific knowledge. But from the reports of their voyages and travels, scholars at home compiled descriptions of the strange new world which stimulated their successors to undertake more systematic enquiries. One of the earliest English expeditions to be despatched for scientific research was that of William Dampier on the *Roebuck,* which was sent out by the Admiralty in 1699 to examine the coasts of North-west Australia. In the 18th cent. British explorers were at work mainly in the Pacific Ocean, with the object of breaking the Spanish monopoly of trade. Capt. James Cook sailed thither in 1769 to observe first the transit of Venus at Tahiti, and then to search for the alleged great southern continent. On this voyage he discovered and charted much of the coasts of New Zealand and the east coast of Australia. On his second voyage he was the first to sail across the Antarctic Circle, and he showed that the southern continent was much smaller than had been supposed. By 1800 the general outlines of the continents, except for Antarctica were known, and explorers in the 19th cent. were largely engaged in opening up the interiors. In Africa British explorers solved two problems which had puzzled men for centuries: Mungo Park and Richard Lander established the true course of the River Niger, and Sir Richard Burton, J. H. Speke, Sir Samuel Baker, and others revealed the true sources of the Nile. The greatest African explorer of that age was undoubtedly David Livingstone, the missionary, who in three great journeys explored the Zambesi and the region of the Great Lakes, spreading the Gospel, fighting the slave trade, and opening up the interior to settlement and trade. In North America Alexander Mackenzie was the first to cross the main breadth of the continent from sea to sea. In Asia motives were also mixed; men like Charles Doughty, who explored in Arabia, and Sir Francis Younghusband, who journeyed from China to India across the Gobi and the Himalaya, were impelled by a love of adventure and the quest for knowledge, but political considerations were often involved. In recent years, with the main features of the world's surface known, exploration has become more intensive. Teams of scientists go out to study restricted areas in detail. An Antarctic expedition can contribute to our knowledge of world weather, or by biological research into the life history of whales, can help to improve our food supplies. Similarly, expeditions in Africa can help to check the loss of valuable agricultural land through soil erosion, or to develop areas of settlement by schemes for irrigation and power. And there are still great areas to be adequately mapped. All these problems are inter-related, and in solving them the modern explorer can call on many improved techniques and instruments—the aeroplane, the aerial camera, tracked motor vehicles, radio, in fact all the resources of modern science. But the human element is still vital, and for those with the old explorers' spirit there will always be problems left to solve.

Explosives, substances which burn violently to produce gases in such volume that an explosion is induced. Gunpowder was the first explosive to be used; Roger Bacon's powder, consisting of charcoal, sulphur, and saltpetre, was the only effective explosive until the 19th cent., but it was difficult to control. Nitroglycerine (glyceryl trinitrate) was first compounded in 1847 by adding glycerine to a mixture of sulphuric acid and nitric acid. In 1866 Alfred Nobel discovered how to make dynamite by absorbing nitroglycerine in the fine sand kiesulguhr. Cordite was the joint invention of Sir Frederick Abel and Sir James Dewar (1889). It came into general use as a propellant. High explosives, providing bursting charge for shells and bombs, include TNT (trinitrotoluene), picric acid, cyclonite (RDX) and many others. Slurry explosives can be pumped on to the site and therefore offer advantages in transportation and safety; they are also waterproof. Chemical explosives have been eclipsed by nuclear explosives which have developed from the first atom bomb (dropped on Hiroshima 6 August 1945) to the 100-megaton hydrogen bomb.

Expressionism, a modern art movement confined primarily to the non-Latin countries of Europe which sought to give expression to intimate and personal emotions by means of distortions of line and colour and simplified style which carried a greater impact in terms of feeling. Broadly speaking, this has been characteristic of northern art in general. (*See* Gothic.) The term is usually used of the modern movement which influenced the Post-impressionists and subsequent movements in France. Tired of the naturalism of the Impressionists, such artists as van Gogh, Gauguin, Matisse, and Rouault together with the Fauvists (*q.v.*) made use of simple outlines and strong colours. Apart from Toulouse-Lautrec, the principal Expressionists were Norwegian, like Munch, or German, like the painters of *Die Brücke* and *Der Blaue Reiter* groups. Individual artists were Ensor, Kokoschka, Nolde, Rouault, and Soutine.

F

Fabian Society. *See* J18.

Fables are fictitious narratives intended to enforce some moral precept, and may be either in prose or verse, and deal with personified animals and objects or with human beings. Aesop in ancient times and Hans Christian Andersen and the Brothers Grimm (in many of their stories) in later days, have given fables. Mention must also be made of La Fontaine's and Krylov's fables.

Faience, a kind of decorated glazed earthenware invented in Faenza, Italy, about the end of the 13th cent. Wedgwood-ware is a notable example of modern faience.

Fairs were established in mediæval times as a means of bringing traders and customers together at stated periods, and formed the chief means of distribution. The great English fairs of early times were those of Winchester and Stourbridge near Cambridge. Traders from the Netherlands and the Baltic gathered there with the great merchants of London, and goods of every kind, wholesale and retail, were sold. The British Industries Fair is the modern counterpart of the mediaeval trade fair. One of the biggest trade fairs was at Nijni-Novgorod, founded in the 17th cent.; other big continental fairs are those of Leipzig (founded in the 12th cent.), Lyons, and Prague.

Fairy Rings are the circles caused in grassland by certain fungi. The circles expand outwards as the fungus spreads, the fruiting bodies being at the periphery. Farther inward where the fungi are decaying the grass grows more strongly, fertilised by the nitrogen released from the rotting fungi. In olden times these rings were held to be the scene of fairy dances.

Falcon, name given to diurnal birds of prey which belong to the same family, *Falconidae,* as the hawk, eagle, buzzard, kite, and harrier. They are swift of wing and feed on birds and small mammals. These birds have long, pointed wings, strong, hooked and notched bill, long, curved claws, and an eye of great power. They are found all over the world. Those that breed in Britain are the Kestrel (the most common), Hobby (one of the swiftest of European birds),

Merlin, and Peregrine, a swift and magnificent bird with slate-grey back, blackish crown, black "moustache" and whitish breast. Other members of the family are the Gyr Falcon from northern latitudes, Iceland and Greenland, which is a winter visitor to Britain, the Lanner, Saker, Eleonora's falcon, Red-footed falcon, and the Lesser Kestrel. The Gyr Falcon and the Peregrine were used in the sport of falconry in olden times. Because of its fearlessness and larger size, the female bird was used. When the quarry was sighted, the bird was unhooded, set free, and after mounting high into the air would dart swiftly down to strike the prey. The heron was the usual victim.

Fall-out. Radioactive material produced by nuclear explosions which may cause bodily and genetic damage. (1) *Local fall-out,* due to the return to earth of larger particles, occurs locally, and within a few hours after the explosion; (2) *Tropospheric fall-out,* due to particles which remain in the troposphere and come down within a month or so, possibly all over the world, but within the altitude in which the explosion occurred; (3) *Stratospheric fall-out,* which comes from fragments taken up into the stratosphere and then deposited, in the course of many years uniformly all over the globe. The two radioactive materials which have given rise to the greatest concern for the health of the individual are strontium-90 and iodine-131. Both these materials are liable to become concentrated in certain parts of the human body, strontium-90 in bone and iodine-131 in the thyroid gland. Radiation exposure may produce genetic effects, that is effects which may show up in succeeding generations. An extensive survey has been carried out by scientists of the U.S. Atomic Energy Commission on the islands of the Bikini atoll, site of some 23 nuclear tests, 1946–58. Their records, published in 1969, reveal that the intensity of radioactivity underneath the point of explosion is still exceedingly high. Most of the radiation remaining is due to the radioactive isotope caesium-137. The variation in intensity from one place to another seems to be correlated with the variations of vegetation: where there was little vegetation weathering had been rapid. (The nuclear test ban treaty, 1963, applies to all nuclear tests except those held underground.)

Fantail, a variety of the domestic pigeon; also a genus of Australian birds of the *Muscicapidae* family. A small New Zealand bird is called a fantail.

Fan Tracery, a complicated style of roof-vaulting, elaborately moulded, in which the lines of the curves in the masonry or other material employed diverge equally in every direction. It is characteristic of the late Perpendicular period of Gothic architecture, and may be seen in St. George's Chapel at Windsor and the Chapel of Henry VII. at Westminster Abbey.

Farmer-General, the name given to the financiers who in the days of the old French monarchy farmed certain taxes, contracting to pay the Government a fixed sum yearly, on condition that the specified taxes were collected and appropriated by themselves. The revolution of 1789 swept Farmers-General away.

Fascism. *See* J19.

Fata Morgana, the name given to a curious mirage often observed over the Straits of Messina, attributed to the magic of the fairy Morgana, half-sister of King Arthur, who was fabled to live in Calabria.

Fathers of the Church were early writers who laid the foundations of Christian ritual and doctrine. The earliest were the Apostolic Fathers, (*q.v.*). The Four Fathers of the Latin Church were St. Ambrose, St. Jerome, St. Augustine, and St. Gregory the Great. The Four Fathers of the Greek Church were St. Basil, St. Gregory Nazianzen, St. John Chrysostom, and St. Athanasius.

Fathom, a nautical measure, the six-foot stretch of a man's arms. It is to be replaced by the metre on British Admiralty charts, but will continue on yachtsmen's coastal charts.

Fats are important foodstuffs. In physiology they constitute a valuable form of reserve food. They contain carbon, hydrogen and oxygen; chemically they are described as esters of

glycerol (glycerine). Commonest fats are stearin, palmitin, and olein, esters formed by the combination of glycerol with stearic, palmitic, and oleic acid respectively. Fats are converted into soap by alkali; this process (saponification) also releases glycerol.

Fault, a term designating a breakage coupled with displacement of geological strata.

Fauvism (Fr. *fauve* = wild beast), a term contemptuously applied to the work of a group of French painters led by Matisse who exhibited at the Salon d'Automne in Paris in 1905. Their belief was that a painting must be not only a consistent and harmonious decoration but the expression of an idea or feeling. Forms and colours are emotive in their own right. The objects painted by the Fauves, though simplified, distorted, and often violently coloured, are easily recognisable. Inspiration for their highly decorative canvasses came from many sources: Byzantine and Persian art in the case of Matisse; German Expressionism in the case of Derain and Vlaminck. The Fauves paved the way for the Cubists (Braque joined Picasso in 1909) who approached nature in more arrogant mood, from a more intellectual point of view.

February, the second month of the year, contains in ordinary years 28 days, but in leap years 29 days. When first introduced into the Roman calendar by Numa *c.* 700 B.C. it was made the last month of the year, preceding January, but in 452 B.C. the position of the two months was changed, February following January.

Federation. *See under* Confederation.

Félibrige, a movement founded in 1854 to revive the ancient glories of Provence, initiated by the French poet Frédéric Mistral.

Felspar, the name given to a group of minerals, silicates of aluminium with some calcium and sodium, or potassium, which make up probably more than half of the earth's crust. It is formed in granite and other rocks, both igneous and metamorphic.

Fenestella, the niche set apart on the south side of the altar for the piscina in Roman Catholic churches.

Fermentation, the action of chemical ferments or *enzymes* in bringing about chemical changes in the materials of living animals and plants, *e.g.*, the breaking-down of sugar by yeast into alcohol.

Ferret, a carnivorous animal of the Pole-cat family, with a pointed head and long sinuous body, well adapted for following rabbits and game into their burrows and hiding-places, it being kept in this country for that purpose. It is a native of Spain and Africa, and does not exist in England in a condition of natural freedom. *See* Z12.

Ferrites are compounds containing iron, oxygen, and one or two of a certain range of other possible metallic elements. Ferrites have recently become very important technically, because, unlike ordinary magnetic materials, they combine strong magnetism with electrical insulating properties. Ferrite-rod aerials are now common in portable radios, and ferrite devices are used in radar. *See* F20(1).

Feudalism. *See* J20.

Fieldfare, the largest member of the thrush family, a regular winter visitor to Britain from Scandinavia. It is brown in colour with a lighter spotted breast and a grey head.

Field-Marshal, the highest ranking title in the British army, and only bestowed on royal personages and generals who have attained great distinction. The first British Field-Marshal was created in 1736, when John, Duke of Argyll, had the title conferred upon him by George II.

Fifth Column. When Franco, the Spanish dictator, revolted against the Spanish Republic in 1936 and attacked Madrid with four armies, he declared that a group of fascists within the city was assisting the besiegers. The term is used to describe a body of spies behind a fighting front.

Fighting-Fish, small pugnacious Siamese fish with long caudal and ventral fins. They are kept in glass globes in Siam, and when brought into contact will fight to the death, these encounters being the occasion of much gambling.

Filibuster, a name first given to pirates and buccaneers in the 17th cent. who took possession of small islands or lonely coast lands, and there maintained themselves apart from any governing authority. In later times the term was used to specify men taking part in expeditions whose object was to appropriate tracts of country, and settle upon them in disregard of international law. The most notable expeditions of this kind in modern times were those of Narcisco Lopez against Cuba in 1850–51, and of William Walker against Nicaragua, between 1855 and 1860. Both leaders were captured and executed. The term is also used to express the right of a minority in the United States Senate for unlimited debate, which is used on occasions to delay legislation.

Finches, a large family of small birds belonging to the Passerine or perching order of birds. There are about 200 species, including greenfinch, hawfinch, chaffinch, goldfinch, siskin, bullfinch, crossbill, linnet, twite, and buntings.

Fir, a cone-bearing tree with small evergreen leaves and of considerable use as timber. There are two types: the Silver Firs and the Douglas Firs numbering about 25 species. All these firs attain to a considerable height, and all yield turpentine or other resinous material.

Fire-damp. *See* Methane.

Fire-Fly, a small winged insect of the *Eleteridae* family, is able to throw out a strong phosphorescent light in the dark. There are some remarkable specimens in tropical countries.

Fire of London, of 1666, extended from East to West, from the Tower to the Temple church, and northward to Holborn Bridge. It broke out in a baker's shop in Pudding Lane, and lasted four days, and destroyed 87 churches, including St. Paul's Cathedral, and many public buildings, among them the Royal Exchange, the Custom House, and the Guildhall. In the ruins were involved 13,200 houses and 400 streets. About 100,000 people were made homeless yet in about 10 years all the houses had been rebuilt. The plague had not disappeared from London when the fire occurred.

Firkin, a former measure of capacity, the fourth part of a barrel, now only used in reference to a small cask or tub for butter, lard, tallow, etc.

Fischer-Tropsch Process. A process for making synthetic petrol from carbon monoxide and hydrogen. The synthesis is accelerated by cobalt-thoria and nickel-thoria catalysts.

Fish Louse. Parasitic crustacea found on marine and fresh-water fishes and whales.

Fission, Nuclear. A nuclear reaction in which the nucleus of an atom (*e.g.*, uranium 235, plutonium) captures a neutron, and the unstable nucleus so produced breaks into two nearly equal fragments and throws out several neutrons as well. In biology the term fission is applied to reproduction by fragmentation of a single-cell organism, as in amœba. *See* F12(1).

Flagella, single hair-like projections found on many micro-organisms. Their sole function is, by complicated motion, to move the organism about. They are longer and less versatile than cilia (*q.v.*).

Flag Officer, a British naval officer who enjoys the right of carrying a flag at the mast-head of his ship, and is of the rank of Admiral, Vice-Admiral, or Rear-Admiral.

Flagship, the ship that flies the Admiral's flag, and from which all orders proceed.

Flamingo, a strangely beautiful, extremely slender wading bird of white and rose-pink plumage with long, slender legs and neck and a long, down-curved bill with which it rakes the mud and obtains its food of worms and molluscs. The wings are bright crimson, bordered with black, and a flock in flight is a picture of singular beauty. There is a large and famous colony in the Camargue.

Flash-Point. This is found by heating an oil in a special cup and taking the temperature at which sufficient vapour is produced to ignite when a small flame is applied. It is an index of the inflammability of oils.

Flea. Fleas are small parasitic insects belonging to the order *Aphaniplera* (so called because these creatures have no wings). They obtain their food by sucking blood from their host. They are laterally compressed, which immediately distinguishes them from lice. The human flea

(*Pulex irritans*) is able to jump vertically a distance of over 7 in.

Fleet Prison, a noted debtors' prison that stood in Farringdon Street, London, where the Congregational Memorial Hall now stands, taking its name from the Fleet Ditch. Notorious for the cruelties inflicted on prisoners. It was pulled down in 1846.

Fleet Street, a famous thoroughfare in London, now the centre of journalism and newspaperdom, though it was long celebrated for its taverns where the literary coteries of the day were wont to meet. It takes its name from the Fleet stream which used to run from Hampstead through Holborn to the Thames at Blackfriars.

Flemings, the people of Flanders, whose ancestors of mediaeval times excelled in the textile arts; England owes its early eminence as a manufacturing nation to the migration of numbers of Flemings to this country in the 16th and 17th cent. *See also* Walloons.

Fleur de Lis, the former national emblem of France, the flower of the lily. It was superseded by the Tricolour in 1789, but is still adhered to by the supporters of the old French royalties.

Flint, consists of granular chalcedony with some opaline silica, and occurs as nodules and bands in the Chalk. It is hard and has a conchoidal fracture, so enabling it to be used in making cutting implements in prehistoric times. Before the invention of lucifer matches, it was used along with steel for striking lights.

Flint implements are objects found in the younger geological strata, and constituting evidence of the condition and life of the period. They include knives, clubs, arrow-heads, scrapers, etc., used as weapons, tools and possibly as surgical instruments and in religious ceremonies. At the end of the Neolithic Period and the beginning of the Bronze Age a people using a new type of stone axe became evident in Europe, advancing towards the south and central regions, and supposed by many to be the ancestors of the present European stock, or Aryans. Similar to prehistoric specimens are the flint and obsidian implements of some of the primitive peoples of today. Ritual weapons and sacrificial knives continued to be made of stone long after the introduction of metals for practical purposes.

Flounder, one of the most familiar of the smaller flat fishes common round the British coasts, and seldom attaining a weight of over three pounds.

Fluorine, a chemical element, member of the halogen family, symbol F, it is found in combination with calcium in fluorspar, and occurs in minute quantities in certain other minerals. Discovered by Scheele in 1771, it was first obtained by Moissan in 1886. A pale yellow gas, it is very reactive and combines with most elements except oxygen. Its acid, hydrogen fluoride, etches glass, the fluorine combining with the silicon to form volatile silicon fluoride. Organic fluorine compounds have found use as very stable polymers which resist a wide variety of chemical actions.

Fluorescent Lamp. *See* Electric Light and Ultra-Violet Rays.

Fluorspar, a mineral; chemically, calcium fluoride. Can be colourless, green, or yellow, but is most commonly purple. Blue fluorspar under the name of Derbyshire "blue John" has been used for ornamental purposes.

Fly, the popular name for a large number of insects with one pair of wings and a proboscis terminating in a sucker through which fluid substances can be drawn up. The best-known species are the common house-fly, the blue-bottle, and the blow-fly. In the larval form flies are maggots, and feed upon decaying substances, animal flesh, etc. Flies are able to walk upon ceilings or upright surfaces by having suckers at the soles of their feet. *See* Diptera.

Flycatcher, a large family of small birds, the Muscicapidae. They are insect feeders, catch their food in the air, and are distributed over most countries of the world. The spotted and the pied nest in Britain, which they visit from April to September.

Flying Fish are frequently to be seen in southern waters, and are capable of gliding considerable distances without touching the water. To build up speed for its "take-off" the fish swims rapidly, to break the surface at 15–20 miles an hour. Maximum air speed is about 40 m.p.h.

Flying Fox, a member of the bat family, but of much larger size, and confined to the tropical and sub-tropical Old World. Like the bats, it is nocturnal, but it feeds entirely on fruits.

Flying Lemur. *See* Colugo.

Flying Lizard, or *Draco,* an Asiatic lizard, possessing wing-like projections from each side, which enable it to make flying leaps through the air, though not sufficient for continuous flight.

Flying Saucers, the name given to certain saucer-like shapes which have on occasion been seen travelling through the atmosphere. For some time speculation was rife, especially in America, but it is now believed that when not hallucinations, meteorological or cosmic-ray balloons, they are nothing more than atmospheric phenomena like mirages or mock suns caused by unusual atmospheric conditions. Described by Dr. Menzel, astrophysics professor at Harvard, "as real as rainbows are real, and no more dangerous". It has been suggested that the study of some of the people who report the sighting of unidentified flying objects (UFOs) would be more rewarding than the investigation of what they saw! *See also* J20.

Flying Squirrel, rodents of which there are several species in Europe, Asia and America. It possesses a parachute-like fold of skin by means of which it projects itself through the air. In appearance they are much like ordinary squirrels, to which they are related. The African flying squirrels belong to a different family.

Fog is caused by the presence of particles of condensed water vapour or smoke in the surface layers of the atmosphere, the term being applied meteorologically when the resulting obscurity is such as to render objects invisible at distances of up to 1 km. Fogs are frequently formed when the air near the ground is cooled below its dew-point temperature by radiation on a still, cloudless night; by flowing over a relatively cold land or water mass; or by mixing with a colder air stream. An accumulation of smoke over a large city may cause a high fog cutting off the daylight and producing gloom. *See* Pollution *and also* Aerosol.

Foliation, a geological term applied to rocks whose component minerals are arranged in parallel layers as the result of strong metamorphic action.

Folio, a printing term for a sheet of paper folded once, a half sheet constituting a leaf.

Folklore concerns itself with the mental and spiritual life of the people—both civilised and primitive—as expressed in the traditional beliefs, customs, institutions, and sayings that have been handed down from generation to generation by word of mouth, and with the observation, recording, and interpretation of such traditions. (The word *folklore* itself was first suggested and used—as two words *Folk Lore*—by W. J. Thoms in the *Athenæum* of August 22nd, 1846, and was at once absorbed into the English language.) Traditional lore of the kind included in the term folklore takes many forms and ranges from omens of good and bad luck (spilling the salt, breaking a mirror, dropping an umbrella, etc.) and the wearing of amulets or the possession of talismans (such as the horse-shoe) as protection against misfortune, to elaborate ceremonial dances such as the Abbots Bromley Horn Dance, the Hobby horses of Padstow and Minehead, the Northern sword-dances, and the Christmas mummers' plays. Especially important are the beliefs and customs associated with birth, babyhood, marriage, and death such being occasions when the individuals concerned require special protection or when unusual happenings can be used for foretelling their future. The child born on a Sunday will be the luckiest; rocking an empty cradle will ensure the speedy arrival of a new baby; throwing an old shoe after a newly-married couple brings them luck; the bride should be carried over the threshold of the new home; on the sea-coast, death is believed to take place at the ebb-tide; the bees must be told of the death of the master of the house, or they will leave the hive. Another very large section of the subject deals with the traditional sayings and practices associated with particular days and seasons of the year—calendar customs, as they are called. The eating of pancakes on Shrove Tuesday; Mother Sunday customs and the simnel cake; Good Friday as the right day for planting potatoes, but emphatically the wrong day for washing clothes or cutting one's finger-nails; the necessity of wearing something new on Easter Sunday; the children's maypole dances and May garlands; midsummer fires; All Hallowe'en as the most favourable occasion for divining the future—especially in respect of marriage—and for games and sports such as apple-bobbing; the numerous practices accompanying the harvest. All these are examples of calendar customs; their full story would occupy several volumes. Folklorists are interested in all such oral tradition because they think that to a large extent it represents what folk have mentally stored up from the past and transmitted to their descendants throughout the centuries, and because therefore it is able to assist other historic methods—ethnographical linguistic, archaeological, etc.—in the elucidation of the early story of man. In those countries with a great diversity of peoples in all stages of culture, a knowledge of folklore and what it can teach of the mind of man is of great importance to administrators. The Folk-Lore Society was founded in 1878, and that part of the subject represented by song and dance has now its own organisation in the English Folk Dance and Song Society.

Force, as a term in physics, signifies an influence or exertion which, when made to act upon a body, tends to move it if at rest, or to affect or stop its progress if it be already in motion. In the c.g.s. system, the unit of force is the dyne; in the foot-pound-second system, the poundal; in the SI system, the newton.

Formaldehyde. Chemically it lies between methyl alcohol and formic acid; oxidation of methyl alcohol yields formaldehyde, and oxidation of formaldehyde produces formic acid. It is used as a disinfectant, in silvering mirrors, and in the manufacture of phenol-formaldehyde plastics (of which bakelite is the best-known example). Solutions of formaldehyde in water, formalin, are used to preserve biological specimens.

Forme, a body of letterpress type, composed and secured for printing from; or a stereotype or electrotype. The former is used more for newspaper formes and the latter in good book work.

Formic Acid can be obtained from a colourless fluid secreted by ants and other insects and plants. It is a strong irritant. Commercially it is obtained from sodium formate, which is synthesised by the absorption of carbon monoxide in caustic soda. It is used in the electroplating, tanning, and textile industries.

Formula, in mathematics and physics a statement of certain facts in symbolical form. In chemistry a representation of the composition of a compound.

Fossils. Remains of animals and plants, or direct evidence of their presence, preserved in rocks. They include petrified skeletons and shells, leaf imprints, footprints, etc.

Four Freedoms, a phrase coined by President Roosevelt in January, 1941, embodying what should be the goal of the Allies. They were (1) Freedom of speech and expression; (2) Freedom of every person to worship God in his own way; (3) Freedom from want; (4) Freedom from fear.

Fox, carnivorous animal of the canine family, found in considerable numbers in most parts of the world. The common fox *Vulpes vulpes* of Europe is a burrowing animal of nocturnal habits, living upon birds, rabbits, and domestic poultry, in the capture of which it displays much cunning. The fox in Britain is preserved from extinction chiefly for hunting purposes. Among other notable species are the Arctic fox and the red fox of North America, of which the valuable silver fox, coveted for its fur, is a variety.

Fox-Shark, *or* Thresher Shark, a large species of shark common in the Atlantic and in the Mediterranean. It is very destructive to small fish, but although it attains a length of 15 ft. it is not dangerous to man.

Franciscans. *See* Friars.

Franco-German War (1870–71) was opened by a declaration of war by Napoleon III., but the Germans who were better prepared than the French, won victory after victory. In September Napoleon and the whole French army were made prisoners at Sedan, a republic was then proclaimed, and Paris sustained a four months' siege. In the end France ceded Alsace and part of Lorraine to Germany, who claimed a war indemnity of over £20 million.

Francolin, a genus of birds closely related to the common partridge, belonging to Africa. It includes the spur-legged partridge, and the black partridge which ranges from Cyprus to Assam.

Frankincense is of two kinds, one being used as incense in certain religious services and obtained from olibanum, an Eastern shrub, the other is a resinous exudation derived from firs and pines, and largely used in pharmacy.

Franklin, the name given in feudal times to a country landowner who was independent of the territorial lord, and performed many of the minor functions of local government, such as serving as magistrate.

Fresco, a painting executed upon plaster walls or ceilings, a technique which has remained unchanged since it was practised by the great Renaissance artists.

Freshwater Shrimp, a small crustacean abounding in British streams, and feeding on dead fish or other decomposing matter. Although of shrimp-like form it is not closely related to salt-water shrimps. Its generic name is *Gammarus*.

Friars, members of certain mendicant orders of the Roman Catholic Church. The four chief orders are the Franciscans or Grey Friars, the Dominicans or Black Friars, the Carmelites or White Friars, and the Augustinians (Austin Friars).

Friday, the 6th day of the week, named after Frigga, the wife of Odin. It is the Mohammedan Sabbath, a general abstinence day of the Roman Catholic Church, and according to popular superstition, an unlucky day.

Friends, The Society of. *See* **J21.**

Frigate-Bird, a web-footed bird widely distributed over tropical latitudes, and deriving its name from its great expanse of wing and forked tail, resembling the shape of a swift vessel. It feeds on flying fish mostly, being unable to dive and also steals from other birds. A frigate-bird was found dying on the Hebridean island of Tiree in July 1953: only twice previously had one been recorded in Europe—the first on the German coast in 1792, and the second on the coast of France in 1902.

Frog, a familiar amphibian, breathing through gills in the earlier (tadpole) part of its existence, and through lungs later. It remains three months in the tadpole stage. The frog hibernates underwater in the mud during the winter.

Frost occurs when the temperature falls to, or below, 0 °C., which is freezing point. Hoar frost is applied to the needles or feather-like crystals of ice deposited on the ground, in the same manner as dew. Glazed frost is the clear icy coating which may be formed as a result of rain falling on objects whose temperatures are below the freezing point. These layers of ice, often rendering roads impassable for traffic, damaging overhead power and communication systems and endangering aircraft, can also be caused by condensation from warm, damp winds coming into contact with very cold air and freezing surfaces.

Froth-Hopper *or* Frog-Hopper. A family of bugs (belonging to the insect order *Hemiptera*) which in the larval stage surround themselves with a protective mass of froth (" cuckoo spit "). These insects, which suck the sap of plants, bear a faint resemblance to frogs, and the adults possess great leaping powers.

Fuel Cells. A recent development is a type of battery into which the active chemicals are fed from external fuel tanks. This is the *fuel cell*, which is being developed in a number of versions in several countries. One was demonstrated in action when in 1959 Bacon of Cambridge University used his fuel cell to drive a fork-lift truck and a welding machine. The Bacon fuel cell consists of two electrodes of porous nickel dipping into a solution of caustic potash in water. One electrode is supplied with hydrogen gas from an outside cylinder and the other with oxygen. These gases, forming layers on the nickel, are the active chemicals. The oxygen combines with water to make two negatively charged ions, each consisting of an oxygen and a hydrogen atom joined together (a hydroxyl ion). The hydroxyl ions travel through the solution to the hydrogen electrode, where they combine with hydrogen to form neutral water. Their negative charge (one electron per ion involved) has now arrived at the hydrogen electrode and is ready to flow back to the other electrode through any outside circuit that is provided. This flow constitutes the useful electric current, and it has been provided at the expense of creating water out of the original hydrogen and oxygen. The water can be removed in the form of steam. What is the advantage of all this? In the first place the fuel gases are easy to make and to store in cylinders. Supplying a new gas cylinder is easier and quicker than recharging an ordinary accumulator. Furthermore, a fuel cell is lighter for a given power than an accumulator; satellite designers have found them useful. The fuel cell is not damaged by heavy overloading, and this is valuable for application to vehicle driving. Fuel-cell-driven buses could combine the advantages of diesel buses and trolleybuses. Fuel cells are still in the development stage. It is not certain how they will compete with combustion engines or, in the oil-less future, with improved ordinary batteries.

Fulani, a non-Negro people of Hamitic stock widely distributed in N.W. Africa, chiefly in Nigeria. There are two main branches: the dark-skinned Fulani, settled farmers and city dwellers, Moslem in religion, and the light-coloured Bororo'en who are semi-nomadic herdsmen. The Fulani are different from any tribe in W. Africa though they resemble in some ways the Masai of E. Africa. The Fulani conquered the Hausa states at the beginning of the 19th cent. which passed under British suzerainty after 1903. Sokoto, built in 1810, was capital of the Fulani empire.

Fuller's Earth, a special kind of clay or marl possessing highly absorbent qualities, originally used in the " fulling "—that is, cleansing and felting—of cloth. Now used in clarifying oils. Deposits in America and in south of England.

Function. In mathematics, one quantity y is said to be a function of another quantity x, written $y = f(x)$, if a change in x results in some corresponding change in y. Thus $\sin x$ or $\log x$ are functions of x. If y depends not only on x but on several other quantities as well, y is called a function of many variables.

Functionalism, in architecture, a movement originated by Le Corbusier, Swiss-born French architect and town-planner, who applied the austere principles of the Purist movement in painting to his own art. From about 1924 he designed in concrete, steel, and glass, buildings in which every part had a significance in terms of function on the theory that objects created to carry out their particular function to perfection cannot help being beautiful. " A house is a machine for living in." The style was in vogue between the two wars, and although its severity became somewhat modified, it is still the basis of most modern architecture.

Fungi, a class of simple plants, which reproduce from spores and lack the green colouring matter *chlorophyll*. It includes moulds, rusts, mildews, smuts, mushrooms, etc. Potato blight is a fungus disease which caused the failure of the potato crop in Ireland in 1846. 50,000 different fungi are known. *See also* **F39**(2), **P8**(1).

Furniture Beetle (*Anobium punctatum*). The common furniture beetle is responsible for 80 per cent of all woodworm damage and is the great pest of the comparatively modern house, causing damage in the main to softwood roofing and flooring timbers. Adults one-eighth of an inch long. The grub tunnels for about 33 months. *See also* **Woodworm, Death Watch Beetle.**

Futurism, the only important modern art movement to arise outside France, initiated by Marinetti, an Italian writer and mountebank friend of Mussolini at a later period. Its origin took the form of a manifesto published in Paris in 1909 in which Marinetti glorified violence, war, and the machine age. In its aggression it favoured the growth of fascism. One of the distinctive features of Futurist art was the use of the principle of " simultaneity " in which the same figure (*e.g.*, a woman descending a flight of stairs) is represented in successive positions like film " stills " superimposed on each other. In spite of two further manifestos it was not until 1911 that the first examples of Futurist painting and sculpture appeared by the artists Severini, Balla, and Boccioni. Apart from the principle of simultaneity, Futurism derived from Cubist and Post-impressionist techniques. The movement faded out early in first world war.

G

Gabardine, a long, loose, coarse, over-garment, worn by men of the common class in the Middle Ages, and prescribed by law as the distinctive garment of the Jews. The name is now given to a closely woven cloth of wool and cotton used to make raincoats.

Gabbro, a kind of igneous rock, often very coarse-grained, containing a good deal of plagioclase felspar, and monoclinic pyroxene; it may occasionally also include biotite, magnetite, ilmenite, and hornblende. A gabbro containing nickel at Sudbury in Canada is one of the richest sources known of that metal.

Gadfly, a widely distributed family of flies with only one pair of wings, including the horse fly. The females are very voracious, being able to bite through the skin and suck the blood of animals. The males are harmless.

Gadolinium. An element belonging to the rare-earths metals discovered in 1886 by Marignac. It is strongly magnetic.

Gaelic, relating to the Gaels and their language, a term now applied only to the Celtic people inhabiting the Highlands of Scotland, but formerly also to the Celts of Ireland and the Isle of Man.

Galago, " Bush Babies," related to the lemur, native to Africa, large-eyed, in keeping with its nocturnal characteristics.

Galaxy *or* **Milky Way Galaxy** is the huge disk-shaped cloud of gas and stars (some 100,000 million, one of which is the sun) that is turning in space like a great wheel, with a diameter of about 100,000 light years. The Milky Way (that part of the heavens in Milton's words " powdered with stars ") is really only a small part of this disk, and every star in the galaxy is moving round the centre under the gravitational control of the whole. The sun and planets lie near the edge of the disk, and it takes them about 250 million years to travel once round. The number of stars that can be seen with the unaided eye is about 3,000, and they all belong to the Milky Way Galaxy, as do most of the stars that can be seen with anything but the greatest telescopes. With the large modern optical and radar telescopes many other systems, similar in size and weight to our galaxy, have been discovered, scattered more or less uniformly through space, and the universe is said to include at least 10,000 million such galaxies. *See also* **F3–6.**

Gale, a high wind now technically defined as one of at least Beaufort force 8. Between thirty and forty gales a year occur on the north and west coasts of the British Isles and only about half of this number in the south-east. At St. Ann's Head, Pembroke, the anemometer registered a gust of 113 m.p.h. on Jan. 18, 1945, which is a record for these islands. Gusts exceeding 70 m.p.h. are rarely experienced in London. Gale warnings are issued for specified areas by the Meteorological Office, the warnings taking the form of radio broadcasts and the hoisting of storm signals at certain points on the coast. *See* Beaufort Wind Scale, **Section N.**

Gall, abnormal vegetable growths caused by insects, mites, bacteria, or fungi, found on all parts of the plant. Oak-apples, Robin's pin-cushion (on wild rose), " witches brooms " (on trees) are examples. Some are useful commercially, *e.g.*, oak apples yield tannic acid and the black oak gall is used in America as animal food.

Galleon, the name given to the old three-decked Spanish treasure vessels employed in conveying the precious minerals from the American colonies to Spain. The term is often applied to any large, especially stately, sailing vessel.

Galley, an oar-propelled sea-boat used by the ancient Greeks and Romans for transport purposes, manned by slaves. Boats of a similar class were used by the French down to the middle of the 18th cent., and manned by convicts.

Gallic Acid, obtained from gall nuts, sumach, tea, coffee, and the seeds of the mango, is used in the manufacture of inks and as an astringent in medicine. It was discovered by C. W. Scheele (1742–86), a Swedish chemist.

Gallium, a white metal, symbol Ga, related to aluminium, but which can be cut with a knife. It was discovered spectroscopically by L. de Boisbaudran in 1875. Long before Mendeleyev had predicted that an element with its properties would be found to fill the then existing gap in the Periodic Table; this gap came immediately below aluminium, so he suggested the name " eka aluminium " for it.

Gallup Poll, a system, introduced by Dr. Gallup of the United States, for testing public opinion on topical subjects by taking a test poll on questions framed to elicit opinions.

Galvanised Iron is iron coated with zinc. The name comes from the fact that such a coat protective against rust could be deposited electrolytically. Electrodeposition is sometimes used, but the cheaper and more common process depends on dipping the iron in a bath of molten zinc.

Gamboge, a resinous gum obtained from the sap of *Garcinia morella*, a tree native to Thailand, Cambodia, and Ceylon, and used as a yellow pigment in paints and also as a purgative.

Game is the term applied to wild animals which are protected from indiscriminate slaughter by Game Laws. In the United Kingdom game comprehends deer, hares, pheasants, partridges, grouse, black game, moor game, woodcocks, bustards, and certain other birds and animals of the chase. Game can only be killed with few exceptions) by persons holding game licences. Occupiers of land and one other person authorised by them in each case are allowed to kill hares and rabbits on their land without licence. Game cannot be sold except by a person holding a proper licence. There is a " close time " prescribed for the different classes of game; for instance, the selling or exposing for sale of any hare or leveret during March, April, May, June, or July is prohibited by law. Grouse cannot be shot between Dec. 11 and Aug. 31; partridges between Feb. 2 and Aug. 31; pheasants between Feb. 2 and Sept. 30; and black game between Dec. 11 and Aug. 10. In regard to foxes, stags, and otters, custom and not Parliament prescribes a certain law which sportsmen rigidly adhere to. Game reserves are legally protected areas where natural vegetation and wild life are allowed to remain unmolested by sportsmen or those who might destroy for economic ends.

Gaming, *or* **Gambling**—*i.e.*, staking money on the chances of a game—differs from betting in that it depends upon the result of a trial of skill or a turn of chance. The Betting and Gaming Act of 1959, passed by the Macmillan administration, replaced all the old laws on gaming, which went back to an Act of 1541 entitled " An Acte for Mayntenance of Artyllarie and debarringe of unlauful games," under which some games were unlawful if played for money in any circumstances. Roulette and any game of dice were among such games. Under the 1959 Act any game was lawful, subject to certain conditions. Since then the Betting, Gaming and Lotteries Act, 1963, and the Gaming Act, 1968, have been passed, to deal with unlawful gaming and to prevent the exploitation of gaming for commercial interests. The playing of bingo is now restricted to clubs licensed for bingo only.

Gammexane, a powerful insecticide, used particularly to kill the tsetse fly and mosquito.

Gangue. Useless minerals associated with metallic ores.

Gannet, a fish-eating bird which dives on its prey from a great height, swallowing it under water; is found in large numbers off the coast of Scotland, and has breeding stations in the Hebrides, St. Kilda, Ailsa Craig, the Bass Rock, Grassholme Island, and on Ortac and Les Etacs (rocks off Alderney). It is a bird of white plumage, black tips to long narrow wings and wedge-shaped tail, and weighs about 7 lb. The gannet breeds in colonies on ledges of steep, rocky, island cliffs. Related to the cormorants, pelicans, and frigate-birds.

Garden Cities in England were founded by Ebenezer Howard (1850–1928), and his ideas were put forward in his book *Tomorrow—A Peaceful Path to Real Reform* (later re-issued as *Garden Cities of Tomorrow*). New towns should be so placed and planned as to get the best of town and country life, an adaptation of the model villages of certain industrial philanthropists such as Salt, Richardson, Cadbury, Leverhulme, and others. The Garden City Association (later the Town and Country Planning Association) was formed in 1899, and the first garden city was begun at Letchworth in 1903 and successfully established. Welwyn Garden City was also Howard's foundation, established in 1919.

Gardener-Bird, a bird possessing many of the characteristics of the bower-bird, and found only in Papua–New Guinea. *See also* **Bower Bird.**

Gargantua, the giant hero of Rabelais' satire, of immense eating and drinking capacity, symbolical of an antagonistic ideal of the greed of the Church.

Gargoyle, a projecting spout for carrying off water from the roof gutter of a building. Gargoyles are only found in old structures, modern waterpipe systems having rendered them unnecessary. In Gothic architecture they were turned to architectural account and made to take all kinds of grotesque forms—grinning goblins, hideous monsters, dragons, and so forth.

Garlic, a bulbous plant of the same genus as the onion and the leek, and a favourite condiment among the people of Southern Europe. It possesses a very strong odour and pungent taste and its culinary use is agelong.

Garnet, a group of minerals; chemically they are orthosilicates of the metals calcium, magnesium, titanium, iron, aluminium. Garnets can be coloured yellow, brown, black, green, or red; the blood-red garnet is an important gemstone.

Garrotte, a method of strangulation used as capital punishment in Spain, and consisting of a collar which is compressed by a screw that causes death by piercing the spinal marrow. Garroting was also applied to a system of highway robbery common in England in 1862–63, the assailants seizing their victims from behind, and by a sudden compression of the windpipe disabling them until the robbery was completed.

Garter. The Most Noble Order of the Garter was founded (*c.* 1348) by King Edward III., and is the premier order of knighthood in Great Britain. The traditional story associating the garter and the motto with the Countess of Salisbury, who it was said dropped her garter while dancing with the King, who remarked " honi soit qui mal y pense " cannot be accepted. The order was originally limited to the Sovereign and 25 knights, but the number has been extended, and it may now be bestowed on royal personages and leading representatives of the British peerage. The insignia of the order are the garter of dark-blue velvet with the motto in letters of gold, the mantle of dark-blue velvet lined with white silk, the surcoat and hood, and the gold-and-enamel collar. The garter is worn on the left leg below the knee and by women as a sash over the left shoulder. *See* **Knighthood.**

Gas is an elastic fluid substance, the molecules of which are in constant rapid motion, and exerting pressure. The technique whereby gases are liquefied depends on increasing pressure and diminishing temperature. Each gas has a critical point; unless the temperature is brought down to this point no amount of pressure will bring about liquefaction. Last gas to be liquefied was helium (1908) which boils at —209 °C. *See* **F17(1).**

Gas from coal was first used as an illuminating agent by William Murdoch towards the end of the 18th cent. in Birmingham, and about 1807 was introduced in London, one side of Pall Mall being lighted with it. It became widely used as an illuminant, and for space heating and cooking. In the United Kingdom there has been increasing attention paid to the possibility of using a primary fuel—natural gas—instead of producing gas from coal or oil. *See* Gas, Natural.

Gas, Natural, natural mixture of gases often present with deposits of petroleum, found issuing from the ground in many parts of the world—in the oilfields of Venezuela and the Caucasus, in China, Saudi-Arabia, but chiefly in North America. Its chief component is methane. Large industrial centres have made use of this gas since the latter part of the 19th cent., but much of this valuable fuel still goes to waste. Pipelines have been constructed to deliver the gas to where it is wanted. Britain began to ship liquid methane from the Saharan oilfield in 1964. Some of the world's largest natural gas fields have recently been discovered in the North Sea and are being actively exploited. Domestic gas appliances have to be modified if the natural product is substituted for ordinary town gas because the burning characteristics are different.

Gas Turbine. In this kind of engine mechanical movement is produced by a jet of gas impinging on a turbine wheel; used in aeroplanes, locomotives, and ships. These engines are mechanically simple compared with internal combustion engines, and require less maintenance. It has been stated that the jet-propelled Comet cruises at 450 m.p.h. burning less than ½ lb. of kerosene per passenger mile.

Gauge, a standard dimension or measurement, applied in various branches of construction. Thus, the standard railway gauge is 4 ft. 8½ in. in the United Kingdom, United States, Canada, France, Germany, Austria, Holland, Egypt, Belgium, Denmark, Italy, Hungary, Sweden, Switzerland, and Turkey. In India, Ceylon, and Spain the gauge is 5 ft. 6 in. In Soviet Russia and Finland, 5 ft., Ireland, 5 ft. 3 in. Narrow railway gauges of different standards are in use on very steep inclines in various countries. Other standard gauges are fixed in building and gun-boring.

Gauls were inhabitants of ancient Gaul, the country which comprised what is now France, Belgium, and parts of the Netherlands, Switzerland, and Germany.

Gault, a stratum of blue clay between the Lower Greensand and the Chalk. A typical section of the Gault can be seen at Folkestone.

Gauss, a unit of magnetic induction in the c.g.s. system, named after the great German mathematician and astronomer, K. F. Gauss.

Gavelkind, an old English custom of land tenure in Kent and other places in England, whereby on the death, intestate, of a property owner, his property is divided equally among his children and not according to the law of primogeniture. Abolished by the Law of Property Act, 1922, and the Administration of Estates Act, 1925.

Gazelle, an animal of the antelope family, of small and delicate shape, with large eyes and short cylindrical horns. It is of a fawn colour, a native of North Africa, and easily domesticated.

Gecko, the name of a family of drab lizards common in or near the tropics. They are nocturnal, insectivorous, and harmless.

Geiger Counter, an electrical device, invented by Geiger, which can detect individual atomic particles, *e.g.,* electrons, protons, etc. It often consists of a tube of gas at a few cm. Hg pressure, fitted with two electrodes—a cylinder and an axial wire. A high voltage is kept across the electrodes, and the passage of a charged particle through the gas releases ions which permit a momentary discharge between the electrodes. Electronic circuits register this discharge as a " count." Geiger counters are widely used to detect and measure radioactivity and cosmic rays, both for technical and research purposes.

Gelatine, a transparent, tasteless, organic substance obtained from animal membranes, bones, tendons, etc., by boiling in water. It is of various kinds, according to the substance used in making it. Isinglass, the purest form of it, is made from air-bladders and other membranes of fish, while the coarser kind—glue—is made from hoofs, skin, hides, etc. Its constituents are carbon, hydrogen, oxygen, and nitrogen. Gelatine is applied to an immense variety of purposes, from the making of food jellies to photographic materials.

Gemsbok, a large South African antelope, with long straight horns and tufted tail. Light fawn in colour, it has a black streak across its face, and is very fleet of foot.

General, a military title next in rank to that of Field-Marshal, the highest officer in the army. Ranking below full General are Lieutenant-General, Major-General, and Brigadier.

Generation, a time-measure reckoned at about 30 years when children are ready to replace parents; also the body of persons existing at the same time or period.

Generation, Spontaneous. *See* Abiogenesis.

Genes, the elementary units of heredity. They exist as highly differentiated regions arranged along the length of the chromosomes which the nuclei of cells carry. A chromosome may carry hundreds or even thousands of genes, each with its own particular structure and specific properties. The position of a particular gene on a chromosome is called its locus. The material of the gene is DNA (*q.v.*). *See* Cell Division, F30(2).

Genesis, the first book of the Pentateuch, compiled in the 5th cent. B.C. from earlier documents which carries the scriptural narrative from the creation to the death of Joseph. Sometimes there is disagreement, as in the story of the creation, Gen. i and ii. Gen. i reflects the views of the ancient Greek scientist Thales (*c.* 640–546 B.C.) and may be said to be the first scientific account of the creation of the world. The conditions described around the figures of Abraham, Isaac, Jacob, and Joseph have a genuine historical basis.

Genet, one of the smaller carnivorous animals, about the size of a cat, but with longer tail and spotted body. It is a native of Southern Europe, North Africa, and Western Asia.

Genetic Code. The elucidation of the structure of DNA (*q.v.*) for which Crick, Wilkins, and Watson were jointly awarded the 1962 Nobel Prize for medicine, revealed the code or chemical dictionary out of which messages serving as blueprints for living structures can be made. *See* Protein synthesis, F29(2).

Geneva Convention, an agreement made by the European Powers at Geneva in 1864, establishing humane regulations regarding the treatment of the sick and wounded in war and the status of those who minister to them. All persons, hospitals, hospital ships are required to display the Geneva cross—a red cross on a white ground. A second conference held at Geneva in 1868 drew up a supplementary agreement. An important result of this Convention was the establishment of the Red Cross Society in 1870.

Genouillieres, ancient metal caps for covering the knees of an armed man; an example may be seen on the Black Prince's monument in Canterbury Cathedral.

Gentian, the name for plants of the *Gentiana* genus. many of which have intensely blue flowers. The gentian-root of *G. lutea* is used in pharmacy.

Genus, a term applied in biology to designate a group of similar species. A group of similar genera is called a family.

Geodesy, the science of calculating the configuration and extent of the earth's surface, and determining exact geographical positions and directions, with variations of gravity, etc. Land-surveying is a branch of geodesy.

Geography, the science which describes the earth's surface, its physical peculiarities, and the distribution of the various animals and plants upon it. It is usual to divide the subject into two main branches—physical geography, which deals with the composition of the earth's surface and the distribution of its living occupants, animate and inanimate; and human geography, which includes economic, political, and social geography.

Geology, the science which deals with the condition and structure of the earth, and the evidence afforded of ancient forms of life. The geological strata are classified in the following categories: *Primary* or *Palaeozoic* (the oldest fossil-bearing rocks including the Cambrian, Ordovician, Silurian, Devonian, Carboniferous, Permian); *Secondary* or *Mesozoic* (Triassic, Jurassic, Cretaceous); *Tertiary* or *Cainozoic*

(Eocene, Oligocene, Miocene, Pliocene, Pleistocene); *Post tertiary* (most recent rocks). *See* F44.

Geometrical Progression is a term used to indicate a succession of numbers which increase or decrease at an equal ratio—as 3, 9, 27; or 64, 16, 4.

Geometry is the branch of mathematics which demonstrates the properties of figures, and the distances of points of space from each other by means of deductions. It is a science of reason from fundamental axioms, and was perfected by Euclid about 300 B.C. The books of Euclid contain a full elucidation of the science, though supplemented in modern times by Descartes, Newton and Carnot. Of recent years non-Euclidean geometry has been developed.

Geophysics, the branches of physics which are concerned with the earth and its atmosphere. Meteorology, geomagnetism, aurora and airglow, ionosphere, solar activity, cosmic rays, glaciology, oceanography, seismology, nuclear radiation in the atmosphere, rockets, and satellites—all these are geophysical subjects. The object of the International Geophysical Year, 1957–58, was to investigate the physical phenomena occurring on and around the earth by means of carefully co-ordinated observations made simultaneously all over the globe.

George-Noble, a gold coin, so called from St. George and the dragon depicted on its obverse. First issued in the reign of Henry VIII.

German Silver, an alloy of copper, zinc, and nickel, and used in the manufacture of table-ware, such as spoons, forks, etc.

Germanium. A grey, hard, brittle chemical element, symbol Ge, chemically related to silicon and tin. Discovered by Winkler in 1886. Its richest ore is germanite containing 6% of the metal. Coal is also a relatively rich source. Since 1948 it has assumed great importance as a semi-conducting material for making transistors (*q.v.*). Because of this it has been so intensively studied that more is known about its physical properties than about those of any other element.

Gesta Romanorum (Latin = deeds of the Romans), a mediaeval collection of Latin stories of unknown authorship which circulated widely in Europe during the Middle Ages. First printed in the 15th cent. The stories were used by Chaucer, Shakespeare and other writers who found many romantic incidents and legends which they were able to turn to good account.

Gestation, the carrying of young in animals during pregnancy, varies considerably in its length. In the case of an elephant, the period is 21 months; a camel, 12 months; a cow, 9 months; a cat, 8 weeks; a horse, 48 weeks; a dog, 9 weeks; and a pig, 16 weeks. Hens " sit " for 21 days; geese, 30; swans, 42; turkeys, 28; pigeons, 18.

Geysers, hot springs of volcanic origination and action, are remarkable for the fact that they throw out huge streams of boiling water instead of lava as in the case of a volcano. The most famous geysers are those of Iceland, which number over a hundred, the principal one having an opening 70 ft. in diameter and discharging a column of water to a height of 200 ft. There are also geysers in the Yellowstone region of America, and some in New Zealand. Also a device now in common domestic use for heating running water quickly by gas or electricity.

Ghost-Moth or **Ghost Swift**, an interesting nocturnal insect (*Hepialus humuli*), common in England, possessing in the male a white collar and known for its habit of hovering with a pendulum-like action in the twilight over a particular spot where the female is concealed.

Giambeaux, metal armour for the legs and shins, worn by the warriors of Richard II.'s reign.

Gibbon, the name of a long-armed ape mainly inhabiting S.E. Asia. It is without tail, and possesses the power of very rapid movement among the trees of the forests.

Gin, a well-known spirit distilled from malt or barley and flavoured with the juniper berry. The principal varieties are the English and American, known as " Gin " or " Dry Gin ", and the Dutch, referred to as " jenever " or " Hollandse jenever ". In Germany and Austria it is called " Schnapps ". The word " Gin " is an abbreviation of " Geneva ", both being primarily derived from the French genièvre (juniper).

Ginger is obtained from a reed-like perennial plant grown in tropical countries. There are two varieties, black ginger and grey ginger. The former is obtained by peeling and drying the root, the latter by scalding and drying. Ginger is largely used as a condiment.

Giraffe, the tallest of existing animals, reaching a height of from 18 to 20 ft. when full grown. Its sloping back and elongated neck seem to be the natural evolution of an animal that has to feed on the branches of trees. It is a native of Africa, is of a light fawn colour marked with darker spots, and has a prehensile tongue.

Giralda, a beautiful and remarkable example of Arabian art, erected in 1195 at Seville, still in existence. Minarets similar to the Giralda are to be found at Morocco, Tunis, and Tetuan.

Glaciers form in the higher Alpine ranges, and are immense consolidated masses of snow, which are gradually impelled by their force down the mountain-sides until they reach a point where the temperature causes them to melt, and they run off in streams. From such glaciers the five great rivers, the Rhine, the Po, the Rhône, the Inn, and the Adige, have their source. The longest of the Swiss glaciers is the Gross Aletsch, which sometimes extends over 10 miles. Some of the glaciers of the Himalayas are four times as long. The Muir in Alaska is of enormous magnitude, and that of Justeldals Brae in Norway is the largest in Europe.

Gladiators were professional athletes and combatants in ancient Rome, contesting with each other or with wild beasts. At first they were drawn from the slave and prisoner classes exclusively, but so much were the successful gladiators held in esteem that men came to make a profession of athletics, and gladiatorial training schools were established. When a gladiator was vanquished without being killed in combat, it was left with the spectators to decide his fate, death being voted by holding the hands out with the thumb turned inward, and life by putting forth the hands with the thumb extended. Gladiatorial shows were the chief public displays in Rome from the 3rd to the 4th cent. A.D.

Glass, a substance obtained from the fusion of silica (sand) with various bases, and is more or less transparent. There are numerous kinds of glass, but they group themselves under one or other of the following classifications:—Flint glass, or crystal, whose components are potash, silica, and oxide of lead; window glass, made from soda, lime, and silica; Bohemian glass, containing potash, lime, and silica; and bottle glass, composed of soda, lime, alumina, silica, and oxide of iron. Heat-proof glasses used for making cooking utensils contain boron. Glass was made by the Phoenicians, and was familiar in ancient Egypt. The Egyptians introduced it into Rome. In the Middle Ages Venice was famed for its glass manufactures, but after the 17th cent. Bohemia acquired pre-eminence. English glass reached its highest level of artistic design in the 17th and 18th cent. Window glass was not used in this country for dwellings until the end of the Middle Ages.

Glass-Snake, genus, *Ophisaurus*, of legless lizards with long fragile tails capable of re-generation when broken. Six species are known; in S.E. Europe, S.W. Asia, Indo-China, and N. America. Attains a length of about 2 ft.; main colouring, green, with black and yellow markings.

Glauconite. A green mineral, chemically a hydrated silicate of potassium and iron. Commonly found in marine sands (hence these rocks are known as " greensands ") and sandstones.

Glaucus is a curious genus of sea slugs often called the Sea Lizard belonging to the molluscs. It is without shell and has a soft body, with horny mouth and four tentacles. It is a native of the Atlantic, and is not more than 12 in. in length.

Glee, an unaccompanied piece for three or more voices. Glee-singing was popular in England during the 18th and early 19th cent. and glee-clubs are still in existence.

Globigerina, an oceanic unicellular animalcule with a perforated shell, and occurring in certain parts of the Atlantic in such vast numbers as to form a bed of chalk ooze with their empty shells.

Glockenspiel, an instrument composed of metal bars each of which is tuned to a note. The bars are struck by hand-hammers and give forth chiming sounds.

Gloria in Excelsis (" Glory to God in the highest ") is the opening of the Latin hymn adapted from Luke ii. 4, and the most prominent hymn of the ecclesiastical rites in the Christian liturgies.

Gloria Patri, the lesser Doxology, with which chants are generally concluded in the English Church service—" Glory be to the Father, and to the Son."

Glow-worm, a beetle, possessing the power (much stronger in the female than the male) of emitting phosphorescent light from the hind end of the body. The female is wingless.

Glucinium. See Beryllium.

Glucose, Dextrose or **Grape Sugar** is a carbohydrate (q.v.). It is produced by hydrolysis from cane sugar, dextrine, starch, cellulose, etc., by the action of reagents. It also occurs in many plants, fruits, and honey. For brewing purposes glucose is prepared by the conversion of starch by sulphuric acid. Malt also converts starch into glucose.

Glutton or **Wolverine**, the biggest animal of the weasel family, inhabits the northernmost parts of Europe and America. In build it resembles the bear, and is rather larger than a badger. Its fur is of a brown-black hue, but coarse.

Glycerine or **Glycerol**, occurs in natural fats combined with fatty acids, and is obtained by decomposing those substances with alkalies or by superheated steam. It is colourless and oily and sweet, and is put to a variety of commercial uses, being widely utilised for medicaments, for lubricating purposes, and in the manufacture of nitro-glycerine.

Glycols. Organic compounds containing two alcohol groups. Ethylene glycol is the most widely known example: it is used as an antifreeze in motor-car radiators on account of its property of greatly reducing the freezing point of water. Also used in the manufacture of " Terylene ". See Esters.

Glyptodon, an extinct species of gigantic armadillo, fossil remains of which have been discovered in S. America. It was some 9 ft. long, carried a huge tortoise-like shell, and had fluted teeth.

Gneiss, a metamorphic rock usually containing quartz, felspar, and mica. It is banded, the light-coloured minerals being concentrated apart from the dark minerals.

Gnosticism. See J22.

Gnu, an animal of the antelope family, combining the characteristics of the buffalo in its head and horns, the ass in its neck and mane, and the horse in its long and bushy tail. There are two species, the common and the brindled, and they are about the size of an ass. They abound in Africa and congregate in herds.

Goat-Moth (Cossus cossus), a large moth of the Cossidae family, common in Britain, evilsmelling, and very destructive in the larval stage to trees of the poplar and willow genus, into the wood of which the caterpillar bores during its three years' period of development.

Goats are horned ruminant quadrupeds, indigenous to the Eastern Hemisphere, but now domesticated in all parts of the world. Though related to the sheep, they are a much hardier and more active animal. The male has a tuft of hair under the chin. Many species, including those of Cashmere and Angora, are valuable for their hair, which is used for fine textile fabrics. The milk of the goat is nutritive, and goat-skins are in good demand for leather for gloves, shoes, etc.

Gobelin Tapestry was originated by a family of dyers named Gobelin in the 15th cent. in Paris. The Gobelin establishment, which produced this beautiful tapestry, made of silk and wool, or silk and cotton, was taken over by the Government of Louis XIV., in 1662, and since then has been the French national factory for that class of fabric.

God and Man. See J22.

Gog and Magog, two legendary City of London giants, supposed to be the offspring of certain wicked daughters of the Emperor Diocletian and a band of demons. They were brought captive to London and made to serve as prisoners at the Palace of Brute, which stood on the site of Guildhall. Effigies of the giants have stood in Guildhall since the time of Henry V. They were destroyed in the Great Fire of 1666, replaced in 1672, and used to be carried through the streets of London in the Lord Mayor's Show. The present figures, newly carved in lime wood by Mr. David Evans, replaced those carved in 1708 by Richard Saunders, which were destroyed in an air raid during the last war.

Gold. Metallic element, symbol Au (Latin Aurum) related to silver and copper, the coinage metals. The greatest amount of gold is obtained by treating gold-bearing quartz by the cyanide process. The gold is dissolved out by cyanide solution, which is then run into long boxes filled with zinc shavings when the gold is precipitated as a black slime. This is melted with an oxidising agent which removes the zinc.

Gold-Beaters' Skin is the outside membrane of the large intestine of the ox, specially prepared and used by gold-beaters for placing between the leaves of gold while they beat them. This membrane is of great tenacity, and gets beaten to such extreme thinness that it is used to put on cuts and bruises.

Gold Standard. Under the gold-standard system, which was widely prevalent up to 1914, each gold-standard country fixed the value of its currency in terms of a weight of gold of a certain fineness and was, broadly speaking, ready to exchange its currency freely for gold, which could then be exported without restriction. This involved keeping a gold reserve big enough to meet all likely demands and also to serve as a backing for the issue of notes. The gold standard had to be given up during the First World War; and though it was in substance restored in Great Britain in 1925 (when Churchill was Chancellor), the restoration was never complete, as the gold reserve remained too small for complete freedom to export to be practicable. Sterling had to be devalued in the financial crisis of 1931 (which brought about the fall of the Labour Government) and Great Britain was forced off the gold standard. Most of the currencies represented in world trade and payments are now convertible. The monetary crisis of March 1968 led to the present two-tier gold price system. See Section G, Part IV.

Goldeneye, a species of wild duck, widely distributed over Arctic regions. It is a passage-migrant and winter-visitor to the British Isles. Has nested in Cheshire. Distinguished by a large white spot in front of each eye on a dark ground.

Golden Number, the number of any year in the metonic cycle of 19 years, deriving its name from the fact that in the old calendars it was always printed in gold. It is found by adding 1 to the number of the year A.D. and dividing by 19, the remainder being the Golden Number; or, if no remainder, the Golden Number is 19. The only use to which the Golden Number is put was in making ecclesiastical calculations for determining movable feasts.

Goldsmiths Company, one of the richest London City Companies; the official assayers of gold and silver, invested with the power of " hallmarking " the quality of objects made from these metals. First charter granted in 1327.

Gondola, the old regulation black boats so common on the canals of Venice, propelled by a gondolier with one oar who stands at the stern, his passengers being accommodated in a covered space in the centre.

Gonfalon, the pennon affixed to a lance, spear, or standard, consisting usually of two or three streamers, and made to turn like a weather-cock.

Gophers. Rodent mammals. The pocket gophers are stout-bodied burrowers common in the U.S.A. The slender burrowing gophers, also called " ground squirrels," occur in central and western U.S.A. The sisel or suslik is a related European species. They are a great pest among grain crops.

Gordon Riots of 1780 were an anti-popery agitation fomented by Lord George Gordon. Called also " No-Popery Riots."

Gorilla, the largest of the anthropoid apes, found in the forests of Equatorial Africa, and at maturity standing from 4 to 5 ft. high.

Goshawk (Accipter gentilis), a diurnal bird of prey,

fearless and extremely agile; loves wooded country and is very destructive of poultry and game-birds. It resembles the peregrine falcon in appearance, but has shorter, rounded wings. This bird was a great favourite of falconers in mediaeval times.

Gospels are those portions of the New Testament which deal with the life, death, resurrection, and teachings of Christ. They are the gospels of Matthew, Mark, Luke, and John, all compiled in the later part of the 1st cent. The first three are called the *synoptic gospels* because of their general unity of narrative. Mark was the first to be written and John the last, and it is to Mark that one should turn for the most reliable source of knowledge of the life of Jesus. The word *gospel* comes from two Anglo-Saxon words *gode* (good) and *spell* (tidings), a translation of the Greek *euangelion* = evangel, evangelist.

Gothic. A term applied to a style of architecture which followed the Romanesque, appeared in France during the 12th cent., and is typical of northern Europe. It was not generally appreciated south of the Alps. The high and sharply pointed arches, the walls supported outside by flying buttresses, the traceried windows, often filled with stained glass, and the lofty spires are in sharp distinction to the semicircular arches and the massive walls characteristic of the more sturdy Romanesque style. Yet the transition was gradual. The cathedrals of Chartres, Laon, and the Benedictine church of St. Denis just outside Paris are typical of early Gothic. The style found its full expression in the French cathedrals of the 13th and 14th cent.: Reims, Notre Dame, Beauvais, Bourges, and Amiens. From France the style spread to other lands in each of which it developed its own characteristics; thus the English churches tended to have massive towers and delicate spires and, as at Salisbury, were often set in open grounds surrounded by lawns; Flemish and Dutch churches were sometimes built of brick as were those in north Germany and Scandinavia; in Spain the Flamboyant style was followed. The main Gothic cathedral in Italy, that of Milan, although begun in 1386 was not completed until the early 19th cent. The lofty character of Gothic has been attributed by the romantic to pious aspiration, as if the spires were striving towards heaven and this concept may well have played a part. The more concrete reasons however were somewhat different: Romanesque churches were thick-walled, sturdy, small-windowed, and set often in open country or on heights (*a*) because architects had not yet discovered how to support a heavy roof without massive walls; and (*b*) because, being built in dangerous times, they had a defensive function. Gothic churches began to be raised in less troublesome times and were tall for the same reason that New York skyscrapers are tall (*i.e.*, the increasing price of land). Also they were built in growing cities where not much space was available and they were lavish in style because wealth was increasing and rich merchants were willing to contribute. Late English Gothic is seen, for example, at King's College Chapel, Cambridge, Henry's Chapel at Westminister, and St. George's Chapel at Windsor (all *c.* 1500). Gothic is also found in secular buildings, *e.g.*, Little Wenham Hall in Suffolk, the castle at Ghent, the town halls of Louvain and Middelburg, and the streets of Gothic houses in Bruges still in use today. Virtually Gothic as a style (excluding the "Gothic revival" of 19th cent. England) ended at the close of the 15th cent. Gothic art is best seen in the illuminated manuscripts of the 13th and 14th cent. and in the church sculpture. Its characteristic is a complete departure from the cool, perfectionist realism of classical times with distortion to produce emotional effects. The human figures are not ideal forms but recognisable as people we might meet in the street; yet there was also the element of wild imagination, intricate design, and a wealth of feeling which might be grotesque, humorous, macabre, or even obscene. This element of distortion and sometimes wildly "unrealistic" colouring which produced an effect more dramatic than the literal representation of the classic schools remained an important element in German art (*see* Expressionism) right up to modern times.

Goths. A Teutonic people who originally came from southern Sweden (Gotland) and by the 3rd cent. were settled in the region north of the Black Sea. They began to encroach on the Roman Empire and early in the 4th cent. split into two divisions: the "wise" Goths or Visigoths between the Danube and the Dniester (referred to as the West Goths), and the "bright" Goths or Ostrogoths in southern Russia on the Dnieper (referred to as the East Goths). The Ostrogoths were conquered by the Huns *c.* 370, while the Visigoths under Alaric devastated Greece and sacked Rome in 410. Eventually the Visigoths spread to France and Spain and their last king Roderick fell in battle against the Moors in 711. The Ostrogoths regained their independence on the death of Attila in 453 and under their king Theodoric the Great conquered Italy in 493. They lost their identity after Justinian regained Italy, 525–552.

Gourd Family *or* **Cucurbitaceæ.** This family of about 650 species of flowering plants includes the gourds, pumpkins, cantaloupes, cucumber, gherkin, water-melon and squashes. Most abundant in the tropics, the cucurbits are mainly climbing annuals with very rapid growth. The bath-room loofah is the skeleton of one curcurbit fruit, *Luffa cylindrica*. The squirting cucumber is another member of the family.

Governor. A device attached to an engine, turbine, compressor, etc., which automatically controls the engine's speed in accordance with power demand. Most governors depend upon the centrifugal action of two or more balls which are thrown outwards as their speed of rotation increases and actuate a throttle valve or cut-off. The centrifugal governor was invented by Thomas Mead, patented by him in 1787, and used on windmills. Watt adapted it to the steam engine.

Grail, Legend of the Holy, a tale of Celtic origin which became part of Arthurian legend and the subject of many mediaeval quest-romances. According to the Christian version the grail was the cup which Christ used at the Last Supper, brought to England by St. Joseph of Arimathea.

Grand Prix, the "French Derby," was established by Napoleon III., in 1863. It is the chief French race and is an international competition of three-year-olds.

Granite is a coarsely crystalline igneous rock consisting of quartz and alkali felspars plus mica or hornblende. It is a much used ornamental and building stone; it forms the high ground of Dartmoor and Bodmin Moor.

Graphite *or* **Plumbago,** commonly called blacklead, is a form of carbon occurring in foliated masses in marble, schist, etc. It is soft, will make black marks on paper or other plain surfaces, and is mainly used for lead pencils. It is also a valuable lubricant. Pure graphite has found a new use with the construction of atomic piles. Important deposits occur in Siberia, Ceylon, Madagascar, Canada, and the U.S.A.

Graptolites, fossil animals confined to Cambrian, Ordovician and Silurian strata. Once classified as hydrazoa but now considered more likely to be hemichordates.

Grasshopper. There are many species of these leaping insects which are related to the locusts and crickets. Most are vegetarians; some eat flies and caterpillars also. The chirping sound they make is made by scraping the hind legs against the wings; in some species a noise is produced by rubbing the wings together.

Gravitation. One of the four types of force known to physics. The others are electromagnetic forces and two types of nuclear force (F15(2)). Gravitational forces are an attraction that one piece of matter has for another; they dominate astronomical phenomena, but inside the atom they are negligible compared with the other three types of force. Einstein's General Theory of Relativity is the only theory at present extant which attempts to interpret gravitational forces in terms of more fundamental concepts. *See* F15(2).

Graylag, the ordinary wild grey goose of Europe, the species from which domestic geese are derived; frequents fens and marshes; breeds in Iceland, Scandinavia, and Scotland; distinguished by pinkish legs and feet and lack of black markings on bill.

Grayling, a fresh-water fish of the salmon family having a large dorsal fin, and averaging about 1 lb. in weight.

Grebe, a diving bird of beautiful plumage found over a great part of the world on lakes and oceans. The two species familiar in Great Britain are the Dabchick or Little Grebe and the large and handsome Great Crested Grebe, which has a feathery tuft, lost in the autumn, on each side of the head. Grebes have remarkable courtship displays. The breast feathers are of a downy softness and silver lustre, for which they were formerly much hunted.

Greek Art. See Hellenic Art.

Greek Fire, a combustible, supposed to have been composed of sulphur, nitre, naphtha, and asphalt, used with destructive effect by the Greeks of the Eastern Empire in their wars.

Greek Kalends, equivalent to never, as only the Romans, not the Greeks, had kalends.

Green Revolution. The " green revolution " is principally due to the American agricultural expert, Dr. Norman Borlaug, who since the 1940s has been working in Mexico on the development of new improved strains of wheat, rice, maize and other cereals. The application of new plant varieties has transformed the agricultural prospects of India, Pakistan, Ceylon, Mexico, the Philippines and other underdeveloped countries; food importers are turning into exporters. For his pioneering work Dr. Borlaug was awarded the 1970 Nobel peace prize.

Greenwich Mean Time. The first Nautical Almanac, for the use of navigators and astronomers, was published by the Astronomer Royal in 1767. It was based on the meridian at Greenwich, with longitude measured east and west of 0°. A master clock, which still exists, was built at Greenwich Observatory in 1852 to control the railway station clocks and Greenwich Mean Time, or Railway Time as it was sometimes called, prevailed. In 1884 Greenwich was chosen as the prime meridian of the world and GMT became known as Universal Time. See also British Standard Time.

Gregorian Calendar. See Calendar.

Gregorian Chant, ritual music with a system of harmony suitable for church use. First established by Pope Gregory I.

Gresham's Law states that if good money, i.e., money with the higher intrinsic value, and bad money are in circulation together, the bad money will tend to drive out the good money from circulation. For instance, the good money is more likely to be melted down or demanded in payment by foreign creditors.

Gretna Green, a celebrated village in Dumfries, just over the border from England, where runaway marriages were performed from 1754 to 1856, though only completely stopped during present century.

Griffin, in ancient mythology, a winged creature with an eagle's head and the body of a lion, found in ancient sculptures of Persia and Assyria. Its origin is traced to the Hittites.

Grilse, a young salmon that has only been once to the sea.

Grimm's Law, formulated by Jacob Grimm, an eminent German philologist, lays down a principle of consonantal change in the Germanic languages. For instance, Lat. pater, Eng. father, Ger. Vater; Lat. frater, Eng. brother, Ger. Bruder; Lat. decem, Eng. ten, Ger. zehn.

Grogram (French = gros grain), a kind of rough fabric made of wool and some other fibre, such as silk, mohair, or cotton, formerly much used for commoner kinds of wearing apparel.

Grotto, a natural or artificial cave. Among the most famous are the blue grotto of Capri and the stalactite grotto of Antiparos (Cyclades, Aegean).

Ground Wave, that part of the energy emitted by a radio transmitter which travels along the ground; as opposed to the sky wave which is reflected back to earth by the ionosphere. With the lower radio-frequencies, the ground wave can be picked up over several thousand miles; in the broadcasting band, over a hundred or so miles; it is virtually useless at high frequencies.

Grouse, game bird of the northern latitudes where some 20 species occur. They are stout, compact, ground-dwelling birds, protectively plumaged (the willow grouse turns white in winter), the male usually being larger and more brightly coloured than the female. The red grouse of the British moorlands has been introduced into Belgium and W. Germany. Of the same family are the blackcock, ptarmigan, capercaillie, American prairie-hen, and the common partridge. Grouse shooting begins in Britain on Aug. 12.

Guanaco, a large species of llama, common to South America, and utilised as a beast of burden.

Guano, the excrement of sea-birds, found in large quantities on the rocky islands of the western coasts of South America and Nauru Is. It forms a useful fertilising agent, being rich in phosphate and ammonia, and first came into use in 1841, since which time Peruvian guano has been a recognised article of commerce. Beds of guano from 50 to 60 ft. in thickness are not uncommon. Fish guano and bat guano from caves in South America and the Bahamas are also used as fertilisers.

Gudgeon, a small fresh-water fish of the carp family with 2 small barbels on the upper lip.

Guelph and Ghibelline, italianised forms of the German words " Welf " and " Waiblingen," the names of two rival princely families whose conflicts made much of the history of Germany and Italy during the Middle Ages. The feuds between these two factions continued in Italy during the campaigns of Emperor Frederick I., and later developed into the fierce struggles of the 13th cent. between emperor and pope. In Italy the Ghibellines supported the side of the German emperors and the Guelphs the cause of the pope. The present Royal Family of England is descended from the Guelphs, through the ducal House of Brunswick (the name of Windsor was assumed during the first world war).

Guildhall, the place of assembly of the members of a guild, and at one time, when guilds were in full strength, was practically the Town Hall. The London Guildhall is to-day the hall of meeting for the City of London Corporation.

Guilds for the fostering and protection of various trades have existed in England since Anglo-Saxon times, and from the 12th to the 16th cent. exercised great influence and enjoyed many privileges. There were trades' guilds and craftsmen's guilds, and in all large cities and towns there was a guild hall. Their successes in the Middle Ages led to many monopolistic abuses, and in the end it became necessary to free the country from their restrictive power. The City Guilds (Livery Companies of the City of London) derive their name from the distinctive dress assumed by their members in the 14th cent. There are 83 Guilds in existence.

Guild Socialism. See J24.

Guillemot, a genus of sea-birds of the auk family, common in Northern Europe, two species—the Common Guillemot and the Black Guillemot—being natives of our own sea coasts, nesting on the cliffs. Brünnich's Guillemot, an Arctic species, is a rare straggler in the British Isles.

Guinea, an English gold coin of the value of twenty-one shillings, current from 1663 to 1817, and deriving its name from the first guinea coinage having been struck from gold obtained on the coast of Guinea.

Guinea-Pig, a rodent of the cavy family about 10 in. in length and with a tail so short that it does not project outside the body. It makes an excellent pet, though easily frightened. Its ancestors were species of the wild cavy of S. America said to have been domesticated by the Incas of Peru. See Z15(2).

Gules, a heraldic term, denoting a rose of red tincture, indicated by vertical lines drawn of engraved without colour.

Gulf Stream is confined entirely to the western side of the N. Atlantic and is the warm-water current flowing through the Straits of Florida from the Gulf of Mexico parallel to the American coast up as far as Cape Hatteras. From there it continues north-eastwards as a slower, broader, cooler (yet even so, relatively warm) drift of water, merging with the North Atlantic Drift and losing its identity about 40° N. Lat., 60° W. Long. It is a common error to attribute the warmth of the British Isles and Western Europe generally to the Gulf Stream but this has no influence whatever except in so far as it feeds the North Atlantic Drift. Both the Gulf Stream and the North Atlantic Drift owe their movement to the direction of the prevailing winds, and it is the south-westerly airstream coming from warmer regions and passing over the surface waters of the Atlantic Drift that brings the warmth inland to influence the climate of Western Europe.

Gull. An extremely well-known, long-winged seabird with rather short legs and webbed feet. In almost all adults the body and tail are white whilst the back and most of the wings are grey or black. In the majority of cases the plumage of juveniles is partly or entirely dusky. Gulls are omnivorous, and are very useful as scavengers. They follow ships and quickly seize upon any refuse which may be thrown overboard. There are 44 species, which vary in size from moderately small to large. With certain exceptions, such as the Kittiwake in the North Atlantic, they are not found very far from land. They are sociable and mostly breed in colonies on cliff-ledges, on islands, beaches and sandhills, and among vegetation in swamps, sometimes a long way from the sea. The nest is usually substantial, and the eggs generally number from two to three. Of the 29 species breeding in the northern hemisphere, 14 occur in the British Isles. The pure white Ivory Gull is the most northerly of birds. Sabine's and the Swallow-tailed Gull have forked tails. Ross's Gull has a black ring round the neck and one species, Franklin's Gull, migrates from the North, where it breeds, to pass the winter in the Southern hemisphere.

Gums are glutinous compounds obtained from vegetable sources, soluble in cold or hot water, but not in alcohol. There are innumerable varieties. Gum Arabic is exuded from a species of acacia grown in Senegal, the Sudan, Arabia, India and other countries, and is a valuable commercial product, used in dyeing, ink-making, as a mucilage, and in medicine. India-rubber is an elastic gum. Gums are also made from starch, potatoes, wheat, etc., from seeds, bark, roots, and weeds. Many so-called gums are resins.

Gun-Cotton, a powerful explosive manufactured by subjecting a prepared cotton to the prolonged action of a mixture of three parts sulphuric acid and one part of nitric acid. It burns without explosion on ignition, but by percussion explodes with a force five times greater than that of gunpowder.

Gunpowder, also called " black powder," the oldest of explosive mixtures, consists of saltpetre, sulphur, and charcoal, intimately mixed, the proportions being varied for different intended uses.

Gunpowder Plot was a conspiracy by a desperate band of Roman Catholics in the reign of James I, to avenge the harsh treatment to which Catholics were subjected. Barrels of gunpowder were secreted in the vaults underneath the Houses of Parliament, and it was proposed to fire these when the King and his Ministers assembled on Nov. 5, 1605. The plot was betrayed and Guy Fawkes and his co-conspirators were arrested and executed. The date serves to perpetuate the ancient custom of burning the effigy of Fawkes, a custom in which young people are the most enthusiastic participants, with bonfires, fireworks, etc.

Gurnard, a sea-fish, with large, bony head and diminutive body, of which there are some forty species. They are plentiful in British waters.

Gymnasium, originally the name given in ancient Greece to the public places where Greek youth used to exercise and receive instruction. Plato, Aristotle, and other great teachers lectured there. The Greek institution was never very popular with the Romans, and it was not until the 18th and 19th cent. that the cult of combining physical with intellectual activity again found a place in educational systems. In Germany the name was applied to the classical grammar school; in this country and America to the halls where gymnastics were practised.

Gypsies, a nomadic race, believed to be of Indian origin; their language, Romany, is related to the languages of N.W. India. They are spread over many parts of the world, but are most common in Europe where they appeared towards the end of the Middle Ages. The English name *gypsy* comes from the Spanish *gitano* = Egyptian; other European names are *Zigeuner* (Ger.), *zingaro* (It.), *tzigany* (Magyar), all resembling the Persian *zingar* = a saddler. Their history has been one of persecution. Hitler treated them like the Jews. In Britain since the war they have been kept increasingly on the move, but in 1968 Parliament passed a Bill to make the provisions of sites a duty of local authorities. The Netherlands passed a similar Bill in 1918! It is now more usual to speak of gypsies as " travellers." Economic pressure has largely removed their traditional crafts of tinkering, basket-making, peg-making. The majority now deal in scrap-iron, paper, and rags.

Gypsum, a whitish mineral consisting of hydrated sulphate of calcium. The finest gypsum is alabaster. When heated gypsum is converted into the powder called Plaster of Paris; the water it loses can be taken up when the plaster is wetted, and the reconversion of Plaster of Paris into gypsum accounts for the way in which the former sets hard. The name " Plaster of Paris " came from the location of important gypsum quarries in the Montmartre district of Paris. It was found after the flood disasters of Jan. 1953 that gypsum could undo the effect of sea-water. By spreading it for the rain to wash into the soil, thousands of acres of farmland in Holland and Britain were made productive again.

Gyroscope is a symmetrical rapidly rotating object, typically wheel-like, which because of its mass and rotation possesses a lot of the dynamical property known as angular momentum. Basic dynamical laws tell us that angular momentum is conserved and a consequence of this is that the axis of rotation tends to stay pointing in the same direction. Disturbing influences make a gyroscope's motion complicated but the general effect of the presence of a gyroscope attached to any body is to help to stabilise the body's motion. This is made use of in reducing the rocking of ships and in compasses and control systems in aircraft, torpedoes, and missiles.

H

Habeas Corpus, the name given to a writ ordering the body of a person under restraint or imprisonment to be brought into court for full inquiry into the legality of the restraint to be made. The first Habeas Corpus Act was passed in 1679, though nominally such a right had existed from Magna Carta, but some of the more despotic kings had disregarded it. In times of public peril the privilege of *habeas corpus* is sometimes temporarily suspended, many instances occurring in the history of Ireland and during the First and Second World Wars.

Haber Process, the important industrial process for synthesising ammonia from atmospheric nitrogen. Nitrogen and hydrogen are made to combine at high pressure (200 atmospheres or upwards) in an electric arc.

Haddock, one of the best-known fishes abounding in northern seas and averaging about 4 lb. in weight. Related to the cod. Largely used for curing, and sold as " finnan haddies."

Hade of veins, a mining term indicating the particular inclination that any vein, seam, or strata may have from the perpendicular; thus, in Weardale the veins mainly "hade" to the north.

Hadrian's Wall. See Roman Walls.

Haematite, ferric oxide, one of the principal iron ores, containing about 70% of the metal. It is usually found in kidney-shaped masses, and is specular, red or brown, in thin fragments, but greyish in bulk.

Haemocyanin, the respiratory pigment of crustaceans and molluscs. It functions like haemoglobin, from which it differs in containing copper instead of iron and being blue when oxidised instead of red. See F36(2).

Haemoglobin, the pigment containing iron which gives red blood corpuscles their colour. It is a respiratory pigment, having the property of picking up oxygen when the blood passes through the lungs to produce the compound known as oxyhaemoglobin. In other parts of the body the oxyhaemoglobin breaks down, liberating oxygen, which is used in the oxidation process (respiration) that the body tissues carry on. *See* F36(2).

Hafiz, besides being the pseudonym of a famous Persian poet, is a title conferred upon any Mohammedan who has committed the whole of the Koran to memory.

Hafnium, a metallic element discovered by Coster and Hevesy in 1922 and important in the atomic-energy field. It occurs in most zirconium minerals to the extent of about 5 per cent.

Hag-fish, a blind, eel-like parasitic sea-fish with soft backbone; found within the bodies of other fish, and called sometimes the " borer," or " the glutinous hag-fish." Related to the Lamprey.

Hagiarchy, the rule or order of Saints.

Hagiology, a branch of literature that is wholly given up to the history of the saints, and the setting forth of the stories and legends associated with their names.

Hail, hard, roughly spherical balls of ice, consisting of white cores covered by layers of both transparent and opaque ice, frequently falling during thunderstorms. They usually do not exceed 1 in. in size, but hailstones larger than apples and weighing more than 2 lb. have been observed. The general theory of a hailstone is that near the top of a cumulonimbus cloud a raindrop becomes frozen, grows in size by condensation and through collisions with snow particles, and eventually becomes so weighty as to overcome the ascending air currents in the cloud. Falling, it first encounters supercooled water drops, immediately freezing on it, increasing the white core, and then at lower levels ordinary water drops, freezing more slowly, producing a layer of clear ice. Before the hailstone arrives at the ground gusts and lulls may transport it several times up and down both regions, adding alternate coatings of soft white and hard clear ice.

Hake, a fish of the cod family, found in large numbers in the seas of Europe, but not in high favour for the table with fastidious feeders.

Halcyon, a term associated in olden times with the kingfisher and days of soothing calm, " halcyon days " being a frequently used expression. The legend was that the kingfisher laid its eggs on the surface of the sea at the time of the winter solstice when the sea was unruffled. Halcyon is the Greek for kingfisher.

Halibut, one of the largest of the flat fishes, averaging when full grown from 4 to 6 ft. in length, and highly esteemed for the table. Specimens of still larger size occasionally occur. It is plentifully distributed. Its two eyes are on the right side of the head.

Hall-mark. A mark or group of marks, impressed by an assay office on gold or silver articles guaranteeing the standard of fineness of the precious metal used in them. These marks, which have been applied to silver made in London since the beginning of the 14th cent., and perhaps earlier, make it possible to establish the year and place of assay as also the name of the maker. English pieces of silver usually have not less than four marks, viz., (1) town mark; (2) maker's mark; (3) date letter; (4) sterling mark.

The town mark is rarely changed; in London a crowned leopard's head was used from the earliest days until 1820 with only minor modifications, except for the period 1697–1720 when a lion's head erased was substituted; since 1820 the crown has been omitted.

Until the late 17th cent. a symbol was often used as a maker's mark, from 1696 to 1720 the first two letters of the maker's surname, and subsequently the maker's initials. Owing to the destruction of the earlier mark plates at Goldsmiths' Hall no maker's name prior to the late 17th cent. can be identified with certainty.

The London date letter is changed at the end of May each year, so each letter covers seven months of one year and five months of the following. The London date cycle has usually consisted of twenty letters: the alphabet of each cycle is of different style, and the letters are enclosed in shields of different shape.

The sterling mark, the lion passant, was introduced in 1544 and continued in use until 1697, when the higher Britannia standard was introduced in order to discourage the practice current amongst goldsmiths of melting down coin of the realm to make plate. The leopard's head crowned and the lion passant were then replaced by a figure of Britannia and a lion's head erased. Though the regulation imposing the higher standard was withdrawn in 1720, a small amount of Britannia standard silver continued to be made and still is made.

From 1784 until 1890 a plate tax was levied on all silver assayed in Great Britain and an additional duty mark, the sovereign's head, was used during this period. A Jubilee mark bearing the head of George V and of Queen Mary was used in between the years 1933 and 1935, and in 1953 a coronation mark with the head of Queen Elizabeth was introduced.

The tables of hall-marks in **Section N** give the London date letter cycles from 1598 to 1955. The form of town mark and sterling mark used during each cycle is given at the head of each column. Where a major alteration took place in either of these marks during a date-letter cycle, the alternative forms are also shown. The date of the change can be established by reference to the notes above. At the bottom of each page the marks used by the major provincial, Scottish and Irish assay offices are shown. Owing to lack of space, the complete date-letter cycles are not shown, but two examples only from the 17th, 18th or 19th cent. Where a provincial assay office was established in the 17th cent. or earlier, the marks of one year in the 17th and 18th cent. respectively are shown, where the office was not established until the 18th cent., the marks of one year in the 18th and 19th cent. are given.

Halloween (Oct. 31), the eve of All Saints' Day, a time associated, especially in Scotland, with certain pleasing superstitions attractively set forth in Burns's famous poem " Hallowe'en." It is the night when young men and maidens are supposed, by observing certain rites, to have their future wives and husbands disclosed to them.

Hallucinogen, a drug which acts upon the brain to create sensory illusions or hallucinations with a variety of emotional effects. One of the most widely studied is LSD (*q.v.*) which will produce symptoms very similar to those found in some mental disorders. .

Halo, a luminous circle usually of 22° radius, surrounding sun or moon, produced by the refraction and reflection of light by ice crystals of high cirrus cloud. It is a very common occurrence, in the British Isles almost one day in three. The inner side is red and the outer a whitish-yellow colour. " Mock suns," *i.e.*, patches of light at the same elevation as the sun are much rarer occurrences, sometimes being of great beauty and brilliance. Halo is the Greek for threshing-floor. *See* **Coronae**.

Halogens, the group name for the four non-metallic elements fluorine, chlorine, bromine, and iodine. The term " halogen " means " salt-producer."

Halteres, the modified hind-wings of the two-winged flies or *Diptera* (*e.g.*, the house-fly). The equilibrium in flight of these insects depends on the halteres, which are commonly called " balancers."

Hampton Court Conference, presided over at Hampton Court Palace by James I. in 1604 and which brought about his authorised translation of the Bible, had an important bearing on the religious differences of the time. James refused to grant tolerations to the Puritans. This sowed the seeds of civil war. Following the conference three hundred English Puritan clergy were ejected from their livings.

Hanaper Office, a former Chancery office, deriving its name from the fact that its writs and papers were kept in a hanaper (hamper). The Chancellor's officer thus came to be known as the Hanaper. The Comptrollers of the Hanaper were abolished in England in 1842.

Hand, a measure of four inches, the average size of the palm; used in reckoning height of horses.

Handfasting, an informal marriage custom once prevalent in Scotland, whereby a man and woman bound themselves to cohabit for a year and a day, and at the end of that period either confirmed their contract by a regular marriage or separated.

Hansard, the title given to the official reports of Parliamentary debates, so named after Luke Hansard who in 1774 became partner in a firm of printers to the House of Commons. His son T. C. Hansard was first the printer and then the publisher of an unofficial series of parliamentary debates inaugurated by William Cobbett in 1803. In 1909 production was taken over by H.M. Stationery Office and today's volumes contain full, substantially verbatim, reports of what is said in both Houses of Parliament.

Hanseatic League was a confederation of North German towns established about 1241 for purposes of mutual protection in carrying on international commerce. The League became so powerful that it was able to dominate the foreign trade of Norway, Sweden, Denmark, and even to some extent of London. A branch was established in London and had its guild hall in Cannon Street for hundreds of years. The League existed down to the middle of the 17th cent. Hamburg, Lübeck, and Bremen are the only cities which, as free ports, still by commercial courtesy retain the name of Hanse towns. *Hansa* is Old High German for Association or Merchants' Guild.

Hapsburg (*Ger.* Habsburg), the ruling house of Austria, 1282–1918; held title of Holy Roman Emperor, 1438–1806, except for 1740–5. The aggrandisement of the Hapsburg family was mainly brought about by a series of fortunate marriages. In 1521 when the Hapsburg power was at its zenith, Charles V divided his dominions into two branches—Austrian Hapsburg and Spanish Hapsburg. The Hapsburg Danubian Monarchy dates from 1526 when the Hungarian and Bohemian crowns were united with the Austrian patrimony of the Hapsburg. The triple union lasted 400 years. The murder of the heir to the Hapsburg thrones, Francis Ferdinand, at Sarajevo in 1914, provoked the outbreak of the First World War. Francis Joseph's great-nephew, Charles, abdicated in 1918. (Prof. C. A. Macartney's authoritative work, *The Habsburg Empire, 1790–1918*, was published in 1969.)

Hare, species of the *Lepus genus*, distributed widely through the N. hemisphere. Noted for having four upper front teeth, one pair behind the other, short tufted tail, a cleft upper lip and longer ears and limbs than the rabbit. It does not burrow. The young are born with hair and able to see. A swift animal hunted with greyhounds in the sport called "coursing." *See* Game.

Harleian MSS. comprise some thousands of volumes of MSS. and documents, collected by the first Earl of Oxford (1661–1724) and his son Edward. After the death of the latter, his widow handed the MSS. over to the nation for £10,000, and they are deposited in the British Museum.

Harlequin, the buffoon of ancient Italian comedy. As adapted to the British stage, however, harlequin is a pantomime character only, in love with Columbine, appearing in parti-coloured garments and carrying a wand, by which he exercises a magic influence in thwarting the fantastic tricks of the clown and pantaloon.

Harmattan, a dry wind which may blow between January and May across the Sahara to the Gulf of Guinea. Although affording relief from the tropical heat, vegetation withers because of its extreme dryness and much irritation is caused by the clouds of fine dust which it carries.

Harmonic Motion, regular periodic motion of the kind exemplified by a ball bobbing up and down at the end of a spring, and by the piston in a steam engine. It may be simple (simple harmonic motion) or composed of two or more simple harmonic motions. In simple harmonic motion the acceleration is proportional to the distance of the moving body from its original rest position.

Harp-seal, the ordinary Greenland seal, with a dark harp-shaped marking on its back, hence its name. It abounds in Newfoundland waters and further northward towards the Arctic.

Harpy Eagle, a large bird of prey named from the winged monsters of Greek mythology, inhabit-

ing the forest regions of Central and South America. There are eight species, one with handsome grey plumage and large crest which attacks and kills animals much larger than itself, and was called by the Aztecs " winged wolf."

Harrier, a bird of prey of the falcon family; of the various species distributed over the world, three breed in Britain: the moorland Hen harrier, the Marsh harrier, and Montagu's harrier. They are large birds with long tails, long legs, long wings, and gliding flight. They nest on the ground and eat small mammals, frogs, lizards, and small birds.

Hartebeest, common African antelope of a grey-brown colour, with ringed and knotted horns bending backward and tapering to sharp points; gregarious, of large size, and capable of domestication. There are several species.

Harvest Bug, a very small insect, of a dark red colour, which appears in large numbers in the fields in autumn, and is peculiarly irritating to animals and man by the tenacity with which it attaches itself to the skin and burrows underneath. Probably the larvae of spinning mites (Trombidoids). In the U.S.A. they are called " chiggers."

Harvest Moon, the full moon that occurs nearest to the autumn equinox, in September. It rises for several nights running about the same time, and yields an unusually brilliant series of moonlight nights.

Harvestmen are, like spiders, members of the arachnid class but belong to the distinctly different order of Phalangida. They are common in the countryside in autumn and have small oval bodies and eight long slender legs which besides being mere organs of locomotion also act as sense organs. Known as " daddy longlegs " in America.

Hashish, an Arabic word for the narcotic substance prepared from the hemp plant (*Cannabis sativa*). It is known by a variety of names, *e.g.*, bhang in India and marijuana in America.

Hatchment, in heraldry, is a square board, in vertical diagonal position, placed outside a house or on the tomb at the death of a member of a family and so arranged that it indicates the sex and condition of the deceased.

Hawfinch, a well-known European bird of the finch family, having a variegated plumage, a sturdy bill, and black-and-white tail. In England it is found in the Midland and Eastern Counties, and locally in Scotland.

Hawk. This name is applied to almost any diurnal bird of prey other than eagle, falcon, or vulture, but in its strict sense applies only to the *Accipiter* genus—the small Sparrow Hawk and the larger Goshawk, round-winged, long-tailed birds with barred under-parts. They prey upon small birds captured in flight and small mammals.

Hawk-moths, large species of moths, thick of body and strong of wing, which fly with rapid swooping motion, hence its name. There are numerous handsome species in Britain.

Hearth-Money was a tax laid on hearths (in all houses paying the church and poor rates). Charles II. introduced it in 1662, and it was repealed in the reign of William and Mary.

Heat, after prolonged controversy over whether or not heat is a " substance " (formerly called " caloric "), it was established in the 19th cent. that heat is a form of energy; it is in fact the combined kinetic and potential energy of the atoms of which a body is composed. Heat can be turned into other forms of energy, *e.g.*, a red hot body loses heat by radiating it in the form of electromagnetic waves (" radiant heat "—chiefly infra-red rays). Heat may also be transferred from one place to another by conduction and, in fluids, by convection. All three processes occur when a glowing fire heats a room. A unit quantity of heat is the calorie, which is the amount of heat sufficient to raise the temperature of 1 gm. of water by 1° C. In general, adding heat to a body raises its temperature. The number of calories required per gram of material to raise the temperature 1° C is called the *specific heat* of the material. However, adding heat may not raise the temperature but may instead cause a change of state, *e.g.*, from solid to liquid (melting) or liquid to gas (evaporation). The amount of heat required to melt 1 gram of a solid is called the latent heat of melting. Similarly, there is a latent heat of evaporation. Strictly speaking, the specific and latent heats of a substance depend on how much its pressure and volume are allowed to vary during the measurements. Water has a high specific heat, and this makes the oceans a vast heat reservoir, a factor of great meteorological significance. The science of heat is called thermodynamics, and is of great importance in physics and chemistry. *See* **F17.**

Heath, flowering plants of the *Ericaceae* family. Heaths are widely distributed over uncultivated spaces of Europe and Africa. In Britain they are represented by heather (of which there are several species) and ling (*Calluna vulgaris*), which cover thousands of acres of moorland. Some of the African or Cape heaths are very beautiful and much prized by florists. One species of heath (*Erica arborea*) which grows in S. Europe and N. Africa has close-grained woody rootstock used for making briar pipes. *See* **T7(2).**

Heat Wave is a spell of very hot weather, due chiefly in the British Isles to a warm southerly current of air caused by the presence of an anticyclone over western or central Europe at the same time as a depression is stationary over the Atlantic. High humidity increases the discomfort.

Hegira, an Arab term signifying departure or flight, and used in reference to Mohammed's departure from Mecca for Medina, A.D. 622, from which date the Mohammedan era is reckoned.

Helicopter, heavier-than-air aircraft which obtains its lift from blades rotating above the fuselage in windmill-fashion. The first successful helicopters were the Focke-Wulf 61, a German machine (1936), and the VS-300, designed by Igor Sikorsky, flown in 1937. Helicopters can hover, and rise and descend vertically, in addition to being capable of horizontal flight.

Heliotrope, a favourite sweet-scented flowering plant, common in tropical and sub-tropical countries; the Peruvian heliotrope is the " cherry pie " of our summer garden borders. *See* **T9(1).**

Helium, a gaseous element first discovered by means of the spectroscope in the sun's atmosphere. This discovery, made in 1868 by the astronomer Sir Norman Lockyer, was followed in 1895 by Sir William Ramsay's proof that the element existed on earth. He found it in the uranium ore, clevite. Later it was established that helium is formed by the radioactive decay of many elements which emit α-particles (nuclei of helium atoms) and is contained in all radioactive minerals. The largest source of helium is natural gas, the richest in helium being the gas from certain wells in Utah, U.S.A. Next to hydrogen, helium is the lightest gas known, has a lifting power equal to 92% of hydrogen and the advantage that it is inert and non-inflammable. It is used for inflating airships. Ordinary air contains 1 part in 200,000 of helium. It was the last gaseous element to be liquefied, this being achieved by Onnes in 1908 in Leyden. Liquid helium has many remarkable properties only imperfectly understood. As well as being scientifically fascinating it is indispensable in cryogenics (*q.v.*) as a medium for cooling other substances to temperatures near absolute zero. Hydrogen fusion in the " H bomb " produces helium.

Hellebore, a plant of the *Ranunculaceae* (buttercup) family. The best-known British examples are the green and stinking varieties. There is also a garden kind which flowers in December called the Christmas Rose. Hellebore yields a bitter substance which forms a drastic purgative, but is now little used. *See* **T9(1).**

Hellenic Art. The art of ancient Greece may be roughly divided into three periods: the prehistoric period (*c.* 1500–1000 B.C.) of the bronze age Mycenaeans; the archaic period (*c.* 600–500 B.C.); and the classical period (*c.* 500–300 B.C.). Of the first period centred on Mycenae in Peloponnesus but extending to the coasts of Asia and the city of Troy we can mention only the massive stone gateways and the shaft graves of Mycenae, where the archaeologist Schliemann discovered painted vases, gold cups, bronze swords, and ornaments of what had once been a great, if primitive, civilisation. During the

archaic period sculpture was the principal form of art expression. The magnificent male and female figures are reminiscent of Egyptian art, but are distinctive in liveliness of facial expression. The vase-paintings of this period became more elaborate, depicting scenes from mythology or ceremonial events. Typical of classical Greek art is the representation of the beautiful and healthy human body deliberately posed and often carrying out heroic or athletic acts. The vast majority of these statues are known to us only through Roman copies. The *Hermes* of Praxiteles (born *c.* 385 B.C.) is possibly the only existing statue which can be assigned with any degree of certainty to an individual artist. Almost the whole of the Greek genius in architecture was expended on temples which are all basically similar in design—a rectangle with a low-pitched gabled roof resting on side walls. The three orders Doric, Corinthian, and Ionic mainly referred to the type of column used, but naturally the whole building was influenced thereby. Some of the main buildings are on the Acropolis, a hill outside Athens, on which stand the Parthenon (from the outer frieze of which the Elgin marbles, now mostly in the British Museum, were taken), the Erechtheum, famous for its Porch of Maidens, and the gateway known as the Propylaea with its broad flight of marble steps. Apart from that on vases, no Greek painting has come down to us, although Greek painters existed and were noted in their time. All we have are copies in mosaic and fresco made by the Romans, at Naples and Pompeii. Of Greek literature in prose, verse, and the drama little can be said here. To the early period (*i.e.*, the archaic age) belong Homer's *Iliad* and *Odyssey*, Hesiod's long poem *Work and Days*, and Sappho's love poems, and Pindar's Odes. The period of Pericles in the 5th cent. B.C. produced more great literature than any comparable period in history: the philosophical writings of Plato and Aristotle, the tragedies of Aeschylus, Euripides, and Sophocles, the comedies of Aristophanes—all these are still part of the European tradition, and together with Greek architecture played a major part in the Renaissance (*see* **J44).**

Hellenistic Art, the art of the period of Greek civilisation which began with the conquests of Alexander the Great (356–323 B.C.) and lasted until his former empire (which encompassed most of the Middle East and part of North Africa) was conquered by the Romans in 146 B.C. Culturally it was an important period because it spread Greek culture far beyond its original boundaries—even as far as the north of India, and its centres spread from Athens to the cities of Alexandria in Egypt, Antioch in Syria, and Pergamum in Asia Minor. But equally Eastern culture spread to the West: democracy was replaced by absolute monarchy, cosmopolitanism took the place of the Greek tendency to believe that all who were not Greeks were barbarians, and mystical philosophies took the place of Greek rationalism. This was a sensuous, secular, pleasure-loving, rootless society, and these tendencies were reflected in its art. Hellenistic sculpture was sensual, effeminate, and violently emotional, yet it depicted individuals and not always noble or beautiful ones. (Classical Greek sculpture was idealistic, showed types rather than individuals, and appealed to the intellect rather than the emotions.) Some of the best examples came from the school at Pergamum and later from the island of Rhodes, and the titles themselves speak of their nature: *The Dying Gaul, Gaul Slaying his Wife and Himself,* and the famous *Laocoön* (representing Laocoön and his two sons being crushed by two enormous serpents). All these date from about 240 to 50 B.C.—for the culture did not immediately end with the Roman conquest. The enormous frieze of the altar of the temple in Pergamum depicts a battle between gods and giants with tremendous realism and brutal violence far removed from the serene art of classical times. Portrait sculpture is typical of Hellenistic art, where it may almost be said to have been invented, since such ventures in the past had been idealistic rather than realistic. The great Hellenistic cities were geometrically planned and fine public buildings made their appearance in which the slender and graceful Ionic or the ornate Corinthian columns took the place of the more austere and heavy classical ones. Alexandria was famed for its library of 700,000 books and was the centre of philosophical schools such as the Stoics and Epicureans. Here too worked the mathematicians Euclid and Archimedes, the physicians Erasistratus and Herophilus, and the geographer Pytheas. But Hellenistic literature was a pale reflection of the glories of the past and we mention only the comedies of Menander and the pastoral verse of Theocritus of Syracuse.

Hemiptera, the order of insects to which belong the true bugs. Their wing structure is in most species incomplete, hence the term hemiptera. This order includes the familiar water insects, the water boatman and water skater, also the aphids, cicadas, leaf hoppers, scale insects. *See* T29(2).

Hemlock, a plant of the *Umbelliferae* family, growing in all parts of Britain, and containing a strong alkaloid poison. Used medicinally, this alkaline substance is of considerable service, being a powerful sedative. According to Pliny, hemlock was the poison used by the Athenians in putting criminals to death.

Hemp (*Cannabis sativa*), name of a plant native to Asia, now cultivated widely for the valuable fibre contained in the stalk or in some species in the leaves. Hemp fibre has been replaced by cotton for textiles and by jute for sacks and is now chiefly used for cordage and twine. It contains a resinous substance from which the narcotic hashish is made. The seed yields a valuable oil. The term hemp is also used for other fibre plants, including manila hemp from the Philippines, sunn hemp from India, sisal from W. and E. Africa and phorium from New Zealand.

Henbane, a plant found in Britain and other parts of Europe and Northern Asia. It belongs to the potato family *Solanaceae*, grows mostly on waste ground, and bears yellow-brown flowers veined with purple. The leaves yield a poisonous alkaloid substance which, medicinally prepared and administered, is of great use. Tincture of henbane is often preferred to laudanum.

Heptarchy, a word derived from the Greek *hepta,* seven, and denoting the seven kingdoms (*archai*) into which Anglo-Saxon England was divided before 900. The seven were Kent, Essex, Sussex, Wessex, Mercia, East Anglia, and Northumbria.

Heracleum, a plant of the *Umbelliferae* family, common in southern and central Europe, though only one species, the cow parsnip, grows in England. It has a bitter root, and from the juice of the stem an intoxicating liquor is occasionally prepared.

Herald, an officer of state empowered to make formal proclamations and deliver messages from the sovereign or other high personage whom he serves. In the developments which took place in armorial bearings, the herald was the functionary charged with the duty of their proper depiction.

Heraldry, the knowledge of armorial bearings, was mainly the outcome of the love of outward distinction which prevailed in mediaeval times. " Heraldry," says Stubbs, " became a handmaid of chivalry, and the marshalling of badges, crests, coat-armour, pennons, helmets, and other devices of distinction grew into an important branch of knowledge." The *shield,* or *escutcheon,* is the ground upon which armorial signs are traced, the colour of the shield being called the *tincture,* the signs recorded the *charges.* There are seven *tinctures—or* (gold), *argent* (silver), *gules* (red), *azure* (blue), *vert* (green), *purpure* (purple), and *sable* (black). The *charges* are classed as " Honourable " and " Subordinate " ordinaries, comprising lines and geometrical forms; and " Common " ordinaries, which latter includes all representations of natural objects. There is also a system of external signs, such as crowns, coronets, mitres, helmets, mantlings, wreaths, and crests, each having its distinctive significance. For other distinguishing marks see Hatchments, Quartering, Rampant, Pean.

Heralds' College or **College of Arms,** was incorporated by Richard III. in 1483. Its head is the Earl Marshal (an office hereditary in the family of the Dukes of Norfolk), and there are three Kings of Arms, six Heralds, and four Pursuivants. The business transacted is wholly connected with the tracing of genealogies and the granting of armorial bearings. In Scotland the Heraldic functions are performed by the Lord Lyon King of Arms.

Herbarium, a systematically classified collection of preserved plants. One of the largest in the world is at the Royal Botanic Gardens at Kew.

Heredity is the study of the transmission of physical and mental characteristics from one generation to another. Gregor Mendel (1822–84), a great experimenter in the field of inheritance, established the principle embodied in Mendel's law in his work published in 1866. The ideas which he then put forward were forgotten until the early years of this century, but today they form the basis of the modern study of genetics. Genes are the units of heredity; they are contained in the chromosomes of the cell nucleus. In human cells there are 46 chromosomes—22 pairs of characteristic shape and a 23rd (the sex chromosomes) similar in women and dissimilar in men, which unite in the process of fertilisation. An individual can only develop, even under the most favourable surroundings, as far as his inherited characteristics, *i.e.,* his genes will allow him to do so. It is in the development of personality that the interplay between heredity and environment becomes most apparent. *See* **The Evolution of Organisms, F45,** *also* **Q27.**

Hermaphrodite, animals or plants possessing both male and female reproductive organs, *e.g.,* snail, earthworms, most flowering plants.

Hermit Crab, a decapod, with a soft asymmetrical body which it protects by thrusting it into an empty gastropod shell, *e.g.,* whelk, which it carries about, only abandoning it when necessary for a larger one. Found in all seas, many live in commensal relationship with sea anemones, etc.

Heron, a large wading bird with long curved neck and pointed bill, is a member of the *Ardeidae* family, of which there are many species. Egrets and bitterns are included as herons. Herons are to be met with in marsh lands and near rivers and lakes, where they feed on fish and frogs. They nest in trees in large numbers, these colonies being called heronries. The common heron is native to England, and other species from the Continent are frequent visitors.

Herring, a common sea-fish, related to the sardine and pilchard, abounding in northern seas and found in large numbers round the British coasts. The herring fishing is the most important fish industry in this country, a large fleet being engaged in it. The fishing season proper lasts from May to October, the enormous shoals being followed as they move from place to place. The spawning season is about the end of August. One female herring may produce 20 to 50 thousand eggs, which sink to the sea-bed, where they develop.

Hibernation, the dormant condition in which numerous mammals, reptiles, amphibians, insects, plants, etc., pass the winter. The rate of metabolism slows down, and the body temperature drops to that of the surroundings. Work on these low temperatures and their physiological effect has led to improved surgical techniques. Animals of the torrid regions pass through an analogous period (aestivation) during the hot season, when the sources of food are dried up.

Hickory, several species of American tree of the walnut family, remarkable for its very hard, solid, heavy white wood, and bearing an edible, four-lobed nut.

Hieratic Art, a type of art (typified by the major part of the art of ancient Egypt) which is (*a*) exclusively religious, and (*b*) conventionally based on earlier forms and traditions.

Hieroglyphics are the earliest form of pictured symbolic expressions, and are supposed to have been introduced by the ancient Egyptians. They consist of rude depictions of animals, plants, signs, and objects, and in their later examples express, in abridged form, ideas and records from which significant historical information has been gleaned. The deciphering of

Egyptian hieroglyphics long formed an ardent study, but gradually the key to the riddle was discovered, and most of the ancient records can now be understood. Besides the Egyptian there are also Hittite, Minoan and Mayan hieroglyphic scripts. *See* Rosetta Stone.

Hi-Fi means high fidelity, and refers to gramophones, tape recorders, and similar apparatus which will *faithfully* reproduce sounds. It is not too difficult these days to amplify electrical signals without distorting them much; it is more difficult to turn electrical impulses into exactly equivalent sound waves (with a loudspeaker, for example) or *vice versa* (with a microphone or gramophone pick-up). Pick-up and loudspeaker are therefore often the weak links in domestic hi-fi and faults in their design, deficiencies in the electronic amplifiers, imperfect gramophone motors can all contribute to audible results ranging from the tolerable to the execrable. Almost perfect sound reproduction is however available to enthusiasts possessing a suitable combination of discrimination, know-how, and financial resources. There are periodical magazines which provide guidance. *See also* **F62–5.**

Hindi, the official language of India. *See* **M44.**

Hinduism. *See* **J24.**

Hindustani, the spoken form of Hindi (written in Devanagari script) and Urdu (written in Arabic characters).

Hippogriff, a fabulous animal, like a horse in body, but with the head, wings, and front legs and claws of an eagle. The monster frequently appears in the romances of the Middle Ages.

Hippopotamus or "river-horse," the largest living representative of the hog family, widely distributed over Africa, where it lives in herds. It is of immense bulk, attaining a length of 12 ft. and a weight of 4 tons and stands about 5 ft. high. Its skin is hairless and about 2 in. thick, and it has a pair of tusks often weighing as much as 6 lb. It spends most of its time in the water, and lives entirely on vegetation, both aquatic and terrestrial. The pigmy hippopotamus, which occurs in forests and swamps in W. Africa, is only half the size.

Histology is the study of the structure of plant and animal tissues. These mainly consist of groups of cells with similar functions, *e.g.,* muscle, brain tissue.

Hittites, an ancient race (often mentioned in the Old Testament) who inhabited Cappadocia (region of Eastern Asia Minor) from the third to the first millennium B.C. Excavations have revealed that they attained a high level of civilisation round about 1350 B.C. The Hittites were rivals of Egypt, disputing with the Pharaohs the mastery of the Middle East. They were the first to smelt iron successfully.

Hobby, a bird of the falcon family, 12–14 in. long. Local breeding visitor to England and Wales, April–Sept.; irregular visitor to Scotland and Ireland. They winter in Africa.

Hog, the common name of animals of the Suina family, including the wild boar, pig, and sow. The wild boar, *Sus scrofa*, is the common ancestor. The skin of the hog is covered with bristles, the snout truncated, and each foot has four hoofed toes. Hogs are omnivorous feeders and eat almost anything that is given them.

Hogmanay, the Scottish New Year's Eve festival and a national holiday of the country. The custom of demanding Hogmanay bread is still upheld in many parts of Scotland.

Hogshead, a cask of varying capacity, also a specific measure. In the old English measure a hogshead was 63 old gallons of wine (= 52½ imperial gallons). Of beer 54 old gallons make a hogshead.

Hollands, Schiedam, or **Schnapps,** a kind of gin made mostly in Holland from rye and malt, with a flavouring of juniper berries.

Holly, a hardy evergreen shrub, largely grown in England. Its bright dark green prickly curved leaves and clusters of red berries are familiar in all parts of the country, and used as house decoration between Christmas Eve and Twelfth Night, probably a relic from Roman and Teutonic customs. Its wood is white and hard, valued for carved work, while its bark yields a gummy substance which is coverted into bird-lime.

Hologram, a photographic record, taken under special optical conditions, of light reflected from a scene or object. The hologram is typically a piece of film. However it is nothing like a photographic negative of the ordinary kind; for one thing it will show an unintelligible pattern of light and dark patches. Nevertheless if it is illuminated (again under special optical conditions) the light coming through it will form a *three dimensional* image of the original object. Another radical difference between a hologram and an ordinary film is that if the hologram is cut up, each fragment can be used to construct the entire image. Holography, as a method of recording and reproducing photographic information, was conceived by Gabor in 1947 but was only fully realised in practice after the invention of the laser (*q.v.*). The use of laser light is one of the "special conditions" referred to above. Technical applications are being explored in many laboratories.

Holy Alliance, an alliance ostensibly for conserving religion, justice and peace in Europe, but used for repressing popular tendencies towards constitutional government. Formed by Alexander I. of Russia, Francis I. of Austria and Frederick William III. of Prussia, at Paris on Sept. 26, 1815. Subsequently joined by all the sovereigns of Europe, except the Pope and the King of England. It ended after the 1830 revolution in France.

Holy Coat of Treves, a garment preserved in the Cathedral of Trèves and said to have been worn by Christ. It was brought from Jerusalem by the Empress Helena in the fourth century.

Holy Rood, an annual Roman Catholic festival held on Sept. 14 to celebrate the Elevation of the Cross in commemoration of its re-erection in Jerusalem by the Emperor Heraclius in 628 after retaking it from the Persians. Also included in the Church of England calendar.

Holyrood, the ancient royal palace at Edinburgh, dating from the 15th cent., and inhabited by many Scottish sovereigns, notably Mary Stuart, the rooms occupied by her (including the one in which Rizzio was murdered) being still shown. It is now known as Holyrood House and is still used as a royal residence.

Holy Roman Empire, the title which the German Empire received in 962 when Pope John XII. crowned Otto I. at Rome. It endured until 1806 when Francis II. became Emperor of Austria.

Holy Water, water blessed by a priest and kept in small fonts at the entrance to Roman Catholic churches, and used by worshippers going in, and out, or by priests in sprinkling.

Holy Week is the week preceding Easter Sunday, and includes the days of the Sufferings of Christ, ending on Good Friday.

Honey, the sweet syrup formed by bees from the nectar of flowers, the sucrose in the nectar being converted into a mixture of the simple sugars, glucose and fructose. Hybla, an ancient town of Sicily, on the southern slope of Mt. Etna, was famous for its honey.

> "For your words, they rob the Hybla bees
> And leave them honeyless." (*Julius Caesar*).

Honey-eater, an Australian bird (of which there are many species) provided with a long curved bill and tufted tongue. It lives by sucking the "nectar" from the flowers which abound in rural parts of Australia and New Zealand.

Hookah, an Oriental pipe for tobacco smoking, the smoke being drawn through the water of a goblet (commonly a coconut shell) by means of a long flexible tube.

Hoopoe, a remarkably handsome bird with vivid black and white-barred wings and tail and black-tipped crest which opens like a fan. Ranges over Europe, Asia, and Africa. It has bred in England and Wales and occurs in the British Isles in small numbers at all seasons. Other species are confined to Africa, Madagascar, and India.

Hops, the female "cones" of the hop plant used in brewing; their essential oils give beer an aromatic flavour, and their tannin and resin act as a preservative as well as accounting for the bitter taste desired. The hop is a perennial climber belonging to the mulberry family. The male and female organs are on separate plants;

as only the female flower-heads are commercially useful, female plants predominate in a hop garden, only a very few male plants being grown so that the female flowers can be fertilised.

Horizon, the limit of vision, the apparent line where sea and sky, or land and sky meet. This is termed the *sensible* or visible horizon. An ordinary person at the height of 5 feet can see for 3 miles, at 20 feet 6 miles, at 50 feet 9½ miles, and at 1,000 feet 42 miles. The figures are approximate.

Horn or **French Horn**, a brass instrument of the trumpet family (*i.e.*, played by three valves) whose tube is very thin and long (Horn in F = 12 ft.). In consequence the tube is curled in a complicated manner. Owing to the sweet tone it is capable of producing, the Horn sometimes plays as part of the wood-wind.

Hornbill, large bird found in Africa and oriental regions, remarkable for its having an immense horned upward-curved helmet, growing over its downward curved beak. It inhabits tropical regions, and feeds on fruits. When the female has laid her eggs in the hollow of a tree, the male bird stops up the entrance, and keeps her imprisoned until the hatching is completed and the young ones are able to fly. There are about 45 species.

Horneblende, the commonest member of the amphibole group of minerals, a silicate of calcium, magnesium, iron and aluminium, of a dark green colour. It is a constituent of numerous rocks, including diorite, syenite, and hornblende schist.

Horned Viper, a curious African genus of *Viperidae*, with a small pointed bone over each eyebrow; a venomous species, found in Egypt, is thought by some to be identical with the "adder" mentioned in Genesis xlix. 17.

Hornet, a general name for many of the bigger wasps. It usually nests in hollow trees, and despite its rather fiercesome appearance does not sting unless unduly provoked.

Horology, the science of time-measurement, including the construction and management of clocks, watches, etc. Instruments of this kind are not known to have existed before the 12th cent. and until the introduction of the pendulum in the 17th cent., clocks were ill-regulated and inaccurate. The time-recording mechanisms of the present day include (*a*) the *clock*, which shows the hours and minutes by hands, and strikes the hours, and sometimes quarters; (*b*) the *timepiece*, which is not generally a fixture and shows the time, but does not strike; (*c*) the *watch*, which is a pocket time-keeper; (*d*) the *chronometer*, which indicates the minutest portions of time; (*e*) electric timepieces, mains electric clocks; (*f*) the highly accurate quartz-crystal and atomic clocks used for astronomical purposes. *See* Clocks.

Horse Chestnut, one of the large forest trees, with ample branches, and full foliage, and much esteemed for parks and ornamental grounds. The bark and fruit seeds yield substances of commercial value, but the timber is not worth much. The tree came originally from Asia about the 16th cent.

Horse Guards, the building in Whitehall which until 1872 was the headquarters of the Commander-in-Chief of the British Army. The archway is still sentinelled by mounted guards.

Horse Latitudes, the latitudes of the sub-tropical high pressure systems, between the trade winds and the prevailing westerlies, characterised by light variable winds and low humidity.

Hospitallers, Knights, were of the order of St. John of Jerusalem, at first devoted to the aid of the sick, but afterwards military monks, who became prominent figures in the Crusades of the 12th cent. They adopted the Benedictine black habit with the eight-pointed cross worn by the modern St. John's Ambulance Brigade. In 1309 they took Rhodes, but were expelled by the Ottomans in 1522. In 1530 the emperor Charles V gave them the island of Malta, which, as Knights of Malta, they held until 1798, when they were dislodged by Napoleon. The Knights still survive as a sovereign order, with headquarters in Rome. *See* Templars and Teutonic Order.

Hottentots, name given to certain African natives by Dutch settlers in the 17th cent. They used

to occupy the greater part of Cape Colony, and though driven out a number still survive in S.W. Africa. Appear to be related to the Bushmen, though their culture is more advanced. In addition to herding, they practise some farming and know how to smelt iron.

Hounds are dogs that were originally bred and trained for hunting, such as the greyhound, fox-hound, bloodhound, wolfhound, deerhound, beagle, harrier, etc., but now often kept also as domestic dogs. The greyhound, deerhound, and wolfhound hunt by sight, the others, with the bloodhound first in order, track by scent.

Hour-glass, a glass instrument tapering to the middle to a narrow orifice, through which a sufficient quantity of fine sand gravitates to mark an hour of time. When the sand has run through from one end, it can be reversed and made to count the hour in the opposite direction. The same kind of glass with smaller supplies of sand will indicate shorter periods, as an egg-glass, which runs its course in three minutes—time to boil an egg by, or to gauge the length of a telephone trunk call.

House Flies are world-wide and prolific. Their eggs are hatched within 24 hours of being laid, and full maturity is attained in a month. They feed mainly on decayed animal and vegetable matter.

Hovercraft, or air cushion vehicle, is a craft which is lifted on a pad of air underneath it. This pad or cushion must be at a pressure higher than that of the atmosphere and it is made by sucking in air above the craft and ejecting it in a downward stream all round the lower edge. The stream is guided by a flexible skirt and the high pressure air pad is contained partly by the skirt and partly by the air stream itself which forms a continuous air curtain all round the vehicle. Hovercraft are being intensively developed and there are variations in the basic scheme just described and also in the means of propulsion which can be by air or water jets or propellers. Hovercraft were devised by Cockerell in the 1950s and a full-scale example appeared before the British public in June 1959. Craft of over 100 tons are made commercially and much bigger ones conceived. The air pad support means that hovercraft can move over land, water, or marsh. Cross-Channel hovercraft were introduced in 1966.

Howler Monkey, a genus of South American monkey noted for a laryngeal conformation which enables it to emit a loud reverberant noise something between a yell and a howl, as the name suggests.

Huanuco-bark, a medicinal bark, brought from the Peruvian town of that name, and derived from the *Cinchona micrantha* tree. *See* Cinchona.

Huguenots, a name applied to the French Protestant communities of the 16th and 17th cent. Henry of Navarre, by the Edict of Nantes in 1598, granted them religious freedom, but more than a quarter of a century before—Aug. 24, 1572—thousands had been put to death in the massacre of St. Bartholomew. The revocation of the Edict of Nantes by Louis XIV. in 1685 drove thousands into exile in England, Holland, Germany, and America.

Humanism. *See* J25.

Humble-bee or **Bumble-bee**, the common name of the insects of the genus *Bombus*, of the Hymenoptera order. They live in small communities comprising males, females, and drones, their habitations being underground. They do not have one queen bee only like the hive bee, but several females occupy the same nest, and these alone live through the winter, breeding and forming new colonies in the spring. Although this large bee buzzes loudly, it does not sting.

Humidity, the state of the atmosphere with respect to the water-vapour it contains. "Absolute humidity" is defined as the density of the vapour present, while "relative humidity," more frequently employed indicates the degree of saturation, *i.e.*, the ratio of the actual vapour pressure to the saturation vapour pressure at the particular temperature, expressed as a percentage.

Humming Birds are so called because of the humming noise made by the vibration of their wings in flying. They are of radiant plumage, and are among the smallest birds. The smallest bird in the world is the Fairy or Princess Helen's

humming bird of Cuba. The body is 2 in. long and the eggs are $\frac{1}{10}$ in. long. There are from four to five hundred species, and they are confined wholly to North and South America, being most numerous in the tropical latitudes. They have long, slender bills and tubular tongues which reach down into flowers to suck up the nectar on which they feed.

Hummum, the original name for what is now called the Turkish Bath in this country. One of the first of these baths to be established in London was the Hummums in Covent Garden.

Hundred, the ancient divisional name given to a portion of a county for administration or military purposes. It is supposed to imply the territory occupied by a hundred families; or the space of a hundred hides of land, or the capacity of providing 100 soldiers. Each hundred had its hundred court, with powers similar to those of a manor court, but this was abolished in 1867 by County Court Act.

Hundred Days, the interval of time between Napoleon Bonaparte's entry into Paris after his escape from Elba and his departure after his abdication, extending from March 20, 1815 to June 28. During this period occurred the battle of Waterloo, June 18.

Hundred Years' War, a term applied to the almost incessant contest between England and France, lasting from 1338 to 1453, including such famous battles as Crécy, Poitiers, and Agincourt, and engaging successively Edward III., Henry V., and Henry VI., among English kings.

Huns, a fierce Asiatic race which swept over eastern Europe in the 4th cent. Under Attila about the middle of the 5th cent. they obtained control of a large portion of central and eastern Europe, forcing even Rome to pay tribute. Their defeat at Châlons-sur-Marne in 451 by a mixed army of Romans, Goths, and Teutonic tribes, and the death of Attila in 453, terminated their empire.

Hurdy-Gurdy, an Italian rustic so-called musical stringed instrument of the lute order, the sounds of which are produced by the action of a rosined wheel turned by the left hand, the notes being made by the fingering of the right hand.

Hurricane. *See Cyclone and Wind.*

Hydra, an aquatic animal of simple structure, whose body is in the form of a cylindrical tube, with a disc-shaped base by which it attaches itself to any shifting substance. Its mouth is surrounded by tentacles by which it catches its food. The Hydra has the power of reproducing lost parts.

Hydrates are compounds containing water of crystallisation.

Hydraulic Ram, a form of automatic pump, used to raise water to a height by the action of its own falling velocity.

Hydraulics, the science of applied hydrodynamics, or water-machine engineering, ranging from pumps to marine engines.

Hydrocarbons are compounds of carbon and hydrogen. They include the *paraffins,* which are saturated compounds (*e.g.,* methane); the ethylene, acetylene and other series which are unsaturated; compounds with ring structures, *e.g.,* benzene, naphthalene, and anthracene. Petroleum is composed almost entirely of hydrocarbons. *See F23.*

Hydrochloric Acid, a solution of hydrogen chloride gas in water, and resulting in considerable quantities as a by-product of the soda-ash or salt-cake manufacture. Its solution forms the common hydrochloric or muriatic acid of commerce. It is present to the extent of nearly half a per cent. in the digestive juice secreted by the stomach.

Hydrocyanic Acid, cyanide of hydrogen or prussic acid; very poisonous, and of the odour of bitter almonds. It is formed by the action of acids on sodium or potassium cyanide. Used to kill wasps (and in the gas chamber in the U.S.A.). It is a very important chemical on account of the reactions of its derivatives in many synthetic fields. Discovered by Scheele in 1782.

Hydroelectric Schemes.—The sun's energy has been indirectly exploited in the past by harnessing the energy of the winds and rain. The climate is due, essentially, to differential heating of the earth. The resulting convection currents in the air (the motion of which is complicated by the rotation of the earth) give rise to winds.

Moisture is collected from the sea and deposited high up on mountains as rain. Some of the gravitational energy may be collected as hydropower. Simple windmills or waterwheels are so undependable that they have not been used to any extent since the beginning of the Industrial Revolution. However, the modern form of the waterwheel—the hydroelectric generation plant —is extensively used in mountainous countries and about a third of the world's electricity is produced by this means. The essential requirements for a modern hydroelectric scheme are a river with a sufficient flow of water to provide the required power, a large " head " of water so that a cheap, compact turbine can be used and a dam so that water can be stored until it is required. In some cases a hydroelectric scheme is made economic by being associated with an irrigation or drainage scheme. Such multipurpose schemes are especially important in certain Commonwealth countries, notably India and Pakistan, where most hydro projects are of this type. Other well-known examples include the Snowy Mountains Scheme in Australia and the Aswan High Dam in Egypt. Although over 90 per cent of the electricity in certain individual countries, notably Norway, Sweden, Portugal, Switzerland, and Uganda is produced from hydroelectric schemes, only a relatively small fraction of the total potential has been exploited. This fraction varies from about a third in Western Europe to a quarter in the United States to a very small fraction in Alaska, Canada, Africa, and the hinterland of Asia.

Hydrofluoric Acid is obtained by distillation of fluorspar with sulphuric acid, and is a compound of fluorine and hydrogen. Its action is highly corrosive; a valuable agent in etching on glass, and a rapid decomposer of animal matter.

Hydrogen, Symbol H, the simplest element, atomic number (*q.v.*) of 1, colourless, and the lightest of all substances. Cavendish in 1766 was the first to recognise that it was an element. It is 14·4 times as light as air, and is found in a free state in volcanic regions. It can be obtained by the action of metals on acids, and forms an explosive mixture with air, burning with oxygen to form water. Commercially it is used to produce the very hot flame of the oxyhydrogen blowpipe for cutting metals; to fill balloons and airships; to harden certain oils and render them suitable for margarine- and soap-production. The gas can be liquefied, and the presence of the isotope deuterium was detected by Urey in 1931 in the residue of the evaporated liquid. The third isotope, tritium, is very rare. *See also* Deuterium, Tritium, *and* F22, F23.

Hydrography, the science of water measurement, as applied to seas, rivers, lakes, currents, rocks, reefs, etc., and embracing the whole art of navigation.

Hydrometer, an instrument for measuring the specific gravity of liquids, especially for ascertaining the strength of spiritous liquors and solutions. It is usually in the form of a glass bulb, to the lower end of which a smaller bulb, containing mercury, is attached, which forces the instrument to sink into the liquid which it is to test. The larger bulb has a scale fixed to it, and the indication on this scale of the sinking point shows the specific gravity. There are many varieties: Twaddell's—a pear-shaped bulb containing mercury: Beaumé's, of similar construction, but applicable to liquids both heavier and lighter than water: Sykes's, largely employed for determining the strength of alcohol: and Nicholson's, used for taking the specific gravities of solids.

Hydropathy, the method of treating disease with water, either by bathing or drinking. Natural springs of special chemical and therapeutic properties, such as sulphur springs, and other mineral sources, have been used since prehistoric times for this purpose. It is probably one of the most ancient methods of cure. Recently the beneficial effects of pure water treatment have been advocated. Hydropathic establishments have been set up in many health resorts.

Hydroponics, the culture of plants without soil. The plants are grown with their roots dipping into a solution of nutritive mineral salts; or they may be rooted in sand which is watered with such a solution.

Hydrostatics, the science of the pressure and equilibrium of liquids that are non-elastic.

Hydrozoa are a class of water animals of the *Coelenterata* *phylum* to which Hydra (*q.v.*) belongs. In one order of the Hydrozoa, free-swimming colonies showing marked division of labour between the individual units occur; this order includes the Portuguese man-of-war.

Hyena, a nocturnal carnivore with powerful jaws. The striped hyenas inhabit N. Africa, India, and S.W. India. The brown hyenas with long shaggy hair are natives of S. Africa. The spotted, or laughing hyena, noted for the peculiar cry from which its name is derived, is also confined to Africa.

Hygrometer, an instrument for measuring the amount of water vapour in the atmosphere. A simple form of hygrometer, known as the wet-and-dry bulb, consists of two vertical thermometers affixed to a frame. One bulb is exposed to the air, and the other is covered with muslin which dips into a water-bath to keep it moist. If the air is saturated, it takes up no moisture from the wet bulb and the two thermometers read the same. If the air is not saturated, evaporation takes place from the wet bulb, latent heat is absorbed from the air, and the temperature of the wet bulb is lower than that of the dry bulb. Relative humidity and dew-point of the air can then be derived from suitable tables. Hygrometers depending upon the expansion of human hair and gold-beater's skin and the deposition of dew on a polished surface, when cooled sufficiently, are also in general use. *See* Humidity.

Hymenoptera, the order of insects to which bees, wasps, hornets, ants and sawflies belong. They have a well-defined waist, two pairs of membranous wings coupled together, mouth parts modified for biting or sucking; the females possess an ovipositor used for depositing eggs and is sometimes modified for stinging. There are about 70,000 species in this order and many live in highly organised communities. *See also* Ichneumon Fly.

Hyperbola. A curve described by certain comets that go round the sun and never return.

Hypsometer, an instrument formerly used by mountaineers to find the height above sea-level by indirectly measuring the atmospheric pressure by determining the boiling point of water at the particular height. Based on the fact that as pressure decreases with height so the boiling point is lowered. Superseded by the aneroid barometer.

I

Ibex, wild goats of several species found in the mountain regions of Europe, Asia, and Africa. The male has exceedingly large curved ridged horns. The species that lives in the Alps is called the Steinbock or bouquetin.

Ibis, belongs to a family of birds related to the stork. The sacred ibis of ancient Egypt is now extinct in Egypt but is found in the lakes and swamps of the Sudan near the Upper Nile. It has white and black plumage and a long curved beak. Other species are found elsewhere, the Glossy Ibis (black plumage glossed with purple and green) occasionally visiting England.

Ibo, a large tribe of S.E. Nigeria, numbering between 5 and 6 million. Since the end of British rule they have been active in their struggle for national independence and under their leader, Ojukwu, embarked upon the secessionist state of Biafra and the unsuccessful civil war against Federal forces. The Hausa and the Yoruba are the other main Nigerian groups.

Ice is frozen water. It is a colourless, crystalline and brittle solid. Being only 92% as dense as water, it floats on the latter; the expansion which occurs as water changes into ice causes the fracture of water-pipes, though the fracture only becomes obvious when the ice melts and leaks out through the crack. The temperature at which ice forms is 0° C., 32° F. Ice can be melted by pressure, and the ease and smoothness with which one is able to skate on ice depend on this phenomenon.

Ice Ages. Periods during which the continents were partly or largely covered by ice-sheets and glaciers. The present-day ice-sheets of Green-land and Antarctica are relics of the most recent Ice Age, which began in the Pleistocene and ended about 10,000 years ago. Much of the southern hemisphere experienced an ice age at the end of the Carboniferous Period; ice ages are recorded from isolated localities during the Pre-Cambrian, but there is no evidence that these were simultaneous. *See* F9(1), 48(2), A2.

Icebergs are detached masses of glacier which subside into the sea and float as wind or current may take them. About one-ninth of an iceberg is above sea-level. The North Atlantic is the chief home of icebergs, which reach the ocean from the ice-clad plateaux of Greenland. Some of these floating masses of ice are of enormous proportions, and constitute in the spring and early summer seasons a great menace to the safety of ships, as was disastrously shown in the *Titanic* catastrophe of 1912. For some years past these menaces to N. Atlantic shipping have been kept under close observation by vessels specially detailed for this work.

Ice-breaker, a special heavy bow-plated ship for forcing a way through ice and used especially at ports of the Baltic Sea and the Great Lakes region of Canada which freeze during the winter months. The Soviet atomic ice-breaker *Lenin,* the first of its kind in the world, launched in Dec. 1957, is designed to cut a channel through ice of any thickness. Her icebreaking performance will allow the sea-route to the north of Siberia to be kept open throughout the year.

Icelandic Literature, the Old Norse literature, centred about Iceland, which includes numerous works of poetry, mythology, and history of interest and importance. Much of this literature is in the saga form. *See also* Edda.

Iceland Moss, a kind of lichen (*Cetraria islandica*) which grows in great quantities in the mountain regions of Iceland and other Northern countries. It possesses certain nutritive qualities and is of some value in medicine.

Iceland Spar, a colourless form of calcite (calcium carbonate), frequently found in association with metallic ores; it has the power to produce strong double refraction of light so that two images are seen of an object viewed through a piece of Iceland spar. It was formerly used in optical apparatus for producing polarised light.

Iceni, an ancient British race who in early times lived in Norfolk and other parts of Eastern England. Their most famous ruler was Queen Boadicea, who led her people against the Romans in A.D. 61.

Ice Plant, also called "dew plant" and "diamond plant." A South African mesembryanthemum commonly grown in British gardens. Introduced in 1690.

Ice Saints, St. Mamertus, St. Pancras and St. Servatius, so called because of the legendary cold on these Saints' Days, namely, May 11–13.

Ichneumon, the Egyptian mongoose, popularly known as "Pharaoh's Rat." It is of great use in checking the multiplication of reptiles. It is frequently domesticated.

Ichneumon Fly, a numerous group of parasitic hymenopterous insects abounding in many lands, and all having the peculiarity of depositing their eggs in the bodies of other insects. It destroys swarms of caterpillars, which become the unwilling hosts of its progeny.

Ichthyology, the natural history of fishes.

Ichthyosaurus was a gigantic marine reptile of the Mesozoic age. The fossils are mostly found in the lias formation. Some were over 30 ft.

Icons. Icons are religious paintings designed for devotional use either by the individual or in church rituals. In size they range from the very small to large ones in two or three panels on church screens dividing the nave from the chancel (these are known as diptych and triptych respectively). The icon style of painting derives from the tomb paintings of Hellenistic and Roman Egypt, where it had become the custom to leave a portrait of the dead over the mummy's face. Icons of the earlier periods are rare, those of the 6th cent. probably having been destroyed and those of the 9th–12th cent. mostly removed to Russia. They were essentially simple with the Virgin and Child, or the Virgin, Christ, and John the Baptist as subject. From the 13th cent. icons were more complex, dealing with New Testament scenes or scenes from the lives of the saints, and by this time schools of painting, each with their own style, were arising in other countries, including Russia, which accepted the Eastern Church. The 16th-cent. icons begin to show Italian influence just as Italian painting was influenced by Byzantine. Most icons were painted on wood, but mosaic was sometimes used, and some icons were of metal.

Ides, in the ancient Roman Calendar, the 15th of March, May, July, October, and the 13th of all other months; always the eighth day after the Nones.

Idiom, an expression characteristic of a country, district, dialect or language, which usually gives strength and force to a phrase or sentence. The idioms of a language are its distinctive marks, and the best writers are the most idiomatic.

Idris, a famous giant belonging to the myths of Wales, commemorated by a chair of rock on the top of the Cader Idris mountain in Merioneth-shire.

Igneous Rocks are such as have been molten under conditions of great heat at some stage in their history: *e.g.,* granite, basalt. *See* F8(2).

Ignis Fatuus *or* " **Will-o'-the-wisp,**" a phosphorescent light which may often be seen on summer and autumn evenings hovering over marshy ground or graveyards. Its nature is hardly understood, though it is generally believed to be the result of the spontaneous combustion of the gases from decaying organic matter. In olden times when marshy grounds were more common than now, this " dancing light " was very frequently visible and was regarded with superstition.

Iguana, large South American lizards, with a long tail, a scaly back and head, a thick fleshy tongue and a prominent claw-lap in the throat. Specimens of the different species average 4–5 ft. in length, and they live mostly in trees, though they are equally at home on land or in the water. The flesh of some species is good eating, as are also the eggs.

Iguanodon, a genus of extinct dinosaurs, whose fossils are found in the Jurassic and Cretaceous rocks. Iguanodons were 15–25 ft. long, and walked on their hind legs, the front legs being small and adapted for grasping the branches of trees on the leaves of which they fed.

Ilex, mentioned by classical authors, the holm- or holly-oak, which flourishes round the Mediterranean. To botanists Ilex is the genus to which the holly and maté plant belong. *See* T9(2).

Iliad, the great epic poem of ancient Greece attributed to Homer (*c.* 700 B.C.). It consists of ancient folk tale and saga, welded into an artistic unity, having as plot the carrying off of Helen by Paris to Troy and the subsequent siege of Troy. *See* H19.

Illuminated MSS. of great value and beauty of decoration exist in most public museums and in many private collections, some of them being of great antiquity, especially those of ancient Egypt executed on papyri. Greek and Latin specimens are also numerous, and the British Museum contains fine examples of all these kinds and also an extensive collection of mediæval English MSS.

Ilmenite, a mineral widespread in igneous rocks: chemically it is an oxide of iron and titanium. Rich deposits have recently been found in the Allard Lake area of Quebec; the Travancore sands are also a source of ilmenite.

Immortality. *See* J25.

Immortelles are wreaths, crosses, or other designs made from what are called everlasting flowers, which are obtained from certain plants of the Composite order, and retain their colours and compactness for a long time. Immortelles are largely used as mementoes for decorating graves, especially in France.

Impeachment, a special arraignment, usually before Parliament or other high tribunal, of a person charged with some offence against the State. The custom in England was for the impeachment to be made in the House of Commons, and the trial to be before the House of Lords. The first instance occurred in 1376 when Lord Latimer was impeached. With present parliamentary procedure, impeachment is no longer necessary, since the Cabinet is responsible for the individual actions of its ministers, who,

acting as a team, must carry the Commons with them, or resign, when it falls to the Leader of the Opposition to form a new Cabinet. Other famous impeachments were those of the Lord High Chancellor Francis Bacon (1621), Earl of Strafford and Archbishop Laud (1640), Warren Hastings (1788), the last being that of Lord Melville (1805). Under the constitution of the United States public officials may be impeached by the House of Representatives and tried by the Senate. The most famous case was that of President Andrew Johnson.

Imperialism. *See* J26.

Impressionism, the name given contemptuously to the first modern movement in painting, being derived from the title of Claude Monet's picture *Impression: soleil levant,* which showed the play of light on water with the observer looking straight into the rising sun. Although intended to be the ultimate form of naturalism the inspiration of the school had been the scientific study of light with an attempt to render the play of light on the surface of objects. Feeling that putting a line around a form was bound to cause it to look unnatural, they used bright colours corresponding to the spectrum and unmixed on the palette, and noted that an object of any given colour casts a shadow tinged with the complementary one (*e.g.,* red-green, yellow-blue). Hence bright sunlight was represented in clear yellows and orange with violet shadows. The first Impressionist exhibition held in Paris in 1874 aroused derision with its paintings by Monet, Renoir, Sisley, Pissaro, Cézanne, and Degas among others. Impressionism subsequently led to the entirely artistic and anti-naturalist movement of Post-impressionism. Cézanne, who felt that he wanted to produce " something solid and durable, like the art of the museums," was only dubiously impressionist, as were also Degas and Renoir. Of course, in the wider sense of the word (*i.e.,* the recording of an ephemeral impression of a scene), Whistler, Turner, and even Rembrandt used the technique.

Impressment, the forced seizure of persons for military service resorted to by many countries before the establishment of conscription. Press gangs forcibly recruited men for British warships especially during the Napoleonic wars, but such measures were abandoned after about 1850.

Imprimatur, originally an official licence to print, and an important formula in the early days of printing. The term is now used in the wider significance of authority, or endorsement.

Incas, an Indian people who inhabited ancient Peru, founded a great empire, and reached a high level of civilisation: overthrown by the Spaniards in 1533.

Incense, an aromatic resinous substance which, under combustion, exhales a pungent odour, and is used, mixed with certain fragrant perfumes, in the celebration of Mass in Roman Catholic churches. Olibanum or frankincense is ordinarily the leading ingredient.

Incisors, the sharp-edged cutting teeth at the front of mammalian jaws. Rodents have long, sharp incisor teeth. Elephant tusks are modified incisors.

Income Tax, a tax on annual income charged under the following schedules:

Schedule A.—On the beneficial occupation of land (including buildings). Finally abolished as from 1964–65. Rents now assessed under Schedule D.

Schedule B.—Abolished as from 1963–64 on amenity lands (parks, gardens). Restricted to woodlands managed on a commercial basis.

Schedule C.—On dividends, interest, annuities from public revenue. Income Tax deducted at source.

Schedule D.—On profits from trade, profession, or vocation; remittances from abroad; interest on government stocks not taxed at source, Post Office Savings, etc.; sundry profits; short-term gains; rents.

Schedule E.—On salaries, wages, pensions, emoluments, directors' fees, etc. Taxed under P.A.Y.E.

The income-tax year is from April 6 to the following April 5. The standard rate on earnings for 1971–2 is 38·75 per cent (30·14 per cent with earned income relief). *Taxable* income is found by deducting from *Total* income certain allowances.

(1) *Earned Income* allowance of two-ninths to £4,005 and 15 per cent over £4,005.

(2) *Personal* allowance of £325 to single persons and earning wives; to married man living with his wife, or if wife though not living with, is wholly maintained by means of a voluntary allowance, £465. If the wife is maintained under a Court Order or under a binding legal agreement the allowance is reduced to £325. Personal allowances for a parent reduced by £42 for each child for whom family allowance is due. With effect from 1972–3 a married couple may elect to have their earned income charged to tax as if they were single. (Joint income needs to be over £100 a week to bring benefit).

(3) *Child* allowance of £155 for each child under 11; £180 over 11; and £205 over 16 if still being educated. Investment income of minor children (under 18) aggregated with that of their parents. (This provision of the 1968 Finance Act to be repealed with effect from 1972–3).

(4) *Dependent Relative* allowance, £75; for single woman, widow, divorced or separated woman solely supporting dependant relative, £110. (Dependant's income limit: £289 (£312 for 1972–3)).

(5) *Daughter's Services*, necessary owing to old age or infirmity, allowance of £40. .

(6) *Additional Personal* allowance of £100 to widows, widowers, and single women (divorced, unmarried, or separated from husband), who have single-handed responsibility for a young child resident with them.

(7) *Housekeeper* allowance of £75 (certain restrictions).

(8) *Age relief* of two-ninths of total income where taxpayer (or his wife) is over 65 and income does not exceed £1,200. Marinal allowances.

(9) *Life Insurance.* Subject to certain restrictions, relief is given for premiums paid for insurance on taxpayer's life or on his wife's life. Amount of premium must not exceed 7 per cent. of capital sum secured on death, nor one-sixth of net total income. Certain further restrictions on policies taken out after 19 March 1968.

(10) *Retirement Annuity Payments.* Subject to certain restrictions, a deduction is allowed for payments made for the provision of a life annuity in old age. Deduction may not exceed 15 per cent. of non-pensionable earnings, or £1,500, whichever is the less.

Age Exemption: no tax payable by single persons aged 65 or over if income does not exceed £504 (£530 for 1972–3); £786 (£825 for 1972–3) for married couples where either is 65 or over. Appropriate marginal allowances.

Pensions qualify for the earned income relief of two-ninths.

Small Income Relief. All incomes up to £450 are treated as Earned Income.

Surtax is charged only if the surtaxable income exceeds £2,500. On earned incomes surtax begins at about £5,500. *See also* Surtax.

Note: In April 1973 the present income tax and surtax system will be replaced by a single graduated personal tax. This will have a basic rate covering a broad band of income and corresponding to the standard rate less earned income relief (approx. 30 per cent), with a supplementary rate for higher incomes.

Independence Day, commemorates the adoption of the Declaration of Independence on July 4, 1776. July 4 is celebrated as a holiday in the U.S.

Index. The name given to a list of books, prepared by papal authority, which are declared to be dangerous to faith and morals, and therefore forbidden to Roman Catholics, called the *Index librorum prohibitorum.* One of the reforms of the Vatican Council was the closing in 1966 of the Curia office which judged writings for the Church's Index of forbidden books, though the Index itself still remains. The Pope ordered that nothing should be placed on the Index until the author had been given a chance of explaining his views. The first Index was issued by Pope Pius IV, in 1559.

India Office Library (since 1947 called the Library of the Commonwealth Relations Office (Division B)). This is an orientalist library, which specialises in Indian studies. It was founded in 1801 by the East India Company, and contains 20,000 manuscripts in European languages and in Sanskrit, Persian, modern Indian, and other oriental languages, and a quarter-of-a-million printed books, of which three-quarters are in oriental languages. There are also collections of drawings, photographs, and other objects of oriental interest. It was announced in 1965 that a judicial tribunal was to decide on legal ownership of the library.

Indian Mutiny. This turning-point in the history of modern India occurred in 1857–58. The ostensible cause was the serving out to the native troops of cartridges greased with animal fat, for contact with this was forbidden both by the Hindu and Mohammedan faiths. A rebellious feeling, however, had long been developing, and when the Sepoys at Meerut in May 1857 refused to obey the English officers, overpowered and put them to death, the mutiny spread like wildfire. The rebels took Delhi and Lucknow, and for many months terrible massacres and atrocities were committed; men, women and children were slain in thousands. Order was re-established in the autumn of 1858 when the governing power was transferred from the East India Company to the Crown.

Indian Summer is applied to a warm spell of weather occurring in the late autumn.

Indicators, substances which by a marked change in colour are used to indicate the course of a chemical reaction. Litmus paper, for instance, is red with acids and blue with alkalis. In biological work some radioactive substances are used as tracer elements.

Indigo, the substance obtained from the plant *Indigofera tinctoria*, a native of S. Asia, India being the chief producing country. The colouring matter is the result of the decomposition and fermentation of a glucoside contained in the plant. This is afterwards dried and becomes the caked indigo of commerce. Natural indigo has been eclipsed by artificial indigo, a coal-tar dye which came into commercial production at the end of the last century, which is cheaper and more uniform in quality.

Indium, a scarce lead-coloured metal, symbol In, found in zinc blende in Saxony and certain other ores. This element was discovered in 1863 by Reich and Richter. It is an important material in the manufacture of transistors.

Indo-European Languages. *See* M45.

Indulgence. In the Roman Catholic Church the remission granted by ecclesiastical authority to a repentant sinner of the temporal punishment still due after the guilt of sin has been forgiven by God. The indiscriminate sale of Indulgences by Tetzel and other Papal agents in the 16th cent. was one of the grievances which led to the Reformation (*see* J44).

Indulgence, Declaration of, was the proclamation by which James II. suspended the penal laws against Roman Catholics and Dissenters. It was issued in 1688, but the clergy as a body refused to obey, and the trial of the Seven Bishops and their acquittal by a jury followed. An invitation was thereupon sent to William of Orange to become King.

Industrialisation is simply a name for industrial development. It is customarily used in particular to designate the course of events in a hitherto underdeveloped country which is seeking to increase its wealth and productivity by the introduction of more advanced techniques and by the establishment of industries previously not carried on within it. The word usually covers not only the development of modern industrial production but also the provision of electric power-stations, irrigation works, and transport and other developments designed to improve production in any field by methods involving large capital investments. The outstanding example in our time of rapid industrialisation has been the Soviet Union, which, unable to get the capital from abroad, has had to carry it through by ruthless restriction of the people's consuming power so as to achieve an unprecedentedly high ratio of investment to total production. Industrialisation has in practice meant a high concentration on the expansion of the basic heavy industries and of power supply, coupled with much slower development of the industries supplying consumers' goods and of agricultural production; but there is no reason why this should always be the case. It may well be that in most under-developed countries development can but be devoted largely to the industries making consumers' goods and to measures designed to increase agricultural production and productivity.

Industrial Revolution. The name, first given by Engels in 1844, to describe the radical changes that took place in Britain during 1760–1840 to transform a mainly agricultural country into one predominantly industrial. It began with the mechanisation of the textile industry (Hargreave's spinning jenny, 1764, Arkwright's water-frame, 1769, Crompton's mule, 1770, and Watt's steam-engine, 1785), with subsequent major developments in mining, transport, and industrial organisation. It was based on Britain's rich mineral resources, particularly coal and iron ore. With the use of the steam-engine as power, industry became concentrated round the coalfields and the great new industrial towns developed—Birmingham, Manchester, Newcastle and Glasgow. Britain became supreme in constructional ironwork (Telford, George and Robert Stephenson). Canals, bridges, railways, and ships were built, and great advances were made in the practical application of scientific principles. Aided by colonial exploitation Britain became the most prosperous country in the world. The new industrial capitalists began to replace the country squires as ruling class. But the great accumulation of wealth at one pole of society was matched at the other by poverty and misery, for child labour, long working hours, low wages, and slums were features of the industrial revolution in its infancy. As with all great technological developments, the industrial revolution produced related changes in all fields of social life—in politics, art, religion, literature, and morals, and with the rise of democracy, social reforms.

Inertia, a term used in mechanics for the property of matter by which it offers resistance to a change in its state of rest or in its state or direction of motion.

Inertial Navigation, an automatic method of dead-reckoning which at present finds its chief application in guided missiles, submarines, and aircraft. Navigation by this means is carried out with reference to inertial space (*i.e.*, space which is stationary with respect to the fixed stars) and not to the surface of the earth as in normal navigation (latitude and longitude). This is done by means of high-accuracy gyroscopes combined with highly sensitive accelerometers in an apparatus known as the Ship's Inertial Navigation System. The American nuclear-powered submarine *Nautilus* pioneered the new north-west passage under the polar ice pack by this method of dead-reckoning in Aug. 1958.

Inflorescence, a flowering shoot. Many arrangements of the flowers are possible and there are many kinds of inflorescence; *e.g.*, the spike, catkin, umbel, capitulum (in composites).

Inflation. *See* G4(2), 37, 38.

Infra-red Rays *or* **Radiation.** This is the range of rays which come between the visible red rays and the ultra-short Hertzian radiation. The wave-lengths involved range from about 0·00076 millimetre (7,600 Angstrom units) to 0·4 millimetre. Infra-red rays penetrate haze; hence landscapes obscured by haze or cloud can be photographed using plates sensitive to infra-red. Many substances strongly absorb these rays and thereby become hot; this happens in toasting bread. Many industries use infra-red lamps for drying paints and lacquers. Very important to chemists, as a tool in the investigation of the structure of compounds, since various groups of elements absorb infra-red radiation at a characteristic frequency.

Infula, a sacred fillet, of woollen material, worn on the forehead by priests, magistrates and rulers in Roman times, also by persons fleeing for protection to sanctuary. Later, each of the two lappets of a bishop's mitre.

Ingoldsby Legends, a series of whimsical metrical tales full of droll humour written by the Rev. R. H. Barham, and first published in *Bentley's Miscellany* in 1837. The best known is the *Jackdaw of Rheims*.

Ink, a liquid pigment ordinarily made from an infusion of nut-galls, copperas, and gum arabic. Shumac is substituted for nut-galls for inferior inks. An acid is sometimes added to prevent oxidation, and for the blue-black inks a small quantity of solution of indigo serves for colouring. Copying ink contains glycerine or sugar, which keeps the ink moist. Lampblack used to be the leading ingredient in printer's ink but now new methods of manufacturing have been developed. Marking ink is composed of a solution of nitrate of silver, gum, ammonia, and carbonate of soda. For red, blue, and other coloured inks, colouring solutions are used, for example, Prussian blue. The earliest examples of ink writing (on wooden tablets) ever found in Britain were recovered from the well of a Roman villa (3rd cent A.D.) during excavations in 1954 at Chew Stoke, Somerset.

Ink Sac, a glandular organ found in squids and other cephalopods which contains an inky solution. When roused the animal discharges the contents of the ink sac into the water, to make a cloud through which its enemies cannot see. The pigment, sepia, comes from the ink sac of the cuttlefish.

Inlaying is the introduction of one class of substance into another in some artistic or other design, such as silver let into zinc, copper, or lead, and called *bidri*; the insertion of gold and silver into iron or steel, which is *damascening*; the mingling of brass with tortoiseshell, *buhl work*; the inlaying of woods, *marquetry*; of stone, *pietra dura*; and of the arrangement of small pieces of stone, for floors, walls, etc., *mosaic*.

Innocents' Day, a festival day in Roman, Greek, and Anglican Churches in commemoration of the killing of the children of Bethlehem by Herod, Dec. 28.

Inns of Court, the four bodies in London which enjoy the privilege of calling candidates to the bar after they have studied for a certain number of terms and passed certain examinations. The Inns are: the Inner Temple, the Middle Temple, Lincoln's Inn, and Gray's Inn.

Inquisition, a Roman Catholic ecclesiastical court which became a formidable weapon of the Church in the 13th cent. under Pope Innocent III. in dealing with charges of heresy. It was effectively set up in the various Catholic countries of the Continent, obtaining its fullest and most sweeping organisation in Spain in the days of Ferdinand and Isabella, when Torquemada was made Grand Inquisitor, and used its powers with terrible severity. *See* Auto-da-fé. In the 18th cent. its influence began to wane, and the jurisdiction of the Congregation of the Holy Office at Rome was limited to the suppression of heretical literature (*see* Index).

Insectivorous Plants, plants which trap insects with special mechanisms. Plant enzymes or bacteria digest the prey, providing the plants with nitrogen usually scarce in the soil in which they grow. The most common British species are the Sun-dew and the Bladderwort.

Insects. This huge class of invertebrate animals (*see* Arthropods, (F33)) includes about 100,000 species. Insects are ubiquitous except in the sea, only a very few species being adapted to marine existence. Characteristic features are: the body is divided into three parts, head, thorax, and abdomen: the head carries a pair of antennae, the thorax three pairs of legs, and usually two pairs of wings. The most primitive insects constituting the sub-class *Apterygota* are wingless. The other sub-class, *Pterygota*, is divided into the *Exopterygota* (*Hemimetabola*), which have a simple metamorphosis, *e.g.*, cockroach, and the *Endopterygota* (*Holometabola*), with a complex metamorphosis, *e.g.*, butterfly, bee. Although many are parasitic on man, animals and plants, innumerable animals and some plants use them as food, and many flowering plants are dependent on a variety of insects for pollination leading to the development of seeds and fruits. *See* F33(1), 38(2), T28(1).

Insignia, marks or badges of office or honour, such as stars, ribbons, crosses, medallions or other designating objects, worn by members of special Orders or holders of prominent offices.

Instinct.—*See* F38(1).

Institut de France was formed in 1795, and after various modifications was in 1832 organised on its present basis. Its five academies are—the Académie Française, Académie des Inscriptions et Belles-Lettres, Académie des Sciences, Académie des Beaux-Arts, Académie des Sciences morales et politiques. It is restricted to 40 members.

Instruments, Musical. Musical instruments may be classified in a number of ways, but in general they fall into one of the three main classes, String, Wind, and Percussion, according to how the sound is produced. Stringed Instruments are those which produce the sound by the vibration of a string: (*a*) by plucking, as in Harp, Lyre, Psaltery, Zither, Lute, Guitar, Balalaika, Ukelele, Harpsichord; (*b*) by friction (bowed), as in Crwth, Rebec, Viol, Violin, Marine Trumpet, Hurdy-Gurdy; (*c*) by striking (hammered), as in Dulcimer, Pianoforte, Clavichord; (*d*) by wind (blown), as in the Aeolian Harp. Wind Instruments are those in which the air in the instruments is set in vibration: (*a*) by blowing into a tube (flue-voiced), as in Recorder, Pandean Pipe, Flute, Organ; (*b*) by means of reeds (reed-voiced), as in Oboe, Clarinet, Saxophone, Bagpipe, Cor Anglais, Bassoon, Organ reed-stops; (*c*) those in which the sound is produced by the vibration of the player's lips against the mouthpiece (lip-voiced), as in Bugle, Horn, Trumpet, Tuba, Trombone, Saxhorn, Flügelhorn, Cornet. In a modern orchestra these are known as the *Brass*: instruments of the flute, oboe, and clarinet families as the *Woodwinds*. Then there are the Percussion Instruments, which include the Drums, Cymbals, Tambourines, Castenets.

Insulator, a substance that will not conduct electric current. Many solids, liquids, and gases are important insulators—rubber, cotton, silk, plastics, porcelain, glass, air, oil. If the applied voltage is too high, all insulators will "break down", *i.e.*, conduct electricity perhaps with resulting breakage, puncture, or charring. Thermal insulators will not conduct heat; they are usually the same kinds of substance as electrical insulators.

Insulin is a hormone which controls the supply of sugar from the blood to muscles. The breakdown of sugar provides energy. In diabetes there is a lack of insulin, causing a build-up of blood sugar which can be released by the injection of insulin. It is secreted by the islet tissue of the pancreas, from which it was isolated in 1922 by Banting and Best. Dr. F. Sanger of Cambridge won the 1958 Nobel Prize in Chemistry for isolating and identifying its amino acid components. Prof. Dorothy Hodgkin and her team at the Dept. of Molecular Biophysics at Oxford have recently succeeded in determining the structure of insulin, a task which would not have been possible without the electronic computer. The discovery may lead to a better use of insulin.

Intaglio, engraving or carving on a sunken ground, a method frequently adopted in the ornamentation of stones and rings.

Intelligence. Intelligence has been variously defined as the innate potential of a person to learn and understand; to make appropriate judgments; to see the relationships between things; to profit from experience; or to meet adequately new problems and conditions in life. There are many lines of evidence to show that intellectual capacity is closely related to heredity and influenced by environmental factors. The idea of intelligence testing was first devised by the French psychologist Binet at the beginning of this century. He was asked by the French government to invent a test which would weed out backward children in state schools, and thus save public money and avoid holding back the work of the class by teaching children who were incapable of learning at a given standard. Briefly, a series of problems are given to a large number of children and it is thus found out which series can be solved by the average child of a given age-group; if a child of 7 can only pass the tests suitable to the average child of 6, then his mental age is 6. The intelligence quotient

or I.Q. is discovered by dividing his mental age by his chronological age and multiplying by 100. A gifted child can usually be spotted at an early age. Although I.Q. tests are the standard method of estimating intelligence, they are not universally accepted as a criterion; a teacher's general judgment may be the best assessment. High intelligence may be inherited, but fail to develop to the full because facilities for education are not available. Recent research suggests that the growth of the brain may be permanently affected by undernutrition at the time of its fastest growth (the last weeks before birth, and, to a lesser extent, the first weeks after birth). At this vulnerable period even quite minor deprivation can effect the rate and ultimate extent of growth of the brain. This has significance not only for the severely undernourished babies in the poor parts of the world, but for babies of low birth weight in our own communities. *See also* Q28.

Interest is the payment made for the use of borrowed money over time. The rate of interest is the rate per cent per annum charged for such loans. There are many such rates, varying with the plenty or scarcity on borrowable money, with the length of time for which the loans are made, and with the degree of risk, if any, that the loans will not be duly repaid. Short-term loans are usually cheaper than long-term: the lowest rates are usually for " call money " repayable immediately on demand. These are used principally in short-term financial transactions, such as bill discounting. Bank loans, though usually made for fairly short terms, command higher rates. Long-term loans are made chiefly to public authorities, or as bonds or debentures to business concerns. The rates obtained vary with the demand and the supply of such accommodation.

Interferon, the name given to a substance discovered in 1957 by Drs. Isaacs and Lindenmann at the National Institute for Medical Research. It is produced by the interaction of viruses with living cells and has the important property of inhibiting virus reproduction. Its development may lead to a new approach to the therapy of viral diseases.

International Date Line, a line along the 180° meridian marking the difference in time between E. and W. For the westward-bound traveller crossing the line the date would be put forward one day, for the eastward-bound, back one day. To avoid difference of date in adjacent land areas, the line deviates from the 180° meridian where this crosses land.

Introit, the psalm sung by the choir as the priest approaches the alter to celebrate the Eucharist.

Invention of the Cross, a Roman Catholic festival held on May 3, to celebrate the finding of the alleged True Cross at Calvary by the Empress St. Helena in 326. Also included in the Church of England calendar. *See* Holy Rood.

Iodine, a non-metal element, symbol I, member of the halogen family (*q.v.*), a substance formerly exclusively obtained from the ribbon-wrack seaweeds. These were burnt and the ashes (kelp) extracted with water. After concentrating the iodides, these were distilled with manganese dioxide and sulphuric acid to yield iodine vapour which was condensed in stoneware bottles. Nearly all iodine now in use is derived from the iodine salt present in Chili saltpetre (sodium nitrate). Iodine is used in photography, as an antiseptic solution in alcohol or potassium iodide (tincture of iodine), and in medicine. Discovered by Courtois in 1812

Ionic Order of architecture is one of the five classic orders, its leading characteristics being the volute of its capital, which has on each side distinctive curved or scrolled ends.

Ionosphere, a succession of ionised layers of the earth's atmosphere lying above the stratosphere. In this region free electrically charged particles —electrons and positive ions—occur in sufficient concentration to affect substantially the propagation of radio waves through the region. It extends upwards from a height of 60 miles to several hundred miles, being most concentrated at an altitude of 200 miles. The behaviour of the upper atmosphere is strongly influenced by the sun. A great deal of new information about the ionosphere above an altitude of 150 miles (the topside ionosphere) has been obtained by the use of instruments carried in satellites. *See also* **Atmosphere.**

Ions, electrically charged atoms, or groups of atoms. Atoms of the metals lose electrons to become positively charged ions, *e.g.*, the sodium ion (Na$^+$) has one electron less than the atom. The non-metal ions are negatively charged, *e.g.*, the chloride ion (Cl$^-$) has one electron more than the atom. Similarly, a group like the sulphate ion (SO$_4$$^{2-}$) has more electrons than the constituent atoms. Thus, the hydrogen atom without its electron is a hydrogen ion or *proton* and the helium atom without its two electrons is a helium ion or *alpha-particle*. When an electric force is applied to certain solutions, the ions into which molecules of the dissolved substance are broken up are attracted to the oppositely charged electrodes, their movements constituting an electric current through the solution. In the same way gases, including air, conduct electricity by virtue of free ions (*see* **F12(2)**). Combustion, radio-activity, and ultra-violet and cosmic radiations produce ionisation. *See* **F20(2).**

Ipecacuanha, a flowering plant of the Brazilian forests. Various alkaloids are isolated from ipecacuanha, one is emetine, which is used in medicine to cause vomiting and so remove poisons from the stomach. Another is used as an expectorant in cough mixtures.

Iridium, a white and very hard metal, symbol Ir, discovered by Tennant in 1804. It occurs naturally as an alloy with platinum or osmium; tips for fountain-pen nibs have been made from the former native alloy. The former standard metre was composed of platinum–iridium alloy (*see* **Metre**) as are parts of scientific apparatus and surgical tools that must be non-corrodible.

Iris, the typical genus of the botanical order *Iridacae*, with tuberous rhizomes and sword-shaped leaves, many of the family having beautiful flowers. About 100 species of Iris are recorded from the northern temperate zone, the most common species wild in Britain being the yellow flag. Orris root, used in perfumery, comes from another iris species.

Iron is a metallic element, symbol Fe (Latin *ferrum*), occurring widely in nature in such ores as haematite, loadstone (magnetic iron oxide), spathic ore, and iron pyrites. It is extracted by a process known as smelting, with coke and limestone in a furnace. Its many uses are familiar, the most important being in the manufacture of cast- and wrought-iron products and of steels, which are alloys mainly of iron with added carbon and various metals. Iron rust is formed by the action of oxygen and water, and is a coating of iron oxide. *See* **Smelting.**

Ironclads, ships of war cased in iron or steel plates of sufficient thickness to resist projectiles. They were first introduced (1858) in the French Navy, and in 1860 the first British ironclad, the *Warrior*, was launched.

Iron Curtain. In a speech at Fulton, U.S.A., on March 5, 1946, Sir Winston Churchill used this phrase to describe the dividing line behind which, he said, lie all the capitals of the ancient States of Central and Eastern Europe—Warsaw, Berlin, Prague, Vienna, Budapest, Belgrade, Bucarest, and Sofia. These famous cities and the populations around them, said Sir Winston, lie in the Soviet sphere and are subject " to a very high and increasing measure of control from Moscow."

Ironsides were Cromwell's special troopers, so called because of their solidity and firmness in battle.

Irredentists, a political party organised in Italy about 1878 with the object of incorporating within Italy neighbouring regions. Also a person, group, or party advocating policies for the restoration to their country of territory formerly belonging to it but later lost.

Irrigation, an artificial method of providing water for the growth of plants on lands where the natural supply of water is deficient. The science has made immense progress during the last fifty years, and has been the means of bringing into profitable cultivation vast tracts of territory in India and Western America which

had previously been arid wastes. The systems are various and are utilised according to the special conditions of the land to be irrigated, but the success which has attended these experiments has been very gratifying. In fact, irrigated lands are often more productive than lands which receive a fair amount of moisture from the elements; the irrigation supply can be distributed and regulated exactly according to requirements. Irrigation also serves the purpose of supplying *warmth* in winter; *e.g.*, in the English water-meadows, and in the more highly developed Italian *marcite* and winter-meadows, where the water is mostly applied in winter when there is plenty of rain. There are several other functions of irrigation; *e.g.*, washing out of excess salts.

Isinglass, a gelatinous substance manufactured from the swim bladders of certain fish; used to preserve eggs, to keep beer free from sediment, and to make a glue.

Islam. *See* **J26.**

Isobars are the lines drawn on charts linking together points of equal barometric pressure.

Isochasms, lines connecting places at which there is an equal probability of seeing an aurora, taking the average over a number of years, based on the auroral catalogue of Fritz.

Isomers are chemical compounds having the same composition but different structural arrangements, and consequently different physical and chemical properties. For example, ethyl alcohol and methyl ether are isomers, since the molecules of both are built up of two atoms of carbon, six of hydrogen, and one of oxygen, *viz.*, C$_2$H$_6$O; ethyl alcohol, C$_2$H$_5$OH; and methyl ether, CH$_3$OCH$_3$.

Isotherms are lines drawn on charts through points of equal temperature.

Isotopes. When one talks of an element, say, uranium or lead, the name of the element is a generic name for a collection of uranium species and lead species. The different species are called isotopes. For any particular element, the number and arrangement of electrons around the nucleus are the same in all the isotopes, so all the isotopes have the same chemical properties. Soddy has described isotopes as " elements, the atoms of which have similar outsides but different insides." For example, in the nucleus of the uranium isotopes, U 235, U 238, and U 239, there are respectively 143, 146, and 147 neutrons, but all have 92 protons. The isotopes have different atomic weights, in this instance respectively 235, 238, and 239. But all have the same chemical properties. *See* **F10(2)**

Ivory, the dentine substance of which the tusks of the elephant, hippopotamus, walrus, etc., are composed. The tusks of the African elephant sometimes weigh as much as 100 lb., and reach a length of 8 or 9 ft.

Ivory Gull, a small, beautifully shaped sea-bird with striking all-white plumage and black legs which breeds on the rocky shores of the Arctic, being found farther north than any other bird; it occasionally wanders south in the winter.

Ivy, the well-known climbing shrub, chiefly evergreen; furnishing a sudorific, the berries having also emetic properties.

J

Jabiru, the Brazilian name for the giant stork of South America.

Jacamar, from *Jacameri*, the Brazilian name for a smallish bird with long, sharply pointed bill and brilliant plumage which inhabits the tropical regions of South America east of the Andes. These birds are seen sitting motionless on trees, darting off at intervals, like flycatchers, to catch insects on the wing.

Jacana, a tropical bird (the water-hen of Brazil and the warmer parts of America) of wide range, beautiful of plumage, with slim body and narrow wings, and long, pointed beak. It feeds on seeds and insects, inhabits marshy lands, and is related to the plovers.

Jack, a small schooner-rigged vessel, used in the Newfoundland fisheries; a pike; an oscillating lever; a device used in roasting meat.

Jackal, *Canis aureus*, a small wild dog related to the wolf and resembling a fox. The Common

Jackal is found in S.E. Europe, India, and Ceylon; other species inhabit Africa and Egypt. The jackal is a well-known scavenger. It hunts singly or in pairs, unlike the wolf, which usually hunts in packs.

Jackdaw, one of the smaller members of the Crow family. This European bird is typically black with grey collar. It is easily tamed, makes an amusing pet, and delights in making off with and taking to its nest bright objects, such as silverware.

Jacobins, a French revolutionary club or party, formed in 1789, and accustomed to meet at a Jacobin convent, hence the name. It became a controlling force in the Revolution, especially in the movement which led to the Terror. Robespierre was its chief spokesman.

Jacobites, adherents of the Stuart cause after the abdication of James II. First James himself, then his son (the Old Pretender), and later his grandson (the Young Pretender) tried to fan the flame of rebellion in Scotland and Ireland, but after the defeat at Culloden in 1746 the cause was lost. Also the name of the monophysite heretics of Syria (*see* **Section J**), so named after their leader Jacobus Baradaeus in the 6th cent. A.D.

Jade, a green mineral found in China, America, and New Zealand, and used for making vases, bracelets, and other ornamental articles. There are many varieties, and there is evidence that the stone was in common use in prehistoric times for weapons and utensils.

Jaguar, a South American carnivorous animal resembling the leopard, but much larger and more powerful, the largest of the Felidae.

Janeite, a devotee of Jane Austen and her writings.

Janissaries, an élite band of Ottoman foot soldiers who acted as the Sultan's bodyguard. They were conscripts, raised by the " tribute of children " from conquered Christian countries mainly Serbia and Albania. First recruited under Murad I (14th cent.). They were not allowed to marry. They gained great power under the Ottoman Empire. In 1826 the Sultan Mahmud II had them massacred.

January, the first month of the year, named after Janus, the two-faced god of the Romans. It was the *Wolf monath* and *Aefter Yule* of the Saxons.

Jasmine, a graceful climber belonging to the olive family with odoriferous blossom, originally a Persian plant, but now acclimatised in many varieties in almost all parts of the world. Two species of jasmine (the common jasmine and the Spanish jasmine) yield oils used in perfumery.

Jasper, a precious stone of the chalcedony variety, opaque, and coloured red, brown, yellow and sometimes green. It was greatly esteemed by the ancients, the Bible having numerous allusions to it.

Jay, a gaily-coloured bird of the Crow family, of many species—the Blue jay of N. America, the Canada jay, sometimes called " whisky jack," the Siberian jay, and the British jay, fawn-coloured with black and whitish crest and bright blue feathers in the wings. It lives in woods and like the magpie, takes the eggs and young of small nesting birds.

Jazz, a rhythmical syncopated music characterised by a strong element of improvisation in the performance, probably originating among the Negro population of the Southern States of the U.S.A. It became popular during the first world war and, in a commercialised form, has held the popular field ever since. Modern dance music and popular songs are based on the jazz idiom, which has also had a profound effect upon contemporary music of a more serious kind.

Jean, a stout kind of twilled cotton cloth much worn in olden times, and resembling fustian. Blue *jeans*, adopted by American city youngsters from farmworkers, are now the fashion elsewhere and worn not only as overalls by workmen but by both sexes in leisure time.

Jelly-fish. The jelly-fishes, which have gelatinous, translucent bodies fringed at the margin with delicate tentacles, constitute the coelenterate order *Scyphozoa.* The mouth, with a squarish opening, is seen on the underside, and there are four horseshoe-shaped sex organs.

Jerboa, small jumping mammals of the Rodent order. These mice-like animals have long tufted tails and very long hind legs, the front legs not being used for locomotion.

Jeremiad, any utterance or writing in which sorrow or complaint is the chief characteristic, so named as recalling the style of the " Lamentations of Jeremiah," in the Old Testament.

Jerusalem Chamber, a room in Westminster Abbey, deriving its name from the circumstance of its having originally been decorated with a view of Jerusalem. Henry IV. died in this chamber, and the Committee for the Revision of the Bible met there in 1870 and later.

Jesuits, members of the Roman Catholic teaching order founded by Ignatius Loyola in 1534. A long and vigorous course of study is prescribed before they are admitted into the privileges of full membership. They are required to take the vows of voluntary poverty, perfect chastity, perfect obedience, and complete submission to the Pope. The Society played an important part in politics.

Jet, a deep black fossil substance admitting of a high polish and much used for jewellery, ornaments, and trimming. It is a form of lignite, the most important British deposit being found near Whitby, where jet manufacture has been an established industry for a long period.

Jet Engine, an aeroplane engine which derives its thrust from the high velocity of the gases it ejects. The essential units in a jet engine are a rotary compressor and a gas turbine, the latter driving the compressor. The first reliable, high-performance jet propulsion engine for aircraft was invented by Air Commodore Sir Frank Whittle.

Jet Stream, a meteorological term coined in 1946 to describe the relatively narrow belt of strong winds (100–200 m.p.h.) at levels in the atmosphere from 3 to 7 miles. These winds are important in forecasting weather, and can be a valuable aid to aircraft. From the ground, where there may be little wind, the jet stream can sometimes be seen as high cirrus cloud moving across the sky at high speed.

Jew's Harp. The name is believed to be a corruption of " jaws harp." This instrument consists of a metal frame with a central tongue of spring steel. The frame is pressed against the teeth, and the tongue of the harp is twanged with the finger, the mouth acting as a resonating chamber. By altering the shape of the mouth the resonant frequency and therefore the note can be varied.

Jockey Club, the governing body that, although possessing no legal status, frames rules and laws by which horse-racing and turf matters generally are regulated. The club-house is at Newmarket.

John Bull, the typical figure of an Englishman, bluff, big, and burly. Arbuthnot's *History of John Bull* is supposed to have originated the character.

John Dory, a fish found in most temperate seas and common in British waters. It is of a golden-yellow colour (*jaune doré*), has a high dorsal fin with long protractile jaws, and is much valued as a table fish. According to legend the dark spot on each side of its body is the thumbprint of St. Peter who took a coin from the fish's mouth (Matt. XVII. 24–7).

John o' Groat's House, W. of Duncansby Head, Caithness, popularly named as the northern-most point of Scotland. According to legend the house, which has now disappeared, was built in octagonal form by a Dutchman Jan de Groot who came to live there in the 16th cent. The site is marked and an inn was erected near it in 1876.

Jongleurs were minstrels and jesters who wandered from town to town singing songs, playing musical instruments, dancing, and giving entertainments in mediæval France and Norman England. Jongleurs were low-born in contrast to the Troubadours, who were often of the nobility.

Joule, a unit of energy in the SI system of units, defined as the work done when the point of application of a force of one newton is displaced through a distance of one metre in the direction of the force. Named after J. P. Joule (1818–89). The relationship between mechanical energy and heat energy is called the mechanical equivalent of heat and was found by Joule to be 778 ft lbf in lb °F units, or 4.18×10^7 ergs in gram °C units. *See* F17.

Jousts were military tiltings in the nature of tournaments, where the contestants strove against each other on horseback with blunted lances. It was the sport of nobles in feudal times.

Judaism. *See* J27.

Julian Calendar, named after Julius Cæsar, who in 46 B.C., finding the Roman year 90 days in advance of the real time, was the first to adopt the calculation of time by the solar year, the average length being fixed at 365¼ days. There was still an overplus of a few minutes every year, and this was rectified by the Gregorian Calendar, introduced in Italy in 1582 and adopted in England in 1752, from which date what is called the " New Style " begins.

July, the seventh month of the year, named after Julius Caesar. It was the *Maed monath* (Meadmonth) of the Saxons.

June, the sixth month of the year, containing 30 days and deriving its name from Juno. It was the *Sear* (Dry) *monath* of the Saxons.

Jungle-Fowl, birds related to the peacocks and peacock-pheasants. At least four species are known from the jungles of India, Ceylon, and Java. The domestic chicken has been derived from the Red Jungle-Fowl (*Gallus gallus*).

Junkers, name of the ruling class of Prussia, military in spirit, who were the party of reaction and defenders of the landed interests. Supported Bismarck prior to the Franco-Prussian war and helped bring Hitler to power.

Jupiter, the largest planet. It is believed to have a rocky core surrounded by ice layers thousands of miles thick. There is an outer atmosphere containing ammonia and methane, both presumably in the liquid or solid state owing to the very low temperatures of the outer layers (−120° C). In 1610 Galileo made history by discovering the four major satellites of Jupiter, which he named Medicean planets after his patron Cosimo Medici; these are visible with good field-glasses. There are eight others. For distance of Jupiter, etc., *see* F7. Also the supreme mythical deity of the Romans, identified with the Greek Zeus (H38).

Jurassic Formation, a series of rocks (the evidences of which are most marked in the Jura Mountains) coming between the Cretaceous and Triassic groups and including the Oolite and the Lias. It is a formation rich in fauna, abounding in echinoids, lamellibranchs, ammonites, and belemnites: large reptiles, marine and land, are common, as are the plants called cyads. In Britain the Jurassic outcrop extends from the Dorset coast to the Yorkshire moors. *See* F44.

Jury, a body of private citizens chosen and sworn to hear and pass verdict upon evidence brought forward at a trial, inquest, or inquiry. The origin of the English jury is obscure, but it is thought to have been introduced by the Normans. The jurors are the sole judges of the true facts upon the evidence laid before them. Under the Criminal Justice Act of 1967 their verdicts in criminal courts in England and Wales no longer have to be unanimous but by a majority of 10 to 2. In Scotland 45 jurors are summoned in criminal cases, of whom 15 are chosen by ballot, and majority verdicts are accepted: not guilty, not proven, and guilty.

Jute, the name given to the fibre of a plant grown largely in Pakistan in the Ganges delta and used for the manufacture of coarse cloths, cordage, and packs. Calcutta is the biggest jute-manufacturing centre of the world, as Dundee was in the 19th cent.

Jutes, a Low German race who in the 5th cent. invaded the south-eastern part of England, establishing themselves in Kent and making Canterbury their capital.

Juvenile Courts.—This is a special kind of Magistrates' Court to deal with accused persons under the age of seventeen. The Magistrates chosen are specially qualified for the work, and where possible a woman is appointed as one of the Magistrates who constitute the Court (*see* D6). The Court is held in private away from the ordinary court room. The object of the Juvenile Court is to introduce into the trial a plan to reform the offender by providing for the care

and protection which he may need, by removal from undesirable surroundings, and by subsequent education or training. In these objectives the Court has the co-operation of social workers, including Probation Officers (*q.v.*). Radical changes in methods of preventing and treating juvenile delinquency are contained in the Children and Young Persons Act, 1969, the result of the findings of two White Papers, 1965 and 1968. They emphasise the necessity of helping and supporting the child as far as possible in his own family and community, with resort to formal procedures only where he is exposed to moral danger, or control is necessary in the interest of society or of the child. The 1969 Act will be phased into operation and the Government have stated that initially children may continue to be prosecuted. The minimum age for prosecution will be raised to 12 when the Government is satisfied that " local authorities and other services have the necessary capacity to cope with this change ". Children who are below prosecutable age will be dealt with by social casework or by care proceedings. Although the Act places restrictions on the prosecution of 14 to 17 year-olds, so that prosecution would be restricted to categories of offences to be prescribed and only if action by other means were inadequate, the Government have announced that they do not intend to bring these provisions into operation.

K

Kakapo, the Maori name for the New Zealand owl-parrot, a peculiar and interesting species, possessing wings but not able to use them for flight (though it can glide): of sap-green plumage, nocturnal in its habits, and nesting in burrows. Still to be found in the larger forest areas of the South I.

Kangaroo, pouched (marsupial) mammals of Australia and adjacent islands. There are over 20 species, the smaller ones being known as " wallabies." Kangaroos leap in a succession of springy bounds 10–20 ft. long, the forefeet not touching the ground. They can reach a height of over 6 ft. and a weight of 200 lb. First seen by white men when Capt. Cook's expedition visited Australia in 1770. Related genera include the tree kangaroos, rat kangaroos, and the Tasmanian Jerboa kangaroo.

Kaolin *or* **Kaolinite,** a fine clay much used in the manufacture of high-class pottery. It results from the decomposition of felspar, and is found in China, Japan, Devon, Cornwall, at Limoges in France, and in parts of the United States.

Karst, geological formations typical of limestone regions in which the drainage is by underground channels. Rain water carries part of the limestone away in solution, leaving the surface dry and barren and pitted with innumerable hollows. The name comes from the Karst (Slav *Kras*) region of N.W. Yugoslavia where the rocks are massive pure limestone: the barren plateau is characterised by fissures, caves and subterranean rivers.

Katydid, large long-horned insects of the grasshopper family, common throughout the United States east of the Rockies. Their name comes from the sound these insects make.

Kauri Pine, a large coniferous tree yielding a fine copal resin which ranges from Malay to New Zealand. The New Zealand Kauri. *Agathis australis,* is found only in the N. Island. Some of the best Kauri gum comes from fossilised pines and is dug out of the soil far from any living trees.

Keep, the central tower or chief stronghold of an ancient castle, sometimes called the donjon.

Kelvin. Lord Kelvin, an important 19th-cent. physicist, gave his name to the kelvin, symbol K, a measure of temperature on the absolute scale (*q.v.*). The Kelvin scale is a development of the scale invented by Celsius (*q.v.*) for everyday use, long known as the " centigrade " scale: the degree interval on both scales is the same.

Kentish Rag, a fossiliferous clayey limestone of Cretaceous age found in Kent. Used in building.

Keratin, a hard protein material of which horns, nails, claws, hoofs, and reptiles' scales are made.

Kestrel, the most common British falcon, well known for its habit of hovering for minutes at a time with vibrating wings and then swooping down to attack mice and insects. The male has spotted chestnut-brown back, greyish head and tail, which has a broad black band near tip.

Ketones. A class of organic compounds, related to aldehydes, of general formula R_2CO (where R is an organic radical). The simpler ketones, especially acetone, are widely used as solvents for lacquers, synthetic rubber, and polymers, such as cellulose acetate and perspex. More complex ketones occur in nature, and some are used in the perfumery industry, muscone (from the musk deer (q.v.)) is an example.

Kew Gardens, officially known as the Royal Botanic Gardens, are among the most celebrated gardens in the world. They were started in 1759 by Princess Augusta of Saxe-Gotha, widow of Frederick, Prince of Wales, and mother of George III. They remained private property until 1841, when control passed to the Commissioners of Woods and Forests. They now cover 300 acres and are administered by the Min. of Agriculture, Fisheries, and Food. Since 1841 the gardens have been open to the public, and form one of the most attractive resorts near London.

Keys, House of, is the Manx representative assembly. See **Tynwald.**

Keystone, the stone which occupies the centre and highest point of an arch and is usually the last to be inserted.

Khaki, a clay-coloured cloth adopted for uniforms in the British Army in the time of the war with the Boers, and used in the first and second world wars. First used by Indian regiments.

Kilderkin, once a common liquid measure in England, representing 18 gallons.

Kilogramme, unit of mass, defined as the mass of the international prototype kilogramme of platinum-iridium kept at the International Bureau of Weights and Measures at Sèvres. A new determination of the imperial standard pound in terms of the international kilogramme was made recently by the National Physical Laboratory (1 international pound = 0·45359237 kilogramme).

Kilowatt. Unit of power, equal to one thousand watts. See **Watt.**

Kinetic Energy, the energy (q.v.) possessed by a particle or body in virtue of its motion. If the motion is destroyed, e.g., by the impact of the body with an obstacle, the kinetic energy vanishes, being turned into some other form of energy such as heat and sound. If the body has mass m and speed v its kinetic energy (leaving out corrections due to relativity) is $\frac{1}{2}mv^2$.

Kinetic Sculpture, a development of equipoised sculpture (i.e., sculpture independent of gravity in the sense of resting on a base either horizontally, vertically, or obliquely) intended to appear as " a weightless poising of volumes, relationships, and interpenetrations." Since in the literal sense this is impossible, the Constructivists (Pevsner, Gabo, and Moholy-Nagy) used glass and invisible wire as supports, giving the impression that their creations were in fact independent of gravity. However, the American, Alexander Calder, has made constructions of balls and wire which he calls " mobiles," and in this form they are now known to everyone as they delicately dangle and rotate suspended from the ceiling.

King Crab, remarkable arthropods now classified separately from both Arachnids and Crustacea which they resemble, inhabiting the sea coasts of America, Japan, India, and Malay Peninsula, carrying a shield-shaped shell, and having a long pointed spine projecting from the posterior. The body comprises three separate sections articulated together. These crabs—in America known commonly as the horseshoe crab because of their shape—are from 18 in. to 2 ft. in length. Fossil king-crabs are found as far back as the Silurian. There are about six living species.

Kingfisher, a well-known family of brilliant-plumaged birds, found in all continents, comprising some 250 species and sub-species. The British kingfisher, *Aceldo atthis*, haunts the rivers and streams, and is one of the most beautiful of native birds, having iridescent blue-green, white, and rich chestnut in its plumage and bright-red feet. All kingfishers have long, dagger-shaped bills. In the Malayan region, New Guinea, the Moluccas, and Australia the varieties are very numerous. The quaint *Laughing Jackass* of Australia is among the largest of the kingfisher family. The European kingfisher is the bird of the Greek legend of the Halcyon.

King-of-Arms, the name of the chief officials of the Heralds' College. There are several in England —the principal being those of the Garter, Norroy and Ulster, Clarenceux. See Heralds' College.

Kiosk, a word of Russian or Turkish origin meaning a small open pavilion of light construction much used in Eastern countries as a place of shade and rest. Similar structures are common in the streets of Paris as news and advertisement stands, and in London as telephone offices.

Kirimon (*Kiri no go Mon*) and **Kikumon** (*Kiki no go Mon*), the two Japanese imperial crests, the first a design of leaves, stems, and flowers of the Paulownia plant, and the other representing the sixteen-petalled chrysanthemum.

Kite, name of several birds of prey, widely distributed, related to the hawks and eagles, graceful in flight, and distinguished by their long wings and deeply forked tails. The red kite, light chestnut brown, once the most familiar bird of prey in Britain, seen scavenging the streets of London, is now the rarest, and found only in Wales. The Egyptian kite and the pariah kite of India, notorious for their daring thefts, are closely related to the black kite, a smaller European species, with less forked tail and blackish-brown plumage.

Kittiwake, a beautiful white and pearl-grey gull with black legs, dark eyes, and greenish-yellow bill. Its range is wide, and includes the British Isles, where it is a local resident. The flight of this only truly oceanic gull, which excepting in the breeding-season, is generally found offshore is graceful, swift, and buoyant. A triangular black patch, noticeable on the ends of the wings when open, is characteristic of the species, as is the call kitti-wake, from which the bird derives its name. It nests in colonies on the ledges of caves and steep cliffs.

Kiwi, flightless, stoutly-built birds of New Zealand, now very rare and carefully protected by the Government. They are little larger than a domestic hen, and lay astonishingly large eggs for their size. Incubation and care of chicks fall to the male bird. They have rudimentary wings concealed by the plumage, and the feathers are hair-like. They are nocturnal in habit.

Knighthood is a degree of honour or title common in Europe since the Middle Ages, and was at first exclusively a military order. In Great Britain the four main orders of knighthood are those of the Garter, the Bath, the Thistle, and St. Patrick; in addition to which there are several other orders, such as the Order of St. Michael and St. George, the Star of India, etc. There are also Knights Bachelors such as are not associated with any special order. The title is not hereditary, and therefore ranks below that of a baronet, though both are entitled to the prefix " Sir."

Knot, a nautical measure of speed (1 sea mile per hour), and formerly measured by a log-line, divided by knots at equal distances $\frac{1}{120}$ of a geographical mile. The number of knots travelled by the ship in half a minute corresponded to the number of sea miles it travelled per hour. A sea mile is equal to about 1⅛ of a statute mile. Also, a grey and white wading bird, usually a winter visitor to Britain found in flocks on the coast.

Knout, a whip of many thongs, often fatal in its effects, formerly used in Russia for flogging criminals.

Koala, the Australian arboreal marsupial mammal that looks like a toy teddy-bear, with ashy-grey fur, bushy ears, and rudimentary tail. It feeds on the leaves and shoots of certain eucalyptus trees, and is not more than 2 ft. in length.

Kohl, a powder prepared from antimony or burnt almond shells, and in common use by the women of the East for darkening the eyelids.

Koto, a musical instrument in general use in Japan consisting of a series of 13 silken strings stretched across a curved wooden surface, and played with the fingers. Each string is 5 ft. long, and has a separate bridge so fixed as to give the vibration necessary for the note it has to produce. It is a sort of horizontal harp, and in the hands of an expert player is capable of giving forth excellent music.

Kremlin, the citadel or walled city within a Russian city which during the Middle Ages served as an administrative and religious centre and offered protection. That of Moscow, now the headquarters of the Russian government, contains the cathedral where the Tsars were crowned, an imperial palace, and the bell-tower of Ivan the Great. Its walls which are topped with towers were built in the 15th cent.

Krypton, one of the rare gases, symbol Kr, occurring in the air to the extent of 1 part in 20 million. It was discovered in 1898 by Ramsay and Travers. It is used in gas-filled electric lamps.

Kusti, the sacred cord or girdle of the Parsees, consisting of 72 threads—the number of the chapters of the Izashue—and two branches, each branch containing six knots, together standing for the 12 months of the year.

Kyrie Eleison (" Lord, have mercy "), the name of a common form of prayer in the Anglican, Roman Catholic, and Greek Churches; also applied to the English Church responses after the recital of the commandments.

Kyrle Society, named after Pope's " Man of Ross," John Kyrle, founded by Miss Miranda and Miss Octavia Hill in 1875, and having for its object, the decoration of workmen's clubs, hospitals, etc. and the promotion among the poor of a taste for literature, music, and outdoor recreation.

L

Labarum, the standard of Constantine the Great, adopted after his conversion to Christianity, marked with his seal, and represented upon the coinage.

Labourers, English Statute of, was passed 1350–51, with the object of compelling labourers to accept a certain rate of wages and not leave their employers' service, the Plague having rendered labourers so scarce that they were in great demand and had been insisting on higher pay. These enactments were bitterly opposed and led to the " Peasants' Revolt," headed by Wat Tyler.

Labradorite, a felspar rich in calcium and of a pearly lustre on cleavage, found in masses in igneous rocks, the best samples of which come from Labrador.

Labyrinth, or Maze, a combination of roads and passages so constructed as to render it difficult for anyone ignorant of the clue to trace the way to the central part. The Egyptian labyrinth near Lake Moeris had 3,000 rooms, half of them subterranean and the remainder above ground. The labyrinth in Crete, according to Greek myth, was built by Dædalus to house the Minotaur. There was one at Lemnos, renowned for its stalactite columns; and another at Clusium constructed by Porsenna, King of Etruria, about 520 B.C. The labyrinth in which Fair Rosamond was concealed was at Woodstock. Hampton Court maze dates from the 16th cent.

Labyrinthodonts, gigantic fossil amphibians which get their name from the curious labyrinthine structure of their teeth, probably an evolutionary link between fishes and reptiles. They occur in the Carboniferous, Permian, and Triassic formations, and remains have been found in Britain and other parts of Europe. Their heads were several feet long, and their footprints, by which they were discovered, closely resemble the prints of the human hand.

Lac, a resinous matter deposited on the branches of a number of tropical trees by the females of the lac insect, the exudation including eggs and a viscous covering. At the gathering time the twigs are broken off and dried in the sun, when the insects die, and the lac that remains is termed *stick-lac*. From this, by the removal of extraneous accretions and dissolving, *seed-lac* is produced. *Shell-lac* is seed-lac after it has been melted and otherwise prepared, and this is the best known of the lacs, being used in printing and the manufacture of varnishes

and sealing-wax, and for other commercial purposes.

Lace, a delicate fabric of linen, silk, or cotton threads, made by hand or machinery, and worked in various ornamental designs. The kinds of lace are many, deriving their distinctive names either from the method employed in production or from the place where any special variety was originally made. The best-known makes are pillow or bobbin-lace, woven and plaited by hand; needle-point lace, worked by the needle over a traced design; and machine lace, which practically dates from Heathcote's invention of the early part of the 19th cent. Some of the most famed laces are the following: *Alençon*, a needle-point lace; *Brussels*, a very fine kind, with needle-point sprigs and flowers; *Chantilly*, a silk variety with flowers and open-work; *Cluny*, a netlace with darned stitch; *Honiton*, a delicate kind with dainty sprigs and figures; *Mechlin*, generally made in one piece and very varied in design; and *Valenciennes*, or bobbin lace, of great durability, the pattern and ground of which are made at the same time, being one of the best and most costly of laces, now manufactured mainly in Belgium. Nottingham is famous for its lace.

Lace-Wings, insects with frail, transparent, and much-veined wings whose grubs eat large numbers of insect pests such as aphids. The eggs are borne at the ends of threads attached to plants.

Lachesis, a genus of venomous snakes of the rattle-snake family confined to tropical countries, and including the " deadly bushmaster," of Surinam, and several Crotalidae pit-vipers of Guiana and Brazil.

Lacquer, a varnish made from shellac and certain colouring matters, and utilised for imparting lustre to various surfaces of metal or wood. In China and Japan the production of lacquer ware of a decorative character has long been an important industry, bringing into use gold, coral, vermilion, sprinkled, and other lacquers, with pleasing effect.

Ladybird, the common name of a large family of beetles—the *Coccinellidae*. The insect is usually of a red or yellow colour with small black or coloured spots. Ladybirds are of good service to the gardener because their larvae feed on aphids. There are about 2,000 species.

Lady-Day, the day of the festival of the Annunciation of the Virgin Mary, Mar. 25. One of the four English quarter days.

Lagoon, a stretch of shallow water opening out upon the sea. Venice is built on lagoons.

Lake Dwelling, the name given to certain prehistoric habitations which were thought to have stood on platforms over lakes, like villages in certain Pacific islands. Recent excavations at the Lake of Burgäschi in Switzerland show that the prehistoric Swiss pile dwellings probably stood on the shores of lakes, not on platforms over the water.

Lakes are bodies of water collected in depressions of the earth's surface. The most notable lakes are the Great Lake series of North America, including Superior, Michigan, Huron, Erie, and Ontario, all discharging into the St. Lawrence River. Africa has an enormous area of lakes, including the Albert Nyanza and the Victoria Nyanza, forming the sources of the White Nile, Lakes Tanganyika, Nyassa, Tchad, etc. Smaller lakes are numerous in other countries—Switzerland, Germany, Italy, England, Ireland, and Scotland, all having their lake regions, where the scenery is invariably beautiful and romantic.

Lake School, the name given, at first in ridicule, to a distinguished trio of poets—Wordsworth, Coleridge, and Southey—who made their homes in the English Lake District.

Lamellibranchs (Pelecypods), the class of aquatic, bi-valve molluscs to which the oysters, cockles, mussels, clams, and scallops belong. In these animals the body, which is compressed laterally, is enclosed in two hinged shells held together by muscular action. The gills are thin plates hence the name " lamellibranch." *See* **F33(1)** **38(2)**.

Lamination, stratification on a very fine scale, as in shales.

Lammas Day is one of the oldest of the Church festivals, probably derived from the loaf-mass (hlafmæsse) of the Anglo-Saxons. It occurs on August 1. In the olden times it was the day when loaves were given in place of first-fruit offerings.

Lammergeyer, the bearded vulture of alpine regions, resembling an eagle in appearance. It has a white head with black tufts at base of the bill, and its general plumage is dark brown, nearly black. It is found in the remote mountain ranges from Southern Spain to China, and is becoming scarce.

Lampblack, a carboniferous pigment obtained from flame-smoke, and now produced in specially constructed furnaces in which bodies rich in carbon, such as tar, resin, petroleum, etc., are burned. The smoke or soot resulting is collected from the sides of the furnace, and forms lampblack. It finds use in making printer's ink, black paint, etc. Being a very pure form of carbon, it is also utilised in the manufacture of dynamo brushes and arc-lamp carbons.

Lamprey. Eel-like fish having no scales, bones, paired fins, or jaws. They attach themselves by their mouths to fish whose blood they suck. Together with the hagfishes, the lampreys are placed in a special class—the Cyclostomes. There are three British lampreys.

Lancelet. See **Amphioxus.**

"**Lancet**," the name of a noted English medical journal, established in 1823 by Dr. Wakley.

Land Crab, a family of crabs (*Gecarcinidae*) which live mainly on land, though migrating to the sea to deposit their eggs.

Land League, an association formed in 1879, with Parnell as president, for compelling a reduction in the rents of land, and a reconstruction of the land laws in Ireland, and in case of non-compliance refusing to pay rent. For a time this League exercised great political influence and was an important aid to the Home Rule agitation.

Landrail, popularly known as the Corncrake, was a regular summer visitor to Britain two generations ago, but no longer. Its harsh and piercing note was a familiar sound in English cornfields. Still found in Ireland.

Landslip, a sudden downward sliding under gravity of large masses of rock, soil, etc.; often set off by earthquake shock or saturation of a particular stratum with water. Many serious landslides have occurred from time to time. In 1618, an earthfall happened at Plurs, on Lake Como, involving the destruction of many buildings and the loss of numerous lives. In 1806 a portion of Rossberg mountain in Switzerland slipped from its position, and falling into the valley below buried many villages and hamlets and over 800 people. A chalk cliff from 100 to 150 ft. high and three-quarters of a mile long fell at Lyme Regis, in Dorsetshire, in 1839, doing great damage. Over 200 people were killed by a landslip in Naini Tal, in India, in 1880; and at Quebec, in 1889, a rocky eminence called Cape Diamond gave way, many buildings being destroyed and lives lost. Notable landslips in recent times have occurred at Amalfi (Italy) in 1924, at Murchiston (New Zealand) in 1929, and near St. Gervais (France) in 1970.

Langue d'oc and **Langue d'oïl,** the two principal mediæval French dialects, *oc* and *oïl* being their respective words for the affirmative particle (modern French *oui*). *Langue d'oc,* spoken south of the Loire, was the language of the troubadours. Provençal, one of its dialects had a literary revival in the 19th cent. under the influence of the poet Frédéric Mistral. *Langue d'oïl* was spoken in northern France, and it was the dialect of the Paris region which developed into modern French.

Lantern Fly, bugs belonging to the family *Fulgoridae* in which the head is drawn out to form a lantern-like structure. In no instance is the "lantern" luminous, though naturalists used to think it was.

"**Lantern of England.**" Bath Abbey possesses so many windows that it is called sometimes the "Lantern of England." Among numerous interesting monuments Bath Abbey contains that of Malthus, author of *Essay on Population.*

Lanthanum, a metal belonging to the rare earth group of metals, discovered by Mosander in 1839.

Lapis Lazuli, an azure-blue mineral, being a silicate of aluminium and sodium. The pig-

ment ultramarine is made by grinding it, though artificial ultramarine has largely superseded it. The mineral (also called *lazurite*) has been used as a gemstone since ancient times.

Lapwing *or* **Green Plover,** familiar British bird on moors and marshlands with iridescent greenish-black plumage, white underparts, and black crest. Often called "peewit" from its cry. Protected under Protection of Birds Act, 1967.

Larboard is the old nautical term indicating the left-hand side of a ship, and changed by Admiralty order to "port" in 1844. Starboard is the right-hand side.

Larch, a familiar coniferous tree in the mountain regions of northern Europe, and though not native to Britain, the Common Larch is successfully cultivated in various parts of the kingdom. It is one of the best of all turpentine-yielding trees, and the bark is valued for tanning. The larch is an unusual conifer in being deciduous.

Larid, a bird of the *Laridae* or gull family.

Lark, a family of song birds (*Alaudidae*) of many species, some of which—notably the skylark—are famed for their habit of soaring into the air, singing all the while. They build their nests on the ground in the open country and, except for the black lark of Russia, have streaked brown plumage. The skylark and woodlark are the best known British species, while the crested lark and shore lark are among the occasional visitors. Africa has the greatest number of larks; America has only one species, the horned lark.

Larkspur, the common name of the genus *Delphinium*, a favourite flower introduced into British gardens from Switzerland in 1573. The common larkspur is *D. consolida.*

Larva, the undeveloped form of any animal which, before maturity, undergoes metamorphosis, usually different from the adult in structure and habits.

Laser. A remarkable kind of light source that was discovered in 1960. With the laser it is possible to probe the behaviour of matter under the influence of enormous energy densities, range and survey vast distances to microscopic accuracy, and send millions of telephone and television messages between any two points that can see each other with telescopes. Laser light, in contrast to natural light, is coherent and can be expressed as a regular progression of waves carrying energy along a particular path. Thus the essential difference is that laser light is an orderly sort of wave motion in contrast to ordinary light which is inherently unsteady and therefore an inefficient carrier of information in time. The name *maser,* which is the microwave parent of the laser, derives from the expression "*microwave amplification by the stimulated emission of radiation.*" Upon application to light wavelengths the microwave part of the name lost its meaning and the term maser became generally descriptive of any device in which stimulated emission dominates.

Latent Heat is the quantity of heat required to convert 1 gram of a substance from one form into another. For example, when a solid changes into a liquid or a liquid into a gas, the addition of heat to bring about the change produces no rise in temperature, the energy being absorbed in the form of latent heat. An equal amount is released when the process is reversed. The latent heat of fusion of ice is about 79·6 calories per gram, that of the vaporisation of water about 539 calories per gram.

Lateran Councils were the religious conventions held in the Lateran basilica at Rome for deciding important questions of Church doctrine. The most brilliant was that of 1215, which pronounced in favour of a Crusade. *See* **Ecumenical Councils.**

Laterite, a residual deposit formed in the tropics by weathering and decomposition of igneous rocks. It consists mainly of hydrated ferric and aluminium oxides and is difficult to cultivate.

Latin America. The Spanish-speaking, Portuguese-speaking, and French-speaking countries of N. America, S. America, Central America, and the W. Indies. *See* **K93.**

Latitude of a point on the earth's surface is its angular distance from the equator, measured

L70

on the surface of the earth in degrees, minutes, and seconds. Thus the equator is 0° Lat. and the poles 90° Lat. (N. or S.). First determined by Hipparchus of Nicaea about 160 B.C.

Laughing Gas. *See* Nitrous oxide.

Launce *or* **Sand Eel**, a family of eel-like sea fishes found in large numbers on the coasts of North America and Europe. There are two species common to British waters. These fishes are of a bright silvery hue, and live much in the sand underneath the water. They are prized as human food and as bait.

Laurentian Shield refers to the Pre-Cambrian rocks in the region of the Upper Lakes of Canada, nearly 2 million sq. m. in extent. Of enormous importance to Canada on account of the mineral wealth, forests yielding valuable timber and wood-pulp, and water-power.

Lava, the molten rock which is erupted from a volcanic vent or fissure. Also the same material which has cooled and solidified.

Lawn, very fine sun-bleached linen, in olden time called " cloth of Rheims."

Lead, a soft malleable metal, symbol Pb (Latin *plumbum*), occurring in numerous ores, which are easily smelted. Its most important source is the mineral galena which consists chiefly of lead sulphide; rarely is it found free. Lead is largely used in plumbing on account of its pliability, and in nuclear reactors as a shield against radiation because of its very high density. As an alloy element it combines in the formation of type metal, stereo metal, shot metal, pewter, and many other compounds. Oxides of lead are used in some types of glass and in the manufacture of paints (red lead). All lead compounds are poisonous. Leading producers of lead are the United States (Missouri), Australia (Broken Hill) and the Soviet Union.

Leaf Insect, a group of insects related to the locusts, grasshoppers and stick insects which in colour and form closely resemble leaves.

Leaf Miners, insect larvae which tunnel between the upper and lower skins of leaves. Most leaf miners are caterpillars of tiny moths; some sawfly larvae have the same habit.

Leagues, or combinations of kings, countries, communities, have been frequent since the kings of Canaan united against the Israelites. Among the most famous leagues may be mentioned the Holy or Catholic League, which prevented the accession of Henry IV. of France until he became a Roman Catholic; and the League of Augsburg against Louis XIV. of France in 1686.

League of Nations, was founded on Jan. 10, 1920, with the object of promoting international peace and security. The original members were the signatories to the Peace Treaties at Versailles, and membership grew to fifty-three as new nations and ex-enemy States were admitted. Two notable absentees were the United States and Soviet Russia, the latter not being represented until 1934. Germany was a member from 1926 to 1933. The League had an Assembly which met at Geneva every year and a Council which met five or six times a year. The Permanent Court of International Justice sits at The Hague. The final Assembly of the League was held at Geneva between April 8 and 18, 1946. Its place has been taken by the United Nations. The International Labour Organisation, set up by the League of Nations met on April 20, 1944, at Philadelphia and resumed its old quarters at Geneva under the new organisation in 1946.

Leap Year *or* **Bissextile,** was fixed by Julius Cæsar, 45 B.C., the addition of one day in every four years bringing the measure of the calendar year even with the astronomical year, with three minutes per year over. The Gregorian Calendar corrected this by dropping leap year at the centuries not divisible by 400. For instance, 1700, 1800, and 1900 were not leap years.

Learning.—*See* F38(1) Q16–20.

Leather was made in ancient Egypt, Greece, and Rome, and has through succeeding centuries played an important part in the service of man. It consists of the dressed hides or skins of animals after the process of tanning has been gone through. Untanned skins are known as pelts. Leather is classed either according to the skins

from which it is made or the system of preparation employed. The best-known kinds are morocco, kin, Russian, chamois, Cordovan, grained, patent, russet, tan, calf, Hungarian.

Leech, an aquatic blood-sucking worm, mostly found in fresh-water ponds. Each end of the body is provided with a sucker, but that at the head end has jaws and teeth. The medicinal leech has three jaws. The leech attaches itself with avidity to animal bodies and sucks until glutted. Its saliva contains an anti-coagulant.

Leeward, a nautical term, meaning the sheltered side of a vessel—that is, the opposite side to that from which the wind is blowing.

Legion, a body of Roman troops, varying in numbers at different periods. A legion was divided into 10 cohorts, and every cohort into three maniples. Three legions composed the Roman army of occupation in Britain.

Legion of Honour, the French order for distinguished services, military or civil, was instituted by Napoleon I. in 1802, and confirmed and modified under later rules. There are five grades—Grands Croix, Grands Officiers, Commandeurs, Officiers, and Chevaliers.

Legume, the fruit typical of the pea, bean family, or *Leguminosae*.

Lemming, small light-brown rodents with dark spots, abounding in Scandinavian countries and in Siberia, about 5 in. long, with a short stump of a tail. The migrations of the lemming are famous, probably caused by overbreeding when food is plentiful. So insistent is the urge to keep moving that these animals will march on into the sea in their thousands and be drowned.

Lemur, the most primitive member of the Primate order of mammals (to which man, apes, and monkeys also belong). They are noted for having strong pliant toes enabling them to use their feet as hands, and also well-developed thumbs on the hands. They have long squirrel-like tails, fox-shaped heads, and large staring eyes, and are distributed over the tropical parts of the Old World, being most abundant in Madagascar.

Lend-Lease. During the earlier phases of the Second World War the bulk of British investments in the U.S.A. had to be either sold or pledged to Americans in payment for dollar supplies. After the United States entered the war this drain was stopped by the Lease-Lend arrangement, under which Great Britain met the costs of American consumption in Great Britain, while the United States paid for British supplies from America. This arrangement was abruptly terminated on the ending of hostilities; and Great Britain and other belligerent countries found themselves without means of paying in dollars for indispensable American supplies, including the foodstuffs, materials and capital goods needed for economic reconstruction. In these circumstances Great Britain negotiated with the United States and also with Canada a large loan, which was used for buying dollar supplies and played an important part in helping the West European economies to maintain themselves and feed their peoples while they were carrying through the earlier stages of postwar reconstruction. These loans involved large charges for interest and amortisation in future years, but proved far too small to meet the dollar deficit for more than a short period. In face of this situation the United States launched the Marshall Plan (*q.v.*).

Lenses, pieces of transparent material designed to focus an image of an illuminated object. Usually of glass, but plastic lenses are common, and quartz, etc. are used for special purposes. The surfaces of the simplest lenses are parts of spheres. Lenses which are thickest, or thinnest, at the centre are called convex and concave respectively. Lenses of complex shape are often used in microscopes, etc. Electron lenses are arrangements of electric or magnetic fields which focus beams of electrons, *e.g.*, on to television screens.

Lent, the forty days' period of fasting that precedes Easter.

Lepidoptera, the order of insects with scaly wings and bodies, to which the 90,000 butterflies and moths belong.

Leptons. A group of particles which include electrons, neutrinos and muons. All are much lighter than protons or any of the baryons. *See* F14.

Lepus, the constellation of the Hare, situated under the Orion group, and one of the constellations with which the ancients were familiar.

Lettres de Cachet, sealed letters which the kings of France issued to their agents to secure the imprisonment of distrusted or disliked persons without trial. Abolished in 1789.

Levée, a State reception held by the Sovereign or his representative and attended by men only.

Lewis, a contrivance for stone-lifting, the principle of which was known to the ancient Romans; it consists of two dovetail tenons of iron or other metal, expanded by an intervening key in a dovetail-shaped mortice in the stone, and shackled by a ringed bolt to the hoisting chain.

Leyden Jar, the earliest form of electrical condenser. Its invention is usually credited to Muschenbroeck of Leyden (1745). It consisted of a jar coated inside and out with tinfoil for about two-thirds of its height and having its inner coating connected with the top by a brass knob and chain. The jar was charged by connecting it to an electrostatic machine.

Lias, a geological term referring to the lower section of the Jurassic group, and mainly comprising shales and limestones.

Liberalism. *See* J28.

Libraries, before the invention of printing, were few, and collected together at enormous cost. At Nineveh remains of libraries, consisting of tablets of baked clay, have been discovered. There were two libraries at Alexandria containing a vast collection of rolls or volumes, founded by Ptolemy I Soter (367–283 B.C.) and established by Ptolemy II Philadelphus (309–246 B.C.). Among the great libraries of later times may be mentioned the Vatican Library at Rome, moved to its present premises in 1588; the Royal Library in Paris which later became the Bibliothèque Nationale; The Astor Library, New York; and in England, the Bodleian Library, Oxford, and the British Museum Library at Bloomsbury. Since 1850 public libraries have been established in all the chief cities and towns of the kingdom. The first lending library was opened in Edinburgh in 1726. In most villages there is a "county library centre" to which collections of books are sent by the County Library. In Great Britain there are 24,000 centres of this kind in village clubs, halls, shops, schools, and even homes. In some counties there is a library van or the bibliobus, as it has been called by a French writer. This travelling library tours on a pre-arranged time-table so that everyone knows exactly when it will arrive. The British Museum Library in London, the National Library of Scotland, in Edinburgh, that of Wales in Aberystwyth, the Bodleian Library of Oxford and the Cambridge University Library comprise the " copyright " libraries, entitled to receive a copy of each new book published in Britain. Other national libraries are the National Reference Library of Science and Invention (part of the Dept. of Printed Books of the British Museum), the National Lending Library for Science and Technology, under the Department of Education and Science, at Boston Spa, Yorkshire, and the National Central Library, which is responsible for interlending at national and international level. On the future organisation of the national libraries, the Dainton committee, reporting in 1969, foresaw that in two or three decades the larger libraries, laboratories, and industrial firms " will be directly linked through their individual computer terminals " to the computerised catalogue of the national libraries; for loans " direct dialogue between interrogator and computer information source may well have become commonplace "; and " computer storage capacity will begin to be able to cope with the retention of full texts of the world's literature, to process it in response to particular queries, and, if necessary, to display it remotely by facsimile transmission wherever it is needed." The Dainton committee's proposals were followed by a government White Paper, *The British Library*, which contained proposals for the creation of a single national libraries organisation, to be known as the British Library. It would consist of the British Museum Library and National Reference Library of Science and Invention (research and reference facilities to be accommodated in new buildings near the British Museum), the National Central Library and the National Lending Library for Science and Technology (lending facilities at Boston Spa).

Lichens. In every lichen, two plants are associated, one being an alga and the other a fungus. The fungus derives its food from the alga; probably the alga gains too from the association, being protected against desiccation by the fungus (an example of symbiosis). Lichens are the first plants to colonise bare rocks.

Life-Boat was invented by three men, Lionel Lukin who converted a coble into a boat for saving life in 1785; William Wouldhave, who discovered how to make a boat right herself if she capsized, and Henry Greathead, who built a life-boat, partly from Wouldhave's model, in 1789. This boat was stationed at South Shields, which was the first permanent life-boat station to be established. It was not until 1851 that the first life-boat able to self-right was built, and a motor was first installed in a life-boat in 1904. Modern motor life-boats have engines of from twin-18 h.p. to twin-80 h.p., with a speed of nearly 10 knots. All coastal life-boats in this country are maintained by the Royal National Lifeboat Institution founded by Sir William Hillary in 1824.

Light, a particular kind of electromagnetic disturbance capable of travelling through space, and some kinds of matter, and of affecting our eyes to cause vision. Its finite speed was first demonstrated by O. Römer, using observations of the eclipses of Jupiter's satellites in 1675. In 1860 Maxwell showed that light waves are electromagnetic. Since Einstein's theory of relativity (1905) it has been generally realised that the speed of light is a fundamental natural constant. Visible light with wavelengths between about 4 and 6×10^{-5} cm. is only a small part of the electromagnetic spectrum. Subtle modern methods give the speed as $2 \cdot 997930 \times 10^{10}$ cm. per sec. (about 186,000 miles per sec.).

Light Year. A measure of astronomical distance, equal to the distance light travels in the course of a year. A light year is thus 5·88 million million miles. *See also* F3(2).

Lighthouses, to warn ships of dangerous places and indicate coasts, points, harbours, etc., have existed since the building of the Pharos, a tower of white marble 600 ft. high, built by Ptolemy II Philadelphus at Alexandria about 280 B.C. In early lighthouses the lights were simple fires. The most famous and one of the earliest British lighthouses is the Eddystone (*q.v.*). Dungeness lighthouse, opened in 1960, is very modern in design, capable of automatic operation and the first of its kind to incorporate the xenon electric arc lamp as a source of illumination. The electric fog signal consists of sixty loud-speaker units built into the tower just below the lantern, giving a honeycomb effect. The lighthouses of England and Wales, the Channel Islands, and Gibraltar are under the control of Trinity House; Commissioners of Northern Lighthouses control those of Scotland; and the Commissioners of Irish Lights control the coasts of Ireland. Particulars of lights in all parts of the world are published for the guidance of navigation in the *Admiralty Lists of Lights*, compiled annually by the British Admiralty.

Lightning, the flash of a discharge of electricity between two clouds, or between a cloud and the earth, when the strength of the electric fields becomes so great as to break down the resistance of the intervening air. With " forked " lightning the actual path, often branched, is visible, while with " sheet " lightning the flash is hidden by the clouds which themselves are illuminated. " Ball " lightning or fireballs is the name given to the luminous balls which have been seen floating in the air during a thunderstorm. The Boys camera has provided much information regarding the sequence of events in a lightning discharge. It is found that a flash consists of a number of separate strokes, usually four or five, and that the discharge of electricity to earth begins with a faintly luminous "leader" moving downwards and branching at intervals. As the ground is approached a much brighter luminosity travels back along the conducting channels, lighting up the several branches. The multiple strokes which follow in fractions of a second have the same " return " nature and are rarely branched. Lightning flashes to earth damage structures, cause loss of life and endanger overhead power systems, often interrupting electricity supply. Such storms generally affect radio transmissions and present hazards to aircraft. Thunder-clouds may develop energy far exceeding the capacity of our largest power generating stations.

Lightning Conductor, a metal rod, the upper part of which is of copper with a conical point, the lower portion being iron, which extends into the earth. Its effect is to gather to itself the surrounding electricity and discharge it into the earth, thus preventing its falling upon the protected building. In ships, lightning conductors are fixed to the masts and carried down through the ship's keel-sheathing. Benjamin Franklin was the first to realise the possibilities of lightning protection and, in 1752, carried out his famous experiment of drawing electricity from thunder-clouds, with the aid of a sharp-pointed conductor fixed to a kite.

Lillibulero, an old marching song composed by Purcell. With words by Wharton, it is said to have " sung James II. out of three kingdoms." Used by the B.B.C. during the second world war as a station identification signal preceding news bulletins, and still in use to announce the Overseas Service programmes in English.

Lily Family (Liliaceae), one of the largest families of flowering plants, with 200 genera and 2,500 species. It includes the true lilies (*Lilium*), tulips and hyacinths. Vegetables belonging to the family are the onion and asparagus.

Limes, trees of the genus *Tilia*, including some 30 species spread over north temperate regions. The word is a corruption of " linden." Limes native to Britain are the small-leaved *T. cordata* and the broad-leaved *T. platyphyllos*. The hybrid *T. vulgaris* was introduced into Britain from the Continent during the 17th cent. and is frequently seen in streets and parks. Lime-wood was used by Grinling Gibbons for his fruit, flower, and bird decorations.

Limestone is carbonate of calcium. It is found in every geological formation, and is often highly fossiliferous. Marble is limestone that will polish after cutting.

Linen, a textile fabric manufactured from flax fibre, known to the ancient Egyptians, and first manufactured in England under Henry III. by Flemish weavers. The chief seat of the manufacture is Ulster, with Belfast as the centre. Dunfermline (famous for its damasks) and Manchester are also large linen-producing towns.

Ling, a sea-fish common on the coasts of Britain, and abounding in more northern waters. It averages from 3 to 4 ft. in length, and is a voracious feeder, living chiefly on small fish. Ling is also the name applied to *Calluna vulgaris*, the plant which most people called " heather."

Linguistics. *See* M43(1).

Linseed, the seed of the flax plant, containing, apart from its fibrous substance, certain oily and nitrogenous matter of considerable commercial value. This yields linseed oil, and some of the residue is used to make cattle food.

Lion, the most impressive of the Cat family (*Felis leo* or genus *Panthera*). It is chiefly found in open bush country in Africa, being comparatively rare in Asia. Its large square head, its flowing mane (in the males only), and its tufted tail distinguish it. From tip to tip it can reach a length of 10 ft.; a weight of 500 lb. Only weak, old lions are liable to attack man, usually they avoid him.

Lion and Unicorn, the supporting figures of the royal arms of Great Britain, date from the union of Scotland with England at the accession of James I. (James VI. of Scotland), the lion representing England and the unicorn Scotland.

Liqueurs are essences combined with alcoholic liquid, and are of many kinds, named according to their flavourings or place of production, and include Maraschino, Chartreuse, Curacoa, Benedictine, Noyau, Kümmel, etc.

Liquid, the name given to matter in such state that it takes its shape from the containing vessel. The volume it occupies is independent of the container, however. *See* F17, 18.

Litanies were first used in church processions in the 5th cent. The first English litany was commanded to be recited in the Reformed churches by Henry VIII, in 1544.

Lithium, a soft metallic element, symbol Li, similar to sodium. It is very reactive and is stored under paraffin oil. It is the lightest metal element.

Lithography, the art of drawing on stone and printing therefrom, was discovered by Alois Senefelder about 1796, and was introduced into England a few years later. Many improvements in the art have been made in recent years, especially in chromo-lithography and photolithography.

Litre, a metric measure, was abolished in 1964 as a scientific unit of volume, but remains as an everyday unit, *e.g.*, of wine in countries that use the metric system for everyday purposes.

Liturgy, the name given to the Church ritual, though strictly applying only to the portion used in the celebration of the Eucharist or Lord's Supper. The Anglican liturgy is laid down in the Book of Common Prayer (1662). Parliament gave its consent in 1965 for changes in the form of worship.

Liverworts (Hepatics), a class of simple green plants related to the mosses. There is no differentiation into stem and leaves. Liverworts are most common in damp situations, such as the banks of ditches.

Lizard, the name given to a diversified order of reptiles, of which there are about 1,600 species. Included among the lizards are the geckos, chameleons, glass snakes, skinks, and blind worms.

Llama, mammals related to the camels, from which they differ in small size, absence of humps, and more woolly coat. The domestic llama of S. America is used as a beast of burden, also providing wool, meat, and milk. *See also* Alpaca, Guanaco.

Loadstone *or* **Lodestone,** an oxide of iron, found chiefly in Sweden and Norway. Its scientific name is magnetite. It has the power of attracting pieces of iron and served as the first magnets used in compasses. One of the class of non-metallic magnetic materials nowadays known as " ferrites."

Lobby Correspondents are political correspondents of newspapers who do not report the actual proceedings of Parliament—this is done by Parliamentary Correspondents—but interpret political news and events.

Lobsters are marine crustacean animals existing in large numbers in the northern seas of Europe and America, and in fair proportion on some parts of the British coasts, especially in the neighbourhood of the Channel Islands.

Locarno, Treaty of, 1925, whereby Germany, France, and Belgium undertook to maintain their present frontiers and to abstain from the use of force against each other. Hitler broke the pact by re-occupying the Rhineland, the demilitarisation of which had been recognised by Germany.

Locust, insects of the grasshopper family, but much more powerful. They are inhabitants of hot countries, and often make their appearance in untold millions, like clouds, devastating all the vegetation that comes within their course. The locust-tree (*Ceratonia siliqua*) is supposed to have furnished food to St. John the Baptist in the wilderness, and its " beans " have accordingly been styled " St. John's Bread."

Loess, a deposit of silt or marl laid down by wind action. The biggest loess deposits are in Asia, the source of the dust of which they are composed probably being the deserts of Central Asia.

Log, a line used for reckoning the speed at which a ship is travelling. It was first used in the 16th cent. The line is divided into spaces of 50 ft. marked off by knots and measured by a half-minute sand glass, bearing the same proportion to an hour as 50 ft. bear to a mile.

Logarithms, a system of calculation invented by John Napier in 1614, and developed by Henry Briggs a few years later. Thus if a number is expressed as the power of another number, *i.e.*, if $a = b^n$, then n is said to be the logarithm of a to base b, written $\log_b a$. Common logs are to base 10 and Napierian to base 2·7182818..., expressed as e. Their use represents a great saving of time.

Logical Positivism. *See* J28.

Lollards. *See* J28.

Lombards, a German people, originating on the Elbe, who settled in Italy in the 6th cent., occupying northern and central regions, and establishing a kingdom with Pavia as capital. They were conquered by Charlemagne in 774, but left their name to the region of Lombardy. Lombard Street, London, takes its name from the Lombard merchants and bankers who came to settle there in the 12th cent.

London Clay, geological stratum which occupies much of the London Basin and part of the Hampshire Basin. It represents the lower stratum of the Eocene. Outside the metropolis, brickfields utilise the clay for brickmaking. Water held above this impervious stratum is tapped by a number of artesian wells in London. The tunnels of the Capital's underground railways run through the London Clay.

London University comprises nearly one-third of the academic activity of the United Kingdom, and is recognised as one of the great universities of the world. Originated in the foundation of a non-sectarian college in Gower Street in 1828. Among the chief colleges are: University, Kings, Imperial College of Science and Technology, London School of Economics, School of Oriental and African Studies, Queen Mary, Birkbeck, Royal Holloway, Bedford, Westfield, and Queen Elizabeth College. London University was the first to throw open all degrees to women (1878).

Long Distance Routes. The National Parks and Access to the Countryside Act 1949 provided for the establishment in England and Wales of Long Distance Footpaths and Bridleways. The following have been approved but only the Pennine Way has been completed: Pennine Way (a magnificent hill walk of 250 miles from Edale in Derbyshire along the Pennines over the Cheviots to the Scottish border); Pembrokeshire Coast Path; Offa's Dyke Path (168 miles along the marches of Wales); South Downs Way (Beachy Head to Salisbury); South-West Peninsula Coast Path (North Cornwall, South Cornwall, South Devon, Somerset and North Devon, Dorset); Yorkshire Coast and North York Moors. *See also* National Parks.

Longitude of a point on the earth's surface is the angle which the meridian through the poles and that point makes with some standard meridian. The meridian through Greenwich is usually accepted as the standard meridian and the longitude is measured east or west of that line. As the earth revolves through 360° in 24 hrs., 15° longitude represent 1 hour's difference in apparent time.

Long Parliament (1640–60), marked the end of Charles I's 11-year attempt to govern without parliament. It carried through what has come to be called "the English Revolution" and was the parliament of the civil war (1642–49).

Lord Chamberlain. *See* Chamberlain, Lord.

Lord Lieutenant is the Queen's representative in the county, and his office is now largely ceremonial. On his recommendation the magistrates or Justices of the Peace are appointed by the Lord Chancellor. The office was created in 1549 to take over the military duties of the sheriff.

Lords, House of, the Upper House of the British Parliament composed of Lords Spiritual and Lords Temporal. The former consist of the two Archbishops and twenty-four English Bishops and the latter of Peers and Peeresses. The full membership (1970) is 1060. The right of the Lords to veto Bills passed by the Commons is restricted by the Parliament Acts of 1911 and 1949. The Lord High Chancellor presides over the House of Lords. *See* Section C, Part II.

Louse, parasitic insect found on the skin of birds and mammals. The bird or biting lice belong to the order *Mallophaga*; the true or sucking lice to the order *Anoplura*. Two species of lice parasitise man, and one of these, the body louse, is a carrier of typhus.

Louvre, one of the old royal palaces of Paris, was built in its present form partly by Francis, I. and added to by later monarchs, Louis XIV. completing the edifice. Napoleon I. turned it into a museum and enriched it with the plunder of many foreign art galleries. The great extension to the Louvre building begun by Napoleon I. was completed under Napoleon III. in 1857. Much injury was done to the building during the Commune of 1871. Amongst other famous treasures it houses the Venus de Milo and Leonardo da Vinci's masterpiece, *La Gioconda*.

Lovebird, a vivid little bird native to Africa, resembling a parrakeet but with a short, wide tail and short body.

LSD (d-lysergic acid diethylamide). This hallucinogenic drug has achieved wide notoriety because of its use by certain people to give themselves abnormal mental experiences. Doctors have frequently warned against the dangers of its use. It is active in extremely small quantities and a dose as small as a fifty-millionth part of a gram can cause marked disturbances of the mental function in man. LSD has been used in the study of mental disease because it produces symptoms very similar to mental disorders such as schizophrenia.

Luddites, a combination of workmen formed in 1811, in a period of great distress, with the object of destroying the new textile machinery then being largely adopted, which they regarded as the cause of their troubles. Their first outbreak was at Nottingham, and was stated to have been started by a young apprentice named Ned Ludd. Afterwards, serious Luddite riots occurred in various parts of the country, especially in the West Riding of Yorkshire, where many people were killed, mills were destroyed, and numbers of rioters were tried and executed. Charlotte Brontë used the period in her novel, *Shirley*.

Lunar Month. *See* Month.

Lung Fishes *or* Dipnoi. *See* Dipnoi.

Lutecium, element of the rare-earth metal group discovered in 1907 by Urbain.

Lutheranism. *See* J29.

Lynx, cats of sturdy build, with tufted ears and spotted fur, inhabiting many parts of the world, including Northern and Central Europe. They commit serious ravages among sheep and goats and are very fierce.

Lyon King of Arms, the President of the Scottish Lyon Court, and head of the heraldic organisation for Scotland.

Lyre-Bird, a remarkable family of Australian birds, the males of which possess a beautiful lyre-shaped tail. The bird is not more than 15 in. long, but its tail, displayed during its remarkable courtship dance, is 23 in. in length. There are two species: the Superb and Albert's Lyrebird.

M

Macaque. A family of monkeys which include the Barbary ape (specimens of which live on Gibraltar), the Rhesus macaque (the organ grinder's monkey and the one used for experimental work in the investigation of disease), the Bonnet monkey of southern India and Ceylon, the Crab-eating, and the Pig-tailed monkeys of south-eastern Asia.

Macaw, a genus of large parrots with brilliant scarlet and sky-blue plumage, with interminglings of green. Native to South and Central America.

Mace, originally a weapon of offence, now an ensign of authority borne before officers of state and other dignitaries. In the House of Commons the mace is handed to an official of the Crown by the Sergeant-at-Arms at the close of a parliamentary session.

Mach Number. Unit of flight speed. The ratio of speed of flight to speed of sound under same conditions of pressure and density. Speed of sound at sea-level is 762 m.p.h., so flight speed of 381 m.p.h. is equivalent to a Mach Number of $\frac{1}{2}$. At supersonic speeds the Mach Number is greater than 1; subsonic speeds, less than 1.

Mackerel, a familiar sea-fish existing in large numbers in the northern waters of both hemispheres. In May and June immense shoals are to be found round the British coasts.

Macromolecules are very large molecules about 10,000 times or more as heavy as ordinary small molecules like hydrogen. Most are built up from a large number of simple sub-units, *i.e.*, are polymers (*q.v.*). The term macromolecule is often used in biology, *e.g.*, starch and cellulose are biological macromolecules, both built from glucose sub-units. Other important ones are proteins and nucleic acids. The properties of macromolecules depend on the sub-units of which they are composed.

Madder, one of the most important of dye-stuffs, largely used in producing Turkey-red dye, but now superseded by synthetic alizarin. Natural madder is the root of the *Rubia tinctorum*.

Madrier, a term in military engineering for a beam used to support the earth in a mine or fortification, or to receive the mouth of a petard.

Maelstrom, a great whirlpool. The most famous is that off the coast of Norway, between the islands of Moskenēs and Mosken, of the Lofoten group, the power of which has been much exaggerated.

Mafia, a secret Sicilian society formed for purposes of exploitation, intimidation, and violence, prominent about 1860, and since the second world war. It was not until 1962 that the Italian Parliament decided to set up a commission to study it and the means of eradicating it. One of the " unsolved " Mafia murders (that of the Socialist municipal councillor Carmelo Battaglia in 1966) was reopened in 1969 by the parliamentary commission of inquiry. The American branch of the Mafia, the Cosa Nostra, has infiltrated many city governments by bribing officials.

Magellan, Clouds of, the name given to a pair of small galaxies, satellite systems of our own galaxy, visible only from the southern hemisphere. On account of their relative nearness to the earth (186,000 light-years), they are receiving much attention from astronomers.

Magenta, a blue-red aniline dye discovered in 1859 by Sir W. H. Perkin, and named after the great battle of that year between the French and Austrians.

Magic. *See* J29.

Magistrates *or* **Justices of the Peace** preside over courts of petty sessions, and are appointed by the Lord Chancellor on the recommendation of the Lord Lieutenant of the County. Most J.P.s are laymen and are unpaid. In certain big towns a legally-qualified, paid, full-time magistrate is appointed, known as a stipendiary magistrate. In London stipendiaries are known as Metropolitan Stipendiary Magistrates. J.P.s are no longer appointed over the age of 60 and they must retire when they reach 70. There are now arrangements for the training of magistrates. By the Justices of the Peace Act, 1968, *ex officio* J.P.s are abolished, except for the Lord Mayor and aldermen of the City of London. *See* D43, 5, 6.

Magma, molten rock material rich in volatile constituents prior to its eruption at the surface. On eruption and loss of volatiles it becomes lava.

Magna Carta was sealed by King John at Runnymede on June 15, 1215, in obedience to the insistent demands of the barons, and has been confirmed many times by later monarchs. It was not a revolutionary document. It laid down what the barons took to be the recognised and fundamental principles for the government of the realm and bound king and barons alike to maintain them. Its main provisions were that no man should be punished without fair trial, that ancient liberties generally should be preserved and that no demands should be made by an overlord to his vassal (other than those recognised) without the sanction of the great council of the realm.

Magnesium, a metallic element, symbol Mg, first isolated in 1808 by Sir Humphry Davy, who prepared it by electrolysing the chloride. Its chief ores are magnesite and dolomite. Industrially it is obtained by electrolysis. Many important light alloys contain magnesium. The metal burns with a very bright light, and for this reason it is used in photographers' flash bulbs and also in firework manufacture.

Magnetic Pole. Either one of two regions of a magnet where the attraction appears concentrated.

Magnetic Storms, large irregular disturbances superimposed upon the normal magnetic field of the earth. They may occur at any time, but are most frequent during equinoctial months and in years of sunspot maxima. World-wide in extent, magnetic storms are most pronounced in the polar regions, being due apparently to intense electric currents located in the upper atmosphere near to the zones of greatest auroral frequency. One theory attributes the high ionisation of these belts to solar radiation. Magnetic storms cause radio fade-outs and interfere with telegraphic communication.

Magnetism, originally the name given to the quality of attraction for iron possessed by lodestone (*q.v.*). Now known to be a phenomenon inseparably connected with electricity (F18). Strong magnetic attraction is possessed by a comparatively small class of substances; iron, nickel, and cobalt are the most common elements, but there are several less well known, *e.g.*, gadolinium. Many alloys have valuable magnetic properties which make possible numberless technical devices. New magnetic substances are always being developed (*see* Ferrite). The earth acts like a huge magnet with its axis inclined at about 11° to the axis of rotation, the magnetic poles being on the Boothia Peninsula (North Canada) and South Victoria Land (Antarctica). The magnetic field at the surface consists of the regular field of a magnetised sphere with an irregular field superimposed upon it. Variation in the magnetic forces occurs from place to place and from time to time, and maps showing the distribution over the globe of points of the same declination (*i.e.*, the angle which the magnetic meridian makes with the geographical one) are of the utmost importance in navigation. In the southeast of the British Isles, at present, a magnetic needle points 9° and in the north-west 14° west of true north. Little is known regarding the origin of the main (regular) field of the earth, but it is believed that the irregularities are due to the presence of intense electric currents in the upper atmospheres and local magnetisation of rock strata. In 1967 the discovery was claimed of isolated magnetic poles, *i.e.*, north and south magnetic poles existing separately, just as positive and negative electrical charges exist separately. If this is confirmed it will probably rank as one of the most important experimental results of the 20th cent., because of its significance for the theory of electromagnetism and fundamental particles.

Magnetohydro-dynamics. A current-carrying wire always experiences a force if it is in a magnetic field. This is the well-known electrodynamic force, and electric motors work because of it. If the current is carried in a fluid, *e.g.*, a liquid metal or a plasma, these forces cause bodily movements of the fluid, which are in general very difficult to calculate. The forces are then called *magnetohydro-dynamic forces.* Now magnetic fields are themselves produced by electric currents; so a current flowing in a fluid produces a magnetic field, which then reacts on the fluid itself by means of the magnetohydro-dynamic forces. In the Harwell machine Zeta, used in studying the technical problems of thermonuclear reactions, this effect acts so as to constrict the electric discharge on to the axis of the tube and thus keeps it away from the walls. This action is assisted by an extra magnetic field produced by a separate current flowing in metallic conductors outside the tube. Thus the hot plasma is contained by magnetohydro-dynamic forces and not at all by the material tube wall. In practical devices of the future magnetic forces may have to sustain plasma pressures of 60 atmospheres—a pressure for which a thick steel wall would normally be used! *See also* Plasma Physics.

Magnificat, the hymn of the Virgin Mary, given in Luke 1, 46 beginning in the Vulgate with the words "Magnificat anima mea Dominum" ("My soul doth magnify the Lord "), and used in the services of all Christian Churches.

Magnitude in astronomy is a measure of the apparent brightness of a star, which is inversely proportional to the square of its distance. A low number indicates a bright star, and a high one a faint star. The *absolute magnitude* is a measure of *real* brightness, *i.e.*, the brightness a star would have at a standard distance away of 32·6 light years. The distance can be calculated if the apparent and absolute magnitudes are known.

Magnolia, species of the family *Magnoliaceae* comprising many beautiful trees, and shrubs with large and fragrant flowers, and chiefly native to North America and Asia. Introduced in 1688.

Magpie, a well-known bird of the crow family, of glossy black and white plumage, famed for its mischievous propensities.

Magyars, the Hungarian race who came to eastern Europe from S.W. Asia and settled in Hungary in the 10th cent. Their language belongs to the Finno-Ugrian group.

Mahdi, an Arab leader of great influence, invested with powers akin to those of a Messiah in the Mohammedan mind. The title was taken by Mohammed Ahmed, who overran the Egyptian Sudan, and in 1885 captured Khartoum.

Mahogany, a fine hard wood susceptible of a very high polish, and distinguished for the beauty of its colour and markings. Obtained chiefly from the trees of the genera *Swietenia* (Spanish or Cuban mahogany) and *Khaya* (African mahogany) of the family Meliacaea. According to tradition Raleigh had a mahogany table made for Queen Elizabeth.

Maidenhair Tree *or* **Ginkgo.** This tree takes its name from the shape of its leaves, which resemble those of the maidenhair fern. Widely cultivated in China and Japan. It is the only survivor of an order of gymnosperms which flourished in Mesozoic times. Botanically interesting because the male gametes are motile.

Malmaison, château at Rueil-Malmaison, a western suburb of Paris. It derives it name from having been inhabited in the 11th cent. by the Norman brigand Odon, and afterwards, according to the tradition, by evil spirits, exorcised by the monks of St. Denis. It was the residence of Napoleon and of the Empress Josephine after her divorce. She died there in 1814 as the result of a chill caught while showing the Russian Emperor round the grounds. In 1900 it was given to the nation.

Malmsey, a strong, sweet wine originally made in Greece, but now also in Spain, Madeira, and the Azores; known also as Malvoisie.

Maltose, a sugar formed in cereal grains during germination. It is produced by hydrolysis of starch, and further hydrolysis converts the maltose into glucose.

Mamluks, commonly known as Mameluks, were originally—in the 13th cent.—a bodyguard of Turkish and Circassian slaves in the service of the Sultan of Egypt, and attained such influence that in 1250 they were strong enough to appoint one of their own body to the throne of Egypt. After that a succession of Mamluk Sultans reigned down to 1517. Then the Turks annexed Egypt, and the Mamluks were taken into the service of the Beys. They again came to the front after Napoleon's conquest of Egypt, and for a time resumed governmental sway; but in 1811 they were decoyed into the citadel of Cairo and massacred by order of Mehemet Ali.

Mammoth, extinct elephants of gigantic size. In 1799 the first perfectly preserved specimen was found in Siberia in a block of ice. It was in prehistoric times an inhabitant of Britain and other parts of Europe, as well as of Asia and America.

Mammoth Cave of Kentucky, about 10 miles long, is one of a series of spacious caverns formed in the limestone rock formation, and is from 40 to 300 ft. wide and at one point 300 ft. high. Stalactites and stalagmites abound.

Manatee, an aquatic mammal of the sea cow (Sirenia) order of mammals, averaging when full grown from 10 to 12 ft. in length, with shovel-shaped tail, and four limbs and nails which almost give the appearance of arms and hands. In spite of their ungainly aspect, these creatures are believed to have given rise to the legend of mermaids.

Manchus, the original nomadic race inhabiting northern Manchuria who invaded China early in the 17th cent. A Manchu dynasty occupied

the imperial throne of China from 1644 to 1911.

Mandarin, the name given to a powerful Chinese official, civil or military, under the old régime, whose rank was shown by the wearing of a button on the cap. Mandarin is the major language of N. China (*see* **M44**).

Mandible, the lower jaw in human anatomy. The two parts of a bird's beak are known as the upper and lower mandible. The term is also used for biting jaws in arthropods.

Manganese, a metallic element, symbol Mn, discovered by Scheele in 1774. It is silver-white, not very hard (it forms a hard alloy with carbon), brittle, and tarnishes when exposed to air. Its chief ore is pyrolusite (manganese dioxide). Steels containing manganese are very tough, and used for making machine parts.

Maniple, eucharistic vestment worn over left arm.

Manna, a tree of the ash genus, *Fraxinus ornus*, growing in the South of Europe and in the East and exuding a sweet substance which is gathered, boiled, and eaten.

Manometer, instrument used to measure gas pressure. Usually a U-tube containing water or mercury, one end open to the atmosphere, the other to the gas whose pressure is to be measured. More sensitive for small pressures than the Bourdon gauge.

Manors were estates originally granted in Anglo-Saxon times as rewards for knightly service, and included the privilege of a special court with jurisdiction, criminal and civil, within the manorial territory. *See* **Court-Leet.**

Mansion House, the official residence of the Lord Mayor of London, stands opposite to the Bank of England, and was erected in 1739–53 from the designs of George Dance.

Mantis. Large insects belonging to the same order as the locusts and grasshoppers. The manner in which the forelegs are held, as though in suppliance, has gained for these insects the common name of " praying mantis." They are distributed throughout the warmer countries of the world.

Manx, the Celtic dialect (Manx Gaelic) of the Isle of Man, now on the point of extinction.

Maoism. *See* **J30.**

Maoris, the race found in New Zealand at the time of its discovery by Europeans. The Maoris are believed to have migrated from Polynesia about 1350. They number 220,718 (1969), and being very intelligent people have adapted themselves with considerable success to the conditions of civilised life. Until 1870 they were frequently in arms against the Government, but since then have settled down with the Whites as equal citizens.

Maple, trees native to the northern hemisphere. There are over 100 species. The sycamore is the best-known species growing in Britain. The sugar maple abounds in Canada and the eastern parts of the United States. The sugar is tapped by boring holes in the tree in Feb. and Mar., and the juice that escapes is collected and evaporated. The maple-leaf is the Canadian national emblem.

Maquis, name of the dense scrub in Mediterranean France and Corsica, providing good cover for bandits and outlaws. The French resistance movement adopted the name Maquis during the German Occupation, 1940–45.

Marble is limestone in its hardest and most crystalline form. There are many varieties—33 were used in the building of the Paris Opera House—but white is the purest and rarest. White marble was used by the ancient Greeks for their temples and statues. Among the famous marbles of Italy are the Carrara and Siena marbles, which were used by Renaissance sculptors. Devonshire and Derbyshire yield some beautiful marbles and Connemara furnishes a serpentine-marble.

March, the third month of the year, and the first of the old Roman Calendar. It was named after the god Mars, and was the *Hlyd* (storm) *monath* of the Anglo-Saxons.

Mardi Gras, the last day of the Carnival in France, Shrove Tuesday.

Marionettes are puppets moved by strings. They originated in the *Fantoccini* of the 15th cent. which had such a vogue in Italy and elsewhere on the Continent. The English *Punch and*

Judy is a version of Punchinello. Puppet shows were known in the earliest civilisations.

Marl, a rock composed partly of clay and partly of carbonate of lime.

Marlinspike, a pointed iron tool used by sailors to splice wire. The instrument used when rope splicing is called a fid.

Marmoset, small monkeys confined to the New World. Very squirrel-like in appearance, with long bushy tails, and thick woolly fur, they are pretty little animals and the smallest of all monkeys. There are claws, not nails, on their digits, the big toe excepted.

Marprelate Tracts, seditious pamphlets written with great maliciousness by a group of Elizabethan puritans about 1586, and intended to discredit the episcopacy, caused a great sensation in their time, and led to the execution of their supposed author, John Penry.

Marquess *or* **Marquis,** the title next in precedence to that of duke. The first English marquess was Rovery de Vere, Earl of Oxford, who had the honour conferred upon him by Richard II. in 1385.

Marquetry, a kind of inlaying in which thin layers of coloured woods are wrought into a design, and mainly used in ornamental floors.

Mars, the fourth nearest planet to the sun (*see* **F7**). There used to be much speculation among scientists about certain dark lines which some observers had seen on the surface of the planet; photographs gave no support to the theory of an artifically constructed network of canals, but it seemed possible they represented areas covered by some simple form of vegetation of the lichenous type. However, photos taken by *Mariner* 6 and *Mariner* 7, which flew past the planet in 1969, showed no trace of the so-called canals. Like the moon it is pitted with craters and appeared to be a geologically dead planet. Findings showed that its atmosphere is at least 98 per cent carbon dioxide with no trace of nitrogen, without which life, as we know it, could not exist. Atmospheric pressure is low, about 8 millibars compared with the earth's 1,000 millibars. A Viking spacecraft is scheduled to land on the planet in 1973. Mars has two small moons—Phobos and Deimos.

Marseillaise, the French national hymn, written and composed by Rouget de L'Isle, a French engineer officer, who was inspired to write it in 1792 to encourage the Strasburg conscripts. It immediately became popular, and received its name from the fact that it was sung by the Marseillaise troops while marching into Paris.

Marshalsea Prison, a once well-known house of detention in Southwark. It stood near St. George's Church, and was originally a prison for royal servants convicted of offences, but from 1842 to 1849 was a debtors' prison. It was abolished in 1849. Dickens described it in *Little Dorrit.*

Marsh Gas. *See* **Methane.**

Marsh Tortoise, an amphibious animal of the order *Chelonia,* spread over many countries and inhabiting ponds and small rivers. There are 42 species, and they are all carnivorous.

Marston Moor, near York, was the scene of the famous battle between Prince Rupert and Cromwell on July 2, 1644. Cromwell's victory was the turning-point in the Civil War.

Marsupials, members of the order of pouched animals. Except for the oppossums of America, all marsupials occur in Australasia. Well-known marsupials are the kangaroos, wallabies, and wombats.

Martello Towers, circular forts erected on the coasts of England and Jersey early in the 19th cent. as defences against the threatened Napoleonic invasion. So called from the circular fort at Mortella (Corsica), which resisted an English fleet in 1794.

Marten, carnivorous animals of the weasel family, one species of which was once common in Britain, but now seldom met with. Many valuable furs come from martens, *e.g.,* the sable of N. Asia and the marten of N. America.

Martial Law is a term loosely employed to indicate the suspension of the administration of normal civil law and its replacement by military authority when this is rendered desirable by such circumstances as war or rebellion.

Martin, a well-known bird-visitor to Britain. It belongs to the swallow family, and the two species that spend their summers here are the house-martin, which makes its nest of mud under the eaves of houses, and the sand martin, which builds in sandy banks.

Martingale, a long strap or thong of leather, one end of which is fastened to the girth of a horse, between the fore legs, and the other to the bit, or to a thin mouthpiece of its own.

Martinmas *or* **St. Martin's Day,** falls on Nov. 11, and is one of the Scottish quarter days. St. Martin was a popular Saint with our ancestors, and Martinmas was a busy time for the mediæval housewife. It was the date when " Martlemas Beef " was dried in the chimney, and enough bacon and mutton cured to last until the spring, because, owing the the scarcity of winter fodder, fresh meat could seldom be obtained. This diet of dried meat without vegetables caused scurvy, King's evil, leprosy, and other maladies. Originally the goose belonged to Martinmas, not to Michaelmas, the legend being that when Martin was elected Bishop of Tours he hid himself, but was betrayed by the cackling of geese. He died in the 4th cent. The spell of fine weather sometimes occurring at Martinmas is called St. Martin's Summer.

Martyrs. People who suffer death in testimony to their faith. Stephen was the first Christian martyr in 39. The first English martyr was St. Alban, 286, and in Tudor times many eminent churchmen went to the stake at West Smithfield, in London, and at Oxford, where now exists the " Martyrs' Memorial.'' There is a Martyrs' Memorial Church in St. John St., Clerkenwell, near the scene of the Smithfield fires.

Marxism. *See* **J31.**

Mason and Dixon's Line is the boundary line separating the old slave states of America from the free state of Pennsylvania. It was drawn by two English surveyors, Charles Mason and Jeremiah Dixon, between 1763 and 1767.

Masques were light dramatic compositions set to music and performed on special occasions. One of the best-known examples is Milton's "Comus," which was given at Ludlow Castle in 1634.

Mass, the service in the Roman Catholic Church in which are enacted and enshrined Christ's words and actions at the Last Supper. It is high or low, *i.e.,* performed with full choral service, or merely by the rehearsal of prayers without singing. Mass was first celebrated in Latin in the 4th cent., and was introduced into England in the 7th cent. The use of a vernacular language was sanctioned by the Second Vatican Council (1965).

Mass Spectrograph, an instrument for separating isotopes. It works by sorting electrified particles according to their masses; the particles stream through a magnetic and possibly an electric field, and the lightest particles undergo the greatest deflection.

Massorah, a collection of criticisms on the Hebrew text of the Scriptures, and rules for its correct interpretation.

Mast, a long round piece of timber or tubular steel or iron, standing upright in a vessel, and supporting the yards, sails, and rigging in general. The earliest ships had only one mast, carrying a simple sail. The number increased until there were 4 or 5, or even more. Above the lower mast of a sailing-ship comes the topmast, and above that, the topgallantmast and royalmast. The position of each mast is indicated by a prefix, as foremast, foretopmast, foretopgallantmast, foreroyalmast, mainmast, maintopmast, etc. The foremast is in the fore of the ship, the mainmast in the centre, and the mizzen nearest the stern. In large vessels nowadays the mast does not extend to the keel, as it formerly did, but is usually stopped at the second deck.

Master of the Revels was an important Court official upon whom devolved the arrangement of Court festivities. The office is at least as old as the time of Edward III. By 1737 it seems to have died.

Master of the Rolls, one of the English judges, formerly a judge of Chancery, but since 1881 a judge of the Court of Appeal only. In addition he has charge of the rolls or records of Chancery and ranks next to the Lord Chancellor and Lord Chief Justice.

Mastodon, an extinct order of quadruped closely resembling the elephant in structure, but larger.

Materials Science is a blend of science and technology; it is the use of scientific research methods to study and improve materials for practical use. The deeper understanding so obtained enables scientists to design new substances with hitherto unknown combinations of properties that are useful in engineering, aircraft, nuclear power, surgery, etc. Materials science institutes or university departments will usually contain an assortment of chemists, physicists, metallurgists, ceramicists, engineers, and others because materials science brings to bear on materials a great many specialised techniques. The scientific study of materials is bringing continual improvement in metals, ceramics, plastics, fibres, and many valuable combinations of these.

Mathematics is a body of knowledge expressed in a language of symbols. *Pure* mathematics studies the propositions that can be deduced in this language by applying definite rules of reasoning to sets of axioms. In *Applied* mathematics, the mathematical language is used, often with great effect, to discuss problems of the real world, such as mechanics, statistics, and science generally. In range, subtlety, complexity, and depth mathematics is unsurpassed among the intellectual disciplines and its study has attracted some of the most brilliant men in history.

Matins, the first of the canonical hours or services of the day in the Roman Catholic Church and Morning Prayer in the Anglican Church. The daily service in the Roman breviary (*q.v.*) consists of eight offices or " hours," fixed by canon, for prayer and devotion. Formerly, Matins was recited or sung at midnight, Lauds at sunrise, Prime at 6 a.m., Terce at 9 a.m., Sext at midday, Nones at 3 p.m., Vespers at sunset, and Compline before retiring for the night. Lauds are now commonly joined to Matins.

Mau-Mau, a secret, anti-European, terrorist movement which agitated the Kikuyu tribe of Kenya during the years 1953–57. Mau-mau was a symptom of native insecurity and discontent; emergency powers were lifted in Nov. 1959, an large-scale reforms were instituted. Kenya attained independence in Dec. 1963 with Mr. Jomo Kenyatta as Prime Minister.

Maundy Thursday, the day before Good Friday, commemorates the Last Supper. "Maundy" derives from Christ's command (mandatum) to his disciples on that day to love one another. It was the custom in the monasteries for the monks to wash the feet of the poor on this day, and for many centuries the sovereigns of England, through their almoners, have distributed money, food, and clothing to " as many old men and as many old women as the Sovereign is years of age." The Royal Maundy ceremony is still observed, special silver money granted by the Royal Almonry is coined for the occasion and the distribution takes place in Westminster Abbey.

Mausoleum, a special place of sepulture, generally for the reception of the remains of members of a royal or other family of distinction. The name is derived from the tomb of King Mausolus at Halicarnassus, erected about 350 B.C., and forming one of the seven wonders of the world.

Mauve, a colouring matter produced from lichens by Dr. Stenhouse in 1848, but in 1856 obtained from aniline by William Perkin (1838–1907), who gave it the name Mauveen. This was the first synthetic organic dyestuff ever to be produced, which led to the building up of the great synthetic dyestuffs industry (which Germany dominated before the First World War).

May, the fifth month of the year, but the third of the ancient Roman calendar. Supposed to be named after Maia, the mother of Mercury, to whom sacrifices were offered on the first day of this month. In England in former days May Day was made the occasion of many festivities, including the crowning of the May Queen, dancing round the Maypole, etc.

" Mayflower," the name of the ship which in 1620 conveyed the Pilgrim Fathers, 101 in number, from England to America. *See* **Pilgrim Fathers.**

May Fly. *See* **Ephemoptera.**

Mazarin Bible, an edition of the Latin Vulgate, acknowledged as the masterpiece of the Guten-

berg press (1456). It was the first book completely printed from movable types. It is called the Mazarin Bible because the first copy to capture the attention of scholars was found in the library of Cardinal Mazarin, in Paris. Sometimes called the Gutenberg or the 42-line Bible.

Mean. In statistics and mathematics generally understood to be the arithmetic mean. The geometric mean between two quantities is the square root of their product. *See* **Average.**

Mechanical Equivalent of Heat. *See* **Joule.**

Medals, as decorations for military service, were first issued in this country by Charles I., who ordered medals for gallantry to be distributed to certain soldiers in 1643. Medals were also issued to officers and men who were victorious against the Dutch fleet in 1653. After Lord Howe's victory in 1794 a naval medal was instituted. Medals were also struck for the victory of Waterloo, and since that time special medals have been issued in connection with all our wars. The Victoria Cross, a special reward for personal gallantry in the Navy, Army, and Air Force, was instituted in 1856. The George Cross for gallantry instituted in 1940 ranks next to the Victoria Cross. The Military Cross was instituted in 1914.

Median. *See* **Average.**

Medlar, a tree of which the fruit is about 1 in. in diameter and hard fleshed when gathered, but after being stored for a few weeks it softens. It has a peculiar flavour. Its large white flowers give it a decorative appearance.

Meerschaum, a white or yellow-white earthy mineral, found in beds in Asia Minor, Greece, and other places, is a silicate of magnesium allied with water. Its chief use is in making pipe-bowls.

Megalith, a prehistoric monument, consisting of a large single stone or a group of such stones, in a circle as at Stonehenge or in burial chambers as at New Grange, Ireland. Megalithic monuments have been constructed by different peoples in different parts of the world since the third millennium B.C.

Meiosis, a special type of cell division by which the gametes or sex cells are generated, resulting in the sperm or ovum receiving only half the number of chromosomes found in a somatic cell. *See* **Mitosis.**

Mendelian Law. The first statistical rules of inheritance, determining the ratio of variation of characteristics in the offspring of differing individuals, and the classification of characters discontinuously inherited, were first formulated by the Austrian monk Gregor Mendel. The results of his most important experiments in the crossing of peas were published in 1866, and showed that when two races are crossed, the resultant hybrids will exhibit the dominant features of one parent, but the offspring of the second generation will show those of both grandparents. *See* **F47.**

Mendicant Friars, certain religious orders which spread over Europe in the 13th cent., and comprised the Franciscans, Dominicans, Augustines, and Carmelites. Originally they depended entirely on alms.

Mercator's Projection, a method of indicating meridians and parallels of latitudes on maps, introduced by Mercator in the 16th cent., and still universally used in navigator's charts.

Mercury, one of the smaller planets and the nearest to the sun, being 36 million miles distant. It has no satellite. *See* **F7.**

Mercury *or* **Quicksilver,** symbol Hg (Latin *hydrargyrum*) is one of the oldest-known metals, whose chief ore is the sulphide, cinnabar, found in certain parts of Spain, China, Japan, Mexico, and South America. It is liquid at ordinary temperature and is used in the construction of barometers and thermometers. Alloys of mercury are called amalgams. It is also of great value in medicine. The metal is used in the mercury-vapour (or "sunlight") lamp, since the vapour gives a bright yellow-white glow in an electric discharge.

Mercy Killing. *See* **D9(2).**

Meridian, an imaginary circle extending through the North and South Poles and any given place. When the sun is at its midday height at any place it is " on the meridian "; hence the terms ante-meridian (a.m.) and post-meridian p.m.). *See also* **Greenwich Mean Time.**

Merino Sheep were imported into England from Spain in 1788 and had great influence in improving native breeds, especially in regard to the quality of the wool.

Merit, Order of, founded by King Edward VII. in 1902 as a special distinction for eminent men and women without conferring a knighthood upon them. The Order has twenty-four British companions in addition to foreign honorary members limited in number, as the choice of members is, by the Sovereign's pleasure. Lord Kelvin was the founder companion. General Eisenhower (1945), and Dr. Sarvepalli Radhakrishnan (1963) are honorary members. Florence Nightingale (1907) and Professor Dorothy Hodgkin (1965) are the only women to have received this coveted decoration.

Merovingians, the name given to the family that ruled over France from about 500 to 750. Clovis was first of the line and Childeric the last.

Mesons (from Greek *meso* = middle), a family of unstable particles of mass between that of an electron and that of a proton. Some are positive, some negative, some neutral. No stable meson is known, the longest-lived particle having a lifetime of only two-millionths of a second. The first of these particles was discovered in cosmic radiation in 1937 and called the mu-meson or *muon*. In 1947 a heavier type was discovered called the pi-meson or *pion*, which behaved like the meson predicted on theoretical grounds by Yukawa in 1935. The pion is connected with the theory of nuclear forces. *See also* **F13, 14.**

Mesozoic. The geological era which includes the Triassic, Jurassic, and Cretaceous rocks. *See* **F44.**

Metabolism, the general term for the physical and chemical processes occurring within a living organism. *See* **F26.**

Metalloid, an element which has properties intermediate between those of a metal and a non-metal. Arsenic is a metalloid.

Metamorphic Rocks are such geological deposits as have undergone alterations of structure and mineral reorganisation. The most active agents in producing these metamorphic changes are heat, water, and pressure. *See* **F8**(2).

Metamorphosis, period of development from egg to adult, during which the animals have different forms, as found, *e.g.*, in the life histories of frog and butterfly.

Meteorites. The word meteor originally signified any natural phenomenon, but in modern usage meteors are small bodies coming from interplanetary space which become luminous by friction on entering the earth's atmosphere. Popularly called "shooting stars." Larger meteors are known as fireballs. Some of these reach the ground. The object which has been a meteor in flight then becomes a meteorite. In some meteorites iron is the predominating element, others are like rock. The iron meteorites are more common amongst those which have been preserved, but falls of rock-like meteorites occur more frequently. At l'Aigle in France in 1803 from 2000 to 3000 meteorite stones fell; this fall is famous because it convinced scientists that meteorites really came from outside our atmosphere. (The largest meteorite stone actually known to have fallen to earth is one which descended in Emmott County, Iowa, in 1870, weighing 437 pounds.) A meteorite weighing no less than 36½ tons found in Greenland is now in New York. On June 30, 1908, an enormous object fell in Siberia in a sparsely-inhabited region. A hot blast destroyed all trees within a radius of about 5–10 miles, the explosion waves being recorded by barographs as far distant as London, Washington, and Batavia. For the next few nights there was in Europe in the northern sky brilliant illumination due to sunlight falling on clouds of dust at a great height in the atmosphere. Whether this dust had accompanied the object in its journey through space like the tail of a comet or whether the dust had come from Siberia is unknown. (Many Russian astronomers now believe this Siberian meteorite, as it is commonly called, was the nucleus of a small comet.) When the place where the object fell was visited in 1927 some 200 craters were found, but no considerable meteorite has been recovered. Meteorites are possibly débris from the disintegration of a body in the solar system.

Meteorology, the science of the atmosphere considered as a heat engine. Deals with weather, climate, optical phenomena, atmospheric electricity, physical processes such as radiation and precipitation, the dynamics and structure of cyclones, anticyclones, etc. Wide application to problems of aviation, agriculture, commerce and shipping. Meteorological observing stations are in operation all over the world, and on the simultaneous or synoptic reports of their instrument readings and estimates of pressure, temperature, humidity, speed and direction of wind, rain, character and amount of cloud, visibility, etc., forecasts, gale, snow and frost warnings are based. Instruments carried by earth satellites (*e.g.*, *Tiros*, *Nimbus*) outside the atmosphere can make systematic observations on a world-wide basis of the atmospheric circulation, through observation of cloud cover and of the thermal radiation into space from the atmosphere. Such observations together with the use of computers are of great importance for weather analysis and forecasting. The main communications centre for the U.K. is at the headquarters of the Meteorological Office at Bracknell, Berkshire, where the collection, editing, and re-transmission of weather messages continue according to strict schedules day and night throughout the year.

Methane. The simplest hydrocarbon, compounded of one carbon atom and four hydrogen atoms. This gas occurs over marshes and swamps, where it is liberated in the decay of vegetable matter. It is the main constituent of natural gas, and also occurs in coal-mines, where it is called "fire-damp" because of the explosive character of its mixture with air. Formerly this natural gas was removed from the coal seams and ran to waste; now in many countries (including Britain) it is being used for commercial purposes.

Methodism. *See* **J31.**

Methylated Spirit, a mixture of 90 parts by volume ethyl alcohol, 9½ parts wood naphtha (methyl alcohol), ½ part crude pyridine, together with small amounts of petroleum oil and methyl violet dye. Industrial methylated spirit consists of a mixture of 95 parts by volume ethyl alcohol and 5 parts wood naphtha. It is used as a solvent and a fuel.

Metre. *See* **English Verse, M30.**

Metre, unit of length in the metric system; since 1960 the wavelength of the orange-red light of krypton 86 has been adopted as the basis of the international unit of length. Before that (since 1889) the platinum–iridium bar kept at Sèvres was the international prototype metre.

Metric System, the system of weights and measures based on the gramme and the metre, smaller and larger units being decimals and multiples of the primary units respectively. A decimal currency was adopted in France in 1795 and the metric system of weights and measures in 1799. (In that year the quadrant of the earth was surveyed and the standard metre adopted.) Nevertheless the change was accepted slowly, and as late as 1837 the French Government had to pass a law forbidding the use of the old measures. Since then the metric system has been adopted in most of the continental countries and is used universally in scientific work. Although there have been many attempts to get the system adopted in Britain, it was not until 1965 that the Government announced that it was encouraging the adoption of the metric system of weights and measures. The change-over to decimal coinage was made on 15 Feb. 1971, the first of the new coins having been issued in 1968. *See* **Section N** for SI units.

Mezzotint, an engraving from copper or steel produced by instruments which burnish and scrape away portions of the surface, and yield an impression effectually graded in light and shade.

Mica. The mica of commerce is a nearly transparent mineral, which has great heat-resisting power, and can be split into thin plates. The most important micas are muscovite (potassium mica), the commoner variety, phlogopite (mag-

nesium mica), and biotite, the magnesium and iron mica.

Michael, St., and George, St., an order of knighthood originally founded for the Ionian Isles and Malta in 1818, and reorganised in 1869, so as to admit Crown servants connected with the Colonies. The Earl of Derby, Earl Russell, and Earl Grey were the first of the new knights.

Michaelmas Day, the festival day of St. Michael and All Angels, Sept. 29th, one of the English quarter days.

Microbe, a term proposed by Sédillot in 1878 to denote any microscopic organism, vegetable or animal, or found on the borderland between the two great natural kingdoms. The term is commonly used, but not by scientists.

Microelectronics, a rapidly developing technology of the 1960s which reduces entire electronic circuits to minute size and embeds them in tiny chips of solid material. These are then called integrated circuits. A circuit consisting of, say, a dozen transistors and fifty resistors can be built into a small piece of semiconductor (q.v.) measuring not more than a couple of millimetres in any direction. Hundreds of these circuits can be made simultaneously in pennysize wafers of silicon about one-hundredth of an inch thick. There are great advantages in cheapness, reliability, robustness, and speed of electronic performance. The small size is in itself an advantage in space vehicles and medical instruments. Applications to missile control systems, computers, and communications equipment are no doubt only the first fruits of this new achievement of the current technological revolution.

Micrometer, an instrument for measuring minute distances; usually attached to the eye-pieces of a microscope or telescope, and consisting of two very fine hairs or wires stretched across the field of view, one fixed, the other movable. It was invented by William Gascoigne in the 17th cent. and improved by later inventors. Sir Joseph Whitworth made one in 1858 to measure the millionth part of an inch.

Micro-organisms, the collective term applied to several types of organism, the most important of which are fungi, viruses, bacteria, and protozoa. It is a classification of convenience in biological studies. These organisms are generally simple in their environmental requirements (e.g., have simple nutritional needs) and in cellular organisation. This makes them very suitable for modern biological research. Much of the information on the nature of the genetic code (**F31**) was obtained from experiments on these organisms.

Microphone, device for converting the acoustic energy of sound waves into waves of electrical energy, used in sound amplifying systems. Developed independently by Edison (1877) and Hughes (1878).

Microscope, invented about 1590 by Janssen, and improved by Galileo, Fontana, and others, is an instrument which by a lens system magnifies minute objects. Microscopes are simple, compound, and binocular. The more powerful instruments have a magnifying capacity of as much as 10,000 diameters. See also Electron Microscope.

Middle Ages (c. A.D. 400–1500), usually considered to be the period between the decline and fall of the Western Roman Empire and the fall of Constantinople to the Turks (see **A4–7**). The period covers (a) an earlier part ending with the 12th cent. (sometimes called the Dark Ages) when science was dead, when theology was the main preoccupation, and when the language of the learned West was Latin; and (b) a later age of Arabian influence when alchemy and astrology (at that time indistinguishable from astronomy) were central interests, technology was advancing, and Greek learning was transmitted by Arab scholars. Characteristic features of the mediaeval scene were monasticism (**J33**), the Crusades (q.v.), Gothic art (q.v.), feudalism (**J20**), and the supremacy of Islam in the field of learning. The period came to an end with the ushering in of the Renaissance (**J44**).

Midrash, name given to the homiletical interpretation of some of the Hebrew Scriptures in which allegory and legendary illustration were freely used. Compiled by Jewish rabbis from c. A.D. 200.

Millenary Petition was presented to James I. in 1603, on behalf of nearly 1,000 Puritan Ministers against certain of the rites and ceremonies of the Church of England. The Hampton Court Conference was the outcome of this petition.

Millennium, a period of a thousand years. The term is specifically used of the period of a thousand years during which, according to Rev. xx. 1–5, Christ will reign in person on earth. The Millenarians are a sect that interprets the "Millennium" as beginning with the commencement of the 6001st year from the Creation, which, according to Archbishop Ussher (1581–1650), was in 4004 B.C.

Millipede. Arthropods (**F33**) allied to the centipedes, from which they differ in having two pairs of legs to each body segment (except the first three) instead of one pair. Worm-like in shape but with a pair of antennae on the head, they can do much harm to garden plants. See **T29(1)**.

Millstone-Grit, a series of grits and sandstones of deltaic origin underlying the coal measures of the Carboniferous system and attaining in England a thickness in parts of 5,000 ft. It is from this rock that millstones have been made from time immemorial.

Mimicry, protective similarity of an animal to another animal or to inanimate objects. Examples of the former are the hover flies, which mimic wasps and bees; of the latter, leaf insects, stick insects, and caterpillars that look like dead twigs.

Mink. Semi-aquatic mammals closely related to polecats. There is one American species and one European. The fur, which varies light to dark brown, is soft and thick, and is among the most valuable of commercial furs. They now live in the wild in the British Isles.

Minnesingers were minstrel poets of Germany who, during the 12th and 13th cent., composed and sang verses of heroism and love. They were of knightly rank, the counterpart of the French troubadours. See **E3(2)**.

Minnow, a small fresh-water fish of the carp family, abounding in all the waters of Europe; it has a mottled back and silvery belly, and forms a popular bait for trout.

Minstrels were originally specially appointed instrumentalists and singers—pipers, harpers, and gleemen—engaged by barons and manorial lords to amuse their tenants. Later, minstrels assumed nomadic habits, made their way into the houses of the great, and were generally welcome. By Elizabeth's time, however, they were too numerous, and were classed as "rogues and vagabonds," along with actors.

Miracle Plays, popular in England in the 15th cent., were usually religious in character, representing some of the dramatic incidents of the Bible. Staging of plays was one of the many activities of the Guilds of those days. See **M41**.

Mirage, an optical illusion often observed in desert regions when the objects on the surface of the earth often seem some distance away appear as if reflected in a surface of water. Mirage is due to the unequal heating of the different parts of the atmosphere, which bends the light rays, and so produces distorted images.

Mishna, the first part of the Talmud, setting forth the "Oral Law" of the Jews.

Missal, the name of the mass-book of the Roman Church compiled 492–96 by Pope Gelasius I., and revised by Gregory I., 590–604. The present Roman Missal was sanctioned by the Council of Trent 1545–63. In the Anglican Communion the Book of Common Prayer superseded the Missal in 1549.

Mistle Thrush receives its name from its partiality to the mistletoe-berry. Larger than the song-thrush, with spotted breast rather than speckled.

Mistletoe, a parasitic evergreen with white berries used as a decoration at Christmas-time. The familiar mistletoe of Europe is the *Viscum album*, which grows on the boughs of lime, willow, apple, poplar, maple, ash, hawthorn, but seldom on oak-trees. It was sacred to the Druids, and in Norse mythology it was a mistletoe dart that killed the god Baldur.

Mistral, a cold, dry, northerly wind peculiar to the French coast of the Mediterranean.

Mitosis, cell division whereby each daughter cell

receives the same number of chromosomes as the parent cell. When the gametes (sex cells) are formed a special type of division occurs (meiosis) in which the number of chromosomes is halved. *See* F30(2)

Mitre, the twofold pointed head-dress of bishops and certain abbots of the Western Church and occasionally of other ecclesiastics.

Moa, the name for several species of ostrich-like extinct birds related to the New Zealand kiwi. The largest species, *Diornis maximus,* stood 8 ft. 7 in. high. Became extinct about 500 years ago.

Moabite Stone, a stone of the 9th cent. B.C. containing the earliest known inscription in Phoenician characters, and discovered in the highlands of Moab in 1868. It is now in the Louvre, Paris. It records the campaign between Moab and Israel, a differing account of which is given in the Old Testament.

Mode. *See* Average.

Moderator, a material used to slow down neutrons in an atomic pile. Examples of moderators are pure graphite and heavy water. *See* **Nuclear Reactors.**

Mohole Project, a scheme to bore through the earth's crust to take samples of the mantle rocks beneath. Drilling trials, led by an American team of geophysicists, began in 1961 near the island of Guadalupe off the Mexican coast in the Pacific. The project, however, was cancelled in 1966 on account of the escalating cost. Russian geophysicists have already started on a similar experiment, but are boring through land rocks where the digging will have to be much deeper and higher temperatures are likely to be met with. The name " Anti-Cosmos " has been given to the project. The boundary between the earth's crustal and mantle rocks is known as the Mohorovičić Discontinuity, or, more simply, as the Moho. *See* F8(1).

Molasses, sugar-cane juice in its uncrystallised form after boiling. The crystallised part is the raw sugar. Used to make rum.

Mole, a small burrowing animal with long, sensitive nose, about the size of a small rat, with short legs and forefeet armed with strong claws for digging in the earth. Their subterranean dwellings are of curiously ingenious construction, and they do not often leave them except to make raids on mice, frogs, snails, etc. The earth-worm, however, is the mole's chief item of food. Not to be confused with the vole which has a blunt nose.

Mole, or gram molecular weight. *See* F21(2).

Molecular Biology, a rapidly expanding branch of science mainly concerned with cell structure and function at a molecular level, in particular with genes and enzymes and the interaction between the two. Recent work in Britain has led to the unravelling of the structure of DNA, the hereditary substance of the genes, and has played a major part in uncovering the molecular mechanism of the transfer of hereditary information and the nature of the genetic code. Crystallisation of the first enzyme (urease) took place in 1929; the gene as a definite chemical entity was discovered in 1943. *See* F26–32.

Molecule. A group of atoms held together by chemical forces. *See* F12(2), 20, *also* Macromolecule.

Molybdenum, symbol Mo, a fairly hard white metal with properties resembling those of chromium. Its commonest ore is the sulphide, molybdenite. The chief use of the metal is in the manufacture of alloy steels.

Monasticism. *See* J33.

Monazite, a cerium mineral containing some thorium. Occurs as grains, often as sand (" monazite sands "), derived from granites. Deposits occur in India (Travancore), Russia, Norway, Madagascar, S. Africa, Brazil, U.S.A.

Monday, the second day of the week, called by the Anglo-Saxons *Monandaeg* (moon-day).

Mongoose, species of mammals related to the civets, feeding on vermin and reptiles. These animals, which have long tails and short legs, occur in Africa and Asia (especially India). The biggest mongoose is the Egyptian ichneumon, and this has been introduced into the W. Indies because of its ability to kill large poisonous snakes.

Monitor, a family of lizards most resembling dragons. There are about 30 species widely distributed over the tropical parts of Asia, Australia, and Africa.

Monroe Doctrine, a principle of American policy declining any European intervention in political affairs of the American continent, outlined by President Monroe in 1823. At the same time interference was disclaimed with applying European colonies in the Western Hemisphere. The American Civil War hampered the application of the doctrine for some time, but afterwards the United States firmly insisted on it. The Doctrine is not international law, but a national policy of the U.S.A.

Monsoons, regular persistent winds which blow at certain seasons in middle latitudes, mainly in South and East Asia. Their occurrence is related to the great changes of pressure which take place between summer and winter over the land mass. In India the south-west monsoon (June–Oct.) is moisture-laden from its long passage over the sea and in the higher regions, especially there is heavy rainfall. Sudden reversal of the wind results in the cold north-east monsoon (Oct.–March) which is dry on account of the shelter afforded by the mountain ranges to the north. Frequently the term " monsoon " is applied to denote the associated rainfall without reference to the actual winds.

Monstrance, an ornamental transparent receptacle in which the Sacred Host is carried in procession or exposed for adoration.

Month, the 12th part of the calendar year. A lunar month is the interval of new moon to new moon or full moon to full moon; mean length, 29 days, 12 hours, 44 minutes, 2·87 seconds. A sidereal month represents the time of the moon's revolution from a given star back to the same again, 27 days, 7 hours, 43 minutes, 11·5 seconds. In English law, since 1926, a month, unless otherwise expressed, means a calendar month.

Monument of London, a 202 ft. column, overlooking Billingsgate, designed by Wren and erected (1671–77) to mark the starting-point of the Great Fire of London (1666). The original inscription upon it ascribed the fire to " the treachery and malice of the popish faction," which stood down to 1831, when the words were erased as objectionable. The black marble staircase has 345 steps (311 to the balcony).

Moon, the earth's satellite, 2,160 miles in diameter and 238,857 miles distant from the earth. It rotates in the same time as it revolves round the earth (27 days 7 hours 43 minutes), so that the same face is always presented to the earth. The lunar surface is pockmarked by innumerable collisions with solid particles of all sizes. Unlike the earth, it is unprotected by any atmosphere and for aeons of time it has been exposed to every kind of cosmic influence, including the parching effect of solar radiation. All moonlight derives from the sun but on the whole it is a pretty poor reflector. The exploration of the moon by means of rockets began in 1959 when the Russian *Luna 2* crashlanded on the plains of the *Mare Imbrium.* 1969 will be remembered as the year of the U.S. *Apollo* triumphs when man first set foot on the moon. The samples of lunar rock and dust brought back to earth are now being studied by lunar scientists but it is unlikely that the great problem of the history and structure of the moon will be satisfactorily solved until a geologist gets to work with his hammer on the spot. The exploration of the moon at close range by means of spacecraft was made possible only by parallel developments in several branches of technology—rocket propulsion, long-range radio and television transmission, electronic computer control. *See also* F54–7.

Moorhen, a widely distributed bird of the rail family, a common resident in the British Isles. The adult is blackish with white under tail-coverts, a white line on the flanks, and a yellow-tipped bill. The frontal shield and the base of the bill are vermilion. It bobs its head, flirts its tail, and dives well. The nest is usually placed close to the water's edge or on an overhanging branch. In feeding the young the parents are sometimes helped by their offspring of a previous brood of the season. In N. America the bird is known as the Florida Gallinule.

Moors, the name given to the Moslems who live in N.W. Africa and to those who once lived in Spain. In 711 Moorish Arabs invaded Spain and spread beyond the Pyrenees into France, where they were driven back by the end of the century. Spain, however, remained virtually under Moorish domination until the 11th cent., and during that period was the most civilised and prosperous part of Western Europe. In the arts and sciences the impact of Moorish culture was profound and lasting. Examples of the brilliant splendour of Moorish architecture are still to be seen in Toledo, Córdoba, Seville, and Granada. During the long struggle for the Christian reconquest thousands were killed and expelled, and in 1492 Granada, their last remaining kingdom, was forced to surrender. They were virtually exterminated by the Inquisition, and the last were expelled in 1609.

Moose, the largest members of the deer family. The N. American Moose stands 5½–6½ ft. high, and has huge palmate antlers. There is another New World species, occurring in Alaska. The European species is known as the elk.

Morse Alphabet, a system of dots and dashes, intended to be used in combination with the indicator in telegraphy; but usually read by sound, the receiving operator writing down the words in the system as transmitted. This system of signals was invented by the American inventor and artist Samuel Finley Breese Morse (1791–1872) of Charlestown, Massachusetts.

Mosaic, art of arranging small pieces of coloured glass, marble, or other materials in such a fashion as to produce a decorative pattern. Some of the best examples of Byzantine mosaics are to be seen at Ravenna, Rome, Venice, and Sicily.

Mosque, a Mohammedan church, the greatest being that of Santa Sophia at Istanbul, now converted into a museum of Byzantine art.

Mosquito, small two-winged flies with long legs and and slender body. Their larvae are aquatic. The females of some species are blood-suckers, and thus come to transmit the blood parasites which cause malaria and yellow fever for example. *See* **DDT** *and* **Gammexane.**

Mosses. Most mosses live in moist habitats, but there are some species that can withstand desiccation and are adapted to live on rocks and tree trunks.

Moths, of the insect order, *Lepidoptera,* differing from butterflies which have clubbed antennae, in having feathery, sometimes thin, pointed antennae, rarely clubbed. Most are nocturnal, and the pupae are usually brown and enclosed in a cocoon unlike those of the butterfly, which are usually naked. *See also* **Lepidoptera.**

Motion, Laws of. According to Newton: (1) A body continues in its state of rest or uniform motion in a straight line except in so far as it is compelled by external forces to change that state. (2) Rate of change of momentum is proportional to the applied force, and takes place in the direction in which the force acts. (3) To every action there is an equal and opposite reaction. These laws are the basis of almost all engineering and everyday mechanics. Corrections to them have been made by relativity and the quantum theory. *See* **F15, 16.**

Mule, a cross between a male ass and a horse mare; a hinny is a cross between an ass mare and a horse stallion. Also the name of the spinning machine invented by Crompton in 1779 which combined the principle of Hargreaves' spinning jenny with the machine invented by Arkwright.

Mullions, the vertical bars dividing the lights in a window, forming a highly decorative feature in the Tudor period of English Gothic architecture. The cross-beam or horizontal bar of wood or stone in a mullioned window is styled a transom. *See* **Windows.**

Munich Agreement. In Sept. 1938 Mr. Neville Chamberlain and M. Daladier, British and French Premiers, reached agreement with Hitler at Munich for the dismemberment of Czechoslovakia, primarily for the benefit of Germany. Czechoslovakia itself was not consulted, nor Russia who with Britain and France had jointly pledged themselves to uphold the independence of Czechoslovakia. Hitler had been threatening that country for some time, but every concession had been met by further demands. After three visits to Germany, during which Hitler raised his demands, the British and French statesmen gave way. Mr. Chamberlain declared on return that he had secured "Peace in our Time." The Agreement was the subject of much controversy. Hitler seized Czechoslovakia in March 1939.

Muscles. *See* **F34(1).**

Musk Deer, a small deer of the Himalayas, standing about 20 in. high. It is grey in colour, slightly brindled, and carries a small pouch in the abdominal region, containing what is commercially known as musk, an article which is of great value in the manufacture of various perfumes. The active constituent of musk, muscone, is now made synthetically. The species was becoming rare on account of its slaughter for its musk.

Mutton Bird, an Australasian name of controversial origin for a shearwater or petrel, *e.g.,* the Short-tailed and Sooty Shearwaters and the Great-winged, Kermadec, and White-headed Petrels. The young are taken by hand from their burrows for human food.

Myrrh, a resinous substance obtained from a tree of the natural order *Amyridaceae,* growing plentifully in Abyssinia and Arabia. Its use for embalming, medical, and aromatic purposes may be traced back to the most remote times.

Mysteries, Greek, secret mystic ceremonies of the ancient Greeks, religious drama accompanied by dancing, the most well known being the Eleusinian and Orphic ceremonies.

Mystery Plays were mediaeval religious dramas performed by priests at great ecclesiastic festivals, particularly in France and Bavaria, staging the Nativity, Passion, and Resurrection. *See* **M41.**

N

Nadir, one of the two poles of the horizon, the other being the zenith. The nadir is the pole vertically below the observer's feet.

Nahum, one of the books of the Minor Prophets of the Old Testament. It is a prophecy of doom on the approaching sack of Nineveh which fell in 612 B.C. to the Medes and Babylonians.

Nantes, Edict of, was a decree promulgated by Henry IV. of France in 1598, giving full freedom of worship to the Protestants of the country. It was the revocation of this edict in 1685 by Louis XIV. that drove hundreds of thousands of French Huguenots to this country.

Naphtha, a liquid combustible believed to have been one of the ingredients of " Greek fire." Naphtha is a light, highly inflammable oil obtained by distilling petroleum, shale oil, or coal tar. The petroleum naphtha consists of a mixture of paraffins; that from shale contains olefines as well as paraffins. Coal-tar naphtha contains xylol.

Naphthalene is an aromatic hydrocarbon; it is obtained from coal tar, and its derivatives are much used in the manufacture of colours for dyers and printers. " Moth balls " are made of naphthalene.

Narcotic, a medical dictionary definition is that a narcotic is a drug that produces stupor, complete insensibility, or sleep. In terms of drug addiction, a narcotic has been defined as altering and distorting the user's perception of himself and of the external world, being taken primarily for that purpose. *See* **P22–24.**

Nardus, a genus of coarse grasses, growing on bleak upland heaths and hill slopes. *Nardus stricta,* known as " mat-weed," is a British species.

Nargbile, an oriental tobacco pipe so constructed that smoke passes through water and up a long flexible tube before reaching lips of the smoker.

Narrative Art, a type of art popular during the late 19th cent. based on the principle: " every picture tells a story "—*e.g.,* such paintings as the little Royalist boy surrounded by his anxious family and confronted across a table by the Roundheads bearing the title: " When did you last see your father? " The term, although often applied derisively, suitably describes many works of considerable artistic merit: *e.g.,* Hogarth's *Marriage à la Mode,* his series of eight engravings entitled *A Rake's Progress,* the Bayeux Tapestry, and many Babylonian and Egyptian friezes.

Naseby, Battle of, was fought on June 14, 1645, between the Royalists under the command of Prince Rupert and the King, and the Parliamentarians under Fairfax and Cromwell. It resulted in a complete defeat for Charles.

National Anthem, a musical composition with words, officially adopted for ceremonial use as an expression of patriotism and loyalty to a national cause. The national anthem of the United Kingdom is " God Save the Queen " which has been in use since about the middle of the 18th cent. There is some doubt about its origin. It has been variously attributed to Dr. John Bull, Henry Carey, and James Oswald.

National Assembly, the name taken by the body responsible for the opening stages of the French Revolution and subsequently by other sovereign bodies in France and elsewhere.

National Covenant, an oath and declaration subscribed to by the Scottish Presbyterians in 1638 to maintain their religion against Charles I.'s episcopalianising designs.

National Gallery, established in 1824 at Pall Mall, London, with the Angerstein Collection of 38 pictures, purchased for £60,000 as a nucleus. The existing building which was opened in 1838 has been enlarged several times. The National Gallery at Millbank, the Tate Gallery, was given to the nation by Sir Henry Tate in 1897.

Nationalisation is the taking over by the State of the ownership and operation of an industry or service—*e.g.*, coal-mining, railway transport, gas, and electricity. Where this is done without revolution, compensation is usually paid to the previous owners at what is regarded as a fair market price; the compensation is sometimes paid in cash, but more often in fixed-interest-bearing bonds issued either by the State or by the administration of the nationalised service, which is usually a publicly appointed Board or Corporation acting, with greater or lesser autonomy, under the direction of a Minister responsible to Parliament. In some cases the State becomes a partner with private investors in the ownership of a particular enterprise, *e.g.*, oil companies, such as the former Anglo-Iranian and some recent French examples. Nationalisation is usually brought about by a separate Act of Parliament relating to each industry or service taken over. These Acts, in Great Britain, include provision for joint consultation at all levels between the administering boards or commissions and the workers employed and their Trade Unions. When, as in the Soviet Union, nationalisation occurs as an outcome of social revolution no compensation is paid to the dispossessed owners.

National Parks. Under the National Parks Act 1949 a National Parks Commission was set up to create National Parks in England and Wales. Ten have been established: Peak District, Lake District, Snowdonia, Yorkshire Dales, Exmoor, Brecon Beacons, Dartmoor, Pembrokeshire Coast, North Yorks Moors, and Northumberland. They cover an area of some 5,260 square miles, or 9 per cent of the total area of England and Wales. It is not intended to change the character of these territories but to control their development so as to harmonise with the two dominant principles: (*a*) that the characteristic beauty of the landscape within the Park area shall be preserved and (*b*) that the visiting public shall have ample access and facilities for recreation and enjoyment. The National Parks Commission also has power to designate areas in England and Wales outside the national parks as "areas of outstanding natural beauty." Twenty-seven areas had been designated by 1971: Gower, Quantock Hills, Lleyn, Surrey Hills, Dorset, Northumberland Coast, Cannock Chase, Shropshire Hills, Malvern Hills, Cornwall, N. Devon, S. Devon, E. Devon, E. Hampshire, Isle of Wight, Forest of Bowland, Chichester Harbour, and Solway Coast, Chilterns, Sussex Downs, Cotswolds, Anglesey, South Hampshire Coast, Kent Downs, Norfolk Coast, Dedham Vale and Suffolk Coast and Heaths. Under the Countryside Act, 1968, the National Parks Commission has been reconstituted as the Countryside Commission. *See also* Long Distance Routes.

National Physical Laboratory, situated at Teddington, is one of the world's largest and best-

equipped laboratories. It was first established in 1900 under the control of the Royal Society. In 1964 it became part of the Ministry of Technology. It conducts research in its three main groups: Measurement, Materials, and Engineering Sciences, and maintains British primary standards and physical units.

National Portrait Gallery, established in 1856, and now located in a building in St. Martin's Lane adjoining the National Gallery. Contains portraits of eminent people in history, literature, art, etc., and a valuable collection of medals and autographs.

National Trust, founded in 1895. " A non-profit-making organisation incorporated by Act of Parliament for the purposes of promoting the permanent preservation of lands and buildings of historic interest or natural beauty for the benefit and access of the people." As a consequence of gifts of public-spirited individuals the Trust now owns many acres of magnificent scenery and property, including mediaeval castles, bird sanctuaries, ancient monuments, birthplaces and homes of famous men, and classic examples of domestic architecture, preserved for the enjoyment of present and future generations. Since 1946 lands and houses of interest to the nation may be given to the National Trust in lieu of death duties.

Nativity. There are three nativity festivals of the Christian Church:Christmas, 25 Dec., festival of birth of Christ; the birthday of the Virgin Mary (8 Sept.); and of St. John the Baptist (24 June).

Natterjack, a curious warty, prominent-eyed, brown toad (*Bufo calamita*), having a bright yellow line down the middle of its back. It utters a muttering sort of croak, hence its name.

Natural Law. *See* J35.

Naturalism in painting has been defined as " a direct and spontaneous approach to nature " —to landscape primarily. Constable, Turner, and Boudin were among the great naturalist painters of the 19th cent. *See* Section I for naturalism in drama.

" Nautical Almanac," published under the authority of the Admiralty, is always issued four years in advance, and contains information specially prepared for the use of navigators and astronomers. It first appeared in 1767.

Nautilus, a term now applied only to the pearly-shelled nautilus, the sole surviving example of the four-gilled section of the *Cephalopoda*. Its fossil relatives are called Ammonites. The spiral shell is divided into a number of compartments, the animal living in the last and largest chamber. There are three or four species, all living in tropical seas. The Paper Nautilus is not related to the Pearly Nautilus, belonging to the same order as the octopus.

Nave is the body or main open portion of a cathedral or church, and extends from the chief entrance to the choir, or chancel, and is usually flanked by aisles. A nave, in mechanics, indicates the " hub " or central part of a wheel.

Neandertal, the name of the valley lying between Düsseldorf and Wuppertal, where in a limestone cave a now famous skull of a very early species of prehistoric man was discovered in 1856. Fossils of Neandertal man have been found over a wide area, and from archaeological evidence he began to disappear from Europe during the last Ice Age, about 40,000 B.C. *See* F48(2).

Necromancy, " the black art," was in olden times much believed in, and supposed to be an occult power by which its practitioners could converse with the spirits of the dead and learn the future.

Negroes are the dark-skinned, woolly-haired races, natives of tropical Africa, or descendants of such natives. There are many different racial types, including the Ashanti of Ghana, the Kikuyu of Kenya, the Yoruba of Nigeria, the Pygmies (nomadic hunters living in the equatorial forests), the Bushmen of the Kalahari Desert, the Hottentots of South Africa (who have largely lost their identity), the so-called Bantu peoples of Central and Southern Africa, and many others. Their culture is rich in folklore, and they have great artistic gifts in music, dancing and sculpture. About 25 million people of Negro descent are in N. and S. America, the European slave trade having taken them there from their homes in W. Africa. *See also* African Languages,M43.

Negus, the name given to any mixture of wine and water, and said to have been named after Colonel Francis Negus about 1714. The sovereign of Abyssinia is styled the Negus.

Nekton, term used to differentiate actively swimming aquatic organisms (*e.g.*, fishes) from the " drifters " or plankton.

Nelson Column, in Trafalgar Square, London, designed by Mr. William Railton, was chosen from among a number of designs—temples, obelisks and various sculptural groups—sent in as a result of a competition held in 1839. The erection of the column was begun in 1840. Twenty-six years later the lions designed by Landseer were set up at the foot of the completed column. The statue of Nelson himself was made by E. H. Bailey and the bronze reliefs at the base executed by Carew, Woodington, Ternouth, and Watson, representing the Battles of the Nile, St. Vincent, Copenhagen, and Trafalgar. Height 170 ft., executed in Portland stone instead of granite, as originally planned, at a cost of £46,000.

Néné or Hawaiian Goose. At the Severn Wildfowl Trust at Slimbridge Mr. Peter Scott has saved this bird from extinction.

Neo-Classical School of Art, a French school of painting and sculpture belonging to the late 18th and early 19th cent. and founded by Jacques David, the Academician, republican, and later admirer of Bonaparte. His classicism probably arose from his republican sympathies, which caused him to paint such works as the *Oath of the Horatii* (Louvre) drawing analogies between revolutionary France and Rome. Because of these views he revolted against the romantic and sensual art of Watteau and Greuze and equally against the realism of Chardin. Among his many famous pupils was Ingres, who later assumed leadership of the school.

Neodymium, an element belonging to the rare earth metal group. Discovered by Welsbach in 1885.

Neo-Impressionism, a development of Impressionism (*q.v.*) by Seurat and Signac during the 1880s who devised the method of painting known as *pointillism* (the application of pure colours in minute touches to form a composite whole, based on a knowledge of the laws of colour and optics). One of the best-known examples of this technique is Seurat's *Sunday Afternoon on the Grand Jatte.*

Neon, inert gas present in air to the extent of about 1 part in 65,000. The crimson glow produced when an electric discharge passes through the gas is familiar in advertising signs.

Neoprene, generic name for a class of synthetic rubbers made from acetylene.

Nepotism, the bestowal of patronage by reason of relationship rather than of merit. It had its origin in the custom of certain Popes to enrich their families out of the offices of the Church.

Neptune. Apart from Pluto this is the most distant of the planets, estimated to be about 2,793 million miles from the sun, and taking about 165 years to revolve around it. Discovered by the German astronomer Galle on Sept. 23, 1846, after its existence had been predicted by Leverrier and Adams.

Neptunium, element 93, one of the four new elements discovered during the progress of the atomic bomb project in the second world war. Neptunium is formed when a neutron enters a nucleus of Uranium 238, and it decays radioactively to yield plutonium.

Neutrino, a neutral particle which carries energy and spin and although possessing little or no mass plays an important part in the interaction of other fundamental particles. The discovery that there are in fact two distinct neutrinos, each with its counterpart, was discovered in 1962 as a result of an experiment made with the 30,000 million-electronvolt proton accelerator at Brookhaven. *See* **F14.**

Neutron, a neutral particle present in all atomic nuclei except the hydrogen nucleus which is a single proton. In the development of nuclear science and technology the neutron has played a most important role and neutrons produce the radioisotopes now widely used in medicine, agriculture, and industry. Neutrons and protons are termed nucleons. *See* **F10, 14.**

New Deal. The measures taken by President Roosevelt in U.S.A. in 1933 to overcome the great economic crisis which broke out at the end of 1929 and to restore the social security threatened by it. The measures were drawn up by a group of experts called a Brains Trust and they provided for recovery by a programme of public works, including large-scale construction of houses and large-scale assistance to farmers. Loans were granted and authorities formed to stimulate activities which reduced the workless from 17 millions to between 7 and 10 millions. Unemployment relief was regulated and enlarged; and social insurance (which for decades had been a subject of dispute, being held to be contrary to American principles of self-help) was introduced. Many of the changes have become a permanent part of American legislation though some laws were repealed by the U.S. Supreme Court as being unconstitutional.

Newgate Prison, now pulled down and replaced by the Central Criminal Court, opened in 1907, was situated near the point where once stood one of the old London city gates. There is a record of a prison upon this spot in the 13th cent. Later a new one was built by the executors of Richard Whittington, but this was destroyed by the Great Fire in 1666. Still another new prison on this site was erected between 1778 and 1780. In the Gordon Riots of the latter year it was destroyed by fire and re-erected. It was not used as a prison after 1880.

News Letters were an early form of newspaper, popular in the time of Charles II. They consisted of items of news and gossip collected at the various coffee-houses and other places of public resort. They often included blank pages on which readers wrote their private letters.

Newspapers. The first news-books to be published at regular intervals in Britain appeared in 1662 with news of what was going on abroad translated from German and Italian news-sheets. Licence to print was obtained from the Star Chamber, which until its abolition in 1641 allowed only the printing of foreign news. With the lifting of the ban on domestic news the Press became free. In the reign of Queen Anne English newspapers employed writers of great intellectual power and versatility. Despite the newspaper tax introduced in 1712, the number of newspapers published in London in 1776 had increased to 53, though the standard of writing was below that of earlier times. The development of the Press was greatly assisted in the 19th cent. by the abolition of the " taxes on knowledge," by the introduction of the cheap postal system, and by improvements in printing, distribution, collection of news, and advertising. The *London Gazette,* founded in 1665 (and still appearing twice weekly as the official organ of the Government), is the oldest newspaper living. *The Times,* known throughout the world, began as the *Daily Universal Register* in 1785, and adopted its present title in 1788. The *Manchester Guardian* (renamed *Guardian* in 1959), once a provincial but now a national newspaper with a world-wide reputation, began as a weekly in 1821, and became a daily in 1855. The *Scotsman,* founded as a weekly in 1817 and established as a daily in 1855, and the *Glasgow Herald,* which began as the *Glasgow Advertiser* in 1783, are the leading Scottish newspapers. The London Press, which is national, publishes 10 daily, 2 evening, and 7 Sunday newspapers.

Newt, amphibians of lizard shape and mottled markings. There are three British species, the largest being the Great-Crested Newt (*Triturus cristatus*), which attains a length of 6 in.

Newton, the unit of force in the SI system of units. Under its influence a body with a mass of 1 kilogramme will accelerate at a rate of 1 metre per second each second.

Newton's Rings. Concentric circular rings, due to the phenomenon of interference, which are seen around the point of contact of a slightly convex lens with a flat plate of glass.

New Towns. The new towns in Britain established under New Town Acts, 1946, 1959, and 1965, with dates of designation are: Basildon (1949), Bracknell (1949), Corby (1950), Crawley (1947), Cwmbran (1949), East Kilbride (1947), Glenrothes (1948), Harlow (1947), Hatfield (1948), Hemel Hempstead (1947), Newton

Aycliffe (1947), Peterlee (1948), Stevenage (1946), Welwyn Garden City (1948); Cumbernauld (1956), Dawley (1963), Irvine (1966), Livingston (1962), Milton Keynes (1967), Newtown (mid-Wales) (1967), Peterborough (1967), Redditch (1964), Runcorn (1964), Skelmersdale (1961), Washington (1964); designated under Town Development Act 1952 Killingworth (1959) and Cramlington (1963); designated under New Towns Act of N. Ireland 1965 Craigavon (1965), and Antrim/Ballymena (1967). In addition a new regional city is to be built in the Preston–Leyland–Chorley area of Lancashire and the new town of Dawley with neighbouring Wellington and Oakengates forms the new town of Telford. It is also proposed to expand Ipswich, Northampton, and Warrington and to build cities along the Tay, Solway, and Humber estuaries.

New Year's Day, Jan 1. The first New Year's festival of which we have record is that constituted by Numa 713 B.C., and dedicated to Janus.

Nibelungenlied, the German epic of the early 13th cent. comprising numerous mythical poems or sagas of which several English translations exist. Wagner's *The Ring of the Nibelungs* was based largely on Norse legends and on the Niebelungenlied.

Nicene Creed, a summary of the principles of Christian faith, first issued in 325 by the Council of Nicaea (summoned by the emperor Constantine the Great) for the purpose of thwarting the Arian heresy and asserting the godhead of Christ. Date of Easter fixed at Council of Nicaea.

Nickel, silver-coloured metal, symbol Ni, fairly soft though harder than iron. Chief source of the metal is the nickel sulphide in iron–copper pyrites deposits in Ontario. Chief uses are: in electroplating, in coins, as an element in alloy steels. A novel method of making pure nickel (by treating the metal with carbon monoxide and heating the resulting liquid, nickel carbonyl) was developed in 1890 by Mond. This discovery led to many technical advances in industrial chemistry, one of which is the production of catalysts for a variety of processes.

Niello Work was in considerable vogue in the Middle Ages, and is said to have suggested the idea of engraving upon copper. It was produced by rubbing a mixture of silver, lead, copper, sulphur, and borax into engravings on silver, and some highly decorative results were obtained.

Night Heron, a stocky, short-legged heron of black and white plumage, red eyes, and yellowish legs, crepuscular except in breeding season, and an occasional visitor to Britain.

Nightingale, a familiar singing bird which visits the southern counties of England every summer, and is sometimes found as far north as Yorkshire. It is a shy, brown bird, not often seen, but the song of the male, usually heard in the late evening or at early morn, is of remarkable sweetness and variety. After its wooing period is over its song ceases.

Nightjar, nocturnal, insectivorous bird, owl-like in appearance, with mottled brown plumage of "dead leaf" pattern, and a churring song. It is a common breeding visitor to the British Isles, Apr. to Sept., and lays its eggs on bare ground.

Niobium is a metal element, symbol Nb, related to vanadium. Technical development has been slow because of its rare occurrence, although niobium is now used in ferrous alloys to increase resistance to corrosion and produce steel which can be used at high temperatures.

Nitre *or* **Saltpetre,** is now mostly manufactured by the double decomposition of sodium nitrate and potassium chloride. Its chief use is the manufacture of gunpowder and fireworks. It has been manufactured in England since 1625.

Nitrogen, a non-combustible gaseous element, symbol N, devoid of taste or smell, and constituting nearly four-fifths of the atmospheric air. Nitrogen compounds are essential to plants and animals, and are used in fertilisers.

Nitro-Glycerine, an explosive yellow fluid produced by mixing small quantities of glycerine with a combination of one part of nitric acid and two parts of sulphuric acid. By itself it is a dangerously explosive substance to handle. In 1867, Nobel produced dynamite, a safe explosive made by absorbing nitro-glycerine in kieselguhr.

Nitrous Oxide, a compound of nitrogen and oxygen possessing mild anaesthetic power. Termed "laughing gas" on account of its exhilarating effect. It is still used in dentistry, and for minor operations and has proved useful in a new technique for finding leaks in water mains.

Nobel Prizes. The Nobel Foundation was established at the beginning of the century to give effect to the wishes expressed by Alfred Nobel in his Will. By the terms of the Will the judges are the Swedish Academy of Science, the Caroline Medico-Surgical Institute, the Swedish Academy, and five members of the Norwegian Storting. The award of a Nobel Prize is accepted as the highest form of international recognition in the field in which it is given: physics, chemistry, medicine, literature, peace, and, since 1969, economics. *See* L126-8.

Nones were dates of the Roman calendar which fell on the 5th of each month, excepting Mar., May, July, and Oct., when they fell on the 7th.

Non Nobis Domine! (" Not unto us, O Lord! "), a musical canon, sung as a grace at public feasts (traditionally attributed to Byrd).

Norman Architecture is English Romanesque (*q.v.*), which flourished from the time of the Norman Conquest and was gradually superseded through a transition period (*c.* 1175–1200) by the introduction of the pointed arch characteristic of the Early English (first Gothic style). Typical of Norman churches are the round arches, thick walls, massive cylindrical columns, with throughout the basic pattern of the square and the circle. Some churches (*e.g.,* the Temple church in London or the chapel at Ludlow Castle) are wholly circular. Roofs in the early days were flat and towers, usually placed at the "crossing," were square but occasionally round; the spires of all these towers have perished, but it seems likely that they were squat and pyramidal.

North-East Passage, from the North Atlantic to Bering Strait has been rapidly developed by the U.S.S.R. in recent years as a northern sea route to render accessible vast areas of northern Siberia. Attempts to find a north-east passage were made by Englishmen and Dutchmen in the 16th cent. but they were always defeated by the ice, for the sea is completely frozen for some 3,000 miles for 9 months of the year. A Swede succeeded in sailing from Europe to Japan via the Arctic in the late 19th cent. *See also* Arctic Exploration.

North-West Passage, from the Atlantic to the Pacific through the Arctic Seas, has been the dream of navigators for centuries. Attempts to find it were made in the 16th and early 17th cent. by John and Sebastian Cabot, Frobisher, Gilbert, Davis, Hudson, and Baffin. Two centuries later Ross, Parry, Franklin, and others made the attempt; but it was not until 1903–5 that Amundsen, discoverer of the South Pole, made the complete voyage in the *Gjoa*. The Canadian icebreaker *Labrador* was the first deep-draft vessel to traverse the North-West Passage (1954) and the U.S. tanker *Manhattan* was the first commerical vessel to do so (1969).

Notre Dame, the famous Paris cathedral, was founded in 1163, and is one of the finest specimens of Gothic architecture in Europe. The best descriptions of the buildings are to be found in Victor Hugo's *Hunchback of Notre Dame*.

November, the 9th month of the year originally, but from *c.* 700 B.C., when Numa added Jan., and Feb., it became the 11th month.

Nuclear Energy. Atomic nuclei consist of protons and neutrons joined in various proportions (**F10**). The heaviest naturally occurring nucleus contains 238 particles (92 protons, 146 neutrons) and is uranium 238 (U^{238}); the lightest is hydrogen, which consists of 1 proton. Neutrons and protons attract one another by very strong forces which are not at all well understood; they are called *nuclear forces*. Consequently it requires energy to be supplied if a nucleus is to be pulled apart into its constituent particles. The energy is required to overcome the attractions of the nuclear forces. Conversely, when the particles rush together to form a nucleus, energy is released in the form of heat or radiation. The energy released when protons and neutrons coalesce to form a nucleus is called *Binding Energy.* The binding energy of a nucleus divided by the number of particles involved is called the binding energy per particle, which we will call B. It is very difficult to overestimate the importance of B to the human race. B varies from nucleus to nucleus, and the exact form of its variation is only roughly understood at the present time. But the most significant thing is that B is greatest for elements of medium atomic weight and lowest at the heavy (uranium) and light (hydrogen) ends of the periodic table. This means that if middleweight nuclei can be formed either from heavy ones or from light ones, B increases and *energy is released in either case.*

Nuclear Fission. *See* F12(1).

Nuclear Fusion. If light nuclei are hurled at high speeds into intimate contact they sometimes coalesce and release binding energy (*see* Nuclear Energy). This has been studied in laboratories where powerful and energy-consuming machines accelerate small numbers of particles for purely experimental purposes. If useful amounts of energy are to be gained these fusion reactions will have to occur on a bigger scale in an apparatus from which the resulting heat can be extracted in a controlled way. The one " useful " fusion device so far made is the thermonuclear bomb (" H-bomb "). Thermonuclear is the important word. If a suitable gas can be raised to a very high temperature the nuclei are stripped of their electrons and all particles move with very high speeds. The gas is then called a plasma. High enough temperatures will make speeds great enough for fusion reactions to occur and nuclear energy to be released. This is a thermonuclear reaction. For example, in deuterium gas, at temperatures over a million degrees Centrigrade, the deuterium nuclei (*i.e.,* heavy hydrogen nuclei consisting of 1 proton joined to 1 neutron) interact to produce helium nuclei. To obtain a net gain in energy from this process, the temperature must be raised to about 300 million degrees C and maintained long enough; otherwise the energy released is less than that required to heat the fuel and to make up for heat losses. Many attempts to study the staggering technical problems are being made, and fusion research is very active in Britain, the U.S.A. and Russia.

Nuclear Power Stations. Britain generates about 12 per cent of her electricity in nuclear power stations and the proportion is expected to rise to about 25 per cent by the mid-1970s. Britain has so far produced as much electricity by nuclear power as the rest of the world put together. The Atomic Energy Authority has five main stations at Calder Hall, Cumberland, Chapelcross, Dumfriesshire, the AGR station at Windscale, Cumberland, the experimental fast breeder station at Dounreay, Caithness, and the Steam Generating Heavy Water Moderated Reactor (SGHWR) at Winfrith, Dorset. The nine nuclear power stations operated by the electricity authorities are at Berkeley (1962), Bradwell (1962), Hinkley Point (1964, Hunterston (1964), Trawsfynydd (1964), Dungeness " A " (1965), Sizewell (1965), Oldbury (1967), and Wylfa, in Anglesey (1970). They have all been developed from the classic Calder Hall type, burning natural uranium inserted in a graphite moderator and cooled by carbon dioxide gas. They are called Magnox stations because the fuel elements of natural uranium rods are encased in magnesium alloy cans. The second nuclear power programme for 1970–75, is based on the advanced gas-cooled reactor system. Dungeness " B " is due to begin operating in 1972. Three further stations, Hinkley Point " B " (1972), Hunterston " B " (1973), and Hartlepool (1974), are under construction. The third programme planned for the end of the 1970s is to be based on the fast breeder reactor.

Nuclear Reactors are pieces of apparatus designed to permit nuclear chain reactions to occur under controlled conditions. (Uncontrolled chain reactions are dangerous, *e.g.,* atomic bombs.) The success of a reactor depends on the neutrons reaching the U^{235} nuclei to produce more fissions and not being wasted in irrelevant processes or simply escaping through the wall of the appa-

ratus (neutrons are quite difficult to contain). The neutrons leaving the scene of fission are rapidly moving, and they stand more chance of causing another fission if they are slowed down. Consequently a material other than the uranium has to be present to facilitate this, and it is called a moderator. A useful moderator is pure graphite. Thus a reactor may consist of alternate blocks of uranium and graphite. If the reactor is too small so many neutrons escape that there are not enough to keep the chain reaction going. The reactor must therefore be greater than a certain *critical size.* In order to intensify or damp down the chain reaction, it is arranged for pieces of neutron-absorbing material, such as cadmium, to be inserted or withdrawn as required. While the chain reaction is proceeding countless numbers of fissions are occurring, each one liberating energy which turns into heat. The temperature therefore increases, and to prevent a catastrophic rise, cooling has to be provided. The reactor therefore has cooling pipes through which a fluid coolant is pumped. The coolant carries the heat away and, in a reactor designed to produce electrical power, the heat is taken to steam-raising boilers and the high-pressure steam is led to turbines which drive the electric generators. What has been briefly described is the type of reactor first used for serious power production at Calder Hall. This is a graphite-moderated, gas-cooled reactor using as fuel natural uranium (*i.e.,* fissile U^{235} greatly diluted with U^{238}). It is also possible to make reactors work without slowing the neutrons with a moderator; these are called *fast reactors.* The design of the prototype fast reactor (PFR) at Dounreay, due for completion in 1971, is based on experience gained with the Dounreay experimental fast breeder reactor which was the first in the world to produce electricity on a commercial scale (1962) and has achieved the highest power output of any of its type in the world. These fast reactors can produce new nuclear fuel in the course of their operation and therefore offer great economies. The British-designed advanced gas-cooled reactor (AGR) successfully developed at Windscale and chosen for the new Dungeness " B " and Hinkley " B " nuclear power stations, promises to produce electricity more cheaply than conventional sources. The alternative method to nuclear fission is nuclear fusion (*q.v.*). The problem of achieving a controlled thermonuclear reactor is one of the outstanding challenging problems of applied physics and although considerable understanding of the phenomena involved has been gained, the 'solution is still as distant as ever. *See also* Breeder Reactor.

Nucleic Acids. Living matter is built up of cells, each of which has a nucleus surrounded by cytoplasm. Cell nuclei are composed chiefly of substances called nucleoproteins, which consist of a protein attached to a nucleic acid (this original name is still used, although nucleic acids are found in the cytoplasm as well as the nucleus). Nucleic acids are complex organic structures made up of chains of compounds called nucleotides (**F29(1)**). Nucleotide molecules have a sugar group attached to a nitrogenous base and a phosphate group. Only two sugar groups are found in the nucleotides, ribose, giving rise to ribonucleic acids (R.N.A.s, found mainly in the cytoplasm) and deoxyribose, which forms deoxyribonucleic acids (D.N.A.s, found mainly in cell nuclei). Seven different nitrogenous bases have been isolated, so that a number of different nucleotides are possible. A repeating, regular pattern of nucleotides is linked by the phosphate groups, forming nucleic acids. The functions of nucleic acids are of fundamental importance. They are concerned in the process of transmission of inherited qualities in reproduction and in building up body proteins. Lord Todd of Cambridge University was awarded the 1957 Nobel Prize in Chemistry for his work on the structures of nucleic acids; the 1962 Nobel Prize in Medicine (*see* L128) was awarded for the discovery of the molecular structure of D.N.A. *See* F28(2), 29.

Nuremberg Trial. On Nov. 21, 1945, an International Military Tribunal, consisting of

L86

one American, one British, one Russian, and one French member, began the trial of twenty-four Nazi leaders. There were four counts: the conspiracy of Nazism; wars of aggression; war crimes; and crimes against humanity. Twelve were condemned to hanging of whom ten were hanged on Oct. 16, 1946. Goering committed suicide; Bormann has never been found; Papen, Schacht, and Fritsche were acquitted. The rest received varying terms of imprisonment.

Nuthatch, name of a number of tree-creeping birds, plump, with short tail, bluish-grey plumage, and black stripe under eye. Nest in holes and wedge nuts in bark of trees, hammering them to get a kernel. There are three European species, one, *Sitta europaea*, resident in England.

Nylon, a generic term for any long-chain synthetic polymeric amide which has recurring amide groups as an integral part of the main polymer chain, and which is capable of being formed into a filament in which the structural elements are orientated in the direction of the axis. The first nylon of commerical interest was made in 1935, and the world's first nylon factory—in the United States—began production in 1940.

O

Oak, a tree of the genus *Quercus,* including some 300 species distributed over the northern hemisphere and into the tropics. Two species are native to Britain, where the oak is the commonest tree (1 in 3)—*Q. petraea,* more common in the west and north on shallower, lighter soils, and *Q. robur,* more common in the south on deeper, heavier soils. Oak timber is much prized for its strength and durability, and from the time of the Spanish Armada to Nelson's day was in great demand for naval construction. It has always been used for building, flooring, furniture, and cabinet work. The oak is attacked by many insects, the round nut-like oak galls, or oak-apples, being produced by the sting of certain minute gall wasps.

"Oaks," a famous race for three-year-old fillies run at Epsom two days after the "Derby."

Obelisk, a tapering monolithic column, square at the base and pyramidal at the top, regarded by the ancient Egyptians as a sacred stone and usually found at the entrance to the sun temples. Many were transported from Egypt and set up at various times: there is one in the Place de la Concorde in Paris, and one on the Thames Embankment in London—Cleopatra's Needle—originally erected at Heliopolis, centre of the sun-cult, by Tuthmosis III *c.* 1500 B.C.

Observatories existed in ancient Babylon and Egypt. They were erected on tombs and temples. The most famous observatory of Egypt was that of Alexandria, erected by Ptolemy Soter, 300 B.C. It was not until the 16th cent., however, that an observatory adequately equipped for astronomical investigations was built. This was at Cassel. Tycho Brahe's observatory at Uranienburg was erected in 1576. The Royal Observatory at Greenwich was completed in 1675. Mount Wilson Observatory in California has had a 100-in. reflector telescope working since 1917 but Mount Palomar Observatory, also in California, has a 200-in. reflector—the largest in the world, completed in 1949—which can reveal remote galaxies out to a limiting distance of 2,000 million light years. It is known as the *Hale* telescope in memory of Dr. George Ellory Hale, the founder of the Mount Wilson Observatory. The 98-in. telescope, the *Isaac Newton,* for the Royal Greenwich Observatory at Herstmonceux Castle was completed in 1967. A number of observatories are devoted to meteorological and geophysical work, the most important in the British Isles being those at Eskdalemuir (Dumfries), Kew, Lerwick, and Valencia (Eire). *See also* Astronomy *and* Telescopes.

Occam's Razor. *See* J37.

Occultation, in astronomy, refers to the concealment of a celestial body by the passing before it of some other heavenly body. The most frequent occultation is the eclipse of a star or planet by the moon.

Ocean, comprises the great body of water which

covers five-eighths of the surface of the earth, and has an average depth of 2 miles. The principal oceans are the Pacific, Atlantic, Indian, and Arctic. *See* F8(2).

Ocean Currents are well-defined streams running over certain portions of the ocean and caused mainly by wind-friction, slope of the sea surface and differences in density of the water, all movements being influenced by the deflective forces due to the earth's rotation. The climatic importance of the great ocean currents is that they constitute one of the means whereby heat is transferred from lower to higher latitudes.

Ocelot, the most common wild cat of S. America. It is about 4 ft. in length, including tail, and of a grey or tawny colour and spotted. Closely related to the Leopard cats.

Octane Number, the index of the knock-rating of petrol. It is based on the arbitrary scale in which iso-octane (which does not cause "knocking") has a value of 100, and normal heptane (which is prone to "knocking") has a value of 0. A good fuel for modern cars must have an octane number greater than 80.

Octarch, the kings of the English heptarchy, Hengist (455) being the first, and Egbert (800) the last.

October, the 10th month, but the 8th in the old Roman calendar. It was held sacred to Mars.

Octopus, a genus of marine molluscs with eight tentacles that bear suckers.

Odyssey, Homer's epic setting forth the incidents of the wanderings of Odysseus on his way back to Ithaca after the Siege of Troy. *See* H23.

Œil-de-bœuf, meaning bull's eye, is the name of a small octagonal vestibule lighted by a small round window in the palace of Versailles. The term is used in architecture for a small round or oval window in friezes, roofs, or domes of buildings.

Oersted, a unit of magnetic-field intensity in the c.g.s. system.

Ohm's Law, propounded by G. S. Ohm in 1826, is expressed in the equation: electromotive force (in volts) = current (in amperes) × resistance (in ohms). The ohm is the unit of electrical resistance in the metre-kilogram-second system.

Oil. The great expansion in energy demand over recent years has been met to a large extent by petroleum oil. This contains a wide range of hydrocarbon molecules of varying complexity. The various components are separated from each other by making use of their different boiling points. Crude oil is heated in the base of a fractionating tower; the various components condense at different temperatures in trays at different levels of the tower. The fraction of a given composition can be increased by "cracking" or breaking down the heavier hydrocarbons into lighter ones. The total world reserves of petroleum oil are still uncertain since large parts of the world are still not fully prospected. However, such information as exists suggests that total reserves from all sources may be between 5×10^{11} and 10^{12} tons of oil.

Okapi, nocturnal ruminant mammal, smaller than the giraffe, chestnut brown in colour with zebra-striped legs, native to the African Congo.

Olbers' Comet was discovered in 1815 by Olbers the German astronomer. Olbers also discovered the asteroids Pallas and Vesta (1802–07).

Old Red Sandstone, the continental rocks formed during the Devonian. *See* F44.

Olefines, a series of hydrocarbons, in which the hydrogen atoms are double the number of carbon. The first member of the series is ethylene.

Oleic Acid, an important fatty acid present in lard and olive- and cotton-seed oils. Used in soap-making. Olein is the ester formed by the reaction of oleic acid and glycerine.

Oléron Laws or Judgments, were a code of maritime laws, introduced into England in the reign of Richard I. in the 12th cent. Oléron is an island off the west coast of France, opposite the mouth of the Charente.

Olive. This small tree, whose fruit yields olive oil, is a native of the eastern Mediterranean countries, but has been introduced into cultivation elsewhere. Its oil is used for cooking, in packing sardines, and in soap making; the green unripe fruit is pickled for table olives.

Olympiads were periods of four years which elapsed between each celebration of the Olympic games, held at Olympia in honour of Zeus. These festivals included competitions in literature, art, drama, rhetoric, music, and gymnastics, and they were continued, with intervals, from 776 B.C. to A.D. 394. Athletic revivals have taken place at Athens 1896, Paris 1900, St. Louis 1904, London 1908, Stockholm 1912, Antwerp 1920, Paris 1924, Amsterdam 1928, Los Angeles 1932, Berlin 1936, London 1948, Helsinki 1952, Melbourne 1956, Rome 1960, Tokyo 1964, Mexico City 1968, and it is planned to hold the 1972 Olympic Games at Munich. *See* U33, 36.

Onomasticians are scientists who study the fascinating subject of names—names of places and names of people—to find out their origins. They tell us, for example, that Cambridge is an Anglo-Norman corruption of *Grantabrycg* = bridge over the Granta; that Harrow-on-the-Hill was an early Anglo-Saxon settlement— " heathen temple on the hill "; that we owe the ridings of Yorkshire to the Vikings (Old Norse *thrithungr* = third part); that in Scotland *-ton* and *-toun* indicate not a town but a hamlet or village. Onomasticians are also concerned with the international standardisation of place names.

Onyx or **Sardonyx**, a variety of chalcedony built up of different-coloured layers, which are parallel and straight (not curved as in agate).

Oolite, a geological term for the Jurassic oolitic limestone existing through a long stretch of country extending from Yorkshire to Dorsetshire. It abounds in fossils of molluscs and reptiles. The term " oolite " derives from the fact that these rocks are made of egg-shaped particles of calcium carbonate.

Opal, a mineral consisting of hydrous silica, occurring in numerous varieties and colours. Precious opal displays a beautiful internal opalescence, the result of the interference of light waves on the surfaces of layers differing in their water-content. Opal miners are called gougers. Chief source, the Andamooka and Coober Pedy fields of South Australia.

Opera. *See* Section E.

Opium was known to the ancients, and used by them as a medicine. It is obtained from the poppy (*Papaver somniferum*), the unripe " head " or seed capsule of that flower yielding a juice which when dried becomes the opium of commerce. The poppy is cultivated in India, Persia, Turkey, Macedonia, and China for the sake of this juice, which yields various alkaloids, such as morphine, narcotine, codeine, etc. These days the drug is rarely used medicinally. *See also* P22(2).

Opossum, marsupial mammals found in the more southerly of the United States, South America, and Australasia. They are arboreal except for the water-opossum, which eats fish.

Optics, the branch of physics which investigates the nature and properties of light and the phenomena of colour. Burning lenses were known to the ancient Greeks and Ptolemy wrote a treatise on optics A.D. 150. Lenses as visual aids were known in ancient China but eyeglasses were not in use until the 13th cent. Spectacles were in more general use after the invention of printing in the 15th cent. The camera obscura was invented in the 16th cent. and the telescope and microscope at the beginning of the 17th cent.

Oracles were in ancient times supposed to be words spoken by the gods, and it was the custom on important occasions to consult them about the future. The Greeks had the Oracles of Zeus at Dodona, and Apollo at Delphi, while the Romans consulted the Oracles of Mars, Fortune, and others.

Orange, a fruit growing in most sub-tropical climates and in universal demand. It is grown on an evergreen tree that attains a height of about 20 ft. at maturity.

Orang-utan, one of the largest of the anthropoid apes, found only in the swampy forests of Borneo and Sumatra. When full-grown it stands over 4 ft. in height and weighs about 150 lb.

Orchestra, a group of instruments and instrumentalists whose playing is under the direction of a conductor. The composition of a typical symphony orchestra is as follows: STRINGS: 1st Violin (16), 2nd Violin (16), Viola (12),

Violoncello (12), Double Bass (8). WOOD-WIND: Flute (3–4), Piccolo (1), Oboe (3), Cor Anglais (1), Bass Oboe (1), Clarinet (3), Bass Clarinet (1), Bassoon (3), Contra-bassoon (1). BRASS: Horn (6), Trumpet (5), Trombone (3–4), Tuba (2). PERCUSSION: Timpani (3–6), Side Drum (1), Bass Drum (1), Cymbals (1), Harp (2).

Orders in Council are issued by the sovereign on the advice of a few selected members of the Privy Council. They must not seriously alter the law of the land. Another class of Orders in Council are issued by authority of an Act of Parliament for the carrying out of its provisions.

Ordination, the ceremony of installing ministers or clergymen in clerical offices, has existed from the earliest times. In the Anglican and Roman Catholic Churches the rites of Ordination are performed by bishops; among Nonconformists the power of ordination rests with the governing bodies of the different Churches.

Organ is a musical wind instrument of ancient origin whose tones are produced by the vibrations of air in pipes of varying length. Basically, an organ consists of a number of pipes grouped in rows or ranks according to their special tone-character. The air is fed by bellows or, in modern organs, by a rotary fan, electrically driven. Each rank is controlled by a slider, and the knob that controls the slider is called a stop. The organist pulls out the stops to give the tones he wants, the other pipes being kept out of action by the slider. When a particular note on the keyboard is depressed the player may hear, by pulling out the appropriate stop, not only the normal pitch but the note in several octaves. A stop of which the notes are of normal pitch is called an 8-foot stop, a 16-foot stop would give an octave lower, a 4-foot stop an octave higher, and a 2-foot stop two octaves higher. The hand keyboard is called a manual, and the foot keyboard the pedal board. The basic tone of an organ is its diapason tone, and is normally of 8-foot length and pitch. Most large organs have four manual keyboards and one pedal board. The most important manual is the great organ which comprises the majority of basic stops. The next in importance is the swell organ, so called because the pipes are enclosed in a box fitted with movable shutters operated by a swell-pedal. The effect provides a controlled crescendo or diminuendo. The tone of a typical English swell has a reedy character. The third manual controls the choir organ— a collection of stops suitable for vocal accompaniment. The fourth manual controls the solo organ—a group of stops which, singly or in combination, may provide a solo melody which the remainder of the organ accompanies. The pedal keyboard controls most of the bass stops. In some very large organs there is a fifth manual controlling the echo organ. This is a small group of stops usually set high in the roof of the building to give the effect of distant music. Most church organs have two or three manuals. Modern cinema organs may have some normal stops but rely chiefly on a number of effects unknown to the straight organ.

Organic Chemistry. The chemistry of compounds containing carbon and usually associated with living organisms. *See* F24–5.

Oriel Window is a window projected from the front of a building, rectangular, triangular, or pentagonal. The ordinary bay window and bow window are varieties of Oriel. When an Oriel window does not reach to the ground it usually rests upon moulded sills supported by corbels.

Oriflamme, the name of the original banner of the abbey of St. Denis, and adopted by Louis VI. as his standard. It remained the national emblem of France for three centuries. The flag was of red silk, the outer edge being cut in the form of flames.

Original Sin, according to Christian doctrine the corruption that is born with us, as a result of Adam's fall.

Orioles, brilliantly coloured birds, members of the passerine family *Oriolidae*, found in the tropical regions of Asia, Africa, and Australia. The golden oriole, perhaps the most beautiful of them all, with brilliant yellow plumage, black wings and tail, winters in Africa, visits England and is known to have nested here.

Orion, a famous constellation of the heavens, comprising nearly a hundred stars, all visible to the naked eye. It contains three stars of the second magnitude in a line, and these are called "Orion's Belt."

Ormer, a shellfish (*Haliotis tuberculata*) which occurs in the Channel Islands and on parts of the French coast. It is considered a great delicacy.

Ornithology, the scientific study of birds.

Ornithorhynchus. *See* **Duckbill.**

Orogeny, large-scale earth movements, including faulting and folding and sometimes igneous activity, which produce a linear belt of mountains, *e.g.,* the Alpine orogeny in Europe which produced the Alps.

Orphism. *See* **J33, H117–128.**

Orphrey, the name of an ornamental border of gold and silver embroidered on ecclesiastical vestments.

Orrery, an instrument used in the 18th and early 19th cent. which showed the motions of the planets round the sun and the satellites round their primaries. The first orrery made was named after Charles Boyle, Earl of Orrery.

Orthodox Eastern Church. *See* **J37.**

Osborne House, near Cowes, in the Isle of Wight. Queen Victoria's favourite winter-residence, and where she died. It was given to the nation by Edward VII., and is now a convalescent home.

Osier, a species of willow growing in damp soils and yielding branches utilised in basket-making.

Osmium, a very hard, bluish-white metal, symbol Os, of the platinum group and one of the heaviest of known metals. It is obtained from certain sands of South America, California, Australia, and Russia. The alloy of osmium and iridium (osmiridium) provides long-wearing tips for gold fountain-pen nibs.

Osmosis, The process by which absorption of liquids through semi-permeable membranes takes place. A solution exerts osmotic pressure (O.P.) or suction in proportion to concentration but also depending on kind of dissolved substance. The roots of the higher plants are covered with fine root-hairs, within the cell-walls of which the sap is normally of a higher concentration than the dissolved matter in the surrounding soil. The root-hairs, therefore, draw into themselves these weaker salt-solutions. (The explanation of water and salt exchanges is complicated by the selective ability of some cells (*e.g.,* roots) to accept or reject particular dissolved substances along with the water. The absorption of salts by a plant is selective, each plant selecting through the semi-permeable membranes of its root-hairs those substances which are most suited to itself.)

Osprey (*Pandion haliaëtus*), a large and magnificent bird of prey, dark brown above and nearly white below. The head is whitish with a dark band from eye to nape. To the British Isles it is a rare passage migrant. In 1959, thanks to the energy and vigilance of the Royal Society for the Protection of Birds, a pair nested in a Scots pine in Inverness-shire and reared three young. Since then more young ospreys have been safely fledged in this sanctuary. The food consists almost entirely of fish, which the bird seizes with its talons. The so-called osprey plumes do not come from this bird but from the egret.

Ostrich, the largest living bird, related to the rhea, emu, and extinct moa, now found only on the sandy plains of Africa and parts of S.W. Asia. The male has beautiful white plumes on wings and tail. The wings are useless in flight, but the birds have a fleetness of foot exceeding that of the swiftest horse. An ostrich's egg weighs 3 lb.

Otary, any seal which has external ears (as opposed to the *true seals* which lack them). The eared seals make up the family *Otariidae,* which includes the Sea-Lion and the Fur-seal of the N. Pacific.

Otter, an aquatic carnivorous mammal widely distributed over Europe, and at one time very common in England and Wales. The otter averages about 2 ft. in length, exclusive of tail, has web-feet, and is a very expert swimmer. Otters are harmless and their hunting is a cruel and senseless blood sport.

Ounce, a carnivorous member of the cat family, spotted like a leopard and having a long bushy tail. It is only found at high altitudes on the Himalayas, and is often called the "snow leopard."

Outcrop. Where a bed of rock appears at the surface of the ground, there is an outcrop of the particular rock. Outcrop coal is surface coal; the mining of such coal is called open-cast mining.

Oviparous, a zoological term referring to animals which lay eggs to be hatched outside the body of the parent.

Ovipositor, the organ by means of which female insects lay their eggs.

Owls, nocturnal birds of prey, distributed over the greater part of the world. Their forward-looking eyes, embedded in rings of feathers, give them a characteristic "owl-like" appearance, and their plumage, usually a mottled blend of browns and greys, is so soft that their flight is almost noiseless. Owls live on small mammals, reptiles, birds, insects, and fish, and are very valuable birds to the farmer. British owls include the barn owl (screech owl), short-eared owl, long-eared owl, tawny owl, little owl. Snowy owls have recently nested in the Shetland Is.

Ox, the popular name of the mammals included in the genus *Bos.* They are hollow-horned ruminants and hoofed quadrupeds, and include the various classes of domestic cattle as well as the different wild species. The adult male is called a bull, the female a cow, and the young a calf. The best-known breeds of domesticated cattle are the Durham or Shorthorn, the Angus, the Jersey, Ayrshire, Suffolk, and Hereford.

Oxalic Acid, an organic acid obtained from numerous plants, such as sorrel and rhubarb, and produced artificially for commercial purposes from sawdust, treated with caustic potash or caustic soda. It combines with metals to form oxalates; used in the manufacture of ink.

Oxford Clay, a geological formation consisting of a bed of blue clay hundreds of feet thick, and forming the lower portion of the Upper Jurassic. It makes good bricks.

Oxford University. The early history of the university is obscure. There was a school at Oxford as early as 1115 and it is known that Robert Pullen, a theologian from Paris, lectured there in 1133. Allusions to Oxford as the most celebrated centre of learning in England occurred in a work of Gerald of Wales in 1184–5. The earliest colleges to be founded were University College (1249), Balliol (about 1263), Merton (1264). In 1571 the university was reorganised and granted a Charter of Incorporation by an Act of Elizabeth. Other colleges and halls with their dates of foundation are: All Souls (1438), Brasenose (1509), Christ Church (1546), Corpus Christi (1517), Exeter (1314), Hertford (1874), Jesus (1571), Keble (1868), Linacre (1962), Lincoln (1427), Magdalen (1458), New College (1379), Nuffield (1937), Oriel (1326), Pembroke (1624), Queens' (1340), St. Antony's (1950), St. Catharine's (1962), St. Cross (1965), St. Edmund Hall (1270), St. John's (1555), St. Peter's (1929), Trinity (1554), Wadham (1612), Wolfson (1965), Worcester (1714), Campion Hall (1962), St. Benet's Hall (1964), Mansfield (1886), Regent's Park (1958), Greyfriars Hall (1953). The women's colleges are:—Lady Margaret Hall (1878), Somerville (1879), St. Hugh's (1886), St. Hilda's (1893), St. Anne's (1952). Women were not admitted to degrees (though allowed to sit for examination) till 1920.

Oxygen is the most abundant of all terrestrial elements, symbol O. In combination, this gaseous element forms about 46% of the earth's crust; one-fifth of the atmosphere; eight-ninths by weight of all water. Discovered independently by Scheele (c. 1773) and Priestley (1774). It is colourless, tasteless, and odourless, and forms the chief life-supporting element of animal and vegetable life.

Oyster, a bivalve mollusc, of the genus Ostrea, having very numerous species and abounding in nearly all seas. The shell is rough and irregular. Oysters are exceedingly prolific, spawning in May and June. In England and Scotland deep-sea oysters are not allowed to be sold between June 15 and Aug. 4, and other kinds between May 14 and Aug. 4. In Ireland, no oysters may be taken between May 1 and Sept. 1, except in certain waters. The Whitstable oyster beds have existed since pre-Roman times; " clocks " are dead oysters.

Oystercatcher, a wading bird with black-and-white plumage and long, orange bill, inhabiting estuaries and sea-shores. Feeds on mussels, shell fish, etc., but not oysters.

Ozone, a modified form of oxygen, containing three atoms of oxygen per molecule instead of two. It is prepared by passing oxygen through a silent electric discharge. When present in air to the extent of 1 part in 4 million parts of air it kills bacteria, and has been used for this purpose in ventilating systems, *e.g.,* that of underground railways. It is present in extremely small quantities in the lower atmosphere but is comparatively plentiful at heights of about 20 miles. The belief widely held that seaside air is particularly rich in ozone is untrue. As ozone absorbs ultra-violet light of certain wavelengths spectroscopic methods, involving the analysis of sunlight. are chiefly used in ozone determinations. *See also* **Atmosphere.**

P

Paca, a genus of large rodents found in Central and South America, and resembling the guinea-pig. It is of nocturnal habits, has a streaked and spotted fur, and lives on fruits and plants.

Pacific Ocean. The first European to recognise the Pacific as distinct from the Atlantic was the Spanish explorer, Vasco Nuñez de Balboa, who discovered its eastern shore from a peak in Panama in 1513. The first European to sail upon it was Magellan, who entered it by the strait that bears his name in 1520. Sir Francis Drake was the first Englishman to sail upon it in 1577. The world's greatest ocean depth (6,297 fathoms or just over 7 miles) was established by a British survey ship in 1962 in the Mindanao trench in the Philippine Sea.

Pagan, a person who does not worship God; a heathen. The word is derived from the Latin *paganus* (a countryman or uncultivated person). In the Middle Ages the term was used largely to describe Mohammedans (Moors, Saracens, etc.).

Pagoda, the name given in China, India, and other Asiatic countries to a high pyramidal tower, usually, but not necessarily, connected with a temple.

Palaeontology, the science which is devoted to the investigation of fossils: animal (palaeozoology) and plants (palaeobotany). By studying the markings and fossils of living things in the stratified rocks, palaeontologists have been able to establish with astonishing accuracy a record of the evolution of life through geological time. The geologist at the same time with the evidence of the fossils has been able to work out the order and the age of the rocks. *See also* **F44.**

Palatinate, a term formerly applied to two German electorates or provinces, the Upper and Lower Palatinates. They are now provinces of Bavaria.

Pale, the name given to the part of Ireland colonised by the English and comprising portions of the counties of Louth, Dublin, Meath, and Kildare. The Anglo-Saxon rulers were styled " Lords of the Pale."

Palimpsests are ancient MSS. or parchments which have been partly effaced and used for fresh writings. Many valuable MSS. were thus lost, but sometimes the second writing has been washed out, enabling the original writings to be deciphered. Among such restorations are a dialogue of Cicero's, a portion of a book of Livy. etc.

Palladium, a scarce metallic element, symbol Pd, similar to platinum, with which it is usually found. It is an expensive metal, with desirable properties as a catalyst in reactions involving hydrogen, since it has a remarkable capacity for absorbing this gas; for example, coal gas and air will inflame in the presence of palladium at room temperature. It forms a silver-white alloy with gold, and this is used in some kinds of jewellery. It is used in expensive watches to make non-magnetic springs.

Pallium, a vestmental ornamentation of white wool presented by the Pope to archbishops on their appointment, and the sign of Papal confirmation.

Palm, a large straight-trunked plant or tree common to tropical countries, and usually fruit yielding, such as dates, coconuts, etc. Many commodities useful to man are obtained from plants of the Palm family (*Palmaceae*).

Palm Sunday, the Sunday before Easter, upon which occasion it is customary to carry palms to the churches in some countries, in commemoration of Christ's entry into Jerusalem for the Feast of the Passover, when the people went forth to greet Him with palm branches.

Panama Canal. In 1903 the United States signed a treaty with Panama (which had previously seceded from Colombia) which gave the United States rights in perpetuity over a ten-mile-wide strip of land extending across the isthmus for the purposes of building and running the canal. The canal connects the Atlantic and Pacific Oceans, is just over fifty miles long (with sea approaches), and the depth varies from 41 to 85 ft. It is constructed above sea-level, with locks, and has been available for commercial shipping since Aug. 3, 1914. Studies are in progress for the building of a new sea-level canal to replace the present one.

Panda, *or* **Cat-Bear,** is related to the Raccoon, Dogs and the Bear. There are two kinds, the Red or True Panda, resembling a large domestic cat, which lives in the eastern Himalayas and S.W. China, and the Giant Panda, which is more like a bear in appearance and inhabits the mountains of western China. Both frequent the dense bamboo forests of these regions.

Pangolin, the scientific name of the " scaly ant-eater," a toothless mammal, found in W. Africa and S.E. Asia. It has a long extensible tongue which it uses in catching ants and termites, its chief food. When attacked the pangolin rolls itself into a ball, and its scales assume the form of sharp spikes. Pangolins have an Order of their own—the Pholidota, the scale-bearers.

Pantagruel, the leading character in one of the satires of Rabelais.

Pantheon, the famous temple in Rome, originally consecrated to the gods, built by Agrippa in 27 B.C. and rebuilt in the 2nd cent. by Hadrian. Its splendid dome and portico make it one of the most interesting architectural monuments of ancient days. Since the 7th cent. it has been used as a Christian church.

Panther, another name for the leopard, *Panthera pardus,* related to the lion, carnivorous, active climber, found in India, and other parts of Asia, also in Africa.

Papal Infallibility. *See* **J38.**

Paper has been known in one form or another from very early times. The papyrus reeds of the Nile swamps served the ancient Egyptians for sheets upon which to inscribe their records. The Chinese and Japanese, centuries later, were using something more akin to modern paper in substance, an Asiatic paper-mulberry, yielding a smooth fibrous material, being utilised. With the spread of learning in Western Europe the necessity of a readier medium made itself felt and paper began to be manufactured from pulped rags and other substances. The first known English paper-mill was Sele mill near Stevenage, built about 1490, which produced the paper for an edition of Chaucer in 1498. Other mills were set up under Elizabeth, using linen and cotton as raw material. Other papermaking staples were later introduced such as surat, esparto grass, and wood-pulp. The chief raw material in the world paper industry is wood-pulp, the main exporters being the timber-growing countries of Canada, Sweden, and Finland. Canada is the world's chief producer of newsprint and supplies a large proportion of U.S. requirements.

Papier mâché means pulped-paper and is a composition of paper pulp and other substances, to which, when moulded into form, coatings of japan, with gilt and coloured inlayings, are added. Elegant and decorative objects are made of papier-mâché. A ceramic papier-mâché is very durable.

Papyrus, the earliest known paper made in Egypt at a very remote period from a large species of reed, *Cyperus papyrus.* This plant is to be found all over tropical Africa, especially in the " sudd " region of the White Nile.

Parachute, the umbrella-shaped safety device used in emergency by the crew and passengers of aircraft. The first parachute descent from a great height was made in 1797 by André Garnerin who dropped 3,000 ft. from a balloon. *See also* **Parachute Jumping, U21.**

Paraclete (the Holy Ghost, or Comforter), the name used in the English translations of St. John's Gospel, and adopted by Abelard to designate the convent in Champagne founded by him, and of which Héloïse became the abbess.

Paradise, a Persian word used by the translators of the Old Testament to designate the Garden of Eden, and since meaning any place of happiness.

Paraffin, a mixture of hydrocarbons of higher boiling point than petrol. Paraffin was first obtained by distillation of coal, the process being discovered about 1830. About 1848, Mr. James Young procured it from mineral oil, and Irish peat also yielded it. The main source of paraffin supply to-day is crude petroleum. It is largely used in the manufacture of candles, for waterproofing, and numerous other purposes.

Parakeets, various small parrots of vivid plumage native to Australia, Polynesia, Asia, and Africa. One of the loveliest of the parakeets is the budgerigar of Australia. *See* **Z21, 23.**

Parallax, the change in direction of a body caused by a change in position of the observer. If the parallax is measured (in degrees of angle) and the distance between the two observation points is known the distance of the observed body can be calculated. The distance of heavenly bodies has been found this way. The first stellar distances were so obtained in 1838 by Henderson, Struve, and Bessel. Stellar distances are so great that even when the two observations are made at opposite points of the earth's orbit round the sun the parallax is always less than 1·0″ of arc. *See* **Aberration.**

Parchment, made chiefly from the skins of animals, usually of goats and sheep, was employed in olden times before printing was invented and superseded papyrus as writing material. Vegetable parchment, invented by W. E. Gaine in 1853, though not equal in strength and durability to skin parchment, is about five times stronger than ordinary paper. Vellum is parchment made from the skins of young calves or lambs.

Paris University, of which the Sorbonne forms a part was founded in the 12th cent. and is one of the greatest educational institutions of Europe.

Parliament, is the name given to the supreme legislature of the United Kingdom. It consists of the Queen, the Lords spiritual and temporal, and the Commons. It meets in two houses: the House of Lords (the Upper or Second Chamber) and the House of Commons. It derives from the Anglo-Saxon *Witans* (*see* Witan). The Statute of Westminster (1275) first uses " parlement " of the Great Council in England, which comes from the French word meaning discourse. *See* **Central Government, Section C,** *also* **D8.**

Parliamentary Correspondents sit in the Press Gallery of the House of Commons and describe its proceedings for newspapers either by impressions or a summary of the debate.

Parquetry, the name of a style of flooring consisting of small rectangular wooden blocks laid down according to geometrical pattern.

Parrot, the popular name of a widely distributed family of tropical birds, including the African grey parrot, the green parrot of South America —both familiar cage pets in this country—and the various parakeets, cockatoos, macaws, lories, etc. Many of these birds possess a remarkable gift of imitating sound, especially that of the human voice.

Parsec, unit of distance used by astronomers for expressing distances between stars; equivalent to about three and a quarter light-years.

Parthenogenesis. The development of animals from unfertilised eggs. The drones of the honey bee are parthenogenetic, and the phenomenon is also common among aphids.

Parthenon, the famous Temple of Athena on the Acropolis at Athens, was built under the rule of Pericles between 447 B.C. and 432 B.C. It was made wholly of marble without mortar. The famous sculptured friezes, known as the Elgin Marbles, are now in the British Museum.

Partridge, a well-known British game bird. Close time: Feb. 2 to Aug. 31. Two species are common in Britain.

Passeriformes, the order of perching birds which includes about half the known species.

Passport is an official document issued to a person by his own government, certifying to his citizenship and permitting him to travel abroad. Passports to British subjects are granted by the Foreign Office, authorise bearer to leave the country and guarantee him the state's protection. Passports now cost £2.—and are issued for a period of 10 years. Passports for children under 16 are issued for 5 years in the first instance, renewable then for a further 5 years without fee on production of new photographs, etc. A simplified form of travel document (British visitor's passport) is issued for British subjects wishing to pay short visits to certain foreign countries for a fee of 7s. 6d., valid for 12 months.

Patricians, the aristocracy of ancient Rome.

Paul's Cathedral, St., is the third cathedral church to be built on the site. It was preceded by a Norman building which was practically destroyed by the Great Fire in 1666. This followed a Saxon church which was burnt in 1086. The present building was designed by Sir Christopher Wren. The foundation stone was laid in 1675 and the structure was completed in 1710. It cost a little under £748,000. Its central feature is the dome, crowned by its cupola and lantern with the golden ball and cross. It escaped serious damage during the air raids of the second world war, but many of the surrounding buildings were laid waste.

pC Value, introduced by Dr. C. L. Whittles in 1935 as a measure of salinity of aqueous solutions (soil extract, irrigation water, etc.); defined as the negative logarithm of specific electrical conductivity in reciprocal ohms. Alone or joined with pH (below) is useful as an index of osmotic pressure (*see* Osmosis) and related hindrance to plant growth resulting from excess of fertiliser or soil salts. If manuring is balanced, growth is best about pC 3.3.

Peacock, a bird of large size and beautiful plumage, its characteristic feature being a tail of brilliant " eyed " feathers, which it can erect and spread out, the males possessing resplendent feathering to a much greater extent than the females. It is related to the pheasant; one species is found wild in the forests of India, and another inhabits Burma and the Malayan regions, in Africa there is the Congo Peacock.

Pean, a term in heraldry indicating one of the furs borne in coat armour, the ground of which is black, with ermine spots of gold.

Peanut, Ground Nut *or* **Monkey Nut.** A member of the pea family native to S. America, but now cultivated in many parts of the world. After pollination, the flower stalk bends down and buries the pod containing the peas (" nuts ") in the ground. The oil from these " nuts " can be used for margarine manufacture.

Pearl is produced by certain shelled molluscs, chiefly the oyster. The inner surface of the shells of the pearl oyster yield " mother-of-pearl," and distinct pearls are believed to be morbid secretions, caused by some external irritation. Many fine pearls are found in the actual body of the oyster. The Persian Gulf, Ceylon, the north-west coast of Western Australia, many Pacific islands, and the Gulf of Mexico are among the most productive pearl-fishing grounds. In ancient times Britain was renowned for its pearl fisheries, the pearls being obtained from a species of fresh-water mussel. Western Australia has produced a 40-grain pearl, the finest the world has seen. The largest pearl ever found was the " Beresford-Hope Pearl," which weighed 1,800 grains, over six times as much as the oyster that produced it.

Peat, decayed vegetable matter found mostly in marshy positions, and common in Ireland and Scotland. Peat is coal in its first stage of development; burnt for fuel in many cottage homes.

Peccary, a pig-like animal native to the Americas. There are two species: the collared peccary and the white-lipped peccary, the latter being a vicious and dangerous animal.

Pelican, a genus of bird with long depressed bill pouched underneath, thus able to hold fish in

reserve. It has immense wings and webbed feet. Eight species.

Pemmican, venison or other meat, sliced, dried, pounded and made into cakes, used by explorers and others when out of reach of fresh meat.

Penguin, a genus of flightless, fish-eating sea-birds of the southern hemisphere. They are stout-bodied, short-necked, and of small, moderate, or large size. The Emperor and King Penguins make no nest but protect and incubate the single egg by carrying it in the down feathers between the feet and the body. Other species brood in the usual way and may lay as many as three eggs. Penguins use their flippers for swimming under water. All 17 species are bluish-grey or blackish above and white below. They are very sociable and breed in colonies.

Penicillin. An antibiotic drug produced by the mould *Penicillium notatum,* and discovered by Sir Alexander Fleming in 1928. It is one of the most effective chemotherapeutic agents known. The mould produces a number of penicillins, all of which are effective antibiotics. *See* P4(2), 9(1).

Peninsular War lasted from 1808 to 1814. Fought in Spain and Portugal (the Iberian peninsula) by the British, Spanish, and Portuguese forces, chiefly under Wellington, against the French. The latter were defeated.

Pentagon, government office in Washington (the largest in the world), housing many thousands of military and civilian workers in the War Department of the United States (Army, Navy, and Air Force).

Pentateuch, the first five books of the Old Testament—Genesis, Exodus, Leviticus, Numbers, and Deuteronomy. Referred to in the Gospel of Mark as " the book of Moses."

Pepys Diary, by Samuel Pepys, was first published in 1825. It gives a picture of the social life of the period 1 Jan. 1660 to 31 May 1669. He bequeathed the manuscript, together with his library, to Magdalene College, Cambridge.

Perch, a well-known family of fresh-water fish, with dark striped sides. The common perch of British rivers and lakes falls an easy prey to the angler because of its voracity.

Perfumes are essences or odours obtained from floral and other substances. The chief flower perfumes are those obtained from rose, jasmine, orange flower, violet, and acacia. Heliotrope perfume is largely obtained from vanilla and almonds. Among the aromatic herbs which yield attractive perfumes are the rosemary, thyme, geranium, lavender, etc., while orange peel, citron peel, musk, sandalwood, patchouli, and other vegetable products are largely drawn upon. In recent times chemistry has been called into play in aid of the perfumer, and many of the popular perfumes of to-day are chemically prepared in simulation of the scents of the flowers or other natural substances the names of which they bear. *See* Musk Deer.

Periclase, a mineral form of magnesium oxide.

Perigee. The moon or the sun is said to be in perigee when it is at its least distance from the earth. The opposite of apogee (*q.v.*).

Perihelion. That point in a planet's orbit when it is nearest to the sun. The opposite of aphelion.

Peripatus, an animal which stands as a link between the annelid worms and the arthropods. Wormlike with short unjointed legs it breathes by a system of air tubes like those in insects. Certain other points of internal structure point to a relationship with annelid worms. There are some fifty species, the best known being the S. African *Peripalus capensis.*

Perjury, the offence of giving false evidence. The ancient Romans threw the perjurer from the Tarpeian Rock, and after the Empire was Christianised, those who swore falsely upon the Gospel had their tongues cut out. The usual punishment in England from the 16th to the 19th cent was the pillory, fine, and imprisonment.

Permian Formation, a group of rocks lying between the Trias and the Carboniferous strata. It has three subdivisions. Upper, Middle and Lower Permian. *See* F44.

Per Procurationem signature means that the subject of the correspondence has been put into the writer's care by his principal for him to use his personal judgment in the matter, and that he is authorised to sign on behalf of his principal. Normally contracted to *per pro* or *p.p.*

Peruke, the name given to the wigs worn by men in the latter half of the 18th cent. The custom of wearing wigs was gradually superseded by powdering the natural hair. Wigs are still worn by the Speaker of the House of Commons, judges, and barristers.

Petrel, the name given to a member of a large, widely-distributed family of sea-birds of great diversity of size and colouring and distinguished by tube-like external nostrils. They usually skim low over the waves, and some, for this reason, are known as shearwaters. The storm petrel or Mother Carey's chicken occasionally patters along the surface, and is often called Little Peter—a reference to St. Peter walking on the water. Except when breeding, petrels are always at sea. They mostly nest in holes and crevices on islands and lay one egg, which is invariably white. The storm petrel, Leach's petrel, Manx shearwater, and the fulmar petrel are resident in the British Isles. *See also* Mutton Bird.

Petroleum. *See* Oil.

Pewter, alloy of tin and lead formerly used for making household utensils and ornaments.

pH **Value.** Introduced in 1909 by the Danish chemist Sørensen to indicate hydrogen-ion concentration on the basis of electrical conductivity and a view of ionisation since discarded; is now taken as a logarithmic scale of acidity or alkalinity of aqueous solutions: acidity 0–7, neutrality at 7·0, alkalinity 7–14. The pH of blood is about 7·6 (faintly alkaline). *See* F22.

Phalanger, pouched marsupial mammals. They are arboreal and superficially resemble squirrels. There are two genera of flying phalangers or flying squirrels, which have a remarkable membrane along each side of the body enabling the animals to glide through the air. The members of the phalanger family are confined to the Australasian and oriental regions.

Phalangid, a member, of the arachnid family Phalangida: popularly known as " harvesters."

Phalanx, a name applied by the ancient Greeks to a body of troops drawn up in close array, with overlapping shields, and eight, ten, or more rows deep. The Macedonians stood sixteen deep. A Greek phalanx consisted of 8,000 men.

Pharisees and Sadduces. *See* Judaism, J27.

Pharmacopoeia, an official publication containing information on the recognised drugs used in medicine. Each country has its own pharmacopoeia. The British Pharmacopoeia (B.P.) is published under the direction of the General Medical Council. The Pharmaceutical Society issues the British Pharmaceutical Codex (B.P.C.); there is also an International Pharmacopoeia (2 vols.) which is issued by the World Health Organisation.

Pharos, the name of the first lighthouse, built by Ptolemy II. about 280 B.C., on the Isle of Pharos, at the entrance to the harbour of Alexandria. It was 600 ft. high, and one of the " seven wonders."

Pheasant, game birds related to the partridges, quails, peacocks, chickens, and turkeys, distinguished by their brilliant plumage and long tapering tail. First found by the Greeks in Georgia where the River Phasis flows through to the Black Sea. Close time: Feb. 2 to Sept. 30.

Phillippics, the orations delivered by Demosthenes, 352–341 B.C., against Philip of Macedon—remarkable for their acrimonious invective. The word was also used for Cicero's speeches against Antony. In modern use, any impassioned invective.

Philosopher's Stone. *See* Alchemy, J3.

Phosphorus is a non-metal element, symbol P. Most familiar as a waxy, yellow solid which is spontaneously inflammable in air. It has chemical similarities to arsenic, like which it is very poisonous. It was discovered by Brandt in urine in 1669. It is found in most animal and vegetable tissues. It is an essential element of all plants and of the bones of animals. In combination with various metals it forms different phosphates, which are largely utilised as manures. The chief commercial use of phosphorus is in the preparation of matches.

Photoelectric Cell, a device which gives a useful electrical response to light falling on it. There are several kinds depending on the different effects which light may have on a suitably

L92

chosen solid (usually a semiconductor), viz., the emission of electrons from the surface (" photo-emissive cell "); change in electrical resistance (" photoconducting cell "); generation of electric current from a specially designed sensitive structure (" barrier layer " or " photo-voltaic cell ", " solar battery "). Different cells respond differently to lights of various wavelength and must be chosen for each application. See also Solar Battery.

Photogrammetry, the science of measurement from photographs taken from an aircraft. Aerial photography has many uses and is of great value to military intelligence and for map-making.

Photon. When light behaves like a stream of discrete particles and not like waves, the particles are called photons. See F13(1), 14.

Photosynthesis. See F28.

Phrenology. See J38.

Phylloxera, a genus of plant-lice related to the aphids, which attacks the grape vine. Many vineyards of France, in common with the rest of Europe, were replanted with native vines grafted on immune stocks from California in 1879 after being ravaged by the insect (which came from America). Curiously enough, the remedy also came from America, the vine stocks there being immune to *phylloxera*.

Picts, inhabitants of Scotland in pre-Roman times, are held by some historians to be a branch of the old Celtic race, by others to have been of Scythian origin. They occupied the north eastern portion of Scotland, and were subdued by the Scots in Argyll in the 9th cent., Kenneth Mac-Alpin becoming king of a united kingdom of the Picts and Scots—the kingdom of Alban.

Pike, a familiar fresh-water fish abundant in the temperate regions of both hemispheres. It forms good sport for the angler in rivers and lakes, and sometimes attains a weight of from 20 to 30 lb. It is extremely voracious, is covered with small scales, and has a ferocious-looking head

Pilchard, a fish of the herring family, but with smaller scales and more rounded body. It appears off the Cornish coasts in vast shoals every summer.

Pilgrimage, the undertaking of a journey to a distant place or shrine to satisfy a religious vow or secure spiritual benefit, was resorted to in early Christian times The first recorded pilgrimage is that of the Empress Helena to Jerusalem in 326. In the Middle Ages pilgrimages became common, and were undertaken by monarchs and people of rank in all Christian countries. Moslems have been making pilgrimages to Mecca since the death of the Prophet, such duty being enjoined by the Koran. Among the great centres of Christian pilgrimages are Jerusalem, Rome, the tomb of Becket at Canterbury, and the holy places of Lourdes and La Salette in France.

Pilgrim Fathers, the 101 English Puritans, who, after living some years in exile in Holland, to escape persecution in their own country, set sail for America in the *Mayflower*, Sept. 6, 1620, landing at Plymouth, Mass., Dec. 4. They founded the settlement of Plymouth, and are regarded as the pioneers of American colonisation although 13 years earlier a small Virginian colony had been established.

"Pilgrim's Progress," Bunyan's famous allegory, written in Bedford gaol. The first part was issued in 1678. It is the greatest work of its kind. See M40(1).

Pillory, a wooden instrument of punishment in use in England until 1837. It consisted of a pair of movable boards with holes through which the culprit's head and hands were put, and was usually erected on a scaffold. While a person was undergoing this punishment the mob generally pelted him with stones and rubbish, sometimes to his serious injury. People convicted of forgery, perjury, or libel were often condemned to the pillory, but from 1816 to 1837 the only offence for which it could be inflicted was perjury.

Pine, a conifer of the genus *Pinus*, which flourishes all over the northern hemisphere and includes 80–90 species, which afford valuable timber and yield turpentine and tar. The Scots Pine, *Pinus silvestris*, with its blue-green, short

needles, set in pairs, and its rosy-orange branches, is native to Britain, as it is to the whole of Europe. It provides the red and yellow deal in everyday use.

Pipa, a species of toad inhabiting Guiana, and not found elsewhere. It is of considerable size, and is remarkable for the fact that the female carries its eggs on its back until they are hatched, herself depositing them in that position. Generally known as the " Surinam toad."

Pitcairn Islanders were originally the mutineers of the *Bounty*. They took possession of the island in 1790, and it was not until 1814 that their whereabouts was ascertained, accidentally, by a passing ship. The mutineers, under their leader, Adams, had settled down to a communal existence, married Tahitian women, and increased so in numbers that in the course of years they were too many for the island to support, and in 1856 they were removed by the British Government to Norfolk Island. A small number returned to Pitcairn.

Pitchblende *or* **Uraninite,** a relatively scarce mineral. It is nearly all uranium oxide, but lead, thorium, etc., are also present. Pitchblende from Joachimstal in Czechoslovakia was the material in which radium was discovered by the Curies. Pitchblende also occurs in Saxony, Rumania, Norway, Cornwall, the Congo, and at Great Bear Lake in Canada.

Plainsong, a style of musical composition sung in unison (all voices singing the same tune without harmony), familiar in the Western Church from very early times and still performed, principally in the Roman Catholic Church. Though restrained and contemplative in spirit, it is capable of expressing deep emotion. See E3(2).

Planetarium, a complex optical system which projects into the interior of a dome a replica of all the phenomena of the sky that can be seen by the naked eye, *e.g.*, sun, moon, planets, stars, comets, meteors, aurora, eclipses, and clouds There is a planetarium in the Marylebone Road, London, and another (opened in 1966) at Armagh Observatory, N. Ireland.

Planets, the name give to such celestial bodies as revolve round the sun in elliptical orbits. The name was first used by the Greeks to indicate their difference from the fixed stars. There are nine planets, Mercury, Venus, Earth, Mars, Jupiter, Saturn, Uranus, Neptune, Pluto. Many important questions can be answered by means of probes sent to the neighbourhood of the planets. These include the measurement of the magnetic field, if any, of the planets, the study of their atmospheres, much of which can be done without actually penetrating to the surface. With instruments landed gently on the surface it is possible to investigate surface conditions and composition by many methods. Even without a soft landing information on these questions can be obtained by photography and subsequent transmission of the picture back to earth by some form of television scanning. For example, the American Mars probe, *Mariner IV.* transmitted pictures of the Martian surface in 1965 when it was at its closest approach to the planet, and the Russian *Venus IV* in 1967 made a soft landing on Venus. See F7, also under their names.

Plankton, a word which first came into biological use in 1886 to describe the usually microscopic plants and animals floating, swimming, and drifting in the surface waters of the sea. To be distinguished from *nekton* (swimming animals like fishes and squids) and *benthos* (plants and animals living on the sea bottom, like fixed algae, sponges, oysters, crabs, etc.). Of great economic importance, providing food for fish and whales.

Plantagenets, the kings who reigned in England between 1154 and 1485 and included the Houses of Lancaster and York. More correctly they are styled Angevins, from Anjou, of which Geoffrey, father of Henry II., was Count, and whose badge was a sprig of broom (*Planta genista*).

Plasma Physics is the physics of wholly ionised gases, *i.e.*, gases in which the atoms initially present have lost practically the whole of the electrons that usually surround their nuclei, so that the gas consists of a mixture of two components, positively charged ions and negatively charged electrons. The physical properties of a *plasma* are very different from those of an unionised gas. In particular, a plasma has a high electrical conductivity and can carry large currents. *See also* **Nuclear Fusion.**

Plastics, a broad term covering those substances which become plastic when subjected to increased temperatures or pressures. The Plastics Industry is based on synthetic organic examples of this group. There are two classes of plastics: the *thermoplastic*, which become plastic every time they are heated (*e.g.* cellulosic plastics) and *thermosetting*, which undergo chemical change when heated, so that once set they cannot be rendered plastic again (*e.g.* Bakelite). Plastics are composed of long-chained molecules, *e.g.*, polyethylene.

Platinum, a metal element, symbol Pt. It is a scarce white metal generally allied with iridium, osmium, ruthenium, and palladium. It can only be melted in an oxyhydrogen or electric furnace, but can be rolled out into a film-like sheet, or drawn out to the finest wire; being resistant to acids it is termed a noble metal.

Platonic Solids, five regular solid figures known to the ancient world. They are: the tetrahedron (4 triangular faces), cube (6 square faces), octahedron (8 triangular faces), dodecahedron (12 five-sided faces), icosahedron (20 triangular faces). All the faces and angles of each solid are identical.

Plebeians were the ordinary citizens of Rome as distinct from the patricians. There was a long struggle between the two orders for political equality.

Pleiades, famous cluster of stars in the constellation of Taurus. Of the seven principal stars in the group, one is rather faint, and many myths have sprung up about this "lost pleiad".

Pleistocene the geological period that succeeded the Pliocene. During the Pleistocene, also known as the *Great Ice Age*, there were four cold periods, when the ice sheets covered northern Europe and N. America, separated by warm periods when the glaciers drew back into the mountains. From recent studies based on rock magnetic measurements the transition to Pleistocene took place about 1,850,000 years ago.

Pliocene, the geological period preceding the Pleistocene, and the last major division of the Tertiary strata. It began about fifteen million years ago. *See* **F44.**

Plough Monday, the first Monday after the Epiphany, when in olden times the rustic population returned to work after the Christmas festivities.

Plover, wading birds, widely distributed over marshy places of Europe. Several species occur in Britain, including the Golden-plover, which breeds on the moors of Devon, Somerset, Wales, N.E. Yorkshire, and Scotland, and the Ringed plover, Kentish plover, and Dotterel.

Pluto, the last planet to be discovered; existence established by C. W. Tombaugh at the Flagstaff Observatory in Arizona in Jan. 1930 from reckonings made by P. Lowell in 1914. It is the most distant of all the known planets; diameter about 3,650 miles. Mean distance from the sun estimated at 3,671 million miles.

Plutonium, a chemical element, symbol Pu, capable of nuclear fission in the same way as Uranium 235. Not until after it had been synthesised in atomic piles during the second world war was it shown to occur in infinitesimally small traces in nature. Its synthesis in the atomic pile depends on the capture by Uranium 238 nuclei of neutrons; immediate product of this reaction is the element neptunium, but this undergoes rapid radioactive disintegration to plutonium. Because of its explosive power and poisonous character, an American scientist once remarked: "If ever there was an element which deserved a name associated with hell, it is plutonium."

Poet Laureate is the poet attached to the royal household, an office officially established in 1668, though its origins go back to the early Middle Ages, when minstrels were employed at the courts of English kings. Chaucer, Skelton, and Spenser, though not court poets, were all unofficial poets laureate. Ben Jonson has been called the first "official laureate" (1616), but the office was not officially recognised until 1668, when Dryden was formally granted the office. It is customary for the poet laureate to write verse in celebration of events of national importance. Cecil Day-Lewis succeeded John Masefield as poet laureate in 1967.

Pogrom. Russian word meaning "destruction." First used to describe the Tsarist attacks on the Jews in 1881 in Russia. In 1938 Hitler ordered a general pogrom in Germany: all synagogues were destroyed and nearly all Jewish shops and homes, Jewish hospitals and children's homes suffered. During the subsequent war Jews of central Europe were systematically exterminated in cold blood by the Nazis.

Poitiers, Battle of, was fought on Sept. 19, 1356, during the Hundred Years' War, when Edward the Black Prince gained a complete victory over John, King of France who was taken prisoner and brought to London.

Polecat, an animal of a dark-brown colour, about 18 in. in length, exclusive of tail; the ears and face-markings are white or light brown. It is carnivorous and belongs to the weasel family. Like the skunk, it emits an offensive odour.

Pole-Star is of the second magnitude, and the last in the tail of the Little Bear constellation. Being near the North pole of the heavens—never more than about one degree from due north—it always remains visible in the Northern hemisphere; hence its use as a guide to seamen.

Police, a regular force established for the preservation of law and order and the prevention and detection of crime. The powers they have vary from country to country and with the type of government; the more civilised and democratic the state, the less police intervention. England, compared with countries abroad, was slow to develop a police force, and it was not until 1829 that Sir Robert Peel's Metropolitan Police Act established a regular force for the metropolis, later legislation establishing county and borough forces maintained by local police authorities throughout England and Wales. Up to that time police duties were discharged by individual constables and watchmen appointed by local areas in England and Wales. Under the Police Act, 1964, the former 121 regular police forces in England and Wales have been reduced, by amalgamation, to 47. In Scotland there are 20. In England and Wales the forces are defined according to area of responsibility:

1. County forces, under a Police Committee.
2. Borough forces, under Watch Committees, elected by the borough councils.
3. Combined forces covering more than one county or borough, under a body representing the constituent areas.
4. The Metropolitan Police Force, covering a 15-miles radius from Charing Cross, under the control of the Home Secretary.
5. The City of London force, under a committee of the Common Council.

In Scotland there are county forces, burgh forces, and combined forces. The Metropolitan Police, with an establishment of about 25,000 are unaffected by the current changes. Apart from the amalgamation of police forces in the interest of efficiency, other reforms recently introduced include the centralisation of criminal records, the introduction of personal radios, and the organisation of the neighbourhood beat system under which officers in cars can patrol their areas. Central authority rests with the Home Secretary in England and Wales and the Secretary of State for Scotland in Scotland. In Northern Ireland the police force is controlled by an Inspector General, who is responsible to the N.I. Government. (The security forces in N.I. are under the control of the British Army).

Pollution of the atmosphere is due chiefly to the incomplete combustion of fuels, especially coal, large particles of soot being deposited fairly quickly close to their place of origin and smaller particles (including smoke) remaining suspended in the air for a long time. Corrosion of exposed objects and damage to buildings result from the production of sulphuric acid. The introduction of more efficient furnaces, the washing of flue gases and the introduction of smokeless zones have assisted in the abatement of smoke and other forms of pollution. Atomic weapon tests add to the load of pollution in the atmosphere (*see* Fall-out). "Smog" (smoke-laden fog) which reduces visibility to zero and affects the respiratory organs, is liable to occur when the air near the earth is cooled below the dew-point temperature by radiation on a still, cloudless night when an accumulation of smoke over a large city cuts off daylight and produces gloom, and absence of wind or vertical currents prevents the lower layers of the air from getting away. Such conditions are associated with the smoke-laden atmosphere of large industrial towns during a winter anticyclone. During the great London smog of 1952 there were 2,000 deaths over and above those expected for the time of year. Since the Clean Air Act of 1956 pollution by smoke and sulphur dioxide has continued to diminish in London, winter sunshine has increased by 50 per cent., and fish now live in the Thames. In 1969 a special Secretaryship of State was created to deal with pollution of the environment (air, waters in rivers and around coasts, noise, pesticides harmful to food and wildlife), and a standing Royal Commission on Environmental Pollution has been appointed. In his 1969 Reith lectures Dr. Fraser Darling said "most pollution comes from getting rid of waste at the least possible cost."

Polonium, a radioactive element, symbol Po, discovered by Madame Curie in 1898, and named after her native land of Poland.

Poltergeist. *See* J39.

Polymerisation is the linking together of small molecules to make a large long-chain molecule. The general name for polymers of ethylene is Polythene, a wax-like plastic solid which because of its special qualities is used in a variety of ways today.

Polytheism. *See* God and Man, J22.

Pomology, the science of fruit-growing.

Pontifex, the title assigned in ancient Rome to members of the college of pontifices. "Pontifex maximus" was the official head of Roman religion. It was as "pontifex maximus" that Julius Caesar revised the calendar in 46 B.C., and when after the rise of Christianity the popes took over the title the revision fell to them.

Pope, The, the head of the Roman Catholic Church, recognised by that Church as the lawful successor of St. Peter. He is elected by the body of Cardinals. Since 1870, when the King of Italy deposed the holder from temporal power, no pope had left the Vatican between appointment and death until 1929, when peace was made between the Church and State in Italy and compensation was paid to the Holy See for the loss of temporal power. Cardinal Montini, Archbishop of Milan, was elected Pope Paul VI in 1963 on the death of Pope John XXIII.

Porcelain. The word is thought to be derived from the Italian *porcellana*, indicating the texture of a piglet. The majority of porcelain made on the continent was of "hard-paste", or true porcelain, similar to that discovered by the Chinese as early as the T'ang Dynasty (A.D. 618–907). It was composed of *kaolin* (china-clay) and *petuntse* (china-stone) which when fired in a kiln at a temperature of *c.* 1300° C. became an extremely hard and translucent material. The recipe of "hard-paste" porcelain remained a secret of the Chinese until 1709, when it was re-discovered in Europe by Johann Böttger of the Meissen factory (popularly known as Dresden). Aided by disloyal Meissen workmen, factories were later established at Vienna, Venice and in many parts of Germany. Plymouth and Bristol were the only English factories to produce this type of porcelain, from 1768 to 1781. Elsewhere, both in England and France, the material manufactured was known as "soft-paste" or artificial porcelain which was made by blending varying white-firing clays with the ingredients of glass. The French factory of Sèvres began to make some hard-paste porcelain by 1768 and by the 19th cent. such porcelain was the only type being made throughout the whole of the continent. In England Josiah Spode is credited with the introduction of "bone-china" about 1794. This hybrid-paste was quickly adopted by many other factories and today remains the most popular type of English porcelain. *See* Pottery and Porcelain Marks, Section N.

Porcupine, a rodent whose back is covered with long, sharp, black and white spikes, which form a powerful means of defence. There are two families of porcupines; one is confined to the Old World and the other contains the American porcupines.

Porphyry, a form of crystalline rock of many varieties that in ancient Egypt was quarried and used for the decorative portions of buildings and vessels. The term is applied generally to the eruptive rocks in which large well-formed crystals of one mineral are set in a matrix of other minerals.

Porpoise, a highly intelligent marine mammal of the dolphin and whale family, and a common inhabitant of northern seas. Porpoises travel in shoals, their progression being marked by constant leapings and plungings. Their average length is from 4 to 5 ft. There are several species, nearly all being confined to northern oceans.

Port, a special kind of red Portuguese wine, taking its name from Oporto. It was little known in England until the Methuen Treaty of 1703, when it was permitted to be imported at a low duty.

Portcullis, a strong, movable timber or iron grating let into the wall of the gateway to a feudal castle, and capable of being lowered or raised at will. It formed an effective protection against attack in the days before firearms.

Portland Vase, one of the most renowned specimens of ancient art, long in the possession of the Portland family. In 1810 it was loaned to the British Museum. Here it was shattered in 1845 by a stone from a maniac's hand, but has been skilfully restored. It is said to have been found in the 17th cent. in an ancient tomb near Rome. It was purchased from the Barberini family in 1770 by Sir Wm. Hamilton, subsequently sold to the Duchess of Portland. The vase, which is actually a two-handled urn, stands about 10 ins. high, is of transparent dark blue glass, ornamented with figures cut in relief in overlaid white opaque glass. It was purchased by the British Museum in 1945.

Portreeve in olden times was an official appointed to superintend a port or harbour, and before the name of mayor was used the chief magistrate of London was styled the Portreeve.

Positivism. *See* J39.

Positron, the "positive electron," an atomic particle having the same mass but an electric charge equal but opposite to that of an electron. It was discovered in 1932. *See also* F14.

Post-Impressionism, a term introduced by Roger Fry to describe the exhibition of paintings sponsored by himself in London (1910–11) officially entitled "Manet and the Post-Impressionists." The exhibition included paintings by Manet, Cézanne, Gauguin, Van Gogh, Seurat, Signac, works by Matisse, Rouault, and the *Fauves* (*q.v.*), and sculpture by Maillol. In a second exhibition, held in 1912, Picasso and the Cubists were also represented. The term therefore refers to the movement in modern art which reacted against the transient naturalism of the Impressionists by concerning itself primarily with colour, form, and solidity. Most artists today would include Cézanne, Van Gogh, and Gauguin as the main Post-Impressionists and maintain that it prepared the way for Fauvism, Cubism, and Expressionism.

Potassium, a metal, symbol K (German *Kalium*). It is similar to sodium, like which it reacts violently with water. It was discovered by Sir Humphry Davy in 1807, and now generally obtained by the electrolysis of fused potassium hydroxide or chloride/fluoride mixture. Its principal minerals are carnallite and kainite, and it is relatively common in rocks, accounting for about 2¼% of the earth's crust. An essential element for healthy plant growth; the ashes of plants are relatively rich in potassium.

Potsdam Agreement was signed by Truman, Stalin, and Attlee in Aug., 1945. By this Agreement a Council of Foreign Ministers was established, representing the five principal Powers: China, France, Soviet Russia, the United Kingdom, and United States of America, with the task of drawing up the peace treaties for submission to the United Nations. It laid down, *inter alia* that German militarism and Hitlerism should be destroyed; that industrial power should be so reduced that Germany would never again be in a position to wage aggressive war; that surplus equipment should be destroyed or transferred to replace wrecked plant in allied territories; that Germany should be treated as an economic whole; and that local self-government should be restored on democratic lines as rapidly as was consistent with military security. The Potsdam Agreement became a dead letter with the creation of a communist régime in the Russian zone of Germany, and marked the beginning of the " cold war."

Prado Gallery, the great public picture collection of Madrid, containing a superb collection of paintings by Velasquez, Murillo, Raphael, Titian, Dürer, Van Dyck, Rubens, Holbein, etc.

Pragmatism. *See* **J40.**

Prefect, chief magistrates in ancient Rome. The title is now applied to the chiefs of administration of the departments of France.

Pre-Raphaelite Brotherhood was the name given to their school of thought by three British artists, Dante Gabriel Rossetti, J. E. Millais, and W. Holman Hunt, who in 1848 revolted against the academic art of their time and advocated a return to the style of the Italian painters prior to Raphael—the simple naturalism of the Primitives, such as Botticelli, Fra Angelico and Fillipo Lippi. Thus they avoided the use of heavy shadows and painted on a white ground in bright colours—a technique which aroused the ire of those used to the dark and murky canvases of the contemporary romantic artists. Although they held these principles in common the three members of the " P.R.B.", as it was popularly called, were really quite different in other respects. Thus Rossetti (who for some reason is always thought of as the typical Pre-Raphaelite) produced works of a highly romanticised mediaevalism which, apart from certain aspects of technique, bear not the slightest resemblance to the sentimental naturalism of Millais or the much more dramatic realism of Holman Hunt (*e.g.*, in *The Scapegoat*). The Brotherhood was later joined by a number of lesser artists, but its works are not commonly accepted with enthusiasm to-day when the general feeling is that they are sentimental and religiose rather than the product of deeply-felt emotions. Ruskin in his writings defended their work but the movement came to an end in 1853.

Presbyterianism. *See* **J40.**

Press-Gang, a body of sailors employed to impress men into naval service, frequently resorted to in England, especially during the war with France in the early 19th cent. Press gangs were not used after about 1850.

Primitive Art. The word " primitive " has a number of different meanings: (1) the art of prehistoric communities (*e.g.*, the famous animal cave-drawings of the Aurignacians, c. 25,000 B.C., at Altamira in Spain); (2) the art of modern primitive communities (*e.g.*, Bushman rock-paintings); (3) child art; (4) peasant art which springs from a spontaneous desire to impart beauty to objects of daily use and shows a tendency towards abstraction. Peasant art has many features in common the world over, the woodcarving of the Norsemen being almost indistinguishable from that of the Maoris; (5) the modern school of primitive painting in which naïveté of presentation is either the aim of a highly sophisticated mind (*e.g.*, the self-taught French painter Le Douanier Rousseau (d. 1910)), or arises naturally from a simple one (the American " grandma " Moses (d. 1961) who began to paint in her seventies).

Printing by movable types was first used in Europe in 1454 by Johann Gutenberg, a citizen of Mainz. The invention is also claimed for Laurens Koster of Haarlem. It was introduced into England by Caxton, who set up a printing press in Westminster in 1476. Gothic characters were first used, being superseded by Roman letters in 1518. In 1798 Earl Stanhope replaced the wood printing press by one of iron. In 1814 Friedrich Koenig applied the principle of steam power to the press. Mr. John Walter, of *The Times* newspaper, was the first to use the steam press. Improvements were introduced

by Applegarth and Cowper in 1828 and great strides were made in 1858 when the Hoe machine was put on the market. Then came the Walter press in 1866 which printed on continuous rolls of paper from curved stereotyped plates. The Monotype machine casts single letters and the Linotype whole lines. The term letterpress is used for all printing methods using plates where the characters stand in *relief*. The other main printing methods are *intaglio* and *planographic*.

The Privy Council is the Sovereign's own council, consisting of about 300 persons who have reached eminence in some branch of public affairs (Cabinet ministers must be Privy Counsellors), on whose advice and through which the Sovereign exercises his or her statutory and a number of prerogative powers. From it have sprung many organs of the constitution and many of our government departments have grown from committees of the Privy Council. For example, the Judiciary or courts of justice have grown from the Sovereign's Council sitting as a Court of Justice, and today the Judicial Committee of the Privy Council is a body of distinguished lawyers acting as a Court of Appeal from courts of the Commonwealth.

Probation Officers are attached to particular Courts, sometimes a Magistrates' or a higher court. Sometimes an offender is not sentenced to punishment, but is released " on probation," that is on the condition that he behaves well and follows directions given by the Court or by a probation officer. Such an officer is a trained man (or woman) who advises, assists, and befriends people who are placed under his supervision by a court of law. The probation officer, by his assessment of the social background of the offender, can advice the court upon the wisdom of putting the offender on probation. The probation officer by his understanding can so befriend an offender as to provide a basis for his rehabilitation. He undertakes the " after care " of those released from prison or Borstal. A juvenile offender, or in need of care, may be made subject to supervision by a probation officer or local authority. *See also* **Juvenile Courts.**

Productivity. Physical productivity is the output of products during a time unit, *e.g.*, so many products per man hour, or day, or year. Total productivity is the sum of all the units of product created during the given time. Labour productivity is the part of the total that is attributed to labour as a factor of production. Productivity of capital is the element attributed to capital as a factor. Productivity of land is the element attributed to the natural powers of the soil, as distinct from what is contributed by the application to it of capital or labour. The term productivity is also used to refer not to the quantity of output, but to its money value.

Propane, a colourless inflammable gas made of carbon and hydrogen; formula C_3H_8. It is easily liquefied and transported liquid in cylinders and tanks. In this form it is familiar as a " portable gas supply " for domestic and industrial uses. It is sometimes mixed with butane (*q.v.*) for this purpose. Propane occurs in natural gas and is a by-product of oil refining.

Proteins are the main chemical substances of living matter: they are a part of every living cell and are found in all animals and plants. Proteins have many functions, and occur in structural matter such as bones, tendons, skin, hair, and hoof, and in some vitamins and hormones. Lean meat, fish, and eggs are almost entirely proteins. Their composition varies with the source, but all proteins are basically constructed of carbon, hydrogen, oxygen, and nitrogen, and some contain sulphur, phosphorus (nucleoproteins), and iron (haemoglobin). Proteins are built up of very long chains of amino-acids connected by amide linkages (the synthetic polymers such as " nylon " and casein plastics (from milk) are built up of the same linkages). Enzymes, which bring about chemical reactions in living cells, are proteins having specific properties. *See* **F27(1).**

Proton, a basic constituent of the atomic nucleus, positively charged, having a mass about 1836 times that of the electron. It is a positive hydrogen ion. *See* **F10(2), 14.**

Prout's hypothesis. The English chemist William

Prout (1785–1850) advanced the idea that all atoms are made of hydrogen, and their weights are exact multiples of the weight of a hydrogen atom. With the modification that neutrons as well as protons occur in the nucleus, Prout's belief, though rejected for many years, has been substantially vindicated.

Provost, a Scottish official similar in rank to an English mayor. The Provosts of Edinburgh, Glasgow, Aberdeen, Perth, and Dundee are styled Lords Provost. The title of provost is also given to the heads of certain colleges.

Prud'hommes (Prudent Men), **Councils of,** were French trade tribunals, of masters and workmen, formed to decide on disputes. Originally a mediaeval institution, they were revived by Napoleon in 1806, and were carried on by the Third Republic.

Psalms, Book of, for many years attributed to David, but present-day scholars are of opinion that the psalms were written by a series of authors at different times and for different purposes, and that few, if any, were written by David. The Holy Scriptures contain 150.

Psychedelism. *See* **J40.**

Psychic Research. *See* **J41.**

Psychoanalysis. *See* **J42.**

Ptarmigan, birds of the grouse family, one species of which inhabits the Scottish Highlands. In the winter the bird assumes a white plumage.

Ptomaines, amino acids produced during the putrefaction of proteins of animal origin. Not a cause of food poisoning, as was once generally supposed, which is almost invariably due to certain specific bacteria.

Publicans, under the Roman Empire, were people who farmed the public taxes. It is this class of officials that is alluded to in the " publicans and sinners " phrase in the New Testament.

Public Corporations, statutory bodies which operate major industries and services in the public interest, *e.g.,* UK Atomic Energy Authority, Bank of England, B.B.C., Electricity Authorities, Gas Council, National Coal Board, British Steel Corporation, British Railways Board. They are accountable to Parliament but their staffs are not civil servants. The Post Office became a public corporation in 1969, responsible to the Minister of Posts and Telecommunications.

Public Schools. The Public Schools Act of 1864 named nine " public " schools: Eton, Harrow, Rugby, Winchester, Westminster, Shrewsbury, Charterhouse, St. Paul's, and Merchant Taylors. Today the term embraces many more, and can be applied to all those schools which are financed by bodies other than the State and whose headmasters belong to the Headmasters' Conference as distinct from the Headmasters' Association. There are about 200 such schools in Britain, including among others: Bedford School (founded 1552); Brighton College (1845); Charterhouse School, Godalming (1611); Cheltenham College (1841); Christ's Hospital, Horsham (1553); City of London School (1442); Clifton College, Bristol (1862); Dulwich College (1619); Eton College (1440); Felsted School (1564); Haileybury College (1862); Harrow School (1571); King Edward's, Birmingham (1552); King's School, Canterbury (600); Lancing College (1848); Malvern College (1865); Manchester Grammar School (1515); Marlborough College (1843); Merchant Taylors' School (1561); Mill Hill School (1807); Oundle (1556); Radley (1847); Repton School, Derbyshire (1557); Rugby School (1567); St. Paul's School (1509); Sevenoaks School (1418); Sherborne School (1550); Shrewsbury School (1552); Stonyhurst College (1593); Tonbridge School (1553); Uppingham School (1584); Wellington College (1859); Westminster (1560); Winchester College (1382); and Warwick (914). Public schools for girls include: Christ's Hospital, Hertford (1552); Cheltenham Ladies' College (founded by Miss Beale in 1853), North London Collegiate School (founded by Miss Buss in 1850), Roedean (1885), Wycombe Abbey (1896).

Pulsars, cosmic objects discovered in 1967 by the radio astronomy group at Cambridge; of great scientific interest because they are probably made of highly compressed matter. Unlike quasars (*q.v.*) they are near objects—all are contained in the Milky Way. *See* **F5.**

Puma, a carnivorous mammal of the cat family found in the New World from Canada to Patagonia.

Pyramids of Egypt, on the west bank of the Nile, are vast stone or brick-built structures with inner chambers and subterranean entrances, built by the Pharaohs as royal tombs and dating from about 3000 B.C. The most celebrated are at Giza built during the 4th dynasty. The largest, originally 481 ft. high, is called the Great Pyramid, one of the seven wonders of the world, built by the Pharaoh Khufu, better known as Cheops, and there he was buried. 100,000 men, according to Herodotus, being employed for 20 years upon it. Chephren, successor of Cheops, erected the second pyramid, and the third was built by Mycerinus, a son of Cheops. The pyramid at Meidum built by King Snefru, founder of the 4th dynasty, is the most imposing of all. American and Egyptian scientists are cooperating in a project to X-ray (by means of cosmic rays) the interior of the Pyramid of Chephren.

Pythons, large snakes, non-poisonous, and destroying their prey by crushing it. Some species average 30 ft. in length, and prey upon deer and other small mammals. Found in Asia, Africa, and Australia. They lay eggs.

Q

Quadrant, an astronomical instrument for measuring altitudes, superseded for navigational purposes in modern times by the sextant. It consists of a graduated arc of 90° with a movable radius for measuring angles on it.

Quai d'Orsay. An embankment in Paris where the French Foreign Office is situated.

Quail, an edible bird of the partridge family, of which only one species, the Common Quail, is found in England. It is not more than 8 in. long. It is found in most of the warmer regions of the world. In England and Wales the Quail is covered by the Wild Bird Protection Acts.

Quair, an old name for a pamphlet or little book.

Quantum Theory. The rapid development of quantum theory has been almost entirely due to the experimental and theoretical study of the interactions between electromagnetic radiation and matter. One of the first steps was taken when it was discovered that the electrons emitted from metals due to the action of ultraviolet radiation have an energy which is not related to the intensity of the incident radiation, but is dependent on its wavelength. Einstein showed in 1905 that this could only be explained on the basis that energy is transferred between radiation and matter in finite amounts, or *quanta*, which are inversely proportional to wavelength. *See* **F13(1).**

Quarks are hypothetical subnuclear particles recently postulated by theoretical physicists concerned with the so-called elementary particles. There are supposed to be three kinds, all carrying electrical charges which are fractions of those carried by familiar particles like electrons and protons. This and other special properties of quarks make them suitable for explaining the existence of the large number of other particles referred to on **F13, 14.** The physical existence of quarks may be demonstrated by experiment at any time and if this happens it will be an exciting truimph for speculative theoretical physics.

Quartering, in heraldry, is the disposition of various escutcheons or coats of arms in their proper " quarters " of the family shield, in such order as indicates the alliances with other families.

Quartermaster, a military officer charged with the provisioning and superintendence of soldiers in camp or barracks, and holding the equivalent rank to a lieutenant. The Quartermaster-General is an officer who presides over the provisioning department of the whole army. A Quartermaster in the Navy is a petty officer responsible to the Officer of the Watch; at sea for the correct steering of the ship and in harbour for the running of the ship's routine.

Quarto, a sheet of paper folded twice to make four leaves, or eight pages; abbreviated to " 4to."

Quartz is a common and usually colourless mineral, occurring both crystallised and massive. In

L97

the first form it is in hexagonal prisms, terminating in pyramids. When pure its specific gravity is 2·66. It is one of the constituents of granite, gneiss, etc. Among the quartz varieties are *rock crystal* (colourless), *smoky quartz* (yellow or brown), *amethyst* (purple), *rose quartz* (pink), and *milky quartz* (white). Quartz veins in metamorphic rocks may yield rich deposits of gold. Mining for gold in the rock is termed quartz-mining.

Quasars, or in preferred terminology, quasi-stellar radio-sources, form a new class of astronomical object, first identified in the period 1960 to 1962. They have enormous energy output, and are at vast distances. Many are strong sources of radio waves and fluctuate in intensity. Their nature and cosmological significance presented the major astronomical problem of the 1960s. In the view of Professor Philip Morrison, of the Massachusetts Institute of Technology, quasars are the condensed remains of entire galaxies, while pulsars (*q.v.*) seem to be the ashes of a star that has exploded. Both, he suggests, contain a core of highly concentrated magnetised material. *See* F5.

Queen Anne's Bounty, established by Queen Anne in 1704 for the augmentation of the maintenance of the poor clergy. Since April 1, 1948, Queen Anne's Bounty and the Ecclesiastical Commissioners ceased to exist and became embodied in the Church Commissioners for England.

Queen's (or King's) Speech is the speech prepared by the Government in consultation with the Queen and delivered by Her Majesty in person or by her deputy, at the opening or closing of a Parliamentary session.

Quicksilver. *See* **Mercury.**

Quinine, a vegetable alkaloid obtained from the bark of several trees of the *Cinchona* genus. It is colourless and extremely bitter. The drug, sulphate of quinine, is one of the most valuable medicines, forming a powerful tonic. It is antiperiodic, antipyretic, and antineuralgic. In cases of malaria it is the most efficacious remedy of natural origin known.

Quirinal, one of the seven hills of Rome.

Quisling, term which came into use during the second world war to denote traitor, collaborator, or fifth-columnist. After Vidkun Quisling, who became head of the puppet government after the German invasion of Norway in 1940.

Quorum, the number of members of any body or company necessary to be present at any meeting or commission before business can be transacted. The House of Commons needs a quorum of 40, the Lords a quorum of 3.

R

Rabbi, a Jewish term applied to specially ordained officials who pronounce upon questions of legal form and ritual, and also generally accorded to any Jewish scholar of eminence.

Rabbit. *See* **Z17.**

Raccoon, plantigrade carnivorous mammals common to the American continent. There are several species. The common Raccoon (*Procyon lotor*) is about 2 ft. long, with a bushy ringed tail and sharp snout. Its skin is valuable.

Race. In the old text-books anthropologists were much concerned with the differences between the various races of Man: they described the Black Man (Negro), the Yellow Man (Mongol), the Red Man (American Indian), the Brown Man (Indian), and the White Man (European). Those who study Man from this point of view further subdivide each group into others. Thus White Man may be divided into Nordic, Alpine, and Mediterranean; Black Man into Hamitic, Bushman, and so on. Each of these groups tends to have physical traits which its members hold in common, although, of course, there are no *pure* racial types. All existing races have been fairly thoroughly mixed. What, in view of recent experience, is really important, is that races or even nations do not have psychological traits—at least not *innate* traits. Anthropology dismisses all theories of a superior race as unscientific: there is not the slightest evidence that one race differs in any way from another in its psychological

potentialities. Jews, Irish, Scots, Italians do differ (so do the inhabitants of Edinburgh and London): but their differences are due to their situation and not to anything inborn. *See* F49.

Raceme, an inflorescence in which the main stem bears stalked flowers, *e.g.*, lupin, foxglove. The youngest flowers are at the tip of this axis.

Radar. The basic principle of radar is very similar to that of sight. We switch on a light in the dark, and we *see* an object because the light waves are reflected from it and return to our eye, which is able to detect them. Similarly, the radar station *sees* an object because the invisible radio waves sent out from the transmitter are reflected from it and return to the receiver, which is able to detect them. Thus radar is the use of radio signals that man broadcasts.

The utilisation of radio waves for the detection of reflecting surfaces began with the classical experiment of the late Sir Edward Appleton in 1925, which he conducted in order to demonstrate the existence of the Heaviside layer in the upper atmosphere. During the course of the last war developments took place which tremendously improved the methods and instruments used. As in the case of so many of the inventions primarily developed for the purpose of waging war, many useful applications have been found for radar in times of peace, and, in particular, it has proved of great service as an aid to aerial and marine navigation, and in meteorology and astronomy. Radar astronomy investigates the solar system with the echoes of signals sent out from the Earth.

Radiation, energy emitted in the form of a beam of rays or waves, *e.g.*, acoustic (sound) radiation from a loudspeaker, radiant heat from a fire, β-radiation from a radioactive substance. The radiation of electromagnetic waves from a body depends on its temperature, the amount of energy radiated per second being proportional to the fourth power of the absolute temperature. The hotter the body, the shorter the wavelengths of the radiation; thus the colour of a glowing body depends on its temperature. Of paramount importance to us is radiation from the sun. Amongst other radiations, the sun sends ultra-violet, visible, and infra-red (heat) waves. The principal gases of the atmosphere are transparent to practically all of the solar and sky radiation and also that which the earth re-transmits to space. Carbon dioxide and water vapour, however, strongly absorb certain types, the latter, as clouds, playing an important rôle in regulating the temperature of the globe. The cooling of the ground on a clear night is a result of the outgoing long-wave radiation exceeding that coming down from the sky; at sunrise cooling ceases as the incoming radiation becomes sufficient to compensate for the loss of heat.

Radiation, Cosmic. *See* F3(2).

Radio. The theory of electromagnetic waves—of which the radio wave is one—was originated by the British physicist James Clerk Maxwell (F12). He showed that both electrical and optical phenomena in space are essentially similar in character, and that the waves if short in wavelength are those of light, and if of longer wavelength those of radio waves. Heinrich Hertz made many useful discoveries about the waves themselves, and about their behaviour under differing conditions, and also about the apparatus for producing them. Marconi developed the use of radio waves as a practical means of communication.

Radio methods are vital for the transmission of observed data from space vehicles back to earth, a process known as "telemetering." This is done by converting the observations into electrical pulses which actuate a suitable radio transmitter so that it radiates a signal, in coded form, which can be received at a ground station and decoded. The transmission of such a signal can also be remotely controlled by means of signals from the earth. Photographic and television techniques may also be employed for obtaining the desired information and sending it back to earth, as in the case of the Russian picture of the reverse side of the moon and the American pictures of the lunar surface. The information may be stored within the spacecraft for a time, and then, upon receipt of a particular radio signal from the earth transmitted by the spacecraft at a time convenient for its reception. Soviet scientists, by a special technique, were able in the case of their *Venus IV* probe (Oct. 1967) to parachute an instrumented canister from the spacecraft so that it could descend slowly to the surface of the planet—a feat described by Sir Bernard Lovell, who was recording the enterprise at Jodrell Bank, as "an experiment of classic elegance." *See also* Radio Astronomy, Telemetry.

Radioactivity is the spontaneous transformation of atomic nuclei, accompanied by the emission of ionising radiations. It was discovered in 1896 by Becquerel, who noticed that salts containing uranium sent off radiations which, like X-rays, can blacken a photographic plate. Two years later Marie and Pierre Curie discovered several new chemical elements which possessed the same property, but many times more intense than uranium, the most important of these was radium. Shortly afterwards it was established, mainly by Rutherford, that three types of radiations called α-, β-, and γ-rays, are emitted from radioactive substances. It was also Rutherford who, jointly with Soddy, deduced that the emission of the radiations is associated with the spontaneous disintegration of atoms which result in the transformation of one radioactive substance into another. A series of such transformations ends when a stable element is produced. All of the heavy radioactive elements can be arranged in three radioactive series, called, the uranium, thorium, and actinium series. Initially, radioactivity was thought to be a property confined only to a few elements occurring in nature. In 1934, however, Irene and Frederick Joliot-Curie discovered that ordinary elements can be transformed into radioactive forms by subjecting them to bombardment with α-particles. Following this, it was found that beams of other fast particles produced in accelerators can also render ordinary substances radioactive. Nowadays it is known that radioactivity is a general property of matter; any chemical element can be produced in one or more radioactive forms, or isotopes. *See* F11.

Radio Astronomy. The science of radio astronomy makes use of radio apparatus and techniques for the observation of events occurring in far distant parts of the universe, and, in so doing, is able to enlarge upon the observational field of optical astronomy in a remarkable way. By means of radio telescopes it is possible to observe parts of the universe so far distant that the radio waves received have taken thousands of millions of years to travel from their source to the earth, and thus to observe happenings which may have occurred near the beginning of the history of the universe. Thus radio astronomy works with signals that are broadcast by objects in space.

There are two main types of radio telescope. The first, known as the interferometer, uses aerials spaced at large distances so as to cover a wide tract of ground. This has a high "resolution" but suffers from the disadvantage that it can "observe" only a very limited area of the sky overhead, as the earth turns upon its axis. The second, and "steerable," type, is that of the radio telescope at Jodrell Bank, Cheshire, which consists of an enormous concave metal bowl, with the radio aerials at its centre. This, though it has a lower "resolution," can be directed or "steered" on to any part of the sky which is above the horizon, and so can undertake a much more comprehensive observational programme. It can be used either to receive radio waves coming from desired sources or to transmit them and then pick up the echo from, for example, the moon or a planet, as in radar.

One source of radio waves which can be detected by radio telescopes is our own sun, whose behaviour under "quiet" and "abnormal" conditions can be observed in this way. Some of the planets also appear to emit radio waves from parts of their surface. But much more remarkable are the waves which are received from quasars (*q.v.*).

Radiosonde, a weather station in miniature carried

aloft by a free balloon to heights normally in the neighbourhood of 10 miles. Signals representative of values of atmospheric pressure, temperature and humidity are transmitted simultaneously by radio to ground receiving apparatus. The position of the balloon at any instant can be determined by radar, enabling the speed and direction of the upper winds to be deduced.

Radium, a radioactive metal, symbol Ra, discovered by Marie and Pierre Curie in 1898. Atomic weight 226. The Radium Institute, founded and equipped by Lord Iveagh and Sir Ernest Cassel, was opened in 1911 for the treatment of patients and research into the effect of radium on the human system. Radiotherapy (use of X-rays from radium) is used in the treatment of cancer.

Radon, a radioactive gaseous element, symbol Rn, formed by radioactive decay of radium. Its discovery completed the series of elements known as the inert (or rare) gases.

Rail, a well-known genus of the *Rallidae* family, including the Water Rail, the Moorhen, Corncrake, and Coot, resident in the British Isles.

Rain. When moist air rises into lower temperatures and becomes saturated, condensation takes place on the numerous hygroscopic particles present in the atmosphere. If the temperature is above freezing a cloud of small droplets is formed, and as the air continues to rise they grow in size until the weight is great enough to make them fall to the earth as rain. The formation of large raindrops has been attributed to coagulation of smaller drops of different sizes, while another mechanism depends upon the presence in the cloud of ice crystals as well as water drops. In temperate latitudes snowflakes falling from the freezing level melt in the warmer air below, producing large raindrops which grow in their flight through the lower part of the cloud.

Rainbow, a beautiful colour effect visible to an observer with back to the sun and facing a rain shower, caused by the refraction and reflection of sunlight in minute water-droplets in the air. From high in the air it would be possible to see a rainbow as a complete circle, but from the ground the most that can be seen is a semicircle when the sun is just on the horizon; the higher the sun is, the smaller the arc of the rainbow. When conditions are suitable two bows are seen, the secondary with the colours of the spectrum reversed. The colours of the rainbow are seven: red, orange, yellow, green, blue, indigo, and violet—the colours of the spectrum. *See also* Aurora.

Raingauge, an instrument consisting of a deep metal funnel whose stem dips into a graduated glass jar from which the depth of the rain water collected can be read. Continuous records of rainfall are provided by self-registering instruments.

Rain Making is a facility long desired by mankind, especially in the drought-ridden regions, and attempted throughout history by numerous non-scientific means. Since the Second World War it has been proved that clouds can sometimes be made to rain or snow by dropping into them from an aeroplane very cold particles of solid carbon dioxide or certain chemicals. This makes the moisture of the cloud form tiny ice crystals which grow big and finally fall out of the cloud. The process is quite complicated and not fully understood and the practical exploitation is somewhat chancy at present, but experiments have been made in many countries and the United States has a considerable programme of study. As well as scientific there are commercial and legal problems; premature commercial exploitation has resulted in disillusionment in some cases.

Rambouillet, a royal French château (14th cent., rebuilt 18th cent.), near Paris, and the official summer residence of the President of the French Republic. Also the name of the famous literary salon of the Marquise de Rambouillet (1588–1665).

Rampant, in heraldry, is a term applied to the figure of an animal with forelegs elevated, the dexter uppermost. When the animal is shown side-faced it is *rampant displayed*, when full-face, *rampant guardant*; when looking back, *rampant reguardant*: and when in sitting position *rampant sejant*.

Rape, a cruciferous plant yielding coleseed or rapeseed, extensively grown in all parts of Europe and India. Rape oil or colza is made from the seeds, and the leaves and refuse are used for sheep-food. Rape oil is a yellow, thick oil, of considerable commercial importance as a lubricant and for other purposes. It was at one time much used as an illuminant.

Rare Gases (also called **Inert Gases**). These are a group of elements which are chemically inert, comprising helium, neon, argon, krypton, xenon, and radon. Cavendish in 1785 noticed that there was in air some gas which was not oxygen, nitrogen, or carbon dioxide, but it was not until 1894 that the first of the rare gases was found by Rayleigh and Ramsay. This they called argon (inert). After the discovery of helium in 1895 Kayser, Rayleigh and Travers soon isolated the other gases except radon, which was later detected as a radioactive decay product of radium. Some of these inert gases are used to fill electric-light bulbs, and helium is used in balloons, since it is very light.

Rat, a well-known order of rodent embracing many species. The *brown rat* appeared in Europe early in the 18th cent., coming from the East and entering by way of Russia; now it is widespread and met with in Britain and all parts of the Continent. The *black rat*, which was the common rat before the arrival of the brown species, is a smaller animal and now comparatively scarce. There are numerous other kinds, all of them gross feeders, and existing in such numbers in many places as to constitute a pest. *See* Z13.

Rationalism. *See* J43.

Rattlesnake, venomous snakes which obtain their name from the possession of a rattle in the end of their tail, consisting of horny pieces so arranged that when vibrated they make a rattling sound. They are only found in N. and S. America.

Raven, a black-plumaged bird of the crow family, with raucous voice and massive bill. Occurs in many parts of Europe, Asia, and America. Ravens are easily domesticated and form interesting pets. Dickens had one which he described in *Barnaby Rudge*.

Ray, fish with a very flat body and broad and fleshy pectoral fins, related to the sharks. There are about 140 species. In Britain they are generally called *skate*.

Razorbill, a sea-bird of the auk family, having a high, furrowed bill and black-and-white plumage. It inhabits rocky cliffs during the breeding season, and at other times is mostly out on the open sea.

Realism is a vague term. For its use in philosophy *see* J44(1). As a movement in art it can be said to have started with Gustave Courbet in the mid-19th cent. in his revolt against the classicism of Ingres and the romanticism of Delacroix. He was a man of strong radical views, and like Zola, Balzac, and Flaubert in literature, turned to the actuality of everyday life, recording it with frankness and vigour. Some young English painters, notably Bratby, of the "kitchen sink" school, practise what some describe as social realism. In another sense, realism is an attitude concerned with interpreting the essential nature of the subject, revealing truths hidden by the accidentals of ordinary visual appearance. Thus form becomes more significant than content. Beginning with Cézanne and Van Gogh this trend passes on to Cubist and Abstract painting.

Record Office, in Chancery Lane, London, the place where the Public Records of England are preserved, including Domesday Book, the various Rolls of Charters, and important historical documents.

Rectifier, an electrical device which will allow electric current to flow in one direction only and can therefore be used for turning alternating current into direct current. Since electricity is usually supplied in alternating form and frequently needed in direct form, rectifiers are of very common use both in industry and the home, for example in radio and television and for battery chargers. Rectifying properties are possessed by a number of different devices, one of which is a thermionic diode (*see* Valve).

Very large valves filled with mercury vapour are often used for rectifying heavy currents for industrial purposes. Many other rectifiers use semiconductors in close contact with metals or with other semiconductors because such junctions have the property of passing electric current easily only in one direction.

Recusants, people who refused to attend the Anglican Church or to acknowledge the ecclesiastical supremacy of the Crown in the 16th and 17th cent.

Red Crag, the name given to a strata of gravel or sand, containing certain fossil mollusc deposits, found on the Suffolk and Norfolk coasts.

Red Cross. *See* Geneva Convention.

Red-Letter Day, a Church festival day indicated in the Prayer Book by red letters, now a popular term for any day of special significance.

Redstart, a small bird of the Thrush family of handsome plumage and striking song. Two species visit Great Britain; the Common Redstart, with bright chestnut rump and tail, white forehead, and black cheeks, favours wooded country, and the Black Redstart, with black breast and throat, chestnut tail and white wing bars, prefers rocky ground or bombed buildings, and has recently begun to breed in S. England.

Redwing, a bird of the Thrush family which finds its way to this country for the winter. Resembles the song thrush, but distinguished by smaller size, buffish-white eye-stripe, chestnut flanks and underwings. It has bred in Scotland and on Fair Isle.

Redwood *or* **Sequoia.** This genus of coniferous tree comprises two species of Redwoods occurring in N.W. America. Specimens of one species, the Giant Redwood, reach a height of over 300 ft. and a thickness of 36 ft. The age of the largest, the General Sherman tree, is put at 3,500 years.

Referendum and Initiative, two methods by which the wishes of electors may be expressed with regard to proposed legislation. It is developed to the highest extent in Switzerland. In a referendum some specific matter is referred to the electors. The Initiative is the means by which electors can compel their representatives to consider a specific issue. After consideration by the legislature it must then be submitted to the electorate for approval (*i.e.*, a referendum). Gen. de Gaulle made use of the referendum in seeking the consent of the French nation for his policies. In a democracy a referendum should be preceded by a programme of education and public debate.

Reformation. *See* J44, 29.

Reform Bills. The principal Bills have been passed for the reform of the Parliamentary franchise. The first was the great Reform Bill of 1832, introduced by Lord John Russell and enacted under the Whig administration of Lord Grey. In addition to a sweeping redistribution of seats, this Act greatly extended the franchise but still left many people without the right to vote. The second Bill, passed by Disraeli in 1867, by giving the vote to workers in towns, established household suffrage. A third Bill, passed in 1884 under a Gladstone ministry, removed the distinction between borough and county franchises, enfranchised agricultural workers, and thus gave the vote to all men over 21. Women had to wait until 1918 to get the vote at the age of 30. The Representation of the People (Equal Franchise) Act, 1928, gave them the right to be registered as Parliamentary electors at the age of 21, thus making England into a true democracy. The Representation of the People Act, 1948, abolished the representation of the universities and the separate representation of the City of London and the business-premises vote.

Refraction. The change of direction which light rays and other rays undergo when passing from one medium to another. The phenomenon is due to the fact that in different media light (and other forms of radiation) has different speeds.

Refractory, a substance capable of standing high temperatures and therefore useful for making furnaces and allied apparatus. Some insulating refractories are fire-clay, alumina, porcelain, carborundum, graphite, and silica. Some refractory metals are platinum, molybdenum,

tungsten, tantalum, and the alloys nichrome, chromel, alumel.

Reindeer, a genus of deer horned in both sexes, occurring only in northerly regions. It has an average height of 4 ft. 6 in., is very fleet of foot, and the Laplanders utilise it for draught purposes and for food.

Relativity. The laws of relativity have been substantially proved and have revolutionised our ideas as to the nature of space, time, matter, and energy and forced us to think along new lines. In 1949 a new theory by Einstein was announced which sets forth in a series of equations the laws governing both gravitation and electromagnetism, which is said to bridge the gap that separates the universe of the stars and galaxies and the universe of the atom. At present the one is explained by relativity, and the other rests on the quantum theory. *See* **F15.**

Relief in sculpture is of three kinds—high relief (*alto-relievo*), in which the figures stand out to the extent of one-half of their natural proportions, low-relief (*basso-relievo*) when the figures project but slightly; and middle-relief (*mezzo-relievo*), when the projection is intermediate.

Renaissance. *See* **J44.**

Republican Party of the United States was born by the fusion in 1854 of the group who called themselves National Republicans, having split from the Democrats over tariffs in 1825, and the northern Democrats, both of them being opposed to slavery. It came to power when Abraham Lincoln was elected President in 1860 and won 14 of the 18 presidential elections held between 1860 and 1932. It was defeated in 1932 largely as a result of the economic depression and reached its lowest ebb in the years of Roosevelt's New Deal (*q.v.*). The Party went on being defeated every four years until Eisenhower's victory in 1952. Nixon narrowly failed to defeat Kennedy in 1960 and Goldwater was decisively beaten by Lyndon Johnson in 1964. In 1968 Nixon was successful in winning the Presidency. The Party has its interventionist and its isolationist wings, its hawks (conservatives) and its doves (liberals). The symbol of the party is an elephant, the invention of Nash, a cartoonist, in 1874.

Requiem. Properly a mass for the dead, the term is extended to cover musical settings by Palestrina, Mozart, Verdi, and others.

Reredos, the ornamental screen at the back of the altar or communion table. It is often of a highly decorative character and is an architectural feature in many churches in Spain. Other examples are to be found in the following cathedrals in England: Southwark, St. Albans, Winchester, Durham, and Liverpool.

Resins, natural resins are vegetable compounds largely employed in the industrial arts. They comprise india-rubber, amber, mastic, copal, etc. "Synthetic resins" is a term sometimes used as a synonym for "plastics."

Reuter, an international news agency, organised since 1941 as a trust and owned by the newspapers of Britain, Australia, and New Zealand, founded by Baron J. de Reuter in 1849.

Rhea, a large flightless bird, the "ostrich" of S. America, distinguished from the ostrich proper by smaller size, longer beak, larger wings, no tail and 3 toes instead of 2. There are 2 species.

Rheology, the science of flow. *See* **F17(2).**

Rhesus Factor. *See* Index to Section P.

Rhinoceros, a large hoofed quadruped, of which there are nine existing species native to the river and marsh regions of Africa, India, Borneo, and Java. It is remarkable for its thick hide and upturned snout, from which springs a long horn. The white rhinoceros, which is scarce, is the biggest species, attaining a length of 10–12 ft. and a height of from 5 to 6 ft.

Rhodium, a metallic element, symbol Rh, discovered by Wollaston in 1804. It is found in platinum ores in small amounts, generally less than 2 per cent. With platinum it gives a very hard and durable alloy. It is also used, instead of silver, in putting the reflecting layer on a mirror.

Ribbon Fish *or* **Oarfish,** a deep-sea fish, deriving its name from its ribbon-like shape. Though many feet in length, it is only an inch or two thick. The ribbon fish is rarely met with because of its habitat, and most of what is

known about it has been learnt from specimens occasionally cast ashore during storms.

Rice, a grain-yielding grass, of which thousands of strains are known today, extensively cultivated in China, India, and certain parts of America, and forming the main food of the peoples of China, Japan, India, and the Malayan regions. Some 95 per cent. of the world's rice is produced and consumed in the Orient. The grain with the husk is known as "paddy." Arrack, an alcoholic liquor, is made from fermented rice seeds.

Rime, a crystalline deposit of ice formed on objects exposed to wet fog at the same time as frost.

Rinderpest *or* **Cattle Plague,** is a highly contagious disease affecting cattle, sheep, and other ruminants. In Europe the disease has been eradicated, but it was formerly very widespread and caused great loss of life amongst cattle. The disease is caused by a filtrable virus, and is attended by fever and congestion of the mucous membranes.

Ring Dove *or* **Wood Pigeon,** a blue-grey bird, distinguished from other pigeons by larger size (16 in.), white wing-bar, glossy green-and-purple neck, and white half-collar. It is very common in Britain.

Rituale, the book of rites used in the Roman Catholic Church for the administration of certain sacraments and other church ceremonies. Like the Roman breviary, it dates in its present form from the Council of Trent.

RNA. (Ribonucleic Acid). *See* **Nucleic Acids.**

Roaring Forties, name applied to the prevailing westerly winds over the oceans in the temperate latitudes of the Southern Hemisphere.

Robin (or Redbreast). A small bird with olive-brown upper parts and orange-red forehead, throat, and breast; both sexes look alike. The young are speckled, lacking the red breast. Its wide European distribution includes the British Isles, where it is the national bird. It also occurs in N. Africa and W. Asia. The nest is placed in a great variety of situations including holes in banks, trees, and walls; in sheds, amongst ivy, and sometimes in old tins. Nesting-boxes are readily adopted, but care should be taken to ensure that the entrance-hole is small enough to exclude starlings. Robins are pugnacious and defend their territories with vigour. Their attractive appearance, trustful disposition, engaging ways, and sweet song make them extremely popular. The name robin is also applied to a number of very different birds, one of which, the American Robin, occasionally wanders to Europe.

Rock Dove, the grey pigeon *Columba livia* of Europe and Asia, ancestor of the domestic pigeons as Darwin was the first to show.

Rockets for use in war were first studied by Sir William Congreve early in the 19th cent., and proved very destructive in siege operations. They were invented by the Chinese as long ago as the 11th cent. The Germans devised the huge V2 rocket, carrying a ton of explosive, which was used near the end of the war to bombard London. Rockets are propelled by the burning of fuel (*e.g.*, oxygen or nitric acid), the exhaust, being ejected at high velocity, thrusts the rocket forward. For the study of the properties of the atmosphere vertical sounding rockets are used. Rocket flight in outer space was first presented as practicable by the Russian rocket expert, K. E. Tsiolkovsky, in 1903. The provision of sufficient launching velocity involves the use of rocket motors with adequate thrust. To launch a satellite into an orbit circulating within a few hundred miles of the surface a velocity of 18,000 m.p.h. must be imparted. This may be done by using a multi-stage launching system. When the first-stage motor has burned out it drops off, so that, when the second-stage motor ignites, it does not have to support the weight of the first-stage, and so on. If the launching velocity is increased to 25,000 m.p.h. the vehicle will not return to the neighbourhood of the earth but pass out of the range of the earth's gravitational pull completely. Unless the launching velocity reaches 100,000 m.p.h. it will not escape from the sun and will become an artificial planet. *See also* **Space Research.**

Rock Magnetism. The study of naturally occurring magnetism in rocks is a subject which has gained considerable importance in recent years.

There are two principal reasons for this. One is that this so-called " fossilised magnetism " may be able to tell us more about the past history of the earth's magnetic field. The other is that after many years of heated dispute between geologists rock magnetism promises to settle once and for all the controversy as to whether or not the continents have changed their relative positions in past times (continental drift theory (*q.v.*)). This branch of geophysical research, in addition to its academic interest, may well have important economic consequences. It might, for instance, become possible to locate mineral deposits once accumulated under special conditions at certain latitudes but now drifted to other places. Salt and similar deposits formed by the continuous evaporation of solutions in hot countries are one example; oil may well be another. There has been a *steady* change in rock magnetisation direction with geological time. It is now known with some accuracy that the most recent reversal took place 700,000 years ago. It has been found that the older the rock, the farther removed is its fossil magnetisation from the present field. *See* F59(2).

Rococo, an architectural style which was, in effect, the final stage of Baroque (*q.v.*). The name first came into use about 1830 to describe the period 1720–70 and means " shell-shaped " (French *Rocaille*), since the shell was a favourite motif in Rococo ornamentation. About the beginning of the early 18th cent. the heavy older type of Baroque began to show even less restraint than had characterised it in the past; it became still less utilitarian, and showed a kind of playful lighthearted vitality which manifested itself in a wealth of ornamental invention. Baroque was flamboyant and robust, Rococo frivolous. In architecture Rococo is naturally found in those areas where the Baroque had flourished, *i.e.*, Munich, Prague, Vienna, and Dresden. In painting, the best expressions of Rococo are to be seen in the works of the French painters Watteau (d. 1721), Boucher (d. 1770), a favourite of Mme de Pompadour, and famous as a decorator of boudoirs, and Fragonard (d. 1806). (As in the case of Baroque, it was typical of Rococo that the sculpture, painting, and the decorative arts of a building all expressed the same spirit.)

Roe, popular name given to organs in fish which produce eggs and sperms. " Hard roe " is that of the female and consists of eggs; that of the male is the soft roe or milt.

Roebuck, a deer that was formerly common in the forests and parks of Britain, but is now only found at large in the northern parts of Scotland.

Roller, a tropical Old World bird of the *Coraciidae* family, related to the hoopoe, kingfisher and bee-eater, of strikingly brilliant blue, chestnut, greenish-blue plumage. There are fifteen species, one of which breeds in the far north and visits the British Isles on its migrations to and from its winter quarters in Africa.

Romanesque Architecture, prevailed throughout Europe from the mid-10th to the 13th cent., and implies an art which developed from that of the Romans. Notable in Romanesque style were the rounded arch and masonry vaulting. Romanesque led to the graceful and more complex Gothic (*q.v.*). The Italians never regarded Gothic highly and Romanesque churches, generally based on the basilican plan (oblong with double colonnades and a semi-circular apse at the end), continued to be built there until the beginning of the 15th cent. Some of the best examples can be seen at Pisa (11th cent.), Florence (San Miniato, 1013), Lucca (12th cent.), and Milan (the 12th cent. San Ambrogio, most famous of all). In Germany Romanesque architecture flourished longer than in France or England; the most famous churches are in the valley of the Rhine, at Cologne (completely destroyed during the second world war), Mainz and Speyer. In France Romanesque churches are found in Burgundy, Provence and Normandy. For English Romanesque *see* Norman Architecture.

Roman Roads, highways constructed by the Romans. They were of great durability. The best known British roads were Ermine Street (London, Lincoln, York), Fosse Way (Lincoln through Leicester, Cirencester, Bath, Exeter), Watling Street (London to Shropshire).

Romanticism, a term for a movement in the arts—whether in music, painting, sculpture or literature—which seeks to give expression to the artist's feelings about his subject rather than to be concerned with form or reality. The romantic view is that art is nature seen through a temperament; the realist view is that art is a slice of life. In painting Delacroix (1798–1863) is the romantic artist par excellence with his uncontrolled expression of the passions and love of the exotic. In literature the Romantic movement reached its finest form in the works of Goethe, Schiller, and Heine; in the poetry of Byron, Keats, Wordsworth, Shelley and Blake; and in the writings of Victor Hugo. Since Romanticism is partly a matter of temperament in the artist just as Classicism is, it may be found at all times and places, although whether or not it becomes predominant depends on contemporary taste. Cubism, for example, with its attention to form is classical, whereas Surrealism with its attention to content is romantic. *See also* Romantic Movement. J45.

Roman Walls were built as frontier barriers under the Emperors Hadrian (76–138) and Antoninus Pius (86–161). Hadrian's works, linking Wallsend-on-Tyne with Bowness-on-Solway, comprised a twenty-foot stone wall, ditches, turrets, " milecastles," fortresses, and a double earthen mound, or " Vallum." Impressive ruins are still visible at Chesters and Housesteads. Antoninus Pius, Hadrian's successor, made a further advance, but the turf wall which he built between Forth and Clyde was soon abandoned. Septimius Severus (146–211) restored Hadrian's wall after the assassination of Commodus and the subsequent civil wars. It was finally abandoned between 380 and 390.

Rood Screen, an ornamental partition, separating the choir from the nave in a church, and supporting a crucifix or rood.

Rook, a member of the crow family, abounding in most parts of the British Isles and found in Europe, Asia, and N. Africa. It has been introduced into New Zealand. Rooks usually nest in colonies in tall trees. They are highly intelligent birds, and their ways have long been the subject of much careful study.

Rosary, a circular chain of beads, used by Catholics when reciting a particular form of sustained prayer. Each bead represents an entire prayer, and the combined prayers constitute the Rosary.

Roses, Wars of the (1455–85), between the rival houses of York and Lancaster, for the possession of the English crown, began in the reign of Henry VI. and ended with the death of Richard III. on Bosworth Field. The emblem or badge of the Lancastrians was the red rose and of the Yorkists the white rose. All rivalry between the Roses ended by the marriage of Henry VII., the Lancastrian, with the Princess Elizabeth, daughter of Edward IV., the Yorkist.

Rosetta Stone, discovered in 1799 by the French at Rosetta in Egypt, and deposited in the British Museum. It is a piece of black basalt about 3 ft. long, and contains a decree of the Egyptian priests of Ptolemy V. Epiphanes (205–181 B.C.) in (1) hieroglyphics, (2) demotic, and (3) Greek characters. It was by means of the three different inscriptions on the same stone that hieroglyphic writing was first able to be deciphered.

Rotten Row, a corruption of *route de roi* (king's drive), the famous riding resort in Hyde Park.

Rouge et Noir, a well-known gambling card game played on a table divided into two sections and marked with two black and two red lozenges. Any number of players can take part, and the money is staked on the red or black spaces. The cards are dealt out, first to Noir, until the pips aggregate more than 30; then in like manner to the Rouge, and the packet coming nearest to 31 wins the stakes.

Roulette, a gambling game played on a table carrying a revolving wheel divided into 37 compartments. Each compartment bears a number, 0 (zero) and 1 to 36. The numbers are mixed and do not follow any particular order. Of these 37 numbers 18 are black and 18 are red, whereas zero is green. The players stake their money on any compartment, colour, or combination of numbers they please.

The wheel is whirled round and a ball is set rolling in the opposite direction, dropping finally into one of the compartments, thus deciding the winning number and colour.

Roundhead. In the reign of Charles I. and later, a Puritan or member of the Parliamentary party who wore his hair cut short. It was originally a term of derision applied by the Royalists, who usually wore ringlets.

Round Towers, high circular towers with conical roof and massive masonry walls, built during the early Middle Ages (c. 10th cent.) It is believed that they served as refuges and lookouts. These buildings are numerous in Ireland, and three remain in Scotland, including that at Brechin which is attached to the church.

Royal Academy of Arts was founded in London in 1768, under the patronage of George III. The early exhibitions of the Academy were held first in Pall Mall, and after in Somerset House, where the exhibitions continued to be held until 1836, when the National Gallery being built, the Academy moved its quarters to that building. In 1869 the present Royal Academy at Burlington House was opened. The Academy numbers 58 R.A.s and about 30 A.R.A.s. List of presidents: Sir Joshua Reynolds (1768), Benjamin West (1792), James Wyatt (1805), B. West (1806), Sir Thomas Lawrence (1820), Sir M. A. Shee (1830), Sir C. Eastlake (1850), Sir F. Grant (1866), Lord Leighton (1878), Sir J. E. Millais (1896), Sir E. J. Poynter (1896), Sir Aston Webb (1919), Sir F. Dicksee (1924), Sir William Llewellyn (1928), Sir E. Lutyens (1938), Sir A. J. Munnings (1944), Sir Gerald F. Kelly (1949), Sir A. E. Richardson (1954), Sir Charles Wheeler (1956) and Walter T. Monnington (1966). The Academy holds an exhibition of pictures, statuary, and architectural designs every summer.

Royal Hospital, Chelsea, built by Wren, was opened in 1694 as an institution for invalid soldiers.

Royal Institution, established 1799, and incorporated by Royal Charter in 1800 for " the promotion, extension, and diffusion of Science and of Useful Knowledge." It was in the building of the Institution that Faraday conducted his experiments. It supports four professors: natural philosophy, astronomy, chemistry, and physiology. Famous also for its Christmas lectures designed for a juvenile audience.

Royal Society was founded in 1660 and incorporated by Royal Charter in 1662, Viscount Brouncker being named the first president. Its *Philosophical Transactions* date from 1665. Among those who served as president of the Royal Society are Sir Christopher Wren, Pepys, Sir Isaac Newton, Sir Joseph Banks, Sir Humphry Davy, Prof. T. H. Huxley, Lord Rayleigh, Sir Archibald Geikie, Sir J. J. Thomson, O.M., Prof. Sir C. S. Sherrington, O.M., G.B.E., Lord Rutherford, O.M., Sir William Henry Bragg, O.M., Sir Henry Dale, O.M., Sir Robert Robinson, O.M., Lord Adrian, O.M., Sir Cyril Hinshelwood, O.M., Lord Florey, O.M., Lord Blackett O.M. (1965), Professor A. L. Hodgkin (1971).

Rubber, produced from the juice of certain trees and shrubs of tropical countries, is in such extensive demand now for tyres and other purposes that rubber plantations have been established in almost every part of the world where rubber can be grown, particularly in Malaysia and Indonesia. The best kinds come from the Amazon valley. In recent years great advances have been made in the production of synthetic rubber.

Rubicon, a small river falling into the Adriatic, and forming one of the Italian boundaries, the crossing of which anciently involved decisive action and constituted a declaration of war. Thus the phrase " crossing the Rubicon ", denoting an act from which there is no withdrawal.

Rubidium, a metallic element, symbol Rb, most closely resembling potassium. It is silver-white and very soft, and was discovered in 1861 by Bunsen and Kirchhoff, using the spectroscope. It is rare, occurring in small amounts in the mica called lepidolite and in potash salts of the Strassfurt deposits in Germany.

Rubrics are instructions in regard to the ceremonies of the Church, appearing in red in the Prayer Book.

Ruby is a deep red variety of Corundum (aluminium oxide); one of the most valued of precious stones. Burma yields some of the finest, and rubies of inferior colour are found in Siam, Ceylon, South Africa, and Brazil.

Rudd, a fresh-water fish of wide distribution, plentiful in the rivers of Britain, and found in most other parts of Europe, also in Asia Minor. It is of a reddish-gold colour, with a greenish-blue beard.

Ruff, a bird related to the common sandpiper, at one time common in the Fen districts. The males have a ruff of feathers round the neck in the breeding season. The female is the Reeve.

Ruffe *or* **Pope,** a small fresh-water fish common in most parts of central Europe, and similar in appearance to the ordinary perch. It is found in British rivers.

" **Rule, Britannia !** " the national sea-song of England, was written by James Thomson (1700–48), the author of the " Seasons," and set to music by Dr. Arne about 1740. The poet's words were " Britannia, rule the waves! " but it is usually rendered " Britannia rules the waves."

Rum, an ardent spirit distilled from molasses, and containing from 40 to 50 per cent. of alcohol. It is chiefly manufactured in the West Indies, and derives its special flavour from a volatile oil.

Ruminants, animals that chew the cud, being provided with a compartmented stomach, enabling them to swallow food, and later to bring it back to the mouth for mastication; *e.g.,* sheep, goats, oxen, etc. While in the rumen, or storage compartment, some digestion of food, especially cellulose, takes place by bacterial action.

Runcible spoon, a kind of fork used for pickles having three broad prongs. The word was used by Edward Lear about 1870 as a nonsense word and may be derived from *Rouncival* meaning large or huge from the bones said to have been dug up at *Roncesvalles* where Roland fell. Rouncival peas are the large peas called " marrowfats."

Runes, certain characters of an alphabet found in inscriptions in the Germanic languages, discovered cut upon stone monuments and implements found in many parts of Europe, including England. The runic alphabet originally had 24 letters. Scholars agree that some of the runes derive from Greek and others from Latin.

Ruskin College, the first residential college for working people, founded at Oxford in 1899 by Mr. Walter Vrooman, an American.

Rusts, parasitic fungi, some common species of which have reddish spores which in a mass have a rusty appearance. A well-known species is the Wheat Rust (*Puccinia graminis*), which has an alternative host in the barberry.

Ruthenium, a greyish-white metallic element, symbol Ru, discovered by Claus in 1845. It is harder and more brittle than platinum, in whose ores it occurs.

Rutile, mineral titanium dioxide. It is found in many igneous rocks, and in gneisses and schists. Its commonest colour is reddish-brown.

S

Sabaoth, a Hebrew word, meaning an army or host, and applied sometimes to the Supreme Being, *e.g.,* " the Lord of Hosts " (Rom. ix. 29).

Sabbath and Sunday. Sunday, or the Lord's Day, is the first day of the week in the Christian year. It was substituted for the Jewish Sabbath in the 1st cent. A.D. as the Christian day of worship in commemoration of the Resurrection. The Sabbath, in the Jewish system, was the last day of the week (Saturday in the Christian calendar), designated as the day of religious rest in the fourth commandment of the Decalogue. It was the Puritans at the time of the Reformation who applied the term Sabbath to the Christian Sunday and the two terms have been used indiscriminately ever since.

Sabbatical Year was instituted by the Jews in ancient times for the purpose of giving the soil a rest from cultivation. This was every seventh year. In universities a sabbatical year is a year of absence from duty for the purpose of study and travel, granted to professors at certain intervals.

Sable, a furred mammal of the weasel family

mainly inhabiting Siberia. It is bright brown in colour, and has a long, bushy tail. American sable is a marten.

Saccharin, a white crystalline solid manufactured from toluene, 550 times as sweet as cane sugar. It is used as a sweetening agent; as a substitute for sugar when sugar is forbidden, as in certain diseases, or when there is a shortage. It has no value as a food.

Sack, the white dry wines of Spain and Madeira, canary being the most popular.

Safety Lamp, as used in coal mines, was invented by Sir Humphry Davy in 1816. The flame is enclosed in a cage of fine-meshed wire which allows air to enter and promote burning, but conducts away the heat generated in combustion so that no product of combustion escapes at a temperature high enough to ignite explosive gases in the mine.

Sainfoin, a widely cultivated forage plant, especially adapted for sheep. It is of strong, leafy growth and bears bright red flowers. It belongs to the same family of flowering plants as peas and beans.

St. Elmo's Fire, a glowing brush-like discharge of electricity which takes place from sharp-pointed objects on mountains or the masts of ships exposed to the intense electric fields of thunder-clouds.

Saints' Days. In the liturgy of the Roman Catholic church a saint is commemorated and his intercession sought on a special day (saint's day), usually the anniversary of his death. Pope Paul has decreed that from 1 January 1970 the following saints are to be dropped from the calendar: Christopher, Catherine of Alexandria, Alexis, Pudenzia, Susan, Margaret, Viviana, Eustace, Martina, Venantius, and Domitilla. Many others, including our own Saint George, and Nicholas (Santa Claus) have been demoted though they may be worshipped locally. There are now only 153 saints' days in addition to those in honour of the Apostles, Saint Joseph and the Virgin Mary. The festival of All Saints is on 1 November.

Salamanders are amphibia superficially resembling lizards, from which they differ in having a moist skin and no scales.

Salic Law was probably instituted in France in the 5th cent. for the purpose of excluding females from inheriting the Crown. The Bourbons introduced the same law into Spain, but this was abolished by decree in 1830 to enable Isabella II. to succeed.

Salmon, a familiar fish notable for its habit of ascending rivers from the sea in the autumn and there depositing its spawn, not returning to the sea until the early spring. The salmon fishing season varies from place to place.

Saltpetre. *See* **Nitre**.

Salvarsan, the organic arsenical compound arsphenamine, which Ehrlich discovered was able to kill inside the human body the spirochæte germ that causes syphilis. Also known as "606." It has been superseded by neosalvarsan.

Salvation Army. *See* **J45**.

Sanctuaries were places where offenders against the law were free from arrest, and previous to 1697, when sanctuaries were suppressed, several parts of London were treated as sanctuaries. The chief of these refuge localities was in White-friars. There were others in the Minories, Mitre Court, the Savoy, Westminster, and the Mint. Other sanctuaries were at Beverley and at St. Burian's in Cornwall.

Sanderling, small wading bird of sandpiper family; breeds in tundra regions of far north, and is seen on sandy beaches of Britain as a winter visitor. Conspicuous white wing stripe and, like Curlew, Sandpiper, Knot, Dunlin, and other members of sandpiper family, has marked change of plumage between winter and summer.

Sandpiper, small- to medium-sized wading birds of several species whose migratory powers are so great that they are found in most parts of the world. They include the Common Sandpiper, a bird about 7 in. long, greenish-brown head and back, white under-parts; beak long and slender. Other species met with in Britain are the Green, Purple, Wood, and Curlew-Sandpipers.

Sans-culottes (French = without knee breeches), a term applied by the French aristocrats to the revolutionary leaders during the French Revolu-

tion who wore long trousers instead of knee breeches.

Sanskrit is the language of ancient India, spoken by the Brahmins, and existing in early Oriental literature. It was the language of literature and government and is now confined to temples and places of learning. Its relationship to the modern Indian languages is rather like that of Latin and Greek to modern European languages. *See also* **M45(1)**.

Saponin. The term is a generic one applied to a range of organic compounds which produce frothy, soapy solutions. Saponins are extracted from the soapwort root, horse chestnut seeds, etc. Saponin is the basis of the "foam" used for fire fighting; it can be used like soap to make insecticides and fungicides adhere to the leaves of plants. Also used as detergents.

Sapphic Verse, a form of verse said to have been invented by Sappho, the lyric poetess of Lesbos, who flourished about 600 B.C.

Sapphire, a valuable deep blue variety of Corundum (aluminium oxide) found mostly in India, Ceylon, and Northern Italy. Synthetic sapphire is often used for gramophone styli.

Saracen, the name given in classic times to the Arab tribes of Syria and adjacent territories. In the Middle Ages the current designation among the Christians for their Muslim enemies.

Sarcophagus, the name given to a stone coffin, such as was used by the ancient Egyptians, Greeks, and Romans, for receiving the remains of their famous dead. These sarcophagi were often decorated with rich carvings and sculptures.

Sardonyx. *See* **Onyx**.

Sassanides were a dynasty of Persian rulers descended from Artaxerxes from 226 to 652.

Satellites are small planets revolving round the larger ones. The moon is the earth's only satellite. Jupiter has twelve; Saturn, nine; Uranus, five; Mars, two; and Neptune, two. Of the 1,750 objects in orbit round the earth in mid-1969, 371 were artificial earth satellites.

Satin-Bird, one of the bower birds of Australia; the male is silky blue-back and the female greyish green. *See* **Bower bird**.

Satinwood, the timber of a tree plentiful in India and Ceylon, and valued for cabinet work. It is of fine grain and very hard. Varieties also exist in the West Indies, Florida, and Tasmania.

Satrap, the name given in ancient times to a Persian Governor of a Province.

Saturday, the seventh day of the week (the Jewish Sabbath), derived its name from Saturn, or, as some hold, is called after the Saxon idol, Saterne, which was worshipped on this day.

Saturn, a planet, the sixth from the sun, from which it is distant about 886 millions of miles, and around which it makes a revolution in about twenty-nine and a half years. It is about 71,500 miles in mean diameter, or nine times as large as the earth, and rotates on its axis in ten and a quarter hours. It is surrounded by a series of rings composed of myriads of tiny satellites. It has nine small satellites. *See* **F7**.

Saturnalia, festivals held in ancient Rome in honour of the god Saturnus. They were made the scene of the most boisterous festivities, and were continued for several days at the end of December.

Sawfish, a large marine ray found in tropical America and Guinea, whose snout often attains the length of several feet, and is provided with saw-like teeth. This "saw" is swung from side to side among a shoal of fish which form the food of this ray.

Sawfly. These insects are considered to be the most primitive members of the order (*Hymeno-ptera*) to which the bees and wasps belong. In appearance they resemble somewhat the latter, but there is no waist separating thorax and abdomen. The ovipositor is never used as a sting; usually it is saw-like so that the female can use it to make incisions into tissues of plants where the eggs are laid. The larvae look like caterpillars of butterflies and moths. One of the commonest species occurs on gooseberry bushes.

Saxons, a Teutonic race originally inhabiting what is now Holstein. By the 7th cent. they had, with the Angles and Jutes, conquered and colonised most of England.

Scald, the name of the Norse poets, who were

similar to the bards of Wales. They had to celebrate the achievements of their warriors and leaders.

Scallop, marine bivalve molluscs of the genus *Pecten,* which is widely distributed. The scalloped edge to the shell results from a pattern of radiating grooves. Related to the oyster.

Scandium, a metal element, symbol Sc. It was discovered in 1879 by Nilson, and occurs in small quantities in certain rarer minerals such as wolframite.

Scapular, a vestment hanging from the shoulder to the knees, worn by members of certain Roman Catholic orders. The name is also given to two small pieces of cloth worn over the shoulders by lay members of the Church in honour of the Virgin.

Scarabaeidae, a family of beetles (Scarabs) widely distributed through Africa and Asia and the inner parts of Europe. It is to this genus that the " Sacred Beetle " of the Egyptians belongs, and numerous representations of it are found on ancient monuments.

Sceptre, the staff or rod constituting the symbol of supreme authority. Tarquin, the elder, was the first Roman to assume the sceptre in 468 B.C. The French kings of the 5th cent. made a golden rod their sceptre.

Schism, an ecclesiastical term for division in a church. The Great Schism was the separation of the Greek Church from the Latin, finally established in 1054. The Western Schism was the division in the Roman Catholic Church from 1378 to 1417, when there were two lines of popes, one at Rome and one at Avignon, which arose over the election of Urban VI. and Clement VII. to the papacy and was more a matter of persons and politics than a question of faith.

Schist, the geological name of certain metamorphic rocks composed for the most part of minerals with thin plate-like crystals (*e.g.,* mica) so that the layers of a schist are closely parallel. Quartz occurs in schists, and where it preponderates the term "quartz schist" is applied.

Scientific Units. The International Bureau of Weights and Measures at Sèvres near Paris, is the custodian of accurate scientific measurement in terms of internationally agreed units. Methods of measurement are continually being improved and measurements of new kinds coming into use. In defining units certain principles have evolved which can be expressed as a statement of priorities:

(i) units should be so defined that measurements made in one laboratory should be reproducible in another with as much consistency as possible;

(ii) units of all kinds should, so far as practical, form an interrelated system based on as few fundamental units as possible;

(iii) the fundamental units adopted should have a natural basis, independent of particular man-made objects such as metal bars or weights. An invariable universal natural standard was achieved for the metre in 1958 when it was defined in terms of the wavelength of a line in the spectrum of krypton–86. *See* **S.I. Units.**

Schoolmen, the great scholastic philosophers of the Middle Ages who devoted themselves to the study and exposition of questions of religious inquiry, and attempted to reconcile the teaching of the Church with that of Aristotle. The chief Schoolmen were Archbishop Anselm, Albertus Magnus, Thomas Aquinas, Peter Lombard, Duns Scotus. *See also* **J46.**

Scorpion. The scorpions constitute an order of the arthropods. Distinctive features are the pair of powerful claws at the head and a "sting" at the tail, which curves over the back in attack or defence so that it points forwards. The poison injected by the sting is potent, causing instant death in spiders, centipedes, etc., and acute discomfort to humans. The idea that a cornered scorpion can sting itself to death is a myth; scorpions are immune to their own poison.

Scorpion Fly. The scorpion fly, of which there are less than 500 species, constitute a separate order of insects, the *Mecoptera.* They have 2 pairs of membranous wings, and gain their popular

name because in some species the end of the abdomen is turned up, though it does not function as a sting.

Scree *or* **Talus,** the mass of loose, angular rock fragments which accumulate towards the bottom of hill-sides and mountain-sides. These fragments have been detached by weathering processes, in particular frost action.

Scythians, nomadic conquerors and skilled horsemen of ancient times (9th–3rd cent. B.C.) who inhabited much of Southern Europe and Asiatic Russia.

Sea Anemones *or* **Actinaria,** an order of marine animals of the cœlenterate class *Anthozia.* They form a large and varied group of about 1,100 species and occur in many beautiful colours, flower-like in form.

Sea Butterfly, marine molluscs which propel themselves by two "wings," or side expansions of the foot. They constitute the order called *Pteropoda.*

Sea Cow. *See* **Manatee.**

Sea Cucumbers *or* **Holothurians.** These animals constitute the class of echinoderms called *Holothuroidea.* They are elongated and worm-like, with a ring of about twenty tentacles round the mouth. There are about 500 species.

Sea Eagle, a genus of flesh-eating birds related to the true eagles, kites, and other birds of prey. Examples are the Bald Eagle, emblem of the U.S.A., White-tailed Eagle (Grey Sea Eagle), and Steller's Sea Eagle of the Pacific coast of Asia. Last known in Britain in 1911.

Sea Elephant *or* **Elephant Seal,** a curious genus of seal, the males of which possess a proboscis a foot or more in length that suggests an elephant's trunk. They are found on the coast of California and in certain parts of the Southern Ocean; their blubber has a commercial value.

Sea Gravimeter, a new instrument to determine the density of the earth's crust beneath the oceans of the world. Designed by Dr. A. Graf of Munich and Dr. J. Lamar Worzel of Columbia University, it can detect changes of one-millionth of the value of gravity at the earth's surface and is being used in the oceanographical research programme of the I.G.Y.

Sea Hare, a genus of molluscs (*Aplysia*), so-called because of resemblance to a crouching hare. The shell is thin curved plate largely sunk in the animal's body. They have four tentacles, occur in Britain in the laminaria or ribbon-wrack zone, and discharge a purple fluid when molested.

Sea Horse, a sea-fish (*Hippocampus*), very numerous in the tropics and comprising some twenty species. Their bodies are ringed and they have prehensile tails. Their heads are horse-shaped, and they swim in a vertical position.

Sea Lily. A class of echinoderms, the sea lilies may be roughly described as "stalked starfishes." There are about 400 living species, and several thousand extinct species are known. Otherwise called Crinoids.

Sea Mouse, a genus of marine worms called *Aphrodite,* oval in shape, 8 or 9 in. long, iridescent, covered with fine bristles.

Sea Squirts *or* **Tunicates.** These animals are placed in the sub-phylum called *Urochorda;* found growing in rounded, jelly-like masses on rocks near low-water level. They get their name through the water jets they discharge.

Sea Urchin, species forming the class *Echinoidae.* The body is globular and covered with spines which may be used for both defence and locomotion. The main organs of locomotion are, however, the tube feet, as in starfishes. Much has been learnt of recent years by marine biologists from experiments with the purple sea-urchin *Arbacia.*

Seasons comprise the four natural divisions of the year, and are due to the inclinations of the earth's axis to the plane of the elliptic. *See* **Section N.**

Secondary Sexual Characters. Characters of animals which are distinctive of sex, but have no direct connection with the reproductive process. Examples are: the mane of the lion and the antlers of some deer.

Secretary Bird, so called because of the quill-like plumes about its ears, is a bird of prey related to the eagles and vultures; common in Africa, and of considerable service as an exterminator of snakes. It is a large bird about 4 ft. in height.

Sedimentary Rocks. See **F8**(2).

Seismology, the branch of geophysics devoted to the study of earthquakes and other earth movements. The instruments used for the registration of earth tremors are termed seismographs and consist in principle of a pendulum system, the supporting framework following the ground movement and the bob remaining at rest, thus setting up a relative movement between two parts. In order to record the displacements completely, at one station, three seismographs are necessary to show the two horizontal and the vertical components of the motion. Apart from detection and study of waves from earthquakes, sensitive seismographs are now widely used in geophysical prospecting, particularly in the search for possible oilfields.

Selenium, a non-metallic element, symbol Se, related to sulphur, it is a dark red colour, and solid, found associated with sulphur, iron, pyrites, etc., though only in small quantities. It is a semiconductor (*q.v.*) and its special electrical properties have led to its use in photoelectric cells and rectifiers. Selenium is widely used in the chemical industry as a catalyst (*q.v.*) in producing aromatic hydrocarbons from less useful hydrocarbons. Also used in making some types of glass.

Semiconductors, substances with numerous special and useful electrical properties a few of which are:

(i) they conduct electricity much better than do insulators, but much less well than metals (hence their name);

(ii) their power to conduct depends strongly on their temperature—which makes them useful for temperature sensitive devices;

(iii) they are sensitive to light—hence their use in photoelectric cells and solar batteries;

(iv) when in contact with metals, or with other suitable semiconductors, they form a boundary layer which conducts electricity much better one way than the other—this is the basis of many rectifiers some of which, called crystal diodes, are an important component in radios and electronic devices;

(v) their electrical properties can be greatly influenced by putting in minute amounts of impurity, this enables semiconductor devices, especially transistors, to be made with carefully selected properties.

Semiconductors were known to Faraday, but the semiconductor age really arrived with the invention of the transistor (*q.v.*) in 1947. The ubiquitous transistor is only one of very many semiconductor devices which perform a variety of functions in technical apparatus of all kinds. Semiconductors used in technology are usually small crystals, frequently of germanium or silicon, and their robustness and small power consumption often make them superior to other devices, such as thermionic valves, which they often replace. Other semiconducting materials are cadmium sulphide, selenium, lead telluride, indium antimonide. See also **F19**.

Senate, the higher governing Assembly of a Legislature. The word, applied primarily to the Roman council, is also used to denote the upper chamber in the legislatures of France, the United States, and other countries. In certain universities the governing body is also called the Senate.

Sensitive Plant. A species of Mimosa (*Mimosa pudica*), whose leaves are extremely sensitive to touch, shaking, and burning.

Sepia, the " ink " of the cuttlefish. See **Ink Sac.**

September, the ninth month of the year, and the seventh of the old Roman calendar; hence the name, from Septimus. The designation was several times changed by the Emperors, but none of the new names survived for long.

Septuagesima Sunday, the third Sunday before Lent.

Septuagint, the Greek translation of the Old Testament made by Alexandrian Jews between 250 B.C. and 100 B.C. from Hebrew texts now lost. There are many differences between the Septuagint and the Massoretic version (A.D. 900), and

therefore it is of great value for textual criticism. The symbol for the Septuagint is LXX.

Serfs, the name given to the slaves formerly existing in Russia, who answered to the condition of the feudal " villeins " of England. They were attached to the soil and were transferred with it in all sales or leases. Serfdom existed in Prussia until 1807 and in Russia until 1861.

Serpentine, a mineral: chemically a hydrous silicate of magnesium. Green serpentine is used as an ornament stone. Fibrous serpentine is called asbestos.

Serval, a small carnivorous animal of the lynx order, with black spots on a tawny ground. It is numerous in Africa, preys upon the smaller animals of the deer family, and is sometimes styled the " Tiger Cat."

Set, both in everyday speech (as in tea set, chess set) and in mathematics, a set is a collection of things. The members of the set can be specified by listing them or by describing the properties necessary for membership of the set, *e.g.*, the set of ginger-haired boxers. Set theory is a very important branch of mathematics founded by a great mathematician, Georg Cantor (1845–1918). Its development has influenced many other branches of mathematics. Perhaps one reflection of its fundamental nature is to be found in the fact that many schoolchildren, even of tender age, are now learning set theory and confounding parents who did not hear of it at school twenty years ago.

Settlement, Act of, passed in 1701, assigned the Crown to the House of Hanover in case of Anne's death without children. The decision represented the determination of the squires and the Anglican Church never again to trust themselves to a Roman Catholic king.

Seven Champions of Christendom, as set forth in mediæval literature, were St. George of England, St. Andrew of Scotland, St. Patrick of Ireland, St. David of Wales, St. James of Spain, St. Denis of France, and St. Anthony of Italy.

Seven Churches of Asia, referred to in the Revelation of St. John, were those of Ephesus, founded by St. Paul in 57, Smyrna, Pergamos, Thyatira, Sardis, Philadelphia (Lydia), and Laodicea (Phrygia), all in W. Asia Minor.

Seven Wonders of the World were: 1, the Pyramids of Egypt; 2, the tomb of Mausolus, King of Caria (hence the word mausoleum); 3, the Temple of Diana at Ephesus; 4, the Walls and Hanging Gardens of Babylon; 5, the Colossus at Rhodes; 6, the Ivory and Gold Statue of Jupiter Olympus; and 7, the Pharos, or Watch Tower, built at Alexandria by Ptolemy Philadelphus, King of Egypt.

Seven Years' War was waged by Frederick the Great and England against Austria, France, and Russia, from 1756 to 1763. It resulted in the secession of Silesia to Prussia, of Canada to England, and in the strengthening of our Indian Empire.

Sexagesima Sunday is the 2nd Sunday before Lent.

Sextant, an instrument which has superseded the quadrant as a measurer of angles between distant objects. It is of special importance in navigation and surveying, and contains 60 degrees described on a graduated arc. A small telescope is attached and there are also a couple of mirrors which reflect the distant objects so as to enable them to be accurately observed. The invention is attributed to John Hadley, and to Thomas Godfrey independently, about 1730. Even today it is still the best instrument for telling where you are at sea.

Shad, a marine fish belonging to the same genus as the herring. It is found along the Atlantic Coast of the U.S.A., and ascends rivers to spawn.

Shagreen, shark's skin: also untanned leather of peculiar grain made from skins of wild asses, camels, and horses.

Shalloon, a kind of cloth manufactured from wool and worsted, and used chiefly for women's dresses and coat linings. It gets its name from the fact that it was originally made at Chalons.

Shamrock, the three-leaved clover-like plant native to Ireland and its national emblem.

Shark, a large and powerful ocean fish, comprising many species, very widely distributed, but most numerous in tropical seas. They have formidable teeth and are the most carnivorous of all fishes. They usually attain a large size, the whale-shark being often of a length of 50 ft. Commercially the shark yields shagreen from its skin, the fins are made into gelatine, and an oil is obtained from the liver.

Sheep, a well-known family of ruminants of great utility as wool-producers, and for food. From the earliest times sheep have been a source of wealth to England. So much were they valued in the 15th and 16th cent., that their exportation was frequently prohibited. Sheep are classified under (1) longwools; (2) shortwools; and (3) mountain breeds. Most of the longwools carry Leicester blood in their ancestry and the shortwooled Down breeds carry the blood of the Southdown. The Southdown produced the present Suffolk, one of the most popular breeds. Cheviot is an important mountain breed. Of the foreign breeds the most valued are the Merino sheep of Spain, which yield a fine long wool. Australia, U.S.S.R., Argentina, India, U.S.A., New Zealand, and S. Africa are the chief wool-producing countries in the world.

Shelduck, a handsome genus of surface-feeding ducks, one of which, the common shelduck, is an inhabitant of this country. It is a beautiful white-and-chestnut plumaged bird with dark-green head and neck and red bill. Another species, the ruddy sheldrake, appears in Britain only occasionally.

Shellac. This resin is the secretion of the lac insect (*Coccus lacca*), which occurs in forests of Assam and Siam. It is used for making varnish and in the manufacture of gramophone records. *See also* **Lac.**

Sherardizing. Process for coating steel or iron parts with zinc to prevent corrosion; this is done by heating the parts in a closed rotating drum containing zinc dust.

Shilling has been an English coin from Saxon times, but it was not of the value of 12 pence until after the Conquest. It is interchangeable with the 5 new pence decimal piece which came into circulation in 1968.

Ships have existed from prehistoric times. There is mention of one that sailed from Egypt to Greece in 1485 B.C., and in 786 B.C. the Tyrians built a double-decked vessel. No double-decked ship was known in England, however, before the *Royal Harry* was built by Henry VII., and it was not until the 17th cent. that ship-building was carried on in this country as a prominent industry.

Ship-worm. *See* **Teredo.**

Shoddy, the name given to a kind of cloth mainly composed of woollen or worsted rags, torn up and re-fabricated by powerful machinery. It was first made at Batley in Yorkshire about 1813, and became a very important industry employing many thousands of people at Batley and the neighbouring town of Dewsbury.

Shot, the name given to solid projectiles fired from guns. In the time of Henry V. stone shot was used, later leaden shot, then iron shot, and finally steel shot, introduced by Sir Joseph Whitworth.

Shrike, a large and varied family of birds of hawk-like behaviour found in all continents except S. America. The Red-backed Shrike, which winters in Africa, is a breeding visitor to England and Wales. It is commonly called the "Butcher Bird" from the way it impales its prey (small birds and insects) on thorn-twigs. The other species on the British list are the Great Grey Shrike, the Lesser Grey Shrike, the Woodchat Shrike, and the Masked Shrike.

Shrove Tuesday, the day before the first day of Lent, receiving its name from the old custom of shriving, or making confession, on that day. In England the day has always been associated with the making of pancakes.

Sicilian Vespers, the term applied to the terrible massacre of French people in Sicily in 1282. The French under Charles of Anjou were then in occupation of the island, and had been guilty of many cruelties. It began at Palermo on Easter Monday at the hour of vespers and resulted in the expulsion of the French king and the introduction of Spanish rule.

Silence, Tower of, or *dakhma,* a tower about 25 ft. high, built by the Parsees for their dead. The corpse is taken inside by professional corpse-bearers and left to be consumed by vultures.

Parsees do not burn or bury their dead, and the *dakhma* is to protect the living and the elements from defilement.

Silhouette, a form of black profile portrait, invented by Etienne de Silhouette in 1759, and formed by an outline cutting made with scissors or other sharp instrument from cloth, paper, or other flat substance.

Silicon, an important non-metallic element, symbol Si, it is related to carbon. Next to oxygen, it is the most abundant constituent of the earth's crust (27% by weight). It occurs in many rocks, and its oxide occurs in many forms (*e.g.*, quartz, sand, flint, agate, chalcedony, opal, etc.). Coming into use as a semi-conducting material for making transistors and similar devices.

Silicones are synthetic organic derivatives of silicon which because of their high resistance to heat and moisture have special uses, *e.g.*, lubricants, heat-resistant resins and lacquers, and water-repellent finishes. Silicones are compounds in which the molecules consist of chains of atoms of silicon and oxygen alternately. Silicones were developed in the United States from discoveries first made by Prof. F. S. Kipping at Nottingham University. Manufacture began in Britain in 1950, and in the form of fluids, resins, rubbers, and greases they find wide use in industry. The largest plant in Europe is in Glamorgan.

Silk, the name given to a soft glossy fabric manufactured from the fine thread produced by the silkworm. It was known to, and highly prized by, the ancients, being at one time paid for, weight for weight, with gold. The manufacture of silk was carried on in Sicily in the 12th cent., later spreading to Italy, Spain, and the south of France. It was not manufactured in England before 1604; but when certain French refugees established themselves at Spitalfields in 1688, the industry was developed and became of importance. In the 18th cent. the Lombes of Derby achieved great success in this industry. Japan, China, Italy, Korea, and the Soviet Union are the chief silk-producing countries.

Silkworm, the larva of a species of moth, *Bombyx mori.* It is native to China, and has been cultivated with success in India, Persia, Turkey, and Italy. The silkworm of commerce feeds on mulberry leaves and produces a cocoon of silk varying in colour from white to orange. The cocoon is the silken habitation constructed by the worm for its entrance upon the pupal condition, and to obtain the silk the pupa is killed by immersion in hot-water.

Sill, a sheet-like mass of igneous rock which has been intruded parallel with the stratification of the country rock, cf. a dyke.

Silurian. This geological period is one of the major subdivisions of the Palaeozoic era. Its beginning is estimated at 440 million years ago, and the period lasted about 40 million years. Maximum thickness of the Silurian strata in Britain measures 15,000 ft. *See* **F44.**

Silver, a white precious metal, symbol Ag (Latin *argentum*), found in a free state, also in certain combinations, and in a variety of ores. The chief silver-producing regions are the Andes and Cordilleras. Peru, Bolivia, and Mexico have yielded vast supplies of the metal since the 16th century, and Colorado and Nevada in the United States have also been very prolific in silver yield. In England standard silver (that used for coinage) formerly contained 92½ per cent. fine silver and 7½ per cent. alloy, but when the price rose to 89½d. per oz. and the coins became worth more than face value, the Coinage Act of 1920 was passed, reducing the fineness to half. To provide silver bullion for industry and for a fund towards the redemption of our silver debt to America, it was decided in 1946 to replace the United Kingdom silver coinage by one made of cupro-nickel (75 per cent. copper, 25 per cent. nickel). Maundy money, however, is of the original silver standard. Silver chloride and bromide are light-sensitive compounds and are used in photography.

Simony, the offence of trading in church offices, has been contrary to English law since the time of Edward VI. Elizabeth also promulgated laws against simony. In 1879 a Royal Commission reported on the law and existing practice as to the sale, exchange, and resignation of benefices. The position is now controlled by the Benefices Act 1898, the Amendment Measure 1923, and the Benefices Rules 1926.

Sinn Fein (*Irish* = ourselves alone), Irish nationalistic movement founded in 1905 which developed into a mass republican party and triumphed in the establishment of the Irish Free State. A small extremist group has survived which represents politically the outlawed I.R.A.

Sins, The Seven Deadly or Capital Sins are pride, avarice, lust, anger, gluttony, envy, sloth.

Sirius, the dog-star, so called because of its situation in the mouth of the Dog (Canis Major): it is the brightest of all the fixed stars, and is also one of the nearest to us.

Sirocco, a warm, southerly, often dust-laden, wind blowing across Mediterranean lands from the Sahara, in advance of an eastward-moving depression over the Mediterranean.

Siskin, a small bird of the finch family, common in Northern regions, nesting in Britain. The common Siskin has a yellow-green colour and is a lively, swift-flying bird with a stout bill.

Sistine Chapel, the chapel of the Pope in the Vatican, renowned for its frescoes by Michelangelo.

S.I. Units (Système International d'Unités) form an internationally recognised system of metric units for scientific and technical quantities. The basic units of length, time, mass, electric current, temperature, and luminous intensity are, respectively, the metre, second, kilogramme, ampere, kelvin (*see* **Absolute Temperature**), and candela. The S.I. was recommended for general adoption by a number of international organisations such as the General Conference on Weights and Measures (1960). Many countries have made or are making the S.I. the only legally recognised set of units. Gt. Britain's intention to "go metric" will bring widespread use of S.I. units in its train. These units command the widespread though not absolutely unanimous support of industrialists, technologists, and scientists. Many have urged that their adoption will be a triumph of commonsense and end the confusing multiplicity of units on the world scene. *See* **Section N.**

Six Articles, The Statute of the, was passed in 1539 for compelling adhesion to the chief doctrines of Roman Catholic faith: transubstantiation, communion in one kind only for the laity, vows of chastity, celibacy of the clergy, private masses, and auricular confession; those who refused to subscribe to the Articles were treated as heretics. The Act was repealed in 1547.

Skate, a genus of sea-fishes related to the Rays.

Skink. The skinks constitute a large family of lizards with large smooth scales, under each of which is a bony plate. The largest species, found in Australia, is about 2 ft. long. Some skinks have adopted a burrowing habit and degeneration of the limbs is associated with this. The Common Skink is a small species about 5 in. long, living in the deserts of N. Africa.

Skua, falcon-like marine birds related to the gulls, found throughout the world. Known as "Robber Birds" because they steal not only the young and eggs of other birds (including penguins) but also their food, which they force them to disgorge in mid-air. The Arctic Skua breeds as far south as Scotland. The Great Skua breeds in both Antarctica and Arctica. Other species are the Pomarine, the Long-tailed, and McCormick's Skua.

Skunk, a North American mammal of the weasel family, with short legs and long bushy tail. All fifteen species are black and white, some being striped and the rest spotted. It secretes and ejects at will a foul-smelling fluid.

Sky. The blue colour of the sky on a summer's day is the result of the scattering of light waves by particles of dust and vapour in the earth's atmosphere. Blue light having almost the smallest wavelength in the visible spectrum (0·00004 cm.) is scattered laterally about 10 times as much as the red (0·00007 cm.).

Skyscraper. Owing to lack of ground space, increasing cost of land, and growth of modern cities, buildings are being made higher than broader; hence the name. The structures are constructed of a steel framework usually clothed in concrete or reinforced concrete. Among the highest New York skyscrapers are the Empire State Building (102 stories, 1,250 ft.), Chrysler (77 stories, 1,046 ft.), the Rockefeller Center (70 stories, 850 ft.), and the World Trade Center (1,350 ft.), due for completion 1972. The tallest building in Britain is the 580 ft. Post Office radio tower (basic diameter 52 ft.) near Tottenham Court Road, London. Japan's first skyscraper is the Kasumigaseki building (36 stories) in Tokyo.

Slate, fine-grained clayey rocks which have undergone metamorphism. They cleave easily, and it is this property of cleavage which makes them a valuable source of roofing material. Important quarries producing mainly green slate are in the Coniston–Ambleside area of the Lake District.

Slavery. In its earlier forms, as in the times of ancient Greece and Rome, in the feudal ages, when vassalage and villeinage existed, and in the serfdom of Russia and other northern nations, slavery was attended by many inhumanities and evils; but perhaps in the negro slavery system which prevailed in the British colonies for upwards of 200 years and in certain parts of the United States up to 1865, it attained its highest point of cruelty. In 1883 the Act of Emancipation was passed, emancipating all slaves in British territories, though slavery continued to be tolerated in northern Nigeria, Sierra Leone and in the Anglo-Egyptian Sudan long after that date. Even today slavery and forced labour are still prevalent in some parts of the world.

Slide Rule, an instrument which consists of two logarithmic scales sliding alongside each other. By its use multiplication, division, extraction of roots, etc., are speedily carried out.

Sloth, a curious family of mammals, only found in Central and South America. They dwell almost entirely in the trees, proceeding from branch to branch with their bodies hanging downwards, their weight being supported by their large hook-like claws. They eat foliage.

Slow-Worm, a species of lizard found in Britain which lacks legs. Silver with longitudinal brown stripes, it lives almost entirely on slugs.

Smelting. The process of heating an ore with a reducing agent to convert ore into metal, and with a flux to convert rocky impurities into a slag that will float on top of the molten metal. Slag and metal can then be tapped separately. An example is iron smelting; the reducing agent is coke, and limestone is added as the flux; the smelting is carried out in a blast furnace.

Snake. The snakes constitute the important reptilian order *Ophidia*. Snakes have a scaly, cylindrical, limbless body, lidless eyes, forked tongue, and the upper and lower jaws joined by an elastic ligament. Their locomotion is accomplished by means of the excessive mobility of their numerous ribs. All snakes have teeth used for seizing prey, and the poisonous varieties are furnished with poison fangs in the upper jaw. These fangs are hollow modified teeth and the venom passes into them from a special gland situated behind the angle of the mouth. Some 2,500 species of snakes are known, divided into 13 families. There are 3 British species—the grass-snake, smooth-snake, and adder.

Snipe, a wading bird, long-legged, with long, slender, straight bill, brown plumage, and zigzag flight. The Common Snipe breeds locally throughout Britain; the Great Snipe and small Jack Snipe are occasional visitors. The close season is Feb. 1 to Aug. 11.

Snow. When water vapour condenses at high levels at a temperature below freezing, a cloud of ice particles is formed. If these frozen droplets are small, they fall slowly and gradually assume a feathery crystalline structure, reaching the earth as snowflakes if the temperature remains below freezing.

Socialism. *See* **J47.**

Soda, carbonate of sodium, is now mainly obtained by certain processes of manufacture from common salt. It was formerly obtained from the ashes of plants. Bicarbonate of sodium is the primary product in the Solvay or Ammonia-soda method for commercial manufacture of soda; it is also formed when carbon dioxide is passed into strong soda solution. The bicarbonate is used in medicine and in the preparation of baking powder.

Sodium, a metallic element, symbol Na (Latin *Natrium*), first obtained by Sir Humphry Davy in 1807 from caustic soda by means of the electric battery. Its chloride is *common salt*; the deposits of salt (*e.g.*, in Cheshire and at Stassfurt) have come into existence through the drying up of inland seas. Salt occurs in sea-water to the extent of about 3 per cent.; the Dead Sea contains about 22 per cent. The blood of animals is maintained at a level of about 0·6% sodium chloride. That there is sodium in the sun's atmosphere was confirmed in 1859 by Kirchhoff from his spectroscopic observations. Liquid sodium metal has properties which make it suitable as a coolant in some nuclear reactors. A technique of handling this very reactive liquid has had to be developed.

Solar Battery, one of the innumerable devices made possible by the development of semi-conducting materials, notably germanium and silicon. This device creates an electric current from light falling on it. The current can be put to use or stored in storage batteries. The energy of the current is derived from the sunlight, and the solar battery is thus an *energy converting* apparatus. Solar batteries have provided power for the instruments in satellites. In London in 1960 a car (developed in the U.S.A.) was demonstrated running on the power from sunlight and solar batteries.

Solar Wind, a continuous stream of electrically charged particles blowing outwards from the sun, supplemented from time to time by intense outbursts from particular regions of the sun's surface. These streams of protons and electrons on encountering the earth's magnetic field distort it and cause magnetic storms and aurorae.

Soldering is a means of joining together two pieces of material, usually metals, by melting a third metal (the solder) into the joint. The solder solidifies in the pores of the other metals and holds them together. The materials to be joined are not themselves melted so the technique requires less heat than welding. Solders are alloys; there are many kinds depending on the materials to be joined and the strength of joint desired. *See* Welding.

Solstice, an astronomical term indicating the point at which the sun is most distant from the equator. *See* Seasons, Section N.

Soundings at sea, to determine depth at any point, have been taken in all seas, and with considerable accuracy. A deep reading was that of the *Challenger* expedition in 1873, near St. Thomas's in the North Atlantic, when 3,875 fathoms were sounded. In 1851 H.M.S. *Challenger* recorded the then maximum ocean depth in the Marianas Trench (W. Pacific) by echo-sounding as between 5,882 and 5,940 fathoms. Another deep was located in the S. Pacific in 1952–53 of 5,814 fathoms in the Tonga Trench, 180 miles S. of Tonga Tabu. Since then even greater depths have been recorded, in the Marianas Trench and the Mindanao Deep. *See* Pacific Ocean.

Southern Cross, popular name of *Crux*, a constellation of the Southern hemisphere, consisting of four bright stars in the form of a Latin cross. It has been called the pole-star of the south and is indispensable to seafarers.

South Sea Bubble, the name given to a series of financial projects which began with the formation of the South Sea Company in 1711 and ended nine years later in disaster after a mania of speculation. The idea behind the parent scheme was that the state should sell certain trading monopolies in the South seas in return for a sum of money to pay off the National Debt (which stood at £51,300,000 in 1719 when the scheme started). The idea fascinated the public, fabulous profits being dreamt of, and the price of the stock rose out of all proportion to the earnings of the Company. Many dishonest speculative ventures sprang up in imitation with the inevitable result that thousands were ruined. All classes had joined in the gamble and a Committee of Secrecy set up by the House of Commons in Dec. 1720 to investigate the affairs of the Company proved that there had been fraud and corruption on a large scale in the affairs of the Company. Sir Robert Walpole who had been an opponent of the scheme from the outset dealt with the crisis.

Space Flight. The Soviet Union was the first country to launch a man into space and bring him safely back to earth. This epoch-making event took place on April 12, 1961, when Yuri Gagarin, tragically killed in an air crash in 1968, circled the earth in a spaceship weighing about 4¾ tons. It was launched by rocket in an elliptical orbit with greatest height 187 miles and least 109 miles. The inclination of the orbit to the equator was 65 deg. 4 min. and the period of revolution was 89 min. 6 sec. Since then, the Russian *Vostok* cosmonauts Titov (17 orbits), Nikolayev (64 orbits), Popovich (48 orbits), Bykovsky (81 orbits), Tereshkova, the first woman space traveller (48 orbits), the *Voskhod* cosmonauts Komarov, Feoktistov and Yegorov (16 orbits), Belyaev and Leonov (17 orbits), the American *Mercury* astronauts Glenn (3 orbits), Carpenter (3 orbits), Schirra (6 orbits), Cooper (22 orbits), the *Gemini* astronauts Grissom and Young (3 orbits), McDivitt and White (62 orbits), Cooper and Conrad (120 orbits), Borman and Lovell (206 orbits), Schirra and Stafford (15 orbits), Armstrong and Scott (6·6 orbits), Stafford and Cernan (44 orbits), Young and Collins (43 orbits), Conrad and Gordon (44 orbits), Lovell and Aldrin (60 orbits) were among the first to complete successful missions in space. Leonov was the first to perform the extra-vehicular (EVA) experiment (1965), *i.e.*, to leave an orbiting spaceship and float freely in space. Russia was the first to achieve an automatic docking (link-up) between two unmanned spacecraft in orbital flight (Oct. 1967), and of two manned spacecraft (Jan. 1969). The American *Apollo* mission was accomplished when Armstrong and Aldrin became the first men to set foot on the moon. This milestone in manned space flight took place on July 20, 1969. *See also* Sputniks, Space Research.

Space Research. By space research we mean scientific research work which can only be carried to otherwise inaccessible observing locations by rocket propulsion. Such propulsion does not rely on the presence of an atmosphere to provide oxygen so that it is capable in principle of conveying objects to unlimited distances. The subject of space research is, therefore, one which is concerned with scientific applications in various fields of a single highly specialised and powerful technique. It is not a single discipline, but can provide data of great importance for many such as the physics of the earth, the sun, moon, and other bodies of the solar system, astronomy, geodesy, and the study of gravitation. The prospect of investigating the biological conditions on different planets such as Mars and Venus is also opened, as well as that of experimental biological studies under conditions of zero gravity. Although the results of many aspects of space research are vital for those concerned with the practical realisation of manned travel in space, space research is largely a branch of pure science, independent of any applications which may stem from it. The major technical problems involved in space research are:

    (*a*) Launching of the instrument-containing vehicle with the necessary velocity.

    (*b*) Guidance and control of the vehicle so it pursues the desired path.

    (*c*) Tracking the vehicle to determine its actual path and the position on the path at any time.

    (*d*) Transmission of the data, recorded by the instruments, back to the earth.

    (*e*) Satisfactory operation of scientific instruments in the environment within the vehicle.

    (*f*) Provision of adequate power supplies to operate the equipment within the vehicle for sufficiently long periods.

It is important to distinguish three distinct types of vehicle—the vertical sounding rocket, the artificial earth satellite, and the deep space probe. The track of a vertical sounding rocket is mainly vertical, and the whole path to the highest point and back is traversed in a few minutes only. An earth satellite circulates in an orbit round the earth in the same way as does our natural satellite, the moon. If it approaches the earth at any point within 100 miles of the surface the air resistance causes the path to spiral in so rapidly that the vehicle is eventually burnt up by air friction within the dense atmosphere after an orbital life of a few months only. It follows that artificial satellite vehicles are only useful as instrument containers if the distance of closest approach (the perigee distance) is not much less than 100 miles. For the study of the properties of the atmosphere at lower altitudes down to the limit (20 miles) attainable by balloons, vertical sounding rockets must be used. It is a great advantage for work at higher altitudes to use satellites, as it is then possible to make systematic observations for months at a time from a great number of positions relative to the earth. The successful space flights achieved by manned satellites also suggest that it should not be long before manned observatories become practicable. Deep space probes include vehicles which pass out to great distances from the earth and may leave the neighbourhood of the earth for ever to become artificial planets. Such probes may pass close to, or soft land on, the moon or planets or may merely pursue paths well out into interplanetary space.

Spanish Civil War, 1936 to 1939. The war commenced by a revolt by the Fascist General Franco against the Republic which had succeeded the Monarchy in 1931. Germany and Italy aided the rebels who besieged Madrid for over 2 years. An International Brigade was formed to help the Republic, but the Spanish Government was faced by the greater part of the Army, and very effective assistance from Italy and Germany. Those powers seized the opportunity to have a curtain-raiser to the world conflict which they intended to precipitate. After a total loss of a million men the Fascists overpowered the Republic.

Sparrow, name given to finch-like birds found in most parts of the world, of which the House Sparrow *Passer domesticus*, is the most familiar of British birds. Also native to Britain is the rural Tree Sparrow, distinguished from the male House Sparrow by its chestnut crown. Other European species are the Italian, Spanish and Rock Sparrows.

Specific Gravity, defined as the ratio of the mass of a particular volume of a substance to the mass of an equal volume of water at 4 °C. *See* Hydrometer.

Spectroscopy. Newton's arrangement with the prism was the first spectroscope; its function was to separate out the colour components of a source of light. Two hundred years elapsed before this apparatus was developed into a precise scientific instrument, capable of measuring both the wavelength and intensity of each colour component. In this form it is called a spectrometer. All atoms and molecules have well defined characteristic spectra which can be used to recognise them. In order to produce emission spectra it is necessary to energise the material under investigation by some means, such as by heating in a flame. The resulting radiation then consists largely of sharp bright lines, characteristic of the material. Absorption spectra are produced by interposing the experimental material between a white light source and the spectrometer. Then dark lines are seen, corresponding to absorptions of energy, in exactly the same places as the bright lines are observed in the emission spectra. Spectroscopic techniques have now been developed to such an extent that accurate measurements of wavelength and intensity are possible not only in the visible region, but over almost the whole of the electromagnetic spectrum. Not only does spectroscopy play an important rôle in probing the structure of matter, but it can be applied in the field of astronomy. The use of radio wave spectroscopy has led to the discovery of several new types of stellar object, and this data is now producing a complete reappraisal of our understanding of the universe.

Sphinx, in Greek mythology, a winged creature with a woman's head and a lion's body. The sphinx of ancient Egypt represented the pharaoh in a divine form.

Spiritualism. *See* J47.

Spirituals, negro melodies with religious inspiration

and which are still spontaneously created, but have also passed into art-music.

Sponge, *See* Porifera, F33(1).

Spoonbill, a long-legged, marsh bird, closely related to the ibis and stork, remarkable for its snow-white plumage and broad, flat, spoon-shaped bill. The European species has not bred in England since the beginning of the 17th cent., but is still a regular summer visitor from Holland, where it nests in colonies in reed-beds and islets.

Sputniks, the name of the Russian earth satellites first launched during the period of the International Geophysical Year. *Sputnik I*, launched 4 Oct. 1957, became the first man-made earth satellite. *Sputnik II*, launched a month later, carried a dog as passenger. *Sputnik III*, launched in May 1958, and weighing well over 2 tons, became the first fully-equipped laboratory to operate in space. The father of space travel with rockets was a Russian—Konstantin Eduardovich Tsiolkovsky—the centenary of whose birth practically coincided with the launching of the first earth satellite.

Squirting Cucumber, *Ecballium elaterium*, so named from the fact that when ripe it breaks from the stalk and ejects its seeds and juice from the hole made by the breakage.

Stainless Steel. The development of stainless steel for cutlery manufacture, etc., began with the discovery of Harry Brearsley in 1912 that steel containing 12 per cent. of chromium is rust-proof.

Stalactites are deposits of calcium carbonate formed on the roofs and sides of limestone caves, and in tunnels, under bridges, and other places where the carbonic acid of rain-water percolates through and partly dissolves the limestone, resulting in the growth of icicle-like forms that often assume groupings. The water that drops from these may deposit further calcium carbonate, which accumulates and hardens into a series of sharp mounds or hillocks called stalagmites.

Starch is an organic compound occurring in granules in nearly all green plants, and especially in the seeds of dicotyledonous and cereal plants, potatoes, etc. In its pure form starch is a tasteless, odourless white powder, and is a carbohydrate consisting of carbon, hydrogen, and oxygen.

Star Chamber, an ancient tribunal of State in existence in 1487 and possibly earlier, charged with the duty of trying offences against the Government, unfettered by the ordinary rules of law. It was in effect a Privy Council entrusted with judicial functions. Under Charles I. the Star Chamber was used by the King and his party to persecute opponents; and in 1641 a Bill carried in both Houses abolished it.

Starling (*Sturnus vulgaris*), a well-known European bird now common in many parts of the world. It has handsome iridescent blackish plumage and nests in holes and crevices. Flocks of starlings are often seen wheeling in the air; thousands roost on buildings in the heart of London. Other European species are the Spotless and Rose-coloured starlings. The latter sometimes wanders to the British Isles.

States-General, national assembly in which the chief estates of the realm were represented as separate bodies. The name, though not the institution, has survived in the Netherlands, where the two houses of parliament are known as states-general. In France the states-general consisted of three orders, clergy, nobility, and commons. Philip IV. first summoned it in 1302 to support him in his quarrel with Pope Boniface VIII. While absolute monarchy was establishing itself it met rarely, and not at all from 1614 until 1789, when it was convoked as a last resort by Louis XVI. But when it met it declared itself the National Assembly which marked the beginning of the revolution.

Statistics is a science that deals with the collection of numerical facts and the evaluation of their significance. The word is also used to refer to the facts themselves as in " trade statistics." This important science gives precise meanings to words like " average " and to statements like " this set of data is significantly different from that." In a world in which more and more information is becoming available in numerical form (I.Q.s, examination results, tax yields, health records, road accidents, etc.) the proper—as opposed to the misleading—use of statistics cannot be over-emphasised. Many young people can now study statistics at school and college, and governments and industries employ many statisticians. See Average.

Statute of Westminster, 1931. An Act of parliament which gave a basis of equality to the British Dominions. The Dominions as well as the United Kingdom were defined by the Balfour Memorandum of 1926 as " autonomous communities within the British Empire, equal in status, in no way subordinate one to another in any aspect of their domestic or external affairs, though united by a common allegiance to the Crown, and freely associated as members of the British Commonwealth of Nations." The Statute was the sequel. The Dominions are sovereign States governed solely by their own Parliaments and Governments. See also K189.

Steam Engine, a machine whereby steam becomes the active agent of the working of machinery, and of very wide application. The leading types of steam engine are: (a) condensing, or low-pressure engines, where the steam is generated by a boiler; (b) non-condensing, in which the cylinder exhausts its steam into the open air. Engines of the latter type are used where portable engines are required

Steam Hammer, invented by the Scottish engineer James Nasmyth (1808–90) in 1839, which proved of great utility in the development of the iron trade. The hammer itself, which is fixed to the end of a piston-rod passing through the bottom of an inverted cylinder, often weighs as much as 80 or 100 tons, and is so perfectly controlled by the steam power that its action can be so accurately gauged that it could be made to crack the glass of a watch without actually breaking it, or brought down upon a mass of molten iron with a force representing many hundreds of tons.

Stearin is the portion of fatty matters and oils which remains solid at an ordinary temperature, and is a compound of stearic acid with glycerine. It is largely used in the manufacture of candles. With caustic soda stearin forms a soap (sodium stearate), which is present in most commercial soaps which contain sodium palmitate and oleate in addition.

Steel, an alloy of iron and carbon, with varying proportions of other minerals. The famous blades of Damascus and steels of Toledo were made by the cementation and crucible method. The metal produced by the " Bessemer process " (q.v.) is of the highest value for structural purposes, rails, etc. In recent years the technique known as continuous casting has been developed which bypasses some major steps in the conventional process of steel-making. See also Stainless Steel.

Stereophonic Broadcasting. A person having normal hearing is able to determine the direction from which a sound reaches him by virtue of the fact that he has two ears, and, therefore, the sound will reach one of them a fraction of a second before it reaches the other. This difference in arrival time allows the brain to calculate direction. It will, therefore, be apparent that if the same person listens to, say, an orchestral concert in a large hall he will be able to determine—even with his eyes shut—the approximate position of a particular instrument with respect to the rest of the orchestra. If, however, he listens at home to a broadcast of the same concert, then, due to the fact that he hears the music after it has been picked up by a single microphone located at one point and radiated over a single-channel transmission system, he will be unable to allocate a definite position to any instrument. The aim of stereophonic broadcasting or sound reproduction, therefore, is to restore the listener's ability to locate the position in space of the various sources of sound and to follow movement. To do this it is necessary to use two microphones in the studio—to simulate the two human ears—and to transmit their outputs, through two similar, but separate, chains of equipment, to two radio receivers and their two loudspeakers, which must be placed some distance apart, in the listener's home. See also F.64(2).

Stereotype, a metal cast taken from movable type

which has been set up in the ordinary way. The first to introduce the process in practical form in this country was William Ged, of Edinburgh, who made stereotype plates in 1730. An impression of the type matter is first taken by means of a mould of prepared plaster of Paris or moistened sheets of specially prepared paper, and when molten stereo metal is poured upon the mould and allowed to cool and harden, the stereo plate is formed, and can be printed from as a solid block for some time.

Steroids. A class of structurally related compounds, based on a system of condensed rings of carbon and hydrogen, which are widely distributed in animals and plants. Included in the steroid family are sterols, found in all animal cells, vitamin D, sex hormones, bile acids, and cortisone, a drug used in the treatment of rheumatic fever.

Stibnite, the chief ore of antimony; chemically it is antimony sulphide. Steely-grey in colour.

Stickleback, a family of small spiny-finned fish widely distributed in both fresh and salt water. Male constructs roofed nest held together by sticky secretion from glands near kidneys. Several females deposit eggs therein which he jealously guards until after young are hatched.

Stirrup, a loop of metal U-shaped strap suspended from the sides of the saddle, used for mounting and to support the horseman's foot. Some authorities allege their use as far back as the early Iron Age, and it is generally believed that they were used in battle in A.D. 378, when the Gothic cavalry defeated the legionaries of the Emperor Valens at Adrianople. Stirrups relieved the tension on the rider's knees and so enabled him to be armed from top to toe.

Stoat, a slender, carnivorous mammal with short legs, related to the weasels. The stoat is distinguished from the latter by its longer tail, which has a black tip. The black tip is retained even in the winter when the animal turns white, the fur then being known as " ermine." It is found in northern latitudes, and is abundant in Arctic America.

Stoma (pl. stomata), microscopic pores on the surfaces of leaves through which gaseous exchanges take place and water is lost. It has been estimated that a single maize plant bears 200 million stomata, usually closed at night.

Stone-Flies, comprise the order of insects called Plecoptera, which includes some 700 species, of which about thirty occur in Britain. The wings are membranous, and two long, thread-like feelers protrude at the tail end. The larvae are aquatic.

Stonehenge, a remarkable collection of Bronze Age monuments arranged in two circles, 340 ft. in diameter, standing on Salisbury Plain, Wiltshire. Modern archaeological research dates origin back to between 1860 and 1500 B.C. There is some evidence to suggest that the monument may have been built for astronomical purposes, providing a method of keeping a calendar for predicting the seasons and foretelling eclipses of sun and moon. See also J15(1).

Stork, a family of heron-like birds with long bills, freely distributed over Europe, Asia, Africa, and S. America. The White Stork is an occasional visitor to England and, more rarely, the Black Stork; these are the only two European storks.

Stratosphere, a layer of the earth's atmosphere, which begins 6–7 miles above the earth. The attraction of the stratosphere as a medium for air travel rests upon the absence of storms; indeed weather phenomena as commonly understood do not occur, there being no vertical temperature gradient in the stratosphere and no convection currents.

Stratum (pl. strata), a bed or layer of rock.

Strontium. This silver-white metallic element was discovered by Hope and Klaproth in 1793, and isolated by Sir Humphry Davy in 1808. The chief strontium minerals are celestite (sulphate) and strontianite (carbonate). Compounds of strontium give a brilliant colour to fireworks and signal flares. Radioactive isotopes of strontium (strontium-90) are formed as fission products in nuclear explosions and tend to collect in bone on account of the chemical similarity of strontium and calcium (q.v.). This genetic hazard is a cause of great alarm. See Fall-out.

Sturgeon, a large fish found in northern seas and

rivers with five rows of bony plates along the back and sides and pointed mouth with four barbels. Caviare is prepared from sturgeon ova. The rights of the Crown to certain wild creatures, including sturgeon, caught off the coasts of Britain and held since the time of Edward II, were abolished in 1970.

Sublimation, when a solid substance is heated and turns into vapour without passing through the liquid stage and then condenses as a solid on a cold surface, it is said to "sublime" and the process is called "sublimation". Iodine behaves in this way, and sublimation is used as a method of purifying it.

Submarine, the first submarine the *Nautilus*, was designed by Robert Fulton and tried out in the river Seine and in the sea off Brest in 1801. The idea was too revolutionary to find acceptance and it was not until electricity for under-water propulsion became available that the submarine underwent extensive development. Britain became interested about 1900 and the Germans developed it and made it into an instrument of warfare. The first voyage under the North Pole was made in 1958 by the American nuclear-powered submarine *Nautilus* (*q.v.*). The Royal Navy's nuclear submarine fleet includes 4 Polaris vessels—HMS *Resolution*, which became operational in 1968. *Renown* (1969), *Repulse* (1969). *Revenge* (1970), each armed with 16 missiles with nuclear warheads. and 6 nuclear-powered Fleet submarines, including *Dreadnought*, *Valiant*, *Warspite*, *Churchill*, and *Conqueror*. A further 3 Fleet submarines were under construction in 1971.

Subpœna (L. = under a penalty), a writ commanding a witness to appear before a court of law.

Suez Canal, connecting the Mediterranean and the Red Sea, was built by the French engineer Ferdinand de Lesseps and opened in 1869. An Egyptian company, *Canal Maritime de Suez*, was formed in 1866 with a capital of 200 million francs. The British Government acquired 176,602 shares out of a total of 400,000 for £4 million (value Mar. 31, 1956, £28,982,544). Its length is 101 statute miles, minimum width 196 ft. 10 in. (navigation channel). Under the Convention of 1888 all nations were granted freedom of navigation without discrimination in peace or war. The right was recognised by Egypt in the Anglo-Egyptian Agreement of 1954, under which Britain agreed to give up the Suez base. The Suez Canal Company was nationalised by the Egyptian Government without warning on July 28, 1956, since when it has been widened and deepened and the average time of transit reduced. The Canal has been barred to Israeli ships since the creation of the state of Israel in 1948, and to all shipping since the Middle East war of 1967.

Suffragette. member of the Women's Suffrage Movement who in the early part of this century agitated to obtain the parliamentary vote. The movement ended in 1918, when women of 30 were given the vote. In 1928 a Bill was passed which granted equal suffrage to men and women. The leaders of the Women's Suffrage Movement were Mrs. Pankhurst and her two daughters, Sylvia and Dame Christabel, Mrs. Fawcett, Nellie Kenny, and others.

Sugar, to the chemist the term is a generic one covering a group of carbohydrates, including cane sugar (sucrose), glucose, fructose, and maltose. In ordinary parlance sugar means sucrose, which is obtained from the sugar cane, sugar beet, or sugar maple.

Sulphur, an elementary, brittle, crystalline solid, symbol S, abounding in the vicinity of volcanoes. It is yellow in colour. It occurs in combination with other elements, as sulphates and sulphides, and allied with oxygen, hydrogen, chlorine, etc., is of great commercial utility. Used in its pure state it constitutes the inflammable element in gunpowder; it is also used for matches and for making sulphuric acid.

Sulphuric Acid, a compound of great commercial importance, used in a variety of manufactures, and composed of sulphur, oxygen, and hydrogen. Extremely corrosive.

Sun, one of the millions of stars in the universe, the centre of the solar system, estimated to be distant from the earth 93,004,000 miles, to have a diameter of 865,000 miles, and a volume

S (80th Ed.)

a million times that of the earth. It rotates on its axis from east to west, though not as a solid, the solar equator turning once in about 25¼ days and the poles in about 34 days. Large spots are observed on the sun—varying in size from 30,000 miles in diameter—which form and disappear at irregular intervals. The area of the disc covered by the spots, however, reaches a maximum roughly every 11 years, when the sun's heat seems rather greater than usual and magnetic storms more frequent (sunspot cycle). Spectrum analysis show that the sun is composed of many elements found in the earth. Its surface temperature is about 6,000° C. Observations made in 1964–65 (Year of the Quiet Sun) complemented those obtained during the International Geophysical Year 1957–58, when the sun was remarkably active. The earth is in the outer atmosphere of the sun and subject to its winds and storms. The apparently inexhaustible heat of the sun, which has maintained life on the earth for millions of years, is derived from the destruction of matter, involved in the transmutation of hydrogen nuclei into helium nuclei, in which process about four million tons of matter is destroyed every second. At this rate of conversion the sun will go on radiating for 30,000 million years. The Soviet space rocket *Lunik I*, fired on 2 Jan. 1959, became the first artificial planet of the sun. *See also* **F7**.

Superconductor, a metal in a state in which its electrical resistance has entirely vanished so that electric currents can flow indefinitely without generating heat or decreasing in strength. The superconducting state of metals was first discovered in mercury by Onnes in Leiden in 1911. There are many magnetic and thermal properties associated with superconductivity and the phenomenon as a whole has proved to be of great scientific interest; it resisted explanation till about 1957. In the meantime many metals and alloys were found to show the property but only at very low temperatures—below *c.*−260°C. There is a growing number of practical applications, *e.g.*, coils of superconducting wire (kept very cold by liquid helium) can be made to carry enough electric current to produce strong magnetic fields. Such fields are very constant and do not require the large supply of electrical power that ordinary electromagnets need.

Supersonic Speed, a speed greater than the speed of sound (in air at sea-level sound waves travel at about 760 m.p.h.). When a body travels at a speed which is greater than the speed at which disturbances themselves can travel, a mechanism exists for the generation of waves of enhanced intensity. Thus aircraft travelling at supersonic speeds produce shock waves in the air somewhat analogous to the bow waves of fast-moving ships. These shock waves are regions of intensely disturbed air which produce the sonic boom effect so distressing to people living near supersonic routes. *Supersonic* is not to be confused with *ultrasonic* (*q.v.*).

Surface Tension. The surfaces of fluids behave in some respects as though they were covered by a stretched elastic membrane. This property is called "surface tension." The action of detergents may be attributed in part to a reduction in the surface tension of water, allowing it to wet the surface of dirty articles.

Surrealism. The aim of the Surrealist school of painting and sculpture is to overcome the barriers between conscious and unconscious mind, the real and unreal worlds of waking and dreaming. As such it has a long and respectable ancestry, although the term was not in use until 1922 when it was picked by André Breton from Guillaume Apollinaire who had used it in connection with works by Chagall. However, Bosch in the 15th cent., Fuseli and Goya in the 18th, and many other purveyors of the weird and fantastic were the forerunners of modern Surrealism. The modern movement has broadly speaking taken two different directions: the first was towards complete fantasy and absurdity which took the form of "found objects" —*e.g.* a bird-cage filled with sugar-cubes and a thermometer, a bottle-dryer, a bicycle wheel, or abstract works with strange and apparently irrelevant titles such as Paul Klee's *Twittering*

L112

Machine; the second towards highly detailed and realistic paintings of objects placed in strange juxtapositions—*e.g.*, Salvator Dali's trees with limp watches drooping over their branches or Georgio de Chirico's deserted and classical-looking streets with long arcaded perspectives and a lone statue or a bunch of bananas in the foreground. On the whole Surrealism has spent its initial force and become almost respectable; its idea of strange juxtapositions, now widely commercialised, finds a place in advertisement illustrations and in the more sophisticated forms of window-dressing.

Surtax, an additional duty of income tax, chargeable on total income in excess of £2,500 (after deduction of certain allowances). The starting level on *earned* income is £5,000 or more depending on personal allowances. Payable on Jan. 1 following year of assessment, so that surtax for 1971–2 is payable on Jan. 1, 1973. The net sum is charged on a sliding scale. In April 1973 the present income tax and surtax system will be replaced by a single graduated personal tax. This will have a basic rate with a supplementary rate for higher incomes and will be less discriminatory against investment income. *See* Income Tax, *also* G42(2).

Swans, large, graceful birds which together with the ducks and geese form the family Anatidae. There are three European species with white plumage; the Mute Swan, distinguished by its orange bill with black knob (less prominent in female), a familiar sight on the rivers and ornamental lakes of this country. Two wild swans are winter visitors here, the Whooper and Bewick's Swan. The "pen" (female) and "cob" (male) mate for life and the young swans are called "cygnets."

Swan-upping. The annual marking of the Thames swans which takes place during the third week of July. This ancient ceremony dates back to the 15th cent. when all the Thames swans were declared to be Royal birds owned by the Crown. Two city guilds—the Vintners' and Dyers' Companies—own one third of the 600 swans now on the Thames. This privilege was granted to them by King Edward IV. in return for money grants. Vintners' birds are marked with a nick on each side of the bill, the Dyers' with a nick on the right side only. The Queen's birds are unmarked.

Sweet Potato. This plant (*Ipomoea batatas*), which is a climbing perennial belonging to the convolvulus family, has thick roots that are rich in starch, and are eaten like potatoes. A native of the W. Indies and Central America, new varieties of sweet potato have been bred which stand cooler climates and can be grown as far north as Cape Cod. The sweet potato of New Zealand is called the Kumara.

Swift, a bird so-called from the extreme speed of its flight, resembling a swallow but related to the humming-bird. It has long, scythe-like wings, sooty-black plumage and greyish-white chin. There are several species inhabiting most parts of the world, particularly the tropics. The British breeding bird is among the latest to return from Africa and the earliest to go. Swifts are the only birds to use saliva for their nests. One oriental species builds its nest entirely from saliva.

Sword, weapon used in personal combat, originally made of bronze. The Romans introduced the iron sword, 20 in. long. During the Middle Ages the most famous blades were those made by the Arabs at Damascus and those made at Toledo.

Symbiosis. When two organisms live together and both derive mutual benefit from the association, the partnership is known as symbiosis. An example is the symbiosis of an alga and a fungus in lichens; another is the ordinary pea plant and the bacteria which live in the nodules on the pea's roots.

Synapse is the point of association between one nerve cell and another. The nervous impulse travelling along one nerve has to be transmitted to the next across a minute gap. This is the synaptic gap. The mode of transmission is chemical though it was at first thought to be electrical. The impulse arriving at the synapse releases a chemical transmitter which diffuses across the gap and stimulates an impulse in the adjacent nerve cell.

Syndicalism. *See* J49.

Synoptic Charts. These are meteorological charts used in forecasting on which weather conditions at a network of stations, at a standard hour of observation, are recorded, using symbols of the international weather code. Surface weather maps have been drawn regularly for more than a hundred years and the modern advance is the drawing of other maps showing conditions in the upper air.

Synoptists. The writers of the first three Gospels whose narratives in the main agree, though Matthew and Luke add material not found in Mark (written first); all three differ from John's Gospel.

T

Tabard, a cloak or outer garment worn in mediæval days by the peasantry. The name was also applied to a garment worn by knights over their armour.

Tailor-Bird, name of a small group of warblers, familiar in India and China, and remarkable for their habit of sewing leaves together to enclose their nests. The bill is used as needle, vegetable fibre as thread, and a knot is tied to prevent it slipping.

Taj Mahal, the white marble mausoleum built at Agra by Shah Jehan in memory of his favourite wife who died in 1629. Over 20,000 men were occupied for over twenty years in its erection.

Takahe or Notornis, large New Zealand bird of the rail family which for many years was believed to be extinct. Small colony found in 1948 in remote valley of mountainous part of the S. Island. The bird is strictly protected.

Take-over Bid describes an offer made to all the shareholders of a company to purchase their shares at a named price and conditional upon acceptance by the holders of a named proportion of the total share issue. If accepted the purchaser thus gains control of the company.

Tallage, in Norman times, were taxes levied by the Crown upon lands of the royal demesnes. The levying of tallage was taken away by a statute of 1340 which required the consent of Parliament for all direct taxes.

Tally Office, in the Exchequer, was the department of the Government in which tallies were kept, representing the acknowledgment of moneys paid or lent; in 1834 the Houses of Parliament were burnt down through the overheating of a stove with discarded Exchequer tallies.

Tambourine, a light, small, single-headed drum with loose metal discs let into the side of the hoop so that they jingle when the tambourine is shaken. An older name for it is the timbrel.

Tammany, a New York democratic organisation, sprang out of an old benevolent society named after an Indian chief, and has exerted a powerful influence over political movements in New York. The leaders of the organisation have used their power when their party has been successful at the polls to appoint their nominees to every prominent office, and have exacted bribes for concessions and privileges, and generally Tammany rule has meant wholesale corruption. Of this there is ample evidence in the disclosures of the Tweed and other Tammany frauds, and in the fact that the "Boss" usually contrived to make himself wealthy.

Tannins are chemical substances obtained from a variety of plants and trees, from oak-bark, and from galls. They are used in the leather trade, the tanning process making the skins resistant to decay.

Tantalum, a scarce bluish metallic element, symbol Ta, discovered by Ekeberg in 1802. Chemically related to vanadium and niobium, it is usually associated with the latter in nature. For several purposes it can be used in place of platinum, and it finds application in the making of surgical instruments. Tantalum is very hard, and resistant to acids (other than hydrofluoric acid); it is used in alloys.

Taoism. *See* J49.

Tapestry, a fabric largely used in former times for wall decoration and hangings. It was known to the ancient Greeks, but in its modern form came into prominence in the 15th and 16th cent., when it was manufactured in a marked degree of excellence by the weavers of Flanders, especially those of Arras. The manufacture was introduced into England early in the 17th cent., and was attended by considerable success. At the present day the term is applied to worsted cloths for furniture coverings, and there are also various kinds of tapestry carpets now made. The most famous tapestries of olden times were the Aubusson Tapestry and the Savonnerie. The Gobelin Tapestry factory, originated in Paris in the reign of Francis I., is still a national establishment. *See also* Bayeux Tapestry.

Tapirs. The tapirs constitute a family close to the horse family and the rhinoceros in the Ungulate order. They have four toes on the front feet and three on the hind. The snout is drawn out into a short trunk. The largest tapir is the Malayan tapir, which stands 3½ ft. at the shoulder. Four species occur in Central and S. America.

Tar is a dark viscid product obtained from the destructive distillation of wood, coal, peat, etc. Wood tar is acid owing to the presence of acetic acid (" pyroligneous acid "). The highest proportion of coal tar goes into road making. Distillation of coal tar yields many valuable compounds, including benzene, phenol (carbolic acid), naphthalene, and creosote; the final residue after distillation is pitch. Based on the chemical manipulation of compounds from coal tar is the preparation of many perfumes, food essences, drugs, antiseptics, and plastics.

Tarantula, the name given to a large range of big hairy spiders. Music was supposed to cure their sting, hence the Tarantella dance.

Tarpeian Rock at Rome received its named from the tradition that Tarpeia, the daughter of the Governor of the Citadel who betrayed the fortress to the Sabines, was crushed to death by their shields and buried beneath the rock. From this height persons guilty of treason were hurled to death.

Tartaric Acid is prepared from tartar (potassium hydrogen tartrate) deposited in wine vats during fermentation. " Cream of tartar " is purified potassium hydrogen tartrate, which is incorporated in baking powder. Tartaric acid is also used in the manufacture of effervescent salts.

Tate Gallery, named after its founder, Sir Henry Tate, at Millbank, S.W., was opened in 1897; Sir Henry Tate bore the cost of the building (£80,000) and also contributed the nucleus of the present collection. "The Turner Wing," the gift of Sir Joseph Duveen, was added in 1910. The collection is thoroughly representative of British art and has been extended several times to include modern foreign art.

Tay Bridge spans the Tay at Dundee, opened for rail traffic on 20 June 1887. A previous bridge, completed in 1877, was blown down on 28 Dec. 1879, as a train was passing over it. A new bridge was opened on 18 August 1966 for road traffic, 7,356 ft. in length, the longest road bridge in Britain.

Tea was introduced into England about the middle of the 17th cent., when it was a great luxury, and fetched from £6 to £10 a pound. It is an Asiatic plant, native properly to China, Japan, and India. Up to about 1885 most of the tea imported into this country came from China; the bulk now comes from India and Ceylon.

Teal, the smallest of the European ducks and next to the Mallard the commonest British species. It is a handsome bird and a very swift flier, but not as swift as the Garganey or Summer Teal.

Te Deum, the song of praise (" Te Deum laudamus "—" We praise Thee, O God "), is supposed to have been the composition of St. Ambrose in the 4th cent. and is used in Roman Catholic and English Church services.

Telecommunications. The sending of messages over a distance. The term is generally applied to the sending of messages by telegraph, telephone, radio, television or radar. The first submarine telegraph cable between England and France was laid in 1850 and, following Hertz's investigations into electric waves, Marconi's invention led to Britain being linked with Europe by wireless telegraphy in 1899. The first permanently successful telegraph cable across the Atlantic was laid in 1866. The first telephone service between London and Paris was opened in 1891. The electro-magnetic telephone was invented by Alexander Graham Bell, a Scottish-born American, in 1876. The first submarine telephone cable to span the Atlantic was laid in 1956 connecting Britain with Canada and the United States, and many submarine telephone cables have since been laid, including the Commonwealth cable system completed in 1967. The spectacular advances in space research depended on the new tools of work provided by parallel developments in telecommunications, *e.g.,* long-range radio and television transmission, electronic computer control. The performance of *Telstar* in July 1962 and of *Early Bird* in April 1965 showed that intercontinental communication by satellites in space is practical. *See also* Radar, Radio, Television.

Telemetry, measurement at remote distances by means of a radio-link from the object (missile or satellite) to the ground. The third Russian sputnik, for instance, carried apparatus for measuring, among other things, the pressure and composition of the atmosphere, and the intensity of different kinds of radiation from the sun. Its radio transmitter, powered by solar-energy batteries, sent out the information in coded form by means of uninterrupted signals at 20·005 megacycles with a duration of 150–300 milli-seconds. Radio telemetry from inside the body is being increasingly used in medical and biological research; miniature radio transmitters can be swallowed or implanted in man or animal to detect various physiological conditions.

Telepathy and Clairvoyance. *See* J50.

Teleprinter, a telegraph transmitter with a typewriter keyboard, by which characters of a message are transmitted electrically in combinations of 5 units, being recorded similarly by the receiving instrument, which then translates the matter mechanically into printed characters. The telex or public teleprinter service provides direct person-to-person transmission of written messages.

Telescope, an optical instrument for viewing objects at a distance, " the astronomer's intelligencer." Lippershey is credited with construction of the first in 1608; Galileo constructed several from 1609 and Newton was the first to construct a reflecting telescope. The ordinary telescope consists of an object-glass and an eyelens, with two intermediates to bring the object into an erect position. A lens brings it near to us, and the magnifier enlarges it for inspection. A refracting telescope gathers the rays together near the eye-piece and is necessarily limited as to size, but the reflecting telescope collects the rays on a larger mirror, and these are thrown back to the eye-piece. The world's largest reflectors are at Mount Palomar Observatory, California (200 in.), Mount Wilson Observatory, California (100 in.), the McDonald Observatory at Mount Locke, Texas (82 in.), and the Victoria B.C. Observatory (72 in.). At the Royal Observatory, formerly at Greenwich, now at Herstmonceux, Sussex, a 98 in. *Isaac Newton* telescope has been installed. The *Hale* 200 in. telescope at Mount Palomar is the largest ever made and has revealed objects never before photographed; it is able to probe space and photograph remote galaxies out to a limiting distance of 2,000 million light years. The *Schmidt* telescope at Mount Palomar has been used to make a huge photographic map of the universe. The giant steerable radio telescope built by Manchester University at Jodrell Park, Cheshire, has a 250 ft. reflector with a beam width of 12 minutes of arc. Early in its career it tracked the Russian earth satellites and the American lunar probes. Another instrument of radio astronomy is the interferometer which consists of two spaced aerials. *See also* Observatories.

Television, or the transmission of images of moving objects by radio. To understand the problems of television it is necessary to consider the action of the human eye. Basically the eye consists of a lens which projects an image of the scene before it upon the retina, a light-sensitive screen at the back of the eye. The retina is made up of several millions of tiny light-sensitive elements, each quite separate and distinct from its neighbours, and each separately connected to the brain by an individual fibre in the optic nerve. Thus the eye is a very complex organ, and it is able to pick out numbers of tiny details from a scene and convey each detail separately and simultaneously to the brain. It does not send a blend of different points of light and shade in the same way that the ear sends a blend of different sounds; if it did the brain would receive a completely unintelligible blur. From this it is clear that a television system which transmitted a mixture of detail would be useless; it must transmit all the details in a scene separately, yet almost simultaneously, and re-assemble them at such a speed that the eye cannot observe the building-up process. A means of doing this was provided by Nipkow in 1884, when he invented his famous scanning disc, and later Weiller invented the mirror drum for the same purpose. Such mechanical devices as these held the field for many years and in 1923 Baird in this country and Jenkins in America were both using them for the experiments which, in 1925, led to the successful transmission of shadows and simple outlines. It was not until 1926, however, that the first practical demonstration of television, as we understand it, took place when Baird transmitted by radio moving pictures of living human faces over a short distance. The B.B.C. began television broadcasts in 1930; the I.T.A. in 1955. The first television exchange across the Atlantic was made in July 1962 by way of the *Telstar* satellite.

Tellurium, a relatively scarce element, symbol Te, discovered in 1782 by Reichenstein. Chemically it behaves rather like sulphur; its salts are known as tellurides. It occurs chiefly combined with metals in ores of gold, silver, copper, and lead. It is a semiconductor, and some of its compounds (also semiconductors) are coming into use in technical devices.

Templars were soldier knights organised in the 12th cent. for the purpose of protecting pilgrims in their journeyings to and from Jerusalem, and obtained their name from having had granted to them by Baldwin II. a temple for their accommodation. At first they were non-military, and wore neither crests nor helmets, but a long wide mantle and a red cross on the left shoulder. They were established in England about 1180. During the crusades they rendered valuable service, showing great bravery and devotion. In the 12th cent. they founded numerous religious houses in various parts of Europe and became possessed of considerable wealth. It was this that caused their downfall. Kings and Popes alike grew jealous of their influence, and they were subjected to much persecution, and Pope Clement V. abolished the Order in 1312. Edward II. in 1308 seized all the property of the English Templars. The English possessions of the Order were transferred to the Hospitallers of St. John, afterwards called the Knights of Malta. *See also* **Hospitallers, Knights, Teutonic Order.**

Temple, a building dedicated to the worship of a deity or deities. Those built by the ancient Greeks at Olympia, Athens, and Delphi were the most famous. The Temple of Diana at Ephesus was another. The Temple of Solomon at Jerusalem was destroyed and rebuilt several times; Herod's Temple was destroyed by the Romans in A.D. 70.

Temple Bar, an historic gateway that until 1879 stood at the western entrance to Fleet Street near the bottom of Chancery Lane. In olden times it was the custom to impale the heads of traitors over this gateway. It has been at Theobald's Park, Cheshunt, since 1888.

Terbium, an element, symbol Tb, discovered in 1842 by Mosander, belonging to the group of rare-earth metals.

Teredo, the scientific name of the ship-worm, a peculiar bivalve mollusc, which lodges itself when young on the bottoms of wooden ships and bores its way inwards, causing much injury.

Termites, also known as *White Ants,* though they are not related to the true ants and are placed in an entirely different insect order (*Isoptera*). They abound in the tropics and also occur in temperate countries, though only two species are common in Europe. There is no British species. They live in colonies and their nests take the form of mounds of earth and

wood, cemented together with saliva, and up to 20 ft. in height. Five separate castes are recognised, three of them being capable of reproduction, and the other two are sterile.

Tern. This slender, gull-like bird has long pointed wings, a deeply-forked tail, pale grey and white plumage, black cap, and is a very graceful flier. There are several species, some of which are summer migrants to Britain. The Arctic tern winters in the Antarctic, returning to find a nesting place in the spring.

Terrapin, a kind of fresh-water tortoise. There are several species widely distributed in the Northern Hemisphere.

Tertiary Rocks, in geology the rocks formed during the Caenozoic era comprising the Eocene, Oligocene, Miocene, and Pliocene periods. *See* **F44.**

Teutonic Order, of German military knights, was founded in the Holy Land at the end of the 12th cent. for succouring the wounded of the Christian army before Acre. They were dispersed in the 15th cent. but the Order continued to exist until 1809, when Napoleon I. confiscated its properties. In 1840 the order was resuscitated in Austria as a semi-religious knighthood. *See also* **Hospitallers, Knights, Templars.**

Thallium, a blue-grey metallic element, symbol Tl, discovered by Crookes in 1861. It is obtained from the flue dust resulting from the burning of pyrites for sulphuric acid manufacture.

Thanksgiving Day, a national holiday in the United States, observed since 1864 on the last Thursday in November; instituted by the Pilgrim Fathers in 1621 to celebrate their first successful harvest.

Theodolite. The instrument used by surveyors for measuring angles in the horizontal and vertical planes; also used in meteorology for following balloons to measure the speed and direction of wind.

Therm. The charges for gas for lighting and heating (formerly reckoned at per cubic foot) are now based on the calorific, or heat, value of the gas, and the unit used is termed a therm. The therm is 100,000 British thermal units.

Thermionic Emission is the departure of charged particles from matter under the influence of heat. The higher the temperature the greater the flow of escaping particles. The most common example is the emission of electrons from red-hot electrodes—this is the basic phenomenon made use of in thermionic valves (*see* **Valve**). If the hot electrode (the cathode) is enclosed in an evacuated or gas-filled bulb, the emitted electrons can be collected at another electrode (the anode) and will flow through an external circuit back to the emitter. Thus an electric current has been generated by heat.

Thermodynamics, a term first applied by Joule to designate that branch of physical science which treats of the relations of heat to work. What is called the first law of thermodynamics is thus stated by Clerk Maxwell: " When work is transformed into heat, or heat into work, the quantity of work is mechanically equivalent to the quantity of heat." In one of its many formulations, the second law asserts that " the heat tends to flow from a body of hotter temperature to one that is colder, and will not naturally flow in any other way." *See* **F17(1).**

Thermo-electric Devices. If two wires of different materials are formed into a loop and if the two joins are kept at different temperatures a current flows in the loop. This was discovered by Seebeck in 1822, and the device is called a thermocouple. The electric current could in principle be made to drive some useful machine, and the energy comes from the heat that is absorbed by the thermocouple—if one part of the thermocouple is not hotter than the others it will not work. It has long been realised that this is a device that converts heat directly into electricity without raising steam and driving dynamos as in a power-station. However, until recently nobody has used thermocouples for much besides temperature measurement, for which they are exceedingly useful. The new development is the manufacture of semiconductors (*q.v.*); for the thermoelectric effects of these new materials are much greater than those of metals. A material much studied in this connection is a compound of bismuth and tellurium, bismuth telluride. It now seems practicable to generate useful electricity from suitably designed thermocouples. For example, the U.S.S.R. produces a thermoelectric device which uses the heat from the chimney of a domestic oil-lamp to produce enough electricity to work a radio. Presumably this is very useful in remote parts with no electricity supply. But the possibilities do not stop there. Indeed, an eminent Russian authority has stated that thermocouples could produce electricity direct from the warmth of sunlight on a scale and at a cost comparable with conventional fuel-burning power-stations. Even if solar energy cannot be so used, it might be possible to use the heat of nuclear reactors, but this means that the thermoelectric devices would have to stand up to very heavy radioactivity and still work. It is not surprising, however, that many firms are showing great interest in thermoelectricity these days.

Thermometer, an instrument by which the temperature of bodies is ascertained. The most familiar kind of thermometer consists of a glass tube with a very small bore, containing, in general, mercury or alcohol. This expands or contracts with variation in the temperature, and the length of the thread of mercury or alcohol gives the temperature reading on a scale graduated in degrees. Various forms of thermometer are used for particular purposes.

Thermonuclear Reactions. See **Nuclear Fusion.**

Thirty-nine Articles. See **Articles.**

Thistle, Order of. See **Knighthood.**

Thorium, a scarce, dark grey, metal element, symbol Th, discovered by Berzelius in 1828. All substances containing thorium are radioactive. Chief source of thorium is monazite sand, big deposits of which occur in Travancore (India), Brazil, and the U.S.A. Considered important as a potential source of atomic energy since the discovery that it can be transmuted into U233, which is capable of fission like U235.

Thrush, a large family of song-birds of the *Passeriform* order, distributed all over the world. The British species include the robin, redstart, nightingale, song-thrush (or mavis), blackbird, mistle-thrush, ring-ouzel of the mountains, and large numbers of migrant fieldfares and redwings from northern Europe are winter visitors.

Thunder, the sound heard after the occurrence of a lightning flash. It is due to vibrations of the air along the path of the flash, which are set up by the sudden heating (and expansion) followed by the rapid cooling (and contraction) to which the air is subjected. It is unusual for thunder to be heard more than 10 miles away, the distance being estimated roughly by allowing 1 mile for every 5 seconds which elapse between seeing the flash and hearing the thunder. Continued rolling of thunder results from the zig-zag nature of the flash and the multiple strokes of which it is composed, variations in the energy developed along the path, and echo effects. Thunderstorms are caused by powerful rising currents of air within towering cumulonimbus clouds and are most frequent during the afternoons and evenings of sunny summer days.

Thursday, the 5th day of the week, named after Thor, the Scandinavian deity. To the ancient Romans Thursday was *dies Jovis*, or Jupiter's day.

Tidal Power. The principle of exploiting the energy of the tides is similar to hydro-power since it involves the harnessing of falling water. A barrage across a bay or estuary is filled during flow tide and closed during ebb tide creating a difference in level. When the water is allowed to fall towards the lower side of the barrage it operates a turbine which drives a generator. More sophisticated schemes would incorporate pumped storage facilities. An essential requirement is a large tidal range in order to get a sufficient head of water. Although a 240MW scheme has recently been completed on the River Rance in France, it is believed that the economics of tidal power are generally insufficiently favourable for the method to be widely used. *See also* **Hydroelectric Schemes.**

Tides, the periodical rise and fall of the waters of the ocean and its arms, are due to the gravitational effect of the moon and sun. Newton was the first to give a general explanation of the phenomenon of the tides. He supposed the ocean to cover the whole earth, and to assume at each instant a figure of equilibrium, under the combined gravitational influence of earth, sun, and moon, thus making and controlling the tides. At most places there are two tides a day, and the times of high- and low-water vary according to the positions of the sun and moon relative to the earth. When earth, moon and sun are in line (at full moon and new moon) the gravitational pull is greatest and we get "spring" tides. When sun and moon are at right angles (first and third quarters of the moon's phases) we get the smaller "neap" tides.

Tiers Etat, the lowest of the three estates of the realm as reckoned in France—nobility, clergy, and commons (*tiers état*)—prior to the Revolution.

Tiger, a powerful carnivorous animal of the cat family, which occurs in India and certain other parts of Asia. Its skin is of a tawny yellow, relieved by black stripings of great beauty of formation. Some tigers attain a length of from 9 to 12 ft.

Time. The measurement of time has become of increasing importance to man with the advance of civilisation. It was at first almost inevitably based on the succession of night and day, the waxing and the waning of the moon, and on the changing seasons of the year, and the astronomical observation of these three periodic effects has served as the basis of time measurement until recent years. The precision of the observations has continually increased, and clocks have been developed for dividing the day into smaller units. The clocks were adjusted so as to keep in step with the rotation of the earth on its axis, but during recent years an atomic standard of time has been developed, and clocks are now adjusted so as to keep in step with the natural period of an atomic vibration. See **Clocks, Greenwich Mean Time, British Standard Time.**

Tin is a white, metal element, symbol Sn (Latin *Stannum*), whose commonest ore is cassiterite (tin oxide), which occurs in Malaya, Indonesia, Bolivia, Congo, Nigeria, and Cornwall. It protects iron from rusting, and the tin coating on tinplate is applied by dipping the thin steel sheet in molten tin or by electrolysis. Tin alloys of importance include solder, bronze, pewter, and Britannia metal.

Tit *or* **Titmouse,** a small insectivorous bird of the woodlands and forests, bright of plumage and very active and agile, often seen hanging upside down searching for food. There are over fifty species, eight of which occur in Britain: the Great and Blue Tits, familiar in gardens and countryside, the Cole Tit, Marsh Tit, Willow Tit, Bearded Tit, Long-tailed or "Bottle" Tit, and the Scottish Crested Tit.

Titanium, a scarce metal, symbol Ti, difficult to extract from ores, found in association with oxygen in rutile, anatase, and brookite, as well as with certain magnetic iron ores. It combines with nitrogen at a high temperature. Discovered by the Rev. William Gregor in 1791. Titanium alloys, being very resistant to stress and corrosion, and combining strength with lightness, are finding wide application not only in marine and chemical engineering but in the building of aircraft, rockets, and the nuclear-energy field. Titanium dioxide is now widely used in making paints.

Tithes, an ecclesiastical tax consisting of a tenth part of the annual produce known to the ancient Jews, and first imposed by Christian authorities in the 4th cent., although not made compulsory in England before the 9th cent. Tithes derived from land are termed "praedial," those derived from cattle being styled "mixed," while others are personal. After the passing of the Tithes' Commutation Act of 1836, tithes were gradually converted into rent charges, and today the old form of tithes exists only to a small degree. Consult Tithe Act of 1936.

T.N.T. (Trinitrotoluene). A high explosive formed by the action of a mixture of nitric and sulphuric acids on toluene. Not highly sensitive to shock, it can be used in shells without danger, and is exploded by a time, or detonator, fuse. Apart from wartime applications, it is used in blasting in quarries and mines.

Toad, an amphibian, differing from the frog in having a dry, warty skin, a heavier, squat build and shorter limbs. It has a similar metamorphosis, is largely nocturnal, and will wander far from water after the breeding season. Two toads occur in Britain, the Common Toad and the Natterjack. The latter can be identified by the narrow light stripe running down the middle of the back.

Tobacco is made from the leaves of various narcotic plants of the *Nicotiana* family, which contain a volatile oil and an alkaloid called nicotine. Tobacco is largely grown in America, India, Japan, Turkey, Greece, Canada, Italy, Indonesia, Bulgaria, Philippines, France, Congo, China, Rhodesia, Zambia, S. Africa, S. America, and other countries of a warm climate. It undergoes various processes of preparation. The leaves are first dried, then cut into small pieces, moistened and compressed, and in this form it is known as cut or "shag" tobacco; when moistened with syrup or treacle and pressed into cakes, it is Cavendish; when twisted into string form, it is "twist" or "pig-tail." For cigars the midribs of the dry leaves are removed, and what is left is moistened and rolled into cylindrical shape. For snuff, the tobacco leaves are moistened and allowed to ferment, then dried, powdered and scented. *See* Section P (Respiratory System) for the connection between tobacco-smoking and lung cancer.

Tolls. Payments for privileges of passage were first exacted in respect of ships passing up rivers, tolls being demanded on the Elbe in 1109. Tolls for land passage are said to have originated in England in 1269, toll-bars being erected at certain distances on the high-roads in the 17th cent., where toll had to be paid for all vehicles passing to and fro. After about 1825 they began to disappear, but still linger on some country roads and bridges. Tolls on London river bridges ceased in 1878–79.

Tonic Sol-Fa, a system of musical notation in which monosyllables are substituted for notes. Thus the major diatonic scale is represented by Doh, Ray, Me, Fah, Soh, La, Te, Doh. The system was invented by a Miss Glover of Norwich in about 1840 and has proved of great assistance in the teaching of music in schools.

Tonsure, the shaven part of the head of a Roman Catholic ecclesiastic, dates from the 5th or 6th cent. In the Roman Catholic Churches only a circle, or a crown, is shaved, while in the Greek Church shaving is forbidden.

Topaz, a transparent mineral gem, being a silicate and fluoride of aluminium and generally found in granitic rocks. Its colour is yellow, but it also occurs in pink and blue shades. The best kinds come from Brazil.

Topiary, the art of clipping and trimming trees, shrubs, etc., into ornamental shapes. In Britain this art goes back before Elizabethan times when gardens were formal and the shapes simple and symmetrical. By the end of Queen Anne's reign topiary had become much more elaborate, and all kinds of fanciful shapes were produced. Pliny in his *Letters* tells how box hedges were clipped into different shapes in Roman times.

Tornado, a violent whirlwind, characterised by a black, funnel-shaped cloud hanging from heavy cumulonimbus. Usually tornadoes are only a few hundred feet in diameter and occur frequently in the Mississippi region of the U.S.A., where it has been estimated that the wind speeds within them may exceed 200 m.p.h. In West Africa the term is applied to thundery squalls.

Tortoises and Turtles, are cold-blooded reptiles, four-footed, and encased in a strong shell protection, the shells of some species being of beautifully horny substance and design, in much demand for combs, spectacle frames, and ornamental work. It is the custom to designate the land species as tortoises and the aquatic kinds as turtles. The green turtle, so called because its fat has a green tinge, is in great demand for soup. Together the tortoises and turtles make up the reptilian order called *Chelonia*, the biggest representatives of which are the giant land tortoises of the Galapagos Islands, reaching a weight of 500 lb. and living a century. Some of these giant tortoises are even said to have reached 200 or 300 years of age.

Toucan, a South and Central American family of brilliantly coloured birds, remarkable for their huge bills. Toucans live on fruit, are of arboreal habits, and nest in holes. There are about 37 species.

Touchstone, a kind of jasper called by the ancients "Lydian stone," of economic value in testing the quality of metal alloys, especially gold alloys. The testing process is very simple. The alloy is drawn across the broken surface of the Touchstone, and from the nature of the mark or streak it makes the quality of the alloy can be ascertained.

Tourmaline, a mineral occurring in different colours in prismatic crystals. It is a well-known example of a pyro-electric crystal, *i.e.*, one that has a permanent electric polarisation. It is a double silicate of aluminium and boron, and occurs in Cornwall, Devon, South America, and Asia.

Tournaments were equestrian contests between military knights and others armed with lances, and frequent in the Middle Ages. The Normans introduced them to England.

Tower of London was built as a fortress by William the Conqueror. It was a royal palace in the Middle Ages and later used as a garrison and prison. Many distinguished prisoners were executed there, including Anne Boleyn, Catherine Howard, Lady Jane Grey, the 2nd Earl of Essex, and Sir Walter Raleigh. The Chapel Royal of St. Peter and Vincula in the Tower was built in 1105 and took its present shape in the reign of Henry VIII. The Crown Jewels are kept at the Tower, and in the Armoury a fine collection of armour is preserved. The attendant staff are called Yeomen Warders of the Tower. Their style of dress is of the Tudor period.

Trade-Mark, a mark used in relation to goods for the purpose of indicating a connection in the course of trade between the goods and some person having the right, either as a proprietor or registered user, to use the mark. Trade-marks can be registered, the registration holding good for 7 years and being renewable thereafter indefinitely for periods of 14 years. Infringement of a registered trade-mark renders the infringer liable to damages.

Trade Winds form part of the circulation of air round the great permanent anticyclones of the tropics and blow inwards from north-east and south-east towards the equatorial region of low pressure. Atlantic trades are more regular than those of the Pacific. The belts may extend over 1,500 miles of latitude and, together with the Doldrums, move north and south in sympathy with the seasonal changes in the sun's declination, the average annual range being about 5 degrees of latitude.

Trafalgar, Battle of, was fought off Cape Trafalgar on Oct. 21, 1805, between the British under Nelson and the French and Spanish under Villeneuve and Gravina. It was a complete victory for the British, but Nelson was killed.

Trafalgar Square. The site has often been referred to as the finest in Europe. It was conceived originally as a square by John Nash (1752–1835) when the project was considered of linking Whitehall with Bloomsbury and the British Museum. It was to be named after the new monarch as King William the Fourth's Square but on the suggestion of George Ledwell Taylor (a property owner near the site) alteration to the more popular name Trafalgar Square was agreed to by the King. On the north side the National Gallery was planned by Nash and erected by William Wilkins on the place of the Royal Mews—a work of William Kent a century before. The lay-out was the idea of Charles Barry but he did not approve the erection of the Nelson column (which see). His idea was for the square to have a grand flight of steps from the north side with sculptural figures of Wellington and Nelson but the Commons decided otherwise and the column as designed by William Railton was begun in 1840. The two fountains by Barry were supplanted in 1948 by ones designed (1938) by Sir Edwin Lutyens. Executed in Portland stone they are flanked by some bronze sculptures. In the same year memorial busts by Lords Jellicoe and Beatty were placed by the north wall.

Transept, the portion of a church which extends across the interior between the nave and the choir.

Transistor. An electronic device consisting of a small piece of semiconducting solid (usually germanium or silicon) to which contact is made at appropriate places by three wires. The three parts resemble in function (not construction or behaviour) the cathode, anode, and grid of a thermionic valve, and transistors can perform many of the operations that valves have hitherto been used for in radio, television, etc. They possess several advantages over valves since there is no need for evacuated glass bulbs nor for a heated emitter to give off electrons. This leads to much greater compactness and economy as well as to a much longer life. Nevertheless, there are certain limitations to their use, and they are not yet suitable as substitutes for valves in all cases. The device was invented by the Americans Bardeen, Brattain, and Shockley in 1948.

Transubstantiation. *See* **J50.**

Treasure-Trove, a legal term applying to treasure (coin, bullion, gold or silver articles) found hidden in the earth or other place, for which no owner can be discovered. The treasure legally belongs to the Crown, but it is the practice to return to the finder all articles not required for national museums and to reward him with the full market value of such as may be retained. It is the duty of the finder to report to the Coroner for the district in which the find is made who holds an inquest to find whether the discovery be treasure-trove or no. In England concealment is a criminal offence. *See also* **Wreck.**

Tree Frog, occurs most commonly in America and Australasia. The common European tree frog is a brilliant green animal, the adhesive discs at the tips of its fingers and toes enabling it to cling to trees, etc., with ease.

Tree Shrew, an arboreal insectivorous mammal of Asia belonging to the family *Tupaiidae.* Tree shrews are related to the shrews, though in appearance they resemble squirrels except for their sharply pointed snout. They occur in Borneo, Siam, China, and Malaya. Some zoologists classify them as primitive primates.

Trent, Council of, the longest and one of the most important in the history of the Roman Catholic Church, was convened to combat the doctrines of Martin Luther. It first sat in 1545, the last sitting being in 1563. At this Council the general policy, principles, and dogmas of the Roman Catholic Church were authoritatively settled.

Triassic *or* **Trias,** the earliest geological period in the Mesozoic era, which began some 225 million years ago. Triassic formations 25,000 ft. thick occur in the Alps. Modern insects were appearing, and also small reptile-like mammals. Other important Triassic animals were: dinosaurs, ichthyosaurs (marine reptiles), and pterosaurs (flying reptiles). *See* **F44.**

Tribunes, name assigned to officers of different descriptions in ancient Rome. The original tribunes were the commanders of contingents of cavalry and infantry. The most important tribunes were the tribunes of the plebs, first elected in 494 B.C. as the outcome of the struggle between the patrician and the plebeian orders. They held the power of veto and their persons were sacred.

Trichoptera. This is the insect order comprising the Caddis-flies. These are moth-like insects, having hairs on the wings. They are usually found fluttering weakly near water. The larvae are aquatic and are remarkable for the cases (caddis cases) which they build out of sticks, small stones, sand grains, and shells.

Tricolour, the flag of the French Republic since 1789, consisting of three nearly equal vertical bands of blue, white, and red (ratio 90 : 99 : 111).

Trilobites, extinct marine arthropods, most abundant in the Cambrian and Ordovician systems. Their appearance may be roughly described as resembling that of a woodlouse,

and like that animal the trilobites were capable of rolling their bodies up into a ball.

Trinity. The Christian doctrine that God exists in three persons, all co-equal, and indivisible, of the same substance—God the Father, God the Son (who became incarnate as Jesus), begotten of the Father, and God the Holy Ghost, proceeding from Father and Son. The system denying the Trinity is Unitarianism (*see* **J51**).

Trinity House, on Tower Hill, London, was incorporated in 1514 as an association for piloting ships, and has ever since been entrusted with various matters connected with the regulation of British navigation. Since 1854 the lighthouses of the country have been under its supervision. The acting Elder Brethren act as Nautical Assessors in Marine causes which are tried by the High Court of Justice.

Triptych, a picture, carving, or other representation, with two swing doors, by which it could be closed in; frequently used as an altar-piece. Also a writing tablet in three parts, two of which folded over the one in the centre.

Trireme, an ancient vessel with three rows of oars of great effectuality in early naval warfare. Mentioned by Thucydides. It was a long, narrow vessel propelled by 170 rowers. The Romans copied it from the Greeks.

Trisagion ("thrice holy"), an ancient Jewish hymn, still regularly sung in the service of the Greek Church. A version of it—"Tersanctus"—also forms part of the Anglican Eucharistic service.

Tritium, a radioactive isotope of hydrogen which has three times the weight of the ordinary hydrogen atom. It is produced by bombarding an isotope of lithium with neutrons and has a half-life of 12½ years, decaying with the emission of β-particles (electrons).

Triumvirate, a term used to denote a coalition of three persons in the exercise of supreme authority. The first Roman triumvirate was that of Pompey, Julius Caesar, and Crassus, 60 B.C.; the second was that of Mark Antony, Octavus, and Lepidus, 43 B.C.

Tropic-Bird, a long-tailed sea bird, of which there are 3 species (the Red-billed, the White-tailed, and the Red-tailed), frequenting the tropical regions of the Atlantic, Pacific, and Indian oceans. They are commonly called Bo'sun Birds.

Troposphere. The atmospheric layer which extends from the earth's surface to the stratosphere. As a general rule the temperature in the troposphere falls as altitude increases. *See* **Atmosphere.**

Troubadours, lyric poets who flourished from the 11th to the end of the 13th cent., chiefly in Provence and the north of Italy. They were often knightly amateurs, and cultivated a lyrical poetry intricate in metre and rhyme and usually of a romantic amatory strain. They did much to cultivate the romantic sentiment in days when society was somewhat barbaric and helped considerably in the formation of those unwritten codes of honour which served to mitigate the rudeness of mediaeval days. *See also* **Jongleurs.**

Trouvère *or* **Trouveur,** mediaeval poet of northern France, whose compositions were of a more elaborate character—epics, romances, fables, and chansons de geste—than those of the troubadour of the south. Flourished between the 11th and 14th cent.

Truffles are subterranean edible fungi much esteemed for seasoning purposes. There are many species, and they are found in considerable quantities in France and Italy, less commonly in Britain. They are often met with under beech or oak trees, and prefer calcareous soils, but there are no positive indications on the surface to show where they are, and they are not to be cultivated. Hogs, and sometimes dogs, are used to scent them out, the former, by reason of their rooting propensities, being the most successful in the work.

Tsetse, an African dipterous fly belonging to the same family as the house-fly. It is a serious economic pest as it transmits the protozoon causing African sleeping sickness when it pierces human skin in order to suck blood, which forms its food. *See* **Gammexane.**

Tuatara *or* *Sphenodon punctatum,* a primitive lizard found in New Zealand. It has a rudimentary third eye on the top of the head; this is called the pineal eye and corresponds to tissue which in mammals forms the pineal gland.

Tube Foot, the characteristic organ of locomotion of starfishes and kindred animals. They are arranged in pairs along the underside of the arms, and their sucker-like ends can grip a surface very tightly. The action of the suckers depends on hydraulic pressure.

Tudor Period extends from 1485 to 1603. The first Tudor sovereign was Henry VII., descended from Owen Tudor; then followed Henry VIII., Edward VI., Mary, and Elizabeth, the last of the line.

Tuesday, the third day of the week, named from the Saxon deity Tuisto, Tiw, or Teusco. To the Romans it was the day of Mars.

Tuileries, a French royal and imperial palace dating from 1564. It was attacked by insurgents during the outbreaks of 1792, 1830, and 1848, and was burned down during the Commune of Paris in 1871.

Tumulus, a mound of earth raised over the bodies of the dead. The mound of Marathon, enclosing the bodies of the Athenians who were killed in the famous battle with the Persians, is a celebrated tumulus. Such mounds were commonly raised over the tombs of the distinguished dead in ancient times, and sometimes enclosed heavy structures of masonry. The Roman " barrows " were tumuli. Evidences of such mounds are frequent in prehistoric remains.

Tuna or **Tunny,** a large marine fish belonging to the mackerel family, frequenting the warm waters of the Atlantic, Pacific, and Mediterranean. Tuna fisheries are an important industry.

Tundra, the vast barren treeless plains with small lakes and morasses lying in the arctic regions of northern N. America and northern Russia where the winters are long and severe and the subsoil permanently frozen. Sparsely inhabited by nomadic peoples—Lapps, Samoyeds, and Eskimos—who support themselves by hunting and fishing. The reindeer is domesticated and supplies most of their needs.

Tungsten, a hard, brittle metal, symbol W (it was formerly called wolfram), silver to grey in colour. Its chief ores are wolframite (iron and manganese tungstate) and scheelite (calcium tungstate). Tungsten is alloyed in steel for the manufacture of cutting tools; also in the non-ferrous alloy stellite (*q.v.*). Electric lamp filaments are made from tungsten. Tungsten carbide is one of the hardest substances known and is used for tipping tools.

Turbines propelled by steam provide power for the propulsion of many ships, and on land steam turbines are a principal source of power, being used in large central electricity stations, for instance, to convert heat energy into electrical energy. Gas turbines have recently come into use in aeroplanes, and gas-turbine railway locomotives are being developed. The first gas-turbine ship had its trials in 1947, just half a century after the first steam-turbine ship.

Turbot, a large flat fish, highly valued as food. It often attains from 30 to 40 lb. in weight. Its flesh is white and firm. It is confined to European waters, and is caught by line or trawl.

Turkey, a fowl of American origin, brought to Europe from America soon after the discovery of that country. It was a domesticated bird in England in the first half of the 16th cent.

Turpentine, an oily substance obtained from coniferous trees, mostly pines and firs. It is widely used especially in making paints and varnishes, and also has medicinal properties.

Turquoise, formerly called Turkey-Stone, is a blue or greenish-blue precious stone, the earliest and best specimens of which came from Persia. It is composed of a phosphate of aluminium, with small proportions of copper and iron. India, Tibet, and Silesia yield turquoises, and a variety is found in New Mexico and Nevada. It derives its name from the fact that the first specimens were imported through Turkey.

Turtle Dove, a summer visitor from Africa to southern England. It is a small, slender bird with reddish-brown upper parts, pinkish throat, black tail with white edges, and a repeated purring note.

Tweed. A rough-surfaced fabric of the twilled type, usually all-wool, though cheaper kinds may include cotton. Of a soft, open, flexible texture, it may have a check, twill, or herringbone pattern. Harris, Lewis, Bannockburn, and Donegal tweeds are well known. " Tweeds " is said to have been written in error by a clerk for " twills."

Twelfth Night is the eve of the feast of the Epiphany, and in olden times was made the occasion of many festivities. It was the most popular festival next to Christmas, but is now little observed.

Twilight is the light which is reflected from the upper portion of the earth's atmosphere when the sun is below the horizon (before sunrise or after sunset). The term is most usually understood to refer, however, to the evening light; the morning light we call dawn. The twilight varies in duration in different countries, according to the position of the sun. In tropical countries it is short; in the extreme north it continues through the night.

Tyburn, a former small tributary of the Thames, which gave its name to the district where now stands the Marble Arch, Hyde Park. Here public executions formerly took place.

Tycoon, the title by which the commander-in-chief of the Japanese army (virtually the ruler of Japan) was formerly described by foreigners. (In Japanese *taikun* means great lord or prince.) The term is now applied, usually in a derogatory sense, to an influential business magnate.

Tympanum is, in architectural phraseology, the triangular space at the back of a pediment, or, indeed, any space in a similar position, as over window or between the lintel and the arch of a doorway. In ecclesiastical edifices the tympanum is often utilised for sculptured ornamentation.

Tynwald, the title given to the Parliament of the Isle of Man, which includes the Governor and Council (the Upper House), and the House of Keys, the representative assembly. This practically constitutes Home Rule, the Acts passed by the Tynwald simply requiring the assent of the Sovereign.

U

Uhlan, a light cavalry soldier armed with lance, pistol, and sabre and employed chiefly as skirmisher or scout. Marshal Saxe had a corps of them in the French Army; and in the Franco-German war of 1870 the Prussian Uhlans won fame.

Ultramarine, a sky-blue pigment obtained from *lapis lazuli*, a stone found in Tibet, Persia, Siberia, and some other countries. A cheaper ultramarine is now produced by grinding and heating a mixture of clay, sulphur, carbonate of soda, and resin.

Ultrasonics, sound waves of frequency so high as to be inaudible to humans, *i.e.*, about 20,000 cycles per sec. and upwards. Ultrasonic waves are commonly produced by causing a solid object to vibrate with a suitably high frequency and to impart its vibrations to the air or other fluid. The object may be a quartz or other crystal in which vibrations are excited electrically, or a nickel component which is magnetically energised. There are numerous technical applications, *e.g.* submarine echo sounding, flaw detection in castings, drilling glass and ceramics, emulsification. Ultrasonic waves are an important tool of research in physics. Bats produce very loud sounds when they are flying, but at ultrasonic frequencies (20,000 to 100,000 c/s), so that we cannot ourselves hear them.

Ultra-Violet Rays. These are invisible electromagnetic rays whose wavelengths are less than 3,900 A. (Angstrom = one-hundredth of a millionth of a centimetre). The sun's radiation is rich in ultra-violet light, but much of it never reaches the earth, being absorbed by molecules of atmospheric gases (in particular, ozone) as well as by soot and smoke particles. One beneficial effect of ultra-violet light on human beings is that it brings about synthesis of vitamin-D from certain fatty substances (called sterols) in the skin. The wave-lengths which effect this vitamin synthesis also cause sun tan and sun burn. Ultra-violet lamps (which are mercury-vapour discharge lamps) are also used for sterilising the air inside buildings, their rays being lethal to bacteria. Many substances fluoresce under ultra-violet light; for instance, zinc silicate glows green, while cadmium borate throws out red light. This phenomenon is applied practically in fluorescent lamps, the light of requisite hue being secured by judicious mixture of the fluorescent materials which coat the lamp. *See* **Electric Light.**

Umbra, the full shadow of the earth or moon during an eclipse; the half shadow is called penumbra.

Unciae. The Romans took over the Egyptian cubit and divided it into 16 digits as well as into 12 parts called *unciae,* the *uncia* being the origin of the inch.

Unction, the act of anointing with oil, a symbol of consecration practised in the Roman Catholic, Greek, and other Churches, but not in the Protestant. *Extreme unction* is the rite of anointing a dying person with holy oil. This function consists in anointing the eyes, ears, nostrils, mouth, the palms of the hands, and the soles of the feet.

Underdeveloped Countries are countries in which primitive methods of production still largely prevail. Most of the population are peasants, carrying on agricultural pursuits on small-holdings without much use of capital, and the industrial production is largely in the hands of individual craftsmen working without expensive capital instruments. Many of these countries are now trying to carry through large plans of industrialisation but are severely hampered by lack of capital resources, as they need to import capital goods for which they find it difficult to pay with exports, especially when the " terms of trade " (*see* **G6**) are unfavourable to primary producers. The need for capital imposes on such countries the necessity of a high rate of saving out of their national incomes; but this is difficult to enforce in view of the deep poverty of most of the people. They accordingly stand in need of help from the advanced countries, both with capital loans at low interest rates and gifts. *See* **Section G, Part III.**

Unicorn, a fabulous single-horned animal. In heraldry its form is horse-like, with the tail of a lion and pointed single horn growing out of the forehead. In the Middle Ages the unicorn was a symbol of virginity.

Union of Great Britain and Ireland was proposed in the Irish Parliament in Jan. 1799 after the 1798 Rebellion and came into force on Jan. 1, 1801. The troubled history of Ireland, associated with the question of self-government, nationalism, land, and religion, culminated in the Easter revolution of 1916. A treaty giving the 26 southern counties independence in 1921, as the Irish Free State, was followed by a period of internal dissention. In 1937 a new constitution was enacted in Eire in which no reference was made to the Crown. This, however, left in force the External Relations Act of 1936 and with its repeal in 1948, Eire separated itself from the British Crown and thus severed the last constitutional link with the Commonwealth, and became an independent Republic.

Union, Treaty of, was the treaty by which Scotland became formally united to England, the two countries being incorporated as the United Kingdom of Great Britain, the same Parliament to represent both, Scotland electing sixteen peers and forty-five members of the House of Commons. Uniformity of coins, weights, and measures was provided for, Scottish trade laws and customs were assimilated to those of England, and as regards religion and the practices of the law, Scotland was to continue as before. This Act was ratified on May 1, 1707.

United Nations. *See* **Section C, Part II,**

Universe in astronomy means not only the star system (of which the sun and planets are a small part) but all the countless star systems or nebulae which may be separated from each other by millions of light-years. *See* **F3–7.**

Universities are institutions of higher education whose principal objects are the increase of knowledge over a wide field through original thought and research and its extension by the teaching of students. Such societies existed in the ancient world, notably in Greece and India, but the origin of the University as we know it today lies in mediaeval Europe, the word

universitas being a contraction of the Latin term for corporations of teachers and students organised for the promotion of higher learning. The earliest bodies to become recognised under this description were at Bologna and Paris in the first half of the 12th cent.; Oxford was founded by an early migration of scholars from Paris, and Cambridge began with a further migration from Oxford. Other Universities sprang up all over Europe, including three in Scotland—St. Andrews (1412), Glasgow (1451), and Aberdeen (1494)—which were followed by Edinburgh in 1582. These six bodies remained the only Universities in Great Britain until the foundation in 1826–29 of University and King's Colleges in London (resulting in the establishment of the University of London in 1836) and of the University of Durham in 1832. There are (1971) thirty-three Universities in England: Aston, Bath, Birmingham, Bradford, Bristol, Brunel, Cambridge, The City, Durham, East Anglia, Essex, Exeter, Hull, Keele, Kent, Lancaster, Leeds, Leicester, Liverpool, London, Loughborough, Manchester (including Manchester University Institute of Science and Technology), Newcastle, Nottingham, Oxford, Reading, Salford, Sheffield, Southampton, Surrey, Sussex, Warwick, York, in addition to the Royal College of Art, which under Royal Charter (1967) grants the degrees of Doctor, Master, and Bachelor of Art or Design (R.C.A.) and the postgraduate University of Cranfield (aeronautics). Formed from colleges of technology, art and design, commerce, and other institutions, thirty polytechnics have been established in England and Wales as centres of higher education. Wales has one University (The University of Wales with colleges at Aberystwyth, Bangor, Cardiff and Swansea) in addition to St. David's, Lampeter, which confers two degrees (in Arts and Theology), and the Welsh College of Advanced Technology, Cardiff, which is expected to be granted university status. Scotland now has eight: Aberdeen, Dundee (1967), Edinburgh, Glasgow, Heriot-Watt (1966), St. Andrews, Stirling (1967), and Strathclyde (1964), Britain's first technological University. Northern Ireland has two: Queen's University, Belfast, and the New University of Ulster at Coleraine. The number of full-time students in the United Kingdom is expected to reach between 220,000 and 225,000 in 1971, over four times the number at the end of the war. The Open University received its charter in 1969; it provides degree and other courses together with radio and television programmes and began its broadcasts in January 1971. The Republic of Ireland now has three Universities: Dublin, Cork, and Galway. The 19th cent. also saw a wide extension of the University movement throughout the British Empire, the early important foundations being McGill (1821), Toronto (1827), and Laval (1852) in Canada; Sydney (1850) and Melbourne (1853) in Australia; New Zealand (1870); South Africa (1873); Bombay, Calcutta, and Madras in 1857 in India; and the University of the Punjab (1882) in the present Pakistan. Since the war a number of Universities and University Colleges have been instituted in Commonwealth countries—in the West Indies, in East and West Africa and Rhodesia, in Malaysia, India, and Pakistan. In the U.S.A. the development of higher education has left the Universities less sharply defined than in Europe and the Commonwealth, the best-known being Harvard, Yale, Princeton, Columbia, and Chicago. In Britain, Universities receive aid from the State mainly in the form of direct grants from the Treasury made on the advice of the University Grants Committee. But they are self-governing institutions free from State control. In recent years students have increased their contributions to the formulation of university policy.

University Boat-race. *See* **U35.**

Uranium, a metal, symbol U, discovered by Klaproth in 1789 in pitch-blende. It is a white metal which tarnishes readily in air. Great developments have followed the discovery that the nucleus of the uranium isotope U^{235} undergoes fission, and uranium minerals have become very important since it was found that atomic energy could be released controllably by taking advantage of fission. Previous to the second world war the uranium content of all the uranium ores that were mined was estimated at 1,000 tons. Before atomic energy work began to take the major part of the world's output of uranium minerals, the chief users of uranium compounds were the ceramics and textile industries. *See also* Nuclear Reactors, Nuclear Fission, F12(1).

Uranus. This planet was discovered by Herschel in 1781. Its diameter is 32,000 miles and its average distance from the sun is 1,783 million miles. It has five small satellites.

Urea, the final product in mammals of the breakdown of nitrogenous waste, *e.g.*, excess amino-acids. It is very soluble in water and is excreted in urine. In 1828 Wohler synthesised urea from inorganic matter. This was the first laboratory synthesis of an organic substance and refuted the idea that living creatures or life force are necessary to create such substances.

Ursa Major, the Greater Bear, or "Charles's Wain," a constellation familiar to all observers because of the brilliance of the seven stars forming its outline. It never sets in these latitudes.

Ursa Minor, the Lesser Bear Constellation, has, like Ursa Major, seven prominent stars, of which the pole star is the brightest.

Utopias. *See* J51.

V

Valency. A term used by chemists to describe the combining ability of an element with respect to hydrogen. Thus oxygen, which forms water, H_2O, with hydrogen is said to have a valency of two, nitrogen (forms ammonia, NH_3) three, and carbon (forms methane, CH_4) four. Chlorine forms hydrogen chloride, HCl, and is said to be monovalent. This empirical approach cannot account for valency in such compounds as carbon monoxide, CO, which appears to require both elements to have the same valency. With the discovery of the electron it was realised that the concept of valency and chemical bonds is intimately concerned with the electronic structure of atoms, and theories have been advanced to explain why the same element can have different valencies in different compounds. Iron, for example, can have a valency of two ($FeCl_2$, ferrous chloride) or three ($FeCl_3$, ferric chloride). *See* F20(2), F66.

Valentine's Day, the 14th Feb., is a festival in celebration of St. Valentine, one of the Christian martyrs of the 3rd cent. A sweetheart or Valentine is chosen on that day and letters or tokens sent secretly to the object of affection.

Valhalla, in Scandinavian mythology, is the special Paradise to which the souls of warriors slain in battle were transported. The term is also generally used to designate a burial place of great men.

Valkyries, the chosen handmaidens of Odin, appointed to serve at the Valhalla banquets. Their most important office, however, according to the Norse mythology, was to ride through the air at a time of battle and point out the heroes who were to fall. It is one of these Valkyries who is made the heroine of Wagner's opera "Die Walküre."

Valve, an electronic device consisting of two or more metal plates (electrodes) usually enclosed in an evacuated glass bulb. One of the electrodes is heated causing electrons to be emitted. If a positive voltage is applied to the other electrode, the electrons will move towards it and the valve must conduct electricity. The current will only flow in one direction as the electrons are emitted only from one electrode. A valve with two electrodes is called a diode, but by putting in one or more intermediate electrodes the flow of current can be sensitively controlled and the valves are then called triodes, pentodes, etc., according to the total number of electrodes in them. Valves have found extensive applications in amplifiers, rectifiers, oscillators, and many electronic devices, but are now being superseded by transistors in many applications where it is advantageous to have greater reliability, smaller power consumption, and smaller size.

Vampire *or* **Werewolf,** according to ancient superstition, was a spectre in human form which rose from its grave in the night-time and preyed upon the living as they slept, sucking their blood, and then returning to the grave.

Vampire-Bats, blood-eating bats of tropical America. They puncture the skin with their incisor teeth, leaving a wound that bleeds profusely. The blood is lapped up by the bat, not sucked.

Vanadium, a scarce metallic element, symbol V, whose chief ores are carnotite and patronite. Some iron ores contain it. Most of the vanadium commercially produced finds its way into vanadium steels, which are used for tools and parts of vehicles, being hard, tough, and very resistant to shocks. The oxide is used as a catalyst in industry, especially in making sulphuric acid.

Van Allen Belts. One of the most remarkable discoveries made during the I.G.Y., 1957–58, was that the earth is surrounded by a great belt of radiation. Evidence came from *Sputnik II* (which carried the dog Laika) and from the American satellites, *Explorers I* and *III*. The American scientist, J. A. van Allen, was able to explain the puzzling data collected from these satellites. Subsequent observations with deep space-probes showed that there are in fact two zones of high intensity particle radiation surrounding the earth, one concentrated at a distance of about 1,000 miles, the other at about 15,000 miles. A close relation exists between the shapes of the zones and the earth's magnetic field. Recent evidence suggests that Jupiter also is surrounded by a dense belt of trapped energetic particles.

Varnish is of two leading kinds: spirit varnish, made from resinous substances dissolved in spirit; and oil varnish, in which the dissolving agent is linseed oil and turpentine.

Vatican, the Papal residence at Rome, a famous palace on the hill adjacent to St. Peter's. Its museum is a rich treasure-house of literary and artistic objects.

Vauxhall Gardens, a famous London pleasure resort from the early part of the 18th to the middle of the 19th cent. It was here that many great singers appeared, where the earliest balloon ascents were made, and where there were fine displays of fireworks.

Vein. *See* Lode.

Venus, the brightest of all the planets, whose orbit lies between that of Mercury and the earth, second in order from the sun (*see* F7). It can approach the earth to within 25 million miles. In common with all the other planets it moves around the sun in the same direction as the earth, but is the only one that rotates about its axis in the opposite direction. The planet takes just under 225 earth days to complete an orbit round the sun. In 1967 Russia succeeded in soft-landing an instrumented canister from their *Venus 4* research spacecraft. Measurements gave a picture of a very hostile environment—high surface temperature, a very high atmospheric pressure, an atmosphere 15 times denser than on earth of almost pure carbon dioxide. *Venus 5 and Venus 6* made twin landings in May 1969 and sent back data on the planet's mysterious veil of white clouds.

Venus Fly-trap, a well-known insectivorous plant (*Dionaea muscipula*) occurring in Carolina in damp mossy places. It is related to the Sundew. The leaf is the organ that catches the insects. The leaf blade is in two halves, hinged along the centre line. Each half bears three sensitive hairs called "trigger hairs." When an insect touches a trigger, the two halves of the leaf clap together, trapping the insect between them, when it is digested by a secretion (digestive enzymes) from the leaf, which afterwards absorbs the soluble products.

Vernalization. Seeds which, after being exposed to a low temperature, produce plants that flower earlier than usual are said to have been "vernalized." This technique of seed treatment devised by Lysenko is called vernalization. It is claimed to have been widely used in Russia to obtain cereal crops in places where climatic conditions are favourable for only a short season.

Versailles, Treaty of. The Peace Treaty, 1919, ending the first world war. The first half was devoted to the organisation of the League of Nations. Among the territorial changes Germany ceded Alsace-Lorraine to France, Posen and the Corridor to Poland. Germany undertook to disarm, to abolish universal military service, to keep only a small army of 100,000 and a small navy. Her colonies were to be shared out among the Allies under League Mandates. Reparations were to be paid, but were gradually reduced and entirely ceased in 1932. Hitler took unilateral action against the Treaty especially in regard to rearmament and the annexation of Austria. Hitler's attempt to change the eastern frontiers was the immediate cause of the Second World War.

Victoria and Albert Museum, in Kensington, London, was begun in 1852 as the Museum of Ornamental Art at Marlborough House. The present building was completed in 1909, and has the following nine departments: Architecture and Sculpture; Ceramics; Engraving, Illustration and Design; Metalwork; Paintings; Woodwork; Textiles; Library (of books on art) and Book-production; and the Dept. of Circulation. The Bethnal Green Museum is a branch of the V. and A.

Victoria Cross, an order of merit for conspicuous valour, awarded to members of the Army, Navy, and Air Force, was established in 1856. In July 1959 it was announced that all holders of the V.C. for whom the British Government is responsible would receive a tax-free annuity of £100.

Vienna Congress, sat at Vienna from Sept. 1814 to June 1815, and settled the delimitation of the territories of the various European nations after the defeat of Napoleon. The Treaty of Vienna which resulted gave Ceylon, Mauritius, Cape Colony, Heligoland, Malta, and part of Guiana to England; France was not permitted to hold more territory than she had possessed at the outbreak of the Revolution in 1789; Austria took Northern Italy; Russia part of Poland; and Prussia, part of Saxony and the Rhenish province. Except for one or two changes the clauses of the treaty were maintained for over forty years.

Viet-Minh, the Indo-Chinese (Annamite) national movement led by Ho Chi-Minh which resisted French rule from 1945 to 1954, when Vietnam was partitioned as a result of the Geneva Conference. The National Liberation Front of South Vietnam is the political arm of the Viet Cong.

Vikings. Scandinavian pirates who from the 8th to the 10th cent. were the terror of northern waters. Sometimes the Viking raids reached south to the Mediterranean and east to the White Sea. Their leader Rurik founded the first Russian kingdom of Novgorod in A.D. 862. The Icelandic Vikings under Eric the Red discovered Greenland in A.D. 982 and a warm period in world climate allowed many to settle there. Their expeditions took them to Labrador and Newfoundland. The Vikings excelled in shipbuilding, were fine sailors and splendid craftsmen.

Vinegar. This condiment and preservative is a weak solution of acetic acid (3–9%) formed by the oxidation of ethyl alcohol by the action of bacteria on alcoholic liquor (wine, beer, cider, fermented fruit juices, or malted cereals). Wine vinegar is usually red; malt vinegar is brown. The name vinegar is derived from the latin *vinum aigre*, bad wine. *See also* Acetic Acid.

Vinyl Plastics are polymers made from derivatives of ethylene, examples are polyvinyl chloride (P.V.C.), which is used in making plastic pipes and kitchen utensils, among other things; polyvinyl acetate used in the paint industry and in bonding laminated articles like plywood; and polystyrene (poly vinyl benzene) used in making electrical fittings and for lenses.

Viper, a family of poisonous snakes of which there is one example in Britain, the common viper or adder, only found in very dry localities.

Virus. *See* P7, F26(2).

Visibility is defined by the distance at which the farthest of a series of objects, specially selected to show against the skyline or in good contrast with their background, can be distinguished. Visibility depends chiefly upon the concentration of water or dust particles

suspended in the air. Instruments are available to measure the obscurity of the atmosphere more directly, including that at night. A large lapse rate of temperature and a strong wind are favourable to good visibility; a small lapse rate, calm or light wind favourable to bad visibility. Fog is when the visibility is less than 1,100 yds.; mist or haze when it is between 1,100 and 2,200 yds. *See* Pollution.

Viscount, a title of rank coming between that of Earl and Baron. The title originally stood for deputy-earl. The first English Viscount was Viscount Beaumont, created in 1440.

Vitamins, name of a group of organic substances found in relatively minute amounts in certain foodstuffs, essential for growth and the maintenance of normal bodily structure and function. The Hungarian biochemist Szent-Györgyi, who first isolated vitamin C or ascorbic acid, defined the vitamin as " a substance that makes you ill if you don't eat it!" *See* F27(1).

Volcanoes are vents through which magma reaches the surface as lava flows, or as the solid products, *e.g.*, ashes and bombs, of explosive eruption. The vent may be cylindrical or it may be a long fissure. The former type usually builds up cones, *e.g.*, Vesuvius. Notable active volcanoes are Etna, Vesuvius and Stromboli, in Italy; Hekla in Iceland; and Mont Pelée in Martinique. The last-named was in violent eruption in 1902, when the chief town of St. Pierre was completely destroyed. Volcanic eruptions are sometimes linked with brilliant sunset phenomena, *e.g.*, the Pacific island of Krakatoa (1883), whose atmospheric and tidal effects were recorded all over the world, and Agung on the island of Bali (1963), which had been dormant for 120 years. A new fissure volcano (Surtsey) developed off the coast of Iceland in 1963.

Vole. There are three species of British vole; the Field-vole, the Bank-vole, and the Water-vole.

Volt, the electromotive force unit, named after Alessandro Volta (1745–1827), and defined in terms of the coulomb, the second, and the joule.

Vraic, a name for seaweed in the Channel Islands, where it is extensively used as a manure.

Vulgate, a term used to designate the Latin version of the Scriptures sanctioned by the Council of Trent. The work of St. Jerome in the late 4th cent. A.D. and still the official Bible of the Roman Catholic Church.

Vulture, a famous bird of prey of two distinctive groups; that of the Old World, whose nostrils are separated by a bony partition, and the New World vulture, which has no such division. Vultures feed on carrion and are the great scavengers of tropical regions. The European species are the Egyptian vulture, Griffon vulture, Black vulture, and Bearded vulture. Vultures have no feathers on the head and neck.

W

Wading Birds, *Charadriiformes,* an order of migratory, long-legged, long-billed birds, frequenting marshes and shallow waters. They include the plovers, avocets, stilts, oystercatchers, curlews, phalaropes, godwits, dunlins, sandpipers, redshanks, greenshanks, snipe, woodcocks, the pratincole of the Mediterranean, and the sun bittern of tropical America. Many species breed in Britain.

Wagtails, familiar long-tailed small birds, the most common British species being the Pied or Water (with sub-species White) Grey and the Yellow (sub-species Blue.) Wagtails nest in holes and are active of habit.

Walloons, name given to the French-speaking population of the southern provinces of Belgium, in contrast to the Flemings or Dutch-speaking population of the northern provinces. The Walloon areas contain the mining and heavy industries of the country; the Flemish regions are more agricultural. Walloons number *c.* 3 million, Flemings *c.* 5 million. The *Mouvement Populaire Wallon* desires an autonomous Wallonia within the Belgian state.

Walpurgis Night, the night before May 1st, when witches and creatures of evil are supposed to have liberty to roam. Named after St. Walpurgis, an English nun, who went on a mission to Germany in the 8th cent.

Walrus, a very large marine mammal, related to the seals having in the upper jaw two large curved tusks, which average in length from 15 in. to 2 ft. It lives on bi-valve molluscs, and inhabits the Arctic seas. An adult walrus can exceed 12 ft. in length and weigh over a ton.

Wapentake, the ancient name given in the northern counties to territorial divisions corresponding to the Hundreds of southern counties.

Warblers, a family of small, lively song-birds closely related to the flycatchers and thrushes. Represented in Britain by about 36 species, including the chiffchaff, one of the earliest spring visitors, willow-wren, wood-warbler, blackcap, garden-warbler, whitethroats, sedge- and grasshopper-warbler.

Water is the simplest compound of hydrogen and oxygen. It is formed when an electric spark is passed through a mixture of the gases, and is a product of combustion of all hydrogen-containing compounds, e.g., petrol, coal, coal gas, and wood. Water is essential to living matter, and is the medium which carries food to animals and plants. Salts in hard water may be removed by distillation of the water or by a process known as ion-exchange (water softening). Pure water freezes at $0°$ C and boils at $100°$ C and is used as a standard of temperature on this scale. It has a maximum density at $4°$ C. Heating water above $100°$ C. converts it into steam, which is used under pressure to convert heat energy into useful work, as in electrical power stations and steam engines. Water gas is a mixture mainly of carbon monoxide and hydrogen formed by blowing steam and oxygen through red-hot coke: it is used as a fuel. Water is one of the very few compounds which freezes from the surface down rather than from the bulk of the liquid up. This property has important consequences on the preservation of life in rivers and lakes when they are frozen over. See also F23.

Water Hyacinth (Eichhornia crassipes), a beautiful aquatic plant native to Brazil which has spread to other favourable equatorial regions of the world causing havoc on account of its abnormal rate of reproduction away from its natural environment. In recent years it has invaded the Nile and the Congo, forming vast floating carpets which block the channels, clog the paddles of river craft and de-oxygenate the water, killing the fish. It is being held in check by spraying with the herbicide 2,4-D.

Waterloo, Battle of, was fought on June 18th, 1815. The Allies (British, German, and Dutch) under Wellington and Blücher defeated the French under Napoleon. This ended Napoleon's career.

Waterloo Bridge, crossing the Thames, was built by Rennie, and opened in 1817. It had nine arches, each of 120 ft. span, was built of granite, and had a length (including approaches) of 2,456 ft. The present bridge, completed in 1942, and formally opened Dec. 10, 1945, is a fine example of reinforced concrete construction. (Architect, Sir Giles Gilbert-Scott.)

Water-Spider, an interesting little animal which spins a sac of silk on a water-plant, which it uses as a sort of diving bell. Into this bell it introduces bubbles of air, one at a time; thus the spider is enabled to remain below the surface a considerable time.

Waterspout, whirling tornado-like cloud, occurring at sea. It begins as a cone of cloud tapering slowly downwards, the sea surface becoming disturbed; on reaching the centre of the cloud of spray the spout takes on the appearance of a column of water. A number of these vortices may form fairly close together at about the same time, their duration ranging up to 30 minutes.

Watling Street, the name of the old Roman road which ran from the Channel ports by way of London to Shropshire. See also Roman Roads.

Watt. A unit of electrical power equivalent to 1 joule of work per second, named after James Watt (1736–1819).

Wax, the name applied to certain substances or mixtures which are solids having little crystalline form and may be regarded as solidified oils. They are used for various purposes, such as the making of wax candles, bleaching, and making artificial flowers and anatomical models, also in

pharmacy for blending in the composition of plasters, ointment, etc. The best-known natural wax is beeswax, and there are others, such as spermaceti, obtained from the sperm whale, and Chinese wax, which is a cerotyl cerotate.

Waxbill, a small Oriental and African bird of the Estrildidae family, with wax-like bill and beautifully variegated plumage. The Java sparrow, and the Blue-breasted waxbill are attractive, and often find their way into cages.

Wayz-Goose, the name given to a festive gathering of people employed in printing and other works, so called from the fact that in earlier times a goose was the principal dish of the feast.

Weasel. A carnivore mammal found in Britain, smallest member of the group including the Stoat, Polecat, and Pine-marten, about 8 in. long. Its fur is reddish on the upper side of the animal, white on the under side; it may all turn white in winter with the exception of the tail.

Weather, the factors determining to-morrow's weather are so manifold, variable, and complex that the task of the meteorologist is no easy one. There are still people who cling to the idea that weather is determined by the phase of the moon, but their predictions have no scientific backing, and can be dismissed. Changes in temperature, humidity, and speed of air masses can best be measured by instruments designed for the purpose. By taking into account the peculiar character of any part of the country, whether coastal, high- or low-lying, industrial, sheltered, precise forecasts for that particular region can be made up to twenty-four hours ahead and sometimes longer. We need to know more about the heat exchange between oceans and the atmosphere before long-range forecasting is possible. The British Isles lie in the path of depressions moving north-eastward across the Atlantic. It is the frequency, intensity, and speed of these centres of low pressure, which give these islands such changeable weather. On the other hand, when an anticyclone builds up and embraces the British Isles, settled weather is fairly certain, the type of weather, whether dull or cloudless, warm or cold, depending mainly on the direction of the wind in the particular area concerned and the time of year. An American earth satellite, Vanguard II, was launched in Feb. 1959 to serve as the first " weather-eye " in space.

Weather Lore. Before instruments were invented to measure atmospheric conditions, man relied on his own observation of wind and sky, behaviour of birds and animals, and came to associate certain phenomena with types of weather. Many popular weather rhymes have survived the centuries, and as long as forecasting is confined to the next 24 hours there is perhaps something to be said for them, particularly those dealing with the winds. What is very unlikely is that next year's summer can be predicted from this year's winter, or that one month's weather is related to that of another. The study of past records reveals too many exceptions for such predictions to be of much use in forecasting.

Weaver Bird, the popular name for a large group of finch-like birds belonging to the family Ploceidae, found principally in Africa but also in Southern Asia, Australia, and Europe and remarkable for their habit of building nests formed of blades of grass dexterously interwoven and suspended from the boughs of trees.

Weaving has been practised since before any times of which we have record. The Egyptians credit the invention to Isis, the Grecians to Minerva. The main principle of the weaving loom is the same to-day as it was thousands of years ago; a warp extends lengthwise through the loom, the threads being held in separate regular order by being passed through a reed or " slay," while the weft is crossed through alternating threads of the warp by means of a shuttle which holds the weft. Thus the fabric is built up. Weaving was done by hand up to the early part of the 19th cent., when Cartwright's steam-power loom was introduced, and is now in universal use. The Jacquard loom for weaving figured designs dates from 1801.

Wedding Anniversaries are: first, Cotton; second, Paper; third, Leather; fourth, Fruit and Flower; fifth, Wooden; sixth, Sugar; seventh

Woollen; eighth, Salt; ninth, Copper; tenth, Tin; twelfth, Silk and Fine Linen; fifteenth, Crystal; twentieth, China; twenty-fifth, Silver; thirtieth, Pearl; thirty-fifth, Coral; fortieth, Ruby; fiftieth, Golden; sixtieth, Diamond; sixty-fifth, Blue Sapphire; seventieth, Platinum.

Wednesday, the 4th day of the week, derived its name from Woden or Odin, the Norse god of war.

Weights and Measures. *See* **Section N.**

Welding is a means of joining together two pieces of material, often metals, by heating the joint until the substances melt locally, run together, and then solidify. The heating can be by burning gas (*e.g.*, oxy-acetylene welding) or electric current (electric arc welding). Techniques exist for welding anything from hair-like wires to massive steel plates. *See* **Soldering.**

Werewolf, a man or woman, who according to mediaeval belief, could be turned by witchcraft or magic into a wolf, eat human flesh or drink human blood, and turn into himself again. This belief was widely held in Europe, and similar superstitions prevail among most primitive peoples, *e.g.*, the " leopard man " of certain African tribes. Lycanthropy (from Gr. = wolf-man) is a form of madness in which the patient imagines himself a beast.

Westminster Abbey stands on the site of an old church and Benedictine foundation of the 7th cent. It was rebuilt under Edward the Confessor, and again under Henry III., and important additions were made by Edward II., Edward III., Richard II., Richard III. and Henry VII., the latter erecting the beautiful eastern chapel in the perpendicular style which bears his name. The western towers and front were rebuilt by Wren in the 18th cent. It contains tombs of many sovereigns, of the Unknown Warrior, and many other illustrious men are commemorated by monuments.

Westminster Cathedral, seat of the Roman Catholic Archbishop of Westminster. It was designed by J. F. Bentley and built between 1895 and 1910. It is of red brick, in early Christian Byzantine style with a domed campanile, 283 ft. high, and a decorative interior.

Westminster Hall, adjoining the Houses of Parliament, was built as a Banqueting Hall by William Rufus, and many courtly festivals were held there in succeeding centuries. King John established the Law Courts there. It now forms a gigantic hallway, leading to the Houses of Parliament. Charles I., Sir Thomas More, and Warren Hastings were tried there.

Whale, a completely aquatic mammal; the fore-limbs are modified to form fin-like paddles and there is virtually no external trace of the hind-limbs. There are two major groups of whales—the *Toothed Whales,* including the Sperm-whale (Cachalot), Dolphins, Killer-whales, and Porpoises; and the *Whalebone Whales.* In the latter a series of whalebone plates grow down from the roof of the mouth, and, being frayed at their edges into a hairy fringe, together constitute a filtering mechanism. The animal takes in sea water containing minute organisms on which it feeds; the mouth is then closed and the tongue raised when the water is forced out through the filter, on which is left the food. As the tongue is lowered, the whalebone plates straighten up, flicking the food on to the tongue, which transfers it to the gut. Most whale oil is obtained from the thick layer of fat under the skin (blubber), but in the Sperm-whale there is a large reserve of oil in the head. The oil is used for making candles, margarine, and soap. Ambergris used in perfumery comes from the intestine of whales. The number of whales that may be killed in a season is limited by International Convention.

Whimbrel, a bird of the Curlew family, more common in Scotland than in England.

Whinchat, a small migratory bird, a breeding visitor to Britain (Apr. to Oct.); bright brown plumage, with prominent eye stripe.

Whirlwind, a sudden circular rush of opposing winds, which often causes much damage.

Whiskers in physics and materials science (*q.v.*) are tiny rods of crystal, thinner than human hair and perhaps half an inch long. Their importance lies in the fact that such crystals are free from the defects described on **F18.** They are

also free from surface cracks and steps. This means they are immensely strong because failures of strength in ordinary solids are due to imperfections and cracks of one kind or another. Large numbers of whiskers of strong solids like graphite, silicon, or silicon carbide embedded in a matrix of softer matter such as plastic or metal would make a very strong new material. Many laboratories are developing such substances.

Whisky, an ardent spirit distilled from malt or other grain, and containing a large percentage of alcohol. It has a greater consumption than any other spirit, and is of many kinds, Scotch and Irish whiskies being chiefly consumed in this country, and being of pot still or patent still production, or a blend of the two. Whisky is the most heavily taxed product: in 1661 a duty of 4*d.* a gallon was imposed, today (1970) the duty is £19 1*s.* 1*d.* on a proof gallon. American whiskies are mostly distilled from corn (maize), or rye. *See* **Alcohol.**

White Elephant, a term in common use to designate a gift that causes the recipient more trouble or cost than it is worth; derived from an old-time custom of the Kings of Siam who presented a white elephant to a courtier whom it was desired to ruin.

Whitehall Palace, built within sight of Westminster by Hubert de Burgh, Earl of Kent, round about 1240, was the residence of the Archbishops of York until Wolsey presented it to Henry VIII in 1530. Thence-forward to 1697, when it was burned down, it continued to be the favourite town residence of royalty, and to the Stuarts especially it was a great centre of court festivities. In those days, with its grounds, it extended from the Strand to the river. The only portion of Whitehall Palace now standing is the Banqueting Hall built by Inigo Jones, on a scaffold projected from the front of which Charles I was beheaded. A block of new government buildings has recently been built on part of the site of the old Palace.

White House, the official residence at Washington of the President of the United States.

Whitsuntide, the festival celebrating the descent of the Holy Ghost and occurring seven weeks after Easter.

Whydah Bird, the widow-bird of Equatorial Africa. The Paradise Whydah is remarkable for the long tail and handsome black-and-scarlet plumage of the male during mating season.

Widow Bird, certain species of African weaver birds with predominantly black plumage. In the breeding season the male birds are strikingly beautiful, with scarlet and buff markings and long tail feathers. They are social parasites and trick other birds into rearing their young.

Wigeon, a surface-feeding duck of northern Europe, known in Britain more as a winter visitor than a nesting bird. It feeds in flocks in the muddy estuaries and has a characteristic " whee-oo " call.

Willow, a water-side-loving tree of the genus *Salix,* to which the osiers belong. The best cricket-bat blades are made from a white willow, *S. alba* var. *caerulea,* a fine tree with bluish-green leaves, mostly found in Essex. Willow is also used for polo balls. Weeping willow, *S. babylonica,* is native to China and is the willow seen on Old China willow-pattern plates. It was introduced into England at the end of the 17th cent.

Wind, air set in motion by special atmospheric conditions, is of various degrees, from a slight rustling breeze to a hurricane. Winds are *constant,* as in trade winds or anti-trade winds; *periodic,* as in monsoons and other wind-visitations occurring according to influences of season; *cyclonic* and *anti-cyclonic,* when their motion is spiral; *whirlwinds, hurricanes,* and *tornados,* when high temperature and great density induce extreme agitation. Ordinarily, a wind is named from the point of the compass from which it blows, or it may be expressed in degrees from true north. The *sirocco,* the *mistral,* and the *simoom* are local forms of winds of great velocity. A *blizzard* is a biting blast of icy temperature. *See also* **Section N.**

Windmills were in use in the East in ancient times, but were not much seen in Europe before the 13th cent. Wind sawmills were invented by a Dutchman in the 17th cent., and one was erected near the Strand in London in 1633. Great improvements have been made in these mills, especially in the United States, where, by the application of the windshaft principle, much space is saved and the mills can be used for pumping, grinding, and other purposes.

Windows (Old Norse *vindauga* = wind-eye), an opening in a wall of a building to admit light and air, and to afford a view of what is outside. In northern Europe windows, as the derivation of the word implies, were first used for ventilation and glass was not used in private houses before the end of the 12th cent. In early Gothic (12th cent.) windows were still small and narrow, with rounded heads. In Early English (13th cent.) they became longer and the heads pointed. In the Decorated period (14th cent.) windows were mullioned (divided by slender bars into panes) and the pointed heads often traceried. In Tudor times when the Renaissance had found its way to England, windows were larger and the bay-window (projecting from the wall) and the oriel window (*q.v.*) were much in vogue; in the late 18th cent. curved bays (called bow-windows) became fashionable. Sash windows (invented by the English) with wooden frames and divided into equal rectangular panes were used in Queen Anne and Georgian houses. Their design was influenced by a passion for symmetry; they were very efficient ventilators. The French window reaches to the floor and has double casements opening as doors. A Dormer window is a vertical window set on the sloping side of a roof. One of the main features of modern architecture is the large area devoted to windows, a development made possible by improved heating systems. Windows are now mass-produced in stock sizes and patterns.

Windsor Castle, the famous British royal residence on the banks of the Thames, as it now stands, was mainly built by Henry III., though a royal residence had existed there from the time of the Conqueror. Additions were made by Henry VIII., Elizabeth, and Charles II. Windsor Park and Forest comprise over 13,000 acres.

Wine, the fermented juice of the freshly-gathered grape. There are innumerable varieties, each obtaining its distinctive character from the species of wine producing the grape, the locality of the vineyard, method of cultivation, etc. Wines are of three main kinds: *sparkling*, as in champagne, due to their having been bottled before fermentation is complete; *beverage*, when the must has been fermented out before bottling. Such wines include the famous red and white wines of Burgundy, Bordeaux and the Rhone valley and the white wines of the Rhine Moselle and Loire valleys. Wines are *fortified* by the addition of alcohol either after fermentation is complete (*e.g.*, Sherry) or during fermentation (*e.g.*, Port). The principal wine-producing countries are: France, Italy, Algeria, Spain, Portugal, Rumania, Argentine, Yugoslavia, U.S.S.R., Greece, Germany, Hungary.

Wirebird, a species of plover confined to St. Helena where it is protected.

Witan *or* **Witenagemot**, the name given to the king's council of "wise men" in Anglo-Saxon times, composed of the archbishops, bishops, abbots of the greater abbeys, ealdormen, and influential thanes.

Witchcraft. *See* J53.

Woad, a plant (*Isatis tinctoria*) that in olden days was largely used in England for the blue dye obtained from the leaves. It is a biennial plant belonging to the same family (*Cruciferae*) as the wallflower and is still cultivated in some parts.

Wolves, well-known carnivorous animals still found in many parts of Europe, but not existing in Britain since the middle of the 17th cent. They usually hunt in packs.

Women's Liberation Movement. *See* J53.

Woodcock, a wading bird, greatly valued for its flesh. It is a member of the snipe family, and breeds in Britain. The parent bird is able to carry its young between its thigh and body when flying to and from the feeding spots. It is one of the birds protected by the Game Laws.

Woodpecker, a familiar tree-climbing, insectivorous bird of conspicuous plumage, of which three species are found in Britain, the green

woodpecker or yaffle (because of its harsh cry), the great and lesser spotted woodpeckers. They build in the hollows of trees. Yaffle has a long sticky tongue for licking up ground insects, especially ants. The other two obtain insects by digging into tree trunks with strong, chisel-like bills, spearing the insects with a sharp tongue. The metallic drumming sound made by the birds in spring is thought to be caused by their beaks hammering away at some hard resounding substance.

Wood's Metal, an alloy with a very low melting point (65° C., which is under 150° F.) so that a spoon made of it will melt when used to stir a cup of tea. Contains bismuth 4 parts, lead 2 parts, tin 1 part, cadmium 1 part. Its use as a heat exchanger has now been largely superseded by silicone oils, which have a wider temperature range.

Woodworm. Four beetles are mainly responsible for woodworm damage: common furniture beetle (*Anobium punctatum*), powder post beetle (*Lyctus brunneus*), death watch beetle (*Xestobium rufovillosum*), and house longhorn beetle (*Hylotrupes bajulus*). Particular attention should be paid to wood in damp, dark, and out-of-the-way places, and the backs and underneaths of furniture. The most frequent cause of woodworm damage is the common furniture beetle (*q.v.*).

Wool is a fibre, made up of very long protein molecules. It has been largely grown and used in the manufacture of cloth in England since before the Roman invasion. It is grown on the backs of sheep, and is of various kinds, according to the breed of sheep from which it is derived. Wool differs from hair in that it has a wavy, serrated fibre, its curl being a notable characteristic, whereas hair has a smooth surface comparatively free from serratures. Long wools are mostly used for the manufacture of worsted goods, and short wools for woollen cloths, though the improvements in machinery in recent years have enabled manufacturers to utilise short wools to a great extent for dress fabrics as well as for woollens. The finest wools are obtained from the fleece of the Spanish merino sheep. Australia, New Zealand, and the Argentine are the greatest wool-producing countries.

Woolsack, the name given to the seat occupied by the Lord Chancellor in the House of Lords. It is a large square bag of wool, without back or arms, covered with red cloth. At the time when it was first used, in the reign of Edward III., wool was the great staple commodity of the country and, it is said, chosen for the seat of judges as a constant reminder of the main source of the national wealth. The Lord Chancellor is said to be "appointed to the woolsack."

World Council of Churches. *See* J53.

World Population. According to United Nations sources world population is expected to rise from an estimated 3,632 million in 1970 to an estimated 4,457 million in 1980 (3,247 million in the underdeveloped regions and 1,210 million in advanced countries). Thus nearly three-quarters live in the poor countries, half in Asia. Different countries are at different stages in a demographic transition from the stability provided by a combination of high birth rate and high death rate to that provided by a combination of low birth rate and low death rate. Their recent population history and current trend of growth, the age-structure of their population, and consequently their population potential for the near future are all widely different. By the beginning of the Christian era world population is believed to have been 200–300 million, rising to about 500 million by 1650, and it is estimated that about one in 25 of all human beings who have ever lived are alive today.

Wreck, the name given to trove found under water, usually from a maritime wreck. Finds must be brought to the notice of the Official Receiver of Wrecks, an officer of H.M. Customs and Excise.

Wren, a family of small passerine birds possessing upturned tails and most abundant in South America. The British species is an interesting singing bird with a surprisingly loud note for its size.

X

Xenon a rare gaseous element, symbol Xe, occurring in minute quantities in the atmosphere, discovered by Sir William Ramsay and M. W. Travers in 1898. *See* Rare Gases.

X-Rays were discovered in 1895 by Professor Röntgen, of Wurzburg, while experimenting with a Crookes vacuum tube, when the fact was accidentally revealed that a photographic plate, contained in a dark box and exposed to its rays, was affected. To the X-rays the box was transparent. X-ray photographs are now commonly taken to obtain information about objects enclosed within solid bodies; they enable bullets and any solid bodies of metal, as well as bones, etc., in the body to be perfectly located and investigated. The discovery has proved of great advantage in surgical operations. X-rays are used to determine the structure of matter; the atoms in a substance may be located and their relative positions determined by photographing reflections of the X-rays by the specimen. *See* F11(1).

Xylem, the woody tissue of higher plants whose function is to conduct water and mineral salts upwards, and to provide mechanical support.

Y

Yacht, a light vessel now much used for pleasure trips and racing. The first yachting club was the Cork Harbour Club, started about 1720; and in 1812 the Royal Yacht Squadron was founded at Cowes. The Royal Thames Yacht Club dates from 1823. The most famous international yachting trophy is *The America's Cup* (*q.v.*). *See also* U32.

Yak, a curious, long-haired ox, found in Tibet, used as a beast of burden, and also kept for milk and meat.

Yard, a standard measure of 36 in, the word being derived from the Saxon *gyrd*, or rod. The yard and pound are now defined by reference to the metre and the kilogramme: yard = 0·9144 of a metre; pound = 0·45359237 of a kilogramme. By international agreement the metre is defined by reference to the wavelength of Krypton-86 light.

Yellowhammer, a common British bird of the bunting family, of lemon-yellow and brown plumage. Nests on or near the ground.

Yeomen of the Guard are a body of Foot Guards established in the reign of Henry VII. for the protection of the Royal Person. Yeomen are now about 100 in number, and their duties consist in being present on ceremonial State occasions, the yearly distribution of Maundy Money, and the searching of the vaults of the Houses of Parliament on Guy Fawkes' day. "Beefeater" is the nickname of both Yeomen of the Guard and Yeomen Warders of the Tower, and they both wear the style of dress of the Tudor period, but with one distinction, the Yeomen of the Guard wear a cross belt, the Warders do not.

Yeti, opinions differ as to whether this is a mythical inhabitant of the Himalayas, a primitive primate or bear. Evidence to date is inconclusive.

Yoga. *See* J53.

York Minster, one of the oldest and finest of English cathedrals, is 524 ft. long, its nave is 240 ft. broad, and the central tower is 216 ft. high. The present edifice, in parts, dates back to the 12th cent., but a church stood on the site in the 7th cent. In 1829 it was set on fire by a lunatic named Jonathan Martin, and the destruction that then took place cost £60,000 to restore.

Ytterbium, a chemical element discovered by Urbain in 1907; one of the group of rare earth metals.

Yttrium, a chemical element discovered by Mosander in 1842. It is found in a few rare minerals such as gadolinite, xenotine, fergusonite, and euxenite. One of the group of rare-earth metals.

Z

Zamboni Pile, a dry galvanic battery, which can provide small amounts of high-voltage current over a very long time. At Oxford a couple of Zamboni piles have kept a bell ringing for over a hundred years. These piles in the second world war were perfected and produced in quantity, being the most convenient source of current for infra-red signalling devices.

Zebra, an African quadruped of whitish-grey colour, with regular black stripings, perhaps the most beautiful member of the Equine family. Rather larger than an ass and smaller than the horse, it has a tufted tail, is of light build, wild, and fleet of foot. The Zebra is threatened with extinction—already the fate of the Quagga species—because of its slaughter by man for its beautiful skin.

Zen Buddhism. *See* J54.

Zenith, the highest point in the heavens above an observer's head, the opposite pole to the Nadir.

Zero, the cypher signifying nothing. The West is indebted to the Arabs for it, who probably got it from the Hindus and passed it to European mathematicians towards the end of the Middle Ages. The zero has also been found in Babylonian cuneiform. The Greeks had no such symbol, which hindered the development of their mathematics. The use of zero led to the invention of decimal fractions and to the later developments in astronomy, physics and chemistry. For absolute zero on the temperature scale *see* L2.

Zinc, a familiar metallic element, symbol Zn, known to the ancients, and used by them in the making of brass. It occurs as the sulphide, carbonate, etc. The ores of zinc are crushed, roasted, and reduced with coal. In combination with copper it constitutes the familiar alloy called brass, and zinc itself is much used for roofing and other protective purposes. Zinc ores are mined in Canada, the U.S.A., Mexico, Poland, Australia, Russia, Italy, Spain, and many other parts of the world. Zinc smelting is carried on in most industrial countries, including Great Britain.

Zionism. *See* J54.

Zirconium, metallic element, symbol Zr, was discovered by Klaproth in the sand of the rivers of Ceylon in 1789. The crystalline metal is white, soft, and ductile; in its amorphous condition it is a blue-black powder. Zirconium is used in atomic reactors as containers for fuel elements, since it does not absorb neutrons.

Zodiac, an imaginary zone or belt of the sky enclosing the circuit over which the principal planets travel. It is divided into 12 equal spaces of 30 degrees each, comprising respectively the 12 signs of the zodiac—Aries, Taurus, Gemini, Cancer, Leo, Virgo, Libra, Scorpio, Sagittarius, Capricornus, Aquarius and Pisces. The idea of the zodiac originated with the Babylonians about 2000 B.C. and passed by way of the Greeks to the Western world.

Zodiacal Light, a faint cone of light occasionally seen stretching along the zodiac from the western horizon after evening twilight or the eastern horizon before morning twilight. It is believed to be due to the scattering of the sun's light by dust particles in orbit round the sun and extending beyond the earth. Recent observations at the high altitude station at Chacaltaya in the Andes suggest that the dust is travelling round the sun in regular planetary orbits.

Zonda, a warm moist wind in Argentina of great velocity blowing from the north or northwest, and, like the Sirocco in Southern Europe, causes much discomfort. It happens when a depression is moving across the pampas, bringing with it a mass of air from the humid tropics. It is followed by a refreshing wind from the southeast.

Zoological Gardens of London were opened in 1828, and belong to the Zoological Society of London. They contain one of the largest and most varied collections of living animals in the world. The Society maintains an open-air zoo at Whipsnade, on the edge of Dunstable Downs; this was opened in 1931.

Zoology, the science of animal biology, treating of the structure, classification, and distribution of the various members of the animal kingdom.

Zoroastrianism. *See* J54.

NOBEL PRIZE WINNERS (1901–1970)

YEAR.	PHYSICS.	CHEMISTRY.	PHYSIOLOGY AND MEDICINE.	LITERATURE.	PEACE.
1901	W. C. Röntgen (G).	J. H. van't Hoff (D).	E. v. Behring (G).	R. F. A. Sully Prudhomme (F).	H. Dunant (Sw), F. Passy (F).
1902	H. A. Lorentz (D), P. Zeeman (D).	E. Fischer (G).	R. Ross (B).	T. Mommsen (G).	E. Ducommun (Sw), A. Gobat (Sw).
1903	H. Becquerel (F), P. Curie (F), Marie Curie (F).	S. Arrhenius (S).	N. R. Finsen (Da).	B. Björnson (N).	Sir W. R. Cremer (B).
1904	Lord J. W. S. Rayleigh (B).	W. Ramsay (B).	L. P. Pavlov (B).	F. Mistral (F), J. Echegaray (Sp).	Institut de Droit International.
1905	P. Lenard (G).	A. v. Bayer (G).	R. Koch (G).	H. Sienkiewicz (P).	Bertha von Suttner (Au).
1906	J. J. Thomson (B).	H. Moissan (F).	C. Golgi (I), S. R. y Cajal (Sp).	G. Carducci (I).	T. Roosevelt (A).
1907	A. A. Michelson (A).	E. Buchner (G).	C. L. A. Laveran (F).	Rudyard Kipling (B).	E. T. Moneta (I), L. Renault (F).
1908	G. Lippmann (F).	E. Rutherford (B).	P. Ehrlich (G), E. Metchnikoff (R).	R. Eucken (G).	K. P. Arnoldson (S), F. Bajer (Da).
1909	F. Braun (G), G. Marconi (I).	W. Ostwald (G).	T. Kocher (Sw).	S. Lagerlöf (S).	A. M. F. Beernaert (Be), Baron d'Estournelles de Constant de Rebeque (F).
1910	J. D. van der Waals (D).	O. Wallach (G).	A. Kossel (G).	P. Heyse (G).	The Bureau International Permanent de la Paix, Berne.
1911	W. Wien (G).	Marie Curie (F).	A. Gullstrand (S).	M. Maeterlinck (Be).	T. M. C. Asser (D), A. H. Fried (Au).
1912	G. Dalén (S).	V. Grignard (F), P. Sabatier (F).	A. Carrel (A).	G. Hauptmann (G).	E. Root (A).
1913	H. Kamerlingh Onnes (D).	A. Werner (Sw).	C. Richet (F).	R. Tagore (In).	H. la Fontaine (Be).
1914	M. v. Laue (G).	T. W. Richards (A).	B. Bárány (Au).	—	—
1915	W. H. Bragg (B), W. L. Bragg (B).	R. Willstaetter (G).	—	B. Roland (F).	—
1916	—	—	—	V. von Heidenstam (S).	—
1917	C. G. Barkla (B).	—	—	K. Gjellerup (Da), H. Pontoppidan (Da).	Comité International de la Croix-Rouge, Geneva.
1918	M. Planck (G).	F. Haber (G).	—	—	—
1919	J. Stark (G).	—	—	C. Spitteler (Sw).	W. Wilson (A).
1920	C. E. Guillaume (F).	W. Nernst (G).	J. Bordet (Be).	K. Hamsun (N).	L. Bourgeois (F).
1921	A. Einstein (G).	F. Soddy (B).	A. Krogh (Da).	A. France (F).	K. H. Branting (S), C. L. Lange (N).
1922	N. Bohr (Da).	F. W. Aston (B).	A. Hill (B), O. Meyerhof (G).	J. Benavente y Martinez (Sp).	F. Nansen (N).
1923	R. A. Millikan (A).	F. Pregl (Au).	F. G. Banting (C), J. R. Macleod (C).	W. B. Yeats (Ir).	—
1924	M. Siegbahn (S).	—	W. E. Einthoven (D).	W. Reymont (P).	—
1925	J. Franck (G), G. Hertz (G).	R. Zsigmondy (G).	—	G. B. Shaw (B).	Sir A. Chamberlain (B), C. G. Dawes (A).
1926	J. Perrin (F).	T. Svedberg (S).	J. Fibiger (Da).	G. Deledda (I).	A. Briand (F), G. Stresemann (G).
1927	A. H. Compton (A), C. T. R. Wilson (B).	H. Wieland (G).	J. Wagner-Jauregg (Au).	H. Bergson (F).	F. Buisson (F), L. Quidde (G).

NOBEL PRIZE WINNERS (1901–1970), *continued*

YEAR.	PHYSICS.	CHEMISTRY.	PHYSIOLOGY AND MEDICINE.	LITERATURE.	PEACE.
1928	O. W. Richardson (B).	A. Windaus (G).	C. Nicolle (F).	S. Undset (N).	
1929	L. de Broglie (F).	H. v. Euler-Chelpin (S), A. Harden (B).	C. Eijkman (D), F. G. Hopkins (B).	T. Mann (G).	F. B. Kellogg (A).
1930	C. V. Raman (In).	H. Fischer (G).	K. Landsteiner (Au).	S. Lewis (A).	L. O. J. Söderblom (S).
1931		F. Bergius (G), K. Bosch (G).	O. Warburg (G).	E. A. Karlfeldt (S).	Jane Addams (A), N. M. Butler (A).
1932	W. Heisenberg (G).	I. Langmuir (A).	C. S. Sherrington (B), E. D. Adrian (B).	J. Galsworthy (B).	—
1933	P. A. M. Dirac (B), E. Schroedinger (Au).	—	T. H. Morgan (A).	Bunin (R).	Sir Norman Angell (B).
1934	—	H. C. Urey (A).	G. Minot (A), W. Murphy (A), G. Whipple (A).	L. Pirandello (I).	Arthur Henderson (B).
1935	J. Chadwick (B).	F. Joliot (F), I. Joliot-Curie (F).	H. Spemann (G).	—	C. von Ossietzky (G).
1936	V. F. Hess (Au), C. D. Anderson (A).	P. Debye (D).	Sir H. H. Dale (B), O. Loewi (G).	E. O'Neill (A).	C. de S. Lamas (Ar).
1937	C. J. Davisson (A), G. P. Thomson (B).	W. N. Haworth (B), P. Karrer (Sw).	A. v. Szent-Györgyi (H).	R. Martin du Gard (F).	Viscount Cecil of Chelwood (B).
1938	E. Fermi (I).	R. Kuhn (G).	C. Heymans (Be).	Pearl S. Buck (A).	Office International Nansen pour les Réfugiés.
1939	E. O. Lawrence (A).	A. F. Butenandt (G), L. Ruzicka (Sw).	G. Domagk (G).	F. E. Sillanpää (Fi).	—
1940–42	—	—	—	—	—
1943	O. Stern (A).	G. Hevesy (H).	H. Dam (Da), E. A. Doisy (A).	—	—
1944	I. I. Rabi (A).	O. Hahn (G).	E. J. Erlanger (A), H. S. Gasser (A).	J. V. Jensen (Da).	Comité International de la Croix-Rouge, Geneva.
1945	W. Pauli (Au).	A. Virtanen (Fi).	Sir A. Fleming (B), Sir H. Florey (B), E. B. Chain (B).	G. Mistral (Ch).	Cordell Hull (A).
1946	P. W. Bridgman (A).	J. B. Sumner (A), J. H. Northrop (A), W. M. Stanley (A).	H. J. Muller (A).	H. Hesse (Sw).	Emily G. Balch (A), J. R. Mott (A).
1947	Sir Edward Appleton (B).	Sir Robert Robinson (B).	B. A. Houssay (Ar), C. F. Cori (A), G. T. Cori (A).	André Gide (F).	American and British Quaker Organisations.
1948	P. M. S. Blackett (B).	A. Tiselius (S).	P. Müller (Sw).	T. S. Eliot (B).	—
1949	H. Yukawa (J).	W. F. Giauque (A).	W. R. Hess (Sw), A. E. Moniz (Po).	W. Faulkner (A).	Lord Boyd-Orr (B).
1950	Cecil F. Powell (B).	Otto Diels (G), K. Alder (G).	E. C. Kendall (A), P. S. Hench (A), R. Reichstein (Sw).	Lord Russell (B).	Ralph Bunche (A).
1951	Sir J. Cockcroft (B), E. T. S. Walton (Ir).	E. M. MacMillan (A), G. T. Seaborg (A).	M. Theiler (A).	P. Lagerkvist (S).	Léon Jouhaux (F).
1952	E. Purcell (A), F. Bloch (A).	A. J. P. Martin (B), R. L. M. Synge (B).	S. Waksman (A).	F. Mauriac (F).	A. Schweitzer (F).

NOBEL PRIZE WINNERS (1901–1970), continued

Year	Physics	Chemistry	Physiology and Medicine	Literature	Peace
1953	F. Zernike (D).	H. Staudinger (G).	H. A. Krebs (B), F. A. Lipmann (A).	Sir W. S. Churchill (B).	Gen. G. Marshall (A).
1954	M. Born (B), W. Bothe (G).	L. Pauling (A).	J. F. Enders (A), F. C. Robbins (A), T. H. Weller (A).	E. Hemingway (A).	U.N. High Commission for Refugees.
1955	W. E. Lamb (A), P. Kusch (A).	Vicent du Vigneaud (A).	Hugo Theorell (S).	Halldor Laxness (Ic).	—
1956	W. Shockley (A), J. Bardeen (A), W. H. Brattain (A).	Sir Cyril Hinshelwood (B), N. Semenov (R).	A. F. Cournaud (A), D. W. Richards (A), W. Forssmann (G).	J. Ramón Jiménez (Sp).	—
1957	T. Dao-lee (Chi), C. Ning-yang (Chi).	Lord Todd (B).	D. Bovet (I).	A. Camus (F).	L. B. Pearson (C).
1958	P. A. Čerenkov (R), I. M. Frank (R), I. Tamm (R).	F. Sanger (B).	G. W. Beadle (A), E. Tatum (A), J. Lederberg (A).	B. Pasternak (R).	Father George Pire (Be).
1959	E. Segré (A), O. Chamberlain (A).	J. Heyrovsky (Cz).	S. Ochoa (A), A. Kornberg (A).	S. Quasimodo (I).	P. J. Noel-Baker (B).
1960	D. A. Glaser (A).	W. F. Libby (A).	P. B. Medawar (B), Sir M. Burnet (Aus).	A. St. Léger (F).	A. Luthuli (S.A.)
1961	R. Hofstadter (A), R. Mossbauer (G).	M. Calvin (A).	G. von Bekesy (H).	I. Andric (Y).	D. Hammarskjöld (S).
1962	L. Davidovich Landau (R).	M. F. Perutz (B), J. C. Kendrew (B).	F. H. C. Crick (B), M. H. F. Wilkins (B), J. D. Watson (A).	J. Steinbeck (A).	L. Pauling (A).
1963	Maria Goeppert-Mayer (A), J. H. D. Jensen (G), E. P. Wigner (A).	K. Ziegler (G), G. Natta (I).	A. L. Hodgkin (B), A. F. Huxley (B), Sir J. Eccles (B).	G. Seferis (Gr).	International Red Cross Committee and the International League of Red Cross Societies.
1964	C. H. Townes (A), N. G. Basov (R), A. M. Prokhorov (R).	Dorothy Hodgkin (B).	K. E. Bloch (A), F. Lynen (G).	Jean-Paul Sartre (F).	Martin Luther King (A).
1965	S. Tomonaga (J), J. Schwinger (A), P. Feynman (A).	A. B. Woodward (A).	F. Jacob (F), A. Lwoff (F), J. Monod (F).	M. Sholokhov (R).	UNICEF
1966	A. Kastler (F).	R. S. Mulliken (A).	F. P. Rous (A), C. A. Huggins (A).	S. Y. Agnon (Is), Nelly Sachs (Sw).	No award
1967	H. A. Bethe (A).	R. G. W. Norrish (B), G. Porter (B), M. Eigen (G).	R. Granit (S), H. K. Hartline (A), G. Wald (A).	M. A. Asturias (Gu).	No award
1968	L. W. Alvarez (A).	L. Onsager (A).	M. Nirenberg (A), H. G. Khorana (A), R. Holley (A).	Y. Kawabata (J).	R. Cassn (F).
1969	M. Gell-Mann (A).	D. H. R. Barton (B), O. Hassel (N).	M. Dellbrück (A), A. D. Hershey (A), S. E. Luria (A).	S. Beckett (Ir).	The International Labour Organisation
1970	L. E. Neel (F), H. Alfvén (Sw).	L. F. Leloir (Ar).	Sir Bernard Katz (B), U. von Euler (Sw), J. Axelrod (A).	A. Solzhenitsyn (R).	N. E. Borlaug (A).

A = American
Ar = Argentine
Au = Austrian
Aus = Australian
B = British
Be = Belgian
C = Canadian
Ch = Chilean
Chi = Chinese
Cz = Czech
D = Dutch
Da = Danish
F = French
Fi = Finnish
G = German
Gr = Greek
Gu = Guatemalan
H = Hungarian
I = Italian
Ic = Icelandic
In = Indian
Ir = Irish
Is = Israeli
J = Japanese
N = Norwegian
P = Polish
Po = Portuguese
R = Russian
S = Swedish
S.A. = South African
Sp = Spanish
Sw = Swiss
Y = Yugoslav

Note: The first Nobel Prize in the Economic Sciences was awarded in 1969 jointly to J. Tinbergen (D), and R. Frisch (N). The 1970 award was made to P. A. Samuelson (A).

LITERARY COMPANION

This section discusses the modern novel and suggests ways of approaching the poetry of the current century. It contains a guide to versification and to our figures of speech.

TABLE OF CONTENTS

Chinua Achebe   Mary McCarthy
James Baldwin   Norman Mailer
Samuel Beckett   Bernard Malamud
Saul Bellow   Iris Murdoch
Elizabeth Bowen   Vladimir Nabokov
Christine Brooke-Rose   V. S. Naipaul
Alan Burns   Flannery O'Connor
Ivy Compton-Burnett   George Orwell
Lawrence Durrell   Anthony Powell
Ralph Ellison   Alan Sillitoe
William Faulkner   C. P. Snow
William Golding   Wole Soyinka
Nadine Gordimer   Muriel Spark
Graham Greene   William Styron
L. P. Hartley   William Trevor
Ernest Hemingway   John Updike
Dan Jacobsen   Evelyn Waugh
B. S. Johnson   Patrick White
Doris Lessing   Angus Wilson
Malcolm Lowry

I. THE CONTEMPORARY NOVEL

This section discusses novels written in English and published since 1945. It consists of two parts: I. Introduction; II. Directory of Novelists.

We are helped to appreciate the modern novel if we understand how it evolved from that of the nineteenth century. The Introduction that follows therefore summarises some of the important characteristics of English, American, and French novels of the nineteenth and early twentieth centuries and describes some of the literary and intellectual ideas that seem to have affected contemporary fiction.

It is important to remember that every worthwhile novel is an individual work of art that creates its own rules and however strange a writer's techniques or subject-matter may seem, we should try to suspend judgement until we have read his novel for a second or third time. Apart from the obvious difference that plays are written to be performed and novels to be read, the criteria of judgement suggested on I7 are as applicable to modern fiction as they are to contemporary drama.

INTRODUCTION.

The Mid-Nineteenth Century.

(a) English and American Novels.

At this time English novelists were members of a comparatively secure and stable society which possessed generally accepted social and moral standards, and the theme of almost all their writing is the interaction of the individual and the community. Novelists such as George Eliot, Dickens, Thackeray, and Trollope depict characters who progress towards self-knowledge as they learn to discriminate between the genuine and the false, the good and the evil in the people and institutions with which they are brought into contact. Since these writers were as much concerned with the presentation of society as of individuals, most of their work contains naturalistic descriptions of the life and manners of their day and, although the main characters of the Victorian novel are the focal points of its action, as Douglas Hewitt has remarked, they are not central to it in the way that the hero of a tragedy is central, the action is not "orientated towards them."

Most English novels of this period are comparatively loose and episodic in structure. Narrative is chronological and most writers place themselves between the reader and the story, standing apart from the characters, observing, commenting on and judging their actions, and, quite often, addressing the reader directly.

A notable exception to this general pattern is *Wuthering Heights*. In both its techniques and its view of life Emily Brontë's novel has more in common with mid-nineteenth-century American fiction than with the work of her compatriots and is unique among the English novels of its day in its disregard of society and of social and moral conventions.

American novelists, such as Twain, Hawthorne, and Melville, were interested in the presentation of individuals rather than of society. This was natural in a country inhabited by pioneers and exiles and their descendants, who had no common culture. Like the heroes of tragedies, the main characters of mid-nineteenth-century American novels are central to their action, isolated pioneers and exiles who create their own worlds.

American novelists used chronological narrative, but they generally wrote in the first person and their techniques were in other ways different from those of most of their English contemporaries and characterised by the use of allegory and symbolism.

In both countries novelists wrote for a middle-class public and, like their readers, they saw fiction as a mode of entertainment and, or, instruction. However, in France other ideas were being born which were to affect both the form and content of twentieth-century English and American fiction and lead many writers to think of novels as primarily works of art.

(b) French Novels.

Gautier and Æstheticism.

As early as 1825 Gautier had said that a writer must concern himself only with perfecting the style and form of his work and that this was impossible if he considered "the needs of society," "civilization," or "progress." Later, he wrote, "A beautiful form is a beautiful idea," implying that a novelist could treat any subject, no matter how sordid or painful, so long as he embodied it in a beautiful work of art.

Flaubert and Realism.

Flaubert, a leading member of the Realist school, felt that novelists must strive to be impersonal, adapting their style to their subject-matter, for only thus could they write "realistically." He believed that it helped novelists to be objective if they based their work on scientific documentation and said, "It is necessary to discuss the human soul with the [same] impersonality that one uses in [the study of] physical sciences." To the public, who were shocked by Flaubert's unconventional subject-matter, "realistic" became a term signifying moral disapproval.

"Realistic" is now used of (i) novels of working-class life, such as Sillitoe's *Saturday Night and Sunday Morning*; (ii) any frank treatment of the physical aspects of life, or of painful or sordid subjects, as in Mailer's *The Naked and the Dead*. Our use of the term has been influenced by Marxist theory and by the writing of the Naturalists.

Zola and Naturalism.

Zola and his followers called themselves Naturalists because, although they agreed with Flaubert that novelists should aim at objectivity, they wanted to produce "slices of life" rather than "works of art." Zola was stimulated by new scientific ideas and particularly interested in the effects of heredity and environment upon character. He inclined to the theory that character is largely determined by environment and wrote of the former in terms of the latter. Fascinated by the sordid side of nineteenth-century life, he tended to concentrate on it to the exclusion of all else and stimulated interest in the portrayal of moral degradation, brutality, and squalor. In England the National Vigilance Society waged a vigorous, and unsuccessful, campaign against the publication of translations of such "corrupt literature"!

1880–1910.

This period introduced some of the most popular kinds of modern novel: inspired by the work of the Frenchman Verne, H. G. Wells began to write Science Fiction; Conrad's *Secret Agent* introduced the Spy Thriller; and Conan-Doyle developed the Detective Story, invented in 1868 by Wilkie Collins.

The work of the French Naturalists was influential throughout this period, but, although it helped to widen the scope of the novel it found few close adherents among English or American writers who were, and are, more interested in those idiosyncratic aspects of personality disregarded by the Naturalists. The influence of Gautier and, particularly, Flaubert was more important and was first apparent in the work of James and Conrad, both of whom saw themselves as artists, not teachers or entertainers. They have been called the first Modern English Novelists.

(a) Henry James (1843–1916).

James admired the work of Gautier and was much impressed by Flaubert's theory of fiction. Like Flaubert, he strove towards an objective, detailed presentation of character and constantly sought to depict the nuances of feeling more delicately and precisely and to give his novels greater aesthetic unity. Many twentieth-century writers call James " The Master," for the scrupulous care with which he revised and polished the style of his novels and short-stories established an ideal of literary craftsmanship. The artistry and poetic sensitivity of his writing have had a marked effect upon the work of writers such as Elizabeth Bowen and Hartley. James began the process of combining the social novel of the European tradition with the more poetic American novel, a process to be carried much farther by Conrad in *Nostromo*.

(b) Joseph Conrad (1857–1926).

Conrad spent his youth in France and was well read in French literature. The sense of insecurity which permeates his writing is one of the first signs in English fiction of the break-up of the social and moral stability of the nineteenth century. This change appeared earlier on the Continent than in England and it is perhaps significant that Conrad was of Polish birth and always spoke French better than English, but his sense of insecurity was doubtless intensified by the hazards of his early naval career in the days of sailing-ships.

Like the novels of present-day writers such as Beckett, Lowry, and White, Conrad's books are essentially poetic and can be read on a number of different levels. They are as realistic as nineteenth-century French novels, but their every detail bears a significant relation to the plight of their central characters, and in his masterpiece, *Nostromo*, Conrad showed that a novel of great poetic intensity could yet encompass the life of a whole society.

James had been unable to banish the intrusive presence of the author from his novels; Conrad managed to, at times by using a narrator whom is deeply involved in the action, at others by reviving an eighteenth-century technique of telling the story from shifting points of view. At the same time he abandoned chronological narrative for a shifting time sequence, which reinforces his themes by intensifying a feeling of insecurity. Narrative of this kind has been used with similar effect by a number of modern novelists, including Beckett, Bellow, and Naipaul, and, although the use of the shifting time sequence, which marks one of the most obvious differences between nineteenth- and twentieth-century fiction, has been influenced by the writing of Proust and Joyce and by new ideas in theoretical physics and psychology, Conrad was the first novelist to use this kind of narrative.

The Early Twentieth Century.

" On or about December 1910 human nature changed," said Virginia Woolf. She probably chose that date because it marked the opening of the first London exhibition of the paintings of the post-impressionists. The work of these artists expressed a new vision of reality which was characteristic of the intellectual and cultural revolution sweeping Western society in the early decades of the century. The stimulus of this new Renaissance was reflected not only in painting, but in the music of Stravinsky, the dance of the Diaghilev Ballet, the poetry of Pound and Eliot and the novels of Proust, Joyce, and Virginia Woolf herself. The sense of exhilaration felt at this time is vividly suggested in Leonard Woolf's autobiographical work *Beginning Again*.

The stability and formality of nineteenth-century life, which had already been undermined by the ideas of Darwin and Huxley, the growing literacy of the working-classes, and the accelerating technological revolution, was now shattered by the combined impact of psychological theories, the ideas of social anthropologists such as Sir James Frazer and the work of physicists like Planck, Einstein, and Rutherford (*see* F10–13). As a result, novelists could no longer assume that readers' attitudes and values would resemble their own and were obliged to reconsider the nature of the relationship between art and life. The exploration of this relationship becomes one of the major themes of twentieth-century fiction, and after the First World War it is accompanied by an increasing sense of the isolation and insecurity of the individual's life and the inadequacy of words as vehicles for communicating experience.

For most writers the nineteenth-century European novel now seemed inadequate to express the complex and fluid nature of consciousness revealed by psychologists, and narrative consisting of a simple chronological progression of events was felt to give a misleading impression of our experience of time. Novelists were therefore compelled to search for new techniques, and were encouraged to do so by the example of experiments already taking place in art and music and by the example of the French Symbolist poets.

(a) The Influence of Psychological Theories.

The interest in the nature of perception revealed in the work of impressionist and post-impressionist painters had been growing since the turn of the century and was stimulated by the writings of the American William James and the Frenchman Henri Bergson.

In 1890, James, the brother of novelist Henry James, had published *Principles of Psychology*, in which he compared consciousness with a " river or a stream," implying that it carries within it submerged and floating memories and receives a fluid series of impressions of the exterior world. The term " stream of consciousness," derived from James's theory, was later applied to a new literary technique evolved by Joyce.

In *Matter and Memory* (1894), Bergson had suggested that perception is controlled by memory and said that our view of the world changes at every moment, " as though by a turn of a kaleidoscope," suggesting that perception involves an involuntary, creative readjustment of elements of past experience. This idea was to have a profound effect upon the work of Proust, to whom Bergson was related by marriage.

The writings of Freud, which began to be published in English in 1913, drew further attention to details of human experience, stimulating the growing interest in the subconscious mind, in dreams and the symbolic transformation of experience and combining with the influence of the Symbolist writers and the music of Wagner to give new impetus to the use of symbolism in fiction.

The influence of Freudian theory also extended the novel's potential subject-matter in two most important ways.

By emphasising the frail barrier between rational and irrational behaviour Freud made possible an imaginative discussion of neurosis and insanity, which had been regarded as shameful in the nineteenth century. The results of this more sympathetic attitude can be seen in the novels of writers such as Faulkner, Bellow, and White, while novels like Doris Lessing's *The Four-Gated City* (1969) (*q.v.*) and Jennifer Dawson's *The Ha-Ha* (1961), an imaginative study of a schizophrenic, are inconceivable as the work of any pre-Freudian writer.

Perhaps the most influential of all Freud's theories was his suggestion that our attitudes and behaviour are determined primarily by sexual needs and experience. Nineteenth-century novelists had been extremely reserved in their treatment of sexual life and although eighteenth-century writers had been uninhibited they had regarded erotic experience either as merely incidental to their characters' lives, or as a subject for ribald comedy and satire. Freudian theories have encouraged modern novelists to treat sexual experience more freely than it was in the nineteenth century and more imaginatively and seriously than it had been by earlier writers. Indeed it is now unusual for a novelist to treat sex humorously!

Freud's ideas on infantile sexuality also aroused enormous interest in childhood experience and relationships between parents and children, particularly in the ways that these might later affect the adult. Novelists whose work reflects this interest include Ivy Compton-Burnett, Hartley, Styron, and Wilson.

It is interesting to note that, despite the influence of Freud and later psychologists, and writers such as Kinsey, it is only within the last decade that English public opinion has allowed novelists to treat erotic love and sexual deviation as frankly as eighteenth-century writers could. An important date in the restriction of censorship came in 1960, when Penguin Books won their case for the publication of an unexpurgated edition of Lawrence's *Lady Chatterly's Lover*.

b) The Influence of the Symbolists. *See also* M22–3.

The work and ideas of the writers associated with this school, which arose in France in the last decades of the nineteenth century, and included the poets Rimbaud and Mallarmé, have had a far-reaching effect upon modern fiction.

The Symbolists' technical experiments in using verbal association, deliberate ambiguities of phrase and syntax, multiple analogies and esoteric allusion, in poetry, and interior monologue in fiction, suggested means by which modern novelists might attempt to express the subtleties of individual consciousness and to create new forms of novel. The Symbolists' feeling that artists are gifted with a mystical apprehension of Reality, and their consequent belief that, in order to express this apprehension, art should possess the evocative, lyrical qualities of music, not only helped novelists like Proust and Joyce to evolve new forms for the novel, but has had a less happy influence on some other writers, encouraging them to indulge in vague metaphysical musings. Two gifted novelists whose work seems to have suffered in this way are the Austrian Hermann Broch and a writer from Guyana, Wilson Harris, both of whose novels are at times highly evocative, but too often seem to degenerate into meaningless verbiage. (However, the eminent critic George Steiner suggests in *Language and Silence* that Broch's *Death of Virgil* (1945) is one of the greatest novels of the century, comparable only with Joyce's *Ulysses*. Its theme is similar to that of T. S. Eliot's *Four Quartets*, and, like Eliot's poem, it is constructed in the form of four "movements," each based on the "key" of one of the elements, earth, air, fire, and water.)

The Symbolists' dream of producing a "universal poem," an epic myth on the scale of Goethe's *Faust*, has been reflected in the work of many modern novelists, notably in Joyce's *Ulysses* and *Finnegans Wake*, the German Thomas Mann's *Joseph and His Brothers*, Broch's *Death of Virgil* and, more recently, in the novels of Beckett, Golding, Lowry, Styron, and White.

(c) The Influence of Russian Literature.

A subsidiary, but nevertheless important influence upon the novel has come from the writing of the great nineteenth-century Russian authors. Turgenev has been available in English since the 1890s. Tolstoy, Dostoyevsky, and Chekhov began to be translated just before the First World War. Their writing heightened novelists' interest in conveying a more spiritual reality and the work of Turgenev and Chekhov particularly encouraged writers who were moving towards a more lyrical treatment of style and form, while the novels of Dostoyevsky stimulated the interest aroused by Freud in the imaginative presentation of mentally handicapped, neurotic, psychotic, and psychopathic characters. American and English novelists' attitudes to the work of these and other Russian authors can be studied in the anthology *Russian Literature and Modern English Fiction*, edited, D. Davie.

(d) Innovators of Literary Techniques.

Marcel Proust (1871–1922).

In his huge novel *À la recherche du temps perdu* (1913–27) Proust evokes the kaleidoscopic patterns of involuntary memory as they float through his narrator's mind. His work has therefore been called a *roman fleuve*—a river novel. Its plot seems non-existent, but the novel is in fact constructed with the greatest artistry and, just as the Symbolist poets used evocative images with a multiplicity of associations, so Proust introduces the characters and events of his narrative, presenting them from different viewpoints and investing them with new significance each time they are recalled. Proust's work had a notable influence upon the writing of Virginia Woolf and Forster and among more recent novelists Powell is Proust's avowed disciple. A translation of *À la recherche du temps perdu* is now published in paperback by Chatto and Windus.

James Joyce (1882–1941).

Joyce, an Irishman, spent most of his life on the Continent and although his work, like that of all great artists, was highly individual, it owed much to the stimulus of the ideas of Flaubert and the work of the Symbolists. Like Flaubert, Joyce believed that a novel should be objective and rooted in experience of everyday life, and by developing the Symbolists' techniques he achieved an hitherto unparalleled impression of objectivity in his portrayal of character.

Joyce's name is particularly associated with the "stream of consciousness" technique, which he evolved from the Symbolist writer Dujardin's "interior monologue," in order to be able to express the mind's activity—not only the way we receive passive impressions of the exterior world and associate them with past experience, the subconscious distortion and imaginative control exercised by the mind, but also how our sensibility and imagination are involved in an active "dialogue" with the world as we apprehend it. Joyce's use of this technique therefore varies considerably, according to the kind of character he is presenting, and since he attempts to express non-verbal experience, as well as verbal thought, his sentences often have a poetic rather than a discursive logic. Stimulated by Joyce's example, later novelists, including Faulkner and Lowry, have evolved their own poetic forms of the stream of consciousness technique, but most later writers have preferred to use a less poetic version, more akin to the interior monologue, expressing the stream of thought, rather than of consciousness. A contemporary novelist who uses interior monologue in this way is Bellow.

It has been suggested that Joyce, having created a new kind of novel, himself used it in every possible way. In *Portrait of the Artist* (1916) he covered the childhood and adolescence of a writer. *Ulysses* (1922) shows a day in the life of Dublin through the eyes of three people and, at the same time, creates a universal image of man's experience of life. In *Finnegans Wake* (1939) Joyce attempted to express the history of the world by evoking the dreams of a Dublin publican, but, despite its occasional brilliance, *Finnegans Wake* is largely inaccessible to readers who have not spent years studying it. Joyce has, therefore, a twofold significance for later writers: he evolved a new kind of novel and, although he wrote with such skill that others have often despaired of emulating him, his achievements have encouraged novelists to experiment, while *Finnegans Wake* has provided a salutary warning of the dangers of indulging in esoteric mythmaking.

(e) Heirs of the Victorian Tradition.

D. H. Lawrence (1885–1930). *See also Section I.*

Lawrence had a vivid appreciation of the beauty of the natural world and emphasised the importance of the instinctual, as opposed to the intellectual, life. He felt that it was only through basic human experience, particularly through the experience of unselfish erotic love, that we could attain the peaceful self-unity that comes from an apprehension of the sacramental quality of life.

Although he abhorred didactic literature, Lawrence was, therefore, a man with a message, the " flag-bearer of intuition in its interminable struggle against logic and reason "—a true heir of the Romantic movement (*see* **Section J**). Lawrence's attitude to the novel was thus akin to that of Victorian writers and the form of his work has much in common with theirs, although, unlike most Victorians, he made deliberate use of poetic symbolism, which, as Walter Allen has said, " enabled him to render the felt quality of the immediate, instinctive self as it had never been before."

Although no later novelist has equalled Lawrence in the tender poetic expression of unselfish erotic love, his ideas have been widely influential. Doris Lessing is among those later novelists whose work, like Lawrence's, has emphasised the unhappiness and sterility of selfish relationships, and the American writer Baldwin also reflects his influence.

E. M. Forster (1879–1970).

Like Lawrence, Forster was a moralist, primarily interested in relationships between people and used techniques and a novel form that have much in common with those of the Victorians. A much more sophisticated novelist than Lawrence, Forster was, superficially, a writer of social comedy in the tradition of Jane Austen, but he was always aware of the numinous quality of life, and expressed it in his novels through complex symbols. His books explore individuals' attempts to " connect " with each other across " the divisions of daily life " in a mutual quest for truth. These themes, which are stated, rather than successfully conveyed in symbolic terms in his early novels, find perfect expression in his masterpiece, *A Passage to India* (1924).

Forster did not publish any novels after 1924, saying, " I had been accustomed to write about the old-fashioned world with its homes and its family life and its comparative peace. All that went, and though I can think about the new world I cannot write about it."

The " new world " is the theme of Kafka and Huxley.

(f) Important Novelists of the 1930s.

Franz Kafka (1883–1924).

A Czech by birth, Kafka wrote in German. His novels first became known to the English-speaking world on the appearance of a translation of *The Castle* in 1930. It was followed in 1935 by *The Trial*. These haunting parables of a man's nightmare life in a world where everything appears contingent, now seem prophetic, and their influence is apparent in works like Rex Warner's *The Aerodrome* (1941), Orwell's *1984*, Ellison's *The Invisible Man*, and the novels of Beckett. Surrealist techniques, giving an effect of confusion between the world of consciousness and that of dream, had been used before Kafka, but he gave them fresh significance.

His tragic short story, *Metamorphosis*, which tells of a man who wakes one day to find himself transformed into a huge insect, brought new dimensions to serious science fiction.

Aldous Huxley (1894–1963).

Huxley was unique among the novelists of the inter-war years. He declared that nothing deserved to be taken seriously save the suffering men inflict upon themselves by their own crimes and follies, and he criticised both the traditional " social " novel of personal relationships and the more poetic individualism of Joyce, Virginia Woolf, *et al.*, as reflecting conventional values that create suffering and help to perpetuate misery. Although Huxley's highly intelligent satires are very different in style from those of any other twentieth-century writer, his themes look forward to those of some of the more important post-war novelists.

John Dos Passos (1896–1970).

Dos Passos was a member of the group of Radical American novelists which also included Farrell and Steinbeck, all of whom were influenced by the work of the Naturalists. In his trilogy *U.S.A.* (1930–36), which is a panorama of American life between 1910 and 1927, Dos Passos developed the collage techniques he had evolved in *Manhattan Transfer* (1925). The trilogy is composed of short sections: some are written in interior monologue, others consist of extracts from newspaper headlines and articles and snatches of popular song, others are biographies of leading American personalities, written in a kind of " free verse " and yet others consist of extracts from the lives of fictional characters. *U.S.A.* does not form an imaginative whole and has nothing of the power of Proust and Joyce's novels, but Dos Passos's technical experiments have exerted considerable influence, not only on a number of later American novelists, particularly Mailer, but also on French writers such as Sartre.

Recent Developments.

(a) Commonwealth Writers.

Since 1945, the language of the English novel has been invigorated by the work of writers from the Commonwealth. Outstanding among these novelists are Achebe and Soyinka from Nigeria and Naipaul from Trinidad (*qq.v.*). Drawing upon a long tradition of oral story-telling these and other African and Caribbean writers are particularly skilful in their treatment of dialogue. Notable authors from the Indian subcontinent include R. K. Narayan and Zulfikar Ghose, while the Australian Patrick White (*q.v.*) is one of the greatest of contemporary novelists in any language.

Heinemann's have recently introduced a highly recommended, inexpensive series of editions of African Commonwealth fiction.

(b) Le Nouveau Roman.

Some critics consider the most exciting recent developments in the novel's form have been made in France by the heterogeneous group of writers whose work is given the title of *le nouveau roman*. Most of their novels are published by Éditions de Minuit, of which Robbe-Grillet, one of their leaders, is a director, and are available in English translation from Calder and Boyars.

Apart from Robbe-Grillet, the most notable of these novelists include Butor and Nathalie Sarraute. Some of their theories about fiction are to be found in Robbe-Grillet's *For a New Novel*, Butor's *The Inventory* and Sarraute's *The Age Of Suspicion*. Interested readers should also refer to *Writing Degree Zero*, *Mythologies* and *S/Z*, by the influential critic and linguistic philosopher Roland Barthes.

Although the writers of the *nouveau roman* have individual styles, all seek to present a character's state of mind over a brief period of time, while introducing incidental details of his past experience. Their techniques involve the inconsequential repetition of key images and phrases in ever differing combinations and contexts. Such aims may seem new to the French literary scene but they are familiar to English readers of the eighteenth-century Lawrence Sterne (*v*. his *Tristram Shandy*, 1760–7). The techniques of the *nouveau roman*, derived from the Symbolists, Joyce and Proust, are not really new either and, although skilfully deployed, often mask the trivial content of works which have nothing of the power of Samuel Beckett's fables (*qq.v.*), their immediate inspiration.

The only English novelist closely associated with this French group is Christine Brooke-Rose (*q.v.*). The experimental writer B. S. Johnson (*q.v.*) has expressed similar aims to those of authors of the *nouveau roman*, but his novels are very different from theirs.

Conclusion.

Contemporary novelists writing in English are experimenting with a variety of forms, continuing to use and adapt the techniques evolved by writers in the early part of the century, and in general their better work approaches more closely to that of the nineteenth-century American tradition than to that of the Victorian novel. This means that although the novel has gained in dramatic and poetic intensity its vision of the world has generally been restricted to that of one or a few characters. This may partly be a result of the interest in individual experience aroused by psychologists, but it seems more particularly a reflection of life in the contemporary world, in which many men feel exiles. Most modern art, not only fiction, expresses feelings of isolation, bewilderment, and suffering, and not only rebellious students, but eminent thinkers such as Tillich have suggested that life for many people in Western society is virtually life different from that under a totalitarian régime. It is significant that such a view of contemporary life was foreshadowed by Kafka and Huxley and is now reflected most impressively, because it is expressed poetically, in the grimly comic novels of Beckett.

In 1968 and 1969 however, new ways of expressing the dilemmas of contemporary life were suggested. In *The Armies of the Night* (*q.v.*), the American Mailer, following a pattern suggested by "Theatre of Fact" (*see* I6), produced a fascinating documentary novel on the American anti-Vietnam War lobby, and from Russia came *Cancer Ward* and *First Circle*, two painful, yet essentially hopeful novels by Alexander Solzhenitsyn, winner of the 1970 Nobel prize.

II. DIRECTORY OF NOVELISTS.

In this part we discuss the work of some of the more important novelists who have published since 1945. It is inevitably selective. A more detailed treatment of the twentieth-century American and English novel may be found in Walter Allen's *Tradition and Dream* (P). Some helpful studies of individual authors are available in Oliver and Boyd's paperbacked series *Writers and Their Critics*.

Except for the later novels of Beckett, dates quoted are those of the first publication. The dates of the first English-language editions of Beckett's novels are given.

Paperback editions are referred to thus: C: Calder and Boyars. Co: Corgi. F: Faber and Faber. Fo: Fontana. FS: Four Square. M: Mayflower. P: Penguin. Pa: Panther. S: Signet Books.

Chinua Achebe (b. 1930).

Achebe, the Nigerian author of four most elegantly written novels, was awarded the first *New Statesman* prize for African and Caribbean writers in 1965.

Things Fall Apart, 1958; *No Longer at Ease*, 1960; *Arrow of God*, 1964.

These novels are all concerned with the impact of Western society upon Ibo culture in earlier years of the century. Achebe shows a vivid appreciation of the value and dignity of the Ibo's traditional ways of life, but his overriding theme is the need for men to have flexible, receptive minds. The hero of each of these novels comes to a tragic end because he cannot adapt to the demands of a new and unforeseen situation.

The three books are characterised by the grace and dignity of their language and are very different in tone from Achebe's latest novel.

A Man of People. 1966.

This is a fiercely ironic study of the career of Chief Nanga, leading demagogue in a newly independent African state. It has been suggested that the portrait of Nanga is modelled from Nkrumah. Although Achebe presents Nanga as an unscrupulous opportunist he also stresses the attractive qualities of his character and suggests that he is, ultimately, a victim of circumstances. It is interesting to compare this novel with Naipaul's *Mimic Men* (*q.v.*).

James Baldwin (b. 1924). *See also* Section I.

Baldwin emphasises the harsh brutality of contemporary life, particularly for the American Negro. One of his dominant themes is the necessity for honesty about oneself; this includes a frank acceptance of one's sexual nature, whether heterosexual or homosexual. He suggests the brutality of modern life is due to the fact that many people, especially, though not only, White people, are afraid of themselves and therefore incapable of accepting or loving others, but fear them and sadistically exploit and attack them. He shows the tragic effects of such viciousness upon those who suffer it and also upon its perpetrators. Much of the distinction of Baldwin's work comes from the compassionate understanding with which he treats the latter. He acknowledges the discovery and acceptance of oneself may involve great suffering and always requires courage, and suggests it is only possible if one is willing to love others and accept the support of their love.

Go Tell It on the Mountain. 1954. Co.

The novel covers two days in the lives of a Negro family who belong to a strict fundamentalist sect, The Fire Baptised. The members of this fellowship identify themselves with the Israelites in captivity. Baldwin shows how this is a reaction to the harshness of their lives and compassionately reveals the mixture of genuine and deluded religious experience among the sect's members. The language of the novel is permeated by echoes of the Authorised Version of the Bible.

Giovanni's Room. 1956. Co.

This is a tragic story of a young American who fears his homosexual predilections and hideously ruins the lives of his Italian lover and of his own fiancée.

Another Country. 1962. Co.

The novel is centred on the lives of a mixed racial group of Greenwich Village artists and intellectuals. The brutality of New York life is reflected in the crude and obscene language the characters use so casually. At the end of the novel five of its central figures are, as the title suggests, on the verge of a new, though not necessarily easy, life, after their difficult and often bitter quest for love and self-knowledge.

Tell Me How Long the Train's Been Gone. 1968. Co

A star Negro actor looks back on a life dominated by fear and concludes that, for the majority of Black Americans, violence offers the only road to freedom. This is a disappointing novel when compared with Baldwin's earlier ones, for it is less objective and therefore less powerful than they. It is, nevertheless, an important expression of the growing bitterness of Black Americans and constitutes a vehement denunciation of the behaviour of the White community.

In each of these novels Baldwin uses a mixture of straightforward narrative and " flash-back " techniques.

Samuel Beckett (b. 1906). *See also* Section I.

Beckett was awarded a Nobel prize in 1969. The form of his novels has been influenced by the work of his friend Joyce and also, and more particularly, by his study of Proust. An erudite man, Beckett delights to enrich his work with subtle allusions to the writings of other authors and those to whom he most often refers include St. Augustine and Dante. Belacqua, the hero of his first stories, who is often mentioned in the later novels, is a character from the fourth canto of Dante's *Il Purgatorio* (P).

Since Beckett's work becomes progressively more difficult and his later novels contain many references to his earlier ones, readers are advised to begin with the short stories *More Pricks Than Kicks*, 1934, and *Murphy*, 1938 (C). Beckett now writes in French, recreating his works into English. He is said to prefer French because that language is the more precise. This search for precision relates to one of the central themes of his novels, the agonising inadequacy of words to express the truth of the human condition, and links Beckett's work with that of other major twentieth-century writers like Kafka and Ionesco and the philosopher Wittgenstein. All Beckett's heroes are driven to feel that they can only tell lies, and they long to achieve the silence of truth, but since truth always eludes them they continue to tell their stories—" One must go on "—in the vain hope that they may at last *speak* the truth and so be released from the tyranny of words.

Beckett is a supreme exponent of the themes of isolation and bewilderment, imprisonment and suffering that are to be found in the work of so many contemporary writers and of artists like Francis Bacon. Poetic in structure and use of language his latest novels haunt the reader's imagination. Each is the monologue of a crippled old man imprisoned in a terrifying, incomprehensible world where life seems a grotesque, bitter farce directed by an elusive tyrant. Yet, harrowing as they are, these novels have their positive side and their bizarre humour has led one critic to call them " supremely entertaining." Beckett's heroes have the tragic gaiety of clowns and, although, as prisoners are said to, they fear

to achieve their longed-for freedom, they never abandon their quest for it.

Watt. 1953. C.

This transitional work is the last novel Beckett wrote in English and was composed between 1942–4 when he was in hiding as a member of the French Resistance.

Sam, a patient in a mental hospital, tells the story of his fellow inmate Watt, who has been a servant to the mysterious Mr. Knott. Watt's purpose in going to Knott's house is expressed in terms of a religious quest, but while he was there he discovered the impossibility of possessing any certain knowledge. The novel is comic in tone and its style recalls Sterne's *Tristram Shandy*.

The Trilogy—*Molloy,* Eng. pub. 1955, *Mallone Dies,* Eng. pub. 1956 (P), *The Unnamable,* Eng. pub. 1958.

In the first part of *Molloy* the bedridden speaker recounts his compulsive, futile quest for his mother; in the second, the tyrant Youdi sends a messenger, Gaber, to one Moran, ordering him to go and look for Molloy. Youdi's name, derived from the Arabic " Yahudi " (cf. Yahweh), is a French colloquialism for " Jew." " Gaber " suggests " Gabriel." Moran doubts Youdi's existence, but fears to disobey the order. He fails to discover Molloy. Molloy and Moran probably represent aspects of the same personality.

In *Mallone Dies* the bedridden Molloy-Moran-Mallone awaits death, " telling stories " about other personifications of himself.

The harrowing *The Unnamable* continues the hero's fruitless search for some understanding of his own identity.

How It Is. 1964.

Arranged in short passages of unpunctuated prose-poetry, this extraordinary work has the effect of nightmare delirium. The speaker, who is at first anonymous, is, it seems, in the throes of a mortal illness, and imagines himself naked, dumb, crawling through mud with a sack of tinned fish suspended from his neck until he meets another, Pim, in a similar condition. He tortures Pim until the latter speaks. By now the narrator has a name, Bom. Pim deserts Bom, who, posing the idea of life as a circle, or procession, of torturers and victims, awaits his own torturer.

Professor Kermode in *Continuities* has noted the ritual quality of this novel's language and drawn attention to the parallels between Beckett's images and those of medieval allegory, suggesting that Bom's sack may be taken as a symbol of the soul, the burden and support of the body, and that Pim may be interpreted as an image of Christ, the tortured Word Incarnate.

Saul Bellow (b. 1915).

Bellow is a leading American novelist and short story writer. Like Beckett's, his characters engage in purgatorial quests, but whereas Beckett's seek answers to the questions, " Who am I? What is truth?" Bellow's ask rather, " What makes a good life?" For the heroes of Beckett's tragic fables death is both sought as a release from their quest and feared lest the apparant release it offers prove an illusion. For Bellow it is death which above all else gives meaning to life, and only when his heroes face the physical reality of death, which they fear, do they begin to accept that death of the self which will enable them to combine individual freedom with social responsibility. Thus, while Beckett's characters become increasingly isolated in a sterile world, Bellow's move towards escaping from self-absorption into an awareness that the significance of life is to be found " in the ranks with other people " and in selfless love for them. Only in *The Victim* and *Mr. Sammler's Planet*, however, does Bellow show any of his heroes attempting to put this into practice and this last novel is the only one with a wholly convincing conclusion.

Bellow's ethical and social concern, a product of his heritage as the son of Russian Jewish emigrés, links him with the great nineteenth-century European novelists. He feels that although earlier writers' answers to the question of what makes a good life may be inadequate for us who live in an urban, technological society, the question nevertheless remains and he considers that most modern novelists evade it, retreating into ivory towers and concentrating upon the production of formally perfect works of art.

Despite his emphasis upon the importance of a novel's content, Bellow has always striven to improve the style and form of his work. This led him to abandon the "Flaubertian standard" he had adopted for his first two novels, when he discovered it was an inadequate vehicle for his own—very different—experience. The form of the transitional *Augie March* is shapeless and Bellow's style in this book and in *Henderson the Rain King* is sometimes undisciplined, but his later novels are very carefully and skilfully constructed and at its best his writing is vigorously exuberant and often wildly funny.

Bellow is keenly aware of the ugliness and suffering of life, which he vividly portrays in his novels, yet the overall effect of his work is one of hopeful optimism, in contrast to the anguish and wryly stoical endurance of Beckett.

The Victim. 1947. P.

This, Bellow's second novel (his first, *Dangling Man*, appeared in 1944) has a New York setting of purgatorial heat and squalor. Its Jewish hero, Leventhal, a moderately prosperous journalist, has known hard times and fears their return. Alone for a few days while his wife visits her mother, he feels particularly vulnerable. His worst fears become embodied in the person of the Gentile Albee, a former vague acquaintance, who appears declaring that his present misfortunes, the loss of his job and wife, are Leventhal's fault. Only when he is able to admit some responsibility for Albee, and saves him from death, is Leventhal freed from fear.

This concentrated novel still seems one of Bellow's finest.

The Adventures of Augie March. 1953. P.

Originally entitled *Among the Machiavellians*, this is a picaresque chronicle of the fortunes of an illegitimate slum boy as he seeks a way of life which will enable him to combine responsibility towards others with freedom from the Machiavellian "reality instructors" who seek to dominate him and to convince him that life is a rat-race.

Although this prize-winning novel was highly praised on publication its rambling shapelessness now makes it seem Bellow's least successful.

Seize the Day. 1956. P.

This *nouvelle* was first published together with three short stories, *A Father to Be, Looking for Mr. Green* and *The Gonzaga Manuscripts*. Like them it is concerned with the insidious power of money. Broke and out of work, Wilhelm feels he is being strangled by the encircling pressures exerted especially by his separated wife, his swindling friend and his scornful father. On "the day" of which Bellow writes Wilhelm's troubles come to a head, but through them he struggles to regain the sense of "general love" for other people, which is, he becomes convinced, "the right clue" to the resolution of his difficulties.

Henderson the Rain King. 1959. P.

The prodigal Henderson dissipates his massive strength and fortune, creating havoc and misery as he seeks to quell his soul's demand for a meaningful life. Eventually he flees to Africa where he inadvertently becomes the Rain Maker of a primitive tribe and thus heir-presumptive to its king. When the latter's death is contrived by his jealous subjects Henderson, who has already realised that it is his duty to return to his wife, escapes from the tribesmen and begins his journey home, a "fighting Lazarus."

Whereas Henderson escaped to Africa, Herzog, a lecturer in philosophy, retires to bed in the derelict country house to which he has fled, shattered by his wife's desertion and his own inability to hate her new husband, whom he had planned to shoot! Incidents in his past life are interspersed with extracts from the letters Herzog endlessly composes on personal, social and philosophical questions as he seeks to "explain, to justify, to put in perspective, to make amends." Gradually he realises that he has stopped hating his former enemies and that to continue his solitary brooding would be self-indulgent, so, like Henderson, he prepares to return to "our common life," "to share with other human beings as far as possible."

This hilarious novel is constructed with great skill and ingenuity.

Mr. Sammler's Planet. 1969.

Born into a wealthy Polish family, educated at Oxford, denizen of Bloomsbury and later of a concentration camp, from which he miraculously escaped, the 72-year-old Sammler is an interested observer of modern American life, where people seem to him to be frantically seeking to ignore the fact of death and absorbed in illusory attempts at self-fulfilment, rather than in caring for one another. The death of a nephew makes Sammler realise that he too has begun to evade his responsibility towards others.

Elizabeth Bowen (b. 1899).

A stylistic artist in the tradition of James, Elizabeth Bowen is famed for the beauty of her descriptive writing and for her sensitive analyses of feeling. Her finest novels are *To the North*, 1932, *The House in Paris*, 1935, *The Death of the Heart*, 1938 (P).

Of her later novels, the best seems *The Heat of the Day*, 1949 (P), a love story set in war-time London; but her most recent, *Eva Trout*, 1969, was awarded the James Tait Black Memorial prize for the best novel of 1969.

Christine Brooke-Rose (b. 1916).

The writing of Christine Brooke-Rose, a lecturer at the free university of Valenciennes, is associated with that of the French authors of the *nouveau roman* and she has translated the work of Robbe-Grillet, one of their leaders.

Herself the author of eight novels, she now disowns the first five, which are traditional in style and form, acknowledging only her recent, experimental work, the novels *Out*, 1964 (now out of print), *Such, Between* and the short stories *Go When You See the Green Man Walking*, 1970.

She has a poetic gift for creating precise visual images and a comedian's joy in the ambiguity of words, which she delights to place in novel and unexpected juxtapositions, using a form of the stream-of-consciousness technique.

Such. 1966.

This bizarre work may have been inspired by Nathalie Sarraute's *Between Life and Death*, 1965.

The key to its significance seems to lie in the sentence, " Surely man as such puts tremendous effort into moving through space and time." The struggling central consciousness of the book belongs to Laurence/Larry/Lazarus, who at first hovers between life and death, later between consciousness and unconsciousness, then between a continued withdrawal from everyday life and returning to it. An underlying theme is man's effort to distinguish between reality and illusion, honesty and self-deception, truth and falsity.

The novel's imagery is drawn from the world of astrophysics, in which Laurence worked, and also owes something to popular science fiction.

Between. 1969.

The lyrical and often very amusing *Between* expresses a sense of suspended animation and loss of identity in a world devoid of significance, as experienced by a woman interpreter. Of mixed nationality, neither married nor unmarried, neither young nor old, she moves from one meaningless international conference to another in indistinguishable 'planes, stays at indistinguishable hotels, meets indistinguishable people speaking a confused Babel of languages, as she does herself.

The weakness of *Between* is that it expresses rather than explores a state of mind and such expression can be more powerfully and economically conveyed in verse than prose.

Alan Burns (b. c. 1935)

Burns is regarded by some critics as among the *avant garde* of contemporary English novelists and his work has been highly praised by Angus Wilson, a writer in a much more traditional vein. However, Burns's vision of the brutality, hypocrisy and futile materialism of modern life seems to find successful expression only in the early *nouvelle Buster* and in *Celebrations*. Both draw upon his traumatic adolescent experience of the deaths of his mother and brother.

Burns's first book was conceived as a series of snapshots after he had noticed a photograph in a Chancery Lane window. He now writes in two stages, cutting up his draft manuscripts into hundreds of slips of paper and shuffling them so as to achieve new, random associations between their words and images. This " cut-up " technique, it technique it can be called, seems to have been devised by the popular American novelist William Burroughs.

Buster. 1961. C.

Published in Calder's *New Writers I* and later filmed, this short, impressionistic tale is more easily followed than Burns's later novels and throws helpful light upon *Celebrations (q.v.)*.

Its protagonist, Buster, early wins the approval of his conventional father, who designates him as a future Lord Chief Justice, while rejecting his older son, who has repudiated his values. Buster, however, admires his brother. Later he too rebels against their father and deliberately fails his law exams. When, in consequence, he is also rejected, he bursts into the family home and, unexpectedly fulfiling his father's prediction, wreaks " justice " upon Helen, the older man's beautiful, spiteful mistress.

Europe After the Rain. 1965. C.

This novel was inspired by Max Ernst's painting, *Europe After the Rain*, depicting a devastated urban landscape. Inconsequential and dreamlike, the action opens with its narrator, accompanied by a girl, crossing a river into a devastated region which is under martial law. The girl is searching for her father whom, from time to time, she finds. Her quest merges with the narrator's intermittently successful search for her. The novel ends with his return across the river, alone, but satisfied.

Celebrations. 1967. C.

Here, as in *Buster*, the novel centres upon the antagonistic relationships between two brothers, their brutal father and his mistress.

The novel's setting moves erratically between the Arctic and a typical suburban industrial estate. The timing of its action fluctuates in a similarly irregular way between the early part of this century and the present.

Williams, the father, is the head of a factory/ state. His sons work there and when the younger wishes to leave Williams contrives his death. The older son plays a waiting game, eventually wins the hand of his father's mistress and usurps his position.

The parts of this surrealistic novel evoking life in the factory have a nightmare quality. The intervening parodies of state funerals and weddings are bitingly satiric.

Babel. 1969.

Unlike Burns's previous novels this lacks even a skeletal narrative. Most of the book is written in short passages of rhythmic prose, but the rhythms are monotonous and numb one's response to the sense of the words. Each passage opens with a headline quotation. Sometimes this headline stands alone but usually it is followed by a brief meditation or comment. References are made to over two hundred people, alive and dead, including many prominent in various walks of public life. The overall result is confusion and bewilderment, admittedly an appropriate image of Babel, but aesthetically and imaginatively unrewarding. One feels, that Burns might have expressed this disenchanted vision more successfully had he submitted it to the discipline of verse.

Ivy Compton-Burnett (1884–1969).

Miss Compton-Burnett was a highly conscious artist, who knew her limits and never exceeded them. Apart from an early, rejected, work, she published eighteen novels, the first, *Pastors and Masters* in 1925, the last, *The Mighty and Their Fall*, in 1963. Her nineteenth novel, *The Last and the First* was published posthumously, in 1971. Written mainly in dialogue, each of her books deals with the claustrophobic life of a well-to-do middle-class household at the turn of the century. Miss Compton-Burnett's themes are those of Greek tragedy; her formal, decorous language is reminiscent of Jane Austen. The combination can be disconcerting.

Lawrence Durrell (b. 1912).

Durrell's shorter novels are *The Black Book*, *White Eagles Over Serbia*, and *The Dark Labyrinth*. His longer, baroque fantasies have had a mixed reception. Their most appreciative critic is G. S. Fraser.

The Alexandria Quartet—*Justine*, 1956, *Balthazar*, 1958, *Mountolive*, 1958, *Clea*, 1960 (all F).

Some find the Quartet a most enjoyable novel, for others it is all but unreadable.

Its form, says Durrell, is based on the relativity proposition, the first three volumes, which give differing aspects and views of the characters' lives and motives, having a " spatial " relationship, the fourth, which continues the narrative more or less chronologically, representing time. The novel's construction thus resembles that of Faulkner's *The Sound and the Fury*, and has much in common too with works like Cary's Gulley Jimpson trilogy.

Durrell's apparent theme is erotic love, but his underlying interest is the relationship between art and life. He suggests life is significant only when interpreted by art. This attitude, rather than the form of his work, differentiates it from novels like Faulkner's and Cary's.

Durrell's volumes contain splendid passages, but too often in the novel as a whole his sensuous language seems merely florid and pretentious, his characters but flimsy inhabitants of a decadent fairyland.

Tunc. 1968. F. *Nunquam.* 1970.

These two volumes comprise a single novel. Their titles are derived from a line from Petronius's *Satyricon*, " Aut tunc, aut nunquam "— " Then or never." The theme of the work seems to be the individual's struggle for a sense of freedom in a world dominated by international commerce, but, although Durrell's theme is serious, his treatment of it seems not only bizarre but frivolous as he chronicles the career of his protagonist, Charlock, an inventor who is taken captive by the all-powerful international firm of Merlin and eventually becomes its head.

Some passages in *Tunc* describing Athens and Constantinople recall the better parts of *The Alexandria Quartet*, but in *Nunquam* there is a loss of momentum. This second volume is mainly concerned with the creation of a life-like dummy representing the dead film star Iolanthe, with whom Julian, the impotent head of Merlin, falls desperately in love, and dies as he tries to prevent " her " from committing " suicide " by jumping from the gallery of St. Paul's Cathedral.

Ralph Ellison (b. 1914).

The Invisible Man. 1952. P.

Ellison is an American Negro and former musician. This, his only novel, is poetic in its complex symbolism and compelling language, and in the intensity of its feeling.

We learn from the prologue that Ellison's hero is not only " invisible," but an " underground man," living in a cellar. He has affinities with the narrator of Dostoyevsky's *Notes from the Underground*. The novel also recalls Kafka. Like Kafka's, Ellison's hero is anonymous, and his vividly recounted experiences have the quality of bewildering dreams, at times of nightmare. He tells of his life from the night he received a scholarship to the State Negro College, to the night of a terrifying Harlem race riot, when, fleeing from supporters of a deranged Black nationalist, Ras the Destroyer, he took refuge in the cellar.

One of the novel's central episodes is that in a paint factory hospital, where the hero is subjected to torturous experiments and there is talk of castrating him. Among other things, the episode signifies the way in which all the " scientists " he encounters exploit those in their power, attempting to force all life into rigid sterile patterns. " Life," he says, " is to be lived, not controlled." A free society is loving and infinitely various.

The hero realises the " scientists "—politicians, demagogues, and confidence men—are unaware of the limitations of their vision and cannot see they are destroying themselves as well as their dupes and victims. Images of blindness recur throughout the novel. The narrator calls himself " invisible " because he has come to feel people who look at him see only projections of their own imaginations. He realises he has been equally blind. One of the novel's themes is his gradual enlightenment as he learns to understand himself and others better—to see " reality."

William Faulkner (1897–1965).

The American Faulkner received the Nobel Prize for Literature in 1950. Although his last novel was published only three years before his death, most of his best work appeared between 1929 and 1936: *The Sound and the Fury, As I Lay Dying, Light in August* (all P), *Absalom, Absalom!* Together with the comic *The Hamlet*, 1940, these novels are his finest achievement.

Faulkner's post-war novels can be divided into three groups: (1) those which are simply enjoyable stories: *The Town*, 1957, *The Mansion*, 1959, which together with *The Hamlet* form the Snopes trilogy, and *The Reivers*, 1962 (P); (2) *The Intruder in the Dust*, 1948 (P), which is too overtly didactic to be a successful novel, though of great interest to anyone concerned by the racial problems of the South; (3) two ritualistic novels: *Requiem for a Nun*, 1951 (P), and *A Fable*, 1954; the latter, set in France in early 1918, is constructed on an elaborate series of parallels with the events of Holy Week.

Faulkner's work is concerned almost exclusively with the Southern States and set in the mythological Yoknapatawpha County, Mississippi. A Southerner by birth, he is soaked in the history and legendary folklore of Mississippi. Although many of his most memorable characters are bizarre, tragic figures, subnormal poor-Whites, murderers, or other outcasts of society, his work reflects not only the grimness, the callousness and brutality of the South, but also the proud individualism, courage, humour, and vitality of its people. Thus one reads Faulkner with pleasure, despite the difficulties presented by his style.

These difficulties are at times inherent in his subject, as at the beginning of *The Sound and the Fury*, which is told from the viewpoint of a moron; in the touching episode in *The Hamlet*, when the idiot Ike Snopes steals a cow he loves; in the evocation of Charles Mallison's nightmare (*Intruder in the Dust*). Sometimes, however, Faulkner seems needlessly obscure; he indulges in turgid rhetoric; his sentences are often three or four pages long, sparsely punctuated and containing innumerable parentheses, and parentheses within parentheses. The effect of such clumsy syntax is utterly bewildering, and one sympathises with the exasperated critic who declared Faulkner a " genius without talent." Such criticism, however, ignores the comic aspect of Faulkner's work, his gift for racy, demotic humour.

William Golding (b. 1911).

Golding's novels are poetic and, like all poems, cannot be fully appreciated on first reading. Essentially a religious novelist, he aims to write " total myths " illuminating contemporary life. To a remarkable extent he has succeeded.

Golding has enormous technical virtuosity; no two of his works are alike, although they express the same vision—a vision of men without God as tragic figures who " seem unable to move without killing each other "; torture those they love; watch themselves becoming automata. But Golding suggests man can regain freedom and the state of grace in which " everything that lives is holy." Thus all his novels, except *Pincher Martin*, express not only the horror, but also the wonder and beauty of life.

Lord of the Flies. 1954. F. P.

Golding rewrites *Coral Island* in " realistic " terms, as an allegory of the Fall and an image of twentieth-century society that makes and drops atomic bombs.

The Inheritors. 1955. F.

This astonishing *tour de force* shows the advent of *Homo sapiens*, mainly through the eyes of the Neanderthal Lok. The measure of Golding's skill is not simply his brilliant evocation of the largely non-verbal world of Neanderthal Man, but his avoidance of sentimentality. He shows the inevitability of *Homo sapiens'* supremacy, and the tragedy in which it involves him, as well as Lok.

Pincher Martin. 1956. F. P.

This novel chronicles the struggles of a drowned sailor against God's overwhelming love. Made, like all men, in God's image, Martin is named Christopher. Alive he chose to " pinch " everything he could; dead, he refuses abnegation of himself, and therefore continues to exist, in a self-made Hell, on a rock he creates from the memory of a decaying tooth. Martin's struggles for " survival " are heroic, ghastly, futile.

Free Fall. 1959. F. P.

Sammy Mountjoy retraces his life, to discover when he lost his innocent delight in life and its beauty, and how he regained this. Containing fine passages, the novel is marred by the fact that Sammy interprets the significance of events, instead of the interpretation being left to us.

The Spire. 1964. F.

The narrative of this, Golding's masterpiece, centres on the building of the spire of Barchester (Salisbury) Cathedral. The cathedral symbolises three aspects of life: man suffering, crucified; man praying; erotic man.

Jocelyn, the Dean, believing himself divinely appointed to build the spire, presses for its completion with ruthless disregard of the suffering and death he causes. His motives are in fact mixed and largely unconscious. Gradually he recognises his hubris and the mixed motives behind his obsession, realising his wicked folly. Admitting on his deathbed he knows nothing about God, Jocelyn is granted a vision of His glory and the wonder of creation, as he gazes at the transfigured spire.

The Pyramid. 1967. F.

Set in Stillbourne, a small Wiltshire town, the novel is superficially a tragi-comedy of provincial life (its central episode is very funny) but on a deeper level *The Pyramid* is a searching exposure of materialism.

The novel's central images are musical ones. Various tastes in, and ways of performing, music signify various kinds of love and modes of life. The title suggests the social pyramid on which the townsfolk wish to rise, and also a metronome, to whose rhythm, that of a selfish, class-ridden society, they choose to move like robots.

Nadine Gordimer (b. 1923).

The writing of Nadine Gordimer, a South African, is banned in her own country. She has published four volumes of stories and five novels. The last of the novels, *A Guest of Honour*, appeared in 1971. Nadine Gordimer is more successful as a short-story writer than as a novelist, for she seems to lack the power to develop character at any length. One is nevertheless compelled to admire her brave and outspoken criticism of the callousness of the South African régime, which makes the people of that country inhabitants of a " World of Strangers." The latter is the title and theme of her second novel.

Graham Greene (b. 1904).

Greene's best work is *The Power and the Glory,* 1940 (P). Apart from the works he calls " entertainments ", of which the latest is *Travels with My Aunt,* 1969, Greene has published five novels since the War. They are: *The Heart of the Matter,* 1948, *The End of the Affair,* 1951, *The Quiet American,* 1955 (all P), *A Burnt-out Case,* 1961, *The Comedians,* 1966 (P). All have settings of topical interest: war-time London, the Congo, Vietnam, Haiti.

While Greene's work has been influenced by the thriller and the film, his literary master is Conrad and, although Greene's novels often seem rather superficial and, at times, he appears unable to treat his characters objectively, he nevertheless tells a good story and is skilled at evoking the discomfort and squalor of life in the tropics. In his first two post-war novels he failed to achieve artistic resolution between his religious beliefs and his feeling that life is a sordid struggle against impossible odds, but *The Quiet American* and *The Comedians,* which have no overtly religious themes, are more successful.

L. P. Hartley (b. 1895).

Hartley is a professional novelist and craftsman in the tradition of James and Hawthorne, the latter his acknowledged master. Like Hawthorne's, Hartley's themes are moral, illuminated by skilful use of symbolism. In his best novels his style is humorous and gently ironical, but in others he lapses into sentimental melodrama.

Hartley seems at his happiest when writing of children and adolescents: a recurrent figure in his work is the delicate, overprotected, hypersensitive, and introspective boy, as in *Eustace and Hilda,* 1947, *The Go-Between,* 1953, *The Brickfield,* 1964. (The heroes of *The Boat,* 1950 (Co), *The Betrayal,* 1966, and *My Sisters' Keeper,* 1970, are older, less successful versions of the same figure.) Hartley is skilled in evoking the atmosphere and scene of his characters' environment, particularly when the latter is East Anglia in the earlier years of the century, Oxford, or Venice.

Of the fourteen novels he has published, the latest is *My Sisters' Keeper,* 1970. The best are:

The Eustace and Hilda trilogy—*The Shrimp and the Anemone, The Sixth Heaven, Eustace and Hilda.* F.

The novel's theme is symbolised in the opening chapter when Eustace and Hilda, playing on the beach at Anchorstone (Hunstanton) try to rescue a half-eaten shrimp from an anemone. The former is an image of the self-sacrificing Eustace, the latter of his beautiful, possessive sister. " The effort to qualify for Hilda's approval " is the " ruling force in Eustace's life."

Hartley presents his hero with sympathy and humour. The novel follows Eustace to Oxford and Venice and ends with his return to Anchorstone, to the now paralysed Hilda. Counterpointing their mutually destructive relationship is the vital life of their sister, Barbara, and her husband.

The Go-Between. P.

The innocent Leo, staying with the rich family of a school friend, acts as a messenger between the latter's sister and her farmer lover, who, like the rest of the characters, appear to him god-like figures.

A Perfect Woman. 1955.

Save for their children Isabel and Harold have little in common. She finds him dull, but, an ardent reader of novels, believes herself aware of the dangers of indulging in romantic daydreams. Her boredom and dissatisfaction become clear when the handsome novelist, Alec, enters their lives after a chance meeting with Harold. Both wish for Alec's approval and friendship and together scheme to procure for him the barmaid of the local pub.

The voice of Isabel's conscience, symbolised in her son's shouts to his sister, " Janice, go back! ", constantly interrupts her daydreams of Alec, and the children's game with the doll, Pamelia, gives symbolic warning of the dangers of their parents' wicked scheme.

The full irony of Hartley's title becomes clear at the end of the novel, when the publication of

Alec's new book provides another comment on his relationship with Isabel and Harold.

Others of Hartley's novels, *The Boat*, *My Fellow Devils*, 1961, *The Brickfield*, and *The Betrayal*, have very similar themes to that of *A Perfect Woman*, but only in the treatment of Margaret, the heroine of *My Fellow Devils*, does he approach the objective sympathy which characterises his presentation of Isabel and Harold, and in none of these other novels does he make such subtle use of poetic imagery as he does in *A Perfect Woman*, *Eustace and Hilda* and *The Go-Between*.

Ernest Hemingway (1898–1961).

This controversial American was awarded the Nobel Prize for Literature in 1954. Hemingway's language and syntax are of extreme, at times monotonous, simplicity. He writes best of physical activities like hunting and fishing. The theme of all his writing is personal honour and courage, but he tends to romanticise violence and suffering. His finest work is his earliest, the short stories *In Our Time*, 1924, and the novel *A Farewell to Arms*, 1929 (P). Hemingway's last novel, *The Old Man and the Sea*, 1952, the story of an old man's struggle to catch and land an enormous fish, has immediate appeal, but on subsequent readings its language seems contrived and precious.

Originally entitled *The Sea in Being*, *The Old Man and the Sea* was planned as one of four volumes set in the Caribbean. Hemingway intended eventually to weld them into a single novel. Two of the other books he called *The Sea When Young* and *The Sea When Absent*. The other, unnamed one, he considered complete and intended to publish it in 1951, but this plan fell through. Now given the posthumous titles *Bimini*, *Cuba* and *At Sea* these volumes, which have been subjected to the editorial cutting of Mrs. Hemingway and C. J. Schribner Jr., have been collected and published as *The Islands in the Stream*, 1970.

Dan Jacobson (b. 1929).

Jacobson, by birth a South African, now lives in England. He has published six novels, all in a traditional form.

The Trap, 1955; *A Dance in the Sun*, 1956; *The Price of Diamonds*, 1957 (all P).

These are three beautifully precise vignettes of South African life. *The Trap* and *A Dance in the Sun* present the tragic spiritual corruption engendered in those who support *apartheid*. *The Price of Diamonds* is a deliciously comic study of two business partners in a small mining town.

The Evidence of Love. 1959.

Jacobson's first full-length novel, *The Evidence of Love*, lacks the verve and precision of his earlier work. It tells how two protégés of a wealthy South African spinster fall in love and of the difficulties they face due to the fact that one of them is Coloured, the other White. Those parts of the novel which deal with the life of the Coloured Kenneth are often vivid, but Jacobson's presentation of the heroine, Isabel, is rather lifeless.

The Beginners. 1966. P.

Jacobson's novels with a South African setting culminated with this chronicle of the life of a family of South African Jews, evoked through a series of brief snapshots. The career of the novel's central character, Joel, bears some resemblance to Jacobson's own.

The Rape of Tamar. 1970.

A note of cynical despair, a sense that life is futilely repetitive, but faintly discernible in *The Evidence of Love* and *The Beginners*, here becomes predominant. The story of *The Rape of Tamar* derives from 2 *Samuel 13*, but Jacobson's interest lies not in the creation of an historical verisimilitude, but in the presentation of his narrator, the cynical, speculative Yonadab, a ghost conversant with twentieth-century culture, who, like the novelist, feels compelled to recreate his past experience in order to objectify it.

B. S. Johnson (b. 1933).

Johnson's *The Unfortunates* makes very painful reading, but he is otherwise one of the most entertaining as well as one of the most skilful of contemporary *avant garde* writers. The predominant influences upon his work are the novels of Lawrence Sterne and Samuel Beckett.

Johnson prefaces his second novel, *Albert Angelo*, with a quotation from Beckett's *The Unnamable*: " When I think . . . of the time I've wasted on these bran dips, . . . when I had me on the premises . . ." and towards the end of *Albert Angelo*, he says, ". . . im trying to say something about me through him albert . . . when whats the point . . . telling stories is telling lies . . . I want to tell the truth about my experience . . . to reproduce the moment to moment fragmentariness of my life, and to echo it in technique . . ." Unlike Beckett, Johnson seems to feel it is possible to " tell the truth."

His expressed aims as a novelist are those of the French Nathalie Sarraute, but from the time of *Albert Angelo* Johnson would seem to have moved much further than she has towards abandoning the pretence of writing anything but the most thinly disguised autobiography. It is not simply that he *says* he writes about himself and includes in each of his last three novels such common details as references to a childhood in Hammersmith, but that his writing, particularly in the High Wycombe scenes of *Travl* and in almost the whole of *The Unfortunates*, conveys the *feeling* of vividly remembered personal experience rather than of fiction created upon the basis of such experience.

The difference between such apparently autobiographical novels and Mailer's avowedly documentary *Armies of the Night* (*q.v.*) is primarily formal and stylistic, but also derives from the fact that whereas Johnson writes about " private " life, Mailer reports himself as a participant in affairs of national and international importance.

Travelling People. 1963. Pa.

In this prize-winning farcical comedy Henry, a young hitch-hiker, is given a lift by Trevor, a businessman, who offers him a summer job in the luxury Stromboli Club, on the Welsh coast, which Trevor and a friend run as a hobby.

The novel, whose form has been much influenced by Sterne's *Tristram Shandy*, is written in a variety of styles.

Albert Angelo. 1964. Pa.

Here Johnson's protagonist and *alter ego*, Albert, is an aspiring architect who earns his living as a supply teacher in the Angel area of Islington.

Often hilariously funny, the novel is distinguished by the loving precision with which Johnson captures the atmosphere of London's dilapidated inner suburbs and the skill with which he deploys his fragmentary, " collage " techniques.

Travl. 1966.

An unnamed narrator describes his experience as a winter " pleasure tripper " on a North Sea trawler. As the sailors fish, the writer throws a " trawl net " into the " sea " of his memories. By the end of the three-week voyage he has overcome his chronic sea-sickness (literal and metaphoric), and looks forward to reunion with his girl friend, Ginnie, the Virginia of *Albert Angelo*.

The Unfortunates. 1969.

The first and last sections of this book are fixed, the rest bound in loose-leaf so that readers may shuffle them—which seems a gimmick of small value, but enables those so inclined to rearrange the book into two chronological narratives.

Johnson tells of a Saturday in the life of B. S. Johnson (now married to Ginnie), who goes to a Midland town—clearly recognisable as Nottingham—to report a football match. When a student, Johnson visited the town and university as the guest of two friends, Tony and June, to whom, he says, he dedicated his first novel (as indeed the author did). On this, later visit, he is preoccupied by memories of these friends and of Tony's premature, agonising death.

Doris Lessing (b. 1919).

A Rhodesian by birth, Doris Lessing emigrated to England in 1949. She is probably best known as a novelist, but has also published poems, short stories, and plays.

Her novels explore ways in which people are affected by belonging to minority groups. Her subjects include white Rhodesians and South Africans, members of extreme left-wing political parties, and women who resent the fact that ours is still largely a man's world. The objective sympathy which is so distinguishing a feature of her treatment of the first two subjects occasionally deserts her when she writes about the third.

The Grass is Singing. 1950. P.

In this accomplished first novel, set in South Africa, Doris Lessing writes of the tortured lives of Dick and Mary Turner, isolated members of the White agricultural community, and of their relationships with their African servants.

The Children of Violence—*Martha Quest*, 1952, *A Proper Marriage*, 1954, *A Ripple from the Storm*, 1958, *Landlocked*, 1965 (all Pa), *The Four-Gated City*, 1969.

Reading the first two books of this sequence one is constantly reminded of George Eliot. Not only do both novelists employ similar techniques, but they share an intense concern with problems of morality and ethics. Martha Quest, the novel's passionately idealistic heroine, recalls Dorothea Brooke and Maggie Tulliver, and is presented here with the same kind of objective, ironic sympathy that characterises George Eliot's treatment of Dorothea.

In the third and fourth books, however, the portrayal of Martha is almost overwhelmed in a detailed study of the social and political life of Rhodesia during the Second World War. Fascinating as social documents, from a literary viewpoint these volumes at first seemed less satisfying than the earlier ones, but their function within the whole novel became clear upon the publication of *The Four-Gated City*.

In this volume, which is set in England, the political and social questions of the last twenty years play a prominent part, but Mrs. Lessing now emphasises their effect upon the individual as she depicts the mature Martha's gradual realisation of the ways in which a person's life and personality can be distorted by unquestioning acceptance of an ideology, and how this can lead him to damage others, as well as himself, by denying the importance of individuals and dismissing their intuitive and imaginative insights.

This final volume has an appendix whose action is set in the future, after a series of catastrophies have devastated much of the world. This section reads convincingly, but follows rather awkwardly upon the naturalism of the rest of the novel.

The Golden Note book. 1962. P.

The content of this novel is most interesting but its form is awkward. The first part of each of its sections recounts incidents in the lives of the heroine, Anna, and her friends and acquaintances. The rest of the novel consists of extracts from notebooks, some diaries, some stories, in which Anna, a novelist, writes of her feelings about her work and her experiences as a disillusioned member of the Communist Party and as a divorcee who hopes to remarry.

Malcolm Lowry (1909-57).

Under the Volcano. 1947. P.

Readers of this complex novel, one of the century's finest, should see Lowry's own criticism of it in *Selected Letters*, edited: Breit & Lowry (Cape).

Set in Mexico in 1938 and '39, it relates the tragedy of the alcoholic Geoffrey Firmin and his wife, Yvonne, to the world tragedies of war and man's inhumanity to man.

In his neglected garden—a symbol both of his ruined marriage and of the mutilated world— Firmin stumbles on a broken notice-board. On it are the words:

> " Do you like this garden?
>   Why is it yours?
>   We evict those who destroy! "

words repeated at the end of the novel. They recall two of its central images: Eden, signifying the beauty man discovers in Nature and the beauty he creates in loving human relationships: Hell, signifying the agony he suffers and causes others when he rejects love. Lowry sees man as a splendid, noble creature who must struggle incessantly to control sado-masochistic impulses, which he can restrain only when he loves others and is able to accept their love. "Man cannot live without love," is the novel's main theme.

Firmin is a tragic hero in the tradition of Marlowe's Faustus, to whom the novel's imagery relates him. The objectivity of Lowry's portrayal of the tortured world of addiction is remarkable: Firmin always has our sympathy, rarely approval.

This book is not simply a good story, but a great poem, its themes expressed not only through the events of the narrative, the lives and feelings of the characters, but through vivid descriptions of Mexico and its people, through subtle, complex imagery.

Lowry intended *Under the Volcano* to form one volume of a sequence. The stories in *Hear Us O Lord From Heaven Thy Dwelling Place*, 1962 (P), and the unfinished novels *Lunar Caustic*, 1968, and *Dark as the Grave Wherein My Friend is Laid*, 1969, were to have been incorporated in the other volumes.

Mary McCarthy (b. 1912).

The American journalist and critic Mary McCarthy has published five satirical novels on the lives of American artists and intellectuals: *The Company She Keeps*, 1942 (P); *The Oasis*, 1949 (S); *The Groves of Academe*, 1952 (S); *A Charmed Life*, 1955 (P); *The Group*, 1962 (P). Like Simone de Beauvoir and Doris Lessing, Miss McCarthy is particularly interested in the rôle of the educated woman in twentieth-century society. Parts of her novels are very amusing, but in general they seem too cerebral and anaemic.

Norman Mailer (b. 1923).

Mailer, an American, is a journalist and film-director and the author of one book of verse as well as six novels. He sees life as a battlefield between the forces of good and evil and the motive behind the sensationalism of much of his later work seems to be a desire to shock readers into an awareness of the nature of American society, which he feels is obscene and life-denying. Mailer suggests that the majority of Americans are either becoming cogs in the machines of a brutal, totalitarian "technology land," or taking selfish refuge in drugs and nihilism, instead of accepting the dangers of living adventurously and trying to establish creative relationships. Readers interested in Mailer's social philosophy should refer to *Advertisements for Myself*, 1959; *The Presidential Papers*, 1963; *Cannibals and Christians*, 1966; *Miami and the Siege of Chicago*, 1968.

The Naked and the Dead. 1948. Pa.

Many critics feel this novel constitutes Mailer's most successful expression of his view of the human condition. He regards it as "the work of a young engineer." Its subject is the American troops' capture of a Pacific island from the Japanese, but its interest lies in Mailer's treatment of the power structure within the American force, which is presented as a microcosm of society. The mass of the troops, represented by the soldiers of one platoon, are shown as the all but helpless victims of the men of power— the fascist General Cummings and the Platoon Sergeant, Croft. Between the two groups stands the ineffectual liberal, Lieutenant Hearn.

Mailer paints a remorseless picture of the agony of the ordinary soldier's life and of the absurdity of the war, and is very successful in his treatment of the characters of Cummings and Croft. The weakness of the book lies in his characterisation of the lower ranks. These soldiers are obviously intended to represent a cross-section of American society, but, although using techniques derived from Dos Passos, Mailer gives a biographical sketch of each man in the platoon, none of them is clearly differentiated from the others.

Barbary Shore. 1951.

In this turgid allegory of the Cold War, the amnesiac Lovett finds himself involved in a contest between two secret agents, McLeod and Hollingsworth, for the affections of McLeod's wife, the promiscuous Guinevere.

The Deer Park. 1955. Co.

Mailer planned this novel as the first of eight, whose themes were to cover the whole of American life. This was the only one to be finished. Its theme is pleasure and its title comes from D'Angerville's *Vie privée de Louis XV*, which refers to "the Deer Park, that gorge of innocence and virtue in which were engulfed so many victims . . .". Mailer's Deer Park is Desert D'Or, a fictional pleasure resort near Hollywood.

An American Dream. 1965. M.

Both the title and the wild improbability of this novel's action suggest that Mailer intends it to be read as an allegory, showing the narrator, Rojack, resisting the suicidal lure of nihilism presented by the moon and then escaping from the evil forces of American society, personified in his wife, her father, and her maid. The sexual relationships between the characters would thus have symbolic importance.

The novel has its comic moments, but its style is generally sensational and its language often highly obscene.

Why Are We in Vietnam? 1967. Pa.

D.J., an eighteen-year-old Texan, accompanying his parents at a dinner party shortly before leaving to fight in Vietnam, remembers a hunting trip he and his friend and his father took to Alaska two years before.

This scatological novel suggests, with a measure of success, the confused and distorted values of a society whose motto is "Go out and kill." The book is divided into alternating sections of breathless narrative and hysterical commentary, progressing at a speed which leaves the reader feeling rather stunned, but the chief impression is of the relish and gusto with which Mailer wrote the novel.

The Armies of the Night. 1968. P.

Apparently Mailer's finest work since *The Naked and the Dead*, this is an absorbing and at times highly comic reconstruction of the events of the Peace March on the Pentagon in October 1967. It is written in two sections. In the first the protagonist is Mailer himself, described objectively in the third person. In the second part we are helped to understand the motives and feelings of other marchers and the fears of the police and troops who confronted them. The book is notable for its objectivity and humour.

Bernard Malamud (b. 1914).

Malamud's name is often coupled with that of his compatriot Bellow. They have a common Jewish heritage. Malamud's novels are similar in theme to those of Bellow, but his writing is less exuberant. Both men show a keen appreciation of natural beauty, rare in American novelists.

The Natural. 1952. P.

As Earl Wassermann has noted, the events of this novel have a factual basis and its theme is that of the Arthurian regeneration myth. However, this story of a baseball player lacks artistic unity and its hero is never fully convincing.

The Assistant. 1957. P.

Here Malamud found a much more fruitful subject, the quiet tragedy of Morris Bober, an unsuccessful Jewish grocer and, of his Gentile assistant, Frank Alpine. For the sake of Bober and of the latter's daughter, Helen, Alpine, who has made many "false starts" in life, gives up what may well be his last hope of achieving material success. The novel is written with beautiful restraint and Chekhovian irony.

A New Life. 1961. FS. P.

Levin, a reformed drunkard, obtains an English post at a small state college, but eventually sacrifices his hard-won chance of an academic career for the sake of the woman he has loved.

The novel is set in the early 1950s, the period of McCarthyism. Malamud criticises the hysteria pervading American life at this time, exemplified in the academic and social atmosphere of Cascadia College, where Levin, a man of liberal principles, suffers from his colleagues' fears and prejudices.

A New Life is less concentrated than *The Assistant*. It contains elements of picaresque comedy and is at times very amusing, though occasionally its tone seems frivolous and inappropriate.

The Fixer. 1966. P.

Yakov Bok is, like Levin, a victim of hysterical feelings of national insecurity. A Jewish odd-job-man—a fixer—he leaves the Pale Settlement for Kiev, hoping to begin a new, more fruitful life, but is arrested on a trumped-up charge and endures three terrible years' imprisonment awaiting trial.

The inspiration of the novel was the case of Mendel Beiliss, a Kiev labourer arrested in 1911, and falsely charged with the ritual murder of a Christian child. Malamud says the novel is intended to stand "rather as a myth than an isolated case-study." But it lacks the compelling force of myth.

Pictures of Fidelman. 1969.

Parts of this book were published in slightly different forms in Malamud's collections of short stories *The Magic Barrel*, 1958 (P) and *Idiots First*, 1963 (P). It is an episodic work containing six "pictures" on the career of a would-be artist, Arthur Fidelman, who goes to Italy to study the work of Giotto, but soon abandons this project in order to make further attempts to discover where his own talent as an artist lies.

This is an uneven work, but enjoyable for its humour, which is derived as much from Malamud's style as from the ludicrous situations in which he places Fidelman. The best "pictures" are those entitled *The Last Mohoican* and *Portraits of the Artist.* The latter contains an hilarious account of Fidelman as a sculptor of holes.

Iris Murdoch (b. 1919).

A philosophy don, Iris Murdoch has published thirteen novels, the latest being *A Fairly Honourable Defeat*, 1970. A sympathetic study of her work has been written by A. S. Byatt.

Technically, Miss Murdoch's experiments in fiction bear a superficial resemblance to T. S. Eliot's experiments in drama (*see* Sec. I.). Eliot sought, by means of poetic ritual, to give expression to the ultimate themes of man's search for truth and of the conflict between forces of good and evil, and from the time of *The Cocktail Party* he sought to embody his rituals within the conventions of the well-made play. Miss Murdoch seems to be trying to combine ritualistic actions and the conventions of undemanding popular fiction. Despite their sophisticated veneer, few of her novels rise far above the level of this popular mode. All her earlier novels have moments of poetic intensity and beauty, such as the description of Rainborough's feelings as he gazes at a snail, in *The Flight From the Enchanter*, 1956, (P), of Dora's releasing a butterfly, in *The Bell*, 1958 (P), and in the evocation of fog-bound east London, in *Time of The Angels*, 1966 (P), but in her latest book the use of such poetic symbols degenerates into mannerism when she describes the heroine (Morgan)'s, pursuit of a pigeon in Piccadilly Underground Station.

Her first tale, *Under the Net*, 1955 (P), an amusing exitentialist fantasy that recalls Beckett's *Murphy*, remains Miss Murdoch's most satisfying novel. The recent *Bruno's Dream*, 1969, which contains a splendid portrait of old age in the character of Bruno, suggested that her latest book might bring the flowering of her undoubted talents, but *A Fairly Honourable Defeat* proved disappointing.

It shows how the complacent lives of the two liberal progressives, Rupert and Hilda Foster, are shattered by the intrusion of Hilda's younger sister, Morgan, and Morgan's former lover, the amoral Julian. Like Morgan le Fay, this Morgan is an enchantress and together she and Julian destroy Rupert. The greater part of this novel is written in dialogue which is extremely difficult to follow at times, as only one of the characters, and he a minor one, has an individual voice. Perhaps, like *A Severed Head*, 1961 (P), which it resembles, *A Fairly Honourable Defeat* will be adapted for the stage, which would highlight the comic elements of its bizarre narrative.

Vladimir Nabokov (b. 1899).

A Russian by birth, Nabokov came to England during the Revolution, subsequently lived in Germany and France and emigrated to America in 1940.

Translations of his early novels are now becoming available. Those he has written in English

include *Lolita*, 1955 (Co), *Pnin*, 1957, *Pale Fire*, 1962 (Co), *Ada*, 1969. The first of these gained notoriety among the ill-informed who imagined it was pornographic. Nothing could be further from the truth.

Nabokov is a learned writer. His humour, wit, and above all his masterly use of language, make his novels a constant source of delight.

V. S. Naipaul (b. 1932).

This distinguished Caribbean novelist was born in Trinidad of Indian parents. The heroes of all his novels are men who feel an urgent need to give their lives order and significance. Thus although most of his work has a Caribbean setting, its themes are of world-wide interest. Naipaul began as a writer of comedy and all his novels have a comic element although his work has become increasingly sombre in tone as it has increased in complexity.

The Mystic Masseur. 1957. P.

In this delightful comedy of Colonial politics, Naipaul shows the metamorphosis of Ganesh Ramsumair, an insignificant, semi-educated Indian, into G. Ramsey Muir, M.B.E., respected Colonial statesman.

The Suffrage of Elvira. 1958 P.

It was not until a few months before the second General Election in the Elvira constituency of Trinidad that "people began to see the possibilities." Neighbours' feuds, practical jokes, bribery, black magic and marriage-broking all play parts in this campaign, which has an ill-omened beginning for Naipaul's endearing protagonist, Harbans, when he nearly runs over two Jehovah's Witnesses and a black dog! However, after a costly and nerve-wracking campaign, he wins the coveted seat on the island's Legislative Council.

A House for Mr. Biswas. 1961. Fo. P.

This sad story tells of Mr. Biswas's search for independence and security. Inveigled into early marriage, he finds he is expected to become a submissive appendage of his mother-in-law's enormous household. Biswas has no intention of playing this rôle, but he is not a practical man and has little formal education and no trade, so that his first two attempts to establish himself independently soon fail. At last, in his early forties, he manages to buy a house, but dies soon afterwards.

Naipaul makes us feel the dreadful tensions and frustrations of family life in overcrowded conditions where there is never any privacy, but despite its sad theme, the novel is often very funny, for Biswas is an imaginative man who delights in colourful language and has a flair for picturesque invective. His touching pride in his children's intelligence and his growing love and respect for his wife are most sensitively portrayed.

Mr. Stone and the Knights Companion. 1963. FS.

The elderly Mr. Stone is filled with despair at the prospect of his impending retirement. Then he suddenly conceives the idea that active pensioners of his firm should visit the disabled. Organising this scheme gives him new hope and vigour and although these fade the novel ends on a note of subdued confidence.

The Mimic Men. 1967. P.

Singh, the narrator of this fascinating novel, is an exiled politician from a newly independent Caribbean state. Singh analyses the events of his life, which he convincingly suggests is representative of those of all Colonial politicians. Thrust suddenly into power, they are compelled to destroy the former pattern of administration and, having no traditions to guide them, nor any experience of government, inevitably become "mimic-men."

Flannery O'Connor (1925–64).

The work of this novelist and short-story writer from the Southern States of America has a growing reputation in her own country, although it is less well known in England and has until very recently been difficult to obtain.

Flannery O'Connor published two novels, *Wise Blood*, 1952, and *The Violent Bear it Away*, 1960. She writes in a poetic, ruthlessly comic style about isolated eccentrics afflicted with religious mania, who evolve their own grotesque, fundamentalist creeds.

George Orwell (1903–50).

Orwell's post-war novels express feelings apparent in his earlier journalism.

Animal Farm. 1945. P.

The theme of this satirical fable is the futility of popular revolutions. Led by the pigs, the animals of Manor Farm evict their brutal owners. However, one of the pigs, Napoleon, gains absolute power, establishing a police state. The animals are worse off than before.

1984. 1949. P.

This grim nightmare, which Orwell wished to call *1948*—his publisher dissuaded him—develops the ideas of *Animal Farm* in a vision of a totalitarian world whose rulers exploit psychological and technological discoveries to retain and consolidate power.

As a novel it is less successful than *Animal Farm*. It has not the latter's occasional humour, and the presentation of its villain, O'Brien, is unconvincing. Raymond Williams's *Culture and Society* (P) sympathetically relates the novel to Orwell's paradoxical feelings about socialism.

Anthony Powell (b. 1905).

Powell published five novels in the 1930s. The elegance of his style and the fact that he took a comic view of upper- and middle-class society led to his comparison with Waugh.

His sixth work, *A Dance to the Music of Time*, is planned as a set of four trilogies. Ten volumes so far have appeared: *A Question of Upbringing*, 1951, *A Buyer's Market*, 1952, *The Acceptance World*, 1955, *At Lady Molly's* 1957 (all Fon), *Casanova's Chinese Restaurant*, 1960, *The Kindly Ones*, 1962, *The Valley of Bones*, 1964, *The Soldier's Art*, 1966, *The Military Philosophers*, 1968, *Books Do Furnish a Room*, 1971.

In this poetic novel Powell is clearly influenced by Proust. His narrator, Nicholas Jenkins, imagines the passage of time as a formal dance in which people appear and reappear unexpectedly and in surprising combinations. This is the novel's central image.

Jenkins, an extremely intelligent, thoughtful man, is a connoisseur of pictures and a novelist vividly aware of the limitations of our knowledge of others, even of our closest friends, and of the dangers of forming stereotyped ideas of people. He has an insatiable desire to understand what motivates human action, particularly how we are influenced by the thirst for power and by a love of adventure. Jenkin's gradual realisation of the complexity of life is expressed poetically through the references to paintings: as a young man he is usually drawn to Renaissance and Baroque works with classical subjects; as he becomes " less ascetic, intellectually speaking more corrupt per-

haps," and recognises that " individuals live in different ways," that " all human beings . . . seen at close range are equally extraordinary," he refers increasingly to paintings of other periods.

The novel, whose action opens in the early 1920s, with a flashback to 1914, and has now reached the period following the second world war, contains an enormous range and variety of characters. Each volume introduces new figures.

Powell has the most sensitive ear for nuances of speech. His novel, leisurely, but never dull, contains passages of brilliant comedy.

Alan Sillitoe (b. 1928).

Sillitoe's first book, *Saturday Night and Sunday Morning*, 1958 (Pan) is among the better of a number of novels of working-class life which appeared in the late 1950s and early '60s. Others include Keith Waterhouse's *There is a Happy Land*, 1957 (P), *Billy Liar*, 1959 (P), Barstow's *A Kind of Loving*, 1960 (P), and David Storey's *Flight into Camden*, 1960 (P).

Arthur Seaton, the hero of Sillitoe's novel, is a belligerent young worker in a Nottingham bicycle factory. He sees life as a continual battle for survival and feels particular hostility towards the forces of " the Establishment ". Seaton's hero is Boris Karloff, but his deepest satisfaction comes from a quiet day's fishing and a country walk with his girl friend.

The novel is uneven in quality, but its occasionally cheap and sensational language appropriately suggests the influence of Seaton's favourite films, and much of the dialogue is vigorously realistic. The rural scenes reflect the influence of Lawrence, who also came from Nottinghamshire.

Saturday Night and Sunday Morning was followed in 1959 by a volume of stories containing a fine *nouvelle*, *The Loneliness of the Long-Distance Runner*, which gives the book its title. Sillitoe's later novels, which have been generally less favourably received by critics, include *The General*, 1960, *The Death of William Posters*, 1965 (both Pan), *A Tree on Fire*, 1967, *A Start in Life*, 1970.

C. P. Snow (b. 1905).

Strangers and Brothers—11 vols. 1940–70. P.

In the course of this sequence the narrator, Lewis Eliot, rises from humble beginnings to success at the Bar, at Cambridge, and in the Administrative Civil Service. While this is clearly not an autobiographical work, the course of Snow's own career as a scientist, don, and civil servant has followed a similar pattern.

One of the strengths of these volumes derives from the fact that Eliot is an unprejudiced observer of his friends' and colleagues' behaviour. We feel he prefers some men to others, but rarely does he judge any of them.

The volumes follow no strict chronology and only two, *A Time of Hope* and *Homecomings*, are concerned directly with Eliot's personal life. The other books of the sequence are each centred on the life of one of Eliot's friends or acquaintances. The best of them all is *The Masters*, where an account of the election of the Master of a Cambridge college becomes an image of political life. The other volumes have a less perfect form and vary in quality, but all are of documentary interest in that they deal with such subjects as the making of the first atomic bomb and the painful decisions in which scientists and civil servants were involved at that time.

Wole Soyinka (b. 1934). *See also* **Section I.**

The Yoruba poet and dramatist Soyinka has published one novel, which has lately been awarded the *New Statesman's* triennial prize for African and Caribbean fiction.

The Interpreters. 1965. Pa.

In this original, highly enjoyable novel, Soyinka writes about a group of young Nigerian artists and intellectuals. The narrative is arranged in " solo " and " choral " sections, now reflecting the experience of individuals, now that of the group. The work has two main themes, which are expressed through complex symbols. The first is the characters' struggle to discover and express the relationship between their traditional culture and contemporary Nigerian society. The second is the need for a fearless commitment to the search for truth. Soyinka includes some highly comic episodes and sketches of dishonest and selfish people. Particularly memorable are an encounter with a German reporter, who likes to pretend he is American, a party given by the Oguazors, an ignorant, snobbish Nigerian don and his wife, and the ridiculous behaviour of Faseyi, who accuses his charming wife of behaving like " a bush-girl from a London slum." Soyinka takes a poet's delight in vivid and inventive use of words and is particularly skilful in his treatment of comic dialogue.

Muriel Spark (b. 1918).

Since the appearance of her first *nouvelle, The Comforters* (P), in 1957, Mrs. Spark has published eight others, the latest being *The Driver's Seat,* 1970. She has also written one full-length novel *The Mandelbaum Gate,* 1965 (P), short stories, a play, verse, and critical works.

Mrs. Spark is an entertaining writer likely to be enjoyed particularly for the tart economy of her language and for her keen observation of absurd and grotesque behaviour and speech, but most of her work is slight and *The Mandelbaum Gate* suggests that she is indeed unable to treat characters or themes in depth or at any length.

Her early *nouvelles* are strange mixtures of comedy of manners and surrealist fantasy, her later tales melodramatic rather than surrealist. Most of them illustrate Mrs. Spark's interest in violent death, a subject she sometimes treats with naïve callousness. Her most satisfying work to date seems *Memento Mori,* 1957 (P), which chronicles the reactions of a group of elderly people to mysterious telephone calls telling them to " remember you must die." Only in this book and, to a lesser extent, in *The Prime of Miss Jean Brodie,* 1961 (P), does Mrs. Spark show much imaginative sympathy for human weakness. However, Professor Kermode has suggested that her three books *The Prime of Miss Jean Brodie, The Girls of Slender Means,* 1963 (P), and *The Mandelbaum Gate,* " add up to the most distinguished achievement of any British novelist since the war," and perhaps those of us who would question this opinion have not yet learnt to appreciate Mrs. Spark's techniques.

William Styron (b. 1925).

A native of Virginia, one of the former slave states, Styron is particularly concerned with the theme of slavery as an emotional or spiritual condition. He implies that it is responsible for the immaturity, brutality, and ugliness of much American life and suggests that it stems primarily from the Americans' heritage of militant, repressive, and self-righteous Puritanism.

Styron's weakness is his tendency to illustrate rather than to explore his novels' themes and many of his characters are too cerebrally conceived, yet even in *Set This House on Fire,* his least successful work, Styron remains an impressive novelist. The architecture of his books,

three of which are very long, is most skilful and all his work is illumined by a poetic gift for capturing the atmosphere of an event or scene and embodying fleeting visual impressions in vivid, precise images.

Lie Down in Darkness. 1948. Co.

The events of this novel take place on the day of Peyton Loftis's funeral, but most of the book consists of long flashbacks through which we learn about the lives of Peyton and her unhappy parents and come to understand why she committed suicide.

Styron implies that the Loftises' story is symbolic of life in the southern States and that the latter is itself a paradigm of American life in general. However, the novel does not sustain the weight of this interpretation, for although the characters arouse our pity they never attain the stature of representative tragic figures that such a theme demands. Nevertheless, this is a remarkable novel to have been produced by a writer of twenty-three. Its strength comes from Styron's gift for presenting individual scenes, illustrated in the novel's brilliant opening paragraphs and in episodes such as the account of Peyton's wedding.

The Long March. 1952. P.

The narrative of this very short book gives an account of the relationships between two Marines, recalled for service during the Korean war, with which they have no sympathy, and their Colonel, a regular officer, whose avoidance of any sign of emotion has earned him the sobriquet of Old Rocky. Here Styron writes of the slavery of military life and the corruption and brutality it engenders, but his underlying theme is the dilemma of liberals, who " born into a generation of conformists " are thus " trapped in a predicament which personal insurrection could, if anything, only make worse," and yet to acquiesce in it would be to become, " like cannibals, hardly men at all." The passion with which Styron expresses this dilemma makes *The Long March* his masterpiece.

Set This House on Fire. 1960

Themes from the previous books are here combined with a sweeping condemnation of the " moral and spiritual anarchy " of contemporary American life, but the novel remains essentially a *roman a thèse* and of the three main characters only Kinsolving, a drunken artist and ex-soldier, becomes more than a blueprint, and even so the parallels Styron suggests between him and Oedipus seem grotesquely inappropriate. Nevertheless, the novel is well worth reading for its incidental poetry. It contains brilliant evocations of the beauty of the Italian countryside and of rural Virginia, the hideousness of American cities and the langour of New York on a Spring Sunday.

The Confessions of Nat Turner. 1967.

This is an imaginative reconstruction of the life of the leader of an abortive slave rebellion. The story is told in the first person as Nat, awaiting trial, looks back over the events of his life and explains why he decided to murder his White masters. Nat himself is not a fully convincing figure, but minor characters are, and Styron is particularly successful in his portrayal of the liberal Judge Cobb, whose predicament recalls that of the marines in *The Long March.*

William Trevor (b. 1928)

Trevor's most recent novel, *Mrs. Eckdorf in O'Neill's Hotel,* appeared in 1969. It tells how the neurotic Mrs. Eckdorf, a professional photographer searching for material of " human interest ", is led to the run-down O'Neill's Hotel in Dublin. Here, she finds a source of comfort and, she believes, true goodness in Mrs. Sinnot, the deaf and dumb nonagenarian proprietress, who loves and accepts people for themselves, and avoids making any attempt to manipulate or coerce them.

This novel is a development from Trevor's early bizarre comedies, *The Old Boys*, 1964, *The Boarding House*, 1965, and *The Love Department*, 1966 (all P). Like them it is written with delightful elegance and precision, but, whereas in the earlier books Trevor sometimes seemed a rather callous observer of humanity, in *Mrs. Eckdorf in O'Neill's Hotel* he imparts a sense of sympathetic understanding of even his least attractive characters.

John Updike (b. 1932).

Updike, a novelist and short story writer from Pennsylvania, has a genuine and congenial talent for recreating the atmosphere and daily life of rural New England. His early ambition was to be a painter and he retains an artist's eye for precise visual detail, but, unlike Jane Austen, another "miniaturist" of country life, Updike seems to lack a sense of his own limitations as a novelist. He sometimes spoils his work by decorating it with superfluous symbols and fails when he ventures outside the rural American scene which is the source of his inspiration.

The Poorhouse Fair. 1958. P.

Set in an old people's home on the day of its annual fair, this short novel creates a vivid impression of life in the "poorhouse" and of the characters of its inmates and its unimaginative and ambitious young director.

Rabbit Run. 1960. P.

At twenty-six "Rabbit" Angstrom still lives in the imaginative world of his schoolboy triumphs at baseball and flees from his responsibilities to his wife, children and mistress.

Again Updike vividly evokes the atmosphere and scenes of his story and his minor characters are convincingly sketched. The novel's weakness derives from its author's ambiguous attitude towards his protagonist.

The Centaur. 1963. P.

The prize-winning *The Centaur*, which covers two days in the lives of a schoolmaster and his son, displays Updike's greatest strengths and weaknesses. Alternating chapters of the narrative are written like those of a conventional realistic novel. They are vivid and highly comic. In the other chapters all characters are referred to by names drawn from classical myth and, apart from the two main characters, who are always referred to as Chiron and Prometheus, these names are inconsistently applied and serve merely to confuse. As Arthur Mizener has remarked, the realistic sections of the book are so well written that they cannot be connected "in any but the most sterile and mechanical ways" with this mythological superstructure.

Of the Farm. 1965. P.

Here Updike reverts to the wholly realistic manner of his early novels to evoke the tensions which arise when Joey, accompanied by his new, second wife and her son, visits his possessive, elderly mother, who, singlehanded, runs the family farm.

Couples. 1968. P.

This is a sad comedy of the boredom of the lives of a group of middle-class couples who have "retreated" to the country, a boredom they relieve only by sports and frivolous sexual encounters, and are therefore shocked when two of their number have a serious "affair" and are repudiated by their respective partners.

As in Updike's earlier novels, the details of everyday life are beautifully captured, but here his central characters are rather flatly drawn.

Bech: A Book. 1970.

Like Malamud's *Pictures of Fidelman* (q.v.), which it palely resembles, parts of this book have already appeared as short stories. Bech, the protagonist, is a writer on a cultural tour and each chapter finds him in a different country. However, Updike seems to have taken small pains to coordinate these stories and, although parts of the book are amusing, the total impression is of a rather careless pot-boiler.

Evelyn Waugh (1902–66).

Waugh's style is elegant and his novels are often amusing, but they are generally superficial and marred by cruelty and distasteful snobbery. A popular writer of the 1930s, he published nine novels after the War.

The Sword of Honour trilogy (pub. in 3 vols., *Men at Arms*, 1952, *Officers and Gentlemen*, 1955, *Unconditional Surrender*, 1961 (all P), revised and reissued as one book 1965).

Waugh's best novel, this chronicles the experiences of Guy Crouchback during the Second World War. Crouchback welcomes the War, which he feels will give his life the direction and purpose it has lacked since his wife deserted him. The first two volumes of the trilogy give a convincing impression of administrative incompetence during the early stages of the War and are occasionally very funny, but they share the cruelty and snobbery of Waugh's other writing.

The third volume is much better. Crouchback, a cardboard figure until now, comes alive and, in a moving encounter with a refugee woman, is forced to admit he became a soldier in order to evade the difficulties of his personal life, and that he, and others like him, were as responsible as the "enemy" for the horrors of the War.

Patrick White (b. 1912).

White, an Australian, was educated in England, where he took a degree in modern languages, and has travelled widely in Europe and America. He is the author of plays and short stories as well as eight novels.

The first of these, *Happy Valley*, 1939, is now unobtainable, and White seems to regard it as worthless; his second, *The Living and the Dead*, 1941 (P), is an uneven novel, much influenced by the writing of Virginia Woolf, but already displaying the extraordinary combination of visionary intensity and brilliant social comedy which characterises his post-war novels: *The Aunt's Story*, 1948; *The Tree of Man*, 1955; *Voss*, 1957; *Riders in the Chariot*, 1961; *The Solid Mandala*, 1966 (all P); *The Vivisector*, 1970.

Like Golding's novels these are essentially religious poems, but whereas Golding, except in *The Spire*, concentrates on man's loss of grace, White is more concerned with his experience of awareness of "the God above God", who is both immanent and mysteriously transcendent. His vision of life, as reflected in these novels, is similar to that expressed by the existentialist theologian Tillich, (v. *The Courage to Be*, Fo, etc.).

White suggests that the "conformism" of civilised life is inimical to goodness, and exemplifies this in his treatment of the suburb Sarsaparilla, the setting of *The Solid Mandala* and of parts of most of his other novels, one of his plays and several stories. The life of Sarsaparilla is presented variously as comic, sterile, hypocritical, cruel and evil. It is almost always hideous and invariably pitiful.

White's main characters are regarded by most of their acquaintances as odd, or stupid, or mad. They are generally avoided, and often feared and attacked, because their essential innocence presents an intolerable challenge to the self-protective conformism of "normal" people. Notable exceptions are the tragic Nietzschian "superman" Voss and Waldo, one of the two main characters of *The Solid Mandala*, who is isolated by his own ignorance and pride.

All White's heroes and heroines suffer greatly, and some die, but, except in *Voss*, he does not imply that suffering is a necessary condition of goodness, but rather that it is its inevitable concomitant. Joy returns to those who survive, for, all these novels emphasise, though good must endure evil, it never yields to it.

Another of the novels' recurrent themes is the difficulty of communication. White's heroes and heroines have the gift of profound empathetic communion but even the most educated of them find it all but impossible to articulate their experiences of joy and suffering. Most of them try to express themselves in other ways, in painting, music, dance and, increasingly, through a wordless, selfless love for people.

Like that of all major writers, White's style is highly individual and makes challenging demands upon his readers. His idiosyncratic punctuation and, in *The Tree of Man*, his frequent use of "verbless sentences," seem attempts to reflect his characters' fumbling for understanding and expression of their experiences. Sometimes White makes no obvious distinction between his characters' expression of feeling and his own comment upon that expression. In *The Aunt's Story*, such interplay between his own and his character's viewpoint is at times confusing, but in subsequent novels his increasing mastery of technique adds to the subtle, allusive qualities of his style. White takes a poet's delight in the metaphorical ambiguity of words. He is a master of ironic bathos and epigrammatic wit.

To symbolise his main characters' quests for understanding and their progress towards it, White uses the age-old symbols of The Explorer, Traveller, Artist and Wise Simpleton. Other figures who repeatedly occur in his novels are a laundress, a harridan mother and a physically deformed spinster.

His finest novels, *The Tree of Man*, *Voss* and *Riders in the Chariot*, are those inspired by archetypal legends: the stories of the Creation and Fall (*The Tree of Man*), the expedition of the explorer Ludwig Leichardt (*Voss*), and the Crucifixion (*Riders in the Chariot*).

White's novels are by no means faultless. Sometimes his style seems self-conscious, at others emptily rhetorical. Occasionally his symbolism is clumsy and in his last two novels there is a general loss of momentum, combined in *The Solid Mandala* with what seems like gratuitous violence. Nevertheless, White remains one of the most rewarding, if also one of the most demanding of contemporary novelists. Each of his books is extremely complex. To write of them so briefly is to deal summary justice.

Angus Wilson (b. 1913).

Although now best known as a novelist, Wilson first made his name with a volume of short stories, *The Wrong Set*, 1949 (P). He has since published two other collections of stories and a play, as well as six novels.

Wilson is an admirer of Jane Austen and at times the style of *Hemlock and After* is reminiscent of that of her novels. He has also long admired the writings of Zola and Dickens, on which he has published critical studies, and recently he has expressed his growing appreciation for the techni-

cal skill of Virginia Woolf, an appreciation which is apparent in his latest novel, *No Laughing Matter*.

A serious comic novelist, Wilson is merciless in exposing snobbery, hypocrisy, and self-deception. However, he does not always achieve artistic transformation of his material. Thus, although some of the finest parts of his work are in dialogue, some of his virtual conversations are as painful to read as they would be to endure in reality. Like Zola and Dickens, Wilson is horrified, yet fascinated by cruelty and vulgarity. He has been called "morbid" by some critics. There are certainly times, especially in *The Old Men at the Zoo* when the charge seems justified. But Wilson can also be deliciously funny, as in his account of the Historical Association meeting (*Anglo-Saxon Attitudes*).

His chief technical fault is a tendency to overload his novels with characters he has no time to develop. His best works seem to be *The Middle Age of Mrs. Eliot* and *Late Call*; in both his cast is limited. Some of the minor characters, particularly working-class ones, appear caricatures, and variations of the same types recur from one book to another. Wilson is, nevertheless, a writer of immense vitality. Each of his novels is quite unlike the others, although they have certain common themes.

Obviously aware of the stresses imposed by the political and social problems of our century, Wilson was the first contemporary English novelist to write frankly of the homosexual "underworld."

Hemlock and After, 1953 (P), *Anglo-Saxon Attitudes*, 1956 (P), *The Middle Age of Mrs. Eliot*, 1958 (P), *Late Call*, 1964.

Each of these novels opens with the hero or heroine facing a crisis which compels him (her) to reassess his (her) adequacy as a person and in relation to others. Each endures considerable mental suffering. Bernard Sands, the novelist hero of the first book, dies before he can rebuild his life. Geoffrey Middleton, historian, connoisseur of pictures (*Anglo-Saxon Attitudes*), Meg Eliot, widow of a successful barrister, and Sylvia Calvert, retired hotel manageress (*Late Call*), each, in quite different ways, comes to find purpose and meaning in life.

Conversely, Meg's brother, David, who has also suffered bereavement, withdraws to the "petty isolation" of his market garden. David is the most fully drawn of the several figures in Wilson's novels who indulge in ritual self-denial, instead of facing facts (cf. Inge, *Anglo-Saxon Attitudes*; Susan, *No Laughing Matter*).

The Old Men at the Zoo. 1961. P.

A political satire, the novel abounds in images of brutality and sadism. At the beginning of the book, the narrator, Simon Carter, Administrator of the London Zoo, seems more imaginative and sensitive than his colleagues, but he becomes increasingly cold-blooded. The novel is an exploration of megalomania. Each of the Zoo's successive Directors is obsessed with putting his own pet schemes into practice and ruthlessly exploits his colleagues and the animals in his care, all of whom he regards as objects to be manipulated. The book closes, at the end of a British-European war, with Simon's canvassing his own appointment to the Directorship.

No Laughing Matter. 1967.

This ambitious, extremely long novel, written in a variety of styles and containing a short story and several plays, presents a panorama of twentieth-century life. Ultimately, it seems to fail, because, since the narrative is divided among the lives of the six Matthews children and their parents, constantly shifting from one to another, none of the characters is fully realised.

II. TWENTIETH CENTURY POETRY

This section does not profess to be a full account of the poetry of the current century, as that would not be possible within the present compass. The aim is rather to touch upon some aspects of the poetry and to suggest ways of approaching it.

I. INTRODUCTION.

The Poem as an Art Form expressive of Feeling.

There is no short cut to the enjoyment of poetry. The only approach is an attentive reading, poem by poem, remembering always that the poet is attempting to express personal *feeling* through a pattern of words, in which their order, their associations, and their verbal music are all of the utmost significance.

Coleridge described poetry as a more than usual feeling with more than usual order, and the reader may like to turn to the paragraph on the function of dramatic art (**I3**) where reference is made to Susanne Langer's thesis that art gives form to our feeling response to life. By this is meant not only emotion as distinct from reason, but the whole gamut of our response to life as human beings—what it *feels* like to use the senses, to have emotions, even what it feels like to think.

Such feeling response cannot adequately be conveyed by logical discourse. How often we hear the phrases "I mean", "You know", from speakers who implicitly acknowledge that they are incapable of "expressing the inexpressible" through the medium of prose discourse and must rely on the sensitivity of their hearer to interpret their feeling. The artist's task is to translate the inarticulate cry into significant images, patterns and forms which convey their import with precision and beauty.

It is perhaps easier for us to see how the painter, the sculptor, or the musician can do this, and how, like Henry Moore, they may resolutely refuse to say what their work "means," for to limit it to "meaning" is to divert attention from its unique value, its numinous feeling quality. But the poet in his subtle and difficult art must use as his material words and grammatical structures which themselves have meaning from which they cannot be divorced. Although possible meanings of individual phrases must be established, the modern literary critic eschews any attempt to state what the poem as a whole "means." He attempts rather to "explicate" the poem, to unfold its hidden implications, to make clear its significance as a whole. We must remember first and foremost that a poet normally uses words not literally, but with a figurative meaning. He loves to speak of one thing as if it were another. The best approach is first to read the poem as a whole and then re-read it with particular attention for the special import of the individual figures of speech.

Special Difficulties of Twentieth-century Poetry.

Poetry of the current century presents the reader with special difficulties. Hitherto, however strange or elaborate the imagery, in most poems prosaic statements and a rational framework could be discerned, but from about 1910 even these were often discarded, so that an even greater receptivity is demanded of the reader.

Drastic Social Changes in the Era between the Wars.

For a fuller understanding of modern poetry we should return to the vital period between the wars, when the masters, Yeats and Eliot, were developing new insights and techniques and setting standards which have not since been equalled.

Inevitably the poetry of the time reflected contemporary changes in society. The Georgian Books of Verse, 1911–22, illustrate how the familiar rural tradition was becoming outworn and it was now to be maintained by only a few poets, Hardy being the most distinguished and influential. For England was fast becoming a predominantly urban society and the imagery of the countryside, inevitably used by Shakespeare, Wordsworth, and Keats, was becoming no longer relevant, sometimes incomprehensible to the town-dweller.

In France, fifty years earlier, Baudelaire (1821–67) had drawn inspiration from the city, both in his preoccupations and in his imagery. In England it was the genius and originality of Ezra Pound (b. 1885) and T. S. Eliot (1888–1965), with their highly original experiments in theme and style, who now gave direction to a new kind of poetry, urban, sophisticated, and cosmopolitan.

Other social factors had their influence. The horror and futility of the First World War, the Communist revolution, the economic slump, the decline in religious faith, the discoveries of Freud, all contributed to the collapse of the old stable sureties and left poets profoundly shaken and searching for new values and effective modes of expression.

Pound, Eliot, and W. B. Yeats (1865–1939) all repudiated the current bourgeois values of wealth and worldly success, which with the rapid growth of industry, commerce and advertising were becoming ever more deeply entrenched. Stigmatised by Matthew Arnold in *Culture and Anarchy* as "Philistine" in 1869, they are the corrosives of art and cause the poet to feel out of sympathy with society.

Pound and Eliot, and later William Empson (b. 1906) consciously directed their poetry to a select minority. Intellectual and satirical, it makes no appeal to facile emotion. The familiar metres and rhymes have been discarded. The elliptical syntax, the complex organisation of the imagery, the erudite references to other cultures, all make demands. A phrase like Pound's "His Penelope was Flaubert" is not immediately clear. Such poetry is not intended to be lapped up by a complacent bourgeoisie.

Another aspect of the new style was indifference to accepted canons of "respectability", in subject and in diction, a candour about sex (encouraged by the work of Freud), and the use of vernacular and slang, which in the Sixties sometimes degenerated into scurrility.

Aesthetic influences.

(a) *The development of the romantic aesthetic*

One of the prime causes of the change in poetic method is not social but aesthetic, the clarification and evolution of the Romantic concept of poetry.

In *Romantic Image*, Frank Kermode has pointed out that from the time of Coleridge there has been a growing conviction in writers such as Keats, Blake, Pater, and Yeats that the artist, in whom the powers of imagination are allied with a passionate sensibility, has a special quality of apprehension and expresses his intuitions in a unique way. The work of art, according to this theory, is original, essentially whole in itself, an "aesthetic monad" and resists analysis into form and content. Without ulterior purpose or utility, its only *raison d'être* is "to be." The image, Coleridge insisted, is essentially "vital", not mechanistic but organic, and it has itself been presented by organic images, notably that of the tree and the dancer.

(b) *The French Symbolists*

In his *Axel's Castle*, 1931, Edmund Wilson discussed the aims of the French Symbolists and their stimulus to English writers, including Yeats and Eliot.

The Symbolist leader, Stephane Mallarmé, attempted to create a new idiom for poetry. Supremely disinterested, a "saint of literature", he wrote little himself, but at his modest weekly receptions he gently expounded his influential views to such visitors as Whistler, Degas, Laforgue, Valéry, Claudel, Gide, Wilde, George Moore, Yeats, and Debussy.

Influenced by Poe, Mallarmé cultivated in his poetry a suggestive indefiniteness, blurring the distinctions between the actual world and that of dream and reverie. Debussy's well-known translation into music of his *L'Après-midi d'un Faune* wonderfully conveys his evocative and amorphous imagery.

Like Poe, the Symbolists were much concerned to reproduce in their poetry the flow of music and they were much influenced by Wagner. They came even to discard the classical Alexandrine and to develop *vers libre*. In the cult of indefiniteness they would, like Poe, confuse the perceptions of the senses. Poe, for instance, "hears" the oncoming of darkness.

What was the purpose of these experiments in poetic language? The Symbolists were so much preoccupied with the unique quality of individual experience, and with the complex and evanescent nature of consciousness, that they eschewed anything so commonplace as a description or statement as a falsification of experience and endeavoured, instead, to express unique and transitory feelings by suggestive images and symbols fastidiously chosen and patterned with exquisite care. The time-honoured rational framework of poetry was being scrapped so that it was becoming irrelevant to speak of the "meaning" of a poem.

(c) *The problem of objective validity in symbolist art*

The symbolism was not of the commonly accepted kind, such as the dove with the olive branch. Each poet deployed a highly idiosyncratic symbolism peculiar to himself in order to express his own intensely personal feelings. Such symbols were, says Wilson, really "metaphors detached from their subjects." Inevitably such poetry is not easy to interpret. An example easily available in English is Valéry's *Le Cimitière Marin*, translated by our Poet Laureate, Day Lewis, as "The Graveyard by the Sea".

The basic problem for the Symbolist poet is to find an imagery both true to his own unique experience and also in some way significant and communicable. That is the supreme test.

It is fascinating to see how English poets, such as Yeats, Eliot, and Sitwell, stimulated by the French experiments, tackle this problem and give objective validity to an intensely subjective vision.

II. SOME INDIVIDUAL POETS.

1. The Masters of the Decade between the Wars.

W. B. Yeats (1865–1939).

References are to the *Collected Poems* (Macmillan).

Yeats's influence is exerted not by the limp romantic Celtic twilight verses between 1889 and 1904 but by the complex, sinewy poems appearing between 1910 and 1939. Although in traditional verse forms they establish Yeats as a great master of the modern symbolic image.

Brought up by a sceptic father, Yeats had sought from early youth for some significance to life in "heterodox mysticism", such as theosophy and the Kabbala, and above all in Blake. Their highly developed systems of symbols stimulated his innate sensitiveness to this intuitive form of insight and expression and encouraged him to develop his gift for waiting on images as they arose from the deeper regions of his mind. Arthur Symons, whose *The Symbolist Movement in Literature* was published in 1899, introduced him

to the work of Mallarmé and other French symbolists, and confirmed him in his poetic approach which he now realised was part of a European movement.

To give objective validity to highly subjective images he used several techniques. Following Shelley's example, he would repeat the same symbol throughout the body of his work, so that one poem illuminates another. The symbol thus seen in perspective reveals new facets of its significance, sometimes even contradictory aspects.

For example, in early poems the rose signifies not only love and, in its Rosicrucian form, a mystic union, but also Ireland, beauty both sensuous and intellectual, and the beauty of Maud Gonne, with whom Yeats remained hopelessly in love.

A ruined Norman tower which Yeats had converted into a dwelling recurs from 1919 in many poems. Its basic significance is the artist's isolation, but it also suggests Milton's Platonist, Shelley's "visionary prince", Samuel Palmer's "lonely light", and Yeats's own Anglo-Irish heritage. He was greatly concerned to give the symbol solidity and firm outline and stresses the tower's emblematic "winding, gyring, spiring treadmill of a stair" and the "grey stone fireplace with an open hearth" and the "fire of turf" of simple hospitality.

He juxtaposed exalted symbols with the singularly down-to-earth motifs which he deployed with increasing frequency. The indignity of age is "a sort of battered kettle at the heel," or "a tattered coat upon a stick" until in his emblematic protagonist, "Crazy Jane," he presents the ultimate in physical destitution inspired by poetic frenzy.

Yeats also relied on archetypal images from the "Great Memory," to which we respond unconsciously. In *The Two Trees* (p. 54), he follows Blake in his use of the image of the tree, which develops from the Kabbala and the Biblical Tree of Life. To Yeats it came to embody the organic nature both of all life and of the imagination, or reality intuitively perceived by the artist as whole and vital. Yeats, like Blake, contrasted this imaginative vision with the abstractions of the discursive intellect and his most perfect expression of the work of art as an organic and indissoluble unit occurs at the climax of *Among School Children*. Here in a passage of multiple import he marries the image of the tree to that of the dance.

" O chestnut-tree, great-rooted blossomer,
Are you the leaf, the blossom or the bole?
O body swayed to music, O brightening glance,
How can we know the dancer from the dance? "

Yeats's poetry was also supported by a framework of mythology, whether of Gaelic legend, Greek mythology, as in *Leda and the Swan*, or, as in much of his more mature work, that of his own private system, which he expounded in his prose *A Vision*, 1926. For instance, he saw history as opposing cycles of 2000 years, each cycle being a reversal of the previous one. He represented this diagramatically by opposing "gyres", his gyre being the spiral traced on a cone.

But Yeats's finest poems, even when the meaning depends on his private hinterland, are still valid and intelligible in themselves. *The Second Coming* affects us through the singular clarity and force of the metaphors and the controlled energy of the rhythm:

" . . . somewhere in sands of the desert
A shape with lion body and the head of a man,
A gaze blank and pitiless as the sun,
Is moving its slow thighs, while all about it
Reel shadows of the indignant desert birds.
The darkness drops again: but now I know
That twenty centuries of stony sleep
Were vexed to nightmare by a rocking cradle,
And what rough beast, its hour come round at
                                                                    last,
Slouches towards Bethlehem to be born?"

Yeats is the poet of paradox and often quoted

Blake, " Without contraries there is no progression." His own life was one of manifold tensions, especially between contemplation and his active participation in Irish politics and art. (He was Production Manager of the Abbey Theatre and was made a Senator.)

A dominant theme is the dichotomy between sensuous living and the creation of immortal works of art, the latter symbolised by Byzantium in two splendid poems. Here he rejects the " sensual music " of " whatever is begotten, born, and dies " or " the fury and the mire of human veins " for " monuments of unageing intellect," symbolised by Byzantium, with its gold mosaic, the starlit or the moonlit dome and the golden singing bird, a miracle, " in glory of changeless metal," (pp. 217, 280).

Yet in the contemporary *Dialogue of Self and Soul*, p. 265, the poet opts for life, however sordid.

" I am content to live it all again
And yet again, if it be life to pitch
Into the frog-spawn of a blind man's ditch."

Paradoxically the splendour of Yeats is the unresolved conflict. In poem after poem he passionately faces his dilemmas, personal, political, artistic, metaphysical, never to rest in a complacent final solution but forging instead enigmatic and arresting images of universal experience.

T. S. Eliot (1888–1965).

The poems referred to are contained in *Collected Poems 1909–1962* (Faber).

Thomas Stearns Eliot is a poet who makes considerable demands on his readers. To some extent these may be met by using critical works such as George Williamson's *A Reader's Guide to T. S. Eliot*; but a poet who apparently needs to be read with a key is a little daunting, so it is perhaps as well to decide what these demands are and whether they are much heavier than or very different from those made by other poets.

Eliot studied philosophy at Harvard (1906–10) and continued his studies abroad at Munich, the Sorbonne, and later (1914) Oxford. He had been interested for a time in Eastern philosophy but chose not to indulge his inclination as he considered it might hinder his participation in Western culture, and in Western culture from the Greeks onward he was steeped. One must expect from a writer who read so widely in Greek, Latin, French, Italian, and German, as well as English, a range of references beyond what is usually expected of the well-educated arts graduate, and from a poet trained in philosophical disciplines one should further expect subtlety and precision. These expectations are met and the poetry, most of it at least, well repays the effort of the reader, who must follow a technique in which unity is achieved not by a framework of narrative or sensory description or even a logical sequence of thought, but by imaginative association where several layers of thought and feeling are fused.

Eliot's first book of verse, *Prufrock and Other Observations*, was published in 1917, although the title poem *The Love Song of J. Alfred Prufrock* had been published separately in 1915 in America, apparently at Ezra Pound's instigation. This poem is probably one of the easiest to begin with and yet touches on ideas and experiences with which Eliot was continually concerned.

At the head of the poem is a quotation from Dante's *L'Inferno*; it is relevant to the poem in that its speaker says that he has answered Dante only because he believes that his answer cannot be taken back to earth, since no one ever leaves the deep abyss alive. Eliot's character is first seen making his way through a maze of streets, a scene which reflects Prufrock's state of mind. The correlation between the exterior situation and the interior state is suggested clearly:

" Streets that follow like a tedious argument."

He arrives at a party; we hear, at a distance as it were, the sounds made by the guests, but in the foreground are Prufrock's thoughts. He is sadly aware of the impression he makes, the figure he cuts, and this inhibits him so that for fear of being misunderstood he withdraws and does not ask his question. This much is achieved with great delicacy. His fear of being ridiculous, misunderstood, and becoming old, together with the wry mockery of self-depreciation

" Though I have seen my head [grown slightly bald]
    brought in upon a platter,
I am no prophet—and here's no great matter; "

makes him a sympathetic character. But there is more to the poem than the failure of a middle-aged man. Prufrock's city is characterised by fog, smoke, drains, restlessness; its citizens use prepared faces and formulated phrases, perhaps to defend themselves against any contact with reality which might disturb their pleasant but futile lives, measured out with coffee spoons. In this society people may talk of culture but it is the culture of the past; the present remains unproductive and people remain isolated and unable to communicate. The sea images which replace the fog are less picturesque but possibly more emotive; the fog may be understood, as Baudelaire used it, to represent the Unreal City, half dead, but the sea image comes from the English tradition and the Mermaids may recall Donne's satirical love poem *Go and Catch a Falling Star*, while the last three lines remind us of Keats's concluding lines in *Ode to Melancholy*. It is these two recurrent images of fog and sea which form the " framework " of the poem and which suggest the breadth of the poet's intention.

The same loneliness and sense not only of failure but of there being nothing worth succeeding in, is expressed in *Gerontion* perhaps more bitterly. This meditation on approaching death is inconclusive,

" I would meet you upon this honestly,"

but if the speaker is not sure what death means he is even less sure of the meaning or value of human life. The references to " windy spaces " (line 15) and

" Gull against the wind, in the windy straits "

suggest Claudio's speech on the terrifying prospect of existence after life has ended, in *Measure for Measure*. The quotation at the head of *Gerontion* comes from the Duke's speech in that play when he tries to steel Claudio's nerve for his coming execution by proving that life is not worth having. Eliot's Old Man seems to agree, but the Duke's Christian assurance, for he is disguised as a friar, evokes no response in him for Christ, the Word, cannot communicate through the swaddling darkness. Whatever the crucifixion may have once meant has been adulterated beyond recognition and there is nothing to replace it.

The *Waste Land*, published in 1922, established Eliot as a major figure on the contemporary scene. Some reviewers thought it a literary hoax because of the elaborate use of allusion and quotation (in several languages) as well as the lack of any formal structure. Charles Powell in *The Manchester Guardian* dismissed most of it as " so much waste paper." F. L. Lucas thought the " unhappy composition should have been left to sink itself; but it is not easy to dismiss in three lines what is being written about as a new masterpiece." Those who thought it a masterpiece praised its honesty, its emotional unity and above all its projection of twentieth-century malaise " the plight of a whole generation." At all events Eliot's reputation as a poet increased, though controversy may be raised again in a different form now that Eliot's original notebooks are being studied. It has been known for some time that Ezra Pound, to whom *The Waste Land* is dedicated, recommended considerable revisions mostly in the form of cuts which Eliot accepted, but the extent was not known until the John Quinn papers were made public in 1968.

However, the version published in 1922 certainly impresses one with a sense of disillusion and anti-climax. The old pre-war Edwardian world has been destroyed, perhaps it was never very satisfactory, but there seems to be nothing to replace it. The theme is repeated at intervals throughout, in different ways; sometimes as a dead land where the sun beats, a place where the cisterns are empty, the wells exhausted, an empty chapel with dry bones. The crowds on London Bridge walking through the fog are dead, for each is locked within himself. The modern Cleopatra seated in her burnished chair is surrounded by erotic symbols, but the romantic suggestion of the gold Cupidon is disturbed by *synthetic* perfume and destroyed by recollection of the rape of Philomel. This "Cleopatra's" life is pointless and unreal; she can only look forward to a game of chess. At the other end of the social scale there is the prostitution of personal relationship to the level of having a "good time" and instead of new life, abortion. "The nymphs are departed" indeed.

But at the end there is perhaps some hope in

"The awful daring of a moment's surrender
Which an age of prudence can never retract."

At all events it seems particularly relevant to this half of the twentieth century when the possibilities of our producing a waste land seem even greater.

In 1927 Eliot became an Anglican. His poems, *Ash Wednesday, Journey of the Magi, A Song for Simeon,* reflect his new belief and his gift for using allusion is directed towards Christian sources. Thus in *Ash Wednesday* single lines from well-known prayers and responses from the Ave Maria and The Reproaches of the Catholic Good Friday service are used technically in the same way that the repeated and echoed phrases in earlier poems are used to give unity; but as the phrases that Eliot uses are ones that are frequently repeated in the liturgy of the church, the poem provides, for some readers, a kind of ceremony.

His major work after this is *Four Quartets,* where he is concerned with the Christian philosopher's interpretation of time, meaning as expressed through words, and salvation. They are full of paradoxes and though a progression of thought may be traced in the four, each Quartet may be read as a unity in itself. The mood of the second Quartet, *East Coker,* is sombre and the fear of nothingness, the dissatisfaction with the "shabby equipment" of contemporary language recalls parts of *The Waste Land*; but the fourth, *Little Gidding,* named after the home of a seventeenth-century community of Anglican mystics, is more hopeful

"All manner of thing shall be well."

Considerable time needs to be spent on these poems if the complexity of the thought is to be appreciated, but the pattern of the verses, the delicate manipulation of the metre may be enjoyed by the reader who is prepared to listen carefully.

2. Edith Sitwell (1887–1964).

In *The Scarlet Tree* Sir Osbert Sitwell vividly describes his elder sister's early background. She was saturated in English poetry, read Baudelaire at the age of seventeen and her governess, Helen Rootham, translator of Rimbaud, became her lifelong friend.

Sitwell interprets her early verses in *Façade,* 1922, as "abstract patterns in sound" written in reaction against "rhythmical flaccidity" and "verbal deadness." She experimented indefatigably with the effect on rhythm and speed of subtle and elaborate patterns of rhyme, assonance and dissonance, successfully capturing dance rhythms. Some verses were set to music by Walton and accompany the well-known ballet.

Like the French Symbolist writer de l' Isle Adam (author of *Axel*) Sitwell also deliberately juxtaposed words that "clash in a protesting combination". She adopted the synaesthesia practised by Poe and the French Symbolists, transferring the language of one sensation to indicate the experiences of another, as when morning light appears as "creaking" or "whining". In later poems we find such phrases as "the dust brays",

or "purple perfumes of the polar Sun", repeated from Rootham's Rimbaud.

Elegant and mannered, the butterfly verses of *Façade* lack inner significance yet they gave Sitwell the expertise to express intense feeling in her later poetry.

Gold Coast Customs, 1929, is the counterpart of Eliot's *Waste Land.* Both express the poet's revulsion from modern society by finding an objective parallel in primitive ritual. Sitwell, writing during the Depression, was most dismayed by the heartlessness of the city, which she images through the bygone Customs in Ashantee, where once at the death of an important person hundreds of the poor were butchered that their blood might lave his bones. This "Reeling appalling/Cannibal mart" symbolises the contemporary sacrifice of the poor demanded by the spiritually dead, epitomised by Lady Bamburger, "smart plague-cart", massively indifferent to the destitution of the slums, where driven by "Want, a cruel rat gnawing there" the pathetic prostitutes, "The calico dummies/Flap and meet".

The ghastly Customs, the desolate slums violently alternate and reflect each other in the kaleidoscope of nightmare, relentlessly maintained by the rhythm of savage drum beat and fevered pulse.

Although the metre and repetitive phrasing have an obsessive monotony, the impact of the poem which foretells "the sick thick smoke from London burning," is unforgettable.

In *Street Songs,* 1942, Sitwell was in command of images of arresting clarity. Two poems on the Raids are incidentally a clear vindication of Symbolist technique for both are extended "metaphors detached from their subjects".

In the ironic *Lullaby* of despair the Pterodactyl, "the steel bird" which "fouls its nest", has devastated the earth and only the Baboon is left to mother the surviving child.

Still Falls the Rain boldly uses the superbly simple image of rain, heavy reiteration, and a thudding, tolling rhythm, stressing the dark monosyllables:

"Still falls the Rain—
Dark as the world of man, black as our loss—
Blind as the nineteen hundred and forty nails
Upon the Cross."

It is a poem of profound and universal compassion for man and beast and also of religious faith, for the Rain is also Christ's blood shed in suffering, love and illumination.

In later publications Sitwell develops the long ode written from the vantage of the poet-seer matured by suffering. Like Yeats she was now giving her work coherence by playing variations on key symbols. Some images appear strained but the most effective are drawn from familiar sources, as the Bible, history, myth and mankind's most primitive experiences—of sun, earth, beasts, grain, fruit, metals, and of cold and warmth, always emblematic for her of evil and good. On these she sets her idiomatic stamp.

She constantly opposes two kinds of gold. In *Harvest* she celebrates the warm gold of the "laughing heat of the Sun" and "the ripebearded fire/Of wheat," reflecting divine energy and love. In *The Song of the Cold,* 1945, she laments the lust for the cold, destructive metal that possesses Dives and "the saints of Mammon," who "ache with the cold/From the polar wastes of the heart", the cold of hell.

Deeply shaken by Hiroshima, Sitwell wrote *The Shadow of Cain,* 1947. The theme of the title poem is fission and envisages Mankind's migration into the Cold, from Cain's first murder up to Hiroshima, when "the Primal Matter/Was broken," and "to the murdered Sun a totem pole arose of dust in memory of Man." The crisis stirs an obscure prescience of impending calamity, of a profound fission between the two aspects of Man: Lazarus embodiment of gold corn and human suffering and Dives of money and defilement. But the two golds fight and finally unite in a new resolution and hope.

This visionary poem is sometimes declamatory and the bleak *Dirge for the New Sunrise*, with its terse antitheses, is more immediate and moving.

After *The Shadow of Cain*, " haunted ever by the shadow that fell on Hiroshima," she yet continued to write poems that are " hymns of praise to the glory of Life."

3. Some Poets of the Thirties.

Wystan Hugh Auden (b. 1907).

Auden was educated in a small public school, Gresham's, and later went to Oxford. Here he met Stephen Spender, Louis MacNeice, and others who formed temporarily a group of " political " poets most of whom were involved in the Spanish Civil War.

His first book of poems appeared in 1930 and was well received. After the publication of *The Ascent of F6*, a play which he wrote in collaboration with Christopher Isherwood, he was expected to become a major figure in English poetry. However, later books of verse were less well reviewed and in the mid-thirties the *Scrutiny* critics complained of his triviality, irresponsibility, and lack of maturity. He left England in 1939 and has since lived in America and Austria. As Eliot took out British citizenship Auden took out American, and, again, like Eliot, he accepted Christianity though perhaps in a less orthodox form.

Auden's interest in politics and the violence of political struggle is reflected in much of the imagery he uses as well as more directly in such different poems as *The Shield of Achilles* and *Alsono to Ferdinand*. *Let History be my Judge* is an early example of his political verse. Russia's forced collectivisation policy is the event which roused the feeling expressed here, but it is not directly referred to so that, if it were not for the date, the reader would not necessarily associate the poem with that particular policy, but with the harsh repression of any uprising or with the invasion of a weak country: the tragedy of the imposition of impersonal policy on the ignorant and defenceless is suggested and the callous self-justification of the powerful, ironically revealed. A later poem, *The Unknown Citizen*, satirises the omnipresence of the bureaucratic state and possibly the twentieth-century obsession with statistics. It begins with particular people, as in the dramatic monologues and some of the elegies, or poems for Auden's friends. In his less successful poems he tends to be either too clever (like Gratiano's in *The Merchant of Venice*, his reasons are like " two grains of wheat hid in two bushels of chaff ") or too anxious for effect. In the same way his dry humour and use of anti-climax is very effective at times, but sometimes the very ease with which he seems to do it betrays him and the joke becomes irritating.

Apart from anthologies, in some of which he is fairly well represented, the Penguin edition, which is the poet's own selection of verse, makes a good introduction to his work. There is one collected edition of *Collected Shorter Poems 1927–1957* (Faber). Otherwise his large production of verse is to be found in about ten small editions (all Faber). A recording of the poet's reading of his own poems has been made by Caedmon and is well worth listening to.

Stephen Spender (b. 1909).

Collected Poems 1928–1953 (Faber).

Spender's first poems, up to 1933, are mainly concerned with or derived from the ideas of Marxism and Freud. There are the stormy calls

" Oh, comrades, let not those who follow after
  —The beautiful generation that will spring from
                                      our sides

Let them not wonder after the failure of banks
The failure of cathedrals, the declared insanity
                                   of our rulers,
We lacked the Spring-like resource of the
                                      tiger—"

but what the comrades are to do is not clear. One does not expect a political manifesto in a poem, but the vagueness of the sentiment of " equal like the shine from the snow " is irritating. It is difficult to take the optimism of such a poem as *The Funeral* seriously, yet if it is meant to be ironic the wit needs clarifying. Spender's early impact and placing in literature doubtless derived from his political and psychological idiom, but the poems which have stood the test of time are those which are more personal, e.g., *My parents kept me from children who were rough*, which strike a more convincing note.

From 1936 onwards his poems are often about war, first the Spanish Civil War and then the Second World War. He is moved by the fate of the ordinary civilian, particularly the young who became involved in battles they do not understand. The defencelessness of the young soldier is poignantly conveyed and in poems such as *Ultima Ratio Regum* he links the greed of society, particularly the middle classes, with the slaughter of the innocent.

The belief in socialism and the brotherhood of man, rather glibly expressed in the earlier poems, is still present, but the tone of poems from this later period is compassionate. Spender rejects the easy, outright condemnation of either war or the enemy and refuses to glorify war by celebrating heroism. In fact there are no easy answers to the questions proposed in these exploratory poems. In the introduction to his collected volume Spender speaks of them as being " malleable " and possibly this unfinished sense is both their weakness and strength.

C. Day Lewis (b. 1904).

Collected Poems 1954 (Cape) and various short, later volumes.

Of this group of poets, C. Day Lewis is probably the most prolific. He began to publish in 1925 and was associated with Auden and Spender up to the outbreak of the Second World War. His early poems show Auden's influence—the use of colloquialism, the experiment with verse form and the concern with politics. How alien this type of verse was from his own vein may be seen from the symphonic poem *A Time to Dance*, 1935, where, in one section, he parodies the Apocalypse to describe the division of society into the exploiters and the exploited:

" I saw . . .
  The director placing explosives under the
     infant's cradle, the editor keeping a nursery
     for snakes:
  The scientist madly driving against traffic lights,
     the artist studying his acne in a pocket
     mirror: "

Later he imitates the rhythm of popular songs.

As his expectation of a Marxist solution faded and involvement in politics lessened, due at least in part to the Spanish Civil War and then the World War, he developed a quieter tone and used the more traditional verse forms. His work is generally polished, if not particularly vigorous. His translation of Virgil's *Aeneid* in 1952 was generally well received and in addition he has written several books of criticism, as well as detective stories under the pseudonym Nicholas Blake.

Louis MacNeice (1907–63).

The Collected Poems of Louis MacNeice, edited E. R. Dodds, 1967 (Faber).

Louis MacNeice was born in the same year as Auden, published his first book of poems in 1929, and continued writing fairly steadily until 1963. He was actively interested in politics of an idealist, left-wing type and was influenced by the contemporary interest in psychology. In 1937 he joined with Auden in publishing *Letters from Iceland*, but after Auden's departure for America in 1939 the partnership, if so it may be called, dissipated itself. MacNeice continued his work as a lecturer in classics and also wrote several radio scripts for the B.B.C., including the verse drama, *The Dark Tower*.

His longest non-dramatic poem is *Autumn Journal*, which covers events from August to December 1938. Apart from its obvious historical interest—he clearly records his impressions of and fears about the political events of that period —it is an unusually convincing poem. It has an authenticity as of Pepys's diary, but it is pervaded by a philosophical tone which brings details into focus. The verse flows smoothly most of the time, but the metre is not intrusive; in fact as an example of the " art to hide art " it is of its kind hardly bettered.

Observation of significant detail, personal reflection on the political situation as it affects society as a whole, reminiscence and a private transitory reaction are skilfully interwoven. For instance, he has spent most of the night anxiously assessing the possibilities of war breaking out and at six o'clock hears various sounds of people going to work—

" And I notice feathers sprouting from the rotten
    Silk of my black
Double eiderdown which was a wedding
    Present eight years back.
And the linen which I lie on came from Ireland
    In the easy days
. . . .
   . . . and I wonder what the morning
    Papers will say,
And decide to go quickly to sleep for the morning
        already
Is with us, the day is to-day."

Humour, often directed at himself, gives his poetry a sharpness which it might otherwise lack since he seldom seems driven by an overpowering inspiration. His use of colloquialisms and cliché is less frequent than Auden's and, possibly because of this, more effective. The opening to his tribute to his friend in *The Casualty* is a good example of this, and the rest of the poem illustrates MacNeice's gift for characterisation, for expressing admiration and regret without sentimentality.

In spite of disappointments and disillusionments MacNeice remained liberal in outlook, and sympathetic to many views (see, for example, *Bottleneck* and *The Conscript*). He may not be a major poet but he has integrity and a respect of poetry, reflected in his skilful handling of metre, which makes him an honest poet rather than a brilliant dilletante.

4. Dylan Thomas (1914–53).

Collected Poems, 1952 (Dent).

In many ways his poetry could hardly be more different from that of the previous group. Dylan Thomas, as a poet at least, was hardly touched by social concerns, and was uncommitted politically. His poems do not exhibit the intellectual force which Auden's and Eliot's do. If these lastmentioned poets derived their inspiration from metaphysical poets like Donne, then Dylan Thomas may be said to derive his from poets such as Southwell or the visionary Blake.

The theme of much of his poetry is the oneness of all creation, the unity of experience: the human is intermingled with the divine, flesh and spirit are indivisible, and the world we inhabit is not essentially different from us.

" The force that through the green fuse drives
          the flower
Drives my green age; that blasts the roots of
          trees
Is my destroyer."

Death is incipient in birth and so in love—

" The word flowed up, translating to the heart
  First characters of birth and death."

Sometimes death is accepted as in *And death shall*

have no dominion and in *A Refusal to Mourn*; at other times Thomas seeks to defy death by protest:

" Go not gentle into that good night
  Old age should burn and rave at close of day."

The condensed language, particularly the use of verbal nouns and adjectives, reflects, sometimes not very clearly, this sense of the unity of creation.

His use of language though much imitated, remains recognisably his own. He uses cosmic symbols: sun, heaven, stars, sea, fire, and wind; images such as womb, bird, blood, and tomb; colours: green, gold, red, blue, and black. Much of his verse—that is when it is not overloaded with images—evokes kaleidoscopic pictures and the rhythmic metrical pattern is generally strong, which is possibly why he was in his own lifetime a popular poet. He draws too a great deal on biblical symbols and this coupled with the use of formal sound patterns, assonance, rhyme, and alliteration gives his verse an incantatory sound which is quite impressive. Finally he has resuscitated the " transferred epithet technique."

At his best he has produced moving but unsentimental celebrations of childhood, *Fern Hill*, *Poem in October*, *Over Sir John Hill*; some religious poems, for example, the unusual pattern poem *Vision and Prayer* and some " occasional " poems.

Very good recordings of Thomas's readings of his poems have been made by the Caedmon group.

5. The English " Movement " Poets.

Robert Conquest's anthology *New Lines*, 1956 (Macmillan), marks the next stage—sometimes called the " Movement "—in English poetry. In his introduction Conquest remarks that groups of poets typical of their decade were " presented to public fire by anthologies which took up definite positions." His anthology was prepared in the belief that " a genuine and healthy poetry of the new period has established itself." The main objections he makes to criticism published from the beginning of the Second World War is that it encouraged poets " to produce diffuse and sentimental verbiage or hollow technical pirouettes." The poets he chose, apart from being contemporary, have in common only the acceptance that " poetry is written by and for the whole man, intellect, emotions, senses and all," and on the technical side a " refusal to abandon rational structure and comprehensible language." However, in their reaction against the undisciplined expression of emotion, the Movement poets tend to go to the opposite extreme. Their writing is highly intelligent and often witty, but generally seems more cerebral than truly imaginative, lacking the inspiration of passionate feeling. The wry self-mockery and hopelessness of much of Larkin's verse is typical of the work of the Movement as a whole, but some younger poets, notably Gunn and Hughes, who were early associated with the group, have gone on in another, more vigorous direction.

Philip Larkin (b. 1922).

The North Ship, 1945; *The Less Deceived*, 1955; *The Whitsun Weddings*, 1964 (all Faber).

Like Dylan Thomas, Larkin recalls his childhood, but he refuses to romanticise it. In *I Remember, I Remember*, he speaks of Coventry where he was born as a place where his childhood was " unspent " and he lists the crises commonly associated with precocious youth which did not occur. So far the poem is mildly ironic, but its end is disturbing:

" ' You look as if you wished the place in Hell,'
  My friend said, ' judging from your face.' ' Oh
        well,
  I suppose it's not the place's fault,' I said.
  ' Nothing, like something, happens anywhere.' "

The sense of emptiness, of opportunities untaken, of flatness, is a theme of much of Larkin's verse, *e.g.*, *Work*, *Departures*, *Triple Time*, but the self-mockery and irony give the work a pointedness which most elegaic verse lacks; when he reflects on the past he is neither nostalgic nor resentful. A conversational tone is used to attract attention, but the language is a " *selection* of the language really used by men "; he does not indulge in the vague slipshod phrasing of what passes for the conversation of " ordinary people." A good example of his style is *Church Going*, a reflection on the future of churches when they " fall completely out of use," which raises the whole question of belief (in values neither immediate nor material).

Thom Gunn (b. 1929).

Fighting Terms, 1954; *The Sense of Movement*, 1957; *My Sad Captains*, 1961; *Touch*, 1967 (all Faber).

At first glance Gunn's poetry seems as contemporary as the morning paper. Titles such as *On the Move*, subtitled *Man you gotta Go, Black Jackets, Elvis Presley*, suggest, rightly, that his poetry is rooted in the present, but not in such a way that it will be incomprehensible when the present has become the past. He is concerned with violence in the classical world in *The Wound* and *Helen's Rape*, in the sixteenth century in *A Mirror for Poets*, and in the twentieth century in *Claus von Stauffenberg*, in personal relationships as well as public, but it is not an unthinking surrender to mere excitement or admiration of brutality, but a recognition of its necessity:

" In this society the boundaries met
Of living, danger, death, leaving no space
Between, . . .
    . . . Yet at this point they found
Arcadia, a fruitful permanent land."
                    (*A Mirror for Poets*)

In *Saint Martin and the Beggar*, Martin, the saint of man, must learn to fight before he can " grow " and then without hesitating he halves his cloak to cover the beggar. He is justified because his action was natural. The tragedy of modern man lies in his inability to marry instinct, intention, and action:

" One joins the movement in a valueless world,
. . . .
At worst, one is in motion; and at best,
Reaching no absolute, in which to rest,
One is always nearer by not keeping still."
                    (*On the Move*)

Ted Hughes (b. 1930).

The Hawk in the Rain, 1957; *Lupercal*, 1960; *Wodwo*, 1967; *Crow*, 1970 (all Faber). There is also a small book of *Selections* from Hughes and Gunn (Faber).

There is some similarity between these two poets. Both have worked in America; both have developed a concise style which mirrors the toughness of their attitude to experience, their refusal to make the rough places smooth.

This said, the differences become more apparent as their individuality becomes clearer. Hughes, for example, uses animal imagery far more than Gunn. He approaches the human dilemma through the animal, but the animal is not a mere cipher. In *Pike*, for instance, the pike exists in its own right and, since Hughes did collect animals in his boyhood, the incident

" Suddenly there were two.   Finally one

With a sag belly and the grin it was born with "

is probably true. But the recollected " nightmare " at the end of the poem goes beyond a boy's terror. The pond he fished, the eye, the dream darkness are symbolic both of the violence which lay in his own subconscious and that of the human race. The human being too is potentially a killer from the egg.

In other poems Hughes is searching for an identity. In *An Otter*, the otter

" Gallops along land he no longer belongs to;
Re-enters the water by melting."

At one level we have the hunt which loses and then finally catches the otter, but at another level there is the self, " attendant and withdrawn," the individual who " does not take root."

Hughes's descriptive powers are certainly strong and sensuous and there are in his verses for children, *Meet my Folks* and *The Earth Owl*, descriptions of people and creatures some of which are as strange and amusing as those of Edward Lear or Lewis Carrol. In the volume *Poetry in The Making* Hughes gives a fascinating account of the genesis of some of his poems and of his methods of composition.

6. The American " Confessional " Poets.

The term " confessional poetry " seems to have been used first by reviewers of Lowell's *Life Studies*, poems which arose from their author's suffering a mental breakdown. It has since been applied to the work of Sylvia Plath and Anne Sexton, which also derives from the immediate experience of mental illness and, like *Life Studies*, expresses feelings of guilt, bitterness and isolation, the material of the confessional or the psychoanalyst's couch.

The label " confessional " is also used in a more general, though allied sense, to denote work in which the poet makes an uninhibited confession of hatred, addiction, lust or similar experience, about which, usually, most of us are reticent. An extreme exponent of this genre is the Beat writer Allen Ginsberg, a selection of whose verse may be found in *Penguin Modern Poets 5*.

In " confessional " writing the poet's need to objectify his experience, in order to give it artistic validity, presents itself in an acute form. Its resolution demands the rare courage and technical virtuosity that Eliot displayed in *The Waste Land* and Lowell approaches, in a very different way, in *Near the Ocean*.

Robert Lowell (b. 1917).   *See also Section I.*

Poems 1938–1949 (1950); *The Mills of the Kavanaughs* (1951); *Life Studies* (1959); *Imitations* (1961); *For The Union Dead* (1964); *Near the Ocean* (1967); *Notebook*, 1970.   Faber.

In an interview, published in J. Scully's *Modern Poets on Modern Poetry*, Lowell records how he was early drawn to the work of Latin, Elizabethan and Jacobean poets. His own mature writing reflects the continuing influence of these early mentors, with whom he shares an anguished sense of the fragility and transience of beauty and a revulsion from the brutal, vicious materialism of the society in which he lives.

His first important work, *The Quaker Graveyard in Nantucket*, 1945, is an elegy for a cousin drowned while serving in the navy during the Second War. The poem presents this cousin as continuing the brutal tradition of the Quaker whalers of Nantucket, and links him with Ahab, the tragic, deranged hero of Melville's *Moby Dick*. The vigour of the poem's language, the musical skill with which Lowell evokes the sounds and atmosphere of the bleak Nantucket coast and the force of his revulsion from the whalers' obscene cruelty are immediately impressive. As Hugh B. Staples has noted in his valuable reference book, *Robert Lowell—the First Twenty Years*, a central theme of the poem is " human evolution, considered as a part of God's plan." Here, as in much of his later work, Lowell shows the aggressive individualism of men bringing a return to primitive violence. The gentle, pastoral stanza VI presents the ideal, the figure of the Virgin, who, " Expressionless, expresses God." However, this stanza lacks the force of the others. The affirmation of faith in the poem's concluding line is similarly less convincing than Lowell's expression of revulsion from the Quakers' primitive lust for power and wealth.

The poem's images have multiple significance The whale, " IS, the whited monster," is at once a symbol of Being Itself, of the vengeful Jehovah and of Jesu Saviour. It is the victim of the sailors' greed and also the agent of their death and damnation, a whited sepulchre, an image of their corrupt faith. The sea is the god Poseidon, " the earth shaker ", and also the primitive source of life and life itself, " hurt " and " fouled " by man.

These and allied images take on new significance in Lowell's later poems, where they replace the Catholic symbols of his early work, as he strives to achieve a more flexible, resonant style, which will give objective validity to his vision. In his mature work the sea and water continue to symbolise life, particularly the life of the spirit. Fish at times represent the primitive violence man has loosed upon the world, but the fish is also an image of vitality struggling against " the stone and bonecrushing waterfall." Monsters become " grunting " " yellow dinosaur steamshovels ", possessive " dragons " and the Gorgon, a fearsome, yet beautiful and pitiful, " tyrant " and " tyrannicide."

Lowell's use of such images is linked with his frequent evocations of the language and imagery of the Bible, particularly the Old Testament and the Apocalyptic books beloved of the New England Puritans. He applies such language and imagery to the life-denying creeds of the Puritans themselves and to all those who seek to dominate their fellows, driving in " stakes " to " command/the infinite " and creating " God the Logos " in their own image, a tyrant with " bloody hands ". Lowell combines such Biblical allusions with references to Classical myths—particularly that of Perseus and Medusa—to give his work wider significance and fuller perspectives. He uses American place names with religious and historical associations, Mount Sion, Concord, Carthage, and writes of contemporary life in terms of that of Ancient Israel and Rome, as in the following passage, where the insistent rhythm, the punctuation and feminine rhymes accentuate the image of the clumsy military machines irrevocably lurching toward their shattering end:

" Hammering military splendor,
   top-heavy Goliath in full armor—
   little redemption in the mass
   liquidations of their brass,
   elephant and phalanx moving
   with the times and still improving,
   when that kingdom hit the crash:
   a thousand foreskins stacked like trash . . ."
          (*Waking Early Sunday Morning*)

In his early verse Lowell imitated the metrical forms of Elizabethan and Jacobean poetry. His middle period was a time of experiment: the dramatic monologues of *The Mills of the Kavanaughs* are written in more colloquial run-on couplets similar to those of Browning; *Life Studies* and *For the Union Dead* contain a number of poems in free verse. His volume, *Near the Ocean*, marks Lowell's return to stricter metrical forms, using a stanza based on four couplets, which he now deploys with the deceptive skill of a master. His earlier experiments with style and metre and the experience he has gained by writing plays and by recreating poems from Latin and other languages for the volume *Imitations*, now enable him to write with vigorous simplicity and haunting beauty:

" Lost in the Near Eastern dreck,
   the tyrant and tyrannicide
   lie like the bridegroom and the bride;
   the battering ram, abandoned, prone,
   beside the apeman's phallic stone."
          (*Near the Ocean*)

Although the autobiographical poems of *Life Studies* have been among the most widely noted of Lowell's work, his later volumes seem of more lasting importance. They express a complex, tragic vision of life in a " black classic " world of " lost connections." We are all " tyrants "; Mussolini was " one of us." Caligula is our " namesake " and " tyrannicide " itself a most arrogant form of tyranny, bringing widespread suffering and destruction:

" I have seen the Gorgon.
   The erotic terror
   of her helpless, big bosomed body
   lay like slop.
   Wall-eyed, staring the despot to stone,
   her severed head swung
   like a lantern in the victor's hand."
          (*Florence*)

" Pity the monsters! " " Pity the planet, all joy gone/from this sweet volcanic cone."

Lowell's recent poems express the anguish of our almost impossible quest for " asylum, peace ". " We are like a lot of wild/spiders crying together/ but without tears." Innocence, goodness and beauty, life itself, are as fragile as " the orange and black/oriole's swinging nest! " In *For the Union Dead* he suggests we can survive only by having the " angry wrenlike vigilance " which chooses death rather than " savage servility " or the security of " a Mosler safe, the 'Rock of Ages'/that survived the blast." The ultimate test is whether we dare become " alive enough " to " die ".

Like Yeats, Lowell has come to feel that we experience innocent joy only in the creation and contemplation of art. Exploring the frightening " corners of the woodshed ", he creates from its " lumber " poems that give " darkness some control ", evoking joy even while they " sing " " despair."

Sylvia Plath (1932–1963).

The Colossus, (1960); *Ariel* (1965). Faber.

An American of German ancestry, Sylvia Plath was married to Ted Hughes. Some of her early poems, such as *Mushrooms* and *Sow*, have an affinity with his, but the most powerful influence upon her work seems to have been the encouragement she received from Lowell.

Like all poets, she has power to make us see the world as if for the first time, to enhance our awareness of life. She writes of poppies " wrinkly and clear red, like the skin of a mouth," and bells that " soberly bong out their names." Her world has the clarity of a primitive painting, but the poems of *Ariel* make almost intolerably painful reading, for they express the heightened vision and self-mockery, the frangible control of utter hopelessness. Their images are often grotesque and full of menace:

" Dawn gilds the farmers like pigs,
   Swaying slightly in their thick suits,

   White towers of Smithfield ahead."
          (*Totem*)

The moon far from being a symbol of serene agape is a face

"White as a knuckle and terribly upset.
It drags the sea after it like a dark crime; it is
                      quiet
With the O-gape of complete despair."
          (*The Moon and the Yew Tree*)

Plath's world is starkly coloured in red, black, white and the yellow of decay. She combines these images with allied symbols of energy, death and living death: blood, the yew, moonlight, the winding-sheet and the pupa. Her poems are haunted by a black father-figure, the Nazi " panzer man " of *Daddy*. The power with which she expresses her anguished vision derives partly from the simplicity of her metres and verse forms, which often have the insistent quality of nursery rhyme.

Poems like *Daddy* and the allied *Lady Lazarus* are unlikely to be forgotten, but in future others, such as the title poem of *Ariel* and *The Arrival of the Bee Box*, *Sting*, and *Elm* may be valued more highly. Our judgment is distorted by Plath's recent death and the knowledge that the harrowing poems of *Ariel* were the prelude to her second, and successful, attempt at suicide.

Anne Sexton (b. 1928).

Anne Sexton began writing in 1957. *Selected Poems*, 1964, and *Love Poems*, 1969, have been published in England by the Oxford University Press. She acknowledges a debt to Lowell and deals with the same kind of subject as Sylvia Plath.

John Berryman (b. 1914).

Homage to Mistress Bradstreet (1956); *77 Dream Songs* (1964); *Berryman's Sonnets* (1967); *His Toy His Dream His Rest* (1969). Faber.

Berryman is the most distinguished of those poets to whom the label " confessional " is applied in its more general sense. Technically he is a most inventive and ingenious writer and his work has enormous vitality. Some find it undisciplined and pretentious.

The best of his early poems, *Homage to Mistress Bradstreet* is cast in the form of a dialogue between Berryman and the 17th cent. immigrant Anne Bradstreet, a poet manquée, with whom he feels tender affinity: " We are on each other's hands/ who care. Both of our worlds unhanded us."

The total effect of the poem is of a conversation between two aspects of the same personality.

In *77 Dream Songs* and *His Toy His Dream His Rest* Berryman develops the techniques he used in the earlier work to present multiple facets of a protagonist called Henry, " a white American in early middle age, who has suffered an irrevocable loss." These two books form a single work of three hundred and eighty-five lyrics. Together they present a kind of open-ended *Odyssey* of contemporary American life. They are often very amusing, often intensely irritating and their allusions to American society sometimes make them difficult for the English reader to follow, but they are compulsive reading and individual Songs, the painful 29 and 53 and the grotesque 91, for example, remain fixed in our minds.

Berryman's Sonnets is a sequence of poems about an unhappy love affair. It was written during the 1940s and has affinities with Meredith's *Modern Love*.

Conclusion.

Readers who are spurred by their study of the poets discussed here and wish to explore further will discover much to enjoy in the work of writers to whom space precludes more than reference: Robert Graves, Edwin Muir, R. S. Thomas, Peter Redgrove; the Americans Robert Frost, William Carlos Williams, Theodore Roethke, Elizabeth Bishop and Charles Olson. Penguin Books publish good anthologies, *The New Poetry* and *Contemporary American Poetry*, as well as two series: *Penguin Modern Poets*, which includes the work of many lesser English and American writers, and another of major European poetry, *Penguin Modern European Poets*.

III. TRADITIONAL VERSE PATTERNS

The poet's intensely individual music is played on the age-old instrument of metre and rhyme, and the better we understand the instrument, the keener will be our enjoyment of the poet's skill and genius.

Even verse that cannot be called poetry—verse that is mechanical, uninspired, lacking that intensity of insight and expression that we recognise as poetic—even this mediocre verse can teach us something of the poet's instrument. A homely nursery rhyme like " Humpty Dumpty " can help us to appreciate the metre of Ariel's unearthly song, " Where the bee sucks."

It is for this reason that the following guide to versification throws its net wide, gathering together for our consideration patterns as diverse as those of the mediæval ballad and the modern Frenchified triolet, of the flippant clerihew, and the grave blank verse of Wordsworth's " Prelude."

The following account of English verse is illustrated by quotations and by constant reference to the numbered poems in the new edition of " The Oxford Book of English Verse," 1939.

Thus " OBEV 16 " means " Oxford Book of English Verse," New Edition, Poem No. 16.

I. INTRODUCTION. STRESS, METRE, AND RHYME.

If we listen carefully to spoken English, we shall observe that there is a natural tendency to stress

some syllables more than others. In the following sentence, for example, the greater stress normally falls on the syllables whose vowels are marked with an acute accent, which is the usual way of indicating stress.

" The expréss léft Mánchester at séven."

It is obvious that in this sentence the stress falls in a quite haphazard way, and it is for this reason that we recognise the sentence as prose, for the essential difference between English prose and verse is that in prose the stress falls at random, while in verse the stressed syllables occur according to some regular pattern.

If we mark the stressed syllables in the following line from Wordsworth,

" And lóud hallóos and scréams and échoes lóud,"

it is immediately clear that the stress occurs regularly. The line is in fact, composed of a simple stress pattern of an unstressed syllable followed by a stressed (*e.g.*, and lóud) which is repeated throughout.

It is a regular pattern of stress, such as this, that in English verse constitutes what we call " metre." Metre in Greek means simply " measure," and it is always by stress that we measure our verse.

Another feature that distinguishes our verse from prose is the use of rhyme, although rhyme, unlike metre, is not essential to verse.

II. METRE.

Different Kinds of Feet.

In English verse the unit of stress pattern constitutes a foot, the foot of verse being comparable to the bar of music.

English verse uses several kinds of feet, some of two syllables, or disyllablic, some of three syllables or trisyllabic, and occasionally a foot of four syllables.

Disyllabic feet are of four kinds:

The **Iamb**, consisting of an unstressed syllable followed by a stressed, *e.g.* " retúrn."

The **Trochee**, consisting of a stressed syllable followed by an unstressed, *e.g.,* " ríver."

The **Spondee**, consisting of two stressed syllables, *e.g.,* " dóor mát."

The **Pyrrhic**, consisting of two unstressed syllables, *e.g.,* in the phrase " into tówn," " into " is a pyrrhic.

Trisyllabic feet are of four kinds:

The **Anapæst**, consisting of two unstressed syllables followed by a stressed, *e.g.,* " as you wish."

The **Dactyl**, consisting of a stressed syllable followed by two unstressed, *e.g.,* " árchery."

The **Amphibrach**, very rarely used, consisting of a stressed syllable between two unstressed, *e.g.,* " delíghted."

The **Tribrach**, still more rare, consisting of three unstressed syllables, *e.g.,* last three syllables of " incommúnicable."

A four-syllabled foot is very occasionally found:

The **Choriambus**, which may be thought of as a trochee followed by an iamb, *e.g.,* " Tóll for the bráve."

Different Kinds of Metrical Line.

Based on the different kinds of feet are the different kinds of English metre, which may be compared with the " time " in music.

Disyllabic metres may be either iambic or trochaic, for it is impossible to speak at any length using only pyrrhic or spondees, and the most common trisyllabic metres are anapæstic or dactyllic. Examples of different kinds of metrical line follow.

Iambic Line.

" I stróve with nóne for nóne was wórth my strife." [OBEV 584]

Trochaic Line.

" Hóme art góne and tá'en thy wáges." [OBEV 150]

Anapæstic Line.

" With a héy and a hó and a héy noninó." [OBEV 147]

Dactylic Lines.

" Wit with his wántonness,
Tásteth death's bitterness." [OBEV 177]

Amphibrach Lines.

" Most friendship is feigning, most lóving mere fólly
Then héigh ho, the hólly!
This life is most jólly." [OBEV 146]

Choriambic Line.

" Kéntish Sir Býng stóod for his Kíng."

Variations in Metre.

Satisfying poetry is rarely entirely regular. Mechanical regularity is soon wearisome to the ear and is a characteristic of doggerel. The poet satisfies our love of rhythm in a more interesting and subtle way by introducing all kinds of variations and inversions, while at the same time maintaining the throb of the basic metre. An account of the chief variations follows.

Elision.

Elision is the suppression in pronunciation of a vowel or a syllable.
In the anapæstic line,

" The Assýrîan came dówn like a wólf on the fóld "

the second foot appears to have four syllables, but in fact the " i " of " Assýrîan " is elided or dropped before the " a " as shown by the little bracket. The elision of " i," which is pronounced " y " and known as " consonantal y," is especially common, and occurs in such words as "familiar," " opinion." Elision is often shown by the use of the apostrophe as in " heav'n." In " heav'n " we see one of the many conventional elisions of poetry, like " 'tis," " 'twas," " did'st," " o'er," " e'er," " 'gainst," and many more.

Substitution.

Substitution is the use of a foot different from that of the metre in which the poem is written. In the following examples we can see the effect on iambic verse of some common substitutions.

Of a Trochee.

" Stiffen the sínews, súmmon úp the blóod."
Shakespeare, " Henry V."
Here the initial trochee gives force and emphasis.

Of a Spondee.

" Rócks cáves, lákes féns, bógs déns and shádes of déath."
In this extraordinary line of Milton's the spondees slow down and weight the verse.

Of a Pyrrhic.

" They flý forgótten as a dréam "
Here the pyrrhic in the third foot gives lightness to the line.

Of a Dactyl.

" Cháttering his téeth for cóld that díd him chill."
When a dactyl replaces an iamb it is usually in the first foot as in this typical instance from Spenser, where the dactyl gives emphasis and variety to the line.

Of Anapæsts.

" And the cóming wind did róar more lóud
And the sáils did sígh like sédge." [OBEV 562]

The initial anapæsts in these two lines from " The Ancient Mariner " give an effect of hurry and speed.

Additional Syllable.

An additional syllable may be added to either the beginning or end of a line.

Feminine Ending.

A feminine ending is an extra unstressed syllable that is added after the final stressed syllable of a line, giving a gentle falling inflexion. It is often used in blank verse and is a marked characteristic of Shakespeare's later plays, *e.g.*,

" Be not afear'd; the isle is full of noises,
Sounds and sweet airs that give delight and hurt not."

Anacrusis.

Anacrusis is the use of an extra syllable before the first regular foot of the line.

Dropped Syllable.

It sometimes appears that a line is a syllable, or syllables, short, until we realise that a suspense or pause occupies the time that would have been taken by the missing syllable. The dropped syllable can be indicated by the " caret " mark, thus ∧. The following technical terms are used for lines that are short of syllables.

Catalectic Line.

This leaves off in the middle of the last foot, as in the trochaic line

" Éver lét the fáncy róam."

or the dactylic line,

" Rings on her fíngers and bélls on her tóes."

The catalectic line is common in trochaic and dactylic verse, for it is in keeping with the tendency of English verse to end on a stressed syllable.

Acephalous Line.

This omits the first syllable of the line, as in the anapæstic line,

" That hóst with their bánners at súnset were séen."

The Cæsura.

The cæsura is a special kind of pause, quite different from that which indicates a dropped syllable. It is a pause about the middle of a line and is usually indicated by a pause in the sense, *e.g.*,

" Both hungered after death; both chose to win or die."

Two Ways of Describing Metre.

The Classical.

The actual names that we have been using for the different kinds of feet and metres are derived from Greek. It is most important, however, to realise that in the classical languages they had a different meaning, for Greek and Latin verse was written on a quite different principle from ours, and was scanned according to the " quantity " or length of the syllable, and not according to stress. Thus an iamb in Greek and Latin consisted of a short syllable followed by a long, marked thus, ∪ –, and a trochee of a long syllable followed by a short, marked – ∪.

In English verse the length of the syllable is totally irrelevant. For instance, the line,

" Pólly pút the kéttle ón and léts have téa "

begins with five trochees, all consisting of two *short* syllables.

The application of Greek words to English metres is confusing only if we forget that in English verse the criterion is stress.

The Modern.

Some writers, however, prefer new ways of describing our verse, and the most popular method is set out below:

A foot is called a period.
A disyllabic metre is called duple or double time.
A trisyllabic metre is called triple time.
A period with the stress on the first syllable is said to be falling.
A period with the stress on a second or third syllable is said to be rising.

III. RHYME.

Another thing that gives a formal pattern to English verse, and distinguishes it from prose, is rhyme. It is not essential to our verse, much of our verse being rhymeless.

Rhyme is a similarity in sound in words occurring normally at the ends of lines. In true rhyme the last stressed syllable and consonants following it are the same, while the sounds preceding the stressed vowel are different, *e.g.*, " cage/page," " pleasure/treasure."

The Types of Rhyme.

The most familiar division of rhyme is into masculine, feminine, and triple rhyme, but we also distinguish broken and Leonine rhyme.

Masculine, Male, or Single Rhyme.

The final syllable is stressed, *e.g.*, " cage/page," " joy/boy."

Feminine, Female, or Two-syllabled Rhyme.

The syllable before the last is stressed, and the final syllable unstressed, *e.g.*, " pleasure/treasure," " bending/lending."

Triple or Tumbling or Three-syllabled Rhyme.

The antepenultimate syllable is stressed. Triple rhyme is normally found in light or comic verse, like that of W. S. Gilbert. This punning " Epitaph on a Dentist " employs it:

" Stranger! Approach this spot with gravity!
John Brown is filling his last cavity."

In " The Bridge of Sighs " [OBEV 662] Hood dares to use it in a serious poem with such rhymes as " scrútiny/mútiny."

Broken Rhyme.

Broken rhyme, where more than one word is needed to complete the rhyme, is occasionally used, *e.g.*, " estate/their gate."

Leonine Rhyme.

Although rhyme normally occurs at the end of the line, we also find verse where the first half of the line rhymes with the second. This device, known as Leonine rhyme, is frequently used in Coleridge's " Ancient Mariner " [OBEV 562], *e.g.*,

" The ice did split, with a thunder-fit."

Poetic Licence in Rhyme.

The difficulty of rhyming in English is considerable, for many words have not a single rhyming word, some have only one, others very few. Certain licences are therefore allowed to the poet in the following ways:

Eye Rhyme or Printers' Rhyme.

Here words rhyme only to the eye, as " love/move." Keats in " Meg Merrilies " uses " rushes/bushes."

Identical Rhyme.

Here the same syllable or word is used twice so that the line rhymes with itself, e.g., " part/impart " [OBEV 562], " universe/this verse " [OBEV 617]. The use of rhyming words spelt differently but pronounced identically is also a poetic licence, e.g., " wright, write, right."

Cockney Rhyme.

Keats' use of Cockney rhymes has been much criticised, e.g., " mourn/torn," " faces/vases," " briar/attire." There is still considerable difference between Northern and Southern pronunciation of English, and many eminent poets have availed themselves of a Southern pronunciation in rhyming " dawn/morn," although in the North of England the "r" of "morn" would be sounded.

Assonance.

Assonance is sometimes used instead of rhyme, and occurs frequently in early folk poetry and less formal verse. It consists in a similarity in the accented vowels and those which follow, but not in the consonants, e.g., " feet/creep," " skin/swim."

Perversion of Rhyme.

Modern poets, following Wilfrid Owen, have sometimes used a deliberate perversion of rhyme, which should not be confused with assonance. Wilfrid Owen opens his bitter poem " A Terre " with the following stanza:

" Sit on the bed. I'm blind and three parts shell.
Be careful; can't shake hands now; never shall.
Both arms have mutinied against me,—brutes.
My fingers fidget like ten idle brats."

The deliberate falsity of rhymes like " shall/shell," and " brutes/brats " conveys Owen's horror at the disintegration and collapse of the First World War.

Recording of Rhyme Schemes.

The conventional way of noting rhyme schemes is to call the first series a, the second b, and so on. Normally each new series is indented, e.g.,

" Joyful, joyful!	a
When virginity	b
Seeks all coyful	a
Man's affinity.	b
Fate all flowery,	c
Bright and bowery	c
Is her dowery!	c
Joyful, joyful."	a

W. S. Gilbert, " Yeomen of the Guard."

IV. THE STANZA.

Some poems are divided into groups of lines, which strictly speaking are called " stanzas," though in popular language they are often known as " verses." Generally the stanzas of a poem are uniform, but sometimes they are varied as in Milton's " Lycidas " [OBEV 325].

V. ENGLISH VERSE FORMS.

English poetry uses an immense wealth of verse forms, distinguishable from each other by the predominating metre and also by the pattern of rhyme and the kind of stanza—or by the absence of rhyme and stanza. An account of these follows.

Iambic Metres.

The metre most natural to the English language is undoubtedly the iambic.

With Iambic Pentameter as Basis.

The iambic pentameter of five stresses and ten syllables, also called the iambic decasyllabic line, is more used than any other, and is the basis of the following forms.

Blank Verse.

Blank verse, consisting of un-rhymed iambic pentameters, is the metre of Shakespeare's plays, Milton's " Paradise Lost," Wordsworth's " Prelude," and Tennyson's " Idylls of the King." In the hands of such masters it is a most flexible instrument, especially when diversified with the eleven-syllabled line with a feminine ending. Shakespeare used the metre with increasing freedom, though it must be remembered that some apparent variations are due to the different pronunciation of Elizabethan times.

The following lines of blank verse occur in Wordsworth's " Prelude," Book III. He is describing his rooms in St. John's College, Cambridge.

" And from my pillow, looking forth by light
Of moon or favouring stars, I could behold
The antechapel where the statue stood
Of Newton with his prism and silent face,
The marble index of a mind for ever
Voyaging through strange seas of Thought, alone."

Heroic Couplet.

The heroic couplet, consisting of iambic pentameters rhyming in pairs, was in Elizabethan times called " riding rhyme," possibly because it is the metre of The Prologue of Chaucer's " Canterbury Tales," and of many of the tales themselves. It became the most fashionable metre of the eighteenth century when it was used by Pope, Goldsmith, and Johnson. Keats later employed it in " Lamia."

The Closed Couplet was, in the heyday of the couplet's vogue, considered the most polished and correct. Here the sentence form exactly coincides with the couplet and the rhyme has a clinching effect, e.g.,

" True ease in writing comes from art, not chance,
As they move easiest who have learned to dance."

Pope was the supreme master of the closed couplet, and eschewed variations such as enjambement, or the Alexandrine.

Enjambement is a variation used by poets before Pope's time and revived by the Romantic poets. In enjambement the sentence flows over from one line or couplet to the next, and the click of the rhyme is submerged, e.g., Keats' description of Lamia in her serpent form with skin of " dazzling hue."

" And full of silver moons, that, as she breathed,
Dissolv'd or brighter shone, or interwreathed
Their lustres with the gloomier tapestries."
            Keats, " Lamia."

The Alexandrine, another variation, is a line of six iambic feet. Dryden made frequent use of the Alexandrine but Pope parodied it in the brilliant line that serves as a mnemonic.

" A needless Alexandrine ends the song,
That, like a wounded snake, drags its slow length along."

The triplet, another variation, consists of three lines rhyming together. The third line is frequently an Alexandrine.

Rhyme Royal.

Rhyme royal has seven iambic pentameters, rhyming ABABBCC. Used by Chaucer in " Troilus and Cressida " [OBEV 14 and 15] and Shakespeare in " Lucrece," it was revived by Masefield in such poems as " Dauber."

Spenserian Stanza.

The Spenserian stanza has eight iambic pentameters followed by an Alexandrine, rhyming ABABBCBCC. Invented by Spenser in " The Faerie Queene," it was used by Byron in " Childe Harold," Keats in " The Eve of St. Agnes," and Shelley in " Adonais."

Elegaic Stanza. The Elegaic stanza has four iambic pentameters, rhyming ABAB. It is also called the " heroic quatrain," quatrain meaning a four-lined stanza. This form is best known through Gray's " Elegy " [OBEV 465].

"Omar Khayyám" Stanza.

The " Omar Khayyám " stanza receives its name from its use by Fitzgerald in his translation of the " Rubaiyat." It has four iambic pentameters, rhyming AABA.

Ottava Rima. Ottava rima, also called the octave stanza, has eight iambic pentameters, rhyming ABABABCC. It was used by Byron in " Don Juan," and by Keats in " Isabella."

Terza Rima. Terza rima has stanzas of three iambic pentameters with a linking rhyme scheme: ABA, BCB, CDC, etc. The concluding stanza is rounded of with an extra line rhyming with its central line, e.g., DEDE, constituting, in effect, a heroic quatrain. Used by Dante, the verse has been adapted by English poets. Shelley's " Ode to the West Wind " [OBEV 617] uses modified terza rima, the final rhymes being DEDEE.

The Sonnet. A sonnet has fourteen iambic pentameters. Perfected in Italy by Petrarch, who died in 1374, it was introduced into England in the sixteenth century. There are two chief types of sonnet.

The *Petrarchan, or Italian, sonnet* has an " octave " of eight lines, rhyming ABBAABBA, followed by a " sestet " of six lines, where some variety of rhyme schemes is found. The strictest Petrarchan sonnets have either two " tercets " of three lines each, with rhymes CDECDE, or else three pairs of lines rhyming CDCDCD.

An example of sestet rhyming CDECDE is Milton's " On His Blindness " [OBEV 327].

Examples of sestets CDCDCD are Wordsworth's " Upon Westminster Bridge " [OBEV 534] and Keats' " On First Looking into Chapman's Homer " [OBEV 641].

Not all of these examples observe the natural pause between octave and sestet which is characteristic of the strict Italian form, and many of our finest sonnets depart from the original rhyme scheme in both octave and sestet.

A lesser-known Petrarchan sonnet by Keats:

' To one, who has been long in city pent,
  'Tis very sweet to look into the fair
  And open face of heaven,—to breathe a
    prayer
Full in the smile of the blue firmament.
Who is more happy, when, with heart's content,
  Fatigued he sinks into some pleasant lair
  Of wavy grass, and reads a debonair
And gentle tale of love and languishment?
Returning home at evening with an ear
  Catching the notes of Philomel,—an eye
Watching the sailing cloudlet's bright career,
  He mourns that day so soon has glided by:
E'en like the passage of an angel's tear
  That falls through the clear ether silently."

The *Elizabethan, or Shakespearean, sonnet* consists of three quatrains with the rhymes ABAB/CDCD/EFEF/ concluded by a couplet rhyming GG. The couplet often clinches the thought.

Examples are Shakespeare's sonnets [OBEV 155–174], and Keats' last sonnet [OBEV 644].

Other Iambic Metres.

Many of our iambic verse forms use a shorter or longer line than the pentameter.

The Octosyllabic Couplet. The octosyllabic couplet consists of lines of four stresses and eight syllables, and the lines rhyme in pairs. English poets like Marvell have used this metre effectively, e.g., " A Garden " [OBEV 365, see also OBEV 367, 370]. It is the metre of Masefield's " Everlasting Mercy " and " Reynard the Fox."

The Ballad. There are two chief kinds of ballad metre.

(a) *Strict Ballad Form* consists of stanzas of four iambic lines, the first and third with four stresses, and the second and fourth with three, with the rhyme scheme ABCB. The fine old ballads " Sir Patrick Spens " [OBEV 381] and " The Wife of Usher's Well " [OBEV 388] are in this metre. Coleridge, in " The Ancient Mariner " [OBEV 562] shows how many varieties of stanza can be based on the simple ballad stanza.

" *Fourteeners* " is the name given to a form which is simply a re-arrangement of the ballad quatrain as a rhyming couplet of two iambic lines with seven stresses, as in Macaulay's " The Armada."

(b) *Less Strict Ballad Form, or Long Metre,* consists of stanzas of four iambic lines each with four stresses, the rhyme scheme being ABCB or ABAB. Many ancient ballads, such as " Thomas the Rhymer " [OBEV 379], are of this type.

" In Memoriam " Metre. This, the metre of Tennyson's " In Memoriam," is like the less strict ballad metre in having four iambic lines, each with four stresses, but its rhyme scheme is ABBA.

Short Metre. Short metre, rarely used, consists of iambic quatrains, each line having three stresses and the rhyme scheme being ABCB.

English Hymn Metres. Most English hymns are written in short iambic lines, and English hymn-ology names them according to the number of syllables. The most common are:

Common Metre, or 8686, with rhymes ABAB, e.g., " O for a thousand tongues to sing " [" Songs of Praise " 595].
Long Metre, or 8888, with rhymes ABAB, e.g., " When I survey the wondrous cross " [" Songs of Praise " 133].
Short Metre, or 6686, with rhymes ABCB, e.g., " Blest are the pure in heart " [" Songs of Praise " 455].

Double Iambic Metre. When we are accustomed to hearing verse we come to realise that stresses are not always of equal weight. It is possible to distinguish in these " fourteeners " of Masefield a major stress, marked `´´` and a minor stress marked `´`.

" Oh sŏme are fónd of Spănish wine, and sŏme are
  fónd of Frĕnch,
And sŏme'll swăllow tăy and stŭff fit ŏnly fór a
  wĕnch."

Masefield's " Captain Stratton's Fancy "
[OBEV 939]

The lines have in fact four major stresses, and between the major stresses intervene three syllables, of which the middle has a minor stress. It is this alternation in the weight of the stress which gives its characteristic swing to such a poem as Chesterton's " The Rolling English Road " [OBEV 930].

Trochaic Metres.

Pure Trochaic Metre.

English poets seldom use a pure trochaic metre, partly because of the difficulty of rhyming, and partly because the continual feminine ending that it involves is not pleasing to the English ear. A few very short lyrics in this metre can be found, as Browne's Song " For her gait, if she be walking " [OBEV 251], but the only poem of any length is Longfellow's " Hiawatha," and the metre of this *tour de force* tends to sound monotonous. It consists of unrhymed lines, each of four stresses, *e.g.*,

" Like a yéllow léaf in áutumn
Like a yéllow wáter-lily."

Modified Trochaic Metre.

Ever since the Middle Ages our poets have contrived to combine the advantages of a trochaic metre and of a masculine ending by the simple expedient of shortening the last foot of the line to a stressed monosyllable. This catalectic, or shortened, trochaic line is found both in couplets and in stanza forms. *The seven-syllabled trochaic couplet, also called the trochaic tetrameter*, consists of these catalectic, or shortened, lines rhyming in pairs, and is a gay, tripping measure, as in some passages of Milton's " L'Allegro " [OBEV 318].

" Háste thee nýmph and bríng with thée
Jést and yóuthful Jóllity."

Keats uses the metre in " Bards of Passion," and " Fancy " [OBEV 637 and 638].

Lyrics in modified trochaic metre are often found. Herrick uses the seven-syllabled lines rhyming in pairs in " Cherry Ripe " and other lyrics [OBEV 264, 279, 280, 281]. Edmund Blunden, in " Forefathers " [OBEV 965], uses it in a stanza rhyming ABABCC. George Herbert in his lyric " Discipline " [OBEV 291] brilliantly combines five- and three-syllabled lines rhyming ABAB, *e.g.*,

" Thrów awáy Thy ród,
Thrów awáy Thy wráth;
Ó my Gód,
Táke the géntle páth."

Further Variations in Modified Trochaic Metre.

The modified trochaic line is especially subject to further variation.

(a) It is often combined with a pure trochaic line, *e.g.*, in Hunt's poem " Jenny Kiss'd Me " [OBEV 600] where the catalectic and the complete trochaic line alternate regularly.

(b) It often has an extra unstressed syllable preceding it (anacrusis), as in the second of these lines from Keats' poem " Fancy " [OBEV 638].

" Ín a dárk conspíracy
To | bánish Éven fróm her ský."

The line that results might well be taken for iambic, and there are some passages in English poetry, such as lines in Milton's " L'Allegro " [OBEV 318], which can be described either as irregular trochaic or irregular iambic lines! It depends on what the hearer judges to be the *basic* stress.

Double Trochaic Metre.

Corresponding to double iambic metre there is a double trochaic metre. W. S. Gilbert effectively uses it in many of his patter songs, as in " Ferdinando and Elvira," *e.g.*,

" Thén we lét off páper cráckers, eách of which
contáined a mótto,
Ánd she lístened while I réad them, till her
móther tóld her nót to."

These lines, like those in double iambic metre, have four major stresses (marked ") and between the major stresses three syllables, of which the middle carries a minor stress.
A modified double trochaic metre, where the last foot is shortened to a stressed monosyllable, can be recognised in Tennyson's " Locksley Hall," or in Lewis Carroll's verses in " Alice in Wonderland ":

" ' Will you wálk a líttle fáster? ' sáid a whíting
tó a snáil."

Trisyllabic Metres Generally.

Because of the irregularities incident to verse in anapæsts, dactyls, and amphibrachs, it is not easy to distinguish one trisyllabic metre from another. Swinburne, the past master of trisyllabic metres, often passes with great freedom from anapæstic to dactylic lines within the same stanza.

Anapæstic Metres.
Pure Anapæstic.

Anapæstic metre is used only in short poems, and often conveys a sense of speed and urgency. The chief variation is the omission of one or two of the unstressed syllables at the beginning of a line. Some of the best-known examples of anapæstic verse are Byron's " Sennacherib," Flecker's " The War Song of the Saracens," and Lewis Carroll's parodies, " 'Tis the voice of the lobster " and " You are old, Father William," from " Alice in Wonderland."

The Limerick.

The limerick may be defined as a single anapæstic stanza, having the first two lines of three feet, the next two lines of two feet and a concluding line of three feet, with the rhyme scheme AABBA.

The origin of the limerick is uncertain, but it became popular after the appearance in 1846 of Edward Lear's " Book of Nonsense." Lear's limericks differ from the contemporary type in that his final line is normally a repetition, adding nothing to the sense and repeating one of the previous rhyme words.

Most of our modern limericks are passed on by word of mouth, but some that concisely express some intellectual attitudes have appeared in print, as the following, on " Determinism "—

" There wás a young mán who said ' Dámn!
It appéars to me nów that I ám
Just a béing that móves
In predéstinate gróoves,
Not a táxi or bús, but a trám.' "

Dactylic Metres.
Pure Dactylic.

Like pure trochaic metre, pure dactylic metre has a feminine ending to the line, which makes rhyming difficult and does not satisfy the English ear. Very few serious poems keep consistently to a pure dactylic verse, and Robert Graves' " In the Wilderness " is most unusual in this respect, *e.g.*,

" Chríst of His géntleness
Thírsting and húngering
Wálked in the wilderness."

Modified Dactylic Metre.

Normally dactylic metre is modified in that a catalectic line is frequently used, where the final foot is shortened to a trochee or a stressed monosyllable, as in Hood's " Bridge of Sighs " [OBEV 662], the most remarkable dactylic poem in the language, *e.g.*,

" Óne more unfórtunate
Wéary of bréath
Ráshly impórtunate
Góne to her déath."

Shakespeare also uses the catalectic line in the refrain to " Where the bee sucks " [OBEV 140]—

" Mérrily mérrily sháll I live nów
Únder the blóssom that hángs on the bóugh."

It is interesting to note how the catalectic dactylic line of the refrain is matched by the catalectic trochaic line of the verse.

Amphibrach Metres.
Pure Amphibrach Metre.

The amphibrach metre is extremely rare in English, although it occurs occasionally in a few lines, or a refrain, like that to " Blow, blow thou Winter Wind " [OBEV 146]. Laurence Binyon's

" Bablock Hythe " is one of the few poems to use amphibrachs continuously, *e.g.*,

> " Till súnset was rímming
> The Wést with pale flúshes;
> Behind the black rúshes
> The lást light was dímming."

Modified Amphibrach Metre.

The pure amphibrach line can be used alternating with a catalectic line, shorn of its last syllable, as in Goldsmith's drinking song in " She Stoops to Conquer," Act I, Scene 2, *e.g.*,

> " Let schóol-masters púzzle their bráin
> With grámmar and nónsense and léarning."

Choriambic Metre.

There are few poems in pure choriambic metre. Ruskin's quatrain " Trust Thou thy Love " [OBEV 753] is one of the few examples, *e.g.*,

> " Trúst thou thy Lóve; if she be próud, ís she not
> swéet? "

Choriambic effects are often obtained incidentally, especially in blank verse, when the first foot of a line is a trochee.

Lionel Johnson frequently achieves the same kind of effect in lyric verses by substituting a choriamb for two iambs, as in the poem " By the Statue of King Charles " [OBEV 909], *e.g.*,

> " Cómely and cálm, he rídes
> Hárd by his ówn Whitehall."

Sprung Rhythm.

Sprung rhythm was practised by Gerard Manley Hopkins and his followers.

Its distinction lies in the fact that in a foot of verse the first syllable is always stressed, and this stressed syllable may be followed by any number of unstressed syllables from none to three, or even more, as the occasion demands. Hopkins has described sprung rhythm in the Preface to his " Poems."

Quantitative Classical Metres.

Since the Renaissance poets such as Spenser, Coleridge, and Tennyson have from time to time endeavoured to reproduce in English verse the complicated quantitative metres of Greek and Latin verse. The difficulty, if not impossibility, of putting the stress on the long vowel in English has for the most past rendered such experiments interesting only to the scholar.

It should always be remembered that the technical names, such as iamb and trochee, although borrowed from the classics, have in English verse a quite different meaning, referring never to quantity but always to stress.

Metrical Forms of French Origin.

It became fashionable during the last years of the nineteenth century for poets to imitate certain verse forms which had long been practised in France, some of them from the time of the troubadours.

Chaucer and Gower had in the fourteenth century used some of these forms, later English poets had occasionally experimented with some of them, and Swinburne, Austin Dobson, Edmund Gosse, and others did much to adapt and naturalise them, although their intricate rhyming patterns are very difficult to construct in a language so short of rhymes as English. The most popular were the triolet, villanelle, rondeau, ballade, and sestina.

Characteristic of the Anglicised versions are:

1. Freedom as regards metre and length of line.

2. Complicated and exacting rhyme schemes, which permit of no such poetic licence as identical rhyme.

3. A refrain line which recurs in certain stereotyped positions without any alteration of sound, although there may be significant alteration of meaning. Only the sestina is without a refrain.

Triolet.

A triolet is a single stanza of eight short lines. The first line is repeated as the fourth, and the first and second appear again as seventh and eighth. Only two rhymes are used, the scheme being: ABAAABAB.

The triolet was re-introduced into England by Bridges in 1873. Austin Dobson's " A Kiss " is a good example of the form.

> " Rose kissed me today,
>   Will she kiss me tomorrow?
> Let it be as it may,
> Rose kissed me today,
> But the pleasure gives way
>   To a savour of sorrow;—
> Rose kissed me today,—
>   Will she kiss me tomorrow ?"

See also Dobson's triolet " I intended an Ode " [OBEV 828].

Villanelle.

The villanelle has five stanzas, each of three lines, followed by one stanza of four lines. It has a refrain which consists of the first and third lines of the first stanza. These lines alternately form the last lines of the four middle stanzas, and reappear as a concluding couplet to the poem. Only two rhymes are employed throughout. Stanzas one to five rhyme ABA and stanza six ABAA.

Austin Dobson wrote several villanelles including the well-known " On a Nankin Plate." The following of Henley's is both a good example and description of the form.

Villanelle by W. E. Henley:

> A dainty thing's the Villanelle
>   Shy, musical, a jewel in rhyme,
> It serves its purpose passing well.
>
> A double-clappered silver bell
>   That must be made to clink in chime,
> A dainty thing's the Villanelle;
>
> And if you wish to flute a spell,
>   Or ask a meeting 'neath the lime,
> It serves its purpose passing well.
>
> You must not ask of it the swell
>   Of organs grandiose and sublime—
> A dainty thing's the Villanelle;
>
> And, filled with sweetness, as a shell
>   Is filled with sound, and launched in time,
> It serves its purpose passing well.
>
> Still fair to see and good to smell
>   As in the quaintness of its prime,
> A dainty thing's the Villanelle.
> It serves its purpose passing well.

Rondeau.

A rondeau is a short and compact verse form. It has thirteen lines, usually of eight syllables, which use only two rhymes, and in addition a refrain, usually of four syllables, which introduces a third rhyme. This refrain consists of the first half of the opening line and is twice repeated, thus giving the rondeau fifteen lines all told. The rondeau is divided into three stanzas with the following rhyme scheme: AABBA: AAB + refrain, C: AABBA + refrain C.

Austin Dobson wrote many rondeaus to this exacting plan, including the ingenious " You bid me try " and " In After Days " [OBEV 830].

A Rondeau by Austin Dobson:

You bid me try.

You bid me try, Blue-Eyes, to write
A Rondeau. What!—forthwith?—to-night?
　Reflect. Some skill I have, 'tis true;—
　But thirteen lines!—and rhymed on two!
" Refrain," as well. Ah, hapless plight!

Still, there are five lines,—ranged aright.
These Gallic bonds, I feared, would fright
　My easy Muse. They did, till you—
　　　You bid me try!

That makes them eight. The port's in sight:—
'Tis all because your eyes are bright!
　Now just a pair to end in ' oo '—
　When maids command, what can't we do.
Behold!—the RONDEAU, tasteful, light,
　　　You bid me try!

　　　　　　　　　　　1876

Roundel.

The roundel is a variation of the rondeau. Swinburne in his " Century of Roundels " wrote a hundred, and his pattern is usually followed. It consists of nine full lines, plus the refrain (consisting of the opening half of the first line), which is twice repeated, giving eleven lines all told. Only two rhymes are used throughout. The roundel is divided into three stanzas with the following rhyme scheme: ABA + refrain B; BAB; ABA + refrain B.

Swinburne's roundel called " The Roundel " is especially interesting.

Rondel.

The rondel is a form of verse similar to the rondeau. The modern English version consists of fourteen lines all told. Only two rhymes are used, and the initial two lines are repeated as lines 7 and 8 and again as lines 13 and 14. The rondel is frequently arranged in three stanzas with a rhyme scheme as follows: ABBA; ABAB; ABBAAB.

The rondel was revived in the nineteenth century by Bridges, Dobson, Gosse and Henley, and Dobson's " Love comes back to his vacant dwelling " is one of the best known.

Ballade.

There are several kinds of ballade, but the most popular modern form consists of three eight-lined stanzas followed by an envoy of four lines. Each of the stanzas and the envoy end with a refrain. The rhymes of the eight-lined stanzas are ABABBCBC, and of the envoy BCBC.

Austin Dobson wrote several ballades of this kind, the best known being, " This was the Pompadour's fan," and " And where are the galleons of Spain? "

Chaucer's " Balade," " Hyd, Absolon, thy gilte tresses clere," is of an earlier seven-lined type without an envoy.

A ballade by Austin Dobson:

The Ballad of the Thrush.

Across the noisy street
　I hear him careless throw
One warning utterance sweet;
　This faint at first, and low
　The full notes closer grow;
Hark! What a torrent gush!
　They pour, they overflow—
Sing on, sing on, O Thrush!

What trick, what dream's deceit
　Has fooled his fancy so
To scorn of dust and heat?
　I, prisoned here below,
　Feel the fresh breezes blow;
And see, thro' flag and rush,
　Cool water sliding slow—
Sing on, sing on, O Thrush!

Sing on. What though thou beat
　On that dull bar, thy foe!
Somewhere the green boughs meet
　Beyond the roofs a-row;
　Somewhere the blue skies show,
Somewhere no black walls crush
　Poor hearts with hopeless woe—
Sing on, sing on, O Thrush!

Envoy.

Bird, though they come, we know,
　The empty cage, the hush;
Still, ere the brief day go,
　Sing on, sing on, O Thrush!

　　　　　　　　　　　1883

The Chant Royal.

The chant royal is a longer form of ballade. It has five stanzas of eleven lines and an envoy of five lines.

The rhyme scheme is ABABCCDDEDE, and the envoy has rhyme DDEDE.

The Sestina.

The sestina has six stanzas, each of six lines. The end words to the lines of the first stanza are repeated as end words in the other five stanzas, but in a different and stereotyped order. The poem concludes with an envoy.

The first sestina published in English was in Spenser's " Shepheardes Calender " (1579). Swinburne wrote many, including " I saw my soul at rest upon a day."

The Clerihew.

The clerihew is an amusing quatrain, so called after its inventor Edmund Clerihew Bentley. It disdains regular metre and depends on the simple rhyme scheme AABB. The distinctive characteristic of the clerihew is that it is concerned with some eminent person, who is named in the first line and then described in a wilfully fanciful way, the matter being dictated by the exigencies of the rhyme, as in Bentley's clerihew on J.S. Mill.

" John Stuart Mill,
　By a mighty effort of will,
Overcame his natural bonhomie
And wrote 'Principles of Political Economy.' "

We might invent a clerihew for Pears Cyclopædia, and say

" You will find *Pears Cyclopædia*
　A simpler and speedier
Aid in your search for verity
If you do not use it with levity."

Free Verse or Vers Libre.

It is hardly possible to define anything so vague as Free Verse. It is characterised by a greater intensity of feeling and a more elevated language than is usual in prose, and has a rhythm that is different from that of poetry in that it is irregular; it has rhythm but not metre.

Free Verse is arranged in lines, but these lines have an indefinite number of syllables. They have balance but no regularly recurring pattern of stress, and no rhyme.

The best-known writer of Free Verse is Walt Whitman, whose " Leaves of Grass " was published in 1855.

VI. CONCLUSION.

The foregoing account is no more than a description of our traditional verse forms. It in no way implies that verse is written according to rules.

We have only to look at Shakespeare's lyrics [OBEV 133–174] to realise how brilliantly free and inventive the poet can be in devising new and delightful patterns of verse—many of them so subtle as to be very difficult to define All that the students and critics can do is to follow in the poets' wake, endeavouring to understand and elucidate the forms that the maker has created.

IV. FIGURES OF SPEECH

We constantly use figurative language without realising it. When we say that we are " browned off," " fed up," " at the end of our tether," we do not expect to be taken literally. We are in fact employing metaphors.

An understanding of metaphors and other figurative expressions enables us to use our language with greater confidence and effectiveness. It also helps us to understand more fully what others have written. Especially is it valuable when we read a good novel, play, or poem, for to the creative writer figurative language is as natural as the air he breathes.

The following guide to our figures of speech is arranged alphabetically for ease of reference.

Alliteration. A kind of repetition. Two or more words in close succession begin with the same letter, or sound, usually a consonant. Up to the fourteenth century much English verse was written according to an alliterative principle, as in this modernised quotation from " Piers Plowman."

" I had *w*andered me *w*eary so *w*eary I rested me
On a *b*road *b*ank by a merry-sounding *b*urn."

A strong tendency to alliteration still survives in our poetry. Shakespeare ridicules it in the mechanical's play in " A Midsummer Night's Dream " (Act V, Scene 1) in such lines as—

" Whereat, with blade, with bloody blameful blade,
He bravely broach'd his boiling bloody breast."

Anti-climax. See Bathos.

Antithesis. A figure of speech where ideas are so set out that they are in sharp contrast to each other, *e.g.*,

" Better to reign in Hell than serve in Heav'n."
Milton.

" To err is human, to forgive divine."
Pope.

Apostrophe. A figure of speech where the speaker or writer suddenly breaks off and directly addresses some other person who may be present either in the flesh or only in the imagination. Often it is not a person but a thing, abstraction, or personification that is addressed, as in Milton's famous apostrophe, " Hail, holy light " in " Paradise Lost," Book III, line 1. Apostrophe can be used with comic effect, *e.g.*,

" She turns, O guardian angels stop her
From doing anything improper."

(This couplet is also, incidentally, an example of bathos.)

Assonance. (1) Assonance is correspondence of vowel sounds. For instance, in the opening lines of the " fairy song " in " A Midsummer Night's Dream " (Act II, Scene 3) there is a play on only three vowels, and this repetition helps towards the effect of a magic charm, *e.g.*,

" Philomel, with melody, Sing."

In Tennyson's poem " Break, break, break " the repetition of the " o " sound in the second line is like an outcry of grief, *e.g.*,

" On thy cold grey stones, O sea."

(2) Assonance is sometimes used instead of rhyme, especially in early folk poetry. Here there is correspondence of one word with another in the accented vowel and any vowels which follow, but not in the consonants, *e.g.*, in " King Estmere," " Spain " is rhymed with " same," and " barone " with " home."

Bathos or Anti-climax. A figure of speech that consists of a sudden and ludicrous descent from lofty to trivial things. In " The Rape of the Lock " Pope wittily used bathos to satirise the frivolity of the woman of fashion, who lacking all sense of proper feeling, casts the same " screams of horror," and " shrieks to pitying heav'n,"

" When *husbands* or when *lapdogs* breathe their last."

The careless writer may fall to bathos which is unintentionally comic in its effect. The word " bathos " in Greek means " depth."

Climax. A figure of speech where ideas are set out in such a way that each rises above its predecessor in fable. In Greek the word " climax " means a ladder. One of the finest examples is in Shakespeare's " The Tempest " (Act IV, Scene 1) when Prospero says,

" And like the baseless fabric of this vision
The cloud-capp'd towers, the gorgeous palaces,
The solemn temples, the great globe itself,
Yea, all which it inherit, shall dissolve."

Epigram. A concise and pointed saying, effective by its wit and ingenuity. It often uses antithesis. S. T. Coleridge's definition of this form is in itself an epigram, *e.g.*,

" What is an epigram? a dwarfish whole:
Its body brevity, and wit its soul."

Euphemism. A figure of speech where a harsh or distressing expression is replaced by one that is gentler, if less accurate. Thus we may call a lie a " flight of fancy," or a " terminological inexactitude." There is a striking instance of euphemism in "Macbeth" (Act I, Scene 5), when Lady Macbeth, planning the murder of her guest, Duncan, says, " He that's coming must be provided for."

Hypallage or " Transferred Epithet." A figure of speech where an adjective, or adverb, is separated from the word to which it belongs grammatically, and is transferred to some other word in the sentence, its unusual position giving it a kind of emphasis. The word " obsequious " is thus transferred in the sentence " A lacquey presented an obsequious cup of coffee."

Hyperbole. A figure of speech where there is a deliberate use of exaggeration for the sake of effect as in the phrase " tons of money." Lady Macbeth uses hyperbole when she says, " Here's the smell of blood still; all the perfumes of Arabia will not sweeten this little hand " (Act V, Scene 1).

Writers of film trailers frequently indulge in hyperbole.

Innuendo. A figure of speech where something is hinted at, or suggested, but not openly stated. Dickens uses innuendo to suggest Scrooge's stinginess by saying, " Darkness was cheap, and Scrooge liked it."

Irony. (1) A figure of speech where the speaker says one thing but intends the opposite to be understood. Shylock uses the word " courtesies " ironically when he says,

" Fair sir, you spit on me on Wednesday last,
You spurn'd me such a day; another time
You call'd me dog; and for these courtesies
I'll lend you thus much moneys."
" Merchant of Venice " (Act I, Scene 3).

The use of irony can clearly be seen in Shakespeare's " Julius Cæsar " in Antony's well-known speech to the citizens. They gradually realise that when Antony repeats that Brutus and the rest are " honourable men," he is speaking ironically, and intends the opposite. When they fully perceive this they cry, " They were traitors . . . villains, murderers." (" Julius Cæsar," Act III, Scene 2.)

(2) *Dramatic irony* is the use of words which have a second inner significance that is not realised by some of the actors in a scene. For instance, in Sheridan's " School for Scandal," Act IV, Scene 3, Sir Peter admires Joseph Surface's useful screen, and Surface replies, " Oh yes, I find great use in that screen." He and the audience know, but Sir Peter does not, that at that very moment the screen is concealing Peter's own wife who had rashly visited Joseph.

It is helpful to remember that in Greek the word " irony " means " dissimulation."

Litotes. A figure of speech which is really a special kind of understatement (or Meiosis). Instead of making a positive statement (*e.g.*, " This is a difficult task ") we might use Litotes, and say " This is no easy task," thus expressing a positive by the negative of its opposite.

Malapropism. An amusing inaccuracy in vocabulary. Words that have an accidental similarity in sound may become confused in the speaker's mind and the wrong word may come uppermost. Thus Mrs. Malaprop complains that the disobedience of her niece gives her, not " hysterics," but " hydrostatics." It is not surprising that Mrs. Malaprop, of Sheridan's " The Rivals," has given her name to this kind of verbal confusion, though many before her time, including humble folk in Shakespeare's plays, have uttered malapropism. Bottom, in "A Midsummer Night's Dream," says that in the wood they " may rehearse more obscenely " when he means " obscurely."

Meiosis. A figure of speech where a deliberate understatement is made for the sake of effect. English people are especially fond of Meiosis and often use it colloquially, in such an expression as " He made a very ' decent ' contribution," meaning a very " generous " contribution. The full meaning of what we intend is often conveyed by the tone of voice, *e.g.*,

" This is *some* war."

Metaphor. It is helpful to think of the figure of speech, metaphor, as a condensed simile. In metaphor one thing is not merely *compared* to another, as in simile, but is boldly spoken of as if it actually *were* that other. Thus Bacon, in the following metaphor, does not say books are *like* food, but speaks of them as if they actually *were* food, *e.g.*, " Some books are to be tasted, others to be swallowed, and some few to be chewed and digested."

Metaphor is usually defined as the transfer of a name, or descriptive term, to some object to which it is not properly applicable, thus making an implicit comparison. Shakespeare uses nautical terms to describe our human situation when Brutus says,

" There is a tide in the affairs of men which, taken at the flood, leads on to fortune " (" Julius Cæsar," Act IV, Scene 3).

In *Mixed Metaphor* two or more inconsistent metaphors are used of the same object, as when, speaking of a suspicion, someone said, " I smell a rat; I see it in the air; but I will nip it in the bud."

Metonymy. A figure of speech where a person or thing is not named directly, but by some associated thing. Instead of saying, " The prisoner addressed the magistrate," we might use metonymy and say, " The prisoner addressed the bench." Similarly, " a speech from the Lord Chancellor " is sometimes called " a speech from the Woolsack."

Onomatopœia. The use of words which imitate or echo the sounds they suggest, *e.g.*,

" Seas half-frozen slushed the deck with slime."
Masefield.

Oxymoron. A figure of speech where words that are usually contradictory are combined in one expression, *e.g.*, " bitter-sweet."

" I know this is a joyful trouble to you."
" Macbeth," Act II, Scene 3.

Paradox. A figure of speech where a statement is made that at first sight seems contradictory, or absurd, *e.g.*,

" The rule of the road is a paradox quite:
If you keep to the left, you are sure to be right."
and

" The child is father of the man."
Wordsworth.

Pathetic Fallacy. A figure of speech where it is assumed that things of nature have feelings like those of human beings, *e.g.*,

" And daffadillies fill their cups with tears."
Milton.

In Greek " pathos " means " feeling."

Personification. A figure of speech where some abstraction, or some inanimate thing is represented as a person, *e.g.*,

" Rule, Britannia."

" But look the dawn in russet mantle clad
Walks o'er the dew of yon high eastern hill."
Hamlet, Act I, Scene 1.

Personification is really a special kind of metaphor.

Pun. The use of words so as to convey a double meaning, as in Belloc's couplet

" When I am dead, I hope it may be said
" His sins were scarlet, but his books were read.' "

In the three puns that follow there is a suggestion of a banking transaction! " The Egyptians received a check on the bank of the Red Sea which was crossed by Moses." Puns, which were popular in the nineteenth century, especially with Lamb and Hood, are now out of favour.

Simile. A figure of speech which makes a comparison pointing out a similarity between things otherwise unlike. It is usually introduced by " like " or " as," *e.g.*,

" Men fear death as children fear to go in the dark." Bacon.

" His own thought drove him like a goad."
Tennyson.

Spoonerism. An accidental transposition of the sound of two words, so called after Rev. W. A. Spooner, warden of New College, Oxford, *e.g.*,

" You have hissed all my mystery lectures " for " You have missed all my history lectures."

Synecdoche. A figure of speech where the name of a part is used for the whole, or the whole for the part, *e.g.*,

" A fleet of a hundred sail ",

meaning a hundred ships.

Synecdoche is really a special kind of Metonymy.

Transferred Epithet. See Hypallage.

V. LITERARY FORMS

Allegory. A description or story which has a second and deeper significance below the surface. The characters are really personifications, usually representing some vice or virtue. Allegory flourished in the Middle Ages, but the best-known allegory in the world is Bunyan's " Pilgrim's Progress " (1678), which has been translated into over a hundred different languages and dialects. On the surface " The Pilgrim's Progress " is the story of a journey in which the hero encounters many difficulties but at last reaches his destination. Its inner meaning is the progress of the Christian soul through life on earth. Spenser's " Faerie Queene " (1589 and 1596) is a more subtle and complex allegory, capable of several interpretations, religious, ethical, and political. Allegory has been described as extended metaphor. *See* **M39.**

Autobiography. The story of a man's (or woman's) own life, written by himself. The autobiography is becoming increasingly popular, recent excellent examples being Stephen Spender's *World within World*, Richard Church's *Over the Bridge* and Laurie Lee's *Cider with Rosie.*

Ballad. There are two chief types of ballad:

1. A light song, often sentimental, as was the Victorian ballad, or a popular song, often of a personal kind, praising or attacking some notability.

2. A traditional poem, passed on by word of mouth. Many of our traditional ballads date from the 15th century. They tell some stirring tale, as do the many ballads about Robin Hood. Sometimes they record an actual occurrence, like the ballad " The Battle of Otterbourne," which tells of a Border skirmish, fought in 1388. Such ballads are enlivened by lively dialogue, and they use a special kind of stanza, which is described on **M33.**

Ballade. A short highly stylised poem, with a strict verse form. *See* **M37.**

Biography. A narrative telling the life story of some actual person, usually a well known figure. The most famous biographer of classical times was Plutarch, who in the 1st century A.D. wrote his series of parallel " Lives " of twenty-three Greeks and twenty-three Romans. The English translation of this provided Shakespeare with some of the plots of his plays. Boswell's *Life of Samuel Johnson* (1791) is our best-known English biography.

Burlesque. The aim of burlesque is to make us laugh by ridiculing the work of some other writer. Sometimes it treats his serious subject in a mocking way. Sometimes it takes the form of an absurd imitation or caricature of his style. Some of our most successful burlesques are dramatic in form, like Sheridan's " The Critic," produced in 1779. This has a play within a play, called "A Tragedy Rehears'd," a brilliant burlesque of the sentimental, historical plays so popular in his time. Danny Kaye's film, " The King's Jester," is a burlesque of pseudo-historical films.

Chant Royal. A poem of a strictly formal kind, French in origin. *See* **M37.**

Clerihew. A single-stanza verse form, four lines long. *See* **M37.**

Comedy. A play which is happy and amusing in tone, but not necessarily light or superficial. A comedy always has a fortunate conclusion. Shakespeare's " Twelfth Night " and Oscar Wilde's " The Importance of being Earnest " are typical examples.

Drama. A play in verse or prose, where the story is unfolded and the characters represented through the actions and speeches of actors on a stage. It is essential to good drama that there should be some kind of dynamic action and some conflict between the characters. In comedy the conflict is usually open and external. " As You Like It," for instance, begins with a quarrel between Orlando and Oliver. But most of the world's finest tragedies reveal also an inner conflict in the soul of man. In " Hamlet " the hero is at odds with many people, including his mother, the king, Ophelia, Polonius, and Laertes but all these struggles are of secondary significance, compared with the conflict in his own mind. Even a play like " Waiting for Godot," which reduces incident and conflict to a minimum, must make some concession to the demand of the audience for the dynamic. Drama cannot be static. Occasionally poets have written dramas which they knew were not practicable for the stage. Shelley's lyrical dramas, " Prometheus Unbound " and " Hellas," are of this kind. *See* Section I.

Eclogue. In classical literature a brief poem, usually in the form of a dialogue between shepherds. It was a popular form in the time of the Renaissance; Spenser's " Shepheardes Calendar " (1579) consists of twelve eclogues one for each month of the year.

Elegy. A lyric poem of lamentation for the dead. Gray's " Elegy in a Country Church-yard " (1750) is the best-known English elegy. It reflects in a general way on the " destiny obscure " of the humble folk who are buried in a quiet church-yard, probably that of Stoke Poges, but most elegies mourn the death of only one person. Such are Shelley's " Adonais " (1821), on the death of Keats, and Matthew Arnold's " Thyrsis " (1867), commemorating his friend Arthur Hugh Clough. Tennyson's " In Memoriam " (1850) is unusual, in that it is not a single elegy, but a series of elegiac poems, inspired by the poet's grief for the death in 1833 of his friend Arthur Hallam.

Epic. A very long narrative poem, usually consisting of several books. The epic tells of the splendid deeds of some hero of history or legend and is frequently concerned with war. Some of the world's greatest epics are the Greek " Iliad " and " Odyssey," ascribed to Homer, the Latin "Aeneid " of Virgil, the Hindu " Mahabharata," and Milton's " Paradise Lost," whose hero is God himself. The epic is distinguished by its sustained dignity of style.

Epilogue. *See* Prologue.

Essay. The word essay, derived from the French, means literally an " attempt " or " endeavour," and as a literary term it applies to a short prose composition which attempts to present the author's reflections on any subject he chooses. As a literary form the essay derives from the French " Essais " of Montaigne, first translated into English by Florio in 1603. Our first English essayist was Francis Bacon, who published between 1597 and 1625 three volumes of his essays, brief, pithy, and objective in character. In course of time the essay has become more subjective and personal, especially in the hands of Lamb, Hazlitt, and contemporary writers.

Extravaganza. A composition, musical or literary, which uses improbable and fantastic elements and incidents. A good example of narrative extravaganza is Thackeray's *Rose and the Ring* (1855), in which, for instance, Gruffanuff's husband, the footman, is, because of his rudeness, turned into a door-knocker. Extravaganzas are frequently dramatic in form, and most panto-mimes may be regarded as such.

Fable. A very brief story designed to teach some lesson or moral. The characters of the story are often animals, birds, or insects, which converse like human beings. The most famous of all fables are those attributed to Aesop, and those of La Fontaine, the French writer of the 17th century.

Farce. A species of dramatic comedy whose whole aim is to excite laughter. It does not scruple to use improbable characters and incidents and absurd situations. "Charley's Aunt" is a typical farce.

Lampoon. A coarse satire (q.v.) attacking an individual. Lampoons are usually short. The word itself is derived from a French word meaning "drinking song."

Limerick. A single-stanza verse form, 5 lines long and with a formal metre and rhyme scheme. *See* **M35.**

Lyric. In ancient Greece a lyric was originally a poem meant to be sung to the accompaniment of the lyre, a stringed musical instrument rather like a small harp. Later the word was used for a poem with song-like qualities; short, usually divided into verses, and expressing the feelings of the poet. The lyric flourished in England in the Elizabethan age, as witnessed by the lovely lyrics scattered through Shakespeare's plays. Neg-lected in the 18th century, it became popular again with the Romantic poets of the 19th century. Odes, elegies, and sonnets are all species of lyrics.

Mask or Masque. A dramatic entertainment performed by amateurs and originating in the court masquerade. The action or plot of the masque is of the slightest and there is little concern with portrayal of character, for the masque gives pleasure by means of its verse, music, and dancing, and its elegant costume and scenery. It was very popular in the 16th and 17th centuries, and from 1605 Ben Jonson wrote many court masques, for which Inigo Jones designed original costumes and settings. Our best-known examples are Shakespeare's masque in Act IV of "The Tempest" and Milton's "Comus".

Melodrama. There are two meanings of the word melodrama.

1. In the early 19th century a melodrama meant a play, usually of a romantic and sensa-tional kind, in which songs were inserted, and where an orchestra accompanied the action. The musical comedy of today might be regarded as its modern counterpart.

2. Today the word melodrama is used of an inferior kind of play, which deliberately excites the emotions by its sensational and violent hap-penings, but which has a happy ending. We should be careful to distinguish melodrama, which uses violence for its own sake, from serious plays, like "Hamlet" or "King Lear," where violent acts are only incidents necessary to a profound interpretation of human conduct.

Memoirs. The word is normally used of a record of events of which the author has some personal experience or special source of informa-tion.

Miracle Plays. Mediæval verse plays produced from the late 14th to 16th centuries by the town guilds and performed in the market-place, or other suitable open space. They consisted of a series of dramatised stories from the Bible or Lives of Saints. Each scene would be allotted to one of the guilds, which was then responsible for its production on a wheeled stage. As soon as the actors of one guild had completed their scene, their stage would be trundled off, sometimes to another rendezvous, and would itself be succeeded by another stage with its scene, until a whole cycle of episodes had been performed. Four great cycles of miracle plays are still extant, called after the towns where they were probably performed. York, Coventry, Chester, and Wake-field. The Wakefield cycle is often called the Towneley cycle. The plays have not only a strong religious sense but also a lively comic spirit. The Towneley cycle has some especially racy comic scenes. One popular incident shows the noisy quarrel that results when Noah's wife refuses to go into the ark.

Mock Heroic. A species of parody (q.v.), caricaturing some play or poem written in a lofty and high-flown style. "The Rehearsal" (1672), by Villiers, is typical. It is an absurd imitation ridiculing the artificial and high falutin' heroic plays which were then in vogue.

Monody. In Greek literature an ode sung by a single voice, like our solo in music. In English literature it signifies a poem of mourning for someone's death. The elegies "Lycidas," by Milton, and "Thyrsis," by Matthew Arnold, were both called monodies by their authors.

Monologue. Originally a scene where one person of the drama spoke alone. Today it usually means a dramatic composition for a single actor, such as the well-known Lancashire mono-logues presented by Stanley Holloway. The word is also sometimes used as meaning soliloquy.

Moralities or Morality Plays. Mediæval verse plays of an allegorical kind, which attempted to teach lessons of virtue, the persons of the drama usually being not real people, but personifications. Most Moralities date from the 15th century, the best known being "Everyman," which is Dutch in origin. The hero, Everyman, is summoned by Death, and vainly appeals for help to his friends, Fellowship, Kindred, Goods, Knowledge, Beauty, and Strength, but all fail him. Only his own Good Deeds will consent to accompany him on his last journey.

Mysteries or Mystery Plays. Some modern writers use the term "Mystery play" instead of "Miracle play" (q.v.). It is really an alternative title. One critic tried to distinguish between "Mystery plays," as concerned with stories from the Gospels, and "Miracle plays," as concerned with the lives and deeds of Saints, but this dis-tinction is not usually followed.

Novel. A lengthy prose fiction in narrative form, telling a realistic story of people and their doings. Its chief interest is in character and incident. The first English novelist was Samuel Richardson, whose novels, especially *Pamela* (1740-41) and *Clarissa Harlowe* (1747-48), had a European reputation. In the present century writers like James Joyce, and Virginia Woolf have written what have been called novels of the "stream of consciousness," where the interest lies not so much in the incidents as in the mind's response to events, and reflections. *See* M4-21.

Ode. In classical literature an ode was a poem to be sung. In English literature it signifies a lyric poem, usually in rhyme, and is seldom longer than 150 lines. It is usually in the form of an address, and lofty in its feeling and style. The ode was popular with the romantic poets. Some of our best known are Shelley's " Ode to the West Wind," and Keats' " Ode to a Nightingale," " Ode on a Grecian Urn," and " To Autumn," all of them published in 1820.

Parable. A parable is an arresting simile or metaphor from nature or common life, which may be elaborated into a life-like story. It presents a situation which at a certain point implies some correspondence with ethical or religious principle. *See* C. H. Dodd's *The Parables of the Kingdom.*

Parody. A literary caricature, which mimics the themes and style of some other author in such a way as to make his faults seem absurd and laughable. J. C. Squire's *Tricks of the Trade* is an amusing collection of his skilful parodies of such writers as Byron, Wordsworth, and Masefield.

Pastoral. A pastoral poem, romance, or play is one in which the life of shepherds or of simple rustic folk is portrayed in an idealised way. Originating in Greek literature, the pastoral was revived at the time of the Renaissance. Spenser's " Shepheardes Calendar " consists of twelve pastoral eclogues. Shakespeare's "As You Like It " is a pastoral play, Milton's " Lycidas " is a pastoral elegy and his " Comus " a pastoral masque. There is usually in the pastoral a deeper meaning below the surface. A critic has said, " The shepherd's cloak was the acknowledged disguise of the lover, the poet, the courtier, the pastor of souls, the critic of contemporary life." In the pastoral form the charm of a simple setting and deeper significance are combined.

Prologue and Epilogue. Generally speaking, a prologue means a foreword, or preface, and an epilogue an appendix to a literary work, but the terms are often used more specifically when referring to a play. Here the prologue is a short speech in verse or prose spoken to the audience by one of the actors before the play begins, the epilogue a similar speech after its conclusion. The prologue endeavours to put the audience into a receptive state of mind, the epilogue to ask for a kind reception to the play. Shakespeare's " Romeo and Juliet " has a prologue, his " As You Like It " an epilogue, spoken by Rosalind, who says, " Good plays prove the better by the help of a good epilogue." In the 18th century it was customary for a leading actor to speak the prologue and for a leading actress to make a plea for the play in the epilogue.

Romance. The romance of the early Middle Ages was a fictitious tale in verse, telling the adventures of some hero of chivalry, the interest being in the incidents, sometimes of a supernatural kind, rather than in character. The most famous of these early romances is the French " Chanson de Roland " of the early 12th century. In the later Middle Ages a romance might be written in prose. In the 16th and 17th centuries a romance meant a tale in either prose or verse in which the scenes and incidents were remote from those of real life. Sir Philip Sidney's " Arcadia " (1590), written to entertain his sister, is of this type. Today the word romance is rather vaguely used of a tale of somewhat improbable events. Sir Henry Rider Haggard wrote several such romances, including *King Solomon's Mines* (1886) and *She* (1887).

Rondeau. A poem of a strictly formal kind. French in origin. *See* M36.

Rondel. A poem similar in form to the rondeau. *See* M37.

Roundel. A variation of the Rondeau. *See* M37.

Saga. The word saga, which is of Norse origin and means story, is applied to the mediæval prose narratives of Iceland and Norway, especially those concerned with the traditions of Icelandic families and Norwegian kings. William Morris, in his " Earthly Paradise," gives in " The Lovers of Gudrun " a version of the Icelandic Laxdæla Saga.

Satire. A work in either verse or prose attacking folly and vice. Pope's " Dunciad," in verse, published between 1728 and 1743, ridicules contemporary authors and literary follies in a massive attack on dullness and literary hacks. Swift's *Gulliver's Travels* (1726), which on the surface is a series of prose tales of travel to imaginary countries, is actually a comprehensive satire. It begins, in the first book on " Lilliput," with incisive ridicule of the squabbles between English political parties and religious sects, and culminates, in the final book on the Houyhnhnms, in a devastating attack on all that is bestial in human nature. Samuel Butler's *Erehwon* (an anagram of Nowhere), published in 1872, also uses a prose travel tale in his satirical exposure of Victorian convention and hypocrisy. Although not precisely satires, many of Shaw's plays are satirical in spirit. "Arms and the Man " may be considered in one of its aspects as a satire on war.

Sestina. A poem of a strictly formal kind. French in origin. *See* M37.

Skit. A light satire, often in the form of parody.

Soliloquy. In a soliloquy a man talks to himself, or utters his thoughts aloud regardless of the presence of others who may hear him. The word is usually applied to such utterances by a character in a play. The most famous soliloquies in literature are those of Hamlet.

Sonnet. A lyric poem of fourteen lines, with an intricate rhyme scheme. *See* M34.

Squib. A brief, sharp satire (*q.v.*) attacking an individual.

Threnody. A term from the Greek, seldom used today. It means a song of mourning, especially a lament for the dead.

Tragedy. A play, or other literary work, which is preoccupied with the serious and unhappy aspects of life. It is sombre in tone and ends with misfortune. Shakespeare's " Macbeth " and Ibsen's " Ghosts " are typical tragedies.

Tragi-Comedy. The word is used in two different ways:

(*a*) It may denote a play (or very occasionally a story) which combines both tragic and comic elements. Chekhov's " The Cherry Orchard " is a tragi-comedy of this type.

(*b*) It may also mean a play which is for the most part sombre in theme and tone, but which has a happy conclusion, like Shakespeare's " The Winter's Tale."

Trilogy. In Greek literature a series of three tragedies, like Aeschylus' trilogy, the " Oresteia," written when he was nearly seventy, in the 5th century B.C. In modern times the word trilogy is applied to any sequence of three literary works which are related to each other in subject and theme.

Triolet. A single-stanza verse form, eight lines long, and with a very formal pattern, French in origin. *See* M36.

Villanelle. A poem of a strictly formal kind, French in origin. *See* M36.

VI. LANGUAGES

The number of known, living languages exceeds 3,000, the great majority of which can be ascribed to about a dozen main language families. More than half the world's population of 3,632,000,000, however, can be reached by as few as 13 languages.

Languages are related in a distinct group if their ancestry can either be traced back to the same mother tongue or be inferred to derive from an assumed parent language (through comparative linguistic methods, historical records, etc.). The term " family " is used for the largest possible such grouping. Contrary to common belief related languages need not be alike phonetically or grammatically, nor need speakers of related languages have racial or cultural characteristics in common.

The scientific study of the structure and mechanics of language in general is the domain of *general linguistics*, various branches of which connect with other sciences, such as, for example, communication theory. *Comparative linguistics* denotes the study of the history and relationships of individual languages and language groups, and has connections therefore with social studies such as ethnology and historical geography. Modern linguistic study has developed from the study of comparative philology, which dates from the end of the 18th cent. It achieved greater scientific objectivity and exactitude in the last decades of the 19th cent., since when the term *philology* has reverted to its original significance, denoting the study chiefly of written texts: its connections lie therefore rather with literary history and criticism.

Chinese has the greatest number of speakers, followed by English, Hindi, Russian, Spanish, Japanese, German, French, Italian, Malay, Bengali, and Portuguese.

The oldest recorded language is Sumerian, which was spoken by a non-Semitic people who lived in the southern part of ancient Mesopotamia, *c.* 3,500 B.C. It was a language conveyed in cuneiform script with a structure and vocabulary unrelated to any other known language. It lost ground to the Akkadian Semitic language and began to die out in Hammurabi's time.

The oldest living language is Chinese, with a progressive history of 4,000 years during which it has maintained its identity and given shape to ideas. It is not phonetic, *i.e.*, it is not written in groups of letters which represent sounds, but each word is represented as a character. Coptic, a direct descendant of the ancient Egyptian language, has also survived but only as the liturgical language of the Christian Coptic Church. (Modern Egyptian is a dialect of Arabic.)

In grammar and phonetics, the most complex languages are those of the Caucasus, together with North American Indian tongues (including Eskimo), while the simplest is said to be Malay. The native languages of Britain, besides English, are Welsh (with an unbroken literary history since the 6th cent. A.D.), Irish Gaelic (the native tongue of Ireland with a literary history dating back to the 9th cent. A.D.), and Scots Gaelic (which became separate from Irish Gaelic in the 13th cent.,

though for literary purposes classical (Irish) Gaelic was employed in Scotland until the 18th cent.). Manx Gaelic is on the point of extinction. Cornish survived until the 18th cent.

A *lingua franca* is a language which acts as a medium of communication over a large multilingual area, such as Hindi in India, Swahili in southern Africa, Malay in the southwestern Pacific areas.

A *hybrid* language arises when foreign speakers adopt the basic vocabulary of a second language, usually as a commercial medium, and adapt it to their own phonetic and grammatical patterns: *Pidgin English* is English–Cantonese, *Beach-la-Mar* is English–Polynesian, *Papiamento* is Negro–Spanish of Curaçao.

An *artificial* language is one that has been deliberately constructed to act as a universal medium of communication; the best known is Esperanto.

A *standard* language is one recognised by a state as its national language and used for administration, national communications (*e.g.*, radio), and education. It may be one of several languages actually spoken in a particular country; or a particular form or dialect in a state where dialectal differences are acute, *e.g.*, standard Italian is the Tuscan dialect; or a purely written standard, *e.g.*, most Arabic-speaking nations, despite vernacular dialectal differences, employ classical Arabic in books and newspapers. A standard language thus tends to act as a *lingua franca*.

Nine major language-families and 11 major individual languages are listed below:

African Languages. Two linguistic pictures of Africa could be drawn, one showing the native languages and dialects, the other showing a patchwork cover of European languages of colonisation; yet neither would be complete without the other, for the two groups are everywhere in close contact, Many states recognise two or more official languages, both native and colonial in origin.

The principal colonial languages are French, English, Spanish, Portuguese, Italian, German, and Flemish. Dutch is of particular interest, since it has developed into what is virtually a new language, Afrikaans, the standard form of which differs in many respects from the European Dutch standard.

The native languages of North Africa, and of East Africa down to the equator, belong to the Semito-Hamitic family (*q.v.*). The true Negro-African languages number many hundreds, with a profusion of dialects. The southern half of the continent is almost exclusively the domain of the Bantu languages. Of these, the chief representative is Swahili: it boasts a considerable body of literature, has long had currency as a medium of trade and commerce, and is fast thriving as a native *lingua franca* over the whole region. It may have as many as 10 million speakers. The Khoin, or Bushman–Hottentot languages, are spoken in parts of Angola, South West Africa and Botswana. The remaining languages, from Senegal to the Sudan, are roughly described as Sudanic, but they have not been satisfactorily classified and probably include many separate language families. The most significant of these is Hausa: originating in northern Nigeria, it has become, like Swahili in the south, an extensive *lingua franca*, with some 15 million speakers.

Altaic. A family of languages extending from Turkey to Mongolia and to northern Siberia, consisting of three main groups: (1) the Turkic languages, the most important member being Turkish, with about 26 million speakers; (2) Mongolian; (3) Tungusic languages of northern Asia, chiefly represented by the Manchu literary language.

Arabic. The language has a great history—as the evangelising medium of Islam, as the vehicle of a rich imaginative literature, and as the repository of science and philosophy during Europe's " dark ages." Spoken by some 75 million inhabitants of countries south and east of the Mediterranean, it remains one of the great languages of the present day. Countries in which it occupies official status include Algeria, Iraq, Israel, Jordan, Kuwait, Lebanon, Libya, Morocco, Saudi Arabia, Syria, and the United Arab Republic. *See also* **Semito-Hamitic.**

Austro-Asiatic. Family of languages in southern Asia. They include (1) the Mon-Khmer languages, chief representative Cambodian or Khmer, and (2) the Munda or Kolarian languages of Bihar and Orissa in north-east India. Some linguists ascribe to this group the Annamese and Mu'ong languages of Vietnam.

Chinese. As the national language of China's estimated 710 million inhabitants, Chinese is spoken by over twice the number who speak English, the second most widely spoken language in the world. Unlike India, China is not divided linguistically except in the south-eastern maritime provinces where several differing and mutually unintelligible dialects are found, including Cantonese, Wu, Min, and Hakka. In most of the rest of the country the language known in the West as Mandarin is spoken.

Mandarin, as spoken in Peking, is now the standard form of Chinese. This national language is called *p'u-t'ung-hua* (common speech). Mandarin is also the official standard of Taiwan, although the local dialect is Amoy, a variety of Min. The majority of the Chinese people who have settled in the United Kingdom speak Cantonese.

The traditional Chinese script is ideographic, *i.e.*, each character represents the meaning of a word, not its pronunciation, so that speakers of otherwise divergent dialects have always been able to follow the written language. The Chinese Government have recently introduced a system of romanisation, a language reform which will facilitate writing and printing through the replacement of the 4,000 essential characters by the relatively few

letters of the Roman alphabet. Chinese has an attested history of over 4,000 years. *See also* Sinitic.

Dravidian. Family of languages found in southern India. Chief representatives: Telugu (spoken by some 35 million in Andhra Pradesh), Tamil (over 30 million in Madras and eastern Ceylon), Canarese or Kannada (16 million in Mysore) and Malayalam (15 million in Kerala). These are the only four Dravidian languages officially recognised in the Indian Union (*see* Indian languages). They are written in native alphabets which, while ultimately related to the Devanagari script, are so modified as to appear totally different. Tamil and Canarese are well established literary languages.

English. The English language belongs to the Germanic branch of the great Indo-European family of languages. Its closest relatives are Frisian and Dutch. It originated in the various Saxon dialects carried across by invaders during the 4th and 5th cent. A.D. Old English, as it is now known, was essentially a spoken language, but with the rise of Christianity and the influence of Latin writers, it emerged as a literary language. Other influences came from Scandinavian sources (Viking invasions) and French (Norman conquest). Modern English dates from the emergence of Mercian as the dominant dialect during the 14th century. As the major language, through former colonisation of countries in all five continents, and as a world-wide cultural, scientific, and commercial medium, English may have up to 300 million speakers.

French. The official language of France's 48 million inhabitants. It is also one of the two official languages of Belgium (spoken mainly in Brussels and the south by about 4 million), and one of the three official languages of Switzerland, with over 1 million speakers in the western cantons (Geneva, Neuchatel, Fribourg, Valais, Vaud). With French-speaking peoples in many parts of the world, in Canada (Quebec and Ontario) and in countries belonging to the French Community, it may have a total of 80 million speakers. Its derivation from Latin classes it as a Romance language, and it is thus related to Portuguese, Spanish, Italian and Rumanian.

German. The language spoken by over 75 million people in East and West Germany, by 7 million in Austria, and as an official language of Switzerland, by nearly 4 million in 19 of the 25 cantons. In addition there are German-speaking peoples in Hungary, Czechoslovakia, Poland, and other smaller areas of Europe, and in former colonial regions (in Africa and some of the Pacific islands), bringing the total to between 95 and 100 million. The standard, High German, is distinct from the Low German or *Plattdeutsch* colloquial dialects spoken in the lowlands of northern Germany. German and English are the chief representatives of the Germanic group of languages, which also include Dutch and the Scandinavian languages.

Hindi. The official language of India, as laid down in the 1950 Constitution. English also continued as the official language until 1965 and under the Official Language Act, 1963, may still be used in addition to Hindi. Technically, Hindi denotes a group of dialects of which Hindustani is the principal member. It is written in the Devanagari script, but has a variant Urdu, written in Arabic script and considerably influenced by Arabic and Persian vocabularies. There are close on 170 million speakers of Hindi/Urdu. The necessity of establishing an official medium was emphasised by the fact that, according to the 1961 census, the number of languages and dialects spoken in India amounted to 1,652. Hindi is an Indo-Aryan language of the Indo-European family related to Persian and more distantly to the majority of European languages. It is a modern descendant of Sanskrit, the literary language of the Vedic scriptures.

Urdu and Bengali are the two state languages of Pakistan. English continues to be the official language until 1970.

Indian Languages. *See* Hindi, Indo-European, Dravidian, Austro-Asiatic.

Indo-European. Most of the languages of Europe and of a large part of southwestern Asia belong to the Indo-European family. The notable exceptions are Hungarian, Basque, Finnish, Lappish, Turkish, and the Caucasian languages. The major branches and languages are: Germanic (English, German, Dutch, Flemish, Danish, Swedish, Norwegian, Icelandic), Romance (French, Portuguese, Spanish, Italian, Rumanian—all derived from Latin), Celtic (Gaelic, Welsh, Breton), Slavonic (Russian, Polish, Czech, Serbo-Croat, Bulgarian), Baltic (Lithuanian, Latvian), Greek, Albanian, Armenian, Iranian (Persian, Afghan) and Indo-Aryan (Hindi, Rajasthani, Punjabi, Bengali).

Italian. The official language of Italy's 50 million people, and spoken by about half a million in the Ticino canton of Switzerland. With emigrant speakers exceeding 10 million, and as a language of former colonisation in Africa (principally in Libya and Ethiopia), the language is probably spoken by as many as 65 million. Italian is the most direct descendant of Latin and is thus related to French and Spanish.

Japanese. The language spoken by Japan's 95 million people and by some speakers in Korea and Hawaii. Known from the 5th cent. A.D., it has been considerably influenced throughout its history by Chinese, both in speech and script. Nevertheless, it differs markedly in structure and vocabulary from its neighbour, and is more likely to be related to Korean, although such a relationship has not been proved.

Malayo-Polynesian. Family of languages native to the southwestern Pacific area, with the following groups: Indonesian (including Malay, Javanese, Tagalog, and Malagasy), totalling over 120 million speakers, Melanesian (which includes Austromelanesian and Micronesian languages, with just over 1 million speakers), and Polynesian (including Tahitian, Hawaiian, Maori, totalling less than half a million). Malay, with over 65 million speakers, is the official language of Indonesia, and is widespread as a *lingua franca* throughout the eastern archipelago. In Indonesia it is called *Bahasa Indonesia*.

Palaeo-Siberian. Family of languages, now considerably on the decline, spoken in northeastern Siberia and including Chukchee, Koryak, and Gilyak. Ainu, of the southern Sakhalin, may belong to this group, which shows some similarities to native languages of North America.

Russian. The major language of the U.S.S.R. is the mother tongue of over 80 per cent of the R.S.F.S.R.'s 125 million inhabitants. It is the official language throughout the Soviet Union, and, as such, is extensively propagated at all levels of education, although the native languages of most minority groups are also legally recognised. Discounting Byelo-Russian and Ukrainian, which are distinct languages, speakers of Russian number at least 160 million. Russian proper may be said to date from the 11th cent. The standard is Muscovite, and the language is written in Cyrillic script.

Semito-Hamitic. Family of languages chiefly represented by Arabic. Hamitic includes the Berber languages of desert nomads of northern Africa, and the Cushitic tongues of coastal Ethiopia and Somalia (the ancient Egyptian language was also a member of this group). The Semitic languages include Arabic (*q.v.*), Hebrew (official language of Israel and widely used by Jews all over the world), and Amharic (the official language of Ethiopia, spoken by some 5 million). Aramaic, the language spoken by Christ, is still spoken in parts of West Syria.

Akkadian, one of the oldest recorded languages and current throughout the Babylonian Empire, was spoken by the Semitic people who came to Mesopotamia *c.* 2,500 B.C. from the Arabian peninsula. They took over the cuneiform script of the non-Semitic Sumerians, although the two languages had no affinities. Akkadian was gradually replaced by the Aramaic language and alphabet.

Most of the Semitic languages have proved important languages of civilisation during their history, and have a rich literature.

Sinitic. Family of languages of southeastern Asia. The main languages and groups are: Chinese (*q.v.*), Tibetan-Burmese, and Thai. The last-named includes Siamese and Laotian. These and other languages of Thailand are very similar to one another, but the official language is Lao (Laotian). The Annamese language of Vietnam may also belong to the Thai group.

Spanish. The official language of Spain, Mexico and most of the Central American states (except Brazil, Guyana, Surinam, French Guiana) as well as of the Greater Antilles, and widespread as a former colonial medium and an important language of trade, with a total of at least 115 million speakers. Modern Spanish may be said to date from the 10th cent. It is very closely related to Portuguese (Portugal, Brazil, and colonial territories).

Uralian. Family of languages including Finnish (4 million in addition to 90,000 speakers of Finnish in the Soviet Union), Hungarian (over 10 million), Lappish (30,000, mainly nomadic) and Samoyedic languages of the northern coastal regions of the U.S.S.R.

VII. FOREIGN PHRASES

Fr., French. Gr., Greek. Ger., German. It., Italian. L., Latin. Sp., Spanish.

à bas (Fr.), down, down with.

ab extra (L.), from without.

ab incunabilis (L.), from the cradle.

ab initio (L.), from the beginning.

ab intra (L.), from within.

à bon chat, bon rat (Fr.), to a good cat, a good rat; well attacked and defended; tit for tat; a Rowland for an Oliver.

à bon marché (Fr.), cheap, a good bargain.

à bras ouverts (Fr.), with open arms.

absente reo (L.), the accused being absent.

absit invidia (L.), let there be no ill-will; envy apart.

ab uno disce omnes (L.), from one specimen judge of all the rest; from a single instance infer the whole.

ab urbe condità (L.), from the building of the city; i.e., Rome.

a capite ad calcem (L.), from head to heel.

à chaque saint sa chandelle (Fr.), to each saint his candle; honour where honour is due.

à cheval (Fr.), on horseback.

à compte (Fr.), on account; in part payment.

à corps perdu (Fr.), with might and main.

à couvert (Fr.), under cover; protected; sheltered.

ad astra (L.), to the stars.

ad calendas Græcas (L.), at the Greek calends; i.e., never, as the Greeks had no calends in their mode of reckoning.

à demi (Fr.), by halves; half-way.

a Deo et rege (L.), from God and the king.

ad hoc (L.), arranged for this purpose; special.

ad hominem (L.), to the man; to an individual's interests or passions; personal.

adhuc sub judice lis est (L.), the case has not yet been decided.

a die (L.), from that day.

ad infinitum (L.), to infinity

ad interim (L.), in the meantime.

ad libitum (L.), at pleasure.

ad modum (L.), after the manner of.

ad nauseam (L.), to disgust or satiety.

ad referendum (L.), for further consideration.

ad rem (L.), to the purpose; to the point.

ad valorem (L.), according to the value.

affaire d'amour (Fr.), a love affair.

affaire d'honneur (Fr.), an affair of honour; a duel.

affaire de cœur (Fr.), an affair of the heart.

a fortiori (L.), with stronger reason.

à gauche (Fr.), to the left.

à genoux (Fr.), on the knees.

à haute voix (Fr.), aloud.

à huis clos (Fr.), with closed doors; secretly.

à la belle étoile (Fr.), under the stars; in the open air.

à la bonne heure (Fr.), well timed; all right; very well; as you please.

à l'abri (Fr.), under shelter.

à la mode (Fr.), according to the custom or fashion.

à la Tartufe (Fr.), like Tartuffe, the hero of a celebrated comedy by Molière; hypocritically.

al fresco (It.), in the open air; out-of-doors.

al più (It.), at most.

alter ego (L.), another self.

à merveille (Fr.), to a wonder; marvellously.

amor patriæ (L.), love of country.

amour-propre (Fr.), self-love; vanity.

ancien régime (Fr.), the ancient or former order of things.

anguis in herba (L.), a snake in the grass.

anno Christi (L.), in the year of Christ.

anno Domini (L.), in the year of our Lord.

anno mundi (L.), in the year of the world.

annus mirabilis (L.), year of wonders; wonderful year.

ante bellum (L.), before the war.

ante lucem (L.), before light.

ante meridiem (L.), before noon.

à outrance (Fr.), to the utmost; to extremities; without sparing.

à pied (Fr.), on foot.

à point (Fr.), to a point, just in time, exactly right.

a posse ad esse (L.), from possibility to reality.

ariston metron (Gr.), the middle course is the best; the golden mean.

arrière-pensée (Fr.), hidden thought; mental reservation.

au courant (Fr.), fully acquainted with.

audi alteram partem (L.), hear the other side.

au fait (Fr.), well acquainted with; expert.

au fond (Fr.), at bottom.

auf Wiedersehen! (Ger.), till we meet again.

au pis aller (Fr.), at the worst.

au revoir (Fr.), adieu till we meet again.

aut vincere aut mori (L.), either to conquer or to die; death or victory.

a verbis ad verbera (L.), from words to blows.

a vinculo matrimonii (L.), from the bond of matrimony.

à volonté (Fr.), at pleasure.

a vostra salute (It.)
à votre santé (Fr.) } to your health.
a vuestra salud (Sp.)

bas bleu (Fr.), a blue-stocking; a literary woman.

beau monde (Fr.), the world of fashion.

beaux esprits (Fr.), men of wit; gay spirits.

beaux yeux (Fr.), fine eyes; good looks.

ben trovato (It.), well or cleverly invented.

bête noire (Fr.), a black beast; a bugbear.

bon gré mal gré (Fr.), with good or ill grace; willing or unwilling.

bonhomie (Fr.), good-nature; artlessness.

bonne bouche (Fr.), a delicate or tasty morsel.

bon vivant (Fr.), a good liver; a gourmand.

brutum fulmen (L.), a harmless thunderbolt.

canaille (Fr.), rabble.

candida Pax (L.), white-robed Peace.

casus belli (L.), that which causes or justifies war.

causa sine qua non (L.), an indispensable cause or condition.

caveat emptor (L.), let the buyer beware (or look after his own interest).

cela va sans dire (Fr.), that goes without saying; needless to say.

ceteris paribus (L.), other things being equal.

chacun son goût (Fr.), every one to his taste.

cogito, ergo sum (L.), I think, therefore I exist.

comme il faut (Fr.), as it should be.

compos mentis (L.), sound of mind; quite sane.

compte rendu (Fr.), an account rendered; a report or statement drawn up.

conditio sine qua non (L.), a necessary condition.

conseil de famille (Fr.), a family consultation.

consensus facit legem (L.), consent makes the law.

consilio et animis (L.), by wisdom and courage.

consilio et prudentia (L.), by wisdom and prudence.

constantia et virtute (L.), by constancy and virtue.

contra bonos mores (L.), against good manners.

contretemps (Fr.), an unlucky accident; a hitch.

cordon bleu (Fr.), blue ribbon; a cook of the highest class.

cordon sanitaire (Fr.), a line of guards to prevent the spreading of contagion or pestilence.

corpus delicti (L.), the body or substance of a crime or offence.

corrigenda (L.), things to be corrected.

coup de grâce (Fr.), a finishing stroke.

coup d'état (Fr.), a sudden decisive blow in politics; a stroke of policy.

coup de soleil (Fr.), sunstroke.

credat Judæus Apella (L.), let Apella, the superstitious Jew, believe it (I won't); tell that to the marines.

cucullus non facit monachum (L.), the cowl does not make the friar.

cui bono? (L.), For whose advantage is it? to what end?

culpam pœna premit comes (L.), punishment follows hard upon crime.

cum grano salis (L.), with a grain of salt; with some allowance.

cum privilegio (L.), with privilege.

currente calamo (L.), with a fluent pen.

da locum melioribus (L.), give place to your betters.

damnant quod non intelligunt (L.), they condemn what they do not comprehend.

data et accepta (L.), expenditures and receipts.

de bon augure (Fr.), of good augury or omen.

de bonne grâce (Fr.), with good grace; willingly.

de die in diem (L.), from day to day.

de facto (L.), in point of fact; actual or actually.

dei gratia (L.), by God's grace.

de jure (L.), from the law; by right.

de mal en pis (Fr.), from bad to worse.

de novo (L.), anew.

deo volente (L.), God willing; by God's will.

de profundis (L.), out of the depths.

dernier ressort (Fr.), a last resource.

deus ex machina (L.), one who puts matters right at a critical moment; providential intervention.

dies non (L.), a day on which judges do not sit.

distingué (Fr.), distinguished; of genteel or elegant appearance.   [idleness.

dolce far niente (It.), sweet doing-nothing; sweet

double entente (Fr.), a double meaning; a play on words.

dramatis personœ (L.), characters of the drama or play.

dum spiro, spero (L.), while I breathe, I hope.

ecce homo! (L.), behold the man!

eheu! fugaces labuntur anni (L.), alas! the fleeting years glide by.

einmal ist keinmal (Ger.), just once doesn't count.

en avant (Fr.), forward.

en badinant (Fr.), in sport; in jest.

en déshabillé (Fr.), in undress.

en famille (Fr.), with one's family; in a domestic state.

enfant terrible (Fr.), a terrible child, or one that makes disconcerting remarks.

enfin (Fr.), in short; at last; finally.

en passant (Fr.), in passing; by the way.

en plein jour (Fr.), in broad day.

en rapport (Fr.), in harmony; in agreement; in relation.

en règle (Fr.), according to rules; in order.

entente cordiale (Fr.), cordial understanding, especially between two states.

entre nous (Fr.), between ourselves.

en vérité (Fr.), in truth; verily.

e pluribus unum (L.), one out of many; one composed of many.

esprit de corps (Fr.), the animating spirit of a collective body, as a regiment, learned profession or the like.

et sequentes, et sequentia (L.), and those that follow.

et tu, Brute! (L.), and thou also, Brutus!

ex animo (L.), heartily; sincerely.

ex capite (L.), from the head; from memory.

ex cathedra (L.), from the chair or seat of authority, with high authority.

exceptio probat regulam (L.), the exception proves the rule.

ex curia (L.), out of court.

ex dono (L.), by the gift.

exeunt omnes (L.), all go out or retire.

exit (L.), he goes out.

ex mero motu (L.), from his own impulse, from his own free will.

ex nihilo nihil fit (L.), out of nothing, nothing comes; nothing produces nothing.

ex officio (L.), in virtue of his office.   [spective.

ex post facto (L.), after the deed is done; retro-

face à face (Fr.), face to face.

façon de parler (Fr.), manner of speaking.

faire bonne mine (Fr.), to put a good face upon the matter.

fait accompli (Fr.), a thing already done.

fama clamosa (L.), a current scandal; a prevailing report.

faute de mieux (Fr.), for want of better.

faux pas (Fr.), a false step; a slip in behaviour.

festina lente (L.), hasten slowly.

fiat justitia, ruat cœlum (L.), let justice be done though the heavens should fall.

fiat lux (L.), let there be light.

fide et amore (L.), by faith and love.

fide et fiduciâ (L.), by fidelity and confidence.

fide et fortitudine (L.), with faith and fortitude.

fidei defensor (L.), defender of the faith.

fide non armis (L.), by faith, not by arms.

fide, sed cui vide (L.), trust, but see whom.

fides et justitia (L.), fidelity and justice.

fides Punica (L.), Punic faith; treachery.

filius nullius (L.), a son of nobody; a bastard.

finis coronat opus (L.), the end crowns the work.

flagrante bello (L.), during hostilities.

flagrante delicto (L.), in the commission of the crime.

floreat (L.), let it flourish.

fons et origo (L.), the source and origin.

force majeure (Fr.), irresistible compulsion; war, strike, Act of God, etc.

forensis strepitus (L.), the clamour of the forum.

fortuna favet fortibus (L.), fortune favours the bold.

functus officio (L.), having performed one's office or duty; hence, out of office.

gaudeamus igitur (L.), so let us be joyful!

genius loci (L.), the genius or guardian spirit of a place.

gradu diverso, via una (L.), the same road by different steps.

grande parure } (Fr.), full dress.
grande toilette }

guerra al cuchillo (Sp.), war to the knife.

Hannibal ante portas (L.), Hannibal before the gates; the enemy close at hand.

hiatus valde deflendus (L.), a chasm or deficiency much to be regretted.

hic et nunc (L.), here and now.

hic et ubique (L.), here and everywhere.

hic jacet (L.), here lies.

hic labor, hoc opus est (L.), this is a labour, this is a toil.

hic sepultus (L.), here buried.

hoc genus omne (L.), all of this sort or class.

hoi polloi (Gr.), the many; the vulgar; the rabble.

hominis est errare (L.), to err is human.

homme de robe (Fr.), a man in civil office.

homme d'affaires (Fr.), a man of business.

homme d'esprit (Fr.), a man of wit or genius.

honi soit qui mal y pense (O. Fr.), evil to him who evil thinks.

honores mutant mores (L.), honours change men's manners or characters.

hors de combat (Fr.), out of condition to fight.

hors de propos (Fr.), not to the point or purpose.

hors-d'œuvre (Fr.), out of course; out of order.

ich dien (Ger.), I serve.

idée fixe (Fr.), a fixed idea.

id est (L.), that is.

il a le diable au corps (Fr.), the devil is in him.

Ilias malorum (L.), an Iliad of ills; a host of evils.

il penseroso (It.), the pensive man.

il sent le fagot (Fr.), he smells of the faggot; he is suspected of heresy.

imperium in imperio (L.), a state within a state; a government within another.

in actu (L.), in act or reality.   [last struggle.

in articulo mortis (L.), at the point of death; in the

in capite (L.), in chief.

in curia (L.), in court.

index expurgatorius } (L.), a list of books prohibited
index prohibitorius }   to Roman Catholics.

in esse (L.), in being; in actuality.

in extenso (L.), at full length.

in extremis (L.), at the point of death.

in memoriam (L.), to the memory of; in memory.

in nubibus (L.), in the clouds.

in petto (It.), in (my) breast; to one's self.

in re (L.), in the matter of.

in sano sensu (L.), in a proper sense.

in situ (L.), in its original situation.

in vino veritas (L.), there is truth in wine; truth is told under the influence of intoxicants.

ipse dixit (L.), he himself said it; a dogmatic saying or assertion.

ipsissima verba (L.), the very words.

ipso facto (L.), in the fact itself.

ipso jure (L.), by the law itself.

jacta est alea (L.), the die is cast.

je ne sais quoi (Fr.), I know not what.

joci causa (L.), for the sake of a joke.

labor omnia vincit (L.), labour conquers everything.

l'allegro (It.), the merry man.

lapsus linguæ (L.), a slip of the tongue.

lares et penates (L.), household gods.

laus Deo (L.), praise to God.

le beau monde (Fr.), the fashionable world.

lector benevole (L.), kind or gentle reader.

le jeu n'en vaut pas la chandelle (Fr.), the game is not worth the candle; the object is not worth the trouble.

le mot de l'énigme (Fr.), the key to the mystery.

le point du jour (Fr.), daybreak.

lèse-majesté (Fr.), high-treason.

lettre de cachet (Fr.), a sealed letter containing private orders; a royal warrant.

lex loci (L.), the law or custom of the place.

lex non scripta (L.), unwritten law; common law.

lex scripta (L.), written law; statute law.

locum tenens (L.), a deputy.

lucri causa (L.), for the sake of gain.

magnum opus (L.), a great work.

mala fide (L.), with bad faith; treacherously.

mal à propos (Fr.), ill-timed; out of place.

malgré nous (Fr.), in spite of us.

malheur ne vient jamais seul (Fr.), misfortunes never come singly.

malum in se (L.), evil or an evil in itself.

mardi gras (Fr.), Shrove-Tuesday.

mariage de convenance (Fr.), marriage from motives of interest rather than of love.

mauvaise honte (Fr.), false modesty.

mauvais goût (Fr.), bad taste.

mea culpa (L.), my fault; by my fault.

me judice (L.), I being judge; in my opinion.

mens agitat molem (L.), mind moves matter.

mens legis (L.), the spirit of the law.

mens sana in corpore sano (L.), a sound mind in a sound body.

meo periculo (L.), at my own risk.

meo voto (L.), according to my wish.

mise en scène (Fr.), the getting up for the stage, or the putting on the stage.

modus operandi (L.), manner of working.

more suo (L.), in his own way.

motu proprio (L.), of his own accord.

multum in parvo (L.), much in little.

mutatis mutandis (L.), with suitable or necessary alteration.

nervus probandi (L.), the sinews of the argument.

nihil ad rem (L.), irrelevant.

nil desperandum (L.), there is no reason to despair.

noblesse oblige (Fr.), rank imposes obligations; much is expected from one in good position.

nolens volens (L.), willing or unwilling.

nom de guerre (Fr.), a false or assumed name.

non compos mentis (L.), not of sound mind.

non sequitur (L.), it does not follow.

nosce te ipsum (L.), know thyself.

nota bene (L.), mark well.

nudis verbis (L.), in plain words.

obiter dictum (L.), a thing said by the way.

omnia vincit amor (L.), love conquers all things.

ora pro nobis (L.), pray for us.

O tempora! O mores! (L.), O the times! O the manners (or morals)!

oui-dire (Fr.), hearsay.

padrone (It.), a master; a landlord.

par excellence (Fr.), by way of eminence.

pari passu (L.), at an equal pace or rate of progress.

particeps criminis (L.), an accomplice in a crime.

pas de quoi (Fr. abbrev. Il n'y a pas de quoi), don't mention it.

passim (L.), everywhere; in all parts of the book, chapter, etc.

pâté de foie gras (Fr.), goose-liver pie.

pater patriæ (L.), father of his country.

patres conscripti (L.), the conscript fathers; Roman senatore.

pax vobiscum (L.), peace be with you.

per ardua ad astra (L.), through rough ways to the stars; through suffering to renown.

per capita (L.), by the head or poll.

per contra (It.), contrariwise.

per diem (L.), by the day; daily.

per se (L.), by itself; considered apart.

pied-à-terre (Fr.), a resting-place; a temporary lodging.

pis aller (Fr.), the worst or last shift.

plebs (L.), the common people.

poco a poco (It.), little by little.   [called for.

poste restante (Fr.), to remain in the post-office till prima facie (L.), at first view or consideration.

prima facie (L.), at first view or consideration.

primus inter pares (L.), first among equals.

pro forma (L.), for the sake of form.

pro patria (L.), for our country.

pro tanto (L.), for so much; for as far as it goes.

pro tempore (L.), for the time being.

quid pro quo (L.), one thing for another; tit for tat; an equivalent.

qui m'aime, aime mon chien (Fr.), love me, love my dog.   [sent.

qui tacet consentit (L.), he who is silent gives con-

quod erat demonstrandum (L.), which was to be proved or demonstrated.

quod erat faciendum (L.), which was to be done.

quod vide (L.), which see; refer to the word just mentioned.

quo jure? (L.), by what right?   [tence.

raison d'être (Fr.), the reason for a thing's exis-

re (L.), in the matter or affair of.

reculer pour mieux sauter (Fr.), to draw back in order to make a better spring.

reductio ad adsurdum (L.), the reducing of a position to a logical absurdity.

requiescat in pace (L.), may he (or she) rest in peace.

respice finem (L.), look to the end.

respublica (L.), the commonwealth.

revenons à nos moutons (Fr.), let us return to our sheep; let us return to our subject.

re vera (L.), in truth.

sans peur et sans reproche (Fr.), without fear and without reproach.

sans rime ni raison (Fr.), without rhyme or reason.

sans souci (Fr.), without care.

sartor resartus (L.), the botcher repatched; the tailor patched or mended.

sauve qui peut (Fr.), let him save himself who can.

savoir-faire (Fr.), the knowing how to act; tact.

savoir-vivre (Fr.), good-breeding; refined manners.

semper idem (L.), always the same.

seriatim (L.), in a series; one by one.

sic passim (L.), so here and there throughout; so everywhere.

sicut ante (L.), as before.

sine die (L.), without a day being appointed.

sine mora (L.), without delay.

sine qua non (L.), without which, not; indispensable condition.

sotto voce (It.), in an undertone.

spirituel (Fr.), intellectual; witty.

stet (L.), let it stand; do not delete.

sub judice (L.), under consideration.

sub pœna (L.), under a penalty

sub rosa (L.), under the rose; privately.

sub voce (L.), under such or such a word.

sui generis (L.), of its own or of a peculiar kind.

summum bonum (L.), the chief good.

tableau vivant (Fr.), a living picture; the representation of some scene by a group of persons.

tant mieux (Fr.), so much the better.

tant pis (Fr.), so much the worse.

tempora mutantur, nos et mutamur in illis (L.), the times are changing and we with them.

tempus fugit (L.), time flies.

tête-à-tête (Fr.), together in private.

tiers état (Fr.), the third estate; the commons.

to kalon (Gr.), the beautiful; the chief good.

to prepon (Gr.), the becoming or proper.

tour de force (Fr.), a feat of strength or skill.

tout à fait (Fr.), wholly; entirely.

tout à l'heure (Fr.), instantly.

tout de suite (Fr.), immediately.

tu quoque (L.), thou also.

ubique (L.), everywhere.

ubi supra (L.), where above mentioned.

ultra licitum (L.), beyond what is allowable.

ultra vires (L.), beyond powers or rights conferred by law.

urbi et orbi (L.), to the city (Rome) and the world.

utile dulci (L.), the useful with the pleasant.

ut infra (L.), as below.

ut supra (L.), as above stated.

vade in pace (L.), go in peace.

variæ lectiones (L.), various readings.

variorum notæ (L.), the notes of various commentators.

vede et crede (L.), see and believe.

veni, vidi, vici (L.), I came, I saw, I conquered.

verbatim et literatim (L.), word for word and letter for letter.

verbum sat sapienti (L.), a word is enough for a wise man.

ver non semper viret (L.), spring is not always green.

vexata quæstio (L.), a disputed question.

via media (L.), a middle course.

via trita, via tuta (L.), the beaten path is the safe path.

vice versâ (L.), the terms of the case being reversed.

videlicet (L.), that is to say; namely.

vi et armis (L.), by force of arms; by main force; by violence.

vigilate et orate (L.), watch and pray.

vita brevis, ars longa (L.), life is short; art is long.

vivat regina! (L.), long live the queen!

vivat rex! (L.), long live the king!

viva voce (L.), by the living voice; orally.

voilà (Fr.), behold; there is; there are.

voilà tout (Fr.), that's all.

volo, non valeo (L.), I am willing, but unable.

vox populi, vox Dei (L.), the voice of the people is the voice of God.

VIII. ABBREVIATIONS IN COMMON USE

A

a. = area; acre(s); are (100 sq. metres).
A.A. = Automobile Association; Alcoholics Anonymous.
A.A.C.C.A. = Associate of the Association of Certified and Corporate Accountants.
A.A.I. = Associate of the Chartered Auctioneers' and Estate Agents' Institute.
A.A.L.P.A. = Associate of the Incorporated Society of Auctioneers and Landed Property Agents.
A. and M. = Ancient and Modern (Hymns).
A.B. = able-bodied seaman; *Artium Baccalaureus* (Bachelor of Arts).
A.B.A. = Amateur Boxing Association.
A.B.B.A. = Associate of the British Association of Accountants.
A.B.I.C.C. = Associate of the British Institute of Certified Carpenters.
ABM = anti-ballistics missile defence system.
Abp. = Archbishop.
abr. = abridged.
abs. = absolute
a.c. (*or* A.C.) = alternating current.
A.C.A. = Associate of the Institute of Chartered Accountants.
A.C.I.S. = Associate of the Chartered Institute of Secretaries.
A.Comm.A. = Associate of the Society of Commercial Accountants.
A.C.P. = Associate of the College of Preceptors.
ACT = Advisory Council on Technology.
ACTH = adreno-cortico-trophic hormone.
A.C.W.A. = Associate of the Institute of Cost and Works Accountants.
A.D. = *anno domini* (in the year of our Lord).
A.D.C. = Aide-de-Camp.
Adm. = Admiral.
advt. (*or* adv.) = advertisement.
A.F.A.S. = Associate of the Faculty of Architects and Surveyors.
AEA = Atomic Energy Authority (UK).
AEC = Atomic Energy Commission (US).
AERE = Atomic Energy Research Establishment.
aet. (*or* aetat.) = *aetatis* (of age).
A.F.C. = Air Force Cross.
A.F.L. = American Federation of Labour.
A.F.M. = Air Force Medal.
AFRASEC = Afro-Asian Organisation for Economic Cooperation.
A.G. = Adjutant-General.
AGR = Advanced Gas-cooled Reactor.
A.H. = *anno Hegirae* (in the year of the Hegira).
A.I.A. = Associate of the Institute of Actuaries.
A.I.A.C. = Associate of the Institute of Company Accountants.
A.I.B. = Associate of the Institute of Bankers.
A.I.B.P. = Associate of the Institute of British Photographers.
A.I.C.E. = Associate of the Institution of Civil Engineers.
A.I.C.S. = Associate of the Institute of Chartered Shipbrokers.
AID = Agency for International Development (U.S.).
A.I.M.E. = Associate of the Institution of Mining Engineers.
A.I.Mech.E. = Associate of the Institution of Mechanical Engineers.
A.I.N.A. = Associate of the Institution of Naval Architects.
A.Inst.P. = Associate of the Institute of Physics.
A.I.Q.S. = Associate of the Institute of Quantity Surveyors.
A.I.R.I. = Associate of the Institution of Rubber Industry.
A.L.A. = Associate of the Library Association.
A.L.S. = Associate of the Linnean Society.
alt. = altitude.

A.M. = *anno mundi* (in the year of the world); *Artium Magister* (Master of Arts); amplitude modulation.
a.m. = *ante meridiem* (before noon).
A.M.D.G. = *ad majorem Dei glorium* (to the greater glory of God).
AMM = anti-missile-missile.
amp. = ampere(s).
A.M.I.C.E. = Associate Member of the Institution of Civil Engineers.
A.M.I.Chem.E. = Associate Member of the Institution of Chemical Engineers.
A.M.I.E.E. = Associate Member of the Institution of Electrical Engineers.
A.M.I.Mech.E. = Associate Member of the Institution of Mechanical Engineers.
A.M.I.Mun.E. = Associate Member of the Institution of Municipal Engineers.
A.M.T.P.I. = Associate Member of the Town Planning Institute.
A.N.A.R.E. = Australian National Antarctic Research Expeditions.
ANC = African National Congress.
anc. = ancient.
ANF = Atlantic Nuclear Force.
anhyd. = anhydrous.
anon. = anonymous.
ANZAC = Australian and New Zealand Army Corps.
ANZUS = Australian, New Zealand and U.S. Defence Pact (Pacific Security Treaty).
A.O.C. = Air Officer Commanding.
A.P. = Associated Press.
aq. = aqueous.
A.R.A. = Associate of the Royal Academy.
A.R.A.D. = Associate of the Royal Academy of Dancing.
A.R.A.M. = Associate of the Royal Academy of Music.
A.R.B.S. = Associate of the Royal Society of British Sculptors.
ARC = Agricultural Research Council.
A.R.C.A. = Associate of the Royal College of Arts.
A.R.C.M. = Associate of the Royal College of Music.
arch. = archipelago.
A.R.C.O. = Associate of the Royal College of Organists.
A.R.C.Sc. = Associate of the Royal College of Science.
A.R.I.B.A. = Associate of the Royal Institute of British Architects.
A.R.I.C. = Associate of the Royal Institute of Chemistry.
A.R.I.C.S. = Associate of the Royal Institution of Chartered Surveyors.
A.R.P.S. = Associate of the Royal Photographic Society.
A.R.W.S. = Associate of the Royal Society of Painters in Water Colours.
A.S. (*or* AS) = Anglo-Saxon.
A.S.A. = Amateur Swimming Association.
ASDIC = Anti-submarine detector indicator
ASEAN = Association of South–East Asian Nations (Indonesia, Malaysia, Philippines, Singapore, Thailand.)
ASLIB = Association of Special Libraries and Information Bureaux.
A.T.C. = Air Training Corps.
atm. = atmospheric pressure.
ATP = adenosine triphosphate.
A.T.S. = Auxiliary Territorial Service.
ATV = Associated Television Authority.
at.wt. = atomic weight.
A.U.C. = *ab urbe condita* (from the founding of the City (Rome)), *or*, *anno urbis conditae* (in the year of the founding of the City)
av. = average.
AV = Authorized Version.
A.W.O.L. = Absent Without Leave.

B

b. = born; bowled.
B.A. = Bachelor of Arts.
B.A.A. = British Astronomical Association.
BAF = British Athletic Federation.
B.A.O. = Bachelor in the Art of Obstetrics.
BAOR = British Army of the Rhine.
B.Arch. = Bachelor of Architecture.
Bart. (or Bt.) = Baronet.
B.B. = Boys' Brigade.
B.B.C. = British Broadcasting Corporation.
B.C. = before Christ; British Columbia.
B.Ch. (or Ch.B.) = Bachelor in Surgery.
B.C.L. = Bachelor in Civil Law.
B.Com. = Bachelor of Commerce.
B.D. = Bachelor in Divinity.
B.D.A. = British Dental Association.
Bde. = Brigade.
B.D.S. (or B.Ch.D.) = Bachelor in Dental Surgery.
BEA = British European Airways.
B.E.C. = British Employers' Confederation.
B.Ed. = Bachelor of Education.
B.E.M. = British Empire Medal.
B.Eng. = Bachelor of Engineering.
BIM = British Institute of Management.
BIS = Bank for International Settlements.
BISRA = British Iron and Steel Research Association.
B.Litt. = Bachelor in Letters.
B.M. = Bachelor in Medicine; British Museum.
B.M.A. = British Medical Association.
B.M.C. = British Motor Corporation.
B.Mus. = Bachelor in Music.
B.N.C. = Brasenose College, Oxford.
BNEC = British National Export Council
BOAC = British Overseas Airways Corporation.
bor. = borough.
B.O.T. = Board of Trade.
b.p. = boiling point.
Bp. = Bishop.
B.Phil. = Bachelor of Philosophy.
Br. (or Brit.) = British.
Brit.Ass. = British Association for the Advancement of Science.
B.R. = British Railways; British Rail.
B.R.B. = British Rail Board.
B.R.C.S. = British Red Cross Society.
B.R.S. = British Road Services.
B.Sc. = Bachelor of Science.
BSC = British Steel Corporation.
B.S.I. = British Standards Institution.
BST = British summer time.
Bt. = Baronet; Brevet.
B.T.H.A. = British Travel and Holidays Association.
B.Th. = Bachelor in Theology.
Btu = British thermal unit.
B.U.A. = British United Airways.
B.V.M. = Blessed Virgin Mary.
B.V.M.S. = Bachelor in Veterinary Medicine and Surgery.
B.W.B. = British Waterways Board.

C

C. = Centigrade; Conservative.
c. = circa (about); centi- (10^{-2}).
C.A. = Chartered Accountant (Scottish Institute).
CABs = Citizens' Advice Bureaux.
Cal. = Calorie (nutritional kilogram-calorie).
cal. = calorie (gram-calorie used in physics and chemistry).
calc. = calculated.
Cantab. = of Cambridge.
Cantuar. = of Canterbury.
cap. = capital letter; capitulum (chapter).
CARD = Campaign Against Racial Discrimination.
CARIFTA = Caribbean Free Trade Area.
CATs = Colleges of Advanced Technology.
C.B. = Companion of the Order of the Bath.
C.B.E. = Commander of the Order of the British Empire.
CBI = Confederation of British Industry (replaces BEC, FBI and NABM).
C.C. = County Council; County Councillor; Chamber of Commerce.
cc = cubic centimetre(s).
CCPR = Central Council of Physical Recreation.

C.D. = Civil Defence.
C.D.C. = Commonwealth Development Corporation.
C.D.S. = Chief of Defence Staff; Campaign for Democratic Socialism.
CDU = Christian Democratic Union (W. Ger.).
C.E. = Civil Engineer; Christian Era.
CEGB = Central Electricity Generating Board.
CENTO = Central Treaty Organisation.
centi = one-hundreth part (10^{-2})
CERN = European Organisation for Nuclear Research.
CET = Central European Time.
C.F. = Chaplain to the Forces.
cf. = confer (compare).
C.G.M. = Conspicuous Gallantry Medal.
C.G.S. = Chief of General Staff.
cgs = centimetre-gram-second.
CGT = Confédération Générale du Travail (French TUC).
C.H. = Companion of Honour.
Ch.Ch. = Christ Church.
Ch.M. = Master in Surgery.
C.I. = Lady of Imperial Order of the Crown of India; Channel Islands.
CIA = Central Intelligence Agency (US).
CID = Criminal Investigation Department.
C.I.E. = Companion of the Order of the Indian Empire.
Cie = Compagnie (Company).
c.i.f. = cost, insurance and freight.
C.-in-C. = Commander-in-Chief.
CIO = Congress of Industrial Organisations (US).
CIR = Commission on Industrial Relations.
C.L. = Companion of Literature.
C.L.B. = Church Lads' Brigade.
cm = centimetre(s).
C.M.G. = Companion of the Order of St. Michael and St. George.
C.M.S. = Church Missionary Society.
CNAA = Council for National Academic Awards.
CND = Campaign for Nuclear Disarmament.
C.O. = Commanding Officer; Colonial Office; Conscientious Objector.
Co. = County; Company.
c/o = care of.
C.O.D. = Cash on Delivery.
C. of E. = Church of England.
COI = Central Office of Information.
CoID = Council of Industrial Design.
COMECON = Council for Mutual Economic Assistance (East European).
Con. (or C.) = Conservative.
conc. = concentrated.
const. = constant.
corr. = corrected.
COSPAR = Committee on Space Research.
CP = Communist Party.
CPC = Communist Party of China.
C.P.R.E. = Council for the Preservation of Rural England.
CPSU = Communist Party of the Soviet Union.
crit. = critical.
C.R.O. = Commonwealth Relations Office.
crystl. = crystalline.
C.S.C. = Conspicuous Service Cross.
C.S.E. = Certificate of Secondary Education.
C.S.I. = Companion of the Order of the Star of India.
CSP = Council on Scientific Policy.
C.T. = Civic Trust.
C.T.C. = Cyclists' Touring Club.
CTR = Controlled thermonuclear research.
cu. = cubic.
C.V.O. = Commander of the Royal Victorian Order.
cwt. = hundredweight.

D

d. = denarius (penny), denarii (pence); died; daughter.
D.A.R. = Daughters of the American Revolution.
dB = decibel(s).
D.B.E. = Dame Commander of Order of British Empire.
D.C. = District of Columbia.
d.c. (or D.C.) = direct current.
D.C.L. = Doctor in Civil Law.

D.C.M. = Distinguished Conduct Medal.
D.C.M.G. = Dame Commander, Order of St. Michael and St. George.
D.C.V.O. = Dame Commander of the Royal Victorian Order.
D.D. = Doctor in Divinity.
D.D.R. = German Democratic Republic (E. Ger.).
D.D.S. = Doctor in Dental Surgery.
DDT = Dichloro-diphenyl-trichloro-ethane.
DEA = Department of Economic Affairs.
deca = ten times
deci = one-tenth (10^{-1})
del. = *delineavit* (he drew it).
DEP = Department of Employment and Productivity.
D.ès L. = Docteur ès Lettres.
D.ès Sc. = Docteur ès Sciences.
D.F.C. = Distinguished Flying Cross.
D.F.M. = Distinguished Flying Medal.
D.G. = *dei gratie* (by the grace of God).
DIA = Design and Industries Association.
dil. = dilute.
Dip.Tech. = Diploma in Technology.
D.L. = Deputy-Lieutenant.
D.Lit. (*or* D. Litt) = Doctor of Literature.
D.M. = Doctor in Medicine (Oxford).
DM = Deutschemark.
D.Mus. = Doctor of Music.
DNA = deoxyribonucleic acid.
D.N.B. = Dictionary of National Biography.
do. = *ditto* (the same).
D.O.M. = *dominus optimo maximo* (To God, the best, the greatest).
D.P. = Displaced Person(s).
D.P.H. = Diploma in Public Health.
D.Phil. = Dictor of Philosophy.
D.P.M. = Diploma in Psychological Medicine.
Dr. = Doctor; debtor.
dr. = drachm.
D.Sc. = Doctor of Science.
D.S.C. = Distinguished Service Cross.
DSIR = Department of Scientific and Industrial Research (to be abolished and replaced by SRC, IRDA, and NERC).
D.S.M. = Distinguished Service Medal.
D.S.O. = Companion of the Distinguished Service Order.
D.Th. = Doctor in Theology.
D.T.M. = Diploma in Tropical Medicine.
D.V. = *Deo volente* (God willing).
dwt. = pennyweight.

E

EAAFRO = East African Agriculture and Foresty Research.
E. and O.E. = Errors and omissions excepted.
Ebor. = of York.
EC = Electricity Council.
ECA = Economic Commission for Africa (UN).
ECAFE = Economic Commission for Asia and the Far East (UN).
ECE = Economic Commission for Europe (UN).
ECG = electro-cardiograph.
ECGD = Export Credits Guarantee Department.
ECLA = Economic Commission for Latin America (UN).
ECSC = European Coal and Steel Community.
EDC = European Defence Community.
EEC = European Economic Community (Common Market).
EEG = electro-encephalogram.
EFTA = European Free Trade Association.
e.g. = *exempli gratio* (for example).
ELDO = European Launcher and Development Organisation.
EMA = European Monetary Agreement.
EMBO = European Molecular Biology Organisation.
emf = electromotive force.
e.m.u. = electromagnetic unit.
ENEA = European Nuclear Energy Agency.
EPU = European Political Union.
E.R. = Elizabetha Regina, *or* Edwardus Rex.
E.R.A. = Electrical Research Association.
ERNIE = electronic random number indicating equipment.
ERP = European Recovery Programme.
ESC = Economic and Social Council (UN).
ESRO = European Space Research Organisation.

et al. = *et alibi* (and elsewhere); *et alii* (and others).
etc. = *et cetera* (others; and so forth).
et seq. = *et sequens* (and the following).
et sqq. = *et sequentes, et sequentia* (and those following).
E.T.U. = Electrical Trades Union.
Euratom = European Atomic Energy Community.
ex lib. = *ex libris* (from the books of).

F

F. = Fahrenheit; Fellow.
f. = and the following page; ff. = and the following pages.
F.A. = Football Association.
F.A.C.C.A. = Fellow of the Association of Certified and Corporate Accountants.
F.A.I. = Fellow of the Chartered Auctioneers' and Estate Agents' Institute.
F.A.L.P.A. = Fellow of the Incorporated Society of Auctioneers and Landed Property Agents.
F.A.N.Y. = First Aid Nursing Yeomanry.
FAO = Food and Agriculture Organisation of the United Nations.
f.a.s. = free alongside.
F.B.A. = Fellow of the British Academy.
F.B.A.A. = Fellow of the British Association of Accountants.
FBI = Federal Bureau of Investigation (U.S.).
F.B.I.M. = Fellow of the British Institute of Management.
F.B.O.A. = Fellow of the British Optical Association.
F.B.S. = Fellow of the Botanical Society.
F.C.A. = Fellow of the Institute of Chartered Accountants.
F.C.G.I. = Fellow of City and Guilds Institute.
F.C.I.A. = Fellow of Corporation of Insurance Agents.
F.C.I.B. = Fellow of Corporation of Insurance Brokers.
F.C.I.I. = Fellow of Chartered Insurance Institute.
F.C.I.S. = Fellow of the Chartered Institute of Secretaries.
F.C.P. = Fellow of the College of Preceptors.
F.C.W.A. = Fellow of the Chartered Institute of Cost and Works Accountants.
F.D. = *Fidei Defensor* (Defender of the Faith).
Fed. = Federation; Federal.
ff. = folios; and the following pages; fortissimo.
F.F.A.R.C.S. = Fellow of the Faculty of Anaesthetics, Royal College of Surgeons.
F.F.R. = Fellow of the Faculty of Radiologists.
F.G.S. = Fellow of the Geological Society.
F.H. = Fire Hydrant.
F.H.S. = Fellow of the Heraldry Society.
F.I.A. = Fellow of the Institute of Actuaries.
F.I.B. = Fellow of the Institute of Bankers.
F.I.B.P. = Fellow of the Institute of British Photographers.
F.I.C.S. = Fellow of the Institute of Chartered Shipbrokers.
F. Inst.F. = Fellow of the Institute of Fuel.
F.Inst.P. = Fellow of the Institute of Physics.
F.Inst.Pet. = Fellow of the Institute of Petroleum.
F.I.Q.S. = Fellow of the Institute of Quantity Surveyors.
F.I.R.E. = Fellow of the Institute of Radio Engineers.
F.J.I. = Fellow of the Institute of Journalists.
F.K.C. = Fellow of King's College (London).
fl. = *floruit* (flourished).
F.L.A. = Fellow of the Library Association.
F.L.A.S. = Fellow of the Land Agents' Society.
F.L.N. = (Algerian) National Liberation Front.
F.L.S. = Fellow of the Linnaean Society.
FM = Frequency modulation.
FMC = Federal Maritime Commission (US).
F.N.S. = Fellow of the Newtonian Society.
F.O. = Foreign Office.
fo. = folio.
f.o.b. = free on board.
F.O.P. = Friendship Oil Pipeline (E.Europe).
f.p. = freezing point.
F.P.S. = Fellow of the Pharmaceutical Society.
F.Ph.S. = Fellow of the Philosophical Society.

F.R.A.D. = Fellow of the Royal Academy of Dancing.
F.R.A.I. = Fellow of the Royal Anthropological Institute.
F.R.A.M. = Fellow of the Royal Academy of Music.
F.R.A.S. = Fellow of the Royal Astronomical Society.
F.R.Ae.S. = Fellow of the Royal Aeronautical Society.
F.R.B.S. = Fellow of the Royal Society of British Sculptors.
F.R.C.M. = Fellow of the Royal College of Music.
F.R.C.O. = Fellow of the Royal College of Organists.
F.R.C.O.G. = Fellow of the Royal College of Obstetricians and Gynaecologists.
F.R.C.P. = Fellow of the Royal College of Physicians of London.
F.R.C.P.Ed. = Fellow of the Royal College of Physicians of Edinburgh.
F.R.C.S. = Fellow of the Royal College of Surgeons of England.
F.R.C.S.Ed. = Fellow of the Royal College of Surgeons of Edinburgh.
F.R.C.V.S. = Fellow of the Royal College of Veterinary Surgeons.
F.R.E.S. = Fellow of the Royal Empire Society.
F.R.Econ.S. = Fellow of the Royal Economic Society.
F.R.F.P.S. = Fellow of the Royal Faculty of Physicians and Surgeons (Glas.).
F.R.G.S. = Fellow of the Royal Geographical Society.
F.R.H.S. = Fellow of the Royal Horticultural Society.
F.R.Hist.S. = Fellow of the Royal Historical Society.
F.R.I.B.A. = Fellow of the Royal Institute of British Architects.
F.R.I.C. = Fellow of the Royal Institute of Chemistry.
F.R.I.C.S. = Fellow of the Royal Institution of Chartered Surveyors.
F.R.M.S. = Fellow of the Royal Microscopical Society.
F.R.Met.S. = Fellow of the Royal Meteorological Society.
F.R.N.S. = Fellow of Royal Numismatic Society.
F.R.P.S. = Fellow of the Royal Photographic Society.
F.R.S. = Fellow of the Royal Society.
F.R.S.A. = Fellow of the Royal Society of Arts.
F.R.S.C. = Fellow of the Royal Society of Canada.
F.R.S.E. = Fellow of the Royal Society of Edinburgh.
F.R.S.L. = Fellow of the Royal Society of Literature.
F.R.S.S. = Fellow of the Royal Statistical Society.
F.S.A. = Fellow of the Society of Antiquaries.
F.S.M.C. = Fellow of the Spectacle Makers Company.
F.T.I. = Fellow of the Textile Institute.
F.Z.S. = Fellow of the Zoological Society.

G

g. = gram(s).
GATT = General Agreement on Tariffs and Trade.
G.B.E. = Knight (or Dame) Grand Cross of the Order of the British Empire.
G.C. = George Cross; Gas Council.
G.C.A. = Ground Control Approach.
G.C.E. = General Certificate of Education.
G.C.B. = Knight Grand Cross of the Order of the Bath.
G.C.I.E. = Knight Grand Commander of the Indian Empire.
G.C.M.G. = Knight Grand Cross of the Order of St. Michael and St. George.
G.C.S.I. = Knight Grand Commander of the Star of India.
G.C.V.O. = Knight (or Dame) Grand Cross of the Royal Victorian Order.
GDP = gross domestic product.
Gen. = General; Genesis.
GeV = thousand million electron-volts.

G.H.Q. = General Headquarters.
G.I. = American soldier (from army term "Government Issue" applied to kit and equipment).
GLC = Greater London Council.
G.M. = George Medal.
G.M.C. = General Medical Council.
G.M.T. = Greenwich mean time.
GNP = gross national product.
G.O.C. = General Officer Commanding.
G.O.P. = Grand Old Party (US Republican Party).
G.P. = General Practitioner.
G.P.O. = General Post Office.
gr. = grain(s).
G.R.C.M. = Graduate of the Royal College of Music.
G.R.S.M. = Graduate of the Royal Schools of Music (Royal Academy and Royal College).
G.S.O. = General Staff Officer.
GYP = gross domestic income.

H

ha = hectare (100 ares).
H.E. = His Excellency; His Eminence: high explosive.
hecto = one hundred times (10^2).
H.H. = His (or Her) Highness.
hhd. = hogshead.
H.I.M. = His Imperial Majesty.
H.J.S. = Hic jacet sepultus (Here lies buried).
H.M. = His (or Her) Majesty.
H.M.A.S. = Her Majesty's Australian Ship.
H.M.I. = Her Majesty's Inspector.
H.M.L. = Her Majesty's Lieutenant.
H.M.S = Her Majesty's Ship; Her Majesty's Service.
H.M.S.O. = Her Majesty's Stationery Office.
H. of C. = House of Commons.
H. of L. = House of Lords.
Hon. = Honourable; Honorary.
hp = horsepower.
H.P. = Hire purchase.
H.R. = House of Representatives (US).
H.R.H. = His (or Her) Royal Highness.
H.S.E. = Hic sepultus est (Here lies buried).
H.T. = high tension.
HTR = high-temperature reactor (type of nuclear power station).
H.V. = health visitor.
H.W.M. = high water mark.

I

IADB = Inter-American Development Bank.
IAEA = International Atomic Energy Agency (UN).
IATA = International Air Transport Association.
ib. (or ibid.) = ibidem (in the same place).
IBERLANT = Iberian Atlantic Command (NATO).
IBRD = International Bank for Reconstruction and Development (World Bank).
ICAO = International Civil Aviation Organisation (UN).
ICBM = Intercontinental ballistic missile.
ICFC = Industrial and Commercial Finance Corporation.
ICFTU = International Confederation of Free Trade Unions.
ICI = Imperial Chemical Industries.
ICJ = International Court of Justice (UN).
ICSU = International Council of Scientific Unions.
ICT = International Computers and Tabulators.
ICY = International Co-operation Year (1965).
Id. = idem (the same).
IDA = International Development Association.
i.e. = id est (that is)
IFC = International Finance Corporation (UN).
Ign. = ignotus (unknown).
IGY = International Geophysical Year (1957–8).
IHS = Iesus Hominum Salvator (Jesus Saviour of men)—repr. a Greek abbrev. of the word Jesus.

ILEA = Inner London Education Authority.
ILO = International Labour Organisation (UN).
I.L.S. = Instrument Landing System.
IMCO = Inter-Governmental Maritime Consultative Organisation (UN).
IMF = International Monetary Fund (UN).
Inc. = Incorporated.
Incog. = *incognito* (unknown, unrecognised).
inf. = infinitive; *infra* (below).
in loc. (*in loco*) = in its place.
I.N.R.I. = *Iesus Nazarenus, Rex Iudaeorum* (Jesus of Nazareth, King of the Jews).
Inst. = Institute; Institution.
inst. = instant (the present month).
Interpol = International Criminal Police Commission (HQ in Paris).
I.O.M. = Isle of Man.
I.O.W. = Isle of Wight.
IOU = I owe you.
IQ = intelligence quotient.
IQSY = International Years of the Quiet Sun.
I.R. = Inland Revenue.
I.R.A. = Irish Republican Army.
IRBM = Intermediate-range ballistic missile.
IRC = International Red Cross; Industrial Reorganisation Corporation.
IRDA = Industrial Research and Development Authority.
I.S.O. = Imperial Service Order; International Standardisation Organisation.
I.T.A. = Independent Television Authority; Institute of Travel Agents; Industrial Transport Association; Invalid Tricycle Association.
I.T.O. = International Trade Organisation.
I.T.U. = International Telecommunication Union.
ITV = Independent Television.

J

J. = Judge; Jet (aircraft).
J.P. = Justice of the Peace.

K

K = Kelvin.
K. = Köchel numeration (of Mozart's works).
k = kilo = thousand.
KANU = Kenya African National Union.
K.B.E. = Knight Commander of the Order of the British Empire.
K.C. = King's Counsel.
kc. = kilocycle(s).
K.C.B. = Knight Commander of the Order of the Bath.
K.C.I.E. = Knight Commander of the Order of the Indian Empire.
K.C.M.G. = Knight Commander of the Order of St. Michael and St. George.
K.C.S.I. = Knight Commander of the Star of India.
K.C.V.O. = Knight Commander of the Royal Victorian Order.
K.G. = Knight of the Order of the Garter.
KGB = Soviet State Security Service.
kg = kilogram(s).
kilo = one thousand times (10^3).
KJV = King James Version.
K.K.K. = Ku Klux Klan.
km = kilometre(s).
k.o. = knock out (boxing).
K.P. = Knight of the Order of St. Patrick.
K.T. = Knight of the Order of the Thistle.
Kt. = knight.
kV = kilovolt(s).
kW = kilowatt(s).
kWh = kilowatt hour(s).

L

L. (*or* Lib.) = Liberal.
L.A. = Local Authority.
Lab. = Labour.
L.A.C. = London Athletic Club.
LAFTA = Latin American Free Trade Association.

LAMDA = London Academy of Music and Dramatic Art.
lat. = latitude.
lb. = *libra* (pound), *librae* (pounds).
lbf = pound-force.
l.b.w. = leg before wicket.
l.c. = lower case (small letter(s)).
LCC = London County Council.
L.C.J. = Lord Chief Justice.
L.C.P. = Licentiate of the College of Preceptors.
L.D.S. = Licentiate in Dental Surgery.
Lès L. = Licencié ès Lettres.
L.F.B. = London Fire Brigade.
L.H.D. = *Litterarum Humaniorum Doctor* (Doctor of Humane Letters).
Lic.Med. = Licentiate in Medicine.
Lic.S. = Licentiate in Surgery.
Lit.Hum. = *Literae Humaniores* (Study of the Classics).
Litt.D. = *Litterarum Doctor* (Doctor of Letters; Doctor in Letters (Camb.)).
LL.B. = *Legum Baccalaureus* (Bachelor of Laws).
LL.D. = *Legum Doctor* (Doctor of Laws; Doctor in Law (Camb.)).
L.M. = Licentiate in Midwifery.
loc.cit. = *loco citato* (in the place sited).
log. = logarithm.
long. = longitude.
L.R.A.D. = Licentiate of the Royal Academy of Dancing.
L.R.A.M. = Licentiate of the Royal Academy of Music.
L.R.C.M. = Licentiate of the Royal College of Music.
L.R.C.P. = Licentiate of the Royal College of Physicians.
L.R.C.S. = Licentiate of the Royal College of Surgeons.
L.R.C.V.S. = Licentiate of the Royal College of Veterinary Surgeons.
L.S. = *loco sigilli* (place of the seal).
L.S.A. = Licentiate of the Society of Apothecaries.
L.s.d. = *Librae, solidi, denarii* (Pounds, shillings, pence).
LSD = Lysergic acid diethylamide
L.S.E. = London School of Economics.
L.S.O. = London Symphony Orchestra.
L.T.A. = Lawn Tennis Association.
LTB = London Transport Board.
L.Th. = Licentiate in Theology.
Lt.-Gen. = Lieutenant-General.
L.W.M. = lower-water mark.
LXX = Septuagint.

M

M. = Member; Monsieur; mark (German coin); *meridies* (noon); mega (million times).
m = metre(s).
m. = married; masculine; million.
M.A. = Master of Arts.
MAOT = Member of the Association of Occupational Therapists.
M.A.O. = Master in the Art of Obstetrics.
max. = maximum.
M.B. = Bachelor in Medicine.
M.B.A. = Master of Business Administration.
M.B.E. = Member of the Order of the British Empire.
M.C. = Military Cross; Master of Ceremonies.
Mc = million cycles, *or* megacycle.
M.C.C. = Marylebone Cricket Club.
M.Ch. = Master in Surgery.
M.Ch.D. = Master in Dental Surgery.
M.Ch.Orth. = Master in Orthopaedic Surgery.
M.Com. = Master of Commerce.
M.C.S.P. = Member of the Chartered Society of Physiotherapy.
M.C.T. = Member of the College of Technologists.
M.D. = *Medicineae Doctor* (Doctor in Medicine).
M.D.S. = Master in Dental Surgery.
M.E. = Middle English.
mega = one million times (10^6).
MeV = megaelectronvolt(s)
M.F.H. = Master of Foxhounds.
mg = milligram(s).
Mgr. = Monsignor.
MHD = magnetohydrodynamics.
micro = one-millionth part (10^{-6}).

M.I. = Military Intelligence.

M.I.C.E. = Member of the Institution of Civil Engineers.

M.I.Chem.E. = Member of the Institution of Chemical Engineers.

M.I.E.E. = Member of the Institution of Electrical Engineers.

milli = one-thousandth part (10^{-3}).

M.I.Mar.E. = Member of the Institute of Marine Engineers.

M.I.Mech.E. = Member of the Institution of Mechanical Engineers.

M.I.Min.E. = Member of the Institution of Mining Engineers.

min. = minimum.

M.I.N.A. = Member of the Institution of Naval Architects.

M.Inst.Met. = Member of the Institute of Metals.

Min. Plenip. = Minister Plenipotentiary.

Mintech = Ministry of Technology.

M.I.Mun.E. = Member of the Institution of Municipal Engineers.

MIRV = multiple independent re-entry vehicle.

M.Inst.T. = Member of the Institute of Transport.

M.I.T. = Massachusetts Institute of Technology.

M.I.T.M.A. = Member of the Institute of Trade Mark Agents.

M.I.W.M. = Member of the Institution of Works Managers.

M.J.I. = Member of the Institute of Journalists.

MKS = metre-kilogram-second system

MKSA = metre-kilogram-second-ampere (Giorgi) system

MLF = Multilateral Force.

Mlle = Mademoiselle.

MM. = Messieurs.

M.M. = Military Medal.

mm = millimetre(s).

Mme = Madame.

m.m.f. = magnetomotive force.

mmHg = millimetre(s) of mercury.

M.N. = Merchant Navy.

Mods. = Moderations (Oxford).

M.O.H. = Medical Officer of Health; Ministry of Health.

m.p. = melting point.

M.P. = Member of Parliament; Military Police.

m.p.h. = miles per hour.

M.P.S. = Member of the Pharmaceutical Society; Member of the Philological Society; Member of the Physical Society.

M.R. = Master of the Rolls.

M.R.A.S. = Member of the Royal Asiatic Society; Member of the Royal Academy of Science.

M.R.Ae.S. = Member of the Royal Aeronautical Society.

M.R.C. = Medical Research Council.

M.R.C.O.G. = Member of the Royal College of Obstetricians and Gynaecologists.

M.R.C.P. = Member of the Royal College of Physicians.

M.R.C.P.(E.) = Member of the Royal College of Physicians (Edinburgh).

M.R.C.S. = Member of the Royal College of Surgeons.

M.R.C.V.S. = Member of the Royal College of Veterinary Surgeons.

M.R.I. = Member of the Royal Institution.

M.S. = Master in Surgery.

Ms., Mss. = Manuscript, Manuscripts.

M.S.A. = Mutual Security Agency.

M.Sc. = Master of Science.

M.T.B. = Motor Torpedo Boat.

M.T.P.I. = Member of the Town Planning Institute.

Mus.B. = *Musicae Baccalaureus* (Bachelor in Music).

Mus.D. = *Musicae Doctor* (Doctor in Music).

MV = million volts *or* megavolt.

M.V.O. = Member of the Royal Victorian Order.

MW = million watts *or* megawatt.

M.W.B. = Metropolitan Water Board.

N

NAAFI = Navy, Army and Air Force Institutes.

N.A.B.M. = National Association of British Manufacturers.

NADGE = Nato Air Defence Ground Environment Organisation.

nano = one-thousand-millionth part (10^{-9})

NASA = National Aeronautics and Space Administration (US).

NATO = North Atlantic Treaty Organisation.

NATSOPA = National Society of Operative Printers and Assistants.

N.B. = *nota bene* (note well).

NBS = National Bureau of Standards (US).

N.C. = Nature Conservancy.

N.C.B. = National Coal Board.

N.C.L.C. = National Council of Labour Colleges.

N.C.O. = Non-commissioned Officer.

N.C.U. = National Cyclists' Union.

n.d. = no date (of books).

NEDC = National Economic Development Council.

NEL = National Engineering Laboratory.

Nem.con. = *Nemine contradicente* (no one contradicting = unanimously).

Nem.diss. = *Nemine dissentiente* (no one dissenting = unanimously).

NERC = Natural Environment Research Council.

Net. (*or* Nett.) = free from, or not subject to, any deductions.

NHS = National Health Service.

NIBMR = no independence before majority rule.

NIC = National Incomes Commission.

NIRNS = National Institute for Research in Nuclear Science.

NLF = National Liberation Front (political arm of Vietcong in S. Vietnam).

NLL = National Lending Library for Science and Technology.

No. = *numero* (number).

non.seq. = *non sequitur* (it does not follow).

N.P. = Notary Public.

N.P.C. = National Parks Commission.

NPD = National Democratic Party (W. Ger.).

N.P.F.A. = National Playing Fields Association.

NPL = National Physical Laboratory.

N.R.A. = National Rifle Association.

NRDC = National Research Development Corporation.

N.S. = New Style in the calendar (in Gt. Britain since 1752).

N.S.P.C.C. = National Society for the Prevention of Cruelty to Children.

N.T. = New Testament; National Trust.

N.U.R. = National Union of Railwaymen.

N.U.T. = National Union of Teachers.

N.Y. = New York.

N.Z. = New Zealand.

O

OAS = Organisation of American States; Organisation de l'Armée Secrète (the clandestine army of the French colonists in Algeria).

OAU = Organisation of African Unity.

ob. = *obit* (died).

obs. = observed.

O.B.E. = Officer of the Order of the British Empire.

OCAMM = Joint African, Malagasy and Mauritanian Organisation.

OCTU = Officer Cadets' Training Unit.

ODECA = Organisation of Central American States.

OECD = Organisation for Economic Co-operation and Development.

O.E.D. = Oxford English Dictionary.

O.F.M. = *Ordo Fratrum Minorum* (Order of Friars Minor = Franciscan).

O.H.M.S. = On Her Majesty's Service.

O.M. = Member of the Order of Merit.

O.P. = *Ordinis Praedicatorum* (Order of Preachers = Dominicans); opposite to prompter (stage term); out of print.

op. = *opus* (work).

op cit. = *opere citato* (in the work cited).

ORC = Overseas Research Council.

ORGEL = Organique et Eau Lourde (organic liquid and heavy water nuclear reactor).

O.S. = Old Style in calendar.

O.S.B. = *Ordo Sancti Benedicti* (Order of St. Benedict = Benedictines).

O.T. = Old Testament.

O.T.C. = Officers' Training Corps.
Oxon. = of Oxford.
oz. = ounce(s).

P

p = penny, pence (decimal system).
P.A. = Press Association.
PAYE = Pay as you earn (income tax scheme).
P.C. = Privy Councillor; Police Constable.
P.C.C. = People's Caretakers' Council (Nat. movement in Rhodesia).
p.c. = per cent.; postcard.
p.d. = potential difference.
pdl = poundal.
P.D.S.A. = People's Dispensary for Sick Animals.
P.E.N. = Poets, Playwrights, Essayists, Editors and Novelists (Club).
P.E.P. = Political and Economic Planning (Society).
per pro (or p.p.) = *per procurationem* (by proxy).
PFLP = Popular Front for the Liberation of Palestine.
Ph.D. = *Philosophiae Doctor* (Doctor of Philosophy).
PIB = Prices and Incomes Board.
pinx = *pinxit* (he painted).
P.L.A. = Port of London Authority.
PLUTO = Pipe-line under the ocean.
P.M. = Prime Minister; Post master; *post meridiem* (afternoon).
P.M.G. = Postmaster General.
P.M.O. = Principal Medical Officer.
P.N.E.U. = Parents' National Education Union.
P.O. = Post Office; postal order; Petty Officer.
P. & O. = Peninsular and Oriental Steamship Co.
P.O.W. = prisoner of war.
pp. = pages.
P.P.C. = pour prendre congé (to take leave).
P.Q. = Parliamentary Question.
P.P.S. = Parliamentary Private Secretary.
P.R. = Proportional Representation.
P.R.A. = President of the Royal Academy.
P.R.B. = Pre-Raphaelite Brotherhood.
Pro tem. = *pro tempore* (for the time being).
Prox = *proximo* (of the next month).
P.R.S. = President of the Royal Society.
P.S. = *post scriptum* (postscript).
Ps. = Psalm.
Pss. = Psalms.
P.S.W. = Psychiatric Social Worker.
P.T. = Physical Training.
Pte. = Private.
P.T.O. = please turn over.

Q

Q. = Queen.
Q = 10^{18} British Thermal Units ($1 \cdot 05 \times 10^{21}$ joules).
Q.B. = Queen's Bench.
Q.C. = Queen's Counsel.
Q.E.D. = *quod erat demonstrandum* (which was to be demonstrated).
Q.E.F. = *quod erat faciendum* (which was to be done).
Q.E.I. = *quod erat inveniendum* (which was to be found).
q.l. (or q.pl) = *quantum libet* (or *quantum placet*) (as much as one pleases).
Q.M. = Quartermaster.
Q.M.C. = Queen Mary College.
q.s. = *quantum sufficit* (a sufficient quantity).
Q.S. = Quarter Sessions.
QSEs = Qualified Scientists and Engineers (*i.e.,* skilled manpower).
QSSs = Quasars (quasi stellar radio sources).
Q.T. = quiet (slang).
Qto. = quarto (folded in four).
q.v. = *quod vide* (which see).

R

R. = Réaumur; *Rex* (King); *Regina* (Queen); Right (stage direction).
R.A. = Rear Admiral; Royal Academy; Royal Academician; Research Association; Right Ascension (astron.).
R.A.C. = Royal Automobile Club.

RAE = Royal Aircraft Establishment.
R.Ae.S. = Royal Aeronautical Society.
R.A.E. = Royal Aircraft Establishment.
R.A.F. = Royal Air Force.
R.A.M. = Royal Academy of Music.
R.C. = Red Cross; Roman Catholic.
R.D. = Rural Dean; Royal Naval Reserve Decoration; Refer to Drawer.
R.D.C. = Rural District Council
R.D.I. = Designer for Industry of the Royal Society of Arts.
R.E. = Royal Engineers.
Reg. Prof. = Regius Professor.
R.E.M.E. = Royal Electrical and Mechanical Engineers.
Rep. = Representative; Republican.
R.G.S. = Royal Geographical Society.
r.h. = relative humidity.
R.H.S. = Royal Humane Society; Royal Horticultural Society.
R.Hist.S. = Royal Historical Society.
R.I. = Royal Institution; Royal Institute of Painters in Water Colours; Rhode Island; Religious Instruction.
R.I.B.A. = Royal Institution of British Architects.
R.I.I.A. = Royal Institute of International Affairs (Chatham House, London).
R.I.P. = *requiescat in pace* (may he rest in peace).
R.L.O. = Returned Letter Office.
R.M. = Royal Marines; Resident Magistrate.
R.M.C. = Royal Military College, Sandhurst.
r.m.s. = root mean square.
R.N. = Royal Navy.
RNA = ribonucleic acid.
R.N.L.I. = Royal National Lifeboat Institution.
Ro. = *recto* (on the right-hand page).
R.P. = Member of the Royal Society of Portrait Painters.
RRE = Royal Radar Establishment.
rpm = revolutions per minute.
R.S.A. = Royal Society of Arts; Royal Scottish Academician.
R.S.M. = Regimental Sergeant Major.
R.S.P.C.A. = Royal Society for the Prevention of Cruelty to Animals.
R.S.V.P. = *Répondez, s'il vous plaît* (An answer is requested).
R.S.W. = Royal Scottish Society of Painters in Water Colours.
Rt. Hon. = Right Honourable.
Rt. Rev. = Right Reverend (of a Bishop).
R.U. = Rugby Union.
RV = Revised Version.
R.W.S. = Royal Society of Painters in Water Colours.
R.Y.S. = Royal Yacht Squadron.

S

S. = *San, Santa, Santo,* or *São* (Saint); SS. = Saints.
s. = *solidus* (shilling), *solidi* (shillings).
S.A. = Salvation Army; Sex Appeal; South America; South Australia; South Africa; Société Anonyme (Limited).
SACEUR = Supreme Allied Commander Europe.
SACLANT = Supreme Allied Commander Atlantic.
SET = selective employment tax.
Sarum = of Salisbury.
S.C. = qualified to admission to Staff College.
sc. = *scilicet* (namely).
Sc.D. = *Scientiae Doctor* (Doctor in Science).
S.C.F. = Senior Chaplain to the Forces.
S.C.M. = State Certified Midwife; Student Christian Movement.
SEATO = South-East Asia Treaty Organisation.
SALT = Strategic Arms Limitation Talks.
S.G. = Solicitor-General; Scots Guards.
SHAPE = Supreme Headquarters, Allied Powers, Europe.
SI = Système International d'Unités (International System of Units).
sic. = so written.
SINS = Ships Inertial Navigation System.
SISTER = Special Institution for Scientific and Technical Education and Research.
SOS = distress signal (wireless code signal, used especially by ships at sea).

s.p. = *sine prole* (without issue).
S.P.C.K. = Society for the Promotion of Christian Knowledge.
SPD = Social Democratic Party (W. Ger.).
sp. gr. = specific gravity.
sq. = square; *sequens* (the following).
sqq. = *sequentes, sequentia* (those following).
SRC = Science Research Council.
S.R.N. = State Registered Nurse.
SS. = Saints.
S.S. = Steamship.
S.S.C. = Solicitor before Supreme Court (Scotland).
SSCR = Social Science Research Council.
S.T.D. = *Sacrae Theologiae Doctor* (Doctor of Theology); Subscriber Trunk Dialling.
St. = Saint; Street.
Ste = *Sainte* (Saint, feminine).
Stet = Let it stand (printing term).
s.t.p. = standard temperature and pressure.
S.T.P. = *Sacrae Theologiae Professor* (Professor of Divinity, old form of D.D.)
s.v. = *sub verbo* (under the entry).

T

TAB = Technical Assistance Board (UN).
TAVR = Territorial and Army Volunteer Reserve.
T.B. = Tubercule bacillus (tuberculosis).
t.b. = torpedo boat.
T.C.D. = Trinity College, Dublin.
T.C.C.B. = Test and County Cricket Board.
T.D. = Territorial Decoration; Teachta Dála (Representative of the Dáil).
temp. = temperature.
T.F. = Territorial Force.
T.H. = Trinity House.
TNT = trinitrotoluene (high explosive).
Toc.H. = Talbot House.
tr. = transpose.
T.R.C. = Thames Rowing Club; Tithes Rent Charge.
T.T. = tubercular tested; teetotal.
TUC = Trades Union Congress.
TV = Television.
TVA = Tennessee Valley Authority.
T.V.W.B. = Thames Valley Water Board.
TWI = Training Within Industry for Supervisors.
T.Y.C. = Thames Yacht Club; Two-year Old (or Thousand Yards) Course.

U

U.A.M. = Afro-Malagasy Union.
U-boat = German submarine.
UAR = United Arab Republic.
UCL = University College, London.
U.D.C. = Urban District Council.
UDEAC = Central African Economic and Customs Union.
UEAC = Union of Central African States.
UGC = University Grants Committee.
UHF = ultra-high frequency.
U.K. (or UK) = United Kingdom.
UKAEA = UK Atomic Energy Authority.
ult. = *ultimo* (of the last month).
U.N. (or UN) = United Nations.
UNCTAD = United Conference on Trade and Development (UN).
UNEF = United Nations Emergency Force(s).
UNESCO = United Nations Education, Scientific, and Cultural Organisation.
UNICEF = United Nations Children's Fund.
UNRWA = United Nations Relief and Works Agency for Palestine Refugees.
UNTSO = UN Truce Supervision Organisation (Palestine).
U.P. = United Press.
U.P.U. = Universal Postal Union (UN).
U.S. (or US) United States.
U.S.A. (or USA) = United States of America.
USAEC = US Atomic Energy Commission.

U.S.P.G = Universities' Society for the Propagation of the Gospel.
U.S.S.R. (or USSR) = Union of Soviet Socialist Republics (Russia).

V

V = volt(s).
v. = *vide* (see); *versus* (against).
V.A. = Vicar-Apostolic.
VAT = value added tax.
V. & A. = Victoria and Albert Museum, S. Kensington.
V.C. = Victoria Cross.
V.C.H. = Victoria County Histories.
V.D. = venereal disease; Volunteer Officers' Decoration.
v.d. = various dates.
V.E. Day = Victory in Europe Day, 8 May 1945.
Ven. = Venerable (of an Archdeacon).
verb. sap. = *verbum sapienti sat est* (a word to the wise is enough).
Very Rev. = Very Reverend (of a Dean or a Provost).
v.g. = very good.
v.h.c. = very highly commended.
V.H.F. = very high frequency.
V.I.P. = very important person.
viz. = *videlicet* (namely).
V.J. Day = Victory over Japan Day, 15 August 1945.
V.L. = Vice-Lieutenant (of a County).
V.M. = Virgin Mary.
V.M.H. = Victoria Medal of Honour (Royal Horticultural Society).
Vo. = *verso* (on the left-hand page).
V.P. = Vice-President.
V.R. = *Victoria Regina* (Queen Victoria).
v.r. = variant, or various reading.
V.S. = veterinary surgeon; vital statistics.
VTOL = vertical take-off and landing (aircraft).

W

W = watt(s).
W.A. = Western Australia.
Wasps = White Anglo-Saxon Protestants.
WCC = World Council of Churches.
W.E.A. = Workers' Educational Association.
WEU = Western European Union.
WFTU = World Federation of Trade Unions.
WHO = World Health Organisation (UN).
WMO = World Meteorological Organisation (UN).
W.O. = Warrant Officer.
W.R.A.C. = Women's Royal Army Corps.
W.R.A.F. = Women's Royal Air Force.
W.R.N.S. = Women's Royal Naval Service.
W.S. = Writer to the Signet.
W.V.S. = Women's Voluntary Services.

X

X = Christ (X repr. first letter of the Greek word).
X's = expenses (slang).
xd = ex dividend.
Xmas = Christmas.

Y

y. = year(s).
yd = yard(s).
Y.M.C.A. = Young Men's Christian Association.
Y.W.C.A. = Young Women's Christian Association.

Z

ZANU = Zimbabwe African National Union (Nat. movement in Rhodesia).
ZAPU = Zimbabwe African People's Union (Nat. movement in Rhodesia)

GENERAL
COMPENDIUM

A collection of useful tables and data on a variety of unrelated subjects, including silver and china marks, SI units, weights and measures, sunrise and sunset tables, and foreign currencies in relation to the £.

**GENERAL
COMPENDIUM**

TABLE OF CONTENTS

GENERAL COMPENDIUM

ENGLISH MONARCHS

(A.D. 827–1603)

Monarch	Accession	Died	Age	Reigned

I.—BEFORE THE CONQUEST.

SAXONS AND DANES

Monarch	Accession	Died	Age	Reigned
Egbert	827	839	—	12
Ethelwulf	839	858	—	19
Ethelbald	858	860	—	2
Ethelbert	858	865	—	7
Ethelred	865	871	—	6
Alfred the Great	871	899	50	28
Edward the Elder	899	924	54	25
Athelstan	924	939	45	15
Edmund	939	946	25	7
Eadred	946	955	32	9
Eadwig	955	959	18	3
Edgar	959	975	32	17
Edward the Martyr	975	978	17	3
Ethelred II (" the Unready ")	978	1016	48	37
Edmund Ironside	1016	1016	27	Apr.–Nov.
Canute the Dane	1017	1035	40	18
Harold I	1035	1040	—	5
Hardicanute	1040	1042	24	2
Edward the Confessor	1042	1066	62	24
Harold II	1066	1066	44	Jan.–Oct.

II.—FROM THE CONQUEST TO THE PRESENT DAY.

NORMANS

Monarch	Accession	Died	Age	Reigned
William I	1066	1087	60	21
William II	1087	1100	43	13
Henry I	1100	1135	67	35
Stephen, Count of Blois	1135	1154	50	19

PLANTAGENETS

Monarch	Accession	Died	Age	Reigned
Henry II	1154	1189	56	35
Richard I	1189	1199	42	10
John	1199	1216	50	17
Henry III	1216	1272	65	56
Edward I	1272	1307	68	35
Edward II	1307	dep. 1327	43	20
Edward III	1327	1377	65	50
Richard II	1377	dep. 1399	34	22
Henry IV ⎫	1399	1413	47	13
Henry V ⎬ Lancaster	1413	1422	34	9
Henry VI ⎭	1422	dep. 1461	49	39
Edward IV ⎫	1461	1483	41	22
Edward V ⎬ York	1483	1483	13	Apr.–June
Richard III ⎭	1483	1485	32	2

TUDORS

Monarch	Accession	Died	Age	Reigned
Henry VII	1485	1509	53	24
Henry VIII	1509	1547	56	38
Edward VI	1547	1553	16	6
Jane	1553	1554	17	9 days
Mary I	1553	1558	43	5
Elizabeth I	1558	1603	69	44

BRITISH MONARCHS
(1603 to the Present day)

Monarch	Accession	Died	Age	Reigned
STUARTS				
James I (VI of Scotland)	1603	1625	59	22
Charles I	1625	beh. 1649	48	24
COMMONWEALTH DECLARED, MAY 19, 1649				
Oliver Cromwell, Lord Protector . . .	1653–8	—	—	—
Richard Cromwell, Lord Protector . .	1658–9	—	—	—
STUARTS (RESTORATION)				
Charles II	1660	1685	55	25
James II (VII of Scotland)	1685	dep. 1688	68	3
Interregnum Dec. 11, 1688 to Feb. 13, 1689				
William III and Mary II	1689	1702	51	13
		1694	33	6
Anne	1702	1714	49	12
HOUSE OF HANOVER				
George I	1714	1727	67	13
George II	1727	1760	77	33
George III	1760	1820	81	59
George IV	1820	1830	67	10
William IV	1830	1837	71	7
Victoria.	1837	1901	81	63
HOUSE OF SAXE-COBURG				
Edward VII	1901	1910	68	9
HOUSE OF WINDSOR				
George V	1910	1936	70	25
Edward VIII	1936	Abd. 1936	—	325 days
George VI	1936	1952	56	15
Elizabeth II	1952			

SCOTTISH MONARCHS
(1057–1603)

Monarch		Accession	Died
Malcolm III (Canmore)	Son of Duncan I	1058	1093
Donald Ban	Brother of Malcolm Canmore	1093	—
Duncan II	Son of Malcolm Canmore, by first marriage	1094	1094
Donald Ban	Restored	1094	1097
Edgar	Son of Malcolm Canmore, by second marriage	1097	1107
Alexander I	Son of Malcolm Canmore	1107	1124
David I	Son of Malcolm Canmore	1124	1153
Malcolm IV (the Maiden)	Son of Henry, eldest son of David I	1153	1165
William I (the Lion)	Brother of Malcolm the Maiden	1165	1214
Alexander II	Son of William the Lion	1214	1249
Alexander III	Son of Alexander II, by second marriage	1249	1286
Margaret, Maid of Norway	Daughter of Eric II of Norway, granddaughter of Alexander III	1286	1290
John Baliol	Grandson of eldest daughter of David, Earl of Huntingdon, brother of William the Lion	1292	1296
Robert I (Bruce)	Great-grandson of 2nd daughter of David, Earl of Huntingdon, brother of William the Lion	1306	1329
David II	Son of Robert I, by second marriage	1329	1371
Robert II (Stewart)	Son of Marjorie, daughter of Robert I by first marriage, and Walter the Steward	1371	1390
Robert III	(John, Earl of Carrick) son of Robert II	1390	1406
James I	Son of Robert III	1406	1437
James II	Son of James I	1437	1460
James III	Eldest son of James II	1460	1488
James IV	Eldest son of James III	1488	1513
James V	Son of James IV	1513	1542
Mary	Daughter of James V, by second marriage	1542	1587
James VI (ascended the Throne of England 1603)	Son of Mary, by second marriage	1567	1625

BRITISH PRIME MINISTERS

	Party	Served		Party	Served
George I, 1714–27			Viscount Palmerston	Liberal	1859–65
			Earl Russell	Liberal	1865–6
George II, 1727–60			Earl of Derby	Conservative	1866–8
Sir Robert Walpole	Whig	1721–42	B. Disraeli	Conservative	1868
Earl of Wilmington	Whig	1742–3	W. E. Gladstone	Liberal	1868–74
Henry Pelham	Whig	1743–54	B. Disraeli	Conservative	1874–80
Duke of Newcastle	Whig	1754–6	W. E. Gladstone	Liberal	1880–5
Duke of Devonshire	Whig	1756–7	Marquis of Salisbury	Conservative	1885–6
Duke of Newcastle	Whig	1757–60	W. E. Gladstone	Liberal	1886
			Marquis of Salisbury	Conservative	1886–92
George III, 1760–1820			W. E. Gladstone	Liberal	1892–4
Duke of Newcastle	Whig	1760–2	Earl of Rosebery	Liberal	1894–5
Earl of Bute	Tory	1762–3	Marquis of Salisbury	Conservative	1895–1901
George Grenville	Whig	1763–5			
Marquis of Rocking-	Whig	1766	**Edward VII, 1901–10**		
ham			Marquis of Salisbury	Conservative	1901–2
Duke of Grafton	Whig	1766–9	A. J. Balfour	Conservative	1902–5
Lord North	Tory	1770–82	Sir H. Campbell-	Liberal	1905–8
Marquis of Rocking-	Whig	1782	Bannerman		
ham			H. H. Asquith	Liberal	1908–10
Earl of Shelburne	Whig	1782–3			
Duke of Portland	Coalition	1783	**George V, 1910–36**		
William Pitt	Tory	1783–1801	H. H. Asquith	Liberal	1910–15
Viscount Sidmouth	Tory	1801–4	H. H. Asquith	Coalition	1915–16
William Pitt	Tory	1804–6	D. Lloyd George	Coalition	1916–22
Lord Grenville	Whig	1806–7	A. Bonar Law	Conservative	1922–3
Duke of Portland	Tory	1807–9	S. Baldwin	Conservative	1923–4
Spencer Perceval	Tory	1809–12	J. R. MacDonald	Labour	1924
(assassinated)			S. Baldwin	Conservative	1924–9
			J. R. MacDonald	Labour	1929–31
George IV, 1820–30			J. R. MacDonald	National	1931–5
Earl of Liverpool	Tory	1812–27	S. Baldwin	National	1935–6
George Canning	Tory	1827			
Viscount Goderich	Tory	1827	**Edward VIII, 1936**		
Duke of Wellington	Tory	1827–30			
			George VI, 1936–52		
William IV, 1830–7			S. Baldwin	National	1936–7
Earl Grey	Whig	1830–4	N. Chamberlain	National	1937–39
Viscount Melbourne	Whig	1834	N. Chamberlain	War Cabinet	1939
Sir Robert Peel	Tory	1834–5	W. S. Churchill	War Cabinet	1940–45
Viscount Melbourne	Whig	1835–7	W. S. Churchill	Caretaker	1945
			C. R. Attlee	Labour	1945–51
Victoria, 1837–1901			Sir W. S. Churchill	Conservative	1951–2
Viscount Melbourne	Whig	1837–41			
Sir Robert Peel	Tory	1841–6	**Elizabeth II, 1952–**		
Lord John Russell	Whig	1846–52	Sir W. S. Churchill	Conservative	1952–5
Earl of Derby	Tory	1852	Sir A. Eden	Conservative	1955–7
Earl of Aberdeen	Peelite	1852–5	H. Macmillan	Conservative	1957–63
Viscount Palmerston	Liberal	1855–8	Sir A. Douglas-Home	Conservative	1963–4
Earl of Derby	Tory	1858–9	H. Wilson	Labour	1964–70
			E. Heath	Conservative	1970–

PRESIDENTS OF THE UNITED STATES

The terms are for four years; only President F. D. Roosevelt
has served more than two terms.

	Party	Served		Party	Served
1. George Washington	Fed.	1789–97	21. Chester A. Arthur	Rep.	1881–5
2. John Adams	Fed.	1797–1801	22. Grover Cleveland	Dem.	1885–9
3. Thomas Jefferson	Rep.	1801–9	23. Benjamin Harrison	Rep.	1889–93
4. James Madison	Rep.	1809–17	24. Grover Cleveland	Dem.	1893–7
5. James Monroe	Rep.	1817–25	25. William McKinley	Rep.	1897–1901
6. John Quincey Adams	Rep.	1825–9	(assassinated)		
7. Andrew Jackson	Dem.	1829–37	26. Theodore Roosevelt	Rep.	1901–9
8. Martin Van Buren	Dem.	1837–41	27. William Howard Taft	Rep.	1909–13
9. William H. Harrison	Whig	1841	28. Woodrow Wilson	Dem.	1913–21
(died in office)			29. Warren G. Harding	Rep.	1921–3
10. John Tyler	Whig	1841–5	(died in office)		
11. James K. Polk	Dem.	1845–9	30. Calvin Coolidge	Rep.	1923–9
12. Zachary Taylor	Whig	1849–50	31. Herbert C. Hoover	Rep.	1929–33
(died in office)			32. Franklin D. Roosevelt	Dem.	1933–45
13. Millard Fillmore	Whig	1850–3	(died in office)		
14. Franklin Pierce	Dem.	1853–7	33. Harry S. Truman	Dem.	1945–53
15. James Buchanan	Dem.	1857–61	34. Dwight D. Eisenhower	Rep.	1953–61
16. Abraham Lincoln	Rep.	1861–5	35. John F. Kennedy	Dem.	1961–3
(assassinated)			(assassinated)		
17. Andrew Johnson	Rep.	1865–9	36. Lyndon B. Johnson	Dem.	1963–69
18. Ulysses S. Grant	Rep.	1869–77	37. Richard N. Nixon	Rep.	1969–
19. Rutherford B. Hayes	Rep.	1877–81			
20. James A. Garfield	Rep.	1881			
(assassinated)					

WEIGHTS AND MEASURES

Many kinds of measure now in use in the United Kingdom are gradually being converted from Imperial units to SI units. SI is short for "Système International d'Unités" and it is a system of metric units now coming into international use through the agency of such bodies as the General Conference of the International Bureau of Weights and Measures and the International Organisation for Standardisation (ISO) in whose work Britain participates. Information about SI units is available in booklets published by the British Standards Institution, Sales Branch, 101–113 Pentonville Road, London, N.1.

For a transitional period of some years, Imperial and SI units will be in use simultaneously. Important parts of the two systems are given separately below. A selection of useful conversion factors is on N8.

Unit Symbols Used in the Tables

Unit	Symbol	Unit	Symbol
metre	m	kilogramme	kg
yard	yd	gramme	g
foot	ft	pound	lb
inch	in	ounce	oz
mile	mile	hundredweight	cwt
square metre	m²	poundal	pdl
square inch	in²	pound-force	lbf
square mile	mile²	foot pound-force	ft lbf
cubic metre	m³	calorie	cal
cubic inch	in³	British thermal unit	Btu
litre	l	horsepower	hp
gallon	gal	tonne	t

I. IMPERIAL WEIGHTS AND MEASURES

Length.

1 nail	= 2¼ in
1 link	= 7·92 in
12 in	= 1 ft
3 ft	= 1 yd
22 yd	= 1 chain
10 chains	= 1 furlong
8 furlongs	= 1 mile = 1760 yd = 5280 ft

Area.

144 in²	= 1 ft²
9 ft²	= 1 yd² = 1296 in²
484 yd²	= 1 square chain
1210 yd²	= 1 rood
4 roods	= 1 acre = 4840 yd²
640 acres	= 1 mile²

Volume.

1728 in³	= 1 ft³
27 ft³	= 1 yd³

Capacity.

4 gills	= 1 pint
2 pints	= 1 quart
4 quarts	= 1 gallon
2 gallons	= 1 peck
4 pecks	= 1 bushel
8 bushels	= 1 quarter
36 bushels	= 1 chaldron

The gallon, as the capacity standard, is based upon the pound.

1 gal = 277·274 in³

Weight (Avoirdupois).

1 dram	= 27·343 75 grains
16 drams	= 1 oz = 437·5 grains
16 oz	= 1 lb = 7000 grains
14 lb	= 1 stone
28 lb	= 1 quarter
4 quarters	= 1 cwt = 112 lb
20 cwt	= 1 ton = 2240 lb

Troy Weight.

1 pennyweight	= 24 grains
480 grains	= 1 ounce

The only unit of troy weight which is legal for use in trade in Britain is the ounce Troy, and weighings of precious metal are made in multiples and decimals of this unit.

The term *carat* is not a unit of weight for precious metals, but is used to denote the quality of gold plate, etc., and is a figure indicating the number of 24ths of pure gold in the alloy, *e.g.*, a 9 carat gold ring consists of nine parts of pure gold and fifteen parts of base metals.

Nautical Measures.

1 nautical mile = 6080 ft = 1853·18 m
1 knot = 1 nautical mile per hour = 1·151 mile/h

Note.—In future the international nautical mile of 1852 m will be used.

Note.—The British Pharmaceutical Code and the British National Formulary—the official works of medicinal reference—no longer contain the apothecaries' units of measurement since medicine is now measured in metric units. Prescriptions are in 5 millilitre (ml) units; medicine bottles are in six sizes from 50 to 500 ml.

II. SI UNITS

There are six base SI Units.　They are:

Quantity	Name of Unit	Symbol
length	metre	m
mass	kilogramme	kg
time	second	s
electric current	ampere	A
temperature	kelvin	K
luminous intensity	candela	cd

Derived units are normally stated in terms of the base unit. Examples: the SI units of velocity and density are, respectively, the metre per second (m/s) and the kilogramme per cubic metre (kg/m³). Some important derived units have well-established names of their own. They are:

Quantity	Name of SI unit	Symbol	Expressed in terms of SI base-units or derived units
frequency	hertz	Hz	$1\ \text{Hz} = 1/\text{s}$
force	newton	N	$1\ \text{N} = 1\ \text{kg m/s}^2$
work, energy, quantity of heat	joule	J	$1\ \text{J} = 1\ \text{N m}$
power	watt	W	$1\ \text{W} = 1\ \text{J/s}$
quantity of electricity	coulomb	C	$1\ \text{C} = 1\ \text{A s}$
electric potential, potential difference, tension, electromotive force	volt	V	$1\ \text{V} = 1\ \text{W/A}$
electric capacitance	farad	F	$1\ \text{F} = 1\ \text{A s/V}$
electric resistance	ohm	Ω	$1\ \Omega = 1\ \text{V/A}$
flux of magnetic induction, magnetic flux	weber	Wb	$1\ \text{Wb} = 1\ \text{V s}$
magnetic flux density, magnetic induction	tesla	T	$1\ \text{T} = 1\ \text{Wb/m}^2$
inductance	henry	H	$1\ \text{H} = 1\ \text{V s/A}$
luminous flux	lumen	lm	$1\ \text{lm} = 1\ \text{cd sr}$
illumination	lux	lx	$= 1\ \text{lx}\quad 1\ \text{lm/m}^2$

There are special prefixes for forming multiples and sub-multiples of the SI units.　These are:

Factor by which the unit is multiplied	Prefix	Symbol
10^{12}	tera	T
10^{9}	giga	G
10^{6}	mega	M
10^{3}	kilo	k
10^{2}	hecto	h
10	deca	da
10^{-1}	deci	d
10^{-2}	centi	c
10^{-3}	milli	m
10^{-6}	micro	μ
10^{-9}	nano	n
10^{-12}	pico	p
10^{-15}	femto	f
10^{-18}	atto	a

Examples: one thousandth of a metre is one millimetre (1 mm); one million volts is one megavolt (1 MV).　These prefixes are *recommended* but other multiples and sub-multiples will be used when convenient, *e.g.*, the centimetre (cm), the cubic decimetre (dm³).
The following is a selection of special points to note:

(i) The name litre now means 1 cubic decimetre or 10^{-3}m^3 and is a measure of volume.

(ii) Days, hours, and minutes are still used to measure time, though some scientists may prefer to use kiloseconds, etc.

(iii) The SI unit of plane angle is the radian (rad), but degrees, minutes and seconds are still used as well.　$1° = \dfrac{\pi}{180}$ rad; 1 rad $= 57 \cdot 295\ 78° = 57°\ 17'\ 44 \cdot 81''$

(iv) A Celsius temperature, say 15 degrees, is written 15°C; note that 15C would mean 15 coulombs.　*See* L21.

(v) The mole (mol) is important in science as a measure of " amount of substance " and may be adopted as a seventh basic SI unit. 1 mol is the amount of substance of a system which contains as many elementary units as there are carbon atoms in 0·012 kg of ^{12}C.　The elementary unit must be specified and may be an atom, a molecule, an ion, an electron, etc., or a specified group of such particles.　*See* F21(2).

(vi) The SI unit of area is the square metre (m²) but the hectare (1 ha $= 10^{4}\text{m}^2$) will be the normal unit for land measure where we have previously [used the acre.　The are (a) $= 10^{2}\text{m}^2$.

(vii) The SI unit of pressure is the newton per square metre (N/m²), but in some technical fields, notably meteorology, the unit of pressure is the bar which approximates to normal atmospheric pressure;　1 bar $= 10^{5}\ \text{N/m}^2$.

II. SELECTED METRIC EQUIVALENTS FOR IMPERIAL WEIGHTS AND MEASURES

Length.

1 in = 2·54 cm = **0·0254 m**
12 in = 1 ft = 30·48 cm = **0·3048 m**
3 ft = 1 yd = **0·9144 m**
1760 yd = 1 mile = **1609·344 m**

Area.

1 in^2 = 6·4516 × $10^{-4}m^2$
144 in^2 = 1 ft^2 = 0·092 903 0 m^2
9 ft^2 = 1 yd^2 = 0·836 127 m^2
4840 yd^2 = 1 acre = 0·404 68
640 acres = 1 $mile^2$ = 2·589 99 × 10^6m^2

Volume.

1 in^3 = 1·638 71 × $10^{-5}m^3$
1 ft^3 = 0·028 316 8 m^3
1 UK gal = 0·004 546 092 m^3

Velocity.

1 ft/s = **0·3048** m/s
1 mile/h = **0·447 04** m/s = 1·6093 × 10^3 m/h

Capacity.

1 pint = 0·568 *l* or $10^{-3}m^3$
2 pints = 1 quart = 1·136 *l*
4 quarts = 1 gal = 4·546 *l*
8 gal = 1 bushel = 36·37 *l*
8 bushels = 1 quarter = 2·909 × 10^2

Weight.

1 oz = 28·35 g
16 oz = 1 lb = **0·453 592 37 kg**
14 lb = 1 st = 6·350 kg
112 lb = 1 cwt = 50·80 kg
20 cwt (2240 lb) = 1 long ton = 1016 kg
2000 lb = 1 short ton = 907 kg

Note.—1 tonne (t) = 1000 kg

Density.

1 lb/in^3 = 2·767 99 × 10^4 kg/m^3
1 lb/ft^3 = 16·0185 kg/m^3
1 lb/UK gal = 99·7764 kg/m^3

Force.

1 pdl = 0·138 255 N
1 lbf = 4·448 22 N

Pressure.

1 lbf/in^2 = 6894·76 N/m^2

Energy (work, heat).

1 ft pdl = 0·042 140 1 J
1 ft lbf = 1·355 82 J
1 cal = **4·1868 J**
1 Btu = 1055·06 J

Power.

1 hp = 745 700 W

Temperature.

1 Rankine degree = 1 Fahrenheit degree
= 5/9 Kelvin = 5/9 Celsius degree

(The Rankine scale of absolute temperature was developed from the Fahrenheit scale, exactly as the Kelvin scale was developed from the Celsius scale.)

Note.—Figures printed in bold type are exact. Unit symbols are the same in the singular and the plural and do not carry a full point (as a mark of an abbreviation).

INTERNATIONAL PAPER SIZES

Trimmed or finished sizes

"A" Series

(Books and Magazines)

Designation	Size mm	Size in
A0	841 × 1189	33·11 × 46·81
A1	594 × 841	23·39 × 33·11
A2	420 × 594	16·54 × 23·39
A3	297 × 420	11·69 × 16·54
A4	210 × 297	8·27 × 11·69
A5	148 × 210	5·83 × 8·27
A6	105 × 148	4·13 × 5·83
A7	74 × 105	2·91 × 4·13
A8	52 × 74	2·05 × 2·91
A9	37 × 52	1·46 × 2·05
A10	26 × 37	1·02 × 1·46

Note.—The basis of the international series of paper sizes is a rectangle having an area of 1 sq. metre, the sides of which are in the proportion of 1 : √2 (a geometrical relationship, the side and diagonal of a square being in that proportion). In addition there is a series of "B" sizes intermediate between any two adjacent sizes of the "A" series (for posters, etc.) and of "C" sizes (for envelopes).

SIZES OF BOUND BOOKS

Name	Size of untrimmed page in	Size of untrimmed page mm
Foolscap octavo	6¾ × 4¼	170 × 110
Crown octavo .	7½ × 5	190 × 125
Large crown octavo	8 × 5¼	205 × 135
Small demy octavo.	8½ × 5⅝	215 × 145
Demy octavo . .	8¾ × 5⅝	220 × 145
Medium octavo .	9 × 5¾	230 × 145
Small royal octavo.	9¼ × 6⅛	235 × 155
Royal octavo . .	10 × 6¼	255 × 160

Note.—The standard for paperbacks is a trimmed page size of 7⅛ in × 4⅜ in (180 mm × 110 mm).

FOREIGN CURRENCIES IN RELATION TO STERLING

Country	Currency	Parity[1] value to £ at 15.1.71	Approximate rate at 9.3.71 or latest date available
Argentine	Peso		9·68
Australia	Dollar	2·143	2·147
Austria	Schilling	62·40	62·585
Belgium/Lux.	Franc	120·00	120·05
Bolivia	Peso Boliviano		28·125
Brazil	Cruzeiro		12·11[3]
British Honduras	Dollar	4·00	4·00
Burma	Kyat	11·429	11·429
Canada	Dollar	2·595	2·428
Ceylon	Rupee	14·286	14·255
Chile	Escudo		29·59[3 4]
China	Renminbi		5·908
Colombia	Peso		46·50[3 4]
Congo (Kinshasa)	Zaire	1·20	1·200[2]
Costa Rica	Colon	15·90	15·924
Cuba	Peso		2·419
Czechoslovakia	Koruna		17·28[2]
Denmark	Krone	18·00	18·093
Dominican Republic	Peso	2·40	2·419
Ecuador	Sucre	60·00	60·00
Egypt (U.A.R.)	Pound	0·836	1·046
El Salvador	Colon	6·00	6·05
Ethiopia	Dollar	6·00	6·00
Finland	Markka	10·08	10·08
France	Franc	13·33	13·343
French monetary a. terrs. in C. and W. Africa and Malagasy Republic	C.F.A. Franc		667·15
Germany (Fed. Rep.)	D. Mark	8·784	8·783
Greece	Drachma	72·00	72·375
Guatemala	Quetzal	2·40	2·419
Guyana	Dollar	4·80	4·80
Haiti	Gourde	12·00	12·097
Honduras Rep.	Lempira	4·80	4·838
Hong Kong	Dollar	14·545	14·572
Iceland	Krona	211·20	211·30
India	Rupee	18·00	18·04
Indonesia	Rupiah		907·20
Iran	Rial	181·80	184·11
Iraq	Dinar	0·857	0·857
Israel	Pound	8·40	8·40
Italy	Lire	1,500·00	1,506·125
Jamaica	Dollar	2·00	2·00
Japan	Yen	864·00	864·50
Jordan	Dinar	0·857	0·862
Lebanon	Pound	5·26	7·87[3]
Malaysia	Dollar	7·347	7·388
Morocco	Dirham	12·145	12·05
Mexico	Peso	30·00	30·21
Netherlands	Guilder	8·688	8·694
Netherlands W.I.	Guilder	4·526	4·50
New Zealand	Dollar	2·143	2·143
Nicaragua	Cordoba	16·80	16·97[3]
Norway	Kroner	17·143	17·263
Pakistan	Rupee	11·429	11·429
Panama	Balboa	2·40	2·419
Paraguay	Guarani		300·00
Peru	Sol		103·815
Philippines	Peso	9·36	15·585
Poland	Zloty		9·60[5]
Portugal	Escudo	69·00	68·825
Rwanda	Franc	240·00	240·00[2]
South Africa	Rand	1·714	1·716
Spain	Peseta	168·00	168·35
Sweden	Kronor	12·416	12·491
Switzerland	Franc		10·408
Syria	Pound	5·26	11·00
Thailand	Baht	49·92	50·66
Trinidad and Tobago	T.T. Dollar	4·80	4·80
Tunisia	Dinar	1·26	1·255
Turkey	Pound (Lira)	36·00	35·938
U.S.A.	Dollar	2·40	2·419
Uruguay	Peso	17·76	601·00
Venezuela	Bolivar		10·83[3 4]
Yugoslavia	Dinar	30·00	36·00

[1] Established under agreement with the International Monetary Fund which requires that the par value of the currency of each member be expressed in terms of gold or U.S. Dollars.
[2] Official rate.
[3] Free market rate.
[4] Not necessarily the effective rate for all transfers.
[5] Basic rate.

THERMOMETER COMPARISONS

Celsius 100°	Fahrenheit 212°	Celsius 100°	Fahrenheit 212°
95	203	20	68
90	194	15·5	60
85	185	12·8	55
78·9	174	10	50
75	167	7·2	45
70	158	5	41
65	149	1·7	35
60	140	0	32
55	131	− 1·1	30
52·8	127	− 5	23
50	122	− 6·7	20
45	113	− 10	14
42·2	108	− 12·2	10
40	104	− 15	5
36·7	98	− 17·8	0
35	95	− 20	− 4
32·2	90	− 25	− 13
30	86	− 30	− 22
26·7	80	− 35	− 31
25	77	− 40	− 40

To reduce Fahrenheit to Celsius (centigrade), subtract 32 degrees and multiply by 5/9; to reduce Celsius to Fahrenheit, multiply by 9/5 and add 32 degrees.

An alternative method, perhaps easier to remember, is to add 40 to the given figure, multiply by 5/9 (°F to °C) or 9/5 (°C to °F) and subtract 40

ROMAN NUMERALS

I	1	LXX	70
II	2	LXXX	80
III	3	LXXXVIII	88
IV	4	XC	90
V	5	XCIX	99
VI	6	C	100
VII	7	CX	110
VIII	8	CXI	111
IX	9	CXC	190
X	10	CC	200
XI	11	CCXX	220
XII	12	CCC	300
XIII	13	CCCXX	320
XIV	14	CD	400
XV	15	D	500
XVI	16	DC	600
XVII	17	DCC	700
XVIII	18	DCCC	800
XIX	19	CM	900
XX	20	XM	990
XXX	30	M	1000
XL	40	MD	1500
L	50	MDCCC	1800
LV	55	MCMLXX	1970
LX	60	MM	2000

GREEK ALPHABET

A	α	Alpha	N	ν	nu
B	β	beta	Ξ	ξ	xi
Γ	γ	gamma	O	o	omicron
Δ	δ	delta	Π	π	pi
E	ϵ	epsilon	P	ρ	rho
Z	ζ	zeta	Σ	σ	sigma
H	η	eta	T	τ	tau
Θ	θ	theta	Y	υ	upsilon
I	ι	iota	Φ	ϕ	phi
K	κ	kappa	X	χ	chi
Λ	λ	lambda	Ψ	ψ	psi
M	μ	mu	Ω	ω	omega

BANK AND PUBLIC HOLIDAYS

In addition to Good Friday and Christmas Day, there are Bank holidays in most parts of England, Wales and the Channel Islands on Easter Monday, in late Spring and late Summer (see below), and on the first weekday after Christmas (Boxing Day). The Channel Islands also observe New Year's Day and Liberation Day, May 9. Scotland observes New Year's Day, Good Friday, a late Spring and a late Summer holiday (see below) and Christmas Day. In addition most towns in Scotland have locally determined holidays in the Spring and Autumn. Northern Ireland observes all the English holidays and, in addition, has a holiday on St. Patrick's Day, 17 March, and on 12 July, commemorating the Battle of the Boyne (1690). Easter Tuesday is also a customary holiday for industry and trade.

The Queen's birthday (when decreed) is observed in the Customs and certain other Government establishments as a holiday.

| 1971 | Easter Monday | Apr. 12 | *Late Spring | May 31 | *Late Summer | Aug. 30 |
| 1972 | ” | Apr. 3 | ” | May 29 | ” | Aug. 28 |

*Note.—In Scotland: May 3; Aug. 2 (1971) May 1; Aug. 7 (1972)

THE SEASONS

	1972	1973
Vernal Equinox—Spring begins	Mar. 30, 12.22	Mar. 20, 18.13
Summer Solstice—Summer begins	June 21, 07.06	June 21, 13.01
Autumnal Equinox—Autumn begins	Sept. 22, 22.33	Sept. 23, 04.21
Winter Solstice—Winter begins	Dec. 21, 18.13	Dec. 22, 00.08

(These times are in G.M.T.)

THE COUNTRY CODE

GUARD AGAINST THE RISK OF FIRE. Great damage is done every year to crops, plantations, woodlands, and heaths. A match or cigarette thrown away or a pipe carelessly knocked out, picnic fires not properly put out or lighted near dry crops, can quickly start a blaze.

FASTEN ALL GATES. If animals get out of a field they stray. As a result they may do serious damage to crops, suffer injury on the roads, or eat food that is harmful.

KEEP DOGS UNDER CONTROL. Animals are easily frightened, even by small, playful dogs. Stillbirths may be the result.

KEEP TO THE PATHS ACROSS FARM LAND. Crops are damaged by treading; flattened crops are difficult to harvest. Grass is a valuable crop.

AVOID DAMAGING FENCES, HEDGES, AND WALLS. If these are damaged, gaps will be caused. Where a man goes, an animal may follow.

LEAVE NO LITTER. Litter is not just unsightly, but often a danger as well. Broken glass and tins may injure animals and harm machinery.

SAFEGUARD WATER SUPPLIES. Countrymen often depend on wells and streams for water for themselves and for their animals.

PROTECT WILD LIFE, PLANTS, AND TREES. Wild animals should not be disturbed, plants uprooted, or trees treated roughly.

GO CAREFULLY ON COUNTRY ROADS. If there is no footpath, walkers are generally safer on the right, facing on-coming traffic. Care and patience are needed by motorists when passing farm animals.

RESPECT THE LIFE OF THE COUNTRYSIDE. Many of the machines and much of the business stock on which the farmer depends for his livelihood have to be kept in the open. Take care not to damage them.

THE BEAUFORT SCALE OF WIND FORCE

Beaufort number	Wind	Effect on land	Speed	
			M.p.h.	Knots
0	Calm	Smoke rises vertically	Less than 1	Less than 1
1	Light air	Direction shown by smoke but not by wind vanes	1–3	1–3
2	Light breeze	Wind felt on face; leaves rustle; wind vanes move	4–7	4–6
3	Gentle breeze	Leaves and twigs in motion; wind extends light flag	8–12	7–10
4	Moderate breeze	Raises dust, loose paper and moves small branches	13–18	11–16
5	Fresh breeze	Small trees in leaf begin to sway	19–24	17–21
6	Strong breeze	Large branches in motion; whistling in telegraph wires; difficulty with umbrellas	25–31	22–27
7	Moderate gale	Whole trees in motion; difficult to walk against wind	32–38	28–33
8	Fresh gale	Twigs break off trees; progress impeded	39–46	34–40
9	Strong gale	Slight structural damage occurs; chimney pots and slates blown off	47–54	41–47
10	Whole gale	Trees uprooted and considerable structural damage	55–63	48–56
11	Storm	Widespread damage, seldom experienced in England	64–75	57–65
12	Hurricane	Winds of this force only encountered in tropical revolving storms	Above 75	Above 65

SUNRISE AND SUNSET, LONDON 1971–72

(These times are given in G.M.T. throughout.)

Sundays, 1971 Date	Sunrise	Sunset	Sundays, 1972 Date	Sunrise	Sunset	Sundays, 1972 Date	Sunrise	Sunset
July 4	03.49	20.20	January 2	08.06	16.03	July 2	03.48	20.21
11	03.56	20.16	9	08.04	16.11	9	03.54	20.17
18	04.04	20.09	16	08.00	16.21	16	04.02	20.10
25	04.13	20.00	23	07.53	16.33	23	04.11	20.02
August 1	04.23	19.50	30	07.43	16.45	30	04.21	19.52
8	04.34	19.38	February 6	07.33	16.58	August 6	04.32	19.40
15	04.45	19.24	13	07.20	17.11	13	04.43	19.27
22	04.56	19.10	20	07.07	17.23	20	04.54	19.13
29	05.07	18.55	27	06.52	17.36	27	05.05	18.58
September 5	05.18	18.40	March 5	06.37	17.48	September 3	05.16	18.42
12	05.30	18.24	12	06.22	18.00	10	05.28	18.27
19	05.41	18.08	19	06.06	18.12	17	05.39	18.10
26	05.52	17.51	26	05.50	18.24	24	05.50	17.54
October 3	06.03	17.36	April 2	05.34	18.36	October 1	06.01	17.38
10	06.15	17.20	9	05.18	18.47	8	06.13	17.23
17	06.27	17.05	16	05.03	18.59	15	06.25	17.07
24	06.39	16.50	23	04.48	19.11	22	06.37	16.53
31	06.51	16.37	30	04.34	19.22	29	06.49	16.39
November 7	07.03	16.24	May 7	04.22	19.34	November 5	07.01	16.27
14	07.16	16.14	14	04.10	19.45	12	07.14	16.15
21	07.28	16.05	21	04.01	19.55	19	07.26	16.06
28	07.39	15.58	28	03.53	20.04	26	07.37	15.59
December 5	07.49	15.53	June 4	03.47	20.11	December 3	07.47	15.54
12	07.57	15.52	11	03.44	20.17	10	07.55	15.52
19	08.02	15.53	18	03.43	20.21	17	08.02	15.52
26	08.06	15.56	25	03.44	20.22	24	08.05	15.55
						31	08·07	16·01

MOON'S PHASES, 1971–72

1971

New Moon		22	9.57 p.m.
First Quarter		30	6.11 p.m.
Full Moon	July	8	10.37 a.m.
Last Quarter		15	5.47 a.m.
New Moon		22	9.15 a.m.
First Quarter		30	11.07 p.m.
Full Moon	August	6	7.42 p.m.
Last Quarter		13	10.55 a.m.
New Moon		20	10.53 p.m.
First Quarter		29	2.56 a.m.
Full Moon	September	5	4.03 a.m.
Last Quarter		11	6.23 p.m.
New Moon		19	2.42 p.m.
First Quarter		27	5.17 p.m.
Full Moon	October	4	12.20 p.m.
Last Quarter		11	5.29 a.m.
New Moon		19	7.59 a.m.
First Quarter		27	5.54 a.m.
Full Moon	November	2	9.20 p.m.
Last Quarter		9	8.51 p.m.
New Moon		18	1.46 a.m.
First Quarter		25	4.37 p.m.
Full Moon	December	2	7.48 p.m.
Last Quarter		9	4.02 p.m.
New Moon		17	7.03 p.m.
First Quarter		25	1.35 a.m.
Full Moon		31	8.20 p.m.

1972

Last Quarter	January	8	1.31 p.m.
New Moon		16	10.52 a.m.
First Quarter		23	9.29 a.m.
Full Moon		30	10.58 a.m.
Last Quarter	February	7	11.12 a.m.
New Moon		15	12.29 a.m.
First Quarter		21	5.20 p.m.
Full Moon		29	3.12 a.m.
Last Quarter	March	8	7.06 a.m.

New Moon		15	11.35 a.m.
First Quarter		22	2.12 a.m.
Full Moon		29	8.06 p.m.
Last Quarter	April	6	11.45 p.m.
New Moon		13	8.31 p.m.
First Quarter		20	12.45 p.m.
Full Moon		28	12.45 p.m.
Last Quarter	May	6	12.26 p.m.
New Moon		13	4.08 a.m.
First Quarter		20	1.16 a.m.
Full Moon		28	4.28 a.m.
Last Quarter	June	4	9.22 p.m.
New Moon		11	11.30 a.m.
First Quarter		18	3.41 a.m.
Full Moon		26	6.46 p.m.
Last Quarter	July	4	3.26 a.m.
New Moon		10	7.39 p.m.
First Quarter		18	7.46 a.m.
Full Moon		26	7.24 a.m.
Last Quarter	August	2	8.02 a.m.
New Moon		9	5.26 a.m.
First Quarter		17	1.09 a.m.
Full Moon		24	6.22 p.m.
Last Quarter		31	12.48 p.m.
New Moon	September	7	5.29 p.m.
First Quarter		15	7.13 p.m.
Full Moon		23	4.07 a.m.
Last Quarter		29	7.16 p.m.
New Moon	October	7	8.08 a.m.
First Quarter		15	12.55 p.m.
Full Moon		22	1.25 p.m.
Last Quarter		29	4.41 a.m.
New Moon	November	6	1.21 a.m.
First Quarter		14	5.01 a.m.
Full Moon		20	11.07 p.m.
Last Quarter		27	5.45 p.m.
New Moon	December	5	8.24 a.m.
First Quarter		13	6.36 p.m.
Full Moon		20	9.45 a.m.
Last Quarter		27	10.28 a.m.

Reproduced, with permission, from data supplied by H.M. Nautical Almanac Office.
These times are in G.M.T. If B.S.T. is required, add 1 hour.
LIGHTING-UP TIME is from half an hour after local sunset to half an hour before local sunrise throughout the year.

THE LONDON

𝔸	1598	a	1618	B	1638	𝔞	1658	a	1678	𝔞	1697
𝔹	9	b	19	B	39	𝔅	59	b	79	𝔅	97
ℂ	1600	c	20	C	40	ℭ	Chas. II. 60	c	80	𝔠	98
𝔻	1	d	21	D	41	𝔇	61	d	81	𝔡	99
𝔼	2	e	22	E	42	ℭ	62	e	82	𝔢	1700
𝔽	Jas. I. 3	f	23	F	43	𝔉	63	E	83	𝔣	1
𝔾	4	g	24	G	44	𝔊	64	g	84	𝔤	Anne. 2
h	5	h	Chas. I. 25	B	45	𝔥	65	h	Jas. II. 85	𝔥	3
I	6	i	26	I	46	𝔍	66	I	86	𝔦	4
K	7	k	27	K	47	𝔎	67	k	87	𝔨	5
L	8	l	28	L	48	𝔏	68	l	88	𝔩	6
m	9	m	29	M	Cmwth. 49	𝔐	69	m	W. & M. 89	𝔪	7
𝔫	10	n	30	N	50	𝔑	70	n	90	𝔫	8
O	11	o	31	O	51	𝔒	71	O	91	𝔬	9
P	12	p	32	P	52	𝔓	72	p	92	𝔭	10
Q	13	q	33	Q	53	𝔔	73	q	93	𝔮	11
R	14	r	34	R	54	𝔊	74	r	94	𝔯	12
S	15	s	35	S	55	𝔖	75	s	Wm III. 95	𝔰	13
T	16	t	36	d	56	𝔗	76	t	96	𝔱	Geo. I. 14
V	17	v	37	B	57	𝔘	77			𝔳	15

PROVINCIAL SILVER MARKS

BIRMINGHAM . .	1800		1900
CHESTER . . .	1701		1800
EXETER . . .	1601		1800

See also **Hall-mark**, Gen. Information.

SILVER MARKS

A	Geo. I. 1716	a	1736	A	1756	a	1776	A	1796	a	1816

A	Geo. I. 1716	a	1736	A	1756	a	1776	A	1796	a	1816
B	17	b	37	B	57	b	77	B	97	b	17
C	18	c	38	C	58	c	78	C	98	c	18
D	19	dd	39	D	59	d	79	D	99	d	19
E	20	e	40	E	Geo. III. 60	e	80	E	1800	e	Geo. IV. 20
F	21	f	41	F	61	f	81	F	1	f	21
G	22	g	42	G	62	g	82	G	2	g	22
H	23	h	43	H	63	h	83	H	3	h	23
I	24	i	44	J	64	i	84	I	4	i	24
K	25	k	45	K	65	k	85	K	5	k	25
L	26	l	46	L	66	l	86	L	6	l	26
M	Geo. II. 27	m	47	M	67	m	87	M	7	m	27
N	28	n	48	N	68	n	88	N	8	n	28
O	29	o	49	O	69	o	89	O	9	o	29
P	30	p	50	P	70	p	90	P	10	p	Will. IV. 30
Q	31	q	51	Q	71	q	91	Q	11	q	31
R	32	r	52	R	72	r	92	R	12	r	32
S	33	s	53	S	73	s	93	S	13	s	33
T	34	t	54	T	74	t	94	T	14	t	34
V	35	u	55	U	75	u	95	U	15	u	35

PROVINCIAL SILVER MARKS

NEWCASTLE	· ·	1702		1800	K
SHEFFIELD	· ·	1800		1900	h
YORK	· · ·	1700		1800	O

THE LONDON SILVER MARKS

	1836		1856		1876		1896		1916		Ed. VIII. 1936
A	1836	K	1856	A	1876	a	1896	A	1916	A	Ed. VIII. 1936
B	Vic. 37	b	57	B	77	b	97	b	17	B	Geo. VI 37
C	38	c	58	C	78	c	98	c	18	C	38
D	39	d	59	D	79	d	99	D	19	D	39
E	40	e	60	E	80	e	1900	E	20	E	40
F	41	f	61	F	81	f	Ed. VII. 1	f	21	F	41
G	42	g	62	G	82	g	2	G	22	G	42
H	43	h	63	H	83	h	3	h	23	H	43
I	44	i	64	I	84	i	4	i	24	I	44
K	45	k	65	K	85	k	5	k	25	K	45
L	46	l	66	L	86	l	6	l	26	L	46
M	47	m	67	M	87	m	7	m	27	M	47
N	48	n	68	N	88	n	8	n	28	N	48
O	49	o	69	O	89	o	9	o	29	O	49
P	50	p	70	P	90	p	Geo. V. 10	P	30	P	50
Q	51	q	71	Q	91	q	11	q	31	Q	51
R	52	r	72	R	92	r	12	r	32	R	Eliz. II. 52
S	53	s	73	S	93	s	13	s	33	S	53
T	54	t	74	T	94	t	14	t	34	T	54
U	55	v	75	U	95	u	15	u	35	U	55

SCOTTISH AND IRISH SILVER MARKS

EDINBURGH . . .	1700		1800
GLASGOW . . .	1700		1800
DUBLIN . . .	1700		1800

MARKS ON ENGLISH POTTERY AND PORCELAIN

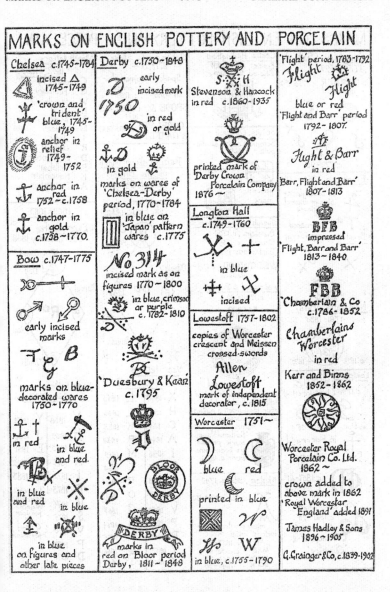

Many of the marks found on ceramics are merely the marks of painters and workman. Even when identified, they are not a sure guide to the place of manufacture, as these people would work in many different factories in the course of their careers. The throwers or "repairers" (the workers who assembled the various parts of figures, etc.) invariably used a mark scratched in the body of the ware prior to the biscuit-firing. These marks when *under* the glaze can safely be treated as genuine. A mark which has been ground in after

firing, in order to deceive, will not have the characteristic burr or raised edge produced when soft clay is scratched.

Painters and gilders would generally use one of the colours in their palette or gilt to mark the wares upon which they worked. This was probably for the benefit of the management as payment was often on a piecework basis.

The marks used on English wares were applied in several different ways—by incising, impressing, painting, or by transfer-printing *under* the glaze

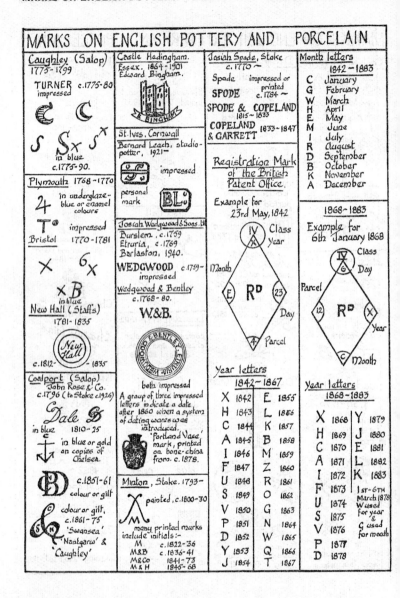

in blue (also in green after 1850). Marking by painting, transfer-printing, or stencilling *over* the glaze in enamel colours is always liable to be fraudulent as these types of mark can be added at any time after the piece has been made.

From 1842–83 many manufacturers' wares were marked with the " diamond-mark ", illustrated above. This was an indication that the design had been registered with the British Patent Office. Ceramics was Class IV, indicated in the topmost section of the mark. This gave copyright protection for three years. After 1883 the mark was written as a number, e.g., Rd. No. 12345.

A further indication of late wares is the inclusion of the word " England " in the mark. This was necessary to comply with the American McKinley Tariff Act of 1891. The full term " Made in England " is an indication of 20th century manufacture.

MARKS ON CONTINENTAL POTTERY AND PORCELAIN

FRANCE

Saint-Cloud
c.1678 ~ 1766

early incised mark

S.C

c.1722 - 66
in blue

Chantilly
1725 ~ 1800

'hunting-horn' mark

red on early wares

blue & other colours from c.1750

Mennecy
1734 - 1806

'D.V' mark for duc de Villeroy

·D·V· in red

in black D·V

D.V. incised.

Sceaux
c.1763 ~ 94

S·X incised

c.1775 ~

Lille 1784 - 1817

stencilled in red

Sèvres
First established at Vincennes c.1738, moved to Sèvres c.1756 ~

early Vincennes marks

mark with date-letter for 1753
letters were used from 1753 until 17th July 1793 to show year of manufacture

A - 1753	V ~ 1774
B ~ 1754	X ~ 1775
C ~ 1755	Y ~ 1776
D ~ 1756	Z ~ 1777
E ~ 1757	AA ~ 1778
F ~ 1758	BB ~ 1779
G ~ 1759	CC ~ 1780
H ~ 1760	DD ~ 1781
I ~ 1761	EE ~ 1782
J ~ 1762	FF ~ 1783
K ~ 1763	GG ~ 1784
L ~ 1764	HH ~ 1785
M ~ 1765	II ~ 1786
N ~ 1766	JJ ~ 1787
O ~ 1767	KK ~ 1788
P ~ 1768	LL ~ 1789
Q ~ 1769	MM ~ 1790
R ~ 1770	NN ~ 1791
S ~ 1771	OO ~ 1792
T ~ 1772	PP ~ 1793
U ~ 1773	(until 17th July)

in blue
1793 - 1804

Sèvres

M.N.ie in red

Sèvres 1803-
—//— 1804
Consular period

Paris factories

rue Thiroux
c.1775 ~ 19th Cent.

blue   red

red

LEVEILLE Rue THIROUX

rue de Crussol
1789 ~ 19th Cent.
Christopher Potter

B
Potter
42

EB   PB
all in blue

rue de Charonne
1795 - c.1840

DARTE
FRERES in red
A PARIS

rue de Bondy
1780 - 1829

gold

Pont-aux-Choux
1743 ~ c.1785

gold

La Courtille 1771-
c.1840

in blue

incised.

Clignacourt
1771 - c.1798

in gold

stencilled in red.

marks on reproductions made by:-

Samson & Co.
1845 ~

on so-called 'Chinese-Lowestoft'

Japanese and Chinese wares

Persian and Hispano-Moresque.

Limousin enamels, Italian wares

Sèvres and terra-cotta

Meissen

French, Italian, Spanish, English porcelain, European enamels

---

It was not until the adoption on Meissen porcelain in 1723 of the "K.P.M." and in 1724 of the cross-swords (from the arms of Saxony) that marks began to be used at all regularly in Europe. The placing of the mark underneath and the use of blue are clear indications that the Chinese model was being followed. The Meissen practice was then adopted by other German and, indeed, by most porcelain factories of repute.

Throughout the 18th century the practice was never regularised, and except for a brief period in France from 1766, and two years later in the Dutch town of Delft, there was no compulsory marking of wares. The factories of repute, proud of their productions, added a recognised mark and even used it, as at Nymphenburg, as part of the decoration. Their imitators left their wares unmarked or employed a mark likely to be mistaken for a more famous one: Weesp and Tournay both adopted a version of the Meissen crossed-swords:

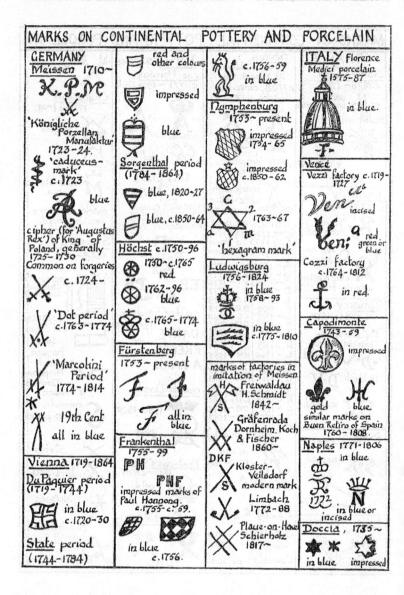

the torches of La Courtille, the hayforks of Rauenstein, the hayforks of Rudolstadt, the "L"s of Limbach, and the "W" of Wallendorf, were all drawn in such a way as to resemble the Meissen mark.

The firm of Samson & Co. was established in Paris in 1845, claiming to make "Reproductions of Ancient Works emanating from the Museums and from Private Collections". When imitating the true hard-paste porcelain of the Far East or the Continent, Samson's wares are difficult to detect, due to their being made from similar materials, whereas his reproductions of such English factories as Bow, Chelsea, and Derby are more easily recognised as fakes. Unfortunately the range of Samson's marks, illustrated above, do not appear to have been regularly used, or, as is sometimes the case, the original mark has been removed by grinding or by etching away with acid, and a replica of a known genuine mark added.

CHINESE REIGN MARKS   MING DYNASTY

洪武
年製

Hung Wu
(1368~1398)

建文
Chien Wên
(1399~1402)

Yung Lo
(1403~1424)
In archaic script

永樂
年製

Yung Lo
(1403~1424)

洪熙
Hung Hsi (1425)

大明宣
德年製

Hsüan Tê
(1426~1435)

In seal
characters

正統
Chêng T'ung
(1436~1449)

景泰
Ching T'ai
(1450~1457)

天順
T'ien Shun
(1457~1464)

大明成
化年製

Ch'êng Hua
(1465~1487)

成
In seal
characters

大明弘
治年製

Hung Chih
(1488~1505)

大明正
德年製

Chêng Tê
(1506~1521)

大明嘉
靖年製

Chia Ching
(1522~1566)

大明隆
慶年製

Lung Ch'ing
(1567~1572)

大明萬
曆年製

Wan Li
(1573~1619)

泰昌
T'ai Ch'ang (1620)

大明天
啟年製

T'ien Ch'i
(1621~1627)

崇楨
年製

Ch'ung Chêng
(1628~1643)

Factory marks in the Western sense are practically unknown on Chinese porcelain wares, while those purporting to record the period of manufacture are so liable to be "commemorative", or even deliberately fraudulent, as to be a frequent cause of dispute among students. Marks of the Ming Chinese Emperors, Hsüan Tê, Ch'êng Hua and Chia Ching are commonly found on wares of the reign of the Ch'ing Emperor K'ang Hsi, while the reign name of K'ang Hsi himself, rare on the abundant porcelain of his period, is chiefly found on 19th- and 20th-century wares.

Under the rule of the Ming Emperors (1368–1644) the Sung ideals in pottery were largely rejected in favour of the vogue for fine-grained white porcelain heralding the beginning of a new period in Chinese ceramic history with its centre in the town of Ching-tê Chên in Kiangsi province where a new Imperial factory was started in 1369 with a prolific output of early Ming blue-and-white

CHINESE REIGN MARKS   CH'ING DYNASTY

治年製 大清順
Shun Chih
(1644~1661)

In seal characters

Tao Kuang
光年製 大清道
(1821~1850)

In seal characters

In seal characters

隆年製 大清乾
Ch'ien Lung
(1736~1795)

緒年製 大清光
Kuang Hsü
(1874~1908)

熙年製 大清康
K'ang Hsi
(1662~1722)

In seal characters

豐年製 大清咸
Hsien Fêng
(1851~1861)

In seal characters

In seal characters

年製 嘉慶
Chia Ch'ing
(1796~1821)

In seal characters

統年製 大清宣
Hsüan T'ung
(1909~1912)

正年製 大清雍
Yung Chêng
(1723~1735)

In seal characters

治年製 大清同
T'ung Chih
(1862~1873)

年製 洪憲
Hung Hsien
(1916)
(Yüan Shih-kai)

Drawn by J. P. Cushion, Victoria and Albert Museum.

and fine enamel-painted porcelain both for the court and later for general use and export.

Following the fall of the Ming Dynasty in 1644 their declining culture was revived by the Ch'ing Emperor K'ang Hsi (1662—1722) who was a great patron of the arts. The European influence of the French and Netherlandish Jesuits at his courts is seen in the Baroque character of the early Ch'ing porcelain.

There was a backward-looking tendency during the reigns of Yung-Chêng (1723–35) and Ch'ien Lung (1736–95) when exact copies of the classical Sung wares and the early Ming painted porcelain were made.

The Imperial porcelain of the 19th century was as a rule carefully and weakly correct in following earlier styles and models. The factory was burnt in 1853 by the T'ai-ping rebels and hardly recovered before the 1911 revolution ended the Dynasty.

MEDICAL
MATTERS

Here we give a brief summary of up-to-date medical knowledge, including some recent developments. It must not be allowed to replace your doctor, who should be consulted immediately if you are worried. An index ensures easy reference.

TABLE OF CONTENTS

MEDICAL MATTERS

PART I. INTRODUCTION.

(a) HOW TO USE THE SECTION.

Diseases do not exist in watertight compartments, but doctors arrange them according either to their cause or the area of the body affected. This plan has been followed here, and at the beginning of each part an account of the group of diseases under discussion is given. Unless you know enough already, you would be wise to read it.

Here is some advice about your attitude to disease in general, and your use of this section in particular.

First of all, and obviously, no book is a substitute for the doctor, and when you are ill you must see him. There are good and bad doctors, competent and incompetent ones, just as in any other profession or trade; so choose a doctor you can trust, *and then believe what he tells you and carry out his advice.* There is no use complaining about the whole medical profession just because you are dissatisfied with your own G.P. If you are, you should change him.

Secondly, *never* believe what you hear from non-medical sources. Literally millions of people are made miserable every year by taking to heart nonsense told them by others, who may well be quite unaware of the harm they do, or even have the very best intentions. In any medical matter ask your doctor, and ignore your next-door neighbour's asked-for or unasked-for advice. Doctors are sometimes wrong, but they are much less likely to be wrong than someone without a medical education. Remember, too, that the statement that there is no cure for a disease does not necessarily mean that it is deadly: and it never means that nothing can be done to make it more tolerable. There is much more to modern doctoring than simply curing the curable.

Thirdly, don't try to diagnose your own trouble or decide what treatment you think you should have. This section will have failed completely in its intentions if it puts you in the position of a character described by an English humourist, who, from a medical dictionary, discovered that he had every disease listed in it with the solitary exception of housemaid's knee. Diseases which appear to the layman to have the "same" symptoms may be vastly different in seriousness: influenza and poliomyelitis, for example, may in, the initial stages, appear very similar. So also may stomach ulcer and cancer of the stomach. No human being is infallible, but it is most important that you should go to the person who is best fitted to know—your doctor.

Lastly, you should not be misled into thinking that you can always tell the seriousness of a disease by the general appearance of the patient. Children, in particular, may have a high temperature, or even be delirious, on one day, and the next be out of bed and wanting to get back to school. On the other hand, many of the most dangerous fevers (as we shall see later) are accompanied by a low temperature and do not appear particularly dramatic in the initial stages. Thus a young woman who may be aware of nothing wrong but lack of energy and getting easily tired may be dangerously ill with tuberculosis of the lungs.

The best rule is to seek medical advice either when you have suddenly become ill with symp-
U (80th Ed.)

toms you don't understand or (and this is equally important) if you have gradually been feeling less fit over a period of time. Perhaps, too, it is wise to call your doctor if you have been ill with *anything* for more than three days. You should *not* call in a specialist before seeing your G.P., as is so often done in America and on the Continent. Specialists are very clever, but are naturally prejudiced in favour of their own subject; for example, an eye specialist will be predisposed to think of your headache in terms of eyestrain, an ear, nose, and throat specialist in terms of sinus trouble, and a psychiatrist in terms of mother-in-law trouble. Therefore you should first have a check from your G.P., who knows a little of all these things and probably a great deal about you and your past history. He will then advise you about a specialist if necessary.

(b) NEW VIEWS ON MEDICINE

(1) Body and Mind. In former times, or, at least during the nineteenth century, the body was regarded as a sort of machine belonging to you in much the same way that you own your watch. You went to your doctor and, in effect, said: " Now what on earth are you going to do about my stomach? "—and you spoke as if, somehow, your stomach didn't have anything to do with the *real* you—it was just an awkward thing that happened to be annoying you. But we know now that this is not so—that your body *is* you, that it is a fort fighting against such enemies as poisons, parasites, germs, cancer, and injuries. The defences are seriously weakened by not enough of the right kind of food, insufficient sleep, or by anxiety. Your anxieties and worries can kill you just as surely as the other agents, and can prevent recovery or retard it when you are already ill.

A stomach ulcer therefore is not just something that is happening to you, you are happening to it. Your fears, your jealousies, your hatreds, your inability to get on in life, can be (in some cases) just as harmful as germs or poisons—in fact, they act by setting free glandular poisons in your blood-stream. Scientists have discovered a reaction which they call the " stress response," and we now know that stress can ultimately lead to sickness or death without any bodily injury at all. Thus, Dr. L. J. Saul, a leading American doctor, writes: " Emotional stress in which there is no physical damage can produce responses which lead to actual damage and even to death." Rats in the laboratory can be killed through long exposure to fear caused by loud noises or other forms of shock without even being touched.

This stress factor is emphasised not because it is more important that the other enemies of the body or mind (it would be better to say body-mind), but because, as we shall see later, it does cause serious diseases, and, secondly, as mentioned already, it influences the process of recovery. A person who is afraid or has no hope is less likely to recover from pneumonia or another disease than one who is hopeful, who has peace of mind and confidence.

(2) New Views about Health. A great deal of nonsense has been talked about the healthy life; at one time we were told to take eighteen chews to each bite, to do deep breathing, to take plenty of exercise, to get lots of fresh air, to eat regularly (or to indulge in peculiar diets). But more recently,

eminent doctors have cast doubt on most of these fancies. Moderate exercise is necessary to health, but athletes who indulge in violent exercise have not always been noted for longevity. Fresh air is pleasant and stimulating, but, where actual breathing is concerned, it is no better than the air in most rooms. Certainly, one of the problems of our time is air pollution by smoke and Diesel fumes, which are highly dangerous, but at present we are considering ordinary fresh air in comparison with the air indoors, and, in this case, the experts say there is little difference so far as health is concerned.

A balanced diet containing correct amounts of the basic food substances is essential, but there is no evidence that when, or at what intervals, you eat makes the slightest difference—unless you are a sufferer from stomach ulcer, in which case it is necessary that the intervals between meals should not be too long. The whole business of having meals at fixed intervals is nothing but a social convention, and in modern life obviously a matter of convenience. See Diet, P40.

Sleep, too, is a necessity. But different people require vastly different amounts of sleep. Some manage on as little as three hours, others seem to believe that they need ten or more. The importance of the dream process is discussed in Sleeping and Dreaming, Part III.

In a number of studies of men and women who lived to a ripe old age it was found that the only factors in common between them were that they had a good balanced diet of healthy food, that they had contented minds, and that they were interested in something which gave them an aim in life. They also came of long-lived families—for living a long and healthy life depends partly upon heredity.

So the main rules of health are: (1) do not think too much about your health unless it gives you trouble; (2) have an interest in life and be prepared to sacrifice a lot for it (nothing useful has ever been done by those who are always "taking care" and being over-cautious); (3) eat a good balanced diet; (4) do not worry, and have a contented mind.

(3) New Drugs. A great surgeon, the first of the moderns, was Ambrose Paré, who died in 1590, and one of his best known sayings was: "I apply the dressing, but God heals the wound." He was quite right; for until about forty years ago, or even less, all the physician could do was to put the patient in as favourable a state as possible to enable his body to cure itself. That is to say, there were hardly any specific drugs—drugs that had a direct effect on the disease. There was quinine, discovered by the Spaniards in America, which was specific for malaria, and there were iron (specific for anæmia) and digitalis (specific for certain types of heart disease), but otherwise nothing until the nineteenth century, when Paul Ehrlich discovered salvarsan, which is specific for syphilis. Ehrlich died in 1914, having conceived the brilliant idea of drugs which he described as "magic bullets"—i.e., drugs which, like bullets, would be aimed at the real cause of the disease. They would, that is to say, be specific.

Since then a large number of such drugs have been discovered. For example, the antibiotics, such as penicillin, discovered in 1928 by Fleming at St. Mary's Hospital, Paddington. Later, Florey and Chain in Oxford, helped in the war years by the vast resources of the American pharmaceutical industry, were able to make penicillin available to the public in sufficient quantities by new techniques of production. Penicillin is practically non-poisonous (although it is possible to become allergic to it, sometimes with serious results). It can kill some germs in a dilu-

tion of one part of pencillin to one hundred million parts of water; it is effective against streptococci, the cause of blood-poisoning, sepsis in wounds, and many other diseases: and also against the germs of anthrax, gonorrhœa, meningitis of some types, syphilis—a whole list of plagues which have troubled man for centuries. Blood-poisoning, whether from wounds or childbirth, used to be almost incurable—now the rate of cure is 80–90 per cent.; anthrax and gonorrhœa have an almost 100 per cent. rate of cure. In pneumonia the rate is about 90 per cent., and early syphilis can be cured in a week, instead of the previous two to three years.

But this was only the beginning. Other antibiotics—streptomycin, tetracycline, erythromycin, and many others—are helping to wipe out the terrible scourges of the human race, in particular, in the case of streptomycin, tuberculosis. The sulpha group of drugs—sulphadiazine, sulphadimidine, etc.—have also proved a great boon. Then there are the new drugs which have created a revolution in psychiatry—the tranquillisers which relieve anxiety, the drugs which clear up certain types of depression, and substances such as chlorpromazine which make it possible to nurse formerly violent patients in the wards of a general hospital. The antihistamine drugs help in many cases of allergy, the anticoagulants prevent further attacks of coronary thrombosis, and every year new and powerful aids in the fight against disease are discovered.

Of course, these potent new drugs are not without their concomitant risks. The doctor is trained to weigh the harm they can do against the disadvantages of not using them in any particular case. He should not use them for every trivial illness in which their only effect may be to shorten slightly the course of a condition which, left alone, would recover of itself. Yet in Britain and other technically-advanced countries indiscriminate prescribing is common, largely because of pressure on the doctor from his patients and the drug firms. The busy mother whose child has a mild sore throat is not going to see the child sweat it out when she knows from past experience that a dose of penicillin can remove the fever and most of the symptoms within twenty-four hours. She is unlikely to listen to the argument that the slower process is capable of increasing the body's resistance to future attacks, or that repeated administration of penicillin may create germs which are insensitive to it in a future emergency, or, worse still, produce an allergy to the drug. The thalidomide tragedy of 1962–3, when a new sedative, hailed as being both effective and safe (cases were quoted of would-be suicides who had taken up to 100 of the tablets without loss of life), resulted in the birth of children with undeveloped arms and legs to mothers who had used the drug in early pregnancy, and prolonged neuritis in some adults, has been quoted as an example of cut-throat competition allowing new preparations on the market before they had been exhaustively tested. But the truth is not quite so simple. There can be no reasonable question that the drug industry needs to be under stricter control; that its methods of advertising its wares to the doctor are wasteful, importunate, and often in bad taste; that different firms put out what is virtually the same drug under various trade names which merely leads to confusion; that the "authorities" quoted in the advertising of some drugs are often obscure individuals in countries not noted for the high standard of their practice of medicine writing in equally obscure journals; and that many drug firms make grossly inflated profits at the expense of our National Health Service. On the other hand, it must be remembered that some of the best drug firms have played a major part in medical progress. But they must constantly check their commercial instincts where these conflict (as they sometimes do) with your interests as the patient-consumer. To be fair about thalidomide, the fact is that nobody previously had seriously considered the possibility of a drug capable of causing deformity in the unborn child, and, if they had done, it is quite likely that the danger would still have been undiscovered, since only certain laboratory animals respond to thalidomide in a similar way to man. The drug had been exhaustively tested by all ordinary methods before being put on the market, and for a number of years (during which, in Germany, it was on sale to the public without prescription because of its apparent safety), millions of people took it without any ill-effects either immediately or subsequently. Its terrible side-effects were, in fact, limited to those mothers who used it in early, not later, pregnancy, and in a lesser degree to a small proportion of adults who developed unpleasant, but not dangerous, symptoms of neuritis.

The taking of any effective drug is always a calculated risk. We have mentioned that the use of penicillin—a drug which is almost completely non-poisonous—may nevertheless cause other germs and fungi to multiply in the body with unpleasant results. This is because penicillin wipes out, not only the disease-producing germs it is being used to destroy, but the penicillin-sensitive harmless germs which hold the other potentially harmful germs at bay. Thus those who keep on sucking penicillin lozenges for a real or imaginary sore throat may develop a black tongue due to the spread of a fungus normally present but kept under control. Other antibiotics, described as " wide spectrum " because they wipe out an even greater variety of germs than penicillin, also kill the organisms responsible for the absorption and possibly the creation of vitamin B in the body, thus causing severe vitamin deficiency. Tranquillisers made by various firms vary from the wholly useless to the very useful, but both can have unpleasant side-effects. One type is prone to lead in a small number of cases to severe depression, others may lower the blood-pressure to a degree that causes fainting attacks, and serious blood and liver diseases are not unknown if not common. Both tranquillisers and the antihistamine drugs can cause some people to become extremely drowsy— an obvious danger if one drives a car or works on heights. Even aspirin causes gastric hæmorrhages which have sometimes been very severe and even lethal, particularly in those with peptic ulceration of the stomach and duodenum. Aspirin, one of the most usefull and safest of drugs, should never be taken for an " upset stomach ", or by people with known stomach trouble. Such patients should be warned that about 150 preparations including some hang-over remedies widely advertised for " upset stomach ", contain large quantities of aspirin (acetyl salicylic acid).

None of this should deter the patient from being advised by a doctor he trusts to use whatever drugs are prescribed; it *should* deter him from putting emotional pressure on his doctor to obtain drugs unwillingly given. It is high time that we gave up the notion that no patient should leave the consulting-room without a prescription for some pill or potion; for something like 40 per cent. of patients simply require advice about the conduct of their life from their diet to their relationships with others rather than medicine of any kind. The housing shortage, a bullying boss, or a nagging mother-in-law cannot be removed by a tranquilliser—in fact, a tranquilliser, by making a man or woman feel better, may prevent them from constructively solving problems which exist in the real world. We should all learn to rely as little on drugs as possible: stop taking tranquillisers or pep pills when we are merely worried about something that any normal person would worry about, or because we are just " fed-up "; stop using antibiotics (which are badly needed elsewhere in the world) for trivial infections in which they are anyhow useless; stop swallowing vitamin pills which do not relieve tiredness and are merely wasted on this overfed nation; stop buying any patent medicine whatever. Modern drugs are potent and effective; they are a dagger to destroy the enemy of disease. But, like a dagger, those who play about with them incompetently and unnecessarily are liable to get badly hurt.

(4) New Methods in Surgery. Only a few years before the Second World War many surgeons were saying that surgery had reached its extreme limits. It was impossible, they believed, to improve on the delicate techniques then reached. But events have proved them wrong. Operations on the heart, for example, which would have been inconceivable a short time ago are now carried out daily—the heart can be opened and defects of the all-important valves made good. " Blue-Babies " or adults with a heart disease which might have led to their death in a few years are now cured by surgery, and it is possible during such operations to cut off all the blood from the heart by deflecting it through tubes to an artificial heart outside the body—a machine which pumps the blood round the body whilst the real heart is at rest.

This however, will be described in more detail later.

Then there are the new anæsthetics, such as Pentothal, which are injected into a vein in the arm instead of being breathed in through a mask, as were ether and chloroform or ethyl chloride. Pentothal is much safer, and avoids the unpleasant after-effects of vomiting and nausea, which usually followed the old type of anæsthetic. Most curious of all anæsthetists use the poison curare. used by South American Indians to poison their arrow-heads. Curare produces paralysis, but in small doses merely gives the degree of muscle relaxation which is so important to the surgeon when he is operating.

Lastly, we might mention the new techniques of plastic surgery. Thus large areas of skin which have been destroyed by severe burns can be replaced by shaving off thin layers from another part of the body. These do not need to cover completely the whole damaged area: small pieces are scattered over the wound and gradually grow together. Corneal disease (the cornea is part of the " window " of the eye, and when it becomes opaque the patient cannot see) is treated by removing the diseased cornea and replacing it by a cornea removed from a dead body, or sometimes from an eye which has had to be removed from a live patient for other reasons. There are, in fact, " cornea banks " where corneas are kept in refrigeration for future use, just as there are " blood banks " for use in blood transfusions. Other advances in surgery will be described elsewhere in the section.

(5) New Approaches in Social Medicine. Medicine has passed through many phases from the time when disease was regarded as a punishment from the gods or a sign of devil possession to the present era, when increasingly there is a tendency to look on society as the patient. Indeed, one commonly hears doctors and sociologists nowadays talking about " the sick society."

The early primitive stage came to an end—at least in one part of the world—when in Greece, five centuries before Christ, Hippocrates and others began to teach that all diseases were due to natural causes. But after the first ray of hope the outlook began to deteriorate when, during the Middle and Dark Ages (that is, from the fall of the Roman Empire right up to the fifteenth century), there was a return to the belief in devil possession and supernatural causes.

Eighteenth-century medicine in Europe was materialistic, regarding the body as a machine. It was founded upon a sort of pseudo-science— although, of course, there were always individual exceptions, physicians such as Sydenham in England, who, avoiding all theories, based their work on observation of the patient. This mechanistic approach persisted right through the nineteenth century, but medicine became more and more truly scientific, and the century saw the most rapid advances in the field ever known until our own times: the discovery of germs by Pasteur, of antiseptics to combat them by Lister, of vaccination by Jenner and anæsthetics by the American Wells and the Scot Simpson. The use of the microscope by Virchow, who was a German, brought great advances in the understanding of disease and Ehrlich, another German, conceived, as we have already seen, the idea of " magic bullets " which would attack the germs at the root of a disease without harming the patient. But one of the greatest of all these great men is perhaps the least known. His name was Edwin Chadwick.

From the earliest period of recorded history human communities had been constantly ravaged by great plagues which swept over their lands year after year, killing untold millions. Such plagues are recorded in the Bible and other ancient books, but, when town life became more and more common, as during the Roman Empire and the Middle Ages in Europe, the overcrowded conditions were even more favourable to the spread of disease. The Black Death of 1348-9 wiped out almost half the population of Europe. But, even in the first quarter of the nineteenth century in London, tens of thousands died from typhus, typhoid, and smallpox—and not only these, for periodically cholera would be brought into the country by travellers from abroad.

In the face of these terrible visitations the individual physician was helpless. He could not treat each one of the many sick even had he known how, and Chadwick's claim to fame rests on the fact that he was the first man to think in terms of *social* control of diseases, by so dealing with their causes that they were prevented from arising at all. In order to wipe out typhoid and cholera, he argued, we must ensure clean water supplies; for these diseases are caused by germs carried in polluted water. In order to attack typhus and plague, one must get rid of the lice which carry the germs of typhus and the rat-fleas which carry the germs of plague (including, of course, the rats, which, in turn, carry the fleas).

In the past, some attempts had been made to segregate the sick to prevent the spread of disease —for example, in the case of leprosy (which, strangely enough, we now know to be less infectious than most germ-borne diseases). But segregating those who are sick with typhoid or cholera is of little use if others are still drinking polluted water, just as it is of little use segregating plague cases if rats with their infected fleas are allowed to run at large. So these early attempts met with little success, due to lack of understanding of how the infections were passed on.

Chadwick was born in a Lancashire farmhouse where the children were washed every day all over, and he ruthlessly drove an obsession with cleanliness into the heads of his countrymen until, later in the century, it was possible for the German philosopher Treitschke to tell his class in Berlin: "The English think soap is civilisation." Although this remark was meant cynically, there is little doubt that soap, if it is not civilisation in itself, has played a greater part in making civilisation possible than many more elaborate remedies. A population riddled with chronic infectious illness has neither the time nor the energy to apply to the arts or sciences, and soap did a great deal to reduce infection.

One of the first Public Health measures was introduced by Chadwick and others when they brought in legislation to purify the water supply of London. Previously, the citizens had used water from the Thames (they still do, but only after it has been filtered and sterilised at the waterworks!), and from filthy, refuse-laden ponds and springs. Later, Chadwick helped to found the Poor Law Commission, and produced a Report in 1842, the principal suggestions of which were: a municipal water supply for all towns; scientific drainage both in town and country; and an independent health service with large powers for dealing with those who endangered the lives of others by polluting water or causing nuisances. He also proposed a national service for interment of the dead; for in those days bodies often remained for days in the overcrowded homes of the poor without burial.

What has the twentieth century contributed to the concept of social health? Well, of course, there has been a great deal of legislation along the lines initiated by Chadwick to control disease, and a great many other measures have been introduced concerned with the idea of positive health—not merely preventing bad health, but trying to bring about the highest possible state of good health. Orange juice, milk, and good meals for school-children have brought about a transformation in child health which has become apparent to the least observant in the last ten or fifteen years. And the National Health Service is in the direct line of descent from early nineteenth-century legislation.

But in future years it is probable that the main achievement of the twentieth century in social medicine will prove to be its extension of the term "social health" to cover every aspect of community life, not only in such subjects as bodily health and its control of social means, but also such problems as mental illness, crime, delinquency, drug addiction, and so on. What we are now asking ourselves is: how far are these problems produced by society itself, and if this is the case, how far can we go in preventing them by social means?

Social medicine takes the view that these problems can never be dealt with solely by moralising and retribution, but only by dispassionately analysing causes and dealing with them. In this century we have developed a social conscience. Not always, it is true, a very well-informed social conscience, but at least this is a good beginning. There are organisations for dealing scientifically with delinquency, for dealing with problem children, for spreading knowledge about cancer in order to show people that it can be successfully treated if taken in time. The organisation known as "Alcoholics Anonymous" has, on the whole, been more successful in treating alcoholics by social means than have any of the individual medical methods. Mental illness is also treated by group methods, which, together with the new drugs, have revolutionised the position in mental hospitals. We can well say with John Donne, who died in 1631, that "no man is an island . . . every man's death diminisheth me; for I am involved in mankind." This is the attitude of twentieth-century social medicine.

Summary. Perhaps we can sum up our progress in the past hundred years more dramatically in terms of hard facts.

One hundred years ago, a surgical operation was never undertaken except under the gravest circumstances. There were no anæsthetics and no antiseptics, and the operation was carried out by a surgeon in a filthy tail-coat, stained with the congealed blood of countless operations (indeed the surgeons of that time took pride in the dirty condition of their coat as showing how much experience they had previously had). Germs and the part they play in producing disease were unknown, and Paul Ehrlich had not yet been born, so there were no "magic bullets" to attack syphilis, or sera for diphtheria and other diseases. The mentally ill were simply locked up with little treatment and subjected to such indignities as the strait-jacket and the padded cell; now they are given treatment which becomes more effective each year, and the padded cell and strait-jacket have gone, and in the more progressive hospitals even the ward doors are not locked.

Only thirty years ago you would very likely have died if you had developed pneumonia, "childbed fever" after the birth of a child, meningitis, dysentery, typhoid, or tuberculosis. With such infections as blood-poisoning you would have had practically no chance at all. Today, the sulpha drugs and the antibiotics have changed all that. Syphilis and gonorrhœa were lifelong tragedies both to the patient and his family, but now they, too, can be conquered.

The National Health Service has brought the possibility of good treatment equally to all, and other bodies—some of them privately run—deal with alcoholism and neurosis, with rehabilitation of the mentally and physically ill, with spastics, birth control, and marriage guidance. It is up to us to see that all these facilities are used to the full by all who need them.

PART II. DISEASES ARRANGED ACCORDING EITHER TO THEIR CAUSE OR THE AREA OF THE BODY AFFECTED.

THE INFECTIOUS DISEASES
INTRODUCTION.

INFECTIOUS diseases are those which are caused by an invasion of the body by organisms from outside (the word " organism " simply means other living things, and we are using this word because, as will be seen later, it is not only what are known as " germs " which can cause infection). We know, too, that what is generally typical about this group is: (a) that the disease can be passed on from one person to another, and (b) that it is usually accompanied by a raised temperature or fever. Now (a), of course, is always true, because the definition of an infectious disease is one that can be passed on to others, but (b) is not always true, because a few infections produce little or no temperature, and also because it is possible to have a raised temperature (again in only a few cases) without any infection. For example, certain types of brain injury, tumour, or hæmorrhage can produce a raised—or lowered—temperature, and so can the injection of some foreign substance such as milk into the muscles. This is known as " protein shock," and was at one time used in the treatment of certain illnesses. Finally, solutions of dead germs, such as the antityphoid vaccine given to protect troops during the War, may lead when injected to very high temperatures. But, by and large, we are entitled to suppose that the patient with a raised temperature is probably suffering from an infection.

Types of Infection.

As we have seen, it is not only germs which cause infections—so from now on we shall give germs their proper name of " bacteria." Here is a list of the chief offenders which are liable to attack our bodies: bacteria, spirochætes, viruses, fungi, amœbæ, worms and other parasites. Of these, bacteria and viruses are by far the most important, but let us look at them all more closely.

Bacteria are tiny living things which can be seen only under a fairly powerful microscope. Some are grouped like bunches of grapes (staphylococci) or in strings or chains (streptococci). They are given these names because " staphylos " is the Greek word for a bunch of grapes, and " streptos " means a chain. Yet others are comma-shaped (such as the cholera vibrio), or shaped like a drumstick—a rod with a small knob at the end (the tetanus bacillus, which causes lockjaw).

It would be a mistake to think that all bacteria are harmful; for without some species we could not survive for long. Bacteriologists divide them according to their behaviour in the human body into three groups: saprophytic, parasitic or pathogenic, and symbiotic. The *saprophytic* organisms are the bacteria normally found in the skin, mouth, and intestines; they do us neither harm nor good. The *parasitic*, or as they are more usually called, pathogenic (*i.e.*, disease-producing) organisms, are the harmful ones with which we are naturally more concerned. Lastly, there are the *symbiotic* organisms, which, whilst taking something from the body, give something in return. For example, cattle would not be able to digest the cellulose of the grass they eat were it not for helpful bacteria in the lower parts of the intestines, and there are certain bacteria in the large intestine of man which build up vitamin B2.

Bacteria have two peculiar characteristics: each reproduces by splitting into two separate individuals as often as every twenty minutes in favourable circumstances like an open wound. If no bacterium were destroyed, one individual could produce a mass of bacteria larger than the whole world in a matter of a few weeks (since each of the offspring also divides into two, which in turn divide again—the progression goes: one gives birth to two, these two to four, the four to eight, eight to sixteen, sixteen to thirty-two, and so on—you will see, if you work it out, that in a short period the figure becomes astronomical). Fortunately, many bacteria have accidents, so for the present the world is safe! The other curious thing about bacteria is that, barring accidents, they are potentially immortal. Under ideal conditions in which no bacteria were killed, none would die; for a bacterium there is no death from old age, no corpse except when it is actively destroyed. It simply goes on dividing, dividing, and subdividing for ever.

How, then, are bacteria destroyed? Briefly, the answer is that most are destroyed by the natural defences of the body of whatever host they are preying on; others are destroyed by antiseptics and the new drugs; and many are destroyed when they are excreted from the body in the sputum or through the bowels and land in places where they are dried up and cannot survive —although some bacteria in such circumstances can form what are called " spores," rather like the seed of plants, so making it possible for them to survive in a state of suspended animation for months on end until picked up accidentally by another unfortunate host. Finally, bacteria, in addition to all these possibilities, face another danger: they may themselves develop disease. This disease is caused by even more minute organisms known as bacteriophages (viruses which affect bacteria), discovered by the French bacteriologist d'Hérelle a good many years ago. Attack by bacteriophage causes whole groups of bacteria (known as " colonies ") to disintegrate and become harmless.

Although bacteriophage has been used in the treatment of some diseases in human beings, this method has now been largely given up, since the new drugs are infinitely more effective.

Spirochaetes. Spirochætes, like bacteria, are minute organisms, but differ in being shaped somewhat like a corkscrew and in being able to move (which many bacteria cannot do). Their progress is produced by a sideways wriggling motion. The two main diseases caused by spirochætes are syphilis and spirochætal jaundice. Spirochætal jaundice is carried by rats, and is common in those who work in mines. It is now rare in Britain, but still occurs in Japan, Egypt, and Malaya; the infection is passed through the skin where the excreta of infected rats mingles with water on damp ground in the mine where miners kneel. Infection may also occur through eating infected food.

Viruses. Unlike bacteria, viruses are too small to be seen under an ordinary microscope. They can, however, be photographed in some cases under an electron microscope, which uses a magnetic field instead of a glass lens and a stream of electrons in place of a beam of light. Viruses cause such diseases as typhus, measles, mumps, poliomyelitis, smallpox, and chickenpox—not to mention such plant and animal diseases as tobacco mosaic disease and foot-and-mouth disease, which often have serious economic consequences. Other virus diseases are psittacosis (an infection of parrots and similar birds which can be transmitted to Man), swine fever in pigs, influenza in Man, and myxomatosis in rabbits. They also cause, it is believed, the common cold.

The main characteristics of viruses are, first, that they can only grow in living cells—unlike bacteria, which readily grow in the laboratory on plates containing a jelly made from meat broth, gelatin, milk, and other delicacies. The scientist, therefore, must keep them in portions of living tissue kept alive outside the body. Secondly, they are so small that they pass through the pores of the finest filter. Thirdly, a first attack usually produces immunity for life. Second attacks of the common virus diseases mentioned above are very rare; but unfortunately, this rule does not apply to influenza or the common cold. Fourthly, there is reason to believe that viruses represent an extraordinary intermediate stage between the living and non-living; they can, for instance, be produced in crystalline form and yet are just as dangerous when " thawed out." Lastly, the virus diseases have proved for the most part to be little affected by the new antibiotics and other drugs, although vaccination in smallpox and the injection of sera from infected patients in other infections may give immunity for longer or shorter periods.

The two great practical problems that doctors face with viruses are: (i) many viruses are unknown because of the difficulty of growing them outside the body in suitable tissue culture. They cannot therefore be conveniently identified in specimens from the patient, as bacteria can; and (ii) they are unaffected by antibiotics like penicillin. It has been a great step forward to grow viruses artificially in tissue culture, in which they are identified indirectly by the effects they have on the cultured cells. But since we do not know exactly how to grow some viruses (like those of infective hepatitis) they have still not been seen.

When we recover from a viral illness like chickenpox, we probably do so by producing virus-killing substances inside our own cells. Scientists are currently searching for these substances in case they can be used, like penicillin, to cure viral disease.

Fungi. Some infections are caused by fungi—that is to say organisms belonging to the same group as moulds, mushrooms, and toadstools. Penicillin and some other antibiotics are produced from moulds, so, as in the case of bacteria, some fungi are helpful; they even help to destroy each other, as bacteria do. For example actinomyces, which can cause infection of the jaw and other tissues, is destroyed by other tissues.

Most fungal infections are trivial and limited to the skin. But, although trivial, they can be unsightly and uncomfortable. Ringworm of the scalp, dhobie itch—an infection of the groin spread by infected underclothing—and so-called " athlete's foot " are caused by a fungus.

Amœbae. Amœbæ are small, single-cell organisms, the largest of which (a harmless type found in stagnant ponds in Britain and elsewhere) is just visible to the naked eye. It is about the size of the head of a pin. Amœbæ move, in the species which are capable of moving, by pushing forward a part of the cell in the appropriate direction and causing the rest to flow into the advancing portion. Like bacteria, they reproduce by dividing into halves, each of which becomes a new amœba.

The main human disease caused by amœbæ is amœbic dysentery (not to be confused with bacillary dysentery).

Parasites. These may live on the skin like lice (which can carry typhus) or fleas (carriers of plague), or the parasites of scabies which burrow into the skin, or they may live part of their time in the blood or other tissues, like malaria. They often have complicated life-cycles involving other hosts (like mosquitoes) at certain stages of development.

Worms. Worms are intestinal parasites, but the only common types found in Britain are threadworms, the tiny thread-like worms which cause irritability and itching in the skin of children, less often in adults; round-worms, somewhat resembling the ordinary garden earthworm, which seldom lead to symptoms; and tapeworms, which may reach a length of 10 or even 20 ft. Many parasitic worms (like parasites elsewhere) lead a double life—they spend part of their life in the human intestine and the other part in the muscles of another animal. The tapeworm, for example, whilst in the human intestine, lays eggs which pass out of the body in the excreta, and are then swallowed by pigs, especially in those parts of the world where human excreta are used as manure in the fields. In the pig, the eggs form cysts in the muscles—meat infected in this way is known as " measly pork "—and when, in turn, the meat is eaten by man, the process in the intestine begins all over again.

Less common types, from our point of view, are the Russian tape-worm (which, as befits a Russian, grows to nearly 30 ft.!); this type is spread by caviare or undercooked infected fish. The small, leaf-shaped liver fluke, lays eggs which are passed into canals or pools in tropical countries in the urine of infected people, hatch out and enter a water snail, and finally leave the snail in the form of small parasites which pierce the skin of bathers, whence they pass to the liver and subsequently the bladder and rectum. This is a serious condition, as is also filariasis (another

tropical disease), for which, unlike bilharzia—caused by the liver fluke—no cure is known. The tropical disease known as loa-loa is caused by a variety of filaria.

How the Infection is Spread.

Infection is spread in many ways, some of which have already been mentioned. In the common fevers found in Europe and elsewhere one of the most frequent ways is by *droplet infection*—that is to say, by minute drops carrying the germs which are coughed or sneezed into the air by someone already suffering from the disease. Such droplets can be projected into the air for 10 ft. or more, and when breathed in by someone within range infection may result. Next commonest mode of spread is perhaps by *infected food, water,* and the dirty hands of those who prepare food: cholera, dysentery, food-poisoning, and typhoid are spread in this way. Spread by *direct contact* is found in the venereal diseases (usually, but not always, spread by sexual intercourse with someone who already has the disease), and, of course, lice, fleas, and other parasites, including the scabies mite, are spread by contact with the infested individual—or sometimes with his clothes or bed linen. Spread through an *intermediary host,* whether it be lice, fleas, or mosquitoes carrying infection, or the various means adopted by worms, has already been described above, so no more need be said. Lastly, the infection may result from *bacteria already within the body;* for example, the bacillus coli which lives in the large intestine is there harmless, but if it gets into the bladder or the ureters (the tubes leading from kidney to bladder) a quite unpleasant result may follow in the form of cystitis or pyelitis.

How the Body Deals with Infection.

The body has many mechanisms of defence against intruders, but suffice it to say here that there are two main ones. First, substances known as antibodies and antitoxins are produced in the blood—the antitoxins to neutralise the poisons produced by the invaders, the antibodies to render them helpless, for example, by causing them to clump together so that they can more easily be dealt with by the second defence mechanism. This second mechanism is provided by the white cells in the blood, some of which (the phagocytes) act like amœbæ and swallow up and destroy the germs. Antibodies and antitoxins can be transferred from one individual to another and are used in medicine both to prevent infection and to cure it. This is known as immunisation, and can be active or passive. Active immunisation is produced by injecting either a solution of dead bacteria, as in the case of antityphoid injections, or by injecting live, but weakened, strains of the organism, as in the case of smallpox vaccination. In both cases the body is stimulated to produce its own immune substances. Passive immunisation is used either for people who have been in recent contact with infection or who are already ill, and in this case the antitoxins produced in another person who has had the illness are injected in the form of serum—*i.e.,* the liquid part of the blood without the blood cells. All these natural defences are inefficient in the ill, the underfed, the very young, and the very old.

Antiseptics.

We have already discussed the other ways in which bacteria are destroyed and now need only make brief mention of antiseptics, and antibiotics. The earliest antiseptic was carbolic acid, used by Lister in his operating-theatre in the form of a fine spray directed throughout the operation on the wound, or sometimes in the form of steam from a kettle containing a solution of carbolic. But carbolic is dangerous, and since Lister's time many more useful antiseptics have been discovered. Acriflavine, thymol, and other old favourites have been discarded too. The various forms of carbolic are still used to disinfect drains, but, to tell the truth, the use of antiseptics nowadays is very limited. In surgery the *antiseptic* method has given way to the *aseptic* method—instead of fighting sepsis we see to it that no possibility of sepsis is present before operating: all instruments, the surgeons' and nurses' hands, the skin, are sterilised—the instruments by boiling, the dressings by dry heat, the hands by soap and water, and almost the only antiseptic used is to clean the patient's skin in the area to be operated on.

Antiseptics are used as first-aid treatment for cuts and wounds, but should be applied only once as a general rule—that is, when the wound is first received. The trouble with antiseptics is that as well as killing germs they also kill the surrounding tissues, which antibiotics never do.

Antiseptic sprays to purify the air of a room or to destroy germs lurking in the dust on the sick-room floor—or any other floor—are practically useless. To quote the *British Medical Journal:* " There is no good scientific evidence that any of the chemical air-disinfectants can control the spread of infection in places such as schools, offices, or cinemas. Nor is there good evidence that any substantial effect on the spread of illness can be obtained by disinfection of dust."

Neither is there any good reason to believe that mouth-washes and gargles have any effect other than making the mouth feel fresher and (temporarily) removing mouth odour—by covering it up with the scent of the antiseptic. Mouth-washes are in contact with the bacteria for far too short a time to have any damaging result, and, in the case of tonsillitis and other diseases, all the important bacteria are hidden far out of any danger from gargles.

Antibiotics.

The antibiotics—penicillin, streptomycin, erythromycin, terramycin, aureomycin, and chloramphenicol—have already been dealt with, and only two important practical points need to be mentioned. These are that although most of such drugs are entirely safe under ordinary conditions, it is extremely dangerous for the layman to use them without medical guidance. If, for example, people get into the undesirable habit of sucking penicillin lozenges for sore throat and keep on doing this every time the sore throat returns, they may become sensitised to penicillin so that, when they become really ill—say, with pneumonia—the serious illness no longer responds to the drug. Or the same habit may make them allergic or hypersensitive to penicillin, and an injection given later may have serious and even fatal results.

Doctors no longer use the lozenges anyway, because of this danger and another one which is that excessive use of antibiotics may kill not only the dangerous bacteria, but also the ones which are helpful to the body. When this happens, other types of organism which are not affected by antibiotics will multiply in the absence of the bacteria which normally keep them under control. Thus chloramphenicol or aureomycin, by killing useful germs in the large intestine, may cause vitamin B deficiency, and when the non-sensitive organisms have their natural enemies removed they may step in and multiply, causing inflammation of the mouth, diarrhœa, and occasionally a fatal bowel infection. Chloramphenicol is too dangerous for general use.

General Treatment of Fevers.

Fevers are ordinarily heralded in by a rise in temperature which is noticeable either by a flushed face or by alternate sensations of heat and cold. A patient with a high temperature may have shivering attacks known as " rigors." Tell the doctor.

A high temperature does not necessarily (especially in a child) mean that the trouble is serious but the lay person should always treat it as such and certainly call a doctor if the patient is a child or an elderly person.

Even the trained physician finds it difficult to tell one fever from another in the early days; for most of the common fevers begin in more or less the same way. It is only when a rash or some other more definite sign becomes evident that a certain diagnosis can be made, and these may not show themselves until the patient has been feeling " run-down " and fevered for some days. Incidentally, although a clinical thermometer is a very useful thing when properly used, many a

doctor must feel that, in unskilled hands, it is a menace. The " fussy " type of mother who is constantly taking her child's temperature whenever it looks in the slightest degree different from usual (probably it is simply feeling justifiably bored with its parents), not only causes anxiety to herself but also gives the habit of anxiety to her child. The child is made to feel that the world is a dangerous place, full of germs and all sorts of causes for fear—as indeed it is, but one needs a sense of proportion, and other dangers which we think much less about are at least as frightening and twice as deadly as most germs. Whatever you do, don't get the thermometer habit; your child, so far as fevers are concerned, is a good deal tougher than you.

Briefly, then, the way to treat a fever in the early stages before the doctor comes, and before one knows exactly what is wrong, is as follows:

(1) Put the patient to bed.

(2) Give little, and easily digested, food; if the patient wants none, give none.

(3) Give plenty to drink—the proprietary preparations containing lemonade and glucose are excellent, but water, weak tea with sugar, or home-made lemonade with squeezed-out lemon juice and sugar, whichever the patient likes best, are at least as good.

(4) Aspirin is useful to relieve headache or other pains and will reduce fever for two or three hours. But it will cure nothing. The patient will be more comfortable, but his illness will not be cured by aspirin except in certain very special cases. Soluble aspirin is best. Do not have special children's aspirins in the house. They are often nicely flavoured, the children are tempted to eat them like sweets, and there have been serious cases of poisoning. For small children, use suitably small quantities of ordinary adult soluble aspirin, having checked the dose with your doctor. Other methods of cooling seriously fevered patients such as bathing, tepid sponging, etc., are strictly for the doctor to prescribe. A patient as hot as that should be in a doctor's hands anyway.

THE INFECTIOUS FEVERS.

The remarks made above apply to the management of *any* fever, and we are now going to discuss particular infectious diseases, beginning with the common childhood fevers, then passing on to less common ones, tropical diseases, and worm and parasitic infestations.

The common infectious fevers are caused by bacteria or viruses, and it is useful to know the meaning of the following terms: *incubation period* is the time which elapses between being infected and developing symptoms; *prodromal period* is the time which elapses between the end of the incubation period and the appearance of a rash; *quarantine period,* the maximum time during which a person who has been in contact with the infection may develop the disease—it is usually two days more than the incubation period; *isolation period,* the time a patient is supposed to be isolated.

Views regarding the common infectious fevers have changed a good deal in recent years. Disinfection of rooms is now regarded as almost useless, and more cases are treated at home. Quarantine in the case of the common fevers is thought by a good many doctors to be a waste of time, since all it can do is to postpone infection from early childhood to early adult life, when it is likely to be more serious. For it is a characteristic of these fevers that they affect the adult much more violently than they do the child. However, on this, and all other points, you will have to be guided by the opinion of your family doctor.

Virus Diseases.

First, we shall take the common virus diseases, measles, chickenpox, and rubella or German measles, then the other virus diseases, mumps, infective hepatitis, virus pneumonia, and some less common conditions which do not always produce a typical rash as in the case of the first three.

In nearly all of these fevers there is a long incubation period, and one infection gives immunity for life.

Measles. The incubation period is 10–11 days. The first sign is the appearance of symptoms rather like a severe cold. The eyes become red, and exposure to light is unpleasant, the nose runs, the throat becomes inflamed, and a dry, harsh cough develops. There may be headache, and the temperature rises to 102° or more. Usually the patient is a child, and especially typical is the development of so-called Koplik's spots, which are small, bluish-white, raised spots seen on the inside of the cheek at the back of the mouth. The rash begins on the fourth day of the prodomal period, *i.e.*, 14 days after the initial infection. It shows on the forehead and behind the ears, spreading within a day downwards over the whole body; in another two days it starts to disappear, but often leaves behind a sort of brownish staining which may last for one to two weeks.

Measles can be serious, especially in very young children because of its complications, such as bronchopneumonia and infection of the ear, which can now be treated with antibiotics. These drugs have no effect on the measles virus, but only on the secondarily invading bacteria which have invaded the lungs and ear during the illness. The illness can be attenuated or lessened by injection of antibodies (gamma globulin) from an immune adult, and this is often worth while in the very young.

Rubella or German Measles. Incubation period 14–19 days. A mild fever, similar to measles except that the rash is usually the first sign that anything is wrong, and the temperature is rarely above 100°. The eyes may be pink, and there are enlarged glands at the back of the neck. The rash disappears completely in thirty-six hours. There are no complications.

German measles, in itself, is harmless, but if a woman gets the disease in the early months of pregnancy malformations in the child may appear at birth. Hence some doctors believe that girls particularly should have the opportunity of contracting German measles before they grow up. There is no special treatment, except the general rules for fevers given above.

Chickenpox. Incubation period 14–15 days, but may be more variable. In children chickenpox is a mild fever which begins with the appearance of tiny blisters on the chest and back. These later spread outwards to the legs, arms and face, and cause itching. Treatment is the general one for fevers already described. Calamine lotion or dusting powder will be helpful for the irritation, and the child's nails should be cut short to prevent scratching and infection of the spots. Whereas children are usually little bothered by chickenpox, young adults may be much more drastically affected—a temperature of 104° is not uncommon, and there may be severe headache.

Mumps. Incubation period 17–18 days. Everyone knows the typical appearance of the patient with mumps—the swelling in the salivary glands in front of the ears which makes the face look full. This causes pain later on, and it may be difficult to open the mouth. Temperature is not usually high (about 101°). Although uncomfortable, mumps is rarely dangerous, but orchitis—swelling of the testicles—is sometimes a complication. Fluid diet should be given if eating is painful, with mouth-washes, and rest in bed.

Infective Hepatitis. "Hepatitis" means inflammation of the liver, and infective hepatitis, which is much the commonest cause of jaundice in young adults, is a virus infection of the liver. In fact, this disease caused serious difficulties during the Italian campaign of 1943, and has probably become more frequent (or, at any rate, more frequently recognised) in this country since the War. The main symptoms are fever, followed by jaundice, which is first noticed in the whites of the eyes as yellow staining, then in the skin. The urine becomes coloured also, and this is most easily noticed if, on shaking in a bottle, the froth shows coloration. If the froth remains white, no jaundice is present. Treatment is a matter for the doctor, but great care should be taken, both by the patient and those in contact with him, to wash the hands thoroughly after urinating or defecating, after handling utensils from the sickroom, and both before and after eating; for the disease is very infectious.

Virus Pneumonia. Pneumonia is usually caused by bacteria, and when we speak of pneumonia, that is the type we ordinarily refer to. Virus pneumonia is known by doctors as " pneumonitis," and is believed to be closely related to influenza. There is no specific treatment so far, and since diagnosis is a specialist matter, little more need be said except that the symptoms in general resemble those of ordinary pneumonia. Psittacosis, another virus disease, can also lead to pneumonia, and although there is no specific treatment for virus infections of the lungs, it is always worth while trying the antibiotics or sulpha drugs in view of the possibility that the lung condition may be caused by a secondary invasion by bacteria.

Influenza. While serious epidemics of influenza take the form of a very dramatic and often fatal disease—for example, the epidemic of " Spanish 'flu " which followed the First World War killed more people than the actual fighting— the milder type more usually seen is difficult to distinguish from the common cold. In fact, many people who complain of " a dose of the 'flu " are suffering from simple colds.

However, a sudden onset, aching in the muscles of the back and legs, and redness of the eyes, would suggest influenza, and especially typical is the depression and weakness which follow influenza but not a cold. The measures suggested above for the general treatment of fever should be applied; but the depression and weakness which follow influenza may need special treatment by the doctor.

Colds. Although everyone thinks he, or she, knows what a " cold " is, the issue is not so simple; for the symptoms of fever, running nose, and a run-down, " headachy " feeling are found in many illnesses. They may be observed, as we have seen, in the early stages of measles before the arrival of the rash, or in a number of other fevers, such as whooping cough. Mild attacks of influenza (see above) may resemble the common cold, and blocking of the nose with discharge and fever may be due to sinusitis—although here there is usually pain above, between, or below the eyes. Colds can be caused by any one of thirty different viruses known as " rhinoviruses " as well as by others which cause influenza, or infect glands (adenoviruses). This is why a single cold does not confer immunity on the sufferer. It is probable that you will not catch a cold from the same virus, at least for the rest of the year, but there are all those others waiting to infect you with other colds in buses, tubes, and other crowded places. Like all infections, do not forget that the best way to avoid them is to keep generally well, and in a good nutritional state. Do not spend money on injections or other vaccines. They do not work, probably because of the multiplicity of viruses involved. It is also unlikely that added vitamins or other expensive additions to the normal diet will do any good at all provided you are eating sensibly. There has recently been a vogue for treating colds with massive doses of Vitamin C. This doesn't work either, as has recently been proved.

Poliomyelitis. "Polio," or infantile paralysis as it used to be called, is a virus infection of the motor nerves—the nerves of movement—at the point where they leave the spinal cord. Fortunately, all the nerves are never affected, but only a few controlling one or more muscle groups.

If these groups happen to be the ones controlling breathing or swallowing (which, fortunately, is not very common) the results may be serious, but ordinarily the muscles affected are those of the legs or arms. Poliomyelitis is almost as common now in adults as in children. Usually it occurs in small epidemics after hot weather, that is in Summer or Autumn, and it often seems to strike at fairly healthy normal people. This, however, is not because healthy people are specially prone as such, but because those living under less hygienic conditions are more likely to have developed immunity. In point of fact, the majority of cases of polio are so mild that they are never discovered at all, and paralysis does not develop; such people are specially dangerous, precisely because they pass unnoticed and spread the disease to others.

Like many other infections, polio begins with sore throat, fever, and sometimes vomiting five to ten days after contact. There may be severe headache and rigidity of the neck muscles. Paralysis is noted about the second or third day after this, and is usually at its maximum from the start, although this is not always the case. This stage lasts two or three weeks, by which time the temperature is down and the paralysis greatly improved, although further improvement may go on up to eighteen months after the acute stage.

This is another disease which has been dramatically reduced and even wiped out in many areas by the widespread use of vaccine. However, when the illness is already present attention is directed to relief of discomfort, resting and splinting the affected limbs, and preventing spread of infection to others. The Kenny method, devised by Nurse Kenny, and much publicised as a means of reducing permanent paralysis, is not believed by most doctors to be any improvement upon orthodox methods. The use of the iron lung is restricted to cases where the muscles controlling breathing are attacked, and any permanent paralysis of the limbs can often be helped by surgical operation.

Encephalitis. This is an infection of the brain caused by a virus, first noted in Vienna in 1916. There was an epidemic in London in 1918, but it is not very common today.

Smallpox. Smallpox was once common in Western Europe, and, as late as the early nineteenth century, was not unknown in Britain. Now, since the introduction of vaccination, it is comparatively rare in industrialised countries, although minor epidemics have occurred here recently. Jenner, who introduced vaccination, noted that dairy-maids who had suffered from the mild disease known as " cow-pox," contracted from the udders of infected cows, and transmitted to the hand of the dairy-maid, did not develop smallpox. In fact, cow-pox is a mild form of smallpox modified by transmission through cattle. Vaccination should be carried out at the age of three months, and repeated at the ages of seven, fourteen, and twenty-one years—also at any time when an epidemic occurs, or when travelling to any part of the world where smallpox is prevalent, or where immigration laws stipulate that it must be done. Many countries insist on an international certificate of recent vaccination before landing. Your family doctor will make out the certificate (he is entitled to charge you for it) and your local Medical Officer of Health will countersign it. Smallpox is one of the diseases which can very readily be spread from countries where it is prevalent because of the great increase in numbers of people travelling about the world by air.

Smallpox attacks people of all ages and is carried by excreta and droplet infection, but particularly by the dried scales on the skins of convalescent patients; it is now most common in the tropics.

Smallpox is similar in many ways to chickenpox. Typical cases are easy for the qualified doctor to distinguish from one another, but one of the difficulties of vaccination (as with Typhoid, and other artificially conferred immunities) is that the typical signs are often modified. Differential diagnosis is a job for the expert, and if your own doctor is in any doubt, he will consult with his local health authorities. The disease begins with shivering, headache, and backache, and the temperature is raised to 102–104°. On the third day a rash appears, which turns into small blisters on the sixth day, and the blisters become filled with pus by the ninth day. On the twelfth day they burst and form crusts. Unlike chickenpox, in which the rash starts in the middle of the body and works towards the outer parts, smallpox produces a rash which begins in the scalp, forehead, wrists, and feet and then moves towards the middle.

Smallpox is a serious disease, and the result depends largely upon whether the patient has been vaccinated within seven years of the attack. Contacts should be vaccinated and kept under observation for sixteen days; the patient must be isolated until all the scabs have separated and the skin healed. An effective drug has recently been announced.

Glandular Fever. This is sometimes called infective mononucleosis, since one of its features is an increase in certain mononuclear white cells and an alteration in their appearance. Another feature is an apparent infectivity. Beyond this the disease is a great mystery, and although it is probably caused by a virus, it may even be related to other (malignant) diseases of white cells. This one, however, is not dangerous although it often causes a lot of trouble by dragging on for many weeks. The main symptoms are fever, enlargement of lymph glands and sore throat. The patient feels very debilitated and often very depressed. Diagnosis is often very difficult, but there is a blood test known as the " Paul-Bunnell " test which is almost specific for the disease. The patient is usually presented as a case known to doctors as " P.U.O.," meaning Pyrexia (fever) of Unknown Origin. He has often been treated with several antibiotics, one after another, without effect, because the causal agent is not affected by these drugs. He is only very mildly infective, and it is unusual to insist on isolation or quarantine.

Typhus. This disease used to be known as " jail fever," because it was frequent in prisons; but overcrowding, poverty, and bad hygienic surroundings anywhere are suitable conditions for epidemics of typhus. Improved conditions in industrialised countries have made it unusual, since typhus is carried by a virus carried from one person to another by lice, and where lice are absent the virus is powerless to enter the human body.

Typhus comes on suddenly with a rise in temperature of about 102°, but within four days it may be as high as 107°. There may, or may not, be a rash at this time, and in the second week, when the temperature is at its highest, there is delirium, weakness, and a feeble pulse. The typical typhus rash appears about the fifth day as reddish blotches on the chest, abdomen, and wrists.

Typhus is, needless to say, very serious but responds to such modern antibiotics as chloramphenicol, aureomycin, and terramycin. Preventive measures are directed towards destroying all lice with D.D.T.

Rabies. Finally, we shall deal very briefly with a number of less common virus diseases, beginning, as is appropriate, with *hydrophobia or rabies*, since it was in this infection that the great French scientist Louis Pasteur (1822–95) showed the possibility of prevention by vaccination. Unlike Jenner, with his ready-made cowpox virus, which we have seen to be the virus of smallpox weakened by natural passage through cows, Pasteur had to weaken the rabies virus by passing it through rabbits. The rabbits were infected, and after death the spinal cord was dried and powdered, a solution passed through another rabbit, and so on until the virus was sufficiently weakened.

Rabies is spread by the bite of infected animals, usually dogs, cats, or wolves, who are driven mad by the disease; in Trinidad, however, it has been spread by vampire bats. Those who are bitten usually show no symptoms for six weeks or more, but sooner or later convulsions and delirium arise, which within four to five days are fatal.

There is no cure once the symptoms have developed, but Pasteur's serum, if given soon after the bite, prevents illness in the vast majority of cases—the sooner after the bite, the better the outlook. Dogs should be muzzled in areas where the disease is common, but quarantining imported dogs has made the infection almost unknown here.

Psittacosis. This is another virus disease which is of interest mainly in that it is spread by birds of the parrot group, such as parrots, love-birds, macaws, and the rest. It occasionally occurs here in people who have been in contact with birds of this type, and is serious both to the bird and its owner. As in the case of rabies, quarantine regulations have greatly reduced the likelihood of infection in Britain.

The symptoms of psittacosis are fever, cough, and bronchitis. The disease is especially danger-ous to old people, but it responds to the same anti-biotics as typhus.

Sandfly Fever, or phlebotomus fever, *Dengue,* or breakbone fever, and *Trench Fever* are all some-what similar conditions in that they resemble influenza and are rarely fatal. They are all due to viruses, spread in the first case by sandflies in tropical climates; in the second by mosquitoes in tropical climates; and in the third by lice in temperate climates. They are all typical " soldiers' diseases "; the first two were common in the Middle East and Far East during the last War, the third during the First World War in France.

Yellow Fever. Of all the virus diseases, only four can be prevented by vaccination—smallpox, hydrophobia, yellow fever, and poliomyelitis. Yellow fever is carried by a mosquito known as Stegomyia, common in South and Central America and in African ports. For its spread, it therefore needs: a hot climate, the stegomyia mosquito, and an infected person.

In 1898 the United States was at war with Spain in Central America, where yellow fever was a serious problem. Following this war the United States, by this time acutely aware of this terrible disease, asked a Dr. G. E. Waring to deal with it in Havana, where it was rife. But Waring died of yellow fever, as had many millions before him, without knowing its cause, and it was left to Walter Reed, who died in 1902, to prove the con-nection between the mosquito and yellow fever. By a vigorous war on the mosquito, the disease has been eradicated from Havana and the West In-dian islands, and Reed's discovery made possible the building of the Panama Canal (Ferdinand de Lesseps, the builder of the Suez Canal, had made a similar attempt in Panama, but had been beaten, amongst other factors, by yellow fever).

In yellow fever there is a sudden high tempera-ture, aching of limbs and head, jaundice, and black vomit; the pulse-rate falls as the fever rises. Previous vaccination seems to be preven-tive if undertaken in time.

Conclusion.

All these virus diseases have this in common: that for many there is no specific cure, although smallpox, rabies, yellow fever, and poliomyelitis can be prevented by vaccination, or by the social control of the creatures carrying the virus. Some of the larger viruses (psittacosis, whooping cough) are destroyed by certain antibiotics. There is usually a long incubation period. Finally the question will sometimes arise of protecting some people from German measles or measles with gamma globulin containing another person's anti-bodies to the disease. This may be considered for measles in very young patients or to protect the foetus in pregnant mothers in contact with German measles.

Bacterial Diseases.

Bacterial diseases differ from virus infections in a number of respects: their incubation period

tends to be shorter; having the disease once does not often confer lifelong protection; and unlike virus diseases, most bacterial diseases respond to one of the antibiotics or sulphonamides. In many cases it is possible to inoculate against the disease to prevent it occurring, as we have seen is possible with only a few of the virus diseases.

Scarlet Fever and Other Streptococcal Infections. In the days, not so long ago, before the arrival of chemotherapy (sulphonamides) and antibiotics, streptococci were very much feared and even caused a high mortality, particularly in such susceptible groups as children, and mothers and babies in maternity hospitals. They are still taken very seriously in the latter and rightly so, although one wonders how much of the mystique is simply a hang over from the days, thirty years ago, when many mothers died from " childbed fever." All signs of infection, such as fever, during the puerperium (the period following child-birth) must be promptly dealt with by a doctor, and only occasionally now is there real cause for anxiety provided treatment is prompt and rigorous.

Scarlet fever is much less common and very much less serious an illness than it used to be, partly because of the effective treatments avail-able today, but also because of a definite but un-explained reduction in its severity. Perhaps the streptococcus has changed, and certainly the im-proved physical condition of people who are now much better fed and housed than they were, has helped to ward off the terrors of this disease as of so many other infections. The classical picture of signs and symptoms is now so rarely seen that it will not be further described.

The importance of streptococcal infections has shifted from the initial infection, such as a sore throat, to some serious conditions which occa-sionally arise as a result of some form of delayed sensitivity to the bacteria. Acute rheumatism or rheumatic fever (not to be confused with ordinary aches and pains nor with rheumatoid arthritis) occasionally arise in people who have had a sore throat a few weeks before. Since the strepto-coccus is not the direct cause of the damage which may consequently occur in the heart or kidney, the antibiotics are no answer except sometimes to keep off further streptococcal invasions.

Diphtheria. This used to be an extremely serious disease, but immunisation has made it almost unknown; it is important, therefore, that all children should be immunised. There are many modern and up-to-date doctors who have qualified since the war who have never seen a case because it has become so rare, and in spite of the propaganda of certain ill-informed people this saving of children's lives is entirely the result of nationwide inoculation during the war and since. The following description is of historic interest only, and will remain so if a high level of inocula-tion is kept up by parents.

In a typical case of diphtheria the incubation period is about three days; the patient is a child who becomes ill and pale-looking (*i.e.,* the onset is not sudden, as in many fevers, but insidious); the temperature is only slightly raised to, perhaps, 99° or 101°, and although there may be no com-plaint of sore throat, examination will reveal in-flammation with—and this is typical of diphtheria —a grey membrane spread over the tonsils, the palate, and the back of the mouth generally. The diphtheria germ does not spread within the body. It stays at the place where it entered (in this case the throat) and sends its toxins through-out the body.

Even after the acute phase is over the patient must not be allowed to walk, because the diphtheria toxin is particularly poisonous to the heart. The ordinary rule is at least one or two months in bed.

Diphtheria also occurs in the larynx—in pre-inoculation days many children choked to death with this form of the infection; in the nose; and, although this is not generally known, wounds can be infected. The so-called " Desert sores " of the North African campaign seem to have been caused by diphtheria-like organisms.

Diphtheria may lead to paralysis of the throat, with difficulty in speaking or swallowing, and paralysis of the eyes or limbs; these are due to neuritis caused by the influence of the toxin on the nerves.

Whooping Cough. For many years whooping cough has been regarded merely as a bother to the patient and a nuisance to others, as, in fact, a trivial disease. Unfortunately, this is not so: because statistics show that it causes more deaths than polio, diphtheria, scarlet fever, and measles all put together.

Whooping cough begins in a child as an ordinary cold with cough and slight fever, and this stage lasts for a week or ten days. Then the "paroxysmal stage" begins as a series of coughs following in rapid succession, during which time the patient is unable to breathe. The "whoop" is caused by the noisy indrawing of breath when the fit stops. The face may become blue and congested. Bronchitis is usually present, and bronchopneumonia may result as a complication, so inoculation of all children before the disease has a chance to strike them is most important.

Once whooping cough has begun, there is no specific treatment, although modern drugs can reduce the frequency of the fits of coughing. The antibiotic chloramphenicol has been used for this disease, but the general opinion is that it is ordinarily of little benefit. Chinese physicians once described whooping cough as the "hundred-days cough," and the cough may, indeed, continue for at least a hundred days.

Food Poisoning Diseases.

Strictly speaking, there is no such thing as "food poisoning" if one is thinking of "poisoning" in terms of anything apart from germs. But not so long ago it used to be thought that decomposition of food in itself produced poisons known as "ptomaines" which were deadly to those who swallowed them. All food poisoning is caused by infection of food with bacteria and by no other cause—unless, of course, we are thinking of the kind of poisoning which is the concern of the lawyer rather than the medical man.

Here we are considering those diseases which are commonly spread by contaminated food or drink. The classification is not scientific, but then no scientific classification has as yet been devised. First, we shall deal with typhoid, paratyphoid, and dysentery—uncommon here in Britain, although Sonné dysentery is fairly frequent. Then there is gastro-enteritis (which means irritation of the stomach and intestines), which is caused by staphylococci and the germs of the salmonella group, and lastly, botulism, which is rare.

Typhoid and Paratyphoid. These diseases are spread by infected water, food, or hands—especially uncooked food, such as milk, salads, oysters, and shellfish. Flies, too, play some part in spreading the disease. Some people are "carriers" and carry and excrete the germs without being themselves affected; for example, "Typhoid Mary," a carrier in the United States in the early years of this century, spent a large part of her life in custody as a public danger, although she did not show any symptoms of typhoid. Nevertheless, this woman caused a great deal of illness in others in her chosen profession of cook.

The influence of Chadwick's propaganda for pure water supplies is shown by the fact that deaths from typhoid, still 332 per 1,000,000 in 1870, fell to 198 per 1,000,000 at the beginning of this century. In the 1920s the death-rate was only 25 per 1,000,000, and now it is even less.

Typhoid fever begins like most fevers with headache, raised temperature, and general feeling of unwellness. This stage lasts about a week, and then the rash appears in the form of rose-red spots on the front of the chest and abdomen and on the back. In the second week there is great weakness, sometimes diarrhœa, flatulence, and mental dullness, together with dry and cracked lips and tongue. The third week is the week, in hopeful cases, of gradual decrease in temperature and other symptoms, and the fourth week is the week of convalescence.

Complications are perforation of the intestine (which needs surgical treatment), delirium, and bronchitis.

Paratyphoid fever is a milder form of typhoid (there are two forms, A and B); ordinarily it can be diagnosed only by scientific tests. The main thing is to inoculate contacts with T.A.B. vaccine and to protect food supplies; treatment is with chloramphenicol.

Dysentery. Dysentery may be caused *either* by a bacterium or an amœba; the first type is known as bacillary dysentery, the latter as amœbic dysentery (which is dealt with under tropical diseases). Infection is spread in much the same way as in typhoid. There is high fever, abdominal pain, and diarrhœa, at first consisting of fæcal matter, then blood and mucus. In severe cases the death-rate used to be over 20 per cent.

Various bacilli cause dysentery. The common tropical types are the Shiga and Flexner groups, but in this country most epidemics are due to the milder Sonné group.

However, in all these infections sulphaguanidine, one of the sulpha drugs, brings rapid relief, but care must be taken to avoid infection of other people.

Diarrhœa and Vomiting. Leaving out typhoid and paratyphoid fevers and dysentery, there is a group of infections known as "D. & V."—diarrhœa and vomiting. In Britain D. & V. is mostly due to:

> (1) Salmonella infection.
> (2) Staphylococcal infections.
> (3) Other bacteria, ordinarily harmless, such as bacillus coli, when present in sufficient quantity.

Salmonella Infections are the most serious of this group; they affect the small intestine and produce vomiting, severe abdominal pain, and diarrhœa. These symptoms occur about one day after eating infected food and usually clear up within about two weeks, but occasionally death results. Salmonella bacteria are most likely to be found in meat, egg powder, vegetables, and ducks' eggs, but staphylococci are liable to grow in milk products, such as ice-cream and cream buns. Food poisoning from staphylococci is seldom severe, and recovery takes place in about a week. Nevertheless, it is extremely infectious, and causes a great deal of lost time in industry and temporary illness in institutions; for it is in such situations that it is most likely to occur.

Staphylococcal Food Poisoning has greatly increased in recent years, so it is important to know what circumstances are likely to cause it. The reason for its increase has nothing to do, as many people suppose, with the greater use of canned foods, but it has much to do with the greater use of communal feeding and canteen meals. It is *possible* for bacterial toxins in infected food to bring about illness even when the canning process has killed the bacteria, but it is certainly extremely rare. Canned foods, in fact, are much safer than so-called "fresh" foods in this respect—except when they have been opened, left about, and then re-heated. The same applies to the re-heating of any kind of food.

The real enemy is the canteen worker with a boil, a discharging nose, dirty hands, or a septic finger. Occasionally food may be infected in the larder by rats or mice, but the sort of canteen or restaurant where this can happen has little to commend it! Frankly, these infections are caused by dirty or stupid people who do not realise that their sore finger or boil can become someone else's diarrhœa and vomiting. Where children are concerned, the outlook is potentially more serious, and in the early part of this century the Summer-time "procession of baby coffins" was all too familiar. Infection is much more common in artificially fed babies or in older children who eat infected ice-cream. However trivial the condition may seem, diarrhœa and vomiting with fever in a child should never be ignored. Those in charge of canteens or restaurants must ensure that staff is supervised, that anyone with a septic infection is put off duty, and that all know about washing after visiting the lavatory and absolute cleanliness.

Bacilli normally present in the intestine, such

as bacillus coli, can cause infections if absorbed in large amounts, or if of a different strain from those in the patient's intestine. They are not usually serious.

Botulism. Now uncommon, this is the disease which used to be known as "ptomaine poisoning" on the theory that it was caused by poisons produced by bad food apart from germs. In the 1920s a party of picnickers at Loch Maree in the Scottish Highlands developed botulism and a number died, with the result that the disease attracted much public attention. Botulism is caused by a germ, the bacillus botulinus, which is peculiar in that, like tetanus, its poison attacks the nervous system rather than the intestines, resulting in fits, double vision, paralysis beginning in the face and spreading downwards, and difficulty in swallowing. It is found in tinned fruits or vegetables containing the toxin even when the germ has been killed, but, as we have already seen, the toxin comes from the bacilli, not from decomposition of food as such (in fact, food does not decompose in the absence of germs). Death is common in botulism, but an antitoxin is now available which, if used in time, can cure the disease.

Tuberculosis. No disease causes more public concern, and no disease is more difficult to describe, than tuberculosis; for, like the streptococcus or the staphylococcus, the tubercle germ can attack many different parts of the body and manifest itself in many ways. Furthermore, it is a widely spread disease, infecting not only humans but also cattle, birds, and reptiles. But here we shall be concerned with those types common to Man—the human and bovine (*i.e.*, the type occurring in cattle which can be spread to man by infected milk).

The tubercle bacillus is particularly hardy, so that when coughed or spat out on the ground it continues to be infectious for a long time. Infection is therefore caused by: (*a*) drinking infected milk; (*b*) droplet infection through having germs coughed in the face; (*c*) breathing in infected dust. In other words, tuberculosis is caused by absorption through either the lungs or the intestines; the former is common in adults, the latter in children.

But there is a good deal more to the problem than this; we know, for example, that over 90 per cent. of people in industrialised countries have been infected with T.B. in early life and have conquered the infection. So the question arises: what conditions predispose to T.B.—why do some people get over the early infection and others not? There are two answers to this question: one is certain—that those who are impoverished and do not get enough food are liable to T.B.; the second is not so certain—that mental stress plays some part. Yet there is reasonably good evidence that such stress as a broken love-affair can cause lowered resistance to breakdown so that when germs are encountered infection will occur.

In children, lung tuberculosis is not common, but tuberculosis of the bones and glands is, as is also infection in the abdomen, the kidney or spine, and, worst of all, tuberculous meningitis. These are often of the bovine type from infected milk. Ordinarily, T.B. in children is less serious than adult infections; but tuberculous meningitis used to be almost invariably fatal until streptomycin was discovered.

Adult tuberculosis usually occurs in the lungs or the pleura—the thin membrane surrounding the lungs. In younger people miliary tuberculosis, which is a form of T.B. blood-poisoning or septicæmia, is a very serious condition, and the infection spreads throughout the whole body in a few weeks.

Lung infection begins gradually in someone who has previously felt unwell. There may be cough, and later blood-stained sputum (although blood which is coughed up does not necessarily prove that T.B. is present). Whatever means of treatment are used, the struggle between disease and patient is likely to be fairly long, but the outlook is now good. The closure of the Swiss sanatoria is due partly to modern disbelief that air in one place is better than that in another, but mainly to improved treatment.

Prevention depends on legal action ensuring tuberculosis-free herds of cattle; on control of spread of the disease by those "open" cases who carry germs in their sputum; on the use of vaccination in childhood with B.C.G. vaccine (which you can ask your doctor about).

Many methods are used in treatment: new drugs, such as streptomycin, isoniazid, and P.A.S., lung surgery, rest, and so on. At any rate, tuberculosis is being got under control, but anyone who is worried can get a free X-ray at the nearest Mass Radiography Centre. For children, there are skin tests to show whether there is susceptibility to T.B.

Septicæmia. Commonly known as "blood-poisoning," is one of those diseases of which textbooks prior to the Second World war used to say: "death usually occurs."

Blood-poisoning occurs generally by spread from some septic area such as a wound (or even a small prick), after childbirth, or any place where certain germs have got admission to the body. The most usual germ is the streptococcus, although the pneumococcus—which ordinarily causes pneumonia—and the staphylococcus may also cause septicæmia.

Fever comes on suddenly and rises rapidly with headaches, sweating, and shivering. The patient is obviously very ill, and later there is wasting and delirium. The white blood cells increase in number. Septicæmia sometimes occurs without any apparent local infection in those who are weak and debilitated.

Pyæmia is a type of septicæmia which leads to the formation of numerous abscesses throughout the body. Its symptoms are the same as described above, except that the causative germ is usually the staphylococcus, and abscesses are found which may need surgical treatment.

However, in both conditions the state of affairs has been revolutionised by the use of the sulpha drugs and antibiotics; cure is now the rule rather than the exception.

Septicæmia should be suspected when any small wound or cut is followed by high temperature and the symptoms described above.

The word "*Toxaemia*" is used when the germs stay in their original position and produce symptoms by spreading their toxins throughout the body. Tetanus, diphtheria, and some kinds of childbirth infection come into this category; the symptoms may vary from mild disturbance to severe illness.

Meningitis means inflammation of the meninges, the covering which, like a layer of plastic, lies over the brain and spinal cord, just as the pleura covers the lungs and the peritoneum covers internal organs in the abdomen. (Hence inflammation of the pleura is known as pleurisy, and inflammation of the peritoneum as peritonitis.)

Various germs may cause meningitis, for example, the bacillus of tuberculosis, the pneumococcus, which ordinarily causes pneumonia, and the streptococcus or staphylococcus, but ordinarily the word refers to *Cerebrospinal Meningitis* or "spotted fever" caused by the meningococcus and occurring at times as an epidemic. It is commonest in the years from infancy to the early twenties, and begins suddenly with headache, vomiting, and fever. The temperature rises quickly, and pain develops in the back and legs; on the second or third day a rash appears on the body, and particularly on the inside of the thighs. Later there is stiffness of the neck, the head may be drawn back, vomiting persists, and the headache can be so severe as to cause the patient to scream with pain.

Fortunately, this type of meningitis (and most of the others) respond to treatment with antibiotics or the sulpha drugs, so the risks are very much less than formerly.

Pneumococcal Meningitis is an unusual complication of pneumonia, and the septic types (*streptococcal or staphylococcal*) arise either following an infected fracture of the skull or from infection of the ear or mastoid.

Tuberculous Meningitis has already been mentioned; originally always fatal, it is now treatable with streptomycin.

All these diseases are very much a matter for

specialist and hospital treatment, but it is worth while mentioning *benign lymphocytic meningitis*, in which, although all the symptoms of meningitis are present, recovery without specific treatment is invariable. Meningitis, which was during the First World War and after what polio is to us now, is no longer common, and when taken in time is easily treated.

Tetanus is usually known as " lockjaw " because there may be difficulty in opening the mouth, although this is simply part of a spasm of all the muscles of the body. The tetanus bacillus is found in rich soil—hence the disease is less common in desert areas—and tetanus resembles rabies in that: (a) it enters at a wound; (b) it affects the nervous system; (c) it results in fits and ultimately death.

However, active immunisation with T.T. (tetanus toxoid) has resulted in the disease becoming uncommon, and even when developed, treatment with antitoxin, anæsthetics, and curare may lead to cure.

The bacillus is anærobic (*i.e.*, does not use oxygen) and is most likely to occur in such situations as when a man digging manure or working in his garden sticks a fork through his foot, or in war-time, when he is wounded in soil contaminated with manure.

Undulant fever, also known as Malta fever or abortus fever, falls into two types: melitensis, which infects goats, and abortus, cattle and pigs. Man gets the disease by reason of close contact with or drinking the milk of infected animals. (The name abortus is given because abortion is produced in cattle and sows.)

In Undulant Fever, as one would suppose, the fever goes up and down for two to three weeks; it may then go down and rise again, persisting for many months. The disease may occur in Britain, but modern drugs are on the whole successful in dealing with it. A striking feature of the disease is the combination of a high temperature with an appearance of relative well-being.

Another disease carried by mammals is *Glanders* or *Farcy*, spread by horses. In glanders there is discharge from the nose and sometimes pneumonia. Occasionally the disease is fatal. In farcy abscesses form, usually along the lymph vessels. Both conditions are very contagious, and treatment is a matter for a specialist; infected horses should be destroyed.

Cholera. Cholera could be classified under the head of food-poisoning, because it is mainly spread by infected water (however, like typhoid, it can also be spread by flies, infected food, and carriers); it could also be classified as a tropical disease, since, although it used to be found in Europe, it is now mainly rife in India.

Also like typhoid, cholera is caused by a bacillus, and can be prevented by early inoculation and care over food supplies—boiling water and milk, washing uncooked foods in chlorinated water, and keeping flies away.

The fever begins in the usual way with a short incubation period, followed by abdominal pain, severe vomiting, and diarrhœa. Later with the loss of fluid from the body there may be cramps in the muscles, diarrhœa increases, and the motions become of the typical " rice-water " type —*i.e.*, there is no solid matter, and the appearance is that of water to which a little milk has been added. This stage is followed by collapse, with low pulse and cold hands and feet. Death, if adequate treatment is not available, results in about 70 per cent. of cases.

Anthrax. The bacillus of anthrax, like that of tuberculosis, can exist outside the body for long periods, and, like that of tetanus, then takes the form of spores or seed-like bodies. It is spread by infected cattle and horses, which get the disease from eating grass containing spores.

In human beings the form the disease takes depends on where the germ alights; sometimes it comes from infected shaving-brushes, when it causes a large sore, like a boil, on the face, known as " malignant pustule "; sometimes it develops in those who inhale the dust from infected hides or wool (hence the name " wool-sorters' disease," which is a form of bronchitis with blood-stained

sputum); lastly it may arise through eating infected meat, when the result is intestinal anthrax.

In all cases the outlook is serious. Death is common, preceded by a high temperature, skin symptoms in the first instance, lung symptoms in the second, and food-poisoning symptoms in the third. Serum and arsenical preparations were formerly used, but now the suplha drugs seem to offer more promise.

Diseases Caused by Fungi.

There are only two important groups of disease caused by fungus: the serious *actinomycosis* and the relatively harmless, if unpleasant, *ringworm*. Ringworm or tinea will be dealt with later; it affects the hair, the body, the groin (dhobie itch, already referred to), and the feet (athlete's foot). Actinomycosis is spread by a fungus in barley and grasses which may reach the human mouth, settle around bad teeth, and thence pass to the lungs, the bone of the jaw, and even to the intestines or brain. Fortunately, this unpleasant fungus, which was once difficult to eradicate, has proved susceptible to penicillin.

The Venereal Diseases.

The venereal diseases are those caused—or at least that is what the name means—by the goddess of love, Venus. Venus, of course, causes a great deal of trouble, but venereal disease is not necessarily the worst she can do. Venereal disease is spread by sexual intercourse with an infected person.

Gonorrhœa is the result of an infection by the gonococcus (*Neisseria gonorrhoea*) and ordinarily comes on after an incubation period of three to seven days. However, babies can get an infection of the eyes, known as ophthalmia, from their mother if she is infected, and gonorrhœa in young children is often the result of being in contact with infected towels or clothes. The disease in adults is evident when there is a thick, creamy discharge from the sexual organs and sometimes pain on passing water; in infants ophthalmia is prevented by the use of silver nitrate eye-drops at birth. Gonorrhœa is fairly easily cured by the use of sulpha drugs or penicillin; but unfortunately venereal disease is increasing in recent years and drug-resistant forms are becoming more common.

Syphilis is a serious venereal disease caused by a spirochete (*Treponema pallidum*). Stories about lavatory seats are simply stories, although it is occasionally possible to get syphilis by other than sexual means: for example, it has happened that a man playing football has been infected through his hand being grazed by the teeth of someone with syphilis. But this is very unusual, although kissing can spread the disease. Children, too, can be born with syphilis (the so-called congenital syphilis).

Adult syphilis begins with a sore, known as a hard chancre, at the point where the sporochæte of syphilis has entered; this may be on the lips, through kissing; on the sexual organs, through intercourse; and very rarely, as explained above, elsewhere. In a short time the chancre disappears and all may seem to be well, but this primary stage is followed by a secondary stage with sore throat, a rash, headache, and enlargement of glands. This, if left alone, also clears up, but is followed by the tertiary stage, in which a chronic infection develops in some part of the body which, presumably, is most susceptible in the particular individual. Thus there may be chronic syphilis of the skin, the bones, the heart, liver, or nervous system.

In the nervous system, the commonest forms are the two diseases of *tabes dorsalis*, in which the spinal cord is infected, and G.P.I. (general paralysis of the insane), in which the brain and mind are affected. These will be discussed under Nervous Diseases.

In congenital syphilis the pregnant mother gives her child syphilis. Such infants are often still-born or premature, they look wizened, like a little old man, and amongst other symptoms are eye disease, "snuffles," a flattened nose, and when the adult teeth appear the front ones may be notched at the biting surface.

The treatment, of course, is very much a matter for a specialist, but diagnosis is usually made through the Wassermann blood test. It was for syphilis that Ehrlich produced his "magic bullet"—an arsenical drug, known as salvarsan, which could attack the organism selectively without harming the body and was the first of the modern specific drugs. Present-day treatment is with penicillin. G.P.I., once hopeless, is now dealt with by malarial therapy with a good deal of success. Penicillin alone is often adequate.

It is important to understand about venereal disease in general: (1) that it happens to many people who are no worse than anyone else; (2) that many patients believe themselves to have V.D. when, in fact, they have not; (3) that the best thing to do is to see your doctor as soon as possible—he is not concerned with your morals, and the sooner you go, the sooner you will get well; (4) every sore in the sexual area need not be V.D. There are other diseases which may be contracted as venereal infections.

Chancroid produces small septic ulcers around the sex organs, with swelling of the local glands in the groin, which may suppurate. It is caused by a bacillus, and can usually be cleared up by sulpha drugs within a week. Scabies and lice often pass from one body to another during sexual intercourse, but are not usually thought of as venereal in origin, although in many cases they are.

Tropical Diseases.

Nothing is more difficult than to define the term "tropical diseases." One might define them as the diseases which occur in tropical climates—but then measles occurs there too; and if they are defined as those diseases which are found *only* in the tropics, the solution is no easier, since leprosy, cholera, smallpox, and typhus are usually listed as tropical diseases, yet were found in this country until fairly recently—and the odd case still is.

But what a story could be told about the conquest of those infections which were—and many still are—the scourge of humanity! One day when generals and dictators are forgotten we shall remember that great international army of physicians and bacteriologists who have saved millions of lives and infinitely reduced human suffering: Koch and Ehrlich of Germany, Pasteur and Roux of France, Ross and Jenner of Britain, Reed of America, Noguchi of Japan, and many others. We shall remember how the Jesuit priests brought quinine from Peru to Europe in 1638, the first drug to save people from malaria; how in tropical heat Ronald Ross (1857–1932) peered for hours through his microscope to discover the connection between malaria and the mosquito until the sweat running from his brow rusted the instrument; how Major Walter Reed's work in Havana (1851–1902) made possible the building of the Panama Canal, and think, too, of the American soldiers who died in helping him to find the cause of yellow fever. In mentioning Jenner once more, we should recall Lady Mary Montagu (1689–1762), who brought the practice of vaccination to England from Turkey—or, rather, the practice of "variolation," which meant inoculating with the pus from smallpox cases. This was, of course, a dangerous practice, but the idea was there. Noguchi, one of the great bacteriologists of the nineteenth century, was the son of a poor peasant. He often had to steal to get enough bread even to keep alive, but was later to help in our understanding of syphilis and many tropical diseases.

Yet there is still much to do. Take, for example, the case of Egypt, one of the world's poorest countries, supporting with the help of water from the Nile about 24 million people. But if the river gives food and drink it does other things; for it carries the disease of bilharzia, which kills thousands of peasants yearly. In the villages of Egypt as many as 90–100 per cent. of the population suffer from this terrible disease. The infantile mortality rate is the second highest in the world—29·5 per cent.—seven times higher than that of Holland; the average expectation of life amongst the lower classes is thirty-one years

of the upper classes fifty to sixty years. The country is ridden with bilharzia, ankylostomiasis, malaria, plague, amœbic dysentry, typhus, tuberculosis, and pellagra. Blindness, due to trachoma and other diseases, affects tens of thousands. Such a situation cannot be treated simply by pouring drugs into the country; what is necessary is social control, to enforce purification of the water supplies, the use of insecticides such as D.D.T. to kill the disease-bearing pests, and removal of the causes of extreme poverty (tuberculosis and vitamin deficiencies which are common in Egypt are diseases of malnutrition).

Relapsing Fever, common in India and Africa, is caused by bad hygiene (rubbing infected lice into the skin); the germ is a spirochæte, similar to that of syphilis, but the disease is non-venereal. Relapsing fever gets its name from the fact that the temperature remains high (103–106°) for about a week, returns to normal for a week, and rises again. There may be three to five relapses of this sort. Cure can be brought about by the arseno-benzol drugs used in syphilis. Lice, of course, should be dealt with.

Epidemic Jaundice (also known as Weil's disease or—if you prefer it—ictero-hæmorrhagica spirochætosis), is also caused by a spirochæte, and spread by rats. Now it is rarely found in Europe, although it occurred in the trenches during the First World War, in men working in sewers, and in the women who worked in the fish market of Aberdeen, which at one time was rat-infested. It is rarely fatal, but leads to high fever and jaundice. Anti-syphilitic drugs are useless, but some of the new antibiotics may help.

Yaws is also a spirochætal disease, common in the tropics and particularly in children. It is unpleasant, but not serious, and tends to clear up in a year or so. There are raspberry-like growths on the skin, which disappear with the drugs used in syphilis (although the condition is non-venereal). The Wassermann reaction, positive in syphilis, is also positive in yaws.

Leprosy. Whereas syphilis, relapsing fever, epidemic jaundice, and yaws are caused by spirochætes, leprosy is caused by a bacillus resembling the bacillus of tuberculosis. Leprosy, in fact, should not be included here at all, for it is non-spirochætal, and not necessarily a tropical infection. Apart from the difficulty of classification, many popular beliefs about the disease are untrue. It is *not* the oldest disease afflicting man; *not* a disease confined to tropical countries; it is *not* very catching; *not* hereditary, *not* incurable; in leprosy the fingers and toes do *not* drop off; it is *not* a divine punishment for wrongdoing. So there are many misunderstandings about this disease, and placing it in the wrong part of the medical section is probably the least.

Leprosy is a serious disease not because of disfiguring light-coloured skin patches and lumps, but because it destroys peripheral nerves. Leprosy may disappear spontaneously, or it may progress until the face is lion-like and the hands and feet wasted and ulcerated. The disease rarely kills, but it is the world's greatest crippler.

Leprosy was once fairly common in colder Western countries, though its extent was exaggerated. The great majority of the 15 million people who suffer from leprosy live in tropical countries, but it still exists in Iceland, Japan, Korea and some of the southern states of the United States. Prolonged and intimate contact with an "open" case is said to be the main mode of infection, but only one infected husband in twenty passes leprosy to his wife.

The sulphone drugs have revolutionised the treatment of leprosy. Given early diagnosis and adequate treatment, the great majority of sufferers could be cured. Established deformity (such as claw hand, drop foot, paralysed eyelids) can be mitigated by reconstructive surgery, although lost sensation cannot be restored.

In the past, only Christian missions were concerned with the plight of the leprosy sufferer. Now, non-sectarian voluntary agencies, Governments and the World Health Organisation have joined in the fight against the disease. Enough is known to control the disease, but not enough is being done, as only one victim in five is at present getting treatment.

Plague is another disease caused by bacteria, common in Europe at one time, but now largely restricted to Asia. Nevertheless, it caused millions of deaths in Europe during the years 1348–49 and 1665 and was the "Black Death," which, indeed, changed the course of history. Interested readers may read Hans Zinnser's *Rats, Lice, and History* about this aspect of the disease. Plague is carried by the bite of the rat flea, but, once people become infected, spread may occur from one to the other by droplet infection—*i.e.*, by coughing and sneezing. After an incubation period of two to ten days, fever develops, rather like severe influenza, and in a day or two the glands in the groin begin to swell, followed perhaps by swelling of the glands elsewhere. This is the usual type of plague, but it is also possible to get disease of the lungs from droplet infection and blood-poisoning from infection of the blood-stream. Both the latter types are almost invariably fatal, and even the glandular type (bubonic plague) has a mortality of about 80 per cent. The vaccine has given place to streptomycin and sulpha drugs which are also used on contacts.

Although we have little space to discuss the subject of plagues and epidemics in general, it is worth noting that serious epidemics have almost always followed wars, revolutions, and economic and political collapse. Thus the Black Death followed the break-up of the Roman Empire, and, in the fourteenth century, accompanied the end of mediæval civilisation. The Napoleonic wars were followed by other epidemics, and the wars of the 1830s in Europe were followed by influenza. In the most widespread outbreak of influenza after the First World War, more people were killed by the disease than in all the fighting of four years. It is a reflection on the peculiar mentality of Man that this devastating epidemic, which affected almost the whole world, occupies little space in his history books—we still, with few exceptions, regard history as the doings of kings, queens, and generals. Yet, in 1918, 20 million men, and women, and children died from influenza, and no cure has, as yet, been found! Later we shall see that many millions of people die yearly from starvation or vitamin deficiencies But these facts—the real facts of life—we rarely hear about.

Protozoal Diseases.

Nearly all the diseases caused by protozoa are tropical diseases, although one of the best-known protozoans is the harmless amœba found in British ponds. Protozoal diseases are caused by these organisms, large in comparison with bacteria which are really one-celled plants. Viruses are neither animals nor plants, and have some distinctive characteristics described elsewhere.

The only important diseases caused by protozoa are sleeping sickness or tryanosomiasis, malaria, and amœbic dysentery (as contrasted with bacillary dysentery), another disease, leishmaniasis—also known by the numerous names of kala-azar, dum-dum fever, and, in milder form, Delhi boil, Oriental sore, or Bagdad sore—will also be mentioned briefly. These infections are few, but important in their influence on Man; for, as Dr. Clark-Kennedy has pointed out, malaria until recently was responsible for one-fifth of all human sickness, sleeping sickness not so long ago caused a large part of Central Africa to be uninhabitable, and in some areas of the tropics there are probably more people with, than without, amœbic dysentery.

Malaria. The word, of course, means "bad air," just as "influenza" means "influence"—in Italian *influenza di freddo*—the influence of cold. Human beings have a natural tendency to suppose that, when two events occur together, then one must be caused by the other. Yet, although malaria and "bad air" may often go together, and influenza and cold, it does not follow that bad air (whatever that may be) causes malaria nor that cold causes influenza. In fact,

the anopheles mosquito carries the amœba of malaria, and the mosquito prefers climates which some people might describe as "bad," but it is the amœba, not the air, which causes the disease. Anyhow, the unfortunate mosquito might well use the phrase honoured by many generations of schoolmasters: "It hurts me more than it hurts you!" For the mosquito, too, is sick, and passes on its sickness to the person it bites.

There are several types of plasmodium—which is the scientific name for this amœba—producing attacks of fever varying in severity and frequency: benign tertian, quartan, and malignant quartan. Entering the body from the mosquito bite, the parasites penetrate the blood cells, multiply there, and finally burst into the blood stream. When this happens the temperature rises, and then they return to the cells to carry out once more the same procedure. Depending on the type, the attacks of fever may be at intervals of three or four days, severe or milder. When someone with malaria is bitten by a mosquito the infection can be transmitted to the next person it meets, but malaria is not infectious from one person to another directly. Quinine, of course, is the time-honoured remedy, but many other drugs are now available: mepacrine, palmaquine, atebrin, and even a sulphonamide derivative known as promin have been tried. The drug must be taken long enough for the infection to die out, otherwise relapses can occur even after leaving a malarial country (but it is only fair to say that, just as some people continue to give themselves the title of "Major" when they have left the Army, so others long in Britain continue to describe attacks of cold or 'flu as "my old malaria again," when, to say the least of it, they are exaggerating).

Important as are the drugs used in the treatment of malaria, even more so is the control of the parasite-bearing mosquito. The eggs of mosquitoes hatch in water, and there the young or larval forms can be attacked by pouring oil on the surface of pools so that they are unable to breathe, or by introducing small fish which have a partiality for them. Adult mosquitoes can be killed by D.D.T. and other insecticides or kept away by nets over beds and skin creams. Finally, antimalarial drugs can be taken in dangerous areas. Whereas anopheline mosquitoes were once well on the way to getting rid of Man, now Man is well on the way to getting rid of mosquitoes.

Blackwater Fever is a sequel to malaria in tropical Africa and some parts of India. Rather illogically, it is described as "Blackwater," although the urine is red and the skin is yellow but the result is due to breaking down of the red blood cells by some malarial toxin. Possibly too much quinine may help in producing the illness. Treatment is to give plenty of fluids and no quinine or any other anti-malarial drugs in the early stages. The death-rate is about 25 per cent.

Trypanosomiasis or sleeping sickness—not to be confused with *sleepy* sickness, which has already been dealt with under the name of encephalitis lethargica—is essentially an African disease (although also found in tropical America) spread by the tsetse fly. Its cause is the type of protozoan known as a trypanosome, almond-shaped with vibrating membranes at the sides which enable it to move through the blood-stream, rather like a flat fish in the water.

There are three stages of the disease: first, the stage of fever with enlarged glands and a rapid pulse, which may continue off and on for three years; secondly, the stage of trembling hands, legs, and tongue, vacant expression, and slow and stumbling speech; thirdly, and lastly, the stage of low temperature, apathy, wasting of the muscles, and possibly death.

Treatment is with arsenical drugs—such as tryparsamide or Bayer 205—which give good results in early cases. Preventive measures in infected areas include the destruction of tsetse flies by insecticide, the cutting down of forests near rivers which are inhabited by tsetse flies, and some authorities have suggested the shooting of big game which may form a "reservoir" of the parasites, whence tsetse flies can carry them to human beings. For similar reasons infected people should not be allowed to move to non-infected areas.

Amœbic Dysentery, also known as *Amœbiasis*, is caused by the *Entamœba histolytica*, an amœba whose cysts are found in food, water, or spread by infected fingers or flies. There is mild fever and diarrhœa which contains blood. The disease may become chronic, and can cause abscesses, usually in the liver but sometimes in the lungs. Amœbiasis is treated and usually cured by injections of emetine hydrochloride, but in the chronic phase the drug known as Yatren is used in the form of an enema.

Leishmaniasis, kala-azar, or dum-dum fever, is another amœbic disease, probably spread in this instance by the bite of sandflies. It is also known as tropical splenomegaly—enlargement of the spleen in ordinary language—since infection results in enlargement of the spleen and liver, low, irregular fever, and death within a year or so. A milder form, affecting the skin, is known as Delhi boil, Oriental sore, or Bagdad sore, does not lead to kala-azar, and is fairly readily cured. The cure for both conditions is to give injections of tartar emetic, which reduces the death-rate from kala-azar from 80 per cent. to about 5 per cent.

Diseases Caused by Parasitic Worms.

Many types of worms infest human beings and other animals. They are interesting for such reasons as their size (which may range from the almost invisible to 30 ft. or more), their life histories, and their serious or trivial consequences on their hosts. We shall mention only a few groups here, and mainly the ones likely to be met with in Europe—the tapeworms, the roundworms, and the threadworms—although some tropical types will be described briefly.

Tapeworms, as we have seen earlier, like many other types of intestinal worm, lead a double life. What usually happens is that the worm breeds in the human intestine, the eggs pass out in the fæces, and are then swallowed by animals eating contaminated material. In the animal the eggs hatch out into larvæ—primitive forms which penetrate the muscle, forming cysts—and Man is infected in turn by eating its meat. Thus *taenia solium* gets into the flesh of pigs, which, if imperfectly cooked (measly pork), causes infestation of the intestine in Man. It reaches a length of about 10 ft. *taenia saginata*, which reaches a length of about 20 ft., is spread in imperfectly cooked beef, and in Baltic countries *dibothriocephalus latus* gets into the human intestine from caviare or undercooked fish. It reaches the awesome length of 30 ft.

Now all the worms we have mentioned so far are found in the human intestine, and the cysts, which are much more dangerous and unpleasant, in the animal's muscles. But in some worms the reverse happens, with the adult in the animal's intestines and the cysts in Man. Thus in Australia the dog tapeworm (*taenia echinococcus*) produces cysts in both sheep and Man. This is known as hydatid disease, and may remain unsuspected until cysts in the lungs, liver, or elsewhere become infected or rupture. *Trichinella spiralis* is similar in action, being found in the intestines of pigs and getting into the muscles or other organs of Man. The main difference is that this worm migrates from the pig's intestines into its muscles, whence it reaches Man in under-cooked pork meat or sausages. The muscular cysts cause swellings and sometimes pain. There are changes in the blood, swelling of the face and leg in the early stages, and fever. A minor epidemic occurred in England in 1941. *Taenia echinococcus* and *trichinella spiralis* are small—not more than ¼ in. in length—but are more serious in their consequences than the large worms. Treatment is very difficult, and ordinarily all that can be done is to deal with individual cysts when they make themselves apparent.

The large tapeworms, *taenia solium* and *saginata* and *dibothriocephalus latus*, produce varying symptoms or none at all. Usually they are not discovered until some segments of the worm are excreted, but there may be mild indigestion, excessive hunger, and occasionally anæmia. However, when the worm is discovered the patient, not unnaturally, is likely to become anxious and uncomfortable at the thought of "having" a tapeworm; these symptoms are caused by the worry rather than the worm.

Treatment is, of course, a matter for a doctor, but purging followed by extract of male fern is usually successful. One has to make sure that the head of the worm has been removed, otherwise it will continue to grow.

Roundworms are similar both in appearance and size to ordinary earth-worms and the eggs reach Man, not from an animal, but from the contaminated fingers of someone else who handles food. They give rise to no symptoms, and are noticed only when discharged in the fæces or occasionally vomited up. They can be removed by the use of santonin.

Threadworms, as the name suggests, are like small ½-¼-inch-long pieces of white thread. They are very common in children, and live mainly in the cæcum—*i.e.*, the part of the large intestine near the appendix. The males, which are the smaller ones, remain there, but the females pass down towards the rectum at night-time and lay their eggs in the area around the anus. Infection is by contaminated hands handling food—especially uncooked food—and water. Threadworms are not serious, and cause few symptoms other than itching around the anus and between the legs, but heavily infected children may show symptoms of anæmia. The nervousness often shown by such children is usually the result of the irritation produced by the worms in the anal region. Infection is not common in adults, and in children tends to disappear at puberty.

Treatment is, in theory, simple; for the worms are easily destroyed by a number of drugs, such as gentian violet, thymol, or one of the proprietary remedies. Ointment is applied to the itching area, and the child should be prevented from scratching. However, since the eggs may lie about the house for some time, reinfection often happens, especially if there are several small children in the home who may pass the disease from one to another.

The idea that intestinal worms in general are likely to cause loss of weight by absorbing food eaten by the patient is largely mistaken: for although it is true that they do live on this food, the amount taken is certainly not enough to be significant.

Tropical Worms. Bilharzia has been mentioned before in connection with its frequency in Egypt, although it is also found in other parts of Africa, Arabia, and Iraq. There are two main types: one infecting the bladder (*schistosomum haematobium*), the other the rectum (*schistosomum mansoni*). Bilharzia is more correctly known as schistosomiasis.

The parasite's fantastic life-history begins when a man bathes in infected water, and the small swimming forms known as cercariæ pierce and enter his skin—or they may enter the body by drinking infected water. From the skin they pass to the portal vein below the liver, remain there six weeks until they become adult and then swim against the blood-stream down to the pelvis, where the female has eggs which have a sharp spine. The eggs penetrate into the bladder or rectum—depending on the type of fluke—and pass out in the fæces or urine. If they enter water they hatch out into small moving forms which seek out a water-snail, develop further in its body, and leave it in the form of cercariæ ready to find a new human victim. The female fluke is slender and round, about 1 in. in length, the male, flat and leaf-shaped, is about ¾ in. long, and, as we have seen, their grisly courting takes place in the portal vein, whence the impregnated female passes to the bladder (hæmatobium) or rectum (mansoni) to lay her eggs.

Infection results in raised temperature and, in the urinary type, blood in the urine; in the intestinal type blood is found in the fæces, and there are symptoms resembling dysentery—e.g., diarrhœa. Treatment in both cases is by injections of antimony tartrate. Needless to say, attempts should be made at prevention by telling people to avoid infected canals (usually easier said than done), and by periodically cutting off the water supply to the canals to kill the snails.

Hookworm Disease, or ankylostomiasis, is found in many parts of the world, especially in miners who work on damp ground. The tiny worm enters the body usually through the feet, passes through the blood-stream to the lungs, eats through into one of the bronchial tubes, climbs the windpipe, and passes down the œsophagus into the stomach to end up in the duodenum. It causes anæmia, can be fairly readily cured, but is occasionally fatal.

Elephantiasis. Some types of parasitic worm are spread by insects. Thus in *Filiariasis* mosquitoes inject by their bites the infantile forms of a tiny worm which enters the lymphatic channels; there the blockade they cause leads to the swelling of the legs and the lower part of the body, known as elephantiasis.

PHYSICAL INJURIES

INTRODUCTION.

In this section we shall inevitably discuss much that could be described as Principles of First Aid. You cannot learn First Aid from a book, even if you read one of the excellent first aid manuals, like those published by the St. John Ambulance Association. The only way is to join one of their many classes of practical and theoretical instruction which are held in all parts of this country and many others. There is much to be said for many more people receiving instruction, to judge by the level of general ignorance and ineffectiveness to be witnessed at most road accidents before the ambulance comes.

The most difficult thing to learn is what *not* to do. When a patient is knocked down in the road, people instinctively seem to want to drag him immediately to his feet, or otherwise pull him on to the pavement away from the traffic. Someone will have entered the nearest shop and be emerging with a chair so that the casualty can sit down. Before long a hot strong sweet cup of tea has arrived, and this or some other beverage is being poured into him. All this is instinctive, and all of it is wrong. Do *not* move the patient until you are sure he has no fracture which will be further aggravated by movement. To take an extreme case, a fractured spine clumsily moved may result in permanent widespread paralysis. Guard your patient from the traffic but only move him when you are certain it is safe to do so. If he has any injury which is likely to require a general anaesthetic on arrival in hospital (and this applies to most fractures) do not give anything at all by mouth. No anaesthetic can be given to a patient who has eaten or drunk anything in the previous three hours, in case he vomits while unconscious and dies of obstruction of his airway. Keep your patient warm (do *not* warm him up artificially) keep his head low, and unless he is bleeding severely or has stopped breathing, do nothing but protect him from the ministrations of the uninstructed until the ambulance comes.

Injuries to the Head and Back.

The head contains the brain, an organ with a number of inconvenient properties from the point of view of injury. Its very great importance is matched by its very great vulnerability as a tissue. Its consistency is that of stiff junket. It is quite incapable of repair once damaged and cannot heal by growing new parts in the way that skin

and bone can. So it has to be totally enclosed by protective bone which means it cannot swell without compressing itself dangerously within its box—and this not infrequently happens after injury. Furthermore, any bleeding into the interior of the skull can only occur at the expense of compressing the brain, since the brain box is already fully occupied by the brain. There is a story in first aid known as " Concussion and Compression." It begins with a knock-out blow to the head and this is known as concussion. The patient struck a hard enough blow to the head will lose consciousness, if only for a short time, due to the brain being shaken up. Even slight knocks would do this if the brain were not cushioned by a thin layer of cerebrospinal fluid. Most concussed patients quickly regain consciousness, and for the great majority that is the end of the affair except for a sore head and a headache for a few days. Unfortunately for a minority, even though there may have been no fracture, the blow that knocked them out will also have damaged a small blood vessel on the surface of the brain. These patients may be indistinguishable from the luckier ones at first. They may have regained consciousness and will be just as anxious to go home. They will often be quite lucid for some hours. Surgeons call this the " lucid interval." However, when more than a certain amount of blood has accumulated in the head, and the brain is sufficiently compressed by it the patient loses consciousness slowly, for a second time, and from this phase of " compression " he will not recover unless something is done. The lucid interval can last some hours. Brain surgeons can relieve the compression and save the life of the patient only if they have him in their care when it occurs. This is why *all* cases of head injury who have once lost consciousness (concussion), for however short a period of time, and however lucid they may subsequently appear, *all* must be seen by a doctor and, if thought necessary, observed overnight in hospital, in case they are bleeding and proceeding to compression. There is no way of saving these avoidable fatalities other than by treating all cases of concussion seriously. Fractured skull is potentially even more serious, because the blow will have been harder and, the brain is therefore more seriously at risk.

The spinal cord can be regarded as an extension of the brain which runs down the middle of the spinal bones of the vertebral column. It has the same delicate consistency, and the same inability to recover from injury as the brain. Injury is usually the result of a fracture-dislocation of the spine. The consequences of injury are due to a permanent interruption of its two main functions. All movements of the voluntary muscles are only possible if they are connected by nerves to the brain. Except for muscles in the head, all these " motor " nerves run in the spinal cord. The nerve pathways leave the skull through a large hole in its base and run down in the spinal cord to the required level. They then emerge between the spinal bones and travel in bundles to reach the muscles. Motor nerves for the arm leave the cord between the vertebrae of the neck. Those for the leg leave the cord in the lumbar region in the small of the back. If the nerve supply is damaged in any part of its course, the muscles being supplied become paralysed and are unable to move. It follows that if the spinal cord is damaged, all muscles below the point of damage have been cut off from the brain, and will be paralysed, and this will be permanent because the cord cannot be repaired. Damage to the nerve pathway *after* it has left the cord can often be repaired. Permanent paralysis is only one of the consequences of cord damage, since there is another whole series of nerves running in the cord which carry sensations from all parts of the body to the brain. Therefore there will be loss of sensation as well as paralysis below the point of injury.

It is emphasised that fracture of the spinal bones can occur without damage to the cord taking place. It is when these bones move one over the other, or " dislocate," that permanent cord damage occurs. It is therefore extremely important that cases of back injury be moved very carefully indeed in order to avoid such a disaster, and special ways of moving such patients are taught in First Aid classes.

Haemorrhage and Shock.

Every part of the body must have a blood supply, or else it will die. It is possible to stop the blood supply to a leg, for example, by fastening a wide rubber bandage tightly around the top of the thigh. This so-called " constrictive bandage " is still mentioned in First Aid books as a desperate means of controlling haemorrhage in a limb. It should hardly ever be used, because by stopping all circulation of blood, the entire limb will die in the course of time. Besides, most haemorrhage can be stemmed by direct pressure on the bleeding point. The tissues of the leg, such as its muscle and skin and bone will begin to die in a little more than half an hour after cutting off the blood supply. The brain, however, will begin to suffer within three *seconds* of its blood supply being cut off, and will die in about three minutes. Thus it can be seen that some parts of the body are more susceptible than others to a failure of the blood supply and the brain suffers earliest of all. Since the brain is where most of the vital functions of the body are controlled, it follows that a shortage of blood to the brain is likely to lead to a " depression of the vital functions "—a state of affairs known to First Aiders as "'shock."

Shock occurs in a number of conditions, but is always due to a failure of the supply of blood to the vital functions of the brain for one reason or another. Its usual causes are:

(1) haemorrhage, when there is a general shortage, but the brain feels it most;

(2) severe burns, in which much fluid is lost from the blood as will be seen later; and

(3) certain medical conditions causing acute heart failure in which there is a failure to pump blood to the brain because the pump has failed.

The treatment for shock consists basically of restoring the blood supply to the brain, and where it is caused by loss of blood or other fluid, the treatment is transfusion. Finally, it must be emphasised that treatment is always urgent, since the brain cannot function for long without its blood supply, and once damaged by the shortage, can never be repaired. No attempt is made here to describe such treatment completely, but the most important things are to keep the head low so as to reduce the work the heart must do to drive blood to the brain; and to avoid artificial heating of the body by hot water bottles, etc., which only diverts blood away from the brain where it is needed, into the skin where it is not.

The treatment of severe haemorrhage is to stop the bleeding, usually by firm, direct pressure, and then to remember above all things that even though the bleeding has stopped, there may be a dangerous state of shock from which the patient could die. This can only be prevented by restoring the circulation to the brain, usually by transfusion; so, having stopped the bleeding drive him fast to hospital for the second part of the treatment which may be as necessary to save his life as the first.

There is great confusion over the use of the word " shock." In the lay mind it is a shake-up of the nervous system caused by a fright, or some bad news, or the sight of something nasty in the woodshed. Even in the medical mind it is sometimes confused, and some of the First Aid books confuse it still further. Too frequently they give the treatment as " loosen all tight clothing from neck, chest, and waist; reassure the casualty and ensure a good supply of air." All this, together with grandmother's hot strong sweet tea is perfectly good enough if the patient is only " shaken-up " by a fright or a fall, but it will be dangerously negligent and time-wasting if he is suffering from true shock due to a failure of blood supply to the brain.

Fainting is a special case which can be prevented by keeping the head low in those who feel faint. It is usually self-curing due to the patient automatically falling into a position in which the head is low. If the faint, however, is due to severe blood loss, this is the same as shock in our proper meaning of the word and must be treated accordingly.

Haemorrhage can therefore be a difficult problem. It is even more so when it is internal. This may be in *medical* cases such as in occasional cases of peptic ulceration in which the blood will be vomited and also passed in the stool. Or it may be *surgical*, in the sense of being caused by injury to internal organs. The blood may emerge from one or other of the various orifices of the body, or it may be entirely concealed within the body. Rupture of internal abdominal organs such as the spleen, kidney and liver can occur with surprisingly little to show in the way of external injury. A fractured thigh bone can pierce the main artery of the leg and cause lethal internal haemorrhage without a drop of blood being visible. In all these cases diagnosis is urgent, followed by emergency blood transfusion if the brain, and hence the patient's life, is to be saved.

Means of detecting the presence of severe haemorrhage without seeing any blood are taught in First Aid Classes as the Signs of Haemorrhage. They are in fact manifestations of the reactions of the body in its attempts to save the failing brain, and are therefore the same as the signs of shock. The main ones are a rapid, feeble pulse, getting more rapid and more feeble as time goes on in a desperate attempt to get the remaining blood to the brain; skin pallor caused by constriction of blood vessels near the surface so that the blood which remains is shunted to the brain away from the less vulnerable skin; and finally, just before death, restlessness and air hunger.

A word of warning about the First Aid treatment of shock due to heart attack (coronary thrombosis). These patients must be transported at complete rest, but many of them react very badly to being made to lie down, since they have great difficulty in breathing in this position. Transport them relaxed, in a sitting position, supported by a large comfortable back rest.

It cannot be too strongly emphasised that with haemorrhage and shock, as with so many First Aid emergencies, the importance of protecting the brain is paramount.

Asphyxia.

The previous section was concerned with maintaining an adequate supply of blood to the brain. This is needed in order to supply the brain's only possible fuel—glucose—and the oxygen with which to burn it. Many different circumstances can conspire to reduce the oxygen content of the blood, and the result in each case is asphyxia. Normally, air is taken into the lungs through the air passages and brought into contact with all the circulating blood. It diffuses from the lungs into the blood, where it enters into a special relationship with the pigment of the red cells—haemoglobin. At the same time, the waste gas carbon dioxide enters the lungs from the blood and is breathed out. The revitalised blood is passed through the heart to build up sufficient pressure to drive it into all the tissues of the body, and in particular into the brain. A special system in the brain—the respiratory centre—controls the complicated machinery of respiration and is itself, of course, kept alive by the products of the very mechanism it controls. This mechanism consists of all the muscles of respiration—those which lift the ribs, the diaphragm and many other so-called accessory muscles. They all have to be finely co-ordinated by means of nerve impulses which begin in the brain, pass down the spinal cord and out to the muscles. Information of many kinds comes along sensory nerve pathways to the respiratory centre so that breathing can be automatically adjusted to the changing needs of the moment. In order that life may continue there must be:

(1) a functioning breathing mechanism to revitalise the blood; and

(2) a circulation to carry the revitalised blood to the brain and other tissues.

In many cases when breathing stops and unconsciousness supervenes as brain function is depressed, the heart will go on beating for some time longer. The aim of First Aid is to restore the breathing by artificial respiration *before the heart stops*. Once the heart stops—and it eventually does so abruptly and without warning—the brain is dead within the usual few minutes unless *both* the heart and the breathing are restarted; and this is a very much more difficult proposition than artificial respiration alone.

For these reasons, a patient whose breathing has stopped must have it started again without any delay. Here, as in the case of severe haemorrhage, it is no use telephoning the doctor or even putting the patient in an ambulance. The First Aider must act himself, because he is on the spot and the only one in a position to save life. Both actions require elementary First Aid training, and even school children can accomplish them if they have been well taught.

Asphyxia is the name given to a failure of the oxygen supply to the brain and is due to a breakdown in some part of the complicated breathing mechanism outlined above. One of its chief causes is a blockage of the airway by (*a*) solids or (*b*) liquids. Any foreign body of the right shape and size will block the airway, as also will the tongue in the unconscious patient. Remember how much more easily the child's airway can become blocked because it is so much smaller. Blockage by a liquid, is of course, drowning. Remember that if a patient drowns in the entire ocean, it is only about half a cupful which is doing him any harm—as it only takes this amount to fill the airway. The same goes for the amount of tea, or vomit, required to kill an unconscious patient if it gets down the "wrong way"—as it will unless someone prevents it.

Another very common cause of asphyxia is carbon monoxide poisoning. Carbon monoxide is a lethal component of car exhaust fumes, incompletely burning and badly ventilated fires and stoves, and domestic coal gas. One of the inconvenient properties of haemoglobin is that it combines with carbon monoxide very much more eagerly than with oxygen. Prolonged contact with even a very slightly contaminated atmosphere can build up a concentration of carbon monoxide in the blood which will prevent the blood from carrying sufficient oxygen—and this is in fact how it kills. It takes a very short time for this to happen if the atmosphere is heavily contaminated. Remember the danger of even a very slight leak of the gas either in the kitchen, or into a car from a faulty exhaust pipe or silencer. Many elderly people die of coal gas poisoning every day because their sense of smell is poor and they do not detect the leak.

Other causes of asphyxia are lack of oxygen in the atmosphere, as occurs at high altitudes; crushing of the chest so that the ribs cannot move; paralysis of the muscles of breathing by interference with their nerve supply, usually in First Aid, as a result of a broken neck and consequent damage to the spinal cord (poliomyelitis can occasionally produce the same effect by attacking the nerves just before they leave the spine); and depressing the respiratory centre in the brain, most commonly nowadays by barbiturate poisoning.

The only really effective method of artificial respiration, which all members of any civilised community should be able to carry out, can be learned in half an hour at a good First Aid class. This is the direct, mouth-to-mouth method, sometimes dramatised by journalists as the "kiss of life." The method is taught with the aid of models and cannot be satisfactorily learned by only reading about it.

In discussing asphyxia, we have again had to consider the particularly vulnerable situation of the brain.

Fractures.

Broken bones are not the most serious possible consequences of injuries causing fractures. It is usually more to be feared that further damage will be done by the broken ends of the bones to tissues and organs in the neighbourhood of the fracture. The First Aid treatment of immobilising the part before transporting the casualty is designed to avoid this.

Six types of fracture are commonly taught, but some of them may co-exist in the same injury and the division is only for descriptive purposes. In addition there are two special fractures of the skull.

A "simple" or "closed" fracture is where only the bone is broken, without damage to surrounding tissues and without a wound. A "compound" or "open" fracture is one in which air, and hence germs, can get at the broken bone. This may be through a wound, in whose depths lies the broken bone; or the bone may have been pushed out through the skin; or a bullet track may lead down to the fracture. All these are examples of compound fracture and the great danger is that the bone will become infected. Even now that infections are less feared than before the days of antibiotics, it is still a grave matter for bone to get infected. However the antibiotic is given, we rely on the blood supply to carry it into the infected tissue, and bone has only a very small blood supply. If the infection is not successfully treated it can smoulder for a long time and become a "chronic osteomyelitis" which might ultimately necessitate amputation of the limb—and all because the original fracture was compound or open.

A "complicated" fracture is one in which the broken ends of the bone have damaged some important organ or tissue in the region. For example, a complicated fracture of the ribs is one in which the lung tissue, close behind the inner surface of the rib, has been pierced, and the patient will be coughing up small amounts of bright red, frothy blood. A "comminuted" fracture is one where the bone is broken into several pieces, and an "impacted" fracture is one in which the broken ends have been driven into each other and are firmly impacted. Finally a "greenstick" fracture occurs sometimes in children because their bones are not brittle and do not always break clean across. They partly break like a green stick.

"Depressed" fracture of the skull is where the vault of the skull has been struck and dinted. Many problems arise, since the brain is inevitably compressed and no dressing of the accompanying wound should be allowed to press on the brain. The dangers of infection here are not only to the broken bone, but to the meninges covering the brain, causing meningitis.

Fractured base of skull often passes through that part of the base through which the internal ear channel runs. Thus it frequently results in blood, or cerebrospinal fluid, or a mixture of both, emerging from the ear. The gravity of this fracture lies in the severity of the impact necessary to produce it, which will probably have also caused great destruction of delicate brain tissue. The outlook is usually very poor.

Remember that most casualties with fractures will require a general anaesthetic on arrival in hospital so that their fracture can be set in plaster or otherwise treated. Avoid giving them things by mouth such as drinks, which will mean a three-hour wait before anaesthetic can be administered.

Burns and Scalds.

The severity of a burn or scald depends largely on its surface area. If a patient dies of a burn, the cause of death is either infection or shock, the latter being due to fluid loss from the surface. Both hazards depend on surface area, since the bigger the surface the more germs are able to enter, and the more fluid can be lost. It follows that the small burn on the hand or arm is seldom a threat to life, however deep the injury; and we shall therefore confine our attention to the larger burns of the whole surface of the limb or trunk. Smaller bodies have a relatively larger surface area, and so a burn of the surface of a child's limb or trunk represents an even greater risk from fluid loss than a corresponding burn in the adult. Everyone has seen the fluid form in the blister of an ordinary small burn. It comes from the fluid part or " plasma " of the blood stream and the loss into such a blister may amount to a thimbleful. This will not hurt anyone. But the loss of similar fluid from the surface of a large burn may amount to many pints. The resultant shock will be partly due to this fluid loss from the blood stream resulting in a reduction in blood supply to the brain. Thus shock from burns has common features with shock from haemorrhage, and it is treated similarly, by transfusion. This time it is not a transfusion of blood but of plasma or some plasma substitute. In practice it is not only water that has been lost but a number of important chemicals dissolved in it as well, so that transfusion solutions have to contain sufficient of each individual substance to restore the deficit. The arrangements for replacing the lost materials are complex and urgent; every bit as urgent as after a haemorrhage and for the same reason. The brain cannot be left too long in need. In general, the First Aid treatment of burns of large surface area is to keep them clean with a dry dressing and get them very quickly to hospital. Life-saving treatment by transfusion cannot start until they arrive. The only permissible delay is in the case of burns caused by corrosive chemicals which must be thoroughly washed off before transport, so that they do not continue to burn the patient on the way.

Unconsciousness.

It is not sufficiently appreciated that the dangers of being unconscious can often far outweigh the dangers from the cause of the unconsciousness. For example it is known that as many as half the deaths from head injuries are due to the airway becoming obstructed and not to the injury itself. The most important thing in managing the unconscious patient from any cause is to preserve an airway. Particularly if the patient is lying on his back it is likely to get blocked:

    (a) by his own tongue as the lower jaw sags backwards;

    (b) by his dentures (so remove them);

    (c) by vomit; and

    (d) by anything anyone may be tempted to give him by mouth.

Nothing whatever should be given by mouth in any circumstances to the unconscious patient, since he cannot swallow and it will inevitably go into his lungs.

Many of these dangers can be very much reduced by not having him on his back. Place him instead in the semi-prone position: half on his side, half on his front, with the upper leg drawn up to prevent him from rolling about. In this position the head will be inclined downwards. The jaw will tend to sag forwards and the tongue with it, away from the back of the throat. Any vomit will also come forwards. If the tongue does get in the way of the breathing the airway can usually be cleared by bending the head backwards as far as it will go and pushing the whole lower jaw forwards, by pushing from behind the angle of the jaw on both sides.

DRUG ABUSE AND DRUG DEPENDENCE.

This section of earlier editions of *Pears* was simply called " Addiction." This word is still much used, but is gradually being replaced by the terms in the present title, because ideas about the nature of the problem and methods of dealing with it are changing. Addiction is a word that conjures up rather 19th century ideas in the minds of readers: opium dens, inscrutable orientals, Sherlock Holmes injecting himself with cocaine— basically a phenomenon of foreign origin, rather frightening if its implications were not literary rather than factual, and not of great significance in Great Britain.

Drug Abuse.

It is now realised by doctors, research scientists, social workers, and the police—if still not by society as a whole—that the truth is quite different. The *abuse* of drugs in this country is at present of large proportions, increasing rapidly and showing no signs of diminishing. It is responsible each year for thousands of deaths by suicide and by accidental overdosage; for an enormous but virtually unmeasurable amount of private suffering; and for the loss to society, in terms of reduced working efficiency, of millions of man-hours every year. It has nothing to do with opium smoking which was never in any case more than the eccentricity of the few. Opium is virtually unused in medicine these days and the amount of smuggling, always small, is now negligible. The problems today arise chiefly from the misuse of drugs given by doctors for their effects on the central nervous system—the pain-killers, sleeping pills, " stimulants," and " tranquillisers."

Drugs and Medicines.

To the doctor, any substance is a drug that can be introduced into the body from outside, and that is capable of producing some detectable effect. Most such substances have a beneficial use. They are " medicines," and as such are given by doctors in suitable cases. Others, for example, nicotine (in cigarettes), alcohol (in beer, wine, or spirits), and carbon monoxide (in coal gas), are of doubtful benefit and of certain harm and are used by doctors, if at all, only under certain very special and usually experimental conditions.

Medicines may be classified under four main headings. First, there are those like quinine, or penicillin and other so-called antibiotics, that actually cure diseases by eradicating the organism (bacteria or other parasites) that cause disturbance of normal bodily function. Second, drugs such as insulin or the steroids overcome in the unhealthy the lack of some necessary substance a healthy body manufactures for itself: they must usually continue to be given for life. Third are the drugs which relieve the signs of disease—for example, there are many new drugs that lower the blood pressure or increase the output of urine—without being able to put right the disturbed basic situation which is the cause of the trouble. Fourth are drugs to relieve the patient's symptoms—which make him feel better, less breathless, take away his pain, help him to sleep, and so on—although we seldom know why they are able to do this. Indeed, in many cases we suspect that they are acting mainly as a token of help from doctor to patient, and so encouraging his body to fight a more successful battle on its own behalf. (There is in fact a fifth class of drugs, which includes the majority of those on the market at any time, the members of which are devoid of any action whatsoever except that of enriching those who manufacture and sell them; but we are not concerned with these at the moment. They constitute a related, but different, kind of problem.)

There is no doubt that the genuine advances in beneficial drugs during the last thirty years have been enormous; but the very successes of the penicillins, tetracyclines, antimalarials, hormones, and so on have bred in the public and in the medical profession itself an attitude of uncritical wonder. There have been relatively few drugs in the first and second categories mentioned above: and in the field of mental health, the importance of which is now so rightly emphasised, there are virtually none. Yet drugs which act upon the brain are often received as if they were curative although they may pose fresh problems rather than solve the old. Thus, although there are many drugs which act upon the mind, few do this in any fundamental sense: they relieve pain and anxiety, bring sleep and lessening of stress, and may allow the patient to recuperate himself during the relief they provide. But often this deeper change does not occur—sometimes because the doctor has not clearly seen his part in helping to bring it about—and then the symptomatic relief may come to be sought for its own sake.

New and old drugs are still prescribed for their effects upon the mind—less so now than even a few years ago, before the thalidomide disaster—without sufficient attention to possible long-term dangers, of which there are in effect four.

Dangers of Long-term Medication with Drugs acting on the Brain.

1. *Toxic effects.* Drugs which act upon the nervous system, like any others, have characteristic toxic or unwanted effects of their own (incidentally, these may become apparent rapidly; even, on rare occasions, after only a single dose). Such effects may have little or nothing to do with the desired effects for which they are being prescribed and taken. For example, it has only come to be realised quite recently that aspirin is liable to cause bleeding, which is occasionally serious, from the lining of the stomach in a large proportion of people who take aspirin regularly; or that phenacetin, another substance very frequently present in pain-killers that can be bought from chemists without prescription, leads (after prolonged use) to kidney damage. Some drugs may cause rashes and other allergic reactions in susceptible subjects; and jaundice, fainting, tremors, and motor disorders are known to occur in some patients taking a variety of other drugs.

2. "*Rebound.*" The body works in such a way, over a variety of its activities, that it tends to return to a "neutral" position after it has departed from this for any reason. For example, over-eating tends to be followed by a lessening of appetite, at least for a time; the runner makes up for his air-deficit during the race by breathing more deeply thereafter; and if, at rest, you breathe for a time more rapidly and deeply than you need, this period will be followed by one in which you breathe *less* often than usual until the balance is restored. These illustrations—and there are others—have nothing to do with drugs: but in a similar way, it seems that if a continued pain, or an unpleasant emotional state such as anxiety or depression is changed into its opposite, or removed altogether by the use of a drug, the prior state may return with increased force when the drug is no longer taken. The "rebound" phenomenon, naturally, encourages the patient to take another dose, and so on.

3. *Habit formation.* This alternation of mood-changed-by-drug with the disturbed mood itself leads to the habit of taking the drug. The patient comes to rely upon it and to take it anyway, even before the unpleasant state has returned. At this stage he is said to be "habituated": he has a psychological need for the drug, and later may become disturbed at the possibility that it will not be available when he needs it. This might not matter so greatly, if it were not that continued use of drugs in this way has physical consequences as well.

4. *Tolerance and habituation.* The body also tends to restore its own balance when drugs are given, too. It "learns" surprisingly quickly how to deal with substances with which it has never before been confronted, so that it eliminates subsequent doses more and more quickly and completely. Thus the effect of each successive dose is smaller and lasts for progressively shorter periods of time. To counter this, the patient tends to increase the dose; and the vicious circle continues. At this point he has become physically dependent upon the drug: and he may suffer physically—sometimes so severely that he dies—if supplies are not continued.

As he increases the dose in this way, so his tolerance of its effects increases, to such an extent that after prolonged use he may be taking doses of a drug that are five or ten times greater than those which will kill somebody not dependent upon them in this way. It sometimes happens that a patient develops a renewed craving at some point after a course of treatment, in which the dose of drug has been reduced without removing the underlying cause of his dependence. He may then obtain and use the dose he habitually took before treatment, not knowing that his body will have lost its tolerance of such doses. That dose is now as high for him as for any other person and so may be lethal. There has been a number of deaths for this reason.

Factors in the Causation of Dependence.

The risk of becoming dependent upon a drug is governed by three main factors: the drug itself, the personality of the individual who takes it, and the circumstances in which it is taken. Most adults have taken alcohol at one time or another, unless it is against their code to do so; yet *relatively* few are dependent upon it (relatively few, but many too many: perhaps half a million in the United Kingdom alone). Many of us have had morphine or some other strong pain-killer for medical reasons, without becoming dependent upon it (whatever so-called addicts say, it is extremely rare for anyone to become dependent on an opiate because he was introduced to it in a medical setting. On the other hand, if we start to take such a drug "for kicks"—as more and more people, particularly teen-agers and young adults are doing—it is extremely probable that we shall become dependent upon it, and sooner rather than later at that. It is also probable that each one of us would become dependent, were he obliged to take it regularly, for long enough, and in sufficient dosage. Thus, although there are personalities—psychopathic, immature, or unstable—that are more prone than others to become dependent if they are exposed to the drug, there are also drugs that are more likely than others to cause such dependence no matter to whom they are given. The extent of the dependence will vary: with some, it is never physiological but remains psychological (but not the less real or disturbing for that). Also, the rate at which dependence develops may vary; and the picture presented by the dependent subject—the extent to which his normal life is impaired, or to which he becomes dangerous to himself or others—varies as well. In a very much oversimplified way, some of these relationships will now be summarised for certain substances.

Heroin, morphine and cocaine are usually injected. Barbiturates (sleeping pills) and Amphetamine ("Benzedrine") are tablets or capsules, and Marihuana ("reefers," hashish) is smoked in cigarettes. Heroin and cocaine are now usually taken together. Combinations of drugs often act differently from their individual constituents and patients dependent upon them are even more difficult to treat. Barbiturate and amphetamine, also, are often mixed (as in "purple hearts"). There is considerable *psychological* dependence on heroin, morphine, cocaine, and amphetamine, but much less with marihuana. *Physiological* dependence is great with heroin and morphine, less with barbiturates, alcohol, and amphetamine in that order, and virtually nil with cocaine and marihuana. Personality plays a greater part in initiating dependence on alcohol, marihuana, and barbiturates than with the others. Heroin, cocaine, and morphine are the cause of more antisocial tendencies in dependent people than alcohol, barbiturates, and amphetamine. The chief danger of marihuana (mere possession of which is illegal) seems to be that the search for it will lead the searcher into localities where his risk of exposure to even more dangerous influences is greatly increased. It is thus sometimes argued that if it were legal to consume marihuana, the number of young people who yearly become dependent upon the other more dangerous drugs would in fact decrease. There is as yet no evidence for or against this proposition. The number of drug dependent people in U.K. is rising fast for heroin and cocaine. This number is very large for alcohol, and is increasing in the case of barbiturates and marihuana. Very few people are dependent on morphine, and the number is not growing.

Treatment.

Exhortations, imprisonment, and other moralistic or legalistic approaches are useless. Treatment of any person dependent upon a drug is a matter for a qualified psychotherapist. It is liable to be time-consuming and frustrating for patient and doctor, and it is frequently unsuccessful. At present, there are too few specialists or centres where treatment can be obtained, although it is to be hoped that this situation will change as the problem is increasingly seen by our society to be of exceptional gravity.

When there is little or no chance of cure, prevention is certainly the best treatment. Drugs should only be taken on the prescription of a doctor; and the patient should remind him from time to time, if this be necessary, that he would like to dispense with his drugs as soon as the doctor thinks it possible. It should also be remembered that there is often no need to reach for the aspirin (or any other drug that anyone can buy from the chemist without prescription) at the first sign of a headache—or to reach for it at all to help one sleep or relax, for which purpose such drugs are in any case pharmacologically useless. A wait for ten minutes is good discipline, and will frequently resolve the problem to an extent that makes a drug unnecessary.

DISEASES OF THE BLOOD

INTRODUCTION.

There are about eight or ten pints of blood in the adult human body. Its main function is to transport nutrient materials to all the various tissues and to carry waste products of tissue activity to organs such as the lungs, kidneys, and liver for disposal. It also helps to maintain a constant chemical environment for the body cells, some of which would be very disturbed in their function if the correct balance of organic and inorganic chemicals were not maintained. The blood also serves a protective function in fighting disease, either with certain of the white cells, or by means of immune antibodies dissolved and carried in the plasma.

A little more than half the volume of blood is the fluid plasma, in which are dissolved all the nutrient materials, organic and inorganic chemicals, hormones and large quantities of protein. The remainder consists of red cells, white cells, and some particles which are not really cells, called platelets. In every cubic millimetre of whole blood, or in every droplet the size of a pin head, there are about 5 million red cells, between 5,000 and 10,000 white cells, and 200,000 platelets as well as half a cubic millilitre of plasma. The red cells suffer a great deal of wear and tear as they are hurled round the circulation, and they only survive for three or four months. There is a red cell factory in the bone marrow which replaces them at exactly the rate they are destroyed, and you have made very many millions of new ones while you have been reading this single paragraph. The function of the red cells is to carry the oxygen from the lungs to the tissues, and to play an important part in carrying the waste gas, carbon dioxide, in the reverse direction. A shortage of red cells, and hence of their oxygen-carrying pigment, haemoglobin, is called anaemia; an excess is called polycythaemia.

There are five kinds of white cells or leucocytes: neutrophils (or polymorphonuclear leucocytes), eosinophils, basophils, lymphocytes, and mono-

cytes. The first three are quite actively motile, like amœbæ, and are capable of ingesting bacteria and other particles by " phagocytosis." There is a great increase in the number of neutrophils (a leucocytosis) during bacterial infections and other inflammatory conditions like appendicitis. Eosinophils are found in larger numbers than usual in allergic conditions like asthma, and in infestations by worms and other parasites, but we do not know why this should be. Lymphocytes are concerned with the manufacture of antibodies. In some infections, particularly tuberculosis and viral infections, there are fewer white cells than usual (leucopenia). Pus consists of the dissolved remnants of inflamed tissue and many dead neutrophils which have become casualties in the battle against infection. It also contains surviving bacteria, and as such is a source of further infection.

Platelets are curious particles, smaller than any of the cells. They are little pieces broken off certain special bone-marrow cells which produce them. They have a role in the stemming of blood loss after injury, partly because they are sticky and adhere to one another and to broken blood vessels and help to plug the open ends of damaged vessels; and partly because they contain a great deal of a substance (thrombokinase) which is necessary to the clotting mechanism of the blood.

Hæmatology, as the study of blood and its diseases is called, is a very complicated subject and only a brief general account will be given here. Diagnosis is usually made by taking small samples of blood (or of the bone marrow where blood cells are made), counting the numbers of the different cells and examining their appearance under the microscope. We shall briefly consider the main diseases involving red cells, white cells, and platelets.

Red Cell Diseases.

These are of two main groups leading to a shortage of red cells (anæmia), or an excess (polycythæmia). The former is much the more common and there are many different kinds. In all of them the shortage of red cells results in a depletion of the capacity of the blood to carry oxygen. This means that the heart must work harder to send more blood than usual to the tissues, and even so the tissues will often go short. The patient will be persistently tired and listless, and if the anæmia is severe the action of the brain and heart will be seriously impeded, even leading to fainting, cardiac pain, and breathlessness on exertion. All these symptoms, however, can be caused by many other conditions. The only way to be sure they are due to anæmia is by a proper examination of the blood, and even this will not lead to the truth if the picture has been spoilt by the patient taking iron tonics and other remedies of his own accord. Therefore do not dose yourself with tonics, in case you really have anæmia. You may make it impossible to arrive at a proper diagnosis later.

Hæmorrhagic Anæmia. Anæmia, a shortage of red cells, may be due to a variety of causes, singly or in combination. One very obvious cause is loss of blood, or hæmorrhage. Following the sudden loss of a pint or two of blood or more, the red-cell-producing bone marrow " factory " will step up its production; but even if it is adequately supplied with all the raw materials such as iron, it may well take many weeks to build up the numbers to normal. A very severe degree of hæmorrhagic anæmia is usually treated by blood transfusion. Milder degrees can be treated by taking extra iron, often over a long period of time. The supply of iron for making new red-cell pigment is nearly always the bottle-neck which limits production. Hæmorrhagic anæmia can commonly occur, however, without a sudden severe hæmorrhage. From what has been said about the constant replacement of red cells as they wear out, it must be obvious that even if there is only a slight failure to keep pace with the numbers lost, several months of such a failure can eventually deplete the numbers to the level of very severe anæmia. This situation is common when small amounts of blood are being continuously or repeatedly lost, and here again it is a shortage of dietary iron which is the usual cause of the failure to replace the lost red cells. Normal menstrual loss in women and girls whose diet is on the border-line of iron deficiency is a common cause of progressive tiredness and lack of energy. Where the menstrual flow is heavier than usual, or where it is frankly excessive in older women due to the various common gynæcological disorders, serious anæmia is surprisingly common. During pregnancy a great deal of iron is lost by the mother to the baby, and this, together with the inevitable blood loss at delivery, often makes for a very tired mother indeed, just at the time when there is an enormous amount of work to be done to manufacture milk and attend to all the extra household tasks of baby care. For these reasons it is almost routinely advisable to build up stocks of iron throughout the pregnancy by remembering to take the pills provided. Men as well as women can lose small amounts of blood continuously in later life from gastro-intestinal conditions such as piles, ulcers, and tropical infestations such as hookworm; and here again the anæmia may be just as severe in the long run as that which inevitably follows a sudden, massive hæmorrhage. One extra word of warning. Do not assume because you are pale that you are anæmic. Pallor is a very poor guide, because it is dependent on so many other things, like the blood vessels in your skin, and its thickness and translucency. Nothing but a blood test (which is so easy for your doctor to do) can really tell you if you are anæmic. And if your anæmia is due to a blood-losing condition, then that too must be treated. So do not be tempted to treat yourself, and never delay seeing your doctor about any excessive or unexplained bleeding, from any source.

Hæmolytic Anæmia occurs when for any reason, there are more blood cells than usual being destroyed in the body. This may be because the cells are abnormally fragile, or because normal cells have been attacked by something to which you are allergic, or rarely because you have become sensitive to your own red cells. Sometimes unborn babies have severe hæmolytic anæmia, due to an incompatability of blood group (Rh factor) between the mother and the baby, and the same sort of thing happens if incompatible blood is given by mistake in blood transfusion. Up to a point, in mild hæmolytic anæmia, the bone marrow can keep pace with the increased loss of cells, but beyond this point anæmia develops. After incompatible blood transfusions a very dangerous situation results from the effects of the destruction of red cells and the liberation of their products into the blood. One form of jaundice is often produced in hæmolytic anæmia, the patient becoming yellow because of the breakdown products of red cells circulating in excess as bile pigments. These latter are normally always present to a small extent due to the normal, comparatively small, rate of destruction of effete red cells

Aplastic Anæmia is the term given to anæmia due to a virtually total failure of the bone marrow red-cell factory. Sometimes this occurs for no obvious reason. It is sometimes due to a heavy dose of radioactivity or X-rays knocking out the cells of the "factory." It may even be due to cancer cells growing in the bone marrow cavity and not leaving sufficient room for the red marrow cells. It is fortunate that aplastic anæmia is very rare, because it can only be treated by blood transfusions every few weeks for the rest of the patient's life. Very occasionally there have been exceptions to this rule, when the patient's marrow has re-awakened for no apparent reason and suddenly begins to make red cells again.

Pernicious Anæmia. This is a fairly uncommon anæmia, which has a very interesting story. The processes by which red cells are manufactured are many and complex, and depend, like so many other bodily activities, on the supply of a vitamin containing cobalt, called vitamin B_{12}. This is nearly always present in more than adequate quantities in the diet, but in order for it to be absorbed from the intestine, there must also be a substance called "intrinsic factor" which is normally made by the lining of the stomach. People with pernicious anæmia have suffered a degeneration of the lining of their stomachs, probably because, for some reason, they have become "sensitive" to this part of their own tissue. This kind of civil war within the body is known as an "auto-immune" disease, and is comparable in type with some forms of hæmolytic anæmia. In other words they destroy their own stomach lining, fail to produce "intrinsic factor," and as a result fail to absorb vitamin B_{12} into the body. Faced with a failure in the supply of this essential substance, the bone marrow produces too few red cells, and the few that are produced are deformed, much too large, and very fragile. In addition to its role in blood formation, vitamin B_{12} is essential to the normal functioning of the spinal cord, and in long-standing cases of untreated pernicious anæmia, there is often a resulting neurological disability.

The cure for pernicious anæmia was discovered about forty years ago, and is a triumph for the scientific investigation of the causes of disease. While treating anæmic dogs, an American scientist named Minot discovered that eating raw liver in large quantities produced a tremendous improvement. Patients with pernicious anæmia were then made to eat vast quantities of raw liver—about one or two pounds a day—and were found to get better, whereas previously they had inevitably died. Raw liver is, of course, very unpleasant to eat, and after a few years it was found possible to prepare crude extracts for injection. Injection had the great advantage that no absorption difficulties arose, and much less liver could be used. Biochemists then began the enormous task of trying to find which of the thousands of substances in liver was the vital factor, and after many years of painstaking chemical fractionation of liver and trying out the various fractions as a cure for the disease, vitamin B_{12} was discovered. The pure substance is one of the most powerful substances known, being active in amounts as small as millionths of a gram. Nowadays pernicious anæmia is treated by small occasional injections of the vitamin, whose other name is cyanocobalamin.

Polycythæmia. Too many red cells per cubic millilitre of blood can be found without there being an increase of the total number of red cells in the body. This occurs in dehydration, when there is a loss of plasma without a comparable loss of cells, and is called hæmo-concentration. Alternatively, the bone marrow can manufacture more cells than usual as a response to living for long periods at high altitudes. The beneficial result can be that the blood can carry normal amounts of oxygen, even though the supply (in the rarefied air) is reduced. Finally there is a red cell disease, analagous to leukæmia (*q.v.*) in which the bone marrow factory gets out of control and produces too many cells with no beneficial results. The number in the blood can be double the normal and the blood becomes so thick that the heart has difficulty pumping it round the body. This disease (*polycythæmia rubra vera*) used to be treated by repeatedly bleeding the patient to reduce the numbers. It is now treated very successfully with carefully judged amounts of radioactive phosphorus or certain other "antimitotic" chemicals which reduce the rate of multiplication of bone marrow cells. Care has to be taken not to knock them out altogether, in which case aplastic anæmia or agranulocytosis (*q.v*) could result.

White Cell Diseases.

These are fortunately much rarer than diseases involving red cells, and are usually much more to be feared.

Agranulocytosis. In this condition the number of those white cells which are responsible for phagocytosis of bacteria falls precipitously. The result is that one of the main bodily defences against infection fails, and the patient may die from an overwhelming invasion of germs and the accompanying high fever. The usual cause is abnormal sensitivity to certain drugs, often those which are in widespread use and only give trouble in the occasional case. One example among hundreds is the antibiotic chloramphenicol which specifically kills typhoid bacteria and is used for that purpose. It is believed that about one case in 60,000 becomes sensitive to it and agranulocytosis often fatally follows. The fact that almost any drug *can* do this to some people and yet be quite safe for the majority, is one good reason not to dose yourself unnecessarily with over-the-counter medicines.

Leukæmia. This is a cancer of the white cells, in which the normal rate of production of any of the white cells gets out of control, leading to a pile-up of abnormal cells at the site of production (bone marrow, lymph nodes, and spleen) or in the blood, or both. In spite of an increase in their numbers, their abnormality renders them unable to combat infection; sepsis and fever result. It is known that this kind of cancer can be caused by the effects of ionizing radiation on the white-cell factory, and it is certain at least in animals, that viruses can also be responsible. Survivors from the atomic explosions in Japan have subsequently suffered from leukæmia far more commonly than the rest of us, as have doctors, nurses, and patients who have been over-exposed to X-rays. At the time of writing, leukæmia is still a uniformly fatal disease, although patients may sometimes survive many years. Their remaining time can nearly always be made more comfortable by various forms of treatment, and one day a cure will be found by the research workers devoting their time to its study. It is difficult not to get very impatient with the slow rate of progress of these studies, particularly when caring for children and young people whose lives are inevitably ended by the disease. The solution, however, as with other forms of cancer, probably depends on the understanding of the nature of life itself, and as long as biological research remains short of the relatively small amounts of money required to tackle these problems at reasonable speed, we have no right to be impatient, except with our elected leaders who spend far more than is needed on less important things.

Hodgkin's Disease, Lymphosarcoma, and Reti-culosarcoma. These are cancerous diseases in many ways similar to leukæmia, in which the cancer process involves cells of the so-called reticulo-endothelial system. Such cells are principally in lymph nodes (which used to be called lymph glands) and the spleen. Hodgkin's disease is named after one of the more illustrious pathologists at Guy's Hospital who first described it nearly a hundred years ago, and whose early specimens of affected lymph nodes are still preserved there; is an even greater puzzle than leukæmia. There are all grades of severity, and although many patients die within six months, many survive much longer, even for twenty years in some cases.

Hæmorrhagic or Bleeding Diseases.

Whenever blood vessels are damaged by injury, there is a remarkable series of mechanisms which automatically come into operation to stem the flow of blood. There is a constriction of all the smaller vessels in the locality. Platelets stick together and release substances which help the vessels to stay constricted as well as others necessary to blood clotting, and yet others which help to bind the clot tightly together. Later, materials appear to prevent too much clotting, and eventually the clot is removed altogether as healing proceeds. There are some very complicated diseases of this blood-conserving mechanism which can lead to abnormal bleeding, sometimes beneath the skin to produce bruising or even smaller leaks; sometimes leading to a greater loss of blood, particularly following a wound. In some kinds of *purpura* (bleeding tendency) the blood vessels are the cause of the trouble, having become fragile and leaky for a number of reasons. This happens in old age (*senile purpura*), in scurvy, or vitamin C deficiency, as an occasional accompaniment to infective diseases, or as an immunological effect on the lining of blood vessels when the patient becomes sensitised to certain substances (*Schönlein-Henoch* or *anaphylactoid purpura*). The latter often follows a streptococcal sore throat, just as rheumatic fever and acute nephritis do; and as well as the purpura there may be joint pains and nephritis. Just as almost any drug or chemical will cause agranulocytosis in some people, so it can also cause anaphylactoid purpura.

Purpura may also be due to a lack of platelets, known as thrombocytopenia (a shortage of thrombocytes or platelets). This can happen if the bone marrow factory is depressed, since this is where platelets too are made. It is therefore a common accompaniment of leukæmia or aplastic anæmia. Or there can be increased destruction of platelets in some diseases of the spleen. Platelets normally last eight to ten days, but their life-span can be shortened in heart failure, and following massive transfusions, or often for no apparent reason ("idiopathic" thrombocytopenia), when removal of the spleen can sometimes help.

Finally, defects of the *clotting mechanism* will lead to a bleeding tendency, and since the mechanism itself is very complex, so is the variety of things which can upset it. The liver provides the blood with many of the substances required for clotting, so it is not surprising that a clotting defect commonly accompanies liver disease. One necessary substance for blood clotting is called "anti-hæmophilic factor" and is missing from people who have inherited the disease *hæmophilia*. These unfortunate people may die of hæmorrhage from quite small cuts or minor surgical procedures like tooth-extraction, and although it is possible to prepare antihæmophilic factor, it is not yet possible to give continuous, life-long treatment with it. In emergencies a transfusion of fresh blood (the factor is destroyed by storing) is sometimes used.

DISEASES OF THE HEART AND BLOOD-VESSELS.

INTRODUCTION.

The heart consists of about three-quarters of a pound of muscle, which makes up the walls of its four chambers. Anatomically the human heart closely resembles the sheep's hearts to be found in a butcher's shop. Indeed it would be an instructive exercise to dissect one of these in the order described below, since there is no other way of properly appreciating what the chambers, valves, etc., are really like. There are two quite separate pumps in the heart—one on the owner's right (or on your *left* if you are looking at the front of someone else), and one on his left. The right heart collects spent, deoxygenated, "venous" blood which returns there from the whole of the body, and gives it the comparatively small push required to drive it through the adjacent lungs. The left heart collects the revitalised, oxygenated "arterial" blood as it trickles away from the lungs, and gives it the enormous push required to build up the arterial blood-pressure, so that it can be forced through all the tissues of the body. As may be expected, the right heart chambers have much thinner walls than the left, since their muscle has much less work to do. This will help you get your bearings with the sheep's heart. The tip, or apex, is the lowest part. The thick-feeling side is the left, the thin the right; and the great vessels are at the top.

The upper chamber on the right, or right atrium, has two large openings into it through which all the spent blood arrives from the upper and lower great veins (the superior and inferior venae cavae). Cut open the thin wall of the right atrium with scissors between these two holes to lay open the interior of the chamber, noting the " auricle " or " dog's ear " that forms a small cul-de-sac. The whole chamber is sometimes, inaccurately, called the auricle. You should be able to push a finger downwards into the lower chamber—the right ventricle—through a communicating hole guarded by the three thin cusps of the *tricuspid valve*. These will not obstruct your finger, since they are designed to permit blood flow in the same direction. When the atrium is full of blood, it squeezes its contents through the tricuspid valve into the right ventricle; and when, a split second later, the ventricle is full and contracts, the three cusps come together to prevent the blood from flowing backwards into the atrium again. Instead the spent blood is driven onwards through the *pulmonary valve* (in the upper part of the right ventricle), through the pulmonary artery, to be delivered to the lungs. The pulmonary valve has three very well-defined cusps which prevent blood from coming back into the ventricle as it relaxes to receive more blood from the atrium before the next contraction or beat. It is possible to pass a blade of the scissors from the opened-out right atrium, through the tricuspid valve towards the tip of the heart, and cut along the right border of the heart through the thickness of the ventricular muscle. Then cut upwards again, passing the scissors blade through the pulmonary valve and open up the *pulmonary artery*. If you have done this successfully you will have followed the path taken by the spent blood through the right heart to the lungs. Notice the thick round bands of muscle lining the ventricle, and notice too that you have not entered the left heart, which has no connection with the right except in some congenital malformations (see later). The same dissection can now be made of the left heart. Open up the *left atrium*, noting its " dog's ear " or " auricle," pass the scissors down into the *left ventricle* through the two rather flimsy cusps of the *mitral valve*. Notice how much thicker is the muscle of the left ventricle, and cut upwards through the three well-formed cusps of the *aortic valve* into the main artery of the body—the aorta. The aorta as it leaves the left heart is distinguishable from the pulmonary artery as it leaves the right, partly by the extreme toughness of the aortic wall (it has to withstand so much more blood-pressure); and partly by the entrances or orifices of the two small branches given off by the aorta, just beyond the valve cusps, which go to supply the heart muscle itself with blood. These are the *coronary arteries* which are so necessary for the heart's own survival.

The amount of blood pumped in unit time, or the *cardiac output*, can be varied a great deal, according to the needs of the moment. This is accomplished by altering both the heart rate and the stroke volume, the amount expelled per beat. Every minute, the healthy adult man at rest shifts about ten pints of blood through the heart—a amount equivalent to all the blood he possesses. When exercise is taken, or in response to anxiety or fear, this is stepped up many times, so that the muscles can receive a greatly augmented supply of the materials required for action. The controlling mechanisms which allow these changes to be made automatically are partly organised in the brain by the so-called *cardiac centre*; and partly by local mechanical and chemical stimuli to the heart muscle itself. The cardiac centre is continuously receiving information through nerves about the physical and chemical state of the circulation, and also from the mind; which is partly how certain emotions make the heart beat faster. All the information is integrated, and a cardiac output continuously arranged which is appropriate for current demands.

Cardiac Neurosis. In ordinary circumstances at rest, most healthy people are not conscious of their heart-beat. However, there are many perfectly healthy people whose hearts slip in an extra beat occasionally. Sometimes their owners are aware of this, and become unnecessarily alarmed.

Their fear causes palpitations (a pounding of the heart) and the tension mounts. An undue anxiety about the tricks played by a healthy heart sometimes leads people to interpret minor pains in the chest, or even indigestion, as grave symptoms of heart disease, and the consequent anxiety leads to still worse symptoms. If you are one of these worried people, take your worries to your doctor, and let him decide for you whether there is anything wrong. A hundred to one there isn't, and then you will have to find something else to worry about, or better still give up the habit altogether. Many people secretly worry about heart disease and high blood-pressure for years, when very often they are worrying unnecessarily. Even if there is cause for worry, so much can be done for these conditions (as it can for cancer) provided medical advice is taken early in the course of the disease. Remember, too, that the slight feeling of giddiness when you get up suddenly from having been lying down, is often experienced by most normal people; but if you get frightened by it you will begin to breathe more quickly and deeply: and this in itself will make you feel even more faint—and so on.

Heart Failure. When the cardiac output of blood is too little for the requirements of the body, a state of *circulatory failure* has arisen, and when this is due primarily to the heart itself being at fault, it is more properly called *heart failure*. As will be seen, heart failure is not a disease, but the common result of a large number of different diseases. The signs and symptoms produced are caused by two sorts of process: (a) tissues of the body have too little blood flow through them and are therefore undersupplied; (b) blood accumulates and stagnates in tissues, causing congestion, since the failing heart cannot move forward the amount of blood presented to it in the great veins. Often the left or right side of the heart fails disproportionately. In *left heart failure* the lungs are congested because they are the territory from which the left heart is failing to move blood. The patient has great difficulty with his breathing, and in advanced cases may not be able to breathe when he lies down horizontally, because the lungs become so congested and waterlogged. In *right heart failure* the main veins are congested and other parts of the body become swollen with excess tissue fluid, mainly in the lower parts such as the legs and ankles. This swelling with fluid is called œdema, and in heart failure is only partly due to the mechanics of the failing heart. It is mainly due to a poorly understood retention of sodium in the body, a situation in which excess water is also retained. Whatever the type of heart failure, it is always likely to be a changing condition, since the amount of failure will depend as much on the demands being made as on the state of the heart. For instance, in mild cases at rest when the required cardiac output is small, there may be no signs or symptoms. These may only appear on exertion. Heart failure will be referred to again later under the various conditions which cause it.

Treatment of heart failure is quite logical. It is aimed at correcting the imbalance between supply and demand of blood, and at the removal of the accumulated excess fluid. We can therefore (a) reduce the body's demand for blood; (b) increase the supply or cardiac output; and (c) promote the excretion of sodium and fluid. Demand for blood is reduced by rest, both physical and mental, and by reduction of weight, since obesity (being overweight) is an additional demand on the cardiovascular system. The cardiac output can be increased by administering a " tonic " to the heart muscle in the form of *digitalis*, which is a powerful heart stimulant derived from foxglove leaf. Fluid (and hence salt) accumulation can be helped by restricting the intake of salt and by giving drugs which promote its excretion by the kidneys (diuretics). Very occasionally, very large accumulations of fluid in the legs, abdomen, or thorax, are tapped and drained physically, with needles. These remarks on treatment, as elsewhere in the Medical Section, are of course very general and must not encourage anyone to treat themselves for such a potentially serious condition as heart failure. Even such a simple measure as doing without salt can be practised quite unnecessarily by many people for years, simply as a result of reading a paragraph like the above. The most they accomplish is to make their food taste horribly dull. If you need to reduce salt intake you should be in your doctor's care, and so please let him decide.

Congenital Heart Disease. It has been estimated that of all the babies born who survive at least one month, there will be about one in every two hundred with some form of congenital heart disease; that is to say that the heart will have failed to develop properly in embryonic life. In some cases this is associated with a virus disease of the mother (commonly rubella, or German measles) or with certain drugs taken by the mother (e.g. thalidomide) at a time, very early in pregnancy, when organs are assuming their adult shape. Parents should see to it that their daughters get German measles before they grow up; and drugs of all kinds should be avoided where possible during early pregnancy. In most cases of congenital heart disease, however, there is no known cause, and it seems that the manner of formation of the embryonic heart is so delicate that it can be thrown out of gear very easily, perhaps even by chance. Scores of different types of defect occur, singly and in combination. Any of the valves may be anatomically defective—either failing to close properly (*incompetence*) or being too tight (*stenosis*); the great vessels (pulmonary artery and aorta) may be switched round, or *transposed*, so that they emerge from the wrong ventricle; there may be defects in the wall (*septum*) which separates the atria or the ventricles on each side (*septal defect*, or " hole in the heart "); or there may be a persistence of the vessel which in the foetus normally by-passes the lungs by joining the pulmonary artery to the aorta (*patent ductus arteriosus*). This vessel normally closes at the time of birth when the first breaths are taken, and subsequently disappears, so that the whole output of the heart is then sent round the lungs. Detecting congenital heart disease early is one of the purposes of routine post-natal check-up examinations of the baby. Exact diagnosis requires very complicated techniques, and sometimes the structural defect can be corrected by surgery, with almost miraculous results.

Rheumatic Heart Disease. Acute rheumatic fever is not to be confused with other forms of rheumatism. Many tissues of the body (particularly the heart) are attacked, as well as the joints, and the trouble is due to a sensitivity which has developed to certain bacteria (*haemolytic streptococci*) which have probably caused a sore throat about three weeks before the onset of the disease. Why acute rheumatism only rarely follows streptococcal sore throat is poorly understood, but this is no consolation to the one per cent or so of the population whose hearts bear its scars. During the acute phase of the illness which usually occurs before the age of fifteen, inflammatory damage occurs to the valves, the heart muscle, and the sac in which the heart lives, the *pericardium*. So there is a *valvulitis* or *endocarditis*, a *myocarditis* and a *pericarditis*. There may be acute heart failure at this stage if the heart is severely affected. The better-known results of rheumatic heart disease, however, are caused in the ensuing years by scarring of the healed valves. The valves are thickened and deformed. They may have lost their elasticity and stretch, so that they do not close properly (*incompetence*); or they may contract and tighten (*stenosis*). In both cases the heart chamber situated next to the affected valve has to work progressively harder, either because it gets no rest in between beats (in *incompetence*); or it has to force the blood through too narrow a hole (in *stenosis*). The end result is some variety of heart failure (P27). Although there are other causes of valvular heart disease which will now be mentioned, rheumatic fever is much the commonest, and much valve trouble can be blamed on rheumatic fever even when the patient has no recollection of ever having suffered

from it. The other, much rarer, causes may be syphilis, congenital valvular anomaly, healed bacterial endocarditis, atherosclerosis, and mechanical injury.

The most commonly affected valve is the mitral, usually causing *mitral stenosis*, in which the opening between the left atrium and left ventricle will sometimes only admit one finger-tip instead of three fingers as it should. In time the left atrium becomes much enlarged as it overworks to force blood through this narrow orifice. Later still a back pressure develops in the lungs causing congestion and breathlessness; and even later the right ventricle is strained as it tries to force blood into the already congested lung. This is a classic example of the march of trouble backwards from the site of the damaged valve involving first the chamber " behind " it (the left atrium), then the territory " behind " that (the lungs), then the pulmonary arteries taking blood to the lungs, and finally the right ventricle trying to send blood to the pulmonary artery. This steady march of events is usually very slow, and can commonly take twenty years or longer from the initial attack of acute rheumatism to the severer symptoms of advanced mitral stenosis. Treatment is both medical and surgical. The heart failure is treated medically as already described. These days surgical reopening of the valve is almost commonplace, either by inserting a finger through the left auricle and breaking down the constriction, or by opening up the heart and re-shaping the valve under direct vision. The latter involves the additional problem of by-passing the heart by the use of some sort of external pump and poses additional problems, even though from other points of view it is obviously more convenient. As always with major surgical procedures much of the problem is in selecting the patients who will benefit from the operation and in whom it is feasible. Quite often there are other valves involved, mainly the aortic or tricuspid or both, and the hydrostatic or " plumbing " problems can be extremely complex. With luck, however, combined with good judgement and good surgery, the lives of incapacitated patients can be transformed by mitral, and other valvular, surgery. The *aortic valve* is stenosed or narrowed by other degenerative processes besides rheumatism. *Tricuspid stenosis* is nearly always rheumatic in origin.

Coronary Heart Disease. This is the term used whenever the blood supply to the heart muscle (through the coronary arteries) is reduced to such an extent that the heart muscle suffers from a lack of supplies. It has a number of causes, but the only really common one is partial obstruction of the coronary arteries by a condition known as *atheroma* or *atherosclerosis*, and sometimes inaccurately called *arteriosclerosis*. This arterial disease is described later (P30). It takes the form of swellings or lumps on the lining of the artery which, if they become large enough to interfere seriously with the flow of blood, produce a blood starvation or *ischaemia* of the tissue being supplied. Obviously, the smaller the artery, the more easily will a lump of given size impede the flow. Equally obviously, the greater the demand for blood, as in exercise, the more blood " starvation " there will be. There are two degrees of coronary artery disease: one in which the blood flow is reduced to the point where the increased demands of hard work cannot be met, and this results in *angina pectoris* due to *coronary insufficiency*; the other is when the coronary artery becomes completely blocked, preventing the flow of blood altogether, usually by a *thrombus* or clot of blood, and this is *coronary thrombosis*.

Angina Pectoris. Whenever activity is increased in any muscle, the demands for oxygen and nutriments from the blood-stream increase, and as these are used up there is an increased production of waste products known as metabolites. To meet these demands for a greater supply and a more efficient waste-disposal, the blood flow through the exercising muscle must always be increased. If sufficient increase does not occur, not only will there be a shortage of supplies, but there will also be a pile-up of metabolites in the muscle which cannot be carried away. It is mainly because of these latter that pain is caused in ischæmic, or blood-starved muscle, and pain is one of the chief symptoms when heart muscle becomes ischæmic. One important mechanism for increasing blood flow normally to exercising muscle is by automatically dilating the vessels concerned. Diseased vessels, such as coronary arteries when they are affected by atheroma, are not so easily dilated, although certain drugs which are powerful dilators of arterioles can accomplish a great deal, albeit temporarily. The measures taken to relieve the pain and blood-starvation of angina are two-fold. The patient can reduce the demands of the heart by a few minutes' rest, and a drug (usually nitroglycerin) can be taken to dilate the coronary vessels of supply. Another obvious long-term way to reduce demands is for the overweight patient to eat less, and reduce the load of extra body weight on his circulation. It is very frustrating, to say the least, that such an incapacitating and often lethal condition should be caused by the narrowing or blockage of only two or three inches of narrow piping about one-eighth of an inch wide. One obvious form of treatment in theory would be surgical replacement of the piping (many larger arteries than these in other parts of the body are commonly replaced already); or surgical removal of the obstruction inside it. It is very likely that surgeons will one day overcome the technical difficulties involved.

Heart Attack or *Coronary Thrombosis.* It should readily be understood from the above description that heart attacks will vary in their severity according to the amount of heart muscle deprived of blood; and this in turn will depend on where in the coronary artery the obstruction occurs. Most usually it is the left ventricular muscle which is cut off from supplies and dies, either in part or in all of its thickness. Since it is the left ventricle which does most of the work of pumping blood to the body, serious heart failure (P27) is to be expected. If too much muscle is killed, the heart will simply stop, and the patient will suddenly die. It is much more usual, however, for enough muscle to be left for survival, albeit with a greatly reduced cardiac efficiency. A heart attack is usually accompanied by severe pain, similar to the pain of angina but more severe, and unrelieved by rest or by the patient's usual drugs. Very occasionally the event occurs apparently without pain, or with so little that it is ignored. These so-called "silent" coronary attacks can make diagnosis extremely difficult. Since the doctor depends very considerably with heart attacks on an exact, spontaneous description of symptoms for his diagnosis, no description will be given here. There are many over-anxious people who will read these words and could be misled into an unspontaneous description of their own symptoms, and this could make the task of treating them such a problem that they could even be mis-diagnosed as a result. If you have the smallest worry that your chest pain is due to your heart, take your anxiety to your doctor without delay. He will almost certainly be able to re-assure you; and if it happens to be your heart after all, you will have taken the first sensible step towards proper treatment. Dangerous as heart attacks are, they are by no means the death warrant that many lay people think, any more than cancer is. The treatment for a true heart attack is urgent and prolonged. Patients must be at complete rest and their pain relieved quickly. The area of heart muscle they have lost must be allowed to heal with a good, firm scar, and this can take three months of rest often in hospital.

Blood-pressure. The blood is normally under great pressure in the arterial system, since it is this which forces it into all the tissues of the body. It is therefore no more meaningful to say you have "blood-pressure" than to say you have a temperature. You would be very badly off without. Blood-pressure which is too high, however, can give rise to problems, though not always. It is

another of those conditions like angina and cancer, which engender much anxiety among people even when they do not suffer from them. For this reason doctors are often unwilling to disclose a patient's blood-pressure and because of this they unjustifiably earn a reputation for unreasonable secrecy. They are themselves to blame for the general public anxiety as the following true story shows. Twenty years ago a lady in her fifties wished to accompany her husband to a post abroad which was to last four years. All arrangements had been made—the husband resigned his previous job, sold the house, etc.—when it was discovered at a routine medical examination that she had a high blood-pressure, and she was very solemnly advised by the rather elderly doctor not to go. There was great consternation and emotional upheaval, not least because of the inconvenience involved. Eventually she was allowed to go at her own risk. The husband's job lasted eight years instead of four, during which the lady was in no way inconvenienced by her blood-pressure; except that she worried interminably about it. On returning home to retire she began to think she had angina, and elaborate hospital investigation revealed that, as might be expected, her arteries were not as young as they used to be. She was undoubtedly suffering from mild angina, but not as badly as she thought. The opportunity then arose, in her late sixties, to go abroad yet again, and this she did, living a quite strenuous life, and one which she enjoyed. At the time of writing she has returned home and, twenty years later, at the age of seventy three is running a home very actively, still with very little inconvenience from her blood-pressure. There is no doubt that it has been very high all this time, and it is also certain that she will one day die, although it may well not be of her blood-pressure. How much better it would have been for her not to have been told it was high twenty years ago and to have avoided all these years of anxiety. It is not being suggested here that high blood-pressure is a trivial condition, but that it is for doctors to worry about rather than patients! If you ever find out your own blood-pressure, never try to work out for yourself what the figures mean. It is much too complicated. Finally, it should be mentioned that high blood-pressure may occasionally be associated with, or "secondary to," certain kidney diseases (*nephritis*) including a strange condition known as *toxaemia of pregnancy*, which lasts only as long as the pregnancy, provided great care is taken. Most high blood-pressure is, however, "primary", and without any known association or cause.

Low Blood-pressure. Some people seem normally to have surprisingly low blood-pressure all the time. There is nothing whatever wrong with this; indeed it may even be beneficial. At least they are unlikely ever to suffer the effects of high blood-pressure. The sudden low blood-pressure of circulatory failure or shock (P27) is another matter and must be urgently treated.

Irregularities of the Heart-beat. How quickly or how slowly the heart beats is largely under the control of the cardiac centre in the brain and the level of certain hormones in the blood. The *regularity* of the beat, however, is controlled by the so-called pace-maker in the wall of the right atrium, and by the way impulses from the pace-maker travel through specialised conducting heart cells (the bundle of His and its branches) to the ventricles. When any part of this elaborate mechanism is upset, either by altering the biochemical or electrical conditions of these specialised tissues, or by killing some of them off by deprivation of blood supply in the course of a heart attack, disordered rhythm can result. Increase (*tachycardia*) or decrease (*bradycardia*) in rate is nearly always a normal response to exercise, or anxiety. Very occasional irregularity, such as the mis-timing of an occasional beat is also quite normal in some people, although many are alarmed by it. Persistent irregularity, however, is abnormal. Its true nature can usually be elucidated by making an electrical record of the heart-beat—an electro-cardiogram. The commonest causes are varieties of coronary artery diseases or rheumatic heart disease.

Pericarditis. The heart beats inside a bag or sac. At every beat its outer surface slides against the lining of the sac, lubricated by a small amount of fluid. This is the pericardial sac, the *pericardium* being strictly the lubricated membrane which lines the sac and which also covers the outer surface of the heart. Sometimes inflammation occurs—*pericarditis*—and the sliding surfaces become roughened and even separated by a fluid effusion. Very occasionally, so much fluid accumulates that the heart's action is seriously impeded. Pericarditis may be due to infection or to rheumatic fever, and it usually overlies the area of damaged muscle after a heart attack. This illustrates something which people rarely appreciate—that inflammation is not by any means always due to infection by bacteria. The last two varieties of pericarditis are quite free from germs (sterile).

Myocarditis. A term loosely applied to disorders affecting the heart muscle. There are lots of very rare causes. The really common ones are due to acute or chronic rheumatic causes or to coronary artery disease, both of which are described above.

Endocarditis or inflammation of the lining of the heart is a term loosely applied to any disorder of the valves or heart lining. All varieties of rheumatic valvular disease (P28) are included. Bacterial endocarditis in its several forms usually involves valves already damaged by rheumatic disease. It is a complication which is still much to be feared, though somewhat less so now that antibiotic drugs are available.

Atheroma or Atherosclerosis. This is the condition referred to above in which lumps arise on the lining of arterial blood-vessels. Although it is therefore a disease of the arteries, its importance lies in the way blood flow is held up, either by the lumps themselves, or by thrombosis ultimately blocking the narrowed portion of the pipework. The effects on the body are therefore those of depriving the tissues of blood. It is an astonishing fact that in England and America, more people die of the consequences of atheroma than of any other single disease, including all forms of cancer put together. Furthermore, cancer is mainly a disease of old age, whereas many of the effects of atheroma on men occur in early middle age. If narrowing of the artery is going to do significant harm it is easy to see that it will be of more consequence in those parts of the body where small-bore vessels are supplying tissues whose functions are necessary for life. Exactly such a situation exists in the heart and in the brain. An additional factor is that the arrangement of the blood supply in these tissues is such that any particular area has only one vessel leading to it. This is unusual among the tissues generally, where several alternative, or " collateral " vessels usually supply an area, and where others can take over if one becomes obstructed. We have, therefore, a situation in which perhaps the most important tissues —the heart and the brain—run the greatest risk of deprivation, and this leads to angina and coronary thrombosis on the one hand, and cerebral thrombosis and hæmorrhage (" stroke illness ") on the other, accounting jointly for about one death in every five. In addition, the effects of atheromatous narrowing are often felt in the legs, where the blood supply to the muscles is inadequate for exercise, leading to intermittent pain comparable with that in the heart in similar circumstances. This is called *intermittent claudication*, or intermittent closing of the leg arteries. In its most severe forms, it leads to the need for amputation, although in most cases early treatment can avoid this. It is small wonder that there is intensive research into the causes of atheroma, as with cancer, but it is probably true to say that we still know rather more about cancer.

A lot of attention has been given to the amounts of certain fats in the circulating blood, particularly cholesterol. This fat is found in large amounts in the blood of sufferers from atheroma, and is also found in the arterial lumps themselves. Efforts have therefore been made to reduce blood cholesterol by modifications of the diet, but it has been extremely difficult to prove that this has done any good. Many other factors are known to contribute to atheroma, and hence to heart attacks and strokes, some of which can be reduced and others not. Such factors are age, obesity, high blood-pressure, and smoking cigarettes. People who lead an active life, like bus conductors, seem to have less trouble than others who are less active, like bus drivers. Sudden severe exercise, however, is bad if you are not used to it. It is better, and life saving, to take regular, moderate exercise. Women have less atheroma than men, until the menopause when they begin to catch up, so that hormones have something to do with it. Serious starvation, such as occurred in the German-occupied territories of Holland and Scandinavia and in the concentration camps conferred one benefit—a freedom from atheroma, but obviously we cannot all starve, and the puzzle remains. Like many of the more important outstanding medical puzzles, there is no single factor responsible, and this is what makes it difficult to solve.

Aortic Disease. The aorta, the main artery of the body, running from the left ventricle down through the chest and abdomen, also suffers from atheroma, but is too wide (about an inch across) to become obstructed. However, weaknesses occur in the thickness of its wall, sometimes due to syphilis but nowadays much more usually due to atheroma, which results in a ballooning out of a part of the vessel, rather like you sometimes see in an old bicycle inner tube. In days gone by these *aneurysms*, as the dilations are called, reached an enormous size, and would wear away the breastbone and ribs, to appear as large pulsating masses on the chest. Now that advanced syphilis is less common, atheromatous aneurysm, with a predilection for the abdominal aorta, is the one most commonly seen; and these days it is treated by replacement of the diseased portion of vessel. *Dissecting aneurysms* of the aorta are another variety in which the blood, under high pressure, somehow finds its way in between the layers of the aortic wall and then suddenly rips up and down the whole length of the vessel, separating (or dissecting) one layer from another in its path. Sometimes it tracks back towards the heart and suddenly fills the pericardium with blood to stop the heart's action altogether.

Embolism. This term refers to any foreign object travelling in the circulation and becoming impacted when it reaches a vessel too small for it to pass through. It may be a thrombus (P31), a collection of cancer cells, a group of bacteria, a chunk of infected pus from an abscess, a collection of fat droplets or even a bubble of air. If it originates in a vein it travels to the right heart and to the lungs. If it comes from the left heart or an artery, it will impact in any part of the arterial tree. Reasonably enough an arterial embolus will commonly end up in those parts of the body with the richest blood supply, like the brain, the kidneys, the liver or the bone marrow. A thrombotic embolus will cause death of the tissue in the area previously supplied by the blocked vessel, a condition known as *infarction.* Perhaps the commonest source of thrombotic embolism is the lining of the heart chambers where a thrombus has occurred at the site of muscle damaged by a heart attack. Massive pulmonary (lung) embolism is usually the result of thrombosis of the leg veins in people kept immobile following surgery or childbirth. That is why postoperative patients are got out of bed for a while as soon as the first day after the operation. The cells of a cancer embolus usually die; but if they survive, a new cancer deposit begins to grow where the embolus impacts, and this is one of the ways cancer may spread. An infected embolus may infect the vessel wall when it impacts, producing a weakness which may give way. Air embolism, if enough insoluble gas enters the circulation, can kill by making so much froth in the heart chambers as to impede the normal pumping action. If bubbles pass the lungs and enter the brain, all sorts of neurological disorders like scores of tiny strokes arise. The same sort of thing happens all over the body in the *"bends"* or *"caisson" disease,* in which the blood literally boils. It is due to a too rapid return to normal pressure from regions of high pressure at great depths or from pressurised chambers. Fat embolism sometimes occurs after fractures due to marrow fat entering damaged veins and being carried away to the lungs.

Thrombosis. This is not quite the same as clotting. It is the mass which arises when platelets adhere to the lining of blood-vessels or heart chambers. Blood clot accumulates among layers of deposited platelets and the thrombus therefore has structure, unlike pure blood clot. Thrombosis usually occurs when the lining of the vessel or chamber is damaged by atheroma or inflammation, or when the circulation becomes very stagnant. One danger is that it will become dislodged and travel as an embolus during the first week or ten days of its existence. After this time it is usually firmly incorporated into the vessel walls by cells which migrate into it from the surrounding tissue. The other danger is, of course, that the tissue previously supplied by the blocked vessel will die before a collateral circulation can be established. As previously explained, this is called infarction. All the technical terms in this section are used elsewhere and can be looked up.

Buerger's Disease or *thromboangiitis obliterans.* This is an inflammation of the arterial wall which leads to blockage by thrombosis. The leg arteries of comparatively young men are most commonly affected, leading to amputation in some cases. Unlike lung cancer, coronary heart disease, and bronchitis, which are known to be associated with smoking, Buerger's disease is only thought to be. There is a horrible tale of a young man who had lost all his four limbs one after another, sitting on the hospital steps begging passers-by to light his cigarette for him.

Reynaud's Disease. This is a strange condition in which the finger tips and in severe cases all the fingers or the whole hand respond in an exaggerated way to cold. The vessels supplying the hand are constricted and the fingers go white as the blood drains from them. Then the capillaries dilate and become distended and filled with blood. But owing to stagnation it is venous and blue, and the fingers are therefore blue. Now we have all experienced this in very cold weather, but sufferers from Reynaud's disease, nearly always women, respond even to very slight cold, like putting their hands into cold water. Even emotional stress will start the process off. In very severe cases the fingers will be so deprived of blood for so long, that sores will develop and fingers can even be lost, but this is very rare, and can be avoided by an operation to cut the nerves which supply the circular muscle of the vessels concerned. In most cases it is sufficient to avoid getting the hands cold.

Frostbite. Strictly speaking, this is literally a freezing of the tissues. Although their freezing point might be expected to be close to that of water, it usually only occurs at temperatures below $-13°$ C ($8°$ F). The patient may feel a pricking feeling at first, and feel an area of firmer, pale skin on the cheeks, nose, ears, fingers, or toes. If these parts are numb with cold, the onset of frostbite may not be felt, and will often only be noticed by others. In countries where extreme cold is prevalent, it is usual for complete strangers to stop each other in the street and point it out when they see it. It is important not to rub the affected part, but contrary to popular belief it must be warmed as *rapidly* as possible. Fingers should be immersed in water as hot as the normal hand can bear (110° F). Many First Aid books still quite wrongly teach that return to warmth must be gradual.

DISEASES OF THE RESPIRATORY SYSTEM

INTRODUCTION.

When air is drawn in during the process of breathing, it is brought into very close contact with the blood passing through the lungs. In this way the air we breathe in, which contains 20 per cent oxygen, is confronted with "spent" blood returning from the tissues which contains much less, and oxygen therefore diffuses into the blood from the air. At the same time, the waste gas, carbon dioxide, passes by diffusion in the reverse direction from the blood into the air, because there is much more carbon dioxide in the returning "spent" blood than the tiny amount in the air we breathe. The blood is therefore continually circulating through the lungs and exchanging carbon dioxide for oxygen from the air we breathe in. When we breathe out, we disperse the carbon dioxide into the atmosphere.

When the air enters the nose or mouth, it passes into the windpipe or *trachea,* through the vocal cords in the pharynx. The trachea is held open all the time by rings of cartilage and is lined by a mucus-secreting membrane covered by millions of tiny "hairs" or cilia. These continuously waft a sheet of sticky mucus upwards, which traps any dust or other small particles we may have inhaled, until a collection of this material in the pharynx stimulates us to cough and expel the phlegm, usually to be swallowed. At its lower end, the trachea or windpipe divides into two, the right and left main *bronchus.* Each main bronchial tube enters a lung, one on each side, and proceeds to divide repeatedly within the lung until the air is being carried by more and more smaller and ever smaller tubes called *bronchioles.* There are many millions of these on each side, and each one ends in a collection of very small balloon-like structures —the air sacs or *alveoli.* If you were to cut across a lung and examine the cut surface in a good light, you would see that it is a spongy tissue, with many millions of tiny holes, each one just visible to the naked eye. These are the air sacs. In their walls run the blood capillaries, each one of which is a branch of the vessels carrying "spent" blood from the right side of the heart. At this stage, the blood is only separated from the air in the sacs by the walls of the capillaries and of the air sacs themselves. Both structures are extremely thin, making for easy diffusion of the gases between blood and air.

The action of breathing is accomplished by two muscular mechanisms. One is by the muscles which move the ribs, and the other by the diaphragm, a sheet of muscle which runs across the body, separating the chest cavity from the abdominal cavity. These muscles are all actuated by nerves, just as all other muscles are. Those running to the muscles of breathing are organised by a mechanism in the brain known as the *respiratory centre.* It is this centre—one of the so-called vital centres of the brain—which receives information from many different sources, and translates it into instructions for the breathing mechanism. Thus, when you run for a bus, you will automatically breathe more deeply and more quickly because the respiratory centre has been informed about all the extra carbon dioxide in your blood which has been produced by the exercising leg muscles. Even the conscious instructions involved when you blow a trumpet, inflate a balloon, or during speaking, all pass first to the respiratory centre. It is the death of the cells of this and other vital centres of the brain that is the ultimate cause of death in everyone who dies.

Bronchitis may be acute or chronic. It is an inflammation of the lining mucous membrane of the larger air passages or bronchi, and results in much more secretion than the amount normally produced, mixed with some pus. The acute form is often caused by viruses, with " secondary " infection from bacteria. It may sometimes be caused by irritant gases, like the sulphur dioxide in smog. The chronic, or long-standing form of bronchitis is often associated with *emphysema,* in which the small air sacs of the lung architecture are destroyed or distorted, leaving larger spaces than normal, often surrounded by fibrous scar tissue. Such an arrangement makes the normal gaseous exchange difficult between air and blood. While the exact cause of chronic bronchitis is difficult to discover, because it is such a mixture of causes, it is mainly associated with older age groups, particularly men, in damp foggy climates like ours in Britain, with polluted town air and especially with smoking. Smoking also makes any existing bronchitis much worse. Patients cough, and produce varying amounts of sputum, or phlegm. They often wheeze like asthmatics. This may go on for many years before the right side of the heart begins to fail (P27). Gradually, during this time, the chest tends to become barrel-shaped. Treatment consists of getting the patient to stop smoking or otherwise contaminating his lungs, preventing infection, particularly during winter months, with germ-killing antibiotics, and breathing exercises. The outlook for chronic bronchitis and emphysema is nevertheless not good, although many patients continue with their disease for many years, provided they take constant care to obey instructions and stop smoking.

Bronchial Asthma (not to be confused with *cardiac asthma*) is a condition in which the finer air passages become constricted due to an allergic response. In addition, an increased secretion tends to obstruct them and the patient wheezes. In many cases it can be shown that he is allergic to a particular component of dust, or, less commonly, a foodstuff. This is the same sort of thing as occurs in the upper respiratory passages in hay fever, but the effect is on a different, lower part of the respiratory system. Many other cases are due to respiratory infection of some sort, probably combined with an allergy to the bacteria causing it. A predisposition to asthma is often inherited. Once a patient has become asthmatic, his attacks will be triggered off by such additional things as emotional stress, changes in temperature (particularly sudden cold), irritating fumes or smoke, and physical exertion. These are secondary factors, and although much of the treatment is concerned with them, it is unlikely that any of them are a sole cause of the condition. Treatment is directed at the relief of the breathing difficulty and of the wheezing, as well as the control of the causative factors. Many useful drugs are available to dilate the contracted air passages and reduce the obstructing secretions. Asthma in children often gets better as the patient grows up. Asthma is another condition made much worse by smoking. Patients should avoid extremes of cold and humidity, particularly outdoor exertion in cold, damp weather. They should also avoid exposure to respiratory infection.

Bronchiectasis. In this condition the bronchial air passages are abnormally and permanently dilated, and the normal structure of the walls destroyed. It is thought to be caused by obstructions of the tubes which lead to dilatation of the parts beyond. Secretions accumulate, and since they cannot easily drain away, they become infected. The infection helps to complete the process of destruction of structures in the bronchial wall. The patient has a chronic cough which often produces large quantities of purulent sputum, and there are often recurrent episodes of pneumonia. Diagnosis is made by a special X-ray examination—a bronchogram—in which a material, opaque to X-rays, is dropped into the air passages. This shows up the dilated and distorted tubes. In some cases, where the disease is localised to one part of the lung, it is often a good idea to cut out that portion, and this is particularly true in young people. Vigorous physiotherapy, involving drainage of the lungs by placing the patient in a suitable posture, together with antibiotic drugs for the infection, are other forms of treatment.

Cystic Fibrosis is an inborn disease which affects chiefly the lungs and the digestive system. It is sometimes called *Fibrocystic disease of the Pancreas*, and sometimes " *Mucoviscidosis* " Until it was medically recognised twenty-five years ago,

children affected usually died from pneumonia in the first year of life. This, of course, was before antibiotics were available for the treatment of infections. Today, cystic fibrosis is known to be the commonest genetically determined disorder affecting children in Britain. One child in 2,000 receives one of the abnormal genes from each parent. Such a child therefore has a double dose of the harmful gene, and will have the disease from birth. One person in 25 of the general population carries only one of these abnormal genes, and such an individual will not have the disease, but will be a carrier of the abnormal gene. If such a seemingly normal carrier marries another carrier, there is a one in four chance of each of their children being affected. The children, therefore, who actually develop cystic fibrosis, have inherited the disease *equally* from both parents, who are carriers, but are themselves unaffected by the disease. Although much has been learned about cystic fibrosis in the past twenty-five years, there remain many unsolved problems, and we still cannot define precisely the biochemical fault which causes it. The prospects for survival into reasonably healthy adult life are steadily improving, but they depend upon early diagnosis and careful management through childhood. In cystic fibrosis most of the damage is caused by the excessive viscidity, or stickiness, of the mucus which is produced in the breathing tubes as a lubricant, and also in the ducts of the pancreatic gland which provides enzymes to help digestion. Being thick and sticky, instead of thin and slimy as in the normal, this mucus tends to block the passages instead of keeping them clear. The pancreatic cells are permanently destroyed. The gland cannot secrete pancreatic enzymes, and the food, especially protein and fat, is not properly absorbed. This deficiency can be compensated fairly well by giving pancreatic extract by mouth with every meal, and by dietary care.

The major clinical problem is in the lungs. The lung passages normally have a thin coating of mucus which is propelled steadily upwards, and is completely renewed in less than one hour. It moves more suddenly on coughing. In cystic fibrosis this upward movement is slowed down and interrupted. There is difficulty in keeping the passages clear, especially when infection with bacteria or viruses greatly increases the amount of mucus. This results in intermittent blocking of the air passages, difficulty in breathing, incomplete use of the lungs, and persistent local pockets of infection. If such infectious processes are not controlled, areas of lung will be destroyed, chronic infection will persist, and multiple lung cavities will develop. These predispose to further infection, interfering with the natural development of the lung—a process not normally complete until halfway through childhood—thus adding to the respiratory problems which the child will face in later life. Unless a correct diagnosis is made, and proper treatment instituted before the first serious lung infection has occurred, the resulting lung damage may well be permanent. The Cystic Fibrosis Research Foundation Trust of Stuart House, 1 Tudor Street, London, E.C.4., was founded in 1964 to raise funds to finance research, and to help and advise parents with everyday problems in caring for these children.

Pneumonia. This is an infection of the lung tissue, rather than of the air passages. The lung is the only internal organ which is directly exposed to the air, and since there are germs of all kinds in the air, it is a source of surprise that pneumonia is not a much more common event in all of us. The answer lies, as with all infections, in the fact that it is not simply (or even mainly) bacteria which cause disease, but our own lack of resistance to them. If we allow germs to thrive and multiply by being unhealthy or run down or undernourished, infective disease will occur. If we are fit, the entry of those same harmful germs into the body causes us no inconvenience, unless we are very young, or very old, or unless the invasion of germs is abnormally overwhelming. This helps to explain why pneumonia is so often quoted as a cause of death. In most cases it is merely a terminal event occurring in the elderly sick, whose normal resistance is so far reduced by their illness that they succomb to an invasion which they would normally not notice. There are two main kinds of pneumonia, and in both the air sacs become filled with inflammatory secretions, making the normally porous lung tissue as solid as liver. In *lobar pneumonia*, a whole segment (or lobe) of the lung becomes solid. In *bronchopneumonia*, areas of lung tissue surrounding the smaller bronchioles become consolidated, leaving normal porous lung tissue in between. Bronchopneumonia is the one which occurs in the rather stagnant lungs of people who are already ill or bedridden. Both forms respond to treatment with the appropriate antibiotics, provided any underlying debility does not interfere with the patient's own resistance. In the terminal bronchopneumonia of fatal illness, it is sometimes considered kinder not to treat the additional pneumonia. *Pleurisy* is a natural complication, and before the days of antibiotic drugs *lung abscess* was very much feared. Another form of pneumonia—*virus pneumonia*—has been referred to on P10(2).

Pneumoconiosis. This is a term which refers to a large group of different diseases, all of which are caused by breathing in some form of dust over a very long period of time. It is therefore an occupational hazard of certain trades. We have already mentioned the mechanisms of mucus secretion in the air passages which normally trap small particles from the air, and prevent them reaching the lung. However, in some occupations there is so much dust breathed in over the months and years that these normal barriers are defeated. About a quarter of the earth's crust consists of silicon, in quartz, flint, or sand. *Silicosis* occurs in people who have worked for many years in trades like mining, stone crushing, sandblasting, or metal grinding, who are often breathing silicon dust in high concentration. When the particles arrive in the air sacs, they set up an irritant chemical reaction which produces nodules of scar tissue. Silicosis for some reason predisposes to tuberculosis (P14(1). Emphysema also occurs and there is a general impairment of respiratory function. Coalminer's pneumoconiosis is similar to silicosis but not identical with it. It is more prevalent in some coalfields than others, owing to the different composition of the dust to which these unfortunate men are daily exposed. It is hoped that modern mining methods will help to reduce this dread disease. Asbestos is a complex silicate of magnesium, calcium, and iron. *Asbestosis* is caused by inhaling its fine fibres. *Berylliosis* is caused by compounds of beryllium, used in the manufacture of fluorescent lamps. *Farmers lung* is a pneumoconiosis caused by inhaling hay and grain dust, and is similar to *bagassosis* and *byssinosis* caused by sugar cane and cotton dust respectively. The newest pneumoconiosis to be reported is *mushroom worker's lung*, caused by something in the compost in which mushrooms are commercially grown.

Pulmonary Embolism. This catastrophic, yet quite common condition has already been briefly referred to (P30(2)). It is a cause of tragic, sudden death in people who have had operations or have given birth to babies some days previously, or who have been bedridden for any other cause. The first event is that the blood in the veins of the legs becomes stagnant, due to the lack of exercise; and together with the tendency to clot which often follows surgery or childbirth, the whole length of a leg vein may be obstructed for twelve inches or more by an elongated clot of blood. This does little harm to the circulation of the leg, since there are plenty of other veins for returning blood to the heart. The danger is that the clot will become dislodged and be swept upwards towards the heart by the flow of returning blood. When this happens it is carried by way of the right auricle and ventricle into the pulmonary vessels which normally carry spent blood to the lungs. Here, for the first time, it enters vessels which are getting smaller as they divide, and it then impacts in the main pulmonary artery. The patient, who may have been recovering very well, suddenly collapses and not unusually dies there and then. At autopsy a long coiled-up mass of clot is found obstructing the pulmonary vessels. It often can be seen to form a cast of the leg vein and even bears the marks of the small venous valves which are present at its site of origin. With the dramatic advances being made in chest surgery, it is now sometimes possible in selected cases to operate to remove the clot. Success clearly depends on the patient's surviving long enough to be taken to the operating theatre for the major operation of *pulmonary embolectomy*. Three quarters of all cases of pulmonary embolism die within two hours, and therefore the best hope would be to prevent the occurrence altogether. This is not at present possible, but clotting in leg veins can be discouraged by early exercise following surgery and childbirth. Patients often resent having to get up the next day because it is so uncomfortable. Herein, however, lies their best hope of avoiding pulmonary embolism.

Haemoptysis. This means coughing up blood or blood-stained material. It must be distinguished from *haematemesis*, in which the blood is vomited from the stomach. It must always be taken seriously because of the underlying lung disease which may be present. No one who coughs up blood, in however small a quantity, should neglect to inform their doctor so that its source can be determined. Haemoptysis occurs in a variety of lung disease, some of which is not serious but much of which must be treated immediately if it is not to become so. This is a suitable place to repeat our general rule that you should see your doctor without delay if you have any unexplained bleeding from any part of the body, however well you feel. And this includes haemoptysis.

Fat Embolism. Liquid fat sometimes enters the bloodstream following extensive crush injuries to soft tissue and bone. It splits up into millions of small globules which are carried to the lungs, and impact in small blood vessels there, producing obstruction of the lung circulation and consequent difficulties in breathing.

Lung Cancer. This is one of the nastiest and most incurable forms of cancer which can occur. It is also probably the easiest to prevent. There has been no reasonable doubt for several years now that it is associated with cigarette smoking, and the evidence is overwhelming. However, in spite of this certain knowledge, smoking continues to increase, and every year there are more and more people dying unpleasantly of lung cancer. It seems that nothing the health authorities can do is able to stop it. Intensive campaigns of public advertising of the dangers, and well organised instruction in schools have so far made no impression whatever on the smoking habits even of people who accept the evidence. The only group of people who are known to have stopped smoking are British doctors, very many of whom have given it up, and it is easy to show that giving it up has saved them from the disease. Their colleagues who have not done so have continued to die. Undoubtedly a large factor contributing to the failure of anti-smoking propaganda is the enormous expenditure by the tobacco manufacturers on very clever advertising, amounting to many millions of pounds each year. Moreover they spend a pitiful fraction of this amount on their own research into the harmful effects of their own product, which has so far discovered nothing which was not already known by research doctors many years ago. Another problem is that it takes a number of years to get cancer. It is not like an infectious disease which is caught a few days after exposure to the bacteria concerned. It may be fifteen or twenty years before the cancer begins, and many smokers are apparently unwilling to look so far ahead. Furthermore, not everyone who smokes dies this way; and so a smoker can gamble with his life and hope it will not be him. The present writer once had to perform a series of post-mortem examinations on people who died of lung cancer, and this helped him to stop smoking completely, having smoked more than twenty cigarettes a day for several years. Not everyone can have this incentive. The main encouragement to smoke probably comes from other people. Schoolboys are easily impressed when their teachers and parents stop smoking. They are not likely to fear the habit when these same people smoke openly. The smoking doctor is also a powerful stimulus to people to carry on smoking.

Lung cancer grows in the wall of a main bronchial air passage. If it grows inwards it can obstruct the air way, choking that part of the lung it is supplying with air. This causes collapse and infection of the lung and may lead to *lung abscess*. The patient will then cough up blood-stained infected and purulent material. Such a case is comparatively lucky, since the disease declares itself early by producing symptoms. In others, the lump may grow outwards into the surrounding lung and produce no symptoms at all in the early stages. Indeed, it may spread to other parts of the body, like brain or bone or liver before causing any trouble to the patient. If this happens he may go to his doctor because of fits, changes of personality, or fracture, only to discover that the origin of the trouble is in the lung.

The chances of cure are negligible, although much can be done to relieve the pain and suffering of the last stages of the illness. Not more than one in twenty cases is alive two years after it is first diagnosed. Surgery, by removing the lung, and irradiation of the growth are the standard palliative treatment. It is not the practice of the Medical Section to alarm the reader unnecessarily, but if only a few are induced to stop giving themselves such a horrible disease, then writing in this way will have been justified.

Secondary Cancer of the Lung. In nearly all forms of cancer, the big problem is that it spreads to other parts of the body. If this were not so it could be eradicated by surgical removal more often than it is. One common way in which it spreads from any part of the body is by entering the bloodstream and being carried as clumps of living cancer cells to distant parts. When these come to rest in smaller blood vessels, they begin to grow and colonise the new environment. Such new colonies are called *secondary deposits* or *metastases*. It so happens that all veins (except portal veins of the liver) lead to the right heart and thence directly to the lungs, and for this reason the lungs are a very common site of *secondary* cancer, which may have begun in the bowel, or breast, or indeed anywhere else in the body. Other common sites of secondary, blood-borne cancer are the brain, liver, bone marrow, and kidney, since all of them have an abundant blood supply, and there is therefore a high chance of the travelling cells arriving there. Secondary cancer of the lung usually consists of several lumps scattered throughout the lung. Lung cancer itself is usually only one growth. One of the main reasons for the success of early diagnosis is that treatment may be possible before blood-borne and other means of spread have occurred. Unfortunately, in the case of primary cancer of the lung, even early diagnosis is of little avail, but in many other common cancers permanent cure is possible if treatment is begun early enough.

Pleurisy. The chest is lined by one layer of a thin membrane called the *pleura.* The lungs are covered and enclosed by a second, continuous layer of this same membrane. When the lungs move during respiration, the pleura covering the lungs rubs against the pleura lining the chest, lubricated by a very thin layer of pleural fluid separating the two pleura. Whenever the pleural surface becomes inflamed, this is known as *pleurisy.* It is nearly always due to inflammatory disease of the adjoining lung, and is therefore not strictly a disease in its own right. For example, pneumonia, tuberculosis, lung cancer, or a lung infarct (P30(2)) will produce a pleurisy if the area of diseased lung adjoins the lung surface. Sometimes the area of inflamed inner pleura will tend to stick to its outer layer or rub painfully against it, producing a sharp pain when the patient breathes. Sometimes a large effusion of fluid is produced which separates the two layers and collapses the

lung by occupying space in the chest which the lung should be occupying. This latter is more usual in tuberculosis or cancer.

The lung can be collapsed by the entry of anything between the normally adjacent layers of pleura. For example, air can be introduced, either deliberately to rest the lung in tuberculosis, or by accidental penetrating wounds of the chest wall, or by accidental rupture of the emphysematous lung (*q.v.*). This condition is called *pneumothorax* or "air in the chest." Bleeding into the cavity between the pleura is called *haemothorax.*

DISEASES OF THE DIGESTIVE TRACT AND LARGE INTESTINE.

INTRODUCTION.

The digestive tract consists of the mouth, pharynx, oesophagus (or gullet), stomach, small intestine, large intestine (or colon), rectum, and anus. The small intestine is very long, and is subdivided into the duodenum, jejunum, and ileum. It ends at the junction of the ileum with the cæcum, where there is a small blind side-tube, the appendix. The cæcum leads into the colon. The whole tract has two main mechanical functions and two main biochemical ones. Mechanically, food has to be chewed in the mouth and further minced up by muscular squeezing, mainly by the stomach. It has also to be propelled along by an orderly series of squeezing movements known as *peristalsis.* While it is still in the digestive tract, food has to be digested. That is to say, it has to be broken down chemically into suitable materials for absorption into the system, and secondly, it has to be absorbed across the wall of the intestine into the blood stream, itself a highly complex biochemical process. The blood stream it now enters is a special part of the circulation, the "portal" system, which travels directly to the liver without first passing to the heart. In the liver the broken-down foods are processed and issued in their new form into the general, or "systemic" circulation, by which they are finally carried to all the tissues of the body.

As the food passes along the digestive tract (or, as it is sometimes called, the alimentary canal), it is mixed with various secretions which are either made in the wall of the tract, or by organs outside the wall connected to the main pathway by small tubes. Examples of the latter are bile, manufactured by the liver and sent into the duodenum through the bile ducts. Also pancreatic juice comes from the pancreas down the pancreatic ducts, also into the duodenum. These secretions are either digestive juices concerned with splitting up the foodstuffs so that they can be absorbed, or they have a lubricant function so that the gut contents slide along easily under the influence of peristalsis. Roughly speaking, it may be said that digestive juices give place to lubricant secretions at the junction between the small and large intestine.

The constituents of the diet are dealt with in a later section. The principle classes with whose digestion we are now concerned are carbohydrates, proteins, and fats.

Carbohydrates are sugars and starches. There are many sugars, which may exist alone, in pairs, or with lots of them stuck together. Alone they are such things as glucose or fructose. Common table sugar is a substance called sucrose, formed by sticking one glucose molecule to one fructose molecule. Starch is lots of glucose molecules all stuck together. Digestion of carbohydrates consists of splitting up sugars and starch into single sugars like glucose, since only single sugars can be absorbed into the system. The splitting is done by digestive *enzymes* which are found in the juices secreted into the digestive tract. Sugar-splitters are found in the saliva of the mouth, in the pancreatic juice of the duodenum, and in the duodenum's own juice from its own wall. On the face of it, you might think it would be better to eat glucose which needs no digestion and can be absorbed in this form, than to eat starch which has first to be split; and so a lot of money has been made out of a gullible public by the sale of glucose drinks and powder. In fact digesting starch is no problem whatever, even for the sick, who can obtain their carbohydrate energy just as easily (and much more cheaply) from potatoes as from expensive glucose. The end result of eating both is the same. The starch-splitting enzyme in saliva is mixed with the food as it is chewed, and it is therefore probably a good idea to chew it well. However, even if the food is bolted it does not seem to matter very much. People without teeth (neither their own nor dentures) seem to digest their carbohydrate quite well, presumably by means of their pancreatic juice at a later stage.

Proteins, which are found in meat, cheese, and eggs, have very large molecules consisting of lots of small ones strung together. Unlike starch, in which all the component glucose molecules are identical, the amino acids of which proteins are composed come in many different types. They all contain nitrogen, and there are about twenty-seven varieties. One protein differs from another in the proportions of the mixture and the order in which they are stuck together. Only single amino acids can be absorbed from the food, and so protein digestion again consists of splitting the material down into its building bricks. There is a strong protein splitting enzyme in the gastric (or stomach) juice called pepsin, whose job it is to split the long amino-acid chains into shorter chains. Several other protein-splitters in the duodenal and pancreatic juice contrive to break the smaller chains into individual amino acids which are then absorbed and sent to the liver for processing.

Fats mainly consist of glycerol to which are attached three fatty acid molecules for each molecule of glycerol. An enzyme in pancreatic juice splits the fatty acids off the glycerol, but would have some difficulty penetrating the globules of fat without the help of bile. One of the constituents of bile (bile salts) has detergent properties like washing-up powder and breaks the fat globules up into a very fine suspension so that the enzyme can get at the fat. Some fat particles of this size can even be absorbed as such, without preliminary splitting.

The processes by which all these enzymic secretions are produced are very finely controlled. They are very expensive to make in terms of energy and raw materials, and so it would be very wasteful to produce them all the time, even when there was no food to digest. And so the body has some very well designed automatic arrangements for sampling the foods as they are eaten and passed on, which ensure that exactly the right kind of juice is waiting in every part of the digestive tract for whatever food arrives. As soon as the food is digested the supply of enzymes is automatically switched off, so that there is very little waste of precious materials. It is, of course, beyond the scope of this account to describe the control mechanisms. Suffice it to say that they are operated partly by nerve reflexes which signal the imminent arrival of food, and partly by special hormones produced in various parts of the gut wall. The best secretion is affected even by psychological factors, so that pleasant company and surroundings, attractive appearance of the food, and an eager anticipation of it all make for good digestion and good health. These psychological factors are all capable of proper scientific investigation and proof. The poor health of those who habitually and irregularly bolt unpalatable food is probably due to such factors as these. So is the failure of appetite in the depressed, the anxious adult, or the scolded child.

Nearly all the digestion which has been described occurs in the stomach and upper part of the small intestine (the duodenum, jejunum, and upper ileum). Almost all absorption of the products of digestion occurs in the small intestine which is long and intricately folded to give it a large surface area for this purpose. The colon, or large intestine, is adapted for conserving water, by removing it from the residual waste material. This has then to be eliminated, and being rather dry its passage has to be lubricated by suitable secretions of mucus.

Constipation. Here, perhaps we had better mention the morbid question of constipation, about which so many people are obsessed and hold such pronounced views. First of all, what is it? For some people it is entirely normal only to pass motions about once or twice a week. For others the normal frequency is once or twice a day. What is abnormal? The answer is that the only thing worth worrying about is any pronounced change of bowel habit, particularly in middle-aged and older people. By a change is meant a change from that individual person's normal routine. Such a pronounced change—either in the direction of constipation or diarrhœa is worth consulting your doctor about if it persists for more than a week or two. Otherwise, forget your bowels and leave them to work naturally as they know best. Many believe that constipation is the root of all evil, that it causes a mysterious condition known to them (although, alas, not to doctors) as " auto-intoxication." Sedulously fostered by the manufacturers of patent medicines, their beliefs range from the notion that headaches, spotty skin, muddy skin, and tiredness are caused by constipation, to the more extreme idea that the whole system is being poisoned and that, if the bowels do not work, the individual will shortly die. Of course, all this is the merest rubbish: for, as Professor Samson Wright, whose *Applied Physiology* is one of the most famous of medical text-books, has pointed out, there is no such thing as absorption of poisonous products from the bowel. There is no such thing as " auto-intoxication." " The symptoms of constipation," he writes, " are largely due to distension and mechanical irritation of the rectum." It has been shown that an enema removes these symptoms *immediately,* which would not be the case if they were due to poisons in the blood, and exactly the same symptoms can be produced by packing the rectum with cotton-wool. Wright mentions the case of a man who went for just over a year without a bowel motion, and at the end of that time, although his abdomen was distended and he felt some discomfort, he was not noticeably ill. Needless to say, telling these facts to the purgative addict will only make him annoyed, but it is as well to note that if no known diseases are due to constipation (although constipation may be a symptom of another disease), the regular use of purgatives *can* cause disease.

Constipation should be treated first by diet containing plenty of roughage—bran and oatmeal are excellent—plenty of stewed and fresh fruits, and at least three pints of fluid should be taken daily. Failing that, one of the best things to take is a proprietary product prepared from senna pods. Never to be taken regularly are liquid paraffin, castor oil, preparations of aloes, Epsom salts, and all the other dreadful stuff that people swill down.

Œsophagus.

The œsophagus, or gullet, is more than a simple tube for taking the food from the mouth to the stomach. It is normally closed except when swallowing, and the act of swallowing is very complicated. When the material to be swallowed arrives in the back of the throat there is an automatic mechanism which opens the top end of the œsophagus to receive it, and from then onwards everything happens automatically. The next portion of the tube opens and the top closes strongly, so that the food (or drink) is propelled forcibly down the next segment. Then the part below this relaxes and the material is squeezed further downwards and so on until it arrives in the stomach. This squeezing (or milking) action is akin to the action known as peristalsis which propels contents in other parts of the gut. Thus when you see someone swallowing a glass of beer very quickly in warm weather, it is not going "down the hatch" under the influence of gravity, however much it may look like it. It is perfectly possible to swallow the same, or any other liquid, standing on your head. Getting into that position is the only difficult part. Sometimes this complicated swallowing mechanism gets out of order, leading to difficulties of swallowing, or *dysphagia*. Another disorder known as *hiatus hernia* occurs at the lower end of the œsophagus as it meets the stomach. At this point the œsophagus has to pass through the diaphragm, the sheet of muscle which separates the chest from the abdomen. The muscular fibres of the diaphragm are normally arranged in a ring around the œsophagus. These help to keep the lower end shut, so that the contents of the stomach do not regurgitate upwards, causing inflammation (*oesophagitis*) or heartburn. A hiatus hernia is when muscle fibres get slack, and the upper end of the stomach can even slide upwards into the chest. People with hiatus hernia get heartburn after meals, and particularly when they bend down or lie down. Except for very severe forms, which need surgical repair, the treatment is to eat less at a time, reduce the acidity with a suitable antacid and reduce weight, so that the weight of the abdomen does not press upwards so much. The other disease of the œsophagus, quite unrelated to the above, is *cancer of the oesophagus*, the cause of which is still unknown in most cases. When cancer occurs in the wall of any tube, it will often encircle the tube and gradually narrow the way through. This is what happens in the œsophagus, leading to difficulty in swallowing, particularly solids. It is a condition, usually, of rather elderly men, although it is sometimes associated with a special form of severe anæmia in women. Treatment is in some way to keep the passage open, either by transplanting a new tube, or more usually, by removing the constricted piece and joining up the remainder.

The Stomach and Duodenum.

By far the commonest diseases of the stomach and duodenum are *gastric ulcer* and *duodenal ulcer*. They are actually the same condition in two different sites and are often classed together as *peptic ulcer* or *acid-peptic disease*. The ulcers, which are rather like sores on the lining of the stomach or duodenum, may be "acute" or "chronic." Acute ulcers tend to be small and there are often several of them. Chronic ulcers are usually single. They may be small, or they may be several centimetres across. Chronic ulcers smoulder for months and even years, like a sore which will not heal, and a great deal of scar tissue forms in their depths. Thus they may in time erode their way right through the wall of the stomach, destroying all its layers, and begin to eat into surrounding structures like the pancreas or liver. The fact that they do not perforate more frequently is due to all the fibrous scar tissue which is formed during the slow eroding process. Healing of such a destructive ulcer is nevertheless common, and the great problem is how to help the natural healing process to win against the ulcer's tendency to erode. Better still would be to discover the cause, and prevent it happening in the first place. This extremely common affliction is confined to the human species and has been known since the earliest times. It does not vary very much with diet or with social class. Although occurring at all ages, it usually begins between the ages of twenty and forty, and is most commonly found in men between forty-five and fifty-five. Gastric ulcer is four times, and duodenal ulcer ten times more common in men than in women. It is always due to an inability of the lining to stand up to the normal digestive activity of the stomach contents. These are normally acid and contain a powerful enzyme for digesting proteins. Again it is perhaps more surprising that we all do not digest our own stomachs, rather than that some unfortunate people do digest small areas slowly. In certain abnormal conditions when the stomach stops making acid, ulcers always heal. However, some ulcers occur without excessive secretion of acid and many heal without the acid being neutralised with antacids. All this points to the main trouble being in the response of the lining to acid, rather than to the acid itself. Nevertheless, the most effective treatment at present known involves regulating gastric secretion, and particularly its acidity. It is also known that peptic ulcers are more common in people whose occupations involve administrative and professional responsibility, competitive effort and nervous tension, long periods of anxiety or frustration. Presumably the higher nervous system influences these events by the same nerves, which normally help to control secretion.

The main symptom of peptic ulcer is pain, and this usually responds well to proper doses of antacids. Many different varieties are available and a lot of money is made from selling them. When indigestion persists for longer than a few days it is always better to see your doctor so that a proper diagnosis can be made and the best remedies begun. Many other causes exist for similar pains, and you should not try to make the diagnosis yourself. It may be necessary to analyse your gastric secretions in the hospital laboratory. Almost certainly you will have a special X-ray examination, and since the stomach cannot easily be seen on a normal X-ray, they will have to show it up by making you drink a white material containing barium. This will be seen as a silhouette of the stomach and duodenal contents. Searching for an ulcer this way is a highly skilled matter and is performed by doctors specially trained in radiology.

Treatment of peptic ulcer is designed to relieve symptoms, heal the ulcer, and prevent complications (see later). Some rest and sedation may help to deal with the psychological influences at work. A special diet may be required. If certain foods cause discomfort they will naturally be avoided, but there is no evidence that any particular foods, like coarse or highly seasoned things retard, or that a soft, bland diet enhances healing. The era of sloppy, milky diets is almost over, for which countless ulcer sufferers will be profoundly thankful. Suitable antacids will be prescribed. Once an ulcer is diagnosed, the time has come to stop treating yourself with antacids from the chemist's counter, and to take the ones your doctor decides are best. Smoking should be stopped by ulcer patients (as, indeed, by everyone else, but that is another matter) because it inhibits healing. Alcohol tends to increase acid secretion and should be avoided. It is also *extremely important* to avoid taking any form of aspirin, even in quite small amounts, since this can lead to very serious bleeding from the ulcer. The ulcer patient should be warned that hundreds of proprietary preparations contain aspirin and all of them are dangerous for him. Search for the formula in small print on the label before taking any remedy, looking particularly for acetyl salicylic acid—the correct name for aspirin. Doctors have been pressing for years for a law which would make it obligatory for patent medicine manufacturers to label aspirin-containing drugs clearly. There is still no such regulation, so that even some widely sold "hang-over" remedies which are sold for "upset-stomach" contain large quantities of aspirin. Some of the patients with "upset stomach" are, of course, ulcer patients, and some even die of haemorrhage following the ingestion of aspirin.

The main complications of peptic ulcer are bleeding, perforation, and a narrowing of the pylorus, or lower part, known as *pyloric stenosis*. Bleeding is caused by the eroding ulcer eating away at one of the many blood vessels in the stomach or duodenal wall. It leads to the passing of "altered" blood in the stool (*melaena*), or to the vomiting of blood (*haematemesis*). When the initial bleeding occurs, the patient may feel suddenly faint, and a little later will notice the black, tarry colour of his stool. This is sometimes confused with a similiar colour when the patient is taking iron. Peptic ulcer is not the only cause of this very serious haemorrhage, which constitutes a hospital emergency whatever its cause. The treatment, like that of every large haemorrhage, is blood transfusion which must be continued until the bleeding stops, or until the patient is sufficiently fit for surgery, should that be deemed necessary. Perforation is perhaps the most serious complication of peptic ulcer, leading to the spilling of stomach contents within the abdominal cavity. Treatment is invariably surgical, either the closure of the perforation or the partial removal of the stomach.

Surgical removal of part of the stomach is often the only way to treat a peptic ulcer which has had its chance to heal in other ways. It is tempting for the patient to " have it out and done with ", but the time for surgery is a matter of fine judgment. So many ulcers heal by medical means if you give them a chance, and operations are for those which persistently refuse, or which become complicated.

Stomach Cancer. The stomach is a fairly common site for primary cancer. There is no known reason for this, and it is particularly important to stress that we know of no connection whatever between the peptic ulcers which have just been discussed and cancer. Stomach cancer used to be the commonest cancer of men, but the current rise of lung cancer has pushed it into second place. There are some strange geographical differences in its distribution. For example, it is much commoner in Japan and Scandinavia than in England or the U.S.A. It is difficult to see any reason for this in dietary habits. In Wales it causes three times as many deaths as in South-East England. All this is very puzzling, as is so much of our information about cancer generally. One of the main problems with stomach cancer is that it often causes the patient no inconvenience and thus produces no symptoms of note until the disease is far advanced and it is difficult to do much. Treatment is by surgical removal of the growth, and even in the most advanced cases a great deal can often be done to make the patient more comfortable.

The Small Intestine.

The small intestine runs from the stomach to the cæcum and comprises the duodenum, jejunum, and ileum in that order. On a more cheerful note it may be remarked that it is very rarely the site of cancer. Its main problems arise in connection with defects in absorption mechanisms, with obstructions, and with a strange inflammatory condition known as *regional enteritis.* Most obstructions are due not to blockages of the tube, but to failures of peristaltic propulsion, the process which is briefly described above under " œsophagus." Such a failure is called *ileus.* When peristalsis stops for any reason, the result is severe dehydration and loss of important chemicals like sodium and chloride from the body. This is because about two gallons of fluid enter the small intestine each day in the form of digestive juices, and all of this has to be pushed onwards to be reabsorbed into the system at lower levels. If peristalsis fails, this bulk of fluid remains in the small intestine, or is vomited. In both cases it is lost to the body itself, leading to serious dehydration and illness. Treatment is by very careful replacement by transfusion of the fluid and the chemicals lost, and by removal of the trapped fluid within the intestine through a tube threaded down through the mouth.

Regional enteritis or *ileitis* is sometimes known as *Crohn's disease.* It is a very mysterious condition in which the normally supple wall of the small intestine becomes inflamed and gradually replaced by thick fibrous scar tissue, so that it looks and feels like a thick garden hose. Loops of inflamed gut stick together, and channels open between them, and if the disease progresses a mass of adherent, thickened intestine results to which everything in the neighbourhood also adheres. However, for some unknown reason some cases do not progress downhill in this way and get better spontaneously. Surgical treatment is necessary for the majority, however, particularly those with advanced disease leading to complications such as obstruction or perforation. Sometimes an early case can be resolved by cutting out the length of affected gut, although recurrences are unfortunately common.

Appendicitis. This must be one of the best known surgical diseases of the intestinal tract.

The appendix is a narrow, blind-ended side tube attached to the cæcum near the end of the small intestine. Appendicitis is when it becomes obstructed, or infected, or both. From its position it is almost predictable that it will get obstructed sooner or later by pieces of fæcal matter which pass its entrance and which are normally infected. The surprising thing is that it does not happen more often. Once this has occurred, however, a closed abscess forms, and as the abscess distends the appendix, it first weakens its wall, making it gangrenous, and then bursts into the abdominal cavity causing *peritonitis* (see later). It would be useless and misleading to describe the symptoms of acute appendicitis in detail, since it is difficult even for experienced doctors to distinguish them from those of several other conditions. Suffice it to say that any severe, persisting pain in the abdomen, whether continuous or intermittent, whether associated with diarrhœa or not, should lead the sufferer to a doctor for a quick diagnosis. Germ-killing antibiotics are useless against appendicitis, and any laxative is extremely dangerous as it may cause an acutely inflamed appendix to perforate.

The Large Intestine or Colon.

The two main serious diseases of the colon are ulcerative colitis and cancer in its various forms. *Ulcerative colitis* is yet another mysterious disease in which severe ulceration of the lining of the colon gives rise most frequently to diarrhœa with the passage of blood and mucus. In fact it can be like dysentery, and it has often been considered to be due to some form of infection. Unfortunately no particular germ can routinely be found in these cases, and the situation is endlessly confused by the presence in the normal bowel of lots of different germs anyway. Nevertheless the ulcerated lining of the bowel certainly does get infected by the germs normally present, and this makes the disease worse. Therefore germ-killing antibiotics are often helpful in alleviating symptoms and can lead to an earlier settling down of the condition, although not to a cure. It has long been known that certain kinds of psychological upset are often associated, but here again the disease is so unpleasant for the sufferer that he is to be forgiven some despondency as a result of, rather than as a cause of, his troubles. It is also suspected that ulcerative colitis may be an auto-immune disease; that is it may represent rejection by the patient of his own colonic lining in a manner somewhat comparable to the tissue rejection which often follows organ transplantation. Some of the more alarming complications are perforation through the wall of the ulcerated bowel, and sometimes massive hæmorrhage occurs. Medical treatment takes the form of keeping the patient in good physical condition in spite of his fluid and blood loss and his frequent lack of appetite. Surgery is often required to relieve obstruction, deal with perforation, remove chronically affected parts of the bowel, etc.

Cancer of the Colon and Rectum. This is another very common form of cancer, which can often be completely cured by surgical removal of the growth provided it is caught in the early stages before it has spread. The commonest symptom is a change in bowel habit, either towards constipation or, more often, towards diarrhœa, in the second half of life. There may be rectal bleeding, or the passage of mucus, and there may be abdominal pain. We cannot too often repeat that any such change of bowel habit, or any unexplained bleeding from any site should lead the patient promptly to his doctor.

Diverticulitis. Some people have small pockets or sacs in the wall of the colon known as diverticula. A minority of these sometimes get inflamed, and this is *diverticulitis.* Occasionally perforation occurs.

Hernia or Rupture. This is a condition in which abdominal contents, usually a loop of intestine, protrude forwards through the muscular wall of the abdomen. The wall consists of a sheet of muscle fibres running in several directions. They normally become tense when we cough, or strain, or in getting up from a recumbent position. There are places in the groin on each side where there is a way through the muscle for the spermatic cord in the male. In many men a weakness can arise at this point, and if it persists, the way through may enlarge and allow loops of bowel to emerge from behind the muscle sheet to appear as a lump under the skin of the groin. On relaxation the lump can be made to disappear by pushing the contents back the way they came; and they will re-emerge when the patient strains. This is an extremely common complaint in men, and it should be treated by an operation in which the muscle wall is repaired. Some men, however, neglect to have their rupture treated until one day it proceeds to "strangulate." This is the time used when the muscle tightens around the neck of the protruding loop of bowel, cutting off its blood supply. From then onwards the loop becomes gangrenous and the intestine is obstructed by having a part of itself nipped outside the abdominal wall. The patient is in severe pain, vomits continously, and quickly is liable to get into such a poor condition that surgical relief is difficult. It is therefore a surgical emergency, and it would have been better to have had the relatively simple repair operation earlier and at leisure. Hernia in the region of the groin is of two types: *inguinal hernia* and *femoral hernia*, the difference between them being technical and of no consequence to the patient. They nearly always occur in men. Other types of hernia less frequently occur in both sexes. *Incisional hernia* is when the muscle wall has been weakened at the site of an old abdominal operation and has failed to heal properly. *Umbilical hernia* occurs owing to the natural weakness of the abdominal wall at the navel, and is so common in babies as to be almost normal. When a baby cries and thereby puts a strain on his abdominal wall, a lump often appears in the region of the navel, and this can be very alarming for the parents. They should of course show it to their doctor who will nearly always be able to reassure them. It is self-healing without operation in the majority of cases.

Peritonitis. The cavity of the abdomen in which the intestines and other organs lie is called the peritoneal cavity, and it is lined by a thin membrane called the peritoneum. When this becomes inflamed the condition is a serious one and is called *peritonitis*. Inflammation may be bacterial, as occurs following a burst appendix and the spillage of bacteria and pus in the cavity. It may be a sterile peritonitis as often follows perforation of a peptic ulcer, when the inflammation is caused by the acid contents of the stomach. It is always very dangerous, probably because of the large surface area afforded by the peritoneum for the absorption of inflammatory toxins.

Hæmorrhoids are simply varicose veins in the rectal and anal regions. They are very common, and are caused probably in about equal degrees by inherited weakness of the veins, strain such as heavy lifting, and constipation (this is one of the very few conditions in which constipation may do some damage, due to the mechanical pressure of hardened faeces in the rectum on the veins). Pregnant women are liable to develop hæmorrhoids or "*piles*," as they are commonly called, owing to the pressure of the baby's head in the pelvis. Hæmorrhoids may be external or internal, the former being in the anal region below the sphincter, the latter in the rectum; the two usually go together. There may be no symptoms, but the veins are liable to bleed, to get thrombosed (*i.e.*, a clot forms within) or to become infected. When clotting or infection occurs the piles enlarge and tend to be pushed out through the anus during defaecation, when they form extremely painful external swellings. Treatment in simple cases may be by the use of suppositories—cones of a firm grease containing suitable medicaments which are inserted in the rectum—in other cases the veins may be injected, as with varicose veins of the leg, in order to close them, but when there is

much bleeding, thrombosis, infection, or interference with bowel movements they should be removed surgically.

DISEASES OF THE LIVER

The liver is the largest organ and has such a wide variety of known functions (to say nothing of the unknown) that it is also one of the most complicated. Nearly all of its functions are biochemical, and it is often called the laboratory of the body. Medical students, when asked to enumerate the functions of the liver, usually stick at about twenty-five, nearly all of them to do with general metabolism: that is the biochemical processing of substances taking part in structure or as body fuel. For example, the liver makes proteins from the amino-acids absorbed from the gut, and breaks down amino-acids and manufactures a waste product (urea) from them. It stores carbohydrates as glycogen, and conducts many of the processes necessary to turn carbohydrates into energy. It manufactures prothrombin with the help of vitamin K, and this is essential for blood clotting. It makes bile and secretes it into the gall bladder and bile ducts (*see later*). The three main constituents of bile (cholesterol, bile pigment or bilirubin, and bile acids) all have to be processed, or metabolised, in the liver during the production of bile. Vitamin B_{12} and iron is also stored and dealt with there, and these are involved in preventing various forms of anaemia (*q.v.*); and in addition to all these things the liver is the place where harmful substances, both from within the body and from outside it, are dealt with and rendered harmless. This last function of "detoxication" is often accomplished by making the offending molecules suitable for rapid excretion by the kidneys, or by altering their chemical shape to make them harmless.

Nearly all of these very different things are done by one single type of cell: the liver cell, and it is one of the remarkable features of the design that this cell can be so versatile. There also have to be some very efficient transport systems in the liver, in addition to the usual blood supply and venous drainage possessed by all other tissues.

One of these is the "portal venous system." Whenever a substance is absorbed across the gut wall from any part of the intestine into the interior of the body it enters the special draining blood vessels of the portal system, which are arranged throughout the length of the digestive tract. All these veins eventually unite in the main portal vein which enters the liver. Everything absorbed from the gut is therefore taken first to the liver to be processed. After this the products are carried away from the liver in the ordinary veins to the heart, and are distributed to the rest of the body by the arterial system. The liver has arteries of its own by which it receives oxygen and nutriment like any other tissue. The fourth transport system collects the bile as it is formed within the liver and delivers it to the gall bladder and bile ducts, which eventually drain it into the duodenum.

Portal Hypertension means high blood pressure in the portal venous system, and is the usual accompaniment to *cirrhosis* (*see later*). When the terminations of the portal veins in the liver are strangled and obstructed by cirrhotic disease, this tends to blow them up, or dilate them with blood. There is a natural escape route for the portal blood where the lower end of the oesophagus or gullet joins the upper end of the stomach. At this place some of the portal veins draining the stomach are connected with the ordinary veins draining the oesophagus so that when pressure rises in the portal system, blood tends to be diverted into these connecting veins, and they in turn become dilated, or varicose. Trouble begins when these dilated connecting veins, which bulge inwards into the oesophagus, are damaged by food particles passing across them and bleed severely into the stomach. The patient vomits large quantities of blood (*haematemesis*) or passes tarry altered blood in the stool *(melaena)*. The other main cause of these is the bleeding which occasionally accompanies peptic ulcer *(q.v.)*.

A second complication of portal hypertension (and hence of cirrhosis) is *ascites*, in which large amounts of a lymph-like fluid accumulate in the abdominal cavity. The fluid contains a great deal of precious protein and salt which is lost to the body economy. Ascites also sometimes accompanies cancerous deposits in the abdomen.

Jaundice means being yellow because there is too much yellow bile pigment circulating in the blood, and there are three main possible causes for this. The term "yellow jaundice," like "gastric stomach" is therefore unnecessarily redundant: there is no other kind.

Bile pigment comes from broken-down red blood cells, which normally come to the end of their time after existing for about 120 days. The breakdown products of red cells can always be found in the blood of normal people, but there is normally insufficient colour to show. Abnormal amounts of colour build up quite logically in any of the following three circumstances:

(1) If too many red cells are being destroyed and even the normal liver cannot deal with the amount of bile pigment produced, it piles up in the blood, and *haemolytic jaundice* is the result. The expression simply means jaundice due to (abnormally large) red-cell destruction.

(2) If the liver cells are themselves sick and unable to cope even with the normal amounts of pigment from normal red-cell destruction. Here too the pigment will pile up and cause *hepatocellular jaundice*, or liver-cell jaundice.

(3) If the bile ducts carrying bile away from the liver are blocked, then bile will pile up behind the blockage and re-enter the blood stream, causing *obstructive jaundice*. In this case the rate of red-cell breakdown is normal, and the liver cells are normal: at least for a time.

It is enormously important for the treatment of jaundice for the doctor to diagnose its type correctly, since the treatment varies from surgical relief of obstruction to the medical treatment of viral infection or of excess red-cell destruction.

The so-called differential diagnosis of jaundice is often exceptionally difficult, and sometimes requires some very sophisticated laboratory tests and X-rays. At other times it is extremely easy and is obvious from a cursory glance at the urine and the stool. In any case all jaundice is a highly technical matter for the doctor who must be consulted early.

There is a special jaundice of newborn babies which resembles haemolytic jaundice and can occasionally have serious consequences for the developing brain *(kernicterus)* if it is allowed to become too severe. When this is threatened, steps are taken to reduce the level of circulating bile pigment by replacement of the baby's blood or by other means.

The commonest cause of hepatocellular jaundice is infective or viral hepatitis. Obstructive jaundice is usually due either to blockage by gallstones *(q.v.)* or by a lump pressing on the bile ducts from an adjacent cancer. This can often be quite satisfactorily relieved by surgery.

Infective Hepatitis. There is a group of disorders affecting the liver which are caused by viruses. The incubation period is often very long, and the sickness and other debility caused is often quite severe and prolonged. One variety, known as serum sickness, is now much less common than a few years ago. It used to be transmitted by using the same needle for injections into several different people, or from transfusing contaminated blood. A greater awareness of the problem, and the use of disposable needles and syringes has cut down the incidence.

Cirrhosis. There are many different kinds of cirrhosis, the commonest of which has already

been mentioned under *portal hypertension* above. In all cases, liver cells are slowly poisoned and are killed off over a long period of time. In response to this, the surviving liver cells undergo cell division, trying to make good the numbers lost, and at the same time fibrous scar tissue replaces the damaged tissue throughout the organ. The result is a hard, knobbly liver. The many "knobs" are spherical areas of regenerated new cells, and they are separated by thickened bands of scar tissue. All of this destroys the normal architecture and leads to the portal hypertension and ascites mentioned above. In some countries *(e.g.,* France and the United States) excessive alcohol is the main cause of the original liver damage which starts it all off. In others *(e.g.,* Bantu South Africa) it seems to be nutritional starvation of the liver. In England much less than half the cases are due to alcohol, and many are thought to be due to a previous episode of infective hepatitis *(q.v.)*, but this is not certain. Infective hepatitis is quite common but cirrhosis is comparatively rare. So that the great majority of people do not progress from one to the other. One day soon the treatment for advanced cirrhosis will be to replace the liver by transplantation, but there are still many problems to overcome before this can become routine.

Cancer of the Liver. Cancer of the liver is quite common, but it is nearly always cancer which has spread in the blood stream from other parts of the body. The liver is a favourite site for such secondary deposits, since it has a large blood supply and will receive a generous helping of anything being carried. It is also a very "fertile soil" for the cancer seedlings to grow in. Primary cancer of the liver is uncommon, and only occurs in a few cases of pre-existing cirrhosis.

Gallstones. These are "stones" formed by some of the major constituents of bile coming out of solution and forming solid bodies. They are very common, and often cause no trouble at all. When they do, it is usually a cholicky intermittent severe pain. This is due to the muscular walls of the bile passages contracting in an effort to expel an obstructing stone into the duodenum. The second common trouble arising from gallstones is obstructive jaundice, described above. It is small consolation to gallstone sufferers that the stones are often very pretty, often being composed of beautiful cholesterol crystals coloured by varying shades of bile. If they contain calcium they will be visible on an X-ray. Otherwise they are not seen. There is a persisting myth in the textbooks that sufferers are usually Females who are Fair, Fat, Forty and Fecund. It is not true. Stones often occur in conjunction with inflammation of the gall bladder, known as *cholecystitis*. The treatment for gallstones is to remove them surgically together with the gall bladder if they are causing persistent symptoms.

The Pancreas.

This is a soft, elongated gland lying behind the stomach; it is about 5 in. long and 2 in. wide. Within its tissues lies the duct, which, when it leaves the pancreas, passes into the duodenum near the point of entry of the bile-duct. This duct transmits the juices containing enzymes which aid in the digestion in the small intestine. The pancreas, however, has two main functions: not only does it manufacture these important digestive juices, but in certain specialised areas, known as the islets of Langerhans, it manufactures insulin, the hormone which makes it possible for the body to utilise sugar. *Diabetes mellitus* or ordinary diabetes is a chronic disorder usually caused by a deficient secretion of insulin. The unused sugar accumulates in the blood and acts as a poison, which, in extreme cases, sends the patient into coma and may—indeed, in former times, usually did—result in death. The treatment of diabetes was revolutionised by the discovery of the hormone insulin by Banting and Best in 1921. On the whole, diabetes is more severe in young people than in the elderly, but with correct treatment it is possible for all cases to lead a perfectly normal life except for dietary restrictions and insulin injections. Not to be confused with *Diabetes insipidus* (P43(2)).

DIET.

When considering diet, and the effect it has on our health and well-being, there is more to it than just the things we eat. We must also know about what our body does with the food, and it would be unscientific not to acknowledge the effects of our psychological make-up and our nutritional beliefs on what we eat, what we do with it, and how well (or ill) we feel as a result.

For example, a deep-rooted conviction that brown eggs or free-range poultry are better for us than white eggs or intensively reared birds is entirely unsupported by any evidence. However, if we believe such a thing sufficiently, we will not only eat the " better " ones, but we will feel happier and more secure afterwards, and this is likely to make us healthier. Food fads can occasionally be dangerous, as when extreme vegetarians become ill through lack of certain vitamins (e.g. B_{12}) which are present only in the foods they exclude. But this is so rare, even among strict vegetarians, that such danger can virtually be ignored. On the whole (and vegetarianism is probably a good example of this) food faddism often leads to a sense of health and well-being in the believer, and should not be attacked by the rest of us for that. It is an accepted fact that personal misfortune, even when it is severe, is more easily withstood by those with strong religious conviction than by others. In the same way, a firm attachment to a theory of what is good for you can produce a feeling of well-being and genuine good health, when another person on exactly the same food intake will not feel so fit. These factors—religious belief, food faddism, or the bedside manner of a kind or persuasive doctor —are commonly dismissed by free-thinking people because they are not " true " or " real." All three, however, can materially affect our health just as can a shock, a personal tragedy. or being in love. The trouble starts, and the magic ceases to work, when adherants declaim their beliefs as *ex cathedra* truths and expect the rest of us to swallow them as wholly (or holy) as they do.

Thus there are genuine *facts* about food, and fallacies too; and as well as these there is a no-man's-land between in which one man's fact is another man's fallacy.

The basic constituents of any diet are protein, fats, carbohydrates, water, vitamins, minerals, salts, and indigestible roughage. All are chemicals whose structure and function are reasonably well understood. Even the mystical differences between fine table wines, so beloved of the connoisseur and gourmet, are reasonably well understood in chemical terms. Perhaps that is a pity.

Much nonsense is talked, especially by nutritionists, about minimal daily requirements. In general terms, however, requirements can be described in terms of how many calories there are in the total intake of proteins, fats, and carbohydrates per day, and how these are distributed between the three classes of food. The other substances mentioned above are only required in trace or small amounts except for water; and roughage is only required as a mechanical stimulus to bowel movement.

During the process of digestion (described on P34-5) all proteins are split into their constituent amino acids; all carbohydrates are split into their constituent simple sugars and most fats are converted into fatty acids and glycerol. At this stage, and not until this stage, all these simpler building bricks derived from the three classes of food are absorbed into the body proper, and taken to the liver and other tissues. Here they are " metabolised." That is to say they are either burned as fuel for the various processes of the body; or they are built up again into proteins, fats, and carbohydrates of the special kinds the body needs. They will either be used to rebuild structures suffering ordinary wear and tear or they will be stored. Many of them will be converted into a different class from the one they came from when they entered the body. For example, excess carbohydrate is converted into fat; or if there is a shortage of carbohydrate, some will be made out of the protein amino-acids which would normally have been used for tissue growth and repair. Thus it is only a generalisation to say that dietary carbohydrates are fuel and proteins are for building bodily structure. The body can convert

one into the other, and spoil the calculation.

There is a great deal of confusion in people's minds about *energy*, and that is why the word *fuel* has been used above in connection with carbohydrates. The lay person uses energy as a term meaning something which allows us to leap about, running and jumping and skipping and dancing, and which keeps us from getting tired and run down. Thus, the food industry tells us, we need potatoes or breakfast cereals for these activities or for a hard day's work. This is a deliberate commercial confidence trick, and the scientist is largely to blame. He originally handed out the word energy to an eager food industry and an unsuspecting public, forgetting to explain that he meant it in the strictly scientific sense of fuel for bodily processes. It simply is not true that more potatoes, or more cornflakes will make you more active. Indeed the reverse is the case, and after a certain point they will only be converted into fat and reduce your activity. The nutritionist measures energy as calories, which are units of heat, and it is certainly true that you must eat enough of these each day if you wish to remain alive, let alone active.

All the three main classes of food provide calories, and in an ordinary well-balanced diet about 15% are provided by protein. Carbohydrates produce most of the remainder. Each gram of fat contains about twice the calories of a similar quantity of carbohydrate. We simply eat less fat than carbohydrate, because fat has a " high satiety value." It takes away the appetite for more. Proteins are mostly found in meat, fish, eggs, cheese, and milk. However, there is quite a lot of protein in many predominantly starchy foods like bread, and such grains as wheat rice, and corn. Carbohydrates are mainly found in bread, potatoes, sugar, pastry, sweets, and so forth. That is one of the words which fortunately seems to be used by both scientists and laymen in much the same sense.

Some substances are absolutely essential to the body if life is to continue, even if they are only needed in trace amounts. These are substances which the body's own factories (like the liver) cannot make for themselves, even if they are provided with the correct ingredients. Unfortunately these essential constituents were given a system of names which grew, like Topsy, as they were discovered, and which has stuck due to common usage, even though more recent knowledge has made a nonsense of most of the words. One whole group of such substances is the *vitamins*. All of these, by definition, are essential and have to be provided for the body in the diet. Vitamins are another gold-mine for the food and pharmaceutical industry. The public know that scientists have discovered these magic substances, only tiny amounts of which are required to keep people healthy. Starting with that piece of " magic " it is not difficult to mislead people into two sorts of erroneous conclusion. The first is that all signs of minor ill-health and tiredness (from which we all suffer at times) are due to lack of these vitamins; and secondly that extra vitamins are the key to " extra " health. The truth is that no one in England who is eating a normal diet is short of vitamins in it; and there are no dividends in " extra " health for taking vitamins above the normal daily intake present in food. It simply is not true that extra vitamin C or D gives protection from colds and other winter ailments. The fate of the extra vitamin intake, however expensive, is the same as the fate of anything else the body cannot use: it finds its way expensively into the lavatory. The money would have been much better spent on wholesome meat or other non-fattening food.

Thankfully, most people buy food because they like it, not because it does them good; and provided they have normal dietary tastes they will usually get a perfectly adequate selection of the things we have spoken of as necessary for good health. The main danger in England is to have a surfeit and become overweight. In addition there are certain times of life when conscious attention should be paid to what is necessary. For example babies and nursing mothers have special dietary needs and will hear about them from their Health Visitor or from their Welfare Clinic or Doctor. Elderly people living alone are also prone to dietary deficiencies for reasons ranging from poverty to loss of appetite or inability to look after themselves properly.

Recent surveys have revealed some interesting facts about people's attitude to food and their knowledge of it. For example, half the people asked knew that meat was a source of protein, a third mentioned eggs and a fifth cheese, fish, and milk. But practically no one knew there was protein in bread. Yet in England about a fifth of our daily protein intake comes from bread, and nearly a third from cereals as a whole. Fish is well known as a source of protein, but did you know that on average we only obtain 4% of our daily protein from fish—less than we get from potatoes (5%)? No one seems to know that potatoes are an important source of vitamin C, although fruit and vegetables are well-known sources. Calcium is recognised in milk, but most people forget its presence in cheese. Most people are very confused about iron. Why does everyone think it is mainly in green vegetables, when these are really such a poor source? Are we indoctrinated by Popeye? For our daily requirement of iron we would each have to eat 2¼ lb. spring greens or peas; or 4½ lb. of sprouts! In fact meat provides one of our best sources, and one-fifth of our daily needs is contained in bread.

Since most of the people who read Pears live in England let us return finally to our commonest nutritional disease, or our commonest form of malnutrition in these islands: obesity. Call it " being overweight " if you like, but acknowledge that it means being fat. Being fat is not only unattractive and unsightly but it is dangerous to health and carries a high mortality. Ask any life insurance company how they view your chances if you are overweight and you will find they are as worried about it as if you had high blood pressure, or smoke heavily. It is a particularly important cause of heart disease. However, it is very important to know exactly what we mean by fatness. Many girls who are not at all fat think they are, and this leads them to diet unnecessarily. On the other hand there are people who do not appreciate they are overweight. Here is a table which shows what your weight should be according to your height.

If you are overweight according to these tables you need to slim, and the question is how? Answer: by will-power. There is no other satisfactory method than to decide to eat less, and to eat as little carbohydrate as possible. For the time being eat as much meat, fruit, green vegetables, and as much fat as you like, but no sugar, starch, sweets, cakes, pastry, or biscuits, and no eating between meals. And cut down on beer and other alcoholic drinks. In case you are tempted to eat " slimming " foods, be aware that there is no such thing. There is nothing you can eat which will cause you to lose weight, in spite of what the advertisement says. In special cases doctors will prescribe tablets to suppress appetite, but they

DESIRABLE WEIGHTS FOR MEN AND WOMEN ACCORDING TO HEIGHT AND FRAME, AGES 25 AND OVER

Men Height (with shoes on— one-inch heels)	Weight in pounds (in indoor clothing)		
	Small frame	Medium frame	Large frame
5' 2"	112-120	118-129	126-141
3"	115-123	121-133	129-144
4"	118-126	124-136	132-148
5"	121-129	127-139	135-152
6"	124-133	130-143	138-156
7"	128-137	134-147	142-161
8"	132-141	138-152	147-166
9"	136-145	142-156	151-170
10"	140-150	146-160	155-174
11"	144-154	150-165	159-179
6' 0"	148-158	154-170	163-184
1"	152-162	158-175	168-189
2"	156-167	162-180	173-194
3"	160-171	167-185	178-199
4"	164-175	172-190	182-204

Women Height (with shoes on— two-inch heels)	Small frame	Medium frame	Large frame
4' 10"	92-98	96-107	104-119
11"	94-101	98-110	106-122
5' 0"	96-104	101-113	109-125
1"	99-107	104-116	112-128
2"	102-110	107-119	115-131
3"	105-113	110-122	118-134
4"	108-116	113-126	121-138
5"	111-119	116-130	125-142
6"	114-123	120-135	129-146
7"	118-127	124-139	133-150
8"	122-131	128-143	137-154
9"	126-135	132-147	141-158
10"	130-140	136-151	145-163
11"	134-144	140-155	149-168
6' 0"	138-148	144-159	153-173

are too dangerous for general use without supervision, and they do not work as well as will-power. At the same time take more exercise. Walk to work. If you make a real and genuine effort for three months without success, you should ask your doctor for advice. Almost certainly you will have to admit you have not really tried. Good luck!

NUTRITIONAL DISORDERS.

Nutritional Deficiency and Malnutrition.—Until quite recently a consideration of malnutrition would have merely led to an account of how too little food, or a deficiency of certain articles in the diet, produced deficiency diseases at the time of the restriction. For example lack of vitamins or various kinds gives rise to such diseases as rickets, scurvy, beri-beri, and pellagra; and an overall shortage of food to general starvation. These may be considered the immediate or concurrent effects of a poor diet. Modern nutritionists, however, are beginning to be concerned with two more kinds of nutritional disorders; and although the study of both kinds is in its infancy, both will be introduced in this account.

The first deals with the effects of comparatively small amounts of harmful constituents in our diet, introduced either voluntarily or involuntarily, and consumed for a long period of time; and the second with the lasting effects on our adult wellbeing of nutritional deficiencies in early life even though they have long since been corrected.

When viewed in this light, one or other of these three kinds of nutritional disorder may at this moment be affecting almost every individual in every part of the world, " privileged " or " underprivileged." Let us first define some terms.

Undernutrition, strictly speaking, means a state of affairs in which the quality of the diet is perfectly good. There is the correct balance of the various dietary constituents and all the necessary components are present: but there is simply too little of it. Many hundreds of millions of people throughout the underprivileged world are suffering and dying from this kind of undernutrition, and the simplicity of the problem must be appreciated: they simply need more food of the kind they are at present getting, and which can often be produced locally.

Malnutrition means an imbalance of the various constituents: a relative lack or excess of one or more of them. It usually leads to conditions which are, from the point of view of medical treatment, much more difficult to deal with. And therefore doctors often class them as "more serious."

The diseases of malnutrition range from the widespread protein deficiencies in other parts of the underprivileged world to obesity in our own better-off industrial countries, which is usually due to excess carbohydrate. Make no mistake about it: obesity (or being overweight) is a widespread disease of nutritional imbalance, and it kills. It is the commonest form of malnutrition in (for example) England and America today, and is a consequence of the sophistication of our diet in modern times. Between one-fifth and one-tenth of the population of the United States is more than 20% overweight, and to be 10% or 15% overweight is almost the rule nowadays in people over thirty. There are high authorities in the world of nutritional science who attribute all this overfed malnutrition to the consumption of refined sugar, or sucrose. They say it is not only the amount of refined sugar we put in our tea or on our breakfast cereals, but also the amount in sweet cakes, biscuits, drinks, chocolates and sweets, and so forth. For some people it adds up to a phenomenal quantity each day. According to this school of thought we are not so much suffering from a surfeit of carbohydrates or starches, but from this single sugar, sucrose. It is interesting to reflect on the recent banning of the artificial sweetener, cyclamate, by many governments. This substance, having been used extensively throughout the world as an apparently harmless non-fattening substitute for sugar, was suddenly banned in America because in very large doses (equivalent to the amount taken in hundreds of cups of coffee per day for a long time) it was found to produce cancer in rats. It has never been shown to do humans any harm, whereas the effects of sugar in producing an overweight population, thereby indirectly kill tens of thousands of British people each year. This is a fascinating example of the difficulties confronting our legislators in making balanced judgments when deciding to ban a foodstuff, a drug, or an artificial fertiliser.

Much the most widespread form of malnutrition, however, is a variety protein-lack which is part of a collection of nutritional diseases known as *Protein-Calorie Deficiency.* In very large underprivileged areas of the world, the childhood population receives such an inadequate diet that children live continuously on the brink of nutritional disaster. It only requires a small extra restriction or stress to topple them over into one of the clinical conditions to be described. At this stage they cease to be merely hungry. They become nutritionally ill. Sometimes the force which produces the disaster is a community catastrophe like a famine, an earthquake, or a war. Sometimes it is a family catastrophe like the loss of a lactating mother or a parental delinquency. Parents abandon young children as often in Africa as anywhere else. Sometimes the clinical nutritional disease is unmasked by a common childhood illness like measles, or gastro-enteritis which the well-fed child would have overcome. The starved child reveals his malnutrition instead and frequently dies. When the precipitating cause of the " epidemic " of malnutrition is a war or other national calamity, our newspapers and television screens carry distressing pictures of thin skeletal, pot-bellied children, and the conscience of a few is touched. It is insufficiently realised that these scenes can be witnessed anywhere in the continents of Africa and Asia, and in large parts of Central and South America any day of the week in normal times. The war has not been the cause, but is only the precipitating factor which has revealed the chronic malnutrition in more children than would normally exhibit it openly.

Protein-Calorie Deficiency is a collection of different kinds of childhood malnutrition. Some are due predominantly to deficiency of protein and are collectively called Kwashiorkor, a West African word meaning " red-haired boy " (see below). Others are mainly due to a severe deficiency of overall foodstuffs and are called *Marasmus.* But in any real-life situation the severe *mal*nutrition of Kwashiorkor exists side-by-side with all gradations between itself and the severe *under*nutrition of Marasmus, so that many intermediate forms of " marasmic kwashiorkor " are described. In kwashiorkor the child is typically listless, apathetic, whining, with a reddish discoloration of the hair, a peeling, scaley skin, and with much extra fluid in his tissues causing oedema. He is so listless as not even to be hungry. In marasmus the child is ravenously hungry. He is extremely thin and " starved " looking and is quite a different picture.

There is good reason to believe that even when protein-calorie deficiency is successfully treated, there will always be some lasting restriction of mental function, particularly if the malnutrition

occurred as early as the first year of life. This is especially true in situations of appalling poverty in towns, where thousands of babies are not breastfed because their mothers are at work. Many of them die. Some of them are no heavier than their birth weight at one year of age. Breast feeding in an underprivileged community is an essential insurance for childhood health and survival.

Two new avenues of nutritional inquiry were mentioned at the beginning of this section. The impact of very long continued intake of refined sugar over many years on our bodily health is an example of one of them. Scientists and others are also becoming alarmed at the effects of modern food additives when taken, even in small amounts, over a long period. These additives include colouring matter, decolourising chemicals, taste " enhancers," and so forth, which are present in everyone's diet in a " civilised community." We are as unable to avoid a constant dosage with them as if they had been added to our water supply. It is, however, difficult to strike a balanced attitude. It is one thing to suspect that these additives are harmful and quite another to prove it. Naturally if any of them are shown to produce harm in animals given reasonable quantities they are invariably withdrawn. But in practice it is extremely difficult for animal experiments to mimic the conditions of human intake, especially as the human life span involves eating the substance concerned in small quantities for several decades. Thus it is easy to postulate the harmful effects of monosodium glutamate (a very common taste enhancer) but practically impossible to prove the question either way. It is not sufficient to condemn " chemicals." All natural foods consist of chemicals, and so do we.

The other new topic in nutrition is more soundly based on animal experiment. It has been repeatedly found that if animals do not grow quickly enough at certain early periods of life, they not only become small, but they remain smaller than they should be even when they are subsequently given as much as they like to eat. This is true of all animals and birds so far studied. For example, if rats are suckled in large families it is found that they are smaller by the time they are weaned (3 weeks of age) than those suckled in small families. The interesting thing is that if they are then given as much as they want to eat for the rest of their lives, the small animals from the larger families never catch up to the others. Whereas if their growth is not restricted until later in their " childhood," full " catch-up " is possible soon after normal diet is resumed. In other words there is a critical time in early life when growth can be permanently affected. At the moment it is difficult to know whether the same is true of humans and, if so, when is our period of vulnerability. There is some suggestion that the corresponding critical period in humans is during the last part of gestation in the uterus, and the first year or so of postnatal life. This new idea may turn out to be very important for world nutrition. Since there will not be enough food for all the children all the time, it may become important to concentrate our aid to underprivileged countries on certain sections of the population only. It may be a good idea to see that pregnant mothers and small babies are specially fed. In this way we may be able to put off the periods of inevitable malnutrition until a time of life when it is recoverable. Such a plan would also go a long way to safeguarding the development of the brain which also occurs mostly at the same early time of life.

We shall now describe some of the better-known nutritional deficiencies, bearing in mind that vitamin deficiencies are virtually unknown in the better-off countries. No one in England need spend money buying vitamins, as has been emphasised in the preceding section. Vitamin deficiency can still occur, however, in elderly people living alone and not having a well-balanced diet. It also occurs for similar reasons in alcoholics, vagrants, etc., and very occasionally in small children.

Beri-beri is a group of diseases usually confined to the Far East where a diet of polished rice results in a poor intake of vitamin B_1 (thiamine). In one form there is oedema (*q.v.*); in another the peripheral nerves are affected leading to tingling and numbness. A similar condition is occasionally seen in alcoholics and diabetics. Treatment is with thiamine, and with other vitamins too, since most sufferers are going short of more than one.

Pellagra is found among maize-eating populations and is due to a deficiency of several vitamins including niacin, another member of the B group of vitamins. There is dermatitis on exposed skin, and soreness of the mouth and tongue, with gastro-enteritis.

Scurvy is due to vitamin C deficiency. In children bone growth is affected. At all ages there is bleeding into the skin (bruising), impaired wound healing, mental depression, and anaemia. Most fresh fruit and vegetables contain vitamin C and a diet containing these prevents the disease.

Vitamin A deficiency is commonly found in children in some underprivileged countries. It causes permanent blindness, with thickening opacity and dryness of the whites of the eyes leading to ulceration of the eye. Beyond a certain stage, therefore, a child's sight cannot be saved. The only real hope is prevention, with an adequate diet.

Rickets, another disease of early childhood, is caused by deficiency of vitamin D. Bones are not properly calcified, and their softness leads to deformities of the legs and many other bones. Vitamin D can either be eaten in the diet or produced under the skin under the influence of sunlight. Therefore rickets commonly occurs when both the diet and the sunlight are inadequate. It was once very common in industrial England, and is still to be seen very occasionally these days in impoverished urban communities in the United States.

DISEASES OF THE ENDOCRINE GLANDS.

Glands are structures or organs which manufacture secretions (except for *lymph glands* which are not glands at all and should be called *lymph nodes*). The secretions are of two main kinds. The first are passed down tubes, or ducts, or are secreted directly into the hollow organs, and act locally. Good examples are the salivary glands which make saliva and pass it down ducts into the mouth for digestion of its contents and lubrication. These are *exocrine glands*. The second kind have no ducts, and secrete their product straight into the blood stream. This secretion is called a *hormone* and it is carried to all parts of the body by the blood where it acts at a distance on some remote part. These are the *endocrine glands* or *ductless glands*, and a number of them will be discussed in this section.

The first hormone, or "chemical messenger," was discovered by the British physiologist Starling in 1904, but the effects of removing some of the endocrine glands were known centuries before when removal of the male testes (castration) was practised to procure a form of manpower safe for the harem, to salvage a good male alto voice for the church choir, or to convert a rooster into a more eatable capon.

Anterior Pituitary.—Many of the endocrine glands do not act as separate autonomous organs in spite of their great differences. They are organised into a well-disciplined band by a "master-gland" called the anterior pituitary. Somebody once called it the "conductor of the endocrine orchestra" and the phrase is still repeated *ad nauseam* in students' examination papers. The pituitary, consisting of its two parts, anterior and posterior, is not much bigger than a pea and it sits right in the middle of the skull, centrally beneath the brain and joined to the brain by a short stalk. This astonishing tiny nodule of tissue produces at least eight important hormones.

One of these is *growth hormone*, which is necessary for normal growth, and also has an influence on insulin. An excess causes *gigantism* and *acromegaly*, often coinciding with diabetes, and

too little results in a form of dwarfism. Three others, known as *gonadotrophic hormones* regulate the cyclical and other activities of the reproductive organs and lactating breast. Another, *thyrotrophic hormone*, regulates thyroid activity, *Adrenocorticotrophic hormone*, or *ACTH*, as its name implies, looks after the activities of another important endocrine gland, the adrenal cortex. And there are several others.

Hypopituitarism, including *Simmonds' disease* and *Sheehan's disease*, results from destruction of the anterior pituitary. It is extremely rare, and is usually associated with difficult childbirth involving very severe bleeding. There are disturbances of all the functions mentioned above, particularly thyroid and adrenal failure (*q.v.*) with upset sexual function. Treatment is by replacing the lost hormones.

Hyperpituitarism, including *gigantism* and *acromegaly*, results from over-activity of the anterior pituitary, and is usually due to a tumour or overgrowth of the gland. In acromegaly the growth hormone is produced in excess over a long period of time in an adult. This results in overgrowth of all the organs except the brain, and it is characteristic to find enlarged extremities—feet, hands, and jaw. In gigantism the same has occurred during childhood before the bones have stopped growing and the result is a person who may be 6 ft. 6 in. tall or more.

Posterior Pituitary. The posterior part of the gland is really a quite separate gland. The main hormone it produces is concerned with the excretion of urine by the kidney (antidiuretic hormone). Deficiency of the hormone results in *Diabetes Insipidus*, not to be confused with *Diabetes Mellitus* or "sugar diabetes." In diabetes insipidus, the patient produces enormous quantities of dilute urine. He consequently has a prodigious thirst and consumes astonishing quantities of fluids. Treatment is by replacing the missing hormone.

Thyroid. The thyroid gland in the neck secretes an iodine-containing hormone called thyroxine. Excess of it causes *hyperthyroidism*, *thyrotoxicosis*, or *Grave's disease.* Lack of it produces *cretinism* in the growing child or *myxoedema* in the adult. Thyroxine is concerned with the metabolic rate of cells throughout the body, or the rate at which they work, as well as with the proper growth of developing tissues, especially the brain. Too much thyroxine as in thyrotoxicosis leads to over-activity, warm sweatiness in an over-excitable patient whose pulse is rapid and who is eating ravenously to try to replace the wasted energy. In spite of his appetite he is very thin, and he often has bulging eyes for a reason not understood. Treatment is by drugs which neutralise the thyroxine or by cutting out some of the gland. A *cretin* is a child usually born with insufficient thyroid. He is destined to grow poorly, and to mental subnormality of a permanent and distressing kind. If the condition is diagnosed soon after birth treatment with thyroxine can avert most of the trouble. In myxoedema, thyroxine is deficient in an adult. They become slow in all their bodily processes, the hair thins and their flesh is puffy with a dry, wrinkled skin. Treatment is by thyroid replacement. *Goitre* simply means enlargement of the gland. It may be accompanied by overactivity or underactivity, or with little functional change. One variety (Derbyshire neck) occurs in areas short of iodine in the soil and drinking water.

Adrenal Cortex. The adrenal or suprarenal glands sit, as the name implies, one on top of each kidney. There are two distinct parts: the cortex or outside which secretes steroid hormones, and the *adrenal medulla*, or core, which secretes adrenalin. There are many different steroid hormones in the adrenal cortical secretion, which look after such divers matters as sodium and potassium balance, sexual function, the reaction of the body to stress, and the regulation of sugar levels. *Addison's disease* (not to be confused with Addisonian anaemia) results from adrenal cortical insufficiency, and is often due to destruction of the gland by tuberculosis. There is weariness, malaise, pigmentation of skin creases and mucous membranes. They are short of sodium and have excess potassium. Treatment is with cortisone (replacement of the missing hormone) and by extra salt by mouth for the lack of sodium. *Cushing's disease* is due to excessive adrenal cortical function, and sometimes also occurs in patients treated with cortisone for other purposes. They have a striking redistribution of fat in the face, neck, and trunk, with stretch marks similar to those acquired by most women during pregnancy. The facial obesity makes them " moon-faced," and female patients may suffer masculinisation with deepening of the voice and hirsutism.

Testis. The male testes, as well as producing sperm are also endocrine glands producing steroid hormones known as androgens. They are mainly concerned with maintaining secondary sex characteristics. At the time of puberty the controlling secretions from the anterior pituitary begin to appear and androgens are produced. There is a whole range of rare disorders, resulting in everything from precocious puberty to delayed puberty. It should be born in mind that the normal time of puberty can vary by several years from one boy to another.

Ovary. The human ovary has two functions: to produce ova, or eggs; and to produce two hormones, oestrogen and progesterone. These functions begin at puberty, one of whose features in the female is the onset of menstruation, or menarche. Just as in boys, the timing of normal puberty is very variable, but on the average, girls achieve puberty before boys. As social conditions improve, the age of menarche is getting younger generation by generation. All the secondary sex characteristics are under the control of the ovarian hormones which are released in response to the appropriate anterior pituitary hormones. The changes which occur in the womb and elsewhere in the intervals between menstrual periods and the periods themselves are controlled by a cyclical or rhythmic secretion, first of oestrogen and then of progesterone, by the ovary. This cycle is upset by pregnancy to allow the development of the embryo. It can also be upset by taking certain combinations of the two hormones by mouth. These can prevent the formation of ova, and are a popular form of contraception. In late middle age, the ovaries lose their function, the menstrual cycles cease to occur, and reproductive life is at an end. This is called the *menopause* or " change of life," and is sometimes accompanied for a time by distressing symptoms due to a temporary imbalance between oestrogen and progesterone. Many sexual functions, however, continue well after the menopause into old age, and these can include a continuing libido or sexual desire.

Parathyroid. Four tiny parathyroid glands are buried behind the thyroid gland and are responsible for regulating the body calcium and phosphate. They are therefore particularly important for the building and maintenance of bones and teeth. Since a proper calcium level in the blood is necessary for muscle (including heart muscle) contraction, and for correct functioning of nerves, disorders of the parathyroids can give rise to muscular spasms as well as loss of bone calcium. The latter can result in fragility and fractures. Overactivity of the glands leads to too much calcium and the formation of stones especially in the kidney.

Pineal. We end this section with a mystery gland. Like the pituitary it is small—about the size of a pea—and sits well back at the base of the brain. It was endowed in ancient times with metaphysical properties all of which remain speculative. In fish and lizards and certain lower vertebrates it is a kind of third eye, and receives light. In higher mammals, like ourselves, it is so far from any source of light that it could scarcely do so. It can be removed without harm. Indeed it normally becomes calcified and

inactive about the time of puberty, and its position seen on X-rays of the skull can be a good guide to whether the brain is being pushed to one side by an abnormal mass.

DISEASES OF THE URINARY SYSTEM.

Everyone knows what kidneys look like—in fact, the term " kidney-shaped " is used to describe other objects. Within the kidneys the blood-vessels carrying waste materials subdivide and finally end up in little coils or glomeruli through which waste products are filtered into the other system, the system of tubes which, beginning as tiny cups around the glomeruli, become larger and larger until they join the ureter passing out at the root of the kidney, the hilum, a point at which both the veins and tubes enter and leave. The kidneys, of course, lie one on each side in the loins, so that if one puts one's hands on the hips and then slides them farther back they will cover the area over the left and right kidney. The ureters pass down on each side to the bladder, which is the storage tank of the products excreted by the kidneys, and lies in the mid-line down low in the abdomen; it is somewhat pear-shaped, and at its base in men there lies the prostate gland— a gland which apparently has few functions but can be a nuisance. Its only known function is that it adds something to the semen from the testes without which the semen would be sterile. Then, from the base of the bladder a single tube, the urethra, passes to the outside. One can, in fact, visualise the urinary system as a capital Y, in which the two upper limbs are the ureters, the place where they meet is the bladder, and the single limb at the foot is the urethra. Clearly, then, there may be diseases of the kidneys, of the ureters, of the bladder, of the prostate gland, or of the urethra.

The amount of urine may be increased or diminished. It is *increased* in the following conditions: after drinking excess of fluids; after taking drugs (known as *diuretics*) which are given to increase the flow; in diabetes of both types—mellitus and insipidus; in some types of chronic kidney disease; and finally, in emotional states of excitement. It is *decreased* in the following conditions: acute nephritis; any disease in which fluid is being lost in other ways, such as diarrhoea or sweating in fevers; when the fluid intake is small; and when both ureters are blocked by stones. Passing a great deal of urine is known as *polyuria*, passing very little as *oliguria*, passing frequent small amounts is simply called *frequency*. Normally, the urine is acid, but in infections of the bladder it may become alkaline owing to decomposition by bacteria. Abnormal substances, or normal substances in abnormal quantities, may occur in the urine and give the doctor an indication of what is wrong. In fact, urine analysis is a very important part of medical diagnosis. Thus urea is a normal content of urine which is increased in fevers, wasting diseases, or diabetes; the amount of urea is to some extent a measure of the degree of tissue breakdown. Uric acid is found in small quantities in normal urine, but the amount is increased in fevers and after an attack of gout (uric acid is important in the causation of gout, but has nothing at all to do with rheumatism in general, so one may disregard the advertisements in the popular Press showing unpleasant pictures of joints with sharp crystals of uric acid which are alleged to cause the pain of rheumatic disease). Oxalates are not ordinarily found in urine, but, since they occur in such foods as rhubarb and strawberries, and some people are unable to deal with them, such individuals may develop oxalate stones or have pain on passing urine after eating oxalate-containing fruits.

Two very important substances which ought not to be in normal urine are albumen and sugar. Albumen is a protein, and its presence in the urine indicates that the filters of the kidney are leaking —they are allowing protein to pass out which ought to remain in the body. Albumen is easily tested for, and its presence may indicate kidney disease or nephritis as it is usually called by doctors. On the other hand, small amounts of albumen occur in fevers and in nervous conditions —*functional albuminuria*. Sugar, too, should not be present, but its presence does not necessarily indicate diabetes; for small amounts may occur in nervous conditions or in some people after taking large quantities of carbohydrate.

Blood in the urine may give it an appearance which varies from bright red to a dark, smoky colour. It is found in many diseases: acute nephritis, stone, tumours, poisoning by certain drugs, infections such as bilharzia or malaria, papilloma (*i.e.*, non-malignant tumour of the bladder), after injury, in high blood-pressure, scurvy, and blood diseases. Sometimes it occurs for no known reason at all.

It will be remembered (or if it is not, you can look it up on p. 28 (1)) that streptococcal infection of the throat may cause in some people disease of the valves in the heart or endocarditis. In such cases, although the germ is found in the throat, it is not found in the heart or indeed anywhere else in the body. *Acute nephritis* occurs in the same circumstances, with the sole difference that the kidneys instead of the heart are affected. The disease appears to be an allergic reaction to the toxins of the streptococcus. The patient, often a child, has a sore throat (and even this may be absent or fail to be noticed) or sometimes the infection may arise in other sites: after scarlet fever, erysipelas, burns, and disease of the ear. A few days later there is headache, vomiting, pain in the loins, slight rise in temperature, and especially typical is *dropsy* or œdema. This begins in the face, first around the eyelids, and then affects the ankles; later it may become more general and affect the rest of the body. Blood and albumen are found in the urine, and the blood-pressure is slightly raised. The outlook is usually good if the kidneys are rested by reducing the amount of protein taken in and also the amounts of salt and water. When this is done, the inflammation soon goes and no permanent harm results. In other cases, however, if treatment is inadequate or the condition severe, the symptoms may go, but the albumen found in the urine persists. This means that permanent damage has been done, and although there may be nothing else to show for many years, *chronic nephritis* develops. In this case, the blood-pressure continues to rise, and since the filters of the kidneys no longer work efficiently, urea, the principal waste-product of the body to be excreted in the urine, is retained in the blood and only small amounts escape from the system. Hence chronic nephritis sooner or later leads to heart failure or hæmorrhage in the brain from the rising blood-pressure, or to the form of poisoning known as *uræmia* which results from the retention of urea in the blood. Uræmia may come on suddenly or gradually, but ends in progressive coma, drowsiness, and unconsciousness. There may be convulsions similar to those of epilepsy, high fever, and difficulty in breathing to complicate the picture.

Another type of nephritis which seems to have nothing at all to do with streptococcal infections, and the cause of which is completely unknown, is *nephrosis*. Developing in early adult life, its onset is insidious, and the patient first shows signs of œdema in his white and puffy face and the swelling of his legs. (It should be said here that if you have swelling of the ankles or elsewhere, you would be foolish to jump to conclusions; for such swelling is common in many diseases—in heart disease, in allergic conditions, in neurotic illness, and even just from hot weather.) When the urine is examined in a case of nephrosis it is found to be full of albumen and, as in chronic nephritis, the blood urea starts to rise. The end-results of nephrosis are the same as those of chronic nephritis and depend upon the damage originally done.

The modern diuretics of the chlorothiazide group help to control the œdema and, provided enough healthy tissue remains, remove both the fluid and the waste-products. In advanced or more serious cases artificial kidneys can be used, but as yet the transplantation of a kidney is largely in the experimental stage.

Pyelitis is an infection of the pelvis of the kidney, that is to say, of the part where the ureter leaves the kidney. It is usually caused by the bacillus coli, which is normally present in the body, or by the streptococcus. These germs may reach the ureter through the blood-stream or may pass upwards from the bladder. Obstruction anywhere in the urinary tract which causes the urine to stagnate is liable to cause pyelitis. Symptoms come on suddenly, with high fever, pain in the loin (the infection is usually on one side only, and is commoner in women), and pain in the abdomen. When urine is passed there is a burning sensation, and it is passed frequently and in small amounts. On examination, the urine is found to be highly acid and full of bacillus coli or whatever the causative germ may be. Pyelitis is fairly readily treated by the antibiotics or sulpha drugs. Plenty of fluids should be given and the urine made alkaline by administration of alkalis.

Cystitis means inflammation of the bladder, either acute or chronic, and its causes are much the same as in the case of pyelitis. There is pain over the lower abdomen, frequency, and sometimes slight fever. The treatment is as for pyelitis. *Urethritis* is an inflammation of the urethra, with burning pain on passing water and frequency. The most serious cause (although it can usually be easily dealt with now) is gonorrhœa. But non-specific urethritis is common, and in this case various germs or none may bring about pain and frequency; there is often a large neurotic element. Urethritis should be regarded as probably due to gonorrhœa, which has already been discussed elsewhere, when there is a thick, creamy discharge from the penis or discharge in women following sexual intercourse with an infected person.

Kidney stones or Renal calculi sometimes form, and, as in the case of gall-stones, what causes them is not certain. They may be caused by disorders of metabolism—that is, in the inability of the body to deal with calcium, proteins, uric acid, and other products; or by vitamin deficiency, obstruction in the urinary tract, and urinary infections. But when a stone or stones are formed various events may occur: thus it may remain in the kidney and cause no symptoms; or it may cause repeated attacks of pain, infection, and blood in the urine (hæmaturia); or it may completely block the passage of urine from the kidney to such a degree that it degenerates and becomes useless; or, lastly, it may pass into the ureter, and when this occurs very severe pain, known as *renal colic*, will occur. A stone passing down the ureter into the bladder may become stuck in the urethra, although this is uncommon, since a stone small enough to get down the ureters is likely to be capable of manœuvring through the rest of the tract. In fact, about 80–90 per cent. of stones are passed spontaneously. Stones not passed spontaneously may have to be removed by operation, but whether this is undertaken or not depends on various factors, such as the general health of the patient, the amount of trouble caused by the stone, and the health of the other kidney —for it is dangerous to operate on one kidney unless one is sure that the other is functioning efficiently.

If a stone blocks the passage of urine on one side for any length of time *hydronephrosis* may result, in which the part where the ureter enters the kidney swells with the retained urine. Ultimately much of the kidney may be destroyed by the back-pressure. The same effect may be produced by kinking of the ureter or anything else which causes obstruction. Sometimes children are born with hydronephrosis, and when the dilation is due to kinking of the tube the condition may be intermittent, with attacks of renal colic during which only small amounts of urine are passed; this is followed with relief and the passage of large quantities.

Tumours and Cysts. The kidney may also be the site of tumours and cysts which produce pain in the loins, sometimes a lump over the kidney which can be felt, and blood in the urine. Cancer of the bladder is a serious condition in which the bladder may have to be removed, so the urinary flow has then to be directed elsewhere. Either the ureters are brought out on to the skin surface, a procedure known as *cutaneous ureterostomy*, or they are implanted in the large bowel, so that the urine flows out with the fæces. This is described as *uretero-colostomy*.

There may also be benign tumours of the bladder or *papillomas*, which are soft and bleed easily; a great deal of blood is passed, but there is usually little or no pain. In this, and similar, diseases of the bladder examination of the inside of the organ is carried out by means of a cystoscope, a thin tube which is passed up the urethra and has a small electric light at the end which enables the surgeon to see what is going on. Instruments may also be passed through the tube, and simple papillomas can be cauterised. Similar instruments are used in the examination of the stomach (gastroscope) and the bronchial tubes (bronchoscope). When some obstruction in the outlet of the bladder or in the urethra occurs the bladder, of course, fills with urine, which cannot be passed, and very painful dilation occurs. In this case an attempt may be made to pass a catheter, a thin rubber tube, into the bladder to relieve the tension, or if this fails a *suprapubic cystomy* is performed—an incision is made in the abdomen over the bladder and a tube inserted into it, through which the urine escapes. This is ordinarily a temporary expedient, and later when the patient's health has improved an attempt will be made to remove the cause of obstruction. The most common cause of such obstruction is *enlargement of the prostate gland* at the base of the bladder, which surrounds this area and the beginning of the ureter. About 40 per cent. of men over sixty have some degree of obstruction due to this cause, and about 20 per cent. of these require operation. The gland is about the size of a walnut, and, as we have seen, its function is to supply part of the fluid which makes up the semen, the male sex secretion. Enlargement of the prostate may be benign or malignant, and, although nobody knows just why, such benign enlargement tends to occur in most men in later life. There may be no symptoms, but characteristically there is frequency during the day and the need to get up at night to pass water. The flow of urine being impeded by constriction of the urethra, the passage is less forceful than normal, and there is a tendency for dribbling to occur. If the obstruction is severe and not relieved the back-pressure may be transmitted to the ureters and kidneys, resulting finally in kidney failure and uræmia. The prostate, except in cases of very mild enlargement, has to be removed either through the abdomen or through the perineum (the part of the body lying between the sex organs and the anus). Sometimes, in less serious cases, it is possible without an incision to cut away the obstructing part by an electrocautery inserted, as is a cystoscope, through the urethra. Prostatectomy was once a serious operation, all the more so because the patient was usually elderly and not in good condition, but new techniques and the use of antibiotics have greatly improved the outlook.

Cancer of the Prostate is always serious, but if discovered in time it can be operated on successfully. The gland, of course, has to be completely removed; in inoperable cases, or in patients unfit to stand operation, the tumour may be treated by means of female sex hormones, which cause it to shrink and may prolong life by some years.

DISEASES OF THE NERVOUS SYSTEM.

The nervous system consists of the Central Nervous System and the Peripheral Nervous System. The brain and spinal cord make up the former. The latter consists of the nerve fibres by which the Central Nervous System is connected to all parts of the body. Human beings have a more complicated brain than any other animal species, but it is only its complexity which makes it different from the brains of other mammals like rats and pigs and cows. We do not have the largest brains, since whales, for example, have much larger ones. Ours is not even the largest for the size of the body. Mice and dolphins and several other creatures have relatively larger brains when compared with body weight. Furthermore the cells and materials of which our brain is composed are virtually identical with those in other mammals, and its living properties are also the same.

Before describing some of the diseases of the nervous system it will be helpful to say a little

about how it is made and how it works. Each human brain probably contains about ten thousand million (10,000,000,000) nerve cells and perhaps four or five times this number of supporting "glial" cells. Each nerve cell has many long thin branching projections, called dendrites, rather like the branches of a tree, leading to many thousands of "twigs" for each single nerve cell. At the end of each "twig" there is a special structure called a *synapse* by which contact is made with other nerve cells. It is through these connections that very large numbers of nerve cells give information (or send impulses) to each other so that they can be co-ordinated. As well as these dendritic branches, each nerve cell gives off one large trunk called the *axon*, down which final messages are sent as the result of all the information it receives from its dendrites. Some axons are many feet long. Some end in another synapse, by which the outgoing message is passed to yet another nerve cell. Some axons, those of the peripheral nerves, end directly on organs like muscles or glands, instructing them and making them work.

Messages are passed along dendrites and axons as electrical impulses. These are generated in the nerve cell " body." They are modified according to information received from other nerve cells and propagated down the axon. It is this superficial resemblance to a series of electrical cables which has given rise to comparisons of the brain with a telephone system or a computer, and as long as it is realised how infinitely more complicated each brain is than any known computer, the comparison is not a bad one. However, the brain generates its own electric power from the fuel brought in its own blood supply; and no spare parts or spare cables are available if the originals should get damaged, except in peripheral nerves. Furthermore the contact of one nerve cell with another through a synapse is not an electrical contact, and neither is the contact between a nerve and the muscle or other organ it is controlling. In both cases the connection is chemical. Thus when an electrical impulse arrives at the end of the nerve fibre, a chemical is released into the gap between it and the next nerve or organ, and it is this chemical which carries the stimulus forward. There is also an arrangement to neutralise the chemical transmitter when the impulse has been transmitted. So the resemblance to a telephone exchange or computer can sometimes be misleading.

Many of the nerve axons which transmit electrical impulses are clothed in fatty *myelin sheaths*, a little like the plastic insulation around an electric wire. Here again the resemblance is only partial, since the myelin sheaths are interrupted at regular intervals and these gaps in the insulation play an important role in transmitting the impulse. One of the important functions of the non-nervous *glial* cells of the brain is to manufacture and maintain the myelin sheaths.

Most of the functions of the brain are quite unknown, and even the ones we know about are very poorly understood. It is assumed to be the organ of higher mental function, of the mind and intellect; but there is surprisingly little evidence for this, and no one has any idea what physical structures or mechanisms subserve these functions. The brain is known to control all bodily functions by means of *motor* and other nerves which carry impulses from the brain outwards to all parts of the body. Sometimes these are under our voluntary control; mostly they are involuntary, reflex or automatic. Reflex actions are the result of impulses passed inwards from the body towards the brain by means of sensory nerves. Information arriving in the brain about the various sensations like heat, pain, touch, position, the need for saliva or gastric juice or even the thought or smell of food, are acted on in the various " centres " in the brain. These send out instructions down the " motor " or " secretary " nerves which instruct the muscles or glands to take appropriate action. Thus a *reflex* has a " sensory ending " which appreciates some sort of sensation. This is converted into an electrical impulse which is sent towards the brain or spinal cord along a sensory or " afferent " nerve. The impulse arrives at a " centre " in the central nervous system which co-ordinates all the relevant information and issues instructions. These travel as impulses outwards, along "efferent" nerves towards "effector" organs like muscles or glands, and an appropriate action occurs automatically. The pathway from sensory ending to effector organ is called a *reflex arc*. Many reflex activities are partly under voluntary control, although mainly automatic. If you touch something hot you will automatically withdraw your hand. But if it is a hot china cup which has cost you a lot of money, you are capable of overriding the tendency to drop it, at least for a time. Breathing is automatic, but it can also be controlled, again at least for a time.

Clearly the brain is a very delicately organised piece of machinery, and its cells are extremely specialised for their job. Achieving this kind of specialised perfection brings many difficulties, however, and the brain cells have become highly dependent on the proper functioning of the other body systems, especially the blood circulation, the respiratory system, and the systems regulating the detailed nutrient composition of the blood. Failure of these systems, even for a very short time, can damage the nerve cells. Nearly all death, from whatever original cause, is produced this way, by an ultimate interference with nerve cell function.

We have already mentioned that the brain and spinal cord are unable to repair or replace any components which get damaged. The vulnerability of the brain is even more obvious when it is realised how easily damage and destruction can occur. For example, unless a rich supply of oxygen and glucose is continuously arriving in the blood stream, brain cells will cease to function in a few seconds and will die in a few minutes, and they can never be replaced. This is in marked contrast to other tissues of the body. The leg, for example, may carry on for over half an hour without any blood at all because the muscle and other cells can find other ways of surviving. Thus the brain can be permanently damaged if the blood contains insufficient oxygen (through asphyxia), insufficient glucose, or if the blood supply is blocked or if the blood pressure falls. All these are likely to happen to any of us at any time, and so there are elaborate mechanisms trying to prevent them occurring. Most of the subject of physiology is concerned with the mechanisms designed to protect the brain, and most of us ultimately die because they eventually fail. One of the clever features of the body design is that all the mechanisms which protect the brain from a supply failure are controlled by the brain itself. Thus the brain has itself been made to control the heart beat and the breathing and the many other systems which are needed for its own survival.

In all that follows concerning disease of the nervous system it will be seen that the effects of neurological disease on the patient are the direct result of something going wrong with one of the structures or mechanisms we have described.

Diagnostic Techniques in Neurology. The doctor has many ways of testing the nervous system, most of which test its various functions as outlined in the introduction. Thus tests of sensation, muscular movement and reflexes of all kinds as well as the special functions of taste, smell, vision, hearing, speech and intellect play a part. *X-rays* only show the skull because it is calcified, the brain not being seen directly. There is, however, a tiny pea-size central structure called the pineal gland which usually becomes calcified with age, and this shows up. If for any reason the brain is pushed over to one side of the skull this can be detected by displacement of the pineal. A great deal can be learned about the brain by *arteriography*. In this test a radio-opaque substance is put into the arteries supplying the brain, and an X-ray picture taken immediately afterwards shows up all the blood vessels. *Ventriculography* is an X-ray examination after gas has been introduced into the brain cavities or ventricles which are normally filled with *cerebrospinal fluid*; *myelography* is an X-ray of the spinal cord after a radio-opaque substance has been injected into the space between the spinal cord and the bony vertebral canal which houses it. All these X-ray procedures are ways of looking for a change in the shape of the brain or its vessels.

Sometimes *radioactive isotopes* are put into the blood stream and carried into the brain where they can be detected from outside the skull by counters. *Electroencephalography* measures the electrical waves generated by the brain by placing electrodes on the scalp. *Electromyography* does the same for muscles.

Consciousness and Unconsciousness (Coma). Everyone knows what consciousness is until he tries to define it. Full consciousness is generally taken to imply not only wakefulness but the total complement of human mental faculties. In clinical medicine, however, something less than this is usually meant. For example a demented person, or one whose memory is lost (*amnesia*), or one whose powers of speech are lost (*aphasia*) may still be "conscious." There is really a continuous gradation between full consciousness and coma, passing through drowsiness and even "stupor" in which condition a patient can be aroused from coma but sinks back into it when left alone. Many different things can cause coma ranging from swelling of the brain, compressing it in its rigid box of bone, to disorders in other body systems resulting in a failure to provide for the brain's needs. Examples of the first are bleeding within the brain or *brain tumours*, both of which occupy space and can only do so by producing compression. In the second category are asphyxia preventing oxygen from reaching the brain, lack of glucose in the blood, circulatory failure in which there is insufficient blood, or insufficient blood pressure. Fainting is a comparatively minor example.

Sleep and Insomnia. Nobody knows what causes sleep, why it is necessary, and how it helps. It is quite different from coma or even stupor, since as much oxygen and glucose is necessary asleep as awake. Insomnia is experienced by everyone at some time, and for some reason is very distressing if it persists. There are three forms: failing to get to sleep, intermittent wakefulness, and awaking early. Nearly all insomniacs sleep more than they think. They should eat light evening meals and avoid stimulants like tea and coffee after mid-day. Elderly people should realise they need less sleep. Being cold or having a full bladder can be a cause. Or simply not being tired. Sedative drugs are a last resort, but they can be useful in "breaking the habit" of wakefulness. Obviously there may be psychological factors such as anxiety and excitement. *Narcolepsy*, or a true inability to keep awake is comparatively rare. Both narcolepsy and insomnia are really extreme examples of what all normal people suffer from occasionally.

Headache is man's most common pain. Here again we must distinguish between the very common varieties of comparatively trivial significance and the rare ones due to serious causes. Some headaches are due to continuous tightness in muscles of the scalp, and are often "nervous" or psychological in origin. Others result from nose blockage and congestion, sinus problems, eye strain, toothache, etc. Migraine is a special kind and will be described below. Very occasionally indeed headache is due to serious disease like brain tumour. Most headache results from "living it up" or being "run down," or both. The headache of alcoholic hangover is probably due to dehydration. It can often be avoided by consuming a great quantity of water (a pint or two) before going to bed, but few people are prepared to do this in the circumstances. Be careful when using aspirin, which is a useful remedy for headache, since it is very dangerous for people with stomach complaints like gastritis or gastric or duodenal ulcer. Occasionally aspirin makes the stomach bleed, and this can be so severe as to kill. A safer pain killer is paracetamol. Be particularly careful in treating "hang-over" headaches by patent fizzy remedies. They are very effective, but often contain large quantities of aspirin described in small print by its proper name as acetyl salicyclic acid.

Migraine. This is a very special variety of "sick headache" and requires special treatment under medical supervision. It has many different forms, but usually there is a definite sequence of events. An attack often starts with some alteration of vision. The patient has shimmering blind spots or other visual disorders. This is followed by a well localised severe headache which may end in nausea or vomiting. The whole thing is caused by a poorly understood disorder of the blood vessels. There are special drugs, mostly derivatives of ergot, which are effective, especially if used when the first signs of an attack appear. Although there is a direct physical cause for an attack, it is also certain that some of the trouble is psychological tenseness. People with migraine are often rather anxious, striving and perfectionist people. Also it has been noticed that attacks are much less frequent when the necessary pills are being carried available for use. However, as with all other conditions which are partly " psychological " in origin they are none the less distressing for the patient. It simply means that the treatment is also partly psychological in encouraging him to come to terms with his problems.

Menière's Disease is one of the conditions in which the organ of balance in the middle ear is affected, giving rise to *vertigo*, a form of giddiness. It usually begins in middle life in the same sort of person who sometimes has migraine. There is buzzing in the ears and some intermittent loss of hearing as well as vertigo. During an attack the patient may be unable to walk because of his loss of balance, and nausea and vomiting are common. Treatment is by special drugs, and occasionally an operation on the ear is necessary.

Epilepsy is a symptom, not a disease, which is common at all ages but especially children. It has been attributed to St. Paul, Julius Caesar, Napoleon, and (with more justice perhaps) to Dostoyevsky. Many varieties of attack occur often in the same patient, the commonest and best known being the *grand mal* or major seizure. In this the patient falls down unconscious and rigid and the jaw is clenched, so that there is danger of the tongue being bitten. This so-called tonic phase is followed, within a minute or so, by a clonic phase in which the limbs contract rhythmically. The attack ends with the patient going limp and gradually recovering consciousness, a process which may take up to an hour. Occasionally the patient has a brief warning, most often an indescribable feeling in the stomach. There are two common forms of minor seizure, one occurring mainly in children and the other more often in adults. The common minor attacks in children are often called *petit mal* or *absence*, which well describes the instantaneous and brief loss of consciousness often unaccompanied by any change in posture. Recovery is equally instantaneous. On the other hand, in the other forms of epilepsy which arise from various parts of the brain, but especially from the lobe under the temporal region, there is often a warning similar to that which may precede a major seizure. In these cases the patient shows only confusion, no definite loss of posture, but automatic activity such as fumbling with buttons, muttering, and grimacing. Following these attacks there may be a quite prolonged period of confusion in which the patient may wander away and occasionally may be violent. Criminal acts are very rarely carried out in this state.

A large number of people have had one or two fits in their lives, particularly at times of physical or psychological stress. " Fever " or " Febrile " convulsions (often called teething fits in the past) are extremely common in young children and are often thought of as something different from epilepsy since the attacks rarely continue in later years. This form of epilepsy and some cases of *petit mal* are the only forms in which hereditary factors are important in the causation, and these are the least serious forms of epilepsy. They are very rarely associated with serious physical or psychological disturbances. Most other forms of epilepsy are due to a scar or other area of brain damage. It is a proportion of these cases which develop the psychological disturbances that are occasionally very serious.

Not every patient who has had one or two fits need necessarily take regular anticonvulsant drugs; that is drugs which damp down the abnormal excessive activity of the brain that leads to the attacks. Many drugs are available of which

the most important are phenobarbitone, phenytoin, succinimides, and troxidones, the last two being effective only against minor seizures. Which one to use and whether to use one at all is, of course, quite a complicated judgment, and must be left to the doctor. Epileptics often find it difficult to get work because of the reluctance of employers to take on someone who may be more prone to accidents and whose signs may distress other workers. Obviously there are some jobs which epileptics should not do because of the danger involved (from, for example, moving machinery), and they should not drive a car. A few cases are so severe that work is almost impossible, but employers have a duty whenever possible to employ these people whose mental health may suffer greatly if they are made to feel outcasts and who ordinarily are as efficient, or even more so, as the next man. It is also hoped that employees will become less prejudiced about epilepsy as the general public become less ignorant about medical matters. In this way epileptics will come to be accepted in all those kinds of employment for which they are well suited. If some of the famous men who have suffered from this disease had had to rely on the charity of some employers today the world would have been much the poorer, although possibly we could have managed without the generals.

Congenital Malformations. The proper shape of the brain and spinal cord is achieved quite early in development by about the thirteenth week after conception. During this time very slight changes in the fetal environment can produce disastrous malformations. The drug thalidomide, for example, operated on other body systems while they were passing through this phase of construction. Some viruses can do the same thing. Most malformations are without known cause, but it is certain that something went wrong at this very early stage, and it only needs a very minor interference with the normal process to do the permanent damage. At about this time the bones of the spine are beginning to enclose, or form a roof over the developing spinal cord. Sometimes they fail to complete the process, resulting in *spina bifida*. If the coverings of the cord protrude through the defect, this is a *meningocele*, and if the cord itself protrudes it is a *meningomyelocele*. The whole protrusion may be covered with skin, but if it is not, the cord soon becomes infected. The effect on the patient is variable, according to the amount of damage to the nerve fibres in the cord, and there are varying degrees of paralysis and loss of sensation below the area involved together with loss of bowel and bladder control. Much help is often obtained from surgical repair, but many cases remain in a distressing condition always, and the only really useful attack on the problem is research to find the cause and prevent it happening. The same is true of the *malformations of the brain.* In one of these, hydrocephaly, the narrow channel is blocked which transmits the cerebrospinal fluid from the chambers within the brain where it is secreted to the outer coverings to be taken back into the blood stream. Blockage of the channel (or aqueduct) results in distension of the brain by fluid, enlargement of the head, and mental retardation. Sometimes a by-pass valve can be inserted to restore normal fluid circulation with very gratifying results. This aqueduct can also be blocked by later disease (meningitis) or injury with the same result. Sometimes the brain fails to form altogether (*anencephaly*), and the child fortunately does not survive after birth.

Cerebral Palsy is a term covering many varieties of *spastic child.* It is thought to be due to brain damage at birth or in early infancy, and is depressingly common. Although a great deal can be done for the spastic (they are often of normal intelligence) the only satisfactory approach is prevention and this means expensive research into its causes. Donations, encouragement, and offers of practical help, please, to the Spastics Society 12 Park Crescent, London W.1.

Motor Neuron Disease. This is a group of distressing diseases usually occurring in people over 40, in whom the parts of the brain and spinal cord degenerate which look after muscular movement. The group includes *Amyotrophic Lateral*

Sclerosis, Progressive Muscular Atrophy, Progressive Bulbar Palsy, and *Primary Lateral Sclerosis.* The results are paralysis or weakness with wasting of the muscles of the body, including those concerned with arms, legs, breathing, speaking, etc. Nothing whatever is known of the cause, and the only treatment is that designed to alleviate the results of the disease. It is uncommon, but this is little comfort to the sufferer.

Parkinson's Disease, paralysis agitans, or the "shaking palsy" is a common condition which begins in later life over the age of 50. It has three classical features: shaking (or tremor), muscular rigidity and loss of those automatic reflexes which look after bodily posture. This results in a stooping shuffling gait. Later there is a mask-like loss of facial expression with diminished eye blinking. It is a progressive disease, but it progresses so slowly that 10 or 20 years may elapse between its onset and incapacity. A good deal can now be done to help these patients with drugs, the most recent of which at the time of writing is DOPA. Occasionally patients have benefited from surgical destruction of small areas of diseased brain. It is important to remember that many elderly people have some tremor of the head or hands called *Senile Tremor,* and this is *not* Parkinson's Disease. It is merely one of the features of achieving advanced seniority as a citizen. *See also* P62.

Chorea. This is a group of diseases in which there is involuntary muscle movement, weakness, and emotional instability. There will be clumsiness, awkward gait, twitching of limbs, face, hands, trunk, or tongue. They include *Acute Chorea* or *St. Vitus' Dance* occurring in children from 5 to 15, *Hereditary or Huntingdon's Chorea* occurring in a well-defined genetic pattern and beginning later, between 35 and 50. *Tics* or habit spasms are not part of these diseases but are often of psychological origin. They are usually eye blinking, head shaking, shoulder shrugging, or any other sudden gesture of limbs or face.

Stroke Illness or Cerebrovascular Diseases. Strokes are due to diseases of the brain's blood vessels which either burst or get blocked. The same blood-vessel disorders cause heart attacks by blocking the coronary arteries supplying the heart. Strokes and heart attacks together kill more people than any other single cause including cancer. They account for one death in every five. Perhaps less is known of the cause of this disease than is known about cancer, and much more research is needed to find out if it is to be prevented. The cause of the commonest cancer (of the lung) is now known and it can be prevented by stopping smoking. Perhaps the prevention of strokes and heart attacks will mean an equally difficult abstinence from all those foods which make us fat. At least it is known that being overweight leads to death from these causes, just as smoking leads to death from lung cancer.

If any artery supplying blood to any part of the brain is blocked, the territory supplied will die; and the bodily functions for which that part of the brain is responsible will cease. The process is called *infarction* of the brain, the dead area being an *infarct.* The blockage is usually due to thrombosis (*see* P31) of the blood within a vessel, a *thrombus* being a rather complicated clot with a structure of its own. The underlying cause is the arterial disease, atheroma (*see* P30) together with stagnation of the circulation. About one blockage in ten is due to a small piece of a much larger thrombus in the heart chambers being flung into the blood stream and impacting in the distant vessel in the brain. This is *cerebral embolism* (*see* P30). If the area of dead or infarcted brain is not too large the patient will recover from his unconsciousness, but will be left with permanent loss of function (paralysis, etc.) related to that part of the brain.

When a blood vessel supplying the brain bursts, this causes *cerebral haemorrhage* or apoplexy. The vessel may be on the surface (*subarachnoid haemorrhage*) or in the depths of the tissue (*intracerebral haemorrhage*). Strokes tend to occur in older people, because the associated arterial disease is a product of age and high blood pressure. Occasionally a subarachnoid haemorrhage occurs in a younger person with an unsuspected malformation of the arteries of the base of the brain known as a *berry aneurysm.* This is a small berry-sized blown-out balloon due to a defect in the wall of the vessel. Berry aneurysms can often be treated surgically. Intracerebral haemorrhage carries a very poor outlook, however, since much brain tissue is often destroyed by the escaping blood, especially the deep tissues responsible for the vital functions. Haemorrhage within the brain cavity can also be caused by injury (*see concussion and compression,* P19).

Inflammatory Diseases of the Nervous System. The membranes covering the brain are called the meninges. Inflammation of these, nearly always by blood-born infection or infection following injury, is called *meningitis.* Cerebrospinal or spotted fever which used to be common and very much feared was only one variety caused by a germ called "meningococcus." It is now rare. Almost any other germ may cause meningitis, and when the germ is susceptible to one of the antibiotics it is usually treatable. It will usually be necessary to identify the germ by taking a sample of cerebrospinal fluid from a convenient space around the spinal cord in the lower back. When the disease is caused by the tubercle bacillus (*tuberculous meningitis*) the problem is more difficult because the patient is often not so obviously ill until the later, less treatable stages. *Cerebral abscess,* or abscess of the brain is very serious because it occupies space in the closed box of the skull and compresses the brain, as well as being a destructive process. It may arise due to an infected piece of tissue or pus being carried to the brain in the blood stream from a distant site in the lungs or heart. When the brain or cord tissue is itself inflamed it is called *encephalitis* (brain) or *myelitis* (cord) or *encephalo-myelitis* (both). These conditions are comparatively uncommon and are often due to infection with viruses rather than bacteria. Some have no known cause, possibly because many viruses are difficult to identify.

Multiple Sclerosis or *Disseminated Sclerosis* or the "creeping paralysis" as it used to be called, is the most important of the "*Demyelinating diseases,*" in which the myelin sheaths wrapped around the nerve fibres disintegrate. This only occurs in small areas, or plaques. It is as if drops of acid have been placed at random throughout the brain and spinal cord and have dissolved away the insulating sheaths over sixpenny (or new penny) sized areas, leaving the wiring (the nerve fibres) running through as before. But this small loss of insulation is enough to spoil the carefully graded electrical impulses; and thus the bodily function subserved by those fibres is lost. So there are apparently random losses of sensation, movement, bowel or bladder control, speech, etc., according to which collection of nerve sheaths happen to have been attacked. Thus it is that no two cases are alike and many are difficult to diagnose. Many have even been labelled malingerers in the early stages, so bizarre are the signs and symptoms. The disease is not a killer. It smoulders on year after year, often beginning in the late teenager and getting steadily more incapacitating over many decades. No one can predict how quickly it will deteriorate, and in some cases many years will go by before yet another episode of more myelin sheath destruction. Neurology has more than its share of completely mysterious diseases. This is perhaps the most mysterious, and it is not very uncommon. The many years of disability in each individual case make it at least as disabling as far commoner diseases which run a much shorter course. There is no more enhumbling disease for the medical scientist, but the faith must remain that, with more and more research, this crippling condition too can be prevented. The Multiple Sclerosis Society, 4 Tachbrook St., London S.W.1, looks after patient welfare, supports research and is very deserving of your donations. As in all other crippling conditions there are countless ways in which you can help the victims at no great expense. Visit them. Help with their shopping and other day-to-day needs. Take them out. And even write to your member of parliament demanding a better deal for the disabled who are still, in spite of recent legislation, among the most downtrodden and deserving of our neighbours.

Myelin sheaths are largely made of fats, so it is small wonder that the brain has its full share of complicated biochemical mechanisms for dealing with fat and manufacturing it. Hand in hand with this is a host of comparatively rare diseases, known as the *lipidoses*, which are basically disorders of fat biochemistry. Among the best known are *Tay-Sachs disease*, *Niemann-Pick disease*, *Gaucher's disease*, and *Hurler's disease*, and it is beyond the scope of *Pears* to describe them in detail.

Brain Tumours. The brain is no exception to the rule that any cell in any tissue of the body can suddenly begin to disobey the body's rules regarding its growth and multiplication. A totally unknown mechanism governs how many cells of a certain type there ought to be and calls a halt to cell multiplication when this number is reached. Every now and then one of them turns a blind eye and goes on dividing, and the result is a tumour, or lump, of anarchic cells which obey no rules. Tumours are commonest in cells which normally go on dividing throughout life, in order to replace those lost by wear and tear. Examples are the cells lining the air passages in the lung, or the alimentary tract in the stomach or large bowel. Fortunately for the brain there is little cell division once it has grown. Nerve cells cannot divide at all in adult life, and the supporting glial cells only do so in response to injury. Therefore primary brain tumours are much less common than those elsewhere. Also many brain tumours like many of those elsewhere, are benign or "innocent" tumours. They are not cancerous, and need only be removed for the patient to be completely cured. The brain, however, is at two major disadvantages compared with other tissues when it comes to tumours. One is that all tumours as they grow take up space, and space in the skull is already fully occupied. Thus even an innocent tumour can compress the brain within its rigid box of bone and become most dangerous until it is removed. The second disadvantage is due to the very large blood supply of the brain. Cancer in other parts of the body spreads partly by sending small pieces of itself to other tissues by way of the blood stream, and those tissues like liver, lung, kidney, and brain which have a big blood supply naturally receive more than their share of other tissues' tumour. These secondary deposits, or *metastases*, cause compression and other trouble in the brain much more frequently than the brain's own primary tumours. Indeed convulsions or other signs of brain disorder may be the first indication that there is a primary tumour in the lung or breast or elsewhere.

Head Injuries are dealt with in the section on Physical Injuries (**P19**), where a great deal of space is given to the effects of most First Aid emergencies on the proper functioning of the brain and spinal cord.

Diseases of Peripheral Nerves. Compared with the nerves of the central nervous system (brain and spinal cord), the peripheral nerves are comparatively rarely affected by disease. They have some similarities of structure with central nerve fibres in that their fibres are often covered with myelin sheaths and are arranged in bundles. A special feature, however, is that they are enclosed by connective tissue sheaths and it is probably these which allow a peripheral nerve to grow again, or regenerate, after it has been cut or damaged. Central nerve fibres are unable to do this. After *injury of a peripheral nerve* the part away from the centre is cut off from its parent cell body and it dies. All function, whether motor or sensory, is lost. But in the course of many months the central surviving part grows into the connective tissue sheaths which act like tubes to guide the new nerve to its destination. Provided the cut ends are close enough together and correctly aligned, and provided enough fibres reach their correct destination, good functional recovery is possible.

A disorder of a peripheral nerve is called a *neuropathy* and means nothing more than that. There are many kinds. One of the most distressing is *trigeminal neuralgia*, again fortunately rare. The trigeminal or fifth cranial nerve has a motor and sensory territory on the face. In this condition there are paroxysmal episodes of extremely severe pain which may resist all treatment except destruction of the nerve itself with consequent facial paralysis and loss of sensation. At the other more trivial extreme are the occasions when a leg "goes to sleep" or gets "pins and needles" after crossing it and pressing on a nerve for too long. *Bell's Palsy* is sudden loss of function of the seventh cranial nerve and there is again paralysis on one side of the face which usually recovers in time. Some bacterial diseases, especially leprosy, invade the nerves themselves. Chronic alcoholism may affect the nerves, as may diabetes, probably by interfering with the nutrition of the nerve cell. So may exposure to arsenic or lead or an unpleasant nerve poison which may contaminate cooking oil known as TOCP, or triorthocresylphosphate.

Muscular Dystrophies. These are a series of diseases of muscle in which there is progressive wasting and weakness of muscle, the causes of which are entirely unknown. They are divided up according to the age of onset and the muscles involved. *Duchenne's muscular dystrophy* occurs in the first decade of life. It affects most of the muscles eventually, including the heart muscle and those concerned with breathing, and so the outlook is not good. Other forms are inherited.

Myasthemia Gravis. This is a strange disorder of the mechanism which transmits instructions from nerve to muscle at the "neuromuscular junction." There is extreme weakness of muscles after they have been used, resembling in some respects the weakness following the administration of curare, or " arrow poison." It is often associated with disorders of the thymus gland. The drug neostigmine reverses the neuromuscular disorder and removal of the thymus is also sometimes effective.

MENTAL DISEASES.

Psychosis.

Mental diseases are divided into psychoses (*i.e.*, insanity) and neuroses (*i.e.*, what is ordinarily known as "nerves"). Psychoses, in their turn, are divided into organic and functional—those due to physical disease and those in which no physical cause has been discovered. In point of fact, the distinction into organic and functional is rather meaningless; for if we accept the modern view of psychosomatic medicine which regards the body and mind as a single unit it is clear that organic disease brings out psychological defects which were already there and that functional disease must, in the final analysis, be the result of physicochemical causes, even if this is brought about by mental stress.

Organic disease results from poisoning of the nervous system by such poisons as alcohol, carbon monoxide, or lead; vitamin deficiencies, as in pellagra; infections such as syphilis; and degeneration of the brain, either primary or as a result of poor blood supply. In all cases its main symptoms are confusion, signs of other disease, and loss of memory. Alcohol leads to various conditions: in *delirium tremens* heavy bouts of drinking end in delirium (" D.T.s"), confusion, hallucination—although not necessarily of pink elephants or rats. It is a serious disease, but the outlook is much improved since it was discovered that injections of concentrated vitamins B and C in the form of " Parentrovite " can help. In more chronic cases *Korsakov's syndrome* manifests itself in the form of mental deterioration and memory defects. There can be little doubt that previously existing mental instability is a predisposing factor in these conditions. The same may be said of *general paralysis of the insane* or G.P.I., and in this case the immediate cause is syphilitic infection of the nervous system. Nevertheless, of all the patients with chronic syphilis, only a small number get syphilis of the nervous system. G.P.I. is typically associated with the usual symptoms of organic disease and delusions of grandeur; for example, a man with this disease may go out and buy several expensive cars in one day. However, it is not uncommon to find G.P.I. associated with severe depression—again the picture depends on the previous personality. The association of the above symptoms with a positive Wasserman test—which proves the presence of the spirochæte in the blood—indicates neurosyphilis. When the lower centres of the nervous system are affected the disease is known as *tabes dorsalis*, in which there is difficulty in passing urine, limb pains, inability to stand when the eyes are closed, and finally difficulty in walking. The patient becomes paralysed and ultimately bedridden. Treatment is with penicillin.

People age at varying rates, so that some are hale and hearty at eighty or ninety whereas others are old at sixty or seventy. They present the typical picture of old age: " second childishness and mere oblivion, sans eyes, sans teeth, sans everything." When this condition, which is caused by degenerative changes in the brain or by defective blood-supply resulting from arteriosclerosis, is pronounced we speak of *senile psychosis*. There is mental confusion, forgetfulness, and delusions, in which the previous personality defects which we all have are accentuated. Such patients may have to be put under special care, but the process is largely irreversible.

The functional psychoses are two in number: schizophrenia and manic-depressive insanity. In *schizophrenia*, which, when it occurs in early adult life, is known (or used to be known) as *dementia præcox*, the symptoms are bizarre. There are delusions and hallucinations, so that the patient often believes himself to be persecuted and hears voices which say objectionable things to him. Sometimes the schizophrenic is wildly excited, and in other cases he goes into a state of stupor which is described as a catatonic state. Although the disease is described as functional, recent discoveries seem to suggest that there is some derangement of the blood chemistry. Treatment by insulin and the new tranquillising drugs has revolutionised the outlook in this admittedly serious disease. Indeed, some cases of psychosis are more easily treated than neurotic patients, since the former respond to physical methods, whereas the latter may require fairly prolonged psychotherapy (psychological treatment) and are less responsive to drugs.

In cases which do not respond to other methods, the brain operation known as *leucotomy* may be performed. Leucotomy is also performed to alleviate intractable pain, as in incurable cancer, but some of the ataraxic drugs (tranquillisers) are probably equally useful for this purpose. Leucotomy involves the severing of the connecting nerve fibres between certain areas of the brain, and the results are often favourable, but in fact the operation should be performed only in cases where the outlook is otherwise very poor; chronic severe neuroses, frequent attacks of manic depressive psychosis, severe chronic depression, and schizophrenia which has not responded to other forms of treatment. The operation reduces anxiety, fear, aggressiveness, and agitation, but may result in the less-desirable symptoms of apathy, impaired judgment, lack of self-control, and loss of initiative.

Schizophrenia developing in later life is likely to be less dramatic in origin, and the delusions tend to be more systematised—that is, they take a persistent form, which does not change from day to day. This type of the disease is known as *paraphrenia*. In those beyond middle age the rare but dangerous condition described as *paranoia* may develop in which there are no hallucinations and the only symptom is a completely systematised collection of persecutory delusions, which on recital may sound entirely convincing even to the ordinary doctor. Such people are dangerous precisely because they are so plausible, and they fill the ranks of the litigious, the troublemakers, and the political and religious eccentrics. One such patient known to the writer spent his life in a mental hospital from which he had parole, employing this to form a society propagating highly eccentric sexual and political beliefs. It says little for the intelligence of the general population that his meetings were invariably crowded out (although, of course, when one reads of the people who apparently believe that the various fictitious families on radio or television—really exist, one need not be surprised at such examples of communal dottiness, even if one may despair of democracy).

Manic-depressive insanity is characterised by mood swings in which the emotions alternate between wild elation without obvious cause and equally causeless depression. However, the picture is not quite as simple as this; for phases of mania or excitement may occur without depression obviously following, or there may be a single attack of depression with no manic phases. The disease may be absolutely incapacitating, or there may be periods of relative normality; typically, then, manic-depressive insanity is a disease of alternating moods. The depression responds to electroconvulsive therapy or E.C.T., but mania is less responsive to treatment. However, it ordinarily remits of itself. Sometimes in middle age *involutional depression* occurs, and this in the vast majority of cases is cured by E.C.T. As in the case of schizophrenia drugs are increasingly used for depression.

Neurosis.

The main neuroses are anxiety neurosis, hysteria, and obsessional neurosis. *Anxiety neurosis* is an illness in which the main symptom (as the name implies) is anxiety. There is fear which rationally the patient knows to be groundless; there may be anxiety attacks, in which the heart pounds, the patient feels he is going mad, is unable to sleep, and worries " for no reason at all." In hysteria, anxiety is largely absent, but there may be apparently physical symptoms ranging from paralysis of the limbs to blindness, deafness, inability to write, and lapses of memory (the so-called hysterical fugues or loss of memory). Typical of *hysteria* is the fact that the patient is less worried by his symptoms than would be expected from their apparent seriousness; this is what the early psychiatrists described as "la belle indifférence." The reason for the indifference is simple—it is that the paralysed individual *wants* to be paralysed, the blind *want* to be blind, the deaf to be deaf (there are none so blind—or deaf—as those who don't want to see, or hear), and the person who doesn't want to write conveniently finds that he cannot.

Generally speaking, neurotic people are suffering from a failure to face up to reality. They are not physically ill and are largely the end result of a faulty upbringing. It is wrong to suppose that the only bad families are those in which the children are ill-treated; much the worst ones are those in which children are spoilt, the parents possessive, and the wrong kind of love is dispensed. Neuroses are the result of a conflict between primitive desires and what the individual has been brought up to believe he should be. For example, before an examination a student may develop a nervous breakdown because he fears failure when he has been brought up to expect success. The excuse, of course, is " overwork "—an entirely non-existent condition. With his breakdown he solves his problem, he avoids the fear of failing and preserves his self-respect: he has been ill. Similarly, the soldier with " shell shock " (another non-existent condition) has a conflict between his sense of duty and his fear of death, which again is solved by becoming ill. Or, to take a final example, a woman feels the duty to look after her ageing mother. But she also wants to get married. So she unconsciously develops a neurosis which says, in effect, " I should like to do my duty in looking after my mother, but unfortunately I am unable to." There is an unconscious rebellion on the part of the mind.

Neurosis, in effect, is not a disease—it is a self-inflicted injury, a form of maladaptation to life. The neurotic, no matter how much he suffers, does not want to get well; he has found some way of getting along, even if a foolish way, and he intends to keep it. Often his symptoms are the sort of excuse that say: " If only I wasn't ill what wouldn't I be able to do! " The neurotic is a person who is different and is afraid to be himself; his problem is a conflict between being " ordinary," " like other people," and being what he was supposed to be.

Obsessional Neurosis is a more severe type of neurotic illness; for although in anxiety neurosis we find such symptoms as phobias—irrational fears of open spaces, closed spaces, animals, and so on—obsessional states are characterised by compulsive feelings that certain acts must be performed or certain thoughts thought. In a mild form we all have obsessions: we feel that we must walk on the spaces between paving-stones, that we must touch lamp-posts, and so on. But when this type of compulsion gets to the stage when we must go back several times to make sure the lights have been put out, when we feel the need to wash our hands every few minutes, become obsessed with numbers on cars or dates on coins, then it becomes a nuisance and requires treatment. The obsessional neurotic is a person who feels that life must be controlled; he is "a creature who moves in predestinate grooves—he's not even a bus but a tram." His symptoms are an attempt to devise self-imposed rules which will control the unconscious desires of which he is so afraid.

Neurasthenia is an entirely imaginary condition allegedly due to exhaustion of the nervous system. Since no such condition exists, we need not bother with it. Neuroses cannot be treated by feeding the nerves (which are perfectly normal). They can be helped by such things as sedatives, but not cured. *Neurosis has nothing at all to do with disease of the physical nerves, so nerve tonics do not exist, and anyone who asserts that they do is a humbug.*

Psychopathic Personality is the term given to anyone who has different standards of behaviour from those generally accepted by society. Some of these unfortunates may be *inadequate*, that is to say, although perfectly intelligent, unable to earn their own living. Others are the *creative* people, who, as in the case of Van Gogh, did many eccentric things but also many productive things— Van Gogh was gifted, or cursed, with an intense sensitivity. Lastly, there are those who have what others regard as peculiar sexual habits. Of the first two classes nothing more need be said, and all that is necessary is to mention certain of the so-called sexual perversions. (When we say so-called the implication is not that none of these forms of behaviour is perverse but that some of them are carried out by otherwise quite ordinary people.) *Sadism* and *Masochism* refer to, in the first place, pleasure in inflicting pain and, in the second, to receiving pain. The pleasure is sexual, and it is incorrect to talk of cruelty in itself as sadism. Sadism is named after the Marquis de Sade, who suffered from this perversion, although he certainly did much less harm in his small way than numerous politicians or generals of our time, and masochism is named after the Austrian novelist Sacher-Masoch, who wrote books which, although unpleasant, were not notably more so than certain Sunday newspapers of today.

Masturbation is sexual self-stimulation. Needless to say, it produces no more *physical* harm than ordinary sexual intercourse—that is to say, none at all, although some people have the strange belief that every act of intercourse weakens the body and it has even been believed that each act shortens life by a specific length of time. This is rather illogical in view of the fact that most of the famous rakes have been noted for their longevity! Masturbation is almost universal in infancy, adolescence, or even in later life when other outlets are not available. It need only be a matter of concern: (*a*) when it is chosen in preference to normal sexual activity, or (*b*) when it is compulsive and excessive, since then it is a sign, not of sexual desire, but of severe underlying anxiety.

Homosexuality is, as presumably most people now know, an attraction between individuals of the same sex. Most people pass through a brief homosexual stage. Ordinarily this comes just before puberty when schoolgirls get "crushes" on older girls or teachers and schoolboys have similar feelings towards their heroes. The disposition, however, may be retained into adult life. Nowadays people take a much more tolerant view of homosexuality, accepting that what adults do (with consent) is their own business and that a male homosexual who seduces a boy under age should be treated in no way differently from the man who seduces an under-age girl. Male homosexual practices are no longer an offence if committed in private between consenting adults. Female homosexual practices have never been an offence.

All that remains to be said is that many of these conditions are treatable or, if not treatable so far as cure is concerned, they can at least be relieved. The world is full of people who are "different"; there are those who are different in the right way, who should take satisfaction from their achievements, and those who are different in the wrong way, who should seek expert advice. Since psychological treatment is time-consuming, it is not very easy to obtain it within the National Health Service, although group treatment has simplified the problem. However, any person with such difficulties would probably benefit from a discussion with his family doctor.

DISEASES OF THE SKIN.

The skin in the course of development before birth is particularly closely associated with the nervous system. It is therefore not surprising that so many skin diseases are influenced by emotional states. Other causes of skin disease are infections, glandular disorders, vitamin deficiencies, and the numerous conditions for which no cause has been discovered, but which presumably are due to metabolic disorders.

One of the commonest skin symptoms is *itching* or *pruritus*. It may accompany many different general diseases, for example diabetes and jaundice. It may also be troublesome during the menopause (the change of life in women), in old age, or in nervous conditions. Sedatives and sex hormones sometimes help the itching during the menopause, and there are ointments which may be useful.

Itching in the region of the anus and genital organs is relatively common. It may be caused by worms, by irritating vaginal discharge, or by sugar in the urine, as in diabetes. The alteration in the normal bacteria of the bowel which follows treatment with various antibiotics also often causes anal pruritus and soreness. In many cases however the itching has some psychological cause. In treatment it is important to avoid ointments and creams which contain a local anæsthetic, because these substances can cause severe allergic reactions if used for longer than a few days, and may thus make the condition much worse. Treatment with a local corticosteroid application is more effective and safer.

Parasites, such as the *scabies* mite or *lice* can cause severe and persistent itching. The scabies mite is very small, and since it burrows under the skin surface, is unlikely to be seen; it is the cause of itching most commonly between the fingers and on the front of the wrists. The itching is worst when the body becomes heated, as in bed. Treatment consists of painting the body from head to foot with benzyl benzoate application, followed the next day by a hot bath. Since scabies is contracted through close personal contact with an infested person it is often desirable for several or all members of a family to be treated at the same time, even though only one of them may be affected. Lice are specialists, one type of which affects the scalp, another the body, and a third the genital area. Head lice are destroyed by lethane, body lice by D.D.T (dicophane) powder, and genital (pubic) lice by shaving off hair and washing. Obviously, the clothes, especially in the case of body lice, should be disinfested, either by the use of D.D.T. or, if this is not available, by using a hot iron over the seams, which lice (for some inexplicable reason) seem to favour. Apart from the discomfort they cause, lice are dangerous as potential carriers of typhus fever.

Baldness, or Alopecia, is a very common condition, as is manifested by the extraordinary number of preparations advertised as curing it. When many preparations are offered for the treatment of one condition it is a fair judgment to assume that none of them is likely to be effective. There are, in fact, two types of baldness; one, which is much the commoner, is hereditary, and cannot be influenced in the slightest by any treatment, the other, *alopecia areata*, is caused by nervous stress, and would recover in most cases by itself, whether one used a solution of soot and water or the most expensive " hair food." There is no such thing as a hair food, any more than there is such a thing as a nerve food, and although it is probable that hair hygiene may delay baldness, it certainly cannot prevent it. All hair tonics and " foods " are useless, and their uselessness is only equalled by their costliness. Those who have lost their hair and find it growing again after using some alleged tonic are people who have had *alopecia areata* and whose hair would have grown back anyhow. In women the hair often thins out soon after a pregnancy, but a few months later it usually returns to normal.

Seborrhœa is a condition in which there is over-activity of the sebaceous glands. The most usual form it takes is *dandruff*. However, it takes other forms, and those who have dandruff may also have rashes on the face, shoulders, and chest. In these areas there is a patchy, greasy, and often itchy, rash which does not clear up until the primary condition in the scalp is dealt with. The scalp should be washed with one of the modern sulphur-containing shampoos at least twice a week, and the affected parts on the face and chest can be dealt with by the use of a sulphur lotion (*not* on any account by greasy ointments). Seborrhœa is not in itself difficult to treat, but, since the condition depends on over-secretion of sebum,˙ the skin lubricant, treatment may have to be persisted in during the years of early adulthood, when it is most active.

Erythema Intertrigo is, quite simply, the sort of irritation which occurs usually from excessive sweating under the armpits, between the legs, and under the breasts in women. All that need be done is to wash frequently and to dust the affected areas after washing with powder. This is the condition which, in the tropics, is known as " prickly heat " and elswhere as a " sweat rash." In some people *hyperidrosis* or *excessive sweating* is a problem, especially when the sweating is accompanied with body odour—the sort of thing that, according to the advertisements " even your best friends won't tell you." There is little use for anyone in these days to suffer in this way: for the cosmetic firms have produced many highly efficient deodorants which not only control odour but also control the amount of sweating. Chlorophyll, which has been much advertised as removing odours, is effective when applied directly to surfaces which give off an unpleasant smell. It is however ineffective when taken by mouth, and does not prevent body odours. Stale sweat smells bad because it is decomposed by bacteria, and this type of body odour can be largely prevented by preparations containing a harmless antiseptic such as hexachlorophane and an antiperspirant such as aluminium chloride (see *Which*, February 1960).

Erysipelas is an infection of the skin caused by the hæmolytic streptococcus. It begins as a red, raised area anywhere on the body where the germs have been able to enter through a small crack or cut in the skin. The red area advances and spreads over the body until the disease is got under control. Erysipelas is very infectious, and those who look after the patient should wash their hands throughly after contact. At one time the disease used to spread as an epidemic throughout the hospital wards, but this is very rare nowadays. Treatment is, of course, a matter for the doctor.

Chilblains are common in cold weather, especially in those with poor circulation. Ordinarily they occur in the toes and fingers, but may appear on the nose and ears. The part affected becomes swollen, dusky, and there is pain and itching, sometimes leading to ulceration. Protection of the body, especially the hands and feet, from cold is the best and the only really effective way of preventing chilblains. Warm lined gloves

and footwear, and warm stockings or trousers should be worn outdoors. Adequate heating of rooms is essential: a temperature between 18° and 21°C is recommended (65°–78°F). Most tablets, medicines, ointments, or creams for chilblains are useless. A skin affection caused by heat is rather grandiosely described as *erythema ab igne*, and is frequently seen on the legs of ladies addicted to roasting their legs before the fire. It takes the form of red patches on the front of the legs and can be removed only by avoiding the cause.

Dermatitis means " inflammation of the skin," and therefore the word could be, strictly speaking, applied to any skin disease. In fact the term is used almost interchangeably with the term *eczema*. There are three main types of dermatitis or eczema. The first, *primary irritant dermatitis* results from injury of the skin by some powerful chemical, such as strong alkali or turpentine. The second, *contact dermatitis* is due to sensitisation of the skin to some substance which is normally liable to cause this type of allergic sensitivity; examples are nickel (in jewellery and suspender buckles), epoxy resins, rubber additives, primulas and chrysanthemums, and even ingredients of cosmetics. Contact dermatitis may continue for a long time, even after the patient is no longer in contact with the offending material. The third type is often called *constitutional eczema*. Although the skin is apt to react adversely to various irritants and sensitisers the major part is played by the personality, and there is often a history of eczema, hay fever or asthma in the family. Treatment is more difficult, but local corticosteroids and tar, sedatives and psychological treatment can be of great help. Infantile eczema also belongs in this category, but in most patients it disappears as the child grows up.

Impetigo is an infectious skin disease caused primarily by the streptococcus, but later often infected with staphylococci. It usually occurs on the face, and takes the form of blisters filled with pus on a red base; when the blisters burst their place is taken by yellow crusts. Impetigo is very infectious and easily spread by the fingers, dirty towels, or cloths; therefore, one of the first necessities is to prevent infection of others or reinfection of oneself by avoiding scratching and using a different towel each day, which must on no account be used by anyone else. Treatment is simple with an antibacterial ointment, so the main issue is prevention of contamination.

Sycosis or " Barber's Rash " occurs in men, and is similarly treated.

Urticaria or *Nettlerash* is a familiar skin disease in which itching weals appear on the skin, usually for no obvious reason. It is not infectious, and can be caused by nervous stress, certain drugs, allergy to some foods, or even exposure of the skin to cold. In some people it is possible to write on the skin with a fingernail: the " writing " appears in the form of weals. This is known as *dermographism*; it occurs in many normal persons as well as in many patients with urticaria. The antihistamine drugs are the most useful in the treatment of urticaria. Urticarial swelling of the tongue or throat must however be relieved at once and is treated by an injection of adrenaline.

Acne, or " *Blackheads*," is a condition found on the face and shoulders; its appearance is so familiar that no description is necessary. Acne is one of those conditions which is the end result of many factors. There is, first, a greasy skin, the result of glandular upset (which is why the disease usually occurs in adolescence); secondly, there is infection of the skin; and thirdly, there is blockage of the sebaceous ducts, which ordinarily allow the grease from the skin to pass out on to the surface. Since the condition starts with excess secretion of grease, ointments should never be used, and probably the best applications are drying lotions containing some sulphur preparation which inhibits secretion of grease. The face should be frequently washed, and it is possible now to obtain detergent solutions which are both antiseptic and prevent grease formation. In severe cases ultraviolet ray treatment may be necessary.

Rosacea. As has already been implied elsewhere, although the wages of sin may be extremely unpleasant, the wages of extreme virtue may be no less troublesome. Thus *rosacea*, in which the nose and cheeks become red and greasy and the skin coarsened, occurs alike in chronic alcoholics and elderly ladies with no vices other than a preference for strong tea. Both cases are associated with indigestion, since, regrettable as it may seem, strong tea and alcohol are about equally liable to cause the gastritis which may be at the root of this complaint. However, in many patients the chronic flushing is caused in other ways and psychological factors are important.

Lichen Planus is one of the numerous skin diseases which seem to be due to nervous states of tension. It may occur on any part of the body, but is most common on the front of the forearms and legs. The rash takes the form of nodules which are lilac in colour and have a dent on the top; when these disappear a stain is left behind. There is severe itching. Treatment is a matter for a doctor, as it also is in the case of *psoriasis*, a very common disease of largely unknown origin, which is extremely resistant to treatment. It tends to run in families. It takes the form of slightly raised papules, usually on the elbows and knees; typically the papules are covered with dry, silvery-looking scales. Apart from the rash, the patient is usually in perfectly good health and there is no itching. Many drugs have been used in psoriasis, notably chrysarobin, and while it is not difficult to cause the rash (which may occur anywhere on the body) to disappear in one area or even in all areas for a time it has a strong tendency to return.

Warts, or *Verrucae* are familiar enough. They are caused by a virus, and are, theoretically at least, contagious (although having removed many warts, the writer has never found them contagious). Most frequently they are found on the hands, but may occur elsewhere. Treatment is best carried out by a doctor, who will use a cautery, a caustic carbon dioxide frozen into " snow ". A curious feature of the common wart is that it can sometimes be caused to disappear by suggestion, which is presumably why so many old wives charms are not necessarily without effect. Different altogether from the common wart is the *plantar wart*, which occurs on the soles of the feet and often causes a good deal of discomfort. It is best dealt with by a chiropodist or in bad cases by a skin specialist since it is highly infectious.

Icthyosis is a disorder of horn formation with which some unfortunate people are born. The oil and sweat-producing glands do not function well and the skin is dry and scaly like the skin of a fish. It is, however, possible to help the condition, which does not affect the general health, by frequent alkaline baths to wash off the scales, and the subsequent use of lanolin to replace the lacking oil. Large doses of vitamin A seem to help in some cases, and there have been reports in the medical Press of cases being helped by hypnosis; this, however, is very much a matter for speculation.

Cancer, Rodent Ulcer, and Cysts. Cancer of the skin occurs mostly in old people, and takes the form of what is described as an *epithelioma*. It is most common on the face or hands, and usually appears as a nodule which breaks down and produces an ulcer. The glands may later be affected, but such cancers can almost invariably be cured unless a considerable time has elapsed during which they have been neglected. *Rodent ulcer* is a form of ulcer which appears on the inner corner of the eye or the side of the nose in old people. It does not spread over the body, but acts by eating into the tissues in the area where it has started. X-ray or operation is necessary, but the outlook is good. *Cysts* on the skin are due to blockage of the sebaceous glands. They may become very large, and are best removed, as they may become infected. They do not turn into cancer, and there is no such thing as " male " and " female " cysts. It does sometimes happen that *moles*, especially of the bluish-black type, may become malignant, so it is perhaps best to have them removed surgically when they exist. *All moles which change in appearance or size should be at once referred to a doctor.*

Skin Grafts.

These are a very complex subject which can be only briefly discussed here. They are used basically for a number of conditions in which large areas of skin have been removed from the body, as in burns or serious accidents. In other cases, as in plastic surgery, grafts may be used to make a new nose, eyelids, and so on. The following are the main types:

Pinch Grafts are small, circular pieces of skin cut from some other part of the body. (The former method of using grafts from another person has been given up almost completely, since such grafts—except in the case of identical twins—never " take.") The small pieces are laid on the area without skin and gradually grow together. *Split-thickness grafts* are grafts removed from another part of the body by an instrument known as a dermatome, which cuts sections about 4 in. by 8 in. containing part of the deep layers of the skin.

In *Full-thickness Grafts*, on the other hand, the whole thickness of the skin is removed from elsewhere and applied to an area which has to bear friction or heavy weights, such as the hand or the foot. Lastly, and this is largely used in plastic surgery, there is the *Pedicle graft*, which, unfortunately, although it is certainly the most exciting type, is rather difficult to describe. Briefly, if one, for example, wants to make a new nose, one cuts an area of skin and underlying fat about 2 in. wide and 5 or 6 in. long in the abdomen. One end, however, remains attached so that it gets adequate blood-supply. The problem is how to get this tissue to the nose, and this is done by a complicated process of leap-frog. First, the free end of the graft is attached to the forearm, whilst its " root " remains in the original site, and when it begins to grow and get its blood-supply from the arm, the original " root " is cut. So we now have a " sausage " of tissue attached to the arm. The arm is then lifted to the face and kept firmly in position there until the new free part becomes attached. It is then detached from the arm, modelled to the correct shape, and grows where the nose used to be!

THE RHEUMATIC DISEASES.

The main rheumatic diseases (or so they are described, although they seem to have little relationship one with the other), are *rheumatic fever*, the acute form, which has already been dealt with (P28); *chorea*, or rheumatism of the nervous system, also mentioned (P49); *rheumatoid arthritis*; *osteoarthritis*; and *gout*. The only thing these diseases seem to have in common is that most seem to be associated with the connective tissues, muscles or joints—this, of course, with the single exception of chorea. Apart from this, there is very little similarity.

Rheumatoid arthritis often starts without evident cause in early adult life, and affects the small joints of the fingers and toes, causing swelling and pain. No infective process has been discovered, yet the disease goes on and on, sometimes better, sometimes worse. It is (and this is all one can say) a disease commoner in women, commoner in temperate climates, commoner following emotional stress. Although, as we have seen, rheumatoid arthritis is a disease characterised by frequent remissions, it takes a considerable time to burn itself out. The most likely explanation for its occurrence is that stress reactions act on the suprarenal glands and the secretion of cortisone is inadequate to play its usual part in preventing the body from responding too severely to injury. However, the injection of cortisone has proved, on the whole, less useful than might have been expected, and there is little reason to suppose that in most cases it is any better than aspirin.

Osteoarthritis is essentially a degenerative disease of old people. The bones affected are ordinarily the larger joints: the shoulders, the hips, or the spine. There is no disease in the ordinary sense, and essentially what has happened is that these joints have got " old " and the bone has overgrown so that movement is less simple than it once was. Osteoarthritis is not curable, but can be relieved by drugs and physiotherapy.

Gout, so far as one knows, has nothing at all to do with rheumatism. It is a metabolic disease caused by the inability of the body to deal with certain protein breakdown substances, such as uric acid.

DISEASES OF THE EYE.

The Eye.

The eye is frequently compared to a camera, and in a general sort of way there is some resemblance. The eyeball consists of 3 coats within which are contained the refraction media: (1) The outermost layer, the main support of the eyeball, comprising the sclera (opaque) and the cornea (transparent, covering the front of the eyeball). The conjunctiva (the part which gets inflamed when you get germs or dust on the surface of the eye) is a thin protective membrane covering the sclera and doubles back to line the inside of the upper and lower lids. It stops at the junction of the sclera and cornea. (2) The middle layer containing many blood vessels which forms the choroid and, in front, the iris (the coloured part of the eye). The muscle in the iris enables its central aperture, the pupil, to contract in bright light, and to dilate in dim light. (3) The innermost layer of nervous tissue, the retina. The retina contains the expanded termination of the optic nerve which is part of the brain. Behind the iris is the lens, which is controlled by a series of muscles which increase or diminish its curvature, and thus produce, according to the nearness or distance of the object, a clear picture on the retina. Some of these parts may, of course, be affected by disease. Here we shall deal only with a few of the more common diseases.

Blepharitis is an infection of the eyelids which is easily recognisable from the red, sore appearance at the margins, the formation of crusts, and the falling-out of the eyelashes. If it has just developed, an attempt may be made to treat it at home with hot bathing and the so-called Golden Eye Ointment, but *blepharitis* is liable to become a chronic disease, and it is wiser to see a doctor. Penicillin cream or ointment can cure the disease, but must *never* be used save under medical advice; allergy to penicillin is commoner in the eyes than anywhere else, and in some cases patients have lost their sight through its use in this way.

Conjunctivitis is the result of infection of the conjunctiva, and the symptoms are the familiar ones of a feeling as if some grit had got into the eye, running from the eye, and frequently gummed-together eyelids in the morning. In some cases it can be treated by hot bathing and eye-baths with one of the proprietary lotions on the market, but it is much wiser to see your doctor, who can supply much more effective remedies and may save you a lot of unnecessary discomfort.

Other Eye Diseases. We can only mention briefly *keratis*, inflammation of the cornea; *iritis*, inflammation of the iris; and *glaucoma*. These are all potentially serious diseases, and should not be diagnosed or treated by the layman. Glaucoma, in particular, may lead to blindness if help is not sought in time. If there is redness and congestion over the eye, dimness of vision, *severe* pain (as contrasted with the irritation caused by conjunctivitis), and perhaps even vomiting, the doctor must be called immediately.

The main disease of the lens is *cataract*, in which the lens becomes opaque and varying degrees of blindness result. Ordinarily, cataract is a condition found in people after middle age, but sometimes it is found in children at birth. The treatment is by operation—one which has been carried out for centuries—in which the opaque lens is removed. The patient thereafter has to wear glasses, but the vast majority of patients obtain good vision.

In *retinitis*, however, where the " screen " at the back of the eye is affected, the general outlook is more serious. This is because, whereas cataract is a localised disease, retinitis often signifies some bodily illness: infection, hardening of the arteries leading to hæmorrhage, diabetes, or kidney disorders. Sometimes the retina becomes detached, leading to blindness. As has been suggested above, except in very minor conditions, such as styes (a localised infection treated in the same way as blepharitis), or conjunctivitis, the doctor should always be consulted. He should be consulted, too, when a foreign body gets into the eye unless it can be removed by very gentle manipulation with a handkerchief, for it must be remembered that such " poking about " on the surface of the eye may do much more harm than the original condition. So, if a couple of minutes fail to remove the grit, give up, and go to the surgery.

DISEASES OF WOMEN.

The *internal sexual organs* of a woman, like the urinary system, can best be described as shaped like a capital Y. At the tips of the arms of the Y are the female sex glands, the ovaries: the two arms running downwards are the Fallopian tubes: the point where the arms meet is the womb or uterus: the single leg of the Y is the vagina. These are the *primary sexual organs* of a woman and they undergo regular cyclical changes in response to the control exercised over them by the pituitary gland, situated in the base of the skull. This control is mediated by chemical messengers (hormones) secreted into the circulation. The ovaries also secrete hormones, œstrogen and progesterone, and a delicate hormonal balance is maintained between the pituitary gland and the ovaries. Each month an egg cell (ovum) matures and is released from the ovary, usually midway between two menstrual periods: the ovum is wafted along the Fallopian tubes by waves of contraction and if fertilised embeds in the lining of the uterus which has been conditioned to nourish it by the ovarian hormones. If it is not fertilised the ovum escapes from the uterus, altered hormone levels then cause the lining of the uterus to be shed (this is menstruation), usually about 14 days after ovulation. After menstruation a new cycle begins; another ovum matures and a fresh lining grows in the uterus. These cyclical changes recur from puberty to the menopause. Menstruation does not occur during pregnancy, of which a missed period is often the first sign. However, women do miss periods even though they are not pregnant, and this usually means that some minor and temporary change has occurred in the hormone balance. If three consecutive periods are missed it is wise to consult a doctor.

The *breasts* are called *secondary sexual organs* and are also under the influence of the ovarian hormones. Two conditions which need treatment are *mastitis* and *cancer of the breast*, both of which are characterised by lumps within the breast tissue. Mastitis may be uncomfortable but is not dangerous and can be treated medically, whereas cancer is more serious. The distinction between mastitis and cancer can only be made by a doctor and any woman who discovers a lump in her breast must seek medical aid *at once.*

Abscesses also occur in the breast, nearly always when the mother is feeding her child. Here again, a lump appears, the breast becomes red and very tender, and the woman may be feverish. Treatment with antibiotics is sometimes successful, especially if the mother consults her doctor quickly, otherwise treatment is by a small operation.

The Ovaries. The two commonest diseases of the ovaries are cysts and disorders arising from hormonal imbalance. The symptoms of ovarian disease are usually abdominal or low back pains, and heavy and painful loss during the periods, which may become irregular. These signs should be taken as a warning to consult a doctor.

The Fallopian Tubes. Infection of the Fallopian tubes is called salpingitis. The membrane lining the tubes is continuous with the lining of the uterus, hence an infection is rarely confined to a circumscribed area in either the tubes or the uterus, and pelvic inflammatory disease is a better name for this condition. Pelvic inflammatory disease often follows an abortion, or childbirth where part of the afterbirth (placenta) has been retained, or can spread from an infection in a nearby organ, for example the appendix. Infection is sometimes conveyed by the blood from another septic source in the body. The gonococcus is another cause of infection. The disease is characterised by pain and tenderness in the lower part of the abdomen, accompanied by fever, general malaise and frequently (but not invariably) a vaginal discharge. The treatment of pelvic inflammatory disease is usually medical and is the same irrespective of the primary site of infection. Before the introduction of antibiotics the disease often became chronic and the Fallopian tubes were frequently blocked by a cicatrising scar, a cause of subsequent sterility.

The Uterus. This is a hollow muscular organ and both its musculature and its lining membrane can be the site of disease. *Fibroids* are non-malignant muscular tumours which develop in many women. The main symptom is a heavy menstrual loss and surgical removal of the uterus (hysterectomy) is often necessary. This is a major operation, but modern anaesthesia and operative techniques minimise the discomfort. Hysterectomy does not impair sexual pleasure, but no more babies can be conceived. Infection of the lining of the uterus is usually part of a generalised pelvic inflammatory disease (*see* Fallopian tubes).

Cancer of the Uterus and Cervical Smears. The uterus is pear-shaped and consists of a body and neck. The wide end is uppermost (the body) and the narrow neck (cervix) projects into the top of the vagina. Cancer of the cervix is commonest in middle-aged women who have married young and have had a large family; cancer of the body of the uterus usually occurs after the menopause and is most common in childless women. The symptoms are variable and it is sufficient to emphasise that any woman who has unexpected bleeding, especially after intercourse, whether her periods have stopped or not, *must* see her doctor at once. The treatment depends on individual circumstances, but is usually by operation. It is now possible to detect cancer of the cervix long before symptoms develop and at a stage when the disease can be eradicated by a relatively small operation. This early detection has been made possible by the development of exfoliative cytology. Cells taken from the cervix (without discomfort to the woman) are examined under a microscope. This test is popularly known as the " cancer test " or " cervical smear." A cervical smear is often taken as part of the routine gynaecological examination by consultants, general practitioners, and family planning doctors, and is also being included in some population screening programmes. It is a big step forward in preventive medicine and may ultimately solve the problem of cancer of the cervix. Every woman between the ages of 25 and 60 should seize any chance to have this test done.

Prolapse means a sagging down of the uterus into the vagina and the cervix may even appear at the outside. It is a result of frequent childbirth and laxness of the ligaments which support the uterus: weakness of the vaginal walls often occurs at the same time. The symptoms of uterine prolapse are low back pain and a heavy dragging feeling in the lower abdomen: these are often overshadowed by the distressingly embarrassing incontinence which results from lax vaginal walls. The stress of only a sneeze, a cough, or a giggle often causes the involuntary escape of urine. The cure is operative and very rewarding.

Dysmenorrhoea or pain with the periods, is very common and most women experience this symptom at some time or another. Very often a girl's first periods are troublefree, but dysmenorrhoea develops after a year or two: this suggests that a psychological element is involved. Dysmenorrhoea is a symptom which has many varying causes, and the sensible thing to do, if pain is troublesome, is to see a doctor.

Amenorrhoea means stopping of the periods in a young woman. It may signify pregnancy or glandular disease _or it can be purely psychological.

Abortion, or its more acceptable name, miscarriage, describes the spontaneous or induced termination of a pregnancy before the foetus (baby) is able to survive. A baby cannot live unless it is born after the twenty-eighth week of pregnancy, though many infants born at this time die. The two main symptoms of abortion are bleeding and abdominal pain. Any bleeding occurring during pregnancy ought to be reported at once. Pain starts in the back and lower abdomen and is usually spasmodic in character, and like colic it works up to a peak and then temporarily passes off. Any pregnant woman with pain and bleeding should go to bed at once and send for her doctor. When doctors are convinced that a pregnancy should be terminated then an abortion by safe surgical means may be performed in hospital.

CONTRACEPTION.

If a couple intends to practice birth control expert advice should be obtained from their family doctor or family planning clinic. The matter of whether or not a baby is born is too important to leave to chance. The method chosen must be effective as well as acceptable to the couple concerned, and the extent of the choice only emphasises the fact that the ideal contraceptive which is best for every couple at all times has yet to be discovered. The only method which is 100 per cent. reliable is abstinence. If the male seed (sperm) fertilises the female seed (ovum) then pregnancy results. Contraception is only effective if this union is prevented. A couple can achieve a measure of contraception without the help of pills or appliances if the husband practices *coitus interruptus* or they rely on the wife's " safe period." *Coitus interruptus* (when the man withdraws before emission occurs) is a thoroughly unreliable method which often leads to psychological difficulties in both partners. The " rhythm " or " safe period " method relies on estimating the time of ovulation and abstaining from intercourse during this time. This is at best unreliable, though its effectiveness can be improved by keeping careful records of the body temperature on waking each morning as the temperature rises once ovulation has occurred. The interpretation of these temperature records needs care and couples who must rely on this method can obtain expert advice from, for example, The Catholic Marriage Advisory Council, or a family planning clinic. *Barrier methods* prevent the sperms from reaching the ovum and can be used by the man (sheath or condom) or woman (cap or diaphragm): the reliability of the barrier is greatly increased if it is used in conjunction with a spermicidal cream, jelly, or pessary. A great many women have found that the *oral contraceptive pill* is ideal for their needs: it is the most aesthetic means of contraception and offers the most complete protection against pregnancy. Oral contraceptive pills contain chemical substances (oestrogen and progestagen) which replace the hormones normally released from the ovary while an ovum is developing. Ovulation does not occur, and without an ovum there can be no pregnancy. Pills must be taken strictly as directed as the dose is the lowest that will provide effective contraception and missing a tablet may result in pregnancy. Side effects sometimes occur (for example, nausea, breast discomfort, headaches,) but usually decrease after a few cycles of medication. Newspaper reports of the deaths of young women taking the pill have caused widespread concern. These tragedies have followed blockage of a blood vessel (by thrombosis or embolism) and have been carefully investigated, and the conclusions are that the number of such deaths is small and does not differ from the number which would probably have occurred in any case. No satisfactory pill for a man has yet been developed. In the newest method of contraception a small plastic *intra-uterine device* (loop, bow, or coil) is inserted into the womb. Once inserted it can be forgotten: a tremendous advantage to many different peoples and societies. It is not as effective as the pill but is more satisfactory than barrier methods. This intra-uterine device is not suitable for all women and is usually not recommended to women who have borne no children or who have very heavy periods. However, careful selection of suitable women has resulted in a high proportion of satisfied users. The search for the ideal contraceptive continues.

Vasectomy (a form of sterilisation) may now be performed under the health service on a husband in the interests of the health of either husband or wife.

PART III. SPECIAL TOPICS

INFANTILE UNDERNUTRITION AND THE BRAIN.

In the last few years, a great deal of attention has been given to the problem of whether malnutrition in early life can result in damage to the developing brain, in such a way as to leave permanent deficits in intellectual capacity persisting into adult life.

This formulation of the problem is, of course, very much influenced by an increasing awareness of the prevalence under normal circumstances of widespread infantile malnutrition throughout the underprivileged world: a situation which is thrown into sharp relief by man-made or natural disaster. Community catastrophes reduce still further the nutritional intake of children who are already struggling for existence below the borderline of minimum requirements. Most people still do not appreciate that the pictures of starving children in disturbed areas, recently given so much publicity by newspapers and television, could easily have been taken in any of the other vast territories where life is still considered normal and undisturbed.

From the limited point of view of scientific investigation, the question is whether physical restriction of supplies can affect the physical development of the brain in a lasting manner, and whether this in turn can lead to deleterious effects on mental function.

For reasons which will be elaborated there are several classes of children in our own more privileged communities whose brains may be equally at risk from perinatal growth restriction, without severe malnutrition.

Two Lines of Approach.

Two main lines of investigation are being followed in current research. At first sight it may not seem difficult to answer the question by making observations on grown-up people in underprivileged communities whose infancy was affected by severe nutritional deprivation. In practice, however, even if one could collect a group of people whose personal histories were so well documented as to comprise a scientifically acceptable sample; and even if one could find a well-fed control group in the same community, with comparable environmental influences on their development; and even if it could be satisfactorily demonstrated that the previously undernourished people were indeed at an intellectual disadvantage compared with the controls, it would still need to be shown that the mental deficits were a direct result of undernutrition restricting the physical development of the brain. And to demonstrate that would assume a knowledge which we do not possess of the connection, if any, between the physical state of the brain and its intellectual function. There might, of course, be innumerable other possible connections between the early undernutrition and the subsequent intellectual deficit such as an inherited constitutional dimness in these particular members of the community which would itself also make them differentially vulnerable to all the ills of poverty, including infective disease, as well as undernutrition.

A second line of approach to the question attempts to reduce some of the complexities by controlled experiments using animals whose normal growth programme is measured in weeks rather than years, and in whom a closer homogeneity of environmental conditions and ultimate products can probably be obtained. It is much more acceptable to impose experimental growth-controlling nutritional regimes on rats, and in particular they can be killed to a pre-designed programme and the physical state of their brains examined. However, the behavioural correlations are at least as difficult to determine in rats as in humans; and digging out the brain and the need to mince it up make longitudinal study of individual animals more difficult. And finally, from the human point of view, we would still be left with the question of how meaningful would be an extrapolation from rats to humans.

Having attempted to show that our original question is scarcely amenable to investigation, and therefore scarcely a question, we will now outline the manner in which we have begun to try to answer it, at least in respect of the physical effects which can be produced on the physical development and ultimate state of the physical brain. It can now be shown that permanent deficits can be produced in the adult brain by quite mild restrictions of bodily growth, provided these are imposed at certain critical limited times in early life.

Just as the body itself does not grow at a uniform rate at all times, but undergoes " growth spurts " at certain stages, so the brain passes through a major " growth spurt " during which it is growing very fast indeed. The brain " growth spurt " occurs in all species in advance of the general bodily " growth spurt." In our own human species this period extends from the last weeks of gestation through the first several months of postnatal life.

The Hypothesis.

The hypothesis which is being investigated proposes that brain development is likely to be most vulnerable to restriction at the time of its most rapid growth; and that restrictions imposed at this time are likely to be to some extent irrecoverable. A corollary to the hypothesis is that the farther away from the period of most rapid growth, the more severe will have to be the deprivation to produce a comparable effect, until in the adult there may be no effect on the physical brain whatever, even from the most severe starvation unto death.

To take the last point first, it is cheating to include the postulate of adult brain invulnerability in a predictive hypothesis, since it has been a partly established fact for at least one century that adult brain weight is unaffected by starvation. This is true even if the individual is slowly starved to death over a long period, and his body and other organ weights are reduced to half their normal values. However, it has probably always been suspected that at least some of the metabolic substances to be found in the adult brain would be diminished or seriously distorted by starvation, just as they are in (for example) the liver. Surprisingly it has recently been established that even the detailed chemical composition of the brain is virtually unaffected by adult starvation, just as is its fresh weight, and this is a very striking example of the old nutritionist's doctrine of " brain sparing." Such is certainly not the case with the *developing* brain which, as will be seen, can suffer quite striking reductions in its chemical and cellular composition as a result of quite mild growth retardation, much milder than the severe starvation imposed on the adult with impunity. Indeed it is sufficient to rear suckling rats in rather large litters to produce irrecoverable deficits in brain size, numbers of cells, and degree of myelination: and some of the evidence for this will be described.

Returning to our hypothesis that lasting effects may be produced in the brain by early growth restriction, there are several theoretical reasons which lend it support. For example, the brain is a tissue in which the adult number of unit cells, or neurons, is achieved quite early. By twenty-five weeks of gestation you probably have as many nerve cells as you will ever have, and these cells are incapable of multiplication or repair after this stage. So the theoretical possibility is easy to accept that early interference at the time they are laid down and growing will have permanent effects. Similarly there is metabolic stability in much if not all of the myelin substance. Myelin is the material derived during the brain growth spurt from the other brain cells, which wrap an insulating sheath around the nerve fibres. The molecules of which this sheath are made do not turn over metabolically throughout life as many other body constituents do. Once laid down in sheath structure during the brain growth spurt, there they probably remain throughout life. It is the inability of myelin to regenerate after injury of the central nervous system which is responsible for failures of recovery in certain chronic human neurological disease. Again it is not difficult to accept the proposition that early restriction of myelin synthesis will lead to irrecoverable deficits in the adult brain.

Experimentally Observed Facts.

Let us now leave theoretical speculation and turn to experimentally observed fact. We know that the principal components of the brain "growth spurt" are:

(1) An increase in the size and number of nerve fibres and other processes growing out of the already established nerve cells, and the consequent vast increase in the numbers of functional connections between them.

(2) An almost explosive multiplication of another important brain cell type—the oligodendroglia. These are the cells which manufacture the myelin sheaths.

(3) The process of myelination, involving the synthesis of myelin materials by the oligodendroglia, and the building of these materials into the insulating myelin sheaths.

We have a convenient way of measuring the second and third of these processes chemically. This is necessary because it would be quite impracticable to count the astronomical numbers of structures involved by any morphological technique. For example, it can be assumed that all the cells contain the same amount of DNA in their nucleus, and therefore a chemical estimation of the increasing amount of DNA in the tissue is an index of cell multiplication. Similarly an estimation of the increasing amount of fatty myelin is possible by estimating a representative myelin fat chemically. Since both nuclear DNA and myelin lipid are metabolically stable, an estimation of each will always represent the extent of development which each has undergone in the brain. It is by such comparatively crude techniques as these that lasting physical effects on the developing brain can be quantitatively measured.

The use of small laboratory animals is thought to be valid at this stage of the investigation. Their brains consist of anatomical units identical with the human; and in their growth and development they pass through a similar sequence of changes. The main difference from the human, apart from the complexity of the eventual product, is the timing of their brain "growth spurts" in relation to birth. Thus the period of fastest growth in the rat brain is entirely postnatal and is encompassed by the normal suckling period. The brain "growth spurt" in the guinea pig is before birth, while that of the domestic pig, like our own, occurs either side of birth. Valid extrapolations from one species to another must therefore take this difference of timing into account.

The rat is a convenient species, since manipulations of growth rate can easily be accomplished

during the suckling period, within which the entire brain "growth spurt" occurs. In one experimental design, two litters of rats born on the same day are taken from their mothers on that day and placed together in a basin. They are then mixed together. Three are awarded at random to one mother, and the balance of fifteen to twenty are given to the other. They are then left to rear their artificially created families and at the time of weaning, at twenty-one days, it is found that the privileged three from the small family are about twice the size of the others. An interesting thing is that their smaller contemporaries from the large litters remain small for the rest of their lives, even when they are weaned to an *ad libitum* diet. Their growth programme has been permanently altered, but this can only be accomplished by restriction at such an early stage. Restriction at a later stage of growth is much more recoverable, and in the mature animal it is usually completely so.

The opportunity now arises of examining the brains of animals pursuing these different growth trajectories. It is also easy to design experiments using different permutations and combinations of periods of growth restriction. For example, large and small weanling animals from small and large litters can both be weaned on to a deficient diet so that their growth is similarly depressed for some weeks after weaning. They are then released to an adequate diet. These two groups are apparently identically deprived at the end of the further period of undernutrition. However, one group has grown its brain under optimal early conditions, whereas the other has been restricted at the time of brain growth. It is found that only the early-restricted group, like all animals suckled in larger litters, have permanent deficits in brain size and composition, resisting all attempts at rehabilitation.

It is important to appreciate that the mature products of early undernutrition which show these lasting deficits have not been severely underfed by being in a large litter. They show no signs of clinical malnutrition at the time, and are not visibly distinguishable from animals at the lower end of the normal range. Nevertheless traces of the experience persist in the brain, as in the body, in marked contrast to the nil effect of severe starvation, even to death, on the adult brain.

The persisting deficits in the brain which have so far been discovered are of three main types:

(1) The weight of the brain is permanently less.

(2) The total number of brain cells is permanently less, to the extent of between 10% and 20%.

(3) The degree of myelination, as determined by estimating myelin lipid per unit weight is permanently less. This latter case is an example of a deficit which is greater than, and independent of, the deficit in brain weight.

The significance of these findings is difficult to assess. Brain weight is dominated by body size during normal growth, although the relationship is not a linear one. It is doubtful if a small brain is any real handicap, provided its size matches the size of the body. Similarly the deficit in cell numbers may simply reflect the reduction in brain size, although we would need to know which cells are missing before being sure, and this we do not yet completely know. Thus the most significant finding so far may be the reduction in myelin which is independent of the brain size. Its significance is not necessarily due to the failure to complete the process of myelination, since even this may not itself matter. In the present state of ignorance, we prefer to consider it simply as a demonstration that this kind of permanent deficit can be produced in developing brain, provided the deprivation is correctly timed to coincide with the brain's "growth spurt"; and thus there may be other similar important deficits which we have not looked for yet.

Further powerful support for the hypothesis comes from the recent finding that of all the regions of the brain, the cerebellum is the most severely affected in the experimental conditions which have been described. Indeed the main brunt of the ultimate cell deficit is borne by the cerebellum, a comparatively small region which in the adult contains as many cells as the rest of the brain put together. Now it has been found in humans as in animals, that this is a part of the brain which grows at an immensely faster rate than any other at the time of the " growth spurt." It is therefore reasonable to predict, on the basis of our hypothesis, that if the growth of the whole brain be restricted at this time, it should be the cerebellum which is hardest hit: and such is indeed the case in experimental animals. Furthermore there is evidence that in these animals there is a detectable impairment specifically of cerebellar function. They are not able to achieve the same fine motor co-ordination achieved by normal controls.

It can now be claimed that considerable evidence is beginning to accumulate in support of our hypothesis that the brain " growth spurt " constitutes a particularly vulnerable period to growth restriction, to the permanent detriment of the brain. If this be true, and if the physical deficits achieved have any functional significance, it remains to consider which human infants will be comparably at risk?

Conclusion.

Unfortunately, before we can guess at the answer, we need to know the timing of the human brain " growth spurt " more precisely. Very little reliable information is available about the changing rate of human brain growth even in terms of whole brain weight. Useful information about the changing composition of human brain is only just coming to hand. From this we are able to say that the vulnerable period probably extends from about the thirtieth week of gestation, throughout the first several months of life. If this in turn be true, there are likely to be four main categories of human babies at risk:

(1) Severely underfed babies in under-privileged communities, often also born of underfed mothers.

(2) Premature babies in our own community, who are born at the very time which is most important for brain growth. Premature babies have to put up with a paediatrician instead of a placenta: and he is not as good.

(3) Babies whose rate of intrauterine growth has been retarded, and who are consequently born small for their gestational age. These " small-for-dates " babies comprise about one-third of all babies of low birth weight.

(4) Babies whose developmental progress has for any other reason been impeded at this vulnerable time.

There is some evidence already that children from all these groups are somewhat less well endowed in later life, though it must be repeatedly and firmly stressed that we are a very long way yet from proving the case.

SLEEPING AND DREAMING.

An alien from some distant planet where biological life had never appeared might be surprised at the strange goings-on he found on earth. He would see creatures of a great variety of shapes and sizes, some cumbersome and armoured, some light and streamlined, others equipped with weapons for biting and tearing, all chasing around trying to eat each other. He would conclude that life on earth was very dangerous, but before going home he might notice a characteristic habit of these creatures seemingly at odds with the relentless duel they appeared to be engaged in. Quite frequently they would drop their neurotic alertness and, almost incredibly, lapse into a period of quiet with sense organs damped down, muscles inactive, and worst of all, their control centres seemingly switched off.

At this point the alien might decide that beings on such a planet which so carelessly let their essential defences drop didn't deserve to survive long, and assume that this dangerous " switch-

off " probably signalled the onset of some internal process, not obvious to the outside observer, which must be of tremendous importance to the creature's well-being. His final surprise might come when he tried to ask the most intelligent of the animals what it was that was so important, and found that they simply didn't know.

And this happens to be the truth, for Man has made amazingly little headway into understanding sleep (which is, of course, the switch-off an alien would have observed), although taken on average he devotes one-third of his life to it. No doubt this is because sleep, by virtue of its own special properties, resists introspection—we cannot study it in ourselves without disturbing it. Furthermore it is a period when *nothing* seems to be happening, barren of thought and memory and yet inherently strange and enveloped in mysteries to which Man has frequently tried to provide answers. In this article we will look at some of these answers, note their general inadequacy, and consider some new facts and a fresh approach, which suggests that one of the main mysteries may be in the process of being unravelled.

Broadly speaking, the various approaches attempting to explain sleep (and, of course, the dream) fall into three main groups that the writer has called: (1) The Commonsense; (2) The Fantastic; and (3) The Psychoanalytic.

The Commonsense.

This theory states that the sole or principal reason for sleeping is to allow us to rest, and, alas for simplicity's sake, it just doesn't happen to be correct. True, there's something very tempting in the idea—after all we do switch into sleep after a period of " feeling tired," and wake in the morning with this feeling altered. What more reasonable than to assume that the point of sleep was to rest the body after the doings of the day? The trouble is that from a physiological point of view sleep is *not* necessary to rest tired muscles and aching bones—a period of relaxation in an arm-chair or stretched out on a bed *without* unconsciousness intervening is quite sufficient to allow the body's physical functions to return to their normal state. In fact during sleep the body engages in a series of postural shifts evidently geared to preventing the musculature seizing-up through disuse. Perhaps then, it is not physical but *mental* rest that is served by sleep.

The brain is the most important organ in the body, working away all day thinking, learning, etc. Should it not have a period of inactivity which ought to be accompanied by a period of unconsciousness or " switch-off "? Unfortunately for this hypothesis, the data from electroencephalography (recording the brain's internal activity by electrodes attached to the scalp) reveal that while there is indeed a significant and very interesting change in the nature of these electrical rhythms during sleep—notably from fast low amplitude to slow high amplitude firing—there is no suggestion that very much *less* is going on. The picture is not one of a run-down of activity, but rather of a shift to activity of a different kind.

So much for the simple commonsense approach —in which, incidentally, dreams are looked on as nothing more than a kind of mistake or error in the system, something to be avoided if a " good night's sleep " is to be had. We do not sleep simply in order to rest (which is not to say, of course, that some rest will not come with sleep).

The Fantastic.

This is the oldest view of all. In many parts of the world it is still the *only* view and while even in our own society large numbers of educated people still believe it, it is really built on an out-of-date fantasy-view of the universe. For this reason we call it " The Fantastic." It has as its main thesis the belief that human beings consist essentially of two distinct parts—the body, which follows the laws of the physical universe; and the mind, soul, or spirit, which is " immaterial." During sleep and in certain other states, this mind or soul may escape the confines of its host body and the normal boundaries of space and time, to roam more or less at will, visiting Australia as easily as crossing a road, and popping into the future for news of the Derby or of the death of a close relation.

Put this way the theory sounds silly rather than just fantastic, but this is not really an unfair representation of a very widely held point of view. The temptation to see sleep as the state of a body with some very important component missing must have been considerable to early philosophers, who, on kicking the body and finding signs of the spirit's return, might then ask the individual where he had been. The reported dream would then be taken as a genuine account of a real experience. For dreams, by this theory, are in part *real* happenings, a hint of the essential spiritual nature of Man and his ability to transcend space and time when the links with the material world are broken.

Support for this point of view comes from the dogma of orthodox religions which say that the soul of man is the true reality, and more enticingly from the strange data of psychical research which nowadays is called parapsychology (**J38**). The Library of the Society for Psychical Research in Kensington, London, has numerous "authentic" accounts of dream visitations from "dead" relatives, to awful pre-visions of disasters in the future. In the 19th cent., Myers and Gurney pooled masses of these accounts into the enormously interesting volume, *Phantasms of the Living*, which would be one of the most important books ever published if one-twentieth of its contents were true. More recently, the mathematician, J. W. Dunne, claimed in his strange work, *An Experiment with Time*, that dreams definitely provided a mirror into the future, a kind of time-telescope which anyone could learn to operate. Today the beliefs of Myers, Gurney, and Dunne seem less acceptable, and the evidence for telepathy (**J43**), patiently gathered by Rhine and co-workers two decades ago, now carries less weight than ever among scientists and philosophers.

The cause of this is tied up with the decline in religious belief and the steady advance of scientific knowledge—both developments which make the "Fantastic" view of sleeping and dreaming progressively less acceptable to most people.

The Psychoanalytic.

The contribution of psychoanalytic theory to an understanding of the mind and its complex rules has been greatly overstressed and also greatly underplayed. In fact, the single insight of the unconscious nature of many of our thought processes and their very real power in determining our behaviour is one of the most important concepts in psychology—or even in science for that matter. The psychoanalytic view of dreams is much to commend it, and in simplified form goes as follows: Man is an animal, with animal drives, emotions, and needs. Society, in exchange for protecting him, requires him to obey certain rules, many of which conflict drastically with his natural inclinations. These dynamic forces, though they may be "denied" by the individual at a conscious level, are merely repressed and retain latent psychic power in the inner rooms of the mind. During sleep, with the force of the social censor diminished, these drives and conflicts burst forth in the form of dreams. Mostly the dream itself is then subject to further repression, thus neatly accounting for the odd tendency we have all noticed to forget our dreams almost immediately we experience them.

Now the strength of this theory is inarguable, and the role of the dream in psychotherapy as a guide to the analyst in deciding the patient's *real* as opposed to his declared problems has proved dramatically fruitful in some cases. The real trouble of course is the pretence, lately being abandoned, that this provides a truly comprehensive theory of dreams—a pretence which has led to some awkward questions being asked and some unsatisfactory answers given.

To take a point, most of us have had dreams in which the subject matter seems devoid of any significance in the psychoanalytic sense. To most analysts this kind of remark is anathema—the truth is, they say, that the real nature of the dream is so appalling or so revolutionary a nature that it cannot even be *dreamt* in its raw form, and must therefore be disguised lest it awake the dreamer. With this escape clause an unshakable, though highly unsatisfactory, comprehensive theory is possible in which all obvious dreams are obvious, and those which are not are disguised.

This of course means that *any* dream can be interpreted in more or less *any* way to suit the interpreter's particular bias and has robbed the psychoanalytic approach of much of its original power. Although it was exceedingly fashionable at one time, the psychoanalytic theory of dreams is not, and is unlikely to become, a comprehensive one.

Sleep Deprivation.

Though a fair bit was known about the mechanics of sleep—blood pressure falls, temperature falls, etc.—scientists seemed, until quite recently, to be getting nowhere in their quest to find the principal reason for sleep. One of the most persistent lines of approach (and one of the least fruitful as it turned out) was the hunt for specific "toxins" or poisons, supposed to accumulate in the body during the day and requiring sleep to eliminate them. The hypnotoxin, when found, would presumably trigger sleep when a sufficient quantity had built up in the body.

Studies of people and animals deprived of sleep for varying periods made it quite clear that sleep was not just a bad habit, wasteful of time and fraught with danger, but an absolute necessity for sanity and life itself. Most of the higher animals die if deprived of sleep for periods of a week or so, showing, en route, signs of excitability and mania. Humans, if the anecdotal evidence of mediaeval Chinese torture chambers is reliable, die after a period as short as ten days, again showing signs of madness prior to death.

The U.S.A. holds most records for prolonged sleep deprivation, of which one of the best documented is that of Peter Tripp, a 32-year-old disc-jockey who stayed awake for over eight days in the window of a store in Times Square in 1959. Tripp suffered a three-month depression to follow his record, which has since been broken by another disc-jockey, Charles Christensen, of radio station KMEN in California, who managed a stretch under medical supervision of 11 days 13 hours in the summer of 1966. All who have subjected themselves to prolonged sleeplessness are united in stating that the process is very unpleasant and rich in hallucinatory adventure—a fact to bear in mind when considering the meaning of the exciting experiments which first began appearing in psychological journals in the 1950s.

In 1952, Eugene Aserinsky, a Ph.D. student in the Physiology Department of the University of Chicago, noticed that babies spent much of their sleeping time making rhythmic bursts of eye movements, which could clearly be observed through the closed lids. He and the distinguished physiologist, Professor Nathaniel Kleitman, who had been studying sleep and dreams for years, then checked with adult sleepers only to find a similar pattern. This observation suggested an interesting experiment—wake up the sleeper during an eye movement burst and see what he reports. This was carried out with the discovery that people woken during these R.E.M. (rapid eye movement) periods stated that they had been dreaming, while others, woken during non-R.E.M. periods rarely, if ever, reported a dream.

Suddenly scientists had in their possession, for the first time, a behavioural index of dreaming, and all sorts of puzzling questions could be answered. How long did dreams last? How many times in a night did one dream? Did everyone dream? What was the depth of sleep at which dreaming occurred? A series of experiments sorted out these problems, and turned up a number of surprising facts—including that we spend up to 25 per cent of the sleep-period in dreaming.

Further experiments in New York and California, notably by William Dement, were even more sensational. Subjects regularly deprived of the opportunity to dream by being woken at the onset of R.E.M. periods began to show psychological disturbance after a few nights, while a control group, woken for the same number of times and for the same amount of time, but during non-R.E.M. periods, were relatively unaffected. In addition, the dream-deprived subjects, when finally allowed to sleep, instead of dropping into a coma-like state of exhaustion, spent significantly more of the sleep-period than average in dreaming! Evidently we need to dream, and perhaps the true function of sleep was to allow us to do so. But if this was true, just what were dreams that they were so vitally important?

Computer Analogy.

One possible explanation has been offered by a psychologist, Dr. Christopher Evans, and a computer engineer, Mr. E. A. Newman, both of the Division of Computer Science at the National Physical Laboratory. The first version of their theory, " Dreaming—an analogy from computers," was published in the *New Scientist* in 1964.

To understand the idea behind the analogy it is necessary to know a little about some aspects of computer functioning. Computers are advanced calculating machines, controlled by sets of programmes. These programmes are instructions to the computer telling it how to use its brain, as it were, and they greatly extend the potential of the system. One programme, for example, might allow the rapid computation of, say, the average of a long string of numbers; another might deal with the preparation of the salaries and wages of a big firm; a third might control the distribution of goods from a warehouse. Technically speaking all the above tasks, and many more, could be handled with ease by a large computer, and which task it was performing at any one moment would be decided by which programme had been selected.

Now computers are developing at a tremendous pace, becoming more complex and powerful in terms of the range of operations they perform. Even at the present moment a certain amount of time has to be routinely set aside for an important series of operations involving the computers. These operations, which are of particular significance to the theory, involve the act of either clearing the system of old programmes, or modifying and up-dating them, and testing *new* programmes. In other words they ensure that the computer is equipped with the latest and most accurate sets of programmes to allow it to do its job properly.

Now it is an interesting fact that the clearance and up-dating must be done when the computer is, to use a technical term, " off-line ", *i.e.*, is uncoupled from any systems that the computer itself is controlling. To give an example, if the computer handles the salary structure of a big firm, then as income tax changes, wages go up, etc., the appropriate programmes have to be modified. If the computer is not " off-line " when these modifications are made and the programme run through, then salaries and wages will be paid at some unsuitable time. Worse, if the computer were controlling the output from some chemical factory, inaccurate or experimental programmes run " on-line " could cause explosions and so on.

It is important to remember that to say a computer is " off-line " does not mean that it is switched off—in fact it may be working like mad, but not coupled to the part of the exterior world it normally controls.

Now the brain is certainly a computer of a special kind, and must be controlled by sets of programmes—though these of course are not fed in by paper or magnetic tape. In addition it is more advanced than most electronic computers because it is *adaptive*, *i.e.*, it continually modifies its own behaviour and capabilities to meet the continually shifting conditions of the world around it. It is with computers such as the brain—and with the increasingly sophisticated man-made devices of the future—that programme revision and clearance processes will be quite vital if the systems are to remain crisply efficient, and more important, are to make the *correct* responses to the changing environment.

In the Evans–Newman analogy, sleep is the state in which the brain-computer is " off-line ", during which time the vast mass of existing programmes are sorted, out-dated ones revised in the light of recent experience, and useless ones or the remnants of modified ones cleared and eliminated. These processes take place for a substantial part of the night, but because the brain is " off-line " and consciousness suppressed

we are mostly not aware of them. However, if for some reason our sleep is disturbed or when we wake in the morning, as the conscious mind " comes to " it catches the programme operations at work, and for a moment has no way of knowing whether the events are internal or external in origin. It sets to work, therefore, to try to make sense of the programme or fragments thereof that are being run through, and the result is what we call a dream—though presumably we should call it an *interrupted* dream.

This approach not only helps to explain the importance of the dream process, but also offers some answers to a number of interesting puzzles. For example, a realisation that the logic of the brain's programming and storage system will follow its own internal rules and not necessarily correspond to the logic of the external world, allows one to understand the Alice-in-Wonderland pattern of our dream life. Programmes might, for instance, deal with quite unexpected characteristics of the material stored in the brain—all events concerned with bicycles or spoked wheels might, to take a completely *ad hoc* idea, be the subject of a special programme and *ipso facto* a dream. Faced with such a weird assembly, the conscious mind would struggle to impose a meaningful " story " on the experience, and do the best it could with the material available.

Try checking this idea by examining the content of your next major dream. The trick, by the way, is to concentrate on the *events* within the dream and not be misled by the apparent fatuity of the story. Without too much effort the origin of these events will click into place—this was something from a magazine, that from a conversation, the other from some private train of thoughts of the previous day. Even the most outrageous absurdities will be revealed as muddled or highly-coloured versions of recent experiences.

The computer-programme analogy predicts that the amount of dreaming (and probably sleeping) is a function of the amount of new *material* (*i.e.*, requiring changes in existing programmes) assimilated in the course of the day. Babies therefore, for whom everything is new, need to sleep and dream the most, while old people, who tend to have inefficient information receivers and very static environments, would require far less.

Similarly there should be a rough equation between cerebral complexity in animals and their dream requirements, and this follows pretty well. Chimpanzees require a fair bit of sleep, though not as much as man; while relatively simple-minded creatures, like sheep, need a good deal less. Even further, with insects, who have no complex adaptive computing systems in their " brains ", sleep as we know it doesn't really occur.

The realisation that one of the main functions of sleep is to allow us to dream makes one think again about the role of drugs, as hypnotic agents. Central nervous system depressants, such as barbiturates or alcohol in large doses, might well not only act as soporifics, but also push the sleeper down too deeply for him to dream properly—with unpleasant long-term effects as a backlog of out-dated programmes builds up. It this were pushed too far, the dream mechanisms might well switch desperately into action when the brain was " on-line " (awake), and the result would be hallucinations of an unpleasantly real kind—such as those which prevail in the delirium tremens of alcoholism.

On the other side of the coin is the suggestion that hallucinogenic drugs, such as LSD, might produce their spectacular effects by kicking the dream mechanism into action, again when the computer is " on-line." This would be contrary to the fundamental rules of cerebral mechanics, and while the inner world of the mind would indeed be revealed to the drug-taker, considerable risk would be involved.

Firstly, one would predict a steady deterioration in his ability to distinguish between " inner " and " outer " reality—a condition reminiscent of the schizophrenic state. Secondly, and no less horrifying, is the possibility that " on-line " dreaming would make one " hyper-programmable "—*i.e.*, any stimuli fed in during this time would be incorporated into a major programme and thus trivial events would assume massive significance to the individual concerned. Incidentally, this feeling of having had a relevation out of trivia is commonly reported by LSD-takers. The real risks, it seems, of LSD and similar drugs may not be in the arguable matter of chromosome damage but rather in its effects on one of the brain's most important functions—the dream.

PARKINSON'S DISEASE.

Recent Advances.

An outstanding advance in drug treatment of this disease has been made by the introduction of levodopa (L-dopa) in 1970. The synthesis and eventual commercial production of this substance by the pharmaceutical industry, notably by the Swiss firm, Hoffmann-La Roche, has in itself been a major undertaking and something of a triumph for the research chemists. It is a matter of interesting historical fact that the compound was first isolated in the laboratories of Hoffmann-La Roche as long ago as 1913. At that time the study of the biochemistry of the nervous system and brain was relatively new and the significance of the compound in terms of neuro-physiology could not have been appreciated.

Parkinson's disease is a chronic, disabling disease of the nervous system that is now, in two out of three cases, effectively controlled by levodopa. To understand and appreciate the years of research by physiologists, pathologists, and biochemists into its causes it is necessary to understand something of the disease itself. It is no exaggeration to say that the use of levodopa has in many instances not only transformed the patient's way of life but that of his family or attendants on whom he has had so much to rely for his daily care.

The Disease.

The disease is *paralysis agitans* or *Parkinson's disease*. The first name means, literally, " shaking palsy "; the eponym is the result of the first clearly documented description of the disease by James Parkinson, a London surgeon, in 1817. The disease is an ancient one. Mention of it can be found in 3rd cent. writings but the classical description of the disease and its course remains that of Dr. Parkinson in his published monograph *An Essay on the Shaking Palsy*, a copy of which can be seen in the British Museum.

The name " shaking palsy " is apt, for the cardinal symptoms are *tremor* with *muscle stiffness* which amounts to a paralysis. The onset is very gradual and the full-blown picture of disease may take months or years to develop. The first symptoms may be a feeling of stiffness or weakness in one part of the body—a wrist joint or fingers. A fine, rhythmical tremor of fingers or hands develops, particularly noticeable while the limbs are at rest. Simple movements such as getting up from a sitting position become not only difficult to carry out, but slow to *start*. The body is held in a rather statuesque manner, with head bent forward, arms and hands held flexed and with a rhythmical tremor of fingers and thumbs characteristic of the movements used in rolling a home-made cigarette.

The difficulty in moving virtually all the muscles leads to a characteristic type of shuffling gait. The feet barely leave the ground and, with the centre of gravity very often over the toes as a result of the bent trunk and forward flexed head and shoulders, the patient tends to totter forward under his own momentum and indeed may actually fall over. His appearance while shuffling thus is as if he were about to break into a little mincing run.

The features become characteristically expressionless, unblinking, and mask-like, with slight drooling at the corners of the mouth. The whole appearance is one of dejection, misery, and immobility. Furthermore, the knowledge that the disease is chronic, disabling, and incurable adds to the general feeling of despair and pessimism in any family unfortunate enough to have an afflicted member. Parkinson's disease affects some 50,000 men and women in Great Britain alone—about one in every thousand. It is a disease of later life, among the age group 50–70, and is twice as common in men as women.

Treatment.

As with any disease of obscure nature and cause, with an inevitably fatal outcome, remedies of every kind have been applied by laymen and doctors alike over the many centuries that the disease has been with us. Parkinson, in his essay mentioned above, was understandably cautious: " until we are better informed respecting the nature of the disease the employment of internal medicine is scarcely warrantable," but that did not stop the purgatives, the arsenic, or the blood letting, favourite empirical remedies of his time.

The first notable advance in treatment was made by the French physician Charcot in the latter part of the 19th cent. He introduced *belladonna*, which had some effect on the excessive salivation and muscle stiffness. Tincture of belladonna was virtually standard treatment by the beginning of the first world war and remained so right up to the 1950s. It was known that the belladonna alkaloids—*atropine* and *hyoscine*—probably exerted their action on those parts of the central nervous system which seemed to be affected in some way by the disease and, gradually, synthetic compounds with similar actions replaced those older remedies. None of these substances did more than ameliorate symptoms—and not particularly effectively at that. Nonetheless, medicine could offer nothing better.

From post-mortem and other studies it had gradually become clear that the seat of the mischief in this baffling disease was in a part of the brain, an area concerned with the maintenance of many bodily activities of which we are never truly aware until something goes amiss. One of these activities concerns the " tone " of musculature generally and the preservation of the right balance between muscles which have opposing actions. It is obviously necessary, when bending the forearm for instance, for the muscles whose action is to straighten the elbow, to *relax* while flexor muscles do their work—or no movement would take place. And when the arm is at rest it is obviously necessary for any tendency for one set of muscles to overcome the other to be corrected—or the arm would not be still. All these co-ordinative activities are controlled below the level of consciousness in an area of the brain which contains the nerve-cell computing centres—the *basal ganglia*. The particular area affected in Parkinson's disease is known as the *corpus striatum*. (The early neuro-anatomists could only describe these different areas of the brain by their naked-eye appearance, only guessing at their probable function.) It is beyond the scope of this article to go further into the detailed pathological changes in those areas of the brain which have been described in subjects dying of the disease. It is sufficient to mention that until the later 1950s the changes described—essentially of loss of nerve cells and degeneration of axons, which are the connecting fibres of such cells—were attributed solely to some type of senile degenerative process associated with age and possibly mediated by arterio-sclerotic types of vascular degeneration in particular (such as atheroma, *see* P30(1)). The incidence of the disease is greatest by far in the 50–70-year age group and that fact gave credence to such views.

However, the general impetus given to medical research by the second world war led in particular to concentrated effort in the field of biochemistry, particularly the biochemistry of " transmitter substances " or hormones. It had been known for a very long time that the opposing states of general bodily physiology—on the one hand, the alert, " fight or flight " state, with blood-flow diverted to muscles, quickened heart beat, raised blood pressure, dilated pupils, and general pallor, and on the other, the relaxed drowsy state of the contented post-prandial dozer, with slowed heart rate, lowered blood pressure, small pupils, and flushed appearance—are basically controlled by the output of adrenalin and acetylcholine respectively. These two states—the " sympathetic " and " parasympathetic "—are mediated and maintained by the actions of the *peripheral* nervous system but are under the master control of the *central* nervous system—the brain and spinal cord.

The idea gained ground that the symptoms of Parkinson's disease—which are predominantly those of parasympathetic, or (acetyl)*cholinergic* activity—might be the result of an essentially *chemical* imbalance between two opposing substances in brain tissue itself. A discovery of major importance was made by three German scientists—Hornykiewicz and his colleagues—in 1961. These workers found that the adrenalin-like neuro-transmitter compound, *dopamine*, was grossly lacking in the basal ganglia of patients with Parkinson's disease. Dopamine and acetyl-choline have the same relationship in the *central* nervous system as adrenaline and acetylcholine have in the *peripheral* system. If dopamine concentrations fall, then cholinergic activity predominates—and this is just what seems to be happening in this disease. Belladonna and its alkaloids exert their action by antagonising acetyl-choline—and hence their use in patients with Parkinson's disease went some way towards restoring the balance and relieving the symptoms.

The *anticholinergic* drugs (now largely synthetic compounds with belladonna-like actions) certainly gave *some* relief but the dose required to do so often meant that side-effects—excessive drying of salivary and bronchial secretions—made life more uncomfortable for the sufferer than his untreated disease. Following on the discovery that dopamine levels in the brain were sub-normal in the disease attempts were made to correct the situation by giving patients dopamine by mouth. Unfortunately dopamine, while readily absorbed by the body, does not get into the brain across the " blood-brain barrier," a physiological brain-protecting mechanism that blocks the entry of many drugs and, indeed, some physiological substances as well.

Dopamine, like many other " chemical messenger " substances in the body, is normally produced on site, as it were, from an inactive precursor. This is *di*hydroxyphenylalanine or " DOPA " which is derived from one of the amino acids, those chemical units which form the complicated molecules of animal and vegetable protein. DOPA crosses the blood-brain barrier readily; dopamine, as has been pointed out, does not. DOPA is readily converted to dopamine in the brain and in early experiments in man in 1962 a Canadian physician, Barbeau, produced quite dramatic but short-lived improvement in Parkinsonian patients by giving small doses of DOPA by mouth. The improvement was mainly in paralysis—the difficulty in *starting* and *maintaining* muscle movement—and was better than had up to then been obtained either with anti-cholinergic drugs or with the highly specialised and sophisticated techniques in brain surgery which had been developed gradually since the early 1950s.

The early attempts to restore dopamine levels in the basal ganglia of the brain by oral DOPA were frustrated by the fact that if more than transient improvement were to be made, much larger doses had to be given. Inevitably, there were unpleasant side-effects. At that time, too, DOPA was difficult and expensive to produce and mainly only available in what the chemists call the *racemic* form. Racemic compounds are mixtures of two *chemically* identical substances whose molecules differ in their spatial arrangements of atoms. One is, in effect, the *mirror image* of the other. Physical chemists are able to distinguish one form from the other by special techniques which enable them to " look " at molecules three-dimensionally. In some examples, polarised light can be used to distinguish one from its " mirror pair " by its ability to rotate the plane of polarised light to the left or to the right when it is passed through a solution. This is true of the " D " and " L " forms of DOPA. (*Dextro* and *Laevo*.)

It was soon realised that the " D " form is not only virtually inactive as a dopamine precursor (it is a form not found naturally in the body) but is toxic. The " L " form, however, seems to be the natural precursor, readily absorbed into brain tissue and much less likely to produce toxic reactions. Furthermore, as equal parts of the " D " and " L " forms are present in the racemic mixture the same effects could be produced with half the dose of substance when the " L " form was used on its own.

Unfortunately, the " L " form proved difficult to synthesise or separate from the racemic form.

Supplies were scarce and costly in comparison to the " DL " form and the early trials, because dosage was kept on the low side, were largely disappointing. The breakthrough came in 1967 when theoretical considerations led to the pioneering use of much larger doses than had been attempted heretofore by Cotzias and his colleagues in the U.S.A. They were forced to use DL DOPA, the " L " form being in extremely short supply and very costly, but built up the dose given to their patients by slow, carefully monitored steps to the maximum that could be tolerated. It was a case of " titrating " the patient to achieve maximum therapeutic effect with the minimum of unwanted side-effects. It was found to be the only way to get to a lasting, effective dose without upsetting the patient in other ways. In some instances as much as 16 grams a day had to be given.

Nevertheless, in spite of careful administration and the slow build-up of dose-levels, there were many side-effects which, if nothing else, were disagreeable to the patient. Not only that, but one patient's blood-cell forming system was affected—a condition known as granulocyto-penia—and this represents a potentially serious hazard.

By this time, as a result of research effort within the pharmaceutical industry, the effective and less toxic " L " form of DOPA became less expensive to produce and relatively less scarce than before. Cotzias and his co-workers undertook a further trial in 1969 using " L " dopa alone. Again, maximum effect was achieved by working up to an optimal dosage; in that trial there were no serious, or potentially serious, side-effects and the solely " troublesome " ones—nausea, vomiting, abdominal pain and the like—were found to be dose-dependent. In other words, they could be avoided by reducing the quantity of " L " dopa used. 28 patients were treated in this trial —and all improved, 20 of them markedly or dramatically.

It will be recalled that the dominant and most distressing features of the disease are the stiffness, the slowness, the difficulty in initiating movements and the tremor. The first three are known to the physician as rigidity, bradykinesia, and akinesia and it is on these that levodopa has its maximum therapeutic effect. *Tremor* may respond after prolonged treatment in some patients, but not all. The effect on the patient when he finds he can get up from his chair or his bed *unaided*, when he begins to *walk* instead of shuffle, when he can cough healthily to clear his throat, when his handkerchief can be kept in his breast pocket instead of being held constantly to drooling mouth, when he can feed like others and feel his face break into a smile, is dramatic. And if he has been somewhat dysphonic (having difficulty in speaking, through stiffness of jaw and tongue muscles), as many patients are, the return of normal or near-normal speech is perhaps the final booster to a morale that has often sunk to its lowest level. His renewed optimism spreads to family and friends. Return to work becomes a reality and restoration of independence naturally follows.

It must be mentioned that some patients fail to respond at all, perhaps something less than one in three. There is as yet no means of predicting response to levodopa. But it should not be forgotten that, although levodopa now tops the list of symptomatic remedies for Parkinson's disease, the others remain—the anticholinergics, amantadine, and, mentioned briefly above, stereotaxic surgery. And most patients can expect some response to one or other of these.

Since 1969 there have been many further clinical studies and it has become abundantly clear that in levodopa physicians have a drug which is as important a step forward in the treatment of Parkinson's disease as the introduction of insulin was in the treatment of diabetes. But it must be remembered that, like diabetes, Parkinson's disease is only symptomatically improved. Its true nature is still not understood and the precise mode of action of levodopa still unknown. The effects of its long-term administration cannot be assessed as yet. And whether this treatment, dramatic though it is in many cases, will have any effect on the *natural history* of Parkinson's disease, is very much an open question.

PART IV. INDEX AND GLOSSARY

Abortion. The termination of pregnancy, from whatever cause, before the child is capable of independent existence.

Abortus fever. An infectious disease known as undulant fever, 15 (1).

Abrasion. Any injury which rubs off the surface skin.

Acidity. *See under* Peptic ulcer, 36 (1).

Acne, 53 (2).

Acromegaly. A state of excessive growth of the body caused by overaction of the pituitary gland in the base of the brain, 43 (2).

Actinomycosis, 15 (2).

Acute chorea or St. Vitus' dance, 49 (1).

Acute nephritis, 45 (1).

Addiction to drugs. *See* Drug abuse, 22.

Addison's disease, 43 (2).

Adenoids, 32 (1).

Adrenal cortex, 43 (2).

Adrenal medulla, 43 (2).

Adrenocorticotrophic hormone (ACTH), 43 (2).

Air we breathe, 4 (1).

Agranulocytosis, 26 (1).

Alcoholics Anonymous, 6 (2).

Allergy. Abnormal sensitivity to any substance which does not affect normal people.

Alopecia, 52 (2).

Amenorrhœa, 56 (2).

Amnesia, 47 (1).

Amœbæ, 8 (1).

Amœbic dysentery, 17 (2).

Amphetamine, 23 (2).

Amyotrophic lateral sclerosis, 48 (2).

Anæmias, 24–25.

Anæsthetic. Any drug used by surgeons to remove pain during an operation.

Anencephaly, 48 (2).

Aneurism, 30 (2).

Angina pectoris, 28 (2).

Ankylosis. Partial or complete fixation of a joint as after some types of arthritis. In other cases deliberately produced by surgery.

Ankylostomiasis, 16 (2).

Anorexia. Loss of appetite.

Anterior pituitary, 43.

Anthrax, 15 (1), 9 (1), 4 (2).

Antibiotics are drugs which act directly against the organism causing the illness by interfering with its growth or some other aspect of its living mechanisms. Of all drugs which are used against bacteria, antibiotics do least harm to the patient's own tissues; some do have unwanted side-effect, but many have none at all. *See* 4, 9, 22.

Antihistamine drugs, 4 (2), 5 (1).

Antiseptics, 8 (2).

Anxiety neurosis, 51 (2).

Aortic diseases, 30 (2).

Aphasia, 47 (1).

Aplastic anæmia, 25 (1).

Appendicitis, 37 (1).

Arteriography, 48 (1).

Arthritis, 54 (2).

Artificial respiration (kiss of life), 21 (1).

Ascites, 39 (1).

Asphyxia, 20 (2).

Aspirin and "upset stomach", 5 (1), 23 (1), 36 (2); *see also* Headache.

Asthma, 32 (1).

Atheroma or Atherosclerosis, 30 (1).

Athlete's foot, 8 (1), 15 (2).

Backache. A symptom which may be caused by many different diseases—sometimes disease of the vertebræ themselves, sometimes strain of the ligaments, and sometimes inflammation or spasm of the surrounding muscles. "Lumbago" is usually due to inflammation of the muscles in the small of the back. Backache from purely local causes may be treated temporarily by applying heat in the form of a kaolin poultice or a rubber hot-water bottle and taking two aspirin tablets a day. On the other hand, many cases of backache are due to disease elsewhere. The most important thing is to find out the cause, and therefore a doctor should be consulted.

Bacteria, 7 (1). **Bacterial diseases,** 12–15.

Bacteriophage, 7 (2).

Baldness, 52 (2).

Barber's rash, 53 (2).

Barbiturates, 23 (2).

Bell's palsy, 50 (2).

Benzedrine. The proprietary name of a drug known as amphetamine. *See* 23 (2).

Beri-beri, 42 (2).

Berry aneurysm, 49 (2).

Bilharzia, 18 (2), 16 (1).

Birth control, 56.

Blackwater fever, 17 (2).

Bladder. *See under* Urinary diseases, 44 (2).

Bleeding diseases, 26 (1).

Blepharitis, 55 (1).

Blood, function of the, 24.

Blood, diseases of the, 24.

Blood Groups. Human blood plasma contains factors which clump, or agglutinate, the red cells of some other people's blood. The main blood groups are called A, B, AB, and O. The plasma of group A blood contains an anti-B factor and *vice versa*, so that people of groups A and B cannot accept each other's blood. Group AB contains neither anti-A nor anti-B factor and people with this group can therefore receive transfusions from both but can give to neither. Group O contains both anti-A and anti-B, and can therefore receive blood only from group O but can donate blood to all groups. It is important that transfused cells should not be agglutinated by the factors in the recipient's plasma. Apart from the so-called ABO system, there are several other blood groupings, one of which is mentioned under Rhesus Factor.

Blood poisoning (septicæmia), 14 (2).

Blood-pressure, 29.

Blood-vessels, diseases of the, 30.

Blue babies, 5 (2).

Botulism, 14 (1).

Brain. *See under* Nervous system, 46, Physical injuries, 19.

Brain tumour, 50 (1).

Breasts, 55 (2).

Bronchial asthma, 32 (1).

Bronchiectasis, 32 (1).

Bronchitis, 31 (2).

Bruises and abrasions, 19 (2).

Bürger's disease, 31 (1).

Burns and scalds, 21 (2).

Cachexia. Extreme wasting due to disease.

Cæsarean operation. When the abdomen has to be opened to remove the child, named after Julius Cæsar, who is said to have been born in this way.

Caisson disease, 31 (1).

Cancer of the breast, 55 (2).
Cancer of the cervix, 56 (1).
Cancer of the colon, 37 (2).
Cancer of the lung, 33 (2), 34 (1).
Cancer of the œsophagus, 36 (1).
Cancer of the rectum, 37 (2).
Cancer of the stomach, 37 (1).
Cancer test (cervical smear), 56 (1).
Carbohydrates. The scientific name for sugars, starches, and cellulose, 34 (2), 40.
Carbon monoxide poisoning, 21 (1).
Carbuncle. A large boil.
Cardiac neurosis, 27 (1).
Cataract, 55 (1).
Cerebral abscess, 49 (2).
Cerebral embolism, 49 (1).
Cerebral haemorrhage or apoplexy, 49 (1).
Cerebral palsy, 48 (2).
Cerebrovascular diseases, see Stroke illness.
Chadwick, Sir Edwin (1800–90). English social reformer, 6.
Chancroid, 16 (1).
Change of life, 44 (1).
Chickenpox, 10 (1).
Chilblains, 53 (1).
Chill. This is not a proper medical word, but refers to the symptoms that occur when one first becomes infected with any germs which cause fever. When such germs enter the body, all the defending processes are mobilised and speeded up. The white cells in the blood increase in number, and the amount of energy used is greater than normal, causing the temperature to rise. This rise in temperature increases the ability of the body to fight back, and, in order to retain heat within the body, the blood-vessels in the skin contract so that less heat is lost by radiation. This makes the skin cold and pale. What is ordinarily called a chill is merely an infection by the germs causing cold and influenza. But a chill may be the preliminary to almost any infectious disease, such as measles, mumps, scarlet fever, pneumonia, and so on. The best treatment when the temperature is raised is to go to bed with as much warmth as possible. Hot drinks and hot-water bottles are helpful. See Colds, 10 (2).
Cholecystitis, 39 (2).
Cholelithiasis, 38 (2).
Cholera, 15 (1).
Cholesterol, 30 (2), 38 (2).
Chorea, 49 (1).
Chronic. A chronic disease is one which is prolonged and relatively mild, as opposed to an acute one which is short and severe.
Chronic nephritis, 45 (1).
Cilia, 31 (2).
Cirrhosis of the liver, 39 (2).
Claustrophobia. A psychological symptom, which causes the individual to be afraid of enclosed spaces. See under Obsessional neurosis, 52 (1).
Cocaine, 23 (2).
Coccyx. The end of the spinal column.
Colds, 10 (2).
Colitis, 37 (2).
Coma, 47 (1).
Concussion, 19 (2).
Congenital heart disease, 28 (1).
Conjunctivitis, 55 (1).
Conciousness and unconciousness, 47 (1).
Constipation, 35 (2).
Contraception, 56–7.
Coronary heart disease, 28 (2).
Coronary thrombosis, 29 (1).
Cortisone. A hormone produced by the suprarenal glands, 54 (2).
Cretin, 43 (2).
Cretinism, 43 (2).
C.S.F. (i.e. cerebrospinal fluid), 48.
Cushing's disease, 44 (1).

Cutaneous ureterostomy, 45 (2).
Cystic fibrosis, 32 (1).
Cystitis, 45 (2).

Dandruff. See Seborrhea, 53 (1).
Deficiency diseases, 41–3.
Demyelinating diseases, 49 (2).
Dengue, 12 (1).
Dermatitis, 53 (2).
Dhobie itch, 8 (1), 15 (2).
Diabetes insipidus, 43 (2).
Diabetes mellitus, 39 (2).
Diarrhœa, and vomiting, 13 (2).
Diet, 40.
Digestive tract, diseases of the, 34.
Diphtheria, 12 (2).
Disseminated sclerosis, 49 (2).
Diverticulitis, 37 (2).
Dropsy, 45 (1).
Drug abuse, 22.
Drug dependence, 23.
Drugs, addiction to, see Drug abuse.
Drugs and medicines, 22 (2).
Drugs, use of the new, 4–5.
Duchenne's muscular dystrophy, 50 (2).
Ductless glands, 43 (1).
Duodenal ulcer, 36 (1).
Duodenum, 36 (1).
Dysentery, 13 (2).
Dysmenorrhœa, 56 (2).

E.C.T. The abbreviated form of the name for a modern type of treatment for certain psychiatric disorders—electro-convulsive-therapy. See under Psychosis, 51 (2).
Ehrlich, Paul (1854–1915). German bacteriologist, 4 (1), 5 (2), 16 (1).
Electro-cardiogram, 29 (2).
Electroencephalography, 48 (1).
Electromyography, 48 (1)
Elephantiasis, 19 (1).
Embolism, 30 (2), 33 (1).
Emphysema, 31 (2).
Empyema. A collection of pus in the lung usually a complication of other diseases.
Encephalitis, 11 (1), 49 (2).
Encephalo-myelitis, 49 (2).
Endemic. Referring to a disease, means prevalent in a particular area.
Endocarditis. Disease of the valves of the heart 30 (1).
Endocrine glands, 43–4.
Enzymes, 34 (2).
Epidemic. Of a disease: widely prevalent among people at a special time and produced by some special causes not generally present in the affected locality. See under Influenza, 10 (2), and also 17 (1).
Epidemic jaundice, 16 (2).
Epilepsy, 48 (1).
Epithelioma (cancer of the skin), 54 (1).
Erysipelas, 53 (1).
Exercise. See New Views about Health, 4.
Exocrine glands, 43 (1).
Eye, disease of the, 55.

Fallopian tubes, 56 (1).
Farcy, 15 (1).
Fat embolism, 33 (2).
Fats. See Diet.
Fevers, general treatment of, 9.

Medicines: classification, 22 (2).

Melancholia. *See* Manic-depressive insanity, 51 (1).

Menières disease, 47 (2).

Meningitis, 14 (2).

Menopause, 44 (1).

Mental diseases, 50.

Metastases or secondary deposits, 50 (1).

Migraine, 47 (2).

Minot, George Richards (1885–1950) American physician and pathologist, specialised in diseases of the blood, 25 (2).

Mitral stenosis, 28 (2).

Montagu, Lady Mary (1689–1762). English wit and letter writer, 16 (1).

Morphine, 23 (2).

Motor nerves, 46 (2).

Motor neuron disease, 48 (2).

Multiple sclerosis or disseminated sclerosis or "creeping paralysis", 49 (2).

Mumps, 10 (1).

Muscular dystrophies, 50 (2).

Myasthemia gravis, 50 (1).

Myelin sheaths, 46 (2)

Myelitis, 49 (2).

Myelography, 48 (1).

Myxœdema, 43 (2).

Narcolepsy, 47 (2).

National Health Service, 6.

Nephritis, acute and chronic, 45 (1).

Nephrosis, 45 (1).

Nerve cells, 46 (2).

Nervous system, diseases of, 46–50

Nettle rash, 53 (2).

Nephrosis, 45 (1).

Neurology: diagnostic techniques, 47 (2).

Neurosis, 51 (2).

Niemann-Pick disease, 50 (1).

Noguchi, Hideyo (1876–1928). Japanese bacteriologist, 16 (1).

Nutritional disorders, 41–3.

Œdema (dropsy), 45 (1), 27 (2).

Obesity. *See* Diet.

Obsessional neurosis, 52 (1).

Œsophagitis, 36 (1).

Olfactory. To do with the sense of smell.

Ophthalmia, 15 (2).

Orthopædics. A branch of medicine dealing with the surgery of bones and joints.

Osteoarthritis, 55 (1).

Ovary, 44 (1), 55 (2).

Palpitation. *See* Tachycardia, 29 (2).

Pancreas, 39 (2).

Papilloma, 45 (1).

Paranoia, 51 (1)

Parasites, 8 (1), 52 (2).

Parasitic worms: diseases, 18 (1).

Parathyroid glands, 44 (1).

Paré Ambroise (*c.* 1510–90). French army surgeon, 4 (1).

Parkinson's disease, 49 (1), 62–3.

Pasteur, Louis (1822–95). French chemist, 5 (2), 16 (1).

Pediatrics. The study of the diseases of children.

Pellagra, 43 (1).

Penicillin, 4 (1), 9 (1), 22 (2).

Peptic ulcer, 36 (1).

Pericarditis, 30 (1).

Peripheral nerves, diseases of, 50 (1).

Peritonitis, 38 (1).

Pernicious anæmia, 25 (1).

Petit mal. *See* Epilepsy, 48 (1).

Physical injuries, 19–22.

Piles. *See* Hæmorrhoids, 38 (1).

Pineal gland, 44 (1).

Pituitary gland, 43 (1).

Plague, 17.

Plastic surgery, 5 (2), 54 (2).

Pleurisy, 34 (1).

Pneumonia, 32 (2).

Pneumoconiosis, 33 (1).

Poliomyelitis, 10 (2).

Polycythæmia, 25 (2).

Portal hypertension, 38 (2).

Posterior pituitary, 43 (2).

Primary lateral sclerosis, 49 (1).

Prognosis. The medical name for the outlook of a disease.

Prolapse of uterus, 56 (1).

Prostate disease, 46 (1).

Protein, 35 (1), 40.

Protein-calorie deficiency, 42 (1).

Protozoal diseases, 17–18.

Pruritus, 52 (2).

Psittacosis, 12 (1).

Psychosis, 50 (2).

Psychosomatic diseases. Psychosomatic diseases are those physical ailments due to emotional causes. They include such complaints as high blood-pressure, gastric ulcer, certain skin diseases, and certain glandular diseases (*e.g.*, exophthalmic goitre). Most physicians now-adays believe that all diseases may show a greater or less degree of emotional causation; that physical and mental factors are both present in all illness. Even in psychosomatic illnesses, heredity and other factors play a large part. Briefly, the main cause of these diseases is worry. The importance of this lies in the fact that they cannot be cured without dealing with the fundamental cause. *See also* New Views on Medicine, 3 (2).

Psychopathic personality, 52 (1).

Pulmonary embolism, 33 (1).

Purpura, 26 (2).

Pyæmia, 14 (2).

Pyelitis, 45 (1).

Pyloric stenosis, 36 (2).

Pyorrhœa. An infection of the gums which causes the edges of the tooth sockets to bleed easily when the teeth are being brushed. There is a constant discharge of pus, which causes the breath to smell and may lead to arthritis and other diseases. Treatment should be carried out by a dentist.

Quarantine period. *See* Infectious Fevers, 9 (2).

Rabies, 11 (2).

Raynaud's disease, 31 (1).

Rectum, cancer of the, 37 (2).

Reducing weight, 41.

Reed, Major Walter (1851–1902). American army surgeon, 12 (1), 16 (1).

Reflex actions, 46 (2).

Reflex arc, 47 (1).

Regional enteritis, 37 (1).

Relapsing fever, 16 (2).

Renal colic, 45 (2).

Respiratory system, diseases of the, 31.

Reticulosarcoma, 26 (1).

Retinitis, 55 (2).

Reynaud's disease, 31 (1).

Rhesus Factor. Apart from the ABO blood group system (*see* Blood Groups) there is another blood group system (designated the Rh-system or Rhesus system). Everybody is either Rh-positive or Rh-negative. Three positive factors (denoted C, D, E) and three negative factors (denoted c, d, e) are involved. This system of blood factors is inherited separately from the ABO group, so that one may be A Rh+ or A Rh−, etc. Both the

AN INTRODUCTION TO PSYCHOLOGY

This section is concerned with the science and study of the human mind, a territory rich in mystery, a glimpse of which we catch through the enigma of memory, and in the misty drama of our dreams. It represents a unique guide to one of the most exciting experimental sciences of today.

TABLE OF CONTENTS

AN INTRODUCTION TO PSYCHOLOGY

The purpose of this section is to provide a general introduction to the young but expanding science of psychology. The topic itself is of course enormously broad and can only be summarised at best. However, it is hoped it will serve to give some idea of the fascinating material that psychologists study and also of their occasionally remarkable, and always interesting findings. The section also aims to dispel some of the illusions that have surrounded the subject and to define its boundaries to the extent that the reader will not only begin to understand what psychology is, but also what it isn't!

I. INTRODUCTION.

What is a Psychologist?

The popular image of a psychologist is a fairly well-defined one—he is a man who treats mental illnesses in the way that a doctor treats physical ones. His principal equipment, apart from a well-furnished "consulting room," is a leather couch for patients to lie on, a well-stocked library, and a cabinet of mysterious drugs of one kind or another to send them off to sleep. He is particularly interested in the dreams of his clients and may use some form of hypnosis to study their "repressed" thoughts and secret emotions. He is probably very wealthy, because of the enormous fees he charges, and may speak with a central European accent.

Silly though the above description may sound, it is nevertheless unfortunately true that it corresponds pretty closely to the kind of picture that most people have of a psychologist and of the kind of work he does. Remote though this description is from the truth—at least as far as the vast majority of psychologists is concerned—the average person can be forgiven for having it firmly lodged in his mind, for in literally hundreds of movies, TV and radio plays, books and novels this is the picture that has been painted. One of the first tasks of this section will be to attempt to straighten out some of these misconceptions so that a clearer idea of the nature of psychology can be given. While the mysterious and, unfortunately, rather glamorous aspect of psychology that concerns itself with mental illness and its treatment is certainly one facet of the topic, there is a good deal more to it than that. Furthermore, the part of psychology which deals not with the abnormal but with the strictly *normal* brain is the area which has best repaid scientific study and, as we hope to show, which has uncovered the most exciting raw material.

This section, therefore, begins with a clarification of the role of the psychologist, and follows with a brief introduction to his principal fields of study—the brain and human behaviour. After this we take in turn the four main areas of study which assist him in his quest for an understanding of human nature. These are Perception, Learning and Memory, Motivation, and finally Personality and Thinking.

One of the main sources of confusion in people's minds arises from puzzlement over the distinction between four commonly used words which, while differing in meaning in important respects, are almost invariably lumped together as one. These are (1) Psychiatry, (2) Psychoanalysis, (3) Psychotherapy, and (4) Psychology. The words do look and sound rather similar but it is not difficult, once the right definitions have been given, to sort the four clearly out in one's mind. Let's take psychiatry first.

(1) **Psychiatry** is the art of *treating* mental diseases or illnesses by medical means and it is a specialist branch of medicine, entered through the medical profession and taught at hospitals or universities. A psychiatrist therefore is quite invariably a doctor of medicine with ordinary medical degrees but with a postgraduate training in mental illness and its treatment. No one may call himself a psychiatrist unless so qualified, and

no one may prescribe drugs or surgery in treating mentally sick individuals unless he is medically qualified. There is an important point of issue here, for in England, and many other countries, people not trained as psychiatrists may nevertheless diagnose and treat mental illnesses—provided that they do not use drugs or surgery to do so.

(2) **Psychoanalysis** is a particular form of examination or diagnosis of an individual's mental state based on the theories of the mind and personality advanced by Sigmund Freud and his colleagues or followers, and the reader may like to turn to the entry on the subject on J42. An interesting feature of psychoanalysis is that, unlike psychiatry, it may be practised without medical or academic qualifications on the part of the analyst. A special training analysis at a recognised institute is normally undertaken by the would-be practitioner, however this is not normally made available to individuals unqualified in medicine or psychology.

(3) **Psychotherapy** is the practice of treating mental diseases or illnesses by more or less *any* means. Thus, strictly speaking, both the psychiatrist and the psychoanalyst are psychotherapists—as are any other individuals using reputable methods who offer therapy for the mind. Once again notice that this implies that one may call oneself a psychotherapist irrespective of whether one has medical or academic qualifications, and it is a word that tends to be adopted, with impunity, by a good many "quacks" and charlatans who can of course do fearful damage in this tricky area.

(4) **Psychology** is literally the study of the mind (or soul) but its area has broadened somewhat in the last century as we have learned that one cannot consider the mind as totally isolated from the body, and it now includes the study of human personality and behaviour. Psychologists also study the behaviour and brain of animals wherever such studies throw light on human behaviour. It is important to realise that psychologists are first and foremost trained as scientists rather than as medical experts and do not necessarily take much interest in abnormalities of the brain and mental processes. Those who do, tend to take postgraduate training in what is known as "clinical psychology," and may add to their knowledge by undergoing training in psychoanalysis.

It is obvious that there is a good deal of overlap between these four aspects of the topic and in the following section we shall be entering the territory of psychiatry and psychoanalysis to some extent, but mainly concerning ourselves with psychology—the science and study of the human mind, personality, and behaviour.

1. The Brain.

From the moment of our birth and emergence from the security of the womb our body is controlled and dominated by a single but complex organ, a library, switchboard, signal-box, computer, and many other things all rolled into one—the brain (see F37(2), P46). Very properly encased in a hard shell of bone and equipped with instruments for detecting food or danger at a distance—eyes, ears, etc.—the brain matures slowly, unlike other bodily organs, reaching its peak of efficiency and potential approximately 18 years after birth. From then onwards, slowly and almost immeasurably at first but with remorseless steadiness, it slides into decline. Its proper functioning determines the "normality" of the behaviour of the individual and the part he can play in society, its efficiency determines to some extent his intelligence and his ability to compete, its storage capacity and information retrieval system, his potential to learn and remember. In addition its computing power determines his creativity and is the primary function which distinguishes between the mature human being and the other animals on earth. No organ or complex of organs is guarded and shielded so carefully.

The brain is the main focus of interest for the psychologist, for there can be little doubt that the key to the understanding of human personality and behaviour lies locked up within it. Its complexity of course is daunting, but thanks to physiological and anatomical studies it is possible to get at least a general idea of what's going on. In the first place the brain acts as the principal co-ordinator of messages coming in from the various sense organs, and then as the dispatch point for the appropriate responses. This co-ordinating centre is easily best developed in man, and is present in most of the "higher" animals. Simpler creatures, however, such as amoeba and certain tiny worms, get along without any important co-ordinator of nervous impulses and respond diffusely to changes in the environment—moving vaguely away from things that "annoy" or damage them and towards food or other "pleasant" things. Such animals are literally the slaves of their environment, incapable of setting up goals to achieve and with no facility for computing the consequences of any action. One important branch of the evolutionary tree shows a steady trend towards increasing brain size and, with it, freedom from this slavery.

In the second place the brain acts as the storehouse of information which the senses have gathered at some time in the individual's life. To us it may seem "obvious" that we have a memory—a device for looking at things that took place in the past—and indeed it is hard to imagine ourselves without one. However, a large number of creatures get by with only the most limited of memory systems, and some with none at all. Clearly a good deal must depend upon how long an animal is to live. If its life-span is to be brief, then it need not set aside much room to store information from its past. If it is to live for many years, survive in a changing and generally rather dangerous environment, and learn by its mistakes and its previous achievements, then this ability to refer back to the past is obviously essential. In human beings mechanisms of learning and memory are of vital importance and we will devote a good deal of this section to discussing the way in which psychologists study these.

The third primary function of the brain is to provide the computing and decision-making processes which dictate so much of human and higher animal behaviour. It is also, in the case of man, the centre of consciousness and at the same time that elusive faculty we call personality.

2. How Does the Brain Divide up its Functions?

Nowadays we rather take for granted that important things such as thinking, remembering, etc., are mediated through the brain and it comes as something of a shock to recall that early philosophers located the majority of such processes in the heart or the stomach! Even today, a good deal of controversy exists over exactly which part of the brain does what and, as we shall see when we discuss the contradictory experimental evidence later, there is even a suggestion that certain processes are dealt with by the brain *as a whole* rather than by some specific part. However, the picture is reasonably clear.

In the first place the brain is composed of a vast number of cells—the building blocks of all living systems—which in this case have become highly specialised and stretched out, rather like telephone lines. These are known as nerve or neural cells or, yet again, as neurones. They act as communication units, receiving electrical signals from other parts of the body. Comparative anatomists are able to trace the routes of whole chains of cells starting at, say, the finger tips and finishing up in a particular slab of the brain where such tactile messages are gathered and interpreted. On the whole messages from the eyes tend to finish up in the back of the brain, or occipital lobes; messages from the ears, nose, etc., on the side, or temporal lobes. In the front exists a large chunk of nervous tissue with a rather mysterious function inasmuch as it seems to be more directly related to the personality and mood of its owner than to any of his senses. In addition there are parts of the brain concerned more with output than input—the so-called motor areas which dispatch the signals commanding various parts of the body to move. Finally there are the parts principally involved in the storage of information, memory, etc.

All these areas we have been talking about up till now are known as the cerebral cortex and they are located on the outer surface of the brain itself—*i.e.*, right up against the inside of the skull. You should by now have gathered that the cortex deals largely with psychological factors closely tied up with consciousness and awareness—seeing, hearing, thinking, remembering, etc. This ties in rather nicely with its alternative name, the neocortex (or new tissue), for in evolutionary terms this part of the brain is "new." In general, the closer that an animal species approximates to man, the greater the proportion of its brain is assigned to neocortex, and the more the particular animal is capable of independent, deliberate and purposeful activity.

Tucked in beneath the cerebral cortex, growing out of the spinal cord, are the so-called lower centres—the old brain. Here in a number of specialised blocks are located the control centres which deal with the most automatic (but no less important) bodily functions such as cardiac activity, respiration, temperature, etc., and which it is unnecessary or inconvenient to keep under conscious control. Damage or injury to these centres is generally very serious, whereas damage to the outer layer of the brain, even when extensive, can have surprisingly little effect on the individual's way of life.

To sum up, we note that the brain is divided into two major functional areas in evolutionary terms—the old and the new. The former largely deals with the vital automatic processes, and the latter with the receiving and interpreting of sensory input and the decision-making processes which guide our interaction with the outside world. Clearly this is an enormously simplified picture (specific aspects of this topic are dealt with in greater detail later) and the brain and central nervous system (CNS) is complicated almost beyond description, with much of its mechanics and rules of operation still poorly understood. How then can one set out to study it properly and unravel its secrets?

3. Methods of Studying the Brain.

Psychologists and physiologists favour many approaches to finding out how the brain works, and while it won't be possible to look at them all in this section it will be worthwhile spending a bit of time on some of the most important lines of attack. These can be classed under the headings (1) comparative anatomy, (2) surgical tissue destruction, (3) electro-encephalography, (4) microelectrode recording, (5) biochemical analysis, (6) behavioural research, and (7) introspection. Some of these are really only possible with animals as the experimental subjects, and others are more suited for research on human beings.

(1) *Comparative Anatomy.*

This is perhaps the most obvious and logical method of all, but it has one serious and insurmountable drawback. Suppose that one wanted to find out how a motor-car engine worked and that one had no prior knowledge of its operation but knew what one looked like from the outside. Failing instruction booklets or advice from motor mechanics, the best method might seem to be to get hold of a complete engine and take it apart to examine its components. Given enough skill one might even be able to put it back together again. The chances are that with a relatively simple device, such as an automobile engine, an intelligent person would begin to see the principles of operation. However, until he had actually watched it at work and studied the effect of, say, depressing the accelerator or pulling out the choke, his comprehension of the device might be limited and he could well come to some funny conclusions about its function and operating habits. This approach is essentially that of the comparative anatomist who sets out to study the brain by examining a dead specimen, peering at it through a microscope, cutting out bits here and there and hoping to work out what each section contributes to the whole. Unfortunately, whereas the average motor-car engine probably contains a maximum of about 1,000 discrete and separate components, some of which are rather large and " obvious," the brain contains a conservative minimum of about *a thousand million* neurones or nerve cells and no large and obvious " moving parts " to give the anatomist useful clues. It is little wonder therefore that while students of the brain adopting post mortem dissection have, in the course of the last few centuries, acquired a pretty clear picture of the way in which the brain is laid out—an anatomical atlas so to speak—most of the principles of cerebral operation are still more or less unknown. One of the great drawbacks of this system, as you will probably have guessed, is the fact that anatomical dissection and analysis can only be done in the dead animal.

(2) Surgical Tissue Destruction.

To return to our rather inexact analogy with the motor-car engine, let us assume that our investigator finds himself with a working, running engine to play with. Let us also assume that he has already made himself pretty familiar with the anatomy of the " dead " engine and has perhaps formed some hypotheses as to what certain parts of it do. For example, he might have a suspicion that the carburettor and the sparking plugs were particularly important, or that a key to the complete device working was that the pistons should move up and down in the cylinders. One of the first things he might do would be to systematically remove what he considered to be important parts of the engine and note how its performance was effected. Using this technique of selective removal he might soon begin to confirm or reject his hunches and a gradual comprehension of the function and capabilities of the engine would build up in his mind. He might find that whereas the removal of one sparking plug did not stop the engine, it would lower its pulling power. Removal of the carburettor in toto would be calamitous, while twiddling with it might have unpredictable effects, making it run better or worse. On the other hand, filing bits off the iron cylinder block would make no difference whatsoever. Once again the psychophysiologist is faced with something immensely more complex when he studies the brain, but there is nevertheless obviously something to be gained by adopting a similar procedure with the working or living system. The systematic removal or destruction of parts of cerebral tissue has, in fact, been one of the most rewarding approaches adopted by brain scientists, though there are naturally severe limitations to the technique. In the first place such surgery cannot be performed on human beings, except where it is a necessary feature of therapeutic brain surgery (*e.g.*, as when removing a brain tumour) and can only be justified in living animals in the interest of serious and clearly defined scientific research. (Despite the assumptions of anti-vivisectionists, no reputable scientist enjoys performing experimental surgery on living animals and these are always conducted in such a way as to cause the creature as little distress and suffering as possible.) In the second place, the very act of surgery itself probably introduces side-effects which serve to complicate the picture. However, this technique, when skilfully used, has led to some informative experiments.

(3) Electroencephalography.

As we have said earlier, the principal building blocks of the brain are the neurones, specialised cells devoted to the transmission of information from one part of the body to the other. This transmission is effected by a change in the electrical potential of the cell along its long stem. The main bodies of cells tend to be pressed up against one another and when a change in potential occurs in one, this tends to trigger off a similar response in a neighbouring cell at a junction point known as a *synapse.* Incidentally, the long stems of the cells (which may be a yard or more in length in certain parts of the body) are covered by an insulating sheath which prevents the electrical " message " leaking out en route and which makes them strangely similar to the kind of electrical wires and cables we use in telecommunications. With a thousand million cells jammed up together in the head, all of them propagating electrical signals in one way or another, it should not surprise anyone to learn that sensitive recording devices can be used to get a picture of the overall electrical activity going on in the brain. Studies of this type (electroencephalography, or EEG for short) couldn't begin until suitable recording machines had been developed and thus, although scientists had been pretty confident that the brain was a potent source of electrical energy since the middle of the 19th cent., it wasn't until the 1920s that anyone was able to get a readable picture of this. The pioneers in this technique were the physiologists Berger and Adrian, who attached little electrodes to the outside of the human scalp and by hooking these up to amplifiers and then to special recording pens were able to get a kind of plot of the electrical activity going on within. To their surprise what emerged was not just a meaningless hodge-podge of electrical " noise " but rather a series of precise and elegant rhythms, the frequency and amplitude of these depending upon the part of the brain where the electrodes were applied, and also—most excitingly —on the individual's mental state at the time of the recording. As time has passed and recording technology has advanced, an immense amount of data has been gathered on these so-called brain waves, and while it is true to say that the high hopes of the pioneers who believed that they were about to unravel the brain's mysteries almost overnight with this technique have not been realised, the EEG has proved its worth in more ways than one. In medicine, for example, certain disruptions of the " normal " brain wave pattern can give clear indications to the expert of the presence of epilepsy or determine the site of otherwise totally inaccessible brain tumours. The EEG can also be enormously useful in evaluating the effectiveness and mode of operation of new drugs and is helping in our understanding of the nature of sleep—the EEG of a sleeping person differs significantly from that of a waking one. Curiously one of the most promising-looking of the many rhythms which the brain emits—and one of the first discovered by the English scientist Adrian, the so-called alpha rhythm, has turned out to be one of the most disappointing. The alpha rhythm, which is generally picked up by electrodes attached to the back of the head (over the occipital or visual cortex), is a beautifully neat and stable wave of about 14 cycles per second frequency. It is present when the individual is relaxed and has his eyes closed. Opening the eyes and looking around, or alternatively keeping them closed and doing a bit of mental arithmetic, causes the rhythm to disappear, and the hypothesis was soon advanced that alpha was a reliable index of the rather abstract mental state known as " attention." Unfortunately for this convenient idea, on further study it was found that the rhythm did not always behave as it should, sometimes doing exactly the opposite to what was expected of it. Furthermore some measurable percentage of humanity—about one in ten of otherwise normal individuals—show no alpha rhythm at all, which has led critics of electroencephalography as a technique to ask sarcastically whether such people were incapable of deciding whether to attend to something or not! All these drawbacks aside, the EEG is still one of the best ways of getting some kind of index as to what is going on inside the head of a human or animal, without resorting to surgery or interfering seriously with normal thought processes.

(4) Microelectrode Recording.

For all practical purposes the record obtained by the EEG is a gross, overall view of the brain at work. The waves and rhythms encountered must, at the least, represent the sum of the activity of literally hundreds of thousands of neural cells, presumably firing more or less in synchrony. Going back once more to the motor-car analogy, the EEG could be likened to a garage mechanic listening with a stethoscope to the pulsing of an engine when running at high speed. Changes of speed, adjustments in carburation or timing, etc., would give characteristically different running sounds, but little if anything could be deduced about the state of activity of an individual component unless it were a very large one. Much the same limitations, only on a gigantic scale, surround the use of the EEG as a device for measuring specific aspects of brain activity. Quite recently, however, an interesting technological development has occurred which allows a more precise and delicate analysis of cortical cell firing to be undertaken—in fact to allow even the output from a single neural cell to be monitored. This technique involves the use of what are known as microelectrodes, tiny slivers of metal, thousandths of an inch in diameter, which when in contact with an electrical source—in this instance the body of a nerve cell or neurone—transmit a pulse of electricity to an amplifier and recording apparatus. Microelectrode recording involves inserting electrodes of this kind in selected areas of the brain of an animal and, by means of a precision adjustment, positioning the electrode so that it is touching up against the body of a single cell. We shall discuss the remarkable findings which have come from experiments of this kind later in the section on "Perception." Microelectrode techniques, incidentally, can on occasions be used with human subjects. In such cases, naturally the opportunity arises when an individual is undergoing brain surgery for, say, the removal of a cerebral tumour. In these circumstances, with the patient's permission, the surgeon may perform experiments to study single cell responses with results which have been of great interest.

(5) Biochemical Analysis.

The fifth major approach to the study of the brain to consider is that of biochemical analysis. For various reasons there has been a growth of interest in the microstructure of cerebral tissue, not just the neural cell but in its basic constituents—in other words at the molecular level. Clearly there is not much hope or point in trying to record the behaviour of molecules by electrode recording or even by microscopic visual analysis, so some other method must be found if one is concerned with this level of analysis at all. This is where the psychologist teams with the biochemist—an example of the kind of interdisciplinary approach which is becoming common in brain research. As with much of the chemical analysis performed in other fields, scientists discover the nature of the substance they are examining by observing its behaviour when mixed with other chemicals or compounds. Crudely speaking, one mixes the unknown substance with some known chemical and simply watches what happens, the reaction which follows giving clues as to the nature of the chemical under study. Now in the case of the brain or the constituents of neurones, it is obvious that one is dealing with more than one single substance so the first problem is how to separate the constituents in order to study them individually. To achieve this biochemists use a number of techniques such as chemical separation, simple heating, and even whirling the material round at great speeds in centrifuges. The biochemical approach to brain research is a bit too complicated to deal with in detail here, but in the view of many it is one of the most promising avenues open to scientists in this field.

(6) Behavioural Research.

Psychologists are interested not merely in the structure of the brain of humans and animals but also of course in their behaviour. By behaviour one means the way in which the individual interacts with its environment and its reasons for doing so. A study of what, when, and how a creature does something can tell one a good deal about the rules that govern behaviour. The way in which a bird builds its nest, a cat rears its kittens, a dog threatens another dog, frequently follow set patterns and presumably have something to do with the way in which at least a part of its brain is organised. Careful study of such behavioural patterns even allows one to make certain predictions about what an animal will do next in a given set of circumstances—and once one is able to predict accurately one has generally discovered something important. Studying animals (or people) " in the wild " is easier said than done and tends to be frustrating because of their tendency to do unpredictable things and their general disinclination to perform to order. Furthermore the range of behaviour that one can study by such methods is limited to the so-called " instinctive " actions which are frequently simple in function and execution. The alternative is to confine the animal in a laboratory and observe its reactions to an experimentally controlled environment. In this way one can study its learning and memory processes, its sensory mechanisms, its intelligence and capacity to "reason," its behaviour under conditions of stress, its preference for various foods, etc., etc. Behavioural research of this kind has turned out to be almost the most important method employed by psychologists in their attempt to understand the brain and while it has its inevitable limitations we will be examining the contribution it has made in more detail under various sub-headings.

(7) Introspection.

The oldest and perhaps most obvious method of studying the brain was simply to think about it! This was the method adopted by early philosophers who believed that if one was sufficiently logical and intelligent one could work out the solution to practically anything. Unfortunately, while the brain, mind, etc., might seem to be an ideal subject for its own thought processes, this method of analysis—known as introspection—just doesn't seem to work in the way that it should. The principal problem is that much of the brain's activities are exceedingly rapid and automatic, as anyone can demonstrate for themselves. For example, turn your head and look at an object on the wall. It will be " perceived " and recognised apparently instantaneously. Even if you can detect a faint lag between the act of inspection and the act of perception, it is quite impossible to describe the steps or stages in the process. Much the same applies to other important mental faculties. One cannot, merely by thinking about it, say how one actually learns something, or how one calls an item up from memory. It was realising the relative hopelessness of this quest which led philosophers interested in the brain to convert themselves, in the middle part of the 19th cent., into psychologists and adopt an experimental rather than an intellectual approach to the problem. However, it should be equally clear (though many psychologists seem to have forgotten this) that there is a whole world of material which does not seem to make itself available to any of the experimental approaches (1–6) which we have described above. The study of language itself is a good example, being part of our mental life and thus of great interest. Similarly, certain features of abnormal psychology ranging from the bizarre thought processes of schizophrenics to the near-mystical states of mind reported by artists and poets, or the distortions of perception and personality induced by the hallucinogenic drugs, are central to the topic of psychology and are clearly only approached in the first instance through some measure of introspection. What too of the raw material of psychoanalysis and the rich glimpse of the interior of our minds granted us through our dreams? These are merely a few examples to highlight a single point that— when studying the brain we should not ignore the mind's power to look in on itself.

This concludes our condensed survey of some of the principal methods used by psychologists and their colleagues in attempting to get to grips with their exciting and challenging field. The reader may have been surprised by a number of things, one of which must surely be how very much wider is the territory covered by psychology than is commonly believed.

4. What do Psychologists Study?

We now come to examine the main areas making up the subject matter of psychology. There are all kinds of ways of breaking this material down and as the topic is so immense (and enlarging quite rapidly) one or two important aspects will have to be left aside. We shall only refer in passing, for example, to the important sub-sections of Child Psychology, Industrial Psychology, and Ergonomics, for these need to be treated separately if they are to be properly understood. Furthermore, much of the material inherent in Sociology will have to be passed over for similar reasons. The reader will also notice some overlap between the various headings which merely confirms what one ought to suspect—that in studying human beings or living animals, it is really impossible to segment the approach completely. A person is an entity and something more than the sum of his various parts.

For the purposes of this Introduction we will consider Psychology as constituting principally the study of four major factors—

(1) Perception, which includes the study of the way information is gathered by the brain and how it is interpreted;

(2) Learning and Memory, which deals with the way the information is stored once it has been gathered and, subsequently, how it is retrieved when wanted;

(3) Motivation, which includes the vital topic of why a human or animal interacts with its environment and why it does one thing rather than another; and

(4) Personality and Thinking, which tackles the abstruse problems concerned with consciousness, self-awareness, and, naturally, disorders of both.

Anyone reading this Introduction seriously will find that in acquiring his first formal background in Psychology he will also have to think at times like a physiologist, a philosopher, an anthropologist, and a good experimental scientist, all rolled into one. This will turn out to be less complicated than one might imagine.

II. PERCEPTION.

(a) Information Gathering and Information Decoding.

The topic of perception itself breaks down into two significantly different headings and it is very important to comprehend the distinction between the two before going any further. These are the processes of *information gathering* and *information decoding*. If these words seem a bit bothersome, they need not be. Information has a meaning in science rather broader than details of train times or facts from history, and it really deals with the influence of one object, person, or thing, on another. For example, when you look at the sun or a bright light, photons from the luminous object strike the retina or sensitive layer at the back of the eye. As the result of this the retina changes its state slightly and in due course passes signals back to the brain. Now the exchange between the sun and the retina, odd though it may seem at first, constitutes an exchange of information, and when the message finally reaches the

brain and the sun is recognised for what it is, the information has flowed all the way from sun to brain. If this appears to be an odd use of the word "information," then this is probably because one has tended to think that information can only be conveyed through words or numbers and "meaningful" conversations. The more one thinks of this limited point of view, however, the less reasonable it seems. If one looks at a painting, which contains neither numbers nor words, but a picture of, say, a ship at sea, then most people will agree that it is conveying information (the artist originating it whenever he painted the picture). In fact we can use this analogy to add that the painting itself can be looked upon as a kind of information store since the artist who set the whole process going could easily be dead and gone, and yet his message continues to be conveyed. If one no longer feels it inappropriate to talk of the sun as an emmitter of information to the eye, then we have made a major advance and can move on into the meat of this sub-section. It is really important to get some grasp of the scientific use of words like information and information storage for they will pop up time and time again and one can make nothing of modern psychology without them. Incidentally, when we spoke of the retina sending signals up to the brain where the sun was "recognised," it should be remembered that what reaches the brain is not a kind of miniature sun but rather a pattern of impulses which need to be interpreted. This interpretation we call information decoding and it is the second important factor in perception which we will come to shortly. But first, how is the information received and gathered?

(b) The Five Senses.

Simple creatures, such as amoeba, react in a vague, generalised way to objects in their environment. The reason for this is that they have no specialised equipment to allow them to detect what is taking place, or about to take place, around them, and no computing centre capable of selecting alternative modes of behaviour. As we ascend the evolutionary scale from jellyfish to worms and up through reptiles, mammals, birds, etc., we note increasing specialisation of the body's cells, the development of devices capable of scanning the external environment and increasingly complex co-ordinating nervous centres (brains). By the time we reach Man and other advanced animals, the individual is not merely reacting to his environment but consciously aware of its flux, able to predict many of its changes before they can effect his body physically, and frequently manipulating it significantly to suit his own ends. This immense versatility is dependent upon information from the environment being fed into the nervous system for processing, and the devices which the body has developed to gather this information are known as the senses—vision, hearing, touch, taste, and smell—roughly in order of importance. Without these senses, the interface between the central nervous system and the world outside, a living creature is nothing more than a helpless vegetable, incapable of survival. For this reason if we are to get anywhere with understanding the operation of the brain we will need to know a fair bit about the sense organs that feed it. We shall spend most time on the two most important—vision and audition.

(c) The Eye.

Perhaps the most useful information from the brain's point of view would be that which concerns the detection of food or a mate at a distance or, of course, the presence of danger in the form of a predator. Consequently, the most vital and remarkably developed of our sense organs are our eyes, which are geared to detecting radiation over a frequency range which we call "light". For those who like this kind of detail, the actual spectrum detected by the eye covers light frequencies whose wavelengths range from about 380 millimicrons to about 720 millimicrons. All this means is that the distance from peak to peak of the waves which constitute the light is a very small amount indeed—far less than a thousandth of a millimetre in fact. Note, however, that not only can the eye detect the 380 and the 720 millimicron waves quite easily but it can also discriminate between them and a whole lot of other wavelengths in between as well. In fact we call the 380 mM waves " violet," the 720 mM " red," those of about 500 mM " green," etc. Remember the minute frequencies involved and you will appreciate that whichever part of the eye handles this kind of information must be very sensitive indeed. This fabulous bit of equipment, one of the most remarkable of all biological systems, is called the retina.

The Retina.

Situated in a layer at the back of the eye the retina is a kind of screen on to which rays of light are focused by the lens after having passed through a window at the front, which is called the cornea. The question now arises as to how the retina detects the light rays and how it then signals the relevant information on to the brain. There are two ways of answering this question, one very complicated and reasonably accurate, the other quite simple and slightly less accurate. We'll choose the simpler and lose a bit of accuracy without worrying too much.

The principle employed is that of energy absorption. The retina is a densely packed mass of neural cells whose speciality is that they contain light-sensitive substances known as " pigments ". These substances change their state rapidly when the photons from a light source strike them, and this change, which is really a high-speed chemical reaction, acts as the trigger which " fires " the cell. This in turn sends a pulse of electrical activity up the neurone's long stem in the direction of the brain. After it has fired, the cell then requires a brief period to recover its normal state and for the minute portion of bleached pigment to regenerate, during which time (known as the refractory period) it will not fire again. Multiply all this by one hundred million, which is the approximate number of cells in the retina, and you will get some idea of the frenzied activity contributing to the process of vision. To complicate matters there are at least two major types of visual receptors, the cones and the rods. To go into their infrastructure in detail is really the province of physiology, but it is necessary to know something about their prime function which is that the cones tend to handle the higher levels of luminance met in daytime and also mediate colour vision, while the rods, which are far more sensitive, tend to come into life in the dusk or dark. The shift from cone to rod vision, which, like most of the body's basic functions, is entirely automatic, is something we all experience regularly in our daily life. Walk out of the sun into a dark room and for a moment one is " blinded." Walk out of a dark room into the sun and again one is " blinded." Actually all that is happening is that the visual system is having to shift from one set of receptors to another and when the change is extreme and rapid, the lag in the switchover is dramatically apparent.

Colour Vision.

Psychologists have known for a long time that the cones, which tend to be packed in the centre or " more useful " part of the retina, have something to do with colour vision, but just how they do this job has been a matter of much debate and argument. One of the most likely bets would seem to be that particular types of cone are equipped with particular types of pigment, one sensitive to light in the " red " range, another to light in the " yellow," another in the " blue," etc. But how many types of cone would one need, therefore, to get the kind of colour vision we enjoy? Would one have a separate type for each subtle shade of hue for example? When thinking such things out scientists always try to see first if they can get by with the smallest possible number of hypothetical elements, and only bring in extra mechanisms when they are absolutely stumped—a principle known as " Occam's razor " and one universally revered in science and philosophy. With this in mind and with a bit of ingenuity, the general view at the moment is that

three separate types of colour receptor are all that are needed to account for human colour vision; this is known as the trichromatic theory which is all we need to know about it for the purposes of this article. But just to show how complicated things are, and yet how interesting for this very reason, we will pause to look at some experiments in human colour vision which show that no matter how neat and simple an explanation is in psychology, there is always a joker hiding in the pack.

Some Experiments in Colour Vision.

To understand these experiments, which were performed by a Swiss psychologist, Dr. Ivo Kohler, we need to know a little bit about the phenomena known as after-images. This information will come in handy again a little later on when we talk about after-images in a slightly different context. You may have observed that if you look at a bright light for longer than a second or two, when you close your eyes you see a continuing image of the object which may persist for quite a while and exhibit a nice range of rather bright colour changes. If you haven't observed this, then you can experiment yourself by just fixing with one eye on the filament of an electric light bulb—not too close to the eye. Count five slowly as you do so, then close your eyes and observe. (Don't do this with the sun, by the way, as it could be dangerous). Now the important point at this stage is the changes in colour you will see taking place, which are generally believed to occur because the bright light has slightly overbleached the retinal pigments and they are taking longer than usual to recover. In the process of recovering they continue to send signals to the brain, which interprets this information as if there was still a light source present and thus the bulb filament is " seen " long after it has really gone. The colour changes themselves are probably due to the fact that some pigments regenerate a bit more quickly than others and thus a sequence of colours is perceived. All this involves lights of greater than average intensity and the question is whether one could get " after-images " with low intensity objects looked at for a long time. The answer is yes, and for anyone who hasn't noticed this before, another simple experiment can be tried. Take a book with a brightish colour binding—say red. Fix on it with one eye, trying to keep your head and eye as still as possible and hold it for about one minute. Now, turn the head away from the book and look at a blank, light wall or other flat surface. What one will see is a rather amorphous image of the book, but coloured green, which will linger for about half a minute before it fades away. This is another version of the first trick, with the after-image being due to the bleaching of the red pigment, and to various other changes that follow in its wake. Now the after-image, as we have noted, soon fades away and no doubt this has something to do with the intensity of the original stimulus. But what would happen if, instead of merely exposing oneself to the colour for a minute or two, one extended the time period to an hour, or a day, or a week, or even longer? This is exactly the question that Kohler set out to answer. To get over the problem of how one could possibly go on looking at something for hours or days on end, he decided on the simple expedient of wearing tinted spectacles and going about his business as usual. For the first experiment, using pink spectacles, he made a number of interesting discoveries. Number one was that although for the first few hours in his experiment the world took on a rosy hue, before the first day was over things were nearly back to normal. After a few days there was no longer any suggestion of a more than normal amount of pink about and his vision appeared to be unaffected—even though, of course, all light was being filtered through the red lenses and thus inevitably tinted. Discovery number two came when he finally took the lenses off to find the whole world tinged with green—the so-called complementary colour of red—a tint which remained for days! His next experiment, apart from doing the whole thing over again with a different set of colours—blue lenses providing a yellow world, green a red one, etc.—was to wear spectacles with one lens red and the other green. This time the position was more complicated. If he closed his right eye, which had the red filter in front of it, then he saw green through the other lens and vice versa. With both eyes open, however, the two colours would 'mix' in his brain and the world appeared through a kind of bluey haze. At this point you might care to try to predict what the scientist found when, after a few weeks of this and after all the colour had washed out, he finally removed the spectacles. In the first place, if he looked at the world through both eyes he saw the complementary to blue (which is yellow) but if he looked through either of his eyes singly he saw the world tinted with the appropriate complementary colour, red or green. Once again the new tints took some time to disperse. All this of course, while exceedingly interesting, could still be reasonably explained on the theory of pigments bleaching away due to long exposure and taking some time to regenerate. Unfortunately for this simple idea, but fortunately for people who like problems, Kohler's next experiment produced a surprise result. For this he had the ingenious idea of segmenting his spectacles so that the right half of each lens was tinted red, the left half green. The position now was that if the wearer looked to the *right* with *both* eyes he saw a red-tinted world, if to the *left* a green-tinted one. Looking straight ahead produced a muddling fusion of both colours. In due course, as one might predict, all spurious colours washed out wherever one was looking. Now came the surprise. On removal of the spectacles Kohler found that when he looked ahead he saw the complementary " fused " colour, but when he looked to the right he saw the complementary of red, which was green. When he looked to the left he saw the complementary of green, which was red. To work out why this was surprising one must think about what was happening in the retina. In the early experiments, with the whole of the right visual field tinted red, say, the persisting perception of the green after-image was felt to be due to some changes in the pigmentation of the cells in the retina. But clearly this will not do in the final experiment, for in this case the same areas of retina seem to be doing two different things. After the glasses had been removed, when the subject gazed to the right he saw a green field and one might assume that this was because the pigment had been changed by overstimulation. But how could this account for the fact that when the subject turned his eyes to the left there was a change of perceived colour to red? Clearly the pigment itself couldn't have changed in that time, nor could it change back when the eyes reverted to the left. Obviously, quite contrary to what one might expect, the colour changes were dependent, in this case, not on the state of the retina but rather on the direction of gaze!

No one has satisfactorily explained Kohler's intriguing results to date, but they do suggest one important point which one is always in danger of neglecting in psychology—that a living organism is not just a collection of parts acting independently of each other. In the drastic situation of wearing tinted lenses for days, or even weeks, changes were evidently taking place not just in the retina of the eye, but also in higher centres of the brain.

More About the Rods and Cones.

Returning briefly to the retina and its constituent cells we might just take a closer look at the rods which, you will recall, come largely into play in conditions of poor luminance.

The extraordinary sensitivity of the rods is the most interesting thing about them. Unlike the cones, which need the brightness of daylight to do them justice, one single rod will be triggered into action by light whose energy is as low as 10 by 10^{-10} ergs, and if that is a value which has no meaning one can get a graphic idea of this sensitivity when one learns that in total blackness the eye could detect the light of a single candle five miles away! Put another way, the amount of kinetic energy used in lifting a pea *one inch* would, if converted to light energy, be enough to give a brief sensation of light to every person that has ever lived on earth! The clustering of cones in

the centre of the retina, the fovea, has been mentioned and the rods consequently tend to be scattered around in the periphery. You can detect this geographical distribution yourself by noticing that whereas in daytime your vision is much better directly in front of you, in very dim light you will be able to see objects on the edge of your visual field rather better. You might also care to note how the periphery of the retina, populated largely by rods and devoid of cones, is remarkably insensitive to colour. Offhand one gets the impression that the whole of one's visual field is richly endowed with colour, but this is far from true. A simple experiment will demonstrate this. Fix, with one eye closed, on a predetermined spot—a mark on a piece of paper will do. Then, slowly bring into your field of vision from the side a small piece of coloured paper drawing it closer and closer to the central spot. Now if you can manage to keep your eye really still and maintain fixation despite the tendency to peek at the incoming paper, you will be surprised how far in the latter will have to be before you can detect its colour with certainty. Try the experiment again with another colour and note that it may be recognised earlier or later. In this way it is possible to plot a simple map of one's own retina, defining the boundaries of the colour sensitive areas and nicely illustrating the division of retinal receptors into two distinct types with different jobs to do—the rods and the cones.

(d) Perception as a Dynamic Process.

Everything we have said in this particular section has reinforced the idea that creatures with complex brains are something far more than automata responding blindly to changes in the environment. Information fed in through the eyes, etc., is processed in some way by the brain, or " decoded ", as we put it earlier. In fact it is this business of decoding and the possible mechanisms which help to achieve it that interest psychologists more than the raw details as to how the senses actually gather the information in the first place. Nevertheless until relatively recently there was a school of thought in psychology that made desperate attempts to deny, or at least reduce, the role of a central integrating process, implying that animal and human behaviour could ultimately be reduced to a great mass of stimulus-response networks, triggering each other into action in a totally mechanical fashion. This " Behaviourist " school, as it was known, had more impact on theories of learning and we shall look at it more closely when we come to the appropriate section, but it also influenced the thinking of psychologists interested in perception. The trouble with this point of view is that it is so obviously inadequate to explain the rich material of perceptual experience. One has only to think of the visual illusions that are experienced when information " correctly " relayed from the eye is " misunderstood " or incorrectly " decoded " in the brain itself. Look at the visual illusion reproduced on the back of the jacket where two lines which appear to be slightly bent are objectively parallel. Clearly it is enormously interesting that all human beings fall prey to illusions, for it suggests that some common mechanism exists which is causing them.

The Gestalt Approach to Perception.

Among the first people to take this up as a general principle and use it as a frontal assault on the Behaviourist view was the so-called " Gestalt school " of psychology, founded in the early part of the century by three talented psychologists, Kurt Koffka, Wolfgang Kohler and Max Wertheimer. In point of fact they looked more closely at other common features or anomalies of perception than at visual illusions, for they believed that the introspective and experimental analysis of human perceptual experience allowed one to deduce the " laws of perceptual organisation " and that these laws must throw light on the fundamental operating procedures of the brain itself. A simple introduction to Gestalt theory is given in Section J so we will confine ourselves here to looking at a few of their more important ideas, most of which are still valid in modern psychology. The first was their insightful statement that in perception *the whole is something more than the sum of its parts*. This principle is nicely illustrated by the fact that a series of dots drawn fairly close together in the shape of a ring are perceived as having a very definite " form "—*i.e.*, that of a circle—despite the fact that all one has actually put on a paper is a collection of dots. Dots are all that are perceived by the retina, and the signals passed up to the brain can only be those arising as the result of the dot stimuli. Look at such a picture, however, and one sees a circle. But where does this come from? From the brain say the Gestalt psychologists, pointing out that the whole (*i.e.* the perception of the circle) is something over and above the sum of its parts (*i.e.* a collection of points or dots). The same thing can be applied to lines, or practically any other shape, and can even apply in the auditory sense (a " tune " is something over and above a collection of separate notes played in sequence). The Gestalt school argued that this was clear evidence for the existence of dynamic forces in the brain whose function was to mould or *structure* the information as it was fed in by the senses. Further examples of this structuring could be seen in other types of visual phenomena, and Koffka and his colleagues formulated a number of " laws of perceptual organisation " which they held were universal and also, probably, innate or " built into " the brain at birth. These laws are a bit too involved for us to discuss in detail but one or two are worth mentioning because the reader can conduct simple experiments for himself. The first, known as " Continuity," is a rather obvious one and similar to the example of a dotted circle that we had earlier. This states that a collection of dots arranged so that they form a " continuous " line, whether straight or curved, would tend to be perceived *as a unit*. In other words, structuring forces within the brain tend to act upon such dots causing them to be perceptually linked despite the fact that they have no true continuity in the physical sense. The age-old perception of the constellations in the sky, formed out of near random stellar patterns, is a good example of the law of " Continuity " in action. Another important law is that of " Similarity." To observe this in operation, scribble on a sheet of paper about twenty small crosses at random. Now, among these crosses again scribble down about 10 small circles. Look at the composite picture and you will probably note that the circles, more or less wherever they are, tend to stand out in isolation from the crosses—the law of " Similarity " in operation. Obvious? Maybe—but why *should* similar things stand out against a dissimilar background? Obviously some important factor in perception must be at work. Yet one more Gestalt " law," that of " Closure," is worth mentioning because its operation is easy to observe experimentally. Koffka and his colleagues believed that the perceptual organising system tended to dislike incomplete or partial figures and where possible would " close " them. This was particularly true, they argued, with neat, simple figures such as circles, triangles, etc. To illustrate this, draw a small neat circle on a piece of paper but leave a small gap in it, say about a tenth of its circumference. Now close your eyes and open them very briefly to give yourself a fleeting glimpse of the figure you have drawn. The chances are that what you will see is a circle—without the gap. Try this on someone else who doesn't know that there is a gap present and it will work even better. Now one might reasonably argue that one has missed the gap because one didn't have time to see it, but that's really no explanation as to why one should see a *complete* circle. The Gestalt argument is that in such fleeting glimpses, the law of Closure within the brain overrides the rather feeble information about the gap that comes up from the retina and the result is the gap just never gets perceived. The effect, incidentally, works for longer looks at patterns viewed in dim light.

A good deal of controversy surrounded the Gestalt approach to perception, much of which has died down in recent years as the Gestalt point of view has gradually fallen out of favour. One of the most controversial facets of the theory was the belief that the so-called laws were innate, or present at birth. In other words if one could somehow question a new-born baby and get a sensible answer out of it we would find that it too had its perceptions modified according to the Gestalt laws of Continuity, Closure, etc. And this brings us to the very interesting question of just what it is that babies can see at birth—if anything.

(e) Learning to See.

Anyone who has spent any time with very young babies will realise that their powers of perception are at best poorly developed. The mother may feel greatly flattered at being " recognised " with a smile, but the harsh facts are that a young baby will produce a charming smile for practically anything—even an absolutely horrific mask—that's placed in front of it. The psychologist William James (brother of the novelist Henry James) actually stated that the world of the newborn baby was a " buzzing, booming confusion "—in other words a mass of sensory data rushing up to the brain with nothing up there to interpret it. This is probably close to the truth—at least as far as human babies are concerned, for there is very good evidence that babies do not come into the world equipped with the ability to perceive the environment in the orderly, clear-cut way that adults do. Incidentally, this is not due to any deficiency in their visual system for the new-born's eyes are physiologically mature with at least the *potential* for detailed colour and pattern vision. What seems to be happening is that in the first few months, perhaps years of life, young humans literally have to *learn to perceive*, as the brain gradually acquires the power to integrate the information sent up by the senses, into a meaningful picture of the environment. There can be no better illustration of the vital distinction psychologists draw between vision (or audition for that matter) and the act of *perception*. One concerns itself with input, the other with its interpretation. Now with animals it is a different story—somewhat. Among the primates, chimpanzees, monkeys, etc., perception at birth is better than with humans but still pretty uncertain and the lower down the animal kingdom (this is called the phylogenetic scale) one goes, in general, the better the creature is equipped at its birth to perceive the environment. Look at it another way and say that the simpler the creature and the less well equipped with cerebral cortex, the more wiring or circuitry is built into it and carried over to every member of the species. This of course is what is meant by instinct—an inherited behaviour pattern or function of some kind which appears in every member of a species at birth. *See also* F38(1)

Instincts are very useful in one sense since the creature endowed with them doesn't have to learn the instinctive task and can perform it at birth (suckling is one of the few human instinctive reflexes). On the debit side, however, is the fact that one can't *unlearn* the instincts either, so that the more of them one has, the more likely they are to get one into trouble if one is a creature likely to change its environment in any radical way. Think, for example, how powerless human beings would be if they were subject to an instinctive desire to hibernate for six months at the onset of each winter. Clearly instincts are good for creatures with limited cerebral capacity, but a big handicap if one wants to respond in a flexible way to the world around one. The big question now is, does the ability to perceive develop as a natural consequence of the maturing brain, or is it dependent upon practice and experience?

Some Investigations.

If one takes kittens and brings them up in total darkness for, say, a month, on being subjected to the light they seem to have normal perception—pretty well equivalent to that of kittens normally brought up. However, if one extends the rearing-in-the-dark for a much longer period, say a year, then the young cat never seems to achieve normal vision on its introduction to a lighted world. Post mortem examination of the brain reveals that certain parts of the visual system seem to have failed to develop in the normal way. Evidently there is a critical period, which when exceeded without visual experience, stultifies the brain so that normal perception can never be achieved. But what of humans? This may seem an impossible question to answer for how could one conduct the necessary experiment—*i.e.*, deprive new-born babies of light for up to a year—without outraging all moral and ethical values? In fact, by an odd and fortunate twist, the necessary data has come to us without the need to perform an impossible experiment. In the 1930s new techniques of surgery allowed the performance for the first time of an operation to graft the human cornea. This, you will recall, is the transparent window on the front of the eye which can, with age or disease, become clouded and opaque. Occasionally the cornea may be opaque at birth with the result that the individual can never achieve the perception of patterns or shapes. Because some light is getting through the milky window, however, he may be able to tell the difference between, say, periods of light and dark. Prior to the 1930s people afflicted with clouded corneas were consigned to a life of effective blindness—the more tragic because in all essentials they were frequently equipped with perfectly operating retinae, optic nerve, etc. With the development of corneal transplant surgery the picture dramatically changed and, while the operation is now usually performed at a relatively early age, there was an initial group of people in middle-age waiting to be treated who had *never had normal vision*. Realising that this provided a unique opportunity for an interesting observational study, the German psychologist Von Senden arranged to follow the progress of the patients with new corneas and record their reactions to the sight of objects which they had hitherto only heard described. Von Senden was set for some surprises—but nothing like the ones that he got. In the first place the newly-sighted patients, far from gazing round in wonder at the marvels of the visual world, were apparently totally incapable of making any sense out of it! This was not, incidentally, a mere failure to recognise subtle differences such as exist between people but a totally inability to tell the difference between most common, everyday objects. Showing the patients large simple drawings, such as a triangle and a square, naming them and then switching their relative position would totally confuse the patients. In order to tell the difference they would have to laboriously trace the outlines of each figure, carefully counting the corners. Notice that they could *see* the outlines, corners, etc.—their eyes were functioning properly—but they were unable to perceive the pattern. Their brains were simply not equipped to recognise shapes and, like young babies, they had to learn the whole process slowly and laboriously. Von Senden's second surprise came when he found that few of the patients seemed to find, at least in the early stages, the gift of sight at all welcome. Some, in fact, literally begged the doctors in the hospital to replace the bandages over their eyes! As with young babies, their visual world was indeed one of " buzzing, booming confusion " and it took some getting used to. There's a happy ending to Von Senden's story. All patients in due course acquired the ability to perceive, slowly at first but with increasing speed and confidence.

The moral of all this is clear, and once again emphasises all the points we have been trying to make about perception. The brain is a device designed to integrate information fed into it by its senses. In due course this integration becomes almost automatic, but this is reached only after a long period of training, which in humans occupies the greater part of infancy and early childhood. How much is actually " built into " human brains at birth in the field of perception? Probably very little, if Von Senden's work is accepted without reservation. Unfortunately there's some curious contradictory work to muddle the issue (as usual) and it concerns experiments with young babies performed by the psychologist J. J. Gibson. His strategy was to take infants and get them to crawl towards what he termed a " visual cliff." This consisted of a sheet or strong glass placed across a kind of trench or ditch in the laboratory, the bottom of which was lined with a chequer

pattern. The children were tempted to cross the trench to come to their mother, this of course involving their venturing out over the glass sheet. Adults might naturally hesitate slightly, pondering perhaps the strength of the glass and the depth of the pit below it. Young babies would of course know nothing of the fragile nature of glass so should not be worried by that. Nor, if they were not equipped with proper pattern recognition mechanisms, should they be able to appreciate the " depth " of the pit or the nature of the visual " cliff " they would have to cross. Gibson found, however, that all children showed exceptional caution when reaching the " cliff " point, and many could not be tempted into apparently empty space. Common sense? Perhaps, but either they have the perceptual mechanism or they don't, and in this case it looks as though the perception of depth, and even some kind of appreciation of the gradients involved in the cliff were at least present in the babies capable of crawling. Does this contradict the work of Von Senden? Not necessarily—perhaps certain vital things (such as the ability to recognise a steep slope) are " instinctive " in humans, while matters such as the perception of patterns like faces, triangles, squares, etc., need to be learned.

(f) The Building Blocks of Perception.

To this point we have been considering (i) how the information is fed into the brain; and (ii) the evidence for the fact that dynamic integrating forces act on this information to mould it in specialised ways. We must now try to consider how this processing might take place. In other words what actually happens inside the brain when a particular pattern or shape is recognised?

Investigation of Individual Nerve Cells.

To get some insight into this we need to take a closer look at one of the latest techniques for studying the brain which we referred to earlier and which is known as microelectrode recording. The principle here is to insert an exceptionally fine electrode into the cortex of an anaesthetised animal, endeavour to place it against the body of a single neural cell and then, via a suitable amplifying system, record the pattern of electrical activity given off by the cell. This technique, which was developed in the 1950s, represents a significant advance over that of electroencephalography (the recording of brain waves from outside the head) inasmuch as instead of being faced with a rather vague pool of electrical activity, possibly coming from numerous cerebral sources, one is able to study the responses of what must surely be the brain's fundamental unit, the neural cell. Studied in this way the activity of a single cell is very interesting. Firstly cells appear to have no period of total inactivity—whether the creature is sleeping or waking and whether stimulated or not, single cells keep up a steady, periodic burst of firing at an average frequency of one burst every few seconds. This has acquired the name of " spontaneous activity," which is another way for saying that psychologists and physiologists don't know what causes it. In the normal, living brain therefore, even when the creature is in a totally relaxed state, millions of cells are bursting periodically into action, a continuous background of electrical noise. This presumably signals the presence of life itself for only with the death of the individual do the brain's cells cease their restless firing. When the animal is stimulated in some way, by light, noise, heat, cold, etc., then measurable changes take place. If the stimulus is visual, cells in the visual cortex of the brain burst into life, while those in areas subserving other senses remain at their spontaneous level. Introduce auditory stimuli, or mixtures of other stimuli and cells perk up in the appropriate areas of the brain. All this is very much as one might expect, backing up our knowledge that different sections of the cortex handle different tasks. But can one focus down rather more sharply? What happens if one studies the behaviour of cells within only one area of the cortex when different stimuli mediated by the same sense are fed in?

This experiment was first performed by the American physiologists, Hubel and Wiesel, with remarkable results. First, they located a cell in the visual cortex of the cat and began to record the output from it when the cat was shown a variety of visual patterns. At first the cell merely exhibited the normal background firing, but when the cat was shown a luminous vertical line, the cell suddenly burst into frenzied life. In the meanwhile other cells in different parts of the visual cortex continued with only background firing. When the vertical bar was slowly rotated so that it was tilted on to the diagonal, the first cell gradually relapsed into background firing but in the meanwhile, another cell began to increase its firing rate. This too " switched off " when the bar was rotated again to a new angle, while yet another cell sprang to life. In this way Hubel and Wiesel, in a memorable series of experiments in the 50s and 60s, began to systematically plot the cat's visual cortex, noting over and over again the fact that individual cells seemed to be specially " labelled " to respond only to specific stimuli. The same applied to cells in the auditory cortex and even—though these were much harder to track down—in other sensory areas. In homely terms what the two Americans had done was to isolate the building blocks of perception, the terminal points in the brain where information being fed in was categorised or classified and where the amazing process of pattern recognition was actually taking place. Similar experiments were soon being performed with a variety of animal species, and also with a range of ages from the infant animal to the totally mature. Here again evidence seemed to imply that with animals higher up the phylogenetic scale, these " perceptual units " tended to be learnt rather than built in, for they were rarely present in the very young animal or the mature animal which had been experimentally deprived of normal environment.

Recent Experiments on the Human Perceptual System.

All this tells one a good deal about the animal brain, but can one make the bald assumption that a recognition system of this kind exists in humans as well? Microelectrode recording with living humans is probably out, except in certain rare surgical cases, so one might expect this to remain an academic question for all time. However, by one of those happy chances which favour scientists from time to time, some recent experiments performed in England suggest that the human perceptual system *does* work along lines similar to that of the animals. These experiments involve a technique which has the rather daunting name of the " stabilised retinal image," but which is a good deal simpler than it sounds at first.

To see the significance of this one needs first to appreciate the relationship between movements of the eyes and the image projected on to the retina. Looking directly at a pattern of some kind, as we have learnt, leads to an image being focused on the retina at the back of the eye, much as an image is projected on to the film at the back of a camera. Now, suppose that the pattern, instead of remaining stationary, moves across the visual field, then clearly the image moves correspondingly across the retina. Conversely, if the object remains fixed, but one moves one's eyes, then the image is again displaced across the retina. Well, what happens if the object remains absolutely stationary and one keeps one's eyes fixed carefully on it? Does the projected image then lock solidly on to the retina? The answer is actually, no, but for no reason more peculiar than that it happens to be physically impossible to keep one's eyes absolutely still. No matter how hard one tries, the eyes continue to move in a fine, trembling motion, barely detectable without specialised instruments. Inevitably the image of any object in the visual field trembles rapidly on the retina at the same time. This might seem to make vision rather imprecise and blurry, but for reasons we haven't the space to go into, this tremor actually serves to *improve* vision—in particular the kind of super-detailed vision which allows us to see minute specks or very fine lines such as spiders' cobwebs. For some time psychologists have been curious about what would

happen to vision if these fine eye movements did not exist, but since they are quite involuntary and automatic the task seemed pretty hopeless. Then someone—the physicist R. W. Ditchburn—had the bright idea of tackling the problem from a different viewpoint. He simply wore a contact lens (which of course acts like a new outer layer to the eye) with a short stalk sticking out of the front of it. On the end of this stalk he fastened a little photograph and a lens to focus the image sharply on the retina. By this trick he had effectively cut out the effect of all movement made by the eye, great or small, because wherever the eye moved now, so the contact lens followed it, and the stalk and photograph followed it too. If you think for a moment you will realise that this means that the projected image of the pattern remains in one position on the retina—the stabilised retinal image. (If you find this difficult to visualise, try sketching the system on a bit of paper—eye, contact lens, stalk, pattern, and of course image on the retina. The logic will immediately be apparent).

With this system Ditchburn made two very interesting observations. Firstly, the " stabilised " pattern disappeared, thus suggesting that the fine eye movements were essential to visual perception. Secondly, he reported that when a pattern disappeared it frequently did so *in part*, rather than washing out as a whole as one would rather expect. Furthermore, the parts that came and went tended to be neat, even sections of the pattern. For example, a cross would alternate between the vertical and horizontal bars, a triangle would break up into one or other of its three sides, etc. A number of experiments have since been performed with human subjects using this ingenious and unusual apparatus, with results which suggest to psychologists that they are dealing with the same kind of perceptual units Hubel and Wiesel found in the cat. The tendency of the lines to appear and disappear as units when viewed as stabilised images seems to imply that basic " line units " are also present in the human brain—the building blocks of perception again.

It so happens that these fascinating fragmentation effects can be observed by a simple experimental method which does not involve wearing specially fitted contact lenses. You will recall that we spoke earlier of after-images, which are temporary changes in the state of the retina caused by a bright light and these are, of course, perfectly stabilised images since they are part of the retina itself. To observe them oneself the best trick is to sit in a rather dark room and stare at the window-frame against the bright sky outside. Do this, keeping one eye closed and the other as still as you can manage, for about thirty seconds. Then close both eyes and *keep them closed.* After a second or so you will see a vivid after-image of the cross-pieces of the window frame and you will note that the vertical and horizontal bars of which it is composed come and go independently of each other. This is something far more than a trick incidentally—as you do it you will be watching your own brain at work processing the pattern locked on to the retina.

We have spent a good deal of time on vision and visual perception because (*a*) it is easily the most important of the sensory channels, and (*b*) because it is the area of perception best charted by psychologists and physiologists. We will now take a less detailed look at the other senses.

(g) The Ear.

The eyes, as we have learnt, are equipped to detect visual radiations within a fantastically fine bandwidth—less than a thousandth of a millimetre. From the brain's point of view this takes care of a good slab of some of the most important sources of energy and radiation within the universe, but a brain equipped only with eyes would be " blind " to a good deal of important information. Therefore we find a complete set of specialised receptors handling other areas of interest, of which by far the most important are the ears. These are tuned to pick up waves and vibrations too, but of air waves rather than light, and in an entirely different range. The absolute spectrum to which the human ear responds is between about 20 and 15,000 cycles a second, with a peak sensitivity between about 1,000 and 6,000 cycles per second. All sounds we can hear, therefore, consist ultimately of vibrations of the air occurring within this frequency range, and in the case of human speech we are dealing with a complex pattern of such vibrations. The ear's method of detecting these and translating them into an electrical code is ingenious and enormously efficient.

Auditory Perception.

The process begins with the outer ears (the flaps of skin on the side of your head!) which serve to catch sound waves coming from the most important direction, which in the case of human beings is in front of them. The importance of these directional indicators is considerable and you can note how strikingly you can change your own auditory perception by flexing the ears with your hand, or cupping your hands so that the "directional indicators" point backwards. Once channelled into the innards of the system, the sound waves are forced down an ever-narrowing tube where they come up against something called the tympanic membrane which is better known as the eardrum. Popular belief seems to be that the auditory process stops here, but from what you have learnt already you can work out that there will need to be much more than this. The translation of the physical vibration of the eardrum into electrical signals will have to take place. In fact the vibrating drum itself sets into motion a beautiful percussive machine in miniature, three tiny and elegant bones known as the hammer, anvil, and stirrup, which carry the message deeper into the ear where they come up against yet another "drum." This is the gateway to a spiral tube called the cochlea, which is filled with a densely packed fluid, and the walls of which are lined with hundreds of thousands of tiny hairs. As the last of the bones in the tiny percussive link beats up against the fluid inside the cochlea, it sets up a series of rapid shock waves which in turn induce complex patterns and rhythms of movement in the hairs linking the cochlear wall—rather like the shifting waves of motion that the sea induces in forests of sea-weeds, only on a faster time-scale. These hairs are themselves hooked up to auditory nerve cells and in some way, at present uncertain to psychologists and physiologists, specific movements of the hairs tend to activate specific cells, the end product being that a series of complex but significantly different patterns of electrical activity make their way up the brain. Here the auditory centres get down to the business of interpreting these electrical signals into "meaningful" sounds.

Thinking of the immense sensitivity of the hairs in the cochlear fluid, it may have occurred to you that it ought to be possible to set them in motion by almost any kind of external vibration—and thus hear without vibrating air waves having moved into the ear. This is quite true. Sound waves can be transmitted through other media than air, including bone, and thus even if the ears are blocked one can hear certain sounds remarkably well. Try it for yourself and you will note that the quality of your hearing changes markedly —your own voice, for example, will sound deeper and barely less loud, yet if you whisper you will not hear yourself at all. The reason for this is that with ears blocked, the sound is being propagated to the cochlea by bone conduction and this acts as a filter, cutting out the high-frequency components almost totally but letting in the lower notes without too much trouble. This is why earplugs are disappointingly ineffective.

This is probably enough about the ear which, if the truth is known, is rather less well understood by psychologists than the eye. Only one major point might be briefly touched on. Why do we have two ears rather than, say, one large one on the top of our head? The answer is that a binaural system allows us to locate sounds rather better; slight differences in the time it takes for sounds to reach each ear (as when one ear is slightly closer to a sound source) cause fractional delays in the arrival of the respective signals to the brain—enough for the magnificent computer there to deduce the sound source's rough location.

(h) Smell, Taste, and Touch.

Olfaction.

Of the remaining three senses, only one is concerned with detecting objects at a distance after the fashion of vision and audition. This is olfaction or, as we generally call it, the sense of smell. Olfaction is particularly interesting because it is concerned with the detection of chemical substances in the air, rather than with wave or vibration analysis. Animals of all kinds make much use of their ability to recognise the chemical changes taking place in plants, other animals, etc., which serve to indicate "good" (*i.e.* necessary for survival) or "bad" (*i.e.* dangerous) objects. These may range from the sweet smell of edible fruit, the characteristic odour of a mate in a sexually receptive state, or the nauseous smell of rotting flesh, riddled with dangerous bacteria. Unlike vision and audition, the olfactory sense mechanism is relatively simple in form, consisting of two small patches of cells situated rather high up in the nasal passages and not in the main line of breathing. This accounts for the animal habit of sniffing to detect smells better, the sniff being a method of pushing air up into the rather inaccessible smell receptors. As with pretty well everything else in the body the olfactory receptors are specialised nerve cells, immune of course to light or air vibration, but incredibly quick to react to a wide range of airborne molecules. The presence of particular molecules on a receptor causes a chemical change to take place in the cell, this in turn inducing an electrical signal to pass up the olfactory nerve. Psychologists have not spent too much time on this sense for it seems to be of relatively low importance to modern man, but have pondered the interesting question as to just how many different kinds of smells human beings can detect. You might try to think about this for yourself and before you say hundreds, you should realise that most smells, like most colours, are probably mixtures of a relatively small number of primaries. There is, as it happens, no definite agreement as there is on the seven colours of the visual spectrum, but an early classification by the psychologist Findley in 1924 has probably not been bettered. His "smell prism" listed six primaries which you may like to compare with your own choice. Each smell is identified with a substance which Findley thought was a typical generator of the odour. (1) fragrant (oil of jasmine), (2) etherial (oil of lemon), (3) resinous (turpentine), (4) spicy (cinnamon), (5) putrid (hydrogen sulphide or rotten eggs) and (6) burned (oil of tar).

Taste.

We now move from the distance senses to the so-called "proprioceptors" which is the name psychologists give to the senses concerned with the detection of things actually in contact with the body. Although it is not classed in this way the logical one to look at next is taste, which has much more in common with smell than most people imagine. Taste in itself is a rather feeble sense, mediated by a number of chemically sensitive receptors on the back and sides of the tongue, and the relative overemphasis of its importance is due to the fact that when people talk about great subtleties of taste they are generally talking about great subtleties of smell, for the latter is vital in any gastronomic treat. The simplest test of this is to sample some particularly good tasting substance, savour its flavour and then hold one's nose. The reduction in taste is dramatic, and one can soon realise how a bad head cold can have such drastic effects on the enjoyment of food and drink. One other remarkable feature of the sense of taste is how quickly it adapts out— a drink which tastes sweet or sour at the first taste, slips into bland neutrality before the glass is emptied. This is another experiment the reader can surprise himself with, particularly if he holds his nose while drinking, thus eliminating the vital smell component. The classification of tastes is somewhat easier it seems than that of smell, with most psychologists settling for four primaries, with which you will probably find yourself agreeing—sour, salt, sweet, and bitter. Anyway the plain fact is that the gustatory sense is a very limited tool in mankind's sensory workshop and poses few experimental questions.

Touch and Sensitivity to Pain

The remaining sense, that of touch, includes under its heading a good deal of sub-senses such as the detection of pressure, heat, cold, and the highly enigmatic pain. Pressure, heat, and cold are fairly well-understood, probably being mediated by a number of different types of specialised cells embedded in the skin. Much controversy surrounds the number of different types of receptors involved and the matter is complicated by the fact that no one has positively identified a "pain" receptor—*i.e.* one which fires only when a potentially dangerous stimulus contacts the body. An early view held that pain was simply the signal the brain received when any kind of stimulus was excessive, but for a number of reasons this will not do. There are also some peculiar factors such as the observation that it is not all that easy for a person, without any other cues, to tell the difference between hot and cold objects. Immersing a finger in icy cold water and in very hot water briefly provokes a generally unpleasant sensation, but it is hard to tell with the eyes closed and without prior knowledge which end of the temperature spectrum is being experienced. Pain itself, the scourge of mankind (and yet his saviour in cases where it keeps him out of danger) is an incredibly mysterious phenomenon and we will not be able to say much about it here except to point out that much of its operation is determined by processes going on in the brain rather than in peripheral parts of the body. Human sensitivity to pain also varies enormously. Among certain rather neurotic people intense pain may be felt at relatively minor physical afflictions, while other people may bear (or learn to bear?) what would generally be accounted as gross physical discomfort with equanimity. The action of pain-killing or analgesic drugs is also very poorly understood. Even the simple miracle of aspirin, one of the most useful drugs known to mankind, works without us knowing why or how. Conversely, doctors have known for centuries that some people's agonising symptoms may be relieved by the administration of a sugar pill. In a later section (Motivation) we shall try to get a little deeper into the psychological mechanisms of pain, or more precisely its "opposite" pleasure and will leave our investigation of the known human senses at this point with, as all psychologists freely admit, vast areas still awaiting exploration and delineation.

(i) Are there any Other Senses?

If we take pleasure and pain as separate senses, which might seem reasonable, then even forgetting about all other possible sub-divisions of sensory detection the traditional five senses are not enough. Most psychologists, however, are content with the traditional categorisation. One important area not particularly well covered by the present human sensory range is that of high energy radiation beyond the ultra-violet. It so happens that until quite recently few living things came much into contact with radiation of this kind—the odd cosmic particles bursting through the earth's envelope of air, while dangerous, are too rare to be worth developing special receptors for. Within the past century, however, man has begun to work regularly with high-energy radiation sources and has suffered a good deal as a consequence. X-rays, for example, were grossly misused in the early days after their discovery, and similarly numerous deaths have been caused by the misapplication of nuclear fission devices. The problem is simply that although the radiation is doing our body mortal harm, we expose ourselves to it because we are not equipped with "radiation detectors" to warn us. Once the pain arising from tissue damage arrives—it may take decades for the damage to become apparent—it is too late to do anything about the original stimu-

lus. This apparent digression is merely to remind one of the tremendous role the senses play in our lives, and how brief our span of life in this dangerous universe would be without them. But what of other senses? A frequently used term is that of the "sixth sense" and many people believe that humans and animals are equipped with some other major sense which allows the creature either to detect some danger at a vast distance—way beyond the range of vision or audition—or alternatively to allow one mind to communicate with another mind. We discuss this problem briefly in the section on Ideas and Beliefs, but it also has a place here since many people believe that the study of extra-sensory perception is a legitimate branch of modern psychology. The first argument against the idea of ESP (you may not feel it is particularly convincing) is that no one has been able to detect any mechanism in any part of the brain which could possibly be transmitting or receiving the messages conveyed by the sixth sense. Believers in ESP reply (a) that one might be discovered at any time, and (b) that perhaps no transmitter or receiver is necessary anyhow. The first point is of course irrefutable, but the second raises a different question and suggests that whatever mind-to-mind contact is, it cannot be looked on in the way we have been attempting to look at either sensation or its necessary complement, perception. There is an even more cogent argument, however, which the vast majority of psychologists today adopt—that there is simply no experimental evidence for the existence of telepathy anyhow. In this case it is quite unnecessary to start looking for mechanisms to mediate it. In experiments conducted to sort out the ESP controversy, psychologists *have* found that people are very much better at gathering information from each other without the use of speech than had hitherto been realised. Tiny changes in facial expression, nervous movements, shifts of eyes, even long periods of unusual silence can all serve to give the trained observer important clues as to what is going on in another person's head. Fortune tellers, detectives, and expert card players have known this for years and are only too aware that they are getting their information by clever and insightful use of their normal senses, but rely on other people's ignorance of just how good these mechanisms really are.

(j) Sensory Deprivation.

Any individual, human or animal, born without a reasonably complete complement of senses would almost certainly be doomed to an early death or a life of relying on other humans for assistance. A few startling souls, such as the late Helen Keller, fought their way out of the solitude of total blindness and deafness to lead full and useful lives, but these are golden exceptions to a fairly inflexible rule. Miss Keller in her autobiography tells of her gradually emerging realisation that the universe consisted of "other things" outside herself and states that it was only through an understanding of this that she began to form the concept of herself as an individual personality. This serves to reinforce the point of view stressed by modern psychology that the individual is a mesh between himself and his environment. True personality has no reality without constant and evolving interplay with the external world.

Some Experiments.

In the early 1950s, as scientists began to see that man would soon be able to make voyages into space, the psychologists began to ponder how well human beings could stand up to the physical and psychological isolation of a space capsule. Man is gregarious, naturally at ease among his fellows, and tends to become eccentric and unbalanced when separated from other humans for any length of time. What, they asked, would be the effect of the extended and rather dramatic isolation imposed on the astronauts of the future? To test this a number of experiments were set up in which people were isolated in sealed chambers under conditions of greatly reduced sensory input for lengthy periods. Initial studies seemed to show that the experience was unexpectedly unpleasant, and, sensing that they were on to something significant, psychologists at McGill University in Montreal, where the pioneering work was done, decided to tighten up their experimental situation. Students were hired at the relatively princely sum (for students) of a dollar an hour and told that they could spend as many hours in isolation as they pleased. They were then placed in stuffed clothing rather like divers' suits, and lowered into chambers of water maintained at body temperature. The helmets of their suits were lightproof and the chamber was sealed and covered to be soundproof. The outcome of all this was that even if the student made a body movement he would feel no apparent response as his body, encased in the bulky clothing, would merely float around in the unresisting water. External vision and sound being eliminated, and with ears plugged to prevent him hearing his own breathing, the subject was in a state of almost total sensory deprivation. His only link with the outside world was a " panic button," which he could press to alert the experimenters if for some reason he wanted to terminate the experiment. What did the psychologists expect? That most students would like nothing better than to do nothing for weeks on end and get paid a solid wage for doing so? The results surprised everyone. Most subjects had had more than enough after only a few hours, and only one stuck it out for more than a day and he suffered a neurotic hangover for his pains. For human beings, total isolation from sensory input is evidently one of the most unpleasant experiences imaginable.

The experiments caused a surge of controversy and a good deal of speculation as to what the results implied. The students' principal objection was that they became oppressed with vivid and bizarre hallucinations, both visual and auditory, apparently comparable in strength and unpleasantness to the hallucinations reported by alcoholics suffering from *delirium tremens* or (more fashionable today) the worst excesses of an LSD trip. These vanished as soon as the subject was removed from the chamber and apparently did not occur again. The first hypothesis advanced was interesting—that living things have a hunger or need for sensory input, comparable, but of greater strength, to the need for food. Furthermore, when the sensory appetite was not assuaged, the brain began in desperation to create its own sensory material, hence the hallucinations. This hypothesis was unchallenged at first, but an alternative point of view has recently been put forward based on the recent discoveries in the field of sleep and dream research (*see* **P59–62**). Many psychologists now believe that humans need to dream and that one of the principal functions of sleep is to allow our brains to undergo a kind of sort-out of the programmes which control the central computer. In this view the hallucinations occurring during sensory deprivation would really be an example of the individual dreaming *while he was awake*, the subject's brain having been fooled into "thinking" that it was asleep by the sharp reduction in sensory input which had occurred. For various reasons the human brain carefully keeps the important process of dreaming separate from the waking state and there is some suggestion that to fully experience our dreams would be a psychologically intolerable experience. If this is correct then the McGill experiments and their successors show not a need for sensory input with consequent hallucinations to feed the sensory appetite, but rather the effects of allowing waking human beings a glimpse of the "inner space" of their minds. Similarly, incidentally, one can look upon both the LSD trip and the alcoholic hallucinations as examples of the same process occurring—except that the tripper has stimulated his dreaming mechanism into action through the drug, while in the case of the alcoholic, his excessive intake of alcohol has led to an inhibition of the normal dream process which bursts into activity when he is awake. Whatever the explanation for the strange experiences of the isolated students, there is no doubt that the human being is not psychologically equipped to face up to total loss of sensory inflow for any sustained period. The adventures of the astronaut have in fact taken place in relatively richly-endowed sensory environments and so the expected problems have not arisen. But what of space voyages lasting for months, or even years?

(k) The Problem of Attention.

We have now really finished with the senses and perception as such, but before moving on to our section on Learning and Information storage, we need to think a little bit about the problems which are posed by the great influx of information to the brain, how it sets about coping with this and how it assigns priorities to the multitude of signals it is faced with. This involves the process which we know as Attention. To get some idea of the task facing the brain, let us take up another simple analogy, even if it isn't 100 per cent accurate to the purist's eye.

The brain can be likened to a complex communications centre, sorting vital information, rather like an air traffic control at an international airport. Information floods in from various sources, with the controller paying attention to the scene through the windows, to radio calls, to messages coming by teleprinter and by hand, etc. One way to sort out the muddle might be to assign one mode of messages to one controller, the second to another, etc., but the problem of co-ordination remains. At some stage the senior controller must select which set of signals he is to work on, switching when appropriate to other sets, and issuing instructions to the aircraft waiting to take off and land. Now there are two ways in which he might select the information. The first would be to cut off the unwanted signals at his desk by refusing to allow the stimuli to reach him, a strategy which might lead to a jam of information such as messengers, bits of paper, telephones off the hook, etc., cluttering up the control room. A second strategy would be to staunch the flow of information in the unwanted channels closer to their source, in this case at the point where they first come into the control tower. Real air traffic centres, fortunately, never get into the kind of muddle we are implying here, and nor, in most cases, does the brain. But which of the above strategies is the closest to that adopted by the brain in attending to one particular set out of a vast pool of competitive information? Until about 10 years ago psychologists tended to favour the idea that the first of the two systems was in operation with every sensory stimulus making its way to the brain to contribute to some great tangle in need of constant sorting out. Confusion and uncertainty under stress were considered to be an example of the tangle getting momentarily too complicated.

The Work of Hernandez-Peon.

This view has now been largely rejected thanks to some brilliant experiments by the outstanding young Mexican psychologist, Raul Hernandez-Peon, who was recently tragically killed in a car crash. Hernandez-Peon's experiment, which many people consider to be the first big breakthrough in the psychological study of attention, was performed first on that most useful of laboratory animals, the cat, but later repeated on other creatures. The first stage was to implant a microelectrode into the cat's brain, specifically in an area known as the cochlear nucleus. You will recall the word cochlea from our section on audition, as being the seat of the translation of the incoming sound waves into electrical signals. Now the cochlear nucleus is the first major junction box at which auditory signals meet before beginning their ascent to the brain. Prior to this there is only the network of neurones springing directly from the tiny hairs in the cochlea itself. By attaching the electrode to an amplifier and looking at the output on a TV screen, the experimenter could watch the electrical impulses from the ear as they passed through the big nucleus. The ticking of a metronome, for example, could be seen as a regular beat in time with the tick. Hernandez-Peon then set about trying to attract the cat's attention away from the metronome and did so by showing it a mouse. The cat, as predicted, gazed interestingly at the mouse whereupon—the electrical signal indicating the still-ticking metronome vanished from the TV screen! This is odder than one thinks at first. Remember that the electrode was planted in the nucleus in the region of the ear, and yet the electrical signals were no longer passing this point. If the metronome was still ticking, then its sound waves should still be activating the ear and should still be trying to send their impulses up the auditory nerve. Clearly then, a gate was being closed not in the brain but right down at the level of the ear—the message to close it, however, presumably being sent down from the brain. How could this gate-shutting message get down to the ear? Evidently there must be neural fibres which send their messages downwards from brain to receptor and not just in the other direction as had hitherto been believed. These corticifugal fibres, as they are called, are now believed to run to other sensory areas, including to the retina in animals and humans, and while they are very difficult to track down by anatomical analysis they are thought to serve a very important function. The facts of the case seem to be that Hernandez-Peon had discovered one of the basic mechanisms of attention, the ability of a creature to filter relevant from irrelevant information. Thanks to his work it now looks as though the brain prevents itself from having to face a muddle of conflicting information by cutting off the unwanted signals actually at the level of the receptor, thus preventing a press of confusing and irrelevant information from flooding in. Once attention shifts again, then the appropriate gates are opened and information flows as before. If this tells us something about the selective filtering of important as against useless information, does it also say something about the way a mother will be undisturbed in the night by the flight of a jet plane and yet wake to her child's slightest cry? Perhaps this is an area which mothers know more about than psychologists ever will.

III. LEARNING AND MEMORY.

(a) How is the Information Stored?

Earlier we discussed the specialist use of the word information that psychologists and other scientists employ and remarked how important it is for an understanding of current work on the brain that one rids oneself of the idea that information can only be conveyed in the form of spoken or written messages. We now need to consider the general problem of the *storage* of information, a concept fundamental to the interesting topics of learning and memory. Most people can readily accept the idea that a book is a store of verbal information as, in a different way, is a gramophone record. In reality in neither case are words actually stored. In books the information is held in the form of coded marks, called printing which need to be decoded by the reader before he can understand the original message. Similarly in the case of the gramophone record the information, which might be the sound of a pop star singing, is coded into the form of a series of ridges on a plastic, the decoding being done by a needle plus amplifying equipment, speakers, etc. Using devices like books, films, and records, information can be held in store for very considerable periods of time, the original message sitting around more or less indefinitely until someone gets down to decoding it. Messages written on the walls of prehistoric caves by our dim and distant ancestors are still passing their information across today, and even the fossils we find in Cambrian rock formations are messages of a kind, though the senders did not consciously originate the signals. In essence then a message consists of an information source, some kind of transmitting medium and a receiver. There may also be a delay built in—storage—in which case some kind of encoding and decoding process will be added to get the message in and out of store. All this preamble leads us now to the point where, having in the previous section considered the information gathering and decoding processes in the brain, we can now consider its role as a storage device. Unlike books and records, which operate on fairly simple lines, the brain chooses immensely complicated and still rather mysterious techniques to do its job.

First, perhaps we should clear up a small point which otherwise will cause confusion—the fact

that psychologists distinguish clearly between the two processes, learning and memory. In fact the distinction is simple, particularly in the light of the principles we have just been considering. Learning is the process of feeding information into store, and memory (or remembering) the process of extracting it once again. The next question is the really big one—in the case of the brain just how is this done?

Returning momentarily to gramophone records and books we can see that the process of information storage implies that the incoming signal has changed the state of the storage device, book, record, or whatever, in some way, either by covering it with marks, ridges, or, in the case of magnetic tape, altering the electrical properties of its surface. Something similar must happen in the brain. Information flows up from the receptors, is processed or interpreted by the perceptual mechanism, and then, depending upon circumstances, fed into some store where it is held until required. What kind of changes could be taking place in the neural circuitry of the brain to constitute the laying down of a memory? Psychologists have been divided on this question for decades, and there are three fairly separate competitive approaches. Without giving too much away we shall probably end up feeling that the true explanation will turn out to be some kind of mixture of all three. The three main suggestions can be summarised as (1) the neurological, (2) the biochemical, and (3) the electrical.

The first suggests that as information is fed in, causing certain patterns of brains cells to be activated, minor changes take place on the structure of these cells, modifying them in a rather gross, physical way. This would be similar in a sense to the changes that take place in the surface of a gramophone record when it is first made. The second argues that such gross changes are unlikely and that the storage must take the form of modification of the biochemical or even molecular structure of the brain, changes taking place *within* rather than on the surface of individual cells. The third view advances the hypothesis that since the brain is a mass of electrical energy, and electricity is the basis of neural activity, then the psychologist should look for changes in the electrical patterns of the brain as an index of the fact that something has been stored. We will look at each point of view in greater detail shortly, but first it will be useful to study the experimental evidence.

(b) Early Studies of Learning.

Experimental psychology started in the latter part of the 19th cent., largely as the result of pioneering work of the German physiologist and psychologist Wilhelm Wundt. No one today gets greatly excited at Wundt's experiments nor at his writings, but he was one of the first people in the world to realise that one could actually subject the raw material of mental activity to the experimental method and in this way he is memorable. Wundt concentrated on perception and similar topics and also conducted the first studies of reaction time—the delays humans make between being given the signal to start a task and actually beginning it. He had little to say about the matter of learning and memory, leaving it to a successor, Hermann Ebbinghaus, to get the ball rolling in this area.

Ebbinghaus's experiments were beautifully simple. He took human beings into his laboratory and set out to teach them lists of words, plotting the success rate (number of words in a sequence remembered) against the number of repetitions that had been given. This may all seem frightfully obvious, particularly when we say that Ebbinghaus found that the more repetitions, the better the list of words were learned. This is exactly what one would expect now, a century later, but at that time things weren't so clear cut. Furthermore, Ebbinghaus showed that when you plotted the rate of learning on a graph, a very characteristic curve emerged, common to all his normal subjects, which indicated a gentle improvement in learning with the first few repetitions of the list, followed in due course by a sharply accelerating rise which in turn tapered off. Finally a point came when the list was either completely learned, or no further improvement was made. The important factor was that while there were individual differences in the final level of achievement, and also in the time taken before the main surge of learning took place, the shape of the curve was very similar for all subjects. In other words, while there were significant differences in the ability of subjects to learn his word lists, the nature of the learning process seemed to be interestingly similar. Ebbinghaus's findings are as valid today as they were then and his learning curve fits rather well to the overall pattern of animal learning as well.

In his quest for objectivity he produced another interesting idea. It seemed to him that if one were to compare the performance of two different people in a learning task, one couldn't deduce much about their respective talents by examining the slope of the learning curve unless one knew something about their previous experience with the subject matter. For example, one person might, because of his job or something, simply have been more frequently exposed to the material featured and this would give him a built-in advantage which confused the issue. How about using foreign languages? Again Ebbinghaus felt that to get absolutely pure learning curves one would have to be certain that the subjects had not received prior exposure to the languages in question, a task almost impossible in principle. This led to his invention of a curious tool in the psychologist's workbox, the nonsense syllable, which is still used today as the standard material for many tests of learning ability. It consists of a word with a meaningful sound and look to it, but which is almost complete nonsense inasmuch as it has no obvious meaningful association. ZAT, BOK, FID, BIJ, HAB are a few examples of this strange vocabulary. Ebbinghaus-type experiments are, as you can believe, immensely boring to perform and subjects today normally have to be paid in order to persuade them to take part! However, his realisation that human learning processes could be brought into a real, if rather dull, laboratory setting was a big step forward. Furthermore he had realised the necessity of separating out performance in one task from the background of past experience, an idea which has had far-reaching consequences on the design of all psychological experiments since and which even touches on the important question of the interplay between heredity and environment which we shall look at in the final section.

(c) Learning Experiments with Animals.

The use of nonsense syllables gets over the problem of past experience in one limited area of experimental psychology only, and if one really wants to know something about the formation of the learning process from scratch then one either has to start with very young babies, or use laboratory animals. One psychologist went so far as to read aloud lengthy passages of Greek prose to his infant son at an age when the baby couldn't even understand English. Years later the psychologist gave his son, by now a young man, a number of passages of Greek prose to learn, among which were the sections the baby had previously heard. The outcome was that the sections to which the child had been exposed as a baby were found to be significantly easier than the fresh material. This odd and very tedious experiment has never been repeated, though it is generally rejected by psychologists today as having been imperfectly controlled. For example, who can say for certain what the young man had or had not learnt in the period between the two phases of the experiment? It nevertheless remains as one of a few heroic efforts to use young babies as subjects in learning experiments and it also highlights some of the great difficulties involved.

By the turn of the century more and more psychologists were beginning to follow the lead given by their physiological cousins in bringing animals into the research laboratory. One of the first and most important figures to do so was the American Edward Thorndike, who began to look at the behaviour of specially bred white rats in laboratory learning experiments. Now with humans the problem of how to get the subject to do what one wants him to—learn nonsense syllables or whatever—is met by simply speaking to him about it. With animals this won't work, so Thorndike decided that they would have to be rewarded in some way if they were to learn anything. Reward can be any one of a lot of things, and for an animal it can be getting out of a situation it doesn't like, such as some kind of maze or puzzle box in which a number of specific moves have to be made in sequence before it can get out. Thorndike found that most animals make strenuous and fairly determined efforts to get out of boxes, mazes, etc., and can follow a fairly elaborate sequence of moves in order to reach their goal. Rats, for example, will learn to press a series of levers in the right order if they will open the door to a box, and they will gradually get better and better with practice. Similarly, when placed in a complicated maze, provided they are rewarded with food or escape at the end, they will soon find their way round it. The crucial point here seemed to be the reward, and while pet owners have known for centuries that a piece of sugar presented at the proper time will make a pet do tricks, it is really not clear why it should. To say that it is because the animal " wants the sugar " is no explanation as to why this trick should be learnt rather than some other pattern of behaviour. But Thorndike found without doubt that an animal would learn a maze or similar task far better if it were rewarded in some way at the completion of the task, and he too couldn't see just why, in physiological terms, the neural events which made up the correct performance of the task should be " built in " simply because the animal was rewarded, while incorrect patterns of behaviour were rejected. Ebbinghaus had come to the conclusion that successful learning was a function of the number of times the task was repeated. Thorndike argued that while practice helped to make perfect, it needed something else as well—i.e. the successful completion of the act. How would one measure success? Well, getting out of a maze or finding sugar at the other end would presumably count, and Thorndike described this principle as the " Law of Effect ", believing that he had discovered two factors necessary for learning to be successful (for the information to be placed into the store), one being *frequency*, the other being *effect*. Psychologists at the time carefully sidestepped the niggling question of how *effect* (something happening at the end of a sequence) could work back in time to establish the sequence in memory by arguing that the reward or reinforcement did not itself cause the sequence to be stored in the memory system. It simply made that sequence more likely to be called up on some future occasion. But, replied the critics, wouldn't that imply that all sequences were stored with both right and wrong behaviour lodged equally firmly in memory? This question is still being hotly debated today, and we will shortly be taking a look at the evidence concerning what is and isn't learnt in an experimental situation. But first a word about one of the most important concepts not only in modern psychology, but also in 20th cent. science—the conditioned reflex.

(d) Pavlov and the Conditioned Reflex.

The great Russian physiologist Pavlov reached the peak of his scientific genius in the early years following the Communist revolution in Russia, where his very physical approach to psychological phenomena found favour with his country's leaders. The reasons were ideological. To many it seemed that Pavlov could explain all behaviour in purely mechanistic terms and thus do away with mystical, metaphysical, and, to Communist thinking, totally out-of-date views of Man's nature. Pavlov, it was felt, was at last exorcising the Ghost out of the Machine. His findings in fact sent ripples across the world, and the face of psychology was changed by them—notably in injecting into it the realisation that a good psychologist must think like a physiologist at least as often as he thinks like a philosopher. On the other hand, his naïvely simple view of the machinery of mind and brain was bound sooner or later to be exposed as only partially adequate, missing many of the richly complicated facets of human behaviour which must be faced up to and not denied. What was Pavlov really saying? At rock bottom his ideas revolved around the notion of the conditioned reflex arc, a concept that all wishing to understand modern psychology must get clear in their minds sooner or later.

The experiments in question were exceedingly simple inasmuch as they confined an animal to a rather limited environment and studied its behaviour in the most fundamental kind of learning situation. Pavlov, who was enormously interested in gastric and salivary secretion, had noticed that some of the animals in his laboratory would respond to the presence of food with copious flows of saliva, while others would not. Some would even respond excitedly when a particular food pan appeared while others again would not. He reasoned that these differences were in some way a function of the particular animal's past experience and set out to study this in detail. Firstly, he devised a method of measuring saliva flow, which would normally be copious when an animal was presented with its food bowl. He then introduced, just prior to the presentation of the food, a buzzer, bell, light, or some other similar stimulus. Initially the preliminary stimulus would yield no salivary response, but after a while, provided that the pairing of the presentations was kept up, the first traces of saliva would begin to appear upon the sound of the bell. If this were reliably followed by food, soon the saliva would appear in full flood to bell alone. Failure to offer up the food, however, if persistent, would lead to a gradual falling off in the amount of saliva until it ultimately dwindled away. Pavlov declared that this must imply that a probably instinctive reflex—salivating to food—had become linked in neural terms with a stimulus which had at first been totally irrelevant, the sounding of a bell. The more frequently the two events were linked and the more closely they were associated in time, the stronger the new reflex arc would be. Lack of association between bell and food would lead to the extinction of the reflex arc. The fact that extinction was not total could be nicely shown by introducing the food again, whereupon things would come rapidly back to normal with the bell producing copious flows of saliva once more. Today this seems a fairly trivial observation, but at the time Pavlov, his co-workers, and psychologists all over the world became immensely excited about the conditioned reflex. The reason was that there seemed to be no reason in principle why the whole of an animal's behavioural responses had not been acquired in just this simple way, with the same argument applying with equal force to humans. At the root of all behaviour lay a simple physiological principle. By employing this properly, all living things could have their behaviour patterns moulded in whatever direction was felt to be appropriate, all psychological malfunctions could be corrected, education made simple, the wild beast tamed, the workings of the brain fully described and comprehended. This, for a brief period, was the golden goal (if one likes to think of it in that way) of the new science of psychology—to see man for what he really was; a complex mass of inherited and conditioned reflex arcs.

If Pavlov and his followers in Russia clung to this dream for decades longer than did less politically committed scientists in other parts of the world, then this is understandable. One of the goals of scientific endeavour is simplification and an explanation of human behaviour in terms of stimulus–response units would certainly meet part of that goal. But on the other hand part of the goal of science is also objectivity—even at the risk of complicating explanations—and before long it became obvious that the animal in the experimental Pavlovian set up was *not* behaving as a complicated automaton. For example, it is possible to condition an animal to lift its foot to avoid an electric shock if a bell reliably signals the imminence of the shock. Now place the animal on its side, ring the bell and—will the animal lift its foot? Yes—but not before getting up to the standing position first. But if the animal is blindly responding to the firing of a neuro-muscular reflex arc, why does it not simply raise its foot while lying down? And how does the standing up act become incorporated into the

reflex sequence without prior training? Such experiments were simply discounted at first as being too inconvenient for the theory, but as time went on the immense oversimplification of the stimulus-response theory of behaviour became obvious. But not before a major movement sprang up in the United States which attempted to make dynamic and imaginative use of Pavlov's findings in an attempt at an all-embracing psychological theory. We now turn to look at this, the so-called Behaviourist School.

(e) The Rise of Behaviourism

Sometime before Pavlov's ideas began to have impact in the West, a spontaneous movement had been developing among psychologists to reject the traditional methods of introspection in experimental research. The interplay of conscious thought and mental activity was felt inevitably to confuse the issue, and workers were urged wherever possible to make objective rather than subjective judgments. One of the hardest advocates of this line was J. B. Watson, who even went so far as to argue that introspective studies of consciousness, etc., were not merely misleading, but positively useless. In principle, Watson proposed, it should be possible to give a total explanation of the subject matter of psychology—whether human or animal—in descriptive, mechanical terms concerning the outward manifestations of behaviour. This implied ultimately taking such extreme points of view as declaring thinking to be merely " sub-verbal speaking," better described in terms of minor twitches of the throat, mouth, and tongue muscles than in patterns of electrical activity in the higher centres of the brain. All that was needed to give the Behaviourist school impetus was Pavlov's discovery of the conditioned reflex, and when this was published it was eagerly incorporated as the prop of Watson's argument. To Watson and his colleagues the only realistic and profitable way to look at human and animal behaviour was in terms of a strictly mechanistic model, the conditioned reflex arcs serving as the vital links in the creature's chain of activity. Now many people might agree that an animal in a highly restricted laboratory situation, trained to salivate to bells, raise its paw to avoid an electric shock, etc., might well be coming as close to a biological machine as one could imagine, but was this a really adequate way of describing its behaviour " in the wild "? Critics of Behaviourism were quick to point out certain peculiarities that they felt could not be handled by Watson's simple system. Take a dog, for example, and face it with a series of doors, behind one of which is to be found food, sometimes one door, sometimes another. Now train the dog to respond to a light switched on briefly as signalling food. Now indicate the door which has food by switching on a light above it, and the dog will soon learn to trot up reliably to the appropriate door. What has happened? Easy say the Behaviourists —the dog has been conditioned to approach a light for food, and the reflex carries over to a light above a door. The dog is not really responding to the door, but to the light which sets the appropriate reflex arc in motion, just as pushing a button can cause a car to start. But what, the critics argued, about the fact that the light is switched on for only a few seconds, and yet even after it is off the dog still moves towards the door? Watson replied that the light caused the animal to look towards the door and it immediately adopted a particular posture, setting its musculature up so that it would set off in the appropriate direction, no longer needing the light for a guide. This might seem fair enough, but for the fact that if, just as the animal is about to set off for the door, you hold it, refusing to allow it to move, it still " shows interest " in the door. Furthermore, if you let go in five minutes time, the chances are that the animal will set off to the correct door—a bit long one would have thought for the reflex arc to have been maintained in suspended animation. Was it not simpler, Watson's critics replied, to face up to the fact that the animal was using the light as a signal and was holding the door in some mental form as a kind of goal to which it could make a delayed response if necessary? So adamant were the Behaviourists that all behaviour could be explained in terms of sequences of conditioned muscular movements that they strove to argue that even during the delay the animal was still maintaining a muscular posture—rather in the way that a hunting dog freezes to point to prey. Furthermore, Watson produced what he believed to be irrefutable evidence for the dominance of the muscular activity, even on a task as complex as learning to run a maze. In this rather cruel-sounding experiment he trained a whole lot of rats to find their way through a rather detailed maze. He then preceded to eliminate by surgery all normal sensory equipment—eyes, ears, smell, etc., leaving only the kinaesthetic, or touch, sense. These grossly deprived animals nevertheless still managed to find their way through the maze, allowing him to conclude that in line with the conditioned-reflex notion, the animals were relying predominantly on a chain of muscle reflexes. For a brief period this dramatic experiment seemed to clinch the Behaviourist case. But then came a counter-experiment, even more drastic. A psychologist called Lashley repeated Watson's experiment, but this time also removed the sense of touch by spinal surgery. The wretched creatures even now managed to stagger through the maze—though they were certainly no longer equipped with proper muscular responses. Lashley, correctly, felt this dealt with the ultra-simple Behaviourist argument and that somehow or other the animals must be retaining some kind of general directional sense, a sort of "notion" as to where the exit lay. At about this time more attacks on Behaviourism came from a rival point of view—the Gestalt school. Watson himself shortly afterwards became involved in a sensational divorce case which forced him, in those less permissive times, to resign from academic life. He ended his brilliant career in, of all things, the advertising profession.

(f) Gestalt Psychologists and Learning.

With its emphasis on such ideas as "the whole is something more than the sum of its parts" and its insistence on the idea that the brain has dynamic organising powers which serve to modify input and intervene between stimulus and response, the Gestalt point of view was clearly about as far removed from the naïve Behaviourist viewpoint as was possible. One of the principal allies of the Gestaltists in its early days was K. S. Lashley, referred to above, a brilliant experimentalist with an eye for the essentials of the problem. Throughout his long research life he remained open-minded about various schools of psychology and unconvinced on the various rival theories concerning the physiological basis of memory. He was, however, quick to see the basic weaknesses in the various brain models that fellow psychologists were always confidently erecting, and the first to feel the sharpness of his attack were the Behaviourists. Lashley swiftly realised that the attractive simplicity of the Pavlov/Watson argument was that the basic unit in learning consisted of a fundamentally simple physiological system, a neural reflex arc. In ordinary terms this could be looked on as a chain of cells connecting from, say, the retina through the higher centres of the brain (where the chain would be forged) down to the muscle or set of muscles which constituted motor output. In other words, a light would strike the retina, a number of cells would fire. These in turn would excite cortical cells which had, by prior conditioning, become linked into a reflex arc. Finally these would, quite mechanically, induce the appropriate muscular response. The memory itself constituted the connecting cells in the cortex, and this memory had been established by the learning or conditioning process. Lashley then realised that a memory unit, or an engram as he named it, must be represented by a particular set of cells in a particular part of the brain. In principle, therefore, one should be able to discover these sets of cells and find out what kind of memory is located in what part of the brain.

Lashley's technique was again that of surgical destruction of tissue and using this he performed one of the most remarkable experiments in the history of modern psychology and physiology. His findings created a shock of disbelief and con-

troversy, and their full implications are still not fully understood today—about 50 years after he performed the experiment. Taking a large number of rats, he trained them until they were highly familiar with a complicated maze. He then proceeded to remove from each rat a small portion of cortical tissue, taking a different area but an equivalent amount from each rat. In due course he had removed from his collection of rats the equivalent of one complete brain, though no individual animal had had more than 5 per cent of its cortical tissue destroyed. He then took another set of rats, trained them in the maze, and again removed the equivalent of a brain, but this time taking 10 per cent from each rat. With a further sample he went through the procedure again, but removed a quarter of each rat's brain, and in his final group he had a limited number of animals, each of which had had half its cortex removed. See if you can work out what he found. Remember that if the memory or engram consisted of a series of linked cells then one might expect that these would be found in one relatively small segment of the brain. Interrupting the chain at any point should presumably destroy or grossly handicap memory. Now from the simple behaviourist point of view, most people would have to predict that one or two rats whose hunk of cortex removed had featured the conditioned reflexes involving the maze, would be completely clueless when placed in it. The engram would have been removed. This would then tell the experimenter, as Lashley had hoped, which part of the brain dealt with such tasks as maze learning. Other animals, who had not lost their maze engram would show no detriment in their performance of this task. To his amazement, and to everyone else's for that matter, Lashley found that his first group of rats, each of whom had lost about 5 per cent of cortical tissue, were apparently totally unaffected by the surgery, running the maze just as well as they did before! The rat with bigger chunks of tissue removed were slightly more affected, but even those with only half a brain left were still able to run the maze fairly competently. The loss of memory seemed to be somewhat proportional to the amount of tissue removed, but *not in any way to the area removed*! In other words, the mysterious engram did not seem to be located in any single spot, and Lashley was forced to conclude that it looked as though learning and memory were a function of the whole brain rather than just part of it.

As could be imagined, these findings were not well received by the conditioned reflex advocates and numerous attempts made to repeat them merely served to support these first findings. They were received enthusiastically by the Gestalt psychologists, who saw them as another example of their argument that the brain must be considered as an integrated whole and not as simply a bundle of conditioned reflexes.

The next strong—perhaps the strongest—anti-Behaviourist argument came from one of the Gestalt school founders, Wolfgang Kohler. His findings were disclosed in his important book, *The Mentality of Apes*, which can be bought in paperback and which everyone interested in psychology should read. Kohler, who was one of those clever scientists who manage to find themselves work in exotic parts of the world, conducted his critical experiments at the Primate Research Station in the Canary Islands. Here he watched with great interest the considerable learning skills of the higher apes, such as chimpanzees, and quickly arrived at the conclusion that conditioned reflex theory was not adequate to explain the scope of their intellectual behaviour. His most famous observation concerned the never-to-be-forgotten chimpanzee, Sultan. Kohler had noticed that chimpanzees will play about with sticks and similar devices in their cage, which they seem to use as toys. He then began to wonder whether the monkeys could ever be induced to use them as tools, so after placing potential implements inside Sultan's cage he then put a banana on the other side of the bars just outside its reach. After a bit of fruitless stretching the ape took one of the sticks and pulled the banana in. Now this in itself is a remarkable achievement, and if the ape had actually "worked out" the solution then it would have been suggestive of very much higher thought processes in the animal than had hitherto been believed possible. However, it could be reasonably argued that the chimpanzee had seen some other person or animal using the stick as a tool and was therefore merely imitating, an action which could, with a bit of latitude, be thought of in behaviouristic terms. Kohler's next step put paid to that point of view. He placed in the cage several sticks of various lengths which could be fitted together to form a longer one, and, taking care not to show this technique to the monkey, again set a banana outside the bars but out of reach of any one single stick. After scratching round fruitlessly with various sticks and making aggrieved noises, Sultan began to play rather aimlessly with the sticks, occasionally fitting them together by chance. Suddenly Kohler, who was watching, saw the chimpanzee fit two sticks together, stare at them for a moment and then, as if making a decision, walk rapidly to the side of the cage and with this new long pole pull the banana in. The moment of comprehension when the ape " realised " what he could do Kohler wittily termed the " ah-ha reflex," a phrase which sums up beautifully a sensation we all understand and which was totally unaccounted for by the Pavlovian approach to the problem.

(g) Later Developments in Learning Theory

You may have the feeling that Behaviourism, conditioned reflex theory, and its attendant experimental studies are more or less worthless and a hindrance rather than a help to the development of modern psychology. This is far from the truth. The point is that despite its vigorous self-confidence and contempt for " introspective " approaches to psychology, Behaviourism really only falls down through its pretentions to providing a *complete* theory of mind and brain. The Behaviourist experiments still work, and there is undoubtedly such a thing as the conditioned reflex, though one has next to no idea, from the physiological point of view, how it is laid down. Throughout the 1930s and beyond, psychologists supporting the Behaviourist position performed thousands of ingenious and often highly imaginative experiments to back up their ideas, these always being subject to counter-attack from the opposition, most of whom were followers of the Gestalt school. For years arguments raged over Kohler's " insight " study with the chimpanzees, and became even hotter when experiments claiming to demonstrate " insight " in lesser creatures, such as rats, were performed. Gradually, under intense pressure, the Behaviourist hard-line softened, the pretence that animals were no more than bundles of totally automatic reflexes was quietly abandoned. Once this occurred, and the Behaviourist method was put to work studying the functioning of living systems, then experimental psychology was set for a boom. Of the most significant features of the conditioned-reflex method, as exemplified by Pavlov's original experiments, was its usefulness for examining the nature of animal perception. Offhand one might wonder how it could be possible to tell what an animal sees, or more exactly, how fine is its capacity for perceptual discrimination. How could one find out whether a rat could tell the difference between a triangle and a square and between one colour and another? One can ask humans, but rats . . .? In the case of colours, what one could do would be to train the creature to respond to a red light, and then gradually alter its hue in the direction of another colour, say blue. If, before one had made much of a change in hue, the animal was ceasing to respond then one would know that it was detecting the change of hue. As for shape perception, the problem is even easier. In the very early days Pavlov conditioned his dogs to respond positively (*i.e.*, with saliva) to a circle, and negatively (*i.e.*, raising paw to avoid shock) when a rather angular ellipse was shown to it. Then he gradually made the circle more and more like an ellipse, and the ellipse more and more like a circle. Up to a point he got clear-cut appropriate responses, until the pattern lay somewhere in between. At this point the dog, poor creature, had a nervous breakdown, which wasn't too nice for it, but which told Pavlov a lot about its sensory and perceptual

processes. While on these slightly macabre topics it might be worth mentioning that today dogs and rats have largely been supplanted for behaviouristic studies by a rather quaint choice of animal—the pigeon. The fact is that pigeons have been found to have quite remarkable powers of sensory discrimination and will peck away at buttons to get food or avoid electric shocks for hours on end. So good is the pigeon at telling the difference between patterns that it was even once proposed for a fantastic rôle in modern warfare—not its traditional job of carrying messages from spies but, believe it or not, as the control centre for a flying bomb! In the early days of guided missiles the kind of electrical equipment available was too bulky, cumbersome and unreliable to be easily put into flying bombs. This was particularly true about the equipment necessary to allow the bomb to select the correct target at the other end. One bright psychologist argued that the pigeon would be an inexpensive, compact, and reliable " pilot " for a flying bomb. The device, complete with pigeon in a little cabin, could be launched off on course and when the bird spotted the target (say an enemy battleship) which it had been previously trained to recognise, it would peck at the appropriate button and that would be that! So far as one can tell the idea was never implemented, which is probably a good thing for us humans—to say nothing of the pigeons. The idea might be described as one of the less fruitful to come from Pavlov's original idea and serves to remind us that psychology, just as any other science, can be properly or improperly used, depending upon circumstances and the individuals involved. But let us now return to the basic question—what is the actual nature of the learning process or the memory trace?

(h) The Nature of the Engram.

Earlier we said that there were three broad approaches to the problem of the memory trace, the neurological, the electrical, and the biochemical.

(1) *The Neurological.*

This is probably the kind of model that Pavlov would put forward today if he were alive. To understand it, remember that the conditioned reflex is essentially a chain of cells running from sense organ to motor-output (finger, paw, eyeblink, whatever). The cells of course were there in the first place, built into the animal from birth. It is the connections between cells, the links in the chain that are forged in the learning process. Fine, but how *are* the connections formed? Why one chain rather than another? A number of attempts have been made to solve this one, perhaps the most ingenious in recent years coming from the Canadian psychologist D. O. Hebb, an architect incidentally of the sensory deprivation experiments, and one of the first psychologists to be elected as a Fellow of the Royal Society. Hebb had been impressed by the discovery that nerve cells were frequently adorned with tiny bumps or knobs which tended to cluster at the points where the cell made contact with other cells—the *synapse.* There was even some suggestion from microscopic studies that these synaptic knobs tended to become larger and more profuse in the brains of more mature animals. Suppose, Hebb argued, that when a nerve cell was fired, it made contact with another via a synaptic knob and thus triggered the second cell into action. Suppose also that each time a synapse was bridged via a contact knob, this knob grew a little, as though through exercise, and thus made better contact. This, as time went on, would significantly raise the likelihood of a nervous impulse crossing at this point. If one can imagine the process repeated with a whole series of cells, then one can see that repeated firings would also increase the likelihood of particular chains of cells being activated, thus wearing a kind of path through the nervous system down which the neural impulse would " prefer " to travel. This Hebb suggested, could be the basis of the conditioned reflex—simply a connection made progressively easier each time the route was travelled.

Hebb's theory attracted a good deal of attention when it was first published over 20 years ago, first because it seemed to fit the known physiological facts (such as they were) and second because it seemed to get over one of the awful difficulties facing any neurological theory of learning—the experiments of Lashley. Recapping briefly, these showed that the memory trace or engram for a particular task was not located in any one small section of the brain. Now Hebb's synaptic knob model implied that the initial path followed by a nervous impulse might be pretty random throughout the cortex, wandering here and there until, with repeated firings, it became established. This would quite possibly be a rather straggly chain and not necessarily the shortest distance between two points. Add to this the fact that the acquisition of a complex habit, such as learning a maze, would obviously depend upon thousands, possibly hundreds of thousands, of these neural links being established, and one can begin to see that Lashley's experimental results no longer seem to fly in the face of reason. Removal of any single chunk of cortical tissue would simply serve to remove a more or less random selection of the neural chains serving as the maze-memory. The more one took out, the worse the memory of the maze would be, but no single piece removed would ever eliminate the whole of the memory! To many people Hebb's theory, crude though it might be, fairly tackles the apparent paradox of Lashley's results. Others are not so sure. Its main default, the intervening years have shown, is that his nice ideas about the growth of synaptic knobs and their significance as contact points between cells are probably no longer valid. Today their function, and even their existence in the form that Hebb discussed, is questioned by many physiologists. Furthermore, for various reasons, there has been a strong shift towards the point of view that whatever form the learning process takes it is unlikely to involve changes in neural tissue—at least of such magnitude. To many psychologists and their colleagues, changes in the molecular structure of the cell must be involved. Before considering the evidence for this hypothesis, we need to examine briefly the Gestalt psychologists' attempt to account for learning and memory.

(2) Electrical Field Theory.

We have been talking of the Gestalt psychologists without pointing out an interesting fact—that the two principal founders were first trained as physicists! Jumping the broad gap between physics and psychology might seem a bit much, but Wolfgang Kohler was one who did it, and in doing so he injected into his theorising some of the ideas basic to his native topic. In the main this involved the concepts of electrical field theory. Without going into this in boring detail, it so happens that an electrical source, either in the form of a battery, a current flowing down a wire or whatever, spouts electrons in its immediate neighbourhood and these constitute an electromagnetic field. As the name implies, the most striking example of such a field is to be seen in the ordinary common-or-garden magnet, and the structure of the field can be observed by placing the magnet in a large mass of iron filings. Now Kohler and his friends argued that the brain was a potent source of electromagnetic energy and ought, therefore, to create a field within and around its tissue. The field would be powerful enough to modify incoming electrical input from the senses and to some extent impose its own pattern on it. Hence the Gestalt " laws " of perceptual organisation. This would be a two-way process, however, for sensory input, no matter how feeble, would impose at least minor changes on the structure of the cerebral field. Such changes, the Gestaltists argued, would constitute the basis of learning. It was a bold, if somewhat implausible point of view, and was treated as a serious alternative to the Pavlovian conditioned reflex ideas for at least a period. It had one or two gross defects, however, which even the Gestalt psychologists found worrying. In the

first place, no kind of recording device seemed able to pick up any signs of permanent or semi-permanent electrical fields surrounding the brain. The EEG seemed to be a rhythmic picture of electrical change within, rather than of a static, powerful field highly resistant to change. Secondly, there is the odd data from electro-shock therapy. This much-maligned method of treating highly-depressed psychiatric patients relies on jolting the brain with a powerful electric shock, a not particularly pleasant process which nevertheless generally brings a notable remission in patients' symptoms. The point here is not to argue the pros and cons of ECT, as it is called, but to indicate that such tremendous shocks should be enough to seriously disturb any electrical fields, no matter how well-established, with presumably drastic effects on memory. In fact, long-term memory is totally unaffected by ECT, though, as the Gestalt supporters were quick to point out, there is short-term amnesia for events immediately preceding the electric shock. Thirdly, and finally, as it happens, there is the clinching experimental work of Lashley—not his tissue-removal experiment, but yet another in the catalogue of his remarkable repertoire. Lashley's procedure was as follows. He first taught a large number of rats a particular maze. Then he inserted in their cortex very fine sheets of gold leaf—a notorious destroyer of electrical fields. He then ran the rats through the same maze again, and found no evidence of any detriment in their performance. He also taught other rats the maze after they had had the gold leaf implanted, and found that they learnt it with no undue difficulty. After this work the Gestalt battle cry never seemed so loud or so convincing again. It is doubtful, actually, whether they ever really believed the electrical field theory, but it was a nice idea while it lasted.

(3) The Biochemical Argument: Some Fresh Surprises.

The memory capacity of the human brain is absolutely enormous. It has been calculated that it is quite capable of storing all the information ever fed into it—in other words there is no need for anything ever to be thrown out of store to make room for fresh material. The real problem in this case is not finding enough room to pump in information, but in finding a sufficiently efficient system to pull it out rapidly. Not only do psychologists believe that the brain has this almost limitless storage capacity, but they also have some evidence that all the information fed in, no matter how trivial, actually *is* stored! Some of the most exciting evidence to back up this belief has come from studies made during human brain surgery. These studies are a trifle gruesome and the squeamish might like to jump a paragraph or two here.

For a particular type of surgery—such as the excision of a brain tumour—it is necessary to remove a portion of the cranium and for various reasons it is advisable to perform the entire operation with the patient fully conscious. This is not so horrific as all that, for the brain itself has no pain-detecting cells and the initial opening can be made with a local anaesthetic. One or two scientifically-minded surgeons, notably Dr. Wilder Penfield, have taken the opportunity presented by this surgical requirement to perform certain experiments which have turned out to be of immense interest. With the patient's permission and co-operation, Penfield stimulated selected exposed portions of their cortex with tiny electric currents. Moving round from sensory area to sensory area he found that his tiny electrical stimuli provoked characteristic sensations from the patients. In the visual areas they might " see " lights, colours, etc., in the auditory areas " hear " sounds, and in the temporal lobes, get impressions of smells, taste, etc. Stranger still, Penfield found that certain parts of the so-called association areas of cortex, when stimulated, led to the patient recalling specific memories, often of apparently forgotten items. One woman got a vivid impression of herself in a kitchen of a former home and hearing the voice of her mother, long since dead. Others reported equally specific memories, sometimes with fragments of speech or conversation attached, quite often of items which the patients reported they "hadn't thought of for years." One possible implication for this exciting work is, as we have said, that *all* information that has ever been put into the brain is stored as memory just in case it should ever be needed again. If this is so, then to most psychologists the idea that the memory trace is laid down in the form of major structural changes in the cell body (such as with synaptic knobs) is no longer tenable. There simply aren't enough cells to cope. But suppose that the engram is laid down *within* the cell, at sub-microscopic level in the form of, perhaps, the rearrangement of the specialised molecular structure. Since no one has ever got a really good look at a molecule, either in the nervous system or out of it, this might seem to be a bit of optimistic guesswork, but there is in fact some strange evidence to back the idea up. To consider this we must acquaint ourselves with one of the lowliest creatures capable of learning— the little flatworm, planaria. There is a good deal of argument about how far down the animal kingdom some form of learning can take place. Some workers even claim to have demonstrated memory mechanism in tiny single-celled creatures such as amoeba or its hairy cousin, paramecia, but you can be sure that any information stored was of the simplest and most rudimentary kind. It is when we get to the simplest form of worms, and planaria is one of these, that something closer to memory in the real sense can be clearly demonstrated. Typical of the kind of task which planaria manage, albeit with a good deal of intellectual effort, is to turn right rather than left at a little junction in order to get food or avoid an electric shock. They can also be conditioned to wince to a light being switched on when this is always followed by an electric shock— rather like Pavlov's dogs. Now planaria has the most rudimentary, almost non-existent central nervous system. It has a front end, shaped rather like an arrow with tiny light-sensitive organs in it, and which is clearly its head. It also has a back end which the charitable would call a tail. The question now is—in what part of the tiny body are memories laid down? The head would seem to be the most likely bet, though you might feel it would be hard to tell for sure. At this point the psychologist makes use of another of planaria's interesting features—its ability to regenerate tissue with ease. Take a knife and slice off planaria's tail and both ends swim away, one rather more efficiently than the other. Now in due course the head section will produce a new tail and—rather fantastically—the tail will produce a new head! Planaria can do other odd things too. Cut down the centre of its head without actually removing any tissue and in due course the two half-heads will regenerate into two full heads, producing a peculiar but rather neat looking creature. If one makes several flaps, instead of just two, you end up with lots and lots of heads on one body and get a very odd-looking planaria indeed. All this is very interesting, but the exercise has more point than this. In the first case, ask yourself a question; suppose you teach planaria a little maze and then slice the head into two. Now, of the regenerating heads, which has got the "memory" of the maze stored in it? Left; right; both; neither? Actually, the answer is both, and this should give some clue as to the answer to the next question. Cut a maze-trained planaria in half (head and tail) and let the respective sections develop again into a full creature. One would certainly expect that the head part plus its new tail would be able to perform its little task without much trouble, but what about the tail with its new head? The answer is that this too can "run" the maze. If this seems to be contradicting everything we've said about learning and the brain in general up to now, then in a way it is. We must remember that planaria is an exceedingly simple creature with no CNS to speak of and no nerve cells of the kind found in higher animals. The engram, wherever it is, is certainly not formed by the development of synaptic knobs or by the modification of complex electrical fields. Furthermore, as it is evidently stored in tail as well as head section, then it must presumably be laid down in most, if not necessarily all, of the animal's body cells. This is the point where the biochemists step in

and argue that it is not the outside but rather the interior structure of the cell that is modified through learning. Odd indeed, but there is odder yet to come. Researchers got a collection of planaria and taught them a particular task— turning right in a simple maze and then took an equivalent number of planaria with no experience of this kind. They then collected the first group and whirled them round in a mixing bowl until all that was left was a homogeneous planaria soup, and repeated the process with the other, untrained group. They now fed the two kinds of soup (planaria will eat more or less anything that's hanging round) to different groups of totally untrained planaria and subsequently trained these in the original right-turn task. This produced an extraordinary result. The planaria who had been fed the soup consisting of trained planaria seemed to learn the maze task significantly quicker than those who had been fed the untrained soup! You will know enough about experimental psychology by now to realise that these results caused immense controversy, and a series of experiments were immediately launched by workers who had found the first result incredible. The controversy, incidentally, still rages as many of the attempts to repeat the experiments have not worked, but the original protagonists still maintain the validity of their results. It is not hard to see why the critics get so hot under the collar, for the implications of the findings, if valid, will throw into question just about every theoretical approach to learning to date. Since the planaria were thoroughly mashed up, no neural connections or even any formal kind of organisation within the system would remain to carry the maze information across to the cannibal planaria. Furthermore, one would have thought that the digestive processes of the cannibals would have completed the process of destruction. How then could the original maze habit, or traces of it, be possibly preserved and carried over? No one on either side of the argument has been able to offer up any convincing explanation, except that if the results are valid, then the maze habit, in the case of planaria at any rate, must be stored right down at molecular level—in other words at such a microscopic level that any mixing and digestion could have little or no effect on it. But even if the planaria results *are* valid, would the same thing necessarily apply to humans? Not necessarily, but if a process works for one living system it could in principle work for another, and we must remember our conclusion that the brain's enormous memory store suggests that modification of the neurone itself would be at too gross a level. It may well be that we shall find the brain puts down information in more than one way. There is reasonable evidence, for example, that many animals and humans are equipped with two kinds of memory store—a short-term, and possibly highly unstable one, and a long-term, more or less perpetual system. Information fed into our brains might go initially to the short-term store where it is filtered for relevance or general usefulness. If unwanted for some reason it might be eliminated, but if wanted, passed on to the longer-term system. Perhaps the short-term memory (the kind that allows you to "momentarily" remember a new telephone number) is electrical and the long-term biochemical, neurological or both. At this moment psychologist and physiologists across the world are concentrating on these exciting problems and perhaps, within the next few years, we shall have some new answers and, quite certainly, some fresh surprises.

(i) Unsolved Problems.

This section has attempted to raise some of the issues confronting psychologists in their attempt to solve one of the main mysteries of the brain— how information is stored and processed within it. Although a fair bit has been learned in the past decades, it has really served to show that the problem is much more complicated than the earlier workers ever imagined. Furthermore, you will have noticed that precious little has been said about how the information is extracted, for the very good reason that precious little is known about this. Curiously some interesting clues are beginning to come from the study of computers, man's own specially-created slave brains. These are already capable of storing quite immense quantities of information, and engineers have been working steadily at improving methods of storing information and of getting it out in a hurry. In recent years the computer engineers and the psychologists have been tending to get together and pool their ideas—with some interesting results (*see* Sleeping and Dreaming, P 59–62). To more and more scientists it has become increasingly obvious that the study of the brain is real ground for interdisciplinary contact, and that contributions to its study can come equally from psychologists, physiologists, physicists, engineers, mathematicians, educationalists, and so on. The recently formed Brain Research Association, for example, is composed of scientists from practically every discipline, with psychologists and physiologists, who are traditionally the kingpins in brain science, making up no more than 25 per cent of its ranks. Perhaps the really big problems in brain research will only come from multi-disciplinary teams of this kind. But this is something of a digression and we must now pass on from learning and memory to the lesser, but no less interesting problem of motivation.

IV. MOTIVATION.

(1) Why Does an Animal Do One Thing Rather Than Another?

This question aptly sums up the problem of animal and human motivation, an important facet of modern psychological research. As is always the case with psychology, perhaps more so than with other fields of science, what initially seem to be straightforward questions, designed to elicit straightforward answers, become steadily more complicated on close inspection. The odd, almost philosophical difficulties surrounding motivation are a good example. Why *does* an animal do one thing rather than another? Because it wants to, is the stock reply—a reply which actually doesn't get anywhere at all. To say that the reason for doing something is because the doer *likes it* is no explanation, merely renaming the problem so that it comes up in a different guise. It so happens that we tend to like doing the things we do, though of course this doesn't always apply. We certainly like to eat, but do we eat principally because we like it or because the food is essential to our survival? Perhaps the key is tied up here somewhere, and the rock-bottom cause for all animal and human behaviour lies in the need to keep the individual creature alive. Well, that will certainly do for food and water, but it clearly doesn't work for other common activities, such as sex. In the long term the survival of all living things depends upon sexual activity but animals certainly don't understand this and humans only found out the link between the sexual act and conception a millenium or so ago. And anyone who believes that people indulge in sex solely to allow the human species to survive is very naïve indeed. Now the situation gets even more complicated. It seems as if we make love because we like it, with the long-term result being that the species survives. But what can be the link, in physiological terms, between liking something and it " doing us good "? And just to complicate matters even more, supposing that we accept this link, how do we explain other common patterns of human behaviour? Why do some people like going to football matches or art galleries? Why don't they go there to eat the footballers or the paintings, and how is the survival of the human species helped by such practices anyway? Having muddled the issue thoroughly—or, rather, showed it up in its true light—we can now go on to see how psychologists have set to work to try to unravel it. They have not got very far, but they have got somewhere.

(2) The Mechanical Tortoise.

The first people to face up to the problems raised above were the Behaviourists. In their gallant attempt to explain human and animal behaviour in mechanistic terms they realised that they would have to account for the tendency of animals to set out to do things rather than simply engage in random, diffuse activity, and they thought this could be fairly simply handled. They were most anxious, of course, to avoid explaining different types of behaviour in terms of different goals—to suggest that an animal had got a goal in mind was to imply that it had a mind and furthermore some kind of " picture of the future " in it. To begin with they took the simplest possible form of mechanical analogy. Imagine a clockwork mouse, which when wound up runs across the floor. What caused it to do so? The clockwork and the energy tied up in the spring, of course, with its direction determined by such matters as the orientation of its wheels, the angle of the floor, etc. Anyone saying that the toy crossed the floor because it wanted to would be being silly. Similarly, the Behaviourists stated, one should be able to avoid the same kind of inference when observing the movements of a real mouse. If the response is that the real mouse can do a good deal more than just run across a floor—can squeak, change direction, avoid cats and eat cheese—then the reply in essence is that one could build a mechanical mouse to do that as well, provided one had the time and ingenuity. The more complicated and versatile the mechanical mouse the harder it would become to tell the difference between the two, and when one had two apparently identical mice, would one still talk about one " wanting " to cross a floor and the other doing it purely automatically? Was there an important difference anyway? Critics of Behaviourism argued that indeed there was a difference. The " real " mouse ate the cheese because it satisfied a need for the food, whereas the mechanical mouse, no matter how many bogus sounds of enjoyment it made as it munched the food, was merely going through an essentially meaningless mechanical process. This is a dangerous argument, for suppose that one decided to power the artificial mouse not by clockwork but by the combustion of cheese and made it so that it would stop when its inner store of cheese ran out . . . one would now have an artificial mouse with a " need " for cheese as great as that of its biological counterpart. If this seems an unlikely step to take, consider the case of Grey Walter's mechanical tortoise. In an effort to replicate some of the conditions of behaviour, the great English psychologist, Dr. Grey Walter of the Burden Neurological Institute, constructed a tortoise which exhibited some of the paramount properties of living creatures. His tortoise—a shell on wheels with no pretentions to looking like an animal—was powered by storage batteries which drove a motor allowing it to run around on the floor. Its movements were far from aimless, for it was also equipped with photocells in its head capable of detecting areas of light or dark. A series of simple switches inside were arranged so that when the tortoise's batteries were fully charged, the device would move towards dark areas of a room, finding its way underneath chairs and tables, carefully working its way round books, human feet, etc., placed in its way. With batteries low, a different switching arrangement would come into operation and the device would now tend to avoid dark areas and seek out light ones—in particular the light inside its " hutch " where a battery charge was conveniently situated. Once inside the hutch Grey Walter's tortoise would connect up to the battery charger, later emerging " replenished " to set out for dark places again! Here the Behaviourist argument emerges most strongly. It is not, of course, that Grey Walter had manufactured a living thing—no one is making that claim—but rather a matter of whether the tortoise's tendency to seek out its battery for recharging, etc., constituted a need in the same sense as does the real mouse's need for cheese. This is a big question which you will probably have to think out for yourself. In the meanwhile let's see how the Behaviourists attempted to translate animal behaviour into similar terms.

(3) Drives and Needs.

The Behaviourist position can be summed up as an attempt at describing animal behaviour in the simplest possible way, and to do this they evolved the concept of " Drive." A drive is described as something which causes an animal to perform a particular act, and the ideal position, from the behaviouristic viewpoint, would be to find that all animal activity could be explained in terms of a limited number of drives. To begin with things looked simple and promising, for it appeared as if a drive could be thought of as something that promoted bodily well-being. For example, when an animal is short of food it is running out of power. This causes a sensation known as " hunger " which signals a bodily " need," and this in turn sets in motion a chain of activity which culminates in eating. When the food has been ingested, the need is satisfied, the hunger vanishes and the drive is reduced. The same argument applies to thirst and, with a bit of modification, to sex. In the latter case if an animal does not engage in sexual activity for a given period of time, certain substances build up in the body, the hormonal system becomes unbalanced, etc., and a need builds up in the body, which gives rise to a drive. This in turn pushes the creature towards sexual activity with a suitable mate. Carry this on just a bit more and include a " need " to escape painful situations and you've practically got the whole of animal behaviour sewn up. What's more it is sewn up in a very convincing way because the needs and drives are not vague and ambiguous, but relate directly to vital bodily processes which if not operating properly will cause the animal's death. All animal behaviour could be explained in terms of a drive to (i) reduce hunger, (ii) reduce thirst, (iii) reduce pain, and (iv) achieve sex. To those who didn't want to talk about " achievement," which seemed to imply that an animal was actually setting out to do something, then the final one could be rephrased (iv) to reduce sexual tension. An animal in a state of need would be activated by some or all of these drives and would continue to " behave " until all drives were reduced. Protagonists of this delightfully simple point of view even showed how learning theory could benefit from drive-reduction ideas; a pattern of behaviour or conditioned reflex would be established, they claimed, if at its conclusion a drive was reduced. If no drive-reduction took place, then the behaviour pattern would not be learned. In the 'thirties and 'forties a number of mathematically inclined psychologists even attempted to express this in the form of sets of equations which looked enormously impressive on paper but which, alas, bore little relationship in practice to the way living animals actually behaved. For example, people soon realised that a bit of a problem emerged for an animal if all its drives were set at maximum, as it were, and all the appropriate drive-reducing stimuli were at hand. Take a rat, severely deprived of food and water, and place it in a cage with both available. What is it going to do first, eat or drink? Presumably it will be pushed in the direction suggested by the strongest drive. Using this as an idea it was decided that it ought to be possible to rank animal drives in order of strength by a simple test. Place a rat deprived of either food, water, or sexual activity in a box facing the necessary drive-reduction stimulus across an electrified grid. Now, how strong an electric shock is the rat prepared to put up with in order to fulfil its need? Experimenters found that thirst was the most effective stimulus, food next, and sex third. This was all fine until they found that rats satiated in all three modes would still occasionally cross the grid even when there was nothing on the other side! Now what kind of drive could be operating here? Furthermore, they found that an animal, again supplied with plenty of food, water, etc., would still run through a complicated maze and learn it pretty well, despite the lack of drive-reduction at the other end! Before long the theorists found themselves rather glumly proposing " exploration " or curiosity-reducing drives to account for the well-known fact that animals like to roam about all over the place. This, naturally, allows one to have a completely comprehensive theory of behaviour and learning in drive-reduction terms, but with the penalty of converting a simple, fairly sharply defined theory, tied closely to describable bodily requirements, into a complicated, diffuse,

and far less convincing one. If any activity not explained in terms of the original drives can now be accounted for in terms of a reduction of an exploratory drive, then one has an " explanation " of the behaviour. But to many people's minds it is no better than those around before the whole concept of drives and needs was introduced. Similarly, there was a certain neatness and utility to the idea that a pattern of behaviour could be learned if at its conclusion a drive such as hunger or thirst was reduced. This neatness vanishes when we are told that an animal has learnt something else because its curiosity was satisfied, or the opposite, that it was not learnt because its curiosity drive was *not* reduced! Clearly the root of all these difficulties lies in the refusal of many psychologists to admit that a creature or a person does something or learns something because it likes it. Fair enough. We have already pointed out how subjective is the idea of an animal doing something because it " wants to," and the job of the psychologist is to try to define behaviour objectively rather than subjectively. What was clearly needed was some definable, describable physiological process which could correspond to " pleasure," and until this was found psychologists could proceed no further in the field of motivation. In 1954 experiments were published which gave them the green light.

(4) The Pleasure Centre.

The arrival of microelectrode recording techniques allowed numerous experimental studies of the animal and even, occasionally, the human brain in action to be made. In a prolonged assault on the inner intricacies of the cerebral cortex and lower control centres psychologists and physiologists began the elaborate job of mapping the brain, defining as rigidly as they could which areas were devoted to what function. In many cases the areas they stimulated seemed to be " silent," *i.e.*, provoking no obvious response from the animal. Others, however, were more dramatically active. In 1956 the American James Olds and the Englishman Peter Milner were studying the responses of rats with electrodes implanted in what is known as the septal area of the brain, a spot beneath a body known as the corpus callosum. Animals stimulated with low voltage electric currents in this area seemed to behave in an odd way—almost as if they were enjoying the experience. For many years it had been known that stimulating the area known as the hypothalamus could produce symptoms of rage in animals, the creatures responding as though angered or threatened, the " sham rage " switching off immediately the electric stimulus ceased. Similarly areas had been found which when stimulated would cause dozy, apparently sleepy behaviour. Now here was something very different and Olds and Milner began to suspect that they had hit on something akin to a " pleasure " centre. To test this they designed a weird electrical circuit, surely one of the oddest ever to be seen in a laboratory. From the electrode in the rat's septal region a wire ran to the battery providing the electrical stimulus. In the rat's cage they placed a lever, and connected this to the battery in such a way that when the lever was pressed the battery emitted a single pulse, thus allowing the rat—if it wanted to—to stimulate this particular area of the brain. Although they had half suspected that the rats might occasionally give themselves a jolt in this " pleasure area," no one had anticipated the extent of the rats' involvement. All animals, once they had discovered the trick of pushing the lever, went into a sustained surge of lever pressing, keeping the activity up for literally hours on end. In fact there was some suggestion that they might have kept it up for ever, had not physical exhaustion sooner or later intervened. Given the choice of alternative levers providing food, water, or the chance to stimulate their septal regions, all rats reliably chose the latter, even those who had been substantially deprived of opportunities to eat or drink for some time. The lack of apparent satiation of the effect was one of the really odd things about the discovery. No human or animal appetite has ever been found which cannot be satisfied, if only for short periods. Only where some severe pathology is involved, such as with a disease or brain tumour, do the normal appetites remain unquenched. But here was something quite different—an appetite which seemed to have boundless depths and which outrode any of the other paramount needs of the animal. It was for this reason that Olds and Milner hypothesised that they had hit on the centre in the brain which mediates the sensation which we humans know of as " pleasure." How surprising is it that some such centre exists? Not very. When we do something we like, be it eating, drinking, or even going to a football match, then the feeling of pleasure that we get must be matched by some parallel process in the brain, and it could well be that this is located in some convenient but specific centre. Olds and Milner, incidentally, found that their animals would very swiftly learn a task if they were rewarded by a session on the pleasure centre, and here perhaps another important point emerges. There has always been some evidence, though the matter is by no means settled, that learning was somehow improved if following the performance of the desired task, a " reward " such as food, drink, sex, etc., was given. The big question is, what kind of signal is given to the memory system to denote when something is to be permanently laid down? Olds and Milner appeared to have provided one possible answer, and one that would have greatly satisfied Pavlov, Watson, and their immediate successors, the reinforcing stimulus—the message that declares that something will be learnt—is a message that has passed through the pleasure centre. The validity of this idea is still uncertain, but it has the merit of answering an age-old question in reasonably simple fashion, and also of helping us towards the solution of an even more venerable philosophical one—the nature of pleasure itself.

(5) Emotion.

This is one of the most misunderstood words in the psychologist's vocabulary and is a source of endless confusion. The trouble is it means so many things to so many different people. To the psychologist, however, it has a fairly specific meaning and we must try to get some idea of what this is. Only by doing so can we avoid falling into such traps as to say, " Animals cannot feel emotions," or " Computers can never think because they have no emotions." First let's attempt to nail the word " emotion " to the wall and try to analyse it. When we talk of people being emotional, what exactly do we mean? That they tend to weep a lot, get easily angered? Sorrow and anger are emotions, that is clear. But is not love an emotion too? Do we mean that emotional people tend to fall in love a good deal? Or do we mean that their love is deeper than others—or perhaps shallower? Already some confusion is creeping in. Let's ask now how we know that someone is emotional, or in an emotional state. The answer is probably that they exhibit a characteristic behaviour pattern which allows us to judge. If they wave their fists, go red in the face and shout, then we might infer that they were angry. Of course they could be acting and merely pretending to be angry, in which case what is the dividing line between the real and the simulated emotion? The answer would seem to be that the latter was not accompanied by an internal *feeling* of a special kind, and this now tells us that there are at least two sides to emotion—subjective psychological state and an external, physiological one. In fact, psychologists find it convenient to consider three aspects. The first is the *behavioural—i.e.* the kind of activity in which the angry or otherwise emotional person engages. This is generally easily detected and is of the waving-arms-around variety. The second is the *physiological*, which consists of considerably more discrete behavioural signs, not always obvious to the observer but which may be detected by suitably sensitive instruments. The third is the *psychological* or introspective, and this refers to the " state of mind " of the individual when he is angry or whatever. This of course cannot be directly sensed by other individuals who rely on the angry person reporting to them " how

he feels." How are these linked together, and what function do they serve?

(a) The Behavioural.

If you fire a pistol behind someone's back they exhibit a very characteristic response, the most common feature of which is that they jump some distance into the air. This may seem desperately obvious, but actually there is a good deal more to the response than that. High speed photography shows that all human beings respond to sudden loud noises by a highly predictable behavioural sequence, of which the jump is just one part, and which bears the name " the startle pattern." It includes a marked hunching of the shoulders, closing the eyes, baring the teeth, and raising the hands in the direction of the face. It doesn't take long to see that these actions, which occur reliably in all human beings, are not random and pointless but serve to help the individual respond rapidly to a dangerous situation. The jump is an alerting response, the eyes are closed to protect them, the hands raised in defence or perhaps to strike, the teeth bared possibly as a threatening or warning sign. Similarly, at a more common emotional level, the waving fists and loud voice of an angry man equip him to some extent for battle. And what of the tears and the cowering posture of a thoroughly frightened individual? Well, these in some way suggest to the aggressor that the battle is over and are signals to him to stop fighting. Men, being natural fighters, tend to do little in the way of crying and will generally scrap on until they are physically incapable of continuing. Women, on the other hand, who are not particularly strong or well-equipped to fight, tend to slip into weeping and submission rather easily, hence the well-known fact that tears are a woman's strongest weapon against a man. (This submissive pattern of behaviour fails dismally of course when the aggressor is a carnivore such as a tiger, when the one submitting is eaten, tears and all.) The very obvious facial expressions made by people in various emotional states led the great Charles Darwin to the view that the type of face made was a good index of what emotion the individual was in the grips of. To test this idea, psychologists took photographs of the facial expressions of people in various emotional states and then asked other people to try to name them. The results were poor, with few people doing better than chance. The only expression reliably recognised and correctly assigned to an emotion was a smile, and even this was occasionally confused with other emotional states such as pain, or even fear. The same experiment performed with movies yielded somewhat better results, and when sound was added results were again improved. The clinching thing, however, seems to be the setting in which the behaviour takes place, for people become very accurate at judging emotions when they see the surroundings in which the other people are behaving. Clearly the external signs of emotion, despite their immediate and rather obvious manifestations, are an unreliable guide to what is going on inside the individual's head. The same argument, incidentally, applies to animals, though somewhat less forcefully. Most animals give pretty explicit signs when they are angry or when they are afraid. One can even detect something suspiciously like guilt in the general pattern of behaviour of a dog which has done something it shouldn't. But can one really talk of a dog " feeling guilty "? If not—why not? Whatever answer you give will be quite as valid as any given by a psychologist.

(b) The Physiological.

The signs and signals we talked about above were all gross, obvious, and yet, as we pointed out, somewhat unreliable. To a large part they seem to be the outward manifestation of an internal process which at the same time serve a useful purpose, as when the startle pattern alerts the individual into a posture suitable for defensive or aggressive action. But what are the finer, physiological manifestations of emotion? These must obviously involve changes in the state of bodily and cerebral activity. Psychologists have pinned down no fewer than 11 distinct facets of human and animal behaviour which give a clear index of changes in emotional states. To give some idea of the complexity of emotional behaviour we will look at each of these briefly.

(1) The first, and perhaps the most obvious, is heart-rate. The heart's job is to pump blood around the body and the blood provides the vital organ supply to the brain. The more intense the activity, the more oxygen is consumed and the more blood needs to be circulated. It should be no surprise therefore to anyone to learn that as activity is stepped up, so heart-rate increases and vice versa. Furthermore, heart-rate tends to accelerate just prior to some important or exciting piece of activity, or even on merely thinking about it, and this means that we have here one index of emotional state. A device known as the electrocardiogram (EKG) can give a very precise picture of heart fluctuations and represents one objective way of plotting this information.

(2) We have already implied another measure, respiration. This increases more or less alongside heart-rate, and is a pretty good index of most emotions. Irregularities of breathing, including variations in the depth of breaths, are a particularly good index of nervousness as most people know and all this can be detected by a suitable instrument.

(3) More or less hand-in-hand with the above come changes in local blood pressure and volume, the facial accompaniments of which—blanching or blushing—are only too obvious. These can be measured by a device known as the pleythsmograph, which is merely a version of the kind of device a doctor uses to measure your blood pressure in a routine medical examination.

(4) A somewhat harder emotional symptom to measure, but very characteristic of most emotional states, is muscle tension and its associate, tremor. In anger, rage, and other aggressive states muscles become tensed to be ready for rapid action and if this is carried too far we get trembling of the limbs—a familiar accompaniment of great nervousness or fright.

All the above are easily discernible indices, amenable to instrumentation but not depending upon it. The remaining manifestations are harder to detect, though just as valuable once one has caught them. Beginning with the most obvious we have:

(5) The pilomotor response, which is a hangover from the days when our ancestors had a good deal more hair than we do today, and which can be seen when a cat's fur fluffs out in rage or fear. In humans today we call it goose-pimples and it is often a precursor to the feeling of full-blooded fear.

(6) Even harder to measure is salivary secretion which is the kind of response Pavlov studied with his dogs. In anxiety or fear the saliva flow tends to be inhibited and we find ourselves with " dry mouths."

(7) An index of emotion which is particularly obvious to the individual is the change in gastrointestinal motility. Movements of the stomach and intestine are brought to a brief but definite halt in strong emotional states with a complementary, and often rather dramatic, surge back to action shortly afterwards. There are plenty of homely and slightly vulgar expressions to describe the consequences of this.

(8) There has been a recent rise of interest in the pupillary response as an index of certain types of emotion. The pupil of the eye tends to dilate in moments of anger or pain with slight dilation occurring during periods of " interest " in something. This has led some clever psychologists who work in the advertising profession to use this as an index of the relative effectiveness of different types of advertisement. All the subjects have to do is look at the subject matter while a recording camera photographs the pupils of their eyes from a distance!

(9) Because the endocrine or glandular system is active in emotional states the chemical constitution of the blood changes markedly as the hormones flow within it, but this index, while potentially useful, is of course abnormally hard to measure directly.

(10) Next we come to the so-called galvanic skin response (GSR) which is in fact nothing more than the electrical resistance of the skin. For various reasons, not properly understood, the resistance of the skin to an electrical current changes with most emotional states, tending to decrease as a function of the intensity of the emotion. This can be detected with a suitable instrument and meter and is perhaps particularly interesting because it is an automatic response which the individual is not consciously aware of. Connect someone up to a GSR meter, tell him that you are going to stick a pin in him and the needle will swing wildly. It is a very effective demonstration of an entirely involuntary response and is generally one of the first experiments that fledgling psychologists perform on each other in their laboratory classes.

(11) Finally there is the EEG, which we referred to earlier on (see Q5). The electrical activity of the brain does change with varying degrees of bodily activity, though what these changes mean is a matter for skilled interpretation.

(c) The Psychological.

You will have noticed that many of the above indices—stomach motility, muscle tension, etc.—have definite physical accompaniments which are only too obvious to the individual experiencing the emotion and it should not be too surprising in the light of all this that an emotional state markedly alters our physical and psychological feelings and sensations. But is this all there is to emotion? Can the age-old human passions of love and hate be reduced to permutations of salivary secretion, blood pressure, pilomotor response and electro-cortical activity? Put so baldly of course the answer is no. Love demands a partner, a setting, a trigger and some temporal span—as does hate. In humans these require the active participation of the complex computer we call the brain, and a background of education, social activity, and some awareness of goals other than the immediate. Nevertheless, the intense physiological and psychological changes which envelop us when we are in love, or when we fight in passion, contribute the better part of the powerful sensations we feel. But which of the three faces of emotion, the behavioural, the physiological, or the psychological is the real or most significant one?

The answer is that no single one predominates for emotion is a complex of all three. When the object of our emotion, be it love, hate, or whatever, is first encountered then mind and body combine to set the individual up for the optimum pattern of responses. This involves some permutation of physical change which, naturally, is reflected in psychological changes of mood. These in turn provoke outward changes on a larger scale which may involve combat or the ritual of love. If this description seems to debase the concept of human emotional response then this is a pity for there is no reason why it should. The powerful forces that thrust men into the numerous passions of the world would have no meaning were they not accompanied by potent changes in bodily state. The artistry that springs from these passions is no fraction diminished because we can identify the physiological and psychological changes that accompany and, to some extent, determine them.

It will have occurred to you that in this section on motivation we have drifted closer and closer to another of the critical areas that psychologists study—the nature of human personality. Psychologists know far less about this area than they would like to, but their century of scientific activity (a small span compared with the history of the more traditional sciences, such as physics) has begun to pay off. In the next and final section we will take a look at what they have done, or have tried to do, in this most fascinating of areas.

V. PERSONALITY AND THINKING.

(1) What Constitutes a Person?

To many people this is the most important single question in psychology and indeed, perhaps, in the combined fields of science and philosophy. What is it that makes up that unique blend of psychological and physiological factors we call "personality"? The answer is, predictably, complicated and before we can even begin to consider it we must attempt to define the problems in the field. In the first place let's consider the most venerable and apparently simplest answer—a person is that thing in the head that thinks, feels, is aware of itself as an individual entity, and which controls a brain and body. This is the answer which probably fits best with the non-technical philosophy of the man-in-the-street and which matches also with a long-standing traditional view fostered by the majority of systems of religious belief. Put another way, it states that human beings are composed of essentially two parts. One of these is physical and consists of the body and its control centre, the brain. The second is non-physical, and is called the mind, soul, spirit, or some similar name. This is a separate entity which controls the body through its brain and while involved in this way must obey the laws of the physical world. It may, however, survive the death of its body (one of the most widespread of religious views of personality) and occasionally, as with telepathy, precognition, etc., may step outside to contact other similar minds in other parts of the world or even take a peek into the future. As we have said, this is an exceedingly widespread view of the nature of personality and it will be the one held by many who read this article. This is now the point where you could ask whether this view is acceptable to psychologists, and that is a fair and proper question. It requires, however, two separate answers. In the first place some psychologists, though certainly not the majority, accept this or some very similar view, but on an entirely personal plane. When they think as scientists, however, most are inclined to disagree with it. Nothing that has been uncovered in the history of experimental psychology, with the possible exception of the very dubious evidence for telepathy, suggests that the human personality is a separate entity to be considered in isolation from brain and body. Psychologists who choose to believe otherwise frankly admit that they do so on the basis of faith or hunch, and argue that even though the scientific facts appear to contradict their beliefs at the moment, perhaps in due course experimental psychology will uncover fresh new material to change the whole picture.

Does "Mind" Exist?

An increasing number of psychologists and brain scientists today take a hard-line on the "spiritual" view of personality, but does this mean that mind does not exist, as the Behaviourists strove so hard to prove? Certainly not. There is clearly a whole range of rich psychological activity which cannot be explained simply in terms of bundles of conditioned reflexes and the like. What seems to have happened in fact is that as animals have evolved via the remorseless processes of evolution, so more and more " power " has been given to the cerebral control centres. At some stage in the evolutionary ladder—it is very hard to say exactly where—the brain ceased to be a purely automatic device and some glimmerings of what we call consciousness began to appear. In the early stages, this probably merely took the form of a " switch " in the brain which allowed the creature to select from one or two alternative modes of action. This capacity would imply

some system within the brain capable of making a " comparison " of the two modes and thus of " standing back from itself." Increase the complexity of the brain and its capacity to select, predict, and determine and you will see that the evolution of a higher control centre capable of " inspecting " ongoing activity will emerge. Thus could the thing we know of as consciousness develop. Incidentally, if you feel that such an abstracting, self-inspecting system could not be conceived in purely mechanical terms then you are wrong, for the latest developments in computer technology have been devoted to achieving this. But before getting caught up in arguments about whether computers could " think " (we'll tackle this briefly later on) let us just summarise the current approach to the problem that most psychologists accept today. Mind is a phenomenon which has arisen almost inevitably as brain complexity and power have increased, and its function is to select alternative activities and compute the consequences. Just as human bodies and brains differ in countless ways, so human minds, subtly moulded over the years from infancy to adulthood, differ too. The result is that the world is populated with a large number of human beings, united as a species, but each one an individual entity, compounded of body, brain, and mind. All three are equally real, equally important—and equally helpless without each other's company. Let us now take a look at the principal forces which serve to mould these individual entities we call people, and some of the essential ways in which they differ.

(2) Interplay of Heredity and Environment.

People and animals differ in a large number of ways, and are alike in others. We share certain features—upright posture, well-developed brains, etc.—with other primates, such as chimpanzees. We also share certain features—binocular vision, mammalian reproduction techniques, etc.—with white rats. We even have a limited amount in common—respiratory systems depending upon oxygen, need to ingest some kind of food, etc.—with creatures as lowly as the earwig, but nothing with cabbages or oak trees, except perhaps a dependence upon sunlight. Now what is it that determines these similarities and differences? The answer is summed up in the word heredity. Creatures of particular species mate with each other and hand on to their offspring, via the genes and chromosomes, the physical characteristics of the species (see **F31**). They may even hand on certain predetermined patterns of behaviour, which we have earlier referred to as instinct (see also **F38**). Broadly speaking, the lower down the phylogenetic scale, the more behavioural information is carried over via the genes, and the less flexible is the creature's ultimate behaviour pattern. Earwigs, for example, come into the world fully equipped to go about their simple business on this planet. They present almost identical faces to the world around them, and taking it all in all they change little from birth to death. Earwigs are largely the product of heredity, the principal forces which mould them lying in the genes of their parents and the incredible long history of their species stretching back for hundreds of millions of years. At the other end of the continuum we have human beings whose physical characteristics and a very limited number of behaviour patterns are inherited, but whose " personalities " and individualities (unlike the earwigs) change significantly throughout the span of their lives. These changes are the consequence of the impact of the environment on the flexible human brain, a flexibility which allows human beings to respond swiftly and intelligently to the changing hazards and opportunities of the world. It should be clear, therefore, that the basic differences that so obviously exist between the personalities of different people, reflect the experiences that each individual has had in his or her lifetime. See a newborn child and search for signs of its personality. You will look for a long time to no avail. But watch a child grow from infancy to adolescence and you will see the personality slowly building and emerging—more or less hand-in-hand with the young person's growing awareness of his own individuality, his strengths and his weaknesses.

Twin Studies.

Striking evidence of the immense influence that the environment has on us comes from the famous studies of identical twins performed in America by Newman in the 1930s. There is a bit of confusion in most people's minds about what actually are " identical " twins as opposed to the ordinary, born-on-the-same-day variety. In the case of the latter—known as fraternal twins— what has happened to produce the happy event is that during conception two of the eggs in the mother have been fertilised and thus two babies are born. Without going into too much detail this means that two quite separate creatures develop, each being equipped with the random genetic mix that follows the meeting of the father's sperm with the mother's egg. The children, when born, may be of different sex, different colour hair, eyes, etc., and are likely to be no more alike than would be brothers or sisters born in different years or even decades. Each, therefore, begins with a different hereditary pattern, as determined by the genes. With identical twins a curious fluke occurs. By some process, after conception and after gene mixing has taken place, the fertilised egg splits, amoeba fashion, and two babies begin to develop—but both have identical gene patterns and thus, up to the moment of birth, can be looked upon as totally identical human beings. This weird identity is, as we all know, frequently carried on throughout the twins' lifetime, even though it is generally noticeable that the similarities become less marked with age. Now to return to Newman's experiment. Nineteen pairs of identical twins were found (a good deal of research was needed) who had for one reason or another been reared apart from an early age and had grown up in different environments. Newman found that while the adult twins maintained a striking physical resemblance, the personalities of the pairs seemed in many cases to have moved apart. In one case, the first of the pair had been successful in worldly terms, had acquired a college education, and was happily married with a stable family, while the second had been less fortunate and was leading a rather unsatisfactory life in an unskilled job in a working-class neighbourhood. Twin " A " seemed optimistic, good-humoured, and more dominant a personality, while twin " B " was morose, lethargic, and lacking in self-confidence. Similar observations were in general noted with other twins, particularly in cases where one of the pair had been reared in a more stable and economically more satisfactory environment. No better illustration of the relative influence of heredity and environment on human personality can be found than in studies of this kind. But is it only physical characteristics that are genetically determined? Is none of the psychological make-up of the individual " built-in " to him at birth? We can answer this by saying that twin-studies have shown that while personality is certainly modified by the environment, there is a good deal of evidence that intelligence is relatively untouched by normal environmental differences. Newman and his colleagues, for example, found that there was a higher correlation between the IQ test scores of identical twins reared apart than there was between fraternal twins reared together—a finding which suggests very strongly that intelligence, whatever that may be, is largely carried over in the genetic system and bequeathed to the individual at his birth. If this seems to be contradictory or terribly unlikely, then there is probably some confusion over the meaning of the word intelligence, and since it is one of the fundamental themes making up the fabric of human personality we will take a closer look at it.

(3) Intelligence and IQ Testing

Psychologists have spent a good deal of time arguing about what exactly is meant by intelligence and it is not worth covering this battle-scarred ground again. One definition which makes a good deal of sense is " versatility of adjustment " which is another way of talking about the kind of flexible response to the environment which is so characteristic of humans. This of course means that we can talk of animals having some degree of intelligence, and most psychologists nowadays would agree that this makes sense. The only problem arises if one considers intelligence to be inextricably tied up with consciousness, thought, language, etc., which of course it is not. Certainly the ability to communicate in linguistic terms and to think in abstract modes are signs of a highly intelligent creature, but some degree of intelligence may be present without those traits. Probably one could even talk of intelligence being present in any animal that could modify its behaviour in response to the environment and repeat this behavioural response at some later date. This means, as you will have gathered, that intelligence is present in any creature that can learn, including our little friend planaria. It is of course a very limited form of intelligence and planaria would not come out with much of an IQ (intelligence quotient) if submitted to human IQ tests. The structure of these tests, incidentally, becomes comprehensible if one sees them as measures of human flexibility rather than of knowledge. The standard IQ test, which forms the basis of the much-reviled 11-plus exam, is an attempt at getting some idea of an individual's general flexibility rather than how much information is actually crammed into his head. Without getting involved in the educational argument here, the point is that a test of the child's inherent capability is more likely to give some index of his fitness for higher education than is a test of his knowledge, and this is what the IQ test attempts to sort out. Hence the relative uselessness of " cramming " to prepare for the 11-plus and the surprise results it sometimes produces. You may think you see a bit of a contradiction here. On the one hand we have said that intelligence, whatever it is, seems to be built in the individual and is something to do with his basic brain power. In this case why are new-born babies not fully intelligent at birth? The paradox is solved by saying that the peak of intelligence is not reached until the brain is fully mature (at about 18 years of age in homo sapiens) after which it begins to decline remorselessly with increasing age. Thus you will find that scores on IQ tests are " weighted " according to age. For very young children considerable allowance is made for age and their " raw " score is upgraded according to a standard scale. So too is the score for older people who inevitably score lower in IQ tests than do 18-year olds. Thus we find that a university professor aged 60 would produce a far lower raw score than a young student of equivalent intelligence—even though the venerable professor's head contains far more knowledge! If this seems odd, remember that it is the individual's potential and general flexibility that the tests are all about and not the depth of his fund of knowledge. The IQ test itself is a rather arbitrary affair and was arrived at in the first place by a group of psychologists selecting a bunch of questions which they felt best tested this rather elusive faculty of flexibility. They then arrived at a scoring system which achieved the result that if you tested a large number of people, drawn randomly from the population, their average score would equal 100. In fact this is exactly what an IQ of 100 means—it is the average score of the population at large. This has led to the sarcastic observation of one psychologist that intelligence was " that faculty that is measured by intelligence tests "! This is a witticism with some truth in it, but nevertheless the IQ has a practical value, notably as a sorter out of the bright from the dull in a situation where environmental or social backgrounds might have intervened to cloud the issue. The 11-plus is one such example, as is the fact that the IQ test taken prior to university entrance is the best-known predictor of success in final degree examinations— at least in the USA. On the other hand, as you may have suspected, social and cultural factors can influence IQ scores, thus suggesting that they are not as pure as might have been hoped. Tests conducted on white and black children in America in the 1930s, for example, showed a marked difference in IQ between the two racial groups— the whites coming out pretty clearly ahead. This was greedily seized on by racialists as demonstrating the innate superiority of the white children until it was pointed out that the selection of the two samples was faulty, the black children had been drawn from rural parts of the south while the whites came from the urban north. When a repeat experiment was performed, drawing the whites from the rustic south and the blacks from the northern cities, exactly the reverse finding emerged, killing one age-old notion and at the same time highlighting the fact that IQ tests were vulnerable to social and cultural factors. Incidentally, for those who like to pursue racial arguments, it is interesting to note that the highest IQ ever recorded by standard tests, a shattering 200, was scored by—a young Negro girl. When considering the world as a whole, however, the fact remains that humans are very heavily divided from each other by a barrier potentially more difficult to surmount than those of race, class, or creed—intelligence. Furthermore the gulf is one that is particularly difficult to bridge because of lack of incentive on either side. A highly intelligent person generally finds the company of a rather dull person quite unacceptable, and the reverse is also true. Also, the differences between high and low IQs are likely to become more apparent in the coming decades as the old barriers of class, etc., which used to mask intelligence, dissolve. From this important aspect of human personality we now move on to consider the nature of one of the processes most characteristic of human brains—thought.

(4) Thinking.

We have suggested that personality is an amalgam of the various faculties which are associated with cerebral activity, and that variations in personality reflect variations in the individual's environmental history. Any creature with a reasonably flexible set of responses to its environment can therefore be said to have some rudimentary personality, and many of us can detect this in our domestic pets. If this seems a peculiar notion then this is only because we have erroneously tended to think of personality as being a solely human trait, rather in the way that people dismiss animals in general as having no intelligence. But what is it that does distinguish us from other animals—do we differ merely in terms of the capacity and computing power of our brains? Probably the answer is yes, though it has to be recognised that the gulf is pretty wide. Yet if one looks at the cerebral equipment of, say, a chimpanzee one gets the feeling that there shouldn't be all *that* difference! Furthermore, if one comes closer to home and looks at some of our ancestors such as Neanderthal or Cro-Magnon Man, it is hard to account for the differences between their primitive lives and ours today. Certainly we exist 100,000 years later in time and it would be a bit pathetic if we hadn't progressed since then. But the same argument surely should apply to chimpanzees, who do not seem to have developed much in the same period, and the whole thing seems even odder when we learn that the now extinct Neanderthal Man had a cranial capacity (brain size) greater than that of modern man. One might explain the vast difference between Man and his rivals on the ground that he was the possessor of an immortal soul or divine spirit. Leaving this rather unsatisfactory explanation aside, let us try to find some other approach. The key lies in the capacity of humans for abstract thought—taking a step back in their minds and "introspecting." With this marvellous facility comes a natural talent to convert the results of these introspections into a code and communicate them to other members of the species. The communicating code is what we call language, and the introspective process, with or without a linguistic component, is known as thinking. Thinking of a kind probably comes in a good deal lower down, at the level where individual animals make "decisions," such as when a dog, faced with a fence blocking it from its food ultimately gives up trying to climb over it and simply walks round it! Kohler's chimpanzee Sultan was certainly indulging in something pretty close to thought when he fitted two

sticks together to reach a banana. Nevertheless, there is rather good evidence that the development of a spoken language, such as only humans have, is the trigger which allows a kind of detached, abstract processing to go on and which has allowed us to build up an immense cultural heritage over the past 10,000 years.

(a) Thought and Language.

How much is thought tied in with speech? You will remember that Watson liked to call thought "sub-verbal speech" and there is some truth in this. Open your mouth and think the word "bubble." You will probably notice a kind of catch in your throat—which shows how the two processes are tied together. On the other hand, think of some visual scene—say a polar bear sitting on an iceberg. Most people can conjure up a pretty reasonable mental picture of scenes like this without too much trouble and certainly without saying, vocally or sub-vocally, either the word bear or iceberg! Incidentally, if you *can't* get a mental image of this kind, don't worry, for about a third of the world's population can't either. This facility for producing "pictures in the mind" has puzzled psychologists for a century—in particular those who can't manage the images themselves, who are inclined to be a bit sceptical about the whole thing. Twist the topic round and consider the case of visual illusions and other perceptual anomalies. For example, take the kind where two lines, objectively the same, look to be of different length. No matter how much measuring with a ruler and how much you tell yourself that the lines are similar, your erroneous percept remains. Here perception and thought are *not* inextricably tied, which disposes of any lingering arguments that thinking was merely a consequence of visual, auditory, or some other input. Incidentally, the link between thought and language is suddenly coming under close study again, almost 50 years after Watson had originally tried to explain one in terms of the other. This arises from the young sub-science known as psycholinguistics, the founder of which is the American mathematician, Noam Chomsky. His thesis, rather seriously over-simplified, is that the structure of language can be used to give us a valuable key to the inner logic of the brain's operation. We can never hope to know directly how the inner mechanics of the brain work, he says, so we must look to find them reflected in some more directly observable process. Chomsky and his followers argue that in addition to its "surface" grammar (the kind of grammar we learn at school) all human languages have a deeper set of rules, closely tied in with the programmes which handle the deepest and most fundamental thought processes. Look closely at language, state and define the logic of the "deep grammar" and you have taken a peek at the brain's deepest secrets. It is an interesting idea, shared by many scientists who hold that similar clues can come from a study of dreams, but it suggests that the problem of defining thinking is even harder than we at first imagined.

(b) Can a Machine Think?

Yet another approach comes from computer scientists, who, concerned with devising computers capable of communicating in linguistic terms with human beings, have been taking a close look at these problems. From one of the pioneers of computer science, the late Alan Turing of Manchester, came a penetrating analysis of the philosophical problems of thought which reopens the discussion again from an entirely fresh angle. He did this by posing the question, "Can a machine think?" Turing pointed out that the almost universal response to this question was "No," but while people felt pretty confident in their opinion, they were seldom able to give a really good reason for it. Typical responses, when they were asked why a machine couldn't think, included, "because you can never get more out a machine than you put into it," "because machines have no souls," and "because only people can think." None of these arguments is valid. In the first place, it is only partly true to say that you can get no more out of a machine than you put in it, and in any case what has that to do with thinking? The second and third points are equally dubious. However, Turing realised that people had a built-in inclination to assume that thinking was a property of humans only, and as a computer engineer who hoped ultimately to see "thinking computers" developed, he was anxious to correct this impression. To do so he rephrased the question this way: "Supposing that you continually built ever more clever computers, how would you know whether one had begun to think or not?" Pointing out that the only evidence we have about whether humans can think (apart from taking their word for it) is the nature of the conversation they have with us, he suggested that one would base one's decision on how well the computer was able to communicate and discourse. Assuming that the fact that the computer was a large metal object with glowing lights, reams of paper tape, etc., would bias people in their judgment of whether it was thinking or not, he proposed that the decision should be based on a simple game. Take one very clever computer which you have reason to suppose may be capable of thought and place it in a room "A." Now take a person in a room "B," and a third in a room "C." Connect up computer "A" and person "B" to person "C" by wires connected to teletypes (special typewriters which allow one to feed information into computers and allow them to respond). Person "C" doesn't know who is on the end of either teletype, "B" or the computer, but he proceeds to try to find out by asking them questions through their respective teletypes. Now if the computer was really dim it would soon give itself away by its dim answers, but if it was really clever it might easily fool "C" into thinking it was the person "B." One important rule of the game, incidentally, is that both "B" and the computer were attempting to fool "C," the object being not to be identified correctly as either human or machine. Now, said Turing, if the point comes where "C" cannot reliably and certainly decide which of his two communicators is which, then to all intents and purposes the computer "A" must be said to be capable of thought! This is really a brilliant approach to the problem even if it seems to be a bit obscure at first. What Turing was really saying was that the *real* evidence that thinking is taking place is evidenced by what the individual, be it human, animal, or computer, actually does, and not what it looks like. (Hence the separation of the three beings in the above guessing game into separate rooms and the elimination of such relatively irrelevant variables as sight and sound.) Consider the case of Sultan the chimpanzee. Most people would agree that his tool-making activities were evidence of at least rudimentary thought processes. This evidence, as we have said, is based on what the creature did—not what he looked like, or whatever prior prejudices one had about apes thinking.

Before leaving this enigmatic topic, consider two recent developments in this area:

(1) A pair of American psychologists, husband and wife, reared a young chimpanzee from birth alongside their new-born son, treating the ape as "one of the family" and rearing it in precisely the same way as they did the child. For the first two years the chimpanzee matured far more rapidly than did the human child, but after the age of two, with the acquisition of speech, the young boy surged ahead. In its last desperate attempts to keep pace, however, the chimpanzee began to make primitive speech sounds including the enunciation of words like "cup" and "water" when it wanted a drink.

(2) In a computer complex in Boston where a number of scientists are connected to a central computer and also to each other via teletypes, two researchers were conversing with each other via the system. The computer was also present as a "third person," assisting them with their calculations. One of the scientists got up to leave the room without telling his friend, who continued conversing quite happily with . . . the computer. Only when the first scientist returned was the unique dialogue between man and computer dis-

rupted. Had the machine passed Turing's test? There are scientists today who argue that it had and, while there are plenty who disagree, quite the majority of computer engineers hold that it will not be long before their charges are capable of clearly demonstrating their capacity to think and not merely to compute.

(5) The World of Inner Space.

We have constantly indicated that psychology is the study of behaviour—the activities of living creatures which respond to a meaningful non-random way to the vagaries of their environment. The key to understanding these patterns of behaviour is of course the brain, and within the brain itself the programmes which control and determine its actions. One important point which all who study the brain swiftly come to realise, and one which this section has attempted to emphasise, is that no living system can be considered as a mechanical assembly of different parts. Each, whether earwig, cat, or human being, is a complex, integrated system functioning as a unit. The further up the phylogenetic scale one rises, the more complex the system and the more sophisticated and elegant its mechanics. At the human level with mental activities and consciousness emerging as super-control systems, the study of psychology reaches its most fascinating point. Here too, it must be admitted, as a science it has made least headway. There are probably good reasons for this, some related to the intrinsically complicated nature of the mind, others to the attitude of the psychologists themselves. The early pioneering work of Wundt, Ebbinghaus, and others seemed to be setting psychology on course as a science in its own right. The work of Pavlov, immensely important and relevant as it was, served to weaken psychology as a discipline and shift its bias drastically in the direction of physiology. Psychologists themselves ceased to think like psychologists and instead attempted to convert themselves into second-hand physiologists, part-time mathematicians, and indifferent clinicians. This trend, which gathered strength in the 1930s, has persisted until quite recently when a growing disenchantment with the relatively meagre results stemming from the millions of behaviouristic experiments involving pigeons, monkeys, and rats has led to an inevitable swing of the pendulum. More now than at any time in this century is the principal creature for psychological study acknowledged to be man himself. Also, for the first time since the turn of the century, "mind" is ceasing to be a dirty word to psychologists. Freud's fabulous and enduring insight—that the mind itself had two vitally important parts, the conscious and the unconscious, each integrated and yet strangely autonomous—is being treated with ever greater respect and understanding today. The realisation that human beings are controlled not merely by their conscious thoughts, wishes, and desires but also by dynamic forces of great power which are *not* under conscious control and barely available to linguistic analysis, is at last becoming a part of even the layman's view of mental life. The tip of the iceberg above the sea, as Freud pointed out, is that part of the mind which is under conscious control. Below the sea, massively enigmatic, lies the great bulk of the unconscious, the repository of the programmes which largely determine the behaviour of man. This is the zone, rich in mystery, which must ultimately be plotted by psychology and its researchers. This is the territory, glimpses of which we catch through the enigma of memory, the hallucinations of dementia, and in the misty drama of our dreams. The controversial English author J. G. Ballard has christened this territory "inner space," in contrast with the vast reaches of outer space that the first human astronauts are today beginning to explore. The explorers of inner space are psychologists, their colleagues in similar disciplines and all who journey along with them. At this stage their voyage has barely begun and, as with the astronauts, has no foreseeable ending. One thing is certain—it will be no less fascinating and no less rewarding. On the one path man seeks to discover his universe; on the other to discover himself.

MODERN GARDENING

A guide for the gardener on all aspects of horticulture particularly in the control of pests and diseases and the eradication of weeds by the latest means.

TABLE OF CONTENTS

MODERN GARDENING

CULTIVATION OF FLOWERS.

Throughout this section the notes must be taken to refer to cultural conditions in the British Isles, although in many cases the information can be adopted to suit the necessity of readers living abroad. Undoubtedly, in many temperate parts of the world interest in gardening has increased enormously during the past decade or so, despite the fact that numbers of large gardens have ceased to exist and that few people can afford to pay for full-time help in their gardens. To counteract this, the all important labour-saving garden has come into its own; shrubby plants have replaced annual bedding schemes and large lawns put down instead of herbaceous borders or beds of particular plants.

In addition, the owner-gardener is anxious to avail himself of the excellent selection of modern tools; thus the conventional hoe is being replaced by the " Swoe " or the Wolf pattern of Dutch weeder, both of which are very easy to use, and digging can be done quickly—and with much less effort—by using a German digger called a " Ter-rex " spade. For grass mowing, the work is easily done with motor mowers like any of the new battery-driven patterns.

For greenhouse work, smaller houses are being used and one, say, 12 ft. by 8 ft., can be run economically with a minimum winter temperature of 40° Fahrenheit by the introduction of trouble-free, thermostatic heaters or the turbo-heaters. At the moment, besides automatic heating, the prototypes for automatic ventilation and watering are making an appearance.

While advocating the use of such appliances, it must be pointed out that there are also to be found tools, sundries, and fertilisers of little value, and many of which have never been properly tested prior to being put on the market. It is, therefore, a good plan to discuss the comparative merits of any appliance or horticultural sundry with a competent horticulturist or to contact a public authority. In particular, many local horticultural societies have special trading facilities, and the merits of most garden things are generally known and discussed among members.

Throughout this Guide the vexed question of change in scientific name has been dealt with as liberally as possible and, whenever necessary, synonyms and cross references are given. In dealing with cultivar names, that is, varietal names like rose ' Peace,' reference is made as recommended in the *International Code of Nomenclature for Cultivated Plants* (1967). By so doing, the references are right up to date and further information on any particular plant or subject is easy to find. For the purpose, a few standard works of reference are given after each section. Normally, all the plants mentioned in the text are available through the usual trade channels.

After each plant listed there is a note on its propagation. Generally, this is the easiest or most efficient way of doing so, but it is not necessarily the only means. Details of the various methods employed are as follows:

Seed. Generally speaking, the early spring is the most suitable time for sowing seeds of trees and shrubs besides those of herbaceous plants and alpines. Where only a few plants are needed, the seed can be sown in pots and a suitable compost made up with 2 parts of soil, 1 part of peat, and 1 part of coarse sand. Before sowing, the pot should be stood up to its rim in water so that the soil is soaked. Then the seed can be sown thinly and covered with a light sprinkling of sifted compost.

For very fine seed, like begonias or azaleas, the seed must have only the merest " sugaring " of sand just sufficient to anchor it. When sown, the pots should be covered with a pane of glass (to prevent evaporation) and kept, if possible, in a warm greenhouse or frame. With this method of propagation it is important to remember that failure will result if the seed is sown too deeply, if the temperature is too low, or if the soil is too dry.

CORRECT PREPARATION OF SEED POTS AND PANS—Note provision for ample drainage and compost to rim of its container. After sowing, the containers are covered with a sheet of glass.

Cuttings. There are two main types of cutting: soft-wood cuttings made from fresh, green shoots in the spring and summer and hard-wood cuttings made of mature or semi-mature woody shoots in the autumn. A soft cutting is taken about 3 in. long, the lower leaves removed and a clean cut made through a node in the stem. These are then inserted in pots containing a light, sandy soil or a rooting medium such as horticultural vermiculite, well watered, and covered with a bell jar or plastic bag. Delphiniums, hydrangeas, and lupins are all propagated in this way.

Hard-wood cuttings are taken in the autumn and made from shoots about 8–12 in. long. These are inserted in a sandy soil out of doors or in a cold frame, and left to develop for a year. Black-currants, forsythia, and roses can be propagated by this means.

Layering. This is one of the easiest ways of propagating the majority of woody plants, and is used to increase stocks of plants like clematis, lilacs, and rhododendrons. Normally, layering is done in the autumn or spring when suitable branches are pegged down. On each of these the young shoots are, in turn, pegged down and tips turned upwards and tied in position. To encourage rooting, gritty sand and peat should be worked around each layer, and usually the young plant can be severed from the parent after about eighteen months.

Division. By this method it is easy to propagate the majority of herbaceous plants, some rock-garden plants, and a few shrubs. A few herbaceous plants, like delphinium and paeony, are slow to get established after moving, and here the method should not be employed. In any case, old plants should not be split up in a wholesale manner; instead, it is far better to select a few young healthy plants, divide these, and replant the best of the young shoots, in the autumn.

ALPHABETICAL LIST OF ORNAMENTAL PLANTS.

Abutilon.—The greenhouse species is often used in public parks for bedding schemes. *A. viti-folium*, with white, mauve, or blue flowers makes a fine wall shrub for warm gardens. If given full sun it will quickly reach 10–15 ft., but is sometimes short-lived. *Prop.*—Easily raised from seed sown in March in a warm greenhouse or frame.

Acer (Maple).—Hardy, ornamental trees; the Norway maple is often planted for its magnificent autumn colour and as a lawn tree. *A. palmatum* and vars. constitute the Japanese maples; all colour brilliantly in the autumn but do not grow freely unless given some shade and a light soil rich in humus. *Prop.*—Seed, layering, or budding.

Achillea (Yarrow).—Grey-leaved perennials for open border or dwarf species, for rock garden. Valued as a cut flower, particularly *A. ptarmica* 'Perry's White,' with double, white flowers and *A. eupatorium* 'Gold Plate,' with large, flat, yellow flower heads. *A. millefolium* is a pernicious weed of turf (T34). *Prop.*—Division in autumn.

Acidanthera.—Scented, bulbous plant introduced from Abyssinia. It is not difficult to grow if the corms are planted in the spring and lifted in the autumn for storing in a frost-proof shed. It requires a sunny position and plenty of water in the summer. *Prop.*—Offsets removed when the old crop of bulbs is lifted.

Aconitum (Monkshood).—Blue-flowered perennial plants particularly useful for lightly shaded positions or full sun; flowers from May to July, height 3–5 ft.; roots poisonous. *Prop.*—Seed or division.

Adiantum.—*See* Ferns.

A WELL-GROWN AGAPANTHUS—In winter the pot should be kept in a cold greenhouse or some protected place; in summer afforded full sun.

Agapanthus.—A bulbous plant, native of South Africa, usually found in seaside gardens and sometimes grown in tubs; flowers blue, violet, or white. It needs winter protection in the form of a covering of bracken or straw and a light soil heavily enriched with manure. Worthy of wider cultivation. *Prop.*—Seed or division in March.

Ageratum.—Blue-flowered carpeting plant. *See* Annuals.

Allium (Flowering Onion).—A genus of nearly 300 species of bulbous plants widely distributed over the Northern Hemisphere. The foliage has the distinctive smell of garlic, but some species are grown for garden ornamentation; in particular *A. roseum*, valuable late-flowering rock plant for dry positions. *Prop.*—Offsets, taken from parent bulbs in the spring.

Alstroemeria aurantiaca (Peruvian Lily).—This tuberous-rooted, herbaceous plant is often grown for cutting. Flowers orange-red and height 2–3 ft.; of easy culture if afforded a sunny position and left undisturbed. For best results apply liquid manure or soot water when growth starts. *Prop.*—Seed or division.

Althaea (Hollyhock).—A truly delightful, old-world plant, but not often seen, as modern hybrids

have given way to rust disease. Best grown in a rich heavy loam. Mulch with manure of any sort and stake as necessary. *Prop.*—Seed in June, thin out, and transfer to flowering position in September. Although a perennial, in some localities the best results are obtained by treating it as a biennial and raising a small supply annually.

Alyssum.—Low-growing annuals and perennials for rock garden and sunny border. The perennial, *A. saxatile*, is deservedly popular by reason of its bright, spring flowers and value as a wall plant. The variety 'Citrinum' is bright yellow and 'Dudley Neville' biscuit-yellow. *Prop.*—Perennial sorts by cuttings in June.

Amaryllis belladonna.—Often this plant is confused with the greenhouse, bulbous plant, *Hippeastrum*. The true amaryllis is a half-hardy bulb for planting at the foot of a warm wall; it has white to pinkish-red flowers. When planting, cover neck of bulb with an inch of soil and leave undisturbed, as the plant resents moving and is slow to get established. Lack of flowering is generally due to planting too deep. Established clumps may be fed with hoof and horn meal at 2 oz. per sq. yd. in July. *Prop.*—Divide and replant clumps in early July.

Amelanchier canadensis.—A large shrub or small tree; valuable for its spring flowers and autumn colour. As it will grow almost anywhere in sun or shade, it makes a good plant for informal screening. *Prop.*—Seed or layers.

Amepelopsis.—*See* **Parthenocissus.**

Anchusa italica.—A blue-flowered perennial with fleshy roots, growing to a height of about 3 ft. Responds to feeding and needs a position in full sun. *Prop.*—Root cuttings in the spring; division in the autumn.

Anemone.—The tuberous-rooted section includes the 'Caen' and 'St. Brigid' strains. These are best grown in an open position in light, rich soil; plant in October, lift and store when foliage dies. The hardy, fibrous-rooted perennials are varieties of *A. hybrida* (syn. *japonica*) and constitute one of the most accommodating of perennials, being particularly useful for damp, shady positions. Worthy of wider attention from gardeners. *Prop.*—Perennial sorts by division in autumn.

Annuals.—These are plants which develop from seed, flower, fruit, and die within a year. Additionally, some perennials, like antirrhinums, may be treated as annuals for the convenience of their cultivation. Sunny borders may be planted solely with annuals, they may be interplanted with perennials, used for window boxes, or, occasionally, in the rock garden. All sorts do best in well-worked, light loam enriched each year with a dressing of fish meal at 3 oz. per sq. yd., ten days before sowing or planting.

In the division of the group Hardy Annuals may be sown in the open ground as soon as conditions permit during March or April where the plants are to flower. Wet or cold soils will give many failures, and fine seed should be covered only with the lightest sugaring of soil. Often surprising—but delightful—results may be obtained by sowing broadcast mixed seed of annuals specially offered by some trade houses.

To raise Half Hardy Annuals, seed may be sown in early March in a warm greenhouse and the seedlings pricked out into boxes. Subsequently, the plants are grown on in a cold frame, gradually hardened off, and then transferred to their flowering positions towards the end of May.

Anthemis tinctoria.—Hardy perennial with feathery, grey foliage and flowers in varying shades of yellow. Height 2–3 ft., needs full sun and good for cutting. *Prop.*—Division in the autumn. *Anthemis nobilis* is the chamomile sometimes unwisely used to make lawns.

Antirrhinum (Snapdragon).—The popular bedding plant requiring a good soil and position in full sun now largely in disfavour owing to rust disease; planting should be restricted to rust-resistant varieties. *See* Annuals.

Aphelandra squarrosa.—An evergreen, perennial plant introduced from Brazil. Often sold as a house plant, albeit a warm temperature and a high humidity are necessary for its cultivation. When grown indoors it is best discarded when the flowers fade and the foliage starts to wither, as it cannot be successfully grown on from year to year under normal conditions indoors.

Aquilegia.—The modern race of hybrids are the result of much interbreeding with wild forms to give a wide range of colours. Best when planted in light shade where soil is naturally moist. *Prop.*—Seed in late spring; transplant to flowering position for following year.

Arabis caucasica.—Once known as *A. albida*, this common rock plant is often used on dry walls. The double-flowered form is particularly good. *Prop.*—Cuttings in July; a fresh stock should be raised regularly as the special forms tend to die out.

Araucaria (Monkey Puzzle).—This tree was introduced from Chile, where it forms large natural forests, and widely planted in Victorian days. Browning of foliage suggests lack of water in the summer or, occasionally, effects of very cold weather. It should be planted in a position protected from the prevailing wind. *Prop.*—Seed in a warm greenhouse.

Armeria maritima.—A hardy perennial with pink or red flowers in the spring; must be grown in full sun where the soil is dry. *Prop.*—Division after flowering.

Artemisia.—A genus of shrubs and perennials suitable for sunny borders or rockeries. *A. lactiflora* is among the best of the herbaceous species, having grey foliage and creamy-white flowers. *A. abrotanum* (lad's love) in the shrubby section has grey, fragrant foliage. *Prop.*—Herbaceous section by division; shrubs by cuttings in the early summer.

Arundinaria.—*See* Bamboo.

Aster (Michaelmas Daisy).—By careful breeding this plant has been improved out of all recognition, and many first-class varieties are available in the trade. Responsive to good cultivation, it is used for its colour late in season and properties as a cut flower, particularly *A. yunnanensis* 'Napsbury' and *A.* 'Barr's Pink.' A wide range of colours are available besides some fine, low-growing forms. In the border one pleasing combination can be made with *A.* 'Harrington's Pink' and *Scabious* 'Dinkie.' *Prop.*—The clumps should be split up *annually* in the spring, and only the plumpest pieces of outer root replanted.

Aster, China or Common.—*See* Callistephus.

Astilbe.—Allied to the *Spiraea* and useful for planting in moist, rich soils; flowers white, pink, and crimson; height 2 ft. *Prop.*—Division of clumps.

Aubrieta.—A name often misspelt. Throughout the country it is used as edging or for dry walls. Many lovely sorts available apart from the commonly found, pale-blue variety. It is a lime lover. *Prop.*—After flowering the plants should be severely trimmed and, as necessary, stock increased by division.

Aucuba japonica.—Much maligned and overplanted shrub, but one tolerant of neglect and sunless or smoky conditions. Interesting variants of the type, like 'Crotonifolia,' may be found in trade lists. *Prop.*—Cuttings rooted in the open in July.

Auricula.—Correctly known botanically as *Primula auricula*. Flowers of alpine auriculas are white or yellow, while in those of florists' auriculas are to be found some of the most delicate colourings among hardy plants. Choice varieties are grown in pots under glass; others in moist,

shady borders. *Prop.*—Seed or division in the spring.

Azalea.—*See* Rhododendron.

Bamboo.—The common name for the large group of woody grasses, reference to which is difficult owing to the confusion in their nomenclature. Often grown for screening and wind breaks, and is a favourite shelter for small birds; the best for home-grown canes are *Phyllostachys viridiglaucescens* and *Sinarundinaria nitida*. An interesting account of bamboo growing is found in the *Jour. Roy. Hort. Soc.* (June 1957). Growth can be encouraged by feeding with sulphate of ammonia and mulching with leaf-mould in the spring. *Prop.*—Division of clumps in late spring; transplants must be kept watered until established.

Begonia.—A genus showing wide diversity of form and much horticultural value. Of particular interest is the tuberous-rooted section, of which many of the loveliest varieties have originated in the nurseries of Messrs. Blackmore and Landon at Bath. For bedding schemes, the tubers are started in boxes of rich soil under glass in late March and planted out 9 in. apart in June. During the summer feed with liquid manure of any sort and keep moist in dry periods. *Prop.*—Cuttings in early spring in a warm case.

Berberis.—An extensive genus of beautiful and easily grown shrubs, evergeen and deciduous; the former used mainly for beauty of flower, and the latter for autumn colouring and ornamental fruits. *B. stenophylla* makes a fine evergreen hedge; invaluable for preventing illicit entry by dogs and, even, unruly children. *B. aggregata* and *B. jamesiana* are among the best berrying kinds. Prune in the winter by removing old wood. *Prop.*—Seed in spring or layering in autumn.

Buddleia.—Deciduous shrubs of easy culture for sunny positions. Varieties of *B. davidii* available in range of colours from purple to white; best when pruned hard by cutting all previous year's growth back to main stems in February. The weeping species, *B. alternifolia*, often grown as a standard; good specimens at R.H.S. Gardens, Wisley. This sort must be pruned in the summer by cutting off the dead flowering stems. *Prop.*—Cuttings in July–August in cold frame.

Cactus.—In the main grown in cool greenhouses or as house plants and, if cultivated well, many will flower every year. As a general guide, plants should be watered fairly freely in the summer and little in the winter, but there are exceptions. A detailed account of growing these fascinating plants will be found in *The Cactus Grower's Guide*, by Vera Higgins (Latimer House), 1946.

Calceolaria.—Seed of the greenhouse biennials sown in June or July for flowering in the following year. Mixed seed provides a wide range of colour. *C. integrifolia* is a half-hardy perennial, raised by cuttings or seed, for greenhouse or bedding work.

Calendula (Marigold).—This common hardy annual is freely raised from seed sown in August. Of easy culture in any sort of soil, although it is worth getting seed of new varieties now available. *See* Annuals.

Callistephus.—The China asters are among the best half-hardy annuals for garden and indoor decoration, but good soil and full sun are necessary for best results. *See* Annuals.

Camellia japonica.—Hardy, evergreen shrub rightly beloved by connoisseurs and cultivated in gardens for many centuries. May be grown in cold greenhouses, woodland gardens, and against north- and west-facing walls; under all conditions camellias must have a moist, acid soil. Best varieties for outdoors are 'Althaeaflora' (dark red), 'Donckelarii' (red, white marbling), and 'C. M. Wilson' (pink). Of recent introduction is the desirable *C. williamsii* bred from *C. japonica* in part; often the subject of television and gardening notes. The dropping of buds is thought due to dryness at the roots at some time or sharp fluctuation in temperature. *Prop.*—Named varieties by cuttings under glass in early July. Otherwise plants easily raised from seeds if sown in the autumn immediately they are ripe, in acidic peat and kept moist.

Campsis grandiflora.—Sometimes found listed as *Bignonia* or *Tecoma*; choice deciduous climber for warm wall, large reddish-orange flowers in autumn. To encourage flowering growth, prune hard back to old growth in spring. *Prop.*—Cuttings in April struck in a warm case.

Canary Creeper.—*See* **Tropaeolum.**

Candytuft.—Hardy annual (*q.v.*) and perennials with white, crimson, blue, or purple flowers. The perennial—*Iberis sempervirens*—is a fine plant for a rock wall. *Prop.*—Seed or, perennials. from cuttings.

Carnation.—*See* **Dianthus.**

Centaurea (Cornflower).—The perennial species are valuable for cutting and border use, and may be found in such colours as pink, crimson, and yellow. *Prop.*—Lift and divide every third or fourth year. The hardy annual, *C. cyanus*, is often sold as a cut flower. *See* **Annuals.**

Chaenomeles speciosa.—This is the correct botanical name for japonica. The species commonly grown is a wide-spreading, rounded shrub, 6–10 ft. in height, and often used against walls. It is a plant of easy culture with best results being achieved by the annual spurring back of the current season's growth in the same way as an apple tree is pruned. All japonicas can be used for making jelly but, for this purpose, the best one is *Chaenomeles cathayensis*, a gaunt shrub about 10 ft. in height which bears fruit up to 8 oz. in weight. To obtain a crop within a reasonable time, two or three plants may be set in a group about 5 ft. apart. If growth or flowering is below par all japonicas should be fed with " Growmore" and mulched with compost.

Cheiranthus cheiri (Wallflower).—Among the finest displays of this biennial are those found each year in the public gardens of Southend-on-Sea, where it is used in conjunction with bulbs and forget-me-nots. *Prop.*—Seed sown thinly in rows in May and seedlings thinned or lined out and then transplanted in late autumn. The so-called Siberian wallflower, *Erysimun asperum*, which has bright orange flowers, is grown in the same way, but it is intolerant of wet soils. Both sorts are lime lovers, and on acid soils plants may receive treatment with 1 oz. of lime in a gallon of water.

Chimonanthus (Winter Sweet).—Hardy, winter-flowering shrub with heavily scented flowers. Although brought to this country from the Far East in the mid-eighteenth century its garden value is not widely appreciated. The large-flowered, yellow sort, *C. praecox*, is particularly fine, but like all the varieties, it is best grown against a sunny wall and where the soil tends to be poor. If growth is excessive and flowering poor, trim back young growth severely in March to encourage short, spur-like shoots. *Prop.*—Easily raised from seed or layers.

Christmas Rose.—*See* **Helleborus.**

Chrysanthemum.—Hardy annual sorts are available in a wide range of colours and give a fine display in the summer months. *See* **Annuals.** There are also a number of perennials such as the shafta daisy and the oxeye daisy for sunny, herbaceous borders; all do well in ordinary soil, but should be lifted and split up about every three years. The plant sold by florists in the autumn is the Japanese chrysanthemum. Many are hardy out-of-doors, but no plant is more responsive to good cultivation and normally is best left to the specialist grower. For ordinary garden work, the best sorts are the Korean and Otley types. Under a brief reference the interesting details of cultivation cannot be dealt with fairly, and reference to specialist books is recommended.

Clematis.—A hardy climber for walls, screens, pergolas, and the like. Best kinds are to be found among named varieties in nurserymen's lists A light, well-drained soil is necessary and if fed annually with a bucketful of manure or compost the plant will thrive for many years. Occasionally plants will be found on north walls, and if grown in full sun some light protection from the sun is desirable for the roots. Varieties which flower on the *current* season's growth, like *C. jackmanii*, should be pruned in late February to within a foot of the ground; other sorts should have sufficient old growth removed, after flowering, to keep them within bounds.

Sometimes the climber is killed by clematis wilt so premature death of young plants should not be automatically blamed on the supplier. Control is by spraying with a copper-containing fungicide. *Prop.*—Layering, by which means one shoot will often give three or four plants.

Convallaria majalis (Lily of the Valley).—Well-known perennial that will thrive in any damp, shady position. For best results lift every four or five years and mulch annually with old manure. *Prop.*—Division when foliage fades.

Coreopsis.—The hardy annuals are found in catalogues under " Callipsis," and all will thrive in ordinary soil. The flowers are mainly bright yellow, and many are good for cutting. *See* **Annuals.** Similarly, the perennials have the same predominant colour and are useful because of their long flowering season and abundance of flower. *Prop.*—Division.

Cornflower.—*See* **Centaurea.**

Cosmos.—Tall-growing, half-hardy annuals that are best grown in full sun in a dryish border. The large, daisy-like flowers can be had in a variety of colours, including white, yellow, pink, and crimson. *See* **Annuals.**

Cotoneaster.—Hardy evergreen and deciduous shrubs or small trees bearing scarlet or sometimes yellow berries in the autumn. All may be grown in ordinary or poor soil and planted in open or shady shrubberies and trailing species used against walls, over banks, or as ground cover. For shrub-berries *C. lacteus* and *C.* ' Cornubia ' with red berries and *C. rothchildianus* with yellow berries are among the best sorts; *C. conspicuus* ' Decora ' is a strong grower for banks, while *C. horizontalis* is an excellent cover for any wall. Planting may be done in the autumn or spring, and no pruning, apart from occasional shaping, is required. *Prop.*—Seeds and layering.

Crataegus (Hawthorn).—There are many good varieties of our British hawthorn, *C. oxyacantha*, worthy of attention, particularly ' Coccinea ' (crimson) and ' Paulii ' (double, red). All will do well on poor soils, and no pruning is required. The common hawthorn makes a stout, impene-trable hedge planted 9 in. apart in a double row 9 in. asunder. *Prop.*—Common sort by seed; choice varieties by budding.

Crocus.—A hardy bulb of great beauty which was studied for many years by one of the best horticulturists of the twentieth century, the late E. A. Bowles. Does best in rich soil planted in bold groups around margins of beds or borders and naturalised in grass. When required, feed in early spring with bone meal at 2 oz. per sq. yd. *C. sieberi* and *C. tomasinianus* flower very early; the large-flowered, garden forms about three weeks later. *C. zonatus* flowers in the autumn and is often naturalised in grass. *Prop.*—Clumps may be lifted and divided about every five years, in July. The so-called autumn crocus is *Colchicum autumnale*. This bears large, lustrous leaves in the summer, followed by mauve or white flowers—of fleeting duration—in the autumn.

Crown Imperial.—*See* **Fritillaria.**

Cytisus (Broom).—Only does really well in dry, poor soils in full sun; choice, procumbent sorts, like *C. kewensis*, used in rock gardens and tall ones in open shrubberies. Pruning is important; shoots should be shortened after flowering, but old wood must never be cut. *Prop.*—Seed and cuttings in August in a sandy soil.

Daffodil.—*See* Narcissus.

Dahlia.—The cultivation of this plant is a special study, and there are probably more garden varieties of it than any other plant. Ordinary soil enriched with manure and an open position is required. Tubers may be planted 3 in. deep in April or young plants in late May. During the summer feed with soot water and liquid manure. After the first frosts lift, dry, and then store tubers in peat or straw in frost-proof place. Many stocks of dahlia are affected by virus (T30), and purchasers should be careful to check source of supply.

Daphne.—Shrubby plants, giving some of the most richly scented of all flowers. In particular, there is *D. mezereum*, which requires a damp soil; failure with the shrub is due usually to root disturbance or virus disease (T31) *D. odora* is one of the evergreen, fragrant species. Some references have suggested that this lovely shrub is not hardy, but there is no evidence to support the supposition. *Prop.*—Seed or layering.

Delphinium.—Hardy annuals and perennials. The latter sorts have gained popularity enormously since the War, due in the main to the activities of the Delphinium Society but also to the introduction of many very fine new varieties. American hybrids, like the 'Pacific Strain,' are very large but tend to die out and, consequently, lack the true, perennial habit of European sorts, albeit some of these have been weakened by the introduction of poor lines. It is important therefore to select stocks of strong constitution. Delphiniums need a deep, rich soil and a sunny position protected from wind. Plant in autumn 3 ft. apart, feed in the summer with liquid soot water, and mulch with decayed compost or manure in the spring. When growth starts, thin out weak growths to leave not more than five stems per plant. In winter take steps against possible slug damage (T29), and on this point it is beneficial to protect crowns with a covering of ashes. *Prop.*—Cuttings in the spring or seed; division of clumps is a poor alternative.

The hardy annual sorts are the well-known larkspurs, which grow to a height of 18 in. to 2 ft. and may be found in a range of colours including pink, red, white, and shades of blue. *See* Annuals.

Deutzia.—Hardy deciduous shrubs thriving in any soil and valuable for their summer flowers of white or whitish-pink shade. To keep the plants vigorous, shoots should be shortened after flowering and old or weak wood cut out. *D. scabra* is of robust habit, reaching about 7 ft., and *D. elegantissima* 'Fasciculata' proves a graceful shrub some 5 ft. tall with clusters of about twenty flowers coloured rosy-pink and each nearly an inch across. *Prop.*—Cuttings made from firm young growths about 10 in. long in sandy soil out-of-doors.

Dianthus.—This name covers a wide range of annual, biennial, and perennial plants. At one time often grown for their fragrance, but to a large extent this has been lost with the introduction of wider ranges of colour. Border carnations and picotees grown out-of-doors need a limy, fairly rich soil in full sun. Plant in the autumn or spring and, as the buds appear, feed with soot water or liquid animal manure, if necessary. These groups are *not* of good perennial habit and should be propagated annually to ensure continuation of stock.

The common pink requires the same soil conditions, and should be propagated when the stock gets weak; good scented varieties should be sought, and include the 'Imperial Pinks,' 'Mrs. Simkins,' and 'White Ladies.' *Prop.*—The best method is by layering in July so that the new plants can be put in their flowering position by mid-September. The lower leaves are pulled off selected shoots and a slit passing through a joint is made in the stem. Each layer is then pegged down with a hair-pin, the pin being placed above the cut. The layers are then covered with an inch of sandy compost and well watered.

In this genus is the sweet william; although truly a perennial, it is generally grown as a biennial and, consequently, the plant is raised from seed in May out-of-doors. In gardens where it is prone to rust disease control is most difficult and it is not worth a place.

LAYERING CARNATIONS—This is a typical example of how many plants can be propagated. A strong, new growth is pegged down into sandy soil after a cut has been made in the stem, at the point of pegging. Once rooted the layer can be severed from the parent and transplanted a week or two later.

Digitalis.—The biennial sort generally found in gardens is the common foxglove, which is grown in light shade in fairly rich, moist soil. In the past many named forms have been offered in the trade, but undoubtedly the best one is *D.* 'Sutton's Excelsior.' *Prop.*—Seed sown in May out-of-doors.

Doronicum.—Hardy perennials with yellow flowers; warrants wider planting, as they are among the earliest perennials to bloom and will thrive in poor soil or in some shade. The best is *D. austriacum* flowering in March, height 9 in. *Prop.*—Division after flowering.

Echinops.—Name appropriately derived from *echinos*, a hedgehog, in reference to the spiny, long scales of the flowers. The plant does well in an open position, where the globular heads of steely-blue flowers can be seen to advantage. *Prop.*—Division in March, but best left undisturbed as long as possible, as it must be moved with care.

Elaeagnus.—Hardy deciduous and evergreen shrubs generally grown in rather dry positions as foliage plants. Of the evergreen sort, *E. pungens* 'Aureo-Variegata' has bright golden variegation, and is therefore valuable for indoor decoration during the winter. *Prop.*—Layering in late summer.

Erica.—The heathers are native plants to Britain, and many variants found in the wild have been introduced into gardens to good purpose. Indeed, heathers have become so popular that special Heather Gardens have been made, and two fine examples may be found in the Royal Gardens, Windsor where the planting is new and the Royal Horticultural Society's Gardens, Wisley. Here, different sorts reaching the dimensions of small trees, dwarf kinds, and many scores of interesting variants, to supply flower throughout the year, will be found.

The Scottish heather is, botanically, *Calluna vulgaris*, and, like all British heathers, it is intolerant of lime or chalk. Where alkaline conditions exist, planters can try *E. carnea*—a winter-flowering heather—or *E. darleyensis*, but the results are usually disappointing. When planting all heathers, clumps must be well firmed and afterwards kept moist; subsequently, mulch all types annually with peat. *Prop.*—Division and layering.

Erigeron.—Hardy perennial for sunny borders; daisy-like flowers freely develop and are good for cutting. *Prop.*—Division in the autumn.

Escallonia.—Slightly tender evergreen and deciduous shrubs. In the Midlands protection of a south wall is necessary; suitable for open shrubbery in the South. Ideal for maritime conditions, and here may be used to good effect as hedges. Many of the best varieties originated in the nursery of Messrs. The Slieve Donard Co. in County Down. *Prop.*—Cuttings under a glass jar in summer; layers in September.

Eschscholzia californica.—A hardy annual of easy culture; height 18 in., flowers mainly shades of orange. *See* Annuals.

Everlasting Flowers.—*See* Helichrysum.

Ferns.—A large number of plants are included under this name and, as they grow wild in many parts of the world, some need hothouse conditions. They are distinguished from flowering plants by their method of reproduction; instead of producing seeds, ferns develop spores, usually on the back of their leaves. The hardy kinds may be grown in equal parts of leaf-mould and soil, and the fronds of leaf-losing kinds should not be removed until the spring, as they offer some protection from the cold. Tender ferns should be repotted when new growth starts in the spring in a compost of equal parts soil, leaf-mould, and sand, using a pot just large enough for the purpose. During the growing season, in particular, keep the roots moist and plants free from a dry or smokey atmosphere. *Prop.*—Division of clumps when growth starts in the spring.

Forget-me-nots.—*See* Myosotis.

Forsythia.—Commonly found in many gardens, as it is of easy culture in any soil. Flowers bright yellow in early spring. To keep in good shape prune directly after flowering by cutting out old wood. *F. intermedia* 'Lynwood' is upright in growth and *F. suspensa* of weeping habit; both types make good wall plants for North aspects. *Prop.*—Cuttings in the autumn.

Foxglove.—*See* Digitalis.

Freesia.—Greenhouse bulbous plant and, if grown for scent, care must be taken to select fragrant varieties. Pot in the autumn in a fairly rich compost and keep as cold as possible until growth is seen. Then bring into a frost-free greenhouse and water freely. When flower stems appear, feed with liquid manure; after flowering, gradually dry-off until time for repotting. Failures almost invariably traced to premature forcing before root growth has been made or growing in excessively high temperature. *Prop.*—Offsets at potting time.

Fritillaria.—The one mainly used in gardens is *F. imperialis*, a handsome, spring-flowering bulb. To grow it *really* well, this species must be given a deep, rich soil and, contrary to some views, it is best lifted every year as soon as the foliage fades. If growth is poor or plants do not flower, feed when growth starts in the following spring with equal parts of bone meal and superphosphate at 3 oz. per sq. yd. *Prop.*—Offsets removed from parent bulb at lifting time. The old bulb should then be replanted at once and any offsets lined out in a nursery row.

Fuchsia.—Greenhouse and tender flowering shrubs. The outdoor sorts (of which *F. riccartonii* is the best) may be grown in light soil in full sun. In the spring prune all growth down to ground level; protect, if necessary, in winter with covering of cut bracken or dry straw. Greenhouse varieties are potted firmly before growth starts in the spring and, when buds burst, all the previous year's growth can be cut back hard. To encourage flowering, feed with a liquid manure, such as dried blood, and syringe foliage in hot weather. During the winter keep plants dry and house in a cool

greenhouse. *Prop.*—Cuttings of new growth taken about 1 in. long and inserted in sand under a plastic cover in the spring.

Gaillardia.—Hardy annuals and perennials 18 in. to 3 ft. high which bear large, richly coloured flowers invaluable for cutting in mid- and late-summer. Unfortunately, on heavy soil the perennials are liable to die after flowering, and even on well-drained soils they cannot be considered long-lived plants. *Prop.*—Normally it is necessary to raise a fresh stock in alternate years; seed is sown in May in a cold frame and the young plants lined out in a reserve border prior to planting in the autumn.

Galanthus (Snowdrop).—Hardy bulbs well worth growing if given a moist, shady position where stock can be left undisturbed. Planting should be done in fairly bold clumps; bulbs are not expensive, and many variants, like double-flowered and tall-stemmed ones, are well worth a trial. *Prop.*—Lift and divide clumps in August.

Gentiana.—The gentians comprise some of the most fascinating of all rock-garden plants partly, perhaps, because some are difficult to manage. In particular, *G. acaulis*—which has true "gentian blue" flowers—is exacting in its requirements, and in many gardens flowering can never be induced. What controls flowering has not been discovered, and the plant can be grown well in acid or limy soils. On the other hand, *G. sino-ornata* must have an acid soil and is best in a position out of the direct sun. Beginners with the genus are advised to start with easily grown sorts, like *G. lagodechina* and *G. septemfida*. *Prop.*—Seed sown in cold frame in March or division in early spring.

Geranium.—The true geranium or cranesbill is a hardy floriferous perennial for rock garden or open border. In the latter case *G. ibericum* (blue flowers) and *G. sanguineum* 'Lancastriense' (rosy-pink flowers) are exceptionally good, and both do well in dry, sunny positions. The so-called "bedding" or "greenhouse" geranium is a pelargonium (*q.v.*). *Prop.*—Seed in March.

Gladiolus.—Dutch hybridists have done much work on this bulbous plant, and many new and lovely varieties are now available. The plant is responsive to good cultivation, and corms may be planted 4 in. deep and 6 in. apart during the spring in well-prepared ground. When the blooms fade remove the dead spikes of flower and lift the corms in September. After a month—and this point is important—pull off the old shrivelled corm and clean the new one. By doing this there is less likelihood of spores of diseases overwintering on the new stock. Finally, the corms should be stored in a dry, frost-free shed, and if given proper attention can be kept for a number of years. *Prop.*—Bulbils, removed when the corms are cleaned, can be sown in the spring in nursery rows and will flower within two years.

Godetia.—Hardy annual of easy culture and tolerant of poor soil conditions and even some shade. There are many varieties, mainly with bright flowers of rosy-pink and crimson. *See* Annuals.

Guernsey Lily.—*See* Nerine.

Gypsophila.—The favourite sort is *G. paniculata*, which is often grown for cutting, together with its double-flowered form, 'Bristol Fairy.' To do well gypsophila must be given a dryish soil which the roots can penetrate undisturbed; if growth is poor mulch in the spring with animal manure. *Prop.*—Generally done by seed in spring; special forms by grafting.

Hamamelis.—A lovely, but little grown, winter-flowering, heavily-scented shrub. The delicate, lemon-coloured flowers appear interminably from December to February. Although it flowers in its young stage, hamamelis is slow to get established and must be left free of root disturbance. The best sort is *H. mollis* introduced from China in 1879. *Prop.*—Usually by grafting; can be layered.

Heather.—See Erica.

Hedera.—Although ivy is seldom planted nowadays, there are a few evergreens to equal it for covering buildings. The large-leaved ivy with golden variegation, *H. colchica* 'Dentato-Variegata,' is invaluable for cold or shady walls. *Prop.*—Cuttings in August in shady border out-of-doors.

Helianthus.—The perennial sunflowers are tall, yellow-flowered plants of vigorous habit. They spread quickly and become a nuisance, and therefore clumps should be lifted and single, rooted pieces replanted every other year. The annual sunflower may reach a height of 10 ft. or so; seed is sown out-of-doors in April or seedlings raised under glass in the spring. When the flower bud appears, feed with soot water. The seed may be used as food for large birds like parrots.

Helichrysum.—Although this is a large group of plants, the most interesting is the half-hardy annual, *H. bracteatum*, the everlasting flower. When the flowers are fully developed they are cut with long stems and hung up to dry for winter decoration. See Annuals.

Heliotropium peruvianum (Cherry Pie).—Scented, shrubby plants used for greenhouse decoration or summer bedding. *H.* 'Sir Edward Fry' is among the scented varieties and *H.* 'Princess Marina' is the best dark-purple variety. For really good results, heliotropes need a rich soil and plenty of water in summer. *Prop.*—Cuttings 2–3 in. long in early autumn or spring, struck in sandy loam in a warm greenhouse.

Helleborus.—The Christmas rose, *H. niger*, should be planted out of the direct sun in a moist soil which has been liberally enriched with leafmould and old manure and here left free from root disturbance. Its large, white flowers appear irregularly from December to February with early flowering encouraged by protection with cloches. The Lenten rose, *H. orientalis*, flowers from February to April, and it is well worth searching nurserymens' lists for varieties with a wide range of colours. *Prop.*—Division of clumps in the spring, with each piece having four or five growth buds; the clumps should not be split into small pieces.

Hemerocallis.—Hardy perennial for moist border either open or slightly shaded. Mulch established clumps in the spring with compost or manure. Many new varieties are coming on the market as a result of introductions from America, where the plant is popular. *Prop.*—Division.

Hibiscus.—The evergreen, shrubby sorts with large exotic flowers are widely grown in the tropics and can be seen under glass in botanic gardens in Britain. *H. syriacus* is a deciduous, hardy species; little pruning is required, and in full sun it will reach 8–10 ft. Normally, it is a free-flowering plant of great beauty and, in cases where the flowers fail to develop, the stock is best replaced with good varieties, like 'Coeleste' (single, blue) and 'Woodbridge' (single, red). *Prop.*—Cuttings under glass; grafting.

Holly.—See Ilex.

Hollyhock.—See Althaea.

Honeysuckle.—See Lonicera.

House Leek.—See Sempervivum.

Hyacinth.—Bulbs generally used for bowl culture; often results are disappointing, but responsibility does not necessarily rest with the nurseryman, as poor cultivation is the most probable cause. Plant in September–early October (not later) in peat, loam, and sand, and keep as cool as possible until growth starts, when bowls may be brought into a warm room. Care must be taken with watering, as the bulbs must not dry out nor the compost allowed to become wet and soggy. After flowering, plant out-of-doors and lift annually in June for replanting in the autumn; for bowls a fresh stock is required every year.

Failures are mostly due to late planting or faulty watering.

Hydrangea.—A favourite shrub introduced from the Far East. Of the many forms, the one offered by florists, *H. macrophylla*, is the most popular. This can be bought in a wide range of shades, from white and pink through to crimson and blue. The colour will depend on soil reaction; in alkaline or neutral soils *only* white and pink shades can be grown, and blue flowers will be found *only* on acid soil. The intensity of colour can be improved by adding lime in the first instance and flowers of sulphur in the second, but it is not possible to make an alkaline garden soil acid in reaction. Lack of flower is generally the result of buds being killed by cold weather. For this reason, hydrangeas are best not pruned until the late spring; then old flower-heads and any weak or unwanted growth can be cut out. During the summer the plants must not suffer from lack of water.

Among the many other sorts are *H. paniculata*, with large, cone-shaped panicles of flower and *H. petiolaris*. The latter plant is a vigorous climber, well suited to cover cold walls or for climbing over dead trees. *Prop.*—Cuttings in July–August in a cold frame.

Iberis (Candytuft).—The hardy annual sorts will thrive in any soil, and may be had in a range of colours. See Annuals. The perennial candytuft (*I. sempervirens*) is a good plant for a rock wall and has white flowers in early spring. *Prop.*—Seeds in spring and cuttings in summer.

Ilex.—The ornamental value of our native holly is rarely fully appreciated, bearing in mind that, on good varieties, the berries sometimes persist until March. The greenish flowers are sometimes bisexual, and sometimes male and female flowers are on *separate* plants. For this reason hollies should be planted in groups, and at least one plant of good berrying habit, like *I. aquifolium* 'Pyramidalis,' grown. Some varieties have yellow berries and gold or silver variegations on their leaves. *Prop.*—Seed; special forms by budding.

Iris.—This plant is divided into two main sections: those types which grow from bulbs and those which grow from fleshy rhizomes, with many subdivisions in each of them. Of the latter type, there are the commonly grown bearded flag irises, which, owing to their ease of cultivation and wide range of colours, are appropriately known as the poor man's orchid. Notwithstanding, these irises respond to good treatment, doing best in well-dug soil to which a little manure has been added and a dressing of rough chalk forked into the surface. The site should be in full sun for preference and one that never lies wet in winter. Planting or division of established clumps is done in July, setting the rhizome on the surface of the soil but firming the roots well. To maintain growth and flower, feed annually in the spring with equal parts of superphosphate and bone meal at 3–4 oz. per sq. yd. Iris gardens are not often found nowadays, but the fine example still maintained at Kew is well worth close inspection.

In the bulbous section the Siberian iris is a graceful plant with delicate foliage, though much smaller-flowered than the flags. They make a fine waterside planting or may be grown in the herbaceous border. The Japanese iris is another water lover, and this has delicate-coloured, clematis-like flowers. On the other hand, for dry, poor, stony soils in full sun the lovely, winter-flowering, Algerian iris, *I. unguicularis* (*stylosa*), is an ideal plant, flowering as it does in December and January. This is a plant which must be left undisturbed after planting in June and if leafy growth is excessive the foliage can be cut back by half in August. Spanish, Dutch, and English types of bulbous iris are often used as cut flowers. These may be planted in ordinary garden soil in the autumn and left undisturbed until signs of deterioration are found.

Japonica.—Common misnomer of *Chaenomeles*. (*q.v.*).

Jasminum.—The yellow-flowered, sweetly scented winter jasmine blooms intermittently from November to February. It grows in any soil, and is best trained up a wall or grown on a trellis. Pruning consists of cutting out the flowering shoots as soon as the blossoms fade. The summer jasmine is a vigorous climbing plant with white, scented flowers. It needs a sunny position and should be well thinned after flowering. *Prop.*—Layering in summer.

Kalmia.—Hardy American shrubs with clusters of waxy, rose or pink blossoms in early summer. Although slow to get established and requiring a damp, acid soil, the plant is well worth growing. It constitutes a feature of the gardens of the National Trust at Sheffield Park, Sussex. *Prop.*—Seed or layering.

Kerria japonica.—A hardy shrub which will thrive in any garden but is best fed with manure to encourage strong growth. When the yellow flowers fade, the stock should be kept vigorous by cutting out old or weak growth. The plant is named after William Kerr, a young man despatched from Kew to collect plants in China. *Prop.*—Division in autumn.

Kniphofia (Red-hot Poker).—Although these plants are so commonly seen, their full value as late-flowering subjects is not often fully explored. There are a number of good varieties worth growing, such as 'Maid of Orleans' (white, 4 ft.), 'Mount Etna' (scarlet, 5 ft.), and 'Royal Standard' (gold and scarlet, 4 ft.). Of equal value is the dwarf variety with grass-like foliage, *K. nelsonii. Prop.*—Division in March; easily raised from seed if so desired.

Laburnum.—Handsome trees with long racemes of yellow flowers the seeds of which are very poisonous. It is not advisable to remove branches, as wounds do not heal well or quickly, and once a specimen shows signs of deterioration it is best replaced with little delay. *Prop.*—Seed or grafting.

Larkspur.—*See* Delphinium.

Lathyrus (Sweet Pea).—For general garden decoration, seed may be sown in pots in a warm greenhouse in early February prior to transplanting out-of-doors in April. When heat is not available sowing can be done in the open in October, setting the seed 4–6 in. apart and 2 in. deep where the plants are to grow. In this case the rows are best protected with cloches. As the plants flower with great freedom and make strong growth, a rich, deep soil is required. During the summer water should be given freely and liquid animal manure or soot water applied weekly when flowering starts. When raised for exhibition, special cultural treatment is necessary. The cause of the condition referred to as bud drop is not known, but it is thought to be connected with low temperature and faulty root action.

There is also the hardy, perennial sweet pea, an old-world plant usually seen at its best in cottage gardens. This plant requires the same cultural conditions, except that the old stems are cut down in the autumn. Three or four different species are available, and all are easily raised from seed sown in the spring.

Lavandula.—The lavender is one of the best known of garden plants. It thrives in full sun in a light soil; old flower heads should be clipped off in the summer, but any cutting back into old growth must be left until the spring. The best garden form is *L. spica* 'Nana Atropurpurea'; it has a neat, dwarf habit, with deep purple flowers, and is available from leading nurserymen. *Prop.*—Cuttings out-of-doors in August–September.

Leucojum.—The spring snowflake flowers in February and is a charming plant for any damp, shady border. Although it has a large flower, it has never become as popular as the snowdrop, despite its ease of culture. It should be grown by everyone who values early spring flowers. *Prop.*—Lift clumps and replant after removing offsets in August.

Lilac.—*See* Syringa.

Lilium.—The lilies constitute a large genus of plants, some of easy culture, some demanding the most exacting of conditions. For a soil containing chalk two of the best lilies are *L. candidum*, the Madonna lily, and *L. regale.* The former is a feature of many gardens in South Wales, where bulbs are planted near the surface of the soil and the clumps eventually left to develop undisturbed. Only the easiest-grown lilies are suitable for the herbaceous border and, here, apart from the Madonna lily, the tiger and martagon lilies should be first choices for beginners in the cultivation of this genus. *Prop.*—Those referred to above may all be raised from seed sown out-of-doors (or in deep boxes in a cold frame) in the spring. In the following April line out into nursery rows prior to transplanting to flowering positions. Also propagated by offsets and bulbils.

Lily of the Valley.—*See* Convallaria.

Lobelia.—The bedding lobelias are perennial plants best raised as annuals (*q.v.*). They do well in a light soil, but should be firmed at planting time to prevent plants dying off during a hot spell. The handsome, tall-growing lobelias with scarlet flowers, like *L. fulgens* 'Huntsman,' may be used in herbaceous borders with great effect, but the roots must be lifted and overwintered in a cold frame. These sorts grow to a height of 2–3 ft. and will do well only on a wet, heavily manured soil.

Lonicera.—The honeysuckles make effective climbing plants if grown on the shady side of arches or tree stumps or against north or west walls. Care should be taken to train young growth before it becomes hard. Old shoots may be cut out each spring to keep the plant within bounds, although space must be available for free development. If growth and flowering is poor mulch the roots in the spring with old manure. *Prop.*—Easily done by layering in late summer.

Lupins.—There are two sorts of lupins, perennial and annual. The herbaceous perennials are among the most colourful of plants as a result of the famous 'Russell' strain being introduced. Of late years, however, the constitution of the plant has been weakened through, perhaps, breeding and virus diseases, and it should be taken for granted that most stocks have to be replaced every two years or even annually in some cases. The plant requires a rich soil and is best in ground free of lime. Conversely, in poor soil the tree lupin thrives and will reach a height of 7–9 ft.; plant in full sun and lightly prune into shape after flowering. *Prop.*—Both sorts are best raised from seed sown in May out-of-doors and transferred to flowering positions in October. The annual lupin may be obtained in a range of colours, and should be grown in full sun. *See* Annuals.

Magnolia.—Rightly said to be one of the most beautiful of all flowering plants. Contrary to popular belief, some kinds are of easy culture, flowering when young and suitable for small gardens. Of course, careful selection is necessary and for a specimen on a lawn *M.* 'Soulangeana' (large, white or white, purple-stained flowers) is ideal. *M. stellata* freely flowers in the young stage, and may be planted in an ordinary border if the soil is lime free. To encourage growth, mulch annually with peat or leaf mould, but never dig near the roots. The evergreen magnolia is often seen as a fine wall plant in old gardens. This is the only species which may be pruned, and long shoots can be cut back hard in April. There are a number of non-flowering strains of the evergreen one, and unsatisfactory plants are best destroyed, as flowering cannot be induced; in buying a replacement care is necessary in order to avoid *another* dud. *Prop.*—Seed sown as soon as it is ripe in October; layering.

Mahonia.—Hardy evergreen shrub of great merit if grown well. *M. aquifolium* is useful as ground cover, thriving in any soil and in shade if protected from cold winds. *M. japonica* has long racemes of lemon-scented flowers in winter; inferior sorts are often listed by nurserymen under this name. Of equal merit is *M.* 'Charity' which by reason of its flowering in November warrants a place in any garden if free from exposure to wind. Foliage sought after by flower arrangement groups. *Prop.*—Seed, suckers, layers, cuttings in August.

Mathiola.—The night-scented stock is a hardy annual with insignificant purplish flowers which open at dusk; grown primarily for its perfume. Conversely, the so-called Ten-Week stocks and a selection of these, the East Lothian stocks, have a wide range of colours. If sown in March they may be used for summer bedding or if sown in August overwintered in a sunny frame and grown as a biennial.

Brompton stocks flower earlier than the other sorts, and are grown as a biennial by sowing seed in June or early July and, after pricking out into boxes, are overwintered in a sunny frame. In

as by careful selection of varieties a long season of flower can be obtained when they are grown in formal borders or naturalised. Thus, a season may be extended with 'Peeping Tom' and 'Covent Garden' (early) and 'Geranium' and 'Buttermilk' (late). The bulbs can be left undisturbed until flowering is affected by over-crowding; the clumps should then be lifted and be divided in the late summer. To maintain vigour, feed annually in February with 2 parts bone meal, 1 part hoof and horn meal, and 1 part sulphate of potash at 2–3 oz. per sq. yd. The chief troubles with narcissi are due to eelworm (T29) and the narcissus bulb fly (T28). For indoor work, plant in bowls in October and keep in cold place until growth is an inch high; failure is invariably due to premature forcing or faulty watering.

Nasturtium.—*See* **Tropaeolum.**

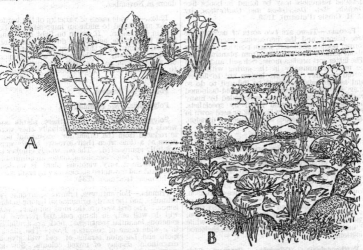

WATER LILIES IN TUBS—Drawing (A) shows a cross-section with correct percentage of water and soil together with water lilies and fish. Drawing (B) illustrates marginal planting with primulas, Japanese irises, and a dwarf coniferous tree.

mild districts, if the soil is well drained, stocks may be planted out-of-doors in the autumn, but a reserve should be kept for filling up gaps in the spring.

Meconopsis.—This genus includes the famous "blue poppy," introduced from the Himalayas. It is not a plant of easy culture, albeit large groups are grown in many woodland gardens where soil conditions permit. After flowering the plants generally die, although an occasional plant may persist. *Prop.*—Seed sown in March.

Michaelmas Daisy.—*See* **Aster.**

Montbretia.—This bulbous plant is of easy culture and has a long season of flowering. Many new varieties with large flowers are now available, and growth can be kept vigorous by lifting and dividing the clumps every three or four years. Plant in early spring 4 in. deep and 6 in. apart and in cold gardens protect clumps in winter with a covering of ashes.

Myosotis.—The forget-me-not is grown as a biennial by sowing seed in May and planting out in the autumn in conjunction with spring-flowering bulbs and wallflowers. Poor varieties freely establish themselves, and these should be destroyed before planting any of the really good sorts offered by seedsmen.

Narcissus.—This botanical name includes plants commonly known as "daffodil" and "narcissus." Although often grown, the wide garden value of these spring-flowering bulbs is not fully realised,

Nepeta (Catmint).—In recent years this edging plant with silvery foliage and mauve flowers has become increasingly popular. When flowering in mid-summer there is no finer display of colour. It grows freely on any light, well-drained soil in full sun. The best sort is *N. faassenii*. *Prop.*—Division of clumps in March.

Nerine.—Lately this lovely bulbous plant has increased in popularity mainly through the varieties introduced from the late Lionel de Rothschild's garden at Exbury. The hardy sort *N. bowdenii* flowers in the autumn and should be planted at the foot of a warm wall in August or September and left undisturbed for many years. As the bulbs gradually multiply and work to the surface, a light dressing of sandy compost, to which has been added a little bone meal, can be applied. *Prop.*—Separation of bulbs in August.

Nicotiana (Tobacco Plant).—This half-hardy annual is grown mainly for its heavily scented flowers, which open in the evening. It is worth remembering that the white-flowered sorts are the best in this respect; scarlets and pinks are very much inferior. *See* **Annuals.** The tobacco of commerce is a different plant, namely, *N. tabacum*.

Nymphaea.—No branch of gardening is more fascinating than the water garden, and for it the chief plant must be the water lily. Basically, the main reason for failure is in the fact that in most pools the *average* depth of water is less than 18 in.; this means that the water is liable to be adversely affected by extremes of temperature. All nymphaeas should be grown in full sun and where the water is still; in streams it is necessary to utilise a little backwater out of the current. Water lilies are planted in May in large wicker baskets with a compost of three-quarters of loam and a quarter of peat; alternatively, planting sites can be built up with bricks to the desired height. If growth is poor, mould "Clay's Fertiliser" into the size of pigeons' eggs and drop one around each clump. To maintain a healthy condition in the water, fish should be introduced as soon as the plants are established. *Prop.*—Division of tuberous roots in late May.

Orchids.—In the main, this large group of plants needs greenhouse conditions and specialised knowledge. Their cultivation has attracted the attention of some of the greatest of horticulturists, and detailed references may be found in books like *Orchids, their Description and Cultivation*, by C. H. Curtis (Putnam), 1950.

Paeonia.—There are two sorts of paeony, the tree paeony and the herbaceous paeony. The former needs a sheltered, warm position and takes about three years to flower from planting time. The latter sort needs a moist, rich soil, and should be mulched annually in the spring with well-rotted manure; some are known not to flower, and as such plants cannot be induced to do so they should be destroyed. The old-fashioned variety of paeony has been superseded by many fine new varieties found listed by specialists. *Prop.*—Tree paeonies by layering or seed sown in the autumn; herbaceous sorts by seed or division.

Pansy.—*See* Viola.

Papaver (Poppy).—The oriental poppy is a hardy herbaceous perennial with striking flowers, intolerant of shade and root disturbance. As it blooms early, it should be set near the back of a border, as the large leaves look untidy later in the year. Apart from the commonly grown, red-flowered sort there are others in shades of crimson, pink, and lavender. *Prop.*—A wide range of colours can be obtained by sowing mixed seeds in May. This is a better method than division. The Shirley poppy is a hardy annual (*q.v.*), while *P. nudicale* is a biennial needing a warm, sheltered position.

Parthenocissus (Virginia Creeper).—This climber, with its brilliantly-coloured leaves, makes a fine sight in the autumn, and there is no better plant for covering brickwork or unsightly buildings with a south or west aspect. It has been suggested (mainly by builders) that the plant will damage stonework or cause dampness. There is little evidence to support these suppositions, and reasons for damage can usually be traced—often without difficulty—to other sources. The plant has had a number of names—*Ampelopsis veitchii* is one—but up-to-date nurserymen are listing it correctly as *P. tricuspidata*. *Prop.*—Cuttings out-of-doors in the late summer; layering.

Passiflora caerulea (Passion Flower).—A south wall in favoured gardens is needed to grow this plant. It is of vigorous habit and, once the framework of branches has been produced, it should be pruned annually in the early spring, by cutting back all the previous season's growth to 2–3 in. of the main stem. *Prop.*—Layering.

Pelargonium (Geranium).—So-called "bedding geraniums," such as 'Paul Crampel,' are really zonal pelargoniums. To maintain a stock, take cuttings in early August and insert in sandy soil around the edge of a pot and overwinter in a frost-free greenhouse. In the spring pot-up singly and use for bedding. Otherwise pot-on after two months and, if early buds are nipped off, plants can be adopted for late flowering indoors. Pelargoniums are easy to grow, but for best results a position in full sun is necessary, and cuttings should be rooted *before* the autumn so that over-wintering constitutes no great difficulty.

Petunia.—Although really perennials, these plants, native of South America, are treated as annuals (*q.v.*). They are sun lovers and do best

on light soils. Petunias make fine plants for sunny window boxes, and particularly happy combinations can be made by planting together varieties such as 'Violacea' (deep violet) and 'Cheerful' (pale pink) or 'Flaming Velvet' (crimson) and 'Cream Star' (pale cream). The violet-flowered sorts are faintly scented.

Philadelphus (Mock Orange).—Although some fine varieties of this shrub are available in the trade, it is not grown as widely as its merit deserves. As a scented shrub it has few equals, while it is tolerant of poor soil conditions and shade. Particularly good sorts worth searching for are 'Albatre' (double), 'Beauclerk' (single), and 'Sybille,' which, at 3 ft., is about half the height of the others. After flowering, prune annually by removing as much old flowering wood as possible. *Prop.*—Hard-wood cuttings out-of-doors in November.

Phlox.—A wide range of varieties of the border phlox are offered to make an impressive display late in the season. If grown on light soils some shade is desirable, as phloxes do well where only the soil is damp. For this reason, mulching should be done annually in the spring with compost or animal manure. Failures are usually due to eelworm (**T**30). *Prop.*—Seeds in autumn: division.

Poppy.—*See* Papaver.

Polyanthus.—*See* Primula.

Polygonum.—In the main these plants are weeds of gardens, although originally they were introduced from the Orient for ornamental purposes at a time when their invasive habits were not fully appreciated. The one woody climber in the genus, *P. baldschuanicum*, makes an admirable cover where a very vigorous plant is wanted. Rampant and unwanted species may be eradicated by hormone treatment (**T**34).

Primula.—Polyanthuses, primroses, greenhouse primulas, and the hardy primulas all belong in this genus. The first two are the most popular; both will do well only in damp soil and respond to generous manurial treatment; both are available in a wide range of colours. *Prop.*—The Blackmore and Langdon strains of seed will give a magnificent display of mixed colours. Sow in warm greenhouse in early March or cold frame in April; prick out into boxes and transfer to flowering positions in the autumn.

Prunus.—A large genus which includes the flowering peaches, Japanese cherries, and flowering almonds. All of them are best left to develop

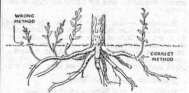

WRONG METHOD

CORRECT METHOD

REMOVAL OF SUCKERS—As illustrated, these must be sawn off into the root or pulled off the root with a sharp tug and never so removed that dormant buds are left.

naturally and are not responsive to pruning or cutting back in any way. A few sorts are overplanted in gardens and as street trees (by Park Superintendents), but anybody wishing to be a little out of the ordinary would do well to see the wide range of some of these lovely trees flowering in April and May in our botanic gardens and many of the large gardens now under the jurisdiction of the National Trust. The selection offered by nurserymen is often strictly along conventional lines. Lack of flower in some seasons can often be traced to bird damage.

Red-hot Poker.—*See* Kniphofia.

Rhododendron.—Greenhouse and hardy, ever-green and deciduous shrubs, including *Azalea*. With something like ten thousand different sorts, it is impossible to deal with individual require-ments. General cultivation; an acidic soil is essential, with adequate moisture in summer. If growth is poor on established plants, mulch liber-ally with animal manure. Beginners should plant from the accepted list of hardy garden hybrids. Since the turn of the century widely planted and fine examples are to be found, for instance, in many gardens of the National Trust. *Prop.*—Seed and layering.

Romneya.—Since its introduction from Cali-fornia in about 1850 the plant has proved a fascina-tion to gardeners, as sometimes it fails completely

will control mildew provided the bushes are well mulched and watered. Captan or maneb should be used immediately after pruning and throughout the summer to control black spot, but thiram for rust control need not be used until the disease appears. Good manurial treatment including foliar feeding will help to *prevent* disease. For control of greenfly *see* **Aphids, T29**.

For a manurial programme, an application of 2 parts of superphosphate and 1 part of sulphate of potash should be applied at 3 oz. per sq. yd. after pruning. Following this, a surface mulch of animal manure, compost, peat, or leaf-mould or a mixture of all of them is given about 2–3 in. thick. Subsequently, if growth is poor, a dressing of nitro-chalk can be made at 1 oz. per sq. yd.

Where soil conditions are poor and disease

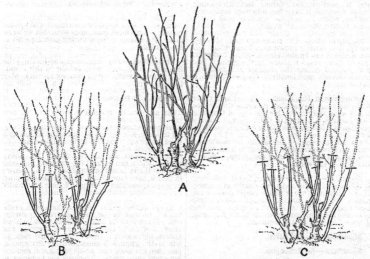

PRUNING ROSES—(A) A vigorous unpruned plant. (B) The same plant pruned for the production of exhibition blooms. (C) and pruned for garden decoration.

or does exceedingly well. It apears to require a light soil and a sheltered position, preferably against a sunny wall, and there is no point in trying to grow a romneya on a heavy, wet soil. Usually the annual stems die off in the winter and may be cut down at ground level in the early spring; if persistent the stems can be cut back to sound growth. The new growth is susceptible to slug damage, and appropriate steps must be taken (T29). *Prop.*—Seed or suckers taken off in the spring.

Rosa (Rose).—Undoubtedly the rose is the most popular of all garden flowers, and it may be found in a multitude of forms. The dwarf roses for bedding may be grown on most soils, but are best on a rich, heavy loam. Planting is done from early November onwards when soil conditions permit and the first pruning carried out in the following spring, when the extent of any winter damage can be seen. Opinions differ sharply on pruning; a sound, general rule is to do the work in March and—unless there are special circum-stances—to prune on the light side. Thus, for Hybrid Teas and the like, reduce strong stems by about one-third of their length, medium ones by a half, and weak ones to within two or three buds of the main stem.

Whatever sorts of soil roses are grown in, feeding is important, but, of course, it is particularly so on poor ones. It is in soils of *low* fertility that diseases such as rust and black spot are most pre-valent and, in some measure, persistence of the disease is due to bad cultivation and lack of treat-ment with fertilisers. Regular dinocap sprays

prevalent, it is important to buy plants only from nurserymen who take special precautions to ensure that their customers have disease-free stock. Likewise, varieties of robust constitution are essential, and a selection list may include: *Hybrid Teas:* 'Ballet' (pink), 'Eden Rose' (magenta pink, 'King's Ransome' (yellow), 'Perfecta' (pink and white), 'Super Star' (coral orange) and 'Wendy Cussons' (rosy red). *Floribundas:* 'Circus' (bicolour yellow/scarlet), 'Dusky Maiden' (crimson), 'Iceberg' (white), 'Queen Elizabeth' (pink) and 'Spartan' (deep salmon).

In most of the modern hybrids scent is almost absent. The true rose perfume is found only in the Old Fashion or shrub roses and, normally, these are planted in a mixed shrub border. For the richest perfume varieties like 'Mrs. John Laing' and 'Conrad F. Meyer' should be sought.

Salvia.—Annuals, perennials, and tender shrubs. The most popular one is the scarlet sort used for bedding. It requires careful attention, and seed should be sown in February in a temperature of 60° Fahrenheit and seedlings put into single pots when large enough. Gradually the young plants are hardened off and finally planted out in rich soil in a sunny bed.

Saxifraga.—A large genus of plants suitable for the rock garden and valued for their bright flowers in the spring. The encrusted saxifrages are cushion-forming plants requiring sharp, surface drainage and an open position out of the direct sun. The mossy saxifrages are mat-forming in growth and of easy culture. In time old clumps develop brown patches and then require splitting up and replanting in the spring.

Scabiosa.—The commonly grown perennial sort is *S. caucasica* and is invaluable as a cut flower. It is not at home on all soils, and only does really well in a deep, rich loam containing plenty of chalk. In addition, it must be grown in full sun and particular care taken against slugs. *Prop.*— Old plants divided in the spring and rooted pieces replanted in their flowering positions. A wide range of shades in white, blue, and purple can be had normally from sowing mixed seed in April.

Sedum.—The stonecrops make up a large group of hardy and tender plants, but comparatively few are of horticultural value. Notwithstanding, *Sedum spectabile* is to be found in most herbaceous borders, where its fine, flat heads of pink flowers are a feature for many weeks. It is beloved by bees and butterflies. *S. sieboldii* was introduced from Japan about 100 years ago and, although hardy, it is usually grown as a house plant. In the winter it can be stood out-of-doors, and every two or three years repotted in the spring; keep well watered during the summer and feed with liquid manure occasionally. *Prop.*—Division in the spring.

Sempervivum (House leek).—These hardy plants with succulent leaves often decorate the crevices of old walls and are regular features of trough or sink gardens. If given a light poor soil and a position in full sun a fascinating collection of house leeks can be built up. The species which gives the plant its common name can be established easily on a sunny roof by planting in a mixture of cow manure and clay during the spring. *Prop.*— Division in the spring.

Skimmia.—A hardy evergreen 2–3 ft. tall which is tolerant of shade and some degree of dryness. If growth is poor water with a liquid manure and mulch with peat or leaf mould. Some forms bear only male flowers and to ensure a good crop of berries plant an hermaphrodite like *S. foremanii*. *Prop.*—Layering in the autumn.

Snowdrop.—*See* Galanthus.

Snowflake.—*See* Leucojum.

Solanum capsicastrum (Winter Cherry).—A berrying plant with bright-red fruits which is often used for house decoration. To maintain the plant in a healthy condition it should be clear of draughts and fumes of gas fires and the foliage kept fresh and free of dust by vigorous syringing. If the stock is to be kept for more than one season water should be given only sparingly in the New Year, and in early March all the side shoots pruned back hard to within a bud or two of the main stems. As new growth develops, water can be given more freely and syringing started when the flowers first appear; liquid manure will prove beneficial when berries develop.

Spiraea.—Hardy deciduous shrubs for open borders; tolerant of poor soil conditions. The commonly grown one is *Spiraea bumalda* (syn. *japonica*). After flowering, a percentage of the old wood should be removed together with any weak growth, and development of new shoots encouraged by mulching with compost or animal manure. *Prop.*—Cuttings rooted in sandy soil under a hand light in summer; suckers thinned out in winter.

Stocks.—*See* Mathiola.

Sunflower.—*See* Helianthus.

Sweet William.—*See* Dianthus.

Symphoricarpos (Snowberry).—Often found existing in deep shade and in competition with roots of overhanging trees, presumably as a result of the generalisation that the shrub is a shade lover. Certainly a useful one in this respect, but it is responsive to good treatment. Given an average soil and if growth is thinned annually in

the early spring, then *S. albus* ' Laevigatus ' is well worth having. Its large white fruits are untouched by birds and hang well into the winter, and are thus beloved by the floral decorator. *Prop.*—Suckers removed in the winter.

Syringa (Lilac).—The botanical name of *Syringa* is often erroneously applied to the Mock Orange, correctly named *Philadelphus* (*q.v.*). A wide selection of first-class varieties are available in nurserymen's lists. To obtain heavy crops of flowers nip off all dead flower-heads as the blossom fades, but do *not* cut back into the old stem, as this will prevent flowering. At the same time any branches causing overcrowding can be removed. Annually feed with " National Growmore " at 2 oz. per sq. yd. and on sandy soils mulch with any sort of manure or compost. *Prop.*—Layering in the autumn.

Tagetes (African and French Marigolds).—Half-hardy annuals of free-flowering habit and easiest culture. Best if fed generously with soot water or other nitrogenous manure during growing season. *See* Annuals.

Tropaeolum.—The common nasturtium and the flame flower (*T. speciosum*) belong to this genus. The former is easily grown from seed sown in May in a sunny position. The latter is a very difficult plant to grow outside the conditions which it demands. To be successful, this perennial climber must be planted in acid soil which is naturally damp and lightly shaded but yet where the new growth can reach full sun. Much disappointment often results from planting it in eastern England, for instance, after seeing it flourishing almost as a weed where the rainfall is high in Ireland and the west of Scotland.

In the genus will also be found the canary creeper, which can be used for screening purposes and will thrive in full sun or shade. Seed is sown in May in open ground and light supports supplied by way of pea sticks or strings; failure is normally due to nothing more than lack of moisture.

Tulipa (Tulip).—Thrives in a deep, rich loam, but will do well for one season in ordinary garden soil. When used for bedding, bulbs must be lifted after flowering, replanted in a trench, and thoroughly watered. Sometimes tulips may be left in the ground *if* conditions are favourable, and then the stock only needs lifting and replanting every three years. To check the incidence of tulip fire plant in late November or early December, covering the bulbs with 4–5 in. of soil and treat the ground with a fungicide like " Botrilex." Before doing so rake in a dressing of 2 oz. superphosphate and 1 oz. sulphate of potash per square yard. A national collection of wild tulips is being got together at Cambridge and grown there in the University Botanic Garden.

Viola.—This name embraces pansies, violas, and violets. Although the viola has not got the rich colours of the pansy (or its attractive markings), it has got a remarkably long season of flower, and for this reason it is invaluable as an edging plant or as ground cover for roses. *Prop.*—Both plants are easily raised from seed sown in a frame in the spring, pricked out, and then transferred to their flowering positions in late May. Alternatively, seed may be sown in July for planting out in October. Named varieties increased by cuttings in a frame in late summer.

Virginia creeper.—*See* Parthenocissus.

Wallflower.—*See* Cheiranthus.

Water Lily.—*See* Nymphaea.

Winter Sweet.—*See* Chimonanthus.

Wistaria.—One of the finest of all climbing plants for south or west walls or stout pergolas. Plants which do not flower, or only do so poorly, are probably seedlings and the true flowering habit cannot be induced; the only solution is to replace with a *grafted* plant of known flowering capacity from a reliable nurseryman. All young shoots not required for the extension of branches should be shortened to within 3 in. of the old stem in the autumn. Wistarias growing over trees do not require pruning. *Prop.*—Layer shoots of current season's growth in the autumn.

Zinnia.—Half-hardy annual, ideally grown on moist, deep loam liberally enriched with well-decayed manure. Mulch with manure after planting and apply liquid fertiliser as buds appear; plants must not suffer from lack of water. *See* Annuals.

Standard References.

Collins Guide to Roses, by Bertram Park (Collins), 1962 (25s.).

Hortus Second, by L. H. Bailey and Ethel Zoe Bailey (Macmillan), 1947 (40s.).

R.H.S. *Dictionary of Gardening*, edited by F. J. Chittenden (Oxford), 1956 (14 guineas).

Sanders' *Encyclopaedia of Gardening*, revised by A. G. L. Hellyer (Collingridge), 1952 (25s.).

The Dictionary of Garden Plants in Colour, Hay and Synge (R.H.S.), 1969 (60s.).

MAKING A LAWN.

In almost every garden the most prominent feature is the lawn, and often a lot of work is put into making one without any great measure of success. Usually, the reason for failure may be found in faulty preparation of the soil or premature sowing, albeit the blame is often placed on bird damage or poor seed.

For anything like a reasonable turf, the site must be thoroughly dug and the content of organic matter increased by incorporating generous quantities of materials like peat, leaf-mould, compost, sewage sludge, and animal manure. A dressing of these ingredients can be applied in a layer 3–4 in. thick and buried in the bottom of the top spit of soil. As the ground is dug to incorporate the organic matter, roots of perennial weeds should be removed.

If the site is one on which water tends to lie or if the soil is heavy, then surface drainage should be sharpened by forking into the top 2 or 3 in. a liberal application of some coarse material such as builders' rubble, road grit, screened ashes, or coarse sand. In some cases this treatment will not be sufficient, and then the installation of land drains must be resorted to. This particular task is not as difficult as is sometimes imagined, but, before a start is made, it is always a good plan to discuss the matter with an experienced man.

After the initial work a fine tilth on the soil may be obtained by thoroughly raking and cross-raking and at the same time establishing a level surface. On this point, it should be remembered that good lawns can be made on undulating ground or on natural slopes, but the things to avoid are the shallow depressions where water will naturally tend to lie. Finally, ten to fourteen days before sowing the subsequent growth of grass can be encouraged by making an application of " National Growmore " at 2 oz. per sq. yd.

Sowing is best done in the late summer at a time when the soil is moist For the purpose, a good mixture of seed should be obtained from a reliable seedsman, and it is worth paying a reasonable price for it, as, by and large, the coarsest and roughest grasses have the largest and heaviest seeds. Opinions differ on rates of sowing, but, with care and in a well-prepared soil, 1 oz. per sq. yd. is ample; heavier rates will give quicker results, but the density of seedlings in such cases often leads to the finer grasses being choked by the coarser ones.

After sowing, the ground should be lightly raked, but not rolled. At this stage the important point is to protect the seed bed from birds by the use of hazel sticks, strings of papers tied to stakes after they have been dipped in lime-wash, and strands of black cotton. Subsequently, annual weeds may appear in quantity; these are of no consequence, and they will be eliminated once the grass is cut regularly. Until a good turf is formed —usually about twelve months after sowing—it is not desirable (or probably necessary) to use hormone weed-killers. *See* T33.

Care of Established Lawns.

Most turf is never manured from year to year, and the soil may seriously lack plant foods. In the first place this can be corrected by making an application annually in the spring of " National Growmore " at 1 oz. per sq. yd. Following this, if growth is below par in the early part of the year an application of sulphate of ammonia can be made at the same rate. To avoid scorching or blackening of the foliage, each fertiliser can be mixed with equal parts of dry soil or sand as a carrier to ensure even distribution and, what is most important, each one should be applied only when the turf is wet and there is the prospect of rain to follow. Linked with this treatment, turf is always responsive to top dressings. A compost for the purpose can be made up with:

2 parts of loam;
1 part of sieved compost;
1 part of fine peat or leaf soil.

This may be used in the spring at 3–5 lb. per sq. yd. and if the soil is heavy 1–2 parts of gritty sand may be added.

With the introduction of new designs in motor mowers, most lawns are seriously overcut, and this has led to a sharp decline in the quality of the grass and the appearance of one or two pernicious weeds. It is appreciated that special turf, such as that found on a bowling green, may be shaved off to $\frac{1}{8}$ in., but if a utility lawn is cut below half to 1 in., then the quality of the grass will deteriorate. Of course, it is a good thing to occasionally cut the grass very short, but, conversely, if the blades of the mower are set as low as possible and left like it throughout the season nothing but harm can result. The reason for this hard fact is that when the turf is cut very close the grasses simply cannot develop and spread, and weeds will gradually establish themselves. Eventually the cultivator will be faced with the difficult problem of trying to deal with such plants as pearlwort, yarrow, and various mosses, all of which are resistant to hormones.

As for the vexed question of whether or not to remove the mowings, there is no doubt that the best turf is found where the mowings are collected up, although in very dry weather they can be left on the surface. If the clippings are not removed the surface of the turf tends to become choked with semi-decayed organic matter, and conditions are brought about which are inducive to the spread of moss.

Finally, it is worth noting that the finest turf is found on acidic—not alkaline—soils. For this reason, lime should not be applied as a general rule, for apart from helping the development of coarse grasses, it encourages the growth of clover. Of course, there are times when lime is necessary, but the occasions are rare and before it is used it is a good plan to test the soil by chemical means.

THE FRUIT GARDEN.

The guidance of an expert is probably more important in the growing of fruit than for most of the commoner vegetables and ornamentals. This is primarily because the majority of fruit trees and bushes are long-lived, and only in the case of strawberries can a change of site or variety be made easily and inexpensively.

Gardens which are low-lying are very prone to damage from spring frosts, and should not have too much space devoted to fruit, as returns may well prove unprofitable. Here, as with the selection of varieties, advice of a local expert is invaluable. Some varieties do better in certain localities and on certain soils than others, although personal preferences will naturally be met where possible. Varieties chosen should cover as long a season as is practicable so that the fruit can be used and enjoyed to the full.

Tree fruits are grown on a rootstock, and for apples and pears special dwarfing stocks make these a possibility for the small garden. It is therefore important to explain to the nurseryman what type of tree is required. As a general rule, however, the smaller gardens will gain by concentrating on currants, gooseberries, raspberries, and strawberries. Plums and cherries have no dwarfing stocks, and should be included only where sufficient room is available.

Apples.—Can be grown on most soils. Manure should not be used when planting, except in sandy and chalky gardens. Obtain trees on dwarfing rootstocks, such as M.IX, M.VII, or MM.106. Always stake trees on M.IX, otherwise this practice is necessary only in exposed sites. The tie must be rigid, with a "cushion" between tree and stake to avoid chafing, and must be renewed annually to avoid constriction. Plant between late October and early March, preferably before Christmas if soil and weather allow. Make the hole large enough to spread the roots evenly; firm thoroughly while filling in and plant level with the nursery soil mark already on the tree. Mulch around each tree with manure or compost, mainly to avoid drying out, and supplement with watering during the summer when necessary.

In the first year any flowers produced are best pinched out to encourage root and shoot development. For walls or fences use oblique cordons or espaliers; these are also useful for flanking paths and lawns. Plant cordons 2½ ft. apart with 6 ft. between rows, and espaliers 12–15 ft. apart. For larger areas use bush trees 12–15 ft. apart.

Manuring for cropping trees should be varied according to growth. Generally apply 1 oz. sulphate of ammonia (or nitro chalk on acid soils) in early March, repeating this in early April if trees are growing in grass. Give ½ oz. sulphate of potash in February and add 3 oz. of superphosphate every third year. The above rates are per square yard, and a complete fertiliser can be used in lieu if preferred.

Young bush trees should have main shoots reduced by half in early years to produce strong branches. Thereafter prune side shoots to three to six buds. For weak growers prune harder, and for strong growers prune less. It is wiser to leave a strong tree unpruned than to prune it too severely, the latter merely encouraging even stronger growth. A few varieties (*e.g.*, 'Bramley's Seedling', 'Worcester Pearmain') fruit at shoot tips, and here a proportion of side shoots should be left unpruned. Summer pruning is advisable on restricted trees, such as cordons; for details see **Pears (T17)**.

Very few varieties are self-fertile, and at least two sorts should be planted to ensure satisfactory crops. Good combinations are 'Cox's Orange Pippin' with 'Laxton's Fortune' and 'Winston' with the cooker 'Lord Derby.' Seek expert advice on pairings if in doubt. Some discerning housewives like apples which break down or fluff on cooking; in this case 'Emneth Early,' 'Lane's Prince Albert' or 'Monarch' may be planted. For those wanting one which stays firm on cooking 'Bramley's Seedling' should be chosen.

Blackberries.—In modern gardens, where space is limited, the best returns in fruit growing are often with the cultivated forms of blackberries and loganberries. Plant at least 10–12 ft. apart against fences and train on wires set 3 ft., 5 ft. and 6 ft. above soil level.

Cropping is dependent on manurial treatment as all are heavy feeders. When planting enrich the site with manure, compost or leafsoil; afterwards mulch the surface with one of them. Annually the ground should be topdressed with compost supplemented with a nitrogenous manure like sulphate of ammonia, chicken manure or dried blood. Also apply sulphate of potash at 1 oz. per sq. yard. Such treatment will show excellent results and, as a bonus, normally ensures a prize at any local Show. After planting, do not lack courage to cut back all growths to within a foot of ground level and keep the soil moist throughout the growing season.

Cherries.—Sweet cherries are unsuited to most gardens. The trees become too large, and *must* be planted in selected pairs to fruit satisfactorily, as all varieties are self-sterile. Large wall spaces are ideal for fan trees, as the fruit can then be protected from birds by the use of nets. Pinch side shoots on fans to four leaves in July; further pruning details being as for plums. Expert advice is essential to ensure that suitable varieties are grown together the factors involved being

complicated. 'Early Rivers' with 'Bigarreau Schrecken' and 'Merton Heart' with 'Waterloo' are good combinations.

Currants, Black.—These are perhaps the most valuable of all hardy fruits, and bushes will give up to 10 lb. and more of currants with correct treatment. Plant from November to February, preferably autumn, at 5 ft. square on clean, heavily manured ground. In the following spring it is important to cut *all* the shoots to within 3 ins. of ground level in order to encourage strong new growth.

Poor results with this fruit are often due to keeping old or worn out bushes when the cropping life is past which, for blackcurrants is around 10 years. Another reason is the lack of feeding. Each spring bushes should be mulched with compost supplemented with a nitrogenous fertilizer like sulphate of ammonia at 1 oz. per sq. yard and superphosphate at double this rate.'

On established bushes prune preferably after fruiting or in winter, retaining strong young wood and cutting out older shoots, where possible from ground level. If necessary, alternate bushes can be cut down completely every other year to maintain vigour, as the bulk of the crop is always borne on young wood. Increase by 8-in. cuttings of one-year-old wood taken in late September from healthy bushes. Remove lower leaves and insert firmly with one bud above ground. Good varieties: 'Boskoop Giant,' 'Wellington XXX.'

Currants, Red and White.—One or two well-grown bushes are usually sufficient for the average household. Plant between November and March at a minimum of 5 ft. square on well-manured ground and mulch each spring. Supplement with fertilisers if necessary, potash being particularly important in the form of sulphate of potash at 1 oz. per sq. yd. in February. Can be grown as cordons or fans against walls or fences, on which the pinching of young side shoots to four leaves in mid-June is essential. Winter pruning of all types simply involves cutting side shoots to one bud and tip pruning branch leaders.

Propagate by 12-in. cuttings of young shoots in late September inserted to half their length with all buds removed except the top four. This enables the bush to be grown on a "leg." A permanent framework of branches is then developed, as, in contrast to the black currant, fruit is borne on spurs on the old wood. Good varieties: 'Laxton's No. 1,' 'White Grape.'

Damson.—*See* Plums.

Figs.—A warm south wall is usually essential, 'Brown Turkey' being one of the few reliable outdoor varieties. Plant in a brick or concrete trough (with drainage holes) about 2½ ft. wide, 5 ft. long, and 2½ ft. deep so that the root run is restricted. This will curb excessive growth (which otherwise is difficult to control) and encourage fruiting.

Plant in March for preference, to avoid frost injury to young shoots, and then train fan-wise. A rich soil is not essential. Figs visible as such in the autumn will never over-winter, and should be rubbed out. Those the size of a pea and less at the tips of short, well-ripened shoots, on the other hand, are the potential crop for the following year, and should be covered in severe weather to avoid frost damage. To encourage the formation of these embryo fruits pinch young shoots back to the fifth leaf in late August. Winter prune in March, removing any wood that is frosted, overcrowded, or worn out; growths should be spaced at about 1 ft. Apply a spring mulch and water freely when required to avoid premature fruit drop.

Gooseberries.—Need conditions and spacing very similar to red currants, but with rather more moisture to ensure ample new wood, as this bears fruit as well as the older wood. Apply sulphate of ammonia and sulphate of potash annually in late February or March at 1 oz. per sq. yd of each in addition to mulching. Can also be grown as cordons, etc., as for red currants. Pruning is also similar, though not quite so severe, as the young wood is productive of fruit. Cuttings are more difficult to root, and for best results should be taken in mid-September, again as for red currants. Good varieties: ' Lancer,' ' Leveller,' ' Whinham's Industry.'

Grapes.—Outdoor vines should be grown against a warm south- or south-west-facing wall. With good cultivation, the grapes should then ripen successfully providing suitable varieties are chosen. In preparing the site ensure that it is well drained and break up the soil to a depth of about 2 ft. Add bone meal to the top few inches at 3–4 oz. per sq. yd. and incorporate mortar rubble, particularly on the heavier soils. Do not dig in any manure except on poor, light soils, but always apply some as a mulch after planting, repeating this every spring. On poor, hungry soils the importation of some fibrous loam is advisable where possible.

Plant in November or, failing this, before early March, with the stem about 6–9 in. away from the wall. Firm well and then wait a further two months before tying to any wires or stakes, in case of soil sinkage. Cut the vine back in winter to well-ripened wood and to just above a bud. The training of subsequent growth will then depend on the space available, single and double cordons being the most convenient. Unwanted shoots should be pinched at about 2 ft. in summer and leading shoots carefully tied in to wire or bamboo supports. The following winter (December) prune leading shoots back to well-ripened wood so as to leave 3–4 ft. of new growth. Then cut all laterals hard back to *one* bud. In spring reduce young side shoots to one at each bud, stop laterals at about 12 in., and pinch any sub-laterals that may develop to the first leaf. Do not allow any crop to develop, except perhaps one bunch if growth is adequate; others should be pinched off. As fruit develops, thinning should be done as required. Winter prune as before, and then in the third summer four or five bunches of grapes can be allowed if the vine is healthy, the crop then increasing annually. Shoots carrying bunches should be pinched to two leaves beyond the bunch. Winter pruning is repeated each year as already described. Sour top-soil should be carefully removed when necessary and replaced with good loam while the vine is dormant. Good varieties: ' Black Hamburgh ' and ' Foster's Seedling.'

Loganberries.—A very popular hybrid berry which should be treated as for blackberries. A thornless form is now available. Suitable for a north wall.

Medlars.—A tree of spreading habit, the peculiar fruits of which are best used for jelly before they are fully ripened. Most soils are suitable, and no pruning is needed except to keep in shape.

Nectarines.—A fruit very closely allied to the peach but with a richer flavour and needing rather more warmth. The skin is smooth, as distinct from the hairiness of the peach. For full details see Peach.

Nuts.—The most important kinds grown are cobnuts, the closely related filberts, and walnuts, but none of these is cultivated to any great extent. The two former kinds flower very early in February, and are therefore predisposed to frost damage; similarly, the young shoots of walnuts are easily injured by spring frosts, and all are therefore inadvisable for frosty areas.

Cobnuts and filberts.—Highly developed forms of the ordinary hazel nut. The nut of a cob is only partially covered by the husk whereas a filbert is completely enclosed by it, this being the essential difference between the two. Will grow on most soils, including the poorer ones, and spacing should be about 15 ft., choosing sites sheltered from the colder winds. Plant during the autumn. Prune established bushes in March cutting back shoots that have borne nuts to two or three buds; strong young shoots are cut back to a catkin near their base, and the weaker ones are left untouched. In August any strong new side growths are " brutted "—that is, broken off—and left hanging until the March pruning. Gather the nuts as they fall and allow to dry. Then store in jars for Christmas use, packing salt and coconut fibre between each layer of nuts.

Walnuts.—Special, grafted varieties are now available which produce early crops compared with the unreliable seedling trees that used to be planted. Plant between October and March and water well in spring and summer. Do not prune, as walnuts bleed badly. Gather nuts in mid-July for pickling. For storing allow to drop naturally and remove outer husk immediately, scrubbing the shell clean and then drying thoroughly. The shells can be bleached if necessary before storing the nuts as for cobs above.

Peaches.—This fruit along with its close ally, the nectarine, is best grown against a warm south or south-west wall, but two varieties of peach, ' Peregrine ' and more particularly ' Rochester,' will succeed as bushes in the open in southern England. The fan-trained peach is one of the most difficult trees to keep in order, as sufficient new shoots must be retained annually to replace old wood. This is essential, as it is only the previous year's shoots which bear fruit. Badly placed shoots are rubbed out when only an inch long, and the principle is to allow one young replacement shoot to develop near the base of each fruiting shoot, pruning back to the former and tying it in as soon as all fruit has been picked. Other shoots may be used to extend the fan where space allows or to replace any branches or parts of them which may have become worn out. Other unwanted shoots are bound to arise during each summer, and these are either removed immediately or pinched to three leaves and then removed when pruning in late summer. Those shoots retained are spaced at about 4 in. apart.

Most peaches are self-fertile, but hand-pollinating on sunny days can improve the set. Excessive feeding should be avoided, varying this according to each tree's performance, but as a general rule a surface mulch of well-rotted manure or compost should always be given each spring, together with sulphate of potash at ½–1 oz. per sq. yd. Prick over and rake off top-soil and replace with good loam every few years. Never allow the sub-soil to dry out—this can quickly occur against warm walls—and water thoroughly when doing so to ensure an even distribution of moisture. On the other hand, drainage must be satisfactory to avoid waterlogging.

There are numerous other essential operations in the growing of trained peach trees (for example, fruit thinning), and it is impossible to deal with these adequately in brief notes. Would-be growers should therefore seek expert advice and obtain literature dealing specifically with the crop rather than risk disappointment. Good varieties for outside wall training include: *Peaches:* ' Peregrine,' ' Bellegarde,' *Nectarines:* ' Early Rivers,' ' Lord Napier.'

Pears.—The requirements for pears are similar to those for apples, but the necessity for adequate summer and autumn warmth rules out many varieties for northern areas. In these less-favoured localities enquire which varieites do succeed, and where possible make use of a warm, south-facing wall. Protection from wind is very important, particularly from the cold easterlies of spring. Many soil types grow pears satisfactorily, providing drainage is good and the trees are looked after. Plant as for apples. Fertiliser requirements are also similar once cropping commences, except that pears may require a little more nitrogen.

Pruning (winter) is comparatively simple, the spur pruning given for apples suiting all except a very few pears. Initial shaping is essential, cutting the stronger shoots selected to form branches by about half their length and keeping the centre of the tree open. For cordons and other restricted forms of tree, to which pears lend themselves particularly well, summer pruning is advisable. This involves shortening all young shoots more than 10 in. in length to about 5 in. from the base. Do this when the base of such shoots is hardening and turning brown in colour, usually late July–early August. Pruned shoots may then be further reduced in winter. Such summer treatment may also be given to trained apple trees with advantage during August.

Only a few pears are self-fertile and ' Conference' is the most reliable if only one tree can be planted. Good pollinating pairings include 'Laxton's Superb' with 'Doyenné du Comice' and 'Conference' with 'Williams' Bon Chrétien.' Early varieties should be picked a little before ripening and used quickly.

Plums.—This general term includes gages and damsons. Numerous varieties are easy to grow but are unsuited to small gardens because of the amount of space required. Unlike apples and pears, there are no dwarfing rootstocks, and a minimum spacing of 14 ft. should be allowed for, growing the trees as half standards, or fan-trained against a south or west wall. Flowering is during April, and frost damage can be serious in some seasons. Plant preferably in the autumn, and by early March at the latest, using no manure unless soil is distinctly poor. Young trees should be staked during their early years, and must not be allowed to rub against the support.

Pruning should be reduced to a minimum, as the spores of silver leaf disease gain entry through wounds such as pruning cuts and stake rubs. Shorten branch leaders on young trees just as buds are bursting, but on older trees prune only when branches become overcrowded. Do this between June and August, when the risk of silver leaf is at a minimum. Cut cleanly and coat the wounds thoroughly with a bituminous paint; treat broken branches similarly immediately they are noticed. Trees fruiting heavily should have the branches supported and the fruit thinned in late June. Side shoots on fans must be cut to four to five leaves in late June and reduced still further following picking if necessary. Feed cropping trees regularly to encourage new growth, by mulching the soil generously with manure, compost, or leafmould in early spring. Some varieties are self-fertile, including 'Victoria,' 'Oullin's Golden Gage,' and 'Merryweather Damson.'

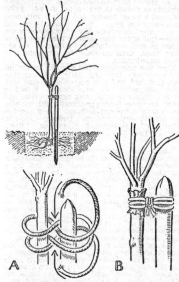

A WELL-PLANTED TREE, illustrating (A) a good method of tying and (B) sapling firmly secured with sacking around the trunk and held with stout cord.

Raspberries.—These are an ideal fruit for the small garden, but because of virus disease always buy certified canes from a fruit nursery. Plant between November and March on clean, well-manured ground, allowing 18 in. between canes and 6 ft. between rows. After planting prune each cane back to 12 in. Do *not* attempt to crop them in their first year, or the production of young canes for the following year's fruit will suffer.

A semi-shaded position will answer, but full sun is preferable for quality fruit. New canes should be looped with string to a post-and-wire fence and later tied individually to each wire when fully hardened. Space them at about 4 in. and remove any weak or diseased canes at ground level. In late February cut each cane to just above the top wire, which is usually 5–6 ft. high. This removes any damaged tips and may encourage fruiting over a longer length of cane. In the second summer a fair crop should result, and netting against birds is essential. Regular watering is imperative in dry weather, and spring and summer mulches of well-rotted manure or compost should always be applied. Supplement this in March with nitrogen and potash (fertilisers) if required, this depending on how well the ground was manured before planting. After fruiting cut out all old canes and tie in the new ones as already described. 'Malling Promise' and 'Lloyd George' are good varieties.

For autumn-fruiting varieties prune all canes to the ground in late February and tie in the best during the summer for cropping in September-October. 'September' is a good variety, and 'Lloyd George' can also be used.

Strawberries.—This is the one fruit that should be included in the vegetable garden. Fresh ground can then be used regularly for establishing new beds. Plants more than two years old are seldom profitable, and the best fruit is always picked from healthy one-year-olds planted the previous August or September. Runners put in later than early October should be deblossomed the following spring, the reward being a much heavier crop in the second year. This wastes ground, however, and early planting is preferable on all counts. Prepare the ground well in advance of planting and dig in plenty of well-rotted manure or compost or both, as this is the key to success.

Because of virus diseases order certified plants from a fruit nursery and burn any unhealthy ones in old beds before planting. Insert firmly with the base of the crown of each plant just at soil level and refirm after winter frosts; space at 20 in. in rows and 2 ft. 6 in. between rows (3 ft. if possible). A mulch of rotted manure or compost is beneficial each autumn, together with an application of sulphate of potash at 1 oz. per sq. yd. In the spring growth can be encouraged by feeling with "Maxicrop"; quick-acting *nitrogenous* fertilisers should normally be avoided.

During flowering cover the plants where possible to guard against frost damage reducing the crop. Keep the ground weed-free and remove runners regularly; a few plants should always be grown away from the main bed, deblossomed and kept purely for runner production, as this then helps to reduce the spread of virus. Ruthlessly burn any plant that remains stunted, including its runners, as this is usually a symptom of virus disease. When the young fruits are just forming spread clean straw underneath them to avoid splashing from the soil; it is a mistake to do this too early, as it increases the risk of frost damage. Net the fruit against birds and remove any rotting specimens when picking.

After fruiting remove and burn all old foliage, weeds, and straw, and feed as already described. Plant a percentage of new, vigorous runners each year on fresh ground, at the same time burning the old ones they are replacing. For flavour, the best variety is still 'Royal Sovereign' of which healthy stocks are available.

Alpine strawberries require similar treatment, preferably with a semi-shaded position, and should be raised from seed. Perpetual fruiting types continue fruiting on and off well into the autumn, and should be treated as for ordinary varieties. In all cases cloches can be used from late February onwards to obtain early fruit.

Standard References:

Tree Fruit Growing by Raymond Bush, revised by E. G. Gilbert. (Penguin) 1962 (12s. 6d.).
The Fruit Garden Displayed (R.H.S.). Revised Ed. 1965 (11s. post free). Available from The Sec., Royal Hort. Soc., Vincent Sq., London, S.W.1.

THE VEGETABLE GARDEN.

The Small Plot.—For some years the trend in gardening has been decidedly towards growing ornamental plants; vegetables have been neglected. This has gone so far that in many instances the vegetable plot has been done away with altogether. As a result, throughout the summer housewives have faced the high cost of buying even such easily grown crops as lettuce or going without them when supplies are short. A further factor promoting a return to home gardening has been the information now available on the toxic properties of some chemicals used freely in commercial horticulture.

To avoid these problems, even a small piece of ground can be used to excellent purpose if first manured and dug over thoroughly. The ideal site is an open, sunny position, sheltered from cold winds with the soil a deep rich loam well supplied with humus; obviously few gardens have such a site but much can be done in most circumstances. Once the ground is ready a few sowings of radishes can be made and lettuce

crops and a suitable succession. The land can be divided into four plots; one is used for the more or less permanent crops, such as asparagus, rhubarb, and globe artichokes, and the other three will provide a rotation. This is used to stop any group of vegetables being grown on the same land more than once in every three years, so preventing the carry-over of some pests and diseases and providing for a full use of the manures in the soil, as different groups of vegetables need more of some nutrients than others. It also allows the clearance of one section to enable winter digging and manuring to be carried out. On this freshly manured plot peas, beans, onions, leeks, and lettuces, all revelling in rich ground, should be grown. The next plot, manured for the *previous* crop, can be used for root crops—early potatoes, carrots, parsnips, and beet. A light dressing of artificial fertiliser such as " National Growmore " should be applied before sowing. On the third plot the green vegetables should be grown; a dressing of fertilisers is desirable, and lime should also be applied.

In the following season the root crops can be

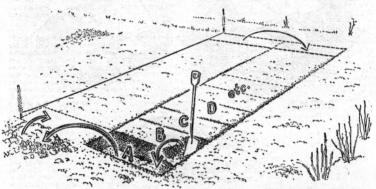

DOUBLE DIGGING.—A sound cultural practice. A trench 2 ft. wide and the depth of a spade is taken out at A and placed as shown. The bottom of trench A is then forked up and filled in with soil from B and the process repeated with C and D, etc. In double digging the sub-soil is *always* left on the bottom and never brought to the surface.

cropped throughout the summer. Other vegetables worthy of consideration are the sowing of spinach and onions grown from sets. Of course, in the small plot, priority should be given to providing a fresh supply of herbs like sage, thyme, chives, parsley and a clump or two of rhubarb.

General Cultivation.—On a new site soil preparation is important as all vegetables do best on ground in good heart. The land should be dug two spits deep (" double digging ") and for this purpose the plot is divided into two longitudinally and a trench 2 ft. wide and 10 in. deep is dug out, as illustrated above. The sub-soil at the bottom of the trench is then broken up and manure or compost added (or turf if grassland is being dug). The next strip is then dealt with in a similar manner and the practice continued down the plot to the last trench which is finally filled in with the loose soil from the first trench. Double digging is not necessary every year and single digging carried out in a similar way without breaking up the second spit, or sometimes a light forking over is sufficient.

Clay soils can be lightened by adding heavy dressings of peat or compost and coarse materials like ashes and road grit. Sandy soils are also improved by addition of humus, in this case to conserve moisture. These soils are less fertile than clay ones but are easier to cultivate, are warmer, and crop earlier. In both cases the addition of lime is only desirable if the ground is too acid; most vegetables, it should be noted, do best on slightly acidic soils *not* alkaline ones. If any doubt exists then it is always best *not* to lime.

The lay-out with vegetables must be designed to provide a succession through the year and to utilise the full capacity of the ground by catch

grown on the plot which was manured the previous year, and the brassicas grown on the land vacated by the root crops. The plot on which the brassicas were growing is double dug and manured ready for the peas, beans, and onions. A system of this type proves very satisfactory, but numerous variations can be devised, and it is really a matter for the gardener to decide his best method. The growing of maincrop potatoes will complicate the system, as a large area is usually required. They are better grown separately in another part of the vegetable garden.

Usually it is wise to have a small piece of ground available for a nursery bed. This should be of good, fine soil in which seeds can be sown to supply the main plot. In all cases seed should be sown very thinly to prevent the necessity for much pricking out, and a slug-killer is often a wise precaution to use before sowing. Sowing dates, as given, are mainly for growers in the South. In the North sowing dates in spring will be generally two weeks or more later and autumn operations the same amount earlier. Any gardener must adjust his work to suit local conditions of soil and climate, and this knowledge is only gained by experience of the particular area.

General cleanliness in the vegetable garden is at all times desirable; weeds and rubbish only harbour pests and diseases, and the hoe should be busy whenever possible. Waste material can be utilised in that essential of the modern garden—the compost heap. See **Manures and Fertilisers** for description.

Frames and Cloches.—The gardener is able to extend the season of many crops by protecting them under frames and cloches; this is particularly useful where spring or early autumn frosts are prevalent. The use of frames is limited, as they are in a fixed position, but nevertheless they are very useful for obtaining out-of-season salad crops, especially if they are heated by electricity or a hot bed.

Cloches have the advantage of mobility and can be used on a number of crops in succession. Essentially, each is a number of pieces of glass in a tent or barn shape held together by wire. Pattern, size, and height vary according to the crop to be covered and the manufacturer's design. A good cloche should be of simple design, rigid and capable of standing up to ordinary winds, easily transported, and well ventilated.

The low barn cloche is probably the most economical type. This is 23 in. wide and 13 in.

to water. Rain seeping under the cloches and a spray directed over them occasionally will provide enough for the crop in normal weather; on dry, sandy soils it may be necessary to spray over the cloches more often. A mulch of compost is also very useful to help retain water.

Dwarf varieties should be used for growing under cloches, although methods of raising the cloches another foot or so have been devised and are on the market, which allow the use of taller growing varieties. Many different vegetables can be helped to some extent in the early stages, besides those crops which can be grown entirely under cloches; the grower must decide what crops he needs and fit a rotation to cover as many crops as possible with the cloches available. This is mainly a matter of experience, but books on the

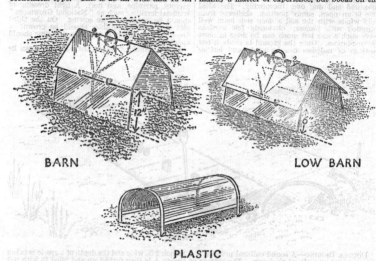

BARN

LOW BARN

PLASTIC

TYPES OF CLOCHES—The most popular is the barn cloche; with 12-in. sides it will cover strawberries and peas and beans in their early stages. The low barn will accommodate three rows of lettuce in winter and cucumbers in the summer. Plastic cloches are growing in popularity, especially those patterns using toughened plastic, and have some decided advantages over glass ones.

high when erected, and will allow two rows of lettuce to be grown, with an intercrop of another vegetable. The large barn or barn cloche of similar design, but with 12-in. side is 19 in. high in the centre, enabling taller crops, e.g., peas and dwarf beans, to be grown on, almost to maturity. The tomato cloche has sides 24 in. square and a basal width of 26 in. Many others of various shapes and sizes are offered; the amateur should buy to suit his own requirements. Other materials have been tried instead of glass with varying success. Plastic cloches are on the market, but their lightness entails very safe anchoring, and at the moment glass still seems to be the best material in most instances.

Gardening under cloches obviously is a subject too large to be dealt with in a few sentences, and the reader would be well advised to refer to one of the books mentioned in the bibliography for fuller information. A few of the main points are mentioned here and also under the individual crops.

Cloche cultivation is an intensive method of production, and this means that the land must be well cultivated and manured to ensure good-quality crops at all times. About ten days before crops are sown or planted the cloches should be put in the position where they are to be used, to warm the soil. The crop is sometimes sown a month before the normal date, and this prewarming ensures that the soil can be cultivated to a good tilth, as well as giving the plants a good start. Watering is a problem that often bothers the amateur. Provided the soil is well watered at sowing time, there should be no need to decloche

subject will suggest many variations that can be tried. Intercropping with quick-maturing crops can also be practised. As instances, radish or mustard and cress can be cropped between two rows of lettuce, or a row of cos lettuce can be grown between two rows of cabbage lettuce.

It must be remembered that the glass of cloches will need cleaning from time to time; the crop still needs the maximum light available, although shading of certain crops may be necessary in hot sun.

Artichokes.—Two different plants are grown as artichokes. One, the Jerusalem artichoke (*Helianthus tuberosus*), is related to the sunflower and is grown for its tuberous roots, which are second in food value only to the potato. It will grow in poor soil, but amply repays good cultivation, and may be placed at the more exposed end of the vegetable plot as a windbreak and screen. Tubers should be planted during February or March, on well-manured ground in drills 4–6 in. deep, and 2 ft. 6 in. apart, with 15 in. between the tubers. Hoe frequently during the summer and cut the stalks down in early winter. The tubers may then be lifted and stored, or better dug as required, reserving a number for replanting the following February.

The other type, the globe artichoke (*Cynara scolymus*), is often grown as an ornamental plant, but is esteemed as a vegetable for its young, fleshy flower-heads, which must be cut before the scales begin to open, after which they become hard and unpalatable. A deep, rich, well-manured soil is required, and after planting in early spring in rows 4 ft. apart, with 2 ft. between the plants, a compost or manure mulch is beneficial. A good crop may be expected for five or six years provided an annual dressing of manure is applied. After this time they should be replaced by young suckrse, planted in a fresh position. A covering of straw or bracken on the crowns is advisable during winter.

Asparagus.—This will grow on most types of soil provided that drainage is good and that plenty of organic matter is available. The site for the asparagus bed should be double dug in the autumn prior to planting, and a generous dressing of about half a barrow load of manure per square yard incorporated. Crowns up to three years old may be bought, but it is found that one-year-old crowns give the best results. Plants may be obtained cheaply by sowing seed in late March in drills 1½ in. deep and 18 in. apart and thinning the seedlings to 4 in. apart. It is thought that male plants produce more stalks of better quality than female plants, but at present no supplies of male crowns alone are available.

Planting may be on the single-row system or the wide-bed system. In the single-row system crowns are planted 18 in. apart in rows 4½ ft. apart; the wide-bed system consists of 5-ft. beds, with three rows of crowns 15 in. apart each way, and 2 ft. between each bed. Planting is best done during April and the plants are placed in a trench 8 in. deep and 1 ft. wide, with a slight ridge at the base, and covered with 3 in. of soil. The remaining soil is worked in during the summer. The roots should never be allowed to dry out.

The following March 2 oz. per sq. yd. of sulphate of ammonia should be applied; in subsequent years 3 oz. per sq. yd. of " National Growmore " applied at the same time, followed by 2 oz. per sq. yd. of sulphate of ammonia in June, after cutting, can be used. Salt, as a fertiliser, is not recommended nowadays. An annual dressing of manure or compost in November is desirable.

No cutting should be done for the first two years after planting and only a light cut taken in the third year. After this a six-to-eight-week season beginning in early May is usual. The spears should be cut when about 4 in. above soil level and severed about 2 or 3 in. below the soil, giving an overall length of 6–7 in. The fronds should be cut in October before the seeds drop, but not during the summer, as the plant is weakened. Weeds should be kept down and in the autumn the plant may be earthed up.

Varieties: 'Connover's Colossal' and 'Kidner's Pedigree.'

Beans. Three types are commonly grown, as follows:

Broad Beans are the hardiest and can, in warm gardens, be sown during autumn to obtain an early crop. Little is gained by this as a rule, and sowing in well-manured ground in February, when the soil is frost free, with successional sowings during March and April, is generally better in most gardens. The soil is broken down, finely raked, and the seed sown 9 in. apart in drills 3 in. deep, with 18 in. between each row. If double rows are sown 10 in. should be left between the rows, and 2 ft. between each pair of rows. Staking may be necessary. Plants from sowings under glass or under cloches in January may be used to obtain an earlier crop; the cloches should be removed in March and a further crop sown, and recloched.

Black aphis was a serious pest, but is now easily checked by pinching out the young tips and applying malathion or lindane as soon as any are seen. The pods may be used before the beans are fully developed and sliced as are runner beans, but normally they are picked when the beans are well formed but not tough.

Varieties: 'Aquadulce' and 'Green Masterpiece.'

Dwarf Beans (which include French, Kidney, and Haricot Beans) may be either used as young pods in a similar manner to runner beans or ripened in the pod for winter use. A rich well-manured soil gives the best results, and seeds sown during the first week in May, 2 in. deep and

6 in. apart, in drills 18 in. apart, may be followed by a second sowing at the end of May. The young plants should be thinned out to 1 ft. apart and small twigs used to stake them. If sown earlier, frost damage may occur. Seeds may also be sown in the greenhouse and the seedlings transplanted, or sown under cloches in the last week in March, provided the soil has been prewarmed.

The plants, as long as the pods are picked over frequently, will continue to bear until the frosts; a little liquid manure will be beneficial during the summer. A late sowing in July, cloched in September, will continue the season into the autumn.

If required for winter use (Haricot varieties) certain plants should be left unpicked and the pods allowed to ripen on the plants. They should not be picked green; if unripe when frosts come, the plants should be pulled up and dried in a shed.

Varieties: 'The Prince' (Cloche), 'Masterpiece,' and 'Comtesse de Chambord' (Haricot).

Runner Beans are the most popular type, and can be grown in two ways: either without stakes, in which case the tips of main and side shoots are regularly pinched out to make a bushy, dwarf plant, a method often used by farmers, or staked, with cross poles, allowing the plants to climb to the tops of the poles before pinching. Seed is sown from early May (mid-April under cloches) until late June, depending on the danger of frost, usually in a double row with drills 15 in. apart, and with seeds 3 in. deep and 6 in. apart in the rows, alternate plants being removed later.

Staking should be done as soon as the first pair of leaves unfolds, and a surface mulch is then applied. If the beans are to be dwarfed the rows should be about 18 in. or 2 ft. apart, and pinching may be required about once a week. A good, well-manured soil is essential, and plenty of moisture is required. The flowers may fail to set in dry weather, and an evening spray of water is helpful in preventing this " running off." Harvesting should be carried out regularly while the pods are young, before the seeds swell; older pods are stringy and seldom worth eating.

Varieties: 'White Czar' (white-flowered, heavy cropper) and 'Streamline.'

Beetroot.—From mid-April onwards varieties of beet may be sown on soil that has not recently been manured but is in good heart; on freshly manured soils coarse, forked roots subject to cracking occur. If in poor condition a light dressing of a complete fertiliser should be given before sowing. Sow in drills 1 in. deep and 12 in. apart and make a first thinning to 4 in. apart when the first rough leaf appears, and a second later, leaving 9 in. between the plants. Transplanting is inadvisable. Early roots for summer pulling may be obtained from a sowing of a Globe type in mid-Apr'l, and the main sowing should be made during May or early June for the winter supply. A sowing under cloches in late February will provide roots for pulling in late May.

On a heavy soil the oval-rooted types are best, but on a lighter soil the long-rooted types may be used. A sowing in late July of the Globe type will provide beet for use at the end of winter. Salad beet from early sowings may be pulled as required; the main crop should be allowed to mature and is lifted in October before the roots become woody and tough. Any damaged roots should not be stored. Twist off the tops just above the roots, shake the soil from the roots, and store in boxes of sand or peat in a frost-free shed. If clamped outside, straw and a thick layer of soil should be used; if frost reaches them they are spoilt.

Varieties: globe—' Detroit Red,' ' Red Globe, and ' Crimson Globe '; oval—' Cobham Early '; long—' Cheltenham Green Top.'

Sugar beet is similar but is white, not red-fleshed, and is mainly a farm crop; if desired it may be grown in a similar manner. Care should be taken in hoeing all beet crops to avoid damage to the small surface roots which feed the swollen rootstock.

Borecole.—See Kale.

Brassica.—A generic name of vegetables usually known to gardeners as " greens." This group includes brussels sprouts, cabbages, cauliflowers, kale, turnips, kohl-rabi, broccoli, and couve tronchuda. As they are all related, similar soil and cultural treatment is needed, and many pests and diseases are common to them. Each is dealt with under a separate heading.

Broccoli.—*See* Cauliflower.

Brussels Sprouts.—Young plants from seed sown thinly in a nursery seed bed during mid-March can be transplanted during May or June. The soil should be firm, well drained, in good heart, and contain adequate lime, some manure preferably having been dug in during the winter; a supplementary dressing of 2 oz. superphosphate and 1 oz. of sulphate of potash per square yard is given before planting. The young plants should be set out 3 ft. apart both ways, planted firmly, and watered in thoroughly Regular hoeing is necessary, and about a month after planting a little soil should be drawn round the stems.

If growth seems weak a top dressing of nitro-chalk should be given and this repeated in early September. As the lower leaves yellow, cut them off and gather the sprouts as they mature, picking from the bottom of the stem. Where space is available a succession of sowings from March to June can be made to lengthen the cropping period.

Club root, the worst disease of brassicas, is kept in check by only using well-limed, well-drained soil, and dipping the roots in 4% calomel before planting, and cabbage root fly, a frequent insect pest, by using lindane.

Varieties: early—'Cambridge No. 1'; mid-season—'Rous Lench' and 'Triumph' (dark foliage, distinct).

Cabbage.—Sowings in March and April for summer use, in May or June for winter use, and in late July or August for spring use will give a succession of cabbages all the year round. Seed is sown thinly in a nursery bed of well-firmed, limed soil, clear of weeds, in drills ¾ in. deep and 6 in. apart, and the seedlings dusted with lindane to check flea beetle attack (prevalent with all brassica seedlings). All cabbages are gross feeders, and a well-drained soil in good heart, with adequate lime, is required.

"Spring cabbage" should be sown during late July (north) and August (south). If sown too early the plants may " bolt " without making a heart. The young plants are set out in mid-September 18 in. apart and with 18 in. between the rows if for hearting, or 9 in. apart with 18 in. between the rows, in which case the alternate plants are cut for " spring greens." On a heavy soil ridging along the rows of plants keeps the soil round the roots drained and helps to prevent loosening by frosts. In cold districts cloches may be used with advantage to help plants through the winter. In early March a dressing of 1 oz. per sq. yd. of sulphate of ammonia or nitro-chalk is a good stimulant.

Seed of "summer" and "autumn cabbage" is sown in March and April and planted during late May and June, 18 in. to 2 ft. each way between the plants, depending on the variety. The plants should be thoroughly watered, both before and after transplanting. A top dressing of 1 oz. per sq. yd. nitro-chalk may be given if required.

"Winter cabbage," maturing from October to February from sowings during May and early June, are set out 2 ft. apart each way in July or early August, usually on ground which has been cropped with early potatoes or peas. No nitrogen fertiliser should be given late in the season, as soft growth, liable to frost damage, is encouraged. A balanced fertiliser, such as "National Growmore," may be used if needed. When the stalks of cabbage are left standing over winter a common practice is to cut across the tops to obtain bunches of leaves, for use as greens during early spring.

"Savoy cabbages" mature during winter and early spring from seed sown in May. Seedlings are transplanted in late July and early August on to land manured for the previous crop, to which a dressing of 2 oz. superphosphate and 1 oz. sulphate of potash per sq. yd. has been applied. The young plants should be set out 2 ft. apart each way; they are exceptionally hardy, and

should be grown in every garden in case of a hard winter.

Varieties: Spring sowing—autumn cutting, 'Greyhound' (early), 'Winningstadt.' autumn sowing—spring cutting, 'April,' 'Wheeler's Imperial.' Savoy 'Ormskirk Late Green.'

Red cabbage is slow to mature; plants from sowings in August are transplanted 6 in. each way in autumn and set out in early spring 18 in. each way. They are ready to cut in late summer.

Cardoon (Cynara cardunculus).—Closely related to the globe artichoke and grown for the blanched hearts. Seed is sown in trenches 18 in. wide and 1 ft. deep; 3 in. of manure is worked into the bottom soil and covered with 3 in. of fine soil. Three or four seeds are dibbled in every 18 in. and covered with a flower pot till visible, and then thinned out, leaving one strong seedling at each station. Protection from sun and late frosts is provided by twigs over the trench, and copious watering is given during the summer.

On a fine day in September the plants are blanched by tying the leaves together and covering with dry hay, 3 in. thick, kept in position by raffia, and earthed up in the same way as celery. Blanching is completed in about a month.

Carrots.—A light, well-drained soil, enriched with decayed organic matter, is suitable for carrots. No fresh manure should be given, but a light dressing of " National Growmore " fertiliser can be applied prior to sowing. The surface is left rough until sowing time and then broken down to a fine tilth. The first sowing is made in early April in drills ¾ in. deep and 12 in. apart, and a succession is obtained by sowing at intervals of a month until the end of July.

On heavy, unfavourable soils stump-rooted varieties are best grown, long-rooted varieties needing a light soil. Thin out the stump-rooted varieties to 4 in. apart and the longer varieties to 6 in. Thinnings should be removed and the soil pressed firmly back to minimise damage by carrot fly. The early sowings are pulled as required, but the later sowings for winter use should be lifted in October and stored in slightly damp sand in a frost-proof shed or clamped in the open.

Frames and cloches are sometimes used to obtain early and late carrots. Seed of a quick-growing variety, such as ' Amsterdam Forcing ' or ' Early Nantes,' sown in late January under cloches or in frames will provide an early crop; the same varieties sown in frames or cloches in early August will provide young carrots for the autumn. Carrot fly is a bad pest, especially on light soils; the seedlings should be dusted in the rows with lindane when 2–4 in. high to prevent the flies from egg laying.

Varieties: globular—'Early Gem '; stump-rooted—'French Short Horn '; intermediate—'Amsterdam Forcing ' and ' Early Nantes '; long—' St. Valery ' and ' Long Red Surrey.'

Catch Crops.—A term used for quick-growing crops interplanted between rows of other crops. Radishes between rows of broad beans, and lettuce between celery rows provide examples. In this way the best use of a limited amount of land can be made.

Cauliflower.—Broccoli is for all practical purposes a hardy winter cauliflower. Seed is sown ¾ in. deep in a nursery bed from mid-April to mid-May, depending on the variety, and transplanted during June and July on to firm soil, well manured for the previous crop. The plants are set out 2 ft. apart each way; 2 oz. superphosphate and ¾ oz. of sulphate of potash per square yard may be hoed in before transplanting. No nitrogenous manure should be given late in the year.

Varieties: cauliflower—'Snowball ' (summer), ' Majestic ' (autumn). Broccoli—' Snow's Winter White ' (winter), ' St. George ' (early spring). Sprouting broccoli—' Nine Star Perennial ' (a many-headed sort).

Sprouting broccoli is very hardy, has a more leafy head, and is cultivated in the same way. Purple- and green-sprouting sorts are grown also.

Summer cauliflowers require a soil which has been limed and manured during w theinter; 1–2 oz. per sq. yd. of superphosphate should be given before transplanting. An early sowing in frames in February or March will provide plants for cropping in June. These should be hardened off and planted in March or April from 18 to 24 in. square, depending on the variety. Seed sown outdoors in April in drills ½ in. deep will give plants for transplanting in May or June, for cropping from late July onwards. If growth is slow a dressing of 1 oz. per sq. yd. of sulphate of ammonia should be given. Leaves broken over the curds will help to prevent any damage from early frosts. Varieties given in previous paragraph.

Celeriac.—A plant allied to celery grown for its edible root, which resembles a turnip but has the flavour of celery; the stems are bitter to the taste and are not eaten. It is used in salads or boiled as other root crops.

Seed is sown in gentle heat in March and seedlings pricked out into seed-boxes, 2 in. apart each way. In June, after hardening off, the seedlings are planted out in shallow drills 18 in. apart, leaving 12 in. between each plant in the row. Water freely during the summer and remove side shoots as they appear. Lift the roots in October or November and store in a frost-free shed.

Celery.—Richly prepared ground is required. A trench 15 in. wide and 1 ft. deep is taken out and manure worked into the bottom of the trench. The soil is then returned to within 3 in. of the ground level. Seed should be sown in early March at about 60° Fahrenheit and the seedlings pricked out in deep boxes 3 in. each way and gradually hardened off. Celery seed is very fine, and care should be taken to cover it with only a fine layer of soil; if covered too deeply it may not germinate.

In late May or June set the plants out in staggered double rows 1 ft. apart, with 10 in. between the plants, and water them in. Frequent watering during the summer is required, and a light dressing of nitrate of soda will stimulate them if growth is poor. Before earthing up to blanch the plants, tie the stems loosely below the leaves and remove any suckers. Earthing up begins when the plants are about 15 in. high; the ground should be moist, and the first earthing should only be slight. The second and third earthings, at intervals of about three weeks, should be more generous, but should never reach higher than the base of the leaves, and no earth should fall into the heart. For exhibition purposes brown-paper collars may be tied round the stalks before earthing. The final earthing should cover all the stems right up to the leaves, and the soil should slope away neatly. In winter litter or bracken spread over the plants will help protect them from frost.

Celery fly is a serious pest, and the brown leaf-blisters should be pinched to kill the maggot inside and lindane applied two or three times at fortnightly intervals. Slugs are a serious pest and must be eradicated. This can be done easily with slug pellets or a liquid formulation of "Slugit." Leaf spot, a seed-borne disease, can be prevented by spraying with May & Baker's, "Bordeaux Mixture."

Varieties: white—' Solid White'; pink—' Clayworth Prize Pink '; red—' Standard Bearer ' self-blanching—' Golden Self-Blanching.'

Chicory.—The young, blanched growths are used in winter salads. Seeds are sown in drills 1 ft. apart in May; the young seedlings are thinned to 8 in. apart and grown on until October or November, when they are lifted and the roots trimmed to 8 or 10 in. long. They are then planted in deep boxes in a moist, sandy soil 5 in. apart each way, leaving 1 in. above the soil surface, and the boxes put in a warm greenhouse or cellar.

No light must reach the crowns; one method sometimes used is to cover the crowns with 6 in. of sand. When the blanched growths show through they are about 6 in. high and ready for cutting.

Chives.—These are like small onions, and the leaves are used for flavouring salads and soups. They are easily grown in window boxes and town gardens. Bulbs can be planted in March 6 in. apart and divided when the clusters become too large.

Corn Salad or Lamb's Lettuce.—Occasionally grown for the leaves, which are used in early spring salads. Seed sown from August to October will provide plants for winter and spring use.

Couve Tronchuda.—A large brassica known as "Portugal cabbage," not generally suitable for smaller gardens. Seed is sown in March and the plants set out 2–3 ft. apart each way. The hearts may be cooked in the same way as cabbage.

Cress.—An annual growing rapidly from seed and used as a salad when only the seed leaves have developed. Seed sown as required, in boxes of light, moist soil and covered with brown paper until germination, when it is removed, will provide salad all the year round. The seed is merely pressed into the soil and the boxes kept moist. Cress may even be grown on damp flannel in a window.

Cucumber.—The cucumber of the shops is grown as a specialist crop under glass. Temperatures of 85° Fahrenheit or more may be required, and only occasionally are they grown by the amateur, although cloche and frame culture is now popular.

Ridge cucumbers, which are smaller and prickly outside, may be grown outdoors in summer. Plants from seed sown singly in pots under glass can be planted during late May on ridges of good, well-manured soil or, alternatively, sown on the ridges 1 in. deep at the same date. Water freely during the summer and cut the cucumbers while young to encourage further production.

If cloches are available greenhouse-raised cucumbers can be planted under them, in mid-April. Frame cucumbers are less hardy, but young plants raised under glass can be planted under cloches in early May.

Varieties: ridge—' King of the Ridge ' and ' Stockwood Ridge '; frame—' Conqueror ' and ' Telegraph.'

Endive.—Used in winter or autumn salads. Seed is sown during April in drills 18 in. apart and the seedlings thinned to 12–15 in. apart. Sowings in June and August will provide a succession. A rich soil and plenty of moisture are the main requirements; before eating blanching is necessary, as the leaves are very bitter. This is achieved by tying the leaves loosely together and covering the plants with inverted flower pots (with the holes blocked) to exclude the light; frost should be kept out by piling litter over the pots in winter. If cloches are used they can be coated inside with lime-wash to achieve the same effect. Alternatively, plants may be lifted in October and blanched in darkened frames.

Varieties: summer—' Green Curled '; winter—' Batavian Broad Leaved.'

Fennel.—A perennial culinary herb used in fish sauces and salads. Blanched stems may also be cooked in the same way as celery. Seed is sown in drills 2 ft. apart in rich soil and the seedlings thinned to 18 in.

French Beans.—See **Dwarf Beans.**

Garlic.—One or two "cloves" planted in February, 9 in. apart, will provide ample garlic for salads, as only a little is required. After growth is complete in summer the bulbs can be lifted, dried, and stored and some saved for re-planting.

Haricot Beans.—See **Dwarf Beans.**

Herbs.—Many herbs are useful in small quantities for flavouring and garnishing, as well as being decorative. If possible, a separate herb garden should be made as a feature in the garden, or they may be used as edging plants. Perennial herbs, of which borage, caraway, chamomile, chives, fennel, garlic, horseradish, lavender, mint, penny-royal, marjoram, rosemary, rue, sage, tansy, tarragon, and thymes are the main types grown, should be given a permanent position. Those grown as annuals—anise, basil, coriander, dill, parsley, purslane, and summer savory—can be used as "fill-ins" on the vegetable garden. Brick and cobble paths associate well with herbs, imparting something of the character of the gardens of bygone days, when herb gardens were considered one of the most important features.

Horseradish.—A deep-rooting perennial herb which appreciates a well-manured, moist soil. It is easily propagated from root cuttings and can become a nuisance, as pieces of root left in the soil will make a new plant; care should be taken to lift the complete root when digging it for use. Straight roots planted in spring with the crowns 6 in. below soil level and 1 ft. apart can be lifted for use in autumn; no further treatment is required, apart from keeping weeds in check. Some of the roots should be kept for planting the following spring.

Kale.—Very useful during a cold winter, when other green vegetables are scarce, because of its hardiness. Seed sown in April or May will provide young plants for transplanting 18 in. apart each way in July or early August, on to a site used for peas or early potatoes, in good heart. A catch crop of lettuce can usually be taken from between the rows. The variety 'Hungry Gap' is usually sown in rows 18 in. apart where it is to mature and thinned, leaving 18 in. between the plants. There are many varieties; which types are grown is a matter of personal preference.
Varieties: 'Cottager's' and 'Hungry Gap.'

Kidney Beans.—*See* **Dwarf Beans.**

Kohl Rabi.—A brassica with a swollen stem base, in flavour and appearance something between a turnip and a cabbage. Seeds sown in April in rows 1 ft. apart are thinned to 1 ft. apart in the rows, and the swollen stem harvested when about the size of a tennis ball. If left to grow it becomes coarse.

Lamb's Lettuce.—*See* **Corn Salad.**

Leeks.—A vegetable which repays planting on a well-manured soil. If they are to follow winter greens, then manure or compost should be dug in after the previous crop is cleared. Leeks may be sown from early March to April in lines 8 in. apart on a prepared seed bed, and the seedlings transplanted as land becomes available during June and July, when about 6 in. high. Thinning in the seed bed should be unnecessary provided the sowing has been correct. The seedlings are set out 9 in. apart in rows 15 in. apart; a hole is made with a dibber, and each seedling dropped in and watered thoroughly. No firming is needed, the watering should tighten the plants sufficiently. Alternatively, drills 4 in. deep and 15 in. apart can be drawn out with a hoe and the plants put in 9 in. apart in the drills.
Regular hoeing is required, and a feed of sulphate of ammonia (1 oz. per gallon of water) can be applied if in poor growth. In September a little earth should be drawn up around the roots, which should, by then, be almost full grown. Leeks are very hardy and can be left in the soil until required for use.
Varieties: 'Lyon' and 'Musselburgh.'

Lettuce.—Two main types are grown: cos lettuce, a summer crop with long, straight leaves that curl inwards naturally or are tied in so that the heart is more or less blanched; and cabbage lettuce, which are broad and spreading, with round cabbage-like hearts, and are grown to supply salad all the year round. Lettuce should be grown on ground manured during autumn or winter, dug and left rough till planting time, when it is broken down and raked to a fine tilth.

This crop is a particularly valuable one for town gardens with restricted space. In these circumstances excellent returns can be had by raising seed indoors and pricking out the seedlings into small peat pots ("Root-o-Pots"). At this stage the plants can be grown on in a "Stewart" propagator which is simply a seed tray covered with a plastic hood, and finally planted out-of-doors in their pots. The practice can be repeated or small sowings made in the open and seedlings thinned to 9 in. apart. Quick, unchecked growth with plenty of moisture is essential; on poor soils peat can be forked into the surface and an application of liquid "Maxicrop" made during the growing season.
Varieties: wide selection available of all types; small, quick maturing sorts include 'Little Gem' ('Sugar Cos') and 'Continuity.'

Maize.—*See* **Sweet Corn.**

Marrows.—Pumpkins, gourds, bush, and trailing marrows all require similar treatment; plenty of sun and water and a rich soil, such as an old hotbed or compost heap, which will provide a porous medium of humus. Seed can be sown singly in pots under glass in March, or outdoors on the site in May. For cloches a bush variety must be used, and greenhouse-raised plants are clocihed in mid-April. Plant four or five seeds in groups about 6 in. apart and 1 in. deep and finally thin to two plants 15 in. apart. Protection from late frosts may be necessary. Water copiously and hoe regularly. Cut marrows when about 12 in. long to encourage further fruits. Some can be left until they are full size and cut before the frosts, for storing in a dry, frost-proof place.
Varieties: bush—'Green Bush' and 'White Bush'; trailing—'Long Green Trailing.'

Melons.—Although usually a glasshouse crop, melons can be grown outdoors under cloches and in frames. Seed is sown under glass in April at 60° Fahrenheit, and seedlings can be set out 3 ft. apart in early May. The soil should be manured generously and the seedlings planted on a mound of compost mixed with soil. The plants must be stopped at the fourth or fifth leaf to encourage laterals. Two can be selected to grow on and, when 18 in. long, pinched out to obtain sub-laterals, which will bear the fruit. The female flowers may require pollinating, and on a sunny day a male flower or rabbit's tail can be used to transfer the pollen; as soon as the young fruits swell, remove all but two or three per plant and pinch back the laterals bearing fruit to two leaves from the melon. A feed of dried blood once a week, with plenty of watering (though not saturation!) will help the developing fruits. Light shading may be necessary.
Varieties: 'Dutch Net' and 'Tiger.'

Mint.—Easily grown from suckers in any soil. For winter use a few pieces can be planted in a frame. A number of varieties—'Apple Mint,' 'Peppermint,' and 'Spearmint'—can be grown besides common mint.

Mushrooms.—Growing mushrooms is really a specialist occupation. For the experimental amateur, beds of composted stable-manure are made up in a warm, damp cellar or disused air-raid shelter. Pieces of spawn are inserted when the temperature of the compost has dropped to about 70° Fahrenheit and the whole bed covered with an inch of inert sub-soil. The air temperature should be from 60° to 70° Fahrenheit, and in a few weeks mushrooms may appear. Full instructions will be given with the spawn, but it is advisable to consult a text-book dealing with the culture, as even for professional growers a crop is never certain.

Mustard.—Grown exactly in the same way as cress, but is ready two or three days earlier. If used together, mustard seed should be sown two or three days after cress. Again it is the seed leaves which are eaten.

Onions.—These respond well to good cultivation. The site is dug deeply in winter, manure incorporated, and left rough until February, when it is broken down to a fine tilth and firmed well. Seed can be sown ¾ in. deep in drills during August and planted in March for exhibition onions, but the usual practice is to sow seed in late February outdoors or under glass in January and transplant during April in rows 12 in. apart with 6 in. between the onions, taking care to keep the bases about ¼ in. below the surface. If sown outdoors and thinned the thinnings may be used in salads. Autumn-sown onions are liable to bolt, but less liable to attack by onion fly than spring-sown plants.

Dressings of a balanced feed can be applied but not after July, and in August the tops are bent over to hasten ripening. The chief pest is onion fly, the larvae of which eat the roots of the seedlings. Control can be maintained by sprinkling the seed drills with Murphy's " Gamma-BHC Dust " or applying a 4-in. band of the dust along the rows at the loop stage.

In small gardens, onion sets are popular. These are small onions grown in the previous summer, stored and replanted the next spring. Plant the bulbils 6 in. apart, leaving only the necks exposed.

Varieties: spring sowing—' Bedfordshire Champion,' ' Best of All,' and ' White Silverskin ' (pickling); autumn sowing—' Giant Zittau,' ' Sutton's Solidity,' and ' White Lisbon ' (salad onions); sets—' Ebenezer ' and ' Stuttgarter Reisen.'

Parsley.—Sow thinly in rows 8 in. apart during March and again in July for a succession of young foliage; thin to 4 in. between plants.

Parsnip.—Grow parsnips on ground manured for a previous crop; if given fresh manure splitting and forked roots occur. Dig the soil deeply, and at sowing time in March, work the soil to a fine tilth. On a soil unsuitable for deep-rooted crops special holes 10–12 in. apart, filled with sifted soil, may be prepared. If this method has to be used four or five seeds are sown per hole; normally drills 15 in. apart and 1 in. deep are made and four or five seeds sown every 9 in. The seedlings are thinned, leaving one at each station. Parsnips should be left in the ground until needed; litter over the rows will ease lifting in frosty weather.

Varieties: ' Evesham ' and ' Student.'

Peas.—Dig the ground well in autumn and add a generous amount of manure or compost. Seed sowing begins at the end of February, and can be continued at three-weekly intervals until early July. Under cloches sowings in January and October will lengthen the season. Both early and late sowings should be of a quick-maturing variety. Seed is sown in drills 6–8 in. wide and 3 in. deep, with 2 ft. between drills; the seeds can be scattered thinly in the drill or spaced 3 in. apart in a treble row. Cover with 2 or 3 in. of soil and as soon as the peas are about 2 in. high stake with twigs.

Failures are often due to attacks by birds and field-mice. The former should be discouraged by netting and the latter by trapping. Pea-sticks will be necessary for the taller varieties which should have 3–4 ft. between the rows. With limited space only the dwarf quick-maturing varieties should be used. A summer mulch will keep the soil moist, and picking should be done regularly.

Varieties: 1½–2 ft.—' Kelvedon Wonder,' ' Kelvedon Triumph,' and ' Meteor ' (cloches); 2½ ft.—' Onward '; 3½–4 ft.—' Gladstone.'

Potatoes.—In general, it is only economic for the amateur to produce an early crop; the main winter supply can be grown if room and labour are available. They should be grown on land well manured the previous season, dressed at planting time with a mixed fertiliser, such as " National Growmore," at a rate of 1½ lb. to a 30-yd. row. The soil should not contain too much lime, as the damage of scab disease is increased.

" Seed " tubers about the size of a large egg are best used, and these can be bought or saved from the previous season's crop. Large potatoes may be cut leaving about three eyes to each part. New stocks should be bought occasionally if the " seed " is home saved to obviate risk of virus. " Seed " should be put in trays during February in a frost-proof shed to sprout, and in early April the " first-earlies " can be planted.

Drills 2 ft. apart and 4–5 in. deep are taken out and the sprouting " seed " planted 12 in. apart in the rows. Maincrop varieties are planted in early May 15 in. apart. The young growths should be protected from frost by earthing up slightly, and a further earthing is done as the potatoes mature. This practice of earthing prevents the tubers near the surface from becoming green when exposed to light, keeps weeds down, and protects the tubers from spores of potato blight, which are washed into the gullies. If growth is poor sulphate of ammonia can be applied at a rate of ¼ lb. per 30-yd. row. Early varieties should mature in late July and later varieties in September and October; when the tops (haulm) turn yellow the crop can be lifted, dried for a few hours (too much light will turn them green), and stored in boxes in a frost-proof shed or clamps.

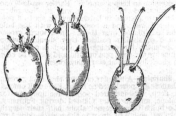

SEED POTATOES—Good seed is essential for first-rate crops. Illustration shows (*left*) a well-sprouted tuber, (*centre*) a large well-sprouted tuber suitable for cutting, and (*right*) a poor, badly sprouted tuber.

Potato blight is a common disease, and control by a spraying with maneb before the leaves touch in the rows is effective. Virus diseases, spread by greenfly, are checked by using " seed " from Scotland, where greenfly is less troublesome because of the lower temperatures. Colorado beetle should be watched for, and if found notified to the Ministry of Agriculture.

Varieties: Discerning growers will find the following well worth growing: ' Edzell Blue ' (violet-coloured skin; excellent cooker), ' Pentland Dell ' (white-fleshed; heavy cropper), ' Red Craigs Royal ' (red-fleshed; heavy cropper), ' Ulster Chieftain ' (white-fleshed, good early variety). Epicureans seeking a first-class potato should grow ' Maris Peer ', a sort understandably gaining in popularity in Scotland, since its introduction. Another interesting sort is the Dutch-raised ' Record ', a yellow-fleshed variety which has a trace of sweetness in its flavour.

Pumpkin.—*See* **Melon.**

Radish.—Although of the easiest culture, it is not grown as much as it should be due probably to the damage done by maggots of the cabbage root fly. This pest can be controlled by dusting the seed drills with Murphy's " Gamma-BHC Dust." Successional sowing can be made in the spring and again in early autumn if desired; summer-sown radish bolt, and are hot and tough.

Varieties: ' French Breakfast ' (cylindrical) and ' Scarlet Globe ' (round).

Rhubarb.—Before planting the ground should be generously manured and deeply dug. Crowns are planted in March, 3 ft. apart each way and mulched, but no rhubarb should be pulled until the following year, when a light pull can be taken. Remove any flowering shoots and give a dressing of sulphate of ammonia if growth is weak. Manure well each winter; if early supplies are needed, some of the crowns can be covered with inverted boxes or barrels and a packing of loose straw or bracken. An established, well-cultivated bed will continue almost indefinitely.

Sage.—A hardy shrub for the herb garden easily raised from cuttings. The leaves are harvested and dried in summer.

Salsify (Oyster Plant).—A winter root rather like a parsnip which requires similar growing conditions.

Savoy.—*See* Cabbage.

Scorzonera.—A winter root cultivated in the same way as salsify. It has a purplish root instead of the yellow-green one of salsify.

Sea-kale.—A perennial plant native to our sea-shores, which can be either grown from seed sown in March and left for two years to produce forcing crowns or from bought thongs, which are planted during March, 9 in. apart in groups of three, leaving 3 ft. between groups. During summer a manure mulch and nitrogenous fertiliser can be applied. When the tops die down in autumn the crowns are covered with boxes to force and blanch the new growths. Crowns can be covered in succession to keep a supply. Earlier sea-kale can be obtained by lifting crowns in November. These are planted in batches five or six to a pot, watered well, and a second pot, with the hole blocked, placed over them. In a warm green-house or similar position they should develop sufficiently for cutting in about three weeks. Slugs are the chief pest outside, and should be kept in check by a proprietary slug-killer.

Shallots.—A popular crop for the small garden. Shallots are purchased as bulbs, like small onions. A deep, well-manured soil is required, as for onions, and they are planted during February, the bulbs being pressed about half their length into soft soil, 6 in. apart in the rows, leaving 1 ft. between rows. In mid-July the little bunches of bulbs can be lifted. Leave them on the surface to dry for a few days and then store in a dry, frost-proof shed. Some, about the size of a shilling, should be kept for planting the following year.

Spinach.—Sowings in February to April on a well-manured soil will provide a succession during the summer. Sow in drills 1 in. deep and 12 in. apart and thin the young plants to 3 in., and then to 6 in., using the second thinning to eat.

When green vegetables are expensive, in winter, the perpetual or prickly spinach is particularly valuable. Sow in August and treat as for the summer variety.

If plants are crowded or suffer from dryness, mildew can be troublesome. Therefore thin seedlings early and water whenever necessary. On poor soils, moisture can be conserved by mulching the rows with peat. Should growth be slow feed with liquid " Maxicrop " and repeat, if required.

Varieties: 'America ' and ' Giant Prickly.'

Sprouting Broccoli.—*See* Cauliflower.

Sugar Beet.—*See* Beetroot.

Swede.—*See* Turnip.

Sweet Corn (Maize).—Gardeners should distinguish between the types of maize used for poultry food and those which supply sweet corn for human consumption. It is wise to use cloches for growing sweet corn, as it is only half-hardy and resents transplanting. Seeds sown under cloches in mid-April in two drills 12 in. apart and 1½ in. deep should be placed 1 ft. apart in staggered positions in the rows. More robust varieties may need 15 in. from plant to plant. A soil well manured for the previous crop is best used, and a mulch can be given as soon as the plants are a few inches high. The first cobs should be ready by mid-July, and should be eaten when the cob is milky.

Variety recommended: ' John Innes Hybrid.'

Tomato.—A sunny, sheltered site is required, otherwise ripening outdoors in our climate is uncertain. Sow seeds under glass in late March and harden off the plants in a cold frame or buy plants for setting out in late May or early June. The soil should be thoroughly dug and some artificial manure applied before planting. Allow 18 in. between plants and 2½ ft. between rows, and put in a strong stake with each plant. Keep to a single stem, pinching out side shoots regularly. When four or five trusses are set pinch out the top of the main shoot.

Feed with a liquid manure during summer. Fruit which fails to ripen outdoors can be gathered and stored at about 50° Fahrenheit or the plants laid flat on the ground and covered with cloches, when the tomatoes should ripen. Under cloches plants can be planted out in mid-April instead of late May, gaining six weeks growing time, and the Cloches removed when they become too large.

Potato blight attacks tomatoes, and a spray of maneb during the first week in August and repeated after fourteen days will give a control.

Varieties: ' Market King ' and ' Money-maker '; some heavy-cropping sorts have little or no flavour and a thick skin.

Turnips.—Ground manured the previous season should be dug well and dressed with 2 oz. super-phosphate per square yard. A good early variety can be sown during April in drills ¾ in. deep and 15 in. apart, followed by successional sowings at three-week intervals as required. The main crop for storage is sown in July and August, and seedlings should be thinned gradually to 10 in. apart. Use when about the size of tennis balls. A sowing can be made in September, left almost unthinned and the tops used as " greens " in spring. In autumn the storage crop is lifted and all undamaged roots put in sand in a shed or clamped. Flea beetle and turnip fly can be checked by lindane at the seedling stage.

Swedes are grown in a similar manner.

Varieties: turnips—' Early Milan ' (summer) and ' Green Top Stone ' (winter storage); swedes—' Purple Top.'

Standard References.

Cloche Cultivation by G. B. Walkden (Colling-ridge) 1955 (9s. 6d.).

The Vegetable Garden Displayed (R.H.S.), 1969 (14s. post free). Available from The Sec., Royal Hort. Soc., Vincent Sq., London, S.W.1.

Vegetables for Garden and Exhibition, by S. M. Gault (Collingridge) 1956 (50s.).

FERTILISERS AND ORGANIC MANURES.

The elements essential for healthy plant growth may be roughly grouped into classes—first, those required in some quantity, the major elements, nitrogen, potassium, and phosphorus; secondly, calcium, magnesium, and sulphur, which are required in lesser quantities; and thirdly, the trace elements, boron, manganese, iron, zinc, copper, and molybdenum, of which only minute quantities are needed. As well as the elements mentioned, others, such as silicon, aluminium, chlorine, nickel, and sodium, are often found on plant analysis, but the evidence that these are essential is inconclusive, though they may be beneficial to certain crops.

It is important to remember, when adding fertilisers to the soil, that different crops may require relatively more of one element than another, but a balance between all the elements is essential. As an instance, brassicas (the cabbage family) are gross nitrogen feeders, while root crops (e.g., carrots) require far less nitrogen, and an excess may be harmful. A further point to notice is that although an element may be present in the soil the plant may be unable to absorb any because it is being kept in an insoluble state by excess of another element. An instance of this is the frequent yellow and sickly appearance of plants on very chalky soils due to lack of iron, which is present, but locked in an insoluble state by too much calcium.

The elements needed by the plant are in the form of various compounds, such as nitrates and phosphates, and may be applied as artificial fertilisers, which are manufactured, or as humus, which contains most of the foods required and also provides the essential soil micro-organisms or bacteria, without which the soil would be inert and no plants would grow. Bacteria break down the complicated animal and vegetable matter of which humus is composed to soluble compounds which plants can absorb. Humus can be supplied as farmyard and poultry manure, leaf mould, compost, sewage sludge, spent hops, and from animal by-products like hoof and horn, dried blood, meat and bone meal, and many others.

Nitrogen is mainly concerned with vegetative growth, encouraging leaf and stem formation. It is also contained in chlorophyll, the green colouring matter of the plant, and one of the symptoms of nitrogen starvation is a pale-green colour to the leaf, indicating a lack of chlorophyll. Most of the nitrogen compounds used are soluble, and it is a wise maxim to apply " little and often "; if given in large doses much is washed through the soil and wasted.

Nitrogenous fertiliser should not be given to any plant late in the season, as sappy growth, easily damaged by winter cold and frosts, is encouraged. Similarly, at no time should large quantities be given to any plant, as this results in an excess of leafy growth, which is very susceptible to disease and adverse conditions of drought and cold; also plants tend to be later flowering.

Sulphate of ammonia is the most used inorganic nitrogenous fertiliser, and is excellent for spring use on seed beds, lawns, and early crops, and it is contained in most fertiliser mixtures. It makes soils acid in reaction, and if both lime and nitrogen are required, nitro-chalk should be used instead. Other nitrogen fertilisers used are potassium nitrate, which has the advantage of supplying two major elements at once, and is very soluble, and nitrate of soda, often used on beet and mangolds. The latter chemical should not be applied in excess, as too much sodium has a bad effect on soil structure. These inorganic fertilisers are all soluble and quick acting.

As a general guide, 1 oz. of the fertiliser to a gallon of water, applied at 1 oz. per sq. yd., is a good summer dressing, given at intervals of two or three weeks. It should always be given after rain or watering, and should be applied to the soil and not to the foliage.

Among organic fertilisers containing a percentage of easily available nitrogen are dried blood, soot, and meat and fish meals. Slower to decompose, and so having a more lasting effect, are shoddy (wool waste) and hoof and horn.

Phosphorus is concerned in the plant with the production of young cells of the root and shoot, and also encourages flower and fruit production and early ripening. Most of the compounds are relatively insoluble (rendering absorption by the plant difficult), and so large amounts can be supplied without deleterious effects, especially on acid soils, where the availability is less than on alkaline soils.

Phosphorus is generally applied to the soil in the form of phosphates, and among these superphosphate of lime is quick acting, and is usually applied at 2–3 oz. per sq. yd. in spring and summer, when the need is greatest. More slow acting is basic slag, a by-product of the steel industry, sold as a fine black powder and containing, besides phosphates, many of the trace elements, as well as a considerable percentage of lime. This is good for application to acid, wet soils, but should not be applied to potatoes owing to the risk of scab disease with the increase in the content of lime. It should not be applied with sulphate of ammonia. Bonemeal is also slow acting and also contains some nitrogen. It is excellent for crops like tomatoes, and is also used extensively for ornamental and pot plants.

Potassium, the third major element, is essential for good flower colour and ripeness in fruits. Dessert apples, potatoes, cereals, and root crops all need potash in some quantity, and if excess nitrogen has been applied a dressing of potash may counterbalance the effect. Sulphate of potash is the main inorganic compound in use. Muriate of potash (potassium chloride), to which some crops are sensitive, is much less used; it should be applied as a winter dressing before the crop is sown to lose the impurities by weathering. Sulphate of potash is purer, and may be applied during the growing season at 1 oz. per sq. yd. on the vegetable plot, and is used in many proprietary fertiliser mixtures.

Wood ash contains variable quantities of potassium, and provided that the ash has not been washed by rain and the potassium leached out, is a useful addition to the soil; bracken, cut during June and July, when large amounts of potassium are present in the foliage, can be composted when green to provide a good supply of the element.

Elements Required in Lesser Quantity.—Calcium, although required in small quantities in the plant, has profound effects on the soil. Its main function in the plant is in the production of the cell walls, but in the soil it helps to bind light soils together and to make the structure of sticky clay soils finer and more workable. Also soils without calcium are acid and tend to lock up some elements in an insoluble form. Addition of calcium changes the acidity, making it slightly alkaline or neutral, and releases the locked elements.

Calcium is applied as some form or derivative of calcium carbonate, commonly known as lime, which can be obtained in various forms. Hydrated or slaked lime (calcium hydroxide) is commonly used on clay soils, and chalk or ground limestone on lighter soils. Calcium is gradually leached from the soil, and it is necessary to replace it, or the soil becomes too acid and many crops will fail to grow. A normal dressing of lime for a vegetable garden is about 4 oz. lime or ½ lb. chalk per square yard every two or three years, and is best applied in autumn as a surface dressing after digging. It should not be applied together with other fertilisers. The amount of lime will depend on the type of soil, but it must be remembered that most vegetables grow best on a slightly acid soil.

Gypsum, or calcium sulphate, is sometimes recommended to supply calcium, but its solubility is negligible, and it is preferable to chalk or limestone only on soils containing salt due to sea flooding. It was used to help reclaim districts of East Anglia flooded by sea-water during the storm surge of January 1953 by improving the soil structure. Sulphur, as sulphates, and magnesium, as an impurity in limestone, are usually present in sufficient quantities for the plants' needs.

Trace Elements.—In the case of the trace elements most soils contain enough for the plant, but in certain circumstances deficiencies occur. Iron on very alkaline soils is insoluble and, as it is essential for the production of chlorophyll, deficiency results in the chlorosis of the leaves. It can be rectified by spraying the leaves with " Sequestrene "; likewise the lack of magnesium and manganese can be remedied where deficient on acidic soils.

Chlorosis in brassicas can be due to a deficiency of both manganese and magnesium. Boron deficiency, often occurring on light, calcareous soils, is responsible for brown heart of cauliflower and several other " diseases," mainly affecting the growing point. It can be rectified by applying borax to the soil at about 1 oz. per 15 sq. yd. Zinc and copper deficiencies are unusual in England, but lack of molybdenum has caused whiptail disease of cauliflower. Only minute quantities of the last three are required; more may be poisonous to plants and animals.

Organic Manures.—It should be noted that most of the deficiencies will not concern the amateur, especially if he keeps the ground in good heart with ample organic manure, which contains all the plant foods necessary. Well-rotted farmyard manure from cows and pigs is by far the best organic food, but is scarce now, good farmers returning it to their own land, and generally the material offered is low in nutrients. Poultry manure, which is rich in soluble nitrogen salts, is excellent either applied direct to the soil (not to the growing crop for fear of damage) or composted with straw.

Many substitutes have been devised to use in place of manure, among them sewage sludge, best applied some time before growing the crop, spent hops from breweries, dried seaweed, excellent for potatoes when supplemented by superphosphate, soot, rich in nitrogen, composted town refuse, and the waste organic animal products mentioned earlier. The organic matter in all these materials is essential for maintaining the soil structure and cannot be replaced simply by artificial fertilisers.

Liquid manure, produced by suspending an old sack of animal manure or soot in water for a few days, is useful for the amateur to apply to pot plants and to individual crops like sweet peas, tomatoes, and chrysanthemums. Leaf mould and peat can be used as a mulch and also to supply organic matter to the soil. Sawdust in a well-rotted condition is also useful for inclusion in compost and as a mulch. It is emphasised that it must be well-rotted, and it is advisable to apply a nitrogen fertiliser, such as sulphate of ammonia, at the same time.

Of the proprietary organic manures, the seaweed one called " Maxicrop " has given good results when used on vegetables and flowers.

Compost-making.—The methods developed for making compost heaps are many and various; they depend on three basic principles, good aeration, plenty of moisture, and a nitrogen supply for the decomposition bacteria. A fairly simple method by which much garden and house refuse can be utilised is as follows. An area about 9 ft. by 4 ft. is marked out and all waste vegetable matter—weeds, lawn mowings, cabbage leaves, pea haulm, straw, dead leaves, and hedge clippings —are put in this area and trodden down. Care should be taken not to use diseased material but grass clippings and weeds which have been recently treated with hormone weed-killers may be applied. When the heap is about 9 in. thick it is sprinkled with sulphate of ammonia and superphosphate, at ½ oz. of each per square yard (2 oz. of each for a 9-ft. by 4-ft. plot) and any wood ash available, and then sprinkled with 4 gallons of water and covered with an inch of soil. This process is repeated with 9-in. layers of rubbish until the heap is about 4 ft. high, when it is better to begin a second heap. A sprinkling of ground lime may be given as each layer is added, but should not be applied until after watering to avoid reaction with the sulphate of ammonia.

The completed heap should be watered occasionally, and after about a month or six weeks, if time permits, it can be turned completely over, watered again, and re-covered with soil. The heap may then be left until rotted, and the compost can be dug in as required; any unrotted material can be used as a basis for a new heap. The time taken for rotting will vary with the time of year and material used, but generally a compost heap made during the summer should be available for autumn use, and one made during the autumn ready for spring use.

There are a number of compounds on the market, known as compost makers, which are said to accelerate the decomposition, but in general a heap made in the way described is eminently satisfactory, and although requiring a certain amount of labour, is the least expensive way of obtaining humus for the garden. This latter point is extremely important nowadays with the scarcity of animal manure and the high costs of both inorganic and organic fertilisers. Prices are, of course, not static, but comparatively the organic manures, such as dried blood, hoof and horn, and guano, are more expensive than the inorganic salts, but these lack humus, which is an essential of a well-cultivated soil.

General Fertiliser.—Many firms supply compound fertilisers containing given amounts of the main nutrients needed, in either liquid or powder form, and some are made up with quantities of nitrogen, potassium, and phosphorus suitable for specific crops like roses, tomatoes, and chrysanthemums. A general fertiliser which can be made up by the amateur is as follows:

7 parts by weight superphosphate.
5 parts by weight sulphate of ammonia.
2 parts by weight sulphate of potash.

Encouraging results have been found with " Maxicrop " a seaweed manure, used as a general feed. In bulk purchase it returns good value for money.

Green Manuring.—Another method of enriching the soil with organic matter is green manuring, which has been practised for some time by farmers and can no doubt be adapted to the gardener's purpose. Green manuring consists of planting a fast-growing catch-crop and ploughing the mature crop back into the soil. Legumes are especially good for this, as certain bacteria in their roots can " fix " the nitrogen in the air. Field peas, sown at 4–5 oz. per sq. yd. and Italian rye grass at 2 oz. per sq. yd are commonly used, while clover and annual lupins are also suitable.

If sown after an early crop on land needing organic matter the green manure may be dug in during late summer. Alternatively, if the land is not being cropped at all during the year two green-manure crops may be grown; an early sowing of field peas in April may be dug in during July, and a further sowing of field peas or Italian rye grass sown immediately after may be dug in following the first few frosts.

New chemicals often appear on the market at exorbitant prices and with fantastic claims as to their value as " soil conditioners " and the like. Contrary to this generalisation, in recent years a chemical known as " Gibberellin " has been used to increase the growth of certain plants. It is now available to the amateur, but should be used with care and mainly in a spirit of experimentation, as no conclusive proof of its efficacy has yet been put forward.

Standard References.

Fertilizers and Manures by Keith Paisley (Collingridge) 1960 (30s.).
Seed and Potting Composts, by Lawrence and Newell (Allen and Unwin) (9s. 6d.).

GARDEN PESTS.

Every garden abounds in insects and other small creatures, but comparatively few species are pests which feed on plants. The great majority are quite harmless, while many are positively beneficial and help to keep the number of pests under control by catching and eating them. Every good gardener should make it his business to be able to differentiate between friend and foe. This is not always easy, but the speed of a creature's movements may often provide a clue. Fast-running, active creatures, such as the black ground-beetle or the centipede, are usually beneficial, while the slow-moving and sluggish ones, e.g., wireworms, aphids and caterpillars, are usually pests. This is by no means an infallible rule, but it is handy to remember when in doubt.

The good gardener should also get to know the pests which are most prevalent in his district and which can be expected to crop up year after year. The first principle of good control measures is to act while an infestation is still in its early stages and before a great deal of damage is done. When one knows what to expect, steps can be taken to prevent an attack or to stop it developing to serious proportions.

Also, from the experience of past years one can often forecast whether a pest is likely to become numerous enough to make chemical treatment worthwhile. Remember, insecticides can become an expensive item, and there is little point in using them if the damage is negligible. In these circumstances insecticides may eventually increase the numbers of pests, since the treatment will also have killed off many of their natural enemies which had hitherto kept the pests under adequate control. In addition, good cultivation and general garden hygiene helps to reduce the numbers of pests.

The common pests of garden plants can be roughly divided into four main groups.

I. **Root Pests.**—These destroy the feeding mechanism of plants or tunnel into fleshy tap roots, tubers, and bulbs. Attacked plants make poor growth, and may eventually wilt and die.

Some insects are general root-feeders. These include (a) Swift Moth Caterpillars, soft, white caterpillars with reddish-brown heads; (b) Chafer Grubs, large, C-shaped, whitish grubs with chestnut-brown heads; (c) Wireworms, long, cylindrical, yellowish-brown grubs with a hard shiny skin; and (d) Leatherjackets, greyish-black grubs with a wrinkled, leathery skin. These are particularly prevalent in recently cultivated grassland or in gardens surrounded by fields, and will attack the roots of a wide range of plants. Chafer grubs, however, are particularly fond of the roots of shrubs, and wireworms will often tunnel in potato tubers and other fleshy roots, whereas leatherjackets prefer the roots of grasses, and may cause browning on large patches of lawn.

Badly infested ground should be dressed with lindane dust when cultivating, working the dust into the top 4 in. of soil. Where this is not possible, i.e., on lawns or around established shrubs, the liquid form of the insecticide should be watered into the soil.

Cutworms are stout, fleshy caterpillars, varying in colour from greyish-brown to dingy green. They feed on roots during the day, but at night come to the surface and feed at the base of the stems of plants, causing them suddenly to collapse and wither. Brassicas and lettuce are commonly damaged in this way and the pests should be removed by hand and killed when the soil is cultivated.

Millepedes are hard-skinned, cylindrical creatures, brown or black, with numerous short, hair-like legs. They are slow-moving and curl up when disturbed. They should not be confused with the active, long-legged centipedes, which are beneficial. Millepedes commonly extend the damage made by other pests, such as slugs and wireworms. They also bore into the sown seeds of peas and beans. During the day they hide in dark, damp places, such as long vegetation or under stones and pieces of wood. Such hiding-places should be removed or dusted with lindane. Drills for pea and bean seed should also be dusted before covering.

Weevil Grubs, small, curved, white grubs, may infest the roots of pot plants and plants in rockeries. Such plants should be removed, the roots cleaned, and replanted in soil which has been dressed or mixed with lindane dust. Where it is not practicable to remove the plants they should be watered copiously with a liquid form of these insecticides and soil dressed properly at the earliest opportunity.

Slugs need no description. They vary greatly in colour. The most destructive are the underground keeled slugs, small, grey-black in colour, which tunnel in roots, tubers, and bulbs. There are also several foliage-feeding species which rasp holes in the top parts of plants. Slugs like wet conditions, and much can be done to control them by ensuring that the soil is well-drained and that long, tangled vegetation is removed.

Poison baits can be bought or made by mixing 1 oz. metaldehyde with 3 lb. bran (or bonemeal for keeled slugs). The bait is sprinkled over the infested ground or distributed in small heaps and protected from the rain. There is also available on the market a metaldehyde spray for dealing with the foliage-feeding types.

Cabbage Root Fly attacks brassicas and wall-flowers. The small white maggot eats away the side roots and tunnels in the main root, causing the plant to wilt and collapse. The roots of young seedlings should be dipped in lindane before planting out. Alternatively, the plants can be given a drench of lindane within four days of planting out.

The maggots also tunnel in radishes and turnips, and this can be avoided by dusting the seed drills with lindane.

Carrot Fly.—The maggot of this fly tunnels in carrots and parsnips. Where the pest is serious it is best to delay sowing until the end of May. If possible, seeds should be sown in exposed,

windy places, which are avoided by the egg-laying flies. Seedlings should be dusted or sprayed when 2–4 in. high with Murphy's " Lindex Garden Spray," an approved chemical.

Onion Fly maggots tunnel into the bulbs of onions, leeks, and shallots, causing the foliage to collapse. Dig out attacked plants carefully, ensuring that parts of them are not left in the soil, and burn them. To prevent attacks dust around the seedlings with lindane when they are at the " loop " stage, i.e., about 1 in. high, and again ten days later.

Narcissus Bulb Flies are serious pests of narcissi and also snowdrops and other bulbous plants. The maggots burrow in the centre of the bulbs, causing them to rot. All soft bulbs should be burned and the remainder immersed for three hours in a solution of lindane containing a wetter. To prevent future attacks and a reinfestation, dust around the necks of growing bulbs with lindane at fortnightly intervals from the end of April until the end of June.

Insects which feed above ground include:

II. Sucking Pests pierce the tissues of plants with needle-like mouth parts and suck the sap. This devitalises the plant, checks growth, and causes wilting. Some species cause distortion of leaves and young shoots, and aphids, suckers, scale insects, and mealy bugs excrete a sugary fluid which disfigures the foliage, attracts ants, and allows the growth of sooty moulds.

Aphids, i.e., blackfly, greenfly, etc., are serious pests which attack almost all plants and multiply rapidly in warm weather. They feed on the shoots and undersides of the leaves, and many species are responsible for the transmission of virus diseases. Infestations should be treated as early as possible. Malathion and nicotine both give excellent results if used properly and thoroughly to both the surface and undersides of the affected foliage. With the advent of these sprays the control of aphids on roses and broad beans, for example, is no longer a serious problem. Tree fruits should be sprayed when the buds are bursting and again when the flower buds are still green. Currants should be treated at the " grape " stage, but lindane should not be used on this fruit. Tar oil, applied to deciduous woody plants while they are completely dormant, will kill the over-wintering stages of these and many other pests. It does not, however, give a good winter control for Woolly Aphid on apples. This pest is best controlled by spraying at the pink-bud stage with B.H.C. with a succinate spreader added. Small colonies on the bark can be eradicated by painting with 10% tar oil.

Some aphids feed underground on roots, particularly of lettuces, currants, and cacti. Where practicable, infested plants should be lifted and the roots cleaned and sprayed before replanting in clean soil. Otherwise water them copiously with malathion or lindane.

Scale Insects are often found in greenhouses, but also occur out-of-doors on trees and shrubs. Flat or dome-shaped, these creatures spend most of their lives immobile, and they do not at all resemble insects, or even appear to be alive. Again tar oil is useful for killing the overwintering stages on deciduous woody shrubs which are dormant. Plants which are in leaf should be sprayed with malathion or nicotine/white oil emulsion two or three times at fortnightly intervals. These substances are more effective if as much as possible of the scale is first removed by means of a sponge, brush, or scraper with water in which soft soap has been dissolved. Mealy Bugs are common pests of greenhouse plants, and should be given the same treatment as scale insects.

Capsid Bugs are very active insects which cause considerable damage to fruit trees and bushes and also to various ornamental plants, principally chrysanthemums and dahlias. They feed on the young leaves, causing distortion and raggedness, and on the buds, which later produce misshapen blooms. These insects, green or reddish in colour, can be controlled by spraying with lindane when the flower buds are still green as, for instance, on fruit trees. Herbaceous plants should be sprayed twice or three times at three-weekly intervals, starting when the plants are young and before the damage is seen. Less persistent insecticides which can be used in this case are malathion and nicotine.

Leafhoppers are small, yellowish-green insects like aphids but much more active. They feed on the undersides of the leaves of a variety of plants, causing them to become speckled with yellow. . Roses are commonly attacked. The treatment given to capsids on herbaceous plants will control these also, the sprays being directed to the undersides of the leaves.

Whiteflies are serious pests in greenhouses, and also occur out-of-doors on rhododendrons and other evergreen shrubs. The adults are like miniature moths with white wings, and the young are small, scale-like creatures, generally greenish in colour, which feed without movement on the undersides of the leaves. To control all whiteflies lindane or malathion should be used as a spray or smoke, two to three applications being given at fortnightly intervals.

Red Spider Mites are extremely small creatures, red or greenish in colour and just visible with the naked eye. They feed on the undersides of the leaves of many greenhouse and outdoor plants, including fruit, causing the leaves to turn sickly yellow. Control is difficult, the most effective materials being malathion, derris, summer ovicides, or azobenzene smoke. The directions on the labels of these products should be followed carefully.

III. Biting Insects have chewing and biting mouth parts which are used to cut away pieces of plants.

Caterpillars (the young stages of moths and butterflies) are the best-known pests in this group. They vary in size and colour according to the species, and most plants are liable to be attacked. These should be sprayed or dusted with derris as soon as the damage is noticed.

On apple and pear trees caterpillars can cause serious trouble and, in this case, treatment should take the form of a pre-blossom spray with trichlorphon.

The greatest problem with caterpillars arises with the well-known large and small white butterflies which in some seasons skeletonise the leaves. The worst damage is in the late summer when the infestation has built up to its highest point. Control is laborious; crush the egg clusters of the large butterfly and remove colonies of caterpillars by hand. As far as chemical control is concerned, this should be restricted to the use of derris up to within two weeks of picking. In recent years various other chemical controls have been suggested and applied on a large scale but their use is not now recommended unless specific approval has been granted. See T31.

Sawfly Caterpillars are very similar to those above, and commonly attack gooseberry and rose foliage. They can be controlled by spraying with malathion or derris.

Attacks by the Apple Sawfly, which burrows in young apples and forms ribbon-like scars on the skin, can be prevented by spraying with lindane seven days after 80% of the blossom has fallen.

Beetles and Weevils which feed on foliage are usually best controlled by spraying or dusting with derris. To kill the tiny Flea-beetles which eat small holes in the seedlings of brassicas and turnips, treat the plants at fourteen-day intervals until they reach the " rough-leaf " stage.

The golden-brown Raspberry Beetle, which feeds on the flowers and whose grub tunnels in the fruit, is best eradicated with derris applied ten days after full bloom and again ten days later. For other common pests in this group, e.g., Vine

Weevil, Clay-coloured Weevil, Pea and Bean Weevil, etc., apply the derris as soon as the damage is first seen.

Earwigs feed at night on the foliage and flower petals of many plants. They hide by day inside flowers, in the folds of leaves, and in nooks and crannies on the ground, under flat stones, etc. These pests are killed by derris applied to the plants (but not to open flowers) and to their hiding-places.

Leaf Miners are very small grubs which tunnel between the upper and lower surfaces of leaves, forming pale blisters, as on lilac, holly, celery, etc., or long, twisting galleries, as on chrysanthemum, pea, and tomato. In small infestations the affected leaves should be picked off and burned. Otherwise spray with lindane as soon as the damage starts, giving three applications at fourteen-day intervals.

IV. Eelworms are microscopic pests which are invisible to the naked eye. They are able to live for very long periods without food and are extremely difficult to eradicate. The most common species are:

Stem and Bulb Eelworm, which infests narcissus, phlox, strawberry, hyacinth, onion, and other plants. Infested plants show distorted foliage and dwarfing and gradually deteriorate. They can only be sterilised by immersion in hot water kept at well-defined temperatures for one to three hours, but expert diagnosis and advice should be obtained before this or any other control is attempted. Infested ground must be kept clear of any host plants for at least three years to starve out the eelworms.

Chrysanthemum Eelworm causes the formation of yellowish blotches between the veins of chrysanthemum leaves, which later turn black and drop off. In severe infestations the blooms are undersized and malformed. Expert advice should be obtained before control measures are attempted.

Potato Root Eelworm is a serious and widespread pest of potatoes, causing the plants to become stunted and sickly, giving very poor yields. The pest can only be kept in check by crop rotation, potatoes being grown on the same ground only once in four years. This is difficult in small gardens, and where land becomes heavily infested the only remedy is to rest it from potatoes for at least five years.

The Purchase and Use of Insecticides.—To ensure that an insecticide will do what the maker claims, it is advisable only to buy brands which have been tested and approved by the Ministry of Agriculture. This can be ascertained from the Approval Mark (T31) on the label. Read the directions and following them carefully. Never apply insecticides to flowers in bloom, otherwise many valuable pollinating insects will be killed.

Standard References.

Encyclopaedia of Garden Pests and Diseases, by van Konynenburg and Lawfield (Collingridge), 1958 (42s.).

Gardening Chemicals. Lists of insecticides, fungicides, herbicides, etc., listed under trade names. Available from The Sec., Royal Hort. Soc., Vincent Sq., London, S.W.1, 1967 (8s. 3d. post free).

Horticultural Pests: Detection and Control, by G. Fox Wilson, revised by P. Becker (Crosby Lockwood), 1960 (25s.).

DISEASES OF PLANTS.

Plant diseases are important because they can cause great loss not only in growing crops but also in the produce after it has been harvested and stored. The skill in growing crops is wasted if they are destroyed by disease, and many people know the wastage of potatoes through blight disease in winter stores and rotting of onions when they decay through neck rot disease. For these reasons the keen gardener must take notice of diseases and use the knowledge available to him in checking them wherever possible.

The most important point to remember about plant diseases is to recognise the first signs so that the remedy can be applied at once. In greenhouses this is of great importance because the atmosphere is warm and moist, and in such conditions diseases flourish. It must also be remembered that the same crop is often grown in the same soil in a greenhouse so that we get a build-up of disease, and this causes the well-known " soil sickness." This means that new soil must be brought in or the old soil enriched and also sterilised by steam or by chemicals. Even frames and propagating pits require periodic cleaning up by a disinfection treatment.

Unlike insect pests, the actual cause of a plant disease cannot be seen with the naked eye, and microscopic examination is required for its detection. The scientists who study diseases are called plant pathologists, and these are stationed

THE APPROVAL MARK—An officially approved crop-protection product shows on its label this design.

at universities and other institutes throughout the country, where they carry out research on various plant troubles and advise on suitable remedies for checking them. It is obviously necessary to understand the exact cause of a disease and how that cause operates before a means of checking the trouble can be devised. The advice can then be passed on to growers, farmers, and the gardening public.

The presence of disease in most cases can only be detected by the symptoms shown by the affected plant, which is called the " host ". The actual cause must then be determined by careful examination in the laboratory, which is done by the pathologist.

Plant diseases in general are divided into three classes as follows: 1. Fungus and Bacterial. 2. Virus. 3. Functional Disorders.

1. Fungus and Bacterial Diseases.—The first kind called fungus diseases are caused by the attack of fungus parasites; examples being the well-known club root of cabbages, potato scab, apple scab, and plum brown rot. These parasitic fungi are microscopic and composed of fine threads, but they attack plants and penetrate them either through wounds (insect bites, hail damage, pruning cuts) or directly through the surface cells (epidermis). The threads grow into the plant, killing the cells and absorbing their contents. There is usually some discoloration or even decay of the tissues around the point of infection, but it is possible for the plant to show distress in one part although the parasite is at work some distance away. Examples are silver leaf in plums and the honey fungus, which kills trees by attacking the roots.

The fungus spreads by means of spores which are equivalent to seeds in flowering plants but which are microscopic in size. These spores are produced on the surface of the plant in enormous numbers and are blown (wind), splashed (rain), or carried (insects, etc.) in all directions to alight on other healthy plants, where they germinate and spread the disease. This occurs in the growing season, but when winter approaches, the parasite forms tough, resting bodies of one kind or another, and these are resistant to extreme cold.

They overwinter in the soil or in the surface of tree bark, etc., so that in the following spring they can germinate and cause disease again. So we get the reappearance of such troubles as damping off in seedlings, scab in apples, brown rot in apples and plums, foot rot in peas, wart disease in potatoes, mildews on all kinds of plants, and so on. This question of soil contamination by overwintering spores is one of the most serious in the fight against plant disease.

The signs of fungus and bacterial diseases are varied, and may show as yellowing, silvering, brown spotting, or blackening of leaves (potato blight, rose black spot, celery leaf spot, antirrhinum rust), as stunting (cabbage wire stem), as pustules and cankers in stems (coral spot, apple canker), as gumming or dieback in branches (rose canker, plum dieback), as galls, warts, witches brooms, or other malformation (club root in cabbages, crown gall, leafy gall, peach leaf curl), as dry or soft rots of fruits, tubers, vegetable bulbs, and corms (gladiolus dry rot, potato dry rot, iris rhizome rot, celery heart rot), and many other abnormal conditions. Sometimes only a part of the plant is affected and can be removed, e.g., branches showing attack by coral spot or one of the large bracket fungi seen on trees, these having gained entrance through a wound.

2. Virus Diseases.—This class of disease is becoming increasingly important as more is discovered about them, although research on them is a comparatively recent development. A virus disease is caused by infection with a virus, and the exact nature of this is not yet clearly understood, but it is so small that it cannot be seen with ordinary microscopes. Its detection is therefore not easy, but when the sap of a virus-diseased plant is injected into a healthy one it causes the disease.

In nature this spread is brought about by biting and sucking insects, which are referred to as Vectors. They transmit the virus by feeding on infected plants and then travelling to healthy ones, on which they feed and so spread the disease. Most viruses are transmitted by aphids (greenflies).

In the garden and nursery they can be carried from plant to plant by pruning knives or by the fingers in the process of trimming plants such as tomatoes, melons, and cucumbers or by the use of the knife in taking cuttings. In general, the virus does not kill a plant quickly but tends to cripple it and cause a slow deterioration. Infected plants cannot recover but remain, sometimes for years, as sources of infection on which insects feed and carry on the disease. So viruses may increase in lily stocks, strawberry beds, and raspberry plantations unless virus-infected plants are removed and aphids strictly suppressed.

The signs of virus disease are of different kinds, but the commonest are those of the type called mosaic, in which the leaves show a mottling with light-green or yellow patches scattered in irregular fashion on the darker green of the leaf. There may be also some reduction in the leaf blades. These symptoms can be seen in the mosaic of cucumber, vegetable marrow, lettuce, cabbage, turnip, tomato, delphinium, primula, dahlia, apple, raspberry, and many other common plants. In some, such as lilies, daffodils, and onions, the mosaic is more in the form of stripes down the leaf blades.

Another virus symptom is flower " breaking," where the normal colour of the petals is broken by streaks and spots of white, and this can be seen in tulip, wallflower, pansy, stocks, or carnations affected by the mosaic virus. Other viruses cause bronzing of the top leaves (as in tomato spotted wilt) or small light-coloured rings arranged in concentric circles (as in dahlia ring spot) or even reduction of leaves until they are tendril like (as in tomato fern leaf). Sometimes there is malformation or even proliferation, producing innumerable stunted shoots, as in blackberry dwarf disease.

The important point to note about these virus diseases is that every part of the plant is quickly infected, so that the sap is infectious to other plants of the same kind. The virus is present in all parts, and for this reason it is useless to propagate from a virus-infected plant. This means that all the scales and offsets from bulbs such as lilies and tulips, all the tubers from potatoes, and all cuttings from herbaceous plants which are taken from a virus-infected plant are useless, because they will carry the virus. They should be destroyed, and the only exception is where the plant is greatly valued, in which case seed can be taken from it before it is destroyed. In general, viruses do not travel in the seed, and only in one or two cases is seed infected, and this only in negligible quantity.

3. Functional Disorders.—This third class of disease is often called non-parasitic, because unlike the previous two kinds there is no parasite involved, and these troubles are therefore not infectious. They are due to faulty cultivation or unsuitable environment, in which soil conditions or climate affect the plants adversely. In this group we include cases of unsatisfactory growth due to waterlogging, drought, frost, high temperature, damage by fumes or atmospheric pollution, or even excess lime.

Perhaps the most important kinds of trouble in this class are the so called Deficiency Diseases, where the plants suffer from shortage of some important food. This may be one of the common food substances, such as nitrogen, potash, or phosphate, and details will be found under the section on manures and fertilisers (T26).

CONTROL OF DISEASES.

1. Garden Hygiene.—The control of plant diseases can be dealt with only briefly, but to begin with we must emphasise the value of good cultivation as an insurance against losses from disease. Robust plants are better able to stand up to disease than sickly ones, and everything in the way of proper drainage, soil aeration, proper spacing, sensible feeding, and so on, will help to keep the plants vigorous, and this is the first line of defence against diseases. Garden hygiene is important, weeds need to be kept down, wounds in trees and shrubs covered with a good paint against infection, new stocks examined carefully, seed bought only from reliable sources, diseased plants burnt, and dead material regularly removed from plants, especially in greenhouses.

2. Soil Sterilisation.—There are other precautions, among which the sterilisation of the soil in greenhouses by means of steam or chemicals is of some importance. Dazomet can be used outside but rotation of crops is a most useful system in helping to avoid disease. Disinfection of frames, propagating pits, and seed boxes by formalin or cresylic acid are other useful measures. All these operations aim at destroying the resting spores of fungus parasites responsible for such diseases as tomato leaf mould, gladiolus dry rot, damping off in seedlings, root rots, and downy mildews of many kinds in young plants such as stocks, cheiranthus, cineraria, tomato, aster, and calceolaria when grown in boxes or pots.

3. Disease Resistant Plants.—The use of disease-resistant varieties of plants is very desirable, but there are not many kinds available, and often the resistant kind does not possess flowers or fruit of such fine quality or flavour as the more susceptible kind. The outstanding success of this kind is that of potatoes immune to the dreaded wart disease, and these can be grown safely in the most heavily infected land. There are antirrhinums resistant to rust disease, and there is resistance in some degree in the case of delphinium mildew, potato blight, tomato leaf mould, and some others. Research goes on to discover still more, because any such plants are always worth a trial.

4. Treatment of Seeds and Bulbs.—For seed-borne diseases seed treatments may be done with captan or thiram seed dressings, or even by immersion of the infected seed in warm water.

In some diseases, for example, tulip fire, we can protect the bulbs from the danger of infected soil by raking in a powder such as "Botrilex" when planting the bulbs, and a similar treatment is done with calomel dust against club root in beds intended for sowing brassica seeds.

5. Fungicides.—Even after all this, a disease may still appear in the crop, and more direct action must be taken. It is then necessary to protect the plants by means of a Fungicide. This is a chemical which is poisonous to fungus parasites but which will not harm the crop plant (host). Fungicides are used as wet sprays or in powder form as dusts, and they are sprayed or dusted all over the plants to protect them from infection by diseases.

The object of the treatment is to cover the plants with a film of the fungicide so as to protect the still healthy ones. To help the spray fluid to spread over and adhere to the foliage another substance, called a wetter, spreader, or sticker, is added to the spray, but sometimes this is already included by the manufacturer.

5. (a) Sprays.—Sprays are applied by means of machines called sprayers which vary from small, hand-syringe types giving a continuous jet of spray to those pumped up to a pressure and carried on the back (knapsack machines), and so on to the large machines driven by a petrol engine, which deliver the spray at a high pressure. It is necessary to have a suitable nozzle giving a fine mist-like cone of spray which settles on the foliage and is not wasted.

5. (b) Dusts.—Dusts are similar chemicals produced in such finely divided form that the powder can be blown over and on the foliage almost like a fog. This is best done after a shower of rain or after a heavy dew. The machines used are far more varied in design than spraying machines. There are small hand dusters worked either like a small pump or like a bellows, of which the "Acme" is a good example, and there are those which are carried on the back and worked as a double-bellows action or on the front of the body with a rotary-fan action. It is important in gardens to clean and dry the machines after use, and small sprayers may be best put upside down to drain for a time after use.

The substances used as sprays and dusts against plant diseases for many years have been copper and sulphur and their compounds. Perhaps the best known copper-containing spray is "Bordeaux Mixture," which is still a good spray, but which has been largely replaced by liquid copper available as "Murphy's Liquid Copper Fungicide" for such diseases as tomato blight, etc. Sulphur is used extensively as lime-sulphur against apple scab and as colloidal sulphur against the powdery mildew diseases. As dusts, copper is mixed with lime to give copper-lime dust and sulphur is used alone either as flowers of sulphur or green sulphur.

5. (c) The Newer Fungicides.—In recent years much research has been carried out in tests to see whether other chemicals have value as fungicides, and the search has been in the field of organic chemistry and among all kinds of these chemicals. Tests of this kind take a long time, but a few substances have already been picked out as showing special promise and we can mention captan which is so good against apple and pear scab, zineb against tomato leaf mould, onion mildew and tulip fire and dinocap against any of the powdery mildews such as American gooseberry mildew, strawberry mildew, vine mildew as well as the same diseases on ornamental roses, delphiniums, michaelmas daisies and other plants.

6. Control of Viruses.—The control of virus diseases is very different, because in this case the only spray treatments likely to be of use are those designed to keep down insects. The other necessary control measure is to remove and destroy the virus-infected plants, which are a danger as sources of infection.

This is best done when the plants are young, so that any young marrows, cucumbers, dahlias, delphiniums, sweet peas, lupins, lilies, etc., which show virus symptoms as commonly revealed in leaf mottling and poor growth should be removed as soon as detected. Propagation should be done carefully, so that young stock is not propagated from stocks of strawberries, raspberries, and all kinds of herbaceous perennials which show signs of virus infection. Even the knife used for taking cuttings should be wiped occasionally on a rag dipped in a good disinfectant.

7. Prevention of Functional Disorders.—In the case of Functional Disorders (non-parasitic diseases) it is not always easy to advise remedies. Where the soil conditions are faulty attention can be directed to improving drainage if necessary or counteracting dryness by digging in humus, irrigating, and general mulching. Dryness at the roots of tomatoes causes loss of fruit, and so does extreme dryness in the air of the greenhouse, but these should be adjusted fairly easily.

Hail damage can spoil many crops, but robust foliage may help a little to lessen the damage. Late frost damage to fruit in some areas can be lessened by various methods of cultivation and planting. The effects of drought can be aggravated by shortage of certain foods, especially potash, so that even here some attempt can be made to avoid loss. Excess liming may cause food shortages by causing the appearance, in the leaves, of a yellowish or even whitish colour, which is known as lime-induced chlorosis. The real reason may be lack of iron or manganese due to the excess lime in the soil, but recently very good results at counteracting this condition have been obtained by using the substance known as " Sequestrene."

Another method of treating these food shortages is to spray the young foliage in early summer with the required element in a very weak solution. They can even be included in sprays used for keeping down diseases or pests. It must not be forgotten that even the ordinary foods, such as nitrogen, potash, and phosphate, may sometimes be in short supply, and the effect can be seen by the trained plant pathologist. In these cases the effect may not always show clearly in the growing crop, but may appear long afterwards in the stored fruits and vegetables, which as a result deteriorate and break down long before they are required for use.

The present-day methods of cultivating large numbers of the same plant in one spot tend to increase the risk of large-scale disease attacks. Modern plants may be highly bred and selected for great purity of strain. Indeed, they have often been chosen for fine quality and flavour, with little regard to their ability to resist disease, so that the gardener must always be ready to give them the protection they may need.

Standard References.

Diseases of Vegetables, by Donald E. Green (Macmillan), 1946 (8s. 6d.).

Plant Diseases, by F. T. Brooks (Oxford), 1953 (38s.).

Insecticide and Fungicide Handbook, Ed. Hubert Martin (Blackwell), 1968 (60s.).

USES OF MODERN WEEDKILLERS.

The eradication of weeds by chemical means is one of the greatest advances of recent years albeit the value of herbicides is still unappreciated by most gardeners. With a planned programme, all cultivated ground and lawns can be kept free of weeds without hoeing or any other sort of manual cultivation.

Occasionally troubles have arisen in not following makers' instructions. Sometimes the damage has been most unfortunate, as the majority of herbicides are toxic, in varying degrees, to a wide range of plant life. In the main, controls are determined by circumstance, as typified in the following cases:

Asparagus Beds.—Annuals and top growth of perennial weeds can be controlled with cresylic acid in the autumn and before the asparagus appears in the spring. In beds free of perennials, a first-class control of weeds can be maintained with Simazine applied in the early spring.

Where annual and perennial grasses predominate, Dalapon or Diquat will give good control. As for bindweed, this may be eradicated by watering the foliage with 2,4-D in late July or August taking care to avoid contact with the asparagus stems and particularly the fern.

Fruit Garden.—Around blackcurrants, gooseberries, raspberries, apples, and pears, grasses can be killed with Dalapon. Once clear of perennial weeds, annuals may be controlled effectively with Simazine. Alternatively, weeds may be killed with Diquat, making applications as necessary throughout the season.

Garden Paths.—On any surfaced path or drive a first-rate control of weeds can be maintained by watering with a residual herbicide such as Simazine. As this preparation is virtually insoluble in water, it does not seep through the soil as sodium chlorate would, and therefore it can be used near garden crops and grass edgings. Further to this, it is not easily washed from the soil and remains active near the surface for up to twelve months. Notwithstanding, the herbicide must be used with proper care.

A dilute solution of sodium chlorate with 4–6 ozs. to a gallon of water may be applied, but it is liable to affect plants near by and, for this reason, application should be confined to the centre of the path, thereby leaving room for the chlorate to seep through the soil.

Lawns.—The majority of weeds in turf can be eradicated easily with formulations of 2,4-D or M.C.P.A. (*see* Finding List). In particular, daisies, dandelions, plantains, and most broad-leaved weeds are susceptible although it may be necessary to repeat the dose after 10 days. The best time to do the work is on a warm, fine day in the spring when the plants are growing actively and there is the prospect of fine weather to follow for twenty-four hours. The action of the herbicides is rapid, and grass may be cut after a couple of days, composting with mowings in the normal way. It appears that the hormones are not injurious to bacterial life in the soil and in a few weeks break down into harmless substances.

Where bulbs are naturalised in grass, steps to control weeds should not be taken until the foliage of the bulbs has died down and the bulbs are dormant. Thus, as a general rule, control measures are best applied throughout July.

To deal with weeds in turf where there arises the danger of the spray—or even a drift from it—touching cultivated plants near by, as, for instance, on grass paths in a rose garden, then one of the plastic canes filled with a solution of hormone can be used to spot-treat weeds. Alternatively a hormone formulated as a powder and appropriately named "Spot," gives good results.

Some weeds are resistant to normal doses of hormones and need special treatment. These are mostly mat-forming plants of low-growing habit which are not cut off by mowing. Typical examples include mosses of all sorts, pearlwort, speedwell or veronica, yarrow, and yellow-flowered clover. Here, the main control must be in the use of lawn sand, a good mixture of which can be made up with:

> 2 parts by weight sulphate of ammonia.
> 1 part by weight sulphate of iron.
> 13 parts by weight LIME-FREE sand.

Where moss is the most prevalent weed, to the mixture should be added sufficient superphosphate to give 1 oz. of it per sq. yd. for the area to be treated. A hundredweight of the lawn sand plus superphosphate can be made up for about 21s. and is sufficient to treat about 450 sq. yds. at 4 oz. per sq. yd.

Applications to patches of the weeds should be made when the turf is damp and there is the prospect of fine weather; if a period of drought follows an application, then water should be applied to avoid serious scorching. Repeat the treatment as necessary throughout the growing season. Linked with this " spot " treatment, the growth of grass must be encouraged, as this will tend to smother low-growing weeds. Thus, in the early spring when the turf is wet, feed with a mixture of equal parts of superphosphate, sulphate of ammonia and dry soil at 2 oz. per sq. yd. over the whole area and repeat after a month, if desirable. In addition, do *not* shave off the grass by close cutting; instead, the blades of the mower should be set reasonably high for a whole season.

Where fertility is low, clovers often predominate in turf. The Dutch clovers with white—or pink—flowers and a white-angled band towards the base of each leaflet, can be eradicated with Mecoprop. Afterwards the turf should be fed with nitrogenous fertilisers like soot and sulphate of ammonia, to discourage clover infestation. Other types of clover found in turf are species of *Trifolium*. Compared to the Dutch clover, these have a tight, bunched habit of growth and yellow flowers. All of them are resistant to hormones and, in addition to manurial treatment, should be treated with lawn sand.

Lakes.—It sometimes happens that aquatic plants with large floating leaves, such as water lilies, get out of hand. Here, control can be established by cutting off the foliage with a long-handled appliance like the "Corypu Water Scythe." The work should be done early in June and repeated as often as any fresh growth is seen.

Bulrushes are difficult to eliminate, but can be destroyed by digging out the roots when the level of the water permits. Dalapon has been found to give a control; applications should be made, with a wetting agent added, when the rushes reach maturity.

Ponds.—Problems of weed control in ornamental ponds are often not easy to solve. Where duckweed is prevalent this small floating plant can be eliminated by sweeping the surface of the water at regular intervals. If this practice is carried out thoroughly much of the vegetative growth will be eliminated, and the plant will not be able to form resting bodies whereby it over-winters. Once a control has been established, further spread of the plant can be prevented by introducing a few moorhens or ornamental ducks.

The most common of unwanted plants in pools is blanket weed. There is no single means of dealing with this plant, for its spread is governed, to a certain extent, by unbalanced plant and anima life in the water. With this fact in mind, water lilies should be established so that their foliage shades about 25 per cent of the water. In addition, a few oxygenating plants should be introduced from local ponds or streams and a supply of goldfish added. Blanket weed is usually found in pools where the water gets overheated in summer; for this reason, the average depth of garden ponds should be a minimum of 2 ft. and preferably a minimum of 3 ft.

Rose Beds.—A complete control of annual weeds among roses can be obtained with Simazine. Here, the salient point is to apply the herbicide immediately after pruning in March *before* any weed growth starts. Alternatively, Diquat can be used in April or early May and the application repeated as necessary.

Shrubberies.—With a shortage of labour, beds of shrubs are often weed infested. Perennials can be eradicated with Diquat and annuals controlled by this treatment as they appear. Alternatively, once the perennials are removed, the ground can be kept clear with Simazine used in the early spring.

Much to check weeds in shrubberies can be done by mulching the surface of the soil with heavy dressings of peat, fallen leaves, or sawdust; if the weeds push through the mulch, a second application should be made at once.

Vacant Ground.—On land free of crops all plants can be killed by watering the herbage with sodium chlorate at 1 lb. to a gallon of water. In some cases repetition may be necessary. When using this method it should be remembered that treated ground will remain toxic to plant life for a period of up to six months; if doubt exists about the persistence of the chlorate in the soil, then it is advisable to wait for the appearance of annual weeds before planting.

Apart from its persistence, sodium chlorate is prone to seep through soil and affect plants for some distance away. To avoid danger of fire from clothes being soaked in a solution of the chlorate and then dried, it is prudent to use a formulation with an additive to reduce the risk of fire. (*See* Finding List.) Where couch grass is predominant then the best control is to be obtained with Dalapon.

SPECIAL PROBLEMS OF WEED CONTROL.

Bindweed.—Probably the most ubiquitous of all garden weeds. Up to the present time the main control has been to carefully fork out the roots as new growth is seen; if this is done methodically the plant can be eliminated within a reasonable time.

Lately, chemicals have come to the fore, and bindweed may now be eliminated by watering or painting the foliage with a formulation of 2,4-D when the annual growth has nearly reached maturity. Thus, first applications can be applied in July and the treatment repeated, if necessary, to good effect. Where the weed is among cultivated plants, the herbicides must be applied with a paint brush or the foliage rubbed with a cloth damped in a solution. When doing this rubber gloves should be worn.

Blanket Weed.—*See* Ponds.

Bracken.—Horticulturally, control is not a big problem, and in limited areas it is easily dealt with by repeatedly cutting the aerial stems with a grass hook as the first fronds open. This practice will exhaust the underground food supply of the plant, and gradually it will die out. The young fronds are rich in plant food and, while still green and fresh, they should be composted. No chemicals will offer a reasonable control of this plant and, indeed, it is best dealt with by cutting and final digging out of the roots.

Couch Grass.—Where the soil is light and tends to be low in fertility, it is often found that this is a difficult plant to eradicate by cultural means. If the long, underground stems are forked out in the conventional manner and left on the surface to dry, the roots may be composted to advantage and a good control established. To prevent reinfestation, manures and fertilisers should be applied generously and the ground kept hoed regularly.

Chemically, couch grass can be killed easily by watering the foliage with Dalapon.

Ground Elder.—Without question this is one of the worst garden weeds and, whether or not the fact is pleasant or acceptable, it is indubitably a weed of neglected ground. In varying degrees it is resistant to hormone weed-killers of all sorts. On ground free of crops it may be reduced by an application of sodium chlorate, as explained in the paragraph Vacant Ground. The first treatment should be made as soon as growth starts in the spring and repeated if the desired effect is not abundantly clear. When ground elder is to be found among herbaceous plants the cultivated plants must be lifted out and the weed removed by repeated hand-forking.

In shrubberies reasonable control can be had by smothering the young growth in the spring with a thick dressing of peat, leaf mould, baled straw, or sawdust. If growth penetrates the surface dressing it will be found that the etiolated shoots are not difficult to remove by hand, or a second layer can be applied to complete the treatment.

Alternatively, the foliage of ground elder can be watered with Diquat and the treatment repeated once or twice during the growing season.

Horsetail.—This is sometimes erroneously called marestail and on poor, sandy soils it is often a common weed. Fortunately, recent experiments have proved that it can be easily controlled by spraying or painting the *mature* growths with a formulation of 2,4-D, taking care, of course, to keep the spray off cultivated plants near by. As the appearance of horsetail is symptomatic of low fertility, manurial treatment should be carried out on a generous scale. Where the weed is growing among cultivated crops, individual stems must be treated separately as recommended for bindweed.

Marestail.—*See* Horsetail.

Moss.—*See* Lawns (T33).

Nettles.—It is difficult to understand why the perennial nettle is so abundant as it is immediately responsive to applications of 2,4-D and 2,4,5-T made any time during the growing season.

The annual nettle is usually proved a denizen of rich, light soils and may be eradicated with cresylic acid, Diquat or 2,4-D.

Oxalis.—Of all weeds this is probably the most difficult to destroy. It is easily identified by its large, trifoliolate leaves like that of clover. Unlike other weeds, oxalis cannot be efficiently removed by hand, as this disturbs the bulbils clustered around the base of the stem of mature plants. On ground free of crops, sodium chlorate can be applied in March (*see* Vacant Ground). Perhaps a second application may be necessary, but, even so, control may not be complete. Among shrubby plants, it may be possible to eradicate the weed by smothering, as suggested in the paragraph on ground elder.

The foliage can be killed with Diquat and, by repeated applications, this may constitute the best means of control.

Speedwell.—*See* Veronica.

Veronica.—This procumbent, blue-flowered weed of turf is sometimes known as speedwell. Being resistant to hormones, its control may only be established with lawn sand. *See also* Lawns.

Woody Plants.—With or without the addition of 2,4-D, these may be killed with 2,4,5-T. This hormone is particularly useful on bramble, gorse, ivy, and other unwanted shrubby plants. It is necessary to thoroughly saturate the foliage of deciduous trees, and the best results are obtainable when the leaves are fully mature but not starting to die off. In the case of ivy, the dormant shoots should be generously sprayed for the best results.

Yarrow.—A weed found in many lawns where its presence often signifies low fertility. Control is with lawn sand. *See* Lawns (T33).

Summary.—From these notes it will be seen that there are many aids for dealing with weeds. The salient point is to get the *right* method for *each* plant. Equally important is to check the reason why certain weeds grow profusely under some conditions. Very often this natural tendency can be counteracted as in the case of phosphatic fertilisers against moss and in the application of organic manures and chemical fertilizers where horsetail and yarrow are concerned. *See* T35.

Standard References.

Chemicals for the Gardener, H.M. Stationery Office, 1965 (1s. 7d. incl. postage).

List of Approved Products for Farmers and Growers (published annually), copies free from Ministry of Agriculture, Fisheries, and Food (Publications), Tolcarne Drive, Pinner, Middlesex.

Weed Control Handbook, issued by the British Weed Control Council (Blackwell), 1965 (32s. 6d.).

HORTICULTURAL SOCIETIES.

There are many specialist societies in Britain. Detailed information on particular plants is normally available from them, and membership is open to all wishing to join. The most prominent societies are:

Alpine Garden Society
Sec. Michael Upward, 58 Denison House, 296 Vauxhall Bridge Road, S.W.1.

Auricula and Primula Society, The National
Sec. A. Marlow, 2 Glebe Close, Thornford, Sherborne, Dorset.

Begonia Society, The National Society of England and Wales
Sec. F. J. Martin, 50 Woodlands Farm Road, Erdington, Birmingham 24.

Cactus and Succulent Society of Great Britain
Sec. D. V. Brewerton, 26 Chester Road, Ilford, Essex.

Camellia Society, The International
Sec. Charles E. Puddle, V.M.H., Bodnant, Tal-y-Cafn, Denbighshire.

Carnation Society, The British National
Sec. E. G. Cook, 1 Evelyn Rd., Worthing, Sussex.

Chrysanthemum Society, The National
Sec. S. G. Gosling, 65 St. Margaret's Avenue, Whetstone, N.20.

Daffodil Society
Sec. D. J. Pearce, College of Ascension, Selly Oak, Birmingham, 29.

Dahlia Society, The National
Sec. P. Damp, 26 Burns Road, Lillington, Leamington Spa, Warwickshire.

Delphinium Society, The
Sec. C. J. H. Topping, B.A., Ph.D., 5 Park Lane, Sevenoaks, Kent.

Floral Arrangement Societies of Great Britain National Association of
Sec. Mrs. F. C. Dobson, 21A Denbigh Street, London, S.W.1.

Fuchsia Society, The British
Sec. W. G. Sharp, Rydal, The Green, Gt. Bentley, Colchester, Essex.

Gladiolus Society, The British
Sec. J. G. Lord, 25 Kimpton Avenue, Brentwood, Essex.

Hardy Plant Society
Sec. Miss B. White, 10 St. Barnabas Rd., Emmer Green, Reading, Berks.

Heather Society, The
Sec. Mrs. C. I. MacLeod, Yew Trees, Horley Row, Horley, Surrey.

Iris Society, The British
Sec. Mrs. D. J. Waters, 87 Raglan Gardens, Oxhey, Watford, Herts.

Pansy and Viola Society, The North of England
Sec. F. C. Marshland, 2 Jubilee Mount, West Lillands, Brighouse, Yorks.

Pansy and Viola Association, The Scottish
Sec. Hugh Campbell, O.B.E., 960 Dumbarton Road, Dalmuir, Glasgow.

Pelargonium and Geranium Society, The British
Sec. Mrs. G. M. Weller, 85 Sparrow Farm Road, Ewell, Surrey.

Pteridological Society, The British
Sec. J. W. Dyce, 46 Sedley Rise, Loughton, Essex.

Rose Society, The Royal National
Sec. L. G. Turner, Chiswell Green Lane, St. Albans, Herts.

Royal Horticultural Society
Sec. John Hamer, M.B.E., B.A., Royal Horticultural Society's Offices, Vincent Square, S.W.1.

Royal Caledonian Horticultural Society
Sec. John Turnbull, D.S.O., D.F.C., C.A., Royal Caledonian Horticultural Society, 44 Melville Street, Edinburgh 3.

Saintpaulia and Houseplant Society
Sec. Mrs. E. A. Robbins, 296 Perth Road, Ilford, Essex.

Scottish Rock Garden Club
Sec. Mrs. L. C. Boyd-Harvey, Boonslie, Dirleton, East Lothian.

Sweet Pea Society, The National
Sec. R. J. Huntley, 431 Wokingham Road, Earley, Reading, Berks.

Vegetable Society, The National
Sec. 283 Northumberland Avenue, Welling, Kent.

FINDING LIST FOR WEEDKILLERS

All the herbicides in this list are first-class chemicals which have been approved by the Ministry of Agriculture and are available in small packs designed for use by amateur gardeners. In case of difficulty in obtaining any of them, the manufacturers should be contacted.

The list may appear unnecessarily long but the pipe dream of multipurpose herbicides is not a reality and the full extent and value of chemical weed controls are only obtained by using herbicides for their specific purposes; as such, they constitute an efficient and economic method of eradicating unwanted plants of all sorts.

Trade names	Chemicals	Manufacturers	Type of action	Plants controlled	Notes and precautions
		WEED KILLERS FOR USE ON TURF			
"Bugges 2,4-D" "Dicotox" "Shell Weed-kill" "Lornox"	2,4-D	Bugges Insecticides Ltd. Sittingbourne, Kent. May and Baker Ltd., Dagenham, Essex. Shell Chemical Co. Ltd. Boots Pure Drug Co. Ltd.	Hormone growth regulator translocated throughout the plant.	Many broad-leafed weeds and some perennial ones. Best hormone type for killing daisies, dandelions and plantains.	Primarily for use on lawns Beware of drift.
"Bugges M.C.P.A." "Weed-a-Lawn" and "Spot" (in powder form)	M.C.P.A.	Bugges Insecticides Ltd., London Rd., Sittingbourne, Kent. Pan Britannia Industries Ltd., Britannia House, Waltham Cross, Herts.	Hormone growth regulator translocated throughout the plant.	Many broad-leafed weeds and some perennial ones. Best hormone type for killing creeping buttercup. Useful against pearlwort with repeated applications.	Primarily for use on lawns Beware of drift; on small areas the powdered formulation in puffer pack can be used.
"Clovotox" "Lawn Clover Killer"	Mecoprop	May and Baker Ltd., Dagenham, Essex. Pan Britannia Industries Ltd., Britannia House, Waltham Cross, Herts.	Hormone growth regulator translocated throughout the plant.	Best control for white-flowered clover, chickweeds and field woodrush. Useful against pearlwort with repeated applications.	Primarily for use on lawns Beware of drift.
Lawn sand "Velvex Lawn Sand" "pbi Calomel Dust"	See T33(2).	Usually home made. Pan Britannia Industries Ltd., Britannia House. Waltham Cross, Herts.	Scorching of annual growth. Of herbicidal and manurial value, in most cases.	Invaluable against weeds resistant or semi-resistant to hormones, like pearlwort, moss, veronica (speedwell), yellow-flowered clover, and yarrow.	See Lawns (T33(2)) for detailed information. The use of calomel dusts should be confined to mosses; of no manurial value.
		WEEDKILLERS FOR GARDEN USE			
"Nova Soil Steriliser"	Cresylic Acid	The Murphy Chemical Co. Ltd., Wheathampsted, St. Albans, Herts.	Contact herbicide.	For destruction of growth of annual weeds and top growth of perennials.	Particularly valuable on asparagus beds and where annual weeds have to be controlled. Also used as a soil sterilant.
"Bugges Dalapon"	Dalapon	Bugges Insecticides Ltd., London Rd., Sittingbourne, Kent.	Translocated throughout the plant, killing vegetation by movement from leaves to roots.	Annual grasses, couch grass, sedges, reeds, and bulrushes.	Delay planting for 40 days after application. May be used, upon makers' instructions as a selective herbicide on asparagus, shrubberies, fruit gardens, etc.
"Weedol"	Diquat Salt	Plant Protection Ltd., Yalding, Kent.	Translocated throughout the plant but with scorching effect similar to contact herbicides.	Kills annual weeds and top growth of perennials. One of the few herbicides to give a good control of ground elder. Selective only by application, i.e., kills all foliage it contacts.	Undoubtedly one of the most valuable and interesting herbicides to be introduced. Inactivated upon contact with soil; no residual effects. Available in small packs. Can be stored from season to season.
"Path Weed Control" "Weedex"	Simazine	Boots Pure Drug Co. Ltd. Fisons Horticultural Ltd., Harvest House, Felixstowe, Suffolk.	Soil acting, killing seedling vegetation by uptake through roots.	Controls germinating seeds of many weeds over a long period.	Apply when ground is wet in early spring on asparagus, apples, pears (not plums), soft fruit, ornamental trees, and shrubs including roses. Slow acting.
"Polybor-Chlorate"	Sodium Chlorate	Borax Consolidated Ltd., Borax House, Carlisle Place, S.W.1.	Translocated throughout the plant and soil acting.	Toxic in varying degrees to all plants except mosses. The best chemical for killing tree stumps.	To a large extent superseded by other chemicals. Can be used on paths, drives, and vacant ground.
"Boots Bramble, Brushwood and Nettle Killer"	2,4,5-T	Boots Pure Drug Co. Ltd., Station Street, Nottingham.	Hormone growth regulator translocated throughout the plant.	Special value in control of woody plants like brambles, brushwood, and ivy. Also good against nettles.	Beware of drift.

GAMES & RECREATIONS

Indoor and outdoor games and leisure activities, alphabetically arranged, together with 4 pages of records, including the 1968 Olympic Games, the 1969 European Championships and the 1970 British Commonwealth Games.

GAMES AND RECREATIONS

PEOPLE have always been fond of playing games and of thinking out ways of spending their leisure time and of celebrating special occasions. The result is a long history of games, recreations, and customs, some of which are described in this section. The arrangement is alphabetical.

One problem that confronts those keen to try some game or recreation is how to set about it. In many cases, the simplest way of finding out what facilities exist in a particular area is to enquire at a local newspaper office, which will have particulars of all sports clubs, dramatic societies, and other recreational bodies in the area. A few addresses that might be useful to those with certain specialised interests appear at the appropriate places in the text, and a valuable source of helpful information on many games and recreations is the Central Council of Physical Recreation, which has English, Welsh, and Northern Irish addresses as follows: England, 26 Park Crescent, London, WIN 4AJ; Wales, 47 Cathedral Road, Cardiff; and Northern Ireland, 49 Malone Road, Belfast. The Scottish Council of Physical Recreation is at 4 Queensferry Street, Edinburgh, 2; Those keen on touring the country at moderate cost might appreciate the services provided by the Youth Hostels Association, which has addresses as follows: England and Wales, Trevelyan House, St. Albans, Herts, with a London office at 29 John Adam Street, W.C.1; Scotland, 7 Bruntsfield Crescent, Edinburgh, 10; Northern Ireland, 28 Bedford Street, Belfast; and the Irish Republic, 39 Mountjoy Square, Dublin.

American Football.

American football is played eleven-a-side on a pitch marked by a line across it every 5 yards, and with goals and a ball resembling those used in rugby football (q.v.), though the ball is smaller. Scoring is by "touchdowns," which are like Rugby tries, but count six; goals after touchdowns, which count one; field goals during play, which count three; and "safeties," which give the attacking side two points if the defenders carry the ball over their own goal-line and touch it down. The ball is advanced by carrying it, forward passing, and kicking. The game consists of a series of "plays" or "downs," the ball becoming dead when the ball-carrier is tackled. A team must advance 10 yards in four downs or give up the ball to their opponents. Players can run ahead of the ball-carrier to protect him by "blocking" opponents. Penalties take the form of distance, usually 5 or 15 yards, lost. A game lasts 60 minutes, divided into four 15-minute quarters.

Angling.

Angling, which is catching fish with rod, line, and hook, goes back to beyond the beginning of history, for it was known to the Greeks and Romans. It is now a recreation, for, though the catch may subsequently be cooked, it is not primarily fishing for the pot. It has its competitive side, with competitions offering prizes for the biggest catch, and there are angling clubs, but many people prefer to use it as a recreation to be enjoyed alone in quiet surroundings. It is actually not so much a recreation as many recreations, for fishing can take place in the sea, rivers, lakes, ponds, and even canals, and there are several entirely different kinds of angling. The most obvious divisions are fresh-water fishing, including coarse and fly-fishing, and sea angling, including fishing from piers and the shore and big-game fishing.

The biggest branch of angling is fresh-water fishing for general or "coarse" fish, which are so called to distinguish them from "game" fish like salmon. Coarse fishing is bait fishing, or, in the case of pike, spinning, groundbait also being thrown in before and during fishing. It covers many varieties of fish, and the bag may be a very mixed one. Certain fish, of course, are known to frequent certain localities or types of locality, but, though the angler may know exactly the kind of fish he is after, he rarely knows if his catch will consist entirely of that kind of fish, or even if it will include any of that kind. Coarse fish do not generally make good eating.

Fly-fishing for salmon and trout differ widely from coarse fishing, and from each other. As the name implies, artificial flies are used, but those used for trout are quite different from those that attract salmon. In the case of trout, a fly is made to resemble a real insect as closely as possible, but, with salmon, this is not necessary. Salmon rarely, if ever, feed in fresh water, and, when in that type of water, they are usually irritable. They will dart wildly at any objects that attract their attention, so salmon flies are simply bright objects designed to draw them on. Fly-fishing is rather an expensive sport, for it means hiring beats on private water. In both coarse and fly-fishing the angler would be well advised to keep out of sight of the quarry as much as possible.

Sea angling is now the most competitive form of angling, with sea-angling festivals and competitions plentiful during the holiday season. It has what might be called its equivalent of fly-fishing with feathers, which attract several kinds of fish.

Big-game fishing takes place from a motor-launch, which is not towed by the hooked fish, but follows it, so that the ensuing fight is between man and fish, and not between the fish and the dead weight of the boat. Such a fight could last for 12 hours, and it is never certain that the angler will win it. Tunny is the only big game found off the British coasts.

Archery. See Old English Games and Customs.

Association Football.

Games that may have resembled football were played by very ancient races, and games that certainly were football of a kind were played in the England of several centuries ago, but the Association football that is the most popular game in Britain, and perhaps the world, to-day had its origins in the games played at English Public Schools in the days before sport became organised.

It was not surprising that some of those who had played football of one kind or another at school should want to go on playing after they left, but, before they could do so, it was necessary to work out a set of rules that would be universally understood and accepted. Meetings were organised by those interested, and, as the universities were natural meeting-places for boys from many schools, it was there, particularly Cambridge, that these took place.

It was soon evident that there was a major difference of opinion between those who wanted handling permitted and those who opposed this. The rival factions proved irreconcilable, so they went their separate ways. The handling enthusiasts based their rules on those in force at Rugby School, and thus pioneered rugby football (q.v.). Those who felt that football should be played primarily with the foot brought into being the game that was to take its name from the Association that was formed, in 1863, to govern it, and became Association football, often called by the abbreviation, " soccer."

Soccer is played with a round ball cased in leather or other approved materials weighing from 14 to 16 ounces, and with a circumference of from 27 to 28 inches, on a pitch marked out as in the accompanying diagram. It is played eleven-a-side, the traditional positions being goalkeeper, two full-backs, three half-backs, and five forwards, though modern position-switching and fluid tactics can make this a 4-2-4 or 4-3-3 disposition—4-2-4, for instance, is four in defence (plus the 'keeper), two in midfield and four attackers or strikers. The object is to score goals by putting the ball between uprights 8 yards apart and under a crossbar 8 feet high. The ball is advanced by kicking or heading, but only the goalkeeper when in his own penalty area may handle it, and he may not carry it while taking more than four steps. A game lasts for 90 minutes, divided into two halves.

He cannot, however, be offside in his own half, from a corner kick, or from a throw-in. If a player in an offside position interferes with the game, a free kick is awarded.

A game is controlled by a referee, who has the assistance of two linesmen. These may signal infringements, but the referee is not bound to act on such signals.

In Britain, soccer is a winter game, the season lasting from August until May, though, in Scotland, it continues even during the short summer season in the form of five-a-side football, known as the " short " game. British soccer is highly organised, ranging from the fully professional Football League of four divisions and the equivalent, though slightly smaller, Scottish League through minor professional leagues to amateur leagues. There are also many cup competitions, from the Football Association

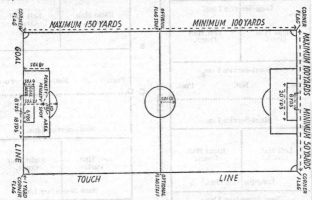

The game is started by a kick-off from the centre, with all the opposing players outside the centre circle and in their own half. The ball must travel at least its own circumference into the opponents' half, and the kicker may not play it again until someone else has done so. The right to kick-off is decided by a toss that gives the winner the option of kicking or choosing which goal he will defend. Ends are changed at half-time, after which the ball is kicked-off by the side that did not do so at the start. The game is restarted in this way after each goal, the non-scorers kicking-off.

If the ball crosses the touch-line it is thrown in by a player of the side that did not put it out, the throw being two-handed. If it crosses the goal-line wide of the goal it is kicked-off by a defender from the 6-yards line if the attackers were responsible, and by an attacker from the intersection of the goal-line and the touch-line if the defenders were responsible.

Infringements are penalised by free kicks, which may be " direct " or " indirect." Direct free kicks, from which a goal may be scored, follow deliberate infringements, indirect free kicks, from which a goal cannot be scored, being for more technical offences. Offences by defenders in the penalty area are generally penalised by a penalty kick, which is a shot from a spot 12 yards out from the centre of the goal, with only the kicker and the goalkeeper in the penalty area, and the goal-keeper barred from moving until the ball has been kicked. However, certain offences in the penalty area, such as excessive carrying by the goalkeeper and obstruction, are penalised only by an indirect free kick.

A player is " offside " if he is nearer the opponents' goal-line than is the ball unless there are two opponents between him and the goal-line, or unless the ball was last played by an opponent.

Challenge Cup, Football League Cup, and the Scottish Cup downwards.

The game has also spread all over the world, being extraordinarily popular in Europe, Asia and South America, and played to some extent almost everywhere else. There is a World Cup competition that is played for every four years, a European Nations Cup, played for every two years, and an annual European Champion Clubs Cup competition played for by the top league club of almost every European country and a European Cup-winners Cup. Soccer is also included in the Olympic Games.

Athletics.

The sport of athletics, which includes running, walking, jumping, and throwing, is probably the most natural of all sports, and certainly one of the oldest.

Modern athletics can be said to have begun in 1849, when the Royal Military Academy instituted a meeting that was followed by a similar meeting at Exeter College, Oxford, and, subsequently, at other Oxford and Cambridge Colleges. The Civil Service were also early in the field; and the first athletic club was the Mincing Lane Athletic Club, now the London Athletic Club. There was also the Amateur Athletic Club, which organised an annual championship meeting, and acted as a governing body for both athletics and amateur boxing.

In 1880 the Amateur Athletic Association was formed as a governing body. Other countries, particularly the United States, took to the sports and in 1896 the first modern Olympic Games were held at Athens. Other international meetings and matches followed, and championships and competitions of all standards were started in many countries. Women came into the sport in the early 1920s, and were included in the Olympic Games in 1928. There is now a long list of internationally agreed standard events, including distances measured in yards and miles, and also their metric equivalents; and including also a major all-round test, the ten-event decathlon.

The longest strictly standard distances are the marathon of 26 miles 385 yards for runners, and 50,000 metres for walkers, but there are regularly held longer races. For runners, the longest annual race is between Durban and Maritzburg, about 55 miles, the longest in Britain being from London to Brighton, about 53 miles; but there are occasional 100-mile and 24-hour events. For walkers, there are annual 100-mile races and fairly regular 24-hour ones.

The marathon commemorates the run of the

Australian Rules Football.

Australian Rules football is played 18 a-side on large oval grounds. At each end, there are four posts seven yards apart; and scoring, which is high, is by goals, counting six points, when the ball is kicked between the two inner posts, and behinds, counting one point, when it is kicked between the outer ones. The ball resembles a rugby ball, but is less pointed. Players must not run more than 10 yards with the ball without bouncing it or touching it on the ground. The ball must not be thrown, but it can be passed by holding it with one hand and punching it with the other, or by kicking. Players in possession can be tackled between the shoulder and the knee or

DOUBLES COURT.

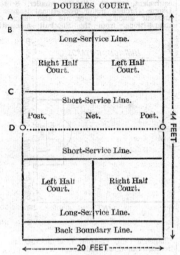

NOTE.—If it is practicable place the posts on the side boundary lines; failing this, place them at any distance not more than 2 ft. outside these lines.
A to B 2 ft. 6 in.   A to C 15 ft. 6 in.
A to D 22 ft.

SINGLES COURT.

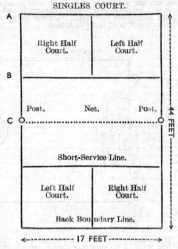

NOTES.—Place the posts on the boundary lines or not more than 2 ft. outside these lines.
The back boundary lines become the long-service lines.
A to B 15 ft. 6 in.   B to C 6 ft. 6 in.

Top of net 5 ft. from ground at centre and 5 ft. 1 in. at posts.
Diagram of Ground as marked out for Badminton.

courier Pheidippides from the battlefield at Marathon to Athens, carrying the news of victory over the Persians (490 B.C.). This run covered about 25 miles but the distance was standardised at 26 miles 385 yards in the 1908 Olympic marathon from Windsor to the White City, London. All marathons commemorate the Battle of Marathon, but the oldest annual marathon, the Boston marathon, also commemorates the Battle of Lexington (the first battle of the American Revolution), and, more particularly, the ride by Paul Revere that preceded it.

Cross-Country. Athletics is mainly a summer sport, but in cross-country running it has an extremely popular winter branch.

Cross-country originated in the traditional runs at various English Public Schools, particularly Rugby and Shrewsbury; and came into wider prominence when it was adopted by the Thames Rowing Club as winter training. It is still used as training by many sportsmen of all kinds, but it is now also a thriving competitive sport in its own right. There is an International Championship, but this is not yet fully representative, being virtually confined to Western European nations. Major cross-country championships are over courses of 9 or 10 miles.

charged. There is no offside and no scrummaging. A game consists of four 25-minute quarters. The game has existed since 1858, and is played to the practical exclusion of all other forms of football in the southern half of Australia and in Western Australia. There are over 3,000 clubs.

Badminton.

Badminton might be described as an indoor version of lawn tennis (*q.v*) in that it is played over a net, and can consist of either singles or doubles. There, however, the resemblance ceases. Only the serving side can score. If the server wins the rally one point is scored; if he loses the next player serves. A game is won by the side first making 15 points (11 for women). Three games make a set. The shuttlecock or " bird " is a small cork hemisphere in which feathers are fixed. All shots are volleys. The major tournament, which has been held for over 70 years, is the All-England Championships.

Bandy. *See* Skating.

Baseball.

The invention of baseball, a summer game played from April until October, and the national game of the United States, is generally credited to an Army officer, its origins being old country games called " One Old Cat " and " Two Old Cat."

Teams are nine-a-side, and bat and field in turn. The main part of the ground, the " diamond," has a " base," marked by a sack, at each corner, the lines from sack to sack being the " base paths." One base is " home," and there the batter stands, by a square of rubber on the ground, called the " plate." The base forward and to the right of a right-handed batter is " first," the one straight ahead of him is " second," and the one forward and to his left is " third," the distance from one base to the next being 30 yards. 20 yards out straight in front of the plate is the pitcher's " mound." The lines from home to first and from home to third are continued beyond these bases, and are the " foul lines."

It is the object of the batting side, using a bat which resembles a long, heavy Indian club with which to hit a hard, white ball weighing 5 ounces, to score runs, one being scored each time a player completes a circuit of the bases, not necessarily from one hit. When a batter leaves the plate, either " out " or to proceed along the base paths, the next man comes in, the team's innings lasting until three men are out. Nine such innings complete the game, and, in each innings, the batting side carries on at the point in the batting order reached in the previous innings. There is no toss for first innings, the visiting side always batting first.

The pitched ball reaches the batter without touching the ground, and, if not hit, it should pass over the plate between the batter's shoulders and knees. If it does so, it is a " strike," and three such strikes dismiss the batter. If it does not, it is a strike only if the batter swings at it; otherwise it is a " ball," and four balls give the batter a free passage to first base, called a " walk." A batter also walks if he is hit by a pitched ball. Other ways in which the batter can be dismissed are by being caught, and by being " put out " while on the base paths by failing to reach the base to which he is running before the ball. When an out is made, the ball does not become " dead." If there is more than one runner on the base paths, then, if the ball can be relayed quickly enough, two, or even three, men can be put out on the same " play."

If the batter hits fairly, he must run, but, to be fair, the hit must be in front of him and between the foul lines. A " foul hit " counts as a strike against him, except that the third strike, which actually dismisses him, must be a clean one across the plate. If a foul is caught, he is out.

The fielding side is divided into three sections, the " battery," the " infield," and the " outfield." The battery consists of the pitcher and the catcher, who stands behind the plate and gives signals indicating the kind of ball he thinks the pitcher should deliver: for, though the pitched ball does not touch the ground, pitchers can produce a wide variety of deliveries, including various kinds of curve. The infield consists of the first baseman, at or near first; the second baseman, between first and second; the short-stop, between second and third; and the third baseman, at or near third. The outfield covers the ground beyond the infield, the three remaining fielders taking the right, centre, and left sections of it. Catchers wear a large glove on the non-throwing hand, a mask, a chest protector, and leg-guards. All the other fielders wear a glove on the non-throwing hand, the first base-man's being larger than the others. The batter wears no protective gear.

Substitutes are permitted, pitchers frequently being changed if they are being hit, and " pinch hitters " being sent in instead of weak batters if a hit is desperately needed. If this happens, the man replaced, often the pitcher, cannot return when his side fields again, though his field replacement need not be the man who batted for him.

As with cricket (q.v.) batting averages are recorded, these being calculated by dividing the number of times at bat into the number of hits. An average of 0·400, referred to as " four hundred," would be exceptionally good. " Hits " mean

safe hits on which the batter achieved one or more bases without giving a chance. If he reaches base because a catch was dropped or a ball mis-fielded, he plays on from there in the usual way, but is not credited with a hit. Pitchers are graded according to the number of games won and lost. Recorded fielding statistics include each man's " put outs," " assists," which are throws from which a team-mate made a put out, and " errors."

In the United States there are clubs and leagues of all standards, from professionals of various classes through semi-professionals to amateurs, called " sandlotters," and boys. The top class of all consists of two major leagues, the National and the American, each with eight clubs. The champions of these two leagues meet in a best-of-seven-games series for the " Championship of the World," always known as the World Series.

Baseball is also the chief summer game of Canada, and it is quite widely played in some other countries, including Australia, Britain, and Japan.

Softball, similar to baseball, is popular in the United States with women as well as men. The ball is not particularly soft, but it is larger than a baseball, and pitching is under-arm. Distances between bases, and between the plate and the mound, are shorter than in the parent game. A modern adaptation is played with a " Frisbee ", a light plastic wheel that has a swerving flight when delivered like a quoit.

Basketball.

Basketball was invented in 1891 by an American Y.M.C.A. official at Springfield, Massachusetts, as a winter team game that could be played indoors. It can be played in almost any gymnasium or hall, and it can also be played outdoors on an asphalt court. In America it is played by teams of all standards from schoolboys to professionals, and it is watched by more spectators than any other game. It has now spread to many other countries and is included in the Olympic Games. It has been established for some years in Britain, where it has been encouraged by the Services and the Y.M.C.A.

Basketball is played five-a-side, substitutes being permitted, with a ball resembling that used in Association football. and goals consisting of a net or basket suspended from a metal ring attached 10 ft above the floor to a backboard. It is purely a handling game, and the ball is advanced by dribbling, which means bouncing, and by passing. Deliberate bodily contact is not allowed. Goals thrown during play count two points, and goals thrown from free throws after infringements one point. Height is an asset in the game, which demands stamina and agility, and which has been highly recommended as an ideal training activity by coaches of other sports, particularly athletics (q.v.).

The Amateur Basket Ball Association, with some 9,300 registered players in 670 clubs, governs the sport in this country; men and women have their local area or county associations; and mini-basketball, with modified rules for under-12s, is becoming increasingly popular in the schools.

Biathlon. *See* Winter Sports.

Billiards.

Billiards, which originated in France, is a game of angles, and of very great skill. It is played on a table measuring 12 feet by 6 feet 1½ inches, having six pockets, one at each corner, and one in the middle of each side. The table is covered with green baize, the edges being of cloth-covered rubber, called " cushions." Across the table, 2 feet 5 inches from the bottom edge, is a line, called the " baulk " line, the space between the line and the bottom of the table being " baulk." On the baulk side of the line there is a semi-circle with a radius of 11½ inches from the centre of the line. Down the centre of the table are four

" spots," one 12⅘ inches from the top, one mid-way between the top and the centre, one in the centre, and one in the middle of the baulk line. Two white balls, one with a spot for identification purposes, and one red one, are used, the balls being played with " cues " that taper down to a striking tip. The remaining equipment includes a long, cue-like stick with a metal cross fixed diagonally on the end, called a " rest " or " jigger," and a special long cue, these being used when the player cannot reach his ball in the ordinary way. Most games are " singles," though " doubles " can be played, the object of the game being to score points according to fixed rules, an agreed number of points making the game.

To decide who is to start, players " string " by playing their balls simultaneously from baulk up to the top cushion, the ball which returns nearer to the bottom cushion winning. At the start, the red ball is " spotted " on the top spot, and players start from the baulk circle. Scoring is three for pocketing, or " potting," the red or going in off the red; two for potting the white, which is, of course, the opponent's ball, or going in off the white; and two for a cannon, which is hitting both the other balls. A player whose shot hits no other balls at all gives one point to his opponent, unless his ball goes into a pocket, when he forfeits three. A player's turn, called a " break," continues as long as he is actually scoring. When the red is potted, it is im-mediately respotted.

Snooker. Also played on a billiard table, and perhaps even more popular, is snooker, which uses 22 balls, positioned as follows: 15 reds in the form of a triangle with its apex on the second spot from the top, and its base at the top end; a black on the top spot; a pink touching the apex ball of the triangle; a blue on the centre spot; a brown in the middle of the baulk line, with a green beside it on the left end of the baulk circle, and a yellow on the right end; and a white, which is the cue-ball to be played. The points values of the balls are from one for red, through yellow, green, brown, blue, and pink, to seven for black. A player's turn continues as long as he scores, his first shot being at a red, when, if he pots one, he plays at one of the other colours, play being at reds and colours alternately as lon as balls are being potted, and as long as there are reds on the table, after which the remaining colours are played in ascending order of value.

A variation of snooker is snooker plus. This uses two additional balls, an orange, placed between the pink and the blue and valued at eight points, and a purple, placed between the blue and the brown and valued at ten points.

Pool, Russian Pool, and Pyramids. Other games played on a billiard table include pool, Russian pool, and pyramids. In pool each player has a ball of a different colour, the order of play being white, red, yellow, green, brown, blue, pink, black. Each player plays at the ball of his predecessor, and tries to pot it, the game start-ing with white spotting his ball on the top spot, so that red is actually the first to play. A player whose ball is potted loses a life, players losing three lives dropping out of the game. A turn continues as long as a player is potting balls, and if he clears all the balls on the table he then spots his own ball for the next player.

Russian pool uses the yellow, green, blue, and black balls, with the white as cue-ball, the black being placed on the top spot, the blue on the centre spot, the green on the left side of the baulk circle, and the yellow on the right side. A player's first shot must hit the black, after which he can play at will. Scoring is by potting balls, by going in off balls, and by cannons, but the black can be used only for the top pockets, the blue for the middle pockets, and the green and the yellow for the bottom pockets. Cannons count two, potting or going in off counting nine for the black, seven for the blue, five for the green, and three for the yellow. A player's turn continues as long as he is scoring, but consecutive cannons on the same balls are limited to 25, and the same ball must not be potted from the same spot more than three times in succession. A complete miss forfeits

three points. A variation of Russian pool adds the pink ball, which is spotted on the second spot from the top, counts six, and can be used after any pocket.

Pyramids uses the 15 reds, starting in their triangle, and a white cue-ball, the object being to pot the reds. A turn continues while a player is scoring, 8 balls potted ending the game.

Bird-watching. *See* Natural History and Field Studies.

Boat Races.

Race rowing is a strenuous sport that makes no pretence of attracting as many active participants as some other sports and games; yet its long history includes races with unusual stories about them; races that are amongst the greatest annual international sporting events; and one race that provides what is probably the most enthusiastically supported free sporting spectacle in the world.

That, of course, is the Oxford and Cambridge University boat race, rowed on the Thames from Putney to Mortlake. First rowed in 1829, it has offered its excited public, which includes thousands of people with no connection of any kind with either university, everything, including runaway victories, dead heats, and even sinking boats. To all intents and purposes, this is a regular annual event, and has been so since 1856; but, in actual fact, every race is the result of a separate special challenge from the losers of the previous race to the winners of it. The race has an interesting parallel in the United States, where Yale University, whose colours are dark blue, annually meet Harvard University, which is at Cambridge, on a river called the Thames.

The Oxford and Cambridge race is the best-known annual race on the Putney–Mortlake stretch of the Thames, but it is by no means the only one. There are other races that attract entries sometimes numbered in hundreds: entries that are far too big to race abreast on the Thames, and so race in single file, with crews following each other at fixed intervals in what are known as the Head of the River races. The biggest of these is for crews of eight, but there are other Head of the River races for women's crews, who cover only part of this famous stretch of water, and for single scullers. Single scullers also cover this course in a straightforward race in the Wing-field Sculls event, which ranks as the English Amateur Championship, and which was first held one year after the first Oxford and Cambridge race, in 1830.

Head of the River races, but with a difference, are also held between the colleges of Oxford and Cambridge, where the Isis and the Cam, respec-tively, are much too narrow to permit straight-forward racing. These are the Bump Races, in which each crew endeavours to catch and bump the crew ahead of it, except for the leading crew, which can concentrate on staying in front. When a bump is achieved, the two crews pull into the bank, and change places for the next day's racing. The racing goes on for four days, and it is, of course, the ambition of each crew, apart from the leaders, to register a bump on each day.

Back on the Thames, but farther down it to-wards the port and docks of London, is the scene of a race that makes the Oxford and Cambridge race and the Wingfield Sculls look like recent innovations. This is the annual race from London Bridge to Chelsea for the Doggett's Coat and Badge, a single sculling event open only to young watermen who are within twelve months of completing their apprenticeship. It was founded in 1715 in honour of the House of Hanover, and to commemorate the anniversary of " King George I's happy accession to the throne of Great Britain," by Thomas Doggett, a Dublin-born actor connected with the Drury Lane and Haymarket theatres, who regularly travelled on the Thames in preference to using the roads, and who left a sum of money to perpetuate the race, which is now controlled by the Fishmongers' Company.

This race is more truly an annual one than almost any other event; for, while most so-called annual races have been subjected to long interruptions because of the two World Wars, those qualified for the Doggett races during those years were subsequently traced, and the races duly decided after the wars. The event is a colourful one, always followed by a barge carrying a batch of past winners wearing the Coat and Badge, and also the cap, breeches, silk stockings, and buckled shoes that go with them. The scarlet, pleated, quilted Coat, with its silver buttons and the large silver arm Badge bearing the White Horse of Hanover and the word " Liberty ", are presented at the Fishmongers' Hall, where the winner is greeted with a salute of trumpets and the tune, " See the Conquering Hero Comes."

For a rowing event of a very different kind, dating back " only " to 1839, one must go up the Thames, far beyond the end of the Tideway, to Henley, for the annual Royal Regatta. This consists of events open to the world and others closed to English colleges and schools for eights, fours, pairs, double sculls, and single sculls, the most famous of its races being the Grand Challenge Cup for eights and the Diamond Sculls.

Soon we are to have our first 2,000-metre international rowing course at the National Water Sports Centre, Holme Pierrepont, near Nottingham. It has been made possible by a Government grant through the Sports Council and will be administered by the Central Council of Physical Recreation.

Competitive rowing in this country is governed by the Amateur Rowing Association, 160 Gt. Portland St. London, W1N 4TB.

Boats. *See* **Canoeing, Cruising, Sailing, Yachting.**

Bobsleigh Riding. *See* **Winter Sports.**

Bowling. *See* **Skittles.**

Bowls.

Bowls, one of the oldest of all games, was once regarded as " an old man's game," but it actually has many devotees of all ages and both sexes, and is played indoors as well as outdoors. It certainly goes back to the thirteenth century, when its popularity made it one of the games legislated against as likely to draw people away from archery. Henry VIII played; and the famous game on Plymouth Hoe, in which Sir John Hawkins stayed to beat Sir Francis Drake even after the Armada had been sighted, if not definitely authenticated, is accepted as fact by several historians. It is interesting to note that, if this game was played, it would have been almost identical with a game of to-day, for it was in that century that the " bias " that is a leading feature of the bowls or " woods " was introduced. A century later, however, Bowls, which was largely played on greens attached to taverns, acquired a reputation as being merely an adjunct to pot-house revelry, but it was revived on a higher level in Scotland, and never again came so near to oblivion.

The English Bowling Association, 2 Roseford Road, Cambridge, is on the International Bowling Board.

There are actually two games of bowls, the rink or level green game and the crown green game, and it is the rinks rather than the objectives that differ. The level green game is the more widely played, and it takes place on a perfectly flat piece of well-cared-for turf. The crown green game, which is popular in the North and Midlands, is played on a green of which the centre is 6 inches or more higher than the corners. The games differ—for instance, in the putting into play of the object ball—but only slightly, so it will be appreciated that the crown green game demands a good deal of experience and skill. It is mainly a singles game, whereas the level green game is played between sides consisting of one, two, three, or four players.

Bowls looks a simple game, the object being simply to place the bowls as near as possible to the object ball, or " jack." The bowls, however, are " biased," and the game is actually one of considerable skill. When bias was introduced, it took the form of weighting with lead, but it is now achieved by turning one side of the bowl less round than the other. Level green bowls weigh up to 3½ lb., but crown green bowls are smaller and less biased. On the crown green, however, the jack, which is played into position by the first player, is also biased.

Players normally use two bowls in a game, or four in singles, and the side with the best record of bowls near the jack wins the " end," and the best record of shots in an agreed number of ends the game.

Bowls is also played on carpet rinks indoors, and the new multi-sports centres usually cater for it.

The French play their *pétanque* or *boule* on gravel, sand, or any other such surface, with steel bowls which are thrown as well as rolled at a wooden jack or *cochonnet*.

Boxing.

Boxing, sometimes called " The Noble Art of Self Defence," though actually aggression is its keynote and defence an incidental, is a modern continuation of the old sport of prize-fighting, which, though always illegal, was popular from the time of the Regency until it was succeeded by the present-day glove-fighting at the end of the nineteenth century.

In prize-fighting bare fists were used, and wrestling holds were allowed. Rounds ended when a fighter went down, and fights continued until, following a knockdown, a man failed to come up to the scratch line in 30 seconds.

In modern boxing, gloves are worn, and no wrestling is allowed. Rounds last for a fixed time, generally 3 minutes with 1 minute between rounds, and fights last only for a fixed number of rounds, never more than fifteen. A knockdown does not end a round, the man who is down having 10 seconds in which to rise. If he fails to do so, his opponent wins by a knock-out. If a man fails to come up at the beginning of a round or if the fight is stopped to save a man from further injury, the victory is by a technical knock-out. If however, both men are still on their feet at the end of the stipulated number of rounds, a decision is given on points. Boxing is therefore technically a contest of skill for points, and, as such, far removed from prize-fights to a finish.

Fights are controlled by a referee, and, in British professional boxing, he is solely responsible for any points decision. In amateur boxing the decision is given by several judges, who sit apart from each other. The difference between a good professional and a good amateur is probably more marked in boxing than in any other sport

Boxing contests are arranged in classes according to weight, the divisions being: fly-weight, up to 8 stone; bantam-weight, up to 8 stone 6 lb.; feather-weight, up to 9 stone; light-weight, up to 9 stone 9 lb.; welter-weight, up to 10 stone 7 lb.; middle-weight, up to 11 stone 6 lb.; light-heavy or cruiser-weight, up to 12 stone 7 lb.; and heavy-weight, any weight. In amateur boxing some of these weights are slightly different, and there are two additional classes, light-welter-weight, up to 10 stone, and light-middle-weight, up to 11 stone.

Prize-fighting was governed successively by " Broughton's Code," the " New Rules of the Ring," and the " London Rules." Then, in 1867, the eighth Marquess of Queensberry and Mr. J. G. Chambers drew up the rules that have been the basis of boxing ever since. British professional boxing has been controlled since 1929 by the British Boxing Board of Control. The Amateur Boxing Association has governed amateur boxing since 1884, when it took over from the Amateur Athletic Club, which had looked after both boxing and athletics.

Bridge.

Bridge is probably about one hundred years old, but though it clearly developed from Whist, its exact origin is unknown. Similar games were played in Denmark, Turkey, Egypt, and Russia, and it first appeared in Britain as Dutch whist in 1884. It was subsequently known as Russian whist and biritch. Then in 1895 the first bridge rules appeared, followed in 1908 by rules for a new version, auction bridge. A third version, contract bridge, was known before the First World War, reached Britain just after it, and acquired international rules in 1929. During the 1930s all three forms were played. The object of each succeeding version was to make the game less one of chance and more one of skill. Contract has now supplanted them all and this is the game we shall describe.

Two partnerships of two oppose each other, and as the names auction and contract imply, the playing of each hand is preceded by an auction in which players bid, or refrain from bidding, on the value of their hands to decide which pair will attempt to make how many tricks with what trumps, or with no trumps.

The suits have different values, the order being spades, hearts (known as major suits), diamonds, clubs (minor suits), but no trumps takes absolute precedence.

Originally, spades were the lowest suit, and when spades bids prevailed players took to throwing in their cards and giving the caller the points rather than play such a low scoring hand. To prevent this, spades were given a value which made them the top suit.

A feature of the actual play is that the member of the pair whose bid prevails who first named the successful suit plays the hand alone, playing both his own cards and his partner's, which are placed face upwards on the table after the first card has been played.

Bridge terms the beginner should know include: *bid*, an offer to make so many tricks in a particular suit or with no trumps; *auction*, the bidding process; *contract*, the last and prevailing bid; *forcing bid*, a bid which forces the player's partner to bid and keep the auction open; *take out*, a bid in a suit other than that bid by the player's partner; *system* or *convention*, the bidding system used by a pair; *the book*, the first six tricks won by a pair, which do not count towards the contract—a bid of one means, in fact, seven; *declarer*, the player of the pair whose bid prevails who first named the successful suit; *dummy*, declarer's partner; *defender*, during the auction, a member of the pair which did not open the bidding, during play, an opponent of the declarer; *game*, 100 points; *rubber*, two games won by a pair; *vulnerable*, a partnership which has won a game becomes vulnerable; *overtrick*, a trick won in excess of the contract; *undertrick*, a trick by which the contract fails; *grand slam*, 13 tricks bid and won; *small slam*, 12 tricks bid and won; *trump*, a card of the contract suit; *ruff*, to trump; *tenace*, two cards not in sequence which may win two tricks, but may win only one. Other terms, not peculiar to bridge, include: *void*, no cards of a suit; *singleton*, one card of a suit; *doubleton*, two cards of a suit; *honour*, ace, king, queen, knave, or ten; *yarborough*, a hand with no honours; *revoke*, failure to follow suit when able to do so.

A bridge score-sheet has a line across it, and points are scored above or below the line. Only points towards game go below the line, these being points for contracts made. Diamonds and clubs count 20 per trick (over six), spades and hearts 30, and no trumps 40 for the first trick and 30 for each subsequent one. When a game is won, points below the line revert to nothing. Above the line go points for tricks won in excess of the contract; for tricks by which opponents fail to make contracts; for winning a rubber; for slams (if bid); and for holding four aces in no trumps or four or five honours in a trump suit in one hand. Being vulnerable affects the points, as does the fact that bids may be doubled by opponents, then redoubled by the bidding pair. It might seem that points for honours in a hand are a gift for a piece of pure luck, but there is more to it than that. A player holding four honours might be tempted to go to almost any lengths to have the hand played in that suit, when, in fact, it might pay him better to play in, or against, another suit and forego the honours bonus.

In addition to rubber bridge, there is duplicate bridge, in which several pairs play the same hands. For those who have reached a certain standard, this is excellent for spotlighting weaknesses in one's play. As there are no rubbers, points are scored for games. Rubber bridge is generally played for money, though the stakes can be quite small, duplicate bridge is not.

Bridge suffers from a certain "mystique" which frightens some people. They hear of "card sense" and fear they might not have it. Actually, the only qualities required are commonsense and concentration; and card sense comes from playing cards. It is fairly widely believed that women make better players than men at all levels up to the very top, where the men take over. The bidding systems or conventions by which players give or request information also frighten people; and, in earlier days, these made supporters of the older versions describe contract as a game for cheats, though, of course, it is not. In addition to the actual laws, there are a number of proprieties which must be observed. Regular partners must not devise their own private bidding system. Only recognised systems may be used, and these must be communicated to the opponents. Unorthodox bids may be made, but not by prior arrangement with one's partner. There are almost countless conventions, and, in the very top class, players have an imposing list beside them. Beginners will soon learn those used in their own circles.

There are professional bridge teachers, and it is also possible (though not easy) to learn from books. Most people, though, learn at home, having a few lessons from friends and then learning by playing. The first thing to learn is how to value a hand, and this is done either by allocating points to cards or, more effectively, by assessing the tricks. Some players assess only honour tricks, but, as honours take, on average, only eight of the 13 tricks, this is not really sufficient. The value given to the hand may have to be readjusted on hearing the partner's bids. It is important to bid up to the full value of the combined hands.

There are countless bridge clubs, many quite small and informal, and some limiting novices to very small stakes until a certain standard has been reached. Eventually, more people will probably learn at school for unlike most card games bridge is encouraged in many schools, and the English Bridge Union runs an annual schools' tournament.

Bumping Races. *See* Boat Races.

Camping.

Camping expresses the townsman's desire to get away from cities and fend for himself in quiet. But some organisation is necessary to provide camping facilities and to maintain high standards. The Camping Club of Great Britain and Ireland has a membership of over 100,000. Its work is twofold: it selects sites suitable for mobile campers and caravanners; and establishes and maintains well-equipped permanent camping grounds. A *Sites List* published annually contains details of

2,000 camp sites. Members agree to abide by the Club's Code of Campers, which stresses the need of the camper to pay full regard to the countryman's way of life and to maintain by country courtesy the goodwill of those among whom he camps. The Club's address is 11 Lower Grosvenor Place, London, S.W.1.

Canadian Football.

Canadian Football resembles American (q.v.), but is twelve-a-side, uses only three downs, and limits blocking.

Canoeing.

Canoeing is both a recreation and an organised competitive sport. Beginners should visit Crystal Palace National Sports Centre for the Canoeing Exhibition each February.

As a recreation, it can take the form either of simply taking a canoe out and " paddling about " for a short period or, by combining it with camping (q.v.), of a lengthy and interesting river trip, the canoe-camper proceeding, of course, at his own pace, and giving as much time as he wishes to sightseeing.

As a sport, canoeing has Olympic Games status. In Britain it has its headquarters on the Thames at Teddington in Middlesex, the governing body being the British Canoe Union, 26 Park Crescent, London, W1N 4DT. There are races for singles and pairs, including events for women. There is also one long annual race for pairs that really combines canoeing with camping. The course is from Devizes in Wiltshire to London, and the competitors have to negotiate a long series of locks.

There are two types of canoe: Canadian canoes, like those used for many years by Red Indians, and kayaks, the very light Eskimo-type canoes, in which an expert, but not a beginner, can turn a complete circle into the water and out again without losing his seat in his craft. Both types are catered for in the Olympic Games, but most of the canoeing in Britain is in kayaks.

Card Games. See Bridge; Patience; Solo Whist; Whist.

Chess.

Chess, greatest of all board games and a game of pure skill, has a known history of some 1500 years. Eastern players, who originated it, reached a high standard, but the game's greatest advances were made in Italy in the fifteenth and sixteenth centuries. In the early days the value of the pieces and their moves underwent periodical changes, but the game we know to-day dates from the sixteenth century.

The board has 64 squares in eight rows of eight, and each player has 16 pieces, one set being white and the other black or red, but always referred to as black. A toss decides possession of white, which always starts. The object is the capture of the opponent's King, no matter how many pieces are lost in doing so, nor how many opposing pieces remain untaken. If the King could be captured on the next move, it is in " check." It must be released from check (by moving, by covering, or by capture of the checking piece), otherwise it is " checkmate " and the game is over. If the King is not in check, but cannot move except into check, and the player has no other pieces he can move, it is " stalemate," and a draw. Games may also be drawn if neither player has sufficient pieces to force a win.

In addition to the King, each player has a Queen, two Bishops, two Rooks—sometimes wrongly called Castles—two Knights, and eight Pawns, and all these move in accordance with rigid rules. The following diagram shows the pieces at the start of a game:

BLACK

(The initial position as seen by White)

Each line of squares across the board is a " rank," and each line up and down the board is a " file."

The permitted moves are as follows:—

The King can move one square at a time in any direction.

The Queen can move in accordance with the powers described below for both Bishops and Rooks.

The Bishops move diagonally as many squares as desired.

The Rooks move straight along the ranks or files as far as desired.

The Knights move as shown in the following diagram:—

(The Knight's Move)

Stationed away from the side of the board, and on a black square, the Knight illustrated can move to any of the numbered white squares. The move is one square along rank or file in the desired direction, and one square diagonally. The Pawns move straight forward, one square at a time, but may move two squares when moved for the first time. They capture by moving one square diagonally forwards. A Pawn reaching the eighth rank may be replaced by any other piece.

Once during a game, a player may " Castle," by moving the King two squares towards the Rook, which is placed on the last square passed over by the King. This move cannot be made if either the King or any of the squares he would pass over are in check. Neither King nor Rook must have moved previously.

Games of chess can be recorded, so players can play over great " Masters " games, and record their own games.

Draughts. Draughts—called checkers in America—is also played on a chess board. Possibly older even than chess, it is much simpler, but not devoid of skill.

Each player has twelve pieces or " men," all alike. Squares of one colour only are used, the men starting on the first three rows on the board. The move is one square diagonally forward, but a man reaching the eighth row becomes a " King," and may then move forward or backward. The object is the capture of all the opposing men by jumping over them. If the arrangement of the men permits it, more than one man may be captured in a single move. A man which can effect a capture but does not do so is removed from the board, or " huffed."

Cricket.

Cricket, traditionally England's national game, has a longer history than most team games. There have been attempts to trace its origin in various games played by ancient races; and, even if some of these derivations are a little far-fetched, it certainly developed from very old country games, and has been played in a form not so very dissimilar from that of to-day for over 250 years. The men of Hampshire, particularly the village of Hambledon, Surrey and Kent were the real pioneers of the cricket of to-day.

Cricket is played by two teams of eleven players, which bat and field in turn. In the centre of the ground are two " wickets," 22 yards apart, and each consisting of three " stumps," joined at the top by two " bails." Bats have a convex striking surface, and the ball must not weigh less than 5¼ ounces nor more than 5¾ ounces.

There is a batsman at each wicket, and their object is the scoring of runs by hitting the ball away, and running before it can be returned, each time the two batsmen cover the length of the pitch counting as one run. Should the ball be hit beyond the boundary line round the ground, it counts four or, if it crosses the line without touching the ground, six.

The ball is " bowled " from one wicket to the batsman at the other, six balls, or, in some cases, eight, which comprise an " over," being bowled from each end in turn. The object of the fielding side is to get the batsmen " out," ten dismissals completing the " innings," as the eleventh man is left without a partner.

A batsman can be dismissed in several ways. If he misses the ball and it hits the wicket, or if he plays it on to the wicket, he is out " bowled." If he leaves his ground, indicated by a line in front of the wicket, misses the ball, and has the wicket " broken " by the wicket-keeper he is out " stumped." If he hits the wicket with his bat he is out " hit wicket." If his hit is caught he is out " caught." If, when running, he fails to reach his ground before the wicket is " broken " he is out " run out." If a ball, when bowled, would have hit his wicket, but hits his leg instead, then, subject to certain provisions regarding where the ball actually pitched, he is out " leg-before-wicket." A batsman may also be given out if he handles the ball or obstructs the fielding side, but these are rare occurrences.

In addition to runs hit by the batsmen, there are certain " extras." If the ball passes the bat, misses the wicket, and goes far enough for the batsmen to run, it is a " bye." If, however, it goes off the batsman's leg it is a " leg-bye," but leg-byes cannot be run unless the batsman was definitely attempting a stroke. If it is bowled so wide that the batsman cannot reach it, it is a " wide." If the bowler comes in front of his wicket before releasing the ball, or if he throws it, it is a " no-ball," in which case the umpire calls

it as quickly as he can, for the batsman can hit such a ball, but he cannot be out to it, unless he is run out. If he does not score, one extra is added.

Of the fielding side, one, of course, is the bowler, and another, placed behind the batsman's wicket, is the wicket-keeper. The others will be placed as the bowler and his captain decide, for there are far more recognised positions than can be occupied at one time. To gain some idea of these positions, imagine a right-handed batsman at the wicket, his left side towards the bowler. The side of the wicket in front of him, nearer to his bat than to his body, is the " off " side; the side behind him, nearer to his body than to his bat, the " leg " side. On the off, behind the wicket and close to it, are the " slips," and, behind them, " third man." Farther round, but still behind the bat and close to it, is " gully." Level with the bat is " point " or, if he is some way from the bat, " deep point." In front of the bat, but in front also of the bowler's wicket, is " cover " and " extra cover." Roughly level with the bowler's wicket is " mid-off," with, behind him, " long off." Similarly on the leg side, where " long on " is the equivalent of " long off," " mid-on " of " mid-off," " mid-wicket " and " deep mid-wicket " of " cover " and " extra cover," " square leg " and " deep square leg " of " point " and " deep point," " short leg " of " gully," " long leg " of " third man," and " leg slip " of " slip."

First-class cricket matches last for three six-hour days or longer, but there are also two-day, one-day, and half-day matches. Matches of two days or more are two-innings games; of one day or half a day, one innings. If the side batting first, which is decided by a toss that gives the winner the choice of batting or fielding first, dismisses the opposing side for a smaller score, the victory is by the number of runs by which the smaller score was exceeded. If the side batting second pass the other total, the game ends, and the victory is by the number of wickets the second side still have standing. In a two-innings match, should the side batting first gain a first-innings lead of a certain size, normally 150 runs in a three-day match, it can require the other side to follow straight on with its second innings, the leading team keeping its second innings in reserve, to be played if needed. If a batting side has sufficient runs, and is anxious to see the other side batting while there is still plenty of time to dismiss it, it can declare its innings closed. In this case, should the second team score enough runs to win, it does, win, even though it may have lost more wickets than had the declaring side.

Cricket is not a fast-moving game, and for years views have been expressed to the effect that it must be " brightened up " if it is not to die out. Periodically, small changes in the rules are made; but, for the most part, the game just goes steadily on, easily retaining a large following that is satisfied with it as it is, and still able, when big international matches take place, to command a place, not only on the sports pages, but on the front pages of the Press.

Until May 1968 the game was ruled by the Marylebone Cricket Club, but although Lord's is still " headquarters," the ruling body is now the Cricket Council, composed of the M.C.C., the Test and County Cricket Board, and the National Cricket Association (representing all grades of cricket up to first-class standard).

Outside England, the development of cricket has been peculiar. Even as near at hand as Scotland and Ireland, the game has never aroused much enthusiasm; and in Continental Europe, where many British games have won great acclaim, cricket has gained a real foothold only in the Netherlands and Denmark. In the United States and Canada it is played, but only to a small extent. However, in Australia, South Africa, New Zealand, the West Indies, India, and Pakistan, it is extremely popular; and the national teams of these countries, together with England, provide the top-class international sides of the game. They meet regularly in " Test Matches," a " rubber " normally being decided in a series of five Tests. *See* U34.

Cricket is rich in technical terms and expressions, which are seen and heard frequently through newspapers, television, and radio when a Test series is in progress. Many of these are almost self-explanatory, but a few never fail to puzzle less-experienced readers, viewers, and listeners. Prominent amongst these are three types of ball used by bowlers, the " yorker," the " googly," and the " chinaman."

A yorker is a fast ball that pitches just in the batsman's block-hole, and often passes under his defensive stroke. The term is believed to have originated in Yorkshire, but the only known explanation of it is that attributed to a Yorkshire cricketer, who, asked why a yorker was so called, replied simply, " Well, what else would you call it ? " There is an answer to that, for the yorker was originally known as a " tice." A googly is an off-break or a leg-break which is disguised, because the bowler has delivered the one with the action of the other. A chinaman is an off-break bowled by a left-handed bowler to a right-handed batsman. These words also lack an authentic derivation.

Cricket has provided one expression that is now heard in many connections. That is " hat-trick," which dates back to the days when cricketers wore top-hats, and any player who took three wickets with three successive balls was presented with a white top-hat. Now, he is usually given the ball.

Croquet.

Croquet originated in France, and has been played in Britain for about a century. The governing body, the Croquet Association, was founded in 1868, with headquarters at Wimbledon. Soon afterwards, this also became the headquarters of

STANDARD SETTING.

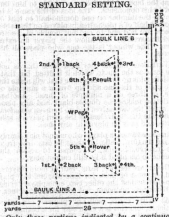

Only those portions indicated by a continuous line need be marked on the court.
The order of making the points is indicated by the arrows.

lawn tennis (q.v.), and it is probable that the rapid growth of that game was a factor that restricted the development of croquet. Croquet, however, still retains a following and, in addition to championships and tournaments it is widely played on private lawns.

The equipment consists of four balls, coloured blue, black, yellow, and red; four mallets, usually marked with the same colours; six hoops; and a peg. The playing area is 35 yards by 28 yards, but this can be reduced, provided that the proportion remains 5 to 4. The hoops, which stand 1 foot out of the ground, and the peg are placed as shown in the diagram. Generally two players, taking the blue and black balls, oppose two using the yellow and red, but singles can be played, each player using two balls, blue being paired with

black, and yellow with red. Each player completes the circuit of hoops twice, finishing by hitting the peg.

Croquet is a game of skill, and players can earn extra turns in various ways, such as hitting another ball with their own or passing through hoops. While making their own circuits, players also concentrate on leaving their opponents at a disadvantage. Handicap matches are possible through the giving of extra turns, or " bisques." A " half-bisque " is an extra turn in which no hoop may be scored.

Croquet can, perhaps, claim some credit for a phrase used in everyday life. " Pegging out " has the rather sinister meaning of " dying " or " finishing," but it is actually the term used for finishing a croquet round by hitting the peg.

Cross-country. *See* **Athletics.**

Cruising on Inland Waterways.

For those who want a touring holiday in Britain away from crowded roads, but who do not want to walk or ride, cruising on inland waterways offers a pleasant and interesting alternative. Facilities are available on a number of canals, rivers, and, of course, the Norfolk Broads; and motor-cruisers can be hired, complete with sleeping accommodation, bed linen, and cooking utensils. At some places, for example, the upper reaches of the Thames, those who prefer to do so can hire cruisers without sleeping accommodation, and spend the nights at riverside inns. The Inland Waterways Association exists to keep the waterways open and, where possible, to re-open others. Particulars of available facilities can be obtained from the Association at 114 Regent's Park Road, London, N.W.1.

Cycling.

As a pleasant recreation, cycling offers a wide range of possibilities. Outings can be for a day or part of a day, or they can be tours of any length the rider wishes, with the overnight halts spent in hotels or hostels or camping (q.v.), which can easily be combined with cycling.

As a competitive sport, governed in this country by the British Cycling Federation, 26 Park Crescent, London, W.1, cycling offers a remarkable variety, for no other form of racing provides events of so many different types. On the Continent, cycle racing is by far the most popular sport, and the leading riders are national heroes. The sport, which caters for both amateurs and professionals, also has a large following in Britain, where it would soon progress still farther if there were more tracks suitable for big events available.

Cycle races are held on banked tracks rather like motor-racing tracks, on flat grass tracks, on cinder tracks, on indoor banked board tracks, on roads, and even across country. There are races at all distances, from short sprints to road tours divided into daily stages lasting for several weeks. There are massed-start races, in which all the competitors start together; races in which competitors are drawn in twos or threes through several rounds up to a final; and time trials, in which each rider starts alone. (Road Time Trials Council, 210 Devonshire Hill Lane, London, N.17).

Track races may be straightforward races or time trials; or motor-paced, with the riders behind motor-cycles; or tandem-paced; or pursuit races, with riders or teams of riders starting on opposite sides of or spaced round the track; or point-to-point, with points awarded to the leaders at the end of each lap; or courses des primes, with a prize for the leader at the end of each lap.; or Madison races, for teams of two, and occasionally three, riding one at a time, and relieving each other at will. There are also races for tandems and tri-cycles; and the sport includes races on both track and road for women as well as men.

In the cross-country side of cycle racing, called cyclo-cross, riders cover a cross-country course of perhaps 10 miles, riding when they can and carrying their machines where riding is impossible. Still another form of cycle racing is roller racing. In this, the cycles are fixed on rollers, and do not move at all, the distance the riders pedal being registered on large dials. There is also cycle speedway, a sport practised only by youths. Events take the form of team matches, generally on rough cinder tracks constructed on waste ground, with pairs of riders opposing rival pairs in a series of races, and points awarded to the leaders in each race. Corners have to be "skidded" round, as they sometimes are in ordinary grass-track cycle racing. Very different, but still competitive in a way, is a form of event that provides a link between the sporting side of cycling and the more purely recreational side, the reliability trial or attempt to achieve a fixed standard.

Cycling also has its team game in bicycle polo, a hard game requiring a high level of cycling skill and considerable nerve, and controlled by the Bicycle Polo Association of Great Britain. The game is divided into six 15-minute chukkas, with five players and one substitute on each side. International matches are played and there are national and local leagues.

There is also an organisation that caters especially for the distance tourist in the Cyclists Touring Club, which keeps a check on premises offering accommodation to cycle tourists, and provides a sign for use on approved accommodation. The address of the C.T.C. national headquarters is Cotterell House, 69 Meadrow, Godalming, Surrey. The office for travel facilities is C.T.C. Travel Ltd., 13 Spring Street, Paddington, London, W.2.

Darts.

Originally just a casual amusement confined almost entirely to public-houses, the game of darts is now one of Britain's most popular pastimes. Public-houses still provide facilities for it, but to-day clubs, canteens, factories, offices, and private houses also have their boards, and there are numerous team and individual competitions, including a National Championship. The prizes rival those of any other game for value, matches are widely reported, and the attendance for the bigger contests is limited only by the size of the hall. This enthusiasm is not misplaced, for the game is a test of skill, and luck plays little part in it. The governing body is the National Darts Association of Great Britain.

The standard circular board has a diameter of 18 inches, and is divided into segments numbered from 1 to 20, but not consecutively. In addition, there are two rings, each ¾ inch wide, that go right round the board and through each segment. These are the "double" ring, at the extremity of the board, and the "treble" ring, near the centre of the board, darts in these rings counting double or treble the value of the segment. In the centre of the board there are two small rings, the "bull" or "dosser," counting 50, and the "outer," counting 25. The bull is 5 feet 8 inches from the ground, and the wooden or metal feathered darts are thrown from a line, called the "hockey," usually 9 feet away.

Matches may be singles, doubles, or between teams of four or eight players. Games are for a certain number of points, usually 101, 201, 301, 501, 801 or 1001, the lower totals being used for individual, and the higher for team contests, and matches are generally the best two out of three games or "legs." Conditions for matches vary, but normally stipulate either "straight start and finish on a double" or "start and finish on a double." In the first case players score from the start, but in the second they do not score until one double has been registered. In both cases they must finish on a double, and they must finish with the exact number they require. Scores are counted downwards, players being told how many they need, rather than how many they have scored.

In addition to the straightforward game, there are many darts variations. In one, "Round the clock," a player has to throw one dart into each segment from 1 to either 20 or the bull, his turn continuing until he throws three darts unsuccessfully. In "Shanghai," players start with a complete throw of three darts at number 1, and continue with a throw at every number up to 9, but players who fail to score at number 5 drop out.

In "cricket," one player "bats," throwing normally, and counting everything over 40, while the other "bowls," throwing only at the bull, and counting one wicket for every "outer" and two for every "bull," five wickets ending his opponent's "innings." In a darts version of shove-ha'penny players have to get three darts in each segment from 1 to 9, and three in the centre. In "Fives," players score only if their total is divisible by five.

Diving. *See* Swimming.

Dominoes.

Dominoes are similar in many ways to cards, in that many games can be played with them with varying degrees of skill. Players play (or *pose* or *down*) in turn from hands. The game was introduced in Europe by way of Italy in the 18th century, though the actual games as they are played today, and also the scoring methods, are of French origin.

The domino itself (called a *card* or *stone*) is oblong with its face divided by a centre line and marked in each half by indented dots. A set normally consists of 28 pieces, respectively marked 6–6 (double six), 6–5, 6–4, 6–3, 6–2, 6–1, 6–0, 5–5, 5–4, 5–3, 5–2, 5–1, 5–0, 4–4, 4–3, 4–2, 4–1, 4–0, 3–3, 3–2, 3–1, 3–0, 2–2, 2–1, 2–0, 1–1, 1–0, 0–0 (double blank). (There are special sets for games consisting of 55 pieces, running up to 9–9, and 85 pieces, running as high as 12–12).

In the common form of the game, using 28 pieces, the dominoes are laid face downwards on the table, each player taking seven, the rest being left as a reserve. A player stands his hand so that the faces of his pieces are visible to him but not to his opponents. The idea of the game is to match the number on one domino-half to that of the free half of a piece already played on the table. Pieces are laid end to end but double pieces are laid transversely and allow the player an extra turn. The winner is the one who plays all his pieces.

Variations include playing a piece that is not the same as the one to which it is fitted, but that, with it, adds up to seven, or one that will make the two ends of the line add up five or a multiple of five, or three or a multiple of three. Another variation makes the double-blank and any piece on which the two halves add up to seven *matadors*. These are the equivalent of the card player's *wild* cards, and may be played at any time.

In some games, a player who cannot play simply misses the turn, while, in others, he may draw from the reserve, having, of course, to retain the domino in his hand if he still cannot play.

Games are for two, three, four or more players; and, in some of those for four players, two play together against the other two, each player trying to block his opponents, but to assist his partner.

As with cards, solitary players can play Patience, and this is a good way for a beginner to learn how to play a hand. The player picks five dominoes from a shuffled set, starts with any piece he chooses, and then continues to play in the normal way. When he cannot play, he draws enough pieces from the reserve to make his hand up to five and carries on, continuing until either he can play out or cannot play at all from the pieces left.

In the more skilful games, as in the more skilful games of cards, a good memory is an asset, as it is essential to remember which player played which piece.

Drama.

Few countries can boast so eager an interest in amateur drama as Britain, and it is estimated that there are some 20,000 groups in the British Isles with half a million membership. The cardinal influence in this enormous movement is the British Drama League, to which some 3,500 groups belong besides over 1,000 private individuals.

The league's influence on drama is exercised in two ways. Its members have the use of the library, which possesses the largest collection of plays and books on the theatre in Great Britain and of its information services, which give help and advice on every conceivable dramatic topic. They can, of course, hire sets of plays (one copy for each character up to twelve.) Then there are the league's training schemes. Courses in production, acting, and décor take place in London all the year round, and there are summer courses in the country. The address of B.D.L. is 9–10 Fitzroy Square, London, W.1.

It was not until the great International Theatre Exhibition at the Victoria and Albert Museum in 1922 that the English public became fully aware of the "new man" who had arrived in the theatre —the "producer" or "director," as the Americans call him. It is the producer who decides how the play is to be produced and sets his signature upon it, very much like the conductor of an orchestra. In this task he unifies the work of the author, actors, designers, and craftsmen of various kinds. The technical side of staging a play is a fascinating one involving problems of the framework (the stage, sight lines, auditorium); curtain settings, lighting, skycloths; the construction of scenery; designing the scenery and the making of scale plans and models; painting the scenery; lighting, and so on.

Television offers new opportunities for the playwriting aspirant, with its need for new methods. In the theatre the playwright and actor must make all things plain to distant members of an audience—whereas the television actor's slightest change of expression is clear to the person sitting within a couple of yards of him. A wink, a nod, a shrug on the television screen suffice for the implications which would be lost in the theatre. The gearing, so to speak, between text and meaning is different. A new field opens, therefore, for the writer for television drama.

Draughts. *See* **Chess.**

Eton Fives. *See* **Fives.**

Fencing.

Fencing can claim a longer history than most sports, for it is the modern equivalent of duelling. In mediæval tournaments mounted knights fought with lances, and, in addition to actual fights to the death, they also met with special, less lethal lances purely for sport. Later, duels were fought dismounted, and with different weapons. In Elizabethan days duellists used a sword, for attacking, in the right hand, and a dagger, for defence, in the left. Later still, the dagger was discarded, and duels were fought, as are fencing bouts to-day, with a sword only.

Duelling declined in Britain during the Regency period, when it became fashionable for gentlemen to learn to fight with their fists, but they continued to learn swordsmanship, and to fence with the practice weapon, the foil. Eventually, duelling became illegal almost throughout the world, but swordsmen of other countries similarly continued to fence with the foil. Even before Britain took to fist-fighting, most of the advances in fencing technique had been made in France and Italy, and the fencers of these and other Continental countries are still the best in the world, countries like Britain and the United States relying largely on fencers of Continental European descent.

Nowadays, widespread class tuition in fencing has opened the sport to anyone.

Modern fencing includes contests with three weapons: the foil, which is the only one used by women; the épée, the real duelling sword; and the sabre, which cuts as well as thrusts. These weapons have "buttons" on the points, but fencers wear a special glove, a padded jacket, and a mask. Fencing requires grace of movement, lightness of foot, agility, strength of wrist and forearm, quick mental reactions, and good eyesight; and it will do much to develop these qualities, including the eyesight. As masks are worn, it is perfectly practicable to fence wearing glasses.

The governing body of the sport is the Amateur Fencing Association, 83 Perham Road, London, W.14.

Figure Skating. *See* **Skating.**

Fives.

There are two games of Fives, Eton Fives and Rugby Fives. They are court games using walls, but an Eton Fives court has the addition of a buttress or "pepper" jutting out from one side wall. The striking implement is the gloved hand. Eton Fives is a doubles game, but both singles and doubles are played in Rugby Fives.

Folk Song and Dance.

Whether or not you play, sing, or dance yourself, you can enjoy the heritage of English folk music, song, and dance. To enable you to enjoy it to the full the story of Cecil Sharp House will be useful. Cecil Sharp went out to collect the folk songs of England in the fields and cottages, in almshouses, and by the roadside. He systematically combed some counties like Somerset. Cecil Sharp and Vaughan Williams joined the English Song Society, which had had Elgar and Parry among its first members. Sharp went on to note down folk dances and to publish details of the steps and figures. In course of time he founded the English Folk Dance Society to restore their traditional dances to the people of England. The two Societies amalgamated in 1932 and, today, Cecil Sharp House (2 Regents Park Road, London, N.W.1) is the home of the English Folk Dance and Song Society, with over 12,000 members.

Scottish Dancing and singing are the primary objectives of special holidays by the Holiday Fellowship at Scottish centres; and Old Time Dancing is enjoyed at an English Centre. Folk dancing is also the feature of special holidays by the Cooperative Holidays Association.

Football. *See* **American Football; Association Football; Australian Rules Football; Canadian Football; Gaelic Football; Public-School Football; Rugby Football.**

Gaelic Football.

Gaelic Football is seldom played by anyone who is not Irish, but it is frequently played outside Ireland, for Irishmen have taken it with them to Britain, the United States, Australia, and South Africa.

Played fifteen-a-side, it is a blend of Association and Rugby football (*q.v.*), the goals having the uprights, cross-bar and net, exactly as in Association, but having the uprights extended above the cross-bar, as in Rugby. If the ball goes under the cross-bar it is a goal, and if it goes over it is a point, a goal equalling three points. The ball is round, and it may be kicked or caught, but not thrown forward, nor carried, though it may be dribbled by bouncing it. In its essentials, it is probably simpler than most other forms of football, but it is fast and involves frequent hard bodily contact. Substitutes are permitted in case of injury.

Gaelic football joins with hurling (*q.v.*) in coming under the old-established Gaelic Athletic Association.

Gliding.

The first serious efforts to develop gliding, which is flying in engineless aircraft or sailplanes making use of natural air currents, took place in Germany in 1919, and were successful enough to lead to experiments in France and England, where it arrived in 1922. At that time, however, it failed to gain much support, and the real history of gliding in Britain dates from a second attempt to encourage it in 1929. Little more than ten years later, gliding had advanced sufficiently to be a real factor in the second World War.

Skilful use of up-currents enables the glider pilot to stay up, and if the air is rising faster than the glider is sinking, the glider will climb.

Gliders can now reach altitudes of over 40,000 feet, stay in the air for over 50 hours, and carry out flights of hundreds of miles. It is an exhilarating sport and certificates for various grades of skill and experience are awarded by the British Gliding Association, 75 Victoria Street, London, S.W.1, to which some 70 clubs are affiliated.

Golf.

Golf, a game of great antiquity, originated in Scotland, and is now widely popular in many countries. It consists of using a set of clubs with which to play a small white ball over a cross-country course of eighteen holes. Each hole will be several hundred yards long, and will have its fixed starting-point and its finish with an actual hole in the ground, the object being to complete the course, which will be several miles long, in as few strokes as possible.

The playing of each hole falls into three sections, driving, approaching, and putting. The starting-point will be a flat piece of ground on which the player will " tee up " his ball on a small rubber peg, or " tee," which he will carry round with him. He will then hit the ball towards the hole, concentrating on achieving distance. From the tee to near the hole is the " fairway," which will consist of fairly smooth ground, not entirely devoid of natural obstacles, and probably containing some sand traps, or " bunkers." On each side of the fairway is the " rough," which may consist of long grass, shrubs, woods, or even roads. The player will continue to play his ball towards the hole, concentrating now chiefly on direction. On the fairway or off it, he should always play his ball where it lies, but, should it be quite unplayable, or even lost, he may drop it or a new one and pay a stroke penalty for the privilege. The actual hole will be on the " green," a rough circle of exceptionally well tended grass, and, once on it, the player will cover the last few yards by the more delicate art of " putting."

There are many different types of club, players being limited to fourteen. The shafts are generally steel, the striking surfaces being iron or, in the case of drivers, wood. The different " irons " have numbers, but golf clubs used to have special names, often descriptive of their functions, for instance, lofter, cleek, mashie, niblick, and even blaster. Originally, most golf courses were by the sea, and these were called " links," a term now loosely applied to any course.

There are two actual methods of competitive play, match play and medal play. Match play is by holes, a player completing any hole in fewer strokes than his opponent winning that hole. Once a player leads by more holes than there are still to play, the game finishes, the victory being by X and Y, where X is the number of holes he is " up," and Y the lesser number of unplayed holes. When a player leads by the same number of holes as there are still to play he is said to be " dormy " so many. Opponents level after eighteen holes proceed to the first hole, and play on until one is one hole up, when he is said to have won at the 19th, 20th, or whatever it may be. Some important match-play events are over 36 holes, or two complete rounds. Medal play is simply stroke play, the result depending on the number of strokes needed to complete the course. This demands a higher level of consistency, for one bad spell can ruin the total, whereas, in match play, it may cost only one hole. In play after the initial drive, the player farthest from the hole normally plays before his opponent.

In match-play championships and tournaments players are drawn against each other, the winners going on to the next round, and so on up to the final. In medal-play events players go round in pairs, but each is, of course, playing against the whole field. Team matches consist of singles and foursomes, in which the partners play shots in turn. Other, less-formal forms of golf are four-ball foursomes, in which each player plays his own ball; best-ball foursomes, in which both partners drive, but, thereafter, play in turn only

at the most successfully driven ball; and three-somes, in which each player plays for himself against the others. During a match, a player must not receive advice from anyone except his " caddie," if he has one, the caddie being an attendant who makes a profession of carrying golfers' clubs round.

Every course has its " bogey " and " par " figures, these being scores, with par representing the higher standard that a first-class player might achieve for the course. By assessing a member's own scores against these figures, clubs can allocate a handicap which indicates the player's standard. There are many minor competitions in which golfers play, not on level terms, but from their handicaps, which also serve as a perpetual incentive to players to improve their game, and therefore their handicaps. The possession of a handicap also makes it easier for players to arrange even matches with strangers. Handicaps are subject to alteration as a player's standard changes, and such alterations may be in either direction. The operation of the handicap in play takes the form of strokes deducted from the actual score at certain holes, in accordance with the arrangements in force at any particular club.

Golf offers a tremendous number of competitions of all standards, as well as championships and team matches. Probably the four most important individual championships are the British Open, the British Amateur, the American Open, and the American Amateur. These are long-established, but the two major international team events are quite new. They are the World Cup, open to teams of two professionals from any country, and the Eisenhower Cup, for teams of four amateurs, the three best scores counting, from any country. Other, much older international team events include the Ryder, Walker, and Curtis Cups, which are contests between Britain and the United States for professionals, amateurs, and women, respectively; though it is interesting to note that the actual inscription on the Curtis Cup indicates that this trophy is open to women golfers of any country.

Golf is ruled by the Royal and Ancient Club of St. Andrews, Scotland, which is recognised all over the world as the game's headquarters. There was an unusual illustration of this widespread recognition when the Eisenhower Cup competition was instituted by the United States in 1958, for, at the special request of the American organisers, the first meeting took place, not in the United States, but at St. Andrews. The Royal and Ancient Club makes the rules of golf, but these are generally supplemented by local rules in force at particular clubs.

The popular expression " rub of the green," used to describe an unexpected and unavoidable mischance, comes from golf, where it is used when a putt fails to take the expected line because of a slight flaw in the normally perfect turf of the green.

Gymnastics.

Gymnastics is a system of exercising with apparatus, and also a competitive sport, the chief items of apparatus used being the horizontal bar, the parallel bars, rings, ropes, ladders, and the vaulting horse. The horizontal bar, the parallel bars, and the rings can all be used for similar exercises, some being fast swings and others slow movements requiring considerable strength. Strength and swinging also come into ladder exercises; and the rope, which can be climbed in several different ways, is a simple form of apparatus that demands, and will develop, strength. The horse can be used for a variety of vaults, in either the lengthways or sideways position, and still others are possible when pommels are fitted to it. In addition to those who specialise in gymnastics, many sportsmen of various kinds regularly attend gymnastic classes as part of their training for their own particular activities.

The trampoline, which is something like a large and very springy mattress, and which has long been used by circus and stage acrobats, has now been accepted as a piece of gymnastic apparatus. gymnasts, divers and other sportsmen use it in training; it is also used in the Services in the training of commandos and parachutists. There are trampoline competitions and championships, in which gymnasts perform many of the acrobatic feats normally performed on the floor.

Head of the River Races. *See* **Boat Races.**

Henley Royal Regatta. *See* **Boat Races.**

Highland Games. *See* **Traditional Games and Customs.**

Hockey.

Hockey originated about three-quarters of a century ago as a game confined to Britain, but with rules that varied in each of the home countries. However, in 1900, England, Ireland, and Wales combined to form the International Hockey Board, with a view to formulating rules that would apply wherever the game was played, and, two years later, Scotland joined the alliance. The game was also taken up with terrific enthusiasm in India, and Indian players became, and remain, the best players in the world. Their enthusiasm extended to what is now Pakistan, so

In play, the ball must be propelled only by the stick, and it must not be stopped with any part of the body except the hand, in which case it must only be stopped, and not caught or knocked forward. These prohibitions, however, do not apply to goalkeepers, who may stop the ball with any part of their body, and also kick it, when in their circle. No part of a player's stick must be raised above the shoulder either at the beginning or end of a stroke, or to stop the ball. Hitting the ball in the air and scooping it are allowed, but deliberate undercutting is not, and umpires can penalise any hit which they judge to be dangerous. Interfering with an opponent's stick, running between an opponent and the ball; and charging or other bodily contact are not allowed. Players must not tackle from the left unless they can play the ball without touching the opponent or his stick.

A player is "offside" if there are fewer than three opponents between him and the goal-line, unless he is in his own half, or unless a team-mate playing the ball is nearer to the goal-line than he is. A player who is offside is put onside if an opponent plays the ball, but not if the ball merely touches or glances off the opponent. Players who are offside are not penalised if they do not interfere with the play.

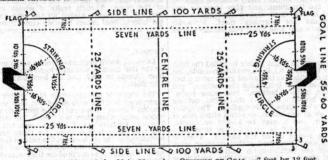

GROUND.—100 yards by 55 to 60 yards. OPENING OF GOAL.—7 feet by 12 feet.
Diagram of Ground as marked out for Hockey.

the division that brought that country into existence also added one more to the list of hockey-playing countries, and without noticeably weakening India's own national team.

Hockey is now played in many other countries, but, for some time, it made little progress on the Continent. Eventually, though, it was tried, liked, and adopted in a number of European countries, and one of these, the Netherlands, has now established a right to a place alongside India, Pakistan, and Britain as the game's top layer. Hockey has, and has long had, Olympic Games status.

Hockey is played eleven-a-side on a pitch marked out as in the accompanying diagram, the normal positions of the players being a goalkeeper, two full-backs, three half-backs, and five forwards, exactly as in Association football (*q.v.*). The white ball can be either sewn, as is a cricket ball, or seamless, and it must weigh from 5¼ to 5¾ ounces. Sticks must weigh from 12 to 28 ounces, and have a handle that can be passed through a ring with an inside diameter of 2 inches. They have a striking surface on the left side only, left-handed sticks not being permitted. A game consists of two 35-minute halves, unless the captains have agreed on a shorter period.

The game is started, and restarted after half-time and after a goal, by a bully at the centre of the ground. The players bullying stand facing the side-line, each with his own goal on his right. Each taps the ground between the ball and his own goal and his opponent's stick over the ball three times alternately, after which one of them must play the ball. At any bully, all the other players must be 5 yards from the ball, and between it and their own goal.

If the ball crosses the side-line it is rolled in by a player of the side that did not put it out. This player must have his hands, feet, and stick outside the field of play, and he must not play the ball again until someone else has done so. All the other players must have their feet and sticks inside the 7-yard line until the ball leaves the roller's hand.

If the ball is sent across the goal-line wide of the goal by an attacker, or, unintentionally, by a defender who is more than 25 yards from the goal-line, the restart is by a bully on the 25-yard line. If it is hit behind unintentionally by a defender who is within 25 yards of the goal-line, a corner is awarded to the attacking side. If it is hit behind intentionally by a defender from any part of the ground, a short, or penalty, corner is awarded to the attacking side. A corner is a hit from a point on either the goal-line or the side-line within 3 yards of the corner flag, while a short corner is a hit from a point on the goal-line 10 yards from the nearer goal-post. At a corner, all the defenders must be behind the goal-line, and all the attackers outside the circle. When the corner hit comes into the circle, attackers are not allowed to take a first-time shot, but must first stop the ball or slow it down. At no time during the game can a goal be scored unless it was hit from inside the circle.

Penalties for infringements outside the circle are generally free hits. Penalties for infringements inside the circle by defenders are short corners, unless they have been deliberately committed to prevent a goal, or have, in fact, prevented a goal, in which cases a penalty bully is awarded. In extreme cases, both short corners and penalty bullies can be awarded for offences anywhere behind the 25-yard line.

In 1963 the penalty stroke was introduced. This replaced the penalty bully, a duel between the offender and one opponent, with all the other players beyond the 25-yard line, that started with a bully 5 yards from the centre of the goal and continued until either a goal was scored or the ball was hit behind the attacker or out of the circle by the defender. If it was hit behind by the defender, the bully was restarted. This was a novel feature, but a not altogether satisfactory one, as the duel was sometimes protracted. The penalty stroke, if less spectacular, is also less complicated. A game is controlled by two umpires, each of whom takes one half of the field and one complete side-line. Substitutes are not permitted in hockey.

Hockey is entirely an amateur game. Until recently most club matches were " friendlies," but the new London League of top clubs seems to be flourishing, plus some rather specialised cup competitions. There are, however, a great many representative games, from county matches to internationals.

A major feature of the hockey season, which normally lasts from October until March (although summer games, usually played in the evening, are becoming increasingly popular) is the end-of-season Easter Hockey Festival. There are several festivals, most of them taking place at seaside resorts. Teams go from many different areas, including the Continent, and play three or four matches in four days against opponents whom they would not normally meet. Six-a-side tournaments also take place occasionally during the season.

Hurling.

Hurling, which might loosely be called the Irish brand of hockey (q.v.), is played fifteen-a-side, and has been described as the fastest game using a ball in the world. The ball, called the " slitter," and the sticks, called " hurleys," bear some resemblance to hockey's ball and sticks, but nothing like hockey's " sticks " rule applies. The slitter may be hit at any height, and with either side of the hurley, and it may be kicked or caught, though it must not be carried more than three steps, nor picked up off the ground. There is no offside, apart from the fact that attackers must not enter the parallelogram marked out near the goal ahead of the slitter. The goals have uprights that are extended above the cross-bar, and scoring is by goals, under the bar, and points, over the bar, a goal equalling three points. There is a good deal of bodily contact, and substitutes are permitted for injured players.

Hurling, rarely played by anyone who is not Irish, but often played by Irishmen outside Ireland, is of great antiquity, and the English authorities in Ireland first tried to suppress it six hundred years ago. It was kept alive, however, and it is very much alive to-day. To Irishmen, hurling and Gaelic football (q.v.) are symbols of nationalism and patriotism. They are governed by the Gaelic Athletic Association, which has a rule that states: " Any member who plays or encourages Rugby, Association Football, Hockey or Cricket by that very fact incurs immediate suspension from membership of the Association."

A form of hurling with slightly different rules, called shinty, is still preserved in another Celtic country, Scotland.

Ice-Hockey. *See* Skating.

Ice Skating. *See* Skating.

Ice Yachting. *See* Winter Sports.

Judo. *See* Wrestling.

Knur and Spell. *See* Old English Games and Customs.

Korfball.

Korfball is a team game with several unique features, the most striking being that it is a mixed game, a team consisting of twelve players—six men and six women. The game resembles basketball (q.v.) in some ways, the goals, which are 11½ feet high, and the scoring of goals being similar. It can be played on any firm surface, the pitch measuring 300 feet by 133 feet, though a smaller pitch can be used, provided that length and width are reduced in proportion. The pitch is divided into three sections, and players do not move from one sector to another during actual play. They must, however, change to another zone after every two goals. This encourages all-round attacking and defensive ability, and ensures that, even in a one-sided match, every player gets a fair share of the game. Four players from each team play in each section, and players always mark opponents of their own sex. Players must not run with the ball which is advanced purely by passing. There is no tackling, and the ball can only pass from one team to the other by interception. Players may not score if there is an opponent within arm's length. A game lasts for 90 minutes, divided into two halves.

Korfball originated in the Netherlands, where it was first played in 1902. It spread to Belgium in 1927, and reached England in 1947. There is an International Board, on which the Netherlands, Belgium, and England are represented. International inter-club matches are a regular feature of the game. Though really a winter game, korfball is actually played all the year round, the international games between clubs from the three korfball countries taking place during the summer.

Lacrosse.

Lacrosse, which originated from a game played by the Red Indians, was introduced into England from Canada in 1867, and has been played here ever since.

The object is the propelling of a rubber ball through goals 6 feet wide and 6 feet high with a wooden " crosse " not more than a foot wide at its widest point, when there is a " mesh " of strings. The goals are from 90 to 110 yards apart, but play can take place behind them, for there are no boundaries to the pitch except the natural borders of the field, unless the captains have agreed otherwise. The only lines required are the centre circle, the goal-lines, and the goal-creases.

In England teams consist of twelve players, but in Canada and the United States the number was reduced to ten some years ago. Players line up right down the field, instead of only in their own half, and there is no offside, except that no attacker may enter the goal-crease before the ball. Should a player leave the field through injury, his opponents must also withdraw a man.

A game consists of four 20-minute periods, but the captains can agree to vary this, either to two 45-minute halves or otherwise. The game is started or re-started after a stoppage by one player from each side " facing " by placing the ball on the ground between the backs of the two crosses, and then drawing them apart, after which the ball is in play. It can then be advanced by running with it on the crosse, throwing it from the crosse, or kicking it, though no goal, except an " own goal," can be scored by a kick. Only the goalkeeper, who can deflect the ball with his hand, but not catch or throw it, may handle the ball. Players can shoulder opponents when trying to get the ball off the ground, and " body check " them by simply standing in front of them to impede them. A player can also check an opponent's crosse with his own crosse if the opponent has the ball. A foul is penalised by giving the non-offending player a " free position," which means that he is given the ball, and the game is then re-started.

Lacrosse demands speed and stamina, and a high level of skill demands practice, but it is basically a simple game. Seven-a-side lacrosse is suitable for school practice—designed to be played in a gymnasium or on a netball court.

It is interesting to note that Lacrosse, which can be one of the roughest of all games, has been made a suitable game for women by very simple measures, such as the elimination of the body check; and that there are now more women playing than there are men.

Land and Sand Yachting. *See* Yachting.

Lawn Tennis.

Originally called Sphairistike—or "Sticky" by those who disliked it—Lawn Tennis was invented in the seventies of the last century as a simplified, outdoor version of real tennis (q.v.), using a net, but no walls. It is now far more widely played than the parent game, being popular almost all over the world. As its name implies, it was originally intended to be played on grass, but it is now also played on hard courts of various surfaces, and indoors on wood.

The court is as shown in the accompanying diagram, the outer long boundary lines being the limitations for doubles, and those parallel to them being the boundaries for singles. Both server and receiver score, four points making a game, six games won a set, and two out of three

Modern Pentathlon.

Imagine a king's messenger riding with an important dispatch, and being hotly pursued. His horse is shot, and he has to engage his pursuers, first with his revolver, and then with the sword. Eventually, he breaks away, swims a river, and finishes his journey on foot and running.

That is the "plot" on which is based one of the most interesting, exciting, and testing of all sporting events, the modern pentathlon. Often wrongly thought to be a part of Athletics, the Pentathlon is a separate sport, but one that actually consists of five different sports: the five activities, in fact, of the king's messenger in the story, riding, revolver shooting, fencing, swimming, and running. True, the pentathlon competitor does not have to carry them out one after the other, but he does have to take part in them in that order, one on each of five successive days, both riding and running being across country, the riding on a horse strange to him.

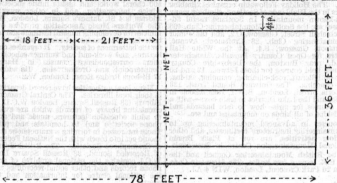

NET:—Height 3 ft. 6 in. at posts, 3 ft. at centre.
Diagram of Ground as marked out for Lawn Tennis.

or three out of five sets won a match. Game points are scored "15," "30," "40," and "Game." The system of "vantage" games and sets is used. This means that, if 40-all—called "deuce"—is reached, a player must gain a clear lead of two points to win the game, the winner of the first point after deuce being said to have the "advantage." If the games reach 5-all, the set continues until one player has a clear lead of two games, though the "tie-break" system—the best of the next 12 points—may soon be more widely adopted.

When the game began, there was considerable discussion before this scoring, which is taken from tennis, was given preference over the straightforward one-two-three system of rackets (q.v.). Much more recently, experiments have been made with the equally straightforward system of table tennis (q.v.), but the tennis system survived these, and remains in force.

Service is almost invariably overhand, and the receiver plays the service after one bounce. Thereafter, strokes may be "ground" strokes, played after one bounce, or volleys, played before any bounce. In doubles, either partner may play the ball, but each must serve in turn.

In addition to being played by thousands of people, lawn tennis attracts large crowds of spectators. The big annual tournaments, such as Wimbledon, Forest Hills, and Paris, are amongst the major sporting events of the year; as are the Davis Cup competition, open to teams of men from every country in the world, and the Wightman Cup, a women's contest between Britain and the United States. Since April 1968 the L.T.A.'s new rule 30 has made it possible for amateurs and professionals to compete against one another in tournaments in this country.

Marbles. *See* Old English Games and Customs.

The pentathlon first appeared in the Olympic Games of 1912, but, in recent years, it has become so popular that, in addition to the Olympic event every four years, there are now annual world championships in many countries, including Britain. The event was originally designed as one suitable for Army officers, and, though present-day Army training is rather different, most pentathlon competitors are still servicemen, though they are not all officers. However, a civilian has won the Olympic event, and, in Britain, the Army authorities are willing to provide training facilities for civilian competitors who show signs of reaching a high standard. Many people believe that the "keys" to success in the modern pentathlon are swimming and running, and that competitors who are good at them can be taught the riding, shooting, and fencing without too much difficulty.

Mountaineering.

Among famous peaks, Mont Blanc was first conquered in 1786, the Jungfrau in 1811, and the Wetterhorn in 1854. By then, mountaineering was becoming organised, and there were systematic assaults on the Alps; in Norway, the Caucasus, and Corsica; in the Rockies and the Andes; in Japan, New Zealand, and Kenya; and, of course, in the Himalayas, where over thirty years passed between the first assault on Everest and its conquest in 1953. There are still unconquered peaks in the Himalayas, but it is not only first ascents that interest the mountaineer; he can find exciting climbing in many parts of the world.

The way to master mountaineering is to accompany and watch experts. Perfect physical and nervous fitness is essential, as is a detailed knowledge of snow, ice, avalanches, glaciers, crevasses, and cornices, and of the different techniques of ascending, descending, and traversing. Also to be learned is step-cutting, which is hard manual labour carried out under difficult conditions, conditions that may make perfect workmanship literally a matter of life or death. Clothing, properly nailed boots, ropes, ice axes, knives, maps, compasses, medical supplies, must be of the best, and yet, at the same time, light.

Mountaineering is generally taken to mean snow- and ice-climbing, but allied to it is rock-climbing, which demands the same perfect physical and nervous condition, and, in place of knowledge of snow and ice, knowledge of several very different kinds of rock. Ascending, descending, and traversing all apply, and so do ropes, and the rock-climber should, in fact, be something of a knot expert. Light, rope-soled shoes replace the mountaineer's nailed boots.

The Youth Hostels Association runs training schools for climbers at all stages in Britain and abroad; and also runs evening classes on rock-climbing in conjunction with education authorities. The Holiday Fellowship organises climbing tours in the Highlands of Scotland, climbing many well-known mountains In Scotland useful addresses are the Scottish Mountaineering Club, 406 Sauchiehall Street, Glasgow, C.2, and the Junior Mountaineering Club, 28 Croftmont Avenue, Croftfoot, Glasgow, S.4. At the White Hall Centre for Open Country Pursuits, Manchester Road, near Buxton, the Derbyshire County Council hold courses for those between 13 and 20 plus on hillcraft, rock-climbing, camping, ski-ing, and canoeing. The Outward Bound Trust, 123 Victoria Street, London, S.W.1, runs schools in Wales and the Lake District to train boys—with a few courses for girls—how to face hazards and hardships of all kinds on mountains and sea.

Courses in advanced mountaineering up to mountaineering instructors' certificates, and other outdoor activities, are run at Plasy Brenin National Mountaineering Centre in Snowdonia.

The British Mountaineering Council and the C.C.P.R. issue a free leaflet, *The Mountain Code*, from 26 Park Crescent, London, WIN 4 AJ.

Music.

One of the most novel changes of the last generation or so has been the widespread diffusion of music not only in this country but all over the world. Twenty or thirty years ago it might have been necessary to travel a long way to hear the performance of a classical musical work; and the opportunity of doing so was only occasional. We can now have a constant flow of such music from wireless and record player. Several things follow from this change. Leisure has been transformed by " high fidelity " and the long-playing record. People listen more easily and frequently than they read; and it is music, rather than literature, which is at the centre of culture. Access to good music does not depend upon training and application to the same extent as access to good literature. It is easier for the tired person to enjoy music than a serious book. " Where the library shelves used to stand," says a commentator, " there are now the record albums, row upon proud and esoteric row." The listener may well be submerged, by the easy flow of music of vastly different kinds; but there is an opportunity for the discerning listener to compare and to select from the music of the different centuries, to study the difference between the classical and romantic masters, the emergence of modern orchestration, choral music, chamber music, opera, and oratorio. We may go on to study other aspects—the study of the personality of the composers; the relation between their work and the problems of the times; knowledge of the different instruments; and how to enjoy reading a musical score. By this means the listener can combine refreshment of spirit with the delights of exercising skills of various kinds.

All through the summer, all over the country there are opportunities for music lovers, whether active musicians or not, to spend a holiday together and pursue some aspect of music. The leader will probably be surprised to learn that there are nearly one hundred such summer schools each year, some for the week-end, others for a week or fortnight. The Rural Music Schools Association at Hitchen, Herts. would help enquirers for particulars. A glance at the annual list shows how wide are the subjects offered: madrigal and other singing, recorder playing, orchestral and chamber music, Russian music, 18th-century music, discussion for wind teachers, the making of musical instruments. These summer schools are in addition to the Music Festivals held at Edinburgh, Bath, Cheltenham, and other places, not forgetting the Three Choirs Festival in the West (British Federation of Music Festivals, 106 Gloucester Place, London, W.1). Details of the various continental festivals can be obtained from the European Association of Music Festivals, 122 rue de Lausanne, Geneva, or 82 Beauchamp Place, London, S.W.3.

Your local public library probably has a music library. The National Operatic and Dramatic Association, 1 Crestfield Street, London, W.C.1, has a library of musical scores and dramatic works. The National Federation of Music Societies publishes a catalogue with practical details of some 500 choral works and assists music societies by advice, information, and in other ways; its address is 4 St. James's Square, London, W.C.1. The Workers Music Association provides opportunities for developing musical instincts and tastes, believing that genuine art moves people to work for the betterment of society. It organises classes, lectures, and week-end and summer schools; and offers correspondence courses in Harmony, Counterpoint, and Orchestration. Its address is 17 Bishops Bridge Road, London, W.2.

Many local authorities have record departments in their local libraries. The Central Gramophone Library (38 Russell Square, London W.C.1) has a circulating library of records which are available to adult education lecturers, music and gramophone societies and to hospitals and prisons. Those interested in forming a gramophone society should get into touch with the National Federation of Gramophone Societies. The British Institute of Recorded Sound, 38 Russell Square London W.C.1 contains the national archives of gramophone records and other sound-recordings and is the national centre for information and documents.

Natural History and Field Studies.

There are nine field centres in England and Wales, at:

Juniper Hall, Dorking, Surrey.
Flatford Mill, East Bergholt, near Colchester, Essex.
Malham Tarn, near Settle, Yorkshire.
Dale Fort, Haverfordwest, Pembrokeshire (including Skokholm Bird Sanctuary).
Preston Montford, near Shrewsbury, Shropshire.
Slapton Ley, Slapton, Kingsbridge, Devonshire.
Orielton, near Pembroke, S. Wales.
Nettlecombe Court, Williton, Taunton, Somerset.
Rhyd-y-Creua, Betws-y-Coed, Caernarvonshire.

The nine centres have been set up by the Field Studies Council in localities selected for their ecological features and for their geological, geographical, archaeological, and artistic interest. Working facilities and expert guidance are available at the Field Centres to all who have a serious interest in the countryside—whether as amateur naturalists or as students or as research workers. They are not reserved for the academic student only. The Council want to encourage and help the beginner and the ordinary person who has an interest in some branch of natural history and wishes to learn of this or allied subjects. The Centres are staffed and suitably equipped to provide residential accommodation and working facilities for numbers ranging up to about sixty persons. Thus field workers enjoy the skilled guidance of the staff, local contacts and information, bench space, tools, maps and records, with something of the intellectual and social life of a small residential college. There are special courses for amateurs, and some of these are less formal than the word " course " suggests. The subjects vary widely including bird study, land structure and scenery, and outdoor painting and sketching.

Juniper Hall, amidst the beautiful chalk hills of the North Downs, is well situated for almost every kind of field study. Flatford Mill is at the head of the Stour estuary, in the countryside of Constable and Gainsborough. The Stour, with its tributary streams, its mill pools and cattle ponds and dykes, provides excellent scope for water biology. Malham Tarn Centre is on the shore of the tarn on the limestone uplands at the head of Airedale in the Yorkshire Pennines. Here is the rich flora of well-drained pastures, screes, and limestone. The tarn itself supports an abundant fauna of invertebrates and fish. Dale Fort at the tip of a narrow peninsula guards the approach to Milford Haven. The flowers on the cliffs in May and June are the envy of the rock gardener. The opportunities for the marine biologist are unsurpassed. But there is no specialisation to the exclusion of any of the many subjects that can advantageously be studied. The Bird Observatory on Skokholm island is a part of Dale Fort Field Centre, and here work on birds has pride of place. Guillemots and razorbills breed on the rocks, and puffins and shearwaters burrow in the edges of the plateau. Preston Montford lies on the banks of the Severn four miles west of Shrewsbury, where geological formations are displayed conveniently for study. In the North Shropshire plain is scope for the study, too long neglected, of the ecology of ordinary English farming country that man has influenced for more than 2,000 years. There are numerous localities of archaeological interest, including the Roman town of Viroconium. At Slapton Ley the 300 acres of Slapton Nature Reserve offer ample scope for interest in most branches of Natural History. The Ley is separated from the sea by a shingle bank. There are moorland and bog: slate and limestone cliffs; lake shores and beaches; and woodlands. Enquiries can be made to the Field Studies Council, Ravensmead, Keston, Kent.

Everyone who *wants* to work in the field can find something useful to do, whatever his natural bent and his training, since the range of research is vast and the problems diverse, with such varying degrees of difficulty. This opportunity has been greatly extended by the increasing importance of ecology, which is a distinctive point of view in the approach to field biology. In its most general sense ecology may be defined as the study of plants and animals as they live *in their natural homes.* The growing popularity of the subject in this country represents a breakaway from the confinement of serious work in biology to the laboratory and museum. These are still, of course, absolutely necessary, but the primary place in which to work at ecology is the field.

Bird-watching. The pleasure of bird-song and the sight of their activities is a common one for most of us. From this point many are prompted to make a closer study of birds and their habits. To get the most pleasure it is a great advantage to turn for advice to those who have had a wide experience. The enthusiast will thus become equipped with some knowledge of methods of bird-watching, how to make field notes and keep records, hides, identification, tables of family likeness, migration, sanctuaries, bird photography, and the structure of the bird.

Bird-watching is not confined to those who live in the country. London has probably more bird-watchers than any other part of Britain. With the possible exception of the parish of Selborne in Hampshire, immortalised by Gilbert White, London, has the longest continuous history of ornithological observation in the British Isles. Groups of enthusiastic naturalists have collected a mass of detail about wild birds and their habits in London. The list of London birds is not only extraordinarily large but also contains many rarities and many birds of great scientific interest, like the black redstart and the little ringed plover. There are also special London problems, like the roosting of starlings in central London and the origin of this starling population. The reservoirs and the river, the commons and woods and park-land around London offer pleasant places for observation. The London Natural History Society (headquarters, the Natural History Museum, Cromwell Road, S.W.7) has, as its chief object, the study and enjoyment of natural history in the London area.

Visiting Nature Reserves. The Nature Conservancy welcome visitors to National Nature Reserves within the limits set by the Conservancy's own responsibilities towards these lands and their plants and wild life. The Reserves are maintained on behalf of the nation to conserve their natural fauna and flora, and so far as possible to enhance their interest and value to science. Many Reserves are accessible without formality; elsewhere a permit is required. A list of the Reserves is obtainable from the Conservancy, 19 Belgrave Square, London, S.W.1, or in Scotland from 12 Hope Terrace, Edinburgh, 9. There are some eighty National Nature Reserves. The largest in Britain is the Cairngorms in Scotland, of nearly 40,000 acres, with fauna rich in variety of species from wild cats to golden eagle and a diverse flora, which includes the arctic-alpine plants of the corries, screes, and exposed summits.

The Council for Nature. If you are interested in any aspect of natural history—for example in plants, birds, rocks, insects, trees, butterflies, or natural history photography—you will have no difficulty in finding the address of your local history society, of which there are a very large number. The local public library would doubtless give you the address you want, or you could enquire from the Council for Nature, Zoological Gardens, Regents Park, London, N.W.1, to which over two hundred organisations belong. These include the Royal Society for the Protection of Birds, The Lodge, Sandy, Beds., which has upwards of 53,000 members and runs the Young Ornithologist's Club for young people interested in bird-watching. It manages over 40 nature reserves, most of which are open to the public, and runs a film library. The Council links amateur and specialist in the study of natural history and the conservation of wild life. It has an Intelligence Unit which is ready to deal with requests for information on field natural history in the United Kingdom and its Film Officer will advise on what natural history films are available and on likely sources for photographs of any British wild animal or plant.

Netball.

Netball, which is played exclusively by women, is similar to basketball (*q.v.*), but it is played seven-a-side, does not allow substitutes, and the goals have no backboards. It is almost always played outdoors on asphalt or grass. Details of school, youth, county and national competition may be obtained from the All England Netball Association, 26 Park Crescent, London, WIN 4DE.

Nine Men's Morris. *See* Old English Games and Customs.

Old English Games and Customs.

The story of England had its beginnings a very long time ago, and many of England's present-day customs, recreations, sports, and games can be traced far back in that story. Some, of course, have undergone very considerable changes, but the links with the past are still clear.

On 1 May, for instance, girls still awake in some villages to the realisation that they are to be May Queens, and to reign for a day, though they may not realise that they are preserving a custom that can point to origins in the days of the Druids and that, in Tudor times, would have sent them and their fellow villagers out to spend the preceding night in the woods, gathering branches of trees and flowers with which to decorate their houses. Maypoles and morris dancers also belonged to May Day, and they can still be seen in England, and not only on that day.

More local, even quainter, but equally traditional is the trial for the Dunmow Flitch of Bacon in the village of Dunmow in Essex. The original conditions offer this award to any married couple who will go to the twelfth-century Augustinian priory, and there kneel on two sharp-pointed stones and swear that they have neither quarrelled nor repented of their marriage within a year and a day of its celebration. This award has lasted into modern times, not annually, it is true; but then it never was given annually, for it was instituted in 1244, and first claimed in 1445.

One annual event that is as traditional as it is strenuous is the Whit Monday cheese-chase at the village of Brockworth, near Gloucester. Records of this go back to the days of the Stuarts, for that was when they started to keep records of a custom that was already old then; so old that its origins are unknown, though they had to do with the villagers' cattle-grazing rights. A massive round cheese is rolled down nearby Coopers Hill, which has a gradient of one in four throughout its 150 yards; and, with a certain amount of risk to life and limb, the chasers tear down after it, the cheese being the prize for whoever catches it. Sometimes, the cheese hits a bump, and literally leaps out of reach over the hedge at the bottom of the hill, but the chase continues, the prize going to the first pursuer to reach the hedge, where " catchers " wait to halt the headlong rush of the runners. Despite the obvious dangers, the records to date mention nothing worse than a sprained ankle.

This brings us to sports and games; and, though today's most popular game, Football, is, in anything like its present form a comparatively recent growth, it can perhaps claim some relationship with Harpastum and Campball, which existed before the Norman Conquest; and it was one of the popular recreations banned in the interests of Archery. The football of those and later days, however, took the form of struggles between whole villages, the players battling en masse over a cross-country course of several miles. People past whose houses the battle was likely to rage prudently barred and shuttered all windows and doors, awaited the cessation of hostilities with anxiety, and probably helped to push this particular custom into oblivion.

The oldest English games are old indeed, and cricket, too, had more remote ancestors, from which the descent to today can be traced more directly. They included Bat and Trap, Creag, Cat and Dog, and Rounders. In Bat and Trap, the batsman hit a ball released from a trap between two posts. His opponent rolled it back underarm at the trap flap. If he knocked it down, the batsman was out: if not, the batsman scored one run and had another hit. This game is still played in Kent. Creag, which was played at the time of Edward II, used a curved stick, called a " cryc," as a bat, and a tree-stump as a wicket. Cat and Dog, which came later, was a game for three, two batsmen defending holes 13 yards apart, and trying to hit away the piece of wood that the third player aimed at the holes, the bats being the " dogs " and the piece of wood the " cat." It is worth noting that Baseball's accepted ancestors are games called One Old Cat and Two Old Cat, which clearly indicates a common origin for Cricket and Baseball. Some of the games in Cricket's ancestry remained popular after Cricket arrived, and Rounders is still a popular children's game.

The beginning of athletics can also be found in old England. Putting the weight and casting the bar, a forerunner of throwing the hammer, were popular with the courtiers in Tudor days, while other events, including javelin throwing, were practised by ordinary people of the same period. Later, the early hammer throwing spread beyond the Court, and was even attempted by women, which modern hammer throwing is not.

Tournaments and jousts were popular from the Middle Ages until Tudor times. These were combats between mounted men, a joust being single combat, while a tournament involved many contestants. They were succeeded by dismounted combats, which still take place today in the sport of Fencing. Those taking part in tournaments and jousts were required to swear an oath to the effect that they were competing purely for sport; and those taking part in the Olympic Games and certain other big sports meetings to-day swear an almost identical oath. Somewhat similar to jousting, but not restricted, as jousting was, to the nobility, was Tilting at the Quintain, which was practised both mounted and on foot, and in which a lance was thrust at a wooden target, which, if not struck accurately, swung round and struck the tilter.

Other old games, clearly the ancestors of modern ones, included Handball, which became Fives, but which is still handball in the United States; Battledore and Shuttlecock, still a children's game, but now developed by adults into Badminton; and Shovelboard, an elaborate game, for the nobility, which consisted of sliding weights down a long table marked with lines, and which is certainly a forerunner of Shove-Ha'penny. Another probable ancestor of Shove-Ha'penny was Squails, in which a coin was placed in the centre of a round table, and players tried to push their " squails," or discs, as close to the coin as possible, distances being measured by an instrument called a " swoggle." Also known as Skayles and Keels, this game appeared in the sixteenth century, lasted into the nineteenth century, and, under the name of Keels, achieved a poetic mention in Sidney's " Arcadia."

Archery. Archery dates back hundreds of years, to the days when the bow was the chief weapon of war, and, because of that, practice shooting and contests were officially encouraged: encouraged, in fact, to the extent that other popular recreations, like Football, Quoits, and Bowls, that might have interfered with it were banned, though the bans were always largely ignored. Eventually, the bow disappeared from the battle-fields, but, to this day, it has remained popular as a means of recreation and sport. Through the centuries, archery contests were generally of three kinds: shooting at a mark, or target; shooting purely for distance, though this was more popular abroad, in countries like Turkey, than in Britain; and shooting at " rovers," in which two or three archers would cover a cross-country course, taking it in turns to select a mark at which to shoot. To-day, archery, which retains enough of tradition in its terminology to remind the archer that he is following in a very long line, consists of shooting at a target containing rings coloured, going from the centre outwards, gold, red, blue, black, and white, the values being respectively, nine, seven, five, three, and one.

Knur and Spell. Knur and Spell belongs to Lancashire and Yorkshire, and originated in a children's game called Trap and Ball. The player uses a wooden club, the striking end of which, called the " pommel," is shaped something like a bottle, though it has a flat hitting surface, with which to hit a small ball, which he himself releases from a trap by means of a trigger. The ball, which is the " knur," weighs ⅞ ounce, measures 1 inch in diameter, and was originally wooden, though, later, porcelain was used. The trap is the " spell," and consists of a small brass cup with a strong spring, which is kept down by the trigger. The fixing of the spell is an elaborate process requiring the use of a spirit level, and, when it is in position, a player is allowed 10 minutes to adjust the tension of the spring. Players generally have their own spells. Each player has five consecutive hits, or " rises," and scores one point for every 20 yards covered.

Marbles. Marbles is supposed to have been played in ancient Egypt, but its popularity, with adults as well as children, in the England of the Middle Ages entitles it to count as an old English game. Marbles are often made of clay, but better ones are glass, and the best are pure marble. These are called " alleys," or " alley taws." There are several games of marbles, but they all involve the aiming of a marble at a target, which may be another marble or an opening, by bowling or " shooting " it along the ground. In shooting, the marble is held between the thumb and forefinger, with the knuckle of the forefinger on the ground, and is then flicked away.

Perhaps the best-known game is Ring Taw, in which players shoot from one circle at marbles placed in another about 6 feet away. Fortifications and Increase Pound use concentric circles, players shooting at marbles in each circle in turn. Three Holes and Handers involve shooting at holes in the ground; Arch Board or Bridge, at arches in an upright board; and Die Shot, at another marble on which a numbered die is balanced.

Nine Men's Morris. Nine Men's Morris is a fourteenth-century game for two, usually played outdoors on a diagram marked on the ground, but sometimes played indoors on a board. The diagram consists of three squares drawn inside each other. In addition to the outlines of each square, there are lines from the centre of each side of the inmost square, through the centre of the sides of the middle square, to the centre of the sides of the outermost square. The corner of each square and the centre of each side are the 24 points of importance in the game. Each player has nine men, often counters, and they play in turn, placing a man at an unoccupied point, and endeavouring to place three men in one row, continuing, when all the men are placed, to try to form rows by moving men along the lines. The completion of a row entitles a player to remove, or " pound," one of his opponent's men, the object of the game being either the capture of all the opposing men or blocking them so that they cannot move. The game has many variations, and many names, including ninepenny morris; fivepenny morris, for a version played with five men; and merils, marls, marrels, morals, morris and miracles, all for a version played with three men.

Pall-Mall. Two London thoroughfares, Pall Mall and the Mall, are reminders that Pall-Mall was once popular. Often described as a forerunner of Croquet, it was really more like a form of Golf, a game that arrived at about the same time, both having a common, if remote, ancestor in the Roman game, Paganica. In Paganica players walked across fields hitting a small, leather ball at trees with a curved stick, the object being to reach the target in the fewest possible strokes. It was played by country people, whereas pall-mall, which achieved rapid popularity in the seventeenth century, was a game for the nobility, though other people played simplified versions of it. Pall-Mall was played in special alleys, sometimes ⅓ mile long, and often surrounded by walls. A boxwood ball a foot in circumference had to be played down the alley, in which were a number of iron arches, in the fewest possible strokes. The player drove off as in golf, but, on reaching the arches, not only changed his club, but also substituted a small steel ball for the boxwood one.

Quoits. Dating back to the fifteenth century, Quoits is one of those ancient games that had the distinction of being banned because its popularity was such that it was believed to be keeping people from archery practice. The ban was not effective, and it continues to this day, though it is now less played than it used to be, Scotland, the North of England and Suffolk being, perhaps, the last main strongholds. The pitch consists of two circles or squares of clay, 18 yards apart, and each having in its centre an iron pin, called the " hub," 1 inch of which remains above the surface. The quoits are iron rings with a diameter that must not exceed 8¾ inches. The weight is not fixed, but is often 3 lb. or more. The object of the game, which can be either " singles " or " doubles," is to throw the quoit over or near the hub from the opposite point, 18 yards away, one point being scored for each quoit nearer the hub than the opponent's quoits, and two being awarded for a quoit that drops over the hub, called a " ringer." No points are awarded if opposing quoits are the same distance from the hub, and none are awarded if each side has a ringer. A game is 11 points in " singles," and 15 points in " doubles." Quoits developed from pitching actual horseshoes, and, to this day, some players make their first practice attempts at it with horseshoes.

Shove-Ha'penny. Shove-ha'penny, an old English game that is still popular, uses a cushioned wood or slate board, divided by parallel lines across it into nine " beds." The " halfpennies " may be actual halfpennies, but are generally round metal discs. The object of the game is to shove the halfpennies into one of the nine beds, the shoving usually being done with the ball of the thumb, though any part of the hand may be used. First turn is decided by shoving halfpennies at the number nine bed, the best attempt winning. A turn consists of five halfpennies, and the winner is the first player to shove three halfpennies into each bed, halfpennies that touch the cushion not counting. Should a player place more than three halfpennies in any bed, his opponent can claim the excess, if he needs them, but cannot win the final point of a game in this way. Push-Penny, a similar game using three coins is played in some parts of the country, mainly in Lincolnshire.

Stoolball. Yet another ancestor of cricket, Stoolball is still a popular girls' game. The wicket is a board a foot square on a pole 4 feet 8 inches high, the bat has a round striking surface, and the ball is rubber. Wickets are 16 yards apart, and eight balls constitute an over.

Orienteering.

A sport long popular in Scandinavia, orienteering as practised in Britain—and it has really caught on—is a combination of walking, cross-country running, and finding one's way about the country by using maps and compasses. Competitively, it is usually played eight-a-side, but plenty of fun can be had at the beginning if played in pairs. It is suitable for people of all ages and details may be obtained from the British Orienteering Federation, 2 Stanley Villas, Hoghton, nr. Preston, Lancashire.

Pall-Mall. *See* Old English Games and Customs.

Parachute Jumping.

Parachute jumping is generally regarded as a last-resort safety measure, to be undertaken only in a supreme emergency, and with considerable anxiety; but it is now also a recreation and a competitive sport, practised entirely voluntarily, and for enjoyment. This form of jumping may be said to have grown out of the Second World War, in which jumping was used to a far greater extent than ever before, and not only for escape in an emergency. Now, international competitions take place, and the sport has an enthusiastic following in Britain.

Parachute jumping as a sport involves jumps of particular kinds, including landings in a certain area, marked by a circle, and demonstrating turns and body control in the air, the parachutist regulating his direction by pulling down the lines of the parachute. Jumps of this kind may be made from about 6000 feet.

The first point that occurs to many people when they think about Parachute Jumping is that it is extremely dangerous. However, those who jump as a recreation maintain that this is not so, and that it is about as dangerous as skiing. Injuries are few and slight, and, in three years, none of the hundred-odd members of the British Parachute Club, of Fairoaks, Surrey, suffered anything worse than a sprained ankle. The parachutes used are so reliable that they still work even if they have been badly packed. A parachute consists of twenty-eight sections, called " gores," each divided into four panels, so that, even if a hole should stretch right across one gore, which is rare, the remainder of the parachute remains intact, and will bring the jumper down safely. As an additional precaution, jumpers wear a small reserve parachute on the chest, but this is hardly ever needed.

Training, which generally takes place at weekends, starts with a period of learning how to fall, how to judge wind direction and speed, and how to pack a parachute. The first actual jumps are from 2,000 or 2,500 feet. Both men and women take part in Parachute Jumping.

Parachutists must be licensed by the Civil Aviation Department of the Board of Trade, and they must produce medical certificates of fitness. Third party insurance is also compulsory, but this is automatically covered by membership of the British Parachute Association. Leading centres of Parachute Jumping are at Blackbushe Airfield, Hampshire; Thruxton, Wiltshire; Manchester; and Gleneagles.

Patience.

Patience is a card game for one person, and, though there are few different games for one, there are countless different forms of Patience. There are some using one pack, and others using two, almost all of them starting with the setting out of the cards on the table according to fixed rules, and having as their object the building up of the four suits on their aces.

The game that might almost be called the basic form of single-pack patience starts with a row of seven cards, only the left-hand one being exposed. Underneath this, and overlapping it, comes a row of six cards with the left-hand one exposed, and so on down to a " row " consisting of only a single exposed card, the exposed cards being left uncovered in each decreasing row. The object is to take out first the aces, and then the cards from two up to king, building each suit on its ace. From the " lay out," exposed cards can be moved when it is possible to put one on a card one pip higher in value of the opposite colour, when any card left uncovered by an exposed card can itself be exposed. The undealt cards can be played three at a time, the top one of each three being " playable," with the one underneath becoming " playable," if the top one is, in fact, played. The undealt cards can be played through three at a time in this manner as often as desired. A slight variation of this game allows the undealt cards to be played through one at a time, but this can be done only once.

Another single-pack game starts with a row of nine exposed cards, with, below it and overlapping, a row of eight, and so on down to one, all the cards being exposed, and the right-hand one being left uncovered in each decreasing row. The remaining seven cards form a separate row at the bottom. The object and the " move " are the same as in the previous game, only one card being moved at a time, and any card being eligible to fill any vacancy that might occur in the top row. Cards in the separate row can be played as required, but, once in the " lay out," they must remain there. This game is called King of the Belgians, and the last seven cards are referred to as the Belgian Reserve.

One to Six is a two-pack game. The player deals out a row of four cards, then discards two to a rubbish heap, and carries on like this until all the cards have been used. If, however, while doing it, he comes across any aces or kings, he takes them out, up to one of each from each suit, subsequently also taking out any that will fit on to these, building up from the aces and down from the kings. Then he goes through the rubbish heap, extracting any cards that will fit on the eight piles. The dealt-out cards, with the rubbish-heap cards, are then dealt again in the same way, the object being to complete the eight built-up suits in three rounds of dealing.

Polo.

Polo, one of the oldest of all games, originated in Persia, then spread in one form or another to China, Japan, and India, eventually being brought from India to England by cavalry officers in the second half of the nineteenth century. Later, it was enthusiastically taken up in the United States and Argentina. Played four-a-side and, mounted, on a pitch that should measure 300 yards by 160 yards, its object is to score goals by hitting a 5-ounce ball through goals 24 feet wide with a

stick consisting of a long cane fixed at a slight angle into a wooden or bambo striking head. The game is divided into periods, called " chukkas," the number of periods varying slightly, as may be agreed for particular games.

Formerly, Polo was a game for the wealthy, for it entailed owning and maintaining a string of trained ponies. In recent years, however, certain stables and riding schools have provided facilities for playing and practising Polo, and these facilities include the hiring out of ponies. This apparently simple and obvious step is actually quite a revolutionary innovation that has brought Polo within the reach of almost anyone who wants to play, and thereby increased the popularity of an ancient and exciting game that might otherwise have died out because of the expense involved.

Pony Trekking.

Pony Trekking as an organised recreation originated in Scotland in 1953, though something similar was known in India before that. The word *trekking* itself is Afrikaans. Chance and coincidence played a part in starting Pony Trekking, at least on a larger scale than might otherwise have been the case. The first trek was at Newtonmore, Inverness-shire, and was partly organised by officials of the Scottish Council of Physical Recreation. At about the same time, at Aberfoyle, Perthshire, *Rob Roy* was being filmed, and many townspeople who came to watch expressed great interest in the horses. This led to the planning of a trek in that area, the organisers of which knew nothing of the Newtonmore venture, though they subsequently heard of it, and received advice from its organisers. The first trek from this second centre took place in 1954. Now, there are about 70 approved centres, mainly in Scotland, Wales, the West Country, and the Lake District, though there are also some in Ireland and on the Continent. " Approved," incidentally, means that they are inspected every year by the Scottish Council of Physical Recreation or the Ponies of Britain Club and hold Certificates of Approval from one or other of those bodies.

Pony trekking consists of riding over the hills and moors, through forests and along ancient tracks at a walking pace: for, if you ride faster than that, you cease to trek and begin to hack (*see* riding). No experience whatever is needed, and the complete novice or child who has never ridden at all can enjoy pony trekking from the start. During the first two days of a trekking holiday, beginners will be given some elementary instruction in saddling, mounting, and starting and stopping the horse; and then they will start with short treks of from five to ten miles.

There are two forms of pony trekking, day trekking and post trekking. Most treks are day treks, consisting of circular, all-day tours starting and finishing at the centre. Post treks last for several days, and include stopping at a different post or centre each night. There are comparatively few post treks, partly because they are only suitable for experienced trekkers and partly because of the difficulty of obtaining accommodation for one night only during the height of the holiday season.

The pony trekking season is mainly from May until September, though some centres are open from March until December, and there is the occasional one that is open all the year round, weather permitting. Details of approved centres, including those especially suitable for children, can be obtained from the Scottish Council of Physical Recreation, 4 Queensferry Street, Edinburgh, 2, the Scottish Tourist Board, 2 Rutland Place, West End, Edinburgh, 1; or the Ponies of Britain Club, Brookside Farm, Ascot, Berks.

Potholing.

Potholing might almost be described as mountaineering in reverse, for it consists in the exploration of underground passages, maybe to depths of several hundred feet. Besides being a challenging recreation, it offers opportunities for specialisation, e.g., diving, photography, surveying, and can yield useful information in connection with water supplies, water pollution and hydroelectric schemes.

The main potholing centres in Great Britain are in Yorkshire, Derbyshire, the Mendips, and South Wales, regions where rainwater, carrying dissolved carbon dioxide from the air, has attacked the massive limestone rocks and the drainage has passed underground. The nature of the passages varies with the geological area. A system containing many horizontal passages is known as a "cave", one with appreciable vertical drops as a "pothole". Drops or "pitches" are comparable to waterfalls in a surface stream and often carry an active stream themselves. A pitch may be over 200 ft. deep, and the system may reach a total depth of 600 ft. or extend for several miles. Potholers make their descents by means of flexible ladders constructed from steel wire and aluminium alloy. Recent developments include the adaptation of skin-diving techniques and equipment to enable the more arduous passages to be explored.

The underground world is far more varied than one would expect. The potholer's headlamp picks out beautiful shapes formed by dripping water containing dissolved limestone—stalactites hanging like icicles, stalagmites growing from the cave floor, curtain-like forms hanging in petrified folds, and smooth pebbles (known as cave pearls) in pure white, orange, green, and black, according to the metallic impurities.

The beginner is strongly urged to join a club, which organises trips and training and provides the proper equipment. Potholing could be dangerous to the novice exploring alone, but as a club member he (she) has the opportunity of taking part in an exciting and exhilarating sport, one of the few left that gives the thrill of original exploration.

Public School Football.

All the forms of football popular to-day grew out of the games played at various English Public Schools a century and more ago. These games differed widely, the rules often depending on purely local considerations imposed by the available space. The Rugby game (q.v.) in its modern form is, of course, still played, both at that school and far beyond it; and other games that still survive at the schools that originated them are the Eton Field Game, the Eton Wall Game, the Harrow Base Game, and Winchester College Football.

Punting.

Punting consists of propelling a long, narrow, flat-bottomed boat with a pole, the punter standing up; and it can be either a pleasant, leisurely recreation or a fairly strenuous competitive sport. The sporting side is governed by the Thames Punting Club, which has headquarters on the Thames at Staines in Middlesex. Women, as well as men, take part in competitive events.

Punting as a sport has the unique distinction of being confined, not only to one country, Britain, but to one river, the Thames; though in some parts of the world boats poled from a standing position are used for various purposes. There have been rumours that Japan has, or had, a similar sport, but these have never been authenticated.

Quoits. See Old English Games and Customs.

Race Walking. See Athletics, Walking.

Rackets.

Rackets is a fast, racket-and-ball game, played on a court measuring 62 feet by 31 feet, and using walls. A game consists of 15 points, unless 13-all is reached, when the non-server can set the game to 3 or 5, or 14-all is reached, when the non-server can set the game to 3, the game going to the first player to score the prescribed number of points.

Only the server scores, the receiver taking over service when he makes a winning shot. When served, the ball must strike the front wall above a line called the "cut" line before striking any other part of the court, but, in play, it may be played either on the volley or after one bounce. If a player impedes his opponent, it is a "let," and the point is re-started.

Real Tennis.

Tennis, sometimes called "Real," "Royal," or "Court" Tennis, is a court game played with rackets and balls that has been called the King of Games, and that was once certainly the game of kings. Henry VIII played at Hampton Court where there is still a fine court and a club; but the first kings to play were of France, where the game originated.

It is a complicated game, and no description could give anyone who had never seen it an accurate idea of what it is like. Most racket-and-ball games use either a net, over which the ball is hit, or walls, against which it is hit, but tennis uses both. Also, in most racket games, players change ends after so many games, but, in tennis, they may do so during a game. Matches are in games and sets, a player winning six games completing a set towards the two out of three or three out of five that will make the match.

There are not many tennis players in the country—there are only about a dozen courts—and very few women have ever played. People who do play, however, most of whom play other games as well, are almost unanimous in voting it the best of all games.

It is said that the term "love," used in so many games to indicate "nought," comes from tennis, the original French term being "l'œuf," which, in that language, actually means "egg": an egg being, of course, something like the figure used for "nought." This derivation is not sufficiently well documented to be accepted as definite fact; but it is interesting to note that, in cricket (q.v.) the term used for a score of "nought" is a "duck," or, in full, a "duck's egg."

Revolver Shooting. See Rifle Shooting.

Riding and Show-jumping.

The almost complete disappearance of the horse from everyday life has been followed by an increase of interest in riding as a recreation. This is at least partly due to the great attention paid in recent years by both Press and television to one particular branch of horsemanship, show-jumping. Before learning to jump, however, it is necessary to learn to ride, and many people never go, and have no wish to go, beyond the ordinary unspectacular riding for pleasure that is called "hacking."

A great deal has been said and written about "correct" riding style, but, in actual fact, there are many different styles. The cavalryman, for instance, bends the leg to some extent; the Red Indian bends it to a much greater extent, more or less in the style that has been adopted by American jockeys; and the cowboy rides with an absolutely straight leg. Yet all these are expert horsemen. To assist in acquiring the normal English style, which is very close to that of the cavalryman, there is an old jingle that is now much less heard than it used to be, but is probably none the less helpful or accurate for that. It runs: "Your head and your heart keep up. Your hands and your heels keep down. Your knees keep close to your horse's sides, and your elbows close to your own." Old or not, anyone who learns it, and then builds up a certain amount of experience of putting it into actual practice is well on the way to becoming a rider.

Those who feel they would like to combine their riding with something competitive might start with gymkhanas, which are sports meetings that generally include mounted equivalents of such novelty events as obstacle races and needle-threading races. For the more ambitious, gymkhanas could even be the first step towards the top-class competitive sport of show-jumping.

Show-jumping. A show-jumping contest is a mounted competition over a circuit of jumps, which the entrants attempt one at a time, each having the field to himself or herself, and being free to concentrate entirely on the jumps, without having to worry about other riders. The jumps, which have to be taken in a certain order, are of many kinds, including fences, double fences, walls, and water. Scoring is by points against, called "faults," so many being debited against an entrant for falling, knocking down an obstacle or displacing part of it, refusing, and other mistakes. Though the event is in no sense a race, there is normally a time limit that must not be exceeded, and, in some events, bonus points are awarded for fast rounds. Show-jumping is not restricted to riders who own their own horses, for some owners do not want to compete themselves, and are only too pleased to let good horsemen take their jumpers round for them. Incidentally, inexperienced riders taking up jumping for the first time will probably find it advisable to make some slight changes in their method of sitting in the saddle. Jumping needs a firm seat, and the novice rider may find it necessary to shorten the stirrups a little.

Allied to show-jumping, and coupled with it in the difficult three-day competitions, is dressage. This is simply a mounted display revealing that the horse is obedient, balanced, supple, and, in a word, trained; and is a simplified form of the better-known "haute école," or highly-schooled riding. Good riders who seek absolute perfection can, if they are willing to pay for it, take an intensive course of haute école riding and all forms of horsemanship at the most famous of all riding schools, the Spanish Riding School in Vienna. Courses, which are conducted in German, consist of eight hours training a day for six months, and informality is not encouraged, the regulation dress for students being a bowler hat, black jacket, and white breeches. Riders who fall are immediately assisted by an attendant armed, not with a stretcher, but with a clothes brush. *See also* pony trekking.

Rifle Shooting.

Considered as a sport, rifle shooting, which might almost be called the modern equivalent of archery, had its origins in virtually the same conditions and circumstances that had popularised the older weapon five hundred years previously; though, unlike archery, it did not enjoy legislation aimed at abolishing other recreations in its favour. Both were encouraged because, in their respective periods, efficiency at them meant, not only success in competitions, but also the most effective defence in time of war, the great period of the rifle's encouragement for this reason being the latter half of the nineteenth century. Archery as a sport survives to the present day, and rifle shooting as a sport continues, though it can no longer be regarded as the most effective weapon.

With a normal rifle, with a calibre of about ·300 inch, competitive shooting is at ranges from 200 yards to 1000 yards, and there are many competitions, the greatest of them being the annual contest at Bisley, Surrey, for the Queen's Prize. Almost equally popular, however, is smallbore shooting, with a calibre of ·22 inch, and this, too, offers many annual competitions.

Revolver Shooting. Revolver shooting, often called pistol shooting, is also a competitive sport, and a very difficult one. Impressions gained from cinema and television screens might lead anyone who has never fired one to think that the revolver is an easy weapon to fire without fuss and with devastating effect. It is the very reverse of this. It is fired, not from the hip, but with the extended arm raised, which is how, in real life, it was generally fired in the old West. It is extremely difficult to hit even a man-size target at 10 yards, and very few people can call themselves good revolver shots, just as few of the old Westerners were good revolver shots. The difficulty is caused by the tremendous "kick" of a weapon that is held, not by both hands and pressed into the shoulder, as a rifle is, but by one hand. Revolvers have sights, but the normal method of aiming is by using the "instinctive pointing sense," which is based on the fact that, if you point at an object in the ordinary way, you do, in fact, point accurately. This applies when pointing a revolver. As with rifles, small-bore target shooting, in which sights are used, is popular.

Rink Hockey. *See* Skating.

Rock Climbing. *See* Mountaineering.

Roller Skating. *See* Skating.

Rowing.

Rowing, meaning simply taking a boat out on the sea or a river for a short period, is a pleasant recreation and a healthy exercise, but competitive rowing is one of the most strenuous of all sports.

A racing oarsman either rows, which means that he uses one oar, or sculls, which means two oars. Races are of various kinds, the best-known being for crews of eight oarsmen with a cox. Then there are races for crews of four with cox, and for crews of four without cox. There are also events for pairs with cox, pairs without cox, double sculls, and single sculls. Eights, fours, and pairs row, while double and single scullers, of course, scull. In fours and pairs without cox, and in all sculling, the oarsmen steer themselves.

Race Rowing is mainly a river sport, but there are races on the sea. For these, crews are usually fours with cox, and they use heavier boats than the normal racing "shell." (*See also* Boat Races.)

Rugby Fives. *See* Fives.

Rugby Football.

As its name implies, Rugby football is based on the game played at Rugby School in the days when football was not organised and various schools played to their own rules. The story of how the Rugby game originated is well known and widely accepted, but it is definitely not accurate and possibly almost entirely apocryphal.

The story is that, in 1823, a boy named William Webb Ellis disregarded the rules of that time by handling the ball, and that handling was subsequently made legal. In fact, handling the ball by catching it was allowed at Rugby before 1823, so, if Ellis was responsible for an innovation, it was not by handling the ball, but by running with it after catching it. Running with the ball certainly became, and remains, the leading feature of Rugby football; but the story that Ellis was responsible, though commemorated by a plaque at the school, was first heard years after Ellis's death, and he never knew of the fame that became his. He was definitely at Rugby at the time, though, and, a few years later, he played in the first-ever Oxford and Cambridge cricket match.

The spread of the game beyond the school that originated it has led to, not one, but two games of Rugby football, Rugby Union and Rugby League. About twenty-five years after the game had become organised, with the Rugby Union as its governing body, there was a dispute on the question of legalising payment for time lost from work by players. The Union would not agree to this, so twenty-two clubs, mainly in Yorkshire, seceded and formed the Northern Union, now the Rugby League. Both bodies originally played the same game, but now, after over sixty years of independent existence, during which each has made various rule changes, there are some important differences.

Rugby was originally played twenty-a-side, but it is now fifteen-a-side in R.U. and thirteen-a-side in R.L., the positions being seven backs and eight forwards in R.U. and seven backs and six forwards in R.L. Played on a pitch marked out as in the diagram, and with an oval ball. Rugby is mainly a handling game, the chief object being the grounding of the ball behind the opponents' goal-line. This is a "try," which counts three points, and entitles the scoring side to an attempt to score a goal by kicking the ball over the crossbar from a point measured in a straight line from where the ball was grounded. Other forms of goal are penalties, which may be awarded anywhere, dropped goals during play, and goals from a "mark," after a player has signalled a "fair catch" of the ball during play by shouting, "Mark." In R.U. goals following tries, called "conversions," count two, and other goals three. In R.L. any goal counts two, but goals from a "mark" are not allowed.

The game is started, and restarted after a score by a kick-off from the centre; and, thereafter, the ball may be advanced by kicking or carrying. It may also be passed from hand, but not forward. Ball carriers may be tackled and thrown down, and they may "hand off" tacklers

though there is a top layer of clubs using part-time professionals.

Sailing.

Mention of sailing tends, perhaps, to conjure up visions of large, graceful yachts, beautiful to see, but clearly to be owned only by the wealthy. Sailing to-day, though, is very different from that. It is mainly sailing in small boats, many of them wholly or partly built by their owners. At first glance the building of a boat might seem a tremendous and highly skilled task, but, in actual fact, it can be as big and as hard or as small and as easy as the builder wishes. Some amateur builders start from the very beginning, acquiring the various materials needed bit by bit, and gradually bringing their boats into being. However, those who either lack the time for this or

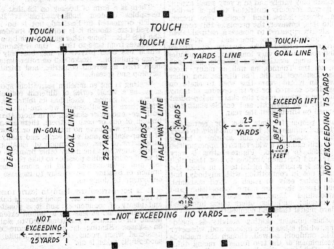

NOTES:—
    ■ Indicates Post with Flag.   Length and breadth of field to be as near to dimensions indicated as possible.
    – – – These broken lines indicate 10 yards and 5 yards from half-way and touch lines respectively.
    Goal dimensions.—10 feet is taken from the ground to the top edge of the crossbar and 18 feet 6 inches from inside to inside of the goal posts.

with the unclenched hand. A frequent method of restarting after a stoppage is the "scrummage," in which the forwards bend down and push against each other, three from each side constituting a front row, and the remainder two subsequent rows. The ball is then put into the tunnel between the front rows, the centre man of each, the "hooker," endeavouring to gain possession by hooking it back into, and generally right through, his "scrum." In R.L. this method of restarting is used whenever the ball goes out over the touch-line; but in R.U. the ball is thrown in straight along a "line out" of both sets of forwards, unless the side whose throw it is demand a scrummage. In R.L. kicking the ball straight out over the touch-line is allowed only from a free-kick, the penalty being a scrummage at the point from which the ball was kicked. The effect of the differences between the two games is that R.L. is faster and more open, and the ball is more continuously in play. A game lasts for eighty minutes, divided into two halves.

In addition to Britain, both forms of Rugby are played in France, New Zealand, and Australia, and R.U. is played in South Africa. Both codes also have other, smaller "outposts" in various European countries, and there are minor R.U. centres in North and South America. R.U. is entirely an amateur game, and R.L. primarily so,

doubt their ability to construct a boat in which they would feel safe on the water can buy complete boat-building kits; and they can buy them at any stage of construction they choose from hardly started to complete except for a coat of paint. It is more economical to build a boat than to buy one complete and ready for launching, and the earlier the stage of construction at which the owner takes over, the greater the saving. Some owners claim that they enjoy the building as much as the sailing, and it is probably true that the owner who has done some work on his boat, however little, takes more interest and pride in the finished article.

The fact that boat-building is now within the reach of practically everyone means, of course, that the end to which it is a means, Sailing, is also within the reach of practically everyone, for few people are far from some suitable stretch of water. Where there is sailing, there are clubs, which the boat owner can join for quite reasonable fees, and which provide either sheltered moorings or "dinghy parks" where the boat can be kept.

Intending boat-owners or builders should visit London's annual Boat Show or the Dinghy Exhibition at Crystal Palace National Sports Centre. For training, young people should get in touch with the Sail Training Association, while for over-

17's we now have the National Sailing Centre at Cowes, run by the R.Y.A. and the C.C.P.R.

Eventually, the small-boat owner may want to try racing his craft, and there are many events for boats of all classes and sizes.

Sculling. *See* Rowing.

Shove-Ha'penny. *See* Old English Games and Customs.

Show-Jumping. *See* Riding and Show-Jumping.

Skating.

At first glance, ice-skating would not appear to be a normal activity for British people, for it is a part of *winter sports* (*q.v.*), which are possible in Britain only rarely and to a very small extent, and it was formerly restricted to brief periods when rivers, lakes, and ponds were frozen. Despite this, however, the people of this country have always appeared to possess a natural talent for it, and they have practised it whenever opportunity offered. The history of British skating goes back a very long way, and includes occasions when skating was possible, and took place, on the Thames, as well as many, more regular instances in the Fen district and other places. In recent years this wish to skate on ice has been catered for by the opening of many indoor rinks, which make the skater independent of weather and daylight, and enable skating to be carried on throughout the year.

Many people ice-skate just for recreation, health, and amusement, but anyone keen to carry skating a stage farther and acquire a higher level of skill can find a wide range of opportunities from which to choose. Figure-skating is very popular and for those anxious to test their skill at it there is a series of medal tests, in which the skater is not in competition with anybody, but is attempting only to reach a fixed standard. Beyond these, there are many competitions and championships. Dancing on skates also attracts many people; and also offers those interested standard medal tests and competitions.

Another popular skating activity is speed-skating, which takes place indoors and, whenever possible, outdoors as well, though the methods and techniques of the two forms of racing differ widely. Outdoors, the skaters normally race in pairs, though each man is timed, and is actually racing against the whole field. Much of the racing is on long, straight stretches of ice. Indoors, skaters race perhaps four at a time, and are directly opposed to those on the ice with them. These races are on small tracks, a lap sometimes being no more than 130 yards. Standard outdoor distances range from 500 to 10,000 metres, while indoor races go from 440 yards to 2 miles. There are also indoor relays, generally of 3 miles, in which teams of four race on the " Madison " method, relieving each other, not at fixed points, but at will. In addition to competitions and championships, speed-skaters also have their standard medal tests.

Ice, however, is not the only surface on which skating takes place for, following an unusual history roller-skating also maintains a large following. Roller-skating was originally introduced long before the arrival of the indoor ice rinks purely to provide ice-skaters with some kind of substitute when no natural ice was available. It progressed by fits and starts, varying from extraordinary " crazes " when it seemed that everybody was roller-skating, to periods when nobody appeared to be doing so. Eventually, it settled down to a steady existence as a popular recreation in its own right that has in no sense been pushed into the background by the increased facilities for ice-skating. The opportunities it offers are almost identical with those of ice-skating, for they include figure-skating, dancing, and speed-skating, with championships, competitions, and standard medal tests in all branches.

Both forms of skating also offer a team game, and in both it is hockey. Ice-hockey, which is called simply hockey in Canada, where it originated, and the United States, is played six-a-side, with substitutes permitted, and with a rubber disc, called a " puck," instead of a ball. It first began to win popularity in Britain soon after the First World War, and since then has had rather a chequered career, helped forward by the semi-professional players from Canada, who play in the National League teams, and held back by the lack of facilities for British youngsters to practise; for practice sessions mean closing rinks to all the other forms of skating for certain periods. The game should, however, survive, for there is a definite demand for it.

Roller-hockey, generally known as rink-hockey, bears a closer resemblance to its parent game, outdoor field hockey, than does ice-hockey. It is played with a ball, and is five-aside, with one substitute permitted. Its popularity is such that it is now played throughout the year.

There is a form of hockey on ice that closely resembles outdoor hockey. This is Bandy, which originated in England, but is no longer played here, though it is popular in Sweden and the U.S.S.R. Some other games have been tried on skates from time to time. One is Badminton, which has been played on ice, but only as a stage exhibition. Basketball on roller-skates has been tried in several countries, and might well develop and spread.

Skating is not so much a recreation, sport, or game as a whole series of different recreations, sports, and games. Each has its following, and, while there are enthusiasts who are interested in both ice- and roller-skating, or in more than one branch of one or both of them, there are many ice-skaters who have no interest in or knowledge of roller-skating, and vice versa, and many keen supporters of just one branch of skating who hardly know that the many other branches exist. It is, of course, quite possible to take part in both ice- and roller-skating, in more than one branch of Skating, and greatly to increase one's enjoyment by doing so.

It is not particularly hard to learn to skate. It requires strong ankles, a good sense of balance, and plenty of confidence; and it is possible to start practising, at least to a limited extent, at home, for instance, by getting used to standing on skates. Skating is probably more easily mastered when young, but many adults have successfully taken it up.

Ski-ing. *See* Winter Sports.

Ski-Joring. *See* Winter Sports.

Ski-Jumping. *See* Winter Sports.

Skittles.

Skittles has been played in England since the 13th century and came from Germany where it was known as *Kegel*. There are several versions, but all consist in throwing a ball down a level alley at a set of pins.

In English skittles, the ball is a flat-sided object called a *cheese*; in German and Dutch Skittles a round ball is used. Both types of ball weigh at least 10 lb. and sometimes as much as 16 lb. Over the years the number of pins has varied between 3 and 17, but the normal number is 9, hence the alternative name of Ninepins, though in some parts of England 10 are still preferred.

English skittles, using nine pins, is played in an alley about 12 yards long and 3 or 4 yards wide. The pins are set up in diamond formation, and players throw the cheese at them from a distance of 6 or 8 yards, being allowed one step forward during the throw. There are several methods of scoring. In one, the object is to score 31 in as few throws as possible, each pin knocked down counting 1, and any throw in which more than the number still required are knocked down not counting. Another method is to knock down as many pins as possible in a fixed number of throws, the highest total winning. Yet another allows each player three throws in each of a fixed number of turns, scoring being 3 if all nine pins are knocked down in one throw, 2 if in two throws, 1 if in three throws, and 0 if any are still standing after the three throws. Pins must be hit by the cheese direct or by another falling pin. Pins knocked down by rebounds do not count.

The Dutch introduced skittles, as played with a round ball and nine pins, to America in the 18th century. The game rapidly became popular but in 1841 it was made illegal because of the betting on it. However, the law specifically mentioned " nine pins ", so the organisers simply added a tenth, and the game survived. As Bowling, it became very popular in 1952 when a machine was invented for replacing the pins automatically and there are now over 30 million players in the United States.

In 1960 this form of the game reached Britain where it soon became easily the most popular version of skittles, there now being well over half a million players. There is a British Tenpin Bowling Association and a Tenpin Bowling Proprietors' Association of Great Britain. The " bowls," some of them converted cinemas, offer many of the facilities of a social club. Competent instructors are available at them, and there are countless competitions and leagues.

Snooker. *See* Billiards.

Snowshoe Running. *See* Winter Sports.

Softball. *See* Baseball.

Solo Whist.

Solo Whist is a card game for four players, who normally act independently. Play is as at Whist (*q.v.*), but the cards are dealt in threes, the final round being dealt singly, and the dealer exposing his last card to indicate trumps.

Players then " declare " in turn, starting with the player on the dealer's left. The lowest call is " I propose," which entails making eight tricks with a partner, any one of the other players being eligible to " accept " in his turn. The next call is " Solo," which requires five tricks to be made unassisted. Next comes " Misère," in which every trick must be lost, and then comes " Abondance," in which nine tricks must be made. Higher still is " Misère Ouverte," in which every trick must be lost with the player's hand exposed, and highest of all is " Abondance Declarée," in which every trick must be made. Any player may " Pass," and, once a call has been made, later callers must make a higher call or pass.

Though calls are made with trumps already nominated, certain calls may alter the trumps; and, with regard to these, there are several views, all quite widely held, as to the rules that should apply. A player calling Abondance can choose his own trumps, though Abondance in the nominated trumps—called Royal Abondance—takes precedence over the same call in another suit. In Abondance one school of thought holds that the first round is played on the nominated trumps, while another takes the view that the first card only is played on the nominated trumps. In either of these circumstances a player making this call should not announce his trumps until the round or card has been played, unless it is necessary to announce Royal Abondance to overcall. There is, however, a third view, and it is the view of the majority of authorities who have actually written about the game, that the new trumps should be announced before the hand starts. Also the subject of differing views is Abondance Declarée, one view being that the caller can choose his own trumps, and another that, in this call, there are no trumps, though both views agree that this call confers the right to lead. A good

player can easily adapt himself to any of these variations, the important thing being to check which versions are being used before starting to play. On the Misère calls there are no trumps, and in Misère Ouverte the player need not expose his hand until the first round has been played.

Speed-Skating. *See* Skating.

Squash Rackets.

This game is played on the same principle as its forerunner Rackets (*q.v.*) but in a smaller court, with a shorter racket and a rubber ball. It is mainly a singles game, though doubles can be played.

The court has four walls with the rear part divided into two service courts, each having a small " service box " down the court by the side wall. The server must have one foot in the box and serve the ball on to the front wall above the " cut " line (6 ft. in singles) so that it comes back diagonally into the other service court. But it need not land direct, or land at all, but may strike the side wall or back wall or both and be volleyed by the receiver. The object of the game is to score points by striking the ball in such a way that the opponent is unable to return it or make a proper shot. Every shot played in a rally must hit the front wall (directly or via another wall) and must be played on the volley or after one bounce. The service ball must always hit the front wall first. Service proceeds from the two boxes alternately. It is important to note that unlike Lawn Tennis (*q.v.*) services that would be faults become good if taken by the receiver. A game is 9 points but if 8-8 is reached the winner is the next to score 2 consecutive points. Only the server scores points, winning shots by the receiver entitling him to take over the service. Players sometimes accidentally impede each other and when this happens it is a " let," and the point is replayed.

The game enjoys great and increasing popularity. The Central Council of Physical Recreation co-operates with the Squash Rackets Association (the game's governing body) in running courses and there are coaches at many clubs. Though many people play purely for exercise and enjoyment, there are many competitive events, both national and international. Internationally, Squash Rackets is largely dominated by the Egyptians and Pakistanis but a rapid rise in popularity, comparable with that in Britain, has brought Australia very close to the top. The game has developed along slightly different lines in the United States, but with the growth of international competition and the formation of an International Federation the differences from the standard game are likely to disappear.

Stoolball. *See* Old English Games and Customs.

Strand-Pulling. *See* Weight-lifting.

Surf Riding. *See* Swimming.

Swimming.

Swimming is an extremely popular pastime that also shares with walking the distinction of being a perfect exercise for health, as it exercises the whole body, and can be carried out as easily or as strenuously as the swimmer wishes. It is also a very useful accomplishment that may at any time put its possessor in a position to save a life.

There are several different swimming strokes, the basic stroke being the breast-stroke, now often seen in an alternative method, the butterfly. Faster strokes include the side-arm, the overarm, the trudgeon, and the crawl, but each of these attempts to speed up progress through the water has really superseded its predecessor, and the crawl is now almost universal. There are also two strokes used in swimming on the back, one being a back equivalent of the breast-stroke, and the other a back crawl. It is possible to swim under the water, using the breast-stroke, and to keep the eyes open while doing so. It is also possible to swim down through the water to retrieve objects that may have been dropped. Ascending through the water is automatic, though it can be hastened by a kick. Remaining stationary in deep water can be achieved either by floating on the back or by treading water, which simply means moving the legs gently up and down.

It is not difficult to teach oneself to swim, and, like cycling, it is an accomplishment which, once learned, is never forgotten. The main thing is confidence, or an absence of any fear of the water. Such fears are quite unnecessary, for water is an element that always tends to keep a human being on the surface, and not to draw him under. Going underneath the water, and staying underneath, requires a definite physical effort, and, if that effort ceases, the swimmer is automatically brought to the surface again. Many non-swimmers who get into difficulties increase these by struggling wildly, for, by doing so, they may easily take and keep themselves under. If they would make only the gentle movements of treading water, they would both stay afloat much longer and present far fewer problems to any swimmer who might be trying to save them.

Saving life in the water is the object of the Royal Life-Saving Society, which teaches the best methods of bringing people who are in difficulties ashore, and also methods of artificial respiration for use in reviving the apparently drowned. Every swimmer should acquire some knowledge of life-saving, for even a strong swimmer may experience considerable difficulty in saving anyone unless he or she has some idea of the best way of setting about it. Many swimmers, for instance, normally use only the crawl and the back crawl, whereas, to save anyone, it is almost essential to use either the breast-stroke or its back equivalent.

Swimming has a well-organised competitive side, with many competitions and championships right up to the Olympic Games. Most races take place in baths, but there are some river and sea events, and the greatest competitive challenge to any swimmer is, of course, the English Channel. Although this has been conquered many times, the swimming of it remains, and will always remain, a wonderful achievement.

Diving. Generally accepted as being akin to swimming, though actually it is quite a different sport, is diving. Competition diving means using boards of various heights, performing certain set dives, and choosing additional ones from an approved list. Diving requires a certain amount of nerve, and also gymnastic ability, including the ability to control the body in the air. Whereas strong swimmers are generally fairly big, divers are often much smaller and more compactly built.

Water Polo. In view of the popularity of swimming, it is not surprising that there is a water team game, this being water polo, in which the object is the scoring of goals, the ball and the goals resembling those used in soccer, though all shots and passes are, of course, thrown. Throughout a history of nearly eighty years, water polo has been beset by rule trouble, and has probably been the subject of more codes of rules than almost any other game. The difficulty is the detection of fouls under the water; the ideal, a game of the basketball type, free of bodily contact.

Surf Riding. Though straightforward swimming, diving, and water polo are the chief competitive water sports, there are other water activities with large and, in some cases, growing followings, some of them also having their competitive side. Fairly old-established is the Hawaiian sport of surf riding, which has been seen though generally in a rather milder form, in many parts of the world. It consists of placing a flat board on the water, and then lying, or, more rarely, kneeling or standing on it, and being carried ashore on the crest of a wave.

Underwater Swimming. Undoubtedly the fastest growing of all swimming activities is underwater swimming, which is a link between ordinary diving and swimming under water, with the swimmer, depending on his own lungs, able to remain below for only a few seconds, and fully-fledged deep-sea diving, with the diver weighed down with equipment and receiving assistance from the surface. The underwater swimmer receives no surface assistance, but he does use light equipment, consisting of an artificial " lung " and breathing tubes, and also a mask and flippers. This type of swimming developed during the Second World War, in which Naval underwater swimmers, called " frogmen," rendered great services. Frogmen can also render useful services in peacetime, in, for instance, the sometimes necessary searching of rivers and canals; in underwater photography; and in exploring wrecks, and even old, lost cities, now under water. There is also a vast amount of knowledge, excitement, and pleasure to be gained from a " close-up " study of the many fascinating aspects of the underwater world.

It might be thought that the first step towards becoming an underwater expert was to become an expert swimmer, but it is not essential for an underwater swimmer to be a surface swimmer of anything like championship class. There are, of course, dangers, and the newcomer to underwater swimming should not go down too deep until he has had a good deal of practice and gained a certain amount of experience. Preferably, the first descents to any depth should not be undertaken alone, and if the swimmer has gone at all deep he should come up slowly, otherwise he risks getting the " bends," which is caisson disease, and means that reduced air pressure has caused nitrogen bubbles to form in the tissues. There may also be danger from large fish, and underwater swimmers should not venture into undersea caverns without a light. It is always advisable to collect as much local information as possible before diving in a strange area. Though all kinds of equipment, including cameras, harpoons, knives, and torches, can be carried, the beginner will make a better start if he dives without encumbrances. Most of the dangers can be avoided or circumvented with care, and the reward for those who master underwater swimming is a whole new world to explore.

Table Tennis.

Originally simply an amusing parlour game known as " Ping-Pong," table tennis is now a serious, world-wide, competitive sport, with many championships and tournaments, and is played on an organised basis by more than 7½ million people in all the continents.

Resembling a miniature game of lawn tennis (*q.v.*), the net is set on a table 9 feet long by 5 feet wide, and the ball is a very light celluloid one. Players serve series of five balls in turn, both server and receiver scoring. The service has to bounce first on the server's side of the net, and then on the other, and, thereafter, all strokes are " ground " strokes, volleying not being allowed. A game is 21 points, and matches are usually the best two out of three or three out of five games. " Vantage " games are played, as, if the score reaches 20-all, each player serves once in turn until one has a clear lead of two points. Both singles and doubles are played.

The English Table Tennis Association state that from September to May each year over 10,000 individual matches are played each evening in England.

Tennis. *See* Lawn Tennis, Real Tennis.

Tobogganing. *See* Winter Sports.

Traditional Games and Customs.

Traditional and unusual sporting events are plentiful in many parts of the world, but few have a longer tradition behind them than the *calcio* that can still be seen in Florence. It is a version of football, based on an ancient Greek game called episkuros and the old Roman game of harpastum. Played twenty-seven-a-side on a pitch rather smaller than an Association football pitch, it was originally restricted to the nobility, and in 1672 a game was cancelled when it was discovered that the selected teams included players who were only "gentlemen." The ordinary people did play, but the game as played by them was called calcio divisi, and was not regarded as the same thing. The playing of calcio in Livrea faded out in 1739, but was revived in 1898, to stop again in 1902, only to be revived once more in 1930. To-day, there are generally two games a year between teams no longer restricted to the nobility and representing the four quarters of Florence. They are wonderful spectacles, for the players, and also numerous officials and attendants, wear fourteenth-century costume, and the games are preceded by ceremonial processions, and by a special address to the most distinguished person present. The trophy for the games is traditionally a white calf.

Another ancient Italian sporting event that still survives is found in Siena, and consists of horse-racing in the city. It is a wild and fierce form of racing in which virtually anything that might further the cause of victory goes on between the riders. Riding events, many of them of great antiquity, figure prominently in countries in which great horsemanship is an age-old tradition. Russia offers kop-karri, a fifteen-a-side mounted game that is a battle for possession of a sheep's pelt. Riders carry their reins in their teeth to leave their hands free for the fight, and anyone who gets the pelt is soon downed in what is one of the roughest and toughest games of all time. Played now by Kazakhs from the Steppes and Tadjiks from the Afghanistan border, this game originated in China, and was brought out of that country by the riders of the Golden Hordes of Genghis Khan. Also found in Russia is the mounted 'kissing game', in which a galloping male horseman seeks to snatch a kiss from a girl rider armed with a whip.

Horses are also prominent in North American Rodeos, which consist of competitions in cowboy skills, such as riding, roping, steer-wrestling, and chuck-wagon racing, which can still be seen annually in rodeos like the famous Stampede at Calgary in Alberta. Rather different are Chilean rodeos, which consist mainly of displays involving horses and young bulls, and the medea-adura, in which two mounted teams push against a long log suspended horizontally between them. Chilean rodeos carefully avoid anything that might harm the animals, which enter into things with excitement and enjoyment. This also applies to the bull races at Pamekasan in the Indonesian island of Madura. Based on the local method of ploughing, these consist of races in which a driver stands barefooted on a small wooden sled harnessed to a pair of bulls, though these need little driving. In India, elephant racing may be as much as a thousand years old, but it is now being allowed to decline because of its reputed "feudal" associations. Recently, there was a not-very-serious attempt to introduce it into the United States, which is, however, more at home with events like Florida's Swamp Buggy Derby, in which vehicles carrying two hunters and their equipment must cover a figure-eight course of a mile within ten minutes.

Differing widely from these events in everything but speed is pelota, or jai alai. Played in Spain, France, Portugal, North Africa, and South and Central America, pelota is a traditional Basque game that developed from a mediæval form of handball that was played against village church walls. To this day, many pelota courts, called "canchas," are next to churches, the wall, or "fronton," which is an integral part of the game being that of the church, and the priest very often being one of the best of the local players. The game, which is very fast and exhausting, can be between two players or between teams of two or three, and consists of playing a ball that is rather smaller than a tennis ball against a wall with either the hand or, in the case of the most popular form of the game, the Grand Chistera, with a long, narrow, wicker basket, called a "chistera," that is strapped to the player's hand and arm.

Personal combat sports have always been popular, and Switzerland has a national sport of this type that had its first big tournament in 1905 in Das Schwingen, which means "The Swinging." It is a form of wrestling, in which the contestants, normally very powerful Alpine herdsmen, wear special belts and shorts by which holds are taken. The traditional prize for the winner of the annual Swiss championship is a two-year-old heifer. Iceland has a rather similar form of wrestling, called glima. Much less similar is the Siamese form of boxing. Competitors in this wear, and use, ordinary boxing gloves, but they are also allowed to use their elbows, knees, and feet, which are bare.

Next, a group of recreations in which the feet are used less lethally, starting with the Netherlands, and the Nijmegen Marches. Over half a century old, these are international long-distance walks that are not races, but reliability trials, in which complete teams must start and finish together within a certain time. The marches take four days, the distance to be covered each day varying between 25 and 30 miles according to the class. Classes catered for include men, women, and also police teams, walking in uniform, and military teams, carrying equipment. The walks, which attract over 10,000 competitors every July, are an unusual and colourful spectacle, and the opening ceremony is as well worth watching as that of the Olympic Games. British walkers, civilian, police, and military, regularly take part. Though called marches, they are really walks; and it is unlikely that many men would consider real precision marching as a recreation. However, women do in at least one country. This is New Zealand, where marching competitions are held between teams of twelve, with a leader, each team wearing a special uniform, and carrying out a three-minute routine to the music of a pipe band. Points are awarded, not only for the marching, but also for the costumes and the leading. Though the competitions are confined to women, teams are generally trained and drilled by men. This type of marching was seen in Britain a few years ago, when the Blair Atholl team toured the country giving demonstrations.

Non-English recreations that English people do not have to travel very far to see are the many and various activities that go to make up Scotland's Highland Games. Highland Games meetings, or gatherings, are sports meetings, but sports meetings with their own definite and extremely colourful and spectacular characteristics. The chief sporting events at them are the "heavyweight" events, including tossing the caber, throwing the hammer in the Scots style, putting and throwing weights of various sizes, and wrestling. In addition, there are competitions in Highland dancing and piping, and often for pipe bands, all playing their parts in a spectacle that can hold its own with any of the many spectacular events that love of tradition and love of sport have combined to produce all over the world. (*See also* Old English Games and Customs.)

Trampoline. *See* Gymnastics.

Tug-of-War.

A Tug-of-War is one of the least complicated and one of the most strenuous events in sport.

It consists of eight men pulling on a rope against another set of eight pulling in the opposite direction, each team trying to pull the other forward across a line, and each helped by a coach, who instructs them when to " heave " and when to concentrate on resisting the opponents' heaves. A pull may be over in a few seconds, or it may take many minutes. Contests are generally the best two out of three pulls, and a competition may involve three such contests in one afternoon. Competitions may be at " catchweights," which means that there is no weight limit, or they may restrict the eight men to a total weight of, say, 104 stone or 100 stone. The tug-of-war requires, and will help to develop, great strength.

A popular event that always arouses great enthusiasm amongst the spectators, the tug-of-war fully merits this position, but it owes some of its success to the fact that it was introduced into the right place at the right time. In the nineteenth century, before athletic sports were really organised, most country sports meetings included events like obstacle races, sack races, and egg-and-spoon races. These, however, though they are found to this day in some children's and local sports, grew less popular, and began to give place to more " serious " ones, a favourite replacement for them being the tug-of-war. Then athletic sports became organised, and the Amateur Athletic Association was founded, and instituted its famous annual championships, including two Tug-of-war championships that still exist, where, a few years earlier, there might have been obstacle-race and sack-race championships.

For years, service units and police forces provided the leading tug-of-war teams, but, more recently, they have been challenged by teams from big firms. A still later development has been the formation of clubs concentrating entirely on the tug-of-war. Organisations and clubs with tug-of-war teams now have their own association, and their own annual championship meeting.

Underwater Swimming. *See* Swimming.

Underwater Watching.

In recent years there has been a considerable increase of interest in the undersea world; and some participation in this has been brought within the reach of those who are unwilling or unable to take part in underwater swimming and diving by the use of glass-bottomed boats, often boats in which the viewer slides back a wooden panel at his feet to reveal the glass viewing panel. Such boats, of course, can only be of use where the water is exceptionally clear and transparent, but, where conditions are suitable, a surprising amount of the life and colour of the world beneath the seas can be seen, and without any of the strain or danger of diving.

Much of the Mediterranean Sea fulfils the necessary conditions of clarity and transparency, particularly, perhaps, the coasts of Corsica, Sardinia, Sicily, and Italy itself. Greek and Egyptian waters are also clear, as are the waters of the Spanish Costa Brava and the Balearic Islands. Going farther afield, there are very transparent waters off parts of the Australian coast, and, of course, in the West Indies.

Volleyball.

Long-established in the United States, and played also in some other countries, volleyball is a comparatively recent arrival in Britain, where it has been encouraged by leading personalities from the sport of athletics, who saw in it an ideal game for maintaining fitness, and formed a governing body to organise and control it. A league started in London owed much of its early success to players of nationalities other than British, but the game took a big step forward when it was adopted by the London Fire Brigade as an effective method of physical training.

Volleyball might be compared with basketball (*q.v.*) in that it is a team game that can be played indoors, though it can also be played on outdoor courts. The actual game, however, differs widely from basketball. Played six-a-side on a rectangular court that should not exceed 60 feet by 30 feet, it consists of " volleying " an inflated ball across a net 8 feet high with the hands, the object being to make it touch the ground in the opponents' court, while preventing it doing so in your own.

Water Polo. *See* Swimming.

Water Ski-ing.

Water Ski-ing originated in the United States in the early nineteen-twenties and actually descends from surf riding (*q.v.*). Surf riding led to Aquaplaning, in which a board was towed by a motor-boat with the rider standing. A further development saw the board giving place to actual skis and water ski-ing was born. It eventually reached France, and then, in 1950, Britain.

In Britain, it rapidly became popular, partly through television, which demonstrated it when it was still in its infancy. This led directly to several new water ski-ing centres being opened up in various parts of the country. Britain now has over 75,000 water skiers and there are about a hundred clubs, most of them affiliated to the British Water Ski Federation. The Federation, which is second in size only to that of the United States, is in turn affiliated to the World Water Ski Union.

Water ski-ing has been described as the ideal family recreation, for, though, at the highest level, it requires great skill and daring, almost anyone including children, can quite easily acquire sufficient skill to enjoy it as a recreation. The more ambitious can, if they wish, proceed to such variations as monoski-ing, using only one ski; slalom, when the skier, generally on one ski, is towed through a staggered arrangement of buoys; jumping, from a ramp between three and six feet high; and tricks, which vary from the quite simple to the very difficult. There are water ski-ing championships, both national and international; these involve slalom, jumping, and tricks.

The Central Council of Physical Recreation holds water ski-ing courses—most of them on Lake Windermere—and there are also coaches at many clubs. Water ski-ing can be practised in a swimming suit, but many skiers wear special rubber suits, or at least jackets.

Walking.

Walking comes so naturally that few people ever think about it. It is, however, worth thinking about, for it is the basis, not only of everyday life, but also of every physical recreation. It has been said that it is impossible to walk too much; and, while those who have done little walking would, of course, have to increase the distance gradually, there is no doubt that a regular, daily two- or three-mile walk would in itself prove an effective method of maintaining health and fitness.

A great deal of pleasure can be added to walking about the countryside by taking an interest in those things which will help you to understand the history of this island. The countryside is rich in churches, historic buildings, ruins, wayside crosses, prehistoric camps, and dykes. Besides a good pair of shoes you need a pencil, a notebook, a 1-in. Ordnance Survey map, a good guide book, and a fund of optimism, imagination, and curiosity. During your rest intervals you can study the map and plan, and read one or more of the many background books to supplement what you have seen and stimulate you to further adventure. Not only is our countryside full of interest, it is remarkably varied. Among the organisations which provide rambling opportunities are the Ramblers' Association, the Holiday Fellowship, and the Countrywide Holidays Association. *See also* Long-distance Routes, Section L.

Weight-lifting.

Weight-lifting is a method of exercising to maintain health and develop strength; a system of training that can usefully be at least a part of the preparation for almost any sport or game; and a highly organised and very popular competitive sport in its own right. Once, quite erroneously, thought to be an over-strenuous and " dangerous " activity, it has now, in more enlightened days, seen the pendulum swing completely in the opposite direction, with professional and amateur sportsmen of all kinds freely admitting how much they owe to it, and a large following of seekers after health and fitness, including women, many of them actresses, models, and others whose work demands a near-perfect figure.

When it is used as exercise and training, the strenuousness of it depends entirely on the wishes of the lifter or his or her adviser; for training with weights does not mean lifting as heavy a weight as possible, but carrying out a certain number of repetitions in various styles with weights well within the lifter's capacity. For those keen to develop the maximum strength of which, according to their build they are capable, weight-lifting is certainly the quickest, and perhaps the only, way of achieving this. One of the charges levelled against it is that it makes one slow, but this is just another fallacy. It does not; and competitive weight-lifters actually make some of the fastest movements known in sport.

As a competitive sport, Weight-lifting is divided into weight classes, and there are many international and national championships and competitions. The sport is popular almost all over the world, and has been firmly established in Britain for many years.

Strand-Pulling. Akin to weight-lifting in that it is a method of keeping fit and developing strength that is also a competitive sport is Strand-pulling, using a steel or rubber expander. Various different " pulls " are possible, and the strength and resistance of the expander can be altered at will. Many people use this old-established system of exercising for health and strength; and, for those interested, there are many strand-pulling championships and competitions.

Whist.

Whist might be called the standard card game. It has never excited quite the furore of Bridge (*q.v.*), but it is long established and popular, both at home and at Whist Drives. It is probably the first card game, apart, perhaps, from a few simple games depending on luck, that most people learn, and it provides a sound foundation for the embryo card player.

It is played by four people, two partnerships of two opposing each other, and with a normal pack of cards. The partners sit opposite each other; and the pack is shuffled, cut for trumps, and dealt out singly. The cards are then played out in thirteen tricks of four each, the player on the dealer's left having first lead, and the winner of each trick leading in the next. Ace counts as the highest card—except in cutting, when it counts as the lowest—and it is followed by king, queen, knave, and then on from ten downwards. The higher card of any suit takes the lower, unless it is trumped by a player unable to follow suit, the tricks being gathered up by the winner as made.

It is necessary to concentrate, to watch the cards played, and to endeavour to " place " the unplayed cards. This comes with experience, as does an understanding of such unwritten rules as " Second in hand plays low " and " Third in hand plays high," and a knowledge of when to disregard these.

Three-handed Whist is possible, one suit being discarded.

Winter Sports.

There are few fields of recreational or sporting activity to which, given the opportunity, British people take more eagerly than Winter Sports. Enthusiasts from Britain were going abroad to find, and in some cases start, them before the turn of the century; and to-day there are probably a hundred travellers for every one who went sixty years ago.

Switzerland is, of course, the traditional objective, but there is actually a wide choice, for facilities exist in Norway, Austria, Italy, France, Germany, and Czechoslovakia. There are opportunities to suit most purses, and to suit both those who want sport and those who want sport combined with entertainment. If the object is simply Ski-ing, the most popular of the winter sports, there is really no need to travel further than Scotland, which provides excellent facilities, and is increasing these every year.

For those whose time and experience are both limited, ski-ing is normally of the downhill variety, rather than the lengthy journeys on the level as well as on hills, and up as well as down, at which many Continental, and particularly Scandinavian, skiers are adept. Greatly increased facilities in the way of ski-lifts enable the holiday skier to work in three times as many descents as the skier of only a few years ago. Almost every resort has a ski-school with an English-speaking instructor, and it is always advisable for a novice to join this. It is also advisable for novices to start training for a ski holiday some time in advance, both by ordinary physical training and by attending a dry ski-school. The air in winter sports resorts encourages more activity than is good for a completely untrained person, and the fitter the skier, the less his chance of being injured. Ski-ing accidents are plentiful, but many of them could be avoided by the exercise of a few simple precautions. Having lessons is one; being fit is another; short skis with safety bindings are still another; and refusing to ski late, which may be any time after four o'clock, is yet another, for, as the light fades, it is replaced by a bluish light that makes uneven patches difficult to see, and the snow tends to ice over. Most winter sports equipment can be hired, but hired or bought, and regardless of the extent to which fashionable ski-ing clothing may be advertised, the most important items are the boots. The winter sports season lasts from December until March, but the snow is sometimes late, and, while Christmas and New Year should be safe enough, February offers the certainty of snow, combined with longer days.

Ski-jumping is a separate sport, and one for experts. The jumper takes-off down a steep slope and over a platform, which he leaves at a speed of about 50 m.p.h., to land something like 150 feet below his take-off, and more than that distance out in front of it. Ski-joring is really ski-racing behind unridden horses, but the term is also applied to quite gentle ski-trips behind ridden horses, horse-drawn vehicles, and mechanical vehicles.

The biathlon is a combination of ski-ing over a 20-kilometre course and rifle-shooting. There is a World Championship, and Britain enters for this, but the leading exponents of this sport are the Scandinavians and the Russians. As with the modern pentathlon (*q.v.*), most British competitors are servicemen, but the sport is in no way barred to civilians.

Bobsleigh riding and tobogganing consist of riding and racing down ice runs at terrific speeds on sleighs, the bobsleigh being for two, four, or five riders, and the toboggan, which takes its name, not from anywhere in Europe, but from a Red Indian language, being for one rider. Bobsleigh crews sit, the first man steering by a wheel or ropes, and the last man operating the brake with which the sleigh is fitted. Toboggan riders lie face downwards, and brake through special spikes on their boots. Both sports are exceptionally thrilling, and both can be dangerous.

Even greater speeds, ranging from 50 to 100 m.p.h., and even greater danger, are to be found in ice-yachting. This sport, or something very like it, has actually been known for hundreds of years, but it is now rarely available in Europe because of the lack of frozen lakes large enough for the modern high-speed yachts. In the United States, however, there are over 3,000 such yachts to be seen during the season, which, as with European winter sports, lasts from December until March. One-man ice-yachts normally carry about 75 square feet of sail, but two-man yachts may carry as much as 650 square feet.

At the opposite extreme from the point of view of speed is the 400-year-old Scottish game of curling, which is played on ice, but not on skates. It resembles bowls (q.v.), but the implements used are curling stones weighing about 35 lb., and having handles. Slow, but still-moving stones are encouraged by sweeping the ice in front of them with brooms.

Not a European winter sport, but nevertheless a snow sport in Canada is Snowshoe Running. Like skiing, this is a useful method of travelling about on snow that has been made the subject of races. The Canadian side of the Atlantic is also the home of Snow Snakes, a Red Indian game that consists of throwing a polished wooden stick along an ice trough in the snow. These "snakes" have been known to go for over a mile and to travel at 120 m.p.h. (*See also* Skating.)

Wingfield Sculls. *See* Boat Races.

Wrestling.

Wrestling, an individual combat in which competitors, using only their bare hands, endeavour to throw each other, is one of the most natural sports, and also one of the oldest. It is practised in many countries, and in many different styles, in most of which the wrestlers are divided into classes by weight.

In Britain, probably the most popular style is Catch-As-Catch-Can, in which the wrestlers start apart, and may try to throw their opponents by grasping them with the hands or by various kinds of trip. During the bout, the competitors may be either on their feet or down on the mat, and the rules contain various provisions to prevent the bout lasting for an indefinite time. Wrestlers reaching a deadlock on the mat may be ordered to stand up and start again, and points decisions after a certain time are also possible. Certain dangerous holds are barred.

Another style is Cumberland and Westmorland wrestling, which is extremely popular in those counties, and in Scotland. In this, the wrestler clasps his hands together behind his opponent's back, and all throwing is done by the legs, the breaking of the opponent's clasp constituting the fall. The initial hold is, therefore, of major importance, and the taking of it often takes longer than the actual bout.

A further form of British wrestling is Cornish wrestling, in which the wrestlers wear canvas jackets, by which all holds are taken. A similar form of wrestling is found in Brittany.

In Græco-Roman wrestling, which has always been very popular on the Continent, though less so in Britain, wrestlers start apart, and may take hold only above the waist. Bouts in this style may take a considerable time. At one time, there were many Græco-Roman handicap matches, in which a top-class wrestler undertook to win a fall, or a number of falls, in a fixed time.

Græco-Roman was formerly the style used in professional wrestling, but, in recent years, professionals have used the "Free" or "All-In" style. This has rules, but it is not always very clear just what they are, and this, combined with widespread suspicions that bouts are not really genuine contests, has led to the quite large following that it retains going to see it more as an amusing "stunt" than as a serious sporting event. All this has, of course, done considerable harm to the reputation of what is really a fine sport and a healthy exercise.

Judo. Wrestling has been popular for centuries in Oriental countries such as India, China, and Japan. Of the various styles, one from Japan has won popularity in many countries, including Britain.

This is Judo, which derives from the more elaborate Ju-Jitsu. Governed largely by rituals, and with wrestlers graded according to ability, Judo is now an international competitive sport; but it is still often taken up as an effective method of defence against a stronger or better-armed attacker. Requiring a knowledge of anatomy, it consists partly of defence by knowing how to fall, and partly of attack by locks which give the opponent a choice between capitulation and a broken bone, and by paralysing nerve centres. The various locks are potentially dangerous, and, when practising, should be released immediately the opponent requests this. Also developed in Japan, though it originated in China, is Karate, a combat system so potentially dangerous that, when practised as a sport, attacking moves must only be indicated, and never pressed home. There are also Kendo (two-handed fencing), and Aikido and Karatedo, both systems of fighting without weapons.

Yachting.

The first recorded sailing contest was a race from Greenwich to Gravesend on 1 October 1661, between Charles II, who won, and his brother, the Duke of York. In those days, such contests generally took the form of manœuvring for positions of advantage, rather than straightforward racing, for the Royal Navy also relied on sailing, and every privately owned vessel was a potentially useful naval auxiliary: a fact that emphasises the appropriateness of the right of England's most famous yacht club, the Royal Yacht Squadron, to fly the White Ensign. The club was founded as the Yacht Club in 1815, becoming the Royal Yacht Club in 1817, when the Prince Regent joined, and taking its present name in 1832. In 1851 the club put up for competition a silver cup that has become the most famous trophy in yachting, and one of the most famous in sport. In that year a schooner of the then famous New York pilot-cutter type, called the *America*, sailed across the Atlantic to compete in a 53-mile race round the Isle of Wight for the new cup, capturing the trophy which now bears her name.

None of the many challenges by yachtsmen from Great Britain, Canada, and, latterly, Australia has been successful, though America's *Resolute* was nearly beaten in 1920 by Sir Thomas Lipton's *Shamrock IV*, which won the first two races and was first to cross the line in the third race, only to lose on corrected time. In 1958, when Britain's *Sceptre* raced the *Columbia*, the rule about sailing the Atlantic to make the challenge was waived.

Land and sand yachting, governed in this country by the British Federation of Sand and Land Yacht Clubs, 151 Highbury Road East, Lytham St. Annes, Lancashire, was started on the Belgian beaches in the 16th cent. The fascination of it is "silent speed" at 50 or 60 m.p.h. in a three-wheeled single-sail craft. Firm, wide beaches and aerodromes are ideal for the practice of this sport.

ATHLETICS

1968 OLYMPIC GAMES WINNERS (HELD AT MEXICO CITY).

100 metres, J. Hines, U.S.A., 9·9 sec.
200 metres, T. Smith, U.S.A., 19·8 sec.
400 metres, L. Evans, U.S.A., 43·8 sec.
800 metres, R. Doubell, Australia, 1 min. 44·3 sec.
1500 metres, K. Keino, Kenya, 3 min. 34·9 sec.
5000 metres, M. Gammoudi, Tunisia, 14 min. 5 sec.
10,000 metres, N. Temu, Kenya, 29 min. 27·4 sec.
Marathon, M. Wolde, Ethiopia, 2 hr. 20 min. 26·4 sec.
4 × 100 metres Relay, U.S.A., 38·2 sec.
4 × 400 metres Relay, U.S.A., 2 min. 56·1 sec.
110 metres Hurdles, W. Davenport, U.S.A., 13·3 sec.
400 metres Hurdles, D. Hemery, U.K., 48·1 sec.
3000 metres Steeplechase, A. Biwott, Kenya, 8 min. 51 sec.
20,000 metres Walk, V. Golubnichiy, U.S.S.R., 1 hr. 33 min. 58·4 sec.
50,000 metres Walk, C. Hohne, East Germany, 4 hr. 20 min. 13·6 sec.
High Jump, R. Fosbury, U.S.A., 7 ft. 4¼ in.
Long Jump, R. Beamon, U.S.A., 29 ft. 2½ in.
Triple Jump, V. Saneyev, U.S.S.R., 57 ft. 0¾ in.
Pole Vault, R. Seagren, U.S.A., 17 ft. 8½ in.
Putting the Shot, R. Matson, U.S.A., 67 ft. 4¾ in.
Throwing the Discus, A. Oerter, U.S.A., 212 ft. 6½ in.
Throwing the Javelin, Y. Lusis, U.S.S.R., 295 ft. 7¼ in.
Throwing the Hammer, G. Zsivotzky, Hungary, 240 ft. 8 in.
Decathlon, W. Toomey, U.S.A., 8193 pts.
100 metres (Women), W. Tyus, U.S.A., 11 sec.
200 metres (Women), I. Szewinska, Poland, 22·5 sec.
400 metres (Women), C. Besson, France, 52 sec.
800 metres (Women), M. Manning, U.S.A., 2 min. 0·9 sec.
4 × 100 metres Relay (Women), U.S.A., 42·8 sec.
80 metres Hurdles (Women), M. Caird, Australia, 10·3 sec.
High Jump (Women), M. Rezkova, Czechoslovakia, 5 ft. 11¾ in.
Long Jump (Women), V. Viscopoleanu, Rumania, 22 ft. 4½ in.
Putting the Shot (Women), M. Gummel, East Germany, 64 ft. 4 in.
Throwing the Discus (Women), L. Manoliu, Rumania, 191 ft. 2½ in.
Throwing the Javelin (Women), A Nemeth, Hungary, 198 ft. 0½ in.
Pentathlon (Women), I. Becker, West Germany, 5098 pts.

1969 EUROPEAN CHAMPIONSHIPS WINNERS (HELD AT ATHENS).

Men

100 metres, V. Borzov, U.S.S.R., 10·4 sec.
200 metres, P. Clerc, Switzerland, 20·6 sec.
400 metres, J. Werner, Poland, 45·7 sec.
800 metres, D. Fromm, E. Germany, 1 min. 45·9 sec.
1,500 metres, J. Whetton, Gt. Britain, 3 min. 39·4 sec.
5,000 metres, I. Stewart, Gt. Britain, 13 min. 44·8 sec.
10,000 metres, J. Haase, E. Germany, 28 min. 41·6 sec.
Marathon, R. Hill, Gt. Britain, 2 hr. 16 min. 47·8 sec.
4 × 100 metres Relay, France, 38·8 sec.
4 × 400 metres Relay, France, 3 min. 2·3 sec.
110 metres Hurdles, E. Ottoz, Italy, 13·5 sec.
400 metres Hurdles, V. Shomorokhov, U.S.S.R., 49·7 sec.
3,000 metres Steeplechase, M. Zhelev, Bulgaria, 8 min. 25 sec.
20,000 metres Walk, P. Nihill, Gt. Britain, 1 hr. 30 min. 49 sec.
50,000 metres Walk, C. Hohne, E. Germany, 4 hr. 13 min. 32·8 sec.
High Jump, V. Gavrilov, U.S.S.R., 7 ft. 1½ in.
Long Jump, I. Ter-Ovanesian, U.S.S.R., 26 ft. 9¾ in.
Triple Jump, V. Sanayev, U.S.S.R., 56 ft. 10¾ in.
Pole Vault, W. Nordwig, E. Germany, 17 ft. 4¾ in.
Putting the Shot, D. Hoffman, E. Germany, 66 ft. 0¼ in.
Throwing the Discus, H. Losch, E. Germany, 202 ft. 10 in.
Throwing the Javelin, J. Lusis, U.S.S.R., 300 ft. 3¼ in.
Throwing the Hammer, A. Bondarchuk, U.S.S.R., 245 ft.
Decathlon, J. Kirst, E. Germany, 8,041 pts.

Women

100 metres, P. Vogt, E. Germany, 11·6 sec.
200 metres, P. Vogt, E. Germany, 23·2 sec.
400 metres, N. Duclos, France, 51.7 sec.
800 metres, L. Board, Gt. Britain, 2 min. 1·4 sec.
1,500 metres, J. Jehlickova, Czech., 4 min. 10·7 sec.
4 × 100 metres Relay, E. Germany, 43·6 sec.
4 × 400 metres Relay, Gt. Britain, 3 min. 30·8 sec.
100 metres Hurdles, K. Balzer, E. Germany, 13·3 sec.
High Jump, M. Rezkova, Czech., 6 ft.
Long Jump, M. Sarna, Poland, 21 ft. 3½ in.
Putting the Shot, N. Chizhova, U.S.S.R., 67 ft. 0¼ in.
Throwing the Discus, T. Danilova, U.S.S.R., 194 ft 6 in.
Throwing the Javelin, A. Ranky, Hungary, 196 ft. 0½ in.
Pentathlon, L. Prokop, Austria, 5,030 pts.

1970 BRITISH COMMONWEALTH GAMES WINNERS (HELD AT EDINBURGH).

Men

100 metres, D. Quarrie, Jamaica, 10·2 sec.
200 metres, D. Quarrie, Jamaica, 20·5 sec.
400 metres, C. Asati, Kenya, 45·0 sec.
800 metres, R. Ouko, Kenya, 1 min. 46·8 sec.
1,500 metres, K. Keino, Kenya, 3 min. 36·6 sec.
5,000 metres, I. Stewart, Scotland, 13 min. 22·8 sec.
10,000 metres, J. Stewart, Scotland, 28 min. 11·8 sec.
Marathon, R. Hill, England, 2 hr. 9 min. 28 sec.
4 × 100 metres Relay, Jamaica, 39·4 sec.
4 × 400 metres Relay, Kenya, 3 min. 3·6 sec.
110 metres Hurdles, D. Hemery, England, 13·6 sec.
400 metres Hurdles, J. Sherwood, England, 50·0 sec.
3,000 metres Steeplechase, A. P. Manning, Australia, 8 min. 26·2 sec.
20 miles Walk, N. Freeman Australia, 2 hr. 33 min. 33 sec.
High Jump, L. Peckham, Australia, 7 ft. 0¼ in.
Long Jump, L. Davies, Wales, 26 ft. 5¼ in.
Triple Jump, P. May, Australia, 54 ft. 10 in.
Pole Vault, M. Bull, N. Ireland, 16 ft. 8¾ in.
Putting the Shot, D. Steen, Canada, 63 ft. 0¼ in.
Throwing the Discus, G. Puce, Canada, 193 ft. 7 in.
Throwing the Javelin, D. Travis, England, 260 ft. 9 in.
Throwing the Hammer, H. Payne, England, 222 ft. 5 in.
Decathlon, G. Smith, Australia, 7,492 pts.

Women

100 metres, R. Boyle, Australia, 11·2 sec.
200 metres, R. Boyle, Australia, 22·7 sec.
400 metres, M. Neufville, Jamaica, 51·0 sec.
800 metres, R. Stirling, Scotland, 2 min. 6·2 sec.
1,500 metres, R. Ridley, England, 4 min. 18·8 sec.
4 × 100 metres Relay, Australia, 44·1 sec.
100 metres Hurdles, P. Kilborn, Australia, 13·2 sec.
High Jump, D. Brill, Canada, 5 ft. 10 in.
Long Jump, S. Sherwood, England, 22 ft. 0½ in.
Putting the Shot, M. Peters, N. Ireland, 52 ft. 3 in.
Throwing the Discus, R. Payne, Scotland, 178 ft. 8 in.
Throwing the Javelin, P. Rivers, Australia, 170 ft. 7 in.
Pentathlon, M. Peters, N. Ireland, 5,148 pts.

THE DERBY

	Horse.	Jockey.	Owner.
1947	Pearl Diver	G. Bridgland	Baron G. de Waldner.
1948	My Love	W. Johnstone	The Aga Khan.
1949	Nimbus	E. Elliott	Mrs. M. Glenister.
1950	Galcador	W. Johnstone	M. Boussac.
1951	Arctic Prince	C. Spares	Mr. J. McGrath.
1952	Tulyar	C. Smirke	The Aga Khan.
1953	Pinza	G. Richards	Sir V. Sassoon.
1954	Never Say Die	L. Piggott	Mr. R. S. Clark.
1955	Phil Drake	F. Palmer	Mme. Volterra.
1956	Lavandin	W. Johnstone	M. Wertheimer.
1957	Crepello	L. Piggott	Sir V. Sassoon.
1958	Hard Ridden	C. Smirke	Sir V. Sassoon.

	Horse.	Jockey.	Owner.
1959	Parthia	H. Carr	Sir H. de Trafford.
1960	St. Paddy	L. Piggott	Sir V. Sassoon.
1961	Psidium	R. Poincelet	Mrs. Arpad Plesch.
1962	Larkspur	N. Sellwood	Mr. R. Guest.
1963	Relko	Y. Saint-Martin	M. F. Dupré.
1964	Santa Claus	A. Breasley	Mr. J. Ismay.
1965	Sea Bird II	P. Glennon	M. J. Ternynck.
1966	Charltown	A. Breasley	Lady Z. Wernher.
1967	Royal Palace	G. Moore	Mr. H. Joel.
1968	Sir Ivor	L. Piggott	Mr. R. Guest.
1969	Blakeney	E. Johnson	Mr. A. Budgett
1970	Nijinsky	L. Piggott	Mr. C. W. Engelhard

CRICKET

TEST MATCHES

England v. Australia.
(first played 1876)

Won: England 68. Australia 80. Drawn: 61.

England v. South Africa.
(first played 1888)

Won: England 46. South Africa 18. Drawn: 28.

England v. West Indies.
(first played 1928)

Won: England 20. West Indies 16. Drawn: 22.

England v. New Zealand.
(first played 1929)

Won: England 20. New Zealand 0. Drawn: 22.

England v. India.
(first played 1932)

Won: England 18. India 3. Drawn: 16.

England v. Pakistan.
(first played 1954)

Won: England 8. Pakistan 1. Drawn: 9.

COUNTY CHAMPIONSHIP

1949	Middlesex and Yorkshire.	1964–5	Worcestershire.	1966	Warwickshire.
1950	Surrey and Lancashire.	1966–8	Yorkshire.	1967	Kent.
1951	Warwickshire.	1969	Glamorgan.	1968	Warwickshire.
1952–8	Surrey.	1970	Kent.	1969	Yorkshire.
1959–60	Yorkshire.			1970	Lancashire.
1961	Hampshire.				
1962–3	Yorkshire.		GILLETTE CUP		
		1963–4	Sussex.		JOHN PLAYER LEAGUE
		1965	Yorkshire.	1969–70	Lancashire.

ASSOCIATION FOOTBALL

WORLD CUP WINNERS

1934	Italy.	1954	Western Germany.	1966	England.
1938	Italy.	1958	Brazil.	1970	Brazil.
1950	Uruguay.	1962	Brazil.		

EUROPEAN CHAMPION CLUBS CUP WINNERS

1959	Real Madrid.	1963	Milano.	1967	Glasgow Celtic.
1960	Real Madrid.	1964	Inter-Milan.	1968	Manchester United.
1961	Benfica.	1965	Inter-Milan.	1969	A.C. Milan.
1962	Benfica.	1966	Real Madrid.	1970	Feyenoord.

EUROPEAN NATIONAL CUP HOLDERS CUP WINNERS

1966	Borussia Dortmund.	1968	A.C. Milan.	1970	Manchester City.
1967	Bayern Munich.	1969	Slovan Bratislav.	1971	Chelsea.

F.A. CUP WINNERS

1951	Newcastle United.	1958	Bolton Wanderers.	1965	Liverpool.
1952	Newcastle United.	1959	Nottingham Forest.	1966	Everton.
1953	Blackpool.	1960	Wolverhampton W.	1967	Tottenham Hotspur.
1954	West Bromwich Albion.	1961	Tottenham Hotspur.	1968	West Bromwich Albion.
1955	Newcastle United.	1962	Tottenham Hotspur.	1969	Manchester City.
1956	Manchester City.	1963	Manchester United.	1970	Chelsea.
1957	Aston Villa.	1964	West Ham United.	1971	Arsenal.

SCOTTISH CUP WINNERS

1951	Celtic.	1958	Clyde.	1965	Celtic.
1952	Motherwell.	1959	St. Mirren.	1966	Rangers.
1953	Rangers.	1960	Rangers.	1967	Celtic.
1954	Celtic.	1961	Dunfermline Athletic.	1968	Dunfermline Athletic.
1955	Clyde.	1962	Rangers.	1969	Celtic.
1956	Heart of Midlothian.	1963	Rangers.	1970	Aberdeen.
1957	Falkirk.	1964	Rangers.	1971	Celtic.

OLYMPIC GAMES WINNERS

1908	United Kingdom.	1932	No Competition.	1956	U.S.S.R.
1912	United Kingdom.	1936	Italy.	1960	Yugoslavia.
1920	Belgium.	1948	Sweden.	1964	Hungary.
1924	Uruguay.	1952	Hungary.	1968	Hungary.
1928	Uruguay.				

RUGBY LEAGUE FOOTBALL

R.L. CUP WINNERS

1951	Wigan.	1958	Wigan.	1965	Wigan.
1952	Workington Town.	1959	Wigan.	1966	St. Helens.
1953	Huddersfield.	1960	Wakefield Trinity.	1967	Featherstone Rovers.
1954	Warrington.	1961	St. Helens.	1968	Leeds.
1955	Barrow.	1962	Wakefield Trinity.	1969	Castleford.
1956	St. Helens.	1963	Wakefield Trinity.	1970	Castleford.
1957	Leeds.	1964	Widnes.	1971	Leigh.

ROWING AND SCULLING

THE UNIVERSITY BOAT RACE

		min.	sec.	Lengths			min.	sec.	Lengths
1950	Cambridge	20	15	3½	1961	Cambridge	19	22	4¼
1951	Cambridge	20	50	12	1962	Cambridge	19	46	5
1952	Oxford	20	23	canvas	1963	Oxford	20	47	5
1953	Cambridge	19	54	8	1964	Cambridge	19	18	6½
1954	Oxford	20	23	4½	1965	Oxford	18	7	4
1955	Cambridge	19	10	16	1966	Oxford	19	12	3¾
1956	Cambridge	18	36	1¼	1967	Oxford	18	52	3¼
1957	Cambridge	19	1	2	1968	Cambridge	18	22	3½
1958	Cambridge	18	15	3½	1969	Cambridge	18	4	4
1959	Oxford	18	52	6	1970	Cambridge	20	22	3½
1960	Oxford	18	59	1¼	1971	Cambridge	17	58	10

DOGGETT'S COAT AND BADGE

1955	J. Goulding.	1959	G. Saunders.	1963	D. Allen.	1967	C. Briggs.
1956	C. Williams.	1960	R. Easterling.	1964	F. Walker.	1968	J. Lupton.
1957	K. Collins.	1961	K. Usher.	1965	A. Collins.	1969	L. Grieves.
1958	R. Crouch.	1962	C. Dearsley.	1966	D. Stent.	1970	M. Spencer

1968 OLYMPIC GAMES WINNERS (HELD AT MEXICO CITY)

Single Sculls, J. Wienese, Netherlands.
Double Sculls, U.S.S.R.
Coxwainless Pairs, East Germany.
Coxed Pairs, Italy.
Coxwainless Fours, East Germany.
Coxed Fours, New Zealand.
Eights, West Germany.

SWIMMING

1968 OLYMPIC GAMES WINNERS (HELD AT MEXICO CITY)

100 metres free-style, M. Wenden, Australia, 52·2 sec.
200 metres free-style, M. Wenden, Australia, 1 min. 55·2 sec.
400 metres free-style, M. Burton, U.S.A., 4 min. 9 sec.
1500 metres free-style, M. Burton, U.S.A., 16 min. 38·9 sec.
100 metres back-stroke, R. Matthes, East Germany, 58·7 sec.
200 metres back-stroke, R. Matthes, East Germany, 2 min. 9·6 sec.
100 metres breast-stroke, D. McKenzie, U.S.A., 1 min. 7·7 sec.
200 metres breast-stroke, F. Munoz, Mexico, 2 min. 28·7 sec.
100 metres butterfly, D. Russell, U.S.A., 55·9 sec.
200 metres butterfly, C. Robie, U.S.A., 2 min. 8·7 sec.
200 metres medley, C. Hickcox, U.S.A., 2 min. 12 sec.
400 metres medley, C. Hickcox, U.S.A., 4 min. 48·4 sec.
4 × 100 metres free-style Relay, U.S.A., 3 min. 31·7 sec.
4 × 200 metres free-style Relay, U.S.A., 7 min. 52·3 sec.
4 × 100 metres medley Relay, U.S.A., 3 min. 54·9 sec.
Highboard Diving, K. Dibiasi, Italy.
Springboard Diving, B. Wrightson, U.S.A.
Water Polo, Jugoslavia.
100 metres free-style (Women), J. Henne, U.S.A., 1 min.
200 metres free-style (Women), D. Meyer, U.S.A., 2 min. 10·5 sec.
400 metres free-style (Women), D. Meyer, U.S.A., 4 min. 31·8 sec.
800 metres free-style (Women), D. Meyer, U.S.A., 9 min. 24 sec.
100 metres back-stroke (Women), K. Hall, U.S.A., 1 min. 6·2 sec.
200 metres back-stroke (Women), P. Watson, U.S.A., 2 min. 24·8 sec.
100 metres breast-stroke (Women), D. Bjedov, Jugoslavia, 1 min. 15·8 sec.
200 metres breast-stroke (Women), S. Wichman, U.S.A., 2 min. 44·4 sec.
100 metres butterfly (Women), L. McClements, Australia, 1 min. 5·5 sec.
200 metres butterfly (Women), A. Kok, Netherlands, 2 min. 24·7 sec.
200 metres medley (Women), G. Kolb, U.S.A., 2 min. 24·7 sec.
400 metres medley (Women), G. Kolb, U.S.A., 5 min. 8·5 sec.
4 × 100 metres free-style Relay (Women), U.S.A., 4 min. 3·5 sec.
4 × 100 metres medley Relay (Women), U.S.A., 4 min. 28·3 sec.
Highboard Diving (Women), M. Duchkova, Czechoslovakia.
Springboard Diving (Women), S. Gossick, U.S.A.

CROSS-COUNTRY

THE INTERNATIONAL CHAMPIONSHIP

1948	Belgium.	1954	England.	1960	England.	1966	England.
1949	France.	1955	England.	1961	Belgium.	1967	England.
1950	France.	1956	France.	1962	England.	1968	England.
1951	England.	1957	Belgium.	1963	Belgium.	1969	England.
1952	France.	1958	England.	1964	England.	1970	England.
1953	England.	1959	England.	1965	England.	1971	England.

HOCKEY

OLYMPIC GAMES WINNERS

1920	Great Britain.	1936	India.	1956	India.	1964	India.
1928	India.	1948	India.	1960	Pakistan.	1968	Pakistan.
1932	India.	1952	India.				

GOLF

WORLD CUP

1956	U.S.A.	1959	Australia.	1962	U.S.A.	1965	South Africa.	1968	Canada.
1957	Japan.	1960	U.S.A.	1963	U.S.A.	1966	U.S.A.	1969	U.S.A.
1958	Ireland.	1961	U.S.A.	1964	U.S.A.	1967	U.S.A.	1970	Australia.

BASEBALL

WORLD SERIES WINNERS

1957	Milwaukee Braves.	1962	New York Yankees.	1967	St. Louis Cardinals.
1958	New York Yankees.	1963	Los Angeles Dodgers.	1968	Detroit Tigers.
1959	Los Angeles Dodgers.	1964	St. Louis Cardinals.	1969	New York Mets.
1960	Pittsburgh Pirates.	1965	Los Angeles Dodgers.	1970	Baltimore Orioles.
1961	New York Yankees.	1966	Baltimore Orioles.		

LAWN TENNIS

DAVIS CUP

1949	U.S.A.	1955	Australia.	1961	Australia.	1966	Australia.
1950	Australia.	1956	Australia.	1962	Australia.	1967	Australia.
1951	Australia.	1957	Australia.	1963	U.S.A.	1968	U.S.A.
1952	Australia.	1958	U.S.A.	1964	Australia.	1969	U.S.A.
1953	Australia.	1959	Australia.	1965	Australia.	1970	U.S.A.
1954	U.S.A.	1960	Australia.				

WIMBLEDON CHAMPIONSHIP WINNERS
Men's Singles

1947	J. Kramer (U.S.A.).	1955	T. Trabert (U.S.A.).	1963	C. McKinley (U.S.A.).
1948	R. Falkenburg (U.S.A.).	1956	L. Hoad (Australia).	1964	R. Emerson (Australia).
1949	F. Schroeder (U.S.A.).	1957	L. Hoad (Australia).	1965	R. Emerson (Australia).
1950	B. Patty (U.S.A.).	1958	A. Cooper (Australia).	1966	M. Santana (Spain).
1951	R. Savitt (U.S.A.).	1959	A. Olmedo (Peru).	1967	J. D. Newcombe (Aus.).
1952	F. Sedgman (Australia).	1960	N. Fraser (Australia).	1968	R. Laver (Australia).
1953	V. Seixas (U.S.A.).	1961	R. Laver (Australia).	1969	R. Laver (Australia).
1954	J. Drobny (Egypt).	1962	R. Laver (Australia).	1970	J. D. Newcombe (Aus.).

Women's Singles

1947	M. Osborne (U.S.A.).	1955	L. Brough (U.S.A.).	1963	M. Smith (Australia).
1948	L. Brough (U.S.A.).	1956	S. Fry (U.S.A.).	1964	M. Bueno (Brazil).
1949	L. Brough (U.S.A.).	1957	A. Gibson (U.S.A.).	1965	M. Smith (Australia).
1950	L. Brough (U.S.A.).	1958	A. Gibson (U.S.A.).	1966	B-J. King (U.S.A.).
1951	D. Hart (U.S.A.).	1959	M. Bueno (Brazil).	1967	B-J. King (U.S.A.).
1952	M. Connolly (U.S.A.).	1960	M. Bueno (Brazil).	1968	B-J. King (U.S.A.).
1953	M. Connolly (U.S.A.).	1961	A. Mortimer (Gt. Britain).	1969	A. Jones (G.B.).
1954	M. Connolly (U.S.A.).	1962	J. Susman (U.S.A.).	1970	B. M. Court (Australia).

RIFLE SHOOTING

Queen's/King's Prize Winners

1947	R. Bennett.	1955	L. Fenwick.	1963	K. Pilcher.
1948	P. Pavey.	1956	G. Twine.	1964	A. Harris.
1949	E. Brookes.	1957	J. Love.	1965	J. Allen.
1950	R. Greig.	1958	R. Fulton.	1966	R. Hampton.
1951	G. Boa.	1959	L. Mallabar.	1967	J. Powell.
1952	A. Kinnier-Wilson.	1960	G. Westling.	1968	A. Parks.
1953	N. McCaw.	1961	N. Beckett.	1969	F. Little.
1954	G. Twine.	1962	P. Hall.	1970	G. F. Arnold.

OLYMPIC ATHLETIC RECORDS

100 metres, 9·9 sec., J. Hines (U.S.A.), 1968, Mexico City.

200 metres, 19·8 sec., T. Smith (U.S.A.), 1968, Mexico City.

400 metres, 43·8 sec., L. Evans (U.S.A.), 1968, Mexico City.

800 metres, 1 min. 44·3 sec., R. Doubell (Australia), 1968, Mexico City.

1500 metres, 3 min. 34·9 sec., K. Keino (Kenya), 1968, Mexico City.

5000 metres, 13 min. 39·6 sec., V. Kuts (U.S.S.R.), 1956, Melbourne.

10,000 metres, 28 min. 24·4 sec., W. Mills (U.S.A.), 1964, Tokyo.

Marathon, 2 hr. 12 min. 11·2 sec., A. Bikele (Ethiopia), 1964, Tokyo.

4 × 100 metres Relay, 38·2 sec., U.S.A., 1968, Mexico City.

4 × 400 metres Relay, 2 min. 56·1 sec., U.S.A., 1968, Mexico City.

110 metres Hurdles, 13·3 sec.
W. Davenport (U.S.A.), 1968, Mexico City.
E. Hall (U.S.A.), 1968, Mexico City.

400 metres Hurdles, 48·1 sec., D. Hemery (U.K.), 1968, Mexico City.

3000 metres Steeplechase, 8 min. 30·8 sec., G. Roelants (Belgium), 1964, Tokyo.

20,000 metres Walk, 1 hr. 29 min. 34 sec., K. Matthews (U.K.), 1964, Tokyo.

50,000 metres Walk, 4 hr. 11 min. 12 sec., A. Pamich (Italy), 1964, Tokyo.

High Jump, 7 ft. 4¼ in., R. Fosbury (U.S.A.), 1968, Mexico City.

Long Jump, 29 ft. 2½ in.. R. Beamon (U.S.A.), 1968, Mexico City.

Triple Jump, 57 ft. 0¾ in., V. Saneyev (U.S.S.R.), 1968, Mexico City.

Pole Vault, 17 ft. 8½ in.
R. Seagren (U.S.A.), 1968, Mexico City.
C. Schiprowski (West Germany), 1968, Mexico City.

W. Nordwig (East Germany), 1968, Mexico City.

Putting the Shot, 67 ft. 10¾ in., R. Matson (U.S.A.), 1968, Mexico City.

Throwing the Discus, 212 ft. 6½ in., A. Oerter (U.S.A.), 1968, Mexico City.

Throwing the Javelin, 295 ft. 7¼ in., Y. Lusis (U.S.S.R.), 1968, Mexico City.

Throwing the Hammer, 240 ft. 8 in., G. Zsivotzky (Hungary), 1968, Mexico City.

Decathlon, 8193 pts, W. Toomey (U.S.A.), 1968, Mexico City.

100 metres (Women), 11 sec., W. Tyus (U.S.A.), 1968, Mexico City.

200 metres (Women), 22·5 sec., I. Szewinska (Poland), 1968, Mexico City.

400 metres (Women), 52 sec.
B. Cuthbert (Australia), 1964, Tokyo.
C. Besson (France), 1968, Mexico City.

800 metres (Women), 2 min. 0·9 sec., M. Manning (U.S.A.), 1968, Mexico City.

4 × 100 metres Relay (Women), 42·8 sec., U.S.A., 1968, Mexico City.

80 metres Hurdles (Women), 10·3 sec., M. Caird (Australia), 1968, Mexico City.

High Jump (Women), 6 ft. 2¾ in., I. Balas (Rumania), 1964, Tokyo.

Long Jump (Women), 22 ft. 4½ in., V. Viscopoleanu (Rumania), 1968, Mexico City.

Putting the Shot (Women), 64 ft. 4 in., M. Gummel (East Germany), 1968, Mexico City.

Throwing the Discus (Women), 191 ft. 2½ in., L. Manoliu (Rumania), 1968, Mexico City.

Throwing the Javelin (Women), 204 ft. 8 in., Y. Gorchakova (U.S.S.R.), 1964, Tokyo.

Pentathlon (Women), 5246 pts, I. Press (U.S.S.R.), 1964, Tokyo.

DOMESTIC PETS

Feeding, management, and diseases
of: aquarium fish — cage-birds —
cats — cavies — dogs — ferrets —
gerbils — golden hamsters —
mice — rabbits — rats — tortoises

DOMESTIC PETS

This section attempts to deal not with all the many hundreds of animals that may be kept as pets, but only with those that are best suited to average homes in Great Britain. The maintenance of monkeys, squirrels, bats, mongooses, and snakes, while quite feasible to those with experience and facilities, requires considerable time or resources at their disposal—in some instances—expense. Those who contemplate such exotic pets should consult works of reference, study the methods adopted in zoological gardens, and discuss the matter with experts. Even in the case of the more common animals, the information provided in the following pages is to be regarded only as a beginning, to be supplemented so far as possible by practical experience, discussions with more knowledgeable owners, and the study of more detailed writings.

Certain considerations are basic. Never keep a pet unless you are really interested in it and are prepared to give it due—and regular—care and attention. Don't keep a pet you cannot afford to maintain in health and comfort. Scrupulous attention to cleanliness is essential, and wise feeding is one of the most important factors in avoiding illness and loss of condition.

Since the passing of the Veterinary Surgeons Act of 1948 it is illegal for anyone to practise the diagnosis and treatment of animal diseases unless he or she is: (1) a veterinary surgeon; or (2) a person whose name has been placed on the Supplementary Veterinary Register. (Certain employees of Animal Welfare Societies are specially licensed, but it is intended that in future all animal treatment shall be given by or under the direct supervision of members of the veterinary profession.) Not even a pharmacist may attempt to diagnose or treat an animal. Anyone may, of course, render " first aid," and an owner may—at his or her own risk—apply treatment. It is, of course, a wise precaution to seek veterinary advice for any ailing animal, and the sooner it is sought the more likely it is that good results will follow.

BREEDS AND VARIETIES OF DOGS.

Of recent years, dog breeding and showing have become specialised occupations, which average people cannot be expected to take up without having adequate time or resources at their disposal. Any amateur who wishes to breed for profit from pedigree animals should seek expert advice before attempting to do so.

Dogs which are intended for shows or for pedigree breeding must be registered, in the name of the owner, with the Kennel Club, 1–4 Clarges Street, Piccadilly, London, W.1.

The following are the breeds of dogs recognised by the Kennel Club for the purpose of separate Registration and Stud Book entries:—

SPORTING BREEDS

Hound Group

Afghan Hounds	Dachshunds (Wire-haired)
Basenjis	Dachshunds Miniature (Wire-haired)
Basset Hounds	
Beagles	Deerhounds
Bloodhounds	Elkhounds
Borzois	Finnish Spitz
Dachshunds (Long-haired)	Foxhounds
Dachshunds Miniature (Long-haired)	Greyhounds
	Irish Wolfhounds
Dachshunds (Smooth)	Rhodesian Ridgebacks
Dachshunds Miniature (Smooth)	Salukis
	Whippets

Gun-dog Group.

English Setters	Spaniels (Clumber)
Gordon Setters	Spaniels (Cocker, American)
Irish Setters	
Pointers	Spaniels (Cocker)
German Short-haired Pointers	Spaniels (Field)
	Spaniels (Irish Water)
Retrievers (Curly Coated)	Spaniels (Springer English)
Retrievers (Flat Coated)	Spaniels (Springer Welsh)
Retrievers (Golden)	Spaniels (Sussex)
Retrievers (Labrador)	Weimaraners

Terrier Group.

Airedale Terriers	Kerry Blue Terriers
Australian Terriers	Lakeland Terriers
Bedlington Terriers	Manchester Terriers
Border Terriers	Norfolk Terriers
Bull Terriers	Norwich Terriers
Bull Terriers (Miniature)	Scottish Terriers
	Sealyham Terriers
Cairn Terriers	Skye Terriers
Dandie Dinmont Terriers	Staffordshire Bull Terriers
Fox Terriers (Smooth)	Welsh Terriers
Fox Terriers (Wire)	West Highland White Terriers
Irish Terriers	

NON-SPORTING BREEDS.

Utility Group

Boston Terriers	Schipperkes
Bulldogs	Schnauzers
Chow Chows	Miniature Schnauzers
Dalmations	Shih Tzus
French Bulldogs	Tibetan Apsos
Keeshonds	Tibetan Spaniels
Poodles	Tibetan Terriers

Working Group

Alsatians (German Shepherd Dogs)	Poodles (Standard)
	Poodles (Miniature)
Bearded Collies	Poodles (Toy)
Boston Terriers	Pyrenean Mountain Dogs
Boxers	
Bulldogs	Rottweilers
Bullmastiffs	St. Bernards
Chow Chows	Samoyeds
Collies (Rough)	Schipperkes
Collies (Smooth)	Schnauzers
Dalmatians	Schnauzers (Miniature)
Dobermanns	Shetland Sheepdogs
French Bulldogs	Shih Tzus
Great Danes	Tibetan Apsos
Keeshonds	Tibetan Spaniels
Mastiffs	Tibetan Terriers
Newfoundlands	Welsh Corgis (Cardigan)
Norwegian Buhunds	
Old English Sheep Dogs	Welsh Corgis (Pembroke)

Toy Group.

Chihuahuas (Long-coat)
Chihuahuas (Smooth-coat)
English Toy Terriers (Black and Tan)
Griffons Bruxellois
Italian Greyhounds
Japanese
King Charles Spaniels

Cavalier King Charles Spaniels
Maltese
Miniature Pinschers
Papillons
Pekingese
Pomeranians
Pugs
Yorkshire Terriers

A separate register, called a Breed Register, is kept by the Kennel Club for each of the above breeds or variety of breeds. A separate register is also kept for the following:—

Setters (Crossbred)
Retrievers (Interbred)
Retrievers (Crossbred)

Spaniels (Interbred)
Spaniels (Crossbred)

A dog which is not eligible for entry in any of the above registers may be entered in one of the following registers kept by the Kennel Club:—

Any Other Variety
Interbred Dogs

Crossbred Dogs

The following breeds, among others, are eligible for entry in the " Any Other Variety " register:—

Alaskan Malamut
Australian Kelpie
Bovier Belge de Flanders
Dachbracke
Groenendaels
Hungarian Kavasz
Hungarian Vislas
Husky
Iceland Dog

Japanese Akita
Maremma (Italian Sheepdogs)
Mexican Hairless
Pedengo Ibicenco
Polish Sheepdogs
Soft-coated Wheaten Terriers
Tibetan Mastiff

Any dog will be accepted for registration in the Obedience and Working Trials Record, irrespective of its ancestry, on condition that it competes only in Obedience Tests and/or Working Trials.

Challenge Certificates are issued by the Kennel Club to certain Championship Shows for each breed or variety of a breed of which a separate register is kept. A dog qualifies for the title of Champion when it has won three Challenge Certificates under three different Judges.

In the limited space available it is impossible to describe the special characteristics of the different breeds. The breeds recognised in Great Britain are subject to constant review by the Kennel Club, and it is probable that the number will continue to be added to from time to time.

The dog was probably the first animal to be domesticated in the true sense of the word, and the uses to which he has been put by man are almost legion. Throughout the world dogs are employed to help protect herds and flocks, and indeed the dog trained for shepherding plays an integral part in sheep management. The names Foxhound, Deerhound, and Otterhound all indicate the specific uses to which dogs have been put in the Chase. Greyhounds and Whippets are used in coursing, and work singly or in pairs, rather than in packs. As their names indicate, the various Setters and Pointers are employed to indicate the exact whereabouts of game, and Spaniels also are widely used as gun-dogs. The other uses to which dogs have been put in field sports include hunting over rough and difficult country by small terriers, and going to earth to kill or hold badgers, foxes, and otters. Fox Terriers, Dachshunds, Dandie Dinmonts, and Scottish Terriers are among the types which have been so employed. Dogs have played their part also in entertainment: thus there are performing dogs, notably the Poodle, and racing Whippets and Greyhounds, while in former times various types of fighting, including the baiting of bulls by Bull-dogs, were to be seen. The use of sledge-dogs is well known, while in Belgium and elsewhere dogs were at one time widely used as traction animals. In coaching days, the Dalmatian was a carriage dog, and modern scientists have recently suggested, as a result of experiments, that the position under or behind a coach which a Dalma-

tian automatically takes is determined by heredity! Perhaps the most exacting use to which man has ever put dog was in China, where the Chow-Chow was once maintained as a source of meat and fur! In Portugal, fishermen employ a race of dog to accompany their fleets. The dogs in question (Portuguese Water Dogs) will dive into the sea to retrieve a broken net or an escaped fish, and will even swim from one smack to another to convey messages! In New Guinea native dogs act as scavengers, while in various countries on the Continent of Europe " truffle dogs " are employed to locate the fungi known as truffles, relished as a table delicacy.

For present purposes it is, however, as a pet or companion that we are considering the dog, and it must be agreed that many of the most successful animals for this purpose are cross-breeds or " mongrels." There are many fallacies or unsubstantiated generalisations regarding the relative merits of pure-breds and mongrels. This is in fact an intricate scientific problem, and probably the simplest way of summarising the true position would be to say that, from the point of view of health and temperament, there are good, bad, and indifferent specimens among pure-bred and cross-bred animals. It is true that within a breed (or within a local community of mongrels for that matter) certain weaknesses or undesirable traits may arise from hereditary defects.

It may be noted that the word "dog" is applied to the whole species, although it is used also to denote the male as opposed to the female, for which the correct term is "bitch." Young animals are referred to as "dog puppies" or "bitch puppies" respectively. A male animal employed regularly for breeding is known as a "stud dog," and the corresponding female as a "brood bitch." In hunting circles the Foxhound is referred to as a "hound," and the term dog and bitch are employed only as prefixes to denote the sex.

CHOICE OF DOG.

However attractive the idea of keeping a dog may be, it is unwise and unkind to purchase or to accept one without very careful consideration. Dogs require regular feeding, grooming, and exercise and, if they are to be allowed to show their full capabilities, constant companionship and attention. Nothing is more pathetic than the unwanted dog, which may have been purchased because of a passing whim, and with which no one appears to have the courage to part. If, on the other hand, one is prepared to give all the necessary time and trouble to the proper care of the dog, the reward will be ample.

The size of the choice is important. Many people keep dogs which are far too large for their houses and for their purses. The smaller the dog, the less food, exercise, and house-room will be need, and the many varieties of terrier provide a range from which suitable choices for most households may be made. In any event, a very large dog should not be chosen unless expert advice has been taken about his feeding and other requirements.

Household dogs of six months of age or over must be licensed. Licences may be obtained from any post office (7s. 6d. at present).

MANAGEMENT OF THE DOG.

Accommodation.—Up till comparatively recently most dogs were kennelled down out of doors. This practice has its advantages, but to-day the majority of pet dogs are allowed more or less the run of the house. A warm sleeping-place, such as a box or basket, should be provided, and should contain removable bedding. Newspaper is an excellent non-conductor of heat. It is a very useful material to place at the bottom of a dog's box; and on two or three thicknesses may be placed a rug or blanket on which the animal may lie. It is astonishing the amount of grit and dust a dog can bring into a house on his limbs and the lower part of his body. His bedding will require frequent shaking out and renewal, and paper is easily changed. The box or basket in which the dog lies should be allowed a place free from draughts, and requires airing daily when the dog leaves its bed in the morning. Wood-wool makes excellent bedding in outhouses or where a special structure is provided by way of dog-kennel, but is inclined to be messy about the house, as a dog will draw portions of it about the room as he leaves his bed. If straw is used, it is best stuffed into a sack and made into a kind of mattress. An odd piece of linoleum forms an excellent foundation to the dog's sleeping-box or kennel; it does not strike cold to the skin, is a slow conductor of heat, and has the advantage of being easily kept clean, particularly during illness, when there may be discharges and messes to be frequently cleaned up, until the animal can once more go out of doors.

Exercise.—Every dog should be exercised regularly, but there is no need to over-exercise, and the practice of allowing a dog (other than a large and athletic animal) to run behind a bicycle for mile after mile cannot be too strongly deprecated. Two or three fairly short walks a day are sufficient for a small terrier, always provided that there is a garden in which he can play on fine days and some open space where he can run freely for a short time. While still in the puppyhood stages, a dog should be trained to walk to heel and to beware of traffic. Even so, it is usually safer to put him on a lead in busy thoroughfares. One point which, to the annoyance of the public, many dog-owners fail to realise, is that their animals would show much less tendency to fight if allowed to investigate one another off the lead. A dog naturally feels aggressive if put on the lead immediately a rival hails in sight. There are, of course, certain dogs which attack others at sight; these are a public nuisance, and should never be allowed loose on the streets.

The practice of allowing a dog to take his own exercise is to be deprecated, especially in towns and suburbs. The animal will be tempted to sniff into dustbins, and, if a male, will tend to follow a bitch in season or to take part in the unsavoury " dog parties " which are so often to be seen. Furthermore, such an animal is usually responsible for the disgusting habit of fouling the pavements and gateways. In this connection, it should be emphasised that dogs may quite easily be trained to defecate in the gutter, or on the grass verge, and so avoid contamination of the pavement or carriage-way. In some districts owners are liable to a fine if their dogs foul the pavement

Training.—Patience combined with the gift of putting yourself in the dog's place is the chief requisite for successful education. It is most important to encourage regularity of habit, as an animal will obviously learn very much more quickly if his daily walks, meals, and grooming take place at fairly constant times. A quiet firmness is the ideal method, and a puppy should learn early that a command *is* a command, and must be obeyed. There is no need to shout and make an exhibition of oneself, or to race in circles after a disobedient puppy; if these things are done, the animal will never become so well trained as it otherwise would. Again, it is rather ridiculous to chastise a puppy *after* he has somewhat belatedly decided to come to heel: quite obviously, he will then be liable to think that he has done wrong in actually coming to heel. Whatever happens, it must never be that the dog becomes master; there is no more unbecoming sight than that of a person with a frankly disobedient dog, and if the animal be large and powerful it may prove a menace to its owner and to the public.

Puppies should be house-trained at an early stage. If care and thought are given to the matter, the animal will soon learn not to make messes in the house. However, it is very stupid to forget all about a puppy or dog for many hours, and then, out of sheer vexation, chastise it for having made a mess. If puppies are let out every two hours or so at first, they will soon learn not to make a mess. Encourage them for performing in the right place rather than scold them for doing so in the wrong one. Physical punishment should be administered only where strictly necessary, and then in a sensible fashion. The most effective

method is to grasp the dog or puppy by the skin of its neck and to shake it.

Grooming and Washing.—Whilst short-haired breeds need little or no attention to the coat, bar an occasional brisk rub down with a brush or rough towel (which incidentally puts a pleasant gloss on the smooth-haired breeds), yet with the long-haired breeds grooming should be carried out regularly, and if the habit is made a daily one it will not be forgotten so readily. Nearly all dogs love this procedure, and most dogs will actually ask for their daily groom by jumping on the table or bench on which it is carried out. Steel combs and brushes are sold by many shops, principally corn chandlers, though some store chemists also provide a suitable range of grooming kit for all breeds. There is a curious fetish current among many breeders that dogs should not be washed. There is no reason why, with a few simple precautions, a dog should not be washed whenever it is socially necessary. The first precaution is to use a soap that does not contain an excess of soda. The strong washing-up soaps, excellent as they are for certain purposes, are too irritant for a dog's skin. While some of the toilet soaps suitable for human use may be employed for dogs, the special dog soaps and shampoos are much better for the purpose. They are more suited to the dog's skin and coat, and have better detergent properties. It is important not to have water that is too hot—as with a baby's bath, it should be possible to dip the point of one's elbow into the water and find that it gives a pleasantly warm sensation but is easily bearable, *i.e.*, it should not be above 95–100° F. On emerging from a bath a dog will shake himself thoroughly, and then, if not curbed, will roll on the floor or ground and speedily cover himself with dust or dirt! It is therefore necessary to give him a brisk rub down with old (but clean) towelling, whereupon he may be allowed to dry off in a warm place free from draughts or, in good weather, put on a lead and taken for a brisk walk. In the case of many of the long-coated breeds it is customary to have them trimmed at the beginning of summer, and this is a sensible precaution that may avoid a good deal of distress during hot weather. The smaller long-haired dogs in particular, such as Scottish Terriers, suffer unduly from the heat if their coats are grown too long.

FEEDING OF THE DOG.

Meat, usually beef, is generally regarded as the staple article of the dog's diet. It must be pointed out, however, that although the dog is naturally a carnivore (flesh-eater), ordinary meat (muscle or " flesh ") is not a completely adequate diet, and lacks certain factors which the wild dog would find in the blood, bones, liver, and other organs of his prey. Furthermore, it has been proved scientifically that dogs can thrive on a meatless diet. In spite of these reservations, however, meat must be regarded as an excellent article of food, and if properly supplemented will prove very satisfactory. In recommendations which have recently been made in America (Dr. S. R. Speelman, of the U.S. Department of Agriculture) it is suggested that meat (beef, lamb, mutton, or horseflesh, providing that the last is fed regularly and not spasmodically) or meat substitutes (fish, milk, eggs, etc.) should constitute one-half of the daily ration, and that the remainder should comprise approximately equal parts of cereal substances (bread, biscuits) and of vegetables (carrots, spinach, onion, beet, etc.). It is pointed out that many dogs do not accept the vegetable material readily. On this basis, the approximate quantities of food required by adult dogs have been calculated as follows:—

Weight of dog.	Total food per day.
1 lb.	2 oz.
10 lb.	12 oz.
25 lb.	1½ lb.
50 lb.	2 lb.
75 lb.	3½ lb.
100 lb.	4½ lb.
150 lb.	5½ lb.
225 lb.	7 lb.

(Weights of up to 10 lb. would include the toy breeds, 25 lb. would correspond to a Fox Terrier; Airedale Terriers and Retrievers would fall into the 50–75-lb. class, and the larger weights would be those of the very big breeds, such as the St. Bernard.) The quantities given are, of course, an *approximation* and no more. Dogs which lead a very active life will require more, while those which take little exercise, or which tend to put on fat easily, will require less. Common sense is necessary, and great care must be taken not to over-feed or to under-nourish.

Meat is probably best fed raw, or lightly cooked, but many animals appear to have a preference (probably through habit) for well-cooked meat. In any event, the meat should not be " over-done," as there is substantial evidence that prolonged heating destroys much of the food value of the meat protein. *Fish* is an excellent substitute. There need be no anxiety about the greed with which a dog swallows lumps of meat and also neglects to masticate them. The teeth of the dog are for tearing meat, he is not concerned with biting his food up small; indeed, his salivary glands contain no digestive ferments, as is the case with some other animals.

Milk is almost essential during pregnancy and lactation (see below), and may well be included in normal dietaries. Whether or not *bones* should be fed is a matter which has been hotly debated, but for mature household dogs the evidence suggests that they are unnecessary. (The teeth of racing greyhounds, which receive a " sloppy " diet, are quite as good as those of the average household dog.) Bone-feeding is responsible for much trouble, including constipation, actual impaction of the rectum, and lodgement of pieces of bone in the mouth or throat. The value of bones is, of course, that they contain large quantities of essential mineral substances, and for this reason the inclusion in the diet of bone-meal, or of steamed *bone-flour*, or, preferably, a mineral supplement, is recommended. Only very small quantities of these substances are required.

Bread is an article of food which is often overlooked in the case of the dog, but there is no doubt that wholemeal bread is very suitable indeed, provided it is not fed to excess.

The answer to the question whether a dog requires vegetables is, in the main, no. From the Vitamin C standpoint they are quite unnecessary, since it has been shown that a dog manufactures this vitamin for itself, but the fact remains that many dogs, particularly of the toy variety, enjoy a few slices of banana or apple, and there is no harm in letting them pander to their taste. Vegetables do help, however, to provide roughage, and cooked (*not* raw) *potatoes* may be used in place of bread or biscuits. The dog—like many other animals—cannot digest raw starch properly. *Flaked maize* and *oatmeal* are other substitutes, but it must be remembered that the energy value of maize is high and that the dogs must never be overfed. *Dog biscuits* are an item that were long is disfavour with some professional people on account of their often having been made from agenised white flour (see section on Canine Hysteria), but now that this factor has been overcome, and the biscuits themselves are being improved in other ways, their use for the non-meat portion of the diet may be recommended.

Clean fresh *water* must be provided at all times. In addition to the diets recommended above, there are on the market several tinned dog foods which claim to be complete, or almost complete, diets for the dog. It must be said that many dogs (including those of the writer) have remained in excellent health when receiving one of these foods as a large part of the diet over long periods. There is, therefore, little that may be said against the widespread use of the better varieties of such products. Again, it is a matter for common sense; if an owner finds that his animal is thriving on such a diet, he is wise to continue to use it.

It is customary to give dogs two meals a day. There is no need to give more than two to healthy adults, for the dog's stomach is exceedingly capacious and adapted to long gaps between meals. Many dogs thrive on only one meal in twenty-four hours. Whatever plan is decided on, regularity should be adhered to, and a meal or meals given at the same times every day.

Dogs require vitamins A and D and B complex. There are several ways of administering these, but the special commercial preparations, including the modern form of condition-powder tablet, are the most convenient.

The *pregnant* and *lactating bitch* require special consideration. The food requirements are very much increased in a bitch which is carrying puppies, especially towards the end of the period. Normally, appetite is not a complete guide to a dog's food requirements, but in pregnancy and lactation the bitch must not be allowed to go hungry. It is quite normal for a heavily pregnant bitch to require over one and a half times her normal amount of food, and in lactation her requirements will increase still further. Milk is a most excellent article of diet at this time; indeed, there is no better way (apart from commercial preparations) of replacing the milk which the bitch is giving to her own puppies.

Up to the age of three weeks or so, *puppies* need have mother's milk only, but at any time after this it is a sound policy to give them additional food, and so spare the mother and also render weaning (at from six to eight weeks) a *gradual* process. At first a little cow's milk or one of the commercial " dog-milk " preparations may be given, and gradually the puppies should be encouraged to eat solid food. Eggs (if they can be spared), wholemeal bread in milk, or even finely minced meat may be given, at first in very small amounts but later in larger quantities. If this process is carefully carried out, there will be far less trouble at and after weaning time. After weaning, puppies should receive five or six meals a day, and this number may be cut down gradually until two or three only are given to the fully grown dog. (The smaller breeds are fully grown at about a year.) *More* meat or meat substitutes and milk, and *less* cereal or vegetable matter, should be fed to the growing dog as compared with the adult. This fact is important, as the substances present in meat and milk are required for laying down the growing tissues. Nevertheless, the energy portion of the ration is important, and the cereal or vegetable should be nutritious and not fibrous. It is possible to rear puppies by hand from birth if the bitch for any reason should die. It requires great patience for the first two or three weeks, as naturally the puppies will require feeding once or twice during the night. Special milks for puppies are to be recommended. Cow's milk requires enriching with fat and sugar to approximate to the composition of bitch's milk. Feeding will have to be done at every two or three hours, and a very useful gadget is a fountain-pen filler attached to cycle-valve tubing. Very small quantities are required for the first two or three days, and a level teaspoonful of milk is more than sufficient for the average terrier at first. Even with the best care in the world hand-fed puppies tend to be weaklings and do not grow as fast as those naturally fed. A foster bitch, if obtainable, is much to be preferred.

BREEDING OF DOGS.

It is natural for adult dogs of both sexes to wish to breed, and in the case of the female especially it is an excellent thing if one can arrange for a suitable mating to take place. Bitches come " into season " or " on heat " (lay terms for œstrus) at approximately six-monthly intervals, but it is not advisable to breed from the first season which occurs usually at about eight to nine months of age, but over a wide range of age according to breed and other factors. The periods of season often occur between January and March and in early Autumn, but there is no fixed rule. Each season lasts for three weeks. For the first seven days, approximately (pro-œstrus), a bitch does not permit mating, though during this time she is a source of strong attraction to all males in the neighbourhood. At about the seventh to the tenth day the blood-stained discharge, which ushers in the heat, stops; this is usually taken by the breeder as an indication that the bitch will stand to service. If possible, it is always better when puppies are wanted to allow mating to occur more than once. Under natural conditions a dog and bitch are usually strictly monogamous and mate for life, and during the period of œstrus will mate many times. A dog and bitch that are kept together all the time will probably behave naturally, but under domestication both dogs and bitches usually become promiscuous. Many bitches will in fact accept service from different males on different days, and the phenomenon of superfecundation, i.e., the production of a litter that is fathered by two males, may occur. It is therefore wise to retain strict control of the bitch throughout the whole of the three weeks or so she is in season. At the end of season the bitch passes into a state of "metœstrus" if she has not conceived.

If a bitch conceives, she carries her puppies for a period of about nine weeks. There is, however, a normal variation of fifty-eight to seventy days, and puppies born before the fifty-eighth day sometimes live. The number of puppies born varies with breed; in the smaller terriers it is usually from four to six, but in Airedales and Alsatians the number may be eight to ten, and the larger breeds tend to have even more offspring at a time. Birth usually takes place fairly easily in the larger breeds, but there is often much difficulty in the case of the short-legged breeds, such as Scottish and Sealyham Terriers, Pekingese and Dachshunds. In some breeds, in fact, the problem is one that is giving serious concern to veterinary surgeons and breeders.

A short while before her puppies are due, a bitch will "make her bed." Owners are often amazed at the destruction of soft furnishings, or even of wall-paper, that a previously well-behaved bitch may carry out at this time; it is therefore by far the best to provide a suitable box (if the animal has not one already). A smooth flooring such as a strip of linoleum serves for the bitch to give birth to her puppies. Her instinct to tear up everything given to her for bedding may lead to suffocation of the puppies by pieces of bedding. Provided labour occurs in a warm room, it is sometimes better—according to the temperament of the bitch—to remove each puppy as it is born, placing a warm bottle underneath, and bring it back to the mother when the last birth has occurred. At this time the bitch should be watched carefully for any discharge from the vulva or for any evidence of straining. If either of these occurs without results, it is advisable to send for help as early as possible, especially in the case of the smaller breeds. Many hundreds of bitches are lost through neglect at this time, and usually because it was not suspected that anything was wrong. If the discharge becomes bloody, or green, help should be obtained at once if no puppy is delivered. Similarly, any great delay between births is a matter for concern. The afterbirth usually follows the puppy within a few minutes, but puppies are sometimes delivered in their foetal membranes, and in this case the latter should be gently but quickly removed. It is quite normal for the umbilical cord to remain attached to the puppy, but the bitch will normally break it by biting through it.

The mother will wash and attend to the new born puppies, and after the last is born it is a good idea to burn all the mess and to provide clean newspaper, but do not worry or frighten the bitch more than is necessary. For the care and feeding of the bitch and her puppies see the sections on Management and Feeding. Puppies, like kittens, are born with their eyes closed, but open them after about nine days—there again being considerable variation.

The phenomenon of pseudopregnancy is common in bitches, and indeed to a minor degree it is probably present in most bitches following an œstrus without conception. In some bitches, however, presumably those with strong maternal drives, the changes in the ovary may be accompanied by external signs of "phantom" or "ghost" pregnancy. These may include not only enlargement but actual functioning of the mammary glands, and the making of a "nest" by the bitch just as if her puppies were really due. The average duration of pseudopregnancy is usually given as about two months, and although variable, it is often sufficiently near to the correct time after œstrus that everyone suspects the bitch to be truly pregnant. The condition may be suppressed with the aid of modern drugs, but in some instances it is not realised that the condition is not real. In many cases only professional advice can solve the mystery, and radiographical examinations have often proved necessary to ascertain the truth, particularly in fat bitches of the heavier breeds. It might be well to note, at this point, that there is another condition of the older bitch that is known as Pyometra. This condition usually reveals itself at the same time as the ghost pregnancy (and is sometimes a pathological extension of it) but is accompanied by considerable disturbance of health, coupled in many instances with purulent discharge from the vagina. A bitch which is off-colour in the weeks following pregnancy, or which develops a discharge from the vulva (especially one which is dark in colour), may well be a pyometra subject. The disease is most serious, and often requires surgical intervention. As the best chance of success is to operate or otherwise deal with early, a veterinary surgeon should be consulted immediately.

DISEASES AND INJURIES OF THE DOG.

Canine Distemper and "Para-distemper" (including so-called "Hard-pad").—It has long been recognised that the commonest and most serious disease of dogs throughout the world is canine distemper. Dogs of all ages and breeds are susceptible, and no dog is free from the risk of infection unless it has recovered from the disease or has acquired an immunity for other reasons (see P8(2). The disease is caused primarily by a minute agent known as a filterable virus (see P7(2), which may be of varying type in that it will attack the body in different ways. Thus some strains of the virus are known as "neurotropic" because they show an affinity for the nervous system. Sometimes a dog will apparently recover from an attack of distemper, only to succumb later to "fits" or other nervous manifestations due to permanent damage to the central nervous system by the virus. Often, however, the virus is not fatal in itself, but will lower the dog's resistance and permit the entry or the activity of bacteria that may lead to pneumonia or other serious effects. These so-called "secondary invaders," as the bacteria are termed, may prove as harmful as the original virus. Indeed, once these bacteria have set to work it is too late to expect the best results from the use of serum, and whether or not the dog will live through will depend upon the severity of the attack, the dog's powers of resistance, and good nursing. It is therefore most important either to prevent the disease by vaccination or to be able to send for veterinary attention (and hence for an injection of serum) immediately an attack is suspected. Any puppy which is listless or off its food, or which may throw a fit, or which is obviously unwell with other symptoms (e.g., cough or diarrhœa) may well be in the early stages of distemper, and it is then (not the next day) that help should be sought. Many thousands of puppies (and older dogs) that have been injected with serum in the early stages of the disease have become perfectly normal within forty-eight hours. On the other hand, the number of dogs that die in Great Britain alone from distemper and distemper-like infections must assume enormous proportions. Distemper is a highly infectious disease, and it is important that the owner of an infected animal should do his best to avoid contact with other dogs, ferrets, or mink. Ferrets and mink are very susceptible to canine distemper. On the other hand, human beings and cats are not susceptible to canine distemper, and the so-called distemper of cats is quite a distinct disease.

A highly satisfactory means of vaccinating puppies against distemper was worked out about 1926–30, and this—named the "Laidlaw-Dunkin" after its two inventors—has since afforded protection to thousands of animals. Modern vaccines are based on a virus which has been modified by growth on developing egg embryos; or, more recently, in tissue culture. Puppies should be vaccinated when they are 10–12 weeks; prior to this age the immunity induced by the vaccine may not develop satisfactorily. After vaccination the puppy requires some time, possibly 2 weeks, before an immunity is established. Sometimes vaccinated dogs suffer distemper or distemper-like signs due to " secondary invaders " causing disease on their own account; or because they were already infected when vaccinated. Variants of distemper of which "hard pad " is an example may also overwhelm a vaccinated dog's immunity, although this is uncommon with modern vaccines, since several distemper strains are used in their production. Hyperimmune serum, which is collected from animals previously hyperimmunised against distemper, is available and can immediately aid the dog suffering from distemper but its effect is short-lived (7-10 days).

Infectious Hepatitis or Rubarth's Disease.— Another virus disease of dogs (and foxes) is known as Rubarth's disease, after one of its discoverers, now known as infectious hepatitis. This disease has been recognised in Sweden ever since the 1930s, but in Great Britain only since the end of the war. The condition is extremely sudden in onset, and an affected dog may be found dead. Many cases are, however, mild, and in some instances only one or two out of a large group of dogs have been affected. The changes seen after death vary, but the findings in the liver cells are usually characteristic. Specific treatment is not yet established as in the case of the distemper-like conditions, although the administration of antibiotics (see P9) may prevent the effects of secondary infection. An effective vaccine is now produced and often combined with the distemper chick embryo vaccine. A dog is thereby protected against both these diseases.

Canine Hysteria (called "fright disease " or " running fits " in the U.S.A.) is an alarming but not necessarily serious condition (in that it can often be cured very readily) which appears to arise from a variety of exciting causes. The affected animal rushes around wildly, often screaming and howling, and obviously loses all sense of whereabouts or ability to recognise people. After a more severe attack (and there are all degrees up to a full epileptiform fit) the dog may appear quite exhausted, but returns to normal. Sometimes there are many attacks in one day. The dog will not wilfully attack people during a bout of hysteria—at least, that has been the experience of the writer—but is very difficult to control. Apart from ensuring that the dog does itself no grievous bodily harm, there is little that can be done until the attack has subsided. Then the animal should be kept as quiet as possible and given a tranquilliser.

Hysteria may be an hereditary taint, derived from one or other parent. In certain circumstances, however, it may arise in apparently normal animals. There are several possible causes (including parasites), but a definite one is the bleaching agent—nitrogen trichloride or " agene "—employed for some years in the manufacture of flour, and hence present in white bread and certain dog biscuits. Indeed, the clear demonstration that agene could set up hysteria in dogs, and subsequent scientific work, has led to the introduction of regulations that have led to its abandonment as a bleaching agent in favour of other methods which have been found not to cause hysteria. There has already been a marked decline in the incidence of hysteria due to dietary factors.

Rabies is a fatal disease of dogs, and is also due to a " filterable virus." It is transmissible to the human being and to many other species, but has fortunately been absent from Great Britain for many years. Stringent precautions are taken to prevent its entry, and dogs which are brought into Great Britain must spend a long period in quarantine. A vaccine is available and people taking dogs to countries where rabies occurs should have their animals protected. Many countries insist on this procedure.

Tonsilitis appears quite frequently in dogs, and seems in many cases to be part of a more generalised infection. It demands expert treatment, but although it may persist for a long time, it usually yields to treatment.

Nephritis.—Inflammation of the kidneys is unfortunately all too common in dogs, and in adult males in particular there is a high incidence of chronic kidney damage. One of the symptoms is a marked thirst. Sometimes this condition is a sequel to an infection known as *leptospirosis*, which calls for prompt veterinary treatment if death or permanent damage is not to follow. It is always worth while seeking professional advice for a dog that drinks excessively or has a somewhat characteristic type of bad breath. A vaccine which gives a good immunity against the two common forms of *leptospirosis* is available.

Anal Glands, which are found in the dog and in other carnivora, often give rise to trouble. Animals which " rub themselves along the ground " are not necessarily affected with " worms," but with impaction of these two little glands, which are situated one on each side of the anus. They secrete a peculiar dark-coloured, very offensive fluid, which sometimes is not discharged properly and causes the animal great discomfort. The glands in such cases should be relieved periodically. Those who do not mind this somewhat dirty task may perhaps learn how to do it themselves. Occasionally, segments of tapeworm are responsible for the impaction, but usually the trouble has nothing to do with worms. Whenever a dog pays considerable attention to his anus, this impaction should be suspected. Actual infection of the glands is also fairly common, and demands expert attention.

Diseases of the Ear, especially of the outer ear, are very common in dogs. The dog's outer ear is somewhat more complicated than is our own, and the drum is set more deeply. Hence it is easy for wax and dirt to accumulate, for various parasites to establish themselves, and for inflammatory conditions to result. The word " canker " (which has no precise scientific meaning) is sometimes applied by lay people to the more serious or chronic forms of inflammation of the outer ear canal. It is not difficult to diagnose " ear trouble," as the affected animal usually shakes its head or worries or scratches its ear and rubs it along the ground. The ears should be inspected regularly to see that there is no great accumulation of wax or dirt. Cotton-wool twisted on to the end of a match-stick or orangestick is quite satisfactory for cleaning out the ear, providing care is taken. A dog which is continually worrying its ear, or which has ears which are obviously diseased, should not be neglected, as the sooner expert treatment is begun the more readily will the condition be cured. Even if the lining of the ear is greatly thickened through inflammatory reaction, and the lumen nearly occluded, it is still possible for a plastic operation to be performed. Many hundreds of such cases have been successfully treated in this way. A percentage of inflammatory conditions of the outer ear is associated with ear mange mites. In such an event treatment with modern antimange preparations should be carried out.

Deafness in certain white dogs (*e.g.*, in some Bull Terriers) appears to be hereditary, and is quite incurable. Old dogs often become deaf, and deafness has been produced experimentally in young puppies by feeding them on a deficient diet.

Diseases of the Eye are very common in dogs, and are often the result of injury. Except for minor discharges from the corners of their eyes (and in younger dogs especially it must be ascertained that these are not a symptom of distemper) any eye disease is sufficiently serious to merit professional advice. Boracic lotion is not suitable for the eyes of dogs. It is slightly irritant, and dogs are apt to scratch and make the eyes raw after application. Colloidal silver eye lotions and ointments are far more suitable pending the advice of a veterinary surgeon. In eye inflammation avoid sunlight and wind. For some days in the early stages of inflamed eyes, the light in the room should be subdued. Pekingese seem to be especially prone to eye disease, but the remarkably un-wholesome appearance of some affected eyes in this breed is not necessarily evidence that recovery is unlikely. Steps should be taken to ensure that the dog does not inflict further injury on an already diseased eye. Cat scratches are a frequent source of inflammatory conditions of the dog's eye. Eyes must never be neglected, for the consequences are serious.

Skin Diseases are common in dogs, and may be contagious. Among the common contagious causes of skin disease are lice, mange mites and fleas. Lice and mange mites (except for demodex) are killed by modern insecticides such as benzene hexachloride (gammexane) although two applications at a 10–14 day interval are required to destroy the young stages which are within the insecticide-resistant eggs at the first dressing. The flea actually on the dog, is only one of four stages in the life cycle of the flea; the others are in the house or dog's bedding. Insecticides used for flea control should therefore be applied every week or 10 days during the summer to kill the young fleas as they hatch and infest the dog. The dog's bedding should be discarded or cleaned. The dog also suffers from other skin diseases caused by systemic disorders for which expert attention is required.

Diseases of the Teeth and Gums are very common in household dogs. A serious systemic disease, such as distemper, may leave the enamel of the teeth permanently pitted, hence " distemper teeth." More serious than this, however, is a form of pyorrhœa, which is really a disease of the gums rather than a primary disease of the teeth themselves. The margins of the gums become red and swollen, and may bleed easily. As the condition progresses the teeth may become loosened. Particles of food become lodged between the teeth or between teeth and gums, and add to the inflammation and to the smell of the breath.

This disease may, if unchecked, become very serious. In many cases extraction of one or more teeth is indicated, but unfortunately it is not always possible to do this. The condition demands expert attention.

Another common condition of dogs' teeth is the deposition around them of " tartar." This should be removed by scaling or by special use of dental forceps. Some breeders and others may themselves have learnt how to carry out these operations with the requisite skill and care, but they are not easy to the amateur, and it is essential that no harm be done to the animal's soft tissues by injudicious use of the instruments. Ordinary dog-owners are strongly advised to take their dogs to a veterinary surgeon in order to have the " tartar " removed.

Most puppies lose their first or " milk " teeth quite regularly between the ages of three and five months, but sometimes there is difficulty and the primary teeth are not shed properly. These cases should be treated by a veterinary surgeon before the permanent teeth are thrown out of their proper alignment.

One hears very much about " teething fits " in puppies, and while these occur, owners should be *very* careful to ensure that a " teething fit " is not a sign of distemper, which often starts with a fit. As puppies of this age are so susceptible to distemper, it is advisable to seek professional advice should any form of fit occur. It may save much time, money, and trouble, and even the animal's life.

Internal Parasites: " Worms."—It is probable that more nonsense has been talked and written about " worms " in dogs than about any other canine subject. According to some people, " worms " are the root of nearly all doggy evil, and so long as a dog is regularly " wormed " all will go well with him. These beliefs are frankly absurd. The real facts are very different, and are stated in as brief a fashion as possible in the following sentences. In this country dogs are infested by a species of " roundworm " (a creature which is a dirty-white colour and in shape somewhat resembles the common earthworm) and by several species of " tapeworm," which are also whitish but which are flat and are made up of many small segments joined to a little " head " which is attached to the lining of the gut. In spite of all that is said, tapeworms as such are rarely responsible for much harm to the dog, although they can, of course, prove debilitating and should be removed. They are a nuisance, and attempts to remove them should be made by administration of the appropriate drug. Occasionally, segments of worm are responsible for impaction of the ducts of the *anal glands* (see above).

The roundworms may be extremely serious in young puppies, in which they cause stunting, " pot-belly," harshness of coat and dangerous or fatal illness. Fortunately, modern anti-roundworm preparations are available for animals of this age. Once over the age of 4–8 months dogs rarely suffer serious illness from roundworms, although these may cause occasional vomiting, or even diarrhœa, and some loss of coat and bodily condition. It is now known that puppies are infected before birth from their mother. It is therefore desirable to keep down the incidence of roundworms in the mother—and in dogs generally—and fortunately the modern preparations are—unlike some of the old-fashioned ones—safe in use and unlikely to cause digestive disturbances. From all that has been said above owners will realise the necessity of taking professional advice about young dogs which are ill, and any signs of " worms " in young puppies—either in the stools or by some obvious intestinal upset or bloated appearance of the belly—should be acted upon. One last word about this aspect of worms—do not assume that your adult dog has " tapeworms " unless you see some evidence in his stools. There are so many " signs of worms " that veterinary surgeons must at times get a little tired of being assured that " My dog has worms " because of some trivial habit connected with appetite.

There is, however, another side to the study of tapeworms, and one which is not generally realised. The tapeworm which is found in the dog represents one stage in the life-cycle. The eggs, which are present in the ripe segment passed by the dog, develop, not in the outside world, but in another animal altogether. Thus one of the commonest tapeworms in this country has an intermediate stage, as it is called, in the flea, and it is when the flea is eaten by the dog that this intermediate stage develops further to become a tapeworm. Another tapeworm has an intermediate stage which develops in the sheep, and a third has one which develops in the ox. There is a fourth tapeworm which has an intermediate stage which *may* develop in man, to set up serious diseases in certain cases. Children may become infected through handling the dog, and so picking up the eggs, which may then be eaten through putting the hands in the mouth. The dogs which are most likely to be infested are those which have the opportunity to eat freshly killed sheep and other food-animals. An ordinary household dog is not likely to be infested, and people should not worry unduly in this connection, provided they do not allow their dogs to stray into the wrong places. It is illegal to allow dogs to enter a slaughter-house, but unfortunately one often sees dogs in such places. The routine worming of dogs is justified if evidence of infection exists, and certainly in country areas where opportunities of tapeworm re-infection may be plentiful.

Tumours, including malignant tumours (" cancers ") are relatively very common in the dog—probably as common as in the human subject. Space does not permit of a detailed account, but the following examples of growths may be mentioned: a proliferation of warts on the skin of puppies (usually disappear spontaneously); a true cancer of the tonsil in middle-aged and older dogs of both sexes; cancer of the mammary glands in bitches (both incurable); fatty growths of the vagina of bitches (amenable to operation). Space does not allow of the discussion of other diseases, but it should be pointed out that dogs are susceptible to human and bovine forms of *tuberculosis*, especially the former. In a household which contains a tubercular person, the dog should be watched for any signs of illness, and the thought entertained that he might be responsible for the further spread of the disease. For a discussion on ringworm see the appropriate heading in the section on the cat (Z12).

Accidents and Injuries.—In these days of swiftly moving motor transport, street accidents to dogs are extremely common. Many could be prevented by training the animal to walk to heel, by the use of a lead in busy thoroughfares, and by not allowing dogs to roam the streets unaccompanied—a thoroughly bad habit. Sometimes the victim escapes with a scare and a few bruises, and at others death is mercifully swift. In the vast majority of accidents, however, a more or less serious injury is incurred, and if the animal is unable to move, the police should be notified immediately. The dog is best left quiet, and it is not recommended that attempts be made to administer brandy or other supposed " stimulants " unless help is markedly delayed. Excessive hæmorrhage may in some instances be prevented by common-sense application of principles learnt in first-aid courses.

One of the commonest accidents to dogs, especially to young dogs, is a fracture involving the head of the femur, or thigh-bone. Inability to put one of the hind legs to the ground, or to bear any weight on this limb, is an indication of such an injury. (This injury may occur also from falling off a chair or wall.) Professional help is, of course, required in such cases.

Cuts and Bruises, if not serious, may be treated at home as in the case of human beings. The indiscriminate use of tincture of iodine is not to be recommended, and spirit alone makes a more satisfactory dressing in most cases. Simple washing and removal of dirt are usually sufficient, combined, perhaps, with modern antiseptic ointments or other preparations. The dog (and also the cat) are very liable to sepsis, and it is best in such cases to send for proper assistance early, or there may be grave trouble. It is probable that in nature many of the flesh-eating animals end their lives as victims of the sepsis following wounds.

Injuries from cat-scratches are exceedingly common, as are bites from other dogs. These are serious, as they more readily result in septic places. The scratch or bite sometimes penetrates quite deeply, leaving a pocket which fills up with pus. This pus may spread under the skin to form sinuses. Never neglect such places.

Conclusion.—There are a few concluding remarks on the treatment of the diseases of the dog:—

(1) It is not correct that " water should be withheld from a sick dog." It is true that an animal which is using water only to vomit, or which is drinking excessively, should have its water intake restricted, but it is wrong to deprive a dog altogether. It may be suffering from diabetes and should be taken to the vet for testing.

(2) There have been such wonderful advances in the field of veterinary anæsthetics that there is nowadays little to fear in this connection from operations to dogs and cats. The records over the past years at the Royal Veterinary College, London and at other centres have been most encouraging, and the anæsthetic risk is now small indeed.

(3) When a dog's life is a burden to him, it is unfair to keep him alive, and he should be put to sleep. It must be realised, however, that putting a dog to sleep is a very skilful task. It is made much easier if an owner will allow his veterinary surgeon to administer an anæsthetic and not allow the animal " to come round," and shooting is also straightforward and painless if *skilfully* carried out. There are no " magical ways " of destroying human or animal life, and an owner must not expect his veterinary surgeon to be able to bring about death merely by holding a pad to the dog's face. It is far better that the task be carried out at a veterinary surgeon's own premises, where there is skilled assistance.

CATS.

Many of the general remarks in the preceding section apply equally to cats, and will not be repeated unnecessarily in the following paragraphs.

BREEDS AND VARIETIES OF CAT.

The following breeds and varieties are recognised for registration purposes by the Governing Council of the Cat Fancy:—

Long-haired Cats.

Black	Tortoiseshell
White (Blue-eyed)	Tortoiseshell-and-White
White (Orange-eyed)	Blue Cream
Blue	Brown Tabby
Red Tabby	Chinchilla
Red Self	Smoke
Cream	Silver Tabby

Short-haired Cats.

Black	Spotted
White	Russian Blue
British Blue	Manx
Cream	Abyssinian
Tortoiseshell	Siamese (Seal-pointed)
Tortoiseshell-and-White	Siamese (Blue-pointed)
Silver Tabby	Siamese (Chocolate-
Brown Tabby	pointed)
Red Tabby	Burmese
Mackerel-striped Tabby	

Pedigree breeding and showing are practised with a very small fraction of the total cat population of Great Britain, and the majority of these remarks will be concerned with the ordinary household cat. Nevertheless, in recent years there appears to have been a considerable increase in pedigree cat breeding. Registration—which is essential for showing and pedigree purposes—is controlled by the Governing Council of the Cat Fancy. Many of the breeds listed above have their own societies, which are affiliated to the Governing Council. The addresses and particulars of these and other cat societies and clubs may be had on application to the secretary of the Governing Council. The two most popular varieties of cat are the Blue Persian and the Siamese, and an exclusive show is held for each of them. In addition to these shows there are five big Championship Shows open to every variety of long- and short-haired cat, while there are classes for cats and kittens at some of the Agricultural Shows.

CHOICE OF CAT.

Although there are, as noted above, many varieties of cat, most people are content to accept an ordinary kitten, and for them the chief points to consider will be: (a) whether to have a long-haired or a short-haired animal, (b) whether to have a male or female, (c) whether or not to have the kitten " doctored " (i.e., castrated or spayed). As a general rule, short-haired cats are probably more suitable for the average household, since their fur does not become shed so noticeably and they probably suffer less from " fur-balling." Nevertheless, many long-haired cats are so attractive that they will obviously be preferred, and there is no reason why they should not be chosen. Sex is a rather more important question, although, as may be seen in the section on management, it is possible to have both males and females " doctored." Male cats which are kept as entires are often a nuisance in that they make abominable smells in the house and spend much of their time in fighting. These characteristics are by no means invariable; but they are so common as to justify the castration of the majority of males. Siamese males in particular may be a liability. Females are generally credited with a greater attachment to the home (although they wander when " in season ") and with being better mousers. The principal objection to females is that they seem to be bearing kittens almost continuously. In normal circumstances it is, of course, quite impossible to prevent cats from mating by keeping the female in confinement during her season, a practice which is frequently adopted in the case of the dog. For one thing, most people are never aware when their female cats are in season.

Whatever animal is chosen, it is essential to pick a healthy and preferably a fairly young—but *not* too young—kitten. It is best not to accept a kitten under about eight weeks of age.

For those who wish for something a little out of the ordinary, Siamese cats make excellent and highly intelligent pets. Siamese kittens are born white, but gradually develop their even pale fawn colour, with cream on belly and chest and with "seal brown" mask, ears, legs, feet, and tail. The coat is very short, and the eyes are blue. There has long been a popular belief that Siamese cats are delicate creatures, but the present writer has seen healthy specimens, kept under ordinary household conditions, living to a mature age. It is not wise to keep a male Siamese as a household pet. The male is a fierce fighter, and is generally a worse offender in the house than the males of other breeds, and should therefore be castrated if it is to be kept as a pet.

Many people find Manx cats attractive. Instead of the normal large number of tail bones, they have but three, and hence appear almost tailless. One should beware against fraudulent amputation of the tail of ordinary cats, which are then described as "Manx."

MANAGEMENT OF THE CAT.

The cat is an independent creature, so much so that one may say that to a large extent it manages its own affairs. This, however, is not true of all cats, and every reasonable attempt should be made to provide the cat with a comfortable and friendly home. Cats are highly intelligent, and if sufficient patience is exercised they will respond to a very great degree to human attention. Kittens should not be neglected, but should be talked to and played with just as are puppies. Many cats, especially young cats, make excellent playmates for children.

In order to prevent to a large extent their nocturnal wanderings, many cats of both sexes are castrated or spayed (the popular lay expression for this is "doctored"). In the male cat the testicles are removed by an operation which is almost always safe and simple if carried out skilfully. From three to four months is a good age at which to have this done. Female cats may also be "doctored." As the female glands or ovaries lie within the body cavity, this operation is a major one, but it is nevertheless quite a straightforward, though a more expensive, procedure if conducted at the right age (about five months). Very many thousands of female cats have been so operated upon and the subsequent health of these cats has been excellent. Indeed, it has been said that a spayed female makes one of the best of all household cats.

Cats may choose to sleep in a variety of places, and will often lie on beds, chairs, mats, and other warm places. It is a sound policy to provide them with a box or basket, and to encourage them to use newspaper as a bedding. Most cats will take well to newspaper. The bed should be placed in a warm site—it is of little use putting it in a cold corner of a room and expecting the cat to lie in it.

Owing to the fact that, even in play, a cat's claws may inflict serious injury, dogs and cats do not always make the best of house companions. Nevertheless, the traditional enmity of cat and dog is often overcome, and if the two are brought up together they often make firm friends, sharing the same basket or hearth-rug and feeding together without serious consequences.

A cat normally attends to its own toilet, and everyone must be aware that a cat devotes long periods each day to cleaning and washing itself. Except in special cases, therefore, bathing is quite unnecessary, while in short-haired cats especially, grooming, too, is superfluous (this does not apply to show-cats). For some reason (and sometimes, apparently, because an owner attempts to assist in the daily grooming) an occasional cat may cease to wash or care for itself. Such an animal is a dejected sight, and should be taken to a veterinary surgeon to have its matted fur cut or combed, and

its dirt removed. Such animals (unless they completely re-acquire their self-respect) must be groomed regularly if they are to be kept at all.

All household cats are accustomed to take their own exercise, and it is advisable (except in any special circumstances) to allow them free access to and from the outer world. Do not shut your cat in the house for a long period and then blame it for making a mess. Cats are clean creatures: they normally dig small holes in which to defecate or urinate, and subsequently cover the deposit with earth. If, therefore, they are for some reason debarred temporarily or permanently from access to a garden, they should be provided with a box or tray containing soil or cinders. Indeed, in many types of houses it is a good plan to encourage kittens to use such a device. (Note the corresponding remarks about puppies.)

It is generally stated that "cats never forget a blow," and for that reason it is recommended that cats are not chastised. It may be said that, if a cat (or dog) be brought up conscientiously and well, it should never, or very rarely, require such punishment. An animal which has been brought up properly seems to develop a fair sense of what is right and what is wrong.

For pedigree cats, or those kept in confinement for other reasons, see the relevent remarks in the section on breeding.

FEEDING THE CAT.

Although most cats are capable of supplementing their diet by catching small rodents or birds, it is unwise to rely on this as a regular source of food. The idea that hungry cats make the best mousers is by no means always correct. Indeed, animals that are in poor condition are less likely to be successful hunters. Moreover, while the riddance of pests is an excellent matter from the human point of view—and one of the reasons why the keeping of cats is economically justified—the "cruel" fashion in which most cats tackle their prey is repulsive to most of us.

It is therefore necessary and desirable to provide regular daily feeding. Kittens should receive several meals a day, but by the time they are six months old the number of daily feeds should be reduced to one, or at most two. Most cats (many Siamese are exceptions) are extremely fond of *milk*, especially if it is creamy, and the cat's love of *fish* is well known. Many *meats*, especially *rabbit meat*, are relished, and a diet high in "animal protein" is indeed the aim, always provided that it contains sufficient "dietary energy." It is significant that cat's milk has a higher content of fat and sugar than cow's milk, *i.e.*, it is a richer source of energy. Some of the proprietary bitch-milk substitutes are nearer to cat's milk in composition than is cow's milk.

Many hundreds of cats have been reared and bred successfully in experimental laboratories on a diet consisting, in the main, of one part of fish or meat and two parts of *cooked potatoes*. This is relatively inexpensive, and may be supplemented by milk and by some of the proprietary cat foods.

Cats are also extremely fond of liver. Some of the proprietary cat foods—the better ones of which are excellent—and vitamin tablets contain liver, which is a rich source of the vitamin B complex.

Within reason a healthy kitten should be fed to appetite, always provided good-quality foods are available. The amount should be restricted when they are adult, however, except for pregnant and lactating cats, which are sometimes referred to as "queens" as opposed to the male "toms." An average daily allowance of solid food for a healthy non-pregnant adult cat should be of the order of $\frac{1}{2}$ oz. per 1 lb. body-weight.

Cats are fastidious eaters; they usually sniff and examine carefully any strange or doubtful food. At the same time they are often greedy, especially with relished food to which they are accustomed, but fortunately they can, like dogs, vomit very readily. Here, incidentally, is one very good tip—an excellent emetic for both cat and dog is a small crystal of washing-soda, given as a pill. People are usually amazed at the way this simple device results in a dog's or a cat's bringing up undesirable food.

It is important not to overfeed cats, and it is

almost equally important to prepare all food in a clean manner, and to make it as attractive as possible. Cats will greatly appreciate this care. While milk is an excellent food for kittens (see under breeding), and is relished by most adult cats, it must be supplemented by solid food.

Clean fresh water should be provided at all times, even if the cat appears to drink it but little.

BREEDING OF CATS.

Pedigree animals are normally confined, and their breeding is strictly controlled. Ordinary household cats are at the opposite extreme and there is little that can be done to prevent their mating. The length and scope of this article does not permit of a discussion of controlled mating.

Scientifically, there is as yet a good deal to learn about the reproductive behaviour of the cat. As an American physiologist has succinctly put it in a description of the reproductive cycle of the female cat, " no two authors agree." In Northern Europe there are two main heat periods a year, in spring and early autumn, but some animals may appear in heat at any time from January to July, and those who keep female cats in confinement describe their charges as " calling " quite frequently if not mated. A cat which is " in season " or " on heat " is often observed to be behaving in a quite characteristic fashion, rolling about on the floor and making peculiar sounds. The periods of heat, which commence usually at about eight months of age, may last for several days, and during this time the female will make every attempt to find a mate.

Gestation lasts about nine weeks, as in the case of the bitch, but here again there is a considerable variation. As most owners are quite unaware of the time at which their cats were mated, it is difficult to talk of " going overtime," but if there is any evidence of trouble during pregnancy, or at birth, veterinary advice should be obtained. As soon as a cat is obviously pregnant, her food allowance should be increased, and she should be allowed plenty of milk. It is highly important to increase her food and milk ration still further after the kittens are born, as lactation is a great drain on the mother.

Cats sometimes choose strange, out-of-the-way places in which to litter, and many healthy litters are born and reared out of doors. Rats are a source of danger, and will often destroy very young kittens during the mother's absence. For this and other reasons it is better in town and suburban areas to have the litter comfortably housed indoors. A wooden box containing newspaper is ideal, provided it is kept in a fairly warm place and out of the way of draughts. An average litter consists of three to six kittens, which are born blind, but which normally open their eyes after eight or nine days. There is no need to be alarmed if the eyes remain closed for a few days longer. Kittens which are born dead should be removed and buried or burnt. If the whole litter is born dead, the mother's food supply should be cut down considerably, and little milk given for a few days. If the mamary glands become inflamed, they may be bathed in a cold solution of alum. The glands normally return to their former size within a short space of time if they are not milked, but if there is persistent trouble veterinary advice should be sought.

While many pedigree owners wean kittens at four to five weeks of age, it is strongly advised that the household cat be allowed to continue to feed her family for a longer period, and eight weeks is not too long if the mother is still in good bodily condition. She *must*, however, be well fed and be allowed plenty of milk. As in the case of puppies, it is an excellent idea to provide the kittens with a little solid food as from a few weeks of age. It is very wrong to remove a kitten from its mother too early, and such an animal is often weakly, develops an intestinal infection, and dies as a miserable bedraggled creature. Moreover, during the period following weaning the mother educates her offspring in the art of living, particularly ratting and mousing.

As many litters are unwanted, some people get rid of all the kittens as soon as possible after birth. Drowning is frequently practised, but it is not recommended as a merciful death. Indeed, a hard blow on the back of the head is more humane if given accurately. It is much better to take the kittens to a veterinary surgeon or clinic.

DISEASES AND INJURIES OF THE CAT.

The principal infectious diseases o cats are still in need of much scientific study. It is now clear, however, that there are at least two major cat plagues. Both have been given many names, and there is much confusion between them.

Feline Enteritis or Panleucopenia.—This is a highly infectious disease, due to a filterable virus. The symptoms include loss of appetite, sometimes accompanied by a rise in body temperature, followed by listlessness, usually vomiting, sometimes diarrhoea, and a marked tendency to show tenderness or pain on being handled. This tenderness or pain is due to a developing peritonitis. The poor animal may become seriously ill, with loss of water from the tissues or dehydration, prostrate and dead within 48 hours or less from the time of the first symptoms. The incubation period of the disease is believed to be from 4 to 8 days, or sometimes longer. There is a fall in the white-cell count of the blood, hence the term " panleucopenia." Some cats recover, the recovery rate in different outbreaks that have been studied ranging from 30 to 80 per cent., and recovered animals are probably immune to further attacks. Cats that are able to take a little food during the early stages of recovery have the best chance of recovery, but require careful nursing. There may be complications during the convalescent stage due to secondary bacterial infections or to vitamin deficiency, and a light nourishing diet, combined with vitamin preparations, is recommended. Fleas may transmit the disease to other cats, as may contact with infected materials. It has been shown that bedding and dirt trays from sick cats were infectious for other cats for up to 16 days. The disease is not transmissible to dogs or to human beings. There is nowadays a protective vaccine, and it is a wise precaution to have your pet vaccinated.

Feline Pneumonitis.—This disease is sometimes called " cat distemper "—as indeed is feline enteritis—but it has no connection with dog distemper, and is not transmissible to dogs or to human beings. Both mild and severe forms occur, and the incubation period varies from 5 to 8 days. The mild form may seem like a cold, and there is a weeping from the eyes and a varying degree of conjunctivitis. There is a thin, clear discharge from the nose, with a characteristic sneezing. Provided that the animals can be made to continue eating, and are kept in warm and dry but ventilated conditions, recovery may be rapid and not entail serious loss of condition. The eyes should be treated with a suitable preparation, such as silver vitellin. There may be secondary bacterial infection in cases that are neglected.

The severe form of the disease has similar, although more severe, commencing symptoms, but the nasal discharge becomes purulent and there is often profuse salivation, with much spreading of the long ropes of saliva. The cat is listless, dislikes strong light, and seems to resent being disturbed. It loses its appetite, and rapidly becomes thinner over a period of from 2 to 5 days or so. Breathing becomes laboured, and a bronchopneumonia develops. There may be a high death rate in young kittens, and pregnant females may abort. Recovery tends to be slow, and is often complicated by bacterial infection. Some of the modern antibiotics appear to be highly effective in the treatment of many cases of this disease, but they must, of course, be given under veterinary supervision.

Tuberculosis.—The cat, like the dog, can contract tuberculosis, but so far as is known only the bovine form has been known to infect it. The infection usually comes, of course, from milk, and the elimination of bovine tuberculosis from this country will stop the incidence of the disease in cats. The disease commences in the abdomen, but may spread to the lungs. There is general wasting.

Skin Diseases.—As in the case of the dog, skin disease in the cat is usually of parasitic origin, and fleas and mange mites are again the chief source of trouble in Great Britain. Cats do so much of their own toilet that the average household cat has probably a cleaner skin than its canine counterpart. When skin disease does develop, it is strongly advised that the animal be taken to a veterinary surgeon for appropriate treatment. As a rule cats greatly resent the interference which must accompany any attempt to bathe or dress an affected place, and for this reason it is usually unwise for an owner to attempt to do other than make an inspection. Very small patches of skin eruption may clear satisfactorily if the surrounding hair is clipped away with curved scissors, but generally speaking skin disease calls for professional attention. The cat flea has a similar life cycle to the dog flea (*see* Z8).

Diseases of the Ear.—The outer ear of the cat is frequently affected, and in a great many cases a form of mange mite is responsible. The animal provides evidence of the trouble by scratching and shaking its ear and generally showing its discomfort. It will not always be possible for an owner to make a thorough examination, as in many cases the cat objects, but if it is possible to look inside the ear it will be seen that there is a dirty and usually brownish mess of tissue, sometimes mixed with dried blood or pus. Not all cases are as bad as this, of course, but if a cat persistently worries its ear it should be taken to a veterinary surgeon. There are satisfactory dressings for this condition, and owners will be able to dress their cats if the latter are docile. Otherwise it is necessary to have the ears dressed by a veterinary surgeon or by one of his staff.

A cat's ear is frequently the site of a blood blister, or hæmatoma. This is usually the sequel to a blow, such as a slamming door, and shows itself as a large, tense swelling, which when opened by the surgeon proves to be an accumulation of serum usually tinged with blood. Some cases become infected at the time of injury, some after with the patient's rubbing. With the greatest surgical skill in the world one must expect a slight deformity, and the cat develops a puckered ear, much the same as the human boxer.

Disease of the Bladder.—The bladder is a common seat of disease in cats, and is frequently affected through the blocking of the natural water-passage by small sand-like calculi. Naturally, male cats are more often affected, as the terminal end of the urinary tracts is wider and more dilatable in females. The urine is unable to escape, and the bladder becomes filled with a mixture of urine and the sandy calcular matter. The condition may be diagnosed quite readily, as the cat usually collapses, or partially collapses, and one may easily feel the distended bladder through the walls of the abdomen (belly). It is necessary to send for professional help immediately, and, while no relief can be guaranteed, it is often possible to relieve the condition by judicious manipulation. Owners should not attempt to do this themselves (unless help cannot be obtained), as they may easily burst the bladder. As the animal is usually in a state of collapse when the condition is discovered, it makes a bad risk for actual operation, and relief by *skilled* pressure is usually to be recommended.

Ringworm.—There are two common kinds of ringworm in the cat (a third, which may also infect the dog, is more rare; it is the *tricho-phyton* which is usually found on cattle). The first kind is acquired from rats and mice, and is most commonly to be found at the bases of the claws, from where it may spread to the ears and face. The individual lesions are circular and yellow in colour, and consist largely of a scabby material. This kind of ringworm is known as "favus."

The second type of ringworm (microsporon) is more important, because it is more readily transmissible to human beings. Whereas this form usually sets up circular scaly lesions in the dog, it often infects cats without there being much naked-eye evidence of its presence. Indeed, in the cat the condition is often unsuspected until the owner himself becomes infected and consults his doctor.

Ringworm should be treated or dealt with by a veterinary surgeon, who will also confirm or refute by special methods the presence of micro-sporon in cats.

Intestinal Parasites—" Worms."—The cat also is subject to both roundworms and tapeworms. The roundworm which parasitises cats in this country is similar to that of the dog (although a different species) and is also much more harmful to the young than to the adult animal. In kittens the symptoms are a general unthriftiness, staring coat, and in some cases diarrhœa and a " pot-bellied " appearance.

The commonest cat tapeworm in this country is one which passes its intermediate stage in the rat or mouse, or sometimes in other rodents. The tapeworm, which, as mentioned under the section on dogs, is dangerous to man, is sometimes found in the cat also.

Accidents and Injuries.—Despite their sagacity and alertness in many ways, cats seem curiously unable, in many instances, to acquire road-sense. They are dazed by a car's head-lights, while if a motorist sounds his horn they tend to stop still in their tracks.

Injuries from traps, *e.g.*, gin-traps, are very common, and it is probable that many thousands of cats annually are maimed in this fashion. Cats suffer injury from shooting, from stoning, and from blows with sticks. Since they are predatory animals, they have often to pay the penalty inflicted on them by wrathful people. Needless to say, cats which survive to return home usually require expert treatment.

Poisoning may be included under this heading. Although there are doubtless many deliberate attempts to poison marauding cats, alleged " poisoning " is often no more than a case of feline enteritis, and owners should not claim glibly that their cats have been poisoned until they have expert evidence to back their judgment.

Fur-balling, as it has been termed, may be mentioned here. Cats, especially the long-haired varieties, must often ingest hair during their toilet, and occasionally serious trouble (a stoppage of the bowels) is brought about by a mass of such hair which has collected in a part of the bowel. There is constipation, loss of condition, and often evidence of considerable pain. Such cats should be taken to a veterinary surgeon.

Bites and scratches are even more common in the cat than they are in the dog, and subsequent sepsis is equally likely.

FERRETS.

Description.—The ferret is probably a domesti-cated form of the pole-cat (*Mustela putorius*), and is known sometimes by that name and sometimes as *Mustela furo*. Most tame ferrets have pink eyes and yellowish-white fur, but there are darker forms believed to have resulted from crossing in previous generations with wild pole-cats. Indeed, these darker forms are popularly termed " pole-cat ferrets." They are of two main kinds, the first having creamy under fur and black guard hairs, and the second being a chocolate-brown colour, with brown upper parts and black under parts, and a few scattered light hairs on the face.

Ferrets are long creatures in relation to their body weight, and when fully-grown may have a body 14 in. long or more and a tail of 5 in. Some strains grow appreciably larger. The main use of the ferret is, of course, in rabbiting, for which purpose they have been employed for many centuries. Although they can become fierce if not accustomed to regular handling or kind treatment, and are capable of inflicting a nasty bite, they may nevertheless be made into docile and highly intelligent pets. It is most important to win their confidence from the beginning and to accustom them to regular handling from the time they are young " kittens."

Accommodation.—Ferrets must have dry, clean accommodation in a room free from draughts but well ventilated. Wood is warmer than metal, but more difficult to clean, and is best lined with hard asbestos sheeting, which is resistant to water. The most suitable accommodation comprises a sleeping compartment of similar proportions to a small kennel, leading by a small doorway or "pop-hole" to a wire-netting exercising run, which should be as large as possible compatible with cleanliness. It is a good idea to have a means of closing the doorway so that the ferret or ferrets may be confined within the sleeping-compartment if necessary. Wood-wool makes an excellent bedding, but if difficult to obtain newspaper may be provided for the ferret to lie on. The floor of the run may have a false bottom or may be sprinkled with sawdust. It is imperative to keep the whole of the accommodation clean and dry, not only to avoid smell but also to prevent the ferrets from developing a very serious necrotic infection of the feet known as "foot-rot."

Feeding.—Many ferrets are unfortunately not fed adequately. It must be appreciated that basically they are carnivorous animals, and that their food requirements are more similar to those of the dog and cat than those of rodents. Indeed, many of the general remarks made about the principles of feeding dogs and cats apply to ferrets also.

Most ferrets like bread-and-milk, and while this is an excellent article of diet, it is in itself inadequate. Up to about 4 oz. of raw meat (minced for younger animals) daily is an excellent basis, and this may be replaced by fish. Liver, especially raw liver, is an excellent source of many factors, and there is good reason to provide some at least weekly if it can be obtained. Failing this, it is advisable to add 1–2 per cent. of whole dry liver to the diet. Once ferrets are grown, one feeding daily—at a fixed time—is sufficient. The female (jill) should have ample supplies of milk just prior to the birth of her young and while she is suckling them.

Breeding.—In the northern hemisphere the female ferret usually comes into œstrus (season) in early March of the year following that in which it is born. If the jill does not conceive during this œstrus she will have a further œstral period in July or August. The desire of the jill to mate is very strong, and if not allowed to do so, some animals sometimes have been found to waste and pine. The act of mating is prefaced by very vigorous behaviour on the part of the male (hob), and anyone not appreciating the performance might think that he was out to kill his mate! The mating act itself is usually prolonged, and may take up to three hours. If left together the hob and jill will probably mate from two to four times during the course of a couple of days. As in the cat and rabbit, ovulation or the shedding of the egg from the ovary takes place as a result of mating, and not spontaneously. The period of gestation is forty-two days, and the numbers of young born usually varies from five to thirteen, the average litter being six to eight. Pseudopregnancy occurs if the jill is not mated, and may become outwardly obvious as in the case of certain bitches.

Males also have a seasonal rhythm, their capacity to fertilise being greatest from early March to August. Young hobs seem to be active about a month earlier than older ones. The length of daylight or, rather, the incrementation in light from day to day, has an important bearing on breeding capacity in both sexes, and by the use of artificial light it has proved possible to induce either œstrus or male activity at different times of the year.

The young are hairless and blind, and weigh on the average under ½ oz. at birth. Their eyes open at about four weeks, and they can then commence to eat small pieces of solid food to supplement their mother's milk. They may be weaned at from six to eight weeks.

Diseases.—The most serious disease of ferrets is *canine distemper,* and the variant known as

"hard pad" (see under dog) is equally capable of infecting ferrets. Such infections can wipe out entire stocks, and every care should be taken to prevent their spread from dogs to ferrets—and vice versa. A veterinary surgeon should be consulted immediately when a ferret becomes ill or out of sorts. Ferrets are also susceptible to some strains of *human* influenza, and should not be tended by persons with colds or with any indications of "flu." The feeding of infected milk may give rise to *tuberculosis* (now unlikely in Britain). *Foot-rot* has already been mentioned, and must on no account be neglected. *Mange* or "scabies" of the back and tail region should be dealt with promptly, employing modern preparations. Abscesses of the neck region are often encountered, and should receive professional treatment if they do not clear up rapidly, for they may spread with dire consequences.

RATS.

Description.—Tame rats are domesticated varieties of the wild Norway or "brown" rat (*Rattus norvegicus*). Such rats are usually albinos or black-and-white, although other colours have been bred. The hooded varieties are those in which the head and foreparts are mainly black or chocolate and the remainder of the body, apart from small patches the same colours as the hood, is white. Tame rats differ materially from wild ones in disposition, and properly managed are extremely tractable. Healthy specimens accustomed to handling bite only when frightened, *e.g.,* when a sudden movement is made in front of them. Males appear to live longer than females, but three years is a good age.

"Black" rats, *i.e.,* the species (*Rattus rattus*) sometimes known as the ship or Alexandrine rat, have been bred in captivity, but tame strains are not generally available.

Housing.—Tame rats require a warm, even temperature—65–70° F. all the year round—and draughts or lowered temperature may precipitate lung disease or other disorders. It is best to have a complete spare set of boxes or cages, and to change to fresh quarters weekly except when the females have unweaned young with them. Empty cages should be cleaned and disinfected thoroughly before being used again. Provided the temperature conditions are suitable—and this is essential—metal cages of the types employed in scientific laboratories are best with wire-mesh false bottoms and trays containing sawdust to catch the droppings. Accommodation should be

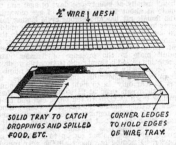

½" WIRE MESH

SOLID TRAY TO CATCH DROPPINGS AND SPILLED FOOD, ETC.

CORNER LEDGES TO HOLD EDGES OF WIRE TRAY.

ample, and even for a pair of pet rats the cage should measure about 30 in. × 18 in. × 18 in. If wooden boxes are employed it may be desirable to line them with hard asbestos sheeting or galvanised metal to prevent damage from gnawing.

Small, dark "shelters" and exercising devices, *e.g.,* wheels or ladders, are appreciated by the rats, but must be kept clean. Wood-wool makes the best bedding.

Feeding.—Rats may take a wide variety of foods, including many of our own, and there are several successful ways of feeding them, including the provision of specially formulated " rat-cubes," of the same type as that described below for mice. A good daily diet is wholemeal bread, mixed cereals (*e.g.*, oats, wheat, hempseed), with about

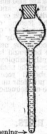

WATER BULB SUITABLE FOR USE WITH PET RODENTS

5 per cent. dried brewers' yeast and milk either fed separately or mixed with the rest of the food. Twice weekly each rat should be given up to ½ oz. or more of meat, liver, fish, or other " animal protein." A little fresh greenfood (even grass) is appreciated, and in winter especially some supplement containing vitamins A and D is desirable. Expectant and nursing mothers should have as much milk as they require. Never overfeed or allow uneaten food residues to remain in the cage. Fresh water (preferably in bulbs or bottles) should be available at all times. Far cleaner than open dishes are the special but simple type of water bulbs suspended on or in front of the cage or box so that the rat can drink from the rounded end of the spout. A simple substitute is a medicine " flat " bottle—or even a ¼- or ½-pint milk-type bottle. This should be fitted with a cork—or, better, a rubber bung—pierced for a piece of bent glass tubing. Provided that the free end of the glass tubing is not sharp, and is chosen so that the aperture is considerably smaller than that of the tube itself, the water will not run out unless sucked out by the rat. The spout should, of course, be within easy access of the rat, which will soon learn to drink from it.

Breeding.—Rats can breed at quite a young age (usually being capable of mating when fifty to sixty days old), but it is better to separate the sexes within a fortnight or so of weaning (weaning being usually at twenty-one days of age) and to mate at about 100 to 120 days of age onwards. the female rat has an œstrous cycle lasting just over four days. One male (buck) may be mated to one female (doe)—this is probably best in the case of pet rats—or with two or three females if preferred, but it is unwise to keep more than one adult male in the presence of females. The gestation period is twenty-one to twenty-two days or occasionally a few days longer. The number born varies considerably, but often it is best to try to rear only six to eight young. The young have their ears open at 2½ to 3½ days, cut their incisor teeth at eight to ten days, can find their way to their mother at about the same time, open their eyes at fourteen to seventeen days, and may leave the nest at twenty-one days. In the case of pet rats it is probably best to leave the young with the mother for up to a week or so longer. Breeding can occur all the year round, but takes place less readily in winter.

Handling.—Rats should not be " tailed," or the skin may slough off. Regular handling after weaning is excellent and promotes docility. The weight of the body should be supported.

Diseases.—On the whole rats are much less liable to disease than mice, provided temperature conditions are suitable. The commonest infection is *broncho-pneumonia*, often precipitated through

draughts or cold. *Mange* (especially of the ear) and infestation with *lice* may occur, and should be dealt with promptly by means of modern insecticides. Avoid contact with wild rodents, or the use of food or bedding that may have been contaminated by wild rats and mice.

MICE.

Description.—Tame mice are descended from the common house mouse (*Mus musculus*), and it is believed that mice have been domesticated for over 3,000 years. Apart from albino or " white mice," there are many varieties that have been bred by the extensive " mouse fancy," and there is a wide range of coat colour and also different types of coat, *e.g.*, long-haired, short-haired, and rex. " Waltzing mice " have an abnormality of that part of the inner ear concerned with balance. Mice may live up to thirty months, and in exceptional cases attain the age of three years or more.

Housing.—Although strains vary, most tame mice require a warm even temperature and the same general remarks concerning temperature range, bedding, and wooden or metal cages apply as in the case of rats. If a solid floor is used, this should be covered with clean sawdust. It is a good plan to change to a clean cage regularly, except when the female (doe) is nursing her young. If the cage is large (as in the case of pet mice it should be, with a floor space of say 24 in. × 12 in. × 12 in. for a group of mice), inner nest-boxes should be provided—one for each doe if breeding is taking place, although two does will often share the same nest-box. (In changing to fresh cages the nest-box, with mother and young inside, may, of course, be moved over.) A " two-storey " cage, with a ladder or " staircase " to the upper part, is an attractive variation, although difficult to keep clean. Mice should be kept well out of reach of wild rodents, from which they may all too readily contract disease.

Feeding.—Mice have not quite such a wide dietary range as rats, but there are several different ways of feeding them, including the provision of special " mouse cubes." These mouse cubes are of varying composition. One of the most successful, devised by workers in the Medical Research Council's laboratories, is known as " Diet 41," and is made up of the following parts by weight: wholemeal flour, 45; Sussex ground oats, 40; fish meal, 8; dried yeast, 1; dried skimmed milk, 3; cod-liver oil, 1; and common salt, 1. Diet 41 has also been employed for rats and monkeys, although for the latter particularly it requires supplementing. It is perhaps worth emphasising that cod-liver oil must not be fed in excess (½% of the diet is quite sufficient, and should not be exceeded), or it may prevent breeding and possibly have other harmful effects. Cubed diets are best fed from a wire basket through which the mice enjoy gnawing and eventually pulling out the pieces. Wholemeal bread is excellent if not allowed to become stale, but it should not form the sole article of diet, and it is a good idea to feed it alternately with a grain mixture (made up of rolled oats, wheat and other cereal grains, or mixed bird seed). Up to about 5 per cent. dried brewers' yeast is excellent, and so is fresh or dried milk, especially for mothers that are carrying or nursing young. Cheese is relished, but may smell if not fed carefully. Mice sometimes like an occasional pinch of marmalade, and it is a good idea to provide lettuce or other greenfood every week or so. There should be a constant supply of fresh water, preferably from bulbs or bottles as described for rats.

Breeding.—Young mice may be weaned at twenty-one days, although it is usually preferable to leave them with their mother for a further week. The age at which mice are capable of mating varies considerably from one strain or individual to another, and while the average is six to eight weeks, it may be much younger. It is therefore desirable to separate the males from the females at or shortly after weaning.

Mice may be mated up at two to three months of age, and the best arrangements are one male (buck) to one or two females. A pair of mice or a "bigynous trio" makes a successful combination. The oestrus cycle is similar to that of the rat, but its length appears to vary with coat colour, being longest in the brown mice and shortest in blacks and albinos. The gestation period is usually from eighteen to twenty days, but may be prolonged if the female was still suckling her previous litter when she conceived. There may be up to twelve or more young in a litter, but the average litter size is from five to seven. The second litter is usually the largest, and subsequent litters tend to decrease in numbers, so that the sixth is usually smaller than the first. Breeding may take place all the year round, although, as with rats, fertility is higher during the summer months.

Handling.—Any rapid or rough movement may frighten mice and cause them to bite through fear. Mice should be lifted by the tail—not too near the tip—and may be held in the palm of the hand, where they may be suitably restrained by keeping the tail between two fingers.

Diseases.—Mice are unfortunately prone to many diseases, although the risks will be much lower if they are kept in suitable surroundings, great care is taken to avoid infection, scrupulous cleanliness is observed, and the standard of feeding is good. One common source of infection is the presence of the excreta of wild rodents on bedding or foodstuffs. A common disease is that sometimes called "*mouse typhoid*," caused by organisms of the Salmonella group. Although some mice recover, they may remain carriers of infection, and once this disease is diagnosed it is best to destroy the affected mice and those in contact with them, and not to employ any of the cages or utensils for fresh mice without adequate sterilisation. There are other septicæmia diseases of mice, and also virus diseases, including certain types of *pneumonia* and a condition known as *infectious ectromelia*. The accurate diagnosis of these calls for expert opinion and often for special bacteriological or other examinations. The mouse-owner should, however, be able to recognise signs of ill-health or departure from normal, one of the commonest being loss of appetite. In young mice the coat should be smooth and glossy. As mice get older there may be loss of pigmentation (in coloured mice) or even loss of fur. A sick mouse usually sits hunched up and has a ruffled coat, while the eyes may be partially closed or have some discharge. A healthy mouse will usually catch on to suitable objects when held by its tail and is capable of pulling quite hard, whereas the pull of a sick mouse is much weaker. If one or more mice die it is best to destroy at once any cage-mates that appear seedy. As in the case of rats, external parasites should be dealt with promptly with the aid of modern insecticidal preparations.

GOLDEN HAMSTERS.

Description.—There are many species of hamsters in the world, and more than one kind can now be bred in captivity. The one referred to, however, is the Golden Hamster (*Mesocricetus auratus*), a delightful little creature of which a full-grown female (females are larger than males) rarely exceeds 7 in. in length. This history of the domestication of the golden hamster is quite remarkable, for prior to 1930 only museum specimens were known. In that year a mother and her twelve young were dug up in a field near Aleppo and were taken to the Hebrew University, Jerusalem, and from that one family have been bred the hundreds of thousands of golden hamsters now employed as pets or as laboratory animals in many parts of the world. The species has taken well to captivity and, although capable of inflicting a nasty little bite if frightened or handled roughly, becomes docile and friendly when properly cared for. Characteristic features are the soft, smooth fur, the large black eyes, the "cheek

pouches" in which food is stored and which may become enormously distended after a meal, the short, stumpy tail, and the extremely loose skin, inside which the hamster can turn round to a considerable degree.

Housing.—The same remarks about accommodation, environmental temperature, freedom from draughts, fittings, and other general considerations (including cleanliness) apply as in the case of rats and mice. For breeding purposes a dark inner chamber or nest-box is desirable. Several hamsters may be kept together, but the introduction of a stranger (or even the re-introduction of a former cage-mate that has been removed for some time) may lead to fighting.

Feeding.—Satisfactory diets include the following: (1) rat cubes (*e.g.*, "Diet 41"), carrots, greenfood, and milk; (2) cereal grains and/or wholemeal bread, carrots, greenfood, and milk; (3) steamed Rangoon beans, wheat, maize meal bread, a little Marmite, and milk. Care must be taken not to allow storage of excess food, which will deteriorate and cause a smell. Grass is a suitable source of greenfood during its growing season. Apples and other fruits are often relished. Water, preferably in bulbs or bottles as described for rats, should always be available.

Breeding.—Golden Hamsters attain puberty at from ten to fifteen weeks of age, or even younger, males being usually earlier. Generally speaking, it is best to defer breeding until after fifteen weeks of age. There is an oestrus cycle of about four days, and the gestation period is very short, averaging sixteen days, although sometimes up to nineteen days. Mating not followed by conception results in phantom or pseudopregnancy. Litter size varies from one to fifteen, but the average is six to seven. Not many females have more than four litters and although both sexes may live up to two years, breeding by the female is rare after nine months. The young are naked and blind at birth. Hair first appears at five days, and covers the whole body at eight days. The eyes open at about eleven days, and soon after this the young begin to take food for themselves and may be weaned at three to four weeks. Care must be taken that the female does not injure the male, and for safety's sake it is probably better to keep only one female and one male together and to remove the male before the young are born.

Handling.—Gentleness is essential, and sudden movements should be avoided. The tail is much too short to use, and the easiest way is to lift them by the loose skin over the back and shoulders. As already noted, they can twist easily within their skins, unless a substantial amount is taken in the hand. After picking up they may be allowed to sit on the palm of the hand.

Diseases.—Several diseases of hamsters are now known, and, like most rodents, they are susceptible to *Salmonellosis* (see notes under "mouse typhoid" and "paratyphoid" in guinea-pigs). One of the most prevalent conditions is *ear mange*, in severe cases of which the condition spreads from the ears to other parts of the body. Modern anti-mange preparations are highly effective.

CAVIES (GUINEA-PIGS).

Description.—Cavies or guinea-pigs (*Cavia porcellus*) are rodents, and are descended from one or more of the several kinds of wild cavy found in South America. They are believed to have been domesticated by the Incas long before Europeans "discovered" that part of the world. They make excellent pets, but are easily frightened, and should be treated gently and quietly. They usually behave quietly, although there may be fighting between adult males ("boars"), while the arrival of food—or the entry of a person into a room, which fact is obviously connected with feeding-time—usually sets up a chorus of chirruping squeaks. There is to-day a considerable cavy "fancy" in Great Britain and other countries, and many varieties are recognised, including rough-coated and smooth-coated types. Among recognised colours are the agouti (banded hairs), brindle, cinnamon, tortoiseshell (tricoloured), and Himalayan (white with attractive black points). The long-haired Peruvian and rosette-haired Abyssinian breeds are popular. Guinea-pigs may live up to two to three years. There is a small tail (composed of from five to seven caudal vertebræ), but usually this is so short that it does not project outside the body. There are four toes on each of the fore-feet and three on each hind foot. An adult guinea-pig may measure up to 10 in. or more in length, and sometimes its weight is well over 2 lb.

Housing.—Guinea-pigs may be kept outside or inside. If outside conditions are favoured, great care must be taken to protect them from dogs, cats, and rats. The last-named may be a danger also in conveying disease. The run should be in a sheltered position away from wind and direct summer sunlight. Tent-shaped waterproof shelters, with wooden floors covered by cleaning trays, have been found satisfactory. Another method is to keep them in hutches of the same type employed for rabbits and when conditions are suitable to let them out into a temporary run on the lawn surrounded by ½ in.-mesh wire-netting that is at least 12 in. high. (N.B. This will keep dogs or cats out.) Guinea-pigs will crop the grass and help to keep the lawn smooth. Great care should be taken not to allow the ground or floor to become so contaminated by guinea-pig excreta that it conveys disease from one animal to another.

If indoor methods are selected, an even, preferably warm temperature is desirable, and there should be freedom from draughts. Guinea-pigs have been found to thrive best at about 65° F. with a humidity range of 45–55 per cent. Provided warm conditions are available, metal cages are easier to keep clean than wooden ones, while a false bottom of wire mesh, above the cleaning tray, is helpful. Wood-wool is again the best bedding. Cages must not be too small, and a pair of pet guinea-pigs should have about 14 sq. ft. of floor space. It is a sound principle, as with rats and mice, to change frequently to a clean cage, the used one being cleaned and disinfected thoroughly before being used again.

Feeding.—Guinea-pigs, like human beings, apes, and monkeys, require a source of vitamin C (ascorbic acid). Normally they obtain this from greenfood, but in winter especially they may not secure enough in this way. The daily requirement of an adult guinea-pig is about 2 milligrammes, and supplies can be obtained from a chemist's shop.

There are many different methods of feeding guinea-pigs. Among cubed or pelleted diets is that known as "Diet 18," which is employed also for rabbits. It contains the following parts by weight: wheat feed, 15; grass meal, 30; decorticated groundnut meal, 15; linseed cake, 10; barley meal, 20; common salt, 1; and chalk, 1. This is fed together with fresh greenfood to supply vitamin C. For feeding without the use of compressed diets a good plan is to provide a daily "concentrate ration" of about 1 oz. per head of a mixture of 2 parts bran and 1 part crushed oats, and to feed in addition ample amounts of cabbage, lettuce or other greenfood, meadow hay of good quality, grass, and raw vegetables. Although guinea-pigs normally derive moisture from fresh greenfood, and may appear to take little or no water for long periods, it is a mistake not to provide a fresh supply, preferably from water bulbs, or from inverted bottles fitted with a stopper and drinking-spout. A little dried brewers' yeast makes an excellent addition to the diet, while for females ("sows") when pregnant or lactating, milk is excellent. Dead foliage should be removed from greenfood, and soil and dirt cleaned off. Frosted greenfood should be soaked in warm water before it is given to guinea-pigs. Unfortunately, hay may be contaminated by wild rodents, but it forms an excellent article of diet. Never allow food residues to remain in the cage.

Breeding.—The lactation period of the guinea-pig is a short one. The gestation period averages sixty-three to seventy-five days, although variations of fifty-eight to seventy-two days are known and the young are born in an advanced state with their eyes already open. They can run freely with their mother shortly after birth. They are able to nibble a little food as early as the second day, and by the time they are two to three weeks old they are completely independent and are neglected by their mother. A sow will often mate again the day the young are born, or shortly after, so that a rapid succession of litters often occurs.

Guinea-pigs are capable of mating from about fifty-five days of age, or even younger in certain circumstances, which include the provision of a high plane of nutrition. The œstrous cycle averages fifteen to seventeen days, although it may vary from thirteen to twenty-five days. The actual period during which mating may occur usually lasts only from about six to eleven hours. One boar may run with as many as twenty sows if so desired, but in the case of pets it is much more interesting to run a boar with only one sow, in which case she need not usually be removed to a separate cage before the young are born. The young guinea-pigs should be separated from the older ones shortly after weaning, and the sexes separated at four to five weeks of age if they are not to breed prematurely. It is better to wait until the animals are approaching six months of age or so before they are mated, for they do not become fully grown and "filled out" until they are between six and nine months.

Handling.—Guinea-pigs are timid creatures, and should be handled gently. They are best picked up with both hands. If a guinea-pig is to be held in order to examine it for any purpose, a good method is to place one hand over the animal's shoulders, with the fingers and thumb around its neck, and to extend its hind limbs with the other hand.

Diseases.—The most important infectious disease of guinea-pigs is, like "mouse typhoid," caused by organisms of the Salmonella group, and it may be contracted from wild rodents or from food or bedding contaminated by them. In guinea-pigs the disease is known usually as "paratyphoid" (or sometimes as "salmonellosis") and it may take an acute form, causing death within a few days, or a more chronic form in which many animals recover to become symptom-less carriers of disease. Outwardly healthy, they may infect susceptible guinea-pigs with which they are placed. Cold or other environmental variations, and faulty feeding, can help to set off an outbreak, for there are few stocks in which the organisms are not lurking in some "latent carriers." Coccidiosis is common, but is a much less serious threat than in the case of rabbits. It has been set up in infected stocks by feeding inadequate diets, and provided that nutrition and hygiene are adequate there is rarely serious trouble from this disease. Infections of the respiratory tract may occur, but are uncommon except when there is overcrowding, high humidity, or damp bedding. Sometimes organisms of the Pneumococcus group cause not only disease of the respiratory tract but also a generalised infection of the serous membranes of the body. When this disease occurs it may produce death without much warning. It is possible that the infection sometimes comes from human beings. The disease known as pseudotuberculosis, and described under rabbits, occurs in guinea-pigs also. Again, environmental conditions and faulty feeding may predispose towards active infection.

With good fortune and sound management, trouble from these serious infections may never occur. External parasites should be dealt with promptly by insecticides. Sometimes non-parasitic skin disorders occur when the diet is faulty, e.g., too dry or lacking in sufficient fresh greenfood of good quality.

RABBITS.

Description.—Domesticated varieties of the wild European rabbit (*Oryctolagus cuniculus*) are now kept in many countries. The wild rabbit is believed to have been introduced into Great Britain in the 12th cent. Tame rabbits have been bred for centuries, and the breeds and strains produced differ appreciably in size, colour, and habits from the common wild form. Some breeds have been specially bred for table purposes, while others (*e.g.*, the Angora, Sitka, and Argente de Champagne) have been developed for their fur. In addition, many varieties are produced for show purposes by the extensive rabbit " fancy." The small hardy Dutch rabbit (usually black and white) is one of the kinds suitable for beginners. Among well-known categories are the English, Japanese, Himalayan, Belgian Hare (really a rabbit), Flemish Giant, Beveren, Blue Imperial, Polish, Havana, Lop, Half-Lop, Chinchilla, and New Zealand White. The Copenhagen rabbit appears to be identical with the New Zealand White. The smaller breeds weigh only 4–6 lb. when fully grown, whereas some specimens of some of the giant breeds attain a weight of 20 lb. or more.

Rabbits and hares were formerly classified with the rodents, but are now placed in a separate Order of mammals, known as the Lagomorphs. Young rabbits (in contrast to leverets or young hares) are blind and helpless for some time after birth. Tame specimens may live for 4–5 years, and individuals have lived for up to 13 years.

Housing.—Since rabbits are kept for commercial purposes, various systems have been devised, including the use of movable ark-huts, with covered runs, that can be moved regularly to fresh ground. If kept indoors rabbits do not need special heating, but freedom from draughts, damp, excessive cold, and access by wild rodents is most desirable. A garage is regarded as an unsuitable place, owing to the susceptibility of rabbits to exhaust or engine fumes. One of the great difficulties of rabbit-keeping is coccidiosis, which is a serious disease in rabbits and hares. (European hares could never be bred successfully in captivity until means of overcoming coccidiosis were discovered.) With young rabbits especially (*i.e.*, those that have left the nest and are able to run about freely) it is a sound principle to move them to a clean floor or fresh ground every two days, so as to " break " the life-cycle of the coccidial parasite. One way of doing this is to have " back-to-back " cages or hutches, from one to the other of which the rabbits may be transferred easily. The empty cage or hutch may then be cleaned and disinfected thoroughly and allowed to dry out before the rabbits are returned to it. Wood-wool makes a suitable bedding material, although the female (doe) will pluck her own fur to line the nest when her litter is due to be born. Wire-mesh floors with a tray beneath are convenient, but if solid floors are used these should be sprinkled with fresh sawdust daily or every other day. Provided the standard of hygiene can be maintained, cages or hutches and their runs should be large. The absolute minimum is " 1 sq. ft. of floor space for each 1 lb. weight of adult rabbit," *i.e.*, if there are two rabbits totalling 12 lb. in weight there must be at least 12 sq. ft. of floor space. If cages or hutches are stacked one on top of the other the lowest should be well clear of the ground, and if there is only one hutch this, for convenience and safety from wild rodents, should be 2–3 ft. off the floor.

Feeding.—The wild rabbit grazes at dusk and dawn, and it is preferable to feed tame rabbits twice daily, while pregnant or lactating does and young rabbits benefit from three meals a day. As in the case of guinea-pigs, the ration may be thought of as consisting of two parts, a concentrate portion and a portion consisting of greenfood and other succulent material. The concentrate portion consists usually of a mixture of cereal grains or of some other form of mash. Successful mashes, of which there are many, include: (1) a mixture of 4 parts cereal grains and 1 part dairy cake; (2) equal parts of bran, weatings, flaked maize—or barley meal—and fish meal. This second is useful for breeding. If materials for the mash are in short supply they may in part be replaced by cooked potatoes. An average daily food allowance for a resting (non-breeding) adult of medium size would be: greenfood (grass, clover, weeds, lettuce, etc.) and/or roots, 12–16 oz.; hay (good quality), 2–3 oz.; and concentrates (cereal grain or meal mash), 2 oz. If cooked potatoes are used they should be fed at the rate of 4 parts to each 1 part of cereal that they replace. For a doe nursing her litter a suitable diet would comprise: greenfood to appetite, hay (good quality and preferably containing clover or other legume), 2–4 oz.; concentrates (preferably with fish meal or some other suitable source of " animal protein "), 4–6 oz.; and common salt at the level of up to 1 per cent. of the ration. A mineral mixture is preferable to salt alone. Excessive greenfood, especially in the form of cabbage and other Brassica plants, may cause polyuria, *i.e.*, the passage of excessive quantities of urine. No matter how much fresh greenfood rabbits may have available, a supply of fresh water should always be provided. The daily water requirement of the rabbit is quite high, and certain bad habits such as urine drinking or even cannibalism may result from an inadequate intake of water. Pots that cannot be overturned or, preferably, water bulbs or bottles as described for guinea-pigs, are the most suitable means of providing water.

" Diet 18," described under guinea-pigs, is one of several types of compressed diet successfully employed for rabbits. Fresh greenfood is preferably fed in addition, while the water requirement with diets of this kind is considerable.

Breeding.—The age of puberty varies with the breed, and also with the time of year at which the individual rabbit was born. Rabbits born in spring are usually capable of breeding at a younger age than those born in the autumn. In Great Britain the wild rabbit has a fairly sharply defined main breeding season, lasting from January to June, but some degree of " out-of-season " breeding may take place at almost all other times. Tame rabbits may not breed freely during the winter months, especially if environmental conditions are cold. Mating may take place as early as four months of age, and although this does not often result in pregnancy, it is accompanied by competition and fighting between individuals of the same sex. Males (bucks) and females should therefore be separated at weaning or at least before they are four months old. Fertile matings may occur at from about 5½ months of age onwards, but it is wise to defer breeding until later—say seven to eight months for most breeds. The female does not ovulate or shed her eggs from the ovary spontaneously as do most domestic mammals, but, like the cat and ferret, does so in response to the act of mating or some other strong stimulus. Even playing between two does may precipitate ovulation, in which case a so-called " phantom pregnancy " (pseudopregnancy) may result, the doe that has ovulated appearing pregnant and even developing lactating mammary glands. There is not therefore an obvious regularly recurring œstrus cycle as in the domestic rat, mouse, and guinea-pig, and in summer at least the doe may be ready to mate at almost any time. Observation suggests, however, that there are fluctuations in the desire to mate. The act of mating in rabbits sometimes causes alarm that all is not well to those that have not hitherto witnessed it, for the buck usually emits a peculiar cry and loses his balance to fall over sideways. It is usually best to separate the buck from the doe before the young are born. The gestation period is usually thirty to thirty-two days. In wild rabbits a high percentage of embryos die and are " resorbed," and are therefore never born. In some populations it appears that about two-thirds of all rabbits conceived (including about 60 per cent. of total litters) are lost before birth in this way. Losses from this cause are probably much less common in domesticated rabbits, especially when the standards of feeding and management are high. Litter size is variable, and depends in part on the breed or strain. In some strains mean litter sizes up to eight or nine have been obtained, but a mean of four or so is more common. Does that do not prepare the nest or ear their young properly should not be selected or further breeding. The doe with her new-born litter should not be disturbed unduly, or she may desert her young, which are blind and helpless at birth and are entirely dependent on her for at least three weeks, after which they begin to nibble food to supplement the milk that they receive from her. The eyes open at about fourteen days. Weaning should be carried out at between six and eight weeks of age, by which time the young should be able to fend for themselves completely.

Handling.—Rabbits should never be lifted by the ears alone. One good way of lifting them is to grip the ears firmly but gently with one hand and to place the other hand under the rump to take the weight of the rabbit's body. Alternatively, one hand may be placed flat under the rabbit's belly, but this requires more care, and may be a risky procedure with pregnant does. Another convenient way to handle rabbits, especially young ones, is to lift them by the loose skin over the shoulders. Rabbits can inflict quite nasty scratches with the nails of the hind feet. It is incidentally a good plan to examine the nails of all four feet and to trim them if they are too long. Care should be taken not to cut back as far as the " quick," i.e., the bluish portion at the base of the nail that contains blood vessels.

Diseases.—As already indicated, *coccidiosis* is a highly important disease of young rabbits. It may be either of the " hepatic type," affecting principally the liver, or the " intestinal type," affecting principally the gut. Even in the case of the hepatic type, however, the coccidial parasites are picked up by mouth and after penetrating the intestinal walls make their way via the blood-stream to the liver. Hygienic measures are the best means of preventing the disease (see under **Housing**), but should it break out, prompt treatment with certain sulphonamides or other anti-coccidial drugs may prove effective. In certain rabbitries in which coccidiosis is a constant problem, protection has been obtained by feeding a dilute solution of one of the soluble sulphonamides in place of drinking-water. There are certain types of digestive disturbance that may resemble coccidiosis, and one of these, the cause of which has not yet been established with certainty, is known as *mucoid enteritis*. Some such cases are probably variations of " bloat " (" the blows ") a condition the cause of which is again not fully established, although there may in fact be several factors. A rabbit may, of course, " blow " after eating fermentative food, but cases of " bloat " can occur independently of this, and some may be due to a virus. " *Snuffles* " is characterised by a nasal discharge, and is not always associated with the same organism. In its milder forms it is not a severe disease, but with the more chronic forms the nasal discharge becomes marked and gives rise to a typical snuffling noise. Severe chronic cases become progressively worse and die of a terminal pneumonia. There is also a severe acute form, in which the rabbit dies so rapidly that the condition is sometimes not recognised. Acute cases that are treated in time with certain sulphonamides may respond well, but chronic snufflers are difficult to treat and go on spreading the infection, and hence are better destroyed. Correct environmental conditions are a great help in preventing this disease. A chronic type of infection is known as *pseudotuberculosis*, which is usually acquired from eating material contaminated by wild rodents or by other infected rabbits. It is caused by quite a different organism from that of true tuberculosis, which is much rarer in rabbits. Clinical cases should be killed, and prevention lies in hygienic measures. Infected wounds or skin abscesses may lead to a disease caused by the " necrosis bacillus " (*Fusiformis necrophorus*) and known sometimes as *necrobacillosis*. It is usually characterised by subcutaneous swellings distributed irregularly over the head and body. Although in the early stages the affected rabbit may remain in apparently good health, the spread of the disease is insidious and usually fatal, and in most instances it is kinder and safer to destroy a case before it progresses too far. There are unfortunately

several other infectious conditions occurring in rabbits, but all call for expert help in diagnosis and treatment.

Among non-infectious conditions *pregnancy toxæmia* is not uncommon in does during the very late pregnancy, and usually proves fatal within two to three days. It is a " metabolic disorder," i.e., it is associated with some functional derangement of the endocrine or ductless glands or with the inability to control properly the utilisation of its food. Faulty feeding is probably a contributory cause.

Among external parasites, *ringworm* is not common, but may be acquired from rodents. Affected rabbits that are to be treated must be isolated. *Ear mange* (known usually as *ear canker*) is common, and may be treated by strict attention to hygiene, with thorough disinfection of the hut or cage, and by dressing with a modern anti-mange preparation. *Body mange* is much less common but far more difficult to treat.

Among internal parasites, so-called " *bladder worms* " i.e., the larval stages of two dog tapeworms (*Taenia pisiformis* and *Taenia serialis*) are quite common, although rarely fatal. The feeding of grass or other greenstuff to which dogs have had access should be avoided, as well as the contamination of the drinking-water with dog fæces.

GERBILS.

Description.—Gerbils, also known as jirds, sand rats and desert rats, are members of the sub-family *Gerbillinae* of the rodent family *Cricetidae*. There are some fourteen genera comprising some 50 species. The genera *Meriones* and *Gerbillus* are the most widely represented (about 14 and 10 species respectively). Virtually unknown in Britain until the mid-1960s, a few species have now been introduced from Asia, Africa and the Middle East, initially as laboratory animals.

Gerbils have now become immensely popular pets, both in schools and in the home, and provided one ensures that a docile species is acquired, one has perhaps the ideal pet mammal. They are virtually odourless, easy to handle and to breed, and pleasing to watch, both in appearance and antics.

Species differ widely in both size and disposition and hence one must take care when acquiring specimens. The Indian gerbil *Tatera indica* is, for example, large, aggressive and virtually untameable. Species recommended include *Gerbillus pyramidum*, *Meriones libycus* and *Meriones unguiculatus* (the Mongolian gerbil). The following advice applies to these species and particularly to the Mongolian gerbil—which is by far the most popular species available in Great Britain and hence the one most likely to be offered.

Housing.—Gerbils appear to tolerate a wide range of temperature conditions. Petter has bred several species (though not M. *unguiculatus*) in outdoor conditions in Paris. There is no evidence to suggest that the Mongolian gerbil is less hardy, though indoor conditions are advised. Precautions against escape should be exercised since they could become feral, and a pest.

Metal cages comprised largely of bars are recommended. Two-storey hampster cages are suitable and these enable one to watch the gerbils' complex and fascinating behaviour. Provide plenty of hay, straw or wood shavings and white paper. The animals shred material to make bedding and "nests." Since the animals are virtually odourless, as too is their urine and faeces, they need cleaning out less frequently than other rodents: once per two weeks suffices.

Either a pair of gerbils may be kept, or two males with two or three females. It is important, however, to introduce only *young animals* from separate litters into the same cage. Adults unused to one another are frequently hostile and aggressive.

Since the animals are burrowers in their natural state, they may be kept in a deep container, e.g., a large aquarium, and supplied with a good depth of peat or a similar material. This method of housing, however, has the drawback that one sees little of the animals.

Pieces of wood provide a gnawing surface: very necessary for most rodents.

Feeding.—Virtually nothing is known of the gerbils' natural foods; still less their nutritional requirements. One must simply provide a range of foodstuffs from which the animals select what is adequate for their needs. Gerbils will take insects, spiders and meat, though they thrive on an entirely vegetarian diet.

Satisfactory foodstuffs include rodent pellets or a coarse seed mixture such as that sold for parrots or for wild birds. Sunflower seeds are taken with avidity as too is germinating grain (i.e., soaked and allowed to grow for a few days to seedling stage). Pieces of raw fruit and vegetable are also consumed.

Water should be provided, though the animals drink little, particularly if vegetables are available.

Breeding.—As indicated under Housing, several adults may be run together.

Mating is rarely observed, though it is said to occur most usually in the late afternoon. Little is known about the breeding cycle.

The duration of pregnancy is about 25 days and the average litter number about 6. Not infrequently the first litter is small in number and the young may be killed by the parents. Second and subsequent litters are usually reared successfully. Hair develops in 6–10 days and the eyes open at about 3 weeks. Varieties of gerbils are beginning to be reported (Parslow 1970).

Handling.—Recently weaned specimens up to some 8 weeks of age require firm "cupping" in the hands since they are prone to jump with little regard for their own safety.

Regular handling over this age ensures a tame yet ever-inquisitive pet. Grasping by the base of the tail is usually necessary to enable one to remove the animal from a cage. Thereafter cupping is to be preferred.

Careless or over-enthusiastic handling of a timid individual sometimes produces a "fright reaction" where the animal lays trembling though otherwise almost inert for a minute or two. However, this soon passes.

Diseases.—Apart from the vulnerability of the first litter these animals are remarkably healthy. The result of fighting between adults from different cages is the only likely injury encountered apart from occasional skin infection around the nose and lips—possibly due to burrowing activity. This condition responds to a mild antiseptic cream.

Old animals may develop a condition where the eyeball tends to protrude. Neither cause nor cure has been investigated.

Any unwanted or infirm animal may be quickly and painlessly killed by the following procedure: put a little ether (diethyl ether) on a generous pad of cotton wool. Introduce this into a screw-cap jar, place the animal in, and fix the cap on firmly. Leave for 20 minutes.

LAND TORTOISES.

Tortoises are popular pets, but although many are kept with great success in Great Britain, the majority of those that are imported each year are never looked after adequately, or fail to thrive for other reasons.

Most land tortoises that are imported into Great Britain for sale through dealers are: (1) the Spur-thighed Mediterranean Land Tortoise (*Testudo graeca*), commonly known as the "Moroccan tortoise" and sometimes as the "Iberian" or "Algerian"; or (2) Hermann's Tortoise (*Testudo hermanni*). The second is distributed in Southern France, Southern Italy, the larger islands of the Western Mediterranean, and parts of Yugoslavia, Albania, and Greece. There is a species found in Greece, the Margined Tortoise (*Testudo marginata*), but while adaptable to life in Great Britain, it is more difficult to acquire. The two common species differ in several ways, the "Moroccan tortoise" having a small bony spur on the back of the thigh. (The upper part of the shell is termed the carapace and the ventral portion the plastron.)

In selecting a tortoise one should ensure that the animal appears healthy. It should be active and withdraw quickly into its shell on being disturbed. Its legs should be firm and not limp, and there should be no abnormal discharge from the eyes or nostrils. The shell and limbs should be uninjured. Females are generally larger and have a shorter tail than the male. The shield above the tail is flat in the former and curved in the male. It is a good idea to obtain a pair or more of tortoises, but not more than can be looked after with care. On being purchased they should be washed in tepid water.

Many tortoises are given free range in gardens, but this is not advised with all, as they eat a wide variety of vegetables and young plants, and being wandering animals are liable to get lost if the garden is not completely fenced or walled. They should be provided with as large a "pen" or "run" as possible, the walls or wire netting of which should be high enough to prevent their climbing over. The practice of tethering tortoises by a hole in the shell should be discouraged. They should always be provided with a box or shelter, the cheapest form being a wooden soap box turned on one side and with a sufficiently wide entrance, the wood being creosoted and covered with roofing felt. It can be lined with asbestos sheeting if desired, and have its floor covered with dry leaves or other bedding material. Some other shelter should also be provided in the run. The tortoises should be bathed during the hot weather. The occasional application of olive oil will keep the shell polished.

Land tortoises must be fed daily, and it is important to allow them to build up good reserves to enable them to hibernate through the winter successfully. Suitable foods include lettuce, young cabbage, peas, clover, dandelions, and a wide variety of green plants and ripe, sweet fruits. Generally bread and milk should be avoided. For young tortoises especially, it is recommended that once weekly or so the food should be sprinkled with powdered cuttlefish bone, or better still a small quantity of powered calcium gluconate or cod-liver oil. Fresh water in a shallow tray, or even a saucer, should always be provided.

One of the most difficult problems in tortoise keeping is hibernation. Some persons avoid allowing their pets to hibernate by transferring them to a warm place, such as a heated greenhouse; if this is done they must be kept well fed and their place maintained at a summer temperature. It is imperative to do one thing or the other—the half-torpid tortoise that is neither hibernating nor kept at summer temperature will die. Moreover, a tortoise that is allowed to hibernate must not be disturbed.

Signs of pending hibernation, including sluggishness and lowered appetite, are usually evident late in September or early in October. Tortoises living in the garden may commence to bury themselves. If this is allowed they must be well covered, else they may be killed by the ensuing frost. It is, though, more convenient and perhaps provides a greater chance of survival, due to the changeable winter conditions in Britain, to place the animal in a large box, which should be packed with straw, leaves, or hay. The box should be stored in a cool but frostproof place, such as out-building, cellar, or attic. It is important not to create conditions that will awaken the tortoise or tempt it to emerge before the following spring. Rats have been known to attack hibernating tortoises, and so due precautions should be taken.

On emerging from hibernation the eyes and nostrils are somewhat sealed, and should be released by bathing with a 4 per cent. boric acid solution and warm water.

Recently imported female tortoises frequently lay eggs, but it is not a common occurrence for pairs to breed freely in Britain. During the early part of the summer the male is sometimes seen butting the shell of the female, this being a courtship action. If eggs are laid it is unlikely that they will be fertile, and less likely that they can be hatched. They have been hatched by placing them on damp sand and storing them in a warm place—a heated greenhouse or airing cupboard. The eggs should not be disturbed or "turned" once incubation has commenced.

Tortoise ticks are often present on freshly imported specimens, and may best be removed by damping the tick with paraffin or methylated spirits and then removing it gently with tweezers. Round worms are very numerous in tortoises, and should they be seen in the faecal matter the remainder may be eliminated by sprinkling up to one grain of powdered santonin on the food once a week for six weeks. Possibly, some of the newer, safe anthelmintic preparations containing piperazine derivatives may be equally effective. Eye infections are common, and are usually remedied by bathing the eye well with a 4 per cent. boric acid solution or warm cod-liver oil. Continuous discharge from the nose indicates lung infection, and as a primary measure the animal should be kept warm. Bleeding can be stopped by using Friar's Balsam, and care should be taken to prevent insects settling on open wounds.

WATER TORTOISES (TERRAPINS)

In Great Britain the tortoises that have become adapted to life in ponds and rivers are usually termed "terrapins," the name turtle being applied to marine forms. In the U.S.A. and Canada, however, not only the marine species but also terrapins and tortoises are all termed "turtles."

Several kinds of terrapin are available and capable of thriving in Great Britain. These include several American species, the European Pond Tortoise (*Emys orbicularis*), the Spanish Terrapin (*Clemmys leprosa*), the Caspian Terrapin (*Clemmys caspica*), and the Reeves' Terrapin (*Chinemys reevesii*), which hails from China and Japan.

The ideal place in which to keep terrapins is a garden pond within an enclosure. The pond should contain an "island" of dry ground on to which the animals can climb easily. The water should vary in depth, and at one point be at least 2 ft. deep. Provided that there is a suitable "island" the boundary walls of the pond can be upright to prevent escape. The final coat of cement should be smooth and mixed with a waterproofing agent. Shade should be available, not only on the island but also in some parts of the water. This may be provided by suitable plants.

Terrapins are almost entirely carnivorous, although the young of some species may take a little lettuce or other vegetable food. Suitable foods include *small* pieces of raw meat, raw liver (this should certainly be given from time to time), fish, and earthworms. Terrapins prefer to take their food in the water, and it is best to feed them individually if there are several, to ensure that each receives his proper share.

Water tortoises also hibernate. Some bury themselves in mud or sand at the bottom of their ponds, others will dig themselves into the earth in the island or banks of their pond, while others again may go to sleep in the box that, as in the case of land tortoises, should preferably be provided for them on part of ther "land." Should they sleep at the bottom of the pond, it is as well to prevent freezing of the water. One means of doing this is to leave a log or logs floating on the surface. Moving these logs on cold mornings will help to break any ice formed and to prevent total freezing.

AQUARIUM FISH.

There are two types of aquaria—the cold-water, for fish from this and other temperate countries, and the heated, for tropical varieties of fish. Apart from the fact that a suitable heating mechanism—usually electric, with thermostatic control—has to be maintained for tropical aquaria, the general principles governing the two types are much the same. There is a certain amount of additional initial expense in setting up a heated aquarium—the running costs are not high—but in some respects tropical fish are easier to maintain than many of the cold-water varieties.

It should be emphasised at the outset that those who want to keep fish should invest in a proper aquarium and not in a "goldfish bowl," unless the latter be very large in relation to the fish to be kept. Far too many fish suffer from overcrowding or from lack of sufficient water

surface. In the case of cold freshwater fish such as carp and goldfish (which need quite different conditions from tropical fish) it has been calculated that every "1 in. of body" requires 1 sq. ft. of water surface in order to obtain sufficient oxygen for respiration. Thus a fish the body of which (*i.e.*, the length minus the tail fins) is 4 in. will require at least 4 sq. ft. of water surface, *i.e.*, an area of 2 ft. × 2 ft. Two such fish will require twice this area, and so on. In *The Right Way to Keep Pet Fish* by R. Dutta (6s.), it is pointed out that a goldfish should normally live for twenty-five years in a suitable pond, and grow to its full length of over 14 in. There are few indoor aquaria capable of supporting many full-grown goldfish in adequate conditions, and indeed it is recommended that domestic varieties of goldfish such as shubunkins, fantails, veiltails, and orandas, which grow more slowly, are far better adapted to cold-water aquaria. Tropical fish of the varieties kept in aquaria are usually much smaller, differ in their oxygen requirements, and can be kept in more crowded conditions. Many have an average body length of only about 1½ in., and eighteen such fish may be maintained in a suitably heated tank with an area of water surface of 18 in. × 12 in.

A beginner should not only read good books on the subject (including *Water Life* publications) but also consult experts and his local aquarist or dealer. Whatever aquarium is chosen, the conditions should be correct *before* any fish are introduced. Should fish be suddenly acquired, before a proper aquarium has been fitted up for them, they should be kept in some temporary (but sufficiently capacious) quarters until the aquarium is ready.

The instructions for installing and fitting up an aquarium are usually supplied, and should be followed carefully. The sand that is usually placed on the bottom should be thoroughly washed, and is best put in a little at a time. Make sure that the inside of the aquarium is thoroughly clean before anything at all is put into it. Ornamental rocks may next be introduced, and great care should be taken to ensure that these are of the correct type, unlikely to harm the fish physically or chemically. Water is then added very gently indeed, and suitable plants set. In the case of large tanks the planting is best done when the tank is only partly filled with water, but in any event the plants themselves should be kept wet all the time, or they may quickly shrivel up. In the case of cold-water aquaria everything may now be left for a few days—preferably a week or more—to ensure that all is well, and to allow certain micro-organisms that help form the food of the fish to develop. In the case of heated aquaria it is necessary also to ensure that the thermostat is working correctly and that the temperature is remaining constant or within very narrow limits. Here again it is advisable to wait at least a week before introducing any fish. Should conditions "go wrong" before or after the fish are introduced, it is best to start filling the tank all over again.

Fish should not be overfed, although regular feeding is essential. Attention must be paid to the feeding instructions issued with prepared fish foods, and to details given by the supplier of "live" foods. Provided fish are neither overcrowded nor overfed, the amount of sediment that accumulates in the tank will not be excessive, but it should be siphoned away gently every month, or more often if necessary. Water lost by evaporation should be replaced, and in the case of heated tanks especially, it is most desirable that the added water be of the same temperature as that already in the tanks.

Certain species of water snail are often placed in aquaria to act as scavengers. It is necessary to ensure that, if snails are kept, they are of the right type, and it is important to consult experts on this matter.

Breeding is an interesting topic, there being both egg-laying and viviparous or "live-bearing" fish. The beginner is well advised to learn first how to keep fish in healthy condition in his aquarium before indulging in any planned breeding, and he should study the relevant information in books on the subject.

An aeration plant is often recommended on the grounds that it will increase the fish-carrying capacity of the aquarium. This is true up to a point, but overcrowding may bring other troubles besides those connected with lack of sufficient oxygen, and the golden rule is never to keep too many fish for the size of aquarium in question. Another factor to be remembered is that should the aerator break down it may leave the fish with less oxygen than their proper requirement. It has been recommended that an aerator is best thought of as a stand-by, to be employed only in emergencies, e.g., when for some reason extra fish have to be added to a tank already holding all or almost all its proper capacity.

There are unfortunately many diseases of fish, and as yet scientific knowledge concerning many of them is far less detailed than it should be. It is clear, however, that environmental factors are responsible for many deaths or cases of unthriftiness, and among the factors concerned may be listed: overcrowding, overfeeding, the provision of a diet that is qualitatively inadequate, lack of "balance" in the aquarium leading to unsuitable conditions, dirt, too strong light, lead paint and noxious substances, that may somehow have come into contact with the water (e.g., from the hands of the person tending them) or been absorbed from the atmosphere. One must be careful of such things as disinfectants, soaps, petrol, etc. In the case of tropical fish the temperature of the water may be incorrect. Should fish troubles occur, therefore, it is as well to consider these various possibilities, although one should not hesitate to seek professional advice where there appears to be a case of infectious disease. An ailing fish should certainly be removed from the tank (assuming that there are other fish present) and given separate quarters of its own if such a course is feasible.

It is not intended to provide a description of the separate diseases, although it may be mentioned that such signs as the appearance of material resembling cotton-wool (actual fungal growths) and "rotting" of the tail or fins, are among those that should lead the owner to isolate affected fish and to seek help immediately.

No attempt is made here to describe any of the many different species and varieties of fish suitable for private aquaria. Some of the "points"

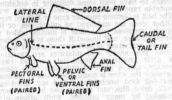

of a fish are shown in the accompanying illustration. Great care must be taken in mixing species, e.g., "hard mouthed" and "soft mouthed" kinds should not be kept together. The temptation to put other species (e.g., newts) with aquarium fish must likewise be avoided.

CAGE BIRDS.

Very many species and varieties of birds are now maintained successfully in captivity, and there exists in Great Britain a large and expanding "cage-bird fancy," that caters for a considerable proportion of the smaller birds adapted to cage or aviary life. The increase in the numbers of budgerigars since the end of the Second World War has been phenomenal, and it was estimated during 1957 that the numbers of the species alone in the United Kingdom exceeded 6 millions, the corresponding figure for the U.S.A.—where the popular name is "parakeets"—being over 18 millions.

The different types and sizes of birds have different requirements, and in the space available it is not possible to do more than cover the general principles and to deal briefly with the special characteristics of the management of the more easily maintained species. The beginner is advised to restrict his attention to one of the better-

known species, e.g., canaries or budgerigars, and not to attempt to maintain exotic varieties until he has acquired considerable experience.

Most species thrive best in aviaries, which may be indoor, outdoor, or of the combined "outdoor-indoor" type. An indoor aviary is usually all-wire and portable. The criticism of many such aviaries is that they tend to be high and narrow, whereas a fairly large floor-space is desirable. They should not be placed in cold or draughty places, nor too near a fire. If sited so as to receive much direct sunlight they must have adequate shelter. The wires must be close together, especially if smaller species are kept, a distance between them of about ⅜ in. being generally suitable. An outdoor aviary—suitable only for some species or at certain times in the case of others—should occupy a sunny position, although it too must include shade, and must be protected from winds. There ought in fact to be a sheltered portion, dry and well protected from the elements. The aviary must be strongly made and safe from all predators, including rats and mice. While it is often considered desirable to allow herbage to protrude through the wire-mesh floor, it is essential that the birds are never in close contact with wild rodents or their droppings. Most birds are highly susceptible to some forms of salmonellosis (see under mice and guinea-pigs), and can contract them in this way. It is advisable also that the roof of the aviary is solid: corrugated asbestos sheeting, projecting well clear of the edges of the uprights so as to prevent water and other matter from entering the interior, is excellent. The droppings of wild birds may be a potent source of bacterial infection or of internal parasites. To prevent close contact otherwise with wild birds, the wire or wire-netting "walls" of the aviary may be double. If an "outdoor-indoor" aviary is employed, there is usually an indoor flight cage, separated from the external portion either by a very light hanging door of suitable size, through which the birds can easily push their way, or by a sliding partition that the owner can operate as required.

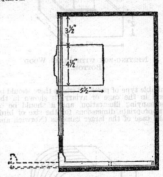

SECTION THROUGH CAGE.

If an aviary is out of the question, then a suitable cage should be purchased or constructed. The cage need not be ornate—indeed simplicity of design usually facilitates the highly important task of keeping everything clean—but it must be large enough. A cross-section through a breeding-cage suitable for canaries, and for many other species, is shown in the accompanying illustration. Such a cage should measure about 40 in. in length × 12 in. wide × 18 in. high. It is constructed of wood or some suitable sheeting except for the front, which consists of vertical wires with horizontal stays, and can be divided into two parts by means of a suitable partition containing a removable section made of wire. By this means the cock and hen canaries can be introduced into the separate sections and develop a courtship before being allowed to be together for actual mating. The cross-section indicates the site and size of the removable portion of the partition, and it shows also the removable tray that is such an excellent fitting for almost any type of cage, and which greatly facilitates cleaning.

Whether an aviary or a cage is employed, it is essential to have proper fittings, including con-

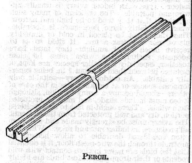

PERCH.

veniently placed drinking-troughs, feeding-trays and bird-baths, and good perches. Much unnecessary discomfort is brought about through the use of unsuitable perches, or ones that are incorrectly situated or not sufficiently "firm."

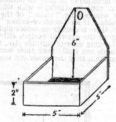

NESTING-BOX WITH PLAIN WOOD BOTTOM.

A suitable type of perch, of which there should be several in the cage or aviary, is shown in the accompanying illustration, and it should be of the appropriate dimensions for the size of bird. In the case of the larger canaries (Norwich and

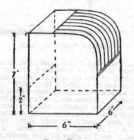

BIRD BATH.

Yorkshire), e.g., the sectional measurements should be ⅜ in. × ¾ in., whereas for a smaller canary (Border) they should be ½ in. × ½ in. The type of perch shown is easy to clean and does not possess awkward corners in which parasites may be harboured. The dimensions of a nesting box a bird-bath, and a feeding-tray suitable for

canaries are also given in the accompanying illustrations.

While wood is a convenient material for aviary and cage construction, it has, of course, several disadvantages. Out of doors it is best creosoted (lead paint must never be used for places in which birds or other small animals are kept), and indoors it is better lined with hard asbestos sheeting. Metal is suitable—provided that it does not rust or corrode and that the environmental conditions are warm enough.

In all cases a supply of clean, fresh water should be available. Strict cleanliness should be observed, and professional advice taken immediately if a bird is not thriving.

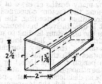

SEED TROUGH.

CANARIES (*Serinus canarius*).—These are domesticated forms of the race of wild serin found in the Canary Islands, and may live up to twenty-five years. Many varieties are known, and although most individuals are "canary yellow," other colours have been developed by fanciers. Many books have been written about the canary, although there is still much to be learned concerning its feeding and diseases—as is indeed the case with almost all cage-birds. The system of feeding generally recommended is based upon a mixture of 2 or 3 parts of canary seed (which is rich in energy, and which is sometimes mixed with a little millet seed) to 1 part of summer rape seed, which is high in fat and protein. There seems to have been some difficulty in obtaining suitable rape seed in some areas since the war. The best is German summer rape or Rübsen rape. Other seeds are employed as substitutes, or for special purposes, e.g., niger is usually added at breeding time, and linseed if there is any indication of premature or soft (out-of-season) moult. Good proprietary seed mixtures are available. A little greenfood should be provided twice weekly, and a piece of cuttlefish bone placed between the wires is a suitable source of calcium. Soft-bill food (containing boiled egg, dried egg yolk, dried flies, and ants' pupæ) is also recommended by many breeders, while others give chopped egg alone. Others again favour milk, especially for young birds.

Breeding is usually started late in March or early in April, but not unless the daily shade temperature is at least 50° F. The pairs should be selected earlier than this and transferred to breeding-cages, with the partition in position. By the middle of February the wire partition may be installed so that the two birds can see one another. A little niger seed is usually added to the diet, while finely ground oystershell or eggshell may be sprinkled on the floor. (Otherwise the floor may be covered with washed sand that is not too fine and is free from dust.) When the birds begin to feed one another through the wire they are ready for mating, and the partition may be removed. The nest-box can then be inserted and suitable nesting materials, e.g., cow hair and moss, placed in the cage. The incubation period is thirteen to fourteen days. After the eggs are laid some owners prefer to separate the cock and the hen, but allow him to rejoin her after the young are all about eight to nine days old and have opened their eyes. If it is desired that all the chicks be hatched together, then one can remove the first three eggs that are laid—usually one egg is laid daily—and keep them in a box at room temperature, substituting dummy eggs for them in the nest-box. On the afternoon of the third day of laying they are returned to the nest-box in place of the dummies.

When the young chicks are able to feed for themselves they should be provided with special food, such as egg and bread crumbs and a little cracked canary seed. If the cock bird interferes with them, or causes the hen to neglect them, he must be returned to his own section. Usually, however, all goes well, and the hen will go to the nest again when the first chicks are almost sixteen days old. Some three or four broods may be raised in a season.

WAXBILLS, FINCHES, AND OTHER SEED-EATERS.—The canary is of course a finch, but most of the other "foreign finches" are considered by dealers and writers together with other types of seed-eating birds. Well over 30 species of *Avadavats, Buntings, Mannikins, Cardinals, Whydahs, Weavers,* and *Finches* of various descriptions have been maintained successfully in captivity in Great Britain. One of the most popular is the *Zebra finch (Taeniopygia castanotis),* from Australia, which has bred so successfully in this country that supplies no longer depend upon fresh importations, and which is already appearing in several varieties. The native bird, and many of its descendants, are grey and white, with red beaks. The male bird has orange cheek-patches, and orange flanks with white markings. The throat has black barring on a white background, and indeed the characteristic markings of the male have been the subject of interesting behaviour studies. The female lacks these special markings. The species is hardy, and is capable of living in outdoor aviaries all the year round, so long as it has shelter from draughts or strong winds and adequate facilities for roosting. If provided with nest-boxes, the birds will attempt—often successfully—to breed all the year round, so to avoid overbreeding it is better to remove these boxes in winter. A mixture of millet and canary seed forms the basis of their diet, which should be supplemented with fresh greenfood, millet sprays, fine grit, and cuttlebone—and, of course, fresh water should be available. Another bird suitable for the relatively uninitiated bird-keeper is the *Bengalese* (a domestic variety of *Munia striata*). It seems that these birds are the result of careful breeding by the Japanese, and may be regarded as fertile hybrids. Three main forms, the Chocolate-and-White, the Fawn-and-White, and the White, have been developed. These birds will thrive in cages or in aviaries. As in the case of Zebra Finches, they will attempt to breed all the year round if provided with nest-boxes. Bengalese are sociable birds, sometimes known in the U.S.A. as Society Finches. They appear to require less additional food than most species, thriving on a mixture of canary and millet seed, together with grit, cuttlebone, and an occasional millet spray or item of greenstuff.

For details of these birds, and of the many others from which a selection may be made, works of reference should be consulted. Three very useful books, all published by Cage Birds, London, are *Foreign Bird Keeping,* by Edward J. Boosey (63s.), *Foreign Birds for Beginners,* by D. H. S. Risdon (10s. 6d.), and *Foreign Birds for Garden Aviaries,* by Alec Brooksbank (10s. 6d.).

BUDGERIGARS.—The increase in the popularity of this bird has been phenomenal, although to those who have experience of other birds as pets the reasons are soon fairly obvious. Apart from the capacity to talk, shown by many birds—especially males—kept alone and trained, there is a liveliness, almost a "cheekiness," and an apparent like of human companionship. The wild green budgerigar (*Melopsittacus undulatus*) exists in large numbers in the grassland and desert shrub regions of Australia. The usual colour is grass green—it is frequently known as the Grass Parakeet—with a yellow mask, with three black spots on either side. As a result of intensive breeding, a considerable number of colour varieties has been produced, and the genetics of colour are a constant source of interest to budgerigar breeders. A vast budgerigar "fancy" has been built up in the United Kingdom, the U.S.A., and other countries and World Budgerigar Congresses are held every few years. Budgerigars will thrive in outdoor aviaries all the year round, but the vast majority

are kept as indoor pets in cages or small aviaries. The cages can be similar to those used for canaries, and care should be taken that the perches are of the correct diameter. If nest-boxes are put up, and the environmental conditions are suitable, budgerigars suitably paired will breed at almost any time of the year. It is customary, however, to restrict breeding to the spring, summer, and early autumn. Overbreeding may lead to difficulties, including the production of "runners" or "French moult." The sexes may normally be distinguished, at any rate in mature individuals, by the colour of the cere at the base of the beak, which is blue in males and brown in females. Males may lose their colour if not in good condition and for other reasons.

There are now many proprietary seeds mixtures, but some owners prefer to make up their own mixtures of millet (usually mixing small yellow and large white varieties) and canary seed. Millet sprays, fresh greenfood, good grit, and cuttlebone are all desirable, and it is important that the correct size and consistency of grit be chosen. Variety in "extras" to the basal seeds diet is probably important, for the captive bird has not the same opportunities as its wild ancestors for ranging widely for, possibly, important trace items of food. Breeding birds secrete a "milk," comparable with the crop milk of pigeons and some other birds, and this is of importance in the early feeding of the young.

Most healthy budgerigars seem to live to the age of 5–7 years or more, and considerably greater ages have been attained in captivity.

Such is the development of the budgerigar fancy that most equipment as well as food can be obtained ready for use. The playful habits of budgerigars have led to their being given table-tennis balls or a variety of small toys to play with, while some forms of food are supplied as budgerigar bells or otherwise in special shapes that seem to amuse the birds as they take the constituent seed from them.

The study of budgerigar diseases is in its infancy, but already some important facts have become realised. French moult is certainly reproducible by overbreeding, and may be linked with deficiencies in the ability of the parent birds to feed their young—or to hand over to them at the time of laying sufficient nutritional reserves to carry them through hatching and parental feeding until the time that they can fend for themselves. A deficiency in the "milk" has been shown in some cases, and may be generally true. Large chicks can be produced by killing off or removing all but a single member of the clutch, and allowing the parents to deal with it alone.

A mite infestation, due to *Cnemidocoptes pilae,* may give rise to *Scaly face, Scaly beak,* or *Scaly leg,* for which veterinary treatment is now available. Another condition, known as *Brown hypertrophy of the cere,* is characterised by thickening and darkening of the surface of the cere. In the early stages it is sometimes thought that the bird is changing its sex. There is no known successful treatment at the time of writing, and if the overgrowth is cut away it will only reform. There are various disturbances of the *digestive tract,* and some of these may be associated with inability to stand properly.

There are many treatises on the budgerigar. A useful little work is *Budgerigar Guide,* by Cessa Feyerbrand (Fond du Lac, Wisconsin: All-Pets Magazine).

LOVEBIRDS AND PARROTLETS are also members of the parrot family, and while they are unlikely to equal the budgerigar in popularity, they are nevertheless interesting birds that are being kept in increasing numbers as pets. Lovebirds, of the genus *Agapornis,* are African in origin, and some six species are commonly kept in captivity. Parrotlets derive from South America, the commonest species being the Guiana Parrotlet, *Forpus passerinus.* Both types of bird are relatively simple to maintain in aviaries or large cages, and their basal diet (which should be supplemented widely) is a mixture of millet and canary seed. They are hardy and vigorous creatures, many details of which are to be found in condensed form in *Lovebirds and Parrotlets,* by C. P. Luke (London: Cage Birds, 8s. 6d.).

CALENDAR FOR 1971.

January
S	M	T	W	T	F	S
.	.	.	.	.	1	2
3	4	5	6	7	8	9
10	11	12	13	14	15	16
17	18	19	20	21	22	23
24	25	26	27	28	29	30
31	.	.	.	.	.	.

February
S	M	T	W	T	F	S
.	1	2	3	4	5	6
7	8	9	10	11	12	13
14	15	16	17	18	19	20
21	22	23	24	25	26	27
28	.	.	.	.	.	.

March
S	M	T	W	T	F	S
.	1	2	3	4	5	6
7	8	9	10	11	12	13
14	15	16	17	18	19	20
21	22	23	24	25	26	27
28	29	30	31	.	.	.

April
S	M	T	W	T	F	S
.	.	.	.	1	2	3
4	5	6	7	8	9	10
11	12	13	14	15	16	17
18	19	20	21	22	23	24
25	26	27	28	29	30	.

May
S	M	T	W	T	F	S
.	.	.	.	.	.	1
2	3	4	5	6	7	8
9	10	11	12	13	14	15
16	17	18	19	20	21	22
23	24	25	26	27	28	29
30	31	.	.	.	.	.

June
S	M	T	W	T	F	S
.	.	1	2	3	4	5
6	7	8	9	10	11	12
13	14	15	16	17	18	19
20	21	22	23	24	25	26
27	28	29	30	.	.	.

July
S	M	T	W	T	F	S
.	.	.	.	1	2	3
4	5	6	7	8	9	10
11	12	13	14	15	16	17
18	19	20	21	22	23	24
25	26	27	28	29	30	31

August
S	M	T	W	T	F	S
1	2	3	4	5	6	7
8	9	10	11	12	13	14
15	16	17	18	19	20	21
22	23	24	25	26	27	28
29	30	31	.	.	.	.

September
S	M	T	W	T	F	S
.	.	.	1	2	3	4
5	6	7	8	9	10	11
12	13	14	15	16	17	18
19	20	21	22	23	24	25
26	27	28	29	30	.	.

October
S	M	T	W	T	F	S
.	.	.	.	.	1	2
3	4	5	6	7	8	9
10	11	12	13	14	15	16
17	18	19	20	21	22	23
24	25	26	27	28	29	30
31	.	.	.	.	.	.

November
S	M	T	W	T	F	S
.	1	2	3	4	5	6
7	8	9	10	11	12	13
14	15	16	17	18	19	20
21	22	23	24	25	26	27
28	29	30	.	.	.	.

December
S	M	T	W	T	F	S
.	.	.	1	2	3	4
5	6	7	8	9	10	11
12	13	14	15	16	17	18
19	20	21	22	23	24	25
26	27	28	29	30	31	.

CALENDAR FOR 1972.

January
S	M	T	W	T	F	S
.	.	.	.	.	.	1
2	3	4	5	6	7	8
9	10	11	12	13	14	15
16	17	18	19	20	21	22
23	24	25	26	27	28	29
30	31	.	.	.	.	.

February
S	M	T	W	T	F	S
.	.	1	2	3	4	5
6	7	8	9	10	11	12
13	14	15	16	17	18	19
20	21	22	23	24	25	26
27	28	29	.	.	.	.

March
S	M	T	W	T	F	S
.	.	.	1	2	3	4
5	6	7	8	9	10	11
12	13	14	15	16	17	18
19	20	21	22	23	24	25
26	27	28	29	30	31	.

April
S	M	T	W	T	F	S
.	.	.	.	.	.	1
2	3	4	5	6	7	8
9	10	11	12	13	14	15
16	17	18	19	20	21	22
23	24	25	26	27	28	29
30	.	.	.	.	.	.

May
S	M	T	W	T	F	S
.	1	2	3	4	5	6
7	8	9	10	11	12	13
14	15	16	17	18	19	20
21	22	23	24	25	26	27
28	29	30	31	.	.	.

June
S	M	T	W	T	F	S
.	.	.	.	1	2	3
4	5	6	7	8	9	10
11	12	13	14	15	16	17
18	19	20	21	22	23	24
25	26	27	28	29	30	.

July
S	M	T	W	T	F	S
.	.	.	.	.	.	1
2	3	4	5	6	7	8
9	10	11	12	13	14	15
16	17	18	19	20	21	22
23	24	25	26	27	28	29
30	31	.	.	.	.	.

August
S	M	T	W	T	F	S
.	.	1	2	3	4	5
6	7	8	9	10	11	12
13	14	15	16	17	18	19
20	21	22	23	24	25	26
27	28	29	30	31	.	.

September
S	M	T	W	T	F	S
.	.	.	.	.	1	2
3	4	5	6	7	8	9
10	11	12	13	14	15	16
17	18	19	20	21	22	23
24	25	26	27	28	29	30

October
S	M	T	W	T	F	S
1	2	3	4	5	6	7
8	9	10	11	12	13	14
15	16	17	18	19	20	21
22	23	24	25	26	27	28
29	30	31	.	.	.	.

November
S	M	T	W	T	F	S
.	.	.	1	2	3	4
5	6	7	8	9	10	11
12	13	14	15	16	17	18
19	20	21	22	23	24	25
26	27	28	29	30	.	.

December
S	M	T	W	T	F	S
.	.	.	.	.	1	2
3	4	5	6	7	8	9
10	11	12	13	14	15	16
17	18	19	20	21	22	23
24	25	26	27	28	29	30
31	.	.	.	.	.	.

CALENDAR FOR 1973.

January
S	M	T	W	T	F	S
.	1	2	3	4	5	6
7	8	9	10	11	12	13
14	15	16	17	18	19	20
21	22	23	24	25	26	27
28	29	30	31	.	.	.

February
S	M	T	W	T	F	S
.	.	.	.	1	2	3
4	5	6	7	8	9	10
11	12	13	14	15	16	17
18	19	20	21	22	23	24
25	26	27	28	.	.	.

March
S	M	T	W	T	F	S
.	.	.	.	1	2	3
4	5	6	7	8	9	10
11	12	13	14	15	16	17
18	19	20	21	22	23	24
25	26	27	28	29	30	31

April
S	M	T	W	T	F	S
1	2	3	4	5	6	7
8	9	10	11	12	13	14
15	16	17	18	19	20	21
22	23	24	25	26	27	28
29	30	.	.	.	.	.

May
S	M	T	W	T	F	S
.	.	1	2	3	4	5
6	7	8	9	10	11	12
13	14	15	16	17	18	19
20	21	22	23	24	25	26
27	28	29	30	31	.	.

June
S	M	T	W	T	F	S
.	.	.	.	.	1	2
3	4	5	6	7	8	9
10	11	12	13	14	15	16
17	18	19	20	21	22	23
24	25	26	27	28	29	30

July
S	M	T	W	T	F	S
1	2	3	4	5	6	7
8	9	10	11	12	13	14
15	16	17	18	19	20	21
22	23	24	25	26	27	28
29	30	31	.	.	.	.

August
S	M	T	W	T	F	S
.	.	.	1	2	3	4
5	6	7	8	9	10	11
12	13	14	15	16	17	18
19	20	21	22	23	24	25
26	27	28	29	30	31	.

September
S	M	T	W	T	F	S
.	.	.	.	.	.	1
2	3	4	5	6	7	8
9	10	11	12	13	14	15
16	17	18	19	20	21	22
23	24	25	26	27	28	29
30	.	.	.	.	.	.

October
S	M	T	W	T	F	S
.	1	2	3	4	5	6
7	8	9	10	11	12	13
14	15	16	17	18	19	20
21	22	23	24	25	26	27
28	29	30	31	.	.	.

November
S	M	T	W	T	F	S
.	.	.	.	1	2	3
4	5	6	7	8	9	10
11	12	13	14	15	16	17
18	19	20	21	22	23	24
25	26	27	28	29	30	.

December
S	M	T	W	T	F	S
.	.	.	.	.	.	1
2	3	4	5	6	7	8
9	10	11	12	13	14	15
16	17	18	19	20	21	22
23	24	25	26	27	28	29
30	31	.	.	.	.	.

CALENDAR FOR 1974.

January
S	M	T	W	T	F	S
.	.	1	2	3	4	5
6	7	8	9	10	11	12
13	14	15	16	17	18	19
20	21	22	23	24	25	26
27	28	29	30	31	.	.

February
S	M	T	W	T	F	S
.	.	.	.	.	1	2
3	4	5	6	7	8	9
10	11	12	13	14	15	16
17	18	19	20	21	22	23
24	25	26	27	28	.	.

March
S	M	T	W	T	F	S
.	.	.	.	.	1	2
3	4	5	6	7	8	9
10	11	12	13	14	15	16
17	18	19	20	21	22	23
24	25	26	27	28	29	30
31	.	.	.	.	.	.

April
S	M	T	W	T	F	S
.	1	2	3	4	5	6
7	8	9	10	11	12	13
14	15	16	17	18	19	20
21	22	23	24	25	26	27
28	29	30	.	.	.	.

May
S	M	T	W	T	F	S
.	.	.	1	2	3	4
5	6	7	8	9	10	11
12	13	14	15	16	17	18
19	20	21	22	23	24	25
26	27	28	29	30	31	.

June
S	M	T	W	T	F	S
.	.	.	.	.	.	1
2	3	4	5	6	7	8
9	10	11	12	13	14	15
16	17	18	19	20	21	22
23	24	25	26	27	28	29
30	.	.	.	.	.	.

July
S	M	T	W	T	F	S
.	1	2	3	4	5	6
7	8	9	10	11	12	13
14	15	16	17	18	19	20
21	22	23	24	25	26	27
28	29	30	31	.	.	.

August
S	M	T	W	T	F	S
.	.	.	.	1	2	3
4	5	6	7	8	9	10
11	12	13	14	15	16	17
18	19	20	21	22	23	24
25	26	27	28	29	30	31

September
S	M	T	W	T	F	S
1	2	3	4	5	6	7
8	9	10	11	12	13	14
15	16	17	18	19	20	21
22	23	24	25	26	27	28
29	30	.	.	.	.	.

October
S	M	T	W	T	F	S
.	.	1	2	3	4	5
6	7	8	9	10	11	12
13	14	15	16	17	18	19
20	21	22	23	24	25	26
27	28	29	30	31	.	.

November
S	M	T	W	T	F	S
.	.	.	.	.	1	2
3	4	5	6	7	8	9
10	11	12	13	14	15	16
17	18	19	20	21	22	23
24	25	26	27	28	29	30

December
S	M	T	W	T	F	S
1	2	3	4	5	6	7
8	9	10	11	12	13	14
15	16	17	18	19	20	21
22	23	24	25	26	27	28
29	30	31	.	.	.	.

THOMAS CLARK

NEWS RECEIPT

w/e Sat. Sep. 3rd

Extras............36